D1605416

WHO'S WHO IN U.S. WRITERS, EDITORS & POETS 1988

WHO'S WHO IN U.S. WRITERS, EDITORS & POETS

A Biographical Directory

1988

Curt Johnson, Editor
Frank Nipp
Consulting Editor

December Press
Box 302, Highland Park, IL 60035

In memory of R. F. "Bud" Dressel
1928-1984
A doer but, much more, a dreamer

Manufactured in the United States of America

December Press
Box 302, Highland Park, IL 60035

WHO'S WHO IN U.S. WRITERS,
EDITORS & POETS

ISSN: 0885-4521
ISBN: 0-913204-21-8
LC Catalog Card Number: 87-648220

Second Edition
1988

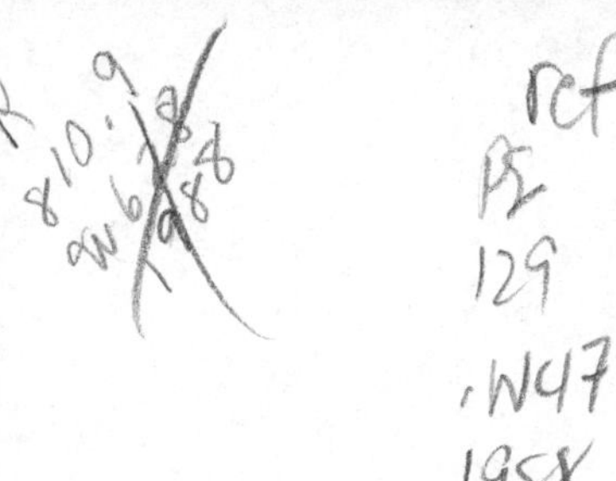

Contents

Preface

This second edition of *Who's Who in U.S. Writers, Editors & Poets* contains the biographies of just under 8,500 poets, novelists, short story writers, editors of journals, periodicals and books, journalists, nonfiction writers, translators, critics, playwrights, scriptwriters, and biographers.

Candidates' names were obtained through research into existing contemporary sources, by solicitation to professional organizations and associations of writers, editors and poets, and through nominations by friends and colleagues. Listings result from independent decisions by the editors and their advisors, who acted under carefully established—if necessarily subjective— standards for gauging national, regional and local reference interest, as those interests could be determined for both the present and the future. Inclusion is considered a mark of literary/publishing distinction and achievement.

So far as we are aware, there is no other single-volume literary directory of the same scope, biographical—and bibliographical—comprehens veness, or currency. The information in *Who's Who in U.S. Writers, Editors & Poets* is intended for use as a reference by other writers, editors, poets, journalists, and publishers, by literary agents, by cultural historians, researchers, and students, and by the general public—as well as by the biographees themselves. The volume is intended also to facilitate communication, referrals and the exchange of information between professionals. The addresses are current. Equally important, the data serve as a confirming and permanent record of the biographees' accomplishments.

The range of facts presented includes date and place of birth of the biographee; names of parents, spouse, and children; details of education; pertinent civic and political activities; military service; professional and social memberships; vocational history; awards, grants, prizes, and other special achievements; current address—and a full publishing and/or editing history.

To ensure accuracy, biographees were given the opportunity to proofread, amend, and update their sketches, which in most instances were prepared from data they themselves provided. If a biographee wished to exclude information that would normally appear in a sketch, that was done.

If you are reading this in a library, or editorial office, or at a friend's, and would like to be considered for inclusion in the next (third) edition of *Who's Who in U.S. Writers, Editors & Poets* (1989), send a SASE to Box 302, Highland Park, IL 60035, and we'll send you a data form. We hope to include a full range of Canadian writers, editors and poets in the next edition. If you find errors in this edition's listings, please let us know what they are.

For their assistance in the preparation of this second edition, the editor thanks the biographees from the first edition and, also, Betty Fox, Carla Hofland, Becky Maley, and (most especially) Frank Nipp.

The editor also thanks John Carlisle of Carlisle Communications, Ltd., Dubuque, IA, and his associate in charge of typesetting for this directory, Donna Frommelt. Through two editions of this annual directory, the people at Carlisle Communications, Ltd., have proven themselves paradigms of expert, efficient, and economical service.

—CLJ

Abbreviations & Acronyms

AAAL American Academy of Arts & Letters
AAEA American Agricultural Editors Association
AAIL American Academy & Institute of Arts & Letters
AAP Academy of American Poets
AARP American Association of Retired Persons
AATE American Association of Travel Editors
AAUP American Association of University Professors
AAUW American Association of University Women
ABBA American Black Bookwriters Association
ABWA Associated Business Writers of America
acad academy
ACEI Association of Childhood Education International
ACLA American Comparative Literature Association
ACLS American Council of Learned Societies
ACLU American Civil Liberties Union
adj adjunct
adminstr administrator
advt advertising
AEA American Editors Association
AESE Association of Earth Science Editors
AFTRA American Federation of Radio & TV Artists
AG Authors Guild
agrl agricultural
AGVA American Guild of Variety Artists
agcy agency
AIM American Institute of Management
AL Authors League
ALA American Library Association
ALMA Association of Literary Magazines of America
ALTA American Literary Translators Association
AMPAS Academy of Motion Picture Arts & Sciences
AMWA American Medical Writers Association
annl annual
anthol anthology
ANWC American News Women's Club
AP Associated Press
APT Association of Professional Translators
ASA American Studies Association
ASBPE American Society of Business Press Editors
ASCAP American Society of Composers, Authors & Publishers
ASCD Association of Supervision & Curriculum Development
ASJA American Society of Journalists & Authors Inc.
ASME American Society of Magazine Editors
assn association
assoc associate
asst assistant
ATA American Translators Association
ATCA American Theater Critics Association
AWP Associated Writing Programs

b born
bd board
biog biographical
BOMC Book of the Month Club
BPW Business Press of America
br branch
bulltn bulletin
bur bureau
bus business
BWAA Bowling Writers Association of America

CAAA Composers, Authors and Artists of America
CAPS Creative Artists in Public Service
CASE Council for the Advancement and Support of Education
CCCC College Conference on Composition & Communication
CCLM Coordinating Council of Literary Magazines
CCNY City College of New York
CEA College English Association
cert certificate
ch church
chmn chairman
chpt chapter
clrk clerk
CLA College Language Association
coll college
com committee
comml commercial
commn commission
commun community
conf conference
cons consultant
contrbd contributed
contrbg contributing
contrbr contributor
coord coordinator
corr correspondent
COSMEP International Association of Independent Publishers (originally, Committee of Small Magazine Editors & Publishers)
CPG Congressional Press Gallery
CRRT Children's Reading Round Table
CWA Crime Writers Association

d daughter
dau daughter
dec deceased
devel development
DG Dramatists Guild
dir director
disting distinguished
div divorced

econ economics
ed editor, edition
edn education
ednl educational
elem elementary
encyc encyclopedia
EPAA Educational Press Association of America
EWA Education Writers Association
exec executive
exhbn exhibition

fdn foundation
fedl federal
fedn federation
FFWA Florida Freelance Writers Association
fgn foreign
FSPA Florida State Poetry Association
FWG Feminist Writers Guild

genl general
grad graduate, graduated

hist historical, historic
hon honorary

IABC International Association of Business Communicators
IBWC International Black Writers Conference
ILA Illinois Library Association
illus illustrated
IMPA International Motor Press Association
ind independent
indsl industrial
info information
inst institute
instr instructor
intl international
intro introduction
IWWG International Women's Writing Guild

JASNA Jane Austen Society of North America
jnl journal
jnlsm journalism
jnlst journalist

lang language
lectr lecturer
LG Literary Guild
lit literature, literary

m married
mag magazine
mem member
meml memorial
mgr manager
MLA Modern Language Association
mng managing
MPA Magazine Publishers Association
mus museum, music
MWA Mystery Writers of America Inc.

NAEYC National Association for Education of Young Children
NAPT National Association of Poetry Therapy
NASW National Association of Science Writers Inc.
natl national
NATVAS National Academy of TV Arts & Sciences
NBCC National Book Critics Circle
NCAC National Coalition Against Censorship
NCTE National Council of Teachers of English
NEA National Endowment for the Arts
NEH National Endowment for the Humanities
NEOWA New England Outdoor Writers Association
NEPC New England Poetry Club
NFPW National Federation of Press Women
NJRWA New Jersey Romance Writers Association
NLAPW National League of American Pen Women
NMPA National Motorsport Press Association
NPW National Pen Women
NWBWA National Women Bowling Writers Association
NWC National Writers Club Inc.
nwsprs newspapers
NWU National Writers Union
NYBPE New York Business Press Editors

ofcl official
OPC Overseas Press Club
orgn organization
OWAA Outdoor Writers Association of America

P&W Poets & Writers Inc.
PEN Poets, Playwrights, Editors, Essayists, and Novelists
philo philosophy
philol philological
photog photographer
PICA Professional Insurance Communicators of America
pres president
prin principal
proc proceedings
prodn production
prof professor
profl professional
proptr proprietor
prtnr partner
PRSA Public Relations Society of America
PSA Poetry Society of America
pub publisher, published
publ publication

qtly quarterly

rec recording
res residence
ret retired
rev revised
rvw review
rvwr reviewer
RWA Romance Writers of America
RNDA Radio/TV News Directors Association
s son
SABEW Society of American Business & Economic Writers
SACUS Southern Association for Children Under Six
SAG Screen Actors Guild
SATW Society of American Travel Writers
SCBW Society of Children's Book Writers
schl school
sci science
secy secretary
sect section
sem seminary
SFWA Science Fiction Writers of America
SMA Society of Midland Authors
SNAP Society of National Association Publications
soc society
spcl special
SPJ Society of Professional Journalists
SPWAO Small Press Writers & Artists Organization
SSP Society for Scholarly Publishing
STC Society for Technical Communication
SUNY State University of New York
supt superintendent
supvr supervisor

TACWT Texas Association of Creative Writing Teachers
tchr teacher
TESL Teaching English as a Second Language
theol theological
treas treasurer

univ university
UPI United Press International

vis visiting
vol volunteer

WALA Western America Literature Association
WBW World Bowling Writers
WD Writer's Digest
WG Writers Guild
WHCA White House Correspondents Association
WIC Women in Communications Inc.
WPA Western Publications Association
wrkg working
wrtr writer
WSJ Wall Street Journal
WWA Western Writers of America Inc.

Alphabetical Practices

Names are arranged alphabetically by surnames first, then by first given name. If two surnames and first given names are identical, the individuals are alphabetized according to their second given name.

Surnames beginning with *De, Des, Du,* however capitalized or spaced, are listed with the prefix preceding the surname and arranged alphabetically, under the letter "D". Surnames beginning with *Mac* and *Mc* are arranged alphabetically under "M". Surnames beginning with *Saint* or *St.* appear after names that begin *Sains*, alphabetically according to the second part of the name. Surnames beginning with *Van, Von* or *von* are alphabetized under "V".

There is properly no history; only biography.

–Emerson

Who's Who in U.S. Writers, Editors & Poets

AAL, KATHARYN MACHAN, b. Woodbury, CT, Sept. 12, 1952, d. Benjamin Angelus and Myra LaVerne (Courtney) Machan; m. William Haputman Aal, Jan. 3, 1976 (div. 1979); m. 2d, Ralph Bonner Thompson, Dec. 21, 1985. Author poetry books: Bird on a Wire (with Kenneth Winchester), 1970, The Wind in the Pear Tree, 1972, The Book of the Raccoon, 1977, Looking for the Witches, 1980, Where the Foxes Say Goodnight, 1981, Conversations, 1982, Seneca Street Poems, 1982, The Raccoon Book, 1982, Writing Home (with Barbara Crooker), 1983, Women: A Pocket Book, 1982, Along the Rain Black Road, 1986, When She Was the Good-Time Girl, 1987, From Redwing, 1987; ed. anthologies: Rapunzel, Rapunzel: Poems, Prose & Photographs by Women on the Subject of Hair (cited by Library Jnl.), 1980, The Wings, the Vines: Poems by Katharyn Machan Aal, Alice Fulton, karen marie christa minns and Sybil Smith, 1983; playwright: The Baffling Boohunk (juvenile); contrbr.: 13th Moon, Paintbrush, Poetry Now, Yankee, other lit mags. Wrkg. on monologues. MA in English Lit., U. Iowa, 1975; PhD in speech, Northwestern U., 1984. Asst. prof. Ithaca (N.Y.) Coll., 1983—; dir. Feminist Women's Writing Workshops, Ithaca, 1983—; coordinator Ithaca Community Poets, 1977-80, 84—. Recipient Celia B. Wagner award PSA, 1982, Cecil Hemley award PSA, 1984. Mem. Feminist Wrtrs.' Guild, AWP, Speech Communication Assn. Office: Box 456 Ithaca NY 14851

AASTRUP, RONDI SUZANNE, b. Stoneham, MA, May 26, 1955; d. Alfred P. and Winona Fern (Kellogg) A. Contrbr. articles to newspapers, newsletters. Ed., contrbr.: Cedar Log, 1978-83, South Lancaster Pioneer, 1983—. B.A., Atlantic Union Coll., 1977; M.A., Andrews U., 1983—. B.A., Atlantic Union Coll., 1977; M.A., Andrews U., 1983. English tchr. Atlantic Union Coll., South Lancaster, MA, 1984, 85-86, 87, South Lancaster Acad., 1981-83, 83—. Active Lancaster Repoertory Co. Mem. Mass. Reading Assn., NCTE. Home: 282 Hudson Rd Bolton MA 01740

ABBE, GEORGE BANCROFT, b. Somers, CT, Jan. 28, 1911; s. Harry Allen Grant and Aida (Kittredge) A.; m. Barbara Rossiter, Sept. 22, 1934. Author: Voices in the Square, 1938, Dreamer's Clay, 1940; Wait for These Things, 1940, Letter Home, 1945; Mr. Quill's Crusade, 1948; The Wide Plains Roarx, 1954, Bird in the Mulberry: Collected Lyrics, 1937-1954, Poetry, the Great Therapy, 1956, The Incandescent Beast, 1957; The Winter House, 1957, One More Puritan, 1960; play The Adomatic Man, 1960; The Collected Poems of George Abbe, 1935-61, 1961, Stephen Vincent Benet on Writing, 1964, You and Contemporary Poetry: An Aid-to-Appreciation, 1964; The Larks, 1965, The Non-conformist, 1966; The Funeral, 1967; Shatter the Day, 1968; Yonderville, 1968; Dreams and Dissent, New Poems 1961–70, 1971; Abbe and Benet, 1973, The Pigeon Lover, 1981; Student, Cushing Acad., 1928; BA, U. N.H., 1933; MA, U. Iowa, 1938. Tchr. lit., writing Mt. Holyoke Coll. Yale, Columbia U., U. Iowa, U. Maine, U. Pitts., Wayne U., Springfield Coll., U. N.H.; co dir. New Eng. Writers Comf, Suffield (Conn.) Acad.; faculty Tchrs. Coll. Conn. New Britain, 1955-57; asst. prof., English Rusell Sage Coll., 1958-64, assoc. prof. 1964-67, resident author, 1958-67; prof. humanities, writer-in-residence State U. Coll., Plattsburgh, N.Y. 1966—; dir. Champlain Writers Conf. Editorial bd.: Book Club for Poetry; adv. editor Poetry Public. Recipient Shelley Meml. award, 1956. Mem. PSA. Address: Box 158 Old Country Rd Dublin NH 03444

ABBEY, EDWARD, b. Home, PA, 1927; s. Paul Revere and Mildred (Postlewaite) A. Author: Jonathan Troy, 1954; The Brave Cowboy, 1956; Fire on the Mountain, 1962; Desert Solitaire, 1968; Black Sun, 1971; The Monkey Wrench Gang, 1975; The Journey Home, 1977; Abbey's Road, 1979; Good News, 1980; Down the River, 1982; Beyond the Wall, 1984; Slumgullion Stew, 1985; One Life a Time, Please, 1987. BA, U. NM, 1951; postgrad. Edinburgh U., 1951-52. Served with U.S. Army, 1945-47. Fulbright fellow 1951; Guggenheim fellow, 1975. AAAL Award, 1987 (declined). Home: Oracle AZ 85623

ABBOTT, JOHN B., JR., b. Plainfield, NJ, Feb. 25, 1956, s. John B. and Clara M. (Anderson) A.; m. Theresa Marie Curcio, Nov. 14, 1981. Regular contrbr. short stories, articles to Untitled, The Home News. BA in English, Rutgers U., 1985. Staff wrtr. The Reporter, South Plainfield, N.J., 1983, The Echoes-Sentinel, Warren, N.J., 1985; ed.-in-chief Untitled, Rutgers U., New Brunswick, N.J., 1984-85; corr. The Home News, New Brunswick, 1985—; freelance wrtr., 1979—. Author murder mystery weekend scripts, "All in the Game," "Two for the Money," and " The Botsford Inn Mystery." Mem. MWA (assoc.). Home: 19 Grochowiak St South River NJ 08882

ABBOTT, KEITH GEORGE, b. Tacoma, WA, Feb. 2, 1944, s. Leonard Elwood and Gertrude Adelaide (Retka) A.; m. Lani Kae Hansen, Aug. 17, 1966; 1 dau., Persephone. Author fiction: Gush, 1975, Rhino Ritz, 1979, Harum Scarum, 1984, Mordecai of Monterey, 1985; author books of poetry: 12 Shot, 1975, What You Know With No Name For It, 1976, The Book of Rimbaud, 1977, Erase Words, 1977, Good News Bad News, 1984. BA, San Francisco State U., 1969; MA, Western Wash. State U., 1970. Wrtr.-in-residence Calif. poet-in-schls. project, 1972-73, Nev. Arts Commn., No. Nev., 1977-78. Recipient Poets Fdn. award, 1972; grantee San Francisco Schl. Dist., 1985. Home: 1020 Cornell St Albany CA 94706

ABBOTT, LEE KITTREDGE, b. Oct. 17, 1947; s. Lee Kittredge and Elaine (Kelly) A.; m. Pamela Jo Dennis, Dec. 20, 1970; children: Noel, Kelly. Collections of stories: The Heart Never Fits Its Wanting, 1980, Love Is the Crooked Thing, 1987, Strangers in Paradise, 1986. Stories pub. in Atlantic Monthly, Ga. Rvw, Ohio Rvw, Ind. Rvw, Epoch, Iowa Rvw, S. Rvw, others. BA, NM State U., 1970, MA, 1973; MFA, U. Ark., 1977. Instr. NM State U., Las Cruces, 1973-75; asst. prof. Case Western Res. U., Cleve., 1977-83, assoc. prof. English, 1983—. Fellow NEA 1979, 85; recipient award for fiction St. Lawrence U., 1981, O. Henry award, 1984, 2est Am. Short Stories award, 1984, Story Qtly. prize for fiction, 1985. Home: 3421 E. Scarborough Rd Cleveland Heights OH 44118

ABBOTT, ROBERT ALVIN, b. Cleve., Apr. 8, 1929; s. Wendell Holmes and Irma (Seibert) A.; m. Sharon Marie Ode, July 6, 1957; children—Christopher Mark, Pamela Ruth Abbott Dillenbeck, John Andrew. Columnist: Quality Progress Mag., 1973-81. Contrbr. articles to profl. jnls., trade mags. B.S. in Engineering Administration, Case Inst. Technology, 1951. Quality assurance mgr. Chemprene Co., Beacon, NY, 1971-73; technical dir. Am. Soc. Quality Control, Milw., 1973-81; quality mgr. Genl. Electric Co., Cleve., 1981—. Home: Unicorn Grove 11546 Caves Rd Chesterland OH 44026

ABBOTT, ROBERT TUCKER, b. Watertown, MA, Sept. 28, 1919; s. Charles Matthew and Frances (Tucker) A.; m. Mary Madeline Sisler, Feb. 18, 1946 (dec. Jan. 29, 1964); children—Robert Tucker, Carolyn Tucker, Cynthia Douglas; m. 2d, Sue Sweeney, Jan. 8, 1966 (dec. Oct. 1976); m. 3d, Cecelia White, May 13, 1977. Author: Am. Seashells, 1954, Kingdom of the Seashell, 1973, (with S.P. Dance) Compendium of Seashells, 1982, numerous others; assoc. ed. Johnsonia, 1941-70; ed.: The Nautilus, 1959-86, Indo-Pacific Mullusca, 1959-77. BS, Harvard, 1946; PhD, George Washington, 1955. Curator, Smithsonian Inst., Washington, 1946-54, Acad. Nat. Sci., Phila., 1953-69; asst. dir. Delaware Mus. Nat. Hist., Greenville, DE, 1969-77; pres. Amer. Malacologists, Inc., Melbourne, FL, 1977—. Mem. AAAS, Explorers Club, hon. mem. 25 shell clubs. Office: Box 5315 Melbourne FL 32902

ABEL, ERNEST LAWRENCE, (E. A. Lawrence), b. Toronto, Feb. 10, 1943; s. Jack and Rose (Tarshes) A.; m. Barbara Ellen Buckley, Sept. 20, 1970; children—Jason, Robert, Rebecca, Rosanne. Author: Ancient Views on the Origins of Life, 1973, The Roots of Antisemitism, 1975, Marihuana, 1980, A Marihuana Dictionary, 1982, Fetal Alcohol Syndrome, 1984, Psychoactive Drugs and Sex, 1985, Fetal Alcohol Syndrome, 1984, Psychoactive Drugs and Sex, 1985, Alcohol Wordlore and Folklore, 1987. B. A., Univ. of Toronto, 1965; Ph.D., U. Toronto, 1971. Acting deputy dir. Research Inst. Alcohol, Buffalo, 1983-85, dir. research, 1985; dir. operations Mott Center, Detroit, 1985—. Office: Mott Center 275 E Hancock Detroit MI 48201

ABEL, ROBERT HALSALL, b. Painsville, OH, May 27, 1941; s. Robert Halsall and Lora Constance (Logan) A.; m. Joyce Keeler, Oct. 31, 1964; 1 child, Charles Robert. Author: (stories) Skin and Bones, 1978; (novels) Freedom Dues, Or a Gentleman's Progress in the New World, 1980, The Progress of a Fire, 1985. BA, Coll of Wooster, 1967; MA, Kans. State Coll., Pittsburg, 1967; MA, MFA in English, U. Mass., 1974. Instr. Kans. State Coll., Pittsburg, 1964-67, Flint Community Coll., Mich., 1969-70, No. Ill. U. De Kalb, 1970-72; ed./wrtr. Contact, U. Mass., Amherst, 1974-78; lectr. Mt. Holyoke Coll., 1986. NEA creative writing fellow, 1978. Mem. AG. Home: Box 223 Lake Pleasant MA 01347

ABERBACH, JOEL D(AVID), b. NYC, June 19, 1940; s. Isidore and Miriam (Meltzer) A.; m. Joan Gross, June 17, 1962; children—Ian Mark, Amy Joyce, Matthew Daniel, Rachel Ann. Author: contrib. Urban Affairs Annual: The Urban Economy and Public Problems, John P. Crecine, ed., 1970, (with Jack L. Walker), Race in the City, 1973, (with Bert A. Rockman), Clashing Beliefs within the Executive Branch: The Nixon Administration Bureaucracy, 1975, (with Robert D. Putnam and Rockman), Bureaucrats and Politicians in Western Democracies, 1981. Contrib. of articles and reviews to prof. jnls., including Law and Contemporary Problems, Am. Pol. Sci. Rev., Urban Affairs Qtly, Am. Jnl. of Pol:. Sci., Am. Behavioral Scientist, and Transaction. AB with honors, Cornell U., 1961; grad. study at Harvard U. and M.I.T., 1962; MA, Ohio States U., 1963, MA, Yale U., 1965, Ph.D., 1967. Univ. of Mich., lecturer, 1967-68, asst. prof., 1968-72, prof. of poli. sci. and public policy, 1977—; research sci., Institute of Public Policy Studies, 1967, research assoc., Center for Pol. Studies, 197-72; sr. fellow, Brookings Institution, 1977-80. Ford Fdn. grant, 1968-72, Natl. Sci. Fdn. grant, 1969-73, 71-73, 78-81, 86-88, Soc. Sci. Res. Cncl. grant, 1971, Natl. Inst. of Mental Health grant, 1971-72. Home: 10453 Colina Way Los Angeles CA 90077

ABRAHAMS, WILLIAM MILLER, b. Boston, Jan. 23, 1919; s. Louis and Wilhelmina (Miller) A. Author: Interval in Carolina, 1945, By the Beautiful Sea, 1947, Imperial Waltz, 1954, Children of Capricorn, 1963, (with Peter Stansky) Journey to the Frontier, 1966, The Unknown Orwell, 1972, Orwell: The Transformation, 1979. BA, Harvard U., 1941. Editor Atlantic Monthly Press, Boston, 1955-77; contrbg. editor Atlantic Monthly, 1968-79, Inquiry mag., 1978—; sr. editor (West Coast) Holt, Rinehart & Winston, 1977-84, E.P. Dutton, 1984—; editor O. Henry Awards annl. vols., 1967—. Served with AUS, 1942-45. Home: 375 Pinehill Rd Hillsborough CA 94010

ABRAMOWSKI, DWAIN MARTIN, (Dwain Martin), b. Muskegon, MI, Mar. 22, 1956; s. Raymond J. and Lorraine (Zynda) A.; m. Christina Ann Hnizdor, June 9, 1979; 1 son, Nathan Andrew. Columnist: Advance Newspapers, 1987—. Contrbr. articles to sailings mags. Wrkg. on children's novel, A Candle on the Moon; short stories for sci. fiction mag. AA, Grand Rapids Jr. Coll., 1976; BS in Edn., Central Mich. U., 1979. Tchr. pre-schl., Grand Rapids, MI, 1979-84; free-lance wrtr., 1984—. Home: 6137 Belrick Ct Belmont MI 49306

ABRAMS, LINSEY, b. Boston, Jan. 4, 1951, d. Orville Christopher and Janis Roslyn (White) Abrams. Novelist: Charting by the Stars, 1979, Double Vision, 1984; contrbr. short stories to Redbook, New Directions anthology, Seattle Rvw, Mademoiselle; contrbr. articles to Miss. Rvw, other publs. BA, Sarah Lawrence Coll., 1973; MA, CCNY, 1978. Adj. lectr. English CCNY, 1978-79, Queens Coll., NYC, 1979-80; mem. fiction wrtg. faculty Sarah Lawrence Coll., Bronxville, N.Y., 1980—. Fiction grantee Creative Artists in Public Service, NYC, 1980. Mem. PEN, AG, ASCAP. Home: 181 Thompson St 24 New York NY 10012

ABRAMSON, MARTIN, b. Bklyn., Jan. 25, 1921; s. Jacob and Bessie (Horwitz) A.; m. Marcia Zagon, May 9, 1948; children— Barry, Jill. Author: The Real Al Jolson, 1956, The Barney Ross Story (Monkey on My Back), 1959, The Padre of Gauadalcanal Story, 1964, Hollywood Surgeon, 1969, Forgotten Fortunes, 1973, The Trial of Chaplain Jensen, 1976, Consumer's Guide to Travel Agencies, 1979; contbr. articles to various mags., including Reader's Digest, Esquire, Parade, Good Housekeeping, Cosmopolitan. BBA., CCNY, 1940; postgrad., Columbia U. Schl. Journalism, 1941, U. Calif., 1942. Syndicated feature writer; feature writer N.Y. Herald Tribune, 1958-67; TV writer; instr. mag. 000ting Nassau Community Coll.; also Congl. press sec.; pub. affairs dir. L.I. Planning Commn., 1974-79. Served with the U.S. Army, World War II. Decorated Bronze Star for outstanding service as corr.; recipient best mag. article award Writers Alliance, 1975, Best Sports Stories award Citadel Press, 1971; pres. Peninsula Public Library. Mem. ASJA (charter), Overseas Press Club. Office: 827 Peninsula Blvd. Woodmere NY 11598

ABSOLON, KAREL B., b. Brno, Czechoslovakia, Mar. 21, 1926; came to U.S., 1948; s. Karel and Valerie (Hauska-Minkusiewicz) A.; m. Mary Joan Bendix, 1954; children: Mary Therese, John Bendix, Peter Henry, Martha Jane. Author: 8 books; contbr. to over 170 publs. MD, Yale U., 1952; MS, U. Minn., PhD, 1963. Asst. prof. surgery U. Minn., Mpls., 1963-66; assoc. prof. surgery Southwestern Med. Schl., Dallas, 1967-70, George Washington U., 1971-76; prof., acad. chmn. U. Ill., Champaign-Urbana, 1977-81; spcl. cons. NIH, Bethesda, Md., 1981-84; cons. intl. health, pres. Kabel Pubs., Rockville, Md., 1985—. Served with M.C., USNR, 1956-58. Fellow ACS; mem. Soc. Arts and Scis. (v.p.), Washington Acad. Scis. Office: Kabel 11225 Huntover Dr Rockville MD 20852

ABT, CLARK C(LAUS), b. Cologne, Ger., Aug. 31, 1929; came to U.S., 1937, naturalized, 1944; m. Wendy Peter, Nov. 3, 1971; children: Thomas Peter, Emily Peter. Author: (with others) The European Arms Control Environment, 1963, Serious Games, 1970, contrib. Short Evaluation Course Evaluation Handbook, 1974, The Social Audit for Management, 1976, ed., The Evaluation of Social Programs, 1977, ed. (with Kenneth J. Arrow and Stephen J. Fitzsimmons), Applied Research for Social Policy, 1979, ed. and contrib., Perspectives on the Cost and Benefits of Applied Social Research, 1979, ed., Problems in American Social Policy Research, 1980, A Strategy for Terminating a Nuclear War, 1985. BS, Massachusetts Institute of Technology, 1951, PhD, 1965; MA, Johns Hopkins U., 1952. Instructor, Johns Hopkins U., 1951-52; sr. staff engineer, Raytheon Co., Bedfored, Mass., 1957-59, mgr. prelim. systems design, Missile and Space Division, 1960-61, mgr. Strategic Studies div., 1962-63, mgr. Advanced systems dept., 1964; founder and president, Abt Associates, Inc., Cambridge, Mass., 1965—. Vis. lecturer, Harvard U., 1968-69, vis. prof. State U. of New York, Binghamton, 1975-76. Founder and pres., Council for Applied Soc. Research, 1977. Mem. bd. dirs., League School of Boston, Inc., 1969, and Theatre Co. of Boston, 1972. Incorporator of Mt. Auburn Hosp., 1980. U.S. Air Force Reserve, 1952-62, active duty as navigator and intelligence officer, 1952-57, to captain. Member: Operations Research Soc. of Am. Thoreau Grand Award for Landscape Arch., 1975, 79. Home: 19 Follen St. Cambridge MA 02138

ABUGEL, JEFFREY, b. Bklyn., Oct. 22, 1952; s. William and Juanita (Stringer) A. Contrbr.: South Bay Mag., 1980, The Argonaut, Atlanta Mag., American Artist. BA, NYU, 1976. Writer, Fairchild Pubns., NYC, 1977-79; mng. ed. Construction Contracting, Redondo Beach, CA, 1979-80, Butane Propane News, Los Angeles, 1980-82; ed./pub. Pacific Surf Mag., Los Angeles, 1982-84; ed. Art material Trade News, Atlanta, 1984-86; ed./pub. Artists Materials Intl., Atlanta, 1986—. Office: Artists Matls 248 Colonial Homes Dr Atlanta GA 30309

ABUSHARIF, IBRAHIM NASEEM, b. Chgo., Sept. 19, 1958; s. Naseem Ibrahim and Zakia (Mahmood) A. Contrbr. article to profl. jnl. Ed.: The Quintesence of the Science of Islamic Jurisprudence, 1986; ed., contrbr.: Islamic Horizons, 1987. BS in Zoology, Southern Ill. U., 1981, BA in Physiology, 1981; MS in Jnlsm., Northwestern U., 1986. Research asst. U. Chgo., 1981-85; co-ed. Islamic Horizons Mag., Chgo., 1987—. Mem. No. Am. Soc. Muslim Jnlsts. Wrtrs. (pres.). Home: 10341 S Lamon Oak Lawn IL 60453

ABZUG, ROBERT HENRY, b. NYC, May 2, 1945; s. Seymour W. and Frances (Wolff) A.; m. Penne L. Restad, Nov. 16, 1980. Author: contrib., Nathan A. Huggins, Maritin Kilson, Daniel Fox, eds., Key Issues in the Afro-American Experience II, 1971, Passionate Liberator: Theodore Dwight Weld and the Dilemma of Reform, 1980, Inside the Vicious Heart: Americans and the Liberation of Nazi Concentration Camps, 1985, ed. (with Stephen E. Maizlish), New Perspectives on Race and Slavery in American, 1986. Contrib. to history jnls. BA magna cum laude, Harvard U., 1967, PhD, U. of Calif. Berkeley, 1977. Instr. in history, U. of Calif., Berkeley, 1976-77, lecturer in history, U. of Calif. Los Angeles, 1977-78, asst. prof., U. of Texas, Austin, 1978-84, assoc. prof. of history, 1984—. Mem. bd. trustees, Carver Museum of Black History, 1981-83, member: Am. Hist. Assn., Org. of Am. Historians, Soc. for Historians of the Early Am. Republic. Office: Dept. History Univ of Texas Austin TX 78712

ACHTERT, WALTER SCOTT, b. Yeadon, PA, May 23, 1943; s. Alfred Carl Robert and Geraldine (Shollenberger) A. AB, Drew U., 1965; MA, NYU, 1966, PhD, 1972. Asst. to exec. dir. MLA, NYC, 1967-72, dir. book publs. and research programs, 1972—; mem. selection jury Common Wealth Award for Lit., 1980—. Author: (with Joseph Gibaldi) MLA Handbook for Writers of Research Papers, Theses and Dissertation, 1977, MLA Style Manual, 1985; editor: MLA Abstracts, 1970-74. Mem. MLA. Home: 166 Bank St New York NY 10014

ACKERMAN, DIANE, b. Waukegan, IL, Oct. 7, 1948; d. Sam and Marcia (Tischler) Fink. Author: On Extended Wings (nonfiction), 1985; The Planets; A Cosmic Pastoral, 1976, 78, Wife of Light, 1978, Lady Faustus (poems), 1983; Twilight of the Tenderfoot (prose memoir), 1980; articles and poetry in lit mags and anthols. Student Boston Univ., 1966-67; BA, Eng., Pennsylvania State Univ., 1970; MFA, Creative Wrtg., Cornell Univ., 1973; MA, Eng., Cornell, 1976; PhD, Eng., Cornell, 1978. NYC slum clearance, 1967; edl. asst., Library Jnl, 1970; lectr., 1978-79, tchg. asst., 1971-78, Cornell; asst. prof., Univ. of Pittsburgh, 1980-83; wrtr-in res., William and Mary, 1982-83; Ohio Univ., 1983; Washington Univ., 1983; Visiting Wrtr, Cooper Union, 1984, 86, Columbia Univ., 1986, NYU, 1986, Cornell Univ., 1987; dir. Writers' Program and wrtr-in-res., Washington Univ. (St. Louis), 1984-86. Pushcart Prize VIII, 1984; Lavan Award, AAP, 1985; NEA Writing Fellowship, 1976, 86. Home: 126 Texas Ln Ithaca NY 14850

ACKERSON, DUANE WRIGHT, JR., s. Duane Wright and Virginia Gale (Rabe) A.; m. Catherine Eleanor McFarland, Aug. 19, 1967; 1 child, Elizabeth Margaret. Author: VA Flight to Chicago, 1971, Works: Edson Benedikt Ackerson, 1972, Old Movie House, 1972, The Lost Refrigerator, 1974, Assembly Room, 1976, Wounds Filled with Light, 1978, The Eggplant & Other Absurdities, 1978; ed. The Dragonfly, 1969-77; co-ed. 54 Prose Poems, 1974; co-translator The Great Mystical Circus (Jorge de Lima), 1978. BA U. Oreg., 1964, MFA, 1967. Instr. English, Salem Coll., Winston-Salem, N.C., 1967-68; dir. creative writing Idaho State U., Pocatello, 1968-74; vis. writer in schls. Artists in Schls. Program, various states, 1974-76; NEA intern, fall 1975; writer-in-residence Willamette U., Salem, Oreg., 1976-78; research analyst Vocat. Rehab. Div., Salem, 1978-79, Oreg. Employment Div., Salem, 1980—. NEA creative writing fellow, 1974. Mem. Sci. Fiction Poetry Assn. (Rhysling award for short poetry 1978, 79). Home: 1850 Corina Dr SE Salem OR 97302

ACKLEY, DANIELLE RENEE, b. Camden, NJ, Apr. 28, 1970; d. Charles Nicholas and Barbara Anne (Ware) A. Author: Taming the Dark, 1985; Mountains and Dark Valleys, 1985; Magic of the Nightworld, 1985. Home: 19 Arbor Meadow Dr Sicklerville NJ 08081

ACKLEY, MARIE, See Wrege, Beth Marie

ACZEL, TAMAS, b. Budapest, Hungary, Dec. 16, 1921, came to U.S., 1966, s. Joseph and Cornelia (Fabian) A.; m. Eva Kadar, Sept. 5, 1948 (div. 1956); m. Olga Anna Gyarmati, Sept. 5, 1959; children—Julia, Thomas George. Novelist: In the Shadow of Liberty, 1949, Storm and Sunshine, 1950, Flames and Ashes, 1953, The Ice Age, 1965, Illuminations, 1981; author: A Song on the Ship (poetry), 1942, Vigilance and Faith (poetry), 1949, In Lieu of a Report (poetry), 1951, On the Secret (poetry), 1956, The Revolt of the Mind: A Case History of Intellectual Resistance Behind the Iron Curtain (with Tibor Meray), 1959, Poetry from the Russian Underground (with Laszlo Tikos and Joseph Langland), 1973, The Literature of Eastern Europe, an Introduction and an Anthology with Bibliography, 1978. BA, U. Budapest, 1948, MA, 1950. Secy. Hungarian Wrtrs. Assn., Budapest, 1950-54; prof. Hungarian Acad. Dramatic Art, Budapest, 1953-56; ed. Star lit. monthly, Budapest, 1951-53, Lit. Gazette, London, 1956-64; prof. English U. Mass., Amherst, 1966—. Recipient Kossuth Prize for Poetry, Budapest, 1949, Stalin Prize for Literature, 1952; NEA fellow, 1976. Mem. PEN-in-Exile (v.p. Am. br.). Home: 34 Amity Pl Amherst MA 01002

ADAMO, RALPH, b. New Orleans, Apr. 28, 1948; s. Joseph and Catherine (Myers) A. Author: The Tiger Who Spoke and Other Poems, 1972, Why We Have Friends, 1975, Sadness at the Private University, 1977, The End of the World, 1979; ed.: Big Easy: An Anthology of New Orleans Poetry, 1978. AB in English, Loyola U., New Orleans, MFA in writing, U. Ark. Prof. English, U. New Orleans, 1975; tchr. English as 2d lang. Assoc. Cath. Charities, New Orleans, 1977-78; tchr. poetry Arts Council, New Orleans, 1978-79; scriptwriter NBC and CBS, NYC, 1979-81; news reporter Gambit Newspaper, New Orleans, 1983—. Mem. WG West, Sal K. Hall Meml. Soc. Home: 6040 Hurst St. New Orleans LA 70118

ADAMS, ALICE, B. Fredericksburg, VA, Aug. 14, 1926; d. Nicholson Barney and Agatha Erskine (Boyd) A.; 1 son, Peter Adams Linenthal. Author: novels Careless Love, 1966, Families and Survivors, 1975, Listening to Billie, 1978, Rich Rewards, 1980, Superior Women, 1984; short story collections Beautiful Girl, 1979, To See You Again, 1982, Return Trips, 1985; contbr. short stories to New Yorker, others. AB, Radcliffe Coll., 1946. Mem. PEN. Address: Knopf 201 E 50th St New York NY 10022

ADAMS, CONSTANCE ALTHEA, b. Westborough, MA, Apr. 10, 1953; d. Luke P. and Helen J. (Goggin) Barton; m. Maynard C. Haskell, July 27, 1973 (dec. Dec. 1, 1974); 1 son, Jerry J. Adams; m. Jay W. Adams, Mar. 5, 1983. Author: (juvenile novel) When Flavias Bloom, 1983; (children's book) Trouble on Birdfeather Hill, 1984; (novel) Peak of Glory, 1985; (screenplay) Image of Glory, 1987, Song in the Night, 1987. Contrbr. articles to mags. Wrkg. on screenplay, novel. Student Way Coll. of Biblical Research and Training, 1979-82. Recipient Happy Heart award Inspirational Romance Wrtrs., 1984. Mem. NWC, SCBW, RWA, Intl. Soc. Dramatists, Northborough Wrtr.'s Group. Home: 8 Myrtle St Westborough MA 01581

ADAMS, ELIE MAYNARD, b. Clarkton, VA, Dec. 29, 1919; s. Wade Hampton and Bessie (Callaway) A.; m. Phyllis Margaret Stevenson, Dec. 22, 1942; children—Steven Maynard, Jill Elaine. Author: The Fundamentals of General Logic, 1954, Logic Problems, 1954, (with others) The Language of Value, 1957, Ethical Naturalism and the Modern World View, 1960, Philosophy and the Modern Mind, 1975, (with others) The Idea of America, 1977; editor: Categorical Analysis: Selected Essays of Everett W. Hall on Philosophy, Value, Knowledge and Mind, 1964, Commonsense Realism, 1966. BA, U. Richmond, 1941, MA, 1944; Colgate-Rochester Div. Sch., (Colgate-Rochesters grad. scholar), 1944; MA, Harvard University, 1947, PhD, 1948. Teaching fellow Harvard U., 1946-47; asst. prof. philosophy Ohio U., 1947-48; asst. prof. U. N.C., 1948-53, assoc. prof., 1953-58, prof., 1958-71, Kenan prof., 1971—, chmn. dept. philosophy, 1960-65, chmn. faculty, 1976-79, chmn. Program in Humanities for Study of Human Values; dir. Curriculum on Peace, War and Defense, 1970-72; adv. com. Natl. Humanities Center, Recipient Thomas Jefferson award, 1971, Outstanding Educator of Am. award, 1971. Mem. Mind Assn., Am. Philo. Assn., N.C. Philos. Soc. (past pres.), So. Soc. Philosophy and Psychology (exec. council 1963-66, pres. 1968-69), Am. Assn. Advancement of Humanities. Home: 813 Old Mill Rd Chapel Hill NC 27514

ADAMS, ELLEN, see Noah, Hope E.

ADAMS, FAY, b. Dinuba, CA; d. Samuel K. and Lulu J. (Harper) Greene; m. William Douglas Adams, Nov. 1, 1924; 1 dau., Marilinda; m. Ernest W. Tiegs, Sept. 1, 1949; m. William S. Noblitt, Mar. 31, 1984. Author: Initiating an Activity Program into a Public School, 1934, Educating America's Children: Elementary School Curriculum and Method, 1954; co-author: Teaching the Bright Pupil, 1928, Man—The Nature Tamer, 1941, Teaching Children How to Read, 1949, Story of Nations, 1952, The Problems of Education, 1938; editor: (with Ernest W. Tiegs) Tiegs-Adams Social Studies Series (books 1-9), 1949, 54, 56, 58, 60, 65, 68, 75-79, 83, Teaching the Social Studies, 1959, 65, California: Your State, 1983. AB, U. So. Calif., 1926, AM, 1929; PhD, Columbia U., 1934. Elementary tchr. pub. schs., Los Angeles, 1924-26, secondary tchr., 1926-29; trng. tchr. U. Calif., Los Angeles, 1929; instr. edn U. So. Calif., 1929-34, asst. prof. edn., also dir. elementary tchr. trng., 1934-40, assoc. prof. edn., 1940-46, prof. edn., 1946—. Mem. Phi Beta Kappa, Kappa Delta, Pi Lambda Theta, Delta Kappa Gamma. Home: 5825 Green Oak Dr Los Angeles CA 90068

ADAMS, HAROLD B, b. Clark, SD, Feb. 20, 1923; s. Lafayette and Wilda W. (Dickey) A.; m. Betty Skogsbergh, Sept. 17, 1949 (div. Apr. 17, 1965); 1 dau., Wendy K. Author: Murder, 1981, Paint the Town Red, 1982, The Missing Moon, 1983, The Naked Liar, 1985, The Fourth Window, 1986, Barbed Wire Noose, 1987, When Rich Men Die, 1987. BA, U. Minn., 1950. Warehouse mgr. Sloan Co., St. Paul, 1953-57; asst. mgr. Better Business Bur., Mpls, 1957-65; exec. dir. Charities Rev., Mpls., 1965—. Trustee, Mpls. Hearing Soc., 1968-70; treas., Natl. Soc. Fund Raising Execs., Mpls., 1973; secy. Health Agcy. Execs., 1975; secy/treas., Minn. United Way Assocs., 1974—. Mem MWA, AG. Address: 12916 Greenwood Rd Minneapolis MN 55343

ADAMS, WILLIAM TAYLOR, b. Phoenix, Jan. 23, 1957; s. John William and Dora Jean (Coe) A. Author training manuals and procedure handbooks; contrbr. articles to profl. and trade publs. Wrkg. on short stories, poems. AA, Glendale Community Coll., 1978; BA in Philosophy, Ariz. State U., 1982. Residence hall dir. Ariz. State U., Tempe., 1982-86; mgr. Tinder box Intl., Scottsdale, Ariz., 1986-87, genl. mgr., 1987—. Home: 8235 N 15th Dr Phoenix AZ 85021

ADAMS-JACOBSON, NANCY, (Nancy Adams) b. Cliffside Park, NJ, Nov. 30, 1952; d. Leo Anthony and Anne Marie (Dombrovska) A.; m. Robert Kirk Jacobson, Apr. 18, 1985. Contrbr. poetry to Anti-War Poems Anthology II, 1986; ed. Antiques Dealer Mag., 1983—. BA, Rutgers Coll., 1980. Editorial asst., R.R. Bowker Co., NYC, 1980-81; asst. ed. Connell Pubns., Miami, FL, 1981-83; ed.-in- chief EBEL-Doctorow Pubns., Clifton, NJ, 1983—. Office: Antiq Dealer 1115 Clifton Ave Clifton NJ 07013

ADAMSON, JOE, b. Cleveland, OH, Dec. 30, 1945; s. Joseph and Janet (Friday) A. Author: Groucho, Harpo, Chico, and Sometimes Zeppo, 1973, Tex Avery: King of Cartoons, 1975, rev. ed., 1985, The Walter Lantz Story, 1985. Contrib., Dictionary of Literary Biography: American Screen writers, vol, 26, 1982; vol. 44, 1986; Byron Haskin, 1984, Stuart Heisler, 1988, both directors Guild of Am. oral histories. Screenplays: Escape to Passion, with James Bryan,

1971: A Political Cartoon, with Jim Morrow 1973; (and editor) The Marx Brothers in a Nutshell, 1982. Author or co-author of other screenplays, including It's an Out of Its Mind World, 1964, The Man Who Owned America, 1965, The Conscience of a King, 1969, Flesh and Blood, 1977. Narration for 14 episodes of Lowell Thomas Remembers. PBS-TV, 1975, seven video presentations, Introduction to Business, 1979, co-author, editor and dir. of W.C. Fields Straight-up, PBS-TV, 1986 (Emmy award for informational spcl.). Work in anthologies, including Film Theory and Criticism, ed. Gerald Mast and Marshall Cohen, 1974, 2d ed. 1979, The American Cartoon, ed. by Gerald and Danny Perry, 1980. Contrib. to many film jnls, including Film Comment, Filmakers Newsletter, Cinema Journal, and American Cinematographer. Attended Gettysburg (Pa.) College, 1963-65, BA cum laude, Univ. of Calif., Los Angeles, 1967, MA, 1970. Instructor, Pennsylvania State Univ., 1970-72, asst. prof. film, 1972-74; freelance writer and film researcher, 1974-80's instructor, Los Angeles City College, 1975, Calif. State Polytechnic Univ., Pomona, 1978, 82, University of Calif., L.A., 1978, 79. Interviewer and historian for Oral History of the Motion Picture in America program, UCLA-American Film Institute, 1968-69 (did Richard Huemer, Fritz Freleng, Dave Fleischer); Office of Special Projects, Directors Guild of America, 1977-79 (did Byron Haskin, Stuart Heisler); Oral History Program of the Astoria Motion Picture and Television Center, 1979. Script reader United Artists, 1978. Asst. to prod. head, Ziv Intl., 1980-81. American Film Inst. Fdn. fellow, 1970. Home: 1210 Washington Ave Santa Monica CA 90403

ADCOCK, ELIZABETH SHARP, (Betty Adcock), b. Fort Worth, TX, Sept. 16, 1938; d. Ralph Lafayette and Sylvia (Hodgins) Sharp; m. Donald Brandt Adcock, June 24, 1957; 1 dau., Sylvia Elizabeth. Author: Walking Out, 1975, Nettles, 1983 (poems), 1983. Lectr., creative writing, Duke U., 1977; wrtr.-in-res., Kalamazoo College, MI, 1983; wrtr.-in-res., Meredith College, Raleigh, NC, 1983—. Awards: NEA fellowship, 1984. Mem. PSA. Home: 817 Runnymede Rd Raleigh NC 27607

ADDAMS, CHARLES SAMUEL, b. Westfield, NJ Jan. 7, 1912; s. Charles Huey and Grace M. (Spear) A.; m. Barbara Day, May 29, 1943 (div. Oct. 1951); m. Barbara Barb, Dec. 1, 1954 (div. 1956); m. Marilyn Matthews, May 21, 1980. Author: Drawn & Quartered, 1942, Addams and Evil, 1947, Monster Rally, 1950, Home Bodies, 1954, Nightcrawlers, 1957, Dear Dead Days, 1959, Black Maria, 1960, The Groaning Board, 1964, The Charles Addams Mother Goose, 1967, My Crowd, 1970, Monster Rally, 1975, Favorite Haunts, 1976, Creature Comforts, 1981. Student, Colgate U., 1929-30, U. Pa., 1930-31, Grand Central Schl. Art, N.Y.C., 1931-32; TV show The Addams Family based on original cartoon characters; drawings in biennial New Yorker Album and The New Yorker War Album, 1942, Mus. Modern Art, NYC. Served with AUS, 1943-46. Recipient Humor award Yale Record, 1954, spcl. award Mystery Writers Am., 1961. Address: New Yorker 25 W 43rd St New York NY 10036

ADDELSON, KATHRYN PYNE, b. Providence, Apr. 22, 1932; d. Joseph Abraham and Catherine (Newton) Etchells; m. Terence Parsons, June 10, 1967 (div.); children—Catherine Casey Pyne, Shawn Pyne; m. 2d, Richard Ullman Addelson, Oct. 31, 1980. AB, Ind. U., 1961; PhD, Stanford U., 1968. Lectr. Bryn Mawr Coll., (Pa.), 1965-66, CCNY, 1966-67; asst. prof. philosophy, U. Ill., Chicago, 1967-72; prof. philosophy Smith Coll., Northampton, Mass., 1972—; assoc. editor Feminist Studies. Contbr. to anthologies and jnls. NEH grantee, 1978-79. Mem. Soc. for Women in Philosophy. Office: Smith College Northampton MA 01060

ADDISON, ERA SCOTT, b. Sparta, TN, Feb. 22, 1933; d. Luther B. and Mattie Mae (Rose) Scott; m. Paul W. Addison, Mar. 31, 1961; children—Valerie p. Sutton, William Zacharay. Columnist Colquitt County Shopper, 1976-79. Contrbr. articles, programs to Church of God Evangel, Herald of Holiness, Peacefinders Yearbook Two, Peacefinders Yearbook Three, Grow and Learn. B.A. in Christian Edn., Lee Coll., 1959; M.A. in Library-Audiovisual Edn., U. Southern Fla., 1972. Spcl. services coord. Southern Ga. Regional Library and Moultrie/ Colquitt-Thomas Co. Library, 1976-79; tchr. Morven Elem. Schl., GA, 1979-80; schl. librarian Quitman Primary Schl., GA, 1981—. Mem. NEA, Ga. Assn. Educators, Brooks, County Assn. Educators. Home: Rt 1 Box 96 Quitman GA 31643

ADDONIZIO, KIM THERESA, b. Washington, July 31, 1954, d. Bob and Pauline (Betz) Addie; 1 dau., Aya Rachel. Author: Crimes of Passion, 1984, Three West Coast Women (with Laurie Duesing and Dorianne Laux), 1987; contrbr. poetry, fiction to Transfer, Poet Lore, Alcatraz 3, Five Fingers Rvw, Across the Generations, Yellow Silk, others; founder Five Fingers Rvw, San Francisco, co-ed., pub., 1982—. BA, San Francisco State U., 1982, MA, 1986. Bookkeeper, Express Auto Parts, San Francisco, 1983—. Mem. Browning Soc., AAP. Office: Five Fingers 100 Valencia St 303 San Francisco CA 94103

ADE, GINNY, b. Corunna, MI, d. Almon L. Calkins and Alice P. (Kelly) Dennis; m. William Ade, Feb. 27, 1949 (div. 1972); children—Terry, Randy, Timothy, Sheryl; m. 2d, C. Richard Sandy, May 1, 1974. Columnist: Sr. World Calif., Sr. World Syndicate, Sr. World of Ariz.; contrbr. travel articles to L.A. Daily News, Home & Away, Herald Examiner Los Angeles, Womens Day, Woodall's Campground Directory, Readers' Digest, Kiwanis Mag., Better Homes & Gardens, Redbook; travel editor Progressive Woman, 1971-74. Mem. SATW, ASJA, OWAA. Home: 9375 Imperial Ave Garden Grove CA 92644

ADLER, C(AROLE) S(CHWERDTFEGER), b. Rockaway Beach, NY, Feb. 23, 1932; d. Oscar Edward Schwerdtfeger and Clarice (Landsberg) Katz; m. Arnold R. Adler, June 23, 1952; children: Steven James, Clifford Paul, Kenneth Gordon. Author: The Magic of the Glits, 1979 (William Allen White award 1982); The Silver Coach, 1979; In Our House Scott Is My Brother, 1980; Shelter on Blue Barns Road, 1981; The Cat That Was Left Behind, 1981; Down by the River, 1981; Footsteps on the Stairs, 1982; The Evidence That Wasn't There, 1982; The Once in a While Hero, 1982; Some Other Summer, 1982; The Shell Lady's Daughter, 1983 (named one of best young adult books of yr. ALA 1983); Get Lost Little Brother, 1983; Roadside Valentine, 1983; Shadows on Little Reef Bay, 1984; Fly Free, 1984; Binding Ties, 1985; With Westie and the Tin Man, 1985; Good-Bye Pink Pig, 1985; Split Sisters, 1986; Kiss the Clown, 1986; Carly's Buck, 1987. BA, Hunter Coll., 1952; MS in Elem. Edn., Russell Sage Coll., 1964. With advt. dept. Worthington Corp., Harrison, N.J., 1952-55; tchr. English, Niskayuna Middle Sch., N.Y., 1969-77. Recipient children's book award NYC Child Study Com., 1986. Mem. AG, Soc. Children's Book Wrtrs. (Golden Kite award for Magic of the Glits, 1979). Home: 1350 Ruffner Rd Schenectady NY 12309

ADLER, CAROL ELLEN, b. Rochester, NY, Dec. 5, 1938, d. Leonard and Helen (Hurvitz) Stalker; m. Samuel Hans Adler, Feb. 14, 1960; children—Deborah Ruth, Naomi Leah. Author poetry books: Arioso, 1975, First Reading, 1984, 1985; contrbr. to: Western Poetry Qtly, Helicon, Facets (featured artist 1975), other lit mags, jnls. AB, U. Mich., 1960. Poet-in-residence Pittsford-Mendon High Schl., Pittsford, N.Y., 1974-75; freelance wrtr., 1974-78; leader workshops ednl. instns., libraries. Winner N.Y. Poetry Forum contest, 1976, Seed-in-Hand contest, 1984. Me. P&W, NY State Lit. Center. Home: 54 Railroad Mills Rd Pittsford NY 14534

ADLER, MARGOT SUSANNA, b. Little Rock, AR, Apr. 16, 1946; d. Kurt Alfred and Freyda (Nacque) A. Author: Drawing Down the Moon; Witches, Druids, Goddess-Worshippers and Other Pagans in America Today, 1979, rev., 1986. Wrkg. on study of religious charisma, annotated 1967 correspondence between Berkeley demonstrator and Vietnam soldier. B.A. in Political Sci., U. Calif., 1968; M.S. in Jnlsm., Columbia U., 1970. Nieman fellow, Harvard U., 1982. Newscaster, Sta. WBAI-FM, NYC 1968-70, talk show host, 1972-77, 78—; Washington bur. chief Pacifica, Washington, 1970-71; reporter Natl. Public Radio, NYC, 1978—. Mem. AG, AFTRA. Home: 333 Central Park W New York NY 10025

ADORJAN, CAROL MADDEN, b. Chgo., Aug. 17, 1934, d. Roland Aloysius and Marie Frances (Toomey) Madden; m. William Walter Adorjan, Aug. 17, 1957; children—Elizabeth M., John M. and Katherine T. (twins), Matthew C. Author: Someone I Know, 1968, Jonathan Bloom's Room, 1972, The Cat Sitter Mystery, 1973, The Electric Man, 1981, Pig Party, 1981; contrbr. short stories to Redbook, N.Am. Rvw., numerous other publs.; author radio and stage plays: Natl. Radio Theater, BBC, Julian Theatre, others. BA, Mundelein Coll., 1956. Artist-in-residence Ill. Arts Council, Chgo., 1982-83, Iowa Arts Council, Dubuque, 1984; leader workshops. Midwest Playwrights Lab. fellow U.Wis., Madison, 1977; grantee IL Arts Council, 1977-78; recipient Ohio State award Radio Group, 1980. Mem. Off Campus Wrtrs. Workshop, Dramatists Guild, P&W. Home: 812 Rosewood St Winnetka IL 60093

AEHEGMA, AELBERT CLARK, see Clark, Albert Carl Vernon

AGNEW, JIM, b. Chgo., Oct. 26, 1945; s. John and Katie (Gallagher) A. Co-author: The Search for James Earl Ray, 1983. Research contributor to numerous books, including Hustlers and Con Men, 1976, Darkest Hours, 1977, Among the Missing, 1979, Murder, America, 1980, Newswordy, 1986. Spcl. assignments for Bill Kurtis, CBS News, Tokyo Rose, 1979, The Chernobyl Project, 1988. Wrkg. on History of the Cherokee Nation and The Trail of Tears with Jack Lesar, UPI. Grad. public schls., Chgo. Mgr., Clark Theatre, Chgo., 1967-69; free-lance researcher, 1969—. Address: 4520 Sheridan Rd Chicago IL 60640

AGNIHOTRI, NEWAL K., b. Balampur, UP, India, Jan. 3, 1941; s. Shriganesh and Kishori

Devi (Tewari) A.; came to U.S., 1971; m. Sukhda, June 1, 1963; children—Anupam, Amita. Ed., Equipment Maintenance and Qualification Nwsltr., 1981—, Nuclear Plant Safety mag., 1983—. MS, Ill. Inst. Tech., 1976. Grad. apprentice, Heavy Electricals, India, 1963-65, maint. engr., 65-71; elect. engr. Sargent & Lundy, Chgo., 1971-76, project engr., 1976-81. Mem. IEEE, ASME, Amer. Nuclear Soc. Office: EQES 779 Roosevelt Rd Glen Ellyn IL 60137

AGOSTINO, JOAN, see Howlett, Joan Gail

A'HEARN, JOAN M., b. NYC, Oct. 10, 1937; d. John Thomas and Kathleen (Nichol) McGee; m. Walter Charles A'Hearn, Jan. 12, 1961 (div. 1978); children—Siobhan, Sheila, Jason. Student NYU, 1958-60, U. Guanajuato, Mex., 1962. Copywriter D'Arcy Advt. Agy., NYC, 1957-59; wrtr. WRSA-Radio, Saratoga Springs, N.Y., 1959-61; wrtr., producer General Electric Co., Fairfield, Conn., 1968—. Mem. Dramatists Guild, AL. Home: 6 West Branch Rd Westport CT 06880

AHERN, THOMAS FRANCIS, (Tom Ahern), b. Holbrook, MA, Aug. 3, 1947; s. Thomas Francis and Hazel (McKay) A. Author: under the name Tom Ahern, The Transcript, 1973, Strangulation of Dreams, 1973, The Sister Pinafore, 1975, A Movie Starring the Late Cary Grant and an As-Yet Unnamed Actress, 1976, The Capture of Trieste, 1978, Hecatombs of Lake, 1984. Contrib. to anthologies, Richard Goldstein, ed., Fresh Meats, 1973, Richard Kostelanetz, ed., In Youth, 1973 and Breakthrough Fictioneers, 1975, Joyce Holland, ed., Alphabet Anthology, 1973, The Poets Encyclopedia, 1979, Richard Peabody and Gretchen Johnson, eds, Fiction 82, 1982. BA, Brown University, 1970 MA, 1973. Publisher, Diana's Press, Providence, R.I., 1972—, co-editor, art director, Eye Witness, 1975—, writing specialist and curriculum coordinator, Center for Career Education in the Arts, Providence, 1976-77, writer, Rhode Island Public Arts Program, 1977, writer-in-residence, Rhode Island State Council on the Arts, 1977-79, dir. of inform., 1981—; journalist, 1979—. Oral historian, freelance graphic designer, programming consultant, Electron Mover (videotape prod. studio), 1979—; consultant to reading series, Providence Parks Dept. National Endowment for the Arts literary fellow, 1980. Home: 71 Elmgrove Ave. Providence RI 02906

AHLSTROEM, G (OESTA) W(ERNER), b. Sandviken, Sweden, Aug. 27, 1918; s. Tage K. J. and Ester V. (Carlsson) A.; m. E. Maria A Brorson Fich, Dec. 20, 1952; children—Parnille (d.), Hans. Author: Psalm Eighty-Nine: Eine Liturgie aus dem Ritual des leidenden Koenigs, 1959, Aspects of Syncretism in Israelite Religion, 1963, contrib. J. C. Rylaarsdam, ed., Transitions in biblical Scholarship, 1968, Joel and the Temple Cult of Jerusalem, 1971, An Israelite God Figurine from Hazor, 1972, contrib., B.A. Pearson, ed., Religious Syncretism in Antiquity, 1975, Royal Administration and National Religion in Ancient Palestine, 1975, In the Shelter of Elyon, ed. by W. Boyd Barrick and John R. Spencer, 1984, An Archaelogical Picture of Iron Age Religions in Ancient Palestine, 1984, Who Were the Israelites?, 1986. Contrib. to encylopedias and profl. jnls. Teol. fil., Univ. of Goeteborg, 1943, Teol. kand., Univ. of Uppsala, Sweden, 1950, Teol. lic., 1954, Teol. Dr., 1959, Fil. kand., 1961. Instructor, Univ. of Uppsala, 1954-59, asst. prof. of Old Testament, Univ. of Chicago, 1959-64, vis. assoc. prof., 1962-63, assoc. prof. 1963-76, prof. of Old Testament and ancient Palestinian studies, 1976—. Annual prof. at W.F. Albright. Inst. of Archaeological Research in Jerusalem, 1969-70. Member of American excavations in Israel, Cyprus, and Tunisia, 1969-77, trustee, 1970-74. Mil. service, Swedish Army, 1939, 41, 44, 60. Member: Amer. Oriental Soc., American Schools of Oriental Research, Archaeological Inst. of Am., Nathan Saederblom Saellskapet (sec. 1960-62), Orphei Drangar, Der Deutsche Verein zur Erforschung Palestinas (pres. (1976-78), Soc. of Biblical Lit., Uppsala Exegetical Soc., Chicago Soc. of Biblical Research. Am. Assn. of Theol. Schls grant for research in Israel and the West Bank, 1969, Guggenheim fellow, 1985-86. Office: Swift Hall U of C Chicago IL 60637

AHO, KATHLEEN GAIL, b. Havre, MT, Feb. 18, 1960; d. Stanley V. and Mary Margaret (Gramlich) Slyngstad; m. Michael Edward Aho, Sept. 1, 1979; 1 child, Johnathon Michael Edward. Contrbr. articles on children and women's topics to Let's Live, East West Jnl., Mil. Lifestyles, Vegetarian Times, Sunday Women Plus. BA in English, U. Mo.-Rolla, 1982. Home: 3405 NW 17th Ave Rochester MN 55901

AIHARA, CORNELLIA, b. Aizu Wakamatsu, Japan, Mar. 31, 1926; d. Hanji and Natsui (Watanabe) Yokota; m. Herman N. Aihara, Dec. 18, 1955; children: Marie and Jiro. Author: (with Herman Aihara) Soybean Diet, 1974, Macrobiotic Child Care, 1979, Calendar Cookbook, 1979, Macrobiotic Kitchen (formerly titled Chico-San Cookbook), 1982, Do of Cooking, 1982, The First Macrobiotic Cookbook, 1984-85. Worker, Chico-San Inc., Chico, Calif., 1962-66; treas. Ohsawa Fdn., Los Angeles, 1966-70, G.O.M.F., San Francisco, 1970-74, Oroville, Calif., 1974—, Vega, Oroville, 1974—. Mem. West Coast Macrobiotic Assn. Home: 2545 Monte Vista Ave Oroville CA 95965

AIHARA, HERMAN, b. Arita, Japan, Sept. 29, 1920; s. Heijiro and Riki (Takayoshi) A.; m. Kazuko Ohtsuka, Feb. 1, 1950 (div. Nov. 1950); m. Cornellia Yokota, Dec. 18, 1955; children: Marie and Jiro. Author: (with George Onsawa) Macrobiotics: An Invitation to Health and Happiness, 1971, (with Cornellia Aihara) Soybean Diet, 1974, Practical Guide to Far Eastern Macrobiotic Medicine, 1976, Learning from Salmon, 1980, Basic Microbiotics, 1985, Acid and Alkaline, 1971, Kaleidoscope, 1986; editor: Book of Judgment, 1980, Sotai Exercise, 1981; also pub. mag. since 1960, currently titled Macrobiotics Today. Wrkg on The Life and Thought of George Ohsawa and Healing at Home. Student G. Ohsawa Macrobiotics Schl., Tokyo, 1944-50; B. of Eng., Waseda U., Tokyo, 1942. Worker, Chico-San, Chico, Calif., 1962-66; pres. Ohsawa Found., Los Angeles, 1966-70, G.O.M.F., San Francisco, 1970-74, Oroville, Calif., 1974—, Vega, Oroville, 1974—. Mem. West Coast Macrobiotic Assn. Home: 2545 Monte Vista Ave Oroville CA 95965

AIKEN, WILLIAM MINOR, b. NYC, Sept. 27, 1932; s. Frank Albert and Margaret (Lloyd) A.; m. Jane Barratt Andrews, Aug. 11, 1962; children—Katherine, Elizabeth, Matthew. Contrbr. articles, poems to popular and lit. mags., anthols. including Wall St. Jnl., Christian Sci. Monitor, Saturday Evening Post, numerous others. Wrkg. on plays. B.A., Trinity Coll., 1954; Ph.D., Boston U., 1976. Instr. to assoc. prof. U. Lowell, MA, 1965-83, prof., 1983—. Home: 807 Preston Ave Blacksburg VA 24060

AINSLIE, TOM, see Carter, Richard

AINSWORTH, CATHERINE HARRIS, b. Elkin, NC, Oct. 5, 1910, d. Edwin Ephram and Catherine Elizabeth (Alexander) Harris; m. Clyde David Eller, Feb. 18, 1931 (dec. 1942); children: Elizabeth Jones, Clyde Harris; m. 2d, Walter Ainsworth, Mar. 29, 1956. Author: Superstitions from Seven Towns of the United States, 1973, Jump Rope Verses Around the United States, 1976, Italian-American Folktales, Black and White and Said All Over-Riddles, 1976, Polish American Folktales, 1977, American Calendar Customs, Vol. I, 1979, Vol. II, 1980, Folktales of America, Vol I, 1980, Vol. II, 1982, Games and Lore of Young Americans (NEA Outstanding Book 1985), 1983, Legends of New York State, 1983, American Folk Foods, 1984, Family Life of Young Americans, 1986. AB, U. N.C., 1931; MA, U. Mich., 1950. Assoc. prof. Niagara County Community Coll., Sanborn, N.Y., 1964-78; mgr. Clyde Press, Buffalo, since 1976. Mem. Am. Folklore Soc., N.Y. Folklore Soc. (past mem. exec. com.), Buffalo and Erie County Hist. Soc. Home: 174 Depew Ave Buffalo NY 14214

AKASHAH, MARY SCOBORIA, b. Bklyn., Jan. 25, 1949; d. Leon Paul and Mary Alice (Ivory) Scoboria; m. Saedeldeen Ahmed Akashah, Sept. 6, 1972 (separated Jan. 22, 1984); children—Mey, Omar. Contrbr. articles to Jnl. Okla. Acad. Scis. Contrbg. ed.: Splash Intl. Mag., 1984—. B.A. in Anthropology, Sociology, Antioch U., 1979; M.S. in Sociology, Okla. State U., 1980. Contrbg. ed. Splash Mag., Sarasota, FL, 1984—, public relations dir., political ed., Splash Mag., 1985-87; copywrtr. Brightill Advt., Sarasota, 1984, 87—. Home: 2460 10th St Englewood FL 34224

AKSYONOV, VASSILY PAVLOVICH, b. Kazan, Volga, USSR, Aug. 20, 1932, came to U.S., 1980, s. Pavel Vassilievich Aksyonov and Eugenia Semionovna (Ginsburg); m. Kira Ludvigouna Mendeleva (div. 1980); 1 son, Alexej; m. 2d, Maya Afanasievna Zmeul, May 30, 1980. Author: The Steel Bird and Other Stories, 1979, The Rendezvous, 1981, The Island of Crimea (novel), 1983, The Paperscape, 1983, The Burn (novel), 1984, Surplussed Barrellware (short stories), 1985, others. Wrkg. on non-fiction book on exile's experience in U.S. MD, Med. Inst., Leningrad, 1956. Wrtr.-in-residence Goucher Coll., Towson, Md., 1983—. Woodrow Wilson fellow, 1981-82. Mem. AL. Home: 4434 Lingan Rd NW Washington DC 20007

ALABISO, ANGELO, (Al), b. Boston, Oct. 19, 1920; s. Vincenzo and Nora (Tabbi) A.; m. Jeanette T., June 3, 1945; children—Vincent J., Nancy J. McLean, Robert, John A. Contrbr. Port Advtg. Handbook; film writer: Boston—Gateway to the West, 1963, Port for New England Export, 1964, Seaward/Westward... Boston, 1966. Stud. N.E. Cons. of Music, 1936-42, Boston U., 1965-66. Ed. Intl. News Svc., Boston, 1941-44; violinist Indpls. Symph., 1944-45, Boston Pops Orch., 1945-48; freelance pub. rel., Boston, 1948-51; pub. rel. mgr. Mass. Port Authority, Boston, 1952-68; ed./pub. Industry Mag., Boston, 1968—. Office: Industry Mag 441 Stuart St Boston MA 02116

ALAZRAKI, JAIME, b. La Rioja, Arg., Jan. 26, 1934, came to U.S., 1962, naturalized, 1973; s. Leon and Clara Antonia (Bolomo) A.; m. Naomi Parver, April 29, 1962; children—Daphne G., Adina Lynn. Author: Poetica y poesiade Pablo Neruda, 1965, La Prosa narrativa de Jorge Luis Borges, 1968, 2d rev. ed., 1974, 3d rev. ed., 1983; Jorge Luis Borges, 1971, El Escritor y la critica: Borges, 1976, ed. (with R. Grass and R. Salmon) and contrbr, Homenaje a Andres Iduarte, 1976, ed (with J. Jvask) and contrbr, The Final Island: The Fiction of Julio Cortazar, 1977, Versiones/ Inversiones/Reversiones: El espejo como modelo estructural del relato en los cuentos de Borges, 1977, Antologia de la novela latino americana, 2 vol., 1987, En busca de unicornio, los cuentos de Julio Cortazar: Elementos para una poetica de lo neofantastico, 1983, Borges and the Kabbalah and Other Essays, 1988. Contrbr to other collections, emcyclopedias, and to profl jnls. BA, Hebrew U. of Jerusalem, 1962, MA, Columbia U., 1964, Ph.D., with honors, 1967. Instructor in Spanish, Columbia U., 1964-67, asst prof, U. of Calif., San Diego, La Jolla, 1967-68, assoc. prof., 1968-71, prof. of Spanish, 1971-77, head of Sp. sec, Dept. of Lit., 1970-74; prof. of romance langs., Harvard, 1977—, head tutor of Span. sec., 1979-82. Vis. prof., U. of Wis., Madison, summer, 1972, and U. of Calif., Los Angeles, 1975-76; vis. fac. mem, Universdad Autonoma de Barcelona, 1985-86. Panelist for summer grant prog., NEH, 1979. Advisor, Guggenheim Memorial Found., 1981—. Member Intl Assn of Hispanists, Intl. Inst. of Ibero-American Lit, MLA, Am. Assn of Tchrs of Span-Port, Argentine Soc. of Writers. Domingo R. Nieto gold medal, Junta de Historia y Litras (La Rioja, Arg.), 1970; Guggenheim fellow, 1971-72, 1983-83, NEH fellow, 1975-76. Home: 324-D Harvard St. Cambridge MA 02139

ALBARELLA, JOAN KATHERINE, b. Buffalo, Sept. 22, 1944, d. John Anthony and Katherine Josephine (DiPasqua) A. Author: Mirror Me, 1973, Poems for the Asking, 1975, Women, Flowers, Fantasy, 1987; ed.: Poetry from the Heart (by Emily Zimpfer), 1979, Husband, Father, Friend (by Ed Martin), 1986. BS, SUNY-Buffalo, 1966,MSEd, 1971. Dir. performing arts Baker Hall, Lacawanna, N.Y., 1980-81; prdn. mgr. Real to Reel TV Show, Buffalo, 1982-83; reporter, photographer WNYCatholic, Buffalo, 1983-86; lectr. SUNY-EOC, 1986—; owner, pub., Alpha Press, Gardenville, N.Y., since 1973; coordinator West Seneca Wrtrs. Club, 1980-85. Named Poet of Yr., Natl. Poetry Press, 1971, 72, 73. Mem P&W, Niagara-Erie Wrtrs., Catholic Press Assn. Home: 3705 Seneca St West Seneca NY 14224

ALBEE, EDWARD FRANKLIN, b. Mar. 12, 1928, Virginia? Adopted s. of Reed A. and Frances Cotter Albee. Plays include The Zoo Story, 1958, The Death of Bessie Smith, 1959, The Sandbox, 1959, The American Dream, 1960, Who's Afraid of Virginia Woolf?, 1961-62, The Ballad of the Sad Cafe (adaptation of Carson McCuller's novella), 1963, Tiny Alice, 1964, Malcolm, 1966, A Delicate Balance, 1966 (Pulitzer Prize winner 1967), Everything in the Garden, 1968, Box, Quotations from Chairman Mao, 1970, All Over, 1971, Seascape, 1975, Counting the Ways, 1976, Listening, 1977, The Man Who Had Three Arms, 1983, The Lady from Dubuque, 1978-79; adaptation of Lolita (Nabokov), 1980. Student, Trinity Coll., Hartford, Conn. Continuity writer WYNC radio station; office boy Warwick & Legles (advt. agcy.); record salesman, G. Schwirmer, Inc., mus. pub.; messenger, Western Union, 1955-58; counterman for luncheonette Manhattan Towers Hotel. Producer with Richard Barr and Clinton Wilder, N.Y. Playwrights Unit Workshop, 1963; dir. of touring retrospective (one-acts) Albee Directs Albee, 1978-79; co-director, Vivian Beaumont Theat., Lincoln Center for the Performing Arts, 1979; founder William Flanagan Center for Creative Persons in Montauk, 1971; mem. of Natl. Endow. grant-giving council. Com. chmn Brandeis U. Creative Arts Awards, 1983, 84. Pres. Edward F. Albee Fdn. Recipient Pulitzer Prize, 1967, 75. Gold medal in Drama AAIAL, 1980. Mem. Natl. Inst. Arts and Letters. Address: 14 Harrison St New York NY 10013

ALBERT, DAVID H., b. Bronx, NY, Feb. 13, 1950; s. Bertram S. Albert and Pearl Toby (Stricker) Harris. Author: Working Toward a New Society and a Critique of American Marxism, 1978, People Power: Applying Nonviolence Theory, 1985; editor: Tell the American People: Perspectives on the Iranian Revolution, 1980; also editor numerous books and articles. Media relations dir. Fellowship Commn., Phila., 1976-85; instr. English and jnlsm. Community Coll. of Phila., 1977-83; lectr. in residence Grandhigram Rural U., Tamil Nadu, India, 1981; pub., chief exec. officer New Soc. Pubs., Phila., 1981—. Founder, bd. dirs. New Soc. Ednl. Found., Phila. 1981—; bd. dirs. Pa. Council to Abolish Penalty of Death, Phila., 1981-87, Natl. Coalition Against Death Penalty, 1982-87, A.J. Muste Meml. Inst., NYC, 1985-87. Carroll Wilson scholar Oxford U., 1971-73; U. Chgo. humanities fellow, 1973-76. Mem. Phila. Pubs. Group; founding member Quakers United in Publishing (QUIP), 1982—. Home: Box 582 Santa Cruz CA 95061

ALBRECHT, PEGGY STODDARD, (Margaret Burgess), b. Indpls., May 2, 1919; d. Albert B. and Ann Louise (Orvis) Burgess; m. Ralph Glenn Albrecht, July 9, 1938; children—Douglas, Ann, Ronald. Author: (young readers novels) Secret of the Old House, 1982, Eyes in the Bombax Tree, 1982, The House Beyond Congo Cross, 1982, The Ainesworth Prowler, 1985. Contrbr. short stories, articles to mags. including the Christian Wrtr., SSI-Student, Upward. Wrkg. on novel for young readers, short story collection. Missionary, United Brethern Ch., Sierra Leone, West Africa, 1958-71; now free-lance wrtr. Mem. Nat. Evangelical Wrtr.'s Soc., Christian WG. Home: 3120 Aloha Ave Englewood FL 34224

ALBRIGHT, GLEN PATRICK, b. Newark, Oct. 12, 1956; s. John Patrick and Natalie (Iarossi) A.; m. Mary Elizabeth Osgoodby, June 12, 1983. Contrbr. poems to Chimaera, Comment, Creative Yrs., The Young American, BA, Seton Hall U., 1980, MA, 1982. Tchr. English, St. Benedicts Prep. Schl., Neward, 1980-82, Seton Hall Prep. Schl., West Orange, N.J., 1985—; tchr. reading Our Lady of Sorrows Schl., South Orange, N.J., 1982-85; tchr. oral communication Seton Hall U., South Orange, 1983—. Home: 942 Liberty Ave Union NJ 07083

ALBRIGHT, NANCY EGGELHOF, b. Indpls., Nov. 3, 1940; d. Ralph Holman and Beulah Edith (Brandon) Eggelhof; m. Robert E. Purdy, Feb. 25, 1967 (dec. Sept. 30, 1967); m. Jack H. Albright, Dec. 9, 1979. Contrbr. poem to lit mag.; articles to mags. Ed.: The Administration of Criminal Justice (Remington), 1969, Crash Course AI (Frenzel), 1986, VM/CMS Handbook (Fosdick), 1987, Mastering Turbo Pascal Files (Swan), 1987. B.M., Ind. U., 1963, M.M., 1965. Ed., Bobbs-Merrill Pub., Indpls., 1968-70, Stone Mag., 1970-72; wrtr., ed., Curtis Publ. Co., Indpls., 1970-72, ed., pub., 1972-79; ed., pub. Design Mag., Indpls., 1972-75, Ind. Bus., Indpls., 1972-79, Demolition Age, Indpls., 1972-79; Ind. Architect, Indpls., 1979-80; EXPO Mag., Indpls., 1979, 81, v.p. The Saturday Evening Post Co., Indpls., 1979; pres. Albright Communications, Inc., Indpls., 1979—; free-lance wrtr., 1979—. Mem. Women in Pub. Office: 2802G Barbary Ln Indianapolis IN 46205

ALCOSSER, SANDRA B., b. Washington, Feb. 3, 1944; d. Karl R. and Bernetta Elaine (Hutson) Weis; m. Murray Alcosser, June, 1972 (div. Oct. 1977); m. 2d, Philip Maechling, May 10, 1978. Author: Each Bone a Prayer, 1982, A Fish to Feed All Hunger, 1986. Contrbr. poems, fiction to lit. mags., popular mags. Editor: Cut Bank, 1979-82. BA, Purdue U., 1966; MFA, U. Mont.-Missoula, 1982. Dir., Poets in the Park, NYC, 1975-77; artist-in-residence, Ia. and Mont., 1977-82; asst. prof. La. State U., Baton Rouge, 1982—; assoc. prof. San Diego State U., Calif., 1985—. Recipient Mary Elinore Smith Poetry prize Am. Scholar, 1983, Syndicated Fiction Project award PEN, 1986; fellow NEA, 1985. Mem. P&W, AWP (Series winner in poetry 1984). Home: NW 5791 W County Line Rd Florence MT 59833

ALDAN, DAISY, b. NYC, Sept. 16, 1923; d. Louis and Esther (Edelheit) A. Author: The Destruction of Cathedrals and Other Poems, 1964, Journey, 1970, 1 plus 1 equals 1 (with Elaine Mendlowitz), 1970, Or Learn to Walk on Water, 1970 (2nd. ed. 1980), Seven: Seven, 1970, The Masks Are Becoming Faces, Breakthrough, 1971, Love Poems of Daisy Aldan, 1978, Stones, 1973, Verses for the Zodiac, 1975, Between High Tides, 1978, A Golden Story (novella), 1979, Poetry and Consciousness, 1979, Contemporary Poetry and the Evolution of Consciousness, 1981, The Art and Craft of Poetry, 1982, In Passage (poetry), 1987, Shakespeare and Spectator Consciousness, 1987; many poems in lit mags U.S. and abroad. Teacher of creative writing and pedagogy NYC, England, Switzerland. Translations from French and German for books. BA, Hunter College; MA, Brooklyn College. Doctorate in Lit, Free University of Pakistan (Karachi). Editor, Folder Editions, NY (also pub.), Tiber Press, Two Cities lit mag (bilingual; publd. Paris), various poetry anthols. Home: 260 W 52 St New York NY 10017

ALDRIDGE, JOHN WATSON, b. Sioux City, IA, Sept. 26, 1922; s. Walter Copher and Nell (Watson) A.; m. Leslie Felker, Dec. 10, 1954 (div. June 1968); 1 son, Geoffrey; children by previous marriages: Henry, Stephen, Leslie, Jeremy; m. Alexandra Bertash, July 13, 1968 (div. Dec. 1982); m. Patricia McGuire Eby, July 16, 1983. Author: After the Lost Generation, 1951, Critiques and Essays on Modern Fiction, 1952, In Search of Heresy, 1956, The Party at Cranton, 1960, Time to Murder and Create, 1966, In the Country of the Young, 1970, The Devil in the Fire, 1972, The American Novel and the Way We Live Now, 1983; editor: Selected Stories by P.G. Wodehouse, 1958. Student, U. Chattanooga, 1940-43; fellow, Bread Loaf Schl. English, summer 1942; BA, U. Calif.-Berkeley, 1947. Lectr. English U. Vt., 1948-50, asst. prof. 1950-53, 54-55; lectr Christian Gauss Seminars Criticism, Princeton, 1953-54; mem. lit. faculty Sarah Lawrence Coll., also New School Soc. Research, 1957; prof. English Queens Coll., 1957; Berg prof. English N.Y.U., 1958; Fulbright lectr. U. Munich, Germany, 1958-59; writer-in-residence Hollins Coll., 1960-62; Fulbright lectr. U. Copenhagen, Denmark, 1962-63; prof. English, U. Mich., 1964—; book critic N.Y. Herald Tribune Book Week, 1965-66, Saturday Review, 1970-79; Staff Bread Loaf Writers Conf., 1966-69; chief regional judge BOMC Writing Fellowship Program, 1966-67; spcl. adviser for Am. studies U.S. embassy, Germany, 1972-73. Served with AUS, 1943-45, ETO. Decorated Bronze Star medal; Rockefeller humanities fellow, 1976-77. Mem. AL and AL of Am., MLA, Natl. Book Critics Circle, PEN. Home: 1050 Wall St Ann Arbor MI 48105

ALDRIDGE, RAY, b. Syracuse, NY, July 6, 1948; s. Raymon Huebert and Muriel June (Rice) A.; m. Nancy Ann Federoff, May 18, 1984. Contrbr.: Writers of the Future (vol. II), Amazing Stories, other publs. Wrkg. on novels. Potter, glass designer, 1973—. Served as sgt. U.S.A.F., 1969-73; Vietnam. Mem. SFWA. Home: 389 N. Gardner Dr Fort Walton Beach FL 32548

ALENIER, KARREN LALONDE, b. Cheverly, MD, May 5, 1947; d. Rona Lee (Bass) Keenan; 1 son, Ivan Ascher Alenier. Author: Wandering on the Outside, 1975, The Dancer's Muse, 1981; editor: Whose Woods These Are, 1983. BA with honors, U. of Md., 1969. Editor, Word Works, Washington DC, 1977—; pres. & chairperson Bd. Dir., Word Works, 1984—.Mem. PSA, Writer's Center of Greater Washington. Home: 4601 N Park Ave Chevy Chase MD 20815

ALES, BEVERLY GLORIA, b. La Place, LA, Aug. 16, 1928; d. William Pinckney and Clementine Marie (Madere) Rushing; m. Warren Vincent Ales, Dec. 29, 1946; children—Merrick Vance, Sherry Ann, Lori Patrice. Poetry in anthologies. Wrkg. on short stories for children. Artist, Owner, dir. Art Gallery, New Orleans and Metairie, 1975-82, Tchr. art & art therapy Magnulia Spcl. Schl. Served as pres. numerous art orgns. Home: 1149 Melody Dr Metairie LA 70002

ALEXANDER, CHARLOTTE ANNE, b. Evansville, IN; d. Carson Gilbert and Ruth Catherine (Bristow) Alexander. Contrbr. poems to popular mags.; editor Outerbridge, 1975—. BA, Indiana U., 1956, MA, 1960, PhD, 1962. Assoc. prof., The College of Staten Island (CUNY), 1967—. CUNY Research Fdn. grants, 1975, 77. Mem. AWP. Home: 112 E 10th St New York NY 10003

ALEXANDER, DIANE, b. Boston; d. Adolphus Lot and Kathryn Glade (Latimer) A. Author: Playhouse (forward by Raymond Burr), 1984, Fitness in a Chair: For the Lazy, the Busy and the Movement-Impaired, 1985. MA in anthropology, U. So. Calif., MPH, U. Calif.-Berkeley. Mem. Intl. Alert, Not Yet New York. Mem. Women's Natl. Book Assn. Founder: Stop Genocide. Office: Dorleac-Macl 5100 Longfellow St Los Angeles CA 90042

ALEXANDER, E. CURTIS, (Mwalima Imara Mwadilifu), b. Norfolk, VA, Sept. 24, 1941; s. Albert T. and Fidellia (Holley) A.; m. Barbara Elaine Johnson, July 2, 1966; children—Kwame, Lesa, Nataki, Ade. Works incl.: Module Curric. Guide—Refer. Wks. of Yosef ben-Jochannan, 1979, Doc Ben Speaks Out, 1980, Axioms & Quots. of Yosef ben-Jochannan, 1981, Elijah Muhammad on Afr. Amer. Educ., 1982, Adam Clayton Powell, Jr., A Black Power Polit. Educator, 1983, Cheikh Anta Diop—An Afr. Scientist, 1984, Richard Allen—The First Exemplar of Afr. Amer. Educ., 1985. EdD, Columbia U., NYC, 1974. Pres., ECG Associates, Chesapeake, VA, 1977—; columnist Norfolk Jnl. and Guide (VA), 1979—; adjunct prof. Vermont Coll. of Norwich U., NYC, 1985—. Home: Box 15004 Chesapeake VA 23320

ALEXANDER, FLOYCE, b. Fort Smith, AR, Dec. 31, 1938; s. Manual Romain and Velma Lorene (Brown) A.; m. Karen Lee Clarke (div. 1983); m. 2d, Margaret Randall, Feb. 1984. Author: Ravines, 1971, Machete, 1972, Bottom Falling Out of the Dream, 1976, Red Deer, 1982; editor: Iron Country: Contemporary Writing in Washington State, 1978. BA, U. Wash.-Seattle, 1962; MA, Wash. State U.-Pullman, 1971; MFA, U. Mass.-Amherst, 1974; doctoral candidate in Am. Studies, U. N.Mex., 1978—. Editor, Wash. State U. Press, Pullman, 1963-70; tchg. asst. English, Wash. State U., Pullman, 1970-71; U. Mass., Amherst, 1972-74; U. N.Mex., Albuquerque, 1975-76, 78-81; free-lance wrtr., ed., Albuquerque, 1982—. Office: 1502 Silver Ave SE Albuquerque NM 87106

ALEXANDER, FRANK SCOTT, b. San Diego, Feb. 20, 1943; s. Claude Emitt and Bette Jane (Wheir) A.; m. Diane Andrea Pettitt, Apr. 12, 1980; 1 son—Jay B. Ed./pub. "movement education" materials for classroom tchrs., P.E. tchrs., curric. dirs., coll. profs., occupl. therapists, and parents. BS in poli. sci., Utah State U., 1965; MA in tchg., Stanford U., 1968. Peace Corps, Colombia, 1965-67, "rural community action"; curric. writer/cslr. Clinton Job Corps, IA, 1968-69; tchr. math & Engl., Tongue Point Job Corps, Astoria, OR, 1969-71; freelance salesperson and rptr. Daily Astorian (OR), 1971-72; ed./writer Prof. Dev. Systems, Berkeley, CA, 1973-74; ed./pub. Front Row Experience, Byron, CA, 1974—. Office: Front Row 540 Discovery Bay Blvd Byron CA 94514

ALEXANDER, LLOYD CHUDLEY, b. Phila., Jan. 30, 1924; s. Alan Audley and Edna (Chudley) A.; m. Janine Denni, Jan. 8, 1946; 1 dau., Madeleine (Mrs. Zohair Khalil). Author: And Let the Credit Go, 1955, My Five Tigers, 1956, Janine is French, 1958, August Bondi, 1958, My Love Affair with Music, 1960, Aaron Lopez, 1960, Time Cat, 1963, Fifty Years in the Doghouse, 1964, (with Dr. Louis J. Camuti) Park Avenue Vet, 1962, The Book of Three, 1964, The Black Cauldron, 1965, Coll and His White Pig, 1965, The Castle of Llyr, 1966, Taran Wanderer, 1967, The Truthful Harp, 1967, The High King, 1968 (Newbery medal 1969), The Marvelous Misadventures of Sebastian, 1970 (Natl. Book award 1971), The King's Fountain, 1971, The Four Donkeys, 1972, The Foundling, 1973, The Cat Who Wished to Be a Man, 1973, The Wizard in the Tree, 1975, The Town Cats, 1977, The First Two Lives of Lukas-Kasha, 1978, Westmark, 1981 (Am. Book award 1982), The Kestrel, 1982, The Beggar Queen, 1984, The Illyrian Adventure, 1986, The El Dorado Adventure, 1987; trans. (Paul Eluard) Selected Writings (1950), (Jean-Paul Sartre) The Wall, 1951, Nausea, 1953, (Paul Vialar) The Sea rose, 1951. Student, West Chester (Pa.) State Coll., 1942, Lafayette Coll., 1943, U. Paris, 1946. Freelance writer and translator, 1946—, cartoonist, pianist, advt. writer, mag. editor, 1948—; author-in-residence Temple U., 1970. Regina Medal, 1986, Helen Keating Ott Award, 1987. Bd. dirs. Carpenter Lane Chamber Music Soc., Phila. Served with AUS World War II. Mem. AL of Am., PEN. Address: 1005 Drexel Ave Drexel Hill PA 19026

ALEXANDER, PAMELA, b. Natick, MA, Apr. 2, 1948; d. Edward Harrison and Muriel Helen (Corliss) A. Author: Navigable Waterways, 1984; contrbr. poems to Epos, The Atlantic, Field, Poetry, Anima, Antioch, Yale rvws, Poetry Now, Ardis Anthology of New Am. Poetry, The U.S. in Literature, 1979, Question and Form in Literature, 1979. BA, Bates Coll., 1970; MFA, U. Iowa, 1973. Reporter Middlesex News, Framingham, Mass., 1973-75; fellow Fine Arts Work Ctr., Provincetown, Mass., 1975-77; ed. Linguistic Systems, Cambridge, Mass., 1977-81; administrv. asst. MIT, Cambridge, 1981-85, instr., MIT, 1985-86; Bunting fellow, 1985—. Recipient Yale Younger Poet award Yale U. Press, 1984. Mem. AAP, P&W. Home: 141 Western Ave Cambridge MA 02139

ALEXANDER, SHANA, b. NYC, Oct. 6, 1925; d. Milton and Cecelia (Rubenstein) Ager; m. Stephen Alexander, 1951 (div.); 1 dau. Katherine. Author: The Feminine Eye, 1970, Shana Alexander's State-by-State Guide to Women's Legal Rights, 1975, Talking Woman, 1976, Anyone's Daughter, 1979, Very Much a Lady: The Untold Story of Jean Harris and Dr. Herman Tarnower, 1983, Appearance of Evil: The Trial of Patty Hearst, Nutcracker: Money, Madness, Murder, 1985. Student, Vassar Coll., 1942-45. With PM, 1944-46, Harper's Bazaar, 1946-47; with Flair, 1950; reporter Life mag., 1951-61, staff writer, 1961-64; writer twice monthly column The Feminine eye, 1964-69; editor McCall's mag., N.Y.C., 1969-71; v. p. Norton Simon Communications, Inc., 1971-72; radio and TV commentator Spectrum CBS News, 1971-72; columnist, contbg. editor Newsweek, 1972-75; commentator CBS 60 Minutes, 1975-79; bd. dirs. Am. Film. Inst. Recipient Sigma Delta Chi and U. So. Cal. Natl. Journalism award, 1965, Los Angeles Times Woman of Year award, 1967, Golden Pen award Am. Newspaper Womens club, 1969, Front Page awrd Newswomen's Club N.Y., 1973, Matrix award N.Y. Women in Communications, 1973-74, Spirit of Achievement award Albert Einstein Coll. Med., 1976; Creative Arts award Natl. Women's div. Am. Jewish Congress. Office: 444 Madison Ave New York NY 10022

ALEXANDER, THOMAS F., b. Ithaca, NY, Apr. 26, 1951; m. Nancy Alexander, Dec. 14, 1979. Editor/pub.: Sinsemilla Tips Magazine, 1980—. BS in Business Admin. U. of New Haven, 1973. Mem. New Pages, COSMEP. Office: Box 2046 Corvallis OR 97339

ALEXANDRE, LEAH, see Seagull, Samantha Singer

ALFRED, WILLIAM, b. NYC., Aug. 16, 1922; s. Thomas Allfrey and Mary (Bunyan) A. Author: The Annunciation Rosary, 1948; verse plays Agamemnon, 1954, Hogan's Goat, 1956, Cry For Us All, 1970, To Your Heart's Desire, 1978, Nothing Doing, 1978; contbr. poems, articles, to profl. jnls.; co-editor: Of Reformation, The Prose Works of John Milton, 1954; assoc. editor: American Poet, 1942-44. BA, Bklyn., Coll., 1948; MA, Harvard U., 1949, Ph.D., 1954. Mem. faculty Harvard U., 1954—, prof. English, 1963—. Served with AUS, 1943-46. Creative Arts Theatre grantee Brandeis U., 1960; Amy Lowell Travelling Poetry scholar, 1956; Natl. Inst. Arts and Letters grantee. Mem. Mediaeval Acad. Am., MLA, Dramatists Guild. Home: 31 Athens Cambridge MA 02138

ALFREDS, JOE, see Callanan, Joseph A.

ALFREDSON, JENS, see Jensen, Dale Alan

ALFS, MATTHEW GERD, b. Duluth, MN, Nov. 2, 1956; s. James Gerd and Diane Marie (Salo) A.; m. Cheryl Ann Gatchell, Apr. 17, 1977; children—Justin Frederick and Stephanie Marie. Author: concepts of Father, Son, and Holy Spirit, 1984. Wrkg. on The "Catalytic" Religion of Jehovah's Witnesses and the Angel Christology:

Christ as Angel in Early Christianity (3 vols.). Owner, operator Old Theology Book House, Mpls., 1978—. Office: Box 11337 Minneapolis MN 55411

ALGER, DEREK S., b. San Francisco, s. Ian Ewart and Elizabeth Joyce (Cannon) A. Author: Confrontation, 1981. BA in poli. sci., NYU, 1977; MFA in fiction wrtg., Columbia U., 1983. Public affairs wrtr. City N.Y. Dept. Genl. Services, 1980-82; reporter The Press Jnl., Englewood, N.J., 1984-85, Co-op City Times, Bronx, N.Y., 1985-86, The Chief, NY, NY, 1986; assoc. ed. City News, Bronx, NY, 1987—; wrtg. instr., Matrix wrkshop., 1986—. Edl. bd., contrbg. ed. New Vision mag., 1987—. Recipient Disting. Achievement in Short Story award Fla. Freelance Wrtrs. Assn., 1984. Mem. AWP. Home: 108 Ottawa Ave Hasbrouck Heights NJ 07604

ALI, AGHA SHAHID, b. New Delhi, India, Feb. 4, 1949, s. Agha Ashraf and Sufia Ashraf (Nomani) A. Author: Bone-Sculpture (poetry), 1972, In Memory of Begum Akhtar (poetry), 1979, T.S. Eliot as Editor (scholarly), 1986, The Half-Inch Himalayas (poetry), 1987. Contrbr. poetry, translations, rvws. to Ariel, Crazyhorse, Helix, Xanadu, numerous other lit mags. Wrkg. on translations of Faiz Ahmed Faiz. MA, Pa. State U., 1981, PhD, 1984; MFA, U. Ariz., 1985. Lectr. English, U. Delhi, India, 1970-75; instr. Pa. State U., University Park, 1976-83; grad. asst. U. Ariz., Tucson, 1983-85; communications ed. JNC Cos., Tucson, 1985—. Breadloaf Wrtrs.' Conf. scholar, 1982, 83; poetry fellow Pa. Council on Arts, 1983. Home: 3801 N Pasatiempo Pl Tucson AZ 85705

ALI, SHAHRAZAD, b. Cin., Feb. 5, 1947, d. Harry and Lucy (Marshall) Levy; m. Solomon Ali, Aug. 17, 1965; children: Pamela, Hassan, Fatima. Author: How Not to Eat Pork (or Life Without the Pig), 1985. Wrkg. on study of polygamy versus monogamy. Student Xavier U., 1964-66, Ga. State U., 1979-80. News and feature ed. Cin. Call Newspaper, 1966-67, Cin. Post, 1966-67; contrbg. ed. Cin. Enquirer, 1965-67, Cin. Herald, 1966-67; ed. Cin. Hi-Lites Mag., 1967-75; nutritionist, freelance wrtr.; mem. staff Temple U., Phila., Clark Coll., Atlanta, GA, Phila. Community Coll. Named one of Top Ga. Authors, Atlanta-Fulton Public Library, 1985. Office: Box 50377 Atlanta GA 30302

ALIESAN, JODY, b. Kansas City, MO, Apr. 22, 1943; d. John David and Minerva Anna (Elliss) Armstrong. Author: Soul Claiming, 1975; as if it will matter, 1978; Desire: Poems 1978-82, 1985; (chapbooks) Thunder in the Sun, 1971, To Set Free, 1972, Doing Least Harm, 1985; contrbr. to anthologies including Iron Country: Contemporary Writing in Washington State, 1978, Leaving the Bough: 50 American Poets of the 80's, 1982, Rain in the Forest, Light in the Trees: Contemporary Poetry from the Northwest, 1983. BA, Occidental Coll., 1965, MA, Brandeis U., 1966, postgrad., 1966-68. Tchr., wrtr., 1968—. NEA lit. fellow, 1978; King Country Arts Commn. grantee, 1979; artist-in-residence Seattle Arts Commn., 1983. Mem. Feminist Wrtrs. Guild, Phi Beta Kappa. Home: Genl Delivery Waldron WA 98297

ALKALAY-GUT, KAREN, b. London, England, Mar. 29, 1945; d. Louis and Doris (Kaganovich) Rosenstein; came to U.S., 1948; m. Nissim Alkalay, July 4, 1967 (div. Mar. 1979); children—Orit, Oren; m. 2d, Ezra Gut, July 30, 1980. Author: Alone in the Dawn: The Life of Adelaide Crapsey, 1988; poetry: Mechitza, 1986, Butter Sculptures, 1983, Making Love, 1980; contrbr numerous mags. BA, U. Rochester, 1966, MA, 1967, PhD, 1975. Lectr., Tel Aviv U., Ramat Aviv, Israel, 1977—; vis. scholar, Columbia U., N.Y.C., 1984—; lectr., U. Negev, Beer Sheva, Israel, 1972-76; instr., SUNY, Geneseo, NY, 1967-70. Arie Dulchin Award, Jewish Agency, Israel, 1985; Travel Award, Fulbright, Austria, 1982. Mem. MLA, PEN, PSA, chmn. Israel Assoc. of Wrtrs. in English, 1982-84. Home: 92 Univ St Ramat Aviv 69345 Israel

ALLARDT, LINDA, b. Brecksville, OH, June 9, 1926; d. Ernst William and Lucile (Clark) A.; m. George A. Gallasch, Apr. 20, 1957; children: Robert George, Margaret Ellen. Author: (poems) The Names of the Survivors, 1979; Seeing for You, 1981; ed. Jnls. and Miscellaneous Notebooks of Ralph Waldo Emerson, Vol. 12, 1976, co-ed., Vol. 15, 1982; co-ed. Poetry Notebooks of Ralph Waldo Emerson, 1986; contrbr. poems to Cin. Rvw, Poetry N.W., Negative Capability, Poetry Now, Chiaroscuro, Cat's Eye, also others. BA, Alfred U., 1948; MA, Middlebury Coll., 1955; PhD, U. Rochester, 1977; Chemist Eastman Kodak Co., Rochester, N.Y., 1948-56; research assoc. U. Rochester, 1970-76, asst. prof. English, 1976—; assoc. ed. State Street Press, Pittsford, N.Y., 1982—. Recipient Borestone Mountain Poetry awards, 1969-75, Hackney Lit. awards, 1973, 74, 80, 81, Elliston spcl. distinction award, 1980, Lilian Fairchild award, 1980. Mem. MLA, AWP. Home: 2 Ann Lynn Rd Pittsford NY 14534

ALLBERY, DEBRA L., b. Lancaster, OH, Mar. 3, 1957, d. James Dean and Janice Darlene (Starr) Allbery. Contrbr. poetry to Poetry, Tendril, Ploughshares, Prairie Schooner, Iowa Rvw, Kenyon Rvw, other lit mags; contrbr. to anthologies: Chester Jones Fdn. Natl. Poetry Competition Winners, 1984, Denny Poems, 1984, The Creative Process: Ten Years at Ragdale, 1986. BA, Coll. Wooster, Ohio, 1979; MFA, U. Iowa, 1982. Poet-in-residence Phillips Exeter (N.H.) Acad., 1985-86. Recipient scholarship Ragdale Fdn., Lake Forest, Ill., 1983, Ind. U. Wrtrs.' Conf., Bloomington, 1984; artist-in-residence, Wis. Arts Bd., 1986-87; NEA fellowship, 1986; George Bennett fellow Phillips Exeter Acad., 1985-86. Mem. AWP, AAP, Phi Beta Kappa. Home: Edgerly- Garrison Rd Durham NH 03824

ALLEN, BEN, see Bell, Victor L.

ALLEN, BLAIR H., b. Los Angeles, July 2, 1933, s. Wendall Boyd and Ethel Rose (Williams) A.; m. Juanita Aguilar Raya, Jan. 27, 1968; children—Theresa A., Geoffery C. Author: Televisual Po-Ums for Bloodshot Eyeballs, 1973, Malice in Blunderland (satire), 1974, N/Z, 1979, The Atlantis Trilogy (poetry), 1982, DreamWish of the Magician (poetry), 1983, Right Through the Silver-Lined 1984 Looking Glass (poetry), 1984, other poetry chapbooks; ed.: The Magical World of David Cole, 1984, Snow Summits in the Sun, 1987. Wrkg. on novels, poetry collections, anthology editing. AA in Social Studies, San Diego City Coll., 1964; student U. Wash., 1965-66; BA in Graphic Art, San Diego State U., 1970. Former book reviewer Los Angeles Times; now spcl. feature ed. Cerulean Press, Kent Publs. Served with USMC, 1953-59; Korea. Mem. Beyond Baroque Fdn., Calif. State Poetry Soc., AAP, The Medina Fdn. Home: 9651 Estacia Ct Cucumonga CA 91730

ALLEN, BUCK, b. Powell County, KY, Nov. 17, 1925; s. Rex and Henrietta (Townsend) A.; m. Misako Furukawa; children—Allen Rex. contrbr. numerous poems to mags., newspapers including Good Old Days, Amazing Stories, others. Wrkg. on rhyming verses. B. S. in Psychology and Edn., William Carey Coll., 1972. Claims representative U.S. Dept. Social Security, Benton Harbor, MI, 1973-82; security guard Burns Security Services, St. Joseph, MI, 1987—. Home: 100 Niles Ave Lot 29 Berrien Springs MI 49103

ALLEN, CAROLYN SESSIONS, b. Salt Lake City, Sept. 22, 1939; d. Dwight Bentley and Audrey Elizabeth (Wolcott) S.; m. Jack Edward Allen, June 15, 1960; children—Michele Diane Merrill, Scott Daniel, Paul Bentley, Jennifer Joy, Wayne Russell. Author: From Here to Maternity, 1987. Contrbr. articles to (Newsletters) Early Morning Alarm, The Sixth Sense, Lane Lines; (mags) Children's Friend, The Ensign, The New Era; (newspapers) Latter-Day Sentinel, The Daily Pilot, Ch. News; designer, developer, ed. (newsletter) The North Stake News. Student U. Southern Calif., 1957-60; B.A. Calif. State U.-Long Beach, 1962. Substitute tchr. Indian Wells Schl. Dist., Ridgecrest, Calif., 1960-61, Ocean View Schl. Dist., Huntington Beach, Calif., 1970-73; asst. ed. Latter-Day Sentinel, Cerritos, Calif., 1983-85, Calif. mng. ed., Huntington Beach, 1985—; pub. communications dir. Ch. of Jesus Christ of Latter-Day Saints, Huntington Beach, 1984—. Mem. Assoc. Latter-Day Media Artists. Home: 6871 Rio Vista Dr Huntington Beach CA 92647

ALLEN, DAVID DUDLEY, b. New Haven, Mar. 6, 1925; s. David Henry Allen and Mary Anna Ptansky/Heske; m. Tula Prauner, Jan. 1, 1960. Author: The Nature of Gambling, 1951, The Price of Women, 1971. Student Yale Drama Schl., 1945-46; MA, U. Chgo., 1951. Pub. The Pampheleeter, New Haven, 1954-55; owner, operator Enhance Fashion Wigs, Bergenfield, N.J., 1960-72; pub. Hyst'ry Myst'ry House, Garnerville, N.Y., 1975-85. Served to 2d lt. USAAC, 1945, ETO. Mem. AG, MWA, Mark Twain Soc. (hon.). Home: One Brush Ct Garnerville NY 10923

ALLEN, GILBERT BRUCE, b. Rockville Ctr., NY, Jan 1, 1951; s. Joseph Aloysius and Marie Dawn (Skocik) A.; m. Barbara Jean Szigeti, Aug. 17, 1974. Author: In Everything: Poems 1972-79, 1982, Conversations with SC Poets, 1986; contbr. poems and essays The Am. Book Rvw, The Am. Scholar, Cumberland Poetry Rvw, Epoch, Kans. Qtly, Pembroke Mag., Shenandoah, Coll. English, other lit mags. BA, Cornell U., 1972, MFA, 1974, PhD, 1977. Asst. prof. English Furman Univ., Greenville, SC, 1977-83, assoc. prof., 1983—. Mem. Amnesty Internatl., Greenville. Recipient Amon Liner award Greensboro Rvw, 1984. Mem. AWP, P&W, PSA. Address: 1 Altamont Terr Travelers Rest SC 29690

ALLEN, HENRY MURIEL, b. Ardmore, OK, Jan. 1, 1952, s. O. M. and Winona (Oxley) A.; m. Wynetta Jean Nikkel, Nov. 22, 1973; children—Christopher, Jeremy. Author: Clinical Laboratory Handbook for Medical Technologists, 1974, Pocket Guide to ECG Interpretation, 1977, 3d ed 1987, The Clinic Laboratory Manual, 1987; contrbr. articles to Okla. Jnl. Forensic Medicine, Yukon Rvw., Patient Care Mag., Okla. State Med. Assn. Jnl., other profl. publs. MT in Med. Technology, Okla. U., 1973, BS in Medicine with distinction, 1976; DO, Univ. Health Scis. Coll. Osteo. Medicine, Kansas City, 1986. Intern Hillcrest Hosp., Oklahoma City,

1986—. Home: 5137 N Sapulpa St Oklahoma City OK 73112

ALLEN, JAMES LOVIC, JR., b. Atlanta, Jan. 2, 1929; s. James Lovic and Effie Grace (Schell) A.; m. Barbara Foster, June 13, 1953 (div.); children—Melinda Sue, Algernon Foster. Author: Locked in: Surfing for Life, 1970, Yeats's Epitaph: A Key to Symbolic Unity in His Life and Works, 1982; editor: Yeats Four Decades After: Some Scholarly and Critical Perspectives, 1979; editorial bd.: 20th Century Lit.; contrbr. articles to profl. publs. BA, Tulane U., 1953, MA, 1954; PhD, U. Fla., 1959. Instr. in English U. Tenn., 1954-56; asst. prof. English Stephen F. Austin State U., Nagodoches, Tex., 1959-60; assoc. prof. English U. So. Miss, Hattaiesburg, 1960-63, U. Hawaii, Hilo, 1963-69, prof., 1969-86, prof. emeritus, 1986—; vis. prof. English Stephen F. Austin State U., 1970-71, U. Tenn., 1976-77, U. Okla., 1986. Served with USN 1946-49. So. Fellowship Fund grantee, 1956-58. Mem. AAUP, MLA, Am. Com. Irish Studies, Phi Beta Kappa. Home: 96-634 Hanile St G-205 Mililani Town HI 96789

ALLEN, MARTHA LESLIE, b. Chicago, IL, Feb. 19, 1948; d. Russell Wykof and Donna Claire (Rehkopf) Allen. Editor: Index/Directory of Women's Media, annually since 1975, The Celibate Woman (jnl.), 1982—, second issue of The Arthemis Pate, A Journal of Self-Transformation, July, 1983; wrkg. on doctoral dissertation, The Development of a Communication Network Among Women, 1963-1983. MA, Howard U., 1978. Editor, typesetter WIFP (DC), 1975—; assoc. dir. Women's Institute for Freedom of the Press (DC), 1978-85, dir., 1985—. Me. Coordination Com. on Wmn. in the Historical Profession. Home: 1910 Calvert St NW Washington DC 20009

ALLEN, RICHARD CHESTER, b. Swampscott, MA, Jan. 24, 1926; s. Chester George and Edith Lydia (Hickford) A.; divorced; children—Steven Richard, Craig Ethan, Scott David. Author: (with Ferster, Weihofen) Mental Impairment and Legal Incompetency, 1968; (with Ferster, Rubin, Readings in Law and Psychiatry, 1968, rev. 1975; Legal Rights of the Disabled and Disadvantaged, 1969, Mental Health in America: The Years of Crisis, 1979; columnist "The Devil's Advocate" Fort Myers Observer, North Fort Myers Observer, Cape Coral Observer, Fort Myers Beach Observer, Island Reporter. Contrbr. numerous chpts., articles to law books, profl. jnls. Assoc. ed. Washington U. Law Quarterly, 1949-50; ed.-in-chief MH, 1972-76. Wrkg. on childrens' stories, political and civil liberties editorials, column on political and social commentary. A.B., Washington U., 1948, J.D., 1950; LL.M., U. Mich., 1963. Attorney, Southwestern Bell Telephone Co., St. Louis, 1952-56, Topeka, KS, 1956-59; prof. law Washburn U., Topeka, 1959-63, Menninger Sch. Psychiatry, Topeka, 1959-63, George Washington U., Washington, 1963-76; dean, prof. law Hamline U., St. Paul, 1976-81; Fulbright visiting prof. U. Swaziland, 1981-84. Served to 1st lt. U.S. Army, 1950-52, USN, 1943-45. Recipient cert. of Appeciation, U.S. Dept. of Health, Edn. & Welfare, Washington, 1969, Rosemary F. Dybwad Intl. award for research and writing in the field of mental retardation and the alw, 1969, cert of Commendation, Supreme Ct. of Minn., St. Paul, 1983. Fellow Am. Acad. Forensic Scis. (Forensic Jurisprudence award 1982); mem. Mo., Kans., Minn. bar assns., ACLU (bd. dirs. Fla. and Minn.), Am. Arbitration Assn. (arbitrator), Nat. Assn. Mental Health (cert. of Commendation 1980). Home: 35 Palmetto Dr Tropicana Fort Myers FL 33908

ALLEN, RICHARD STANLEY, (Dick Allen), b. Troy, NY, Aug. 8, 1939; s. Richard Sanders and Doris (Bishop) A.; m. Loretta Mary Negridge, Aug. 13, 1960; children—Richard Negridge, Tanya Angell. Author: Anon and Various Time Machine Poems, 1971, Overnight in the Guest House of the Mystic, 1984, Regions with No Proper Names, 1975, Flight and Pursuit, 1987; poems, articles, rvws; editor, poetry editor, Mad River Rvw, 1964-68; ed.: Science Fiction: The Future, 1982; co-editor: Detective Fiction: Crime and Compromise, 1974, Looking Ahead: The Vision of Science Fiction, 1975; contrbg. editor: Am. Poetry Rvw; book reviewer: Poetry, Am. Book Rvw, Hudson Rvw. AB, Syracuse U., 1961; MA, Brown U., 1963. Teaching assoc. Brown U., 1962-64; instr. English Wright State U., Dayton, Ohio, 1964-68; mem. faculty U. Bridgeport, (Conn.), 1968—, prof. English, 1976-79, Charles A. Dana prof. English, 1979—, also dir. creative writing. Recipient Union Arts and Civic League Poetry prize, 1971, Assoc. Depts. English-MLA Disting. Teaching award, 1971, San Jose Poetry prize, 1976; Hart Crane Meml. Poetry fellow, 1966, Robert Frost poetry fellow, 1972; Mellon research fellow, 1981; NEA poetry writing grantee, 1984, Ingram Merrill Poetry Fellowship, 1986. Mem. AAUP, P&W, PSA, PEN, Modern Poetry Assn. Home: 74 Fern Circle Trumbull CT 06611

ALLEN, ROBERTA, b. NYC, d. Sol Allen and Jeanette (Waldner) Sanderson. Author: The Traveling Woman (short fiction), 1986; contrbr. to anthols.: Contemporary American Fiction, 1983, Wild History, 1985; contrbr. to mags. Creative wrtg. instr., Parsons Schl of Design, NYC. Mem. P&W. Home: 5 W 16th St New York NY 10011

ALLEN, SAM, See Dougherty, Samuel Allen

ALLEN, WILLIAM DEAN, b. Lake Charles, LA, Dec. 1, 1950; s. William Edward and Hazel Dorothy (Reese) A. Author, pub.: It Ain't Rape Unless You Struggle, 1978, More than a Tax Revolt!, 1982, How to Read the I.R.S. Code, 1985, Introduction to Freedom, 1986. Ed., pub.: (newsletter) The American, 1980—. B.A., Franklin U., 1977. Served to sgt. U.S. Army, 1968-72. Home: Box 2362 Texas City TX 77590

ALLEY, HENRY MELTON, b. Seattle, Jan. 27, 1945; s. Edward Shaw and Johnnie Bernice (Cotton) A.; m. Patricia Grimm, Dec. 21, 1967, 1 dau., Ann. Author: novels, The Lattice, 1986, Through Glass, 1979, verse play, Hameon, 1980, The York Handbook for the Tchg. of Creative Writing, 1979; contrbr. stories to Kans. Qtly, The Widener Rvw, Round Table Rvw, Outerbridge, Virginia Woolf Qtly, Pikestaff Forum, Snapdragon, Sawtooth. BA, Stanford U., 1963-67; MFA, Cornell U., 1967-69, PhD, 1971. Assoc. prof. Schl. of the Ozarks, Point Lookout, Mo., 1972-75, Univ. Idaho, Moscow, 1975-82; asst. prof. Honors Coll., Univ. Ore., Eugene, 1982—. Pres., Lane Lit. Guild, Eugene, 1985-86. Mem. MLA, AWP, Phi Beta Kappa. Home: 48 West 26 Ave Eugene OR 97405

ALLISON, ALDEN GARY, b. Muskegon, MI, May 14, 1956; s. Thurlo Leroy and Joanne Francis (Stratil) A. Contrbr. poetry: Singles Circle Mag.; poetry in anthologies. Wrkg. on poetry collection, short story, fiction. Grad. Muskegon Community Coll. Home: 2400 S Sheridan St Muskegon MI 49442

ALLISON, HARRISON CLARKE, b. West Liberty, KY, Nov. 4, 1917; s. Asher Owen and Florence Olivia (Davis) A.; m. Amy Lee Henry, Mar. 1, 1940 (div. Dec. 1946); 1 son, James Lee (dec.); m. Jessie Hudson, Dec. 16, 1947; children—Anita Charles, Nancy Zarczynski, Elizabeth, Sue Johnson. Author: Personal Identification, 1973, Handbook of Crime Scene Investigation, 1980. Contrbr. articles to mags. Ed.: Book Rvw., Ala. Pcace Officers Jnl., 1970-78, Fundamentals of Criminal Investigation, 1976. Wrkg. on Cogitations of an Old Codger. B.A., Georgetown Coll., 1939; M.S., U. Ala., 1950. Engineer, Sylvaia Electric Products, Lexington, KY, 1944-45; tchr. Marion Military Inst., Marion, AL, 1947-49, 53—. Served to capt. U.S. Army, 1941-44. Named Prof. of Yr., Marion Military Inst., 1983. Fellow am. Inst. Chemists, Am. Assn. Criminology; mem. Intl. Assn. Identification, Int. Assn. Chiefs Police, Ala. Peace Officers Assn. Home: 701 Moore St Marion AL 36756

ALLMAN, JOHN, b. NYC, July 27, 1935, s. John King and Helen (Burghard) A.; m. Eileen Victoria Jorge, Sept. 18, 1962; 1 dau., Jennifer Deirdre. Author: Walking Four Ways in the Wind, 1979, Clio's Children, 1985, Scenarios for a Mixed Landscape, 1986; contrbr. to Am. Poetry Rvw, Ironwood, Paris Rvw, Poetry Now, other publs.; contrbr. to anthologies: Saturday's Children: Poems of Work, 1983, The Pushcart Prize VIII:Best of the Small Presses, 1983, Anthology of Mag. Verse and Yearbook of Am. Poetry, 1985. BA, Hunter Coll., 1963; MA, Syracuse U., 1967. Editorial coordinator Greystone Press, NYC, 1963; instr. Syracuse (N.Y.) U., 1964-67; instr., then asst. prof. Cazenovia (N.Y.) Coll., 1967-71; prof. Rockland Community Coll., Suffern, N.Y., 1971—. Recipient Helen Bullis prize Poetry Northwest, 1976; NEA creative wrtg. fellow, 1984. Mem. AWP, PEN. Home: RD 4 Frances Dr Katonah NY 10536

ALLYN, BARBARA, see Tatelbaum, Brenda Loew

ALMADA, MANUEL, b. New Bedford, MA, Feb. 10, 1912; s. Manuel Salles Almeida and Mary (Medeiros) A. Author: 1296 Giant Steps to Business Survival and Success, 1986. Contrbr. numerous articles, stories to mags., newspapers; author numerous radio plays. Advt. dir. CFW Inc. Co., New Bedford, 1936-64; advt. salesman Standard-Times, New Bedford, 1966-74; v.p. Jacques Advt. Agcy. Inc., New Bedford, 1974—; pres. Alma Day Sales WGH, New Bedford, 1974—. Home: 25 Chancery St New Bedford MA 02740

ALMAND, J.D., b. Cale, AR, Sept. 7, 1917; s. John David and Emma (Burns) A.; m. Louise Bewley, May 3, 1941; 1 dau., Mary Ellen Almand Blount. Author: Magdalene (Scottish Heraldry award CLCB Press, 1985), 1985, A Medal for Thomas. Grad. public schls., Cale. Meat cutter Retail Grocer, Russellville, AR, 1946-55; insurance agent, Russellville, 1956-80, retired. Mem. Chamber of Commerce, Russellville, 1960-80. Home: 27 E Shore Dr Russellville AR 72801

ALMEN, LOWELL GORDON, b. Grafton, ND, Sept. 25, 1941; s. Paul O. and Helen E. (Johnson) A.; m. Sally Arlyn Clark, Aug. 14, 1965; children—Paul Simon, Cassandra Gabrielle. Editor: (curricula) World Religions and Christian Mission, 1967, Our Neighbor's Faith, 1968; mng. editor: The Lutheran Standard, Mpls., 1974-78, editor, 1979—. BA, Concordia

Coll., 1963; MDiv, Luther Theol. Sem., 1967; LittD (hon.), Capital U., 1981. Ordained to ministry Lutheran Ch., 1967. Pastor, St. Peter's Ch., Dresser, Wis., 1967-69; assoc. campus pastor and dir. communications Concordia Coll., Moorhead, Minn., 1969-74. Recipient Disting. Alumnus award Concordia Coll., 1982; Bush Fdn. grantee, 1972. Mem. Associated Ch. Press (bd. dirs. 1981-84), Evang. Press Assn., Minn. Press Club. Home: 1453 Lincoln Terr NE Minneapolis MN 55421

ALMQUIST, MARY REBECCA, b. Red Oak, IA, May 28, 1958, d. Erland Lincoln and Elinor Frances (Chase) Almquist. Contrbr. poetry to: Sketch, Lyrical Iowa, Feelings. BA, Iowa State U., 1980. News ed. Springfield (Minn.) Advance-Press, 1980-81; family living ed. Marengo (Iowa) Pub. Corp. including Marengo Pioneer-Republican, Williamsburg Jnl. Tribune, Belle Plaine Union and South Benton Star-Press; columnist; lectr. on creative writing. Home: 220 W Washington St Marengo IA 52301

ALMQUIST, SHARON KRISTINA, b. Red Oak, IA, Oct. 13, 1962; d. Erland Lincoln and Elinor Frances (Chase) A. Columnist: Cedar Valley Times, Vinton, IA, 1985—. Contrbr. articles to newspapers, mags. B.A. in Jnlsm., Iowa State U., 1985. Feature wrtr. Iowa State Daily, Ames, 1983-85; reporter The Evening Sentinel, Shenandoah, IA, 1984; staff wrtr. Cedar Valley Times, 1985—. Mem. AAUW, Iowa State U. Alumni Assn. Home: 904 W 3d St Apt E Vinton IA 52349

ALPEROVITZ, GAR, b. Racine, WI, May 5, 1936; s. Julius and Emily (Bensman) A.; m. Sharon Sosnick, Aug. 29, 1976; children by previous marriage: Kari Fai, David Joseph. Author: Atomic Diplomacy: Hiroshima and Potsdam, 1965, rev. ed.. 1985, Cold War Essays, 1970, Strategy and Program, 1973, Rebuilding America, 1984, American Economic Policies, 1985. BS in History, U. Wis., 1958; MA in Econ., U. Cal. at Berkeley, 1960; PhD in Poli. Econ. U. Cambridge, Eng., 1964. Congl. asst., 1961-62; mem. U.S. Senate staff, 1964-65; spcl. asst. Dept. State, 1965-66; fellow King's College, Cambridge (Eng.) U., 1964-68, Inst. Politics Harvard, 1966-68, Brookings Instn., 1966, Inst. Poli. Studies, 1968-69; co-dir. Cambridge (Mass.) Inst., 1968-71; pres. exploratory project econ. alternatives, 1973—; pres. Natl. Center Econ. Alternatives, 1978—; guest prof. Notre Dame U., 1982-83. Home: 2317 Ashmead Pl NW Washington DC 20009

ALPERT, HOLLIS, b. Herkimer, NY, Sept. 24, 1916; s. Abram and Myra (Carroll) A. Author: The Summer Lovers, 1958, Some Other Time, 1960, The Dreams and the Dreamers, 1962, For Immediate Release, 1963, The Barrymores, 1964, The Claimant, 1968, The People Eaters, 1971, Smash, 1973, (under name Robert Carroll) A Disappearance, 1974; Editor: The Actors Life-Journals, Charlton Heston, 1978; Lana: The Lady, The Legend, The Truth (with Lana Turner), 1982; Burton, 1986, Fellini, A Life, 1986; contbr. numerous short stories to mags. including Harper's Bazaar. Student, New Schl. Social Research, 1946-47. Book reviewer Sat. Rvw, New York Times, others, 1947-59; film critic Sat. Rvw, after 1950, Woman's Day, 1953-60; mng. editor World Mag., after 1972, film editor, lively arts editor, after 1973; editor Am. Film, 1975—; Algur Meadows Disting. vis. prof. So. Method. U., 1982; past dir. Edward Mac Dowell Assn. Served to 1st lt. AUS, 1942-46. Recipient Critic's award Screen Dirs. Guild Am., 1957. Mem. Natl. Soc. Film Critics (chmn. 1972-73). Address: Box 142 Shelter Island NY 11964

ALPHABET, DR., see Morice, David Jennings

ALPHIN, ELAINE MARIE, b. San Francisco, Oct. 30, 1955; d. Richard E. and Janice Mae (Toler) Bonilla; m. Arthur Brent Alphin, May 9, 1982. Author: The Quest for the Ghost Cadet, 1988. Contrbr. articles, short stories to mags., including Houston City Mag., Children's Digest, other. Dept. ed.: Rice Thresher, Houston, 1975-76. Wrkg. on That Lion!, Children of Glass, Simon Says. B.A., Rice U., 1977. Staff mem. Cornwall Public Library, Cornwall-on-Hudson, NY, 1982-85; free-lance wrtr., 1975—. Named Outstanding Young Woman, 1983. Mem. SCBW, AAUW. Home: Rt 5 Country Estates Madison IN 47250

ALSBROOK, JOSEPH DAVID, b. Clinton, IL, Aug. 2, 1943; s. Clarence Virgil and Margaret Agnes (Hoag) A.: m. Phyllis Kay McVay, Oct. 15, 1964 (div. 1967); 1 son, James Christopher; m. Valerie Tomayko, Aug. 15, 1970; 1 dau., Margaret Louise. Author, ed.: The Flavor of Eureka, 1985, The Flavor of Bella Vista, 1986, The Flavor of the Ozarks, 1986, Somewhere in the Ozarks (essays), 1988. Wrkg. on novel. BA in History, U. Ark., Little Rock, 1975; postgrad., U. Ark., Fayetteville, 1984—. Bus./ mgr. Essence Newspaper, Little Rock, 1970-74; account exec. Ark. Times Mag., Little Rock, 1978-84; pres. Creative Solutions, Inc., Fayetteville, 1984—. Address: Box 1782 Fayetteville AR 72702

ALSCHULER, AL, b. Gary, IN, Jan. 27, 1934; s. Harold Morris and Sarah A.; m. Joy Van Wye, June 28, 1956; children—Mari Lynn, David Van, Mark Jonathan. Ed.: Florida Designers Qtly, 1982-84, On Design, 1983-84, Design South, 1984—; contrbg. ed.: I.D.E.A.S., 1977-82; Interiors & Sources, 1980-82; assoc. ed. Fla. Medical Rvw, 1987—; contrbg. ed. Archit., Design & Development News, 1987; contrbg. writer: Miami Mag., 1979-82, Miami News, 1980-81, Miami Today, 1984—, Good News, 1985—, Miami's Guide to the Arts, 1987—. BA in Jnlsm., U. OK, 1955. V.p. Vanleigh Furniture, NYC, then Miami, FL, 1958-79; pub. relns. consultant & free-lance writer, Miami, 1979-82. Served to Capt., USAF, 1956-58. Mem. SPJ, num. profl. orgns. Office: 9 Island Ave 1604 Miami Beach FL 33139

ALSTON, MARY ELIZABETH, (Beth Alston), b. Culhbert, GA, Mar. 6, 1953; d. Frank Fletcher Jr. and Rebecca (Rutherford) A. Contrbr. to Sirocco, Americus Times-Recorder. B.A. in English, Ga. Southwestern Coll., 1977. News dir. Sta. WDEC, Americus, GA, 1977-79; copywrtr. Metalux Corp., Americus, 1981-84; graphics tchr. Tri-County High Sch., Buena Vista, GA, 1984-85; staff wrtr. Americus Times-Recorder, 1985—. Mem. Ga. Press Assn. (3d place for best personal column on a serious subject 1986). Home: 207G S Lee St Americus GA 31709

ALTA, b. Reno, May 22, 1942. Author: Freedom's in Sight, 1969; Letters to Women, 1970; Burn This & Memorize Yourself, 1971; No Visible Means of Support, 1971; Song of the Wife, Song of the Mistress, 1972; True Story, 1972; Momma, 1975; I Am Not a Practicing Angel, 1976; Pauline & The Mysterious Pervert, 1976; Theme & Variations, 1978; The Shameless Hussy, 1980. Wrkg. on new collection of love poems. Student pub. schls., Castro Valley, Calif. Pub. Shameless Hussy Press, Berkeley, Calif., 1969—; instr. poetry U. Calif. Extension, Berkeley, 1974-79; columnist Plexus, Oakland, Calif., 1975-80. Recipient Am. Book award Before Columbus Fdn., NYC, 1981. Address: Box 3092 Berkeley CA 94703

ALTMAN, IRWIN, b. NYC, July 16, 1930; s. Louis L. and Ethel (Schonberg) A.; m. Gloria Seckler, Jan. 2, 1953; children—David Gary, William Michael. Author: (with J. E. McGrath), Small Group Research: Synthesis and Critique of the Field, 1966, (with D.A. Taylor), Social Penetration: The Development of Interpersonal Relationships, 1973, The Environment and Social Behavior: Privacy, Personal Space, Territory, and Crowding, 1975, Culture and Environment (with M. Chemers), 1980; ed. Human Behavior and Environment: Advances in Theory and Research, vol. 1, 1976, vol. 2, 1977, vol. 3: Children and the Environment, 1978, vol. 4: Environment and Culture, 1980, vol. 5: Transportation and Behavior, 1982, vol. 6: Behavior and the Natural Environment, 1983, vol. 7: Elderly People and the Environment, 1984, vol. 8: Home Environments, 1985, vol. 9: Neighborhood and Community Environments, 1987, vol. 10: Public Places and Spaces, 1988, ed (with Daniel Stokols) and contrbr., Handbook of Environmental Psychology, 1987. Contrbr to other works and monograph series. Contrbr to prfnl jnls and encyclopedias, book reviews. BA, New York U., 1951, MA, U. of Md., 1954, Ph.D, 1957. Asst prof of psych, American U., Washington, D.C., 1957-58; v.p. and res. sci., Human Sciences Research, Inc., Arlingto, Va., 1958-60; assoc. prof of psych and sr. res. psychlgdt, Naval Med. Res. Inst., Bethesda, Md., 1962-69; prof. of psych., U. of Utah, Salt Lake City, 1969-70; adj. prof in dept of commnctns, 1977—, prof in dept. of family and consumer studies, 1987—, chmn psych dept., 1969-76, dean of college of Social and Behav. Scis., 1979-83, v.p. for Academic Affairs, 1983-87, disting. prof. of psychology, 1987—. Adj. prof at U. of Md., 1968-69. Mmbr res. Advisory panel of American Inst. of Architects, 1970-72; mbr Natl. Inst. of Mntl Hlth grant review comm., 1970-73, 74—. Consult. to Battelle Meml. Inst. U.S. Army, personnel psychologist, 1954-56, 1st lt. Member: Intl Assn of Applied Psych., Am. Psychlgl Assn. (fellow; chmn of task force on environment and behavior, 1973-76; ch. of div. for population and environment), AAAS (fellow), AAUP, Soc. for Psychgcl Stdy of Soc. Issues, Soc. of Exper. Socl. Psych. (ch.; mem of exec. com., 1974-76), Soc. of Personality and Soc. Psych (pres), Assn. for Stdy of Man-Environment Reltns, (founder; mbr bd dirs, 1967-73), Environmental Desgn Res. Assn. (mem bd drs, 1976-79), Interior Design Educators Cncl (hon. mem.), Western Psychlcl Assn, Sigma xi. Disting, service awd in soc. scis., Utah Acad. of Scis, Arts, and Letters, 1981; career awd, Environmental Design Rsrch Ass., 1982; superior service awd, Div. of Population and Environmental Psychology, Am. Psychlgcl. Assn, 1985. Home: 2827 commonwealth Ave Salt Lake City UT 84109

ALTMAN, NATHANIEL, b. NYC, Jan. 25, 1948; s. Morris and Sadie (Davis) A.; Author: Eating for Life: A Book about Vegetarianism, 1973, enl. edn, 1977, 84, The Chriopractic Alternative, 1981, Nathaniel Altman's Total Vegetarian Cooking, 1981, Ahimsa: Dynamic Compassion, 1981, Pocket Guide to Vegetarian Restaurants, 1982, The Palmistry Workbook, 1984, Sexual Palmistry, 1986, (with Jose A. Rosa), Power Spots, 1986, (with Andrew Fitzherber), Career, Success and Self-Fulfillment, 1988, The Nonviolent Revolution: Ahimsa in Everyday Life, 1988. Attended U. of Wis., 1966-68, and Universidad de Los Andes, 1968-69, BA, U. of Wis., 1971. Resident staff member, Theosophical Soc. in America, Wheaton, Ill., 1971; registrar and faculty mem, Krotona Inst. of Theosophy, Ojai, Calif., 1972-74. Full-time writer, 1974—. Member: Theosophical Soc., North American Vegetarian Soc. Home: 169 Prospect Park W Brooklyn NY 11215

ALTON, JOHN G., b. Tallassee, AL, June 17, 1954; m. Janet Rock, May 16, 1981. Contrbr. to Writing Ctr. Jnl., Small Pond Mag. of Lit., Dark Horse. BA, U. Ala., 1978, MFA, 1982. Instr. English, Shelton State U., Tuscaloosa, Ala., 1981-82, Va. Inst. Tech., Blacksburg, 1982—. Mem. NCTE, South Atlantic MLA. Home: 504 Sunrise Dr Blacksburg VA 24061

ALVAREZ, RAYMOND P., b. Hollywood, CA. Ed., The Empire State Mason Mag., 1982—. BFA, R.I. School of Design; MS, Boston U. Pres., R. A. Peters Assoc., Valhalla, NY; dir. pub. reins. CIBA-Geigy Corp., Ardsley, NY, Res. World, Div. Amer. Airlines, NYC; acct. exec. B.B.D.O. Agency, NYC; East Div. pub. relns./ sales promo. advisor Tidewater Oil, NYC. One Welwyn Valhalla NY 10595

AMABILE, ANTHONY A., b. Glasgow, Scotland, Aug. 10, 1934, came to U.S., 1935; s. Nunzie J. and Isabella (McGregor) A.; m. Josette Ann Ceglia, Apr. 15, 1977; 1 son, Mark Anthony. Contrbr.: N.Y. Times, U.S. News & World Report, numerous other newspapers and periodicals. Student St. Peters Coll., Jersey City, then Fordham U. Reporter Hudson Dispatch, Union City, N.J., 1956-57; dir. public relations Jersey City Med. Center, 1958-61, Jersey City Bd. Edn., 1967-71; ed. various weekly publs., N.J., 1972-78; pres. Meadowlands Assocs., Inc., Bloomfield, N.J., 1979—; ed. Hudson Forum Mag., Hudson C. of C.; biographer Windsor Publs.; mktg. cons. Tatnic Enterprises, Inc.; campaign mgr., media cons. numerous Democratic party candidates on local and fedl. level, 1957— Office: Meadowlands Assocs 40 Conger St Bloomfield NJ 07003

AMAN, REINHOLD ALBERT, (Uncle Maledictus), b. Fuerstenzell, Bavaria, Germany, Apr. 8, 1936, s. Ludwig and Anna (Waindinger) Aman; came to U.S., 1959; m. Shirley Ann Beischel, Apr. 9, 1960; 1 dau., Susan. Author: Der Kampf in Wolframs "Parzival", 1968; Bayrisch-Oesterreichisches Schimpfwoerterbuch, 1972, 1986; Maledicta, vols. 1-9, 1977-87; editor: Mammoth Cod, 1976; How Do They Do It?, 1983 BS, U. Wis., Milwaukee, 1965; PhD, U. Texas, Austin, 1968. Translator, U.S. Army, Frankfurt, Germany, 1954; chemist, Shell Oil, Montreal, Can., 1957-59; chemist, A.O. Smith, Milwaukee, 1960-62; asst. prof., U. Wis., Milwaukee, 1968-74; editor, publisher Maledicta Press, Waukesha, Wis., 1975—. French-German Award, U. Wis., 1965; NDEA Title IV Fellowship, U. Tex., 1965-68; computer research grants, U. Wis., 1972. Pres. International Maledicta Society, 1976. Home: 331 S. Greenfield Ave. Waukesha WI 53186

AMANUDDIN, SYED, (Un), b. Mysore, Karnataka, India, Feb. 4, 1934 (arrvd. USA 1967), d. Syed Jamaluddin and Shahzadi Begum; m. Ashraf Basith Amanuddin, Feb. 18, 1960; children—Irfan, Rizwan. Author: (poetry) The Forbidden Fruit, 1967, Tiffin State Hospital, 1970, The Children of Hiroshima, 1970, Shoes of Tradition, 1970, Poems of Protest, 1972, Lightning & Love, 1974, The Age of Female Eunuchs, 1976, Adventures of Atman, 1977, Gems & Germs, 1978, Make Me Your Dream, 1984, Poems, 1984, Bhopal Cantos, 1986, (drama) System Shaker and Other Plays, 1972, The King who Sold His Wife, 1978, (fiction) Passage to the Himalayas, 1979, (criticism) Hart Carne's Mystical Quest, 1967, World Poetry in English, 1982; co-ed. New Poetry from Australia, 1973. BA, U. Mysore, 1956, MA, 1957; PhD, Bowling Green State U., 1970. Lectr. English, Osmania U., Hyderabad, India, 1961-67; teaching fellow Bowling Green State U., Ohio, 1967-70; prof. English, Morris Coll., Sumter, S.C., 1970—, chmn. div. humanities, 1972—. Intl. scholar U. London, summer 1972; Lilly scholar in humanities Duke U., 1976-77. Mem. MLA, Sumter Poetry Club (founder, pres. 1974-78), South Asian Lit. Assn. (sec.-treas. 1979-81). Home: 790 McKay St Sumter SC 29151

AMEEN, MARK JOSEPH, (Terrence Harmony), b. Lowell, MA, Aug. 18, 1958, s. Emil Joseph and Shirley Ann (Barnaby) A. Author: A Circle of Sirens (poetry), 1985, Aye, My Dear, I Worry About That (chapbook), 1982, Three New York Poets (with Carl Morse and Charles Ortleb), 1987; contrbr. short story to Gay Sunshine, Mirage. BA, U. Mass., 1980. Actor, Medicine Show, NYC, The Front Line, Inc., NYC; night mgr. Hotel Westbury, NYC. Mem. PSA. Home: 235 E 4th St New York NY 10009

AMERY, DIANE, see Fink, Barbara Arlene

AMES, PATRICK W., b. Toledo, Apr. 4, 1954, s. James White and Katherine (Greenfield) A. Author: A Heaven in the Eye, 1984, Migration, 1985, The Same Sea in Us All, 1985, Voices from an Island, 1985, Time and the White Tigress, 1986. BA in English, Coll. of Wooster, Ohio, 1976. Cons., prin. Ames Pub. Cons., Portland, OR and Seattle, 1983—; editor-in-chief Breitenbush Books, Portland, 1983—; pub. WestMark Books, Seattle, 1986—. Recipient Western States Book award Western States Arts Fdn., 1984, 86. Home: 644 NW 74th St Seattle WA 98117

AMES, STEVEN EDMUND, b. Oakland, CA, July 25, 1940; s. Eldridge Edmund and Eleanor Ruth (Mendenhall) A.; m. Carol Murray Nelson, Aug. 20, 1966; children— Krista, Karen. Contrbr. to numerous mags. including Baseball Digest, Football Digest. BA, San Jose St. U., 1967, MS, 1971; EdD, Nova U., Ft. Lauderdale, FL, 1977. Sports ed. Contra Costa Times, Walnut Creek, CA, 1959-61; reporter, photographer Standard Register- Leader, Sunnyvale, CA, 1965-66; writer Peninsula Living magazine, Burlingame, CA, 1967-68; sports writer The Daily Review, Hayward, CA, 1968-69; journalism instr., Merced (CA) College, 1971-78; dir. of student publs. Pepperdine U., Malibu, CA, 1978—. Served as Spec. 4, U.S. Army, 1961-64. Distinguished Newspaper Adviser Award, College Media Advs., 1985. Mem: College Media Advs./ Soc. of Newspaper Design; Soc. Profl. Jnlsts.; Sigma Delta Chi; Assn. for Edn. in Journalism and Mass Communication. Home: 3376 Hill Canyon Av Thousand Oaks CA 91360

AMETHYST, see Bynum, Cheryl Diane

AMEY, DAVID EDWARD, b. Circleville, OH, Sept. 25, 1947; s. Ralph L. and Annabelle (Shellhammer) A.; m. Karen Lee Predmore, June 14, 1969; children—Angela, Ted. Ed.: Circleville Herald, 1963-77, Broiler Industry, 1986—, Poultry Tribune, 1978-86, Intl. Poultry Trade Show Guide, 1984-86. BS in Jnlsm., Ohio U., 1969. Rptr./photog. Circleville Pub. Co. (OH), 1971-73, city ed., 1974-77; field ed. Watt Pub. Co., Mt. Morris, IL, 1978-80, ed., 80—. Served to SP5, US Army, 1969-71. Office: Box 947 Cullman AL 35056

AMICE, CAROL RIZZARDI, b. Chambersburg, PA, Aug. 11, 1955; d. Carl Joseph and Angela Ann (Zagrosky) R.; m. Thierry Thymen Amice, June 12, 1980. Ed.: Volkssporting News, 1985-86, Shelf Action, 1983—, Comparative Law Yearbook, 1978; author: Quakerism and Feminism, 1977, Oppression of Women in the Catholic Church: Its Origins, Traditions, and Future, 1977. BS, Northwestern U. Medill Schl. of Jnlsm., 1973-78; postgrad. U. MD, Munich (W.Germany) Campus, U. Ill. Chgo. Campus Gen. assignment rptr. var. nwsprs.; copy ed. Stars & Stripes, Griesheim, W. Germ., 1980; asst. ad. mgr./p.r. Chas. Levy Circulating Co., Chgo., 1981-83; merchandising/mktg. coord., Better Homes & Gardens, Des Moines, IA, 1983—. Mem. WIC. Office: BH&G 17th and Locust Des Moines IA 50336

AMMER, DONALD SCOTT, b. Gary, IN, Oct. 23, 1962; s. Rudolph Christian and Dawn Noreen (Klein) A. Contrbr. short stories to popular mags. including Star Hits, Ellery Queen's Mystery Mag. Comml. artist Snickers' Clown Service, Portage, IN, 1982-86; salesclerk Carson Pirie Scott & Co., Merrillville, IN, 1986-87; clerical asst. Hobart Public Library, IN, 1986-87; free-lance wrtr., 1980—. Recipient John & Connie Heckert Writing award Mississippi Valley Wrtr.'s Conf., Rock Island, IL, 1987. Mem. Wrtrs. on Writing Support Group (founder). Home: 638 S Pennsylvania St Hobart IN 46342

AMMONS, ARCHIE RANDOLPH, b. Whiteville, NC, Feb. 18, 1926; s. Willie M. and Lucy Della (McKee) A.; m. Phyllis Plumbo, Nov. 26, 1949; 1 son, John Randolph. Author: Ommateum, 1955, Expressions of Sea Level, 1964, Corsons Inlet, 1965, Tape for the Turn of the Year, 1965, Northfield Poems, 1966, Selected Poems, 1968, Uplands, 1970, Briefings, 1971, Collected Poems, 1951-1971, 1972, Sphere: The Form of a Motion, 1974, Diversifications, 1975, The Selected Poems: Nineteen Fifty One-Nineteen Seventy Seven, 1977, The Snow Poems, 1977, Selected Longer Poems, 1980, A Coast of Trees, 1981, Worldly Hopes, 1982, Lake Effect Country, 1983; poetry editor The Nation, 1963. BS, Wake Forest Coll., 1949; student, U. Calif.-Berkeley, 1951-52. Prin. Hatteras (N.C.) elem. schl., 1949-50; exec. v.p. Freidrich & Dimmock, Inc. (biol. glassware mfg.), Millville, N.J., 1952-61; asst. prof. English, Cornell U., 1964-68, assoc. prof., 1968-71, prof., 1971—, Goldwin Smith prof. poetry 1973—. Served with USNR, 1944-46. Recipient Bollingen prize in poetry, 1973-74; Guggenheim fellow, 1966; traveling fellow Am. Acad. Arts and Letters, 1967; recipient Levinson prize Poetry mag., 1970; Natl. Book award for poetry, 1973; Natl. Book Critics Circle award, 1982. Fellow Am. Acad. Arts and Scis. Address: 606 Hanshaw Rd Ithaca NY 14850

AMORY, CLEVELAND, b. Nahant, MA, Sept. 2, 1917; s. Robert and Leonore (Cobb) A. Author: The Proper Bostonians, 1947, Home Town, 1950, The Last Resorts, 1952, Who Killed Society?, 1960, Vanity Fair (anthology), 1960, Mankind? Our Incredible War on Wildlike, 1974, Animail, 1976; novel The Trouble With Nowadays, 1979, The Cat Who Came for Christmas, 1987; radio syndicated Curmodgeon At Large; TV commentator; syndicated newspaper columnist, Animail. AB, Harvard U., 1939; L.H.D., New Eng. Coll. Newspaper reporter Nashua (N.H.) Telegraph, Ariz. Daily Star, Tucson; then mag. editor Prescott (Ariz.) Evening Courier; assoc. editor Saturday Evening Post, 1939-41; free lance writer, 1943—; editor Celebrity Register, 1959, 63, sr. ed., Saturday Rvw, 1959-72; rvwr., TV Guide, 1963-76; contrbg. ed., Parade, 1981—. Founder, pres. The Fund for Animals. Office: 200 W 57th St New York NY 10019

ANANIA, MICHAEL ANGELO, b. Omaha, Aug. 5, 1939, s. Angelo Michael and Dora (Van Der Berg) A.; m. Joanne B. Oliver, Dec. 22, 1960; 1 child, Francesca. Author: The Color of Dust, 1970, Set/Sorts, 1974, Riversongs, 1978, The Red Menace, 1984, Constructions/Variations, 1985, Two Poems, 1985, The Sky at Ashland, 1986; ed. New Poetry Anthology, 1969. BA, U. Nebr., 1961; postgrad. SUNY, Buffalo, 1961-64. Ed. Audit/Poetry, Buffalo, 1963-66; instr. English, Northwestern U., 1965-68; lit. ed. Swallow Press, Chgo., 1967-74; prof. English, U. Ill., Chgo., 1968—. Recipient poetry prize Friends of Lit., 1970, Pushcart prize, 1980, Author of Yr. award Ill. Assn. Tchrs. English, 1985; Ill. arts Council fellow in fiction, 1980. Mem. PEN, CCLM (chmn., pres. 1972-76). Home: 5755 Sunset La Grange IL 60625

ANAPORTE-EASTON, JEAN BOEHLKE, b. Saginaw, MI, July 19, 1942, d. Otto Joseph and Jean Elizabeth (Adsitt) Boehlke; m. Stephen Whitney Easton, May 6, 1965 (div.); 1 child, Delia Ellen. Contrbr. poetry to Anima, Greenfield Rvw, Anthol Am. Verse, Yellow Silk, Yrbk. Am. Poetry. AB, U. Mich., 1964; MAT, Brown U., 1970; MFA, Cornell U., 1983; DA, SUNY, Albany, 1986. Asst. prof. SUNY, Cobleskill, 1972-78, dir. vis. wrtrs. program, 1975-78; condr. writing workshop Elmira Correctional Facility, N.Y., 1979-80, Mental Health Assn., Albany, N.Y., 1985-86; teaching asst. Cornell U., Ithaca, N.Y., 1978-80; part-time lectr. SUNY, Albany, 1983-86; adj. faculty, Univ. Without Walls, Skidmore College, 1987—. Mem. MLA, AWP, Hudson Valley Wrtrs. Guild, Feminist Wrtrs.' Guild. Home: 220 Green St 5C Albany NY 12202

ANAYA, RUDOLFO A., b. Pastura, NM, Oct. 30, 1937, s. Martin and Rafaelita (Mares) A.; m. Patricia Lawless. Novelist: Bless Me, Ultima, 1972, Heart of Aztlan, 1976, Tortuga, 1979, The Legend of La Llorona, 1984; author: Cuentos: Tales from the Hispanic Southwest, 1980, The Silence of the Llano (short stories), The Adventures of Juan Chicaspatas (epic poem), The Magic Words (essay); co-ed.: Ceremony of Brotherhood (with Simon Ortiz), 1980, Cuentos Chicanos—A Short Story Anthology (with Antonio Marquez), 1984, A Chicano in China, 1986; contrbr. stories: Grito del Sol, Mother Jones, Wrtrs. of the Purple Sage, numerous other lit publs. BA in English, U. N. Mex., 1963, MA in English, 1968; LHD (hon.), U. Albuquerque, 1981, Marycrest Coll., 1984. Prof. U. N.Mex., Albuquerque, 1974—. Recipient Premio Quinto Sol for Bless Me, Ultima, 1971, Mesa Chicana Lit. award, U. N.Mex., 1977; NEA creative writing fellow, 1979. Home: 5324 Canada Vista NW Albuquerque NM 87120

ANAZAGASTY, ANITA DOLORES, b. Bronx, NY, Feb. 29, 1944, d. Francisco and Carmen (Vasques) Anazagasty; m. Julio Ruiz, May 28, 1966 (div. May 1, 1971); children: Julio-Rafael Ruiz and Marisol Ruiz. Author: Love's Inner Secrets (1987); contrbr. to anthols. Wrkg. on novel, biography. Ed. James Monroe H.S. (Bronx); cert. in wrtg., Brentwood H.S. (L.I., NY). Special ed. tchr. aide-adult skills trnr., Adult Skills Trng. Ctr., Bronx, 1975-78; mental hygiene therapy aide, State Hospital (Melville, L.I., NY), 1979-82. Award of Merit (poem), Sacramento, CA, 1984; Golden Poet Award, Reno, 1985. Home: 6 Rosewood St Central Islip NY 11722

ANDAL, MARIAN, see Sevandal, Martiana Asis Sagun

ANDEREGG, KAREN KLOK, b. Council Bluffs, IA Dec. 19, 1940; d. George J. and Hazel E. (Durham) Klok; m. George F. Anderegg, Jr., Aug. 27, 1970. BA, Stanford U., 1963. Copywriter Vogue mag., NYC, 1963-72; copy editor Mademoiselle mag., NYC, 1972-77, mng. editor, 1977-80; assoc. editor Vogue Mag., 1980—. Mem. ASME. Office: 350 Madison Ave New York NY 10017

ANDERS, JEANNE, see Anderson, Joan Wester

ANDERSDATTER, KARLA M., (Karla Margaret), b. San Francisco, April 9, 1938; d. Howard Riley and Daphne (Haugen) Crosier; m. 1960 (div. 1970); children—Jennifer Kathleen Williams, Scott Billings. Author: poetry (under name Karla Margaret), Spaces, 1974, I Don't Know Whether to Laugh of Cry 'Cause I Lost the Map to Where I was Going, 1978, Transparencies: Love Poems for the New Age, 1980, The Rising of the Flesh, 1983, To a Chinese Girl, Singing, 1984, The Girl Who Struggled with Death, 1985; fantasies for children, Witches & Whimsies, Marissa the Tooth Fairy, 1979, Follow the Blue Butterfly, 1980, Anazazi Woman, 1985, The Nevernuff Nasty, 1986; contrb to anthologies: Robert Grumpertz and Diane Brewer, eds., Dream Notebook, 1976, A Shout in the Streets, 1981, also magazines and newspapers, including Haight Ashbury Journal, Maybe Mombasa, Nitty Gritty, Room: A Women's Literary Journal. BA, U. of Calif. at Los Angeles, 1958, MA, 1968. Teacher, part-time lecturer in educ., San Francisco State U. Co-ordinator of Late Summer Poetry Series, No Name Bar, Sausalito; publisher, Open Reader; exhibitor at San Francisco Book Fair; workshops and poetry redings; storyteller; artist-in-residence at Centrum Fdn. Member: COSMEP, American Storytellers, Assn. for Humanistic Psychology, Poets and Writers. Calif. Art Council grantee, 980-83 for storytelling in Marin Co. schools. Home: Box T Sausalito CA 94966

ANDERSON, ALEXANDRA C., b. Boston, May 14, 1942; d. Henry and Marion Ruth (Thompson) Fuller; children: Lafcadio, Genevieve, Oscar. BA, Sarah Lawrence Coll., 1961. Art editor: Village Voice, NYC, 1974-77; features assoc.: Vogue Mag., 1977-78; sr. editor Portfolio Mag., NYC, 1979-83; editor-in-chief: Arts and Antiques Mag., NYC, 1983-84; exec. editor, Am. Photographer, 1985—; author: Anderson and Archer's SoHo: The Essential Guide to Art and Life in Lower Manhattan 1979; freelance writer. Bd. dirs. N.Y. State Small Press Assn. Recipient Art Critics' award NEA, 1978; Japan Fdn. travel grantee,1976. Office: 1515 Broadway New York NY 10036

ANDERSON, ANNETHEA ELIZABETH, b. Chgo., June 4, 1932; d. Theodore Francis and Elizabeth Valentine (Louis) Crawley; m. Paul Edward Anderson, Dec. 31, 1958; children—Darienne E., Brette C., Paula F., Peter Crawley Hill. Contrbr. poems to anthols. B.A. sociology, Rossevelt U., 1954. M.Ed., Loyola U., Chgo., 1972. Caseworker Chgo. Welfare Dept., 1954-57, St. Mary's Home for Children, Chgo., 1957-60; dir head start program Chgo. Youth Centers, 1966-69; instr. child devel. Prairie State Coll., Chicago Heights, IL, 1972—. Mem. Natl. Assn. Edn. Young Children, Black Child Devel. Inst. Home: 364 E 89th St Chicago IL 60619

ANDERSON, BRIAN E., b. Mpls., June 13, 1944; s. Bertil E. and Phyllis M. A.; m. Theresa A. McDonald, June 6, 1970; children—David, Elizabeth. BA, U. MN, 1966. Rptr., Mpls. Star & Tribune, 1966-68, 70-73; legislative aide/speechwriter Sen. Walter F. Mondale, Washington, 1968-70; acct. exec. Carl Byoir & Assocs.,Mpls., 1975-76; editorial v. p., MSP Pubns., & ed. Mpls. St. Paul mag., Mpls., 1977—. Served in US Army Res., 1966-72. Mem. SPJ, MN Press Club, Phi Beta Kappa. Office: MSP Pub 12 S 6th St Minneapolis MN 55402

ANDERSON, BROCKE, see Anderson, Irma Louise

ANDERSON, CAROL JEAN, b. Seattle, Nov. 29, 1946; d. James William and Patricia Helen (Pratt) Hunt. Author: Muddle Puddle, 1983; author, pub.: Alphabet Soup, 1985; author ed.; Northwest Corner Catalog, 1986. Contrbr. articles to popular mags. B.A. in Edn., Western Washington U., 1969, M.A. in Edn. Administration, 1986. Tchr. Bellingham schs., WA, 1969-74, Queen Charlotte sch. dist., Queen Charlotte Island, British Columbia, Canada, 1974-76. Mem. COSMEP, Natl. Council Computers in Edn. Home: Box 5182 Bellingham WA 98227

ANDERSON, CURTISS MARTIN, b. Mols., July 16, 1928; s. Otto and Hilda Marie (Holman) A.; m. Anne Sonopol, Dec. 12, 1953. Author: Collections from the American Past, 1975, (with J.C. Hall) When You Care Enough, 1979. BA, U. Minn., 1951. With Meredith Pub. Co., Des Moines, 1951-60; editor Vacation Ideas book, Home Building Ideas Book, 1951-52, assoc. editor, sr. writer mag., 1956-57, spcl. features editor mag., 1957-60; assoc. editor, staff writer Ladies Home Jnl., Phila., 1960, mng. editor, 1961-62, editor-in-chief, 1962-64; contract writer McCall's mag., 1964; editor Venture—The Traveler's World, 1964-71, v.p., 1967-71; editor Hallmark Cards, Inc., Kansas City, Mo., 1971-72; editor. pub. dir. Diversion Mag., 1972-75; mng. editor Look mag., 1978-79; editor mag. development, Hearst Corp., 1979—; asst. to pub. SF Examiner, 1984—. Served with USN, 1946-48. Recipient award for best article on architecture in non-profl. mag AIA, 1955; named one of ten oustanding young men of year S. Jr. C. of C., 1963. Mem. Am. Soc. Mag. Editors, Sigma Delta Chi. Home: 150 E 69th St New York NY 10021

ANDERSON, DALE, See Anderson, Paul Dale

ANDERSON, DAVID CHARLES, b. Oakland, CA, Apr. 27, 1931; s. Clarence Emil and Alice Smith A; m. Jean Lynn Hess, June 8, 1957; children: Alan R., David Christian, Gregory Leon, Bradley R., Lisa L. Author: From Solomon's Songbook: The Odes, 1984; ed. and compiler: Veterinary serials, 1987. BA, U. Calif.-Berkeley, 1952, BLS, 1953. Libn. local Planning office, State Dept. Finance, Sacramento, Calif., 1957-62; serials cataloger Univ. Calif., Davis, 1962-69, head health sci. cataloging pool, 1969-71, tech. services libn. health sci. library, 1971—. Served to Spec. 3, US Army, 1953-56, Newfoundland. Address: 8732 Rock Springs Rd Penryn CA 95663

ANDERSON, DAVID POOLE, b. Troy, NY,May 6, 1929; s. Robert F. and Josephine (David) A. m. Maureen Ann Young, Oct. 24, 1953; children—Stephen, Mark, Mary Jo, Jean Marie. Author: Countdown to Super Bowl, 1969, (with Ray Robinson) Sugar Ray, 1970, (with Larry Csonka and Jim Kiick) Always On the Run, 1973, Pancho Gonzalez, 1974, (with Frank Robinson) Frank: The First Year, 1976, Sports of Our Times, 1979, The Yankees, 1979, (with John Madden) Hey, Wait a Minute, I Wrote a Book, 1984, (with Madden) One Knee Equals Two Feet, 1986, The Story of Football, 1985; editor: The Red Smith Reader, 1981. BA, Holy Cross Coll., 1951. Sports writer Bklyn. Eagle, 1951-55, New York Jnl-Amer., 1955-56, New York Times, 1966—. Recipient Best Sports Stories award (mag.), 1965; Best Sports Stories award (features), 1972; Page One award for sports features, 1972; Nat Fleischer award for boxing writing, 1974; Pulitzer Prize for commentary, 1981. Home: 8 Inness Rd Tenafly NJ 07670

ANDERSON, IRMA LOUISE, (Brocke Anderson), b. Dothan, AL, Oct. 29, 1941; d. Grady Byron and Wilmot Williams Brock, m. John Heany Hall, Nov. 16, 1960 (div. June 1971); children—Jack Byron, Sandra Lee; m. Daniel Warren Anderson, July 4, 1971; children—Roxanna, Danielle. Columnist Delta Junction Midnight Sun, Alaska, 1970. Contrbr. articles to newspapers. Wrkg. on short story, novel A Coming of Age. A.A., Chipola Jr. Coll, 1985. Recipient 1st place for article Colorado Springs Gazette-Telegraph, 1977, Honorable Mention for fiction NWC, 1985. Home: Rt 1 Box 167 Blountstown FL 32424

ANDERSON, JACK NORTHMAN, b. Long Beach, CA, Oct. 19, 1922; s. Orlando N. and Agnes (Mortensen) A.; m. Olivia Farley, Aug. 10, 1949; children—Cheri, Lance F., Laurie, Tina, Kevin N., Randy N., Tanya, Rodney V., Bryan W. Author: (with Ronald May) McCarthy the Man, The Senator, The Ism, 1952, (with Fred Blumenthal) The Kefauver Story, 1956, (with Drew Pearson) U.S.A. Second Class Power?, 1958, Washington Expose, 1966, Case Against Congress, 1968, (with Carl Kalvelage) American Government—Like It Is, 1972, (with George Clifford) The Anderson Papers, 1973, (with Bill Pronzini) The Cambodia File, 1981, (with John Kidner) Alice in Blunderland, 1983, (with James Boyd), Fiasco (1983). Student, U. Utah, 1940-41, Georgetown U., 1947-48, George Washington U., 1948. Reporter, Salt Lake Tribune, 1939-41; war corr. Deseret News, 1945; reporter Washington Merry-go-Round, 1947—, partner from 1965, owner, from 1969; Washington editor Parade mag., 1954-68, bur. chief, from 1968; Missionary in So. states for Church Jesus Christ of Latter Day Saints, 1941-44. Secy, trustee Chinese Refugee Relief from 1962. Served with U.S. Mcht. Marine, 1944-45; with AUS, 1946-47. Recipient Pulitzer Prize for Natl. Reporting, 1972. Mem. White House Corr. Assn. Club, National Press Club. Office: United Feature 200 Park Ave New York NY 10166

ANDERSON, JACK WARREN, b. Milwaukee, WI, June 15, 1935; s. George William and Eleanore (Forse) Anderson. Author: The American Dance Festival, 1987, Modern Dance: A Concise History, 1986, Selected Poems, 1983, The Clouds of That Country, 1982, The One and Only: The Ballet Russe De Monte Carlo, 1981, The Nutcracker Ballet, 1979, Toward the Liberation of the Left Hand, 1977, The Dust Dancers, 1977, City Joys, 1975, Dance, 1974, The Invention of New Jersey, 1969, The Hurricane Lamp, 1969. BS, Northwestern U., 1957, MA, Indiana U., 1958. Asst. drama critic, Oakland Tribune, Ca., 1960-62; corresp., Ballet Today, London, 1960-70; dance wrtr., Dance Mag., NYC, 1964-78; NYC corresp., The Dancing Times, London, 1971—; dance critic, NY Times, NYC, 1978—. Awards: NEA Fellowship, 1973; Pushcart Prize, 1976-77. De La Torre Bueno Award, 1980. Mem. PSA, Dance Critics Assn. Home: 110 Thompson St New York NY 10012

ANDERSON, JAMES E(LLIOTT), b. Galva, IL, July 6, 1933; s. Albin C. and Amy (Nelson) A.; m. Alberta Hedstrom, June 21, 1953; children: Carrie, Elise, Joel. Author: The Emergence of the Modern Regulatory State, 1962, Politics and the Economy, 1966, compiler, Politics and Economic Policy-making: Selected Readings, 1970, (with Richard Murray and Edward L. Farley) Texas Politics: An Introduction, 1971, 4th ed., 1984, Public Policy-making, 1975, 3d ed., 1984, ed., Cases in Public Policy-making, 1976, 2d ed., 1981, ed., Economic Regulatory Policies, 1976, (with David W. Brady and Charles Bullock III), Politics and Policy in America, 1978, 2d ed., 1984, (with Jared Hazelton), Managing Macroeconomic Policy: The Johnson Presidency, 1986. Cntrbr. to pfnl. jnls. Attended U. of Illinois, 1950-52 and Ill. State Normal U. (now Illinois State U.), 1952-53; BS, Southwest Texas State Teachers Coll. (now Southwest Texas State U.), 1955, Ph.D., U. of Texas, 1960. Instructor Wake Forest College (now University), Winston-Salem, N.C., 1959-60, asst. prof., 1960-64, assoc. prof. 1964-66; assoc. prof., of pol. sci., U. of Houston, Tex. 1966-69, prof. of pol. sci., Texas A & M U., 1986—. Member: Am. Pol. Sci. Assn., Policy Studies Organ. Midwest Poli. Sci. Assn., Southern Poli. Sci. Assn., Southwestern Poli. Sci. Assn. Politics: Democrat. Office: Dept. of Pol. Sci. Texas A & M College Station TX 77843

ANDERSON, JEAN BLANCHE, b. St. Louis, Sept. 13, 1940; d. Clifford George and Blanche Jean (Pell) Schulze; m. Donald Wyckliffe Anderson, Feb. 14, 1961; children—Thomas, Laura. Contrbr. numerous short stories, essays, rvws., poems to lit. mags., anthols., popular mags. Ed.: Permafrost, 1978. A.A., Harris Tchrs. Coll., 1960; B.A., U. Alaska, 1977, M.F.A., 1980. Poet in elem. schls. Fairbanks Arts Assn. of North Star Borough Schl. District, AK, 1981-82; project coord. fiction competition Fireweed Press, Fairbanks, 1984; book rvwr. Fairbanks Daily News-Miner, 1985—. Awarded Individual Artists' Award in Lit., Alaska State Council on the Arts, 1982, PEN syndicated fiction selection, 1985. Home: 509 Aquila St Fairbanks AK 99712

ANDERSON, JOAN WESTER, (Jeanne Anders), b. Evanston, IL, Aug. 12, 1938; d. Theodore Michael and Monica Florence (Noesges) Wester; m. William Henry Anderson, Aug. 20, 1960; children—Christopher, Timothy, William, Brian, Nancy. Author: Love, Lollipops and Laundry, 1976, Stop the World—Our Gerbils are Loose!, 1979, The Best of Both Worlds—A Guide to Home-Based Careers, 1982, Teen Is a Four-Letter Word, 1984, Dear World, Don't Spin so Fast, 1984; (as Jeanne Anders): Language of the Heart, 1985, Leslie, 1987; contrbr. over 600 articles and short stories to: Modern Bride, Modern Maturity, Christian Sci. Monitor, Marriage and Family Living, others. Student Mount Mary Coll., 1956-58. Home: 811 N Hickory St Arlington Heights IL 60004

ANDERSON, JOHN CHARLES, b. Bay City, MI, May 20, 1954; s. Charles James and June Elizabeth (Lepisto) A.; m. Marcia Susan Foster, July 14, 1984. Author: (poems) Cosmic Omelet, 1979. Contrbr. poems to North Am. Mentor, anthol. B.A. in History, U. Mich., 1976; post-grad. Cath. U. Am., 1985—. U.S. Army Civil Svc., 1981—.Served to capt. U.S. Army, 1976-81. Mem. Mensa.. Home: 5903 Mt Eagle Dr 207 Alexandria VA 22303

ANDERSON, JON, b. Somerville, MA, July 4, 1940, s. Charles and Francis Elizabeth (Ladd) Golder; m. Barbara Anne Hershkowitz; 1 child—Bodi Orlen. Author: Looking for Jonathan, 1968, Death & Friends, 1970, In Sepia, 1974, Counting the Days, 1974, Cypresses, 1982, The Milky Way, Poems 1967-82, 1983. BS in Edn., Northeastern U., 1964; MFA, U. Iowa, 1968. Prof. U. Portland, Oreg., 1968-71, Ohio U., Athens, 1971-72, U. Pitts., 1972-74; U. Iowa, Iowa City, 1974-75, U. Ariz., Tucson, 1976—. Guggenheim fellow, 1975, NEA fellow, 1981, 86; recipient Shelley Meml. award, PSA, 1983. Home: 633 N Stewart St Tucson AZ 85716

ANDERSON, KAREN L., b. Pensacola, FL, Aug. 28, 1948, d. Charles Robert and Betty Lou (Christianson) Anderson; m. Robert Spencer Hotchkiss, June 8, 1968 (div. 1984); children—Lanson Spencer, Bree Anders. Author: Building Bridges (with Pauline Paulin), 1972, Always Searching, 1974, Velvet Caves, 1987, Kaleidoscope Truth, 1987; contrbr.: Puerto del Sol, Am. Poetry Anthology, Thoughtprints, Wide Open, numerous others; ed.: Art and the Computer (by Melvin Prueitt), 1984, Braves, 1974-76, Smokesignals, 1978-80, Pegasus, 1985—; author, ed. curricular materials, reports, scholarly papers. BA, U. N.Mex., 1971, MA, 1974, ABA, 1987. Tchr. Los Alamos (N.Mex.) Schs., 1971—; instr. U. NM-Los Alamos, 1981—; cons., ed., Los Alamos, 1982—; ed. AAUW, Los Alamos chap., 1981-82. Mem. AAP, AAUW, Santa Fe Writing Forum, Rio Grande Wrtrs. Assn. Home: 2536 C 36th St Los Alamos NM 87544

ANDERSON, MAGGIE, b. NYC, Sept. 23, 1948. Author: The Great Horned Owl, 1979, Years That Answer, 1980, Cold Comfort, 1986; ed. Trellis, 1971-81; contrbr. poems to Am. Poetry Rvw, Prairie Schooner, Poetry East, N.W. Rvw. AB, W.Va. U., 1970, MA, 1973. Artist-in-residence Marshall County Schls., Moundsville, W.Va., 1978-80, Mercer County Schls., Princeton, W.Va., 1982; vis. poet U. Pitts., 1981, 83, vis. prof. W.Va. Univ., 1986, vis. asst. prof., 1983-84; vis. lectr. Hamilton Coll., Clinton, N.Y., 1985; vis. poet Penn State U., 1986. W.Va. Arts and Humanities Commn. writing fellow, 1980-81; poetry fellow Pa. Council on Arts, 1982, 87, NEA, 1984; fellow MacDowell Colony, 1984. Mem. AWP, PSA. Home: 353 N Porter St Waynesburg PA 15370

ANDERSON, MARIE BARBARA, (Barbara Anderson), b. Detroit, Feb. 5, 1934; d. Frank and Marie (Banyai) Brandstatter; m. G. W. Anderson, 1950 (div. 1979); children—Alan C., Michael D., William J. Author: Touring the Grand, 1987. Contrbr. articles to mags. Wrkg. on Seven Who Lost and The Papal Countess. Student Mich. State U., 1949-50. Secy., clrk. Wurzburg Dept. Store, Grand Rapids, MI, 1950-53; salesperson real estate, Grand Rapids, 1981—. Home:1265 Curwood Ct SE Grand Rapids MI 49508

ANDERSON, MARY JANE, b. Richmond, VA, May 27, 1930; d. Francis Wilber and Margaret Genevieve (Esbrook) A. Pub., The Anderson Report, Foods by Mail, 1973—; contrbr. num.

arts. to food svc. trade books. BS in Jnlsm., Wayne State U., 1952. Var. pub. jobs, Detroit, 1952-54; rptr., Fairchild Pubns., Detroit & Chgo., 1954-67; food svc. ed. Vend May/Billboard Pub., Chg. & NYC, 1967-73; owner/pub. Anderson Pubns., Chgo., 1973—. Office: Anderson Pub 203 N Wabash Chicago IL 60601

ANDERSON, MICHAEL JAMES, b. Temple, TX, Nov. 7, 1943. Contrbr. poetry to Wormwood Rvw, The Cape Rock, Kans. Qtly, numerous other lit mags; contrbr. articles to AP wire service. BA in Journalism, U. Oreg., Eugene, 1965; BA in Community Service, Eastern Oreg. State Coll., La grande, 1976. Ed. Clarke Press, Portland, Oreg., 1968-69; sports ed. Newport (Oreg.) News-Times, 1969-72; freelance wrtr., 1976—. Home: 158 Lincoln St Ashland OR 97520

ANDERSON, MOIRA KATHARINE, b. Santa Rosa, CA, Jan. 1, 1959; d. Victor Roland and Muriel Ann (Drake) Anderson; m. Patrick David Allen, Mar. 17, 1984. Contrbr.: Quilt, 1980, 84, Omni, 1984, Am. Kennel Club Gazette, 1983, 85; synd. stringer News Post News Svc., 1983—; assoc. ed. Cat Fancy, 1985—, Bird Talk, 1985—, Horse Illustd., 1985—; contrbg. ed. Pet Health News, 1985—; mng. ed. Dog Fancy, 1985—. BA in Anthrop., U.CA-Berkeley, 1981. Tech. writer Natl. Inst. Health, Bethesda, MD, 1984; mng. ed. Dog Fancy, San Juan Capistrano, CA, 1985—; freelance writer. Mem. Dog Writers Assn. Am. Home: 17211 Stowers Ave Cerritos CA 90701

ANDERSON, PAUL DALE, (Irwin Chapman, Karl Gustav, Dale Anderson), b. Rockford, IL, Sept. 11, 1944; s. Paul Anders and Winnefred Lisle (Crosby) A.; m. Susan E. Risinger, 1975 (div. 1979); m. Gretta McCombes, June 22, 1985; 1 dau., Tammy Jeanne. Author: The Devil Made Me Do It: Twenty Contemporary Tales of Subtle Horror, 1985; columnist SPWAO Newsletter, 1986-87. Contrbr. short stories, articles, book rvws. to mags. Ed.: 2AM Mag., 1986—. Wrkg. on novels, short story collections, how-to book on writing and marketing contemporary fiction. Student Rockford Coll, 1964-66; B.A. in English, Loyola U., 1975. Account exec. Allstates Promotional Adr. Corp. Skokie, IL, 1984; customer service representative Am. Soc. Clinical Pathologists, Chgo., 1985-87; instr. How to Write Bestsellers workshop U. Ill., Chgo., 1986—. Recipient Voice of Democracy Speech award VFW, Rockford, 1962. Mem. SPWAO (Service award 1987; grievance officer), Horror Wrtrs. Am. (v.p. 1986), Sci. Fiction Research Assn., Soc. Lit. Sci., COSMEP. Adderss: Box 3481 Oak Park IL 60303

ANDERSON, POUL WILLIAM, b. PA, 1926. Degree physics, U. Minn., 1948. Author: Brain Wave, 1954, Planet of No Return, 1956, War of the Wing-Men, 1958, Earthman Go Home!, 1960, jayday Orbit, 1961, After Doomsday, 1962, Let the Spaceman Beware, 1963, Orbit Unlimited, 1963, Is There Life on Other Worlds, 1963, Time and Stars, 1964, Agent of the Terran Empire, 1965, The Trouble Twisters, 1966, The Horn of Time, 1968, Infinite Voyage: Man's Future in Space, 1969, Tall Zero, 1970, Brain Wave, 1970, Circus of Hells, 1970, Guardians of Time, 1970, Seven Conquests, 1970, Tales of the Flying Mountains, 1970, Operation Chaos, 1971, Byworlder, 1971, The Broken Sword, 1971, Hrolf Kraki's Saga, 1973, Virgin Planet, 1973, The Rebel World, 1973, People of the Wind, 1973, Fire Time, 1974, The Many Worlds of Poul Anderson, 1974, The Book of Poul Anderson, 1975, Mirkheim, 1977, The Avatar, 1978, The Merman's Children, 1979, Orion Shall Arise, 1983, numerous others. Recipient Hugo award, Nebula award. Issue of Mag. Fantasy and Science dedicated to him, 1972. Office: Meredith Lit Agcy 845 3d Ave New York NY 10022

ANDERSON, RICHARD, b. NYC, Dec. 27, 1946; s. Arnold Andrew and Isabel (Guilfoyle) A.; m. Deborah Shea, Aug. 21, 1981. Author: William Goldman, 1979, Straight Cut Ditch, 1979, Muckaluck, 1980, Robert Coover, 1981, On the Run, 1986, Arranging Deck Chairs on the Titanic, 1986; ed.: (with Jim Charlton) Sports Quotation Handbook, 1987. MA, CUNY, 1971; PhD, NYU, 1977. Fulbright prof. U. of Bergen, Norway, 1982-83; acting dir. Michael Karolyi Foundation, Vence, France, 1983-84; James Thurber Writer in Resid., Ohio State U., Columbus, 1985—. Home: 2908 S E Tolman St Portland OR 97202

ANDRE, MICHAEL, (T. W. Fretter), b. Halifax, Can., Aug. 31, 1946; arrd. USA, 1968. Author: Studying the Ground for Holes (poetry), 1976; ed. Poets Encyc., 1979. BA, McGill, 1968; PhD, Columbia, 1972. Art critic Art News and Village Voice, NYC, 1971-76; ed. Unmuzzled Ox, NYC, 1971—. Recipient Can. Council award, NYC, 1968-72. Address: 105 Hudson St New York NY 10013

ANDRE, PAUL DEAN, b. Mechanicsville, IA, Sept. 5, 1928; s. Marvin Leonard and Beryl Madge (Anderson) A.; m. Fran Valeria Tjaden, Dec. 27, 1952; 1 dau., Carol Lea Andre Happley. Assoc. farm ed.: Cedar Rapids Gazette, IA, 1955-61; asst. extension ed.: Iowa State U., Ames, 1961-62; ed.: Watt Pub. Co., Mt. Morris, Ill., 1962-64, St. Paul, 1964—. Recipient Top Choice award Colo. Cattle Feeders Assn., 1981. Mem. Livestock Pub. Council (vp, 1985-87, pres., 1987-88; numerous writing and photography awards 1973-85), Am. Agrl. Eds. Assn. (numerous writing and photography awards 1973-85). Home: 18351 W Sioux Vista Dr Jordan MN 55352

ANDREWS, BILLY F., b. Graham, NC, Sept. 22, 1932; s. Dean Franklin and Arlee A. (Byers) A.; m. Fay Rich, Dec. 25, 1953; children—Ann Elizabeth, Billy F. Jr., David Ashley. Ed.: Small-for-Date Infants, 1970, The Newborn, Pediatric Clinics of North America, 1977, Aphorisms, Tributes, and Tenets of Billy F. Andrews, 1986, Sir William Osler in Perinatal Perspective; contrbr. articles and abstracts to profl. jnls., poetry to med. jnls., books and mags. Wrkg. on poetry collection. BS cum laude, Wake Forest Coll., 1953; MD, Duke U., 1957. Pediatrician; dir. Comprehensive Health Care Center for High Risk Infants, Louisville, 1968—; chief of staff Kosair Children's Hosp., Louisville, 1969—; prof., chmn. pediatrics U. Louisville, 1969—. Founding lectr. Jnl. Pediatrics, 1972. Home: Rt 3 Box 547 Floyds Knobs IN 47119

ANDREWS, HEBER J., b. Santa Rosa, CA, Apr 19, 1935; s. Edward Andrews and Hannah Soper Bryant; m. Cheryl Ruth Forbes, Jan. 21, 1967; children: Jeffrey G. and Monica P. Author: Bicycle Owner's Packet, 1980; How To Prevent Bicycle Theft, 1982, How to Avoid Bicycle Theft, 1985. Owner Tacoma Custom Tire, Wash, 1977—, Hands Off Pub. Co., 1979—. Served to sgt. 1st class, US Army, USA, 1953-77. Mem. Bicycle Fedn. Am., League Am. Wheelmen, Bikecentennial. Address: 3517 N Verde St Tacoma WA 98407

ANDREWS, JOHN, see Hegyeli, Ruth Ingeborg Elisabeth Johnsson

ANDREWS, MARCIA STEPHANIE, (M.S. Andrews), b. Portland, OR, Aug. 7, 1947; d. Margaret Mary (Lockhart) A. Author: (novel) A Summer's Tale, 1986; contrbr. poetry and short stories to Antenna, New Mexico, So. Humanities revs., others. BA, Portland State U., 1970; MA, San Francisco State U., 1984. Recipient 2d prize Gertrude Stein Symposium, UCLA, 1984; Ludwig Vogelstein Fdn. fellow, 1985. Mem. NWU. Home: 390 Bartlett St 12 San Francisco CA 94110

ANDREWS, MARY ANITA, b. Hope, Ar, Nov. 8, 1931; d. Webb and Hope (Bennett) Laseter; m. Isaac Raymond Andrews, June 20, 1981. Contrbr. articles to newspapers, mags. including Ark. Democrat, Shreveport Times, True Romance, others. Grad. public shcls., Hope, Ar. Reporter, Hope Star, AR, 1956-74, Sta. KXAR, Hope, 1956-74; free-lance wrtr., 1950—. Recipient numerous awards Ark. Wrtrs. Conf., 1950-87. Home: 2701 Aldersgate Rd 138 Little Rock AR 72205

ANDREWS, MICHAEL DUANE, b. Inglewood, CA, Dec. 15, 1944, s. James Joseph and Ruth Virginia (Elm) A. Author: Poems for Amber, 1975, Xmas Tree Massacre, 1975, 40 Turkeys So What, 1975; editor: Beyond Baroque Foundation, 1975-76; editor-pub.: Alley Cat Reading, 1975-76; pub.: Bombshelter Press, 1976—, River Run, 1977, Machu Picchu, 1979, Riding South, 1982. Wrkg. on The Xmas Kid, 99% Pacified, Gnomes. Student pub. schls., Inglewood, Calif. Programmer analyst Control Data Corp., Saigon, Vietnam, 1969-71, Bell Helicopter, Tehran, Iran, 1975; programmer cons., Hermosa Beach, Calif., 1972-74; poet, printer, artist, Hermosa Beach, 1975-82; v.p. software devel. Sum Data Systems, Inglewood, 1982—. Mem. Mensa. Home: 1092 Loma Dr Hermosa Beach CA 90254

ANDREWS, RAYMOND, b. Madison, GA, June 6, 1934, s. George Cleveland and Viola (Perryman) A.; m. Adelheid Wenger, Dec. 28, 1966 (div. June 1980). Author: (novels) Appalachee Red, 1978, Rosiebelle Lee Wildcat Tennessee, 1980, Baby Sweet's; 1983; contrbr. to Sports Illustrated, Ataraxia. Student Mich. State U., 1956-57. With KLM, NYC, 1958-66; photog. librarian Pix Photo Agcy., NYC, 1967-72; courier Archer Courier, NYC, 1972-84; freelance fiction wrtr., since 1966. Served with USAF, 1952-56, Korea. Recipient James Baldwin award Dial Press, 1979. Home: 2013 Morton Rd Athens GA 30605

ANDRIES, DOROTHY DELACOMA, b. Chgo., Jan. 10, 1937; d. Albert Joseph and Pearl Margaret (Burr) D.; m. Donald Andries, June 14, 1958; chidren—Daniel Albert, Donald Joseph, David Delacoma, Darrill James. BS, Marquette U. Coll. Jnlsm., 1958. Arts ed. Pioneer Press, Wilmette, IL, 1973-78; travel ed. Milwaukee Sentinel, 1978-81; ed. Pioneer Press Qtly, Wilmette, 1982—. Mem. adv. bd. Chicago Catholic newspaper. Home: 926 Wilmot Rd Deerfield IL 60015

ANDROLA, RON, b. New Castle, PA, Aug. 7, 1954, s. Harold Frank and Julie (Abdoe) A.; m. Diane Catherine Shied, Feb. 2, 1979; children—Rachel, Douglas. Author: 14 Poems, The Spirituality of Husbands, T 'n A, Curls Thru the Language, The Kiss, The Taste of Pain, Steam & Garlic, Don't Read this Poem, Morning Philosophy, Power as a Writer, Duck & Suck, Cunt, 1987, You No Me, 1987; contrbr. to Random Weirdness, Gargoyle, Raw Bone, Planet Detroit, other lit mags.; ed. Northern Pleasure mag., Northern Pressure Press, 1982—. BA, Franconia Coll., 1976. Home: 4017 Rilling Ave Erie PA 16509

ANDRZEJEWSKI, MARGARET RUSEK, b. Buffalo, Mar. 4, 1953, d. Eugene F. and Irene (Saramak) Rusek; m. Wayne F. Andrzejewski, May 4, 1979; 1 dau.—Susan Ann. Columnist, advisor INFO, publ. NY State Assn. Two-Yr. Colls. Wrkg. on freelance articles. BA, SUNY, Buffalo, 1976. Officer of Admin., Trocaire Coll., Buffalo, 1973—. Home: 457 Weimar St Buffalo NY 14206

ANGEL, JOHNNY, see Bennett, John J.

ANGEL, RALPH MICHAEL, b. Seattle, May 2, 1951, s. Lee and Margie Luna (Nahmias) A.; m. Killarney Elizabeth Clary, June 12, 1982. Author: History (chapbook), 1982, Anxious Latitudes, 1986. BA, U. Wash., 1973; MFA, U. Calif.-Irvine, 1977. Instr. U. Calif.-Irvine, 1977; vis. instr. Calif. Inst. Arts., Valencia, 1980-81; assoc. prof. U. Redlands, Calif., 1981—. Mem. AWP, AAP. Home: 838 Bank St South Pasadena CA 91030

ANGELL, ROGER, b. NYC, Sept. 19, 1920; s. Ernest and Katharine Shepley (Sergeant) A.; m. Evelyn Ames Baker, Oct. 1942 (div. 1963); children—Caroline S., Alice; m. Carol Rogge, Oct. 1963; 1 son, John Henry. Author: The Stone Arbor, 1961, A Day in the Life of Roger Angell, 1971, The Summer Game, 1972, Five Seasons, 1977, Late Innings, 1982. Grad. Pomfret Schl., 1938; AB, Harvard, 1942. Editor, writer: Mag. X, Curtis Pub. Co., 1946-47; sr. editor: Holiday, 1947-56; fiction editor, genl. contbr.: New Yorker, 1956—. Past com. member New York Civil Liberties Union. Served with USAAF, 1942-46, PTO. Recipient George Polk award for commentary, 1981. Mem. AG, AL, PEN. Home: 1261 Madison Ave New York NY 10028

ANGELL, VALENTINE CHAUNCEY, (V. C. Angell), b. Grand Rapids, MN, Sept. 14, 1941; s. Valentine C., Jr. and Laverne (Leef) A.; m. Joyce K. Sukalski, Nov. 28, 1964 (dec. Aug. 14, 1967); 1 dau., Kathryn L.; m. 2d, Mary Martin Hess, Oct. 11, 1969; 1 son, Valentine. Ed. Advance Jnl, vols. IX and X, 1981-83; author (as ghost writer) 2 how-to-business books; contrbr. business articles to trade mags. Lab. supr. U. Penn., Phila., 1967-79; bus. cons., writer, Bemidji, Minn., 1979-83. Served with U.S. Army, 1963-66, Vietnam. Mem. AG. Home: 712 11th St Bemidji MN 56601

ANGELOU, MAYA, b. St. Louis, Apr. 4, 1928; d. Bailey and Vivian (Baxter) Johnson; 1 son, Guy Johnson. Author: I Know Why the Caged Bird Sings, 1970, Just Give Me a Cool Drink of Water 'Fore I Die, 1971, Georgia, Georgia, 1972, Gather Together in My Name, 1974, Oh Pray My Wings Are Gonna Fit Me Well, 1975, Singin' and Swingin' and Gettin' Merry Like Christmas, 1976, And Still I Rise, 1976. Named Woman of Yr. in Communications, 1976. Ofice: Le Camera L & D Inc 51 Church St Boston MA 02116

ANGER, KENNETH, b. Santa Monica, Calif., 1932. Producer, dir. films Escape Episode, 1946, Fireworks, 1947, Puce Moment, 1949, Eaux d' Artifice, 1953, Inauguration of the Pleasure Dome, 1954, Thelema Abbey, 1955, Scorpio Rising, 1962-64, Kustom Kar Kommandos, 1965, Invocation of My Demon Brother (Lucifer Rising), 1969, Rabbit's Moon, 1971; author: Hollywood Babylon, 1959. Ford Fdn. fellow, 1964. Address: Am Fedn Arts 41 E 65th St New York NY 10021

ANGLE, ROGER, R., b. Wichita, KS, Aug. 2, 1938; s. Roy E. and Alice (Unger) Angle; m. Fontelle Slater, Dec., 1960 (div. 1968); 1 son—Morgan T. Contrbr. to Orange Coast Mag., New West, Waterfront, Plumed Horn, Work, Los Angeles Rvw, Fiction West, other lit mags. BA, U. of Wichita, 1962; MFA, U. Of Calif., 1972. Reporter Newport Ensign (Newport Beach, CA), 1979-82, ed., 1983-85: freelance PR writer, 1986—.Home: 2225 Pacific Ave Apt D Costa Mesa CA 93672

ANGLESEY, ZOE R., b. Forest Grove, OR, June 5, 1941; d. Elmer Anglesey and Lorraine (Peachey) Strong; m. Michael Best; m. Steve Cannon; children: Melanie, Shavahn, Catherine, Chryssa. Author: (poetry) Something More Than Force, 1983, Is It Dangerous, 1987, Central to America, 1987; contrbr. poetry and transls. to Poetry East, New Eng. RVW, Fiction Intl., Mass. Rvw, Ploughshores, others; ed. anthol., IXOK Amar-go: Calif. Women's Poetry. BA, Central Wash. U., AB, Grays Harbor Coll., MA, NYU, 1985. Home: 285 E 3d St New York NY 10009

ANGOFF, MARION BRENDA, b. Cambridge, MA, Mar. 23, 1939; d. Nathan Robert and Evelyn (Kanter) Angoff. Author: An Approach to Achieving Measurable Effective and Efficient Composition Skills in Grades 6-12, 1979; ed. prose and poetry for publ., 1969—. Wrkg. on non-fiction. BA, Wellesley Coll., 1961; MEd, Tufts U., 1962. Assoc. ed. Harvard Med. Alumni Bulltn., Boston, 1962; tchr. English Lexington (Mass.) Public Schs., 1963-88; acct. exec. New Eng. Times Job finder, 1987—. Mem. Lexington Edn. Assn., Mass. Tchrs. Assn., NCTE, New England Poetry Club (organizer poetry readings). Home: 25 Bothfeld Rd Newton MA 02159

ANNE, CLAIR, see Kilbourne, Clara Anne

ANNETT, BRUCE JAMES, Jr., b. Pontiac, MI, May 5, 1952; s. Bruce James and Frances (Bach) A.; m. Amy Walker, July 20, 1985. Ed.: Lawrence Inst. of Tech. Mag., Southfield, MI, 1977—; admissions ed.: DePauw U., Greencastle, IN, 1974-76. B.A., Albion Coll., 1974; student Mich. State U., 1986—. Dir. coll. relations and alumni services Lawrence Inst. of Tech., 1976—. Recipient Spcl. Merit award Council for Advancement and Support of Edn., Washington, 1980; Merit award Natl. Schl. Public Relations Assn., Arlington, VA, 1981, 83, 84, hon. mention award, 1981, award of excellence, 1984. Mem. Engr. Soc. Detroit (past chmn. pub. com.), Detroit Press Club, IABC (merit award 1983, honorable mtn., 1986). Home: 1034 Northlawn Ave Birmingham MI 48009

ANSON-WEBER, JOAN E., (Joan Anson), b. London, Apr. 9, 1927; d. Walter Leslie and Ethel Lilian (Penman) Nichols; m. Ronald G. Kingham Anson, May 29, 1948 (dec. Nov. 1981); children: Michael Gregory, Christopher Martin; m. Richard Conrad Weber, Sept. 30, 1984. Author: Before the Trees Turn Gray, 1981; contrbr. to lit mags, including Small Pond, Wrtr.'s Digest (3d prize, 1975), Darien Rvw, Potpourri Intl, Wings, Canine Chronicle, Nashville Newsletter (1st prize, 1979), Canvass, The Poet, Poetry Scope, Poem, Taurus, Fairpress. Grad. Guildhall Schl. Music, London, 1948, St. James Coll., London, 1946. Med. secy., Darien, Conn., 1968-84; freelance wrtr., 1974—; poet-in-residence Middlesex Jr. High Schl., Darien, 1981—. Recipient Louisa Halporn award Ind. U., 1980. Mem. Conn. Poetry Soc. (medal 1985). Home: 570 Hoyt St Darien CT 06820

ANSTETT, ROBERT EMORY, b. Jersey City, NJ, Oct. 18, 1933; s. Robert Emory and Frances W. (Whiteman) A.; m. Eleanor Pfordte, Oct. 8, 1960; 1 son, Steven. Mng. ed. Citizens Conservation Council Communicator; daily columnist "Our Environment", 1971-83; contrbr. features on pollution to Ingersoll Synd., 1973; poet, Evidence nos. 1 & 2; author 5 plays, 7 short stories. Student acting, playwriting, Lee Strasberg, NYC. Served to PFC, U.S. Army, 1955-57, Europe. U.S. Dept. Agric. award, outstanding contrbn. as environl. jnlst., 1979. Mem. Common Cause, Environmental Action. Authorized adaptor Twain's "The Man Who Corrupted Hadleyburg." Home: 220 Virginia Dr Brick Township NJ 08723

ANTHONY, JOSEPH, b. Norwich, CT, Apr. 7, 1960. Contrbr. articles to mags., newpapers including Washington Post, Changing Times Mag., Nation's Bus., others. B.A. in Jnlsm. and Poli. Sci., George Washington U., 1982; M.A. in Public Policy Jnlsm., Ohio State U., 1987. Assoc. ed. Outlook Mag., Washington, 1985-86; free-lance wrtr., 1987—. Mem. Washington Ind. Wrtrs. Home: 125 16th St 16 Huntington Beach CA 92648

ANTIGNANI, BONNIE PROVENZANO, b. Trumbull, CT, Oct. 25, 1952; d. Joseph and Dorothy (Krosky) Provenzano; m. David Patrick Antignani,'Aug. 24, 1974; children—BonniLee, David Joseph. Poetry in anthologies. Wrkg. on book. Student Bridgeport Hosp. Schl. Surg. Tehnology, 1971-74, U. Bridgeport, 1971-74, N.Y. Schl. Clin. Hypnosis, 1982. Surg. technologist Bridgeport Hosp., 1971-74, St. George Hosp., Cin., 1975-76; counselor, hypnotherapist, Meriden, Conn., 1980—. Mem. NWC, Am. Poetry Soc., World Poetry Assn. Home: 61 Ridgefield St Meriden CT 06450

ANTILA, V. ANNA, see Clark, Viola Anna

ANTIN, DAVID, b. Bklyn., Feb. 1, 1932; s. Max and Mollie (Kitzes) A.; m. Eleanor Fineman, Dec. 16, 1961; 1 son, Blaise Cendrars. Author: Definitions, 1967, Autobiography, 1967, Code of Flag Behavior, 1968, Meditations, 1971, Talking, 1972, Talking at the Boundaries, 1976, Who's Listening Out There, 1980, Tuning, 1984. BA, CCNY, 1955; MA (Herbert Lehman fellow), N.Y. U., 1966. Prof. visual art U. Calif.-San Diego, 1968—; contbg. editor Alcheringa, 1972-80; editorial com. U. Calif. Press, 1972-1976; contbg. editor New Wilderness, 1979—. Recipient Creative Arts award U. Calif., 1972; Guggenheim fellow, 1976-77; NEH fellow, 1983-84. Home: Box 1147 Del Mar CA 92014

ANTONAZZI, FRANK JOSEPH, JR., b. NYC, Oct. 5, 1950; s. Frank Joseph and Louise (Di Benedetto) A.; m. Theresa Sue Lavelle, Nov. 17, 1980. Contrbr. poetry to Choice, Rapport, Green's, also anthologies. BA, SUNY-Buffalo, 1972. Pub. relations cons. Soc. Underprivileged and Handicapped Children, Inc., Alexandria, Va., 1983—; lectr. adult edn. system Fairfax County, Va., 1985—. Mem. P&W. Home: 2239 Farrington Ave Alexandria VA 22303

APODACA, RUDY SAMUEL, b. Las Cruces, NM., Aug. 8, 1939; s. Raymond and Elisa (Alvarez) A.; m. Nancy Ruth Mitcham, Jan. 16, 1967; children: Cheryl Ann, Carla Renee, Cynthia Lynn, Rudy Samuel. Author: (novel) The Waxen Image, 1977; (screenplay) A Rare Thing, 1984. Wrkg. on mystery suspense screenplay, fictional 3-generation family chronicle. BS, N. Mex. State U., 1961; JD, Georgetown U., 1964. Solo practice law, Las Cruces, 1964-86; appellate judge, NM Court of Appeals, 1987—. Served to capt. U.S. Army, 1964-66. Mem. P&W. Home: 2602 Via Caballero del Norte Santa Fe NM 87501

APPEL, ALFRED, JR., b. NYC, Jan. 31, 1934; s. Alfred and Beatrice (Hoffman) A.; m. Nina Schick, Sept. 1, 1957; children—Karen Appel Oshman, Richard James. Author: A Season of Dreams, 1965; Nabokov's Dark Cinema, 1974, Nabokov's Fifth Arc, 1982, Signs of Life, 1983; author and editor, The Annotated Lolita, 1970; editor: John DeForest's Witching Times, 1967; Nabokov (with Charles Newman), 1970; The Bitter Air of Exile (with Simon Kazlinsky), 1977. Cornell U., 1952-54; Columbia U. BA, 1959, MA, 1960, Ph.D. in English, 1962-63; asst. prof. Stanford U., 1963-68; Northwestern U., asst. prof. 1968-69, assoc. prof. 1969-74, prof. 1974—. U.S. Army, 1955-57. Guggenheim fellow, 1972; Rockefeller fellow, 1976; recipient Best Creative Essay award Ill. Arts Council, 1974. Home: 717 Greenleaf Ave Wilmette IL 60091

APPEL, MARCIA FAYE, b. Rock Rapids, IA, May 21, 1950; d. John and Henrietta A.; m. Vincent Charles Giorgi, Nov. 17, 1984; 1 son, Anthony John Giorgi. Ed./rptr. St. Paul Dispatch, 1970-74; Corporate Report Mag., 1974-77; exec. ed. Twin Cities Woman Mag., 1977-79; ed. Corporate Report Goldletter, 1975-76, Twin Cities Mag., 1986—; contrbr. The Future of Amer. Bus., 1985; co-author Jobs of the Future, 1984. BA in Jnlsm., U. MN, 1974. Mem. MN Press Club, WIC. Office: Twin Cities 7831 E Bush Lk Rd Minneapolis MN 55435

APPLE, JACKI, (Jacqueline), b. NYC, Dec. 11, 1941, d. Irving Sidney and Caroline Edith (Gross) Blum. Author: Partitions, 1976, Tracings, 1977, Trunk Pieces, 1978, The Mexican Tapes (LP record), 1980, Alternatives In Retrospect: An Historical Overview 1969-1975 (catalog), 1981, The Art of Spectacle (catalog), 1984, Last Rites after Angkor Wat (radio play), 1984; contrbr. to Media Arts, High Performance, LA Weekly, Artweek, numerous other mags. Student Syracuse U., 1959-60; grad. Parsons Schl. Design, NYC,1960-63. Curator exhbn. and performance Franklin Furnace, NYC,1977-80; host, producer sta. KPFK- Pacifica Radio, Los Angeles, 1982—; instr. Art Coll. Design, Pasadena, CA, 1983—; contrbg. ed. Media Arts, Los Angles, 1983—, Artweek, Oakland, CA, 1983—; contrbg. wrtr. Los Angeles Weekly, 1985—. Bd. dirs. Los Angeles Contemporary Exhbns., 1981-86. Visual arts fellow NEA, 1979, 81; grantee NY State Council on Arts, 1981, NEA, 1984. Mem. So. Calif. Art Wrtrs. Assn., Cactus Fdn. Home: 3827 Mentone Ave Culver City CA 90232

APPLE, WILLIAM MARLAN, b. Little Rock, Oct. 14, 1929; s. William Monroe and Vivian (Marlan) A.; m. Irene Miller, June 24, 1956; children—William M. Jr., Vicki Lynn. Contrbr. articles: Delta Retailing, Consumer Research Mag., Incentive Mktg., Salesman's Opportunity, numerous other trade jnls. and bus. publs. Wrkg. on short fiction, essays, BBA, U. Ark., 1951; JD, Ark. Law Sch., 1956. Ins. agt., cons. W.M. Apple & Co., Little Rock, 1953—. Served to 1st lt. USAF, 1951-53; Korea. Mem. NWC. Home: 6508 Pleasant Pl Little Rock AR 72205

APPLEGATE, DEBRA ANNETTE, b. South Bend, IN, Mar. 15, 1962; d. John Henry and Anna Theresa (DeMaio) A. City ed.: The Pilot-News, Plymouth, IN, 1985—. Wrkg. on freelance projects, novel. B.A. in Jnlsm., U. Mo., 1984. Vol., Marshall County Humane Soc., Plymouth, 1985—. Home: 116 E Adams Plymouth IN 46563

APPLEMAN, PHILIP, b. Feb. 8, 1926; m. Marjorie Haberkora. Author: The Silent Explosion, 1965 and 66, Portuguese trans., 1973; Kites on a Windy Day, 1967; Summer Love and Surf, 1968; Open Doorways, 1976; In the Twelfth Year of the War, 1970; Shame the Devil, 1981, Darwin's Ark, 1984, Darwin's Bestiary, 1986. Editor: The Origin of Species, 1975; An Essay on the Principles of Population, 1976; Darwin, 1970 (2d ed., 1979); founding ed., Victorian Studies, 1957-63; contrbr. to various publns. BS, 1950, PhD, 1955, Northwestern U.; AM, 1951, U. Mich.; postgrad., 1951-52, U. Lyon (France). Teaching asst., Northwestern U., 1953-55; at Indiana U.: English instr., 1955-58; asst. prof., 1958-62; assoc. prof., 1962-67; prof., 1967-82; disting. prof., 1982-86; disting. prof. emeritus, 1986—. Dir., instr. in world lit and philosophy, Intl. Schl. Am., 1960-61, 62-63; vis. prof. lit., St. U. New York, Purchase, N.Y., 1973; vis. prof., Columbia U., 1974. With U.S. Army Air Corps, 1944-45; U.S. Merch. Marine, 1946, 1948-49. Mem. AAUP, MLA, NCTE, PEN, PSA, AAP, AG, Phi Beta Kappa. Co-founder Bloomington, IN, Civil Liberties Union; faculty adviser, Ind. U. Civil Liberties Union. Fulbright Scholar, France, 1951-52; Huntington Hartford Fdn. fellow, 1964; NEA fellow, 1975. Recipient Indiana Authors' Day citation, 1968; Friends of Lit. Soc. Robert F. Ferguson Meml. award; soc. Midland Authors Midland Poetry award, 1969; PSA Christopher Morley Meml. award, 1970, and Alice Fay di Castagnola award, 1975. Home: Box 39 Sagaponack NY 11962

APPLEWHITE, JAMES WILLIAM, b. Stantonsburg, NC, Aug. 8, 1935; s. James William and Jane Elizabeth (Mercer) Applewhite; m. Janis Forrest, Jan. 12, 1955; children, Lisa Ann, James, Jeffrey. Author: Statues of the Grass, 1975, Following Gravity, 1980, Foreseeing the Journey, 1983, Ode to the Chinaberry Tree and Other Poems, 1986, Seas and Inland Journeys, 1985. BA, Duke U., 1958, PhD, 1964. Instr., asst. prof., UNC, Greensboro, 1960-71; asst. prof., Duke, Durham, NC, 1972-75; assoc. prof., Duke, 1975—. Awards: NEA Fellowship, 1973, Guggenheim Fellowship, 1976. Mem. PSA. Home: 606 November Dr Durham NC 27712

ARANDA, CHARLES, b. Las Vegas, Nov. 4, 1931; s. Roman and Eloisa M. (Romero) A.; m. Yolanda Hidalgo, May 20, 1949 (div. 1966); children: Michael, Thomas Lee; m. Bertha Alicia Caso, Apr. 16, 1976; children: Blanca, Patricia, Jose, Carlo. Author: Dichos and Proverbs Translated from the Spanish, 1975, The Pentitewte Papers, 1977, New Mexico Folklore from the Spanish, 1979, The Silva Gang y Sus 40 Bandidos, 1980, Nuevos Dichos, 1982, Dudes or Duds (novel), 1984, Special Collection of Dichos, 1985. Tchr. various elem., jr. high, and sr. high schls. in N.Mex., 1965-85, Espanola High Schl., N.Mex., 1985; guest lectr. U. N.Mex. Served to capt. U.S. Army, 1949-65, Korean War. Mem. VFW. Home: 9100 Hendrix St NE Albuquerque NM 87111

ARAX, CHRISTINE, see Nemetz, Christine Arax

ARCELLA, LISA, b. Westwood, NJ, Mar. 8, 1961, d. Raymond G. and Phil (D'Amico) Arcella. Ed.: Tiger Beat Star, 1983—, Rock! Specials, 1986—, Star Specials, 1983—; wrtr. Sharon Books. BA in Communication Arts and Journalism, St. Thomas Aquinas Coll., Sparkill, N.Y., 1983. Ed. D.S. Mags., Teaneck, N.J., 1983—. Mem. Women in Communications, Natl. Assn. Press Women. Recipient Columbia Scholastic Press Assn. award, 1982. Home: 85 W Shore Ave Dumont NJ 07628

ARCHER, JULES, b. NYC, Jan. 27, 1915, s. Maxwell D. and Fannie A.; widower; children—Mike, Dane, Kerry. Author over 60 books including: Fighting Journalist: Horace Greeley, 1966, Man of Steel: Joseph Stalin, 1965, Hawks, Doves, and the Eagle, 1970, Mao Tse-tung: A Biography, 1972, Thorn in Our Flesh: Castro's Cuba, 1970, Watergate: America in Crisis, 1975, The Plot to Seize the White House, ,73, Jungle Fighters, 1985, The Incredible Sixties, 1986; contrbr. stories, articles: Esquire, New Republic, New Book of Knowledge, many others. BA, CCNY. Served as M/sgt. USAF and GI war correspondent, 1941-45. Address: 404 High St Santa Cruz CA 95060

ARCHER, MYRTLE LILLY, b. Carp Lake, MI, June 14, 1926; d. Henry and Lillian Marie (Craven) A.; m. Howard Paul Spracklin; child—Jay Allen. Author: The Young Boys Gone (yng. adult novel); fiction and poetry in numerous periodicals, including Conquest, Journeys, Health Culture, Bardic Echoes, Ski Mag., New Directions for Women, 2nd Bittersweet. First prize fiction, Natl. Lg. Am. PEN Women, 1975, Yng. Adult Novel, 1978. Mem. Calif. Writers Club, Natl. Lg. Am. PEN Women. Home: 21172 Aspen Ave Castro Valley CA 94546

ARCHER, NUALA MIRIAM, b. Rochester, NY, June 21, 1955; d. Charles Leslie Stewart and Naomi June Therese (Barry) A. Author: Whale on the Line, 1981, contrbtr. numerous poems to Confrontation, Pequod, TLS, Epoch, and other lit mags in U.S., Ireland. Ed.-in-chief, Midland Rvw, 1985—, poetry co-ed., Cimarron Rvw. BA, Wheaton Coll., 1976; Dip., Trinity Coll., Univ. of Dublin, 1977; MA,PhD,Univ. of Wis., Milwaukee, 1978, 1983. Tchg. asst., Univ. of Wis., Milwaukee, 1977-80; lectr., Coll. of Mktg. and Design, Dublin, 1981-83; lectr., Dun Laoghaire Coll. of A&S, Dublin, 1981-83; tchg. asst., Univ. of Wis., Milwaukee, 1983-85; asst. prof., Oklahoma State Univ., 1984—. Brendan Behan Memorial Fellowship, Ireland, 1983. Mem. MLA, Natl. Women's Studies Assoc., Oklahoma Historical Soc. Home: PO Box 754 Stillwater OK 74076

ARDEN, WILLIAM, see Lynds, Dennis

ARDINGER, RICHARD KIRK, b. Pitts., Sept. 26, 1953, s. Albert Herman and Agnes Ruth (Barr) A.; m. Rosemary Powers, Apr. 10, 1976. Author poetry collections: One Place for Another, 1983, Letters from Custer, 1984; ed., pub. The Limberlost Rvw lit. mag., 1976—; ed. What Thou Lovest Well Remains: 100 Years of Ezra Pound. BA, Slippery Rock State Coll., 1975; MA,Idaho State U., 1980. Me. Faculty dept. English Idaho State U., Pocatello, 1977-79, 82-83, U. N.Mex., Albuquerque, 1980-81; sr. ed. Commtek Pub. Co., Boise, Idaho, 1983—. Wrtr.-in-residence Idaho Commn. on Arts, Boise, 1983. Home: HC33 Box 1113 Boise ID 83706

ARGUELLES, IVAN, b.Rochester, MN, Jan. 24, 1939, s. Enrique Sabino and Ethel Pearl

(Meyer) A.; m. Marilla Calhoun Elder, Oct. 27, 1962; children—Alexander, Max. Author poetry collections: Instamatic Reconditioning, 1978, The Invention of Spain, 1978, Captive of the Vision of Paradise, 1982, The Tattooed Heart of the Drunken Sailor, 1983, Manicomio, 1984, Nailed to the Coffin of Life, 1985, What Are They Doing to my Animal?, 1985; contrbr.poetry: American Poetry Rvw, Abraxas, Kayak, Yellow Silk, numerous other mags, jnls and anthols. BA, U. Chgo., 1961; MLS, Peabody U., 1968. Tchr. Scuola Aeronautica, Macerata, Italy, 1967; librarian N.Y. Public Library, NYC,1968-78, U. Calif., Berkeley, 1978—. Winner chapbook poetry contest Silverfish Rvw, 1984, Erotic Poetry contest Yellow Silk, Berkeley, CA, 1986. Home: 1740 Walnut St Berkeley CA 94709

ARIAS-MISSON, ALAIN AUGUST, b. brussels, Belgium, Dec. 11, 1939, came to U.S., 1940, s. Guy Misson and Countess Mary K. Teleki; m. Nela Arias, Mar. 25, 1963; 1 child, Onyx. Author: The Confessions of a madman, murderer, rapist, bomber, thief or A year from the Journal of an Ordinary American (novel), 1975, The Public Poem Book (art book), 1979; editor L'VII New Spanish Writing, 1972, Chgo. Rvw issue on visual poetry, 1974, issue on concretism, 1967, U.S. editor of Lotta Poetica, Italian Art Qtly, 1983—; contrbr.: Once Again, New Directions, The Avantgarde Today, numerous others. BA, Harvard U., 1959. Interpreter UN, EEC, FAO, other orgs., Europe, South Am. and U.S., 1963-68; instr. creative writing Columbia U., NYC,1982-83. Served to 1st lt. Belgian Army, 1960-62. Recipient Visual Arts award N.J. State Council on Arts, 1985. Mem. P&W. Home: Box 24 Clarksburg NJ 08510

ARIYOSHI, RITA CLARE, b. NYC, Feb. 12, 1939; d. James Joseph and Angela Mary (Carew) Gormley; m. James Masaji Ariyoshi; children—Laura, Daria, Clare, Joyce, David Masao, David Bingham. Author: Maui on My Mind; contrbr. photog. to Day In the Life of Hawaii; contrbr. articles to N.Y. Times, Modern Bride, Travel/Holiday, Geo, inflight mags. of Western, United, Amer., Philippines, Singapore airlines. Ed.-in-chief Hawaiian Air Inflight, Honolulu, 1974-76, Davick Pubns., Aloha Mag., RSVP Mag., Honolulu, 1976—; freelance writer. Mem. SATW, NFPW. Home: 4536 Kilauea Ave Honolulu HI 96816

ARK, CONNIE EILEEN, (Connie K. Miller, Connie E. Kimball), b. Springfield, Ohio, Aug. 13, 1951; d. Charles Ralph and Peggy Lou (Slygh) Kimball; m. Bruce Anthony Ark, June 21, 1982. Contrbr. articles: Schl. Library Jnl., Book Report mag., Ohio Media Spectrum; contrbr. book revs. Book Report mag.; poetry in anthologies. BEd, Wright State U., 1975. Freelance wrtr., 1969—; library-media specialist Mad River Twp. Schls., Dayton, Ohio, 1977-87, Springfield (Ohio) City Schls., 1987—; ed. Ohio Media Spectrum jnl., Ohio Ednl. Library-Media Assn., Columbus, 1985-87. Mem. editorial bd. Ohio Ednl. Library-Media Assn., also mem. publs. com., conf. exhibits com. Mem. ALA. Home: Box 284 Enon OH 45323

ARKHAM, GERALD, see Rawlinson, James Scott

ARKIN, JOSEPH, b. NYC, Mar. 28, 1922; s. Hyman A. and Celia (Brown) A.; m. Shirley Guttnetag, Dec. 20, 1947 (div. 1977); m. 2d, Sarah N. Antonoff, Apr. 2, 1978; children—Herbert, Francine. Author: Taxation of Prizes and Awards, 1962; contrbr. articles to trade and profl. mags., newspapers, Wrkg. on bus. articles. BBA, St. Johns U., 1944; MBA, Pace U., 1962. CPA, NYC. Mem. profl. orgns. Home: 761 NE 180th St North Miami Beach FL 33162

ARLEN, GARY O'HARA, (Howard Gray), b. Cleve., Jan. 8, 1945, s. M.N. and C.L. (Lef) A.; m. Bonnie Holland, Sept. 8, 1968; 1 son, Ben. Contrbr. articles to numerous media publs. AB, Washington U., 1967; MS, Northwestern U., 1968. Creative dir. Instarite, Washington, 1970-77; mgr. Am. Film Inst., Washington, 1976-77; ed. VideoNews, Bethesda, Md., 1977-80, Arlen Communications, Inc., Bethesda, 1980—. Mem. profl. orgns. Office: 7315 Wisconsin Ave Bethesda MD 20814

ARLEN, MICHAEL J., b. London, Eng., Dec. 9, 1930; s. Michael and Atlanta (Mercati) A.; m. Ann Warner, 1957, div. 1971; children—Jennifer, Caroline, Elizabeth, Sally; m. Alice Albright Hoge, 1972; stepchildren—Alicia, James Patrick, Robert Hoge. Author: Living-Room War, 1969; Exiles, 1970; An American Verdict, 1973; Passage to Ararat, 1975; The View from Highway 1, 1976; Thirty Seconds, 1980; The Camera Age, 1981. Harvard, 1952. Reporter, Life mag., 1952-56; contrbr. TV critic, The New Yorker mag., 1957—. Recipient, award for television criticism, Screen Dirs. Guild, 1968; Natl. Book award for contemporary affairs, 1976; Le Prix Bremond, 1976. Office: New Yorker 25 W 43d St New York NY 10036

ARMAH, AYI KWEI, b. Takoradi, Gold Coast (now Ghana), 1939. Author: novels, The Beautiful Ones Are Not Yet Born, 1968, repr. 1969, Fragments, 1970, Why Are We So Blest?, 1971, Two Thousand Seasons, 1973, 1980, The Healers, 1978, 1979. Poetry in Messages: Poems from Ghana, ed. K. Awoonor and G. Addi-Mathi, 1970. Cntrbr. short stories to Atlantic Monthly, Harper's, articles to New African and N.Y. Review of Books. BA, Harvard U., attended Achimoto Coll., U. of Ghana, and Columbia U. Translator, Algiers, for magazine Revolution Africaine, scriptwriter, Ghana Television, teacher of English, Naurongo School, Ghana, 1966; ed. and translator, Jeune Afrique (news magazine), Paris, Fr., 1967-68; writer, 1978—. Vis, prof., Teachers Coll., Dar es Salaam U., U. of Mass., Amherst U., U. of Lesotho, U. of Wis.—Madison. Fairfield Fdn. grantee. Address: Third World Press 7524 Cottage Grove Ave Chicago IL 60619

ARMANTROUT, (MARY) RAE, b. Vallejo, Calif., Apr. 13, 1947, d. John William and Hazel Maud (Hackett) Armantrout; m. Charles Korkegian, Sept. 21, 1971; 1 son, Aaron. Author poetry collections: Extremities, 1978, The Invention of Hunger, 1979, Precedence, 1985; contrbr. poetry to BlueFish, Feminist Studies, Partisan Rvw, other lit mags. AB, U. Calif., Berkeley, 1970; MA,San Francisco State U., 1975. Lectr. San Diego State U., 1979-82, U. Calif., San Diego, La Jolla, 1984-86. Home: 3074 Dwight St San Diego CA 92104

ARMER, SONDRA SCHECTER, b. NYC,Sept. 28, 1944, d. Harry and Helen Anna (Mauss) Schecter; m. Jerome Joseph Armer, 1963 (div. 1973); 1 dau., L. Samantha. Contrbr.: Negative Capability, Yet Another Small Mag., Waterways, Alura, Home Planet News, other periodicals. BA, Hunter Coll., 1966; MA,Columbia U., 1967, PhD,1971. Adj. asst. prof. CUNY, 1967-73; tchr. Hunter Coll. High Sch., NYC,1972-74; proofreader Young & Rubicam, NYC,1975-81; freelance indexer, proofreader, 1981—; tchr. creative writing NY Assn. for Blind, 1985-87. Woodrow Wilson Fdn. fellow, 1969; grantee English-Speaking Union, Eng., 1974. Mem. P&W, Wrtrs Community, Feminist Wrtrs.' Guild. Home: 202 Seeley St Brooklyn NY 11218

ARMITAGE, BARRI JUNE, b. Columbus, OH, Oct. 18, 1937; d. Thomas Barry and June Viola (Hardesty) Gotham; m. David Templeton Armitage, Aug. 29, 1959; children—Nancy Elizabeth (dec.), David Templeton. Contrbr. poetry articles to mags.; poems to lit. mags., anthols. Turn. B.A. summa cum laude in Psychology, Muskingum Coll., 1959; M.A. in Elem. Edn., Syracuse U., 1966; postgrad. U. S.C., 1975-76. Poetry ed. Augusta Spectator, GA, 1980-84; poetry tchr. Augusta Arts Council, 1982-84, Barnsley Schl., Rockville, MD, 1985—. Recipient 1st prize for poetry Sand Hills Writing Conf., 1977, 79, 84. Home: 13904 N Gate Dr Silver Spring MD 20906

ARMSTRONG, ALICE CATT, b. Ft. Scott, KS, Feb. 7; d. Charles Harmon and Florence Iles (Packenham) Catt. Author: 17 books, including California Biographical and Historical Series, 1950—, Dining and Lodging on the North American Continent, 1958; And They Called It Society, 1961-62. Ed. 200th Anniversary of California issue, 1968; also radio skits, travel guides, children's stories, poems. LittD, St. Andrews Univ. (England), 1969, St. Paul's Coll. and Sem. (Italy), 1970; six honorary doctorates; 1 son, Gary. Actress Little Theatre groups Pasadena Playhouse, 1942-48; tchr. dramatic arts, Hollywood, Calif., 1946-48; ed.pub. Historical Research Pubns., 1949—. Numerous citations U.S. and England, other countries. Mem. Celebrity Books & Authors Club (Beverly Hills), Children's Society of Books & Authors, Nat. Soc. Magna Charta Dames, Save the Redwoods League. Home: 1331 Cordell Pl Los Angeles CA 90069

ARMSTRONG, PATRICIA KAY, b. Highland Park, MI, Dec. 18, 1936; d. Elzine M. and Vivian B. (Thompson) Stoddard; m. Charles W. Armstrong, Jan. 27, 1955; children—Jacquelin Joy, Rebbecca Raye. Author: Trilogites of the chicago Region, 1962, Summits of the Soul, 1978, Prairie Poetry, 1979, 2d ed., 1981. contrbr. articles on nature subjects, biology edn., backpacking to popular mags., numerous poems to antols., lit. mags. B.A., North Central Coll., 1958; M.S., U. Chgo., 1968. Biology tchr. Washington Jr. High Sch., Naperville, IL, 1960-69; asst. in edn. Morton Arboretum, Lisle, IL, 1970-86; ednl. environmental cons., free-lance wrtr., 1986—. Recipient 2d place for sonnet Natl. Fdn. State Poetry Socs., 1982. Mem. Wis. Fellowship Poets (1st place for powm 1984), Wis. Regional Wrtrs. Home: 612 Staunton Rd Naperville IL 60565

ARNDT, C. C., see Hoeppner, Iona Ruth

ARNER, ROBERT DAVID, b. Lehighton, PA, Jan. 17, 1943; s. George David and Esther Louise (Fairchild) A.; m. Constance Marie Snyr, Aug. 18, 1973; 2 sons, Justin Fairchild and James Robert. Contrbr. articles to NE Qtly, Early Am. Lit., Criticism Qtly, So. Lit. Jnl, So. Folklore Qtly, others; chapters to Am. Lit. Scholarship, 1974-77, Essays on Early Va Lit. . ., 1977, Major Writers of the Am. Revolution, 1977, Puritan Poetry and Poetics, 1985; monographs and pamphlets on Kate Chopin, 1975, James Thurber, 1980, The Lost Colony in Lit., 1985. Wrkg. on book about James Thurber. BS in Ed., Kutztown State Coll., 1964; MA, Pa State U; PhD, 1970. Instr. and asst. prof. English Central Mich Univ., Mt. Pleasant, 1968-71; asst. prof. Univ. Cin., 1971-72, assoc prof., 1972-75, prof., 1975—. Mem. Soc. for Study of So. Lit. Office: Dept Eng Univ Cincinnati Cincinnati Oh 45221

ARNETT, CARROLL (GOGISGI), b. Okla. City, OK, Nov. 9, 1927. Author poetry: Then, 1965, Not Only That, 1967, Like A Wall, 1969, Through the Woods, 1971, Earlier, 1972, Come, 1973, Tsalagi, 1976, South Line, 1979, Rounds, 1982; guest ed Am Indian issue Beloit Poetry Jnl, 1979; co-ed Coyote's Jnl, 1982. BA magna cum laude, Beloit Coll, 1951; MA,U Tex, 1958. Instr. English, Knox Coll, Galesburg, IL, 1958-60, Stephens Coll, Columbia, MO 1960-64; asst. prof. Wittenberg Univ, Springfield, OH, 1964-68; assoc. prof. Nasson Coll, Springvale, ME, 1968-70, prof. English Central Mich Univ, Mt Pleasant, 1970—. Deer Clan Chief Overhill Band, Cherokee Nation, Xenia, Ohio, 1974—. Served USMC, 1946-47, CA. NEA Fellowship, 1974. Address: 5586 Ten-Mile Rd Mecosta MI 49332

ARNINK, DONNA JEAN, b. Corry, PA, Nov. 29, 1946; d. Floyd Leon and Mildred R. (Lines) A. Author: 21, 1968, Farkelberry Magic, 1973, Theatre Crafts, 1985, Dramatics, 1985, 2d ed., 1987, Creative Theatrical Makeup, 1985, Workbench, 1987. B.S., Edinboro U., 1968; M.F.A., Ohio U., 1971. Prof. Penn. State U., State College, 1976-77, Mich. State U., East Lansing, 1971-76, 77—. Mem. U.S. Inst. Theatre Technology, Am. Theatre Assn. Home: 712 N Magnolia Lansing MI 48912

ARNOLD, BOB, b. Adams, MA, Aug. 5, 1952; s. Robert Thomas and Penny (Scott) A.; m. Susan Eileen Paules, Aug. 28, 1974; 1 son— Carson Wesley. Author: Rope of Bells, 1974, Habitat, 1979, Thread, 1980, Back Road Caller, 1985, Sky, 1986, Go West, 1987, Cache, 1987, Long Time Together, 1987; contrbtr. to Coyote's Jnl, Harper's, New Letters, Cold Spring Jnl, other mags; editor/publisher: Longhouse, 1973—, Scout, 1973—. Student Brewster Academy, Wolfeboro, NH. Self- employed stonemason, builder, 1970—; visiting wrtr. Stoneleigh Burnham School (Greenfield, MA), 1977—, Deerfield Academy (MA), 1985. Home: Green River RFD Guilford VT 05301

ARNOLD, CRAIG GLEN, b. Sioux City, IA, Jan. 8, 1949. Author: Euterpe, 1986; ed. trade books: The Day Richmond Died, 1981, Appomattox Commander, 1981, The Dark Side of the Screen: Film Noir, 1981, James Wong Howe: Cinematographer, 1981, A History of the Electric Locomotive, 1981, The Western Maryland Railway, 1981, Rambling Willie, 1981, MG: The Sports Car Supreme, 1982; ed.: Mains'l Haul, 1984—; contrbr. to Seacoast Mag., VFW Mag., Mains'l Haul. Contrbg. wrtr. Seacoast Mag., Encinitas, Calif., 1979-81; ed. Oak Tree Publs., San Diego, 1980-82; freelance ed., wrtr., Cardiff, Calif., 1980-84; ed., librarian San Diego Maritime Mus., 1984—. Home: 2212 Edinburg Ave Cardiff CA 92007

ARNOLD, EDGAR FRANK, JR., b. Madisonville, KY, Sept. 29, 1925; s. Edgar Frank and Caroline (Long) A.; m. Ruby Jarvis Mitchell, June 20, 1948 (div. June 12, 1965); children—Frank E., Gil M., Brian B. (dec.); m. 2d, Jeanne Lavonne Campbell, Mar. 11, 1966. Author: The Arnolds of Gwent, 1985. Student U. Ky., 1946-47. Reporter, then ed. The Messenger, Madisonville, 1946-70; appraiser Ky. Hwy. Dept., Madisonville, 1972-85, chief r/w agt., 1985—. State rep. Commonwealth of Ky., 10th district, 1958-60; mem. Democratic State Central Exec. Com., 1965-71. Served as f/o, U.S. Air Force, 1943-46. Home: 246 Country Club Ln Madisonville KY 42431

ARNOLD, EMILY, see McCully, Emily Arnold

ARNOLD, GARY HOWARD, b. Princeton, IN, Aug. 22, 1942; s. Charles Howard and Ferris (Smith) A.; m. Sue Datz, Dec. 29, 1967; children—Pauline, Jane, Esther. NYU 1959-60, U. Calif. at Berkeley, 1960-63. Film critic: Diplomat mag., 1966; Ind. Film Jnl., 1968-69; Washington Post, 1969-84. Home: 5133 N 1st St Arlington VA 22203

ARNOLD, JACKIE SMITH, b. Bessemer, AL, Oct. 3, 1932; d. Bill Fred and Lillian (McDougal) Smith; m. Fred E. Wakefield, June 22, 1950 (div. 1954); m. 2d, Howard Batts, Jr., Nov. 17, 1956 (div. 1977); children—David Michael, Charles Howard, Thomas Alan; m. 3d, William C. Arnold, Oct. 6, 1979. Author: Kinship is a Relative Thing, 1985; contrbg. author: Fermi-1, New Age 6r Nuclear Power, 1979; Kinship—It's All Relative, 1987. Wrkg. on newspaper column, murder mysteries, poetry, dance history. Student U. Mich. Extension, Detroit, 1960, Macomb Community Coll., 1975. Vice-pres. William Arnold Assocs., Inc., Detroit, 1977—; exec. asst. to pres. Detroit and Wayne County Tuberculosis Fdn., 1978—; wrtr., adminstrv. asst. Burnett Studios, Detroit, 1983-87. Mem. Thumb Area Wrtrs.' Club, Legal Asst. Adv. Bd., 1976-87 McComb CC. Home: 300 Sheridan Ln W Peck MI 48466

ARNOLD, MARGOT, see Cook, Petronelle M.M.

ARNOVITZ, BENTON MAYER, b. Butler, PA, July 21, 1942; s. Paul and Miriam (Shapiro) A. AB, Cornell U., 1964; MA, NYU, 1969; grad., U.S. Army Command and Gen. Staff Coll., 1982. Editor, Macmillan Pub. Co., 1966-73; sr. trade editor, Chilton Book Co., Radnor, PA, 1973-76; exec. editor, Stein and Day Pubs., Briarcliff Manor, NY, 1976—, v.p., 1984—. Captain, U.S. Army, lt. col. USAR. Home: 19 Putman Rd Continental Vill RD 3 Peekskill NY 10566

ARONSON, ARNOLD P., b. Lake Hiawatha, NJ, Mar. 8, 1943, s. Louis and Anna (Gross) A.; 1 son, Isaac Davy. Author: The History and Theory of Environmental Scenography, 1981, American Set Design, 1985; contrbr.: Shakespeare in the South, 1983; contrbr., adv. ed.: Contemporary Designers, 1985; ed.: 1st and 3d Biennial Scenography Exposition Catalogs. PhD, NYU, 1977. Assoc. Prof. U. Va., Charlottesville, 1976-84; vis. assoc. prof. Cornell U., Ithaca, N.Y., 1984-85, NYU, 1984, U. Del., Newark, 1985-86; ed. Theatre Design & Technology, N.Y.C., 1978—. Mem. U.S. Inst. Theatre Tech., Am. Soc. Theatre Research. Office: USSIT 330 W 42d St New York NY 10036

ARONSON, MICHAEL ANDREW, b. Bklyn., Apr. 27, 1939; s. Jesse Besthoff and Marcia (Sacks) A. BA, Johns Hopkins U., 1960. Asst. dir. Ind. U. Press, Bloomington, 1966-69; at U. Chgo. Press: London editor, 1970, sci. editor, 1971-73; editor-in-chief Johns Hopkins U. Press, Balt., 1973-78; genl. editor Harvard U. Press, Cambridge, MA, 1978—. Office: Harvard U. Press 79 Garden St Cambridge MA 02138

ARROWSMITH, WILLIAM AYRES, b. Orange, NJ, Apr. 13, 1924; s. Walter Weed and Dorothy (Ayres) A.; m. Jean Reiser, Jan. 10, 1945 (div. 1980); children—Nancy, Beth. Founding editor Chimera, 1942-44, Hudson Rvw, 1948-60, Arion, Jnl Classical Culture, 1962—; adv. editor Tulane Drama Rvw, 1960-67; adv. bd. Mosaic, 1968—; mem. exec. com. Natl. Translation Center, 1965-70; mem. faculty, mem. bd. Natl. Humanities Faculty, 1972-74; ed. Delos, 1968-70; ed.-at-large APR, 1976—; contrib. ed. Pequod, 1985—. Translator: (Petronius) The Satyricon, 1959, (Euripides) The Bacchae, Cyclops, Heracles, Orestes and Hecuba, 1960, (Aristophanes) The Birds, 1961, Clouds, 1962, (with R. Shattuck) The Craft and Context of Translation, 1962, (with D.S. Carne-Ross) Cesare Pavese) Dialogues with Leuco, 1965, (Cesare Pavese) Hard Labor, 1976; editor: Image of Italy, 1961, Five Modern Italian Novels, 1964; genl. editor: The Greek Tragedy in New Translation (33 vols.), 1973—, Alcestis (Euripides), 1975, That Bowling Alley on the Tiber (Michelangelo Antonioni), 1985, The Storm and Other Things (Eugenio Montale), 1985, The Occasions (Eugenio Montale). BA, Princeton U., 1947, PhD, 1954; BA (Rhodes scholar), Oxford (Eng.) U., 1951, MA, 1958. Instr. classics Princeton U., 1951-53; instr. classics and humanities Wesleyan U., Middleton, Conn., 1953-54; asst. prof. classics and humanities U. Calif., Riverside, 1954-56, mem. faculty U. Tex., Austin, 1958-70, prof. classics, 1959-70, chmn. dept., 1964-66, Univ. prof. arts and letters, 1965-70; vis. prof. humanities M.I.T., 1971; prof. classics, Univ. prof. Boston U., 1971-76; vis. Henry McCormick prof. dramatic lit. Schl. Drama, Yale U., 1976-77; prof. writing seminars and classics Johns Hopkins U., 1977-81; prof. classics, NYU, 1981-83; Kriser Prof. Classics and Comp. Lit., Emory Univ., 1983-86; univ. prof. and prof. of classics, 1986—. Served with AUS, 1943-46. Woodrow Wilson fellow, 1947-48; Guggenheim fellow, 1957-58; Prix de Rome sr. research fellow Am. Acad. Rome, 1956-57; Phi Beta Kappa vis. scholar, 1964-65; Rockefeller fellow in humanities, 1980-81; recipient Longview award criticism, 1960; Bromberg award excellence in teaching U. Tex., 1959; Morris L. Ernst award excellence in teaching, 1962; Piper prof. for disting. teaching, 1966; Harbison award for disting. teaching, 1971; award for lit. AAIAL, 1978. Mem. PEN, Assn. Am. Rhodes Scholars, Phi Beta Kappa, PSA, Acad. Lit. Criticism. Home: 275 Goddard Ave Brookline MA 02146

ARSONE, SARAH, b. Sacramento, CA, Aug. 30, 1940, d. Michael and Edith Brodovsky. Contrbr. to LA Times, LA Herald Examiner, Israel Today, Burbank (CA) Daily Rvw, BACHY, Rara Avis, Aspen Anthology, West Coast Writers' Conspiracy. BA in Spanish, U. So. Calif., Los Angeles, 1962; Journalism Profl. Designation, UCLA, 1984. Freelance writer, Lost Angeles, 1977—; contrbg. editor Israel Today, Northridge, CA, 1978. Mem. NWU. Address: 2850 Ocean Park Blvd 300 Santa Monica CA 90405

ARTHUR, ELIZABETH, b. NYC, Nov. 15, 1953; d. Robert and Joan (Vaczek) Kouwenhoven; m. (1) Robert Gathercole, May 2, 1974 (div. Sept. 1980), (2) Steven Bauer, June 19, 1981. Author: (nonfiction) Island Sojourn, 1980, (novels) Beyond the Mountain, 1983, Bad Guys, 1986; contrbr articles and essays to New York Times, Backpacker, Ski X-C, and other periodicals. Contrbr of poetry to Shenandoah. Attended U. of Michigan, 1971-73, Notre Dame U., Nelson, Brit. Colum., 1976-77; BA with distinction, U. of Victoria, 1978, Diploma in Educ., 1979. Vis. instr creative writing, U. of Cincinnati, 1983-84; asst. prof., cr. writing, Miami (Ohio) U., 1984-85; asst. prof. of English, Indiana U.—Purdue U. at Indianapolis, 1985—. Leader of cr. writing workshop, Sinclair Commuinty Coll., Cleveland, O., 1983; fiction writer-in-res., Northern Ky. U., Ft. Thomas, 1984. Creative prose judge, Loft-McNight awards, Minneapolis, Minn., 1983-84, lit. judge, Individual Artists Grants, Ohio Arts Council, Columbus, O., 1985. Staff member, Bread Loaf Writer's conference, summers, 1984, 87. Member: Poets and Writers, ASPCA, World Wildlife Fund. William Sloane fellow in prose, Bread Loaf, 1980; Ossabaw Island Project writing fellow, 1981, VT. Council on the Arts grant-in-aid, 1981-82, NEA fellow in prose, 1982-83. Home: 14100 Harmony Rd. Bath IN 47010

ARTHUR, ELIZABETH ALDRICH, b. South Bend, IN, Oct. 6, 1923; d. George Ames and Esta Lena (Grantham) Aldrich; m. Laurence Kenneth Arthur, June 17, 1945. Contrbr. crossword puzzles to newspapers, books including Christian Sci. Monitor, Chgo. Sun Times, Chgo. Tribune. B.Sci., Roosevelt U., 1951. Free-lance crossword puzzle constructor, 1984—. Home: 5548 S Blackstone Chicago IL 60637

ASANTE, MOLEFI K(ETE), (Arthur L(ee) Smith, Jr.; name legally changed in 1975); b. Valdosta, GA, Aug. 14, 1942; s. Arthur L. and Lillie (Wilkson) Smith; m. 2d wife, Kariamu Welsh; children: Kasina Eka, Daahoud Ali, Molefi Khumalo. Author: as Arthur Lee Smith, The Break of Dawn (poems), 1964, (with Andrea Rich) Rhetoric of Revolution: Samuel Adams and Emma Goldman, 1970. As Arthur L. Smith, Rhetoric of Black Revolution, 1969, contrbr, Donn Parsons and Wil Linkugel, eds., Television and the new Persuasion, 1970, Toward Tramsracial Communication, 1970, ed. (with Stephen Robb) The Voice of Black Rhetoric, 1971, contrbr (Larry Barker and Robert Kobler, eds.) Speech communication Behavior, 1971, (with Anne Allen and Deluvina Hernandez) How to Talk with Peoples of Other Races, Ethnic Groups, and Cultures, 1971, ed., Language, Communication and Rhetoric in Black America, 1972, Trnasracial Communication and Rhetoric in Black America, 1972, Transracial Communicaiton, 1973; as Molefi K. Asante, The Social Uses of Mass Communication, 1972, (with Jerry K. Frye) Contemperary Public Communication Applications, 1977, ed. (with others) Handbook of Intercultural Communication, 1979, Afrocentricity: The Theory of Social Change, 1980, ed. (with Abdulai S. Vandi) Contemporary Black Thought: Alternative Analyses in Social and Behavioral Science, 1980, ed. (with Kariamu Welsh Asante) African Culture: The Rhythms of Unity, 1985, Epic in Search of African Kings, 1978, Mfecan (novel), 1984. Contrbr spch jnls. Mem. bd. of eds., Black Men in America series, 1969-70; founding ed., Journal of Black Studies, 1969—; ed. assoc., Speech Teacher, 1970-73; contrbng ed., Encore, 1970-72; book reviewer, Journal of Communication, 1970-72; mem. advsry bd., Black Law Journal, 1971-73, and Race Relations Abstract, 1973-77. BA cum laude, Oklahoma Christian College, 1964; MA, Pepperdine College (now University), 1965; Ph.D., Univ. of Calif., Los Angeles, 1968, LHD, Univ. of New Haven, 1976. Instructor, Calif. State Polytechnic Coll. (now University), Pomona, 1966-67; instructor, San Fernando Valley State Coll. (now California State Univ., Northridge), 1967; asst. prof. of communication, Purdue U., Lafayette, Ind., 1968-69; asst. prof., Univ. of Calif., Los Angeles, 1969-70, assoc. prof. of speech, 1971-73, dir. of Center for Afro-American Studies, 1970-73; prof. of communication, State Univ. of N.Y. at Buffalo, 1973-85, chmn. dept., 1973-79; prof. African Studies, Temple U., 1985—. Vis. prof., Howard Univ., Washington, D.C., 1979-80; Fulbright prof., Zimbavwe Inst. of Mass Communication, 1981-82. Chair, Indiana State Civil Rights Commission on Higher Educ. and the Afro-American, 1968-69. Member selection comm., Martin Luther King and Woodrow Wilson fellowships, 1970-72. Member: Intl. Communication Assn., Speech Communication Assn. (mem. legis. assembly, 1971-72), African Heritage Studies Assn. Soc. for Intercultural Education, Training and Research. Education Guild Writer's Award, 1965. Home: 709 Medary Ave Philadelphia PA 19126

ASBELL, BERNARD, . Bklyn.,May 8, 1923; s. Samuel and Minnie (Zevin) A.; m. Mildred Sacarny, Jan. 2, 1944; childred—Paul, Lawrence, Jonathan, Jody; m. Marjorie Baldwin Farrell. June 11, 1971. Author: When FDR Died, 1961; The New Improved American, 1965; What Lawyers Really Do, 1970; Careers in Urban Affairs, 1970; The FDR Memoirs, 1973; pseudonym Nicholas Max: President McGovern's First Term, 1973; Productivity (with Clair F. Vough), 1975; The Senate Nobody Knows, 1978; White Coat, White Cane (with David Hartman). 1978. Editor: Mother and Daughter: The Letters of Eleanor and Anna Roosevelt, 1982; Transit Point Moscow, 1985. Student U. Conn., 1945-44. Reporter Richmond (VA) Times-Dispatch, 1945-47; pub. relations, Chgo, 1947-55; mng. editor, Chgo. mag., 1955-56; tchr. non-fiction writing U. Chgo. 1956-60, Bread Loaf Writers Conf., Middlebury (VT) Coll., 1960. 61, U. Bridgeport, 1961-63; vis. lectr., Yale U., 1979-80, Pa. State U., 1984-85; dir. New Eng. Writers Center, 1979—; writer-in-residence Clark U., 1982; cons. Ednl. Facilities Labs, 1963, U. Ill., 1964, Ford Found., 1965, 1968-69; cons. to sec. HEW, 1965-68, IBM Corp., Carnegie Corp., NY; assoc. fellor Trumbull Coll., Yale U., 1981—. US Army, 1943-45. Recipient Sch. Bell award NEA, 1965; Edn. Writers Assn. 1st prize mag. coverage, 1965; spcl. citation, 1966. Mem. ASJA (pres. 1963, exec. council 1964-66), PEN, AG, Natl. Press Club, Mensa. Address: Box 522 State College PA 16804

ASCHWANDEN, RICHARD JOSEF, b. Silenen, Switzerland, Apr. 20, 1927; s. Karl and Emilie (Egetemeyer) A.; m. Maria Schnieper, Apr.6, 1953; children: Charles, Pia, Alex, Magdalena, Mark, Paul, Mary, Peter, David. Author: (with Maria Aschwanden) A Time of Personal Regeneration, 1983, Escaping Collusion, 1984; editor: Congratulations, America, 1982, If Men Were Men, 1985, Challenging a Humanist, 1986, Space Defenders Do, 1987. Regional chef Slater Food Service, Balt., 1959-62; dist. mgr. ARA Service, Phila., 1962-64; v.p. ARA Service & Holiday Inn, Chgo., 1969-71; chef Minnequa Club, Pueblo, Colo., 1976-83; pub. and editor Rama Pub., Carthage, Mo., 1984—. Served to pfc. U.S. Army, 1950-52. Home: Rt 4 Box 457-Z Carthage MO 64836

ASH, ROBERT W., see Asher, Dustin T.

ASHANTI, BARON JAMES, b. NYC, Sept. 5, 1950; s. David Lancaster and Gladys Carole (Mathews) Foxhall; m. Brenda Cummings, Sept. 8, 1979; children—Marcus Kwazi, Nova Akosua. Contrbr. poems, articles to lit mags, anthols. Student pub. schls., N.Y.C. Organizer African Peoples Party, Phila. and NYC, 1969-81. Served to sgt. USMC, 1967-71. Recipient Killeen prize St. Peters Coll., Jersey City, N.J., 1982; fellow PEN, 1985. Mem. Harlem WG, New Renaissance Wrtrs. Club. Home: 4343 N 9th St Philadelphia PA 19140

ASHBERY, JOHN LAWRENCE, b. Rochester, NY, July 28, 1927; s. Chester Frederick and Helen (Lawrence) A. Author: poems Turandot and Other Poems, 1953, Some Trees, 1956, The Poems, 1960, The Tennis Court Oath, 1962, Rivers and Mountains, 1966, Selected Poems, 1967, Three Madrigals, 1968, Sunrise in Suburbia, 1968, Fragment, 1969, The Double Dream of Spring, 1970, The New Spirit, 1970, Three Poems, 1972, The Vermont Notebook, 1975, Self-Portrait in a Convex Mirror, 1975, Houseboat Days, 1977, As We Know, 1979, Shadow Train, 1981, A Wave, 1984, Selected Poems, 1985, April Galleons, 1987; (with James Schuyler) novel A Nest of Ninnies, 1969; also author plays, numerous articles, translations, contrbns. to lit mags. Grad., Deerfield Acad., 1945; BA, Harvard Univ., 1949; MA, Columbia Univ., 1951; postgrad., NYU, 1957-58; DLitt. hon Southampton Coll. of LIU, 1979. Copywriter Oxford Univ. Press, NYC,1951-54, McGraw-Hill Book Co., 1954-55; art critic European edtn. NY Herald Trib., Paris, 1960-65; Paris corr. Art News, 1964-65; exec. ed. Art News 1966-72; prof. Eng. Brooklyn Coll., 1974—, Disting. prof, 1980—. Ed. Qtly. Rvw. Art and Lit., Paris, 1963-66; art critic, Art Internatnl., Switzerland, 1961-64; ed. Locus Solus, Lans-en¨ercors, France, 1960-62; poetry ed. Paris Rvw., 1976-80; art critic NY Mag., 1978-80, Newsweek, 1980-85. Recipient Yale Series of Younger Poets prize, 1956; Natl. Inst. Arts and Letters Award, 1969; Shelley award PSA, 1973; Pulitzer prize, 1976; Fulbright scholar, 1955-57; Poets' Fdn. grantee, 1960, 64; Ingram Merrill Fdn. grantee, 1962, 72; Guggenheim fellow, 1967, 73; Rockefeller Fdn. grantee, 1979-80; Bollingen Prize in Poetry, 1985; MacArthur Fdn. Fellowship, 1985-90. Fellow AAP; mem. AAIAL. Address: c/o Georges Borchardt Inc 136 E 57th St New York City 10022

ASHCROFT, SHELLEY ALANE, (Elyse Diamond, Joy Elyse), b. Meadville, PA, Dec. 9, 1953; d. Robert Hugh and M. Carolin (Hunsaker) Ross; m. Robert Lloyd Ashcroft, 1975; five children. Author, ed. numerous booklets and newsletters. Student Ricks Coll., 1972-74, Brigham Young U., 1974-76. Ed., writer relig. and ednl. pubns., 1980—; ed. Creative Learning Mag., 1985—. Office: Crtv Lrng Box 37568 San Antonio TX 78237

ASHER, DUSTIN T., (Robert W. Ash, Jackson G. Dorr), b. Sacramento, CA, Apr. 1, 1942, s. Bud William and Lillian Alice (Hardy) A.; m. Sharon Miller; children—Charles, Edward, John. Author: The Telepathic Sender, 1962, The State of Adrenergia, 1973, The Mobile Center of Consciousness, 1978, The Ritual of the Irrational, 1984, Theory of Psi-Plasma Control, 1986, Negative Ion Enrichment on Honey Dew Tomato Production, 1987. BBA, Sacramento State U., 1964. Served to capt. USAF, 1964-68. Home: 2351 Forney St Honeydew CA 95545

ASHFORD, MARY JANE, b. Roseville, OH, Apr. 7, 1948; s. Franklin W. and Henrietta (Gillispie) A. Contrbr. articles to mags. Wrkg. on short stories, novels. J.D., Blackstone Schl. Law, 1985; A.A., Urbana U., 1988. Recipient 1st place, Ohio Pen Artists Showcase, 1987; Ed.'s Choice award Unicorn Lit. Mag., 1987. Home: 27 Hall St Roseville OH 43777

ASHLEY, ROSALIND MINOR, b. Chgo., Oct. 10, 1923, d. Jack and Frances Minor; m. Charles

Ashley; children—S.D., Richard A. Author: Successful Techniques for Teaching Elementary Language Arts, 1970, Activities for Motivating and Teaching Bright Children, 1973, Simplified Teaching Techniques and Materials for Flexible Group Instruction, 1976, Portfolio of Daily Classroom Activities with Model Lesson Plans, 1979, Successful Techniques for Teaching Elementary Language Arts, pb 1981; ed.: Language and How to Use It, Beginning Levels (by Marion Monroe), 1971. BS in Edn., Northwestern U. Tchr. elem. schl. Evanston and Wilmette, Ill., 1962-71; assoc. ed. Scott Foresman & Co., Inc., Glenview, Ill., 1971-73; ed., curriculum cons. Carlsbad (Calif.) Schl. Dist., 1985—; columnist, The Citizen, Del Mar Citizen, and LaCostan. Home: 260 Via Tavira Encinitas CA 92024

ASHLEY, SIMON K., see Kimball, Richard Wilson

ASHTON, DORE, b. Newark; d. Ralph N. and Sylvia (Ashton) Shapiro; m. Adja Yunkers, July 8, 1952; children—Alexandra Louise, Marina Svietlana; M. Matti Megged, 1985. Author: Abstract Art Before Columbus, 1957, Poets and the Past, 1959, Philip Guston, 1960, The Unknown Shore, 1962, Rauschenberg's Dante, 1964, Modern American Sculpture, 1968, Richard Lindner, 1969, A Reading of Modern Art, 1970, Pol Bury, 1971; cultural guide New York, 1972; Picasso on Art, 1972, The New York School: A Cultural Reckoning, 1973, A Joseph Cornell Album, 1974, Yes, But, A Critical Biography of Philip Guston, 1976, A Fable of Modern Art, 1980, American Art Since 1945, 1982, About Rothko, 1983, Out of the Whirlwind, 1987; co-author: Rosa Bonheur, A Life and Legend, 1981; editor: 20th Century Artists on Art, 1985; co-editor: Redon, Moreau, Bresdin, 1961; N.Y. contrbg editor: Studio Intl., 1961-74, Opus Intl. 1968-74, XXieme Siecle, 1955-70, Arts, 1974—; contrbr. to Vision and Value series (Gyorgy Kepes), 1966, The New Art Anthology (Gregory Battcock), 1966. BA, U. Wis., 1949; MA, Harvard, 1950. Assoc. editor Art Digest, 1951-54; assoc. critic N.Y. Times, 1955-60; lectr. Pratt Inst., 1962-63; head humanities dept. (Schl. Visual Arts), 1965-68; prof. Cooper Union, 1968—; art critic, lectr., dir. exhbns.; exec. bd. of PEN. Guggenheim fellow, 1964; Graham fellow, 1963; Ford Fdn. fellow, 1960; NEH grantee, 1980. Mem. Intl. Assn. Art Critics, Phi Beta Kappa. Home: 217 11th St New York NY 10003

ASHTON, ROBIN G., b. Honolulu, Dec. 24, 1949; s. Charles R. and Marjorie (Robbins) A.; 1 son, Daniel Potter Ashton. Editor: Sick, 1978. AB, Shimer Coll., 1971; MA in Comp. Lit., SUNY-Binghamton, 1976. Sports writer, Poughkeepsie Jnl. (NY), 1975-76; rptr. Beacon Free Press (NY), 1976-77; ed. Teach'em, Inc., Chicago., 1977-78; sr. and exec. ed. Restaurants and Institutions, Des Plaines, IL, 1978-82; ed. Foodservice Equipment & Supplies Specialist, DesPlaines, 1982—. Mem. ABP. Office: Cahners Box 5080 DesPlaines IL 60018

ASIMOV, ISAAC, b. Petrovichi, Russia, Jan. 2, 1920; came to U.S., 1923, naturalized, 1928; s. Judah and Anna Rachel (Berman) A.; m. Gertrude Blugerman, Jan. 2, 1942; children—David, Robyn Joan; m. Janet Opal Jeppson, Nov. 30, 1973. Author 363 books, including Pebble in the Sky, 1950, I, Robot, 1950, The Stars, Like the Dust, 1951, Foundation, 1951, Foundation and Empire, 1952, Currents of Space, 1952, Second Foundation, 1953, Caves of Steel, 1954, End of Eternity, 1955, Races and People, 1955, The Naked Sun, 1957; textbook Biochemistry and Human Metabolism, rev. ed, 1957; World of Carbon, 1958, World of Nitrogen, 1958, Nine Tomorrows, 1959, The Words of Science, 1959, Realm of Numbers, 1959, The Living River, 1960, Kingdom of the Sun, 1960, Realm of Measure, 1960, Wellsprings of Life, 1960, Words from Myths, 1961, Realm of Algebra, 1961, Life and Energy, 1962, Words in Genesis, 1962, Fact and Fancy, 1962, Words on the Map, 1962, Search for the Elements, 1962, Words from the Exodus, 1963, The Human Body, 1963, The Genetic Code, 1963, Intelligent Man's Guide to Science, 1960, View from a Height, 1963, Human Brain, 1964, A Short History of Biology, 1964, Quick and Easy Math, 1964, Adding a Dimension, 1964, A Short History of Chemistry, 1965, The Greeks, 1965, Of Time and Space and Other Things, 1965, The New Intelligent Man's Guide to Science, 1965, An Easy Introduction to the Slide Rule, 1965, Fantastic Voyage, 1966, The Noble Gases, 1966, The Neutrino, 1966, The Roman Republic, 1967, Understanding Physics, 1966, Is Anyone There?, 1967, To the Ends of the Universe, 1967, Mars, 1967, Egyptians, 1967, Asimov's Mysteries, 1968, Science, Numbers and I, 1968, Stars, 1968, Galaxies, 1968, A Whiff of Death, 1968, Near East, 1968, Asimov's Guide to the Bible, vol. 1, 1968, vol. 2, 1969, The Dark Ages, 1968, Words from History, 1968, Photosynthesis, 1969, The Shaping of England, 1969, Twentieth-Century Discovery, 1969, Nightfall and Other Stories, 1969, Opus 100, 1969, ABC's of Space, 1969, Great Ideas of Science, 1969, Solar System and Back, 1970, Asimov's Guide to Shakespeare (2 vols.), 1970, Constantinople, 1970, ABC's of the Ocean, 1970, Light, 1970, The Stars in Their Courses, 1971, Where Do We Go from Here?, 1971, What Makes the Sun Shine?, 1971, The Sensuous Dirty Old Man, 1971, The Best New Thing, 1971, Isaac Asimov's Treasury of Humor, 1971, The Land of Canaan, 1971, ABC's of the Earth, 1971, The Left Hand of the Electron, 1972, The Gods Themselves, 1972, Asimov's Guide to Science, 1972, More Words of Science, 1972, ABC's of Ecology, 1972, The Early Asimov, 1972, The Shaping of France, 1972, The Story of Ruth, 1972, Asimov's Annotated Don Juan, 1972, The Shaping of North America, 1973, Today and Tomorrow and, 1973, Jupiter, the Largest Planet, 1973, Please Explain, 1973, How Did We Find Out About Numbers, 1973, How Did We Find Out About Dinosaurs, 1973, The Tragedy of the Moon, 1973, Asimov on Astronomy, 1974, The Birth of the United States, 1974, Before the Golden Age, 1974, Our World in Space, 1974, How Did We Find Out About Germs, 1974, Asimov's Annotated Paradise Lost, 1974, Tales of the Black Widowers, 1974, Earth: Our Crowded Spaceship, 1974, Asimov on Chemistry, 1974, How Did We Find Out About Vitamins, 1974, Of Matters Great and Small, 1975, The Solar System, 1975, Our Federal Union, 1975, How Did We Find Out About Comets, 1975, Science Past—Science Future, 1975, Buy Jupiter and Other Stories, 1975, Eyes on the Universe, 1975, Lecherous Limericks, 1975, Heavenly Host, 1975, The Ends of the Earth, 1975, How Did We Find Out About Energy, 1975, Asimov on Physics, 1976, Murder at the ABA, 1976, How Did We Find Out About Atoms, 1976, The Planet That Wasn't, 1976, The Bicentennial Man and Other Stories, 1976, More Lecherous Limericks, 1976, More Tales of the Black Widowers, 1976, Alpha Centauri, The Nearest Star, 1976, How Did We Find Out About Nuclear Power, 1976, Familiar Poems Annotated, 1977, The Collapsing Universe, 1977, Asimov on Numbers, 1977, How Did We Find Out About Outer Space, 1977, Still More Lecherous Limericks, 1977, The Beginning and the End, 1977, Mars, The Red Planet, 1977, The Golden Door, 1977, The Key Word and Other Mysteries, 1977, Asimov's Sherlockian Limericks, 1977, Quasar, Quasar, Burning Bright, 1978, How Did We Find Out About Earthquakes, 1978, Animals of the Bible, 1978, Life and Time, 1978, Limericks: Too Gross, 1978, How Did We Find Out About Black Holes, 1978, Saturn and Beyond, 1979, In Memory Yet Green, 1979, Opus 200, 1979, Extraterrestrial Civilizations, 1979, How Did We Find Out About Our Human Roots?, 1979, The Road to Infinity, 1979, A Choice of Catastrophes, 1979, Isaac Asimov's Book of Facts, 1979, The Science Fictional Solar System, 1979, The Thirteen Crimes of Science Fiction, 1979, How Did We Find Out About Antarctica, 1979, Casebook of the Black Widowers, 1980, How Did We Find Out About Oil?, 1980, In Joy Still Felt, 1980, Microcosmic Tales, 1980, Who Dun It?, 1980, Seven Deadly Sins of Science Fiction, 1980, The Annotated Gulliver's Travels, 1980, How Did We Find Out About Coal, 1980, In the Beginning, 1981, Asimov on Science Fiction, 1981, Venus: Near Neighbor of the Sun, 1981, How Did We Find Out About Solar Power, 1981, How Did We Find Out About Volcanoes, 1981, Views of the Universe, 1981, The Sun Shines Bright, 1981, Change, 1981, A Glossary of Limericks, 1982, How Did We Find Out About Life in the Deep Sea, 1982, The Complete Robot, 1982, Laughing Space, 1982, Exploring the Earth and the Cosmos, 1982, How Did We Find Out About the Beginning of Life, 1982, Foundation's Edge, 1982, How Did We Find Out About the Universe, 1982, Counting the Eons, 1983, The Winds of Change and other Stories, 1983, The Roving Mind, 1983, The Measure of the Universe, 1983, X Stands for Unknown, 1984, Opus 300, 1984, Banquets of the Black Widowers, 1984, Asimov's New Guide to Science, 1984, Asimov's Guide to Halley's Comet, 1985, Exploding Suns, 1985, Substomic Monster, 1985, Robots and Empire, 1985, The Alternate Asimovs, 1986, The Dangers of Intelligence, 1986, Best Science Fiction of Isaac Asimov, 1986, Best Mysteries of Isaac Asimov, 1986, The Union Club Mysteries, 1983, Norby, the Mixed-Up Robot, 1983, How Did We Find Out About Genes, 1983, The Robots of Dawn, 1983, Foundation and Earth, 1986, Robot Dreams, 1986, Far as Human Eye Could See, 1987, How to Enjoy Writing, 1987. BS, Columbia U., 1939, MA, 1941, PhD, 1948. With Boston U. Schl. Medicine, 1949—, assoc. prof. biochemistry, 1955-79, prof., 1979—. Address: 10 W 66th St 33-A New York NY 10023

ASNEN, ALAN RICHARD, b. NYC, Feb. 29, 1952; s. Norman and Ida (Beckerman) A.; m. Kathleen Bridget Lemke, Dec. 22, 1976 (div. Mar. 12, 1979); m. 2d, Susan Beth Cooperstein, June 27, 1983; 1 son, Roger. Author: In Our Times, 1979, Dictionary of American Sport Biography, 1986, MacMillan's Biographical Companion to the Baseball Encyclopedia, 1987. Student CUNY-N.Y.C., 1970-74, City U. of San Francisco, 1977-79 U. SC, 1987—. Mng. ed. The East Village Other, NYC, 1966-71; reporter The Soho Weekly News, NYC, 1974-75; creative mgr. Creative Concepts, Inc., San Francisco, 1975-77; pub. liaison coordinator Wells Fargo Bank, Inc., San Francisco, 1979-83; advt. copywriter The Sharper Image, Inc., San Francisco, 1983; mgr., creative dir. The Book Dispensary, Inc., Columbia, S.C., 1984-86. Mem. Soc. Am. Baseball Research, S.C. Natural Wrtrs. Cadre (cofounder). Home: 501 Pelham Rd Columbia SC 29209

ASSENSOH, AKWASI B., (Akwasi Bretuo), b. Dunkwa-on-Offin, Ghana, West Africa, Apr. 1, 1946; came to U.S., 1978; s. Opanin Kwabena and Abena (Amoatemaa) A.; m. Irenita Benbow, Mar. 19, 1981; children—Rose Abena, Akwasi B. Jr. Author: Kwame Nkrumah: Six Years in Exile, 1966-72, 1978, Black Woman: An African Story (novel), 1980, Campus Life (three-act play), 1981, Africa in Retrospect, 1985, Martin Luther King, Jr. and America's Quest for Racial Integration, 1987; ed., contrbr.: Essays on Socio-Historical Topics, 1987; contrbr. chaps. to numerous books. Wrkg. on biography, history of Ghana. BA in History and Polit. Sci., Dillard U., 1981; MA, NYU, 1982, PhD, 1984. Asst. ed. Daily Listener, Chronicle, Digest, Monrovia, Liberia, 1968-69, ed., 1969-70; sub. ed. The Pioneer, Kumasi, Ghana, 1970-72; syndicated columnist Compass News Features, Luxembourg, 1986—; dir. honors program & assoc. prof. history Dillard U., New Orleans, 1984—. Recipient numerous fellowships, scholarships. Mem. PEN (London), New Orleans Press Club. Office: Dillard Univ 2601 Gentilly Blvd New Orleans LA 70122

ASTLE, THORA MYRLENE, (Thorne M. Astley), b. Evanston, WY, Oct. 1, 1913, d. Thomas Thorva and Ida Beatrice (Burleigh) Nelson; m. LaFarr P. Astle, June 12, 1937; children—Dianne Gale Astle Stone, Nelson L. Author: Reflections in a Still Key (poetry), 1986, Look Who's Cooking (cookbook), 1966; author teaching materials for Mormon Ch.; contrbr. stories and articles to mags. Wrkg. on novel. BA, Weber State U. Owner, operator Los Medanos Bus. Service, Pittsburg, Calif., 1959—. Mem. Wrtrs. Forum Martinez, Calif. Home: 264 Franklin Ave Pittsburg CA 94565

ASTLEY, THORNE M., see Astle, Thora Myrlene

ASTOR, SUSAN IRENE, b. NYC,Apr. 2, 1946; d. Irving David and Miriam Anne (Plotkin) Miller; m. Stuart Lloyd Astor, Dec. 24, 1967 (div., Nov. 1985); children—Abigail, Joanna. Author: Dame, 1980, Where the Dream Waits, 1984 (editor). Poems in West Hills Rvw, Wisc. Rvw, Poet Lore, other lit mags. Contrbtr. to Monitor Books Anthology of Mag. Verse, 1979-83, Windflower Almanac, 1980, and Portfolio One, 1983. BA, Adelphi U., Garden City, NY, 1967; Poet/tchr., NY City Poet in the Schools, 1981-83; self- empl. poet/tchr., NYC,1983—. Mem. P&W. Home: 113 Princeton St Roslyn Heights NY 11577

ASTOR, MRS. VINCENT, (Brooke), b. Portsmouth, NH; d. John Henry and Mabel (Howard) Russell; m. Vincent Astor. Author: Footprints, Patchwork Child, The Bluebird Is At Home, The Last Blossom on the Plum Tree. LL.D., Columbia U., 1971, Brown U., 1980; H.H.D. (hon.), Fordham U., 1980; hon. Doctor of Law, Brown U., 1980; Doctor of Humane Letters, NYU, 1986, PhD in Biomedical Sci. (hon.) Rockefeller U., 1986. Feature editor House and Garden,; trustee & hon. chmn., N.Y. Public Library,; mem. council of fellows Pierpont Morgan Library, trustee, Metropolitan Museum of Art, trustee, NY Zoological Sol., pres. & trustee, The Vincent Astor Fdn. Office: Astor (The Vincent) Fdn 405 Park Ave New York NY 10022

ATCHITY, KENNETH J., b. Eunice, LA, Jan. 16, 1944, s. Fred J. Sr. and Myrza A.; children—Vincent, Rosemary. Author: A Writer's Time: A Guide to the Creative Process, from Vision Through Revision, 1986, Sleeping with an Elephant, 1978, Homer's Iliad: The Shield of Memory, 1978, In Praise of Love, 1974; ed., Dreamworks, 1987; author intro.: English Lit./ Shakespeare, 1980, Yearbook of Am. Poetry, 1981, Scorpio Rising, 1983; ed., pub. PEN Los Angeles Center Yearbook, 1983; contrbg. ed., mem. editorial bd. Assn. for Study of Dreams Newsletter, 1984; contrbr. Am. Qtly, Classical Philosophy, Folio, Italian Qtly, numerous others. AB, Georgetown U., 1965; MPhil, Yale U., 1969, PhD,1970. Prof. Occidental Coll., Los Angeles, 1970-85; pres. L/A House Entertainment, Pasadena, Calif., 1976—; cons. Los Angeles Times Book Rvw, 1980, UCLA Writers Program Joyce Gay Report, Houston, 1984, Mitchell Energy & Devel., 1984. Grantee Mellon Fdn., 1978; recipient Design award Calif. Inst. Design, 1984. Mem. Greater LA Press Club, PEN. Home: One West California 224 Pasadena CA 91106

ATKINS, RUSSELL, b. Cleve., Feb. 25, 1926, s. Perry Kelly and Mamie Atkins. Author: Phenomena, 1961, Objects, 1963, Heretofore, 1968, The Nail, 1970, Maleficum, 1971, Here In The, 1976, Whichever, 1978; contrbr. to Sixes and Sevens, 1961, Sounds and Silences, 1969, Celebrations, 1977, numerous other anthols; contrbr. to Beloit Poetry Jnl, Wrtrs. Forum, Poetry Now, Cornfield Rvw, many other lit mags. Student Cleve. Inst. Music, 1945-46; LittD (hon.), Cleve. State U., 1976. Ed. Free Lance Mag., Cleve., 1950, 79-80; cons. ETV Television, Cleve., 1969-71; poet-in-schs. Ohio Arts Council-NEA, Columbus, 1973-75; instr. creative writing Karamu Theatre, Cleve., 1973—; lectr., presenter readings colls. and univs., 1963-79; mem. lit. adv. panel Ohio Arts Council, 1973-75. Recipient Karamu Prize and Tribute, Karamu House and Theatre, Cleve., 1971; Ohio Arts Council fellow, 1978; invitee Bread Loaf Conf., Middlebury (Vt.) Coll., 1956; music theory presented Avant-garde Festival, Darmstadt, Germany, 1956. Mem. Poets League Greater Cleve. (trustee). Home: 6005 Grand Ave Cleveland OH 44104

ATKINSON, CHARLES ORA, b. Weymouth, MA, Jan. 11, 1944; s. Clarence O. and Verda D. Atkinson; m. Carolyn Brott, Sept. 7, 1966; children: Nathan, Seth. Contrbr. to lit mags including Beloit Poetry Jnl, Poetry, Prairie Schooner, Va. Qtly, So. S.W. rvws, Quarry West, Amicus Jnl, Coll. English, Anthology Mag. Verse, Kans. Qtly, Denver Qtly. BA cum laude, Amherst Coll., 1966; MA, U. Calif.-Santa Cruz, 1975, PhD, 1979. Tchr. U.S. Peace Corps, Manila, 1966-68, Brookline High Schl., Mass., 1969-70; asst. house-master Hampshire Coll., Amherst, Mass., 1970-72; lectr. U. Calif., Santa Cruz, 1979—. Mem. NCTE. Home: 116 Yosemite Ave Santa Cruz CA 95060

ATKINSON, LUCY JO, b. Cleve., Oct. 13, 1931; d. Arland Carey and Mary (Steele) A. Co-author, Berry & Kohn's Intro. to Operating Room Technique, 6th ed., 1986; ed. Point of View mag., 1966—; contrbr. to books: Surgical Technol.: Basis for Clinical Pract., 1974, Operating Room Mgt., 1984, C.R. Bard trng. manuals, 1968, 72, 75, 77, 83, 85; contrbr. articles to AORN Jnl, Supervisor Nurse, Hospitals, Jnl of Emergency Nursing. BS in Nursing, Case Western Reserve U., 1954; MS, UCLA, 1966. Operating room supr. Childrens Hosp., Pitts., 1957-61; asst. dir. nursing Cedars of Lebanon Hosp., Los Angeles, 1961-66; dir. educ. svcs. Ethicon, Inc., Somerville, NJ, 1966—. Office: Ethicon Inc Somerville NJ 08876

ATLAS, JAMES ROBERT, b. Chgo., Mar. 22, 1949; s. Donald and Nora (Glassenberg) A.; m. Anna O'Conor Sloane Fels, Aug. 2, 1975. Author: Delmore Schwartz: The Life of an American Poet, 1977, The Great Pretender (novel), 1986; contrbr. articles to various natl. mags. BA, Harvard U., 1971; postgrad (Rhodes scholar), Oxford U., 1971-73. Staff writer, Time, 1977-78; NY Times: asst. editor NY Times Book Review, 1978-81; assoc. editor, Atlantic Monthly, 1981-85; contrbg. ed. Vanity Fair, 1985. Home: 40 W 77th St New York NY 10024

ATMA, see Thorne, Rick J.

ATTARD, JANET, b.Roosevelt, NY, Oct. 1, 1944, d. Reuben and Mary Florence (Feeley) Fels; m. George John Attard, Oct. 26, 1969; children—Stephen, Vicki. Author: You Can Organize a Successful Meeting, 1983, Hire the Perfect Employee, 1983, 61 Ready-to-Use Marketing, Advertising and Sales Checklists, 1983, 53 Ready-to-Use Time Management Checklists, 1983, Organize Yourself for Peak Productivity, 1984, 43 Ready-to-Use Office Management Checklists, 1984, Choose the Right Microcomputer, 1985; contrbr.: The New Financial Guide for the Self-Employed, 1981, The Complete Guide for Business Owners, 1982, The Laws of Business, 1983; contrbr. articles: The Profl. Report, Tax Update for Bus., Sidelines for Bus., Crafts Mag., Village Times, Suffolk Sun, Planning Ahead, Bus. Inc. BA in English, SUNY, Stony Brook. Copy editor Suffolk Sun, Deer Park, NY, 1966-68; assoc. editor Chem. Bank, NYC,1968-69; sr. staff editor J. C. Penney Co. NYC,1969-70. Communications specialist Upcountry Consumer Info. Ctr., Mt. Kisco, NY, 1975. Address: 20 Fairway Dr Centereach NY 11720

ATTAWAY, LE ROY BANKS (ROY), JR., b. Walterboro, SC, Sept. 16, 1937; s. LeRoy Banks and Claire (Walker) A.; m. Jane Scott Brown, Feb. 25, 1956 (div. 1975); children—Dorothy Claire, Catherine Jane, LeRoy Banks, III; m. 2d, Robyn Worth Gill, Apr. 24, 1982. Stud., U. NC, 1955-57. Contrbr. arts. & photos. to numerous natl. mags. inclg. Time, Sports Illus., Newsweek, Field & Stream, Outdoor Life, Travel & Leisure, Clipper, Glamour, Golf Digest, Family Circle, Sail, Diversion. Sportswriter, Sunday ed. The News & Courier, Charleston, SC, 1960-66; pub. rel. Olin Corp., NYC, 1966-68; writer Harbinger Prodns., NYC, 1968-69; freelance writer/photog. Hilton Head, SC & NYC, 1969-78; sr. ed. Motor Boating & Sailing, NYC, 1978-81; ed. Boating Mag., NYC, 1981-86; ed. Yachting Mag., Cos Cob, CT, 1986—. Mem. WG, ASME. Home: 424 East 52nd St New York NY 10022

ATTHOWE, JEAN FAUSETT, b. Bklyn., Feb. 26, 1931, d. Lynn and Helen Elizabeth (Wessells) F.; m. John M. Atthowe, Jr., Dec. 17, 1954; children—Helen Elizabeth, John Wessells. Contrbr. short stories to San Jose Studies (best short story of yr. award 1983), West Branch, Bellingham Rvw, Writers Forum, Primavera. BA, U. Utah, 1952; MFA, U. Mont., 1972. Freelance wrtr., Missoula, Mont., 1972-73; tchr. Gill-St. Bernards Schl., Gladstone, N.J., 1974-75; instr. Rutgers U., Newark and New Brunswick, N.J., 1975-84, Middlesex County Coll., Edison, N.J., 1978; adj. instr. Fairleigh Dickinson U., Madison, N.J., 1978-83. N.J. Council Arts fine arts grantee, 1983. Mem. AWP. Home: Box 163 RD 1 Far Hills NJ 07931

ATWATER, RICHARD MERLIN, b. Canton, MS., Oct. 6, 1946; s. David Henry and Eva Viola (Dyer) A. Author: Perspectives on Life (An Anthology of Poetic Variety), 1984, The Rich Atwater Scrapbook of 57 Selected Songs, 1985, Keeper of the Light (one-act play), 1984, Truth, Honor and Freedom (five-act musical), 1984, The Rich Atwater Scrapbook of Not-So-Very-Famous Poetry, 1986. Wrkg. on screenplays. AS, Weber State Coll., 1970, BS in Polit. Sci., 1973; MA in Poli. Sci., Brigham Young U., 1975. Asst. prof. aerospace studies Brigham Young U., Provo, Utah, 1982-85; counter-terrorism analyst Def. Intelligency Agcy., USAF, Washington, 1985—. Home: 7704 Oxon Hill Rd Oxon Hill MD 20745

ATWOOD, JEFFREY B, b. Lake Forest, IL, Mar. 13, 1948; s. Myron Jack and Carol Anita (Barnes) A.; m. Therese M. Rice, Nov. 1, 1969; 1 son Ryan. Contrbr. articles to mags. including Lab. Management Mag., Parapsychology Rvw., Ameri-Asia News, others. Newletter ed. Central Fla. chpt. Am. Soc. Training and Devel. Wrkg. on field investigators handbook of paranormal phenomena. B.S., U. Wis.-Parkside, 1973; M.A., Webster U., 1977; Ed.S., U. Wis.-Stout, 1984. Supvr. Abbott Labs., North Chicago, IL, 1977-79; coord. Gateway Technical Coll., Kenosha, WI,1980-85; v.p. Tobin & Assoc., Inc., Maitland, FL, 1986-87. Served to sgt. USAF, 1968-72. Mem. Fla. Freelance Wrtrs. Assn. Recipient Challenge award Wis. State Bd. of Vocational, Technical and Adult Edn., 1982. Home: 612 Mayfair Dr Altamonte Springs Fl 32701

AUCHINCLOSS, LOUIS STANTON, b. Lawrence, NY, Sept. 27, 1917; s. Joseph Howl and Priscilla (Stanton) A.; m. Adele Lawrence, Sept. 1957; children—John, Blake, Andrew. Author: Reading Henry James, 1975, The Winthrop Covenant, 1976, The Dark Lady, 1977, The Country Cousin, 1978, Persons of Consequence, 1979, Life, Law and Letters, 1979, The House of the Prophet, 1980, The Cat and the King, 1981, Watchfires, 1982, Exit Lady Masham, 1983, others. Yale U., 1939; LL.B., U.Va., 1941; Litt.D., NYU, 1974; Pace U., 1979. NY Bar, 1941. Assoc. firm Sullivan & Cromwell, 1941-51; Hawkins, Delafield & Wood, NYC, assoc. 1954-58, partner, 1958—. Lt., USNR, 1941-45. Mem. Am. Coll. Probate Counsel, Natl. Inst. Arts and Letters, Assn. Bar City NY. Home: 1111 Park Ave New York NY 10028

AUEL, JEAN M(ARIE), b. Chicago, Feb. 18, 1936; d. Neil S. and Martha (Wirtanen) Untinen; m. Ray B. Auel, March 19, 1954; children: RaeAnn, Karen, Lenore, Kendall, Marshall. Author: Earth's Children Series, The Clan of the Cave Bear, 1980, The Valley of the Horses, 1982, The Mammoth Hunters, 1985. Attended Portland (Ore.) State Univ.; MBA, University of portland, 1976; DL, Univ. of Portland, 1983, DH, U. of Maine, 1985, DHL, Mt. Vernon Coll., 1985. Clerk, 1965-66, circuit board designer, 1966-73, technical writer, 1973-74, credit mgr., Tektronics, Inc., Beaverton, Ore., 1974-76; writer. Member: AG Authors League of America, Natl. Women's Forum, PEN, Mensa, Oregon Writers Colony, Willamette Writers Club. Award for Excellence in Writing, Pacific Northwest Booksellers Assn., 1980, Vicki Penziner Matson Award, Friends of Literature, 1981, nomination for best first novel, Amer. Book Awards, 1981; Golden Plate award, Amer. Acad. of Achievement, 1986. Address: Naggar Lit Agcy 336 East 73rd St New York NY 10021

AUGERSON, SCOTT WILLIAM, b. Chgo., Sept. 29, 1949; s. Dale L. and Betty Jane (Boyle) A.; m. Mary F. Norman, Dec. 5, 1968 (div. 1979); children—Jennifer Marie, Kimberly Dale (twins). Contrbr.: Computers in Healthcare, South Fla. Bus. Jnl., Office Mag., other trade and tech. publs. Wrkg. on articles, book. MBA, Northern Colo. U., 1977, MS, George Washington U., 1983. Group product mgr. Siemens Info. Systems, Boca Raton, Fla., 1984—. Mem. IEEE (book reviewer). Home: 11441 Woodchuck Dr Boca Raton FL 33428

AUGUSTINE, JANE, b. Berkeley, CA, Apr. 6, 1931, d. Waldemar Rolf Augustine and Marguerite (St Clair) Radloff; m. Anthony J. Morley, Feb. 2, 1952 (div. June 1975); children—Marguerite, Thomas, Jefferson, Patrick; m. Michael D. Heller, Mar. 5, 1979. Author: (poems) Lit By the Earth's Dark Blood, 1977; represented in anthology Images of Women in Literature, 1985; contrbr. poems to mags. Wrkg. on PhD dissertation on Hilda Doolittle. AB cum laude, Bryn Mawr Coll., 1952; MA,Washington U., St. Louis, 1965. Instr. English, Webster Coll., Webster Groves, MO, 1965-67; instr. speech John Jay Coll., NYC,1970-72; mem. faculty New Schl., 1977-85, Parsons Schl. Design, NYC,1985—; asst. prof. English, Pratt Inst., Bklyn., 1977—. Seven Coll. Conf., scholar, 1948-52; NY State Council on Arts CAPS grantee, 1976, 79. Mem. PSA, MLA, N.E. MLA. Home: Box 981 Stuyvesant Sta NYC 10009

AUSTIN, NANCY ELIZABETH, b. Chgo., Sept. 26, 1953; d. Fletcher and Mary Ellen (Ledwin) A. Prodn. ed., Consumer Guide Mag., 1979-80; exec. ed. Super Service Station Mag., 1980-85; ed. Automotive Prods. Rpt. Mag., 1985—, Home Ctr. Prods. Rpt. Mag., 1986—. BA, U. IL, 1976. Prodn. ed. Consumer Guide Mag., Skokie, IL, 1979-80; ed. Irving-Cloud Pub. Co., Lincolnwood, IL, 1980—. Mem. Intl. Motor Press Assn., Chgo. BPE. Office: Irving-C 7360 N Cicero Ave Lincolnwood IL 60646

AUSTIN, PATRICIA, see Horrigan, Patricia Ann

AUSTIN, PHYLIS ANN, b. Logansport, IN, Oct. 14, 1943; d. Donald Paul and Ollie Ann (Cunningham) A. Author: Natural Remedies, 1982, More Natural Remedies, 1984, Food Allergies Made Simple, 1986, Natural Remedies for the Discomforts of Pregnancy, 1987, Fatigue: Causes, Prevention and Cure, 1987. Ed.: Sci./Health Abstracts, 1982--. Wrkg. on book on childhood diseases. B.S., Southern Coll., 1967. Home: 4118 Brenda Dr Decatur GA 30035

AVERILL, THOMAS FOX, b. Berkeley, CA, Apr. 30, 1949; s. Stuart Carson and Elizabeth Katherine Walter A.; m. Jeffrey Ann Goudie, Jan. 31, 1974; 1 dau., Eleanor Goudie-Averill. Author: (short stories) Passes at the Moon, 1985. Contrbr. short stories, poems, articles to lit mags, newspapers. Editor: Young Kansas Writers, 1983-85. BA, U. Kans.-Lawrence, 1971, MA, 1974, MFA, U. Iowa, 1976. Lectr., U. Kans., Lawrence, 1976-80; asst. prof. English, Washburn U., Topeka, 1980—. Appointed to Kans. Com. for the Humanities, Topeka, 1982—. Grantee, Kans. Com. for the Humanities, 1979-80. Mem. NCTE, Kans. Assn. Tchrs. English, Kans. State Hist. Soc. (life), Kans. Wrtrs. Assn. Home: 628 Webster Topeka KS 66606

AVERY, HELEN PALMER, b. Haverford, PA, Jan. 22, 1910, d. Frederic and Helen (Wallace) Palmer; m. William H. Avery, July 18, 1938; children—Christopher, Patricia Avery Bartlett. Author: (plays) The Ghost of Canterville Hall, 1977, The Palace of the Minotaur, 1978, A Christmas Carol, 1976, The Secret Garden, 1984, The Cricket on the Hearth, 1985. AB, Wellesley Coll., 1932. Exec. secy. Harvard U., 1933-38; exec. secy., asst. dean women U. Md., 1951-57; theatre dir., playwright, Adventure Theatre, Glen Echo, Md., 1961-86. Winner Seattle Jr. Theatre playwriting contest, 1982. Mem. PSA, Am. Theatre Assn. (v.p. Mid-Atlantic dist. 1968-69, pres. 1969-70, spcl. recognition 1973), Children's Theatre Assn. Am. (Charlotte Chorpenning cup 1975), Intl. Theatre Assn. for Children and Youth, American Assn. of Theatre for Youth. Home: 724 Guilford Ct Silver Spring MD 20901

AVERY, KENNETH AUSTIN, b. Haleyville, AL, Nov. 27, 1953; s. Austin and Mary Dean (Lee) A.; m. Pamela Carol Winsett, June 28, 1975; 1 dau., Angela Carol. Contrbr. features to Jnl.-Record, Hamilton, AL and Progress, Hamilton. Wrkg. on serial western for Progress. Grad. public schl., Hamilton. Production mgr. The Jnl.-Record, Hamilton, 1975-84; genl. mgr. The Progress, Hamilton, 1984--. Home: Box 201 Hamilton AL 35570

AVERY, NEIL FRANCIS, b. Buffalo, May 29, 1953; s. Ralph Lynn and Irene Orzechowski A. Editor: Kinesis Jnl. Philo., So. Ill. Univ., 1978-79, The Word, 1985—. BA in Philo., Syracuse Univ. 1978. Tech. writer OAO Corp, Greenbelt, Md., 1980-82; systems engineer Computer Assocs., Munich, W. Ger., 1982-84; info. security analyst Fidelity Union Life, Dallas, 1985-86, sr.systems programmer, 1986—. Address: Box 18235 Dallas TX 75218

AVERY, WILLIAM P., b. Regina, Sask., Canada, Feb. 11, 1918; s. Percival Albert and Ida Eleanor (Wilson) A.; m. Evelyn Ivy Braghetta; children—Carol Lynn, Janice Claire, Gail Anne. Contrbtr. to Mariners Mirror. Student pub. schls., Oakland CA. Switchman-Yardmaster, Alameda Belt Line (CA), 1941-1976. State Leg. Rep., Switchman's Union of N. Amer., State of CA, 1946-52. Mem. Nautical Research Soc., England, 1978, Canadian Nautical Research Soc., 1985. Home: 4111 Stone Rd Box 194 Bethel Island CA 94511

AVGERINOS, CECILY TERESE, b. Bronx, NY, Apr. 16, 1945; d. Salvatore and Susan (Avitable) Grazio; m. Robert Thomas Avgerinos, May 24, 1969 (dec. Jan. 30, 1983); children—Catherine Ann, Christopher James, Matthew Robert. Contrbr. poetry to numerous anthols. BA, NYU, 1966. Retail copywriter Casmir Advt., NYC, 1966-67; advt. sales mgr. Alden's Catalog, NYC, 1967-69; sr. advt. copywriter J.C. Penney, NYC, 1967-74, free-lance writer, 1974-77; free-lance writer Ventura Assoc., NYC, 1984. Vice pres. Hubbard Schl. Orgn., Ramsey, N.J., 1984, mem. publicity com., 1983, chrm. mini-course, 1986, St. Paul's Youth Ministry, 1987. Recipient 15 awards of Merit, World of Poetry, 1984-87, Golden Poet award, 1985, 86, 87. Mem. NYU Alumni Assn. (v.p. 1974). Home: 173 Momar Dr Ramsey NJ 07446

AXELROD, DAVID BRUCE, b. Beverly, MA, July 29, 1943; s. Samuel R. and Irene (Kransberg) A.; m. Joan Carol Hand, May 29, 1966; children—Jessica Ellen, Emily Elizabeth, Daniel Elliott. Author: (books of poetry) Stills from a Cinema, 1972; Myths, Dreams and Dances, 1974, A Dream of Feet, 1976, A Meeting with David B. Axelrod and Gnazino Russo, 1979, The Man Who Fell in Love with a Chicken,

1980, Home Remedies, New and Selected Poems, 1982. BA, U. Mass., 1965; MFA, U. Iowa, 1968; MA, Johns Hopkins U., 1966, PhD, Union Grad. Schl., 1977. English teacher, U. Iowa, 1967-69; prof. English Suffolk Coll., Selden, NY, 1969; pres. Writers Unlimited Agcy, Inc., Rocky Points, NY, 1976—, also dir.; dir. Handy Enterprises Real Estate, Rocky Point, 1980—; dir. vis. writer's program Suffolk Coll., 1972—. Mem. editorial bd. Cross-Cultural Pubs., Merrick, NY, 1979—. Recipient C.W. Post Poetry award AAP, 1979-80; grantee Suffolk County, 1977-79; N.Y. State Council on Arts, 1977-79; SUNY Research fellowship, 1983. Mem. bd. dirs. Com. Against Nuclear Pollution, Shoreham, N.Y., 1969—, East End Arts and Humanities Council, Riverhead (N.Y.), 1976-78; L.I. Writers Conf. (bd. dirs.), Alliance N.Y. Writers and Pubs. (pres. 1978—). PEN Intl., PSA. Home: 194 Soundview Dr Rocky Point NY 11778

AXELROD, MARK RICHARD, b. Phila., Mar. 31, 1946; s. Morris and Doris (Sokolov) A.; m. Greta Gaard. Author: Neville Chamberlain's Chimera, 1980, Clam Chowder, 1983; contrbr. Ardis Anthology of New Am. Poetry, 1977, Bloomsbury Rvw, Am. Book Rvw, Boston Rvw, Mnpls/St. Paul Mag., Mpls. Star, Mpls. Trib., Ia. Rvw, Playboy, Emphasis. BA, Ind. U., 1969, MA, 1977; PhD, U. of Minn., 1987. Tchg. assoc. Univ. Minn., 1978—. Recipient Alliance Francaise Natl. writing award, NYC, 1974-76; Oxford Univ. Scholarship, Intl. Inst. Edn., NY, 1978; Natl. Playwriting award, Western Ill. Univ., Macomb, 1984. Mem. MLA. Address: 2051 Loop St Minneapolis MN 55402

AXINN, DONALD EVERETT, b. NYC, July 13, 1929; s. Michael and Ann (Schneider) A.; m. Joan F.; children—Meredith, Allison, Michael, Jennifer. Author: Against Gravity, 1986, The Hawk's Dream and Other Poems, 1982, Sliding down the Wind, 1978; articles and poems in NYT, Newsday, Poetry Miscellany and others. Spcl. conslt. for New England Rvw/Bread Loaf Qtly. BA, Middlebury College, 1951, MA,Hofstra U., 1975. Vice pres., Axinn & Sons Lumber, Northport, NY 1951-58; chrmn., Donald E. Axinn Co., Jericho, NY, 1958—. Mem. PEN, P&W, Poets House. Address: 131 Jericho Turnpike Jericho NY 11753

AXTHELM, PETE, b. NYC, Aug. 27, 1943; s. Ralph Axthelm and Marjorie Axthelm Scholly; child—Megan. Author: The Modern Confessional Novel, 1967, Tennis Observed (with William F. Talbert), 1969, O.J. (with O.J. Simpson), 1971, The City Game, 1971, The Kid, 1978. BA, Yale U., 1965. Racing writer, columnist, NY Herald Tribune, 1965-66; staff writer, Sports Illus., 1966-68; at Newsweek: sports editor, 1968-73, columnist, contrbg. editor, 1973—; commentator, NBC Sports, NYC, 1979—. Recipient Page One award, Newspaper Guild; Natl. Headliners award; Silver Gavel award, Amer. Bar Assn.; Schick award; Eclipse award. Mem. Natl. Turf Writers Assn., Natl. Pro Football Writers Assn. Office: Newsweek 444 Madison Ave New York NY 10022

AYCOCK, DON MILTON, b. El Campo, TX, Dec. 10, 1951; s. Dewey and Mabel (Stout) A.; m. Carla C. Ricketts, Nov. 17, 1974; children—Ryan and Christopher (twins). Author: The E. Y. Mullins Lectures on Preaching, 1980, Symbols of Salvation, 1982, Walking Straight in a Crooked World, 1987; (with Carla Aycock) Not Quite Heaven, 1981; (with Len Goss) Writing Religiously, 1984 (main selection Wrtrs. Digest Book Club 1985). Editor: Preaching with Purpose and Power, 1982 (main dual selection Religious Book Club 1984); Heralds to a New Age, 1985; editor, contrbr. Apathy in the Pew, 1983. BA, La. Coll., Pineville, 1974; MDiv, Southern Seminary, Louisville, 1976, ThM, 1978; Oxford U., 1979, ThD, New Orleans Bapt. Seminary, 1986. Mem. Am. Acad. Religion. Home: Rt 7 Box 128 Franklinton LA 70438

AYDELOTTE, WILLIAM OSGOOD, b. Bloomington, IN, Sept. 1, 1910; s. Frank and Marie Jeannette (Osgood) A.; m. Myrtle Elizabeth Kitchell, June 22, 1956; children—Marie Elizabeth, Jeannette Farley. Author: Bismarck and British Colonial Policy, 1937, rev. ed., 1970; Quantification in History, 1971. Editor: The Dimensions of Quantitative Research in History, 1972; The History of Parliamentary Behavior, 1977; bd. editors: Am. Hist. Rvw, 1976-78. AB, Harvard U., 1931; PhD, U. Cambridge, Engl., 1934. Asst. in chmn.'s office Fed. Home Loan Bank Bd., Washington, 1934-36; faculty Trinity Coll., Hartford, CT, 1937-43, Smith Coll., Northhampton, MA, 1943-45, Princeton U., 1945-47; U. Iowa, Iowa City, 1947—, prof. history, 1950—, chmn. dept. history, 1947-59, 65-68, Carver prof. 1976-78, emeritus, 1978—; vis. prof. Harvard U., Cambridge, MA, 1966, U. Leicester, Eng., 1971; fellow Center Advanced Study Behavioral Scis., 1976-77. Fellow Royal Hist. Soc.; mem. Am. Hist. Assn., AAUP, Social Sci. Research Council (dir. 1964-70), Natl. Acad. Scis., Iowa Acad. Sci., Social Sci. History Assn.: steering com. 1973—, v.p. 1978-79, pres. 1979-80. Phi Beta Kappa. Home: 201 N 1st Ave Iowa City IA 52240

AYER, ANNE, b. Topsfield, MA, June 23, 1917; d. Frederick and Hilda (Rice) Ayer; m. Edward Ford MacNichol, Jr., Sept. 7, 1940; children—Edward Ford III, Anne MacNichol Brownell. Poetry in: Words of Praise, A Cape Cod Sampler, Voices of the Majestic Sage, American Poetry and other anthologies. Wrkg. on poetry. Student spcl. schl., NYC; pvt. vocal instrn., NYC., Boston, 1937-70. Concert singer, recording artist, 1948-81. Mem. Nat. Soc. Lit. and the Arts. Home: 45 Brewster St Cambridge MA 02138

AYERS, JAMES WILBER, b. Attalla, AL., Apr. 1, 1928; s. Jay and Thelma Elizabeth A. Author: Modest Dove (poetry), 1971, The New Angels (fantasy novel), 1971, Circles of Conquest (sci. fiction novel), 1979. Feature wrtr. Joe Weider Fan Club Newsletter. State record holder for letters to the editors of local area newpapers. Home: 609 1st St Attalla AL 35954

AYLESWORTH, THOMAS GIBBONS, b. Valparaiso, IN, Nov. 5, 1927; s. Carrol Wells and Margaret Ruth (Gibbons) A.; m. Virginia Lillian Boelter, Aug. 13, 1949; children—Carol Jean, Thomas Paul. Author: The Story of Dragons and Other Monsters, 1980, Storm Alert, 1980, Animal Superstitions, 1981, Science Looks at Mythical Monsters, 1982, The Mount St. Helens Disaster, 1983, America This Beautiful Land, 1984, History of Movie Musicals, 1984, others. AB, 1950, MS, 1953; PhD, Ohio State U., 1959. Tchr. Harvard (IL) High School, 1951-52, New Albany (IN) Jr. High Schl., 1952-54; head sci. dept. Battle Creek (MI) High Schl., 1955-57; asst. prof. Mich. State U., East Lansing, 1957-61. Spcl. lectr. Wesleyan U., Middletown, CT, 1961-64. Sr. editor Doubleday & Co. Inc., NYC, 1964-80; pres. Update Pub. Corp., 1976—; editor-in-chief Bison Books Corp., Greenwich, CT, 1981—; vis. prof. Ohio State U., Columbus, 1962, Whitewater State U., WI, 1964. New England editor, Am. Biology Tchr., 1962-64; sr. editor, Current Sci., 1961-64. U.S. Army, 1946-47. Mem. NY Acad. Scis., Natl. Sci. Tchrs. Assn., Natl. Assn. Biology Tchrs., Natl. Assn. Research Sci. Teaching, Am. Assn. Sci. Writers, AG, Phi Delta Kappa. Home: 48 Van Rensselaer Ave Stamford CT 06902

AYRES, ED, b. Summit, NJ, Oct. 11, 1941; s. John V. and Alice (Hutchinson) A.; m. Bonnie Garber (div. 1969); m. 2d, Sharon Lee Talbott, May 5, 1980; 1 dau., Elizabeth Ann. Author: Economic Impact of Conversion to a Nonpolluting Automobile, 1969, What's Good for GM, 1970. Editor, pub. Running Times mag., 1976—. BA, Swarthmore Coll., 1963; postgrad. Columbia U., 1967. English tchr. George Schl., Newtown, Pa., 1963-68; sr. staff IRET, McLean, Va., 1969-76. Recipient Annual Journalism award Road Runners Club Am., 1985. Home: 1950 Old Post Terr Woodbridge VA 22191

AZRAEL, JUDITH ANNE, b. Balt., July 28, 1938; d. Maurice and Altie (Chapel) A.; m. Herbert Greenberg (div.); children: Denise, Jeffrey. Author: (poetry) Fire in August, 1969; Fields of Light, 1974; Antelope Are Running, 1978; Apple Tree Poems, 1978; contrbr. poetry and short stories to The Nation, Western Humanities, Red Cedar, So. Poetry, Laurel, Sunstone, Mendocino, Blackbear, Slackwater, Wormwood, Minn. rvws, Carolina Qtly, December, Voices Intl., Mississippi Mud, Christian Sci. Monitor, numerous others. BA, U. Wis., 1959; MFA, U. Oreg., 1972. Mem. faculty U. Oreg., 1971-72, Coll. of Redwoods, Ft. Bragg, Calif., 1974-77, Western Wash. U., Bellingham, 1977-80, Whatcom Community Coll., Bellingham;, 1981-86, Mendocino College and College of the Redwoods, 1987. Helene Wurlitzer Fdn. fellow, 1974. Mem. AWP. Home: Box 1306 Mendocino CA 95460

BABB, SANORA, b. Leavenworth, KS, Apr. 21, 1907; d. Walter Lacy and Anna Jeanette (Parks) Babb; m. James Wong Howe, 1936 and 1949 (dec. July, 1976). Author: The Lost Traveler, 1959, An Owl On Every Post, 1970, The Dark Earth (stories), 1987; contrbr. poetry Borestone Mountain Awards, 1967, Grub St. Book of Verse, 1928, Spring Anthol, 1932, Anthol Mag Verse, 1984, Yearbook Am. Poetry, 1984; short stories and poems in numerous mags. inclg. Saturday Evening Post, Redbook, Woman's Jnl, New Story, Windsor Qtly, New Masses, San Francisco Rvw, Antioch Rvw, Southern Rvw, Southwest Rvw, New Mexico Rvw, Northwest Rvw, Southwest Rvw, Ariz. Qtly, Prairie Schooner, Dalhousie Rvw, stories in anthologies: Cross Section of Am. Lit, 1945, 48; The Am. Century, 1955; Best Am. Short Stories, 1950, 60; US Stories, 1960; Anatomy of Reading, 1965; Writers in Revolt, 1973. High school diploma. Reporter newspapers Okla. and Kans., 1924-28, KFWB radio, Hollywood, 1929-32; freelance writer national mags, 1929—; lit. editor The Clipper, Hollywood, 1940s, Calif. Quarterly, 1950s; short story tchr. UCLA Extension, Los Angeles, 1959. Recipient Gold Medal for poetry, Mitre Press, London, 1932, Borestone Mountain award, 1967. Wrkg. on a book on the life and work of cinematographer, James Wong Howe. Mem. AG. Address: 1562 Queens Rd Hollywood CA 90069

BABER, ROBERT HENRY, (Bob Henry), b. Mineola, NY, Dec. 15, 1950; s. Troy Nash and Roberta marie (Schwienler) B.; div., 1 dau., Ciara Tess. Author: Assorted Lifesavers & Poems from the Mountains, 1976, Time is an Eightball, 1984, Common Ground, 1986; Broadsides, 1982-83; editor Mucked, 1978, 2d ed., 1984. BA in Creative Writing, Antioch Coll., 1976; PhD, Union for Experimenting Colls. and Us, Cin., 1983. Exec. cons. Appalachian Poetry Project, Lexington, Ky., 1980-81; creative writing instr. Santa Fe Council for the Arts, N.Mex., 1981-83; Poetry Workshop leader Youth Diagnostic Ctr., Albuquerque, 1981-83; Writing Workshop coordinator N.Mex. State Penitentiary, 1983; asst. prof. labor edn. W.Va. Tech., Montgomery, 1984—. Mellon fellow in Appalachian studies, Berea Coll., Ky., 1984-85. Mem. So. Appalachian Writers Coop., W.Va. Writers Inc., Appalachian Writers Assn., Soupbean Poets. Address: Box 413 Richwood WV 26261

BABULA, WILLIAM, b. Stamford, CT, May 19, 1943, s. Benny Francis and Lottie (Zajkowski) B.; m. Karen Gemi, June 19, 1965; children—Jared, Joelle. Novelist: The Bombing of Berkeley and Other Pranks (Ione Burden award Deep South Wrtrs.' Conf.), 1984, St. John's Baptism, 1988; playwright: The Fragging of Lt. Jones: A Vietnam Play in Three Acts (1st prize Gualala Arts Competition), 1983, The Winter of Mrs. Levy, 1984, Creatures, 1987; author: Wishes Fall Out as They're Willed: Shakespeare and the Tragicomic Archetype, Elizabethan & Renaissance Studies, 1975, Shakespeare in Production 1935-1979: A Selective Catalogue, 1981; contrbr. short stories: Mike Shayne Mystery Mag., Gem, Fiction 84 Anthology, others; contrbr. articles: Dalhousie Rvw, South Atlantic Bulltn., Reader's Encyc. Eng. Lit., others. BA, Rutgers U., 1965; MA, U. Calif.-Berkeley, 1967, PhD, 1969. Chmn. dept. English, U. Miami, Fla., 1975-81; dean of Arts and Humanities, Sonoma State U., Rohnert Park, Calif., 1981—. Mem. DG, AL of Am. Office: Sonoma State U Rohnert Park CA 94928

BACH, MARCUS, b. Sauk City, WI, Dec. 15, 1906; s. Louis P. and Albertina (Buerki) B.; m. Lorena Ernest, Aug. 17, 1932. Author: plays, While Mortals Sleep, 1935, Within These Walls, 1936, Champion of Democracy, 1940, Who is Mrs. Chimpsie?, 1940, Common Ground, 1943, Sunrise by Request, 1944; books, The World of Serendipity, 1970, Strangers at the Door, 1971, What's Right with the World, 1973, The Power of Total Living, 1977, I, Monty, 1978, numerous others; contrbr. to encycs. and natl. mags. Student, Wis. Schl. Music, Madison, 1920-22; Mission House Coll. and Sem., Plymouth, WI, 1924-25; U. Ia., AM, 1937, PhD, 1942. Research and study 1933-35, under Rockefeller fellowship, 1934-36. Instr. dramatic lit. Carleton Coll., Northfield, MN, 1937; research among Am. religious and folk groups, 1938-40; assoc. dir. and prof. Schl. Religion, U. Ia., 1942—. Founder, dir., Fdn. for Spiritual Understanding, Intl., Palos Verdes, CA. Recipient Charles Sergel Natl. Playwriting award, 1937, Nicholas Copernicus award, 1943. Mem. Am. Acad. Poli. and Social Sci. Home: 100 Via Alameda Palos Verdes Estates CA 90274

BACHE, ELLYN, (Ellen Mathews), b. Washington, Jan. 22, 1942, d. Herman and Clara (Winik) Olefsky; m. Terrance William Bache, July 5, 1969; children—Beth, Matthew, James, Benjamin. Author: (under pseudonym Ellen Matthews) Culture Clash, 1982; Safe Passage (novel), 1988; contrbr. short fiction to Young Miss, McCall's, Va. Country, So. Humanities Rvw, Ascent, Woman's World, Antietam Rvw. BA, U. N.C., 1964; MA,U. Md., 1967. Freelance journalist Washington Post. Balt. Sun, also others, 1974-85; ed.-in-chief Antietam Rvw, 1982-85; instr. N.C. Wrtrs' Network, Wilmington, 1986—. Home: 2314 Waverly Dr Wilmington NC 28403

BACHEM-ALENT, ROSE MARIE, b. Rhineland, Germany, Jan. 15; to U.S., 1950, naturalized, 1955; d. H.F. Baake and E.C. (Beegen) Baake; m. Peter J. Bachem, July 23, 1947 (div. 1964); children—Yvonne C., Suzanne N.; m. 2d, Mury B. Alent, June 12, 1965. Author: The Companion to Foreign Language Composition, 1972, Beruhmte Franen aus deutschen Landen, 1981. Staatsexamen, U. Berlin, 1946; MA, U. Rochester, 1953, PhD, 1957. At SUNY- Geneseo, from asst. prof. 1956 to prof., 1963-74, disting. teaching prof. comparative lit., 1974—. Home: 39 2d St Geneseo NY 14459

BACKLUND, RALPH THEODORE, b. Hoffman, MN, Aug. 3, 1918, s. Adolph T. and Grace (Sheppard) B.; m. Caroline Hillman Eckel, May 18, 1956; child—Nicholas Sheppard. AB magna cum laude, 1940, U. Minn. Radio newswriter, WCCO, Mpls., 1946-50; producer, news and public affairs, Columbia Broadcasting System, 1950-55; exec. producer, public affairs programs, CBS Radio Network, 1955-58. At Horizon mag., NYC: assoc. editor, 1958-64; mng. editor, 1964-66. Spcl. asst. for arts, Bur. Ednl. and Cultural Affairs, U.S. Dept. State, Washington, DC, 1966-69. At Smithsonian mag.: bd. editors, 1969-76; exec. ed., 1976—. With U.S. Army, 1942-46, 51-52. Recipient Heywood Broun award, Am. Newspaper Guild, 1948. Home: 3827 Massachusetts Ave NW Washington DC 20016

BACON, DAISY SARAH, b. PA; d. E. Ellsworth and Jessie M. Holbrook B. Author: Love Story Writer, 1953, 2nd ed., 1959; Love Story Editor, 1963; The Golden Age at Street & Smith, 1975. Contrbr. articles to mags. Taught by private tutors. Editor: Love Story mag., 1928—; Ainslee's mag., 1934-38; Smart Love Stories, 1937-39; Pocket Love mag., 1937; Detective Story and Romantic Range mags, 1940—; overseas armed forces ed. Detective Story mag. distbd. by U.S. Army, 1942-46. Pub. Gemini Books, 1963—. Compiler four annual prize story anthologies. Spur Awards judge, Western Writers Am., 1967-68. Home: 7 Hillside Ave Port Washington NY 11050

BACON, DONALD CONRAD, b. Jacksonville, FL, Jan. 15, 1935; s. Francis Herbert and Myrtis Ann (Gunter) B.; m. Barbara Lee Barnwell, June 22, 1957; children—Elizabeth, Jennifer (dec.). Author: Congress and You, 1969; co-author: The New Millionaires, 1961, Rayburn: A Biography, 1987. BS Journalism, 1957, U. FL. Staff writer, Wall St. Jnl., 1957-61; Congl. fellow, 1961-62; staff writer, Washington Star, 1962-63. With Newhouse News Service: Congl. corr., White House corr., sr. corr. and columnist, 1962-75. With U.S. News & World Report mag., Washington; assoc. editor, 1972-79; sr. editor, 1979-81; asst. mng. editor, 1981—. Recipient Loeb award, U. Conn, 1961; award for excellence in journalism, Lincoln U., Jefferson City, MO, 1977. Mem. National Press Club, The Society of Professional Journalists, Sigma Delta Chi. Home: 3809 East-West Hwy Chevy Chase MD 20815

BACON, PHILLIP, b. Cleve., July 10, 1922; s. Hollis Phillip and Emma (Schneider) B.; m. Jane Lowrie, Nov. 21, 1980; children (by prev. marriage)—Laura Jane Bacon Brogdon, Phillip Everett. Author: Australia, Oceania, and the Polar Lands, 1961; North America, 1961; Children's Picture Atlas of the World, 1966; Knowing Our Neighbors in the United States (with Norman Carls and Frank E. Sorenson) and Knowing our Neighbors in the United States and Canada, 1966; Regions Around the World, Towns and Cities (with R. R. Boyce), The United States and Canada (with co-authors), and The Story of Latin America (with P. V. Groco—all), 1970; America: in Space and Time (with co-authors), 1976; Exploring Our World, 1982; World Regions (with Donald C. Fairweather), Our World Today (with James B. Kracht), and Our State: California (with M. Evelyn Swartz), all 1983. Editor, Focus on Geography, Key Concepts and Teaching Strategies, 1970. Co-editor, Foundations of World Regional Geography Series, 1970; sr. edl. advisor, Harcourt Brace Jovanovich Social Studies Program, 1988. Attended The Citadel, 1940-42; AB, 1946, U. Miami; MA,1951, Ed.D., 1955, George Peabody Coll. for Tchrs. Tchr. social studies: Castle Heights Mil. Acad., Lebanon, TN, 1946-47; Army and Navy Acad., Carlsbad, CA 1948-53. At Columbia Tchrs. Coll.: vis. asst. prof. geography, 1956-57; asso. prof., 1957-60; prof., 1960-63, 64-66. At George Peabody (now Vanderbilt U.): dean, Grad. Schl., 1963-64; acting dir., Library Sch., 1964. At U. Wash.: prof. geography and social studies edn, 1966-71. At U. Houston: prof. geography, 1971—; chmn. dept., 1973-78. Disting. vis. prof. social studies edn. and geography, Seattle Pacific U., 1977-79. With USNR, 1942-45. Fellow, Royal Geog. Soc. and Explorers Club. Chmn. Publs. com., Assn. Am. Geographers, 1976-78. Pres. (1966) and life mem., Natl. Council for Geog. Edn. Life mem. NEA. Recipient: Distinguished Service award, Natl. Council for Geog. Edn., 1974; Teaching Excellence awards, U. Houston, 1975, 79, 80. Home: 2 Tennis Ct Ln Albuquerque NM 87120

BACON, WALLACE ALGER, b. Bad Axe, MI, Jan. 27, 1914; s. Russell Alger and Mana Wallace) B. Author: Savonarola (verse play), 1950—rec'd. Bishop Sheil award, 1946; William Warner's Syrinx, 1950; Literature as Experience (with Robert S. Breen), 1959; Literature for Interpretation (with Breen), 1961, 2d ed. 1972, 3d ed. 1979; Spoken English (with N. Crame-Rogers and C. V. Fonacier), 1962; The Art of Oral Interpretation (with C. V. Fonacier), 1965; The Art of Interpretation, 1966; Oral Interpretation and the Teaching of Literature in Secondary Schools, 1974; assoc. ed. Performance of Literature in Historical Perspectives, 1983. Contrbr. articles, poetry, monographs to jnls. AB, 1935, Litt. D., 1967, Albion Coll. AM, 1936, PhD,1940, U. Mich. LL.D, 1975, Emerson Coll. Instr. English, U. Mich., 1941-47. At Northwestern U.: chmn, dept. interpretation, Schl. of Speech, 1947-79; asst. prof English and speech, 1947-50; assoc. prof English and speech, 1950-55; prof. speech, 1955-80; prof. emeritus, 1980—. Mem.: Speech Communication Assn, N. Mex. Communication Assn., Western Speech Communication Assn., World Commn. Assn., Malone Soc., AAUP, Phi Beta Kappa. Recipient Hopwood Major award for drama writing, U. Mich., 1936; Alfred Lloyd postdoctoral fellow, U. Mich., 1940-41; Rockefeller fellow, 1948-49; Ford Fdn. fellow, 1954-55; spcl. citation, U. Philippines, 1965, 70; spcl. commendation, Ednl Fdn. Philippines. Home: Box 2257 Taos NM 87571

BADANES, MENKE, see Katz, Menke

BADILLO-SCIORTINO, OLGA ESTHER, b. NYC, May 9, 1941; d. Frank and Guillermina (Rivera) Badillo; divorced; 1 dau., Deborah Lynn Nieves; m. Frank Anthony Sciortino, July 12,

1986. Secy. to ed. Boating Industry Mag., NYC, 1963-76, directory ed., 1968-76, promotion mgr., 1976-77, mng. ed., 1977-83, ed., 1983—; edl. dir. OEM Business and Boating News, 1987-. Recipient Silver M award Marymount Manhattan Coll., NYC, 1983, Econ. Gold medal, 1983, named to Curian Honor Soc., 1983. Mem. ASBPE, Assn. Bus. Pubs. (ed. com.), Boating Wrtrs. Intl. Home: 137-23 80th St Howard Beach NY 11414

BAEHR, TIMOTHY JAMES, b. New Britain, CT, Dec. 29, 1943; s. Arthur J. and Yvonne M. (Robichaud) B.; m. Judith A. Delk, July 3, 1965 (div. 1979; 1 son, Alan; m. Ann S. Landsberg, Dec. 1, 1984; children—James, Max. Contributor to numerous textbooks published by Random House, Macmillan, Scott, Foresman, Houghton Mifflin, Economy, Laidlaw, others; indexes of college and professional books pub. by Little, Brown, Houghton Mifflin, Natl. Acad. of Sciences, others. B.A., U. Mich., 1965, postgrad., 1965-69. Ed. U. Mich., Ann Arbor, 1967-69, Ginn & Co., Lexington, MA 1969-74, Houghton Mifflin Co., Boston, 1974-80; freelance writer and indexer, 1980—. Mem. Bookbuilders of Boston, Freelance Editorial Assn. Home: 21 Eliot St Jamaica Plain MA 02130

BAENDER, MARGARET WOODRUFF, b. Salt Lake City, Apr. 1, 1921, d. Russell Kimball and Margaret Angline (McIntyre) Woodruff; m. Phillip Albers Baender, Aug. 17, 1946 (dec. 1980); children—Kristine, Charlene, Michael Phillip, Russell Richard. Author: Shifting Sands (young adult fiction), 1981, Tail Waggings of Maggie (juvenile fiction), 1982; contrbr. to periodicals. Wrkg. on hist. biographies. BA, U. Utah. Wrtr. The Valley Pioneer, Danville, Calif., 1976-78. Mem. NWC, IWWG, Soc. Children's Book Wrtrs., Wrtrs. Connection. Home: Box 402 Diablo CA 94528

BAEUMER, MAX LORENZ, b. Trier, Germany; to US, 1952, naturalized, 1958; s. Lorenz Max and Helene (Dahm) B.; m. Helene Heine, Jan. 25, 1945. Author: Das Dionysische i.d. Werken W. Heinses, 1964; Heinse-Studien, 1966; W. Heinse, Ardinghello, 1975; Nietzche and the Dionysian Tradition, 1976; Winckelmann, French Classicism, and Jefferson, 1978; Sozialkritische und revolutionäre Literatur der Reformationszeit, 1980; Reformation in Braunschweig, 1981; Nietzsche and Luther, 1985; Luther and the Rise of the German Language, 1984; Goethe as a Critic of Literature, 1984; Was Luther's Reformation a Revolution? 1985; Imperial Germany in Its Máss Festivals, 1985; Klassizität und repúblikanische Freiheit in der Winckelmann-Rezeption, 1986. Chief editor: W. Heinse, Collected Works and Letters, 1980-86; Toposforschung, 1973. Ph.L., 1939, Coll of Trier; postgrad., 1947-49, U. Frankfurt; Ph.D., 1959, Northwestern U. Instr., Northwestern U., 1958-59; asst Prof., Bowling Green State U., 1959-61. At U. Kans., asst. prof., 1961-63, asso. prof., 1963-64 and at U. Wis., Madison, prof. German lit., 1965—; Wisconsin Alumni Research Foundation (-WARF) Senior Distinguished Research Professor, 1984-. Dir., Northwestern U. Summer Inst., Germany, 1963. Fullbright vis. prof., U. Stuttgart, Germany, 1964-65; evaluator NDEA Insts. in Germany, 1963. Vis. prof., 1968, and permanent member, 1972, U. Wis. Inst. for Research in Humanities. Dir., seminar on history and lit. of Reformation, NEH, 1980. Fellow: Deutscher Akademischer Austauschdienst, 1975; Herzog August Bibliothek Wolfenbüttel, 1977, 84. Mem.: Goethe Soc. N. Am, Am. Assn. Tchrs. German, Internatl. Germanist. Verband, Arbeitskreis für Renaissanceforschung, Amer. Soc. 18th Century Studies, Deutsche Gesellschaft zur Erforschung des 18. Jahrhunderts, Internatl. Archiv. f. Sozialgeschichte d. dt. Literatur. Office: Inst for Rsrch in Humanities U Wis Madison WI 53706

BAGAI, ERIC PAUL, b. Cleve., June 10, 1940; s. Joseph Kovach and Leona (Parr) Bagai; m. Judith Ann Eisenstein, June 20, 1968; 1 son, Jeremy Paul. Author (with Judith Bagai), System FORE Handbook, 1977. MA in Special Ed., CSULA, 1971; Natl. Ldrship Trng.: D/HH, CSUN, 1973. Systems anal. Kaiser Permanente, Los Angeles, 1963-65; consult. in specl. ed. Exceptl. Child.'s Fdn., Los Angeles, ,69-71; dir. Diagnostic Schl., Five Acres, Pasadena, CA, 1971-72; spcl. prog. consult. Montebello USD, Montebello, CA, 1972-75; pub./ed. Foreworks Pubs., N. Hollywood, CA, 1975—. Home: 7112 Teesdale North Hollywood CA 91605

BAGDIKIAN, BEN HAIG, b. Marash, Turkey, Jan. 30, 1920; to US, 1920, naturalized, 1926; s. Aram Theodore and Daisy (Uvezian) B.; m. Elizabeth Ogasapian, Oct. 12, 1942 (div. 1972).children—Christopher Ben, Frederick Haig; m. Betty L. Medsger, 1973 (div. 1983); m. Marlene D. Griffith, 1983. Author: In the Midst of Plenty: The Poor in America, 1964; The Information Machines: Their Impact on Men and the Media, 1971; The Shame of the Prisons, 1072; The Effete Conspiracy, 1972; Caged: Eight Prisoners and Their Keepers, 1976; The Media Monopoly, 1983, rev. ed., 1987. Contrbr., The Kennedy Circle, 1961; editor, Man's Contracting World in an Expanding Universe, 1959. AB, 1941, D. Litt., 1963, Clark U.; L.H.D., 1961, Brown U. Reporter, Springfield (MA) Morning Union, 1941-42; assoc. editor, Periodical House, Inc., NYC,1946. At Providence Jnl: reporter, fgn. corr., chief Washington corr. Contbg. editor, Sat. Eve. Post, 1963-67. Proj dir., study of future US news media, Rand Corp., 1967-69. At Washington Post: asst mng. editor for natl. news, 1970-71; asst. mng. editor, 1971-72. Natl. corr. Columbia Journalism Review, 1972-74; M. Lyle Spencer vis. prof., Syracuse U., 1973; prof., Grad. Schl. Journalism. U. Calif., Berkeley, 1977—; Dean, 1985—. With USAAF, 1942-45. Bd. editors, Jnl Investigative Reporters and Editors, 1980—; mem. steering com., Natl. Prison Project, 1974-82. Bd. dirs: Natl. Capital Area Civil Liberties Union, 1964-66; Com. To Protect Journalist, 1981—.Pres., Lowell Mellett Fund for Free and Responsible Press, 1965-76. Acad. adv. bd. Natl. Citizens Com. for Broadcasting, 1978—. Recipient: George Foster Peabody award, 1951; Sidney Hillman Fdn. award, 1956; Most Perceptive Critic citation, Am. Soc. Journalism Administrs., 1978. Ogden Reid Fdn. fellow, 1956; Guggenheim fellow, 1961-62. Home: 25 Stonewall Rd Berkeley CA 94705

BAGLEY TARANTINO, ALICE MARIE, (Anna Joan), b. Fairborn, OH, Feb. 14, 1957; d. Henry Stuart and Mildred (Teater) Bagley; m. Anthony L. Woodward, Aug. 17, 1975 (div. 1977); m. Gary Alan Tarantino, Feb. 14, 1978; 1 son, David Alan. Contrbr. articles, poems to newspapers, anthols. B.A. with honors, Ark. State U., 1981; Cert., Inst. Children's Lit., 1980; Cert. in real estate Career Coll., Fort Worth, 1982. Marketing specialist Century 21, Fort Worth, 1982-85; mgr. Broadway Nursery, Pocahontas, AR, 1985-86; real estate marketing specialist ERA Real Estate, Jonesboro, AR, 1987—. Recipient Natl. Poetry Merit award World of Poetry, 1984. Home: 1405 Alpine Rd Walnut Ridge AR 72476

BAGNAL, KIMBERLY BAUGHMAN, b. Sumter, SC, Dec. 26, 1949; d. Leon Melvin, Sr. and Louise (May) Baughman; children—Melissa Corbett Bagnal, Earle Rowland Bagnal. Ed.: Marching On—the official S.C. ed. of the Vietnam Veterans of America pubn., 1986—; South Carolina College News, 1986, Veterans of Foreign Wars, 1986, South Carolina Youth Baseball Souvenir Book, 1986. Ghostwriter: Handbook of Handwriting Analysis Techniques, 1986. Contrbr. articles to Intercom, South Carolina College News, The State Magazine, The Gamecock. BA, USC 1986; Cert. in COBOL Programming, Midlands Tech. Coll., 1983. Counselor Crisis Intervention, Sumter, 1974-75; legal asst. Levi & Wittenberg, Sumter, 1976-77; purchasing agt. Ellett Bros., Inc., Chapin, S.C., 1978-79; genl. mgr., L. M. Baughman & Assocs., Sumter, 1979-81; ed. Lytle Pub. Co., Columbia, S.C., 1985-86; tech. wrtr., Media Marketing, Columbia, SC, 1986—; free-lance writer, Columbia, 1985—. Media vol. Harbison West Elem. Sch., Columbia, 1985-86, writing instr., 1984-85; vol. counselor Spcl. Olympics Com., Sumter. Mem. Phi Beta Kappa. Home: 1603 Wellspring 500 Harbison Blvd Columbia SC 29212

BAHR, LAREN S., b. New Brunswick, NJ, July 3, 1944; d. Simon A. and Rosaline J. (Cabot) B. Student, 1964, U. Grenoble, France; BA (Branstrom Scholar) MA,1966, U. Mich. Asst Editor: New Horizons Pubs., Inc., Chgo., 1967; Scholastic Mags., Inc., NYC,1968-71. Supervising editor, Houghton Mifflin Co., Boston, 1981; product devel. editor, Appleton-Century Crofts, NYC,1972-74; sponsoring editor, McGraw-Hill, Inc., NYC,1974-75; editor, Today's Secy. mag., 1975-77; sr. editor, Media Systems Corp., NYC,1978. At CBS Coll Pub., NYC: sr. editor, coll. dept., 1978-82; mktg. mgr. fgn langs., dir mktg adminstrn., 1982-83. Dir. devel., Coll div. Harper & Row, NYC,1983—. Home: 444 E 82nd St New York NY 10028

BAILEY, CHARLES WALDO, II, b. Boston, Apr. 28, 1929; s. David Washburn and Catherine Ruth (Smith) B.; m. Ann Card Bushnell, Sept. 9, 1950; children—Victoria Britton, Sarah Tilden. Author: No High Ground (with Fletcher Knebel) 1960; Seven Days in May, 1962; Convention, 1964; Conflicts of Interest: A Matter of Journalistic Ethics, 1984. Contrbr. to: Candidates, 1960, 1959; Exeter Remembered, 1965; The President's Trip to China, 1972. AB magna cum laude, 1950, Harvard U. Reporter, Mpls. Tribune, 1950-54; corr., Washington bur., Mpls. Tribune, Des Moines Register and Look mag., 1954-67; chief Washington bur., Mpls. Tribune, 1968-72; editor, 1972-82; editor, Star and Tribune, 1982. Washington editor, Natl. Pub. Radio, 1984-87. Mem. Standing Com. Corr., Washington, 1962-63; Overseas Writers; Council on Fgn Relations. Trustee, Carnegie Endowment for Intl. Peace, Washington Journalism Ctr. Home: 3001 Albemarle St NW Washington DC 20008

BAILEY, JACKSON HOLBROOK, b. Portland, ME, Sept. 22, 1925; s. Philip R. and Mercy (Holroak) B.; m. Caroline A. Palmer, June 23, 1949; children—Jay Allen, Christopher Holbrook, Bruce Cutler, Linda Arletta. Author: contrbr, Sidney A. Brown, ed., Studies on Asia, 1962, ed. (with A.T. Embree, S. C. Chu, D.V. Hart, and G.A. Lensen) A Guide to Paperbacks on Asia, 1964, rev. ed., 1968, (with others) A New China Policy: Some Quaker Proposals, 1965, contrbr Robert K. Sikai, ed., Studies on Asia, 1965, ed. Japanese Language Teaching in the Seventies, 1972, ed. Listening to Japan: An

Anthology, 1973, co-author Opening Doors, Contemporary Japan, 1977, ed. Japan: The Living Tradition, 1977, ed. Japan: The Changing Tradition, 1978, co-author, First Steps in Japanese, 1979, author "Japan on the World Scene" in Perspectives on Japan, 1983, "Matsukata Masayoshi" in Japan Examined, 1983. Contrbr to Jnl of Asian Studies, Jnl of Liberal Educ. AB, Earlham College, Richmond, Ind., 1950, MA, U of Wis, 1951, Ph. D., Harvard U., 1959; also attended U. of Tokyo, 1957-59. Prog. dir of intl student seminars and work camps in Japan and Hong Kong for Amer. Friends Service, 1951-54; asst prof, Earlham Coll., 1959-63, assoc prof, 1963-68, prof of history, 1968—, Landrum R. Bolling prof of Social Scis, 1979—, chmn dept of history, 1969-70. Vis asst prof, Antioch Coll., Yellow Springs, O., 1960-63, dir Asian studies program, Earlham and Antioch Colls., 1959-63. Traveled and conducted independent study in South and Southeast Asia, 1958; dir U.S. Office of Educ. Center for East Asian Languages and Area Studies, 1965-73; mem task force on implementation of Intl Educ Act, 1966; mem. of adv. com to Ambassador of Japan for Japan Fndn, 1972-75; dir of projet to produce a intructory cowise in Japanese culture and history for public television, 1974-78. Chmn bd dirs, Farm & Wilderness Fndn, 1972-75. U.S. Army Medical Corps, 1944-46. Member: Intl House of Japan (exec. assoc., 1963), American History Assn, Assn for Asian Studies, Midwest Conf on Asian Affairs (v.p., 1966-67'es., 1967-68). Ford Fnd for area training fellow, 1956-59; Fulbright-Hays faculty fellow at Inst for Humanities Studies, U. of Kyoto, 1967-68). Ford Fndn for area training fellow, 1956-59; Fulbright-Hays faculty fellow at Inst for Humanities Studies, U. of Kyoto, 1967-68; Lilly Endowmnt faculty fellow for research in Japan, 1982-83; NEH and Soc Sci Res Cncl grant for research and writing, 1985-86. Religion: Society of Friends (Quakers). Home: 5289 Shoemaker Rd. Centerville IN 47330

BAILEY, JAMES MARTIN, b. Emmetsburg, IA, July 28, 1929; s. Allen Ransom and Kathryn (Ausl) B.; m. Betty Jane Wenzl, June 5, 1954; children—Kristine Elizabeth, Susan Ruth. Author: Windbreaks, 1959; Youth in the Town and Country Church, 1959; Worship with Youth, 1962 and When Youth Plans Worship, 1987 (with Mrs. Betty Bailey, wife), From Wrecks to Reconciliation, 1969; The Steps to Bonhoeffer (with Douglas Gilbert), 1969, "1000 years," 1987. Contrbg. editor, Reformed World, Geneva, Switzerland. BA Journalism, 1951, State U. Iowa; BD, 1954, DD 1966, Eden Theol. Sem., MS Hiyrbakusnm 1956, Medill Schl. Journalism, Northwestern U.; DD. 1967, Lakeland Coll. Ordained to ministry, United Ch. Christ, 1954. Mem. staff Natl. Council Chs., 1954-60. At Internatl. Jnl. Religious Edn., bus mgr., 1954-60; mem. news and info. dept., 1974—. Mem. exec. com. Communications Comn., 1975—. At United Church Herald (later A.D. mag): dir. circulation, advt., and promo., 1960-63; editor, 1963-72; editor A.D., 1973 to discontinuance. Editor Connections, 1984-85. Assoc. Genl. Secy., Natl. Council of Churches, 1985—. Chmn. Interchurch Features, 1969-73. Home: 45 Watchung Ave Upper Montclair NJ 07043

BAILEY, KATHRINE E., (Kay), b. Sauk Rapids, MN, Apr. 16, 1922, d. James Stewart and Martine Kathrine (Larson) Leyerly; m. Boyd A. Bailey, May 6, 1944; children—William Boyd, Penny Marie Bailey Canchari. Author: The Sampler Quilt, 1977, Quilting Stitchery vol. 1, 1978, vol. 2, 1981, vol. 3, 1983, To Make a Quilt, 1979, Quilt Your Christmas, 1980, Record Keeping for the Small Business, 1981. Student St. Cloud (Minn.) Bus. Coll. Freelance cost acctg., tax cons, Maple Plain, Minn., 1960-83, wrtr., 1983—. Served to s/sgt. USAAF, 1942-45. Home: 3145 County Rd 92 N Maple Plain MN 55359

BAILEY, REUBENA WINONA, (BINNIE), b. Chickasha, OK, May 24, 1926; d. Charles Albert and Alta Mae (Morgan) Hargrove; m. Harold W. Bailey, Jan. 20, 1946; 1 dau., Donna Helen. Contrbr. articles: The Vol. Leader, Hosp. Gift Shop Mgmt., other publs. Wrkg. on novels, mgmt. book. Pres. Binnie Bailey Assocs., cons. and tng. firm, Tallahassee, Fla., 1985—. Active hosp. vol. orgns. Mem. Tallahassee Wrtrs. Assn., Natl. Press Women, Fla. Freelance Wrtrs. Assn. Home: 5257 Pimlico Dr Tallahassee FL 32308

BAIN, GERI RHONDA, b. NYC,Aug. 7, 1951, d. Sanford Kenneth and Ruth (Lerman) B. Contrbg. editor: The Travel Agt. Mag., 1981—; contrbr. to Eastern Rvw, Houston Post, Travel Smart, Parents Guide, Dance Pages, Meetings & Convs., Corp. Meetings & Incentives, Robb Report, others. BA in Philosophy, U. Colo., Boulder, 1973; Bus. cert., LIU, 1976. Tchr. English Instituto Guatemalteco-Americano, Guatemala City, 1973-75; prodn. mgr., asst. art dir. Donnelley Travel Mags., NYC,1975-76; assoc. editor Gralla Publs., NYC,1976-80; freelance journalist, 1980—. Mem. NY Bus. Wrtrs. Assn. Address: Apt 1E 9 W 64th St NYC 10023

BAIN, ROBERT ADDISON, b. Marshall, IL, Sept. 20, 1932; s. Ernest A. and Linda Gail (Clark) B.; m. Bonnie Jean Baker, Dec. 27, 1951 (div. 1981); children—Susan E., Robin Anne, Michael A. Author: H. L. Davis, 1974; Intro. H.L. Davis: Collected Essays and Short Stories, 1986. Co-Editor, author: Fifty Southern Writers Before 1900, A Bio-Bibliographical Sourcebook (with Joseph M. Flora), 1987; Fifty Southern Writers After 1900: A Bio-Bibliographical Sourcebook (with Flora), 1987; The Cast of Consciousness: Concepts of the Mind in British and American Romanticism (with Beverly Taylor), 1987; The Writer and the Worlds of Words, 1975; Southern Writers: A Biographical Dictionary, 1979; Colonial and Federalist American Writing (edited with George F. Horner), 1966. Ed. bd., S. Lit. Jnl, 1975—. BS with honors, 1954, Eastern Ill. U.; AM, 1959, PhD,1964, U. of Ill. Tchr., Lanphier High Schl., Springfield, IL, 1954-58. Reporter, Ill. State Jnl, Springfield, 1954-58. Teaching asst., U. of Ill., Urbana, 1958-64. At U. of N. C. Chapel Hill: prof. English, 1964—; dir. Freshman English, 1967-70; asst. dean, The Genl. Coll., 1979-82; Bowman and Gordon Gray Professor of Undergraduate Teaching, 1987. Mem. exec. com., CCCC, 1971-74, NCTE; S.E. Conf. English in Two-Yr. Coll.; S. Atlantic MLA. Home: G9 Ridgewood Apts Carrboro NC 27510

BAINBRIDGE, JOHN, b. Monticello, MN, Mar 12, 1913; s. William Dean and Bess (Lakin) B.; m. Dorothy Alice Hazlewood, June 2, 1936; children—Jonathon, Janet. Author: Little Wonder, or The Reader's Digest and How It Grew, 1946; The Wonderful World of Toots Shor, 1951; Biography of an Idea, 1952; Garbo, 1955; The Super-Americans, 1961; Like a Homesick Angel, 1964; Another Way of Living, 1968; English Impressions, 1981. Contrbr. many articles to The New Yorker and other natl mags, inclg. Gourmet, 1972-. BS, 1935, Northwestern U. Editorial staff member The New Yorker, 1938—. Address: New Yorker 25 W 43d St New York NY 10036

BAIRD, THOMAS (P.), b. Omaha, NE, April 22, 1923; s. Edgar A. and Alice (Kennard) B.: Author: novels, Triumphal Entry, 1962, The Old Masters, 1963, Sheba's Landing, 1964, Nice Try, 1965, Finding Out, 1967, People Who Pull You Down, 1970, Losing People, 1974, The Way to the Old Sailors Home, 1977, Poor Millie, 1978, Finding Fever (juvenile), 1981, Walk Out a Brother (juvenile), 1982, Villa Aphrodite, 1984. BA, Princeton U., 1945, MFA, 1950. Writer. Instructor in art history, Pinceton U., 1949-51, 1953-54; lecturer in art history, Frick Collection, N.Y. C., 1954-57; mem. of curatorial staff, Nat. Gallery of Art, Washington, D.C., 1957-60; assoc. dir., Dumbarton Oaks, Washington, D.C., 1967-70; assoc. prof., Trinity Coll., Hartford, Conn., 1970-77, prof. of art history, 1977—. U.S. Naval Reserve, 1943-46. Home: 293 Oxford St Hartford CT 06105

BAIZER, ERIC WYATT, (Herman Mold, Chester Gully), b. NYC, Mar. 6, 1950; s. Manuel and Mary B.; m. Sharon Gelmark, Apr. 17, 1958; 1 son, Jason. Author: Codger Picnic, 1976, In the Museum of Temporary Art, 1978. Contrbr. poems, satire, articles to numerous mags. Editor: Mus. Temporary Art mag., 1976-79; contrbg. editor: Washington Book Rvw, 1980-82. Wrkg. on non-fiction book. BA, U. Mich., 1972. Vice-pres. Foxworthy Assocs., Washington, 1982-84; dir. pub. relations Alliance of Nonprofit Mailers, Washington, 1984-85; free-lance wrtr., Hollywood, Calif., 1985—. Mem. Am. Film Inst., Sierra Club. Address: 11933 Magnolia Blvd Ste 20 North Hollywood CA 91607

BAKAL, CARL, b. NYC, Jan. 11, 1918, s. William and Esther (Tutelman) B.; m. Shirley Sesser, 1956; children—Stephanie, Emily, Amy, Wendy. Author: Filter Manual, 1953, How To Shoot for Glamour, 1955, The Right to Bear Arms, 1966, No Right to Bear Arms, 1968, Charity U.S.A., 1979; contrbr. popular consumer mags., Encyc. Photography, 1942; Treasury of Tips for Writers, 1965; Photo-journalism columnist, Writers Digest 1956-57; travel editor, Sylvia Porter's Personal Fin. mag., 1984—. BS, CCNY, 1939; postgrad., Columbia, 1949. Advt. mgr. Fotoshop, NYC, 1939-41; editor Fotoshop Almanac, 1939-41. At U.S. Camera: assoc. editor, contrbg. editor, 1939-43; sales promotion mgr. Universal Camera Corp., 1941-43; editorial chief information control div. Mil. Govt., Germany, 1947-48; promotion writer NY Mirror, 1948-50; assoc. editor Coronet mag., NYC, 1950-55; freelance writer, photo-journalist, 1955-57, 58—. Editor, Real, See mags., 1957-58; pub. affairs cons. U. S. Dept. Commerce, 1961-62; sr. assoc. Howard Chase Assoc., NYC, 1962-65; dir. mag. dept. Carl Byoir & Assoc., 1966-68; account supr. Anna M. Rosenberg & Assoc., 1968-84; sr. v.p. Jack Raymond & Co., Inc., NYC, 1984-86; pres. Carl Bakal Assoc., NYC, 1986—; guest lectr. photo-journalism U. Wis., 1953. Served as 1st lt. AUS, 1942-46, 51-52. Recipient 1st prize Popular Photography $25,000 picture contest, 1956. Mem. Violoncello Soc., PEN, Soc. Journalists and Authors, Natl. Council for a Responsible Firearm Policy (founder-v.p.) Home: 225 W 86th St New York NY 10024

BAKER, ALTON FLETCHER, JR., b. Cleve., Nov. 15, 1919; s. Alton Fletcher and Mildred (Moody) B.; m. Genevieve Mertzke, 1947 (div. 1975); m. Jeannette Workman Vollstedt, Feb. 14, 1976; children—Sue Baker Diamond, Alton Fletcher, III, Sara Moody, Robin Louise. AB, 1942, Pomona Coll., Pomona, CA. At Eugene (OR) Register-Guard: reporter, 1946-50; mng. editor, 1950-54; editor, 1954—; pub., 1961-82;

chmn. bd., 1982—. Capt., USAAF, WW II. Chmn., Oregon Press Conf., 1973. Mem. Oregon, national newspaper assns. Office 975 High St Eugene OR 97401

BAKER, CAROLYN CROOM, b. Winston-Salem, NC, Dec. 28, 1946; d. Asa Abraham and Clara (Barger) Croom; m. Carl B. Baker, Aug. 21, 1982. Author: How to Deal with Difficult Men, 1985. BA, Howard U., 1968; MEd, Am. U., 1970. Guidance counselor Duke Ellington Schl. of the Arts, Washington, 1978—. Mem. Am. Assn. Counseling Devel., Natl. Assn. Coll. Admissions Counselors. Home: 2727 29th St NW Apt 122 Washington DC 20008

BAKER, DAVID ALAN, b. Greenville, SC, Aug. 18, 1957; s. Jack Durwood and Mattie Ruth (Sons) B. Contrbr. articles to mags., newspapers. Editor: Daniel Dimensions mag., Gang Box newspaper, 1982—. BA in Journalism, U. S.C., 1979, M.Mass Communication, 1981. Tchg. asst. U. S.C., Columbia, 1981; film critic Pubs. South, Greenville, 1981-84; ed. employee pubs. Daniel Internat. Corp., Greenville, 1982—. Recipient Best Rvw. award S.C. Press Assn., 1979, 80; Excellence in Research award U. S.C. Coll. of Journalism, 1981. Mem. Carolinas Assn. Bus. Communicators (bd. dirs.) Intl. Assn. Bus. Communicators. Home: 104 Mason St Greenville SC 29611

BAKER, DONALD WHITELAW, b. Boston, Jan. 30, 1923, s. Merrill Ellsworth and Ida margaret (Dempsey) B.; m. Natalie Jane Krentz, May 2, 1945; children—Pamela Jane, Alison Jean. Author: Twelve Hawks and Other Poems, 1976, Formal Application: Selected Poems 1960-1980, 1982, Unposted Letters (poetry), 1985; contrbr. to: Atlantic, Beloit Poetry Jnl, Prairie Schooner, Gallimaufry, numerous other publs. Wrkg. on poetry, fiction. AB, Brown U., 1947, AM, 1949, PhD, 1955. Instr. Brown U., Providence, R.I., 1947-53; mem. faculty Wabash Coll., Crawfordsville, Inc., 1953—, prof., 1963—, poet-in-residence, 1960-87, Milligan prof. of English emeritus, 1987. Served to 1st lt. USAAF, 1942-46. NEA fellow, 1974-75; recipient numerous awards, grants. Mem. AWP. Home: 61 Seaway East Brewster MA 02631

BAKER, ELBERT HALL, II, b. Quincy, MA, July 18, 1910; s. Frank Smith and Gertrude (Vilas) B.; m. Betye Martin, May 27, 1936; children—Susanne Baker Bethke, Martine Baker Huesman. Student, 1932, Rensselaer Poly. Inst. With Tribune Co., Tacoma, WA: first pos., 1932; pub., 1960; pres., 1969-77; chmn., 1977—. Served U. S. Army, 1942-46. Mem. The Soc. Profl. Journalists, Sigma Delta Chi. Home: 29 Forest Glen Ln SW Tacoma WA 98498

BAKER, ELIZABETH CALHOUN, b. Boston; d. John Calhoun and Elizabeth Marshall (Evans) B. BA cum laude, Bryn Mawr Coll.; MA, Radcliffe Coll.; Fullbright scholar, Inst. d'Art et d'Arheologie and Ecole du Louvre, Paris. Instr. art history: Boston U., Wheaton Coll., Norton, MA. At Art News, NYC: assoc editor, 1963-65; mng. editor, 1965-73. Editor, Art in Am. mag., NYC, 1973—. Instr. art history, Schl. Visual Arts, NYC, 1968-74. Grantee, NEA 1972. Office; Art in Am 850 3d Ave New York NY 10022

BAKER, FREDERICK WALLER, b. Doylestown, PA, Aug. 1, 1949; s. Robert Wendell and Mary Catherine (Waller) B.; m. Christine Hold, Aug. 9, 1969; children—Mary-Jo, Jennifer, Allyson, Joan Frances. Author: The Harleysville Insurance Cos. Annual Report, 1977-85. Ed., pub.: (mag.) Lines, 1974-77; (newsletter) Inlines, 1975-77, Off the Cuff, 1977-83, All About Us, 1979—, Insights for Employees, 1983—, Insights for Agents, 1983—. Sr. wrtr. Reliance Insurance Cos., Phila., 1974-75. Wrkg. on collection of anecdotes applicable to bus. marketing. B.S. in Communications, Temple U., 1971. Systems analyst Reliance Insurance Cos., Phila., 1972-74, mgr. internal communications, 1975-76, dir. public relations, 1976-77; mgr. communications The Harleysville Insurance Cos., PA, 1977-80, asst. sec., dir. communiations, 1980-85, asst. vp & dir. commns., 1985-. Dir., v.p. North Penn Chamber of Commerce, Lansdale, PA, 1978—; mem. marketing adv. bd. Montgomery County Commun. Coll., Blue Bell, PA, 1983—; mem. exec. com. North Penn United Way, Kulpsville, PA, 1984-85, chmn. public relations, 1984-85. Recipient Gold Quill award IABC, 1975, 76, Pepperpot award Public Relations Soc. of Am., Phila., 1980, Cert. of excellence United Way of Am., 1984. Mem. Penn. Assn Mutual Insurance Cos. (chm. public relations 1978-79, 83-84), Insurance Marketing Communications Assn. (secy., treas, vp, exec. vp exec. com., Best of Show for annual report 1985), Insurance Public Relations Assn. Home: 109 Nightingale Circle Chalfont PA 18914

BAKER, JEANNINE ANN, (Jeannine Parvati, Jeannine Parvati Baker, Jeannie O'Brien Medvin), b. Los Angeles, June 1, 1949; d. Frank Blair and Viola Vicki (Spunt) O'Brien; m. Michael Lee Medvin, July 25, 1969 (div. 1978); children: Loi Caitlin, Oceana Violet, Cheyenne Coral; m. 2d, Frederick Hamilton Baker, Nov. 17, 1978; children: Gannon Hamilton, Quinn Ambriel, Halley Sophia. Author: Prenatal Yoga and Natural Birth, 1974, Hygieia: A Woman's Herbal, 1978, Conscious Conception: Elemental Journey through the Labyrinth of Sexuality, 1986; contbr. to other books in field of health and birth, also mags. including Mothering, New Age, Yoga Jnl, Spiritual Mothering, Homespun, Nurturing, others. BA in Psychology with honors, Sonoma State U. Author, Freestone Pub., Monroe, Utah, 1973—; tchr., lectr. Ctr. for Family Growth, Cotati, Calif., 1973-78, Heartwood Coll., Santa Cruz, Calif., 1978-81; founder Hygieia Coll., Santa Cruz and Monroe, 1980—; speaker at numerous convs., ednl. instns., radio and TV in U.S. and Can. Rep. Calif. Assn. Midwives, 1976-81; tchr. Childbirth Without Pain League, Cotati, 1971-78; planner Sevier Peace Coalition, Sevier County, Utah, 1985-86. Mem. Pre and PeriNatal Psychology Assn. North Am., Utah Midwives Assn., Suzuki Assn. Utah. Home: 960 S Ross Ln Sevier UT 84766

BAKER, JOSEPH EDWARD, b. Ironton, OH, July 29, 1917; s. Edward L. and Sarah B.; m. Mary Elizabeth Fletcher; children—Joseph Edward, Steven Alan. Author: The Right to Participate: Inmate Involvement in Prison Administration, 1974, Kentucky Jailors Management and Operations Manual, 1976, Prisoner Participation in Prison Parole, 1985. Wrkg. on novel. B.S.W., Ind. State U., 1952. With Fed. Bureau of Prisons, 1940-67; warden Penitentiary of NM, Sante Fe, 1967-69; sec. Dept. of Corrections, Sante Fe, 1969-70; deputy commr. Ky. Dept. of Corrections, Frankford, 1970-72; cons., 1972-75; instr. coordinator correctional trng. Ky. Dept. of Justice, Richmond, 1975-76, supr. program development and evaluation, 1976-78; mgr. staff development Ky. Corrections Cabinet, Frankford, 1979-81; retired. Served to sgt. USAF, 1943-46. Mem. Am. Correctional Assn., Ky Council Crime and Delinquency, Natl. Assn. Soial Workers, Assn. Cert. Social Workers. Home: 1730 Airdrie Ln Frankford KY 40601

BAKER, NORMAN LEE, b. Reyno, AR, July 24, 1926; s. Ottis King and Lora Faye (Weaver) B.; m. Lois Constance Shanner, Jan. 1, 1960 (dec. Aug. 22, 1985); children—Gary Kale, Mary Ellen King, Syntha Eleanor. Ed.: Jet Propulsion Mag., 1955-56, Missiles & Rocket Mag., 1957-59, Space Business Daily, 1959, Defense Daily, 1959—, Space Business Week, 1960, Who's Who in Space, 1965, Soviet Space Log, 1967, Soviet Aerospace, 1971—. BSAE, IN Inst. of Tech., 1956. Devel. engr. Boeing Airplane Co., Seattle, 1956-57; assoc. ed. Amer. Aviation Pubns., Washington, 1957-59; ed. Space Pubns., Inc., Washington, 1959—. Served in USNR, 1943-45, PTO, Iwo Jima, US Army, 1951-54, Korea. Mem. National Space Club, NPC, Sigma Delta Chi. Awarded Order of the Silver Slide Rule, IIT, Space Pioneer Award, natl. Rocket Club. Office: Space Pubns 1341 G St NW Washington DC 20005

BAKER, ROBERT LEON, b. Marion IN, Sept. 29, 1920; s. Laurance Milford and Grace Marie (Baird) B.; m. Patricia Ann Petterson, Nov. 28, 1953; 2 sons, Christopher Leon, Kevin Knox. Author: The Best of Impact; contrbr. articles to trade and profl. publs., newspapers; produced and edited publs. for major corps. and orgns. BPE, Purdue, 1947, MS Jnlsm., Northwestern U., 1950. Copy ed. Omaha World-Herald, Nebr., 1950-51; dir. field servs. Standard Oil (Ind.), Chgo., 1951-59; dir. communications Owens-Corning Fiberglass, Toledo, Ohio, 1959-60; pres. Baker & Bowden, Chgo., 1960—; pub. Impact publs., Evanston, Ill., 1959—. Mem. Internatl. Assn. Bus. Communicators (pres. Chgo. chpt. 1956-57). Address: 2020 Hawthorne Ln Evanston IL 60201

BAKER, RUSSELL WAYNE, b. Loudon County, VA, Aug. 14, 1925; s. Benjamin Rex and Lucy Elizabeth (Robinson) B.; m. Miriam Emily Nash, Mar. 11, 1950; children—Kathleen Leland, Allen Nash, Michael Lee. Author: American in Washington, 1961; No Cause for Panic, 1964; All Things Considered, 1965; Our Next President, 1968; Poor Russell's Almanac, 1972; The Upside Down Man, 1977; So This is Depravity, 1980; co-author Home Again, Home Again, 1979; Growing Up, 1982; The Rescue of Miss Yaskell and Other Pipe Dreams, 1983. BA, 1947, D. Litt., Johns Hopkins U.; L.H.D., Hamilton Coll., Franklin Pierce Coll., Princeton U.; LLD, Union Coll.; D. Litt., Wake Forest U. Balt Sun, 1947-54. NY Times Wash. bureau, 1954-62. Author-columnist, Observer, 1962—. USNR, 1943-45. Recipient: Frank Sullivan Meml. award, 1976; George Polk award for commentary, 1979; Pulitzer Prizes for disting. commentary, 1979, and biography, 1983; Elmer Holmes Bobst prize for nonfiction, 1983. Mem. AAIAL. Office: 229 W 43rd St New York NY 10036

BAKER, SAMM SINCLAIR, b. Paterson, NJ, July 29, 1909; s. Simon and Sara (Carlin) B.; m. Natalie Bachrach, June 12, 1937; children—Wendy Baker Cammer, Steven Jeffrey. Author: One Touch of Blood, 1955, Murder, Very Dry, 1956, contrbr, The Mystery Writer's Handbook, 1956, Miracle Gardening, 1958, Casebook of Successful Ideas for Advertising and Selling, 1959, How to be an Optimist and Make It Pay, 1960, How to Be a Self-Starter, 1960, Miracle Gardening Encyclopedia, 1961, Your Key to Creative Thinking, 1962, Samm Baker's Clear & Simple Gardening Handbook, 1964, co-author, 1001 Questions and Answers to Your Skin Problems, 1965, Indoor and Outdoor Grow-It Book for Children, 1966, (with Irwin M. Stillman) The Doctor's Quick Weight Loss Diet, 1967, Vigor for Men over 30, 1967, The Permissible Lie, 1968, (with Stillman) The Doctor's Quick Inches-Off Diet, 1969, (with Natalie Baker) Introduction to Art, 1969, How to Protect Yourself Today, 1970, Gardening Do's and Don'ts, 1970, (with Stillman) The Doctor's Quick Teenage Diet, 1971, The Doctor's Quick Weight Loss Diet Cookbook, 1972; (with James W. Smith) "Doctor, Make Me Beautiful!," 1973, (with Stillman) Dr. Stillman's 14-Day Shape-up Program, 1973, Conspicuous Happiness, 1975, (with Mary Susan Miller) Straight Talk to Parents about School, 1976, (with Jane Boutelle) Lifetime Fitness for Women, 1978, (with Herman Tarnower) The Complete Scarsdale Medical Diet, 1979, (with Leopold Bollak) Reading Faces, 1980, The Delicious Quick-Trim Diet, 1981, Erotic Focus: The New Way to Enhance Your Sexual Pleasure, 1984, Make Money Writing: Writing Nonfition That Sells, 1986, (with Barbara Debetz) The Dr. Debetz Champagne Diet: The Medically Proven Program for Total Weight Control, 1987. BS in economics, U. of Penn., 1929. Part-time and summer work in textile factories, retail stores, and on news-papers to 1930; worked with Rauch Associates, Inc. (adv. agcy), N.Y.C.; copy writer to pres., Kiesewetter, Baker, Hagedorn & Smith, Inc., 1937-55; v.p. an mem exec. staff, Donahue & Coe, Inc. (adv. agcy), 1955-63; self-employed writer and personal business consultant, 1963—. Consultant to firms in advertising, promotion, merchandising, marketing. Teacher in advanced retail copywriting, N.Y.U.; teacher or lec., Columbia U., U. of Penn, Drexel U., Iona College and others. Gardening writer and lec. for Flair, ABC daily network radio program. Member: MWA, Garden Writers of America, AG, Authors League of America. Awards from U.S. Coast Guard and U.S. Treasury Dept. for war-time writing. Address: 1027 Constable Dr. S. Mamaroneck NY 10543

BAKER, SHERIDAN, b. Santa Rosa, CA July 10, 1918; s. Sheridan Warner and Juliet (Shaw) B.; m. Helen Elizabeth Barker, Apr. 6, 1946 (Dig. Aug., 1954); m. Sally Baubie Sandwick, June 17, 1955; children— Elizabeth Baker, Elizabeth Lagler, William. Author: The Practical Stylist, 1962; The Essayist, 1963; The Complete Stylist, 1966; Ernest Hemingway: An Introduction and Interpretation, 1967; The Written Word (I.A. Richards and Jacques Barzun co-authors), 1971; The Practical Imagination (Northrop Frye and George Perkins co-authors), 1980; The Harper Handbook to Literature, 1984. Editor: Mich. Qtly Rvw., 1964-71; Henry Fielding's Writings; Contrbr: poems to New Yorker and other mags. and articles on 18th cent. and modern lit. Student, 1935-37, Santa Rosa (CA) Jr. Coll.; AB, 1939, MA,1946, PhD,1950, U. Calif.-Berkeley. At U. Calif.-Berkeley: teaching fellow, 1946-49; lectr., 1949-50; vis. prof., 1970. At U. Mich.: instr., 1950-57; asst. prof., 1957-61; assoc, prof., 1961-64; prof., 1964—. Lt. comdr., USNR, 1940-46. Recipient U. Mich. Distinguished Service award, 1960. Named to Top Fifty Living Am. Poets, Epoch 15, 1966, Resident Fellow, Rockefeller Fdn., Bellagio, Italy, 1978. Visiting Scholar, U. of Newcastle, Australia, 1986. Pres. Mich. conf. AAUP, 1959-60; pres. Mich. Acad. Sci, Arts and Letters, 1963-64. Pres. Soc. for the Study of Narrative Literature, 1986-87.Home: 2866 Provincial Dr Ann Arbor MI 48104

BAKER, WILLIAM RADCLIFFE, b. Hoboken, NJ, Nov. 13, 1946; s. William Radcliffe and Ruth (Carry) B. Works: Renegotiations, 1982 (short stories), The Natural, 1983 (screenplay), Skin of Light, 1983 (poems), N, 1985 (play), The Fourth World, 1986 (screenplay). MFA, San Francisco State Coll. Consultant, Dept. of Ed., St. Croix, V.I., 1979-80; freelance lectr., 1981-82; tchr./mentor, Columbia Pacific U., San Rafael, CA, 1982—. Office: Hayoka Press 450 Gough San Francisco CA 94102

BAKKEN, DICK, b. Custer County, MT, Aug 24, 1941; children: Eric Michael, Creseyde Donne. Author: Hungry!, 1967, Miracle Finger, 1975, Here I Am, 1979, True History of the Eruption, 1980, Kazuko Shiraishi with Dick Bakken, 1985, The Other Side, 1986, Jesu O Jesu, 1987, How to Eat Corn, 1986; ed. Salted Feathers mag and books, 1964-75; poetry ed., Bisbee Times, 1982, Bisbee Observer, 1985; co-ed. Weed-Free, 1983; poems in Ironwood, Poetry Northwest, Poetry Now, Colo. State Rvw, St. Andrews Rvw, Artspace, Poetry Flash, others. BA in English, Pacific Lutheran U., 1963; MA in English, Wash. State U., 1966. Coordinator Portland Poetry Fest, 1973-74; poet-in-residence Thomas Jefferson Coll., Allendale, Mich., 1975. St. Andrews Presby. Coll., Laurinbrg, NC, 1976, 77, 78; co-founder Poetry Resource Center of Mich., Allendale, 1975; co-dir. Bisbee Poetry Fest, Az., 1981-82; dir. Heart of Carlos Spoken Arts, Bisbee, 1984—. Address: Box BT Bisbee AZ 85603

BALAKIAN, NONA HILDA, b. Istanbul, Turkey; to US, 1926; d. Diran and Koharig (Panossian) B. Author: Critical Encounters: Literary Views and Reviews, 1953-78; editor (with Charles Simmons), The Creative Present: Notes on Contemporary American Fiction, 1963; mem. editorial bd., Ararat Qtly, 1970-79. BA, 1942, Barnard Coll.; MS in Journalism, 1943, Columbia U. Mem editorial bd., NY Times Book Review, 1943—; book reviewer, Sunday and daily NY Times, 1943—. Contrbr.. rvws., articles, essays to lit mags. Mem., book selection com., Books-Across- the-Sea, 1978-86. Mem. Pulitzer Prize jury, non-fiction, 1977; poetry, 1979, 81; Hopwood Award jury, essays, 1979. Mem.: exec. bd., PEN, 1973-80; exec bd., Natl. Book Critics Circle, 1974-78; Authors Guild. Recipient Humanities award, Rockefeller Fdn. 1981. Office: NY Times Book Rvw 229 W 43d NYC 10036

BALAKIAN, PETER, b. Teaneck, NJ, June 13, 1951, s. Gerard and Arax (Aroosian) B.; m. Helen Kebabian, Aug. 16, 1980; 1 dau., Sophia Ann. Author poetry books: Father Fisheye, 1979, Sad Days of Light, 1983, Reply from Wilderness Island, 1987; ed.: Graham House Rvw. BA, Bucknell U., 1973; PhD,Brown U., 1980. Assoc. prof. English Colgate U., Hamilton, NY, 1980—. Winner AAP prize, 1974. Office: Dept Eng Colgate U Hamilton NY 13346

BALAZS, MARY W., b. Cleve., Aug. 2, 1939, d. Philip P. and Emma M. (Zollinger) Webber; m. Gabriel G. Balazs, June 18, 1960; children— Gabriel Bryan, Eliot Loren. Author: The Voice of Thy Brother's Blood (poetry), The Stones Refuse Their Peace (poetry), 1979; contrbr. poetry: Poet and Critic, Kans. Qtly, Small Pond, West Coast Poetry Rvw, others; contrbr. essays: Stone Country, Sunrust, Va. Jnl. Edn., others; co-ed. poetry anthologies: I, That Am Ever Stranger, 1974, Touching This Earth, 1977; guest-ed.: Puddingstone No. 5, 1976. MA in English, Pa. State U., 1962, PhD in English, 1965. Asst. prof. English Va. Mil. Inst., Lexington, 1970—; poet-in-schs., NEA, throughout Va., 1974—; vis. prof. Washington and Lee U., 1973, Randolph-Macon Woman's Coll., 1978. Awarded Best Poem of Issue, Patterns Lit. Mag., winter 1971, Baby John Lit. Mag., 1972, Sam Ragan Poetry Prize, 1987. Mem. AAP, Poetry Soc. Va. Home: 503 Brooke Ln Lexington VA 24450

BALCH, GLENN, b. Venus, TX, Dec. 11, 1902; s. Glenn Olin and Edith (Garrison) B.; m. Faula Mashburn (div. 1935); child—Betty Lou; m. Elise Kendall, May 15, 1937; children—Lynne Kendall, Mary Olin. Author: novels—Riders of the Rio Grande, 1937; Tiger Roan, 1938; Hide-rack Kidnapped, 1939; Indian Point, 1942; Wild Horse, 1946; Viking Dog, 1948; Christmas Horse, 1949; Lost Horse, 1950 (Boys' Club Book Award, 1951); Winter Horse, Squaw Boy, Midnight Colt, Indian Saddle-Up—all 1953; Little Hawk, The Free Horse, 1956; The Brave Riders, 1958; White Ruff, Horses, 1959; Horse in Danger, The Stallion King, 1960; Spotted Horse, 1961; Stallion's Foe, 1962, The Runaways, 1963, Keeping Horse, 1966; The Flaxy Mare, 1967; Horse of Two Colors, 1968; Buck, Wild, 1976; non- fiction—Guide to Western Horseback Riding, 1965, and The Book of Horses, 1966. Student, 1921-23, North Tex. State Tchrs. Coll., Denton, TX, and 1923-24, U. Tex; AB, 1924. Baylor U.; post-grad., 1937, Columbia U. Reporter, Idaho Daily Statesman, Boise, 1925-29; freelance mag. writer and publicist, 1929 (also worked as bank clerk and forest ranger). Lt. col. USAAF, 1941-45, CBI. Recipient Geo. Washington Meml. awards, Freedom Fdn., 1954, 56, 57. Home: 3890 E Victory Rd Meridian ID 83642

BALDANZA, DEB, see Glaefke, Deborah S.

BALDERSTON, JEAN MERRILL, b. Providence, RI, Aug. 28, 1936; d. Frederick Augustus and Helen May (Cleveland) Merrill; m. David Chase Balderston, June 1, 1956. Poetry in Womansong, 1976, Desire, 1980, Amoretica, 1981, Knock, Knock, 1982, and other anthols. BA, U. of CT, 1957; MA, Teachers College, Columbia U., 1965, EdD, 1968. Psychotherapist, private practice, NYC,1968—. Mem. P&W, PSA, The Emily Dickinson Society. Address: 1225 Park Ave New York NY 10128

BALDRIDGE, CHARLENE, b. Evanston, IL, Apr. 26, 1934, d. Charles Edward and Thelma Marie (Good) Stube; m. Robert Ortego, Apr. 1954 (div. 1958); children: Charles Edward, Robert John; m. 2d, Samuel Costales, Jan. 1959 (dec. 1962); 1 dau., Laura Jeanne; m. 3d, Charles Shepard Baldridge, Dec. 1, 1963. Author poetry collection: Wordsperson, 1985; ed.: Cuttings: A Gathering of Six, 1983; contrbr. poetry, criticism, articles to Broomstick, Horizon, Sunrust, Kyriokos, numerous others. Student Mesa Coll., San Diego, 1978-79, Grossmont Coll., El Cajon, Calif., 1979-82. Arts wrtr. Daily Californian, El Cajon, 1979-83; opera critic, Opera Can., Toronto, Ont., 1983—; publicist San Diego Met. Opera Auditions, 1979-82; natl. media, publs. dir. Old Globe Theatre, San Diego, 1981—; freelance wrtr., publicist, poet, ed., 1978—. Winner 1st Place, poetry Orgn. for Women, 1984. Mem. Public Relations Soc. Am., P&W, NY poetry forum (Dorothy Frank award 1980). Home: 3008 Contut Ct Spring Valley CA 92077

BALDWIN, DEIDRA B., b. Erie, PA, June 26, 1945, d. George Andrew and Gladys (Swiderski) Baldwin; m. Thomas Anthony Horne; 1 son— Anthony Baldwin. Author: Gathering Time, 1975, The Emerging Detail, 1977, The Light Shepherd's Absence, An Occasional Suite, 1981; contrbr. poetry to The Unicorn and The Garden, Positively Prince Street, Proteus Mag., other anthols and lit mags. BA, Pa. State U.; MA, Johns Hopkins U., 1976. Poet-in-residence Artists in Edn. Program, Washington, 1974-75, State of Va., 1977-78, State of Md., 1978-81; poetry ed. Woodwind: A Jnl for the Arts, 1972-74; ed., cons. Washington Wrtrs. Pub. House, 1976-81; ed., founder The Word Works, 1975—. Address: 3420 16th St NW Apt 103 Washington DC 20010

BALDWIN, DICK, see Raborg, Frederick Ashton, Jr.

BALDWIN, EDWARD R (OBINSON), (Ned Baldwin) b. Concord, NH, April 30, 1935; s. Henry Ives and Birgit (Svedrup) B.; m. Janet Eldridge, June 6, 1958 (div. 1972); child—Benjamin Huyck. Author: The Cross-Country Skiing Handbook, 1972, 2d ed., 1973, (as Ned Baldwin) The Beginner's Guide to Cross Country Skiing, 1973, The Family Guide to Cross-Country Skiing, 1976, Skiing Cross Country, 1977; also author of doc. film script, Telemark, 1973. BA, Yale U., 1957, M. Arch., 1961. Licensed architect in Conn., N.Y., Mass., Ohio, and Fla. Architet, John Johansen, Architect, New Canaan, Conn., 1961-65; architect, John Andrews Architects, Toronto, Ont., 1966-68, partner, 1969-72; proprietor, Edwin R. Baldwin, Arhitect, Toronto, & Baldwin & Franklin Architets, 1973—. U.S. Army, 1957-58. Member: Royal Architetural Inst. of Can., Ontario Assn. of Architects, Am. Inst. of Architects. Am. Inst. of Arscs. honor awar for design, 1973. Home: 3 Rosedale Toronto Ont. Canada

BALDWIN, JAMES, b. NYC, Aug. 2, 1924; s. David and Berdis Emma (Jones) B. Author: Go Tell It on the Mountain (novel), 1953; Notes of a Native Son, 1955; Giovanni's Room (novel), 1958; Nobody Knows My Name: More Notes of a Native Son, 1960; Another Country (novel), 1962; The Fire Next Time, 1963; Blues for Mr. Charlie (novel); The Amen Corner (play), 1955; Going To Meet the Man, 1966; Tell Me How Long the Train's Been Gone, 1968; No Name in the Street, 1972; One Day When I Was Lost, 1973; If Beale Street Could Talk, 1974; Little Man, Little Man, 1975; The Devil Finds Work. 1976; Just Above My Head, 1979, The Exidence of Things Not Sen, 1985. Secondary schl. ed. Mem. natl. advisory bd., Congress on Racial Equality; Ntl. Comm. for Sane Nuclear Policy; lectr. civil rights. Mem. Actors Studio, NIAL. Deceased Nov. 30, 1987.

BALEY, GENEVE, b. Chgo., Oct. 29, 1923; m. John-Claude Baley; 1dau., Robin-Marie. Author, pub.: Economic Critique, 1971, Economics Without Fear, 1972, A New American Economic System: Excerpts, 1979, A 1974 Collection, 1974; author numerous econ. reports, papers, speeches; contrbr. poetry, essays, short stories to numerous publs. poetry in anthologies. AA, Wright Jr. Coll.; MusM (2), Am. Conservatory of Music; Leo Sowerby, Chgo. Art Inst., Aaron Copland—Chosen scholarship, Berkshire Music Center, Nadia Boulanger, Sorbonne. Freelance polit.-econ. theorist, researcher for UN, U.S. Govt., Ford Motor Co.; composer. Home: 33-54 99th St Corona NY 11368

BALK, ALFRED WILLIAM, b. Oskaloosa, IA, July 24, 1930; s. Leslie William and Clara Irene (Buell) B.; m. Phyllis Lorraine Munter, June 7, 1952; children—Laraine M., Diane Balk Palguta. Author: A Free and Responsive Press 1973; The Free List: Property Without Taxes 1971; co-editor, Our Troubled Press, 1971. Student, 1948-49, Augustana Coll., Rock Island, IL; BS, 1952, MS, 1953, Medill Schl. Journalism, Northwestern U. Reporter, Rock Island (IL) Argus, 1946-50; newswriter-producer, WBBM(CBS), Chgo., 1952-53; reporter, Chgo. Sun-Times, 1956; pub. rel. writer, J. Walter Thompson Co., Chgo., 1957-58. Freelance writer for natl. mags., including spcl. writer, Saturday Evening Post, 1958-66; feature editor, Saturday Rvw, 196-68; editor-at-large, 1968-69. Vis. scholar, Russell Sage Fdn., 1968-69. At Columbia U.: lectr. journalism; editor, Columbia Journalism Rvw, 1969-73. At World Press Rvw: editor, 1974; editor-pub., 1975—. Exec. secy., NY Gov's Com. on Employment of Minority Groups in News Media, 1968-69. Mem. Am. Soc. Mag. Editors (exec. council, 1977-83); The Soc. of Profl. Journalists, Sigma Delta Chi (Wells Meml. Key). Overseas Press Club (gov. 1978-79). Office: World Press Rvw 230 Park Ave NYC 10169

BALL, ANGELA, b. Athens, OH, July 6, 1952, d. Emerson and Virginia (Rheinfrank) B. Asst. ed. Miss. Rvw, 1979—; contrbr. poetry to 2 Plus 2, Poetry, Malahat Rvw, New Orleans Rvw, Adena, Crosscurrents, also articles, rvws., translations. Author: Kneeling Between Parked Cars, 1987; Recombinant Lives, 1987. BA, Ohio U., 1973; MFA, U. Iowa, 1975; PhD, U. Denver, 1979. Asst. prof. English, U. So. Miss., Hattiesburg, 1979-85, assoc. prof., 1985—. Recipient Duncan Lawrie prize Arvon Fdn. Great Britain, 1983; 3d place poetry prize Ind. Rvw, 1985; winner Owl Creek poetry competition, 1986. Mem. AWP, South Atlantic MLA. Office: 105 Cambridge Dr Hattiesburg MS 39402

BALL, DOUGLAS HOWARD, b. Glendale, CA, Dec. 30, 1942; s. Walter E. and Thelma C. (Williams) B.; child by a previous marriage, Michael Douglas; m. Patricia Ann Mooney, June 14, 1970; children—Claire Ann, Douglas H. Contrbr. articles to Countryside, Ariz. Mag., Mother Earth News. Wrkg. on modern western novel, terrorist thriller. Tchr., Sanders Bible Christian Acad., AZ, 1984-85; tchr. computer tehnology St. Johns Public chls., AZ, 1986—. Chmn. Apache County Library, St. Johns, 1983—. Served with U.S. Navy, 1960-80. Mem. Apache County Wrtrs. Roundtable (facilitator 1985—). Home: Box 1128 Saint Johns ZA 85936

BALL, GEORGE WILDMAN, b. Des Moines, Dec. 21, 1909; s. Amos and Edna (Wildman) B.; m. Ruth Murdoch, Sept. 16, 1932; children—John Colin, Douglas Bleakly. Author: The Discipline of Power, 1968; Diplomacy for a Crowded World, 1976; The Past Has Another Pattern, 1982. BA, 1930, J.D., 1933, Northwestern U. Bar: IL, 1934; DC, 1946. Served Genl. Counsel's Office, US Treasury, Wash., DC, 1933-35. Law practice: Cleary, Gottlieb, Steen & Ball, Chgo., 1935-43, Wash., DC, 1946-61; Cleary, Gottlieb, Steen & Hamilton, 1966-69. Assoc. genl. counsel Lend-Lease Adminstrn. and Fgn. Econ. Adminstrn., 1942-44; dir., US Strategic Bombing Survey, London, 1944-45; Genl. Counsel, French Supply Council, Wash., 1945-46; undersecy. of state for economic affairs, 1961; undersecy. of state, 1961-66; US permanent rep. to UN, 1968. With Lehman Bros. Intl., Ltd.: chmn., 1966-68, sr. ptnr., 1968-82. Office: 107 Library Pl Princeton NJ 08540

BALL, IVERN IMOGENE, (Joni Cagle, Ivern Boyette), b. Pocahontas, AR, July 3, 1926; d. Virgil Seigle Cicero and Elise Lanora (Tomlin) Cagle; m. Ivy Lesley Boyette, 1944 (div. 1956); m. Thomas Paul Ball, Nov. 2, 1973. Contrbr. to numerous mags. and newspapers including Sat. Eve. Post, Coronet, Wall Street Jnl, Atlanta Weekly, This Singing Earth poetry anthology; columnist El Paso Times, 1986—; wrtr. for standup comics. Underwrtr. Conn. Gen. Life Ins. Co., Dallas, 1965-75, office supr., 1975-78; underwriting mgr. Combined Ins. Co., Dallas, 1978-85; freelance wrtr., 1985—. Mem. Wrtrs. of Purple Sage (co-chmn.). Home: 700 E Spruce St Deming NM 88030

BALL, ROBERT M., b. NYC,Mar. 28, 1914; s. Archey Decatur and Laura Elizabeth (Crump) B.; m. Doris Jacqueline McCord, June 30, 1936; children—Robert Jonathan, Jacqueline Elizabeth. Author: Pensions in the United States, 1952; Social Security Today and Tomorrow, 1978; and articles on social security, natl. health ins., welfare, and health care. AB, 1935, MA, 1936, Wesleyan U. With Bur. Old Age and Survivors Ins., Soc. Sec. Bd.: staff, 1939-46; asst. dir., 1949-52; acting dir., 1953; dep. dir., 1953-62; commr. of soc. sec., 1962-73. Sr. scholar, Inst. Medicine, Natl. Acad. Scis., 1973-81; Visiting Scholar, Center for the Study of Social Policy, 1981—. Writer, lectr., cons., 1981—. Asst. dir., comm. on edn. and soc. sec., Am. Council on Edn, 1946-49; staff dir. advisory council on soc. sec. to US Senate Finance Comm., 1947-48, chmn. Adv. Council Social Security, 1965, mem. Natl. Commn. Social Security Reform, 1982. Mem. Inst. Medicine, Am. Pub. Welfare Assn., Natl. Council on Aging, other public welfare groups, Phi Beta Kappa. Home: 7217 Park Terr Dr Alexandria VA 22307

BALLANTINE, IAN, b. NYC,Feb. 15, 1916; s. Edward James and Stella (Commins) B.; m. Elizabeth Jones, June 22, 1939; child: Richard. AB, 1938, Columbia U.; student, 1938-39, London Sch. Econs. Gen. mgr., Penguin Books, Inc., NYC,1939-45; pres., dir., Bantam Books, Inc., NYC,1945-52, and Ballantine Books, Inc., NYC,1952—; pres., Greenwich Press, Trumbull, CT; dir., Peacock Press Ltd. Instr. sociology, Columbia U., 1969-70. Mem. Phi Beta Kappa. Home: 60 E 9th St New York NY 10003

BALLARD, EDWARD GOODWIN, b. Fairfax, VA, Jan. 13, 1910; s. James W. and Margaret (Lewis) B.; m. Lucy McIver Watson, Nov. 22, 1938; children—Susanne Ballard Dowouis, Lucy Ballard Armentrout, Edward Marshall. Author: Art and Analysis, 1957; Socratic Ignorance, 1965; Philosophy at the Crossroads, 1971; Man and Technology: Toward the Measurement of a Culture, 1978; Principles of Interpretation, 1983; Philosophy and the Liberal Arts, 1987. Contrbr. to philos. jnls Edit. bd.: So. Jnl Philosophy, 1963-78; Research in Phenomenology, 1969—; Tulane Studies in Philosophy, 1970—. Cons. editor: Continental Thought series, U. Ohio Press, 1979—; Current Continental Research, Univ. Press Am., 1980. BA, 1931, Coll. William and Mary; dipl., 1932, U. Montpelier, France; MA, 1936, Ph.D., 1946, U. Va.; postgrad., 1951, U. Sorbonne, Paris, and 1931-32, Harvard U. Asst. prof. English, 1939-41, VMI; asst. in philosophy, 1941-42, U. Va. At Tulane U.: asst. prof. philosophy, 1946-52; assoc. prof., 1952-56; prof., 1956-77; W. R. Irby Prof. philosophy, 1977-80; emeritus, 1980—. Vis. prof.: Yale U., 1963-64; La. State U. at Baton Rouge, 1969; U. Mo., 1981; U. of South, 1981-82. Mem. selection com., Woodrow Wilson Fellowship, 1966-69; selection panel, Natl. Endowment for Humanities, 1970-74; bd. dirs., Center Advanced Research Phenomenology, 1979—. Comdr. USN, 1942-46; reserve to 1970, PTO. Mem. So. Soc. Philosophy and Psychology (pres. 1967), Am. Philos. Assn., AAAS, Am. Metaphys. Soc., SPEP. Home: Rt 5 Box 102 Lexington VA 24450

BALLENTINE, LEE KENNEY, b. Teaneck, NJ, Sept. 4, 1954, s. George Kenney and Veda Avis Maxine (Havens) B.; m. Jennifer Marie Ursula Moore, Aug. 20, 1983. Author: Directional Information, 1981, Basements in the Musicbox, Xexoxial Editions, 1986; ed.: POLY: New Speculative Poetry, 1985; contrbr. Cerulean Press Anthology, Aliens and Lovers, Abraxas, Pandora, Antithesis, Velocities, Mississippi Mud, Star*Line, Portland Rvw, other lit publs. BS, SUNY, 1976. Ed.-in-chief Ocean View Press, Mountain View. Mem. PEN, MLA, Sci. Fiction Poetry Assn. Address: Box 4148 Mountain View CA 94040

BALLENTINE, RUDOLPH M., b. Ballentine, SC, Aug. 16, 1941, s. Rudolph M. Sr. and Martha B.; m. Pennell Whitney, Aug. 3, 1979; children—Rebecca, Schuyler, Galen. Author: Diet and Nutrition, 1978; co-author: Yoga and Psychotherapy, 1976, Science of Breath, 1979; ed.: Theory and Practice of Meditation, 1975; contrbr. chap. to Acute Coronary Care, 1985. BS, Duke U., 1962, MD, 1967. Mem. faculty La. State U., New Orleans, 1971-72; practice medicine specializing and genl. and psychosomatic medicine, Buffalo, NYC,Chg., Mpls., Pa., 1974—; pres. Himalayan Inst., Honesdale, Pa., 1981—. Office: Himal Inst RR 1 Box 400 Honesdale PA 18431

BALLIETT, WHITNEY, b. NYC,Apr. 17, 1926; s. Fargo and Dorothy (Lyon) B.; m. Elizabeth Hurley King, 1951; children—Julia, Elizabeth, Will; m. Nancy Kraemer, 1965; children—Whitney, James. Author: The Sound of Surprise, 1959; Dinosaurs in the Morning, 1962; Such Sweet Thunder, 1966; Super-Drummer: A Profile of Buddy Rich, 1968; Ecstasy at the Onion, 1971; Alec Wilder and His Friends, 1974; New York Notes: A Journal of Jazz, 1976; Improvising: Sixteen Jazz Musicians and Their Art, 1977; American Singers, 1979; Night Creature: A Journal of Jazz, 1981; Jelly Roll Jabbo and Fats: Nineteen Portraits in Jazz, 1983; American Musicians: 56 Portraits in Jazz, 1986. Contrbr.: poetry to Atlantic, Saturday Rvw, The New Yorker. Originated plan for CBS TV show, Sound of Jazz. BA, 1951, Cornell U. With New Yorker mag.: collator, proofreader, reporter, 1951-57; staff writer, 1957—; columnist on jazz rec., concerts, book reviewer, movie and theatre reviewer, reporter. Sgt., USAAF, 1946-47. Office: New Yorker 25 W 43d St NYC 10036

BALLON, ROBERT J(EAN), b. Laeken, Belg., April 28, 1919; s. Joseph and Emma (Roeykens) B. Author: ed., Doing Business in Japan, 1967, rev ed., 1968, ed. Joint Ventures in Japan, 1967, ed. The Japanese Employee, 1969, ed. Japan's Market and Foreign Business, 1971, ed. (with Eugene H. Lee) Foreign Investment and Japan, 1972, ed. Marketing in Japan, 1973, (with Hideo Inohara), Business Glossary, 1973, Joint Ventures in Jpan, 1973, (co-author) Financial Reporting in Japan, 1976, Nihon-Gata Business no Kenkyu (''Consideration on Japanese-like Business''), 1978, Promotion of Personnel in Japan, 1979, Recruiting Japanese Managers, 1984, Salary Administration in Japan: Regular Workforce, 1985, The Business Contract in Japan, 1985, Labor-Management Relations in Japan, 1986, co-author Financial Behavior of Japanese Corporations, 1988. Also ed. of Bus. series, Inst. of Comparative Culture, Sophia University, Tokyo. Contrbr to Japanese, American, and European jnls. BA, University of Louvain, 1941, MA (philosophy), 1947; MA (econ), Catholic Univ. of American Washington, D.C., 1957. Ast. prof., Sophia U., 1957-63, prof. of econ. and intl. bus., 1963—, dir. of finance, 1958-70, chmn of Socio-Economic Inst., 1970-81, dir of Intl. Mngmnt Devel Seminars, 1981—, counsellor for Belgium's External Trade to Japan, 1980—. Member Eur. Fndn for Mngmnt Development and 21st Century Forum. Conductor of about 30 annual seminars for resident fgn. execs and Japanese execs in frgn corps; participant in conferences of Japanese and intnl business; mngmnt consultant. Member: Indsl Relations Research Assn, Yomiuri Intl Econ Soc, Japan Indsl Relations Researh Asn, Japan Mngmnt Reearch Assn, Japan Society (London), Assn de Tiers-Monde (Paris). Merit citation from U. S. Civil Service Commn, 1962; doctor honoris cause, Universidad Catolica de Cordoba, 1979; chevalier de l'Ordre de la Couronne, 1980. Home: SJ House 7 Kiochicho Chiyoda-ku Tokyo 102 Japan

BALOG, BETTY ENOCKSEN, b. Hammond, IN, Aug. 19, 1932; d. Charles and Helen Margaret (Martine) Enocksen; m. Ernest Andrew Balog, Sept. 19, 1959; children: Mark A., Erik A. Contrbr. poetry and fiction to Cape Rock, Attention Please, Ind. Rvw, Forum, Womankind, Skylark, Whitewater Woman, Streets, MacGuffin. AB in English, Ind. U., 1969, AM in English, 1981. Dir. conservation City of Gary, Ind., 1972-73; tchr. English, Gary Community Schls., 1974-87; adj. instr. English, Ind. U. N.W., Gary, 1986—; resident Millay Colony, Austerlitz, N.Y., 1981, Indiana poet in the Schools, 1981. Mem. P&W, Word Weavers. Home: 264 N Lake St Gary IN 46403

BALSIGER, DAVID WAYNE, b. Monroe, WI, Dec. 14, 1945; s. Leon C. and Dorothy May (Meythaler) B.; m. Robyne Lynn Betzsold, July 10, 1982; children—Lisa Atalie, Lori Faith (by prev. marriage), Jennifer Anne. Author: The Satan Seller, 1972, The Back Side of Satan, 1973, Noah's Ark: I Touched It, 1974, One More Time, 1974, It's Good To Know, 1975, In Search of Noah's Ark, 1976, The Lincoln Conspiracy, 1977, Beyond Defeat, 1978, On the Other Side, 1978, Mister Abe, 1988, 8 Mini Guide Books (travel), 1979, Presidential Biblical Scoreboard, 1980, 84, Candidate's Biblical Scoreboard, 1986, Family Protection Scoreboard, 1987. Movie/TV producer and researcher: Operation Thanks, 1965; The Life and Times of Grizzly Adams, 1976-77; In Search of Noah's Ark, 1976; The Lincoln Conspiracy, 1977; The Bermuda Triangle, 1977. BA, 1977, Natl. U., San Diego; L.H.D., 1977, Lincoln Mem. U., Harrogate, TN. Chief photog., feat. writer, Anaheim (Calif.) Bull., 1968-69; pub/ed. Money Doctor mag., Anaheim, 1969-70; Media dir., World Evangelism, San Diego, 1970-72; dir. mktg., Logos Intl. Christian Book Publishers, Plainfield, NJ, 1972-73; pres., dir., Master Media (advt. agy.), Costa Mesa, CA, 1973-75; pres., Balsiger Lit. Service, Costa Mesa, 1973-78; v.p. communications, Donald S. Smith Assocs., Anaheim, 1975-78; assoc. producer, dir. creative devel., Sunn Classic Pictures, L.A., Salt Lake City, 1976-78 owner, Writeway Profl. Lit. Assocs., Santa Ana, CA, 1978—; pub. Mini Guide Books, Santa Ana, 1979-80; owner, Balsiger Enterprises, Costa Mesa, 1978—; v.p., Donald S. Smith Assocs., Anaheim, 1982-84; vis. prof., Natl. U., San Diego. Received Religion in Media award, 1980, 84, 86; Lit. Hall of Fame, 1977; mem. RAMBO Coalition (fdr.-pres.). Address: Box 10428 Costa Mesa CA 92627

BANDOW, DOUGLAS LEIGHTON, b. Washington, Apr. 15, 1957; s. Donald E. and Donna J. (Losh) B. AA, 1974, Okaloosa-Walton Jr. Coll., Niceville, FL; BS in Econ., 1976, FLA State U.; JD, 1979, Stanford U. Bar: Calif. 1979. Editor Inquiry Mag, 1982-84; natl. columnist Copley News Service, San Diego, 1983—; Wash. corr. Socioeconomics Studies Newsltr, 1983-86. Sr. policy analyst Reagan for Pres. Com., Los Angeles, 1979-80; Office of Pres. Elect, Washington, 1980-81. Spcl. asst to the Pres. for policy devel. White House, Washington, 1981-82. Senior Fellow, Cato Institute, 1984—. Mem. Calif. Bar Assn, ABA, Washington Ind. Writers, Nat. Writers Club. Received Freedom leadership award, Freedoms Fdn., Valley Forge, PA, 1977; cert. for polit. and journ. activities by Freedoms Fdn, 1979. Office: Inquiry Mag 1320 G St SE Washington DC 20003

BANES, DANIEL, b. Chgo., Apr. 19, 1918; s. David and Fanny (Bornstein) B.; m. Helen Mae Richter, Apr. 6, 1941; children—Susan Penny Banes Harris, Ruby Elisabeth Ann Banes Bell, Sally Rachel. Author: Introduction to Regulatory Drug Analysis, 1965; Principles of Regulatory Drug Analysis, 1968; Chemist's Guide to Regulatory Drug Analysis, 1974; Provocative Merchant of Venice, 1975; Shakespeare, Shylock and Kabbalah, 1978. BS, 1938, MS, 1940, U. Chgo; Ph.D, 1950, Georgetown U. With FDA, 1939-73, assoc. commr. for sci, 1968-69; dir. pharm. research and testing, 1969-73; dir. drug standards div. U.S. Pharmacopeia, 1973-79; cons. drug analysis and control. Adj. prof. chemistry, Am. U., 1951—. With USAAF, 1942-46. Recd. Distinguished Service award, HEW, 1964; Harvey W. Wiley award, 1968. Fellow AAAS; mem. Am. Chem. Soc., and Acad. Pharm Scientists. Home: 805 Malcolm Dr Silver Spring MD 20901

BANGS, CAROL JANE, b. Portland, OR., June 22, 1949, d. Howard Eugene and Mary Ellen (McLarty) Berry; m. Stephen Edward Bangs, July 3, 1969 (div. 1972); m. James A. Heynen, Aug. 1, 1973; children—Emily Jane, William Geoffrey. Author: Irreconcilable Differences, 1978, The Bones of the Earth, 1983; contrbr. poetry, criticism, rvws., fiction, and essays to numerous publs. BA, Portland State U., 1979; MA, U. Oreg. PhD, 1977. Mem. faculty U. Oreg., U. Wash., Boise State U., Bellevue Coll., Peninsula Coll., Western Wash. U., 1975—; freelance writer, editor, 1975—; arts adminstr. Centrum Fdn., Port Townsend, Wash., 1981—. Chair Port Townsend Arts Comm., 1980-82. NDEA fellow, 1971-74. Mem. MLA, Philol. Assn. Pacific Coast, PSA. Home: 624 Lincoln St Port Townsend WA 98368

BANKS, CAROLYN, see Rafferty, Carolyn Banks

BANKS, STANLEY EUGENE, b. Kansas City, MO, Nov. 27, 1956, s. George Forge and Maxine Ann (Slaton) B.; m. Sheila Darnell Foster, July 27, 1985; 1 son, Marcus. Author: On 10th Alley Way, 1980; contrbr. poetry to Focus Midwest, Number One Mag., Cottonwood Rvw; contrbr. to Missouri Poets: An Anthology, 1982, Voices from the Interior: Poets of Missouri, 1982. BA in English, U. Mo., Kansas City, 1979; post-grad. Howard U., 1980. Tchr. Kansas City Schl. Dist., 1979-80; research asst., grad. researcher U. Mo., 1981; mediator, investigator Kansas City Human Relations Dept., 1981—; mem. Gov.'s Lit. Adv. Comm. Mo. Arts Council. Recipient Langston Hughes prize for poetry, BookMark Press, 1980. Home: 7120 Indiana Kansas City MO 64132

BARANCZAK, STANISLAW, b. Poznan, Poland, Nov. 13, 1946, came to U.S., 1981, s. Jan and Zofiz (Konopinska) B.; m. Anna Brylka, July 6, 1968; children—Michael, Anna. Author 7 books of poetry and 7 books of criticism published in Polish, 1968-84; translator Am., Eng., and Russian poetry into Polish; contrbr. to New Republic, Partisan Rvw, Paris Rvw, Ploughshares, numerous other periodicals. MA, Adam Mickiewicz U., Poland, 1969, PhD, 1973. Asst. prof. Adam Mickiewicz U., Poznan, 1969-77, 80-81; assoc. prof. Harvard U., Cambridge, Mass., 1981-84, Jurzykowski prof. of Polish lang. and lit., 1984—. Recipient award Koscielski Fdn., Geneva, 1973, Jurzykowski Fdn., NYC,1980. Mem. Am. Assn. Advancement Slavic Studies, Union Polish Wrtrs. Abroad. Home: 8 Brookdale Rd Newtonville MA 02160

BARANOW, JOAN MARIE, b. Cincinnati, Oct. 10, 1958; m. John Suplee, July 2, 1983. Poems in Window, The Little Magazine, and MSS. BA, Hollins College, 1980; MA, SUNY, Binghamton, 1983. Tchg. asst., SUNY, Binghamton, 1981-83; instr., Mohawk Valley Community College, 1982; tchg. asst., Rutgers U., New Brunswick, NJ 19984—. Mem. PSA, MLA, AWP, Amer. Assoc. of Univ. Prof. Home: 10 Suydam St New Brunswick NJ 08901

BARBA, HARRY, b. Bristol, CT, June 17, 1922; s. Michael Hovanessian and Sultone (Mnatsignanian) B.; m. Roberta Ashburn Riley, 1955 (div. 1963); 1 son Gregory Robert; m. Marian Andrea Homelson, Oct. 29, 1965. Author: For the Grape Season, 1960, 3 by Harry Barba, 1967; 3 X 3, 1969; The Case for Socially Functional Education, Art and Culture, 1970-1973, One of a Kind, 1976, The Day the World Went Sane, 1979, What's Cooking in Congress? I, 1979, II, 1982, The Gospel According to Everyman, 1981, Round Trip to Byzantium, 1985. AB, Bates Coll., 1944; MA, Harvard U., 1951; MFA, U. Iowa, 1961, PhD with honors, 1963; post-grad. Boston U., 1950-51, NYU, 1955-56, CCNY, 1956-57, Columbia U., 1957-58, U. Middlebury, 1945. Stringer, feature writer Bristol Press, 1944-45; instr. English and writing Wilkes Coll., 1947, U. Conn., Hartford campus, 1947-49; tchr. English, Seward Park High Schl., NYC, 1955-59; instr. U. Iowa, 1959-63, grad. fellow, 1961-62; asst. prof. Skidmore Coll., 1963-68, assoc, prof., 1968; Fulbright prof., vis. Am. specialist Damascus U, 1963-64; prof. English, dir. writing Marshall U., Huntington, W. Va., 1968-70; Title I Writing Arts dir. W. Va., 1969-70; disting. vis. lectr. contemporary lit., cons. writing SUNY, Albany, 1977-78; pres., pub., exec. editor Harian Creative Books, Ballston Spa, N.Y., 1967—; founder, dir. Skidmore Coll. Writers and Educators Conf., 1967. Skidmore research grantee, 1965-68; N.Y. State Council arts grantee, 1971; U. Iowa writing fellow, 961-62; PEN Syndicated Fiction awardee, 1985. Mem. College English Assn., MLA, AG, Writers League, PEN, COSMEP. Home: 47 Hyde Blvd Ballston Spa NY 12020

BARBANO, FRANCES ELIZABETH, b. Corry, PA, May 28, 1944; d. Franis Joseph and Mercy Elizabeth (Quinn) Dufresne; m. Robert Harkins, Nov. 11, 1967 (div. 1974); children—Matthew Scott, Sheila Marie; m. Duane Louis Barbano, Nov. 18, 1974; stepchildren—Terry Merdanian, Jeff Barbano. Contrbr. numerous articles to sports and fitness mags. inluding Outdoor Life, Angler. Ed.: Southwest Outdoors, 1985—. Cert. in Cosmotology, Phoenix Area Vocational Coll., 1977. Cosmetologist, Carefree Hair Designs, AZ, 1978-84; supvr. Boulders Club Restaurant, Carefree, 1986-87; free-lane wrtr., photography, 1983—. Mem OWAA, Southwestern Outdoor Wrtrs. Assn., NWC. Home 40240 N 69th Pl Box 230 Cave Creek AZ 85331

BARBATO, JOSEPH ALLEN, b. NYC., Feb. 23, 1944, s. Joseph Michael and Florence (Kelly) B.; m. Augusta Ann DeLait, Oct. 23, 1965; children—Louise Jeanette, Joseph DeLait. Fiction ed., co-pub. The Remington Rev. mag., 1972-78; book columnist Change mag., 1977-82, Amtrack Express mag., 1981-83; contrbr. to The Book of the Month (anthol.), 1986; contrbg. ed. Prime Times mag., 1983-87; mem. editorial adv. bd. Small Press mag., 1984-86; contributing editor, Publishers Weekly; contrbr. articles to Smithsonian, N.Y. Times, Christian Sci. Monitor, numerous other publs. Wrkg. on book on alcohol and general health. BA, NYU, 1964, MA, 1969. News wrtr. NYU, 1964- 68, dir. alumni communications, 1969-74, sr. wrtr. devel. office, 1976-78; freelance wrtr., NYC, 1978-86; director of public information, Alcoholism Council of Greater New York, 1986—. Mem. Nat Book Critics Circle, SPJ. Office: 40-13 82d St Elmhurst NY 11373

BARBER, BENJAMIN R, b. NYC,Aug. 2, 1939; children—Jeremy, Rebecca. Author: Totalitarianism in Perspective (with C.J. Friedrich and M. Curtis), 1969, Superman and Common Men, 1971, The Death of Communal Liberty, 1974, Liberating Feminism, 1975, Marriage Voices (novel), 1981, Strong Democracy, 1985, The Conquest of Politics, 1988; ed.: The Artist and Political Vision (with M.G. McGrath), 1982. BA, Grinnell (Iowa) Coll., 1960, LLD (hon.), 1985; MA, Harvard U., 1963, PhD, 1966; cert. London Schl. Econs., 1958. Lectr. Albert Schweitzer Coll., Churwalden, Switzerland, 1963-65; asst. prof. poli. sci., U. Pa., Phila., 1966-69; prof. poli. sci. Rutgers U., New Brunswick, NJ, 1970—. Adviser U.S.A.-UN Assn. Bd., 1982—. Sr. Research fellow Fulbright Fdn., 1976-77, vis. fellow NY Inst. for Humanities, NYC,1980-81, Guggenheim fellow, 1980-81, ACLS fellow, 1984-85. Mem. Authors Lg. of Am., Dramatists Guild, PEN Intl., ASCAP, Am. Philos. Assn., Am. Poli. Sci. Assn. Home: 275 W 96th St New York NY 10025

BARBIERO, DANIEL C., b. New Haven, CT, Oct. 12, 1958; s. Donato and Grace marie (Santagata) B. Contrbr. poetry to Multiples, Gryphon, Ariel, The MacGuffin; transls. The Sun, New Voices, 1985. BS in Fgn. Svc., Georgetown U., 1980. Publs. mgr. Ctr. for Sci. in Public Interest, Washington, 1984—. Mem. AAP, Md. State Lit. Soc., Wash. Independent Writers. Home: 4107 Stanford St Chevy Chase MD 20815

BARBOUR, WILLIAM RINEHART, JR., b. NYC,Mar. 2, 1922; s. William Rinehart and Mary (McKelvey) B.; m. Mary Munsell, Nov. 17, 1951; children—Bruce R., Elizabeth M., Alan W. Student, Mich. State Coll., 1941-42. Employed by Fleming H. Revell Co., 1944-83; pres., 1968-80; chmn, 1980-83. USAAF, 1942-44. Awarded Pub. of Year Religious Heritage Am., 1974. Home: 6809 Turban Fort Myers FL 33908

BARCI, ROBERT JOHN, b. Brooklyn, NY, May 21, 1954; s. Augustine Patrick and Gloria (Morgan) Barci. Author: Spoken Words, 1979, Axis, 1982, Boomerang, 1986. BA in Social Relations, Windham, Patney, VT, 1976. Home: 400 Meacham Ave Elmont NY 11003

BARCUS, JAMES EDGAR, b. Alliance, OH, Oct. 29, 1938, s. James Edgar and Mary (Weizenecker) B.; m. Nancy Ellen Bidwell, May 28, 1961; children—Heidi Anne, Jeffrey Thomas, James Hans. Author: The Literary Correspondence of Bernary Barton, 1966, Shelley: The Critical Heritage, 1975; contrbr. to Fdns. Christian Higher Edn., Tex. A&I Studies, Jnl Aesthetic Edn., Evang. Friend, Ky. English Bulltn., Cithara, His, Wesleyan Advocate, Christian Life, English in Tex., others. BA, Houghton Coll., 1959; MA, U. Ky., 1961; PhD, U. Pa., 1968. Teaching fellow U. Pa., U. Ky., 1959-63; asst. to personnel mgr., acting personnel mgr. ASTM, Phila., 1961-63; vis. prof. Nyack Coll., N.Y., 1963-64; prof. Houghton Coll., N.Y., 1964-79, Baylor U., Waco, Tex., 1980—; ed. Christianity and Lit., 1984—. NEH fellow, Princeton U., 1977. Mem. MLA, NCTE, Conf. Coll. Tchrs. English, Conf. Christianity and Lit., English Inst., Eds. Scholarly Jnls. Home: 8317 Gatecrest St Waco TX 76710

BARD, SUSAN M., b. Trenton, NJ, Apr. 4, 1954; d. Max and Miriam (Marcus) B. Contrbr. articles to business mags. B.A. in Political Si., Douglas Coll. of Rutgers U., 1976; M.S. in Jnlsm., Northwestern U., 1977. Reporter, copy ed., asst. bureau chief Commodity News Services, Chgo., 1977-79; staff wrtr. public relations dept. Chgo. Bd. Trade, 1979-80; local trader, broker MidAm. Commodity Exchange, Chgo., 1980-82; free-lance wrtr., ed., Chgo., 1982; mgr. public affairs dept. Nat. Futures Assn., Chgo., 1982-83; owner, founder Letters Etcetera, Chgo., 1983—. Mem. Intl. Assn. Fin. Planning, Futures Industry Assn. (exec. com. Chgo. div.), NWC. Home: 360 E Randolph St Chicago IL 60601

BARDECK, WALTER PETER, b. New Britain, CT, Oct. 22, 1910; s. Peter and Catherine (Tlustock) B.; m. Olga Marie Marra, June 6, 1942; children—Roland, Eileen Bardeck Przybysz. Author: Poems, 1937, Silver Petals, 1939, Blossoms and Tears, 1942. Contrbr. over 200 poems to anthols and magazines. Wrkg. on novel, The Martyr; Hard-Bread, Stranger than Fiction. Electrical supvr. Conn. Valley Hosp., Middletown, 1944-72, retired. Recipient Golden Poet award World of Poetry, 1985, 86, 87. Mem. Mark Twain Soc. (Schroeder Medal for lit. acheivement 1942), Eugene Field Soc., Henry Longfellow Soc. Home: 619 E Main Middletown CT 06457

BARISANO, JOSEPH, see Barron, Ray

BARKER, BARRY W., b. Ottawa, IL., Aug. 14, 1943; s. J.G. and Carolyn (Wilson) B.; m. Avis Lee Eagleston, Aug. 14, 1966; children—Will, Tom, Alison. Ed.: Earthtrek series books on Peru and Panama. Wrkg. on further Earthtrek documentary travel books. MEd, U. Del., 1968; PhD, Sussex (Eng.) Coll. Tech., 1976. Asst. dean of men, U. Cin., 1968-71; dir. Nat. Inst. Exploration, Champaign, Ill. and Miami, Fla., 1980—. Office: Natl Inst Expl 111 N Market St Champaign IL 61820

BARKER, GARRY G., b. Otway, OH, Nov. 26, 1943; s. James H. and Loval J. (Cox) B.; m. Anita L. Hurst, June 30, 1973; children: Gregory, Elizabeth. Author: Mountain Passage & Other Stories, 1986, Fire on the Mountain, 1983, Copperhead Summer, 1985; contrbr. anthologies: From Seedbed to Harvest, 1985, Harvest from The Hills, 1984, Mountain Ways, 1985, The Uneven Ground, 1985; contrbr. short stories to Appalachian Heritage, The Mountain Spirit, Grab-A-Nickel, Inscape, Cavalier, Delta Scene, Heirloom, Chevron USA, Mich. Living, Ceramics Monthly, others. BA in English, Berea Coll., 1961-65. Asst. dir. So. Highland Handicraft Guild, Asheville, NC, 1965-71; asst. dir. Ky. Guild of Artists and Craftsmen, Berea, 1971-80; communications coordinator Morehead State Univ., Ky., 1984-85; dir. student crafts program Berea Coll., 1985—. Recipient Appalachian Fellowship, Berea Coll, 1982; poetry award Ky. State Poetry Soc., 1985; fiction award Inscape Mag, 1985; best short story award Catholic Press Assn., 1985. Mem. Appalachian Writers Assn. (exec. secy.), Natl. Book Critics Circle, P&W. Address: 110 Holly St Berea KY 40403

BARKER, JAMES, b. Des Moines, IA, Nov. 25, 1946; s. Walter Wilson and Audrey (Lentzinger) Barker; m. Lac Thi Barker, May 12, 1977; 1 dau., Valerie. Author articles publ. in veterans and sports mags.; wrkg. on novel about Viet Nam vet triathletes. BSW, Boise State U., Idaho, 1974; MSW, U.Hawaii, 1977. Mental health specialist, Intl. Catholic Migration Commission, 1985—; priest, Reorganized Church of Jesus Christ, 1969—. With US Army, 1969-72. Home: 3862 Tuers Rd San Jose CA 95121

BARKER, STANLEY ANTHONY, b. Chgo., Nov. 24, 1956; s. George William and Jeanette Genevieve (Francikowski) B. Author: The Signs of the Times, 1984. Contrbr. articles to Mother Earth News, The Artist's Mag. Student Columbia Coll., Chgo., 1973-75, Northwestern U., 1975. Staff writer Kerred Pubs., Chgo., 1975-79; free-lance writer, 1976—; editorial cons. Llewellyn Pubs., St. Paul, 1984; contrbg. ed. The Artist's Mag., Cinc., 1986—. Home: Box 6172 Broadview IL 60153

BARKHAMER, JOSEPHINE RITA, b. Phila., May 18, 1949; d. George Joseph and Josephine (Petrella) Vittolino; m. Robert Jay Barkhamer, Jr., June 3, 1972; children—Jason, Gregory. Author poetry: Glowing Embers, 1984, Ashes to Ashes, 1985, Moods and Mysteries, 1985, Art of Poetry, 1985, Grit, 1985, Words of Praise, 1986, World of Poetry, 1986. Stud. Phila. pub. schls. Statistical typist Farrington Corp., Phila., 1966-69; typist Publishers Corp., Phila., 1969-70; legal typist Redevelopment Authority of Phila., 1970—. Home: 910 Belmont Ave Westmont NJ 08108

BARKHORN, JEAN COOK, (Mrs. Henry C. Barkhorn), b. NYC, Apr. 3, 1931; d. Francis Howell and Janet (McCord) Cook; m. Henry C. Barkhorn, May 14, 1971. BA, Vassar Coll., 1953. With Town and Country mag., NYC, 1954—, exec. dir., 1966-68, mng. editor, 1968—. Home: 36 E 72nd St New York NY 10021

BARKLEY, TAMMINY, see Seagule, Samantha Singer

BARLOW, LOLETE FALCK, b. Mobile, AL, Aug. 23, 1932; d. John Vecil Walter and Bessie Lolete (Clarke) Falck; m. John Woodman Bryan Barlow, May 13, 1952; children—John Bryan, Kimberly Barlow Hoffman, Windsor. Contrbr. poems to anthols., lit mags. Student Fla. State U., 1950-51. Recipient 1st prize Midwest Poetry Rvw., 1981, 87. Mem NLAPW (officer, Della Crowder Miller award 1979). Home: 5403 Ludlow Dr Camp Springs MD 20748

BARLETTA, JOSEPH FRANCIS, b. Punxsutawney, PA, Oct. 1, 1936; s. Michael Albert and Vandolyn R. (Raffetto) B.; m. Marilyn M. Minetti, Feb. 23, 1969. AB, Marietta Coll., 1959; JD, Duquesne U, 1963. Bar: Pa., 1963, Ill. 1975, N.Y. 1981. Practice law, Ellwood City, Pa., 1963-66; labor rel. mgr. Dow Jones & Co., 1966-70; v. p., dir. employee relations, v.p. dir. ops. hgo. Tribune, 1970-76; exec. v.p., gen. mgr. N.Y. Daily News Inc., 1977-81; ptnr. firm Seyfarth, Shaw, Fairweatner & Geraldson, 1981—; pres. San Francisco Newspaper Agcy. (Chronicle & Examiner), 1982—. Home 2222 Hyde St San Francisco CA 94109

BARLOW, WILLIAM EDWARD, b. Indpls., Dec. 6, 1917; s. Edward Stevens and Eva (Eustis) B.; m. Marguerite Emily Holcombe, Oct. 4, 1943 (div. 1975); children—Gloria Barlow Bernhardt, Christopher, James. BS, Hamilton Coll., 1940; postgrad., Williams Coll., 1940. With Pan Am. Airways, 1941-45, Time Intl., 1945-48; founder, pres. Vision Inc., NYC, 1948-75, Middle East Enterprises, 1975-79; owner, pres. M.I.N. Pub., NYC, 1978. First pres. Council of the Americas, 1963-71, v.p. Interam. Council Commerce and Prodn., 1968-70; bd. dirs. Fund for Multinatl. Mgmt. Edn., 1968—, Recipient Maria Moors Cabot Gold award Columbia U. Grad. Schl. Journalism, 1963. Office: 18 E 53d St New York NY 10022

BARNARD, CHARLES NELSON, b. Arlington, MA, Oct. 5, 1924; s. Charles Nelson and Mae E. Johnson B.; m. Diana Lee Pattison, Aug. 6, 1949 (div. Aug. 1970); children—Jennifer Lee, Rebecca, Charles Nelson, Patrick; m. Karen Louise Zakrison, Apr. 18, 1971. Author: The Winter People, 1973, 20,000 Alarms, 1974, I Drank the Water Everywhere, 1975, The Money Pit, 1976, It Was a Wonderful Summer for Running Away, 1977; Editor, A Treasury of True, 1957, Official Automobile Handbook, 1959, Anthology of True, 1962; Contrbr. Encyc. Brit. BJ, U. Mo., 1949. Editor Dell Pub. Co., NYC, 1949; assoc. editor True mag., Fawcett Publs., NYC, 1949-54, mng. editor, 1954-63; sr. editor Sat. Evening Post, NYC, 1964-65; exec. editor True Mag., 1965-67, editor, 1968-70; travel editor Modern Maturity (publs. Am. Assn. Ret. Persons); editorial cons., freelance writer, 1971—. Served from pvt. to sgt. AUS, 1944-46; war corr. Member Alpha Tau Omega, Sigma Delta Chi, Kappa Tau Alpha. Home: 225 Valley Rd Cos Cob CT 06807

BARNES, ANDREW EARL, b. Torrington, CT, May 15, 1939; s. Joseph and Elizabeth (Brown) B.; m. Marion Otis, Aug. 26, 1960; children—Christopher Joseph, Benjamin Brooks, Elizabeth Cheny. BA, Harvard U. 1961. Reporter, bur. chief Providene Jnl., 1961-63; from reporter to edn. editor Washington Post, 1965-73; metro. editor, asst. mng. editor St. Petersburg (Fla.) Times, 1973-75, mng. editor, 1975-84, editor, pres., 1984—Pres. Trend Mags, 1985—'es. Congl. Qtly., 1985—. Served with USAR, 1963-65. Alicia Patterson fellow, 1969-70. Mem. AP Mng. Editors Assn. (bd. dirs. 1983—), Fla. Soc. Newspapers Editors (pres. 1980-81), Am. Soc. Newspaper Editors. Office: 490 1st Ave S Saint Petersburg FL 33731

BARNES, DICK, b. San Bernardino, CA, Nov. 5, 1932; s. Harold and Kathleen B.; m. Catherine Beston; m. 2d Mary Twiss; m. 3d, Patricia Casey, July 30, 1981; children: Elizabeth, Harold, Henry, Jean, Paul, Sarah, Ellen, Richard, Louis. Author: A Lake on the Earth, 1982, A Pentecostal, 1985, Episodes in Five Poetic Traditions, 1972, Three Spanish Sacramental Plays, 1968; ed. The Psalms of David and Others, 1977. AM, Harvard U., 1955; PhD Claremont, 1959. Instr. Univ. Calif, Riverside, 1958-59; prof. Pomona Coll., Claremont, Calif., 1961—, Arthur M. Dole and Fanny M. Dole prof. English. Mem. New Chaucer Soc., Medieval Assn. Pacific, Am. Congress Irish Studies. Address: Dept Eng Pomona Coll Claremont CA 91711

BARNES, JANE ELLEN, b. Bklyn., Dec. 29, 1943, d. Martin D. and Barbara Jane (Krancher) Barnes. Author: Mythologies, 1976, They Say I Talk in My Sleep, 1979, Extremes (poetry), 1981; contrbr. stories to Dark Horse, Voices in the Night, Ascent, other anthologies; contrbr. poetry to Poetry Now, Ploughshares, Hanging Loose, Gargoyle, Harvard Mag., numerous other lit mags, anthols.; founder, ed. Dark Horse poetry and fiction newpaper, 1974-80, Quark Press (1976—) publilshing modern haiku or "minimals"; Blue Giant Press, 1981—. Wrkg. on poetry manuscript, novels, collection of short stories, screenplay. BA, Ga. State U., 1966; MA in Poetry, Fiction, Boston U., 1978. Tech. wrtr. Honeywell/MIT, Cambridge, 1966-72; freelance wrtr., Boston and Cambridge, 1981—; instr. mgmt. program Boston U., 1980; bd. dirs. Boston Book Affair, 1976. Mem. P&W. Home: 24 Concord Ave Cambridge MA 02138

BARNES, JERRY NEAL, (The Prairie Sage), b. Tahona, OK, Apr. 20, 1933; s. Samuel and Mary Magdalene (Smith) B.; m. Jerilynn Marie, Sept. 10, 1971; children—Elizabeth, Jerry N., Susan M., Christopher G., Jannette A. Pearce, Richard J. Pearce. Author: (novel) Thunder Is Its Song, 1984, The New Privateers, 1985; area correspondent St. Joseph Gazette, MO, 1982-85. Contrbr. poetry to lit. mags., newspapers, police mags. B.S., Mo. Western State U., 1982. Police officer City of Olathe, KS, 1966-71, City of Hiawatha, KS, 1975-85. Served to sgt. USAF, 1950-54, sgt. Res., ret. Recipient Golden Poet award World of Poetry, 1985, 86. Mem. Kans. Peace Officers Assn. Home: 406 S First St Hiawatha KS 66434

BARNES, JILL, b. Kenilworth, NJ, Apr. 28, 1953, d. John Howard and Magdalene (Kollar) Barnes; m. John T. Nelson, July 1, 1979, 1 son, Erik J. Contrbr. articles to Sports Parade, Atlantic Salmon Jnl, USA Today, Fur-Fish-Game, numerous other publs. Wrkg. on sports, outdoor and health articles. BA, Ramapo Coll., 1976. Sports reporter Paterson (N.J.) News, 1978-79, The Record, Hackensack, N.J., 1979-83, The Star-Ledger, Springfield, N.J., 1983-86; freelance wrtr. Mem. OWAA, NWC, N.J. Sports Wrtrs. N.J. Outdoor Wrtrs. Home: 26-11 Kipp St Fair Lawn NJ 07410

BARNES, JIM WEAVER, b. Summerfield, OK, Dec. 22, 1933, s. Austin Oscar and Bessie Vernon (Adams) B.; m. Cora FloDell McKown, June 20, 1964 (div. 1972); m. Carolyn Louise Turpin, Nov. 23, 1973; children—Bret, Blake. Author: (poetry) This Crazy Land, 1980, The Fish on Poteau Mountain, 1980, The American Book of the Dead, 1982, A Season of Loss, 1985; translator (from German) Summons and Sign: Poems by Dagmar Nick, 1980; contrbr. to anthologies. BA, S.E. Okla. State U., 1964; MA, U. Ark., 1966, PhD, 1972. Instr. English, N.E. Okla. State U., Tahlequah, 1965-68; prof. English, N.E. Mo. State U., Kirksville, 1970—; ed. The Chariton Rvw, Kirksville, 1975—; ed., dir. The Chariton Rvw Press, 1978—. Recipient transl. prize Columbia U., 1980; NEA poetry fellow, 1978; Canadian Govt. faculty enrichment fellow, 1984. Mem. CCLM. Home: 918 Pine St Macon MO 63552

BARNES, MARY JANE, b. Chinville (town renamed Raceland), KY, Apr. 23, 1913, d. William Ezekial and Neva (Artis) Smith; m. Howard Andrew Beattie, Nov. 11, 1929 (div. 1950); children—Howard Carlton, David Lowell; m. 2d,

Paul Elbert Barnes, June 14, 1953; 1 stepson, Paul Richard. Author poetry: The Opposite Shore, 1961, Delta Portraits, 1962, Song of a Quester, 1964, Puff of Smoke, 1969, Vignettes: American, 1973, Look East of the Mountain, 1976, Rising Tides of Splendor, 1976, Shadows on April's Hills, 1981, Songs from an Islander, 1982, Naomi and Ruth (musical drama in blank verse), 1985. BS, Morehead State U.; MA, Ariz. State U. Tchr. public schls. in Ky., Ariz., Calif., 1933-73. Recipient numerous poetry awards. Mem. Ky. State Poetry Soc., World Poetry Soc., Interfaith Wrtrs. Club, Calif. Fedn. Chaparral Poets, United Poets Laureate Intl., World Academy of Arts and Culture. Home: 425 Pippo Ave Brentwood CA 94513

BARNES, NANCY CAROL, (Nancy C. Coleman), b. Vicksburg, MS, Dec. 18, 1953; m. Jimmy Don Barnes, Sept. 10, 1983; 1 son, John Michael. Author: Veterinary Medicine/Small Animal Clinician, 1980, 3d ed., 1983, Scientifur, 1983. Contrbr. poems to anthols.; newspaper columnist Delta Democrat-Times, 1984-85. BS, Miss. State U.-Starkville, 1976; DVM, Auburn U., 1979. Intern vet. Westside Animal Clinic, Grenada, Miss., 1979; vet. Animal Clinic of Oxford, Miss., 1979-80, Greenville Animal Clinic, Miss., 1980—. Recipient Grand prize for overall writing Vet. Medicine Pub. Co., 1983, 1st prize for surgery article, 1983. Mem. AVMA, Miss. Vet. Med. Assn. Home: Box 129 Glen Allan MS 38744

BARNES, ROBERT GOODWIN, b. Augusta, GA, Sept. 1, 1914; s. John Andrew and Charlotte R. (Jones) B.; m. Helen Z. Jeffries, June 21, 1941; children—Susan Jeffries, John Andrew II, Frances Goodwin. AB, Columbia U., 1937. With Procter & Gamble, 1937-42, B. Heller & Co., 1946-47; with Doubleday & Co., Inc., N.Y.C., 1947-51, 52-69, v.p. 1964-69; pres., dir. Columbia U. Press, 1969-80; acting exec. dir. Am. Assn. Univ. Presses, 1980-81; prin. Mosley Assos., 1981-83; consultant, 1983—. Served to lt. comdr. USNR, 1942-46, 51-52. Mem. Assn. Am. Pubs. (dir 1978-80). Address: Box 94 Cornwall CT 06753

BARNES, WADE, b. Alliance, OH, May 15, 1917, short story. James Ralph and Flora Ellen (Borem) B.; m. Georgene O'Donnell, July 13, 1957. Contrbr. to: TV-Radio Age, Esquire mag., N.Y. Times, others. Student Mt. Union Coll., Alliance, 1934-35, CUNY, 1981. News dir., announcer various radio stas. in N.Y. and Conn., 1966-71; real estate cons. Mid-Fla. Lakes, NYC, 1971-78; chmn., ptnr. Barnes Assocs., NYC, 1978; bd. dirs., dir. public relations Literacy Vols. N.Y., 1981-83. Mem. Natl. Acad. TV Arts and Scis. Home: 20 Beekman Pl New York NY 10022

BARNET, RICHARD JACKSON, b. Boston, May 7, 1929; s. Carl J. and Margaret L. (Block) B.; m. Ann Birnbaum, Apr. 10, 1953; children—Juliana, Beth, Michael. Author: Who Wants Disarmament, 1960, (with Marcus Raskin) After Twenty Years, 1965, (with Richard Falk) Security in Disarmament, 1965, Intervention and Revolution, 1968, The Economy of Dearth, 1969, (with Marcus Raskin) An American Manifesto, 1970, Roots of War, 1972, Global Reach, 1974, The Giants, 1977, The Lean Years, 1980, Real Security, 1981, Alliance, 1983; contrbg. editor: Sojourners mag., 1979—. AB summa cum laude, Harvard U., 1951, LLB cum laude, 1954. Bar: Mass. 1954. Research fellow Am. Law Inst., 1957-58; assoc. firm Choate, Hall & Stewart, Boston; fellow Harvard U. Russian Research Center, 1959-60; spcl. asst. Dept. State, 1961; depy. dir. Office of Pol. Research, U.S. ACDA, 1961-62; fellow Center for Intl. Studies, Princeton U., 1963; co-dir. Inst. for Policy Studies, Washington, 1963-77, sr. fellow, 1977—. Served to 1st lt. JAGC U.S. Army, 1955-57. Recipient Sidney Hillman prize Amalgamated Clothing Workers Am., 1975; U. Mo. Schl. Journalism award, 1981. Mem. World Peacemakers (pres.), Com. for Natl. Security, Council on Fgn. Relations, Com. of Compassion. Home: 1716 Portal Dr NW Washington DC 20012

BARNETT, BILL MARVIN, b. Atlanta, Apr. 15, 1931; s. Henry Claude and Ida Belle (Estes) B.; m. Joan Kitchens, May 28, 1952 (div. 1979); 1 dau., Donna Satin; m. Amy Joseph, May 10, 1981. BA, Auburn U., 1957, MA, 1960. English instr. Auburn U., Alabama, 1958-61; coll. salesman Harcourt Brace Jovanovich, Atlanta, 1961-65, so. regional sales mgr., 1966-70, genl. mgr., San Francisco, 1970-77, dep. dir. San Diego, 1978-81, dir., 1981—, vp, 1983—. Trustee COMBO, San Diego, 1983—. Served with USAF, 1950-54. Recipient Kirkland award, Auburn U., 1955. Mem. Phi Eta Sigma, Phi Kappa Phi. Office: College Dept HBJ 1250 6th Ave San Diego CA 92101

BARNETT, DAVID LEON, b. Savannah, GA, Jan. 21, 1922; s. Jack and Ida (Levy) B.; m. Jeanne Kahn, Dec. 29, 1946; children—Randel, Megan, Jane. BS with honors in Govt., Harvard U, 1943; MS, Columbia U., 1947. Mem. staff Richmond (Va.) News Leader, 1947-54, chief statehouse bur. and polit. corr., 1950-51, asst. city editor, 1951-54; regional corres. Business Week mag., 1951-54; Washington corres. N. Am. Newspaper Alliance, 1954-55, chief Washington bur., colunist 1955-65; Washington news editor Hearst Newspapers, 1966-76; asst. mng. editor U.S. News & World Report, Washington, 1976—. Served with USAAF, 1943—46. Mem. White House Corr. Assn. Home: 7218 Beechwood Rd Alexandria VA 22307

BARNETT SCHARF, LAUREN ILEENE, b. Chgo., May 9, 1956; m. Craig Allen Scharf, Apr. 8, 1979. Author: Stand-Up Poems: A Comic Book of Poetry, 1975, Book of the Monthly, 1985, Book of the Monthly: No. 2, 1985, The Big Book of the Monthly, 1986; editor and contbr. to 40-plus Lone Star periodicals, 1981—; contbr. to periodicals, including Jnl of Irreproducible Results, Innerview, Woman's World, Computer World, others; producer, director and ed. Lone Star Humor Survey (TV, 1986). BA in English, Conn. State U., 1980. Mem. Assn. Comedy Writers, Soc. Ethical and Profl. Publishers of Lit. Office: Box 29000 No. 103 San Antonio TX 78229

BARNHART, CLARENCE LEWIS, b. nr. Plattsburg, MO, Dec. 30, 1900; s. Franklin Chester and Frances Norah (Elliott) B.; m. Frances Knox, Feb. 21, 1931; children—Robert, David. Ph.B., U. Chgo., 1930, postgrad., 1934-37. Editor Scott, Foresman & Co., 1929-45, War Dept., 1943, Random House, 1945-48; founder Clarence L. Barnhart, Inc.; Hon. research assoc. Inst. Pschol. Research, Columbia, 1945, 46. Author: (with Leonard Bloomfield) Let's Read: A Linguistic Approach, 1961; author (with R. Barnhart), Let's Read 1, 2, 3, 1963, 4, 5, 6, 1964, 7, 8, 1965, 9, 1966, Let's Look series 1-9, 1966, (with S. Steinmetz and R.K. Barnhart) The Barnhart Dictionary of New English from 1963, 1973, The Second Barnhart Dictionary of New English, 1980; Editor: Thorndike Century Junior Dictionary, 1935, 42, Thorndike Century Senior Dictionary, 1941, Dictionary of U.S. Army Terms, 1943, American College Dictionary, 1947, Thorndike-Barnhart Comprehensive Desk Dictionary, 1951, Thorndike-Barnhart Junior Dictionary, 1952, Thorndike-Barnhart High School Dictionary, 1952, New Century Cyclopedia of Names, 1954, New Century Handbook of English Literature, 1956, Thorndike-Barnhart Advanced Junior Dictionary, 1957, Thorndike- Barnhart Beginning Dictionary, 1964, Thorndike-Barnhart Intermediate Dictionary, 1971, Thorndike-Barnhart Advanced Dictionary, 1973; editor: (with Robert K. Barnhart) The World Book Dictionary, 1976. Recipient War Dept. certificate appreciation, 1946. Mem. Am. Dialect Soc., Linguistic Soc., Modern Lang. Assn., NCTE Am. Name Soc. (past pres.), Phi Beta Kappa. Office: Box 250 1 Stone Pl Bronxville NY 10708

BARNHART, DAVID KNOX, b. Oak Park, IL, May 15, 1941; s. Clarence Lewis and Francis (Knox) B. Editorial contbr. to World Book Dictionary, Thorndike-Barnhart Dictionaries, Barnhart Dictionary of New English Since 1963, Second Barnhart Dictionary of New English, TROIKA—The TROIKA Introduction to Russian Letters and Sounds, Dictionary of Bahamian English, The Barnhart Dictionary Companion. AB, Syracuse, U., 1964. Editor, C. L. Barnhart, Inc., Bronxville, N.Y., 1966-80; proprietor, Lexix House Pubs., Cold Spring, N.Y., 1980—. Mem. Int. Linguistic Assn., Am. Dialect Soc., Linguistic Soc. Am., MLA, Dictionary Soc. Am., NCTE, Comm. on English Lang. Home: Rt 9-D Garrison NY 10524

BARNIDGE, MARY SHEN, b. March AFB, CA, June 22, 1948; d. Thomas Brake and Myrna (Shen) Barnidge. Author: Parties and Poets in Whitewater, Milw., DeKalb, Phila., Okinawa and Chgo., 1978; Piano Player at the Dionysia, 1984. BA, Wis. State U.-Whitewater, 1970; postgrad, U. Ill-Chgo., 1976-79. Mem P&W. Address: 1006 West Dakin St Chicago IL 60613

BARNOUW, ERIK, b. The Hague, Holland, June 23, 1908; came to U.S., 1919, naturalized, 1928; s. Adriaan Jacob and Anne Eliza (Midgley) B.; m. Dorothy Maybelle Beach, June 3, 1939; children—Jeffrey, Susanna, Karen. Author: 3 act play Open Collars, 1928, Handbook of Radio Writing, 2d ed., 1947, Handbook of Radio Production, 1949, Mass Communication, 1956, The Television Writer, 1962, (with S. Krishnaswamy) Indian Film, 1963, 2d ed., 1980, A History of Broadcasting in the U.S.: A Tower in Babel, vol. 1, 1966, The Golden Web, vol. 2, 1968, The Image Empire, vol. 3, 1970 (Bancroft prize 1971), Documentary: A History of the Nonfiction Film, 1974, rev. ed., 1983, Tube of Plenty: The Evolution of American Television, 1975, rev. ed., 1982, The Sponsor: Notes on a Modern Potentate, 1978, The Magician and The Cinema, 1981; Editor: Radio Drama in Action, 1945. Writer, adapter radio and TV series Theatre Guild, 1945-61; writer, producer: series Decision, Natl. Ednl. TV, 1957-59. AB, Princeton, 1929. Radio writer and dir. Erwin Wasey & Co. (advt.), 1931-35, Arthur Kudner (advt.), 1935-37; writer, editor CBS, 1939-40; script editor NBC, 1942-44; commentator overseas br. OWI, 1943-44; supr. edn. unit Armed Forces Radio Service, War Dept., 1944-45; mem. faculty Columbia, 1946—, prof. dramatic arts in charge film, radio and TV, 1964-69; editor Center for Mass Communication, Columbia U. Press, 1948-72; chief motion picture, broadcasting and recorded sound div. Library of Congress, Washington, 1978-81; fellow Woodrow Wilson Center for Scholars, 1976; cons. communications

USPHS, 1947-50. Recipient Gavel award for Decision films Am. Bar Assn., 1959, Eastman-Kodak gold medal, 1982; Fulbright Research fellow, India, 1961-62; Guggenheim fellow, 1969; JDR 3d fellow, 1972; Indo-Am. fellow, 1978-79. Mem. AL Am., Radio Writers Guild Am. (chmn. 1957-59), WG Am. (chmn. 1957-59), Acad. TV Arts and Scis. (bd. govs. 1966-68), ACLU, PEN Club, Intl. Film Seminars (pres. 1960-68), Phi Beta Kappa. Home: 39 Clarement Ave New York NY 10027

BARNSTONE, WILLIS, (Robert Barnstone), b. Lewiston, ME, Nov. 13, 1927; s. Robert Carl and Dora E. (Lempert) B.; m. Helle Phaedra Tzalopoulou, June 1, 1949; children—Akiki Dora, Robert Vassilios, Anthony Dimitrios. Author: From This White Island, 1960, Eighty Poems of Antonio Machado, 1960, Sappho, 1964, Greek Lyric Poetry, 1963, The Poems of Saint John of the Cross, 1969, Spanish Poetry, 1971, A Day in the Country, 1971, China Poems, 1976, New Faces of China, 1973, Poems of Mao Tse-tung, 1972, The Unknown Light: The Poems of Fray Luis de Leoc, 1979, Overheard, 1979, A Snow Salmon Reached the Andes Lake, 1980, Borges at Eighty: Conversations, 1982, A Bird of Paper: Poems of Vicente Aleixandre, 1982, The Poetics of Ecstasy: Varieties of Excess from Sappho to Borges, 1983, The Other Bible, 1984, Five A.M. in Beijing, 1987; editor, Modern European Poetry, 1966, Eighteen Texts, 1973; contrbg. editor, Books Abroad. BA cum laude, Bowdoin Coll., Lewiston, 1948, D.Litt. (hon.) 1981; MA with high honors, Columbia U., 1956; PhD with distinction, Yale U., 1958. Tchr. Amavrita Acad., Athens, Greece, 1949; instr. French U. Md. overseas program, Perigueux, France, 1955-56; asst. prof. Spanish, Wesleyan U., 1958-62; mem. faculty Indiana U., Bloomington, 1962—, prof. comparative lit., Spanish, Portuguese, 1968—, prof. comparative lit. and Latin Am. studies, 1972-75; Fulbright lectr. Professorado de Avenida de Mayo, Buenos Aires, 1975-76, Fgn. Lang. Inst. Peking, 1984-85. Served with U.S. Army, 1954-56. Guggenheim fellow, 1961-62; ACLS fellow, 1969-70; NEH fellow, 1979-80; recipient Cecil Hemley Meml. award Poetry Soc. Am., 1969, Lucille Medwick Meml. award, 1978. Mem. PEN. Address: Dept Lit Indiana U Bloomington IN 47401

BAROLINI, HELEN, b. Syracuse, NY, Nov. 18, 1925, d. Anthony S. and Angela (Cardamone) Mollica; m. Antonio Barolini, July 26, 1950 (dec. 1971); children—Teodolinda, Susanna, Nicoletta. Author: Umbertina, 1979, Love in the Middle Ages, 1986, 1988; intro. to The Dream Book: an Anthology of Writings by Italian American Women, 1985; contrbr. to Love Stories by New Women, 1982; contrbr. articles, stories, rvws., poetry and translations to Paris Rvw, Cosmopolitan, Prospetti, Antigonish Rvw, numerous other Am. and Italian publs.; translator 7 books from Italian to English. BA, Syracuse U., 1947; MLS, Columbia U., 1959. Tchr. Trinity Coll. Abroad, Rome, 1971-72, Kirkland Coll., Hamilton, NY, 1973-74; reference librarian Chappaqua (NY) Public Library, 1984—. Town historian, Ossining, NY, 1977-79. Recipient Marina- Velca award, Italy, 1970, grantee NEA, 1976, Lit. award Am. Comm. on Italian Migration, 1982, Lit. Arts award Americans of Italian Heritage, 1984, Am. Bk. Award, 1986. Mem. PEN, AG, Am. Italian Hist. Assn., The Hudson Group. Address: Scar Manor Box 307 Scarborough NY 10510

BARON, CAROLYN, b. Detroit, Jan. 25, 1940; d. Gabriel and Viola (Petlanski) Cohn; m. Richard W. Baron, Nov. 14, 1975. BA in Liberal Arts, U. Mich., 1961. Editor, editorial prodn. dir. Holt, Rinehart & Winston, NYC, 1965-71; mag. editor E. P. Dutton, NYC, 1971-74, exec. editor, 1974-75; adminstrv. editor Pocket Books, Simon & Schuster, NYC, 1975-78; v.p., editor-in-chief 1978-79, Crown Pubs. NYC, 1979-81; v.p., pub. Dell Pub., NYC, 1981-86; St. Martin's Press, 1986; v.p. Bantam Books, 1986. Author: The History of Labor Unions in the U.S., 1971, Re-Entry Game, 1974, Board Sailboats: A Buying Guide, 1977; contrbr. articles to mags. Mem. Women's Media Group. Home: Shelter Island Heights NY 11965

BARON, MARY KELLEY, b. Providence, RI, Nov. 18, 1944; d. Richard Lawrence and Mary Elizabeth (Reynolds) Kelley; children—Cordelia Baron, Kiernan Baron, Miranda Anawrok (dec.). Author: Letters For the New England Dead, 1974, Wheat Among Bones, 1980. AM, U. of Mich., 1969; PhD, U. of IL, 1973. Asst. prof., Tufts U., Medford, MA, 1973-75; assoc. prof., Hartwick College, Oneonta, NY, 1976-78; prof., dept. head, U. of Alaska, Fairbanks, 1978-87; prof., dept. chair, U. of N. Florida, Jacksonville, 1987—. Address: Dept Lang 4567 St. John's Bluff Rd S Jacksonville FL 32216

BARONE, DENNIS, b. Teaneck, NJ, Mar. 11, 1955; s. Alfred D. and Shirley M. (Lawson) B.; m. Deborah Ducoff, Aug. 21, 1977. Author: Echo of the Imperfect, 1982, The House of Land, 1986, Unfold the Mid- Point Now, 1987; editor and founder: Tamarisk, 1975-85; editorial bd. Confrontation, 1985-86; poetry to Some Other Magazine, Boundary 2, The Difficulties, Exquisite Corpse, Star-Web Paper, Paper Air, others; also interviews and rvws. in Partisan Rvw, Tri-Quarterly, Phila. Inquirer, Am. Book Rvw, Ninth Decade, others.; essays on Am. lit. in anthologies. BA, Bard Coll., 1977; MA, U. Pa., 1979, PhD, 1984. Teaching fellow and lectr. dept. history U. Pa., Phila., 1979-84; tchr. LaSalle Coll. High Sch., Phila., 1983-85; instr. English dept. Temple U., Phila., 1981-83, Phila. Coll. Performing Arts, Phila., 1981-83; lectr. English dept. C. W. Post-L.I.U., Greenvale, N.Y., 1985-86; asst. prof. English & Am. Studies, Saint Joseph Coll., 1986—. Committeeman, Democratic Party, Phila., 1983-84. CCLM/NEA/Pa. Council Arts grantee, 1978-83; Pa. Council Arts fellow, 1985. Mem. Library Co. Phila., MLA, Am. Studies Assn. Office: Saint Joseph College West Hartford CT 06117

BARONE, ROSE MARIE PACE, b. Buffalo, Apr. 26, 1920; m. John A. Barone, Aug. 23, 1947. Contrbr. articles, play: Bus. Edn. World; contrbr. article: Columbia Press; asst. to ed.: Philosophy and Phenonenological Research Jnl., U. Buffalo; asst. ed. Avi Pub. Co., Westport, Conn.; contrbr. poetry, articles to area newspapers. BA, U. Buffalo, 1943; MS, U. So. Calif., 1950. High schl. tchr., Angola, N.Y., 1943-46, Puente, Calif., 1946-47, Lafayette, Ind., 1947-50, Bridgeport, Conn., 1954-80. Mem. Natl. League Am. Pen Women (state pres. 1986-88, recipient Natl. Historian award 1976), Conn. Poetry Soc. (festival chairperson 1987), Natl. Federated Women's Poetry Award, state awards in poetry, short story, playwriting, local acting award. Home: 1283 Round Hill Rd Fairfield CT 06430

BARR, TINA, b. NYC, Apr. 13, 1955, d. Dudley Riggs and Laura Prugh (Hays) Barr. Author poetry chapbook: At Dusk on Naskeag Point, 1984; contrbr. poetry: Beloit Poetry Jnl, Prairie Schooner, Ploughshares, other jnls., anthols. Editorial asst. fiction dept. Good Housekeeping Mag., NYC,1978-79; instr. Villanova (Pa.) U., 1982-84, Temple U., Phila., 1982-85. Recipient fellowship Pa. Council on Arts, 1984, Temple U., 1985-86. Mem. P&W, MLA, AWP. Home: 738 Mildred St Philadelphia PA 19147

BARRETT, HAROLD FRANCIS, JR., (Hal Barrett), b. Dayton, OH, Dec. 13, 1919; s. Harold F. and Carolyn (Kaesemann) B.; m. Grace Ethel Dressler, June 9, 1946 9div. 1963); children—Margaret Ann, Paul Harold; m. Kathryn Mae Lohrentz, Mar. 1, 1969; stepchildren—William H. Ehrstine, Gale Ann Worman. Author: (poems) The Song of My Heart, 1944; (biography) To Natalie: In Memoriam, 1954; (newsletter) Brimberg Phases, 1960-61; (poems with haroal sketches) The Wanderer, 1975; (text) (with Joseph Corcoran) Refrigeration, 1960; (text) A Labor Guide to Labor relations, 1983; Principles of Church Newsletter Planning, Design, Writing, Production (with Maury Wyckoff), 1987; author curricular material for all courses in labor studies A.A. program at Sinclair Commun. Coll. Contrbr. essays, poems, news features to labor mags., newspapers; numerous letters-to-ed. in Dayton Jnl.-Herald; curricular religious plays, stories, games to mags. Creator, ed.: 1548 Forward newsletter, 1953-55, Federal Machinist News, 1957-60, The Labor Angle mag., 1960-62, Twinbrook Times newspaper, 1960-61, PWP Chapter 60 Newsletter, 1964-67; creator, ed., contrbr.: The Illuminator newsletter, 1982-87; creator, contrbr.: The Single Parent mag., 1966. Wrkg. on handbook on ch. newsletter planning, design, editing and pub.; compilations of life work in poetry, essays an editorials, musical compositions. Student Occidental Coll., 1945-52; A.A., Pasadena City Coll., 1950. Field representative U.S. Dept. Labor, San Francisco, 1962-63; exec. secy. Natl. Advisory Com. on Equal Opportunity in Apprenticeship and Training, Washington, DC, 1963-67; grand lodge representative Intl. Assn. Machinists and Aerospace Workers, 1967-77; chmn., founder labor studies dept. Sinclair Commun. Coll., Dayton, 1977-83, retired. Mem. Sigma Zeta Psi (honorary mem. for creative writing 1950). Home: 212 Marathon Ave Dayton OH 45405

BARRETT, JAMES LEE, b. Charlotte, N.C., Nov. 19, 1929; s. James Hamlin and Anne (Blake) B.; m. Merete Engelstoft, June 1960; children—Jessica, Penelope, Birgette, Christian David. Edn. Furman U., Pa. State U., Columbia U., Art Students League. Screenwriter, 1955: motion picture D.I. (Marine Corps Combat Corrs. Assn. award), The Greatest Story Ever Told, Bandolero, The Undefeated, Shenandoah, tick . . . tick . . . tick, The Cheyenne Social Club, The Green Berets, Something Big, Fools' Parade, Hank, Smokey and the Bandit; TV film The Awakening Land (Am. Women in Radio and TV cert. commendation), Belle Starr, Stubby Pringle's Christmas (Humanities nomination), The Day Christ Died, Angel City, Mayflower: The Pilgrim Experience, Vengeance, Stagecoach (Wrangler Award from Western Heritage Soc. & Natl. Cowboy Hall of Fame), Poker Alice, April Morning; playwright: Shenandoah (Tony award for best musical book). Served with USMC, 1950-52. Mem. WG, Am., Dramatists Guild, Acad. Motion Picture Arts and Scis. Address: Box 5407 San Luis Obispo CA 93403

BARRETT, LYN, see Heath, Lyn Barrett

BARRICELLI, JEAN-PIERRE, b. Cleveland, OH, June 25, 1924; s. Giovanni A. and Orfea (Malpezzi) B.; m. Norma Gaeta, Oct. 19, 1957;

children—Marco A., Laura C., Franca R. Author: (with Leo Weinstein) Ernest Chausson: His Life and Works, 1955, Dodecahedron (poems), 1956, Demonic Souls (on Balzac), 1964, The Prince: An Ananysis of Machiavelli's Treatise on Power Politics, 1975, Alessandro Manzoni, 1976, Crocuses through the snow (short stories), 1984, Giacomo Leopardi, 1986, Melopoiesis: Approaches to the Study of Literature and Music, 1987; ed: Alfred de Vigny, Chatterton, 1967, Chekhov's Great Plays: A Critical Anthology, 1981, (with Joseph Gibaldi) Interrelations of Literature, 1981; transl.: Giacomo Leopardi, Poems, 1963, Wergeland, Poems, 1974, Virgil, Aeneid I, 1975. Ed Italian Quartly, 1969-75, Heliconian, 1975—, Modern Philology, 1983—; forum ed Fantasy Studies, 1987—; assoc ed Comparatist, 1984—, Selecta, 1983—, Studies in Interdisciplinarity, 1986—. BA, Harvard U., 1947, MA, 1948, Ph. D., 1953. Lectr in Spanish and French, Western Reserve U. (now Case Western Reserve U.), Cleveland, Ohio, Summers, 1946-50; teaching asst. in French an Italian, Harvard, 1948-50, 1951-53; asst prof of romance langs and compar lit and dir. Wien Intl Scholarship Program, Brandeis U., Waltham, Mass., 1953-62; prof. of humanities and compar lit, U. of Calif., Riverside, 1963—, chmn dept of lits and langs, 1976-81. Conductor of Waltham Symphony Orch. and Cafarelli Opera Assn, 1955-60. Lctr in music at Cambridge (Mass.) School of Adult Educ, 1954-58; vis prof, Norwegian School of Econ and Bus Admin and at U. of Bergen, 1962-63, NY U., summer, 1978. Military Service: U.S. Army, in psychological warfare and mil govt, 1943-46, European Theatre, assumed rank of major; received five Bronze Stars. U.S. Army Reserve, 1946-50. Member: Intl Compar Lit Assn, MLA (mem of exec comm on lit and other arts), American Comp Lit Assn (mem adv. bd, 1976-79), Dante Soc of America, Natl Assn for the Advancement of the Rumanities, Law and Humanities Inst. (mem bd. govs, 1980), Phi Beta Kappa. Fulbright fellow, 1950-51, 62-63; U. of Calif Humanities Inst awards, 1968, 69; outstanding educator of America, 1974; disting teaching award, U. of Calif., Riverside, 1975; Ken2n Disting Prof of Humanities, College of William & Mary, 1988-89. Home: 5984 Windermere Way Riverside CA 92506

BARRINGTON, JUDITH M., b. Brighton, Sussex, UK, July 7, 1944; arr. U.S. 1976; d. Reginald Jack Christie and Violet Elizabeth (Lambert) Barrington; m. R. E. Gundle, July 9, 1979. Author poetry: Trying to Be An Honest Woman, 1985; contrbr. poetry and essays var publs. BA, Maryhurst Coll., 1978; MA, Goddard Coll., 1980. Dir. Utilair Ltd, London, 1968-73; instr. Portland State Univ, 1978-82; founder and tchr. The Flight of the Mind, OR, 1983—; freelance writer, Portland, 1982—; poet in the schsl., 1985—. Recipient Jeanette Rankin award Natl. Women's Political Caucus, OR, 1983, grant for poetry readings Met Arts Comm., Portland, 1985, 86. Mem. Feminist Writers Guild, Natl. Bk. Critics Circle. Address: 622 SE 28th Portland OR 97214

BARRIO, RAYMOND, b. West Orange, NJ, Aug. 27, 1921, s. Saturnino and Angelita (Santos) B.; m. Yolanda Sanchez, Feb. 2, 1957; children—Angelita, Gabriel, Raymond Jr., Andrea, Margarita. Author: The Big Picture, 1967, Experiments in Modern Art, 1968, Art: Seen, 1968, The Plum Plum Pickers (novel), 1969, Selections from Walden, 1970, Prism/67, 1970, The Fisherman's Dwarf, 1970, Mexico's Art and Chicano Artists, 1975, The Devil's Apple Corps, 1976, A Political Portfolio (essays), 1985; contrbr. articles to art mags., fiction to lit mags. BA, U. Calif.-Berkeley, 1947; BFA, Art Center Coll., Los Angeles, 1952. Mem. faculty Ventura (Calif.) Coll., 1961-62, U. Calif.-Santa Barbara, 1963-64, Skyline Coll., San Bruno, Calif., 1965-68, Foothill Coll., Los Altos, Calif., 1974-77, Sonoma State U., Rohnert Park, Calif., 1985—; owner, pub. Ventura Press. Served with U.S. Army, 1943-46; ETO. Address: Box 1076 Guerneville CA 95446

BARRON, RAY, (Joseph Barisano), b. Boston, Sept. 11, 1925; s. Patrick and Antonette (Morello) B.; m. Marilyn Baretta, Nov. 13, 1953; children—Karen, Robyn. Columnist, contrbr.: Boston Herald, 1982—; columnist Ad Week, 1978-85, Ad East, 1985-87. Author: Forties: When We Were Dreamers of Dreams, 1987, Pick Up the Beat, 1988. Contrbr. articles to newspapers, mags. Wrkg. on Italianization of Am., memoirs from fifties and sixties. B.A., Burdett Coll., 1949. Copywriter ad agys., Boston, 1951-53; pres. BH & M, Boston, 1953—. Founder Nahant Arts Assn., MA, 1967, Friends of Library, Nahant, 1968. Mem. Italian-Americans in Communications (dir.), New England Broadcast Assn., Advt. Club of Boston. Home: 43 Pleasant St Nahant MA 01908

BARRY, BEN, see Reynolds, Benjamin J.

BARRY, EDWARD WILLIAM, b. Stamford, CT, Nov. 24, 1937; s. Edward and Elizabeth (Cosgrove) B.; m. Barbara Helen Walker, Sept. 14, 1963; children—Wendy Elizabeth, Neil Edward. BA with honors, U. Conn., 1960. Pres. The Free Press, 1972-82, Oxford U. Press Inc., 1982—; sr. v.p. Macmillan Pub. Co., 1973-82. Mem. Phi Alpha Theta. Home: 62 High Rock Rd Stamford CT 06903

BARRY, JAN, b. Ithaca, NY, Jan. 26, 1943; m. Paula Kay Pierce, 1973; children—Chris, Nikolai. Ed., Peace is Our Profession, 1981; co-ed. (with others) Winning Hearts & Minds: War Poems by Vietnam Veterans, 1973, (with W.D. Erhart), Demilitarized Zones: Veterans After Vietnam, 1976; contrbr. Everything We Had: An Oral Hist. of the Vietnam War by 33 Am. Soldiers Who Fought It, 1981, Carrying the Darkness—Am. Indochina: The Poetry of the Vietnam War, 1985. Cadet U.S. Milit. Acad., resigned 1964. Writer, jnlst, poet, 1965—. Mem. P&W. Home: 75 Gates Ave Montclair NJ 07042

BARRY, JOHN ABBOTT, b. Nashua, NH, Mar. 1, 1948; s. Fred Leon and Jane (Abbott) Barry; m. Eva Katherine Langfeldt, June 1, 1985. Editor: InfoWorld's Essential Guide, 1984; co-author: The Unofficial I Hate Computers Book, 1984, Computers and the Decline of the English Language, 1984; author: The Sexual Connotations of Computer Terminology, 1985. Co-author: Desktop Publishing, 1986. BA, Keene State Coll., 1971. Editorial svcs. mgr. Sun Microsystems, 1985—; Managing Ed. InfoWorld Books (Menlo Park, CA), 1983-1984, InfoWorld Mag., 1980-1983, Microcomputing Mag. (Peterborough, NH) 1977-1980. Home: 283 Nimitz Ave Redwood City CA 94061

BARRY, MIMI NEAL, (Miriam L. Barry), b. Sunflower, MS., d. John Thomas and Elizabeth Wilson (Butler) Lancaster; m. Edward Ford Neal, Dec. 24, 1943 (div. 1968); children: Keith Lancaster Neal, Patricia Neal Pryor, Elizabeth Neal Cameron; m. 2d, William Patrick Barry, Feb. 28, 1970 (div. 1984). Contrbr. to Miami Mag., Thunderhead Lit. Mag., Miss. Poetry Jnl. Wrkg. on novel, poetry book, cookbook. Student Millsaps Coll., 1941-43, U. Va., 1946. Women's ed. State Times, 1955-56; food ed. Jackson (Miss.) Daily News, 1956-57; staff wrtr., AP, 1958-60. ed. Chekpoint Newsletter, 1969-71, Quest Mag., 1969-71; asst. ed. The Legal Link, 1986. Recipient awards for feature articles, editorials, and poetry. Mem. Miss. Poetry Soc., Mensa, Assocs. of the Univ. Press of Mississippi. Home: 1217 Linden Pl Jackson MS 39202

BARRY, RICHARD FRANCIS, III, b. Norfolk, VA, Jan. 18, 1943; s. Richard F. and Mary Margaret (Perry) B.; m. Carolyn Ann Kennett, Aug. 7, 1965; children—Carolyn Michelle, Christopher David. BA, LaSalle Coll., 1964; JD, U. Va., 1967. Bar: Va. 1967. Assoc. firm Kaufman, Oberndorfer & Spainhour, Norfolk, 1967-71, partner, 1972-73; corp. secy. Landmark Communications, Inc., Norfolk, 1973-74; pres., genl. mgr. Roanoke (Va.) Times & World-News, 1974-76, The Virginian-Pilot and the Ledger-Star, Norfolk, 1976-78, pub., 1983—; pres., chief operating officer, dir. Landmark Communications, Inc., Norfolk, 1976—, chief exec. officer, 1984—. Office: 150 W. Brambleton Ave Norfolk VA 23510

BARTEL, PAULINE C., b. Poughkeepsie, NY, May 7, 1952, d. Joseph Anton and Mary Frances Bartel. Author: Biorhythm: Discovering Your Natural Ups and Downs, 1978; contrbr. nonfiction to Boys Life, Mademoiselle, Seventeen, Christian Science Monitor, numerous other mags. BA, Coll. St. Rose, Albany, 1983. Freelance wrtr., ed., Waterford, NY, 1976—; instr. SUNY Albany, 1981-85, Hudson Valley Community Coll., Troy, NY, 1985—. Mem. Women's Press Club, The Writing Group, Delta Epsilon Sigma, Kappa Gamma Pi. Home: 12-1/2 Division St Waterford NY 12188

BARTH, JOHN SIMMONS, b. Cambridge, Md., May 27, 1930; s. John Jacob and Georgia (Simmons) B.; m. Harriette Anne Strickland, Jan. 11, 1950; children—Christine Anne, John Strickland, Daniel Stephen; m. Shelly I. Rosenberg, Dec. 27, 1970. Author: The Floating Opera, 1956, The End of the Road, 1958, The Sot-Weed Factor, 1960, Giles Goat-Boy, 1966, Lost in the Funhouse, 1968, Chimera, 1972 (Recipient Natl. Book award in fiction 1973), Letters, 1979, Sabbatical: A Romance, 1982, The Friday Book, 1984, The Tidewater Tales, 1987. BA, Johns Hopkins U., 1951, MA, 1952. From instr. to assoc. prof. English Pa. State U., 1953-65; prof. English SUNY, Buffalo, 1965-73; prof. English and creative writing Johns Hopkins U., 1973—. Office: Writing Seminars Johns Hopkins Baltimore MD 21218

BARTH, R(OBERT) L(AWRENCE), b. Covington, Ky, June 7, 1947; m. Susan Helen Albers, Jan. 10, 1970; 1 dau., Ann Elizabeth. Author: Forced Marching to the Styx., 1983, Anniversaries, Hours and Occasions, 1984, Looking for Peace, 1985; ed. Selected Latin Poems of Samuel Johnson Trans. by Var. Hands, 1986. BA, No. Ky. U., 1973; MA (Wallace Stegner fellow), Stanford, 1980. Instr. English Xavier Univ., Cin., 1983—. Served to sgt. E5, USMC, 1966-69; Calif., Vietnam. Home: 14 Lucas St Florence KY 41042

BARTHELME, DONALD, b. Phila, Apr. 7, 1931; s. Donald and Bechtold B.; m. Marion Knox, May 26, 1978; children—Anne, Katharine. Author: Snow White, 1967; short stories Come Back, Dr. Caligari, 1964, Unspeakable Practices, Unnatural Acts, 1968, City Life, 1970, Sadness, 1972; stories Guilty Pleasures, 1974; novel The Dead Father, 1975; stories Amateurs,

1976, Great Days, 1979, Sixty Stories, 1981, Overnight to Many Distant Cities, 1983. Recipient Natl. Book award, 1972, Natl. Inst. Arts and Letters award, 1972; Guggenheim fellow, 1966. Mem. AG, PEN, AAIAL. Office: New Yorker 25 W 43rd St New York NY 10036

BARTKOWECH, RAYMOND A., (Randy Larson), b. New Brunswick, NJ., Feb. 7, 1950, s. Adam Paul Bartkowech and Anna (Perrone) Brooks. Author: Backpacking, 1979, The Illustrated Backpacking Dictionary, 1981; contrbr. poetry, stories to Oyez, Zahir, N.D. Qtly, Quarry West, numerous other publs. BA, philo., U. Colo.-Boulder, MA, English Lit./Creative Writing. Freelance wrtr. 1969—; author Montalvo Arts Center, Saratoga, Calif., 1985. Mem. AWP, PSA, P&W, AAP. Home: 10 Day St. Cambridge MA 02140

BARTLETT, BRUCE ALLEN, Akron, June 6, 1948; s. Robert Mead and Elizabeth (Hawes) B.; m. Joleen Jane Kamm, May 19, 1973; children—Olivia, Tom. Author: Introduction to Professional Recording Techniques, 1987, PZM Theory and Application Guide, 1987; (pamphlet) PZM Boundary Booklet, 1986. Contrbr. articles to communications mags. including Stereo Rvw., Modern Recording' & Music, db, Recording Engineer/Producer. Ed.: Mike Memo, 1983—Sonics, 1984—. Student Akron U., 1976-77; B.A. in Physics, Coll. Wooster, 1970. Microphone engineer Astatic Corp., Conneaut, OH, 1976-79; technical wtr, microphone engineer, Shure Brothers, Inc., Evanston, IL, 1979-82; technical wrtr., microphone engineer Crown Intl., Elkhart, IN, 1982—. Mem. Audio Engineering Soc. Office: Crown Intl 1718 W Mishawaka Rd Elkhart IN 46517

BARTLETT, BYRON ALLAN, b. Las Vegas, Feb. 14, 1940; s. Byron Edwin and Yvonne Marie (Lodwick) B. Author: By Wave & By Wire, 1974 Contrbr. articles to Audio-Visual Communications, E-ITV, TehTrends, Current. B.A., Ariz. State U., 1962; M.A., U. Denver, 1966. Producer, Sta. KAET-TV, Tempe, AZ, 1963-65; producer, instr. Southern Ill. U., Carbondale, 1966-71; instructional TV specialist Ill. State Bd. Edn., Springfield, 1971—. Chmn. City Commn. Com. on Cable TV, Springfield, 1984. Served with U.S. Army, 1963. Recipient 2d place Swathout Awards, 1962. Mem Springfield Ednl. Communications Assn. (secg.-treas. 1974, pres. 1978), Natl. Assn. State Ednl. Media Profls., NWC. Home: 520 S 2d St 1102 Springfield IL 62701

BARTLETT, ELIZABETH, b. NYC, d. Lewis Winters and Charlotte Field; m. Paul Bartlett, April 19, 1943; 1 son, Steven. Works include: Poems of Yes and No, 1952, Behold this Dreamer, 1959, Poetry Concerto, 1961, It Takes Practice Not to Die, 1964, Threads, 1968, The House of Sleep, 1975, In Search of Identity, 1977, Address in Time, 1979, Memory is No Stranger, 1981, The Gemini Poems, 1984, Candles, 1986; contrbr. to New Voices, 1955, American Scene, 1963, Where Is Vietnam, 1969, Poets West, 1976, Encounters, 1985, many other anthologies. BA, Teachers College, Columbia U. Editor, ETC, San Fran., 1963-76, prof., San Diego State U., Ca. 1978-80; prof. U. of San Diego, C. 1979-81; poetry editor, Crosscurrents, Westlake Village, Ca., 1983—. Mem. PEN, PSA, AG, AL, Intl. Women's Writing Guild. Home: 2875 Cowley Way San Diego CA 92110

BARTLETT, HELEN BUCK, b. Washington, May 28, 1959, d. Charles Leffingwell and Martha (Buck) B.; m. Anthony Cecil Hass, June 22, 1985. Contrbr. articles to Ladies' Home Jnl, Good Housekeeping, Bklyn. Heights Press, N.Y. Beat; contrbr. poems to Mass. Rvw, Kans. Qtly, Columbia: Mag. of Poetry & Prose, Great Contemporary Poems. Editorial asst. Paris Rvw, 1984, contrbg. ed., Los Angeles, 1985—; feature wrtr. N.Y. Beat, NYC, 1984-85; dir. devel. Tony Bill Prodns., Los Angeles, 1985—; condr. poetry reading Mount Holyoke Coll. Home: 469 Landfair Ave Los Angeles CA 90024

BARTLETT, LEE ANTHONY, b. Berkeley, CA, Mar. 4, 1950, s. Lebaron Albert and Marian Elizabeth (Peters) B.; m. Mary Leona Dougherty; children—Katy, Jennifer, Emma, Marisa. Author: William Everson: A Descriptive Bibliography, 1977, Letters to Christopher: Stephen Spender's Letters to Christopher Isherwood, 1980, Karl Shapiro: A Descriptive Bibliography, 1980, Birth of a Poet: The Santa Cruz Meditations of William Everson, 1982, The Beats: Essays in Criticism, 1982, William Everson, 1985, Red Scare, 1985, Talking Poetry: Conversations in the Workshop with Contemporary Poets, 1986; contrbr. articles, poetry and rvws. to Paideuma, Sagetrieb, Am. Lit., Am. Book Rvw, Western Am. Lit., Poetry, Am. Poetry, Am. Lit. Scholarship, Calif. Qtly, N.Y. Qtly, others; co-ed. Am. Poetry: A Critical Tri-Qtly; gen. ed. Am. Poetry Contemporary Bibliography Series. AB, U. Calif., Berkeley, 1974; PhD, U. Calif., Davis, 1979. Tchr. prep. schl., Galt, Calif., 1974-76; lectr. U. Bordeaux, France, 1978-79, U. Calif., Davis, 1979-80; asst. prof. Pikeville Coll., Ky., 1980-81; asst. prof., assoc. prof. U. N.Mex., Albuquerque, 1981—, Presdl. lectr., 1984-86. Mem. MLA, Western Am. Lit. Assn. Home: Box 250 Placitas NM 87043

BARTLETT, LYNN CONANT, b. Bethlehem, PA, Dec. 14, 1921; s. Fay Conant and Marie Agnes (McGuiness) B.; m. Margaret Emma Johnson, June 29, 1946; 1 dau., Anne Elston. BA, Lehign U., 1943; AM, Harvard U., 1947, Ph. D., 1957; B. Litt., Oxford U., Eng., 1952. Instr. English Lehigh U., 1946; teaching fellow Harvard, 1948-50; instr. Vassar Coll., 1952-57; asst. prof., 1957-62, assoc. prof., 1962-70, prof., 1970—, asst. dean coll., 1958-61, secy. coll., 1966-70. Editor: (with W.R. Sherwood) The English Novel, Background Readings, 1967. Served with AUS, 1943-46. Decorated Bronze Star. Mem. Phi Beta Kappa, Sigma Phi Epsilon. Home: 170 College Ave Poughkeepsie NY 12603

BARTLETT, STEVEN JAMES, b. Mexico City, Mexico, May 15, 1945; s. Paul Alexander and Elizabeth Roberta (Winters) B.; m. Karen Margo Love, June 5, 1970. Author: Phenomenology and New Rhetoric, 1970, Validity, 1973, Metalogic of Reference: A Study in the Foundations of Possibility, 1975, Patterns of Problem Solving: A Study of Problem Solving Instruction at the University Level, 1977, Conceptual Therapy: An Introduction to Framework-Relative Epistemology, 1983, (with Peter Suber)/Self-Reference: Reflections on Reflexivity, 1987, When You Don't Know Where to Turn: A Self-Diagnosing Guide to Counseling and Therapy, 1987. Mem. advisory bd.: Metholodgy and Sci., 1976—. B.A., Raymond College, Univ of the Pacific, 1965; M.A., U. Calif.-Santa Barbara, 1968; Ph.D. U. Paris, 1971. Fellow, Ctr for Study of Dem. Instns., 1969-70; asst. prof., U. of Florida, 1971-72; asst. prof. U. Hartford, CT, 1972-74; visiting research logician Max-Planck-Institut, Starnberg, West Germany, 1974-75; prof. St. Louis U., 1975-84. Mem. Am. Philosophical Assn. Symbolic Logic. Home: 5550 Bethel Hts NW Salem OR 97304

BARTLEY, ROBERT LEROY, b. Marshall, MN, Oct. 12, 1937; s. Theodore French and Iva Mae (Radach) B.; m. Edith Jean Lillie, Dec. 29, 1960; children—Edith Elizabeth, Susan Lillie, Katherine French. BS, Iowa State U., 1959; MS, U. of Wis., 1962; LL.D., Macalester Coll., 1982. Reporter Grinnell (Ia.) Herald-Register, 1959-60; staff reporter Wall Street Jnl, Chgo., 1962-63, Phila., 1963-64, editorial writer, NYC, 1964-70, Washington, 1970-71, editor editorial page, NYC, 1972-78, editor, 1979—,v.p., 1983—. Served to 2d lt. USAR, 1960. Recipient Overseas Press Club citation, 1977, Gerald Loeb award, 1979, Pulitzer prize for editorial writing, 1980. Mem. Am. Soc. Newspaper Editors, Natl. Conf. Editorial Writers, Am. Poli. Sci. Assn., Council on Fgn. Relations, Sigma Delta Chi. Office: 200 Liberty St New York NY 10281

BARTLEY, SHIRLEY KAY, b. Indpls., Jan. 15, 1955; d. Albert James Bartley and Rosella Grace (Wilbur) Robey. Editor-in-chief: Boca Raton Mag., 1985—. BS, Emerson Coll., Boston, 1977; MA, Ind. U.-Bloomington, 1979; PhD, Temple U. 1983. Researcher SIRS, Boca Raton, Fla., 1983-84; instr. Coll. Boca Raton, 1984; research asst. Natl. Enquirer, Lantana, Fla., 1984-85. Mem. Fla. Mag. Assn., Nat. Wrtrs. Club. Office: Box 820 Boca Raton FL 33429

BARTMAN, JEFFREY, b. Paterson, NJ, Mar. 1, 1951; m. Elizabeth Hanson, June 1981. Author: The Cave of Night, 1978, Habit Blue, 1981. BA, Emerson, Coll., 1972; MFA, U. Mass.-Amherst, 1976. NEA fellow, Washington, 1976; Bread Loaf Writers Conf. fellow, 1977. Corp. comm. mgr., Data Genl. Corp., 1981—. Address: 4 Radcliffe St Holyoke MA 01040

BARTON, BRETT, see Sand, George X.

BARTON, COLLEEN, (Pat Barton), b. Blackwell, OK., Dec. 16, 1923; d. M.L. and Fay (Minor) Opperud; children—Barbara Lee Barton Theobald, Billie Ann Barton Ketchum, Charles W. Contrbr. poetry, articles. BA, U. S.D., 1947. Reporter Plain Talk, Vermillion, S.D., 1946-52; mem. advt. staff Midwest Outdoor, Sioux Falls, S.D., 1956-58; ed. Daily Leader, Madison, S.D., 1958-63, Daily Sentinel, Woodstock, Ill., 1963-68; tchr. English Schl. Dist. 156, McHenry, Ill., 1968-87. Reipient Best New Poet award, APA, 1986, 87. Home: 5118 W Willow Ln McHenry IL 60050

BARTON, FREDRICK PRESTON, b. Alexandria, LA, Jan. 15, 1948, s. Vernon Wayne Barton and Joeddie (Whisenhunt) Harris. Author: (novels) The El Cholo Feeling Passes, 1985, Courting Pandemonium, 1986; film ed. Gambit, 1980—. MA, CPhil, UCLA, 1975; MFA, U. Iowa, 1979. Teaching/writing fellow U. Iowa, 1978-79; prof. English, U. New Orleans, 1979—; film columnist Gambit newspaper, New Orleans, 1980—; resident film critic Sta. WWNO, New Orleans, 1980—, WDSU-TV, 1982-85, WLAE, 1986—. Recipient excellence in critical rvw. award New Orleans Press Club, 1982, 83, 86, 87; Alex Waller Meml. award, 1984; excellence in column writing, 1985. Mem. AG, AWP, Soc. for Cinema Studies. Home: 825 Dublin St New Orleans LA 70118

BARTON, PAT, see Barton, Colleen

BARTON, ROGER, b. Chgo., Oct. 17, 1947; m. Pamela J. Strahl; 1 son, Ian Jacob. Contrbr. poetry: Once Upon a Poet, Tidings to a Tick, vol. I, Sunshine and Butterflies, vols. I and II, numerous other collections and anthologies. BA in Music Theory, DePaul U., 1970, MA in English, 1975. Media librarian DePaul U., Chgo., 1971-78; mgr. membership records Am. Public Works Assn., Chgo., 1987— Home: 277 W 16th Pl Chicago Heights IL 60411

BARTON, THOMAS FRANK, SR., b. Cornell, IL, Dec. 3, 1905; s. Frank Douglas and Martha (Gamlin) B.; m. Erselia M.A. Monticello, Sept. 26, 1931; 1 son, Thomas Frank Monticello. Author: Living in Illinois, 1941, Patrick Henry: Boy Spokesman, 1960, John Smith: Jamestown Boy, 1966, Lyndon Baines Johnson: Texas Boy, 1973, (with others) Southeast Asia in Maps, 1970, (with Sidman P. Poole and Clara Belle Baker) Through the Day, 1947, From Season to Season, 1947, In Country and City, 1947, (with Poole and Irving Robert Melbo) The World About Us, 1948; co-author: Geography of the North American Midwest, 1955, Curriculum Guide for Geographic Education, 1963, Methods of Geographic Instructions, 1968, An Overall Economic Development Study of Southeastern Indiana, 1970, World Geography, 1972, Southeast Asia: Realm of Contrasts, 1974; senior author: An Economic Geography of Thailand, 1958; assoc. editor, Jnl. of Geography, 1940-45; asst. editor, 1948-50; editor, 1950-65, land surface wall map series 1952, including world, U.S., Europe, S.A., Africa, Eurasia, N.A. Editor: series maps and globes Pictorial Relief with Emerging Color. Contrbr. chpts. tech. publs., articles profl. jnls. Diploma, Ill. State U., 1929, B.Ed., 1930, LL.D. (hon.), 1977; PhM, U. Wis., 1931; PhD, U. Neb., 1935. Rural schl. tchr., 1925-27; grad. teaching asst., dept. geography U. Wis., 1930-32, U. Neb., 1932-34; assoc. prof. social studies Neb. State Tchrs. Coll., 1934-35; prof. geography, head geography-geology dept. So. Ill. U., 1935-47; assoc. prof. Ind. U., 1947-51, prof. geography, 1951—, vis. prof. geography and social studies Sri Nakharinwirot U., Bangkok, Thailand, 1955-57; supr. U.S. Airway Weather Sta., So. Ill. U., 1941-47; secy. Intl. Geog. Union Commn. on Teaching of Geography in Schls., 1952-55; ednl. motion picture collaborator and adviser. Instr. Army A.C. Tng. Program, all 1942-43. Recipient Distinguished Alumni award Alumni Assn. Ill. State U., 1975, Rocking Chair award Sigma Delta Chi of Ind. U., 1976, Distinguished Service award Geog. Soc. Chgo., 1978. Fellow AAAS, Ind. Sci., Natl. Council Geog. Edn. (distinguished service award 1965), Natl. Council Geography Tchrs. (pres. 1935), Ill. Council Geography Tchrs. (pres. 1939-40), Ind. Council Geography Tchrs. (pres. 1961-62), Ill. Acad. Social Sci., Ind. Acad. Social Sci. (pres. 1972-73), Ill. Edn. Assn., Ind. State Tchrs. Assn., Assn. Am. Geographers, Royal Geog. Soc., AAUP. Home: 940 S Jordan Ave Bloomington IN 47401

BARTOW, STUART ALLEN, JR., b. Danbury, CT., Mar. 17, 1951; s. Stuart Allen and Mary Christine (Hanley) B.; m. Susana Yalovi Naqura, Nov. 17, 1976; 1 son, Stuart Allen III. Author: (poetry) Sleeping through Seasons, 1984; poetry in numerous lit mags including Atavist, Blue Unicorn, Lit. Rvw, South Fla. Rvw, U. Wis. Rvw, Gargoyle, New Voices, Minotaur; also in anthology Snow Summits in the Sun, 1987. BA, Rider Coll., 1973. Home: 164 S. King St Danbury CT 06811

BARWOOD, LEE, see Satter, Marlene Yvonne

BARZUN, JACQUES, b. Creteil, France, Nov. 30, 1907; came to U.S., 1920, naturalized, 1933; s. Henri Martin and Anna-Rose B.; m. Mariana Lowell, Aug. 1936 (dec. 1979); children—James Lowell, Roger Martin, Isabel; m. Marguerite Davenport, June 1980. Author: Darwin, Marx, Wagner, 1941, Teacher in America, 1945, Berlioz and the Romantic Century, 1950, 3d edit., 1969, Pleasures of Music, 1951, 2d edit., 1977, God's Country and Mine, 1954, Music in American Life, 1956, The Energies of Art, 1956, Of Human Freedom, 2d edit., 1964, Race: A Study in Superstition, 1937, The Modern Researcher, 1957, 4th edit., 1986, The House of Intellect, 2d edit., 1975, Classic, Romantic and Modern, 1961, Science: The Glorious Entertainment, 1964, The American University, 1968, A Catalogue of Crime, 1971, On Writing, Editing and Publishing, 1985, The Use and Abuse of Art, 1974, Clio and the Doctors, 1974, Simple and Direct, 1975, Critical Questions, 1982, A Stroll with William James, 1983, A Word or Two Before You Go, 1986, editorial bd.: The American Scholar, 1946-76, Ency. Brit. 1979—; editor: Selected Letters of Lord Byron, 1953, Nouvelles Lettres de Berlioz, 1954, The Selected Writings of John Jay Chapman, 1957, Follett's Modern American Usage, 1966. Ed. Lycee Janson de Sailly, Paris; AB, Columbia U., 1927, MA, 1928, PhD, 1932. Lectr. history Columbia U., 1927, instr., 1929, asst. prof., 1938, assoc. prof., 1942, prof., 1945, dean grad. faculties, 1955-58, dean faculties and provost, 1958-67, Univ. prof. emeritus, also spcl. adviser on arts, 1967-75; lit. adviser Scribner's, 1975—. Trustee N.Y. Soc. Library; bd. dirs. Council for Basic Edn., Am. Friends of Cambridge U., Peabody Inst.; adv. council U. Coll. at Buckingham. Decorated Legion of Honor; Extraordinary fellow Churchill Coll., U. Cambridge (Eng.). Fellow Royal Soc. Arts; mem. Am. Hist. Assn., Am. Philo. Soc., Mass. Hist. Soc. (corr.), AAIAL (pres. 1972-75, 77-78), Am. Acad. Arts and Sci., Phi Beta Kappa. Address: 115 Fifth Ave New York NY 10003

BASART, ANN PHILLIPS, b. Denver, Aug 26, 1931; d. Burrill and Alberta Mayfield Phillips; m. Robert David Basart, Jan 29, 1955; children: Kathryn, Nathaniel. Author: Listening to Music (with Richard Crocker), 1971, Serial Music: A Bibliog. of Twelve-Tone Music, 1961 (reprinted, 1980), Perspectives of New Music: Index, 1984; The Sound of the Fortepiano: Discography, 1986; editor, newsletter UC-Berkeley library, 1976—. BA in Music UCLA, 1954; MLS, UC-Berkeley, 1958, MA in Music, 1961. Ref. libn. music library Univ. Calif., Berkeley, 1960-61, 70—; music instr. San Francisco Coll. Women, 1963-66; pub. Fallen Leaf Press, Berkeley, 1984—. Fulbright fellow, 1956-57, Florence, Italy. Mem. Music Library Assn. (citation for newsletter), Intl. Assn. Music Libns., Am Musicolog Soc. Address: Box 10034 Berkeley CA 94709

BASHINSKY, SLOAN YOUNG, II, b. Birmingham, AL., Oct. 7, 1942; s. Sloan Young and Nelle (Major) B.; m. Dianne Lawson, July 4, 1964 (div. 1973); m. Jane Shea, June 14, 1975; children: Nelle Major, Alice Lawson. Author: Home Buyers: Lambs to the Slaughter?, 1984; Selling Your Home, $weet Home, 1985; Kill All the Lawyers? A Client's Guide To Hiring, Firing, Using and Suing Lawyers, 1986. Wrkg. on med. malpractice crisis in Am. BA, Vanderbilt U., 1965; JD, U. Ala., 1968, ILM in Taxation, 1979. Dir., v.p. Golden Flake Snack Foods, Inc., Birmingham, 1969-73; prtnr. firm Kracke, Bashinsky, Woodward & Thompson, Birmingham, 1973-82; sole practice law, Birmingham, 1982-85; wrtr., 1983—. Home: 949 Acequia Madre Sante Fe NM 87501

BASIL, DOUGLAS CONSTANTINE, b. Vancouver, B.C., Canada, May 30, 1923; s. William and Christina (Findlay) B.; m. Evelyn Margaret Pitcairn, 1950; 1 dau., Wendy Patricia. Author: Executive Development, 1964, (Paul Cone, John Fleming) Effective Decision Making Through Simulation, 1972, Organacao E Controls Da Pequena Empresa, 1968, La Direccion de la Pequena Empresa, 1969, Managerial Skills for Executive Action, 1970, Leadership Skills for Executive Action, 1971, Women in Management: Performance, Prejudice, Promotion, 1972, Autorite Personnelle et Efficacite des Cadres, 1972, Conduccion y Liderazgo, 1973, Developing Tomorrow's Managers, 1973, Management of Change, 1974, others. B. Commerce, U. B.C., 1949; BA, 1949; PhD, Northwestern U., 1954; postgrad. London Schl. Econ., 1950. Instr. Marquette U., 1951-54; asst. prof. Northwestern U., 1954-57; assoc. prof. U. Minn., 1957-61; prof. mgmt. U. So. Calif., 1961—; cons. mgmt. devel.; intl. lectr. Served to capt. Canadian Army, 1943-46. Home: 2201 Warmouth St San Pedro CA 90732

BASKERVILL, JANE GIBBS, (Jane Baskerville), b. New Bern, NC, Feb. 1, 1955; d. Robert Dortch and Jane Douglas (Gibbs) B. Author: The Sky's the Limit, 1982; contrbr. The Clef, Sun Jnl, The Pilot, Ursus, prof. jnls. Wrkg on novel, The Joy Ride, in collaboration with Elizabeth Mills. BA, hum., North Carolina State Univ., 1977; MA, ed., East Carolina State Univ., 1984. Tchrs. aide, W. Havelock (NC) Elem. Schl., 1979-81; coord. River Park Environ. Awareness Ctr. (Greenville, NC), 1982-83; salesperson, Upstairs Gallery (New Bern), 1984-85; spinner of yarns, Tryon Palace (New Bern), 1984—. Mem. NC Writers' Conf., English Spkrs. Union, Natl. Wildlife Fedn., Sea Coast Spinners & Weavers Guild. Home: 226-A Change St New Bern NC 28560

BASS, DEBORAH LIVINGSTON, b. Montmorenci, SC, July 17, 1956; d. Max Livingston and Maybelle Mundy; m. John A. Bass, Feb. 24, 1983; 1 child, Alexis Jean. Author: Serving Him 150 Years, 1980; Reflections, 1985; College Catalog, 1985; A Readership Study of The South Carolina Market Bulletin, 1982; editor, South Carolina Equine, 1980; asst. editor: South Carolina Market Bulletin, 1979-81. Contrbr. articles to Southern Christmas Show, 1980; Retiring in South Carolina, 1980; South Carolina Food Jnl, 1980; Impact, 1983, 84, 85; photos to South Carolina Fresh Fruit and Vegetable Assn., 1980. BA, U.S.C., 1977, MA, 1982. Advt. mgr. Rambler Pubs., Aiken, S.C., 1977-78; pub. info. specialist S.C. Dept. Agrl., Columbia, S.C., 1979-81; dir. info. services Aiken Tech. Coll., 1983-85; writer, pub. relations cons. Farmward Enterprises, Inc., Salley, S.C., 1985—; freelance writer, Salley, 1975-77. Named Gregg-Graniteville scholar Graniteville Co., 1973-77. Mem. Intl. Rdg. Assn., Sigma Delta Chi. Home: Rt 2 Box 4 Salley SC 29137

BASS, DOROTHY ELIZABETH, (Dorothy Ussery Bass), b. Charleston, SC, Aug. 22, 1931; d. Hugh Dudley and Minnie Beatrice (Jones) Ussery; m. William Merritt Bass, Aug. 22, 1953; children—William Dudley, Elizabeth Carol, Joe David. Contrbr. poems var. mags. inclg. The Lyric, Hoosier Challenger, Old Hickory Rvw, The Smith, Hollins Critic, Roanoke Rvw, Maelstrom, NY Qtly, others; contrbr. local newspapers. Student, Queens Coll., 1949-51; BS, Va. Tech., 1951-53. Lab. tech. Blacksburg, Va., 1953-54; sub. tchr. Farmville, Va., 1967-76. Chmn. history comm., Sharon Baptist Ch., Rice, Va.,

1983—. Address: Rt 1 Box 64 Rice VA 23966

BASS, ELOISE, b. Panama City, FL, Aug. 2, 1935; d. Alford Lee and Marie (Martin) Patterson; m. Willie Fred Bass, June 28, 1985. Contrbr. poems to anthols. Grad. public schls., Blountstown, FL. Recipient Golden Poet award World of Poetry, 1986, 87, Honorable Mention, 1986. Home: Box 914 Wewahitchka FL 32465

BASS, MILTON RALPH, b. b. Pittsvield, MA, Jan 15, 1923; s. Philip and Lena (Brunell) B.; m. Ruth Mary Haskins, May 27, 1960; children—Michael Jon, Elissa Allen, Amy Brunell. Author: Jory, 1969, Force Red, 1971, The Doctor Who Made House Calls, 1973, Mistr Jory, 1974, Not Quite a Hero, 1976, The Moving Finger, 1986, Dirty Money, 1986, The Bandini Affair, 1987, Sherrf Jory, 1987, Gunfighter Jory, 1987. BS, U Mass, 1947; MA Smith Coll, 1948; Columbia U., 1948-50. Entertainment ed. Berkshire Eagle, Pittsfield, 1951—. Moderator, Town of Richmond, Mass, 1981-84. Served to Pfc, US Army Infantry, 1942-44; ETO. Mem. AG, PEN, Am Theatre Critics Assn., SATW. Address: View Drive Rt 49 Pittsvield MA 01201

BASSETT, ELIZABETH EWING (Libby), b. Cleve., July 22, 1937, d. Ben and Eileen Grace (Ewing) Bassett. Author/editor: The World Environment Handbook, The Growth of Environment in the World Bank, Environment and Development: Africa and the Middle East, numerous articles. AA, Bradford Jr. Coll., Mass., 1957. Girl Friday Time-Life, others, 1957-63; asst. producer, stage mgr. NY State Pavilion at NY World's Fair, 1963-64; reporter/writer/editor AP, NYC, 1965-72; resident correspondent, Newsweek, Nairobi, 1973; ABC Radio, Voice of America, UNICEF, Addis Ababa, 1973-74; Newsday, ABC Radio and TV, Cairo, 1974-77; director, Publications & Communications, World Environment Center, NYC, 1978-85; consultant writer/editor, UN Environment Programme, NYC, 1986—. Guest lecturer, American U. Cairo, Columbia U., LIU, Rutgers U., UN Association. Member, Sigma Delta Chi, World-WIDE, Soc. Intl. Development. Office: 521 E 14th St 4F New York NY 10009

BASTIAN, LISA ANN, b. Cin., May 14, 1958; d. Frank Xavier and Elizabeth Ann (Kitt) Steinker; m. Edward Charles Bastian, Nov. 12, 1983; 1 son: Nicholas Francis, b. April 5, 1986, Public relations director Communique Prodns., Ind., Hamilton, OH, 1987—; Account executive Dan Pinger Public Relations Inc., Cincinnati, 1986-87; assistant editor St. Anthony Messenger magazine, 1981-1986; sr. ed. Cincinnati Scene mag., 1985-87; contrbg. ed. The Meeting Mgr. magazine, Dallas, 1985-86; senior ed. Cincinnati Bride & Groom magazine, 1986; pub. relns. coord. Solarcrete Corp., Erlanger, KY, 1980-81; company owner Doubletake Communics., Fairfield, OH, 1984—. BA in English lit., U. Cin., 1980; Scripps-Howard jnlsm. scholarship, 1980; Lee Evans jnlsm. scholarship, 1979. Mem. Cin. Eds. Assn., 1981—; writer/ed. Communique nwsltr., board member, 1985-86. Home: 5633 Valley Forge Dr Fairfield OH 45014

BASU, TAPENDU KUMAR, b. Munger, India, Sept. 7, 1944; came to U.S., 1967; naturalized, 1978; s. Bijoy Gopal and Maya B.; m. Kalpana Royhowdhury, Dec. 7, 1967; children—Anirban, Reshmi. Author: (poems) Me and Mine and Other Nuances, 1986. Wrkg. on short stories, novel, poetry. Intermediate science, Calcutta Univ., 1961; M.D., Calcutta U., 1967. Asst. prof. medicine Loyola U., Maywood, IL, 1973-74; dir. hemodialysis unit St. Mary's Hosp., Kankakee, IL, 1975—. Home 14 Inverness Dr Bourbonnais IL 60914

BATE, WALTER JACKSON, b. Mankato, MN, May 23, 1918; s. William G. and Isabel (Melick) B. Author: Negative Capability, 1939, The Stylistic Development of Keats, 1945, From Classic to Romantic, 1946, Criticism: The Major Texts, 1952, The Achievement of Samuel Johnson, 1955, Prefaces to Criticism, 1959, Writings of Edmund Burke, 1960, John Keats, 1963 (Pulitzer Prize, 1964), Coleridge (1968), The Burden of the Past and the English Poet, 1970, Samuel Johnson, 1977 (Pulitzer Prize 1978, Natl. Book Award 1978, Natl. Book Critics Circle Award 1978); co-editor: Biographia Literaria for the Collected Works of Coleridge, 1982, British and American Poets, 1986. Contrbg. editor: Bollingen edit. of Collected Coleridge, Yale edit. of Johnson. AB, Harvard U., 1939, MA, 1940, PhD, 1942; LHD, Ind. U., 1969, U. Chgo., 1973; LittD, Merrimack Coll., 1970, Boston Coll., 1971, Rutgers U., 1979, Colby Coll., 1979. Mem. faculty English Harvard, 1946—, prof. 1956—, chmn. dept. history and lit., 1955-56, chmn. dept. English, 1956-63, 66-68, Abbott Lawrence Lowell prof. humanities, 1962-79, Kingsley Porter Univ. prof., 1979—. Guggenheim fellow, 1956, 65. Mem. Am. Philo. Soc., Brit. Acad., Am. Acad. Arts and Scis., Phi Beta Kappa (Christian Gauss award lit. history and criticism 1956, 64, 70). Home: Warren Hs Harvard U Cambridge MA 02138

BATES, LAURA MAE, b. New Concord, OH, Dec. 5, 1933; d. Elbert Seward and Evelyn Elfreda (Barr) Williams; m. Everett Earl Bates, June 29, 1952; children—Randall Earl, Jon Seward, Steven Douglas. Contrbr. articles to newspapers; author travel scripts, commls., videos. Wrkg. on ancestral history, portfolio. Grad. public schls., new Concord. Script wrtr. Sta. WILE, Cambridgee, OH, 1952-58, 68-81; freelane wrtr., producer, 1981—. Pres. Ohio Arts & Crafts Fdn., Cambridge, 1983-87 publicity wrtr. Salt Fork Arts Festival, Cambridge, 1971—; bd. dirs., secy. Cambridge Performing Arts Centre, 1982—. Recipient Civic Service award Jr. Chamber of Commerce, Cambridge, 1974; named Person of Yr., Daily Jeffersonian Paper, Cambridge, 1983. Home: 6310 Friendship Dr New Concord OH 43762

BATES, SCOTT, b. Evanston, IL, June 13, 1923, s. Alfred Ricker and Eleanor (Fulcher) B.; m. Phoebe Strehlow, Apr. 17, 1948; children—Robin Ricker, Jonathan Reed, David Scott, Samuel Jackson. Author: Guillaume Apollinaire, 1967, Petit Glossaire des Mots libres d'Apollinaire, 1975, The ABC of Radical Ecology, 1982, Lupo's Fables, 1983; ed.: Poems of War Resistance, 1969, The Ecology Papers, 1970-72; contrbr. poetry and articles to numerous jnls. BA, Carleton Coll., 1947; MA, U. Wis., Madison, 1948, PhD,1954. Prof. French, U. of the South, Sewanee, Tenn., 1954—; prof. film, 1969—. Served as cpl. U.S. Army, 1943-45, ETO. Fulbright scholar, France, 1951-53. Home: Box 1263 Sewanee TN 37375

BATIN, CHRISTOPHER MICHAEL, b. Dayton, OH, June 6, 1955; s. William James and Sara Jane (Rosati) B.; m. Adela Grace Johnson, Nov. 27, 1982. Author: How to Catch Alaska's Trophy Sportfish, 1984, Hunting in Alaska: The Complete Guide, 1986. Alaska ed.: Western Outdoors Mag., The Hunting Report, The Bird Hunting Report; contrbg. author Successful Goose Hunting; outdoor columnist: Anchorage Daily News, Fairbanks Daily News-Miner; contrbr. num. pubns. Stud. U. AK, Anchorage Commun. Coll. Freelance writer, Anchorage, 1976-79; assoc. ed. Alaska Outdoors, Anchorage, 1979, ed., 1979—; ed/pub. Alaska Angler Pubns., Fairbanks, AK, 1984—. Served to SSgt. E/6, USAF, 1973—79. Mem. OWAA, Northwest OWAA, Amer. Soc. Mag. Photogs. Alaska rep. for Intl. Gamefish Assn. Home: Box 82222 Fairbanks AK 99708

BATLIN, ALFRED ROBERT, b. San Francisco, Aug. 24, 1930; s. Philip Alfred and Lavenia Mary (Barnes) B.; m. Diane Elise Giblin, July 4, 1956; children—Lisa, Philippa. BA, Stanford, 1952, MA, 1954. Reporter San Bruno Herald, 1952-53; copy editor, then dept. editor San Francisco News, 1956-59; dept. editor San Francisco News-Call Bull., 1959-65; feature editor San Francisco Examiner, 1965-74, arts editor, 1974-85, asst. style editor, 1985—. Served with AUS, 1954-56. Mem. Sigma Delta Chi. Home: 91 Fairway Dr Daly City CA 94015

BATSON, LARRY FLOYD, b. Aguilar, CO, Feb. 17, 1930; s. Ernest C. and Myrtle Mae (Diskin) B.; m. Laurel A. Larson, Apr. 19, 1951; children—Ernest, William, James. Student, U. Nebr. Reporter, news broadcaster, editor Star Herald, Scottsbluff, Nebr.; asst. mng. editor Omaha World Herald; news and sports editor Mpls. Tribune, columnist, currently natl. correspondent. Contrbr. articles to mags.; works include numerous juvenile books and The Hills Are Theirs, 1978. Served with USAF, 1950. Mem. Sigma Delta Chi. Home: 3501 Buchanan St NE Minneapolis MN 55418

BATT, ALLEN EDWARD, b. Albert Lea, MN, Mar. 16, 1949, s. George Edward and Lucille Edna (Cook) B.; m. Gail Marie Nelson, Sept. 6, 1970; 1 son, Brian Douglas. Contrbr. to newspapers, mags. columnists, comedians, radio and TV personalities, others. Wrkg. on comic strips, novel. Office: Rt 1 Box 56A Hartland MN 56042

BATTEN, FRANK, b. Norfolk, VA, Feb. 11, 1927; s. Frank and Dorothy (Martin) B.; m. Jane Neal Parke; children—Frank, Mary, Dorothy. AB, U. Va., 1950; MBA, Harvard U., 1952. Asst. sec., treas., v.p., dir. Norfolk Newspapers, Inc., 1952-54; chmn. bd., Landmark Communications, Inc., 1966—; pub. Norfolk Virginian-Pilot, Norfolk Ledger-Dispatch, 1954—, Portsmouth Star, 1954—; chmn. Greensboro (N.C.) Daily News, Greensboro Record, 1965—, WTAR Radio-TV Corp., 1966—, Roanoke Times and World-News, Tele Cable Corp., Landmark Community Newspapers, Inc.; vice chmn. AP, 1977-82, chmn., 1982-87, Newspaper Advt. Bur., 1972-74. Vice-chmn. State Council Higher Edn. for Va., from 1977; chmn. bd. Old Dominion U., 1962-70; trustee, pres. Norfolk Acad.; trustee Hollins Coll., 1969-75. Office: 150 W Brambleton Ave Norfolk VA 23510

BATTEN, JAMES KNOX, b. Suffolk, VA, Jan. 11, 1936; s. Eugene Taylor and Josephine (Winslow) B.; m. Jane Elaine Trueworthy, Feb. 22, 1958; children—Mark Winslow, Laura Taylor, Taylor Edison. BS, Davidson Coll., 1957; M. Pub. Affairs, Princeton, 1962. Reporter Charlotte (N.C.) Observer, 1957-58, 62-65; corr. Washington bur. Knight Newspapers, 1965-70; editorial staff Detroit Free Press, 1970-72; exec. editor Charlotte (N.C.) Observer, 1972-75; v.p. Knight-Ridder Newspapers, Inc., Miami, Fla., 1957-80, sr. v.p., 1980-82, pres., 1982—; dir. AP. Trustee Davidson Coll., U. of Miami. Served with AUS, 1958-60. Recipient George Polk Meml. award for regional reporting, 1968; Sidney Hillman Fdn. award, 1968. Office: One Herald Plaza Miami FL 33101

BATTIN, WENDY J., b. Wilmington, DE, May 27, 1953, d. Harry E. and Mary V. (McGovern) Battin. Author: In the Solar Wind, 1984; contrbr. poetry to: Ga. Rvw, Tendril, Poetry Northwest, Epoch, numerous other periodicals; contrbr. to New Voices 1979-83, Extended Outlooks: The Iowa Rvw Collection of Contemporary Women Wrtrs., other anthologies. BA, Cornell U., 1975; MA in Creative Writing, U. Wash., 1981. Lectr. Suffolk U., Boston, 1984, Boston U., 1984—. Fine Arts Work Center fellow, Provincetown, Mass., 1976-78. Mem. AWP, New Eng. Wrtrs. for Survival. Office: Dept Engl Boston U Boston MA 02215

BATTLE, JEAN ALLEN, b. Talladega, AL, June 15, 1914; s. William Raines and Lemerle McLemore (Allen) B.; m. Lucy Troxell, Aug. 25, 1940; 1 dau., Helen Carol Battle Salmon. Author: Culture and Education for the Contemporary World, 1969, (with others) The New Idea in Education, 1974, Choices for an Intelligent and Humane School and Society, 1981, Education: The Fate of Humanity, 1982, rev. ed., 1983. Student, Birmingham So. Coll.; BS, Middle Tenn. State U.; MA, U. Ala.; EdD, U. Fla; postgrad., Oxford U. Dept. chmn., dean students Fla. So. Coll., dean coll.; dean Coll. Edn. U. South Fla., Tampa, currently prof. higher edn.; guest lectr. Rewley House, Oxford U., Oxford, Eng.; editor, pub. Tenn. Valley News; mem. Fla. Tchrs. Edn. Adv. Council, Fla. Continuing Edn. Council; mem. courses study com. Fla. Bd. Edn.; mem. Tampa Bay Com. on Fgn. Affairs; adv. com. Hillsborough County Hosp.; bd. dirs. Fla. Univ. System Honduras Program, World Trade Council, Tampa, Poynter Fdn., St. Petersburg, Fla., Harold Benjamin Fdn. U. Md.; bd. dirs., v.p. Southeastern Edn. Lab., Atlanta. Served to capt. USAAF. Recipient Disting. Service awards Fla. So. Coll., Fla. Citizenship Clearing House; Outstanding Alumnus award Middle Tenn. State U., Murfreesboro, Tenn. Mem. SAR, Fla. Hist. Soc., NEA, Fla. Edn. Assn. (co-chmn. tchr. recruitment com.), Tampa C. of C. (edn. com.), Acad. Polit. Sci., Omicron Delta Kappa, Pi Gamma Mu, Kappa Delta Pi, Phi Delta Kappa, Sigma Alpha Epsilon. Home: 11011 Carrollwood Dr Tampa FL 33618

BATTLE, WILLIAM ROBERT, b. Nolensville, TN, Dec. 25, 1927; s. william Robert and Cleo (Smith, B.; m. Elizabeth Qgilvie, Dec. 23, 1948; children—Valerie Elizabeth, William Robert III. Student, George Pea-body Coll., 1946-49. With Nashville Banner, 1943—, police beat, county polit. beat, 1943-53, city editor 1953-64, mng. editor, 1964-71, exec. editor, 1971-75, asst. to editor, 1975-78, regional editor, 1978-80, sr. editor, 1980-84, vp, bus. ed., 1984—. movie columnist, 1955-72; editor Hurst Constrn. News; corr. Natl. Enquirer, Lantana, Fla.; staff writer Country Style mag.; bd. dirs. Women's Execs. Intl. Appeared as newspaperman in film, Teacher's Pet, 1957, also in country music on Broadway, 1963; contrbr. numerous artic- to nat. publs. Home: 4108 Crestridge Dr Nashville TN 37204

BATTLES, BRIAN JAMES, b. Hartford, CT, Dec. 16, 1957; s. Carroll Victor Battles and Ruth Constance (Robert) Lombardo; m. Stephanie Jean Haynes, July 18, 1981;children—Ian, Jillian. Contrbg. ed.: Modern Recording and Music Mag., 1984-86, dB—The Sound Engineering Mag., 1985—; disc jockey various stations, 1975—. Student U. Conn., 1975-78. Marketing dir. Royal Ice Cream Co., Manchester, CT, 1985; mgr. natl. sales Sun Hill Corp., Manchester, 1985-86; mgr. audio production Careertrack, Boulder, CO, 1986—. Recipient Boli award Long Island Advt. Club, 1981, Big Apple award Intl. Radio Festival of N.Y., 1982, Clio award, 1982, NYMRAD, N.Y. Market Radio Advt. Bur., 1983. Mem. Audio Engineering soc.; amateur radio technicien WA1YUA. Home: 2160 Spencer St Longmont CO 80501

BATTLES, (ROXY) EDITH, b. Spokane, WA, Mar. 29, 1921, d. Rosco Jiriah and Lucile Zilpha (Jacques) Baker; m. Willis Ralph Dawe Battles, May 2, 1941; children—Margaret Elizabeth Battles Holmes, Ralph Willis, Lara Lucile. Author: Over the Rickety Fence, 1967, The Terrible Trick or Treat, 1970, 501 Balloons Sail East (Natl. Sci. selection), 1971, The Terrible Terrier (Jr. Lit. Guild selection), 1972, One to Teeter Totter (also pub. in Danish, Swedish, German), 1973, Eddie Couldn't Find the Elephants, 1974, What Does the Rooster Say, Yoshio? (UN featured book), 1978, The Secret of Castle Drai, 1980, The Witch in Room 6, 1987. Wrkg. on children's novel series. BA, Calif. U.-Long Beach, 1958; MA, Pepperdine U., 1976. Tchr. Torrance (Calif.) Unified Schls., 1959—; extension instr. Pepperdine U., Los Angeles, 1975-80. Mem. SW Manuscripters, Surfwrtrs. Home: 560 S Helberta Ave Redondo Beach CA 90277

BATY, VICKI LOUISE, b. Ottumwa, IA, Feb. 24, 1948; d. Don K. and Normagene L. (Mellott) Robertson; m. James R. Baty, Oct. 10, 1966 children—James R., John R. Columnist: (newspaper) The New Girl on the Block, Moravia Union, Moulton Tribune, 1983—. Contrbr. news articles, editorials to newspapes. Ed., pub.: Moravia Union, IA, 1983—, Moulton Tribune, IA, 1983—. Bd. dirs. Moravia Arts Council, 1985—; active Appanoose County Emergency Med. Services Council, Centerville, IA, 1985—. Mem Iowa Newspaper Assn. Home: RR 2 Moravia IA 52571

BAUER, MALCOLM CLAIR, b. Enterprise, OR, Mar. 19, 1914; s. John Jacob and Lucile (Corkins) B.; m. Roberta Moody, July 11, 1937; children—Bette-B, Mary, Kent, Roberta Jean. Author: Profile of Oregon, 1971. BS, U. Oreg., 1935; Nieman fellow, Harvard, 1950-51; Journalism fellow, Stanford U., 1968. News editor Eugene (Oreg.) Register Guard, 1935-36; news editor Pendleton East-Oregonian, 1936; with The Oregonian, Portland, 1936—, city editor, 1941-51, assoc. editor, 1951—, book editor, 1951—, editor editorial page, 1977-79 (ret. 1979); lectr. journalism Portland State College, 1956—. Served from 1st lt. to col. AUS, World War II. Decorated Bronze Star medal, Legion of Merit with oak leaf cluster Order Brit. Empire. Mem. Am. Soc. Newspaper Editors, Oreg. Hist. Soc. (past pres.), Phi Delta Phi, Phi Beta Kappa, Phi Delta Theta. Home: 1641 SW Englewood Dr Lake Oswego OR 97034

BAUER, STEVEN ALBERT, b. Newark, Sept. 10, 1948; s. Albert Henry and Alice Marian (Horrocks) B.; m. Bonnie Smolen, July 26, 1977 (div. Sept. 1981); m. 2d, Elizabeth Arthur, June 19, 1982. Author: (novel) Satyrday, 1980; The River, 1985; stories from teleplays for TV series Amazing Stories, 1986; contrbr. poetry to Ascent, Mass., Seattle, N.Am., Chariton, Chgo. rvws., Poetry Now, Denver Qtly, Prairie Schooner, MSS. BA in English, Trinity Coll., Hartford, Conn., 1970; MFA in English, U. Mass., 1975. Instr. Colby Coll., Waterville, Maine, 1979-81, asst. prof., 1981-82; asst. prof. English, Miami U., Oxford, Ohio, 1982-86, assoc. prof., 1986—. Fellow Mass. Council on Arts and Humanities, 1978, Bread Loaf Wrtrs.' Conf., 1981, Ossabaw Island Project, 1982. Mem. AWP, PSA, P&W. Home: 14100 Harmony Rd Bath IN 47010

BAUER-PATITZ, D., see Patitz, Dolores R.

BAUGHMAN, DOROTHY, b. Prattville, AL, July 13, 1940; d. Charles Ross and Thelma Florine (Cooper) McCartney; m. James Baughman, Apr. 22, 1960; children—Jimmy, Vicki, Toni. Author: Piney's Summer, 1976; (Gothic mysteries) Ghost of Aronov Point, 1979, Secret of Montoya Misson, 1980, Icy Terror, 1982, Secret Wishes, Secret Flars, 1987. Contribr. short stories to children's mags. including Highlights for Children, Jr. Discoveries, others articles to mags. including Women's Circle, Cappe's Weekly, True Story, others. Wrkg. on mystery and Civil wr novels. Grad. public schls., Eclectic, AL. Laboratory se. Elmore County Hosp., Wetumpka, AL, 1986—. Councilwoman, Eclectic, 1976-80. Home: Box 176 Eclectic AL 36024

BAUGHMAN, J. ROSS, b. Dearborn, MI, May 7, 1953; s. Charles T. and Patricia Jane (Hill) B. BA cum laude, Kent State U., 1975. Staff photographer, writer Lorain (Ohio) Jnl, 1975-77; contract photographer, writer AP in Africa and Middle East, 1977-78; co-founder Ind. Visions Internat., Inc., 1978; pres. Visions Photo Group, NYC, 1978—; mem. faculty New Schl. for Social Research, NYC, 1979—, NYU, 1980-82; co-founder, program dir. Focus Photography Symposiums, NYC, 1981; adj. prof. U. Mo. Grad. Program in Journalism, NYC, 1984—. Recipient Pulitzer prize in journalism for feature photography 1978. Author: Graven Images: a thematic portfolio, 1976, Forbidden Images: a secret portfolio, 1977. Mem. Natl. Press Photographers Assn., Photographers Gallery, Am. Soc. Mag. Photographers (sustaining 1984—), Sigma Delta Chi. Office: 105 Fifth Ave New York NY 10003

BAUMAN, GEORGE DUNCAN, b. Humboldt, IA, Apr. 12, 1912; s. Peter William and Mae (Duncan) B.; m. Nora Kathleen Kelly, May 21, 1938. Student, Loyola U., Chgo., 1930-35; JD, Washington U., St. Louis, 1948; LittD (hon.), Central Meth. Coll.; LLD (hon.), Maryville Coll.; LHD (hon.) Mo. Valley Coll., 1981, St. Louis Rabbinical Coll., 1981. Reporter, Chgo. Herald Examiner, 1931-39; archtl. rep. Pratt & Lambert, Inc., St. Louis, 1939-43; reporter, rewriter, asst. city editor St. Louis Globe-Democrat, 1943-51, personnel mgr., 1951-59, bus. mgr., 1959-67, pub., 1967-84. Home: 37 Conway Close Rd St Louis MO 63124

BAUMBACH, JONATHAN, b. NYC, July 5, 1933; s. Harold M. and Ida Helen (Zackheim) B.; m. Georgia Anne Brown, June 14, 1968; children—David, Nina, Noah, Nicholas. Author: The Landscape of Nightmare, 1965, A Man to Conjure With, 1965, What Comes Next, 1968, Reruns, 1974, Babble, 1976, The Return of Service, 1979, Chez Charlotte and Emily, 1979, My Father More or Less, 1982, The Life and Times of Major Fiction, 1986. Editor: Writers as Teachers, 1970, (with others) Moderns and Contemporaries, 1965, Statements 2, 1977. Film critic: Partisan Rvw, 1974. AB, Brooklyn Coll., 1955, MFA, Columbia U., 1956; PhD, Stanford U., 1961. Asst. prof. English Ohio State U., 1961-64; asst. prof. N.Y.U., 1964-66; Bklyn. Coll., CUNY, 1966-69, assoc. prof., 1970-72, prof., 1972—, dir. MFA in creative writing, 1974—; vis. prof. Tufts U., 1969-70, U. Wash.,

1978-84. Recipient Young Writers Award, 1961; Woodrow Wilson fellow, 1961; NEA fellow, 1968; Guggenheim fellow, 1978-79, Ingram Merrill, 1984-85. Mem. PEN, Natl. Soc. Film Critics, Fiction Collective. Office: Dept Eng Brooklyn College Brooklyn NY 11210

BAUMGARTNER, DANIEL BENTON, b. Mt. Pleasant, MI, Jan. 5, 1944; s. Luther Leroy and Elizabeth Benton B; m. Billie Dawn Spies, Sept. 8, 1966; 1 dau, Jessica Taylor. Author: The Park Ave. Money Diet, 1983 (paper, 1984). BA, Tex Lutheran Coll, 1965; M Music, U. So. Calif., 1971. Music tchr. Punahou High Schl., Honolulu, 1971-72, Quartz Hill High Schl., Lancaster, Calif., 1972-74; realtor Coldwell Banker, Lancaster, 1974—. State dir., Calif. Assn. Realtors, Lancaster, 1977, 78, 81-84; secy. Antelope Valley Bd. Realtors, 1981, vice pres., 1982, pres., 1983, ombudsman, 1986, 87. Mem. Natl. Assn. Realtors. Address: 41514 Mission Dr Palmdale CA 93551

BAUSCH, RICHARD CARL, b. Ft. Benning, GA, Apr. 18, 1945; s. Robert Carl and Helen Louise (Simmons) Bausch; m. Karen Sue Miller, May 3, 1969; children—Wesley, Emily, Paul. Author novels: Real Presence, 1980, Take Me Back, 1981, The Last Good Time, 1984, Spirits, and Other Stories, 1987; contrbr. stories The Atlantic Monthly, Ploughshare, Numen, New Writing from the South. BA, George Mason U., 1974; MFA, Univ. Iowa, 1975. Lectr. George Mason Univ, Fairfax, Va, 1975-78, asst. prof., 1980-85, assoc. prof., 1986—. Grantee, NEA, 1982; Guggenheim fellow, 1984. Mem AWP. Address: 4428 Naoma Ct Fairfax VA 22030

BAVOTA, MICHAEL FRANCIS, (Michael Ryan), b. Balt., Feb. 16, 1952; s. Roland P. and Thelma (Baier) B.; m. Elizabeth Anne Lindblade, July 21, 1973; 1 son, Ryan. Contrbr. articles, short stories to mags. including Hudson Valley Mag., Our Family, Coins, New Eng. Grocery. Corp. perishable sector mgr., Carrefour (USA) Secacus, NJ, 1987—. Recipient Cert. of Achievement for short story, Writer's Digest, 1983. Home: 2432 Steiner Rd Lakehurst NJ 08733

BAYARD, JEAN, b. Chgo., Aug. 21, 1923, d. Gerhardus James and Elsa (Post) Holwerda; m. Robert T. Bayard, Feb. 25, 1945; children—Dona, David, Bernard, Thomas, Lynda. Author: How to Deal with Your Acting-Up Teenager, 1981, Attachment: Toward the Liberation of the Essential Person, 1985. Wrkg. on book for peace workers. PhD, U. Pitts., 1955. Staff psychologist U. Pitts. Med. Schl., Staunton Clinic, 1965-75; pvt. practice clin. psychologist, Santa Clara, Calif., 1975—. Home: 10120 Crescent Dr Cupertino CA 95014

BAYER, CARY STUART, b. NYC,May 22, 1953; s. Samuel and Lillian (Ehrlich) Bayer. Author: The Short Report: Good News for Guys 5'7'' & Under (with Bob Levine), 1983, Fire Island Fried (With Robert Romagnoli), 1985. BA in English, SUNY at Buffalo, 1975. Pub. Rel. Manag. Doyle Dane Bernbach, New York, NY, 1980-83; Ed/Pub. Fire Island Snooze, (NY), 1984, 1985; Pres. Bayer Comm., New York, NY, 1983—. Home: 59 W 12th Street New York NY 10011

BAYES, RONALD HOMER, b. Freewater, OR, Jul. 19, 1932; s. Floyd Edgar and Mildren (Cochran) Bayes. Poet: collections include—The Casketmaker, 1972, Tokyo Annex, 1977, Fram, 1979, A Beast in View, 1985. BS, East Oregon State Coll., 1955, MS, 1956; ABD, U. of Penn, 1960. Assoc. prof., English, East Oregon State Coll (LaGrande) 1955-56, 1960-66, 1967-68; lecturer, English, U. of Maryland (Col. Park) 1958-59, 1966-67; prof, English, St. Andrews Coll. (Laurinburg, NC) 1968—. Chmn. Scotland Co. (NC) GOP, 1984-85; Vice Chmn. Anderson for Pres. Com., 1980. Corp., US Army, 1956-58, Iceland. Woodrow Wilson Fellow, 1960. Mem. PEN, PSA. Home: Box 206 Laurinburg NC 28352

BAYLER, LAVON ANN BURRICHTER, b. Sandusky, OH, Jan. 17, 1933; d. Emil John and Elsie Lydia (Dickel) Burrichter; m. Robert L. Bayler, June 26, 1958 children—David Allen, Jonathan Robert, Timothy Norris. Author: Fresh Winds of the Spirit, 1986, Whispers of God, 1987. Contrbr. to Bread for the Journey, 1982, Flames of the Spirit, 1985. Wrkg. on book. B.A., Iowa State Tchrs. Coll., 1955; M.Div., Eden Theol. Seminary, 1959. Pastorates in Ohio and Illinois, 1959-72; Pastor First United Church of Christ, Carpentersville, IL, 1973-79; area conf. miniter Ill. Conf. United Church of Christ, DeKalb, 1979—. Mem. Profl. Assn. Clergy (officer). Home: 2251 Tara Dr Elgin IL 60123

BAYLOR, MURRAY, b. What Cheer, IA, Apr. 8, 1913; s. John Thomas and Elizabeth (Murray) B.; m. Elisabeth Anne Barbou, Sept. 1, 1937; children—Denis A. Michael G., Stephen M. Ed.: Scriabin: Selected Works for the Piano, 1974, Satie: Three Gymnopedies and Three Gnossiennes, 1985, Rachmaninoff: Selected Works for the Piano, 1985, Rachmaninoff: Fantasy Pieces, op. 3, 1986, Schubert: Moments Musicaux, op. 94, 1987, Schubert: Impromptus, op. 90, 1987, Schubert: Impromptus, op. 142, 1987. Wrkg. on Rachmaninoff: 10 Preludes, op. 23 and 13 Preludes, op. 32; Prokofieff: Visions Fugitives. B.A., U. Iowa, 1934, M.A., 1936, Ph.D., 1950. Prof. musi Knox Coll., Galesburg, IL, 1942-80. Mem. Phi Beta Kappa, Pi Kappa Lambda. Home 1187 N Cherry St Galesburg IL 61401

BAXTER, KAREN GRIMSLEY, b. Dothan, AL, Oct. 9, 1949; d. George Harold Grimsley; m. Terrance Moran Baxter III, Aug. 18, 1968; children—Ted, Brent, Kay. Poetry in anthologies, So. Poetry Rvw. BS in Edn., then postgrad., Troy State U. Tchr. elem. schls. Headland, Ala., 1972-73, Columbia, Ala., 1973-74; tchr. Abbeville (Ala.) Christian Acad., 1980-86; tchr. 2d grade, Columbia, Ala. Home: Rt 1 Box 62 Columbia AL 36319

BAXTER, MICHAEL JOHN, b. Terre Haute, IN, July 5, 1944; s. Victor LeRoy an Wilda Ione (Davis) B.; m. Joanne Kay Stohlman, July 5, 1966⇆ildren—Bradley Scott, Jeffrey John, Michael Vitor Martin, Matthew John. BA, U. Nebr., 1967. Reporter Lincoln (Nebr.)Evening Jnl, 1962-68; staff wrtr. Tropic mag.,1969; reporter Miami (Fla.) Herald, 1968, 70-76, city editor, 1976-80, dep. mng. editor, 1981—85. Served with USAR, 1967. Recipient George Polk Meml. award L.I.U., 1973, A.P. Mng. Editors' Pub. Service award, 1974; Investigative Reporting award Fla. Soc. Newspaper Editors, 1974; Pub. Servie award, 1974; Distinguished Achievement award U. Nebr., 1975; Distinguished Journalist award, 1975. Mem. Kappa Tau Alpha. Home 13631 SW 103d Ave Miami FL 33176

BAYS, EDRIE HILL, b. Bedford, VA, Mar. 3, 1949; d. Hill Goodman and Elizabeth Edrie (Craghead) Bays; m. Jack Anderson Holland, Feb. 14, 1981. Contrbr. articles to profl. jnls., newspapers, poetry in Artem is. B.A., Longwood Coll., 1971; M.A. in Liberal Studies, Hollins Coll., 1984. Tchr. Cave Spring High Schl., Roanoke, VA, 1971—. Bd. dirs., copy ed. Artemis, 1983—, elimination judge poetry contest, 1984—. Mem. NCTE, Va. Assn. Tchrs. English (Service award 1985), Tchrs. Wrtrs. Collaborative, AAP, AWP. Home: 1889 Richland Hills Dr Salem VA 24153

BEAGLE, PETER SOYER, b. NYC, Apr. 20, 1939; s. Simon and Rebecca (Soyer) B.; m. Enid Nordeen, May 8, 1964 (div. 1980); children—Vicky Lynn, Kalisa, Daniel Nordeen. Author: A Fine and Private Place, 1960, I See By My Outfit, 1965, The Last Unicorn, 1968, The California Feeling, 1969, (with Pat Derby) The Lady and Her Tiger, 1976, The Fantasy Worlds of Peter Beagle, 1978, The Garden of Earthly Delights, 1982, The Folk of the Air, 1987; screenwriter: The Dove, 1974, The Greatest Thing That Almost Happened, 1977, The Lord of the Rings: Part One, 1978, The Last Unicorn, 1982; freelance writer for: Ladies Home Jnl, Saturday Evening Post, Holiday, others. BA, U. Pitts., 1959; student Stanford U., 1960-61. Vice chmn. Santa Cruz chapt. ACLU, 1968-69. Home: 5517 Crystal Springs Dr NE Bainbridge Island WA 98110

BEAL, WINNONA MARIE, (Wyn), b. Thayer, KS, Mar. 5, 1938, d. Earle Cecil and Marie Helen (Witty) Lander; children—Julie, Paige. Contrbr. poetry to Our World's Most Beloved Poems, 1984. Student Emporia State Coll., 1956-57. Office coordinator Ozark Guidance Center, Bentonville, Ark., 1984—. Recipient Golden Poet award World of Poetry, 1985, Silver Poet award, 1986. Home: 925 S 26th St Rogers AR 72756

BEALE, IRENE ALLEMAN, b. Pitts., Sept. 3, 1920, d. Dudley and Irene (Simpson) Alleman; m. Richard Alden Beale, Sept. 2, 1960; children—Jane, Martha. Author: William P. Letchworth: A Man for Others, 1982, Genesee Valley People 1743-1962, 1983, Genesee Valley Women 1743-1985, 1985, Genessee Valley Events, 1668-1986, 1986. Wrkg. on Genesee Valley history. BA, Wheaton Coll., Norton, Mass., 1942; MA, Union Theol. Sem. NYC,1956. Wrtr., pub. Chestnut Hill Press, Geneseo, 1977—. Home: 5320 Groveland Rd Geneseo NY 14454

BEAMAN, JOYCE PROCTOR, b. Wilson, NC, Apr. 27, 1931; d. Jesse David and Pauline P.; m. Robert H. Beaman, Aug. 17, 1952; 1 son, Robert David. Author: Broken Acres, 1971, All For The Love of Cassie, 1973, Bloom Where You Are Planted, 1975, You Are Beautiful: You Really Are, 1981. BS, East Carolina U., 1951, MA, 1952. English, French tchr. Snow Hill, NC, 1953-60, Saratoga, NC, 1960-78; librarian Elm City (NC) Middle School, 1978-82; retired, 1982—. Terry Sanford Award, NCAE, Raleigh, NC, 1977. Mem. NEA, Delta Kappa Gamma, Kappa Delta Pi. Home: Rt 2 Box 424 Walstonburg NC 27888

BEAR, (CLARA) ANN, (The Mama Bear), b. Piedmont, OH, Jan. 18, 1937; d. John William and Ila Virginia (Cash) Brokaw; m. Glenn Heywood Bear, July 7, 1954; children—Debra, Rick, Pat, Teddy, Tim, Kim, Jim, Annette. Author: Hitch in Hell—Hitch in Hell, 1967. Contrbr. articles, poetry, songs (words and music) to mags., newspapers. Grad. public schls., Freeport, OH. Reporter, The Freeport Press, 1957-70, The Times-Reporter, New Philadelphia, OH, 1961-74, Daily Jeffersonina, Cambridge, OH, 1961-74, Leader, Martins Ferry, OH, 1964-74, Harrison News-Herald, Cadiz, OH, 1970-74; computer typesetter, proofreader Freeport Press, 1973-85. Home: 109 Main St Freeport OH 49373

BEAR, , see Hayes, James Russell

BEAR, G., see Wall, Thomas J.

BEAR, SUN, b. White Earth Reservation, MN, Aug 31, 1929. Author: At Home in the Wilderness, 1968; Buffalo Hearts, 1970; The Bear Tribe's Self-Reliance Book, 1978; The Medicine Wheel; Earth Astrology, 1980; Sun Bear: The Path of Power, 1983. Founder and pres. Bear Tribe Medicine Soc., 1970—; tchr. and curriculum dev. Tecumseh Indian Studies program Univ. Calif., Davis; tech. cons. tv and films, Hollywood, Calif.; community action with Indian community, Reno, Nev. Address: Box 9167 Spokane WA 99209

BEAR, THE MAMA, see Bear, Clara Ann

BEASLEY, CONGER, JR., b. St. Joseph, MO, Aug. 21, 1940; s. Conger and Ardus (Albrecht) B.; m. Elizabeth M (McCoy), June 18, 1966; children—Ardus, Tony. Author: (novel) Hidalgo's Beard: A California Fantasy, 1979, The Ptomaine Kid: A Hamburger Western, 1981; (poems) Over DeSoto's Bones, 1979, Looking Up from the Bottom of the World, 1986; (stories) My Manhattan, 1986. Editor: The Hermitage Journals of John Howard Griffin, 1981, Missouri Short Fiction, 1985. BA, Columbia U., 1962; MA, NYU, 1964. Ed. Universal Press Syndicate, Kansas City, Mo., 1970-82. Home: 5900 Ward Pkwy Kansas City MO 64113

BEASON, ROBERT GAYLE, b. Prescott, KS, May 21, 1927; s. Henry M. and Ruth (Herman) B.; m. Sylvia Elizabeth Toulouse, Nov. 18, 1950; 1 son, Drew. Author: Hanging On (novel), 1984. Student, U. Nebr., 1945-46; BJ, U. Mo., 1949, BA, 1950. News editor Rolla (Mo.) Daily Herald, 1950; sports editor Moberly (Mo.) Monitor-Index, 1950-51; reporter, then copy editor Kansas City Star, 1951-54; promotion editor, then asst. editor Mechanix Illus. mag., 1955-60; editor Electronics Illus. mag., 1960-63, Mechanix Illus. and Electronics Illus. mags. (mags. merged to Mechanix Illus. 1972), NYC, 1963-79; freelance writer, editor, 1980—; adj. lectr. creative wrtg., U. of Ct. at Stamford, 1985. Served with USNR, 1945-46. Mem. Electronics Press Club (pres. 1965-67), Inst. High Fidelity (pubs. com.), Intl. Motor Press Assn. (pres. 1977-78), ASME, Tau Kappa Epsilon, Sigma Delta Chi. Home: Chestnut Hill Rd Stamford CT 06903

BEATTIE, ANN, b. Washington, Sept. 8, 1947; d. James and Charlotte (Crosby) B. Author: Chilly Scenes of Winter, 1976, Distortions, 1976, Secrets and Surprises, 1979, Falling In Place, 1980, Jacklighting, 1981, The Burning House, 1982, Love Always, 1985. BA, Am. U., 1969; MA, U. Conn., 1970. Vist. asst. prof., U. Va., Charlottesville, 1976-77; vis. writer, 1980; Briggs Copeland lectr. English Harvard U., 1977. Recipient Distinguished Alumnae award Am. U., 1980, award in lit. AAIAL, 1980; Guggenheim fellow, 1977. Mem. PEN, AG. Office: c/o Lynn Nesbit 40 W 57 New York NY 10019

BEATTIE, MELODY LYNN, b. St. Paul, May 26, 1948; d. Jean Harold and Izetta Bernice (Lee) Vaillancourt; m. David Anthony Beattie, Dec. 19, 1976 (div. June 1986); children—John Steven Thurik, Nichole Marie Beattie, Shane Anthony Beattie. Author: (with Carolyn Owens) A Promise of Sanity, 1982, Denial, 1985, Codependent No More, 1986, Crack, the Facts, 1987, 5 audio tapes, 1987; 1987 member Minn. media delegation touring Minn. Natl. Guard activities in Central America; contrbr. 200-plus feature/news articles to nwsprs., mags. Stud. pub./pvt. schls., Mpls./St. Paul. Legal secy., Mpls., 1970-74; chem. dep. cslr./admin., Mpls., 1974-79, 81-85; freelance writer, Mpls. & Stillwater, MN, 1979—. Sherwood E. Wirt award for excell. in writing, Billy Graham Evang. Assn., 1981. Address: 615 Nightingale Blvd Stillwater MN 55082

BEATTY, JACK J., . Cambridge, MA, May 15, 1945; s. John J. and Frances C. (Parks) B.; m. Lois Masor, Sept. 3, 1976; 1 son, Aaron. Lit. editor The New Republic, Washington, 1978-83; sr. editor The Atlantic, Boston, 1983—. Poynter fellow, Yale U., 1980. Mem. Natl. Book Critics Circle. Home: 25 Bowker St Brookline MA 02146

BEATTY, PATRICIA JEAN, b. Portland, OR, Aug. 26; d. Walter Marcus and Jessie Pauline (Miller) Robbins; m. Carl G. Uhr, July 31, 1977; 1 dau. by previous marriage, Ann Alexandra Beatty Weiner. Author: (with John Louis Beatty) At the Seven Stars, 1965, Campion Towers, 1966, (with others) Who Comes to King's Mountain, 1975, Hail Columbia, 1970, A Long Way to Whiskey Creek, 1971, Red Rock Over the River, 1973, Something to Shout About, 1976, By Crumbs, It's Mine, 1976, I Want My Sunday, Stranger, 1977, Wait for Me, Eula Bee, 1978, Lacy Makes a Match, 1979, That's One Ornery Orphan, 1980, Lupita Manana, 1981, Eight Mules From Monterey, 1982, Jonathan Down Under, 1982, Melinda Takes a Hand, 1983, Turn Homeward, Hannalee, 1984, The Coach That Never Came, 1985. BA, Reed Coll., 1944. Tchr. English and history Coeur d'Alene (Idaho) High Schl., 1947-50; librarian Dupont Co., Wilmington, Del., 1952-53; mem. library staff Riverside (Calif.) Public Library, 1953-57; tchr. creative writing UCLA, 1968-69, U. Calif., Riverside, 1967-68. Recipient 9 awards for books. Mem. Soc. Children's Book Writers. Home and Office: 5085 Rockledge Dr Riverside CA 92506

BEAUDET, EUGENE (GENE) CHARLES, b. NYC., June 24, 1924, s. Raymond Julius and Anastasia Florence (Powell) B.; m. Elinor Ruth Mutke, Aug. 25, 1948; children—Christine Anne Beaudet McGovern, Patricia, Elizabeth J. Beaudet Gates. BA in Social Sci., St. John's Coll. Iron Age mag., Radnor, Pa., ed., 1963-68, ed.-in-chief, 1968-87, assoc. pub., Metalworking News, 1987—; contrbr. to Encyc. Britannica. Recipient awards Am. Bus. Pubs., 1964-76. Mem. Washington Press Club Home: 975 Mill Rd Bryn Mawr PA 19010

BEAUFORD, FRED, b. Neptune, NJ, Nov. 11, 1940; s. Robert Beauford and Louise (Morton) Scott; m. Dorenda Jophes, Feb. 14, 1960 (div. Mar. 1, 1973); m. 2d, Cindy Martinez, Nov. 11, 1977; children—Danielle, Fred, Tama, Alexis. BS, NYU, 1971. Ed./fdr.Black Creation, NYC, 1969-73; ed./pub. Neworld Mag., Los Angeles, 1973-83; ed. Crisis Mag., NYC, 1984—. Served to PFC, US Army, 1958-60. Home: 1290 Grove St 501 San Francisco CA 94117

BEAUFORT, JOHN DAVID, b. Edmonton, Alta., Can., Sept. 23, 1912; came to U.S., 1922, naturalized, 1943; s. Ernest and Margaret Mary (Crawley) B.; m. Francesca Bruning, June 28, 1940. Author: 505 Theatre Questions Your Friends Can't Answer, 1982. Student, Boston U., 1930-33, 35-39, Rollins Coll., 1933-35. With Christian Science Monitor, Boston, 1930-33, 35—, asst. reviewer, 1937-39, NYC drama and film critic, 1939-43, war corr. for Pacific, 1943-46, chief NYC news bur., 1946-50, arts and mag. editor, 1950-51, NYC drama and film critic, 1951-58, 59-61, arts-entertainment editor, 1959-61, chief London bur., 1962-65, feature editor, Boston, 1965-70, NYC drama critic, 1971-74, contrbg. drama critic, feature writer, 1975—. Recipient Critics award Dirs.Guild Am., 1961. Mem. NY Drama Critics Circle. Am. Theatre Critics Assn., New Drama Forum Assn., Critics Circle of London (hon.), Natl. Theatre Conf. (hon.). Home: 424 E 52d St New York NY 10022

BEAUREGARD-BEZOU, MARION JOSEPH, b. New Orleans, Aug. 6, 1914; s. Andrew Ralph and Lydia Marie (Bouligny) Bezou; m. Alexandra Kay, June 1949. Contrbr. poetry to Kaleidoscope, numerous periodicals and anthology. BA, Wayne State U., 1949, MA, 1952, Edn. Splty., 1964. Art tchr. Detroit Public Schs., 1949-81; instr. U. Detroit, 1950-53, Wayne County Community Coll., 1970-80, Detroit Coll. Bus., 1966-80; art instr. Crystal Lake Art Center, Frankfort, Mich., 1982—. Founding mem., past pres. Benzie Area Arts Council, Frankfort. Fellow Intl. Acad. Poets. Home: Box 183 Elberta MI 49628

BECHER, PAUL RONALD, b. Columbus, OH, Oct. 16, 1934; s. Charles Cleveland and G. Irene (Smith) B.; m. Leitsa Pauline Katsampes, Aug. 8, 1965; children—Lori Sue, Lynne Marie. BFA, Ohio State U., 1956. Textbook salesman Charles E. Merrill Pub. Co., Columbus, 1960-61, product mgr. bus. and econ. series, 1962-67, mgr. book prodn., 1967-69, editor-in-chief coll. div., 1970, dir. coll. div., 1971-72, exec. v.p. pub., 1973—. Mem. adv. bd.: Personnel Mgmt. Abstracts Jnl, 1964—. Mem. adv. bd. Friends Ohio State U. Libraries, 1976—. Served to 1st lt. USAF, 1957-59. Mem. Assn. Am. Pubs., Sigma Chi. Home: 2080 Cheshire Rd Columbus OH 43221

BECK, ALAN M(ARSHALL), b. Bklyn, Aug. 15, 1942; s. Manny and Esther (Stettin) B.; m. Carol Rosenblum, July 23, 1967 (div. 1979); children: Gillian Emily, Andrea Carey. Author: contrbr M. W. Fox, ed, Ecology and Social Behavior of Canids, 1972, The Ecology of Stray Dogs: A Study of Free-Ranging Urban Animals, 1972, contrbr, A.W. Stokes, ed, Animal Behavior in Laboratory and Field, 1973, contrbr, F. Stearns and T. Montag, eds, The Urban Ecosystem: A Holistic Approach, 1975, contrbr Proceedings of the Seminar on Environmental Pests and Disease Vector Control, 1975, contrbr M. W. Fox, ed, The Wild Canids, 1975, author of introd., I. Nowell, The Dog Crisis, 1978, ed Animal Encyclopedia: Companion Animals, 1983, ed (with A.H. Katcher) and contrbr New Perspectives on Our Lives with Companion Animals, 1983, (with Katcher) Between Pets and People: The Importance of Animal Companionship, 1983, contrbr W. J. Kay and others, eds, Pet Loss and Human Bereavement, 1984. Contrbr to scholarly jnls and popular periodicals, including Natural History, Amer. Midland Naturalist, Jnl of Mammology, and Nation's Cities. Mem ed review bd, Pet News, 1976-80, Animal Regulation Studies, 1979-81, and Pet Care Reports, 1982—. BA, Brooklyn Coll. of the City Univ. of N.Y., 1964; MA, Calif. State Coll. (now U.), Los Angeles, 1968; Sc. D., Johns Hopkins U., Baltimore, Md., 1972. High School biol tchr, N.Y.C., 1964-66; research assoc, Center for Biology of Natural Systems and chmn urban ecological task force, Washington U., St. Louis, Mo., 1972-74; dir NYC Dept, of Health, Bureau of Animal Affairs, 1974-79; adj assoc prof of animal ecology and dir, Center for the Interaction of Animals and Society, U. of Penn, School of Veterinary Med., 1979—. Consultant to the Center for Disease Control and the U.S. Public Health Service. Lectr on ecological problems and public health aspects of urban animals. Mem. Am. Soc. of Mammology, AAAS, Delta Soc (corr. secy, 1981—), Expolorer's Club. Home: 155 Merion Ave Narberth PA 19072

BECK, ART, see Dybeck, Dennis Joseph.

BECK, JAMES (HENRY) BECK, b. NYC, May 14, 1930; s. Samuel and Margareth (Weisz) B.; m. Darma Tercinod, Apr. 9, 1956; children—Eleonora M., Lawrence C. Author: Mariano di Jacopo detto il Taccola, "Liber tertius," 1969, Jacopo della Quercia e San Petronio, 1970, Michelangelo: A Lesson in Anatomy, 1975, Raphael, 1976, Masaccio, the documents, 1978, Leonardo's Rules of Painting: An unconventional approach to modern art, 1979, Italian Renaissance Painting, 1981. BA, Oberlin Coll., 1952; MA, NYU, 1954; PhD, Columbia U., 1963. Asst. prof. U. Ala., Tuscaloosa, 1958-59; asst. Prof. Ariz. State U., Tempe, 1959-61; faculty Columbia U., NYC, 1961—, prof. art history, 1972—, Chmn., 1984—; vis. assoc. prof. Princeton U., 1970. Recipient grants-in-aid Am. Philo. Soc., 1969, 72, 75; Herodotus fellow Inst. for Advanced Study, Princeton U., 1967; fellow Harvard U. Center for Italian Renaissance Studies, 1967-68, 72; vis. scholar Harvard U. Center for Italian Renaissance Studies, 1983; Guggenheim fellow, 1973-74. Mem. Renaissance Soc. Am., Mediaeval Acad. Am., Coll. Art Assn. Home: 435 Riverside Dr New York NY 10025

BECK, JOAN WAGNER, b. Clinton, IA, Sept. 5, 1923; d. Roscoe Charles and Mildred (Noel) Wagner; m. Ernest William Beck, Sept. 9, 1945; children—Christopher, Melinda. Author: How to Raise a Brighter Child, 1967, (with Dr. Virginia Apgar) Is My Baby All Right?, 1973, Effective Parenting, 1976, Best Beginnings, 1983. BJ cum laude, Northwestern U., 1945, MS in Journalism, 1947. Radio script writer O.W.I. Voice of Am., 1945-46; copy writer Marshall Field & Co., 1947-50; feature writer Chicago Tribune, 1950—, writer syndicated column about young people, 1956-61, syndicated column about children, 1961-72, editor daily features sect., 1972-75, mem. editorial bd., 1975—; syndicated editorial page columnist, 1974—. Portal House award Chgo. Com. on Alcoholism, 1955; AP award for best newspaper feature series award, Ill., 1964; best feature, 1966; Alumni merit award Northwestern U., 1965, 77; Alumnae award, 1977; Natl. award of Achievement Alpha Chi Omega, 1966; 1st place award Penney-U. Mo., 1973; Woodrow Wilson Fdn. vis. fellow, 1983. Home: 905 Castlegate Ct Lake Forest IL 60045

BECK, ROBERT NELSON, b. Ft. Dodge, IA, Sept. 27, 1924; s. Victor E. and Elizabeth (Nelson) B.; m. Gladys E. Johnson, Mar. 28, 1942; children—argaret E. (Mrs. Richard B. Knowlton), JoAnne M. (Mrs. John H. Gottcent), Ronald N. Author: The Meaning of Americanism, 1956, Perspectives in Philosophy, 1961, American Ideas, 1963, C.J. Bostrom's Philosophy of Religion, 1962, Perspectives in Social Philosophy, 1967, Ethical Choice, 1970, Ideas in America, 1970, (with R.H. Lineback) Page Composition Costs of Philosophy Journals, 1976, Handbook in Social Philosophy, 1979; founder, editor: Idealistic Studies. BA, Clark U., 1947, AM, Boston U., 1948, PhD, 1950. Prof. philosophy, Clark U., 1948—, chmn. dept., 1957—, Univ. prof., 1980—; Carnegie intern Yale, 1955-56; prof. philosophy U. So. Calif., 1967-68; Moderator Town of Leicester, Mass., 1953-67; trustee Leicester Jr. Coll., 1966-68, Upsala Coll., 1975—. Served with AUS, 1943-46. Mem. Am. Philo. Assn., Assn. Philosophy Jnl Editors (pres. 1972-80), Metaphys. Soc. Am., Phi Beta Kappa. Home: 25 Brentwood Dr Holden MA 01520

BECKENSTEIN, MYRON, b. Cleve., Mar. 11, 1938; s. Irwin and Rachel (Miller) B.; m. Charlotte Hunt, Oct. 17, 1970; 1 dau, Stacey Amanda. BS, Northwestern U., 1959, MS, 1960. Mem. staff Chgo. Daily News, 1959-78, Balt. Sun, 1978—. Served with AUS, 1961-64. Mem. Upper Patuxent Archeol. Group, Sigma Delta Chi. Home: 6281 Tufted Moss Columbia MD 21045

BECKER, GEORGE JOSEPH, b. Aberdeen, WA, Apr. 19, 1908; s. George Joseph and Ella (Fox) B.; m. Marion Kelleher, Aug. 25, 1932; children—John, Dennis, Michael. Author: John Dos Passos, 1974, Shakespeare's Histories, 1977, Realism in Modern Literature, 1980, D.H. Lawrence, 1980, Master European Realists of the 19th Century, 1982, James A. Michener, 1983; also articles on Am. novelists of social criticism; translator: Jean-Paul Sartre, Anti-Semite and Jew, 1948; editor, translator: Documents of Modern Literary Realism, 1963, Paris Under Siege, 1870-71, 1969, Paris and The Arts, 1851-96, 1971. BA, U. of Wash., 1929, MA, 1930, PhD, 1937. Mem. faculty Immaculate Heart Coll., Los Angeles, 1934-39, Los Angeles City Coll., 1939-42; translator War Dept., 1942-45; mem. faculty Swarthmore Coll., 1945-70, chmn. dept. English, 1953-70, Alexander Griswold Cummins prof. English, 1961-70; mem. faculty Western Wash. U., Bellingham, 1970-74, acting chmn. dept. English, 1973; Fulbright lectr. Am. lit. and civilization U. Bordeaux, U. Lille, 1956-57; Fulbright research grantee to Spain, 1963-64. Mem. AAUP, Phi Beta Kappa. Home: 2225 Niagara Dr Bellingham WA 98226

BECKER, LESLEE ANN, b. Plattsburgh, NY, May 14, 1945, d. John Herman and Mary Veronica (George) Becker. Contrbr. short stories to Nimrod, The Atlantic, Iowa Rvw. BA in English, Cortland (N.Y.) Coll., 1966; MA in English, U. Vt., 1972; MA, Hollins Coll., 1980; MFA, U. Iowa, 1984. Instr. English, U. Vt., Burlington, 1978-79, Johnson (Vt.) State Coll., 1981-82; teaching-writing fellow Iowa Wrtrs.' Workshop, Iowa City, 1983-84; James Michener writing fellow, 1985-86; Stegner writing fellow Stanford U., Palo Alto, Calif., 1984-85. Winner Katherine Anne Porter Fiction prize, Nimrod Mag., 1983. Home: 714 Kirkwood Ave Iowa City IA 52240

BECKER, SCOTT RANDAL, (Scooter), b. Austin, MN, Sept. 9, 1962; s. David Eugene and Donna Ione (Youngmark) B. Contrbr. poetry to numerous anthols. Cook, Hardees Restaurant, La Crosse, Wis., 1983-84, Village Chef, La Crescent, Minn., 1985-86; prodn. foreman Formel Molding, Rushford, Minn., 1984; cashier Montgomery Ward, La Crosse, 1984-85; free-lance writer, Rushford, Minn., 1985—. Home: 1035 Tyler LaCrosse WI 54601

BECKER, STEPHEN, b. Mt. Vernon, NY, March 31, 1927; s. David and Lillian (Kevitz) B.; m. Mary Elizabeth Freeburg, Dec. 24, 1947; children—Keir, Julia, David. Author: The Season of the Stranger, 1951, Shanghai Incident, 1955, Juice, 1959, Comic Art in America, 1959, Marshall Field III, 1964, A Covenant with Death, 1965, The Outcasts, 1967, When the War Is Over, 1969, Dog Tags, 1973, The Chinese Bandit, 1975, The Last Mandarin, 1979, The Blue-Eyed Shan, 1982. BA, Harvard U., 1947; student, Yenching U., Peking, China, 1947-48. Free-lance writer, 1948—; tchr. Tsing Hua U., Peking, 1947-48; faculty Brandeis U., 1951-52, U. Alaska, 1967, Bennington Coll., 1971, 77-78, U. Iowa Writers Workship, 1974. Paul Harris Fdn. fellow, 1947-48; Guggenheim fellow, 1954. Home: East End Tortola British Virgin Islands

BECKERMAN, BERNARD, b. NYC, Sept. 24, 1921; s. Morris and Elizabeth (Scheftel) B.; m. Gloria Brim, Aug. 21, 1940; children—Jonathan, Michael. Author: Shakespeare at the Globe, 1599-1609, 1962, Dynamics of Drama, 1970, also articles, rvws. SS, CCNY, 1942; MFA, Yale U., 1943; PhD, Columbia U., 1956. Mem. faculty Hofstra Coll., 1947-65; organizer, dir. Ann. Hofstra Shakespeare Festival, 1950-64, chmn. dept. drama and speech, 1957-65; mem. faculty Columbia U., 1957-60, 65—, prof., chmn. dept. theatre arts, 1965-81, Brander Matthews prof. dramatic literature, 1976—, chmn. dept. English and comparative lit., 1983—, dean, 1972-76; Fulbright lectr. U. Tel-Aviv, 1960-61. Bd. dirs. L.I. Arts Center, 1963-64. Served with infantry, AUS, 1943-45, ETO; decorated Bronze Star. Recipient 7th Annl. award Am. Shakespeare Festival and Theatre Acad., 1962. Fellow Am. Theatre Assn.; mem. L.I. Speech Assn., N.Y. Dist. Theatre Conf. (pres. 1961-62), ANTA (dir., 1963-68), Am. Soc. Theatre Research (dir., chmn. 1973-79), Natl. Theatre Conf. (trustee), Shakespeare Assn. Am. (trustee, pres. 1981-82). Home: Redwood Rd Sag Harbor NY 11963

BECKETT, HENRY S.A., see Goulden, Joseph Chesley

BECKETT, THOMAS L., b. Battle Creek, MI, Jul. 20, 1953; s. John A. and Nancy J. (Johansen) Beckett; m. Barbara Ann Bakos, Oct. 16, 1976; children—Mischa Ann, Rachel Claire. Author: The Mandala Book, 1978, Dump, 1982, Soluble Sexes Census, 1984, Except by Talking, 1986; editor: Viscerally Press, 1977—; The Difficulties, 1980—; contrbr. to Gallery Works, Chicago RVW, Sun & other lit mags. BA in Poli Sci Kent State U., 1974. Home: 596 Marilyn St Kent OH 44240

BECKSTEAD, LUCILLE, b. Hazelton, ID, Oct. 28, 1920; d. Hyrum and Lorilla (Shepherd) Johnson; m. Frank L. Beckstead, Aug. 8, 1943. Columnist: The Colorado Leader, 1970-82, Brooks Towers News, 1970-82. Contrbr. numerous articles to regional and natl. mags. Wrkg. on hist. novel, futuristic novel. A.A., Idaho State U., 1940; B.S. in Jnlsm., U. Colo., 1969. Instr. Natl. Wrtrs. Sch., Aurora, CO, 1971-83, dir., 1983—; free-lance wrtr., 1960—. Mem. NWC (bd. dirs.). Home: 3505 Miller Ct Wheat Ridge CO 80033

BECKSTEAD, ROBERT DALE, b. Massena, NY, Sept. 8, 1959, s. Robert Dean and Jean Helen (Rusaw) B.; m. Brenda Lee Sypin, July 26, 1980; children—Robert Dale II, Aaron Douglas. Author numerous articles for U.S. Army publs. Student public schls., Massena; grad. Army's Defense Info. Schl., Fort Benjamin Harrison, IN, 1978. Enlisted in U.S. Army, 1977, staff wrtr., ed., photographer various locations to 1984, sr. journalist, supr. Ft. Dix., N.J., 1984-85, pub. affairs supr. 2d support command, 1985—. Recd. Dept. of Army's Keith L. Ware Award for jnlsm. excellence. Address: Box 257 APO New York NY 09160

BECKWITH, MERLE RAY, b. East Grand Rapids, MI, July 16, 1942; s. Elwood DeWerff Beckwith and Lessie Lorena (Cherry) Hartzler;

m. Barbara Jean Cutler, June 19, 1982. Author: Nature and Love, 1980; Nature, 1980; contrbr. poetry to books and lit. mags. including Manna, Broken Streets, Golden Dreams, Poets, Glowing Embers, Secrets of the Poetic Vision. BA, Western Mich. U., 1964; postgrad. UCLA, 1966-68. Peace Corps vol., Nigeria, 1964-66; clk. Assn. Retarded Citizens, Santa Barbara, Calif., 1983—. Recipient award of merit World of Poetry, 1983-87, Golden Poet award, 1985, 86,87. Home: 3732 Monterey Pine Apt A 109 Santa Barbara CA 93105

BEDARD, PATRICK JOSEPH, b. Waterloo, IA, Aug. 20, 1941; s. Gerald Joseph and Pearl Leona (Brown) B. BS in Mech. Engring, Iowa State U., 1963; M. Automotive Engring., Chrysler Inst. Engring., 1965. Product engr. Chrysler Corp., Highland Park, Mich., 1963-67; tech. editor Car and Driver mag., NYC, 1967-69, exec. editor, 1969-78, editor at large, 78—; tchr. race driving, cons. in field; freelance writer. Mem. Soc. Automotive Engrs., Intl. Motor Sports Assn., Sports Car Club Am., Pi Tau Sigma. First driver to win profl. road race in N. Am. in Wankel-powered car, 1973; first driver to exceed 200 mph at Indy in stockblock-powered car, 1984. Home: Rt 1 Box 779 Port St. Joe FL 32456

BEDE, SYLVESTA, see Des Marais, Louise M.

BEDINI, SILVIO A., b. Ridgefield, CT, Jan. 17, 1917; s. Vincent and Cesira (Stefanelli) B.; m. Gerda Hintz, Oct. 20, 1951; children—Leandra, Peter. Author: Ridgefield in Review, 1958, The Scent of Time, 1963, Early American Scientific Instruments and Their Makers, 1964, (with F.R. Maddison) Mechanical Universe, 1966, (with W. von Braun and F.L. Whipple) Moon, Man's Greatest Adventure, 1970, The Life of Benjamin Banneker, 1972, (with others) The Unknown Leonardo, 1974, Thinkers and Tinkers, 1975, The Spotted Stones, 1978, Declaration of Independence Desk: Relic of Revolution, 1981, Thomas Jefferson and His Copying Machines, 1984, Clockwork Cosmos, 1985. Ed. Columbia U., 1935-42; LLD U. Bridgeport, 1970. Curator div. mech. and civil engring. U.S. Natl. Mus., Smithsonian Institution, Washington, 1961-65; asst. dir. Mus. History and Tech., 1965-71, dept. dir., 1971-78, keeper rare books, 1978—; Mem. exec. council Soc. History Tech., 1963—. Fellow Washington Acad. Scis.; mem. Am. Philo. Soc., Am. Antiquarian Soc., Soc. Am. Historians, Soc. History Discoveries, History Sci. Soc., Scientific Instrument Soc. (London), Astrolabe Soc. (Paris). Home: 4303 47th St NW Washington DC 20016

BEEBE, F. LISA, b. b. Rastatt, Baden, Germany, Dec. 29, 1952 (arrvd. USA 1955), d. Herbert and Elfriede (Ganz) Schnepf; m. Clark Andrew Beebe, Nov. 29, 1975 (div. July 1984). Contrbr. to Wash. Post, Bangkok Post, Private Clubs, Am. Way, Signature, MD Mag., Silver Kris, Mabuhey, Off Duty, Computer Decisions, Insight Guide: Continental Europe, Insight Guide: Spain, Fielding's Economy Europe, 1984; columnist and contrbg. ed., R&R; contrbg. wrtr., Business Jnl. of NJ. BA in English, Moravian Coll., 1974; MA in English, Lehigh U., 1979. Tchr. English, Saucon Valley Jr. High Schl., Pa., 1974-75; freelance wrtr./ed., Bangkok, Madrid and NYC,1977—; prof. bus. Spanish and Spanish translation Schiller U., Madrid, 1982-84 Mem ASJA, Travel Jnlsts. Guild, ATA. Home: 505 E 79 St New York NY 10021

BEECHCROFT, WILLIAM, see Hallstead, William F.

BEELER, MYRTON FREEMAN, b. Winthrop, MA, Apr. 27, 1922, s. Myrton Freeman Beeler and Helen Gray (Scott) Allen. Author: Clinical Microscopy (with J.A. Freeman), 1974, Interpretations in Clinical Chemistry, 1978, Laboratory Medicine-Urinalysis and Medical Microscopy (with Freeman), 2d ed., 1983, How to Analyze Clinical Research Reports (with R.W. Sappenfield), 1986; contrbr. articles to profl. jnls. AB, Harvard U., 1945; MD, N.Y. Med. Coll., 1949. Dir. labs. Ochsner Clinic, New Orleans, 1958-67; prof. pathology La. State U., New Orleans, 1967—; ed.-in-chief Am. Jnl Clin. Pathology, New Orleans, 1980—. Home: 1421 Chartres St New Orleans LA 70116

BEELER, THOMAS TAYLOR, III, b. Oklahoma City, May 22, 1944; s. Thomas Taylor and Virginiia (Klein) B.; m. Susan Jane O'Connor, July 24, 1965; children—Ethan Thomas, Emily Susan. BA, Columbia U., 1966, MA, 1967, PhD (Jethro Robinson fellow in Am. lit., Woodrow Wilson dissertation fellow), 1974. Cross-reference editor Am. Heritage Pub. Co., NYC., 1968; editorial cons. Garret Press, NYC, 1968-69, editorial dir., v.p., 1969-71; editor Gregg Press div. G. K. Hall & Co., Boston, 1972-73; exec. editor, 1974-78, also exec. editor, 1973-78; pub. G. K. Hall & Co., 1978—. Co-editor, bus. mgr.: Little Mag, 1965-71. Mem. MLA, Am. Studies Assn., Bibliog. Soc. Am. Home: King St Hampton Falls NH 03844

BEEM, JANE A., b. Forest City, IA, Aug. 6, 1934; d. Frank S. and Elsie A. (Anderson) Engels; m. W. Wayne Beem, Nov. 29, 1952; children—Gregory W., Timothy S., Pamela J. Gustafson, Angela L. Ashmore. Contrbr. articles to Ill. English Bulltn., Lit.: News that Stays News. B.A., Carthage Coll., 1970; M.A., Northwestern U., 1977. Tchr., Warren Township High Sch., Gurnee, IL, 1970—, chair English dept., 1985—. Mem. NCTE, Ill. Assn. Tchrs. English. Home: 10923 W Wadsworth Rd Zion IL 60099

BEEMAN, MARSHA LYNN, b. Pontiac, Mich., Feb. 5, 1959; d. William Wesley and Catherine Almeda (Paul) Beeman. Poetry in anthologies. Wrkg. on Mich. hist. book, poetry, AA, Oakland Community Coll; BA in Psychology, Oakland U. Freelance wrtr., photographer The Mature Am., Bloomfield Hills, Mich., 1985-86, The Reminder, Clarkston, Mich., 1985-86; sales agt. Hester Realty, Pontiac, Mich., 1985-87; freelance wrtr., 1984—. Home: 3035 Beacham Dr Pontiac MI 48055

BEERMAN, HERMAN, b. Johnstown, PA, Oct. 13, 1901; s. Morris and Fannie (Toby) B.; m. Emma N. Segal, May 13, 1924. AB, U. Pa., 1923, MD, 1927, ScD (Med.), 1935. Diplomate: Am. Bd. Dermatology, 1935. Asst. Dept. Agr., Phila., 1925-26; intern Mt. Sinai Hosp., Phila., 1927-28; resident Hosp. U. Pa., 1929-33, asst. chief dermatology clinic, 1938-65, Abbott fellow in chemotherapeutic research, 1932-46; with U. Pa. Schl. Medicine, 1929—, prof. dermatology, 1951-70, prof. emeritus, 1970—, grad. schl. med., prof. 1947-67, chmn., 1949-67; assoc. seriolgy Pepper Lab., 1949—; asst. dir. Inst. Study Venereal Disease, 1939-54; physician out-patient dept. Pa. Hosp., 1929-36, hosp. dermatologist, chief, 1935-45, assoc. dermatologist, 1946-47, dermatologist, head dept., 1947-67, cons. dermatologist, 1967—; asst. dermatologist radium clinic Phila. Gen. Hosp., 1938-40, dermatologist, 1940-53, active cons. dermatology, 1953-68, hon. cons. in dermatology, 1968; cons. lab. Children's Hosp. Phila., 1949—; cons. VA Hosp., Phila., 1953-66; cons. pathology U.S. Naval Hosp., Phila., 1954—; cons. dermatology VA Hosp., Coatesville, Pa., 1967-79, USPHS, 1937—; pvt. practice, Phila., 1933—; mem. panel venereal diseases subcom. infectious disease, chemotherapy NRC, 1954—; Sigmund Pollitzer lectr. NYU, 1963; Irving Wershaw Meml. lectr., Israel, 1967; Pusey Meml. lectr. Chgo. Dermat. Soc., 1968; Ruben Nomland Meml. lectr. U. Iowa, 1968; Samuel M. Bluefarb lectr., Chgo., 1973; treas., trustee Inst. Dermatologic Communication and Education, 1963—. Editorial bd.: Jnl Investigative Dermatology, 1948-53, Am. Jnl Med. Scis., Intl. Jnl Dermatology, Jnl Cutaneous Pathology, 1978—; mem. bd. editors sect.: XIII-Dermatology and Syphilology, Excerpta Medica, 1950-75; contrbr. articles to profl. jnls. Mem. Am. Med. Wrtrs. Assn. Home: 2422 Pine St Philadelphia PA 19103

BEERS, VICTOR GILBERT, b. Sidell, IL, May 6, 1928; s. Ernest S. and Jean (Bloomer) B.; m. Arlisle Felten, Aug. 26, 1950; children—Kathleen, Douglas, Ronald, Janice, Cynthia. Author: A Child's Treasury of Bible Stories, 4 vols., 1970, Family Bible Library, 10 vols., 1971, The Book of Life, 23 vols., 1980. AB, Wheaton Coll., 1950; MRE, No. Baptist Sem., 1953, MDiv, 1954, ThM, 1955, ThD, 1960; PhD, Northwestern U., 1963. Prof. No. Baptist Sem., Chgo., 1954-57; editor Sr. High Publs., David C. Cook Pub. Co., Elgin, Ill., 1957-59, exec. editor, 1959-61, editorial dir., 1961-67; pres. Books for Living, Inc., Elgin, 1967—; editor Christianity Today, 1982-85.Home: Rt 1 Box 321 Elgin IL 60120

BEETLER, DIANNE LYNN, (Lynn Edwards, Edward Francis), b. Galesburg, IL, May 17, 1951; d. Donald Edward and Mary Frances (Brown) B. Contrbr. articles to popular mags. including Modern Mturity, Ladies' Home Jnl., Wrtr.'s Digest, others. Contrbr., ed. Abingdon Pottery Collectors Newsletter, 1987, BEST News, 1987. B.A., Bob Jones U., 1973. Tchr. Beaver Marsh Christian Sch., Chemult, OR, 1973-74; free-lance wrtr., 1974—. Corr. secy. Abingdon Pottery Collectors, IL, 1987. Recipient 1st place, Honorable Mention, Ill. Press Assn., 1983; Hon. Chpt. Farmer degree ROVA FFA chpt., Oneida, IL, 1985. Mem. Knox County Genealogical Soc. Home: Rt 1 Box 29-A Altona IL 61414

BEGALLA, PATRICIA, b. London, Oct. 25, 1936; d. Arthur Charles and Mary Maureen (Clare) Hall; came to U.S. 1961; m. George Edwin Copping, Aug. 16, 1963 (div. June 18, 1969); 1 son—Stephen Charles Copping; m. 2d, Leonard J. Begalla, May 29, 1976 (dec. Oct. 1985). Ed./pub.: Published!, 1985—. Student grammar, secondary, and business schls., London. Owner/off. mgr. Ad Rem Advert., Phoenix, 1964-67; legal sec'y. Ariz. Land Corp., Phoenix, 1967-69; ed. asst./off. mgr. Irving Wallace, Los Angeles, 1969-78; owner Platen Pub. Co., Sylmar, CA, 1979—. Mem. COSMEP. Home: 14240 Bledsoe St Sylmar CA 91342

BEGELL, WILLIAM, b. Wilno, Poland, May 18, 1928; came to U.S., 1947, naturalized 1953; s. Ferdin and Liza (Kowarski) Beigel; m. Esther Kessler, May 27, 1948; children—Frederick Paul, Alissa Maya. B. Ch. E., Coll. City N.Y., 1953; M. Ch. E., Poly. Inst. Bklyn., 1958; postgrad., Columbia U., 1958-59. Engring. mgr. heat transfer research facility dept. chem. engring. Columbia U, 1953-59; co-founder, exec. v.p. Scripta

Technica, Inc., Washington, 1959-74; founder, pres. Hemisphere Publishing. Co., Washington, 1974—; lectr. pub. George Washington U., Washington, also N.Y.U.; cons. Heat Transfer Research Lab., Columbia U.; cons. in field. Editor 7 books; contrbr, numerous prof. jnl. articles. Mem. natl. adv. bd Center of the Book, Library of Congrss; chmn. exec. council Profl. and Scholarly Pubs. Mem. AAAS, Am. Inst. Chem Engrs., Am. Soc. for Engring. Edn., ASME (policy bd.), Assn. Am. Publishers (dir.), N.Y. Acad. Scis. (publs. bd.), Washington Book Publishers (founder), Am. Assn. Engring. Socs. Home: 46 E 91st St New York NY 10028

BEGGS-UEMA, MARCK LEWIS, b. Alameda, CA, Mar. 6, 1958; d. Conrad Lary and Audrey Dell (Fraser) Beggs; m. Masae Uema, Aug. 11, 1984. Contrbr. poetry Natl. Forum, Intro 15, Manhattan Poetry Rvw. BA in English and Women's Studies, U. Ark.-Little Rock, 1984; MFA in Creative Writing, Warren Wilson Coll. Assoc. poetry editor Crazyhorse, Little Rock, 1983—. Mem. AAP, Phi Kappa Phi. Address: 7000 Sparks Rd Little Rock AR 72210

BEHLEN, CHARLES WILLIAM, b. Slaton, TX, Jan. 29, 1949, s. Robert Stanislaus (Stinson) B. and Oleta Elizabeth (Brake) Tanner; 1 dau., Laura Behlen-McKenzie. Author: Perdition's Keepsake, 1978, I Am Part of All that I have Met, 1984, My Grandfather's Hammer, 1985; contrbr.: Bitterroot, Chowder Rvw, Cedar Rock, Sulphur River, other periodicals, Anthology of Mag. Verse and Yearbook of Am. Poetry, 1985, other anthologies. Student N. Mex. Jr. Coll., 1968-70. Poet-in-residence Tex. Commn. on Arts, 1983—, N. Mex. Arts Div., 1985—; ed., pub. Chawed Rawzin Press, San Antonio, since 1974. Home: 905 S. Bridge Apt B Victoria TX 77901

BEHM, RICHARD H, b. Tiffin, OH, Oct 14, 1948; s. Delmer Hess and Jayne Ellen Wolph B.; m. Susan Marie Sperl Apr. 6, 1971 (div. Aug. 1, 1983); 1 dau., Jessica Jayne; m. 2d, Mary Ellen Norby, Apr. 27, 1984. Author poetry: Letters from a Cage & Other Poems, 1976, This Winter Afternoon of Angels, 1978, The Book of Moonlight, 1978, Simple Explanations, 1982, When the Wood Begins to Move, 1982; contrbr. poetry Kenyon Rvw, So. Poetry Rvw, Sewanee Rvw, Qtly West, So. Humanities Rvw, Spoon River Qtly, others; ed. and pub. Song/Song Press, 1975—. BA, Coll. of St. Thomas, 1970; MFA, Bowling Green State Univ., 1973, PhD, 1976. Prof. English Univ. Wis., Stevens Point, 1976—. Served to lt. USAF, 1970-72, USA. Recipient Creative Writing fellowship, Wis. Arts Bd, 1983, 85. Mem CCLM, AWP, NCTE. Address: 1333 Illinois Ave Stevens Point WI 54481

BEHN, ROBERT DIETRICH, b. Washington, Sept. 5, 1941; s. Victor Dietrich and Nona (Hefley) B.; m. Judith Howe, May 4, 1968; 1 son, Mark Dietrich. Author: (with others) Quick Analysis for Busy Decision Makers, 1982; editor: The Lessons of Victory, 1969; contbr. articles to mags. and profl. jnls. BS in Physics, Worcester Poly. Inst., 1963; M.S.E.E., Harvard U., 1965, Ph. D. in Decision and Control, 1969. Research dir. The Ripon Soc., Cambridge, Mass., 1968-69, exec. dir., 1970-72; asst. to gov. Commonwealth of Mass., 1969-70; lectr. Harvard Bus. Sch., 1972-73; assoc. prof. Inst. Policy Scis. and Pub. Affairs, Duke U., Durham, N.C., 1973—, dir. 1982—; cons. RAND Corp., Santa Monica, 1966, Urban Acad., N.Y.C., 1978-79, Ford Found, 1977. Home: 1607 Cotherstone Dr Durham NC 27712

BEHRENDT, DAVID FROGNER, b. Stevens Point, WI, May 25, 1935; s. Allen Charles and Vivian (Frogner) B.; m. Mary Ann Weber, Feb. 4, 1961; children—Lynne, Liza, Sarah. BS, U. Wis., 1967, MS, 1960. Reporter Decatur (Ill.) Review, 1957-58; re-porter Milw. Jnl., 1960-70, copy editor, 1970-71, editorial writer, 1971-84, editorial page editor, 1984—. Recipient Am. Polit. Sci. Assn. award for distinguished reporting pub. affairs, 1963, Natl. Council for Advancement Edn. Writing award for best newspaper series on edn., 1968; Recipient 1st prize for editorial writing Natl. Edn. Reporting award, 1981. Home: 1928 Hillside Ct Delafield WI 53018

BEHRMAN, DANIEL, b. NYC., June 20, 1923; s. Emanuel and Miriam (Adleson) B.; m. Lida Schechtmann, 1947 (div.) 1 son, Dan; m. Madeleine de Sinety, July 28, 1975; children—Thomas, Peter. Author: The New World of the Oceans, 1969, The Man Who Loved Bicycles, 1973, Solar Energy—The Awakening Science, 1976, Assault on the Largest Unknown—The International Indian Ocean Expedition, 1981. Contrbr. articles to newspapers. Wrkg. on book on windjammers of Penobscot Bay. B.A., U. Mich., 1943. Sci wrtr. Unesco, Paris, 1950-80; free-lance wrtr., 1980—. Served to corporal U.S. Army, 1943-45. Home: Box 859 Rangeley ME 04970

BEIDEL, HYUN SOOK, b. Tientsin, China, of Korean parents, Aug. 23, 1935; d. Hwa Young Lee and Shin Kyoung (Park) Lee; m. Donald George Beidel, May 19, 1962; children—Sophia LeeAnn, David Lee. Author: The Story of Susie Lee, 1984; wrkg. on sequel to The Story of Susie Lee. BA, College of Staten Island, 1978. Asst. unit head, OEO, NYC Bd. of Educ., Brooklyn, 1978-85, real estate broker, 1986—. Home: 22 Androvette St Staten Island NY 10309

BEILKE, MARLAN, (Linomarl), b. Wausau, WI, 1940; s. Lyle and Sally B.; m. Irene, Aug. 6, 1966; children—Laura, Diane Theodore. Author: Shining Clarity: God and Man in the Works of Robinson Jeffers, 1979. AB U. of Calif., 1963; MA U. of Tasmania, 1973. Publisher/printer Quintessence Publications (Amador City, CA), 1976—; Curator of Quintessence Working Press Room Museum. Home: 356 Bunker Hill Mine Rd Amador City CA 95601

BEIM, NORMAN, b. Newark, NJ; s. Herman and Freida (Thau) B.; m. Virginia Rapkin (div.). Playwright: works include The Deserter, 1979, Success, 1983, Pygmalion and Galatea, 1983. Student, Ohio State U., Hedgerow Theatre Schl., Phila., Inst. Contemporary Art, Washington. Actor: Broadway play Inherit the Wind, 1956-58; off-Broadway play Coriolanus, 1953, Black Visions, 1973; natl. touring production Tribute, 1980. Served with F.A. U.S. Army. Mem. Actors Equity Assn., Screen Actors Guild, AFTRA, Dramatist Guild Am. Home: 425 W 57th St New York NY 10019

BEL GEDDES, JOAN, b. Los Angeles, Dec. 2, 1916; d. Norman and Helen (Sneider) Bel G.; m. Barry Ulanov, Dec. 16, 1939 (div. 1968); children—Anne, Nicholas, Katherine. Author: Small World: A History of Baby Care from the Stone Age to the Spock Age, 1964, How to Parent Alone: A Guide for Single Parents, 1974, To Barbara With Love—Prayers and Reflections by a Believer for a Skeptic (Catholic Press Assn. award, 1974), (with others) Art, Obscenity and Your Children (1969), American Catholics and Vietnam, 1970, The Future of the Family, 1971, Holiness and Mental Health, 1972, The Children's Rights Movement, 1977, And You, Who Do You Say I Am?, 1981; translator: (with Barry Ulanov) Last Essays of Georges Bernanos, 1955; editor: Magic Motorways (Norman B. Geddes), 1940, Earth: Our Crowded Spaceship (Isaac Asimov), 1974; editor-in-chief: My Baby mag., 1954-56, Congratulations mag., 1954-56. BA, Columbia U., 1937. Researcher and theatrical asst. to Norman Bel Geddes, Inc., NYC, 1937-41; publicity dir. Compton Advt., Inc., NYC, 1942, new program mgr., 1943-47; pub. info. officer UNICEF, 1970-76, chief of editorial and publs. services, 1976-79, edl. cons., 1979—; tchr. of drama Birch Wathen Schl., NYC, 1950; mem. faculty of Inst. on Man and Sci., Rensellaerville, N.Y., 1969. Interviewer-hostess: weekly radio program Religion and the Arts, NBC, 1968. Mem. AL of Am., Natl. Soc. of Lit. and the Arts, Am. Theilard de Chardin Assn., Municipal Arts Soc. N.Y., Am. Film Inst., Thomas More Soc. Home: 60 E 8th St New York NY 10003

BELCHER, GRACE (RUTH) DALEY, b. Rochester, NY, Oct. 5, 1902; d. Frederick and Cynthia Ada (Amos) Daley; m. Wilbur Leith Belcher, Feb. 21, 1954 (dec. Dec. 14, 1972). Author: musical plays for elementary grade pupils and Fortnightly Club of Rockville Center (L.I., NY). BA, Hofstra Univ. Teacher, elementary grades, Rochester and Long Island, NY, 1922-65. Playwright award, Long Island Federation of Women's Clubs, 1983. Home: 380 Union Hewlett LI NY 11557

BELDON, SANFORD T., b. Scranton, PA, Nov. 9, 1932; s. Benjamin and Evelyn (Jacobson) B.; m. Jeanne Sherman, June 25, 1967; children—Mary, Kenneth, Emily. BBA, CCNY, 1955; postgrad., NYU Grad. Schl. Bus., 1956-57. Publicist Prentice-Hall, Inc., NYC, 1956-59; publicity dir. Fawcett Publs., Inc., NYC, 1959-62; asst. dir. public relations Crowell-Collier-Macmillan, NYC, 1963-65; dir. advt. and public relations, edn. group Litton Industries, White Plains, N.Y., 1966-68; dir. promotion Baker & Taylor div. W.R. Grace Co., 1968-71; dir. mktg. Book div. Rodale Press, Inc., Emmaus, Pa., 1971-74; dir. advt. Organic Gardening mag., 1974-78, group v.p., 1974—, pub., 1978-86; pub. Prevention mag., 1986—. Office: 33 E Minor St Emmaus PA 18049

BELFIELD, JUDITH ANN, b. Davenport, IA, Oct. 18, 1946; m. John V. Belfield, Jan. 8, 1966; children—Jonathan D., Jennifer M. Contrbr. numerous poems to lit. mags. St. Francis Acad., 1964; postgrad. Joliet Jr. Coll., 1979—. Comml. artist Shelby Craftco Corp., Joliet, 1964-70; waitress Sheridan Restaurant, Joliet, 1970-72; genl. clerical Joliet Jr. Coll., IL, 1979—, sec. lit. mag., 1981—. Recipient 4th prize White Rock Rvw., 1983; 3d prize Manna mag., 1984, 1st prize, 1985; Spcl. Recognition, Calif. State Poetry Soc., 1985. Mem. P&W (Honorable Mention 1983, 1st prize 1984, 2d prize 1985), Home: 804 Vine St Joliet IL 60435

BELITT, BEN, b. NYC, May 2, 1911; s. Joseph and Ida (Lewitt) B. Author: poems The Five-Fold Mesh, 1938, Wilderness Stair, 1955, The Enemy Joy: New and Selected Poems, 1964, Nowhere But Light: Poems, 1964-69, 1970, The Double Witness: Poems 1970-76, 1977, Possessions: New and Selected Poems, 1938-85, 1986; prose School of the Soldier, 1949; essays Adam's Dream: A Preface to Translation, 1978; editor and translator: Four Poems by Rimbaud: The Problem of Translation, 1947, Poet in New York (Federico Garcia Lorca), 1955, 1983, Selected Poems of Pablo Neruda, 1961, Juan de Mairena and Poems from the Apocryphal Songbooks (Antonio Machado), 1963, The Selected Poems of Rafael Alberti, 1965, Pablo Neruda, A New Decade; Poems, 1958-67, 1969, Poems from the Canto General, 1968, To Painting (Rafael Alberti), 1972, Splendor and Death of Joaquin Murieta (play, Pablo Neruda), 1972, New Poems: 1968-70 (Pablo Neruda), 1972, Five Decades: Poems 1925-70 (Pablo Neruda), 1974, Skystones (Pablo Neruda), 1981; contrbr. to: The Selected Poems of Federico Garcia Lorca, 1955, Cantico, Selections (Jorge Guillen), 1965, Selected Poems (Eugenio Montale), 1965, Jorge Luis Borges: Selected Poems, 1923-67, 1972. BA, U. Va., 1932, MA, 1934, postgrad., 1934-36. Asst. lit. editor Nation, 1936-37; prof. English Bennington (Vt.) Coll., 1938—; mem. faculty dance summer schls. Bennington Coll., Mills Coll., 1939, Conn. Coll., 1948-49. Recipient Shelley Meml. award in poetry 1936, Oscar Blumenthal award in poetry 1956, Chgo. Civic Arts award 1957, Brandeis Creative Arts award in poetry 1962, natl. Inst. Arts and Letters award in poetry 1965. Served with AUS, 1942-44. Guggenheim fellow, 1946; NEA grantee, 1967-68; Ben Belitt lectureship endowment Bennington Coll., 1977; Russell Loines award for poetry AAIAL, 1981, Rockefeller grant, 1984, Williams/Derwood Award for Poetry, 1986, Fellow Vt. Arts and Scis.; mem. PEN, AG, Phi Beta Kappa. Address: Bennington College Bennington VT 05201

BELL, CHARLES GREENLEAF, b. Greenville, MS, Oct. 31, 1916; s. Percy Bell and Nona Oliver (Archer) B.; m. Diana Mason, July 23, 1949; children—Carola M. Birnbaum, Sandra M.; children by previous marriage: Nona D., Charlotte C., Margaret Delia. Author: verse Songs for a New America, 1953, rev. ed., 1966, Delta Return, 1956, rev. ed., 1969, Five Chambered Heart, 1986; novels The Married Land, 1962, The Half Gods, 1968; author: film The Spirit of Rome, 1965; 38 slide-tape studies Symbolic History, The Human Arts: Through Sight and Sound; contrbr. numerous poems to Harper's mag, New Yorker, Atlantic Monthly and other lit publs; contrbr. short stories and articles to lit jnls. BS, U. Va., 1936; BA, Oxford (Eng.) U., 1938; LittB, 1939, MA, 1966. Instr. English Blackburn Coll., Carlinville, Ill., 1939-40; instr. English Iowa State Coll., 1940-43, asst. prof., 1943-45, asst. in physics, 1943-45; research asst. in physics, Princeton, 1945, asst. prof. English, 1945-49; asst. prof. humanities U. Chgo., 1949-56; tutor math., sci., langs. Great Books Seminars, St. John's Coll., Annapolis, Md., 1956-67, western br. Santa Fe, 1967—; dir. Grad. Preceptorial on dimensions of history, 1972-73; lectr. history of western arts adult edn. Springfield (Ill.) Pub. Library, 1939-40; lectr. cultural history Black Mountain Coll., N.C., summer, 1947; guest prof. U. Frankfort, Germany, 1952, U. P.R., Mayaguez, 1955-56, dir. honors program, 1955-56; Fulbright prof. Technische Hochschule Munich, Germany, 1958-59; writer-in-res., lectr. modern poetry U. Rochester, N.Y., spring 1967; guest prof. SUNY, 1970. Rockefeller grantee, 1948; Ford Fdn. fellow, 1952-53. Home: 1260 Canyon Rd Santa Fe NM 87501

BELL, CHARLOTTE DOROTHY, b. Chgo., June 8, 1931; d. Jeanette (Staller) and Samuel Bell. Author poetry books: The Quiet Ways, The Gentle Moments, 1984, The Right Words, 1984, The World of the Winds, 1986, A Signature of Love, 1986; poetry in anthologies. Wrkg. on chapbooks. Home: 1516 Missouri St Unit 2 San Diego CA 92109

BELL, ELISE STONE, b. Detroit, MI, d. Mead Wilmer and Elise (Seeman) Stone; m. Charles Robert Bell, Sept. 13, 1941; children—Jean, Wendy Bell Bjorkan, Robert Mead. Author: Television & Teamwork, 1962; contrbr. to numerous mags., newspapers, television programs. BA, Swarthmore College, 1939. Ed. Doubleday Publ., NYC, 1939-41; script writer, Enrichment Records, NYC,1950-75; ed. Ideas for Teachers, Nassau TB Assn., Roslyn, NY 1953-58; Freelance Wrtr., 1975—. Freedom Fdns. Award, Valley Forge, PA, 1971; Best Children's Record List, The NY Times, 1968. Home: 100 E Broadway Roslyn NY 11576

BELL, HARRISON B., b. Bangor, ME, May 9, 1925; s. Charles Edward and Dorrice Clement (Robinson) B.; m. Martha Louise Denton, Aug. 7, 1948; children: Sally R. Bell Fink, Martha M., Judith L. Author: Spelling for You, 1958; editor schl. text series: Short Stories (by E. H. Sauer and Howard M. Jones), Drama (by John Gassuer and M. Sweetkind), Understanding Poetry (by John Theobald); editor: Hancock Pointers on Cooking, 1984, The Vice of Verses and Other Slanderous Rhymes, 1984. Mng. editor Holt Rinehardt, NYC, 1960-66; v.p., editor-in-chief Noble & Noble, NYC, 1966-69, Silver Burdett, Morristown, N.J., 1969-75; v.p., pub. Harper & Row, NYC, 1975-80; asst. to pres. AMSCO, NTC, 1981-82; pres. Ten-Thirty Corp., Jackson Heights, N.Y., 1983—. Treas. Council for Bd. of Edn., Greenwich, Conn., 1967-69; pres. Hancock Point Library Assn., Maine, 1971-75. Served with USNR, 1944-56, World War II, Korean War. Mem. COSMEP, Network Ind. Pubs. (chmn. 1985-86), Delta Chi. Home: 7000 Boulevard East Guttenberg NJ 07093

BELL, JAMES ADRIAN, b. Altoona, KS, Nov. 12, 1917; s. George Andrew and Fay (Commons) B.; m. Virginia Gray, July 8, 1941; children—Jane Gray, George Edward. Grad., Brent Schl., Baguio, Philippines, 1936; AB, U. Kans., 1940. Reporter Topeka Daily Capital, 1940-42; corr. Chgo. bur. Time Inc., 1942-48; White House corr. Washington bur., 1948-50; chief N.Y. bur., 1950; war corr. Tokyo bur., 1950, Middle East bur. chief, 1951-54, Central European bur. chief, 1954-56; chief China and Southeast Asia bur., Hong Kong, 1956-59, Africa bur., 1959-61, Central European bur., Bonn, Germany, 1961-66, N.Y. bur., 1966-68, London bur., 1968, Rome bur., 1968-73, Atlanta bur., 1973-76, sr. corr., 1976—. Served from pvt. to 2d lt., Signal Corps AUS, 1942-45. Mem. Delta Tau Delta. Office: Time 399 Boylston St Boston MA 02116

BELL, JANE MATLACK, b. Washington, June 27, 1949; d. Harry H. and Mildred Harriet (Post) B.; m. Douglas Matthew Davis, Dec. 12, 1970; stepchildren—Laura Katharine, Mary Elizabeth; 1 dau., Charlotte Victoria. BA, Bennington (Vt.) Coll., 1971, Ecole Intl., Geneva, 1967. Public affairs assoc. N.Y. Cultural Center, 1973-74, acting dir. dept public affairs, 1974; revs. editor, then contbg. editor Arts mag., 1973-76; editorial assoc. Artnews mag., 1979—; cntrbg. editor N.Y. Arts Jnl., 1978—; assoc. editor Art Express, 1980-81; sr. editor The Art Economist, 1980-82; bd. dirs. Intl. Network Arts, 1979—; founding mem. Ho TV, 1976-77, Artists TV Network, 1978-80; co-tchr. Advanced Video Workshops, Brooklyn. Mus. Art Schl., 1978, SUNY, Purchase, 1979, Phila. Coll. Art, 1979, Pratt Inst., 1979, Osaka U. Arts, 1980, Alexander Mackie Coll., Sydney, Australia 1980. Grantee Kosciuszko Fdn., 1976. Mem. Intl. Assn. Art Critics. Address: 80 Wooster St New York NY 10012

BELL, LINDA R., b. Columbia, TN., Nov. 13, 1949; d. William F., Jr., and Dorothy (Cecil) Rainey, Jr.; m. Dennis L. Bell, 1971 (div. 1980); m. 2d, T. Martin Warren, 1983. Author: Love Puzzles, 1982; January Summers, 1982; The Red Butterfly, 1983; contrbr. poems to World Poet Press, Am. Poetry Anthology, Lyrical Treasures, Phoenix, Suwannee Poetry, The Poetry, Proof Rock, Sojourner, Parnassus, Poetic Justice, Satori, also articles in periodicals including Lic. Practical Nurse, Creative Crafters Jnl., Natl. Gardening. BS in Chem. Engring. cum laude, U. Tenn., 1971, MSE magna cum laude, 1972. Design engr. Olin Corp., Charleston, Tenn., 1975-78; environ. engr. TVA, Knoxville, Tenn., 1978-85; instr. writing U. Tenn., Knoxville, 1985—; freelance wrtr./photographer, 1982—. Address: Box 24 Columbia TN 38402

BELL, MADISON SMARTT, b. Nashville, Aug. 1, 1957, s. Henry Denmark and Allen (Wigginton) B.; m. Elizabeth Spires, June 15, 1985. Author: The Washington Square Ensemble, 1983, Waiting for the End of The World (novel), 1985, Straight Cut (novel), 1986, Zero DB (stories), The Year of Silence (novel), 1987; contrbr. to anthologies: Best Am. Short Stories, Best of Intro, Homewords: Tennessee Wrtrs., New Stories from the South; contrbr. to Harper's, Hudson Rvw, Crescent Rvw. AB, Princeton U., 1979; MA, Hollins Coll., Roanoke, Va., 1981. Freelance wrtr., 1979-85; lectr. in fiction Goucher Coll., Balt., 1984-86; vis. lectr. Wrtrs. Workshop, Iowa City. Mem. AWP, AG, PEN. Home: 3005 Cresmont Ave Baltimore MD 21211

BELL, MICHAEL STEVEN, b. Joplin, MO, July 4, 1946; s. Vernon Leigh and Alpha Marie (Russell) B.; children by previous marriage: Mercury, Shannon, Ororah, Justin. Contrbr. to Junction, Bardic Echoes, Intermedia, Artweek, Visionary Art News, other periodicals. BFA, Calif. Inst. Arts, Valencia, 1970; MFA, U. Ky., 1972. Curatorial asst. Oakland Mus., Calif., 1975-76, art registrar, 1976-80; dir. Midland Art Council, Mich., 1980-82; curatorial asst. San Francisco Mus. Modern Art, 1982-84; asst. dir. San Francisco Arts Commn., 1984-87, curator visual art access, 1987—. Served with USAF, 1963-66. Mem. Bay Area Art Wrtrs. Guild. Address: 685 McAllister 212 San Francisco CA 94102

BELL, WILLIAM JOSEPH, b. Chgo., Mar 6, 1927; s. William Jennings and Gertrude (Oteman) B.; m. Lee Phillip, Oct. 23, 1954; children—William James, Bradley Philip, Lauralee Kristen. Student, U. Mich., 1944, DePaul U., 1947-49. Co-editor Hi-Shopper Pub. Co., Chgo, 1948-49; writer, producer CBS, 1949-53; account exec. McCann-Erickson, advt., 1953-56, Cunningham & Walsh, 1956-57; co-owner NBC-TV show Another World, 1964—; pres. Bell-Phillip TV Prodns., Inc., 1970—, Miss Lee Flowers, Inc., 1972; corp. dir. Graphic Pictures, Inc., Dramatic Serials, Inc.; prtnr. Bell Dramatic Serial Co., 1983—; owner Sunset Ridge Farm, Casa del Suena, Lake Geneva, Wis. Coauthor TV show Guiding Light, 1957, As the World Turns, 1958-67, Our Private World, 1965; story editor, head writer: Days of Our Lives, 1966—; creator, head writer: The Young and the Restless, CBS-TV, 1973—; exec. producer, CBS-TV, 1982. Served with USNR, 1945-46. Recipient Emmy award for best show, 1974, 83, Award for Best Writer, 1976. Mem. Acad. TV Arts Scis. Home: 209 E Lake Shore Dr Chicago IL 60611

BELL, VICTOR LEROY, (E. M. Frickert, Linda Oliver, Ben Allen, Enrique Shaw-Galvez), b. Columbus, OH, Sept. 12, 1935; s. Benjamin Allen and Clara Jen (Hatfield) B.; m. Sandra Lee Wylie, Apr. 1, 1960; children—Karen, Kenneth. Contrbr. articles to electronic mags. Ed.: Electronic Technician Mag., 1961-64, Electronic Engineering and Maintenance Mag., 1961-63. Wrkg. on short stories; planning jnl. of U.S. malcontents and cynics. Student Ohio State U., 1953, 54, 58, Akron U., 1985, 86. Ed. Ojibway Press, Duluth, MN, 1961-64; chief service engineer Sylvania Corp., Batavia, NY, 1964-67; dir. technical services Diebold, Inc., Canton, OH, 1967-73; free-lance wrtr., 1973-79; mgr. field service SmithKline Beckman, Phila., 1979—. Served to staff sgt. U.S. Air Force, 1954-58. Home: 505 E Porter St Box 338 Malvern OH 44644

BELLAMY, JOE DAVID, b. Cincinnati, Dec. 29, 1941; s. Orin Ross and Beulah Pearl (Zutavern) B.; m. Connie Sue Arendsee, Sept. 16, 1964; children—Lael Elizabeth, Samuel Ross Carlos. Book reviewer Sat. Review, 1975—, NY Times Book Rvw, 1975—, Washington Post, 1975—. Editor: Apocalypse: Dominant Contemporary Forms, 1972, Superfiction, or the American Story Transformed, 1975, Moral Fiction, 1980, New Writers for the Eighties, 1981, Love Stories/ Love Poems, 1982, American Poetry Observed, 1984; author: The New Fiction, 1974, Olympic Gold Medalist, 1978. Student, Duke U., 1959-61; BA, Antioch Coll., 1964; MFA, U. Iowa, 1969. Editor The Antiochian, 1965-67; instr. English Pa. State Coll., Mansfield, 1969-70, asst. prof., 1970-72; asst. prof. English St. Lawrence U., Canton, N.Y., 1972-74, assoc. prof., 1974-80, prof. English, 1980—; pub., editor Fiction Intl. mag. and Press, 1972-83; cons. editor U. Ill. Press, Champaign, Ill., 1974—; program cons. NEH, 1976—. Grantee NEH, 1974, NEA, 1985. Mem. Natl. Book Critics Circle, CCLM (pres., chmn. bd. dirs. 1979-81). Home: 14 Jay St Canton NY 13617

BELLI, MELVIN LOURON, b. Sonora, CA, July 29, 1907; s. Caesar Arthur and Leonie (Mouron) B.; m. Betty Ballantine, 1933; children—Richard R., Melvin Mouron, Jean, Susan; m. Joy Maybelle Turney, May 3, 1956; 1 son, Caesar Melvin; m. Lia G.T. Triff, June 3, 1972; 1 dau., Melia. Author: Modern Trials and Modern Damages, 6 vols., 1954, abridged ed., 1962, 2d ed., 1981, Ready for the Plaintiff, 1956, Trial and Tort Trends, 14 vols., 1954-62, The Adequate Award, 1953, Demonstrative Evidence and The Adequate Award, 1955, Malpractice, 1955, Modern Trials (student edition), (with Danny Jones) Belli Looks Life and Law in Russia, 1964, (with Maurice Carroll) Dallas Justice, 1964, The Law Revolt, 2 vols., 1968, Melvin Belli My Life on Trial, 1976, The Belli Files: Reflections on the Wayward Law, 1983; assoc. editor, Am. Trial Lawyers Assn. Law Jnl, 1950—; adv. editor, Negligence and Compensation Service, 1955—; legal adv. bd.: Traumatic Medicine and Surgery for the Atty., 1958—; mem. bd. editors: Trial Diplomacy Jnl; mem. editorial bd., The Common Law Lawyer; bd. dirs.: Am. Jnl Forensic Psychiatry. AB, U. Calif.-Berkeley, 1929; LLB, Boalt Hall, 1933; JD (hon.) New Eng. Schl. Law. Bar: Calif. 1933. Sr. partner Belli Law Offices, San Francisco, 1940—; condr. Belli Seminars in Law, 1953—; pres. Belli Fdn. Lectrs., 1960—; provost Belli Soc.; Mem. Calif. Bldg. Standards Commn.; Bd. dirs. Disability & Casualty Inter-Ins. Exchange, N.W. Affairs Council; mem. exec. bd. Western State U. Coll. Law. Named dean emeritus Coll. Law, Riverside U.; decorated grand ofcl. St. Brigidian Order. Fellow Internatl. Acad. Trial Lawyers (dir., past dean); mem. Authors Guild, Am. Acad. Forensic Scis., Tuolumne County Hist. Soc., Inter-Am. Bar Assn. ABA, Calif. Bar Assn., San Francisco Bar Assn., Fedl. Bar Assn., Intl. Bar Assn. (patron), Intl. Legal Aid Assn., San Diego, Hollywood, Beverly Hills bars, Am. Trial Lawyers Assn. (past pres.), Barristers Club San Frasncisco (past dir.), La Asociacion Nacional de Abogados Mexico (hon.), Societe Driot (pres.), Phi Delta Phi, Delta Tau Delta. Office: Belli Bldg 722 Montgomery St San Francisco CA 94111

BELLOW, SAUL, b. Lachine, Quebec, Can., June 10, 1915; s. Abraham and Liza (Gordon) B.; children—Gregory, Adam, Daniel. Author: Dangling Man, 1944, The Victim, 1947, The Adventures of Augie March, 1953 (Natl. Book award 1953), Seize the Day, 1956, Henderson the Rain King, 1959, Herzog, 1964 (James L. Dow award 1964, Internatl. Lit. prize 1965, Natl. Book award 1965, Soc. Midland Authors Fiction award 1976), Mosby's Memoirs and Other Stories, 1968, Mr. Sammler's Planet, 1969 (Natl. Book Award 1970), Humboldt's Gift, 1975 (Pulitzer prize 1976), To Jerusalem and Back, 1976; short stories Him With his Foot in His Mouth, 1984; contrbr.: fiction to Esquire and lit mags; criticisms appear in New Leader, others; short story to Atlantic's 125th Anniversary edit., 1982. Student, U. Chgo., 1933-35; BS, Northwestern U., 1937, LittD, 1962; LittD, Bard Coll., 1962, Harvard U., 1972, Yale U., 1972, McGill U., 1973, Brandeis U., 1974, Hebrew Union Coll.-Jewish Inst. Religion, 1976, Trinity Coll., Dublin, Ireland, 1976. Tchr. Pestalozzi-Froebel Tchrs. Coll., Chgo., 1938-42; faculty Princeton, N.Y.U., U. Minn.; faculty English dept. U. Chgo., 1963—, mem. com. on social thought, 1973—, chmn. com. on social thought, 1970-76, now Raymond W. and Martha Hilpert Gruiner Distinguished Services prof.; Tanner lectr., Oxford U. Decorated Croix de Chevalier des Arts et Lettres, France, Comdr. Legion of Honor, France; recipient Natl. Inst. Arts and Letters award, 1952; Friends of Lit. Fiction award, 1960; Communicator of the Yr. award U. Chicago Alumni Assn., 1971; Nobel prize for literature, 1976; Medal of Honor for lit. Natl. Arts Club, 1978; O.Henry prize for short story A Silver Dish, 1980; Guggenheim fellow, 1955-56; Ford Fdn. grantee, 1959-61. Mem. Am. Acad. Arts and Scis. Address: U Chgo 1126 E 59th St Chicago IL 60637

BELL-TENEKETZIS, BARBARA, b. Newton, MA, Aug. 22, 1947; m. Doros Byron Loizou, May 20, 1972 (dec. 1974); m. 2d, Demosthenis Teneketzis, Nov. 18, 1979. Contrbr. articles Ann Arbor (Mich.) News; poetry in anthologies. Wrkg. on novel, poetry collection. Assoc. Applied Sci., Chamberlayne Jr. Coll., 1967. Freelance orgn. cons., Watertown, Mass., 1982-83; freelance wrtr., Ann Arbor, 1984—; vol. in writing project Pattengill Sch., Ann Arbor, 1987—. Mem. Com. for Human Rights in Cyprus, 1978; NOW, 1984—; Mich. Women's Campaign Fund, 1986—; League of Women Voters, 1987—; NAACP, 1987—; asst. dir. of publicity, Bd. of Dirs., Faculty Women's Club, U. of Mich. (Ann Arbor), 1987. Home: 1201 Marlborough Dr Ann Arbor MI 48104

BELNAP, DAVID FOSTER, b. Ogden, VT, July 27, 1922; s. Hyrum Adolphus and Lois Ellen (Foster) B.; m. Barbara Virginia Carlberg, Jan. 19, 1947. Student, Weber Coll., Ogden, 1940. Asst. city editor Seatle St2, 1945-47; bur. chief UP Assns., Helena, Mont., 1947-50, Honolulu, 1950-52; regional exec. Pacific N.W., 1952-55, dir. Latin Am. services, 1955-67; Latin Am. corr. Los Angeles Times, 1967-80, asst. fgn. news editor, 1980—. Recipient Overseas Press Club Am. award for best article on Latin Am., 1970, Maria Moors Cabot prize, 1973. Mem. Overseas Press Club Am. Clubs: Am. of Buenos Aires; Phoenix of Lima (Peru). Home: 1134 W. Huntington Dr Arcadia CA 91006

BELOOF, ROBERT LAWRENCE, b. Wichita, KS, Dec. 30, 1923; s. P.A. and Ida (Dungan) B.; m. Ruth Madeleine LaBarre, June 14, 1946 (div. 1972); children—Marshall H., Laird D., Douglas E., Grant L. Author: The One-Eyed Gunner, 1956, The Performing Voice in Literature, 1966, Good Poems, 1973, The Children of Venus and Mars, 1974; also poetry, articles; co-author: The Oral Study of Literature, 1966; editor record performer of hist. anthology of Am. poetry, 2 vol. LP, 1965. Student, Haverford Coll., 1944, Swarthmore Coll., 1945; BA, Friends U., 1946; MA, Northwestern U., 1948, PhD, 1954; MA, Bread Loaf Schl. English, Middlebury, Conn., 1948. Faculty U. Calif., 1948—, lectr., asst. prof., then assoc. prof., 1948-64, prof., 1964—, chmn. dept. speech, 1964-68; Fellow Inst. Advancement Edn., 1951-52, Inst. Creative Arts, 1963-64; Fulbright prof., Italy, 1959-60. Mem. Speech Communication Assn. Office: Dept Rhetoric U Calif Berkeley CA 94720

BELTON, BETTY ROSE, (Kepka Hochman Belton), b. Wilson, KS., Mar. 11, 1934; d. Frank and Rose Betty (Kepka) Hochman; m. Glen S. Belton, June, 1969 (div. 1973); 1 dau., Risa-Marie. Author: School Arts, 1971, Christmas on a Matchstick, 1974, Kepka's Egg Lap-Studio and Batiking Method for Making Czechoslovakian Kraslice, 1984. Contrbr. art books, popular mags. including Womans Day. Wrkg. on books on Czechoslovakia, folklore, motifs and Kraslice. BS in art edn., Emporia State U., 1956; MS in art, Ft. Hays State U., 1966. Art tchr. Linn pub. schls., Kans., 1966-69, Parsons Jr. High Schl., Kans., 1974-75, Wilson Pub. Schls., Kans., 1979—; free-lance wrtr., artist, inventor, 1969-79, Known as "Czech Egg Lady." Recipient Art Enhancer award, Kans. Art Educators, 1985; NEA grantee, 1984-85, 86. Home: 1007 N. Grand Ellsworth KS 67439

BELTON, KEPKA HOCHMAN, see Belton, Betty Rose

BELTZ,, WILLIAM ALBERT,, b. Meriden, CT., Aug. 24, 1929; s. Albert Henry and Marie Adelade (Heusel) B.; m. Beverly Sawyer, May 31, 1958; children-John, Jane, Kurt, Adam. AB, Tufts U., 1951. With Bur. Natl. Affairs, Inc., Washington, 1956—, assoc. editor, then exec. editor, 1965-80, pres., chief exec. officer, 1980—; dir. Fisher-Stevens, Inc., Totowa, N.J., 1978—. Mem. White House Corrs. Assn. Info. Industry Assn. (dir.). Club: Natl. Press (Washington). Home: 1001 Herbert Springs Rd Alexandria VA 22308

BENBOW, CHARLES CLARENCE, b. Moore Haven, FL, Feb. 23, 1929; s. Clarence Oliver and Rosalie Florence (King) B.; m. Lois Chandler, Oct. 10, 1954; children—Margot Britton, Claudia King. B. Applied Arts, U. Fla., 1951; MS in Art Edn., Fla. State U., 1961, postgrad., 1965-66. Art dir. sta. WJXT-TV, Jacksonville, Fla., 1955-58; tchr. art Duval County (Fla.) Pub. Schls., 1958-62; instr. humanities U. Fla., 1962-65; writer-critic St. Petersburg (Fla.) Times, 1966-86. Co-author Fla. state guide for art in secondary schls.; contrbr. articles to profl. jnls. Served with USN, 1951-55. Named Best Architecture Critic in Fla. Fla. Assn. Am. Inst.

Architects, 1978, 80. Home: 205 19th Ave SE St Petersburg FL 33705

BENCHLEY, PETER BRADFORD, b. NYC, May 8, 1940; s. Nathaniel Goddard and Marjorie Louise (Bradford) B.; m. Winifred B. Wesson, Sept. 19, 1964; children—Tracy, Clayton. Author: Time and a Ticket, 1964, Jonthan Visits the White House, 1964, Jaws, 1974, The Deep, 1976, The Island, 1979, The Girl of the Sea of Cortez, 1982, Q Clearance, 1986; screenplay Jaws; co-author; The Deep, 1976, The Island, 1980; writer narrator: shows Am. Sportsman, ABC-TV. BA cum laude, Harvard U., 1961. Genl. assignment reporter Washington Post, 1963; assoc. editor Newsweek mag., 1964-67; staff asst. to Pres. White House, Washington, 1967-69. Free lance writer, 1969—. Served with USMCR, 1962-63. Address: ICM 40 W 57th St New York NY 10019

BENDER, ELEANOR M., b. Schenectady, July 26, 1941, d. George Henry and Dorothy Emma (Branahl) Shufelt; m. Robert Morton Bender, Oct. 5, 1963 (div. 1985); children—Alyssa, Gillian, Jessica. Ed. All of Us are Present (with Nancy Walker and Bobbie Burk), 1984; ed., pub., founder Open Places, 1966—. BA, U. Mich., 1963. Instr. dept. English Stephens Coll., Columbia, Mo., 1971-84, dir. devel., 1986—. Recipient numerous grants. Mem. CCLM. Office: Stephens Coll Box 2035 Columbia MO 65215

BENDER, ESTHER LOUISE, b. Meyersdale, PA, Mar. 14, 1942; d. Alton N. and Rhoda Viola (Brenneman) Miller; m. Ezra Paul Yoder, July 3, 1960 (div.); children—Renatta, Ramona; m. O. Jason Bender, June 11, 1983; stepchildren—Wendy, Robin, Brandi. Contrbr. articles to mags., newsletters. Ed.: Perspective newsletter, 1985-86. Wrkg. on editing Casselman Chronicle, children's books, teen novel, articles. B.S. in Early Childhood Edn., Frostburg State U., 1974, M.S. in Edn., 1981. Tchr. public schls., Grantsville, MD, 1974—. Mem. NEA, Tri-State WG (co-pres.). Home: Rt 2Box 33-H Grantsville MD 21536

BENDER, THOMAS, b. Redwood City, CA, Apr. 18, 1944; s. Joseph Charles and Catherine Frances (McGuire) B.; m. Sally Hill, June 8, 1966 (div. Oct. 1983); 1 son, David William; m. 2d, Gwendolyn Wright, Jan. 14, 1984; 1 dau., Sophia Wright. Author: Toward Urban Vision, 1975 (Frederick Jackson Turner prize 1975), Community and Social Change in America, 1978, (with Edwin Rozwenc) The Making of American Society, 1978, (editor) Democracy in America, 1981, New York Intellect: A History of Intellectual Life in New York City from 1750 to the Beginnings of Our Own Time, 1987. BA, U. Santa Clara, 1966; MA, U. Calif.-Davis, 1967, PhD, 1971. Asst. prof. history and urban studies U. Wis., Green Bay, 1971-74; asst. prof. history NYU, NYC, 1974-76; assoc. prof. history, 1976-77, prof. history, 1977—, Samuel Rudin prof. humanities, 1977-82, Univ. prof. humanities, 1982—. Editor, Intellectual History Group Newsletter, 1978-85. Bd. dirs. Muni. Art Soc. N.Y., 1983-84. Guggenheim fellow, 1980-81, Rockefeller Fdn. Humanities fellow, 1984-85, fellow N.Y. Inst. Humanities. Mem. Am. Hist. Assn., Orgn. Am. Historians, Soc. Am. Historians. Home: 54 Washington Mews New York NY 10003

BENDERSON, BRUCE, b. Syracuse, NY., Aug. 6, 1946; s. Jacob and Ida Mae (Olsen) B. Co-ed. Capstan, 1976; contrbr. fiction to Between C & D, Dreamworks, Benzene, Sebastian Quill, Red Dust; film criticism to Mulch, 1,000 Eyes, Fangoria; translator from French (with U. Molinaro), Manuscript Painting at the Court of France (F. Avril), 1978, The Golden Age (M. Thomas), 1980, Event (Philippe Sollers), 1986; Sun & Shadow (Jean-Pierre Aumont), 1977. BA, SUNY-Binghamton, 1969. Freelance wrtr., ed., translator, 1975—. HOME: 81 St Marks Pl Apt 2W New York NY 10003

BENDINER, ROBERT, b. Pitts., Dec. 15, 1909; s. William and Lillian (Schwartz) B.; m. Kathryn Rosenberg, Dec. 24, 1934; children—David, William, Margaret. Author: The Riddle of the State Department, 1942, White House Fever, 1960, Obstacle Course on Capitol Hill, 1964, Just Around the Corner, 1967, The Politics of Schools, 1969, The Fall of the Wild, The Rise of the Zoo, 1981, TV documentary NBC White Paper Series, The Man in The Middle, The State Legislator, 1961. Student, CCNY, 1928-33. Mng. editor The Nation, NYC, 1937-44, assoc. editor, 1946-50, freelance writer, 1951-68, 78—; lectr., program chmn. Wellesley Summer Inst. Social Progress, 1946-53; mem. Faculty Salzburg Sem. in Am. Studies, 1956; vis. lectr. pub. affairs Wesleyan U. (Conn.), 1983. Contrbg. editor: The Reporter, NYC, 1956-60; U.S. corr.: New Statesman, London, 1959-61; mem. editorial bd.: N.Y. Times, 1969-77. Served with AUS, 1944-45. Guggenheim fellow, 1962-63; recipient Benjamin Franklin Mag. award U. Ill., 1955, School Bell award NEA, 1960. Mem. Natl. Press Club, PEN Am. Center. Home: 45 Central Pkwy Huntington NY 11743

BENEDETTO, DONNA A., b. Bklyn., Jan. 23, 1962, d. Thomas V. and Nancy Marie (Petz) Benedetto. Contrbr. to Kaleidoscope, Spectrum, Seawanhaka, Here's Brooklyn, Medica. BA in English, LIU., 1984. Contrbg. editor Here's Bklyn., 1983-84; tchr.-guide wrtr. Warner Books, NYC, 1984; editorial asst. Medica Mag., NYC,1984-85; prodn. asst. Marcel Dekker, Inc., 1985—; contrbg. wrtr., Status, 1986—. Recipient Albert Berman Meml Wrtg. award LIU., 1983. Home: 6830 Ridge Blvd Brooklyn NY 11220

BENEDICT, ELINOR DIVINE, b. Chattanooga, TN, June 4, 1931; d. Thomas M. and Mary M. (Faxon) D.; m. Samuel S. Benedict, Oct. 3, 1953; children: Samuel, Jonathan, Kathleen. Author: Landfarer, 1978, A Bridge to China, 1983; editor lit mag Passages North. BA in English, Duke U., 1953; MA in English, Wright State U., 1977; MFA, Vermont Coll., 1983. Staff writer Times Publs., Kettering, Ohio, 1969-76; instr. Bay de Noc Community Coll., Escanaba, Mich., 1977—. Recipient Coll. Fiction award Mademoiselle mag., 1953, Creative Artist award Mich. Council for Arts, 1984; AAUW grantee, 1981. Mem. AAUW, P&W, Poetry Resource Ctr. of Mich. (bd. dirs. 1985—). Home: 8627 S Lakeside Dr Rapid River MI 49878

BENEDIKT, MICHAEL, b. NYC, May 26, 1935; s. John and Helen (Davis) B. Contbg. editor: Am. Poetry Rvw, 1973—; editor: poetry The Paris Rvw, 1974-78; author: The Body, 1968, Sky, 1970, Mole Notes, 1971, Night Cries, 1976, The Badminton at Great Badminton, or Gustave Mahler and the Chattanooga Choo-Choo, 1980; (subject) Benedikt: A Profile, 1978; editor: drama anthologies Theatre Experiment, 1968, Modern Spanish Theatre, 1968, Post-War German Theatre, 1967, Modern French Theatre, 1965; editor poetry anthologies The Poetry of Surrealism, 1975; The Prose Poem: An International Anthology, 1976; guest poetry and fiction editor: Chelsea, 1968; guest poetry editor: Modern Poetry Studies, 1971; mng. ed. Locus Solus, 1960-62; contrbr. poetry to 50 anthols, articles on literature and the arts to numerous critical anthologies, also scholarly, popular and lit mags inclg. Poetry, APR, Partisan Rvw, Paris Rvw, The London Mag., ABR, Iowa Rvw, Science '86, numerous others. BA in English and Journalism, NYU, 1956; MA in Comparative Lit., Columbia U., 1961. Assoc. editor Horizon Press, NYC, 1959-61; N.Y. corr. Art Intl. 1965-67; editorial assoc. Art News mag., NYC, 1962-72; assoc. prof. Bennington Coll., 1968-69, Sarah Lawrence Coll., 1969-73, Hampshire Coll., 1973-75; Sexton prof. poetry Boston U., 1975, vis. prof. English and creative writing, 1977-79; vis. prof. Vassar Coll., 1976-77; judge Natl. Book award in translation, 1974; judge CCLM, 1970, 73, judge Lamont Poetry awards Acad. Am. Poets, 1970-72; mem. CAPS panel in mixed media, 1976, Mass. Arts and Humanities Fdn. panel in poetry, 1977. Recipient Hokin award for best poems in single year Poetry Mag., 1969; Guggenheim fellow in poetry, 1968-69; NEA prize for single poem, 1970; Fels award for excellence in mag. editing, 1975; CAPS poetry grantee, 1975; NEA fellow in poetry, 1979-80. Mem. MLA, PEN, PSA, Am. Assn. for Advancement of the Humanities. Home: 315 W 98th St New York NY 10025

BENET, THOMAS CARR, b. Paris, Sept. 28, 1926; s. Stephen Vincent and Rosemary (Carr) B.; m. Joan Gregory, Aug. 27, 1952; children—Rebecca Benet Sawyer, Alice. BA, Yale U., 1949. Reporter San Francisco Chronicle, 1950-60, asst. city editor, 1968-78, editorial writer, 1978—. Served with AUS, 1945-47. Recipient Christophers award Christophers Orgn., 1954. Mem. San Francisco Com. on Fgn. Relations, Century Assn. Office: SF Chronicle 901 Mission St San Francisco CA 94119

BENFEY, OTTO THEODOR, b. Berlin, Oct. 31, 1925; U.S., 1946, naturalized, 1952; s. Eduard and Lotte (Fleischmann) B..; m. Rachel Elizabeth Thomas, Aug. 28, 1949; children—Stephen, Philip, Christopher. Author: From Vital Force to Structural Formulas, 1964 (also partial Chinese transl.), Classics in the Theory of Chemical Combination, 1963, The Names and Structures of Organic Compounds, 1966 (also Portuguese transl.), Introduction to Organic Reaction Mechanisms, 1971 (also German and Japanese transls.), From Intellectual Scaffolding to the Elixir of Life, 1978 (also Japanese transl.), Friends and the World of Nature, 1981; co-editor and contrbr. to Perspective on the 17th Century World of Viscountess Anne Conway, 1986; also articles, intros., and chapts. books; translator: (Ernst Cassirer): Determinism and Indeterminism in Modern Physics, 1956; editor: Chemistry, 1963-78; editorial bd.: Revista Iberoamericana de Education Quimica, 1966-78, Current Contents/Phys. Scis, 1974—; The Scientist, 1986—. BSc, Univ. Coll., London, 1945, PhD, 1947. Postdoctoral research fellow Columbia U., 1947-48; from instr. to assoc. prof. Haverford Coll., 1948-55; research fellow Harvard U., 1955-56; from assoc. prof. to prof. chemistry and history of sci., Earlham Coll., Richmond, Inc., 1956-73; Dana prof. chemistry and history of sci. Guildord Coll., Greensboro, N.C., 1973—, clrk. faculty, 1977-79; lectr., cons. in field; vis. scholar Tokyo U., 1982; vis. prof. Intl. Christian U., Tokyo, 1985-86. Pres. Soc. Social Responsibility in Sci., 1951-53. Mem. AAUP, History of Sci. Soc., ACLU, Assn. Harvard Chemists, Assn. Asian Studies, Am. Chem. Soc., Sigma Xi. Home: 801 Woodbrook Dr Greensboro NC 27410

BENFORD, GREGORY ALBERT, b. Mobile, AL, Jan. 30, 1941; s. James Alton and Mary Eloise (Nelson) B.; m. Joan Abbe, Aug. 26, 1967; children—Alyson Rhandra, Mark Gregory. Author: novels Deeper than the Darkness, 1970, Jupiter Project, 1975, If the Stars are Gods, 1977, In the Ocean of Night, 1977, The Stars in Shroud, 1978, Find the Changeling, 1980, Timescape, 1980, Against Infinity, 1983, Across the Sea of Suns, 1984, Artifact, 1985, Heart of the Comet, 1986, In Alien Flesh, 1986, Great Sky River, 1987; also research papers on plasma physics, astrophysics, solid state physics. BS, U. Okla., 1963; MS, U. Calif., San Diego, 1965, PhD, 1967. Research asst. U. Calif., San Diego, 1964-67; post-doctoral fellow Lawrence (Calif.) Radiation Lab., 1967-69, research physicist, 1969-71; prof. physics U. Calif., Irvine, 1971—; cons. in field. Woodrow Wilson fellow, 1963-64; grantee Office Naval Research, 1975—, NSF, 1972-76, Army Research Orgn., 1977-82, Air Force Office Sci. Research, 1982—; recipient Brit. Sci. Fiction award, 1981; Australian Ditmar award for intl. novel, 1981; John W. Campbell award for best novel, 1981. Mem. Am. Phys. Soc., Royal Astron. Soc., SFWA (Nebula award 1975, 81). Home: 1105 Skyline Dr Laguna Beach CA 92651

BENINGTON, GEORGE BEAUBIEN, b. Santa Monica, Calif., Sept. 30, 1959, s. Herbert Davidson and Merithew (Hills) B. Ed.: Women Who Marry Houses (Jo McDougall), 1983, Three American One-Act Monologues (Dan Domench), Rainmakers (Deborah Ward), 1984, Kaisa Kilponen (Rebecca Cummings), 1985, The Wildman (Martin Steingesser), 1985, An Abridged Field Guide to the Maine Writer, 1984. BA in Human Ecology, Coll. of Atlantic, 1982. Exec. dir. Maine Wrtrs. and Pubs. Alliance, 1982-85; mng. ed. Coyote Love Press, Portland, Me, 1982—; book designer Anthoensen Press, Portland, 1985—. Grantee Me. State Commn. on Arts and Humanities, 1984, 85; recipient Design award Me. State Commn. on Arts and Humanities, 1984, 85. Mem. Baxter Soc. Office: 294 Spring St Portland ME 04102

BEN-ISRAEL, SHABTAI, see Gormezano, Keith Stephen

BENJAMIN, DAVID, see Slavitt, David Rytman

BENJAMIN, MARY LYNN, b. Atlanta, Feb. 15, 1942; d. Herman Victor and Gertrude Edna (Mikkola) Everett; m. William Edward Fallon (div.); children—Shelley Arlene, Shaun Paul; m. Clifford Charles Benjamin, May 14, 1983. Contrbr. feature articles to mags., newspapers. Wrkg. on book, Red Wing Has Spoken. Staff wrtr. 4 Seasons Travelers Guide, Windham, ME, 1986-87; free-lance wrtr., 1987—. Home: Box 154 7 Tenney Hill Rd South Casco ME 04077

BENJAMIN, ROBERT L., b. Indpls., Oct. 23, 1923; s. Albert Allen and Frances Louise (Wright) B.; m. Alice Lorene Sanders, June 16, 1950; children—Bruce Elliott and Robin Ann Benjamin Hastings. Ed.: Agents News, 1950—, Crier (and its forerunners), 1952—, Mutual Insur. Companies Assn. of IN Legislative Bulletins, 1950's—; author numerous news stories & press releases, 1945—. BS in Jnlsm., Butler U., 1945. Rptr./writer Indpls. Star, 1945-49; pub. relns. dir. Indpls. Real Estate Reassessment Proj., 1949-50; p.r. dir. IN Farmer's Insur. Group, Indpls., 1950-79, v.p./p.r., 1979—; exec. v.p./ genl. mgr. Mutual Insur. Co.'s Assn. of IN, 1961—. Presidential award from U.S. Pres. Jimmy Carter, 1980, Award of Excellence, Agents News, PICA, 1985, num. others. Mem. Indpls. Press Club, PRSA, IN Soc. Assn Execs., Insur. Advtg. Council. Home: 7524 Kimberly Dr Indianapolis IN 46256

BENJAMIN, ROBERT SPIERS, b. Bklyn., Aug. 17, 1917; s. Harry Asher and Alice (Spiers) B.; m. Dorothy Calhoun, Apr. 25, 1945 (dec. 1961); children: Robert C., Gordon R. (twins), Geraldine Benjamin Ameriks, Alan; m. Sarah Graves (Nov. 7, 1970); 1 dau. Diana Lee. Author: Call to Adventure, 1934, (sever-fgn. edits.) Call to Adventure, The Vacation Guide, 1940, The Inside Story, 1940, Europa Para Todos, 1973; editor: Eye Witness, 1940, I'm An American, 1941; assoc. editor: New World Guide to the Latin American Republics, 1943; Student Schl. Journalism, Rutgers U., 1940. Staff writer Panama Star & Herald, 1940; asst. editor Dodd, Mead & Co., 1941; chief publs., office coordinator Inter-Am. Affairs, Dept. State, Washington, 1942-43; chief Time-Life bur., Santiago, Chile, 1946-47, Buenos Aires, Argentina, 1947-48, Mexico City, 1949-51; corr., dir. Latin Am. ops. Vision Mag., 1951-56; stringer N.Y. Times, Mexico, 1951-56; founder, chief exec. officer Robert S. Benjamin & Assocs., Mexico City, 1957—. Served with CIC U.S. Army, 1943-46. Mem. Over-seas Press Club (founder, hon. life mem.), Explorers Club, Pub. Relations Soc. Am., Interam. Fedn. Pub. Relations Assns. Home: Homero 1933-2P Mexico City 11560 Mexico

BENJAMIN, RUTH, see Rosenblatt, Ruth

BENNER, MARY D., b. Philadelphia, Apr. 22. Author of Winged Moments, 1969; contrbr. poems to Am. Haiku, The Unsung, Candor, Ideals, Dragonfly, other lit mags., N. Phila. newspaper. Wrkg. on book of poetry and novel. Student Community Coll., Temple U., Phila. Admin. positions with U.S. Govt., Phila., 30 years. Secy. Nat. Shut-in Soc., 1968-69. Mem. Phila. Writers Conf. Home: 2101 Chestnut St Philadelphia PA 19103

BENNETT, ALLYSON JOY, b. Milw., May 1, 1965; d. Ernest E. and Beverly S. (Reynolds) B. Author: (chapbook) Creatures in our Blood, 1985. Contrbr. poems to lit. and popular mags., anthols. including Wis. Rvw., Souwester, others. Ed.: Wis. Rvw., 1986-87, From the Tongue of the Crow: Wis. Rvw. Anthol., 1987. Wrkg. on chapbook, Winter on Asylum Bay. Student U. Wis. Oshkosh, 1983—. Home: 3263 Shorewood Dr Oshkosh WI 54901

BENNETT, ANNA ELIZABETH, b. Bklyn, July 18, 1914; d. Walter Scott and Francis Livermore B. Author: Little Witch, 1953; Cantabile (poems), 1954; contrbr. fiction, poetry many mags. AB, Adelphi U., 1931-35; LSB, Pratt Inst., 1936-37. Asst. children's library NYC Pub., 1937-38, Lansing public, Mich., 1938-42; children's libn., Morristown, NJ, 1942-44; post libn. US Army, Cambridge, Ohio, 1944-46; cataloger Bklyn. public library, 1946-50; children's libn., Northport, NY, 1956-65. Recipient Helen Dean Fish Meml prize, Lippincott Pubs., 1954, Leitch Meml. prize, Lyric Mag., 1975. Address: 90 Inlet Rd Hampton Bays NY 11946

BENNETT, BERNICE SPITZ, b. Boston, Sept. 4; d. Marx and Lena (Shaller) Spitz; m. Jack Bennett, June 5; children—Victor Paul, Laura Marian. Wrkg. on autobiographical novel. Former student Boston U., Simmons Coll., Brandeis U. Columnist Newton (Mass.) Graphic; contrbr. Confidential Chat column, Boston Globe. Mem. Nat. Profl. Wrtrs.' Union. Address: 9 Ithaca Circle Newton MA 02162

BENNETT, CARL EDWARD, b. Slidel, LA, May 18, 1918; s. Carl Edward Bennett and Ettie (Sally) Randall; m. Gertrude Weiner, Sept. 24, 1944, (dec.); m. 2d, Helen Bryant, Feb. 11, 1969; children—Carol, Robert, Stuart. Contrbr. poems to numerus anthols. BA, Northwestern U., 1950. Copywriter, Montgomery Ward & Co., Chgo., 1945-52, buyer, 1952-57; self-employed mfg. rep., Atlanta, 1957-68. Served to sgt. USMC, 1937-45. Home: Rt 1 Box 341 State Line MS 39362

BENNETT, CAROLYN LINDA, b. Bklyn., Feb. 21, 1950; d. Richard and Louise (Yodice) B. Author poetry: The Everyday Way, 1985. Wrkg. on: book of poetry, Looking For Cold Mountain, children's book, Catula. BA, Bklyn Coll., 1975; MA, CCNY, 1985. Commun. arts cons. Midwood-Kings Hwy. Dev. Corp., Bklyn., 1979-80; sales co-ord. Berlitz Pubs., NYC, 1981-83; prod. supr. MacMillan Book Clubs, NYC, 1983; pub. Gull Books, Prattsville, NY, 1980—. Address: Box 273A Prattsville NY 12468

BENNETT, GARY LEE, b. Twin Falls, ID, Jan. 17, 1940, s. Joseph Albert and Adelaide Phillipa (Leonard) B.; m. Cleo Sue Guetschow, Sept. 14, 1961; 1 stepson, Bruce Norman McMurtrie. Author: The Star Sailors (novel), 1980; contrbr. articles: Popular Sci., Astronomy, Technology Rvw, Aviation Space, other mags. AA, Boise State U., 1960, BS, U. Idaho, 1962, MNuclear Sci, 1966; PhD,Wash. State U., 1970. Safety mgr. AEC, Germantown, Md., 1971-74; tech. asst., bur. chief Nuclear Regulatory Comm., Silver Spring, Md., 1974-80; div. dep. dir. U.S. Dept. Energy, Germantown, 1980—. Mem. SFWA, Small Press Wrtrs. and Artists Orgn. Home: 704 Carr Ave Rockville MD 20850

BENNETT, GLADYS JENKINS, b. Tuscaloosa, AL, Nov. 13, 1929; d. Malcolm Dewey and Lena Arizona (Extine) Jenkins; div. 1967; children—Carol Diane, Clifford Daniel, Michael David, Peggy Lynne. Contrbr. articles: Natl. Examiner, Mesa Mag., Spur-Shopper, Education Computer News, various other local news organs. Wrkg. on young adult novels. BS in Journalism, Ariz. State U., 1982. Freelance wrtr., 1977-81; mng. ed. Sch. Sci. and Math. Jnl., Tempe, Ariz., 1981—. Mem. NWC, Ariz. Authors Assn. Home: Box 509 Queen Creek AZ 85242

BENNETT, IRVING, b. Bridgeport, CT, June 11, 1923; s. Isadora B. and Dorothy Mae (Sheer) B.; m. Trude Friesem, July 5, 1945; children—Linda Mae, Donald Walter. D. Optometry, Pa. State Coll. Optometry, 1944. Practice of optometry, Beaver Falls, Pa., 1946—; pres. Advisory Enterprises, Inc., 1971-87, OptiFair, Inc., 1977-87. Editor: Jnl of Am. Optometric Assn., 1957-64; American editor, Optica International, 1964-70; editor: Optometric Mgmnt., 1971-81; contrbg. collaborator: Dictionary of Visual Science.Home: 3307 7th Ave Beaver Falls PA 15010

BENNETT, JOHN FREDERIC, (Sean Garrigan), b. Pittsfield, MA, Mar. 12, 1920, s. John Frederic and Lauretta (Simpson) Garrigan; m. Bertie Evelyn Verschleisser, Apr. 11, 1944 (div. 1956); m. Elizabeth Mary Jones, Aug. 20, 1960; children—Catherine Jeremy, Jennifer Nora. Author: Melville's Humanitarian Thought, 1956, (poems) The Zoo Manuscript, 1968, Griefs and Exultations, 1970, The Struck Leviathan, 1970, Knights and Squires, 1972, Echoes from the Peaceable Kingdom, 1978, Seeds of Mustard, Seeds of Tare, 1979, Fire in the Dust, 1980, Beyond the Compass Rose, 1983, The Nixon Rubaiyat, 1984, The Holy Unicorn, 1985, A Book of Trousered Apes, 1987. BA, Oberlin Coll., 1942; MA, U. Wis., 1950, PhD, 1956. Instr. English, Ind. U., Jeffersonville, 1953-58; asst. prof. Beloit Coll., Wis., 1958-59; prof., chmn. dept. English, Rockford Coll., Ill., 1959-68; disting. prof. English, St. Norbert Coll., De Pere, Wis., 1968—, poet-in-residence, 1979. Recipient Devins Memorial Award, 1970, poetry award Soc. Midland Authors, 1970, 78. Mem. Melville Soc. Home: 526 Karen Ln Green Bay WI 54301

BENNETT, JOHN J., (Johnny Angel), b. Bklyn., Aug. 8, 1938, s. John J. and Margaret E. (Kiefer) B. Author: Anarchistic Murmurs from a High Mountain Valley (prose poems), 1975, The Night of the Great Butcher (stories), 1976, The Party to End All Parties (stories), 1976, La-La Poems, 1977, The Adventures of Achilles Jones (novel), 1979, Whiplash on the Couch (stories, poems), 1979, Crazy Girl on the Bus (poems), 1979, The White Papers (essays, 4 vols.), 1982, 83, Tripping in America (mixed genre), 1984, Survival Song (mixed genre), 1985, Infant of the Aftermath (novel), 1985, Crime of the Century (social commentary), 1987; contrbr. to anthologies: Poets West, 1975, Pushcart Prize Anthology, 1976, Vagabond Anthology, 1978, Iron Country Anthology (1st prize in fiction), 1978, Editor's Choice Anthology—Best of the Small Presses, 1965-77, 1980, Fiction-82, 1982; contrbr. rvws., essays: Clinton St. Qtly, San Francisco Rvw of Books, Small Press Rvw, others; contrbr. to: Crab Creek Rvw, Pulpsmith, Poetry Now, Litmus, other lit mags. Ed., pub. Vagabond Press, 1966—. Recipient William Wantling award, 1985. Address: Box 395 Ellensburg WA 98926

BENNETT, JOHN M., (Nick L. Nips, The Spitter, Johnee), b. Chgo., Oct. 12, 1942; s. John William and Kathryn (Goldsmith) B.; m. Janifer H. (div.); child—William E.; m. C. Mehrl, July 4, 1980; child—Benjamin K. Author: more than 35 bks. and chapbks., including White Screen, 1976, Found Objects, NY, 1973, Meat Watch, 1977, Nips Poems, 1980, Puking Horse, 1980, Time Release, 1978, Jerks, 1980, Some Blood (With C. Mehrl Bennett), 1982, Blender, 1983, Burning Dog, 1983, Antpath, 1984, No Boy, 1985, 13 Spits, 1986, Ax Tongue, 1986, The The Poems, 1987; poetry, graphics, word art, articles, reviews, and translations to lit mags; ed. Lost and Found Times, 1974—; pub.-ed., Luna Bisonte Prods, 1974—. BA, Washington Univ., 1966; PhD, UCLA, 1970. Asst. prof., Ohio State Univ., 1969-76; Latin America Ed., OSU Library, 1976—; ed. dir., Ohio Poetry Therapy Ctr. and Library (Columbus), 1981—. Mem. Natl. Assn. for Poetry Therapy. Home: 137 Leland Ave Columbus OH 43214

BENNETT, LERONE, JR., b. Clarksdale, MS, Oct. 17, 1928; s. Lerone and Alma (Reed) B.; m. Gloria Sylvester, July 21, 1956; children—Alma Joy, Constance, Courtney, Lerone III. Author: Before the Mayflower: A History of Black America, 1619-1964, 1962, rev. 1964, 82, The Negro Mood, 1964, What Manner of Man, A Biography of Martin Luther King, Jr., 1964, Confrontation: Black and White, 1965, Black Power U.S.A., 1968, Pioneers in Protest, 1968, The Challenge of Blackness, 1972, The Shaping of Black America, 1975, Wade in the Water, 1979; contrbr. to: New Negro Poets: USA, 1964, American Negro Short Stories, 1966. BA, Morehouse Coll., 1949, D.Letters, 1966; D.Hum., Wilberforce U., 1977; D.Litt., Marquette U., 1979, Voorhees Coll., 1981, Morgan State U., 1981; LHD, U. Ill., 1980, Lincoln Coll., 1980, Dillard U., 1980. Reporter Atlanta Daily World, 1949-51, city editor, 1952-53; assoc. editor Ebony mag., Chgo., 1953-58, sr. editor, 1958—; vis. prof. history Northwestern U., 1968—69. Recipient Patron Saints award Soc. Midland Authors, 1965; Book of Year Award Capital Press Club, 1963; AAAL Acad.-Inst. lit. award, 1978. Mem. Black Acad. Arts and Letters, Phi Beta Kappa, Kappa Alpha Psi, Sigma Delta Chi. Office: Ebony Mag 820 S Michigan Ave Chicago IL 60605

BENNETT, LIBBIE ANN, b. Moscow, OH; d. Thomas S. and Margaret (Davis) Neftzer; m. Thomas W. Bennett, Oct. 10, 1970; children—Michael, Alicia. Contrbr. articles to newspapers, magazines, poems to anthols. Grad. public schls., Felicity, OH Recipient Golden Poet award World of Poetry, 1987, Honorable Mention, 1987. Home: 1600 N Altman Rd New Richmond OH 45157

BENNETT, NORMAN E., b. Saugus, MA, Aug. 15, 1917; s. Elmer A. and Mildred J. (Smith) B.; m. Eleanor Teel, Dec. 3, 1942; children—Roger, Jeffrey, Alison. Student, N.Y. U., 1937-40. Dir. bus. relations, v.p. Natl. Better Bus. Bur., 1946-51; with P.F. Collier, Inc., NYC, 1951—, sr. v.p., 1960-65, pres., 1965-68, chmn. bd., 1968-71; v.p. Crowell-Collier & MacMillan, Inc., 1961-67, sr. v.p., 1968-73; chmn. bd. Merit Students Ency., Inc., NYC, 1968-71; pres. P.F. Collier Ltd., Toronto, Ont., Can., 1965-68, chmn., 1968-71; chmn. bd. Crowell Intl., 1970-72. Served to lt. col., ord. dept. AUS, 1941-45. Home: Box 607 Center Harbor NH 03226

BENNETT, PATRICIA ANN WORK, b. Houston, Feb. 27, 1947; d. Otis James and Laura (Irwin) Work; m. Richard Carl Bennett, Oct. 27, 1972; children—Matthew, Elizabeth, Kimberly, Timothy. Author: (with husband) Stepfamilies: The Freedom to Be, 1983. Contrbr. articles to Nurturing News, Working Mother. Ed.: Leadership News, 1976—, Stepfamilies & Beyond, 1980—. Cert. as Registered Nurse, Methodist Hosp. of Dallas, 1968. With public relations Listening Inc., Gary, IN, 1978—; free-lance wrtr., 1985—. Office: Listening Inc 8716 Pine. Ave Gary IN 46403

BENNETT, PAUL (LEWIS), b. Gnadenhutten, OH, Jan. 10, 1921, s. John Emerson and Mary Eva (Gehring) B.; m. Martha Jeanne Leonhart, Dec. 31, 1941; children—Charles Kirby, William David. Author: Robbery on the Highway (novel), 1961, The Living Things (novel), 1975, A Strange Affinity (poetry), 1975, The Eye of Reason (poetry), 1976, Building A House (poetry), 1986. Follow the River (novel), 1987. BA, Ohio U., Athens, 1942; MA, Harvard U., 1947. Mem. faculty Denison U., Granville, Ohio, 1947—, Lorena Woodrow Burke chair of English, 1978-86, poet-in-residence, 1986—; profl. gardener, orchardist, Granville, 1948—. Served to lt. (j.g.), USNR, 1942-45. NEA fellow, 1974. Home: 1281 Burg St Granville OH 43023

BENSINK, JOHN ROBERT, (John Robertson), b. Corry, Pa., Aug. 7, 1948; s. John Robert and Grace Marie (Frisina) B.; m. Lauren Pesich, Aug. 5, 1972; 1 dau., Elizabeth Sharon. Co-author (as John Robertson, with Brett Rutherford): Piper (novel), 1987; contrbr. articles: New York Mag., MONEY, Playboy, other publs.; short stories in anthologies and mags. Wrkg. on non-fiction, screen writing, short story collection. Student Edinboro State Coll., 1968-70. Ed. Nat Assn. Printers and Lithographers, NYC., 1976-78; copywrtr. New Sch. Social Research, NYC., 1979-80; exec. ed. Twilight Zone Mag., NYC., 1981-86; ed. Country Inns-Bed & Breakfast Mag., NYC., 1986-87; freelance wrtr., Los Angeles, 1987—. Mem. WGA Agent: Shorr, Stille 800 S Robertson Blvd Los Angeles CA 90035

BENSKO, JOHN, b. Birmingham, AL, Nov. 28, 1949; s. John and Patricia Frances (Blanton) B.; m. Rosemary Collins, May 1980; 1 son, Thomas. Author: Green Soldiers, 1981; contrbr. poetry numerous publs. inc. Poetry, Critical Qtly, Carolina Qtly, The Morrow Anthology of Younger Am Poets, The Best of INTRO, Shenandoah, Black Warrior Rvw. BA, U Ala, 1973, MFA, 1979; PhD, FLA State U, 1985. Tching. asst., writing fellow and instr. U. Ala., Tuscaloosa, 1974-80; instr. Old Dominion Univ, Norfolk, Va, 1980-82; univ. fellow Fla. State U., Tallahassee, 1982-85; asst. prof. Rhodes Coll., Memphis, Tenn., 1985—. Mem. MLA. Address: Rhodes Coll 2000 N Parkway Memphis TN 38112

BENSON, CLARA MAYS, (Rusta"B"), b. Sharon Hill, PA, Feb. 3, 1932; d. Jesse Arthur and Ida Catherine (Wyatt) Mays; m. Floyd Stephen Benson, Dec. 20, 1958; 1 son, Stephen Eugene. Contrbr. poems, short stories to newspapers, anthols. Wrkg. on books of spontaneous poetry, short stories for children, holiday crafts; adaptation of A Gumper Christmas. B.Fine Arts, Edn., Phila. Coll. Art., 1954; M.Ed., Temple U., 1962. Tchr. art public schls., Phila., 1956-67, substitute tchr. art public schls., Ayer, MA, 1975-78, Rockville, MD, 1984-86; administrative asst. MSSI, Gaithersburg, MD, 1985—. Coord. arts Harvard Bicentennial Com., MA, 1975-76; bd. dir. Nashoba Art Assn., Littleton, MA, 1976-78. Named Best New Poet, Am. Poetry Assn., 1986, 87. Mem. Natl. Museum Women in Arts. Home: 22600 Fitzgerald Dr Gaithersburg MD 20879 Mailing Address: Box 1583 Rockville MD 20850

BENSON, LARRY DEAN, b. Sioux Falls, SD, June 20, 1929; s. Joseph Robert and Elsie (Ellis) B.; m. Margaret Owens, Jan. 5, 1951; children—Cassandra, Gavin, Amanda, Geoffrey. Author: Art and Tradition in Sir Gawain and the Green Knight, 1965, (with T. M. Andersson) The Literary Context of Chaucer's Fabliaux, 1971, King Arthur's Death, 1974; editor: The Learned and the Lewed, 1975, Malory's Morte D'Arthur, 1976, (with J. F. Leyerle) Chivalric Literature, 1980, (with S. Wenzel) Wisdom of Poetry, 1982; asst. editor: Speculum, 1965—. AB, U. Calif. at Berkeley, 1955, AM, 1957, PhD, 1959. Lectr. English U. Calif. at Berkeley, 1958-59; instr. Harvard, 1959-62, asst. prof., 1962-65, assoc. prof., 1966-69, prof. 1969—, chmn. dept. English and Am. lang. and lit., 1980—; Allston Burr. sr. tutor Quincy House, 1963-65. Served with USMCR, 1946-48, 50-51. Guggenheim fellow, 1965. Fellow Medieval Acad. Am., Am. Acad. Arts and Scis. Home: 24 Woodland Rd Lexington MA 02173

BENSON, STEVE, b. Princeton, NJ, June 14, 1949, s. Paul Roy and Rachel Anne (Walker) B. Author: As Is, 1978, Blindspots, 1981, The Busses, 1981, Dominance, 1985, Briarcombe Paragraphs, 1985; contrbr.: In the American Tree anthology, 1986. BA, Yale U., 1971; MFA, U. Calif., Irvine, 1973. Home: 2325 McKinley Ave Berkeley CA 94703

BENTLEY, ERIC, b. Eng., Sept. 14, 1916; s. Fred and Laura (Eveleen) B. Author: A Century of Hero-Worship, 1944, The Playwright as Thinker, 1946, Bernard Shaw, 1947, In Search of Theatre, 1953, The Dramatic Event, 1954, What is Theatre?, 1956, The Life of the Drama, 1964, The Theatre of Commitment, 1967, What Is Theatre and Other Reviews, 1968, A Time to Die, 1970, The Red White and Black, 1970, Are You Now?, 1972, The Recantation, 1972, Theatre of War, 1972, Expletive Deleted, 1974, Memoirs of Pilate, 1977, Rallying Cries, 1977, Lord Alfred's Lover, 1978, Wannsee, 1979, The Brecht Commentaries, 1981, Concord, 1981, The Fall of the Amazons, 1982, The Kleist Variations, 1983, Monstrous Martyrdoms, 1985, The Pirandello Commentaries, 1986, Thinking About the Playwright, 1987; author-editor: Thirty Years of Treason, 1971; editor: The Importance of Scrutiny, 1948, From the Modern Repertoire, 1949-56, The Modern Theatre, 1955-60, The Classic Theatre, 1958-61, The Theory of the Modern Stage, 1968, The Great Playwrights, 1970, Eric Bentley's Dramatic Repertoire (4 vols.), 1985-86; adapter, translator: plays A Man's a Man, 1962, Mother Courage, 1963, others. BA, Oxford (Eng.) U., 1938, LittB, 1939; PhD, Yale U., 1941; DFA (hon.), U. Wis., 1975; LittD (hon.), U. East Anglia, 1979. Brander Matthews prof. dramatic lit. Columbia, 1953-69; dramatic critic The New Republic, 1952-56; Norton prof. poetry Harvard U., 1960-61; artist-in-res. Ford Fdn. Berlin, 1964-65; Katharine Cornell prof. theatre SUNY, Buffalo, 1974-82; prof. comparative lit. U. Md., College Park, 1982—. Co-producer of DMZ, a political cabaret, 1968; recipient: George Jean Nathan award, 1966, Obie Award, 1978. Guggenheim fellow, 1948-49, 67-68; Fulbright scholar in Yugoslavia, 1980. Mem. Am. Acad. Arts and Scis. Address: 194 Riverside Dr New York NY 10025

BENTLEY, SEAN SINGER, (Siobhan Bugatti), b. Seattle, Apr. 15, 1954; s. Nelson and Beth Rita (Singer) B. m. Robin Smith, June 21, 1986. Author: Instances, 1979, Into the Bright Oasis, 1976. Contrbr. stories, poems to anthols., Poetry Northwest, Another Chicago Magazine, Cincinnati Poetry Rvw, others. Editor: Catawampus mag., 1978-79, Maniac mag., 1980; co-ed. Fine Madness mag., 1984—. BA cum laude in Cinema, U. Wash.-Seattle, 1980. Walk Don't Walk, 1980— asst. ed., Madrona Pub., Seattle, 1986—. Recipient Dearborn award U. Wash., 1976. Club: Ephemerists (pres. 1979-80). Home: 6511 16th Ave NE Seattle WA 98115

BENYO, RICHARD STEPHEN, b. Palmerton, PA, Apr. 20, 1946; s. Andrew Joseph and Dorothy Rita (Herman) B.; m. Jill Wapensky, Apr. 29, 1972 (div. 1979). Author: The Grand National Stars, 1975, The Book of Richard Petty, 1976, Superspeedway, 1977, Return to Running, 1978, The Indoor Exercise Book, 1980, Advanced Indoor Exercise Book, 1981, (with Kym Herrin) Sexercise, 1981, Masters of the Marathon, 1983, (with Elaine LaLanne) Elaine LaLanne's Complete Fitness Diary, 1984; editor: The Complete Woman Runner, 1978, Running for Everybody, 1981. BA in English lit., Bloomsburg State U., 1968. Mng. editor Times-News, Lehighton, Pa., 1968-72; editor Stock Car Racing mag., Alexandria, Va., 1972-77, sr. editor, 1977—; exec. editor Runner's World mag., Mountain View, Calif., 1977—; editorial dir. Skiers mag. and Fit mag., Mountain View, 1980—,Anderson World Books, 1980—, Strength Trng. for Beauty mag., 1983—; editor Corporate Fitness Report, Mountain View, 1980—, Natl. Health Fitness Report, 1982—, Runner's World Qtly, 1982—; v.p. J. R. Anderson Enterprizes, Inc., 1982—; pres., pub. Specific Publs., Inc., 1983—; program dir. PTVC-TV, Palmerton, Pa., 1969-72. Mem. Am. Auto Racing Writers and Broadcasters Assn. (1st pl. award for tech writing), Intl. Motor Press Assn., Athletic Congress, U.S. Ski Writers Assn., N.Y. Road Runners Club, Natl. Sportcasters and Sportstwriters Assn., Track and Field Writers of Am., Intl. Sports Press Assn. Home: PO Box 4432 Mountain View CA 94040

BERBRICH, JOAN D., b. Richmond Hill, NY, May 12, 1925, d. John Adam and Dorothy C. (Scharen) Berbrich. Author: Three Voices from Paumanok, 1969, Sounds and Sweet Airs, 1970, Heritage of Long Island, 1970, 101 Ways to Learn Vocabulary, 1971, The Women, Yes, 1973, Stories of Crime and Detection, 1974, Heaven and Hell, 1975, Wide World of Words, 1975, Writing Practically, 1976, Writing Creatively, 1977, Writing Logically, 1978, Writing About People, 1979, Writing About Fascinating Things, 1980, Writing About Curious Things, 1981, Writing About Amusing Things, 1982, Reading Today, 1983, Reading Around the World, 1985, Thirteen Steps to Better Writing, 1986, Fifteen Steps to Better Writing, 1987. BA, SUNY, 1946; MA, Columbia U., 1949, PhD, NYU, 1956. Tchr. Mineola High Schl., Garden City Park, N.Y., 1949-75; freelance wrtr., 1975—. Home: 5 Owen Ave Glens Falls NY 12801

BERCK, MARTIN GANS, b. NYC, Feb. 5, 1928; s. Samuel M. and Florence (Gans) B.; m. Lenore Fierstein, July 12, 1953; children—Jonathan, Judith, David. AB, NYU, 1947; MS in Journalism, Columbia U., 1953, Russell Sage fellow, 1968. Newsman, AP, 1953-56; successively reporter, polit. writer, UN corr., natl. editor N.Y. Herald Tribune, 1956-66; writer, editor, producer NBC News, 1966-72; editorial writer, UN Bur. chief, fgn. editor Newsday, L.I., N.Y., 1972—; adj. prof. journalism NYU, 1975—. Book editor; contrbr. articles to mags. Served with AUS, 1950-52. Mem. UN Corrs. Assn., Sigma Delta Chi, Kappa Tau Alpha. Home: 604 Ramapo Rd Teaneck NJ 07666

BERCOVITCH, HANNA MARGARETA, b. Chgo., Sept. 5, 1934; d. Sven Victor and Elizabeth (Rubin) Malmquist; m. Sacvan Bercovitch, July 29, 1956; 1 son, Eytan. Student, St. Thomas More Coll., 1960, Sir George Williams Coll., Montreal, 1960-61. Acquisition librarian Honnold Library, Claremont, Calif., 1961-62, acting rare book librarian, 1962-63, spcl. project staff, 1963-64; asst. editing Partisan Rvw, Congress Monthly, Rutgers U., N.Y.C., 1974-75, 78-80; free-lance rearch assoc. Columbia U., NYC., 1965-80; sr. editor Library of Am. Literary Classics, NYC., 1980—; guest curator Melville Whitman Exhibit, NY. Pub. Library, 1982; cons. Parkman Exhibit, NY. Hist. Soc., 1983, Henry James and Washington Squre Exhibit, NY Public Library, 1983. Office: Lib Am Lit Classics 14 E 60th New York NY 10022

BERESFORD, ELIZABETH, see Faber, Inez McAlister

BERG, ABBY MARVIN, b. NYC, July 23, 1928, d. Benjamin and Sandra (Goldfield) Marvin; m. Eugene B. Berg, Apr. 14, 1948 (div. 1979); children—Richard, Jack, David, Daniel. Contrbr. to Modern Bride, Lions Mag., Liberty News, Modern Maturity Mag., River Reporter, Between the Rivers mag., numerous other publs. Wrkg. on sociological novel. Student Pratt Inst., Bklyn., 1946-48, Abbey Inst., Manhattan, N.Y., 1946-48. Freelance ed., wrtr., pub. relations wrtr., newspaper colmnst., Bayonne, N.J. and N.Y., 1946-78; freelance wrtr., artists' rep., NYC, 1979—. Recipient Non-fiction award Wrtr.'s Digest mag., 1979, 85. Mem. Am. Women's Econ. Devel., Catskill Art Soc., Delaware Valley Arts Alliance. Address: Star Rt Box 23 Kenoza Lake NY 12750

BERG, DAVID, b. Bklyn., June 12, 1920; s. Morris Isaac and Bessie (Friedman) B.; m. Vivian Lipman, Mar. 3, 1949; children—Mitchel Ian, Nancy Anne Iva. Student, Cooper Union, Pratt Inst., U. Wis., New Schl., Iona Coll., Rochelle, N.Y., Coll. New Rochelle; ThD (hon.), Reconstructionist Rabbinical Coll., 1973. Artist-writer Will Eisner Prodns., NYC, 1940-41; assoc. editor Timely Comics, 1945—; artist-writer Fawcett Publs., NYC, 1941—, Warner Books, also Signet Books, 1956—, Mad. mag.; also contrbr. regular feature Lighter Side of; creative cons. NBC-TV, 1979—; guest tchr. Westchester (N.Y.) Schls., lectr. colls. and univs., 1968—. Author, artist: books My Friend God, 1972, Roger Kaputnik and God, 1974; also series of 11 Mad books, 1964—. Served with USAAF, 1941-45. Named to Chair of Great Cartoonists UCLA student body, 1975; David Berg Day named by Westchester County, N.Y., May 7, 1978. Mem. AL, Writers Guild West, Natl. Cartoonists Soc. Home: 14021 Marquesas Way Apt 307C Marina Del Rey CA 90291

BERG, JEAN HORTON, b. Clairton, PA, May 30, 1913; d. Harry Heber and Daisy Belle (Horton) Lutz; m. John Joseph Berg, July 2, 1938; children—Jean Horton, Julie Berg Blickle, John Joel. Author 50 books for children and young people, 1950—, articles, stories, poems for young people, articles for adults. BS in Edn., U. Pa., 1935, AM in Latin, 1937. Tchr. creative writing, 1968—; speaker in field of creative writing. Recipient U. Pa. Alumni award of merit, 1969; Follett award for beginning-to-read book, 1961; medallion City of Phila.; Friends' Central Schl. Distinguished Alumna award, 1978. Mem. AG, AL, ASCAP, Natl. League of Am. Pen Women, Phila. Childrens Reading Round Table. Home: 207 Walnut Ave Wayne PA 19087

BERGAMINO-FREY, GINA MARIE, b. Long Island, NY, Dec. 11, 1961; d. Anthony and Diane (DeSibio) Bergamino; m. Hardy A. Frey, July 28, 1984. Contrbr. over 200 poems to lit. mags., anthologies, newspapers. Wrkg. on nonfiction. BA, U. Tampa, 1986. Home: Box 952 Rantoul IL 61866

BERGE, CAROL, b. NYC; d. Albert and Molly Peppis; m. Jack Berge, June 1955; 1 son, Peter. Author: A Couple Called Moebius, 1972, Acts of Love: An American Novel, 1973, Timepieces, 1977, The Doppler Effect, 1979, Fierce Metronome 1981, Secrets, Gossip and Slander, 1984; (poetry) From a Soft Angle: Poems About Women, 1972, The Unexpected, 1976, Rituals and Gargoyles, 1976, A Song, A Chant, 1978, Alba Genesis, 1979, Alba Nemesis, 1979; editor: CENTER Press, 1970-84, Miss. Rvw, 1977-78; contrbg. editor: Woodstock Rvw, 1977—, Shearsman mag., 1980—. Disting. prof. lit. Thomas Jefferson Coll., Allendale, Mich., 1975—; tchr. fiction and poetry U. Calif. extension, Berkeley, 1976-77; assoc. prof. U. So. Miss., Hattiesburg, 1977-78; vis. prof. U. N. Mex. Honors Centr., 1978-79; vis. lectr. Wright State U., 1979, SUNY, Albany, 1980-81, U. New Mexico, 1987; tchr. Poets and Writers, Poets in the Schls. (N.Y. State Council in Arts). CAPS/NY State Council Fellow, 1974; NEA fellow, 1979-80. Mem. PEN, Am. Pen, AL, AG, PEW, MacDowell Fellows Assn., N. Mex. Press Women. Address: c/o Menza Agcy 237 W 11th St New York NY 10014

BERGER, AMY H., b. Bklyn., May 25, 1942; d. Leon and Betty Isabelle (Buchuael) Swersey; m. Murray J. Berger, Oct. 28, 1962; children—Laurel Heather, Peter Glen. Writer monthly Achievers feature, Bus. Jnl. of NJ; former ghost writer bi-monthly fashion beauty expert's mag. column; contrbr. articles to mags. & nwsprs. inclg. The NY Times, The Sunday NY News, The New Tribune, Good Housekeeping, Seventeen, US, Woman, Woman's World, Doll Reader, Metro Newark. Student Bklyn. Coll. Correspondent, The News Tribune, Woodbridge NJ, 1980-84; freelance writer, 1973—; contrbg. ed. Bus. Jnl of NJ, Jamesburg, 1985—, Woman's World, 1986—, Wooman, 1987—. Mem. NFPW, NJPW. Adress: 1 Scheid Dr Parlin NJ 08859

BERGER, ERIC, b. NYC, Dec. 18, 1906; s. David and Mary (Friedenberg) B.; m. Isabelle Gronich, Jan. 5, 1935; 1 son, Neil. Student, N.Y. U., 1924-25; LLB, St. John's Coll., Bklyn., 1928. Reporter Bklyn. Daily Eagle, 1929-31, Bklyn. Times, 1931-33; editor Natl. Sci. Publs., Inc., NYC, 1934-39; freelance writer and editor, 1940-41; with Scholastic mags., Inc., NYC, 1941—; editor Sr Scholastic, 1941-59, World Week, 1942-43, Lit. Cavalcade, 1948-55; editorial dir. Science World, 1960-70, Science Tchrs. World, 1959-70, dir. sci. dept., 1963-70; editor-in-chief high schl. div., 1968-70, assoc. publ. schl. div., 1970-72, editorial cons., 1973—. Served with AUS, 1943-45. Recipient Freedom Fdns. award for articles on democracy, 1953. Mem. Natl. Assn. Sci. Writers, AAAS. Home: 127 W 96th St Apt 9-D New York NY 10025

BERGER, THOMAS LOUIS, b. Cin. July 20, 1924; s. Thomas Charles and Mildred (Bubbe) B.; m. Jeanne Redpath, June 12, 1950. Author: novels Crazy in Berlin, 1958, Reinhart in Love, 1962, Little Big Man, 1964, Killing Time, 1967, Vital Parts, 1970, Regiment of Women, 1973, Sneaky People, 1975, Who Is Teddy Villanova?, 1977, Arthur Rex, 1978, Neighbors, 1980, Reinhart's Women, 1981, The Feud, 1983, Nowhere, 1985, Being Invisible, 1987; play Other People, performed 1970. BA with honors, U. Cin., 1948; postgrad., Columbia U., 1950-51. Litt. D. (hon.) LIU, 1986. Librarian Rand Schl. Social Sci., NYC,1948-51; staff mem. N.Y. Times Index, 1951-52; assoc. editor Popular Sci. Monthly, 1952-53; film critic Esquire 1971-73; writer in residence U. Kans. 1974. Distinguished vis. prof. Southampton Coll., 1975-76; vis. lectr., Yale U., 1981, 82; lectr., U. of Calif. Davis, 1982. Served with AUS, 1943-46, ETO. Recipient Rosenthal award Natl. Inst. Arts and Letters, 1965, Western Heritage award, 1965; Dial fellow, 1962, Ohioana Bk Award, 1982. Mem. Authors Guild, Phi Alpha Theta (hon.). Office: Congdon 111 Fifth Ave New York NY 10003

BERGERON, KATHLEEN YVONNE, b. Visalia, CA, Dec. 19, 1953, d. Harold and Ida Darlene (Atchley) Rollins; m. Lawrence Paul Bergeron, June 5, 1976; children—Jeffrey Lawrence, Leilani Darlene, Shoshana Kathleen. Contrbr. poetry, articles to Home Life, Cat Fancy,Cornerstone, Virtue, Natl. Enquirer,numerous other genl. interest publs.; columnist: The Majove Desert News, 1986—. BA in History, Calif. State U., Fresno, 1976. Home: 16537 Koch St Mojave CA 93501

BERGES, MARSHALL WILLIAM, b. Chgo; s. Charles and Beatrice (Marin). B Ed, Marquette U, U. of Chicago. Columnist Los Angeles Times Author: Corporations and the Quality of Life, 1972, The Life and Times of Los Angeles, 1984. Served with USNR Office: LA Times, Times Mirror SQ Los Angeles CA 90053

BERGL, NANCY, b. Oak Park, IL, Dec. 17, 1959; d. Harold Joseph and Dorothy Frances (Bergl). Co-editor: The Publicity Club of Chicago Media Guide, 1987. Contrbr. to Image mag. B.A. in Econ., U. Ill., Chgo., 1985. Free-lance wrtr. Chgo. Sun-Times, 1984-85; sports ed. City News Bur., Chgo., 1985-86; ed., public relations asst. Ill. Coll. of Optometry, Chgo., 1986—. Mem. Publicity Club Chgo. Home: 1590 Oak St Evanston IL 60201

BERKMAN, HAROLD W(ILLIAM), b. Bdlyn, Feb. 22, 1926; s. Abel A. and Rose (Garfinkel) B.; m. Muriel Siegel, Feb. 3, 1950; children: Gary Keith, Karen Ann. Author: (with T. J. Young) The Human Relations of Management, 1974, 2d ed, 1980, (with Young) Cases and Issues: The Human Relations of Management, 1975, ed (with B.R. Armandi and J.J. Babe2) and contrbr Contemporary and Classical Readings in Human Relations, 1975, (with Christopher C. Gilson) Consumer Behavior: Concepts and Strategies, 1978, 3d ed, 1986, (with Ivan R. Vernon) Perspectives in International Business, 1979, (with Gilson) Advertising Today: Concepts and Strategies, 1980, 2d ed, 1987, (with Armandi and Barbora) Organizational Behavior: Contemporary and Classical Readings, 1982, (with V.V. Bellur and H.F. Lau) Readings in Advertising Management, 1986, (with Bellur) Readings in Marketing Management, 1986, (with Linda Neider) Human Relations in Organizations, 1987. Ed of Proc., contrbr to jnls, including Business Critique, Jnl of the Acad of Marketing Sci, (mem ed bd) and Jnl of Marketing. BBA, U. of Ga., Athens, 1949; MBA, St. John's U., Jamaica, N.Y., 1969, Ph. D., 1971. Adj asst prof of bus admin, Long Island U., C.W. Post Center, Greenvale, N.Y., 1969-70, adj assoc prof of sociology, 1970, assoc prof, 1970-75, prof of management and marketing, 1975-77; prof. of bus. mngment and organization, U. of Miami, Coral Gables, Fla., 1977—, dir. of executive and spcl programs, 1977-80, assoc dean of Sch of Bus Admin, 1980-83, assoc dean and dir of grad programs and research admin, 1983-87; spcl. advisor to the dean & prof. of mgmt., 1987—. Vis prof, St. John's U., 1971, vis. prof mngment, N.Y. Inst of Technology, 1976. Former pres. and mem bd of dirs of Hastings and Berwick Ltd (importers and exporters of French wines) and Jarub Realty Corp. Pres and dir Valencia Liquor Shops, Inc., 1950-77; or partner and dir Halmor Management Co., 1960-77. Military service: U.S. Army, infantry 1943-46, Eur. theatre. Mem: Acad of Intl Bus, Assn for Consumer Research, Acad of Marketing Sci (exec v.p. and dir, 1971—), Amer. Marketing Assn, Amer. Management Assn, Money Management Inst., Delta Mu Delta, Delta Sigma Pi, Beta Gamma Sigma. Award for merit. service from Fed. of Jewish Philanthropies, 1963-64; cwrt. de merite from Le Comite des Vins de France, 1967; award for disting. service from Acad of Marketing Sci, 1972; conferee, Saint-Etienne of Alsace-France, 1973; Outstanding Faculty Scholar of the Year award, C.W. Post School of Business, 1974; Danforth Assn fellow, 1976; U. of Miami award for significant writing activity, 1978; Acad. of Marketing Sci Leadership award, 1979; Excellence in Published Writing award, Schl of Bus, U. of Miami, 1979; World Marketing Congress award, 1983, for leadership and scholarly contrib to marketing. Home: 5882 Southwest 105th St Miami FL 33156

BERKOV, WALTER, b. Allentown, PA, July 19, 1922; s. Hyman and Marion (Labg) B.; m. Janet Louise Smith, June 14, 1949; children—Ellen, Amy. BA in Journalism, Pa. State U., 1942. Reporter Pitts. Post-Gazette, 1949; wire editor Middletown (Ohio) Jnl, 1950-52; copy editor Atlantic City Press, 1953; wire editor, Sunday editor Columbus (Ohio) Citizen, 1953-57; copy editor, asst. fgn. and natl. editor Cleve. Plain Dealer, 1957, now book editor. Mem. Natl. Book Critics Circle. Home: 3723 W 230th North Olmsted OH 44070

BERKOW, IRA HARVEY, b. Chgo. Jan. 7, 1940; s. Harold Grosswald and Shirley (Halperin) B.; m. Dolores Case, Apr. 18, 1978. Author: Oscar Robertson: The Golden Year, 1971, (with Walt Frazier) Rockin' Steady, 1974 (ALA Best Books of Year 1975), Beyond the Dream, 1975, Maxwell Street, 1977, The DuSable Panthers, 1978, (with Rod Carew) Carew, 1980 RED: A Biography of Red Smith; The Man Who Robbed the Pierre, 1987; writer: TV documentary Champions of American Sport, 1983. BA, Miami U., Oxford, Ohio, 1963; MS in Journalism, Northwestern U., 1965. Reporter Mpls. Tribune, 1965-67; sports columnist, sports editor Newspaper Enterprise Assn., NYC, 1967-76, sports columnist and feature writer N.Y. Times, 1981—. Recipient Page One Award Newspaper Guild, Mpls., 1966, Scripps-Howard Feature award, 1969, N.Y. Public Library commendation, 1978, AP Sports Editor award, 1982. Mem. Baseball Writers Assn., Am. Basketball Writers Assn. Office: NY Times 229 W 43 St New York NY 10036

BERKWITT, GEORGE JOSEPH, b. Springfield, MA, Feb. 14, 1921; s. Louis Harry and Lillian B.; m. Gilda King, Oct. 1, 1948; 1 dau., Randi Lynn. BS in Journalism, N.Y.U., 1949. Journeyman tool and diemaker Springfield Armory, 1941-44; promotional writer Air Reduction Inc., 1949-53; assoc. editor Metalworking mag., 1953-58; indsl. mktg. editor Printer's Ink, 1958-61; spcl. feature editor Mill & Factory mag., 1961-65; sr. editor Dun's Rvw, 1965-73; exec. editor Modern Industry mag., 1967-69; chief editor Indsl. Distbn. mag., 1973—; editorial bd. Am. Bus. Press, 1975-76. Pres. Council, mem. bd. dirs. Hudson Guild Settlement House, 1973-75. Served with U.S. Army, 1944-45. Mem. Soc. Advancement Mgmt. Home: 280 9th Ave New York NY 10001

BERLES, JAMES JOHN, b. Fort Wayne, IN, Jan. 8, 1957; s. John James Berles and Daisy L. (McCarty) Headford. Contrbr. articles to Ocean Industry, Hydrocarbon Processing, World Oil, Petroleum Mgt., 1981—. BA, IN U. Campaign co-ord. Indiana Democratic Party, 1979-81; prodn. ed. Gulf Pub. Co., Houston, 1981-82; asst. ed. World Oil, Houston, 1982-84; news ed. & writer Petroleum Mgt., Houston, 1984—. Home: 2100 Winrock 68 Houston TX 77057

BERLINER, DON, b. Columbus, OH, July 3, 1930; s. Abe H. and Helen(Kolitz) B. Author: Scale Reference Data: World War II Jet Fighters, 1982, Victory over the Wind: A History of the Absolute World Air Speed Record, 1983, Record-Breaking Airplanes, 1985, Unusual Airplanes, 1986. Juveniles: Airplane Racing, 1979, Home-Built Airplanes, 1979, Aerobatics, 1980, Yesterday's Airplanes, 1980, Scale-Model Airplanes, 1982, Flying-Model Airplanes, 1982 Personal Airplanes (illus. with photos), 1982, Helicopters, 1982. Author of Competition Scene, monthly column in Air Progress, 1965-73. Contrb ed of Airplanes of the World, 1976. B. Sc., Ohio

State U., Columbus, 1953; grad. study at Ohio U., Athens, 1958. Reporter and photographer, Painesville (O.) Telegraph, 1959-62; staff writer and ed, Science Trends, 1962-65; staff writer Natl Invest. Comm. on Aerial Phenomena, 1965-68; freelance aviation writer, 1969—. Military service: Ohio Air Natl. Guard, 1948-50; U.S. Air Force, 1950-51; became staff sgt. Men: Intl Aerobatic Club, Intl Soc of Aviation Historians, Experimental Aircraft Assn. Home: 1202 S Washington St Alexandria VA 22314

BERLITZ, CHARLES FRAMBACH, b. NYC, Nov. 22, 1914; s. Charles L. and Melicent (Berlitz) Frambach; m. Valerie Anne Seary, Jan. 28, 1950; children—Lin Maria, Marc Daniel. Author: Berlitz Method Spanish, 1947, Berlitz Method English, 1947, Berlitz Method French, 1954, Berlitz Self Teacher French, 1949, Berlitz Self Teacher Spanish, 1949, Berlitz Self Teacher Italian, 1949, Berlitz Self Teacher German, 1949, 50, Berlitz Self Teacher Russian, 1951, Berlitz Self Teacher English, 1951, Berlitz Self Teacher Portuguese, 1953, Berlitz Self Teacher Hebrew, 1953, Phrase Books and Pocket Dictionaries—French, German, Spanish, Italian, 1954, Berlitz Self-Teaching Record Course: French, 1956, Spanish, 1957, German, 1957, Italian, 1958, Language Teaching Films, 1962, World Language Phrase Book, 1962, The Mystery of Atlantis, 1969, Mysteries from Forgotten Worlds, 1973, The Bermuda Triangle, 1974 (Dag Hammarskjold Intl. prize for Lit. 1976), Without a Trace, 1976, The Philadelphia Experiment, 1978, Doomsday 1999 A.D., 1981, Native Tongues, 1982, Atlantis the VIII Continent, 1984, Passport to Language, 1986, The Lost Ship of Noah, 1987. Grad. Riverdale County Schl., 1932; BA magna cum laude, Yale U., 1936. Dir. Berlitz Schls. Langs. NYC, Balt., Boston, Chgo. and S.A., 1937-41, v.p. 1944-67, Berlitz Publs., 1947-66, pres., 1966-67; v.p. Berlitz Schls. East Asia. Served as maj. intelligence officer AUS, WWII, lt. col. ret. Mem. Res. Officers Assn., Mil. Order of World Wars. Office: Doubleday 245 Park Ave New York NY 10017

BERMAN, ANN MURIEL, b. Montreal, Quebec, Canada, Apr. 25, 1951, came to U.S., 1974; d. Samuel and Regina (Kaps) Berman. contrbr. Poetry Press, American Poetry Anthology, 1985. BA in Counseling Psych. City U of NY, 1978; MA in Psychol/Psychometrics, Columbia U., 1980. Psychometrician/Counsl. Project Find (New York), 1977-81; Educational Serv. Inst. of Electric. & Electron. Engineers (New York), 1981-83; Independ. Contract. (New York), 1983—. Third Prize, Poetry Press, 1985. Mem. American Personnel & Guidance Assoc, 1981—, NWU. Home: 644 Amsterdam Ave New York NY 10025

BERMAN, EDGAR FRANK, b. Balt., Aug. 6, 1915; s. Isaas Isaac and Sarah (Katz) B.; m. Phoebe Rhea, Nov. 22, 1952. Author: Teilhardian Philosophy, 1966, The Unchanging Woman, 1967, Population and Foreign Policy, 1965, Population and Politics, 1969, The Politician Primeval, 1974, The Solid Gold Stethoscope, 1976, Hubert—The Triumph and Tragedy of the Humphrey I Knew, 1979, The Compleat Chauvinist: A Guide for the Bedeviled Male, 1982, In Africa with Schweitzer, 1986; editor: The Carroll County Times, 1964-70; columnist: N. Am. Newspaper Alliance, 1970-71, USA Today. MD, U. Md., 1939. Diplomate: Am. Bd. Surgery. Intern Sinai Hosp., Balt., 1939-40, resident in surgery, Lutheran Hosp., Johns Hopkins Hosp.; cons. surgeon to Albert Schweitzer Hosp., Lambarene, Gabon, 1960, Med. Aspects of Community Devel., Columbia, S. Am., 1961; coordinator rural health projects, Central Am., AID, 1962-65, Nat. Physicians Com. for Johnson and Humphrey, 1964; chief cons. to State Dept., AID on Lat. Am. Health, 1962-67; dir. Haiti Med. Pilot Project, 1960-61; cons. to White House Task Force, Medicare, 1962-62; dir. of med. survey southeast Asia, 1960-61; Adviser to the Vice President of U.S., 1965-69. Served to lt. USN, 1943-46. Fellow ACS; mem. AMA, Natl. Pub. Health Assn., Internat. Coll. Surgeons (regent 1957-62), N. Y. Acad. Scis. Address: 1116 Valley Rd Lutherville MD 21093

BERMAN, RONALD STANLEY, b. NYC, Dec. 15, 1930; s. Herman and Jean (Wolfson) B.; m. Barbara Barr, Aug. 27, 1953; children—Andrew, Julia, Katherine. Author: Henry King and the 17th Century, 1964, A Reader's Guide to Shakespeare's Plays, 1965, Henry V: A Collection of Critical Essays, 1968, America in the Sixties: An Intellectual History, 1970. BA, Harvard U., 1952; PhD,Yale U., 1959. Instr. Columbia U., 1959-61, asst. prof. 1961-62; assoc. prof. Kenyon College, Gambier, Ohio, 1962-65, U. Calif. at San Diego, 1965-68, prof. Renaissance lit., 1968-71, 77—; chmn. Nat. Endowment for Humanities, 1971-77, Fedn. Council on Arts and Humanities, 1975-77. Editorial assoc. Kenyon Rev., 1963-70. Served to lt. USNR, 1952-56. Home: 2965 Ariane Dr San Diego CA 92117

BERMAN, SANFORD, b. Chgo., Oct. 6, 1933; s. Samuel and Dorothy (Feinman) Berman; m. Lorraine Oliver, May 31, 1968; children—Marlise Jill, Paul. Consulting/contributing editor: New Pages, Interracial Books for Children Bulletin, Collection Building, Technicalities, other profl. jnls., editor: ALA/SRRT Newsletter, 1973-75, HCL Cataloging Bulletin, 1973-79; contrbr. to Library Journal, Reference Librarian, Utne Rdr, Shmate other prof. and popular jnls; author, editor, bibliography and technical for fields of library science/alternative press including Prejudices and Antipathies, 1971, Joy of Cataloging, 1981, Alternative Library Literature, 1984, Subject Cataloging, 1984, Cataloging Special Materials, 1986, Alternative Library Literature, 1987. Periodicals librarian UCLA Res. library (Los Angeles), 1964-68, U. of Zambia library (Lusaka, Zambia), 1968-70; librarian Makerere Inst. of Soc. Res. (Kamoala, Uganda), 1971-72; head cataloger Hennepin County Library (Minnetonka, MN), 1973—. SP3 US Army, 1955-57, West Germany. Bd. member Minnesota Reviews, Inc. Mem. NWU, Librarians for Nuclear Arms Control, ALA Social Responsibilities Round Table, Am. Humanist Assn., New Jewish Agenda. Office: Hennepin County Library 12601 Ridgedale Dr Minnetonka MN 55343

BERMANT, CHARLES MARK, b. Bklyn., Mar. 27, 1954; s. Oser I. and Lilian (Maringer) B. Contrbr. The President And The Press, 1984, and numerous newspapers. BS, Boston U., 1977. Reporter, Rio Grande Sun, Espanola, NM, 1977-78, Carlsbad (NM) Current Argus, 1978-79; assoc. Jack Anderson Ent., Washington, DC, 1980-84, assoc. ed. PC Magazine, 1984-86; sr. ed. Infoworld, 1986-87. Home: 727A Waller St San Francisco CA 94117

BERNARD, DAVID KANE, b. Baton Rouge, Nov. 20, 1956; s. Elton David and Loretta (Artigue) B.; m. Connie Jo Sharpe, June 6, 1981; 1 son, Jonathan David. Author: In Search of Holiness, 1981; The Oneness of God, 1983; The New Birth, 1984; Pratical Holiness: A Second Look, 1985; Essentials of Oneness Theology, 1985; The Message of Romans, 1986. Contrbr. to religious books. BA magna cum laude, Rice U., 1978; JD with honors, U. Tex.-Austin, 1981. Bar: Tex. 1981. Ordained minister United Pentecostal Ch. Intl. Dean of students Jackson Coll. of Ministries, Miss., 1981-82, dean of missions, 1981-85, asst. v.p., 1982-86; assoc. ed. United Pentecostal Ch. Internat., Hazelwood, Mo., 1986—. Order of Coif, U. Tex., 1981; recipient Chancellors award U. Tex., 1981. Mem. Phi Beta Kappa. Home: 143 Mission Walk Ct Florissant MO 63031

BERNARD, KENNETH, b. Bklyn, May 7, 1930; s. Otis and Mary (Travaglini) B.; m. Elaine Ceil Reiss, Sept. 2, 1952; children--Lucas, Judd, Kate. Author: plays Night Club and Other Plays, 1971, Two Stories, 1973, The Moldive Chronicles, 1987. BA, CCNY, 1953; MA, Columbia U., 1956, Ph.D., 1962. Faculty, English dept. L.I.U., N.Y.C., 1959—.; profl. Cons N.Y. Creative Artists Pub. Service Program, 1973-75, Mass. Arts and Humanities Found., 1975—, Wis. Arts Bd., 1975; v.p. N.Y. Theater Strategy, 1972-79; adv. editor Confrontation 1973-75, asst. editor, 1976, fiction editor, 1979-85; cons Md. Arts Council, 1978. Served with AUS, 1953-55. Recipient Arvon Poetry prize, 1980; Office for Advanced Drama research grantee U. Minn., 1971; N.Y. State Creative Artists Pub. Service grantee, 1973, 76; Rockefeller grantee, 1975; Guggenheim fellow, 1972-73; NEA grantee in fiction, 1978. Home: 800 Riverside Dr New York NY 10032

BERNARD, ROBERT, see Martin, Robert Bernard

BERNAUER, CAROL CANDICE, b. Cleve., Nov. 12, 1956; d. Nelson Clarence and Lois Carol (Calmer) B. Author chapbooks: Modern Day Beasties I, 1983, Modern Day Beasties II, 1984. Contrbr. poems to anthols. B.F.A., Clev. Inst. Art., 1979; M.B.A., Baldwin Wallace Coll., 1987. Advt. coord. Ferro Corp., Cleve., 1980—. Home: 1304 W 105 St Cleveland OH 44102

BERNAYS, ANNE, b. NYC,Sept. 14, 1930; d. Edward L. and Doris E. (Fleischman) B.; m. Justin Kaplan, July 29, 1954; children—Susanna, Hester, Polly. Novels: Short Pleasures, 1962, The New York Ride, 1965, Prudence, Indeed, 1966, The First to Know, 1975, Growing Up Rich, 1975, The School Book, 1980, The Address Book, 1983; numerous non-fiction pieces and rvws. Wrkg. on novel under contract. BA, Barnard Coll., 1952. Mng. editor Discovery mag., NYC,1953-56; staff extension program Harvard U., Cambridge, Mass., 1977—; vis. writer U. Mass., Boston, 1985. Mem. panel Mass. Council Arts and Humanities, Boston, 1972-74. Mem. PEN; exec. bd. PEN American Center; chair PEN/New England. Recipient Edward Lewis Wallant award, 1976, Matrix award Women in Communication, 1981. Home: 16 Francis Ave Cambridge MA 02138

BERNE, KARIN, see Karni, Michaela Jordan

BERNE, STANLEY, b. Port Richmond, S.I., NY, June 8, 1923; s. William and Irene (Daniels) B.; m. Arlene Zekowski, July 1952. Author: (fiction) A First Book of the Neo-Narrative, 1954; The Dialogues, 1962; The Multiple Modern Gods and Other Stories, 1964; The Unconscious Victorious and Other Stories, 1969; The Great American Empire, 1981; (criticism) with A. Zekowski) Cardinals & Saints . . . On the aims and purposes of the arts in our time, 1958; Future Language, 1977; (poetry) The New Rubaiyat of Stanley Berne, 1973. BS, Rutgers U. 1947; MA, NYU, 1949, Grad. fellow La. State

U., Baton Rouge, 1954-59; assoc. prof. English, Eastern N. Mex. U., Portales, 1960-80, research prof. English, 1980—; host, co-producer TV series Future Writing Today, Sta. KENW-TV, PBS, 1984-85. Served as 2d lt USAAF, 1945-49; decorated Philippine Liberation medal, 1949; served with General McArthur, occupation of Japan 1948-49. Recipient lit. research awards Eastern N. Mex U., 1966-76. Mem. PEN, COSMEP, New Eng. Small Press Assn., Rio Grande Wrtrs. Assn., Santa Fe Wrtrs. Coop. Home: Box 4595 Santa Fe NM 87502

BERNELL, SUE, (Karin Berne, Diana Burke), b. Balt., Aug. 9, 1942; d. Jerome Herbert and Estelle (Seigel) Levy; m. Gordon Zelman Bernell, Mar. 15, 1964; children: Julie Elaine, David Allen. Author: (novels) Heart of the Matter, 1980, Impoverished Heiress, 1981, Bare Acquaintances, 1985, Shock Value, 1985. False Impressions, 1986; contrbr. to New America, Singles Scene Mag., Southwest Sports. Student U. Md.-Silver Springs, 1960, Balt. Jr. Coll., 1961. Scriptwriter Jerry Goffe Prodns., Albuquerque, 1977-81. Pres. Hadassah, Albuquerque, 1972-75; program dir. weekly show sta. KZIA, Albuquerque, 1975-78; corrections vol. County Detention Ctr., Albuquerque, 1984-86; research coordinator Turning Point Halfway House, Albuquerque, 1986. Home: 7916 Sartan Way NE Albuquerque NM 87019

BERNEY, BETTY LOU, b. Phillipsburg, KS, March 23, 1932; d. Roy Ethan and Cora Grace (Frazer) Munyon; m. Nat Berney, Jr., Dec. 28, 1951; children—LaRhonda Kaye, Rand Curtis, Lisa Gaye. Contrbr. poetry to Teammate Mag., Sunflower Petals, Phillips County Rvw, Logan Republican (KS), Hays Daily News (KS), Graybeards (Korean Veterans pubn.); articles to Salina Jnl, Phillips County Rvw, Hays Daily News; lyric awards for songwrtg. Ed. pub. schls., adult ed. classes, Colby Community Coll., Colby, Kans. Clrk. Philipsburg Sales Co., 1952-83; depty. clrk. District Court, State of Kansas, Phillips Co., 1977-83. Mem. Kansas Authors Club, Nashville Songwriter's Assn., Kansas Poetry Assn., Kansas Wrtr., Progressive Songwrtrs. Home: RR 2 Box 10 Phillipsburg KS 67661

BERNHARD, ARNOLD, b. NYC,Dec. 2, 1901; s. Bernhard and Regina (Steigelfest) B.; m. Janet Marie Kinghorn, Dec. 21, 1929; children—Jean Haxton (Mrs. Edgar M. Buttner), Arnold Van Hoven. BA, Williams Coll., 1925; LL. D.; LH.D., Skidmore Coll., U. Bridgeport. Newspaper reporter, 1926-28, securities analyst, 1928-31, investment counsel, 1931—; founder, chief exec. officer Arnold Bernhard & Co., Inc., 1935. Editor and research chmn. The Value Line Investment Survey, N.Y., 1936—, The Value Line Over-the-Counter Spcl. Situations Service, 1951—, The Value Line Convertibles Service, 1967—; pres., portfolio mgr. The Value Line Fund, 1950—, The Value Line Spcl. Situations Fund, 1956—; chmn. The Value Line Leveraged Growth Investors, Inc., 1972—, The Value Line Cash Fund, 1979—, The Value Line Tax Exempt Fund, The Value Line Bond Fund, 1981—. Pres. Mid-Century Book Society, 1955-65; life trustee U. Bridgeport. Mem. Phi Beta Kappa, Delta Signma Rho, Delta Upsilon. Home: 21 N Sylvan Rd Westport CT 06880

BERNSTEIN, BURTON, b. Boston, MA, Jan. 31, 1932; s. Samuel Joseph and Jennie (Resnick) B.; m./Ellen Louise Hora-Siccama, 1960 (div. 1977), Jane Ewen Anderson, 1984; children: (1st marriage) Karen, Michael. Author: The Grove, 1961, The Lost Art. 1963, The Sticks, 1970, Thurber: A Biography, 1975, ed and contrbr Look, Ma, I'm Kool! and Other Casuals (anthol.), 1977, Sinai: The Great and Terrible Wilderness, 1979, Family Matters: Sam, Jennie, and the Kids, 1982, Plane Crazy, 1985. Author of TV scripts. Contrbr of fiction and articles to magazines. AB, Dartmouth Coll.; MS, Columbia U., 1954. Writer, DuMont Television, NYC, 1956; writer, New Yorker, 1957—.Military service: U.S. Army, 1954-56. Office: New Yorker 25 West 43rd St New York NY 10036

BERNSTEIN, CARL, b. Washington, Feb. 14, 1944; s. Alfred David and Sylvia (Walker B.; m. Nora Ephron, 1976 (div.); children—Jacob Walker, Max Ephron. Copyboy to reporter, Washington Star, 1960-65; reporter Elizabeth (N.J.) Jour., 1965-66, Washington Post, 1966-76; Washington bur. chief ABC, 1979-81; corr. ABC News, 1981-84. Author: (with Bob Woodward) All the President's Men, 1974, The Final Days, 1976. Student, U. Md., 1961-64; LL. D., Boston U., 1975. Served with AUS, 1968. Recipient; Drew Pearson prize for investigative reporting of Watergate, 1972; George Polk meml. award; Worth Bingham prize; Heywood Broun award Intl. Newspaper Guild; Sigma Delta Chi Distinguished Service award; Sidney Hillman Fdn. award; gold medal U. Mo. Schl. Journalism, 1972.Address: Nesbit 40 W 57th St New York NY 10019

BERNSTEIN, CHARLES, b. NYC, Apr. 4, 1950; m. Susan Bee; 1 dau., Emma Bee. Author: Shade, 1978, Controlling Interests, 1980, Resistance, 1983, Islets/Irritations, 1983, The Sophist, 1987, Contents Dream: Essays 1975-84, 1986, others; contrbr. poems to lit. mags, anthols; editor: L-A-N-G-U-A-G-E, 1978-81, Language Sample, 1982, The L=A=N=G=U=A=G=E Book, 1984, 43 Poets (1984), 1986. AB, Harvard Coll, 1972. Dir. intelligence services Segue Found., NYC, 1978—; dir. research Dysraphic Studies Ctr., NYC, 1982—. Poetry fellow NEA, 1980, Guggenheim fellow, 1985. Home: 464 Amsterdam Ave New York NY 10024

BERNSTEIN, HERBERT J., b. Bklyn., Sept. 26, 1944, s. David and Dorothy (Ashery-Skupsky) B.; m. Frances C. Turnheim, Apr. 7, 1968; children—Michael Edward, Daniel Julius. Author (with others): Four High Level Extensions of FORTRAN IV, 1972; author tech. reports and papers for publ. in profl. jnls. BA magna cum laude with honors in maths., NYU, 1964, MS, 1965, PhD, 1968. Computer scientist; sr. research scientist Courant Inst. Math. Scis., NYU, 1983—. Mem. profl. orgns. Home: 5 Brewster Ln Bellport NY 11713

BERNSTEIN, JANE, b. Bklyn., June 10, 1949; d. David and Ruth (Levinson) Bernstein; children—Charlotte Claire, Rachel Alexa, Glynn. Author: Shadow and Light, 1988, Seven Minutes in Heaven, 1986, Departures, 1979; contrbr. stories to Mademoiselle and Prairie Schooner. BA, NYU, 1971; MFA Columbia U., 1977. Instr. jnlsm. Rutgers Univ., 1977-79; seminar instr., N.J., 1980-83; screenwriter. Fellow (fiction) NJ State Council on the Arts, 1981-82; NEA fellow, 1982. Mem. WGA (East). Address: 29 Cowperthwaite Pl Westfield NJ 07090

BERNSTEIN, MASHEY MAURICE, b. Dublin, Ireland, Sept. 13, 1946, came to U.S., 1971, naturalized, 1985; s. Solomon and Bertha (Saperstein) B. Contrbr. articles in mags. including Newsweek, U.S. West, Flex, Midstream. BA, Trinity Coll., Dublin, 1970; PhD, U. Calif.-Santa Barbara, 1977. Dir edn. Kehilath Israel Synagogue, Overland Park, Kans., 1977-87; prin. Community Religious Schl., Prairie Village, 1978-86; free-lance wrtr., 1986—. Recipient Simon Rockower award for excellence in Jewish jnlsm., Am. Jewish Press Assn., 1985. Mem. MLA. Home: 7414 Chadwick Shawnee Mission KS 66208

BERNSTEIN, ROBERT LOUIS, b. NYC,Jan. 5, 1923; s. Alfred and Sylvia (Bloch) B.; m. Helen Walter, Nov. 23, 1950; children—Peter Walter, Tom Alfred, William Samuel. Grad. Lincoln Schl., NYC,1940; BS, Harvard U., 1944. Genl. sales mgr. Simon & Schuster, Inc. NYC,1946-57; with Random House, Inc., 1976—, Helsinki Watch, 1970—; Bd. dirs. Am. Book Pubs. Council, 1967-70, Dr. Seuss Fdn. Writers and Scholars Intl.; chmn, U.S. Helsinki Watch, Fund for Free Expression. Served with USAAF, 1943-46. Mem. Assn. Am. Pubs. (chmn 1972-73, chmn. com. Soviet-Am. public relations, 1973, com. on intl. freedom to pub., 1975-76), Council on Fgn. Relations, Soc. Fellows N.Y.U. Office: 201 E 50 St New York NY 10022

BERNSTEIN, SIDNEY RALPH, b. Chgo, Jan. 29, 1907; s. Charles and Jennie R. (Greenblatt) B.; m. Adele Bass, Oct. 5, 1930; children—Janet Bernstein Wingis, Henry. Author: This Makes Sense to Me, 1976. Student, U. Ill., 1924-25; MBA, U. Chgo., 1956. Assoc. editor and mng. editor Hosp. Mgmt., 1925-31; mng. editor Advt. Age, Chgo, 1932-38, editor, 1939-57, editorial dir., 1958-64, pub., 1964-70; dir. research and promotion Crain Communications Inc. (formerly Advt. Pubs., Inc., Chgo), 1938-39, v.p., 1938-60, exec. v.p., gen. mgr., 1961-64, pres., 1964-73, chmn. exec com., 1973—; pres Red Tag News Publs., Chgo, 1971-77; chmn. bd. Crain Automotive Group (formerly Mktg. Services, Inc.), Detroit, 1973—, Am. Trade Mags, Chicago, 1973—; lectr. U. Coll., U. Chgo, Mich. State U., 1950-58; bd. dirs. Am. Bus. Press, 1970-73, Mag. Pubs. Assn, 1970-76. Sigma Delta Chi, Chgo. Press Club. Home: 3450 Lake Shore Dr Chicago IL 60657

BERNUTH, ERNEST PATRICK, JR., b. NYC, Nov. 17, 1939; s. Ernest Patrick and Sophie Josephine (Kilbreth) B. Contrbr. to NY Magazine, Washington Post, Natl. Observer. BA, Princeton U., 1962; MBA, Columbia U., 1972. With Fairhurst Tech. Intl., Tehran, 1964-67, Sanderson & Porter, mgmt. cons./ engrs., NYC,1968-70; bus. mgr. Field and Stream mag., NYC,1972-74; editor, gen. mgr Field and Stream Book Club, NYC,1974-76; dir. administrn. Holt, Rinehart & Winston, NYC,1976-77; pub. Praeger Pubs., NYC,1977—. Served with USAR, 1963-64. Mem. Assn. Am. Publ. Home: 562 West End Ave New York NY 10024

BERRIGAN, DANIEL, b. Virginia, MN, May 9, 1921; s. Thomas and Frieda (Fromhart) B. Author: Time Without Number, 1957 (Lamont Prize), The Bow in the Clouds, Man's Covenant with God, 1961, World for Wedding Ring, 1962; No One Walks Waters, 1966, Consequences: Truth &, 1967, Go From Here, A Prison Journal, Love, Love at the End, 1968, They Call Us Dead Men, 1968, Night Flight to Hanoi, 1968, The Trial of the Catonsville Nine, 1970, False Gods, Real Men, 1969, Trial Poems, 1970, Nor Bars to Manhood, 1970, Dark Night of Resistance, 1971, America is Hard to Find, 1972, Conversations after Prison, 1972, Jesus Christ, 1973, Prison Poems, 1974; Selected and New Poems Lights on in the House of the Dead, 1974, (with Thich Nhat Hanh) The Raft is Not the Shore, 1975, A Book of Parables, 1977, Uncommon Prayer, a Book of Psalms, 1978, Beside the Sea of Gass, the Song of the Lamb, 1978, The Discipline of the Mountain, 1979, We Die Before We Live, 1980, Conversations with the Very Ill, 1980, Commandments for the Long Haul, 1981. Edn., Woodstock (N.Y.) Coll., West Coll. Joined Soc. of Jesus, 1939; ordained priest Roman Catholic Ch. 1952; tchr. St. Peter's Prep. Schl., Jersey City, 1945-49, French and philosophy Bklyn. Prep. Schl., 1954-57; prof. N. T. studies Le Moyne Coll., Syracuse, N.Y., 1957-63; became dir. United Religious Work Cornell U., 1967; prof. theology Woodstock Coll.; vis. lectr. U. Man., 1973; religious dir. Walter Farrell Guild, 1954-57; founder Catholic Peace Fellowship; with OEO, 1967; active anti-Viet Nam War movement, peace, antinuclear movement. Served as aux. mil. chaplain, 1954. Address: 220 W 98 St 75 New York NY 10025

BERRIGAN, PHILIP FRANCIS, b. Two Harbors, MN, Oct. 5, 1923; s. Thomas William and Frida (Fromhart) B.; m. Elizabeth McAlister; two children. Author: No More Strangers, 1965, Punishment for Peace, 1969, Prison Journals of a Priest Revolutionary, 1970, Widen the Prison Gates, 1974, Of Beasts and Beastly Images, 1979. AB English, Holy Cross Coll., 1950; BS Secondary Edn, Loyola U. of South, 1959; MA, Xavier U., New Orleans, 1961. Ordained priest Roman Catholic Ch., 1950; prof. English and religion, also student counselor St. Augustine High Schl., New Orleans; asst. pastor St. Peter Claver Ch., Balt.; worked and demonstrated with So. Christain Leadership Conf., NAACP, CORE, SNCC; co-founder, co-chmn. Catholic Peace Fellowship, Balt. Interfaith Peace Mission; lectr. on race, peace, poverty; active anti-Viet Nam War movement, peace, anti-nuclear movement. Served with inf. AUS, World War II, ETO. Address: Baltimore MD

BERRY, BETSY E., Dr. Ernest C. Berry; m. Casimer F. Sajdak, May 1, 1982. Author: New Hampshire Profiles, 1981. MA, U. of VT, 1971. Mem. PSA, VT Historical Soc. Home: Spaulding Hill Rd Dummerston Center Putney VT 05346

BERRY, HENRY ARNOLD, JR., b. Bridgeport, CT, Mar. 7, 1945; s. Henry Arnold and Helene Marie (Ciglar) B. Author: Pathways to Restoration-The Revitalization of the American Spirit, 1983, (pamphlet) El Salvador-Fragment of the Future, 1984. BA in philosophy and English, Fairfield U., 1972; MA in philosophy, Georgetown U., 1976. Tchr. Fairfield Bd. of Edn., Conn., part-time 1977-80; free-lance writer, Fairfield, 1979—; ed., pub., owner Greenfield Press, Southport, Conn., 1983—; cons. in writing, pub., 1984—; ed., pub., The Small Press Book Rvw. Served with USAF, 1965-69. Recipient 3rd place Joseph E. Brodine award, Conn. Poetry Assn., 1976. Mem. COSMEP, bd. directors, 1987-89; SMPG, AG. Home: 5225 Main St Trumbull CT 06611

BERRY, JOHN, b. Fullerton, Calif; m. Ynez Johnston. Author: Krishna Fluting, 1959, (story collection) Flight of White Crows, 1961; contrbr stories var mags and collections inclg Best m Short Stories, 1959-61, Take Along Treasury, 1963, Best from Fantasy and Sci Fiction, 1962, Writingcraft, 1976, Busy Signal, 1978, Prairie Schooner, 1976, Mass Rvw, 1979, Denver Qtly, 1981, Short Story Internat, 1982, Chelsea 44, 1985; wrkg on short stories and poetry. Recipient MacMillan Fiction award, MacMillan Co, 1959, Ingram Merrill award for Poetry, 1962; Guggenheim Fellow, 1960; Fulbright fellow (India), 1965. Address 579 Crane Blvd Los Angeles CA 90065

BERRY, JOHN NICHOLS, III, b. Montclair, NJ, June 12, 1933; s. John Nichols and Matian Petrea (Chase) B.; m. Louise Parker, June 5, 1982; children—Elizabeth Ann, John Nichols IV. Contrbg author: Library Issues The Sixties, 1970; editor: Directory of Library Consultants, 1969, Bay State Librarian, 1962-64 (ALA/H.W. Wilson Library Periodical Award, 1962); contrbr. articles to profl. jnls. AB in history, Boston U., 1958; MS in LS, Simmons Coll., Boston, 1960. Youth-reference librarian Reading (Mass.) Pub. Library, 1959-60; reference librarian Simmons Coll., 1960-62, asst. dir. library, 1962-64; lectr. Schl. Library Sci., 1961-64; asst. ed. Library Jnl., R. R. Dowker Co., NYC, 1964-66, editor book editorial dept., 1966-68, editor-in-chief Library Jnl, 1969—. Served with AUS, 1955-57. Home 41 Chester St Stamford CT 16905

BERRY, JOYCE CHARLOTTE, b. Chgo, Feb. 12, 1937, d. George Carlisle and Myrtle Dorothy (Olsen) B. BS, U. Colo., 1958; cert. Institute de Touraine and U. Grenoble, France, 1961-61; diploma in French studies, The Sorbonne, Paris, 1962; postgrad., Columbia U, 1964-65. Cartographic map editor Corps Engrs, San Francisco, 1958-60; assoc. ed. Grolier Inc., NYC,1963-65; sr. editor Oxford U. Press, NYC,1965—. Office: Oxford University Press 200 Madison Ave NYC 10016

BERRY, LINDEN FARRAR, b. Washington, May 11, 1944, d. McCarthy Jr. and Marjorie (Eddy) Hanger; 1 son—Joshua. Editor: Life mag., 1969, One-Pot Cooking, 1978, Women's Sports Mag., 1983-84; contrbr. Collegiate Career Women, 1984. AB, Vassar Coll., 1966. Devel. officer East Harlem Block Schls., NYC,1969-71; corp. pub. relations mgr. Levi Strauss & Co., NYC,1977-82; prin. Berry Communications, San Francisco, 1982—. Mem. Women's Fdn. Address: 1711 Baker St San Francisco CA 94115

BERRY, RICHARD LEWIS, b. Greenwich, CT, Nov. 6, 1946; s. John William and Dorothy May (Buck) B.; m. Eleanor Flagg von Auw, July 6, 1968. Author: Build Your Own Telescope, 1985, Discover the Stars, 1987; ed., Astronomy Mag., 1976—, Telescope Making Mag., 1979—; contrbr. to books & mags. inclg. Photoelectric Photometry of Variable Stars, 1982, Microcomputers in Astronomy, 1982, Microcomputers in Astronomy II, 1984, Astronomy, Odyssey, Telescope Making, Deep Sky. BA, U. VA, 1968; MSc, York U. (Canada), 1972. Clifford W. Holmes award, Astronomy for Am., 1982. Mem. Intl. Amateur/Profl. Photoelectric Photometry. Office: AstroMedia 1027 N 7th St Milwaukee WI 53233

BERRY, WENDELL, b. Henry County, KY, Aug. 5, 1934; m. Tanya Amyx, May 29, 1957; children—Mary Dee, Prior Clifford. Novels: Nathan Coulter, 1962, A Place on Earth, 1967, The Memory of Old Jack, 1974; poetry: The Broken Ground, 1964, Findings, 1969, Openings, 1968, Farming: A Handbook, 1970, The Country of Marriage, 1973, Clearing, 1977, A Park, 1980, The Wheel, 1982, Collected Poems, 1985; essays: The Long-Legged House, 1969, The Hidden Wound, 1970, The Unforeseen Wilderness, 1971, A Continuous Harmony, 1972, The Unsettling of America, 1977, Recollected Essays, 1965-80, 1981, The Gift of Good Land, 1981, Standing by Woods, 1981; short stories: The Wild Birds, 1986. AB, U. Ky, 1956, MA, 1957. Mem. faculty U. Ky, 1964-77, Disting. prof English, 1971-72. Home: Port Royal KY 40058

BERSSENBRUGGE, MEI-MEI, b. Beijing, China, Oct. 5, 1947, d. Robert J. and Martha W. Berssenbrugge. Author: Fish Souls, 1971, Summits Move with the Tide, 1974, Random Possession, 1979, The Heat Bird, 1984, Hiddeness, 1987, Empathy, 1987; ed. Walking Ink III, 1983; contrbr.: Partisan Rvw, Pequod, River Styx, Unmuzzled Ox, Conjunctions, other lit mags and anthologies. BA, Reed Coll., 1969; MFA, Columbia U., 1973. Artist-in-schls. N.Mex. Arts Div., 1977—, Arts Alaska, 1981—; instr. English Inst. Am. Indian Art, Santa Fe, N.Mex., 1983—; mem. lit. panel N.Mex. Arts Commn., 1980-83; bd. dirs. Segue Fdn., Tooth of Time Press; mem. adv. bd. Center for Contemporary Arts of Santa Fe, 1983—, Inst. Am. Indian Art Press, 1983—. Grantee NEA, 1976, 81; recipient Am. Book award, 1980, 84; Yaddo Colony fellow, 1984, 85, 87. Mem. PSA, Rio Grande Wrtrs. Assn. Office: Inst Am Indian Art St Michael's Dr Santa Fe NM 87501

BERST, BARB JO, b. Richland, WA, Sept. 23, 1957; m. Mark Perkins, July 1, 1978. Author/illus.: I Love Softball, 1985; contrbr. various mags. including Nitty Gritty, Pandora, Seventeen, Balls & Strikes, Young Am. BA and MA in children's lit. and art. Typographer, Westinghouse Art Dept., Richland, 1977-78; paste-up artist and editor-writer for weekly paper and monthly newsletter, Kennewick, Wash., 1978-80; graphic artist Graphic Arts Agcy., Kennewick, 1980-82, mgr. art dept., 1982-83; children's author-artist, Anacortes, Wash., 1983—. Coach girls softball, city recreation, 1982—. AA in Journalism, Spokane Falls Coll., 1978. Mem. Soc. Children's Book Writers, Pacific Northwest Writers. Office: 2310 17th Anacortes WA 98221

BERTO, GENE, see Enderlin, Lee

BERTOLINO, JAMES D., b. Hurley, WI, Oct. 4, 1942, s. James and Doris (Robbins) B.; m. Lois Ann Behling, Nov. 29, 1966. Author poetry books: Employed, 1972, Soft Rock, 1973, Making Space for Our Living, 1975, The Gestures, 1975, The Alleged Conception, 1976, New & Selected Poems, 1978, Precinct Kali and The Gertrude Spicer Story, 1982, First Credo, 1986; author chapbooks, pamphlets; contrbr. poetry: Paris Rvw, Foxfire, Painted Bride Qtly, Ironwood, numerous other lit mags; ed.: Northwest Poets Anthology, 1968, Stone-Marrow Press, 1970-76, Abraxas Press, 1969-72, anthologies, chapbooks and lit mags; contrbr. to: Small Press Rvw, The Spirit That Moves Us, Carrots & Peas, other mags. BS in English, U. Wis.-Oshkosh, 1970; MFA in Creative Writing, Cornell U., 1973. Mem. faculty U. Cin., 1974-84; instr. Skagit Valley Coll., Mt. Vernon, Wash., 1984—. Recipient Discovery award Poetry Center, NYC, 1972, Betty Colladay Book award Qtly Rvw Lit., 1986; NEA fellow, 1974, Ohio Arts Council fellow, 1979. Mem. AWP. Home: PO Box 1157 Anacortes WA 98221

BERTOLINO, ROSALEEN, b. San Francisco, May 20, 1956; c. John Pasquale and Marjorie Louise (Lyons) Bertolino; m. Thomas Mitchell Cowardin. Author: (with Janet Wondra and Laura Johnson-Brickford) Emerging Island Cultures: A Collection of Stories and Poems, 1984. Contrbr. stories to mags. Wrkg. on Emerging Island Cultures II. B.A. in Environmental Planning, 1979; M.A. in English/Creative Writing,

San Francisco State U., 1982. Ed., Emerging Island Cultures Press, Fairfax, CA, 1984—.Recipient Honorable Mention, James D. Phelan award, 1984. Home: 130 Ridge Rd Fairfax CA 94930

BESS, ROBERT WADE, b. Roanoke, VA, Sept. 25, 1958; s. Jack Gilman and Margaret Ann Chaney B.; m. Janet Dean Stacy, May 29, 1982. Author: Domestic Birds (Chapbook), 1986; contrbr. poetry and rvws. to Inlet, Roanoke Rvw, Hollins Critic, others; ed., Artemis mag. BA, Roanoke Coll., 1976-80; MA, Hollins Coll., 1980-81. Back chainman JGB Land Surveying Co, Roanoke, 1973-80; messenger Colonial Am. Natl. Bank, Roanoke, 1980-81, vault teller, 1981—. Director Roanoke Writers' Workshop. Address: Box 3021 Roanoke VA 24015

BESSOM, MALCOLM EUGENE, b. Boston, Sept. 27, 1940; s. Harold Eugene and Mina (Townley) B. Author: Supervising the Successful School Music Program, 1969, Teaching Music in Today's Secondary Schools, 1974, 2d edit., 1980, How to Sell Your Songs Like Professionals Do, 1978; contrbg. author: This is Music for Today, Books 6, 7, 8, 1970-71; editor: Music in Special Education, 1972, Music in World Cultures, 1972, Careers and Music, 1977; contrb. articles, columns, musical arrangements to profl. publns. and recordings. BMus, Boston U, 1962, postgrad, 1962-63. Dir. vocal music Pub. Schls., Chelmsford, Mass., 1963-67; asst. editor Allyn & Bacon Inc., Boston, 1967-68, assoc. editor, 1968-70; asst. editor Music Editors Jnl, Washington, 1970-71, editor, 1971-77, 79-81, Reston, Va., 1975-77, 79-81; dir. pubns. Music Educators Natl. Conf, Reston, 1976-77, 79-81; pres. David Allen Press, Washington, 1978-81; dir. pubns. Am. Theatre Assoc., 1984. Recipient Distinguished Achievement Award in journalism Ednl. Press Assn. Am., 1973, 74, 75, 76, 78, 81. Home: 2314 Huidekoper Pl NW Washington DC 20007

BEST, MARY SUE, b. Jackson, MS, Dec. 18, 1930; d. Joseph Revell and Susie Jeanette (Kethley) Smith; m. David B. H. Best, Dec. 27, 1956; 1 dau., Melanie Sue. Author: technical training books; Columnist: The Indpls. Star, 1978-82. Contrbr. articles to newspapers, mags. including Saturday Evening Post, Christina Sci. Monitor, Grit, Woman's Circle, others. Ed.: Compare and Save mag., 1984-86. B.A., Millsaps Coll., 1952; M.A., U. Miss., 1954. Prof., Miss. Coll., Clinton, 1955-57, Ind. U., Purdue U., Indpls., 1962-68; free-lance wrtr., 1968—; free-lance public relations, 1976—. Recipient award for essay and short story, Miss. Arts Festival, 1969, award for short story, 1972; award for essay Miss. Arts Commn., 1970; award for TV script Miss. Ednl. TV, 1971. Mem. Intl. Platform Assn., Natl. Soc. Arts Letters, NLAPW, Fortnightly Lit. Club (pres. 1986-87). Home: 5402 Washington Blvd Indianapolis IN 46220

BEST, WINFIELD JUDSON, b. Dillon, MT, Oct. 1919; s. Floyd and Margaret (Pearson) B.; m. Lois Gustafson, 1948; children—Charles, Mark, Constance. Author: (with Alan F. Guttmacher and Frederick S. Jaffe) The Complete Book of Birth Control, 1962, Planning Your Family, 1964, Birth Control and Love, 1969, (with Everett S. Lee and David L. Birch) America's Lands and Cities: Challenge of Transition; contrbr. articles on population, sex, conservation, bus. mgmt. and corp. communications, problems of youth and aging to natl. mags.; Ency. Brit. BS summa cum laude, Northwestern U., 1943. Editorial assoc. Pub. Adminstrn. Clearing House, Chgo., 1946-48; dir. pub. relations Am. Mcpl. Assn., 1948-50; dir. research publs. HHFA, Washington, 1951-52; pub. relations dir. Planned Parenthood Fedn. Am., 1952-63; exec. v.p. Planned Parenthood-World Population, NYC, 1963-69; exec. dir. Businessmen's Ednl. Fund, 1969-72; dir. communications and planning Carolina Population Ctr., U. N.C., Chapel Hill, lecturer population and ecology, 1972-78; founder Winfield Best Communications, 1976; freelance writer; communications and TV producer, cons. Communications Research Fdn., 1980—. Served with AUS, 1943-46. Mem. Natl. Assn. Sci. Writers, Am. Pub. Relations Soc., Population Assn. Am. Office: Box 148 Chapel Hill NC 27514

BETCHKAL, JAMES JOSEPH, b. Racine, WI, Mar. 11, 1936; s. Herbert M. and Frances (Cetrano) B.; m. Ann Vernon, June 23, 1956; children—Janet Ann, Mark James. BS, U. Miami, 1956; postgrad., U. Wis., 1957, Northwestern U., 1959. Asst. editor Actual Specifying Engr., Chgo, 1956-58; mng. editor Nation's Schls. Mag., Chgo, 1959-563; editor The Record, Oak Park, Ill., 1963; exec. editor Pioneer Newspapers, Inc., Oak Park, 1964-68; editor, pub. Am. Schl. Bd. Jnl., Washington, 1968-79; editor-in-chief, pub. The Exec. Educator and assoc. exec. dir. nat. Schl. Bds. Assn. Am., Washington, 1978—. Recipient Editorial award Ill. Press Assn., 1966, All-Am. award Ednl. Press Assn. Am., 1970, 71, 72, 75, 76. Mem. ASME, Soc. Natl. Assoc. Pubns., Edn. Writers Assn. Home: 4927 McArthur Blvd NW Washington DC 20007

BETHEL, C. A., see Foy, Catherine Anthony

BETTERSWORTH, JOHN KNOX, b. Jackson, Miss., Oct. 1909; s. Horace Greely and Annie McConnell (Murphey) B.; m. Ann L. Stephens, Oct. 28, 1943; 1 dau. Nancy Elizabeth. Author: The People and Policies of a Cotton State in Wartime, 1943, People's College: A History of Mississippi State, 1953, Mississippi: A History, 1959, Mississippi in the Confederacy: As They Saw It, 1961, Your Old World Past, 1960, Mississippi: Yesterday and Today, 1965, New World Heritage, 1968, Your Mississippi, 1975, People's University, The Centennial History of Mississippi State, 1980, Mississippi: The Land and the People, 1981; co-author: This Country of Ours, 1965, South of Appomattox, 1959; contrbg. author: A History of Mississippi, 1973; contrbr. articles to profl. publs.; founder, pub. The Miss. Qtly, editor, 1946-56. BA magna cum laude, Millsaps Coll., 1929, PhD,Duke U., 1937. Instr. Jackson (Miss.) Central High Schl., 1930-35; grad. fellow Duke U., 1935-37, vis. prof., summer, 1940; vis. instr. Asheville (N.C.) Normal, summer 1937; instr. history Miss. State U., Mississippi State, 1937; asst. prof. 1938-42, assoc. prof. 1945-48, prof., 1948—, head dept. history and govt., 1948-61; dir. Social Rearch Sci. Center, 1950-60; asso. dean lib. arts Schl. Arts and Sci., 1956-61, acad. v.p., 1961-77, dean faculty, 1966-77, spcl. cons. to pres., 1977-79, prof. and v.p. emeritus, 1978—. Home: 401 Broad St Starkville MS 39759

BETTLEHEIM, BRUNO, b. Vienna, Austria, Aug. 28, 1903; came to U.S. 1939, naturalized 1944; s. Anton and Paula Seidler) B.; m. Trude Weinfeld, May 14, 1941; children—Ruth, Naomi, Eric. Author: (with Morris Janowitz) Dynamics of Prejudice, 1950, Love is Not Enough: The Treatment of Emotionally Disturbed Children, 1950, Symbolic Wounds, 1954, Truants from Life, 1955, The Informed Heart, 1960, Dialogues with Mothers, 1962, The Empty Fortress, 1967, The Children of the Dream, 1969, A Home for the Heart, 1974, The Uses of Enchantment, 1976 (with Karen Zelan) on Learning to Read: The Child's Fascination with Meaning, 1982, Freud and Man's Soul, 1983, Surviving, 1979, A Good Enough Parent, 1987; contrbr. articles, essays to popular, profl. publs., PhD, U. Vienna, 1938. Research assoc. Progressive Edn. Assn., U. Chgo., 1939-41; assoc. prof. psychology Rockford (Ill.) Coll. 1942-44; asst. prof. ednl. psychology U. Chgo, 1944-47, assoc. prof, 1947-52, prof. 1952-73, Stella M. Rowley Distinguished Service prof. edn., prof. psychology and psychiatry, 1963-73; head Sonia Shankman Orthogenic School, 1944-73. Home: 718 Adelaide Pl Santa Monica CA 90402

BETTS, DORIS JUNE WAUGH, b. Statesville, NC, June 4, 1932; d. William Elmore and Mary Ellen (Freeze) Waugh; m. David Lowry Betts, July 5, 1952; children—Doris LewEllyn, David Lowry, Erskine Moore II. Author: (story collections) The Gentle Insurrection, 1954, Beasts of the Southern Wild, 1973; (novel) Tall Houses in Winter, 1957 (Sir Walter Raleigh award for best fiction by Carolinian, 1957), Scarlet Thread (Sir Walter Raleigh award, 1965), The Astronomer & Other Stories, 1966, The River to Pickle Beach, 1972, Heading West, 1981; contrbr. stories to anthols; editor: Young Writer at Chapel Hill, 1968. Student, Woman's Coll., U.N.C., 1950-53, U.N.C., 1954. Newspaperwoman Statesville Daily Record, 1950-51, Chapel Hill (N.C.) weekly and News-Leader, 1953-54, Sanford Daily Herald, 1956-57; edtiorial staff N. C. Democrat, newspaper, 1961-62; editor Sanford (N.C.) News Leader, 1962; lectr. creative writing, English dept. U. N.C., Chapel Hill, 1966—, dir. Freshman-Sophomore English 1972–76, assoc. prof., 1974-78, prof., 1978—, Alumni Disting. prof., 1981—, dir. Fellows program, 1976-76, asst. dean Honors program, 1979-81, chmn. faculty, 1983—; vis. lectr. creative writing Duke U, 1971, mem. bd. AWP; mem. lit. panel NEA, 1979-81, chmn, 1981. Recipient short story prize Mademoiselle mag., booklength fiction prize G. P. Putnam-U. N.C., 1954; N. C. medal for lit, 1975; Guggenheim fellow, 1958-59. Member N.C. Writers Assn. Office: Dept English U NC Chapel Hill NC 27514

BEVERIDGE, GEORGE DAVID JR., b. Washington, Jan. 5, 1922; s. George David and Lillian Agnes (Little) B.; m. Betty Jean Derwent, June 6, 1944; children—Barbara J., Deborah A., David C. Student, George Washington U, 1939. Copy boy Washington Star, 1940, news reporter, 1942-63, editorial writer, 1963-74, asst. mng. editor, 1974-75, ombudsman, 1976-81, assoc. editor, 1980-81; asst. chmn. Albritton communications Co., Washington, 1981-84; Sr. v.p. communications Riggs Watl. Bk., 1984—. Served to 1t., AUS, 1942-46. Recipient Pulitzer prize for reporting in local news category, 1958. Home: 9302 Kingsley Ave Bethesda MD 20814

BEVILL, EVANGELINE STONECIPHER, b. Haynesville, LA, May 30, 1928; d. George Clawson and Eva Caroline (Bond) Stonecipher; m. Benjamin Loyd Bevill, Jan. 20, 1946; children—George Bryan, Benjamin Wyatt, Susan Melinda. Author: Melinda, 1980, Communicating, Here and Beyond, 1984. Wrkg. on novel. Student public schs., Haynesville. Active civic and religious orgns. Home: 716 Mesquite Dr Cottonwood AZ 86326

BEVINGTON, DAVID MARTIN, b. NYC,May 13, 1931; s. Merle Mowbray and Helen (Smith) B.; m. Margaret Bronson Brown, June 4, 1953;

children—Stephen, Philip, Katharine, Sarah. Author: From Mankind to Marlowe, 1962, Tudor Drama and Politics, 1968, Action is Eloquence, Shakespeare's Language of Gesture, 1984; editor: Medieval Drama, 1975, The Complete Works of Shakespeare, 3d ed., 1980, The Bantam Shakespeare, 1988. BA, Harvard U., 1952, MA, 1957, PhD,1959. Instr. English Harvard U., 1959-61; asst. prof U. Va, 1961-65, assoc. prof., 1965-66, prof., 1966-67; vis. prof U. Chgo, 1967-68, prof., 1968—. Served with USN, 1952-55. Guggenheim fellow, 1964-65, 81-82; sr. fellow Southeastern Inst. Medieval and Renaissance Studies, summer 1975; sr. cons. and seminar leader Folger Inst. Renaissance and Eighteenth-Century Studies, 1976-77, 87-88. Mem. MLA, Renaissance Soc. Am., Shakespeare Assn. Am. (pres. 1976-77), AAUP. Home: 5747 S Blackstone Ave Chicago IL 60637

BEVINGTON, HELEN S., b. Afton, NY, Apr. 2, 1906; d. Charles W. and Elizabeth N. (Raymond) Smith; m. Merle M. Bevington, June 1, 1928 (dec.); children—David, Philip. Poet: numerous works include, Doctor Johnson's Waterfall and other Poems, 1956, When Found, Make a Verse of, 1961, A Book and a Love Affair, 1968, Beautiful Lofty People, 1974, Along Came the Witch, 1976, The Journey is Everything, 1983. PhB, U. of Chgo., 1926; MA, Columbia U., 1928. Instructor, Asst. Prof., Assoc. Prof., Prof. Prof. emeritus, Duke U. (Durham, NC), 1943-77. Roanoke-Chowan Poetry Award, NC Histor. Soc., 1956 & 1962; Governors Award Distinguished Achievement, State of NC, 1976. Home: 4428 Guess Road Durham NC 27712

BHARATI, AGEHANANDA, b. Vienna, Austria, Apr. 20, 1923; came to U.S., 1956, naturalized, 1968; s. Hans and Margarete Helene (von May) Fischer. Author: The Ochre Robe, 1963, A Functional Analysis of Indian Thought and Its Social Margins, 1964, The Tantric Tradition, 1966, The Asians in East Africa: Jayhind and Uhuru, 1972, The Light at the Center: Context and Pretext of Modern Mysticism, 1976, Great Tradition and Little Traditions: Indological Investigations in Cultural Anthropology, 1978, Hindu Views and Ways and the Hindu-Muslim Interface, 1981; editor: Tibet Soc. Bulltn, 1974—; co-editor: World Anthropology, 1973. Contrbtr. book rvws. and articles on cultural anthropology, religion, and the history of Occidental and Oriental philosophy to lit. mags. and scholarly Am., Brit., and German jnls; contrbr. numerous book chaps. on Oriental religion and cultural anthropology. AB in Ethnology and Indology, Oriental Inst., U. Vienna, 1948; Acharya (PhD), Samnyasa Mahavidyalaya, India, 1951. Lectr. in German Delhi (India) U., 1951; hon. reader in philosophy Benares Hindu U., India, 1951-54; guest prof. comparative religion Nalanda (India) Inst. Postgrad. Buddhist Studies, 1954-55; vis. prof. comparative religion Mahamukuta Royal Buddhist Acad., Bangkok, Thailand, 1955-56; Asia Fdn. vis. prof. U. Tokyo, 1956-57, Kyoto, Japan, 1956-57; research assoc. Far Eastern Inst., U. Wash., Seattle, 1957-60; asst. prof. anthropology Syracuse (N.Y.) U, 1961-64, assoc. prof, 1964-68, prof., 1968—, chmn. dept. anthropology, 1971—; ordained to Hindu Samnyasi Order of Monks, India, 1951. Home: 1209 Harrison St Syracuse NY 13210

BIAL, RAYMOND STEVEN, b. Danville, IL, Nov. 5, 1948; s. Marion John and Catherine Louise (Jackse) B.; m. Linda Marie LaPuma, Aug. 25, 1979; 1 dau., Anna Marie. Author: Ivesdale; A Photographic Essay, 1982, In All My Years; Photographs of Older Blacks in Champaign-Urbana, 1983, Upon a Quiet Landscape; The Photographs of Frank Sadorus, 1983, There Is a Season, 1984, (with Kathryn Kerr) First Frost, 1985, In All My Years, rev. ed. 1985, Common Ground; Photographs of Rural and Small Town Life, 1986; editor: (with Linda LaPuma) Illinois Small Press Directory, 1984; contrbr. articles to popular and scholarly publs. including Commonweal, America, Studies in Visual Communication; also photographs pub. in numerous jnls. BS, U. Ill., 1970, MS, 1979. Librarian Parkland Coll., Champaign, Ill., 1980—; freelance writer/photographer, 1973—; editor, pub. Stormline Press, Inc., 1985—. Cert. of commendation, Am. Assn. of State and Local History, 1986., Award of Superior Achievement, Ill. State Hist. Soc., 1985. Mem. ALA, Ill. Library Assn. Home: 403 E Washington St. Urbana IL 61801

BIANCOLLI, LOUIS, b. NYC,Apr. 17, 1907; s. Carmine and Achilla (Montesano) B.; m. Edith Rattner, 1933 (dec. 1957); 1 dau., Margaret (Mrs. Murray Weissbach); m. Jeanne Mitchell, 1958; children—Lucy, Amy. Author: (with Robert Bagar) The Concert Companion (1947), The Book of Great Conversations, 1948, The Victor Book of Operas, 1949, The Analytical Concert Guide, 1951, (with Mary Garden) Mary Garden's Story, 1951, (With Kirsten Flagstad) The Flagstad Manuscript, 1952, The Opera Reader, 1953, The Mozart Handbook, 1954, (with Herbert F. Peyser) Masters of the Orchestra, 1954, (with Ruth Slenczynska) Forbidden Childhood, 1957, (with Roberta Peters) A Dubut at the Met (1967); Translator: Boris Goudonoff libretto from Russian, 1952, 64; in blank verse Dante's Divine Comedy, 1966, (with Thomas Scherman) The Beethoven Companion, 1972; libretto: Italian opera Ezio (Handel), 1972, Poro (Handel), 1977, Introduction to Am. ed. Greek collection of letters of Dimitri Mitropoulos, 1972; contrbr. articles to mags., music brochures. AB, N.Y. U., 1935, A.M., 1936, postgrad., Columbia U., 1936-38. Am. Council Learned Socs. grant for studies Russian, Intensive Lang. Programs, 1943. Music critic, N.Y. World-Telegram and Sun, 1928-66; annotator, N.Y. Philharmonic Soc., 1941-49. Mem. Music Critics Circle, Phi Beta Kappa. Address: New Preston CT 06777

BIARDO, JOHN CHARLES, b. Chgo., July 28, 1950; s. David C. and Mary Ann (Cannella) B. Author: The World's Greatest Television Trivia Quiz Book, 1985, 501 Patio Party Cocktails, 1986. BA, Triton Coll., 1972. Sales rep. DeMoon Realty, Chgo., 1974-85; pres. Elmwood Pk. Publishing, Ill., 1985—. Me. Am. Assn. Handwriting Analysts. Address: 2907 N 72d Ct Elmwood Pk IL 60635

BICKEL, WILLIAM JON, (Bill), b. NYC,July 8, 1955, s. Benno and Sheila Linda (Farber) B.; m. Robin Carol Becker, Mar. 18, 1979. Contrbr. sci. fiction, fantasy and mystery stories to Universe Anthology, Isaac Asimov's Science Fiction Mag., Tomorrow's Voices, numerous others. BA, Amherst Coll., 1977. Freelance wrtr.; assignments ed. Sci. Fiction and Fantasy Workshop. Office: Box 266 Hillside NJ 07205

BIDDLE, LIVINGSTON LUDLOW, JR., b. Bryn Mawr, PA, May 26, 1918; s. Livingston Ludlow and Eugenia (Law) B.; m. Cordelia Frances Fenton, Mar. 15, 1945 (dec. May 1972); children—Cordelia Frances, Livingston Ludlow IV; m. Catharina Van Beek Baart, Nov. 3, 1973. Author: Main Line, 1950, Debut, 1952, The Village Beyond, 1956, Sam Bentley's Island, 1960. AB, Princeton, 1940; LHD (hon.), Mt. St. Mary's Coll., NY, 1978, DFA (hon.), U. of Cincinnati, 1979, DFA (hon.) U. of L.I., 1979, LLD, Catholic U., 1979, Providence Coll., 1980, U. Notre Dame, 1980, DL, Drexel U., 1980. Reporter Phila. Evening Bull., 1940-42; with Am. Field Service, Middle East, N. Africa, Italy, France, Germany, 1942-45; spcl. asst. to U.S. Senator Claiborne Pell, 1963-65; depy. chmn. Natl. Endowment for Arts, Washington, 1965-67; chmn. div. arts Liberal Arts Coll., Fordham U., Lincoln Center, NYC,1967-70; spcl. asst. to Senator Claiborne Pell, 1973-74; liaison dir. Natl. Endowment for the Arts, Washington, 1974-75, chmn., 1977-81; Staff dir. subcom. on edn arts and humanities U.S. Senate, 1975-77. Recipient Phila. Athenaeum Best Novel Award, 1956. Home: 3050 P St NE Washington DC 20007

BIED, DAN, b. Burlington, IA, Nov. 21, 1925; s. George C. and Lynda M. (Danielson) B.; m. Millie Stodgell, Sept. 11, 1973. Author 2 vols. World War II expers., 3 vols. hist. Burlington, IA, 1 vol. hist. West Burlington; contrbr. wkly. articles to local nwsprs., occasional articles to The Des Moines Register. BA, Burlington Commun. Coll. Rptr., Sunday ed., assoc. ed. Burlington (IA) Hawk Eye, 1957-68; house organ ed. Iowa Army Ammunition Plant, Middletown, 1978—. Served to Cpl., U. S. Army, 1944-45 ETO, USA. Home: 151 Holiday Terr West Burlington IA 52655

BIEHL, VICKI, b. Suffern, NY, June 8, 1956, d. Richard Earl and Dorothy May (Hall) Biehl. Author: Mystery of the Kinnaird House Ghost (juvenile fiction). BA, SUNY-Albany, 1977. Library clrk. Nanuet (N.Y.) Public Library, 1980—. Mem. NWC, Phi Beta Kappa. Home: 60 Pinto Rd Pearl River NY 10965

BIEN, PETER ADOLPH, b. NYC,, May 28, 1930; s. Adolph F. and Harriet (Honigsberg) B.; m. Chrysanthi Yiannakou, July 17, 1955; children—Leander, Alec, Daphne. Author: L. P. Hartley, 1963, Constantine Cavafy, 1964, Kazantzakis and the Linguistic Revolution in Greek Literature, 1972, Nikos Kazantzakis, 1972, Antithesis and Synthesis in the Poetry of Yannis Ritsos, 1980; (with others) Demotic Greek I, 1972, Demotic Greek II, 1982; translator: The Last Temptation, 1960, Saint Francis, 1962, Report to Greco, 1965 (all by Nikos Kazantzakis), Life in the Tomb (Stratis Myrivilis), 1977; co-editor: Modern Greek Writers, 1972; Assoc. editor: Byzantine and Modern Greek Studies, 1975-82, jnl. Modern Greek Studies, 1983—. Student, Harvard U., 1948-50; BA, Haverford Coll., 1952; MA, Columbia U., 1957, PhD,1961; postgrad. (Fulbright fellow), Bristol (Eng.) U, 1958-59, Woodbrooke Co.., Eng., 1970-71. Lectr. Columbia U., 1957-58, 59-61; instr. dept. English Dartmouth Coll., 1961-62, asst. prof., 1963-65, assoc. prof., 1965-68, prof., 1969—. Geisel prof., 1974-79; vis. prof Harvard U., 1983, U. Melbourne, 1983. Mem. Modern Greek Studies Assn., MLA. Home: 12 Ledyard Ln Hanover NH 03755

BIENEN, LEIGH BUCHANAN, b. Berkeley, CA, Apr. 24, 1938; d. Norman Sharpe Buchanan and Janet (Saniter) Buchanan Arnold; m. Henry S. Bienen, Apr. 28, 1961; children—Laura, Claire, Leslie. Author: Jurors and Rape, 1980; contrbr. articles to legal jnls, stories to lit mags and anthologies. BA, Cornell U., 1960; MA, U. of Iowa Writers Workshop, 1963; JD, Rutgers-Newark Schl. Law, 1975. Bar: N.J., 1975, U.S. Dist. Ct. N.J., 1975, Pa., 1977, N.Y., 1982, U.S. Supreme Ct., 1982, D.C., 1983. Research atty. Center for Rape Concern, Phila.,

1975-76; law assoc. U. Hall, U. Calif., Berkeley, 1976-77; lectr. U. Pa. Schl. Law, Phila., 1981; asst. dep. public defender, Dept. Public Defender, Trenton, N.J., 1977—; lectr. Princeton U., 1977, 82, 84, 87, Recipient fiction prize O'Henry Prize Stories 1983; Am. Philo. Soc. grantee, 1981-82; fellow MacDowell Colony, 1979, 82, Yaddo, 1984; NJ State Concil on Arts grantee, 1986-87. Bd. dirs. NJ ACLU, 1982—; bd. dirs. Womens Rights Law Reporter, 1977—. Mem ABA, Lawyers Com. for Human Rights. Office: Spcl Projects CN-850 Justice Complex Trenton NJ 08625

BIERBRIER, DOREEN, b. Montreal, Quebec, Canada, Nov. 21, 1946; arrived in US 1953; d. Paul and Fay (Horowitz) Bierbrier. Author: Living with Tenants: How to Happily Share your House with Renters for Profit and Security, 1983, Managing Your Rental House for Increased Income, 1985. BA Brandeis U., 1968; MPH U. of Michigan, 1974. Volunteer Peace Corps (Philippines), 1968-70; dir. Family Planning (Visalia, CA), 1970-73; project officer US Dept. Health & Human Svcs. (Washington, DC), 1976-82; wrtr./lecturer (Arlington, VA), 1982—. Home: 5002 N 14th St Arlington VA 22205

BIERDS, LINDA LOUISE, b. Wilmington, DE, Apr. 20, 1945, d. Henry Walter and Edith (Patterson) B. Author: Snaring the Flightless Birds: The Legends of Maui, 1982, Flights of the Harvest-Mare, 1985, Off the Aleutian Chain, 1985; contrbr. New Yorker, Fine Madness, Owl Creek Press Anthology, numerous other lit mags and anthols. BA, U. Wash., 1969, MA, 1971. Recipient Dearborn Award Seattle Music and Arts Fdn., 1970. Mem. AAP, PW, PSA. Home: 832 NE 127th St Seattle WA 98125

BIERSTEDT, ROBERT, b. Burlington, IA, Mar. 20, 1913; s. Henry F. and Bertha (Strauss) B.; m. Betty MacIver, Dec. 26, 1939; children—Peter, Karen, Robin. Author: The Social Order, 1957, 4th ed., 1974, (with others) Modern Social Science, 1964, Emile Durkheim, 1966, Power and Progress, 1974, American Sociological Theory, 1981. Editor: The Making of Society 1959, (with others) Florian Znaniecki, 1969; adv. editor: Intl. Jnl Sociology and Social Policy; contrbr. articles to profl., lit. jnls. AB, U. Iowa, 1934; AM, Columbia U., 1935; PhD,1950; asst. prof. Wellesley Coll., 1946-47, U. Ill., 1947-51, assoc. prof., 1951-53; prof., chmn dept sociology and anthropology Coll. City N.Y., 1953-59; Fulbright lectr. U. Edinburgh, Scotland, 1959-60; head dept. N.Y.U., 1960-66, prof. sociology, 1960-72; Fulbright lectr., The London Schl. of Economics, 1966-67; mem. Center Advanced Studies, U. Va., 1972-74, prof. sociology, 1972-82, Commonwealth prof., 1982—, prof. emeritus, 1983—; Bd. dirs. Am. Council Learned Socs., 1979-87. Served from lt. (j.g.) to lt. USNR, 1943-46. Mem. Am. Sociol. Assn., Sociol. Research Assn., AAUP, ACLU, Phi Beta Kappa. Home: 9 Old Farm Rd Charlottesville VA 22901

BIEWEN, ROBERT L., b. Austin, MN, July 15, 1936; s. W. J. and Dona C. Biewen Gahagan; m. Catherine E. Jelinek, June 24, 1967; children—Jennifer, Mary. BA, St. John's U., Collegeville, Minn., 1958; postgrad., U. Minn., 1958-60. Exec. editor, college Harcourt, Brace, Jovanovich, 1970-72; dir. college div. Acad. Press, 1972-76, sr. v.p. mktg., 1976-78; exec. v.p., chief exec. officer Springer Verlag N.Y. Inc., 1978-80; exec. v.p. McGraw- Hill Book Co., 1980—. Me. Assn. Am. Pubs. Office: McGraw-Hill Book Co 1221 Ave of Americas NYC 10020

BIGGART, ELEANOR MARIE, b. Moulton, AL, Sept. 30, 1926; d. Walter Henry and Jennie Bunneta (Hadley) Porter; m. Elza Dick, Nov. 13, 1948 (div. 1964); children—Henry Dick II, Nola Marie Dick Hadley, Paul Kenneth, Barbara Susan Dick Washburn;; m. 2d, Thomas Biggart, Nov. 21, 1976; stepchildren—Lynette Biggart Kuhns, Robert Stuart, David Thomas. Editor: Introduction to Automated Office Practice, 1968, Mathematics for Business and Finanace, 1969, Century 21 Accounting, First Year Course, 1972, Executive Decisions, 1976, Administrative Office Management, 1978, Economics—Principles and Applications, 1978, Operations Management, 1979, Real Estate Investment and Taxation, 1981, Effective Selling, 1981, Production and Operations Management, 1984, also workbooks, practice sets, tchr. manuals. Freelance wrtg.: wrkg. on articles, book proposal. AB, Wilmington (Ohio) Coll., 1948; MBA, U. Cin., 1975. Editorial assoc. South-Western Pub. Col, Cin., 1961-74, ed., 1974-82; mgr. Husman House Condominiums, Cin., 1983-84; registered rep. First Investors Corp., Cin., 1985-87; broker Cornwall Securities, Cin., 1987—. Mem. Adminstrv. Mgmt. Soc. (newsletter ed., 1979-80, dir. 1980-83). Home: 6249 Raytee Terrace Cincinnati OH 45230

BIGGERS, ANN PEEPLES, b. Meridian, MS, Feb. 15, 1943; d. Lewis Terry and Frances (McCoy) Peeples; m. James Aaron Biggers, June 15, 1965; children—Lewis, Sarah. Contrbr. articles to mags. Co-ed.: Montage, 1986—, mem. editorial bd., 1982—. Wrkg. on short stories, poetry, essays. B.A., Miss. Coll., 1965; M.Edn., La. State U., 1968, postgrad., 1980-86. Tchr. Eden Park Elem. Schl., Baton Rouge, LA, 1981-82, McKinley Middle Magnet Schl., Baton Rouge, 1982—. Recipient 3d prize State Times-Morning Advocate, Baton Rouge, 1987. Fellow La. State U. Writing Project (tchr., cons.); mem. Natl. Writing Project, NCTE (cert. of Achievement East Baton Rouge Parish Council 1984, 85, 86, 87), Capital Area Reading Council. Home: 529 Centenary Dr Baton Rouge LA 70808

BIGGS, ABRAHAM LINCOLN, b. Limon, Costa Rica, Mar. 4, 1909, came to U.S., 1977, s. Robert and Ethel (Brown) Biggs; m. Betsy Reid, 1936 (dec. 1948); 5children—Vera, Rehoboam, Alexander, Jenetta, Buster, Delia, Shirley, Esperanza; m. 2d, Thazarbell McKenzie, Mar. 5, 1950; children—Valrie Mae, Carol Joy, Narciso, Lavona, Davilmar. Author: The Layman's Guide to Personal Bookkeeping for Credit Cards, Charge Accounts and Loans to Fight Inflation, 1984. Wrkg. on non-fiction. Ed., Panama and Costa Rica. Home: Calle 9 A y W Casa 16 Alto Panama 10 Republic of Panama

BIGGS, MARGARET KEY, b. Needmore, AL, Oct. 26, 1933; d. Samuel Elbert and Maggie Lee (Jackson) Key; m. Wayne Saunders Biggs, Apr. 1, 1956. Author poetry: Swampfire, 1980, Sister-to-the-Sun, 1982, Magnolias and Such, 1982, Petals from the Womanflower, 1984, Plumage of the Sun, 1986; contrbr. poetry, short stories, essays, interviews, revws. to mags. and anthologies. B.S. in English, Troy State U., 1954; M.A. in Humanities, Calif. State., 1979. Tchr. Port St. Joe jr. and sr. high schls., FLA., 1954-86. Recipient more than 70 natl. and intl. awards for writing inclg. Natl. League Am. PEN Women awards, Pulitzer Prize nominee, 1986, FLA. State Poets Assn., 1984, The Pensters, 1985. Mem. FLA. State Poets Assn., Ala. Writers Conclave, Ala. Poets Assn. Address: Box 551 Port St Joe FL 32456

BIGGS, MARY, b. NYC, Feb. 8, 1944, d. Magnus Clyde and Ruth Irene (Murray) Gleason; m. Robert Heron Mancuso, Dec. 14, 1963 (div. 1977); children—Nicholas H., Nathan G.; m. 2d, Victor Clayton Biggs, July 8, 1978. Contrbr.: Jnl Library History, Jnl Higher Edn., 13th Moon, other publs.; editor Publishers and Librarians: A Foundation for Dialogue, 1984; co-ed. Editor's Choice II, 1987; ed. Library Qtly, 1985-88; co-ed. Primavera, 1979-83, Editor's Choice II: Poetry and Fiction from the U.S. Small Press, 1978-83, 1986; contrbg. ed.: New Pages: News and Reviews of the Progressive Book Trade, 1981-84. BA, SUNY-Albany, 1972; MA, SUNY-Buffalo, 1976, MLS, 1977; PhD, U. Chgo., 1986. Public svc. libn., U. Evansville (Ind.), 1977-79; editorial asst. U. Chgo. Press, 1979-81, chair info. services Bowling Green (Ohio) State U., 1983-84; instr. Grad. Library Schl., U. Chgo., 1982-83, 84-85, asst. prof., 1985-87, prof., Columbia U., 1987. Mem. ALA, Soc. Scholarly Publishing, Assn. Library and Info. Sci. Educators. Home: 37 Schraalenburgh Rd Haworth NJ 07641

BIGGS, WELLINGTON ALLEN, b. Platteville, CO, Mar. 9, 1923; s. Wellington H. and Adeline (Brown) B.; m. Laura Jean Mowrey, Dec. 7, 1951; children—Catherine, Joseph, Lorraine, Louise, Jeffrey. BA, U. Colo., 1949. Asst. editor Brighton (Colo.) Blade, 1949-50; editor Haywood Pub. Co., Chgo., 1950-52; asst. editor Alamosa (Colo.) Daily Courier, 1952, Wyo. State Jnl, Lander, 1952; dir. publs. U. Colo., 1952-56; editor Rocky Mountain Teamster, Denver, 1956-61; pub. relations cons. Colo. Freedom to Bargain Com., 1958; dir. pub. relations, editor Intl. Teamster mag., Washington, 1961-81; sr. editor Editorial Consultancy, Silver Spring, Md., 1981—. Served with USNR, 1942-46; PTO. Home: 500 Valleybrook Dr Silver Spring MD 20904

BIGLER, MARY JAYN, b. Poplar Bluff, MO, Aug. 5, 1958; s. A. Jay and Pam (Manus) B. Contrbr. articles, poems to mags., newspapers, anthols. including Children's Playmate, St. Louis Globe-Democrat, others. Ed.: Pine Hills Rvw., 1983-84. Wrkg. on screenplay, mag. articles. Student William Woods Coll., 1976-79, Southern Ill. U., 1980. Society ed., advt. mgr. The Gazette-Democrat, Anna, IL, 1980-85; sales representative Southern Illinoisan, Carbondale, 1985-86; travel agent Trio Travel Center, Cape Giraudeau, MO, 1986; office mgr. Linguists Unlimited, Carbondale, Ill., 1987—. Home: Rt 2 Anna IL 62906

BIGUENET, JOHN JOSEPH, b. New Orleans, Mar. 9, 1949. Contrbr. to No. Am. Rvw, Ploughshares, Ga. Rvw, Mundus Artium, others; ed. New Orleans Rvw, 1977—, Foreign Fictions, 1978; intl. ed. bd. , Transl. Rvw, 1980—; founder and ed. Black & White: An Intl. Rvw of the Arts (merged with New Orleans Rvw), 1975-77. BA, Loyola U-New Orleans, 1971, MFA, U Ark, 1975. Poet-in-residence, Univ. Ark., Little Rock, 1974-76, (vis.) Univ Tex, Dallas, 1980; asst. prof. Loyola Univ., New Orleans, 1977-80, assoc. prof., 1981-86, prof., 1987. Bd. dirs., Arts Council of New Orleans, 1981—. Recipient Mag Writing award, Harper's Mag, NYC, 1970. Mem ALTA. Address Dept Eng Loyola Univ New Orleans LA 70118

BIKE, WILLIAM STANLEY, b. Chgo., Apr. 9, 1957; s. William F. and Jean A. (Smolen) B.; m. Anne M. Nordhaus, May 10, 1986. Ed.-in-chief: Berwyn-Cicero News, 1981, Oak Park News, 1981, Loyola World, 1984—, Loyola

Mag., 1985—, Loyola Law, 1987—. B.A., DePaul U., 1979. Editorial asst. Crain Communications, Chgo., 1979-81; ed.-in-chief Sanford Pub. Co., Oak Park, IL, 1981; assoc. ed. Irving-Cloud Pub. Co., Skokie, IL, 1982-84; v.p. Near West Gazette, Chgo., 1983—; pubs. mgr. Loyola U., Chgo., 1984—. Home: 3530 N Damen Chicago IL 60618

BILL, J(OHN) BRENT, b. Columbus, OH, May 11, 1951; s. John Henry and JoAnn (Shields) B.; m. Sharon ReVell Deming, Mar. 6, 1971; children—John Benjamin, Timothy Alan. Author: David B. Updegraff: Quaker Holiness Preacher, 1983, Rock and Roll: Proceed with Caution, 1984, rev., 1988, Stay Tuned: A Guide to Critical Viewing, 1985, Lunch is my Favorite Subject, 1987. Contrbr. to The Group Retreat Book, 1983; articles, photographs to mags., newspapers including Quaker Life, Friends Jnl., Christianity Today, others. A.A., Chatfield Coll., 1977; B.A. magna cum laude, Wilmington Coll., 1978; M.A., Earlham Schl. Religion, 1980. Assoc. minister 1st United Methodist, Hillsboro, OH, 1976-79; pastoral minister Jericho Friends Meeting, Winchester, IN, 1979-81; dir. christian edn. Western Yearly Meeting of Friends, Plainfield, IN, 1981—. Home: 869 Cragwood CT Plainfield IN 46168

BILLINGS, HAROLD WAYNE, b. Cain City, TX., Nov. 12, 1931; s. Harold Ross and Katie Mae (Price) B.; m. Bernice Schneider, Sept. 10, 1954; children: Brenda, Geoffrey, Carol. Author: Edward Dahlberg: American Ishmael of Letters, 1968, A Bibliography of Edward Dahlberg, 1972; editor, The Leafless American (2d ed.), 1986, other books in field; mem. editorial bd.: Library Chronicle, 1970—. BA, Pan Am. Coll., 1953; MLS, U. Tex., 1957. Mem. ALA Office: Univ of Tex Austin TX 78712

BILLITER, WILLIAM OVERTON, JR., b. Cin., Sept. 3, 1934; s. William Overton and Laura Louise (Dorsey) B.; m. Maureen Ann Flanagan, June 22, 1962; children: Suzanne, Stephen, Mary, Patrick. Reporter New Orleans Times-Picayune, 1959-61; reporter, polit. editor Louisville Courier-Jnl., 1965-74; editorial writer, columnist Louisville Times, 1974-77, city editor, 1977-78; reporter Los Angeles Times, 1978—. B.A., U. Ky., 1956; M.S., U. Louisville, 1970. Served with USAF, 1956-59. Mem. Soc. Profl. Journalists. Home:9522 Telhan Dr Huntington Beach CA 92646

BILLMAN, IRWIN EDWARD, b. Manhattan, NY, July 7, 1940; s. Herman Frank and Ruth (Dutchen) B. Asst. controller Whelan Drug Co., 1965-66; v.p., treas. Curtis Circulation Co., Phila., 1966-71; exec. v.p., Chief operating officer Penthouse Omni and Forum mags., 1971-81; pres., publisher Oui Mag., NYC, 1981-82; pres. Billman Media Group; ptnr. Mag. Communications Cons. B.S. in Econ, Wharton Sch., U. Pa., 1962. Mem. Periodical and Book Assn. Am. (pres. 1977-81). Home: Box 350 Westhampton NY 11977

BILLS, SHERYL JEAN, b. Rushville, IN, Aug. 4, 1945; d. Robert Jackson and Mary Elizabeth (Kehl) B.; m. John M. Heckler, Nov. 30, 1985. Mem. staff Cin. Enquirer, 1967-82, asst. mng. editor features, 1979-80, mng. editor, 1980-82; planning editor USA Today, Gannett Newspapers, 1982-83, mng. editor life, 1983-85, sr. editor, 1985—; lectr. in field. Recipient writing award Ohio Newspaper Women's Assn., 1971, 74; Ohio AP award for enterprise in journalism, 1974, award mag. covers-Outdoor Writers Ohio (Ohio Press Photographers Assn., 1976), Penney-Mo. award for newspaper lifestyle sect., 1978. Mem. Women in Comunications, AP Mng. Editors Assn., ASNE. Office: Kelvedon Box 1772 Middleburg VA 22117

BINGHAM, HIRAM A., b. London, Sept. 24, 1935, s. Hiram and Rose (Morrison) B.; m. Anne Elisabeth Buswell, Aug. 4, 1965; children—Hiram Edward, Olivia Tiffany, Matthew R.A. Author: The Dawnwatchers, 1984. BA, Yale U., 1957; LLB, Columbia U., 1963. Exec. v.p. Intl. Stratford of Tex., Houston, 1972-74; tchr. Emerson Coll., Sussex, Eng., 1974-75; pres. Caithness Corp., NYC, 1976—. Home: 8 Ullman Terr Monsey NY 10952

BINGHAM, SALLIE, b. Louisville, Jan. 22, 1937; d. George Barry and Mary (Caperton) Bingham; m. Timothy C. Peters, June 15, 1983; children: Barry Ellsworth, Christopher Iovenko, William Iovenko. Author: (novel) After Such Knowledge, 1959, (novella and short stories) The Touching Hand, 1968, (short stories) The Way It Is Now, 1972, (autobiog.) Passion and Prejudice, 1988; contrbr. to anthologies and mags. including Atlantic Monthly, Ladies Home Jnl, Redbook, McCalls. BA magna cum laude, Radcliffe Coll., 1958. Faculty U. Louisville, 1977-78, 79-81, 83, 85. Fellow Yaddo, 1980, 83, Va. Ctr for the Creative Arts, 1981, MacDowell Colony, 1979, 82; recipient Greensboro Rvw award for short story, 1986, Open Circle Theater award for play, 1986. Mem. AG, DG, PEN. Office: Am Voice Heyburn Bldg Louisville KY 40202

BINIEK, JOSEPH PAUL, b. Avon, MN, June 23, 1922; s. Peter B. and Mary (Cichy) B.; m. Margaret C. Krantz, Feb. 18, 1950; children—Joseph, Michael, Margaret, Stephen, Patrick, Katherine. Author: History and Future of Spark Ignition Engines, 1973; Potential Effects of Application of Air & Water Quality Standards on Agricultural and Rural Development, 1975; Pollution Taxes, Effluent Charges & Other Alternatives for Pollution Control, 1977; Agricultural and Environmental Relationship, Issues and Priorities, 1971; Status of Environmental Economics, an Update, 1982; Controversies in Environmental Policy, 1986. B.S., U. Minn., 1949, M.S., 1960. Economist, Economic Research Service, U.S. Dept. Agrl., Washington, 1960-72; Specialist Congressional Research Service, Library of Congress, Washington, 1972-82. Recipient Letter of Commendation, U.S. Study Commn., 1962, Recognition of Vauable Services award, 1963; Letter of Commendation, Sec. of Agrl., 1971; Superior Service award, Library of Congress, 1982. Home: 808 Capri Isles Blvd 216 Venice FL 34292

BINKLEY, JANET RAMAGE, b. Prescott, AZ Mar. 18, 1930; d. Russell A. and Elva Caroline (Brobst) R.; m. Thomas Eden Binkley, Nov. 1953 (div. 1964); 1 dau., Christina Kreider Binkley. MA, U. CO, 1964; PhD with distn., U. KS, 1975. Advt. asst. Readers Digest Intl., NYC, 1952-53; ed. U. of IL Press, Urbana, 1954-60; asst. prof. Foreign Lang., Stephens Coll., Columbia, MO, 1963-69; asst. prof. German, KS State U., Emporia, 1969-74; journals ed. Intl. Reading Assn., Newark, DE, 1975—. Mem. EWA, SSP. Home: 933 Rockmoss Ave Newark DE 19711

BINSTOCK, ROBERT HENRY, b. New Orleans, Dec. 6, 1935; s. Louis and Ruth (Atlas) B.; m. Martha Burns, July 27, 1979; 1 dau., Jennifer. Author: America's Political System, 4th edit., 1984, Feasible Planning for Social Change, 1966; editor: International Perspectives on Aging: Population and Policy Changes, 1982, Handbook of Aging and the Social Sciences, 2d ed., 1984. AB, Harvard U., 1956, PhD, 1965. Ford Fdn. fellow, 1959-60. Fellow Gerontol. Soc. Am. Office: Brandeis Heller Bldg Waltham MA 02254

BINZEN, PETER HUSTED, b. Montclair, NJ, Sept. 24, 1922; s. Frederick William and Lucy Beckwith (Husted) B.; m. Elisabeth Virginia Flower, June 12, 1951; children: Lucy Binzen Wildrick, Jennifer Binzen Cardoso, Jonathan Peter, Katherine Lorna. Author: Whitetown U.S.A., 1970, (with Joseph R. Daughen) The Wreck of the Penn Central, 1971, The Cop Who Would Be King, 1977. BA in Poli. Sci., Yale U., 1947; postgrad (Nieman fellow), Harvard U. 1962. Reporter UP, NYC, 1947, Passaic (N.J.) Herald-News, 1947-50; reporter, editor Phila. Bull., 1951-82; reporter Inquirer, 1982-86; columnist, 1986—. Served with AUS, 1943-45. Decorated Bronze Star. Office: Phila Inq 400 N Broad St Philadelphia PA 19101

BIRD, CAROLINE, b. NYC, Apr. 15, 1915; d. Hobart Stanley and Ida (Brattrud) B.; m. Edward A. Menuez, June 8, 1934 (div. Dec. 1945); 1 dau., Carol (Mrs. John Paul Barach); m. John Thomas Mahoney, Jan. 5, 1957; 1 son, John Thomas. Author: The Invisible Scar, 1966, Born Female, 1968, rev. edit., 1970, The Crowding Syndrome, 1972, Everything a Woman Needs To Know To Get Paid What She's Worth, 1973, rev., 1982, The Case Against College, 1975, Enterprising Women, 1976, What Women Want, 1979, The Two-Paycheck Marriage, 1979, The Good Years, 1983; chief writer: The Spirit of Houston, 1978 Student, Vassar Coll., 1931-34; B.A., U. Toledo, 1938; M.A., U. Wis., 1939. Desk editor N.Y. Jour. Commerce, 1943-44; editorial researcher Newsweek mag., NYC., 1942-43, Fortune mag., NYC., 1944-46; with Dudley-Anderson-Yutzy, pub. relations, NYC., 1947-68. Mem. ASJA, Women in Communications. Home: 31 Sunrise Ln Poughkeepsie NY 12603

BIRD, ROBERT BYRON, b. Bryan, TX., Feb. 5, 1924; s. Byron and Ethel (Antrim) B. Author: (with others) Molecular Theory of Gases an Liquids, 2d printing, 1964, Transport Phenomena, 39th printing, 1987, Spanish ed., 1965, Czech edit., 1966, Italian ed., 1970, Russian ed., 1974, Een Goed Begin: A Contemporary Dutch Reader, 1963, 2d ed., 1971, Comprehending Technical Japanese, 1975, Dynamics of Polymeric Liquids, Vol. 1, Fluid Mechanics, Vol. 2, Kinetic Theory, 1977, 2d ed., 1987; Reading Dutch: Fifteen Annotated Stories from the Low Countries, 1985; also numerous research publs.; Am. editor: (with others) Applied Sci. Research, 1969—; adv. bd. Indsl. and Engring. Chemistry, 1970-72; editorial bd. Jour. Non-Newtonian Fluid Mechanics, 1975-86. Student, U. Md., 1941-43; B.S. in Chem. Engring, U. Ill., 1947; Ph.D. in Chemistry, U. Wis., 1950; student, U. Amsterdam, 1950-51; D.Eng (hon.), Lehigh U., 1972, Washington U., 1973, Tech. U. Delft, Holland, 1977, Colo. Sch. Mines, 1986; Sc.D. (hon.), Clarkson U., 1980. Served to 1st lt. AUS, 1943-46. Decorated Bronze Star; Fulbright fellow Holland, 1950; Fulbright lectr., Holland, 1958, Japan, 1962-63; Guggenheim fellow, 1958; recipient numerous awards including Natl. Medal of Science, 1987. Mem. N.Y. Acad. Scis., Am. Acad. Arts and Scis., Wis. Acad. Scis., Natl. Acad. of Engineering, Arts and Letters, Royal Dutch Acad. Scis. Office: 3004 Engring Bldg 1415 Johnson Dr U Wis Madison WI 53706

BIRD, SARAH ANN, Ann Arbor, MI; d. John Aaron and Colista Marie (McCabe) Bird; m. George Roger Jones. Author: Do Evil Cheerfully, 1983, Alamo House: Women Without Men, Men Without Brains (novel), 1986; contrbr.: Mademoiselle, Savvy, Pursuits, other publs. MA, U. Tex.-Austin, 1977. Assoc. ed. Third Coast mag., Austin, 1980—. Mem. Austin Wrtrs. League, Pro Group. Home: 1203 Alegria St Austin TX 78757

BIRMINGHAM, STEPHEN, b. Hartford, CT, May 28, 1931; s. Thomas J. and Editha (Gardner) B.; m. Janet Tillson, Jan. 5, 1951 (div.); children—Mark, Harriet, Carey. Author: Young Mr. Keefe, 1958, Barbara Greer, 1959, The Towers of Love, 1961, Those Harper Women, 1963, Fast Start, Fast Finish, 1966, Our Crowd: The Great Jewish Families of New York, 1967, The Right People, 1968, Heart Troubles, 1968, The Grandees, 1971, The Late John Marquand, 1972, The Right Places, 1973, Real Lace, 1973, Certain People: America's Black Elite, 1977, The Golden Dream: Suburbia in the 1970's, 1978, Jacqueline Bouvier Kennedy Onassis, 1978, Life at the Dakota, 1979, California Rich, 1980, Duchess, 1981, The Grandes Dames, 1982, The Auerbach Will, 1983, The Rest of Us, 1985, The LeBaron Secret, 1986; contrbr. articles to periodicals. BA cum laude, Williams Coll., 1950; postgrad., Univ. Coll., Oxford (Eng.) U., 1951. Advt. copywriter Needham, Harper & Steers, Inc., 1953-67. Served with AUS, 1951-53. Address: c/o Brandt & Brandt 1501 Broadway New York NY 10036

BIRNBAUM, STEPHEN NORMAN, b. NYC, Mar. 28, 1937; s. Louis M. and Ruth L. (Kreisel) B.; m. Alexandra Mayes, Dec. 28, 1972. Creative dir. DePerri Advt., Inc., NYC, 1967-72; mng. editor Fodor's Travel Guides, NYC, London, 1972-75; editor Diversion Mag., Titusville, N.J., 1975-76, editor, pub., NYC, 1976—; travel editor Golf Mag., 1973—, Esquire, 1976-79, N.J. Monthly Mag., 1977; travel Commentator CBS Radio Network, 1977—; CBS Morning News, 1986—; travel editor Today Show, NBC, 1977-79, Good Morning America, ABC, 1982-86; editor Stephen Birnbaum Travel Guides pub. by Houghton Mifflin Travel Guides, 1977—; author/commentator Birnbaum Audio Travel Guides, 1985—; syndicated columnist Chgo. Tribune/N.Y. News Syndicate, 1978—; editorial dir. Sojourn mag., 1978—, Fair Lanes mag., 1979—; Direct mag., 1981-84; travel commentator Ind. Network News, 1981; travel editor Playboy mag., 1979-82, 84-85, Good Housekeeping mag., 1982-84, 85—. BA, Columbia U., 1957. Served with USCG, 1958-66. Mem. Soc. Am. Travel Writers, N.Y. Travel Writers, Golf Writers Am. Office: Diversion Mag 60 E 42d St New York NY 10017

BIRNSTEIN, ANN, b. NYC, May 27, 1927; d. Bernard and Clara (Gordon) B.; m. Alfred Kazin, June 26, 1952 (div. 1981); 1 child, Cathrael. Author: (novels) Star of Glass, 1950, The Troublemaker, 1955, The Sweet Birds of Gorham, 1966, Dickie's List, 1973, American Children, 1980; (3 short novels) Summer Stiuations, 1973; (biography) The Rabbi on Forty-seventh Street, 1982; co-ed., The Works of Anne Frank, 1959; contrbr. stories, articles, essays, and rvws. to Book World, Confrontation, Geo, Inside, Mademoiselle, McCalls, N.Y. Times Book Rvw, The New Yorker, The Reporter, Vogue, other mags.; film critic Vogue, 1966-72. BA, Queens Coll., 1948; postgrad. Sorbonne, 1951-52. Wrtr.-in-residence CCNY, 1970; vis. lectr. Iowa Wrtrs. Workshop, 1973, 76; adj. assoc. prof. English, Barnard Coll., N.Y.C., 1981—; lectr. Columbia U., 1985—. Dodd, Mead lit. fellow, 1950; Fulbright fellow, 1951-52; NEA grantee, 1981-82. Mem AG, PEN, MacDowell Colony Fellows (pres.). Home: 1623 3d Ave Apt 27 SW New York NY 10128

BIRSH, ARTHUR THOMAS, b. Englewood, NJ, Oct. 6, 1932; s. Abraham S. and Mary (Levinsohn) B.; m. Judith Rosenberg, June 29, 1955 (div. 1982); children: Andrew, Philip, Joanne; m. Joan Alleman, 1983. Engaged in sales Western Pub. Co., Poughkeepsie, N.Y., 1956-58; founder Cross Road Press, Hyde Park, N.Y., 1958, pres., 1958-60; with Playbill mag., NYC, 1961—, publisher, 1965—; exec. v.p. Am. Theatre Press, Inc., 1961—, publisher, 1965—; exec. v.p. Am. Theatre Press, Inc., 1961-68, pres., 1974—; group v.p. Metromedia, Inc., 1968-73. Grad., Lawrenceville N.J. Schl., 1950; B.A., Yale, 1954. Serverd with AUS, 1954-56. Home: 71/2 Leroy St New York NY 10014

BISHER, JAMES FURMAN, b. Denton, NC, Nov. 4, 1918; s. Chisholm and Mamie (Morris) B.; divorced; children—Roger, James Furman, Monte. Author: With A Southern Exposure, 1962, Miracle in Atlanta, 1966, Strange But True Baseball Stories, 1966, Arnold Palmer—The Golden Year, 1971, Aaron, 1974, The College Game, 1974, The Masters, 1976, also numerous articles; contrbr. to anthologies including Best Sports Stories of Year, 23 times. AB in Journalism, U. N.C., 1938. Editor Lumberton (N.C.) Voice, 1938-39; reporter High Point (N.C.) Enterprise, 1939-40; reporter, state editor Charlotte (N.C.) News, 1940-42, sports editor, 1946-50, Atlanta Constn., 1950-57, Atlanta Jnl, 1957—; columnist The Sporting News, St. Louis; moderator weekly TV show, Football Rvw, 1950-68. Served to lt. Air Corps USNR, 1943-46. Recipient Ga. AP and UPI Sports Writing award, numerous times; recipient Turf Writing award Fla. Thoroughbred Breeders Assn., 1972, 75; others. Mem. Natl. Sportscasters and Sportswriters Assn. (pres. 1974-76), Football Writers Assn. Am. (pres. 1959-60). Home: 3135 Rilman Rd NW Atlanta GA 30327

BISHOP, ANNE, b. Amasya, Turkey, May 1, 1912; came to U.S., 1947, naturalized, 1950; d. Kevork an Zabel (Isburian) Avakian; m. Jacques Bruyere, June 6, 1940; 1 son, Christian Georges; m. John Bishop, 1950; children: John, Elizabeth. Author: Franklin in Paris, 1937; opera Hripsime, 1974, Spirit of 76, 1974, Western Spirit of '76, 1975, A Nation of Dreamers, 1975, Queen Elizabeth's Silver Jubliee, 1977, World Who's Who of Armenians, 1977-80, Gerontology Outreach Affiliated Library System, 1978, Volunteers International Education, Adv. Council 5-year Ann., 1974-79, 1980, Upon Attaining Immortality, 1980, The Kingdom of Heaven, 1980. Student, Oxford U., 1935-37, Sorbonne U., 1937-41, Ecole Univerelle de Paris, 1944, Ecole Orientale, 1946, Calif. State U., Northridge, 1978; D.D. (hon.), Christ U., 1980. Paris Bur. chief London Daily Mirror, 1935; fgn. and war corr. UPI, N.Y. News, Chgo. Tribune, 1935-46; freelance writer Social Studies mag., Life and Time mag., Lit. Tabloid, 8-Ball, Armenian Reporter, Armenian Observer, Nor Gyank, Armenian Mirror, Sptator, 1947—. Named World's Greatest War Corr. N.Y. News-Chgo. Tribune Syndicate, 1946. Mem. ALA (life), Am. Soc. Composers and Producers, Nat. Soc. Lit. an Arts. Home: 615 S Manhattan Pl Los Angeles CA 90005

BISHOP, PIKE, see Obstfeld, Raymond

BISHOP, STEPHEN RICHARD, b. Camden, NJ, Dec. 1, 1953; s. William Harry and Edith (Williams) B. Poet: Lust is a Four-Letter Feeling, 1983; contrbr. to Am. Poetry Anthol. Stud. pub. schls., Medford & Wildwood, NJ. Driver, Colson Lumber, N. Wildwood, NJ, 1983-84; self-employed, 1985—. Served to E-4, U.S. Army, 1974-76. Mem. Cabin Fever Cafe. Home: 407 Central Ave North Wildwood NJ 08260

BISHOP, WENDY S., b. Fukuoka, Japan, Jan. 12, 1953; d. Robert Loomis and Lillian (Hagen) Bishop; m. Marvin E. Pollard, May 10, 1985; 1 child, Morgan Pollard Bishop. Author: Second Nature, 1980; poetry in Calif. Qtly, Chariton Rvw, Cutbank, other lit mags. MA, U. Calif., Davis, 1976, 1979. Lectr., Bayero, Kano, Nigeria, 1980-81; instr., Navajo Comm. College, Tsaile, AZ, 1984-85; vis. prof., U. of AK, Fairbanks, 1985-86. Mem. AWP, PSA, NCTE. Home: Box 146 UAF Fairbanks AK 99775

BISKIN, MIRIAM MARCIA NEWELL, b. Cohoes, NY, May 17, 1920, d. Eli and Bessie (Fishman) Newell); m. Irving Biskin, May 17, 1946; children—Anne Biskin Rothenberg, Deborah Biskin Levine. Author: Pattern for a Heroine (biography), My LIfe Among the Gentiles (essays), Three Spinning Fairies (play), The Enchanted Shirt (play), Landmarks of Old Troy (history); contrbr. stories, plays, poems, articles to The Friend, Highlights for Children, The Torch, Times Record Newspapers, others. BA, SUNY-Albany, 1941, MA, 1946. Educator; cons. N.Y. State Dept. Edn. Home: 2507 16th St Troy NY 12180

BISSELL, LECLAIR, b. Ft. Monroe, VA, May 18, 1928; d. Clayton Lawrence and Louise LeClair (Gaillard) B. Author: (with Richard Watherwax) The Cat Who Drank Too Much, 1982; (with Paul W. Haberman) Alcoholism in the Professions, 1984, (with James E. Royce, SJ) Ethics for Addiction Professionals, 1987, (with Eleanor Sullivan and Etta Williams) Deadly Diversion: The Chemically Dependent Nurse, 1988; also numerous articles on alcoholism counseling and addiction/alcohol problems among profl. populations. BA, U. Colo., 1950; MS in LS, Columbia U., 1952, MD, 1963. House officer, physician Roosevelt Hosp., NYC, 1963-79; Founder Smithers Alcoholism Treatment & Tng. Ctr., 1968; pres., chief exec. officer Edgehill-Newport Alcoholism Treatment Ctr., R.I., 1979-81; author, researcher, cons., lectr., NYC, 1982—. Home: 130 W 16th St Apt 63 New York NY 10011

BITA, LILI, b. Zante, Greece, Dec. 23, 1935; came to U.S., 1959; d. George and Eleni (Makri) Bitas; m. Robert Zaller, Jan. 19, 1968; children: Philip, Kimon. Author: Steps on the Earth, 1955; Lightning in the Flesh, 1968; Furies, 1969; Zero Hour, 1971; Blood Sketches, 1973; Sacrifice, Exile and Night, 1976; Fleshfire: New and Selected Love Poems, 1980; trans. A Spy in the House of Love (Anais Nin), 1974; contrbr. to anthologies City Lights, Contemporary Greek Women Poets, numerous others. Instr. Emporia Coll, Kans., 1960-62, U. Toledo, Kans., 1963-65; guest lectr. master classes Bklyn. Conservatory Music, 1970—, univs. in U.S. and Europe, 1970—; performer in classic theater. Mem. Southeastern Theater Conf., Am. Tchers. Music. Home: 5901 SW 51st St Miami FL 33155

BITTEL, LESTER ROBERT, b. East Orange, NJ., Dec. 9, 1918; s. William Frederick an Helen (Korte) B.; m. Muriel Albers Walcutt, May 8, 1972. Author: (with others), Practical Automation, 1956, What Every Supervisor Should Know, 1959, 5th ed, 1984, Management by Exception, 1964, (with Robert Craig) Training and Development Handbook, 1967, The Nine Master Keys of Management, 1972, Improving Supervisor Performance, 1976, Shenandoah Management Games for Supervisors, 1978, Encyclopedia of Professional Management, 1979, Introduction to Business in Action, 1980, 3d ed., 1988, Essentials of Supervisory Management, 1981, (with Ronald Burke) Introduction to Management Practice, 1981, (with Jackson C. Ramsey) Handbook for Professional Managers, 1984, Executive Skills Program, 1981, Leadership, 1984, Complete Guide to Supervisory Training and Development, 1987. Author of film senario The Case of the Snarled Parking Lot, 1981. BS in industrial engineering, Lehigh U., 1940; MBA, James Madison U., 1974. Field engineer, Leeds & Northup Co., Philadelphia, Pa., 1940-46; industrial engineer, Western Electric Co., Kearny, N.J., 1947; plant supt., Koppers Co. Inc., Kearny, 1947-52, training dir., Pittsburgh, 1952-54; ed of Fatory, McGraw-Hill Book Co., NYC., 1954-70, dir. of information systems, 1971-72; instr in management, Lord Fairfax Community Coll., Middleton, Va., 1972-74; prof of management, James Madison U. Harrisonburg, Va., 1975—. Member: Amer. Soc. of Mech. Engs. (fellow), Amer. Soc. for Training and Development, Institute of Certified Professional Mgrs. (sec-treas, 1981—), Overseas Press Club, Phi Kappa Phi. Jesse Neale Awd of Merit, Amer. Bus. Press, 1957, 59, 60, 61, 69; cit. from Amer. Soc. of Meh. Engs., 1967 for outstanding engineering leader-ship; G. M. Loeb award, Amer. Financial Inst., 1968, for disting. bus and financial journalism; William McFeeley award, Intl Management Cncl, 1978, for contribs to mangmnt and educ; Centennial Award and Frederick W. Taylor Award, Amer. Soc. of Mech Engrs, both 1980; Virginia Eminent Scholar, 1986. Military Service: U.S. Army Air Fores, 1942-46; became first lt. Home: 106 Breezewood Ter Bridgewater VA 22812

BITTLER, KERRY ANDREW, b. Mankato, MN, June 7, 1958; s. Edward Clifford and Mary Jo (Miller) B.; m. Virginia Denise Walrath, May 12, 1984. BS in Jnlsm., U. OR, 1980. Writer, then ed. North American Gold Mining Associates, Ltd., Wilsonville, OR, 1983—. Office: NA Gold Mining Assoc 8565 S W Salish Ln Wilsonville OR 97070

BIXBY, ROBERT JAY, b. Mt. Pleasant, MI, Nov. 9, 1952, s. Edgar Allen and Betty Jean (Sprague) B.; m. Kathleen Mae Beal, July 30, 1971; children—Jennifer Marie, Steven Jay. Contrbr. stories to Redbook, Gargoyle and other periodicals. B.S., Central Mich U., 1978; M.S.W., Western Mich U., 1980. Social worker VAMC Battle Creek, Mich, 1980-87; asst. ed. COMPUTE! Books, 1987—. Served USN, 1972-76. Home: 3006 Stonecutter Greensboro NC 27405

BIXLER, HOWARD, see Bixler, Paul

BIXLER, PAUL, (Howard Bixler), b. Union City, MI, Oct. 27, 1899; s. Miles Fred and Lida (Gillett) B.; m. Norma Hendricks, Oct. 6, 1926; children: Giles Norman, Jon, Mark Frederick. Author: chpts. The Administration of the College Library, 1944, Mexican Library, 1969, Southeast Asia: Bibliographic Directions, 1974; editor: Antioch Rvw Anthology, 1953, Freedom of Communication, 1954; contbr. articles to profl jnls. A.B., Hamilton Coll., 1922; student, U. Pa., 1922-23; M.A., Harvard U., 1924; B.L.S., Western Res. U., 1933. Police reporter Cleve. Press, 1926-27; mem. editorial bd. Antioch Rvw., 1941-42, 58—, chmn., 1943-58, editor, 1974-77. Judge Nonfiction Natl. Book Award, 1955; Ford Fdn. grantee for bibliog. research S.E. Asia, 1962-63. Mem. ALA, ACLU. Home: 1345 Rice Rd Yellow Springs OH 45387

BLACIK, STEPHEN MARK, (Ray Ureform), b. St. Paul, Mar. 2, 1951; m. Ann Hoagland, Sept. 17, 1983. Author: Withdrawal Pains, 1974; Spiritmen, 1976; Three Cherries and a Banana, 1981. BA, Carleton Coll., 1973. Spcl. asst. Congressman Abouaezk, Washington, 1972, U.S. RRB, Chgo., 1973-80; programming analyst Prudential Life Ins. Co., Plymouth, Minn., 1981—. Pres., Rice Lake Woods Homeowners Assn., Maple Grove, Minn., 1984—; active Citizens Long-Range Improvement Com., Maple Grove, 1986—. Mem. Maple Grove Reviewers (founder), North Hennepin Guild. Home: 13727 86th Ave N Maple Grove MN 55369

BLACK, BRADY FORREST, b. Lawrence County, KY, July 31, 1908; s. Fred Nixon and Melissa (Cornwell) B.; m. Edra Dailey, Sept. 17, 1930; children: Brenda Gayle, Brady Brent, Lisa Anne. Sports editor Ashland (Ky.) Ind., 1927-38, city editor, 1959-64, v.p., editor, 1964-75; syndicated newspaper columnist, 1976-80. Student pub. schls. Mem. Inter Am. Press Assn. Home: 1009 Park Crest Park Hills KY 41011

BLACK, CATHLEEN PRUNTY, b. Chgo., Apr. 26, 1944; d. James Hamilton and Margaret (Harrington) B. Advtg. sales rep. Holiday mag., NYC., 1966-69, Travel & Leisure mag., NYC., 1969-70; advt. sales rep. New York mag., 1970-72, assoc. pub., 1977-79, pub., 1979-83; pres. USA Today, 1983—; advt. Dir. Ms. mag., 1972-75, assoc. pub., 1975-77. B.A., Trinity Coll., 1966. Home: 325 E 72d New York NY 10021

BLACK, CREED CARTER, b. Harlan, KY, July 15, 1925; s. Creed Carter and Mary (Cole) B.; m. Mary C. Davis, Dec. 28, 1947 (div. 1976); children: Creed Carter, Steven D., Douglas S.; m. Elsa Goss, Dec. 9, 1977. Reporter Paducah (Ky.) Sun-Democrat, 1942-43, 46; editor Daily Northwestern, 1947; copy editor Chgo. Sun-Times, 1949, Chgo. Herald-Am., 1950; editorial writer Nashville Tennessean, 1950-57, exec. editor, 1957-59; v.p., exec. editor Savannah (Ga.) Morning News and Savannah Evening press, 1959-60, Wilmington (Del.) Morning News and Evening Jour., 1960-64; mng. editor Chgo. Daily News, 1964-68, exec. editor, 1958-69; asst. sec. for legislation HEW, 1969-70; editor Phila. Inquirer, 1970-77; chmn. bd., pub. Lexington (Ky.) Herald-Leader, 1977—. B.S. with highest distinction and honors in Polit. Sci., Northwester U., 1949; M.A., U. Chgo., 1952. Served with 100th Inf. Div. AUS, World War II, ETO. Deorated Bronze Star. Mem. Am. Newspaper Pubs. Assn., So. Newspaper Pubs. Assn. (pres. 1987), Am. Soc. Newspaper Editors (dir.; pres. 1983), Natl. Conf. Editorial Writers (pres. 1962). Home 1932 Blairmore Rd Lexington KY 40502

BLACK, HARRY GEORGE, b. Hammond, IN, Jan. 31, 1933, s. Harry Howard and Theresa (Grebb) B.; m. Marilyn Gaye Gibbons, June 21, 1961 (dec. 1984); children—Gaye Jeane, Robin. Author: The Lost Dutchman Mine: A Short Story of A Tall Tale, 1975, Survival in the Wilds, 1977, Trails to Hoosier Heritage, 1981, Trails to Illinois Heritage, 1982, Pictorial Americana: The National Road, 1984, Historic Trails and Tales of Northwest Indiana, 1985; contrbr. articles to newspapers, mags. BA in Sociology, Roosevelt U., Chgo., 1959. Tchr. Hammond (Ind.) Pub. Schls., 1964-74; author, 1974—; pub. HMB Publs., Hammond, 1980—. Served as cpl. U.S. Army, 1953-55. Mem. Duneland Hist. Soc., Hammond Hist. Soc., Historic Landmarks Fdn. Ind. Office: HMB Publs 7406 Monroe Ave Hammond IN 46324

BLACK, HILLEL MOSES, b. NYC., Apr. 8, 1929; s. Isidor and Ida (Feldstein) B. Author: B. Author: The Watch Dogs of Wall Street, Buy Now, Pay Later, The American Schoolbook. B.A., U. Chgo., 1949, M.English and Fgn. Langs., 1952. Copy boy N.Y. Times, 1952-53; reporter AP, Pitts., Newark and NYC., 1954-58; freelance writer, NYC., 1959-65; editor Saturday Evening Post, 1966-67; sr. editor William Morrow & Co., NYC, 1967-77, editor-in-chief, 1977-82; pub. gen. books div. Macmillan Pub. Co., NYC, 1982—. Office: Macmillan 866 3d Ave New York NY 10022

BLACK, SANDRA KAY, b. Springfield, IL, Nov. 30, 1942; d. David Patrick Sulverski and Mary Louise (Sullivan) Sulverski Anderson; m. Les James Black, Feb. 20, 1965; childrn—Shawna Adrienne, Breann Danielle. Contrbr. poetry: Moods & Mysteries Anthology, The Art of Poetry: A Treasury of Contemporary Verse, other publs.; contrbr. short stories: Showcase 6, Dark Regions, The Creative Urge, others. Wrkg. on short stories, novel, anthology. Student Ill. State U., Normal, 1960-61. Mem. Small Press Wrtrs. and Artists Orgn. Home: 401 W Main St Pleasant Plains IL 62677

BLACK, THEODORE MICHAEL, b. Bklyn., Oct. 3, 1919; s. Walter Joseph and Elsie (Jantzer) B.; m. Barbara A. Somerville, Nov. 10, 1956; children: Walter Joseph II, Theodore Mihael Black; stepchildren: Mrs Beverly A. Pavlak, Mrs. Dorothy B. Scharkopf. Author: Know Your Stamps, 1934, Democratic Party Publicity in the 1940 Campaign, 1941, How to Organize and Run a Citizens' Committee for Your Candidate, 1964, Straight Talk About American Education, 1982. With Walter J. Black, Inc., 1945—, v.p., 1952-58, pres., 1958—, treas., 1958-80, chief exec. officer, 1980—; genl. partner Black's Readers Service Co., 1949-58, pres., 1958-68. A.B. summa cum laude, Princeton U., 1941; grad., Inf. Officers Candidate Sch., Ft. Benning, Ga., 1943; Litt.D. Honoris causa, Siena Coll., Loudonville, N.Y., 1971. Served from pvt. to capt., CIC AUS, 1941-45; lt. col. Army res. ret., 1967. Decorated Bronze Star with cluster (U.S.) Belgian, French Fourragere; recipient medal SAR. Home: 8 Terrace Dr Port Washington NY 11050

BLACKBURN, BARBARA ANN, b. Buffalo, Mar. 23, 1942; d. Lester Lon and Dorothy Elizabeth (Baker) Breeding; m. Alan Porter Blackburn, June 21, 1969; children—Ann Petrina, Bradford Alan. Author: Old West Cookbook, 1985, Herbs from "A" to "Z", 1981, contrbr. to True West, Frontier Times and Real West. BS, Buffalo St. U. College, 1964, MS, 1967. English tchr. Clarence Jr. High, NY, 1964-66, Lancaster H.S., 1966-67; Reading tchr. Leeward Community College, HI, 1967-69; adult edn. tchr. Williamsville Edn. Center, NY, 1982—. Gold Belt Buckle, Western Publs., Stillwater, OK, 1983; Chef-in-Residence, Artpark, Lewiston, NY, 1985. Mem. Natl. Outlaw & Lawman Assn.; Western Writers Assn. Home: 31 Reist St Williamsville NY 14221

BLACKER, HARRIET, b. NYC., July 23, 1940; d. Louis and Rebecca (Siegel) B.; m. Roland Algrant, Aug. 6, 1970 (div. Jan. 1981). Exec.

asst. Nat. Book com., N.Y.C., 1965-67; dir. publicity Hawthorn Books, N.Y.C., 1967-69, Coward-McCann & Geoghegan, N.Y.C., 1969-74; exec. dir. publicity Random House, N.Y.C., 1980-81; v.p. pub. relations Putnam Pub. Group, N.Y.C., 1981-85; pres. Harriet Blacker Inc., Public Relations, N.Y.C., 1986—. B.A., U. Mich., 1962. Mem. Publishers Publicity Assn. (sec. 1973-75, treas. 1982-83, pres. 1983-85), Women's Media Group. Home: 310 E 75th St New York NY 10021

BLACKFORD, STAIGE D., b. Charlottesville, VA, Jan. 3, 1931; s. Staige D. and Lydia H. (Fishburne) Blackford; m. Bettina Balding, Nov. 1, 1958; children—Linda, Sheila. Research Director in charge of all publications Southern Regional Cncl. 1962-64; pol. report. and editorial wrtr. Norfolk Virginian Pilot, 1964-69; editor: Virginia Qtly Rvw, 1975—; editorial consltnt: White Burkett Miller Cntr. of Pub. Affairs, 1980—. BA, U. of Virginia, 1952; BA, Oxford U. 1954 (Rhodes Scholar). Intelligence Officer CIA, 1954-58; Time Inc. (NYC), 1958-59; Grolier, Inc. (NYC), 1960-62. 1st Lt, USAF, 1955-57. Home: 1857 Westview Road Charlottesville VA 22903

BLACKLIDGE, RICHARD HENRY, b. Kokomo, IN, June 7, 1914; s. Kent H. and Bernice (Kautz) B.; m Marian Reinertsen, Jan. 5, 1938. With Kokomo Tribune, 1936-83, chief exec. officer, pub., 1968-83; exec. com., dir. Union Bank and Trust Co., Kokomo, 1942-84; dir. Pub. Service Ind. B.S. in Chem. Engring., Purdue U., 1936. Served with USAAF, 1944-45. Mem. Inland Daily Press Assn. (pres. 1960-61), Hoosier Press Assn. (pres. 1956, dir.), Am. Newspaper Pubs. Assn. (dir., pres. 1970-72, chmn.; past v.p. and dir. researh inst.), Internat. Fedn. Newspaper Editors and Pubs. (v.p. 1970-76). Home: 814 Maplewood Dr Kokomo IN 46901

BLACKMAN, DOROTHY LOYTE, b. Lynn, MA, Sept. 11, 1935; d. Harvey William and Marion (Hooper) Loyte; m. John A. Blackman; children—David, Deborah, Karen, Kathy. Author: The Long Sleep, Zeke (juveniles); contrbr. fiction to mags. including Seventeen, Salome; Mohawk Valley USA. Student Gordon Coll., Wenham, Mass. Substitute tchr. Clifton Fine Central Schl., Star Lake, N.Y., 1962-64, Edmeston Central Schl., N.Y., 1964—; dir. Edmeston Free Library, 1982—; field rep. NY State Alcohol Edn., 1966-76. Dir., coordinator Reading is Fundamental, Edmeston, N.Y., 1982, 83. Home: 9 North St Edmeston NY 13335

BLACKMON, ANTONIA A., b. Ogdensburg, NY. d. Glenn F. and Barbara (Marsh) Ireton. Contrbr.: Scriptwriter News, PRSA Journal, The Businesswoman, Gannett Newspapers, Intl. Altrusian, Congresl. Record, columnist/wrtr. agric. and transport. mags.; novelist, A Woman of Bad Character. BA Lib. Arts U. of Toronto; Postgrad. Advertis. Wrtg. Southeastern U., 1953-56. Dir. Women's Activ. Amer. Truck. Assns. (Wash., DC), 1965-71; Writer, Assoc. Ed. Movie/TV Marketing mag. (NY), 1969-81; Playwrt., Dir., Prod., Guys in the Truck (NY), 1978, It's About Time (NY) 1980, Go Into the Kitchen (NY) 1981; fiction, humor workshop leader, freelance ed., writer, playwright, 1965—, Chapt. Pres., Nat'l Bd. Mem., NOW (Wash., DC), 1967-71; Unusual Merit-First Place, Industr. Ed. Assn., 1965. Mem. Dramatists Guild, Intl. Women's Wrtg. Guild, AL of America. Home: 49 Elm Ave Mt Vernon NY 10550

BLACKSHEAR, HELEN FRIEDMAN, b. Tuscaloosa, AL, June 5, 1911; d. Samuel and Annie Laurie (Longshore) Friedman; m. William Mitchell Blackshear, Apr. 21, 1934 (dec. Sept. 26, 1986); children—Ann Spragins-Harmuth, Sue Blackshear-Bowen, Helen M. Stevenson. Author: Robert Loveman: Belated Romanticist, 1932, Tuscaloosa Sketches, 1967, Mother Was a Rebel, 1973, rth ed., 1986, Creek Captives and Other Alabama Stories, 1975; (poems) With a Quiet Mind, 1974, Along Alabama Roads, 1979; (essays) Southern Smorgasbord, 1981. Contrbr. articles, poems to mags. B.A., Agnes Scott Coll., 1931; M.A. U. Ala., 1932. English tchr. public schs., Tuscaloosa and Montgomery, AL, 1942-73. Mem. Ala. Assn. Retired Tchrs., Ala. Wrtrs. Conclave (pres.), NLAPW (branch pres.), Ala. Poetry Soc. (Poet of Yr. 1983). Home: 334 Felder Ave Montgomery AL 36104

BLACKSMITH, SARA, see Jones, Nancy Joy

BLACKTREE, BARBARA, see Coultry, Barbara A.

BLACKWELL, EARL, b. Atlanta, May 3, 1913; s. Samuel Earl and Carrie (Lagomarsino) B. Author: Crystal Clear, 1978, Skyrocket, 1980; play Aries is Rising, 1939. Student, Culver Mil. Acad., 1928; A.B., Oglethorpe U., 1933; student, Columbia U Co-founder, Celebrity Service Inc. (NYC., London, Paris, Rome, Hollywood), pres., 1939-85, chmn., 1985—; editor-in-chief Celebrity Register; contrbg. editor Town & Country mag., 1964—, editorial cons; lectr. on celebrities, 1963—. Office: 171 W 5th St New York NY 10019

BLACKWELL, LINDA CHRISTINE, b. Detroit, Apr. 19, 1953; d. Edward Norman and Gladys Louise (Adrian) B. Contrbr. articles to lit. mags. Project ed.: Business Communication for the information Age, 1987; asst. ed. ACI, Detroit, 1979-81, Harcoutr Brace Jovanovich, Orlando, FL, 1984—. B.S. in Humanities, Lawrence Tech., 1978; M.A. in Jnlsm., Mich. State U., 1983. Founder, Arbiter Press, 1986. Applegate scholar Mich. State U., E. Lowing, 1983. Home: 740 Jamestown Dr Winter Park FL 32792

BLADES, ANN, b. Vancouver, B.C., Can., Nov. 16, 1947; d. Arthur Hazelton and Dorothy (Planche) Sager. Author, illustrator: Mary of Mile 18, 1971 (Can. Assn. Children's Librarians Book of Year award 1972), A Boy of Tache, 1973, The Cottage at Crescent Beach, 1977, By the Sea: An Alphabet Book, 1985; illustrator: Jacques the Woodcutter, 1977, A Salmon for Simon (Can. Council Children's Lit. award for illustration 1979), 1978 (Amelia Frances Howard-Gibbon award 1979), Six Darn Cows, 1979, Anna's Pet, 1980, Pettranella, 1980, A Candle for Christmas, 1986, Ida and the Wool Smugglers, 1987. Teaching cert., U. B.C., 1971; R.N., B.C. Inst. Tech., 1974. Mem. Writers Union Can. Address: Writers Union Can 24 Ryerson Ave Toronto ON M5T 2P3 Canada

BLAIR, CLAY DREWRY, b. Lexington, Va, May 1, 1925; s. Clay Drewry and Marie Louise (Barreto) B.; m. Agnes Kemp Devereux, Nov. 25, 1960 (div. 1969); children: Marie Louise, Clay Drewry III, Joseph Devereux (dec.), Sibyl Devereux, Kemp Devereux, Robert August Drewry, Christopher Ryan; m. Joan Rutledge West, Nov. 11, 1972. Author: The Atomic Submarine and Admiral Rickover, 1954, (with James R. Shepley) The Hydrogen Bomb, 1954, Beyond Courage, 1955, (for Maj. Ward M. Millar) Valley of the Shadow, 1955, (with Comdr. William R. Anderson) Nautilus 90 North, 1959, Diving for Pleasure and Treasure, 1960, (with A. Scott Crosfield) Always Another Dawn, 1960, The Board Room, 1969, The Strange Case of James Earl Ray, 1969, The Archbishop, 1970, Pentagon Country, 1971, Survive, 1973, Silent Victory: The U.S. Submarine War Against Japan, 1975, (with Joan Blair) The Search for J.F.K., 1976, MacArthur, 1977, Scuba!, 1977, Combat Patrol, 1978, Return from the River Kwai, 1979, Mission Tokyo Bay, 1980, Swordray's First Three Patrols, 1980, (with Omar N. Bradley) A General's Life, 1983, Ridgeway's Paratroopers, 1985. Student Tulane U., 1946-48, Columbia U., 1948-49. Corr. Time mag., 1949-55; mil. corr. Life mag., 1955-57; assoc. editor Saturday Evening Post, 1957-61, asst. mng. editor, 1961-62, mng. editor, 1962, editor, 1963-64; v.p., editorial dir. Curtis Pub. Co., 1962, sr. v.p., editor-in-chief, 1963-64, exec. v.p., dir., 1964. Served with USNR, 1943-46. Decorated Submarine Combat insignia, Address: Meredith 845 Third Ave New York NY 10022

BLAIR, DIANA, b. Los Angeles, May 16, 1947; d. Sheldon Lee Farber and Joyce Marilyn (Johnson) Jackels; children—Daniel Thomas Blair, Deborah Dawn Blair. Author: How to Understand Your Spanish Babysitter/Maid and Speak to Her . . . In Minutes!, 1986. Contrbg. editor: Valley Entertainer Mag. Student Pierce Coll., Woodland Hills, Calif. Dir. music, disc jockey KCSN radio, Northridge, Calif., pub. relations Diamonds On Rodeo, Beverly Hills, Calif., Judge, C. of C., Mission Hills, Calif., 1985. Mem. Broadcast Music, Country Music Assn., Am. Guild Variety Artists, Acad. Country Music. Home: Box 7947 Van Nuys CA 91409

BLAIR, SAMUEL RUFUS, b. Dallas, Sept. 26, 1932; s. James Everette and Edna Glenn (Miller) B.; m. Karen Klinefelter, Oct. 1, 1970; children: Jason Everette, Collin Miller. Author: Dallas Cowboys: Pro or Con?, 1970, (with Roger Staubach and Bob St. John) Stauback: First Down, Lifetime to Go, 1974, (with Grant Teaff) Grant Teaff: I Believe, 1975, Earl Campbell: The Driving Force, 1980, (with Lee Trevion) Super Men, 1982; works included in annl. anthology Best Sports Stories. BJ, U. Tex. at Austin, 1954. Mem. sports staff Dallas Morning News, 1954—, writer, copy editor, 1954-61, 79—, columnist, 1961-53, daily columnist, 1964-78, asst. sports editor, 1966-68, sports editor, 1968-81. Served with USAF, 1955-57. Winner Tex. Sports Writers Competition, 1963, 66, 71, 78, 79, 80, 81, Golf Writers Am. Competition, 1964, 66, 67, 69, 70, 71, 74, 78, 80, UPI Competition, 1975, AP Competition 1978, Pro Football Writers of Am. Competition, 1978, Mem. Football Writers Am., Golf Writers Am., Baseball Writers Am., Tex. Sports Writers Assn. Home: 6843 North Ridge Dallas TX 75214

BLAIS, MADELEINE HELENA, b. Holyoke, MA, Aug. 25, 1949; d. Raymond J. and Maureen M. (Shea) B.; m. John Strong Miner Katzenbach, May 10, 1980. Reporter Boston Globe, 1971-72, Trenton (N.J.) Times, 1974-76; staff writer Tropic Mag., Miami Herald, 1979-87. BA, Coll. New Rochelle, 1969; MS, Columbia U., 1970. Nieman Fellow, Harvard, 1986; assoc. prof., Dept. Jnlstc. Studies, U. of Mass. Amherst, 1987—. Recipient Pulitzer Prize, 1980. Office: Tropic Mag Miami FL 33101

BLAISE, CLARK LEE, b. Fargo, ND, Apr. 10, 1940, s. Leo Romeo and Anne (Vanstone) Blaise;

m. Bharati Mukherjee, Sept. 19, 1963; children—Bart Anand, Bernard Sudhir. Author: (stories) A North American Education, 1973, Tribal Justice, 1974, (non-fiction) Days and Nights in Calcutta, 1977, (novels) Lunar Attractions, 1979, Lusts, 1983, (autobiog) Resident Alien, 1986; co-ed. Here and Now, (with Bharati Mukherjee) The Sorrow and the Terror, 1987; contrbr. numerous articles, rvws., stories to various publs. BA, Denison U., 1961; MFA, U. Iowa, 1964. Prof. English, Concordia U., Montreal, 1966-78, York U., Toronto, 1978-80, Skidmore Coll., Saratoga Springs, N.Y., 1980-81, 82-83; vis. prof. U. Iowa, 1981-82, Emory U., 1985, Columbia U., 1986. Fellow Can. Council, 1973-74, NEA, 1981-82, Guggenheim Fdn., 1984-85. Mem. PEN (Can. Ctr.). Home: Markson Agcy 44 Greenwich Ave New York NY 10011

BLAKE, JANE SALLEY, b. Tallahassee, Sept. 3, 1937; d. George Lawrence Salley and Eleanor (King) Hookham; m. Arthur Copeland Blake, Jr., Sept. 5, 1959; children—Arthur Copeland, Tarrant Salley. Pub., exec. editor: The Kentucky Center for the Arts Mag., 1983—; Beaux Arts Mag., 1980-84. BA in fine arts and journalism, Fla. State U., 1958. Exec. sec. Historic Homes Fdn, Louisville, 1975-76; chmn. Ky. Heritage Bicentennial Celebration, 1976; founder, pres., chair of bd., Arts Forum, Inc., Louisville, 1978-84, pres., prin. The Ctr. Mag., Inc., Louisville, 1986—, J. S. Blake & Assoc., Inc., Louisville, 1986—. Mem. Pub. Relations Soc. Am., Entrepreneur Soc., Advt. Club of Louisville (6 Gold and 7 Silver Louie awards 1981-85), Sigma Delta Chi, Sigma Tau Delta, Women in Communications. Home: 2006 Round Ridge Rd Louisville KY 40207

BLAKE, JOHN BALLARD, b. New Haven, Oct. 29, 1922; s. Francis Gilman and Dorothy Palmer (Dewey) B.; m. Jean Place Adams, Apr. 2, 1949; children: Catherine Curtis, John Gilman, Ann Ballard, James Adams. Author: Benjamin Waterhouse and the Introduction of Vaccination: A Reappraisal, 1957, Public Health in the Town of Boston, 1630-1822, 1959; editor: Medical Reference Works, 1967, Education in the History of Medicine, 1968, Safeguarding the Public, 1970, Centenary of Index Medicus, 1879-1979, 1980. BA, Yale U., 1943; MA, Harvard U., 1947, PhD, 1954. Fellow history of medicine Johns Hopkins, 1951-52; research fellow history of medicine Yale, 1952-55. Served as 1st lt. USAAF, 1943-46. Home: 3038 Newark St NW Washington DC 20008

BLAKE, RENEE, see Blakeman, Beth Renee

BLAKE, ROBERT JAMES, b. Valparaiso, IN, Aug. 25, 1946; s. James Harry and Thelma Louise (Bull) B.; m. Sharon Kay Winter, July 11, 1970; 1 son, Thomas Robert. Author: To Find a King, 1985, The Bane of Llywelyn, 1985, The Wrath of Olympus, 1987, Town of Baldwmar, 1987. Wrkg. on non-fiction on retail pharmacy. BS in Pharmacy, Purdue U., 1969. Pharmacist, Hook Drugs, Valparaiso, 1970. Home: 358 E Soon St Valparaiso IN 46383

BLAKE, VERONICA ELIZABETH, b. Ft. Smith, AR., Dec. 20, 1953; d. Cecil Eugene and Ortencia Elizabeth (Gonzales) Bettger; m. Leonard Allen Blake, June 14, 1980; children—Jason, Tiffany, Brian. Novelist: Texas Rose, 1987, Desperado Desire, 1988. Wrkg. on novel. Student public schs., Steamboat Springs, Colo. Mem. NWC. Home: Box 771073 Steamboat Springs CO 80477

BLAKELY, ROBERT JOHN, b. nr. Ainsworth, NB, Feb. 24, 1915; s. Percy Lee and Mary Frances (Watson) B.; m. Alta M. Farr, 1964; 3 children. Author: Adult Education in a Free Society, 1958, Toward a Homeodynamic Society, 1965, Knowledge Is the Power to Control Power, 1969, The People's Instrument: A Philosophy for Public Television, 1971, Fostering the Growing Need to Learn, 1974. To Serve the Public Interest, 1979. BA with highest distinction, State U. Iowa, 1937; scholar, Harvard Grad Schl., 1937-38. Editorial writer Chgo. Daily News, 1964-67, editor schl. page, 1967-68; with Register and Tribune, Des Moines, 1938-42, 46-48, editorial page editor St. Louis Star Times, 1948-51; author scripts for films. Served from pvt. to 1st lt. USMCR, 1943-46. Home: 5418 S Blackstone Ave Chicago IL 60615

BLAKEMAN, BETH RENEE, (Renee Blake), b. Yonkers, NY, July 7, 1951, d. Charles Bruce and Gladys (Chapman) Blakeman. Contrbr. articles: Steppin' Out Mag., Phila. Inquirer, Daytona Beach News Jnl, AP, numerous other publs. Wrkg. on book on radio. AB, Goddard Coll., Plainfield, Vt., 1973. Program dir. Sta.-WPRY, Perry, FLA., 1981; news anchor WHLY-FM, Orlando, FLA., 1981-83; news dir. WJYO-FM, Orlando, 1983-86; program dir. WKXL, AM/FM, Concord, NH. Address: Box 6574 Penacook NH 03303

BLAKER, CHARLES WILLIAM, b. Pitts., Mar. 4, 1918; s. William Henry and Mame Belle (Jolley) B.; m. Elozabeth Isabel Duncan, Aug. 30, 1941; children—Jeffery Scott, Jon Alan, Charles Lynn. Contrbr. numerous articles, poems, features to mags., newspapers including Popular Sci., Grit., Okla. Today, others. Columnist: Cecil County Democrat, 1975-76, Columbus Ledger, 1984-85. Ed: Sales Training Manual - Tom's Foods, 1986. Wrkg. on collection of short stories, articles, Bible game of knowledge. B.S. in Electrical Engineering, U. Pitts., 1937; Th.M., M.Div., Pitts. Theol. Seminary, 1949. Headmaster, Brandon Hall Schl., Atlanta, 1966-69; organizing dir. Bell and Howell Schl., Atlanta, 1969, Ednl. Advisory Service, Atlanta, 1969-70; organizing headmaster Woodlawn Acad., Chatham, VA, 1970-74; head sci./drama Brookstone Sch., Columbus, GA, 1974-76, dir. upper sch., 1976-81, chair philosophy/religion, 1981-85; instr. speech/communication Columbus Coll., 1980, 82; retired, 1985. Mem. Phila. Headmasters' Assn., Balt. Pvt. Sch. Assn., nat., Ga. assns. secondary sch. principals, nat., southern assns. coll. admissions counselors. Home: 6203 Jane Ln Columbus GA 31909

BLAKESLEE, ALTON LAUREN, b. Dallas, June 27, 1913; s. Howard Walter and Marguerite Alton (Fortune) B.; m. Virginia Boulden, July 3, 1937; children—Dennis, Carolyn Sandra. Author: Polio and the Salk Vaccine, 1956, What You Should Know About Heart Disease, 1957, Your Heart Has Nine Lives (Blakeslee award Am. Heart Assn. 1964), 1963 (Lasker award 1965). Student, Duke, 1931-33; AB, Columbia, 1935. Reporter Jnl Every Evening, Wilmington, Del., 1935-39; mem. staff AP, 1939—, journalist, Balt., 1939-42. N.Y. fgn. news staff, 1942-46, sci. reporter, 1946, sci. editor, 1969-78; AP corr. U.S. Navy Antarctic Expdn., 1946-47. Recipient George Westinghouse sci. writing award AAAS, 1952, Lasker Med. Journalism award, 1954, 62, 64; Sci. Writers' award ADA, 1967; Robert T. Morse Writer's award Am. Psychiat. Assn. 1973; Disting. Journalism award Am. Heart Assn., 1978. Mem. Natl. Assn. Sci. Writers (pres. 1954-55). Home: 13 Vista Way Port Washington NY 11050

BLANCHETTE, RITA T. BILLINGS, b. Marinton, IL., July 21, 1913; d. William and Delvina (Degree) Billings; m. Everal Leo Blanchette (dec. 1985), Oct. 10, 1932; children—Joyce, Kenneth, JoAnn, Janet, Kerry, Kathleen, Karen. Contrbr. articles to numerous newspapers; poetry in anthologies. Wrkg. on autobiography, articles, poetry. Student Holy Family Acad., Beaverville, Ill. Mem. Am. Poetry Assn. Golden Poet Award, 1985, 86, 87. Home: Monticello Health Care Ctr 1120 N Main Monticello IN 47960

BLANCOS, ROBERTO, see Queenan, Joseph Martin, Jr.

BLANK, FRANKLIN, b. Phila., Oct. 19, 1921; s. Louis Julius and Anna (Liefer) B.; m. Annette Evelyn Chotin, Dec. 25, 1952, 1952; 1 dau., Emily Celia. Contrbr.: People in Action, Dog Fancy, VFW Magazine, Grit, Emergency, numerous other publs. Wrkg. on allegory. BBA, Southeastern U., 1956; AA, U. Balt., 1966. Medical coding clk. Social Security Adminstrn., Balt., 1971-86; stringer Nat. Enquirer, Jewish Post, Opinion, 1979-80. Fellow World Lit. Acad., (Life) Intl. Biographical Assn.; mem. Am. Biog. Inst. (natl. research bd. adviser 1986 —), AG, European Acad. Arts, Scis. and Humanities. Home: 5477 Cedonia Ave Baltimore MD 21206

BLANK, WANDA, see Morgenstern, Frieda Homnick

BLANKENSHIP, JOHN L., b. Parkersburg, WV, June 27, 1948, s. Bryan D. and Mary F. (Miller) B. Author: The Apple House, 1984, The Gradebook System (software documentation), 1984, Robotic Arm Projects for the Apple II, 1985, Structured BASIC Programming for the IMB PC-with Technical Application, 1987, BLANKENSHIP BASIC (software documentation), 1987. B.S.E.E., Va. Tech. Inst., 1970; M.B.A., Ga. State U., 1979. Engr. Western Electric Co., Greesnboro, N.C., 1970-72; prof. DeVry Inst., Atlanta, 1972—. Address: Box 47934 Atlanta GA 30362

BLANKENSHIP, J. RANDALL, b. Hampton, SC, Jan. 16, 1953; s. James Ernest and Nellie Ernestine (Thomas) B.; m. Judith Ann Judy, Mar. 10, 1984; 1 son, Michael W. Judy. Author: Parental Guide to Drug Abuse, 1980, Florida State Law Enforcement Wage and Fringe Benefit Survey, 1980, Contrct Administration, 1981, Police Career Development, 1983, OUC: An Investigative Report. Wrkg. on instructional guide, poetry, literary criticism. AA, Valencia Coll., 1986; BA, U. Central Fla., 1987. Patrol officer Oviedo Police Dept., Fla., 1972-79; instr. asst. Valencia Coll., Orlando, Fla., 1985-87; mng. ed. Police: Today 'n' Tomorrow, 1978—83. Home: 2858 Silver Spur Ln Orlando FL 32822

BLASER, CATHY B., b. Cleve., Oct. 31, 1950; d. Charles Walton and Mary Therese (Lengel) B. Editor, pub. Stage Managers Directory, 1983-84, 84-85, 85-86 editions, New York Theatrical Sourcebook, 1984-85, 85-86 editions. Workg. on Stage Managers Directory, 1986-87 edition, New York Theatrical Sourcebook, 1986-87 edition. BFA in Theatre, U. Detroit, 1973; MA in Theatre, William Patterson Coll., 1975. Prodn. mgr. various Broadway shows, NYC, 1975-84; editor, pub. Broadway Press, NYC, 1983—. Recipient nomination George Freedely award Theatre Library Assn., 1985, 86. Mem. Stage Mgrs. Assn. Home: 350 W 85th St 67 New York

NY 10024

BLASS, GERHARD ALOIS, b. Chemitz, Germany, Mar. 12, 1916; came to U.S., 1949; s. Gustav Alois and Anna Marie (Mehnert) B.; m. Barbara Leonore Siegert, July 16, 1945; children—Andrew, Marcus, Evamaria, Annamaria, Peter. Author: Theoretical Physics, 1962, Weil Hiersein viel ist (poetry), 1987. Advanced degree, Universitat Leipzig, 1943. Prof. physics Coll. St. Thomas, St. Paul, 1949-51, U. Detroit, 1951-81; now retired; chmn. Lapeer County (Mich.) Commn. on Aging, 1987—. Fellow AAAS; mem. Soc. Asian and Comparative Philosophy, Am. Esperanto League. Home: 4441 Stewart Rd Metamora MI 48455

BLATE, SAMUEL ROBERT, b. Bklyn., July 20, 1944; s. Bernard Joseph and Sonya Frances (Sroelov) B.; children—Alex B., Andrew H. Author novel, Spirals, 1988. Contrbr. book rvws., essays, fiction, photographs to jnls. Ed.: Potomas Appalachian Mag., 1974, Md. Landlord-Tenant Law, Practice, and Procedures, 1983, Software Success, 1985, My Roosevent Years, 1987, Understanding Organic Chemistry, 1987; ed., pub.: Assn. Editorial Businesses Newsletter, 1982-83; editorial staff: The Carolina Qtly, 1963-65, Potomas Appalachian Mag., 1973-76. A.B., U. N.C., 1966; M.A., Goddard Coll., 1984. Prof. English, Montogomery Coll., Rockville, MD, 1967—; pres. Samuel R. Blate Assocs., Gaithersburg, MD, 1978—. Mem. Assn. Editorial Bus., Inc. (sec. 1983-84), Washington Ind. Wrtrs., Washington Area Wrtrs., SSP, NWU. Home: 10331 Watkins Mill Dr Gaithersburg MD 20879

BLATNER, BARBARA ANN, b. Albany, NY, Aug. 31, 1949; d. Henry Leroy and Elizabeth (Mendleson) B. Author: (poems) The Pope in Space, 1985; contrbr. poems to Groundswell, NY Qtly, Nadir, Green Horse, Cafeteria, fiction to Albany Tricentennial Rvw, Nadir; plays produced by Albany City Arts Office Playwrights' Workshop. BA, Vassar Coll., 1971; DA, SUNY-Albany, 1984. Lectr. writing Jr. Coll. Albany, 1979-85, SUNY-Albany; publs. asst. MIT, Cambridge, 1986—. CETA grantee, 1975-79, also various hon. mentions. Mem. Stage Source. Home: 12 Elston St Somerville MA 02144

BLATTY, WILLIAM PETER, b. NYC, Jan. 7, 1928; s. Peter and Mary (Mouakad) B.; children: Christine Ann, Michael Peter, Mary Joanne. Author: Which Way to Mecca, Jack?, 1959, John Goldfarb, Please Come Home, 1962, I, Billy Shakespeare, 1965, Twinkle, Twinkle "Killer" Kane, 1966 (Golden Globe award as best movie screen play 1981), The Exorcist, 1970, I'll Tell Them I Remember You, 1973, The Exorcist: From Novel to Film, 1974, The Ninth Configuration, 1978, Legion, 1983; writer screenplays: The Man From the Diner's Club, 1961, John Goldfarb, Please Come Home, 1963, Promise Her Anything, 1962, The Great Bank Robbery, 1967, Gunn, 1967, What Did You Do In the War, Daddy?, 1965, A Shot In The Dark, 1964, Darling Lili, 1968, The Exorcist, 1973. AB, Georgetown U., 1950, George Washington U., 1954, LHD, Seattle U., 1974. Editor: USIA, 1955-57. Served to 1st lt. USAF, 1951-54. Recipient Academy award Acad. Motion Picture Arts and Scis., 1973; Gabriel award and blue ribbon for Insight TV series script Am. Film Festival, 1969. Office: S&S 1230 Ave of Americas New York NY 10020

BLAUNER, LAURIE ANN, b. NYC,May 4, 1953, d. Richard Blauner and Renee Lewis-Bolton; m. Sheldon Glassberg, Nov. 23, 1983. Author: Other Lives, 1984 (poetry). BA, Sarah Lawrence Coll., 1974; MFA, U. Mont., 1980. Coordinator social service City of Missoula, Mont., 1980—. Home: 9705 Rustic Rd Missoula MT 59802

BLAUVELT, RALPH, (Ralph Jay), b. Suffern, NY, Oct. 1, 1942; s. Theodore and Helen (Cramer) Blauvelt; m. Frances Riley Aug. 5, 1953; children—Colette. Contrbr. to The Journal-News, OP Magazine, Sound Choice, Option. BM, Manhattan School of Music, 1964; MM, Manhattan School of Music, 1967; PhD (a.b.d.), State U. of NY, Buffalo, 1972. Tchr. and Adminstrn., Community Music Schl., Spring Valley, NY, 1977-82. Music Coord., Rockland, NY Arts Council, 1979-80; Instr., Rockland CC, 1980—; Music Tutor, Empire State College, Nanuet, NY, 1983—; Music Critic, The Journal-News, West Nyack, NY 1977-85. Home: 41 S Madison Ave Spring Valley NY 10977

BLAZEK, DOUGLAS DAVID, b. Chgo., Dec. 31, 1941; s. Harry and Josephine (Siwe) Blazek; m. Alta Arlene Judd, June 27, 1961; children—Nathan, Aaron. Author: All Gods Must Learn to Kill, 1968, Edible Fire, 1978, Exercises in Memorizing Myself, 1976, Flux and Reflux, 1970, Skull Juices, 1970. Editor: Ole, 1964-67, Ole Anthology, 1968, Open Skull, 1968-69, A Bukowski Sampler, 1968, Hard Pressed, 1976-79, Landing Signals, 1986; contrbr. poetry, essays, rvws to numerous journals. Student, North Central College, Naperville, IL. Publisher, Open Skull Press, 1965-70; freelance writer, 1967—, instr. poetry workshops, CSUS, 1984—. Mem. PSA. Home: 2751 Castro Way Sacramento CA 95818

BLAZEK, JOSEPH LAWRENCE, b. Valparaiso, IN, July 19, 1957; s. Joseph Charles and Cecilia Barbara (Norton) B. Contrbr. poems, short stories to lit. mags., anthols. Ed.: Opposum Holler Tarot, 1982—. Wrkg. on Axxays the Dead, collection of poems, Adventures of Addua Dauzia, short stories, poems. Grad. public schls., Valparaiso. Shoreler, Ft. Worth Shooting Club, 1980; packer Taylor Industries, St. Louis, 1981. Home: Rt 2 Campellsbury IN 47108

BLEHERT, (MAURICE) DEAN, b. St. Paul, Apr. 4, 1942, s. Henry David and Esther (Goldish) B.; m. Pamela Rhianon Coulter, Apr. 3, 1983. Author: Dear Reader (poetry), 1976, Family Pictures (poetry chapbook), 1979, The Naked Clowns (poetry), 1982; poetry ed. Epoch Mag., 1967-68; contrbr.: Kans. Qtly. Rev., Dark Horse, Crosscurrent, numerous others; pub. Deanotations poetry letter; 3 computer programming workbooks, 1985. BA in Math. and English, U. Minn., 1963; MA, Stanford U., 1966, postgrad. 1963-67. Asst. prof. English Cornell U., Ithaca, N.Y., 1967-69; mem. ministerial, counseling staff Ch. of Scientology, NYC and Los Angeles, 1969-79. Mem. Bethesda Wrtrs. Center. Home: 11919 Moss Pt Ln Reston VA 22094

BLEIBERG, ROBERT MARVIN, b. Bklyn., June 21, 1924; s. Edward and Frances (DuBroff) B.; m. Harriet Evans, May 1948 (div. Mar. 1953); 1 dau., Ellen; m. Sally Diane Veverly, Oct. 25, 1956; 1 son, Richard Beverly. V.P. Dow Jones & Co., Inc. Asso. editor: Prudden's Digest of Investment and Banking Opinions, N.Y.C., 1946; assoc. editor: Barron's Natl. Bus. and Financial Weekly, NYC, 1946-54; editor, 1955-81, pub., 1980—, eidtorial dir., 1981—. B.A., Columbia, 1943; M.B.A., N.Y. U., 1950; D.C.Sc., Hillsdale, Coll., 1977. Served with inf. AUS, 1943-45, PTO. Decorated Purple Heart. Mem. N.Y. Fin. Writers Assn. Home: 25 Central Park W New York NY 10023

BLEIWEISS, HERBERT IRVING, b. Bklyn., July 26, 1931; s. Oscar and Anna (Fliegel) B.; m. Rachel Newman, Apr. 6, 1973; children: Jeffrey, Richard. Design cons. Syska & Hennessy Engrs.; tchr. mag. design Parsons Schl. Design. Designer, Ehrlich, Newirth Advtg., NYC, 1952-57, art dir., C.J. Herrick Advtg., 1957-59, Irving Serwer Advt., 1959-61, DKG Advtg., 1961-62, McCalls mag., 1962-67; exec. art dir.: Ladies Home Jnl., 1967-75; also art dir.: Good Housekeeping mag., 1975—; art dir.: Country Living; Photographer for: books A Patchwork Point of View, 1975, Redo-It Yourself, 1977, The Pillow Book, 1979. Student, Cooper Union, 1948-50. Served with AUS, 1950-52. Recipient numerous Art Dirs. awards and Gold medals (N.Y., Los Angeles, London Art Dirs. Clubs), numerous Art Dirs. awards and Gold medals Soc. Illustrators. Mem. Soc. Publ. Designers, Art Dirs. (N.Y.) Office: 959 8th Ave New York NY 10019

BLEWETT, STEPHEN DOUGLAS, b. Bremerton, WA, Feb. 21, 1942; s. Wesley Edgar and Christina (Ball) B.; m. Judith Marie Mohr, June 17, 1967; children—Mark Joseph, Christina Marie, Susan Renee. Contrbr. articles to lit. mags. including Spokane Mag., The Inland Register, The Illuminator. Wrtr., ed.: The Spokesman-Rvw., Spokane, 1969-73; pub. coordinator: Wash. Water power, Spokane, 1973—. B.A. in Journalism, Eastern Washington State Coll., 1969; M.A. in English, Eastern Washington U., 1981. Visiting instr. Spokane Commun. Coll., 1978-79. Eastern Wash. U., Spokane, 1981-86. Mem. lay staff Immaculate Heart Retreat House, Spokane, 1983—. Served with USAF, 1961-65. Mem. IABC (bd. dirs. Metro Spokane chpt. Awards: IABC, Gold Quill, Silver Six, Accredited Business Communicator, NELPA Service Award. Home: E 1818 35th Spokane WA 99203

BLISS, CORINNE DEMAS, b. NYC,May 14, 1947. Author: That Dog Melly (juvenile), 1981, The Same River Twice (novel), 1982, Daffodils or the Death of Love (short-story collection), 1983. BA, Tufts U., 1968; PhD,Columbia U., 1980. Asst. prof. English Mt. Holyoke Coll., South Hadley, Mass., 1978-84, assoc. prof., 1984—. NEA fellow, 1978, 83, Andrew W. Mellon Fdn. fellow, 1982. Mem. AG, PEN. Office: Dept English Mt Holyoke Coll South Hadley MA 01075

BLISS, RONALD GENE, b. Atwood, KS, Aug. 12, 1942; s. Wilbur Cyril and Mary Lucille (Makings) B.; m. Margarget Jane Keeler, July 25, 1965; children: Eric Dean, Kirk Ronald. Author: Indian Softball Summer, 1974; Eagle Trap, 1983; Child of the Field, 1984; contrbr. short stories to Farm Women, Wyo. Rural Electric, articles to VFW Mag., TV Guide, Runner's World, Farm Women, Sign of Times, Grit, also numerous regional publs. BA, Kans. State U., 1964; MA, U. Mo., 1969. Reporter Sta. KSNW-TV, Wichita, Kans., 1969-84; freelance wrtr., 1984-85; wrtr. Boeing Co., Wichita, 1985. Recipient numerous awards for TV documentaries Kans. Assn. Broadcasters, 1972-84. Home: 701 James St Maize KS 67101

BLIVEN, BRUCE, JR., b. Los Angeles, Jan. 31, 1916; s. Bruce and Rose (Emery) B.; m. Naomi Horowitz, May 26, 1950; 1 son, Frederic Bruce. Author: The wonderful Writing Machine, 1954, Battle for Manhattan, 1956, Under the Guns, 1972, Book Traveller, 1975, Volunteers, One and All, 1976, The Finishing Touch, 1978, New York: A Bicentennial History, 1981; juveniles The Story of D-Day, 1956, The American Revolution, 1958, From Pearl Harbor to Okinawa, 1960, From Casablanca To Berlin, 1965, (with Naomi Bliven) New York: The Story of the World's Most Exciting City, 1969. A.B., Harvard U., 1937. Reproter Manchester (Eng.) Guardian, 1936; editorial asst. New Republic mag., 1937-38; editorial writer N.Y. Post, 1939-42; contrbr. to New Yorker 1946—; Tchr. Ind. U. Writers Conf., 1955, 66. Served from pvt. to capt. F.A. AUS, 1942-45. Decorated Bronze Star with oak leaf cluster. Mem. ASJA, AG (council, 1970—), PEN. Office: The New Yorker 25 W 43d St New York NY 10036

BLOCH, ROBERT ALBERT, b. Chgo., Apr. 5, 1917; s. Raphael A. and Stella A. (Loeb) B.; m. Eleanor Alexander, Oct. 16, 1964; 1 dau. by previous marriage, Sally Ann. Author: numerous books of fantasy and suspense fiction, 1945—; latest being The King of Terrors, 1977, The Best of Robert Bloch, 1977, Out of the Mouths of Graves, 1978, Strange Eons, 1979, Such Stuff as Screams Are Made Of, 1979, There is a Serpent in Eden, 1979, La Boite a Malefices de Robert Bloch, 1981, Mysteries of the Worm, 1981, Psycho II, 1982, Le Scene Finale, 1982, Parlez-moi d'horreur, 1982, Le Demon Noir, 1983, Dr. Holmes Murder Castle, 1983, Twilight Zone-The Movie, 1983, Les Yeux de la Momie, 1984, The Night of the Ripper, 1984, Recitsde Terreur, 1985, L'Homme qui Criah au Loup, 1985, Out of My Head, 1986, Unholy Trinity, 1986, Midnight Pleasures, 1986, Lost in Time and Space (with Lefty Feer), 1987, Selected Short Stories of Robert Bloch, 1987, Abominations, 1987, Abonomations II, 1987; screenplays: The Couch, 1961, The Cabinet of Caligari, 1962, Straitjacket, 1963, The Night Walker, 1964, The Psychopath, 1965, (with Anthony Marriott) The Deadly Bees, 1966, Torture Garden 1967, The House That Dripped Blood, 1970, Asylum, 1972; also numerous radio scripts and teleplays; contbr. numerous short stories to various mags. and lit. jnls.; Editor: The Best of Fredric Brown, 1977. Student public schs., Maywood, Ill and Milw. Freelance writer, 1934-42, 53—; copywriter Gustav Marx Advt. Agy., Milw., Wis., 1942-53; lectr. various schs. and community orgns., 1946—. Recipien E.E. Evans Meml. award, 1958; ScreenWriter's award, 1960; Inkpot award for Sci. Fiction, 1964; Award for Service to Field of Sci. Fantasy, Los Angeles Sci. Fantasy Soc., 1974; Fritz Leiber Fantasy award, 1978; World Sci. Fiction Conv. Hugo award, 1958, Lifetime Achievement award, 1984; Edgar Allan Poe Scroll, 1960; Trieste Film Festival award, 1964; Reims Festival award, 1979; Lifetime Career award Atlanta Fantasy Fair, 1984; Twilight Zone Dimension award, 1985. Mem. Writers Guild Am., Sci. Fiction Writers Am., Mystery Writers Am. (pres. 1970-71), Acad. of Motion Pictures Arts and Scis. Office: Shapiro-Lichtman 8827 Beverley Blvd Los Angeles CA 90067

BLOCK, JANET LOU, b. Algona, IA, Oct. 5, 1937; d. Arthur C. and Neola Mae (Eggleston) Henry; m. James Block, Apr. 20, 1958; children—John James, Jolene Amy. Author: (poems) The National Poetry Anthology, 1986; The American Poetry Anthology, 1986. Wrkg. on articles, religious and inspirational poetry. Home: RR Rolfe IA 50581

BLOCK, JULIAN, b. Chgo, July 8, 1934; s. Nathan and Ruth (Rubinstein) Block; m. Zelda Miller, Aug. 23, 1964 children—Robert, Nadine. Author: Julian Block's Guide to Year-Round Tax Savings, 1981-86; What the New Tax Law Means to You, 1986; The Tax-Wise Way to Buy, Own and Sell Your Home, 1987; syndicated col. The Tax Report, 1985—. BSC, Roosevelt U., 1956; JD DePaul U. Law School, 1962; LLM (Tax) NY U. Grad. School of Law, 1969. Attorney IRS (NY & Wash. DC), 1962-68; Superv. Ernst & Whinney (NY and DC) 1968-73; Man. Ed. Research Inst. of Amer. (NY), 1973-85; senior tax consult. Prentice-Hall (Paramus, NJ) 1985—. PFC, U.S. Army, Mar. 1956-Dec. 1957, Japan and Korea. Mem. ASJA. Home: 3 Washington Sq Larchmont NY 10538

BLOCK, LAWRENCE, b. Buffalo, June 24, 1938; s. Arthur Jerome and Lenore (Nathan B.; m. Loretta Ann Kallet, 1960; children—Amy Jo, Jill Diana, Alison Elspeth. Author: among others, Death Pulls a Double Cross, 1961; The Girl with the Long Green Heart, 1965, The Triumph of Evil, 1971, The Burglar Who Liked to Quote Kipling, 1979, Eight Million Ways to Die, 1982, When the Sacred Ginmill Closes, 1986. Recipient Nero Wolfe award, 1980. Student Antioch Coll., 1955-59. Editor Scott Meredith Inc., 1957-58; Whitman Pub. Co., Racine, Wis., 1964-66; freelance wrtr. 1957—. Address: Burger 39½ Washington Sq New York NY 10012

BLOCKSMA, MARY, b. Chgo., Jan. 19, 1942; d. Ralph and Ruth (Enss) Blocksma; m. Bruce W. Schadel; 1 son, Dylan Kuhn. Author: easy-to-read children's books, and Easy-to-Make Spaceships that Really Fly, 1983, Marvelous Music Machine, 1984, Water Toys, 1985, Space Crafting, 1986, Amazing Mouths and Menus, 1986, Action Contraptions, 1988, The Numbers Survival Book: How to Read Numbers in American Life, 1988, Time Traveler's Catalog: Ticket to the Twenties, 1989. Contrbr. stories, poems, articles to mags. BA. Wheaton, College, 1963; MA, Johns Hopkins U., 1964; MLS, U. Mich., 1968. Peace Corps, Nigeria, 1965-67; Dr. Albany County Public Library, Laramie, WY, 1970-76; staff wrtr. Addison-Wesley Reading Program, Menlo Park, CA, 1977-80; free-lance wrtr., 1980—. Mem. SCBW, Author's League. Home: 1440 Univ Healdsburg CA 95448

BLOMSTER, ADELHEID, (Heidi Blomster), b. St. Gallen, Switzerland, Aug. 8, 1930, came to U.S., 1955, naturalized, 1959; d. Johann Pankraz and Elisabeth (Plattner) Woerz; m. Wesley V. Blomster, July 4, 1955 (div. Jan. 13, 1982); 1 son, Thomas Alvin. Contrbr. poems, short stories to lit. mags., anthols. Diploma in music, Music Acad., Zurich, Switzerland, 1950; MA in German, U. Colo., 1966. Instr. music U. Montana, Billings, 1958-59; chapel organist Colby Coll., Waterville, Maine, 1961-62; instr. German and humanities U. Colo., Boulder, 1962-77. Recipient Cert. of Merit, N. Am. Mentor, 1982, 84, 85, Am. Poetry Assn., 1984. Mem. Delta Phi Alpha. Home: 901 Sherman 114 Denver CO 80203

BLOMSTER, HEIDI, see Blomster, Adelheid

BLOOD, OPAL SUE, (Opal Sue Saunders Blood), b. Lecompte, LA, mar. 25, 1939; d. Elmo Darius and Oddie (Broussard) Saunders; m. James Franklin Blood, June 29, 1958; children—David Wayne, James F. (dec.), Marvin Lee. Contrbr. hist. and news articles, feature stories to newspapers, mags. Contrbr., ed.: Cooking with the Belles, 1982; ed.: Journal Recipe book, 1984, Historic Cheneyville, 1984. Wrkg. on cookbook an hist. ch. history book. Cert., Avoyelles Vocational-Technical Coll., 1981. Columnist, Gazette Newspaper, Ville Platte, La., 1975-77; women's ed., advt. representative, Bunkie Record Weekly Paper, LA, 1981-83, columnist, 1975-81; staff wrtr., advt. representative Avoyelles Jnl., Marksville, LA, 1983-84, Weekly News, Marksville, 1984-85; staff corr., Alexandria Daily Town Talk, 1984—; Bd. dirs., mem. Am. Businesswoman's Assn., 1979—; public relations com. Le Theatre des Bon Temp, Bunkie, LA, 1979-86. Address: Rt 1 Box 102-A Saint Landry LA 71367

BLOOM, EDWARD ALAN, b. Michigan City, IN, May 24, 1914; s. Robert and Tillie (Leibovitz) B.; m. Lillian Doris Blumberg, June 17, 1947. Author: Samuel Johnson in Grub Street, 1957 (with C.H. Philbrick, E.M. Blistein), The Order of Poetry, 1961, (with L.D. Bloom) Willa Cather's Gift of Sympathy, 1962, The Order of Fiction, 1964, Joseph Addison's Sociable Animal, 1971, Satire's Persuasive Voice, 1979; also articles on 18th-century and contemporary English and American lit. problems. Editor: Shakespeare 1564-1964, 1964, Frances Burney's Evelina, 1968; editor: English and Am. lit Blaisdell Pub. Co., 1964-70, (with L.D. Bloom) The Variety of Fiction, 1969, Anthony Collins, A Discourse concerning Ridicule and Irony, 1970, Camilla, 1972, Fanny Burney's Journals and Letters, 1978, Addison and Steele Critical Heritage Series, 1980; co-editor (with Philbrick and Blistein) The Variety of Poetry, 1964; sr. editor: Novel: A Forum on Fiction, 1967—; contrbr. book reviews short stories to natl. and internatl. jnls. BS in Journalism, U. Ill., 1936, MA, 1939, PhD in English, 1947; AM (hon.), Brown U., 1957. Newspaper reporter, corr., editor Midwestern Papers and Press Service, 1936-38; also freelance mag. writer; asst. instr. English U. Ill., 1939-42, 46-47; faculty dept. English, Brown U., 1947—, prof. English, 1959—, chmn. dept., 1960-67, Nicholas Brown prof. oratory and belles lettres, 1960-67; dir. NEH Summer Seminars, 1978, 80. Served from pvt. to capt. AUS, 1942-46; decorated Bronze Star. Huntington Library fellow, 1963-64, 67-68, 72; Guggenheim fellow, 1969-70; Huntington Library-NEH fellow, 1977-78; NEH grantee, 1980—; Huntington Library fellow, 1981. Mem. AAUP, MLA, Am. Soc. 18th-Century Studies, The Johnsonians (chmn. 1980), Sigma Delta Chi. Home: 480 S Orange Grove Pasadena CA 91105

BLOOM, HAROLD, b. NYC, July 11, 1930; s. William and Paula (Lev) B.; m. Jeanne Gould, May 8, 1958; children: Daniel Jacob, David Moses. Author: Shelley's Mythmaking, 1959, The Visionary Company, 1961, Blake's Apoclypse, 1963, Commentary to Blake, 1965, Yeats, 1970, The Ringers in the Tower, 1971, The Anxiety of Influence, 1973, Wallace Stevens: The Poems of Our Climate, 1977, A Map of Misreading, 1975, Kabbalah and Criticism, 1975, poetry and Repression, 1976, Figures of Capable Imagination, 1976, The Flight to Lucifer: A Gnostic Fantasy, 1979, Agon: Towards a Theory of Revisionism, 1981, The Breaking of the Vessels, 1981, Freud: Transference and Authority, 1984, Poetics of Influence: New and Selected Criticism, 1984, B.A., Cornell U., 1951; Ph.D., Yale U., 1955; L.H.D., Boston Coll., 1973, Yeshiva U., 1976. Melville Cane award PSA, 1970; Zabel prize Am. Inst. Arts and Letters, 1982; numerous others; Guggenheim fellow, 1962; Fulbright fellow, 1955. Mem. Am. Acad. Arts and Scis. Home: 179 Linden St New Haven Ct 06511

BLOOM, HERBERT, b. Boston, Nov. 23, 1930; s. Albert and Rose (Swartz) B.; m. Arlene Perlis, Aug. 17, 1958; children—Sarah, Kenneth.

BA, Brandeis U, 1952, AM, Harvard U., 1954; MLS, Simmons Coll., 1959. Librarian, Lowell (Mass.) State Coll., 1959-63; Librarian So. Ill. U., Carbondale, 1963-67; sr. editor ALA, Chicago, 1969—. Contbr. articles to profl. publs. Served with AUS, 1954-57. Home: 1430 Western Ave Flossmoor IL 60422

BLOOM, JANET K., b. Tucson, AZ, d. Christina Affeld and Dr. Benson Bloom. Author: Alice, 1976, (chapbook); staff wrtr.: Architectural Forum, Architectural Record, Holiday. Contrbr. poetry, articles, lit. interviews, lit. rvws. to anthols., American Poetry Review, Poetry Now, New York Qtly, Parnassus, Contact II, Teachers & Writers, Mag., Journal of Gerontological Social Work, others. B.A., Bennington Coll.; M.F.A. Goddard Coll.; C.T.I., Image Institute. Teaches imaging, nature imaging and writing to all ages at workshops, conferences, camps and schools. Office: 6425 Broadway 7C Riverdale Bronx Ny 10471

BLOOM, LARY ROGER, b. Cleve., Nov. 13, 1943; s. Abraham William and Helen miriam B.; 1 child, Amy. Reporter Akron (Ohio) Beacon Jnl., 1967-68, mag. writer, 1969-70; editor Beacon mag., 1971-78, Tropic mag. Miami (Fla.) Herald, 1978-81, Hartford Courant mag., 1981—; chmn. editorial bd. Met. Sunday Newspapers, Inc., 1982—. B.S. in Journalism, Ohio U., 1965. Served with AUS, 1965-67. Office: 285 Broad St Hartford CT 06115

BLOOM, LYNN MARIE ZIMMERMAN, b. Ann Arbor, MI, July 11, 1934, d. Oswald T. and Mildred (Kisling) Zimmerman; m. Martin Bloom, July 11, 1958; children—Bard, Laird. Author: Doctor Spock: Biography of a Conservative Radical, 1972, Strategic Writing, 1983, Fact and Artifact: Writing Nonfiction, 1985; co-author: The New Assertive Woman, 1975, American Autobiography, 1945-1980: A Bibliography, 1982; ed.: Forbidden Diary: A Record of Wartime Internment, 1941-45 (by Natalie Crouter), 1982, The Essay Connection, 1984, 88, The Lexington Reader: Readings in Nonfiction, 1986, Forbidden Family: Margaret Sams Wartime Memoir, 1942-45, 1989; co-ed.: Bear, Man, and God: Seven Approaches to William Faulkner's 'The Bear', 1964, 71, Symposium, 1969, Symposium on Love, 1970. BA, U. Mich., 1956, MA, 1957, PhD, 1963. Asst. prof., then assoc. prof. Butler U., Indpls., 1970-74; assoc. prof. U. N.Mex., Albuquerque, 1975-78, Coll. William and Mary, Williamsburg, Va., 1978-83; prof. English Va. Commonwealth U., Richmond, 1982—; vice-pres. Council Wrtg. Program Adminstrs.; chmn. Com. on Status of Women in Profession, Coll. Composition and Communication. NEH fellow, 1986-87; George Mason U. Wrtg. Center fellow, 1982; Coll. Assessment Program Evaluation fellow, 1985; grantee NEH. Mem. MLA, NCTE. Home: 302 Mill Neck Rd Williamsburg VA 23185

BLOOM, PAULINE, d. Max and Meta (Landau) Bloom. Author: Toby, Law Stenographer, 1959; contrbg. author: Mystery Wrtrs. Handbook, 1956, Handbook of Short Story Writing, 1970, Handbook of Mystery Writing, 1970; contrbr. articles and short stories to numerous natl. mags. Ed. Columbia U., Bklyn. Coll. Mem. AL of Am. (past council mem.), MWA (past bd. dirs.). Home: 20 Plaza St Brooklyn NY 11238

BLOOMINGDALE, TERESA, b. St. Joseph, MO, July 26, 1930, d. Arthur Victor and Helen (Cooney) Burrowes; m. Arthur Lee Bloomingdale, July 2, 1955; children: Lee, John, Michael, James, Mary, Daniel, Peggy, Ann, Timothy, Patrick. Author: I Should Have Seen It Coming When the Rabbit Died, 1979, Up a Family Tree, 1981, Murphy Must Have Been a Mother, 1983, Life Is What Happens When You Are Making Other Plans, 1985, Sense and Momsense, 1986. Au of A Mother's Meditation, syndicated humor column and a weekly column in Our Sunday Visitor. Contrbr to magazines, including Good Housekeeping, Catholic Digest, SET, LHJ, and Family Circle. Contributing ed. of McCall's, 1982-85. BA, Duchesne Coll., Omaha, Neb. Legal sec., Creighton U., School of Law, Omaha, Neb., 1952-54; teacher, Webster School, St. Joseph, Mo., 1954-55; writer. Serves on coms, including Friends of Boytown, 1979-82, Madonna School Board, 1985—, Com on Religius and Civil Rights (bd mem). Mem: AG, AL of America, Nebraska Writers Guild, Omaha Press Club, St. Joseph Women's Press Club, Associated Alumnae of the Sacred Heart, Alpha Sigma Nu. Address: Bach Lit Agcy 747 Third Ave New York NY 10017

BLOS, JOAN W., b. NYC, Dec. 9, 1928; m. Peter Blos, Jr., 1953; 2 children (dec.). Author: "It's Spring!" She Said, 1968, (with Betty Miles) Just Think!, 1971, A Gathering of Days: A New England Girl's Journal, 1830-32, 1979 (Newbery Medal, ALA, and Am. Book award 1980), Brothers of the Heart: A Story of the Old Northwest, 1837-38, Martin's Hats, 1984, Old Henry, 1987. BA, Vassar College, 1950; MA, CCNY, 1956. Assoc. publs. div., mem. tchr. edn. faculty Bank St. Coll. Edn., NYC, 1958-70; lectr. Schl. Edn., U. Mich., Ann Arbor, 1972-80; U.S. editor Children's Literature in Education, 1976-81. Office: Curtis Brown 10 Astor Pl New York NY 10003

BLOSSOM, BETH, b. Babylon, NY, June 14, 1926, d. Sumner Newton and Edna (Stroh) Blossom; m. Robert Roy Metz, Aug. 16, 1952 (div. 1976); children—Robert Sumner, Christopher Roy. BA. U. N.H.; postgrad. Am. Acad. Dramatic Arts, NYC. Editorial asst. Celebrity Service, Inc., 1948; producer, wrtr. sta. WNBC, NYC, 1949-52; wrtr., publicist press dept., NBC, NYC, 1952-56; public relations cons., ptnr. Public Library Prodns., Inc., 1965-73; assoc. dir. communications center Population Inst., 1974-77; dir. public relations Toy Mfrs. of Am., 1978-82, Recording Industry Assn. Am., 1982; now freelance public relations cons., wrtr., NYC. Recipient Clio award, 1967, 68, Intl. award Hollywood Radio and TV Soc., 1968, Silver award Intl. Film and TV Festival, 1980. Mem. Public Relations Soc. Am., Women in Communications. Home: 62 Revere Dr Sayville NY 11782

BLOUGH, GLENN ORLANDO, b. Edmore, MI, Sept. 5, 1907; s. Levi and Catherine (Thomas) B. Author: Monkey With a Notion, 1948, Beno The Riverburg Mayor, 1949, The Tree on the Road to Turntown, 1953; Jr. Lit. Guild selections Not Only for Ducks, The Story of Rain, 1954, Lookout for the Forest, 1955, After the Sun Goes Down, 1956, Who Lives in This House, 1957; When You Go to the Zoo, 1957, Young Peoples Book of Science, 1958, Soon After September, 1959, Discovering Dinosaurs, 1959, Who Lives in This Meadow?, 1960, Christmas Trees and How They Grow, 1961, Who Lives at the Seashore, 1962, Bird Watchers and Bird Feeders, 1963, Discovering Plants, 1966, Discovering Insects, 1967, Discovering Cycles, 1973, Elementary School Science and How To Teach It, 1978, 84, LL.D., 1950; B.A., U. Mich., 1929, M.A., 1932; postgrad., Columbia, summers 1935-37, U. Chgo., 1938. Served as lt. comdr. USNR, World War II. Award for contrbn. to lit. of natural history Am. Nature Study Soc., 1980. Mem. NEA. Home: 2820 Ellicott St NW Washington DC 20008

BLUE, PERCIE, see Martinez, Georgina V.

BLUESTEIN, DANIEL THOMAS, (Daniel B. Thomas) b. Bronx, NY, Jan. 20, 1943, s. Abraham and Selma (Cohen) B.; m. Marta Figueroa, Feb. 11, 1984. Author: Momma I Know Why, 1974, Fast Changes, 1979, Testament, 1986; contrbr. poetry: Kans. Qtly, Stonecloud, Croton Rvw, other lit publs. BA, CCNY, 1966; MBA, Baruch Coll., 1971. Counselor Bridge Plaza Treatment for individuals who are opiate-dependent, NYC, 1974-78, adminstr., 1978-85. Treas. Croton Council on Arts, Croton-on-Hudson, N.Y., 1977—. Mem. NWU. Home: 12 Park Trail Croton on Hudson NY 10520

BLUH, BONNIE, b. NYC. Author: Woman to Woman: European Feminists, 1974; Banana, 1976; The "Old" Speak Out, 1979; book reviewer for Soho News and other newspapers. Mem AG, AL, NWU. Home: 345 Riverside Dr 55 New York NY 10028

BLUM, GEOFFREY CARL, b. NYC, Apr. 15, 1951; s. Constantin Andrew and Prudence Mary (Lewis) B. Ed., contrbr. The Carl Barks Library, 1983—; contrbr. criticism and poetry to Jnl Irish Lit., Blue Unicorn, Nemo, Am. Artist, Comics Buyer's Guide. Wrkg. on mystery novel set in Victorian Eng., bibliography of James Stephens, transls. European Walt Disney comic books. AB, U. Calif., Berkeley, 1972; MA, Ind. U., 1973; C. Phil., UCLA, 1977. Freelance wrtr., 1981—; assoc. ed. Another Rainbow Pub., Inc., Scottsdale, Ariz., 1983—. Mem. Phi Beta Kappa. Home: 1700 Julian Ct El Cerrito CA 94530

BLUMBERG, LEDA, b. Mt. Kisco, NY, July 19, 1956, d. Gerald and Rhoda (Shapiro) Blumberg; m. Thomas Todd Volk, Sept. 4, 1983; 1 child, Dana Lyn. Author: The Horselover's Handbook, 1984, The Complete Book of Horses, 1987, Pets, 1983; co-author: Simon and Schuster's Book of Facts and Fallacies, 1983; co-author, photographer: Lovebirds, Lizards and Llamas, 1986; contrbr.: Disney's My First Encyclopedia, 1981; contrbr. articles, photographs: Chronicle of the Horse, Pet Lovers' Gazette, Cobblestone, others. Student Franconia (N.H.) Coll., 1974-76. Asst. naturalist Teatown Lake Nature Reservation, Ossining, N.Y., 1974; riding instr., horse trainer, 1974—; vet. asst., Westchester County, N.Y., 1979; freelance wrtr., photographer, 1980—. Mem. AG. Home: Baptist Church Rd Yorktown Heights NY 10598

BLUMBERG, NATHAN(IEL) BERNARD, b. Denver, Apr. 8, 1922; s. Abraham Moses and Jeannette B.; m. Lynne Stout, June 1946 (div. Feb. 1970); children: Janet Leslie Blumberg Knedlik, Jenifer Lyn Blumberg Loeb, Josephine Laura Blumberg Loewen; m. Barbara Farquhar, July 1973. Author: One Party Press?, 1954; The Afternoon of March 30: A Contemporary Historical Novel, 1984, also articles in mags. and jnls.; co-editor: A Century of Montana Journalism, 1971; editor: The Mansfield Lectures in International Relations, Vols. I and II, 1979; reporter Denver Post, 1947-48; assoc. editor Lincoln (Nebr.) Star, 1950-53; asst. to editor Ashland (Nebr.) Gazette, 1954-55; asst. city editor Washington Post and Times Herald, 1956; from asst. prof. to assoc. prof. journalism U. Nebr., 1950-55; asso. prof journalism Mich. State U., 1955-56; dean, prof. Sch. Journalism, U. Mont., 1956-

68, prof. journalism, 1968-78, prof. emeritus, 1978—; pub. Wood FIRE Ashes Press, 1981—. B.A., U. Colo., 1947, M.A., 1948; D.Phil. (Rhodes scholar), Oxford (Eng.) U., 1950. Founder: Mont. Journalism Rvw, 1958—. AUS, 1943-46. Decorated Bronze Star medal. Mem. Assn. Am. Rhodes Scholars, Natl. Conf. Editorial Writers. Home: Box 99 Big Fork MT 59911

BLUME, JUDY SUSSMAN, b. Elizabeth, NJ, Feb. 12, 1938; d. Rudolph and Esther (Rosenfeld) Sussman; m. John M. Blume, Aug. 15, 1959 (div. Jan. 1976); children—Randy Lee, Lawrence Andrew; m. George Cooper, June 6, 1987. Author: fiction books including Are You There God It's Me, Margaret (outstanding children's book 1970), Then Again, Maybe I Won't, 1971, It's Not the End of the World, 1972, Tales of a 4th Grade Nothing, 1972, Otherwise Known as Sheila the Great, 1972, Deenie, 1973, Blubber, 1974, Forever, 1976, Superfudge, 1980, Tiger Eyes, 1981, Smart Women, 1984, others; novel Wifey, 1978. BA in Edn., NYU, 1960. Mem. AL & Guild, Soc. Children's Book Writers. Office: Harold Ober 40 E 49th St New York NY 10017

BLUMENSON, MARTIN, b. NYC, Nov. 8, 1918; s. Louis and Dorothy (Reicher) B.; m. Genevieve Aldebert, May 20, 1947; child: John. Author: contrbr Kent Roberts Greenfield, ed., Common Decisions, 1959, Breakout and Pursuit, 1961, Duel for France: 1944, 1963, Anzio: The Gamble That Failed, 1963, Kasserine Pass, 1967 (pub. in England as Rommel's Last Victory: The Battle of Kasserine Pass, 1968), Sicily: Whose Victory?, 1969, Salerno to Cassino, 1969, Bloody River: The Real Tragedy of the Rapido, 1970 (pub in England as Bloody River: Prelude to the Battle of Cassino, 1970), Eisenhower, 1972, The Patton Papers, vol. 1, 1885-1940, 1972; vol. 2, 1940-45, 1974, (with James L. Stokesbury) Masters of the Art of Command, 1975, The Vilde Affair: Beginnings of the French Resistance, 1977, Liberation, 1978, Mark Clark: Last of The French Resistance, 1977, Liberation, 1978, Mark Clark: Last of the Great World War II Commanders, 1984, Patton: The Man behind the Legend, 1885-1945, 1985. Contrbr to books on military matters and to encyclopedias. Contrbr to books on military matters and to encyclopedias. Contrbr to Yale Rvw, American Heritage, Amer. Hist. Rvw, Jnl of m. Hist, Military Rvw, other periodicals. AB, Buchnell U., Lewisburg, Pa., 1939 MA, 1940; MA, Harvard U., 1942; Litt. D., Acadia U., 1972, Bucknell U., 1976. Instr in history, U.S. Merchant Marine Acad., Kings Point, N.Y., 1948-50; lectr in history, Hofstra Coll. (now U.), Hempstead, N.Y., 1950; historian, Dept. of the Army, Office of Chief of Mil. Hist., Washington, D.C., 1957-67; vis prof of mil and strategic studies, Acadia U., Wolfville, N.S., 1969-71; held Ernest J. King chair, Naval War College, Newport, R.I., 1971-73; Mark W. Clark Vis Prof of Mil History, The Citadel, Charleston, S.C., 1974-75; Harold McKeith Johnson chair, Army War College, Carlisle, Pa., 1975-76; professorial lectr in intl affairs, George Washington, U., 1981; adj prof, National War coll., WAshington, D.C., 1983-84; writer. Military service: U.S. Army, 1942-46, 1950-57; became lt. col. and historian. Mem. Amer. Hist. Assn, Amer. Mil. Inst., AAUP, Assn of the U.S. Army , Authors Guild, Authors League of Amer., Phi Beta Kappa, Phi Alpha Theta. Alumni Award for Meritorious Achievement, 1973, Bucknell U. Home: 3900 Watson Pl NW Washington DC 20016

BLY, CAROL McLEAN, (Ann Reynolds), b. Duluth, MN, Apr. 16, 1930, d. Charles Russell and Mildred (Washburn) McLean; children—Mary, Bridget, Noah, Micah. Author: One Down (novel transl. from Danish), 1975, Letters from the Country, 1981, Backbone, 1985, Soil and Survival, 1986, Bad Government and Silly Literature, 1986; contrbr. essays and stories to New Yorker, The Nation, Tri Qtly, Milkweed Chronicle, others; 3 short stories on American Playhouse TV, 1988. BA, Wellesley Coll., 1951. Cons., Natl. Farmers' Union, 1978-81, Land Stewardship Project, 1981-83; prof. Hamline U., St. Paul, 1985—; prof. U. Minn., 1987—. Grantee Minn. State Arts Bd., 1980, Bush Fdn., 1981. Mem. The Loft—Wrtrs. Ctr. Home: Rt 2 Box 546 Sturgeon Lake MN 55783

BLY, MARK JOHN, b. Sioux Falls, SD, Feb. 1, 1949; s. Myrle Sylvester and Lois (Bergen) B. Ed. The Guthrie Theater Program/ Mag., 1981—; contrbg. ed. Theater (Yale Sch. Drama), 1985—; contrbr. to Theater Jnl, Speech Jnl, Review of Books and Religion, Boston Herald American Sunday Book Section, The Mpls. Star and Tribune. MFA, Yale Schl. Drama, 1980. Asst. literary mgr. Yale Repertory Theater, New Haven 1979-1980; assoc. lit. mgr. Arena Stage, Washington, 1980-81; assoc. dramaturg/lit. mgr. The Guthrie Theater, Mpls., 1981-83, dramaturg/lit. mgr., 1983—. Mem. Lit. Mgrs. and Dramaturgs of Am., on-site evaluator, NEA, 1984-86. Office: Guthrie 725 Vineland Pl Minneapolis MN 55403

BLY, ROBERT ELWOOD, b. Madison, MN, Dec. 23, 1926; s. Jacob Thomas and Alice (Aws) B.; m. Carolyn McLean, June 24, 1955 (div. 1979); children—Mary, Bridget, Noah Matthew Jacob, Micah John Padma; m. Ruth Ray, June 27, 1980. Author: (poems) Silence in the Snowy Fields, 1962, The Light Around the Body, 1967; (prose poems) The Morning Glory, 1970; (poems) Sleepers Joining Hands, 1973, Jumping Out of Bed, 1973, Old Man Rubbing His Eyes, 1975; (criticism) Leaping Poetry, 1975; (prose poems) This Body Is Made of Camphor and Gopherwood, 1977; (poems) This Tree Will Be Here for a Thousand Years, 1979, (poems) Loving a Woman in Two Worlds, 1987. Editor: (prose poems) Forty Poems Touching on Recent American History, 1967; A Poetry Reading Against the Vietnam War, 1966; author: The Sea and the Honeycomb, 1966, News of the Universe, 1980, Man in the Black Coat Turns, 1981; translator (from Swedish) Selma Lagerlof The Story of Gosta Berling, 1962; Gunnar Eikelof I Do Best at Night Alone, 1968; (from Norwegian) Knut Hamsun Hunger, 1967; (from German) Twenty Poems of Georg Trakl, 1961; (from Spanish) Twenty Poems of Cesar Vallejo, 1963, Forty Poems of Juan Ramon Jiminez, 1967, Twenty Poems of Pablo Neruda, 1967; (from Swedish) Twenty Poems of Tomas Transtromer, 1972, Night Vision (Tomas Transtromer), 1972; (from Spanish) Lorca and Jiminez: Selected Poems, 1972; (from Swedish) Friends, You Drank Some Darkness: Three Swedish Poets, Martinson, Ekelof and Transtormer, 1975; (From Hindi and English) The Kabir Book: 44 of the Ecstatic Poems of Kabir, 1977; (from Norwegian) Twenty Poems of Rolf Jacobsen, 1977; (with Lewis Hyde) (from Spanish) Twenty Poems of Vincente Aleixandre, 1977; (from German) Selected Poems of Rainer Maria Rilke, 1980; (from Spanish) Time Alone: Selected Poems of Antonio Machado, 1982. Student, St. Olaf Coll., 1946-47; AB, Harvard, 1950; MA, U. Iowa, 1956. Editor, pub. Fifties, Sixties, Seventies Press, Madison, 1958—; co-chmn. Am. Writers vs. Vietnam, War, 1966—. Served with USNR, 1944-45. Recipient award Natl. Inst. Arts and Letters, Natl. Book award in poetry, 1968; Fulbright grantee, 1956-57; Amy Lowell fellow, 1964-65; Guggenheim fellow, 1965-66, 72-73; Rockefeller Fdn. fellow, 1967. Address: 308 1st St Moose Lake MN 55767

BLY, STEPHEN ARTHUR, b. Ivanhoe, CA, Aug. 17, 1944, s. Arthur Worthington and Alice Pearl (Wilson) B.; m. Janet Chester, June 14, 1963; children—Russell, Michael, Aaron. Author: Radical Discipleship, 1981, God's Angry Side, 1982, Devotions with a Difference, 1982, Questions I'd Like to Ask, 1982, The President's Stuck in the Mud, 1982, Quality Living in a Complicated Age, 1984, Trouble at Quartz Mountain Tunnel, six- book series of novels, The Crystal Books, 1986, How to be a Good Dad, 1986. BA, Calif. State, U., Fresno, 1971; MDiv, Fuller Theol. Sem., Pasadena, Calif., 1974. Ranch mgr. Bly Farms, Ivanhoe, Calif., 1965-74; pastor 1st Presbyn. Ch., Woodlake, Calif., 1974-78, 1st Presbyn. Ch., Fillmore, Calif., 1978-81; pastor wrtr. Winchester (Idaho) Community Ch., 1981-82; sr. pastor Fillmore Bible Ch., 1982—. Named Wrtr. of Yr., Mount Hermon Christian Wrtrs. Conf., 1982. Home: 736 Tighe Ln Fillmore CA 93015

BLYTH, MYRNA GREENSTEIN, b. NYC, Mar. 22, 1939; d. Benjamin and Betty (Austin) Greenstein; m. Jeffrey Blyth, Nov. 25, 1962; children—Jonathan, Graham. Author: novels Cousin Suzanne, 1975, For Better and For Worse, 1978. BA, Bennington (Vt.) Coll., 1960. Sr. editor Datebook mag., NYC, 1960-62, Ingenue mag., 1962-70; book editor Family Health mag., 1972-73; book and fiction editor, then assoc. editor, 1978-81; editor-in-chief Ladies' Home Jnl., 1981—; freelance writer, contrbr. mags., 1965—. Office: Ladies' Home Jnl 100 Park Ave New York NY 10017

BOB, INDIANA, see Novak, Robert L.

BOCCIO, KAREN CORINNE, b. NYC,Nov. 18, 1954; d. John Joseph and Josephine (Steingoetter) Herceg; m. Paul Alexander Boccio, Dec. 4, 1978; children—Alexander David, Justin Paul. Contrbr. poetry Poets Celebrate Am., Valhalla 6, Mati, New Leaves and other publs.; author: Inner Sanctions. BS magna cum laude, Columbia U, 1982. Writer and poet, NYC,1977—. Mem. PW. Address: c/o First East Coast Theatre POB A244 Village Sta NYC 10014

BOCK, GORDON HONOLD, b. Bryn Mawr, PA, Sept. 30, 1952; s. Harry Honold and Virginia (Porter) B.; Contrbr. articles to numerous mags. and newspapers, including The Old-House Jnl, Yachting, The Woodworker's Jnl, Small Boat Jnl., Road Rider. BA Boston Coll.; AAS, Westchester Community College, Valhalla, NY, 1983. Marine Electronics Technician, Griffith Marine Navigation Inc., New Rochelle, NY, 1977-84, Bock Marine Systems, Inc., 1986—; freelance writer, 1984—. Home: 7 Clove Rd N White Plains NY 10603

BOCK, RUSSELL SAMUEL, b. Spokane, WA, Nov. 24, 1905; s. Alva and Elizabeth (Mellinger) B.; m. Suzanne Ray, Feb. 26, 1970; children: Beverly A. Bock Wunderlich, James Russell. Author: Guidebook to California Taxes, annually, 1950—, Taxes of Hawaii, annually, 1964—. B.B.A., U. Wash., 1929. Office: 1398 Plaza Pacifica Santa Barbara CA 93108

BODDINGTON, CRAIG THORNTON, b. Kansas City, KS, Nov. 12, 1952, s. Edward

Mosely and Jeanne Estes (Popham) B.; m. Paula Lynn Merriman, Mar. 3, 1984; 1 dau., Brittany Lynn. Ed.: America—The Men and Their Guns that Made Her Great, 1981; author: Campfires and Game Trails—Hunting North American Big Game, 1985, From Mt. Kenya to the Cape: Ten Years of African Hunting; contrbr.: Outdoor Life, Hunting, Gun World, Safari, other outdoors publs. BA, U. Kans.-Lawrence, 1974. Vice-pres. Internatl. Hunting Cons., Santa Monica, Calif., 1978-79; ed. Guns & Ammo Spl. Publs., Los Angeles, 1979-83, Hunting mag., Los Angeles, 1983—. Served to maj., USMCR, 1974—. Mem. Outdoor Wrtrs. Assn. Am. Office: Petersen's Hunting Mag 8490 Sunset Blvd Los Angeles CA 90069

BODE, CARL, b. Milwaukee, Mar. 14, 1911; s. Paul and Celeste Helene (Schmidt) B.; m. Margaret Lutze, Aug. 3, 1938 (dec.); children—Barbara, Janet, Carolyn; m. Charlotte W. Smith, 1972. Author: The Sacred Seasons, 1953, The American Lyceum, 1956 (pb 1968), The Man Behind You, 1959, The Anatomy of American Popular Culture, 1840-1861, 1959 (repub. as Antebellum Culture, 1970), The Half-World of American Culture, 1965, Mencken, 1969, Highly Irregular (newspaper columns), 1974, Maryland: A Bicentennial History, 1978; Practical Magic, 1981; Maryland, 1983; editor: Collected Poems of Henry Thoreau, 1943, enlarged ed., 1964, The Portable Thoreau, 1947, rev. ed., 1964, American Life in the 1840s, 1967, The Selected Journals of Henry David Thoreau, 1967, (hardcover, The Best of Thoreau's Journals, 1971), Ralph Waldo Emerson, A Profile, 1969, Midcentury America: Life in the 1850's, 1972, The Young Mencken, 1973, The New Mencken Letters, 1977, Barnum, Struggles and Triumphs, 1982, Alger, Ragged Dick & Struggling Upward, 1985; co-editor: American Heritage, 2 vols., 1955, The Correspondence of Henry David Thoreau, 1958, American Literature, 3 vols., 1966, The Portable Emerson, 1981; editor and contrbr.: The Young Rebel in American Literature, 1959, The Great Experiment in American Literature, 1961. Contrbr. articles to encys., poetry and rvws. to Brit. and Am. jnls; columnist, Balt. Evening Sun. PhB, U. Chgo., 1933; MA, Northwestern U., 1938, fellow, 1940-41, PhD, 1941. Tchr. Milw. Vocat. Schl., 1933-37; asst. prof. English UCLA, 1946-47; prof. English U. Md., College Park, 1947-82, exec. secy. Am. Civilization program, 1950-57; cultural attache Am. embassy London, 1957-59; Mem. Md. State Arts Council, 1971-79, chmn., 1972-76; mem. Md. Humanities Council, 1981— chmn., 1984-86; Marshall Scholarship Adv. Council, 1960-69. Served with AUS, 1944-45. Ford Fdn. fellow, 1952-53; Newberry Library fellow, 1954; Guggenheim Fdn. fellow, 1954-55. Fellow Royal Soc. Lit. U.K. (hon.); mem. AAUP (council 1965-68), Am. Studies Assn. (founder, 1st pres., 1952), MLA, Thoreau Soc. Am. (dir. 1955-57, pres. 1960-61), Popular Culture Assn. Am. (v.p. 1972-75, pres. 1978-79), Mencken Soc. (founder, 1st pres. 1976-79), Phi Beta Kappa (hon.); Alpha Tau Omega. Home: 7008 Partridge Pl Col Hght Estates Hyattsville MD 20782

BODEK, NORMAN, b. NYC, Aug 12, 1932; s. Samuel Lewis and Dorothy Jaffe B, m. Marilyn Stern, June 6, 1954; 2 daus: Phyllis Miriello, Beth Simone. Ed. Data Entry Mgmt Newsletter, 1976—. BA, NYU, 1954. Acct. Bodek, Heitner and Co, NYC, 1957-61, vp Data Utilities, NYC, 1961-67, Intl. Systems, 1967-71; pres. Key Universal Ltd., Greenwich, Conn., 1971-79; pres. and ed. Productivity Inc., Stamford, Conn., 1979—. Served to cpl, US Army, 1955-57, USA. Address: Box 16722 Stamford CT 06905

BODEY, RICHARD ALLEN, b. Hazelton, PA, Nov. 27, 1930; s. Allen Z. and Marie F. (Smith) B.; m. Ruth L. Price, Sept. 10, 1955; children—Bronlynn Beth Spindler, Richard Allen. Author: You Can Live Without Fear of Death, 1980, Good News for All Seasons, 1987, Zondervan Pictorial Bible Encyclopedia, 1975, Encyclopedia of Christianity, vols. 1-3, 1962-72. Contrbr. articles to religious mags. including Christianity Today, Moody Monthly, Jnl. of Evangelical Theological Soc. Ed.: Voices, 1980—, Student Munlenberg coll, 1948-49; A.B., Lafayette coll., 1952; M.div., Princeton Theol. Seminary, 1955; Th.M., Westminster Theol. Seminary, 1972, D.Min., Trinity Evangelical Divinity Sch., 1984; postgrad. Wycliffe Coll., 1961, Seabury-Western Theol. Seminary, 1985. Ordained to ministry, Presbyterian Church USA, 1955. Head of staff First Assoc. Reformed Presbyterian Ch., Gastonia, NC, 1973-79; dir. Gastonia Sch. of Biblical Studies, 1979; assoc. prof. practical theology Trinity Evangelical Divinity Schl., Deerfield, IL, 1979-87, prof., 1987—; instr. in preaching Moody Bible Inst. Correspondence Sch., Chgo., 1982-86. Recipient Gaston Evangelical Assn. award, 1979. Mem. Evangelical Theol. Soc., Acad. Homiletics. Home: 36443 N Beverly Ave Gurnee IL 60031

BODIE, IDELLA FALLAW, b. Ridge Spring, SC, Dec. 2, 1925; d. Grady and Grace Fallaw; m. James E. Bodie, Aug. 15, 1947; children: Susanne, Edwin, John, Beth. Author: (juveniles) Secret of Telfair Inn, 1971, Mystery of the Pirates' Treasure, 1973, Ghost in the Capitol, 1976, Stranded!, 1984; SC Women: They Dared to Lead, 1978; A Search for Life's Extras, the Story of Archibald Rutledge, 1980; contrbr. to Guideposts. BA, Columbia Coll., S.C., 1946; postgrad. U.S.C., 1957-62. Tchr. English, chmn. dept. Aiken High Sch., S.C., 1960-84; freelance writer, 1969—. Mem. S.C. Poetry Soc., Caroliniana Hist. Soc. Home: 1113 Evans Rd Aiken SC 29801

BOERSTLER, RICHARD WILLIAM, b. Boston, Feb. 14, 1923. Author: Letting Go: A Holistic and Meditative Approach to Living and Dying, 1982. B.S., Tufts, 1947; PhD,Columbia Pacific U., 1984. Investigator Liberty Mutual Ins., Boston, 1948-76; psychotherapist, 1977—. Mem. Assn. Humanistic Psychology. Home: 115 Blue Rock Rd South Yarmouth MA 02664

BOETIG, DONNA BYRNES, b. Norwalk, CT, June 28, 1950; d. John Francis and Ethel Pearl (Kiska) Byrnes; m. Allen Kenneth Boetig, July 8, 1972; children—Scott Allen, Bradley John, Ryan Robert. Contrbr. articles to mags., newspapers including Saturday Evening Post, Catholic Digest, others. Student Wroxton Coll., Oxfordshire, England, 1971; B.A. in Jnlsm., Pace U., 1972. Staff wrtr. The Hampton Union, NH, 1980-82, Portsmouth Herald, NH, 1982-83; corr., feature wrtr. The Union Leader, Manchester, NH, 1980-82; free-lance wrtr., 1985—. Home: 610 Woodsman's Way Crownsville MD 21032

BOGEN, DON, b. Sheboygan, WI, May 27, 1949; s. Howard Leopold and Evelyn Mae (Childs) B.; m. Cathryn Jeanne Long, Sept. 5, 1976; children: Anna Cathryn, Theodore Donald. Author poetry: After the Splendid Display, 1986; contrbr. poems to New Republic, The Nation, Paris Rvw, Am. Poetry Rvw, Poetry, Ploughshares, Kenyon Rvw, No Am Rvw, Stand, others; rvws. of poetry in The Nation, Threepenny Rvw, other jnls; transls. in Antaeus and others; critical articles on modern poetry in English Lit. History, Papers on Lang. and Lit. and other jnls. AB, U. Calif.-Berkeley, 1971, MA, 1974, PhD, 1976. Asst. prof. English Univ. Cin., 1976-82, assoc. prof., 1982—. Recipient Edwin Markham award, Eugene V. Debs Fdn., 1976, Discovery/The Nation award, The Nation Mag., 1980; Grand Prize/Anniversary awards, AWP, 1982; Ohio Arts Council grantee, 1985. Mem. AWP, AAUP, NBCC. Address: 209 Atkinson St Cincinnati OH 45219

BOGEN, LAUREL ANN, b. Los Angeles, Mar. 27, 1950, d. Max Martin and Helen Marguerite (Ramsay) Bogen. Author: The Woof and the Warp, 1974, Six by Laurel Ann Bogen, 1976, The Disappearing Act, 1978, The Night Grows Teeth and Other Observations, 1980, Origami: The Unfolding Heart, 1981, Do Iguanas Dance, Under the Moonlight?, 1984, The Great Orange Leonard Scandal, 1984, The Projects, 1987; contrbr. poems and short stories to numerous lit mags and anthols. BS, USC, 1971; postgrad. U. Ariz., 1972-73. Poetry dir. George Sand, Books, L.A., 1977-78; poetry dir. Hyperion Theater, L.A., 1978-80; exec. dir. L. A. Poetry Theater, 1980-84; contrbg. ed. Madrona, L.A., 1982-85; instr. creative wrtg. workshops, L.A., 1982—. Advisory bd. mem, lit. arts prog., Social & Public Arts Resources Center, L.A., 1983. AAP Coll. Award, USC, 1968; poetry scholarship, Squaw Valley Wrtrs. Conf., 1980. Mem. PSA, PW. Home: 520 S Hauser Blvd Los Angeles CA 90036

BOGENSTADT, LUDWIG VON., see Lewis, Monte Ross

BOGGS, MARCUS LIVINGSTONE, JR., b. Birmingham, AL., Dec. 19, 1947; s. Marcus Livingstone and Sarah Alice (McFarland) B.; m. Elizabeth Ruth Bell, June 12, 1977. Author: Scissors, Paper, Stone, 1981. A.B., Princeton, U., 1970. Editor Oxford Univ. Press, NYC, 1977-83, Harcourt Brace Jovanovich, San Diego, 1983—. Home: 1335 Torrance St San Diego CA 92103

BOGGS, ROBERT NEWELL, b. Denver, Sept. 14, 1930; s. John Irwin and Rowena Opal (Newell) B.; m. Gwendolyn Carol Lee, June 18, 1955; children: Kerrie Kim and Kristi Kay (twins), Kevin Clarke, Karole Lee. Writer Gates Rubber Co., Denver, 1959-63; asst. editor Design News, Denver, after 1963, then assoc. editor, sr. editor, 10 1971, mng. exec. editor, Boston, 1971—. B.S.M.E., U. Colo., 1958. Served with USAF, 1950-54. Mem. Am. Soc. Bus Press Editors (founding pres chpt. 1974-75, dir. 1979-82, 1st, v.p. 1983-84). Home: 288 Holly Rd Marshfield MA 02050

BOGUE, LUCILLE MAXFIELD, b. Salt Lake City, UT, April 21, 1911; d. Roy Douglas and Maude Ethel (Callicotte) Maxfield; m. Arthur Ellsworth Bogue (dec.) Dec. 25, 1935; children—Sharon Kay, Bonnie Gale. Author: Typhoon! Typhoon! 1969, Eye of the Condor, 1975, Bloodstones/Lines from a Marriage, 1980, Salt Lake, 1982, Windbells on The Bay, 1983, Dancers on Horseback: The Perry-Mansfield Story, 1984. BA, U. of North Colorado, 1934; MA, San Francisco State, 1972. Tchr., Col pub. schls., 1934-62; founder/pres., Yampa Valley College, Steamboat Spg., Col., 1962-66; dir. of guidance, Am. Schl. In Japan, Tokyo, 1966-68; dean, Anna Head Schl. for Girls, Oakland, Ca., 1968-71; instr., Colegio Americano, Guayaquil, Ecuador, 1974-75; freelance wrtr., Ca., 1972—. Awards: Woman of the Year Natl. Lg. of Am. PEN

Women, 1984. Mem. Cal. Writers Club, Natl. Lg. of Am. PEN Women, Ina Coolbrith Poetry Circle. Home: 2611 Brooks El Cerrito CA 94530

BOHLE, BRUCE WILLIAM, b. St. Louis, July 21, 1918; s. Edward F. and Emma W. (Fricke) B. BA, Washington U., St. Louis, 1939. Film critic St. Louis Star-Times, 1946-51, drama and music critic, 1950-51; asst. mgr. St. Louis Symphony Orch., 1951-53; assoc. editor Grolier Soc., NYC, 1960-64. Editor Theatre Arts mag., 1953-63; usage editor: Am. Heritage Dictionary, Am. Heritage Pub. Co., NYC, 1964—; editor: The Home Book of American Quotations, 1967; editor: International Cyclopedia of Music and Musicians, 10th ed., 1975, 11th ed., 1985. Served with USAAF, 1942-46; PTO. Recipient Harvard Book prize, 1935. Mem. Phi Beta Kappa. Home: 260 Audubon Ave New York NY 10033

BOIARSKI, PHILIP S., b. Wheeling, WV, Nov. 6, 1945, s. Anthony Daniel and Teofila Ann (Miloszewski) B.; m. Kaye White Knore, Nov. 1, 1970; children—Sean Luke, Clarissa, Juliana. Author: Black Polacks: The Human Crowd, Coal & Ice, Cornered; contrbr. poetry to Aspen Anthology, Ohio Jnl, Minn. Rvw, Paris Rvw, other lit mags. BA, Ohio State U., 1968; MFA, Goddard Coll., 1980. Wrtr.-in-Schls., Ohio Arts Council, 1970-80; creative dir. Swink, Kight, Haunty, Columbus, Ohio, 1980-83; wrtr., producer Ohio Dept. Devel., Columbus, 1983—. Bd. dirs. Days of Creation Arts Program, Columbus, 1980—. Ohio Arts Council fellow, 1978, grantee, 1980. Mem. AAP (Walt Whitman finalist 1977), Yellow Pages Poets (founder 1975). Home: 839 Lakefield Dr Galloway OH 43119

BOISCLAIR, JOAN, b. Denver, Nov. 1, 1956, d. John Burnett and Bette Jane (Anderson) B. One son: Nathan Tincher-Boisclair. Contrbr. poetry and articles to Feminist Poetics, Transfer, Calyx, Birthstone, other lit mags. BA in Poli. Sci., U. Oreg., 1977; MA in Creative Writing, San Francisco State U., 1983. Freelance wrtr., 1979—; lectr. creative writing San Francisco State U. 1984-86; prin. wrtr., ed. for texts Pub. Mgmt. Inst., 1979-84; tech wrtr. Apple Computer, 1984-86; Weyerhauser Mortgage Co., 1987—. Mem. AWP, Phi Beta Kappa, Media Alliance. Home: 1635 Calif St Berkeley CA 94703

BOLAND, MARTY, see Ellis, Margaret Boland

BOLLEN, PETER DOUGLAS, b. Lynn, MA, Mar. 24, 1948; s. James W. and Frances L. Bailin B. Ed: Handbook of Great Labor Quotations, 1983; Nuclear Voices, 1986; contrbr. Lynn Item, North Shore: Sunday, labor jnls, Fed. Times, Boston Globe. Student No. Shore Comm. Coll, 1970-71. Printer Court Square Press, Boston, 1965-73; clk. US PO, Lynnfield, Mass., 1974—; staff Lynn Newpaper, 1974-79. Bd. dirs., Lynn Mental Health Citizens Adv Comm, Union Hospital, Lynn, 1985; pres., Am Postal Workers Union No. 6077, Lynnfield, 1985-86. Recipient Tools of Your Trade award, Lynn Tchrs. Assn., 1965; letter of commendation, US Postal Service, Framingham, 1974. Address: Box 601 Lynnfield MA 01940

BOLLINGER, TAREE, b. Forks, WV, Dec 21, 1949; d. Francis Lloyd and Vir Nadean Dyer Harrison; m. Robert Patrick Bollinger, May 5, 1979; children: Cassandra Jo, Robert Jacob. Author: The Baby Gear Guide, 1985; contrbr. Baby!, Expecting, Family Circle, Baby Talk; ed The Jnl. of Forms Mgmt., 1981—, Today's Home and Investment, 1985—, News & Views, 1984—, InsidePocatello (booklet), 1985. Student Wash. State Univ., 1967-71. Adv. copy writer Sears, Seattle, 1971-73; procedure/forms mgr. and writer Airborne Freight Corp., Seattle, 1973-79; off. mgr. Stan Wiley Real Estate, Portland, Ore, 1979-81, free lance publ. services, Moorpark, CA, 1981—. Mem. AG, AL Am., Soc. of Children's Book Writers. Address: 6431 Linville Ct Moorpark CA 93021

BOLTE, CHARLES GUY, b. NYC, Jan. 19, 1920; s. Guy Willard and Marian (Stewart) B.; m. Mary Brooks Elwell, Aug. 1, 1943; children: Guy Willard II, John Cox, Brooks. Author: The New Veteran, 1945, The Price of peace: A Plan for Disarmament, 1956, Libraries and the Arts and Humanities, 1977; editor: (Mary Bolte) Portrait of a Woman Down East, 1983. A.B., Dartmouth Coll., 1941, L.H.D., 1970; M.Litt. (Rhodes scholar 1947), Oxford (Eng.) U., 1949. Newspaper reporter, 1937-41; spcl. writer O.W.I., 1943-44; mil. corr. The Nations, 1944; exec. sec. Am./ book Pubs. Council, 1952; v.p. Viking Press, 1956-61, exec. v.p., 1961-66; editor Am. Oxonian, 1977; writer, cons., 1973—. Served as lt. Brit. Army, 1941-43. Home: Dresden Me 04342

BOMBECK, ERMA LOUISE, b. Dayton, OH, Feb. 21, 1927; d. Cassius Edwin and Erma (Haines) Fiste; m. William Lawrence Bombeck, Aug. 13, 1949; children: Betsy, Andrew, Matthew. Author: At Wit's End, 1967; Just Wait Till You Have Children of Your Own, 1971; I Lost Everything In The Post-Natal Depression, 1974; The Grass Is Always Greener Over The Septic Tank, 1976; If Life is a Bowl of Cherries, What Am I Doing in the Pits?, 1978; Aunt Erma's Cope Book, 1979; Motherhood: The Second Oldest Profession, 1983; Family—The Ties That Bind. . .and Gag!, 1987. B.A., U. Dayton, 1949. Syndicated columnist Newsday Syndicate, 1965-70, Pubs.-Hall Syndicate, 1970-85 (now North Am. Synd.); Los Angeles Times Syndicate, 1985—; contrbg. editor Good Housekeeping Mag., 1969-74. Mem. Am. Acad. Humor Columnists. Office: LA Times Synd Times Mirror Sq Los Angeles CA 90053

BOND, HAROLD HERANT, b. Boston, Dec. 2, 1939, s. Khorin and Ovsanna (Avakian) B.; m. Ruth Thomasian, June 6, 1981 (div. 1985). Author poetry books: 3x3 (with Harry Barba, Leo Hamalian), 1969, The Northern Wall, 1969, Dancing on Water, 1970, The Way It Happens to You, 1979, Other Worlds; contrbr. poetry to Beloit Poetry Jnl, Lit. Rvw, Ploughshares, Shenandoah, Sumac, other jnls, anthologies; contrbr. articles, interviews, to Am. Lit. Rvw, Little Rvw, other mags. AB in English-Journalism, Northeastern U., 1962; MFA in Creative Writing, U. Iowa, 1967. Asst. ed. Horizon House, Dedham, Mass., 1962-65, Allyn and Bacon, Boston, 1967-69; copy ed. Boston Globe, 1969-71; ed. Ararat mag., Saddle Brook, N.J., 1969-70, mem. editorial bd., 1971—; tchr. poetry seminars; mem. faculty Cambridge Center for Adult Edn., 1968—; poet-in-schls. Mass. Council on Arts and Humanities, 1971-74, N.H. Commn. on Arts, 1973-76, Artists Fdn. Mass., 1977-79, Poets Who Teach, Mass., 1974-80, Inst. for Arts., Mass., 1983—. Winner poetry prize Armenian Allied Arts Assn. Am., 1963, 64, 65, Kansas City Star, 1967, 68; NEA fellow, 1976, PEN and AL Am. grantee. Home: 11 Chestnut St Melrose MA 02176

BOND, VIRGINIA F., b. Greeley, CO. Apr. 13, 1919; d. John Merton and Florence Belle (Dorey) Gross; m. Frank L. Bond, Feb. 16, 1941; children—David, Jess, Carol. Author—poetry: Denver Post, Branches of Coral, Grade Teacher, other publs.; children's plays: plays Magazine, Grade Teacher; guest editorialsit: The Greeley Tribune; contrbr. articles: Grade Teacher, Instructor. Wrkg. on children's plays, poetry collection. AB in Elem. Edn., U. No. Colo., 1953, MA in Elem. Edn., 1958. Tchr, public schs., Kersey, Colo., 1950-57, Greeley, Colo., 1957-81. Mem. Greeley Poetry Club (pres.), numerous profl. orgns. Home: Box 147 Kersey CO 80644

BONE, BRENDA KAY, (Christina Shannon, Brenda Chutes, Courtney Shell, Kay Chandler), b. Columbus OH, Dec. 10, 1960; d. Jerry R. and Marjorie Louise (Shannon) Chutes. Contrbr. short stories, articles to mags., lit. mags. Wrkg. on hist. novels, horror novel. Cert. in Creative Writing, Inst. Children's Lit., 1982. Shipping clrk. Oasis, Columbus, 1977-79; legal secy., Fishman Legal Svcs. Columbus, 1983—; freelance wrtr., 1979—. Mem. RWA. Home: 13230 Havens Corners Rd Pataskala OH 43062

BONETTI, KAY JACQUELINE, b. Monroe County, MO, Dec. 1, 1940; d. James Stuart and Hazel Beatrice Palmer Callison; m. Edward Michael Bonetti, Feb. 1, 1969 (div. Feb., 1972); m. 2d, Michael Lee Naughton, Jan 11, 1975; 1 dau., Dora. Contrbr. criticism Chouteau Rvw; poetry to Westport Trucker, Chariton Rvw; interviews Mo. Rvw, Saturday Rvw. BM, Central Methodist Coll., 1963; MA, U. Mo.-Columbia, 1968. Instr. Univ. Mo., Columbia, 1966-74, Ctr. Ind. Study, 1976-83; dir. Am. Audio Prose Lib., Columbia, 1980—. Bd. dirs. Columbia Commn. on the Arts, 1983—, chmn., 1985—; mem. exec. comm., Columbia Regional Arts Council, 1985—; vp, New Wave Corp., Columbia, 1978-80; mem. and coord., Cen. Mo. Humane Soc. Edn. Comm., Columbia, 1970-83. Recipient award Choice Mag, 1982; Ohio State award for Ednl. Broadcasting, 1985; Community Radio award Natl. Fedn. Community Broadcasters, 1983. Mem. MLA. Address: 600 Crestland Ave Columbia MO 65203

BONHAM, GEORGE WOLFGANG, b. Free City of Danzig, Aug. 12, 1924; came to U.C., 1938, naturalized, 1943; s. Walter C. and Kate M. (Selbiger) B.; children: Mary Faith, Mark David. Editor: Inside Academe, 1972, On Learning and Change, 1973, Colleges and Money, 1975, The Future of Foundations, 1978, In the Public Interest, 1978, The Communications Revolution and the Education of Americans, 1980; Contbr. articles to nat. mags. B.A., Ohio State U., 1948-49, D.H.L. (hon.), 1975, LL.D. (hon.), 1977. Editor-in-chief, pub. Change mag., 1969-81. Served with 44th Div. M.I. AUS, 1943-45. Home: 371 Cypress Point Rd Half Moon Bay CA 94019

BONINA, MARY, b. Worcester, MA, Nov. 2, 1950; d. Biagio John and Mary Cecilia (Feeherry) Bonina; m. Mark Pawlak, Aug. 21, 1982; 1 stepchild, andrai Pawlak Whitted. Contrbr. poems to lit. mags. Ed., contrbr. short fiction, articles, poems: The Little Apple, 1975-82. Wrkg. on collection of short stories, novel. B.A. in English, Anna Maria Coll., 1972; M.F.A. in Creative Writing, Warren Wilson Coll., 1985. coord. Piedmont Center for Arts, Worcester, MA, 1975; tchr. English, City Public Schs., Worcester, 1978-81; tchr. communication skills, English, devel. studies Quinsigamond Commun. Coll., Worcester, 1981; housing research specialist commonwealth of Mass., Boston, 1982-86. Recipient Achievement in Poetry award Ednl. Assn. Worcester, 1980; grantee Worcester County Poetry Assn., 1974; award winner, Boston Subway Station Permanent Poetry Installation, Urban Arts, Inc., 1987. Home: 173A Ridge Ave Cambridge MA 02140

BONINI, VICTOR LOUIS, b. NYC, Sept. 8, 1958; s. Victor Louis and Maureen E. (Smith) B.; m. Donna Kathryn Willson, July 10, 1983. Contrbr.: The Mountaineer, The Horse, The Force, Children & Animals, numerous others. AA, AS in Journalism, Mt. San Antonio Coll. Ed. The Mountaineer, Walnut, Calif., 1985-86, mng. ed., 1986; mng. ed. Nat. Assn. Advancement of Humane Edn., East Haddam, Conn., 1986—. Mem. Ednl. Press Assn. Am. Home: 30 Terrace Ave Taftville CT 06380

BONNER, THOMAS, JR., b. New Orleans, Sept. 19, 1942; s. Brigadier General Thomas and Mercedes Mary (Vulliet) B.; m. Judith Ann Hopkins, Aug. 27, 1966; children—Ashley Elizabeth, Laura Vulliet. Author: William Faulkner: William B. Wisdom Collect., 1980, A Kate Chopan Companion, 1987; contrbr. to books: The History of Southern Lit., 1985, Southern Writers: A Biographical Dictionary, 1979, South. Lit. in Transition, 1983, In Old New Orleans, 1983; contrbr. to numerous jnls inclg. Mississippi Qtly, New Laurel Rvw, Louisiana Lit., Explicator, Blue Grass Lit. Rvw. BA, Southeastern LA U., 1965; MA, Tulane U., 1968, PhD, 1975. Prof. Engl., Xavier U. of LA, New Orleans, 1971—; book reviewer The Times-Picayune, New Orleans, 1980—; ed. Xavier Review, New Orleans, 1982—; sr. writer/researcher WYES-TV, New Orleans, 1982—. Mem. MLA, SSSL. Home: 6202 Marshal Foch New Orleans LA 70124

BONNETT, KENDRA R., (I. M. Pooka), b. Greenwich, CT, June 11, 1955; d. Dovell Nicholas and Rosemary (Buehrig) B. Author: (with Gene Oldfield) The Everyone Can Build a Robot Book, 1984; ACT It Use Your Computer to Improve Your Grades, 1984, The Creative Print Master, 1985. Contrbr. articles to bus., computing mags., electronics books. Contrbr., ed.: WEECN Newsletter, 1980; contrbr., founding ed.: RAP: Resources and Practice, 1983, ETC: Ednl. Technology & Communications, 1982-84, Digit Mag., 1983-84. B.A. with honors in History, Ariz. State U., 1974; M.A. in History, Coll. William & Mary, 1976. Dir. technical learning, sr. wrtr., ed. Far West Laboratory, San Francisco, 1979-84; owner, free-lance wrtr. Bonnett Communications, Greenwich, 1984—; marketing wrtr. Info. Builders, Inc., N.Y.C., 1987—. Recipient Honorable Mention for fiction Wrtrs. Digest, 1982. Mem. IABC. Home: 225 Byram Shore Rd Greenwich CT 06830

BONOMELLI, CHARLES JAMES, b. Raton, NM, July 5, 1948; s. James and Carmelita (Serna) B.; m. Mary Ann Harvey, May 31, 1936. A.A., Trinidad State Jr. Coll., 1969; B.A., U. Southern Colo., 1970. Correctional officer Colo. State Peniteniary, Canon City; police officer Pueblo Police Dept., CO. Recipient Cert. of Achievement, Potpourri Intl. Press, 1984, 5th prize, 1985; Honorable Mention, ursus Press, 1985. Home: 2133 Sherwood Ln Box 1102 Pueblo CO 81005

BOONE, LALIA PHIPPS, b. Tehuacana, TX, Apr. 19, 1907; d. John Ardis and Mattie Ida (Johnson) Phipps; m. Joe Floy Boone, Sept. 10, 1927 (div. 1953); children—Joe Ardis, Martha Nell, Doris Anne. Author: Petroleum Dictionary, 1951; Communicative Arts 9-12, 1961; (textbook) Word Study, books 7-9, 1961; A Creative Approach to the Teaching of Spelling, 1964; Books Recommended for Junior-High Libraries, 1972; Checklist for Language Skills, K-3, 1972; Post Offices of Latah County, 1978; (dictionary) From A to Z in Latah County, 1984. Contrbr. articles to Am. Speech, Southern Folklore, Idaho Place Names, Boston U. Studies in English, Modern Lang. Notes. MA, U. Okla, 1947; PhD, U. Fla., 1951. Tchr. Navarro County pub. schl, Currie, Emhouse, Tex., 1925-32; tchr., prin. pub. schl, Wortham, Tex., 1928-44, 44-46; instr. English, U. Okla., Norman, 1946-49; asst. prof. U. Fla., Gainesville, 1949-59, assoc. prof., 1959-65; prof. English, U. Id., Moscow, 1965-72, prof. emeritus, 1972—. Active Lewis & Clark Trial Heritage Fdn., 1986—. Grantee Assn. for Humanities in Id., 1984, John Calhoune Smith Fund, 1984, Kaypro Co., 1983. Fellow ACLS; Penrose fellow Am. Philo. Soc.; mem. Latah County Hist. Soc., Natl. League Am. PEN Women (1st place in tech. art 1963), AAUW, Am. Dialect Soc., Am. Name Soc., MLA. Home: 10000 Brunswick Ave 302 Silver Spring MD 20910

BOORSTIN, DANIEL J., b. Atlanta, Oct. 1, 1914; s. Samuel and Dora (Olsan) B.; m. Ruth Carolyn Frankel, Apr. 9, 1941; children—Paul Terry, Jonathan, David West. Author: The Mysterious Science of the Law, 1941, Delaware Cases, 1792-1830 (3 vols.), 1943, The Lost World of Thomas Jefferson, 1948, The Genius of American Politics, 1953, The Americans: The Colonial Experience, 1958 (winner Bancroft award 1959), America and the Image of Europe, 1960, The Image or What Happened to the American Dream, 1962, The Americans: The National Experience, 1965 (Francis Parkman prize 1966), The Landmark History of the American People, 2 vols., 1968, 70, The Decline of Radicalism, 1969, The Sociology of the Absurd, 1970, The Americans: The Democratic Experience, 1973 (Pulitzer prize 1974; Dexter prize 1974), Democracy and Its Discontents, 1974, The Exploring Spirit, 1976, The Republic of Technology, 1978, (with Brooks M. Kelley) A History of the United States, 1981, The Discoverers, 1983 (Watson Dairo Prize, 1986); editor: An American Primer, 1966, (with Brooks M. Kelley) American Civilization, 1972, Am. history, Ency. Brit., 1951-55; Author articles, book rvws. AB summa cum laude, Harvard U., 1934; BA with first class honors (Rhodes scholar), Balliol Coll., Oxford U., 1936, BCL, 1937; post-grad., Inner Temple, London, 1934-37; JSD (Sterling fellow), Yale U., 1940; LittD (hon.), Cambridge U., 1967; numerous other hon. degrees. Bar: Admitted as barrister-at-law Inner Temple 1937, Mass. bar 1942. Instr., tutor history and lit Harvard and Radcliffe Coll., 1938-42; lectr. legal history Harvard Law School, 1939-42; asst. prof. history Swarthmore Coll., 1942-44; asst. prof. U. Chicago, 1944-49, assoc. prof., 1949-56, prof. Am. History, 1956-64, Preston and Sterling Morton Disting. Service Prof., 1964-69; Walgreen lectr. Am. instns., 1952; dir. Natl. Mus. History and Tech., Smithsonian Instn., Washington, 1969-73, sr. historian, 1973-75; librarian of congress Library of Congress, 1975—; Fulbright vis. lectr. Am. history U. Rome, 1950-51, Kyoto U., Japan, 1957; cons. Social Sci. Research Center, U. P.R., 1955; lectr. for U.S. Dept. State in Turkey, Iran, Nepal, India, Ceylon, 1959-60, Indonesia, Australia, New Zealand, Fuji, 1968, India, Pakistan, Iceland, 1974, Philippines, Thailand, Malaysia, India, Egypt, 1975; 1st incumbent of chair Am. history U. Paris, 1961-62; Pitt prof. Am. history and instns. U. Cambridge, 1964-65; Shelby and Kathryn Collom Davis lectr. Grad. Inst. Intl. Studies, Geneva, 1973-74; sr. fellow Huntington Library, 1969; mem. Commn. on Critical Choices for Ams., 1973—, Dept. State Indo-Am. Joint Subcommn. Edn. and Culture, 1974-81, Japan-U.S. Friendship Commn., 1978—; mem. Am. Revolution Bicentennial Commn.; sr. attorney Office Lend Lease Adminstr., Washington; Fellow Trinity Coll., 1964-65. Recipient Bowdoin prize Harvard, 1934, Jenkins prize, Younger prize, Balliol Coll., 1935, 36. Mem. Colonial Soc. Mass., Orgn. Am. Historians, Am. Acad. Arts and Scis., Am. Philo. Soc., Am. Antiquarian Soc., Am. Studies Assn. (pres. 1969-71), Intl. House Japan, Honorary Fellow Am. Geographical Soc., Royal Hist. Soc. (corr. fellow), Phi Beta Kappa. Home: 3541 Ordway St NW Washington DC 20016

BOOTH, DIANE ELIZABETH, b. Balt., Jan. 16, 1948; d. Albert August and Mary Anna (Deasel) Scheper; m. David Edgar Booth, May 27, 1967; children—Jan, Cynthia, David. Contrbr. articles to mags., newspapers. Wrkg. on mag. articles, true story book, newspaper stories. Student Notre Dame Coll., 1981-83. Researcher, Balt. Bus. Jnl., 1982-83; staff reporter Harford County Sun, 1984-85; contrbg. wrtr. Warfield's Mag., Balt., 1986—. Mem. Intl. Women's Writing Guild, Wrtr.'s Center. Home: 3607 Lord Baltimore Way Monkton MD 21111

BOOTH, PHILIP, b. Hanover, NH, Oct. 8, 1925; s. Edmund Hendershot and Jeanette-Challis (Hooke) B.; m. Margaret Tillman, Aug. 3, 1946; children—Margot, Carol, Robin. Author: Letter from a Distant Land, 1957, The Islanders, 1961, Weathers and Edges, 1966, North by East, 1968, Margins, 1970, Available Light, 1976, Before Sleep, 1980, Relations, Selected Poems 1950-85, 1986; editor: The Dark Island, 1960, Syracuse Poems, 1965, 70, 73, Syracuse Stories and Poems, 1978, 1981. BA, Dartmouth Coll., 1948; MA, Columbia U., 1949; Litt D (hon.) Colby Coll., 1968. Instructor Bowdoin Coll., 1949-50; asst. to dir. admissions Dartmouth, 1950-51, instr. in English, 1954; instr. to asst. prof. Wellesley Coll., 1954-61; assoc. prof. Syracuse (N.Y.) U, 1961-65, prof, 1966-1986. Served with USAAF, 1944-45. Recipient Hokin prize Poetry mag., 1955, Lamont prize AAP, 1956, Saturday Rvw Poetry award, 1957, Phi Beta Kappa Poet Columbia, 1963, Emily Clark Balch prize Va. Qtly Rvw, 1964, creative writing award Natl. Inst. Arts and Letters, 1967, Theodore Roethke prize, 1970. Guggenheim Meml. fellow, 1958-59, 65; Rockefeller fellow, 1968; NEA fellow, 1980, fellow of the AAP, 1983. Mem. Dennett's Wharf Hist. Soc., Phi Beta Kappa. Home: Main St Castine ME 04421

BOOTS, SHARON G., b. Grand Rapids, MI, May 5, 1939; d. Robert Thomas and Roma Marguerite (West) Gray; 1 dau., Katherine Margaret. Contrbr. articles to profl. jnls. & texts. BA in Chem., U. WI, 1960; PhD, Stanford, 1963. Research assoc., Dept. of Chem., Stanford U., 1978-81; in environmental toxicology, U. WI., 1981-82; ed. Jnl. Pharmaceutical Scis., Washington, 1982-86; mng. ed., Anal. Chem., 1987—. Mem. Am. Chem. Soc., Council of Biol. Eds., AAAS, Phi Beta Kappa. Office: ACS 1155 16th St NW Washington DC 20036

BORDEN, WILLIAM VICKERS, b. Indpls., Jan. 27, 1938, s. Harold Rudolph and Elizabeth Margaret (Vickers) B.; m. Nancy Lee Johnson, Dec. 17, 1960; children—Andrew, Sara, Rachel. Author: Superstoe, 1968; plays produced in NYC, Los Angeles, Denver, Mpls., Kansas City, Louisville. AB, Columbia U., 1960; MA, U. Calif., Berkeley, 1962. Asst. prof. dept. English, U. N.D., Grand Forks, 1967-70, assoc. prof.,

1970-82, prof., 1982—; playwright-in-residence Playwrights Center, Mpls., 1981-85, core playwright, 1985—, bd. dirs., 1981-82. Winner Midwest Playwrights Program, 1981, Towngate Theatre Playwriting Contest, 1982, Unicorn Theatre Playwriting Contest, 1982, Midwest Radio Theater Workshop, 1982, 85, Performing Arts Repertory Theatre Contest, 1983. Mem. PEN, Dramatists Guild, AWP. Home: 307 Princeton St Grand Forks ND 58201

BOREL, YOGI, see Sapiro, Leland

BORENSTEIN, EMILY RUTH, b. Elizabeth, NJ, May 6, 1923; d. Louis and Jennie (Molowitz) Schwartz; m. Morris Borenstein, June 27, 1942; children—MJanet Brickner, Sandra Guskin Jennings, Marc. Author: Woman Chopping, 1978, Finding My Face, 1979, Cancer Queen, 1979, Night of the Broken Glass, 1981. Contrbr. poems to anthols., lit. mags. BS in comparative lit., Columbia U., 1964, MS in social work, 1984; MA in English, NYU, 1972. Piano instr., Middletown, N.Y., 1972-82; social worker psychiat. clinic Middletown Psychiat. Ctr., 1984—. Trustee, Homemaker Service of Orange County, Middletown, 1985—, Family counseling Service of Orange County, 1985—, Temple Sinai, Middletown, 1986—. Recipient Annual Poetry award Jewish Currents Mag., 1978. Mem. P&W, PSA, AAP, Natl. Assn. Social Workers. Home: 189 Highland Ave Middletown NY 10940

BORESI, ARTHUR PETER, b. Toluca, IL, s. John Peter and Eva (Grotti) B.; m. Clara Jean Gordan, Dec. 28, 1946; children: Jennifer Ann Boresi Hill, Annette boresi Pueschel, Nancy Jean. Author: Engineering Mechanics, 1959, Elasticity in Engineering Mechanics, 3d ed., 1987, Advanced Mechanics of Materials, 4th ed., 1985; also articles. Student, Kenyon, Coll., 1943-44; B.S. in Elec. Engring, U. Ill., 1948, M.S., 1949, Ph.D., 1953. Served with AUS, 1944-46. Office: Box 3295 Univ Sta U Wyo Laramie WY 82071

BORG, GAVIN, see Queenan, Joseph Martin, Jr.

BORICH, MICHAEL, b. Waterloo, IA, May 16, 1949, s. Milo Anthony and Dorothy Elizabeth (Mulholland) B.; m. Lynn McClintock, June 6, 1969; children—Aeron Michael, Shawn Mark. Author: The Black Hawk Songs (poetry), 1975, Nana's Ark (novel), 1984, A Different Kind of Love (novel), 1985. BA in English, U. No. Iowa, 1971; MFA in Writing, U. Calif., Irvine, 1979. Lectr. U. Calif., Irvine, 1977-79, U. Wis., Green Bay, 1979-81; instr. Kirkwood Community Coll., Cedar Rapids, Iowa, 1981-84, Broward Community Coll., Ft. Lauderdale, Fla., 1984-85, asst. prof. of commns, Evangel Coll., Springfield, Mo., 1986—. Recipient Books-Across-The-Sea award English Speaking Union, London, 19756. Home: 1415 S. Pickwick Springfield MO 65804

BORIS, ROBERT ELLIOT, (Robert Elliot), b. Salem, MA, July 21, 1947; s. Stanley Henry and Emilie (Czajkowski) B. contrbr. articles to newspapers, mags. including The Boston Globe, The N.Y. Times. Ed.: The Salem Evening News, 1970-71, The Beverly Times, 1971-72, The M.P.A. Sentinel 1973-75; feature ed.: Essex County Newspapers, Beverly, MA, 1971-72; mng. ed.: Eustis News, 1981-85, Tavares Citizen, 1981-85, Mt. Dora Topic, 1981-85. B.A., Boston U., 1969. Producer, WHDH-TV, Boston, 1968-70; producer, dir. WXPO-TV, Lowell, MA, 1970-72; field producer ABC-TV, NYC, 1973-75; pres., producer Media-Arts Assocs., Eustis, 1975—; pres. Central Fla. Broadcasting, Inc. Home: 705 East Key Ave Eustis FL 32726

BORN, EMILY MARIE, b. Lawton, OK, Oct. 2, 1959; d. George Arthur and Sumiko (Nagamine) B. Author: Power to the People: A History of Rural Electrification in Indiana, 1985; feature wrtr.: the News-Sentinel, Fort Wayne, IN, 1981-83. Wire ed.: The Daily Ledger, Noblesville, IN, 1983; staff wrtr., mng. ed., ed.: Electric Consumer, Indpls., 1983—. Wrkg. on editing tabloid mag. for Ind. Statewide Assn. Rural Electric Cooperatives, also communications. Mem. IABC (Silver Quill award of excellence 1985), Cooperative Communicators Assn., Natl. Electric Cooperative Eds. Assn. Office: Assn REC 720 N High Schl Rd Indianapolis IN 46214

BOROWITZ, ALBERT IRA, b. Chgo., June 27, 1930; s. David and Anne (Wolkenstein) B.; m. Helen Blanche Osterman, July 29, 1950; children—Peter Leonard, Joan, Andrew Seth. Author: Fiction in Communist China, 1955, Innocence and Arsenic: Studies in Crime and Literature, 1977, The Woman Who Murdered Black Satin: The Bermondsey Horror, 1981, A Gallery of Sinister Perspectives: Ten Crimes and a Scandal, 1982, The Jack the Ripper Walking Tour Murder, 1986, The Thurtell-Hunt Murder Case: Dark Mirror to Regency England, 1987; contrbr. articles to profl. jnls. BA in Classics (Detur award 1948) summa cum laude, Harvard U., 1951, MA in Chinese Regional Studies, 1953, JD (Sears prize) magna cum laude, 1956. Bar: Ohio 1957. Assoc. firm Hahn, Loeser, Freedheim, Dean & Wellman, Cleve., 1956-62, partner, 1962-83, Jones, Day, Reavis & Pogue, partner, Cleve., 1983—. Recipient Cleve. arts prize for lit., 1981. Mem. Am. Law Inst., Am. Bar Assn., Ohio State Bar Assn., Bar Assn. Greater Cleve. Office: 1700 Huntington Bldg Cleveland OH 44115

BOROWSKY, BEN A., b. Bklyn., Nov. 17, 1930, s. Boris M. and Mina (Zivilik) B.; m. Joan J. Polsky, Oct. 20, 1957; children—Alice, Deborah, Beth. Edn., U. Wis.-Madison, CCNY. Sports ed., mng. ed. Bucks County Courier Times, Levittown, Pa., 1954-71; ed. Burlington County Times, Willingboro, N.J., 1971-77; press secy. Gov.'s Office, Trenton, N.J., 1977; public info. dir. N.J. Casino Control Commn., Trenton, 1978-83; ed., pub. Casino Chronicle, Cherry Hill, NJ, 983—. Home: 1412 Chanticleer Cherry Hill NJ 08003

BORRELLI, PETER R., b. Somerville, MA, Feb. 9, 1943; m. Jane Tomlinson Roberts, Oct. 22, 1967; children—Marcus, Justin. Author poetry collection: Other Minds, 1970; contrbr. poetry to mags, anthols; ed.: The Catskills, Land in the Sky, 1975, The Strip Mining of America, 1971, Energy, 1972, The Catskill Center Plan, 1974, On the Mountain, In the Valley, 1974. Student, Harvard U., 1961-65. Reporter, ed. Berkshire Eagle, Pittsfield, Mass., 1966-67; reporter Springfield (Mass.) Union, 1965-66; corr. Time-Life News Service, Washington, DC, 1967-70; eastern dir. Sierra Club, San Francisco, 1970-73; exec. dir. Catskill Ctr. Conservation and Devel., Arkville, N.Y., 1973-77, 79-81; spcl. asst. N.Y. State Dept. Environment and Conservation, Albany, 1977-79; ed. Amicus Jnl, Natural Resources Defense Council, NYC, 1979—. Home: 20 Vischer Ferry Rd Rexford NY 12148

BORTON, JEANETTE, (Jeanette Aloi Borton), b. Fairmont, WV, July 22, 1948; d. Tony Aloi and Katherine Chickovitch Leary; children—Catherine Elizabeth, Michael D. Contrbr. articles, short stories, poems to mags., newspapers, anthols. Student Cuyahoga Commun. Coll., 1977-78, Inst. Childrens Lit., 1981-82. Ed., wrtr. P.T.A. Newsletter, Bedford, OH, 1978; columnist The Bulltn., Twinsburg, OH, 1978-79; salesperson, wrtr. Blackberry Press, Macedonia, OH, 1985. Mem. Poetry in the Park. Home: 10091 Valley View Rd Macedonia OH 44056

BORUCH, MARIANNE, b. Chgo., June 19, 1950; d. Edward James Boruch and Martha Jeannette (Taylor) Augliera; m. David Leroy Dunlap, Aug. 15, 1976; 1 son, Will Nottingham. Author: View from the Gazebo (poetry), 1985, Descendant, 1988; poetry and essays in Am. Poetry Rvw, Partisan Rvw, Antioch Rvw, The Little Mag., New Letters, others. BS, U. Ill., 1972; MFA, U. Mass., 1979. Lectr. English, Tunghai U., Taichung, Taiwan, 1979-81; instr. English, U. Wis., Madison, 1982-84; artist-in-res. Wis. Arts Bd./Wayland Acad. Beaver Dam, Wis., 1982-83; asst. prof. dept. lang. and lit. U. Maine, Farmington, 1984-87; assoc. prof. Eng., Purdue Univ., 1987—. Individual artist project grantee Wis. Arts Bd., 1983; creative writing fellow in poetry NEA, 1984; Cecil B. Hemley award, PSA, 1986. Mem. AWP, PSA. Home: 415 Maple St West Lafayette IN 47906

BOSS, LAURA, b. NYC, April 20, 1938; d. Leonard D. Ziegler and Sadie (Rakowsky) Vamos; m. Lawrence S. Boss, July 1, 1958 (div. 1980); children—L. Barry, Jeffrey. Author: Stripping, 1982, On the Edge of the Hudson, 1986. BA summa cum laude, Fairleigh Dickinson U., 1975, MA, 198O. Sr. editor, Lunch Mag., Rutherford, NJ, 1977-79; instr., Fairleigh Dickinson U., Rutherford, NJ, 1977-83; instr., Montclair State College, Montclair, NJ, 1984-85; editor-in-chief, Lips Magazine, Montclair, NJ, 1981—. Mem. PSA P&W. Home: 7000 Blvd East Guttenberg NJ 07093

BOSTON, BRUCE, b. Chgo., July 16, 1943; s. John Edmund Joseph and Lillian (Rose) B. Author: Jackbird, 1976, She Comes When You're Leaving, 1982, All The Clocks Are Melting, 1984, Alchemical Texts, 1985, Nuclear Futures, 1987; contrbtr. poetry and fiction to New Words, 1976, Pushcart Prize Anthology, 1976, New York Times Magazine, Isaac Asimov's Science Fiction Magazine, and numerous other mags. and anthologies. BA, U. of California, Berkeley, 1965, MA, 1967. Prof., John F. Kennedy U.. Orinda . Ca.. 1978-82; fiction editor, Berkeley Poets Workshop & Press, 1980-85. Mem. Sci. Fi. Poetry Assoc., SFWA. Home: 1819 9th Street Berkeley CA 94710

BOSTWICK, BURDETTE EDWARDS, b. Washington, Mar. 31, 1908; s. John Wilson and Harriet Caroline (Edwards) B; m. Betty Bannister Brown, Sept. 19, 1936; children—Burdette E., Sherry Bostwick Bishka. Author: Resume Writing: A Comprehensive How-to-do-it Guide, 1974, How to Find the Job You've Always Wanted, 1976, 101 Techniques & Strategies for Getting Interviews, 1978. AA, Rutgers U., 1932, LLB (JD), 1935. First v.p. J. Wiss & Sons Co., Newark, 1927-70; pres. The B. E. Bostwick Co., NYC, 1973-82; writer, 1974—. Home: 292 Short Hills Ave Springfield NJ 07081

BOSWORTH, DAVID, b. Northampton, MA, Mar. 4, 1947; m. Jacqueline Wayne, 1970; 2 sons, Alexander, Gabriel. Author: The Death of Descartes, 1981, From My Father, Singing, 1986; contbr. stories, rvws. to lit mags. AB, Brown U, 1969. Sr. lectr. Univ. Maine, Orono, 1983-84; asst. prof. Univ. Washington, Seattle, 1984—. NEA fellow, 1979, Ingram Merril fellow, 1983; recipient Drue Heinz prize, Univ. Pitts Press. 1981, citation, Ernest Hemingway Fdn. and PEN, 1982, Eds'. Book award Pushcart Press, 1984. Mem. PEN, P&W, AWP. Address: Dept English Univ Washington Seattle WA 98195

BOTSHON, ANN, b. NYC, June 2, 1942; d. Sam and May (Winter) Lichman; m. Richard Botshon, Sept. 27, 1966; children—Lisa, Ellen. Ed., Garden Mag., 1977—. AB, Radcliffe, 1963; MA, U.CA- Berkeley, 1965. Asst. ed. W.A. Benjamin, Inc., NYC, 1966; sci. ed. Columbia U. Press, NYC, 1973-75; medical writer Learning Technology, Inc., Albany, NY, 1975-77; ed. Garden, NY Botanical Garden, NYC, 1977—. Award of achievement, Amer. Assn. of Museums, 1983. Office: NY Botanical Garden Bronx NY 10458

BOTTARI, GEORGE L., b. NYC, Nov. 3, 1919; s. George A. and Johanna (Albonese) B.; m. Nora Nagle, Dec. 28, 1974; stepchildren: Fern, Barbara, Mimi. Author: (novels) Of Mabel and Men, 1952; Off Limits!, 1953; Untamed Passion, 1960; also short stories. Wrkg. on novels. Student Columbia U., 1937-38. Assoc ed., article wrtr. Indsl. Distbn. mag., NYC, 1952-59, advt. sales mgr., 1959-64; dir. sales trng., mgr. classified advt. McGraw-Hill Pub. Co., NYC, 1964-69; v.p. corp. purchasing and graphic arts McGraw-Hill, 1969-82, v.p. corp. resources planning, 1982-84; ret., 1984. Served with AUS, 1942-45; ETO. Mem. Carolina Wrtrs. Guild. Home: 79 Myrtle Bank Rd Hilton Head Island SC 29928

BOTTEL, HELEN ALFEA, b. Beaumont, CA; d. Alpheus Russell and Mary Ellen (Alexander) Brigden; m. Robert E. Bottel; children: Robert Dennis, Rodger M., R. Kathryn bottle Bernhardt, Suzanne V. Bottel Peppers. Author: To Teens With Love, 1969, Helen Help Us, 1970, parents Survival Kit, 1979. A.A., Riverside Coll. Calif.; student, Oreg. State U., 1958-59, So. Oreg. coll., 1959. Editor Illinois Valley News, Cave Junction, Oreg.; writer Grants Pass (Oreg.) Courier, Portland Oregonian, Medford (Oreg.) Mail Tribune, 1952-58; columnist King Features Syndicate, NYC, 1958-83. contbg. editor, columnist, Real World mag., NYC, 1978-84, freelance mag. writer, author, lectr., 1956—; weekly columnist: Yomiuri Shiumbun, Tokyo, 1982—; columnist Sacramento Union, 1986—. 1st place award for books Calif. Press women, 1970; Sacramento Regional Arts Council Lit. Achievement award, 1974. Mem. ASJA, Calif. Writers. Home: 2060 56th Ave Sacramento CA 95822

BOTTIGLIER, JANET ELLEN, b. Lakewood, OH, Feb. 23, 1952; d. Arnold Herman and Lucille (Rollin) Reisland; m. Richard Allen Bottiglier, Apr. 4, 1985. Author poetry: Mountain Harbors, 1985. B.S., U. Wy., 1976. Asst. to dentist, Fairview Park, OH, 1980-85; retailer Castle of Treasures, Lakewood, 1985—. Home: 1588 Lakeland Ave Lakewood OH 44107

BOUCHARD, LYNDA M., b. St. Albans, VT, July 6, 1956; d. L. Paul Bouchard. Author: Poetry, 1978, Public Relations Soc. of Am. Research and Development Handbook, 1982; editor: The Nautilus, 1974-78. BA, Salve Regina Coll., 1978; MS, Boston U., 1982. Public relations asst. WNEV-TV, Boston, 1980-82; flight attendant Piedmont Airlines, Norfolk, Va., 1982—. Publicist Va. Orchestra League, Norfolk, 1982—. Mem. Public Relations Soc. Am., Acad. Motion Pictures and TV Arts and Scis., Sigma Phi Sigma. Address: 2309 Kingbird Ln Virginia Beach VA 23455

BOUDREAU, EDNA MAE, (Edie), b. Chgo., May 29, 1935, d. Julian Clifford and Mae Lucille (Owens) Albright; m. Gordon Joseph Boudreau, June 13, 1953 (div. 1978); children—Cynthia Ann, Tina Marie, Mark Gordon, Brenda Jean, Brett Paul. Author: History of Southern California (5 vol. biography collection), 1964; contrbr. articles to numerous management and general interest publs. Wrkg. on screenplay. AA in English, Orange Coast Coll.; BA in Communications, Calif. State U.-Fullerton. Publs. ed. Ford Aerospace Co., Newport Beach, Calif., 1975—; publs. ed. Gen. Dynamics Co., Pomona, Calif., 1978-82, sr. publs. coordinator in public affairs, ed. employee pubn., 1982—; freelance wrtr., 1978—. Mem. Natl. Mgmt. Assn. (public relations mgr.), Public Relations Soc. Am., Women in Communications (past sec., treas.), Intl. Assn. Bus. Communicators. Home: 13715 Westward Dr Fontana CA 92335

BOUGHAN, THOMAS ROBERT, b. Chinhae, Republic of Korea, Oct. 14, 1953, came to U.S., 1956, naturalized, 1965; s. John Lawrence Arthur and Jong Ae (Yoo) B. Contrbr. poems to antohls. Wrkg. on poems, short stories, novels. B.A. in Anthropology, Mich. State U., 1976. Farm hand Corey Lake Orchards, Three Rivers, MI, 1980; orderly Three Rivers Manor, 1981—. Recipient 3d prize for poem World of Poetry, 1982, Honorable Mention, 1983, Golden Poet award, 1985, Silver Poet award, 1986. Home: 57952 Lockport Dr 106 Three Rivers MI 49093

BOUGHNER, HOWARD ROBERT, b. Cadillac, MI, Dec. 16, 1908; s. Robert Arthur and Emma Gene (Teachout) B.; m. Dorothy Marie Peterson, July 1, 1938. Author: Cartooning Jobs for Beginning Cartoonist, 1952, Posters, 1952, Posters, 1962, Dictionary of Things to Draw, 1979. Contrbr. features to comic books, calendars, children's mags. including Jack & Jill, Treasure Chest, others; games, comml. cartoons. Cert. in Cartooning, Detroit Art Acad. Staff cartoonist Natl. Edn. Assn. Service, Cleve., 1936-46; free-lance wrtr., 1946—. Mem. Natl. Cartoonist Soc. Home: 12525 Edgewater Dr Lakewood OH 44107

BOUNDY, DONNA J., b. Framingham, MA, Dec. 4, 1949: d. Dean M. and Esther M. (Phillips) Boundy. Contrbr. New York Times, 1984-85. BA, U. of CT, 1971; MSW, Hunter College, 1981; student, SUNY, 1983-84; student, New School for Social Res., 1984-85; student, Intl. Center of Photography, 1985. Counselor, Drug Help Inc. Waterbury, CT, 1975-77; asst. dir., Liberation Clinic Drug Program, Stamford, CT, 1977-80; Mental health asst., Einstein College of Med., Bronx, NY, 1980-81, couns., Briarcliff H.S., NY, 1981-85: freelance writer of A/V and other educ. materials, 1984—. Mem. NWU, Intl. Womens Writing Guild. Home: Box 1208 Woodstock NY 12498

BOURASAW, NOEL V., b. Middletown, MO, Aug. 9, 1944; s. Victor and Hazel Kirks B.; m. Terry Rustan, June 22, 1985; 1 dau., Jennifer. Contrbr. Calif. Winelands, Wines of Am., Wine West, Napa Sonoma Rvw, Country Almanac, Redwood City Almanac. BS, W. Wash. U., 1969. Pub. Northwest Wine Almanac, Seattle, 1983—; exec. dir. Wash. Wine Inst., Seattle, 1983-85. Served to Spcl4, US Army, 1963-66, W. Ger. Address: Box 85595 Seattle WA 98145k

BOURDIN, THOMAS FRANCIS, (Courtenay Frank), b. Pass Christian, MS, Nov. 25, 1931; s. William and Alice (Courtenay) B. Contrbr. articles to fin. mags., popular mags. Editor newsletters for Am. Inst. Banking, Pass Christian Yacht Club. Mississippi Gulf Coast rep. Dolphin Pres, Inc. B. Journalism, U. Tex.-Austin, 1959. Advt. officer Hancock Bank, Gulfort, Miss., 1959-85, retired. Mem. Pass Christian Library Assn. (chmn. 1976), Miss. Library Assn. Home: 126 Seal Ave Pass Christian MS 39571

BOURDON, DAVID, b. Glendale, CA, Oct. 15, 1934; s. David Joseph and Marilyn Edythe (Casale) B. Author: Christo, 1972, Carl Andre Sculpture 1959-77, 1978, Calder, 1980; contrbr. Christo: Running Fence, 1979, Christo: Surrounded Islands, 1986; contrbr. articles to numerous mags. BS, Columbia U., 1961. Asst. editor Life mag., NYC, 1966-71; assoc. editor Smithsonian mag., Washington, 1972-74; art critic The Village Voice, NYC, 1964-66, 74-77; sr. ed. Geo, 1981-83; sr. editor Vogue mag., 1983-86. Home: 315 W 23d St Apt 3C New York NY 10011

BOURJAILY, VANCE, b. Cleve., Sept. 17, 1922; s. Monte Ferris and Barbara (Webb) B.; m. Bettina Yensen, 1946; children—Anna (dec.), Philip, Robin. Author: The End of My Life, 1947, The Hound of Earth, 1953, The Violated, 1958, Confessions of a Spent Youth, 1960; (non-fiction) The Unnatural Enemy, 1963; The Man Who Knew Kennedy, 1967, Brill Among the Ruins, 1970; (non-fiction) Country Matters, 1973; Now Playing at Canterbury, 1976, A Game Men Play, 1980. AB, Bowdoin Coll. Newspaperman, TV dramatist, playwright, lectr.; prof. U. Ariz., U. Iowa Writers Workshop, 1958-80; co-founder, editor Discovery, 1951-53. Served with Am. Field Service, 1942-44; served with AUS, 1944-46. Address: Morris Agcy 1350 Ave Ams New York NY 10019

BOURNE, DANIEL CARTER, b. Olney, IL, Mar. 2, 1955; s. Carter Wheeler and Wanda Lea (Umfleet) B.; m. Karen Marie Kovacik, Dec. 10, 1983. Author: Boys Who Go Aloft, 1987. Contrbr. Poems to anthols. Translator poems from Polish in lit mags. Editor: Artful Dodge, 1979—. BA, Indi. U., Bloomington, 1979, MFA, 1987. Mem. Polish Inst. Arts Scis., Phi Beta Kappa. Home: 3441 Franklin Highland IN 46322

BOUVARD, MARGUERITE GUSMAN, b. Trieste, Italy, Jan. 10, 1937; m. Jacques Bouvard, Nov. 25, 1959; children—Pierre Christian, Laurence Anne. Author: Voices From an Island, 1985, Landscape and Exile, 1985, Journeys Over Water, 1982, The Intentional Community Movement: Building a New Moral World, 1975, The Labor Movements in the Common Market, 1972, MA, Harvard, 1960, PhD, 1965; MA, Boston U., 1977. Prof., Regis College, Weston, MA 1966—. Mem. PSA, Women West of Boston. Home: 6 Brookfield Circle Wellesley MA 02181

BOVOSO, CAROLE IONE LEWIS, b. Washington, May 28, 1937; d. Hylan Garnet Lewis and Leighla (Whipper) Ford; divorced; children: Alessandro, Snaiago, Antonio. Author: The Coffee Table Lover, 1976; Piramida Negra, 1983; Private Pages: American Womens Journals 1830s-1970s, 1986. Bennington Coll., 1959. Ed., pub., Letters Mag., 1974—; contrbg. ed. Essence Mag., 1981-83; poet-in-residence N.Y. State

Poets in Schls. dir. wrtrs. in performance series Manhattan Theatres Club, 1985—. S.C. Humanities Commn. grantee, 1984; fellow Edward Albee Found., 1985, Brookdale Ctr., CUNY, 1985, MacDowell Fdn., 1986. Home: HC 2 Box 81 Olive Bridge NY 12461

BOWART, WALTER HOWARD, (Tom Kirby, A Kalid Rah, Maxwell Riddle, Carolyn Cahones), b. Omaha, May 14, 1939; s. Walter Herman and Fenna Jeanne (Wheeler) B.; m. Peggy Mellon Hitchcock, Dec. 31, 1969 (div. 1978); children—Wolfe, Sophia, Nuria; m. 2d, Rebecca Suzanne Fullerton, Nov. 24, 1983; 1 son, Wythe Kalan Bowart. Author: Essential Changes, 1972, The High Way, 1973, Deck of Changes, 1973, Women's Lip, 1974, Operation Mind Control, 1978; ed. pubns.: Aspen Daily News, 1981, Port Townsend Daily News, 1982, Palm Springs Life, 1983—, Indio Mag., Palm Desert Mag., Guestlife Series. Student, Oklahoma U., New School for Soc. Research. Ed.-in-chief/fdr. The East Village Other, NYC, 1965-68; ed./pub. Omen Press, Tucson, 1970-74; mng. ed. Aspen Daily News (CO), 1981; ed Port Townsend Daily News (WA), 1982-83, Desert Pubns., Inc., Palm Springs, CA, 1983—. Mem. Desert Press Club, So. CA Writer's Conf. Office: Desert Pub 303 N Indian Ave Palm Springs CA 92262

BOWDEN, JESSE EARLE, b. Altha, FL, Sept. 12, 1928; s. Jesse Walden and Earline (Rackley) B.; m. Mary Louise Clark, Feb. 4, 1951; children: Steven Earle, Randall Clark. Author: Always the Rivers Flow, 1979, Iron Hores in the Pinelands, 1982. Reporter, columnist Panama city (Fla.) News-Herald, 1950; sports editor Pensacola (Fla.) News-Jour., 1953-57, news editor, 1957-65, editorial page editor, 1965-66, editorial cartoonist, 1965—, editor-in-chief, 1966—; prof. journalist U. West Fla. B.S. in Journalism and Polit. Sci. Fla. State U., 1951; D.H.L., U. West Fla., 1985. Served to capt. USAF, 1951-53. Natl. award editorial writing Freedoms Fdn. at Valley Forge, 1967, 68, 69, 70, 72, 74; awards for editorials and cartoons, 1967, 68, 69, 72; U. West Fla. Found. fellow, 1982. Mem. ASNE, Natl. Conf. Editorial Writers, Fla. Soc. Newspaper Editors (pres. 1970). Home: 3725 Bonner Rd Pensacola FL 32503

BOWERSOCK, GLEN WARREN, b. Providence, Jan. 12, 1936; s. Donald Curtis and Josephine (Evans) B. Author: Augustus and the Greek World, 1965, Pseudo-Xenophon, Constitution of the Athenians, 1968, Greek Sophists in the Roman Empire, 1969, Julian the Apostate, 1978, Roman Arabia, 1983; editor: Philostratus' Life of Apollonius, 1970, Approaches to the Second Sophistic, 1974, (with J. Clive, S. Graubard) Edward Gibbons and the Decline and Fall of the Roman Empire, 1977. AB, Harvard U., 1957; BA, Oxford U., Eng., 1959 and DPhil, 1962. Lectr. ancient history Oxford U., 1960-62, vis. lectr., 1966; instr. Harvard U., 1962-64, asst. prof., 1964-67, assoc. prof. classics, 1967-69, prof. Greek and Latin, 1969-80; chmn dept classics, 1972-77, assoc. dean faculty arts and scis., 1977-80; prof. hist. studies Inst. Advanced Study, Princeton, N.J., 1980—; sr. fellow Center for Hellenic Studies, Washington, 1976—; syndic Harvard U. Press, 1977-81. Rhodes scholar, 1957-60. Fellow Am. Acad. Arts and Scis., Am. Numis. Soc.; mem. Am Philol. Assn., Archeol. Inst. Am., Leschetizky Assn. Am., Soc. Promotion Roman and Hellenic Studies, German Archaeol. Inst., The Johnsonians, Phi Beta Kappa Office: Inst Adv Study Princeton NJ 08540

BOWKETT, GERALD EDSON, b. Sacramento, Sept. 6, 1926; s. HArry Stephen and Jessie (Fairbrother) B.; m. Norma Orel Swain, Jan. 1, 1953; children: Amanda Allyn, Laura Anne. Radio wire editor UP, Washington, 1956-57; reporter, columnist Anchorage Daily Times, 1957-64; spl. asst., press sec. to Gov. William A. Egan, 1964-66; pub. Alaska Newsletter, 1966-68; juneau bur. chief Anchorage Daily News, 1967-68; editor S.E. Alaska Empire, Juneau, 1969-71; mgr. news sservice U. Alaska, 1971-82. B.A., San Francisco State Coll., 1952; post-grad., Georgetown U., 1954. Served with USMC, 1944-46, PTO. Cited for outstanding news and feature writing, editorial works Alaska Press Club, 1962, 64, 73, 77, 79. Address: Box 80666 Fairbanks AK 99708

BOWLES, PAUL, b. NYC, Dec. 30, 1910; s. Claude Dietz and Rena (Winnewisser) B.; m. Jane Sydney Auer, Feb. 1938. Author: poetry: Two Poems, 1933, Scenes, 1968, The Thicket of Spring: Poems, 1926-69, 1972, Next to Nothing, 1976; novels: The Sheltering Sky, 1948, Let It Come Down, 1952, The Spider's House, 1956, Up Above the World, 1966; Without Stopping, An Autobiography, 1972; travel essays: Yallah, 1957, Their Heads Are Green and Their Hands Are Blue, 1963; stories: The Delicate Prey, 1950, A Little Stone, 1956, The Hours After Noon, 1959, A Hundred Camels in the Courtyard, 1962, The Time of Friendship, 1967, Pages from Cold Point, 1968, Three Tales, 1975, Things Gone and Things Still Here, 1977, Collected Stories, 1939-1976, 1979, Midnight Mass, 1983, Points in Time, 1984; translations: from the French, Jean-Paul Sartre, No Exit, 1946, Isabelle Eberhardt, The Oblivion Seekers, 1975; from Maghrebi: Driss ben Hamed Charhadi, A Life Full of Holes, Mohammed Mrabet, 1963, Love with a Few Hairs, 1967, The Lemon, 1969, M'Hashish, 1969, The Boy Who Set the Fire, 1974, Hadidan Aharam, 1975, Look and Move On, 1976, Harmless Poisons, Blameless Sins, 1976, The Big Mirror, 1977, The Beach Cafe, 1980, The Chest, 1983, Marriage with Papers, 1986. Composer: mus. scores for Roots in the Earth, for Soil Conservation Service, U.S. Dept. Agr., Watch on The Rhine, Jacobowsky and the Colonel, The Glass Menagerie, Cyrano de Bergerac, Summer and Smoke, In the Summer House, Yerma, Sweet Bird of Youth, The Milk Train Doesn't Stop Here Any More; ballets Sentimental Colloquy, Yankee Clipper, 1936, Pastorela, 1941; opera The Wind Remains. Student at U. of Va.; studied with Aaron Copland, NYC, Berlin, 1930-32; with Virgil Thomson, Paris, 1933-34. Guggenheim fellow, 1941; Rockefeller grantee, 1959. Address: c/o Wm Morris Agcy 1350 Ave of the Americas New York NY 10019

BOWMAN, BOB, b. Anderson County, TX, June 3, 1936, s. Elvis Weldon and Annie Mae (Milligan) B.; m. Doris Fay Shaddock, Feb. 14, 1958; children—Neil, Jimmy. Author: This Was East Texas, 1966, The Towns We Left Behind, 1972, They Left No Monuments, 1975, The Best of East Texas, 1978, If I Tell You A Hen Dips Snuff, 1981, The Lufkin That Was, 1982, The Best of East Texas II, 1983, Say . . . Do You Know A Good Place to Eat?, 1984, I Ain't Sure I Understand Everything I Know About This, 1985, The Best of East Texas III, 1986; ed.: Land of the Little Angel, 1976. Ed. Tyler (Tex.) Jr. Coll. Wrtr. Tyler Courier-Times, 1955-57; city ed. Lufkin (Tex.) News, 1957-62; bur. chief Houston Chronicle, 1962-66; mgr. public relations Southland Paper Co., Lufkin, 1966-77; southwest public relations mgr. St. Regis Paper Co., Lufkin, 1977-82; corp. communications mgr. DeltaUS Corp., Tyler, 1982-85; pres. Bob Bowman & Assocs., Lufkin, 1985—. Mem. Public Relations Soc. Am., Am. Mktg. Assn. Office: 400 S 1st St Lufkin TX 75901

BOWMAN, JAMES HENRY, b. Chgo., Dec. 29, 1931, s. Paul Clarke and Kathryn (O'Connell) B.; m. Winifred Marie Moore, July 12, 1969; children—Angela, Katie, Maggie, James Henry Jr., Peter, Marietta. Author: What A Modern Catholic Believes About Prayer, 1971; Booz, Allen & Hamilton (a history), 1984, More Than a Coffee Company: The Story of CFS Continental, 1986, Good Medicine: The First 150 Years of Rush-Presbyterian-St. Luke's Medical Center, 1987. Wrkg. on corp. histories. AB, Loyola U., Chgo., 1955, MA, 1961; PhL, Loyola U., West Baden, Ind., 1957, STL, 1964. Member Jesuit Order, 1950-68. Reporter Chgo. Daily News, 1968-78; freelance wrtr., 1978—. Recipient Best Fiction for Young People short story award Catholic Press Assn., 1962. Mem. Soc. Midland Authors, Chicago Press Veterans. Address: 220 N. Harvey Oak Park IL 60302

BOWMAN, MARY ANN, b. Crawfordsville, IN, Aug. 15, 1940; d. David and Mary (Lindley) Wells; m. Joel P. Bowman, July 26, 1962; 1 child, Joel David. Author: Books on Business Writing and Technical Writing in the University of Illinois Library, 1975; Western Mysticism: A Guide to the Basic Works, 1978; Library and Information Science Journals and Serials: An Analytical Guide, 1985; co-author: Written Communication in Business: An Annotated Bibliography, 1977. BA, Coll. of Wooster, 1961; MLS, UCLA, 1963; MA, Western Mich. U., 1979. Bibliographer U. Ill., Urbana, 1969-70, gift and exchange librarian, 1970-74; reference librarian U. Fla., Gainesville, 1974-75; vis. prof. Sch. Librarianship, Western Mich. U., Kalamazoo, 1976-77, instr. dept. communication, 1979—. Mem. AAUP. Home: 2317 Outlook St Kalamazoo MI 49001

BOWSER, JAMES WILLIAM, b. Indiana, PA, Jan. 16, 1929; s. Kenneth William and Thelma Byrd (Smith) B.; m. Dorothy Messing, Aug. 7, 1971. Author: Doomsday Vendett, 1968, The Glass Cypher, 1968, Death of the Falcon, 1974, A High Yield in Death, 1976, Starring Elvis, 1977, No Sanctuary, 1987. Reporter Johnstown (Pa.) Tribune-Democrat, 1947-54; editor Dell Pub. co. Inc., N.Y.C., 1956-79; editorial dir. Bonomo PUbls., Inc., N.Y.C., 1980-81; editorial/publs. cons., 1981—. Mem. Soc. Profl. Journalists. Address: Rivercross Roosevelt Island New York NY 10044

BOYARSKY, BENJAMIN WILLIAM, b. Berkeley, CA, Oct. 21, 1934; s. Herman and Naomi (Heimy) B.; m. Nancy Elaine Belling, July 21, 1956; children—Robin Ann, Jennifer Lynn. Author: The Rise of Ronald Reagan: Backroom Politics, 1974, (with wife) Ronald Reagan: His Life and Rise to the Presidency, 1981. AB, U. Calif. at Berkeley, 1956. Copy boy, reporter Oakland (Calif.) Tribune, 1953-60; reporter, editor AP, San Francisco, 1960, Sacramento, 1960-70; pol. writer Los Angeles Times, 1970-75, natl. pol. writer, Washington, 1975-76, writer met. staff, 1976-78; chief city-county bur., 1978—. Office: LA Times Times Mirror Sq Los Angeles CA 90012

BOYCE, WAYNE, b. Tuckerman, AR, June 20, 1926; s. Edward Wayne and Sylla Jo (Harvey) B.; m. Phyllis Elayne Williams, Oct. 29, 1951; children—Martha Elayne B. Zellmer, Edward Wayne. Ed.: The Stream of HIstory, 1981—.

J.D., 1951. Lawyer, Boyce & Boyce, Newport, AR; vice chmn. edn. bd. Law Notes for Gen. Practice, 1968-78. Trustee, Epscpal Theol. Seminary of Southwest, Austin, TX, 1985—, Bd. Dirs. Baptist Med. Ctr. Fdn., Little Rock, 1983—. Served with U.S. Army, 1944-47. Fellow Ark. Bar Fdn.; mem. Southern Conf. Bar Pres., Am. Law Inst., ABA, Ark. Bar Assn. (pres. 1978-79). Home: 7 Pickens St Newport AR 72112

BOYD, CATHERINE EMMA, (K. T. Boyd), b. Dixon, IL, Jan. 24, 1918; d. Carl Albert and Regina Barbara (Haas) Buchner; m. Allan J. Boyd, Oct. 12, 1940 (div. 1964); children—James A., Barbara M. Author: ATR, Airline Transport Pilot, 1969, ATP, Airline Transport Pilot, 1970, 3d ed., 1988, Weather or Not, A Pilot's Eye View of Weather (citation Aviation/Space Wrtrs. Assn. 1976), 1975, ATP-FAR 135, Airline Transport Pilot, 1983. Contrbr. articles to mag., newspapers. B.A., MacMurray Coll,. 1939; postgrad. Northern Ill. U. Dir. course devel. Accelerated Ground Schls., Atlanta, 1973-81, Traveling Aviation Seminars, Columbus, OH, 1981-83; asst. to pres. Olentangy Assocs., Columbus, 1983—. Mem. NLAPW (treas. Columbus br.), Aviation/Space Wrtrs. Assn. Home: 1301 Old Henderson Rd Columbus OH 43220

BOYD, MALCOLM, b. Buffalo, June 8, 1923; s. Melville and Beatrice (Lowrie) B. Author: Crisis in Communication, 1957, Are You Running with Me, Jesus?, 1965, Free to Live, Free to Die, 1967, Book of Days, 1968, As I Live and Breathe: Stages of an Autobiography, 1969, The Fantasy Worlds of Peter Stone, 1970, Human Like Me, Jesus, 1971, The Lover, 1972, When in the Course of Human Events, 1973, The Runner, 1974, The Alleluia Affair, 1975, Christian, 1975, Am I Running with You, God?, 1977, Take Off the Masks, 1978, Look Back in Joy, 1981, Half Laughing/Half Crying, 1986, Gay Priest: An Inner Journey, 1986, Are You Running with Me, Jesus? II, 1987; plays Boy, 1961, Study in Color, 1962, the Community, 1964; editor: On the Battle Lines, 1964, The Underground Church, 1968; contrbr. Gay Spirit: Myth and Meaning, 1987; book reviewer: Los Angeles Times; contrbr.: articles to numerous magazines and newspapers. BA, Univ. Ariz., 1944; BD, Ch. Div. Schl. Pacific, 1954; postgrad., Oxford (Eng.) U., 1955; STM, Union Theol. Sem., NYC, 1956. Vice pres., gen. mgr. Pickford, Rogers & Boyd, 1949-51; ordained to ministry Episcopal Ch., 1955; rector in Indpls., 1957-59; chaplain Colo. State U., 1959-61, Wayne State U., 1961-65; natl. field rep. Episcopal Soc. Cultural and Racial Unity, 1965-68; resident fellow Calhoun Coll., Yale U., 1968-71, assoc. fellow, 1971—; writer-priest-in-res. St. Augustine-by-the-Sea Episcopal Ch., 1982—; dir. Institute of Gay Spirituality and Theology, 1987—; Theology, 1987—≤ctr. World Council Chs., Switzerland, 1955, 64; columnist Pittsburg Courier, 1962-65; resident guest Mishkenot Sha'ananim, Jerusalem, 1974. Active voter registration, Miss., Ala., 1963, 64. Malcolm Boyd Collection and Archives established Boston U., 1973; recipient Integrity Intl. award, 1978; Union Am. Hebrew Congregations award, 1980. Mem. Natl. Council Chs., PEN (pres. chpt. 1984-87), Los Angeles Center, AG, Integrity, Natl. Gay Task Force, Fellowship of Reconciliation (natl. comm.), Clergy and Laity Concerned (natl. bd.), NAACP, Episc. Peace Fellowship, Los Angeles City/County AIDS Task Force. Address: 1227 4th St Santa Monica CA 90401

BOYETTE, IVERN, see Ball, Ivern Imogene

BOYLAN, ROGER BRENDAN, b. Miami, FL, July 20, 1951, s. E. B. and E. R. Boylan. Translator: Great Mysteries of Lost Treasures, 1978, Sumer: The First Great Civilization (by Amar Hamdani), 1980; short stories in lit mags. Student U. Ulster, Northern Ireland, 1971-72; BA with honors Edinburgh (Scotland) U., 1976. Copy ed., translator Gotham Lit. Agcy., 1978-81; freelance translator, wrtr., 1981-85; lang. instr. Natl. Inst. Lang., 1985—. Mem. Am.-Irish Hist. Soc. Home: 211 E 14th St New York NY 10003

BOYLE, JOHN DAVID, b. NYC,May 22, 1946, s. John Joseph and Alice Elizebeth (Davies) B.; m. Cynthia McCoy, June 17, 1967; 1 son, Christopher Stephen. Co-author: History of the Sacramento Police Department, 1983; contrbr. articles to Eagle, Grit, Police Product News, Sacramento Sports, numerous other publs. AA, Am. River Coll., Sacramento, 1971; BA, Calif. State U., Sacramento, 1974. Sergeant, speechwrtr. Sacramento Police Dept., 1971—. Served as sgt. U.S. Army, 1965-68; Vietnam. Mem. Calif. Wrtrs. Club. Home: 6849 Thunderhead Circle Orangevale CA 95662

BOYLE, JOHN E. WHITEFORD, (Whiteford) Vanderbylt), b. Milw., Mar. 8, 1915, s. Hermann Edward Whiteford and Margaret Lauretta (Casey) B., m. Renee Kent Colin, Feb. 2, 1950; children—Vanessa V. Whiteford Boyle Wayne, Christopher Whiteford, Andrea Renee Boyle Heller, Mara Alexandra. Author: Beyond the Present Prospect: The Impact of the XXth Century Revolutions in Science on the Varieties of Religious Experience, 1977, The Indra Web: The Renewal of Ancient Oriental Concepts in Modern Western Thought, 1983, Graffiti on the Wall of Time: Thirty Poems Celebrating the Triumph of Western Heresy. PhB, Marquette U., 1937; MA, Harvard, 1947; Licencie en Arts et Lettres, Persanes Institut Franco-Iranien U. Tehran, 1961. Wrtr. Hearst Mags., NYC, 1937-38; ed. Chesterton (Ind.) Tribune, 1938; wrtr. Milw. Jnl., 1938-40; exec. officer and agt. CIA, Washington, Germany, Iran and Tunisia, 1947-67; pres. Fgn. Services Research Inst., Washington, 1974—. Mem. Acad. Ind. Scholars (v.p. 1983—). Office: Box 0317 Washington DC 20015

BOYLE, KAY, b. St. Paul, MN, Feb. 19, 1903; d. Howard Peyton and Katherine (Evans) B.; m. Richard Brault, June 24, 1923 (div.); m. Laurence Vail, Apr. 2, 1931 (div.); m. Baron Joseph von Franckenstein (dec. 1963); children—Sharon Walsh, Apple-Joan, Kathe, Clover, Faith Carson, Ian Savin. Author: short stories, Wedding Day, 1930, Plagued by the Nightingale, 1930; novels Year Before Last, 1932, Gentlemen I Address You Privately, 1933, My Next Bride, 1933, Death of a Man, 1936; short stories The White Horses of Vienna, 1936; novel Monday Night; three short novels The Crazy Hunter, 1938; poems A Glad Day, 1938; novels Primer for Combat, 1942, Avalanche, 1944; poem American Citizen, 1944; novel, a Frenchman Must Die, 1946; Thirty Stories, 1946; novels 1939, 1947, His Human Majesty, 1949; short stories The Smoking Mountain, 1951; novels The Seagull on the Step, 1955, Three Short Novels, 1957, The Youngest Camel, 1959, Generation without Farewell, 1960; Collected Poems, 1962; Breaking the Silence, 1962; short stories Nothing Ever Breaks Except the Heart, 1966; juvenile Pinky the Cat Who Liked to Sleep, 1966; edited The Autobiography of Emanuel Carnevali, 1967; memoirs (with Robert McAlmon) Being Geniuses Together, 1968; juvenile Pinky in Persia, 1968; poems Testament for My Students, 1970; essays The Long Walk at San Francisco State, 1970; novel The Underground Woman, 1970, Fifty Stories, 1980; poems This Is Not a Letter, 1985; essays Words That Somehow Must Be Said, 1985. Contrbr. short stories to mags. Student, Ohio Mechanics Inst., 1917-19. Mem. faculty San Francisco State U. Recipient O. Henry Meml. prize, 1936, 41; San Francisco Art Commn. award, 1978; Guggenheim fellow, 1934, 61; NEA sr. citizen grantee, 1980. Mem. Am. Acad. Arts and Letters. Address: Watkins-Loomis 150 E 35 St New York NY 10016

BOYLES-SPRENKEL, CAROLEE ANITA, b. Hollywood, Fl, May. 15, 1953; d. William J. and Marjorie Faye (Smith) Boyles; m. Richard K. Sprenkel, Jan. 25, 1981. contrbr. articles to mags. including The Fla. Naturalist, Fla. Wildlife, Fla. Grower & Rancher. B.S. in Biology, Fla. State U., 1975; M. Forest Resources and Conservation, U. Fla., 1978. Adj. asst. Fla. 4-H Dept., Gainesville, 1975-76, 78-81; host WFSU-TV, Tallahassee, 1982, 84; free-lance wrtr., 1981—. Treas., Wetumpka Area Vol. Fire Dept., Quincy, FL, 1987. Mem. Tallahasse Wrtrs. Assn. (pres.), Fla. OWAA. Home: Rt 3 Box 2180 Quincy FL 32351

BOYLSTON, SAMUEL LIONEL, b. Springfield, SC, May 8, 1923; s. Raymond Powell and Lillie (Boylston) B.; children—Norma Cheatham Brown, Robin Cheatham Caldwell. Ed., Motor Transportation Hi-Lights, 1963—; author From Horses to Horsepower, 1982. LLP, U.SC, 1950. Lawyer, Springfield, SC, 1950-56; dir. SC Warehouse Div., Columbia, 1956-61; self-employed, Columbia, 1961-62; ex. v.p. Motor Transp. Assn. of SC, Inc., Columbia, 1963—. Mem. S.C. General Assembly, 1951-56. Office: Box 50166 Columbia SC 29250

BOZZA, LINDA SUSAN, b. NYC, Dec. 9, 1949, d. Abraham and Loraine (Aunkofsky) Serebransky; m. John Anthony Bozza, Sept. 16, 1972; children—Ilyssa, Michael. Contrbr. to Newsletter of Poetry, Entrepreneur, East Northport Voice, Choices, others. BA, SUNY-Albany, 1971; MA, NYU, 1972. Rehab. counselor Human Resources Center, Albertson, N.Y., 1972-75, cons., 1975-78; freelance wrtr., 1975—. feature wrtr. East Northport (N.Y.) Voice, 1985—. Cultural arts coordinator Fifth Ave. Schl., East Northport, 1984—. Home: 3410 Beech Trail Clearwater FL 33519

BRABEC, BARBARA, b. Buckley, IL, Mar. 5, 1937, d. William Jonas and Marcella Eliza (Williams) Schaumburg; m. Harry J. Brabec, Aug. 15, 1961. Author: Creative Cash—How to Sell Your Crafts, Needlework, Designs and Know-How, 1979, rev. ed., 1986; The Handcrafts Business, 1981; Homemade Money—The Definitive Guide to Success in a Home Business, 1984, rev. ed., 1987; Crafts Marketing Success Secrets, 1986; contrbr. Women Working Home, 1983, The Complete Guide to Writing Nonfiction, 1983; columnist Crafts mag., 1979—. Student public schls., Buckley (Ill.). Pub., ed. Artisan Crafts mag., 1971-76, Guide to the Craft World, 1974-75, Craftspirit '76, 1976; pub., gen. mgr. book div. Barrington (Ill.) Press, Inc., 1979-81; pub. Natl. Home Bus. Report (formerly Sharing Barbara's Mail), Naperville, Ill., 1981—. Mem. ASJA, NWC. Home: Box 2137 Naperville IL 60565

BRACKEN, JEANNE MUNN, b. Poughkeepsie, NY, Apr. 15, 1946; d. Richard Earl and Laura (Prentice) Munn; m. Raymond Ronald Braken, May 16, 1970; children—Lisa Jeanne, Mollie Howland. Columnist, contrbr. Beacon Communications, Acton, MA, 1979—; author: children with Cancer: A Comprehensive Reference Guide for Parents, 1986. Contrbr. articles, short stories to mags., newspapers including Working Mother, Denver Post, Boston Globe, others. B.A., U.N.H., 1968; M.S. in Library Sci., Simmons Coll., 1971. Research librarian Arthur D. Little, Inc., Cambridge, MA, 1969-76; asst. reference librarian Acton Meml. Library, 1978—; free-lance wrtr., 1980—. Trustee Reuben Hoar Library, Littleton, MA, 1981-84. Recipient Excellence in Cancer Communications award Am. Cancer So., 1981, Best Editorial award Mass. Press Assn., awards for columns, feature stories New England Press Assn., 1985, 86. Mem. SCBW (assoc.). Home: 305 Goldsmith St Littleton MA 01460

BRADBURY, RAY DOUGLAS, b. Waukegan, IL, Aug. 22, 1920; s. Leonard Spaulding and Esther Marie (Moberg) B.; m. Margueurite Susan McClure, Sept. 27, 1947; children—Susan Marguerite, Ramona, Bettina, Alexandra. Author: Dark Carnival, 1947, The Martian Chronicles, 1950, also screenplay, 1964; The Illustrated Man, 1951, The Golden Apples of the Sun, 1953, Fahrenheit 451, 1953; play The Meadow, 1947; screenplay Moby Dick, 1954; juvenile Switch on the Night, 1955; The October Country, 1955, Dandelion Wine, 1957, A Medicine for Melancholy, 1959; screenplay Icarus Montgolfier Wright, 1961; stories R Is for Rocket S Is for Space, 1962; novel Something Wicked This Way Comes, 1962; plays The Anthem Sprinters, 1962, The Machineries of Joy, 1963; The World of Ray Bradbury, 1965; stories The Vintage Bradbury, 1965, The Autumn People, 1965; play The Wonderful Ice Cream Suit, 1965; paperback edit Tomorrow Midnight, 1966; illus. stories Twice Twenty-Two, 1966; radio drama Leviathan '99, 1966; screenplays The Picasso Summer, 1968, The Halloween Tree, 1968; play Any Friend of Nicholas Nickleby's is a Friend of Mine, 1968; stories I Sing The Body Electric, 1969; The Small Assassin, 1973; Mars and the Minds of Man, 1973, Zen and the Art of Writing, 1973; poems When Elephants Last in the Dooryard Bloomed, 1973; play Pillar of Fire, 1975; Long After Midnight, 1976, Where Robot Mice and Robot Men Run Round in Robot Towns, 1977, The Mummies of Guanajuato, 1978, The Stories of Ray Bradbury, 1980, About Norman Corwin, 1980, The Last Circus, 1980; poems The Haunted Computer and the Android Pope, 1981; The Ghosts of Forever, 1981; others; prodns. one act plays, Royal Shakespeare Festival Theatre, The Pandemonium Theatre Co., 1963. Student pub. schls. Mem. Screen Writers Guild, Sci. Fantasy Writers Am., Pacific Art Fdn., WG Am. (mem. screen writers bd.) Address: Bantam Bks 666 5th Ave New York NY 10103

BRADEN, DENNIS RAY, b. Los Angeles, Nov. 10, 1949, s. Ray Christopher and Opal Virginia (Gile) B.; m. Jill Jeanette Braden, Dec. 19, 1970. Author: (chapbook) In Things Completed, 1986; contrbr. poems to Epos, Nova, Colo.-North Rvw, Your Own Poets, Dacotah Territory, Sojourners, Limberlost Rvw, Broken Streets, others; ed. Colo.-North Rvw, 1975-76, Poetry-North Rvw, 1978-80. BA, U. No. Colo., 1976; MA, U. Colo., 1980. Resident in writing Edward F. Albee Fdn., 1984. Mem. AWP. Home: 212 Croyden Ave Rockville MD 20850

BRADFORD, MARJORIE ODELL, (Gigi), b. Frankfurt, W.Ger., July 14, 1952 (arrvd. USA 1953), d. Joseph Odell and Alison (Kimball) B.; m. James J. Stanford, July 11, 1982; 1 child, Cynthia Miller. BA, Trinity Coll., Hartford, Conn., 1974; MFA, U. Iowa, 1980. Exec. dir. AAP, NYC, 1981-82; dir. poetry programs Folger Shakespeare Library, Washington, 1984—; adj. prof. U. Va.; bd. dirs. Poetry Com. for Greater Washington Area, 1985—. Mem. AAP. Office: Folger Sh Library 201 E Capitol St SE Washington DC 20003

BRADFORD, RICHARD ROARK, b. Chgo., May 1, 1932; s. Roark and Mary Rose (Sciarra) B.; m. Julie Dollard, Sept. 15, 1956 (div.); 1 son Thomas Conway; m. Lee Head, June 25, 1977. Author: Red Sky at Morning, 1968, So Far from Heaven, 1973. BA, Tulane U., 1952; D. Litt., N. Mex State U., 1979. Staff Writer, editor N.M. Tourist Bur., 1965-69, New Orleans C. of c., 1959-61, Zia Co., Los Alamos, 1963-65; research analyst N. M. Dept. Devel., 1967-68; screen-writer Universal PIctures, 1968-70. Served with USMC, 1953-56. Mem. Edouard Manet Soc., Sigma Chi, Quien Sabe (Santa Fe). Home: Box 1395 Santa Fe MN 87501

BRADLEE, BENJAMIN CROWNINSHIELD, b. Boston, Aug. 26, 1921; s. Frederick J. and Josephine (deGersdorff) B.; m. Jean Saltonstall, Aug. 8, 1942; 1 son, Benjamin Crowninshield; m. Antoinette Pinchot, July 6, 1956; children: Dominic, Marina; m. Sally Quinn, Oct. 20, 1978; 1 son, Quinn. Author: That Special Grace, 1964, Conversations with Kennedy, 1975. A.B., Harvard U., 1943. Reporter N.H. Sunday News, Manchester, 1946-48, Washington Post, 1948-51; press attache embassy, Paris, France, 1951-53; European corr. Newsweek mag., Paris, 1953-57, reporter Washington bur., 1957-61, sr. editor, chief bur., 1961-65; mng. editor Washington Post, 1965-68, v.p., exec. editor, 1968—. Served to lt. USNR, 1942-45. Home: 3014 N St NW Washington DC 20007

BRADLEY, DAVID HENRY, JR., b. Bedford, PA, Sept. 7, 1950, s. David Henry and Harriette (Jackson) B. Author: South Street, 1975, The Chaneysville Incident, 1981; contr. to: While Someone Else Is Eating, 1980, In Praise of What Persists, 1983, From Mt. San Angelo, 1984, Our Roots Grow Deeper than We Know, 1986. BA in Creative Writing, U. Pa., 1972; MA in U.S. Studies, U. London, 1974. Asst. ed. trade books J.B. Lippincott Co., Phila. and NYC, 1974-76; asst. prof. English, Temple U., Phila., 1976-80, assoc. prof., 1980—. Recipient Acad. award AAIAL, 1982, Faulkner award, 1982. Mem. WG, PEN/Faulkner. Home: 759-B Noth Ringgoll St Philadelphia PA 19130

BRADLEY, FLORENCE FRANCES, b. Phila., May 13, 1934; d. James Francis Sr. and Florence Anna (Eder) Ryan; m. James Howard Bradley, Jan. 28, 1956; children: Kathleen, James Jr. (Brad), Susan Anni, Scott, Penny, Patti. Compiler, editor: (poetry anthology) Best of the Editor's Desk; past editor Atlantic City ed. Where mag.; compiler, pub., 7 poetry anthologies; writer, pub. monthly writer's mag. BA, Atlantic Community Coll., N.J. Freelance writer, 1956—; reporter/photographer Atlantic City Press, 1971-76; editor-in-chief Editor's Desk, Ocala, Fla., 1982—. Pres. Editor's Desk Writer's Orgn., Ocala, 1985-86; past pres. Women's Council Realtors, Ocala, 1982-83. Home: 709 SE 52nd Ave Ocala FL 32671

BRADLEY, MARION ZIMMER, b. Albany, NY, June 3, 1930; d. Leslie Raymond and Evelyn Parkhurst (Conklin) Zimmer; m. Robert Alden Bradley, Oct. 1949; 1 son, David Stephen Robert; m. Walter Breen, Feb. 14, 1964; children—Patrick Russell Donald, Moira Evelyn Dorothy. Author: (Darkover novels) Planet Savers, 1962, The Sword of Aldones, 1962, The Bloody Sun, 1964, The Winds of Darkover, 1970, The World Wreckers, 1971, Darkover Landfall, 1972, The Spell Sword, 1972, The Heritage of Hastur, 1975, The Shattered Chain, 1976, The Forbidden Tower, 1977, Stormqueen, 1978, The Bloody Sun (rewrite), 1979, Two to Conquer, 1980, The Keeper's Price, 1980, Sharra's Exile, 1981, Sword of Chaos, 1982, Hawkmistress, 1982, Thendara House, 1983, City of Sorcery, 1984, (other sci. fiction, anthologies, gothics); (mainstream novels) The Catch Trap, 1979, The Mists of Avalon, 1983. BA, Hardin Simmons U., 1964; postgrad., U. Calif.-Berkeley, 1965-67. Home: Box 352 Berkeley CA 94701

BRADY, DAN PHILLIP, (T.W. Tell); b. NYC, Aug. 16, 1952; s. Charles and Thelma (Belloumoni) B. Author: (chapbook) In Twilight, the Rising Moon, 1979, Cast the LIne, 1980. contrbr. poems to lit. mags., anthols. Ed.: Enclosed Broadside, 1978. Wrkg. on sci. fiction short stories, poetry, study of conversation as an art. B.A., San Francisco State U., 1973. Home: 425 Irving St San Francisco CA 94122

BRADY, FRANK R, b. Bklyn., Mar. 15, 1934; s. James Joseph and Beatrice Adele (Mignery) B.; m. Maxine Kalfus, Mar. 31, 1963; children—(from 1st marriage) Sean, Erin. Author: Chess: How to Improve Your Technique, 1973, Profile of a Prodigy, 1973, Hefner, 1974, Onassis, 1977, Favorite Bookstores, 1978, Streisand, 1979, Orson Welles, 1984. BS, SUNY, 1954; MFA with honors, Columbia U., 1976; MA, NYU, 1980, postgrad. 1980—. Assoc. producer The Secret People WPIX-TV, NYC, 1964; producer, broadcaster The Hip 400 Pacifica network, 1964; editor Playboy mag., Chgo., 1965-70; pub. Avant Garde mag. NYC, 1970-71; tchr. drama, Reid Intl. Schl., Ibiza, Spain, 1971; account exec. Metromedia Corp., 1971-72; editorial dir. Hammond, Inc., 1976-78; mem. faculty English dept. and Washington Sq. Writing Center N.Y.U., 1978-81; mem. communications faculty St. John's U., 1980—; mem. English faculty Bernard Col., CCNY, Columbia U., 1980-82. Producer: Study in Black and White, BBC, Reykjavik, Iceland, 1972; broadcaster, ABC-TV Wide World of Sports, 1972, Public Broadcasting Service, Natl. Public Radio, 1972-75. Elected Intl. arbiter Fedn. Internationale des Echecs, Skopje, Yugoslavia, 1972. Mem. AL, AG, Marshall Chess Club, U.S. Chess Fedn., PEN, Natl. Acad. TV Arts and Scis., ASJA, Soc. Profl. Journalists, Overseas Press Club. Address: 175 W 72d St New York NY 10023

BRADY, HENRY GRADY, (Henry O' Grady); b. Columbia, SC; s. Henry Brady and Juanita (Perry) B.; divorced. Author: Research Needs in Adult Education, A Survey of Selected Professor in U.S.A., 1982. Contrbr. articles to ednl. mags., poems to numerous publications. Ed.: (with Dr. I. Johns) The Adult Basic Education Curriculum & Its Development. Wrkg. on books, poems, articles. B.S., Clemson Univ., 1954; M.Ed., U. Fla., 1964; Ph.D., Fla. State U., 1969. Prof., U. South Fla., Tampa, Fla., 1964-69, Fla. State U., Tallahassee, 1964-69; coord. graduate studies in adult edn. U. South Fla., 1969-87; cons. in adult learning and program planning, 1984—. Served as col. U.S. Air Force, 1951-62. Mem. Air Force Edn. Fdn., Am. Assn. Adult Continuing Edn., Commn. Profs. of Adult Edn. Address: 1351 Gulf Blvd 109 Clearwater FL 34630

BRADY, HOLLY WHEELER, b. Evanston, IL, Apr. 28, 1947; d. Warren Calvin and Doris (Wise) W.; m. C. Townsend Brady, Apr. 12, 1969; 1 dau., Meredith Caitlin Brady. Contrbg. ed. Learning mag., 1981-84; ed. Classroom Computer Learning, 1983—. BA, Stanford U., 1969; MA, Miami U. of Ohio, 1971. Advtg. writer Rike-Kumler Co., Dayton, OH, 1974-76; editorial mngr. Mazer Corp., Dayton, 1976-81; ed. Curriculum Product Review, Palo Alto, CA, 1981-83; contrbg. ed. Learning Mag., Belmont, CA, 1981-84; ed. Classroom Computer Learning, Belmont, 1983—. Mem. EWA, EPAA, Jean Piaget Soc. Lawrence B. Johnson award for edl. wrtg., 1986, disting. achievement award, EPAA, 1984, 85, 86. Home: 384 Riviera Dr San Rafael CA 94901

BRADY, MARY GERARD, b. NYC, Dec. 4, 1959, d. Maron Blaise and Concetta-Sophia (Anziano) Brady. contrbr. Newsday, 1982-83. BA, Adelphi U., Garden City, N.Y., 1981; MS, Columbia U., 1983. Editor Starrett City Sun, Bklyn., 1981-82; assoc. editor Sportswise Mag., NYC, 1983-84; wrtr. Parliamentarians for Global Action, NYC, 1985—. Recipient Jacqueline Radin award Newsday,1982. Home: 96 Fifth Ave 7G New York NY 11011

BRADY, MAUREEN, b. Mt. Vernon, NY, June 7, 1943, d. Francis J. and Margaret C. (Hughes) Brady. Author: Give Me Your Good Ear, 1979, Folly, 1982, The Question She Put to Herself, 1987; contrbr. stories to So. Exposure, Kaliedoscope, Sinister Wisdom, Conditions, other mags. and anthologies. BS, U. FLA., 1965; MA, NYU, 1977. Phys. therapist various hosps. and clinics, 1965-76, pvt. practice, N.Y., 1978—; instr. Hunter Coll., N.Y.C., 1976-78, Russell Sage Coll., Albany, N.Y., 1976-78; tchr. writing workshops; co-founder Spinsters, Ink Pub. Co., Argyle, N.Y., 1978. Grantee N.Y. State Council on Arts, 1979, writer-in-residence, 1986; recipient 1st Place award Lesbian Community Theatre, Lansing, Mich, 1981, residency McDowell Colony, Peterborough, N.H., 1983, Briarcombe Fdn., Bolinas, Calif., 1983. Mem. PW. Home: 427B Spillway Rd West Hurley NY 12491

BRADY, PHILIP, (Favour Brady), b. Boston, Oct. 27, 1916; s. Edward John and Dora Pierce (Favor) B.; divorced: children—Philip, David W., Dennis A.; m. Eleanor Marie Garland, June 29, 1974. Author: 100+ Ways to Improve Every Graphic Project, 1988. Wrkg. on children's fiction. B.B.A., Northeastern U., 1950, M.B.A., 1956. Mem. SCBW. Home: 8 Atwood St Mansfield MA 02048

BRADY, STEVEN ROY, b. Spokane, WA, July 3, 1951; s. Roy Arthur and Beverly Anne (Blick) B.; children—Alisson and Melissa. Contbr. poetry Bellingham Rvw, Soundings East, Tausus, Dog River Rvw, Lucky Star, Coydog; contbr. stories Center, Willow Springs, Miss. Mud, contrbr. rvws. Western Am Lit; ed Cache Rvw, 1981—. BA Phi Beta Kappa, U Ariz, 1973. Library clrk. and secy. Univ Ariz Library, Tucson, 1983—. Mem. Phi Kappa Phi. Address: 3142 E Fairmount Tucson AZ 85716

BRAINBEAU, J.C., see Lemon, George Edward

BRALEY,, ROBERT BRUCE,, b. Wilkinsburg, PA, Oct, 1957; s. William Francis and Doma Louise (Bell) B.; m. Barbara Gail Uth, Dec. 27, 1986; 1 daughter, Elizabeth Anna. Author: (playscript) A Creation Story, 1984, (with Chris Catledge) Brought to You by Arlo, 1982; (television script) Crosslink, 1985; (radio scripts) The Adventures of Captain United Sound, 1984-86; (comic strips) Rab/The Adventures of Rab, 1977, 82-85. B.A. in Communications, Bowling Green State U., 1979; M.Div., United Theol. Seminary, 1986. Home: 2938 Urwiler Ave Cincinnati OH 45211

BRAM, ELIZABETH, b. NYC,Dec. 5, 1948; d. Joseph Bram and Jean (Rhys) Bram. Author: The Door in the Tree, 1976, A Dinosaur is Too Big, 1977, The Man on the Unicycle, 1977, I Don't Want to Go to School, 1977, One Day I Closed My Eyes and the World Disappeared, 1978, Woodruff and the Clocks, 1980, There Is Someone Standing on My Head, 1979, Saturday Morning Lasts Forever, 1978. Student Silvermine College of Art, New Canaan, CT, 1969-71. Freelance wrtr. and artist. Mem. AG. Home: 4 Prospect St Baldwin NY 11510

BRAMAN, SANDRA, b. MN, Aug. 30, 1951; d. Donald William and Sally Lou (Davidson) B.; m. Douglas Woolf, July 1976 (div. 1980). Author: (poetry) The One Verse City, 1976, Geretschky, 1978, spokesheards, 1983; (prose) A True Story, 1985; contrbr. poems, stories, plays, interviews, critical archtl. and mass media works, scholarly articles to Credences, Truck, River Styx, Sun & Moon, Hills, Island, Bezoar, Tree, Brilliant Corners, Mpls. Star & Tribune, City Pages, Twin Cities Reader, Jnl Communication Inquiry, others. BA, U. Minn., 1974, MA, 1984. Self-employed wrtr., 1974—; instr. U. Minn., 1982—; profl. storyteller. Silha Ctr. for Study Media Ethics and Law fellow U. Minn., 1986-87. Home: 19 S 1st St Minneapolis MN 55401

BRAMANN, JORN K., b. Wuppertal, Germany, Dec. 21, 1938; came to U.S., 1967. Author: Capital As Power: A Concise Summary of the Marxist Analysis of Capitalism, 1984, Wittgenstein's Tractatus and the Modern Arts, 1985, Sunny Side Up: Industrial Strength Poetry, 1985, The Water Woman: An Elegy (video drama), 1985, Walden Zero, 1987; ed.: Self-Determination: An Anthology of Philosophy and Poetry, 1983, Nightsun: A Literary, Interdisciplinary Yearbook, 1981—. PhD, U. Oregon, 1971. Assoc. prof. philo., Frostburg State Univ., Frostburg, MD, 1972—. Fellowship for Coll. Tchrs., NEH, Princeton, NJ, 1975-76, Irvine, CA, 1981, Los Angeles, 1984. Office: Frostburg St Univ Dept Philo Frostburg MD 21532

BRAND, STEWART, b. Rockford, IL, Dec. 14, 1938. BS in Biology, Stanford, 1960. Formerly with Merry Pranksters; founder Am. Needs Indians; spcl. cons. Edmund G. Brown, Jr. (gov. of Calif.), 1976-78. Editor/pub.: The Last Whole Earth Catalog, 1968-71 (Natl. Book award), Whole Earth Epilog, 1974, The Next Whole Earth Catalog, 1980-81, The Co-Evolution Qtly, 1974-85; editor-in-chief: Whole Earth Software Catalog, 1983; author: Two Cybernetic Frontiers, 1974, The Media Lab, 1987. Founder Uncommon Courtesy, Schl. of Compassionate Skills, 1982. Vis. sci., MIT, 1986; cons., Royal Dutch/Shell, 1986—. Fellow Lindisfarne Assn. Address: 27B Gate 5 Rd Sausalito CA 94966

BRANDER, JOHN MORRAN, b. San Francisco, Jan. 26, 1932; s. George Morran and Blodwen (Hancock) B. Author: The Fractured Horizon, 1984. Editor: (with others) Orange County Poetry Anthology, 1983-; Calif. State Poetry Quarterly, 1985—; San Miguel Rvw., 1986—; assoc. editor: Electrum, 1981-85. BSc, Univ. Coll., Cardiff, UK, 1954; LLM, Georgetown U., 1971; MA in Govt., U. San Francisco, 1980. Atty., U.S. Dept. Agrl., Washington, 1974-76, Calif. Dept. S & L, Los Angeles, 1976-78; sole practice, San Francisco and Santa Ana, Calif., 1978-86; pub. Ars Poetica Press, Santa Ana, 1986—. Recipient Golden City award for lit. arts edn. Santa Ana, 1984. Mem. PEN. Home: 1200 E Ocean Blvd 64 Long Beach CA 90802

BRANDI, JOHN, b. Los Angeles, Nov. 5, 1943. Author: Desde Alla, 1970, Y Aun Hay Mas, 1972, Diary from a Journey to the Middle of the World, 1980, Narrowgauge to Rio Bamba, 1975, The Cowboy from Phantom Banks, 1982, Rite for the Beautification of All Beings, 1983, That Crow That Visited was Flying Backwards, 1984, Poems at the Edge of Day, 1984, Zuleikha's Book, 1984, That Back Road In, 1985, Hymn for a Night Feast, 1987; ed.: Chimborazo, 1976, Dog Blue Day, 1985. BFA, U. Calif., Northridge, 1965. Vol. Peace Corps, 1965-68; ind. research, Alaska, 1969, Mexico, 1972, India, 1979; poet-in-schls., N.Mex. Arts Div., 1973-88; ind. research, India, Nepal, Burma, Thailand, 1981. Grantee PEN, 1973, 85, Witter Bynner Fdn., 1984; NEA poetry fellow, 1979. Home: PO Box 2553 Corrales NM 87048

BRANDT, ALVIN GEORGE, b. Union City, NJ, Jan. 3, 1922; s. Henry William and Mabel (Webb) B.; m. Josephine Marion Baldessari, Oct. 21, 1950; children—Andrew Curtis, Elizabeth Joan. Author: Drama Handbook for Churches, 1964. Editor: AGVA News, 1957-66; The Churchcaster, 1965-83. Contrbr. articles to mags., jnls., brochures, newsletters, press releases, theatre playbills. With Am Natl. Theatre & Acad., NYC, 1947-49; AG Variety Artists, N.Y.C., 1949-69; Dover Gen. Hosp., Dover, N.J., 1969-87. Pres. Dover Little Theatre, 1984-86. Served to tech. sgt. U.S. Army, 1942-46. Mem. Wharton Hist. Soc., Episcopal Actors Guild. Home: 33 Columbia St Wharton NJ 07885

BRANDT, ANDREW CURTIS, b. Jersey City, NJ, Aug. 9, 1951; s. Alvin George and Josephine (Baldesarre) B. Contrbr. articles to newspapers. Program book ed.: Shreveport Symphony, 1986—; ed.: The Leading Tone, 1986—. B.Music Edn., Baldwin-Wallace Coll., 1973; M.Music with Distinction, Ind. U., 1979. Prin. bassoonist Shreveport Symphony, LA, 1979—, Longview Symphony Orchestra, TX, 1979—; pres. Baroque Artisits of Shreveport, 1980—, music dir., 1984—; instr. bassoon Centenary Coll., Shreveport, 1980—. Home: 218 Boulevard St Shreveport LA 07885

BRANDT, EDWARD NEWMAN, JR., b. Oklahoma City, OK, July 3, 1933; s. Edward Newman and Myrtle (Brazil) B.; m. Patricia Lawson Brandt, Aug. 29, 1953; children—Patrick James, Edward, Rex Carlin. Contrbr. articles to profl. pubs., monographs, book chpts. in field; ed. profl. proceedings. Assoc. ed.: Continuing Edn. for the Family Physician, 1973-74, ed., 1974-77. B.S. in Mathematics, U. Okla., 1954; M.S. in Mathematics, Okla. State U., 1955; M.D., U. Okla. Med. Center, 1960; Ph.D., U. Okla. Med Center, 1963. Prof. epidemiology and preventive medicine U. Md., Balt., 1985—, prof. family medicine, 1985—, chancellor, 1985—; asst. secy. for health U.S. Dept. Health and Human Services, Washington, 1981-84. Home: 3112 Old Ct Rd Baltimore MD 21208

BRANNON, JEAN MARILYN, b. Chgo., d. John Raymond and Charlie Marie (Holliday) Brannon. Author: The Negro Woman, 1967, Blacks and the American Revolutionary War,

1976. Edn., Woodrow Wilson Jr. Coll., Chgo. Tchers. Coll. Ed. Let's Save the Children, Chgo.; print media ed. Coronet Instrnl. Media, Chgo.; freelance ed. Johnson Pub. Co., Chgo.; mng. ed., editor-in-chief, ShopTalk-Simply YOU, Chgo., 1981—. Mem. Chgo. Assn. Black Journalists. Home: 407 S Dearborn Suite 1500 Chicago IL 60605

BRANSON, BRANLEY ALLEN, (Rogers MacGowan McNair), b. San Angelo, TX, Feb. 11, 1929; s. Branley Allan and Era Elizabeth (Rogers) B.; m. Mary Louise Lewis, July 11, 1964; 1 son, Rogers MacGowan. Author: Fishes of the Red River, Kentucky, 1972. Contrbr. numerous articles, essays, poems tomags, jnls. Editor: Ky. Acad. Sci. BS, Okla. State U.-Stillwater, 1956, MS, 1957, PhD, 1960. Asst. prof. biology Kans. State U., Pittsburg, 1960-65; prof. biology Eastern Ky. U., Richmond, 1965—. Served with USN, 1948-52, Korea. Fellow AAAS; mem. Ky. Acad. Sci. (Disting. Scientist 1985). Home: 100 Walnut Hills Richmond KY 40475

BRANT, WILLIAM MORTON, b. Elmira, NY, Nov. 21, 1937; s. Glen and Marjorie (Sykes) B.; m. Catharine Polcez, Feb. 11, 1972; children: Steven, William. Author: (textbooks) Practical Time Management, 1980, Administrative Planning, 1982; How To Develop and Train Your Managers, 1981; ed., pub. Packascope USA Newsletter, 1979-81; contrbr. to mgmt. newsletters of Alexander Hamilton Inst., 1974-80. BA, U. Fla., 1959, MA, 1962; MBA, U. Pitts., 1964, PhD, 1968. Dir. Orgn. devel. Phila. Quartz, 1970-73; prof. bus. Trenton State Coll., N.J., 1973-80; dir. edn. Adminstrv. Mgmt. Soc., Willow Grove, Pa., 1980-82; dir. mgmt. curriculum Am. Coll., Bryn Mawr, Pa., 1982—. Home: 61 Apple Ct Marlton NJ 08053

BRASFIELD, JAMES, b. b.Savannah, GA, Jan. 19, 1952; s. Williamson Glover and Marion (Luke) B.; m. Charlotte A. Holmes, Mar. 7, 1983; 1 son, Williamson Stanhope. Author: Chapbook, 1983; contrbr. poet to numerous mags. BA, Armstrong St. College, Savannah, GA, 1975; MFA, Columbia U., 1979. Ed., reporter The True Citizen, Waynesboro, GA, 1976-77; editorial asst. The Paris Review, 1981-82; English instr. Western Carolina U., 1983—. Mem. PSA, AWP, AAP. Home: Box 291 Cullowhee NC 28723

BRASHERS, (HOWARD) CHARLES, b. Martin County, TX, Dec. 11, 1930, s. George A. and Sallie Louise (Whitaker) B.; m. Kerstin B. Brorson, June 13, 1959 (div.); children—Erik, Bart, Perry. Author: The Other Side of Love (novellas), 1963, The Life of America, 1965, Introduction to American Literature, 1965, Creative Writing: Fiction, Drama, Poetry, The Essay, 1968, Creative Writing for High School Students, 1968, The Structure of Essays, 1972, Whatta Ya Mean, 'Get out o' that Dirty Hole'? I LIVE here! (poems and cartoons), 1974, Developing Creativity, 1974, A Snug Little Purchase, 1979, Creative Writing Handbook, 1984, Creative Processes, 1987; contrbr.: Blue Cloud Qtly, Sewanee Rvw, Conradiana, other lit publs. U.S. and Scandinavia. BA, U. Calif.-Berkeley, 1956; MA, San Francisco State U., 1960; PhD, U. Denver, 1962. Fulbright lectr. Am. studies Royal U. Stockholm, 1962-65; mem. faculty U. of Mich., 1965-68, San Diego State U., 1968—, prof. English, 1973—. Home: 8785 Navajo Rd Apt 11 San Diego CA 92119

BRAUDY, LEO BEAL, b. Phila., June 11, 1941; s. Edward and Zelda (Smith) B.; m. Dorothy McGahee, Dec. 24, 1974. Author: Narrative Form in History and Fiction: Hume, Fielding, and Gibbon, 1970, Jean Renoir: The World of His Films, 1972, The World in a Frame: What We See in Films, 1976, The Frenzy of Renown: Fame and Its History, 1986; editor: Norman Mailer: A Collection of Critical Essays, 1972, Focus on Truffaut's Shoot the Piano Player, 1972, (with Morris Dickstein) Great Film Directors: A Critical Anthology, 1978. BA, Swarthmore Coll., 1963; MA, Yale U., 1964, PhD, 1967. Instr. English Yale U., New Haven, 1966-68; asst. prof. Columbia U., NYC, 1968-70, assoc. prof., 1970-73, prof., 1973-76; prof. English Johns Hopkins U., Balt., 1977-83; prof. English, chmn. U. So. Calif., Los Angeles, 1983—, Leo S. Bing Prof. of Lit., 1985—. Mem. editorial bd.: ELH, 1976, PMLA, 1979-82, Qtly Rvw of Film Studies, 1976, Raritan Rvw, 1979, Prose Studies, 1979. Guggenheim fellow, 1971-72; ACLS grantee, 1971; NEH, 1978, 79, 86. Mem. MLA, Am. Soc. for Eighteenth-Century Studies. Office: Dept Eng U So Calif Los Angeles CA 90089

BRAUN, CLAIRE S., b. East Orange, NJ, Jan. 1, 1931; d. William Kenneth and Mary Cecilia (Gorman) Sims; m. Thomas Braun, Dec. 27, 1952 (div. Nov. 1963); children—M. Colleen Braun O'Dell, Thomas, Caron Braun Toth. Author Greystone Park Psych. Hosp. pubns.: Bulletin, Psychogram, deptl. manuals, trng. materials; Nutrition News, 1964—; contrbr. book Enjoying Your Restricted Diet; author and illustrator children's series Adventures with Caitlin. BS Mary Washington Coll., U. VA, 1952; postgrad. St. Elizabeth Coll., 1971-75. Admin. dietitian II Greystone Park (NJ) Psychiatric Hosp., 1964—. Home: 5 Stony Brook Rd Morris Plains NJ 07950

BRAUN, HENRY, b. Olean, NY, July 25, 1930; s. Josiah Henry and Evelyn (Kelly) B.; m. Joan Lapedos, June 16, 1956; children—Jessie, Sarah. Author: (Poems) The Vergil Woods, 1968. BA, Brandeis U., 1955, MA, 1957; postgrad. Boston U., 1960-62. Instr. English, U. Maine, Orono, 1963-65; instr. to asst. prof. English, Temple U., Phila., 1965-86, assoc. prof., 1986—. Mem. War Resisters League, AAUP. Home: 737 N 3 Philadelphia PA 19123

BRAWLEY, ERNEST CHARLES, b. Los Angeles, Oct. 8, 1937, s. Ernest Calvin Brawley and Helen (Wasson) Polnik; m. Chiara Coletti, June 8, 1969; 1 child, Lucia. Author: (novels) The Rap, 1974, Selena, 1979, The Alamo Tree, 1984. BA, San Francisco State U., 1962, MA, 1969. Instr. U. Hawaii, 1969-70; lectr. NYU, 1985-86. Music Corp. Am. fellow in creative writing, 1966-67. Mem. AG. Home: 335 Greenwich St New York NY 10013

BRAWLEY, PAUL HOLM, b. Granite City, IL, Sept. 27, 1942; s. Paul Virgil and Lucille Melba (Holm) B. Recs. librarian Boston Pub. Library, 1965-66, audio-visual librarian, 1966-68; nonprint revs. editor Booklist (A.L.A.), Chgo., 1969-73, editor-in-chief, art dir., 1973—; Guest lectr. library sci. Kent State U., L.I. U., Dalhousie U., Halifax, N.S., Syracuse U., U. Wash., Seattle. B.A. in English, So. Ill. U., 1965; M.S. in L.S., Simmons Coll., Boston, 1968. Mem. ALA. Address: 50 E Huron St Chicago IL 60611

BRAZELTON, EUGENIA LOUISE, b. Groesbeck, TX, Sept. 4, 1919; d. Richard Oliver and Mary Elsie (Kierbow) B. Author: Guide to Selecting a Group Tour, 1984; articles for mags and newspapers, tour brochures. AA, Pasadena City Coll., 1943, student N.Y. Schl. Interior Design, 1944, UCLA, 1945-46. Freelance designer Los Angeles, 1945-47; staff designer, Barker Bros. Co., Los Angeles, 1948-58; owner, designer Interiors by Louise, Newport Beach, Calif., 1960-62, designer with several firms in Orange Co., 1962-82; cons., freelance writer; instr. Glendale Jr. Coll., 1953-55, Orange Coast Coll., 1960-66. Mem. Am. Soc. Interior Designers. Home: 512 Tustin Ave Newport Beach CA 92663

BREAKEY, JEFFREY M., b. Ann Arbor, MI, Jan. 15, 1959; s. Barry A. and Myra (Townsend) Breakey. Publisher/editor Sprouting Publications 1980-85, Waternews Bulletin; owner Health Essenhals, 1985—. Office: Bx 339 Ashland OR 97520

BRECHER, EDWARD MORITZ, b. Mpls., July 20, 1911; s. Hans and Rhodessa (Roston) B.; m. Ruth Ernestine Cook Stilson, Dec. 27, 1941 (dec/ 1966); children: William Earl, John Samuel, Jeremy Hans. Author: (with Ruth E. Brecher) Medical and Hospital Benefit Plans, 1961, (with Ruth E. Brecher and others) Consumers Union Report on Smoking and the Public Interest, 1963, (with Ruth E. Brecher) An Analysis of Human Sexual Response, 1966, The Rays: A History of Radiology in the U.S. and Canada, 1968, The Sex Researchers, expanded edit., 1979, Licit and Illicit Drugs, 1972, Mehadone Treatment Manual, 1973, Health Care in Correctional Institutions, 1975, Treatment Programs for Sex Offenders, 1977, Love, Sex, and Aging: A Consumers Union Report, 1984; assoc. editor consumer Reports, 1947-51; editor Tech. Assistance Adminstrn., UN, 1951-52; freelance writer, 1952—. Student, U. Wis. Exptl. Coll., 1928-30; B.A. Swarthmore Coll., 1932; M.A., U. Minn., 1934; postgrad., Brown U., 1934-35. Writer Compton's PIctured Encyc., chigo., 1936-37. Recipient George Polk Meml. award, Robert T. Morse Meml. award Am. Psychiat. Assn., 1971, Ellie award ASME, 1975, Albert Lasker Meml. award Lasker Fdn., 1963. Fellow Soc. Sci. Study of Sex; mem. Natl. Assn. Sci. Writers, ASJA. Address: Yelping Hill West Cornwall CT 06796

BREEN, ANN E., b. Phila., May 6, 1940, d. John Mathias and Mary (Mallon) Breen; m. Ross E. Cowey, Aug. 8, 1964 (div. 1981); children—John F., Sara S., David F., Catherine A. Co-ed. (with Dick Rigby) Urban Waterfronts'83: Balancing Public-Private Interests, 1984, (with Dick Rigby) Caution: Working Waterfront/The Impact of Change on Marine Enterprises, 1985, Urban Waterfront '84: Toward New Horizons, 1985, (with Dick Rigby) Fishing Piers: What Cities Can Do, 1986, (with Dick Rigby) Urban Waterfronts '85: Water Makes a Difference, 1986, (with Dick Rigby) Urban Waterfronts '86: Developing Diversity, 1987. BA, Trinity Coll., Washington, 1961; M.Urban Planning, George Washington U., 1976. Policy analyst Dept. Commerce, Washington, 1975-83; co-dir. The Waterfront Center, Washington, 1981—; ed. Waterfront World newsletter. NEA grantee, 1984 Home: 1536 44th St NW Washington DC 20007

BREEN, TIMOTHY HALL, b. Cin., Sept. 5, 1942; s. George E. and Mary B.; m. Susan Carlson April 5, 1963; children—Sarah, Bant. Author: Character of the Good Ruler, 1970, Shaping Southern Society, 1975, Puritans and Adventurers, 1980, America: Past and Present, 1983, Tobacco Culture: The Mentality of the Great Tidewater Planters, 1985. BA, Yale U., 1964,

MA, 1966, PhD, 1968. Asst. prof. history and Am. culture, Yale U., 1968-70; assoc. prof. Northwestern U., 1970-75, prof. history and Am. culture, 1975-86, Wm. Smith Mason Prof. of Am. History, 1986—, dir., American Culture Program, 1975-78. Awardee Guggenheim Fdn., 1975, Inst. Advanced Study, 1980, Natl. Humanities Center, 1983; ACLS fellow, 1971; Fowler Hamilton Research Fellow, Christ Church, Oxford, 1987-88. Assoc. Newberry Library; council of Early Am. History and Culture; bd. of eds. Am. Qtly. Office: Hist Dept Northwestern Evanston IL 60201

BREEZE, GRACE WILKIE, b. Purcell, OK, June 6, 1934; d. James Henry and Zena Fay (Rock) W.; m. Bobby Gene Breeze, June 6, 1953 (div. Mar. 1985); children—Carmen Anita,Bobby Gene, Jr., Melanie Diane, Amy Suzanne, Pamela Gail. Ed., Fort Worth Star-Telegram Junior Mag. and Weekly Chaser; contrbr. articles to: Fort Worth Star-Telegram, Cap Cities/ABC Ink, The Texas Woman, Yale Law Rvw, United Way, Baylor Alumni Mag. BA, U. Texas at Arlington, 1979, MA, 1981. Engl. Tchr. U. Texas, Arlington, 1979-82; special sects. writer Star-Telegram, Fort Worth, 1982-84, co. pubns. ed., 1984—. Mem. AAUW, IABC. Office: Star-Tele 400 W 7th St Fort Worth TX 76102

BREGGIN, PETER ROGER, b. Bklyn., May 11, 1936; s. Morris Louis and Jean (Weinstein) B.; m. Sally Ann Friedman, 1959 (div. 1971); m. Phyllis Jean Lundy, Oct. 13, 1972 (div. 1983); m. Ginger Ross, 1984; children—Linda Karen, Sharon Jane, Benjamin Jay. Author: (with C. Umbarger, J. Dalsimer, A. Morrison) College Students in a Mental Hospital, 1962, The Crazy from the Sane, 1971, After the Good War: A Love Story, 1972, Electroshock: Its Brain-Disabling Effects, 1979, The Psychology of Freedom: Liberty and Love as a Way of Life, 1980, Psychiatric Drugs: Hazards to the Brain, 1983; intl. com. contbrs.: Spirali: Mensile Internazionale di Cultura, contrbr. articles to profl. jnls. BA with honors, Harvard U., 1958; MD, Case Western Reserve U., 1962. Diplomate: natl. Bd. Med. Examiners. Intern State U. N.Y., Upstate Med. Center, Syracuse, 1962-63, resident in psychiatry, 1964-66; psychiat. resident Mass. Mental Health Center, Boston, 1963-64; teaching fellow Harvard Medical Schl., Boston, 1963-64; full-time NIMH cons. in bldg. and staffing mental health centers, Charlottesville, Va., 1966-67, full-time cons. NIMH in edn., Chevy Chase, Md., 1967-68, pvt. practice medicine, specializing in psychiatry, Washington and Bethesda, Md., 1968—; staff Psychiat. Inst., Washington, 1968—; faculty Washington Schl. Psychiatry, 1968-72; cons. Antioch-Putney Grad. Schl. Edn., 1968-70, U. Md. Grad. Schl. Edn., 1968-70; dir. Project to Examine Psychiat. Technology, Washington Schl. Psychiatry, 1971-72; field faculty Humanistic Psychology Inst. Washington, 1975-78; exec. dir., founder Center for Study of Psychiatry, Washington, 1972—. Mem. fellowship adv. com. Center for Libertarian Studies; Mem. adv. bd. Libertarian Intl.; Natl. Comm. Libertarian Party, 1985—; adv. bd. San Diego Humanist Fellowship. Served to lt. comdr. USPHS, 1966-68. Mem. Am. Psychiat. Assn., Assn. for Humanistic Psychology, Am. Acad. Psychotherapists, Am. Assn. Abolition of Involuntary Mental Hospitalization, Am. Humanist Assn., Libertarian Health Assn. (founding mem.) Libertarian Party. Address: 4628 Chesnut St Bethesda MD 20814

BREITMAN, RICHARD D(AVID), b. Hartford, CT, March 27, 1947; s. Saul Harold and Gloria (Salz) B.; Carol Rose; 1 child: David Russell. Author: German Socialism and Weimar Democracy, 1981, (with Walter Laqueur) Breaking the Silence, 1986, (with Alan M. Kraut) American Refugee Policy and European Jewry, 1933-45, 1987. Contrbr to history jnls. BA, Yale U., 1969; MA, Harvard U., 1971, Ph. D., 1975. Asst prof, American U., Washington, D.C., 1976-81, assoc. prof, 1981-85, prof of history, 1985—. Mem: Amer. Hist. Assn. Carnegie fellow, Yale U., 1969-70. Home: 127 Quincy St Chevy Chase MD 20815

BREMKAMP, GLORIA HOWE, b. Hugo, OK, Sept. 14, 1924; d. Robert Scott and Lucinda (Sapaugh) H.; m. James Karl Bremkamp, Dec. 23, 1950 (dec. Oct. 24, 1977); 1 son, James Patrick. Author novels: Rahab, 1985, Merari—The Woman Who Defied Jezebel and the Pagan Gods, 1986, A Woman of ourage—Mary of Jerusalem, 1988. Ed. newsletter: Scanner, 1978—. Student Okla. City U., Okla. U., U. London. House mag. ed. George Knox Assocs., Oklahoma City, OK, 1948-53; v.p., public relations dir. Lowe Runkle Co., Oklahoma City, 1964-78; public relations counselor, 1954-64, 78—; free-lance wrtr., 1978—. Recipient Leadership award Direct Mail Marketing Assn. Am., 1973, 75, Outstanding Byliners' award WICI, 1980. Mem. Okla. Hosp. Public Relations Dirs. Soc. (charter mem., 1st pres. 1969; Disting. Service award 1969), Am. Women in Radio Television, AL. Home: 8012 W Lakeshore Dr Oklahoma City OK 73132

BRENER, ROCHELLE, see Squire, Rochelle Brener

BRENNAN, DAVID DANIEL, b. Hartford, CT, June 16, 1938; s. Eugene S. and Yolande M. (Auclair) B.; m. Elizabeth Ann Schuster, Aug. 31, 1960; children— Kathleen Mary Brennan Griffin, Tracey Ann. Ed., Precision Shooting mag., 1982—; contrbr. articles to sport shooting mags. Student parochial schl., Bloomfield, CT, 1953-57. Pres., Hilb, Rogal & Hamilton of Conn., Inc., Manchester, CT, 1962—. Served to S/Sgt. E6, Army N.G., 1959. Home: 37 Burnham St East Hartford CT 06108

BRENNAN, JOSEPH PAYNE, b. Bridgeport, CT, Dec. 20, 1918, s. Joseph Payne and Nellie Wilkerson (Holborn) B.; m. Doris May Philbrick, Oct. 24, 1970. Author: poetry collections: Heart of Earth, 1950, The Humming Stair, 1953, The Wind of Time, 1962, Nightmare Need, 1964, Edges of Night, 1974, As Evening Advances, 1978, Webs of Time, 1979, Creep to Death, 1981, Sixty Selected Poems, 1985; short story collections: Nine Horrors and a Dream, 1958, The Dark Returners, 1959, Scream at Midnight, 1963, The Casebook of Lucius Leffing, 1973, Stories of Darkness & Dread, 1973, The Chronicles of Lucius Leffing, 1977, The Shapes of Midnight, 1980, The Borders Just Beyond, 1986; author: (with Donald M. Grant) Act of Providence, 1979, Evil Always Ends, 1982. Student Jr. Coll. Commerce, New Haven, 1936-37. Book evaluator Yale U. Library, New Haven, 1946-85, ret., 1985. Served as cpl. U.S. Army, 1943-46, ETO. Recipient Poetry award Clark Ashton Smith Fdn., 1978, Life Achievement award World Fantasy Conv., 1982. Mem. PSA (Leonora Speyer Meml. award 1961) Home: 26 Fowler St New Haven CT 06515

BRENNAN, KAREN, b. New Rochelle, NY, Dec. 30, 1941; d. James Thomas and Margot Madeleine (Zimmer) Morley; m. Thomas John Brennan, June 6, 1964 (div. 1973); children—Margot Karen, Thomas Christopher, Geoffrey Bernard, Rahel Elizabeth; m. John Francis Palumbo, Dec. 22, 1979. Author: Here on Earth, 1988. B.A., Newton Coll. of Sacred Heart, 1963; M.F.A., Goddard Coll., 1979; postgrad U. Ariz., 1981—. Asst. to dir. Tucson Women's Commn., 1979-81; tchr. composition, creative writing, bus. and tehnical writing U. Ariz., Tucson, 1981—. Recipient Poetry award U. Ariz. an Am. Acad. Arts, 1986. Home: 1320 E Lester Tucson AZ 85719

BRENNER, BARBARA JOHNES, b. Bklyn., June 26, 1925; d. Robert Lawrence and Marguerite (Furboter) Johnes; m. Fred Brenner, Apr. 16, 1947; children: Mark, Carl. Author: Somebody's Slippers, Somebody's Shoes, 1957, Barto Take the Subway, 1960, A Bird in the Family, 1961, Amy's Doll, 1963, The Five Pennies, 1964, Career and Opportunities in Fashion, 1964, Beef Stew, 1965, The Flying Patchwork Quilt, 1965, Nicky's Sister, 1966, Summer of the Houseboat, 1968, Faces, 1970, A Snake-Lover's Diary, 1970, A Year in the Life of Rosie Bernard, 1971, If You Were an Ant, 1973, Bodies, 1973, Hemi: A Mule, 1973, others, including A Killing Season (YA), 1982, Mystery of the Disappearing Dogs, 1982, A Dog I Know, 1983, Love and Discipline (adult nonfiction), 1983, The Snow Parade, 1984, The Gorilla Signs Love (YA), 1984. Student Rutgers U., 1942-44. Clrk. Prudential Ins. Co., Newark, 1942-45, writer, 1945-46; artists agt. freelance, NYC, 1947-53; freelance writer, 1953—; editor Bank Street Coll., NYC, 1980—. Chmn. SANE, N.Y., 1960's. Recipient Outstanding Sci. Book award Natl. Sci. Tchrs. Assn. and Children's Book Council, 1974, 75, 77, 79, 80, ALA Notable Book award, 1970, 78. Mem. Soc. Children's Book Writers, PEN, Wayne-Pike Audubon Soc. Home: Box 1826 Hemlock Farms Hawley PA 18428

BRENNER, ROBERT CHARLES, b. Wayne, MI, Oct. 22, 1941; s. Charles E. Brenner; m. Carol Ann Berry; children—Daniel Robert, Laura Ann, Edythe Sue, Dawn Marie. Author: Thc Apple II Plus/IIe Troubleshooting and Repair Guide, 1984, The Commodore 64 Troubleshooting and Repair Guide, 1985, The IBM PC Troubleshooting and Repair Guide, 1985, MILCOM 85 Proceedings, 1985, VCR Troubleshooting and Repair Guide, 1986. MSSM, U. of So. Calif., 1977; MSEE, Naval Postgrad. School, Monterey Ca., 1979; Electronics technician, US Navy, 1961-70; naval officer, US Navy, 1970-84; author/consultant, Brenner Microcomputing, Inc., San Diego. 1984—; mktg. mgr., lectr., TRW, San Diego, 1984—. Mem. IEEE, World Future Soc. Home: 9282 Samantha Ct San Diego CA 92129

BRESLIN, JIMMY, b. Jamaica, NY, Oct. 17, 1929; s. James Earl and Frances (Curtin) B.; m. Rosemary Dattolico, Dec. 26, 1954 (dec. June 1981); children—James and Kevin (twins), Rosemary, Patrick, Kelly, Christopher; m. Ronnie Myers Eldridge, Sept. 12, 1982; stepchildren—Daniel, Emily, Lucy Eldridge. Author: Can't Anybody Here Play This Game?, 1963, The Gang That Couldn't Shoot Straight, 1969, World Without End, Amen, 1973, How the Good Guys Finally Won, 1975, Forsaking All Others, 1982, Table Money, 1986; co-author Forty-Four Caliber, 1978. Student, L.I.U., 1947-48. Syndicated columnist N.Y. Herald-Tribune, Paris Tribune, New York Daily News. Recipient Pulitzer Prize for disting. commentary, 1986; George Polk award for reporting, 1986; award for natl. reporting Sigma Delta Chi, 1964, Meyer Berger award for local reporting, 1964, N.Y. Reporters Assn. award reporting, 1964. Mem. Screen Actors Guild, AFTRA, WG Am. Office: NY Daily News 220 E 42nd St New York NY 10017

BRETT, PETER D., b. Jackson, MI, Apr. 23, 1943; s. Benjamin Thomas and Fanchon (Eidelman) B.; m. Hazel Zeldes, Aug. 21, 1983; 1 child, Rebecca. Books: Crossing Paradise, 1972, Ghost Rhythms, 1978, Gallery, 1979, Borrowing the Sky, 1980. BS in Biology, Wayne State U., 1965. Freelance writer, San Rafael, CA, 1971—. Mem. Sierra Club. Recipient Hopwood award U. Mich., 1971. Office: Box 697 Ross CA 94957

BRETTON, BARBARA, b. NYC, June 25, 1950, d. Melvin Cassen and Viola (McNaught) Fuller; m. Roy Bretton, Sept. 8, 1968. Novelist: Love Changes, 1983, The Sweetest of Debts, 1984, No Safe Place, 1985, Star Fire, 1985, The Edge of Forever, 1986, Promises in the Night, 1986, Shooting Star, 1986; contrbr. N.Y. Times, Seventeen mag., Personal Romances, others. Student Queens Coll. Computer programmer Cross Country, Syosset, N.Y., 1974-82. Mem. NWC, Romance Wrtrs. Am. Home: 81 Carlls Path North Babylon NY 11703

BRETUO, AKWASI, see Assensoh, Akwasi B.

BREUR, LESTER MONS, b. Butte, MT, April 15, 1939, s. Ralph Alfred and Lorraine (Hedral) B. Author: A Tax Guide for Drinkers, 1978, A Soak's Tithe for Dunkers, 1983, A Lax Guild of Drunkards, 1983, Boose Whose?, 1986. AA, Boise Jr. Coll., 1959; BA, U. of Idaho, 1961. Tchr. H.S. jnlsm. 1965-73; pub. rel., Rupert, ID, 1974-78; ski shop mgr., 1978-82. Mem. AG, DG, SABEW. Address: Box 302 Highland Park IL 60035

BREWER, (GRACE) DIANE, b. Birmingham, AL, Feb. 4, 1948; d. William Ellis and Sybil Lois (Willis) Woodward; m. John Richard Brewer, Mar. 8, 1968; 1 dau., Sybil Ellisha. contrbr.: Coronet, Good Housekeeping, Jack and Jill, Humpty Dumpty mag., others. Wrkg. on short stories, children's stories, screenwriting. Freelance wrtr., 1966—. Mem. Ala. Wrtrs.' Conclave. Home: 143 Poetercrest Rd Graysville AL 35073

BREWER, JOHN ISAAC, b. Milford, IL, Oct. 9, 1903, s. John H. and Edna (Ishler) B.; m. Ruth Russell, June 2, 1928; 1 son, John Vernon. Author: Gynecology, 1950, Textbook of Gynecology, 1953, 5th edit., 1967, Gynecologic Nursing (with Doris Molbo and A.B. Gerbie), 1966; contrbr. articles to profl. jnls. MD, U. Chgo., 1928, PhD, 1935. Practice medicine specializing in gynecology; ed. Am. Jnl. Ob-Gyn., St. Louis, 1956-70, ed.-in-chief, 1970—. Mem. numerous profl. orgns. Home: 860 N Lake Shore Dr Chicago IL 60611

BREWER, KENNETH WAYNE, b. Indpls., Nov. 28, 1941, s. Ulyss and Edna Juanita (Virt) B.; m. Carol Ann Hayton, Aug. 20, 1964 (div. 1977); children—Kimberley Diane, Jonathan Keith; m. 2d, Roberta Stearman, Sept. 22, 1978. Author: Places, Shadows, Dancing People, 1969, Sum Of Accidents, 1977, Round Again, 1980, The Collected Poems of Mongrel, 1981, To Remember What is Lost, 1982. PhD,U. Utah, 1973. Tchr. Las Cruces (N.Mex.) High Schl., 1967-68; assoc. prof. English Utah State U., Logan, 1968—. Winner long poem div. competition Utah Arts Council, 1978. Office: Dept Eng Utah State Univ Logan UT 84322

BREWSTER, BERNADETTE HEIDT, b. Bismarck, ND, Feb. 1, 1942; d. Adam and Clara (Jacobson) Heidt; m. Alton C. Morton, Mar. 22, 1963 (div. 1982); children—Lori Ann, Daniel Carl, Michael Adam Robert; remarried. Contrbr. articles to Channel 22 TV Guide, Trumpet Newspaper. Wrkg. on non-fiction murder mystery. Grad. public schls., Mandan, ND. Deputy dir. Children's Rights of Am., Largo, FL, 1982-84; v.p., exec. dir. Sun Bay Recovery, Largo, 1984—. Bd. dirs. Fla. Gulf Coast Fine Arts Soc., Belleair, FL, 1985—. Home: 12800 Sophia Circle Largo FL 34644

BREWSTER, TOWNSEND TYLER, b. Glen Cove, NY, July 23, 1924; s. Townsend and Sara Frances (Tyler) B. BA, Queens Coll., 1947; MA, Columbia U., 1962. Koussevitzky Fdn. scholar Berkshire Music Festival, 1947; translator, adaptor NBC TV Opera, 1950-51; questionnaire processor Alfred Politz Research, 1953-58; copywriter Hicks & Greist, NYC, 1958-62; librarian Lennen & Newell, NYC, 1962-67; lectr. theatre dept. CCNY, 1969-73; editor Harlem Cultural Rvw, 1973—. Theatre critic for Denver Qtly, Showbus., Amsterdam News, Players, Big Red, Routes; librettist: operas The Tower, 1957; playwright, translator: Please Don't Cry and Say No, 1972; playwright: Black High, 1977, Arthur Ashe and I, 1979; translator num. French works, 1984-87; radio appearances on shows on black theatre, Danmarks Radio, Copenhagen, 1972; consultant Apollo Opera and Drama Co. Recipient Louise Bogan Meml. prize in poetry N.Y. Poetry Forum, 1975. Jonathan Swift award for satire Commonwealth U., 1979;; Natl. Theatre Conf. Playwrights fellow, 1947; William Morris Playwriting scholar Am. Theatre Wing, 1955; NEA librettists' grantee, 1977. Mem. DG, Outer Critics Circle, Harlem Cultural Council, Intl. Brecht Soc., Maple Leaf Soc., ASCAP, BMI Musical Theatre Workshop. Home: 171-29 103 Rd Jamaica NY 11433

BRICE, JANET KAY, b. Reedsburg, WI, Jan. 28, 1954; d. Ora Thomas and Esther Lillian (Johnson) Brice. Author: (poems) Sweet and Flaky, 1984. Contrbr. Poems to mags, anthols. Assoc. Applied Sci., Western Wis. Tech. Inst., 1975. Operator, Wis. Telephone Co., Baraboo, Wis., 1971-73; secy. Edwards Agri-Supply, Baraboo, 1975-78; secy., agt. Baraboo-Portage Ins. Agy., 1979-86. Recipient Cert. Merit, N. Am. Mentor, 1982, 85, 1st place WSEY-radio, Sauk City, Wis., 1984; Hon. Mention, ByLine, 1985, 86. Mem. Unicorn Hunters. Home: 400 3d Ave Baraboo WI 53913

BRICKLIN, MARK HARRIS, b. Phila., Apr. 13, 1939; s. Arthur Benjamin and Rose (Gaurd) B.; m. Alice Goddard Terry, Apr. 26, 1963 (div.); children—Deirdre, Brendon; m. 2d, Rita Baker, June 4, 1987. Author: The Practical Encyclopedia of Natural Healing, 1976, Lose Weight Naturally, 1979, Natural Healing Cookbook, 1981, Rodale's Encyclopedia of Natural Home Remedies, 1982. BA, Temple U., 1960, postgrad., 1961-62; postgrad., Boston U., 1960-61. Teaching fellow English Boston U., 1960-61; city editor Phila. Tribune, 1962-71; freelance writer, photographer, 1962-71; with Rodale Press, Emmaus, Pa., 1971—, v.p., 1975—; exec. editor Prevention mag., 1974—; founding editor, editorial dir. Spring mag., 1982—; editorial dir. Walker's World, 1986—; jnlsm. preceptor Pkwy. Exptl. program Phila. Schl. Dist.; cons. book pub. Home: 520 N Glenwood St Allentown PA 18104

BRIDGE, PETER J., b. Passaic, NJ, Dec. 27, 1935, s. Charles Anthony and Alita Mary (Frobose) B.; widowed, 1984; children—Rebecca Anne, Jennifer Marie. Co-author: The Mafia Talks, 1969; contrbg. author, Megacities, 1970; ed., Valentines, 1973; contrbr. articles to various natl. publs. BS, Syracuse U. Reporter Endicott (N.Y.) Bulltn., 1960, Oneonta (N.Y.) Star, 1960-61; reporter, ed., bur. mgr. Newark News, 1961-72; freelance wrtr., Belleville, N.J., 1972—; co-adj. prof. journalism Rutgers U. Newark, 1986; jailed for refusing to testify before grand jury as a reporter, 1972. Served with U.S. Army, 1953-56. Recipient journalistic awards. Home: 136 Beech St Belleville NJ 07209

BRIDGERS, SUE ELLEN, b. Greenville, NC, Sept. 20, 1942; d. Wayland Louis and Elizabeth (Abbott) Hunsucker; m. Ben Oshel Bridgers, Mar. 17, 1963; children—Elizabeth Abbott, Jane Bennett, Sean MacKenzie. Author: Home Before Dark, 1976, All Together Now, 1979, Notes for Another Life, 1981, Sara Will, 1985, Permanent Collections, 1987. BA, Western Carolina U, 1976. Bd. dirs. Jackson County Lib., Sylva, NC, 1985—, NC Ctr. for Pub. TV, Chapel Hill, N.C., 1984—, Western Carolina Tomorrow, Cullowhee, 1980-82. Recipient Hornbook Boston Globe, honor book, 1979, Christopher award, 1979, Alan award, Assembly on Adolescent Lit, 1985. Mem. AG, AL. Address: 64 Savannah Dr Sylva NC 28779

BRIDGES, PATRICIA ANN, b. St. Louis, June 20, 1952, d. Ernest and Edna Alberta (Cleary) Morton; m. David Edward Suwal; children—Aaron Cheston Ian Bridges, Ian Christian Bridges. Contrbr. articles, poetry and short stories to lit mags and anthologies, including Humanities News, Another Small Mag., Amaranthus. BS, Grand Valley State Coll., Allendale, Mich., 1982; MFA, U. Oreg., 1986. Asst. ed. mag. Haworth Corp., Holland, Mich., 1980-81; research asst. Council on Fgn. Relations, NYC, 1982-84; proofreader/ed. Pantheon Books/ Random House, NYC, 1983-84; grad. teaching fellow U. Oreg., Eugene, 1985-86; adjunct faculty English, Grand Valley State Coll., 1986—. Recipient C. Cahn Meml. Poetry prize Anhinga Press, 1985; AAUW Ola Love fellow, 1985-86. Mem. AWP, Intl. Soc. for Gen. Semantics, Phi Kappa Phi, NCTE, Natl. Museum, Women in the Arts. Home: 76 Union SE Apt 205 Grand Rapids MI 49503

BRIDGFORD, KIM SUZANNE, b. Moline, IL, Aug. 8, 1959; d. Kenneth Lyle and Carole Suzanne (Nelson) Bridgford. Contrbr. poetry to Altadena Rvw, Antigonish Rvw, Ascent, The Cresset, Event, Kans Qtly, Mundus Artium, Negative Capability, New Orleans Rvw, Tar River Poetry, Queen's Qtly, Texas Rvw, West Hills Rvw. BA in English, U. Iowa, 1981, MFA in Creative Writing, 1983; MA in English, U. Ill., 1985. Recipient 1st place award Natl. Career Awards Competition in Poetry, Natl. Soc. Arts and Letters, 1983. Address: 507 East White 3 Champaign IL 61820

BRIDWELL, MARGARET, see Jones, Margaret Bridwell

BRIEDIS, LAURA MARIJA, b. North Olmsted, OH, May 22, 1964; d. Imants and Ausma B. Translator: Fearless in Search of Fear, 1986. Contrbr. articles to mags., newspapers. B.A. in Jnlsm., Ohio State U., 1986. Newspaper reporter Lorain County Times, OH, 1986; asst. ed. Harcourt Brace Jovanovich, leve., 1987—; free-lance wrtr., 1987—. Home: 24338 LeBern

Dr North Olmsted OH 44070

BRIEGEL, WILLIAM EUGENE, (Willis Washington), b. Ft. Wayne, IN, Nove. 25, 1949, s. Arnold Eugene and Ida S. (Sanders) b., m. JoAnn Ostermeier, June 28, 1986. contrbg. ed.: Essays for Free Republic, 1985-87, The Savant, 1985-87. B.A., Purdue U., 1975; M.S., Ind. U., 1978. dir. devel. Purdue U., Ft. Wayne, Ind., 1975-79; pres. Briegel & Assocs., Ft. Wayne, 1981—. Home: 4809 Calumet Ave Fort Wayne IN 46806

BRIGGS, CHARLIE IRWIN, (Fay Irwin), b. Paducah, KY, July 10, 1927; d. Frank and Ora Lee (Lipford) Irwin; m. Andrew Jackson Briggs, June 7, 1948; children—Clark Hamilton, Charles Anthony. Author: My Orphans of the Wild, 1974, Two Writers Tell You How to Sell Your Writing, 1972; (anthol.) When Boys Meet Girls, 1965. Contrbr. articles, short stories to popular mags., newspapers including Ladies Circle, Southern Living, Tampa Tribune. Columnist: Transylvania Times, Brevard, NC, 1956-60; columnist, ed.: Charlotte Chronicle, Port Charlotte, FL, 1972, Norht Port News, FL, 1972, Venice Gondolier, 1986-87; ed., pub.: Venice Community Mag., 1978-84. Wrkg. on The Mabry Family in Triggs County, Ky. Student U. Ky., 1946-47. Tchr. writing Manatee Commun. Coll., Venice, FL, 1981-87. Recipient Algernon S. Sullivan award U. Ky., Lexington, 1947. Mem. Wrtrs. Alliance of Venice, Etc. (dir., pub. The Seagull). Home: 420 S Harbor Dr Venice FL 34285

BRIGGS, JOHN GURNEY, JR., b. High Point, NC, Feb. 17, 1916; s. John Gurney and Hazel Irene (Harmon) B.; m. Elizabeth Balee Westmoreland, Dec. 23, 1938; children: Robert Ragan, Mary Curtis. Author: The Collector's Tchaikovsky, 1959, Leonard Bernstein: The Man, His Work and His World, 1961, The Collector's Beethoven, 1962, Requiem for a Yellow Brick Brewery, 1969; contbr. articles and short stories to mags. Music editor, NBC, 1938-40; music critic: N.Y. Post, 1940-49; editor: Etude music mag., 1949-52; N.Y. Times, 1952-60; sr. writer, Smith, Kline & French Labs., Phila., 1961-70; writer: Camden (NJ) Courier-Post, 1970—program annotator, Phila. Orch., 1963-71. Student, U. N.C., 1932-35; grad., Curtis Inst. Music, 1938. Home: Cooper River Plaza Pennsauken NJ 08109

BRIGGS, PATTY ANN, see Eakins, Patricia

BRIGHT, NANCY ELIZABETH, b. Tupelo, MS, Dec. 29, 1944; d. Leland William and Marguerite (Ashe) B. Author: Southern Voices, 1974, The Aura Review, 1986, The Long Story, 1987, Kaleidoscope, 1987. Columnist: The Pearl Preaa, Pearl, MS, 1972-82; book rvw.: Clarion Ledger, Jackson, MS, 1987—. Home: 2305 Old Brandon Rd Pearl MS 39208

BRILEY, JOHN MARSHALL, JR., b. NYC, Oct. 9, 1940; s. John Marshall and Dorothy (DeWolf) B.; m. Ilona Diane Lucas, May 27, 1967; children—Kelly, Erin, Kathleen. Author: Pediatric Ward, 1985; columnist Mauian Moe., 1982—. Contrbr. short stories to mags. A.B., Harvard Coll., 1963; M.D., Columbia Coll. Physicians & Surgeons, 1967. Intern, Boston City Hosp., 1967-68, resident, 1968-70; pediatrician Maui Meical Group, Lahaina, HI, 1970—. Home: 258 Alu Rd Wailuku Maui HI 96793

BRILL, ERNEST, b. Bklyn., June 17, 1945. Author: (short stories) Sunbury, River Styx, Crazy Hattie Enters The Ice Age (adapted for public television), I Looked Over Jordan and Other Stories, 1980; poetry ed. Toward Revolutionary Art mag., 1972-76; contrbr. poems to Heirs, Toward Revolutionary Art, Foolkiller, Poetry for the People, Working Classics, Going for Coffee, short stories to Quindaro mag., essay to The 60s without Apologies. BA, San Francisco State Coll., 1971, MA, 1974. Ward clrk., chart researcher Kaiser Hosp., San Francisco, 1973-78; indsl. medicine drug counselor Albert Einstein Coll. Medicine, Bronx, N.Y., 1981—. N.Y. State Council for Arts creative arts grantee in fiction, 1981. Mem. P&W, NWU. Home: 51 Marks Pl Apt 9 New York NY 10003

BRINDEL, JUNE RACHUY, b. Little Rock, IA, June 5, 1919; d. Otto Louis and Etta Mina (Balster) Rachuy; m. Bernard Brindel, Aug. 26, 1939; children: Paul, Jill. Author: (juvenile) Luap, 1971 (Jr. Lit. Guild selection 1972); (novels) Ariadne, 1980, Phaedra, 1985; (short stories) Nobody Is Ever Missing, 1984; contrbr. short stories and poetry to Iowa, Mississippi Valley, Barat, Wascana rvws., Mss, Story, Kans., Carolina, Spoon River qtlys., others. BA, U. Chgo., 1945, MA, 1958. Prof. English, Chgo. City Coll., Wright Campus, 1958-82. Recipient prize Chgo. P&W, 1965; Wilmette Children's Theatre, 1970; C. S. Lewis prize Ind. U., 1973; award Ill. Arts Council, 1984, 85, lit. award, 1985; PEN Syndicated Fiction award, 1986. Mem. PEN, AG, P&W, Soc. Midland Authors. Home: 2740 Lincoln Ln Wilmette IL 60091

BRINGHURST, ROBERT, b. Los Angeles, CA, Oct. 16, 1946; s. George H. and Marion (Large) B.; m. Miki Cannon Sheffield, June 3, 1974 (div. 1981). Author: The Shipwright's Log, 1972, Cadastre, 1973, Deuteronomy, 1974, Eight Objects, 1975, Bergschrund, 1975, Jacob Singing, 1977, The Stonecutter's Horses, 1979, Tzuhalem's Mountain, 1982, the Beauty of the Weapons: Selected Poems 1972-82, 1985, ed (with others) Visions: Contemporary Art in Canada, 1983, Ocean/Paper/Stone, 1984, (with Bill Reid) The Raven Steals the Light, 1984, Tending the Fire, 1985, The Blue Roofs of Japan, 1986, Pieces of Map, Pieces of Music, 1986, Shovels, Shoes and the Slow Rotation of Letters, 1986. Contrbr to anthologies: The New Oxford Book of Canadian Verse, 1982, Oxford Anthology of Canadian Literature in English, 1983, The Penguin Book of Canadian Verse, 1984. Guest ed. of Arabic lit. and Greek issues of Contemporary Lit. in Transl, 1974, 1976; contrbg ed, Fine Print, 1985—. Attended Mass. Inst. of Tech., 1963-64, 1970-71, and U. of Utah, 1964-65; BA, Indiana U., 1973, MFA, U. of British Columbia, 1973. Journalist, Beirut, Lebanon, 1965-66, Boston, Mass., 1970-71; dragoman in Israel and Palestine, 1967-68; law clerk in Panama Canal Zone, 1968-69; vis lctr, U. of B.C., Vancouver, B.C., 1975-79, mem. Eng. dept. faculty, 1979-80; poet-inOres., School of Fine Arts, Banff, Alta, 1983; part-time lectr, Simon Fraser U., Vancouver, 1983-84; writer-in-res., U. of Winnipeg, Manitoba, 1986. Presented lectures and seminars at universities in Australia, New Zealand, Fiji, and Japan, 1985; participated in Ojibway and Cree Cultural Centre writing workshops in Ont., 1985-86. Home: Box 280 Bowen Island British Columbia VON 1GO Canada

BRINK, WILLIAM JOSEPH, JR., b. Indpls., Feb. 29, 1916; s. William Joseph and Emma Elizabeth (Schell) B.; m. Jenny Lou Dwyer, May 24, 1947; children—Timothy, John, William Allen, Robert. Author: (with Louis Harris) The Negro Revolution in America, 1962, Black and White, 1966. BA, Ind. U., 1940. With U.P.I., Detroit, Chgo., 1945-55, night mgr., Chgo., 1950-55; writer natl. affairs, genl. editor Newsweek, 1956-63, sr. editor, 1963-69; asst. mng. editor N.Y. Daily News, 1969-74, mng. editor, 1974-81. Served with USAF, 1942-45; MTO. Decorated Air medal with oak leaf cluster. Mem. Am. Soc. Newspaper Editors, Sigma Delta Chi. Home: 11 Birchwood Ln Westport CT 06880

BRINKLEY, WILLIAM CLARK, b. Custer, OK, Sept. 10, 1917; s. Daniel Squire and Ruth (Clark) B. Author: Quicksand, 1948, The Deliverance of Sister Cecilia, 1954, Don't Go Near the Water, 1956, The Fun House, 1961, The Two Susans, 1962, The Ninety and Nine, 1966, Breakpoint, 1978, Peeper, 1981. Student, William Jewell Coll., 1936-37; BA, U. Okla., 1940; spcl. student Yale Drama Schl., 1961-62. Reporter Daily Oklahoman, Oklahoma City, 1940-41, Washington Post, 1941-42, 49-51; successively corr., asst. editor, staff writer Life mag., 1951-58. Served to lt. USNR, 1942-46. Mem. Phi Beta Kappa. Address: 500 Wichita St No 79 McAllen TX 78501

BRINNIN, JOHN MALCOLM, b. Halifax, N.S., Can., Sept. 13, 1916; s. John Thomas and Frances (Malcolm) B. Author: (poetry) The Garden is Political, 1942, The Lincoln Lyrics, 1942, No Arch, No Triumph, 1945, The Sorrows of Cold Stone, 1951, Skin Diving in the Virgins, 1970; (biography) Dylan Thomas in America, 1955, The Third Rose: Gertrude Stein and Her World, 1959; (juvenile) Arthur, The Dolphin Who Didn't See Venice; (criticism) William Carlos Williams, 1963; The Selected Poems of John Malcolm Brinnin, 1963; (autobiography) Sextet: T. S. Eliot, Truman Capote & Others, 1981; editor: (with Kimon Friar) Modern Poetry: American and British, 1951, A Casebook on Dylan Thomas, 1960, The Poems of Emily Dickinson, 1960, Selected Operas and Plays of Gertrude Stein, 1970, The Sway of the Grand Saloon: A Social History of the North Atlantic, 1971, Beau Voyage: Life Aboard the Last Great Ships, 1981. BA, U. Mich., 1941; postgrad., Harvard U., 1941-42. Dir. Poetry Center, NYC, 1949-56; prof. English emeritus Boston U. Recipient Gold medal for disting. service to poetry, PSA, 1955. Mem. Natl. Inst. Arts and Letters. Home: King Caesar Rd Duxbury MA 02332

BRISBY, STEWART PAUL, b. Bronx, N.Y., Feb. 3, 1945, s. Clarence and Mattie (Wynne) B. Author poetry: Urinating in the Pool (chapbook), 1974, A Death in America, 1986; ed.: Born Into a Felony, 1978, A Letter Full of Roses, 1981; contrbr. to Callaloo, Manna, Cicada/Amelia, Tandava, numerous other mags. and anthologies. TV producer, dir. Syracuse (N.Y.) Cablesystems, 1979-82; coordinator, tchr. N.Y. State Poets in the Schls., NYC, 1982-85; pub. Wolverine Press, NYC. Grantee NEA, 1978, CAPS, 1981. Office: Box 962 Hell Gate Sta New York NY 10029

BRISTOW, ROBERT O'NEIL, b. St. Louis, Nov. 17, 1926; s. Jesse Reuben and Helen Marjorie (Utley) B.; children by previous marriage—Cynthia Lynn, Margery Jan Wu, Gregory Scott, Kelly Robert. Author: Time for Glory, 1968, Night Season, 1970, A Faraway Drummer, 1973, Laughter in Darkness, 1974. BA in Journalism, U. Okla., 1951, MA, 1965. Asst. advt. mgr. Altus (Okla.) Times Democrat, 1951-53; freelance writer Altus, 1951-60; prof. English Winthrop Coll., Rock Hill, SC, 1960—. Served with USNR, 1944-45. Recipient award for literary excellence U. Okla., 1969, award for novel

Friends of Am. Writers, 1974. Home: 321 Aiken Ave Rock Hill SC 29730

BRITE, MARY ALICE, b. Drumright, OK, June 28, 1930; d. Leo and Bessie A. (Murphy) Bowers; m. Charlie P. Venable, June 4, 1950 (dec. Jan. 1, 1967); children—Daniel, Kathlyn, Ruth, David; m. Robert N. Brite, Dec. 26, 1969. Author: Top of the Valley, 1976, Triumph Over Tears, 1979, Armadillo: Fact & Fiction, 1983. Wrkg. on life of Mary, Mother of Jesus, children books. B.S. in Elem. Edn., Okla. State U., 1955. Tchr. public elem. schls., NE, OK, CO, 1955-69. Recipient Sherwood E. Wirt award for Christian writing Billy Graham Schl., 1975, 1st prize Warner Press, 1975. Mem. Okla. Wrtrs. Fedn. Home: 2836 E 84th St Tulsa OK 74137

BRITT, LEIGH, see Hardenbrook, Yvonne Imogene

BRITTAIN, RASA, (Rasa Kaye), b. NYC,Jan. 2, 1960, d. Anthony A. and Danute A. Bobelis; m. Ross Brittain, Feb. 20, 1982. Contrbr. to numerous publs. including Glamour, NY Times, Seventeen, BA, Hofstra U., 1981. Acct. exec., Epoch 5 Marketing, Huntington, NY, 1980-81; reporter, WABC-AM Radio, NYC,1981-83; news director/wrtr., WEZB-FM Radio, New Orleans, 1983, prod./wrtr., Troika Productions, NYC,1984; news director/wrtr., WLTW-FM Radio, NYC,1984—. Awards: Best publ. affairs prog., NY State Broadcasters, 1985; Emmy, Natl. Acad. of TV Arts and Sci./NY, 1985; silver medal, Intl. TV Festival of NY, 1984. Mem. Intl. Radio & TV Soc., NY Press Club, Radio and TV News Directors Assn. Home: 30 W 63rd St New York NY 10023

BRITTAIN, WILLIAM E., b. Rochester, NY, Dec. 16, 1930; s. Knox and Dorothy (Sunderlin) B.; m. Virginia Ann Connorton, Feb. 6, 1954; children—James, Susan. Author: (children's books) All the Money in the World, 1979, Devil's Donkey, 1981, The Wish Giver, 1983, Who Knew There'd Be Ghosts, 1985, Dr. Dredd's Wagon of Wonders, 1987. Short stories pub. in Ellery Queen Mystery Mag. and Alfred Hitchcok's Mystery Mag., 1964-86. BS in Edn., Brockport State Tchrs. Coll., 1952; MS in Ednl. Adminstrn., Hofstra U., 1959. Tchr. LeRoy Central Schl. Dist., NY, 1952-54; tchr. English and reading Union Free Schl. Dist. No. 15, Lawrence, NY, 1954-86. Mem. MWA, NY State PW, Soc. Children's Book Writers. Recipient Charlie May Simon award State of Ark., 1982, Newberry Honor Book award ALA, 1984. Home: 17 Wisteria Dr Asheville NC 28804

BRITTON, JANET LORENE, b. Jamestown, PA, May 14, 1947; d. Albert G. and Shirley M. (Julian) Duney; m. Roland Rex Britton, July 8, 1967; children—Renae Marie, Neil Albert. Author non-fiction: To Live Eah Moment, 1984. Contrbr. articles to religious mags. Wrkg. on novel on marriage. B.S. in English Edn., U. Maine, 1970; M.A. in English, Youngstown State U., 1981. English tchr. Badger High Schl., Kinsman, OH, 1973-86, Pymatuning Valley High Schl., Andover, OH, 1986—. Mem. NEA, NCTE. Home: 5128 Stanhope-Kelloggsville Rd Andover OH 44003

BROADCORENS, YVONNE RAMAUT, b. Grammont, Belgium, Feb. 17, 1905, came to U.S., 1909, naturalized, 1921; d. Alfons and Clementine (Van Damme) Ramaut; m. Gustaf Broadorens, Aug. 17, 1930 (dec. Jan. 1937); 1 dau., Joan Nathalie. Contrbr. articles to mags. Wrkg. on articles. B.S. in Jnlsm., Boston U., 1929; student Harvard extension, New Schl. of Research, N.Y., 1952. Production staff CBS, WEEI, Boston, 1940-42; ed. Along the Line, New Haven Railroad, 1942-44, Textron Tide, 1944-47; assoc. ed. Modern Materials Handling, 1947-50; dir. publicity Simmons Coll., 1950-64, dir. public info., 1964-70, spl. instr. photojnlsm., 1970—; photography instr. Dennis Youmouth High Schl., MA, 1973-82. Mem. Profl. Wrtrs. Cape Cod, Mass. Indsl. Eds. Assn., Boston Press Club, Am. Coll. Public Relations Assn. (dir. N.E. dist. 1969-70), Edn. Wrtrs. Assn., Publicity Club, N.E. Women's Press Assn., New England Weekly Press Assn., Am. Women Radio and Television. Home: 38 Captain Perival Rd South Yarmouth MA 02664

BROBST, WILLIAM KEPLINGER, b. Canton, OH, Oct. 19, 1928, s. John Carlisle Brobst and Zelma (Keplinger) Karl; m. Mona Dalene Cope, Jan. 23, 1949 (div.); children—Joy Evelyn Brobst Garrison, Mark William; m. 2d, Judith Margaret Balogh, Dec. 16, 1974. Contrbr Poetry N.Am. Mentor. Published in numerous vols. APA. U.S. Army (Sgt.) sve. Korean Theatre, 1951-53. Tool and machine designer; maintenance tech. Fortune Savings Bank.Seminole, Fla., 1983—. Home: 10000 Park Blvd Lot 634 Seminole FL 34647

BROCK, JAYNE, b. Toccoa, GA, June 11, 1959; d. Harold Lamar and Dorothy Anne (Yearwood) Brock; m. Stephen C. Wyche, Nov. 5, 1977 (div. 1981); 1 dau., Jessica Lynn. Contrbr. poems to anthols., Wide Open Magazine. Wrkg. on poems, custom greeting cards. Grad. public schls., Chamblee, GA. Operations clrk. Sun Data Inc., Norcross, GA, 1983-86; operations mgr. Mtn. Capital, Tucker, GA, 1985-86, Park Financial, Norcross, GA, 1986—. Treas., Stone Mountain Jaycees, GA, 1986-87. Recipient Golden Poet award World of Poetry, 1986, 87, 4 Honorable Mentions, 1986-87. Mem. Ga. State Poetry Soc. Home: 921 Wilton Ln Lilburn GA 30247

BROCK, RANDALL J., b. Colfax, WA, Nov. 24, 1943; s. Homer Clarence and Roberta (Keith) B. contrbr. chapbooks: Mouse Poems, 1971, Poems and Photographs, 1979, I am Poems, 1982, Pockets of Origin, 1983, Shadows of Seclusion, 1983, The Goat Poems, 1984, Solid Blue, 1985; contrbr. Crow's Nest, Central Park, Rvw '76, Pigiron, Last Cookie, Gypsy, Sepia, Small Pond, other lit mags. AB, Eastern Wash Univ., 1970, BA, 1970, MFA, U. Oreg., 1973. Tchr. Christian Action Ministry, Chgo., 1967; mail clrk. and porter, Yellowstone Natl. Park, Wyoming, 1968; janitor Goodale & Barbieri, Spokane, 1978-79; bookstore clrk A-1 Old Book Trader, Spokane, 1981. Mem. United World Federalists, Pullman Wash., 1964, Future Spokane, 1982. Recipient Centrum scholarship, Port Townsend, Wash., 1977. Address: 1214 W Sprague 22 Spokane WA 99204

BRODER, DAVID SALZER, b. Chicago Heights, IL, Sept. 11, 1929; s. Albert I. and Nina M. (Salzer) B.; m. Ann Creighton Collar, June 8, 1951; children—George, Joshua, Matthew, Michael. Author: (with Stephen Hess) The Republican Establishment, 1967, The Party's Over: The Failure of Politics in America, 1972, Changing of the Guard: Power and Leadership in America, 1980. BA, U. Chgo, 1947, MA, 1951. Reporter Pantagraph, Bloomington, Ill., 1953-55, Congressional Qtly, Washington, 1955-60, Washington Star, 1960-65, N.Y. Times Washington bur. 1965-66; reporter Washington Post, 1966-75, asso. editor, 1975—; syndicated columnist. Served with AUS, 1951-53. Recipient Pulitzer prize in journalism, 1973. Home: 4024 N 27th St Arlington VA 22207

BRODERICK, JOHN CARUTHERS, b. Memphis, TN, Sept. 6, 1926; s. John Patrick and Myrtle Vaughn (Newson) B.; m. Kathryn Price Lynch, Sept. 10, 1949; children—Kathryn Price, John C. Author: Whitman the Poet: Materials for Study, 1960. Contrbr. articles to profl. jnls., books. Ed.: Henry David Thoreau, Jnl., 1981, 84. A.B. Southwestern U., 1948; M.A., U. N.C., 1949, Ph. D., 1953. Asst. chief mansucript Library of Congress, Washington, 1965-74, chief, 1975-79, asst. librarian research services, 1979—; adj. prof. English, George Washington U., Washington, 1964-84. Served with U.S. Army, 1945-46. Mem. MLA, Bibliographical Soc. Am. Home: 8005 Inspection House Rd Rockville MD 20854

BRODEY, JIM, b. Bklyn., Nov. 30, 1942, s. Arnold and Regina (Miles) Dolmatz; m. Tandy Martin, June 29, 1968 (div. May 1978); m. 2d, Kathy Foley, June 26, 1980. Author: (poems) Fleeing Madly South, 1964, Identikit, 1966, Long Distance Quote, 1967, Blues of the Egyptian Kings, 1975, Unless, 1976, Piranha Yoga, 1977, Judyism, 1980, Heart of the Breath, 1986, (prose) Last Licks, 1972, Laughingstock, 1972; ed. Clothesline 1, 1965, 2, 1970; contrbr. to anthologies including The World Anthology, Another World, An Anthology of N.Y. Poets; contrbr. articles to Poetry Project Newsletter, Circus mag., Los Angeles Free Press, N.Y. Times, also others. Wrkg. on 11 book series of 1100 poems written 1983-1985. BA in Am. Poetry, NYU, 1964. Record rvw. ed. Rolling Stone, 1968, Crawdaddy, 1969; assoc. ed. Rock mag., 1969; entertainment ed. N.Y. Herald, 1979-81. Recipient Dylan Thomas poetry prize New Schl. for Social Research, 1964; grantee Poet's Fdn., 1965, 67, Change Fnd., 1976, PEN Club Am., 1976. Mem. PW. Home: 73-12 35th Ave Jackson Heights NY 11372

BRODINE, KAREN HARRIET, b. Seattle, June 14, 1947; d. Val Daniel and Mary (Pierce) B. Author: (poetry) Slow Juggling, 1975; Workweek, 1977; Illegal Assembly, 1980; Woman Sitting at the Machine Thinking, 1987; contrbr. to numerous mags including Ironwood, Greenfield Rvw, Firewood, Heresies, Conditions, New Lesbian Writing. BA in Dramatic Arts, U. Calif.-Berkeley, 1972; MA in Creative Writing, San Francisco State U., 1974. Instr creative writing San Francisco State U., 1975-81. Mem. NWU, Natl. Women's Studies Assn. Home: 2661 21st St San Francisco CA 94110

BRODOVSKY, SUE, see Arsone, Sarah

BRODSKY, IOSIF ALEXANDROVICH, b. Leningrad, USSR, May 24, 1940; expelled from Russia and came to U.S., 1972; s. Alexander I. and Maria (Volpert) B. Works include: (poetry) A Christmas Ballad, 1962, Elegy for John Donne, 1963, Isaac and Abraham, 1963, Verses on the Death of T. S. Eliot, 1965, Song Without Music, 1969, Selected Poems, 1973, A Part of Speech, 1980; (essays) Less than One, 1981. Student, Russian secondary schls. until 1956. Poet-in-res. U. Mich., Ann Arbor, 1972-73, 74-79; vis. prof. Smith Coll., Amherst Coll., Queens Coll., Hampshire Coll.; fellow N.Y. Inst. Humanities, NYU; assoc. Russian Inst., Columbia U. John D. and Catherine T. MacArthur Fdn. fellow, 1981; Nobel Prize, literature, 1987. Mem. AAAL. Office: Dept Slavic Lang U. Mich Ann Arbor MI 48109

BRODY, HARRY PHILIP, b. Ottumwa, IA, Dec. 4, 1952, s. Ernest Earl and Betty (Johnson) B.; m. Janet Alabach, June 8, 1979; children—Hagen, Margot. Author: As One to Birth I Went Now I Am Taken Back, 1982, Darkness Is Skin, 1984, Milk from a Lioness, 1986, Fields, 1987; contrbr. to Chariton Rvw., Poetry Now, Conn. Poetry Rvw., Painted Bride Qtly., Aileron, New Collage, Permafront, others. BA, New Coll., Sarasota, Fla., 1982; JD, Duke U., 1985. Assoc. Caudle & Spears, P.A., Charlotte, N.C., 1985—. Home: 119 Manning Dr Charlotte NC 28209

BRODY, JACQUELINE, b. Utica, NY, Jan. 23, 1932; d. Jack and Mary (Childress) Galloway; m. Eugene D. Brody, Apr. 5, 1959; children—Jessica, Leslie. AB, Vassar College, 1953; postgrad., London Schl. Econs., 1953-56. Assoc. editor Crowell Collier Macmillan, NYC, 1963-67; writer Council on Fgn. Relations, NYC, 1968-69; mng. editor Print Collector's Newsletter, NYC, 1971-72, editor, 1972—. Office: 72 Spring St New York NY 10012

BRODY, JANE ELLEN, b. Bklyn,. May 19, 1941; d. Sidney and Lillian (Kellner) B.; m. Richard Engquist, Oct. 2, 1966; children: Lee Erik and Lorin Michael Engquist (twins). Author: (with Richard Engquist) Secrets of Good Health, 1970, (with Arthur Holleb) You Can Fight Cancer and Win, 1977, Jane Brody's Nutrition Book, 1981, Jane Brody's The New York Times Guide to Personal Health, 1982, Jane Brody's Good Food Book, 1985. B.S., N.Y. State Coll. Agr., Cornell U., 1962; M.S. in Journalism, U. Wis., 1963. Reporter Mpls. Tribune, 1963-65; sci. writer, personal health columnist N.Y. Times, 1965—. Recipient numerous writing awards, including; Sci. Writer's award ADA, 1978; J.C. Penney-U. Mo. Journalism award, 1978. Office: 229 W 43d St New York NY 10036

BROHAUGH, WILLIAM EDWARD, b. Dec. 5, 1953; s. Earl Robert and Hazel Florence (Goff) B.; m. Susan Jill McTavish, June 10, 1978; 1 son, Christopher William. Ed., Writer's Digest, 1982—, Just Open a Vein, 1987; author Professional Etiquette for Writers, 1986; contrbr. to The Rangefinder, Word Processing News, Play Meter, Success, Popular Computing, Cincinnati Enquirer Sunday, others. BA, U. WI, 1976. Staff positions F&W, Cincinnati, 1976-79, asst. ed. Writer's Digest, F&W, 1979-82, ed., 1982—. Office: F&W Pub 1507 Dana Ave Cincinnati OH 45207

BROIDA, HELEN, b. St. Louis, d. Max and Jennie (Cohen) B.; children—Vicki Ward, Ronna Frank. Author: Coping with Stroke, 1979. Contrbr. Archives of Phys. Medicine and Rehab. Wrkg. on novel. PhD, U. So. Calif., Los Angeles, 1962. Speech pathologist St. John's Hosp., Santa Monica, Calif., 1964-67, VA Hosp., West Los Angeles, 1967-72; VA Hosp., La Jolla, 1972-82; wrtr. 1978—. Home: 5362-0 Algarrobo St Laguna Hills CA 92653

BROKAW, R. MIRIAM, b. Kobe, Japan, June 15, 1917; came to U.S., 1930; d. Harvey and Olivia (Forster) B. BA, Wilson Coll., 1937, Litt, 1966. Proofreader Westminster Press, Phila., 1937-44; freelance editor Prentice-Hall, NYC, 1944-45; proofreader Princeton U. Press, N.J., 1945-48, editor, then mng. editor, 1948-65, assoc. dir., editor, 1966-85; English editl. advisor U. Tokyo Press, 1965-66. Mem. Am. Hist. Assn., Assn. Am. Univ. Presses (pres. 1975-76), Intl. Assn. Scholarly Pubs. (secy.-gen. 1967-70). Home: 4674 Province Line Rd Princeton NJ 18540

BROMBERT, VICTOR HENRI, b. Nov. 11, 1923; U.S., 1941, naturalized, 1943; s. Jacques and Vera B.; m. Beth Anne Archer, June 18, 1950; children—Lauren Nora, Marc Alexis. Author: The Criticism of T.S. Eliot, 1949, Stendhal et la Voie Oblique, 1954, The Intellectual Hero, 1961, The Novels of Flaubert, 1966, Stendhal: Fiction and the Themes of Freedom, 1968, Flaubert par lui-meme, 1971, La Prison romantique, 1975, Eng. trans., The Romantic Prison: French Tradition, 1978, Victor Hugo and the Visionary Novel, 1984; editor: Stendhal: A Collection of Critical Essays, 1962, Balzac's La Peau de Chagrin, 1962, The Hero in Literature, 1969, Flaubert's "Madame Bovary," 1986; contrbg. author: The World of Lawrence Durrell, 1962, Ideas in the Drama, 1964, Instants Premiers, 1973, Romanticism, 1973, Literary Criticism, 1974, Die Romanische Novelle, 1977, The Author in His Work, 1978, Essais sur Flaubert, 1979, Writers and Politics, 1983, Flaubert and Postmodernism, 1984, Writing in a Modern Temper, 1984, Hugo le Fabuleux, 1985. BA, Yale U., 1948, MA, 1949, PhD, 1953; postgrad., U. Rome, 1950-51; HHD (hon.), U. Chgo., 1981. Faculty Yale U., New Haven, 1951-75, assoc. prof., 1958-61, prof., 1961-75, Benjamin F. Barge prof. Romance lits., 1969-75, chmn. dept. Romance langs. and lit., 1964-73; Henry Putnam Univ. prof. Romance and comparative lit. Princeton U., 1975—; dir., Christian Gauss Seminars in Criticism, 1984—. Served with M.I. AUS, 1943-45. Home: 187 Library Pl Princeton NJ 08540

BROMIGE, DAVID M., b. London, Oct. 22, 1933, emigrated to Canada, 1953, came to U.S., 1962, s. Harold Thomas and Ada (Cann) B.; m. Joan Shirley Peacock, Dec. 21, 1961 (div. 1970); 1 son, Christopher Kenneth; m. 2d, Cecelia Therese Belle, Jan. 3, 1981; 1 dau., Maggie. Author: The Gathering, 1965, Please, Like Me, 1968, The Ends of the Earth, 1968, The Quivering Roadway, 1969, Threads, 1970, 3 Stories, 1973, 10 Years in the Making, 1973, Birds of the West, 1974, Tight Corners, 1974, Out of My Hands, 1974, Spells and Blessings, 1975, Credences of Winter, 1976, Living in Advance, 1976, My Poetry, 1980, P-E-A-C-E, 1981, In the Uneven Steps of Hung-Chow, 1982, The Melancholy Owed Categories, 1984, You See, Parts 1 and 2, 1986, Red Hats, 1986, Bromige No. of The Difficulties, 1987, Desire, 1987; ed.: Raven, 1961-62, Rx CxLion, 1966-67, Open Reading, 1970-76; poetry ed. NW Rvw, 1962-64. BA, U. B.C., 1962; MA, U. Calif., Berkeley, 1964, ABD, 1969. Instr. Calif. Coll. Arts and Crafts, 1969-70, U. Calif., Berkeley, 1969-70; prof. English, Sonoma State U., Rohnert Park, Calif., 1970—. Recipient Discovery award NEA, 1969, NEA Poetry award, 1979-80, Poetry award Can. Council, 1976-77, Pushcart Prize, 1980. Home: 461 High St Sebastopol CA 95472

BROMMER, GERALD F(REDERICK), b. Berkeley, CA, Jan. 8, 1927; s. Edgar Carl and Helen Christine (Wall) B.; m. Georgia Elizabeth Pratt, Dec. 19, 1948. Author: Wire Sculpture and Other Three-Dimensional Construction, 1968, Relief Printmaking, 1970, Drawing: Ideas, Materials, and Techniques, 1972, rev ed, 1978, Transparen Watercolor: Ideas and Techniques, 1973, Space (juvenile), 1974, Movement and Rhythm (juvenile), 1975, (with George F. Horn) Art in Your World (juvenile), 1977, rev ed, 1985, (with Horn), Art: Your Visual Environment (juvenile), 1977, rev ed, 1985, Landscapes, 1977, The Art of College, ed by Horn and Sarita K. Rainey, 1978, Discovering Art History, 1981, rev ed, 1987, Careers in Art: An Illustrated Guide, 1984, Watercolor and Collage Workship, 1986, Exploring the Art of Painting (high school text), 1987, Exploring Drawing (high school text), 1987. Editor: Jack Selleck, Faces, 1977, Albert W. Poeter, The Art of Sketching, 1977, Joseph A. Gatto, Cities, 1977, Gatto and others, Exploring Visual Design, 1978, rev ed, 1987, Mary Korstad Mueller, Murals: Creating an Environment, 1979, Albert W. Porter, Creative Watercolor Painting, 1982, Norman Fullner, Airbrush Painting, 1982. Contrbr of articles to periodicals, including School Arts, Southwest Art, Today's Art, and Art and Activities. BA, Concordia Coll., Seward, Neb., 1948; MA, U. of Nebraska, 1955; further grad. study at Chouinard Art Ints., 1955, U. of Calif., Los Angeles, 1956-57, Otis Art Institute, 1958-59, and U. of Southern Calif., 1959-61. D. Litt., Christ Coll. Irvine, Calif. Artist and author. Teacher, St. Paul's Lutheran School, North Hollywood, Calif., 1948-55; chmn of art dept, Lutheran H.S., Los Angeles, Calif., 1955-73; chief designer, Daystar Designs, Inc., Van Nuys, Calif., 1963-73. Work exhibited in numerous group shows and more than 100 one-man shows. Work in permanent collections of N.Y. State U., Utah State U., Alan Hancock Coll, in State of California Collection, TRW, Pacific Telesis, Las Vegas Hilton Hotel, and HOward Ahmanson collection. Member: Natl. Watercolor Soc (treas., 1963, v.p., 1965-66 and 1982-83; pres, 1966-67 and 1982-83), Watercolor U.S.A. Honor Society, West Coast Water Color Soc., Artists for Economic Action, Natl. Art Educ Assn, Artists Equity, Rocky Mountain Natl Watercolor Soc. Named alumnus of the year by Concodia Teachers Coll, 1975. Home: 11252 Valley Spring Lane North Hollywood CA 91602

BRONSON, WOLFE, see Raborg, Frederick Ashton, Jr.

BRONTE, LOUISA, see Roberts, Janet

BROOKE, AMANDA, see Mayer, Jane S.

BROOKE, AVERY ROGERS, b. Providence, May 28, 1923; d. Morgan Witter and Lucy Avery (Benjamin) Rogers; m. Joel Ijams Brooke, Sept. 14, 1946; children: Witter, Lucy, Sarah. Author: Youth Talks with God, 1959, Doorway to Meditation, 1973, How to Meditate Without Leaving the World, 1975, Plain Prayers for a Complicated World, 1975, Roots of Spring, 1975, As Never Before, 1976, Hidden in Plain Sight, 1978; (under pseudonym Alice Benjamin) Cooking With Consciene, 1975. Editor: The Vineyard Bible, 1980, Celtic Prayers, 1981, Trailing Clouds of Glory: Spiritual Values in Children's Books, 1985 (with Madeleine L'Engle). Student, R.I. Sch. Deign, 1942-45; B.F.A., Union Theol. Sem., 1970. Founder, pres. Vineyard Books, Inc., Noroton, Conn., 1971—; pub., v.p. Seabury Press, N.Y.C., 1980-83. Mem. Women in Communication, AG, Am. Acad. of Religion. Home: 129 Nearwater Ln Noroton CT 06820

BROOKS, BEN, b. Washington, Nov. 20, 1948; s. Leon Richard and Esther Helen (Levin) B.; m. Nancy Ellen Hall, Dec. 26, 1971; children—Liana Kristin, Luke Orion. Author: The Ice box, 1987; contrbr. short stories numerous publs. inclg. Willmore City, Story Quarterly, Shankpainter, Confrontation, Sewanee Rvw, Chicago Rvw, Mississippi Rvw, Denver Qtly, Davidson Misc., Greensboro Rvw, Alchemy, Outerbridge, Ala Qtly Rvw, Other Voices, Prize Stories: O. Henry Awards, 1982; contrbr. essays on art Fall Arts Fest Catalogue, 1980, Permanent Collection Catalogue, 1978, Days Lumberyard Studios Exhibition Catalogue, 1978. BA cum laude in Eng., Harvard, 1970; MFA in Writing, U Iowa, 1975. Writer/archivist Provincetown Art Assn., Mass, 1977-78; dir. Cape Cod Fall Arts Fest, Provincetown, 1980; writer-in-residence Mass. Arts Fdn., 1978-83; communications coord. Anderson DeBartolo Pan, Inc, Tucson, 1984—. Fellow Fine Arts Work Ctr, Provincetown, 1975-76, 76-77, Mass Artists Fdn., 1978, Ossabaw Island Project, Ga, 1982, Ingram Merrill Fdn., 1984, Ariz. Arts Commn., 1984; grantee, Friendship Fdn, NYC,1981; recipient O. Henry award, 1982 (3d prize). Mem. NWU. Address: Box 40804 Tucson AZ 85717

BROOKS, FRANK PICKERING, b. Portsmouth, NH, Jan. 2, 1920, s. Frank Edwin and Florence Isabel (Towle) B.; m. Emily Elizabeth Marden, July 5, 1942; children—William B., Sally E., Robert P. Author: The Control of Gastrointestinal Function, 1970, Diseases of the Exocrine Pancreas, 1980; ed. books: Exocrine Glands (with Sy Botelho and W. Shelley), 1969, Endocrinology of the Gut (with W. Y. Ehey), 1974, Nerves and the Gut (with P. W. Evers), 1977, Gastrointestinal Patho-physiology, 1974, 2d ed., 1978, Peptic Ulcer, 1985; ed. jnls.: GI Abstracts and Citations, Digestive Diseases and Sciences, 1982—; mem. editorial bd. Am. Jnl. Physiology, 1962-68, Proceedings of Soc. Exptl. Biology and Medicine, 1974-80, Pancreas, 1986—. Wrkg. on non-fiction. AB, Dartmouth Coll., 1941; MD, U. Pa., 1943. Mem. faculty dept. medicine U. Pa. Med. Schl., Phila., 1952—. Served to lt. (jg) USN, 1946-48. Mem. numerous med. orgns. Home: 206 Almur Ln Wynnewood PA 19096

BROOKS, GWENDOLYN, b. Topeka, June 7, 1917; d. David Anderson and Keziah Corinne (Wims) B.; m. Henry L. Blakely, Sept. 17, 1939; children—Henry L., Nora. Author: poetry A Street in Bronzeville, 1945, Annie Allen, 1949; novel Maud Martha, 1955; for children Bronzeville Boys and Girls, 1956; poetry The Bean Eaters, 1960, Selected Poems, 1963, In the Mecca, 1968, Riot, 1969, Family Pictures, 1970, Aloneness, 1971, To Disembark, 1981; autobiography Report from Part One, 1972, The Tiger Who Wore White Gloves, 1974, Beckonings, 1975, Primer for Blacks, 1980, Young Poet's Primer, 1981. Grad. Wilson Jr. College, Chicago, 1936; LHD, Columbia Coll., Chgo., Northeastern Ill. State Coll.; Mem. Illinois Arts Council. Named One of 10 Women of the Year Mademoiselle mag., 1945; recipient award for creative writing Am. Acad. Arts and Letters, 1946; Guggenheim fellow for creative writing, 1946, 47; Pulitzer prize for poetry, 1950; Anisfield-Wolf award, 1969; named Poet Laureate of Ill., 1969. Consultant in Poetry to the Library of Congress, 1985-86. Mem. Soc. Midland Authors. Home: 7428 S Evans Ave Chicago IL 60619

BROOKS, JOHN, b. NYC, Dec. 5, 1920; s. John Nixon and Bessie (Lyon) B.; m. Anne Curtis Brown, Mar. 6, 1948 (div. 1952); m. Rae Alexander Everitt, Aug. 15, 1953 (div. 1975); children—Carolyn, John Alexander; m. Barbara Smith Mahoney, Jan. 29, 1982. Author: The Big Wheel, 1949, A Pride of Lions, 1954, The Man Who Broke Things, 1948, The Seven Fat Years, 1958, The Fate of the Edsel, 1963, The Great Leap, 1966, Business Adventures, 1969, Once in Golconda, 1969, The Go-Go Years, 1973, Telephone, 1976, The Games Players, 1980, Showing Off in America, 1981, The Takeover Game, 1987; also articles and rvws.; editor: The One and the Many, 1962, The Autobiography of American Business, 1974. AB, Princeton U., 1942. Contrbg. editor Time mag., 1945-47; staff contrbr. New Yorker mag., 1949—. Trustee N.Y. Pub. Library, 1978-84. Served with AUS, 1942-45; ETO. Poynter fellow Yale, 1974-75. Mem. AG Am. (pres. 1975-79), PEN (v.p. 1962-66), Soc. Am. Historians (v.p. 1984, pres. 1987—). Home: 41 Barrow St New York NY 10014

BROOKS, TERRY, b. Sterling, IL, Jan. 8, 1944; s. Dean Oliver and Marjorie Lantha (Gleason) B.; m. Barbara Ann Groth, Apr. 23, 1972; children—Amanda Leigh, Alexander Stephen. Author: The Sword of Shannara, 1977, The Elfstones of Shannara, 1982. AB, Hamilton Coll., 1966; LLB, Washington and Lee U., 1969. Bar: Ill. Mem. Besse, Frye, Arnold & Brooks, Sterling, 1969—. Mem. Am., Ill., Whiteside county bar assns. Am. Trial Lawyers Assn. Home: 1310 Sinnissippi Rd Sterling IL 61081

BROOKS, VIRGINIA K., b. Springfield, Mass., Nov. 28, 1953, d. George Bard and Dorothy Jane (Irwin) Brooks. AS, Mitchell Coll., 1974; BS, Bridgeport (Conn.) U., 1976. Wrtr. Stanley Home Products, Westfield, Mass., 1978-79; ed. Natl. Grange Mut., Keene, N.H., 1979. Home: 119 Butternut Dr Keene NH 03431

BROSMAN, CATHARINE SAVAGE, b. Denver, June 7, 1934, d. Paul Victor and Della L. (Stanforth) Hill; m. Patric Savage, Apr. 7, 1955 (div. July 1964); m. 2d, Paul William Brosman, Jr., Aug. 21, 1970; 1 child, Katherine Elliott. Books: Andre Gide: l'evolution de sa pensee religieuse, 1962, Malraux, Sartre, and Aragon as Political Novelists, 1964, Roger Martin du Gard, 1968, Jean-Paul Sartre, 1983. Poetry collections: Watering, 1972, Abiding Winter, 1983. Contrbr. critical articles to French Rvw., Studies in Romanticism, Symposium, Australian Jnl. of French Studies, Essays in French Lit., Claudel Studies, French Forum, Lang. and Style, Modern Lang. Rvw, Forum for Modern Lang. Studies, South Central Rvw, Folio, Papers in Romance, Critique, Jnl of Peace Studies, others. Contrbr. to Columbia Dictionary of Modern Lit., A Critical Bibliog. of French Lit., The Twentieth Century, Litterature et gastronomie, 1985, Approaches to Teaching "The Plague," 1985, others. Mng. ed. French Rvw, 1977-80. Contrbr. poems to So. Rvw, Sewanee Rvw, Va. Qtly Rvw, Southwest Rvw, Tex. Qtly, Colo. Qtly, Prairie Schooner, Shenandoah, others. Wrkg. on critical study of writer Jules Roy, Dictionary of Lit. Biography, French novelists of 20th century (2 vols.), study of Simone de Beauvoir, crit. bibliog. of works on André Gide, also poetry. BA, Rice U., 1955, MA, 1957, PhD,1960. Instr. French, Rice U., Houston, 1960-62; asst. prof. French, Sweet Briar Coll., Va., 1962-63, U. Fla., Gainesville, 1963-66; assoc. prof. French, Mary Baldwin Coll., Staunton, Va., 1966-68; assoc. prof. French, Tulane U., New Orleans, 1968-72, prof. French, 1972—.Mem. MLA, Am. Assn. Teachers of French, South Central MLA, South Atlantic MLA. Recipient 3rd place poetry award Best Poems of 1973, Palo Alto, Calif., 1974. Home: 7834 Willow St New Orleans LA 70118

BROUGHTON, JAMES, b. Modesto, CA, Nov. 10, 1913; s. Irwin Reece and Olga (Jungbluth) B.; m. Suzanna Hart, Dec. 8, 1962 (div. 1978); children: Serena, Orion; m. Joel Singer, July 23, 1978. Author: The Playground, 1949, Musical Chairs, 1950, True and False Unicorn, 1957, A Long Undressing, 1971, Seeing the Light, 1977, Odes for Odd Occasions, 1977, The Androgyne Journal, 1977, Graffiti for the Johns of Heaven, 1982, Ecstasies, 1983; contrbr. numerous anthologies; writer and dir. films: Mother's Day, 1948, Loony Tom, 1951, The Pleasure Garden, 1953, The Bed, 1968, This Is It, 1971, Dreamwood, 1972, Testament, 1974, (with Joel Singer) Devotions, 1983; many other books and films. BA, Stanford U., 1936; DFA, San Francisco Art Inst., 1984. Prof. San Francisco State U., 1965-76, San Francisco Art Inst., 1968-82, fellow Guggenheim Fdn., 1971, 73; grantee NEA, 1976, 82; recipient Cert. of Honor, City of San Francisco for artistic contrbns. to community for 40 yrs., 1983. Office: Box 183 Mill Valley CA 94942

BROUGHTON, PAMELA KAY, b. Oklahoma City, OK, Apr. 5, 1946; d. David A., Sr. and Mary Eloise (Earp) Wood; m. Nick Lucas Woodard, Sept. 21, 1965 (div. Aug. 1971); 1 son, Addison Lucas; m. John L. Broughton (div. June 1985); children—Jonathan David, Christopher A. Author: The Creation, 1985, Noah's Ark, 1985, Joseph and the Coat of Many Colors, 1986, Jesus at the Temple, 1986, The Prodigal Sun, 1986, The Miracle of the Loaves and Fishes, 1986, David and Goliath, 1986, The Story of Jonah, 1986, The Life of Jesus, 1986, Moses in the Bullrushes, 1987. Wrkg. on adult novel set in 1920's. B.A. in English, U. Okla., 1982, M.A. in Jnlsm., 1984. Lectr., wrtr. U. Okla., Norman, 1984-86; free-lance wrtr., 1974-84, 87—. Mem. SCBW, SPJ. Home: 3400 N Virginia Ave Oklahoma City OK 73118

BROUGHTON, T. ALAN, b. Bryn Mawr, PA, June 9, 1936; s. T. Robert and Annie Leigh (Hobson) B.; m. Laurel Ginter; children—Shannon Leigh, John Camm, Travers Nathaniel. Author novels: A Family Gathering, 1977, Winter Journey, 1980, The Horsemaster, 1981, Hob's Daughter, 1984; poetry: Preparing To Be Happy, 1987, Dreams Before Sleep, 1982, Far From Home, 1979, In the Face of Descent, 1975, The Others We Are, 1979, Adam's Dream, 1975. BA, Swarthmore College, 1962; MA, U. of Washington, 1964. Instr., Sweet Briar College, Sweet Briar, Va., 1962-64; prof., U. of Vermont, 1964—. Awards: NEA fellowship, 1976-77, Guggenheim fellowship, 1982-83. Home: 406 South Winooski Ave Burlington VT 05401

BROUMAS, OLGA, b. Hermoupolis, Greece, May 6, 1949; arr. US, 1967; d. Nicholas Constantine and Claire Antoinette (Pendeli) Broumas; m. Stephen Edward Bangs, Aug. 2, 1973 (div. 1979). Author: Black Holes, Black Stockings (with Jane Miller), 1985, Pastoral Jazz, 1983, Soie Sauvage, 1980, Beginning with O, 1977, Restlessness (in Greek), 1967; translator. What I Love (Odysseas Elytis), 1986; contrbr. poetry numerous publs. inclg. Zyzzyva, APR, Calyx, Parnassus, The Iowa Rvw, An Anthology of Women Poets from Antiquity to Now. BA, U. Pa, 1970; MFA, U. Ore., 1973. Assoc. Fac. Goddard Coll., Plainfield, Vt., 1979-81; poet-in-residence Women Writers Ctr., Cazenovia, N.Y., 1981-82; founder and dir. Freehand Inc., Provincetown, Mass., 1982—. Recipient Yale Younger Poets award, 1977; NEA grantee, 1978, Ore. and Vt. Arts Comm, 1978, 80; Guggenheim fellow, 1981. Mem. PSA. Address: Box POB 806 Provincetown MA 02657

BROWER, CHERYL DIANE, b. Yuma, CO, Mar. 3, 1958; d. Walter Earl Rogers and Mardell Marie (McDonald) Rogers White; m. Stephen Wayne Brower, June 26, 1976; children—Cassandra Ellen, Adrian Wayne. Contrbr. poems to anthols. Student Morgan Commun. Coll. Recipient (5) Honorable Mention, World of Poetry, 1984, 85, 86, Spcl. Mention, 1985, (2) Golden Poet awards, 1985, 86. Home: 14530 Hwy 34 15 Fort Morgan CO 80701

BROWN, AUBREY NEBLETT, JR., B. Hillsboro, TX, May 6, 1908; s. Aubrey Neblett and Virginia Rose (Sims) B.; m. Sarah Dumond Hill, Oct. 4, 1932; children: Aubrey Neblett III, Zaida English, Julia Haywood, Virginia Sims, Eleanor Berkeley, William Hill, Ernest Thompson, Katherine Purdie. Editor Presbtyn. Outlook, Richmond, Va., 1943-78, Going-to-College Handbook, 1946-79, Church Publicity Book, 1986. A.B. Davidson Coll., 1929; B.D., Union Theol. Sem., Va., 1932; Litt.D., Southwestern at Memphis, 1950; D.D., Maryville Coll., 1961; Litt.D., Davidson Coll., 1979. Recipient Editorial citation Asso. Ch. Press, 1952. Home: 3213 Brook Rd Richmond VA 23227

BROWN, AUDREY, see du Chemin, Audrey May

BROWN, BARBARA BLACK, b. Eureka, CA, Dec. 11, 1928; d. William Marion and Letitia (Brunia) Black; m. D. Vinson Brown, June 18, 1950; children: Tamara, Roxana, Keven. Editor: Tapestries in Sand (by David Villasenor), 1963, Warriors of the Rainbow (by Vinson Brown), 1963, Exploring Pacific Coast Tidepools (by Brown and Braun), 1966, Exploring and Mining Gems and Gold in West (by Ryerson), 1967, Natural Remedies for Better Health (by Ingrid Sherman), 1970, Lord of the Dawn, Quetzalcoatl (by Tony Shearer), 1971, Country Land and Its Uses (by Howard Orem), 1975, Broken Pattern (by Vada Carlson; co-editor, K. Meilicke), 1984. BA, Western State Coll., 1950. Co-owner, mgr. Naturegraph Pubs., Los Altos, Calif., 1950-54, co-owner, proofreader, editor, San Martin, Calif., 1954-60, Healdsburg, Calif., 1960-76, Happy Camp, Calif., 1976—. Office: Naturegraph 3543 Indian Creek Rd Happy Camp CA 96039

BROWN, BERNARD E(DWARD), b. Bayonne, NJ, Sept. 17, 1925; Author: American Conservatives: The Political Thought of Francis Lieber and John W. Burgess, 1951, (with Roy C. Macridis) The DeGaulle Republic: Quest for Unity, 1960, ed (with Macridis) comparative Politics: Notes and Readings, 1961, 6th ed, 1986, New Directions in Comparative Politics, 1962, (with others) Government and Politics: An Introduction to Political Science, ed by Alex N. Dragnich and John C. Wahlke, 1966, contrbr, Cases in Comparative Politics, 1960, 2d ed (ed. with James B. Christoph), 1969, 3d ed, 1976, ed (with Wahlke) The American Political System: Notes and Readings, 1967, rev. ed, 1971, Protest in Paris: Anatomy of a Revolt, 1974, ed. Eurocommunism and Errosocialism: The Left Confronts Modernity, 1978, Intellectuals and Other Traitors, 1980, Socialism of a Different Kind: Reshaping the Left in France, 1982, ed., Great American Political Thinkers, 2 vols., 1983. Contrbr to profl jnls. B.S.S., City College (now City College of the City University of N.Y.), 1945; MA, Columbia U., 1946, Ph.D., 1950. Instr. in govt., City College, NYC, 1951-53; asst prof. of poli. sci. Michigan State U. of Agri. and Appl. Scis. (now Michigan State U.), East Lansing, 1954-56; asst prof to assoc prof of poli. sci., Vanderbilt U., Nashville, Tenn., 1959-65; prof of poli. sci., Brooklyn Coll. of the City U. of N.Y., 1965-74; prof of poli. sci at the Graduate School and University Center and Herbert H. Lehmann Coll., City U. of N.Y., 1974—. Vis prof McGill U., U. of Delhi, and U. of Daker; Smith Mundt Prof, U. of Saigon. Member: Amer. Pol. Sci. Assn. Fulbright research grantee, U. of Paris, 1956-57, 1979; Rockefeller Fdn Hum. fellow, 1980; NEH fellow, 1986. Address: Dept. POli. Sci. CUNY 33 West 42nd St New York NY 10036

BROWN, BETH, see Frio, Mary Oliver Brown

BROWN, CHARLINE HAYES, b. Cotton Valley, LA, Dec. 13, 1919; d. Howard R. and Flora Sue (Davis) Hayes; m. Joseph Cecil Brown, Jr., Sept. 30, 1945; children—Joe Howard, Susan Carol Brown Thorn, Terry Ann. Author poems: Brief Lightning, 1979. Contrbr. poems to anthols. Wrkg. on collection of poems. B.S. in Bus. Administration, La. State U., 1941. Sey., treas. Lumbermen's Supply Co., Inc., Monroe, LA, 1953-85; estate administr. Estate of H. R. Hayes, Monroe, 1977-78, Estate of Sue D. Hayes, Monroe, 1983-84; mgr. Hayes Co., Monroe, 1978—. Mem. NLAPW, La. State Poetry Soc. (4-1st prizes 1955, 2d place 1969), Miss. State Poetry Soc. Home: 5200 Bon Air Dr Monroe LA 71203

BROWN, CHERRI LOUISE, b. Santa Monica, CA, Jan. 18, 1949; d. James Andreani and Alma Louise (Naughton) Shaw; m. David Alexander Brown, Jr., Nov. 7, 1972; children—John Pierce, David, Jyl Marie. Food columnist: Hollywood Sun Tattler, 1984, West Kendall Gazette, 1984—, San Juan Star, 1986—. Contrbr. features to newspapers. Student U. Tampa, 1967-69. Co-owner Cherri's Kitchen, 1973—; operator/co-owner La Buenamesa, 1981-82; food stylist for TV; feature wrtr. La Coqueta, 1984-85. Home: 9120 SW 134th Pl Miami FL 33186

BROWN, CHRISTINE, see Stevens, Christine Hyde

BROWN, DAVID, b. NYC, July 28, 1916; s. Edward Fisher and Lilliam (Baren) B.; m. Liberty LeGacy, Apr. 15, 1940 (div. 1951); 1 son, Bruce LeGacy; m. Wayne Clark, May 25, 1951 (div. 1957); m. Helen Gurley, Sept. 25, 1959. Editor: I Can Tell It Now, 1964, How I Got That Story, 1967. Author: Brown's Guide to Growing Gray, 1987. Contbr. to Journalists in Action, 1963. Contrbr. to Am. mag., Collier's Harpers, SEP. A.B., Stanford U., 1936; M.S., Columbia U., 1937. Apprentice San Francisco News, also Wall St. Jnl, 1936; night editor, asst. drama critic Fairchild Publs., 1937-39; editorial dir. Milk Research Council, 1939-40; assoc. editor exec. editor, editor-in-chief Liberty mag., 1943-49; editorial dir. Natl. Edn. Campaign, A.M.A., 1949; assoc. editor, story editor, 20th Century-Fox Film Corp. Studios, Beverly Hills, Calif., 1952-56; editorial v.p. New Am. Library World Lit., Inc., 1963-64; v.p., dir. story operation 20th Century Fox Film Corp., 1964-69, exec. v.p. creative operations, 1969-70; exec. v.p. creative operations, dir. Warner Bros., 1971-72. Served as 1st lt., M.I. AUS, World War II. Mem. Acad. Motion Picture Arts and Scis., Producers Guild Am., Am. Film Inst. (vice-chmn., trustee, mem. exec. com.). Final judge best short story pub. in mags. ann. Benjamin Franklin Mag. awards 1955-58. Office: Zanuck/Brown 200 W 57th St New York NY 10019

BROWN, DEE ALEXANDER, b. LA, 1908; s. Daniel Alexander and Lulu (Cranford) B.; m. Sara B. Stroud, Aug. 1, 1934; children—James Mitchell, Linda. Author: Wave High the Banner, 1942, Grierson's Raid, 1954, Yellowhorse, 1956, Cavalry Scout, 1957, The Gentle Tamers: Women of the Old Wild West, 1958, The Bold Cavaliers, 1959, They Went Thataway, 1960, (with M. F. Schmitt) Fighting Indians of the West, 1948, Trail Driving Days, 1952, The Settler's West, 1955, Fort Phil Kearny, 1962, The Galvanized Yankees, 1963, Showdown at Little Big Horn, 1964, The Girl from Fort Wicked, 1964, The Year of the Century, 1966, Bury My Heart at Wounded Knee, 1971, The Westerners, 1974, Hear That Lonesome Whistle Blow, 1977, Tepee Tales, 1979, Creek Mary's Blood, 1980, The American Spa, 1982, Killdeer Mountain, 1983, Conspiracy of Knaves, 1987; editor: Agricultural History, 1956-58, Pawnee, Blackfoot and Cheyenne, 1961. BS, George Washington U., 1937; MS, U. of Ill., 1951. Librarian Dept. Agr., Washington, 1934-42, Aberdeen Proving Ground, Md., 1945-48; agrl. librarian U. Ill. at Urbana, 1948-72, prof., 1962-75. Served with AUS, 1942-45. Mem. AG, Soc. Am. Historians, Western Writers Am., Beta Phi Mu. Home: 7 Overlook Dr Little Rock AR 72207

BROWN, DIANA, b. Twickenham, Middlesex, England, Aug. 8, 1928, came to U.S., 1949, d. Antranik and Muriel Violet Florence (Maynard) Magarian; m. Ralph Herman Brown, Dec. 31, 1964; children—Pamela Hope, Clarissa Faith. Author: The Emerald Necklace, 1980, Come Be My Love, 1981, A Debt of Honour, 1981, St. Martin's Summer, 1981, The Sandalwood Fan, 1983, The Hand of a Woman (named outstanding title 1984 ALA Booklist), 1984, The Blue Dragon, 1988. MLS, San Jose State U., 1976, MA, 1977. Research librarian Signetics Corp., Sunnyvale, Calif., 1978-79, NASA-Ames Research Center, Moffett Field, Calif., 1979-80, Univ. Phoenix, San Jose, Calif., 1984-86. Mem. AG, Phi Kappa Phi. Home: 1612 Knollwood Ave San Jose CA 95125

BROWN, DROLLENE MAE, b. South Charleston, WV, Sept. 24, 1939; d. Wilson William and Evelyn Augusta (McCluer) Plattner; m. Charles Ray Tittle, Aug. 29, 1961 (div. May 21, 1975); children—Mark Alan, Shauna Kay; m. Albert Joseph Brown, Jr., May 28, 1982. Author: Sybil Rides for Independence, 1985 (a Child Study Assn. of Am. Children's Bk of Yr), Belva Lockwood Wins her Case, 1987. Contrbr. articles to mags., newspapers. Wrkg. on history of mayors of Boca Raton, FL, screenplay about South Am. adventurer. B.A., Ouachita Baptist Coll, 1961; M.A., U. Tex., Austin, 1963. Mgr. The Quote Bookstore, Ft. Lauderdale, FL, 1978-79; br. mgr. Am. Savings of Fla., Boca Raton, 1979-81; v.p. A. J. Brown, Inc., Boca Raton, 1981—. Address: 1132 SW 4th St Boca Raton FL 33486

BROWN, DUART VINSON, b. Reno, CA, Dec. 7, 1912; s. Henry Alexander and Bertha (Bender) B.; m. Elizabeth Braedon, May, 1939 (div. 1944); children—Kirby, Jerry; m. Barbara Black, June 18, 1950; children—Keven, Tamara, Roxana. Author 36 books including: Amateur Naturalist's Handbook, 1947, Warriors of the Rainbow, 1952, Voices of Earth & Sky, 1974, Rocks and Minerals of California, 1955, Handbook of California Birds, 1961, John Paul Jones, a Schl. Reader, 1950, Secret Languages of Animals, 1955. Nature columnist: Gilroy Dispatch, 1946-50, Healdsburg Tribune, 1950-68, Sonoma Index Tribune, 1950-87. Wrkg. on books: Wildlife and Common Plants of Texas, Oklahoma and the Southern Great Plains. A.B., U. Calif., Berkeley, 1939; M.A., Stanford U., 1946. dir. Amateur Naturalist Club, Berkeley, 1936-41; lectr. Natl. Schl. Assembly, Los Altos, CA, 1949-50; co-owner, pres. Naturograph Pubs., Healdsburg and Happy Camp, CA, 1950-78. Served to sgt. U.S. Army, 1944-45. Home: Box 1045 Happy Camp CA 96039

BROWN, HELEN GURLEY, b. Green Forest, AR, Feb. 18, 1922; d. Ira M. and Cleo (Sisco)

Gurley; m. David Brown, Sept. 25, 1959. Author: Sex and the Single Girl, 1962; Sex and the Office, 1965, Outrageous Opinions, 1966, Helen Gurley Brown's Single Girl's Cook Book, 1969, Sex and the New Single Girl, 1970, Having It All, 1982. Student, Tex. State Coll. for Women, 1940, Woodbury Coll., 1940-42. Exec. secy. Music Corp. Am., 1942-45, William Morris Agcy. 1945-47; copywriter Foote, Cone & Belding, Los Angeles, 1948-58; advt. writer, account exec. Kenyon & Eckhardt, Hollywood, Calif., 1958-62; editor-in-chief Cosmopolitan mag., 1965—; editorial dir. Cosmopolitan intl. edits. Recipient Francis Holmes Achievement award for outstanding work in advt., 1956-59; distinguished achievement award U. So. Cal. Schl. Journalism, 1971; spcl. award for editorial leadership Am. Newspaper Woman's Club, Washington, 1972; disting. achievement award. in Journalism Stanford U., 1977; named 1 of 25 most influential women in U.S. World Almanac, 1976-81. Mem. AL Am., ASME, AFTRA, Eta Upsilon Gamma. Office: Cosmo 224 W 57th St New York NY 10019

BROWN, JACK, b. Los Angeles, Aug. 6, 1927; s. George Wesley and Harriet Elizabeth (Barton) B.; m. Arlyne Reddick, Nov. 28, 1952 (div. 1962); children—Gregg (dec.), Jan Patrice, Jeffrey; m. 2d, Patricia Willard, July 28, 1964 (div. 1975); 1 child—Jack Jr.; m. 3d, Lynn Reese Johannsen-Brown, July 4, 1986; stepchildren—Eric, Julia, Rebecca Johannsen. Mng. ed. Western Outdoor, 1981—; ed. 52 Fishing Hotspots, 1985. BS, UCLA, 1951. Asst. polit. ed. The Examiner, Los Angeles, 1948-62; exec. asst. mayor of Los Angeles, 1962-69; polit. ed. Herald- Examiner, Los Angeles, 1970-77; assoc. pub. Metropolitan News, Los Angeles, 1977-81; mng. ed. Western Outdoors, Costa Mesa, CA, 1981—. Served to Y3/c US Navy, 1945-46, PTO. Mem. OWAA, Northwest OWA, Southwest OWA, OW of CA. Maggie awards, Western Pubns. Assn., 1985, 86. Home: 3515 Landsford Way Carlsbad CA 92008

BROWN, JAMES MICHAEL, b. San Jose, CA, Nov. 14, 1957, s. Donald Bernard and Vivien (Agrillo) B.; m. Heidi Ann Whited, June 12, 1983; 1 son, Andrew James. Author: Going Fast (novel), 1977, Hot Wire (novel), 1985, Final Performance (novel), 1988; contrbr. short fiction to So. Calif. Anthology, other mags. Wrkg. on novel. BA in English, San Francisco State U., 1980; MFA, U. Calif., Irvine, 1986. Instr. fiction writing, Cal. State Hayward, 1986—.Fiction scholar Squaw Valley Wrtrs.' Conf., Calif., 1983, 84; Margaret Bridgman fellow in fiction Bread Loaf Wrtrs. Conf., 1985; Djerassi Fdn. artist-in-residence, 1987. Home: 1150 Pierce St Apt 3 Santa Clara CA 95050

BROWN, JEAN MC BRAYER, b. Kiowa, KS, Dec. 9, 1908, d. Charles Henry and Rena May (Mackey) McBrayer; m. Kenneth Eugene Brown, May 12, 1940 (dec. 1962); 1 son, Charles Eugene. Author: A History of Kiowa, Old and New, on the Cowboy-Indian Frontier, 1979; contrbr.: True West, Frontier Times, Kansas, Heritage of Great Plains, Kanhistique, numerous daily and weekly newspapers. Wrkg. on historical book, articles. BA, U. Okla., 1932; postgrad., Northwest Okla. State U., 1965. Librarian Kiowa (Kans.) Public Library, 1962-73; med. records librarian Kiowa Dist. Hosp., 1966—. Mem. Kans. Authors Club (recipient J. Donald Coffin award 1980). Home: 418 N 6th St Kiowa KS 67070

BROWN, KENNETH H., Author: My Seed Grows Wilder (poetry), 1964, Through A Cage Brightly (poems), 1965, The Narrows (novel), 1970; contrbr. articles to City Lights Jnl, N.Y. Times, Village Voice, Evergreen Rvw, other publs.; playwright: The Brig, 1963, Nightlight, 1973, numerous produced but unpublished plays. Resident playwright, tutor Yale U., 1966-69; mem. faculty dept. theater Hollins (Va.) Coll., 1969, Hunter Coll., 1969-70, U. Iowa, 1971. Guggenheim fellow, 1965, Rockefeller fellow, 1966, ABC-Yale U. fellow, 1967, 68; grantee NEA, 1972, CAPS, 1974. Address: 150 74th St Brooklyn NY 11209

BROWN, KENT LOUIS, JR., b. Cleve., Nov. 23, 1943; s. Kent L. and Elizabeth (Myers) B.; m. Jolyn Taylor; children: Maj Turi, Boyd Benjamin, George Kent. Asst. editor Highlights for Children, Honesdale, Pa., 1971-76, mng. editor, 1976-78, editor, 1978—, dir., 1976—. Student, U. Hawaii, 1963-65; B.A. in English, Hobart Coll., 1967; postgard., SUNY-Oswego, 1969; M.S. in English Edn., Syracuse U., 1971. Served with AUS, 1963-65. Recipient Craftsmanship award Printing Industries of Am., 1979. Mem. ASME, Ednl. Press Assn. Am. (pres. 1986), Natl. Press Club. Home: Boyd Mills Rd Milanville PA 18443 Office: Highlights 803 Church St Honesdale PA 18431

BROWN, LESTER L., (Les), b. Indiana Harbor, IN, Dec. 20, 1928, s. Irving Harry and Helen (Feigenbaum) B.; m. Jean Rosalie Slaymaker, June 12, 1959; children—Jessica, Joshua, Rebecca. Author: Televi$ion: The Business Behind the Box, 1971, Electric Media, 1972, The N.Y. Times Encyc. of Television, 1977, Keeping Your Eye on Television, 1979, Les Brown's Encyc. of Television, 1982, Fast Forward: The New Television and American Society, 1983. BA in English, Roosevelt U., 1950. Reporter, reviewer Variety, Chgo., 1953-55, 57-65; assoc. ed. Down Beat mag., Chgo., 1955-56; TV-radio ed. Variety, NYC, 1965-72; TV corr. N.Y. Times, 1972-80; ed.-in-chief Channels Mag., NYC, 1980—. Recipient Pub.'s award N.Y. Times, 1975, Louis Cowan award Aspen Inst., 1979; Poynter fellow in modern journalism, Yale U., 1977. Home: 131 N Chatsworth Ave Larchmont NY 10538

BROWN, MARY OLIVER, (Kaze Utada, Beth Brown), b. Cleve., Mar. 7, 1953, d. James Beaty and Jeannette (Glover) Oliver; m. Yukio Utada; m. 2d, Alan Frio, Dec. 2, 1985; 1 son, Otis W. Brown III. Author: Lightyears: 1973-76, 1982, Blue Cyclone, 1982, Kaze, 1985, Satin Tunnels, 1988; five cassette bks. with Overtone Series; contrbr. articles, poems, rvws., stories to numerous publs. AB, Bryn Mawr Coll., 1976, MFA, Goddard Coll., 1981; EdD, Temple U. Contrbg. ed. Forum on Medicine, Am. Coll. Physicians, 1978; editorial asst. Painted Bride Qtly, 1982; mem. book rvw. staff Phila. Inquirer, 1982. Tchr., pvt. tutor, 1971—; mem. faculty Pan African Studies Community Edn. Program, Temple U., Phila., 1984—. CBS fellow in writing U. Pa., 1981-82; recipient AAP award, 1981. Home: 4238 Chestnut St 4 Philadelphia PA 19104

BROWN, NATALIE JOY, b. McKeesport, PA, Apr. 18, 1962, d. George Walker and Joanne Mitchell (Wood) Brown. Author: Crossing Seasons (poetry), 1984, On the Way to the River (poetry), 1985; ed.: Broadsides lit. rvw, 1981-82, Manchester Coll. Rvw lit mag, 1982-83, WCR lit mag, 1983-84. Student, Oxford (Eng.) U., 1982-83; BA, Washington Coll., 1984; MA, Johns Hopkins U., 1985. Teaching asst. Johns Hopkins U., Balt., 1984-85, U. Del., Newark, 1985—. Recipient numerous awards, Washington Coll., 1981-84. Mem. Intl. Thespians, AWP, MLA. Office: Dept Eng U Del Newark DE 19716

BROWN, RITA MAE, b. Hanover, PA, Nov. 28, 1944. Author: The Hand that Cradles the Rock, 1971, Rubyfruit Jungle, 1973, Songs to a Handsome Woman, 1973, A Plain Brown Rapper, 1976, Six of One, 1978, Southern Discomfort, 1982, Sudden Death, 1983, High Hearts, 1986; TV shows I Love Liberty, ABC-TV, 1982, The Long Hot Summer, NBC, 1985, My Two Loves, ABC, 1986. BA, NYU, 1968; PhD, Inst. Policy Studies, 1976. Lectr. Fed. City Coll., 1970-71; mem. faculty Goddard Coll., 1973—; mem. lit. panel NEA, 1978-81; Hemingway judge for 1st fiction PEN Intl., 1983. Recipient award WG Am., 1982. Office: J Bach Agcy 747 3d Ave New York NY 10017

BROWN, ROBERT HUGH, b. Miami, FL, Oct. 11, 1959; s. Charles Vicotr and Ermine (Parker) B. Contrbr.: Cinefantastique, Amazing Stories, Minnesotan Science Fiction Reader, Bookdealers Profile, other publs. BA, U. South Fla., 1980. Paperbacks mgr. Moderne Book Shop, Miami, Fla., 1981-83; asst. mgr. Waldenbooks, Fort Myers, Fla., 1984—. Address: Box 334 Fort Myers FL 33902

BROWN, ROSALIE, see Moore, Rosalie

BROWN, SCOTT KEITH, b. Torrance, CA, Nov. 22, 1960, s. Allan and Akiko (Shibuya) B. Author screenplay: Walker's Blues, 1983; songwriter: Terminal Time, Meet the Mirror, Full Circle, The Beat Street, Celluloid Electric Atmosphere, Wild Ones, 1983-85; contrbr. LA Weekly, Hollywood Reporter, Picture Week, Mainstream, Century City News; contrbg. author: The Hip Guide to Los Angeles, 1985. Wrkg. on screenplay, book. BA in Journalism, U. So. Calif., Los Angeles, 1983, BA in Cinema, 1983. Asst. editor US Contact, Los Angeles, 1983; co-editor Paperwork Mag., Los Angeles, 1982-83; film editor Rock Mag., Los Angeles, 1982-85; newswriter KNBC Teletext, Burbank, Calif., 1984-85; editorial asst. NBC Network News, Burbank, 1985—; stringer Time mag., 1985—. Recipient Cinema Circulus award, U. So. Calif., 1981, Harold Lloyd Fdn. award, 1982. Mem. Mensa. Home: 29848 Wistaria Valley Canyon Country CA 91351

BROWN, SHARON, b. Toronto, Ont., Can. Co-author: To See Ourselves: Five Views on Canadian Women, 1975; contrbr. articles: Chatelaine mag., Exec. mag., Spectator, numerous others; ghostwrtr. fin. articles. BA, York U. Reporter, ed. Bus. Week mag., NYC, 1968-73; project mgr. Govt. of Can., Ottawa, Ont., 1974-75; freelance wrtr., ed., 1976-77; mng. ed. Los Angeles (Calif.) County Med. Assn., 1978-81, dir. publs., 1981—; mem. editorial bd. Med. Execs. mag., Chgo. Recipient Sandoz award for med. journalism, 1978, 79, 80, 81. Mem. Women in Communications, Intl. Assn. Bus. Communicators (Golden Quill award 1972, 79), Western Publs. Assn. (Maggie award 1979, 86). Office: LA Cty Med Assn 1925 Wilshire Blvd Los Angeles CA 90057

BROWN, SPENCER, b. Hartford, CT, Oct. 16, 1909, s. Walter Spencer and Anna Geraldine (Hall) B.; m. Elizabeth Boyle, Dec. 23, 1935; children—Thomas Sheill, Margaret Spencer. Author poetry collections: My Father's Business, 1956, Looking into the Fire, 1967, Child's Game, On a Journey, 1979; contrbr. poetry to

New Yorker, Partisan Rvw, Sewanee Rvw, numerous others; contrbr. articles to Commentary, N.Y. Times Mag., Harper's, Sports Illustrated, others. BA, Harvard U., 1930, MA, 1932. Tchr. pvt. schls. Conn., NYC,1930-65; prin. Fieldston Schl., NYC,1965-71; vis. prof. Colo. Coll., Colorado Springs, summer 1964, 65. Home: 189A Bedford Rd Pleasantville NY 10570

BROWN, STEVEN FORD, b. Florence, AL, Sept. 11, 1952, s. Ford M. and Gloria (Peters) B. Author: Erotic Mask: Prose Poems, 1984, Available Angel: A Decade of Prose Poems 1976-86; Editor: Contemporary Literature in Birmingham: An Anthology, 1983; Editor of The American Poets Profile Series, critical studies of American poets—Dave Smith, John Logan, Andrew Glaze, Paul Zimmer, Carolyn Kizer, Donald Hall; translator (with Pedro Gutierrez Revuelta) of 15 Poems of Angel Gonzalez, 1987; Tchr. U. Ala., Birmingham, 1980-83; Poet-In-Residence Birmingham, Alabama, city middle schools, 1979; Southside Community School, 1979-81; Indiana University, Honors Division, Nov., 1981; ed., pub. Ford-Brown & Co., Publishers, Houston, 1983—. NEA Small Press grantee, 1981, 83. Address: Box 600574 Houston TX 77260

BROWNE, ALICE PAULINE, (A. P. Sweeney), b. Topeka, KS, June 26, 1918; d. James Paul Sweeney and Alice Bertha (Crabb) Young; children—Gerald, Raymond, Jonathan, Patricia Smetzer. Contrr. articles to legal and accounting jnls., mags., newspapers including Wall St. Jnl., Bus. Week, others.; poems to anthols. Wrkg. on autobiography, My Name is Pauline; The Beauty of Africa, In the Footsteps of Van Gogh. B.B.A., U. Miami, 1976; J.D., Atlanta Law Schl., 1980. Owner, Sweeneys Tax Service, 1985—; owner, operator Smetzer Flying Service, Catalia, OH, 1948-58, Greenwood Inn, Castalia, 1955-56. Pub. letter to prisoners, 1982—. Home: 4735 Roswell Rd NE Apt 40-F Atlanta GA 30342

BROWNE, MICHAEL DENNIS, b. Walton-on-Thames, Eng., May 28, 1940; came to U.S., 1965, naturalized, 1978; s. Edgar Dennis and Winifred Margaret (Denne) B.; m. Lisa Furlong McLean, July 18, 1981; children: Peter David Denne McLean-Browne, Mary Julia Hughes McLean-Browne. Author: The Wife of Winter, 1970; Sun Exercises, 1976; The Sun Fetcher, 1978; Smoke from the Fires, 1985; wrtr. texts for composers David Lord, John Foley S.J., and Stephen Paulus. BA with 1st class honors, Hull U., Eng., 1962; MA, U. Iowa, 1967. Vis. lectr. U. Iowa, Iowa City, 1967-68; adj. asst. prof. Columbia U., N.Y.C., fall 1968; mem. faculty Bennington Coll., Vt., 1969-71; asst. prof. to prof., U. Minn., Mpls., 1971—. Recipient Borestone prize, 1974; prize for poetry NEA, 1977, for libretto, 1978; Loft McKnight wrtr.'s award, 1986; Bush Fnd. fellow, 1981. Mem. Am. PEN, PSA. Home: Box 8 Benedict MN 56436

BROWNE, MORGAN TREW, b. Chestertown, MD, Nov. 22, 1919; s. Morgan and Mary Groome (Trew) B.; m. Ann Elizabeth Riley, Feb. 14, 1949; children: Elizabeth, Morgan. Mgr. Sci. Book Club, Religious Book Club, 1945-46; mng. editor Tide mag., 1946-53, editor, 1950-53; exec. v.p., gen. mgr., pres., editorial dir. Bill communications; Dir. periodicals N.A.M., 1949-51. Student, Balt. City Coll., 1934-37, Johns Hopkins, 1937-40. Home: 1057 Hillsboro Mile Hillsboro Beach FL 33062

BROWNELL, DAVID WHEATON, b. Fall River, MA, Feb. 17, 1941; s. Frank W. and Mary K. (Coughiin) B.; m. Mary E. Chute, Sept. 24, 1966. Ed.: Old Cars, 1971-78, Special-Interest Autos, 1978—, Hemmings Motor News, 1984—, Hemmings Vintage Auto Almanac, 34rd, 4th, 5th, 6th eds.; chief writer Heritage Plantation Auto Collectn. Book, 1986; contrbr.: Bentley Drivers Club Review, 1984, Standard Catalog of Amer. Cars, 1805-1942, SCAC, 1946-75. BS in Visual Design, Durfee Coll., 1964. Ed. Krause Pubns., Iola, WI, 1971-78, Watering, Inc., Bennington, VT, 1978—. Mem. Guild of Motoring Writers (UK), Intl. Motor Press Assn. Mem. selection comm. Automotive Hall of Fame, 1980—; Soc. Automotive Wrtrs. (pres., 1980). Home: White Creek Rd No Bennington VT 05257

BROWNELL, JAMES GARLAND, b. Valparaison, IN, July 29, 1933; s. Walter Ezra and Floy and Gladys (Binyon) B. With Scholastic Mags., Inc., N.Y.C., 1961—; asst. to asso. editor Sr. Scholastic, 1961-64; mng. editor World Week mag., 1964-66, Sr. Scholastic, 1966-68; editor Jr. Scholastic, 1975-77, editorial dir., 1977-85, dir. product prodn., 1985—. B.A. in Poli. Sci. Ind. U., 1955; diploma, Internat. Grad. Sch. for English Speaking Students, U., Stockholm, Sweden, 1956; postgrad., Valparaiso U. Law Sch., 1959-60. Served to 1st lt. AUS, 1957-59. Home: Upper Kent Hollow Rd RFD 1 Kent CT 06757

BROWNELL, JOYCE E. TARRIER, b. Ashland, KY, July 22, 1942; d. Owen Theodore and Mariah Adelaid (Maholm) Tarrier; m. Thomas Heath, June 21, 1969; children: Nathan Owen Brownell, Anthony Wayne Brwonell. Adapted works of Tolstoy, Victor Hugo for Readers' Theater, Big Rapids, Mich. BA, Wittenberg U.; MA in Dramatic Arts, Brigham Young U. Reporter Caldeonian Record, St. Johnsbury, Vt., 1969-71, 78-80; mem. faculty Ferris State Coll., Big Rapids, Mich., 1983—. Mem. Mecosta County Council for Humanities (bd. dirs., sec.), Mecosta County Council for Arts (bd. dirs.), NCTE. Home: 404 Maple St Big Rapids MI 49307

BROWNING, ELIZABETH, b. Madera, CA, Nov. 19, 1933, d. John Henry and Marie (Koop) Foth; children—Carol Lockwood, Charles Ramsel. Contrbr. poetry to Am. Poetry Anthology, 1982, Hearts On Fire. Wrkg. on novel, short stories. Student West Hills Coll., 1977-80, Fresno City Coll., 1980-86. Real estate broker, Fresno, Calif., 1980-86. Home: 4287 N Emerson St Fresno CA 93705

BROWNING, PAMELA, (Pam Ketter, Melanie Rowe), b. Evanston, IL, Apr. 25, 1942; children—Neill, Bethany. Author: Sands of Xanadu, 1982, One on One, 1983, Wish for Tomorrow, 1983, Sea of Gold, 1984, Stardust Summer, 1984, Touh of Gold, 1985, Cherished Beginings, 1985, Handyman Special, 1985, Through Eyes of Love, 1985, Interior Designs, 1985, Ever Since Eve, 1986, Forever Is a Long Time, 1986, To Touch the Stars, 1986, The Flutterby Princess, 1987, Ice Crystals, 1987. Contrbr. fiction and non-fiction to mags. including Highlights for Children, Child Life, Newsday Sunday Mag. Mem. RWA, Washington Romance Wrtrs. Office: 2129 Lyndale Dr S Hartsville SC 29550

BROWNING, TAMARA NADINE, b. Quincy, IL, Jan. 4, 1959; d. Wayne Gilbert and Norma Jean (Nixon) Mahr; m. Ronald Browning, Dec. 4, 1982; 1 son, Nathanael. Asst. editor: Religious Broadcasting Mag., 1985-86; editor: Inside NRB, 1985-86. Contrbr. articles to East Orange Record, Religious Broadcasting Mag., The North Jersey Herald-News. BA, Culver-Stockton Coll., 1981. Free-lance writer Bloomfield C. of C., N.J., 1983-84, East Orange Record, N.J., 1983-84; stringer North Jersey Herald-News, Passaic, 1984-85; edl. asst. State Jnl.-Register, Springfield, IL, 1986—. Recipient Honorable Mention for writing competition Writer's Digest, 1985. Mem. AAUW. Home: 1974 S 18th St Springfield IL 62703

BROWN MICHELSON, LINDA, b. Santa Monica, CA; d. Vernon Charles and Harriett Catherine (Weber) Brown; m. Gajus Michelson, Mar. 21, 1976; 1 son, Shawn Anthony. Editor: Crosscurrents, A Quarterly, 1980—. Wrkg. on anthol. BA magna cum laude in English, Calif. State U.-Northridge, 1975; MA in English, UCLA. Mem. Pubs. Mkgt. Assn., Ventura Arts Council, CCLM. Office: CC 2200 Glastonbury Rd Westlake Village CA 91361

BROWNMILLER, SUSAN, b. Bklyn, Feb. 15, 1935. Student, Cornell U., 1952-55, Jefferson Schl. Social Science. Reporter NBC-TV, Phila., 1965; network newswriter ABC-TV, N.Y.C., 1965-67; former researcher Newsweek mag.; former staff writer Village Voice. Freelance writer mags., newspapers; author: books including Shirley Chisholm, 1970, Against Our Will: Men, Women and Rape, 1975. Founder Women Against Pornography. Office: S & S 1230 Ave of Americas New York NY 10020

BROWNSON, CHARLES, b. Aug. 16, 1945. Author: Guide to the Marshall Family Papers, 1975, Passages: Library Instruction for Lifelong Enrichment, 1978, Ancestors, 1984, Im Uz, 1985. Wrkg. on novel. MFA, U. Oreg., Eugene, 1969; MLS, U. Calif., Berkeley, 1972. Spcl. curator SUNY-Oswego, 1972-76; instr. librarian Christopher Newport Coll., Newport News, Va., 1976-80; lit. specialist Ariz. State U. Libraries, 1980-84, humanities coordinator, 1984—. Office: Hayden Library Ariz State Univ Tempe AZ 85287

BROWNSTONE, DAVID M., b. NYC, Aug. 7, 1928; s. m. (1) Lilla Goldman, 1949 (div. 1967); children: Douglass, Gregory; (2) Irene M. Franck, Jan. 20, 1969. Author: Successful Selling Skills for Small Business, 1978, Sell Your Way to Success, 1978, (with Gorton Carruth) Where to Find Business Information, 1979, 2d ed., 1982, (with Gene R. Hawes) How to Get the Money to Pay for college, 1978, rev ed as The College Money Book, 1984, (with Irene M. Franck and Douglass L. Brownstone) Island of Hope, Island of Tears (oral history of Ellis Island), 1979, (with Irene M. Franck and Gorton Carruth) The VNR Business and Finance Dictionary, 1980, (with Hawes) The Complete Career Guide, 1980, (with I.M. Franck) The VNR Investor's Dictionary, 1980, (with Jacques Sartisky) Personal Financial Survival: Guide for the Eighties and Beyond, 1981, (with I.M. Franck) The VNR Real Estate Dictionary, 1981, (with I.M. Franck) The Manager's Advisor, 1983, (with I.M. Franck) The Sales Professional's Advisor, 1983, (with I.M. Franck) To the Ends of the Earth: The Great Travel and Trade Routes of Human History, 1984, (with I.M. Franck) The Self-Publishing Handbook, 1985, The Saver's Guide to Sound Investments, 1985, Moneywise, 1985, (with Sartisky) The Manager's Lifetime Money Book, 1986, (with I.M. Franck) the Silk Road: A History, 1986, (with I.M. Franck), The AMA Handbook of Key Management Forms, 1986, (with I.M. Franck), The Great Historic Places of America, 1987, the IRA Survival Guides, 1987, Planning to Win with the New

Tax Law, 1987. Work Throughout History Series with I.M. Franck: Artists and Artisans, 1986, Builders, 1986, Communicators, 1986, Clothiers, 1986, Financiers and Traders, 1986, Leaders and Lawyers, 1986, Harvesters, Healers, Helpers, and Aides, 1987, Manufacturers and Miners, 1987, Performers and Players, 1988, Scholars and Priests, 1988, Scientists and Technologists, 1988, Restauranteers and Innkeepers, 1988, WArriors and Adventurers, 1988. America's Ethnic Heritage Series with I.M. Franck: The Chinese-American Heritage, 1988, The Jewish-American Heritage, 1988, The Scandinavian-American Heritage, 1988, The German-American Heritage, 1988, The Irish-American Heritage, 1988, The Italian-American Heritage, 1989. Genl. ed, Small Business Series, 1977-80. Co-ed. Film Review Digest, 1975-77. BA, Brooklyn Coll. (now of the City U. of N.Y.), 1948. Marketing repr., commerce Clearing House, N.Y.C., 1957-61; pres., Institutional Publishing Co., N.Y.C., 1961-62; v.p. and genl. mgr, Tax Research Inst. of America, N.Y.C., 1962-72; founder, pres. of Institute for Intl Research, Ltd., N.Y.C. and creator of International Tax Report and International Investment Advisor in N.Y.C. and London, Eng., 1972-74; principal, Hudson Group (an independent gorup of writers and editors), Pleasantville, N.Y., 1974—. Pres., Temeraire Enterprises, Inc., Chappaqua, N.Y. Member: Authors Guild, Authors, League of America. Best management and business book of the year, Assn. of American Publishers, 1979, for Where to Find Business Information; travel book award, Geographical Soc. of Chicago, 1984. Office: 201 Millwood Rd. Chappaqua NY 10514

BROX, ELEANOR ANDREA, b. Lowell, MA, Sept. 24, 1959; d. Frank Arthur and Eleanor Maybel (Kelly) B. Contrbr. articles to mags., newspapers. B.A., Marquette U., 1981; M.S. in Jnlsm., Northwestern U., 1983. Reporter, Construction Data Bulltn., Cambridge, MA, 1981-82; sr. wrtr. Sportscape, Inc., Brookline, MA, 1984-87; free-lance wrtr., 1982-84, 87—. Recipient Honorable Mention for non-technical feature articles ASBPE, 1986, 2d place for non-technical feature articles, 1986. Home: 180 Winchester St Brookline MA 02146

BROYLES, WILLIAM DODSON, JR., b. Houston, Oct. 8, 1944; s. William Dodson and Elizabeth (Bills) B.; m. Sybil Ann Newman, Aug. 15, 1973; children: William David, Susannah. Author: Brothers in Arms, 1986; editor: Tex. Monthly, Austin, 1972-80; editor-in-chief, 1981—, Newsweek Mag., 1982-84; columnist U.S. News and World Report, 1986—. B.A. in History, Rice U., 1966; B.A. in Politics, Philosophy and Econs., Oxford U., 1968, M.A., 1971. Served with USMCR, 1969-71. Decorated Bronze Star. Mem. Tex. Inst. Letters. Office: 2400 N St NW Washington DC 20037

BRUCCOLI, MATTHEW JOSEPH, b. NYC, Aug. 21, 1931; s. Joseph M. and Mary (Gervasi) B.; m. Arlyn Shuey Firkins, Oct. 5, 1957; children—Mary Firkins, Joseph Matthew, Josephine Arlyn, Arlyn Barbara. Author: The Composition of Tender is the Night, 1963, The Last of the Novelists, 1977, The O'Hara Concern, 1975, Scott and Ernest, 1978, Selected Letters of John O'Hara, 1978, Just Representations: A James Gould Cozzens Reader, 1978, Correspondence of F. Scott Fitzgerald, 1980, Some Sort of Epic Grandeur: The Life of F. Scott Fitzgerald, 1981; James Gould Cozzens, 1983; editor: lit. works Fitzgerald/Hemingway Annual, 1969-79; series editor Dictionary of Literary Biography, 1978—, Lost Am. Fiction, 1972—, Pittsburgh Series in Bibliography, 1971—. BA, Yale U., 1953; MA, U. Va., 1956, PhD, 1961. Prof. English U. S.C., Columbia, 1969—, Jeffries prof. English, 1976—; dir. Center for Editions of Am. Authors, 1969-76; pres. Bruccoli Clark Publishers, 1976—. Guggenheim fellow, 1973. Home: 31 Heathwood CR Columbia SC 29205

BRUCE, DEBRA, b. Bristol, CT, Apr. 4, 1951, d. Willard Arthur and Mary Elizabeth (Conlin) Bruce; m. thomas Richard Kinnebrew, Aug. 21, 1981. Author: Dissolves, 1977, Pure Daughter, 1983, Sudden Hunger (poetry); contrbr. to Selections, 1980, A Century in Two Decades: A Burning Deck Anthology, 1982, Anthology of American Verse, 1984, Yearbook of American Poetry, 1985; contrbr. poems to Am. Poetry Rvw., Calyx, Cutbank, numerous other lit mags. MA, Brown U., Providence, R.I., 1976; MFA, U. Iowa, 1978. Instr., Old Dominion U., Norfolk, Va., 1978-81; asst. prof. Northeastern Ill. U., Chicago, 1984—. NEA grant for creative writing, 1982; NEH grant for scriptwriting, 1983; AAP Poetry prize. Mem. AWP, PSA, AAP. Office: Dept of Eng Neastern Ill Univ 5500 N St Louis Ave Chicago IL 60625

BRUCE, ROBERT VANCE, b. Malden, MA, Dec. 19, 1923; s. Robert Gilbert and Bernice Irene (May) B. Author: Lincoln and the Tools of War, 2d edit., 1973, 1877: Year of Violence, 2d edit., 1970, Bell: Alexander Graham Bell and the Conquest of Solitude, 1973, Lincoln and the Riddle of Death, 1982, The Launching of Modern American Science, 1987. Student, MIT, 1941-43; BS, U. NH, 1945; MA, Boston U., 1947, PhD, 1953. Instr. U. Bridgeport, Conn., 1947-48; master Lawrence Acad., Groton, Mass., 1948-51; research asst. to Benjamin P. Thomas, Washington, 1953-54; mem. faculty Boston U., 1955—, assoc. prof. history, 1960-66, prof., 1966-84, emeritus, 1984—; visiting prof. U. Wis., Madison, 1962-63. Served with AUS, 1943-46. Guggenheim fellow, 1957-58. Home: Evans Rd RFD Durham NH 03824

BRUCIE, THOMAS JAMES, b. Corning, NY, Mar. 20, 1947, s. Vincent Rocco Sr. and Kathleen (Carrick) B.; children—Theresa, Jason, Derrick, Heather. Author: Residential Construction Costs, 1982, The Dangerous Risk; contrbr.: The Poet, Deros, Earthwise, others. Edn.: St. John's Sem., Montour Falls, N.Y. Served with U.S. Army, 1966-69; Vietnam. Home: Fresno CA

BRUGGER, HEIDI NACK, b. Norristown, PA, Mar. 10, 1950, d. Byron Ferdinand and Virginia (Huber) Nack; m. Read DeBow Brugger, Apr. 16, 1977; children—Jonah, Eleanor. BA in English, U. Mass.-Amherst, 1974. Asst. ed. div. parish services Luth. Ch. Am., Phila., 1974-76; copy ed. Cahner's Pub. Co., Newton Corner, Mass., 1977-83; mng. ed. Farmstead Press, Freedom, Me., 1983—. Office: Farmstead Box 111 Freedom ME 04941

BRUMBAUGH, ROBERT SHERRICK, b. Oregon, IL, Dec. 2, 1918; s. Aaron John and Marjorie Ruth (Sherrick) B.; m. Ada Zarbell Steele, June 5, 1940; children—Robert Conrad, Susan Christianna, Joanna Pauline. Author: (with N.P. Stallknecht) The Spirit of Western Philosophy, 1950, Plato's Mathematical Imagination, 1953, The Compass of Philosophy, 1954, Plato on the One, 1960, Plato for the Modern Age, 1961, (with Nathaniel Lawrence) Philosophers on Education, 1963, The Philosophers of Greece, 1964, Ancient Greek Gadgets and Machines, 1966; co-editor: Plato Manuscripts: A catalogue of the Plato Microfilm Project, Yale University Libraries, Parts I and II, 1962, Part III, 1974, (with Nathaniel Lawrence) Philosophic Themes in Modern Education, 1973, The Most Mysterious Manuscript: The Voynich "Roger Bacon" Cipher Manuscript, 1978; contrbr. to jnls. and encys. AB, U. Chgo., 1938, MA, 1938, PhD, 1942. Faculty Bowdoin Coll., 1946-49, Ind. U., 1949-52; faculty Yale, New Haven, 1951—, prof. philosophy, 1961—; research fellow Am. Schl. Classical Studies, Athens, Greece, 1962-63; Fulbright vis. prof. Hebrew U., Jerusalem, 1967. Morse fellow, 1954-55; Guggenheim fellow, 1976-77. Mem. Metaphys. Soc. Am. (councillor 1961-65; pres. 1966), Am. Philo. Assn., Soc. Ancient Greek Philosophy, AAUP, Phi Beta Kappa. Home: 150 Ridgewood Ave North Haven CT 06473

BRUMME, MARJORIE VIVIAN, b. Chgo., Feb. 25, 1917, d. Joseph Henry and Nanny (Lindroth) Danielson; m. Howard Lee Brumme, Sept. 2, 1938; children—Nancy (dec.), Richard, Larry (dec.), James, Stephen, John. Contrbr.: Union Gospel Press, Scripture Press, Eternity Mag., Regular Baptist Press, others. Student Moody Bible Inst., 6 yrs. Home: Rt 2 Box 151B Oskaloosa KS 66066

BRUMMEL, MARK JOSEPH, b. Chgo., Oct. 28, 1933; s. Anthony William and Mary (Helmreich) B.; BA, Cath. U. Am., 1956, STL, 1961, MS in L.S., 1964. Joined order of Claretians, Roman Cath. Ch., 1952, ordained priest, 1960; librarian, tchr. St. Jude Sem., Momence, Ill., 1961-70; assoc. editor U.S. Cath. mag., Chgo., 1971-72, editor, 1972—; dir. Claretian Publs., Chgo., 1972; bd. dirs. Eastern Province Claretians, 1973-86; pres. bd. dirs. Claretian Med. Center, 1980—; bd. dirs. 8th Day Center, 1980—. Editor: Today mag., 1970-71. Home: 3200 E 91st St Chicago IL 60617

BRUNER, RICHARD WALLACE, b. Burlington, IA, June 26, 1926; s. Eugene Floyd and Dorothy Katherine (Gavin) Bruner; m. Rosemary Holahan, June 14, 1947 (div. Nov. 1981); children—Sean, Susan, Richard; 2nd m. Virginia Leddy, Dec. 30, 1983. Author: Black Politicians, 1971, Whitney M. Young, 1972; contrbtr: Labor & Amer. Politics, 1967, Profile of Amer. Politics, 1960. BA U. of Minnesota, 1949. Writer Alex Drier, NBC News (Chgo) 1957-58, NBC (NY) 1958-66; Freelance wrtr., 1966—. PRC, U.S. Army Air Corps, 1944-46, U. S. and Japan. Mem. DG, AG, WG. Home: Box 605 West Shokan NY 12494

BRUNSTING, MELODY ANN, b. Santa Ana, CA, Sept. 19, 1955, d. Wallace Charles and Colleen Adelene (Baker) Huber; m. Calvin Henry Brunsting, Aug. 18, 1974. Author: Get Wired, 1986, Return to Duckcake (a ballet), 1986, Dance of the Wildflowers, 1987; contrbg. wrtr.: Gemco Courier, 1980; ed.: Do-It-Yourself Humor (by Stew McKinley), 1985. B, Calif. Poly. U., 1980. Assoc. ed. Community Woman, Anaheim, Calif., 1977-80; ed. TV Digest, Pomona, Calif., 1980-81; mng. ed. Butterfield Bull., Temecula, Calif., 1981-83; ops. mgr. Bargain Bull., Temecula, 1983—; owner, mgr. Trainable Type publs. cons. firm, Wildomar, Calif., since 1983. Publs. chmn., Temecula Valley Chbr. Comm., 1987-88. Mem. Calif. Presswomen, Natl. Fedn. Presswomen. Home: 21705 Como St Wildomar CA 92395

BRUSIN, JOYCE HELENA, b. Tampere, Finland, Sept. 26, 1958 (arrvd. USA 1959), d. Roy and Hertta Orvokki (Viita) B. Contrbr. poetry to Riprap 4, Union Daily, Visions of Peace. BA, Calif. State U., Long Beach, 1980; MFA, U. Mont., 1985. Admissions coordinator Schl. Nursing, Calif. State U., 1980-82; asst. ed., co-ed., CutBank, 1983-84, fiction ed., mng. ed., 1984-85; adminstrv. aide dept. fgn. langs. U. Mont., Missoula, 1985—. Mem. AWP.Home: 340 S 5th W Missoula MT 59801

BRUSTEIN, ROBERT SANFORD, b. NYC, Apr. 21, 1927; s. Max and Blanche (Haft) B.; m. Norma Ofstrock, Mar. 25, 1962 (dec.); children: Phillip Cates (stepson), Daniel Anton. Author: The Theatre of Revolt: Studies in the Modern Drama, 1964, Seasons of Discontent: Dramatic Opinions 1959-65, 1965, The Third Theatre, 1969, Revolution as Theatre: Notes on the New Radical Style, 1971, The Culture Watch, 1975, Critical Moments, 1980, Making Scenes, 1981, Who Need Theatre, 1987; editor: The Plays and Prose of Strindberg, 1964. BA, Amherst Coll., 1948, LittD.; postgrad., Yale Drama Schl., 1948-49, U. Nottingham, Eng., 1953-55; MA, Columbia U., 1950 PhD, 1957. Drama critic New Republic, 1959-67, 78—, contrbg. editor, 1959—; guest theatre critic London Observer,1972-73; contrbr. to N.Y. Times, 1972—. Served with U.S. Mcht. Marine, 1945-47. Recipient George Jean Nathan award dramatic criticism, 1962, George Polk Meml. award outstanding criticism, 1965, Elliot Norton award, 1985, others. Fulbright fellow, 1953-55; Guggenheim fellow, 1961-62; Ford Fdn. fellow, 1964-65, Senior Fulbright Fellow to Spain, 1987. Mem. AAAs. Office: Loeb Drama Center Cambridge MA 02138

BRYAN, COURTLANDT DIXON BARNES, b. NYC, Apr. 22, 1936; s. Joseph III and Katharine (Barnes) O'Hara; m. Phoebe Miller, Dec. 28, 1961 (div. Sept 1966); children: J. St. George III, Lansing Becket; m. Judith Snyder, Dec. 21, 1967 (div. July 1978); 1 dau., Amanda Barnes. Author: P. S. Wilkinson, 1965 (Harper prize novel), The Great Dethriffe, 1970, Friendly Fire, 1976, The National Air and Space Museum, 1979, Beautiful Women; Ugly Scenes, 1983. Grad., Berkshire Schl., 1954; BA in English, Yale U., 1958. Writer-in-res. Colo. State U., winter 1967; vis. lectr. writers workshop U. Iowa, 1967-69; editor Monocle mag., 1961—; spcl. cons. editorial matters Yale U., 1970; fiction dir. Writers Community, NYC, 1977—. Served with AUS, 1958-60, 61-62. Home: 719 Podunk Rd Guilford CT 06437

BRYAN, JOSEPH J., b. Cleve.; s. Matilda (Payle) Bodnar. Columnist: (auto racing) Medina Gazette, 1971, Brunswick Times, 1973; (hobby) Car Model Mag., 1974, Scale Modeler Mag., 1981. Wrkg. on western novel, Ford Country. Student Western Technical Coll., 1963-65. Auto racer reporter Medinda Gazette, OH, 1971, Brunswick Times, OH, 1973; hobby columnist Tonto Pub., Phoenix, 1974; free-lance wrtr., 1963-74, 75-86. Home: Box 652 Brunswick OH 44212

BRYAN, SHARON, b. Salt Lake City, Feb. 10, 1943; d. Glen and Shirley (Storrs) Allen. Author: Salt Air, 1983; Objects of Affection, 1987. BA, U. Utah, 1965; MA, Cornell U., 1969; MFA, U. Iowa, 1977. Ed. numerous pubs., Boston, Denver, Seattle, 1969-80; mem. faculty Marlboro Coll., Vt., 1977-78, U. Wash., Seattle, 1980-87; assoc. prof. and ed. Memphis State Rvw, 1987—. Recipient Discovery award, The Nation, 1977; Gov.'s award State of Wash., 1985; prize The Observer, London, 1985, NEA, 1987. Mem. AWP. Home: 845 Bellevue Pl E 206 Seattle WA 98102

BRYANT, DAVID ERNEST, b. Appanoose County, IA, Feb. 14, 1922; s. David Reo and Bessie Bly (Harl) B.; m. LeVergne C. Bookwalter, June 5, 1965; children: Marilyn K., Virginia L., David W. Farm editor Globe-Gazette, Mason City, Iowa, 1950-51; field editor Wallaces farmer, Des Moines, 1951-57; editor Iowa Rural Electric News, Des Moines, 1957-64; asso. editor mng. editor Today's Farmer, Columbia, Mo., 1964-71, editor, 1971-80. Ag Newsletter Service, Des Moines, 1980—. B.S. in Agrl. Journalism, Iowa State U., 1950. Served with AUS, 1942-46. Mem. Am. Agrl. Editors Assn. (pres. 1977), Coop. Editorial Assn. U.S.A. (Klinefelter award 1973). Home: 1129 11th St W Des Moines IA 50265

BRYANT, EDWARD WINSLOW, JR., b. White Plains, NY, Aug. 27, 1945, s. Edward Winslow and Anne Harter (Van Kleeck) B. Author: Among the Dead, 1973, (with Harlan Ellison) Phoenix without Ashes, 1975, Cinnabar, 1976, Wyoming Sun, 1980, Particle Theory, 1981; ed. (with Jo Ann Harper) 2076: The American Tricentennial, 1977; author film and TV scripts. BA, U. Wyo., 1967, MA, 1968. Wrtr., 1968—; participant numerous writing confs. and workshops, also wrtr.-in-residence. Recipient Top Hand award Colo. Authors League, 1984, 85. Mem. SFWR (Nebula award 1979, 80), AL, Soc. Children's Book Wrtrs. Home: 2535 E 14th Ave 10 Denver CO 80218

BRYANT, GAY, b. Newcastle, Eng., Oct. 5, 1945; came to U.S., 1970; d. Richard King and Catherine (Shiel) B.; m. Charles Childs, Apr. 10, 1982. Author: The Underground Travel Guide, 1973, How I Learned To Like Myself, 1975, The Working Woman Report, 1984. Student, St. Clare's Coll., Oxford, Eng., 1961-63. Sr. editor Penthouse Mag., NYC, 1968-74; assoc. editor Oui mag., NYC, 1974-75; founding editor New Dawn mag., NYC, 1975-79; exec. editor Working Woman mag., NYC, 1979- 81, editor, 1981-84; editor, v.p. Family Circle mag., NYC, 1984—; adj. prof. Schl. Journalism, NYU, 1982—. Mem. Women's Media Group, Women in Communications, ASME. Home: 34 Horatio St New York NY 10014

BRYANT, G. PRESTON, b. Cullman, AL, Mar. 26, 1933; s. James Arthur and Bernice (Cruce) B.; m. Gloria Elaine Glasgow, June 7, 1960 (div. 1985); children—Robyn Renee, Shannon Lee, Heather Marie, Brooke Elizabeth. Editor: Artificial Intelligence: A User Friendly Introduction, 1985, Evolution of the Cruise Missile, 1985, Low Intensity Conflict and Modern Technology, 1986, Bear Tracks in Indochina, 1987, The Tactical Air Control System, 1987, Wrkg. on tech. and tng. books. MS, Auburn U., 1966; JD, Jones Law Sch., 1980. Civilian employee U.S. Air Force, 1974—, text devel. specialist, Maxwell AFB, Montgomery, Ala., 1978-80, wrtr.-ed., 1980—. Recipient numerous awards U.S. Air Force. Home: Box 892 Montgomery AL 36101

BRYANT, KATHY ANN, b. El Paso, TX, Feb. 16, 1942; d. Arthur James and Katherine Louise (Pollock) Lingle; m. Gene C. Bryant; children—Christopher, Sean. Contrbr. to various newspapers and mags, 1973-83. Art reviewer Register (Santa Ana, CA) 1982-83; mng. ed. Orange Cty. mag. (Costa Mesa, CA), 1982-84; ed. Newport Beach (Irvine, CA) 1984-85; wrtr. Orange Cty. Register, 1985; freelance wrtr., 1985—. BA, Denver U., 1963. Mem. Women's Political Cauc., MWA, Indep. Wrtrs. So. Calif. Home: 20361 Kelvin Grove Ln Huntington Beach CA 92646

BRYANT, SYLVIA LEIGH, b. Lynchburg, VA, May 8, 1947; d. Mr. and Mrs. Hundley Bryant. Contrbr. poetry to The Poet, Modern Images, Adventures in Poetry Magazine, Hoosier Challenge, other lit mags, anthols. DLit, World University, 1981. Gold Medal, Accademia Leonardo da Vinci. Editor/publisher, The Anthology Society. Home: 106 Garford Rd Madison Heights VA 24572

BRYANT, TAMERA SUE, b. Gainesville, TX, Sept. 19, 1955; d. William Troy and Ellen Irene (Lillard) B.; 1 son, Ashley Lillard. Contrbr. poetry to anthols., lit. mags.; articles to newspapers. Ed.: Apr. Perennial Mag., 1981, Maturity, 1987št. ed.: Hypatia, 1986—. B.A. in English and Sociology, Tex. Woman's U., 1983. Copyeditor, Gainesville Daily Register, 1982-83; resident advisor Job Corps Center, McKinney, TX, 1983-84; literay recruiter Lewis & Clark Library System, Edwardsville, IL, 1986-87; free-lance wrtr., ed., 1987—. Fundraiser, speaker Literay Link, Edwardsville, 1986-87. Recipient 1st prize for poetry Cooke County Coll., Gainesville, 1978, 79, 80, 81, 2d prize for poetry U. Tex., San Antonio, 1981; grantee Tex. Woman's U., 1981-82, Ill. State Library, 1986-87. Mem. Wrtrs. Roundtable, Intl. Reading Assn. Home: 600 N Buchanan Edwardsville IL 62025

BRYK, WILLIAM, b. Troy, NY, Mar. 12, 1955, s. William Zygmundt and Joy Kathleen (Hart) Bryk. Contrbr. to Newsday, Talking Turkey, Revolver, Manhattan Coll. Qtly. BSc, Manhattan Coll., 1977; postgrad. Fordham Law Schl., 1985—. Coordinator spl. programs Office of Comptroller, City of N.Y., 1977-81, wrtr., ed., 1981-82; asst. to pres. Borough of Manhattan, 1982-85; exec. asst. to NYC Councilman, 1986; asst. to NYC Council pres., 1987. Candidate for Congress, 1980, 1983. Home: 335 E 58th St New York NY 10022

BUCHAN, VIVIAN EILEEN, b. Eagle Grove, IA, May 19, 1911; d. Arum LeRoy and Frances Ma (Cline) Eaton. Author: Cat Sun Signs, 1983; Your Star Child. Contrbr. numerous articles, poems, columns to mags. and jnls. including Healthways, Modern Living, Living with Preschoolers, Toastmaster, others; Sara Teasdale bibliog. pubd. by Bulltn. of Bibliog., 1967-68. BA, Coe Coll., 1933; MA, U. Ill.-Urbana, 1958. Instr. U. Ia., Iowa City, 1959-67. Pres. Iowa City Pub. Library, 1976, bd. dirs. 7 years. Recipient Merit award Coe Coll., Cedar Rapids, Ia., 1983. Mem. Natl. League Am. PEN Women, Natl. Fedn. Press Women, NWC. Home: One Wellesley Way Iowa City IA 52240

BUCHANAN, HUBERT A., b. Denver, Aug. 5, 1905; s. Wylie Franklin and Josephine (Smith) B.; m. Ruth Stubblefield, June 1932 (dec. 1968); m. Sarah Jane Radley, JUne 1, 1976 (dec. 1980); stepchildren—Richard Radley, Jane Radley; m. Odin Waugh, Sept. 13, 1981; stepchildren—John Waugh, Phyllis Waugh. Author: Winnowing Winds (short stories), 1984. Wrkg. on fiction. AA, PUeblo Jr. Coll.; BBA, Univ. So. Colo. Ins. underwriter N.Y. Life Ins. Co., 1932-84. Home: 209 W 19th St Pueblo CO 81003

BUCHANAN, MAGGIE, see Gilman, Julia M.

BUCHEK, KATHLEEN A., b. Chgo., Apr. 24, 1958; d. Lawrence S. and Ann B. (Krhounek) B. Contrbr. to Contemporary Poets of America, Black Creek Rvw, Celebration, Seams Spring/ Fall, Our Western World's Greatest Poems, Our

World's Best Loved Poems, Am. Poetry Anthology, Am. Poetry Showcase, American Poetics, American Muse, Poems of the Century, From the Heart of a Poet, Sands of Time, others. Student pub. schls., Chgo. With Sears, Roebuck & Co., Chgo., 1981; freelance wrtr., 1982—. Recipient cert. of merit Yes Press, 1985; Golden Poets award World of Poetry Press, 1985, Silver Poets award, 1986. Mem. Songwriters Club of Am. Home: Box 87234 Chicago IL 60607

BUCHWALD, ART, b. Mt. Vernon, NY, Oct. 20, 1925; s. Joseph and Helen (Kleinberger) B.; m. Ann McGarry, Oct. 11, 1952; 3 children. Author: Paris After Dark, 1950, Art Buchwald's Paris, 1954, The Brave Coward, 1957, A Gift From the Boys, 1959, More Caviar, 1958, Un Cadeau Pour Le Patron (Prix de la Bonne Humeur 1958), Dont' Forget to Write, 1960, Art Buchwald's Secret List to Paris, 1963, How Much Is That in Dollars?, 1961, Is It Safe to Drink the Water?, 1962, I Chose Capitol Punishment, 1963, And Then I Told the President, 1965, Son of the Great Society, 1966, Have I Ever Lied to You?, 1968, The Establishment Is Alive and Well in Washington, 1969, Counting Sheep, 1970, Getting High in Government Circles, 1971, I Never Danced at the White House, 1973, The Bollo Caper, 1974, I Am Not a Crook, 1974, Irving's Delight, 1975, Washington is Leaking, 1976, Down the Seine and Up the Potomac, 1977, The Buchwald Stops Here, 1978, Laid Back in Washington, 1981, While Reagan Slept, 1983, You *Can* Fool All of the People All the Time, 1985, I think I Don't Remember, 1987. Student, U. So. Calif., 1945-48. Syndicated columnist, Los Angeles Times Syndicate. Served as sgt. USMCR, 1942-45. Recipient Pulitzer prize for outstanding commentary, 1982; elected member AAIAL, 1986. Office: 2000 Pennsylvania Ave NW Washington DC 20006

BUCHWALD, SARA P., b. Quitman, GA, Nov. 21, 1941; d. Paul W. and Nadine (Heeth) Patrick; m. Timothy R. Buchwald, Oct. 5, 1961 (div. 1969); children—Cynthia D., Andrea D.; m. Bill Wathen, Nov. 2, 1985. Author video documentaries, film scripts; contrbr.: Indpls. Woman Mag., Indpls. Star, Ind. Bus. Mag., others. Wrkg. on short-story collection, drama screenplay, documentary script. BS, Valdosta State U., 1964; MA, Ga. State U., 1970. Advt. mgr. Ransburg, Inc., Indpls., 1972-75; account exec. McQuade Bloomhorst, Indpls., 1975-79; v.p. McGill Ross Advt., Indpls., 1979-80; wrtr., exec. producer, owner The Alvarez Group, Indpls., 1986—; freelance wrtr. Grantee Lilly Meml. fund, St. Paul's Episcopal Ch., 1987. Mem. Am. Film Inst., Central Ind. Wrtrs. Center. Home: 1430 E Ohio St Indianapolis IN 46201

BUCKHOLTS, CLAUDIA, b. Ardmore, OK, Dec. 29, 1944, d. Paul O. and Lillian (Biard) Buckholts. Author: Bitterwater (poetry), 1975, Traveling Through the Body (poetry), 1979, The Book of Q (fiction), 1987; contrbr. Back Bay View, Gargoyle, Zeugma, Aeon, numerous other lit mags. Wrkg. on novel, poetry. Student Vassar Coll., 1962-63; BA, U. Mich., 1967. Editorial asst. Houghton Mifflin Co., Boston, 1968-70; dir. Cambridge Poets Workshop, Mass., 1973-83; founder, ed. Gargoyle poetry mag., Cambridge, 1975-82; mem. staff fgn. rights dept. Harvard Univ. Press., Cambridge, 1979—. Recipient Hopwood award for poetry, U. Mich., 1965, for fiction, 1967, Grolier Poetry Prize, Cambridge, 1976, Sri Chinmoy award for spiritual poetry, 1977, 78; Mass. Artists Fdn. fellow, 1981. Mem. NWU. Home: 505 Green St Cambridge MA 02139

BUCKLER, BEATRICE, b. NYC., Nov. 4, 1933; d. S. and Ida (Frost) B.; m. Edgar I. Gotthold, Nov. 20, 1955; 1 dau., Jessica Frost. Assoc. service editor, Good Housekeeping, 1961-63; assoc. editor articles, Parent's mag., 1966-69; writer-editor Woman's Day, 1963-66; with Family Circle mag., 1969-75, exec. editor, 1970-77; v. p. (1st woman) Family circle, Inc., N.Y. Times Co., 1973-75; founder, editor-in-chief, pub. Working Woman, 1975-78; editorial cons., 1978-79; cons. editor Prime Time mag., 1980; cofounder, editor Hers mag., 1981—. Recipient N.Y. Women in Communications award, 1977, for founding Working Woman. Home: 137 E 36th St New York NY 10016

BUCKLEY, PRISCILLA LANGFORD, b. NYC, Oct. 17, 1921; d. William Frank and Aloise (Steiner) B. Copy girl, sports writer U.P., N.Y.C., 1944, radio rewrite, 1944-47, corr., Paris, France, 1953-56; news editor Sta. WACA, Camden, S.C., 1947-48; reports officer CIA, Washington, 1951-53; with Natl. Rvw., 1956—, mng. editor, 1959-86, sr. editor, 1986—. Columnist: One Woman's Voice Syndicate, 1976-80. B.A., Smith Coll., 1943. Mem. U.S. Advisory Comm. on Public Diplomay, 1983—. Office: Natl Rvw 150 E 35th St New York NY 10016

BUCKLEY, VIRGINIA LAURA, b. NYC, May 11, 1929; d. Alfred and Josephine Marie (Manetti) Iacuzzi; m. David Patrick Buckley, July 30, 1960; children: Laura Joyce, Brian Thomas. Author: State Birds. Copy editor World Pub. Co., NYC, 1959-69; children's book editor Thomas Y. Crowell, NYC, 1971-80; editorial dir. Lodestar Books, E. P. Dutton, Inc., NYC, 1980—. BA, Wellesley Coll., 1950; MA, Columbia U., 1952. Mem. ALA. Office: Dutton 2 Park Ave New York NY 10016

BUCKLEY, WILLIAM FRANK JR., b. NYC, Nov. 24, 1925; s. William Frank and Aloise (Steiner) B.; m. Patricia Taylor, July 6, 1950; 1 child, Christopher T. Author: God and Man at Yale, 1951, (with L. Brent Bozell) McCarthy and His Enemies, 1954, Up from LIberalism, 1959, Rumbles Left and Right, 1963, The Unmaking of a Mayor, 1966, The Jeweler's Eye, 1968, The Governor Listheth, 1970, Cruising Speed, 1971, Inveighing We Will Go, 1972, Four Reforms, 1973, United Nations Journal, 1974, Execution Eve, 1975, Saving the Queen, 1976, Airborne, 1976, Stained Glass, 1978, A Hymnal, 1978, Who's On First, 1980, Marco Polo, If You Can, 1982, Atlantic High, 1982, Overdrive, 1983, The Story of Henri Tod, 1984, See You Later Alligator, 1985, Right Reason, 1985, High Jinx, 1986, Racing Through Paradise, 1987, Mongoose, R.I.P., 1987; editor: The Committee and Its Critics, 1962, Odyssey of a Friend, 1970, American Conservative Thought in the Twentieth Century, 1970; contbr. to Racing at Sea, 1959, The Intellectuals, 1960, What is Conservatism?, 1964, Dialogues in Americanism, 1964, Violence in the Streets, 1968, The Beatles Book, 1968, Spectrum of Catholic Attitudes, 1969, Great Ideas Today Annual, 1970, Essays on Hayek, 1976; also periodicals. Student, U. Mexico, 1943; B.A., Yale U., 1950. Assoc. editor Am. Mercury, 1952; editor-in-chief Natl. Rvw, 1955—; syndicated columnist, 1962—. Served to 2d lt. inf. AUS, 1944-46. Recipient Bellarime medal, 1977; Am. Journalism award Friends of Haifa U., 1980; Creative Leadership award NYU, 1981. Fellow Soc. Profl Journalists. Office: 150 E 35th St New York NY 10016

BUCKMAN, REPHA JOAN, b. St. Paul, KS, Aug. 18, 1942; d. Francis Albert and Leona Myrtle (Aronholdt) Glenn; m. Larry Dean Buckman, Jan. 15, 1961 (div. Jan. 15, 1978); children—Eric Dean, Alan Glenn, Martin Lance. Author: (non-fiction) Critter Crossin', 1978; (poetry) Repha, 1986, Women Writers in Kansas, 1981, Cleaving the Surface, 1980, Seeker, 1980, Winfield Daily Courier, 1980, Puppetry, Lang. and the Special Child, 1984, Kansas English, 1984, Odessa Poetry Rvw, 1986; editor: Blasdel, Buckman and Barnes on Barns, 1983; Kate's Taming of the Cooks Book, 1983; Center is Being, 1983, The Teacher's Edition, 1986. BA, Southwestern, Winfield, Kans., 1970; MA, Fort Hays State U., 1978. Tchr., Burton Unified Schl. Dist., 1970-74, Sterling USD, Kans., 1974-79, Hutchinson Community Coll., Kans., 1985-86; artistic dir. Tri-Crown Family Theatre, Sterling, 1983-86; artist-in-edn. Kans. Arts Commn., 1982-86, 86-87. Bd. dirs. Kans. Pub. TV Sta., Wichita, Kans., 1982-86, Hutchinson Theatre Guild, Kans., 1983-85, Bob Woodley Fdn., Topeka, Kans., 1986—; pres. bd. dirs. Tri-Crown Enterprises, Inc., Sterling, 1984—. Recipient Honorable Mention award Rocky Mountain Poetry Soc., 1980; Kans. Com. for Humanities grantee. Mem. Assn. Kans. Theatres (Best Program Design, Set Design, Costume Design, Best Actor, Best Overall Concept 1983), Assn. Kans. Writers, Friends of Humanities, Kansas Author's Club. Home: Rt 1 Box 35 Sterling KS 67579

BUCKNER, SALLY BEAVER, b. Statesville, NC, Nov. 3, 1931; d. Henry George and Foda Leigh (Stack) Beaver; m. Robert Lynn Buckner, Aug. 21, 1954; children—George Robert, Sally Lynn, Theodore Warren. Playwright: Encounter at the Corner, 1966; author poetry collect. Strawberry Harvest, 1986; contrbr. poet to numerous mags. including Southern Poetry Rvw and Woman's Day. AB, UNC-G, 1953; MA, NC St. U., 1970; PhD,U. NC, 1980. Tchr., Gastonia (NC) City Schools, 1953-54, Goldsboro (NC) City Schools, 1959-60, The Protestant School, Goldsboro, 1962-65; reporter Raleigh Times, 1966-68; prof. Peace College, Raleigh, 1970—. First place poetry, Crucible, Wilson, NC, 1978, Windhover, Raleigh, NC, 1968. Mem. NC Writers Conference, NC English Tchrs. Assn., NC Wrtrs. Network. Home: 3231 Birnamwood Rd Raleigh NC 27607

BUCKVAR, FELICE, b. Bklyn., Oct. 14, 1938; d. William and Ruth (Marcus) Spitz; m. Morton Buckvar, Dec. 25, 1957; children—Eric, Tod, Lynn. Author: All The Way, 1980, Happily Ever After, 1980, Ten Miles High, 1981. BA, Bklyn Coll, 1958; MA, L.I. U, 1976. Freelance reporter Newsday, L.I., N.Y., 1970—, The N.Y. Times, Westchester, 1981—; instr. NY Inst. Tech., L.I., 1981—. Mem AG, PW (keynote speaker, 1980, 81, 84). Address: 43 Juneau Blvd Woodbury NY 11797

BUDY, ANDREA HOLLANDER, b. Berlin, Fed. Republic Germany, Apr. 28, 1947, came to U.S., 1948, naturalized, 1962; d. Milton Henry and Blanche (Simon) Hollander; m. Todd Budy, July 18, 1976; 1 son, Brooke. Author: Living on the Cusp, 1981. Contrbr. poems to anthols, lit mags, including Ga Rvw, Plainsong, Third Rail, Negative Capability, Rhino, Cache Rvw, Chariton Rvw, Keener Sounds, 1987. BS, Boston U., 1968; MA, U. Colo.-Boulder, 1972, doctoral candidate, 1974-77. Asst. prof. U. Colo., Denver, 1974-77; owner, innkeeper Comml. Hotel, Mountain View, Ark., 1982—; instr. U. Central Ark., Conway, 1984-85. Active Stone County Council on Tourism, Mountain View, 1983—. Mem. P&W, AAP. Home: Box 1107 Mountain View AR 72560

BUEHLER, ROBIN MARIE, b. Camden, NJ, Dec. 7, 1969; d. Robley S. Buehler and Marjorie Marie (Kruckner) Hagquist. Contrbr. poems to anthols. Wrkg. on novel. Tchr. asst. Sunday schl. Holy Communion Lutheran Ch., Berlin, N.J., 1985—. Recipient hon. mention World of Poetry, 1985. Home: 169 Taunton Rd RFD 3 Berlin NJ 08009

BUEHRER, BEVERLEY BARE, b. Hanley, Stoke-on-Trent, Eng., Feb. 12, 1947, d. Duward Joseph and Vera (Price) Bare, m. Carl Howard Buehrer, Aug. 21, 1971. Contrbr. articles to Women's Circle Home Cooking, Video, Filmfax, numerous other publs. B.S., No. Ill. U., 1969, M.S., 1972. Freelance wrtr., 1980—; tchr. Kishwaukee Community Coll., Malta, Ill. 1985—. Recipient prize for poetry Am. Graniteware Assn., 1981. Mem. Ill. Wrtrs., Wordwrights. Home: 106 Wendell St DeKalb IL 60115

BUELL, FREDERICK HENDERSON, b. Bryn Mawr, PA, Nov. 17, 1942; s. Clarence Addison and Marjorie (Henderson) B.; m. Jill V. Pettinato, Oct. 30, 1983; 1 child, Alexander Silvano. Author: Theseus and Other Poems, 1971; The Social Poetry of W. H. Auden, 1973; Full Summer, 1978; contrbr. articles to Iowa, New Eng., Cornell rvws., Boundary 2, Coll. English; contrbr. poems to Poetry, Hudson, New Eng. rvws, The Little Mag, Epoch, Matrix. BA, Yale U., 1964; PhD, Cornell U., 1970. Instr. English, Queens Coll., Flushing, NY, 1970-71, asst. prof., 1971-73, assoc. prof., 1973-78, prof., 1978—. NEA fellow, 1972-73. Mem. MLA. Home: 72 Amity Rd Warwick NY 10990

BUETTNER, DEBORAH ANNE, (Debi Buettner), b. Cleve., Oct. 28, 1957; d. Robert Kreilick and Annette Catherine (Hook) B. Author chapbooks: Fantasy Dreaming, 1985, No More Dreams, 1986. Contrbr. poems to anthols. B.A., Coll. Wooster, 1979. Sales asst. Top Market TV, Cleve., 1979-82; sales engineer Thompson & Assoc., Cleve., 1982—. Recipient Golden Poet award World of Poetry, 1985, 86, 87. Mem. Am. Poetry Soc. Home: 6501 Marsol Rd 106 Mayfield Heights OH 44124

BUFFIN, CAROL, b. Norwich, CT, Mar. 30, 1957; d. Edward Joseph and Beatrice Agnes (Clocher) Maruniewicz; m. Robert Alexander Buffer, Jr., June 5, 1976 (div. Oct. 7, 1981). Contrbr. articles to sports mags. including The Wrestling News, Ring Wrestling Mag., WWF Mag. Grad. private & public schls., Jewett City, CT. Mem. Wrtr.'s Digest Book Club. Home: 10 Blossom Ln Jewett City CT 06351

BUGATTI, SIOBHAN, see Bentley, Sean Singer

BUGBEE, HELEN LOUISE, b. Spring Valley, WI, Oct. 18, 1909, d. George Julian and Sarah Ethel (Schumann) Bugbee. Author: Their Revolution or Ours: The American Way to a More Abundant Life; contrbr. to The Freeman, Modern Age, Partners, The Humanist. AB, U. Iowa, 1928. Wrtr., Kemper Ins., Chgo., 1942-45, Sheldon- Claire Co., Chgo., 1949-59; wrtr., ed. Commerce Clearing House, Chgo., 1960-69; ed. numerous med. orgns. Home: 525 Hawthorne Pl Chicago IL 60657

BUGEJA, MICHAEL JOSEPH, b. Hackensack, NJ; s. Michael Carl and Josephine (Apap) B.; m. Diane Faye Sears, Sept 15, 1979; 1 dau., Erin. Author: Feature Writing for Newspapers and Mags, 1985, How-To Newswriter, 1986; ed SW Cultural Heritage Essays, 1984; more than 150 poems in jnls including Ga. Rvw, Antioch Rvw, Kenyon Rvw, New England Rvw; fiction in Intro, Kans Qtly, SD Rvw, dzns of articles in Writer's Digest, Ed. and Pub. and Jnlsm. Edr. among others; lit crit in Ga. Rvw, Ala. Qtly Rvw, Qtly West; book rvws. in Ga. Rvw, Hollins Critic and So. Humanities Rvw. BA, St. Peter's Coll., 1974; MS, S. Dakota State, 1976; PhD, Okla. State-Stillwater, 1985. State ed. UPI, Sioux Falls, SD, 1976-79; assoc. prof. Okla. State Univ., Stillwater, 1979—; poetry ed. Cimarron Rvw. Recipient AAP Univ prize, 1983; Amelia award, 1985, AWP Award, 1985; AMOCO award for tchg., Amoco Fdn., 1985; Writer's Digest Grand Prize, 1986. Address: Scripps Schl Jnlsm Ohio Univ Athens OH 45701

BUGH, MARY LOU, b. Omer, MI, Feb. 10, 1942; d. Victor and Rose Josephine (Swiecicki) Trombley; divorced; children: Paul Wilson, harles Edward, Annette Marie, James Dale. Contrbr. articles, poems to mags., newspapers, anthols. B.A., Saginaw Valley State Coll., 1972; M.A., Mich. State U., 1978. Elem. Tchr. Pinconning Schls., MI, 1972—. Recipient 1st prize for short story Mid-Mich. Wrtrs., 1983. Home: 3404 Senske Standish MI 48658

BUGLIOSI, VINCENT T., b. Hibbing, MN, Aug. 18, 1934; s. Vincent and Ida (Valerie) B.; m. Gail Margaret Talluto, July 21, 1956; children: Wendy Suzanna, Vincent John. Co-author: Helter-Skelter, The True Story of the Manson Murders, 1974, Till Death Us Do Part; a true murder mystery, 1978. B.B.A., U. Miami, Fla., 1956; LL.B., UCLA, 1964. Served to capt. AUS, 1957. Office: 9300 Wilshire Blvd 470 Beverly Hills CA 90212

BUHAGIAR, MARION, b. NYC, Oct. 27, 1932; d. George and Mae (Pietrzak) B.; 1 dau., Alexa Ragozin. Bus. reporter Time mag., 1957-59; assoc. editor Fortune mag., 1960-73, story devel. editor, 1970-73; text editor Time-Life Books, 1973-76; v.p., editor Boardroom Reports, NYC, 1977—; exec. editor Bottom Line/ Personal, NYC, 1980—. BA cum laude, Hunter Coll., 1953; postgrad., Mt. Holyoke Coll., 1954. Office: Boardroom Reports 500 5th Ave New York NY 10110

BUKOWSKI, CHARLES, b. Andernach, Ger., Aug. 16, 1920; came to U.S., 1923; (div.); 1 dau., Marina Louise. Author: novels Post Office, 1971, Factotum, 1975, Women, 1978, Ham on Rye, 1982; short stories Confessions of a Man Insane Enough to Live with Beasts, 1965, All the Assholes in the World and Mine, 1966, Notes of a Dirty Old Man, 1969, Erections, Ejaculations and General Tales of Ordinary Madness, 1972, South of No North, 1973, You Kissed Lilly, 1978, Hot Water Music, 1983; poetry Flower, Fist and Bestial Wail, 1960, Poems and Drawings, 1962, It Catches My Heart in Its Hands, 1963, Crucifix in a Deathhand, 1965, Cold Dogs in the Courtyard, 1965, The Genius of the Crowd, 1966, A Terror Street and Agony Way, 1968, Poems Written Before Jumping Out of an 8 Story Window, 1968, The Days Run Away Like Wild Horses Over the Hills, 1969, Fire Station, 1970, Mockingbird Wish Me Luck, 1972, Me and Your Sometimes Love Poems, 1972, While the Music Played, 1973, Burning in Water, Drowning in Flame, 1974, Africa, Paris, Greece, 1975, Scarlet, 1976, Maybe Tomorrow, 1977, We'll Take Them, 1978, Love is a Dog from Hell, 1978, Play the Piano, 1979, Dangling in the Tournefortia, 1981, Horsemeat, 1982; screenplay Barfly, 1979; travel book Shakespeare Never Did This, 1979; narrator: documentary film Poetry in Motion (Ron Mann), 1983; film produced from short stories: Tales of Ordinary Madness (Marco Ferreri), 1982. Student, Los Angeles City Coll., 1939-41. Editor: Laugh Literacy and Man the Humping Guns, 1970. NEA grantee, 1974. Address: Box 3993 Santa Barbara CA 93105

BULBUL, see Pilgrim-Guracar, Genevieve

BULNES, SARA MARIA, b. Havana, Cuba, Sept. 20, 1954, came to U.S., 1962; d. Jose Ramon and Maria (Prego) B. Contrbr. poems to anthols. A.A., Miami Dade Commun. Coll., 1978; student U. Miami, 1983—. Recipient 5 Honorable Mentions, World of Poetry, 1986-87, Golden Poet award, 1986, 87; Honorable Mention, Am. Collegiate Poets, 1986, 3d place, 1987; Honorable Mention, Am. Poetry Anthol., 1986, 87. Home: 421 SW 13th Ave Miami FL 33126

BUMPUS, JERRY DON, b. Mt. Vernon, IL, Jan. 29, 1937; s. Carl Lester Bumpus and Opal Irene (Gibbs) Chapman; m. Bettie Ann McShane Nov. 11, 1961; 2 daus.: Margot, Prudence. Author: (novels) Anaconda, 1967, The Worms Are Singing, 1974, (short story collections) Things in Place, 1975, Special Offer, 1980, Heroes and Villains, 1986; contrbr. short stories to lit mags and comml. mags. BA, U. of Missouri, 1958; MFA, U. of Iowa, 1960. Instr. Ariz. State U., Flagstaff, 1961-62, Canadian Academy, Kobe, Japan, 1962-63, Midwestern U., Wichita Falls, Tex., 1963-66, Colorado Schl. of Mines, Golden, 1966-67, Eastern Kentucky U., Richmond, 1967-68; asst. prof., Eastern Wash. U., Cheney, 1968-71; prof. of English, San Diego State U., San Diego, 1971—; exchange prof., Wuhan U., Wuhan, People's Republic of China, 1985-86. Home: 5545 Morro Way Q11 La Mesa CA 92042

BUNNELL, PAUL JOSEPH, b. Amesbury, MA, July 28, 1946; s. James Henry, Sr. and Lorraine Muriel (Violette) B.; m. Leslie Diane White, May 10, 1969; children—Matthew Paul, Jeannine Marie. Author: Thunder Over New England, 1987, History of Marion County, 1986, Bunnell/Bonnell Genealogy, 1986. Wrkg. on novel, Best Friends. Tumbleweed, Insane Love, geneology. Govt. property admin. (Hughes Aircraft, Canoga, Calif., 1966-75. Owner, The World of Books, Inc., Wareham, MA, 1975-77; br. mgr. Westinghouse Corp., Portland, OR and Boise, ID, 1977-79; warehouse supvr. Augat Inc., Mashpee, MA, 1979—; free-lance/profl. genealogist, 1977—. Home: 31 Timber Ln West Barnstable MA 02668

BUNTING, ANNE EVELYN, (Eve Bunting), b. Maghera, Ireland, Dec. 19, 1928; came to U.S., 1958, naturalized, 1969; d. Sloan Edmund and Mary (Canning) Bolton: m. Edward Davison Bunting, Mar. 26, 1951; children: Christine Ann, Sloan Edward, Glenn Davison. Author: numerous children's books, including Barney the Beard, 1975 (Honor book Chgo. Book Clinic), One More Flight, 1976 (Golden Kite award, Outstanding Sci. Book award), Ghost of Summer, 1977 (jr. Lit. Guild selection), The Big Cheese, 1977, Winter's Coming, 1977, (with Glenn Bunting) Skateboards, How to Make Them, How to Ride Them, 1977, If I Asked You, Would You Stay? 1985 (ALA best book award 1985). Student, Meth. Coll., Belfast, Ireland, 1935-45, Queen's U., 1945-47. Lectr. U. So. Calif., Pasadena City Coll., Sierra Writing Camp. Mem. PEN, AG, Soc. Children's Book Writers, Calif. Writers Guilid, So. Calif. Council on Writing for Children and Young People. Home: 1512 Rose Villa St Pasadena CA 91106

BUNTING, EVE, see Bunting, Anne Evelyn

BURACK, SYLVIA E. KAMERMAN, b. Hartford, CT, Dec. 16, 1916; d. Abraham and Augusta (Chermak) Kamerman; m. Abraham S. Burack, Nov. 28, 1940 (dec.); children—Janet, Susan, Ellen. Editor and publisher Plays, The Drama Mag. for Young People, also the Writer Mag., 1978—. Mem. Natl. Book Critics Circle, LWV, Friends of Library at Boston U. (dir., pres., 1981-83), Phi Beta Kappa. Editor: Little Plays for Little Players, 1952, Blue Ribbon Plays for Girls, 1955, Blue Ribbon Plays for Graduation, 1957, A Treasury of Christmas plays, 1958, Children's Plays from Favorite Stories, 1959, Fifty Plays for Junior Actors, 1966, Fifty Plays for Holidays, 1969, Dramatized Folk Tales of the World, 1971, On Stage for Christmas, 1978, Christmas Play Favorites for Young People, 1982, Holiday Plays Round the Year, 1983, Patriotic and Hist. Plays for Young Peoples 1987; (adult) Writing the Short Short Story, 1942; Book Reviewing, 1978; The Writer's Handbook, 1987, Writing and Selling Fillers, Light Verse and Short Humor, 1982; Writing and Selling the Romance Novel, 1983, Writing Mystery and Crime Fiction, 1985, Plays of Black Americans, 1987. BA magna cum laude, Smith Coll., 1938. Home: 72 Penniman Rd Brookline MA 02146

BURBANK, JAMES CLARKE, (Jim), b. Denver, Nov. 24, 1946; s. John Allen and Marian (Rasmussen) B.; m. Sharon Maxine Niederman, July 5, 1973. Ed. Los I & II, 1971, 75, Energy (nine vols), 1975, Loka Anthology, 1976; contrbr. more than 100 articles, short stories, poems in var. publs. inclg. Active Anthology, Malebolges, Retelling Am, Boundary II, Tarasque, NY Times, Natl. Real Estate Investor, Financial Trend. BA, U Colo, 1970; postgrad. San Francisco State, 1971. Mng. ed. Denver/Boulder mag., 1978-79; contrbr. ed New Mex. Bus. Jnl, Albuquerque, 1984-85; freelance writer and ed., Albuquerque, 1985-86. Bd. dirs. Rio Grande Writers Assn., 1984; arts panelist in grants, New Mex Arts div., Santa Fe, 1984. Recipient NEA publg. grant, 1978. Address: 302 Alamosa NW Albuquerque NM 87107

BURCH, MARIEL RAE, b. Ishpeming, MI, Apr. 3, 1934; m. Kate Anne Bishop, Mar. 19, 1981. Editor, Together—The Only Mag. for Lesbian Couples, 1985. BA, Ind. U., 1979; MSW, U. Mich., 1981. Dir. Lesbian Edn. & Counseling, Santa Rosa, Calif., 1981-85; editor Lesbian Inciter newspaper, San Francisco, 1985—. Mem. Natl. Women's Polit. Caucus, Santa Rosa and Ann Arbor, Mich., Natl. Urban League, Ft. Wayner, Ind. Mem. Ntl. Assn. Social Workers, Feminist Writers Guild, NOW (membership chmn. 1983-85). Home: 22 Higuera Ave San Francisco CA 94132

BURCHARD, RACHAEL C., (Gowan (Ballenger), b. Hendersonville, NC, Aug. 27, 1921; d. Henry Homer and Olive (Gowan) Ballenger; m. Waldo W. Burchard, May 24, 1945; children—Gina Michel, Petrea Celeste, Stuart Gregory, Margot Theresa. Author: John Updike: Yea Sayings, 1971, Green Figs and Tender Grapes, 1985, play Hallelujah Hopscotch, 1986 (1st prize 1984-85 Play Writing, Indiana U./Purdue U.), poetry in Midwest Poetry Rvw., Miss. Valley Rvw, The Hollins Critic, Spoon River Qtly, other lit mags; contrbr. reviews to Masterplots, 1982-84. BA, Linfield College, 1945, MA, Northern IL. U., 1966. Tchr., Cal. publ. schls., 1945-53; instr., Northern Il., U., Dekalb, IL, 1958-60, 1965-72, 1978-80; instr., Rock Valley College, Rockford, IL, 1974-77, freelance wrtr., 1958—. Mem. PSA, Amer. Theatre Assoc., Dekalb Arts Comm., Children's Community Theatre, Ill. Writers, Inc. Home: 907 Sharon Dr Dekalb IL 60115

BURDELL, BILL, see Welsh, William Francis Anthony

BURDEN, JEAN (PRUSSING), b. Waukegan, IL, Sept. 1, 1914; d. Harry Frederick and Miriam (Biddlecom) Prussing; m. David Charles Burden, 1940 (div. 1949). Author: Naked as the Glass, 1963, Journey Toward Poetry, 1966, The Cat You Care For, 1968, The Dog You Care For, 1968, The Bird You Care For, 1970, The Fish You Care For, 1971, A Celebration of Cats, 1974, The Classic Cats, 1975, The Woman's Day Book of Hints for Cat Owners, 1980; poetry editor: Yankee Mag., 1955—; pet editor: Woman's Day Mag., 1973-82. BA, U. Chgo., 1936. Editor, copywriter Domestic Industries, Inc., Chgo., 1941-45; editor Stanford Research Inst., South Pasadena, Calif., 1965-66; prop. Jean Burden & Assocs., 1966-72; supr. poetry workshop Pasadena City Coll., Calif., 1961-62, 66, U. Calif. at Irvine, 1975. Recipient 1st prize Borestone Mountain Poetry award, 1963. Mem. PSA, AAP, AG. Address: 1129 Beverly Way Altadena CA 91001

BURDEN, NANCY CASWELL, b. Waterloo, NY, Mar. 7, 1946; d. Charles Irving and Margaret Ida (Fellows) Caswell; m. David George Burden, July 1, 1977; children by previous marriage—Jeffrey Charles Somerville, Margaret Lynn Somerville. Ed.: Breathline, 1983-87, Fla. Med. Jnl., 1987; assoc. ed.: Jnl. Post Anesthesia Nursing, 1985-87. Contrbr. articles to med. jnls. Diploma in nursing Commun. Gen. Hospital, 1967. Mem. Am. Soc. Post Anesthesia Nurses (5th place in natl. jnlsm. 1985). Home: 83 Flamingo Pl Safety Harbor FL 34695

BURDICK, ARIANE NEIMAN, b. Denver, Feb. 18, 1945; d. Gilbert and Margaret (Goodwin) Neiman; separated; children—Lilia, Serena. Author: Small Cloud, 1984. Wrkg. on novel, Minotaurs in Clarion: non-fiction book on edn., collection of poetry. B.A. in History, Philosophy, Alaska Pacific U., 1967. Receptionist Anthony Tucker, Greenfield, MA, 1972-73; owner D.B.A. Light Lunches, Millers Falls, MA, 1976—. Home: 9 Church St Millers Falls MA 01349

BURDSALL, CLARICE W., b. Stilesville, IN, Apr. 13, 1909; d. Clarence Clay and Iva M. (Wallace) Whicker; son: Carroll W. Burdsall Columnist: Plainfield Messenger (Ind.), 1978—. Student Central Normal College, 1928-29. Recipient 1st prize for column on horticulture, 1st prize for column on birds State Garden Soc., 1985. Home: Rt 1 Box 175 Stilesville IN 46180

BURGER, HENRY G., b. NYC, June 27, 1923; s. B. William and Terese R. (Felleman) B. Author: Telesis, 1967, Ethno-Pedagogy, 1968, Ethnic Live-In: A Guide to Penetrating and Understanding a Cultural Minority, 1969, Ethno-Strategy: A Guide for Analyzing a Foreign Culture, 1st ed., 1972, 2d ed., 1976, 3d ed., 1987; author chpt. in The Concept and Dynamics of Culture (editor Bernardo Bernardi), 1977; compiler and editor: The Wordtree: A Transitive Cladistic for Solving Physical and Social Problems, 1984. BA, Columbia U., 1947, MA in anthropology, 1965, PhD in anthropology, 1967. Indsl. engr. and mfrs. rep. various orgns., Chgo. and NYC, 1947-55; social sci. cons., NYC, 1956-67; staff anthropologist Southwestern Coop. Edn. Lab., Albuquerque, 1967-69; assoc. prof. anthropology and edn. U. Mo., Kansas City, 1969-73, prof., 1973—; editor, pub. The Wordtree, Merriam, Kans., 1984-86, Overland Pk., 1986—. Fellow Royal Anthro. Inst. (life), European Assn. Lexicography, World Acad. Art and Sci.; mem. Dictionary Soc. North Am. (life), Academie europeenne des sciences, des arts, et des lettres (corr.), Phi Beta Kappa. Pulitzer scholar Columbia U.; NSF faculty research grantee, 1970. Home: 10876 Bradshaw Overland Park KS 66210

BURGER, ROBERT EUGENE, b. Yerington, NV, June 21, 1931; s. Edmund Ganes and Rose Catherine (Kobe) B.; m. Mary Theresa Dunne, June 26, 1954; children: Eileen, Marlene, Robert, Diane, Elisabeth, Joseph, Daniel, John, Clare, Christopher. Author: Where They Go to Die, 1968, McCarthy, Words to Remember, 1969, Out From Under, 1970, Twilights Believers, 1971, Pietro on Wine, 1972, The Love Contract, 1972, Ego Speak, 1973, The Simplified Guide to Personal Bankruptcy, 1974, The Chess of Bobby Fischer, 1975, Inside Divorce, 1975, Forbidden Cures, 1976, Jogger's Catalog, 1978, The Polish Prince, 1978, The Jug Wine Book, 1979, The Whole Life Diet, 1979, Meganutrition, 1980, The Courage to Believe, 1980, Meganutrition for Women, 1982, The Healing Arts, 1986.BA, U. Calif.-Berkeley, 1953, MA, 1955. Writer, 1968—. Mem. AG Am. Office: 802 Montgomery St San Francisco CA 94133

BURGESS, CRAIG E., b. Camden, NJ, Oct. 8, 1944; s. Edward Russell and Ruth Eleanor (Quinn) B. Contrbr. poetry to num. anthols. including Am. Poetry Anthol. 1983, Our Western World's Greatest Poets, 1983, Our World's Best Loved Poems, 1984, Our World's Most Beloved Poems, 1985, Our World's Most Cherished Poems, 1986, Hearts on Fire, 1985, 1986. BA, Rutgers U., 1967; MS, U. PA, 1971. Tchg. fellow U. PA, Phila., 1967-68; Spanish instr. Cherry Hill (NJ) H.S. East, 1968—. Office: Cherry Hill HS E Kresson Rd Cherry Hill NJ 08003

BURGESS, EDWARD FRANCIS, VIII, b. Scotia, CA, Oct. 30, s. Edward Francis and Gwyneth (Langdon) B.; m. Sandi Smith; children—Tommy, Dae, Ronnie, Chelsea, Eddie. Author: The Grand Parade: an American Poetry, 1980; contrbr.: Poets Anonymous, Hard Pressed, Primal Urge, numerous other periodicals; ed., Poems from a Class Five Target, 1986. Wrkg. on poetry books. BA and MA in English, Calif. State U.-Sacramento. Instr. English, Sierra Coll., Rocklin, Calif., 1985—, Sacramento City Coll., 1980—; lectr. English Calif. State U., Sacramento, 1981—. Office: CA State Univ 6000 J St Sacramento CA 95819

BURGESS, MARGARET, see Albrecht, Peggy

BURK, A.R., see Burke, Ruth

BURKE, (CAROL) ELIZABETH, b. Great Bend, KS, June 23, 1946, d. Robert Merle and Virginia Mae (Jaworski) Burke; m. Harry Gottesfeld, Oct. 23, 1985; adopted dau., Gina Faye Burke. Author: The Rose and The Sunflower, 1984, Mrs. Wigglesworth, 1984, The Oogle, 1984, Power, Affiliation and Self Fulfillment, 1985, Improving the "Who Are You" Test, 1985, Power and Perception, 1986. BA in Communications, SUNY-Buffalo, 1971, J.D., 1974. Sr. prtnr. Elizabeth Burke Law Firm, N.Y., Tex., Hawaii, 1974—; legal expert KHOU-TV, Houston; news film maker AFTRA, NYC,1985—. Home: 10 Waterside Plaza New York NY 10010

BURKE, DIANA, see Karni, Michaela Jordan

BURKE, EDGAR PATRICK, (Ned Burke), b. Scranton, PA, May 20, 1944; s. Edgar J. and Rita Marie (Sweeney) B.; divorced; children—Donna, Patrick, Kevin. Author: How to Start Your Own Publication on Less than a Shoestring, 1986, Best of Burke's corners, 1987. Ed., pub. Yesterday's Magazette, 1973—, New Wrtr.'s Magazette, 1986—. Student LaSalle U., 1966-68, U. Scranton, 1962-66, Palmer Wrtrs. Schl., 1968-70. Ed., North Port News, FL, 1979-81, Winter Park Sun Herald, FL, 1981-83, Weekender Mag., Sarasota, FL, 1984-86, DeSoto Times, FL, 1983-84, Fla. Banner, Longwood, 1983-86, ed., pub. Ind. Pub. Co., Sarasota, 1973—; founder Desktop Pub., Sarasota, 1986—. Office: Box 15126 Sarasota FL 34277

BURKE, RUTH, (A.R. Burk, Silver Morgan), b. Los Angeles, Jan. 16, 1933; d. Thomas Arthur and Bertha Ann (Morgan) King; m. Benjamin Burke, Dec. 19, 1951 (div. 1969); children—Julian, Alan, Carol, MIchael, Laurel, Abram. Author: How to Live on Nothing While Writing the Great American Novel, 1977, Snowbird's Nest (trailer park guide), 1984; contrbr. to: Catholic Digest, Ebony, Mother Trucker, News, National Enquirer, Mother Earth News, Wall Street Journal, Grit, Reader's Digest, numerous other publs. Wrkg. on non-fiction. AB in History, San Diego State U. Asst. ed. True Romance-True Experience, Macfadden-Bartell Pub. Co., N.Y.C., 1970; tchr. Yuma LaPaz and Maricopa County (Ariz.) Schs., 1970—; bookmobile driver Yuma, City-County Library, 1981-84; instr. English Reed Christian Coll., Compton, Calif., 1985. Home: Box 604 Salome AZ 85348

BURKE, NED, see Burke, Edgar P.

BURKET, HARRIET, (MRS. FRANCIS B. TAUSSIG), b. Findlay, OH; d. John Franklin and Betty (Hoege) B.; m. Maurice C. Reinecke, Sept. 24, 1935 (div. Apr. 1952); 1 dau., Rosalind; m. Francis Brewster Taussig, Oct. 8, 1960 (dec. 1970). Assoc. editor Arts and Decoration, 1933-35, Creative Design, 1935-37; assoc. editor House and Garden, 1937-44, home furnishings mdse. editor, 1952-55, exec. editor, 1955-58; editor-in-chief, 1958-70; partner Editors Inc., 1970—; interior design editor Woman's Home Companion, 1944-52. Editor: House & Garden's Complete Guide to Interior Decorating, 7th ed., 1970, House & Garden's Complete Guide to Creative Entertaining, 1971. AB, Vassar Coll., 1931. Home: 14 Sutton Pl S New York NY 10022

BURKHART, ROBERT EDWARD, b. Pitts., Jan. 11, 1937; s. Edward Wendelin Burkhart and Violet Elizabeth (Reichel) Fay; m. Sylvia Carol Davis, June 11, 1966; 1 dau. Heather Ellen. Author: Perspectives on Our Time, 1970, Shakespear's Bad Quartos, 1975. Contrbr. articles, rvws., stories, poems to lit. mags., profl. jnls. Ed.: (jnl.) Language Today, 1975-77. Wrkg. on short stories, novels, articles on Shakespearean topics. B.B.A., U. Pitts., 1958, M.A., 1963; Ph.D., U. Cin., 1967. Instr., U. Ky., Lexington, 1965-67; asst. prof. to prof. Eastern Ky. U., Richmond, 1967-71, prof., 1971—, chair English dept., 1979-86. Active, Concerned Citizens of Madison County, Richmond, 1986. Served to 1st lt. U.S. Army, 1959-61. Fellow NEH, 1981. Mem. Intl. Shakespeare Assn., Shakespeare Assn. Am., MLA, Hemingway Soc., South Atlantic MLA, Southeastern Renaissance Conf., Ky. Philological Assn. Home: 123 Buckwood Dr Richmond KY 40475

BURKIN, MARY, b. Kansas City, KS, d. Francis Earl and Marjorie Ann (Tarry) B. Playwright: Today/Today, 1985, Louisa May Alcott, 1979, Susan B. Anthony: 50 Years, 1981, Clara Barton, 1981, Victoria Woodhull, 1983, Love and Friendship: An Evening with Jane Austen, 1978, Up the Coast, 1984, The Road Show, 1986, I Lift My Lamp, 1987. BA U. So. Calif., Los Angeles; MA, Calif. State U., Long Beach. Mng. dir. Am. Living History Theatre, Hollywood, Calif., 1982—; bd. dirs. Women in Theatre, Los Angeles, 1983-84, workshop dir., 1984-86. Recipient Dramalogue award, 1981, Achievement award Women in Theatre, 1984. Mem. NOW, Acad. Arts and Scis. Home: Box 176 Altadena CA 91001

BURLEY, KATHLEEN MARY, b. Minot, ND, Jan. 17, 1942, d. Harry Jerome and Cathern (Doyle) Brickner; m. Henry Richard Burley, Dec. 27, 1966. Author: Who You Are, Where You Are?, 1987, Looking Back, Book One (poetry), 1987; contrbr. poetry to numerous publs. BS in Music and Edn., Minot State U. 1963; MA in Edn., Ariz. State U., 1966; Cert. Instr., Children's Lit., 1981; MBA, U. Phoenix, 1984. Tchr. schl. systems Ariz., Germany, Idaho and Saudi Arabia, 1963-81; bus mgr. BCD Enterprises, Linden, MI, 1981-82; payroll admin. Fairchild Control Syst., Manhattan Beach, CA, 1983-84; cons., trng. rep., customer trng. splst., Ewing/Northrop Corp., Hawthorne, Calif., 1984—. Included Best New Poets of 1986, Amer. Poetry Assn.Mem. Am. Soc. Trng. and Devel., Natl. Assn. Female Execs. Home: 1419 W 179th St Gardena CA 90248

BURNES, CAROL GANSON, b. Boston, Mar. 31, 1942; m. James N. Burnes, Aug. 30, 1969; children—Hannah, Jamie. Author: Roots and Wings, 1986; contrbr. to Sail, 13th Moon, Connections, Little Mag., Christian Sci. Monitor. Tchr. writing Boston U., schls. in New Eng. and Europe; tech. writer various small cos., New Eng. and Eng. Recipient various prizes for poetry. Mem. PSA, New Eng. Poetry Club. Home: Box 364 Weston MA 02193

BURNESS, DON, b. Hartford, CT, May 9, 1941; s. Manuel and Frances B.; m. Mary-Lou Fisher, Oct. 23, 1965. Author: Shaka King of the Zulus in African Literature, 1976, Fire: Six Writers from Angola, Mozambique and Cape Verde, 1977, Wanasema: Conversations with African Writers, 1985, (poems) Safari, 1984, (poems) The Other Side of Sorrow, 1986; translations of poems in books. Contrbr. poems to lit. jnls. Editor: Critical Perspectives on Lusophone African Literatures, 1981; assoc. editor: A New Readers Guide to African Literature, 1983. BA, U. Mich., 1963; MA, U. Ia., 1968. Prof. English, Franklin Pierce Coll., Rindge, N.H., 1968—; vis. prof. U. Port Harcourt, Nigeria, 1982-83. Mem. African Lit. Assn., Assn. L'Etude de Litteratures Africaines. Home: Box 344 Rindge NH 03461

BURNESS, WALLACE B(INNY), (Tad), B. Berkeley, CA, July 11, 1933; s. Thomas B. and Wallea Tormey (Draper) B.; m. Sandra Kay Chapman, JUly 9, 1967; children: Tammy Lynn. Author: under name Tad Burness: Cars of the Early Twenties, 1968, Auto Album, vol. 1, 1969, vol. 2, 1976, Cars of the Early Thirties, 1970, Indianapolis 500 Winners, 1974, The Auto Album, 1983. The Spotters Guide Series: American Car Spotters Guide, 1940-65, 1973, rev ed, 1978, American Car Spotter's Guide, 1920-1939, 1975, American Truck Spotter's Guide, 1920-1970, 1978, Imported Car Spotter's Guide, 1979, American Car Spotter's Guide, 1966-1980, 1981, Chevy Spotter's Guide, 1920-80, 1981, Ford Spotter's Guide, 1920-1980, 1981, Pickup and Van Spotter's Guide, 1945-1982, 1982, American Truck and Bus Spotter's guide, 1920-1985, 1985. Contrbr of articles on automobiles and mobile homes to magazines. Attended San Jose State coll (now U.), 1951-58. In real estate and property management, San Jose, Calif., 1956-63; civil service in Calif., 1960-65; United Feature Syndicate, New York City, syndicated weekly column, Auto Album, 1966—. Radio announcer in San Jose, 1955-61; automotive history consultant. Member: Intl Edsel Club, Antique Automobile Club of America, Soc. of Automotive Historians, Edsel Owners Club, Contemporary Historical Vehicle Club, Metropolitan Owners Club, WPC Club (Walter P. Chrysler-Chrysler Products Restorers Club). Address: UF Syndicate, 200 Park Ave New York NY 10017

BURNHAM, CRISPIN REED, b. Lawrence, KS, Oct. 4, 1949; s. Albert Dwight and Lillian Gray (Reed) B. Contrbr. and ed. Spoor Anthology 2 (with Edward P. Berglanod), 1974, Dark Messenger Reader, Eldritch Tales, Crypt of Cthulhu, Cinefan. Ed. and pub. Eldritch Tales, Lawrence, 1975—. Mem. Small Press Writers & Artists Orgn. (v.p. 1983), Assoc. mem. Horror Writers of Am. Address: 1051 Wellington Rd Lawrence KS 66044

BURNHAM, GREGORY ALAN, b. Elgin, IL, Aug. 31, 1954; s. Joseph Andrew and Ruth Merrifield (Drover) B. Contrbr. short stories to San Jose Studies, Ind. Rvw, Telescope, Central Park, Pulpsmith, other lit mags. Student Morningside Coll., Sioux City, Iowa, 1972-73; BA in English composition, Beloit Coll., 1976. Free-lance wrtr., 1980—. Recipient 2d place award for fiction Ind. Rvw, 1983. Home: Box 129 Burton WA 98013

BURNHAM, SOPHY, b. Balt., d. George Cochran and Sophy Tayloe Snyder Doub; m. David B. Burnham (div. 1984); children—Sarah Tayloe, Molly Bright. Author: The Art Crowd, 1973, Threat to Licensed Nuclear Facilities, 1975, Buccaneer, 1977, The Landed Gentry, 1978, The Dogwalker, 1979; (plays and films) The Smithsonian's Whale, 1963, The Leaf Thieves, 1964, Penelope, 1976, The Study, 1979, 84, The Witch's Tale, 1978, Beauty and the Beast, 1979, The Emperor and the Nightingale, 1980; contrbr. articles to New York, N.Y. Times mag., Esquire, others; represented in anthologies Crime in the Cities, 1970, Cities in Trouble, 1970. BA cum laude, Smith Coll., 1958; cert. U. Florence, 1957. Self-employed wrtr./ed., 1964—. Recipient best mag. feature award, Natl. Steeplechase and Hunt Assn., 1969, Daughter of Mark Twain, 1974, 3d prize Episcopal Drama award Natl. Episcopal Chs., 1979; best children's radio play award Natl. Assn. Community Broadcasters, 1980; award of excellence Communications Arts mag., 1980; 1st prize Women's Theatre, 1981. Mem. AG, DG, Washington Ind. Wrtrs. Home: 1405 31st St NW Washington DC 20007

BURNS, ALAN, b. London, Dec. 29, 1929; arr. US, 1977; s. Harold and Ann (Marks) B.; m. May 5, 1956 (div. 1980), children—Danny, Shamin; m. 2d, children—Katherine. Author novels and non-fiction: Buster, 1961, Europe After the Rain, 1965 (US, 1970), Celebrations, 1967, Babel, 1969, Dreamerika!, 1972, To Deprave and Corrupt, 1972, The Angry Brigade, 1974, The Day Daddy Died, 1982, The Imagination on Trial, 1982, Revolutions of the Night,

1986. Barrister at law, called to the bar, Inns of Court, London, 1956. Writing fellow Univ. East Anglia, Norwich, UK, 1971, City Lit. Inst., London, 1976; sr. tutor West Australian Inst. Tech., Perth, 1975; prof. Univ. Minn., 1977—. Recipient writing fellowships Henfield fund, 1971, C. Day, Lewis, London Arts, 1973, Arts Council Great Britain, 1976-77, Bush Fdn., MN, 1984-85. Address: Univ Minn Lind Hall Mpls MN 55455

BURNS, GERALD PATRICK, b. Detroit, Mar. 16, 1940, s. Stan and Sheila (Middler) B. Author: Boccherini's Minuet, 1969, 2d ed., 1981, Letters to Obscure Men, 1975, A Book of Spells, (first third), 1979, Toward a Phenomenology of Written Art, 1979, A Book of Spells II, 1985, Twenty-Four Gnomic Poems, 1986; contrbr. to: L-A-N-G-U-A-G-E 13, Sulfur, Boxcar, Menu, other publs. BA, Harvard U.; MA, So. Meth. U. Instr. So. Meth. U., Dallas, 1965-69, NYU, 1969-70; assoc. prof. Nassau Community Coll., Garden City, N.Y., 1970-75; vis. lectr. Simon Fraser U., Burnaby, B.C, Can., 1984; poet-in-res. Millersville U. of Pa., 1985. Grantee NEA, 1985. Home: Box 411 Thompson CT 06277

BURNS, PATRICIA HENRIETTA, b. L.I. City, NY, Dec. 9, 1934; d. Henri Jacob and Rolanda Katherine (Berger) Verwayen; m. John Christopher Verwayen-Burns, Oct. 3, 1953 (dec. Jan. 3, 1977); children—Stephanie, David, J. Henri. Author: The Book of Revelation Explained, 1982. Securities license, Phoenix, 1974; computer programming cert., Lamson Business Coll., Tempe, 1980. Advt. mgr. W.T. Grant Co., Phoenix, 1970-74; securities salesperson Waddell & Reed, Inc., Phoenix, 1974-76; criminal/probate clrk. Superior Ct., Phoenix, 1976-80; pres. The Nondenominational Bible Prophecy Study Assn., Tempe, 1982—. Office: BRE Pubs 339 E Laguna Dr Tempe AZ 85252

BURNS, PHYLLIS ANN, b. Martinsville, IL, Feb. 2, 1935; d. Burl LeRoy and Gwendolyn Euretta (Seaton) Dill; m. Olin Baker; m. 2d, Bob Henry Burns, Feb. 29, 1961; children—Carrie Lynne Ford, Steve, Scott. Publs. include. The Brighton Primrose and Cattlemen's Gazette, 1977-81, Inside Joke, Byline, Secrets, True Experience, Empire State Realtor, True Romance and others. A.A. in Edn., Trinidad Jr. Coll., 1956. Energy Conservation educator, Colo. State Univ., Brighton, 1977-78; techology vol. ACCEPT, Brighton, 1981-82, project coord., 1982; ed. and pub. Handicap News, Brighton, 1984—. Mem. Adams County Hist. Soc. Home: 3060 E Bridge 342 Brighton CO 80601

BURNS, RICHARD KEITH, b. Black Mountain, KY, Jan. 9, 1935, s. Judge Mitchell and Louise Mary (Cooke) B.; m. Frances Mary Forgione, 1959 (div. 1982) children—Judge Keith, Nina Louise. Ed.: Court House Histories of Virginia, 1967, Virginia Librarian, 1965, Come-All-Ye⇈tr., ed. Libraries at Large, 1968; contrbr., reviewer Library Jnl, 1960-68. BS, Morehead U., 1959; MS, U. Ill., 1960. Dir. Falls Church (Va.) Public Library, 1960-71; ed. Legacy Books, Hatboro, Pa., 1971—; wrtr., researcher White House Commn. on Libraries, Washington, 1968. Mem. ALA, Sonneck Soc. Home: 12 Meetinghouse Rd Hatboro PA 19040

BURNS, ROBERT EDWARD, b. Chgo., May 14, 1919; s. William Joseph and Sara (Foy) B.; m. Brenda Coleman, May 15, 1948; children: Maddy F., Martin J. Author: The Examined Life, 1980, Catholics on The Cutting Edge, 1983. Student, DePaul U., 1937-39; PhB, Loyola U., Chgo., 1941. Exec. editor U.S. Cath. mag.; gen. mgr. Claretian Publs., Chgo., 1949-84. Home: Rt 2 Box 277J Montello WI 53949

BURNS, STUART L, b. Ellsworth, IA, Oct 17, 1932; s. Robert Russell and Pearl Violet (Case) B; m. Suzanne Kay Holdefer, June 12, 1960; children: Sheila Kaye, Becky Jo, Theron Joseph. Author: Whores Before Descartes, 1980, Stressing and Unstressing in a Tent, 1987. MA, Drake U., 1960; PhD, U. Wis., 1964. Prof. English Drake Univ., Des Moines, Ia, 1963—; editor and pub. Wash Launderan Press, Des Moines, 1980—. Mem AWP. Address: 5804 Ingersoll Ave Des Moines IA 50312

BURNS, VIRGINIA LAW, b. Redford, MI, May 23, 1925; d. Alvin John and Leola Wadley Law; div.; children: James S. Ritchie, Duncan L. Ritchie, Margaret M. Ritchie. Author: The Way It Was In Bath; William Beaumont—Frontier Doctor; Lewis Cass—Frontier Soldier; First Frontiers; Tall Annie; contrbr. mags and newspapers; ed. mags and newsletter; reporter Lansing State Jnl. BA in edn., MSU, 1956. Tchr. Mich. elem. schls., 1952—; pub. Enterprise Press, Bath, Mich., 1978—. Mem. Mich. Hist. Soc. Address: 5631 Cade St Haslett MI 48840

BURR, GRAY, b. Omaha, Mar. 20, 1919, s. Alfred Earnest and Geraldine (Gray) B.; m. Carol Taber, Sept. 8, 1943; children—Elizabeth, Rebecca, Katherine; m. 2d, Ellen Jean Krohn, Aug. 10, 1961; 1 child, Martha. Author: A Choice of Attitudes, 1969, (chapbook) Sea Marks, 1978, The Moon by Day, 1984; contrbr. to Mass. Rvw, New Yorker, NY Times, New World Writing, Poetry, Harvard mag, others; appeared in numerous anthologies, including Sports Poems, 1972, Western Wind, 1974, New Coasts and Strange Harbors, 1974, Lit. Reflections, 1976, Poems That Storm Inside My Head, 1977, Dryad Anthology, 1978. AB, Harvard U., 1943, MA, 1949. Instr. Tufts U., Medford, Mass., 1950-54; asst. prof. Wheaton Coll., Norton, Mass., 1954-61; assoc. prof. SUNY-New Paltz, 1961-82. Served to lt. USN, 1943-45, PTO. Recipient Ingram-Merrill award Ingram Merrill Fdn., 1976. Home: Box 575 Truro MA 02666

BURRELL, NANCY BRADBURY, b. Evanston, IL, June 12, 1948; d. David Hamlin and Nancy Bradbury (Blunt) B. Contrbr. to Library Jnl., Directory of Health Services & Practitioners in Sarasota County. Wrkg. on health-related articles, poems. B.S. magna cum laude, Boston U., 1970; M.S. in Library Sci., Case Western Reserve U., 1974. Dir. library services U. Sarasota, FL, 1979-81; librarian Sarasota County, Venice, FL, 1981-82, U. Southern Fla., Sarasota, 1986—; cons. IBID, Inc., Sarasota, 1982-86. Mem. Southern Health Assn., ALA. Home: 5139 Windward Ave Sarasota FL 34242

BURRIS, THELMA RUTH, b. Nampa, ID, Sept. 29, 1921; d. Samuel Biren and Margaret Eva (Potter) McCroskey; m. Hugh Edward Burris, Nov. 18, 1939; children: Norvan Lance, Kevan Ray. Author: autobiography. Wrkg on short stories for children, Secundus. Edn. Boise H.S., Idaho. Home: 3417 Barcelona SW Albuquerque NM 87105

BURROUGHS, WILLIAM SEWARD, b. St. Louis, Feb. 5, 1914; s. Perry Mortimer and Laura (Lee) B.; m. Joan Vollmer, 1945; 1 son, William Seward. Author: Junkie: Confessions of an Unredeemed Drug Addict, 1953, re-issued, 1977, Naked Lunch, 1959, The Exterminator, 1960, Minutes to Go, 1961, The Soft Machine, 1961, The Ticket That Exploded, 1962, Dead Fingers Talk, 1963, (with Allen Ginsberg) The Yage Letters, 19663, Nova Express, 1964, (with Daniel Odier) The Job, 1969, Wild Boya, 1971, Exterminator!, 1973, White Subway, 1974, The Last Words of Dutch Schultz, 1975, (with Brion Gysin) The Third Mind, 1978, Ah Pook Is Here, 1979, City of the Red Night, 1981, The Burroughs File, 1984, Queer, 1985. AB, Harvard U., 1936; postgrad. in ethnology and archeology; med. student, U. Vienna. Formerly newspaper reporter, now full-time writer. Served with AUS, World War II. Address: Grove Press 107 W Houston St New York NY 10014

BURROWAY, JANET GAY, b. Tucson, Sept. 21, 1936, d. Paul McKenzie and Alma May (Milner) Borroway; m. Walter Eysselinch, Mar. 18, 1961 (div. 1973); children—Timothy Alan, Tobyn Alexander. Author: Descend Again (novel), 1960, But to the Season (poems), 1961, The Dancer from the Dance (novel), 1965, Eyes (novel), 1966, The Buzzards (novel, nominated for Pulitzer Prize 1970), 1969, The Truck on the Track (children's book), 1970, The Giant Jam Sandwich (children's book), 1973, Raw Silk (novel), 1977, Material Goods (poems), 1980, Writing Fiction: A Guide to Narrative Craft, 1982, 2d ed., 1987, Opening Nights (novel), 1985. BA, Barnard Coll., 1958; BA, Cambridge (Eng.) U., 1960, MA, 1965. Assoc. prof. Fla. State U., Tallahassee, 1972-77, prof., 1977—; FSU Fdn. Prof. of English, 1986—. NEA creative writing fellow, 1976; grantee Fine Arts Council Fla., 1983-84; winner Fla. Poetry Contest, 1983. Mem. MLA, AWP. Home: 240 DeSoto St Tallahassee FL 32303

BURSTEIN, JOHN, (Slim Goodbody), b. Minela, NY, Dec. 25, 1949; s. Herbert and Beatrice (Sobel) B.; m. June Beznover, June 26, 1976. Author: Mr. Slim Goodbody Presents the Inside Story, 1977, Slim Goodbody: Your Body, Health and Feelings, 1978, Slim Goodbody's Healthy Days Diary: Activity Book, 1983. Under pseudonym Slim Goodbody, The Get-Well Hotel, 1980, Lucky You!, 1980, The Force Inside You, 1983, The Healthy Habits Handbook, 1983. Folm strips: Slim Goodbody and Your Body, 1978, Slim Goodbody's World of Animals and Plants, 1981, Slim Goodbody's World of Weather and Climate, 1983. Sound recording: The Inside Story. BA, Hofra U., 1972. One-man health education musical performer in U.S. elem. schls, under stage name Mr. Slim Goodbody, 1974—. Starred in The Adventures of Slim Goodbody in Nutri-City, biweekly feature on Captain Kangaroo program, CBS-TV. New Jersey Authors Award, N.J. Inst. of Technology, 1978, for Mr. Slim Goodbody Presents the Inside Story. Address: Box 773 New York NY 10013

BURT, NATHANIEL, b. Moose, WY, Nov. 21, 1913; s. Struthers and Katharine (Newlin) B.; m. Margaret Clinton, Aug. 5, 1941; children—Margery Burt Smith, Christopher Clinton Burt, Andara Smith, Elijah Smith. Novels: Scotland's Burning, 1954, Make My Bed, 1957, Leopards in the Garden, 1968; poetry collections, Rooms in a House, 1947, Question on a Kite, 1950; nonfiction: The Perennial Philadelphians 1963, War Cry of the West, 1964, First Families, 1970, Palaces for the People, 1977, Jackson Hole Journal, 1983. BS in Music Ed. New York U, 1939; MFA in Music, Princeton U., 1949. Asst. Instructor, Princeton U. (NJ), 1939-41. Mem. PEN, AG, PSA, Soc. of Amer. Historians, Century Assn. Home: 13 Campbelton Crcl Princeton NJ 08540

BURTON, DONNA M., see Mainster, Donna Marie

BURTON, MARY ALICE, (Morales), b. Greenwood, SC, Feb. 9, 1954, d. Annie M. Burton Pinckney. Contrbr. poetry to anthologies including World of Poetry (seven awards); songwriter, comedy writer, singer. Student SUNY-Binghamton, 1974-77. Student counsellor SUNY-Binghamton, 1977; asst. lifeskills specialist Catholic Guardian Soc., NYC, 1978-79; communications technician NYC Police Dept., 1983—. Home: 2940 Kingsland Ave Bronx NY 10469

BUSCAGLIA, (FELICE) LEO(NARDO), b. Los Angeles, Mar. 31, 1924; s. Tulio and Rosa (Cagna) B. Author: Because I Am Human, 1972, Love, 1972, The Way of the Bull, 1973, The Disabled and Their Parents: A Counseling Challenge, 1975, rev. edit., 1983; Personhood: The Art of Being Fully Human, 1978, Human Advocacy: P.L. 94-142 & Mainstreaming, 1979, Living, Loving & Learning, 1982, The Fall of Freddie the Leaf, 1982; Loving Each Other: The Challenge of Human Relationships, 1984, Seven Stories of Christmas Love, 1987. A.B., U. So. Calif., 1950, M.A., 1954, Ph.D., in Lang. and Speech Pathology, 1963. Served with USN, 1941-44. Office: Box 686 South Pasadena CA 91030

BUSCH, FREDERICK, b. Bklyn., Aug. 1, 1941; s. Benjamin and Phyllis Toby (Schnell) B.; m. Judith Burroughs, Nov. 29, 1963; 2 sons, Benjamin, Nicholas. Author (novels): I Wanted a Year Without a Fall, 1971, Manual Labor, 1974, The Mutual Friend, 1978, Rounds, 1979, Take This Man, 1981, Invisible Mending, 1984, Sometimes I Live in the Country, 1986; stories: Breathing Trouble, 1973, Domestic Particulars, 1976, Hardwater Country, 1979, Too Late American Boyhood Blues, 1984; criticism: Hawkes, 1973; essays: When People Publish, 1986. AB, Muhlenberg Coll., 1958-62; MA, Columbia U., 1967. Prof. English Colgate Univ., Hamilton, NY, 1966—. Fellow NEA, 1976, Guggenheim Fdn., 1980, Ingram Merrill, 1981; recipient Jewish Book Award in fiction, 1984. Address: Box 31A RD 1 New Trnpk Rd Sherburne NY 13460

BUSH, ANITA MARIE, b. Chgo., Nov. 18, 1951; d. Edward Steven and Anita Marie (Zasadil) Kozanecki; m. Lawrence Edward Mullen, Jr., May 12, 1970 (div. 1971); 1 son, Edward Vaughn; m. 2d, Christopher Thomas Bush, Mar. 3, 1984. Ed.: A Critical Care Handbook (by B. Czopek), 1984; contrbr. articles: Heart & Lung, The Jnl. of Critical Care, Dimensions of Critical Care Nursing, Technology and the Scientist, numerous other profl. publs.; author monographs. Wrkg. on short stories, articles. AS in Nursing, SUNY-Albany, 1980. Staff nurse, Fairbanks Meml. Hosp., Alaska, 1981—. Served as sgt. U.S. Army, 1974-77. Mem. Am. Assn. Critical care Nurses (newsletter ed. 1982—). Address: Box 10461 Fairbanks AK 99710

BUSH, JOHN CHARLES, b. Century, FL, Mar. 8, 1938; s. William Ernest and Anna Lee (Vaughn) B.; m. Sara Lucile Fulton, Dec. 18, 1959; children—Michael David, Janet Lucile. Author: Disaster Response: A Handbook, 1979, the Right to Silence, 1983. Contrbr. articles to religious mags., newsletters. Exec. pub., (newspaper) Intercom. BA, Samford U., Birmingham, Ala., 1960; MDiv, Midwestern Bapt. Sem., Kansas City, Mo., 1963; DMinistry, San Francisco Sem., 1976. Ordained to ministry 1956. Pastor, United Presbyn. Ch., Americus, Kans., 1963-67, Grand River Parish, Butler, Mo., 1968-70; exec. dir. Interchurch Council, Clinton, Mo., 1970-73, Ky. Council of Chs., Lexington, 1973—. Home: 1021 Claiborne Way Lexington KY 40502

BUSHNO, LILA JOAN, b. Pomona, MO, Aug. 9, 1931; d. Orval Ulysses and Lois Elaine (Bottom) Goyer; m. John Busho (div.); children—John, Deanne, Rose Marie, Mark, Elizabeth Kay; m. Edward R. Williams (dec.); children—Edward R., Sherra A. Contrbr. poems to anthols, newspapers, articles, photos to newspapers, mags. Wrkg. on photo stories, hist. articles, poems. A.A., Black Hawk Coll., 1980. Certified Nurse Asst., Henry County, IL, 1977-87. Recipient numerous poetry awards including Golden Poet award World of Poetry, 85, 86, 87; Best New Poets of 1986 award Am. Poetry Assn., 1986. Mem. Midwest Songwrtr.'s Assn., New England Genealogical Soc. Home: 714 E 5th St Kewanee IL 61443

BUSSEY, CHARLES DAVID, b. Edgefield, SC, Dec. 8, 1933; s. Alex William, Sr. and Mattie Lou (Phillips) B.; m. Andra Lee Holmes, Nov. 7, 1956 (div. Apr. 24, 1965); m. Eva Lois Gray, July 1, 1967; children—Terri Lyn, Tonia Marie, Charles Frederick. Contrbr. articles to military mags. and daily newspapers. B.S. in English, N.C. A & T State U., 1955; M.A. in Jnlsm., Ind. U., 1970, M.S. in comm. Sci., Shippensburg State, 1974. Commissioned 2d lt. U.S. Army, 1955, advanced through ranks to major general, 1984—. Mem. PRSA. Home: 6302 Martins Ln Lanham MD 20706

BUSWINK, ANTHONY ALLEN, b. Dearborn, MI, Jan. 17, 1940; s. Alexander Mathew and Delma Lorraine (Sutton) B. Contrbr. articles to profl. jnls., chpts. to books including Steroid Hormone Action and Cancer, 1976, Principles of Medicinal Chemistry, 1981. A.A., Pasadena City Coll., 1962; B.A., Calif. State Coll., 1965. Research assoc. U. Mich., Ann Arbor, 1970-82; computer analyst Oceanic Inst., Waimanalo, HI, 1982-83; technical wrtr. Avco Everett Research Lab., Puunene, HI, 1983-85; free-lance technical wrtr., 1985—. Mem. Am. Physical Soc. Home: 750 Amana St 1402 Honolulu HI 96814

BUTCHER, GRACE, b. Rochester, NY, Jan. 18, 1934; d. Lyman Lorenzo and Mary Hyndman (Spencer) Lamb; m. Robert C. Butcher, Dec. 15, 1951 (div. 1967); children—Robert Claar, Daniel Charles. Author: (poems) The Bright Colored Dark, 1966, More Stars than Room For, 1966, Rumors of Ecstasy . . . Rumors of Death, 1971, 2d edit., 1981, Before I Go Out on the Road, 1979. Columnist Rider mag., 1979-85. BA, Hiram Coll., 1966; MA, Kent State U., 1967. Instr. English, Cleve. State U., 1967-68; assoc. prof. English, Kent State U. Geauga Campus, Burton, Ohio, 1968—. Recipient Vachel Lindsay prize Hiram Coll., 1963, 64, 66; grantee NEA, 1969, Ohio Arts Council, 1979. Mem. AAP. Home: Box 274 Chardon OH 44024

BUTHMANN, EDNAH JONES, (Ednah Jones), b. Weymouth, MA; children—Richard, Lawrence, Robert, Thomas. Contrbr. articles to mags., newspapers. Wrkg. on articles on antiques and inspirational topics. Interpreter, Museum of Am. Textile History, North Andover, MA, 1986-87, Trustees of Reservations, Ipswich, MA, 1986-87, Longyear Hist. Soc., Brookline, MA, 1987; owner Antique & Appraising Bus., North Andover, 1985—. Home: 156 Chestnut St North Andover MA 01845

BUTLER, JOSEPH PATRICK, b. Washington, DC,July 24, 1957, s. Edward Joseph and Dorothy May (Raleigh) B.; m. Diane Marie Williamson, Nov. 15, 1980; children—Joseph Patrick, Jr., Kenneth James. Contrbr. poetry to Suwanee Poetry Rvw, Sartori Jnl, Poetalk, other lit mags and anthologies; articles to Wide Open mag., Nursing Life, Writer's Bloc mag., Boston newspapers; contr. columnist horror nwsltrs. Wrkg. on short stories, articles, poetry. Asst. ops. mgr., emergency med. technician Stavis Ambulance Service, Brookline, Mass., 1977—; dep. sheriff Norfolk County, Dedham, Mass., 1981—; mental health worker Arbour Hosp., Jamaica Plain, Mass., 1984—news corr. Daily Transcript, Dedham, Mass., 1987—. Author courses, lecturer acute psychiatric crisis intervention, Mass. Off. Emergency Med. Svcs., 1987. Mem. World Poetry Soc. Home: 108 Park St West Roxbury MA 02132

BUTLER, NATHAN, see Sohl, Jerry

BUTLER, ROBERT FRANCIS, b. Fall River, MA, Oct. 7, 1935; s. Nicholas Francis and Ellen Dolores (Griffin) B.; m. Beatris Rosa children—Ellen, Nicholas, Laura, Robert, Daniel. Contrbr. short stories, editorials, essays to mags., newspapers. A.A., Manchester Commun. Coll., 1973; B.A., U. Conn., 1975. Manufacturing supvr. Jacob's Manufacturing Co., Bloomfield, CT, 1984—. Served to sgt. U.S. Army, 1953-67. Recipient citation for short story New Breed Mag., 1987. Mem. NWC. Home: 295 High Path Rd Windsor CT 06095

BUTLER, ROBERT OLEN, b. Granite City, IL, Jan. 20, 1945, s. Robert Olen and Lucille Frances (Hall) B.; m. Carol Supplee, 1968 (div. 1972); m. 2d, Marylin Geller, 1972; 1 son, Joshua Robert; m. 3d, Maureen Donlan, Aug. 7, 1987. Novelist: The Alleys of Eden, 1981, Sun Dogs, 1982, Countrymen of Bones, 1983, On Distant Ground, 1985, Wabash, 1987. BS, Northwestern U., 1967; MA, U. Iowa, 1969. Ed., reporter Electronic News, NYC, 1972-73, reporter, Chgo., 1974-75; ed.-in-chief Energy User News, NYC, 1975-85; asst. prof. McNeese State U., Lake Charles, La., 1985—. Mem. PEN. Office: Box 935 McNeese State U Lake Charles LA 70609

BUTTACI, SAL ST. JOHN, b. Corona, NY, June 12, 1941, s. Michael S. and Josephine (Amico) B.; m. Susan Linda Gerstle, Mar. 9, 1974. Author: Stops & Pauses on the Scrapbook Express (poetry), 1974, In Praise of Grandpa: Memory Poems, 1976, Bread and Tears & 35 Other Poems, 1986; ed. New Worlds Unlimited, 1974—, pub. annl. anthologies. BA in Communication Arts, Seton Hall U., 1965; MBA, Rutgers U., 1981. Tchr., adminstr. pub. schls. in N.J., 1966-80; dir. mail mktg. exec. Hugo Dunhill, Inc., NYC, 1980—; certified graphologist. Winner 1st Prize for Sci. Fiction Poem, Karmic Runes mag., 1977. Mem. ASCAP, COSMEP, N.J. Poetry Soc., N.Y. Poetry Forum, Songwrtrs. Guild, Am. Handwriting Analysis Fdn. Office: Box 556 Saddle Brook NJ 07662

BUTTERFIELD, YITZHAWK, see Sachs, Edward K.

BUTTERICK, GEORGE F., b. Yonkers, NY, Oct. 7, 1942, s. George W. and Kathleen T. (Byrnes) B.; m. Colette Marie Hetzel, June 19, 1965; children—George Adam, Aaron. Author: The Norse, 1973, Reading Genesis by the Light of a Comet, 1976, A Guide to the Maximus Poems of Charles Olson, 1978, Editing the Maximus

Poems, 1983, Rune Power, 1983, The Three-Percent Stranger, 1986, Repartee with the Mummy, 1987; ed.: (with D. Allen) The Post-moderns, 1982, The Maximus Poems (Charles Olson), 1983, The Collected Poems (Charles Olson), 1987. Contrbr. poetry, essays, rvws. to Credences, Sagetrieb, Sulfur, Am. Poetry, numerous other publs. BA, Manhattan Coll., 1964, PhD, SUNY-Buffalo, 1970. Asst. prof. English U. Conn., Storrs, 1970-72, curator lit. archives, lectr. English, 1972—. Bicentennial Fund grantee Swedish Info. Service 1985. Mem. NWU. Home: 194 North St Willimantic CT 06226

BUXTON, BARRY MILLER, b. Blowing Rock, NC, Aug. 5, 1949; s. Carrie (Miller) B.; m. Deborah Keyes, June 15, 1985; 1 son, Loren. Ed.: The Many Faces of Teaching, 1986,The Blue Ridge Pkwy, 1986, The Appalachian Experience, 1984, Critical Essays in Appalachian Life and Culture, 1983, National Directory of Sociol. of Edn., 1975-77; contrbr. articles var. publs. BA magna cum laude, Appalachian State U., 1973, MA, 1973; PhD,U. Nebr., 1976. Dean instrn. Southeast Community Coll., Lincoln, Nebr., 1977-80; adj. faculty U. Nebr., Lincoln, 1978-80; exec dir. and dir. press Appalachian Consortium, Boone, NC, 1980—; adj. faculty, Appalachian State Univ., Boone, 1982—. Mem. Nebr. Comm. Humanities, Lincoln, 1977-79. Home: Rt 1 Box 55 Blowing Rock NC 25605

BUZAN, NORMA JEANNE STEPHENS, b. Independence, MO, Oct. 30, 1924; d. Vernon Regalia Stephens and Evelyn Emma (Courier) Curran; m. Leroy Roderick Buzan, Mar. 25, 1945; children: Christopher Reid, Randall Douglas. Author: Bed and Breakfast North America, 1982, 4th ed., 1987; Bed and Breakfast in Michigan and Surrounding Areas, 1985. BS in Edn., Wayne State U., 1960, MLS, 1976. Librarian, Farmington Hills Pub. Library, Mich., 1976-78, Troy Pub. Library, Mich., 1978-81; owner Betsy Ross Publs., Bloomfield Hills, Mich., 1981—. Trustee, Bloomfield Township Pub. Library, 1970—. Recipient Trustee Citation of Merit, Mich. Library Assn., 1972. Mem. Am. Library Trustee Assn. (2d v.p. 1986-87), AAUW, LWV. Clubs: Birmingham/Bloomfield Book and Author. Home: 3057 Betsy Ross Dr Bloomfield Hills MI 48013

BUZBEE, RICHARD EDGAR, b. Fordyce, AR, Aug. 16, 1931; s. Edgar Andrew and Helen Koester (Darling) B.; m. Marie Palmer, Apr. 16, 1955; children: Robert Edgar, William Bruce, James Palmer, John Richard. Mgmt. intern Harris Newspaper Group, Chanute (Kans.) Tribune, Burlington (Iowa) Hawk-Eye, also Olathe (Kans.) News, 1957-63; editor, pub. Olathe News, 1963-79, Hutchinson (Kans.) News, 1979—. B.J., B.A., U. Mo., 1954. Served to lt. (j.g.) USNR, 1954-57. Mem. Am. Soc. Newspaper Editors, Internat. Press Inst., Inland Daily Press Assn. Home: 4 Crescent Blvd Hutchinson KS 67501

BUZZELLI, ELIZABETH KANE, b. Detroit, Mar. 5, 1936, d. John Anthony and Dorothy Luella (Deveines) Kane; m. Antonio Buzzelli, Jan. 8, 1955; children—Kathryn, Patricia, Antonio, David, Cynthia. Author: Gift of Evil, 1983; contrbr. articles to Det. News, Observer Newspapers, Pace Mag., Emily Dickinson Bull. BA, Oakland U., 1974. Self-employed wrtr. Recipient award of merit Mich. Hist. Soc., 1978. Mem. Detroit Women Wrtrs. (pres. 1983-85). Home: 60185 Lamplight Ct Washington MI 48094

BYER, KATHRYN STRIPLING, b. Camilla, GA, Nov. 25, 1944; d. Charles M. and Bernice Campbell Stripling; m. James E. Byer, Mar. 21, 1970; 1 dau., Corinna. Author: (poems) Search Party, 1979, Alma, 1983, The Girl in the Midst of the Harvest, 1986. BA, Wesleyan Coll., Macon, Ga., 1966; MFA, U. N.C.-Greensboro, 1968. Instr. English, Western Carolina U., Cullowhee, N.C., 1968—. Recipient prize AAP, 1968, Anne Sexton prize Miami U., 1978; series award AWP, 1985-86; fellow N.C. Arts Council, 1986. Home: Box 489 Cullowhee NC 28723

BYLINSKY, GENE MICHAEL, b. Belgrade, Yugoslavia, Dec. 30, 1930; s. Michael Ivan and Dora (Shadan) B.; m. Gwen Gallegos, Aug. 14, 1955; children: Tanya, Gregory. Author: The Innovation Millionaires, 1976, Mood Control, 1978, Life in Darwin's Universe, 1981, High Tech Window on the Future, 1985. BA in Journalism, La. State U., 1955. Staff reporter Wall St. Jnl, Dallas, 1957-59, San Francisco, 1959-61, NYC, 1961; sci. writer Natl. Observer, Washington, 1961-62, Newhouse Newspapers, 1962-66; member, bd. of editors, Fortune Mag., NYC, 1966—. Served with AUS, 1956. Recipient 21st Annl. Albert Lasker Med. Journalism award, 1970; Med. Journalism award, AMA, 1974; Claude Bernard Sci. Journalism award Natl. Soc. Med. Research, 1973, 74; others. Mem. Natl. Assn. Sci. Writers, N.Y. Acad. Scis. Office: Time and Life Bldg Rockefeller Cnt New York NY 10020

BYNUM, CHERYL DIANNE, (Amethyst), b. Fountain, NC, July 21, 1960; d. William Earl and Bertha (Mitchell) Bynum. Author: Intense Awakenings to Ordinary Magic; contrbr. to Aspects, Essence, New Woman. Student NC State U., 1980-81. Sub. teacher Edgecombe Co. Bd. of Ed. (Tarboro, NC), 1984-85; clerk/typist Edgecombe Co. Dept. Soc. Serv. (Tarboro, NC), 1984—. Hon. Ments. Ursus Press, 1984; Cert/ Love and Cert./Humor The Writer's Ink Guild, 1984. Mem. NC Poetry Soc., Piedmont Literary Soc. Home: Rt 1 Box 18B Macclesfield NC 27852

BYRD, JAY, see Hopper, Jeannette M.

BYRD, ODELL RICHARD, JR., (Jitu Tambuzi), b. Richmond, VA, s. Odell Richard and Lottie (Fountleroy) B.; m. Rosetta Walker, Jan. 8, 1984 (div. Jan. 1986). Author: (under pseudonym Tambuzi) (poetry) A Voice Within, 1979, (play) Tomorrow Be Gone, 1978; ed. (with Jeff Elzinga) Contemporary Prison Writings, U.S.A., 1980; contrbr. to Yearbook of Modern Poetry, Bitterroots Intl. Poetry Qtly., Black Books Bulltn. Wrkg. on two poetry manuscripts of socio-psycho attitudes and moods. BA, New Paltz Coll., 1978; postgrad. Va. Commonwealth U. Ed.-wrtr. Tambuzi Publs., Kingston, N.Y., 1974-82; tchr. Richmond Pub. Schls., 1982-86; antique dealer Pack Rat II Antiques, Richmond, 1985—. Recipient outstanding contrbn. to lit. award Break-Thru in Arts, 1978. Fellow Intl. Acad. Poets; mem. PW. Home: 2310 Gordon Ave Richmond VA 23224

BYRD, ROBERT J., (Bobby), b. Memphis, Apr. 15, 1942, s. William Hudson Byrd and Charlotte (Stanage) Grider; m. Lee Kingston Merrill, Apr. 17, 1969; children—Susannah Mississippi, John William, Andrew Merrill. Author: The Black Poems, 1969, Places Is/& Memphis Poems, 1971, Here, 1975, The Bright Sun, 1975, Pomegranates, 1984, Art in America, 1985, Get Some Fuses For the House, 1987; ed. From a Window poetry mag., 1965-67, Rio Grande Wrtrs. Newsletter, 1983-84; contrbr. to anthologies The Temple of Baseball, The Face of Poetry, Coyote's Jnl, The Rio Grande, Desert Rvw Anthology. BA in English Lit., U. Ariz., 1965; MA in English Lit., U. Wash., 1967. Tech. wrtr. Intercon Systems, El Paso, Tex., 1978-86; founder Cinco Puntos Press, 1985; dir. New El Paso Poetry Series, 1980-85. Mem. Rio Grande Wrtrs. Assn. (pres. 1982-83). Home: 2709 Louisville St El Paso TX 79930

BYRD, WILLIAM AARON, JR., b. Newark, May 4, 1958; s. William Aaron and Shirley (Moody) B. Columnist: Atlanta Daily World, 1982. Contrbr. poems to anthols. Wrkg. on book of poetry. B.A., Clark Coll., 1982. Entertainment ed. Atlanta Daily World, 1982-85; reservationist Days Inn of Am., Atlanta, 1985-87; police officer Ga. State U., Atlanta, 1985-87. Home: 2671 Laurens Circle Atlanta GA 30311

BYRNES, FREDERICK JOSEPH, b. Huntington, NY, s. Frederick Joseph Sr. and Helen Francis (Stubbolo) B. Author: Luck and Other Poems, 1985, No One to Sing Praises (poetry), 1986; contrbr. to Broadside Mag., Evolution Mag., Riverrun Mag., others. BA in English, Dowling Coll., 1986. Tutor Suffolk Coll., Selden, N.Y., 1983; tchr. creative writing Dowling Coll., Oakdale, N.Y., 1984-86; poetry ed. Riverrun Mag.; lectr. on poetry, various ednl. instns., TV appearances. Mem. P&W. Home: 17 Koster Ct Huntington NY 11746

BYRNES, ROBERT FRANCIS, b. Waterville, NY, Dec. 30, 1917; s. Michael Joseph an Pauline (Albeker) B.; m. Eleanor Frances Jewell, June 6, 1942; children: Shaun, Sheila Byrnes Bowles, Sally Byrnes Neylon, Susan Byrnes Wallace, Robin Byrnes Huntington, Charles, James. Author: Anti-semitism in Modern France: The Prologue to the Dreyfus Affair, 1950, 2d ed., 1969, Bibliography of American Publications on East Central Europe, 1945-57, 1959, The Non-Western Areas in Under-graduate Education in Indiana, 1959, (with others) The College and World Affairs, 1964, Pobedonostev: His Life and Thought, 1967, The United States and Eastern Europe, 1967; editor: (with others) East-Central Europe under the Communists, 7 vols., 1956-57, Germany and the East: The Collected Essays of Fritz Epstein, 1973, Communal Families in the Balkans: The Zadruga Essays by Philip E. Mosely, 1975, Soviet-American Academic Exchanges, 1958-1975, 1976, Awakening American Education to the World: The Role of Arhibald Cary Coolidge, 1982, After Brezhnev: Sources of Soviet Conduct in the 1980s, 1983; contbr. articles to profl. jnls. B.A., Amherst Coll., 1939, D.H.L., 1964; M.A., Harvard U., 1940, Ph.D., 1947; sr. fellow, Columbia U., 1948-50; LL.D., Coe Coll., 1964; D. Litt., St. Mary's Coll., 1967. Fellow Inst. Advanced Study, 1950, Netherlands Inst. for Advanced Study, 1976-77; fellow Inst. of History, Soviet Academy, 1963, 1978. Civilian service M.I., AUS, 1944-45. Guggenheim fellow, 1953; ACLS fellow, 1962-63, 78; sr. fellow Ctr. for Advanced Russian Studies, summer 1985. Fellow, History of Ideas Unit, Australian Natl. Univ., 1987-88. Home: 402 Reisner Dr Bloomington IN 47401

BYRON, STUART, b. NYC, May 9, 1941, s. Irving and Mary (Citronbaum) B. Contrbr. to books: Favorites Movies: Critics' Choice, 1973, Lavendar Culture, 1978, Orgasms of Light: The Gay Sunshine Anthology, 1977, Out of the Closets: Voices of Gay Liberation, 1972, Seeing through Shuck, 1972, Voices Against the Wilderness: The 1983 Black Cardinal Anthology of Gay Poets; co-ed.: Movie Comedy, 1977; contrbr.

articles to December, N.Y. Times, Film Qtly., others; contrbr. poetry to Gay Sunshine, Fag Rag, Mouth of the Dragon, others. BA, Wesleyan U., 1963; postgrad. Columbia U., 1963-64. Reporter, interviewer Variety mag., 1967-69; dir. devel. Natoma Prodns., NYC,1969-70; film critic, film ed. The Real Paper, Cambridge, Mass., 1973-74; contrib. ed. Film Comment, 1975-78; columnist Village Voice, NYC,1979-84; freelance wrtr. Home: 1625 Rendall Pl Los Angeles CA 90026

CABARCAS, ELINA, b. Ciénaga, Magdalena, Colombia, Jan. 16, 1932; d. Antonio and Vicenta (Hernandez) Cabarcas; came to U.S., Feb. 1983. Transl. into Spanish: William Wallace of China (J. Fletcher), Things I Would Like to Know (Emma Viola Hollinger), (with Crea Ridenour) Devotionals for Every Occasion (Virginia Whitman); ed. Nuestra Tarea; ed./transl.: El Libro de Action Misionera, Planes de Trabajo de la UFM 1985-86, 1986-87. MRE, Southwestern Th. Seminary, Fort Worth, 1966; Lic. Lenguas Modernas, Universidad del Valle, Cali, Colombia, 1976. Ed., El Colaborador, Colombia WMU, Cali, Colombia, 1952-55, 59-63; tchr. Engl. & res. supr. Baptist Theol. Sem., Cali, 1967-83; writer, La Estrella & La Ventana mags., Spanish Pub. House, El Paso, TX, 1963-83; ed. Nuestra Tarea, Birmingham, AL, 1983—. Office: Box C-10 Birmingham AL 35283

CABRAL, OLGA MARIE, b. Port of Spain, Trinidad, B.W.I., Sept. 14, 1909 (arrd. U.S. 1919); d. Anthony Ferreira and Marie Lourdes (Baptista) C.; m. Aaron Samuel Kurtz June 27, 1951 (widowed May 30, 1964). Author: Cities and Deserts, 1959, The Evaporated Man, 1968, Tape Found in a Bottle, 1971, Occupied Country, 1976, The Darkness in My Pockets, 1976, In the Empire of Ice, 1980 (poetry); The Seven Sneezes, 1948, The Four-in-One Book, 1948, Tony the Tow Car, 1949, So Proudly She Sailed, 1981 (juveniles); contrbr. numerous literary jnls, 30 poetry anthols in U.S. and Europe. Just completed: Such a Pretty Girl as I (juvenile historical novel). Emily Dickinson Award, PSA, 1971; Lucille Medwick Award, PSA, 1976. Mem. Authors Guild, PSA, NWU. Home: 463 West St Apt H-523 NYC 10014

CABRINETY, PATRICIA BUTLER, b. Earlville, NY, Sept. 4, 1932; d. Eugene Thomas and Helen Sylvester (Fulmer) Butler; m. Lawrence Paul Cabrinety, Aug. 20, 1955; children—Linda Anne, Margaret Marie, Stephen Michael. Contrbr. articles to local newspapers; poetry in anthologies. Wrkg. on poetry. BS in Elem. Edn. and Music, SUNY-Potsdam. Tchr. music, 1960-79; pres. Superior Software, Inc., Mpls., 1981—; freelane poet, illustrator, 1981—. Recipient poetry awards. Mem. Natl. Wrtrs. Assn., Worcester County Poetry Assn., Fla. Freelance Wrtrs. Assn., numerous profl. orgns. Home: 925 Pearl Hill Rd Fitchburg MA 01420

CACCAVALE, JUDITH LANSDOWNE, b. Jersey City, Feb. 12, 1941, d. Brinley Morgan Evans and Marion Elizabeth (Miller) Lansdowne; m. Philip Peter Caccavale, Apr. 11, 1965; 1 dau., Amy Bronwyn. Contrbr. feature articles to numerous genl. interest publs. Wrkg. on mystery novel, Italian cookbook. BA in English, Montclair State Coll., 1962, postgrad., 1964-66. Tchr. English North Bergen (N.J.) High Schl., 1962-68, Middlesex County Vo-Tech High Schl., Woodbridge, N.J., 1982-86; East Brunswick High, 1986—; contrbg. ed., food columnist N.J. Living mag., 1983—. Mem. profl. orgns. Home: 13 Pitt Rd East Brunswick NJ 08816

CACKENER, HELEN ELIZABETH LEWIS, b. Elmira, NY, July 4, 1926, d. Norman Pratt and Grace Genevieve (Oakes) Lewis; m. Daniel Glyndwr Lewis, June 17, 1950 (div. 1959); children—Deborah Anne, Elizabeth Laura, Margaret Grace; m. 2d, Robert Millard Cackener, Apr. 17, 1960. Folklore and local hist. columnist Glen Falls Today mag., Saratoga Style mag., 1986—; contrbr. articles to Delta Kappa Gamma Bull., English Jnl. BA magna cum laude, Oberlin (Ohio) Coll., 1948; MAT, Harvard U., 1950. Tchr. English Westbrook Coll., Portland, Me., 1949-50, Schenectady City high schls., 1950-51, 60, Hudson Falls (N.Y.) Sr. High Schl., 1960-85. Mem. N.Y. Folklore Soc. Home: 895 W River Rd Gansevoort NY 12831

CADY, JACK, b. Columbus, OH, Mar. 20, 1932; s. Donald Victor and Pauline Lucille (Schmidt) C. Author: The Burning and Other Stories, 1972, Tattoo and Other Stories, 1978, The Well, 1981, Singleton, 1982, The Jonah Watch, 1982, McDowell's Ghost, 1983, The Man Who Could Make Things Vanish, 1984. BSc, U Louisville, 1961. Asst. prof. U Washington, Seattle, 1968-73; freelance writer, 1973-78, 78-84; sr. lectr. Pacific Lutheran Univ, Tacoma, Wash, 1984—; newspaper columnist The Daily News, Port Angeles, Wash., 1976-84. Served to PO2c, USCG, 1952-56. Recipient the Atlantic Monthly First award, Atlantic Monthly, Boston, 1966, Natl. Literary Anthology award, Natl. Council on the Arts, 1971, Washington Gov's award, Wash. state, 1972, Univ. Iowa prize for short fiction, 1972. Mem. PEN, AG, Sigma Delta Chi. Address: 315 Logan St Port Townsend WA 98368

CAFFERATA, ROXANE, b. Corpus Christi, TX, Aug. 20, 1955; d. Harold and Frances Elizabeth (Masarick) C. BA, Harpur Coll., 1977. Editorial asst. Medical Exam Publishers, Garden City, NY, 1979-80; assoc., then sr., ed. Medical Times & Staff Physician, Port Washington, 1980—; mng., then exec., ed. Surgical Rounds, Port Washington, 1980—. Mem. AMWA, IABC. Office: R & P Pub 80 Shore Rd Port Washington NY 11050

CAGLE, JONI, see Ball, Ivern Imogene

CAHONES, CAROLYN, see Bowart, Walter Howard

CAINE, SHULAMITH W., b. Dayton, OH, Apr. 18, 1930, d. Pinchas and Sonia (Dlugach) Wechter; m. Burton Caine; children—Uri, Sara, Gidon. Contrbr. poetry to various jnls., revs. MA, U. Pa. Instr. Drexel U., Phila., 1978—. Co-chair poetry com. YM/YWHA, Phila., mem. film festival com.; lectr. USIA, India, 1983, Taiwan, 1984; mem. exec. com. Nat. Assn. Holocaust Edn.; mem. program com. Nat. Mus. Am. Jewish History; mem. planning com. poet-scholar program Reconstructionist Rabbinical Coll. Home: 122 Grasmere Rd Cynwyd PA 19004

CALHOUN, HARRY L., b. Connellsville, PA, Sept. 27, 1953; s. Harry G. and B. M. (Moore) C.; m. Julie Ann McCauley, Oct. 5, 1985. Author: (poems) Coming to Light, 1985. Contrbr. articles to mags. including Wrtr.'s Digest, Private Clubs, Natl. Enquirer, others; poems to over 100 lit mags; book rvws. to mags, including Gargoyle, Pitts. Press. Editor: Pig In a Poke jnl., 1982—; mng. editor: Alternative Housing Builder, 1985-86. BA in history, Pa. State U.-State College, 1980. Dir. creative services NBS Inc. Career Ctrs., Pitts., 1983-85; free-lance wrtr., 1980—. Home: 5562 Hobart St Apt 208 Pittsburgh PA 15217

CALIP, ROGER E., b. Manila, Sept. 19, 1941, s. Generoso and Paula (Echalar) C. Contrbr. articles: Hartford Courant, N.Y. Times. Licence Es Lettres LittB in Journalism, U. Santo Tomas, 1961; U. Paris, Sorbonne, 1968; MA in Sociology, U. Conn., Storrs, 1972, MA in French, 1977. Ed. pub. relations office Hotel Filipinas, Manila, 1961-63; ed. Philippine Trade & Travel Guide, 1961-63, Orient Tours Mag., 1961-63; contrbg. ed. Business Times, Rocky Hill, Conn., 1986—. French-English interpreter/translator, Interpreters and Translators, Inc., Manchester, Conn., 1986—; adj. prof. French, Univ. of Hartford, 1986—. Mem. NWC. Home: 35 Owen St 303 Hartford CT 06105

CALISHER, HORTENSE, (MRS. CURTIS HARNACK), b. NYC, Dec. 20, 1911; d. Joseph Henry and Hedvig (Lichtstern) C.; m. Curtis Harnack, Mar. 23, 1959; children by former marriage: Bennet Hughes, Peter Heffelfinger. Author: short stories In the Absence of Angels, 1951, False Entry; novel Tale for the Mirror, 1961; novella and short stories Textures of Life, 1962; novel Extreme Magic, 1963; novella and short stories Journal from Ellipsia, 1964; novel The Railway Police and The Last Trolley Ride, 1965; novellas The New Yorkers, 1966; novel Queenie, 1969, Standard Dreaming, 1971, Herself, 1972; novel Eagle Eye, 1972; The Collected Stories of Hortense Calisher, 1975; novel On Keeping Women, 1977, novel Mysteries of Motion, 1984, Saratoga Hot (little novels), 1984, The Bobby-Soxer (novel), 1985, Age (novel), 1987; contbr.: short stories, articles, rvws. to Am. Scholar; anthologies, others. AB, Barnard Coll., 1932; LittD (hon.), Skidmore Coll., 1980. Guggenheim fellow, 1952, 55; Dept. of State Am. Specialist's grantee to S.E. Asia. 1958; recipient Acad. of Arts and Letters award, 1967, Natl. Council Arts award, 1967, pres. Am. Acad. & Inst. of Arts and Letters, 1987; pres. PEN Am. Ctr. Office: Donadio 111 W 57th St New York NY 10019

CALL, JACK STANLEY, b. Hico, TX, Apr. 11, 1949, s. Cleo Cox and Clare Helen (Huffstutter) C.; m. Mary Jo Minkler, Dec. 10, 1972; children—Stanley, Aaron. Author: The Latest Roundup, 1984. BA, Calif. State U., Los Angeles, 1971. Home: 12431 Camilla St Whittier CA 90601

CALLANAN, JOSEPH ALFRED, (Joe Alfreds), b. Washington, Aug.4, 1920; s. Joseph P. Callanan and Agnes M. (Buckley) Ledwidge; m. Edith S. (Hamn), Aug. 14, 1943. Author: The School Administrators Guide Book, 1967, Energy and the Schools, 1975, An Executive's Guide to Efective Writing, 1980, Communicating, 1984, Sales Management and Motivation, 1987; (with Charles Healey) Discovering You, 1976; (with Leo Pachett and Harold Smiley) Criminalistics and the Law Enforcement Officer, 1977; (with Brooks Fenno) Dynamic Ideas in Marketing, 1982. Contrbr. articles on bus. subjects, edn., travel to mags. Project ed.: This Sceptered Isle, 1964. Mng. ed. Medford Mercury, MA, 1946-48; ed. Fiction House, N.Y.C., 1948-50; wrtr., ed. The Lamp, N.Y.C., 1950-59; project ed. Natl. Geographic Soc., Washington, 1060-64; mgr. pubs. Digital Equipment Corp., Myanard, MA, 1976-79; free-lance wrtr., 1964—; lectr. jnlsm. and public relations Conn. U., Northeastern U., Simmons Coll., Boston U. Recipient Cultural Writing award All-Ohio Conf. of Eds. and Communicators, 1973, Silver Bowl award Francis W. Hatch, 1981. Men. IABC (1st place award for Marathon World 1973). Home: 12 Simpson Rd Wayland MA 01778

CALLAWAY, KATHY JEAN, b. Holyoke, MA, Feb. 19, 1943; d. Raymond Leonard and Shirley Joan (Wedlock) C. Author: (novel) The Bloodroot Flower (Second prize Friends of Am. Wrtrs. 1983, Round Table award 1983), 1982; (poems) Heart of the Garfish, 1982. Contrbr. poems, articles to lit. mags., anthols., popular mags. including The Nation, The Iowa Rvw., The Pushcart Prize: Best of the Small Presses; scriptwriter daytime TV Dramas, 1969-77. B.A., U. Montana, 1978, M.F.A., 1979. Instr., U. Montana, Missoula, 1978-79, Schl. of Visual Arts, NYC, 1981-82; wrtr.-in residence, asst. prof. lit. Mankato State U., MN, 1982-84; visiting wrtr. U. Northern Iowa, 1983, 84, UCross Fdn., Wy., 1984. Fellow NEA, 1984; recipient Loring Williams prize for poetry AAP, 1979, New Wrtr. award PEN, 1980, Agnes Lynch Starrett award for poetry U. Pitts. Press, 1981. Mem. WGA East. Home: 1403 4th Ave So Moorhead MN 56560

CALLENBACH, ERNEST, b. Williamsport, PA, Apr. 3, 1929; s. Ernest William and Margaret Isabel (Miller) C.; m. Christine Leefeldt, May 19, 1978; children: Joanna, Hans. Author: Living Poor with Style, 1971, Ecotopia, 1975, Ecotopian Encyclopedia for the Eighties, 1981, Ecotopia Emerging, 1981; co-author: The Art of Friendship, 1979, A Citizen Legislature, 1985, Humphrey the Wayward Whale, 1986. PhB, U. Chgo., 1949, MA, 1953. Editor, Film Qtly, U. Calif. Press, Berkeley, 1958—, editor books, 1958—. Mem. NWU. Office: U CA Press 2120 Berkeley Way Berkeley CA 94720

CALLICO, JEFF SCOTT, b. Louisville, KY, Jan. 21, 1963; s. James Ellis and Carole Elaine (Calvert) C.; m. Stacey Lynn Dupree, Mar. 14, 1986. B.A., Carson-Newman Coll., 1985. Contrbr. poems to anthols. Wrkg. on novelette, In the Key of Life. Telemarketer, Dial America, Atlanta, 1986; reporter Marietta Daily Jnl., GA. 1986-87, ed., 1987—. Recipient Honorable Mention, World of Poetry, 1987, Golden Poet award, 1987. Mem. Commun. Alliance Stage and Theatre. Home: 4445 Wood Hollow Ct Douglasville GA 30135

CALLIS, VICTORIA D., b. New Castle, IN, Nov. 28, 1953; d. Franklin D. and Patricia Mae (Brenner) C. Contrbr. poems to anthols., lit. mags. Grad. public schls., Cambridge City, IN. Product number ed. Belden, Richmond, IN, 1975-77. indsl. engineering rate clrk., 1977-86, data entry clrk., 1986-87, time study clrk., 1987—. Recipient award for writing excellence Tin Penny, 1986, award of Merit, Creative Enterprises, 1987, Honorable Mention, World of Poetry, 1986, 87, Runner-Up award Jessee Poet, 1987, Home: Box 568 Dublin IN 47335

CALLOWAY, DAWN KELLY, b. Jasper, AL, Jan. 31,1958; d. Watus Wilson and Vaudie Frances (Burrow) Rooks; m. Carl Hubert Calloway Jr., Jan. 1, 1981; 1 child, Kinsey Wade. Contrbr. poetry: Riders of the Rainbow, Words of Praise, numerous anthologies. Wrkg. on poetry collection, novel, short stories. Student public schs., Arley, Ala. Police officer Jasper (Ala.) Police Dept., 1980-81' freelance wrtr., 1986—. Home: Rt 8 Box 511 Jasper AL 35501

CALNON, GUIN CORINNE, b. Owosso, MI, April 29, 1943; d. Wilbur LaVergne and Brandon (Richardson) Dyer; m. Dan Michael Calnon, June 7, 1969; children: Paul Michael, David Timothy, Angela Rose, Jonathan Jack, Mark Richard. Author: Tulips of Love, 1987. Wrkg on stories for children. Edn. Bob Jones Univ., Layton Schl of Art (Milwaukee). Secretary, Bob Jones Univ., 1966—. Mem. Foothills Writers' Club. Home: 108 Creighton Dr Taylors SC 29687

CALORE, JAMES JOHN, b. Phila., July 9, 1948; s. Carmen John and Geraldine Mary (Murphy) C.; m. Linda Teresa DiRenzo, Feb. 26, 1972; children—Danielle, Kristen, Kevin. Works incl.: Technical Trade School Text, 1982, Electronic Game Repair, 1986, Troubleshooting Wells Gardner, 1987, Electronic Monitors, 1987, Laser Disc Applications in Entertainment, 1984; ed. Star Tech Jnl, 1979—. Student, Ryder Tech. Inst. Customer svc. mgr. Atari Inc., Piscataway, NJ, 1977-78; dept. mgr. Active Amusements, Phila., 1978-80; consultant Banner Specialty, Phila., 1980-81; dir. Technical Trade School, Phila., Balt., Pitts., 1982-83; pub./ed. Star Tech Jnl, Merchantville, NJ, 1979—. Served to Sgt., USAF, 1967-70. Office: Box 1065 Merchantville NJ 08109

CALVERT, PATRICIA, (Peter J. Freeman), b. Great Falls. MT, July 22, 1931; d. Edgar C. and Helen P. (Freeman) Dunlap; m. George J. Calvert, Jan. 27, 1951; children: Brianne L. Calvert Elias, Dana J. Calvert Holbert. Author: contrbr, Lyle L. Miller, ed., Developing Reading Efficiency, 4th ed, 1980, The Snowbird (juvenile), 1980, The Money Creek Mare (juvenile), 1981, The Stone Pony (juvenile), 1982, The Hour of the Wolf (juvenile), 1983, Hadder MacColl (juvenile), 1985, Yesterday's Daughter (juvenile; Junior Lit. Guild selection), 1986, Stranger, You and I (juvenile), 1987. Contrbr more than 100 articles and stories to children's magazines (sometimes under pseudonym Peter J. Freeman), incl. Highlights for Children, Friend, Junior Life, and Jack and Jill. BA, Winona (Minn.) State U., 1976, grad study, 1976—.Laboratory clerk, St. Mary's Hosp., Great Falls, Mont., 1948-49, clerk typist, General Motors Acceptance Corp, 1950-51; cardiac lab. technician, Mayo Clinic, Rochester, Minn., 1961-64, enzyme lab tech, 1964-70, senior edit. asst in section of publications, 1970—. Member: Am. Med. Writers Assn., Children's Reading Round Table, Soc. of Children's Book Writers, Soc. of Midland Authors. Best book award, ALA, juvenile fiction award from Soc. of Midland Aus., and juvenile award Friends of American Writers, all 1980, for The Snowbird; William Allan White award, 1987, for Hadder MacColl. Home: Foxwood Farm RR 2 Box 91 Chatfield MN 55923

CAMARGO, MARTIN J., b. Flushing, NY, July 23, 1950; s. Mario and Veronica (Burg) C. Contrbr. articles to Speculum, Viator, Genre, Studies in Philology and other jnls. AB, Princeton U., 1972; PhD in English, U. Ill-Urbana, 1978. Asst. prof. Univ. Ala., Tuscaloosa, 1979-80, Univ. Mo., Columbia, 1980-85, assoc. prof. English, 1985—; essays editor Missouri Rvw, 1982—. Fulbright fellow, Paris, 1974-75, research fellow ACLS, 1983-84, Alexander von Humboldt fellow, Tubingen, 1987-88. Mem. MLA, Medieval Acad. Am., Intl. Soc. History Rhetoric. Address: 607 Donnelly Ave Columbia MO 65203

CAMERON, ELEANOR FRANCES, b. Winnipeg, Man., Can., Mar. 23, 1912; d. Henry and Florence Lydia (Vaughan) Butler; m. Ian Stuart Cameron, June 24, 1934; 1 son, David Gordon. Author: The Unheard Music, 1950, The Wonderful Flight to the Mushroom Planet, 1954, A Room Made of Windows, 1971 (ALA Notable Book); The Court of the Stone Children, 1973 (ALA Notable Book), The Green and Burning Tree: On the Writing and Enjoyment of Children's Books, 1969 (Commonwealth Lit. award 1969), Julia and the Hand of God, 1977 (ALA Notable Book), A Spell is Cast (Commonwealth award), Beyond Silence, 1980, That Julia Redfern, 1982 (ALA Notable Book), others. Student, UCLA, 1931-33, Mem. editorial bd. Cricket Mag., LaSalle, Ill., 1973—, Children's Lit. in Edn., 1982—. Recipient Natl. Book Award for Court of the Stone Children 1973. Mem. AL, PEN Intl. Address: EP Dutton 2 Park Ave New York NY 10016

CAMERON, LOU, b. San Francisco, June 20, 1924; s. Louis Arnold and Ruth (Marvin) C. Author: Angel's Flight, 1960, The Big Red Ball, 1961, The Sky Divers, 1962, The Empty Quarter, 1962, Not Even Your Mother, 1963, The Bastard's Name is War, 1963, The Black Camp, 1963, The Green Fields of Hell, 1964, The Block Busters, 1964, adaptor, None But the Brave (novel based on film of same title), 1965, The Amphorae Pirates, 1970, Spurhead, 1971, Cybernia (sci. fiction), 1972, adaptor, Californea Split (novel based on film of same title), 1974, The Closing Circle, 1974, Barca, 1974, Doc Travis, 1975, North to Cheyenne, 1975, (under pseud. Julia Cameron) Devil in the Pines, 1975, and The Darklings, 1975; The Spirit Horses, 1976, The Guns of Durango, 1976, Code Seven, 1977, adaptor, How the West Was Won (based on stories and teleplays by Calvin Clements), 1977, The Big Lonely, 1977, The Cascade Ghost, 1978, (under pseud. Mary Louise Manning) The Last Chronicles of Ballyfungus, 1978; The Wilderness Seekers, 1979, This Fever in My Blood, 1980, The Track Stalker, 1980, The Subway Stalker, 1980, The Hot Car, 1981, (under house pseud. Tabor Evans) Longarm in Boulder Canyon, 1982, and Longarm and the Great Train Robbery, 1982. Also au of over 100 additional fiction, mystery, sci. fiction, and western books, including Behind the Scarlet Door, The First Blood, Good Guy, Hannibal Brooks, Mistress Bayou Labelle, Mud War, Outside, Tipping Point, Tunnel War, The Girl with the Dynamite Bangs. Under house pseud. Tabor Evans author of other books in the Longarm series, and under pseud. Ramsay Thorne of books in the Renegade series. Contrbr of about 300 short stories and articles to mags. Attended Califonia School of Fine Arts, 1940-41. Variosly employed as movie extra, private detective, ranch hand, and trucker; freelance commercial artist for pulp publs, comics and mags, 1950-60; full-time writer, 1960—.Military service: U.S. Army, 1941-50, served as artillery scout and combat instructor, Eur. theatre during World War II; became tech. sgt.; received Bronze Star, Purple Heart, three battle stars. Thomas Edison award, best historical comic book, 1956, for Life of Columbus; Spur award, Western Writers of America, 1976, for The Spirit Horses. Address: c/o Lowenstein 250 West 57th St New York NY 10107

CAMP, MARCIA CLAIRE, b. Little Rock, Aug. 19, 1931; d. Carl Samuel and Clara (Morgan) Cloud; m. Leon Ray Camp, June 1949 (div. Jan. 1985); children—Valerie Claire, Drew Christopher, Angela Carlin, Shawn Clayton. Contrbr. articles, poetry, short stories to mags., newspapers including True Romance, Ark. Bus., Ark. Times Mag., others. Secy., treas. Ray Camp, Inc. Consulting Foresters, Little Rok, 1954—; exec. secy. Ark. State Bd. of Registration for Foresters, 1969—. Recipient 1st place for short story Am. Mothers Assn., 1985. Mem. Poets Roundtable Ark. (Sybil Nash Abrams Poetry award 1984; 1st v.p.). Home: 75 Robinwood Dr Little Rock AR 72207

CAMPA, JOSEPH FRANK, b. Trenton, NJ, Nov. 18, 1955; s. Joseph Paul ad Margaret Mary (Chasarick) C.; m. Elaine Nancy-Matz, Aug. 20, 1978; children—Joseph, Arlan, Aaron, John. Reporter: Natl. Enquirer, 1985—. Contrbr. articles and photos to newspapers, popular mags., lit. mags. including Newsweek, Silver Kris, Newlook Mag., Northwest Viewmas. Wrkg. on articles on sister city projects between U.S. and Nicaragua. Coll. of Redwoods, 1984-85. Mem Am. Soc. Mag. Photographers. Home: 2552 Old Arcata Rd Bayside CA 95524

CAMPBELL, EWING, b. Alice, TX, Dec. 26, 1940; s. James Vernon and Marie (Crofford) C. Author: Weave It like Nightfall, 1977, The Way of Sequestered Places, 1982, The Rincon Triptych, 1984; Piranesi's Dream (stories), 1986. Co-ed.: The Plaza of Encounters, 1979. BBA, No. Tex. State U., 1968; MA, U. So. Miss., 1972; PhD,Okla. State U., 1980. Lectr. U. Tex., Austin, 1981-82, Okla. State U., Stillwater, 1982-83; instr. Wharton Jr. Coll., Tex., 1983-84; asst. prof. Tex. A&M U., College Station, 1984—. Home: 1003 S Magnolia Hearne TX 77859

CAMPBELL, JANE, see Edwards, Jane Elizabeth

CAMPBELL, JOANNA, see Simon, Jo Ann

CAMPBELL, LIBERTY, b. Danbury, CT, Apr. 5, 1918, d. George Leslie and Lillian Dorothea Elizabeth (Schofield) Campbell; children—Barbara Kortemeyer, Alexandra Hays. Author: Pelicans are Scarce, 1981, Blue Dawn, Blue River, 1981, Up to my Neck in Haiku, 1982, Lanternes, Cinquains, Cameos, 1983, Haiku of Old Japan, 1983, To a Far Province with Basho, 1983. BS, Columbia U. Nurse various orgns., 1942—. Served to Capt., Nurses Corps, U.S. Army, World War II; NATOUSA, ETO. Winner 1st prize Am. Verse Wrtrs.' Guild, 1982. Home: Draper Hall 67 1918 1st Ave New York NY 10029

CAMPBELL, LOUISE, (Wendy, Louise Ware-Campbell), b. Henryetta, OK, Oct. 11, 1937; d. Elvin Otis and Myrtle Elizabeth (Wood) Ware; m. Paul Gordon Campbell, June 23, 1956; children—Kim Renee, Kena Louise, Kristen Melissa, Jeremy Aaron. Contrbr. numerous poems, articles to anthols. Grad. public schls., Henryetta. Tchr.'s aide Ryal Schl., Henryetta, 1980-83; free-lance wrtr., 1983—. Recipient Golden Poet award World of Poetry, 1987, Honorable Mention, 1987. Home: 709 W Moore Henryetta OK 74437

CAMPBELL, PAT, see Campbell, Patricia Ann

CAMPBELL, PATRICIA ANN, (Pat Campbell), b. Pocatello, ID, Sept. 27, 1941; d. John Woodrow and Wilma Ruth (Mecham) Keaton; m. George Alexander Campbell, Sept. 1, 1962; children—Nancy Kay Britton, Evan John. Author: Pages of Time, 1975, A Bamboo Cage, 1985, Reflections, 1985. Contrbr. poems and prose to anthols., lit. mags., newsletters. Studied comml. art, Id. State U.-Pocatello, 1959-60. Asst. tech. librarian Phillips Pet Co., Idaho Falls, Id., 1961-63; asst. librarian Blackfoot Pub. Library, Id., 1972-74; farmer,Blackfoot, 1970-76; cook Jefferson County Schl. Dist., Rigby, Id., 1980-82; free-lance wrtr., Rigby, 1982—. Mem. Id. Wrters. League (Poet of Yr. 1984), Western World Haiku Soc. Home: 201 W Main St Rigby ID 83442

CAMPBELL, R(OBERT) WRIGHT, b. Newark, NJ, June 9, 1927; s. William James and Florence (Clinton) C.. Author: The Spy Who Sat and Waited, 1975, Circus Couronne, 1977, Where Pigeons Go to Die, 1978, Killer of Kings, 1979, Malloy's Subway, 1981, Fat Tuesday, 1983, The Junkyard Dog, 1986, In La-La Land We Trust, 1986, Thr 600 Pound Gorilla, 1987, Hip-Deep in Alligators, 1987, Alice in La-La Land, 1987. Screenplays: Five Guns West, 1955, Naked Paradise, 1957, Gun for a Coward, 1957, Quantez, 1957, Man of a Thousand Faces, 1957, Machine Gun Kelly, 1958, A New World, 1958, Teenage Caveman, 1958 (released in England as Out of the Darkness), The Night Fighters, 1960, The Young Racers, 1963, The Masque of the Red Death, 1964, The Secret Invasion, 1964, Hells Angels on Wheels, 1967, Captain Nemo and the Underwater City, 1969, Also au of film scripts for television programs, including Medic, Maverick, Cheyenne, Mr. Garland, Twelve O'Clock High, Loretta Young, Star and the Story, Marcus Welby, M.D., and Born Free. Attended Pratt Inst., 1944-47. Artist, novelist, screenwriter. Freelance illustrator, 1947-50. Military service: U.S. Army, 1950-52. Academy Award nom., 1957, for Man of a Thousand Faces; Edgar award for The Junkyard Dog, 1987. Home: Box 412 Carmel CA 93921

CAMPBELL, SHARON LYNN, b. Denver, Sept. 23, 1955, d. Frank B. and June J. (Wallace) Sauter; m. Gerald R. Campbell. Contrbr. articles to Toastmaster, News and Views Am. Cncl. on Sci. and Health, Nursing '84, EEO Rvw, Communications Briefings, Backstage, others. BS, U. Colo., 1977; MA, NYU, 1980. Med. technologist Mercy Med. Center, Denver, 1977; environ. health coordinator Columbia U., NYC, 1980-83; pres. S.L.C. Communications, NYC, 1983—. Home: Box 8R 39-65 52d St Woodside NY 11377

CAMPION, DANIEL RAY, b. Oak Park, IL, Aug. 23, 1949, s. Raymond Edward and Wilma Frances (Dougherty) C. Author: Calypso, 1981; co-ed.: Walt Whitman: The Measure of His Song, 1981; contrbr. articles to: Lit. Mag. Rvw., Hispanic Jnl, Chgo. Tribune, Chgo. Reader; contrbr. poetry: Ascent, Poet Lore, The Spirit that Moves Us, other lit mags. AB, U. Chgo., 1970; MA, U. Ill., Chgo., 1975. Prodn. ed. Encyc. Britannica, Inc., Chgo., 1972-74; children's book ed. Follett Pub. Co., Chgo., 1977-78; teaching and research asst. U. Iowa, Iowa City, 1978-84; test specialist Am. Coll. Testing Program, Inc., Iowa City, 1984—. Recipient Festival of Arts poetry award U. Chgo., 1967, All- Nations Poetry Contest award Triton Coll., River Grove, Ill., 1975, Poetry award Ill. Arts Council, 1979. Mem. MMLA, NCTE. Home: 1700 E Rochester Ave Iowa City IA 52240

CAMRON, ROXANNE, b. Los Angeles, May 16; d. Irving John and Roslyn (Weinberger) Spiro; m. Robert Camron, Sept. 28, 1969; children: Ashley Jennifer, Erin Jessica. West Coast fashion and beauty editor, Teen mag., Los Angeles, 1969-70, sr. editor, 1972-73, editor, 1973—; freelance writer. BA in journalism, U. So. Calif., 1967. Mem. Women in Communications. Address: 8831 Sunset Blvd Los Angeles CA 90069

CANAN, JANINE BURFORD, b. Los Angeles, Nov. 2, 1942. Author: Of Your Seed, 1977, Daughter, 1981, New Directions 42, 1981, Who Buried the Breast of Dreams, 1982, Shapes of Self, 1982, Her Magnificent Body, 1985. BA, Stanford, 1963. Psychiatrist, Berkeley, 1979—. Mem. PSA. Home: 68 Avis Rd Berkeley CA 94707

CANFIELD, DEBORAH ANN, b. Utica, NY, Aug. 24, 1953; d. George Leland and Betty Ann (Taylor) C.; m. Rory More Houlihan, Mar.9, 1974 (div. May 1984); children—Kelly More. Contrbr. poems to lit. mags., articles to Star Advocate and Tribune. Wrkg. on poems. A.A.S. in Early Childhood Edn., SUNY-Cobleskill, 1973; A.A. in Genl. Edn., Brevard Commun. Coll., 1987; student U. Central Fla., 1987—. Genl. mgr. Desperados Restaurant, Cocoa Beach, FL, 1980-86; waitress IntraCoastal Dispensing Co., Melbourne, FL, 1986—. Home: 494 S Atlantic Ave 211 Cocoa Beach FL 32931

CANFIELD, JOAN GILTNER, (Austelle Arriaynne Hawtre), b. Des Moines, Nov. 22, 1921; d. Wrenn Manly and Martha Ann (Giltner) C. Author: All About Pan, 1960, Ming Plate, 1972, Laughing New Orleans, 1980. Student num. colls. Served in hosp. corps, USN, 1941-45. Mem. NPW. Home: 4815 Harwood Dr Des Moines IA 50312

CANN, RACHEL P., b. Medford, Mass., Nov. 25, 1942; d. Paul Komewchuk and Henrietta (Stathacopoulos) Komenchuk Moran; div., 1976; 1 son, Sean Philip. Contrbr. short stories: Oak Square, New Black Mask, Anemone, Green Feather, Ripples, numerous other lit. mags. Wrkg. on novel, film script. BA, U. Mass.; MEd, Boston State Coll. Tchr. public schs., Malden, Mass., 1966-71; driver Towne Taxi Co., Boston, 1985-86; freelance wrtr. Mem. IWWG, Feminist Wrtrs.' Guild, NWC. Office Box 1723 Brookline MA 02146

CANNIFF, KIKI, b. Danville, IL, Oct. 26, 1948; d. Richard L. and Peggy E. (La Zier) Smith. Author: The Northwest Golfer; A Guide to the Public Golf Courses of Washington & Oregon, 1987, Free Campgrounds of Washington & Oregon, 1985, Washington Free, 1984, Oregon Free, 1986; contrbr. to Redbook, Pacific Skipper, Decorating & Crafts, Northwest, other mags. Student Phoenix Coll., 1967-68. Mem. Northwest Assn. Book Pubs.,PASCAL/PMA, Book Publicists Northwest, Oregon Wrtrs. Colony, Willamette Writers. Office: Box 13322 Portland OR 97213

CANTOR, ELI, (Gregory A. Douglas), b. NYC, Sept. 9, 1913; s. Sol M. and Bertha (Seidler) C.; m. Beatrice Mink, Oct. 4, 1942; children: Ann, Fred. Author: Enemy in the Mirror, 1977; Love Letters, 1977 (also screenplay Forever Yours); (under pseudonym Gregory A. Douglas) The Rite, 1979, The Nest, 1980; contrbr. poetry to Poetry Mag., Yearbook of American Poets, stories and articles to Esquire, Coronet, Story, Accent, Reader's Digest, others; author plays Candy Store, 1948, The Golden Goblet, 1986, also TV plays for Armstrong Circle Theatre. BS, NYU, 1934, MA, 1935; JD, Harvard U., 1938. Mem. legal staff CBS, NYC, 1938-39; mem. editorial staff Esquire Mag., Chgo., 1939-41; ed.-in-chief Research Inst. Report, NYC, 1941-61; pres. Composing Room Typographers, NYC, 1961-71. Yaddo Artists' Colony fellow, also Eli Cantor fellow in lit. established there. Mem. PEN, P&W. Home: 384 N Washington Dr Sarasota FL 34326

CANZONERI, ROBERT, b. San Marcos, TX, Nov. 21, 1925, s. Joe and Mabel (Barnett) C.; m. Dorothy Mithcell, June 10, 1950 (div.); children—Tony, Nina; m. 2d. Candyce Barnes, Nov. 10, 1972. Author: "I Do So Politely": A Voice from the South, 1965, Watch us Pass, 1968, Men with Little Hammers, 1969, Barbed Wire and Other Stories, 1970, A Highly Ramified Tree, 1976; contrbr.: Harpers, Southern Rvw, Antioch Rvw, Best Little Mag. Short Stories, Contemporary Am. Poets, other lit. publs. MA, U. Miss., 1951; PhD,Stanford U., 1965. Prof. English Ohio State U., Columbus, 1965—. Recipient Henry W. Bellamann award, 1965, Ohioana award Ohioana Library, Columbus, 1976; grantee Danforth Fdn., 1960, 63, 64; Ohio Arts Council fellow, 1978, 80. Home: 195 Cornell Ct Westerville OH 43081

CAPEK, ANTOINETTE A., (Ann T. Nett), b. Cornell, WI, May 26, 1926; d. Anton Frances and Lillian (Fuchs) C. Contrbr. poems to anthols. Wrkg. on Family Favorite Recipe Book, book of poetry, Art for Fun book, Decoration Made with Used Stamps. Grad. public schls., Cadott, WI. Free-lance photo colorist, 1956-59, cake decorator, 1960-84, wrtr., 1986—. Recipient cert. of Merit, Song Festival, 1981; cert. of Ahievement, Wrtr.'s Digest, 1985; (6) Honorable Mention, World of Poetry, 1984-85, Golden Poet award, 1985, 86. Home: 11S 100 Carpenter St Lemont IL 60439

CAPICE, PHILLIP, see Deverevx, John

CAPLAN, JUDITH SHULAMITH LANGER, (Shulamith Surnamer), b. Bklyn., Feb. 3, 1945, d. Samuel and Gladys (Surnamer) Langer; m. Neil Howard Caplan, June 28, 1970; children—Hillel Nathaniel, Baruch Ian. Contrbr.: Sandsounds, Crosscurrents, Shofar, New Traditions. Earth's Daughters, Wrkg. on poetry collection, short-story collection, Jewish holiday anthology. BA in English, Bklyn. Coll., 1966; MS in Radio-TV, Syracuse U., 1968. Tchr. various schls., N.Y.C. Bd. Edn., 1966—; poetry ed. Sandsounds, L.I., 1983—; co-founder Proetica creative writing workshop, 1982. P&W grantee, 1983, 84. Mem. L.I. Poetry Collective, Intl. Women's Writing Guild. Home: 27 W Penn St Long Beach NY 11561

CAPORALE, PATRICIA JEANE, (Cass Hauseman), b. Camden, NJ, Nov. 27, 1947; d. Cassius Floyd and Dorothy Amanda (Hauseman) Senior; m. Joseph Emil Caporale, May 28, 1968; children—Mark Andrew, Michael Charles, Lawrence Joseph; Jessica Kristine. Contrbr. to: My Weekly Mag. in Scotland, Good Housekeeping, Ladies' Home Jnl, Equilibrium. AS in Soc. Svcs., Camden County Coll., 1978. Assoc. ed. Town Crier Herald, Haddonfield, NJ, 1978-79; ed. Record Breeze, Berlin, NJ, 1979-80; mng. ed. Cam-Glo Nwsprs., Blackwood, NJ, 1980-82; news ed. Haddon Gazette, Haddonfield, 1982-83, Cherry Hill (NJ) News, 1983-86; mng. ed. & news ed. Suburban News Group, Cherry Hill, 1984-86; You're Invited to Florida's Space Coast mag., 1986—. Mem. NJ Press Assn. Num. profl. awards, NJ and Phila. Press Assns., 1979-86; profl. excell. award, SPJ, 1985, 86. Home: 1310 Ebb Tide Ave Merritt Island FL 32952

CAPOSSELA, JAMES P., (Jim), b. Tarrytown, NY, Feb. 7, 1949; s. Carmen N. and Josephine Z. C. Author: How to Catch Crabs by the Bushel, 1982, Part Time Cash for the Sportsman, 1984, How to Write for the Outdoor Mags., 1984, Good Fishing Close to NYC, 1985; ed. Great Fishing in Lake Ontario & Tributaries, 1986; contrbr. to outdoor mags. incld. Field & Stream, Outdoor Life, Sports Afield. BA, Mercy Coll., 1973. Copywriter, Dancer- Fitzgerald-Sample Inc., NYC, 1976-80; freelance writer, 1974—; copy supr. Spectravideo Inc., NYC, 1982-84; pres. Northeast Sportsman's Press, Tarrytown, NY, 1982—. Address: Box 188 Tarrytown NY 10591

CAPPELLO, ROSEMARY C., b. Llanerch, PA, Oct. 8, 1935; d. John and Rose (Arcaro) Petracca; m. Oct. 29, 1955 (div. June 1983); children: Joseph, Anthony, Mary. Contrbr. over 250 poems in numerous publs. including Painted Bride Qtly, Poetry of Parkway Anthology, Quoin, Pearl; also over 200 articles. Wrkg. on Italian-Am. poetry. BA, Widener U., Chester, Pa., 1983. Sec., 1953-56, 83—; ed., pub. Phila. Poets, 1980—. Home: 1919 Chestnut St Apt 1701 Philadelphia PA 19103

CAPUTO, PHILIP JOSEPH, b. Chgo., June 10, 1941; s. Joseph and Marie Ylonda (Napolitan) C.; m. Jill Esther Ongemach, June 21, 1969 (div. 1982); children: Geoffrey Jacob, Marc Anthony.; m. Marcelle Lynn Besse, Oct. 30, 1982 (div. 1985). Author: A Rumor of War, 1977, Horn of Africa, 1980, Del Corso's Gallery, 1983, Indian Country, 1987. BA in English, Loyola U., Chgo., 1964. Mem. staff Chgo. Tribune, fgn. corr., Rome, 1972-74, Beirut, 1974-76, Moscow, 1976-77. Served with USMCR, 1964-67; Vietnam. Recipient award Ill. Assoc. Press, Ill. United Press; Overseas Press Club award; Pulitzer prize; others. Mem. AG, NWU. Address: Priest Lit Agcy 565 5th Ave New York NY 10017

CARAM, EVE, b. Hot Springs, AR, May 11, 1934, d. Raymond Briggs and Lois Elizabeth (Merritt) La Salle; m. Richard G. Caram, Apr. 19, 1965; 1 dau., Bethel Eve. Author: The Palm Reader's Daughters (short-fiction collection), 1987; contrbr. short fiction, poetry to Wis. Rvw, Cottonwood Rvw, Epos, other lit mags. AB in Comparative Lit., Bard Coll., 1956; MA in English, U. Mo., Columbia, 1977. Lectr. English, Stephens Coll., Columbia, Mo., 1980-82, Wrtrs.' Program, UCLA Ext., 1983—, Calif. State U.-Northridge, 1983—; dir. studies Profl. Wrtg. Program, U. So. Calif. Residency grantee, Ossabaw Island (Ga.) Project, 1978, Wurlitzer Fdn., Taos, N.Mex., 1978; Yaddo fellow NEA, 1976, 82; recipient Manuscripts Intl. award, 1984; Ragdale Fdn., 1985. Home: 3400 Ben Lomond Pl 125 Los Angeles CA 90027

CARBERRY, JOHN A., see Morgenstern, Frieda Homnick

CARD, LEWIS, see Vinacke, W. Edgar

CARDILLO, JOE, b. Norwich, NY, Aug. 1, 1951, s. Alfio and Josephine (Pino) C. Author poetry: Delicate Passions and Madnesses (chapbook), A Legacy of Desire, 1983, Turning Toward Morning, 1984, No Denials, 1986, Artifact, 1988; contrbr. poetry: Crab Creek Rvw, Rolling Stone, Iron, other lit mags; adv. bd.: Esprit—A Mag. for the Humanities, 1983—. BA, Siena Coll., Loudonville, N.Y., 1973; MA, SUNY-Albany, 1978. Asst. prof. English and creative writing Hudson Valley Community Coll., Troy, N.Y., 1978—; presenter public readings, workshops; wrtr.-in-residence various instns., 1978—. Home: RD2 2 Heather Ridge Averill Park NY 12018

CAREY, MARGARET STANDISH, b. Albany, OR, Nov. 28, 1926, d. John K. Standish and Helen C. (Collins) Rasmussen; mn. Robert Everett Carey, Sept. 3, 1949; children—William R., Elizabeth R. Author, pub. (with Patricia Hoy Hainline): Brownsville: Linn County's Oldest Town, 1976, Halsey: Linn County's Centennial City, 1977, Shedd: Linn County's Early Dairy Center, 1978, Sweet Home in the Oregon Cascades, 1979, Northwest Passages newsletter, 1986—. Student Cascade Coll., 1944, Multnomah Jr. Coll., 1948-49. Ptnr., author, ed. Calapooia Publs., Brownsville, Oreg., 1976—; ptnr., columnist Times Pub. Co., Brownsville, 1976-85; news corr. Brownsville Times, 1960-67, historical (Past Times) columnist, 1976—. Mem. Willamette Wrtrs., WWA, Fellowship of United Methodisto in Workship, Music and Other Arts. Home: 32865 Lake Creek Dr Halsey OR 97348

CARGAS, HARRY J(AMES), b. Hamtramck, MI, June 18, 1932; s. James H. and Sophia (Kozlowski) C.; m. MIllie Reider, Aug. 24, 1957; children: Martin de Porres, Joachim James, Siena Catherine, Manon Theesa, Jacinta Teilhard, Sarita Jo. Author: I Lay Down My Life: Biography of Joyce Kilmer, 1964, ed, Graham Greene, 1968, ed (with Thomas P. Neill) Renewing the Face of the Earth: Essays on Contemporary Church-World Relationships, 1968, ed The Continuous Flame: Teilhard in the Great Tradition, 1969, Religious and Cultural Factors in Latin America, 1970, ed (with Ed Erazmus) English as a Second Language: A Reader, 1970, ed (with Ann White) Death and Hope, 1970, Daniel Berrigan and Contemporary Protest Poetry, 1972, Harry James Cargas in cinversation with Elie Wiesel, 1976, The Holocaust: An Annotated Bibliography, 1978, Keeping a Spiritual Journal, 1980, A Christian Response to the Holocaust, 1981, When God and Man Failed, 1981, The Holocaust, 1986. Gen. ed Christian Critic series. Author of book columns for Way, Friar, Catholic Book Reporter, and Catholic Library World. Contrbr of articles and book reviews to Jubilee, America, New York Times, Catholic World, Ave Maria, and other publs. Ed-in-chief, Catholic Book Reporter, 1960-61, and Queen's Work, 1963-64; assoc ed, Holocaust and Genocide Studies. Attended Aquinas coll, 1955-56; BA, U. of Michigan, 1957, MA, 1958; Ph. D., St. Louis U., 1968. English tchr and athl dir, St. David's School, NYC, 1958-61; instr in English and athl coach, Montclair Academy, Montclair, N.J., 1962-63; instr in English, St. Louis, 1969—. Staff editor, Simon & Schuster; freelance ed, Herder & Herder. Moderator and occasional producer TV program The Church Is You; host of book review program Booking Ahead, KWMU for ten years. U.S. Holocuast Meml. Concl, natl. dir Community Outreach Programs, and presidential appointee. Consulting ed, Catechetical Guild, Natl Cncl of Catholic Men, and Natl Catholic H.S. Reading Program. Member: Yad Vashem (Jerusalem). Micah Award, Amer. Jewish Comm., 1980; Human Rights Award, UN Assn, 1980; Eternal Flame Award, Anne Frank Inst. Home: 127 Park Ave Kirkwood MO 63122

CARLI, AUDREY MARILYN, b. Bessemer, MI, Mar. 14, 1932; d. Henry Peter and Helen Karen (Niemi) Johnson; m. David John Carli, Feb. 2, 1952 (dec. Jan. 10, 1984); children—Debra, Glenn, Lynn, Lori. Author: Jimmy's Happy Day, 1967, When Jesus Holds Our Hand, 1987. Contrbr. articles to anthols. Wrkg. on Tears to Cheer meditations. Cert. in Creative Writing, Iron County Commun. Schl., 1963. Pres. A. M. C. Pub. Co., Stambaugh, MI, 1987—; free-lance wrtr., 1963—. Mem. NWC. Home: Box 158-807 Jefferson Ave Stambaugh MI 49964

CARLILE, HENRY DAVID, b. San Francisco, May 6, 1934, s. Aurelio Antonio Prieto and Grace Edna (Harris) Carlile; m. Sandra Jean McPherson (div. Nov. 1985); 1 child, Phoebe. Author: The Rough-Hewn Table, 1971, Running Lights, 1981; contrbr. poems, articles and book rvws. to numerous publs., including Anthology of Mag. Verse and Yearbook of Am. Poetry,

Poetspeak, Six Poets, Six Poems, Strong Measures: Recent Am. Poems in Traditional Forms, A Geography of Poets, Am. Poetry, Antioch, Chowder, Iowa, Malahat, Mo., N.W., Ohio, Portland, S.D., Tampa Poetry, Western Humanities rvws, Antaeus, The Nation, New Yorker, Parnassus, Poetry, Poetry Bag, Poetry N.W., Poetry Now, Tar River Poetry. BA, U. Wash., 1962, MA, 1967. Instr. Portland State U., Oreg., 1967-69, asst. prof., 1969-71, assoc. prof., 1972-80, prof., 1980—; vis. lectr. Iowa Wrtrs. Workshop, Iowa City, 1978-80. Recipient syndicated fiction award PEN, 1983, 86, Pushcart, 1986; NEA grantee, 1970, poetry fellow, 1976; Ingram Merrill Fdn. fellow, 1985. Mem. PSA, AWP NWU. Home: 7349 SE 30th Ave Portland OR 97202

CARLISLE, JOYCE ELLEN, b. Findlay, OH, Dec. 21, 1954, d. Edward Lester and Myrtle Marie (Roberts) M.; m. Joel Edward Carlisle, Feb. 5, 1983; 1 dau., Marie Margaret. Author: The Avocado Lovers' Cookbook, 1985. Student public schls., Findlay. Sole proptr. Foliage Factory, San Jose, Calif., 1973-76; ptnr. ICare Vitamin Products, San Jose, 1976-81; sole proptr. Blue Ribbon Pubs., Santa Barbara, 1982—. Mem. Pubs. Mktg. Assn. Home: 150 El Sueno Rd Santa Barbara CA 93110

CARLSON, ARTHUR BRUCE, b. Omaha, Apr. 16, 1934; s. Rudie Julius and Alma (Vold) C.; m. Marilyn E. Tucker, June 8, 1958; children—Alan Bruce, Lisa Ann. Author: Ghosts of Lee County, Iowa, 1986; Ghosts of Des Moines County, Iowa, 1986. BS in chemistry and edn., Western Ill. U., 1956. Research chemist U.S. Dept. Agrl., Peoria, Ill., 1956-58; engr. Sheaffer Pen Co., Fort Madison, Ia., 1958—. Served as pvt. U.S. Army, 1956-58. Mem. Burlington Area Writers' Club (v.p.).Home: RR 1 Box 135A Wever IA 52658

CARLSON, LANETTE ANNE, b. Geneseo, IL, Apr. 12, 1952; d. Albert C. and Lucille M. (Eeckhout) Buysse; m. James Andrew Carlson, Feb. 12, 1972; children—Alissa Ann, Blaine PAtrick. Contrbr. articles to mags., newspapers including Farm & Ranch Living, Ranger Rick, Antique Rvw., Daily Dispatch. Student Western Ill. U., 1971; Diploma, Inst. Children's Lit., 1980. Sec., treas. Henry County Fair Assn., Cambridge, IL, 1979-83; news correspondent Daily Dispatch, Moline, IL, 1982—; free-lance wrtr., photographer, 1983—. Chmn. public relations Parents Club of Cambridge Elementary Sch., 1986-87; trustee Cambridge Library District. Named Hon. Chpt. Farmer, Future Farmers Am., Cambridge, 1985. Mem. RWA. Home: Rt 3 Box 21 Cambridge IL 61238

CARLSON, NATALIE SAVAGE, b. Winchester, VA, Oct. 3, 1906; d. Joseph Hamilton and Natalie Marie (Villeneuve dit Vallar) Savage; m. Daniel Carlson, Dec. 7, 1929; children: Stephanie Natalie (Mrs. Robert David Sullivan), Julie Ann (Mrs. Walter Erskine McAlpine). Author: The Talking Cat and Other Stories of French Canada, 1952, Alphonse, That Bearded One, 1954, Wings Against the Wind, 1955, Sashes Red and Blue, 1956, Hortense, the Cow for a Queen, 1957, The Happy Orpheline, 1957, The Family Under the Bridge, 1958 (Newbery honor book), A Brother for the Orphelines, 1959, Evangeline, Pigeon of Paris, 1960, The Tomahawk Family, 1960, The Song of The Lop-Eared Mule, 1961, A Pet for the Orphelines, 1962, Carnival in Paris, 1962, Jean-Claude's Island, 1963, The Empty Schoolhouse, 1965, Sailor's Choice, 1966, Chalou, 1967, Luigi of the Streets, 1967, Ann Aurelia and Dorothy, 1968, Befana's Gift, 1969, The Half Sisters, 1970, Luvvy and the Girls, 1971, Marie Louise and Christophe, 1974, Marie Louise's Heyday, 1975, Runaway Marie Louise, 1977, Jaky or Dodo?, 1978, The Night the Scarecrow Walked, 1979, King of the Cats and Other Tales, 1980, A Grandmother for the Orphelines, 1980, Marie Louise and Christophe at the Carnival, 1981, Spooky Night, 1982, Surprise in the Mountains, 1983, The Ghost in the Lagoon, 1984, Spooky and the Ghost Cat, 1985, Spooky and the Wizard's Bats, 1986. Student, parochial schls., Calif. Newspaper reporter Long Beach (Calif.) Sun, 1926-29. Home: 3220 Hwy 19 N Lot 17 Clearwater FL 34621

CARLSON, WENDELL R., b. Dayton, IA, Sept. 7, 1936; s. Kenneth Frances and Agnes Arvida (Malmberg) C; m. Violet Lorraine Wolf, June 7, 1959; children—Dawn, Brian. Field ed. Waterfowlers World; contrbr.: Waterfowl U.S.A. mag., Shotgun Sports. Student Electronics, Air Force Tech. Schl., 1959. V.P./gen. mgr./part owner Reeder Radio/TV, Cedar Rapids, IA, 1958-84; owner Carlson Championship Call Co., Cedar Rapids, 1971—; outdoor writer, 1981—. Prizewinning waterfowl custom call maker. Home: 1200 College St Cedar Rapids IA 52401

CARMAN, JUANITA CHENAULT, b. Mt. Sterling, KY, Oct. 6, 1923; d. Charlie Henry Chenault and Viola Angela (Young) Chenault Grubbs; m. Luby Elton Carman, Mar. 22, 1948; children—Anita Yvonne Carman Walker, Viola Grace Carman Hubbard. Author, pub. Reach-Out series for youths: Who Are You?, Short Essays, Poems and Prose, Children's Stories, Teen-Agers' and Young Adults' Stories, Poetry for All; ed.: Annual Letters series of Letters to schl. children through newspaper eds.. Wrkg. on children's stories, poetry. BBA, Ky State U., 1945-47, Chgo., 1969-78, 79-81, St. Thomas, V.I., 1978-79; presenter freelance writing workshop for continuing edn. program U. Toledo, Southfield, Mich., 1984. Participant poetry readings. Mem. P&W, Mich. Council of Arts, Internat. Black Wrtrs. Conf. Home: 29434 Fall River Rd Southfield MI 48076

CARMAN, SUSAN LEA, b. Freeport, NY, Feb. 21, 1952, d. Sanford George and Aura M. (Himes) Carman. Contrbr. to: Earthshine, Glowing Embers, Am. Poetry Anthology, other publs. Wrkg. on short stories, poetry. Freelance lyricist, N.Y., 1968—; mem. internal distbn. Darby Group Co., Rockville Centre, N.Y., 1977—. Mem. Soc. Lit. Designates (life mem.; Dane title of merit 1971). Home: 37 Clinton Ave Rockville Centre NY 11570

CARMELL, PAMELA LEE, b. Kansas City, MO, Sept. 11, 1950, d. William Edward and Betty Anne Carmell. Contrbr. translations of poetry and fiction to Choutean Rvw, Colo. State Rvw, Poetry Miscellany, Nimrod, other lit mags. BS in Edn., U. Mo., 1972, MA in Spanish, 1977; MFA in Translation, U. Ark., 1984. Advt. mgr. Helicon 9 mag., Kansas City, 1979-80; promotion mgr. U. Ark. Press, 1983-84; asst. prof. English, U. Ark., Fayetteville, 1984—, ed. agr. publs., 1985-86. Mem. ALTA. Home: 901 Hargrove 20A Tuscaloosa AL 35405

CARMEN, MARILYN ELAINE, (Aisha Eshe), b. Harrisburg, Pa., Nov. 23, 1941; d. James Alvin and Geneva (Felton) Scruggs; children: Crystall Lynn, Michele, John, Michael. Author: (play) Don't Lose Your Soul, 1983; (poems) I Usta Be Afraid of the Night, 1985; contrbr. poetry to Black Voice, [illegible] Poet Lore, Mwendo, Poetry Jnl, Black Poetry Jnl, also articles and short stories. AA, Harrisburg Area Community Coll., 1975; BA, Pa. State U.-Middleton, 1977, MA, Iowa State Univ., 1987. Tchr., 1978—. Home: 872 Pammel Ct Ames IA 50010

CARNELL, JUDITH M., b. Whittier, CA, July 7, 1943; d. Kenneth and Margaret Lillian (Telford) Carnell. Contrbr. poetry: Winter Solstice, On Stage, other publs. AA, El Camino Coll., 1963; BA, Calif. State U.-Long Beach, 1965. Tchr. public high schl., San Luis Obispo, Calif., 1966-85; theatical cons., 1986—. Recipient theatrical and teaching awards. Home: 3257 W Charleston St Phoenix AZ 85023

CARNEVALL, DORIS L(ORRAIN), b. Seattle, d. Helmer and Hannah (Anderson) Scholin; m. Armando Carnevali; children: Nick, Jeffrey. Author: (with Dolores Little) Nursing Care Planning, 1969, 3d ed, sole author, 1983, ed (with Maxine Patrick) Nursing Management for the Elderly, 1979, 2d ed, 1986, (with others) Diagnostic Reasoning in Nursing, 1984. Contrbr: Edith M. Lewis, ed, The Clinical Nurse Specialist, 1970, Margaret Auld and Linda Birum, eds, The Challenge of Nursing, 1973, Joan P. Riehl and Joan Wilcox McVey, eds, The Clinical Nurse Specialist, 1973, Pamela Mitchell, ed, Concepts Basic to Nursing, 1973, 3d ed, 1981, Marjorie V. Batey, ed, Copmmunicating Nursing Research, vol. 8, 1975, Ann Mariner, ed, The Nursing Process: A Scientific Approach to Nursing Care, 1975, Judith Walter, Geraldine Pardee, and Doris M. Molbo, eds, Dynamics of Problem Oriented Approaches, 1976, Craven, Himle, Fundamentals of Nursing, 1988. Contrbr of about 30 articles to nursing jnls. Diploma, Swedish Hosp. Schl of Nursing, Seattle, Wash., 1943; B.S.N., U. of Washington, Seattle, 1947, M.N., 1961. Staff nurse, Swedish Hosp, 1944-45, head nurse, 1945-46, clinical instr, 1947-51; instructor, U. of Wash Schl of Nursing, 1947-51; supervisor, VA Hosp. Seattle, 1951-53; asst. exec. sec., Washington State Nurses Assn, 1953-55; instr., U. of Wash. Schl of Nursing, 1961-66, asst prof, 1966-69, assoc prof, 1969-82, emeritus, 1982—. Hon. mention from American Jnl of Nursing for best feature article, 1968; Book of the Year award from Amer. Jnl of Nursing, 1969, 79, 86. Member: Sigma Theta Tau (charter member of Psi chapter). Home: 3250 36th Ave SW Seattle WA 98126

CARNEY, CHARLES SEYMOUR, b. Pierson, IA, July 12, 1920; s. Charles and Florence Margaret (Seymour) C.; m. Dorothy Eleanor Bigelow, Mar. 31, 1922; children—Charles, James, Michael, Carol, Cynthia. Ed. NMEA News, 1982-86. BSEE, IA State U., 1950. Dir. maritime mktg. Collins Radio, Dallas, 1950-74; v.p. mktg. Communication Assoc., Huntington, NY, 1974-82; ed. NMEA News, Oronoco, MN, 1982-86. Served to Lt., USNR, 1937-45, PTO. Mem. IEEE. Office: Natl Maritime Elec 15 2d Ave SW Oronoco MN 55960

CARPATHIOS, NEIL EMMANUEL, b. Columbus, OH, Mar. 4, 1961, s. John and Mary (Volas) C. Contrbr. poetry: Crab Creek Rvw (Pushcart Prize nominee), Parnassus, Ripples, Studia Mystica, other lit mags; contrbr. fiction to Pig Iron Press Anthology. BA, Ohio State U., 1983; MFA, U. Iowa, 1986. Poetry therapist Hubbard House, Columbus, Ohio, 1982-83; arts rep. Iowa Arts Council, Iowa City, 1985-86, poet-in-schls., 1985-86. Recipient Poetry Press prize, 1982, Community of Poets award Ohio Arts Council, 1984. Mem. Natl. Assn. Poetry Therapy. Home: 376 49th St NW Canton OH 44709

CARPENTER, BEN, b. Cincinnati, OH, Oct. 23, 1936; s. Russell and Carmelia (Farris) Carpenter. Author: Moments, Moods & Memories, 1979, Summer Sunsets, 1984; poetry to various publications. Student Woodward U. Mem. Poets of Am. Home: 4407 Crocker St Los Angeles CA 90011

CARPENTER, JOHN RANDELL, b. Cambridge, MA, Apr. 14, 1936, s. Frederic Ives and Lillian Moore (Cook) C.; m. Bogdana Marie-Magdalena Chetkowska, Apr. 15, 1963; children—Michael Randell, Magdalena Maria-Anna. Author: Creating the World: Children, Art and Poetry, 1986, Poetry and Space, 1979, Egret, 1979, Gathering Water, 1972, Hammering, 1984; translator, author intro.: Selected Poems of Zbigniew Herbert, 1977, Report from the Besieged City (by Zbigniew Herbert), 1985. BA, Harvard U., 1958; Doctorate, U. Paris-Sorbonne, 1965. Freelance translator, ed., Berkeley, Calif., 1966-74; poet-in-residence, tchr., lectr. U. Wash., Seattle and Seattle Public Schls., 1975-76, 77-80; asst. prof., lectr. U. Mich., Ann Arbor, 1982—. Commr. Berkeley Arts Commn., 1969-74. NEA fellow, 1976-77, 79, 80-81; recipient Witter Bynner poetry translation award PSA, 1978, Islands and Continents translation award, Setawket, NY, 1979. Mem. PW. ALTA. Home: 1606 Granger Ave Ann Arbor MI 48104

CARPENTER, PATRICIA, (Kit Patrick), b. Detroit, May 16, 1920; d. William H. and Kathryn Virginia (Dix) Humphrey; m. Warren H. Carpenter, Mar. 29, 1958. Author: Fire & Magic: Poems by Patricia Carpenter, 1983; plays—The Capuchin Caper, 1986, The Phoenix Folly, 1987. Contrbr. poems to anthols., lit. mags. Ed.: (with P. Ahren, H. Olmsted) Kaleidoscope: Miscellany by Livingstone County Wrtrs., 1986. Wrkg. on mystery The Magic Shop. A.B., Oberlin Coll., 1941; B.S. in Library Sci., Western Reserve U., 1943; M.A., Wayne State U., 1958, Ph.D., 1961. Psychologist, Clinic for Child Study, Wayne County Juvenile Court, Detroit, 1959-63, dir. psychological service, 1963-81; clinical psychologist Psychological Service for Youth, Brighton, MI, 1981—. Mem. Livingston County Wrtrs. Home: 3875 W Coon Lake Rd Howell MI 48843

CARPENTER, WILLIAM, b. Cambridge, MA, Oct. 31, 1940, s. James M. and Dorothy (Sauer) C.; m. JoAnne Carpenter, Aug. 19, 1962; 1 child—Matthew. Author: The Hours of Morning, 1981, Rain, 1985; contrbr. poems to New Eng. Rvw, Am. Poetry Rvw, Poetry, Black Warrior Rvw, Pequod, others. BA, Dartmouth Coll., 1962; PhD,U. Minn., 1967. Mem. faculty U. Minn., Mpls., 1963-67, U. Chgo., 1967-73; mem. faculty Coll. of the Atlantic, Bar Harbor, Me., 1973—, dean of faculty, 1983—; mem. lit. panel ME Humanities Commn., 1985—; project dir. A Spirit of Place, Me., 1982. Recipient Pablo Neruda award U. Tulsa, 1979, AWP Series Award, 1980, Morse prize, Northeastern U., 1985; NEA fellow, Italy, 1985. Mem. AWP, Me. Wrtrs. & Pubs. Alliance, MLA. Address: Box 1297 Stockton Springs ME 04981

CARR, ALBERT BERNARD, b. NYC, Nov. 29, 1930; s. Albert B. and Sarena (Scaffa) C.; m. Norma Gomez, Dec. 26, 1954; children—Lorrie, Linda, Kevin, David. Author: Islands of the Deep Sea, 1966, The Black Box, 1969, Junior High School Science Textbook Series, 1969, Black Is a Word, 1972, I Wonder Why Science Readers, 1972, Science for Micronesia, 1973, Early Experiences in Learning, 1974, Samoan Curriculum in Science, 1975, Science: Process and Content, 1980, Sealive Park Fun Book, 1985, Energy Activities, 1986. Wrkg. on sci., energy, health, technology curriculum materials. B.S., Iona coll., 1950; M.A., Columbia U., 1951; Ed.D., 1958. Tchr. sci. public schs., NYC, 1951-58; prof. sci. edn. U. Hawaii, Honolulu, 1958—; sr. author in residence Encyc. Britannica Ednl. Corp., Chgo., 1967-68; cons. sci. and energy edn., 1960—; scholar-in-res., IBM, Atlanta, 1987. Fellow Am. Assn. Advancement Sci.; mem. AAUP, ACLU, Am. Fed. Tchrs., Assn. Edn. Tchrs. Sci., Council Elem. Sci. Intl., Hawaiian Acad. Sci., Hawaii Sci. Tchrs. Assn. NEA, Nat. Sci. Tchrs. Assn., Phi Delta Kappa. Home: 461 Hao St Honolulu HI 96821

CARR, DANIEL PAUL, b. Cranston, RI, Aug. 24, 1951, s. Daniel Paul and Emma Louise (Very) C.; m. Julia Ann Ferrarie, Apr. 17, 1982. Author: Li Po's Sandalwood Boat, 1975, Living in Fear, 1975, Notice the Star, 1976, Antediluvian Dream Songs, 1978, Transmissions of the Mist, 1979, The Ennead of Set-Heru, 1983, Mysteries of the Palaces of Water, 1985. BA, Clark U., 1974. Co- proptr. Four Zoas Night House, Boston and Ashuelot, N.H., 1971—; co-founder, ed. Four Zoas Press, Hardwick, Mass. and Boston, 1972-79; co-proptr. Golgono Letter Foundry, Boston, 1979-82, Ashuelot, N.H., 1982—. Mem. Guild Bookworkers, Am. Typecasters Fellowship. Home: 30 Main St Ashuelot NH 03441

CARR, GERALD FRANCIS, b. Pitts., Dec. 29, 1930; s. James Patrick and Hannay (Sweeney) C.; m. Irmengard Paula Rauch, June 12; children—Christopher James, Gregory Conrad. Author: Linguistic Method: Essays in Honor of Herbert Penzl, 1979. Contrbr. articles to profl. jnl. Ed.: (with others) The Signifying Animal: The Grammar of Man's Language and His Experience, 1981, Language Change, 1983. Wrkg. on grammar of Old Saxon, edition of articles on Semiotics. B.Ed., Duquesne U., Pitts., 1960-62, 65-68; teaching asst. U. Wis., Madison, 1962-65; prof. German, Eastern Ill. U., Charleston, 1968—. Mem. MLA, Linguistic Soc. Am., Am. Assn. Tchrs. German. Home: 1534 3d St 6 Charleston IL 61920

CARR, PAT, b. Grass Creek, WY, Mar. 13, 1932; d. Stanley and Beatrice (Parker) Moore; m. Jack Esslinger, June 4, 1955 (div. July 5, 1970); m. 2d Duane R. Carr, Mar. 26, 1971; children—Stephanie, Shelley, Sean, Jennifer. Author: The Grass Creek Chronicle, 1976, Bernard Shaw, 1976, Mimbres Mythology, 1979, The Women in the Mirror, 1977, Night of the Luminarias, 1986, In Fine Spirits, 1986; contrbr. stories Southern Rvw, Yale Rvw, Best Am. Short Stores, Kans. Qtly, others; contrbr. articles Western Humanities Rvw, Modern Fiction Studies, Modern Drama, Critique, New Scholar. BA, Rice U., 1954, MA, 1955; PhD,Tulane U., 1960. Asst. prof. Tex. So. Univ., Houston, 1956-58, New Orleans Univ., 1961-62, 65-69; prof. Univ. Tex., El Paso, 1969-79. Grantee NEH, 1973, Ark. Endowment for Humanities, Little Rock, 1985; recipient short fiction award, Iowa Schl. of Letters, 1977, Tex. Inst. Letters, 1978; Library of Congress Marc IV, 1970. Mem. IWWG, P&W. Address: Pinnacle Star Rt Elkins AR 72727

CARR, RICH, see Krutenat, Richard Carroll

CARRANCO, LYNWOOD, b. Samoa, CA, April 2, 1921; s. Filberto and Cecilia (Ysais) C.; m. Ruth Cannam, June 12, 1947; children: Robert, Donald. Author: Fundamentals of Modern English, 1963, rev ed, 1977, The Redwood Country: History, Language, and Folklore, 1971, (with John Labbe) Logging the Redwoods, 1975, (with Estle Beard) Geoncide and Vendetta: The Round Valley Wars of Northern California, 1981, The Redwood Lumber Industry, 1981, College of the Redwoods: The First Nineteen Years, 1985, The Redwood Country, 1986, (with Henry L. Soenson) Steam in the Redwoods, 1987, (with John Labbe) Logger Language: A Dictionary of the Lumber Industry. Contrbr of articles to jnls. AB, Humboldt State Coll (now U.), 1949; MA, Columbia U, 1951; grad. study U. of Southern Calif., 1959-60 and Ball State U., 1951; grad. study U. of Southern Calif., 1959-60 and Ball State U., Muncie, Ind., 1967-68; Ph. D., U. of Sarasota (Fla.), 1973. Public school tchr of languages, Arcata, Calif., 1951-56; asst prof, Humboldt State coll, 1956-58, assoc prof, 1959-64; assoc. prof, College of the Redwoods, Eureka, Calif., 1964-68, prof of English, 1968-82. Member: Humboldt County Historical Soc (pres, 1975), Redwood Council of English Tchrs (pres, 1964) Western Writers of America. Home: 2778 Buttermilk Ln Arcata CA 95521

CARRIE, JACQUES FELIX, b. Nimes, France, Aug. 5, 1939, came to U.S., 1959, s. Marc and Josephine (De Sicilia) C; m. Eva Tuyor, July 26, 1987. Author: The Bridge of Movie Producer Louis King (novel), 1981, Intrepid Visions (short stories), 1985, VV (novel), 1986. Wrkg. on novel. BSEE, Tex. A&M U., 1968. Sr. wrtr. Geophysical Systems Corp., Pasadena, Calif., 1981-82, Mattel Corp., Hawthorne, Calif., 1982-83, MAI Basic Four Co., Tustin, Calif., 1983-85, Ashton-Tate Co., Culver City, Calif., 1985, Hamilton/Avnet Co., Culver City, 1986—. Novel nom. Intl. Prize, Satire. Selected as guest wrtr. to represent U.S. in 6th Intl. Festival Humor & Satire, Com. for Culture, Gabrovo, Bulgaria, 1983. Mem. P&W, AFTRA, STC. Home: 430 S Westminster Ave 200 Los Angeles CA 90020

CARRIER, CONSTANCE VIRGINIA, b. New Britain, CT, July 29, 1908, d. Lucius Alonzo and Lillian Miriam (Jost) Carrier. Author: The Middle Voice, 1955, Poems of Propertius, 1961, Poems of Tibullus, 1967, The Angled Road, 1973; contrbr. to Five Roman Comedies, 1970, Complete Comedies of Terence, 1974, Aesopus Hodie, 1985; contrbr. poetry to mags. and lit jnls. Working on verse-renderings of Aesop's fables. BA, Smith Coll., 1929; MA, Trinity Coll., Hartford, Conn., 1942. Tchr. English, French and Latin, public schls., Conn., 1929-75; mem. summer staff Tufts Coll., 1964-72. Recipient Lamont award AAP, 1955. Address: 225 W Main St New Britain CT 06052

CARRINGTON, ELIZABETH ELLEN, b. Indpls., July 5, 1943; d. Herbert Wesp and Mildred Louise (Dean) Thomas; m. Robert Allen Carington, May 28, 1966 (div. May 20, 1987); children—Paul, Gail, Ryan, Adam. BS, Ind. State U., 1983. Reporter Ind. Statesman, Terre Haute, IN, 1980-83, Terra Haute Tribune/Star, 1985—; field interviewer Simmons Market Research Bur., N.Y.C., 1986—; cons. in advt., promotion, design of logos, mag. writing. Mem. Am. Marketing Assn. (publicity chmn. chpt. 1983). Home: 621 Woodland Dr Rockville IN 47872

CARRINGTON, GRANT CLARK, b. New Haven, June 4, 1938, s. Alfred Otis Carrington and Margaret Louise (Frey) Jackson. Novelist: Time's Fool, 1981; contrbr. articles to Is, Diversity, Woodwind, Thrust, Corpus Colossum, other publs.; contrbr. book rvws. to: Locus, New

Look Thrust, other publs.; Playwright: U.F.O.!, 1982, A Gentleman of Stratford, 1984, Topanga, 1985; contrbr. short stories to Amazing, The Arts and Beyond, Weirdbook, numerous other publs. BA, NYU, 1962; MA, U. FLA., 1970. Computer programmer U. FLA., Gainesville, 1976, Savannah River Ecology Lab, 1977-80; software engr., Westinghouse Co., Balt., 1980-85. Address: Box 320 Greenbelt MD 21218

CARROLL, JANE HAMMOND, b. Greenville, SC, May 15, 1946; d. Charles Kirby and Margaret Edwards (Cooper) Hammond; m. Robert Lindsay Carroll Jr., Feb. 3, 1968; children—Jane Gower, Robert Lindsay. Author: Intimate Moments, 1986, Grace, 1987. Wrkg. on book illustrations. BA, U.S.C., 1968. Wrtr., illustrator winston Derek Pubs., Nashville, NY, 1985-87; artist, exhibitor, merit states Atlanta Artists Club, 1984-87; gallery participant Rag, Ribbon, Rainbow, Atlanta and Phila., 1985-87. Mem. Natl. League Am. Pen Women, (exec. bd. Atlanta branch). Home: 2979 Majestic Circle Avondale Estates GA 30002

CARROLL, JUDITH ANN, b. Oswego, KS, Jan. 11, 1947; d. Byron David and Ruth Marcel (Thomas) Jones; m. John Daniel Carroll, Nov. 28, 1970; children—Katherine, Barbara, Gregory, Joseph. Columnist: Up the Family Tree, Neodesha Sun-Register, 1984-86, Cherryvale Gazette, 1985—, Girard Press, 1985, Cherryvale Citizen, 1985; contrbr. articles to mags. BS in Bus., Emporia State U., 1969. Exec. dir. Independence Arts Council, Kans., 1984-85; legal secy. Scovel, Emert, Heasty and Chubb, Independence, 1986—. Lit. chmn. Independence Arts Council Bd., 1986—. Mem. Kans. Authors Club (1st place for non-fiction 1985, hon. mention for fiction 1985). Home: Rt 2 Box 220-A Independence KS 67301

CARROLL, JONATHAN, b. NYC, Jan. 26, 1949; s. Sidney and June (Sillman) C.; m. Beverly Schreiner, June 19, 1971; Children: Ryder Pierce. Author: The Land of Laughs (novel), 1980, Voice of Our Shadow (novel), 1983, Bones of the Moon (novel), 1987. Contrbr of short stories to periodicals, including Transatlantic Review, Sport, Cimarron Review, Folio, Christian Sci Monitor, and Four Quarters; book reviews in St. Louis Globe-Democrat, Cleveland Plain Dealer. BA (cum laude), Rutgers U., 1971; MA, U. of Va., 1973. English tchr, North State Acad., Hickory, N.C., 1971-72; Eng. tchr, St. Louis (Mo) Country Day Schl, 1973-74; Engl. tchr, americam Intl Schl, Veinna, 1974—. Emily Clark Balch fellow in creative writing, U. of Va., 1972. Book of the Year citation from Washington Post, 1983, for Voice of Our Shadow. Address: c/o Ober 40 E 49th St New York NY 10017

CARROLL, PATRICIA L, b. Mineola, NY, Mar. 17, 1958; d. George J. and Barbara (Fitzgerald) Fuchs, m. Robert B. Carroll, Sept. 15, 1984. Contrbr. to books on nursing: Procedures, 1983, Immune Disorders, 1985, Respiratory Care Handbook, 1988; also contrbr. articles, commentary to nursing publs. A.A.S., SUNY-Upstate Med. Ctr., Syracuse, 1977; B.S., Charter Oak Coll., 1983; A.S., Greater Hartford Community Coll., 1984. Nurse, respiratory therapist, tchr., 1975-86; cons., Middletown, Conn., 1986—. Mem. numerous profl. nursing orgns. Home: 21 Keefe Lane Middletown CT 06457

CARROLL, THEODUS CATHERINE, b. Conway, PA, Sept. 26, 1928; d. Randolph Waite and Eleanor Marie (Scanlon) Foster; m. Francis Edwar Carroll, Nov. 3, 1948 (div.); children—Michael James, Randolph Francis. Columnist: Health Care Product News, 1966-75; author: (young adult novel) Evil is a Quiet Word, 1976; (children's books) Firsts Under the Wire, 1978, The Lost Christmas Star, 1979, Mystery of the Body Clocks, 1979. Contrbr. short stories to mags. including Ingenue, Datebook, Family Herald; rewriter adult plays, books, stories. Student Duquesne U., 1947-49, Carnegie Mellon U., 1947-49. Ed., Health Care Product News, New Canaan, CT, 1966-75, Hanson pub. Group, Stamford, CT, 1985—; sr. ed. Garrard Pub., New Canson, 1976-80. Home: 22B Umpawang Redding CT 06896

CARRUBBA, SANDRA J. MCPHERSON, b. Buffalo, Dec. 21, 1943, d. David and Ruth Elizabeth (Remington) McPherson; m. Joseph Carrubba, June 24, 1967; children—Lisamarie, Joanne P. Contrbr. articles to Nursery Days, The Young Crusader, Home Life, Animal Lovers' Mag., numerous other adult and juvenile publs., also genl. interest newspapers. BS in elem. edn., SUNY-Oswego, 1965. Tchr. Ken-Ton Schls., Kenmore, N.Y., 1965-69; freelance wrtr., Kenmore, 1975— stringer Western N.Y. Catholic Visitor, Buffalo, 1979-81; tchr. adult writing Carnegie Cultural Center, Tonowanda, N.Y., 1979-82. Mem. Natl. League Am. Pen Women, AAUW. Home: 86 Chalmers Ave Buffalo NY 14223

CARRUTH, GORTON VEEDER, b. Woodbury, CT, Apr. 9, 1925; s. Gorton Veeder and Margery Tracy Barrow (Dibb) C.; m. Gisele Leliet, Dec. 28, 1955; children: Gorton Veeder III, Hayden III, Christopher Leliet. Author: Encyclopedia of American Facts and Dates, 7th rev. ed., 1978; co-author: Where to Find Business Information, 1979, 2d ed., 1982, Oxford Am. Dictionary, 1980, The VNR Dictionary of Bus. and Fin., 1980, The Oxford Literary Guide to the United States, 1982, The Encyclopedia of Historic Places, 1984, The Complete Word Game Dictionary, 1984. PhB, U. Chgo., 1948; BA, Columbia U., 1950, MA, 1954. Editor ref. books Thomas Y. Crowell Co., 1954-63; exec. editor McGraw-Hill Book Co., 1963-68; editor-in-chief Funk & Wagnalls, 1968-71; pres. Morningside Assocs., Pleasantville, N.Y., 1971—. Home: Box 168 Pleasantville NY 10570

CARRUTH, HAYDEN, b. Waterbury, CT, Aug. 3, 1921; s. Gorton Veeder and Margery Tracy Barrow (Dibb) C.; m. Sara Anderson, Mar. 14, 1943; 1 dau., Martha Hamilton; m. Eleanore Ray, Nov. 29, 1952; m. Rose Marie Dorn, Oct. 28, 1961; 1 son, David Barrow II. Author: The Crow and the Heart, 1959, Journey to a Known Place, 1961, Norfolk Poems, 1962, Appendix A, 1963, North Winter, 1964, Nothing for Tigers, 1965, Contra Mortem, 1967, After the Stranger, 1965, For You, 1970, The Clay Hill Anthology, 1970, The Voice That is Great Within Us, 1970, The Bird Poem Book, 1970,, From Snow and Rock, from Chaos, 1973, Dark World, 1973, The Bloomingdale Papers, 1975, Loneliness, 1976, Aura, 1977, Brothers, I Loved You All, 1978, Almanach du Printemps ViVarois, 1979, Working Papers, 1982, The Mythology of Dark and Light, 1982, The Sleeping Beauty, 1982, If You Call This Cry a Song, 1983, Effluences from the Sacred Caves, 1983 Asphalt Georgics, 1984, The Oldest Killed Lake in North Am., 1985, Lighter Than Air Craft, 1986, Selected Poetry of Hayden Carruth, 1986, Sitting In: Selected Writings on Blues, Jazz, and Related Topics, 1986; mem. editorial bd.: Hudson Rvw, 1971—. AB, U. N.C., 1943; MA, U. Chgo., 1948. Editor-in-chief Poetry mag., 1949-50; assoc. editor U. Chgo. press, 1950-51; project administr. Intercultural Publs. Inc., NYC, 1952-53; poetry editor Harper's mag., 1977—; poet-in-res. Johnson State Coll., 1972-74. Recipient Annual Poetry award Brandeis U. 1959, Harriet Monroe Poetry prize U. Chgo. 1960, Vachel Lindsay prize, 1954, Bess Hokin prize, 1956, Levinson prize, 1958; Helen Bullis prize U. Seattle, 1962; Carl Sandburg prize, 1963; Emily Clark Balch prize, 1964; Shelley award PSA, 1978, Lenore Marshall prize, 1979. Fellow Bollingen Fdn, 1962, John Simon Meml. Guggenheim Fdn., 1965, 79, Mrs. Gary Whiting Fdn., 1986; NEA grantee, 1967, 74; Morton Zabel prize, 1968. Office: Dept Eng Syracuse U Syracuse NY 13210

CARSON, RONALD FRANK, Logan, UT, Sept. 15, 1947; s. Edwin and Verna Irene (Mertz) C.; m. Georgia Elaine Craig, June 14, 1969; 2 sons, Nicholas George, Colin Edwin. Author: Betrayed by F. Scott Fitzgerald, 1977 (paper, 1984), Truants, 1981, The News of the World, 1987; ed The Hotchkiss Alumni Mag, 1972-81; contrbr. Best of the South, 1986, Best American Short Stories, 1987. BA, U. Utah, 1970, MA, 1972. English tchr. the Hotchkiss Schl., Lakeville, Conn., 1971-81; instr. Univ. Utah/Extension, Salt Lake City, 1982-86; wrtr.-in-res., Ariz. State Univ., 1986-87; artist-in-ed., UT, ID, AK, 1982-88; creative wrtg. dept., Ariz. State Univ., 1987—. Fiction grantee Conn. Commn. on the Arts, 1978, NEA, 1985. Mem. AG, Park City Writers Conf., 1985—. Address: 2132 E Yale Dr Tempe AZ 85283

CART, DOROTHY CARIKER, b. Kingston, AR, Dec. 22, 1923; d. Howard E. and Sara Etta Garton; m. Ken Cariker, May 24, 1946 (de. 1970); children—Lynn Cariker Reeves, Kenneth Mark, Carla Cherie Blackshaw; m. 2d, Bob G. Cart, Sept. 6, 1974. Author 8 novels, 20 short stories; contrbr. short stories: Live Mag., other publs.; ed. Renal Reminiscences, 1986; poetry in anthologies, including Best New Poets of 1986. Wrkg. on sreenplay, novel. BBA, U. Okla., 1971. Ed. Central Div. News, Humble Oil Co., Oklahoma City, 1956-70. Served to cpl., USAF, 1944-46; U.S. and India. Mem. Okla. Wrtrs. Home: Rt 1 Box 164 A Binger OK 73009

CARTER, BEAR, see William Jay Carter

CARTER, CURTIS HAROLD, JR., b. Augusta, GA, May 19, 1939; s. Curtis Harold and Sara (Milligan) C.; m. Florence Broome, Sept. 12, 1958; Children—Mary Elizabeth Carter Brewer, Curtis H. Author: Charleston History Tour, 1968, Great Plans (Do-It-Yourself) Manuals (4), 1985. Contrbr. articles to newsletters, mags., corporate and co. image brochures including The Osmose Report, Weekend Gardener, others. Wrkg on corporate brochure. B.F.A., U. Ga., 1961. Recipient Governor's Travel award S.C. Dept. of Parks, 1968; Gold award Building Supply & Home Ctr. Mag., 1985, Silver award, 1985. Mem. IABC. Home: 102 Summit Dr Griffin GA 30223

CARTER, DARLE LYNN, b. Oakland, CA, Sept. 22, 1935; d. Edward William and Winifred Mae (Fox) Smith; m. Ross Westerlund Carter, Dec. 31, 1978; children—Ferryl Scott, Aaron Goertzen. Contrbr. poems to Our Twentieth Century's Greatest Poems, and American Poetry Anthology. BA, San Fran. State U., 1961; MA, Sonoma St. U., 1976. Tchr., California publ. schools, 1961-68, reading spclst., 1968-75. Home: 22200 Callayomi Rd Middletown CA 95461

CARTER, ERSKINE, b. Oxford, England, June 4, 1948; came to U.S., 1973; naturalized; s. Erskine and Verna (Andrews) C.; m. Christine (Evans), Jan. 7, 1984; 1 dau., Bryonie Anne. Contrbr. short stories, poems. to mags. Ed.: Ouroboros Mag., 1985d—. Wrkg on novels. B.A., Trinity Coll., 1978; M.A., U. Conn., 1986. Tchr. St. Edwards Sch., Vero Beach, FL, 1978-80, U. Conn., Storrs, 1981-87; assoc. prof. Black Hawk Coll., Moline, IL, 1987—. Home: 3216 13th Ave Rock Island IL 61201

CARTER, JARED, b. Elwood, IN, Jan. 10, 1939; s. Robert Alton and Cleva Lois (Hackett) Carter; m. Diane Haston, June 21, 1979; 1 daughter, Selene Burack Carter. Poet: Early Warning, 1979, Work, for the Night Is Coming, 1981, Fugue State, 1984, Pincushion's Strawberry, 1984, Millennial Harbinger, 1986. Author: (with photographer Darryl Jones) Indiana, 1984, (with Richard Balkin) A Writer's Guide to Book Publishing, 1977. BA, Goddard College, Plainfield, VT, 1969; student, Yale U., 1956-59, 1960-61. Journalist, Huntington, IN. Herald-Press, 1959-60; Kokomo, IN. Morning Times, 1966; ed. Bobbs-Merrill College Div., Indpls., 1969-76; wrtr., lectr. 1976—. Served as Spec. 4 in U.S. Army, 1962-64. Walt Whitman Award, Acad. of Am. Poets, NY, 1980; Fellowship, NEA, 1981; Guggenheim Fellowship, 1983. Mem. PEN Am. Center. Home: 1220 N State Ave Indpls IN 46201

CARTER, JOYCE LEE, (Peaches Stone), b. Chillicothe, TX, May 11, 1929; d. John D. and Katy Myrtle (Marlow) Tallant; widowed June 18, 1968; children—Carlee, Candy, David. Contrbr. poems and short stories to news jnls. and periodicals, including Star News and Senior Life, Inky Trails and Hoosier Challenger. Educated public schls. Missionary nurse and writer (Calif. and Japan), 1964—; counselor Joyce Carter's Open Christian Hs., Chula Vista, CA, 1964-83. Asst. ed., Senior Life, 1982-83. Home: 957 Agua Tibia Chula Vista CA 92011

CARTER, LAURA STEPHENSON, b. Princeton, NJ, Jan. 24, 1952; d. Kennard Frierson and Ann Katharine (Elmore) Stephenson; m. Geoffrey Corbin Carter, Sept. 4, 1976; children—Sarah, Emily. Contrbr. scripts for corp. slide presentations, press releases to local newspapers. Editor newsletter for Edmund Niles Huycle Preserve. BA, Upsala Coll., 1974. Asst. to chief Fed. Reserve Bank of N.Y., 1974-80. Home: 81 Oakview Terr Short Hills NJ 07078

CARTER, LIANE KUPFERBERG, b. Flushing, NY, July 21, 1954; d. Jesse Michael and Joan Florence Shiller) Kupferberg; m. Marc David Carter, May 31, 1981. Contrbr. (fiction, reviews, articles) to Cosmopolitan, The Worcester Telegram, New Directions for Women, Washington Market Rvw, Jewish World, The Villager, Womensports; wrkg. on a novel and collection of short stories. BA Brandeis U., 1976; MA NYU., 1981. Publicity Assist. William Morrow & Co. (NYC), 1978-79; Publicist-copywrtr. Pocket Books (NYC), 1979-80; freelance publicist, 1980-82; director, publicity and promo. Pilgrim Press (NYC), 1982-84; freelance wrtr. 1984—. Mem. Wmn. in Commun., Inc. Home: 7 Lexon Pl Scarsdale NY 10583

CARTER, MARY ARKLEY, b. Coos, Bay, OR; d. Robert Pickering and Elizabeth May (Holzlin) Arkley; children: William P. Lyon Carter, Robert A. Lyon Carter. Author: (novels) A Fortune in Dimes, 1963; The Minutes of the Night, 1965; La Maestra, 1973; A Member of the Family, 1974; Tell Me My Name, 1975; contrbr. rvws., articles and columns to N.Y. Times, Holiday, Vanity Fair, stories to lit mags, Redbook, McCall's, Sat. Eve. Post, others. Student U. Oreg., Pitzer Coll., Claremont, Cal. Mem vis. faculty Boston U., 1971-73, 78, 80-81, acting dir. creative writing, spring 1981; wrtr.-in-residence Coll. William and Mary, 1979-80; dir. creative writing U. Ariz., Tucson, 1981—. Resident fellow MacDowell Colony, 1972-85, Va. Ctr. for Creative Arts, 1972-73, Ossabaw Fdn, Ga., 1973, Foundation Karolyi, France, 1974-77; NEA fellow, 1986. Mem. PEN, AWP (program dirs. steering com.), AAUP. Address: Eng Dept Mod Lang Bldg U AZ Tucson AZ 85721

CARTER, RICHARD, b. NYC, Jan. 24, 1918; s. Samuel J. and Alice (Kulka) C.; m. Gladys Chasins, Oct. 20, 1945; children: Nancy Jane, John Andrew. Author: The Man Who Rocked the Boat, 1956, The Doctor Business, 1958, The Gentle Legions, 1961, Your Food and Your Health, 1964, Breakthrough: The Saga of Jonas Salk, 1966, Superswine, 1967, (with Curt Flood) The Way It Is, 1971, (under pseudonym Tom Ainslie) The Compleat Horseplayer, 1966, Ainslie's Jockey Book, 1967, Ainslie's Complete Guide to Thoroughbred Racing, 1968, 79, 86, The Handicapper's Handbook, 1969, Theory and Practice of Handicapping, 1969, Ainslie's Complete Guide to Harness Racing, 1970, Ainslie's Complete Hoyle, 1975, Ainslie's Encyclopedia of Thoroughbred Handicapping, 1978, How to Gamble in a Casino, 1979, (with Bonnie Ledbetter) The Body Language of Horses, 1980. BA, Coll. City N.Y., 1938. Music editor Billboard mag., 1940-46; staff organizer N.Y. Newspaper Guild, 1946-47; writer N.Y. Daily Mirror, 1947-49; N.Y. Daily Compass, 1949-52; contrbr. mags., 1952—; pres. Millwood Publs., Inc., 1971—. Served with USAAF, 1942-45; PTO. Recipient George Polk Meml. award, 1952. Mem. AG, Nat. Assn. Sci. Writers. Address: 165 Pinesbridge Rd Ossining NY 10562

CARTER, WILLIAM JAY, (Bear), b. Blackburn, OK, May 16, 1921; s. John Ernest and Mary Katherine (Schumacher) C.; m. L'Aleen Gloria Kramer, Sept. 12, 1943 (div. Dec. 16, 1986); children—Angella Zepeda, Dr. John, Dr. Joseph, William Jay, Walter. Author: Pediatric Dentistry Lab. Procedures, 1956, Dental Collectibles & Antiques, 1984; pub. Dental Jnl (monthly); contrbr. over 60 articles to sci. press. B.S., Okla. State U., 1943; D.D.S., U. Mo., 1946; M.S., Georgetown U., 1951. Asst. dental research USN, Wash., 1949-51, dir., 1951-54; prof. dentistry U. Mo., Kansas City, 1954-60; private practice, Kansas City, 1960-70, Overland Pk., Kans, 1970-80. Served to lt., USN, 1942-54. Mem. ADA, Greater Kans. City Dental Soc., Kans. Dental Assn., Am. Soc. History Dentistry. Am. Assn. Dental Eds. Home: 7612 W 95 St A Overland Park KS 66212

CARTLAND, BOB, see Heyment, George

CARUS, A. ROSS, see Gallant, James T.

CARVER, RAYMOND, b. Clatskanie, OR, May 25, 1938; s. Clevie Raymond and Ella Beatrice (Casey) C.; m. Maryann Burk, June 7, 1957 (div. Oct. 1982); children: Christine LaRae, Vance Lindsay. Author: (poetry) Near Klamath, 1968, Winter Insomnia, 1970, At Night The Salmon Move, 1976, Where Water Comes Together with Other Water, 1985, Ultramarine, 1986, In a Marine Light; (short stories) Put Yourself in My Shoes, 1974, Will You Please Be Quiet, Please?, 1976, The Furious Seasons, 1977, What We Talk About When We Talk About Love, 1981, Cathedral, 1983, Where I'm Calling From: New and Selected Stories, 1988; essays, poetry, short stories, Fires, 1983. AB, Humbc'dt State U., 1963, MFA, U. Iowa, 1966. Lectr. creative writing U. Calif., Santa Cruz, 1971-72, vis. prof. English, Berkeley, 1972-73; vis. lectr. Writers' Workshop, U. Iowa, 1973-74; mem. faculty writing program Goddard Coll., 1977-78; vis. disting. writer U. Tex., El Paso, 1978-79; prof. English Syracuse (N.Y.) U., 1980-83. Recipient Strauss Living award AAIAL, 1983—; NEA fellow in poetry, 1971; fellow in fiction, 1980; Wallace Stegner fellow, 1972-73; Guggenheim fellow, 1979-80. Mem. PEN, AG. Home: 602 B St Pt Angeles WA 98362

CARY, EMILY PRITCHARD, b. Pitts., Sept. 6, 1931; d. Ernest Markwood and Adelaide Elizabeth (Stuart) Pritchard; m. Boyd Balford Cary Jr., Sept. 28, 1953; children—Matthew Roger and Roland Mylles. My High Love Calling, 1977, The Ghost of Whitaker Mountain, 1979 (both transl. Ger. Dutch and Danish, 1984); Our Psychic World; articles in natl. periodicals inclg. NY Times, Phila. Inquirer, Pitts. Press, Washington Times, Washington Star, Cleve. Plain Dealer. BA, U. Pa., 1952; MA, Kean Coll., 1975; doctoral student in ed./communication, U. Md. Tchr. vocal music Pittsford Central schls., NY, 1967-71; tchr. pub. schls., Millburn-Short Hills, NJ, 1971-79; music reviewer Tchr. Mag., 1972-81, and feature writer Jnl. Newspapers, Washington, 1981—; tchr. of gifted, pub schls., Fairfax County, Va, 1979—. Bd. dirs. Intl. Bell Soc., 1986-88. Mem. NEA, Alpha Delta Kappa, Phi Delta Kappa. Finalist Tchr. in Space, NASA. Address: 12013 Gary Hill Dr Fairfax VA 22030

CARY, JAMES DONALD, b. Douglas, AZ, Oct. 7, 1919; s. Leon Barker and Ruth Fauver (Dunlap) C.; m. Norma Frances Goben, Dec. 18, 1942; 1 son, James Christopher. Author: Japan Today: Reluctant Ally, 1962, Tanks and Armor in Modern Warfare, 1966. Contrbr. articles to mags. including Ariz. Highways, Ariz. Sportsman, Am. Mercury. Wrkg. on novel, And Then Came the Puritan. B.A. in Jnlsm., U. Ariz., 1942; M.S., Northwestern U., 1948. Reporter Miami Beach Evening Sun. 1945, Miami Daily News, 1945-46; state house corr. Ariz. Times, Phoenix, 1947-49; reporter, desk ed. AP, Phoenix, Tokyo, Washington, 1949-65; diplomatic-White House corr. Copley News Service, Washington, 1965-73, Washington bur. chief, 1973-78, sr. corr., 1978-81, retired. Served to Capt. U.S. Army, 1941-46. Recipient awards for feature news Ariz. Press Club. Phoenix, 1951, 53, Ring of Truth award Copley Press, Washington, 1968, 72; Disting. Service award Brigham Young U., Provo, 1983-84. Mem. Sigma Delta Chi, Fla. Freelance Wrtrs. Home: 269 SW 29th Ave Delray Beach FL 33445

CASADA, JAMES ALLEN, b. Bryson City, NC, Jan. 28, 1942; s. Commodore Andrew and Anna Lou (Moore) C.; m. Elizabeth Ann Fox, June 3, 1967; 1 dau., Natasha Lea. Author: Dr. David Livingstone and Sir Henry Morton Stanley, 1976, Sir Harry H. Johnston: A Bio-Bibliographical Study, 1977, Recent Trends and Interpretations in African and Afro-American History, 1978. Editor: (series) Themes in European Expansion: Exploration, Colonization, and the Impact of Empire, 1981—; contrbg. editor: Sporting Classics mag., 1983—; contrbg. ed., Fly Fishing Heritage and The Fly-fisher, 1987—; columnist, Virginia Fins and Feathers, 1986—; outdoor columnist, The Herald (Rock Hill, SC), 1986—; editorial bd. Premier Press,

1984—, Briar Patch Press, 1985—. BA, King Coll., Bristol, Tenn., 1964; MA, Va. Polytechnic Inst. & State U., 1968; PhD, Vanderbilt U., 1971. Instr., Hargrave Mil. Acad., Chatham, Va., 1964-67; prof. history Winthrop Coll., Rock Hill, S.C., 1971—; gen. series ed. Garland Pub., N.Y.C., 1980—. Named Disting. Prof., Winthrop Coll., 1983; John Hay Whitney Opportunity fellow, 1971; fellow U. Edinburgh, 1977; grantee Am. Philo. Soc., 1977, 79, 83. Fellow Royal Geog. Soc.; mem. OWAA, Phi Alpha Theta, Phi Kappa Phi. Home: 1250 Yorkdale Dr Rock Hill SC 29730

CASE, L.L., see Lwein, Leonard C.

CASEWIT, CURTIS W., b. Mannheim, Ger., March 21, 1927; came to U.S. in 1948; s. Theodor and Elsa C.; m. Charlotte Fischer-Lamberg, Feb 1954 (div.); children: Carla, Stephen, Niccolo. Author: Accent on Treason, 1954, Ski Racing: Advice by the Experts, 1963, 2d ed, 1969, Adventure in Deepmore Cave, 1965, How to Get a Job Overseas, 1965, 3d ed, 1985, Ski Fever: How to Master the Fastest-Growing Winter Sport, 1965, United Air Lines Guide to Western Skiing, 1967, (with Bob Beattie) Bob Beattie's Learn to Ski, 1967, (with Richard Pownall) The Mountaineering Handbook: An Invitation to Climbing, 1968, Ski Racer, 1968, The Hiking-Climbing Handbook, 1969, The Adventures of Snowshoe Thompson, 1970, The Skier's Handbook: Advice from the Experts, 197f1, Overseas Jobs: The Ten Best Countries, 1972, A Guide to Western Skiing, 1972, Mountain Troopers: The Story of the Tenth Mountain Division, 1972, publ. as The Saga of the Mountain Soldiers, 1981, Colorado, 1973, (transl) Karl Schranz, The Kaarl Schranz Seven-Day Ski System, 1974, Freelance Writing: Advice form the Pros, 1974, rev ed, 1985, Anerica's Tennis Book, 1975, Skiing Colorado: A Complete Guide to Anerica's Number One Ski State, 1975, The Mountain World, 1976, The Complete Book of Mountain Sports, 1978, The Stop Smoking Book for Teens, 1980, Freelance Photography: Advice fromthe Pros, 1980, The Graphology Handbook, 1980, Making A Living in the Fine Arts: Advice from the Pros, 1981, The Deary: A Complete Guide to Journal Writing, 1981, The Complete Guide to Stopping Smoking, 1983, Foreign Jobs: The Most Popular Countries, 1984. Colorado: Off the Beaten Path, 1987. Contrbr of short stories and articles to more than 100 newspapers and magazines in seven countries. Attended Florence (Italy) Language School, 1933-38; u. of Denver and U. of Colo. Freelance writer, 1964—. May Dept. Store, Denver, bookbuyer, 1959-64; teacher of creative writing, Denver Opportunity Schl, 1961—; instr. in non-credit writing courses, U. of Colo, Denver, 1965—. Translator in German, French, and Italian. Member: Travel Journalists Guild, Soc. of Magazine Writers, Amer. Soc. of Jrnlsts and Authors, Colorado Authors League, Colorado Mountain Club. Short story contest award, Writer's Digest, 1955; Edgar Allan Poet (Edgar) award, Mystery Writers of America, 1956, for best book reviewing; Dutton award for articles published in Best Articles of 1964 and Best Articles of 1965. Military service: French Army, 1940-43, British Army, interpreter, 1945-47; became sergeant. Home: Box 19039 Denver CO 80219

CASEY, GERALD WAYNE, b. Pangburn, ARm Jan. 1, 1940; s. Max and Ruth (Edwards) C.; m. Bettye Ritchie, Dec. 11, 1960; children—Brian, Laura Greta. Author: Thou Shalt Worship the Lord Thy God, 1969, God and Government, 1972. Contrbr. articles to Del. English Jnl. Wrkg on profl. articles in English edn. B.A., Harding U., 1961, M.A.T., 1965; postgrad. U. Del., 1981-86. English tchr. Red Clay Consolidated Sch. Dist., Wilmington, DE, 1965-86, coord. of English, 1986—. Named Outstanding Secondary Educators of Am., 1974. Mem. NCTE, NEA (life), Del. Assn. Tchrs. English, Del. Assn. Sch. Adminstrs. Home: 12 Gates Circle Hockessin DE 19707

CASEY, JOHN DUDLEY, b. Worcester, MA, Jan. 18, 1939, s. Joseph Edward and Constance (Dudley) C.; m. Jane Barnes, June 17, 1967 (div. 1981); children—Maud, Eleanor; m. 2d, Rosamond Pinchot Pittman, June 26, 1982; 1 child—Clare. Author: An American Romance, 1977, Testimony & Demeanor, 1979; contrbr. stories and articles to The New Yorker, Sports Illustrated, Esquire, Ploughshares, numerous others. BA, Harvard U., 1962, LLB, 1965; MFA, U. Iowa, 1968. Assoc. prof. U. Va., Charlottesville, 1972—. Adviser Fiction Syndicate, Fiction Network, San Francisco, 1982—, wrtr.-in-residence comm. St. Albans Schl., Washington, 1982—. Guggenheim fellow, 1979-80, NEA fellow, 1982; recipient Friends of Am. Wrtrs. prize, Chgo., 1980. Home: 1326 Rugby Rd Charlottesville VA 22903

CASHEN, ERIC, see Darling, William Ritchie

CASO, ADOLPH, b. Naples, Italy (b. U.S. citizen), Jan. 7, 1934, came to U.S. 1947; s. Ralph and Prisca (De Luca); div.; children—Richard, Robert, Liana. B.A., Northeastern U., 1957; M.A., Harvard, 1964. Dir. bi-lingual dept. pub. schls., Waltham, Mass., 1964-82; ed. and pub. Branden Pub. Co., Brookline, Mass., 1982—. Pres., Dante Univ. of Am. Found., Weston, Mass., 1976. Recipient Harvard Fellowship, 1962, Fulbright Fellowship, 1967, Cavaliere award Republic of Italy, 1978. Home: 158 Hickory Rd Weston MA 02193

CASPER, LEONARD RALPH, b. Fond du Lac, WI, July 6, 1923: s. Louis and Caroline (Eder) C.; m. Linda Velasquez-Ty, June 2, 1956; children: Gretchen Gabrielle, Kristina Elise. Author: Robert Penn Warren: The Dark and Bloody Ground, 1960, The Wayward Horizon: Essays on Modern Philippine Literature, 1964, New Writing from the Philippines: A Critique and Anthology, 1966, A Lion Unannounced: 12 Stories and a Fable, 1970; editor: Six Filipino Poets, 1955; editor: With T. A. Gullason) The World of Short Fiction: An International Collection, 1962; editor: Modern Philippine Short Stories, 1962; contbg. editor: Panorama, Manila, 1954-61, Drama Critique, 1959-62, Solidarity Manila, 1966-78, Literature East and West, 1969-81, Aquila, 1975—; poetry in lit mags and rvws. BA, U. Wis., 1948, MA, 1949, PhD, 1953. Served with F.A., AUS, 1943-46. Stanford creativing writing fellow, 1951-52; Bread Loaf creative writing scholar, 1961; research grantee ACLS-Social Sci. Research Council, 1965; grantee Asia Soc., 1965; research travel grantee Am. Philo. Soc., 1968-69; Natl. Council on Arts award, 1970. Mem. Natl. Cath. Playwrights Circle. Home: 54 Simpson Dr Saxonville MA 01701

CASSADY, MARSH GARY, b. Johnstown, PA, June 12, 1936; s. Clarence and Hazel (Spahn) Cassady; m. Pat Mizer (dec.); children—Kathi, Kim, David, Beth, Heather. Author: Theatre: A View of Life, 1982, Songs of My Soul, 1984, Playwriting Step by Step, 1985, Characters in Action, 1985, The Book of Scenes for Acting Practice, 1985, Storms of Meaning, 1986, Melinda: A Survivor, 1987. BA Otterbein Coll.; MA and PhD Kent State. Mem. San Diego Writers/ Ed. Guild (pres. 1987), Natl. Wrtrs. Club, DG. Home: 8455 Kingsland Rd San Diego CA 92115

CASSELL, DANA KAY, b. Hornell, NY, d. Robert William and Mayadell Louise (Reubens) Amacher; m. Leslie John Cassell, Jan. 14, 1967 (d. June 25, 1977); children—William, Denise, Jody, Robert; m. Donald Thomas Cuddy, July 2, 1983. Author: How to Advertise and Promote Your Retail Store, 1983, Making Money with Your Home Computer, 1984; publ. more than 1100 articles in more than 150 publications. Copywriter Sta. WTOC-TV, Savannah, Ga., 1965-67; ins. agt. Liberty Natl Life Ins. Co., Savannah, Ga., 1967-70; dist. mgr. LaSalle Extension U., Fla., 1972; mgr. Stuart Domestic Service (Fla.), 1974-75; pres. Cassell Communications Inc., Ft. Lauderdale, Fla. 1977—. Served with USAF, 1960-61. Mem. Natl. Writers Club, Fla. Freelance Writers Assn. (founder 1982, exec. dir. 1982—), Natl. Assn. Female Execs., Fla. Mag. Assn., ASJA, AG, COSMEP, American Consultants League, Natl. Assn. of Ind. Publishers (advisory bd). Mensa. Office: Box 9844 Fort Lauderdale FL 33310

CASSELLS, CYRUS CURTIS, b. Dover, DE, May 16, 1957; s. Cyrus Curtis Jr. and Mary Isabel Williston C. Author: The Mud Actor, 1982 (Natl. Poetry Series award); trans: To the Cypress Again and Again (Salvador Espriu); contrbr. poems, translations and rvws. to lit mags: Callaloo, So. Rvw, Seneca Rvw, Translation, Sequoia, Quilt, Shankpainter. BA in Communications, Stanford U., 1979. Fellow Mass. Artists Fdn., Mass. Arts Council, 1985; NEA grantee, 1986. Mem PEN, PSA. Address: 116B Pembroke St Boston MA 02118

CASSIE, see Fox, Catherine Mary

CASSILL, KARILYN, (KAY), b. IA; m. R. V. Cassill; 2 sons, 1 dau. Author: The Complete Handbook for Freelance Writers, 1981, Twins: Nature's Amazing Mystery, 1982; contrbg. ed.: Foxy Lady Mag.; contrbr. poetry, fiction to N.Am. Rvw, Quixote, Iowa Poetry Day Annual, others; contrbr. articles to N.Y. Times Syndicate, Christian Sci. Monitor, numerous other newspapers and mags.; spcl. corr. People mag., 1975—. Wrkg. on novel, television and radio scripts. BA with honors in English, U. Iowa, 1953; postgrad. Academie de la Grande Chaumier, Paris, 1956, New Schl. Social Research, NYC, 1960-67, U. Iowa, 1965-70; mem. Iowa Wrtrs. Workshop. Research asst. edn. and arts div. Ford Fdn., NYC; exec. sec., bd. dirs. AWP; lectr. Providence Coll., U. R.I.; interviewer ASJA workshops; cons. in field; judge Va. Commonwealth U. poetry contest, 1974. Founder and pres., The Twins Fdn., 1983—. Recipient Martha Foley Distinctive Short Stories award, 1976, Penney-Missouri Journalism award, 1975, Iowa Poetry Day award. Mem. ASJA, AG, AWP, Women in Communications, New Eng. Woman's Press Assn., Overseas Press Club, Intl. Assn. Bus. Communicators, Am. Med. Wrtrs. Assn. Address: 22 Boylston Ave Providence RI 02906

CASSILL, RONALD VERLIN, b. Cedar Falls, IA, May 17, 1919; s. Howard E. and Mary (Glosser) C.; m. Karilyn Kay Adams, Nov. 23, 1956; children—Orin, Erica, Jesse. Author: Eagle on the Coin, 1950, Clem Anderson, 1961, Pretty Leslie, 1963, The President, 1964, The Father, 1965, The Happy Marriage, 1966, La Vie Passionnee of Rodney Buckthorne, 1968, In An

Iron Time, 1969, Doctor Cobb's Game, 1970, The Goss Women, 1974, Hoyt's Child, 1976, After Goliath, 1985, also short stories; editor: Norton Anthology of Short Fiction, 1977, Labors of Love, 1980, Flame, 1980. BA, U. Iowa, 1939, MA, 1947. Tchr. Writers Workshop, U. Iowa, 1948-52, 60-66; prof. Brown U., 1966—; reviewer for N.Y. Times, Book Week, Chgo. Sun Times. Served to 1st lt. AUS, 1942-46. Recipient Rockefeller grant, 1954, Guggenheim grant, 1968; Atlantic "First" prize, 1947, O. Henry Prize Stories, 1956. Mem. AWP (organizer, president 3 years), Phi Beta Kappa. Home: 22 Boylston Ave Providence RI 02906

CASSINGHAM, RANDY C., b. Burbank, CA, April 1959; m. Michele Ann Wolf, July 12, 1986. Author: The Dvorak Keyboard, 1986. BA, Humboldt State U., 1985. Ed., Dvorak Developments Newsletter, Upland, CA, 1985—; pub. and ed. Freelance Communications, Upland, 1985—. Mem. COSMEP. Office: Box 1895 Upland CA 91785

CASTANEDA, CARLOS, b. Sao Paulo, Brazil, Dec. 25, 1931; s. C. N. and Susana (Aranha) C. Author: The Teachings of Don Juan: A Yaqui Way of Knowledge, 1968, A Separate Reality: The Phenomenology of Special Consensus, 1971, Journey to Ixtlan, 1974, Tales of Power, 1975, The Second Ring of Power, 1977, The Eagle's Gift, 1982. BA, U. Calif. at Los Angeles, 1962, MA, 1964, PhD, 1970. Address: U CA Press 2223 Fulton St Berkeley CA 94720

CASTEEL, BETTE, b. Ft. Wayne, IN, Nov. 27. 1920; d. John Graham and Ruth Rebecca (Roebuck) Dickson; m. Robert Earl Casteel, Feb. 26, 1945; 1 child, Douglas. Author: The Roebuck Family in America, 1969; Edwards Heirs' Index, 1979; Edwards—Who, Was, Where, When, 1983. Student Duluth State Tchrs. Coll., 1939-42, U. N.Mex., 1956-57, 59-60, 61-62. Profl. potter, Albuquerque, 1960—; propr. antique shop, Albuquerque, 1976—. Home: N Star Rt Box 1121 Corrales NM 87048

CASTILLO, RAFAEL C., b. San Antonio, TX, Dec. 30, 1950; s. Jose and Rosa (Cruz) Castillo; m. Hope Rodriguez, Nov. 20, 1972. Founding Editor: Palo Alto Review; assoc. editor: Saguaro; adv. editor, English Literature; contrbr. to Imagine Jnl, Arizona Qtly, Nuestro, New Mexico Humanities Rvw, other lit jnls. BA St. Mary's U., 1975; MA U. of Texas, 1977. Teacher/writer Northside Independent Schl. Dist. (San Antonio, TX), 1981-85; prof./wrtr. Palo Alto Coll. (San Antonio), 1985—; wrtr.-in-residence, TX Commn. on the Arts, 1981-82; editor ViAztlan Journal (San Antonio), 1982—. Mem. TX Assn. of Chicanos in Education. Sp4, US Army, 1970-76, TX. English Journal Writing Award, NCTE, 1985. Mem. NCTE Task Force on Racism and Bias in Literature, National Hispanic Wrtrs. Gld. Home: 246 Chesswood San Antonio TX 78228

CASTRO, JAN GARDEN, b. St. Louis, June 8, 1945; d. Harold and Estelle (Fischer) Garden; 1 son, Jomo Jemal. Contrbr: San Francisco Rvw of Books, 1983; co-founder, dir. Duff's Poetry Series, St. Louis, 1975-81; founder, dir., River Styx P. M. Series, St. Louis, 1981-83; editor River Styx Mag., St. Louis, 1976-86; author: books include Mandala of the Five Senses, 1975, The Art and Life of Georgia O'Keeffe, 1985, co-ed., Margaret Atwood: Vision & Forms, 1988. Student Cornell U., 1963-65; BA in English, U. Wis., 1967; cert. in pub. Radcliffe Coll., 1967; MAT, Washington U., St. Louis, 1981. Life cert. tchr. in secondary English, speech, drama and social studies, Mo. Tchr., writer, St. Louis, 1970—; lectr. Lindenwood Coll., 1981—; exec. dir. Big River Assn., St. Louis, 1980-85. Mem. University City (Mo.) Arts and Letters Commn., 1983. Mem. MLA. Home: 7420 Cornell Ave St. Louis MO 63130

CASWELL, DONALD EUGENE, b. Miami, FL, Feb. 20, 1948; s. Eugene Theodore and Thelma Rebecca (Dyer) C.; m. Julia Sullivan, Feb. 28, 1976 (div. Dec. 1, 1979); 1 child—Dugan Sullivan Caswell; m. 2d, Kathleen Mickleberry, Mar. 15, 1985. Author poetry: Watching the Sun Go Down, 1977, A Nail in My Boot, 1982; ed. Apalachee Quarterly, 1976-77. BA, Fla. State U., 1977; MA, U. Fla., 1979. Dir., Poets-in-the-prisons, Raiford, FL, 1975; poet-in-classroom Poets in the School, Tallahassee, 1976-77; instr. Fort Valley State Coll., Fort Valley, GA, 1980, 84, Fla. State U., Tallahassee, 1981-82, Fla. A & M, Tallahassee, 1984—; dir. Anhinga Press, Tallahassee, 1981—. Mem. AAP. Office: Box 10423 Tallahassee FL 32302

CATALA, RAFAEL ENRIQUE, b. Las Tunas, Cuba, Sept. 26, 1942; came to U.S., 1961; s. Rafael Enrique and Caridad de las Mercedes (Gallardo) C. Author: Caminos/Roads, 1973; Circulo cuadrado, 1974; Ojo sencillo/Triqui-traque, 1974; Copulantes, 1980, rev. edit., 1985; Cienciapoesia, 1986, Para una lectura americana del barraco mexicano: Sor Juana Y Siguenza-y-Gongora, 1987; (with others) Cinco aproximaciones a la literatura hispoanoamericana, 1977; (with J. D. Anderson) Index of American Periodical Verse, 1981—; ed. Romanica, 1973-75; co-ed. Soles emellis, 1983; contrbr. to N.Y. Times, Ideologies & Lit., Revista Iberoamericana, Impacto, Critica, Dialogos, Wrtrs. Workshop, Hoy, Latin Am. Lit. Rvw, numerous others, also chaps. in books. BA, NYU, 1970, MA, 1972, PhD, 1982. Instr. Lafayette Coll., Easton Pa., 1976-78, asst. prof., 1985-87; asst. prof. Seton Hall U., South Orange, N.J., 1983-84; dir. Racata Lit. Workshop, CUNY, spring 1983. Penfield fellow NYU, 1975; Cintas Fnd. fellow, 1984-85. Mem. MLA, N.E. MLA, Intl. Inst. Iberoam. Lit., Am. Assn. Tchrs. Spanish and Portuguese, Latin Am. Studies Assn. Home: Box 38 New Brunswick NJ 08903

CATES, EDWARD WILLIAM, b. Manchester, NH, Mar. 11, 1952, s. William and Helen Mary (Niemiec) C. Author: Geopolitics, 1979, Remember Your Dreams (libretto), 1983; ed. Small Moon Intl., 1974-78. Wrkg. on translations from Polish. BA in English Lit., Boston U., 1974. Social worker Boston Center for Older Americans, 1973-75, Boston Family Service Assn., 1975-77; daycare tchr. various schls., Mass., 1977-84; asst. tchr. English as second lang., IndoChinese Refugee Assn., Somerville, Mass., 1985—; wrtr., reviewer Am. Friends Service Com., Cambridge, Mass., 1983—. Grantee Mass. Council for Arts, Coordinating Council Lit. Mags., 1974-78; Mass. Fdn. for Arts and Humanities poetry fellow, 1977; recipient Best of Small Presses award, Pushcart Prize, 1978-79. Mem. New Eng. Wrtrs. for Survival, New Eng. Poetry Club. Home: 78 Summer St Sommerville MA 02143

CATHCART, MARGARET E., b. San Diego, Aug. 16, 1945, d. Harry I. and Margaret (Eller) Biszmaier; m. John G. Cathcart, May 22, 1971. Author: Guidelines for Contractor-Prepared Publications, 1984, Guidelines for Processing Publications, 1984; contrbr. articles to tech. and profl. publs. BA, San Diego State U., 1967. Tech. wrtr., ed. Naval Electronics Lab., San Diego, 1968-70; tech. wrtr., ed. Naval Undersea Ctr., San Diego, 1970-73, mgr. reports group, 1973-77; mgr. reports br. Naval Ocean Systems Ctr., San Diego, 1977-79, mgr. publ. div., 1979—. Mem. Soc. Tech. Communication. Home: 5370 Wilshire Dr San Diego CA 92116

CATHERWOOD, C. CUMMINS, see Morrow, William L.

CAULFIELD, CARLOTA, b. Havana, Cuba, Jan. 16, 1953, came to U.S., 1981, naturalized, 1987; d. Francis and Ada (Rob) Caulfield; m. Servando Gonzalez, May, 1974; 1 son, Franco. Author: Fanaim, 1984, Sometimes I Call Myself childhood, 1985, Oscuridad Divina, 1985, El Tiempo Es una Mujer que Espera, 1986, 34th Street and Other Poems, 1987. B.A. Instituto del Vedado, 1974; M.A. in History, Havana U., 1979; M.A. in Spanish, San Francisco State U., 1986. Ed., researcher Ministry of Culture, Havana, 1975-80; Spanish tutor, 1981; lectr. San Francisco State U., 1983-85; ed., pub. Ediciones el Gato Tuerto, San Francisco, 1984—. Recipient Honorable Mention, Mairena, 1983, CINTAS fellowship, 1987-88. Mem. Intl. PEN, Gruppo Internazionale di Lettura, MLA, Poetry Assn. Home: 205 16th Ave 6 San Francisco CA 94118

CAVAIANA, MABEL, b. Manley, IA, Sept. 12, 1919; d. Bret G. and Ida (Hall) Sniffin; m. Charles Cavaiana, April 14, 1950. Author: The Low Cholesterol Cookbook, 1972, (with Audrey Ellis) Farmhouse Kitchen, 1973, (with Muriel Urbashich) Simplified Quantity Recipes: Nursing-Convalescent Homes and Hospitals, 1974, rev ed, 1986, The High-Fiber Cookbook, 1977,(with Urbashich and Frances Nielsen) Simplified Quantity Regional Recipes, 1979, (with Urbashich and Nielsen) Simplified Quantity Ethnic Recipes, 1980, Low Cholesterol Cuisine, 1981. The New Diabetic Cookbook, 1985, The High-Fiber Diabetic Cookbook, 1987. B. Sci., Iowa State U., 1940; grad study at St. Xavier's Coll., Chicago. Registered dietitian; in restaurant mngmnt, Chicago, 1940-61; dietitian, U.S. Army Research Center, Chicago, 1961-63; dietitian, U.S. Fook Service Center, Menu Planning Div, Chicago, 1963-71, Army rep. on Armed Forces Recipe Service Com, 1967-71. Mem bd trustees, Oak Lawn Public Library, 1968-71; mem bd, Wadena Public Library, 1980-85. Consultant to nursing homes and programs for the elderly, 1974-86. Home: Box 66 Wadena IA 52169

CAVALIERI, GRACE, b. Trenton, NJ, Oct. 3, 1932, d. Angelo and Annette (Zoda) Cavalieri; m. Kenneth Clegg Flynn, Oct. 31, 1953; children—Cynthia Ann, Colleen Patricia, Shelley Anne, Angela Beth. Author poetry books: Why I Cannot Take a Lover, 1974, Body Fluids, 1976, Swan Research, 1978, Creature Comforts, 1982, Bliss, 1986; contrbr. poetry over 200 periodicals. BS in Edn. and English, N.J. State 1954; MA in Writing, Goddard Coll., 1975. Wrtr.-in-residence Antioch College writing programs, 1970-75. Producer sta. WPFW Pacifica Radio, Washington, 1976—, producer poetry program since 1976; poet, Am. Program, Antioch Coll., Oxford U., Eng., 1978; assoc. dir. PBS, Washington, 1978-82; program officer NEH, Washington, 1982—; lectr. Harvard U., Cambridge, Mass., 1985; presenter poetry readings Library of Congress, Washington, 1985, 86; mem. poetry bd. Folger Shakespeare Library, adv. bd. Living Stage, Watershed, Kidbits TV, Multicultural Resource Center Los Angeles. Poetry and radio fellow D.C. Commn. on Arts, 1985. Mem. MLA. Home: 1813 16th St NW Washington DC 20009

CAVAN, ANN M., b. Worcester, MA, Nov. 25, 1955; d. David J. and Mildred D.C. Author: Energy Resources in Southern Africa: A Select Bibliography, 1981, PURPA Rates: Annual State Update, 1985-87. Abstracter: Hist. Abstracts, 1986—. Contrbg. ed.: Hydro Rvw., 1984-85; ed.: PURPA Lines, 1985. B.A. in History, Boston Coll., 1977; M.Sc. in Intl. Relations, London Schl. Econs., 1979; Cert. as pub. Specialist, George Washington U., 1982. Info. specialist African Bibliographic Center, Washington, 1979-82; info. coord. Natl. Hydro Corp., Boston, 1982-84; freelance wrtr., ed., 1982—. Mem. Freelance Editorial Assm. Office: Box 341 Newburyport MA 01950

CAVE, GEORGE PATTON, b. Washington, Sept. 17, 1948, s. William Jones and Betty Barker (Patton) C. Contrbr. to Ethics and Animals, Agenda, Environ. Ethics, Intl. Jnl for Study of Animal Problems, other profl. publs. BA, Dickinson Coll., 1970; Cert. Higher European Studies, Inst. Am. Univ, Aix-En-Provence, France, 1971; MA, Bryn Mawr Coll., 1972, PhD, 1978; postgrad. Univ. Strasbourg, 1973-74; MA in English, Pa. State U., 1981. Pres. Trans-Species Unlimited, Williamsport, Pa., 1981—, ed. One World mag. Office: Box 1553 Williamsport PA 17703

CAWS, PETER JAMES, b. Southall, Eng., May 25, 1931; came to U.S., 1953; s. Geoffrey Tulloh and Olive (Budden) C.; m. Mary Ann Rorison, June 2, 1956; children: Hilary, Matthew. Author: The Philosophy of Science, Systematic Account, 1965, Science and the Theory of Value, 1967, Sartre, 1979; editor: Two Centuries of Philosophy in America, 1980; editorial bd.: Jnl Enterprise Mgmt., 1976—. BS, U. London, 1952, MA, Yale U., 1954, PhD, 1956. Editorial bd. Philosophy Documentation Center, 1969—; bd. dirs. CCLM, 1969-70; mem. editorial bd. Environment, 1972-78. ACLS fellow, Paris, 1972-73; Rockefeller Fdn. humanities fellow, 1979-80. Fellow AAAS (v.p. 1967).Home: 140 E 81st St New York NY 10028

CECALA, KATHY PETERSEN, b. Hartford, CT, Sept. 26, 1956; d. Michael B. and Valerie (Moskey) P.; m. Francis Dominic Cecala, May 24, 1981. Contrbr. fiction, McCall's mag. BA in jnlsm., St. Bonaventure U. Editorial prodn. asst. Woman's Day, NYC, 1978-80; copy co-ord. Vogue/Butterick, NYC, 1980-81; copy ed. McCall's, NYC, 1981-83; freelance ed., NYC, 1983-85; indexer/writer NY Times Info. Bank, Parsippany, NJ, 1985—. Home: 77 Maple Ave Morristown NJ 07960

CECIL, PAULA B., b. Renwick, IA, July 14, 1927; d. Samuel Henry and Oneida (Badgely) Klassie; m. William Joe Cecil, Mar. 27, 1954 (div. 1965); 1 dau., Michelle Elayne Cecil. Pubns. include: Word Processing in the Modern Office, 1976, 1980; The IBM Memory Typewriters, 1977, The Observer, 1979—, Mgt. of Word Processing Ops., 1980, Power Typing on Word Processors, 1981, Intelligent Typewriters, 1981, The IBM Electronic Typewriters, 1982, AT & T, Rolm & IBM PBX Systs., 1982, The Microcomputer Reference Guide, 1983, Office Automation Concepts & Applics., 1984, The IBM Displaywriter, 1984-85. BA, State U. of IA, 1949; MA, U. of Redlands, 1980. Customer systs. supp. rep. IBM Corp., San Jose, CA, 1966-72; cust. supp. mgr. Trendata Corp., Sunnyvale, CA, 1972; sales analyst Xerox Corp., Rochester, NY, 1972-73; consultant/author/pub./instr. Automated Office Resources, Aptos, CA, 1973—. Mem. Assn. of Info. Systs. Profls. Home: 812 Via Tornasol Aptos CA 95003

CECIL, RICHARD THOMAS, b. Balt., Mar 14, 1944; s. Louis Marvin Cecil and Dominica May (Costa) Tiller; m. Maura Stanton, Apr. 10, 1972. Author poetry: Einstein's Brain, 1986. MA, U. Iowa, 1972; MFA, Ind. U., Bloomington, 1985. Instr. J. Sgt. Reynolds Community Coll., Richmond, Va, 1973-77, Humboldt State Univ., Arcata, Calif., 1977-78, Pima Community Coll., Tucson, Ariz., 1979-81; Germana CC, Fredericksburg, Va., 1981-82; assoc. instr. Ind. Univ., Bloomington, 1982-85; poet-in-res. Univ Louisville, Ky, 1985-86, asst. prof., Lock Haven (PA) Univ., 1986-87; assoc. prof., Indiana Univ., 1987—. Mem. AWP, MLA. Address: 912 East First St Bloomington IN 47401

CEDERING, SIV, b. Overkalix, Sweden, Feb. 5, 1939; came to U.S., 1953, naturalized, 1958; d. Hilding and Elvy (Wikstrom) C.; children: Lisa, Lora, David. Author: poems and photographs Cup of Cold Water, 1973, Letters from the Island; poems, 1973, Letters from Helge, 1974, Two Swedish Poets, Gosta Friberg and Goran Palm (transl. from Swedish), 1974, Mother Is, 1975, How to Eat a Fortune Cookie, 1976, The Juggler, 1977, Color Poems, 1978, The Blue Horse; children's poems, 1979, Leken i Grishuset, 1980, Oxen, 1981, Grisen som Ville Bliren, 1983, Twelve Poems from the Floating World, 1983, Letters from the Floating World: New and Selected Poems, 1984, Polis, Polis, Potatisgris, 1985, Grisen Ville Bli Julskinka, 1986, Grisen Far Till Paris, 1987; books transl. into Japanese, Swedish.; editor, translator: Det Blommande Tradet (The Flowering Tree, collection Am. Indian and Eskimo lyrics), 1974, You and I and the World, Poems by Werner, Aspenstrom, 1980; poems and prose published in periodicals, including, Harper's, New Republic, Partisan Rvw, Paris Rvw, Qtly Rvw Lit. Cons. CCLM, 1972-75. Recipient William Marion Reedy award PSA, 1970, John Masefield Narrative Poetry award, 1969; Annapolis Fine Arts Festival poetry prize Md. Fine Arts Council, 1968; Borestone Mountain Poetry award, 1974; Emily Dickinson award, 1978; NY State Council on Arts fellow, 1974; Swedish Writers Union stipend, 1979, NY Fdn. fellow, 1985, Rhysling Award, 1985. Mem PSA, PEN. Address: Box 800 Amagansett NY 11930

CENSABELLA, LAURA MARIA, b. Bklyn., July 27, 1959, d. Arturo Thomas and Victoria Louise (Avidano) C. Author: (plays) Jazz Wives Jazz Lives, 1985, Abandoned in Queens, 1986; contrbr. short stories to Time Capsule and Salome: Lit. Dance Mag. BA in Philosophy, Yale U., 1981. Winner Natl. Playwright's Conf., Eugene O'Neill Meml. Theater, Waterford, Conn., 1985, 86. Mem. DG, Playwrights Unit of Puerto Rican Traveling Theatre. Artist-in-res. NYC public schls, 1987—. Home: 34 S Oxford St 3B Brooklyn NY 11217

CERDA, GABRIELA, see Zentella, Yoly Gabriela

CERNY, JANICE LOUISE, (Jan Cerny), b. Falls Church, VA, Mar. 6, 1947; d. George Anthony and Julia Virginia (Driggers) Cerny; m. Douglas R. Pennington, Apr. 28, 1979 (div. 1981). Author poetry: The Lasting Rose, 1984. Contrbr. articles to mags., poems to anthol. Ed.: The Pulsetter, 1985. Wrkg. on Haiku collection, God Loves a Nurse. Student Ga. State U., 1965-67. Private duty nurse Western Med., Atlanta, 1981-84; dir. nursing Nursecare of Atlanta, 1984-85, MAS Nursing of Ga., Atlanta, 1985—. Recipient Silver Poet award World of Poetry, 1986, Poet's Market award Trouvere Co., 1986, Sixth Sense award Ed.'s Desk, 1986. Mem. Atlanta Wrtrs. Club, Ga. State Poetry Soc., NLAPW. Home: 21D Cedar Run Rd Dunwoody GA 30350

CERRI, LAWRENCE J., (Lawrence Cortesi), b. Troy, NY, Aug. 6, 1923, s. Vincent and Assunta (Cortesi) C.; m. Frances Barringer; children—David, Diana, Richard, Catherine, Elizabeth. Author 34 books including: Trouble on the Big Tusk, 1983, Operation Friday the 13th, 1981, Operation Huon Gulf, 1982, Gunfight at Powder River, 1980, The Last Outlaw, 1979, 14-book World at War series, 1980-86, Operation Rome, 1978, Take the 505 Alive, 1986; biographer; playwright: The Adorable Imp, 1973, For Services Due, 1974, Grim Reapers, 1985; contrbr. over 200 works to mags. BA Siena Coll., Loudonville, NY,; MA, Albany State Coll., NY, 1950. Reporter Albany Times, 1951-57; tchr. Watervliet (NY) schls., 1957-76; freelance wrtr., 1976—. Served as sgt. USAAF, 1943-45. Recipient Best Children's Books award Child Study Assn., 1973. Mem. Watervliet Hist. Soc. (past pres.) Home: 79 Boght Rd Watervliet NY 12189

CERTO, DOMINIC NICHOLAS, (Jason D. Loran), b. New Brunswick, NJ, Mar. 14, 1950; s. Patrick and Concetta (D'Angolini) C.; divorced; children—Dominic Jason, Laurann Marie. Author: The Valor of Francesco D-Amini, 1979; Success, Pure and Simple, 1984. Assoc. Tech., Northwest Mo. State U., 1976. Regional mgr. N.Y. Life Ins. Co., Edison, N.J., 1972-76; regional dir. ARA Services, White Plains, N.Y., 1976-81; dir. mkgt. Service Am. Corp., Roseland, N.J., 1981—. Served to E-4, U.S. Marines, 1968-71, Vietnam. Recipient Vega award for prose, 1979; knighted Order of St. John Knights of Malta, 1986. Mem. AG, Intl. Fedn. Bodybuilders. Home: P O Box 385 Keasbey NJ 08832

CEYNAR, MARVIN EMIL, b. Fairfax, IA, Sept. 30, 1934; s. Emil Vincent and Mary Helen (Roshek) Ceynar; m. Barbara Jeanette Shepard, Dec. 18, 1957; children—Susanna Barbara Karagoez, John Marvin. Author: Creativity in the Communicative Arts, 1975; Iowa Bicentennial Mailbag series, 1983-84; Writing for the Religious Market, 1986. Editor: IRWA Newsletter, 1981—; History of Mason City District U. Methodist Churches, 1984. Creator Lincoln as a Social Prophet, Natl. Ednl. Radio, 1968. BA, State U. Ia., 1957, MA, 1965, MDiv, Garrett Theol. Seminary, 1962. Ordained to ministry, 1962. Prof. speech communication Northern Ill. U., DeKalb, 1966-73; pastor United Meth. Ch., Nichols, Ia., 1962-66, Williamsburg, Ia., 1975-79, Waterloo, Ia., 1979-80, Dumont, Ia., 1980-86, Moville, Ia., 1986—. Chmn. Chgo. CORE, 1960-61; counselor, advocate Ia. Farm Crisis Network, Moville, 1986—; mem. Dist. Bd. of Ordained Ministry. Recipient Walker scholarship State U. Ia., 1957. Mem. Interstate Religious Writers Assn. (pres., founder 1981), Moville Ministerial Assn. Home: 419 Pearl St Box B Moville IA 51039

CHAFETZ, MARION CLAIRE, b. Lawrence, MA, June 17, 1925; d. William Edward and Molly (Byrnes) Donovan; m. Morris Chafetz, Sept. 2, 1946; children—Gary, Marc, Adam. Author: Health Education, 1981; ed. numerous health edn. materials; contrbr. chap. to Encyc. Britannica Ann., 1986. Student Wayne U., 1948-49, Boston U., 1967-69. Ed.-in-chief Health Edn. Fdn., Washington, 1976—. Home: 3129 Dumbarton St NW Washington DC 20007

CHAFFEE, C. DAVID, b. NYC, Dec. 13, 1951, s. Hubert and Charlotte Eleanor (Hess) C.; m. Margot Elizabeth Bride, Apr. 20, 1985. Contrbr. Country Gentleman Mag., Purchasing Mag., Optics News, other publs. BA, Conn. Coll., 1973; MA in Journalism, U. Md., 1979. Ed. Nuclear Waste News, Silver Spring, Md., 1979-82; sr. and group ed. Phillips Pub., Inc., Potomac, Md., 1982—. Home: 3006 Flag Marsh Rd Mount Airy MD 21771

CHAFFIN, LILLIE D., (Lila Day, Lena Winston, Randall Chaffin), b. Varney, KY Feb. 1, 1925; d. Kenis V. Dorton and Farabelle Kelley; m. Thomas W. Chaffin, 1 son, Thomas R.; m. 2d, Dr. Vernon O. Kash. Works include: Waiting For Love, 1982, We Be Warm Till Springtime Comes, 1980, Appalachian History & Other Poems, 1980, Eighth Day Thirteenth Moon, 1979. Contrbr. fiction, non-fiction, poetry to numerous publs., anthologies. BS, Pikeville College, Pikeville, KY 1958; MA, Eastern KY U., Richmond, 1972. Freelance wrtr. and edit. Mem. PSA, KY State Poetry Society, Fla. State Poetry Assn. Home: 2284 Spanish Dr Clearwater FL 33575

CHALIP, ALICE GRACE, (Grace Morrison), b. Los Angeles, June 30, 1930; d. Morris Getz and Mary Margaret (Cornell) Grace; m. Bernard Rogers Chalip, July 13, 1949; 1 son, Laurence Hilmond; 4 foster children. Author: (documentary) Summit Up, 1964; (play) A Moment to Courage, 1965; contrbr. to Teaching General Semantics (ed. Mary Morain), 1969, Anthology of Alameda Poets and Artists, 1972, Know What I Mean?, 1972, Conference in Rhetorial Criticism Papers, 1972, A Descriptive Study of the Group conversation Method of Rachel Davis DuBois, 1974, To Love and Let Go, 1984. Contrbr. articles to newspapers. BA in English, U. Calif.-Berkeley, 1954; MA in rhetoric, Calif. State U.-Hayward, 1974. Feature and news wrtr. Kofman Newspapers, Alameda, Calif., 1969-71; arts critic Berkeley Daily Gazette, 1971-83; lectr. in speech Calif. State U., Hayward, 1972-73; instr. Peralta Community Coll., Oakland, Calif., 1973-83; wrtr., ed. Pillar Press, Alameda, 1983—. Mem. Intl. Soc. Gen. Semantics (bd. dirs., past v.p.), COSMEP, Natl. Foster Parents Assn. Home: 636 Tarryton Isle Alameda CA 94501

CHALLEM, JACK JOSEPH, (Jack Joseph, Joseph Jackson), b. Montreal, Que., Can., May 29, 1950; s. Alex and Sara Bella (Novak) C.; m. Renate Lewin, Sept. 30, 1977. Author: What Herbs Are All About, 1980, Vitamin C Updated, 1983; contrbg. ed. Bestways Mag., 1975-79, N. Mex. Ind., 1979-84, Let's Live, 1979—; contrbg. assoc. Your Good Health Rvw, 1979-83, Health Qtly, 1979-83; contrbr. over 300 articles to Albuquerque Jnl, New Mexican, Healthways Digest, Am. Forests, Am. Chiropractor, Sexology Today, Denver Post, also poetry to mags. Student Wright Jr. Coll., Chgo., 1968-70; BA in Sociology, Northeastern Ill. U., Chgo., 1972. Advt. mgr. J. R. Carlson Labs., Arlington Heights, Ill., 1973-78; ed.-in-chief Physician's Life, Evanston, Ill., 1978; graphics mgr. Eberline Instrument Corp., Sante Fe, 1979-81; wrtr.-ed. Los Alamos Natl. Lab., 1981—. Home: 2779 Villa Caballero del Sur Santa Fe NM 87505

CHALLONER, ROSEMARY REGINA, see Wilkinson, Rosemary

CHALMERS, CATHERINE FAYE, b. Calgary, Alberta, Can., Feb. 22, 1959; d. Hugh Alexander and Roxana Marguerite (Wheaton) C.; came to U.S., Aug., 1971. Contrbr. to Cellular Television Business Mag., Satellite Communics. BS, Western State Coll., 1981. Acct. exec. Satellite Communics. Mag., Englewood, CO, 1981-83; assoc. ed. Communications Mag., Englewood, 1983-84; ed. Global Communics. Mag., Englewood, 1984—, Cellular Marketing, Englewood, 85—. Mem. Soc. of Satellite Professionals. Office: Cardiff Pub 6530 S Yosemite St Englewood CO 80111

CHAMBERLAIN, DONALD WILLIAM, b. Green Bay WI, Nov. 28, 1905; s. Elmer Ellsworth and Nellie (Hayes) C.; m. Artha Kwoni Littel, Aug. 9, 1945; children—Frank, Ellen, Elizabeth. Contrbr. articles, chpts., bulltns. to profl. jnls. B.A., St. Norbert Coll., 1929; M.A., U. Wis., 1943, Ph.D., 1943. Instructor in horticulture, U. of Wis., 1943-45; asst. agronomist U. Ky., Lexington, 1945-46; plant pathologist U.S. Dept. Agriculture-U. Ill., Urbana IL, 1946-75, retired. Recipient Excellence in Agricultural Jnlsm. award Am. Soc. Agronomy, 1966, Alma Mater award for profl. attainments St. Norbert Coll., DePere, WI, 1973. Mem. Am. Phytopathological Soc., Sigma Xi, Phi Sigma. Home: 2022 Boudreau Dr Urbana IL 61801

CHAMBERLAIN, DONNA JON, b. El Paso, TX, Jan. 30, 1937; d. John Roosevelt and Eleanor Mary (Sweeney) Brindley; m. Albert Robert Chamberlain, May 19, 1959; childen—Judith Lee, Jon Robert. Author: (poems) Waif's Messenger, 1984. Contrbr. poems to anthols., articles to newspapers. Wrkg. on poems, short story, biographical jnl. Student Bryn Mawr Hosp., 1957-58, Ga. State Coll., 1958, Brigham Young U. (corr. div.), 1966-67. Commun. nurse Bahamian Government, Staniel Cay, 1959-70; tchr. Westwood Hills Christian Acad., Gainesville, FL, 1979-81. Media coord. Bread for the World, Coral Springs, FL, 1984-85. Office: Airways Rsvtn Ctr 4250 SW 11th Terr Fort Lauderdale FL 33315

CHAMBERLAIN, KAREN, b. Hartford, CT, Dec. 1, 1942; d. Frederick E. and Dorothy Hannah (Battersby) Recknagel; m. Robert Matheiu Chamberlain, Sept. 24, 1977. Contrbr. poetry and essays to The Nation, Denver Qtly, Hawaii Rvw, Aspen Anthology, Poetry Northwest, Mountain Gazette and others. BA, U. N. Mex-Albuquerque; MFA Warren Wilson Coll. Scriptwriter Wild America, PBS-TV, Marty Stouffer Pdns., Aspen, Colo., 1983—; dir. Aspen Writers Conf., 1986—. Letter writer, Amnesty Intl. Recipient Discovery prize, The Nation, 1983. Address: 221 Teal Ct Aspen CO 81611

CHAMBERLAIN, MARISHA ANNE, b. Sarasota, FL, Jan. 6, 1952; d. Charles Martin and Judith (Cooper) C. Author: Powers; contrbr. to Burns Mantle Yearbook: Best Plays of '84-'85, Scheherazade; Warm Jnl, Ironwood, Prairie Schooner, Great River Rvw, Dacotah Territory. BA, Macalester Coll., 1972; MFA in Poetry, Goddard Coll., 1980. Wrtr.-in-residence Compas, St. Paul, 1979-81; playwright-in-residence The Playwrights' Ctr., Mpls., 1980-83, The Cricket Theater, Mpls., 1981-87; mem. adj. faculty Macalester Coll., St. Paul, 1983—, U. Minn. Writing Program, Mpls., 1985—, Carleton Coll., 1986. NEA fellow, 1976; Bush. Fdn. fellow, 1981; Loft/McKnight fellow, 1982; Rockefeller Fdn. fellow, 1985-86. Mem. DG, Playwrights' Ctr. Home: 1049 Goodrich Apt 5 St Paul MN 55105

CHAMBERLAIN, VELMA, see Richeson, Cena Golder

CHAMBERS, JOHN DARBY, b. Halifax, Nova Scotia, Canada, Sept. 19, 1939, came to U.S., 1977; s. Robert William and Grace Majory (Fraser) C.; m. Judith May Tarnpoll, May 29, 1977; 1 son, Joshua Matthew. Contrbr. articles, chpts. to mags., profl. jnls., books including Conn. Mag., Fate Mag., Fairfield County Mag., others. Wrkg. on humorous spiritual auto biography, Journey in Search of the Self, or, Memoirs of a New Age Groupie. B.A. with honors, Dalhousie U., 1960; M.A. in English, U. Toronto, 1970. Assoc. ed. McGraw-Hill, NYC, 1981-83, asst. ed., 1985-86; asst. ed. Intl. Thomson, NYC, 1983-84, assoc. ed., 1987—; ed.-in-chief Beyond Avlcon Quarterly, Bridgeport, CT, 1986—; free-lance wrtr., 1980—. Home: 93 Jackson Ave Bridgeport CT 06606

CHAMLEE, KENNETH D., b. Greenville, SC., Oct. 6, 1952; s. Robert G. and Marjorie (Hinsdale) Chamlee; m. Priscilla Anne Canupp, April 19, 1975. Poetry in Appalachian Heritage, Writer's Forum, College Eng, The Lyricist, Arts Jnl, and other mags. BA, Mars Hill College, NC, 1974; MA, Colorado State U., Fort Collins, 1976. Instr., Greenville TEC, Greenville, SC, 1977-78; assoc. prof., Brevard College, Brevard, NC, 1978—. Mem. NCTE, AWP, NC Poetry Society. Home: 123-H Yesteroaks Way E Greensboro NC 27408

CHAMPION, ELIZABETH HOLLIS, b. Americus, GA, Apr. 29, 1945; d. Mr. and Mrs. James Perry Champion, Jr. Feature wrtr.: Periscope, 1965-67; ed.: Argo, 1967, Challenge Chatter, 1973-76; illustrator, indexer: Echoes of the Past (by Jane Luthy Champion). 1986; contrbr. articles to jnls., ed. jnl. article. Wrkg on hist. articles, transcriptions, illustrations, poetry collection. BA, Shorter Coll., 1967; MLS, La. State U., 1969. Asst. serials librarian U.S.C., Columbia, 1969-71; asst. librarian Albany Jr. Coll., Ga., 1971-73; freelance wrtr. Home: 905 2d Ave Albany GA 31701

CHANCE, JANE, (Jane Chance Nitzsche), b. Neosho, MO, Oct. 26, 1945; d. Donald William and Julia (Mile) Chance; m. Dennis Carl Nitzsche, June 15, 1966 (div. Mar. 12, 1969) 1 dau, Therese Chance; m. 2d, Paolo Passaro, May 2, 1981; 2 sons, Antony Damian, Joseph Sebastian. Author: The Genius Figure in Antiquity and the Middle Ages, 1975, Tolkien's Art, 1979, Woman as Hero in Old English Lit, 1986; ed. Mapping the Cosmos (with R. O. Wells, Jr.), 1985, Approaches to Teaching Sir Gawain and the Green Knight, 1986. BA, Purdue, 1967; AM, U. Ill-Urbana, 1968 PhD,1971. Asst. prof. Rice Univ., Houston, 1973-77, assoc. prof., 1977-80, prof., 1980—. NEH fellow, London, 1977-78, Guggenheim fellow, 1980-81; Mem. Medieval Acad. Am., New Chaucer Soc., MLA. Address: 12510 Ashling Dr Stafford TX 77477

CHANDLER, KAY, see Bone, Brenda Kay

CHANDONNET, ANN FOX, b. Lowell, MA, Feb. 7, 1943; d. Leighton Dinsmore and Barbara Amelia (Cloutman) Fox; m. Fernand Leonce Chandonnet, June 11, 1966; children—Yves, Alexandre, Maxim. Author: Incunabula (collection of poems), 1968, The Wife and Other Poems, 1977, The Wife, Part Two, 1979, The Complete Fruit Cookbook, 1972, The Cheese Guide and Cookbook, 1973, Ptarmigan Valley, 1980, Auras, Tendrils, 1984, At the Fruit-Tree's Mossy Root (poems), 1984, On the Trail of Eklutna (history of an Alaskan Athapascan village), 1986. Ed. Alaskan Arts and Writing issue of Northward Jnl, 1981. Poems in anthologies: Black Sun,

New Moon, 1980, Sun-Catcher, Children of the Earth, 1982, Hunger and Dreams: The Alaskan Women's Anthology, 1983, In the Dreamlight: 21 Alaskan Writers, 1984. BS, Lowell U., 1964; MS, U. Wis.-Madison, 1965. English tchr Kodiak High Schl., Alaska, 1965-66; instr. English Lowell U., Mass., 1966-69; secy. 1st Enterprise Bank, Oakland, CA, 1971-72; freelance writer, 1972-82; feature writer Anchorage Times, 1982—. Mem. AK Press Club. Home: 6552 Lakeway Dr Anchorage AK 99502

CHANEY, DEBORA ANNE, b. Lafayette, IN, Feb. 7, 1965; d. Dennis Allen and Evelyn Anne (Bracy) Chaney; m. Charles Martin O'Donnell, Oct. 10, 1987. Contrbr. poems to anthols. Wrkg. on book of poems. Diploma in Cosmetology, Bernard's Schl. Hair Fashion, 1985. Owner, cosmetologist db's Shear Magic, Damariscotta, ME, 1986—. Recipient Golden Poet award World of Poetry, 1985, 87, Silver Poet award, 1986. Office: Box 417 Damariscotta ME 04543

CHANG-RODRIGUEZ, EUGENIO, b. Trujillo, Peru; s. Enrique and Pergrina (Rodriguez) Chang. Author: Literatura politica de Gonzalez Prada, Mariategui y Haya, 1957, ed (with H. Kantor) La America Latina de Hoy (anthology), 1961, ed (with G. MacEoin and M. Luz) The Hemisphere's Present Crisis, 1963, (with Alphonse G. Juilland) Frequency Dictionary of Spanish Words, 1965, (with L. Poston and others) Continuing Spanish, 5 vols, 1969, The Lingering Crisis: A Case Study of the Dominican Republic. 1969, (with C. Smith and M. Bermejo) Collins Spanish Dictionary, 1971, ed, Spanish in the Western Hemisphere, 1982, Poetica e ideologia en J.C. Mariategui, 1983, Latinoamerica: Su Civilization y su Cultura, 1983, Opciones politicas peruanas, 1985, rev ed, 1987. Assoc ed, Hispania, 1963-65; ed, Boletin de la Academia Norteamericana de la Lengua Espanola, 1976—, and Word, 1983—. Ph. B., U. of San Marcos (Peru), 1946; BA, William Penn College, 1949; MS, U. of Arizona, 1950; MA, U. of Washington, Seattle, 1952, Ph.D., 1956. Instr in Spanish and asst to dean of Coll. of Arts and Scis., U. of Wash., 1950-56; asst prof of Romanance langs and lits, U. of Penn, Philadelphia, 1956-61; asst prof to prof of Romance langs, Queens Coll. of the City Univesity of N.Y., Flushing, 1961—, chmn Latin American Area Studies, 1969-80. Vis prof, U. of Southern Calif., summers, 1950, 61, 62; lectr., Columbia U., Barnard Coll., and other schls.; hon. prof., Matl. U. of San Marcos, Peru, 1980—. Mem. White House Conf on Intl Cooperation, 1966; chmn organizing com, Natl Conf on Linguistics, N.Y., 1967; chmn Columbia Seminar on Latin America, 1974-80; mem jnt com on Latin Ameican Studies, Soc. Scis Research Council, 1976-79. Advisory ed, Charles Scribner's Sons, N.Y., 1965-66. Mem: Intl Linguistics Assn (pres, 1969-72, 87-88), Intl League for the Rights of Man (council chmn, 1970—), Associacion Internacional de Hispanistas, Instituo Internacional de Literatura Iberoamericana, North American Acad of the Spanish Language, MLA, UN Correspondents Assn, American Assn of Teachers of Spanish and Portuguese (chpt pres, 1954-56), Latin American Studies Assn (chmn, Consortium of Latin American Studies, 1980), Linguistic Soc of America, Hispanic Soc. of America. Hispanic Inst. Home 60 Sutton Place S New York N.Y. 10022

CHAPMAN, CAROLYN NELSON, b. Chgo., Jan. 26, 1925; d. Edward Samuel and Mildred Mary (McNeill) Nelson; m. Robert Arthur Chapman, Dec. 16, 1944; children-Diana Carolyn Miller, Victoria Christina Forness. Author: Know Your County, St. Clair County, IL, 1965, rev., 1977, A Survey of Health Services in St. Clair County, 1971. Contrbr. articles to mags. Student U. Chgo., 1942-44. Chmn., St. Clair County Mental Health Bd., Belleville, IL, 1969-81, mem., 1985—. Recipient Oscar G Thalinger Verse Play award St. Louis Poetry Ctr., 1971. Mim. MLAPW. Home: 5937 Memory Ln Belleville IL 62223

CHAPMAN, CINDY LORRAINE FARR, (Cindy Farr), b. Jackson, MS, Sept. 13, 1952; d. Joseph White and Johnnie Ruth (Beasley) F.; m. Richard Alan Chapman, Aug. 18, 1986. Contrbr. poetry to numerous anthols. AD, Hinds Jr. Coll., Raymond, Miss., 1985; AD in nursing, Hinds Jr. Coll., Jackson, 1987. Recipient 2d place (3) Hinds Jr. Coll, 1986, Miss. Jr. Coll. Creative Writing Assn./Hinds Jr. Coll., 1986. Mem. Natl. Student Nurse's Assn., Orgn. Advancement Assoc. Deg. Nursing, Student Nurse's Assn. (v.p.), Phi Theta Kappa. Home: 401 E College St Apt C-3 Clinton MS 39056

CHAPMAN, CONSTANCE ANN, (KanKan), b. Detroit, June 21, 1935, d. Conway Clayton and Ann Elizabeth (Byrd) Chapman; 1 stepchild, Matu. Contrbr. poetry, stories, articles to numerous mags., newspapers and jnls. Wrkg. on novel, short stories. MA, Columbia U., 1974. Tchr. public schls., Detroit and N.Y., 1957-67; instr. John Jay Coll., NYC, 1969-74, adj. prof., 1981-84; lectr., U. W.I., Kingston, Jamaica, 1974-78; adj. prof. Malcolm-King Coll., NYC, 1982-84. Mem. NCTE, Intl. Reading Assn., N.Y. State Reading Assn., Kappa Delta Pi. Home: 2186 Fifth Ave 2L New York NY 10037

CHAPMAN, IRWIN, see Anderson, Paul Dale

CHAPPELL, FRED, b. Canton, NC, May 28, 1936; s. James Taylor and Ann (Davis) Chappell; m. Susan Elizabeth Nicholls; 1 son—Christopher Heath. Author: It is Time, Lord, 1963, The Inkling, 1965, Dagon, 1970, The World Between the Eyes, 1971, The Gaudy Place, 1971, MidQuest, 1982, Moments of Light, 1982, Castle Tzingal, 1984, I am One of You Forever, 1985, Source, 1985. BA Duke U., 1961, MA 1964. Engl. teach. U. of NC, Greensboro, 1964-85. Sir Walter Raleigh Prize, State of NC, 1980; Best Foreign Novel, Academie Francaise, 1973; Bollingen Prize in Poetry, Yale U., 1985. Home: 305 Kensington Rd Greensboro NC 27403

CHAR, CARLENE MAE, b. Honolulu, Oct. 21, 1954; d. Richard and Betty C. Ed./pub. Computer Book Review, 1983—; ed./pub. Maeventec Software Review, 1983—. BA in Econ., U. HI, 1977; MA in Bus. Admin., Columbia Pacific U., 1984, PhD in Jnlsm., 1985; BGS in Computer Sci., Roosevelt U., 1986. Certified Office Automation Profl. Office: Box 37127 Honolulu HI 96837

CHARNEY, DAVID H., b. NYC,July 30, 1923; m. Louise C. Verrette; children—Beth Esther, Steven, Kenneth. Author: Magic Quadrangle, 1976; Sensei, Charter Ace, 1982; Sensei II: Swordmaster Charter, 1984. Wrkg. on naval expedition novel. BFA, Cooper Union, 1977. Sr. v.p., exec. art dir. R.A. Becker, Inc., NYC,1962—. Served to 1st lt., USAAF, 1942-45; PTO. Home: 341 Scarsdale Rd Crestwood NY 10707

CHARTERS, ANN D., b. Bridgeport, CT, Nov. 10, 1936; d. Nathan and Kate (Schultz) Danberg; m. Samuel Barclay Charters, Mar. 14, 1959; children—Mallay, Nora. Author: Bibliography of Works by Jack Kerouac, Olson/Melville, Scenes Along the Road, Nobody, Kerouac: A Biography, I Love, The Beats, The Story and Its Writer, Beats & Company. BA, U. Calif.-Berkeley, 1953-57; MA, Columbia U., 1960, PhD, 1965. Lectr. Columbia Univ., NYC, 1964-65; instr. Colby Jr. Coll., New Hampshire, 1961-63; asst. prof. NYC Community Coll., Bklyn., 1967-70, assoc. prof. U. Conn., Storrs, prof. English, 1974—. Address: Dept Eng Univ Conn Storrs CT 06268

CHASE, ELAINE RACO, b. Schenectady, Aug. 31, 1949, d. Ernest Salvatore and Helen Nancy (Scavia) Raco; m. Gary Dale Chase, Oct. 26, 1969; children—Marlayna, G. Marc II. Author: Rules of the Game, 1980, Tender Yearnings, 1981, A Dream Come True, 1982, Double Occupancy, 1982, Designing Woman, 1982, No Easy Way Out, 1983, Video Vixen, 1983, Calculated Risk, 1983, Best Laid Plans, 1983, Special Delivery, 1984 (Walden Book Award, 1985, for topselling novel), Lady Be Bad, 1984, Dangerous Places, 1987, Dark Corners, 1988. contrbr. to Love's Leading Ladies and How To Write a Romance (Kathryn Falk) Lovelines (Rosemary Guiley) So You Want a TV Career (T.E. Hollingsworth), Bankable Ladies of Paperback Romance (Marilyn Lowery). Student pub. schls., Rotterdam, N.Y. Audio-visual librarian Sta. WGY- WRGB-TV, Schenectady, 1968-70; copywrtr. Beckman Advt., Albany, 1970-71; author, 1978—. Mem. PW, MWA, Romance Wrtrs. Am. (past pres. Fla. chpt., current pres. Bay Area chpt., Texas). Home: 15703 Cavendish Rd Houston TX 77059

CHASE, NAOMI FEIGELSON, b. Pitts., May 26, 1932, d. Henry and Rachel (Savage) Ellenbogen; m. Eugene Feigelson, Aug. 30, 1960 (div. 1967); children—Elizabeth, Jonathan; m. 2d, Gordon Chase, July 3, 1974 (dec. 1980). Author: The Underground Revolution: Hippies, Yippies & Others, 1970, A Child is Being Beaten, 1974, Listening for Water, 1980; contrbr. poetry: Primavera, Terra Poetica, Dark Horse, Xanadu, numerous other publs.; contrbr. articles: Wall St. Jnl, N.Y. Times, others; contrbr. fiction: Dancy, others. Wrkg. on non-fiction. BA, Radcliffe Coll., 1954; MA, Brandeis U., 1956. Reporting The Village Voice, NYC, 1964-74; dir. public info. N.Y.C. Dept. Consumer Affairs, 1968-69, N.Y.C. Health Services Adminstrn., 1970-72; pres. Naomi F. Chase, NYC, 1984-86; dir. communications JFK Schl. Govt., Harvard U., Cambridge, Mass., 1986—. Grantee Maurice Falk Med. Fdn., Pitts., 1966, Ford Fdn., 1971, 77; MacDowell Colony fellow, 1979, 81, 84. Office: JFK Schl Govt 79 JFK Blvd Cambridge MA 02139

CHASE, OTTA LOUISE, b. Salem, MA, July 8, 1909; d. Benjamin Franklin and Reta Townes (Young) Graffam; m. Hunter Ellsworth Chase, Feb. 17, 1929; children—Donald Clayton, Nancy Lee, Charles Frederick. Author: November Violets, 1973, Tender Vines, 1986. Student, Everett, Mass. publ. schls. Town treas., Sweden, ME, 1957-58, town clerk, 1959—. Mem. PSA, Poetry Soc. of NH, Poetry Fellowship of ME, KY State Poetry Soc., PA Poetry Soc. Home: RFD 2 Box 1502 Harrison ME 04040

CHATTERTON, ROYLANCE WAYNE, b. Franklin, ID, July 14, 1921, s. Jesse Ray and Josephine (Hill) C.; m. Ardath Louise Lefler, July 19, 1945. Author: Vardis Fisher: The Frontier and Regional Works, 1972, Nelson Algren (with Martha Heasley Cox), 1975, Alexander Woollcott, 1978, Irvin S. Cobb, 1986; contrbr.

to A Literary History of the American West, 1987. Wrkg. on Western writing series, collection of Irvin S. Cobb. BS, Brigham Young U., 1945, MA, 1946; PhD, U. Utah, 1963. Assoc. prof. lit. Coll. Idaho, Caldwell, 1949-68; prof. English and Am. lit., Boise State U., 1968-82, prof. emeritus, 1982—. Co-ed. Boise State U. Western Wrtrs. Series, 1972—. Served with USMC, 1942-44; PTO. Mem. Western Lit. Assn., MLA (hon. life mem. Rocky Mountain chap.), NWC. Home: 2589 Westminster Ln Boise ID 83704

CHAYAT, SHERRY, b. Bklyn., Oct. 2, 1943; d. Leonard Corlan and Sylvia (Wasserman) Chayat; adopted d. Maxwell Chayat; m. Louis D. Nordstrom, Sept. 2, 1967 (div. Jul. 1979); 2nd m. B. Andrew Hassinger, Nov. 11, 1979; 1 son—Jesse Leonard. Contrbr. to Syracuse Guide, Collier's Encyc. Year Book, Art News, Tamarack, American Ceramics, Lilitn, Syracuse Post-Standard, Ceramics Monthly, New York Alive, Art in America, Present Tense, Herald-American, Jewish Observer. BA Vassar Coll, 1965; postgrad NY Studio School, 1966-67. Fine arts & relig. ed. Syracuse U. News Bureau (NY), 1976-78; dir. pub. relat. LeMoyne Coll. (Syracuse, NY), 1978-80; ed.-in-chief Jewish Observer (Syracuse, NY), 1980-85; adj. instr. contemp. art Univ. Coll. of Syracuse U., 1985—; art critic Herald- American 1985—. Founder, first VP Millay Colony for Arts (Austerlitz, NY), 1973-75; board member, VP Society for New Music (Syracuse), 1978-80. Mem. Syracuse Press Club. Home: 111 Concord Pl Syracuse NY 13210

CHEATHAM, K. FOLLIS, see Cheatham, Karyn Elizabeth

CHEATHAM, KARYN ELIZABETH, b. Oberlin, OH, Jan. 30, 1943, d. Benjamin Curtis and Elizabeth Virginia (Blackburn) Follis; m. Eugene C. Cheatham, III, July 17, 1965; children—Nisah, Onika. Author: Spotted Flower & The Ponokomita, 1977, Life on a Cool Plastic Ice Floe, 1978, Bring Home the Ghost, 1980, The Best Way Out, 1982; contrbr. to Front Street Trolley, Knoxville Lifestyle, Emrys Jnl, Minorities & Women in Business, Wind Lit. Jnl, Sojourner: The Women's Forum, Phoenix. Student Ohio State U., 1960-63, 65-68. Research analyst Battelle Meml. Inst., Columbus, Ohio, 1965-69; adminstrv. asst. Environ. Simulation Lab., Ann Arbor, Mich., 1969-70; freelance craftswoman, poet, speaker, Raleigh, NC, 1973-77; profl. wrtr., 1977—. Recipient award for notable children's trade book in social studies field Children's Book Council and Natl. Council for Social Edn., 1983. Mem. WWA, P&W, Nashville Wrtrs. Alliance. Home: 784 Blevins Dr Nashville TN 37204

CHENG, FRED NAI-CHUNG, b. Los Angeles, Aug. 30, 1970; s. I-Fan and Chih-Liuh (Lee) C. Contrbr. essays to Mpls. Star & Tribune, telescript and dramatic script to Scholastic, Inc., dramatic script to Young Playwrights Festival. Recipient Honorable Mention, Scholastic, Inc., 1985, Jewish Community Ctr., St. Paul, 1984. Mem. Playwrights' Center. Home: 7432 Lee Ave N Brooklyn Park MN 55443

CHENOWETH, DELLZELL, see Schricte, Dellzell

CHERNER, ANNE, see Whitehouse, Anne Cherner

CHERRY, ETHEL JOHNNSON, b. Jan. 13, 1898, Leavenworth, KS; d. Joseph Henry and Hattie (McClanahan) J.; m. Jacob Ward, June 8, 1922 (div. 1949). Author: Cross My Heart, 1956, Don't Call My Number, 1956, Pasadena Profiles, 1959, Curly, 1985; contrbr. Christian Home, NY Village, NY Daily News, Los Angeles Eagle (col.). Humanitarian Award, Pasadena City, 1968. Baptist, Methodist. Home: 411 Ottawa St Leavenworth KS 66048

CHERRY, KELLY, b. Baton Rouge, LA, Dec. 21, 1940; d. J. Milton and Mary S. Cherry; m. Jonathan Silver, Dec. 23, 1966 (div. 1969). Author: Sick and Full of Burning, 1974, Lovers and Agnostics, 1975, Relativity: A Point of View, 1977; Augusta Played, 1979, Conversion, 1979, Songs for a Soviet Composer, 1980, In the Wink of an Eye, 1983, The Lost Traveller's Dream, 1984, Natural Theology, 1987. MFA, U. of North Carolina, 1967. Disting. wrtr.-in- residence, Western Washington Univ., Bellingham, WA, 1981; disting. vis. prof., Rhodes College, Memphis, TN, 1985; prof., U. of Wisc., Madison, 1977—. Awards: Best American Short Stories, 1972, NEA Fellowship 1979. Mem. PEN, PSA, AG, NBCC. Home: 211 Highland Madison WI 53705

CHERTKOW, FERN, b. Chgo., May 14, 1951; d. Nathan and Sara (Benjamin) Chertkow. Contrbr. to Nimrod, Dan River Anthology, Day Tonight/Night Today, Prism, a Jnl of Ideas, GPU News. MA, Ind. U.-Bloomington; PhD (Neff fellow), U. Utah. Assoc. instr. Indiana Univ., Bloomington, 1976-78; tchg. fellow Univ. Utah, Salt Lake City, 1980-85; legal secretary Watkiss & Campbell, Salt Lake City, 1979-86. Recipient Clarice Short tchg. award, Univ. Utah, 1983. Mem. AWP. Address: 305 Third Ave Salt Lake City UT 84103

CHERVIN, RONDA, b. Los Angeles, April 24, 1937; d. Ralph and Helen (Winner) DeSola; m. Martin Chervin, July 9, 1962; children: Carla, Diana, Charles, Author: Church of Love, 1973, The Art of Choosing, 1975, Prayer and Your Everyday Life, 1976, The Spirit and Your Everyday LIfe, 1976, Love and Your Everyday Life, 1976, The Way and the Truth and the Life, 1976, Why I Am a Catholic Charismatic, 1977, Christian Ethics and Your Everyday Life, 1979, (with Mary Neill) The Woman's Tale, 1980, (with Neill) Bringing the Mother with You, 1982, Victory Over Death, 1985, Feminine, Free, and Faithful, 1986; ed. The Ingrafting: Stories of Hebrew-Catholics, 1987. BA, U. of Rochester (N.Y.), 1957; MA, Fordham U., 1959, Ph.D., 1967. Lectr., Fordham U. Extension, U. of Calif., Irvine Extension, Chapman Coll, and St. Joseph's Coll, 1967-69; asst prof, Loyola Marymount U., Los Angeles, Calif., 1969-73, assoc. prof. of philosophy, 1973-86; prof of philosophy, St. John's Seminary, Camarillo, Calif., 1986—. Home: 7612 Cowan Ave Los Angeles CA 90045

CHESSLEY, BARA, see Donhess, Barbara M.

CHESROW, CATHLEEN GWEN, b. Chgo., Jan. 16, 1947; d. Marguerite (Rosenbaum) Gras, step-d., Dr. Vernon Gras; m. Eugene Joseph Chrsrow (div. 1979); children: Albert John, Alexis Maria. Author: poetry to anthologies, song lyrics, genl. interest articles to newspapers. BFA, Art Inst. Chgo.; student Univ. Chgo. extension. Instructor horsemanship, Treasurer, Larkspur Corp. (Larkspur Riding School), LaPore, Ind., 1978-82. Address: Box 1675 LaPorte IN 46350

CHESTER, EDWARD WILLIAM, b. Richmond, VA, Nov. 9, 1935; s. Edward William and Mary Elizabeth (Lewis) C. Author: Europe Views America: A Critical Evaluation, 1962, Issues and Responses in State Political Experience, 1968, Radio, Television and American Politics, 1969, Clash of Titans: Africa and U.S. Foreign Policy, 1974, Sectionalism Politics and American Diplomacy, 1975, A Guide To Political Platforms, 1977, The U.S. and Six Atlantic Outposts: The Military and Economic Considerations, 1980, U.S. Oil Policy and Diplomacy, 1983; contbr. articles to profl. jnls. AB summa cum laude, Morris Harvey Coll., 1956; MA, U. Pitts., 1958, PhD, 1961. Summer research grantee Earhart Fdn, 1977, 78. Home: 800 Tanglewood Ln Arlington TX 76012

CHICAGO, JUDY, b. Chgo., July 20, 1939; d. Arthur M. and May (Levenson) Cohen. Author: Through the Flower: My Struggle as a Woman Artist, 1975, The Dinner Party: A Symbol of Our Heritage, 1979, Embroidering Our Heritage: The Dinner Party Needlework, 1980, The Birth Project, 1985. B.A., U. Calif. at Los Angeles, 1962, M.A., 1964. Address: Box 834 Benicia CA 94510

CHICHETTO, JAMES WILLIAM, b. Boston. Author poetry books: Poems, 1975, Dialogue: Emily Dickinson and C. Cauldwell, 1977, Stones, A Litany, 1980, Gilgamesh and Other Poems, 1983, Victims, 1985; contrbr. to Blood to Remember: American Poets on the Holocaust, 1986, Night House Anthology, 48 Younger American Poets, 1982; contrbr. to Boston Globe, Gargoyle, Manhattan Rvw, numerous others. BA, Stonehill Coll.; MA, Wesleyan U. Poetry ed. Conn. Poetry Rvw, New Haven, 1985—. Grantee NEA, 1980, 83; recipient Sri Chinmoy Poetry award, 1984. Mem. NWU. Home: Box 136 South Easton MA 02375

CHILCOTE, RONALD H., b. Cleve., Feb. 20, 1935, s. Lee Alfred and Katherine (Hodell) C.; m. Frances Tubby, Jan. 6, 1961; children—Stephen, Edward. Author: Latin America: The Struggle with Dependency and Beyond (with Joel Edelstein), 1974, Theories of Comparative Politics: The Search for a Paradigm, 1981, Theories of Development and Underdevelopment, 1984, Latin America: Capitalist and Socialist Perspectives of Development and Underdevelopment (with Joel Edelstein), 1986; ed.: Protest and Resistance in Angola and Brazil, 1972, Brazil and its Radical Left: An annotated Bibliography of the Communist Movement and the Rise of Marxism, 1922-72, 1980, Dependency and Marxism: Toward a Resolution of the Debate, 1982, Theories of Development: Mode of Production or Dependency (with Dale Johnson), 1983; mng. ed. Latin American Perspectives qtly jnl, 1974—. BA, Dartmouth Coll., 1957; MBA, Stanford U., 1959, MA, 1963, PhD, 1965. Mem. faculty Univ. Calif., Riverside, 1963—, prof. dept. poli. sci., 1975—. Grantee OAS, 1971, Social Sci. Research Council, 1971, 75; Fulbright sr. lectr. Council on Edn., Washington, 1983, 85. Mem. Am. Poli. Sci. Assn., Latin Am. Studies Assn. Office: Dept Poli Sci U Calif Riverside CA 92521

CHILD, ROSS, see Shanstra, Carla Ross

CHILDRESS, WILLIAM DALE, (Chilly, Ozark Chilly), b. Hugo, OK, Feb. 5, 1933; s. J.W. and Viola Lorraine (Couch) C.; m. twice; children—Diane Marie, Christopher, Jason, David. Poetry in December, Poetry Now, Poetry, Kenyon Rvw, Harpers, The Nation, New Repub, Mademoiselle, Southern Rvw, many other mags.; fiction and non-fiction in Southern Rvw, Smithsonian, Sports Afield, Saturday Evening Post, Holiday,

BH&G, Gourmet, many other pop. and lit mags and anthologies. MFA, U. of Iowa, 1968. Freelance wrtr./photog., 1972-81; columnist, St. Louis Post Dispatch ("Out of the Ozarks"), 1981—. Corporal, US Army, 1951-58, paratroops; USAF, 1959. Stephen Vincent Benét award, Poet Lore, 1970; Story Anthology award (Whit/Hallie Burnett), 1970; Devins award, 1972; Ill. Arts Cncl. award, 1974; Pulitzer Prize nomination, 1985. Mem. PSA. Home: Rt One Box 312 Anderson MO 64831

CHILDS, SISTER MARYANNA, (C. Sand Childs), b. NYC, Jan. 16, 1910; d. James Michael and Clara Henrietta (Sand) C. Author: The Littlest Angel and Other Legends, 1942, My Little Book of Thanks, 1957, My Mary Book, 1959, With Love and Laughter, 1960, My Little Book of Manners, 1963, With Joy and Gladness, 1964, The Sounds of Ireland, 1969, Lovesongs: 1930-1980, 1980. Contrbr. poems, articles, stories to numerous mags. B.A., St. Mary of the Springs, 1942; M.A., Catholic U., 1948. Prof., Ohio Dominican Coll., Columbus, OH, 1946-86, chmn. English dept., 1947-85, prof. emeritus, 1986—. Grantee Am.-Irish Fdn., 1965, Ohio Arts Council, 1980; recipient Grand prize World of Poetry, 1986. Mem. MLA, Verse WG, Ohio Poetry Day Assn. Home: 1216 Sunbury Rd Columbus OH 43219

CHILLY, see Childress, William Dale

CHIN, DARYL, b. NYC, Nov. 2, 1953; s. Kaimno and Lolly (Jarm) C. Playwriter, designer, dir. (with Larry Qualls): The Dialectic of Enlightment, 1982, Act and the Actor, 1984, Narco-cism, or the Drug of Self-Love, 1985, Aspersion Cast, 1985. Mng. ed.: Film Cultrue, 1975-76; cons. ed.: VRI, Imperial Beach, CA, 1984—; ed.: (VRI Theater Series) Vol. 1: Ice Station Zebra (Mosakowski), 1986, Vol. 2: Nuit Blanche (Chong), 1986, Vol. 3: A Walk Out of Water (Driver), 1986, Vol. 4: Thin Wall (Sutton), 1986, Vol. 5: The White Crow (Freed), 1986, Vol. 6: The Team (Feely), 1987, Vol. 7: Because Pretty Girls Aren't That Smart (Lynch), 1987, Vol. 8: Bodacious Flapdoodle (Wellman), 1987; Art & Cinema (new series), 1986-87. Wrkg. on editing for VRI Theater Series. B.A., Columbia U., 1974. Film critic The Soho Weekly News, NYC, 1976-77; free-lance critic, 1969—, free-lance playwright, 1976—. Co-founder Asian-Am. Film Festival, NYC, 1978, Asian-Am. Video Festival, N.Y.C., 1982; co-organizer Asian Cinevision "Talk 'N' Cheap" Series NYC, 1987. Mem. DG. Home: 141 Wooster St New York NY 10012

CHIN, MARILYN MEI LING, b. Hong Kong, Jan. 14, 1955, came to U.S., 1961, d. George G. G. and Rose (Wong) Chin; m. Robert Nadler. Author: Dwarf Bamboo (poems), 1986; ed.: Writing from the World, 1984; co-translator: The Selected Poems of Ai Qing, 1984, Devil's Wind: Poetry by Gozo Yoshimasu, 1981; contrbr. poetry: Yearbook of Am. Poetry, Kayak, MS, Seneca Rvw, other publs. BA, U. Mass., 1977; MFA, U. Iowa, 1981. Instr. U. Iowa, Iowa City, 1978-82; translator, ed. Intl. Writing Program, Iowa City, 1978-82; guest ed. The Iowa Rvw, 1982-83; bilingual counselor Crestwood Psychiatric Hosp., Vallejo, Calif., 1982-83; Wallace Stegner fellow in poetry, Stanford, 1984-85; NEA fellow, 1985. Mem. AWP, P&W, AAP. Home: 3144 Anza St San Francisco CA 94121

CHING, CHAUNCEY T. K., b. Honolulu, July 25, 1940, s. Robert C. and Elsie L. C.; m. Theodora Ying Lam, July 7, 1962; children—Donna, Cory. Author: Simple Computing, 1984, Computer Applications in Agriculture, 1985, Production Economics, 1985. AB in Econ., U. Calif., Berkeley, 1962; PhD in Ag. Econ., U. Calif., Davis, 1967. Prof. Coll. Agr., U. Nev., Reno, 1972-80, Coll. Trop. Agr. and Human Resources, U. Hawaii, Honolulu, 1980-84; dir. Hawaii Inst. Tropical. Agr., Honolulu, 1984—. Commr. Nev. State Duty Commn., 1977-79. Home: 1239 Alewa Dr Honolulu HI 96817

CHING, LAUREEN, see Kwock, Laureen C.

CHOCK, ERIC EDWARD, b. Honolulu, Aug. 8, 1950; s. Edward Y. T. and Shigerko Miyagi C. Author: Ten Thousand Wishes, 1978; ed. Talk Story Anthol., 1978; Bamboo Ridge, The Hawaii Writers' Qtly, 1978—; Small Kid Time Hawaii, Poems by Hawaii's children, 1981. BA in sociol., U. Pa., 1971; MA in English, U. Hawaii, 1977. Poet in the schl; Dept Edn, Honolulu, 1973—; coordinator, 1974—. Commissioner, City Commn. on Culture and the Arts, Honolulu, 1982-84 (poetry award, 1977). Bd. dirs. Hawaii Lit. Arts Council (pres., 1980). Address: 1665 Piikoi St No 4 Honolulu HI 96822

CHOHN, MIJAEL, see McCormick, Patrick M.J.

CHOMSKY, AVRAM NOAM, b. Phila., Dec. 7, 1928; s. William and Elsie (Simonofsky) C.; m. Carol Doris Schatz, Dec. 24, 1949; children: Aviva, Diane, Harry Alan. Author: Syntactic Structures, 1957, Current Issues in Linguistic Theory, 1964, Aspects of the Theory of Syntax, 1965, Cartesian Linguistics, 1966, Topics in the Theory of Generative Grammar, 1966, (with Morris Halle) Sound Pattern of English, 1968, Language and Mind, 1968, American Power and the New Mandarins, 1969, At War with Asia, 1970, Problems of Knowledge and Freedom, 1971, Studies on Semantics in Generative Grammar, 1972, For Reasons of State, 1973, (with Edward Herman) Counterrevolutionary Violence, 1973, Peace in The Middle East?, 1974, Logical Structure of Linguistic Theory, 1975, Reflections on Language, 1975, Essays on Form and Interpretation, 1977, Human Rights and American Foreign Policy, 1978, (with Edward Herman) The Political Economy of Human Rights, 2 vols., 1979, Rules and Representation, 1980, Lectures on Government and Binding, 1981, Towards a New Cold War, 1982, Concepts and Consequences of the Theory of Government and Binding, 1982, Fateful Triangle, 1983, Turning the Tide, 1985, Knowledge of Language, 1986, Barriers, 1986, Pirates and Emperors, 1986, On Power and Ideology, 1987. BA, U. Pa., 1949, MA, 1951, PhD, 1955. Jr. fellow Soc. Fellows, Harvard, 1951-55; research fellow Harvard Cognitive Studies Center, 1964-67. Fellow AAAS; corr. fellow Brit. Acad.; mem. Natl. Acad. Scis., Am. Acad. Arts and Scis., Linguistic Soc. Am. Home: 15 Suzanne Rd Lexington MA 02173

CHOPP-SCHEUERMANN, JOAN JANET, (Joan), b. Detroit, Feb. 28, 1931; d. Roy and Ann (Sibincic) Chopp; m. Robert Henry Scheuermann, June 4, 1953; children: Michael, Teresa, David, Susan E., Thomas, Sara. Contrbr. poetry: Poetry Press, Yes Press, Hieroglyphics Press, Suwanee Poetry Rev., numerous other lit. mags., anthologies. Wrkg. on poetry collection, haiku collection. BA, Siena Heights Coll., 1953. Freelance artist, art tchr. Home: 4 Hanover St Pleasant Ridge MI 48069

CHORLTON, DAVID, b. Spittal-an-der-Drau, Austria, Feb. 15, 1948 (arrvd. USA 1978), s. Frederick and Ernestine (Eder) C. M. Roberta Jeanne Elliott, June 21, 1976. Author: Corn Dance, 1978, Poetry by David Chorlton, Stephanie Myers, Agnese Udinotti, 1980, No Man's Land, 1983 (chapbooks) Allegiance to the Fire, 1984, Old Water, 1985, The Skin Beneath, 1986, Without Shoes, 1987; contrbr. poems to numerous lit mags, including Poet Lore, Permafrost, Abraxas, Pikestaff Forum, Mississippi Mud, Slipstream, Webster, Taurus, Pteranodon. Mem. Rio Grande Wrtrs. Assn. Home: 118 W Palm Ln Phoenix AZ 85003

CHOW, TSE-TSUNG, b. Kiyang, Hunan, China, Jan. 7, 1916; s. P'eng-Chu and Ai-Ku (Tsou) C.; m. Nancy N. Wu; children: Lena Jane, Genie Ann. Author: Election, Initiative, Referendum and Recall: Charter Provisions, in Michigan Home Rule Cities, 1958, The May Fourth Movement: Intellectual Revolution in Modern China, 1960, Research Guide to The May Fourth Movement, 1963, Hai-yen (Stormy Petrel) (collected poems), 1961, On the Chinese Couplet, 1964, editor: Wen-Lin: Studies in the Chinese Humanities, 1968, A New Study of the Broken Axes in the Book of Poetry, 1969, An Index to Mathews' Chinese-English Dictionary with a New Method of Arranging Chinese Words, 1971; On Wang Kuo-Wei's Tz'u Poetry, 1971; Chinese transl. Rabindranath Tagore's Fireflies, 1971, Stray Birds, 1971, Odyssey (1st part), 1972; Papers on Dream or the Red Chamber, 1982, Ancient Chinese Shamanistic Medicine and the "Six kinds of Poetry": A Study of the Origin of China's Romantic Literature, 1986; ed., Wen-Lin, vol. 2, 1987. BA, Cheng-Chih U., 1942; MA, U. Mich., 1950, PhD, 1955. Editor-in-chief New Understanding monthly, Chungking, China, 1942-43; editor-in-chief City Govt., monthly, 1943-44; editor New Critic monthly, 1945. Guggenheim fellow, 1966-67. Mem. MLA, The Island Society of Singapore (hon. pres.), Singapore Assn. Writers (hon. pres.). Home: 1101 Minton Rd Madison WI 53711

CHOYKE, PHYLLIS MAY, (Phyllis Ford, Phyllis Ford-Choyke), b. Buffalo, Oct. 25, 1921, d. Thomas Cecil and Vera (Buchanan) Ford; m. Arthur Davis Choyke, Jr., Aug. 18, 1945; children—Christopher Ford, Tyler Van. Ed. Gallery Series-Poets, vols. 1-5, 1967-77, (with Jessie Kashmar and Helen Winter) Apertures to Anywhere (poems), 1979; contrbr. poetry: Rhino, Voices Israel, Poetry Northwest. BS, Northwestern U. Reporter City News Bur., Chgo., 1942-43, Chgo. Tribune, 1943-44; feature wrtr. Office War Info., N.Y.C., 1944-45; secy. Artcrest Products Co., Inc., Chgo., 1951-63, v.p., 1963—. Grantee CCLM, 1972. Mem. Soc. Midland Authors, Chgo. Press Vets. Assn., Women in Dir.'s Chair. Home: 29 E Division St Chicago IL 60610

CHRISTENSEN, PAUL, (NORMAN), b. West Reading, PA, Mar. 18, 1943; s. Kenneth Serenus and Ann Theresa (Tramuta) C.; m. Jane Tee Flowers, Jan. 2, 1964 (div. June 1968); 1 child, Sean Oliver; m. Catherine Ann Tensing, Aug. 30, 1970; children: Maxine Elizabeth, Signe Laura, Cedric Owen. Author: Old and Lost Rivers, 1977; Charles Olson: Call Him Ishmael, 1979; The Vectory, 1981; Signs of the Whelming, 1983; Weights and Measures, 1985; The Gulfsongs, 1986; ed. Osiris at the Roller Derby (J. Edgar Simmons), 1984; A Citadel of Breathless Wonder (Judson Crews), 1986. BA, Coll. William and Mary, 1967; MA, U. Cin., 1970; PhD, U. Pa., 1975. Prof. English, Tex. A&M U., College Station, 1974—. Grantee Tex. Commn. on Arts, 1983-84. Mem. MLA, P&W. Home: 206 S Sims

St Bryan TX 77803

CHRISTIAN, PAULA, b. Nashville, July 24, 1953; d. Leonard Paul and Tommie (Wilson) Christian; m. Glenn Gallaher, Jan. 7, 1980. Author poetry collection, Blood Lines, 1985; contrbr. poetry to Samisdat, Miss. Valley Rvw, Poem, Hiram Poetry Rvw, Yarrow, Dragonfly. BA, Memphis State U. Freelance writer, Waynesboro, Tenn., 1977—; pub. Wayne County Herald, 1983-85. Mem. MENSA. Address: Box 91 Waynesboro TN 38485

CHRISTIAN, REBECCA ANNE, b. Des Moines, Oct. 7, 1952; d. George Edward and Rena Raye (Ballenger) C.; m. Russell Jeff Thompson, Jan. 22, 1977; children—Kate, Nicholas, George. Co-author: Vocational Biographies, 1977, 78, 79, 80; How to Get the Best Health Care for Your Money, 1979; The Prevention Guide to Surgery and its Alternatives, 1980. Author: Cooking the Spanish Way, 1985. Contrbr. articles to Travel/Holiday, Prevention, Seventeen, Woman's World, numerous others. BA, Ia. State U., 1974. Reporter Mason City Globe Gazette, Mason City, Ia., 1974-75; pub. relations dir. State Library, Des Moines, 1976-77; editor/writer Rodale Press, Emmaus, Pa., 1977-78; contrbg. ed. The Iowan, Des Moines, 1984—; correspondent Des Moines Register, Des Moines, 1984—. Vice pres. Crest Area Arts Council, Creston, Ia., 1984-86. Recipient Essay Contest award Verbatim Mag., 1983, honorable mention Redbook Mag., 1981, News Reporter award Ia. Bd. Realtors, 1975, 1st prize for short story Seventeen Mag., 1973. Mem. Talented Gifted Edn. Assn., Midwest Travel Writers Assn. Home: 1003 W Adams Creston IA 50801

CHRISTIAN, ROLAND CARL, (Bud), b. LaSalle, CO, June 7, 1938, s. Roland Clyde and Ethel Mae (Lattimer) C.; m. Joyce Ann Kincel, Feb. 15, 1959; children—Kathleen Christian-Davis, Kristine Christian Sweet. Author: Be Bright! Be Brief! Be Gone! A Speaker's Guide (textbook), 1983, Potpourrivia, A Digest of Curious Words, Phrases and Trivial Information, 1986, Nicknames in Sports: A Quiz Book, 1986; contrbr.: Ways We Write (by George Gates), 1964, Family Treasury of Great Poems, 1982, Our Twentieth Century's Greatest Poems, 1982, Anti-War Poems: Vol. II, 1985-86, World Poetry Anthology, 1986, Impressions, 1986, other anthols. BA in English, Speech, Colo. State Coll., 1962; MA in English, U. Northern Colo., 1966. High schl. tchr., 1962-67; prof. English, poetry, speech, lit. Northeastern Jr. Coll., Sterling, Colo., 1967—, also lit. advisor New Voices art and lit. mag. Mem. NCTE, Poets of the Foothills. Home: 1027 Park St Sterling CO 80751

CHRISTIANSON, KEVIN EARL, b. Racine, WI, Jan. 30, 1948; s. Earl Owen and Geraldine Esther (Grube) C.; m. Lisa Anne Washburn. Author: Figs & Raisins, 1971, Seven Deadly Witnesses, 1971. Contrbr. poems to lit mags. BA, U. Wis.-Madison, 1974; MA, U. Wis.-Milw., 1979, PhD, 1986. Instr., Lynchburg Coll., Va., 1984-86, asst. prof., 1986-87; asst. prof. Eng. Schl of the Ozarks (MO), 1987—. Mem. SAMLA, Sigma Tau Delta. Address: Eng Schl of the Ozarks Pt Lookout MO 65726

CHRISTMAN, ELIZABETH A., b. St. Louis, Jan. 18, 1914, d. Edwin Roy and Genevieve (Templeman) Christman. Author: A Nice Italian Girl, 1976, Flesh and Spirit, 1979, A Broken Family, 1981. AB, Webster Coll., Webster Groves, Mo., 1935; MA, NYU, PhD, 1972. Lt. agt. Harold Ober Assocs., NYC, 1946-69; asst. prof., then assoc. prof. DePauw U., Greencastle, Ind., 1969-76; assoc. prof. Am. studies U. Notre Dame (Ind.), 1976—. Served to lt. (j.g.), USN, 1944-46. Office: Am Studies U N D Notre Dame IN 46556

CHRISTMAN, HENRY MAX, b. Kansas City, MO, Jan. 21, 1932; s. Henry Max and Irene Blanche (McBride) C. Author: The Public Papers of Chief Justice Earl Warren, 1959, The Mind and Spirit of John Peter Altgeld, 1960, A View of the Nation, 1960, Walter P. Reuther—Selected Papers, 1961, This Is Our Strength-Selected Papers of Golda Meir, 1962, Walt Whitman's New York, 1963, Peace and Arms-Reports from the Nation, 1964, The South As It Is, 1965, One Hundred Years of the Nation, 1965, The Essential Works of Lenin, 1966, The American Journalism of Marx and Engels, 1966, Communism in Practice: A Documentary History, 1969, The State Papers of Levi Eshkol, 1969, The Essential Tito, 1970, Neither East Nor West: The Basic Documents of Non-alignment, 1973, Indira Gandhi Speaks: On Democracy, Socialism, and Third World Nonalignment, 1975, Mahout, 1982; editor: (Myers) The History of Bigotry in the United States, 1960, (La Guardia) The Making of an Insurgent, 1961, (Garland) A Son of the Middle Border, 1962. BA in history and govt., U. Mo. at Kansas City, 1953; PhD, U. Belgrade, 1971. Home: 435 FDR Dr New York NY 10002

CHRISTOPHER, MATTHEW FREDERICK, (Matt Christopher), b. Bath, PA, Aug. 16, 1917; s. Fred and Mary Rose (Vass) C.; m. Catherine Mary Krupa, July 13, 1940; children—Martin Allan, Pamela Jean, Dale Robin, Duane Francis. Author: Basketball Sparkplug, 1957, Wing T. Fullback, 1960, Crackerjack Halfback, 1962, Catcher with a Glass Arm, 1964, Mystery on Crabapple Hill, 1965, The Year Mom Won the Pennant, 1968, The Kid Who Only Hit Homers, 1972, The Fox Steals Home, 1978, The Dog That Stole Football Plays, 1980, Tight End, 1981, Drag Strip Racer, 1982, Return of the Headless Horseman, 1982, The Dog that Called the Signals, 1982, Dirt Bike Runaway, 1983, Favor for a Ghost, 1983, The Great Quarterback Switch, 1984, Supercharged Infield, 1985, The Hockey Machine, 1986, Red Hot High-Tops, 1987, numerous others. Contrbr. articles, short stories to numerous mags. Active Administrative Council Boy Scouts Am., Syracuse, N.Y., 1950-54; bulltn. ed. Lansing Lions Club, N.Y., 1961-73. Recipient Short-short Story award in writing contest Wrtr.'s Digest, 1936, 48, Article prize, 1964, 65, scriptwriting prize, 1983. Mem. Soc. Children's Book Wrtrs. Home: 1830 Townes Ct Rock Hill SC 29730

CHRISTOPHER, MAURINE BROOKS, b. Three Springs, TN; d. John Davis and Zula (Pangle) Brooks; m. Milbourne Christopher, June 25, 1949. Author: America's Black Congressmen, 1971, Black American's in Congress, 1976. BA, Tusculum Coll., 1941. Reporter, feature writer Balt. Sun, 1943-45; TV radio Advt. Age, 1947-51, sr. editor, head broadcast dept., 1951-77, dep. exec. editor, NYC, 1977-79, dep. exec. editor, Videotech columnist, 1979—; roving ed., member edl. bd., 1984—. Home: 333 Central Park W New York NY 10025

CHRISTOPHERSON, LEROY OMAR, b. Spring Grove, MN, Apr. 25, 1935; s. Ephriam Roy and Ladice May (Chase) C.; m. Alice Marie Nelson, June 19, 1954; children—Alan Lee, Tony Russell, Tloa Marie. Author scripts for training, how-to-do-it films including Zellwood, 1978, The Viking, 1982, Strawberry Spring, 1980, Orlando Garden Show, 1983, Psalms in Our Life, 1982, Volkswagon, The Car Nobody Wanted, 1983, Reunion '84, 1984. contrbr. articles to trade mags. Grad. public schs., Mabel, MN. Owner, E-Z Baby Portrait Plan, Orlando, FL, 1962-65, Christopherson's Studio, Orlando, 1965-72; wrtr., producer LAC Productions, Orlando, 1973-80; wrtr., photographer Alice Christopherson & Assoc., Orlando, 1980—. Head of beautification Merchant's Assn., Orlando, 1967-68; mem. better bus. bur. Orlando Area Chamber of Commerce, 1967-69. Mem. Fla. Profl. Photographers (Ed.'s award 1974, 75, 76, Sections Pres. award 1979.) Profl. Photographers Soc. Central Fla (Outstanding Service award 1976, Pres.'s award 1978). Home: 2606 Grassmere Ln Orlando FL 32808

CHUBB, HILKKA AILEEN, b. Bessemer, MI, May 11, 1930; d. John Lottanen and Hilda Marie (Ranta) Korhonen; m. William Robert Chubb, Mar. 16, 1950 (dec. Nov. 23, 1969); children—Susan, Karen. Author: Learning Today for Tomorrow, 1978; (films) Finnish Immigrant Lives, 1982, Tradition Bearers, 1982. Wrkg. on two novels. B.S., Northern Mich. U., 1961, M.A., 1966. Translator, ed., rsearcher Northern Mich. U., Marquette, 1980-82, sr. secy., 1982-86; freelance wrtr., 1973—. Mem. WD Book Club. Home: 1205 Gray Marquette MI 49855

CHUNN, LEONA HAYES, b. Croton, OH, May 1, 1885, d. John Henry Riggs and Altha Jane (Weaver) Hayes; m. Perry Edwin Chunn, 1915 (dec. 1973). Author: Rouse with the Dawn, 1965, Verse in Blythe Spirit, 1975; contrbr. to Chgo. Tribune, Christian Sci. Monitor, Unity Mag., Penwomen, other publs. Recipient numerous awards N.C. Poetry Soc., Fla. Fedn. Women's Clubs, Poetry Council N.C., Ohio Poetry Day Assn., N.C. Poetry Council. Mem. Penwomen N.C., Fla. Penwomen. Home: 1616 Cedar St Lawrenceville IL 62439

CHURCH, JOHN IRWIN, b. Boise, ID, Oct. 23, 1919, s. Elmer Edmund and Vivian Elma (Irwin) C.; m. Bette Isobel Elliott, Apr. 10, 1943 (dec. Oct. 1972); children—John Robert, Elizabeth Ann; m. Marguerite Chien Eng, Nov. 2, 1974. Author: Hoosier College Poet, 1984. BA, DePauw U., 1940; MA, U. Oreg., 1948. Instr. U. Oreg., 1949-51; officer U.S. Dept. State, 1954-73. LTC, U.S.Army, Rtd. ACLS advanced grad fellow, 1951. Home: Box 1215 McLean VA 22101

CHUTE, MARCHETTE, b. Wayzata, MN, Aug. 16, 1909; d. William Young and Edith Mary (Pickburn) C. Author: Rhymes About Ourselves, 1932, The Search for God, 1941, Rhymes About the Country, 1941, The Innocent Wayfaring, 1943, Geoffrey Chaucer of England, 1946, Rhymes About the City, 1946, The End of the Search, 1947, Shakespeare of London, 1950, An Introduction to Shakespeare, 1951, Ben Jonson of Westminster, 1953, The Wonderful Winter, 1954, Stories from Shakespeare, 1956, Around and About, 1957, Two Gentle Men: The Lives of George Herbert and Robert Herrick, 1959, Jesus of Israel, 1961, (with Ernestine Perrie) The Worlds of Shakespeare, 1963, The First Liberty: A History of the Right to Vote in America, 1619-1850, 1969, The Green Tree of Democracy, 1971, PEN American Center: A History of the First Fifty Years, 1972, Rhymes About Us, 1974. AB, U. Minn., 1930; LittD, Western Coll. for Women, 1952, Carleton Coll., 1957, Dickinson Coll., 1964. Recipient Author Meets the Critics award for best non-fiction of, 1950; Chap-Book award PSA, 1954; N.Y. Shakespeare Club award, 1954; Secondary Edn. Bd. book award, 1954. Fellow Royal Soc. Arts, Soc. Am. Historians. Mem. PEN (pres. 1955-57), Am. Acad. Arts and Letters, Renaissance Soc. Am. Home: 450 E 63d St New York NY 10021

CHUTES, BRENDA, see Bone, Brenda Kay

CIABATTARI, JANE DOTSON, b. Emporia, KS, Mar. 27, 1946, d. William Francis and Dorothy Lea (Bruner) Dotson; m. G. Mark Ciabattari, Jan. 7, 1967; 1 son—Scott Antony. Contrbr. short stories to The North Am. Rev., Redbook, Kans. Women Wrtrs., articles to Working Woman, Threepenny Rvw, Glamour, Dial, others; novella condensed in Redbook, 1980. BA in Creative Writing, Stanford U., 1968; MA in Creative Writing, San Francisco State U., 1984. Mng. ed. Calif. Living, San Francisco Examiner & Chronicle, 1973-82, Redbook, NYC,1982-83; exec. ed. mag. devel. projects CBS Publs., 1983; ed.-in-chief Dial, 1983-85; contrbg. ed. Parade mag., 1985—, Working Woman; adj. prof. journalism NYU, 1985-86; Columbia, 1985—. Press chair Mont. gov.'s Commn. on Status of Women, 1972-73. Mem. AG, ASME, Women's Media Group. Home: 36 W 75th St New York NY 10023

CIHLAR, CHRISTINE CAROL, b. Milw., Feb. 25, 1948; d. Peter J. and Sylvia I. (Sunstrom) Cihlar; m. Frederick L. Rippy, Jr., July 25, 1981. Contrbr. articles to profl. jnls. Ed.: Luther Coll. Chips, 1967-68, Luther Mag., 1972-78, Luther coll., 1974-78. B.A., Luther Coll., 1970. Asst. ed. Colo. Leader, Denver, 1971-72; dir. public info. Luther Coll., Decorah, IA, 1972-78; founder, owner The Emporium, Deorah, 1975-77; regional sales representative food service div. Hormel Co., Charlotte, NC, 1978-80; dir. public affairs St. Mary's Coll. of Md., St. Mary's City, 1980—. Mem. CASE, EWA, Am. Numismatic Assn. Home: 29 White Elm Ct California MD 20619

CIRCUS, ANTHONY, see Hoch, Edward D.

CIRINO, LEONARD JOHN, b. Los Angeles, Sept. 11, 1943, s. Herbert and Marjorie C. Author chapbooks: The Extension of Olson's Arm, 1978, From His Own Bridge Into the River, 1979, gd god, 1979, Umbilical, 1980, A Small Book of Changes, 1988; contrbr. to Small Pond, Plains Poetry Jnl, Stone Country, numerous other lit mags. BA in English, Sonoma State U., 1977. Poetry instr. Coll. of Redwoods, Ft. Bragg, Calif., 1980—. Home: Box 591 E Rd N Albion CA 95410

CISSOM, MARY JOAN, (M. J. Rebecca Riley), b. Ripley, MS, Feb. 27, 1941, d. Jim R. and Lars Etta (Riley) Turner; m. William Howard Franks, Aug. 25, 1956 (div. 1958); 1 son, William Allen; m. 2d, William Melvin Cissom, Nov. 28, 1964. Contrbr. to Alsop's Tables, Mountain Breeze, Message mag., Ideals mag., So. Sentinel, other publs., Edn. Northeast Miss. Jr. Coll. Freelance wrtr., 1961—; columnist So. Sentinel, Ripley, Miss., 1986; Oxford Times, Miss., 1986—. Wrkg. on novel. Home: Rt 1 Box 110-B Blue Mountain MS 38610

CITINO, DAVID JOHN, b. Cleveland, March 13, 1947; s. John David and Mildred Rita (Bunasky) Citino; m. Mary Helen Hicks, July 26, 1969; children—Nathan John, Dominic John, Maria Ann. Author: The Gift of Fire, 1986, The Appassionata Doctrines, 1986, The Appassionata Lectures, 1984, The Appassionata Poems, 1983, Last Rites and Other Poems, 1980; editor: Cornfield Review, 1974-84, The Ohio Journal, 1985—, 73 Ohio Poets, 1978, Poetry Ohio: An Anthology of Ohio Poems, 1984. BA, Ohio U., 1969; MA, Ohio State U., Columbus, PhD,1974. Asst. prof., Ohio State, Marion, 1974-85; assoc. prof., Ohio State, 1985—; poetry ed., Ohio State Univ. Press, 1986—. Mem. MLA, AWP, Verse Writers Guild of OH, Poets' League of Greater Cleveland. Home: 278 Huber Village Blvd Westerville OH 43081

CLAIBORNE, CRAIG, b. Sunflower, MS, Sept. 4, 1920; s. Lewis Edmond and Kathleen (Craig) C. Author: Classic French Cuisine, 1970, Cooking with Herbs and Spices, rev. ed., 1970, New York Times International Cook Book, 1971, Craig Claiborne's Kitchen Primer, 1972; editor: New York Times Cook Book, 1961, New York Times Menu Cook Book, 1966, (with Virginia Lee) The Chinese Cook Book, 1972, Craig Claiborne's Favorites From The New York Times, Vol. I, 1975, II, 1976, III, 1977, IV, 1978, (with Pierre Franey) Time/Life Books' Classic French Cookery, 1970, Veal Cookery, 1978, The New New York Times Cook Book, 1979, The Gourmet Diet Cook Book, 1980, A Feast Made for Laughter, a memoir with recipes, 1982. BJ, U. Mo., 1942; student, Ecole Hoteliere, Lausanne, Switzerland, 1953-54. With ABC, Chgo., 1946-49; now food editor N.Y. Times. Served to lt. USNR, 1942-45, 50-53. Decorated chevalier Ordre du Merite Agricole. Home: 15 Clamshell Ave East Hampton NY 11937

CLAIRE, ELIZABETH, b. NYC, Apr. 6, 1939; d. Albert Rudolph and Anna (Gregor) Eardley; m. Edward Simms, 1957 (div.); children—Jon Arthur, James Allen; m. 2d, Richard Buehler, May 31, 1969 (div.). Author: A Foreign Student's Guide to Dangerous English, 1980, A Foreign Student's Introduction to American Humor, 1984, Hi! English as a Second Language for Children, 1985, ESL Teacher's Activities Kit, 1987. BA magna cum laude in Spanish, CCNY, 1966; MA in TESOL N.Y. U., 1968. Tchr. NYC pub schls., 1966-73; Fort Lee pub. schls., N.J., 1977—; lectr. Weight Watchers Intl. Inc., 1975; salesperson Reader's Digest Ednl. Div., 1976; pub., wrtr. Eardley Pubs., N.J., 1980—. Experienced Tchr. fellow NYU, 1967. Mem. Natl. Tchrs. English to Speakers Other Langs., N.J. Tchrs. English to Speakers Other Langs., Wrtrs. Anonymous Northern N.J., Mensa, Phi Beta Kappa. Home: 302 Nedellec Dr Saddle Brook NJ 07662

CLAIRE, WILLIAM, b. Northampton, MA, Oct. 4, 1935; s. William Cahil and Vena Marie (Lasonde) Claire; m. Sedgley Mellon Schmidt, Nov. 24, 1973; 1 son—Mark-Andrew. Editor: Publishing in the West, 1974, Essays of Mark Van Doren: 1924-1972, 1981, Literature and Medicine; contrbr., American Scholar, Antioch Rvw, The New Republic, The NY Times, others. BA, Columbia College, 1958; MLS, Georgetown U., 1980. Dir., Wash. office, Amer. Paper Institute, 1964-68; exec. dir., World Federalists, USA, Wash. DC, 1969-71; dir., Wash. office, State Univ. of New York, Washington, DC, 1971-83; pres., Washington Resources, Inc., 1984—; editor, Voyages: A national Literary Magazine, 1967-73. Mem. PSA, PEN. Home: 4705 Butterworth Pl NW Washington DC 20016

CLAMPITT, AMY KATHLEEN, b. New Providence, IA, June 15, 1920; d. Roy Justin and Lutie Pauline (Felt) Clampitt. Author: Multitudes, Multitudes, 1974, The Kingfisher, 1983, A Homage to John Keats, 1984, What the Light Was Like, 1985, Archaic Figure, 1987. BA with honors, Grinnell College, 1941, LHD, 1984. Awards: Guggenheim fellow, 1984, lit. award, AAIAL, 1984; fellowship award, AAP, 1984; elected mem. of Inst., Am. Acad. and Inst. of Arts and Letters, 1987. Home: c/o Alfred A Knopf 201 E 50th St NYC 10022

CLARK, ALBERT CARL VERNON, (Aelbert Clark Aehegma), b. White Plains, NY, Apr. 21, 1947; s. Frederic Ralph and Virginia Alma (Mehne) C.; children—Michelle, Diana, Alexander, Arrien. Author: No Poems, 1972, Revolutionary Danbury: The Romance and the Reality (also ed.), 1976, Turtle Dance: Poems of Hawaii and translations from the Hawaiian Creation Chant: The Prologue to the Night World of the Kumulipo, 1984; author multi-media performances: In Search of the Mythical Beast, 1980, The Night World, 1983, Aloha Opera, 1985. AS, Norwalk (Conn.) Community Coll., 1969; BA in English, Central Conn. State Coll., 1972; MA in Multi-media, Beacon Coll., Washington, 1980. Printer, pub., ed., feature wrtr. Danbury News Times, Gen. Print, Western Printing, Danbury Advocate, Occult Jnl., 1969-79; poet-in-schls., Fairfield, Conn., 1975-77; poet-in-residence Children's Mus., Fairfield, 1976-79; freelance poet, multi-media artist, N.Z. and Hawaii, 1980—. Grantee Conn. Commn. for Arts, 1977; recipient Lloyd Preston Jones award Ky. Poetry Soc., 1978, 1st place poetry award Ka Huliau Mag., 1984. Mem. P&W, West Hawaii Wrtrs., The Artery (founder, dir.), Artist Guild (founder, dir.), Conn. Artists' Confedn. (founder, chmn. 1978); Pacific Museum Studios (founder, dir.). Home: Box 156 Na'alehu HI 96772

CLARK, DIXIE DUGAN, (Dixie Dugan), b. De Ridder, LA, May 6, 1940; d. John William and Minnie Lou (Reeve) Dugan; m. Albert Lee Clark, Dec. 7, 1986; children—Lillie, Robert, Charles McEntire. Author, ed.: Health Care Study for Older Americans, 1985; columnist Ark. Mag., 1987—. Founded Mellow Pages, 1980; ed. Mellow Pages, 1981-82, writer, 1980-87. Ed.: Lincoln Ledger, Star City, AR, 1966-67. Wrkg. on update of health care study. B.A. in English, Jnlsm., La. Coll., 1964; Cert., N.Y. U., 1977; M.A. Certificate, Gerontology, U. Ark., 1980-85. Reporter, Alexandria Daily Town Talk, LA, 1964; program analyst Fed. Council on Aging, Washington, 1984-85; exec. dir. Central Ark. Area Agcy. on Aging, Inc., 1979-84,85—. Mem. Gov.'s Advisory Council on Aging, Little Rock, 1987-88. Recipient cert. of Merit, State of Ark., 1985, Leadership award Ark. Assn. Area Agcys. on Aging, 1983; Exemplary Svc. Award, Chamber of Commerce, 1983, 86. named Outstanding Arkansan, Ark. Genl. Assembly, 1985, State of Ark., 1986. Mem. Ark. Assn. Area Agys. Aging (pres. 1983-84, 87-88), Natl. Assn. Area Agcys. Aging (state liaison 1986-87), Southwest Soc. Aging (past bd. dirs.). Address: Box 5988 North Little Rock AR 72119

CLARK, ELEANOR, b. Los Angeles; d. Frederick Huntington and Eleanor (Phelps) C.; m. Robert Penn Warren, Dec. 7, 1952; children: Rosanna, Gabriel. Author: novels The Bitter Box, 1946, Baldur's Gate, 1971, Dr. Heart, A Novella and Other Stories, 1975, Gloria Mundi, 1979, Camping Out, 1986; for children The Song of Roland, 1960; non-fiction Rome and a Villa, 1952, expanded ed., 1975, The Oysters of Locmariaquer, 1964, Eyes, Etc., A Memoir, 1977, Tamrart: 13 Days in the Sahara, 1983; translator: Dark Wedding (R. Sender), 1943; contbr. stories, essays and rvws. to numerous publs. BA Vassar Coll. Served with OSS, 1943-45. Guggenheim fellow, 1946-47, 49-50; recipient

Natl. Book Award, 1965. Mem. Natl. Inst. Arts and Letters (award 1946). Address: 2495 Redding Rd Fairfield CT 06430

CLARK, LAVERNE HARRELL, b. Smithville, TX, June 6, 1929; d. James Boyce and Belle (Bunte) Harrell; m. L. D. Clark, Sept. 15, 1951. Author: The Deadly Swarm and Other Stories, 1985, Focus 101, 1979, Re-Visiting Mari Sandoz' Plains Indian Country, 1977, They Sang for Horses: The Impact of the Horse on the Folklore of the Navajo and Apache, 1966, 1971, pb ed. 1984; ed. The Face of Poetry, 1979; contrbr. short stories Southwest, The Pawn Rvw, Sands, Vanderbilt Rvw, Pembroke, St Andrews Rvw, Cache Rvw. Adv and sales Columbia Univ. Press, NYC,1951-54; news writer Bulletin Mag., NYC,1959-60; dir. Poetry Ctr. of Univ. Ariz., Tucson, 1962-66; freelance writer, photographer and lectr., 1966—. Am Philos. Soc. grantee, 1969; recipient Julian Ocean Lit. prize Triple P Publs., Boston, 1984, Univ. Chgo. Folklore prize, 1966, 1st Place Fiction (for Deadly Swarm), 1986, Biennial Am. PEN Women. Mem. Rio Grande Writers Assn., Am. PEN Women, Soc. Southwestern Authors, WWA. Address: 4690 N Campbell Ave Tucson AZ 85718

CLARK, MARGARET GOFF, b. Oklahoma City, Mar. 7, 1913; d. Raymond and Fanny (Church) Goff; m. Charles Robert Clark, Sept. 2, 1937; children: Robert Allen, Marcia Clark Noel. Author: The Mystery of Seneca Hill, 1961; The Mystery of the Buried Indian Mask, 1962; Mystery of the Marble Zoo, 1964; Mystery at Star Lake, 1965; Adirondack Mountain Mystery, 1966; Mystery of the Missing Stamps, 1967; Danger at Niagara, 1968; Freedom Crossing, 1969; Benjamin Banneker, 1971; Mystery Horse, 1972; Their Eyes on the Stars, 1973; John Muir, 1974; Death at Their Heels, 1975; Mystery of Sebastian Island, 1976; Mystery in the Flooded Museum, 1978; Barney and the UFO, 1979; Who Stole Kathy Young?, 1980; Barney in Space, 1981; Barney on Mars, 1983; The Latchkey Mystery, 1985; also over 200 short stories, mostly juveniles, 50 poems. BS in Edn., State Univ. Coll., Buffalo, 1936. Freelance wrtr., 1942—. Mem. MWA, Natl. League Am. Pen Women, AG, Assn. Profl. Women Wrtrs. (past pres.). Home: 5749 Palm Beach Blvd Lot 334 Fort Myers FL 33905

CLARK, MARY HIGGINS, b. NYC, Dec. 24, 1929; d. Luke J. and Nora C. (Durkin) Higgins; m. Warren Clark, Dec. 26, 1949 (dec. Sept. 1964); children: Marilyn, Warren, David, Carol, Patricia. Author: Aspire to the Heavens, A Biography of George Washington, 1969, Where Are the Children, 1976, A Stranger is Watching, 1978, The Cradle Will Fall, 1980, A Cry in the Night, 1982, Stillwatch, 1984, Weep No More, My Lady, 1987. BA, Fordham U., 1979. Recipient Grand Prix de Litterature Policiere, France, 1980. Mem. MWA (dir., pres, 1987), AL, ASJA, Acad. Arts and Scis. Office: 210 Central Park S New York NY 10019

CLARK, MASON ALONZO, b. Ladysmith, WI, Aug. 13, 1921, s. Lester A. and Edith Viola (Clark) C.; m. Mary Violet Deacon, Feb. 2, 1923; children—James, Thomas. Author: The Healing Wisdom of Doctor P. P. Quimby, 1982, The Official Guide to Winning at Kensington, 1983. BS, Northwestern Inst. Tech., Evanston, Ill., 1947; MS, Northwestern U., Evanston, 1949. Vice-pres. Microwave Assocs., West Sunnyvale, Calif., 1968-70; mktg. mgr. Micromanipulator Co., Sunnyvale, 1983—. Home: 836 Starlite Ln Los Altos CA 94022

CLARK, MATT, b. Chgo., Feb. 3, 1930; s. Matthew and Kathryn (Speckman) C.; m. Ellen Ann Mitchell, Aug. 23, 1952 (dec. 1978); children: Thomasin, Geoffrey Beach, Douglas Mitchell. Reporter Boston Traveler, 1953-56, sci. editor, 1956-58; writer Med. News, NYC, 1958-61; medicine editor Newsweek mag., 1961—; freelance contrbr. to publs. in field, 1958—. Grad., Hill Schl., 1947; A.B., Wesleyan U., Middletown, Conn., 1951. Served with USNR, 1951-53. Recipient Albert Lasker Med. Journalism award, 1964, 67; Editorial award Assn. Advancement Med. Instrumentation, 1967; Penney-Mo. mag. award in health, 1967-71, 75; med. journalism award AMA, 1969; Claude Bernard Sci. Journalism award Natl. Soc. for Med. Research, 1971; Page One award Newspaper Guild N.Y., 1974, 83; Media award (mag.) Am. Cancer Soc., 1976; N.Y. Deadline Club award, 1977; Am. Med. Writers Assn.-Searle Labs journalism award, 1983. Fellow AAAS; mem. Natl. Assn. Sci. Writers. Home: 201 E 87th St 12-K New York NY 10028

CLARK, THOMAS WILLARD, b. Oak Park, IL, Mar. 1, 1941, s. Arthur Willard and Rita Mary (Kearin) C.; m. Angelica Louise Heinegg, Mar. 21, 1968; 1 dau.—Juliet Lee. Author numerous books of poetry including: Stones, 1969, Air, 1970, John's Heart, 1972, At Malibu, 1975, When Things Get Tough on Easy Street: Selected Poems 1963-78, 1978; Heartbreak Hotel, 1981, Paradise Resisted: Selected Poems 1978-84, 1984, The Border, 1985, Disordered Ideas, 1987; author: Champagne and Baloney: The Rise and Fall of Finley's A's, 1976, No Big Deal (with Mark Fidrych), 1977, The World of Damon Runyon, 1978, One Last Round for the Shuffler, 1979, The Great Naropa Poetry Wars, 1980, Jack Kerouac, 1984, Late Returns: A Memoir of Ted Berrigan, 1985, Kerouac's Last Word, 1987; fiction works include: Who is Sylvia?, 1979, The Master, 1979, The Last Gas Station and Other Stories, 1980, Property, 1985, The Exile of Celine, 1986. BA, U. Mich., 1963; MA, Cambridge (Eng.) U., 1965, U. Essex, Eng., 1967. Poetry ed. Paris Rvw., 1963-74; instr. Am. poetry U. Essex, 1966-67; ed. Boulder (Colo.) Monthly, 1979-80; book reviewer San Francisco Chronicle, Los Angeles Herald Examiner, others, 1977—; instr. U. Calif. Extension, Berkeley, 1985—. Fulbright fellow, 1963-65; grantee Rockefeller Fdn., 1968-69, Guggenheim Fdn., 1970-71, NEA, 1985-86. Home: 1740 Marin Ave Berkeley CA 94707

CLARK, VIOLA ANNA, (V. Anna Antila), b. Calumet, MN., Dec. 1, 1930, d. Swanti and Anna (Mursu) Antila; m. Eugene Burton Clark, Apr. 11, 1950; children—Kathleen, Jennifer, Thomas, Patricia, Ronald. Contrbr. to Loonfeather. Wrkg. on historical novel, children's fiction. Student public schls., Coleraine, Minn. Freelance market research interviewer, 1963—; owner, operator Four Flags Gift Shop, Nisswa, Minn., 1970-75; freelance wrtr. Home: Star Rt 2 Box 190 Pequot Lakes MN 56472

CLARK, WALTER H., b. Pittsfield, MA, Oct. 6, 1931; s. Walter H. and Ruth (O'Brien) C.; m. Francelia Mason, Oct. 14, 1967; 1 dau., Alison. Author: Nineteen Poems, 1967, View from Mount Paugus, 1976, 2d ed., 1979, nominated Lamond award; contrbr. Reading in Philosophy of Edn., 1970, Aesthetic Concepts and Edn., 1970, Tchg. Environmental Lit., 1985. BA with honors, Swarthmore Coll., 1954; PhD, Harvard, 1957-65, MAT. Assoc. prof. English U. Mich., Ann Arbor, 1965—; co-founder Mich. New England Lit. Program. Served to Sp-3, US Army, 1954-56, W. Ger. Recipient Fulbright lectureship, Graz, Austria, 1971-72; Silver medal of Merit, Carl Francis Univ., Graz, 1972. Mem. Am. Soc. Aesthetics, Council Tchrs. English, MLA. Address: 122 Chapin St Ann Arbor MI 48103

CLARKE, JOHN R., b. St. Paul, Apr. 15, 1913; s. John R. and Anne (Murphy) C.; m. Opal Emmons, Dec. 16, 1939; children—Carol, John, Dale, Richard, Susan. Author: Executive Power—How to Use It Effectively, 1979; contrbr. numerous articles to trade publs. AB, U. Puget Sound, 1938; MS, Purdue U., 1939. Psychologist B.F. Goodrich Co., Akron, Ohio, 1939-45; dir. indsl. relations Stewart-Warner Corp., Chgo., 1945-60; v.p. Outboard Marine Corp., Waukegan, Ill., 1960-75; cons., Boca Raton, Fla., 1987—. Mem. Fla. Freelance Wrtrs. Assn. Home: 411 SW 7th Ave Boca Raton FL 33486

CLARKE, LA VERNE ALEXIS EVANS, b. Bklyn., Aug. 25, 1955, d. Alexander William and Geneva Mable (White) Evans; m. Mark Judson Clarke, Aug. 21, 1981; 1 child, LeMarr Evan. Contrbr. to N.Y. Poetry Soc. Anthology. BA, Bklyn. Coll., 1978, MS, 1984. Tchr. public schls., Bklyn., 1978—. Home: Brooklyn NY

CLASSON, LOUISE LAURETTE, b. Berlin, NH, Sept. 21, 1948; d. Laurier Napoleon and Aline (Landry) Renaud; m. Kenneth Harry CLasson, June 6, 1970; children—Brian, Christopher. contrbr. articles to mags., newspapers. B.A. in Sociology, Rivier Coll., 1970. Staff wrtr. Building & Grounds Maintenance, 1986—, Maintenance & Modernization Supervisor, 1986—; ed. Petroleum Marketing Management, 1986—, Allied Landscape, 1986—. Mem. Intl. Wrtr. Data Bank. Address: 8212 Langport Terrace Gaithersburg MD 20877

CLAUSEN, WENDELL VERNON, b. Coquille, OR, Apr. 2, 1923; s. George R. and Gertrude (Johnson) C.; m. Corinna Slice, Aug. 20, 1947; children: John, Raymond, Thomas; m. Margaret W. Woodman, June 19, 1970. Editor: Persius, 1956, Persius and Juvenal, 1959, Appendix Vergiliana, 1966; editor, contrbr.: The Cambridge History of Latin Literature, 1982; assoc. editor: Am. Jnl Philology, 1976-81; contbr. articles in classical philology. AB, U. Wash., 1945; PhD, U. Chgo., 1948; AM (hon.), Harvard U., 1959. Fellow Am. Acad. in Rome, 1952-53, ACLS, 1962-63; fellow commoner Peterhouse, Cambridge, Fellow Am. Acad. Arts and Sciences. Home: 8 Kenway St. Cambridge MA 02138

CLAY, DISKIN, b. Fresno, CA, Nov. 2, 1938; s. Norman and Florence Patricia (Diskin) C.; m. Sara Christine Clark, Oct. 28, 1978; children: Andreia, Hilary, Christine. Author: Oxyrhynchan Poems, 1973, (with Stephen Berg) Oedipus the King, 1978, Lucretius and Epicurus, 1983; mem. editorial bd.: Jnl of Modern Greek Studies, 1983-86; contrbr. articles on Greek lit. and philosophy to profl. jnls.; mem. editorial bd.: Am. Jnl Philology, 1975—; editor, 1982-87; founding ed., Am. Jnl of Philoology Monographs in Classical Philology, 1986—. BA, Reed Coll., 1960; postgrad. (Fulbright fellow), France, 1960-61; MA (Woodrow Wilson fellow), U. Wash., 1963; PhD, Am. Schl. Classical Studies, Athens, Greece, 1963-64. ACLS fellow, 1975; NEH fellow, 1974-75. Home: 206 Hawthorn Rd Baltimore MD 21210

CLAYTON, JAY, b. Dallas, July 11, 1951; s. John B. III and Margaret (Fooshee) C.; m. Ellen

Wright; 1 son, James Wright. Author: Romantic Vision and the Novel, 1987; contrbr. stories, essays and interviews to So. Rvw, Southwest Rvw, Kans Qtly, ELH, Contemporary Lit. Assoc. ed., Contemporary Literature. BA, Yale U., 1974; PhD, U. Va., 1979. Asst. prof. Univ. Wis., Madison, 1979-86, assoc. prof., 1986—. Fellow Wis. Arts Bd., 1980, ACLS, 1981-82. Mem. MLA, AWP. Address: Dept Eng Univ Wis White Hall Madison WI 53706

CLAYTON, JOAN, see Guy, Carol Ann

CLAYTON, JOHN J., b. NYC, Jan. 5, 1935, s. Charles and Leah (Kaufman) C.; m. Marilyn Hirsch; children—Laura, Josh; m. 2d, Marlynn Krebs; 1 child—Sasha; m. 3d, Sharon Dunn. Author: Saul Bellow: In Defense of Man, 1968, 79,What Are Friends For? (novel), 1979, Bodies of the Rich (short fiction collection), 1984; ed. D.C. Heath Introduction to Fiction, 1977; contrbr. short fiction, essays to Playboy, Antioch Rvw, Va. Qtly Rvw, Mass. Rvw, others. BA, Columbia U., 1956; MA, N.Y. U., 1959; PhD, Ind. U., 1966. Instr. U. Victoria, B.C., Can., 1962-63; lectr. U. Md. European campus, 1963-64; asst. prof. Boston U., 1964-69; mem. faculty U. Mass., Amherst, 1969—, now prof. NEA fellow, 1980. Mem. PEN. Home: 12 Lawton Rd RFD 3 Amherst MA 01002

CLEARY, MICHAEL, b. Schenectady, NY, Feb. 27, 1945; s. Gerald P. and Mary Elizabeth (Baker) C.; m. Kay Alexander, Aug. 24, 1968; children—Beth, Brian. Contrbr. articles to books: Fifty Western Writers, 1982, Twentieth Century Western Writers, 1982, Shane: The Critical Edition, 1984; contrbr. numerous articles and poems to var. jnls.; ed., The South Florida Poetry RVW, 1983-86. BA, SUNY at Potsdam, 1967; MS, SUNY at Plattsburgh, 1971; DA, Middle Tenn. State U., 1978. Eng. tchr. Queensbury H.S., Glens Falls, NY, 1968-75; Eng. prof. Broward Commun. Coll., Ft. Lauderdale, FL, 1978—. 1st place, Artemis Poetry Contest, Artemis Lit. Mag., 1984. Mem. WALA, S. Fla. Poetry Inst. Home: 1037 SW 49th Terr Plantation FL 33317

CLEAVER, VERA ALLEN, b. Virgil, SD, Jan. 6, 1919; d. Fortis Alonzo and Beryl Naiome (Reininger) Allen; m. William Joseph Cleaver, Oct. 4, 1945. Author: (with Bill Cleaver) Ellen Grae, 1967, Lady Ellen Grae, 1968, Where the Lilies Bloom, 1969, Grover, 1970, The Mimosa Tree, 1970, I Would Rather Be a Turnip, 1971, The Mock Revolt, 1971, Delpha Green & Company, 1972, Me Too, 1973, The Whys and Wherefores of Littabelle Lee, 1973, Dust of the Earth (WWA Spur award Best Western Juvenile Novel, Lewis Carroll Bookshelf award), Trial Valley, 1977, Queen of Hearts, 1978, A Little Destiny, 1979, The Kissimmee Kid, 1981. Student pub. schls. Freelance pub. accountant, 1945-54. Served with USAF, Tachikawa, Japan, 1954-56, Chaumont, France, 1956-58. Address: Bantam Books 666 5th Ave New York NY 10103

CLEDE, EMILE WILLIAM, JR., (Bill Clede), b. Fort Worth, TX, Nov. 26, 1927; s. Emile W. and Evangeline (Hagler) C.; m. Mildred C. Holloway, Dec. 5, 1946 (div. 1963); children—Emile W., Michael W., Edward R.; m. Lois C. Stone, Nov. 25, 1965. Author: Police Handgun Manual, 1985, Police Shotgun Manual, 1986, Police Nonlethal Force Manual, 1987. Contrbr. articles to trade, popular mags. including Law & Order, Field & Stream, Sports Afield, Dog World. Outdoor ed. Hartford Times, CT, 1962-76. B.A., U. Md., 1951. Promotion specialist Winchester-Western, New Haven, 1957-62; outdoor dir. Sta.-WTIC, Hartford, 1967-76; mem. public relations Chas. Palm/Moroton Advt., Bloomfield, CT, 1976-84; free-lance wrtr., Wethersfield, CT, 1984—. Served to capt. USAF, 1951-53. Recipient numerous jnlsm. awards. Mem. OWAA (past pres.), SPJ, Boating Wrtrs. Intl. Home: 272 Ridge Rd Wethersfield CT 06109

CLEM, WENDY LEE, (Wendy Stevenson Clem), b. Lansing, MI, Feb. 13, 1950; d. William John and Charlotte May (Simpson) Stevenson; m. Mark Stephen Clem, Sept. 11, 1971; children—Paul, Beth, Todd. Contrbr. articles, short humor to mags. newspapers, Woman's Day Mag., others; sport catalogs, brochures. Contrbg. ed. & researcher: The Brainstorm Book, 1986-87, heritage Mag., 1986. Wrkg. on humor-related material, non-fiction article, cartoon gags. Student Wayne State U., 1968-71. Humorist/satirist Springbrook Pub., Inc., St. Clair Shores, MI, 1979-80; wrtr., co-owner Art-Beats Unlimited, Roseville, MI, 1981-85; freelance wrtr., 1979—. Home: 19235 Skyline Roseville MI 48066

CLEMENT, DALLAS BRENT, b. Rigby, ID, Dec. 2, 1940; s. Victor Floy and Belva (Heilison) C.; m. Ann Ellen Mitchell, Nov. 23, 1966; children—Dallas, Vaughn, Cameron, Nicole, Candace, Christopher. Ed.: Potato Grower of Idaho, 1972-75, Cutter and Chariot Racing World, 1972-75, Idaho East, 1974-75, Ag Marketer, 1975-85, Agri-Equipment Today, 1976—, Onion World, 1984—, Potato Country, 1985—. AA, Ricks Coll., 1961; BA, Brigham Young U., 1966, MA, 1968. Tech. ed. Allied Chemical, Idaho Falls, ID, 1968-70; writer/ed. Deseret News, Salt Lake City, 1970-72; ed. Harris Pub. Co., Idaho Falls, ID, 1972-75; ed/owner Columbia Pub., Yakima, WA, 1975—. Mem. AAEA. Home: Rt 3 Box 3765 Selah WA 98942

CLEMENT, GREGORY VANCE, b. McAlester, OK, May 24, 1928; s. Albert Bittick and Mary Agnes (Hamilton) C.; m. Sharon Ferguson, July 1, 1950; children: Chris, Pat, Steve. Contrbr. articles: Marine Bus., Small Boat Jnl., numerous other publs. Attended U. Okla., 1951. Yacht broker, Young's Yacht Sales, New Orleans, 1970-72, self-employed, Guntersville, Ala., 1972-80; tchr. Jefferson Parish Schs., New Orleans, 1980—. Mem. NWC, New Orleans Wrtrs. Network. Home: 5701 Chopin Ct Metairie LA 70003

CLEMENTS, ARTHUR L., b. Bklyn., Apr. 15, 1932; m. 2d, Susan A. Hauptfleisch, May 5, 1983; children—Margaret, Stephen, Michael, Thomas. Author: The Mystical Poetry of Thomas Traherne, 1969, Common Blessings (poems), 1987; ed. John Donne's Poetry, 1966; contrbr. poems and essays to various jnls. Wrkg. on Poem Sequences, Modern and Metaphysical Poets (criticism). AB, Princeton U., 1954; PhD,Syracuse U., 1964. Assoc. prof. English, SUNY, Binghamton. Recipient Poetry Ctr Prize, 1986; poetry prize Sri Chimoy Poetry Fdn., 1980; NEH fellow, 1967-68; Research Fdn. SUNY fellow, 1973, 74, 78. Mem. PSA, AAP, MLA. Office: RD 7 Box 35 Binghamton NY 13903

CLEMENTS, FRED PRESTON, b. Mar. 27, 1954; s. Fred Preston and Virginia Louise (Vaughn) C.; m. Julie Ann Bruce, Apr. 10, 1982. Ed., contrbr.: Manhattan Beach News, El Segundo Herald, 1974-76, The Beach Reporter, 1977-80, The Beverage Bulletin, 1980-81; Motorcycle Dealernews, Aftermarketing Mag., 1982—. AA in Jnlsm., El Camino Coll., 1974; BA in Jnlsm., San Jose State U., 1976. Staff writer/ed. Beach Cities Nwsprs., Hermosa Beach, CA, 1974-76; ed. The Beach Rptr., Manhattan Beach, CA, 1977-80; sr. ed. Beverage Bulletin, Beverly Hills, CA, 1980-81; ed./assoc. pub. HBJ Pubns., Santa Ana, CA, 1982—. Mem. WPA. Office: HBJ Pub 1700 E Dyer Rd Santa Ana CA 92705

CLEVELAND, CEIL MARGARET ELLEN, b. Olton, TX, Jan. 10, 1938, d. James Donaldson C. and Margaret Ellen (Gowdy) Slack; m. Donald Waldrop; children—Wendy Ellen, Jay Hardy, Tim Owen; m. 2d, Jerrold K. Footlick, Sept. 25, 1984. Ed.: English Musical Culture, 1975, Management of Power, 1981; ed., contrbr.: We Have Something to Say, 1976, Syzygy, 1974, Columbia Jnl; contrbr. Aspen Inst. Reader, consumer mags. and newspapers. Wrkg. on short fiction, novel, TV and film scripts. BA, magna cum laude, Whitworth Coll., Spokane, Wash., 1969; MA (honors), Midwestern U., Wichita Falls, Tex., 1972; adj. prof. Eng. Columbia U., 1977-85; U. Cin., 1972-75; ed. Horizons, U. Cin., 1975-77, Syzygy, a Jnl. of Poetry and Prose, 1973-77; ed.-in-chief Columbia mag., NYC,1977-85; communications cons., NYC, since 1976; assoc. vp for publns. and media affairs, SUNY, Stonybrook, NY, 1986—; panelist profl. meetings, presenter symposia. Trustee Council Advancement and Support of Edn. (ed. Top Ten Univ. mag., 1981, 82, 83, 84, 85, 87, Best Articles in Higher Edn. award 1982-87), Women in Communications, Woodrow Wilson Fellow, Ivy League Eds. Group, Sibley Soc. Disting. Eds. Office: 320 Admin SUNY Stony Brook NY 11744

CLIFT, G.W., b. Winfield, KS, May 27, 1952; s. W.S. and J.L. (Marsh) C.; m. D.C. Collins, May 26, 1975. Contrbr. to Vanderbilt RVW, 1980, Manhattan Mercury, 1985, Twister, 1986. BS in Hist., Kansas State U., 1974, MA in Engl., 1979. Instr., Engl. dept., Kansas State U., Manhattan, KS, 1975—; ed. Touchstone, Manhattan, 1978, The Manhattan Project, 1984, 85; ed. Literary Mag. Rvw, Manhattan, 1982—; assoc. dir. Conf. for H.S. Writers, Manhattan, 1984-85, 87, dir., 1986. Mem. KSU Writers Soc., AWP, JASNA. Office: Eng Dept KSU Manhattan KS 66506

CLIFTON, LINDA JANE, b. Bklyn., July 31, 1940; d. Harry George and Sophie (Shapiro) Robinson; m. Kyle Clifton Jr., 1963 (div. 1973); 1 dau., Cynthia Leigh. Editor Crab Creek Rvw, 1983—; contrbr. poems, short stories to Calyx, Visions, Tinderbox, Ellensburg Anthology; also articles in English Jnl, Wash. English Jnl. BA, U. Wash., 1962, MA, 1982. Tchr. various schl. dists. in Wash., 1963-83, Northshore Schl. Dist., Bothell, Wash., 1984—; asst. dir. Puget Sound Writing Program, Seattle, summer 1983—. Trustee, Central Wash. U., Ellensburg, 1977-82; pres. Wash. Women United, Olympia, 1980-82. Mem. Wash. State Council Tchrs. of English (rec. sec.), NCTE. Home: 806 N 42nd Seattle WA 98103

CLIFTON, MERRITT ROBIN, b. Oakland, CA, Sept. 18, 1953; s. Jack William and Phyllis Jean (Stoner) C.; m. Pamela June Kemp, Nov. 29, 1976. Author: (novels) 24x12, 1975, A Baseball Classic, 1978, (novella) Betrayal, 1980; (essays) Freedom Comes from Human Beings, 1981, The Pillory Poetics, 1975, 3rd ed. 1981; (exposes) The Asbestos Line, 1981, Learning Disabilities: What the Publicity Doesn't Tell, 1981; (poetry) From the Golan Heights, 1975, Vindictment, 1977, From the Age of Cars, 1980, Live Free or Die!, 1982; (short stories) Two from Armageddon, 1976, Baseball Stories for Girls and Boys,

1982; many others; editor Samisdat (lit mag and chapbook series), 1973—, The Reed, 1971-73, Those Who Were There (bibliography of Vietnam War), 1984. Wrkg. on novel, also history of Vietnam War resistors in Quebec. BA in creative writing, San Jose State U., 1974. Editor, pub. Samisdat, Richford, Vt., 1973—; environ. journalist, art critic, sports writer The Record, Sherbrooke, Que., Can., 1978-86; environ. journalist The Townships Sun, Lenoxville, Que., 1977; contrbg. editor The Small Press Rvw, 1975—. Corr. sec. Eng of the Line, Sutton, Que., 1981—; publicity dir. Tour du Lac Brome, Knowlton, Que., 1982—; contrbg. wrtr., The Animals' Agenda, 1986—; columnist, Innings, 1986—. Phelan Fdn fellow, 1971-75; recipient 1st place local angle natl. story Centre for Investigative Journalism, 1979-80, 2d place Dumont-Frenette Writing prize Assn. Quebec Regional English Media, 1983, 1st place Concours de Reportage, Environment Quebec, 1984. Mem. Soc. Am. Baseball Research, Brome Lake Runners, Coureurs Au Pied de Sherbrooke, Missisquoi Runners, Quebec Press Council. Office: Box 129 Richford VT 05476

CLINE, CHARLES (WILLIAM), b. Waleska, GA, Mar. 1, 1937; s. Paul Ardell and Mary Montarie (Pittman) C.; m. Sandra Lee Williamson, June 11, 1966; 1 son, Jeffrey. Poet: Crossing the Ohio, 1976, Questions for the Snow, 1979, Ultima Thule, 1984; contrbr. to numerous mags. AA, Reinhardt College, Waleska, GA, 1957; BA, Peabody College, Nashville, TN, 1960; MA, Vanderbilt U., 1963. Asst. English prof. Shorter College, Roma, GA, 1963-64; English instr. W. GA College, 1964-68; manuscript procurement ed. Fideler Co., Grand Rapids, MI, 1968; assoc. English prof. Kellogg Community College, Battle Creek, MI, 1969-75; English prof., resident poet 1975—. Grant to edit Bicentennial anthology, MI Council for the Arts, 1975; Two first places, Poetry Soc. of MI, 1975; Resolutions of Appreciation, MI Senate and House, Kalamazoo City Commission, 1981; Intl. Acad. of Poets, Publication Prize, 1983; World Institute of Achievement, Literary Award, 1985. Home: 9866 S Westnedge Ave Kalamazoo MI 49002

CLINE, RICHARD ALLAN, (Rich Cline, Allan Lichti), b. Santa Monica, CA, June 30, 1961, s. Ronald Allan and Barbara Ann (Lichti) C. Author: Mine (poetry), 1985; wrtr., dir. screenplay: War and Peace, 1983; wrtr., ed., pub.: Writing on the Wall newsletter, 1985—, Shadows on the Wall (film rvws.), 1985—; ed., Around the World mag., 1987—. Wrkg. on book of poetry, novel, screenplays, articles, short stories. BA in Journalism cum laude, Azusa Pacific U., 1983. Mng. ed. The Clause, Azusa, Calif., 1981-83; account rep., copy wrtr. Treasure Chest Advt., Glendora, Calif., 1983-85; wrtr., Focus on the Family, 1985-86; publs. ed. HCJB World Radio, Opa Locka, Fla. and Quito, Ecuador, 1986—. Mem. Am. Film Inst. Office: Box 553000 Opa Locka FL 33055

CLINE, TIM, b. Portland, IN., Jan. 30, 1942; s. Meredith L. and Maribel (Borton) C.; m. Ann Marie Brown, Dec. 31, 1979; children—Shannon, Tim, Brock, Mary. Columnist: Sports Car Mag.; contrbr. articles to popular mags., newspapers including Car & Driver, Road & Track, Washington Post Mag. Pub.: The Stage Times newsletter. BS, Southern Ill. U., 1970. Pres., Ampersand Communications, Washington, 1980—. Served to sgt. USAF, 1963-67. Mem. Intl. Motor Press Assn., Washington Automotive Press Assn. Office: Ampersand 3636 16th St NW Washington DC 20010

CLINGAN, ROBERT KEITH, (Gerry Clinton), b. Jackson, MS, June 9, 1961; s. Alton B. and Margaret Ann (Webb) C. Staff wrtr. Northside Sun, Jackson, 1985; columnist Lifestyles, Jackson, 1985. Sports editor: Miss. State U. Reflector, 1982-84, Picayune Item, 1985—; mng. editor: Miss. State U. Bulldog, 1983. B.Bus. Adminstrn., Miss. State U.-Starkville, 1984. Mem. Miss. Press Assn., Miss. Sports Wrtrs. Assn., Picayune Jaycees (dir. 1985-86). Home: 2801 Cooper Rd Picayune MS 39466

CLINTON, D., see Clinton, Lloyd DeWitt

CLINTON, DOROTHY LOUISE, b. Des Moines, Apr. 6, 1925; d. Gilbert H. and Carrie Randle; m. Moses S. Clinton, June 17, 1950; 1 son, Jerome Boyd. Contrbr. poetry to Magic of the Muse, Carousel Qtly, Am. Poetry Assn., Iowa Poetry Assn., other publs. Wrkg. on play, poetry. BFA, Drake U., 1949. Home: 1530 Maple St Des Moines IA 50316

CLINTON, GERRY, see Clingan, Robert Keith

CLINTON, LLOYD DeWITT, b. Topeka, Aug. 29, 1946, s. John Jarrett and Natalie (Mathews) C.; m. Jacqueline Fay Hollebeek, July 14, 1973; 1 stepchild, Melissa Elizabeth Sobin. Author: The Conquistador Dog Texts, 1976, The Rand-McNally Poems, 1977, The Coyot. Inca Texts, 1979, Night Jungle Bird Life, 1983, Das Illustrite Mississippithal Revisited, 1983, Furnace: A Ballet Performance, 1984, (under pseudonym Witt Lowidski) Active Death: Unholy Rhymes, 1986; ed. Salthouse, 1975—; co-ed. An Americas Anthology: A Geopoetics Landmark, 1983; ed., Eleven Wisconsin Poets, 1987; contrbr. to anthologies Winning Hearts and Minds, 1972, Itinerary 2: Poetry, 1975, Heartland II: Poets of the Midwest, 1975, Poetry Ohio: Art of the State, 1984. Wrkg. on The Collected Writings of Our Lady of Cortez, Furnace (journeys with Coronado). BA, Southwestern U., Winfield, Kans., 1968; MA, Wichita State U., 1972; MFA, Bowling Green State U., 1975, PhD,1981. Teaching asst. Wichita State U., Kans., 1970-72; teaching fellow Bowling Green State U., Ohio, 1973-75, 78-81; instr. Wayne State U., Detroit, 1975-77; lectr. U. Wis.-Whitewater, 1981-85, asst. prof., 1985—. Served with U.S. Army, 1968-70, Vietnam. Recipient hon. mention Elliston Book Award, U. Cin., 1976; CCLM publ. grantee, 1975-82; Mich. Council for Arts creative artist grantee, 1981. Mem. AWP, CCLM, MLA. Home: 3567 N Murray Ave Shorewood WI 53211

CLOTHIER, PETER D., b. Newcastle, UK, Aug. 1, 1936; arrd. US, 1964; s. Harry L. and Peggy Williams C.; m. Elizabeth Foot, Feb. 17, 1960 (div. 1970); 2 sons, Matthew, Jason; m. 2d, Ellen Blankfort, Nov. 11, 1972; 1 dau., Sarah. Author: Aspley Guise, 1969; Parapoems, 1974; Chiaroscuro, 1985. BA, Cambridge Univ.-England, MA; PhD, U. Iowa. Asst. prof. in comparative lit. USC, Los Angeles, 1968-76; dean/acting dir. Otis Art Inst., Los Angeles, 1976-79; dean of arts Loyola Mary Mount Univ., Los Angeles, 1980-84. NEA fellow, 1976-77; Rockefeller fellow, 1980. Mem. Coll. Art Assn., Los Angeles County Mus. Art, Mus. Contemporary Art of Los Angeles. Address: 2341 Ronda Vista Dr Los Angeles CA 90027

CLOUD, DAVID EUGENE, b. Wichita, KS, Oct. 29, 1934; m. Georgianna K. Albright, Dec. 6, 1958; children—Mark, Julie, Gary. Author: Youth and Sex Education, 1968, Preparing for Marriage and Home Life, 1968, Studies of Genesis, 1970, The Gospel of Luke, 1971, The Gospel According to Paul, 1973, The Layman's Introduction to the Old Testament, 1975, My Space, Your Space, 1979. Contrbr. articles to mags., jnls. Editor: The Protestant Herald, 1967-68. Wrkg. on short stories, plays, children's books, religious non-fiction books. BA, Friends U., Wichita, 1958; MRE, Central Bapt. Theol. Sem., Kansas City, Kans., 1962. Ordained to ministry, 1962. Minister of edn. Am. Bapt. Chs., Minn., Kans., Colo., Ind., Ill., 1962-74; pastor Am. Baptist Chs., Illinois, KS, 1974-84; substitute tchr. pub. and pvt. schls., Ill. and Kans., 1972-86; supr. Herbalife, Internat., Wichita, 1983-86; tchr. English/writing Bethel Life Schl., Wichita, 1984-85; free-lance wrtr., 1965—. Mem. PSA, Pub. Fellowship, Christian Poetry Assn., Kansas Author's Club. Home: 2312 Fairchild Wichita KS 67219

CLOUSTON, JUDITH KAY, b. Liberal, KS, Jan. 20, 1940; d. Oliver Scott and Doris Evelyn (Thompson) Brown; m. Paul S. Jones, July 4, 1963 (div. Dec., 1968); m. 2d, Peter L. Clouston, Mar. 21, 1975. Contrbr. non-fiction to newspapers and mags. including Tucson Citizen, Columbus Dispatch, Kansas City Star, Marriage & Family Living, Amelia, Poet's Corner. Student Colo. Woman's Coll., 1957-59; BA in Journalism, U. Ariz.-Tucson, 1964. Free-lance ct. reporter, metro Kansas City, 1970-72; official ct. reporter Cir. Ct., Jackson County, Mo., Kansas City, 1972-74, Dist. Ct., Johnson County, Olathe, Kans., 1974-80; free-lance writer, 1980—. Vol. The Whole Person, Inc., Kansas City, 1978—; docent Nelson-Atkins Mus. Art, Kansas City, 1982—. Mem. Women in Communications. Home: 8005 Nall Ave Prairie Village KS 66208

CLOUTIER, DAVID EDWARD, b. Providence, RI, Apr. 20, 1951; s. Maurice Roger and Adeline Alice (Abbott) Cloutier; m. Anne Frances Greene, Jun. 11, 1972; 1 son— Perrin Taliesin. Poetry collections: Soft Lightnings, 1982, Tongue and Thunder, 1980, Tracks of the Dead, 1976, Ghost Call, 1976. Translations of work of Jean Laude, and Claude Esteban. MA Brown U., BA, 1974. Teaching assoc. Brown U., 1981; asst. ed. Copper Beech Press (Providence), 1975-83; creative wrtg. specialist RI State Arts Council, 1970-75. Home: 51 Methyl St Providence RI 02906

CLOW, BARBARA HAND, b. Saginaw, MI, Feb. 14, 1943; d. Eugene Albert and Catherine (Wallace) Hand; m. John Collet Frazier, Aug. 4, 1962 (div. 1972); children—Thomas Frazier, Matthew Frazier; m. 2d, Gerald Cudahy Clow, June 22, 1974; children—Christopher, Elizabeth. Author: The Stained Glass Manual, 1976, Eye of the Centaur: A Visionary Guide into Past Lives, 1986; contrbr. to mags. inclg. Creation Mag., Pursuit Mag., Catastrophism and Ancient History. Student, U. Mich., 1961-63, Seattle U., 1964-66; MA, Mundelein Coll. Jewelry designer Deja Vue Jewelry, San Francisco, 1968-72; stained glass window designer Leverett Stained Glass Studio, Levgrett, Mass., 1972-76; acq. ed., 1983-86, mng. ed., Bear & Co., Santa Fe, 1986—. Office: 506 Agua Fria Drawer 2860 Santa Fe NM 87504

CLUNE, HENRY W., b. Rochester, NY, Feb. 8, 1890, s. George H. and Hattie (Bruman) C.; m. Charlotte Boyle; children—George, Peter, William, Barry. Attended pvt. schl. Author: (novels) The Good Die Poor, Monkey on a Stick, By His Own Hand, The Big Fella, Six O'Clock Casual, O'Shaughnessy's Cafe, (nonfiction) Main Street Beat, The Genesee, The Rochester I

Know, I Always Liked It Here; contrbr. to Monsey's N.Am. Rvw., Collier's, McClure's, also others. Columnist Gannet Newspapers, 1926-68. Served with U.S. Army, 1917-18. Recipient lit. award Rochester Pub. Library. Address: Box 31 Scottsville NY 14546

CLYNE, PATRICIA EDWARDS, (Allison Parker, P. E. Edwards), b. NYC, May 2, 1935, d. Ray Augustus and Neta Helen (Bohnsack) Edwards; m. Francis Gabriel Clyne, June 11, 1960; children—Christopher, Francis, Ray; 1 son by previous marriage: Stephen Paul DeVillo. Author: The Corduroy Road, 1973, Tunnels of Terror, 1975, Patriots in Petticoats, 1976, Ghostly Animals of America, 1977, Strange and Supernatural Animals, 1979, Caves for Kids in Historic New York, 1980, The Curse of Camp Gray Owl, 1981; editorial asst. on Collected Works of Edgar Allan Poe, vol. I, 1969, vols. II and III, 1978. BA in Journalism, Hunter Coll., 1958. Newspaper reporter, trade jnl. ed., ed. for book pubs., various locations to 1970; freelance wrtr., ed., 1970—; sr. ed. Library Research Assn., Monroe, N.Y., 1985—. Home: Box 147 Circleville NY 10919

COBB, WILLIAM, b. Green County, AL, Oct. 20, 1937; s. Edwin Sledge and Inez Susan (Land) C.; m. Loretta Douglas, Aug. 15, 1966; 1 child: Meredith. Author: Coming of Age At the Y, 1984, The Hermit King, 1986; plays Sunday's Child, Recovery Room; contrbr. essays and short stories to var. publs. inclg. Story, The Arlington Quarterly, Arete, Comment. Wrkg. on two plays. BA, Livingston Coll., 1961; MA, Vanderbilt U, 1963. Prof. English and writer-in-residence Univ. of Montevallo, Ala., 1963—. Fellow, NEA, 1978, Atlantic Ctr. for the Arts, Fla., 1985. Mem. DG. Address: Rt 2 Box 51 Montevallo AL 35115

COCHRANE, SHIRLEY GRAVES, b. Chapel Hill, NC, Mar. 5, 1925; d. Thornton Shirley and Mary Margaret (White) Graves; m. William McWhorter Cochrane, June 3, 1945; children: William Daniel, Thomas McWhorter. Author: (poems) Burnsite, 1979, Family & Other Strangers, 1986; co-ed.: The Good Doctor and Other Selections from the Essays and Addresses of William DeBerniere MacNider, 1953, New Eyes for Old: Nonfiction Writings by Richard McKenna, 1972, (fiction anthology) Through the Saloon Doors, 1982; co-ed., contrbr. (poetry anthology) The Other Side of the Hill, 1979; ed. Faces: Thirty Poems by Riley Hughes, 1981. AB, Agnes Scott Coll., 1946; MA, Johns Hopkins U., 1970. Ed. U. N.C. Press, Chapel Hill, 1946-52; lectr. Am. U., Washington, 1974—; instr. Georgetown U., Washington, 1978—; v.p. Washington Wrtrs. Pub. House, 1980, 83—, pres., 1981-82, 1987—; co-ord. Wash. Prize, Word Works. Recipient award Washington Wrtrs. Pub. House, 1979. Mem. Wrtr.'s Ctr., Washington Ind. Wrtrs., Phi Beta Kappa. Home: 127 7th St SE Washington DC 20003

CODDINGTON, JOSEPH, JR., b. Long Branch, NJ, Oct. 30, 1939; s. Joseph and Margaret (Reynolds) C.; m. Kathleen Backshall, Aug. 15, 1969; children—Kim, Joseph, Mary. Author: (novel) Sting of the Scorpion, 1980. Foreperson, Sandoz, Inc., East Hanover, N.J., 1966—. Served as pvt. U.S. Army, 1957-64. Home: Twin Oak Terr Tannersville PA 18372

CODRESCU, ANDREI, (Ames Claire, Tristan Tzara, Julio Hernandez, Alice-Henderson Codrescu), b. Sibiu, Romania, Dec. 20, 1946; came to U.S., 1966; s. Baron Julius Von Hunyadi and Eva (Bruckenthal) Geller; m. Alice Henderson; children: Lucian, Tristan. Author: (poetry) License to Carry a Gun, 1970, A Serious Morning, 1973, The History of the Growth of Heaven, 1973, For the Love of a Coat, 1978, The Lady Painter, 1979, Necrocorrida, 1982, Selected Poems: 1970-80, 1983; (fiction) Monsieur Teste in America, 1976, The Repentance of Lorraine, 1976, Samba de Los Agentes, 1982; (autobiography) The Life and Times of an Involuntary Genius, 1975, In America's Shoes, 1983; (chapbooks) Why I Can't Talk on the Telephone, 1972, the, here, what, where, 1972, Grammar and Money, 1973, Secret Training, 1973, A Mote Suite for Jan and Anselm, 1976, Diapers on the Snow, 1981; (translation) For Max Jacob, 1974; poetry in over 200 mags; other fiction and translations; author newspaper columns for Balt. Sun, 1979-84; editor, founder Exquisite Corpse: A Monthly Review of Books and Ideas, 1983—; contrbg. editor The American Book Rvw and San Francisco Rvw of Books. BA, U. Bucharest, Romania. Assoc. prof. La. State U., Baton Rouge, currently. NEA grantee, 1973, 83, 85; recipient Pushcart prize, 1980, 83, A.D. Emmart Humanities award, 1982, Towson Univ. prize for lit., 1983. Office: La State U Dept Eng Baton Rouge LA 70803

CODY, JAMES MARION, b. Springfield, MO, Feb. 5, 1945; s. Joseph Fincher and Josephine Alice (McDaniel) C. Author: (prose) Colorado River, 1972; (poetry) Return, 1976, 81, Ritual Songs, 1982, Prayer to Fish, 1984, A Book of Wonders, 1986, The Canyon/Eagle: First Sweat/Ritual Songs, 1986; transl. Oib, The Celtic Dawn, The Revival of Celticism in America, 1986; ed. Wood Ibis lit. jnl., 1974—; Blood Root (Alma Villanueva), 1976, 82; Hablando de brujas y la gente de antes (Jim Sagel), 1981; Breeds (Roxy Gordon), 1984; The Return of the Inca, 1986, numerous other vols. BA in philosophy, U. Tex., Austin, 1970. Ed.-pub. Place of Herons Press, Austin, 1974—; rehab. technician Brackenridge Hosp., Austin, 1983—. NEA grantee, 1976, 77, 78, 80. Mem. AAP. Home: Box 1952 Austin TX 78767

COE, JOE ANN, (Joan Langham-Coe, Jack Ofhand, Joan Langham), b. Wesley, AR, Dec. 14, 1934, d. George Clarence and Katie Ernest (Counts) Langham; m. Kenneth Sewell Coe, Jr., Oct. 19, 1958; children—Leslie Ann, Kenneth Sewell III, Todd Andrew. Author children's books: The Country Road, 1981, The Real Story of Christmas, 1985; author poetry: I Cry in the Wilderness, 1975; contrbr. poetry genl. interest publs. Wrkg. on novel, family history. BA in Art, Calif. State U.-Stanislaus, 1975; postgrad. Calif. State U.-Fresno, 1975-77. Chmn. Merced Country (Calif.) Refugee Adv. Com., 1985—; mem. planning commn. City of Atwater, Calif., 1983—. Mem. United Amateur Press. Address: 260 Elm Ave Atwater CA 95301

COE, MARIAN (ZIPPERLIN), b. Birmingham, AL, Mar. 12, 1931; d. Will and Susan Gray (Jones) Riddle; m. David Coe, Sr., (dec.); children—Carol Coe Abdo, David; m. Paul R. Zipperlin, July 7, 1985. Author: On Waking Up, 1979, Women in Transition, 1984. Contrbr. articles to newspapers. Wrkg. on psychological suspense novel, travel features. Reporter, Montgomery Advertiser, Ala. Jnl., 1954-56, Evening Ind., St. Petersburg, FL, 1956-62, St. Petersburg Times, 1963-84. Mem. NFPW, Fla. Press Women, Fla. Freelance Wrtrs. Assn. Home: 2812 Park St N Saint Petersburg Fl 33710

COFER, JUDITH ORTIZ, b. Hormigueros, Mayaguez, PR, Feb. 24, 1952, came to U.S., 1960, d. J. M. and Fanny (Morot) Ortiz; m. John Cofer, Nov. 13, 1971; 1 dau., Tanya. Author: The Native Dancer (poetry chapbook), 1981, Peregrina (winner Riverstone Intl. Poetry Chapbook Competition 1985), 1986, Reaching for the Mainland (poetry), 1986; contrbr. poetry: Prairie Schooner, New Letters, So. Poetry Rvw, Poetry Miscellany, other lit mags. BA in English, Augusta (Ga.) Coll., 1974; MA in English, Fla. Atlantic U., 1977. Instr. English Broward Community Coll., Hollywood, Fla., 1977-80, U. Ga., Athens, 1984—; lectr., U. Miami, Fla., 1980-84; poetry ed. Fla. Arts Gazette, 1979-83; panelist Fine Arts Council Fla., 1982, Ga. Council for Arts, 1986—. Fine Arts Council Fla. fellow, 1981. Mem. Ga. Wrtrs. Forum (chmn.), MLA. Office: Ga Univ Sta Box 2418 Athens GA 30612

COFFEN, RICHARD WAYNE, b. Stoneham, MA, Nov. 19, 1941; s. George Albert and Dorothy Cowan (Hayward) C.; m. Rosalia Jane Clausen June 9, 1963; children—Robert, Ronald. B.A., Atlantic Union Coll., 1963; M.A., Andrews U., 1964. Book ed. Southern Pub. Assn., Nashville, 1970-80; book ed., v.p. Rvw. and Herald Pub. Assoc., Hagertown, MD, 1980—. Mem. Soc. Biblical Lit., Assn. Adventist Eds. Home: 25 Bittersweet Dr Hagerstown MD 21740

COFFEY, MICHAEL JOHN, b. NYC, Nov. 11, 1954; d. John Frederick and Eleanor Elizabeth (Reynolds) C.; m. Oralia Briones, Aug. 7, 1976 (div. June 1981); 1 son, Joshua Brian; m. Brenda Marsha Cullom, May 31, 1985. BA in English, U. Notre Dame, 1976; MA in Anglo-Irish, Leeds U., Eng., 1977. Editorial asst. IEEE, NYC, 1978; editor Elsevier North-Holland, NYC, 1980-82; mng. editor Station Hill Press, Barrytown, N.Y., 1982-84; editor Bergin & Garvey, South Hadley, Mass., 1985—. Home: Box 178 Hatfield MA 01038

COFFIN, LYN, b. NYC,Nov. 12, 1943, d. Richard Guild and Susan Knowles (Sims) C.; children—Jan Thomas Miksovsky, Christopher Alois Miksovsky, Schuyler Lyn Hibbard. Author: The Poetry of Anna Akhmatova, 1983, The Poetry of Wickedness, 1981, Elegies, 1980, The Plague Monument, 1980, Human Trappings, 1979; contrbr. fiction and poetry to Poet Lore, Poetry Now, Intl. Poetry, Mich. Qtly, So. Humanities, Lit., N.E., Green River, Portland, S.W. rvws., Bits, Wind, Denver Qtly, Descant, Paunch, Kans. Qtly, Aspen Leaves Anthology, Best American Short Stories. MA, U. Mich., 1971. Recipient prize AAP, 1981, Hopwood award U. Mich., 1981; Mich. Council for Arts artists grantee, 1985. Home: 3315 Stone School Rd Ann Arbor MI 48104

COGGINS, KATHLEEN BOBRICH, b. Chgo., Mar. 29, 1958, d. Steve and Dolores (Stasch) Bobrich; m. Jeffery Randall Coggins, Sept. 22, 1984. Contrbr. articles to Rock 'n Roll News, Music Phase, Aardvark, others. Student Calif. State U., Sacramento, 1976-77, 78-79. Library asst. Sacramento Public Library, 1982-83; clrk. Sacramento Dist. Atty., 1985—. Home: 5233 Andrea Blvd Sacramento CA 95842

COHAN, ANTHONY ROBERT, b. NYC, Oct. 28, 1939; s. Philip and Mary Helen (Foster) C.; m. Ruthane Capers, Nov. 1, 1964 (div. June 1971); 1 child, Maya; m. Masako Takahashi, June 1, 1974. Author: (stories) Nine Ships, 1975, (novel) Canary, 1981, (essays) The Flame, 1983, (novel) Opium, 1984; ed., contrbr. Outlaw Visions anthology, 1977. BA, U. Calif.-Santa Barbara, 1961. Mem. Pen, AG, Natl. Assn. Rec. Artists and

Scientists. Home: Box 480277 Los Angeles CA 90048

COHEN, BARBARA ANN, b. Bethpage, NY, Feb. 9, 1958; d. Samuel William and Harriette (Sherman) C. Author poems, short stories, publ. in various mags. Student, Drake Business School, Flushing, NY, 1977. Admin. asst. Actors Studio; asst. ed. Gastronome mag., 1985—. Home: 47-30 61 St Woodside NY 11377

COHEN, IRA H., b. NYC, Feb. 3, 1935, s. Lester and Faye (Koch) C. Author: 7 Marvels, Kathmandu, 1973, From the Divan of Petra Vogt, 1975, Gilded Splinters, 1976, Poems from the Cosmic Crypt, 1976, The Stauffenberg Cycle, 1980, On Feet of Gold, 1986; ed., pub. Gnaoua, 1964; ed. Great Society, 1967; contrbg. ed. Ins & Outs mag., 1977-80, Third Rail, 1982—. Also photographer, filmmaker. Home: 225 W 106th St New York NY 10025

COHEN, KEITH, b. Quantico, VA, Apr. 10, 1945; s. Maxwell Lewis and Dolores Theresa (Keith) C.; m. Paula Sue Bassoff, Aug. 21, 1967; children—Alex, Marc, Benjamin. Author: A First Reader in Contemporary American Short Fiction, 1971, The Young American Writers, 1971, Tri Quarterly, 1977, Sub-Stance, 1977, The Classic American Novel & The Movies, 1977, Film and Fiction: The Dynamics of Exchange, 1979, Beyond Amazement: New Essays on John Ashbery, 1980, (novel) Natural Settings, 1981. Contrbr. articles to mags. BA, Columbia U., 1967; PhD, Princeton U., 1974. Asst. prof U. Wis., Madison, 1974-79, assoc. prof., 1979—, chmn. dept. comparative lit., 1980-83. Mem. MLA, P&W, Comparative Lit. Council. Home: 7402 N Seneca Rd Milwaukee WI 53217

COHEN, LILA BELDOCK, b. NYC, Apr. 1, 1927; m. Marshall J. Cohen, Oct. 28, 1956; children—Tamar, Howard. Author: (children's play) Rumpelstiltskin, 1978. Contrbr. articles, short stories to mags., newspapers including N.Y. Times, Northeast/Hartford Courant, others. B.A., U. Conn., Owner, operator Paperback Alley, South Windsor, CT, 1981—. Home: 19 Cushman Dr Manchester CT 06040

COHEN, MARION DEUTSCHE, b. Perth Amboy, NJ, 1943, d. Jacob David and Sylvia (Katz) Deutsche; m. Jeffrey M. Cohen; children—Marielle, Arin, Kerin, Bret, Devin. Author: The Weirdest Is the Sphere, 1979, The Temper Tantrum Book, 1983, An Ambitious Sort of Grief, 1983, She Was Born She Died, 1984, The Shadow of an Angel, 1986, A Garden Flower, 1987; ed.: Mother/Poet, 1984, The Limits of Miracles, 1985, Tuesday Nights, 1977. Wrkg. on poetry collections, articles, MA, Wesleyan Univ., 1966, PhD,1970. Assoc. prof. Community Coll. Phila., 1974; N.J. Inst. Tech., Newark, 1969-75, Drexel U., Phila., 1976-77, 78, 80; facilitator workshops Temple U. Center City, Phila., 1975—. Mem. Feminist Wrtrs. Guild, Sigma Xi, Phi Beta Kappa, Am. Math. Assn. Home: 2203 Spruce St Philadelphia PA 19103

COHEN, ROBERT L., b. NYC, Feb. 19, 1947; s. Sol E. and Lorraine S. (Sterling) C. Contrbr. articles Newsday, Phila. Exponent, Balt. Jewish Times, Moment, Columbia, Sport, Jerusalem Post; lexicographer contrbr. Random House Dictionary; created and produced Yedid Nefesh radio program, WEVD, NYC, 1975-80; scriptwriter for One People, Many Voices: Jewish Music in Am. for Natl. Pub. Radio. Ed. Cornell U, class of 1967. Freelance writer and ed. NYC. Mem. Ed Freelancers Assn. Address: 640 E 2d St AA2 Brooklyn NY 11218

COHN, JANET STONE, b. NYC, Sept. 5, 1909; d. Louis and Bessie d. (Charles) Stone; m. Yale Cohn, June 10, 1933; children: Barbara Cohn Gordon, Deanne Cohn Stone. Author: Poems for All Seasons, 1971; contrbr. poetry to newspapers and mags. Ed. public schls., NYC and Rockville, Conn. Sec.-tres. Bostonian Fishery, Inc., Hartford, Conn., 1950—. Home: 131 Ardmore Rd West Hartford CT 06119

COHN, JAN KADETSKY, b. Cambridge, MA, Aug. 9, 1933; d. Allan Robert and Beatrice (Goldberg) Kadetsky; children—Cathy Rebecca, David Seth Solomon, m. 2d William Henry Cohn, Mar. 9, 1969. Author: The Palace or the Poorhouse: The American House as a Cultural Symbol, 1979; Improbable Fiction: The Life of Mary Roberts Rinehart, 1980, Romance and the Erotics of Property, 1987. BA, Wellesley Coll., 1955; PhD, U. Mich.-Ann Arbor, 1963. Asst. prof. Univ. Toledo, Ohio, 1963-68; assoc. prof. Univ. Wis., Whitewater, 1968-70, Carnegie-Mellon Univ., Pittsburgh, 1970-79; prof. George Mason Univ., Fairfax, Va., 1979-87; dean of faculty, Trinity coll., Hartford, Conn., 1987—. Fellow ACLS, 1973, NEH, 1973-74, Danforth, 1974. Mem. MLA, Popular Culture Assn., NCTE. Address: 71 Vernon St Hartford CT 06106

COHN, JIM, b. Highland Park, IL, Apr. 17, 1953. Author poetry: Green Sky, 1980; Mangrove, 1981; Divine April, 1955; pub. and ed. Action mag; Moorish Jnl, Third Congress. Cert. poetics, Jack Kerouac Schl. Disembodied Poetics, 1976-80; MEd, Deaf U. of Rochester, 1984-86. Gandy dancer Burlington-No. RR, Wyo-Nebr, 1979; sign lang. interpreter Off. Vocat. Rehab., Rochester, NY, 1984; Engl. poetry tchr. Schl. without Walls, Rochester, 1985; tchr. of deaf, Rochester, Toronto and NY, 1985; ed. and pub. 21st Sensual Press, Rochester, 1983—. Recipient Walt Whitman award, Abrams pub. Mem. TESA, Natl. Coalition Alternative Schls. Address: 47 Erion Crescent Rochester NY 14607

COKER, WILLIAM R., b. Cedartown, GA, May 9, 1936, s. William A. and Virginia (Boyles) C.; m. Martha O'Bryant, Dec. 20, 1959; children—Heather, Richard. Contrbr. to Airline Exec. mag., Modern Paint and Coating Mag., numerous other trade publs. BA in English, Journalism, Ga. State U. Ed. Mobile-Modular Housing News, Covington, Ga., 1970-73; dir. advt. and public relations A&U Enterprises, Blacksburg, Va., 1973-75; dir. public relations Ga. Mcpl. Assn.,Atlanta, 1975-77; group ed., assoc. pub. Communication Channels, Atlanta, 1978—. Home: 3817K Brockett Trail Clarkston GA 30021

COLANDER, VALERIE NIEMAN, b. Jamestown, NY, July 6, 1955; d. Warner and Eleanor (Aiken) Nieman; m. John O. Colander, Jr., May 20, 1978. Contrbr. poetry to Laurel Rvw, Tar River Poetry, Star Line, Proof Rock, Yet Another Small Magazine, other lit mags. BA in Journalism, W.Va. U., 1978. Reporter/ed. Daily Athenaeum, Morgantown, W.Va., 1976-78; pub. relations wrtr. W.Va. U., Morgantown, 1977-78; reporter Dominion-Post, Morgantown, 1978; reporter/arts and entmt. ed., Times-West Virginian, Fairmont, 1979—. Mem P&W, SFWA, W.Va. Wrtrs. Homes: Box 1614 Fairmont WV 26554

COLBURN, ROBERT DICKINSON, b. Wilmington, DE, May 1, 1962, s. Robert Marshall and Dorothy Middleton (Rowlett) C. Contrbr. to: The Progressive, Washington Post Mag., Poetry In Sci. '85, The Other Side. BA, Columbia U., 1984. Database ed. IEEE, NYC,1985—. Home: 316 W 95th St New York NY 10025

COLBY, EDITH LUCILLE, (Lucille Cribbens), b. Rochester, NY, July 6, 1917; d. Joseph Albert and Nellie May (Hall) Spros; m. George Colby (dec.), May 8, 1942; one child. Contrbr. poems to Ram, Hoosier Challenger, Midwest Poetry, other lit mags, anthols. Wrkg. on novel. Ed. Rochester (NY) H.S.; nurse, 1930-50. Mem. Natl. Wrtrs. Club. Home: 572 Lake Ave—108 Rochester NY 14613

COLDSMITH, DON(ALD CHARLES), b. Iola, KS, Feb. 28, 1926; s. Charles I. and Sara (Willett) C.; m. (1) Barbara A. Brown, Aug. 1949 (div. 1960), (2) Edna E. Howell, Nov. 6, 1960; Children: Carol Coldsmith Edwards, April Coldsmith Mann, Glenna Coldsmith Young, Leslie, Connie. Author: Horsin' Around (articles), 1975, Horsin' Around Again, (articles), 1981. Spanish Bit series (historical novels): Trail of the Spanish Bit, 1980, Buffalo Medicine, 1981, The Elk-Dog Heritage, 1982, Follow the Wind, 1982, Man of the Shadows, 1983, Daughter of the Eagle, 1984, Moon of Thunder, 1984, Sacred Hills, 1985, Pale Star, 1986, River of the Swans, 1986, Return to the River, 1987. Author of Horsin' Around, a self-syndicated weekly newspaper column. Contrbr. to medical jnls and equestrian mags. Contrib ed., Horse of Course. AB, Baker U., 1949; MD, U. of Kan., 1958, Youth dir., YMCA, Topeka, Kan., 1958-59; private practice of medicine in Emporia, Kan., 1959—. Adj. prof of English, Emporia State U Member: AMA, Western Writers of America (officer), Appaloosa Horse Club, Natl. Rifle Assn., Kan. Med. Soc, Flint Hill Med Soc, Kiwanis. Military service: U.S. Army, 1944-46, served in the Philippines and Japan. Home: Rt 5 Box 150 Emporia KS 66801

COLE, ANN MARIE, b. Comfort, TX, Nov. 24, 1937; d. Chester Paul and Veta Marie (Culpepper) Heinen; m. Donald Robert Cole, Dec. 30, 1960; children—James Robert, Charles Allen, Steven Layne. Ed., Extension Today, 1981—, numerous agric. pubns. including Endangered Marine Turtles of the Gulf Coast, 1981 (Superior Award, Agric. Communicators in Edn., 1982). BS, Southwest Texas State U., 1959; MEd, Texas A & M, 1972. Jnlsm./Engl. tchr. Snyder (TX) Ind. Schl. Dist., 1959-62, 64-65, 68-69; asst. ed./pubns. Texas Agric. Ext. Svc., College Station, 1969-73; pubns. engr. Lockheed Electronics Co., Clear Lake City, TX, 1973-76; communics. spclst. Texas Agric. Ext. Svc., College Station, 1976—. Texas Superior Svc. Unit award, Texas Agric. Ext. Svc., 1981. Mem. IABC (pres., Brazos Valley chapter), CASE. Office: 107K Reed McDonald Bldg Texas A&M College Station TX 77843

COLE, DOUGLAS, b. NYC, July 25, 1934; s. Ronald and Helen Elizabeth (Bladykas) C.; m. Virginia Ann Ford, Nov. 28, 1957; children: David, Stephen, Karen, Kristin. Author: Suffering and Evil in the Plays of Christopher Marlowe, 1962; editor: 20th Century Views of Romeo and Juliet, 1979, Renaissance Drama XI: Tragedy, 1980; contrbr. numerous articles to profl. jnls. BA, U. Notre Dame, Ind., 1957; MA, U. Chgo., 1957; PhD (Woodrow Wilson fellow, Danforth fellow), Princeton U., 1961. Morse fellow, 1966-67. Office: Eng Dept Northwestern U Evanston IL 60201

COLE, E(UGENE) R(OGER), (Nicholas R. Noble, Peter Lorcee), b. Cleve., Nov. 14, 1930,

s. Bernard James and Mary Luise (Rogers) C. Author: Kecharitomene (monograph), 1958, Which End, the Empyrean? (play), 1959, April Is the Cruelest Month (play), 1970, Falling Up: haiku and senyru, 1979, Act & Potency: poems, 1980, Ding an sich: anapoems, 1985, Uneasy Camber: early poems & diversions, 1943-50, 1986; ed.: Grand Slam: 13 Great Short Stories About Bridge, 1975, In the Beginning, 1978, Grand Slam Doubled: A Second Collection of 13 Great Bridge Stories, 1988; assoc. ed. The Harvester,, 1955; guest ed. Experiment: An Intl. Rvw, 1961; editorial participant This Is My Best, 1970; contrbr. Sat. Rvw, La Voix des Poetes, Dalhousie Rvw, Light Yr., over 60 jnls. and anthologies. BA, St. Edward's Sem., 1954; MDiv. Sulpician Sem. of Northwest, 1958; BA, Central Wash. U., 1960; MA, Seattle U., 1970. Ordained priest Roman Catholic Ch., 1958. Chmn. dept. English Central Cath. High Schl., Yakima, Wash., 1959-66, Marquette High Schl., Yakima, 1966-68; poetry critic Natl. Wrtrs. Club, Denver, 1969-72; freelance wrtr., ed., researcher, 1969—; founder, Godspeople, 1985—. Recipient Haiku Comment award, Dragonfly, Portland, Oreg., 1974, Annl. Mentor Poetry award, N.Am. Mentor, Fennimore, Wis., 1974. Mem. PSA, AG, AAP, P&W. Address: Box 91277 Cleveland OH 44101

COLE, ELAINE GENEVA, b. Jamestown, N.Y., Oct. 9, 1932, d. Fernando Charles and Lillian Edith (Wright) Smith; m. William Ethan Cole, Aug. 4, 1950; children—Vicki, Kim, Debra, Kevin, Todd. Contrbr. articles to Augsburg Pub. House, Regular Baptist Press. Diploma Christian Writers Inst., Wheaton, Ill. Freelance wrtr., 1965—; corr. Post Jnl, Jamestown, 1973–78, wrtr. feature articles, 1974-84; columnist, corr. Chautauqua News, Westfield, N.Y., 1976—; columnist Kitoti Paper, 1982; wrtr. feature articles Erie Times News, 1984—. Mem. N.Y. State Press Assn., Chautauqua County Christian Wrtrs. Club. Home: Locust Haven North Clymer NY 14759

COLE, JUSTINE, see Phillips, Susan Elizabeth

COLE, RICHARD, b. Denton, Tex., Nov. 17, 1949, s. Richard Carlton and Janice (Holland) C.; m. R. Lauren Cole, Oct. 20, 1984. Author poetry collection: The Glass Children, 1986; contrbr. poetry to The New Yorker, Hudson Rvw., Chgo. Rvw, The Westering Experience anthology, others. BA, U. Tex., 1971; postgrad., U. Calif.-Berkeley, 1971-78. Freelance wrtr., Mpls., 1978-83; copywrtr., SSCI, NYC,1983-86. Recipient Eisner award, U. Calif., Berkeley, 1976, Mentor prize The Loft, Mpls., 1978; Bush Fdn. fellow, 1981; grantee Minn. State Arts Bd., 1982, NEA grant, 1986. Home: 540 E 6th St New York NY 10009

COLE, RUTH ELENA, b. nr. Terry, MT, Mar. 27, 1918, d. Elias Knutson and Lena (Johnson) Rusth; m. Robert Lee Cole, Aug. 30, 1939; children—Robert Lee, Jr., Jacqulynn, Kristine, Michael. Contrbr. articles to Grit, Gospel Carrier, PHP Intl. (Japan), United Methodist Reporter, others; contrbr. children's stories: Pacific Press, Little Pathfinder Mag. Student Portland State Coll., West Valley Calif. Coll. Tchr. adult edn. San Jose, Calif., 1967-69; freelance wrtr., 1972—; ed. house organ Pine Mountain Lake Assn., Groveland, Calif., 1978—. Mem. Calif. Wrtrs. Club. Home: Star Rt Box 5723 Groveland CA 95321

COLEMAN, ELLEN SCHNEID, b. NYC, June 17, 1943; d. Martin Leo and Sylvia Ruth (Klein) Schneid; m. Earl Maxwell, Aug. 19, 1973. Asst. editor Clarkson & Potter, Inc., NYC, 1966-68; journal co-ord. editor Plenum Pub., NYC, 1968-73; editor Jelfrey & Norton Pub., NYC, 1973-75; mng. editor Sci. Assoc. Intl., NYC, 1975-78; sr. editor/prodn. Earl M. Coleman Enterprises Inc., Croton-on-Hudson, N.Y., 1978-84; sr. editor, prodn. mgr. Nat. Pubs. of Black Hills, Inc., Elmsford, N.Y., 1984—. Office: Nat Pubs 47 Nepperhan Ave Elmsford NY 10523

COLEMAN, JAMES N., b. Cleve., Jan. 27, 1931, s. James A. and Dorothy (Verne) C.; m. Thelma F. Pruitt, 1976; 1 son—Gary. Author: The Null Frequency Impulser, 1965, Seeker from the Stars, 1968. BS, Finn Coll., Cleve, 1947. Mem. SFWA, MWA, Writers & Editors Guild San Diego. Address: 6781 Pilot Way San Diego CA 92114

COLEMAN, JANE C., b. Pitts., Jan. 9, 1939, d. Joseph R. and Sophia (Weyman) Candia; m. Bernard D. Coleman, Mar. 27, 1965. Contrbr. poetry to Yankee, West Branch, Tar River Poetry, Cottonwood, Backcountry, Plainswoman, Footwork, Hyperion, Xanadu, also others, fiction to Plainswoman, Crosscurrents, Pa., Gila, Chowder, Antietam rvws, Sewickley mag. BA, U. Pitts., 1961. Ed. Biophys. Research Lab., Pitts., 1961-66; feature wrtr. Pitts. New Sun, 1979-81; wrtr.-in-residence Carlow Coll., Pitts., 1981-84, dir. writing ctr., 1985-86. Recipient 1st prize for fiction Plainswoman, 1983, Sewickley mag., 1985; Pa. Council for Arts writing grantee, 1986. Mem. WWA, Intl. Poetry Forum (bd. dirs. 1983—). Home: Box 29 Hereford AZ 85615

COLEMAN, MARY ANN, b. Marion, IN, Jan. 3, 1928; d. William Henry and Helen Elizabeth (Jeffrey) Braunlin; m. Oliver McCarter Coleman, Jr., Mar. 4, 1955; 2 sons, Jeffrey Boyer, Christopher Braunlin. Author: disappearances (chapbook), 1978; contrbr. poetry to Lit. Rvw, Commonweal, Kans Qtly, So. Poetry Rvw, Ga. Rvw, Poetry Now, Poets On:, Pembroke, NY Herald Trib., Remington Rvw, Hiram Poetry Rvw, Ga. Jnl, Sun Dog, Diamond Anthology (PSA) others. Student Ind. U., 1945-49; BS in Edn., Auburn U., 1949-50. Tchr., Pompano Beach, Fl., 1950-51, East Point, Ga. 1952-55; welfare worker, Atlanta, 1951. Ga. Cncl. for Arts grantee, 1986. Mem. PSA (Consuelo Ford Meml. award, 1974), Ga. State Poetry Soc. Address: 205 Sherwood Dr Athens GA 30606

COLEMAN, NANCY C., see Barnes, Nancy C.

COLEMAN, ROSA LEE, b. Premier, WV, June 10, 1916; d. Charles Henry Clemons and Fannie Estelle (Hirston) Coles; m. Luther Eugene Coleman, Dec. 22, 1948 (div. Apr. 27, 1967). Wrkg. on short stories, poems. Grad. public schls., Montgomery, WV. Clrk., Dept. of Motor Vehicles, Hartford, CT, 1956-66; distrbution clrk. U.S. Postal Service, Hartford, 1966-81, retired. Recipient Commendation, U.S. Postal Service, 1981, cert. of Merit, World of Poetry, 1987. Home: 8 Bestor Ln 30 Bloomfield CT 06002

COLEMAN, STEPHEN M., b. Chgo., Aug. 27, 1911; s. Robert A. and Edith B. (Robinson) C.; m. Corinne Rosenberg Coleman, Mar. 19, 1950; children—Mitchell, Joshua, Adam. Author: Smootchie (The Dog Who Likes Bubble Gum) and Don't Flush the Toilet, I'm Taking a Shower, Syndicated columnist: Senior Talk, 1985—. B.Sc. in Bus. Administration, U. Ill., 1936. Office mgr., wrtr., Little Technical Library, Chgo., 1938-41; announcer, wrtr. Sta. WEDC, Chgo., 1946-50; owner Coleman Advertising, Dayton, 1950-81. Mem. Wayne State U. Wrtrs. Club. Home: 409 Red Haw Rd Dayton Oh 45405

COLEMAN, WANDA, b. Los Angeles, Nov. 13, 1946, d. George and Lewana (Scott) Evans; m. Austin Straus. Author: (poems) Art in the Court of the Blue Fag, 1977, Mad Dog Black Lady, 1979, Imagoes, 1983. Co-host The Poetry Connexion, Sta. KPFK. Recipient Emmy award natl. Acad. TV Arts and Scis., 1976; NEA lit. grantee, 1981-82; Guggenheim Fdn. poetry fellow, 1984. Mem. PEN. Home: Box 29154 Los Angeles CA 90029

COLES, ROBERT, b. Boston, Oct. 12, 1929; s. Philip and Sandra (Young) C.; m. Jane Hallowell; children: Robert, Daniel, Michael. Author: Children of Crisis: A Study of Courage and Fear, 1967, Dead End School, 1968, Still Hungry in America, 1969, The Grass Pipe, 1969, The Image is Yours, 1969, Wages of Neglect, 1969, Uprooted Children: The Early Lives of Migrant Farmers, 1970, Teachers and the Children of Poverty, 1970, Erik H. Erikson: The Growth of His Work, 1970, The Middle Americans, 1970, Migrants, Sharecroppers and Mountaineers, 1972, The South Goes North, 1972, Saving Face, 1972, Farewell to the South, 1972, A Spectacle Unto the World, 1973, Riding Free, 1973, The Darkness and the Light, 1974, The Buses Roll, 1974, Irony in the Mind's Life: Essays on Novels by James Agee, Elizabeth Bowen and George Eliot, 1974, Headsparks, 1975, The Mind's Fate, 1975, Eskimos, Chicanos and Indians, 1978, Privileged Ones: The Well-Off and The Rich in America, 1978, Women of Crisis Lives of Struggle and Hope, (with Jane Hallowell Coles), 1978, Walker Percy: An American Search, 1978, Flannery O'Connor's South, 1980, Women of Crisis: Lives of Work and Dreams, 1980, The Moral Life of Children, 1986, (with Ross Spears) Agee: His Life Remembered, 1986, Dorothy Day: A Radical Devotion, 1987, Simone Weil: A Modern Pilgrimage, 1987; contrbg. ed: The New Republic, 1966—, Am. Poetry Rvw, 1982—, Aperture, 1974—, Lit. and Medicine, 1981—, New Oxford Rvw, 1981—; mem. editorial bd.: Integrated Edn., 1967—, Child Psychiatry and Human Devel., 1969—, Rvw of Books and Religion, 1976—, Internat. Jnl Family Therapy, 1977—, Jnl Am. Culture, 1977—, Grants mag., 1977, Learning mag., 1978—, Jnl Edn., 1979—; bd. editors: Parents' Choice, 1978—; editor: Children and Youth Services Rvw, 1978—. AB, Harvard U., 1950; MD, Columbia U., 1954. Recipient Ralph Waldo Emerson prize, 1967; Pulitzer prize, 1973 (all received for Children of Crisis, Vols. II, III); MacArthur prize fellow, 1981; numerous others. Fellow Davenport Coll., Yale U., 1976—; fellow Am. Acad. Arts and Scis., Inst. Soc. Ethics and the Life Scis., member bd. dirs., Medical Education for South African Blacks, 1985. Home: 81 Carr Rd Concord MA 01742

COLGAN, WILLIAM B., b. Quitman, GA, Dec. 1, 1920; s. John Perry and Margie (Phillips) C.; m. Anita Lamae Allen, July 24, 1943; children—Sandra, William b., Jr. Author: Fishing Scene in Northwest Florida, 1978, World War II Fighter-Bomber Pilot, 1985. Wrkg. on war history book. Ret. col., USAF, served in World War II, Korea, Vietnam; ret., 1972. Mem. mil. orgns. Address: Box 313 Shalimar FL 32579

COLLIER, JANE, see Collier, Zena

COLLIER, ZENA, (Jane Collier, Zena Shumsky), b. London, Jan. 21, 1926, came to U.S., 1946, d. Ben and Rebecca (Capinsky) Feldman; m. Louis Shumsky, May 3, 1945 (div. 1967) children—Jeffrey A. (dec.), Paul E.; m. 2d, Thomas M. Hampson, Dec. 30, 1969. Author: (as Jane Collier) The Year of the Dream, 1962, First Flight (as Zena Shumsky, with Lou Shumsky), 1962, Shutterbug (as Zena Shumsky, with Lou Shumsky), 1963, A Tangled Web (as Jane Collier), 1967, Seven for the People: Public Interest Groups at Work (as Zena Collier), 1979, Next Time I'll Know (as Zena Collier), 1981; contrbr. short stories to McCall's, Alfred Hitchcock's Mystery Mag., Woman's Day and lit jnls. Resident fellow Yaddo, 1978, 80, Va. Centre Creative Arts, 1982, 85, 86, Alfred U. Summer Place, 1983, 84. Mem. P&W, AWP, MWA. Home: 83 Berkeley St Rochester NY 14607

COLLINGS, MICHAEL ROBERT, b. Rupert, ID, Oct. 29, 1947; s. Ralph Willard and Thella Marie (Hurd) C.; m. Judith Lynn Reeve, Dec. 21, 1973; children: Michael-Brent, Erika Marie, Ethan Hunt, Kendra Elayne. Author: (poetry) A Season of Calm Weather, 1974; (with wife) Whole Wheat Harvest, 1981; Brian W. Aldiss: A Reader's Guide, 1985; Piers Anthony: A Reader's Guide, 1983; Stephen King as Richard Bachman, 1985; (with Engebretson) The Shorter Works of Stephen King, 1985; (poetry) Naked to the Sun: Dark Visions of Apocalypse, 1985; The Many Facets of Stephen King, 1986, The Films of Stephen King, 1986, The Annotated Guide to Stephen King, 1986, The Stephen King Phenomenon, 1987; contrbr. articles to Death and the Serpent, The Scope of the Fantastic, Hard Science Fiction, Extrapolation; poetry ed. Dialogue: A Jnl of Mormon Thought, 1984; ed. The Lamp Post of So. Calif. C.S. Lewis Soc., 1981-83, Reflections on the Fantastic, 1986. BA, Whittier Coll., 1969; MA, U. Calif.-Riverside, 1973, PhD, 1977. Assoc. in English, U. Calif-Riverside, 1973-79; instr. English, San Bernardino Valley Coll., Calif., 1976-79, UCLA, 1978-79; assoc. prof. English, Pepperdine U., Malibu, Calif., 1979—. Mem. Sci. Fiction Research Assn., Sci. Fiction Poetry Assn., Intl. Assn. for Fantastic in Arts. Home: 1089 Sheffield Pl Thousand Oaks CA 91360

COLLINS, DAVID RAYMOND, b. Marshalltown, IA, Feb. 29, 1940; s. Raymond Amby and Mary Elizabeth (Brecht) C. Author: Kim Soo and His Tortoise, 1970; Great American Nurses, 1971; Walt Disney's Surprise Christmas Present, 1972; Linda Richards, America's First Trained Nurse, 1973; Harry S. Truman, People's President, 1975; Football Running Backs, 1975; Abraham Lincoln, 1976; Illinois Women: Born to Serve, 1976; Joshua Poole Hated School, 1977; Charles Lindbergh, Hero Pilot, 1978; A Spirit of Giving, 1978; If I Could, I Would, 1979; Joshua Poole and Sunrise, 1979; The Wonderful Story of Jesus, 1980; A Special Guest, 1980; The Only Thing Wrong With Birthdays, 1980; George Washinton Carver, 1981; George Meany, Mr. Labor, 1981; Dorothy Day, Catholic Worker, 1982; Thomas Merton, Monk with a Mission, 1982; Super Champ! The Story of Babe Didrikson Zaharias, 1983; (with Evelyn Witter) Notable Illinois Women, 1983, The Golden Circle, 1983; The Game of Think, 1984; Florence Nightingale, 1985, Johnny Appleseed, 1985, Not Only Dreamers, 1986; Junior Nature Book Series, 1987, Ride a Red Dinosaur, 1987, Lyndon Baines Johnson—No Ordinary Man, 1987. Wrkg. on youth biographies, adult novel. B.S., Western Ill. U., 1962, M.S., 1966. English instr. public schls., Moline, IL, 1962—; founder, dir. Miss. Valley Wrtr.'s Conf., 1973—, Children's Lit. Festival, 1979—; secy. Quad Cities Arts Council, 1971-75; pres. Friends of Moline Public LIbrary, 1965-66. Recipient writing award Wrtr.s Digest, 1967, wrtr. of yr. award Wrtr.'s Studio, 1971, award Bobbs-Merrill Pub. co., 1971, wrtr. of yr. award Quad-Cities Wrtrs. Cub, 1972, writing awards Judson Coll., 1971, Jr. Lit. Guild awards, 1980, 82. Mem. Natl. Ill., Moline (dir. 1964-67) Edn. Assns., Wrtrs. Studio (pres. 1967-71), Children's Reading Roundtable, AG, SCBW, Juvenile Forum, Quad-Cities Wrtrs. Club (pres. 1973-75, 77-78), Am. Amateur Press Assn., Book Lures, Inc., Schoolmasters, NCTE, Blackhawk Reading Council. Home: 3403 45th St Moline IL 61265

COLLINS, GARY ROSS, b. Hamilton, Ontario, Canada, Oct. 22, 1934; came to U.S., 1959; naturalized, 1985; s. Harold Arthur and Vera (Stanger) C.; m. Julie Heinze, July 18, 1964; children—Marilynn, Janice. Author books, 1969—, including Handling the Holidays, 1982, Spotlight on Stress, 1982, Give Me a Break: The How to Handle Pressure Book for Teens, 1982, Beyond Easy Believism, 1982, Getting Started, 1984, The Sixty-Second Christian, 1984, The Magnificent Mind, 1985, Innovative Approaches to Counseling, 1986, Getting Your Life Out of Neutral, 1987, Can You Trust Psychology?, 1988. contrbr. numerous articles, book rvws., columns to jnls., mags., newspapers. Wrkg. on rev. of Christian Counseling: A Comprehensive Guide. B.A., McMaster U., 1956; M.A., U. Toronto, 1958; Ph.D., Purdue U., 1963. Assoc. prof. & dept. chmn., Bethel Coll., St. Paul, 1964-68; prof. of counseling and dir. of clinical trng., Conwell Sch. Theol., Phila., 1968-69; prof. of psychology (Dir. chmn., 1969-83), Trinity Divinity Schl., Deerfield, IL, 1969—. Mem. Am. Psychological Assn., Am. Scientific Affiliation (past pres.). Home: 20720 N Meadows Ct Kildeer IL 60047

COLLINS, JENNY LOU GALLOWAY, b. Cumberland, KY, Sept. 5, 1950, d. Estill Galloway and Lena (Maggard) Carubba; m. Bobby Joe Collins, May 6, 1967; children—Norman, Robbie, Jason. Contrbr.: Appalachian Heritage, Hill & Valley, Fine Arts Press, Truckers, U.S.A., other publs. Student Southeast Community Coll., Cumberland, Ky. Asst. ed. Mountain Rvw, Whitesburg, Ky., 1980-81; ed. Poet's Corner, Tri-City News, Cumberland, 1981-83; feature storyteller Harlan (Ky.) Daily, 1983—; project dir. Appalgrafics, Whitesburg, Ky., 1983-84; assoc. ed. Pine Mt. Sand & Gravel, Whitesburg, 1984-86; freelance wrtr. Recipient Award of Merit, World of Poetry, 1984, Golden Poet award, 1985. Mem. Ky. State Poetry Soc., So. Appalachia Wrtrs. Co-op. Home: HC 87 Box 1400 Thornton KY 41855

COLLINS, JOSEPH THOMAS, b. Crooksville, Ohio, July 3, 1939; s. Joseph Thomas and Luvadelle Bernice (Aichele) C.; m. Suzanne L. Ryse, Dec. 12, 1984. Author: Amphibians and Reptiles in Kansas, 1974, Fishes in Kansas (with F. B. Cross), 1975, Turtles in Kansas (with J. P. Caldwell), 1981, A Review of the Diseases and Treatments of Captive Turtles (with J. B. Murphy), 1983, Natural Kansas, 1985, Snakes: Ecology and Evolutionary Biology (with R.A. Siegel and S.S. Novak), 1987; ed. Reproductive Biology and Diseases of Captive Reptiles (with J. B. Murphy), 1980. Wrkg. on Peterson Field Guide to Reptiles and Amphibians. A.A., U. Cin., 1967. Zoologist and ed. U. Kans., Lawrence, 1968—. Served to E-4 US Army, 1963-68. Pres. Soc. for the Study of Amphibians and Reptiles, 1978, Kans. Herpetolog. Soc., 1983, Kans. Assn. Biology Tchrs., 1980-81, Univ. Kans. Classified Senate, 1984. Home: 1502 Medinah Circle Lawrence KS 66046

COLLINS, MARTHA, b. Omaha, NB, Nov. 25, 1940; d. William E. and Katheryn (Essick) Collins. Author: The Catastrophe of Rainbows, 1985; editor: Critical Essays on Louise Bogan, 1984; poetry in Pushcart Prize, Anthol. of Am. Verse, Am. Poetry Rvw, Virginia Qtly and other anthols and lit mags. AB, Stanford U., 1962; MA, U. of Iowa, 1965, PhD,1971; asst. prof., NE Missouri State, Kirksville, 1965-66; instr., U. of Mass., Boston, 1966-71, asst. prof., 1971-75, assoc. prof., 1975-85, prof., 1985—. Awards: NEH Fellowship, 1977-78; Pushcart Prize, 1985, Mary Carolyn Davies Award, PSA, 1985. Mem. AWP, PSA, New England Writers for Survival. Home: 881 Mass Ave Cambridge MA 02139

COLLINS, MICHAEL, see Lynds, Dennis

COLLINS, PEGGY ANN, b. Denver, Dec. 5, 1948; d. Arthur Roland and Lanita Elaine (Pitts) C. Contrbr. articles to Med. Center News, Health Services Management Jnl., Jnl. Operating Room Research Inst., Health Lit. Rvw. Contrbr., ed.: Medinform, Denver, 1981—; assoc. ed.: Am. Jnl. Sports Medicine, 1980-81. B.S., Metropolitan State Coll., 1976. Administrative clrk. U. Colo. Health Sci. Center, Denver, 1986—. Mem. AMWA (past pres. Rocky Mountain chpt.), Council Biology Eds. Home: 4324 Eaton St Denver CO 80212

COLSON, CHARLES WENDELL, b. Boston, Oct. 16, 1931; s. Wendell Ball and Inez (Ducrow) C.; m. Nancy Billings, June 3, 1953; children: Wendell Ball II, Christian B., Emily Ann; m. Patricia Ann Hughes, Apr. 4, 1964. Author: Born Again, 1975, Life Sentence, 1979, Crime and The Responsible Community, 1980, Loving God, 1983, Who Speaks for God?, 1985, Kingdoms in Conflict, 1987. A.B., Brown U., 1953; J.D., George Washington U., 1959; Served to capt. USMCR, Korean Conflict. Office: Box 17500 Washington DC 20041

COLTER, CYRUS, b. Noblesville, IN, Jan. 8, 1910; s. James Alexander and Ethel Marietta (Bassett) C.; m. Imogene Mackay, Jan. 1, 1943. Author: The Beach Umbrella (U. Iowa Schl. Letters award for short fiction 1970); (novels) The Rivers of Eros, 1972, The Hippodrome, 1973, Night Studies, 1979. JD, Ill. Inst. Tech. Chgo. Kent Coll. Law, 1940; LittD (hon.), U. Ill., 1977. Served to capt. F.A. AUS, 1942-46; ETO. Home: 1115 S Plymouth Ct Chicago IL 60605

COLVIN, THOMAS STUART, b. Columbia, MO, July 17, 1947; s. Charles Darwin and Miriam (Kimball) C.; m. Sonya Marie Peterson, Sept. 11, 1982. Contrbr. articles to Wallaces Farmer, Successful Farming, Ia. Farm Bur. Spokesman, Agrl. Engring., Trans. Am. Soc. Agrl. Engrs. Wrkg. on articles on conservation tillage and agrl. mgmt. BS, Iowa State Univ., 1970, MS, 1974, PhD in Agrl. Engring., 1977. Research assoc. Iowa State U., 1972-77; agrl. engr. U.S. Dept. Agrl., Agricultural Research Svc., Ames, 1977—. Mem. Am. Soc. Agrl. Engrs., Soil Conservation Soc. Am., Ia. Acad. Sci., Alpha Epsilon, Gamma Sigma Delta, Sigma Xi. Home: RR 1 Box 185 Cambridge IA 50046

COMBERIATE, JOSEPHINE BERTOLINI, (Jo B. Comberiate, "Jay Bee C."), b. Washington, D. C., March 11, 1917; parents: Anthony

Oreste and Catherine Mary (Gardella) Bertolini; husband: Michael Bruno Comberiate, Nov. 25, 1945; children—Catherine Mary, Michael Anthony, Anthony B. Taught piano 1934-44; recd. certificates and awards for misc. courses and club memberships; member ASCAP; Composer/Author/Publisher; music book of 139 songs, "Love, Life, and Liberty", 1979; almost 200 songs (wds., music, & harmony), record album and other recordings, greeting cards, published poems. Received honors in piano, harmony, and academic stuides; diplomas with honors from Comptometer School, 1935, and from Strayer College (Secretarial/Accounting), 1937; student Catholic U., 1950; Univ. of MD., 1977-79. Recd. gold watch for safety slogans (Natl. Safety Council) 1955; Home: 13973 4-Wheel Dr Rt. 108 Highland MD 20777

COMBS, MAXINE RUTH SOLOW, b. Dallas, June 14, 1937; d. Eugene Maxwell and Sayd Frances (Travis) Solow; m. Edouard Gauthier, Dec. 27, 1959 (div.); m. 2d Bruce Combs, June, 1967 (div.); children—Bella, Wayne. Contrbr. poems Piedmont Lit. Rvw, Whose Woods These Are, Finding the Name, Dog River Rvw, Round Table, Iris, Backbone, So. Fla. Poetry Rvw; short stories in Wooster Rvw, Coe Rvw, Antietam Rvw, others; reviews in Northwest Rvw, Far Point, Wash Rvw, Wash. Times, Gargoyle, Poet Lore, Columbia Road Rvw, Small Press Rvw, Belle Lettres. BA, Mills Coll., 1958; PhD, U. Oreg., 1967. Instr. Idaho State Univ., Pocatello, 1963-65, Lane Community Coll., Eugene, Oreg., 1966-69; asst. prof. Am. Univ., Washington, 1970-74, George Mason Univ., Fairfax, Va., 1979-80, Univ. D.C., Washington, part-time 1973—. Address: 3730 R St NW Washington DC 20007

COMBS, RICHARD ALEXANDER, b. Los Angeles; s. Leroy O. and Ramona (Castellanos) C.; m. Rita Winona Cranston, Feb. 19, 1964; 1 son, Richard Arthur. Contrbr. articles to mags. including Truckers/USA, Rock & Gem, Farm & Ranch Living, others. Home: HC 62 Box 15132 Pinetop AZ 85935

COMEY, JAMES HUGH, b. Phila., Dec. 18, 1947, s. John Joseph and Mary Agnes (Waters) C.; m. Patricia Ann Borda, Dec. 20, 1969; children—Jennifer Tricia, James Hugh Jr., Colleen Patricia (dec.). Author: Death of the Poet King, 1975. BS, West Chester (Pa.) U., 1969, MEd, 1972; adminstrv. cert. U. Pa., 1977. Instr. Delaware County Community Coll., Media, Pa., 1975-82; tchr., adminstrv. asst. Upper Darby (Pa.) Sch. Dist., 1974-86; dir. Comcy Dynamic Improvement, 1986—. Mem. AG. Home: 105 Treaty Rd Drexel Hill PA 19026

COMMINS, MICHAEL WILLIAM, b. San Francisco, May 15, 1948; s. William R. and Caroline D. (Boone) C.; m. Susan D. Litke, Jan. 1, 1977 (dec. Feb. 23, 1982); m. 2d, Karen E. Zahora, Mar. 20, 1985. Contrbr. articles to Ski Patrol mag. Student Idaho State U.-Pocatello, 1972-1974. Dir. ski patrol Grand Targhee Resort, Alta, Wy., 1976—. Bd. dirs. Teton County Hosp., Driggs, Idaho, 1986-87. Home: Rt 1 Box 1578 Tetonia ID 83452

COMMIRE, ANNE, b. Wyandotte, MI; d. Robert and Shirley (Moore) C. Author: plays Shay, 1973, Put Them All Together, 1978, Transatlantic Bridge, 1977, Sunday's Red, 1980, Melody Sisters, 1983, Mariette: Alone, at Last, 1986, Starting Monday, 1987; teleplay Rebel for God, 1980, Hayward's, 1980; editor: Something About the Author, 1970—, Yesterday's Authors of Books for Children, 1977-78. B.S., Eastern Mich. U., 1961; postgrad., Wayne State U., NYU. Recipient Eugene O'Neill Theatre award, 1973, 78, 83; Creative Artists Program grantee, 1975; Rockefeller grantee for playwriting, 1979. Mem. Dramatists Guild, Writers Guild Am. Home: 81R Oswegathie Rd Waterford CT 06385

COMO, WILLIAM MICHAEL, b. Williamstown, Mass., s. Michael and Janet Antoinette (Caporale) C. Ed., Am. Acad. Dramatic Arts. Sales mgr. Dance Mag., NYC, 1954-60, advt. mgr., 1960-69, ed.-in-chief, 1969—; ed.-in-chief After Dark mag., NYC, 1968-80. Wrkg. on autobiography. Office: Dance Mag 33 W 60th St New York NY 10023

CONCAISON, JOHN SILVA, b. New Bedford, MA, June 5, 1963; s. Michael John and Jovina (DaSilva) C. Wrkg. on short stories, novellas. B.A., Southeastern Massachusetts Univ., 1985. Corr., The Standard-Times, New Bedford, 1985—. Home: 79 Easton St New Bedford MA 02746

CONDRY, DOROTHEA JUNE, b. El Reno, OK, June 20, 1935; d. Edgar Newton and Pearl Lee (Upton) Douglass; m. Garland Garnett, Sept. 12, 1953; 2 daus., Deborah, Ellen. Contrbr. poetry chapbooks The Sign, The Latter Days, The Four Phases of the Moon, Corporate Security; articles to Okla. Pub. Co., Rural Newspapers and Coops; poetry and fiction in var. pubs. inclg. Thirty-Seven Okla. Poets, A Territory of Oklahoma Publication, Now Mag; wrkg. on a novel, Wheat; a fact book, To Love is an Infinitive; To Do is an Imperative. BA in English, CSU, 1968, MA in Profl. Writing, 1974, Assoc. in Engring. Instr. Canadian County Schls., El Reno and Calumet, Okla., 1969-77; assoc. prof. Okla. City Southwestern Coll., 1978-80; adminstrv. asst. Control Data Subsidiary MPI, Okla. City, 1980—; private tutor language arts, 1980—. Youth Council organizer, Canadian County, 1974-76; arts council organizer, Canadian County, 1976-78. Mem. Okla. Ind. Artists, Central State Univ. Alumni Assn., AWP, Intl. Platform Assn. Address: Rt 2 Box 7 Calumet OK 73014

CONE, RUBY, see Prater, Ruby Marian

CONKLE, DONALD STEVEN, b. Martin's Ferry, OH, Nov. 26, 1948; s. Donald Ralph and Annabel (Herriman) Conkle. Author: Tree Zen, 1978, Re: vision, 1984; Neon (play), 1986; editor: The Back Door Anthology; contrbr. poems, short stories, essays, reviews, to lit mags, jnls, and anthols; bk. critic Columbus Dispatch and Small Press Rvw, 1986—. BA, Oberlin, 1970; MA, OH St. U., 1973. Freelance poet, wrtr., journalist, 1975—; asst. editor, The View After Dark, Columbus, OH, 1985-86; co-dir., ed., Pebbles, Reynoldsburg, OH, 1984—; dir., sr. edit., The Broken Stone, 1984—, dir., sr. edit., The Forces of Magic, 1977—; prof., Ohio Dominican Coll., Columbus, OH, 1985-86. Mem. MLA, COSMEP, PSA. Address: Box 246 Reynoldsburg OH 43068

CONN, CAROL, b. Atlanta, May 21, 1952, d. Richard Lee Conn; m. Walter F. Maibaum, Sept. 9, 1984. Ed.: Pathways Mag., 1976, Weight No More (by Karen Darling), 1983; contrbg. wrtr.: Antiques World and Am. Crafts Mag., 1979-80, Pleasures, 1984. Wrkg. on book and TV documentary on the art business. BA, George Washington U., 1975. Wash. Post feature wrtr., arts columnist weekend sect., 1972-79; freelance wrtr., NYC, 1979-80; project dir., speechwrtr. PRA, Inc., San Francisco, 1981-82; assoc. dir. Swan Lake & Delancey Mus., San Francisco, 1985—. Office: 2064 Green St San Francisco CA 94123

CONN, CHRISTOPHER, b. Columbus, OH, Aug. 4, 1948. Columnist: Harding Hosp. Newsletter, 1986—. Contrbr. articles to mags., poems to lit. mags., anthols. Wrkg. on poetry, humor, short stories. B.A., Ohio State U., 1970. Psychiatric counselor Harding Hosp., Worthington, OH, 1973—. Served to 1st lt. U.S. Army, 1966-72. Mem. NWC, P&W. Home: 1526 Melrose Ave Columbus OH 43224

CONN, SANDRA, b. Evanston, IL, Mar. 29, 1944, d. Edward Newman and Etta Evelyn (Fulton) Hickey; m. Richard Howard Hytken, Nov. 22, 1967 (div. 1975); m. 2d, Laurence Lewis Conn, Dec. 31, 1979. Author art exhbn. catalogs, 1979—; contrbr. to Chgo. History, 1979-80, Chgo. Reader, Crain's Ill. Bus., Crain's Chgo. Bus., other publs. BA, Northwestern U., 1966; MA, U. Louisville, 1971, ABD, 1972. Freelance wrtr., Chgo., 1975-77; lectr. U. Louisville, 1970-75, U. Wis. Center System, Madison, 1977-81, Mundelein Coll., Chgo., 1981-82; dir. Sandra Conn Assocs., Chgo., 1982—. Home: 2551 N Clark Chicago IL 60614

CONNELL, EVAN SHELBY, JR., b. Kansas City, MO, Aug. 17, 1924; s. Evan Shelby and Elton (Williamson) C. Author: The Anatomy Lesson and Other Stories, 1957, Mrs. Bridge, 1959, The Patriot, 1960, Notes From a Bottle Found on the Beach at Carmel, 1963, At the Crossroads, 1965, The Diary of a Rapist, 1966, Mr. Bridge, 1969, Points for a Compass Rose, 1973, The Connoisseur, 1974, Double Honeymoon, 1976, A Long Desire, 1979, The White Lantern, 1980, St. Augustine's Pigeon, 1980, Son of the Morning Star: Custer and the Little Bighorn, 1984. Student, Dartmouth, 1941-43, U. Kans., 1946-47, Stanford U., 1947-48, Columbia U., 1948-49. Editor Contact mag., 1959-65. Served as naval aviator, 1943-45. Eugene Saxton fellow, 1953; Guggenheim fellow, 1963; Rockefeller Fdn. grantee, 1967. Address: 487 Sherwood Dr Sausalito CA 94965

CONNELLY, ROBERT BOURKE, (Bob Connelly), b. Boston, Sept. 27, 1935; s. Matthew J. and Dorothea (Knothe) C.; m. Linda Kathryn Steinert, Nov. 30, 1971. Author: The Silent Film, 1986 (vol. 10, The Motion Picture Guide); contrbr. consumer mags; (play) Little Orphan Nannie, 1968. BA, Fordham Univ., 1959. Entertainer, New Wine Singers, 1960-65; screenwriter, Metro Goldwyn Mayer, Calif., 1965-67; composer/performer, Folkways Records, NYC, 1965; actor, San Francisco, 1968; columnist, editor, Chicagoland Magazine, 1968-69; script writer & composer for the "Music Game" TV program; freelance wrtr., editor, Chgo., 1970—. Pvt. E2, Natl. Guard, NYC, 1959-64. Mem. ASCAP, Am. Fedn. Musicians, Club d'Ronde. Address: 1715 W. Balmoral Chgo IL 60640

CONNER, CINDY DIXON, b. Phila., MS, Dec. 6, 1951; d. Robert Myatt and Maxine (Rivers) D.; m. Charles Stockton Conner, July 24, 1976; children—Robert Stockton, Jonathan Rivers. Ed.: Pro Bass Mag., 1975-76, Delta Scene Mag., 1976, Waterfowler's World Mag., 1977—, HRDC Trends, 1985, Flagship News, Number One, Newsbreak. BA, U. MS, 1973. Ed. Daily News, Memphis, 1976, Holiday Inns, Inc., Memphis, 1976-78; asst. dir. Univ. Relations, U. TN, Memphis, 1978-84; pubns. cons., numerous orgns., Memphis, 1984-86; commun. spclst. Federal Express, Memphis, 1986—; pub. Waterfowler's World Mag., Germantown, TN,

1977—. Office: Box 38613 Germantown TN 38183

CONNER, DON R., b. South Bostoa, VA, Jul. 19, 1949. Editor: Proofrock, Literary Arts Jnl; contrbr. to Amelia, American Wrtrs. Jnl, Center Stage, Poetry Rvw, Piedmont Lit Rvw, Pig in a Poke, The White Rock Rvw, Winewood Jnl, Zenos (UK), other lit mags. BA Averett Coll., 1972; MA Longwood Coll., 1978. English teacher Volens Schl. (Nathalie, VA), 1973—. Mem. Piedmont Literary Soc., Pres., 1984-85. Home: Box 607 Halifax VA 24558

CONNIE, see Lapham, Constance Sumner,

CONNOR, J. ROBERT, b. NYC, Jan. 31, 1927; s. Joseph M. and Ethel May (Ball) C.; m. Marie Louise Zolezzi, Sept. 6, 1952; children: Jeanne Marie, Robert Brian, Ellen Louise. Author: A Job With A Future in Automotive Mechanics, 1969, (with Heinz Ulrich) The National Job-Finding Guide, 1981; contrbr. numerous articles to popular mags. BA, Hunter Coll., 1951. Copy editor, sports desk, N.Y. Mirror, 1950-52; mng. editor, Mechanix Illustrated Mag., NYC, 1953-70; editor-in-chief, Motor Mag., NYC, 1972-77; editor, Construction Contracting, 1978-79; editor-in-chief, Graduating Engr. McGraw-Hill, Inc., 1979-81; Housing mag., 1981—; editor, new prod. devlop., Bus. Week, 1981—, editor, Bus. Week Almanac, 1981—, editor-in-chief, Bus. Week's Guide to Careers, 1982—. Served with AUS, 1945-46. Mem. Intl. Motor Press Assn. (pres. 1966-67), ASME. Home: 8 Woodvale Ln Huntington NY 11743

CONNOR, JOHN ANTHONY, b. Manchester, Eng., Mar. 16, 1930; came to U.S., 1967, naturalized, 1982; s. John and Dorothy Mabel (Richings) C.; married, June 21, 1961 (div. 1972); children: Samuel, Simon, Rebecca. Author: poems With Love Somehow, 1962, Lodgers, 1965, Kon in Springtime, 1968, In the Happy Valley, 1971, Memoirs of Uncle Harry, 1974, New and Selected Poems, 1982, Spirits of the Place, 1986; numerous plays. MA, U. Manchester, 1967, Wesleyan U., Middletown, Conn., 1972. Served with Brit. Cavalry, 1948-50. Fellow Royal Soc. Lit. Home: 44 Brainerd Ave Middletown CT 06457

CONNOR, SEYMOUR VAUGHAN, b. Paris, TX, Mar. 4, 1923; s. Aikin Beard and Gladys (Vaughan) C.; 1 son, Charles Seymour. Author: Preliminary Guide to Texas Archives, 1956, Peters Colony of Texas, 1959, A Biggers Chronicle, 1961, Adventure in Glory, 1965, Texas: A History, 1971, (with Odie Faulk) North America Divided: The Mexican War, 1846-48, 1971, (with W.C. Pool) Texas, the 28th State, 1971, (with Odie Faulk) La Guerra de Intervencion, 1846-1848, 1975, Texas in 1776, 1975, (with J.M. Skaggs) Broadcloth and Britches: The Sante Fe Trade, 1976; editor: Panhandle-Plains Historical Rvw, 1953-57, Texas Treasury Papers (3 vols.), 1955, The West Is for Us, 1957, Builders of the Southwest, 1959, Saga of Texas (6 vols.), 1965, Dear America, 1971, Texas Tech Museum Jnl, 1975-78; contrbr. articles to profl. jnls. BA, U. Tex., 1948, MA, 1949, PhD, 1952. Archivist, Panhandle-Plains Museum, 1952-53; Texas State Archivist, 1953-55; prof. of history, Texas Tech Univ., 1955-79; prof. emeritus, 1979—. Served with AUS, 1943-45; ETO: Served with USAR, 1946-55. Fellow & past pres., Texas State Hist. Assn. Home: 3503 45th St Lubbock TX 79413

CONNORS, THOMAS E., b. Waltham, MA, Jan. 21, 1929; s. Thomas Patrick and Elizabeth (Forrestal) Connors; m. Feiga Hollenberg June, 1956; children—Thomas, David, Sarah. Author: Abstract Relations (short stories), 1980; fiction in many literary jnls, including Literary Rvw, North American Rvw, Perspective. BA, Brandeis U., Waltham, Mass., 1956; MA, Boston U., 1957. Prof., Suffolk U., Boston, 1957—. Served with USMC, 1946-48. Home: 320 Tappan St Brookline MA 02146

CONOLEY, GILLIAN, b. Austin, TX, Mar. 29, 1955; s. Graham Gillis and Billie Tom (Curby) C.; m. Domenic Stansberry, Mar. 22, 1986. Author: Woman Speaking Inside Film Noir, 1984, Some Gangster Pain, 1987. Contrbr. poems to lit. mags. Editor: Black River Press, 1984—; Willow Springs, 1987—. BFA, Southern Meth. U., 1977; MFA in Poetry, U. Mass., 1983. Instr. creative writing Smith Coll., Northampton, Mass., 1983; instr. U. New Orleans, 1984-87; visiting lectr. in lit. Tulane U., New Orleans, 1985-87; artist-in-res., Eastern Wash. Univ., 1987—. Mem. AWP, AAP, MacDowell Colony Fellows Orgn. Home: 1230 W Sprague 14 Spokane WA 99201

CONROY, CATHRYN DEVAN, b. Bryn Mawr, PA, Mar. 9, 1954; d. Christopher Bartram and Margaret Elizabeth (Brice) Devan; m. Michael John Conroy, JUly 16, 1977; children—Kevin Michael, Christopher Patrick, Megan Elizabeth. Contrbr. articles to mags., newspapers. Contrbg. ed.: Online Today, 1982—, Online Access Guide, 1986—. B.A., Cleve. State U., 1976; M.A., Ohio State U., 1983. Dir. public relations Lakewood Public Library, OH, 1977-79; asst. dir. public relations St. Anthony Hosp., Columbus, OH, 1979-82; free-lance mag. jnlst., 1982—. Recipient Bronze Quill award IABC, 1985. Mem. Washington Ind. Wrtrs. Home: 8905 Alliston Hollow Way Gaithersburg MD 20879

CONROY, DONALD PATRICK, b. Atlanta, Oct. 26, 1945; s. Donald and Frances Dorothy (Peek) C.; m. Lenore Guerewitz, Mar. 21, 1945; children: Jessica, Melissa, Megan, Gregory, Emily. Author: The Citadel, 1967, The Boo, 1970, The Water Is Wide, 1972, The Great Santini, 1976, The Lords of Discipline, 1980, The Prince of Tides, 1986. BA in English. Ford Fdn. Leadership Devel. grantee, 1971. Mem. AG Am. WG, PEN. Address: Old NY Book Shop 1069 Juniper St Atlanta GA 30309

CONROY, JACK, (John Wesley Conroy), b. Moberly, MO, Dec. 5, 1899; s. Thomas Edward and Eliza Jane (McCollough) C.; m. Elizabeth Gladys Kelly, June 30, 1922 (dec. Oct. 17, 1981); children—Margaret Jean (Mrs. James Walter Tillery, dec.), Thomas Vernon (dec.), Jack. Author: The Disinherited, 1933, reissued 1963, A World to Win, 1935; (with Arna Bontemps) The Fast Sooner Hound, 1942, They Seek a City, 1945, Slappy Hooper, The Wonderful Sign Painter, 1946, Sam Patch, The High, Wide and Handsome Jumper, 1951, Anyplace But Here, 1966; The Jack Conroy Reader (edited by Jack Salzman and David Ray), 1980; The Weed King and Other Stories (edited by Douglas C. Wixson), 1985. Editor: (with Ralph Cheyney) Unrest, 1929-31, 1931; Midland Humor: A Harvest of Fun and Folklore, 1947, (with Curt Johnson) Writers in Revolt: The Anvil Anthology, 1973. Student, U. Mo., 1920-21; LHD, U. Mo. at Kansas City, 1975. Editor The Rebel Poet 1931-32, The Anvil, 1932-35; The New Anvil, 1939-41; assoc. editor Nelson's Encyc. and Universal World Reference Encyc., 1943-47; sr. editor New Standard Encyc., Chgo., 1947-66; dir. Standard Information Service, 1949-55; lit. editor Chicago Defender, 1946-47, Chgo. Globe, 1950; instr. fiction writing Columbia Coll., 1962-66. Guggenheim fellow, 1935; recipient James L. Dow award Soc. Midland Authors, 1966; award Literary Times, 1967; Lit. award Mo. Library Assn., 1977; Mark Twain award Soc. for Study Midwestern Lit, 1980; Louis M. Rabinowitz Fdn. grantee, 1968; NEA grantee, 1978. Soc. Midland Authors Award, 1986. Mem. Soc. Midland Authors (v.p. Mo.), Intl. Platform Assn. Home: 701 Fisk Ave Moberly MO 65270

CONROY, JOHN WESLEY, see Conroy, Jack

CONSTANTINE, JEAN M., see Koran, Connie Jean

CONTURSI, PAUL, b. Bklyn., Sept. 5, 1953; s. Gaetano and Julia (Gratta) Contursi. Contrbr. articles to science pubs. including Astronomy, 1981-82. BA, Michigan Tech., Houghton, 1976. Freelance wrtr., NYC,1976-83; tech. wrtr., STAC, NYC, 1983-84; sr. tech. wrtr., Dean Witter Reynolds, NYC,1984—. Home: 145 72nd St Brooklyn NY 11209

CONWAY, ALICE FRANCES, b. Highland Park, IL, Nov. 13, 1907; d. Michael Francis and Catherine Amanda (Hanlon) Curley; m. Carroll Joseph Conway, June 8, 1940 (dec. Oct. 5, 1961); 1 stepdau., Patricia Conway Higgins. Contrbr. articles to mags., newspapers including Good Old Days Mag., Modern Maturity, Chgo. Daily News, Chgo. Tribune. Wrkg. on novels, short stories. Grad. pvt. schls., Highland Park. Teller, First Nat. Bank, Highland Park. Teller, First Nat. Bank, Highland Park, 1926-74, retired. Mem. NWC. Home: 855 N McKinley Rd Lake Forest IL 60045

CONWAY, JOHN R., b. Monticello, NY, Oct. 11, 1952, s. John J. and Ida Mae (Fredenburgh) C. Author: Trifles & Poppycock, 1984; contrbr. to Mechanix Illustrated, Popular Science, MG Publs., Wrtr.'s Yearbook, other publs. Wrkg. on trivia book, automotive articles. Student Ga. Inst. Tech., Atlanta, 1970-75. Sports ed. Atlanta Scene, 1976; sports dir. sta.-WREK, Atlanta, 1977; news reporter sta.-WSUL, Monticello, N.Y., 1978, news dir., ops. mgr., 1979-80; freelance wrtr., 1980—. Home: Box 94 Rock Hill NY 12775

COOK, ALBERT SPAULDING, b. Exeter, NH, Oct. 28, 1925, s. Albert Spaulding Cook and Adele (Farrington) Ventura; m. Carol Rubin, June 19, 1948; children—David, Daniel, Jonathan. Author criticism: The Dark Voyage and the Golden Mean: A Philosophy of Comedy, 1949, The Meaning of Fiction, 1960, The Classic Line: A Study of Epic Poetry, 1966, Prisms: Studies in Modern Literature, 1967, The Root of the Thing: A Study of Job and the Song of Songs, 1968, Enactment: Greek Tragedy, 1971, French Tragedy: The Power of Enactment, 1981, Shakespeare's Enactment, 1976, Myth and Language, 1980, Changing the Signs: The Fifteenth Century Breakthrough, 1985, Thresholds, a study of some aspects of Romanticism, 1985, Figural Choice in Poetry and Art, 1985; author poetry: Progressions, 1963, The Charges, 1972, Adapt the Living, 1981; playwright: Double Exposure, 1958, Night Guard, 1962, Big Blow, 1964, Check, 1966, The Death of Trotsky, 1971; author textbooks: Oedipus Rex: A Mirror for Greek Drama, 1963, Plays for the Greek Theatre (with E. Dolin), 1972, The Odyssey: A Critical Edition, 1972; contrbr. poetry, criticism: Clio, Helios, Costerus, Kenyon Rvw, numerous periodicals. AB,

Harvard U., 1946, MA, 1947, postgrad., 1947-48, jr. fellow Soc. of Fellows, 1948-51; Fulbright fellow U. Paris, 1952-53. Educator, English, classics, comparative lit., 1955—; prof., Brown U., Providence, R.I., 1978—, Ford Fdn. prof., 1986—. Recipient numerous academic awards, fellowships. Office: Box E Marston Hall Brown Univ Providence RI 02912

COOK, DAVID CHARLES, III, b. Elgin, IL, June 11, 1912; s. David Charles, Jr. and Frances Lois (Kerr) C.; children: Margaret Anne, Martha L., Bruce L., Gregory D., Rebecca. Author: Walk the High Places, 1964, Invisible Halos, 1975. Student, Occidental Coll., 1930-32; PhB, U. Chgo., 1934; LitD, Judson Coll., 1965. Chmn. bd. David C. Cook Pub. Co. (founded by grandfather 1875), Elgin, Ill., 1934, editor-in-chief of its 35 curriculum publs. Office: 850 N Grove Ave Elgin IL 60120

COOK, EILEEN MARIE, b. Pitts., Mar. 10, 1950; d. Francis R. and Helen M. (Martin) Wuenstel; m. Jim Warren, June 21, 1969 (div. May 25, 1975); children—Valerie, Angela; m. Dan E. Cook, Apr. 18, 1980. Author: Guilt Mirror, 1986, When Dragons Dream for Little Girls (2d place for sci. fiction FFWA, 1987), 1987, Vivaldi's Strain, 1987. Contrbr. interviews to newspapers. Wrkg. on anthol. of short stories. A.A., Hillsborough Commun. Coll., 1986. Costumer, Epcot, Orlando, FL, 1981-83. Mem. FFWA. Home: 9715 Redwood Blvd Tampa FL 33635

COOK, FRED S., b. Alameda, CA, May 20, 1915; s. Frederick A. and Anna C. (Stuart) C.; m. Mitzi Mayfair, June 1960 (div. 1972). Author over 100 local histories of Western U.S. . Wrkg. on local history. Student Oakland Jr. Coll., 1933-34. Makeup ed. N.Y. Daily Mirror, 1939-50; asst. to pub. Publs. Rolland, Mexico, 1950-60; ed. Calif. Traveler, Volcano, 1961-76. Served RCAF, then maj. USAAF, 1941-44; ETO. Home: Box 3071 Parker AZ 85344

COOK, GEOFFREY ARTHUR, b. Cleve., Apr. 9, 1946; s. Arthur William and Donna Kay (Christy) C. Author: Tolle Lege, 1974, Love & Hate: Selected Translations from the Carmina of Gaius Valerius Catullus, 1975, A Basket of Chestnuts: From the Miscellanea of Venantius Fortunatus, 1981. Contrbg. ed.: Margins, 1975-78, La Mamelle Art Contemporary, 1977-81. Wrkg. on translation of Cathemerinon of Aurelius Prudentius Clemens. Student Kenyon Coll., 1964-67; B.A., U. Calif., Berkeley, 1982, M.A., 1987. Mem. PEN, ALTA, Wrtrs. Union. Home: Box 4233 Berkeley CA 94704

COOK, PETRONELLE MARGUERITE MARY, (Margot Arnold), b. Plymouth, England, May 16, 1925, came to U.S., 1950; naturalized, 1953; d. Harry Alfred and Ada Wood (Alford) Crouch; m. Philip R. Cook, Jr., July 20, 1949 (div. 1979); children—Philip R., Nicholas E.A., Alexandra M. L. Author: The Officer's Woman, 1973, The Villa on the Palatine, 1975, Marie, 1978, Exit Actors, Dying, 1979, Cape Cod Caper, 1980, Zadok's Treasure, 1981, Death of a Voodoo Doll, 1982, Lament for a Lady Laird, 1982, Death on the Dragon's Tongue, 1983, Affairs of State, 1984, Love Among the Allies, 1985, Desperate Measures, 1986, Sinister Purposes, 1988. Contrbr. chpt. to book, short stories in anthols. B.A. with honors, U. Oxford, England, 1946, M.A. with honors, 1950. Lectr. archaelogy and anthropology U Md., Rome, Italy, 1971, Cape Cod ommun. Coll., Hyannis, MA, 1972—. Mem. NWC. (fiction prize 1984), Boston Author's Club. Home: 11 High Schl Rd Hyannis MA 02601

COOK, RODNEY EDWIN SR., (Many Trails), b. Amesbury, MA, Feb. 9, 1937; s. Roland Francis and Mabel May (Butland) C.; m. Janet Lee Fowler, June 22, 1959; children—Susan Lee, Marie Alice, Darlene Janet, Tammy Ellen (dec.), Rodney Edwin, Bambi Lynne, Tula Jean, Troy Andrew. Contrbr. articles to newspapers, mags. including Boston Globe, others. Wrkg. on poetry, fishing articles. A.A. in Liberal Arts, Northern Essex COmmun. Coll., 1978. Machine operator Owens-Ill., Newbury Port, MA, 1982—. Home: 142A S Main St Seabrook NH 03874

COOKE, AUDREY, (April Frazier), b. Brklyn.; d. Harold Francis and Anna (Frazier) C. Contrbr. poems to lit. mags., anthols. Wrkg. on Roman Ruins and Other People. Marymount Coll. (NY), 1948; M.A. in English, Breadloaf Schl. English, 1971; Ph.D. in French, Catholi U., 1960. Sr. fellow English/French, Mackinac Coll., Mackinac Island, MI, 1967-69; dept. chair French St. Margaret-McTernan High Sch., Waterbury, CT, 1969-78; tchr. French and English, St. Thomas Aquinas High Sch., Ft. Lauderdale, FL, 1983—. Recipient Honorable Mention, Wrtrs. Digest, 1968, 83, 1st prize for religious poem N.Y. Poetry Forum, 1983, Golden Poet award World of Poetry, 1985, 86. Mem. FFWA, South Fla. Poetry Inst. (1st prize for Irish poem 1986), Am. Assn. Tchrs. French, Modern Lang. Tchrs. Assn. Home:4159 SW 67th Ave Apt 208-A Davie FL 33314

COOK-LYNN, ELIZABETH, (Liz Cook), b. Crow Creek Sioux Indian Reservation, Ft. Thompson, SD, Nov. 17, 1930, d. H. Jerome and Hulda (Petersen) Irving; m. Malvin P. Traversie Cook (div.); children—David, Mary, Lisa, Margaret; m. 2d, Clyde J. Lynn. Author: Then Badger Said This (poetry collection), 1978; contrbr. short stories, poetry, rvw.: Indian Historian, Ethnic Studies Jnl, Prairie Schooner, New Native American Novel, numerous other periodicals; author articles, research papers; ed.: Wicazo Sa Rvw, Jnl of Native Am. Studies, 1985—. BS, S.D. State Coll., 1952; MEd, S.D. U., 1970; postgrad. U. Nebr., Black Hills State Tchrs. Coll., U. N. Mex. Mem. faculty Eastern Wash. U., Cheney, 1970—, assoc. prof. English (Indian Studies), 1980—. Grantee NEH, 1980. Office: Dept Eng E Wash Univ Cheney WA 99004

COOLER, AMANDA JEFFERS, b. Ridgeland, SC, Sept. 27, 1955; d. Julian Emerald, Jr. and Estelle Ann (Crosby) Jeffers; m. Jerry Everett Cooler, July 14, 1978; 1 dau., Jennifer Anne. Contrbr. book rvws. Low County Weekly, 1984-87. Wrkg. on contemporary western romance novel, Apache Love. Librarian, Hardeeville Commun. Library, SC, 1976-80. Home: Box 1114 Hardeeville SC 29927

COOLEY, JOHN R., b. Oneonta, NY, Oct. 26, 1937; s. Philip Cooley and Helen (Ryder) Courtney; m. Barbara Zschiesche, July 16, 1960; children—Carolyn, Meredith. Author: Savages and Naturals: Black Portraits by White Writers in Modern America, 1982. Contrbr. articles in lit. mags., profl. jnls. Editor: Celery, 1976-82. BA, Syracuse U., 1959, MA, 1960; PhD, U. Mass.-Amherst, 1970. Asst. prof. to prof. English, Western Mich. U., Kalamazoo, 1969—; research fellow U. Sussex, Brighton, England, 1975-76; vis. prof. U. Exeter, England, 1982-83. Fellow, NEH, 1985. Mem. MLA, Am. Culture Soc. Home: 2504 Crescent Dr Kalamazoo MI 49001

COOLEY, PETER JOHN, b. Detroit, Nov. 19, 1940, s. Paul John and Ruth Esther C.; m. Jacqueline Marks, June 12, 1965; children—Nicole, Alissa, Joshua. Author: The Company of Strangers, 1975, The Room Where Summer Ends, 1979, Nightseasons, 1983, The Van Gogh Notebook, 1987; poetry ed. N.Am. Rvw, 1970. BA, Shimer Coll., 1962; MA, U. Chgo., 1964; PhD, U. Iowa, 1970. Asst. prof. U. Wis., Green Bay, 1970-72, assoc. prof., 1972-75; asst. prof. Tulane U., New Orleans, 1975-77, assoc. prof., 1977-83, prof. English, 1983—. Creative writing fellow State of La., 1981, Robert Frost fellow Bread Loaf Wrtrs.' Conf., 1982. Mem. PEN, P&W, PSA. Home: 241 Harding St Jefferson LA 70118

COOLS, ALTA MARIE, b. Elmhurst, IL, May 25, 1941; d. Joseph an dLorraine Josephine (Cahill) Cools; m. James Rufus Halama, Oct. 10, 1987. Columnist: Photo Weekly, NYC, 1974-76. Feature ed.: Photographic Trade News, Woodbury, NY, 1978-81, Photo Weekly, 1982-86; contrbg. ed.: Photo Bus., NYC, 1986—. B.A., U. Ill., 1963. Pub. For Your Info., Glen Ellyn, IL, 1981—. Home: 440 Raintree Ct Glen Ellyn IL 60137

COOMBE, JACK D., b. Baltic, MI, Mar. 1, 1922; s. Harry Coombe and Susan Ruth (Brown) Coombe Moyle; m. Margaret Caroline Manfred, Aug. 26, 1947. Author: Consider my Servant, 1956, The Temptation, 1985; contrbr. articles to mags.; scriptwrtr. for TV, radio, films. BA, Northwestern Coll.; postgrad., Roosevelt U. Freelance wrtr. Creative Writing Services, Northbrook, Ill., 1976—; wrtr.-in-residence High Sch. Dist. 225, Northbrook, 1987—. Served with USN, 1940-46; PTO. Home: 1704 Maple Ave Northbrook IL 60062

COOMER, JOE, b. Ft. Worth, Nov. 3, 1958; s. Rufus and Linda Loyce (Dennis) C. Author: The Decatur Road, 1983; Kentucky Love, 1985; A Flatland Fable, 1986. BA, So. Methodist U., 1981. Recipient Jessie Jones fiction award Tex. Inst. Letters, 1983. Home: 101 Ash Creek Dr W Azle TX 76020

COONEY, ELLEN, b. St. Louis, June 23, 1948, d. Robert Paul John and Hildegarde (Bramman) Cooney. Author poetry collections: The Silver Rose, 1979, The Quest for the Holy Grail, 1981, House Holding, 1984. BA, Lone Mountain Coll., 1970. Home: 919 Sutter St San Francisco CA 94109

COONFIELD, ED, b. Bartlesville, OK, Mar. 24, 1941; s. Kenneth Alden and Maxine Marie (Stroud) C.; m. Lois Ann Vermillion, May 8, 1964; 1 son, Dustin Edward. Author: Enduro Secrets Revealed, 1985, Arizona Ghost Town Map, 1976. Customer engr. M.A.I., Calif., 1965-67, D.P.A., Calif., 1967-70; antique shop owner Treasure Chest, Colo., 1971—; freelance writer, 1970—. Home: Box 924 Salida CO 81201

COOPER, ARTHUR MARTIN, b. NYC, Oct. 15, 1937, s. Benjamin Albert and Elizabeth (Sadock) C.; m. Amy Beth Levin, June 9, 1979. Contrbr. articles: The New Republic, Playboy, Mademoiselle, Sat. Rvw. BA, Pa. State U., 1959. Corr. Time mag., NYC, 1966-67; assoc. ed. Newsweek mag., NYC, 1967-76; ed. Penthouse mag., NYC, 1976-77, Family Weekly, NYC, 1978-83; ed.-in-chief Gentlemen's Qtly, NYC, 1983—. Served to lt. (j.g.) USN, 1960-63. Named Ed. of Yr., AdWeek mag., 1985; profl. journalism fellow Stanford U., 1970-71. Mem. ASME. Office: G Qtly 350 Madison Ave New York NY

10017

COOPER, BARBARA MARY, b. Willimantic, CT, June 11, 1949; d. Anthony Joseph and Mary Ann (Kement) Meglin; m. James Elmer Cooper, Dec. 29, 1973. Ed.: The Mariner, 1970-73, Eleven, 1979-82, Leader Letter, 1979-82, Horizons, 1983-86. BA, Marquette U., 1970. Pub. relns. dir. St. Mary's Hosp., Milw., 1971-73; adv. asst. Wisconsin Telephone, Milw., 1973-79; mgr. internal communics. Rexnord, Milw., 1979-83; ed. Allen-Bradley, Milw., 1983—. Silver Trumpet award, Publicity Club Chgo., 1985; IABC awards, 1983, 85. Mem. IABC. Office: Allen-B Co 1201 S 2nd St Milwaukee WI 53204

COOPER, BARBIE PERKINS, b. Columbus, GA, Aug. 22, 1950; d. Walter Woodrow and Sybil Gertrude (Hunter) Perkins; m. Phillip Ray Cooper, Sr., Aug. 2, 1968; 1 son, Phillip Ray. Contrbr. poems to anthols. Diploma in Interior Design, Adrian Hall Shl. of Design, 1982. Freelance designer, 1977-84; free-lane wrtr., 1987—. Recipient 1st place for fiction Florence Wrtrs. Seminar, SC, 1984; Honorable Mention, World of Poetry, 1986, Golden Poet award, 1986. Mem. RWA. Home: 641 Palmetto St Mount Pleasant SC 29464

COOPER, BILLY NORMAN, b. Jonesboro, AK, June 4, 1937; s. Bill and Gladys (Brinkley) C.; m. Zelma Vanhorn, May 9, 1957; children—Billy Ray, Anthony Royce. Author: Poems by a Patriot, 1964, Men of Honour, 1987. Contrbr. numerous articles and poems to Keesler AFB Newspaper. Wrkg. on collection of patriotic children's poems. Student Commun. Coll., Biloxi, MS, 1982. Advanced through grades to chief master sgt. USAF, 1957—. Vice pres. POW/MIA Council, Keesler AFB, 1987—. Home: 15908 Orange Dr North Biloxi MS 39532

COOPER, EDGAR S., see Hoeppner, Iona Ruth

COOPER, JEFFREY B., b. Bronx, N.Y., Nov. 14, 1950, s. Melvin and Miriam (Cohen) C.; m. Rhonda Solomon, Jan. 23, 1973; 1 child, Sara. Author: How To Make Love to an Extraterrestrial, 1983, Bonnie's Blues, 1985, Robin in the Apple, 1986, The Nightmares on Elm Street, 1987, The Nightmare on Elm Street Companion, 1987, Finny in Love, 1987. BA in English, Hunter Coll., 1971. Home: 79 New York Ave Sound Beach NY 11789

COOPER, JOHN CHARLES, (Charles E. Greene III), b. Charleston, S.C., Apr. 3, 1933, s. Chauncey Miller and Margarete Anna (Gerard) C.; m. Clelia Ann Johnston, June 6, 1954 (div. 1986) children—Martin C., Catherine M., Cynthia A., Paul Conrad; m. 2d, Deborah Karen Moroz, Dec. 30, 1986. Author: Wine in Separate Cups, 1967, Mark: Gospel of Action, 1963, The Roots of Radical Theology (translated into Braille, Brit., Dutch, Italian, Spanish, Swedish, German and Japanese), 1967, Radical Christianity and Its Sources, 1968, The New Mentality (book club selection), 1969, The Christian and Politics, 1969, The Turn Right, 1970, Celluloid and Symbols, 1970, Religion in the Age of Aquarius (book club selection, translated into Japanese), 1971, Getting It Together, 1971, Paul for Today, 1981, Amos: Prophet of Justice, 1972, A New Kind of Man, 1972, The Recovery of America, 1972, Religion After Forty, 1973, Finding a Simpler Life, 1974, Fantasy and the Human Spirit, 1975, Your Exciting Middle Years (book club selection), 1976, Living, Loving and Letting Go (book club selection), 1977, Why We Hurt and Who Can Heal (book club selection), 1978, The Deacon, 1979, Not for a Million Dollars, 1980, Love Within Love, 1980, The Joy of The Plain Life, 1981, Religious Pied Pipers, 1981, Dealing with Destructive Cults (book club selection), 1984, Throwing the Sticks, 1985, All the Flora of the Bible, 1986; contrbg. author: Humanistic Psychology, 1981, Writing to Inspire, 1982, The Future of Lutheran Higher Education, 1984, Abingdon Dictionary of the Bible and Religion, 1985; contrbr. articles, rvws: Luth Qtly, Jnl of Ohio Acad. Religion, Augustinian Studies, Clergy Jnl, numerous other publs. Leader wrtrs. conferences, Ohio, Illinois, Wis., Pa., Ontario, 1970—. AB cum laude, U. S.C., 1955; MDiv cum laude, Luth. Theol. So. Sem., 1958, MA, U. Chgo., 1964, PhD in Christian Theology, 1966. Ordained minister Luth. Ch. Am., 1958. Educator, 1961—; prof. systematic theology, dean acad. affairs Winebrenner Theol. Sem., Findlay, Ohio, 1971-82; prof. religion, chmn. dept. philosophy and religion Susquehanna U., Selinsgrove, Pa., 1982—. Served as sgt. USMC, 1950-52; Korea. Office: RD 1 Box 64 Mifflinburg PA 17844

COOPER, JUDITH, b. Phila. Contrbr. stories to Midway Rvw, Louisville Rvw, Permafrost, Black Warrior Rvw. BA, U. Pa., 1972; MFA, U. Iowa, 1976. Winner fiction contest Midway Rvw, 1984; Ill. Arts Council fellow, 1985. Mem. NWU, central region VP, 1986-87. Home: 6620 N Glenwood Ave Chicago IL 60626

COOPER, KATHY NELLE, b. Greenville, SC, July 10, 1956, d. Palmer Dee and Anne Rosemond (Long) Cooper. Author: Lost Love, 1984, Love, 1985. Wrkg. on horror novel, sci. fiction. BA in English Edn., U.S.C., 1978; MA in Edn., Furman U., 1980; currently student pre-vet medicine, Clemson Univ. Tchr. public schls., Fountain Inn, S.C., 1978-84, Piedmont, S.C., 1984—. Mem. NEA. Home: Rt 6 Box 278 Piedmondt SC 29673

COOPER, KENNETH CARLTON, b. St. Louis, May 2, 1948; s. George Carlton and Mary Frances (Kavanaugh) C.; m. Susan Ann Bujnak, Sept. 6, 1969; children: Jeffrey Carlton, Daniel Steven, Mara Elizabeth. Author: Nonverbal Communications for Business Success, 1979, World's Greatest Blackjack Book, 1980, Bodybusiness, 1981, Always Bear Left, 1982, STOP IT NOW, 1985. Wrkg. on Common Mistakes All Salespeople Make (book). BS, U. Mo., 1970, MS, 1971; PhD, Columbia Pacific U., 1984. Mktg. rep. IBM, St. Louis, 1971-76; pres. Ken Cooper Communications, St. Louis, 1976—. Registered profl. engr., Mo.; cert. adminstrv. mgr. Adminstrv. Mgmt. Soc.; cert. speaking profl. Natl. Speakers Assn. Mem. Am. Soc. Trng. and Devel. Home: 16408 Brandsford Pt Chesterfield MO 63017

COOPER, SANDRA LENORE, (Sonni Cooper), b. NYC, July 9, 1934; d. Edward Emmanuel and Mollie (Hantman) Kleeman; m. Ralph Sherman Cooper, Jan. 10, 1956; children: Laurie Mara, Brett Edward. Author: (sci. fiction novel) Black Fire, 1983; (soap operas and serials) Forbidden Passions, 1986, Love Trap, 1986. BFA, U. Colo. Pres. Creative Enterprises, Long Beach; v.p., chmn. bd. Apogee Research Corp., Long Beach. Mem. SFWA, SAG, SEG. Home: 76 Santa Ana Ave Long Beach CA 90803

COOPER, SONNI, see Cooper, Sandra Lenore

COOPER, WYN, b. Detroit, Jan. 2, 1957, s. William Wendell and Maree (Falls) Cooper. Author: The Country of Here Below, 1987. Contrbr. poetry: Black Warrior Rvw, Prairie Schooner, Sun Dog, Tar River Poetry, numerous other publs. BA in English, U. Utah, 1979; MA in Wrtg., Hollins Coll., Roanoke, Va., 1981. Freelance wrtr., Salt Lake City, 1981—; ed.-in-chief Qtly. West, Salt Lake City, 1983-85; teaching fellow U. Utah, Salt Lake City, 1982—; ed.-in-res. Bennington (Vt.) Coll., 1983-85; ed. Utah Wilderness Assn. Rvw, Salt Lake City, 1981-86. Mem. MLA. Home: 834 5th Ave Salt Lake City UT 84103

COOPERMAN, HASYE, b. NYC, Feb. 2, 1909; d. Ephraim and Miriam (Scholar) Cooperman; m. N. B. Minkoff (dec.), October 1931; children—Amram, Eli. Works include: The Aesthetics of Stephane Mallarme, 1933, rev. ed., 1971; The Chase, 1932, Men Walk the Earth, 1953, The Making of a Woman, 1985; 3 radio cassettes on Yiddish lit., 1979-80; contrbr. poetry and articles to various mags. BA, Hunter College; MA, Columbia U., PhD,Columbia U. Editorial researcher, World Publishing Co., Cleveland, 1937-43; instr., City College, NYC,1939-41; prof., New School for Social Research, 1950—, Chairman, Lit. Dept., 1960-67. Mem. PSA, AAUP. Home: 334 West 85th St New York NY 10024

COPE, DAVID EDGE, b. Detroit, Jan. 13, 1948; s. Robert Edge and Jean Elizabeth (Hamilton) C.; m. Suzanne Marie Schneider, Aug. 21, 1970; children: Anne, Jane. Author: Quiet Lives, 1983, On the Bridge, 1986; ed. and pub. Big Scream Mag.; contrbr. poetry to City Lights Jnl No. 4, New Directions No. 37, The Pushcart Prize II, Dial-a-Poem, Blind Alley, In the Light, Windows in the Stone, Delirium, The World, Roof, Bombay Gin, New Blood, Ferro Botanica, The Refinery, Wonderland, other lit. mags.; essays in St. Mark's Poetry Project newsletter, Mich. Council Tchrs. of English Monthly. LSA, U Mich. Factory worker Miller Metals Products Corp, Grandville, Mich., 1970-73; custodian Grand Rapids pub. schls., Mich., 1973—. Marcher in anti-war causes, Mich., 1966-70; conducted anti-nuclear tch.-ins, Grand Rapids area, 1979-80; sponsored emigration of Vietnamese family to US, 1979. Mem. Ed. & Pub., Nada Press. Address: 2782 Dixie SW Grandville MI 49418

COPPOLA, CARLO, b. Wooster, OH, Oct. 1, 1938; s. Carlo and Flavia Marie (Gasbarre) C.; m. Alicia Teresa Villarreal, Sept. 1, 1963 (div. 1980); children—Johanna Melanie, Carlo; m. 2d, Patrice Elizabeth Gerard, Mar. 21, 1981 (div. 1986). Ed. Marxist Influences and S. Asian Lit., 2 vols., 1974, An Anthology of Mohan Rakesh, 1976; asst. ed., Jnl. Asian Studies, 1978-80. BS, John Carroll U., 1960; MA, U. Chgo., 1961, PhD,1975. Instr. Ind. Univ., Gary, 1966-67; lectr. Oakland Univ., Rochester, Mich., 1968-70, asst. prof., 1970–76, assoc. prof. 1976-82, prof., 1982—; co-founder and ed. Jnl. S. Asian Lit. Program dir. WQRS-FM, Detroit, 1969-74; devel. dir. Christopher Ballet, Rochester, 1973-75, Mich. Lyric Opera Co., W. Bloomfield, Mich., 1976-81; instr., Culinary Arts, Schoolcraft Coll., 1984—. Mem. MLA, S. Asia Lit. Assn. Home: 2760 Upper Ridge Dr Rochester MI 48063

CORBETT, (WINFIELD) SCOTT, b. Kansas City, MO, July 27, 1913; s. Edward Roy and Hazel Marie (Emanuelson) C.; m. Elizabeth Grosvenor Pierce, May 11, 1940; 1 dau., Jane Florence. Author: over 60 books, latest being The Case of the Silver Skull, 1974, The Great Custard Pie Panic, 1974, The Case of the Burgled Blessing Box, 1975, The Boy Who Walked on Air, 1975, The Great McGoniggle's Gray Ghost, 1975, Captain Butcher's Body, 1976, The Black Mask Trick, 1976, The Hockey Girls, 1976, The Great McGoniggle's Key Play, 1976, The Hangman's Ghost Trick, 1977, Bridges, 1978, The Discontented Ghost, 1978, The Mysterious Zetabet, 1979, The Donkey Planet, 1979, Home Computers, 1980, The Deadly Hoax, 1981, Grave Doubts, 1982, Down with Wimps, 1984, The Trouble with Diamonds, 1985, Witch Hunt, 1985. BJ, U. Mo., 1934. Served with infantry, AUS, 1943-46. Recipient Edgar Allan Poe award MWA, 1962, Mark Twain award, 1975. Mem. AL Am. Address: 149 Benefit St Providence RI 02903

CORDASCO, FRANCESCO, b. NYC, Nov. 2, 1920; s. Giovanni and Carmela (Madorma) C.; m. Edna Vaughn, Oct. 22, 1946; children: Michael, Carmela. Author: Research, 1948, 15th edit., 1974, Junius Bibliography, 1949, rev. ed., 1974, 18th Century Bibliographies, 1950, Adam Smith: A Biblographical Checklist, 1950, Bohn Libraries, 1951, Daniel Coit Gilman and the Protean Ph.D.: The Shaping of American Graduate Education, 1960, A Brief History of Education, 1963, 5th ed., 1981, Educational Soiology, 1965, Education in the Urban Community, 1969, School in the Social Order, 1970, Puerto Rican Community an its Children, 1968, 3d ed., 1982, Jacob Riis Revisited: Poverty and the Slum in Another Era, 1968, Minoritie in the American City, 1970, Teacher Education in the United States: A Guide for Foreign Students, 1971, Puerto Ricans on the U.S. Mainland, 1972, Italians in the United States, 1972, Puerto Rican Experiene, 1973, Italian American Eperience, 1974, Equality of Educational Opportunity, 1973, The Puerto Ricans, 1973, The Italians: Social Backgrounds of an American Group, 1974, Studies in Italian American Social History, 1975, Bibliography of American Educational History, 1975, Bilingual Schooling in the United States, 1976, Immigrant Children in American Schools, 1976, Spanish for Hospital and Medical Personnel, 1977, Tobias G. Smollett, M.D., 1978, Sociology of Education, 1978, Bilingual Education in American Schs., 1979, Medical Education in the U.S., 1979, American Ethnic Groups, 1980, The White Slave Trade and the Immigrants, 1981, American Medical Imprints, 1820-1910: A Bibliography, 1983, Crime in America, 1985, Immigrant Woman in North America, 1985, Junius and His Works, 1986. Editor: Social History of Poverty, 15 vols., 1968-70, Puerto Rican Experience, 33 vols., 1975, Italian American Experience, 39 vols., 1975, Bilingual Education in the U.S., 40 vols., 1981. B.A., Columbia, 1942; M.A., N.Y. U., 1945, Ph.D., 1959; student, U. London, U. Salamanca. Served with AUS, World War II. Home: 6606 Jackson St West New York NJ 07093

CORDNER, DENISE FRANCOISE, b. Tripoli, Libya, Dec. 5, 1961; came to U.S., 1979; naturalized 1961; d. Barton C. and France J. (Burthe-Mique) Bruce. Contrbr. poems to anthols. B.A. in Psychology, Coll. Sante Fe, 1983. Sec. productions Mobil Oil Exploration, Stavanger, Norway, 1979-80; treatment counselor Denver Children's Home, 1983—. Recipient Golden Poet award World of Poetry, 1986, award of Merit, 1986. Home: 1571 Newton St Denver CO 80204

CORDNER, JACQUELINE WILLINGHAM, b. Sparkill, NY, Feb. 28, 1922; d. John Young and Elizabeth (Clucas) Telfer; m. Harold J. Willingham, Feb. 15, 1943 (dec. Oct. 1943); m. 2d, Dr. Harold J. Cordner, Jr., MD, Nov. 24, 1969. Author: Logic of Operating Room Nursing, 1962, 3d edit., 1984, Manual of Operating Room Management, 1982. RN, Roosevelt Hosp. Sch. Nursing, N.Y.C., 1942; BA, Jersey City State Coll., 1970. Asst. supr. operating rm. Roosevelt Hosp., 1950-54; dir. operating rm. Hackensack Med. Ctr., N.Y., 1955-74; dir. operating rm., recovery rm. Riverside Gen. Hosp., Secaucus, N.J., 1975-81; cons. operating rm., 1982-85. Mem. Assn. Operating Rm. Nurses. Home: Lynn Ct Woodcliff Lake NJ 07675

COREY, STEPHEN DALE, b. Buffalo, Aug. 30, 1948; s. Dale B. and Julienne B. (Holmes) C. Books of poetry: The Last Magician, 1981, Fighting Death, 1983, Gentle Iron Lace, 1984, Synchronized Swimming, 1985. BA, SUNY-Binghamton, 1971, MA, 1974; PhD, U. Fla., 1979. Newswriter, sportswriter Post-Jnl., Jamestown, NY, 1972-75; instr. English, U. Fla., Gainesville, 1979-80; ed. The Devil's Millhopper, Gainesville and Columbia, S.C., 1977-83; asst. prof. English, U. S.C., Columbia, 1980-83; assoc. ed. The Ga. Rvw, Athens, 1983—. Mem. P&W, South Atlantic MLA. Individual artist's fellow Fine Arts Council Fla., 1979-80, lit. fellow S.C. Arts Commn., 1981-82, John Atherton fellow in poetry Bread Loaf Writers Conf., 1981; artist-initiated grantee in poetry Ga. Arts Council, 1985-86. Home: 357 Parkway Dr Athens GA 30606

CORKERY, CHRISTOPHER JANE, b. Spokane, WA, Jan. 7, 1946; d. Robert Joseph and Eleanor Cecilia (Dunn) Corkery; m. Thomas Seymour Hart, Mar. 17, 1979; 1 son, Patrick Harrington Corkery Hart. Author: Blessing, 1985; contrbr. poetry to numerous lit jnls including Southern Poetry Rvw, Poetry. BA, Manhattanville College, Purchase, NY, 1967; Postgraduate diploma, Trinity College, Dublin, Ireland, 1971. First reader Harvard U. Press, 1977-79; freelance ed. 1977-83; instr. Lesley College, Cambridge, MA, 1985; Harvard U., 1984—. Artists Fdn. Fellowship, Boston, 1978, Ingram Merrill Fdn. Grant, 1983. Mem: PSA. Home: 20 Kenwood St Dorchester MA 02124

CORLL, VIVIAN MORGAN, b. Brunswick, GA, Feb. 12, 1940; d. John Thomas and Vivian Estelle (Helmey) Morgan; m. Paul R. Corll, Aug. 5, 1961; children—Helen Marie, Mary Elaine. Contrbr. articles on parenting, education, devotions, science, short stories to popular, profl. mags., jnls. including Home Life, English Jnl, Dolphin Los. B.A. in English, Stetson U., 1961; M.A. in English, Ohio U., 1965. Tchr. English, creative writing, rhetoric, coll. rvw. Broward County Sch. System, Ft. Lauderdale, FL, 1961—. Recipient awards Southeastern Wrtrs. Assn., Atlanta, 1981, 85, 86. Mem. SCBW. Home: 3681 NW 17 Terrace Fort Lauderdale FL 33309

CORMAC, C. D., see Hopes, David Brendan

CORMAN, AVERY, b. NYC, Nov. 28, 1935; s. Maurice and Ruth (Brody) C.; m. Judy Lishinsky, Nov. 5, 1967; children: Matthew, Nicholas. Author: Oh, God!, 1971, The Bust-Out King, 1977, Kramer Versus Kramer, 1977, The Old Neighborhood, 1980, 50, 1987. Contrbr. articles to natl. mags.; screenwriter for ednl. films. BS, NYU, 1956. Mem. AG, WG Am., PEN. Address: Donovan ICM 40 W 57th St New York NY 10019

CORMAN, CID, b. Boston, June 29, 1924; s. Abraham and Celia (Kravitz) C.; m. Shizumi Konishi, Feb. 14, 1965. Author: numerous poetry books, including In Good Time, 1964, Sun Rock Man, 1962, Words for Each Other, 1967, And Without End, 1968, Plight, 1969, Living Dying, 1970, Out and Out, 1972, O/I, 1974,'S, 1976, Antics, 1977, Auspices, 1978, Tabernacle, 1980, Aegis: Selected Poems 1970-80, 1983; editor: Word for Word: Essays on the Art of Language, 1977, At Their Word: Essays on the Art of Language, 1978, Origin mag (Japan), 1951—.AB, Tufts U., 1945; post-grad., U. Mich., 1946-47, U.N.C., 1947, U. Paris, 1954-55. Tchr. poetry, 1981; lectr. in field. Fulbright grantee, 1954; CCLM grantee, 1970-71, 78-79. Office: Sta Hill Press Station Hill Rd Barrytown NY 12507

CORMIER, ROBERT EDMUND, b. Leominster, MA, Jan. 17, 1925; s. Lucien Joseph and Irma Margaret (Collins) C.; m. Constance B. Senay, Nov. 6, 1948; children: Roberta Susan, Peter Jude, Christine Judith, Renee Elizabeth. Author: Now and At the Hour, 1960, A Little Raw on Monday Mornings, 1963, Take Me Where the Good Times Are, 1965, The Chocolate War, 1974, I Am the Cheese, 1977, After the First Death, 1979, Eight Plus One, 1980, The Bumblebee Flies Anyway, 1983, Beyond the Chocolate War, 1985; contrbr. short stories to Redbook, McCalls, Saturday Evening Post, Sign, St. Anthony Messenger. Student, Fitchburg (Mass.) State Coll., 1943-44, LittD (hon.), 1977. Script/comml. writer radio sta. WTAG, Worcester,Mass., 1946-48; reporter, columnist, assoc. editor Fitchburg Sentinel & Enterprise, 1955-78; writing coach, cons. Worcester Telegram & Gazette. Recipient Best News Story in New Eng. award AP, 1959, 74; K.R. Thomson Prize Thomson Newspapers, Inc., 1974. Home: 1177 Main St Leominster MA 01453

CORN, ALFRED DEWITT, b. Bainbridge, GA, Aug. 14, 1943; s. A. D. and Grace (Lahey) C.; m. Ann Rosalind Jones, July 24, 1967 (div. 1971). Author: All Roads at Once, 1976, A Call in the Midst of the Crowd, 1978, The Various Light, 1980, Notes from a Child of Paradise, 1984, The Metamorphoses of Metaphor, 1987. BA, Emory U., 1965; MA, Columbia U., 1970. Free-lance writer, NYC, 1971-77. Recipient award NEA, 1979, Levinson prize Poetry mag., 1982, Spcl. award AAIAL, 1983; fellow Ingram Merrill Fdn., 1974. Mem. PEN, Natl. Book Critics Circle, PSA. Home: 54 W 16th St New York NY 10011

CORNELIUS, KAY OLDHAM, b. Memphis, Jan. 14, 1933; d. George Evertson and Annie Mai (Whitehead) Oldham; m. Donald W. Cornelius, Sept. 19, 1951; children: Kathryn Amy Cornelius Parvin, Kevin Oldham. Author: Love's Gentle Journey, 1985; contrbr. to: Ala. Writing Tchr., Event, Wrkg. on articles, novel. BA, George Peabody Coll. for Tchrs., 1954; Med, Ala. A&M U., 1978. Tchr. public schs. Tenn., 1956-58, Huntsville, Ala., 1968—. Mem. Natl. League Am. Pen Women, NCTE, other profl. orgns. Home: 1212 Huntsville Hills Dr Huntsville AL 35802

CORNISH, EDWARD SEYMOUR, b. NYC, Aug. 31, 1927; s. George Anthony and Elizabeth Furniss (McLeod) C.; m. Sally Woodhull, Oct. 12, 1957; children: George Anthony, Jefferson Richard Woodhull, Blake McLeod. Author: The Study of the Future, 1977; editor: Resources Directory for America's Third Century, 1977, The Future: A Guide to Information Sources, 1977, 1999: The World of Tomorrow, 1978, Communications Tomorrow, 1982, Careers Tomorrow, 1983, Global Solutions, 1984, The Computerized Society, 1985; editorial cons.: Natl. Goals Research Staff, 1970, White House report Toward Balanced Growth, 1970. Diplome d'etudes, U. Paris, France, 1948; AB, Harvard U., 1950. Copy boy, cub reporter Evening Star, Washington, 1950-51; staff corr. U.P. Assn., Richmond, Va., 1951-52, Raleigh, N.C., 1952-53, London, 1953-54, Paris, 1954-55, Rome, 1956; staff. writer Natl. Geog. Soc., 1957-69; creator, editor The Futurist Mag., 1966—; editor World Future Soc. Bulln., 1968-77. Mem. Intl. Sci. Writers Assn. Home: 5501 LincolnSt Bethesda MD 20817

CORNWELL, ILENE JONES, b. Spartanburg, SC, Sept. 27, 1942; d. Thurmond Glasgow and Elizabeth Norrie (Furber) Jones; m. James H. Cornwell, Mar. 2, 1963 (div. 1976); 2 sons, James David, Robert Grant. Author: Natchez Trace Parkway: A Microcosm of America (60-minute film), 1986 (PBS broadcast, 1988); Travel Guide to the Natchez Trace Parkway, 1984, Nancy Ward, 1979, Footsteps Along the Harpeth, 1970, 76, Ruskin!, 1972; ed. vols. inclg. Nashville: 200 Years of Hospitality, Deserted Sycamore Village of Cheatham Co., Tenn., Legal Terms For the Genealogist. Women in Action, The Genesis Connection; compiler-ed., Biographical Directory of the Tenn. Genl. Assembly, 1901-31, vol. III, 1987, vol. IV (1931-51), 1988.. Student U. Tenn., 1971-73, 75-78. Freelance artist, Nashville, 1969-71; feature wrtr., Tennesee Conservationist, 1969—; feature wrtr. and artist Suburban News, Nashville, 1970-74, Westview, 1978-80; pub. info. officer Tenn. Hist. Commn., Nashville, 1974-78; publs. cons. Vanderbilt Univ., Nashville, 1978-81; owner, CEO Southern Resources Unlimited, Nashville, 1981—. Pres., Natchez Trace Assn. Tenn., Nashville, 1975-78; founder and pres. Bellevue-Harpeth Hist. Soc., 1970-74. Recipient Tenn. Outstanding Young Woman award, 1975; first place award Am. Assn. Med. Colls., 1979; Vintage '80 award Intl. Assn. Bus. Communicators, 1980; MacEachern award AHA, 1981. Mem. Natl. League Am. PEN Women, Womens Press and Authors. Home: 5632 Meadowcrest Ln Nashville TN 37209

CORNYN-SELBY, ALYCE P., b. Dayton, OH, Nov. 22, 1946; d. William Bain and Alice Ruth (Kill) Sellers; 1 child, Kelly Cornyn Alexandre. Author: The Man Who Ran Out of Words, 1985, Procrastinator's Success Kit, 1986, Take Your Hands Off My Attitude, 1987; contrbr. articles to mags., newspapers; author multi-media film scripts. BA, Maryhurst (Oreg.) Coll. Mag. prodn. mgr. Port of Portland, Oreg., 1976-84; pres. AEnterprise, Portland, 1979—. Recipient writing and photography awards Internat. Assn. Bus. Communicators. Mem. Oreg. Wrtrs. Colony, Willamette Wrtrs., Northwest Assn. Book Pubs. Address: 1928 SE Ladd Ave Portland OR 97214

CORRIGAN, CFX, JOHN THOMAS, b. Bklyn., Feb. 28, 1936; s. William Michael and Ann Elizabeth (Rafter) C. Works include: Librarian/Educator Interdep., 1976, The Relationship of the Lib. to Instructl. Systs., 1978, Today's Youth/Today's Librarian, 1980, Archives the Light of Faith, 1981, What Today's Youth is Reading and Why, 1981, Anglo-Amer. Cataloging Rules II, A Year Later, 1982, Periodicals for Relig. Edn. Ctrs. and Parish Libraries, 1976, Guide for the Orgn. and Operation of a Relig. Resource Ctr., 1977. BA, Catholic U., 1960; MSLS, St. John's U., 1967. Librarian, Nazareth HS, Bklyn., 1962-71, Spalding Coll., Louisville, KY, 1971-73; ed. Catholic Lib. World, Haverford, PA, 1973-86; ex. dir. Catrolic Lib. Assn., 1987—. Mem. Natl. Council Lib./Info. Assns., Cath. Lib. Assn., Natl. Info Standards Orgn. Home: 503 Old Lancaster Rd Haverford PA 19041

CORRINGTON, JOHN WILLIAM, b. Memphis, Oct. 28, 1932; s. John Wesley and Viva Lillian (Shelley) C.; m. Joyce Elaine Hooper, Feb. 6, 1960; children: Shelley Elaine, John Wesley, Robert Edward Lee, Thomas Jonathan Jackson. Author: (poetry) Where We Are, 1962, The Anatomy of Love, 1964, Mr. Clean and Other Poems, 1964, Lines to the South, 1965, Southern Writing in the Sixties: Poetry (anthology edited with Miller Williams), 1967; (novels) And Wait for the Night, 1964, The Upper Hand, 1969, The Bombardier, 1970, Shad Sentell, 1984, So Small a Carnival, 1986, A Project Named Desire (with Joyce H. Corrington), 1987, All My Trials, forthcoming; (anthology) Southern Writing in the Sixties (edited with Miller Williams), 1966; (short fiction) The Lonesome Traveller and Other Stories, 1968, The Actes and Monuments, 1978, The Southern Reporter and Other Stories, 1981; also numerous screen plays and TV prodns. BA, Centenary Coll., 1956; MA in Renaissance Drama, Rice U., 1960; DPhil, U. Sussex, Eng., 1965; JD, Tulane U., 1975. Bar: U.S. Supreme Ct., 1977. Asst. prof. La. State U., Baton Rouge, 1960-66; assoc. prof. Loyola U., New Orleans, 1966-72; visiting prof. U. Calif.-Berkeley, 1968; atty. Plotkin & Bradley, New Orleans, 1975-78; writer Corrington Prodns., Ltd., New Orleans, 1978—, head writer for various CBS, ABC, and NBC TV series, 1978—. La. State U. research grantee, 1963, 65; recipient Charioteer Poetry award, 1961, NEA Award in fiction, 1967, outstanding tchr. award Loyola U., 1967, best nonfiction award Natl. Cath. Press, 1969; inclusion in Best American Short Stories, 1973, 76, 77, O. Henry Award Stories, 1976. Mem. La. State Bar Assn., WG (nominated for outstanding serial script 1981, 82). Home: 1724 Valence St New Orleans LA 70115

CORRODY, CAROL ANN, b. Glen Cove, NY, Nov. 18, 1957, d. George William and Lucy Barbara (Glashesky) Corrody. Contrbr. to Gourmet Newsletter, freelance wrtr. BBA, Hofstra U., Hempstead, N.Y., 1980. Advt. asst. Dance Mag., NYC, 1981; editor PTN Pub. Corp., Woodbury, N.Y., 1981-85; co-editor newsletter GIT Industries, N.Y.C., 1985–86. Address: 12 4th St Bayville NY 11709

CORSERI, GARY STEVEN, b. NYC, Mar. 31, 1946; s. Casper and Estelle Ruby (Kaplan) C.; m. Yoko Kagawa. Contrbr. poetry, fiction, translations, essays, rvws., and articles to N.Y. Times, Redbook, Ga., Fla. (1st prize 1975), Cold Mountain, Oconee, Intl. Poetry, Washout, U. Tampa Poetry, Webster, Louisville rvws., Poetry N.W., Poet Lore, Fla. Qtly, Pyramid, Calamus and Winds (Japan), Poetry View, Poetry Nippon, others. BA, U. Fla., 1967; MAT, Harvard U., 1969. Tchr. English pub. schls., Wayland, Mass., 1968-69, San Francisco, 1969-70; instr. English, U.Fla., Gainesville, 1971-74; sr. lectr. Hokusei Gakuen Coll., Sapporo, Japan, 1978-81; lectr. Aoyama Gakuin U., Tokyo, 1984-86. Recipient Stephen Vincent Benet narrative poetry prize, 1973; Harvard-Fla. scholar, 1967; Ga. Council for Arts and Humanities grantee, 1977; Fla. State U. fellow, 1986, 87. Mem. AWP, Phi Beta Kappa, Phi Delta Kappa. Home: 1101 NW 58th Terr Apt 404 Sunrise FL 33313

CORSI, DEBORAH ERANDA, b. McKeesport, PA, May 6, 1953; d. Adolph Joseph and Francesca Sylvana (D'Arliano) C.; m. William Vaughan Jenkins, Aug. 31, 1985. Ed., Smithsonian Press, 1984-85; proj. dev. ed. Smithsonian Surprises: An Ednl. Activ. Bk. for Child., 1985. AAS, N. VA Commun. Coll., 1980; BA, Marymount Coll., 1984. Editorial asst., Smithsonian mag., Washington, 1981-82; edit./mkt. asst., Smithsonian Press, 1982-83, ed., 84-85; freelance ed. scholarly manuscripts, Colonia, NJ, 1986—; asst. ed., Jnl of Alcohol Studies, 1986—. Home: 4306 Warner Ln Chantilly VA 22021

CORSI, PIETRO, b. Casacalenda, Italy, Aug. 3, 1937, came to U.S., 1968, s. Giovanni and Teresa (Vincelli) C.; m. Elsa Gama, Jan. 11, 1963; children—Giampiero, Giancarlo. Novelist: Ritorno a Palenche, 1966, 2d ed., 1985, Due Rapporti, 1967, 2d ed., 1982, Sweet Banana, 1984, Un Certogiro di Luna, 1986, L'uomo-Dio, 1986; author: Cooking with Flair, 1984, You and Your Guest, 1984, You and Your Table Guest, 1984, The Princess Cruises Bar Guide, 1984, Cooking with Fruits and Wines, 1985. Ed. in Italy. Sr. v.p. Princess Cruises, Los Angeles, 1968—. Knight order of Cavaliere, Italy, Chevalier du Tastevin, Burgundy, France. Mem. Am. Translators Assn. Home: 4404 Sherman Oaks Ave Sherman Oaks CA 91403

CORSINI, RAYMOND JOSEPH, b. Rutland, VT, June 1, 1914; s. Joseph August and Evelyn Carolyn (Lavaggi) C.; m. Kleona Rigney, Oct. 10, 1965; 1 dau., Evelyn Anne. Author: Methods of Group Psychotherapy, 1957, Roleplaying in Business and Industry, 1961, Roleplaying in Psychotherapy, 1966, The Family Council, 1974, The Practical Parent, 1975, Role Playing: A practical Manual, 1980, Give In or Give Up, 1981, Individual Psychology: Theory and Practice; Editor; Critical Incidens in Psychotherapy, 1959, Adlerian Family Counseling, 1959, Critical Incidents in Teaching, 1965, Critical Incidents in School Counseling, 1972, Critical Incidents in Nursing, 1973, Current Psychotherapies, 1973, Current Personality Theories, 1978, Readings in Current Personality Theories, 1978, Great Cases in Psychotherapy, 1979, Alternative Educational Systems, 1979, Theories of Learning, 1980, Comparative Educational Systems, 1981, Handbook of Innovative Psyhotherapies, 1981, Adolescence: The Challenge, Encyclopedia of Psychology, 1984, Encyclopedia of Aging, 1986, Condensed Encyc. of Psychology, M87, Jnl. Individual Psychology, 1974, 76. B.S., CCNY, 1939, M.S. in Edn., 1941; Ph.D., U. Chgo., 1955. Address: 140 Niuki Circle Honolulu HI 96821

CORSO, GREGORY NUNZIO, b. NYC, Mar. 26, 1930; s. Fortunato and Michelina (Colonna) C.; m. Sally November, May 7, 1963 (div.); 1 dau. Mirandia; m. Belle Carpenter, 1968; 1 dau., Cybelle Nuncia; 1 son, Max-Orphe. Author: poems The Vestal Lady on Brattle, 1955, Gasoline, 1958, Bomb, 1958, Marriage, 1959 (Longview Fdn. award), The Happy Birthday of Death, 1960, Long Live Man, 1962, Selected Poems, 1962, Elegiac Feelings American, 1970; novel The American Express, 1961, The Mutation of the Spirit, 1964, There is Yet Time to Run Back Through Life and Expiate All That's Been Sadly Done, 1965, 10 Times a Poem, 1967; play This Hung-Up Age, 1955, The Little Black Door on the Left, 1968, Poesy: Heirlooms from the Future, 1978; co-editor: Young American Poetry, 1961. With Los Angeles Examiner, 1951-53; poetry readings in East and Midwest, mid-1950's. Address: Phoenix Bookshop 18 Cornelia St New York NY 10014

CORTESI, LAWRENCE, see Cerri, Lawrence J.

CORTINOVIS, DAN, b. St. Louis, Sept. 4, 1947, s. Robert F. and Irene E. (Killian) C.; m. Susan

Cortinovis, Sept. 3, 1982; 1 dau., Lisa. Author: Controlling Wastewater Treatment Processes, 1984, Pass Your Wastewater Operator Exams, 1985. BA in Chemistry, Calif. State U., Hayward, 1978; MS in Civil Engring., San Jose State U., 1983. Prin. engr. Brown & Caldwell, Walnut Creek, Calif., 1978-84; project engr. Harris & Assocs., Lafayette, Calif., 1984-85; consulting engr., Lafayette, 1985—. Home: 1136 Orchard Rd Lafayette CA 94549

CORY, JIM, b. Oklahoma City, Sept. 7, 1953, s. Donald and Olive Gayle (Brantseg) C. Contrbr. to The Drummer, Mickle Street, Painted Bride Qtly, Treetop, numerous other publs. BA, Pa. State U. Sr. features ed. Hardware Age, Radnor, Pa., 1979—. Recipient Jesse Neal award Am. Bus. Press, 1979, 83, 84. Mem. Natl. Book Critics Circle. Home: 2300 Pine St Apt 12 Philadelphia PA 19103

COSBY, BILL, b. Phila., July 12, 1937; s. William Henry and Anna c.; m. Camille Hanks, Jan. 25, 1964; children: Erika Ranee, Erinn Charlene, Ennis William, Ensa Camille, Evin Harrah. Author: The Wit and Wisdom of Fat Albert, 1973, Bill Cosby's Personal Guide to Power Tennis, Fatherhood, 1986, Time Flies, 1987. Student, Temple U.; Ph.D. in Edn., U. Mass. Served with USNR, 1956-60. Address: 151 El Camino Beverly Hills CA 90212

COSNER, SHAARON LOUISE, b. Albuquerque, Feb. 10, 1940; d. Roy Francis and Jewel Louise (Brian) Bigelow: m. Ronald Jerome Cosner, Mar. 3, 1962; hildren—Robert, Victoria. Author: American Windmills, 1977, American Cowgirls, 1978, Masks Around the World, 1979, How to Be Your Own Weather Forecaster, 1981, Special Effects in Movies & Television, 1985, The Light Bulb, 1985, Rubber, 1986, Paper Through the Ages, 1984, War Nurses, 1988. B.A., Ariz. State U., 1965, M.A., 1979. Tchr. orona Del Sol High Schl., Tempe, AZ, 1980—. Home: 1116 E Watson Tempe AZ 85283

COSTA, HELEN MARIE, b. Burbank, CA, Aug. 27, 1951; d. Larry and Betty Lee (Kesling) Costa; m. George Joseph Beaudet, May 2, 1981 (div. Mar. 16, 1983); m. William Yon Regan, June 8, 1985; stepchildren—Vesla Dannielle, Andria orinne. Author: (with Betty Costa) A Micro Handbook for Small Libraries and Media Centers, 1983, rev. ed., 1986; Adult Literacy/Illiteray in the United States: A Handbook for Reference and Research, 1987. Contrbr. to Wilson Library Jnl., A+ Mag. Ed.: SCBW Newsletter, 1986-87. Student Occidental Coll., 1969-71, Metropolitan State oll., 1987—. Staff wrtr. Denver Monthly Mag., 1980-81; creator, program dir., head wrtr. Sound-Off Syndicated Radio Show, Los Angeles, 1981-82; free-lance wrtr., technical wrtrs., 1982—. Mem. SCBW. Home: 12255 W Ohio Pl Lakewood CO 80228

COSTLEY, BILL, (Boles Kulik), b. Salem, MA, May 21, 1942, s. William Kirkwood and Mary Stefania (Kulik) C.; m. Joan Helen Budyk, June 6, 1964 (div. 1985); children—Maya, Alex William. Author poetry books: Knosh I Cir (Selected Poems, 1964-75), 1975, Rag(a)s, 1978; contrbr. poetry, book rvws to numerous mags. in U.S., U.K., Can., Japan, W.Ger., including Antigonish Rvw, Poetry Nippon, Ploughshares, The (Last) Glasgow Mag., Gargoyle, Pulpsmith, West End, Small Pond; producer, program host sta. WZLY-FM, Wellesley (Mass.) Coll., 1982-84, 86—. AB in English, Boston Coll., 1963; MFA in Creative Wrtg., Boston U., 1968. Public info. officer Cambridge (Mass.) Model Cities Program, 1968-73; tech. wrtr. Digital Equipment Corp., Marlboro, Mass., 1976-79, tech. wrtr., ed., Andover, Mass., 1982-84, mktg. wrtr., Marlboro, Mass., 1987—; instrnl. wrtr. Data Gen. Corp., Westboro, Mass., 1979-82; part-time staff Barnes & Noble Books, Wellesley, Mass., 1986—; recording sec. Wellesley Council for Arts, 1981-83. Mem. New England Wrtrs. for Surrival, 1983—, Wellesley Comm. for a Nuclear Weapons Freeze, 1983—,NWU (past mem. steering com. Boston sect., now European rep. in U.K., France), Edinburgh Playwrights Workshop, Fife Wrtrs. Group. Home: 1 Sunset Rd Wellesley Center MA 02181

COTTERILL, SARAH L., b. Mineola, NY, Mar. 16, 1948; d. S. Sanford and Evelyn Joy (Wing) Sproul; m. Philip Glenn Cotterill, 1969. Author: (poems) The Hive Burning, 1983; contrbr. poems to Am. Poetry Rvw, Poetry N.W., Carolina Qtly, Nimrod, Kans. Qtly, Minn. Rvw, other jnls. BA, Swarthmore Coll., 1970; MFA, U. Iowa, 1978. Teaching-writing fellow Iowa Wrtrs.' Workshop, U. Iowa, Iowa City, 1976-78; tchr. creative writing Bethesda Wrtrs.' Ctr., Md., 1986—. Yaddo fellow, 1979, 84, 85; Md. Arts Council grantee, 1985; recipient judge's prize Nethers Farm Retreat, Va., 1981; Laurel prize Arts Wayland Ctr., Natick, Mass., 1983. Mem. AWP, P&W. Home: 9624 Evergreen St Silver Spring MD 20901

COTTS, CYNTHIA L., b. Washington, Jan. 4, 1958; d. Arthur Clement and Doris Lee (Granger) C. Author: (short stories) Gold Beads, 1984, Lessons, 1984, The Exchange, 1984, A Civil Transaction, 1984. BA, Oberlin Coll., 1980; MA, Johns Hopkins U., 1983. Book reviewer Columbus Dispatch, Ohio, 1985—. Wrtr.-in-residence St. Albans Schl., Washington, 1983-84; residency MacDowell Colony, 1984. Mem. P&W. Home: 60-38 Putnam Ave Ridgewood NY 11385

COUGHLAN, (JOHN) ROBERT, b. Kokomo, IN, July 7, 1914; s. William Henry and Lucile DeNevers (Ernsperger) C.; m. Patricia Ann Collins, June 30, 1939; children: John Robert, Brian Christopher, Kevin Brooks, Cynthia Davis. Author: The Wine of Genius, 1951, The Private World of William Faulkner, 1954, Tropical Africa, 1962, The World of Michelangelo, 1966, Elizabeth and Catherine, 1974, (collaborated with Rose Kennedy on memoirs) Times to Remember, 1974; contrbr. anthologies, newspapers, mags. BS, Northwestern U., 1936. Mem. staff Fortune mag., 1937-43, assoc. editor, 1938-43; text editor Life mag., 1943-49, mem. editorial staff as writer-editor, 1943-70; editorial assoc. Kennedy Fdn., 1971-73. Recipient Benjamin Franklin award, 1953; Lasker award for med. journalism, 1954, 59; Benjamin Franklin citation, 1954; citation for excellence Overseas Press Club, 1957; Sigma Delta Chi award for Distinguished Service to Journalism, 1959; merit citation Natl. Edn. Writers Assn., 1961; Heywood Broun citation Am. Newspaper Guild, 1963; Annl. Book award Natl. Assn. Ind. Schls., 1967. Address: Madison St Sag Harbor NY 11963

COULTER, N(ORMAN) ARTHUR, JR., b. Atlanta, Jan. 8, 1920, s. Norman Arthur and Carabelle (Clark) C.; m. Elizabeth Harwell Jackson, June 23, 1951; 1 son, Robert Jackson. Author: Synergetics: An Experiment in Human Development, 1955, Group Tracking: an Introduction to Synergetics, 1956, Analytical Procedure (with Ben Keller), 1968, Synergetics: An Adventure in Human Development, 1976; ed.: Change: Jnl. of Synergetic Soc., 1954—, Vital Signs, 1984—; contrbr. numerous articles to profl. jnls in physiology, biophysics, biomed. engring., systems theory. BS, Va. Poly. Inst., 1941; MD, Harvard U., 1950. Postdoctoral fellow in biophysics Johns Hopkins U., Balt., 1950-52; mem. faculty dept. physiology, Ohio State U., Columbus, 1952-65; mem. faculty U. N.C., Chapel Hill, 1965—, prof. surgery and biomed. engring., 1986—, chmn. biomed. engring., 1969-82. Served to maj. U.S. Army, 1941-46, Aleutians. Mem. Biophys. Soc., Am. Physiological Soc., Biomed. Engring. Soc. Home: 1825 N Lake Shore Dr Chapel Hill NC 27514

COULTRY, BARBARA A., (Barbara Blacktree), b. Athens, NY, Aug. 18, 1945, d. Benjamin and Dorothy (Edelhertz) Wolkomir; m. Thomas Edward Coultry III, June 18, 1977; 1 son, Benjamin. Author: Ariel's Song, 1985; contrbr. to Women's Home Cooking, 1976, Times Union, 1977. Wrkg. on mystery novel. BS, Syracuse U., 1967. Home: 1 Rhode Island Ave Rensselaer NY 12144

COURSEN, H. R., b. Newark, Mar. 28, 1932. Author poetry collections: Storm in April, 1973, Survivor, 1974, Lookout Point, 1974, Inside the Piano Bench, 1975, Fears of the Night, 1976, Walking Away, 1977, Hope Farm: New and Collected Poems, 1979, Winter Dreams, 1982, War Stories, 1985; fiction: After the War, 1982. BA, Amherst Coll., 1954; PhD, U. Conn., 1965. Mem. Faculty Bowdoin Coll., Brunswick, Me., 1964—. Served to capt. USAF, 1951-62. Office: Bowdoin Coll Brunswick ME 04011

COURT, WESLI, see Turco, Lewis Putnam

COURTNEY, DAYLE, see Goldsmith, Howard

COUSINS, LINDA, b. Knoxville, TN, Jan. 19, 1946; 1 child, Nadage Amia. Ed.: Our Ancient Legacy (Black history quiz series), 1984-86, Universal Black Wrtr. Mag., 1979-83, Black and In Brooklyn: Creators and Creations, 1983, Ancient Black Youth and Elders Reborn—The Poetry, Short Stories, Oral Histories and Deeper Thoughts of African-American Youth & Elders, 1985; contrbr. poetry to A Rock Against the Wind, 360 Degrees of Blackness, Jnl of Black Poetry, other jnls, PBS-TV prodn. of poetic works If Hell Freezes Over I'll Skate. BS, U. Tenn., Knoxville, 1969. Pub., ed. The African-American Traveler Newsletter; Universal Black Wrtr. Press, Bklyn., 1979—. Recipient numerous publishing grants. Mem. Collective of African-Am. Pubs. (founder), CCLM (Ed.'s award 1984), COSMEP. Office: Box 5 Radio City Sta New York NY 10101

COUSINS, NORMAN, b. Union Hill, NJ, June 24, 1915; s. Samuel and Sara (Miller) C.; m. Ellen Kopf, June 23, 1939; children: Andrea, Amy Loveman, Candis Hitzig, Sara Kit. Author: The Democratic Chance, 1942, Modern Man Is Obsolete, 1945, Talks with Nehru, 1951, Who Speaks for Man?, 1952, In God We Trust; The Religious Beliefs of the Founding Fathers, 1958; editor: A Treasury of Democracy, 1941, (with William Rose Benet) Anthology of the Poetry of Freedom, 1943, Writing for Love or Money, 1949, Doctor Schweitzer of Lambarene, 1960, In Place of Folly, 1961, Present Tense, 1967, The Improbable Triumvirate, 1972, The Celebration of Life, 1975, Anatomy of An Illness, 1979, The Human Option, 1981, The Physician in Literature, 1981; editorial supr.; March's Dictionary-Thesaurus, 1980. Lit. editor, mag. editor Current History mag., 1935-40; editor Saturday Rvw, 1940-71, 73-77, chmn. bd. editors, 1978, editor emeritus, 1980—; editor U.S.A.; mem. editorial bd. Overseas bur. O.W.I., World War II. Recipient Thomas Jefferson award for Advancement of Democracy in Journalism, 1948; Benjamin Franklin citation in mag. journalism, 1956; Overseas Press Club award, 1965; nat. mag. award Assn. Deans Journalism Schls., 1969; Carr Van Anda award for contrbns. to journalism Ohio U., 1971; Gold medal for lit. Natl. Arts Club, 1972; Journalism Honor award U. Mo. Schl. Journalism, 1972; Irita Van Doren Book award, 1972; Henry Johnson Fisher award as mag. pub. of yr. Mag. Pubs. Assn., 1973; Author of Yr. award ASJA, 1981. Mem. PEN, Natl. Acad. Scis. Home: 2644 Eden Pl Beverly Hills CA 90210

COUTS, SHIRLEY ASHLEY, (Ashley Couts), b. Minot, ND, Dec. 19, 1943; d. Donald W. and Frances L. (Latta) Ashley; widowed; children—Steven Eric Seats, Susann Elayne Couts. Contrbr. articles, fiction to mags., anthols. including Genesis, Indpls. Monthly, Sagamore News Mag., others. Ed.: The Chronical, 1978-80, Music Sheet, 1982-83, And All That Piano (Anita Speer Smith), 1984. Student in Art, Ind. U., Herron Schl. of Art, 1984—. Staff wrtr. Hamiltonian Mag., Carmel, IN, 1975-76; news producer Sta. WHYT, Noblesville, IN, 1976-78; ed. Zionsville Pubs., IN, 1979-80; pub. Music Sheet Mag., Indpls., 1982-83. Mem. Wicl, Assoc. Wrtrs. Ind. (pres. 1984), Ind. Wrtrs.' Center (pub. designer 1985—). Home: 209 Vail Ct Indianapolis IN 46280

COVINA, GINA, b. Janesville, WI, May 13, 1952, d. Charles Albert Robertson and Olga (Kowal) Bodinar. Author: The Ouija Book, 1979, The City of Hermits, 1983; co-ed.: The Lesbian Reader (with Laurel Galana), 1975, The New Lesbians (with Laurel Galana), 1976. Wrkg. on novel, non-fiction interview book. BFA, Calif. Coll. Arts and Crafts, Oakland, 1973. Ed., pub. Amazon Press, Berkeley, Calif., 1972—, Barn Owl Books, 1983—. Grantee Intersection Fdn., San Francisco, 1982-86. Mem. P&W. Office: Box 7727 Berkeley CA 94707

COVINO, MICHAEL, b. NYC. Author: The Off-Season (short stories), 1985, Unfree Associations (poetry), 1982. Assoc. editor, East Bay Express, 1978—; contrib. ed., Calif. Mag., 1986—. Awards: NEA fellowship, 1981; Aga Khan Fiction Prize, Paris Rvw, 1985. Mem. AFI, PSA. Home: Box 4631 Berkeley CA 94704

COWLEY, JOSEPH GILBERT, b. Yonkers, NY, Oct. 9, 1923; s. Joseph Gilbert and Gertrude Claire (Hersey) C.; m. Ruth Muriel Wilson, Feb. 28, 1948 (div. Nov. 22, 1983); children—Barbara, Charles, Jennifer, Joseph. Author: The Executive Strategist, 1969, The Chrysanthemum Garden, 1981. Wrkg. on novels, short stories, play. B.A., Columbia Univ., 1947, M.A., 1948. Sales promotion Home Life Insurance, NYC, 954-56; ed. Research Inst. of Am., NYC, 1956-82, retired. Home: 96 Mound St Lebanon OH 45036

COX, CAROL MOORE, b. Washington, Apr. 22, 1946, d. Robert Edgar and Caroline (Harrison) Moore; m. Fletcher Cox, Dec. 28, 1969. Author: Woodworking and Places Near By (poems), 1979, The Water in the Pearl (poems), 1982; contrbr. to Mountain Moving Day anthology, 1973. BA with honors in English, U. N.C., Chapel Hill, 1968. Secy. Eng. Dept., Columbia Univ., NYC,1968-70; tchr. Wyo. Indsl. Inst., Worland, 1970-72; secy. Tougaloo (Miss.) Coll., 1972-75; craftsperson Cox Woodwork, Tougaloo, 1975—. Home: Box 188 Tougaloo MS 39174

COX, JACK R., b. Muncie, IN, Nov. 26, 1930, s. Charles R. and Martha L. (Wurtzler) C.; m. Shirley A. Royster, Feb. 25, 1956; children—Erin Cox Holmes, Bret R. BA, Baldwin Wallace Coll., 1953. Ed. Gemac Corp., Redlands, Calif., 1963—, Gems and Minerals mag., Jeweler's Bench mag. Office: Gemac Pub. 555 Cajon St Redlands CA 92373

COX, JAMES ANDREW, b. Los Angeles, Nov. 6, 1942, s. Luther Andrew Bell and Elizabeth (Moore) Bell-Cox; m. Carol Scheiss, June 1, 1959 (div. 1969); m. 2d, Nancy Lorraine Stubbs, Oct. 31, 1970; children—Lee, Jared, Micah, Canon, Bethany. Author: Social Contributions of Joseph Smith to Plural Marriage, 1964; editor, The Midwest Bookwatch, 1980—. BA, Brigham Young U., 1964; M.S.W., U. Wis., Madison, 1977. Editor Madison Rev. of Books, Wis., 1973–80, Midwest Book Rvw, Oregon, Wis., 1980—. Mem. Nat. Assnl. Local Cable Programmers, Natl. Fedn. Community Broadcasters, Soc. Study and Furtherance of Sci. Fiction and Fantasy. Office: 278 Orchard Dr Oregon WI 53575

COX, JOSEPH MASON ANDREW, b. Boston, July 12, 1930; s. Hiram and Edith (Henderson) C. Author: Land Dimly Seen, New and Collected Poems, Great Black Men of Masonry (vols. 1 and 2), Collected Poetry of Joseph Mason Andrew Cox, Profound Reality and Fantasy Remembered. LLD, Columbia Univ., 1952; PhD,World Univ., 1972. Prof., CUNY, 1976-80; TV prod., Fedl. Community Protection Corp., 1981—. Mem. PSA, Authors Lg. of Am., Intl. Acad. of Poets (London), Intl. Acad. of Letters, Arts, Science (Rome). Home: 801 Tilden St Bronx New York NY 10467

COX, JUSTIN BRANTLIN (JACK), b. Seagrove, NC, Jan. 27, 1934; s. Justin Brantlin and Ruth (Farlow) C.; m. Golda Rae Garner, Dec. 28, 1958. Ed., The Vintage Airplane, 1973-75, Sportsman Pilot, 1981—; ed.-in-chief Sport Aviation, 1970—. AB, High Point Coll., 1955. Tchr., Siler City pub. schls. (NC), 1955-56, Asheboro pub. schls. (NC), 1958-69; pub. relns. Wings & Wheels Mus., Santee, SC, 1969-70; ed.-in-chief Sport Aviation, Experimental Aircraft Assn., Oshkosh, WI, 1970—; ed. Sportsman Pilot, Oshkosh, 1981—. Served to PN3, US Navy, 1946-58. Office: EAA Wittman Airfield Oshkosh WI 54903

COX, WILLIS FRANKLIN, b. Newport News, VA, Jan. 24, 1927, s. Willis Franklin and Beulah (Fowler) C.; m. Rosemary Coates, July 15, 1950; children—Beulah Elizabeth, Perrien Fowler. Author: Tidbits for Thought, 1983, Conversations About God, 1985, Phillip's Daffodil, 1987. Wrkg. on profile of politics. BA in Poli. Sci., Christopher Newport Coll., 1973. Owner, operator Cox Fuel and Hardware, Newport News, Va., 1947-74, W. F. Cox Gen. Mdse., James Store, Va., 1974—; postmaster U.S. Postal Service, James Store, 1974—; vice-mayor City of Hampton, Va., 1971-74. Served with USN, 1945-46. Home: Box 47 James Store VA 23080

COY, DAVID LAVAR, b. Powell, WY, Apr. 24, 1951, s. Vernon and Dorothy Dean (Ellis) C.; m. Eileen Pearl Dryer, Dec. 19, 1975; children—Hanna Avriel, Nile Adrian. Contrbr. poetry to Spoon River Qtly, Plainsong, Jumping Pond, other lit mags. BA, U. Wyo., 1975; MFA, U. Ark., 1983. Asst. prof. English, Southwest Mo. State U., Springfield, 1983—. Recipient award AAP, 1982. Mem. AWP. Home: 803 N Grant St Springfield MO 65802

CRADER, REBECCA JANE, (Becky Paterson), b. Topeka, Dec. 20, 1951; d. Robert Samuel and Patricia Louise (Anno) Crader; m. James Thomas Patterson, July 2, 1981 (div. July 31, 1987). Contrbr. poems to anthols. BA in Psychology, Washburn U., 1988. Secy., Topeka Police Dept., 1969-77, M.D. Anderson Hosp. and Tumor Inst., Houston, 1978-81; clrk./typist V.A. Hosp., Houston, 1978; secy./receptionist Menninger Fdn., Topeka, 1982-85: research asst. psychology dept. Washburn U., Topeka, 1986-87; receptionist Robert Proctor, PhD., Topeka, 1986—. Home: 1820 E 6th St Topeka KS 66607

CRAIG, JAMES DUHADWAY, (James Younger James, J.C. Younger), b. Kansas City, MO, Aug. 21, 1943; s. Gilbert Frank and Mary Jean (Duhadway) C. Works include: Luis & Les Deux Coins, 1976, The Antiquated American, 1976. BA, SMU, 1965; MA, UCLA, 1966. Address: Box 42 17 Mile Dr Pebble Beach CA 93953

CRAIG, M. S., see Craig, Mary Francis Shura

CRAIG, MARY FRANCIS SHURA, b. Pratt, Kans., Feb. 27, 1923; d. Jack Fant and Mary Francis (Milstead) Young; m. Daniel Charles Shura, Oct. 24, 1943 (dec.); children: Marianne Francis Shura Sprague, Daniel Charles, Alice Barrett Craig Stout; m. Raymond C. Craig, Dec. 8, 1961 (div. 1894); 1 dau., Mary Forsha. Author: (adult and children's books as Mary Francis Shura, Mary Craig, M.S. Craig) Simple Spigott, 1960, Garrett of Greta McGraw, 1967, Mary's Marvelous Mouse, 1962, Nearsighted Knight, 1963, Run Away Home, 1964, Backwards for Luck, 1968, Shoeful of Shamrock, 1965, A Tale of Middle Length, 1967, Pornada, 1969, The Valley of the Frost Giants, 1971, Topcat of Tam, 1972, The Shop on Threnody Street, 1972, A Candle for the Dragon, 1973, Ten Thousand Several Doors, 1973, The Cranes of Ibycus, 1974, The Riddle of Ravens Gulch, 1975, The Season of Silence, 1976, Gray Ghosts of Taylor Ridge, 1978, Mister Wolf and Me, 1979, The Barkley Street Six-Pack, 1979, Chester, 1980 (Pinetree award 1983), Happles and Cinnamunger, 1981, Eleanor, 1983, Jefferson, 1984, The Search for Grissi, 1985, The Josie Gambit, 1986, The Chicagoans, Dust to Diamonds, 1981, Were He a Stranger, 1978, To Play the Fox, 1982, Lyon's Pride, 1983, Pirate's Landing, 1983, Gillian's Chain, 1983, The Third Blonde, 1985, Flashpoint, 1987, Don't Call Me Toad! 1987; contrbr. fiction to popular mags., 1969—, poetry to popular mags., 1960—; weekly columnist: "Scrapbook from Shuranuff Farm," 1960-64. Creative writing tchr., summer conf. U. Kans., Lawrence, 1961—; tchr. creative writing Avila Coll., U. N.D., Calif. State U., U. Kans., Central Mo. State U., N.E. Mo. State U. Mem. AG, AL Am., Soc. Children's Bookwriters, MWA, Childrens Reading Round Table, Crime Writers Great Britain. Home: 301 Lake Hinsdale Dr Apt 112 Clarendon Hills IL 60514

CRAM, DONALD JAMES, b. Chester, VT, April 22, 1919; s. William Moffet and Joanna (Shelley) C.; m. Jane Maxwell, Nov. 25, 1969. Author: (with S.H. Pine, J.B. Hendrickson and G.S. Hammond) Organic Chemistry, 1960, 4th ed., 1980, Fundamentals of Carbanion Chemistry, 1965, (wth John H. Richards and G.S. Hammond) Elements of Organic Chemistry, 1967, (with J.M. Cram) Essence of Organic

Chemistry, 1977; contrbr. chpts. to Applications of Biochemical Systems in Organic Chemistry; also articles in field of host-guest complexation chemistry, carbonium ions, stereochemistry, mold metabolites, large ring chemistry. BS, Rollins Coll., 1941; MS, U. Nebr., 1942; PhD (Natl. Research fellow), Harvard, 1947, U. Uppsala, 1977, DSci, U. So. Calif., 1983. Am. Chem. Soc. fellow, 1947-48; Guggenheim fellow, 1954-55. Mem. Natl. Acad. Scis., Am. Acad. Arts and Scis. Home: 1250 Roscomare Rd Los Angeles CA 90077

CRAMER, MARIAN H., b. Frankfort, SD, Sept. 22, 1934; d. George E. and Aletta Laura (Hilkemeier) Hull; m. Delmar H. Cramer, Sept. 12, 1954; children: Roger, Laurie, Leanne. Author: Country Shadows, 1982, Lantern Glow, 1984, Pasque Petals, 1976-86; work also pub. in various mags. Student Huron Coll., 1953. Elem. tchr. in rural schl., Hitchcock, S.D., 1953-54; tchr. aid Willow Lake Schl., S.D., 1967-73, music tchr., 1978—. Winner 2d place for hist. paper Dakota State Coll. History Conf., 1980, 3rd place, 1981. Mem. S.D. State Poetry Soc. Home: Rt 1 Box 147 Bryant SD 57221

CRAMER, TERESA LYNN, b. Rochester, NY, Dec. 3, 1964; d. Lawrence Everett Cramer and Sharon Eileen (Whitney) Cramer-Van Eps. Contrbr. poems to anthols., record co. Wrkg. on collection of poetry. Grad. public schls., Phoenix. Sales person Artcraft, Phoenix, 1986-87, key operator Alphapraphics, Phoenix, 1987—. Recipient awards Redwood Acres Fair, Eureka, CA, 1986; Honorable Mention, World of Poetry, 1986, Golden Poet award, 1987. Mem. Ariz. Commn. Arts., Lit. Markets. Home: 2601 E Clarendon 14 Phoenix AZ 85016

CRANDAL, JACK, see Grimmett, Gerald Glen

CRANDALL, CHARLES JORDAN, b. Wayne, MI, Oct. 27, 1958; s. Carles William and Loretta Carol (Frazer) C. Ed., pub.: Splash Mag., 1984—. Wrkg. on Spontaneous Combustion. Student U. Fla., Gainesville, 1978-81, Tracy Roberts Sch. Theatre, 1982-83. Office: Splash Mag 561 Broadway 4B New York NY 10012

CRANDALL, GILBERT ALBERT, (Gil Crandall), b. Annapolis, MD, July 1, 1915; s. Lawrence Albert Crandall and Lillian Marie Leddy; widowed; 1 dau., Linda Rawson. Columnist: The Publick Enterprise, 1980—. Contrbr. articles to mags. including Reader's Digest, Motor Boating, others. Ed.: Sr. Sentinel, 1982—. B.A., St. John's Coll., 1936; postgrad. Duke U., 1936-37. Public affairs officer Puerto Rico Develop. Administration, N.Y.C., 1955-61; dir. tourism State of Md., Annapolis, 1961-73, state agriculture public affairs officer, 1973-77. Recipient award IABC, 1983. Mem. PRSA (Silver Anvil award 1970). Mason-Dixon Outdoor Wrtrs., OPC, Md. Press Club. Home: 24 Spa View Circle Annapolis MD 21401

CRANDALL, JOHN KARL, b. Salt Lake City, Apr. 20, 1931; s. Karl Kent and Vesta (Anderson) C.; m. Ruby G. Cook, June 14, 1963; children—Cynthia C. Oliphant, Karl, Brian. Columnist: Management Digest, 1987. Contrbr. article to Data Processing for Management Conf., 1968. B.A. with high honors, U. Utah, 1954; postgrad. U. Pa., 1980. With Mountain Bell, Salt Lake City, N.Y.C., Phoenix, Denver, 1957, then genl. mgr., 1987, retired. Home: 7205 W. Clifton Ave Littleton CO 80123

CRANDALL, NORMA RAND, b. NYC; d. Edward Herman Crandall and Marie Vanderveer Hall. Author: Emily Bronte: A Psychological Portrait, 1970-77; reviews, poetry, and essays in The New Republic, The NY Times, The Humanist, other mags. An Evening with the Brontes, presented by The Library Players in 1960s, 70s; an illus. talk about Emily Bronte given NYC in 1970s, 80s.Student, Barnard College, NYC. Editor, Harcourt, Brace, NYC,1939-40; freelance edit., cons., NYC,1940—. Mem. PSA, The Bronte Soc. of England. Home: 44 East 63rd St Apt 1B NYC 10021

CRANE, BURTON, see Swartz, Burton Eugene

CRANE, TERESA YANCEY, b. Durham, NC, Mar. 18, 1957; d. Henry Alexander and Janet (Brady) Yancey; m. W. Carey Crane III, Sept. 27, 1980; 1 son, Judson Alexander. Correspondent, The Richmond Newsleader; pub. LINC; ed. Issue Mgt.: Origins of the Future; ed./pub. Corporate Public Issues and Their Mgt. BA in Econ., Randolph-Macon Woman's Coll., 1978. Staff pub. relns., Reynolds Metals, Richmond, VA, 1978-79; bus. mgr. Howard Chase Ent., Stamford, CT, 1979-82; fndr., pres. Issue Action Pubns., Stamford, 1982—. Office: Issue Action 105 Old Long Ridge Rd Stamford CT 06903

CRASE, DOUGLAS, b. Battle Creek, MI, July 5, 1944, s. Norman Ward and Margaret Fuller (Walmsley) C. Author: The Revisionist, 1981. AB, Princeton U., 1966. Indsl. speechwriter, free-lance, 1971—; visiting lectr. English, U. Rochester, N.Y., 1976-77; sub. assoc. prof. English, Brooklyn Coll., 1983. Editor, Political Reform Commn., Mich. Dem. Party, 1969; speechwriter, Levin-for-Governor Comm., Detroit, 1970. Ingram Merrill Fdn. Award, 1979; Witter Bynner Prize for Poetry, AAIAL, 1983; Guggenheim Fellowship, 1984; Whiting Fdn. Writer's Award, 1985. Fellow, NY Inst. for the Humanities, 1983-86, MacArthur Fdn. Fellowship, 1987. Home: 470 W 24th St New York NY 10011

CRAVEY, ROBIN T., b. Houston, Apr. 27, 1951, s. Robin and Leatrice Elaine (Bell) C.; m. Jane Eileen Kurzawa, Nov. 19, 1977; children—Emma Leah, Molly Colleen. Author: Diverging: Poems by Robin Cravey, 1983; contrbr. to The Gar, Tex. Observer, Town Crier, Tilted Planet Tales, numerous other jnls. and mags. BA in Am. Studies, U. Tex., Austin, 1981. Ed., pub. Ecology in Texas, Austin, 1970-73; editorial asst. Daily Texan, Austin, 1974-75; county ed. The Highlander, Marble Falls, Tex., 1978, Stevenson Press, Round Rock, Tex., 1980, Onion Creek Free Press, Buda, Tex., 1981-82; pub. Tilted Planet Press, Austin, 1983—, ed. Tilted Planet Poems, 1986; publs. coordinator Morgan Printing & Pub., Austin, 1985-86; prodn. supvsr. Alpha Graphics Downtown, 1987—. Recipient editorial-writing award Tex. Press Assn., Austin, 1982, Austin Book award Tex. Circuit Austin Arts Commn., 1985. Mem. Austin Wrtrs. League, Tex. Pubs. Assn., Texas Circuit. Office: PO Box 8646 Austin TX 78713

CRAWFORD, GARY WILLIAM, b. Baton Rouge, Jan. 1, 1953; s. William Harris and Betty Jean (Stutzman) C. Ed. Gothic Jnl, 1979—; contrbr. Horror Literature, Dark Horizons, Survey of Modern Fantasy Literature, Nyctalops, Romantist, Star Line, Discovering Stephen King, Discovering Modern Horror Fiction, Fantasy. BA, La. State U., 1975; MA, Miss. State U., 1977. Mgr. Omega Theaters, Inc., Baton Rouge, 1971-75, 78—. Mem. Small Press and Artists Orgn., Sci. Fiction Research Assn., MLA. Home: 4998 Perkins Rd Baton Rouge LA 70808

CRAWFORD, JOHN F., b. Long Beach, CA, June 5, 1940. Contrbr. poetry to Sunbury, Unmuzzled Ox, River City, So. Calif. Anthology; ed.: The Girl (by Meridel Le Sueur), 1978, Hard Country (by Sharon Doubiago), 1981, A Nation of Poets (Nicaraguan poems), 1985, numerous other books. BA, Pomona Coll., 1962; PhD, Columbia U., 1970. Ed., pub. West End Mag., N.Y.C., 1971-76; ed., pub. West End Press., Cambridge, Mass., Mpls. and Los Angeles, 1976—; ed., pub., Peoples Culture, 1988—; lectr. Eng., Univ. of New Mexico, 1984— Home: Box 27334 Albuquerque NM 87125

CREA, SAMATHA, see Liddle, Catherine Diane

CREAGER, MAUREEN, b. Youngstown, OH, Mar. 23, 1931; m. Charles Q. Creager, Jan. 31, 1953; children—Kevin, Sue, Mark, Allyson, Marla. Travel columnist to numerous newspapers, 1969-79. Contrbr. articles to mags. Wrkg. on hist. novel. B.A. in Writing, Vt. Coll., postgrad. Northeastern U. Travel columnist The Times Pub. Co., Niles, OH, 1969-75, The Record Pub. Co., Ravenna, OH, 1971-79, Phoenix Pub., Inc., Niles, 1975-79; travel wrtr. Things to Do in Oh., Akron, 1978-79; cons. ed. Fischer Pub. Inc., Canfield, OH, 1983-84; owner, ed. WordPro, Canfield, 1984—. Mem. Youngstown Area Assn. Women Wrtrs., Youngstown State Univ. Wrtr.'s Group. Home: 106 E Main St Canfield OH 44406

CREED, NELLIE ANNE, b. Columbia, SC, May 9, 1955; d. Smyrl Alvin and Nellie (Watts) C.; m. Ronald John Giess, July 13, 1985. Author: (plays) Ladies in Waiting, 1984; Sharecroppers, 1985; contrbr. to Savvy, S.C. State Mag., Columbia Record, The State. BA in English, Queens Coll., Charlotte, N.C., 1977; MBA, U. Pa., 1979. Supt. Turner Constrn. Inc., Phila., 1979-80; designer Legacy Designs Inc., Columbia, 1981-83; pres. Creed Constrn., Inc., Columbia, 1983—. Newsletter ed. Sertoma Club, Columbia, 1986. Mem. DG. Office: Box 9006 Columbia SC 29290

CREELEY, ROBERT WHITE, b. Arlington, MA, May 21, 1926; s. Oscar Slade and Genevieve (Jules) C.; m. Ann McKinnon, 1946 (div. 1956); children—David, Thomas, Charlotte; m. 2d, Bobbie Louise Hall, Jan. 27, 1957 (div. 1976); children—Kirsten, Sarah, Katherine; m. 3d, Penelope Highton, 1977; children—William, Hannah. Author: Le Fou, 1952, The Immoral Proposition, 1953, The Kind of Act of, 1953, The Gold Diggers, rev. ed., 1965, All That is Lovely in Men, 1955, If You, 1956, The Whip, 1957, A Form of Women, 1959, For Love, Poems, 1950-60, 1962, The Island, 1963, Poems 1950-65, 1966, Words, 1967, The Finger, rev. ed., 1970, The Charm, 1968, Numbers, 1968, Pieces, 1969, A Quick Graph, 1970, A Day Book, 1972, Listen, 1973, A Sense of Measure, 1973, Contexts of Poetry, 1973, Thirty Things, 1974, Backward, 1975, (with Marisol) Presences, 1976, Selected Poems, 1976, Mabel: A Story, 1976, Myself, 1977, Hello, 1978, Was That a Real Poem & Other Essays, 1979, Later, 1979, Robert Creeley and Charles Olson: The Complete Correspondence, vols. 1 and 2, 1980, vol. 3, 1981, vol. 4, 1982, vol. 5, 1983, vol. 6, 1985, vol. 7, 1987,Mother's Voice, 1981, Echoes, 1982, Collected Poems, 1945-75, 1983, Mirrors, 1983, Collected Prose, 1984, Memory Gardens, 1986; editor: Black

Mountain Review, 1954-57, (with Donald M. Allen) New American Story, 1965, The New Writing in the U.S.A., 1967, Selected Writings of Charles Olson, 1967, Whitman: Selected Poems, 1973. BA, Black Mountain Coll., 1954; MA, U. N. Mex., 1960. Instr. Black Mountain Coll., 1954-55; vis. lectr. English U. New Mex., Albuquerque, 1961-62, lectr., 1963-66, vis. prof., 1968-69, 78-80, SUNY, Buffalo, 1966-67, prof. English, 1967—, Gray prof. poetry and letters, 1978—; lectr. U. B.C., Vancouver, 1962-63; lectr. creative writing San Francisco State Coll., 1970-71. Served with Am. Field Service, 1944-45, CBI. Recipient Levinson prize Poetry mag., 1960, Blumenthal-Leviton award, 1965, D.H. Lawrence fellow, 1969; Guggenheim fellow, 1964, 71; Rockefeller grantee, 1965; Shelley Meml. award PSA, 1981; NEA grantee, 1982; DAAD grantee, 1983, Leone d'oro Premio Speciale, Venice, 1985; inducted Am. Acad. and Inst. of Arts and Letters, 1987; Frost Medal, PSA, 1987. Home: Box 384 Waldoboro ME 04572

CRESS, FLOYD CYRIL, (Cy), b. Lowpoint, IL, March 10, 1920; s. Floyd Henry and Alma Elizabeth (Prenevost) C. Contrbr. poems to Arena, Colo. Quarterly, others, short stories to books including More Parades, Best of Audubon (Literary Guild Selection), mags. including Adam, Argosy, Cavalier, Empire, Family Handyman, Farm Journal, Travel, others. Editor: First Port Reporter, Sugro, Colorado Green, others. Films: Sugarbeet Industry, Ship Salvaging in Caribbean, Denver's Greenways. BFA, U. Denver, 1950; postgrad. U. of New Zealand, 1951. Address: 414½ S. Silver St Deming NM 88030

CRETZMEYER, STACY MEGAN, b. Phila., Oct. 27, 1959, d. Charles Henry and Patricia Anne (Walsh) Cretzmeyer. Playwright: The Willis Family Preserved, 1984; author: One Step Ahead (memoir of Ruth K. Hartz), 1987. BA, Hollins Coll., Roanoke, Va., 1981, MA, 1982. Playwright-in-residence U. New Orleans, 1984; reviewer Georgetown (S.C.) Times, 1984; freelance wrtr., researcher, Charleston, S.C. and Phila., 1985—. Recipient AAP prize, 1981, numerous awards Hollins Coll. Home: Box 246 Pawley's Island SC 29585

CREWS, FREDERICK CAMPBELL, b. Phila., Feb. 20, 1933; s. Maurice Augustus and Robina (Gauder) C.; m. Betty Claire Peterson, Sept. 9, 1959; children—Gretchen Elizabeth, Ingrid Anna. Author: The Tragedy of Manners, 1957, E.M. Forster: The Perils of Humanism, 1962, The Pooh Perplex, 1963, The Sins of the Fathers, 1966, The Patch Commission, 1968, The Random House Handbook, 1974, 5th ed., 1988,Out of My System, 1975 The Borzoi Handbook for Writers (co-author), 1985, Skeptical Engagements, 1986; editor: Red Badge of Courage (Crane), 1964, Great Short Works of Nathaniel Hawthorne, 1967, Starting Over, 1970, Psychoanalysis and Literary Process, 1970, The Random House Reader, 1981. AB, Yale, 1955; PhD, Princeton, 1958. Faculty U. Calif., Berkeley, 1958—, instr. in English, 1958-60, asst. prof., 1960-62, assoc. prof., 1962-66, prof., 1966—; mem. study fellowship selection com. ACLS, 1971-73; mem. selection com. summer seminars NEH, 1976-77. Fulbright lectr., Turin, Italy, 1961-62; ACLS fellow, 1965-66; Center for Advanced Study in Behaviorial Scis. fellow, 1965-66; Guggenheim fellow, 1970-71; recipient Essay prize NEA, 1968. Mem. MLA, NCTE. Home: 636 Vincente Ave Berkeley CA 94707

CREWS, HARRY EUGENE, b. Alma, GA, June 6, 1935; s. Ray and Myrtice (Haselden) C.; m. Sally Thornton Ellis, Jan. 22, 1960; children—Patrick Scott, Byron Jason. Author: novels The Gospel Singer, 1968, Naked in Garden Hills, 1969, Karate is a Thing of the Spirit, 1971, This Thing Don't Lead to Heaven, 1970, Car, 1972, The Hawk is Dying, 1973, The Gypsy's Curse, 1974, A Feast of Snakes, 1976, A Childhood: The Biography of a Place, 1978, Blood and Grits, 1979, Florida Frenzy, 1982; columnist: Esquire mag. BA, U. Fla., 1960, MEd, 1962. Mem. faculty Broward Jr. Coll., Ft. Lauderdale, Fla., 1962-68; assoc. prof. English U. Fla. at Gainesville, 1968-74, prof., 1974—. Served with USMC, 1953-56. Recipient Am. Acad. Arts and Scis. award, 1972; NEA grantee, 1974. Home: 1800 NW 8th Ave Gainesville FL 32601

CRICHTON, JOHN MICHAEL, b. Chgo., Oct. 23, 1942; s. John Henderson and Zula (Miller) C. Writer, dir. film: Westworld, 1973, Coma, 1978, The Great Train Robbery, 1979, Looker, 1981, Runaway, 1984. Author: The Andromeda Strain, 1969, Five Patients, 1970, The Terminal Man, 1972, The Great Train Robbery, 1975, Eaters of the Dead, 1976, Jasper Johns, 1977, Congo, 1980, Electronic Life, 1983, Sphere, 1987, Travels, 1988. AB summa cum laude, Harvard U., 1964, MD, 1969. Postdoctoral fellow Salk Inst., La Jolla, Calif., 1969-70. Recipient Edgar award MWA, 1968, 80; named med. writer of year Assn. Am. Med. Writers, 1970. Mem. AG, WG Am. West, Dirs. Guild Am., PEN Am. Center, Acad. Motion Pictures Arts and Scis., Phi Beta Kappa. Office: 2049 Century Park East 4000 Los Angeles CA 90067

CRINER, JOHN LAWRENCE, b. Winston-Salem, NC, Sept. 20, 1960, s. Edie Arnold and Dolores (Holmes) Criner. Poetry and fiction ed., contrbr. Inscape mag., 1981-82; ed.: Towzie Tyke newsletter, 1981; freelance wrtr. Axlon Games, 1984. Wrkg. on short stories, poetry. BA in English Lit., Central Meth. Coll., Fayette, Mo., 1982; cert. in tech. wrtg., San Jose State U., 1984. Co-op. tech. wrtr. IBM Corp., San Jose, Calif., 1983-84; game wrtr. Axlon Games, Sunnyvale, Calif., 1984; tech. wrtr. McDonnell Douglas Corp., Long Beach, Calif., 1984—. Home: 17052 Green St 40 Huntington Beach CA 92649

CRINITI, MARY PAULINE, b. Yonkers, NY, July 14, 1931; d. John and Assunta (De Lorenzo) Trombone; m. Joseph Ralph Criniti, July 12, 1952; children—David Joseph, Robert Dominic, Susan Lisa. Poetry in anthologies. Wrkg. on poetry. Ed., E.C. Goodwin Tech. Coll. Gen. clk. New Britain Machine, Conn., 1977— Home: 39 Shweky Ln Southington CT 06489

CRITCHLEY, LYNNE, See Radford, Richard Francis Jr.

CRITES, DOROTHY ADELE, (Dorothy A. Dele), b. Ill, Feb. 5, 1919; d. Joseph and Minnie M. (Law) Cook; m. Merle D. Crites, June 20, 1936; children—Rochelle Crites Pampe (dec.), Lynn, Robert, Phillip. Contrbr. poetry: Am. Poetry Anthology, Masterieces of Modern Verse, World Poetry Anthology, others. Wrkg. on poetry, short stories, books. Student pub. schs., Taylorville, Ill. Sec. to art dir. Sangamon Greeting Card Co., Taylorville, 1968-70; county office asst. Farmers Home Adminstrn., Taylorville, 1970-85. Home: Rt 1 Box 106 Taylorville IL 62568

CRITTENDEN, TOYA CYNTHIA, b. Detroit, Dec. 19, 1958; d. Willie and Sarah (Lott) Crittenden. Poetry in anthologies. Wrkg. on poetry collection, juvenile poetry. Ed. Wayne State U. Pre-school teacher, Detroit, 1980-86. Home: 9403 Kentucky St Detroit MI 48204

CROBAUGH, EMMA ADELIA, b. Harriman, TN, Jan. 24, 1903, d. James Edgar and Hattie Elizabeth (Milburn) DeLozier; m. Edward Bleckner (dec.); 1 son, Edward Jr.; m. 2d, Clyde Julian Crobaugh (dec.). Over 1,000 poems published in natl. and intl. mags., many translated into fgn. langs. Recipient numerous awards from state poetry socs. and lit. orgns. including Tex. Poetry Soc., N. Am. Mentor, Galaxy of Verse. Mem. AAP, Am. Poetry League, Assn. Poetry Therapy, 20 state poetry socs. Address: 3300 S Ocean Blvd Highland Beach CA 33431

CROCKETT-SMITH, D. L., see Smith, David Lionel

CROES, KEITH JOHN, b. Port Huron, MI, July 27, 1952; s. Jack Waldrop Croes and Paula Gertrude (Dettling) McNight; m. Pamela Ruth Lutz, July 25, 1983; children—Christopher Mazzoli, Kenneth John Croes. Ed.: County Lines Mag., 1979-82, Orthopedics Today, 1982-84, Fine Times Mag., 1986, Ocular Surgery News, 1982—. Student, Penn. State U., 1970-71, 77-78; Defense Info. Schl., 1974. Rptr., Harrison Post, Indpls., 1975-77; ed. County Lines Mag., West Chester, PA, 1979-82, Slack Medical Pubns., Thorofare, NJ, 1982—. Served to E4, USArmy, 1974-77. Mem. AMWA. Home: 1260 Allerton Road West Chester PA 19382

CROMWELL, SHARON LEE, b. Danbury, CT, Oct. 31, 1947; d. James F. and Dorothy May Cromwell; m. Edward D. Canade, July 1, 1967 (div. July 1968); m. 2d, Arthur Ray Henick, July 5, 1981. Reporter: Bank Advt. News, North Miami, Fla., 1967-77, Danbury News-Times, 1978-81. Editor: Hartford Courant, Conn., 1981-82; Topics, 1984-86. BA in English, Western Conn. State U., 1975; student, Emerson Coll. Mgr. pub. relations and communications Union Trust Co., New Haven, 1984—. Active Friends of Chester Library, Conn., 1984-86. Recipient Hon. Mention for newspaper feature Sigma Delta Chi, 1979, award for newspaper feature ACS, 1979. Mem. IABC. Home: 11 High St Chester CT 06412

CROOKER, BARBARA, b. Cold Spring, NY, Nov. 21, 1945, d. Emil and Isabelle Charlotte (Smith) Poti; m. Michael James Gilmartin, Aug. 1967 (div. 1975); 1 dau., Stacey Erin; m. 2d, Richard McMaster Crooker, July 26, 1975; children—Rebecca Cameron, David MacKenzie. Author: Writing Home, 1983, Moving Poems, 1987; contrbr. poetry to anthologies, lit mags: Poetry Rvw, Beloit Poetry Jnl, Blue Unicorn, Hiram Poetry Rvw, Poets On. BA, Douglass Coll., 1967; MSEd, Elmira Coll., 1975. Instr. Elmira (N.Y.) Coll., 1975, Tompkins-Cortland Community Coll., Dryden, N.Y., 1975-76, Corning (N.Y.) Community Coll., 1974-76, County Coll. of Morris, Dover, N.J., 1978-79, Cedar Crest Coll., Allentown, Pa., 1982—; contrbg. ed. River World, Mountain View, Calif., 1978-79. Lit. fellow Pa. Council on Arts, 1985; recipient Laureate award Am. Amateur Press Assn., 1985. Mem. PSA. Home: 28 Woodsbluff Run Fogelsville PA 18051

CROOKES, JOYCE FUDA, b. Albany, NY, Mar. 18, 1941; d. George Everett and Elsie Martha (Hildenbrand) Fuda; m. C. James Crookes, June 2, 1962; children—Christopher, Jennifer. Contrbr. poems to lit. mags., anthols. B.S. in Edn., Russell Sage Coll., 1962. Tchr. Riverhead Schl. Dist., Aquebogue, NY, 1962-63; copy wrtr.

Scott, Foresman, Pubs., Chgo., 1963-65; free-lance wrtr. Home: 15268 N 52d Dr Glendale AZ 85306

CROSBY METZGER, LISA M., b. Schenectady, Mar. 25, 1960, d. Kenneth Nathan and Bertha May (Tenace) Crosby; m. Ronald Paul Metzger, Dec. 9, 1984. Contrbr. to Guide to Natural Places of the Northeast: Inland, 1983-84. BA, Skidmore Coll., 1982. Circulation mgr. Salmagundi, 1979-82; editorial asst. St. Martin's Press, 1982-83; publs. dir. Adirondack Mountain Club, Glens Falls, N.Y., 1984—; mem. editorial rev. bd. Skidmore Coll. Alumni Mag., 1986. Office: Adirondack Mt Club 174 Glen St Glens Falls NY 12801

CROSS, MARY FRANCES, b. Warren, OH, Feb. 13, 1956; d. Okey Theodore and Shirley Ann (Tilley) C.; 1 son, Michael Chrisopher. Contrbr. numerous poems to anthols., newsletters. Ed.: Help Me Newsletter, 1985-86. Wrkg. on poems, collection of poetry, children's coloring book on childhood sexual abuse. Student Kent State U., 1979-80. With Buckeye News and Rvw., Farmington, OH, 1972-74, Native Am. Indian Rights Assn., Kent, OH, 1979-80; pres. Michael Christopher Advt. Co., Warren, 1982-83; dir. art dept., darkroom asst. Park Studies, Warren, 1984-85; newsletter ed., dir. art dept. Help Me Orgn., Warren, 1985-87; free-lance technical wrtr., artist, 1987—. Recipient award for poem, Native Am. Indians, 1986; 1986; named Bet New Poet of Yr., Am. Poetry Assn., 1987. Home: 266 N St NW Warren OH 44483

CROSS, RONALD ANTHONY, b. Hollywood, CA, Sept. 12, 1937; s. Leonard Seth Cross and Virginia Maria (Romeo) Gibson; m. Barbara Susan Traurine, July 16, 1965; 1 son, Gideon Kane. Author: Prisoners of Paradise, 1988. Contrbr. short stories to numerous sci. fiction mags. Mem. SFWA. Home: 1103 16th St Santa Monica CA 90403

CROUSE, KAREN JEAN, b. St. Louis, Nov. 19, 1962; d. James E. and Patricia J. (Kessing) C. Sports wrtr. Peninsula Times Tribune, CA, 1987—. Assoc. ed.: Swimming World Pubs., Los Angeles, 1984-86. B.A. in Jnlsm., U. Southern Calif., 1984. Mem. Ga. Sportswriters Assn. (award 1986). Home: 2692 Tuliptree Ln Santa Clara CA 95051

CROUT, TERESA ELIZABETH KOCHMAR, b. Jersey City, NJ, May 20, 1945; d. Joseph Edward and Emma Elizabeth (Norrmann) Kochmar; m. John Charles Crout, July 12, 1969 (div. Apr. 22, 1986); 1 son, Douglas Terence. Contrbr. non-fiction to newspapers, mags. including TV Guide, Woman's World, Baby Talk, Woman Exec.'s Bulltn. BS in Nursing, Carlow Coll., Pitts., 1967; MEd, Xavier U., 1973. Instr. psychiatric-mental health nursing Christ Hosp. Schl. Nursing, Cin., 1970-71, chmn. psychiatric-mental health area, 1971-73, faculty coordinator, 1973-82; free-lance wrtr., 1983—. Served as lt. j.g. USNR, 1967-70. Home: 719 Meadow Wood Dr Apt 12 Crescent Springs Ky 41017

CROW, DONNA FLETCHER, b. Nampa, ID, Nov. 15, 1941; d. Leonard Samuel and Reta Lee (Book) Fletcher; m. Stanley Dean Crow, Dec. 14, 1963; children—Stanley D., Preston Fletcher, John Downing, Elizabeth Pauline. Author: Recipes for the Protein Diet, 1972, Frantic Mother Cookbook, 1982, Professor Q's Mysterious Machine, 1983, Dr. Zarnof's Evil Plot, 1983, Mr. Xanthu's Golden Scheme, 1985, General Kempthorne's Battle Strategy, 1987, others; (plays) Called Unto Holiness, 1978, Because You Ask Not, 1984, A Rumor of Resurrection, 1983, An Upper Room Experience, 1983, Puppets on Parade, 1985, Resolved to Conquer, 1987. Contrbr. articles to mags., books. BA, Northwest Nazarene Coll., 1964. English tchr. Nampa High Schl., 1963-64, Lexington Christian Acad., Mass., 1965-66, Boise High Schl., Id., 1967-68. Named Wrtr. of Yr., Mt. Hermon Wrtr.'s Conf., Calif., 1983. Mem. Romance Wrtrs. Am. (Best Inspirational Novel, hon. mention 1985), Id. WL. Home: 3776 La Fontana Way Boise ID 83702

CROWDUS, GARY ALAN, b. Lexington, KY, Jan. 2, 1945, s. Charles Dallas and Bessie May (Rice) C. Contrbr. to Quinze ans de cinema mondial, 1975, Conflict and Control in the Cinema: A Reader in Society, 1977, The Documentary Tradition, 1979, Cineaste Interviews, 1983. BFA, NYU, 1969. Assoc. ed. Film Soc. Rvw, 1969–72; ed. Cineaste, NYC, 1967—, VP Tri-Continental Film Ctr., 1972–80; VP The Cinema Guild, 1981—. Mem. NY Film-Video Cncl., Assn. Ind. Video and Filmmakers.Home: 116 Saint Marks Pl New York NY 10009

CROWE, JOHN, see Lynds, Dennis

CROWE, RONALD GIRARDEAU, b. Atlanta, Aug. 17, 1932, s. Hubert E. and Betty Lee (Girardeau) C.; m. Clarynn Sentker, Feb. 16, 1961 (div. 1968); 1 son, Ronald Craig; m. 2d, Candace Lee Kiel, Aug. 5, 1977. Author: Crowe's Compleat Guide to Fairbanks (satire and poetry), 1979, Fireweeds (poetry), 1981, Crowe's Compleat Guide to Anchorage (satire), 1982, Two in the Bush (novel), 1984; contrbr. to Anthology of Magazine Verse and Yearbook of American Poetry, 1981, 85. BA in Journalism, U. Ala., 1959; MFA in English, U. Alaska, 1977. Tech. wrtr. various cos., 1959-68; ed. Battelle, Richland, Wash., 1969-72; ed. Inst. Social and Econ. Research, U. Alaska, 1972—. Recipient McCrackin Award for Poetry, U. Alaska, 1974, 76, Lucille Medwick award, N.Y. Qtly, 1978. Home: Box 111022 Anchorage AK 99511

CROWLEY, CAROL LEE, b. Coggon, IA, Feb. 18, 1931; d. Earle Lewis and Harriette Elizabeth (Church) Hinton; m. Paul Howard Crowley, Nov. 18, 1950; children—Michael Paul, Thomas Daniel, Sharon Elizabeth. Contrbr.: Quilter's Newsletter Magazine, Quiltmaker, Reflections lit. mag., Friend mag., Rocky Mountain News, Denver Post, numerous others. Wrkg. on mystery novel, play, book revs. BA, Regis Coll., 1982. Ed., Regis College Bulletin, 1982-83; Program coordinator Passages, Inc., Denver, 1983-84; free-lance ed., 1984-85; genl. ed., book reviewer Quilter's Newsletter Magazine, Wheatridge, 1985—; mng. ed. Quiltmaker mag., Wheatridge, 1987—. Mem. Hayna Wrtrs. Home: 2384 W 23rd Circle Golden CO 80401

CROZIER, OUIDA G., b. Clermont, FL, Oct. 21, 1947; d. Charles Edward Sr. and Ouida Rhea (Hinson) C. Contrbr. poems and short stories to books and magazines including A Woman's Touch, The Crucible. BA in Psychology, U. Fla., 1969; MEd in Counselling, U.S.C., 1973. Psychotherapist in pvt. practice, tchg. and consulting. Mem. Defenders of Wildlife, Natl. Wildlife Fedn., People for Ethical Treatment of Animals, Minn. Women in Psychology, Assn. Lesbian and Gay Psychologists, Women's Psychol. Assn. Home: 3708 12th Ave S Minneapolis MN 55407

CRUMLEY, JAMES, b. Three Rivers, TX, Oct. 12, 1939, s. Arthur Roland and Ruby Jewel (Crisswell) C.; m. Maggie Spittler, Nov. 23, 1968 (div. 1972); children—Mary, Elizabeth, David; m. 2d Bronwyn G. Pughe, Dec. 30, 1982; children—Conor, Kyle. Novelist: One to Count Cadence, 1969, The Wrong Case, 1974, The Last Good Kiss, 1978, Dancing Bear, 1982. BA in History, Tex. A&I, 1964; MFA in Fiction, Univ. of Iowa, 1966. Asst. prof. U. Ark., Fayetteville, 1969-70, Colo. State U., Ft. Collins, 1971-74, U. Tex.-El Paso, 1981-84; vis. wrtr. Carnegie Mellon Inst., Pitts., 1979-80; pres. Hellgate Prodns., Missoula, Mont., 1985—. Served with U.S. Army, 1958-61. Mem. WG, AWP, Tex. Inst. Letters. Home: Box 9278 Missoula MT 59807

CRUMP, JUDY GAIL, b. Huntington, WV, Jan. 12, 1955; d. Raymond and Lulu Mae (Lewis) Lowe; m. Charles Crump, Apr. 12, 1969; 1 son, David. Author: (novel) Love in a Stranger's Arms, 1982, (play) Away Down South, 1981. Student pub. schls., Paris, Ky. Machine operator Ky. Textiles, Paris, 1973-86. Home: 1455 High St Apt 1 Paris KY 40361

CRUSE, IRMA RUSSELL, b. Hackneyville, AL, May 3, 1911; d. Charles Henry and Nellie (Ledbetter) Russell; m. J. Clyde Cruse, Dec. 22, 1931 (dec. 1963); children—Allan B., Howard Russell. Contrbr. articles: Home Life, Vista, Woman's Touch, Mature Living, Link, numerous other publs.; playwright two published plays. AB in Journalism, U. Ala., 1976; AM in English, Samford U., 1981, AM in History, 1984. With South Central Bell Telephone Co., Birmingham, Ala., to 1976, ed. Bama Bulltn., 1960-76; free-lance wrtr., copy ed., public relations wrtr. Recipient Freedoms Fdn. Award for Bama Bulltn., 1967, 68, 69. Mem. Ala. Wrtrs.' Conclave (pres. 1973-74), Ala. State Poetry Soc. (ed. The Muse Messenger 1976-78), Women in Communications (pres. 1970-71), Natl. League Am. Pen Women. Home: 136 Memory Ct Birmingham AL 35213

CRUTCHER, CHRISTOPHER C., b. Cascade, ID, July 17, 1946; s. John William and Jewell (Morris) C. Author: Running Loose, (Best Books for Young Adults, ALA, 1983), 1983, STotan (Best Books for Young Adults, ALA, 1986), 1986, The Crazy Horse Electric Game, 1987. Contrbr. articles to Spokane Mag. B.A. in Sociology and Psychology, Eastern Wash. State Coll., 1968, Cert. in Edn., 1970. Tchr., coordinator Kennewick Dropout Sch., WA, 1971-72; dir. Lakeside Sch., Oakland, CA, 1973-82; child and family therapist Commun. Mental Health, Spokane, 1983—. Home: W 730 Carlisle Spokane WA 99205

CRUTCHFIELD, JAMES ANDREW, b. Nashville, May 16, 1938; s. Sam Shaw, Sr. and Frankie Alfreda (Whitworth) C.; m. Regena Arlene Hawkins, May 13, 1965. Author: The Harpeth River: A Biography, 1972, Early Times in the Cumberland Valley, 1975, A Primer of Handicrafts, 1976, Footprints Across the Pages of Tennessee History, 1976, Williamson County: A Pictorial History, 1980, Yesteryear in Nashville, 1981, A Heritage of Grandeur, 1981, Timeless Tennesseans, 1984, The Natchez Trace: A Pictorial History, 1985, The Tennessee Almanac, 1986, A Primer of the North American Fur Trade, 1986. Contrbr. articles to mags. Editor: America's Headlines, 1985, Your Tennessee, 1979, Tenn. Valley Hist. Rvw, 1972-74. Student U. Tenn.-Nashville, 1959, Vanderbilt U., 1960. Served with U.S. Army, 1961-66. Chmn. and pres., Williamson Sales and Prte. Co., Franklin, TN. Bd. dirs. Pioneers' Corner, Franklin, Tenn., 1986—, past pres. Recipient Commendation,

Am. Assn. for State/Local History, 1973, Best Writing award Tenn. Bi-Centennial Com., 1976. Mem. WWA, Williamson County Hist. Soc. (past pres.), Am. Legion. Home: 1012 Fair St Franklin TN 37064

CUDWORTH, MARSHA ELIZABETH, b. Paterson, NJ, Mar. 6, 1947; d. Warren Philip and Helen Elizabeth (Pinter) DeMauro; m. John Cudworth, Aug. 31, 1969 (div. 1977); 1 son, John. Author: Victorian Holidays Guide to Inns, Guesthouses and Restaurants of Cape May, NJ, 1982; Self-Guided Archtl. Tours of Cape May, NJ, 1985. BA, Montclair State Coll. Art tchr., Bergenfield, NJ, 1968-70, Manahawkin, NJ, 1976—; freelance craft designer, 1970-75; artist/author Bric-A-Brac Book Works, Forked River, NJ, 1982—. Address: 613 Beach Blvd Forked River NJ 08731

CULLEM-KRISTIAN, FLORENCE MARY, b. NYC, Jan. 3, 1922; m. James Cullem, May 1, 1942 (dec. 1969); children—James, Daniel, John, Thomas, Catherine, Margaret; m. 2d, Stanley Kristian, May 3, 1976 (dec. 1984). Founder Bethpage (N.Y.) Tribune, 1966, ed., pub. to 1979; feature wrtr., columnist numerous genl. interest publs. including Levittown (N.Y.) Tribune, Observer Newspaper, Massapequa, N.Y.; public relations coordinator Displaced Homemakers, Nassau County, N.Y., 1979-83, Hope for Youth, Nassau County, 1982-84; freelance wrtr. Recipient several awards as pub. of Bethpage Tribune. Home: 32 Horizon Ln Levittown NY 11756

CULLEN, MARGARET, b. Glover, VT, Feb. 6, 1924; d. Armour John and Frances (Hastings) Smith; m. John Paul Cullen, Aug. 22, 1948 (dec. Sept. 27, 1983); children—Brian John, Cynthia Marie. Translator: Latin-Am. poetry for Whales: A Celebration, 1983; translation Chap. IX, Book V of Histoire de ma vie by George Sand; comml. and technical translations. A.B. in Romance Langs., Tufts U., 1946; M.A. in French, Assumption Coll., 1974. Tchr. French and Spanish, Acton-Boxboro Regional High Schl., Acton, MA, 1967-80; free-lance translator, 1980—. Mem. ATA (1st prize for French poetry translation 1982), ALTA. Home: 41 Linda Ave Framingham MA 01701

CULLER, JONATHAN DWIGHT, b. Cleve., Oct. 1, 1944; s. Arthur Dwight and Helen Lucille (Simpson) C.; m. Cynthia Chase, Dec. 27, 1976. Author: Flaubert: The Uses of Uncertainty, 1974, Structuralist Poetics: Structuralism, Linguistics and the Study of Literature, 1975, Saussure, 1976, The Pursuit of Signs: Semiotics, Literature, Deconstruction, 1981, On Deconstruction: Theory and Criticism after Structuralism, 1982, Roland Barthes, 1983. Advisory editor: New Literary History, 1972—, PTL, 1976-79; mem. advisory bd., Publs. MLA, 1978; mem. editorial bd.: Diacritics, 1974—, Poetics Today, 1979—. BA, Harvard U., 1966; BPhil, St. John's Coll., Oxford (Eng.), DPhil, 1972. Fellow, dir. studies in modern langs. Selwyn Coll., Cambridge U., 1969-74; vis. prof. English and comparative lit. Yale U., 1975; fellow Brasenose Coll. and univ. lectr. French, Oxford U., 1974-77; prof. English and comparative lit Cornell U., Ithaca, N.Y., 1977—; dir. Soc. for the Humanities, 1984–90. Recipient James Russell Lowell prize MLA, 1975; Rhodes scholar, 1966-69; Guggenheim fellow, 1979-80, NEH Fellow, 1987–88. Home: 643 Jacksonville Rd Jacksonville NY 14854

CULLINAN, ELIZABETH, b. NYC, June 7, 1933; d. Cornelius G. and Irene (O'Connell) C. Author: House of Gold, 1970, The Time of Adam, 1971, Yellow Roses, 1977, A Change of Scene, 1982; also short stories pub. in New Yorker mag. BA, Marymount Coll., NYC, 1954. Recipient new writer's award Great Lakes Colls. Assn., 1970; Houghton Mifflin literary fellow, 1970; NEA grantee, 1974; Carnegie Fund grantee, 1978. Address: 34 E 68th St New York NY 10021

CUMMING, PATRICIA ARENS, (Ann Cummings), b. NYC, Sept. 7, 1932; d. Egmont Arens and Camille (Davied) Rose; m. Edward Cumming, June 6, 1954 (dec. Feb. 1960); children: Julie, Susanna. Author: (poems) Afterwards, 1974, Letter from an Outlying Province, 1976; (with others) Free Writing, 1976; author gardening articles as Ann Cummings; contrbr. poetry to lit. mags. and anthologies. BA magna cum laude, Radcliffe Coll., 1954; MA, Middlebury Coll., 1956. Co-producer Theatre Co. of Boston, 1963-65; editorial assoc. Daedalus jnl., Cambridge, Mass., 1966-69; instr., asst. prof., assoc. prof. MIT, Cambridge, 1969-80. Old Dominion grantee MIT Humanities Dept., 1977; Danforth Fdn. faculty fellow, 1978. Mem. NWU, Feminist Wrtr.'s Guild, Phi Beta Kappa. Home: Box 251 Adamsville RI 02801

CUMMING, ROBERT, b. Davidson, NC, Dec. 15, 1935. Contrbr. poems, short stories, articles to lit. mags., anthols. Translator, editor: (with Deborah Cumming, Montri Umavijani) A Premier Book of Contemporary Thai Verse, 1985. BA, Harvard U., 1957; MPhil, Oxford U., 1960. Staff wrtr. N.C. Fund, Durham, 1966-68; tchr. CCNY, 1968-73, Lander Coll., Greenwood, S.C., 1974—. J. F. Kennedy Fdn. fellow in Thailand, 1981-82, Artist fellow in writing, S.C. Arts Commn., 1982-83. Home: Rt 1 Box 308 Greenwood SC 29646

CUMMINGS, ANN, see Cumming, Patricia Arens

CUMMINGS, BETTY SUE, b. Big Stone Gap, VA, July 12, 1918; d. Howard Lee and Hattie J. (Bruce) C. Author: Hew Against the Grain (Finalist, Natl. Book award 1978, Intl. Reading Assn. Honor book 1978, 3d place for adult novels NLAPW 1978), 1978, Let a River Be, 1979, Now, Ameriky, 1980, Turtle, 1981, Say These Names (3d place NLAPW 1986), 1984. Wrkg. on The Dummy Line. B.S., Longwood Coll., 1939; M.A., U. Wash., 1949. Tchr. public schs., Norton, VA, 1939-41, Richmond, VA, 1941-42, Thermopolis, WY, 1949-57, Titusville, FL, 1957-73; free-lance wrtr., 1973—. Mem. NLAPW, AG. Home: 3980 Alpine Ln Titusville FL 32780

CUMMINGS, JEAN, b. Charles City, IA, Apr. 19, 1930; d. William Kinsey and Eathel Jean (Gibson) Carr; m. Dwain W. Cummings, Feb. 2, 1951; children—Bruce, Beth, Brenda. Author: Why They Call Him the Buffalo Doctor, 1971, Alias the Buffalo Doctor, 1980. Contrbr. articles to mags., newspapers including Redbook, others. Wrkg. on 2 hist. novels, 1 young adult novel. Student Carleton Coll., 1948-49, U. Iowa, 1949-51; B.A., Drake U., 1953. Editorial asst. Fruitport Area News, MI, 1985—. Bd. dirs. Muskegon County Library, MI, 1973-86. Mem. NWC (6th place for novel 1983). Home: 2609 E Fruitport Rd Spring Lake MI 49456

CUMMINS, WALTER (MERRILL), b. Long Branch, NJ, Feb. 6, 1936; s. Jacob and Pearl (Lichtenstein) Caminsky; m. Judith Gruenberg, Jun. 14, 1957 (div. Jan., 1981); children—Pamela, Jennifer; 2nd m. Alison Elizabeth Cunningham, Feb. 14, 1981. Editor-in-chief: The Literary Review, 1984—; co-editor: The Other Sides of Reality, 1972; author story collections: Where we Live, 1983, Witness, 1975; novels: A Stranger to the Deed, 1968, Into Temptation, 1968; short story contrbr. to Virginia Qtly Rvw, Florida Rvw, other lit mags. BA, Rutgers U., 1957; PhD,U. of Iowa, 1965. Editor General Electric Co. (Schenectady, NY), 1957-59; instructor U. of Iowa (Iowa City), 1962-65; asst.-full prof. Fairleigh Dickinson U. (Madison, NJ), 1965—. Pvt. Army Reserve, 1959-65. Fiction fellowship NJ State Cncl. on the Arts, 1983. Mem. College English Assoc., NCTE. Office: Dept Eng Fairleigh Dickinson U Madison NJ 07940

CUNNEEN, JOSEPH, b. NYC,Feb. 21, 1923, s. John James and Mary Margaret (Beha) C.; m. Sally McDevitt; children—Michael, Peter, Paul. Ed. Cross Currents of Psychiatry and Catholic Morality, 1964, Looking Toward the Council; contrbr. to Commonweal, Esprit, Christianity and Crisis, The Nation, other jnls; translator Plays by Gabriel Marcel, BA, Holy Cross Coll., 1942; MA, Catholic U. Am., 1947, LHD, Coll. New Rochelle, N.Y., 1981; LLD (hon.), Coll. of the Elms, Chicopee, Mass., 1982. Mem. faculty Fordham U., Bronx, N.Y., 1948-52, Coll. of New Rochelle, 1953-57, Mercy Coll., Dobbs Ferry, N.Y., 1976—; sr. ed. Holt Rinehart, Winston, N.Y.C., 1962-74; ed.-in-chief Cross Currents, West Nyack, N.Y., 1950—. Served with U.S. Army, 1943-46, ETO. Home: 103 Van Houten Fields West Nyack NY 10994

CUNNINGHAM, DEBORAH LYNN, b. Hot Springs, AR., May 20, 1954; d. William Rufus and Zelma Harriett (Featherston) Simpson; m. James Clarence White, 1973 (div. 1974); m. 2d, Phillip Charles Cunningham, Dec. 2, 1981; children: Donald, Leland, Geoffrey and Jennifer (twins). Contrbr. articles to mags. Student U. Alaska, 1983—. Served as sgt. USAF, 1974-83. Home: 8672 Augusta Circle Anchorage AK 99504

CUNNIGHAM, E. V., see Fast, Howard

CUNNINGHAM, JULIA WOOLFOLK, b. Spokane, Oct. 4, 1916; d. John George and Sue (Larabie) C. Author: (juveniles) The Vision of Francois the Fox, 1960, Dear Rat, 1961, Macaroon, 1962, Candle Tales, 1964, Drop Dead, 1965, Violet, 1966, Onion Journey, 1967, Burnish Me Bright, 1970, Wings of the Morning, 1971, Far in the Day, 1972, The Treasure Is the Rose, 1973, Maybe a Mole, 1974, Come to the Edge, 1977, Tuppenny, 1978, A Mouse Called Junction, 1980, Flight of the Sparrow, 1980, The Silent Voice, 1981, Wolf Roland, 1983, Oaf, 1986. Grad., St. Anne's Schl., Charlottesville, Va., 1933. Mem. AG. Home: 33 W Valerio St Santa Barbara CA 93101

CUNNINGHAM, MARCIA LYNN, (Marci Cunningham), b. Connellsville, PA, July 9, 1955, d. Richard Thomas and Hazel Laverne (Marietta) McGuinness; m. Alan Joseph Cunningham, Mar. 17, 1982; children—Brynn Estella and Tara Lynn (twins). Author: Natural Remedies, 1985, Unforgettable Poems for Everyday People, 1985, The Deerhunters' Guide to Success: From the Woods to the Skillet, 1985, Natural Remedies, Recipes & Realities, 1986, Don't Be Mistreated, 1987, Twin Care, 1987.Pub., author, prin. Backwoods Books, Gibbon Glade, Pa., 1981—. Mem. Am. Bookdealers Exchange, COSMEP, PMA. Home: Box 9 McClellan Ln Gibbon Glade PA 15440

CUOMO, GEORGE (MICHAEL), b. NYC, Oct. 10, 1929, s. John and Lillian (Vogt) C.; m. Sylvia Epstein, Aug. 15, 1954; children—Celia, Douglas, Gregory, Rosalind, Michael. Author: Becoming a Better Reader, 1960, Jack Be Nimble (novel), 1963, Bright Day, Dark Runner (novel), 1964, Among Thieves (novel), 1968, Sing, Choirs of Angels (stories), 1970, The Hero's Great Great Great Great Great Grandson (novel), 1971, Geronimo and the Girl Next Door (poems), 1974, Pieces from a Small Bomb (novel), 1976, Becoming a Better Reader and Writer, 1978, Family Honor (novel), 1983. BA, Tufts U., 1952; MA, Ind. U., 1955. Prof. English, Calif. State U., Hayward, 1965-73, U. Mass., Amherst, 1973—. NEA fellow, 1976, Guggenheim fellow, 1983. Mem. WG, AWP, Phi Beta Kappa. Office: Dept English Univ Mass Amherst MA 01003

CURLEY, THOMAS F., b. Boston, Mar. 12, 1925, s. Thomas Francis and Mary Elizabeth (Morrissey) C.; divorced; children—Thomas, Mark. Novelist: It's a Wise Child, 1960, Past Eve and Adam's, 1963, Nowhere Man, 1967, Camp Meeting, 1979. MA, Boston Coll. Served as sgt. USMC, 1943-45, PTO. Home: 88 East End Ave New York NY 10028

CURRAN, CHARLES (EDWARD), b. Rochester, N.Y., March 30, 1934; Author: Christian Morality Today: The Renewel of Moral Theology, 1966, A New Look at Christian Morality, 1968, ed. Absolutes in Moral Theology, 1968, (with others) The Responsibility of Dissent: The Church and Academic Freedom, 1969, ed. Contraception: Authority and Dissent, 1969, (with Robert E. Hunt and others), Dissent in and for the Church, 1970, Contemporary Problems in Moral Theology, 1970, ed. with George J. Dyer, Shared Responsibility in the Local Church, 1970, Catholic Moral Theology in Dialogue, 1972, Politics, Medicine and Christian Ethics: A Dialogue with Paul Ramsey, 1973, New Perspectives in Moral Theology, 1974, Ongoing Revision: Studies in Moral Theology, 1975, Themes in Fundamental Moral Theology, 1977, Issues in Sexual and Medical Ethics, 1978, Transaction and Tradition in Moral Theology, 1979, ed. with Ricarad P. McCormick, Moral Norms and Catholic Tradition, 1979, The Distinctiveness of Christian Ethics, 1980, Morality and the Magisterium, 1982, The Use of Scripture in Moral Theology, 1984, Official Catholic Social Teaching, 1986, Moral Theology: A Continuing Journey, 1982, American Catholic Social Ethics: Twentieth-Century Approaches, 1982, Critical Concerns in Moral Theology, 1984, Directions in Catholic Social Ethics, 1985, Directions in Fundamental Moral Theology, 1985, Faithful Dissent, 1986, Toward an American Catholic Moral Theology, 1987. BA, St. Bernard's Seminary and College, Rochester, N.Y., S. T.B., 1957, S.T.L., Gregorian Univ., Rome, Italy, 1959, S.T.D., 1961; S.T.D., Academia Alfensiana, Rome, 1961. Ordained Roman Catholic priest, 1958, prof. of moral theol., St. Bernard's Sem., 1961-65; asst. prof., Catholic University of America, Washington, D.C., 1965-67, assoc. prof, 1967-71, prof. of Moral Theol., 1971—; visiting prof., Cornell U., 1987. Sr. res. scholar, Kennedy Center for Bioethics, Georgetown, U., 1972. Member: Am. Soc. of Christian Ethics (pres. 1971-72), Am. Theol. Soc., Catholic Theol. Soc. of Am. (v.p. 1968-69, pres. 1969-70), College Theol. Soc. Office: Dept. Theol Catholic Univ Washington DC 20017

CURRAN, MADELINE MC GRATH, b. Staten Island, NY, July 11, 1947; d. John Joseph and Catherine Ruby (Lindou) McGrath; m. Lawrence Thomas Curran, Dec. 20, 1969; children—Christopher, Melynda, Eric. Contrbr. articles to mags., newspapers including Boston Globe, others. Wrkg. on book on Boston's arson fires. B.A. in English, U. Mass., 1971, M.A. in English, 1976. English tchr. public and pvt. schls., MA, 1971-81; free-lance wrtr., 1981—. Home: 1389 Main St Lynnfield MA 01940

CURRELLEY, LORRAINE, b. NYC, Feb. 27, 1951, d. William Gillard and Annie (Daniel) Currelley. Contrbr. poetry numerous anthologies, lit. publs. Student Herbert H. Lehman Coll. Performance poet, Gaptooth Girlfriends: The Third Act; lectr., performer ednl. instns.; founder, dir. Growing Theatre, Inc., NYC, Poet's Cafe, NYC; dir. Intl. Women's Poetry Festival, NYC. Mem. P&W, Feminist Wrtrs.' Guild (steering com. N.Y.C, chpt., newsletter ed.). Home: Box 562 Coll Sta New York NY 10030

CURREY, RICHARD, b. Parkersburg, WV, Oct. 19, 1949; s. Allen Eugene and Mary Kay (Dulaney) C.; m. Aiko Allen, June 12, 1976; 1 dau., Aja. Author: Crossing Over: A Vietnam Journal (nominated for Pulitzer prize 1980, named Best Title of Yr., Library Jnl, 1980), 1980, Fatal Light, 1988; contrbr. poetry: Blue Unicorn, Aleph, Clown War, other lit mags; contrbr. short stories: N.Am. Rvw, Qtly West; prose anthologized: First Person Intense, 1979. Cert. physician asst. Howard U., 1979. Freelance wrtr., 1972—; wrtr.-in-residence D.H. Lawrence Ranch, Taos, N.Mex., 1981; columnist Belen (N.Mex.) News-Bull., 1984–86. Served with USN, 1968-72, Vietnam. Recipient Santa Fe Festival of Arts Poetry Prize, 1979, Coll. Poetry Prize, AAP, 1981, Short Fiction award AWP, 1984; D.H. Lawrence fellow U. N.Mex., 1981, NEA fellow, 1982, 87. Mem. NWU. Address: 160 Washington SE 185 Albuquerque NM 87108

CURRY, DAVID LEE, b. Springfield, IL, Jan. 10, 1942; s. George Bruce and Jessie Lee (Ebel) C. Author poetry: Here, 1970, Theatre, 1973, Contending to Be the Dream, 1979. Wrkg. on Certain Flowers (poems) and Blue Psalm. Advt. dir. OGR Ser. Corp., Springfield, 1965-76; ed. and pub. Apple, Springfield, 1967-76; public info. officer Ill. Capital Devel. Bd., 1977-81; admin. asst. Office of Ill. Atty. Genl., Chicago, 1983—. NEA fellow, 1976. Address: 2045 N Dayton Chicago IL 60614

CURRY, ELIZABETH R., b. Evanston, IL, Jan. 31, 1934; d. William George and Alice Mary (Martel Fisher) Reichenbach; m. Stephen Jefferis Curry, June 10, 1958; 1 son, Geoffrey Stephen. Contrbr. scholarly articles to numerous publs.; ed. service publs. for Slippery Rock U. Pa.; poetry in anthologies. Wrkg. on poetry, scholarly articles, editing. BA, Northwestern U.; PhD, U. Wis.-Madison. Mem. faculty Slippery Rock U. Pa., 1969—, prof. English, 1976—. Winner poetry competitions. Home: 218 W Cooper St Slippery Rock PA 16057

CURRY, JANE LOUISE, b. East Liverpool, OH, Sept. 24, 1932; d. William Jack and Helen Margaret (Willis) C. Author: (juveniles) Down from the Lonely Mountain, 1965, The Change-Child, 1969, The Daybreakers, 1970, Over the Sea's Edge, 1971, The Lost Farm, 1974, Parsley Sage, Rosemary and Time, 1975, The Watchers, 1975, The Magical Cupboard, 1976, Poor Tom's Ghost, 1977, The Birdstones, 1977, Ghost Lane, 1979, The Wolves of Aam, 1981, Shadow Dancers, 1983. The Great Flood Mystery, 1985, The Lotus Cup, 1986, Back in the Beforetime, 1987, others. Student, Pa. State U., 1950-51; BS, Indiana U. of Pa., 1954; postgrad., UCLA, 1957-59; AM, Stanford U., 1962, PhD, 1969, U. London, 1961-62, 65-66. Tchr. art East Liverpool Schls., 1955, Los Angeles Schls., 1956-59; teaching asst. dept. English Stanford U., 1959-61, 64-65, acting instr., 1967-68; lectr., 1987. Address: McElderry Bks 866 Third Ave New York NY 10022

CURRY, MARY EARLE LOWRY, b. Seneca, SC, May 13, 1917; d. Ullin Sidney and Mary Sloan (Earle) Lowry; m. Peden Gene Curry, Dec. 25, 1941; children: Eugene Lowry, Mary Earle (dec.). Author: (poetry) Looking Up, 1949; Looking Within, 1961; contrbr. to anthologies, including Yearbook of Modern Poetry, Poets of America, Poetic Voice of America, We, The People, Poetry Digest; contrbr. to S.C. Christian Adv., Wesleyan Christian Adv., Living in S.C., also newspapers. Student Furman U., 1945. Home: R-5 Box 371 Seneca SC 29678

CURTIS, HALLIE VEA, b. Slick, OK, Oct. 27, 1930; d. Earnest and Ada (McCargo) Kellum; m. Earl Tottress, Oct. 17, 1947 (div. Feb. 5, 1957); children—Earl E., Antoinette H., James P., Jacobus O., David E.; 2nd m. Raymond Edward Curtis, Jun. 19, 1965. Author: The Silent Strangler, 1981. BA in Sociol. CA State U., 1972. Acct. clerk Conn. Gen. Insur. Co. (Los Angeles), 1972-73; tchr. Manchester Baptist Elem. Schl. (Inglewood, CA), 1973-78; ed. Abigail, Inc. (Los Angeles), 1982—. Home: 8806 S Van Ness Ave Los Angeles CA 90047

CURTIS, LINDA LEE, b. Stafford, KS, Apr. 18, 1950; d. Robert Lee and Donna Leatrice (Joy) Herren; m. Ronald Benson Curtis, June 8, 1979. Author: The Cheaters Almanac, 1976, Midnight Echoes, 1976, Sonnets and Sunbonnets, 1976, Smoke Rings, 1977, More Than My Share, 1979, Intermission, 1982, Money-Making Ideas for Poets, 1984; contrbr. poems to Soundboard, Pudding Mag, Ariz. Women's Voice, Inago Anthology, Bittersweet, Mallife. AA, Barton County Community Coll., 1978. Staff poet Soundboard Mag., Phoenix, 1983—. Mem. P&W. Address: 1919 W Adams Phoenix AZ 85009

CURZON, DANIEL, b. Illinois, Mar. 19; s. Russell E. and Ida V. (Billingsley) B. Author: Something You Do in the Dark, 1971, Human Warmth and Other Stories, 1981, The World Can Break Your Heart, 1985, Murder of Gonzago (play), 1986.PhD, Wayne State U, 1969. Lectr, Univ. Calif., Fresno, 1974-76, City Coll. of San Francisco, 1980—. NEA grantee for radio drama, 1982. Mem. DG. Home: 511 Capp St San Francisco CA 94110

CUSSEN, JUNE, b. South Bend, IN, Mar. 28, 1944; d. Thomas and Rose (Stephens) Miller; m. David M. Cussen, July 11, 1977. BA, Northwestern U., 1966; MA, San Francisco State U., 1967; MS, U. Calif., 1969. Exec. edit. and co-pub. Pineapple Press, Englewood, FL, 1982—. Founding mem. Pub. Assn. of the South. Office: Box 314 Englewood FL 33533

CUTLER, BRUCE, b. Evanston, IL, Oct. 8, 1930, s. Richard S. and Dorothea L. (Wales) C.; m. Tina Cirelli, July 3, 1954; children—David, John, Ann. Author: The Year of the Green Wave, 1960, A West Wind Rises, 1962, Sun City, 1964, A Voyage to America, 1967, The Doctrine of Selective Depravity, 1980, The Maker's Name, 1980, Nectar in a Sieve, 1983, Dark Fire, 1985; ed.: The Arts at the Grass Roots, 1968, In That Day, 1969. BA summa cum laude, U. Iowa, 1951;

MS, Kans. State U., 1957. Mem. faculty Wichita (Kans.) State U., 1960—, now Adele Davis disting. prof. English, dir. creative writing program. Mem. AWP. Home: 150 N Quentin St Wichita KS 67208

CUTLER, JANE, b. Bronx, NY, Sept. 24, 1936; d. Emanuel and Beatrice (Drooks) Cutler; divorced; children—Frances, David and Aaron Nudelman. Contrbr. fiction to popular, lit. mags; biographies for young adults. Editing med., tech., text, other. BA, Northwestern U., Evanston, Ill., 1958; MA, San Francisco State U., 1982. Recipient Herbert Wilner award for short fiction, 1982; winner, PEN short fiction contest, 1987. Mem. PEN, Media Alliance. Home: 352-27th St San Francisco CA 94131

CUTTER, MARGARET MEAD, b. Camden, NJ, Oct. 11, 1953; d. Samuel, Jr. and Barbara (Niland) Mead; m. Howard Moore Cutter, Jr., July 6, 1974; 1 son, Howard M. Contrbr. articles to popular mags. including Horseman Mag., Horses All, Eastern Rodeo News, Roundup; to newspapers including Phila. Inquirer, Atlantic City Press, Atlantic County Record; poems to anthols. BA, Glassboro State Coll., 1974. Recipient 1st prize for mag. articles Editor's Desk Wrtrs. Conf., 1985, 2d prize for juvenile writing, 1985, hon. mention for journalism, 1985. Mem. NWC. Home: RD 4 Box 8 Millville Rd Mays Landing NJ 08330

CUTTER, RALPH FREDERICK, b. Walnut Creek, CA, Jan. 25, 1955; s. John W. and Francis (Carter) Cutter; m. Lisa Marie Whittet, Dec. 29, 1975; children—Teal Skye, Haley Crystal. Author: Sierra Trout Guide, 1984. Student U. of Southern Calif. Researcher, Calif. Dept. of Fish and Game, 1980-84; guide, instructor, Bristol Bay Lodge, Alaska, 1984-85, pres., Calif. School of Flyfishing, 1983—. Mem. Outdoor Writers Assoc. Clubs: Sierra Club, Tahoe Truckee Flyfishers, Federation of Flyfishers. Home: Box 6402 Tahoe City CA 95730

CUZZORT, R. P., b. Cin., Dec. 1926; s. James Middleton and Clara Gertrude (Wolfhorst) C.; m. Phyllis Evelyn Taylor, Dec. 23, 1951 (dec. 1972); 1 dau., Barbara Rochelle. Author: (with Otis and Beverly Duncan) Statistical Geography, 1961, Humanity and Modern Social Thought, 1969, (with E. King) 20th Century Social Thought, 3d ed., 1980. BA, U. Cin., 1951, MA, 1951; PhD, U. Minn., 1955. Research assoc. Population Research and Tng. Cntr., U. Chgo., 1956-57; asst. prof. sociology U. Kans., Lawrence, 1957-62; assoc. prof. U. Ill., Champaign, 1965-66; prof. U. Colo., Boulder, 1966—, chmn. dept. sociology, 1982-84, research assoc. Inter-Univ. Com. on Superior Student, 1963-65. Served with USN, 1945-46. Fellow Ford Fdn., 1955. Mem. Western Social Sci. Assn. (editor 1983—), Am. Sociol. Assn., AAUP, Assn. Humanistic Sociology. Home: 1300 Elder St Boulder CO 80302

CYGANOWSKI, CAROL KLIMICK, b. Chgo., Apr. 12, 1949; d. John Nick and Olga (Kushta) Klimick; m. Daniel Robert Cyganowski, June 20, 1970; 1 dau., Claudia. Author: Magazine Editors and Professional Authors in Nineteenth Century America: The Genteel Tradition and The American Dream, 1988; Am. lit. cons., contrbr.: Women's Studies Encyc., 1988; asst. to ed., contrbr.: Encyc. Handbook of American Women's History, 1988. Wrkg. on lit. history of women wrtrs in Am. mags. MA in English, U. Chgo., 1970, PhD in English, 1980. Instr. Roosevelt U., Chgo., 1975-80; asst. prof. DePaul U., Chgo., 1981—. Mem. MLA (exec. com. women's caucus, Midwest region 1985, 86). Home: 72 Chestnut Ave Clarendon Hills IL 60514

CYMET, TYLER CHILDS, (Naftali Tzimet), b. Smithtown, NY, Jan. 30, 1963; s. Seymour Harvey and Sabina (Childs) C. Contrbr. articles to profl. jnls. Columnist, asst. editor Visions Mag., 1978-80; editor-in-chief The Voice, 1981-84; asst. editor Student D.O.ctor Mag., 1984-85, editor-in-chief, vol. 7, nos. 1,2 1985; bd. contrbrs. Med. Anthropology Quarterly, 1986. BA in anthropology/Hebrew lit., Emory U., 1984, BS in Psychology, 1984; postgrad in Osteo. Medicine, Southeastern Coll. Osteo. Medicine, 1984—. Admitting rep. Meml. Hosp., Hollywood, Fla., 1977-80; instr., lectr. ARC, Hollywood, 1977-86; free-lance wrtr., 1983—. Dir. youth services Intl. Aquanaut Fdn., Hollywood, 1978-80; vol. coordinator South Fla. Spcl. Olympics, Dade County, 1979-80; mem. Am. Israel pub. affairs com. Youth Leadership Div., 1979—; coordinator, wrtr. Am. Zionist Youth Fdn., Atlanta, 1980-84; Dorot Fdn. grantee Ungerleider-Mayerson Fdn., 1981. Fellow Fla. Acad. Sci.; mem. Am. Osteo. Assn. (student), Fla. Osteo. Med. Assn., Am. Osteo. Acad. Sports Medicine, Am. Anthrop. Assn., Am. Pub. Health Assn., Natl. Undergraduate Am. Acad. Osteo. (bd. dirs.), Soc. Collegiate Journalists, Omicron Delta Kappa, Lambda Alpha, Phi Sigma Gamma, Phi Sigma Iota. Home: 4450 N Hills Dr Hollywood FL 33021

DACEY, (JOHN) PHILIP, b. St. Louis, May 9, 1939; s. Joseph M. and Teresa Veronica (McGinn) D.; children—Emmett, Austin, Fay. Author: How I Escaped from the Labyrinth and Other Poems, 1977, The Boy Under the Bed, 1981, Gerard Manley Hopkins Meets Walt Whitman in Heaven and Other Poems, 1982, Fives, 1984, Strong Measures: Contemporary American Poetry in Traditional Forms, 1985, The Man with Red Suspenders, 1986. MA, Stanford U., 1968; MFA, U. Iowa, 1970. Prof. English, Southwest State U., Marshall, Minn., 1970—; Vis. Disting. Poet-in-Res., Wichita State U., 1985. Fellowships: NEA, 1975, 1980; Bush Fdn., 1977. Address: English Dept SSU Marshall MN 56258

DADDONA, PATRICIA ANN, b. Waterbury, CT., Nov. 8, 1960; d. Francis Nicholas and Juanita Angela (Cosmo) Daddona. Poetry in literary mags and anthologies. BA, Connecticut College, New London, CT. Edit. asst. Town Times, Watertown, CT, 1983-84; edit. asst., book rvwr., Litchfield County Times, New Milford, CT, 1984—. Mem. AAP. Home: 217 Scott Road Apt. 3B Waterbury CT 06705

DAHL, BARD, b. Seattle, July 26, 1926; s. John and Emelia (Brakney) D. Editor lit. qtly. Pangloss Papers, Los Angeles, 1982—. Real estate entrepreneur. Served as pfc. U.S. Army, 1945-46, ETO. Office: Box 18917 Los Angeles CA 99018

DAHLBERG, JOYCE KAREN, b. Mpls., Sept. 30, 1943, d. Elon Clinton and Adelynne Elizabeth (Mitchell) Tuttle; m. Curtis Leroy Dahlberg, Dec. 23, 1967; children—Eric Curtis, Curtis Elon. Contrbr. poems, children's stories, to The Friend, Communique, Marriage and Family Living, other publs.; wrtr., ed. newsletters for various orgns., trng. manuals, operations and software manuals, public relations and advertising brochures and materials; newspaper and magazine articles, videotape scripts; tchr. of wrtg. and spkr. on creativity and wrtr. BA cum laude, Hamline U., 1965. Freelance wrtr., ed., Mpls., 1975—; pres. Challenge Communications, 1987—. Mem. Women in communications, Freelance Communicators Network. Home: 205 Rice Creek Blvd NE Minneapolis MN 55432

DAHLBERG, RLENE H, b. Detroit, May 16, 1925; d. Robert E. and Lee L. (Meyers) Howell; m. Edward Dahlberg, Oct. 14, 1950 (div. 1967). Author: Twelve from the Cemetery of Saller, 1977, Emma Goldman, 1983. AA, Stephens Coll., 1948; MA, U. Chgo., 1950. Asst. to curator Met. Mus. Art, NYC, 1949-51; tchr. English, NYC, 1956—; pub Pequod Press, NYC. Address: 344 Third Ave New York NY 10010

DAHMS, JANET H., (Janet Bassett), b. Blue Earth, MN, Dec. 12, 1919, d. William and Rosina Julia (Poirier) Bassett; m. Arthur Edwin Dahms, Dec. 19, 1942 (dec.); children—A. Stephen, Robert D., Gregory S., Douglas G., Janine M., Nanette L., Susanne R. Contrbr. articles on science satire, history and humor to popular mags., newspapers; also poetry. Artist, portrait, genre, abstract; illustrated no. of own manuscripts. Attended Mankato State U., ed. major 1937-39, U. of MN, arts ed. 1951-58. MN teacher private and public schools at Winnebago, Albert Lea, 1939-42, St. Paul, 1967-78. Active in Boy Scout Indianhead Council and school groups 1956-78. Mem. Teacher's Retirement Assn., Natl. Retired Tchrs. Home: 85 W Thompson 311 West St Paul MN 55118

DAIGLE, PIERRE VARMON, b. Church Point, LA, Nov. 23, 1923; s. Leo and Odelaise (Doucet) D.; m. Hilda Sonnier, July 1, 1945; children—Carlos, Brenda, Phyllis, Timothy, Todd. Author: Tears, Love, and Laughter; The Story of Cajuns and Their Music, 1972, 2d ed., 1987, How to Teach Creative Writing to Junior and Senior High School Students, 1973; (hist. novel) Plow, Sword and Prayers, 1977; (novel) The Echo of their Cries, 1978; (play) A Bilingual Celebration (1st prize Deep South Wrtrs. Conf., 1971), 1984. B.A. in Edn., U. Southwestern La., 1956. Tchr. public schls., Rayne, LA, 1956-80. Served to sgt. U.S. Army, 1943-45, PTO; U.S. Air Force, 1947-52. Home: Rt 4 Box 470 Church Point LA 70525

DAIGON, RUTH, b. Winnipeg, Man., Can., March 3, 1933; d. Nathan and Rose (Levin) Popeski; m. Arthur Daigon, April 11, 1952; children—Tom, Glenn. Author: Learning Not to Kill You, 1976, On My Side of the Bed, 1979, A Portable Past, 1986; poetry in numerous lit mags. BA, U. of Manitoba, Winnipeg, 1950; student Royal Conservatory of Toronto, 1950-52. Profl. singer, 1950-75; cast member, CBS, Camera Three, 1952-54; ed. and pub., Poets On Mag., 1976—. Mem. PSA, P&W, COSMEP, CCLM. Home: Box 255 Chaplin CT 06235

DAILEY, JANET, b. Storm Lake, IA, May 21, 1944; m. William Dailey; 2 stepchildren. Author: No Quarter Asked, 1974, After the Storm, 1975, Sweet Promise, 1976, The Widow and the Wastrel, 1977, Giant of Mesabi, 1978, The Bride of the Delta Queen, 1979, Lord of the High Lonesome, 1980, Night Way, 1981, This Calder Sky, 1981, This Calder Range, 1982, Stands a Calder Man, 1983, The Lancaster Men, 1981, Silver Wings Santiago Blue, 1984, The Glory Game, 1985, The Great Alone, 1986, Heiress, 1987. Student pub. schls., Independence, Iowa. Secy. Omaha, 1963-74. Recipient Golden Heart award Romance Writers Am., 1981, Golden Pen Award, 1987. Home: Star Rt 4 Box 2197 Branson MO 95616

DALE, MAE, see Donchess, Barbara M.

DALE, VERONICA, see Treutel, Lucile Veronica

DALE, TIMOTHY, see Patterson, Timothy Dale

DALEY, JOHN, b. Buffalo, Sept. 4, 1948, s. Francis V. and Evelyn Primrose (Notley) D.; m. Debora Ott, Mar. 18, 1972; children: Sabina, Alice. Author: (poetry) Roadie, 1984; contrbr. to Intrepid, B.C. Monthly, Beloar, Rolling Stock, Brilliant Corners, other lit mags; ed. Ink, 1980, 81, 82, 83. BS, Cassius Coll., Buffalo, 1970; JD, SUNY-Buffalo, 1973. Sole practice, Buffalo, 1974-85. recipient Genl. Electric. Fdn. award CCLM, NYC, 1984. Office: 111 Elmwood Ave Buffalo NY 14202

DALLMAN, ELAINE GAY, b. Sacramento, CA, Mar. 8; d. Vernon Selig and Etta Evangeline (Hornstein) Dallman; m. Willard B. Ross, Dec. 18, 1954 (div. 1970); children—Willard Dallman Ross, Laurel Alyce Neesan. Author: A Parallel Cut of Air, 1986; ed.: Woman Poet—The West, 1980, Woman Poet—The East, 1982, Woman Poet—The Midwest, 1985, Woman Poet—The South, 1987. BA, Stanford U.; MA, San Francisco State U., 1969; PhD, Southern Illinois U., 1975. Tchr., SIU, Eng. Dept., Carbondale, 1970-74; lectr. U. Nev., Eng. Dept., Reno, 1978; seminar/workshop ldr., Nev. State Arts Council, 1979-82, Poet-in-Res., 1979; fdr. and pres. ARRA Intl., Reno, 1981—; fdr. and pres. Women-in-Literature, Reno, 1978—. Mem. MLA, AAUP, Am. Assoc. of Univ. Women, P&W. Home: Box 60550 Reno NV 89506

DALLOWAY, MARIE, b. Ballston Spa, NY, May 9, 1945; d. Charles Robert and Dorothy Winifred (Wilsey) Shortsleeves. Contrbr. articles to Ariz. Running News, Sportsweek USA, Ariz. Rd. Racers, Women's Sports and Fitness. B.A., Wheaton Coll., 1967; M.S., U. Mass., 1971, Ph.D., 1977. Research dir. Phila Geriatric Ctr., 1977-78, A.R.E. Clinic, Phoenix, 1979-80; co-dir. Wellness Research Assocs., Phoenix, 1980-82; dir. Optimal Performance Inst., Phoenix, 1983—. Mem. Natl. Speakers Assn. Home: 2636 N Dayton St Phoenix AZ 85006

DALRYMPLE, RONALD GERALD, b. Denver, Nov. 24, 1949; s. Claeton Gerald and Norma Ethel (Shaffer) D. Author: Keys to Genius, 1978, Richard the Liar-Hearted, 1979, Mind Wars, 1981, Increase Your Power of Creative Thinking in Eight Days, 1985, The Inner Manager, 1987. B.A., U. Md., 1971; M.A. in Psychology, U. Md., 1982, Ph.D. in Psychology, 1984. Pres. Celestial Gifts Pub., Chester, MD and Estes Park, CO, 1976—; exec. dir. Bay Area Psychological Services, Chester, 1987—. Home: Box 414 RD 1 Box 80F Chester MD 21619

DALRYMPLE, RONALD GERALD, b. Denver, Nov. 24, 1949; s. Claeton Gerald and Norma Ethel (Shafer) D. Author: Keys to Genius, 1978, Richard the Liar-Hearted, 1979, Mind Wars, 1981, Couples Counseling Treatment Program for Alcohol and Drug Referred Clients, 1985, Increase Your Power of Creative Thinking in Eight Days, 1985. MA, U. Md., 1982, PhD (Md. fellow), 1984. Pub. Celestial Gifts Pub. Co., Estes Park, Colo. and Chestertown, Md., 1978—. Bd. dirs., Midshore Council on Family Violence, Denton, Md., 1985. Mem MENSA, Am. Psychol. Assn., Md. Psychol. Assn. Address: Box 414 RD 1 Box 80F Chester MD 21619

DALTON, DOROTHY, b. NYC,Sept. 25, 1915; d. John and Mae (Ferris) Dalton; m. Roy E. Kuehn; children—Christine, Stephanie. Author: Poems, 1967, Midnight and Counting, 1973, The Moon Rides Witness, 1978, Unfinished and Holding, 1984; poetry in Abraxas, Christian Science Monitor, Forum, Poet Lore, River Bottom, Yankee, and many other lit mags and anthols. BSA, U. Wis., Green Bay; postgrad, Columbia U., NYC. Editor, Poetry View/Poetry Scope, 1970-82. Corporal, US Army, 1943-45. Mem. PSA, AAP. Home: 1125 Valley Rd Menasha WI 54952

DALTON, LOUISIANA, b. Dallas, Nov. 24, 1936; divorced; 4 children. Author: (plays) Life's a Gamble, 1986, The Audition 1987. Contrbr. articles to mags. including Southern, others. Ed.: Chin Chat, 1973-74, Bright Ideas, 1976-79, Scoop, 1984-86. Wrkg. on play, article about ancestoral memory. Home: 5406 Hawthorne Pl New Orleans LA 70124

DALY, JANET MORGAN, (Janet F. Morgan), b. White Plains, NY, Jan. 14, 1937; d. William George and Laura Elizabeth (Josten) Russell; m. Hugh Thomas Morgan, Jr., June 27, 1959 (div. Oct. 1976); 1 son, Hugh Thomas Morgan; m. 2d, Alan Frederick Daly, Oct. 4, 1985. Student Wash. Sq. Coll., 1954-55. Assoc. pub. & ed. dir. Earnshaw's Review, Small World mags.; mng. ed. Yes books; editorial prodn. ed. Seventeen Mag.; editorial asst. The Catholic News; contrbg. ed. Baby & Kinder. Sr. ed. Men's Wear magazine, NYC, 1975-79, Chain Store Age, NYC, 1979-80, HFD, NYC, 1980-84; v.p. mktg. Dan River, NYC, 1984-85, Gear, Inc., NYC., 1985; ed. Floor Covering Weekly, NYC, 1985—; instr. Parsons Schl. of Design; home furnishings seminar leader, 1986-87; Natl. Home Fashions League, pres. NY chpt. 1985. Office: Flr Cvrg Wkly 919 3d Ave New York NY 10022

DALY, SARALYN R., b. Huntington, WV, May 11, 1924; d. John Ross and Ruth (Kaufman) Daly. Author: Katherine Mansfield, 1965, reissue update 1979, (verse trans.) Book of True Love (Juan Ruiz), 1978; (novels) In the Web, 1978, Love's Joy, Love's Pain, 1983; fiction in lit mags including Western Humanities Rvw, Beyond Baroque, others. BA, Ohio State U., 1944, MA, 1945, PhD, 1950. Instr. English, Ohio State U., 1947-49; prof., chmn. dept. English, Coll. of Emporia, Kans., 1949-50; prof. English, Midwestern U., Wichita Falls, Tex., 1950-61, Tex. Christian U., Fort Worth, 1961-62, Calif. State U., Los Angeles, 1962—; Fulbright prof. Am. U. Beirut, 1964-65, Tsuda Coll. and Tokyo Gakugei U., 1967-68, U. Bujumbura, Burundi, 1970-71; exchange prof. U. de Aix-en-Provence, France, 1986, Tubingen Universitat-en Provence Tubingen, W.Ger., 1986-87, exchange prof. U. of Ottawa, Ont., Canada, 1987-88. Recipient Henry Morton Landon trans. award AAP, 1980; NEH research fellow, 1980-81. Mem. Med. Acad. Am., MLA. Home: 6211 Gyral Dr Tujunga CA 91042

DAME, EDNA GENEVIEVE OTTO, b. Suttons Bay, MI., Apr. 13, 1906; d. Fredrick William and Martha D. (Mahn) Otto; m. Guyles M. Dame, Sept. 22, 1928. Author: Echoes from the Past (poetry), 1985; contrbr. poetry: Odessa Poetry Rev., A New Day, Whisper of Dreams, Basenji mag., numerous other publs. and anthologies. Wrkg. on poetry. BS, Mich. State Normal Coll., 1925; B. Phys. Edn., Am. Coll. Phys. En., 1939. Tchr. various schs. throughout Mich., 1925-72. Recipient poetry awards. Home: 10885 N Shore Dr Northport MI 49670

D'AMBROSIO, CHARLES A., b. Chgo., Aug. 31, 1932. Author: Bulls, Bears, and Bucks: An Elementary Guide to Personal Investing, 1967, A Guide to Successful Investing, 1970, My Stockbroker is a Bum, 1971, The Portable Investor, 1975, The Portable Financial Manager, 1975, Principles of Modern Investments, 1976, The Theory of Business Finance, 2d edit., 1976, Study Guide to Accompany Principles of Corporate Finance, 1984, Modern Investment Practice, 1985. BS, Loyola U.-Chgo.; PhD, U. Ill. Prof. finance U. Wash., Seattle, 1960—; cons. ed. McGraw-Hill Book Co., NYC, 1970—; ed.-in-chief Fin. Analysts Jnl, NYC, 1982—, CFA Digest; dir., The Research Fdn. of the Inst. of Chartered Financial Analysts. Mem. profl. fin. orgns. Home: 3604 42d Ave NE Seattle WA 98105

D'AMBROSIO, VINNIE-MARIE, b. NYC; d. Melvin Mix and Lucille (De Marco) Aguanno; m. Richard D'Ambrosio (div.); 1 dau., Cynthia. Author: Life of Touching Mouths, 1971; contrbr. to numerous anthologies. BA, Smith College; PhD, New York U. Poet-in-res., San Diego State U., 1981; prof. Brooklyn Coll., City Univ., U. of NY, 1972—. Award: Christopher Morley Award, PSA. Mem. PSA, MLA, AAUW, NCTE, PEN & Brush, Medieval Club of NY. Home: 405 Parkside Ave Brooklyn NY 11226

DAME, ENID, b. Beaver Falls, PA, June 28, 1943; d. Morton Jerome and Bernice (Levenson) Jacobs. Author: (chapbooks) Between Revolutions, 1977, Interesting Times, 1978, Confessions, 1982; (book) On the Road to Damascus, Maryland, 1980; co-editor: Making Contact anthol.,1978, Home Planet News; poetry in N.Y. Qtly, Confrontation, Pivot, 13th Moon, others; story in Confrontation. MA, CCNY, 1973; PhD, Rutgers U., 1983. Tchr. Balt. pub. schls., 1965-67; caseworker N.Y. Dept. Social Services, NYC, 1967-71; instr. Rutgers U., New Brunswick, N.J., 1973—. Mem. Shorefront Peace Com., Bklyn., 1984—. recipient 3 Arts of Homeland award, 3 Arts Club of Homeland, Md., 1963; CAPS award N.Y. State, 1982; Louis Bevier award Rutgers U., 1982. Mem. PSA. Home: 3047 Brighton 1st Place Brooklyn NY 11235

DAMON, CONSTANCE TIFFANY, b. Waynesboro, GA; d. Robert Clyde Manley and Judith (Rittenhouse) Burgess; divorced. Contrbr. articles to newspapers, mags. including Wrtrs. Digest, Army Trainer, Signal Intl. Mag., others. Wrkg. on collection of poems, Songs Without Music, and book, Childfree. B.S. in Edn., Ga. Southern Coll., 1972, M.S. in Sci., 1974. Commissioned lt. U.S. Army, 1984—. Recipient Honor cert. Freedoms Fdn. of Valley Forge, 1985; named Disting. Military Graduate, Ga. Southern Coll., 1982, Stringer of Yr., Info. Systems Command, Ft. Huachuca, AZ, 1986. Mem. Intl. Training Communications (v.p. 1986-87), Armed Forces Communications Electronic Assn. (publicity chmn. 1986-87). Home: 6111 Woodmont Blvd Norcross GA 30092

DAMON, JOHN D(REW), b. Akron, OH, Dec. 25, 1926, s. Howard Burton and Dorothy (Drew) D.; m. Barbara Brunner, Aug. 17, 1963 (div. 1982); children—Karen, Laura, Suzanne, Christine. Ed.: Design for Freedom (by Theodore J. Carlson), 1982; contrbr. to Police Detective, Fawcett Christmas Ideas, Woman's Day Home Modernization Guide, Wrtr.'s Digest. Wrkg. on non-fiction. BA in English Composition, Northwestern U., 1952. Editorial asst. Phila. Inquirer, 1952-53; promotion wrtr. Disston, Phila., 1953-54; energy mktg. ed. Electrical World, NYC,

1958-68; mgr. public relations Edison Electric Inst., NYC, 1968-79, ADT, NYC, 1980-81; freelance wrtr., 1981—. Served with U.S. Army, 1945-46; Japan. Home: 601 Park Ave Huntington NY 11743

DAMON, VALERIE HUBBARD, b. Roswell, NM, Sept. 27, 1945; d. Richard James and Alice Lillard (Dobson) Hubbard; m. David Stanley Damon, Aug. 26, 1969; children: Cara, Brook, Emily. Author: Grindle Lamfoon and the Procurnious Fleekers, 1979, Creative Teacher's Guide to Grindle Lamfoon, 1981, Willo Mancifoot and the Mugga Killa Whomps, 1985, Creative Teacher's Guide to Willo Mancifoot, 1987, The Fire Ferret Town, 1987. BA in Art, Fla. Co. Coll., 1967. Designer, Hallmark Cards, Kansas City, Mo., 1967-73; freelance writer, 1973-76; pub., author, illustrator Star Publs., Kansas City, 1977—. Pan Ednl. Inst. grantee, 1986. Home: Box 22534 Kansas City MO 64113

DANA, JAYNE, see Gassman, Jayne Dana

DANDREA, CARMINE, b. Elmira, NY, July 30, 1929; s. Carmine Salvatore and Mary Elizabeth (DePietto) D.; m. Nancy McMan, Jan. 1, 1976; children—Michael, Karen, Anne, Jane. Author poetry: Heart's Crow, 1972. Contrbr. poems to lit. mags., anthols. Wrkg. on 2 book-length poetry manuscripts: A Journey to India and Am. Still Life. B.A. summa cum laude, Hobart Coll., 1956; M.F.A., Cornell U., 1969. Instr., Lake Mich. Coll., Benton Harbor, 1973-75, assoc. prof., 1975, prof., 1976—. Served to to sgt. U.S. Marine Corps. Recipient Natl. Poetry award N.Y. Poetry Center, 1969. Mem. N.J. Poetry Soc. Home: 153 Windsor Rd Benton Harbor MI 49022

DANIEL, HARDIE WILLIAM, b. Detroit, June 17, 1933; s. George and Mary (Hill) D.; children—Michelle, Adrienne. Author: A Poem in Beauty, 1967, The Love Poet, 1978, Magnificent Poet, 1985. AA in Police Sci., Ohio Christian Coll., 1970; B Indsl. Security, Eastern FLA. U., 1972. With U.S. Post Office, Detroit, 1958-67; mem. security staff Montgomery Ward, Detroit, 1967-68, Highland Park (Mich.) High Schl., 1968-69, St. Joseph Hosp., Detroit, 1969-70; security supr. Sinai Hosp., Detroit, 1971—. Served to lt. USAF, 1952-56. Recipient Popular Songwriting award ASCAP, NYC, 1970, cert. of achievement Music City Song Festival, Nashville, 1982, cert. of merit Am. Song Festival, Hollywood, Calif., 1982, Golden Poet award World of Poetry, Sacramento, 1985. Mem. AAP. Home: 30064 Annapolis Circle Inkster MI 48141

DANIELS, CELIA ANNETTE, b. Oklahoma City, OK, Sept. 8, 1958; d. Stephen and Elizabeth Jean (Badders) D. Contrbr. articles to profl. jnl., lit. mag.; poems to anthols., lit. mags. Ed: Inscape, 1981, 84, Spoken Across a Distance (Cynthia Pederson), 1982, Goat's House (Gene DeGruson), 1986, Kitestrings (Marilee Means), 1987, Electricity (Thomas Reynolds), 1987. B.A., Washburn U., 1981; M.H.A.M.A. in Hist. Administration and Museum Studies, U. Kans., 1987. Research asst., Washburn U., Topeka, KS, 1985-86; public edn. coord. Kans. U. Museum of Anthropology, Lawrence, 1986—. Recipient Carruth Poetry award U. Kans., 1985. Home: 1521 Coll Ave Topeka KS 66604

DANIELS, GEORGE GOETZ, b. Bklyn., Aug. 17, 1925; s. George Bryant and Katherine June (Goetz) D.; m. Doris Alden Billings, Dec. 19, 1965; 1 dau., Katherine Billings; children by previous marriage—Peter, Michael, Robert, Geoffrey. BA cum laude, Harvard U., 1949. Corr., Time mag., Detroit, 1949-50, contbg. editor, 1950-56, assoc. editor, 1956-60, sr. editor, 1960-71; editor Time-Life Records, 1971-73; series editor Time-Life Books, 1973-82, exec. editor, 1982-; dir. Main-Pearl Corp., Buffalo. Served to 1st lt. USAAF, 1943-46. Mem. Am. Ornithologists Union, Am. Birding Assn. (dir.). Home: Pleasant Hill Dr Potomac MD 20854

DANIELS, GLADYS ROBERTA STEINMAN, (Mahala Garrison), b. Grafton, Ill., Oct. 20, 1912; d. Robert Olean and Gladys Mears (Fuller) Steinman; m. Frank Eugene Daniels, July 20, 1971 (dec. 1983). Author: Order and Art in Exact Memory, 1961; contrbr. articles and poetry to numerous publs. AB in English, MacMurray Coll., 1934; MA in English, U. Ill., 1940. Tchr. public schs. various cities in Ill., 1934-54; mem. faculty State Coll., Cape Girardeau, Mo., 1944-46, U. Mo., Columbia, 1946-51, Monticello Coll., Godfrey, Ill., 1954-57; instr., then asst. prof. English So. Ill. U., Edwardsville, 1957-73, emerita assoc. prof., 1983—. Home: 707 N State 2St Jerseyville IL 62052

DANIELS, HOPE MARY, b. Perth Amboy, NJ, Feb. 24, 1947; d. Thaddeus H. Daniels and Virginia Joan (Sotak) Huhndorf; m. Walter A. Sadowski, Apr. 22, 1972 (div. Dec. 23, 1981). BA in Jnlsm., Rutgers, 1970. Feature ed., The News Tribune, Woodbridge, NJ, 1972-78, Phila. Bulletin, 1978-82, Detroit Free Press, 1982, Balt. Sun, 1982-84; ed. Military Lifestyle, Washington, 1984—. Mem. SPJ. Office: Downey Comm 1732 Wisconsin Ave NW Washington DC 20007

DANIELS, JIM, b. Detroit, June 6, 1956. Author: Factory Poems, 1979, On the Line, 1981, Places/Everyone, 1985; contrbr. poetry to Paris, Mich. Quar., Ohio, Agni, Cin. Poetry rvws, New Letters, Carolina Qtly, Tar River Poetry, also numerous other jnls. BA in English and Spanish, Alma Coll., 1978; MFA in Creative Writing, Bowling Green State U., 1980. Asst. prof. English, Carnegie-Mellon U., Pitts., 1981-85, assoc. prof., 1986—. Winner poetry contest Passages North mag., 1983; recipient award for outstanding contrbns. to lit. arts Warren Cultural Commn., Mich., 1983; Brittingham prize for poetry U. Wis. Press, 1985; NEA creative writing fellow, 1985. Office Engl Dept Carnegie-Mellon U Pittsburgh PA 15213

DANIELS, SHOURI, see Ramanujan, Molly

DANIELS WEINERT, PATTI MARIE, (Leslie Young, Patti Daniels W.), b. MI, Apr. 1, 1932; d. Leslie Anson and Betty (Opal) Daniels; married; children—Robert, Gail, Kimberly. Author: (poems) Collections of You and Me. Contrbr. numerous poems to anthols., lit. mags. Student Wrtrs. Digest Schl., 1980. Salesperson, 1987—; free-lance wrtr., 1980—. Recipient K. Mendoza award Sounds of Poetry, 1986, Golden Award, World of Poetry, 1986-87. Home: 3701 Schlee St Lansing MI 48910

DANKY, JAMES PHILIP, b. Los Angeles, Oct. 3, 1947; s. Philip Harper and Elizabeth (James) D.; m. Christine I. Schelshorn, Aug. 23, 1980; 1 son, Matthew Philip. Author: Undergrounds, 1974, Women's History, 1975, Genealogical Research, 1979, Black Newspapers and Periodicals, 1979, Hispanic Americans in the United States, 1979, Asian American Periodicals and Newspapers, 1979, Women's Periodicals and Newspapers, 1982, Alternative Materials in Libraries, 1982, Alternative Library Literature, 1982, 2d ed., 1984, Native American Press in Wisconsin and the Nation, 1983, Native American Periodicals and Newspapers, 1984. Wrkg. on right-wing press and German-Am. labor press in Am. AB, Ripon Coll., 1970, MA in Library Sci., U. Wis.-Madison, 1973. Order librarian State Hist. Soc. of Wis., Madison, 1973-76, librarian newspapers and periodicals, 1976—. Treas., Cooksville Community Ctr., Wis., 1980—. Home: 261 Hwy 138 S Stoughton WI 53589

DANN, JACK M., b. Johnson City, NY, Feb. 15, 1945, s. Murray I. and Edith (Nash) D.; m. Jeanne Helen Van Buren, Jan. 1, 1983; stepson, Jody Scobie. Author: Starhiker (novel), 1977, Christs and Other Poems, 1978, Timetipping (short stories), 1980, Junction (novel), 1981, The Man Who Melted (novel), 1984; ed.: Wandering Stars of Jewish Fantasy and Science Fiction, 1974, Faster Than Light (with George Zebrowski), 1976, Future Power (with Gardner Dozois), 1976, Immortal, 1978, Aliens! (with Dozois), 1980, More Wandering Stars, 1981, Unicorns! (with Dozois), 1982, Magicats! (with Dozois), 1982, Bestiary! (with Dozois), 1985, Mermaids! (with Dozois), 1986, Sorcerers! (with Dozois), 1986, In the Field of Fire (with Jeanne Van Buren Dann), 1987, Damons! (with Dozois), 1987. BA, SUNY-Binghamton, 1968, postgrad., 1971—; postgrad. St. John's Law Schl., 1969-70. Instr. writing and sci. fiction, Broome Community Coll., Binghamton, 1972, 74; asst. prof. Cornell U., Ithaca, N.Y., 1973; lectr. Sci. Fiction Wrtrs. Speakers Bur., 1971—. Mem. SFWA, World Future Soc. Home: 825 Front St Binghamton NY 13905

DANNA, CARL, b. Bklyn., Feb. 25, 1930, s. Dominick and Lucy (Macaluso) D.; m. Mary T. Eigner, Aug. 24, 1957 (div. 1974); children—Stephen, Susan, Janice, Laura, Peter, Kristen. Author: Scholastic Teacher, 1962; ed.: Long Island Union teacher, 1965, It's Never Too Late to Start Over, 1984, How to Win the Job Interview Game, 1985. BA in English, Bklyn. Coll., 1956; MLS, Palmer Grad. Library Schl., Greenvale, N.Y., 1968. Tchr., Hicksville (N.Y.) High Schl., 1958-70, media specialist, 1970—; ed. Palomino Press, NYC, 1984—. Served with U.S. Army, 1948-49. Grantee Fed. Govt. Inst., 1978. Mem. NWU. Home: 230 Marcellus Rd Mineola NY 11501

DANNENMANN, OTTO KARL, b. Kornwestheim, Germany, Mar. 11, 1915, came to U.S., 1949, s. Georg and Margarete (Sachs) D.; m. Erika Julchen Busch, July 1, 1939, 1 dau., Jutta Margarete. Contrbr. poetry to Milw. Deutsche Zeitung, Fennimore Times, Boscobel Dial, N.Am. Mentor. Wrkg. on autobiography. Ed. Germany. Chef Gimbels, Milw., 1950-79, ret. Served to sgt. maj. German Army, 1932-45. Home: 1685 Madison St Apt 8 Fennimore WI 53809

DANTE, ROBERT DAVID, b. Lytham-St. Annes, England, Feb. 12, 1953; arrd. U.S., 1966; m. Wendy Aldwyn. Contbr. articles to Houston Art Scene, In Art Mag; poetry in Haiku Mag., Port of Galveston Mag., En Passant, Intoxicated Typewriter, Seven Stars, Travois, Shadwell Sampler, other lit mags. Student U. Houston. Co-ed., Wings Press, Houston, 1976-78; apprentice to Allen Ginsberg, Naropa Inst., 1978; regional coordinator Poetry on the Buses, Houston, 1980; ed. Horizons Mag., 1984-85; series coordinator Writers in Performance, 1985-86. Mem. Mensa, Motion Picture Council of Houston,NWU. Address: Box 66341 Houston TX 77266

DANTES, EDMUND, see Welsh, William Francis Anthony

DANTO, ARTHUR COLEMAN, b. Ann Arbor, MI, Jan. 1, 1924; s. Samuel Budd and Sylvia (Gittleman) D.; m. Shirley Rovetch, Aug. 9, 1946 (dec. July 1978); children—Elizabeth, Jane; m. Barbara Westman, Feb. 15, 1980. Author: Analytical Philosophy of Knowledge, 1968, What Philosophy Is, 1968, Analytical Philosophy of History, 1965, Nietzsche as Philosopher, 1965, Analytical Philosophy of Action, 1973, Mysticism and Morality, 1972, Jean-Paul Sartre, 1975, The Transfiguration of the Commonplace, 1981, (Lionel Trilling Book prize 1982), Narration and Knowledge, 1985, The Philosophical Disenfranchisement of Art, 1986, The State of the Art, 1987; editor: Jnl Philosophy, 1965—; art critic, The Nation, 1984—. BA, Wayne State U., 1948; MA, Columbia U., 1949, PhD, 1952; postgrad., U. Paris, 1949-50. Instr. U. Colo, 1950-51; mem. faculty Columbia U., 1952—, Johnsonian prof. philosophy, chmn. dept., 1979—, co-dir. Center for Study of Human Rights, 1978—. Bd. dirs. Amnesty Intl. 1970-75, genl. secy. 1973, natl. adv. council, 1975—. Served with AUS, 1942-45. Fulbright fellow, 1949, Guggenheim fellow, 1969, 82; ACLS fellow, 1961, 70; Fulbright Disting. prof., Yugoslavia, 1976; George Polk Meml. Award for Criticism, 1985. Fellow Am. Acad. Arts and Sci.; mem. Am. Philo. Assn. (v.p. 1969, pres. 1983). Office: 710 Philosophy Hall Columbia New York NY 10027

DANTON, REBECCA, see Roberts, Janet

DARACK, ARTHUR J., b. Royal Oak, MI, Jan. 1, 1918; s. Edward Charles and Sonia (Resnikov) D.; m. Jean Claire Puttmyer, May 28, 1942; children—Glenn Arthur, Brenda Lee. Author: Outdoor Power Equipment, 1977, Consumers Digest Automobile Repair Book, 1979; co-author: The Great Eating, Great Dieting Cookbook, 1978, Playboy's Book of Sports Car Repair, 1980; author: syndicated column Buy Right, 1977-81; contrbg. editor, columnist: The Money Letter, 1979—. MusM, Cin. Conservatory, 1949; PhD, Ind. U., 1951. Mus. editor Cin. Enquirer, 1951-61, feature writer, columnist, 1961-62, book and art editor, 1962-63; editor Dimension, Cin. monthly mag., 1963-65; assoc. editor Encyc. Brit., Chgo., 1967-70; sr. editor Actual Specifying Engr. (monthly mag.) 1971—; editor Consumers Digest mag., 1972-78; pres. Consumer Group Inc., 1978—. Program annotator Cin. Symphony Orch., 1952-61; adj. asso. prof. music Coll. Music, U. Cin. Served with AUS, 1941-45. Mem. Pi Kappa Lambda. Home: 9018 Sleeping Bear Rd Skokie IL 60076

DAREFF, HAL, b. Bklyn., May 8, 1920; s. Barnett and Bessie (Littman) D.; m. Gladys Wilkowitz, Sept. 12, 1944; children—Scott, Brooks. Author: The First Microscope, 1962, Man in Orbit, 1962, Jacqueline Kennedy: A Portrait in Courage, 1965, Fun with ABC and 1-2-3, 1965, The Story of Vietnam, 1966, From Vietnam to Cambodia, 1971. Ed., New Schl. Social Research, NYC, Washington and Lee U. Freelance writer and editor, 1946-52; editor Children's Digest of Parents' Inst. and Better Reading Fdn., 1952-67; genl. editor Dell Seal books, Dell Pub. Co., 1963-65; also editorial cons. pub. co.; contrbg. ed. Parents' mag., 1965-66; editor-in-chief juvenile and young adult books Grosset and Dunlap, NYC, 1967-69; v.p. pub. Greenwood Press, Inc.; also affiliate Negro Univs. Press, Westport, Conn., 1969-70; pub. cons. New American Library, Inc., 1970—; pres., pub. Hyperion Press, Inc., 1972—; pub. cons., 1983—. Served with AUS, 1941-45. Mem. AG, Artists and Writers Assn., AL Am. Home: RFD Box 4186 Beaucaire Ave Camden ME 04843

D'ARGNAC, JESSE, see Harsen, Edward Charles

DARLING, WILLIAM RITCHIE, (Eric Cashen), b. Washington, May 6, 1933, s. Henry Maurice and Frances (Clarke) D.; m. Susan Solomont, Dec. 24, 1954; children—Sarah Christie, Kate Elizabeth. Contrbr. to numerous mags. including December, Trace, Neon, Black Mountain Rvw, others. BA, Goddard Coll., 1958, Windham Coll., 1963; MA, Johns Hopkins U., 1959. Mem. faculty Worcester (Mass.) Jr. Coll., 1960-61, Dartmouth Coll., Hanover, N.H., 1963-65, U. Mass., Amherst, 1968-69, Franklin Pierce Coll., Rindge, N.H., 1969—; co-coordinator New Eng. Small Press Assn., 1969-80; ed., pub. Green Knight Press, Rat & Mole Press, No. New Eng. Rvw. Press; pub. No. New Eng. Rvw, 1973—. Home: 45 Hillcrest Pl Amherst MA 01002

D'ARPINO, TONY, b. Mt. Holly, NJ, Sept. 20, 1951; s. Anthony Bernard and Ann (Feeney) D'A.; m. Paula von Loewenfeldt, Mar. 20, 1985; children: Gwen, Deva, Ian. Author: (poetry) The Tree Worshipper, 1983; ed. Two/Poetry, 1976; Phosphenes, video mag., 1977-78; SOON 3: Renaissance Radar, 1981. Student Burlington Community Coll., Pemberton, N.J., 1969-70, Rutgers U., 1970-71. Freelance wrtr., Phila., 1973-75, San Francisco, 1986—; account exec. San Francisco Rvw of Books, 1975-78, advt. dir., 1983-84; adminstrv. dir. SOON 3 Theatre, San Francisco, 1978-83; ed. Western Pub., San Francisco, 1984-86; ed. San Francisco Rvw of Books, 1986—. Mem. NWU, Media Alliance. Home: Box 591012 Golden Gate Sta San Francisco CA 94159

DARR, ANN RUSSELL, (Ann Darr), b. Bagley, IA, March 3, 1920; d. Henry Horton and Lessle Rebecca (Hooper) Russell; m. George C. Darr, 1941 (div. 1981); children—Elizabeth, Deborah, Shannon. Author: St. Ann's Gut, 1971, The Myth of a Woman's Fist, 1973, Cleared for a Landing, 1978, Riding with the Fireworks, 1981, Do You Take This Woman, 1986. Contrbr. poetry to Paris Rvw, New Republic, Western Hum. Rvw, Hollins Critic, other lit mags, and 22 anthols. BA, State U. of Ia., 1941. Writer/perf., NBC, NYC, 1941-43; wrtr./perf., ABC, NYC, 1946; poet-in-the-classroom, MD, VA, DC pub. schools, 1974-79; poet-in-res. with Am. Wind Symphony Orch. on Rivers of Eastern U.S. and Jamaica, 1976-84; adj. prof., American U., Wash. DC, 1982-88; instr., The Writer's Center, Bethesda, MD, 1981-88. Pilot U.S. Army Airforce, 1943-44. Awards: NEA Fellowship, 1976; Discovery Award, 1970, NY Poetry Ctr; Bunting Fellowship, Radcliffe, 1979-80, fellowships Yaddo and MacDowell, 1979. Mem. PSA, AAP, AWP, Phi Beta Kappa. Home: 4902 Falstone Ave Chevy Chase MD 20815

DARROW, TERRI LYNN, b. Ft. Sill, OK, Mar. 3, 1955; d. Jackie G. and Bette Lou (Wilmoth) Brooks; divorced; 1 son, Jason Dewane. Contrbr. articles to mags., newpapers including Okla. Home & Garden, Dramatics Mag., Ford Times, others. Wrkg. on articles and books on arthritis in young women, travel, golf courses in Okla. Student Central State U., (year attended?) 1982-85. Reporter, photographer Mustang Enterprise, OK, 1982-84; publicity dir. Lyric Theatre of Okla., Oklahoma City, 1984; with T. L. Darrow & Assoc., Yukon, OK, 1981—, free-lane wrtr., publicist, photographer, 1973—. Mem. WIC, NWC, Intl. Wrts. Databank, SPJ. Home: 4717 Sky Trail Yukon OK 73099

DASSANOWSKY-HARRIS, ROBERT, (Robert Harris), b. NYC, Jan. 28, 1956; s. Baron Leslie Harris de Erendred and Baroness Elfriede Maria (von Dassanowsky). Author: Telegrams from the Metropole, 1987; ed Politicus Jnl, 1984-85; ed. Rohwedder Intl. Arts Qtly, 1986—, New German Rvw, 1987—; Contrbr. articles to E. European Qtly. Criticon (W.Ger.), Germanic Notes; contrbr poetry to Poetry/LA, The LA Weekly, Dreamworks, Rohwedder, Crosscurrents, Mod. Poetry Studies, Gryphon, Osiris, Cottonwood, Wind Jnl, S. Fla. Rvw, Calif Qtly, other lit mags, art jnls. Grad., Am. Acad. Dramatic Arts, 1977; BA in Poli. Sci. and Ger. Lit., UCLA, 1985; MA, UCLA, 1987. Actor/dir., LA/NYC, 1977—; co. dir. Theatrical Prdn. Co., Los Angeles, 1981—; freelance playwright, poet, writer, Los Angeles, 1980—. Mem Ger.-Am. Congress, Ill, 1983—, Paneuropa Union, W. Ger./Austria, 1980—; bd. advs., Comm. Art for Olympia, NY, 1984—Recipient outstanding scholar award, UCLA Alumni Assn., 1984-85, playwright award, Beverly Hills Theatre Guild, Calif, 1984. Mem. DG., Screen Actors Guild, P&W, Heinrich von Kleist Gesellschaft, W. Ger., Goethe Soc. of North Am. Address: 4346 Matilija Ave 27 Sherman Oaks CA 91423

DAUNT, JON, b. Columbus, OH, March 1, 1951; s. John G. and Mary (Powell) D.; m. Ruth Harzula Dec. 16, 1979. Contrbr. poetry (and fiction and criticism) to Folio Intl. (England), Mississippi Rvw, Prairie Schooner, Coydog Rvw, Malahat Rvw, Denver Qtly, Crawlspace, other lit mags. BA, Stanford Univ., 1973; MA, Univ. of Calif., Davis, 1983. Foreman, Soho, Inc. (Boston), 1974-78. Celeste Turner Wright Poetry Award, AAP, 1984; Black Bear Poetry Prize, 1985; Wildwood Prize in Poetry, 1985; Alice Sherry Meme. Prize for Humorous Poem, 1985. Mem. PSA, Natl. Audubon Society. Home: 609 D St Davis CA 95616

DAVENPORT, GUY MATTISON, b. Anderson, SC., Nov. 23, 1927; s. Guy Mattison and Leila Marie (Fant) D. Author: The Intelligence of Louis Agassiz, 1963, Flowers and Leaves, 1964, Carmina Archilochi, 1964, Sappho: Songs & Fragments, 1965, The Iliad, A Guide, 1967, The Odyssey: A Guide, 1967, Tatlin!, 1974, Da Vinci's Bicycle, 1976, Eclogues, 1981, The Geography of the Imagination, 1981, Trois Caprices, 1982, Herakleitos and Diogenes, 1982, The Resurrection in Cookham Churchyard, 1982, Archilochos, Sappho, Alkman, 1984, Apples and Pears, 1984, The Mimes of Heronda, 1984, Cities on Hills: Pound's Cantos I-XXX, 1984, The Bowmen of Shu, 1985, The Bicycle Rider, 1985, The Medusa, 1985, Maxims of the Ancient Egyptians, 1985, Thasos and Ohio, 1986, Jonan, 1986, August, 1986, Every Force Evolves a Form, 1987, The Jules Verne Steam Balloon, 1987.BA, Duke U., 1950, BLitt, Oxford, 1952, PhD,Harvard, 1961. Instr. Washington Univ., St. Louis, 1952-55; asst. prof. Haverford Coll., Pa., 1961-63; prof. Univ. Ky., Lexington, 1964—. Rhodes schol., 1948; Recipient Blumenthal prize Poetry Mag., 1976, Zabel prize for fiction, Am. Acad. Arts and Scis., 1981. Address: 621 Sayre Ave Lexington KY 40508

DAVENPORT, GWEN, (Mrs. John Davenport), b. Colon, C.Z., Oct. 3, 1910; d. James Farquharson and Gwen (Wigley) Leys; m. John Davenport, Feb. 5, 1937; children—Christopher, John Farquharson, Juliet Rathbone (Mrs.

Bertrand Gilbert). Author: A Stranger and Afraid, 1943, Return Engagement, 1945, Belvedere, 1947; motion picture prodn. Sitting Pretty, 1947, Family Fortunes, 1949, Candy for Breakfast, 1950, The Bachelor's Baby, 1957, The Wax Foundation, 1961, Great Loves in Legend and Life, 1964; contrbr. short stories to natl. mags. AB, Vassar Coll., 1931. Home: 308 Penruth Place Louisville KY 40207

DAVENPORT, KAREN ODOM, b. Chgo., Apr. 3, 1953, d. Emwood Earl Odom and Ruth (Price) Wooldridge; m. Randall Louis Davenport, June 19, 1978 (div. 1980); 1 child, Dedan. Contrbr. to Essence, Chgo. Sun-Times, Chgo. Tribune, Black Enterprise, Ebony Jr! Wrkg. on children's book, mag. articles. BA, Brown U., 1973; MS in Journalism, Northwestern U., 1974. Mng. ed. Ebony Jr!, Chgo., 1976-77; cons., wrtr. Chgo. Bd. Edn., 1978-80; ed., wrtr. James H Lowry & Assocs., Chgo., 1980-81; assoc. ed. IBM, White Plains, N.Y., 1981-83, ed. HQ mag., 1983-84, trade press ed., 1984—. Home: 111 E Hartsdale Ave 4D Hartsdale NY 10530

DAVID, BRUCE EDWARD, b. El Paso, TX, Jan. 18, 1952; s. Raymond and Joyce (Albright) D. Author: A Shoestring Approach to Profitable Advertising, 1982, Shortcuts to AAA Credit—Even after Bankruptcy, 1984, Successful Self-Publishing on a Shoestring, 1985; contrbr. articles to In-Business, Sideline Business, Video Times, Marketing Today, New Clevel. Woman, Crain's Cleve. News, BookDealers World,, others. Student Kent State U., 1972-74, Ariz. State U., 1974-75. Account exec. Cox Syndicate, Tempe, Ariz., 1974-76, ComCorp., Cleve., 1979-82; Midwest advt. mgr. Harcourt Brace Jovanovich, Cleve., 1982-85; pub. Worthprinting Ltd., Twinsburg, Ohio, 1985—; Akron Business Rptr. Mem. Am. Book Dealers Assn. Home: 1791-D Rolling Hills Dr Twinsburg OH 44087

DAVID, MARTIN A., b. Bklyn., Feb. 28, 1939; s. Jacob Carl and Judith (Greenstein) Rosen. Author: The Dancer's Audition Book, 1983; dance critic Hollywood Drama-Logue, 1978-86; ed.-in-chief Dance West Mag., 1979-81; contrbr. to Los Angeles Times, Calif. Mag.; ed., Dance Teacher Now, 1986—; author stage and radio plays. Wrkg. on book on prevention and treatment of dance injuries. BA in Theatre Arts, Bklyn. Coll., 1961. Freelance wrtr., artist, performer, 1964—; mem. artistic adv. panel Los Angeles Area Dance Alliance, 1980-85; panelist Calif. Arts Council, Sacramento, 1981—. Mem. Soc. Dance History Scholars, 1987,Bay Area Media Alliance. Recipient Dance Critics fellowship Am. Dance Festival, Durham, N.C., 1981, Dance Recognition award Dance In Action, So. Calif., 1986. Home: 2402 24th St San Francisco CA 94110

DAVIDSON, CHALMERS GASTON, b. Chester, SC, June 6, 1907; s. Zeb Vance and Kate (Gaston) D.; m. Alice Graham Gage, Mar. 20, 1937; children—Robert Gage, Alice-Davidson Sims, Mary Davidson Pennington. Author various works, 1949—, latest being The Generations of Davidson College, 1955, 64, 72, 80, The Last Foray, the SC Planters of 1860, 1971, The Plantation World Around Davidson, 1969, 73, 82. AB summa cum laude, Davidson (NC) College, 1928; MA, U. Chgo., 1936; PhD, Harvard U., 1942. Instr., Chamberlain-Hunt Military Acad., Port Bigson, MS, 1928-29, Blue Ridge School for Boys, Hendersonville, NC, 1933-34, The Citadel Military College of SC, Charleston, 1934-45; history prof., library dir. Davidson College, 1936-76, prof. emeritus, archivist, 1936—. Served in USN, 1944-46. Charles A. Cannon award for contributions to NC history, 1951, NC Soc. of County & Local Historians Award of Merit, 1971, SC Daughters of Colonial Wars Tchr. of the Year, 1972. Mem: NC Writers Conference, NC Literary & Hist. Assn. Home: Beaver Dam Concord Rd Davidson NC 28036

DAVIDSON, ROBERT LEE III, b. Nevada, MO, May 10, 1923, s. Robert Lee Jr. and Nancy Helen (Manker) D.; m. Lorena Elizabeth Turner, June 13, 1950; children—Roberta Anne, Curtis Lee. Author: Successful Process Plant Practices, 1958, Manual for Process Engineering Calculations (with others), 1962, Petroleum Processing Handbook (with others), 1966, Business Week's 1972 Report on Business and the environment (with others), 1972, Handbook of Water-Soluble Gums & Resins, 1980; assoc. ed. Petroleum Processing mag., 1954-57; sr. ed. Petroleum Week mag., 1957-59; ed.-in-chief Petro/Chem Engineer mag., 1964-66; mng. ed. Chem. Engring. mag., 1966-75; ed.-in-chief Business Books, McGraw-Hill Book Co., 1975-80; dir. Book Pub. Ctr., McGraw-Hill Pub. Co., 1980-82; communications cons. and ed., 1982—. BS, U. Mo., 1944, MS, 1947; JD, Fordham U., 1978. With McGraw-Hill Pub. Co., NYC, 1966-82; sole practice law, Princeton, N.J., 1981—; freelance sci. and tech. wrtr., ed., Princeton, 1982—. Served to 1st lt. U.S. Army, 1942-46. Address: 45 Patton Ave Princeton NJ 08540

DAVIES, ROBERT ALLAN, b. Cambridge, MA, Oct. 15, 1928; s. Frank and Theresa (Spitzer) D.; m. Jane Haas, June 18, 1959; children: Alexey J., Katherine A. Author: Love in Four Keys, 1955, Timber, 1979, Timber 1st addition, 1982; co-editor: Where Did I Wake Up (Stanislaw Baranczak), 1978, Peckerneck Country (Walt Curtis), 1978, Under My Own Roof (Baranczak), 1980, Only the Birds Protest (Mario Azzopardi), 1980, Citizen R.K. Does Not Live (Ryszard Krynicki), 1985, Columbus Names the Flowers (Mr. Cogito anthology), 1985; co-editor Mr. Cogito mag., 1973—. AB, U. Mass., 1952; MA, U. Mich., 1953. English master Cardigan Mt. Schl., Canaan, N.H., 1953-54, Kimball Union Acad., Meredin, N.H., 1954-55; instr. U. Idaho, Moscow, 1955-58, S.D. State Coll., Brookings, 1958-59; prof. Pacific U., Forest Grove, Oreg., 1959—. Served as pvt. U.S. Army, 1946-47, ETO. Home: 2417 18th Ave Forest Grove OR 97116

DAVIS, A. JANN, b. Shattuck, OK, Sept. 1, 1941, d. William I. and Mildred A. (Shaw) Fletcher; m. Charles D. Davis, Dec. 27, 1961; children—Kristen M., Charles W. Author: Please See my Need, 1981, Listening and Responding, 1982; contrbr. numerous articles to nursing and med. publs. Diploma, Wesley Med. Center, 1962; MA, U. No. Iowa, 1979. Nurse, educator, 1962—; owner, dir. Satellite C.E., Inc., Charles City, Iowa, 1979—; columnist Am. Jnl Nursing, 1983-85; presenter workshops, seminars. Mem. profl. orgns. Home: 706 2d Ave Charles City IA 50616

DAVIS, ALLEN, III, b. Cin., Mar. 9, 1929, s. Allen and Rose (Gershon) D., Jr. Author: (children's plays) Rocco, The Rolling Stone, Leroy and the Ark, 1967; produced plays The Head of Hair, 1968-70, The Rag Doll, 1970-74, Where the Green Bananas Grow, 1972, Bull Fight Cow, 1976, Montezuma's Revenge, 1979. Wrkg. on two new plays. BA, Syracuse U., 1950; MFA, Yale U. Drama Schl., 1956. Gen. mgr. Santa Fe Theatre Co., 1967-68; wrtr.-in- residence U. Alaska, Anchorage, 1975; adminstr. P.R. Traveling Theatre, NYC, 1970-74, 76-78, dir. playwright's workshop, 1980-86. Winner playwright contest Milw. Repertory Theatre, 1968; CAPS grantee N.Y. State Council on Arts, 1980; NEA playwright grantee, 1978. Mem. Lit. Mgrs. and Dramaturgs Am., DG, Actors Equity Assn., New Dramatists (1968-78). Home: 484 W 43d St 20-F Nnew York NY 10036

DAVIS, ANN-MARIE, b. Pasadena, CA, Oct. 9, 1951, d. John Benadict and Catherine Ann (McGee) Kiernan; m. Robert Albert Davis, Sept. 14, 1974; children—Patrick, Brendan. Contrbr. short stories to Sequoya Rvw, Louisville Rvw, Passages North, Home Words: A Book of Tennessee Writers. BA, Sacramento State Coll., 1977; postgrad. in writing Vt. Coll. Tchr. St. Judes Schl., Hixon, Tenn., 1978-70, Dade County Schl. System, Lookout Mountain, Ga., 1980-81. Recipient 1st prize for fiction Tenn. Wrtrs. Guild, 1984, 3d prize for short short fiction AWP, 1985. Home: 212 N Hermitage Ave Lookout Mountain TN 37350

DAVIS, EDWARD JOSEPH JR., b. Detroit, Feb. 10, 1930; s. Edward Joseph and Agnes Hildagarde (Leary) D.; m. Wilda Yvonne Bazinet, July 17, 1951; children—Cynthia Ann, Sharon Elizabeth, Edward Joseph III. BS, R.I. Coll., 1978. Owner, operator Davis Press, Tiverton, R.I., 1954-71; ed., pub. Stamp Bus. Mag., 1965-73, Basic Stamp Dealing, 1966, Essentials of Stamp Investment, 1967, How to Start your Own Local Post, 1985; graphics art instr. R.I. Dept. Edn., 1971-73; tchr. Fall River (Mass.) Schl. Dept., 1973—. Served as sgt. U.S. Army, 1950-53; Korea. Wrkg. on philatelic column for Providence Jnl. Bulltn. Home: 847 Old Main Rd Tiverton RI 02878

DAVIS, CHRISTOPHER, b. Phila., Oct. 23, 1928, s. Edward and Josephine (Blitzstein) D.; m. Sonia Fogg, June 6, 1953; children—Kirby G., Katherine H., Emily F., Sarah B. Author: (novels) Lost Summer, 1958, First Family, 1959, A Kind of Darkness, 1962, Bellmarch, 1964, The Shamir of Dachau, 1966, Ishmael, 1967, 69, A Peep Into the 20th Century, 1971, The Sun in Mid-Career, 1975, Suicide Note, 1977; The Producer (nonfiction), 1972, Waiting for It (nonfiction), 1980; Sad Adam-Glad Adam (children's book), 1966, A Peep into the 20th Century (play). BA, U. Pa., 1955. Lectr. creative writing Bryn Mawr (Pa.) Coll., 1976—. Grantee NEA, 1967-68, 74, Guggenheim Fdn., 1972-73, Pa. Council on Arts, 1983; Yaddo fellow, 1978, 79, 81, 86. Mem. AG, DG, PEN. Address: Curtis Brown 575 Madison Ave New York NY 10022

DAVIS, GREGORY TODD, b. Keesler, MS, July 3, 1959; s. James W. and Judith M. (Less) D.; m. Gayle A. Musolf, July 14, 1979; children, Erin B., Justin L. Contrbr. articles to bulltn. B.A. in English, U. Mich., 1981. Reporter, The Mich. Daily, Ann Arbor, 1976-77; reporter, photographer Winkler County News, Kermit, TX, 1981-83; ed. Rumford Falls Times, ME, 1983—. Recipient Jr. Best of Show award Tawas Bay Art Show, MI, 1975; 2d place for photo Oct. Affair Arts, Kermit, 1981; 1st place for feature series Maine Press Assn., 1984, Honorable Mention for feature, 1984. Mem. New England Press Assn. Home: Ridge Rd West Peru ME 04290

DAVIS, HOPE HALE, (Hope Hale), b. Columbus Junction, IA, Nov. 2, 1903; d. Hal and Frances (MacFarland) Hale; m. Claud Cockburn, Feb. 18, 1932 (div. 1934); 1 dau., Claudia Flanders; m. 2d, Robert Gorham Davis, Sept, 3, 1939; children—Stephen Hale, Lydia Brooks. Author: The Dark Way to the Plaza, 1968. Contrbr. stories, rvws., articles to mags, including New Yorker, Saturday Rvw., The New Leader. Editor: Consumers Guide, 1933-37. Mary Ingraham Bunting fellow, Radcliffe Coll.; vis. scholar, Radcliffe, 1984-85, mem. faculty, Seminars, 1985-86, 86-87, 87-88.Mem. PEN, Natl. Book Critics Circle. Home: 1600 Mass. Ave 704 Cambridge MA 02138

DAVIS, IRVIN, b. St. Louis, Dec. 18, 1926; s. Julius and Anna (Rosen) D.; m. Adrienne Bronstein, Apr. 25, 1968; 1 dau., Jennifer Alison. Works include: Richman, Poorman, Room for Three, Compreh. Study for The Field of Advt. & Pub. Relns., Today's Manager, Use It In Good Health, Charlie, Family Album. BSBA, Washington U., 1950; MBA, St. Louis U., 1955; PhD (hon.), National Coll., Evanston, IL, 1983. Pres. Clayton-Davis & Assocs., Inc., St. Louis, MO, 1953—. Served US Army Air Force. Recipient numerous awards, incl. Freedoms Fdn. Award, Valley Forge, 1975, Emmy Award, NATAS, 1980, 81. Trustee, NATAS; mem. PRSA, Intl. Soc. of PR Cslrs., AMWA. Office: 8229 Maryland Ave St Louis MO 63105

DAVIS, J(AMES) MADISON (JR.), b. Charlottesville, VA, Feb. 10, 1951, s. James Madison Davis and Alma Lucille (Tate) Blue; m. Simonne Evelyn Eck, May 22, 1977; children—James Madison III, Jonathan Tyler. Author: Critical Essays on Edward Albee, 1986, Stanislaw Lem, 1987, Blackletter, 1986; contrbr. fiction to Miss. Rvw, Pulpsmith, Swallow's Tale, other lit mags; contrbr. non-fiction to Miss. Folklore Register, New Orleans Rvw, Shakespeare Qtly, others; co-ed.: Intro 14. MA, Johns Hopkins U., 1975; PhD, U. So. Miss., 1979. Instr. Allegany Community Coll., Cumberland, Md., 1975-77, U. So. Miss., Hattiesburg, 1977-79; asst. prof. Pa. State U., Erie, 1979-84, assoc. prof., 1984—; bus. mgr. Studies in Am. Drama, Erie, 1985—. Va. Center Creative Arts fellow, 1974, 81, Ragdale Fdn. fellow, 1982, Pa. Council of Arts fellow, 1984. Mem. P&W, AWP, Miss. Philol. Assn. Office: Behrend Coll Pa St U Erie PA 16428

DAVIS, JAMES PAXTON, b. Winston-Salem, NC, May 7, 1925; s. James Paxton and Emily (McDowell) D.; m. Wylma Elizabeth Pooser, June 6, 1951 (div. 1971); children—Elizabeth Keith, Anne Beckley, James Paxton III; m. Peggy Painter Camper, July 21, 1973. Author: Two Soldiers, 1956, The Battle of New Market, 1963, One of the Dark Places, 1965, The Seasons of Heroes, 1967, A Flag at the Pole, 1976, Ned, 1978, Three Days, 1980. Student, Va. Mil. Inst., 1942-43; AB, Johns Hopkins, 1949. Reporter Winston-Salem Jnl., 1949-51, Richmond (Va.) Times-Dispatch, 1951-52, Twin City Sentinel, Winston-Salem, 1952-53; faculty Washington and Lee U., 1953-76, prof. journalism, 1963-76, chmn. dept., 1968-74; vis. scholar Cambridge U., 1973. Book editor: Roanoke (Va.) Times & World News, 1961-81; contrbg. editorial columnist, 1976—. Served with AUS, 1943-46, CBI. Mem. Phi Beta Kappa, Omicron Delta Kappa. Home: Box 33 Fincastle VA 24090

DAVIS, JON EDWARD, b. New Haven, CT, Oct. 28, 1952, s. Harris Everett Davis and Joan Elizabeth (Carney) Somers; m. Terry Lynne Layton, Jan. 8, 1978. Author: West of New England, 1983, Dangerous Amusements, 1986; contrbr. to: Poetry, Georgia Rvw, Tendril, other lit mags; contrbr. to anthologies: Anthology of Mag. Verse and Yearbook of Am. Poetry, 1985, Crossing the River: New Poets of the American West, 1986, Snow Summits in the Sun, 1986. BA in English, U. Mont., 1984, MFA in Creative Writing, 1985. Editor CutBank, Missoula, Mont., 1982-85. Winner Conn. Poetry Circuit, 1980; recipient Merriam Frontier award, U. Mont., 1982, AAP prize, 1983, 85; NEA wrtrs. fellow, 1986, Fine Arts Work Ctr. fellow, 1986-87. Mem. AWP, P&W. Home: 824 Glen Rd Orange CT 06477

DAVIS, KEVIN ADAM, b. Evanston, IL, Sept. 24, 1962; s. Marc I. and Judy L. (Axelrod) D. Contrbr. wrtr. to Dallas Morning News, Chgo. Tribune. Wrkg. on short stories. BS, U. IL, 1985. Reporter, intern, Dallas Morning News, 1984, Ft. Lauderdale News & Sun-Sentinel, 1985—. 3rd place AP Award, IL, 1983, 8th place William Randolph Hearst Award, 1984, 1st place Robert F. Kennedy Journalism Award, student, Washington, DC, 1985. Mem: Sigma Delta Chi, Kappa Tau Alpha. Home: 1204 NE 13th Ave Fort Lauderdale FL 33304

DAVIS, KEVIN R., b. Milw., Jan. 9, 1945, s. Emmett Mathew and Mary Ruth (McCarten) D.; m. Karen Susanne Veley, Nov. 9, 1963 (div. 1979); children—Christopher, Cameron. Author screenplays: The Jail, 1969, The Hoax, 1970, The Heirhunters, 1971, The Heirhunter, 1985, Great Adventure, 1973, The Campus Town Rapist, 1974; librettist: Run-Through (musical play), 1978; contrbr. to TV series Owen Marshall, Counselor at Law, 1974. Wrkg. on screenplay. BS, U. Wis.-Madison, 1967. Computer salesman IBM Co., Madison, Wis., 1967-69; computer programmer, analyst Hughes Aircraft Co., Culver City, Calif., 1969-75; real estate investor Davis Mgmt. Corp., Los Angeles, 1975—. Mem. WGA. Home: 456 S. Spalding Dr Beverly Hills CA 90212

DAVIS, MARALEE G., see Gibson, Mary Elizabeth G.

DAVIS, MARC I., b. Chgo., Nov. 12, 1934, s. Sol Aaron and Rose Anne (Schwartz) D.; m. Judy Lee Axelrod, Mar. 15, 1961; children—Kevin, Laura. Novelist: Spector, 1970; author: Man's History of Law, 1974; ed.: Highlights of the Warren Report, 1964; contrbg. wrtr.: Encyc. Britannica, Compton's Encyc.; book reviewer: Chgo. Tribune, Chgo. Sun-Times. Student, U. Ill., Chgo., 1952-55, NYU, 1957-59. Wrtr., sports statistician Chgo. Tribune, 1952-55; feature ed., columnist, Ft. Bliss News, El Paso, Tex., 1955-57; police reporter Chgo. City News, 1957; genl. assignment reporter El Paso Herald Post, 1959; ed. Physician's Mgmt., Chgo., 1960-63; freelance wrtr., Chgo. and Tex., 1963-80; senior copywriter, Bradford Exchange (plate division; new business; Hammacher Schlemmer), 1980—. Served AUS, spec4, 1955-57. Recipient ECHO Award, Direct Mail Assn., 1987. Mem. AG, Am. Newspaper Guild. Home: 4350 Bluebird Ct Gurnee IL 60031

DAVIS, MARGARET A., b. Havana, Cuba, July 17, 1952; came to U.S., 1962; d. Rodolfo M. Cordero and Nelsa (Duardo) Gomez; m. Donald E. Davis, Nov. 27, 1971 (div. 1984); 1 son, Seth Jon. Ed.-at-large: Helm mag., 1971; co-author, ed.: It's Easy to Avoid Probate, 1983; contrbr. articles, editorials: LCN Express, Other Paths, other publs. Wrkg. on children's books in Spanish and English, metaphysical study guides, human rights commentaries. Student U. South Fla., Miami-Dade Coll., Coll. of Charleston, numerous workshops and institutes. Owner, pres. Unique Services, Orlando, Fla., 1984—; lectr./tchr. writing, human rights. Home: 1365 Hibiscus Ave Winter Park FL 32789

DAVIS, ROD, b. Columbus, OH, Dec. 13, 1946, s. Donald E. and Melba Janell (Lutz) D.; m. Deborah J. Cooper, Oct. 12, 1975 (div. 1984); 1 dau., Jennifer. Contrbr. to Tex. Monthly, Playboy mag., Southern mag., America, Farmers Almanac, Houston City, numerous other publs. BA cum laude, Southwest Mo. State U., 1968; MA, La. State U., Baton Rouge, 1970. Reporter AP, Dallas, 1972-74, Rocky Mountain News, Denver, 1978; asst. dir. Tex. Film Commn., Austin, 1975-76; ed. Tex. Observer, Austin, 1980-81; lectr. dept. English U. Tex.-Austin, 1981-85; sr. ed. Houston City mag., 1985—; freelance wrtr. NDEA fellow, 1969; DuPont fellow U. Va., 1970; Yaddo Colony resident, Saratoga Springs, N.Y., 1978; recipient Bryant Spann prize Eugene V. Debs Soc., Indpls., 1981. Home: Box 49156 Austin TX 78765

DAVIS, RONALD WAYNE, b. Jacksonville, Fla., Jan. 25, 1954; s. James Randall and Audrey Lee (Sweat) D.: m. Sue Wilcox, June 8, 1980. Author: Tennessee Educational Leadership, 1984, Behavioral Disorders, 1985, The Directive Teacher, 1986. Wrkg. on developmental book. PhD, Ga. State U., 1986. Social worker Comprehensive Deel. Services, Valdosta, Ga., 1978-81; tchr. Lowndes County schs., Valdosta, 1981—; tng. mgr. South Ga. Industries, Valdosta, 1985—. Sec. Valdosta Council for Exceptional Children, 1986; bd. dirs. Nat. Assn. for Retarded Citizens, 1986. Mem. profl. orgns. Office: South Ga Ind 1016 W Gordon St Valdosta GA 31601

DAVIS, S. YANA, see Davis, Samuel Dale

DAVIS, SARAH IRWIN, b. Louisburg, NC, Nov. 17, 1923; d. Marian Stuart and May (Holmes) D.; m. Charles Goodrich, Nov. 18, 1949 (div. 1953). Contrbr. articles in lit. maga. including Studies in Short Fiction, Studies in the Novel, Nathaniel Hawthorn Jnl. A.B., U. NC, 1944, M.A., 1945; Ph.D. NY U., 1953. Ed., McGraw-Hill, NYC, 1955-60; prof. English, Randolph-Macon Woman's Coll., Lynchburg, VA, 1963—. Mem. MLA, Am. Studies Assn., Coll. English Assn. Home: Box 3183 Lynchburg VA 24503

DAVIS, SONIA, see Williams, Alberta Norine

DAVIS, STEPHEN W., (Steve), b. Dallas, May 23, 1953. Author: Programs for the TI Home Computer, 1983, Programs for the PCjr, 1984, The Electric Mailbox, 1986, The Writer's Yellow Pages, 1987. Edited: 7 other trade non-fiction titles. BFA, SMU, 1974; MS, NTSU, 1976. Owner, Steve Davis Publishing, Dallas, 1982—. Office: Box 190831 Dallas TX 75219

DAVIS, SUSAN JEAN, b. Flushing, NY, d. Samuel Davis and Helen (Gutterman) Turner. Contrbr. to High Tech Mktg., N.Y. Post, Calyx, Self, other publs. BA, U. Buffalo, 1976; MA in Journalism, NYU, 1981. Asst. ed. Macmillan Co., NYC, 1980-81; freelance wrtr., NYC, 1981—; ed. Vertical Mkt. Report, NYC, 1985; ed.-in-chief Globecon Group, NYC, 1986—. Mem. Phi Beta Kappa. Address: Globecon 71 Murray St New York NY 10007

DAVIS, TERRY MICHAEL, b. St. Peter, MN, July 28, 1957, s. Merritt Lyle Sr. and Lorraine Elizabeth (Chadderdon) D. BA, Mankato (Minn.) State U., 1979. Sports ed., mng. ed. Sheldon Publishing Co., Sheldon, Iowa, 1980-85; reporter, photographer Hutchinson (Minn.) Leader, 1985—; public info. officer Minn. div. Am. Cancer Soc., McLeod County, 1985-87. Home: 975 Jefferson St 4 Hutchinson MN 55350

DAVIS, WALTER, b. Los Angeles, June 14, 1912, s. Isaac and Rose (Bierman) D.; m. Eleanor Einhorn, Sept. 13, 1943; children—Marilyn Jo, Stephen Ian. Contrbr. articles, publicity and public relations items to numerous newspapers, mags.; copywrtr. TV and radio commls., mag. and newspaper advertisements, dir. mail advt. materials. Wrkg. on novel. Student Otis Art Inst., Los Angeles, 1938-41, UCLA, 1969—, Calif. State U., Northridge, 1975—. Pres. Advertisers Workshop, Burbank, Calif., 1946-55, Davis & Blackwell, Inc., North Hollywood, Calif., 1955-67; advt. and public relations cons., North Hollywood, 1968-70; pres. Walter Davis Advt. and Public Relations Agcy., North Hollywood, 1970-85; coll. instr. mktg., advt. and art, 1970—. Public relations, publicity mgr. Maxwell for Gov. campaign, 1962. Address: 3853 Blanton Rd Eugene OR 97405

DAVIS, WILLIAM VIRGIL, b. Canton, OH, May 26, 1940, s. Virgil Sanor and Bertha (Orth) D.; m. Carol Ann Demske, July 17, 1971; 1 child, William Lawrence. Author: (poetry) One Way To Reconstruct the Scene, 1980 (Yale Series Younger Poets' award 1979), The Dark Hours, 1984 (Calliope Press Chapbook prize 1984), also fiction and other 700 poems in lit mags and other periodicals; ed. George Whitefield's Journals 1737-1741, 1969; contrbg. ed. Theodore Roethke: A Bibliography, 1973. AB, Ohio U., 1962, MA, 1965, PhD, 1967; MDiv, Pitts. Theol. Sem., 1965. Asst. prof. English, Ohio U., Athens, 1967-68, Central Conn. State U., New Britain, 1968-72, U. Ill., Chgo., 1972-77; prof. English, Baylor U., Waco, Tex., 1977—, wrtr.-in-residence, 1977—. Sr. Fulbright fellow U. Vienna, 1979-80, U. Copenhagen, 1984. Home: 2633 Lake Oaks Rd Waco TX 76710

DAVIS ASPINWALL, GAIL ANN, b. Los Angeles, CA, July 16, 1959; d. Milton M. and Alice (Goldman) Davis; m. William Aspinwall, Nov. 1, 1986. Ed.: Progress Report, 1983-84, AMI Now, 1981-85; contrbr. to AMI Focus, Marketing Quarterly, Occupational Healthline. BA in Jnlsm. Cal. State U., 1981. Ed. asst. Am. Med. Intl. (Beverly Hills), 1981-82, wrtr./ed. 1983-85, editorial services manager, 1985—. Kappa Tau Alpha, Cal. State, 1981. Mem. Intl. Assoc. Bus. Communicators. Office: Med Intl 414 N Camden Dr Beverly Hills CA 90210

DAVISON, PETER HUBERT, b. NYC, June 27, 1928; s. Edward and Natalie (Weiner) D.; m. Jane Auchincloss Truslow, Mar. 7, 1959 (dec. July 4, 1981); m. Joan Edelman Goody, Aug. 11, 1984; children—Edward Angus, Lesley Truslow. Author: poems The Breaking of the Day, 1964, The City and the Island, 1966, Pretending to Be Asleep, 1970, Dark Houses, 1971, Walking the Boundaries, 1974, A Voice in the Mountain, 1977, Barn Fever and Other Poems, 1981, Praying Wrong: New & Selected Poems,1957-84, 1984; editor: Hello Darkness: The Collected Poems of L. E. Sissman, 1978, The World of Farley Mowat, 1980. AB magna cum laude, Harvard, 1949, St. John's Coll., Cambridge (Eng.) U., 1949-50. Page U.S. Senate, 1944; asst. editor Harcourt, Brace & Co., 1950-51, 53-55; asst. to dir. Harvard U. Press, 1955-56; assoc. editor Atlantic Monthly Press, 1956-59, exec. editor, 1959-64, dir., 1964-79, sr. editor, 1979-85; consulting editor Houghton Mifflin Co., 1985—; poetry editor, Atlantic Monthly, 1972—; mem. adv. bd. Natl. Transl. Center, 1965-68; policy panelist in lit. NEA, 1980-83. Trustee Fountain Valley Schl., 1967-75; mem. corp. Yaddo, 1978—. Served with AUS, 1951-53. Winner competition Yale Series Younger Poets, 1963; recipient poetry award Natl. Inst. Arts and Letters, 1972; Michener Award, Academy of American Poets 1981 and 1985. Mem. Phi Beta Kappa. Office: 2 Park St Boston MA 02108

DAWKINS, CECIL, b. Birmingham, AL, Oct. 2, 1927; s. James Toliver and Lucile-Hannah (Thiemonge) D. Author: (novels) The Live Goat, 1971, Charleyhorse, 1986; (stories) The Quiet Enemy, 1963; The Disciple and Person (play), 1967; contrbr. short stories to Paris, S.W., Sewanee, Ga. rvws, McCall's, Redbook, Pacific Spectator, Charm, Sat. Eve. Post, Martha Foley's Best Am. Short Stories. BA, U. Ala., 1950; MA, Stanford U., 1953. Wrtr.-in-res.Stephens Coll., Columbia, Mo., 1973-76, Sarah Lawrence Coll., Bronxville, N.Y., 1979-81. Recipient Harper Saxton prize Harper and Row, 1971; Stanford U. fellow, 1952-53; Guggenheim fellow, 1966; NEA grantee, 1976. Address: Literistic 264 5th Ave New York NY 10001

DAWKINS, VICKIE LYNN, b. Long Beach, CA, July 31, 1960; d. James Albert and Bettye Lou (Edrington) Anderson. Contrbr. feature articles to mags., newspapers. Public relations coord. Leake Devel., Tulsa, OK, 1985-86; public relations asst. The Williams Co., Tulsa, 1986—; free-lance wrtr., 1985—. Program chmn. Okla. Best Sellers Seminar, Tulsa, 1987. Recipient 1st place for feature writing North Eastern State U., Tahlequah, OK, 1977, 1st place for editorial writing, 1977. Mem. Tulsa Nightwrtrs. (v.p.), Okla. Wrtrs. Fedn. (fellow). Home: 2870 E 51st St Apt F Tulsa OK 74105

DAWSON, GEORGE AMOS, (Mark Freeman), b. Akron, OH, July 5, 1924; s. Lloyd Sherrif and Mary Charlotte (Freeman) D.; m. Sue Virginia Evans, Oct. 12, 1946; children—Shirley Looney, David, James, Deborah Pickens, Charlotte. Author: Book of Scramble Puzzles, 1987. Contrbr. articles to religious mags. BA, Hiram Coll., 1951. Ordained minister July 22, 1951, Ch. of Christ. Minister various Christian chs., in Ohio, Ky., N. Mex., Colo., La., 1948-1986, Baker Ch. of Christ, La., 1986—. Home: 1807 Debra Dr Baker LA 70714

DAWSON, MARY MARTHA, b. Anderson, IN, Aug. 30, 1908; d. Earl R. and Elena Elizabeth (Hill) Morgan; m. John Franklin Dawson, Apr. 18, 1950 (dec. Jan. 6, 1976). Contrbr. articles, poems, fiction to mags., newspapers including Denver Post, Aspire Mag., others. DSB, DSD, Brooks Divinity Schl., 1972; student U. Colo.-Boulder, 1927-1930. Counsellor, Divine Sci. Ch., Denver, 1969—, minister, 1972—; freelance wrtr., 1935—. Mem. Colo. Poetry Soc. (past pres., Poetry award 1950, 60), Denver Woman's Press Club (past pres.). Home: 1255 19th St Apt 710 Tamai Towers Denver CO 80202

DAY, AUDREY, see True, June Audrey

DAY, GEORGE R., b. Salem, MA, July 22, 1950; s. Frederic L. Day, Jr. and Barbara (Walker) D.; m. Rosa Hennessy, Jan. 25, 1975; children—Simon, Timothy. Ed., Trawler Cruiser Yacht, 1980-83, Cruising World, 1983—; author Out There, 1984. BA, Boston U., 1972. Office: Cruising 524 Thames St Newport RI 02890

DAY, LILA, see Chaffin, Lillie D.

DAY, RICHARD CORTEZ, b. Covington, KY, July 19, 1927; s. Cortez Fernando and Queen Angela (Ballard) D.; m. Bonnie Schwinnen, Oct. 26, 1952 (div.); children: Cort, Alexa, Elizabeth. Author: When in Florence, 1986; contrbr. Dec. Mag. Stories for the Sixties, Mass. Rvw, Kenyon Rvw, Redbook, Qtly West (reprinted Pushcart Prize IV), Mundus Artium, Carolina Qtly, NER/BLQ. BS, U Mich. Ann Arbor, 1950. MA, 1952; PhD, U IA, 1960. Prof English Humboldt State Univ, Arcata, 1959—. NEA grantee, 1985. Address: Box 947 Arcata CA 95221

DAYTON, IRENE CATHERINE, b. Lake Ariel, PA, Aug. 6, 1922; d. Florance B. and Effie (Wargo) Glossenger; m. Benjamin Bonney Dayton, Oct. 16, 1943; children—David Bonney, Glenn Charles. Author poems: The Sixth Sense Quivers, 1970, The Panther's Eye, 1974, Seven Times The Wind, 1977, In Oxbow of Time's River, 1978; contrbr. poetry to numerous lit jnls and anthologies, U.S. and Europe.AA, Roberts Wesleyan College, Rochester, NY, 1942. Poet-in-residence, poetry cons. NY State Arts Council, Rochester, 1971-73; instr. Blue Ridge Tech. Coll. Adult Edn., Flat Rock, NC, 1978-85, Opportunity House, Hendersonville, NC, 1982-85. Disting. Submissions Award, Dellbrook Wrtrs. Conf, Shenandoah Valley Acad. of Lit., 1979, Guinness Award, Cheltenham Festival of Lit., Britain, 1963, 1st prize Rochester Festival of Religious Arts, 1959, 60. Meme: P&W, PSA, NY Poetry Soc., NC Poetry Soc., Intl. Acad. of Poets. Home: 209 S Hillandale Dr E Flat Rock NC 28726

DEAGON, ANN, b. Birmingham, Ala., Jan. 19, 1930; d. Robert Fulton and Alice Turpin (Webb) Fleming; m. Donald David Deagon, June 29, 1951 (dec. 1985); children—Andrea Webb, Ellen Lathrop. Author: Carbon 14 (poems), 1974, Poetics South (poems), 1974, Indian Summer (poems), 1975, Women & Children First (poems), 1976, There is no Balm in Birmingham (poems), 1978, The Flood Story (fiction), 1981, Habitats (short stories), 1982, The Diver's Tomb (novel), 1984, The Pentekontaetia (fiction, autobiography), 1985. AB, Birmingham So. U., 1950; MA, U. N.C., Chapel Hill, 1951, PhD,1954. Asst. prof. Furman U., Greenville, S.C., 1954-56; prof. classics, wrtr.-in-residence Guilford Coll., Greensboro, N.C., 1956—; ed. The Guilford Rvw, Greensboro, 1976-84; dir. Poetry Center Southeast, Greensboro, 1980—. NEA fellow 1981-82. Mem. AWP, PSA, AAP, Vergilian Soc., Classical Assn., Am. Philol. Assn. Home: 802 Woodbrook Dr Greensboro NC 27410

DEAL, SHIRLEY MAE HERD, (Shirley Herd), b. Wichita, KS, Sept. 13, 1935, d. James R. and Dorothy Mae (Powell) Herd; children—Michael James DeGood, Mark William DeGood. Author: Cruising Cook, 1977, Easy Spanish for the Traveler, 1982, Blimey, Limey! What'd He Say?, 1983. BS in Edn., U. Kans., 1957. Pres. S. Deal & Assocs. pub. co., San Diego, 1975—; book reviewer SEA, San Diego Union, 1975—; columnist SEA mag., Costa Mesa, Calif., 1975—, freelance wrtr. Winner 1st place column award Natl. Fedn. Press Women, 1979, 80. Mem. Boating Wrtrs. Intl., San Diego Eds. and Wrtrs. Guild, Book Publicists San Diego. Home: 1629 Guizot St San Diego CA 92107

DEAL, SUSAN STRAYER, b. Lincoln, NE, Feb. 21, 1948; d. Gayle David and Eileen (Karre) Strayer; m. Steven Lee Deal, Feb. 29, 1968. Author: No Moving Parts, 1980, The Dark Is A Door, 1984; anthology All My Grandmothers Could Sing, 1984, Adjoining Rooms, 1985;

contrbr. poems NW Rvw,Crosscurrents, Mid-Am. Rvw, Black Warrior Rvw, Prairie Schooner, Ohio Jnl, S. Fla. Poetry Rvw, Sun Dog, others. BA, Kearney State Coll.; MA, Univ. Nebr.-Lincoln. Instr. Blackhawk Coll., Moline, Ill., 1982-85, St. Ambrose Coll., Davenport, Iowa, 1982-85, Augustana Coll., Rock Island, Ill., 1982-85, Univ. Nebr., Lincoln, 1985—, library asst., 1986—. Recipient Writers' Choice award, Pushcart Fdn., Wainscott, NY, 1984-85; Poetry in Motion award, Univ. Nebr., Omaha, 1984; All Nations Poetry Contry winner award, Triton Coll., 1982. Address: 1721 Harwood Lincoln NE 68502

DEAN, CYNTHIA BAILEY, b. Wilmington, NC, Aug. 5, 1956; d. James Warren and Rosa Elizabeth (Sneeden) Bailey; m. David Allan Dean, June 10, 1986; 1 son, Daniel Paul. Sports wrtr.: Park City Daily News, Bowling Green, KY, 1978-79; columnist; Down Home, 1985-86. Ed.: North Warren Observer, Smiths Grove, KY (Info. award for 4-H coverage Ky. Assn. of 4-H Agts. 1986), 1985—. B.S. in Horticulture Sci., NC State U., 1978; M.S. in Recreation, Western Ky. U., 1980. Wrtr. for Frontier Graphics, 1987. Home: 864-G North Elm St Hopkinsville KY 42240

DEAN, ROSEMARY, see Hamilton, Rosemary Ann

DEANE, JAMES GARNER, b. Hartford, CT, Apr. 5, 1923; s. Julian Lowrie and Miriam (Grover) D. BA, Swarthmore Coll., 1943. Mem. editorial staff Washington Star, 1944-60, edn. editor, 1952-57, classical records critic, 1952-60; ind. researcher, vol. in conservation activity, 1961-68; assoc. editor, Natl. Parks Mag., 1968-69, editor, 1969; asst. editor The Living Wilderness, Washington, 1969-71, exec. editor, 1971-75, editor, 1975-81; editor Defenders mag., Washington, 1981—; Washington corr. Mus. Courier, 1945-55; contrbg. editor High Fidelity mag., 1953-55; mem. com. transp. environ. rvw. process Transp. Research Bd., National Research Council, 1974-77; Am. co-chmn. Can. U.S. Environ. Council, 1975—. Bd. dirs. Arctic Intl. Wildlife Range Soc., 1979—; trustee Com. of 100 on Federal City, 1967—, 1st vice chmn., 1967-69; chmn. Potomac Valley Conservation and Recreation Council, 1967. Served with AUS, 1946-47. Recipient award Edn. Writers Assn., 1956, Public Service award Washington Newspaper Guild, 1956, Charles Carroll Glover award Natl. Park Service, 1967. Home: 4200 Cathedral Ave NW Washington DC 20016

DE BOARD, JANEEN SLOAN, b. Washington, Feb. 1, 1953; d. Warren Keith and Janice Ellen (Denison) Sloan: m. J. Kent, Dec. 1973 (div. 1979); 1 dau., Cynthia Janeen; m. Scott Michael DeBoard, Feb. 6, 1982. Contrbr. articles in equine mags. Student Southwest Tex. State U., 1971-73, Tex. A&M u., 1974. Data processor State of Ohio, Columbus, 1979-81, inquiry asst., 1981-83, programmer/analyst, 1983—. Home: 623 Franshire Dr W Columbus OH 43228

DE BRUIN, JEROME EDWARD, b. Kaukauna, WI, July 10, 1941; s. Joseph Henry and Margaret (Hughes) DeB.; m. Nancy Carol Knaack, Aug. 17, 1968; 1 son, Todd. Author: Creative Hands On Science Experiences, 1980, 2d ed., 1986, Young Scientists Explore Nature, 1986, Young Scientists Explore Rocks and Minerals, 1986, Young Scientists Explore Light and Color, 1986, Scientists Around the World, 1987, Eugene DeBruin (in First Heroes, by R. Colvin), 1987. Wrkg. on Look to the Sky, The Science of Cycles. B.S., U. Wis.-Stevens Point, 1966; M.Ed., U. Ill., 1969, Ph.D., 1972. Asst. prof. to assoc. prof. U. Toledo, 1972-75, prof., 1978—. Mem. NWC, Natl. Sci. Tchrs. Assn. (Search for Excellence in Sci. Edn. award 1986), Natl. Assn. Research Sci. Teaching, Am. Ednl. Research Assn. Home: 7321 Gwenn Ct Sylvania OH 43560

DE CAMP, L(YON) SPRAGUE, b. NYC, Nov. 27, 1907; s. Lyon and Emma Beatrice (Sprague) de C.; m. Catherine Adelaide Crook, Aug. 12, 1939; children—Lyman Sprague, Gerard Beekman. Author: about 100 books, including popularizations of science and technology (The Ancient Engineers, 1963, The Day of the Dinosaur, 1968); history (The Great Monkey Trial, 1968, Great Cities of the Ancient World, 1972), textbooks (Inventions, Patents, and Their Management, 1937, Science Fiction Handbook, Revised, 1977) historical novels (The Dragon of the Ishtar Gate, 1961, An Elephant for Aristotle, 1958), science fiction (Lest Darkness Fall, 1941, Rogue Queen, 1951, The Bones of Zora, 1984), fantasy (The Incomplete Enchanter, 1941, The Reluctant Shaman, 1970), juvenile non-fiction (The Story of Science in America, 1967, Darwin and His Great Discovery, 1972), biography (Dark Valley Destiny: The Life of Robert E. Howard, 1983, Literary Swordsmen and Sorcerers, 1976), and verse (Heroes and Hobgoblins, 1978). Editor of anthologies (Warlocks and Warriors, 1970, 3,000 Years of Science Fiction and Fantasy, 1972) and symposia (The Conan Swordbook, 1969, The Blade of Conan, 1969). Collaborated with wife Catherine Crook de Camp, Lin Carter, Willy Ley, Fletcher Pratt, and Alf K. Berle. Over 400 articles and stories in periodicals and encyclopedias; about 75 radio scripts. Stories and articles in about 90 periodicals and 50-odd anthologies and symposia. Works translatd into 10 or more foreign languages and have translated stories from French and Italian. BS, Calif. Inst. Tech., 1930; MS, Stevens Inst. of Tech., 1933. Instr. Inventors Fdn., 1933-36; prin. Schl. Inventing and Patenting, Intl. Corr. Schls., 1936-37; editor Fowler-Becker Pub. Co., 1937-38; asst. editor, ASME, 1938; freelance writer, 1938-42, 46—. Served from lt. to lt. comdr. USNR, 1942-46. Recipient Pat Terry Award, Sydney Sci. Fiction Fdn., 1973, Tolkien Fantasy award, World Sci. Fiction Conv., 1976, Nebula award, SFWA, 1979, World Fantasy award, World Fantasy Conv., 1984. Mem. Univ. Mus. U. Pa., Phila. Acad. Natl. Scis., Hist. of Sci. Soc., Soc. History of Tech., Fellows in American Studies, Sci. Fiction Writers, Am. AG, Assn. Phonétique Internationale. Address: 278 Hothorpe Ln Villanova PA 19085

DECKER, MARY LOCHER, b. Peoria, IL, Mar. 16, 1936; d. Ross Emil and Irene F. (Johnson) Locher; m. Donald Milton Decker, Aug. 20, 1961; children—Catherine, Thomas. Contrbr. to various newsps. and mags; co-author: Reflections on Elegance: Pasadena's Huntington Hotel Since 1906, 1984; co-ed. books include Life's Fulfillment: Memoirs of Beatrice Whittlesey, 1985, How I Spent the Twentieth Century, 1985; A Celebration of Family: The Johnsons of Pekin, IL (co-author), 1985. BA, Cal. State U, 1958. Assoc. in poli. sci. U. of Cal. (Davis), 1961-63; secondary sub. Stockton unified schl. dist. (CA), 1977-79; asst. dir. financial aid U. of the Pacific, (Stockton), 1981-83. Chair United Methodist Nursery schl., 1970-75. Mem. Los Escribientes, Cal., Hist. Soc., Pres. niversity Women (Stockton). Home: 29451 Drydock Cove Laguna Niguel CA 92677

DECKER, VIRGINIA ANN, b. Hillsboro, OR, June 13, 1942; d. Willis P. and Mattie Rebecca (Cox) Pyle; m. Larry Edward Decker, Sept. 1, 1962; children: Weston Edward, Wendy Ann. Contrbr. Community Edn. Jnl, Comm. Involvement for the Classroom Tchr., Adminstrs. and Policy Makers Views of Comm. Edn., The Funding Process, Learning Comm. Connections, Capacity Building Alts. for Serving Language Minority Pops. BA, U. Oreg, 1964, MBA, 1965. Research asst. Bur. Govt. Res. and Bur. Bus. and Econ. Res., Eugene, Oreg., 1964-68, instr. Lane Comm Coll., 1968-70; freelance writer and tech. ed, Charlottesville, VA, 1970—, mng. ed. Comm. Collaborators, 1977—; book rvw. ed. Natl. Comm. Edn. Assn., Alexandria, Va, 1982—. Edn. Comm. League Women Voters, Charlottesville, 1980—; middle schl. evaluation comm., Albermarle County pub. schls., 1984-85, redistricting comm., 1983-84. Mem. Va Community Edn Assn (bd dirs, 1984, disting. service award, 1981), Natl. Community Edn. Assn. (bd dirs, 1981-84; natl. conf. co-chair, 1986). Address: 106 Cannon PL Charlottesville VA 22901

DE CORMIER-SHEKERJIAN, REGINA, d. Robert R. and Selma F. (Stigberg) deCormier; m. Haig Shekerjian; children—Tor, Jean-Rene. Author: Discovering Israel, 1960, Growing Toward Peace (with Eleanor Roosevelt), 1961; poetry anthols: Believing Everything, 1980, Pioneer Letters, 1981, Peace is Our Profession, 1981, The Denny Poems, 1982, Anti-War Poems, 1985; Changes (anthol.), 1987; contrbr. poetry to Mass Rvw, Poetry Rvw, Commonweal, Northwest Rvw, Pacific Rvw, The Little Magazine,Tendril, others; ed.: A Book of Ballads (with H. Shekerjian), 1966, A Book of Christmas Carols (with H. Shekerjian), 1978. Recipient Natl. Jewish Book award, Jewish Book Council, N.Y., 1961, 1st Prize in Poetry, Conn. Writers League, 1982, Pablo Neruda Award, Arts & Humanities Council, Tulsa, 1984; fellow Millay Colony for the Arts, Austerlitz, N.Y., 1983. Mem. AG, P&W, Natl. Lg. of Am. Pen Women. Home: 4 Sparkling Ridge New Paltz NY 12561

DE CRESCENTIS, JAMES, b. Rochester, NY, May 29, 1948, s. Liborio and Lena (Recchia) de C. Author poetry chapbooks: The Space Out Back, 1977, Last Minute Notes About Deep Terror, 1984; contrbr. poetry: New Letters Cloud Chamber, Greenfield Rvw, Ragged Oaks, other lit publs. BA in English, SUNY-Geneseo, 1971; MFA in Creative Writing, Bowling Green (Ohio) State U., 1984. In-camp tchr. N.Y. State Migrant Center, Geneseo, 1971-74; spcl. lectr. English, St. John Fisher Coll., Rochester, 1985-87; in charge of poetry reading series 1985-87; poet-in-residence Alternative Lit. Programs in Schls., Albany, N.Y., 1985-87. Mem. P&W. Home: 1 Girton Pl Rochester NY 14607

DECROW, KAREN, b. Chgo., Dec. 18, 1937; d. Samuel Meyer and Juliette (Abt) Lipschultz; m. Alexander Allen Kolben, 1960 (div. 1965); m. Roger Edward DeCrow, 1965 (div. 1972). Author: (with Roger DeCrow) University Adult Education: A Selected Bibliography, 1967, The Young Woman's Guide to Liberation, 1971, Sexist Justice, 1974, The First Women's State of the Union Message, 1977; (with Robert Seidenberg M.D.) Women Who Marry Houses: Panic and Protest in Agoraphobia, 1983; Editor: The Pregnant Teenager (Howard Osofsky M.D.), 1968, Corporate Wives, Corporate Casualties (Seidenberg), 1973; contrbr. articles to Chicago Sun-Times, N.Y. Times, Los Angeles Times, Boston Globe, Vogue, Mademoiselle, Miami

Herald; other newspapers, mags.; columnist: Syracuse Post-Standard; BS, Northwestern U., 1959; JD, Syracuse U., 1972. Bar: N.Y., U.S. Dist. Ct. (no dist.) N.Y. Resorts editor Golf Digest mag., Evanston, Ill., 1959-60; editor Am. Soc. Planning Ofcls., Chgo., 1960-61; writer Center for Study Liberal Edn. for Adults, Chgo., 1961-64; editor Holt, Rinehart, Winston, Inc., NYC, 1965, L. W. Singer, Syracuse, N.Y., 1965-66; writer Eastern Regional Inst. for Edn., Syracuse, 1967-69; Pub. Broadcasting System, 1977; tchr. women and law, 1972-74; natl. bd. mem NOW, 1968-77, natl. pres., 1974-77, also natl. politics task force chmn.; cons. affirmative action, lectr. corps., polit. groups, colls. and univs., internationally; natl. coordinator Women's Strike for Equality, 1970; N.Y. State del. Intl. Women's Year, 1977; candidate for mayor, Syracuse, 1969; originated Schls. for Candidates; mem. chancellor's affirmative action com. Syracuse U.; mem. N.Y. State Ct. Arbitration Program, 1980; bd. advisorsWorking Women's Inst.; participant DeCrow-Schafly ERA debates, 1975—. Hon. Trustee Elizabeth Cady Stanton Fdn. Mem. Am. Arbitration Assn., Dist. Attys. Adv. Council, ACLU, N.Y. State Women's Bar Assn. (chpt. dir.), N.Y. State, Onondago County bar assns. Address: 7 Fir Tree Ln Jamesville NY 13078

DECTER, MIDGE, b. St. Paul, July 25, 1927; d. Harry and Rose (Calmenson) Rosenthal; m. Norman Podhoretz, Oct. 21, 1956; children—Rachel, Naomi, Ruth, John. Author: The Liberated Woman and Other Americans, 1971, The New Chastity, 1972, Liberal Parents, Radical Children, 1975; Contrbr. articles to popular publs. Student, U. Minn., 1945-46, Jewish Theological Sem. Am., 1946-48. Asst. editor Midstream mag., 1956-58; mng. editor Commentary, 1961-62; editor Hudson Inst., 1965-66, CBS Legacy Books, 1966-68; exec. editor Harper's mag., 1969-71; book review editor Saturday Review/World mag., 1972-74; sr. editor Basic Books, Inc., 1974-80; exec. dir. Com. for Free World, 1980—. Bd. dirs. Heritage Fdn. Mem. Council Fgn. Relations. Home: 120 E. 81st St New York NY 10028

DEEDY, JOHN GERARD, JR., b. Worcester, MA, Aug. 17, 1923; s. John G. and Grace R. (McDonough) D.; m. Mary M. Noonan, Apr. 20, 1949; children—Mary Joan, John J., Justine A., Paul V. Author: (with Jack Frost) The Church in Worcester New England, 1957, (with Martin Marty, David Silverman) The Religious Press in America, 1963, Eyes on the Modern World, 1965, The Vatican, 1970, What A Modern Catholic Believes About Conscience, Freedom and Authority, 1972, (with Philip Nobile) The Complete Ecology Fact Book, 1972, What A Modern Catholic Believes About the Commandments, 1975, Literary Places: A Guided Pilgrimage, New York and New England, 1978, Seven American Catholics, 1978, Apologies, Good Friends; An Interim Biography of Daniel Berrigan, S.J., 1981, The New Nuns: Serving Where the Spirit Leads, 1982, Your Aging Parents, 1984, The Catholic Fact Book, 1986 American Catholicism: And Now Where, 1987. AB, Holy Cross Coll., 1948; cert., Institut du Pantheon, Paris, 1949; AB, Trinity Coll., Dublin, 1949, MA, 1957. Reporter, corr. Boston Post, Boston Globe, Worcester Telegram, 1940-51; founding editor Cathl Free Press, Worcester, 1951-59; editor Pitts. Cath., 1959-67; mng. editor Commonweal, NYC, 1967-68. Served with USAAF, World War II. Recipient Pro Ecclesia et Pontifice, Pope Pius XII, 1954. Home: 28 Granite St Rockport MA 01966

DEEDY, JOYCE, b. New London, CT, Feb. 16, 1928; m. Donald G. Deedy, Oct. 30, 1948; children—Elaine Deedy-Sincali, D. Thomas, Diane, Deborah Deedy-Dazzi. Author: Spots and Splashes, 1985, A Million Butterflies, 1985; The Rabbit Under the Wisteria Bush, 1986. Contrbr. comic tale to anthol., poems to anthols. Diploma, Inst. of Children's Lit., 1978. Bd. dirs. Deedy Construction Co., Inc., 1955—.Recipient Golden Poet award World of Poetry, 1985, 86, 86. Mem. SCBW. Home: 113 Old Colchester Rd Quaker Hill CT 06375

DEEMER, BILL, b. Norfolk, VA, Mar. 4, 1945, s. Charles Robert and Florence Isabel (Lear) D.; m. Toby Joy Murray, Mar. 4, 1966. Author: Poems, 1964, Diana, 1966, The King's Bounty, 1968, A Few for Lew, 1972, A Few for Lew & Other Poems, 1974, All Wet, 1975, This Is Just to Say, 1981, Subjects, 1984, A Few for Lew, 1986. NEA grantee, 1968. Home: 92400 River Rd Junction City OR 97448

DE FORD, SARA WHITCRAFT, b. Youngstown, OH, Nov. 9, 1916; d. Union Corwin and Grace (Whitcraft) de Ford. Author 7 books, also poems; contrbr. articles to professional jnls. AB, MA, Mt. Holyoke Coll., 1936, 1938; PhD,Yale, 1942. Instr., Eng., Barnard Coll., 1942-46; asst. prof. Goucher Coll., 1946-50, assoc. prof., 1950-57; prof. 1957-81; prof. emeritus, 1981—. Eugene F. Saxton Fellowship, 1948; Fulbright lectr., Japan, 1954-55, 61-62. Mem. Medieval Acad. Am., AAUP, AAUW. Mem. Soc. of Friends. Home: 1961 S Josephine Denver CO 80210

DEFREES, MADELINE, (formerly Sister Mary Gilbert); b. Ontario, OR, Nov. 18, 1919; d. Clarence Chesterfield and Mary Teresa (McCoy) DeFrees. Author: Springs of Silence, 1953, Later Thoughts from the Springs of Silence, 1962, From the Darkroom, 1964, When Sky Lets Go, 1978, Imaginary Ancestors, 1978, Magpie on the Gallows, 1982. BA, Marylhurst College, 1948; MA, U. of Oregon, 1951. Prof., Holy Names College, Spokane, Wash., 1950-67; prof., U. of Mont., Missoula, MT, 1967-79; prof., U. of Mass., Amherst, MA, 1979-85. Awards: Guggenheim Fellowship, 1981-82; NEA Fellowship, 1982; Litt. D., Gonzaga U., 1959. Mem. PSA, NOW, PEN. Home: 7548 11th Avenue NW Seattle WA 98117

DE GARMO, SHERLY FRANCES, b. Manchester, CT, Apr. 11, 1952; d. John Peter and Beatrice Alice (Cooley) DeG.; m. Arthur Edward Ashwell, Jr., Nov. 14, 1970 (div. Sept. 28, 1973); 1 dau. Michelle Lee Ashwell. Contrbr. poems to anthols. Grad. public schs., Manchester, CT. Recipient 14 Merit awards World of Poetry, 1983-87, Golden Poet award, 1985, 86, 87; Natl. Amateur Poet Search award Johnson Pub. Co., 1986. Home: 1114 Boston Turnpike Coventry CT 06238

DE GRUSON, GENE, b. Girard, KS, Oct. 10, 1932, s. Henri Dieudonne and Clemence (Merciez) DeG. Author: Kansas Authors of Best Sellers, 1970, That Printer of Udells: A Dramatization of Harold Bell Wright's Novel, 1975, Goat's House: Poems, 1986; ed.: The Library Bulln., 1968-74, Little Balkans Rvw, 1980—; contrbr. to Crazy Horse, Bitterroot, Kans. Qtly, other publs. BS in Edn., Kans. State Coll., 1954, MS, 1958; postgrad., U. Iowa, 1958-60. Asst. prof. English, Pittsburg (Kans.) State U., 1960-68, spcl. collections librarian, 1968—. Mem. Kans. Wrtrs. Assn., Bibliographical Soc. Am., Kans. Library Assn. Home: 601 Grandview Hts Terr Pittsburg KS 66762

DE HAVEN, TOM, b. Bayonne, NJ, May 1, 1949, s. Clarence Richard De Haven and Margaret (O'Hare) Hussey; m. Santa Sergio, June 26, 1971; children—Jessie Ann, Kate Marie. Novelist: Freaks' Amour, 1979, Jersey Luck, 1980, Funny Papers, 1985. BA in Sociology, Rutgers U., 1971; MFA in Creative Writing, Bowling Green (Ohio) State U., 1973. Mng. ed. Mag. Assocs., NYC, 1973-76; ed. Freelance mag., 1977-80; adj. prof. creative writing Hofstra U., Hempstead, N.Y., 1981—; evaluator prose and lit. orgns. panel N.J. State Council on Arts, Trenton, 1986—. NEA fellow, 1979, 86, N.J. State Council on Arts fellow, 1980. Mem. PEN, AG, P&W. Office: Wasserman 137 E 36th St New York NY 10016

DEHMLER, MARI LYNCH, b. Lincoln, IL, Dec. 29, 1953; d. Irwin Ray Lynch and Eugenia Rae (Martin) Lynch; m. Martin Charles Dehmler, Oct. 10, 1981; 1 son, Nathan Lynch. Editor (with others): Family Life Education: Resources for the Elementary Classroom (DeSpelder and Strickland), 1980; contrbr. "Nutrition Update" column Santa Cruz Sentinel, 1979; edl. assistant and writer, natl. mag. Well-Being, 1979. Editing dreams/journaling book, elder care book, sickle cell anemia book, humor pieces, short stories. President's Scholar So. Ill. U.-Carbondale, 1971-72, So. Ill. U.-Edwardsville, 1974. Editorial asst. Well-Being Productions, Santa Cruz, Calif., 1979; editor Planned Parenthood, Santa Cruz, 1980-81; freelance editor, writer, 1981—. Legis. Adv. sustainable agriculture groups, 1979—; nuclear disarmament groups, 1979—. Club: Monterey Peninsula Writers. Home: 20 Oxton Rd Monterey CA 93940

DEIMER, LORENA RUTH MURRILL, (Sylvia Drake), b. Thermopolis, WY, Jan. 11, 1926; d. Charles Edward Murrill and Lela Emma (Gilmore) Murrill Ernest; m. Richard R. Schoenewald, Feb. 15, 1946 (div. Dec. 21, 1958); children: Charles R., Helen Frances Schoenewald Hodgins; m. Marshall Fredrick Deimer, Feb. 21, 1959. Contrbr. articles to Mags.,/newspapers including Ladies Home Jnl., Modern Romances, Denver Post, others. Wrkg. on From Magnolia Blossoms to Sage, Murder in the Church, Elisia. Student, Casper Jr. Coll., 1956-57. Recipient Golden Poet award World of Poetry, 1987. Mem. NWC, Metro Natl. Workshop. Home: 1164 Macon St Aurora CO 80010

DE JONGH, JAMES LAURENCE, b. St. Thomas, V.I., Sept. 23, 1942; s. Percy Leo and Mavis Elizabeth (Bentlage) de J. Author: City Cool, 1978, Do Lord Remember Me, 1983. BA, Williams Coll., 1964; MA, Yale U., 1967; PhD, NYU, 1983. Assoc. prof. CCNY, 1970—. Named Outstanding Musical Creator, AUDELCO, 1984; fellow N.Y. State Arts Council, 1977, NEA, 1978, NEH, 1986. Mem. DG, WG, Harlem WG. Home: 6 Fordham Hill Oval 9D Bronx NY 10468

DEKKER, CARL, see Lynds, Dennis

DE KOVNER-MAYER, BARBARA, b. Boston, Jan. 7, 1938, d. S. Edward Davidson and S. Dolly (Franks) Schneider; m. Alan De-Kovner, 1956 (div. 1964); children—Michael, Mari; m. 2d, John Mayer, 1968 (dec. 1981); 1 son, Greg; m. 3d, Godfrey Harris, 1984. Coauthor: From Trash to Treasure (with Godfrey Harris), 1985. Student Mus. Fine Arts, Boston, 1950-51, UCLA, 1971-73. Solo entertainer stage, movies, TV, 1944-84; asst. to ed. Buzza-Cardozo Greeting Cards, Los Angeles, 1955-56; features ed. Am. Pub. Co., Encino, Calif., 1973-77; polit. affairs analyst Israel Today, Van Nuys,

1977—; host, co-producer The Female Connection, sta.-KIEV, Glendale, Calif., 1985—; creator, moderator "Female Connection" seminars tchg. women art of attracting men, 1985—. Mem. AFTRA, AGVA, Screen Actors Guild. Address: Box 12 Encino CA 91316

DE LAND, MICHELLE KAREN, b. Grosse Pointe, MI, Sept. 30, 1954; d. G. William and Nina Bell (Wilson) DeLand.BA in journalism, Wayne State U., 1976. Editorial Asst. The Detroit News, 1976-80; ed. pubs. K-mart Corp., Troy, Mich., 1980—; owner, pres., ed. Classic Furniture Restoration, Warren, Mich., 1982—; freelance for Heritage jnl, Grosse Pointe, 1986—. Home: 27597 Hoover Warren MI 48093

DE LA ROSA, EDNA ELNORE, (Edna Dewberry), b. Newton, MS, Nov. 29, 1918; d. Sam Brown and Kate Elnora (Martin) Lovett; m. Enoch Arden Dewberry, July 10, 1937 (dec.); children—Iris Edwina Walk, Stanley Ray; m. Raul De La Rosa, Nov. 24, 1980. Contrbr. numerous poems to anthols. Author: Christmas Poems. Wrkg. on book of poetry. Diploma in Practical Nursing, Chgo. State Schl., 1963. Practical nurse, 1968-69; food service worker Skokie Country Club, Glencoe, IL, 1974—. Recipient cert. of Merit, Intl. Clover Poetry Soc., 1974. Mem. Ill. State Poetry Soc. (cert. of Merit 1973), Ariz. Wrtr.'s Club (secy. 1968, treas. 1969). Home: 1710 W Erie Chicago IL 60622

DELAUNE, (JEWEL) LYNN (DE GRUMMOND), b. Centerville, LA, d. Will White and Lena (Young) de Grummond; m. Richard K. Delanne, March 1, 1952; children: Richard K. Jr., Linden Marjorie, Jonathan Ernest. Author: biographies with her mother: Jeff Davis: Confederate Boy, 1960, Jeb Stuart, 1962, repr 1979, Babe Didrikson: Girl Athlete, 1963, Jean Felix Piccard: Boy Balloonist, 1968; Giraffes Can Be a Trouble, 1955. Contrbr to World Book Encyclopedia yearbooks, 1969-78. BA, Louisiana State, Baton Rouge, BS, MA. Layout artist, Army and Navy Publ. Co., Baton Rouge, one year; grad asst in history, Louisiana State U., two years, affiliated with library acquisitions dept, circulation librarian, one year; area librarian, Special Services (civilian personnel), U.S. Army, Sendai, Japan, two years; lectr, College of William and Mary, Williamsburg, Va., 1966-70, asst prof of education, 1971-81 Home: 316 Burns Ln Williamsburg, VA 23185

DELAURA, DAVID JOSEPH, b. Worcester, MA, Nov. 19, 1930; s. Louis and Helen Adeline (Austin) DeL.; m. Ann Beloate, Aug. 19, 1961; children—Michael Louis, Catherine, William Beloate. Author: Hebrew and Hellene in Victorian England: Newman, Arnold, and Pater, 1969; editor: Victorian Prose: A Guide to Research, 1973. AB, Boston Coll., 1955, AM, 1958; PhD, U. Wis., 1960. Mem. faculty U. Tex. at Austin, 1969-74, prof. English, 1968-74; Avalon Fdn. prof. humanities, prof. English U. Pa., Phila., 1974—. Mem. MLA (annl. award for outstanding article 1964), AAUP. Home: 31 Orchard Ln Villanova PA 19085

DE LAURENTIS, LOUISE BUDDE, b. Stafford, KS, Oct. 5, 1920; d. Louis and Mary (Lichte) Budde; m. Mariano Anthony DeLaurentis, Mar. 26, 1948; 1 son Delbert Louis. Author: Etta Chipmunk, 1963; contrbr. poetry: Epoch, Kans. Qtly, WomanSpirit, Christian Century, other publs.; contrbr. stories: Outerbridge, Kans. Qtly, Cricket, others. BA, Ottawa (KANS) U., 1942. Air traffic controller FAA, various locations, 1943-54; freelance wrtr. Home: 983 Cayuga Heights Rd Ithaca NY 14850

DELBANCO, NICHOLAS F., b. London, Aug 27, 1942; arrd. U.S., 1948; s. Kurt and Barbara G. (Bernstein) D.; m. Elena C., Sept. 12, 1970; 2 daus., Francesca Barbara and Andrea Katherine. Author: The Martlet's Tale, 1966, Grasse, 3/23/66, 1968, Consider Sappho Burning, 1969, News, 1970, In The Middle Distance, 1971, Fathering, 1973, Small Rain, 1975, Possession, 1977, Sherbrookes, 1978, Stillness, 1980, Group Portrait: Conrad, Crane, Ford, James and Wells, 1982, About My Table and Other Stories, 1983, The Beaux Arts Trio: A Portrait, 1985; ed. Stillness and Shadows, Two Novels by John Gardner. BA, Harvard U., 1959-63; MA, Columbia U, 1964-66. Prof Bennington Coll, Vt., 1966-85; Univ Mich., Ann Arbor, 1985—. Founding dir., The Bennington Writing Workshops, Vt, 1977-85. Recipient NEA Creative Writing award in fiction, 1973, 83; NEA composer & librettists fellowship, 1976; Guggenheim fellow, 1981. Mem AL, AG, PEN. Address: 428 Concord St Ann Arbor MI 48104

DELE, DOROTHY A., see Crites, Dorothy Adele

DELFANO, M. M., see Flammonde, Paris

D'ELIA, MICHAEL JOSEPH, b. Bklyn., May 28, 1955. Technical manuals inclg. DDC Diffusion Furnace Process Troubleshooting Manual, 1984, CV Plotting Trouble Shooting Guide, 1984, Universal Test Structure Manual, 1985. Student, Marist Coll., 1978. Sr. Process eng. Fairchild Corp. (Wappingers Falls, NY), 1982-85; proc. eng. Harris Semiconductor (Poughkeepsie, NY), 1979-82; chemist Tau Labs (Poughkeepsie), 1978-79. Mem. NY State Civ. Defense Comm., 1979-85. Home: 25 Royal Crest Dr Marlboro MA 01752

DE LILLA, CELINA S., b. Belen, NM, June 11, 1934; d. Ernesto and Anita (Gonzalez) Sanchez; m. Luigi De Lilla, July 3, 1965; children—Margherita, Ernesto, Michele, Giovanni. Author: (script adaptations) The Magic Flute (W. A. Mozart), 1984, The Marriage of Figaro (W. A. Mozart), 1985, Die Fledermaus (J. Strauss), 1986. Contrbr. poems to anthols. Wrkg. on collection of poems, adaptation of Madame Butterfly, children's stories. B.Music Edn., Millikin U., 1956, M.Music Edn., 1961. Editorial sec. Doubleday & Co., Inc., N.Y.C., 1962-74; freelance singer, 1975—; free-lance organist, 1981—. Recipient Citizenship medal for essay Daus. of Am. Revolution, 1952. Home: 4618 Constitution NE Albuquerque NM 87110

DE LIMA, SIGRID, b. NYC, Dec. 4, 1921; d. Andrew Lang and Agnes de Lima; m. Stephen Greene, Dec. 24, 1953; 1 child, Alison. Author: Captain's Beach, 1950; The Swift Cloud, 1952; Carnival by the Sea, 1954; Praise a Fine Day, 1959; Oriane, 1968. BA, Barnard Coll., 1942; MS in Journalism, Columbia U., 1944. Recipient prix de Rome Am. Acad. Arts and Letters, 1953-54. Home: 408-A Storms Rd Valley Cottage NY 10989

DELLINGER, DAVID, b. Wakefield, MA, Aug. 22, 1915; s. Raymond Pennington and Marie E. (Fiske) D.; m. Elizabeth Peterson, Feb. 4, 1942; children: Patchen, Ray, Natasha Peterson. Author: Cuba: America's Lost Plantations, 1961, More Power than We Know, 1975; editor: (with Michael Albert) Beyond Survival: New Directions for the Disarmament Movement, 1983; contbr.: Seeds of Liberation, 1964, Nonviolence in America, 1966, Telling It Like It Was—The Chicago Riots, 1969, Against the Crime of Silence, 1969, Collected Essays—Revolutionary Nonviolence, 1970, Nonviolent Action and Social Change, 1979. BA, Yale,, 1936; student, Yale U. Div. Schl., 1937-39, New Coll., Oxford (Eng.) U., 1936-37; grad. secy., Dwight Hall, Yale U., 1937-39; student, Union Theol. Sem., 1939-40. Prtnr. Libertarian press, workers coop., Glen Gardner, N.J., 1946-67; editor and pub. Liberation, 1956-75; editor Seven Days Mag., 1975-80. Poynter fellow journalism Yale, 1969. Office: South End Press 302 Columbus Ave Boston MA 02116

DELMORE, DIANA, see Nollet, Lois Sophia

DE LOACH, ALLEN WAYNE, b. Jacksonville, FL, Aug. 21, 1939; s. Robert Earl and Wyalen Lavina (Sweat) De L.; m. Barbara Aggler, May 27, 1960 (div. Oct. 1979); children—Allen Wayne, Karsten Devin; m. 2d, Joan Ford, July 5, 1981 (div. Oct. 1983). Author: (poetry) Elegy: For Walt Whitman, 1967, From Maine, 1970, Third Part Unordered, 1970, Planting Pahos, 1978, Mudhead Kachina: Poems and Photographs of Hopi Land, 1985; (prose) Buffalo Cold Spring Precinct 23 Bulletin, 1971, Literary Assays: Portraits of Major Writers, 1984 (photography); editor: We Are All Poets, Really, 1968, Of Love, Abiding Love, 1970, The East Side Scene, 1972, Intrepid Anthology, A Decade and Then Some, 1977 Editor, Intrepid Press, also Intrepid mag., Buffalo, 1964, Beau Fleuve Series, chapbooks contemporary prose, poetry, and literary criticism, 1970. BA with honors, SUNY, 1967, postgrad. through 1971. Teaching asst. SUNY, Buffalo, 1967-70; asst. prof Am. Studies and lit. Empire State Coll., SUNY, Buffalo, 1971-78. Producer video tapes, records; exhbns. paintings, multi-media shows in U.S. Also gallery exhbns. photographs; rep. in anthologies; contrbr. to mags. Served USMC Res., 1957-65. Mem. COSMEP (conf. dir. 1970). Address: 951 W Perry St Buffalo NY 14209

DELON, FLOYD G(URNEY), b. Shirley, IN, Aug. 7, 1929; s. Horace L. and Reola (Phelps) D.; m. Elizabeth Taylor, May 29, 1949; children: Laura Delon Stephens. Author: Contrbr, Warren E. Gauerke and Jack R. Childress, eds, The Theory and Pratice of School Finance, 1967, (with Lee O. Gerber) The Law and the Teacher in Missouri, 1971, 3d ed, 1982, Substantive Legal Aspects of Teacher Discipline, 1972, new ed, Legal Controls on Teacher Conduct: Teacher Discipline, 1977, ed, The Yearbook of School Law, 1974, Administrators and the Courts: Update 1977, 1977, School Officials and the Courts: Update 1979, 1979, School Officials and the Courts, Update 1981, Legal Issues in the Dismissal of Teachers for Personal Conduct, 1982. Contrbrs to Handbook of Contemporary Education and to educ. jnls. BS Ed, Ball State Teachers College (now U.), Muncie, Ind., 1951; MS, Butler U., Indianapolis, Ind., 1954; Ed. D., U. of Arizona, 1961. High School teacher of mathematics, Arlington, Ind., 1951-54; principal of public schools, Hillsboro, Ind., 1954-56, and Mays, Ind., 1956-60; asst prof of educ., Northwest Missouri State Coll (now U.), Maryville, 1961-62; assoc prof of educ, U. of Mo.—Columbia, 1962-67; dir., South Central Region Educational Laboratories, Little Rock, Ark., 1967-69; prof of educ. and assoc. dean of Coll. of Educ., U. of Mo.-Columbia, 1969—. Fulbright lecturer in Iran, 1975-76, and in Cyprus, 1983, 1987. Member: Natl. Org. on the Legal Problems of Educ. (pres., 1981), American Assn of School Administrators (mem bd dirs, 1973-75),

Missouri State Teachers Assn, Phi Delta Kappa, Kappa Delta Pi. Home: Rt. 1 Box 230, Rocheport, MO 65279

DELORIA, VINE VICTOR, JR., b. Martin, SD, Mar. 26, 1933; s. Vine Victor and Barbara (Eastburn) D.; m. Barbara Jeanne Nystrom, June 1958; children: Philip, Daniel, Jeanne Ann. Author: Custer Died for Your Sins, 1969, We Talk, You Listen, 1970, Of Utmost Good Faith, 1972, God Is Red, 1973, Behind the Trail of Broken Treaties, 1974, The Indian Affair, 1974, Indians of the Pacific Northwest, 1977, The Metaphysics of Modern Existence, 1979, Red Man in New World Drama, 1972, American Indians, American Justice, 1983. BS, Iowa State U., 1958; MTh, Lutheran Schl. Theology, 1963; JD, U. Colo., 1970; DH LItt., Augustana Coll., 1971. Served with USMCR, 1954-56. Mem. AG, Colo., Authors League. Office: Dept Poli Sci U Ariz Tucson AZ 85721

DELP, MICHAEL W., b. Greenville, MI, Dec 21, 1948; s. William and Francis (Kipp) D.; m. Janel Ross, Sept. 12, 1971 (div. June 1976); m. 2d, Claudia Elmasian, Apr. 19, 1980; 1 son, Jaime. Author: A Dream of the Resurrection, 1976, A Short Guide to the Wilderness, 1976, Languages, 1984; contrbr. poems to So. Poetry Rvw, The Small-Towner, Passages North, The Third Coast; contrbr. articles to Playboy, Detroit Mag, Wonderland Mag. BA, Alma Coll., 1971. Tchr. Grayling High Schl., Mich. 1971-84; dir. creative writing Interlochen Arts Academy, Mich, 1984—Recipient Poem of the Year award, Passages North, 1983; Creative Artist grant Mich Council for the Arts, Detroit, 1984. Mem. Poetry Resource Center (trustee). Address: Interlochen Arts Academy Interlochen MI 49043

DEL REY, LESTER, b. Saratoga, MN, June 2, 1915; s. Franc and Jane (Sidway) del R.; m. Judy-Lynn Benjamin, Mar. 21, 1971. Author: sci. fiction and children's books including Marooned on Mars, 1952, Attack from Atlantis, 1953, Mission to the Moon, 1956, Step to the Stars, 1954, Cave of the Spears, 1957, Mysterious Earth, 1960, The Mysterious Sea, 1961, Moon of Mutiny, 1961, Mysterious Sky, 1964, Outpost of Jupiter, 1963, Runaway Robot, 1965, Infinite Worlds of Maybe, 1966, Rocket from Infinity, 1966, Tunnel Through Time, 1966, Prisoners of Space, 1968, The Eleventh Commandment, 1970, Nerves, 1970, Pstalmate, 1970, Gods and Golems, 1973, Early del Rey, 1975, Police Your Planet, 1975, The World of Science Fiction: 1926-76, 1980, others; editor: Fantastic Science-Fiction Art, 1926-54, 1975, Garland Library of Science Fiction, 1975, The Best of John W. Campbell, 1976. Student, George Washington U., 1931-33. Author, 1937—; author's agent Scott Meredith Lit. Agcy., NYC, 1947-50; tchr. fantasy fiction NYU, 1972-73; former editor sci. fiction mags.; editor Best Sci. Fiction Stories of Yr. E. P. Dutton & Co., 1971-75; fantasy editor Ballantine Books, 1975—. Home: 310 E 46th St New York NY 10017

DEL VECCHIO, LAURA, see Schmidt, George Neil

DEMARIS, OVID, b. Biddeford, ME, Sept. 6, 1919; s. Ernest J. and Aurore (Casavant) D.; m. Inez E. Frakes, May 15, 1942; children: Linda Lee, Peggy Ann. Author: Ride the Gold Mare, 1957, The Hoods Take Over, 1957, The Lusting Drive, 1958, The Slasher, 1959, The Long Night, 1959, The Extortioners, 1960, The Enforcer, 1960, The Gold-Plated Sewer, 1960, Lucky Luciano, 1960, The Dillinger Story, 1961, The Lindbergh Kidnaping Case, 1961, Candyleg, 1961, Chip's Girls, 1961, The Parasites, 1962, (with Ed Reid) The Green Felt Jungle, 1963, The Organization, 1964 (reissued as Fatal Mistake 1966, The Contract, 1970), (with Garry Wills) Jack Ruby, 1968, Captive City, 1969, America the Violent, 1970, Poso del Mundo, 1970, The Overlord, 1972, Dirty Business: The Corporate-Political Money-Power Game, 1974, The Director: An Oral Biography of J. Edgar Hoover, 1975, Judith Exner: My Story, 1976, Brothers in Blood: The International Terrorist Network, 1977, The Last Mafioso: The Treacherous World of Jimmy Fratianno, 1981, The Vegas Legacy, 1983, The Boardwalk Jungle, 1986. AB, Coll. Idaho, 1948; student, Syracuse U. Law Schl., 1948-49; MS, Boston U., 1950. Reporter Quincy (Mass.) Patriot-Ledger, 1949-50, Boston Daily Record, 1950, Boston bureau UP, 1950-52; advt. copy chief Los Angeles Times, 1953-59. Freelance writer, 1959—. Served with USAAF, 1940-45. Address: Box 6071 Santa Barbara CA 93160

DE MASI, JACK BERNARD, b. Bklyn., Oct. 26, 1946; s. Giacome Salvatore and Bernardine Pauline (Damen) DeMasi; m. Maryann Havrilak, April 25, 1970 (div. Apr. 25, 1980); m. 2d, Susan Beth Rubenstein, Aprl. 3, 1958; children—Alexander James, Ariel Colleye. Nonfiction to various mags. since 1960's: poetry in Hyn, Bitterroot, The Periodical, Basement Review. MA in English, CCNY,1969; MA in Cinema Studies, NYU, 1977. Senior ed. Eastern Basketball Mag. (W. Hempstead, NY), 1977—; mus. ed. NY Nightlife mag. (DeerPark, NY), 1982—; pres. Alpha Media (Huntington, NY), 1982—; tchr. NY Inst. of Tech. (Old Westbury, NY), 1970; Media Co-ord. Syosset schl. dist. (NY), 1979—. E5, NY State Nat'l. Guard May 1969-May 1975. Mem. Sigma Delta Chi, Univ. Film Assn., Am. Film Inst. Home: 22 Dobie Ave Huntington NY 11743

DEMBY, BETTY J., (Betty Jeffries), b. Chgo., Sept. 19; d. Herman and Sarah Jaffe; m. Dr. Emanuel H. Demby, May 15, 1955. Feature articles in various publs. including Seventeen Magazine, Filmakers Newsletter, Variety, NY Times, NY Daily News, NBC Monitor and Washington Star. BA, U. of Chgo. Writer and editor, DAI Newsletter, 1982—. Address: Demby Assoc, Inc 141 E 44 St NYC 10017

DE MILLE, NELSON RICHARD, b. NYC., Aug. 22, 1943, s. Huron and Antonia (Lombardo) DeM.; children—Lauren, Alex. Author: By the Rivers of Babylon, 1978, Cathedral, 1981, The Talbot Odyssey, 1984, Word of Honor, 1985. BA, Hofstra U., 1970. Served to 1st lt. U.S. Army, 1966-69; Vietnam. Mem. MWA, AG. Office 233 7th St Garden City NY 11530

DEMING, ALISON HAWTHORNE, b. Hartford, CT, July 13, 1946; d. Benton Hawthorne and Travilla (MacNab) Deming. One dau., Lucinda Williams. Contrbr. poetry to New Letters, Firehouse, Penumbra, Kennebec, Maine Times, Portland Rvw of the Arts, Louisville Rvw, Beloit Poetry Jnl, Nimrod, Tendril, Great River Rvw, Calliope, Shankpainter, others. MFA in Writing, Vt. Coll., 1983. Cons. to Health and Human Services Agencies, 1978—; adj. faculty Univ. So. Maine, Portland, 1983—. Recipient Pablo Neruda prize, 1983; Fine Arts Work Center fellow, 1984-85; Wallace Stegner Fellow, Stanford Univ., 1987-88. Address: 1002 Sawyer Rd Cape Elizabeth ME 04107

DEMOTT, BENJAMIN HAILER, b. Rockville Centre, NY, June 2, 1924; s. D. Gerard and Janet (Sanders) DeM.; m. Margaret Jane Craig, June 22, 1946; children: Joel, Thomas, Benjamin, Megan. Author: novels The Body's Cage, 1959, A Married Man, 1968; essays Hells & Benefits, 1962, You Don't Say, 1966, Supergrow, 1969, Surviving the Seventies, 1972, Scholarship for Society, 1974, America in Literature, 1977; Bd. editors: College English, 1964-70; contrbg. editor: Sat. Review, 1972-73, Atlantic Monthly, 1977—. BA, George Washington U., 1949; PhD, Harvard, 1953; MA, Amherst Coll., D. Litt., Franklin and Marshall Coll., 1970. Columnist Harper's, 1962-64, 81—, Am. Scholar, 1962-64, Atlantic Monthly, 1973-80; writer Nat. Ednl. TV, 1964. Mem. Soc. Mag. Writers; exec. com. Tchrs. and Writers; Collaborative, NYC. Guggenheim fellow. 1964, 69. Mem. PEN, Natl. Book Critics Circle, MLA. Address: U Mass Coll Fine Arts Amherst MA 01003

DENNIS, (MARY) RUTH, b. Bloomfield, IA, July 16, 1907, d. Claude Charles and Nora Jane (Townsend) Atwood; m. Donald A. Dennis, Sept. 11, 1932 (div. 1955); children—Lawrence Whitney, Mary Jo Dennis Bousek. Author: Homes of the Hoovers, 1986; contrbr. articles to Encyc. of Library and Info. Sci., numerous newspapers. Wrkg. on Wit and Wisdom of Hoover. Student U. Iowa, 1928, 56; cert. in library sci. U.S. Dept. Agr. Grad. Schl., 1964. Asst. librarian U.S. Dept. Agrl. Research and Devel., Peoria, Ill., 1964-66; librarian Herbert Hoover Presds. Library, West Branch, Iowa, 1966-72; freelance researcher, indexer, wrtr. Home: Main Street Pl Apt B2 West Branch IA 52358

DENNISON, SALLY ELIZABETH, b. Bartlesville, OK., Nov. 18, 1946; d. George Lovell and Elizabeth Ruth (Armstrong) Sneed; m. Gene Paul Dennison, July 12, 1969; children: Ted, Jean Marie. Author: Alternative Literary Publishing: Five Modern Histories, 1984; ed.: Caenis: A Mother-Myth (Schuett) 1979; Prairie City (Debo), 1985; Cleora's Kitchens: Eight Decades of Great American Food (Butler), 1985; White Knuckles Log (McAlpine), 1986; Back to the Damn Soil (Gubser), 1986. Wrkg. on fgn. fiction in English translation. MA, U. Tulsa, 1975, PhD, 1982. Teaching fellow U. Tulsa, 1975-79; owner/pres. Chrysalis House, Tulsa, 1979-82; gen. prtnr. Council Oak Books, Tulsa, 1984—. Home: 1324 E 26 St Tulsa OK 74114

DENTINGER, STEPHEN, see Hoch, Edward D.

D'EON, LEONARD JOSEPH, b. Boston, July 1, 1929; s. Maximin J. and Anna C. d'E.; m. Barbara Trant; children—Ann Mary, Leonard Joseph, Karyn Marie, Christopher Edward. Novel: The Cavalier, 1987. Wrkg. on novel. B.A., Boston Coll., 1951; M.B.A., Babson Coll., 1956. Home: 6330 E Lincoln Dr Paradise Valley AZ 85253

DE PALMA, ANTHONY ROBERT, b. Hoboken, NJ, June 16, 1952; s. Anthony Charles and Phyllis (Montenino) DeP.; m. Miriam Zebina Rodriques, May 25, 1975; children—Aahren, Laura Felice, Anthony Andres. Contrbr. articles to mags. and newspapers including N.Y. Times, Woman's Day, Sportstyle, N.J. Outdoors, Trenton Mag. Wrkg. on real estate column for N.Y. Times. B.A., Seton Hall U., 1975. Producer, N.J. Pub. TV, Trenton, N.J., 1975-78; mng. editor N.J. Reporter Mag., Princeton, N.J., 1979-81; free-lance writer, Montclair, N.J., 1981—. Mem. Sigma Delta Chi. Home: 88 Edgemont Rd Montclair NJ 07043

DE PAOLIS, ROSEMARY, b. Easton, PA, Sept. 8, 1962; d. John P. and Barbara Ann (Piazza) DeP. Contrbr. to North Am. Poetry Rvw, Impressions—A Collect. of Poetry, Blue Mountain Arts, Inc., The Express, The Woman's Nwspr. of Princeton. BA in jnlsm., Douglass Coll., 1984. Freelance writer/photog., Phillipsburg, NJ, 1983—; asst. ed. A.M. Best Co., 1986—. Home: 894 Wilbur Ave Phillipsburg NJ 08865

DE'PAZZI, ELLEN E, (e.e. de'pazzi), b. Elcador, IA, Apr. 7, 1915; d. Benjamin Harrison and Cecelia Hartlee (Gilman) Bosley; m. Pazzino, Aug. 17, 1940 (dec. Aug. 25, 1983); children: Cosimo H., Victor A. Contbr. poetry to various publs. including Sound Waves, Tap Roots, Poetry Corner, Poetry Anthology, others. Assoc. Degree, Suffolk Community Coll., 1987; postgrad. Ind. U., 1935-37. Chmn. Westhampton Outdoor Art Show, Westhampton Beach, N.Y., 1960-75; active Girl Scouts U.S.A., Washington, 1941-45. Portraits of 3 Presidents comm. Am. Freedom Fdn., 1962; recipient Gold medal Academia Italia Delle Art e Del Lavoro, 1982, World Culture prize Centre Studie, Italy, 1985. Mem. DAR (publicity chmn. 1980-82), Southfork Craftsmen Guild (publicity chmn. 1962-86), Hampton Ctr. Gallery (dif.-founder artist-poet group 1975—). Home: 44 Bayfield Ln Westhampton Beach NY 11078

DER HOVANESSIAN, DIANA, b. U.S.A. Author: How to Choose Your Past, 1978, Inside Green Eyes, Black Eyes, 1986, About Time, 1987; editor: Come Sit Beside Me and Listen to Koutchag, 1985, (also transl.) For You on New Year's Day, 1986; co-editor and transl.: Anthology of Armenian Poetry, 1978, Sacred Wrath, 1980, The Arc, Land of Fire, 1986; contrbr. Poemmaking, Twentieth-Century Literature. AB in Liberal Arts, Boston U.; postgrad. Harvard U. Visiting poet Mass. Council on Arts and Humanities, 1972—; tchr. workshops and seminars at various universities. PEN/American Translation Center award, 1977; Mary Carolyn Davies Award, PSA, 1977; Kolligan Award for Transl., Natl. Assn. of Armenian Studies and Research, 1980; Barcelona Prize for a Poem for Peace, Phoenix Ed. Ent., Barcelona, Spain, and Orbis Mag., England, 1985; Columbia Transl. Ctr. Van de Bovencamp Award for literary excellence in translating, 1986. Mem. PSA, New England Poetry Club (pres.), PEN, ALTA. Home: 2 Farrar St Cambridge MA 02138

DERHAM, MATTHEW JOSEPH, b. Feb. 3, 1928, s. Matthew Joseph and Catherine (Pinkham) D.; children—Kerin, Stephen. Ed., NYU. Vice-pres., account exec. Donnelly Bros., 1954-64; exec. v.p., chief exec. officer Automobile Club Underwrtrs. Acgy., Florham Park, N.J., 1964—; pres., chief exec. officer N.J. Automobile Club, Florham Park, 1973—, ed., pub. Driving mag., 1973—. Served with USN, 1946. Mem. Intl. Assn. Bus. Communicators. Office: Auto Club 1 Hanover Rd Florham Park NJ 07932

DERRICOTTE, TOI M., b. Detroit, Apr. 12, 1941, d. Benjamin Sweeney Webster and Antonia (Baquet) Dyrsu; m. Clarence Reese, July 1, 1962 (div. 1965); m. 2d, C. Bruce Derricotte, Dec. 30, 1967; 1 son—Anthony. Author: The Empress of the Death House, 1978, Natural Birth, 1983, Creative Writing, A Manual for Teacher, 1985; contrbr. poetry An Introduction to Poetry, 1986, Pequod, Iowa Rvw, Ironwood, Northwest Rvw. BA, Wayne State U., Detroit, 1965; MA, NYU, 1984. Poet-in-Schl., N.J. Council on Art, Trenton, 1974—, master tchr., 1984—; poetry tchr. Writers Voice, Manhattan West Side Y, N.Y.C., 1985—; writer-in- residence Cummington Community, Mass., 1986. Poetry fellow MacDowell Colony, N.H., 1982, N.J. State Council on Arts, 1983; creative writing fellow NEA, 1985. Mem. PEN, PSA, AAP. Home: 7958 Inverness Ridge Rd Potomac MD 20854

DERRINGER, STEELE, see Steward, Nanncy J.

DE SAINT PHALLES, THERESE, b. NYC, March 7, 1930; d. Alexandre and Helen Georgia (Harper) de S.P.; m. Jehan de Drouas, Dec. 30, 1950; children: Henri. Author: La Mendigote, 1966, La Chandelle, 1967, transl, The Candle, 1968, Le Tournesol, 1968, transl. The Sunflower, 1970, Le Souverain, 1970, La Clairiere, 1974, transl The Clearing, 1978, Le Metronome, 1980, Le Programme, 1985. Also author of opera libretto, Les Noces Rhymiques; five television plays. Contrbr to Le Monde and other periodicals. Attended the Sorbonne, University of Paris. Mem of editorial staff, Fayard, Paris, 1948-63; editor, Presses de la Cite (publisherssss, Paris, 1963-70; editor, Flammarion, Paris, 1971-84; gen. mgr, Stock (publishers), Paris, 1984—. Novelist. Awarded Prix le Bec et la Plume for La Mendigote. Home: 46 blvd Emile Augier 75116 Paris France

DES MARAIS, LOUISE MERCIER, (Sylvesta Bede), b. Cambridge, MA., Feb. 28, 1923; d. Louis Joseph Alexander and Zoe (Lassagne) Mercier; m. Philip Hubert Des Marais, Aug. 12, 1950 (separated May 1977); children—Monica, David (dec.), Louis (dec.). Author: For Goodness Sake, 1966, Signs of Glory, 1975. Contrbr. articles, poems to mags., newsletters. Editor speeches from Natl. Congresses of Confraternity of Christian Doctrine. AB in English, Emmanuel Coll., Boston, 1944. Secy., ed. Natalie Springarn, Eleanor Dulles, Washington, 1977-85; secy. Georgetown U., Washington, 1982—. Family Affairs Chmn. Natl. Council of Cath. Women, Washington, 1967-71. Mem. Washington Ind. Wrtrs., Washington Area Wrtrs. Home: 1529 44th St NW Washington DC 20007

DESMOND, WALTER THOMAS, JR., b. Meriden, CT. March 24, 1953; s. Walter Thomas Desmond and Joanne Marie (Casabon) Elkins; m. Cindy Marie McBey July 26, 1980 (div. July 1982); children—Daniel Grant. Poetry in Poet Lore, Blue Unicorn, The Writer, Orphic Lute, Rhino, other lit mags. Wrkg on book- length poetry ms. and essay on Franco-American novelist Julien Green. BA, Eng., Southern Conn. State Univ.; MA, Engl., Fordham Univ. Freelance wrtr. 1974-75; tchg. asst., Fordham, 1980-82; freelance, 1983-84; tchr., Oakland School (Boyd Tavern, Va.), 1985—. Mem. Poe Society. Home: 1505 Rugby Ave Charlottesville VA 22901

DETJEN, GUSTAV HEINRICH HUGO, JR., b. Altona, Elbe, Germany, Jan. 20, 1905, came to U.S., 1926, s. Gustav Heinrich Nicholaus and Martha (Lueders) D.; m. Marion Louise Kirby, Sept. 16, 1944; children—Christine Detjen Westendorf, Theodore, Louise Detjen Agne, James. Editor: Fireside Chats, F. D. Roosevelt Philatelic Soc., 1963—, The Philatelic Journalist, 1971—, Japos Bull., 1974—. Student, Pace U., 1933. Treas. Jay Dreher Corp., N.Y.C., 1930-38; pres. Detjen Corp., 1938-80. Home: 154 Laguna Ct Saint Augustine Shores FL 32086

DETZ, JOAN MARIE, b. Lancaster, PA, Aug. 13, 1951; d. Vernon Gerald and Mary Jane (McLaughlin) Detz. Author: How to Write and Give a Speech, 1984, You Mean I Have to Stand Up and Say Something?, 1986. BA in English, Millersville (Pa.) State Coll., 1973; MA in English, Coll. William and Mary, 1975. Account mgmt. trainee Wells, Rich, Greene Advt., N.Y.C., 1976-80; speech and script wrtr. Bklyn. Union Gas, 1980-85; speechwriting cons., Bklyn., 1985—. Mem. ASJA, Intl. Women's Writing Guild, Intl. Assn. Bus. Communicators. Home: 573 2d St Brooklyn NY 11215

DEUR, LYNNE A., b. Jamestown, NY, Mar. 14, 1941; d. Milford L. and Bessie H. (Peterson) Adams; m. Paul A. Deur, June 8, 1963 (div. 1984); children—Vincent, Sara. Author: Indian Chiefs, 1972, A Lumberjack's Story, 1982, Explorers and Traders, 1986, others. BA, Hope Coll., 1963. Editor Lerner Publications (Minneapolis, MI), 1965-67; freelance wrtr. 1967-80; publisher River Road Publications (Spring Lake, MI), 1980—. Office River Road Pub 830 East Savidge Spring Lake MI 49456

DE VINCK, JOSE M., (BARON DE VINCK), b. Brussels, Belgium, Mar. 31, 1912, came to U.S., 1948; s. Baron Marcel A. and Emma de Wouters d'Oplinter de V.; m. Catherine Kestens, Feb. 1, 1945; children—Bruno, Oliver, Anne—Catherine, Christopher, Jose, Maria. Author: Images, 1940, Le Cantique de la Vie, 1943, The Virtue of Sex, 1966, The Yes Book, 1972, The Words of Jesus, 1981, Revelations of Women Mystics, 1985; (with J. Raya) Byzantine Missal for Sundays & Fest Days, 1958, Byzantine Daily Worship, 1969; translator: The Works of Bonaventure, 5 vols., 1962-72. Greco-Latin Humanitics Certificate, Coll. St. Michel, Brussels (Jesuits), 1929. Candidate in Philo. and Letters (undergrad.), St. Louis Inst., Brussels, 1931. Doctor of Laws Louvain Univ., 1935; Prof. philosophy, Seton Hall U., South Orange, NJ, 1950-54; ed., translator St. Anthony Guild, Paterson, NJ, 1955-72; wrtr., owner Allelulia press, Allendale, NJ, 1972—. Recipient Poetry award Belgian Royal Acad. of Lit., Brussels, 1943. Home: 672 Franklin Turnpike Allendale NJ 07401

DE VIRI, ANNE, see Gunderson, Joanna

DE VITA, SHARON LOUISE, b. Chgo., June 19, 1950; d. Alan Henry and Endurance (Partee) McFeely; m. Anthony De Vita, Dec. 6, 1969; children—Jeanne, Ann Marie, Anthony Joseph. Author: Heavenly Match, 1986, Lady and the Legend, 1987, Kane and Mabel, 1987, Baby Makes Three, 1988, Sherlock's Home, 1988, Italian Knights, 1988. Grad. public schls., Hillside, IL. Mem. Natl. Soc. Arts Letters (3d v.p. Chgo. Chpt. 1984—), RWA (treas. Chgo. chpt. 1984-87; Best Unpublished Novel award 1985). Home: 3210 Saratoga Downers Grove IL 60515

DE VITO, JOSEPH ANTHONY, b. NYC, Aug. 1, 1938; s. James and Theresa (DeMartino) DeV. Author: The Psychology of Speech and Language, 1970, General Semantics, 1971, 74, Psycholinguistics, 1971, The Interpersonal Communication Book, 1976, 4th ed., 1986, Human Communication (formerly titled Communicology), 1978, 4th ed., 1988, The Elements of Public Speaking, 1981, 3d ed., 1987, The Communication Handbook: A Dictionary, 1986; editor: Communication: Concepts and Processes, 1971, 3d ed., 1981, Language: Concepts and Processes, 1973. BA, Hunter Coll., N.Y.C., 1960; MA, Temple U., Phila., 1962, PhD, U. Ill., Urbana, 1964. Mem. faculty Hunter-Lehman Coll., Bronx, N.Y., 1964-68, Lehman Coll., 1968-71, Queens Coll., Flushing, N.Y., 1971-85, Hunter

Coll., 1985—. Mem. Speech Communications Assn., Intl. Communications Assn., Intl. Soc. Gen. Semantics. Home: 140 Nassau St Apt 3C NYC 10038

DE VORE, MARY ALICE, (Madelyn Dohrn), b. Greenfield, OH, Dec. 16, 1940; d. Robert Garrett and Elsie Irene (Erskine) Anderson; m. James Harry DeVore, June 12, 1960; 1 s., Christian James. Author: The Best Defense (as Madelyn Dohrn), 1987. BS summa cum laude, Bloomsburg U., 1967; MA, Bowling Green State U., 1974. Profl. asst., dir. communications skills center Ohio No. U., Ada, 1977—; speaker on writing to local orgns. Mem. Writing Centers Assn., Romance Wrtrs. Am. Home: 126 W Montford St Ada OH 45810

DE VORE, SHERYL LYNN, b. Chgo., Aug. 20, 1956; d. Raymond J. and Dolores Faith (Wyszynski) Osterman; m. Karl W. Devore, Aug. 11, 1979. Contrbr. articles to newspapers, mags. including Suburban Tribune, The Ind. Register, Pioneer Press Newspapers, Ill. Mag., Sch. Musician, Great Lkes Travel & Living Mag. Asst. ed. Pioneer Press Spl. Section, Apr. 1987; ed. Northshore Concert Band Newsletter, 1985—; ed. Executive Image Newsletter, 1987—. B.S. in Edn., Northern Ill. U., 1978. Wrtr. Ind. Register, Libertyville, IL, 1982-83; staff wrtr. Pioneer Press Newspapers, Wilmette, IL, 1983—. Recipient Best-in-State award for feature story Ill. Coalition Against Domestic Violence, 1985, Best Feature award, Pioneer Press Newspapers, 1986, 87. Home: 967 Braeburn Rd Mundelein IL 60060

DE VRIES, PETER, b. Chgo., Feb. 27, 1910; s. Joost and Henrietta (Eldersveld) De V.; m. Katinka Loesser, Oct. 16, 1943; children: Jan, Peter Jon, Emily, Derek. Author: No But I Saw the Movie, 1952, The Tunnel of Love, 1954, Comfort Me with Apples, 1956, The Mackerel Plaza, 1958, The Tents of Wickedness, 1959, Through the Fields of Clover, 1961, The Blood of the Lamb, 1962, Reuben, Reuben, 1964, Let Me Count the Ways, 1965, The Vale of Laughter, 1967, The Cat's Pajamas and Witch's Milk, 1968, Mrs. Wallop, 1970, Into Your Tent I'll Creep, 1971, Without a Stitch in Time, 1972, Forever Panting, 1973, The Glory of the Hummingbird, 1974, I Hear America Swinging, 1976, Madder Music, 1977, Consenting Adults, or The Duchess Will be Furious, 1980, Sauce for the Goose, 1981, Slouching Towards Kalamazoo, 1983, The Prick of Noon, 1985, Peckham's Marbles, 1986. AB, Calvin Coll., 1931; student, Northwestern U., summer 1931. Editor community newspaper, Chgo., 1931, free-lance writer, 1931; assoc. editor Poetry Mag., 1938, co-editor, 1942; mem. editorial staff New Yorker Mag., 1944—. Mem. AAIAL. Home: 170 Cross Hwy Westport CT 06880

DE WESTBROOK, CICERO, see Martin Jack Rosenblum

DEWEY, BARBARA, b. Los Angeles, Dec. 21, 1923; d. Edward Russell Dewey and Elenore (Stratton) Van Fliess; children: Carol Whitnah, David Whitnah, Robert Wehrman, Catherine Wehrman Federico, Wendy Wehrman Turner. Author: As You Believe, 1985, The Creating Cosmos, 1985, The Theory of Laminated Spacetime, 1985. BA, Smith Coll., 1946. Peace, ecology, civic activist. Home: Box 634 Inverness CA 94937

DEWEY, DONALD WILLIAM, b. Honolulu, Sept. 30, 1933, s. Donald William and Jean (Jackson) D.; m. Sally Rae Dewey, Aug. 7, 1961; 1 dau., Wendy Ann. Author: Radio Control From the Ground Up, 1970, Flight Training Course, 1983, For What it's Worth, 1973; ed., pub. Starfish, Sea Urchins and their Kin, Baby Discus. Student Pomona Coll., 1953-55. Freelance photojnlst., 1951-53; TV script wrtr., 1953-54; pres., chmn. bd. dirs. R/C Modeler Corp. and RCM Publs., Sierra Madre, Calif., 1963—, ed., pub. R/C Modeler Mag., 1963—, Freshwater and Marine Aquarium Mag., 1978—, Pit Stop Mag., 1970-71. Creative wrtr. and contrbr. to numerous jnls. Home: 410 W Montecito Ave Sierra Madre CA 91024

DE WULF, KATHRYN COLLEEN, b. Des Moines, July 27, 1959; d. Ralph Wayne and Venita Elizabeth (Ehlers) Rorick; m. Kelly Phillip DeWulf, Mar. 22, 1980. Contrbr. poetry to anthols. Recipient 4 hon. mentions World of Poetry, 1985-87, Golden Poet Award, 1986. Mem. Ia. Poetry Assn. Home: RR 1 Wheatland IA 52777

DEXTER, JERRY D. (HAL WAYNE), b. Long Beach, CA, July 4, 1947; s. Sylvanus P. and Velma G. (Johnson) D.; m. Jennifer J. Holdaway, Apr. 10, 1976; 1 dau., Melissa Jean. Ed. & contrbr.: Street Rodding Illustrated, 1980-82, Street Rodder Mag., 1980-82, Custom Rodder Mag., 1980-83, The Best of Street Rodder, 1982, Popular Cars Mag., 1983-86, Camaro Trans Am, 1983-86, Rodder, 1985, Mustang Illustrated, 1986, Corvette Illustrated, 1986. BA, Cal. State Long Beach. Ed., McMullen Publishing, Anaheim, CA, 1980-82, editorial dir., 1982-85, group assoc. pub., 1986—. Served to Cpl., USMC, 1967-71. Office: McMullen 2145 W LaPalma Ave Anaheim CA 92801

DEYO, STEVEN MARK, b. Rochester, MN, July 10, 1957; s. Willet Ladd and Dieta Ortrud (Buchholz) D.; m. Maureen McGowan, Apr. 26, 1986. Writer: Catholic Bulletin, 1985-86; contrbr. to Mythcon XVI Proceedings, 1985 XVIII, 1987, & var. periodicals. BA in Span. & Theol. magna cum laude, Coll. of St. Thomas, 1978; MA in Jnlsm., U.MN, 1987. Ed.-in-chief Minnesota Technolog, Mpls., 1979-81; owner/agent and ed./pub. Crown Communications (pub. Mythos and Good News: Christians in Journalism), St. Paul, MN, 1981—. Office: Box 11626 St. Paul MN 55111

DIAMAN, N. A., (Nickolas Antony), b. San Francisco, Nov. 1, 1936; s. Petros Diamantides and Eva (Gemellas) Chrisopoulos. Author: (novels) Ed Dean Is Queer, 1978, The Fourth Wall, 1980, Second Crossing, 1982, Reunion, 1983, Castro Street Memories, 1987.BA, U. So. Calif., Exec. dir. Antares Fdn., San Francisco, 1976-79; pub. Persona Press, San Francisco, 1978-83, pres., chief exec. officer, 1983—.ess: Box 14022 San Francisco CA 94114

DIAMOND, ELYSE, see Ashcroft, Shelley Alane

DIAMOND, OLIVIA HARRIET, b. Chgo., Sept. 19, 1947; d. Clyde Garland and Alice (Dzierzgowski) Diamond; m. Abdu Sowayan, Mar. 29, 1969 (Div. Sept. 14, 1981); children—Leila, Khalid. Contrbr. poems to lit. mags., anthols. B.A., Northern Ill. U., 1969; M.A., U. Mo., 1971. Instr. U. Riyadh, Saudi Arabia, 1977-79; claims representative Social Sec., Rockford, IL, 1979— . Mem. Ill. Wrtrs. Inc. (coord. press table 1987), Rockford WG (program chmn., v.p.). Home: 1602 Latham St Rockford IL 61103

DIBNER, MARTIN, b. NYC., Oct. 5, 1911; s. Charles William and Ann Barbara (Schwam) D.; m. Nancy Cushman, Feb. 24, 1945 (div.); children: Eric, Steve. Author: (novels) The Bachelor Seals, 1948; The Deep Six, 1954 (made into film); Showcase, 1958; A God for Tomorrow, 1960; Sleeping Giant, 1962; The Admiral, 1967; The Trouble with Heroes, 1972; Ransom Run, 1980; Devil's Paintbrush, 1984; (non-fiction) The Arts in California, 1966; Seacoast Maine, People & Places, 1972, 1987; also numerous short stories, articles. BA in econ., U. Pa., 1933; postgrad. Rollins Coll., 1947-48. Exec. dir. Calif. Arts Comm., Sacramento, 1964- 66; founding dir. Joan Whitney Payson Art Gallery, Portland, Maine, 1970-74; commentator WMTW, ABC-TV, Auburn-Lewiston, Maine, 1985- 86. Served to lt. comdr. USN, 1941-45; PTO. Fellow 20th Century- Fox, 1945, Rosenwald Fdn., 1947, Huntington Hartford Fdn., 1961, Breadloaf Wrtrs., 1963, Baxter Soc.; mem. Mark Twain Soc. Home: Mayberry Hill Casco Village ME 04015

DICKINSON, JANET, (Jan), b. Cleve., Oct. 2, d. Richard Fisher and Gizella (Keplinger))Fisher Webster; m. Roy Huddleston Nicolai, Apr. 6, 1956 (div. 1961); m. 2d, Rodney Earl Dickinson, June 18, 1965 (div. 1976); 1 dau., Kimberly Cae. Author: Complete Guide to Family Relocation, 1983, Spouse Employment Assistance, 1984, Building Your Dream House, 1984, The Group Move/Corporate Relocation, 1983, Cookin' on the Move, 1983, Caveat Emptor—Let the Relocation Buyer Beware, 1984, Portland Facts Book, 1984, We're Moving! A Coloring Book, 1984, Quick Guide for the Not-So-Frequent Flyer, 1985, Establishing an Effective Relocation Department, 1983; contrbr.: Mobility Mag., SAVVY, People's Express Air mag., numerous other publs.; newsletter ed. Wrkg. on relocation books. Vice-pres. Art Lutz Co. Realtors, Oreg., Wash., Idaho, 1975-79; ind. relocation cons., Portland, Oreg., 1979-84; owner, pres. The Relocation Center, Portland, 1984—. Office: Reloc Ctr 6175 SW 112 Ave Beaverton OR 97005

DICKSON, JOHN, b. Chgo., July 10, 1916; s. John and Josephine (Stanley) D.; m. Virginia Weatherby; children—Susan Jane, Judith Anne, Patricia Jo. Author: Victoria Hotel, 1979 (Friends of Lit. Poetry award 1980), Waving at Trains, 1986; contrbr. short stories to Atlantic, Prairie Schooner, Denver Qtly., Tex. Qtly., U.S. Catholic, Topper, Rogue, Yankee, Progressive, Silver Foxes; contrbr. poetry to numerous popular and lit. publs. Student, Furman U., Greenville, S.C., 1935-36. Ptnr. John W. Dickson Co., Chgo., 1945-79. Presenter poetry shows, readings, Evanston Lighthouse Poetry Series, Loyola U. Poetry Day, Mus. Contemporary Art, Newberry Library, Mensa Soc., others. Named Poesia Gradara, Italian govt., 1971; recipient Editor's award Ill. Arts Council, 1984. Mem. Poetry Club Chgo., Poets & Patrons Chgo., North Shore Creative Writers. Address: 2249 Sherman Ave Evanston IL 60201

DIDDLE, DEBORAH KAY, b. Indpls., Mar. 21, 1949; d. Robert Alpheus and Lucinda Edna (Heisterberg) D. Contrbr. articles to Crown Point, Indiana-1934-1984, Hoosier United Methodist, Hoosier Homemaker, The Times Newspaper, Hammond, IN, 1981—. Wrkg. on short stories, articles, book on life in Ind. in 1800's. B.S. in Elem. Edn., Valparaiso U., 1973. Public info. officer Lake County Extension Homemakers, Crown Point, 1987—; active Lake County Hist. Soc. Home: 623 1/2 W South St

Crown Point IN 46307

DIDION, JOAN, b. Sacramento, CA., Dec. 5, 1934; d. Frank Reese and Eduene (Jarrett) D.; m. John Gregory Dunne, Jan. 1964. Author: novels Run River, 1963, Play It As It Lays, 1971, A Book of Common Prayer, 1977, The White Album, 1979; essays Slouching Towards Bethlehem, 1969; co-author screenplays for films The Panic in Needle Park, 1971, A Star Is Born, 1976. BA, U. Calif., Berkeley, 1956. Assoc. feature editor Vogue mag., 1956-63; former columnist Saturday Evening Post; former contrbg. editor National Review. Recipient 1st prize Vogue's Prix de Paris, 1956; Breadloaf Writers Conf. fellow, 1963. Address: Wallace & Sheil 177 E 70th St New York NY 10021

DIEBEL, DONALD RAY, b. Galveston, TX, June 12, 1947; s. Clarence William Diebel and Earlene June (Bowen) Henson; m. Sandra Gail Keeling, Jan. 26, 1974 (div. Dec. 12, 1978); 1 dau.—Erica Nicole. Author: How to Pick Up Women in Discos, 1980, The Complete Guide to Meeting Women, 1982, The Complete Guide to Meeting Men, 1986. Lab. tech. S.W. Chem., Seabrook, TX, 1969-72, Hercules, Inc., Pasadena, TX, 1973-80; ICI, Pasadena, 1981—; pub. Gemini Pub. Co., Houston, 1978—. Office: Gemini 11543 Gullwood Dr Houston TX 77089

DIECKMANN, ED(WARD) JR., b. San Diego, CA., Feb. 20, 1920; Se Edward Adolph and Martha Susan (Agnew) D.; m. Charlotte L. Peltcher, March, 1943; Children: Christopher M. Author: Volcano Mondo, 1977, The Secret of Jonestown: The Reason Why, 1981, Beyond Jonestown: Sensitivity Training and the Cult of the Mind, 1986. Contrbr. to history jnls and popular magazines, including Esquire, True, Coronet, American History Illustrated, and Civil War Times. Contrbg. ed., American Merury. BA in English (with distinction), San Diego State Coll (now U.), 1960. Patrolman, San Diego Police Dept., 1945-54, deputy marshal, 1954-56; parole agent in charge of Downey Parole and Probation Employment Project, State of California, Huntington Park, 1962-68; freelance writer and public speaker, 1969—. Mem.: Mystery Writers of America (hon. mem), Gamma Psi. Shared award from Argosy, 1943, for essay What Kind of America Do I Want to Come Back To? Military service: U.S. Army, paratrooper, 1939-45; served in Pacific Theater. Address: 3120 East Third St. Long Beach, CA 90814

DIERNISSE, VILLY, b. Denmark, Feb. 11, 1928. Author: Plastics Forming: New Technology, New Economics, New Potential, 1980, Plastics in Food Packaging, 1980, Retort Pouch: New Growth Industry, 1981, Word Processors and Typewriters Worldwide: Opportunities and Pitfalls, 1984; contrbr. articles to trade and consumer mags., 1948—. BSME, Polytechnic U., Bklyn., 1961. Address: 9 Kaufman Dr Westwood NJ 07675

DI FRANCO, ANTHONY M., b. NYC, Aug. 29, 1945, s. Theodore John and Josephine (Greco) Di F.; children—Allyson, Elizabeth, Dorothea, William. Author: Pope John Paul II: Bringing Love to a Troubled World, 1983, Italy: Balanced on the Edge of Time, 1983, Ardent Spring (novel), 1987. The Streets of Paradise (novel), 1984. BA, Fordham U., 1966, MA, 1969. Prof. English Suffolk Community Coll., Selden, N.Y., 1974—. Winner 1st prize fiction, Catholic Press Assn., 1982, O. Henry award, 1986. Office: Suffolk CC 533 Coll Rd Selden NY 11784

DIGGES, DEBORAH LEA, b. Jefferson City, MO, Feb. 6, 1950, d. Everett Dornbush and Geneva Ione (Van Dyke) Sugarbaker; m. Charles William Digges V, Aug. 23, 1969 (div. Dec. 1980); children—Charles William VI, Stephen Phillip; m. Stanley Ross Plumly, July 11, 1985. Author: (poetry) Vesper Sparrows, 1986; contrbr. poetry to New Yorker, Antaeus, The Nation, Am. Poetry Rvw, Field, Ga. Rvw, Antioch Rvw, others. BA, U. Calif., Riverside, 1976; MA, U. Mo., 1981; MFA, Iowa Wrtrs. Workshop, 1984. Asst. prof. English, Tufts U., Medford, Mass., 1986. Breadloaf Wrtrs. Conf. scholar, 1980, fellow, 86; teaching- writing fellow U. Iowa Writers Workshop, 1984; Ingram Merrill Fdn. fellow, 1985-86. Mem. PSA. Home: 84 Winthrop St Brookline MA 02146

DIGGS, ELIZABETH FRANCIS, b. Tulsa, OK, Aug. 6, 1939; d. James Barnes and Virginia (Francis) Diggs; m. Will Mackenzie, June 8, 1961 (div. 1963); 1 dau., Jennifer. Author plays: Close Ties, 1980, Dumping Ground, 1981, Goodbye Freddy, 1983, American Beef, 1987. B.A., Brown U., 1961; M.A., Columbia U., 1963, Ph.D., 1980. Asst. prof. Jensen City State Coll., NJ, 1972-77; adj. prof. N.Y.U., 1987; playwright-in-residence Portland Stage Co., 1985, N.Y. Stage Co. Am., 1987. Mem. DG. Home: Rural District Box 212 Chatham NY 12037

DIKMEN, NED F., b. Istanbul, Turkey; s. Edip and Roza (Devli) D.; came to U.S., 1961. MS, U. MI, 1965, PhD, 1969. Pub./ed.-in-chief Great Lakes Boating Mag., Chgo., 1981—. Mem. Chgo. Press Club. Office: Great Lks Boating 830 N State Chicago IL 60610

DILL, EDITH PALLISER, b. Bklyn., Mar. 21, 1925; d. Charles Henry and Edith Adelaide Palliser; m. John W. Dill, Aug. 31, 1963; children—Donna R. Nunn, Susan E. McDuffie. Contrbr. poems to anthols., newspaper. Assoc. ed., graphic artist: A History of Altoona and its Surrounding Area, 1987. Student Packer Collegiate Inst., 1945. Swim coach Bell Haven Park, Miami, 1952-69; rural carrier U.S. Postal Service, Umatilla, FL, 1973-80, retired. Recipient Honorable Mention, World of Poetry, (2) 1986, Golden Poet award, 1987. Home: Meadowind Farm Box 52 Altoona FL 32902

DILL, MICHELE ANDRUS, b. CA, Aug. 18; d. James C. and Diana (Lincoln) Andrus; m. Michael N. Dill, Feb. 22, 1980. Assoc. ed. Seattle Business, 1985—; ed. Pacific Banker, 1985—. BA summa cum laude, Brigham Young U., 1982. Feat. writer/rptr. Las Vegas (NV) Sun, 1979-81; asst. features ed. Ogden (UT) Standard-Examiner, 1982-84; copy ed. Seattle Times, 1984-85; assoc. ed. Seattle Business, 1985—; ed. Pacific Banker, Seattle, 1985—. Mem. SPJ. SPJ awards, 1983, 85, 86, 87, AP awards, 1984, 85, Intl. Assn. of Business Communicators Award of Excellence, 1987. Office: Vernon Pub 109 W Mercer Seattle WA 98119

DILLARD, ANNIE, b. Pittsburgh, April 30, 1945; d. Frank and Pam (Lambert) Doak; m. Gary Clevidence, April 12, 1980; children—Carin, Shelly, Cody Rose. Author: poetry Tickets for a Prayer Wheel, 1974; Pilgrim at Tinker Creek, 1974 (Pulitzer Prize for genl. nonfiction); Holy the Firm, 1977; Living by Fiction, 1982; Teaching a Stone to Talk, 1982; Encounters with Chinese Writers, 1984, An American Childhood, 1987. Wrkg. on Writing a Book. BA, Hollins Coll., 1967, MA, 1968. Lectr. Hollins Coll., 1974; Distinguished Visiting Professor, Western Washington Univ., 1975-78; prof., Wesleyan Univ., 1979—; prof. and wrtr.-in-res., 1987—. Columnist The Living Wilderness, The Wilderness Soc., 1973-75; contrbg. ed. Harper's, 1973-81. NY Presswomen's award for excellence, 1975. Phi Beta Kappa Orator, Harvard Univ., 1983. Mem. PSA, AG, Natl. Citizens for Public Libraries, Phi Beta Kappa. Address: Gregory 2 Tudor City Pl New York NY 10017

DILLARD, EMIL LEE, b. Langdon, KS, Mar. 14, 1921, s. Oscar Winfield and Mabel Dolly (Brooks) D.; m. Leona Mae Sneed, Sept. 12, 1942. Contrbr. poetry: Adelphi Qtly, Descant, Quoin, Scimitar & Song, other lit. mags.; author: Nouns and Pronouns: I and Others (selected Poems), 1974. Wrkg. on poems. BA, Emporia State U., 1946; MA, Columbia U., 1948, MPhil, 1974. Mem. faculty U. Oreg., Eugene, 1948-50, Hunter Coll., NYC., 1953; mem. faculty Adelphi U., Garden City, N.Y., 1954—, prof. emeritus, 1984—. Served to 1st lt. USAF, 1942-46; PTO. Mem. AAUP, MLA, P&W, AAP, PSA, LI Poetry Collective. Home: 74 Rutland Rd Hempstead NY 11550

DILLINGHAM, DANIEL JAY, b. Greenville, MI, Apr. 6, 1958; s. Allen J. and Barbara Jean (Carlton) D. Contrbr. articles to profl. jnls., lit. mags. B.A. Grand Valley State Coll., 1986. Counselor spl. services program Grand Valley State Coll., Allendale, MI, 1986—. Recipient E. W. Oldenburg Writing award Grand Valley State Coll., 1982, 84. Home: 132 Lafayette Grand Rapids MI 49503

DILLMANN, NANCY CAMERON, b. Durham, NC, Nov. 11, 1947; d. William Eccles and Elizabeth Jane (Scott) Huff; m. Joseph Michael Dillmann, July 3, 1986. Contrbr. poetry: Quill Books, Green Valley Pub., Am. Poetry Assn., New Worlds Unlimited, numerous others. Diploma, St. Joseph's Sch. Nursing, 1969. RN, Ill. Staff nurse St. Joseph's Hosp., Alton, Ill., 1969-77, Condell Meml. Hosp., Libertyville, Ill., 1983-86, Hawthorn Place Surg. Center, Libertyville, 1986—. Golden Poet Award, 1987. Home: 526 Oak St Libertyville IL 60048

DILLON, BRANDY, see Dillon, Debra Jean

DILLON, DEBRA JEAN, (Brandy Dillon), b. Dewitt, IA, Nov. 23, 1952; d. Daniel Bunce and Lucille Viola (Jurgensen) Faber; children—Michelle Lee, Tara LeeSan. Contrbr. poems to anthols., mags. Wrkg. on book of poetry, novel. Student Bradley U., 1976. Home: RT 1 Box 125 Wheatland IA 52777

DILLON, MILLICENT, b. May 24, 1925; d. Ephraim and Clara (Millman) Gerson; children—Wendy Lesser, Janna Lesser. Author: Baby Perpetua and Other Stories, 1971, The One in The Back Is Medea, 1973, A Little Original Sin: The Life and Work of Jane Bowles, 1981; ed.: Out in the World, 1985. NEH fellow, 1977. Mem. PEN, AG. Address: 72 Sixth Ave San Francisco CA 94118

DILLON, RICHARD HUGH, b. Sausalito, CA., Jan. 16, 1924; s. William T. and Alice M. (Burke) D.; m. Barbara A. Sutherland, June 9, 1950; children: Brian, David, Ross. Author: Embarcadero, 1959, The Gila Trail, 1960, Shanghaiing Days, 1961, California Trail Herd, 1961, The Hatchet Men, 1962, Meriwether Lewis, 1965, J. Ross Browne, 1965, The Legend of Grizzly Adams, 1966, Fool's Gold, 1967, Humbugs and Heroes, 1970, Burnt-Out Fires, 1973; Exploring the Mother Lode Country, 1974 (Spur award WWA, 1974), Siskiyou Trail, 1975,

We Have Met the Enemy, 1978, High Steel, 1979, Great Expectations, 1980, Delta Country, 1982, San Francisco, 1983, North American Indian Wars, 1983, Iron Men, 1984, North Beach, 1985, Impressions of Bohemia, 1986. AB with honors in history, 1948, MA, 1949, BS in L.S., 1950. Served with inf. AUS, World War II; ETO. Decorated Purple Heart; recipient award Am. Assn. State and Local History for all-around research and pub. Fellow Calif. Hist. Soc.; ex- pres. Book Club Calif. Home: 98 Alta Vista Ave Mill Valley CA 94941

DIM, see Murphy, Diana Sue Grogan,

DIMEO, R. STEVEN, b. Portland, OR, Sept. 27, 1945, s. Frank Angelo and Josephine Ann (Giglio) D.; m. Laura Lea Fiasca, Dec. 17, 1965 (div. 1976); m. 2d, Nettie Elaine Schermer, Nov. 20, 1976. Contrbr. short stories, poetry to Crosscurrents, Descant, Gusto, Blue Unicorn, numerous other lit mags. BA, U. Oreg., 1967; MA, U. Utah, 1968, PhD with distinction, 1970. Asst. prof., acting chmn. dept. English Mayville (N.D.) State Coll., 1970-72; Fulbright jr. lectr. Am. lit. Gesamthochschule Duisburg, W. Ger., 1974-75; ed. Transition Lit. Mag./New Oreg. Rvw, Hillsboro, 1976—; film reviewer Cinefantastique, 1978—. Mem. NWC, P&W, CCLM. Home: 537 NE Lincoln St Hillsboro OR 97124

DIMLER, GEORGE RICHARD, b. Balt., Oct. 21, 1932; s. George Herbert and Gertrude Helena (Kelly) D. Author: Friedrich Von Spee's Trutznachtigall: German Studies in America, 1973, Friedrich Spees Trutznachtigall, 1981; editor: Issues of Life and Death, 1982, Special Issue on Violence, 1981; translations and articles pub. in numerous scholarly jnls. MA, Middlebury Coll., 1966; PhD, UCLA, 1970. Asst. prof. Loyola Coll., Balt., 1970-72; assoc. prof. Fordham U., Bronx, N.Y., 1972-81, prof., 1981—; editor-in-chief Thought Mag., Bronx, 1978—. Grantee NEA, 1974, ACLS, 1975, Fordham U., 1973, 76, 77, German Acad. Exchange Service, 1976, 77, Jesuit Writers Fund, 1975, Huntington Library, 1983. Mem. Editors of Learned Jnls., Am. Assn. Teachers of German, Soc. for German Renaissance and Baroque Lit., Renaissance Soc. Am., MLA, Catholic Press Assn., Soc. Scholarly Publ., German Soc. of Md., Soc. Emblem Studies. Office: Fordham U Loyola Hall 607 Bronx NY 10458

DINARDO, MARILYNN, (Mary Lynn Lesti), b. Cleve., Dec. 4, 1937; d. Tom S. and Lillian A. (Drdek) Dinardo; m. John Lesti, Aug. 30, 1969 (dec. June 20, 1985); stepchildren—Sandy, Lisa, Michael, Anthony. Columnist: Crusader News, 1985-86; columnist, contrbr.: Liberty News & Views, 1985—. Contrbr. numerous articles, interviews to newspapers. B.S., Fenn Coll., 1961; M.A., Western Reserve U., 1963. Tchr. public schls., Cleve., 1961—. Mem. SPJ, SDX, Cleve. Press Club, Ohio Press Women, NFPW. Home: 22440 Sandalwood Rd Bedford Heights OH 44146

DI NICOLA, ALBERT, b. Brittoli, Italy, Apr. 28, 1917, came to U.S., 1924; naturalized, 1943; s. Ettore and Carina (Di Benedetto) Di N.; m. Theresa Patricia Lento, Jan. 6, 1946; children—Albert F., Claudia M. Rufo. Author: Making Good Marriages, 1954, 2d ed., 1986, Dear David, 1983, Take a Break!, 1984, 2d., 1986. JD, Northeastern U., 1942; J.D., Suffolk U., 1948. Served with U.S. Army, 1942-45. Home: 1310 Highland Glen Rd Westwood MA 02090

DINTENFASS, MARK, b. NYC., Nov. 15, 1941; s. Sidney and Gerri (Berger) D.; m. Phyllis Schulman, June 10, 1962; children: David, Nathan. Author: (novels) Make Yourself an Earthquake, 1969; The Case Against Org, 1970; Figure 8, 1974; Montgomery Street, 1978; Old World, New World, 1982; The Loving Place, 1986. BA, Columbia U., 1963, MA, 1964; MFA, U. Iowa, 1968. Prof. English, Lawrence U., Appleton, Wis., 1968—. Mem. AG, PEN. Home: 738 E Eldorado St Appleton WI 54911

DINUSCHEONNIA, see Walker, Lorraine,

DIOMEDE, MATTHEW, b. Yonkers, NY., June 8, 1940; s. Frank and Josephine (Carione) D.; m. Barbara Ruth Rogers, June 29, 1968. Contrbr. poems, prose and fiction to Phylon, Voyeur, S. W. Rvw, Bardic Echoes, other lit. mags. BA in English, Fordham U., 1962, MS, 1965; MA in English, L.I. U., 1975. Coordinator communications U. Mo., St. Louis, 1979-82; teaching fellow in English, Harris Stone State Coll., St. Louis, 1983-85; lectr. English Parks Coll. of St. Louis U., Cahokia, Ill., 1982-85, asst. prof. English, 1985—; instr. English, Belleville Area Coll., Ill., 1983-85. Served with USMC, 1959-65. Recipient alumni poetry award L.I. U., 1978; 2d prize Maine Wrtrs. Conf., 1970. Mem. NCTE, CCCC. Home: 815 Bourbon Red Dr Des Peres MO 63131

DIORIO, MARGARET TOARELLO, b. NYC; d. James and Marie (Locke) Toarello; m. David Diorio; children—Juliette, Christopher. Poems in many lit mags. and anthols including U. of Windsor Rvw, Beloit Poetry Jnl, Wisconsin Rvw; books: Bringing in the Plants, 1980, Listening, 1970, Morning Fugues, 1960. Student, Columbia Univ., New York. Edit. and publ., Icarus, Balt., MD, 1973-82. Home: 1015 Kenilworth Dr Towson MD 21204

DI PASQUALE, EMANUEL (PAUL), b. Ragusa, Italy, Jan. 25, 1943; came to U.S., 1957; s. Serafino and Raffaella Di P.; m. Mari Kula, Jan. 14, 1965; children—Paul, Laura. Book: The Dynamics of Student Writing, 1984. Book of poems: Genesis, 1987. Poems have appeared in texts: Literature, Tygers of Wrath, An Intro. to Poetry, Easter Poems, Thanksgiving Poems, others. BA, Adelphi U., 1965; MA, NYU, 1966. Instr. Elizabeth City U., N.C., 1966-68; asst. prof. Middlesex County Coll., Edison, N.J., 1968—. Mem. NCTE. Home: 34 Westminster Pl Edison NJ 08817

DI PRIMA, DIANE, b. NYC, Aug. 6, 1934; d. Francis and Emma (Mallozzi) diP.; children—Jeanne, Dominique, Alexander, Tara, Rudi. Coeditor: The Floating Bear, 1961-63; editor: Kulchuir, 1960-61, Signal mag., 1963; editor, pub.: (with Alan S. Marlowe) Poets Press, NYC, 1964-69; books include Dinners and Nightmares, 1961, New Handbook of Heaven, 1963, Earthsong: Poems, 1957-59, 1968, Hotel Albert, 1968, Revolutionary Letters, 1969, The Book of Hours, Loba, pt. I, 1973; pub.: Eidolon Edits., San Francisco, 1972-76; dir.: N.Y. Poets Theatre, 1961-65; author: This Kind of Bird Flies Backward, 1958; (play) Murder Cake, 1960, Paideuma, 1960, The Discontent of a Russian Prince, 1961, Like, 1964; (poetry) The Monster, 1961, Poets Vaudeville, 1964, Haiku, 1967, The Star, The Child, The Light, 1968; (novel) Memoirs of a Beatnik, 1969, L.A. Odyssey, 1969, New As..., 1969, Notes on a Summer Solstice, 1969, Prayer to the Mothers, 1971, So Fine, 1971; (novel) The Calculus of Variation, 1972; Poems for Freddie, 3 vols., 1972-78, Selected Poems, 1956-75, 1975; editor: (with LeRoi Jones) The Floating Bear: A Newsletter, Nos. 1-37, 1974, War Poems, 1968, Various Fables from Various Places, 1960; Loba, pt. II, 1976, Selected Poems, 1956-1976, 1977, Loba, pts. I-VIII, 1978, Spring and Autumn Annuals, 1979, Poetry Road, 1979; ed. anthol. Realm of the Mothers, 1979. Natl. Inst. Arts and Letters grantee, 1965; NEA grantee, 1966. Address: Box 15068 San Francisco CA 94115

DITCHOFF, PAMELA JANE, b. Lansing, MI, Sept. 21, 1950; d. Ronald Ernest and Beatrice Watson (Porter) Reed; m. Paul Alexander Ditchoff, Mar. 28, 1983; children—Dean Reed, Joshua Judson, Deborah Kristine. Contrbr. to So. Fla. Poetry Rvw, Yet Another Small Mag, Rhino, Sonora Rvw; author made-for-tv documentary, 1983. BA, Mich. State U., 1982, MA, 1985. Copywriter/creative cons. WFSL-TV, Lansing, Mich., 1982-84; writing instr. Mich. State Univ. and Lansing Community Coll., 1984—; freelance media writer, East Lansing, 1984—. Recipient Mich. Addy award for Excellence, Am. Advertising Fedn., 1984. Address: 2457 Lk Lansing Rd East Lansing MI 48823

DITTMER, STEVAN W., b. Cin., Jan. 23, 1952; s. Wayne M. and LaVerne M. (Brookbank) D.; m. Debra Ann Smith, Sept. 1974; 1 son, Chris. BS with honors, Ohio State U., 1974. Communications dir. Nebraska Stock Growers, Alliance, NE, 1974-76; exec. dir. Nebraska Beef Industry Fdn., Gibbon, NE, 1976-83; ed. & pub. Calf News Mag., Riverdale, NE, 1983—. Mem. Natl. Cattlemen's Assn., Nebraska Stock Growers Assn., Livestock Publs. Council. Home: Rt 1 Box 27A Riverdale NE 68870

DIVOK, MARIO J., b. Benus, Czechoslovakia, came to U.S., 1970, s. Jozef and Anna (Citterberg) D. Author: The Relations, 1975, The Voice, 1975, The Wind of Changes, 1978, Equinox, 1978, The Collection, 1978, I Walk the Earth, 1980, The Blind Man, 1980, Looking for the Road to the Earth, 1983, The Birthday, 1984, Forbidden Island Complete Works: Two, 1986. Ed. in Czechoslovakia; MPA, Calif. State U.-Long Beach, 1977. Tchr. history of art and lit. Atenisi Coll., Tonga, Peace Corps, 1976. Recipient Schlossar award for play, Hall Pubs., Switzerland, 1980, Potpourri Intl. award, London, 1980; winner One-Act Play competition One Way Theatre, San Francisco, 1980, Orange County Poetry Contest, Laguna Poets, 1981, others. Home: 5 Misty Meadow Irvine CA 92715

DIXON, STEPHEN, b. NYC, June 6, 1936; s. Abraham Mayer and Florence (Leder) Ditchik; m. Anne Frydman, Jan. 17, 1982; 2 daus., Sophia, Antonia. Author: No Relief, 1976, Work, 1977, Too Late, 1978, Quite Contrary, 1979, 14 Stories, 1980, Movies, 1983, Time To Go, 1984, Fall & Rise, 1985, Garbage, 1987. BA, CCNY, 1958. Bartender/waiter, NYC,1975-76; lectr. NYU, NYC,1979-80; assoc. prof. Johns Hopkins Univ., Balt., 1980—. Stegner fellow, Stanford Univ., 1964-65, Guggenheim fellow, 1985; NEA grantee, 1975; recipient Am. Acad. Inst. Arts and Letters award in Lit, 1983. Address: 2103 Sulgrave Ave Baltimore MD 21209

DOBBS, ROSALYNE BROWN, b. Little Rock, Aug. 20, 1933; d. Hervey Alger and Vera (Crow) Brown; m. John Allen Dobbs, Aug. 25, 1954; 1 dau., Cheryl Anne Dobbs Wikman. Contrbr. articles: Am. Horticulturist, Am. Rose Mag., Pediatric Newss, Progressive Farmer, Organic Gardening, numerous other publs. Wrkg. on articles, gardening book. BA, La. State U., 1954.

Freelance wrtr., 1973—; columnist Am. Rose Mag. Mem. NASW. Home: 10934 Effringham Ave Baton Rouge LA 70815

DOBELL, (ELEANOR) MERCY, b. Columbus, OH, Sept. 21, d. Edwin Bishop and Eleanor (Mobroe) Dobell; m. George H. Wolfe, Nov. 8, 1958. Am. corr. and feature wrtr., Die Linie, 1975—; contrbr. articles to: Japanese mag., Body Fashions mag. Wrkg. on fantasy stories. BA cum laude, Ohio State U., MA, cum laude. Ed. Haire Pub. Co., 1949-66, Harcourt, Brace, Jovanovich, 1966-75. Mem. Pen & Brush. Home: 20 W 10th St New York NY 10011

DOBELL, BYRON MAXWELL, b. Bronx, NY., May 30, 1927; s. Jacob and Marie (Schaeffer) D.; m. Edith Spielberg, 1952 (div. 1957); m. Ande Rubin, 1958 (dec. 1967); 1 dau., Elizabeth; m. Elizabeth Rogers Dempster, 1969. Picture editor U.S. Camera, 1952-55; assoc. editor Popular Photography, 1956-57; feature editor Pageant, 1957-58, This Week, 1958-60; sr. editor Time-Life Books, 1960-62, assoc. dir. editorial planning, 1971-72; mng. editor Esquire mag., NYC., 1962-67; 79-82, editor- in-chief, 1977; ed.-in-chief Book World (weekly lit. supplement Chgo. Tribune and Washington Post), 1967-69; ed.-in-chief book div. McCall Pub. Co., 1969-71; editorial dir. New York mag., 1972-77; sr. editor Life mag., 1978-79; editor Am. Heritage mag., 1982—; AB, Columbia U., 1947. Editor: Life Guide to Paris. Served with AUS, 1946-47. Mem. PEN. Home: 150 E 69th St New York NY 10021

DOBRIN, ARTHUR BARRY, b. Bklyn., Aug. 22, 1943; s. Moe and Anne (Slavin) Dobrin; m. Lyn Beth, Aug. 30, 1960; children—Eric Simba, Kikora Anana. Author: A History of Black Jews in America, 1965, The Role of Cooperatives in the Development of Rural Kenya, 1968, Sunbird, 1976, Getting Married The Way You Want, 1975, The God Within, 1977, Little Heroes, 1977, Saying My Name Out Loud, 1978, Gentle Spears, 1980, Out of Place, 1982, MA, NYU, 1971. Peace Corps vol., Kenya, 1965-67; leader, Ethical Humanist Society of Long Island, Garden City, NY, 1968—. Mem. Am. Assoc. of Family Therapists, PSA, Amnesty Intl. Home: 613 Darmouth ST Westbury NY 11590

DOCTOROW, EDGAR LAWRENCE, b. NYC., Jan. 6, 1931; s. David Richard and Rose (Levine) D.; m. Helen Esther Setzer, Aug. 20, 1954; children: Jenny, Caroline, Richard. Author: Welcome to Hard Times, 1960, Big as Life, 1966, The Book of Daniel, 1971, Ragtime, 1975; (play) Drinks Before Dinner, 1979; Loon Lake, 1980, Lives of the Poets, 1984. AB in philo. with honors, Kenyon Coll., 1952. Editor New Am. Library, NYC., 1960-64; editor-in-chief Dial Press, 1964-69, pub., 1969; creative writing fellow Yale Schl. Drama, 1974-75; writer-in-res. U. Calif., Irvine, 1969-70. Served with AUS, 1953-55. Recipient Arts and Letters award Am. Acad. and Natl. Inst. Arts, 1976; Guggenheim fellow, 1973; CAPS fellow, 1973-74. Mem. AG, AAIAL, Am. PEN, WG AM. Address: Random HS 201 E 50th St New York NY 10022

DODD, ANNE WESCOTT, b. Bangor, ME, Apr. 24, 1940; d. Arhie Hanson an Felicia (Ferrara) Wescott; m. James H. Dodd, Feb. 26, 1965; children—Vickie Gehm, Suzan de los Heross. Author: Write Now, 1973, From Imagess to Words, 1986, Practical Strategies for Taming the Paper and People Problems in Teaching, 1987. Contrbr. articles to ednl. jnls., newspapers, mags. B.A., U. Maine, 1961, Certificate of Advanced Study, 1982; M.A., Calif. State U., Los Angeles, 1967. Prin., Freeport Middle Schl., ME, 1981-83; lectr. Bates Coll., Lewiston, ME, 1984—; visiting lectr. Colby Coll., Waterville, ME, 1986—. Mem. NCTE, Maine Council English Lang. Arts (prs.), SCBW. Home: 3095 Mere Pt Rd Brunswick ME 04011

DODD, DONALD BRADFORD, b. Manchester, AL, Feb. 6, 1940; s. Benjamin Garland and Alta Savanna (Weaver) D.; m. Sandra Ellen Dodd, June 18, 1961 (div. 1984); children—Donna Ellen, Donald Bradford, Jr.; m. 2d, Amelia Jane Bartlett, Dec. 7, 1986; 1 dau., Anna Lorene. Author: Historical Atlas of Alabama, 1974; co-author: Winston (Mountain Unionism in Confederate Alabama), 1972, Historical Statistics of the South, 1973, Historical Statistics of the Midwest, 1976, Simulations in Urban and Contemporary Affairs, 1977, USAF Victory Credits, World War II, 1978, State and Local Government Administration, 1985, numerous pamphlets and bibliographies; ed. pamphlets on mil. and diplomatic affairs. BS, U. N. Ala., 1961; MA, Auburn U., 1966; PhD, U. Ga., 1969. Prof. History Auburn U.-Montgomery, Ala., 1969—. Col. USAF Res. Grantee, seminar and workshop leader NEH, 1977-85. Mem. numerous profl. orgns. Home: 6012 Pinebrook Dr Montgomery AL 36117

DOHERTY, JOHN PATRICK, b. Chgo., May 21, 1947; s. John and Mary (McGing) D. Contrbr. articles on AIDS, support services to mags., trade jnls. Wrkg. on book, AIDS: Caring for the Caregiver. BA, philosophy, Niles Coll., Loyola Univ., 1965; M.Div., U. St. Mary of the Lake, 1969. Clinical supvr. Gateway Fdn., Chgo., 1983-85; dir. support services Howard Brown Clinic, Chgo., 1985-87, counseling coord., 1981—. Mem. Ill. Pediatric AIDS Task Force, Ill. Oncology Social Workers AIDS Task Force, Ill. Alcohol & Addiction AIDS Task Force. Home: 3420 N Janssen 2 Chicago IL 60657

DOHRN, MADELYN, see DeVore, Mary Alice

DOHRN, MADELYN, see Dornbusch, Joan Louise Falquet

DOLAN, G. KEITH, b. Los Angeles, June 14, 1927; s. George K. and Ruth B. (Brookhart) D.; m. Florence Campbell, Apr. 8, 1952 (div. Dec., 1982); children—Diana, Clarice, Daniel, Carole; m. 2d, Brenda Maddox, Feb. 18, 1984. Author: Sports Almanac—USA, 1984. BA, Pepperdine U., 1950; Ed.D., UCLA, 1962. Prin. La Mesa Jr. High Schl., Calif., 1956-60, San Bernadino High School, 1960-67; prof. Calif. State Univ., San Bernadino, 1967—. Pres. YMCA, San Bernadino, 1964-66; v.p. Calif. Faculty Assn., 1985-86. Served in USN, 1945-46. Recipient Outstanding Educator Alumni award Pepperdine Univ., Los Angeles, 1962, Outstanding Tchr. (Univ.) award, 1970. Mem: La Mesa-Spring Valley Tchrs. Assn., San Bernadino Adminstrs. Assn. Home: 3946 Ironwood San Bernadino CA 92404

DOLLEN, CHARLES JOSEPH, b. April 14, 1926; s. Charles Joseph and Cecelia Margaret (Pfeiffer) D. Author: Bibliography of the United States Marine Corps, 1963, ed and translator, A Voice Said Ave.! 1963, Jesus Lord, 1964, Civil Rights: A Source Book, 1964, rev ed, 1966, John F. Kennedy, American, 1964, Toward Responsible Parenthood, 1964, ed. C. Marmion, Fire of Love, 1964, ed St. Augustine, The Trinity, 1965, Index to Sixteen Documents of Vatican II, 1966, Mademoiselle Louise: The Life of Louise de Marillac, 1967, African Triumph, 1967, Ready or Not, 1968, Vatican II: A Bibliography, 1969, Messengersss to the Americas, 1975, co-ed, The Catholic Tradition, 14 vol, 1979, The Catholic Church in the West, 1981, ed Prayerbook of the Saints, 1984, Prayers for the Third Age, 1985, Prophecies Fulfilled, 1986, Rosary: Power and Mystery, 1987; ed. The Book of Catholic Wisdom, 1986. Contrbr of articles and book rvws to magazines. Contrbng ed., Priest, 1968—. BA, St. Bernard's Seminary and Coll., Rochester, N.Y., 1948; advanced study, New Melleray Abbey; MS in Lib. Sci., U. of Southern Calif., Los Angeles; M. Theol., St. Bernard's Institute, Colgate-Rochester, 1985. Employee Eastman Kodak Co., Rocheter, N.Y. before entering seminary to study for Roman Catholic priesthood; ordained May 5, 1954; Rev. Msgr., 1985; lib. dir., U. of Dan Diego, 1954-65; parish asst. in San Diego, 1954-65, and acting chaplain to Sisters of Social Service, 1957; pastor, St. Louise de Marillac Parish, El Cajon, Calif., 1965-68; founding pastor, St. Gabriel's Church, Poway, Calif., 1973—, honorary prelate, 1985—. Acting librarian, St. Francis Coll., 1965-73. Mem bd trstees, Poway Unified School District, 1977-81. Military service: U.S. Naval Reserve, chaplain, 1957-64. Mem Catholic Library Assn (chmn of college section, 1964-65), Calif. Lib. Assn, Knights of Columbus, Legion of Mary. Address: Box 867 Poway CA 92064

DOMAC, DRAGUTIN CHARLES, (Dragutin Petrovic), b. Yugoslavia, came to U.S., 1940; m. Lois Cherrington, July 13, 1942; children—Jane, Julie, Jacqueline. Contrbr. articles to Monterey Life, San Francisco Chronicle, Christian Sci. Monitor, The Nation, Boston Globe, Politika (Belgrade); contrbr. short stories to Modern Reading, London, various Yugoslav publs., The Mariner. Wrkg. on novel. Ed., Yugoslavia. Marine Surveyor, Los Angeles, 1954-69; vis. prof. High Maritime Schl., Rijeka, Yugoslavia, 1969-70. Address: 115 17-Mile Dr Pacific Grove CA 93950

DOMINOWSKI, ROGER LYNN, b. Chgo., Feb. 21, 1939; s. Frank and Annette (Bochniak) D.; m. Nancy Ricketts, May 27, 1961 (div. Mar. 1976); children—Barbara, Andrew, Tracy, Matthew; m. Carol Jean DeBoth, Sept. 19, 1984. Author: Research Methods, 1980; (with L. E. Bourne, B. R. Ekstrand) Psychology of Thinking, 1971; (with L. E. Bourne, E. F. Loftus) Cognitive Processes, 1979; (with L. E. Bourne, E. F. Loftus, A. F. Healy) Cognitive Processes, 2d ed., 1986. Contrbr. chpts. to profl. books. Cons. ed. Jnl. Experimental Psychology, 1970-84, Memory and Cognition, 1974-81. Wrkg. on Practical Problem Solving, Coping with Life's Conflicts. B.A., DePaul U., 1960, M.A., 1963; Ph. D., Northwestern U., 1965. Asst. prof. DePaul U., Chgo., 1964-66; asst. prof. U. Ill., Chgo., 1966-68, assoc. prof., 1968-73, prof., 1973—. Mem. Psychonomic Soc., British Psychological Soc., Sigma Xi. Home: 1142 Wenonah Oak Park IL 60304

DONALDSON, STEPHEN REEDER, b. Cleve., May 13, 1947; s. James R. and Mary Ruth (Reeder) D.; m. Stephanie Rae Boutz, Sept. 20, 1980. Author: Lord Foul's Bane, 1977, The Illearth War, 1977, The Power That Preserves, 1977, The Wounded Land, 1980, (as Reed Stephens) The Man Who Killed His Brother, 1980, The One Tree, 1982, White Gold Wielder, 1983, Daughter of Regals, 1984; (as Reed Stephens) The Man Who Risked His Partner, 1984, The Mirror of Her Dreams, 1986. BA, Coll. of Wooster, 1968; MA, Kent State U., 1971. Acquisitions editor Tapp- Gentz Assos., West Chester, Pa., 1973-74; instr. Ghost Ranch Writers Workshops, N. Mex., 1973-77. Recipient John W. Campbell award for best new writer World Sci. Fiction Conv., 1979, Best Novel award Brit. Fantasy Soc., 1979, Balrog award for best novel, 1981, 1983, Balrog award for best collection, 1985, Saturn award for best fantasy novel, 1983. Office: Del Rey 201 E 50th St New York NY 10022

DONALLY, KEITH, b. Ionia, MI, Sept. 28, 1948; s. Donald Glenn and Berniece D.; m. Judith Ann, Nov. 24, 1966 (dec. June 5, 1981); children—Kelly, Keith, Kimberly; m. Nancy DeLarosa, Aug. 11, 1984. Author technical manuals, bulltns. A.A., Lansing Commun. Coll., 1973; B.A., Mich. State U., 1976. Systems analyst State of Mich., Lansing, 1977-79, asst. div. chief, 1980-83, training coord. dept. natural resources, 1983—. Served with U.S. Army, 1968-69. Home: 2707 Rockdale Ave Lansing MI 48917

DONATH, ROBERT E., b. Bklyn, Dec. 11, 1945; s. Robert W. and Helen D.; m. Patricia L., Mar. 21, 1968 (div. 1979); 1 son, Gregory Wayne; m. Marianne C. Paskowski, Aug. 14, 1982. BS in Jnlsm., Northwestern U., MBA. Assoc. ed. Advertising Age, NYC, 1974-78; columnist N.Y. Daily News, NYC, 1978-79; ed. Business Marketing Mag., NYC, 1979—. Mem. NY Fincl. Writers Assn. Neal award, ABP, 1980, 82. Office: Bus Mktg 220 E 42 St New York NY 10017

DONAVEL, DAVID FRANK, b. Rochester, NY, Aug. 10, 1946; s. Frank Nicholas and Joan Marie (Barber) D.; m. Gene Elizabeth Landis; children—Mason, Tess, Bonnie (previous marriage). Contrbr. to Skin Diver, Nautica, Essex Life, Accent, Sea Frontiers, Diver, Dolphin Log, Wind, Firelands Rvw, Kans. Qtly, Tendril, Wittenberg Rvw, Anthology of Am. Verse and Yearbook of Am. Poetry, others. BA with honors, Denison U., 1968; MA, Case Western Reserve, 1970. English tchr. high schls. Brockton, Mass., 1973-76, Topsfield, Mass, 1976—. Secy., Masconomet Tchrs. Assn. Address: 54 Pearl St Amesbury MA 01913

DONCHESS, BARBARA M., (Bara Chessley, Mae Dale), New Bedford, MA, Sept. 26, 1922; d. Carleton Church and Alice T. (Dale) Briggs; m. Kalman Donchess, Apr. 19, 1947; children—Ann, Carleton, Christine. Author: How to Cope with His Horoscope, 1975, In Other Women's Houses, 1978. Contrbr. articles to astrology mags. Wrkg. on book on London and book on occult. Student Kinyon's Bus. Coll., 1941. Owner, pub. Perky Pubs., Canton, MA, 1975—. Address: 5 South ST Canton MA 02021

DONELSON, KENNETH L., b. Holdrege, NE, June 16, 1927; s. Lester Homer Irving and Minnie Irene (Lyons) D.; m. Virginia Juanita Watts, May 24, 1948 (div. Nov. 1969); m. 2d, Annette Whetton, June 5, 1970 (div. Feb. 1983); m. 3d, Marie Elizabeth Smith, May 30, 1983; children—Sherri Lynette George, Kurt Allen, Jennie. Mag. ed.: Arizona English Bulletin, 1969-76, English Journal, 1980-87; author: The Student's Right to Read, 1972, (with Dwight Burton et al.) Teaching English Today, 1974, (with Alleen Nilsen) Literature for Today's Young Adults, 2d. ed., 1985. BA, U. IA, 1950, MA, 1951, PhD, 1963. Tchr. speech & Eng., Glidden HS (IA), 1951-56; tchr. Eng., Thomas Jefferson HS, Cedar Rapids, IA, 1956-63; asst. prof. Eng., Kansas State U., Manhattan, 1963-65; assoc. prof. Eng., Arizona State U., Tempe, 1965-70, prof. 1970—. Served to Cox BM3rd, USN, 1945-46. Mem. NCTE, Freedom to Read Fdn. Office: Engl Dept AZ State U Tempe AZ 85287

DONNELLY, MARGARITA PATRICIA, b. Caracas, Distrito Federal, Venezuela, Mar. 9, 1942; d. Harry Francis and Mary Catherine (Donnelly) Donnelly; came to U.S. 1953; 1 dau.—Angelique Xochime Brady. Ed.: Calyx, A Jnl of Art & Lit. by Women, 1980—, ed. Calyx Books (founded 1985), var. anthols. & novels. BA in Anthro., San Francisco State U., 1966; MEd in Cslg., OR State U., 1974. Prog. co-ord. Spcl. Svcs. Prog., OR State U., Corvallis, 1973-78, cslr./program co-ord., Women's Studies, 1978-81; managing ed. Calyx, Inc., Corvallis, 1976—; ed. Eric Clearinghouse, Eugene, OR, 1983—. Recipient CCLM Editor's Grant, 1985. Bd. mem. CCLM. Office: Box B Corvallis OR 97339

DONOHUE, IRENE MARY, see Jurczyk, Irene Donohue

DONOVAN, DIANE C., b. San Francisco, Jan 13, 1956; m. William R. Donovan, May 24, 1976. Contrbr. Day Tonight/Night Today, Amelia Mag, Kudzu, Bookwatch, other publs. BS, San Francisco State U., 1976. Ed. The Bookwatch, San Francisco, 1986—. Mem. Media Alliance. Home: 166 Miramar Ave San Francisco CA 94112

DONOVAN, GREGORY EDWARD, b. Mammoth Springs, AR., July 8, 1950, s. Thomas August and Barbara Ruth (Friedrich) D. Contrbr. to MSS, Cimarron Rvw, New Virginia Rvw, others. MA, U. Utah, 1977; PhD, SUNY-Binghamton, 1983. Asst. prof., coordinator MFA creative writing program Va. Commonwealth U., Richmond, 1983—. Home: 400 N Lombardy St. Apt 6 Richmond VA 23220

DONOVAN, MARK, b. Detroit, Apr. 24, 1960. Author: Pieces, Patches and Songs of the Country, 1983; Fresh Dessert and Other Leftovers, 1984; God Bless America, 1984; contrbr Howling Dog Mag. BA in English, Mich. State U., 1981; MA in tech writing, NM State U., 1984. Writer N. Mex. Solar Energy Inst., Las Cruces, 1982-84, Comtec, Inc., Farmington, Mich, 1985—; writer/ed. FisherBody div. Genl. Motors, Warren Mich., 198485; ed. Howling Dog mag, Detroit, 1985—. Address: Parkville 10917 W Outer Dr Detroit MI 48223

DORAY, ANDREA WESLEY, b. Monte Vista, CO, Oct. 4, 1956; d. Dant Bell and Rosemary Ann (Kassap) Slack; m. Paul Dean Doray, Nov. 25, 1978. Contrbr. poetry: Voices in Poetics, Riders of the Rainbow, others; contrbr. fiction: Metrosphere. BA, U. No. Colo., 1977. Contrbg. ed. Colorado Springs Bus. Mag., 1984-86; advt. instr. Pikes Peak Community Coll., Colorado Springs, 1983-86; pres., creative dir. Doray Doray, Monument, Colo., 1985-87; dir. account services Praco, Ltd., Colorado Springs, 1987—; contrbr., ed. numerous newsletters; creative wrtr. World Cycling Championships, Colorado Springs, 1986. Mem. Pikes Peak Advt. Fedn. (past pres.), Am. Advt. Fedn. (Silver Medal award winner Colorado Springs chap. 1986). Office: Praco Ltd 511 N Tejon St Colorado Springs CO 80903

DOREN, KONSTANTIN (CORKY), b. Paterson, NJ, Dec. 9, 1956; s. George and Elisabeth (Gittler) D. BA in jnlsm., Glassboro State, 1979. Assoc. ed., Beverage Retailer, Wayne, NJ, 1979-83, ed., 1983-84; mng. ed. American Bicyclist, NYC, 1984—. Home: 458 W 20th St New York NY 10011

DORIA, CHARLES, b. Cleve.; s. Louis and Alice Rose (Farinacci) D.; div. 1972; 1 child, Diana. Author: The Game of Europe, 1982; Short, 1982; Short r, 1984; Shortend, 1986; ed., translator: Origins: Creation Myths from the Ancient Mediterranean, 1976; ed., contrbr.: The Tenth Muse: Classical Drama in Translation, 1980; assoc ed., contrbr. A Big Jewish Book: Poems and Visions of the Jews from Tribal Times to the Present, 1978; contrbr. to Technicians of the Sacred, rev. ed., 1985. Wrkg. on 1st English translation of Giordano Bruno's De imaginum . . . compositione, 1591. BA, Western Res. U., 1960; MA, Harvard U., 1963; PhD, SUNY-Buffalo, 1970. Owner, pub. Assembling Press, Bklyn., 1980—; vis. lectr. Mason Gross Schl. Arts, Rutgers U., New Brunswick, N.J., 1985—. Home: Box 1967 Brooklyn NY 11202

DORNBUSCH, JOAN LOUISE FALQUET, (Madelyn Dohrn), b. Cin., July 14, 1932; d. Louis Alexander and Marguerite Fay (Cummings) Falquet; m. Clyde Henry Dornbusch, Aug. 21, 1953; children—Paula Joan, Neal Clyde. Author: The Best Defense, 1987. Wrkg. on romances with Mary DeVore. B.A., DePauw U., 1955; M.A., Miami U., 1968. Tchr. public schs., Cin., 1953-55; part-time coll. instr. Ohio Northern U., Ada, 1968-78, part-time profl. asst. communication skills ctr., 1977—. Mem. AAUW (One of Ten Best award for short story 1971), RWA. Home: 111 S Park Dr Ada OH 45810

DORR, JACKSON G., see Asher, Dustin T.

DORR, JAMES SUHRER, b. Pensacola, FL, Aug. 12, 1941; s. Frank J. and Betty (Suhrer) D.; m. Ruth Michelle Clark, Aug. 16, 1975 (div. 1982). Contrbr. poems to lit. mags., anthols.; fantasy and sci. fiction to mags., anthols.; numerous articles on bus., consumer topics, humor, sci./technology to mags. Assoc. ed.: Bloomington Area Mag., IN, 1983-86. B.S., Mass. Inst. Technology, 1964; M.A., Ind. U., 1968. Technical wrtr. Wrubel Computing Ctr., Bloomington, 1969-74, chief technical wrtr., 1974-79, ed., 1979-81; wrtr., marketing cons. The Stackworks, Bloomington, 1982; free-lance wrtr., 1982—. Mem. Bloomington Traffic Commn., 1974-86. Mem. NWC, SPWA, Am. Assn. Advancement Sci. Home: 1404 E Atwater Bloomington IN 47401

DORSET, GERALD HENRY, b. Sofia, Bulgaria, Aug. 9, 1920; s. Stoyan Iliya Vidinski and Teresa (Petcova) Rilska; came to U.S., 1947; m. Julia Balan, Sept. 9, 1944, (div. Oct. 1947); m. 2d., Edna Mae Badgely, May 1, 1950. Author: Love You, 1965, City Poems, 1969, Time Music, 1974. LLB, St. Clement U. Law School, Sofia, Bulgaria, 1946; MSS, Catholic U., 1972. Scriptwriter, Voice of Am., NYC,1949-53, Free Europe Radio, NYC,1953-55, BBC, London, England, 1955-61; prof. U. HI, 1962-65; librarian Library of Congress, 1966-70. Mem. ALA. Home: 45 Tudor City 1903 NYC 10017

DORSETT, MARTHA JANETTE, b. Lufkin, TX., Aug. 21, 1943, d. C. B. and Dorothy (Smith) Dorsett. Contrbr. poetry: Am. Poetry Anthology, Masterpieces of Modern Verse, Form and Focus (textbook), other publs.; contrbr. stories: Rainbow Collection. Wrkg. on stories, poems, illustrations, articles. BS in elem. edn., Stephen F. Austin State U., 1964, MEd with Supervisory Cert., 1969. Tchr. Kinlichee Boarding Schl., Ariz., 1964-67, Chuska-Tohatchi Consol. Schl., N.Mex., 1967—. Recipient Golden Poet award World of Poetry, 1985, 87, Silver Poet award, 1986. Home: Box 155

Tohatchi NM 87325

DORSETT, MARY JANEEN, b. Lufkin, TX., Aug. 21, 1943, d. C. B. and Dorothy (Smith) Dorsett. Contrbr. articles to educational and Indian affairs newsletters; contrbr. stories: Form and Focus (textbook), Rainbow Collection; contrbr. poetry: Hearts on Fire: A Treasury of Poems on Love, Masterpieces of Modern Verse, Our World's Most Cherished Poems, numerous other poetry collections. Wrkg. on stories, poems, news and educational articles. BS in elem. edn., Stephen F. Austin State U., 1964, MEd with Supervisory Cert., 1969. Tchr. Kinlichee Boarding Schl., Ariz., 1964-67, Chuska Boarding Schl., Tohatchi, N.Mex., 1967-84, Chuska-Tohatchi Consol. Schl., 1984—. Recipient Golden Poet award World of Poetry, 1985, 86, 87. Celebrate Literacy award Intl. Reading Assn., 1985. Home: Box 155 Tohatchi NM 87325

DORSEY, JAMES WILKINSON, JR., (Jacek, Jaz Dorsey, Strada), b. Atlanta, Dec. 31, 1953; s. James Wilkinson and Harriett Hand (Callaway) D. (Please list plays written and dates of production) Author: plays—Alice in America, 1987, Songs from the Cafe Escargot, 1986, Destiny Calls Collect, 1985. B.A. in German, French, U. N.C.-Chapel HIll, 1978. Acting instr. The Learning Annex, Atlanta, 1984-86; artistic dir. The Bauhaus, Atlanta, 1984-87; free-lance wrtr. Mem. Atlanta Wrtrs. Club, Actors in Renascance, Artforce (founder). Home: 99 Peachtree Battle Ave Atlanta GA 30305

DOSEDEL, JAMES ANTHONY, b. St. Paul, Dec. 14, 1951; s. John Frank and Joan Ardel(Sybers) D. Business editor: Jnl of Bus. and Psychology, 1986—. BS in biology, U. Minn.-Mpls., 1975; MA in tech communication, U. Minn.-St. Paul, 1984. Assoc. producer KSTP-TV, Mpls., 1977; supr. advt., copywriter Domain, Inc., New Richmond, Wis., 1978-80; creative dir. Agmark,Inc., Bloomington, Minn., 1980; tech. rschr. PBS-TV, Mpls., 1983-84; tech. wrtr. info svcs. mgr., St. Paul Cos., St. Paul, 1984—. Artist, keyliner Ronald McDonald House, Mpls., 1980-85; dir. Northwest St. Croix County Credit Union, New Richmond, 1978-79; dir. W-3 wrtrs. workshop, 1987. Mem. Soc. Tech. Communicators. Home: 2038 Pinehurst Ave Saint Paul MN 55116

DOSKEY, JOHN STANLEY, b. Cleve., Dec. 19, 1927, s. Daniel Frement and Agnes (Marks) D.; m. Rosemary Bartuccio, May 17, 1952; children—Ellen Marie, Janice Clare, Carol Ann. Author: Media Equipment: A Guide and Dictionary (with Kenyon C. Rosenberg), 1976; ed.: The European Journals of William Maclure, 1987. Wrkg. on editing The Correspondence of William Maclure and Marie D. Fretageot, 1820-1833. BA, Ohio State U., 1950; MA, San Jose State U., 1970. Tchr. public schls., Los Angeles and Lafayette, Calif., 1956—. Research and editing grantee NSF, 1972-73, 80-81, Am. Philo. Soc., 1976. Mem. Assn. Documentary Editing. Home: 355 Mount Washington Way Clayton CA 94517

DOTSON, RAYMOND PAUL, b. Phelps, KY, Jan. 28, 1933; s. Andy and Mary D.; m. Geraldine Litton, July 19, 1953; children—Paul Jeffrey, Cheryl Ann. Contrbr. to various tech. mags including Sextant, Remark, Microcomputing; also poetry in lit mags. Student, Morehead U., KY, 1951-54. Owner/manager, Array Enterprises, Goldsboro, NC, 1975—. Served USAF, 1954-76. First place poetry, NC Poetry Society, 1987. Home: 606 S Taylor St Goldsboro NC 27530

DOTY, CAROLYN HOUSE, b. Tooele, UT, July 28, 1941; d. Oran Earl and Dorothy (Anderson) House; m. William Doty, Feb. 2, 1963 (div. 1982); children—Stuart W., Margaret E.; m. 2d, Gardner H. Mein, June 16, 1986. Author: A Day Late, 1980, Fly Away Home, 1982, What She Told Him, 1985. Wrkg. on a novel Free the San Francisco Six, also a collection of short stories, Gallery. BFA, U. Utah, 1963; MFA, U. Calif.-Irvine, 1979. Teaching assoc. U. Calif.-Irvine, 1977-79; lectr. San Francisco State U., 1980, U. Calif.-Irvine, 1984-86; fiction dir. Squaw Valley Community of Writers, Calif., 1980—; asst. prof., U. Kansas, 1986—. Dir. Day Care Ctr. for Retarded Children, Berkeley, Calif., 1970-75, Camping Unltd. for Retarded Children, Berkeley, 1971-76. Mem. AG, P&W, Squaw Valley Arts Soc. (adv. bd.). Squaw Valley scholar Squaw Valley Community of Writers, 1975, 76; recipient hon. mention Henry Jackson award, 1976; semi-finalist S.B. Goldwyn award, 1979; U. Calif. teaching fellow, 1977-79. Office: Eng Dept U KS Lawrence KS 66045

DOTY, RUTH, b. Louisiana, Jan. 15, 1947, d. Robert Charles and Bertha (Cook) Cudd; m. Mark A. Doty, Sept. 12, 1972 (div. 1980). Author: Empire of Summer, An Alphabet; contrbr. to numerous mags. BA, U. Houston, 1968; MFA, U. Ariz., 1972. Prof. Drake U., Des Moines, 1972—. Recipient Borestone award, 1976, 77, Pushcart prize, 1982. Mem. AWP. Home: 1215 25th St Apt F Des Moines IA 50311

DOUGHER, COLLEEN MARIE, b. Salem, NJ., Apr. 9, 1962; d. Thomas Peter and Sheila Agnita (McCormack) Dougher. Contrbr. poetry: Inky Trails, Hob-Nob Annual, Manna Prose-Poetry, Parnassus Lit. Jnl., numerous other lit. mags. and anthologies. Student Broward Community Coll. Editorial asst. Fort Lauderdale (Fla.) News & Sun Sentinel, 1984—. Home: 1748 SW 20th St Fort Lauderdale FL 33315

DOUGHERTY, JAY EDWIN, b. Accokeek, MD, May 4, 1959; s. Edwin Loomis and Evelyn Virginia (Burdette) Dougherty. Book: Coveringdeertrackswithwords, 1984, Conversations from Another Planet, 1987; contrbr. to Wallace Stevens Jnl, Explicator, D.H. Lawrence Rvw, Bogg, Gargoyle, Poetry East, Wormwood Rvw, other lit mags; editor: Clock Radio. BA, U. of Maryland, 1982; MA, 1984. Instr. U. of Maryland (College Park), 1982-84, Mainz U. (FR Germany), 1984-85, U. of Connecticut (Storrs), 1985—. Fulbright Scholar, West Germany, 1987. Address: Flewelling 1807 Aquasco Rd Brandywine MD 20613

DOUGHERTY, SAMUEL ALLEN, (Sam Allen), b. Helper, UT, Dec. 25, 1917; s. Charles Wooten and Mary Alma (McComb) D.; m. Betty Alene Rosette, May 6, 1942; children—Mari Ann Holder, John Samuel. Author: Call the Big Hook, 1984, Rudolf Diesel's Legacy 1982, Sandhouse Christmas, 1983, The Gold Watch, 1984, Working on the Railroad, 1985. Contrbr. articles to Colo. Old Times. Grad. public schls., Price, UT. Locomotive engineer Denver & Rio Grande Western Railroad, Denver, 1937-78, road foreman of equipment, 1963-78. Mem. NWC. Home: 1230 W Battlement Pkwy H-103 Parachute CO 81635

DOUGLAS, CATHIE M., see Montgomery, Cathie Marion

DOUGLAS, GREGORY A., see Cantor, Eli

DOUGLAS, LALETTE, (Hammett Lalette); b. Clarksburg, WV, Dec. 5, 1931; d. Myron Jackson and Bess Beatrice (Criss) Hammitt; m. Paul Lee Douglas, Jr., Nov. 22, 1950 (dec. Dec. 17, 1984); children—David, John, Kathy, Valerie, Diane, Paul. Author: The Captain's Doxy, 1980, 3d ed., 1988. Wrkg. on Rogue's Realm, The Wiles of a Vixen. Student Commun. Coll. of Denver. Mem. RWA, NWU. Home: 6000 Ottowa Way Box B Red Feather Lakes CO 80545

DOUGLAS, LEE, see Robertson, Howard Wayne

DOUGLAS, WADE, see Hall, D. Elaine

DOULIS, THOMAS JOHN, b. Vandergrift, PA, Dec. 31, 1931; s. John Stamatis and Argiro (Stradis) D.; m. Nancy Barnes Ritter, July 8, 1962; children—John (Yianni) Randolph, Dion Argent. Author novels: Path for our Valor, 1963, The Quarries of Sicily, 1969; critical biography, George Theotokas, 1975; histories: Surge to the Sea, 1977, Landmarks of Our Past, 1983; ed. and intro. Journeys to Orthodoxy, 1986. Wrkg. on trilogy of novels on the Americanization of a Greek immigrant family. BA, La Salle Coll., 1955; MA, Stanford, 1957. Tchr. Friends' Select Schl., Phila., 1960-62; instr. to asst. prof. Phila. Coll. Art, 1962-68; freelance writing Greece and England, 1968-72; assoc. prof. Portland State Univ., Ore., 1972-77, prof., 1977—. Served to cpl. US Army, 1957-59, USA. Pres., Hellenic Univ. Club, Phila., 1967; vice-pres. Holy Trinity Greek Orthodox Church, Portland, 1984. Fulbright grantee, Athens, Greece, 1968-70, grantee, Ore. Comm. for Humanities, Portland, 1978; fellow Am. Council Learned Socs, UK, France, Greece, 1980-81. Founding mem. Modern Greek Studies Assn.; mem. AAUP, AWP. Address: 2236 NE Regents Dr Portland OR 97212

DOUSKEY, FRANZ THOMAS, b. New Haven, Dec. 2, 1941, s. Stanley Anthony and Wadia (Mekdeci) D.; m. Sarah Sedgwick Heath, July 4, 1977. Author: Indecent Exposure, 1976, Sitting Across from Death, 1980, Rowing Across the Dark, 1981, Archeology of Night, 1986; contrbr. to N.Y. Qtly, Rolling Stone, Kayak, Abraxas, numerous others. BA, Goddard Coll., 1973, MA, 1975. Assoc. prof. So. Central Community Coll., New Haven, 1977—. Mem. AWP, PEN, PSA. Home: 50 Ives St Mount Carmel CT 06518

DOUTHWAITE, GRAHAM, b. Johannesburg, Transvaal, South Africa, Oct. 27, 1913; s. Walter Slade and Alice; m. Beatrice Maude Gillen, May 17, 1947; children—Mary, Penny, Patricia, Susan, Gregory, Alice, Katherine. Author: Restitution, 1977, Unmarried Couples and the Law, 1979, Jury Instructions on Medical Issues, 3d ed., 1986, Jury Instructions on Damages in Tort Actions, 1981. Jury Instructions in Automobile Negligence Actions, 1986, Jury Instructions on Product Liability, 1987. BA, Witwatersrand U., Johannesburg, South Africa, 1934, LLB, 1936, BCL, Oxford (Eng.) U., 1940. Fgn. service officer Govt. of South Africa, London, 1946-49, Rome 1951-55; prof. U. Santa Clara, Calif., 1959-79. Mem. Phi Alpha Delta. Home: 610 Monroe St Santa Clara CA 95050

DOVE, RITA FRANCES, b. Akron, OH, Aug. 28, 1952. Author: Ten Poems, 1977, The Only Dark Spot in the Sky, 1980, The Yellow House on the Corner, 1980, Mandolin, 1982, Museum, 1983, Fifth Sunday, 1985, Thomas and Beulah, 1986. BA, Miami U., Oxford, OH, 1973; MFA, U. of Iowa, 1977. Res. asst., U. of Iowa, Ia.

City, 1975; tching. asst., U. of Iowa, 1976-77; asst. prof., Arizona State U., Tempe, 1981-84; wrtr.-in-res., Tuskegee Inst., Ala., 1982; assoc. prof., AZ State U., 1984-87, prof., 1987—. Awards: NEA fellowship, 1978; Guggenheim fellowship, 1983, Lavan Award, AAP, 1986, Pulitzer Prize for Poetry, 1987.Mem. AWP (pres 1986), AAP, PEN Club. Home: 631 W 15th St Tempe AZ 85281

DOVE, WHITE, see Behymer, Claudia Sue

DOWBENKO, URI, b. Chgo., IL, Dec. 1, 1951; s. Rostyslaw and Katherine (Reshetnyk) Dowbenko; m. Barbara Louise Geary, Apr. 4, 1983. Author: Homegrown Holography—How to Make Holograms in Your Own Studio, 1975, Marijuana Doubletake, 1983; contrib. editor: Kodak's Encyclopedia of Practical Photography, 1975; contrbr. to Yoga Jnl, Los Angeles Herald Examiner, CEO, Uri Dowbenko Advertising Photography & Design, 1980—. Mem. ASMP, AIGA,Direct Mrktg. Creative Guild. Home: Box 207 Emigrant MT 59027

DOWLING, JAMES STEPHEN, b. Effingham, IL, Apr. 9, 1951; s. Jack Maynard and Rose Elizabeth (Thies) D. Technical ed. U. Ill., Champaign, 1981-82, assoc. ed., 1982-84, pubs. ed., 1984—; ed: Library Trends, 1981—, Annual Proceedings of the Allerton Park Insts., 1985—, Occasional Papers, 1985—, monograph series on library and info. sci. topics for U. Ill., 1985—. Mem. Soc. Collegiate Journalists. Home: 1415 W Kirby 4 Champaign IL 61821

DOWNARD, BOB HANSON, b. Orange, CA, Sept. 11, 1946; s. Marshall Clem and Dorothy Mae (Hanson) D.; m. Teresa Lee Morgan, May 31, 1984. Author: (plays) Roundheads, 1976, Evening Shadows (Critics' award Dramalogue 1978), 1977, The Princess and the Dragon, 1979, Celebration of the Angels, 1980; (opera) Martin Avdeich: A Christmas Mericle, 1986. B.A., Calif. State U., 1968; M.A. in Music, U. Southern Calif., 1970. Staff accompanist Los Angeles City Coll, 1980-83; instr. Loretto Heights Coll., Denver, 1983—; free-lance musician, tchr., 1962—. Mem. Natl. Wrtrs.' Club, DG. Home: 768 Ogden 5 Denver CO 80218

DOWNIE, LEONARD, JR., b. Cleve., May 1, 1942; s. Leonard and Pearl Martha (Evenheimer) D.; m. Barbara Lindsey, July 15, 1960 (div. 1971); children: David Leonard, Scott Leonard; m. Geraldine Rebach, Aug. 15, 1971; children: Joshua Mark, Sarah Elizabeth. Author: Justice Denied, 1971, Mortgage on America, 1974, The New Muckrackers, 1976. BA, Ohio State U., 1964, M.A., 1965. Reporter, editor Washington Post, 1964-74, metro. editor, 1974-79, London corr., 1979-82; natl. editor Washington Post, 1982-84, mng. ed., 1984—. Alicia Patterson Fdn. fellow, 1971-72. Office: Wash Post 1150 15th St NW Washington DC 20071

DOWNS, ROBERT C. S., b. Chgo., Nov. 23, 1937, s. Norbert Henry and Laura Catherine (Smith) D.; m. Barbara Lewry, Sept. 6, 1968; children—Christina, Susan. Novelist: Going Gently, 1973, Peoples, 1974, Country Dying, 1976, White Mama, 1980, Living Together, 1983; author screenplay: White Mama, 1980. AB, Harvard U., 1960; MFA, U. Iowa, 1965. Asst. prof. Colby Coll., New London, N.H., 1968-73; assoc. prof. U. Ariz., Tucson, 1973-79; prof. English Pa. State U., State College, 1980—. Guggenheim Fdn. fellow, 1979-80, NAACP Image Award, 1980. Home: 764 W Hamilton Ave State College PA 16801

DRAHOS, LESLIE ANN, b. Cleve., Dec. 11, 1942, d. Robert Powell and Kathryn (Hughes) Evans; m. Dean F. Drahos, Aug. 6, 1965. BS, Case-Western Res. U., 1964. Wrtr., ed. Printing Prodn., 1971-74, Newspaper Prodn., 1971-74, Vet. Econs., 1975-77, Handling & Shipping Mgmt., 1977-81, Govt. Product News, 1981—. Bd. mem. Am. Soc. Bus. Press Eds. (dir., recipient 21 citations), Cleve Press Club (writing awards, 1984, 85, 86), Women in Communications (Editorial award 1986). Home: 24000 Rainbow Dr Olmsted Township OH 44138

DRAIME, CHARLES DOUGLAS, (Jake Wild), b. Vincennes, IN, Feb. 23, 1944, s. Charles Elroy and Lenore Louise (Lynch) D.; m. Beth Ann Partlow, Dec. 28, 1976 (dec. 1979); m. 2d, Lora Louise Stewart, Dec. 17, 1980; children—Aaron, Shawn; 1 stepson, Adrian. Contrbr.: Black/White, Prairie Poetry, Pulpsmith, LA Wkly, The Other Side, Northwest, other lit mags, newsletters. Student U. Chgo., 1962-63. Served as sgt. U.S. Army, 1964-66. Home: 2571 E Evans Creek Rd Rogue River OR 97537

DRAKE, CHRISTINE SPATA, b. Beverly, MA, Nov. 23, 1946; d. Anthony Paul and Anna Rita (Stella) Spata: m. David Wade Drake, Aug. 26, 1972. Contrbr. articles on art, humor, business to newspapers and profl. jnls. B.A. in History of Art, Mt. Holyoke Coll., 1970; M.A. in History of Art, Mich. State U., 1971. Head art Slide library U. Ga., Athens, 1975-76; technical wrtr. King & Spalding, Atlanta, 1981-85; free-lance wrtr., 1981—. Home: 1205 Gail Dr NE Atlanta GA 30319

DRAKE, DAVID ALLEN, b. Dubuque, IA. Sept., 24, 1945; s. Earle Charles and Maxine Dorothy (Schneider) Drake; m. Joanne Mary Kammiller, Jun. 5, 1967; 1 son—Jonathan. Author: Hammer's Slammers, 1979, The Dragon Lord, 1979, Time Safari, 1982, From the Heart of Darkness, 1983, Cross the Stars, 1984, At Any Price, 1985, Bridgehead, 1985, Ranks of Bronze, 1986, Lacey and His Friends, 1986, Counting the Cost, 1987, (with Janet Morris) Kill Ratio, 1987. BA U. of Iowa, 1967; JD Duke U., 1972. Mem. SFWA. Home: Box 904 Chapel Hill NC 27514

DRAKE, NICHOLAS, see Stearns, Jon Rod

DRAKE, SYLVIA, see Deimer, Lorena Ruth Murrill

DRANOW, JOHN THEODORE, b. Passaic, NJ., Dec. 29, 1948; s. Nathan Dranow and Betty Jane (Coleman) Ranney; m. Louise Gluck, Jan. 1, 1977; 1 child, Noah. Author: Life in the Middle of the Century, 1987; contrbr. to Goddard Rvw, New River Rvw, Kans. Qtly., December, New Eng. Rvw. BA, Boston U., 1971; MFA, MA, U Iowa, 1974. Instr. U. Iowa, 1973-74, U. Mo., 1974-76, Radford Coll., 1976-77; dir. summer writing program Goddard Coll., Plainfield, Vt., 1977-79; v.p., co-founder New Eng. Culinary Inst., Montpelier, Vt., 1979—. Recipient 1st prize in novel competition Va. Highlands Lit. Festival, 1977; 1st prize Boston U. Alumni Wrtr.'s Contest, 1983; Iowa teaching-writing fellow, 1973; Vt. Council on Arts grantee, 1977. Home: Box 1400 RD 2 Plainfield VT 05667

D'REALO, DUKE, see McBee, Denis

DRELLICH, KAREN KINNEY, (Karen Drellich), b. Berkeley, CA, May 27, 1942; d. Willard A. and Barbara Janette (Sheridan) Kinney; m. Mark Folger Emerson, Oct. 23, 1964 (div. Sept. 1973); 1 son—Folger Mark; 2nd m. Kenneth Morton Drellich, Apr. 26, 1974; 1 dau—Kinney Rutherford. Author: It's your Baby, 1979; contrbr. to Media: An Introductory Analysis of Am. Mass Commun., 1972, Sew News. Reporter/ed. Oakland Trib. (CA), 1963-75; tchr. The Seven Hills Schl. (Walnut Creek, CA), 1984. Fdn. Pres., Contra Costa Ballet, 1979-81. Mem. Am. News Women's Club. Home: Box 4068 Walnut Creek CA 94596

DRENNAN, JANICE S., b. Grenada, MS, Dec. 29, 1950; d. Henry Bardie an Ruby Josephine (Taylor) Scarbrough; m. Carl Stephen Evans, Jan. 1, 1972 (div. 1981); m. 2d, Jimmy A. Drennan, May 29, 1982; 1 dau., Dee Anna. Contrbr. to: Horizons: 100 Arkansas Women of Achievement, 1980. BA in English, Ark. State U., 1972, MA in English, 1973. Public info. officer Ark. Dept. Local Services, Little Rock, 1979-81; public relations officer, ed. Ark. Telephone Times, Southwestern Bell Telephone Co., 1981-83; public info. officer Ark. Dept. Edn., Little Rock, 1985-87; freelance wrtr., ed., Little Rock, 1987—. Recipient Bronze Quill award Intl. Assn. Bus. Communicators, 1986, 87, Golden Achievement award Natl. Schl. Public Relations Assn., 1987. Mem. Ark. Press Women (central dir. 1987-88). Home: 719 N Van Buren St Little Rock AR 72205

DRENNEN, MARCIA SIMONTON, b. Columbus, OH, July 19, 1915, d. Mark E. and Susannah Belle (Gunning) Simonton; m. Everett Drennen, Jr., Jan. 1939 (div. 1946); 1 son, Everett III. Contrbr. to Am. Poetry Anthology, Plains Poetry Jnl, Poetry Press, Scimitar and Song, others. Wrkg. on novel. BA, Ohio State U., 1936. Reporter, newswrtr. numerous orgns., 1943-56; sr. ed. Reader's Digest Condensed Books, N.Y., 1958-80. Recipient Am. Poetry Assn. award, 1985. Home: 11 W 9th St New York NY 10011

DREW, DEREK C., b. Stamford, CT, April 24, 1956; s. Robert Lincoln and Rue (Faris) Drew. BA, NYU., 1981. Senior Editor, Institutional Investor, newsletter div., NYC,1981, managing editor, 1981-82, exec. editor, 1983-85; editor-in-chief, Investment Dealers' Digest mag., NYC,1985—. Home: 487 Columbus Ave 3R New York NY 10024

DREW, DR., see Exler, Andrew Ross

DREW, GEORGE, b. Greenville, MS., Nov. 3, 1943. Author poetry book: Toads in a Poisoned Tank, 1986; anthol. North Country, 1986; contrbr.: Anthology of Mag. Verse and Yearbook of Am. Poetry, 1985, Thames Poetry, Wormwood Rvw, Pulpsmith, numerous other lit publs. BA, SUNY-Albany, 1967; MA, Western Wash. U., Bellingham, 1969. Asst. prof. English Hudson Valley Community Coll., Troy, N.Y., 1971—. Mem. Council Lit. Sponsors Northeastern N.Y. (exec. bd.), AWP. Home: Box 286 Sand Lake NY 12153

DREWRY, GUY CARLETON, b. Stevensburg, VA, May 21, 1901; s. Samuel Richard and Julia Harriett (Pinckard) D.; m. Margaret Elisabeth McDonald, April 12, 1942; children—Dr. Barbara Louise Whitney,Guy Carleton (called David). Author: Proud Horns, 1933, The Sounding Summer, 1948, A Time of Turning, 1951, The Writhen Wood, 1953, Cloud Above Clocktime, 1957, To Love That Well, 1975; contrbr. to Sat. Rvw., Nationa, NY Times, New Repub., Yale Rvw. and other periodicals and authols; assoc. ed. The Lyric, 1929-54; ed. Southern issue

Voices, 1954. Poet Laueate of the Commonwealth, Virginia, since 1970. Honorary Vice Pres., PSA. Mem. Poetry Soc. of Va., Poetry Soc. of Am., Va. Writer's Club. Home: 2395 Maiden Lane SW Roanoke VA 24015

DRIESSEL, A. BERKLEY, (Wittig Keane), b. Milwaukee, WI, Aug. 21, 1937; s. Arthur Francis and Amber Jean (Groth) Driessel; m. Diane Keane, Oct. 9, 1961 (div. Nov. 1972) 2nd m. Marilyn Louise Landro, Dec. 31, 1982. Contrbr. to Peninsula Times Tribune, San Francisco Examiner, Marquette Business Rvw, Jnl. of Comm., The Party Line; contrbr. author: New Dimensions of Catholic Higher Ed., Communications Spectrum 7. MA, Marquette U., 1963; postgrad. Stanford U., 1968. Commissioner Santa Clara Co. (San Jose, CA), 1964—; rvwr. Travel Quest. Commun. consult./wrtr. 1980—. Alternate mem. Dem. central comm., Santa Clara Co. Sgt. USAR, 1961, Ft. Lewis, WA. Kellogg Fellow., Kellogg Fdn., 1964. Home: 2555 Homestead Ave Santa Clara CA 95051

DRINNON, DORIS JEAN, b. Gray, KY, Apr. 29, 1930; d. Stonewall Jackson and Margaret (Sevier) Grace; m. Ralph Elmo Drinnon, Dec. 28, 1947; children: Cheryl Jean Drinnon Butler, Jackie Leah Drinnon Wert, Garfield Robert. Poetry in anthologies; book, 1985. Ed. Lincoln Meml. Cordele Wrtrs. Club. Home: 902 17th Ave E Cordele GA 31015

DRINNON, ELIZABETH MCCANTS, b. Butler, GA, Apr. 17, 1925; d. Jonathan Morgan and Leila Booth McCants; m. Everett Gostin Drinnon, Oct. 9, 1949; children—Licia Drinnon Jackson, Lauren Drinnon Leskosky. Contrbr. articles, short stories to mags., newspapers, anthol. Student Mercer U., 1947-48, Wesleyan Conservatory, 1948-49. Feature wrtr. Macon Telegraph, Macon, GA, 1947-49; prtnr. Zenith Publicity Agcy., Macon, 1949; dir. public relations YWCA, Macon, 1960-72; asst. dir., then dir. public relations Mercer U., 1972—. Recipient Gold Addy award Middle Ga. Advt. Club., 1986; named Wrtr. of Yr., Macon Quill Club, 1961. Mem. Baptist Public Relations Assn., CASE. Home: 2441 Kensington Rd Macon GA 31211

DRISCOLL, JACK, b. Holyoke, MA, Mar. 7, 1946; s. John Francis and Teresa (Rheaume) D. Author: The Language of Bone, 1980, Fishing the Backwash, 1984. BA, Windham Coll., 1969; MFA, U. Mass.-Amherst, 1972. Tchr. Interlochen Arts Acad., Interlochen, Mich., 1975-87. NEA fellow, 1982. Mem. APS, AWP. Address: Box 29 Interlochen MI 49643

DRISCOLL, MARY HARRIS, b. Worcester, MA, June 6, 1928, d. E. Paul and Mary Teresa (Boyle) Harris; m. Joseph F. Driscoll, June 21, 1952; children—Catherine, Mary, Lisa, Eileen, Joseph, Daniel, Timothy, Jane, Gabriel. Contrbr. poems to Phoenix, Night Sun, Anemone, Worcester, Grey Ledge, Joycean Lively Arts, Manhattan Poetry, Shadow Graphs, Dark Horse, The Little Apple, The Lobe, others. AB magna cum laude, Smith Coll., 1949, MA, Wellesley Coll., 1952. Tchr. Millbury High Schl., Mass., 1949-52; instr. English, Assumption Coll., Worcester, 1959-63, Anna Maria Coll., Worcester, 1960-61; owner, treas. Harris Oil Corp., 1963—, Green Gold Tree Co., 1954—, Singletary Produce, 1982— (all Millbury). Mem. PSA, New Eng. Poetry Club (Leighton Rollins prize 1985). Home: 206 W Main St Millbury MA 01527

DROWN, MERLE, b. York, ME, Jan. 14, 1943, s. Merle and Hazel (Gallagher) D. Author: Plowing Up a Snake, 1982. BA, Macalester Coll., St. Paul, 1965; MFA, Goddard Coll., Plainfield, Vt., 1978. Home: 60 W Parish Rd Concord NH 03301

D'ROYCE, JERIC, see Friggle, Judith Ann

DRUMM, CHRIS, b. Stamford, CT., Sept. 15, 1949; s. Howard Victor and Phyllis Ann (Streit) D.; m. Amy Rose Garrett, July 17, 1974; 1 child, Neil. Ed., pub. Drumm Booklet series, 1983—; compiler, pub. bibliographies of Hal Clement, Mack Reynolds, Thomas M. Disch, Algis Budrys, R. A. Lafferty, Larry Niven, James Gunn, Richard Wilson. BA, U. Mo., 1972. Owner Chriss Drumm, Books, Polk City, Iowa, 1982—. Mem. Sci. Fiction Research Assn. Home: Box 445 Polk City IA 50226

DRUMMOND, LA VENA MAY, b. Arcola, MO, June 23, 1931; d. John Raymond and Dora Beatrice (Fry) Hastings; m. Jack Wilbur Drummond, July 15, 1949; children—Jackie LaVerna, James Lester. Contrbr. poems to anthols. Student Pittsburg State U. Rancher, J & L Ranch, Severy, KS. Recipient Golden Poet award World of Poetry, 1985, 86, 87. Home: J & L Ranch Box 142 Severy KS 67137

DRURY, ALLEN STUART, b. Houston, Sept. 2, 1918; s. Alden Monteith and Flora (Allen) D. Author: Advise and Consent, 1959, A Shade of Difference, 1962, A Senate Journal, 1963, That Summer, 1965, Three Kids in A Cart, 1965, Capable of Honor, 1966, "A Very Strange Society," 1967, Preserve and Protect, 1968, The Throne of Saturn, 1971, Courage and Hesitation, 1971, Come Nineveh, Come Tyre, 1973, The Promise of Joy, 1975, A God Against the Gods, 1976, Return to Thebes, 1976, Anna Hastings, 1977, Mark Coffin, U.S.S., 1979, Egypt: The Eternal Smile, 1980, The Hill of Summer, 1981, Decision, 1983, The Roads of Earth, 1984, Pentagon, 1986. BA, Stanford U., 1939. Editor Tulare (Calif.) Bee, 1940-41; county editor Bakersfield Californian, 1941-42; mem Senate staff UPI, Washington, 1943-45; free-lance corr., 1946; nation editor Pathfinder mag., 1947-53; natl. staff Washington Evening Star, 1953-54; mem. congl. staff NY Times, 1954-59; poli. contbr. Reader's Digest, 1959-62. Served with AUS, 1942-43. Recipient Pulitzer prize for fiction Advise and Consent, 1960; Sigma Delta Chi, natl. award for editorial writing 1941. Address: Doubleday 245 Park Ave New York NY 10167

DUBERSTEIN, HELEN LAURA, b. NYC, June 3, 1926; d. Jacob M. and Beatrice (Lieberman) D.; m. Victor Lipton, April 10, 1949; children—Jacqueline Frances, Irene Judith. Author: Arrived Safely, Changes, The Voyage Out, Succubus/Incubus, The Human Dimension (poetry); fiction, articles, reviews published in lit mags, periodicals. BS, ed., CCNY. Librarian, teacher K-8, teacher of emotionally disturbed, workshop leader, playwright-in-res., Goucher Coll., Hunter Coll.; rdgs. various schls., festivals. Home: 463 West St 904D New York NY 10014

DU BOIS, BARBARA RATTRAY, b. Yonkers, NY., Oct. 2, 1926; d. Alexander Albert and Ana Henrietta (Theboult) Rattray; m. Frederick Williamson DuBois, June 19, 1946; children—Samuel Michael, Alfred Joseph, Kathryn Helen. Contrbr. articles, poems to mags., anthols. BA, U. Mich., 1948, MA, 1952. English instr. Los Alamos Natl. Lab., N.Mex., 1974—, Northern N. Mex. Community Coll., Los Alamos, 1977-80, U. N.Mex., Los Alamos, 1980-86; head humanities div. U. N.Mex., Los Alamos, 1981-86; English instr. New Mex. Inst. of Mining and Tech., 1986. Mem. Mesa Pub. Library Bd., Los Alamos, 1962-67, chmn., 1964-65; secy. Pajarito Elem. Schl. PTA, Los Alamos, 1964-65; buyer AAUW Playschool, Los Alamos, 1960-64. Mem. MLA, NCTE, Soc. Tech. Communication, Toastmasters (pres. 1984), Phi Beta Kappa, Phi Kappa Phi, Delta Kappa Gamma. Home: Star Rt 2 Box 153 Socorro NM 87801

DUBOIS, CHRISTINE, b. Richmond Heights, Mo., Dec. 30, 1956; d. Edward Neely and Jean Charlotte (Hall) Dubois; m. Steven Edward Bourne, Sept. 16, 1979. Contrbr. more than 300 articles to: V.S. Catholic, Sunday Digest, Living Church, Seek, numerous other publs. BA magna cum laude in Communications, U. Wash., 1979. Prod. asst. weekend assignment ed. KING-TV news, Seattle, 1978-81; freelance wrtr., Seattle, 1981—; co-ed. Washington Christian News, Seattle, 1979-83; ed. Olympia Churchman, Episcopal Diocese of Olympia, Seattle, 1983-85; sr. ed. View Pub. Group Health Co-op., Seattle, 1986—; natl. columnist, The Episcopalian, 1986; communications tchr. North Seattle Community Coll., Shoreline Community Coll. Mem. Wash. Press Assn. (recipient writing, editing, photography awards), Episcopal Communicators. Home: 4416 Linden Ave N4 Seattle WA 98103

DUBOIS, JEAN CHARLOTTE, b. Denver, Jan. 4, 1926; d. Forest R. and Meyrtle Christina (Aker) Hall; m. Edward N. Dubois, Aug. 21, 1947; children—Christine Bourne, Katherine Reed, William Edward. Author: A Galaxy of Stars: America's Favorite Quilts, 1976, The Colonial History Quilt, 1976, Ann Orr Ptchwork, 1977, Bye Baby Bunting, 1979, Patchwork Quilting in Wool, 1985. Contrbr. numerous articles, book rvws. on quilting, genl. interest, short stories, poems to mags., newspapers. Ed.: LaPlata Rvw., Greeley, CO, 1984-86, LaPlatta Letter, Greeley, 1981-83. Wrkg. on novel. B.A., U. Wyo., 1947; M.A., Penn. State U., 1963. Dir., LaPlata Press, Greeley, 1975-86. Home: Box 1430 Golden CO 80402

DUBUQUE, CHERYL ANNE, b. Oswego, NY., Nov. 24, 1952, d. Fred E. and Genevieve A. (Muscalino) D. Author: Leaders, 1981, Tranquility, 1982, I Wish You Love, 1982, The Snow Lay Softly, 1984, Wild Flower, 1984, Reflections, 1985; contrbr. to American Poetry Anthology, 1983, other collections. Wrkg. on screenplay. Publicist Best of the West Prodns., Simi Valley, Calif., 1983—. Recipient Poetry award Campbell Publs., 1982, 85. Home 15233 Dickens St Sherman Oaks CA 91403

DU CHEMIN, AUDREY MAY, (Audrey Brown), b. Ardmore, Okla., June 7, d. Robert Louis and Josephine (Kearney) Brown; 1 dau., Elisabeth Frey. Co-author: India—Land of Mystery and Enchantment, 1984, Gujarat of Gandhi, 1985; contrbr. articles and short stories to natl. and intl. mags. and newspapers; contrbr. to newsletters. BA, U. Denver, 1928; postgrad., UCLA, 1952-54, U. So. Calif.-Los Angeles, 1955-56. Freelance wrtr., 1935-42, 75—; news ed. El Monte (Calif.) Herald, 1942-44; ed. employee publs. TRW-West Coast, Bell, Calif., 1944-54; jnl. ed. Alumni Assn. Loma Linda U. Schl. Medicine, Los Angeles, 1959-76. Dir. ednl. projects Los Angeles United Way, 1956-59. Named Indsl. Ed. of Yr., So. Calif. Indsl. Eds. Assn., 1952, Ed. of Yr., Los Angeles United Way, 1953,

Top Ten Ed., Am. Alumni Council, 1959; recipient various editorial awards. Home: 3220 Broad St Newport Beach CA 92660

DUDLEY, BOBBY G., b. Wichita Falls, TX, Dec. 8, 1928; s. George Sherril and Verna M. (Emmons) D.; m. Doris Jean Roberts, Oct. 3, 1951. Co-author, ed. 70 books on chess; ed. var. state and local chess mags. Instr., USAF, Sheppard AFB, TX, 1951; officer, USAF, 1951-71; prof. Robert Morris Coll., Pitts., 1971—; owner/ed. Chess Enterprises, Coraopolis, PA, 1978—. Home: 107 Crosstree Rd Coraopolis PA 15108

DUDLEY, PEGGY LOUCELLE, (Pennetta Penn) b. Valley City, N.D., Sept. 2, 1943; d. Charles Butler and Violet Loucelle (Lacy) Brown; m. Larry Dee Dudley, Feb. 2, 1961; children—Larry, Ronald. Contrbr. poetry: Impressions, 1986, Hearts on Fire, 1987, Kids, Cats and Puppydogs II, 1987, other publs. Wrkg. on poetry collection. Student public schs., Pomona, Calif. Home: White Oak Shores Rt 1 Box 657 Eufaula AL 36027

DUDLEY, SHERRI DENISE, b. Vandenberg, CA, Nov. 12, 1965; d. Leland Eugene and Madge Louise (Hitt) Biser; m. Thomas Lawrence Dudley, Apr. 27, 1984; 1 son, Thomas. Contrbr. poems to anthols., lit. mags. Wrkg. on poetry. Recipient Honorable Mention, World of Poetry, 1985, Golden Poet award, 1986. Home: 4490 Lewis/Clark Meridian ID 83642

DUEMER, JOSEPH, b. San Diego, May 1951, s. Louis R. and Evelyn (Tuttle) D.; m. Mady F. Lund, Dec. 15, 1973 (div. 1980). Author: The Light of Common Day (poetry), 1986, Fool's Paradise (poetry), 1980, Customs (poetry), 1987. BA in English, U. Wash., 1978; MFA in Poetry, U. Iowa, 1980. Ed. Energy Times, Seattle, 1980-81; lectr. Western Wash. U., Bellingham, 1981-83; instr. San Diego State U., 1983—. Grantee NEA, 1984, NEH, 1985. Mem. AWP (anniversary award 1985). Home: 4975 Brighton Ave San Diego CA 92107

DUER, DAVID EDWARD, b. Akron, OH, July 29, 1954; s. John David and Rose Marie (Trares) D.; m. Patricia Lyn Schmid, Dec. 5, 1981; children—Sierra Soleil, Emma Claire, Jesse Paul. Author: To Bread (chapbook), 1986, Attitude Kingdom (chapbook), 1987. Ed., Luna Tack Mag., 1981—; contrbr. poems to numerous mags.; contrbr. reviews to North Am. Rvw, Daily Iowan, Prairie Sun. BGS, U. Iowa, 1981. Assoc. ed. Coffee House Press, West Branch, IA, 1981-85; clerk, U. Iowa Hospitals, 1986—. Mem. CCLM. Address: Box 372 West Branch IA 52358

DUERR, PAULA CUMMING, b. San Antonio, Feb. 22, 1929, d. Arthur August Jannasch and Lura Myrtle (Cumming) Jannasch Leonard; m. Edward Harold Duerr, July 17, 1953; children—David Laurence, Amy Louise. Author: The Culturally Handicapped Child, 1966, Beginning Entomology, 1978, Entomology Resource for Leaders, 1978, Three-Level Approach to Learning, 1973; contrbr. articles to 4-H Leader, Key to Christian Edn., Christian Home, San Antonio Express, numerous other publs. Wrkg. on parent-child education books, stories. AA, San Antonio Coll., 1948; BS, Trinity U., 1952. Tchr. numerous schls. throughout Tex. and Calif., 1948-54. Home: 841 Willard Ct Gilroy CA 95020

DUFFY, YVONNE HELEN PATRICIA, b. Toronto, Ontario, Canada, Nov. 29, came to U.S., 1964, naturalized, 1976; d. Prederick Paul and Yvonne Helen Margaret (Garvin) D. Author: All Things Are Possible, 1981, Meeting the Challenge: A Guide to Barrier-Free Learning, 1981. Contrbr. chpts. to books. B.A. in English Lit., U. Mich., 1973. Research asst. U. Mich., Ann Arbor, 1973-77, student services asst., 1973-77; free-lance jnlst., 1978—. Mem. Natl. Women's Studies Assn., Intl. Women WG, Am. Assn. Disability Communicators. Home: 720 E Ann St Ann Arbor MI 48104

DUFOUR, DARLENE, (Marilyn Long), b. Alexandria, LA, May 26, 1944; d. W. T. and Beatrice (Thompson) Long; m. Sidney L. Dufour, Nov. 15, 1969; children—Michael, Ray. Author: (study guides, self-checks, tests, tchr.'s key) Gregg Shorthand for Colleges, vol. 2, 1981; Student Handbook for Typewriting I, 1987. Contrbr. articles to lit. and popular mags., edn. books including Redbook, Country, others. Features ed.: North Rapides Express, 1984-85. Wrkg. on fiction novel, non-fiction articles for mags. B. S. in Bus. Edn., La. Coll., 1974; M.S. in Bus. Edn., Northwestern State U., 1978, Specialist in Edn., 1980. Instr. Alexandria Vocational-Technical Inst., 1980-86; tchr. Oak Hill High Schl., Elmer, LA, 1986—. Recipient 7th place for non-fiction WD, 1985, 1st place for unpublished non-fiction Reader's Digest, 1986, 1st place La. Wrtr.'s Conf., 1986. Mem. RWA, NWC, La. Press Women (3d prize for news reporting). Home: 178 Moss Ridge Pineville LA 71360

DUGAN, DIXIE, see Clark, Dixie

DUGGER, JULIA BURNS, b. Watertown, NY, Dec. 26, 1942; d. Thomas Eugene and Katherine (Burns) Nicholson; m. John Edwin Dugger; children—Katherine, Anne, Sarah, Thomas. Author: relig. articles, bklet.; co-author tchrs. manual, That They Might Have Life Through The New Testament; writer/prod. wkly. puppet show, Morris Cablevision, 1976-77. AA, Pierce Coll., 1962; BS in Jnlsm., Gonzaga U., 1964. Freelance writer, 1965—; profl. puppeteer, 1975-81; freelance ed. Benziger Pub., Mission Hills, CA, 1985—. Home: 125 Morris Turnpike Randolph NJ 07869

DUGGER, RONNIE E., b. Chgo., Apr. 16, 1930; s. W. O. and Mary (King) D.; m. Jean Williams, June 13, 1951 (div. 1978); children: Gary McGregor, Celia Williams.; m. Patricia Blake, June 29, 1982. Author: Dark Star: Hiroshima Reconsidered in the Life of Claude Eatherly of Lincoln Park, Texas, 1967, Our Invaded Universities, Form, Reform, and New Starts, A Nonfiction Play for Five Stages, 1974, The Politician: The Life and Times of Lyndon Johnson, 1982, On Reagan, The Man & His Presidency, 1983; Editor: Three Men in Texas, Bedicheck, Webb and Dobie, 1967. BA, U. Tex., 1950, postgrad., 1954; student, Oxford U., 1951-52. Journalist Tex. newspapers, 1947-52; editor Tex. Observer, 1954-61, 63-65, 81, pub., 1965—; Rockefeller fellow, 1969; Research fellow Inst. Indsl. Relations, U. Calif. at Los Angeles, 1969-70; NEH fellow, 1978; fellow Woodrow Wilson Intl. Ctr. for Scholars, 1983-84. Mem. AG, PEN, Tex. Inst. Letters. Home: Box 1466 Austin TX 76767

DUGGIN, LORRAINE JEAN, b. Omaha, Sept. 21, 1941, d. Frank Jr. and Sidonia (Bodlak) Jansky; m. Jack A. Kiscoan Dec. 19, 1964 (div. 1975); children—Eric, Susan; m. 2d, Richard C. Duggin, July 16, 1977 (div. 1983). Co-ed (with Richard Duggin); Annex 21 No. 2; contrbr. to Smackwarm, Prairie Schooner, Phoebus, Bellwether, others. BA, U. Omaha, 1965; MA, U. Nebr.-Omaha, 1979. Instr. U. Nebr.-Omaha, 1974-82, acting chair wrtrs.' workshop, 1982; wrtr., adminstrv. asst. to pres. Bellevue (Nebr.) Coll., 1983-85; resident artist Nebr. Arts Council, 1983—. Recipient John H. Vreeland Grad. award in Wrtg., U. Nebr.-Lincoln, 1981, Mari Sandoz Prairie Schooner fiction award, 1984, AAP prize, 1982. Mem. P&W. Home: 932 N 74th Ave Omaha NE 68114

DULTZ, RON WILLIAM, b. Apr. 24, 1943; s. Marvin and Josephine (Klissner) D. Author: Hello World, 1969, The Collected Poetry of Ron Dultz, 1984, Educating the Entire Person, 1984, Hainesville, 1985; contrbr. to Woodstock 69, 1970, A Technique of Oral Interp., 1973, Portland Review, 1984; creator: The Greeting Cards of Ron Dultz (line of cards avail. at retail), 1986. Student pub. schls., Reseda, CA. Author/pub. Ron Dultz Publishing, Reseda, CA, 1978—. Home: 7502 Canby Reseda CA 91335

DUMOUCHEL, J. ROBERT, b. North Adams, MA., Dec. 22, 1936; s. Antoine and Gabrielle (Phoenix) D.; re-married Mary C. Braithwaite Nov. 7, 1986; children—Philip, Monica, Natalie, Denise. Author: Dictionary of Development Terminology, 1975, European Housing Rehabilitation Experience—A Summary and Analysis, 1978, The Commissioner's Dictionary of Housing and Community Development Terminology, 1985, Government Assistance Almanac 1985, 86, 87.Student Georgetown U., 1957-61; MA, Goddard Coll., 1977. Pub., founder Foggy Bottom Pubs., Washington, 1984; cons. housing and community devel., 1968—. Office: Box 23462 Washington DC 20026

DUNBAR, LESLIE WALLACE, b. Lewisburg, WV., Jan. 27, 1921; s. Marion Leslie and Minnie Lee (Crickenberger) D.; m. Peggy Rawls, July 5, 1942; children: Linda Dunbar Kravitz, Anthony Paul. Author: A Republic of Equals, 1966; co-authr, editor: Minority Report, 1984. MA, Cornell U., 1946, PhD, 1948. Guggenheim fellow, 1954-55; United Negro Coll. Fund scholar-at-large, 1984-85. Poli. Sci. faculty, Emory Univ. and Mt. Holyoke Coll., 1948-51, 1955-58; U.S. AEC, 1951-54; exec. dir. and dir. research, So. Regl. Council, 1958-65; exec. dir., Field Fdn., 1965-80. Home: 56 Benedict Pl Pelham NY 10803

DUNCAN, JULIA ERIN NUNNALLY, b. Marion, NC, Apr. 16, 1956, d. Charles Otto and Madeline Julia Esther (Davis) Nunnally; m. Charles Stephen Duncan, Mar. 30, 1973. Contrbr. stories to Mendocino Rvw, Now and Then, Wrtrs.' Forum; contrbr. poetry: Piedmont Lit. Rvw, Old Hickory Rvw, Lyrical Fiesta, Visions. BA, Warren Wilson Coll., Swannanoa, N.C., 1982, MFA, 1984. Prof. English Warren Wilson Coll., 1985; instr. English McDowell Tech. Coll., Marion, N.C., 1986—. Fiction scholar Duke U., 1985. Home: Rt 4 Box 981 Marion NC 28752

DUNETZ, LORA E., b. NYC. Poetry in New York Times, Georgia Rvw, Poet Lore, Icarus, Anthology of American Magazine Verse, other mags and anthologies. Edl. staff, Without Halos. MA, Teachers College, Columbia U., 1943; OTR, New York U., 1945. Reg. occup. therapist, Baltimore County Bd. of Ed., 1964-75. Mem. PSA, New Jersey Poetry Soc., Am. Occupational Therapy Assn. Address: Box 113 Whiting NJ 08759

DUNGEY, JOAN MARIE, b. Seattle, Nov. 24, 1944; d. Richard Allan and Bonita Florence (Slane) Ostrholt; m. Ronald E. Dungey, July 21,

1969; children—Keenan, Philip. Author: What We've Learned the Hard Way: Language Development Grades 7-12, 1980, A Handbook for Using the Newspaper in the Eighth Grade Classroom, 1981, Bible Studies for New English Speakers, 1982, 2d ed., 1986, Summer Spelling Fun Booklets, Grades 3, 4, 5, 6, 1982, The Reading Teacher, 1983, Teaching English in the Two Year College, 1984, Innovations, 1984, Videotape and Viewers' Guide: Teaching the Bible to New English Speakers, 1986, Using Fairy Tales and Fantasy to Motivate the Reluctant Reader, 1987. Contrbr. articles to profl. jnls. B.A., U. Wash., 1966; M.Ed., Seattle Pacific U., 1983. Science tchr. Bellingham, Wa., 1967-69; Seoul, Korea, 1969-70; English rdg., ESL tchr., Plainview, Texas., 1979-81; evaluator English as a second lang. Northshore Schl. District, Bothell, WA, 1982-83; technical wrtr. Computer Financial Services, Bellevue, WA, 1983-86; ednl. cons., 1980—. Mem. Intl. Reading Assn., NCTE, Tchrs. of English to Speakers of Other Langs., Laubach Literay Advance. Home: 126 N Walnut Yellow Springs OH 45387

DUNHAM, SHERRIE ANN, b. Kalamazoo, MI, July 3, 1949; d. George Willis and Gladys Marie (Lambert) D. Author plays: The Witch & the Scarecrow, 1981, Wanted: One Fair Damsel, 1983. Contrbr. article, chpt. to secretarial mag., creative writing textbook. B.A., Western Mich. U., 1971. Asst. to office mgr. oncology & Hematoloty, P.C., Kalamazoo, 1973-79, 82-85; secy. Leonard Hill Real Estate, Lawton, MI, 1985-87; free-lance designer scenic notepaper, 1985—. Address: 30032 County Rd 354 Lawton MI 49065

DUNKEL, TOM RICHARD, b. Summit, NJ, June 18, 1950; s. Wilbur Elbert Dunkel and Norma (Huber) Karle. Contrbr. articles to Wash. Journalism Rvw, Soho News, N.J. Monthly, Sport Mag., N.Y. Times, Oakland Tribune, Travel & Leisure, airline mags. BA, Muhlenberg Coll., 1972; MA in Journalism, NYU, 1982. Media coordinator U.S. Com. for UNICEF, NYC., 1977-78; mgr. trade media relations Am. Soc. of Travel Agents, NYC, 1978-80; freelance print and broadcast wrtr., Montclair, N.J., 1980-85; staff wrtr. N.J. Monthly mag., Morristown, 1985—. Recipient William Allen White commendation for commentary City and Regional Mag. Assn., 1986, 1st place investigative reporting, NJ chpt. Soc. Profl. Jnlsts., 1987. Home: 1135 Gresham Rd Plainfield NJ 07062

DUNLAP, JOE EVERETT, b. Delaware, OH, May 11, 1930; s. Arthur Calvin and Mary Irene (Jones) D.; m. Mary Susan King, June 17, 1959; children—Marlene, Todd, David, Sherrie, Dru. Author: Surviving in Dentistry, 1977, The Beginning of Dental Practice, 1978, 2d., 1983, Stress, Change, & Related Pains, 1982, Keeping the Fire Alive, 1983, 10 Trends, 1986. Acquisition ed.: PennWell Pub. Co., Clearwater, FL, 1984-86. Wrkg. on novel, articles for trade pubs., book on dental cost containment. D.D.S., Ohio State U., 1959. Dentist, Clearwater, 1961-81; genl. mgr. operations Sheppard Dental Ctrs., FL and TX, 1981-84; free-lance wrtr., 1987—. Home: 1816 Lombardy Dr Clearwater FL 34615

DUNLEAVY, JANET EGLESON, (Janet F. Egleson, Janet Frank), b. New York, Dec. 16, 1928; d. Christian J. and Evelyn (Aron) Frank; m. Gareth W. Dunleavy, July 25, 1971. Author: (under name Janet F. Egleson; with Jim Egleson) Parents without Partners, 1961, (under name Janet F. Egleson) Design for Writing, 1970; George Moore: The Artist's Vision and the Storyteller's Art, 1973, (with Gareth W. Dunleavy) The O'Conor Papers, 1977, contrbr, Herbert Fackler, ed, The Irish Novel since James Joyce, 1980, contrbr, John Halperin, ed, Trollope Centenary Essays, 1981, ed. Anthony Trollope, Castle Richmond, 1981, contrbr, P.J. Drudy, ed, Anglo-Irish Studies, 1979, Ralph Aderman, ed, The Quest for Social Justice, 1983, ed George Moore in Perspective, 1983, contrbr, Bernard Oldsey, ed, Dictionary of Literary Biography, vol 15, British Novelists 1930-59, 1983; contrbr James Kilroy, ed, The Irish Short Story, 1984, contrbr, Melvin J. Friedman and Beverly Lyon Clark, eds, Flannery O'Connor, 1985; ed (with G. Dunleavy) Selected Plays of Douglas Hyde, 1988. Under name Janet Frank, juveniles: Daddies, 1954, Davy Crocket and the Indians, 1955, Happy Days: What Children Do the Whole Day Through, 1955. Also au of two more children's books. Contrbr to Treasurey of Little Golden Books. Editorial consultant to encyclopedias and university presses. Contrbr to prof. jnls, including Victorian Studies, Irish University Review, Eire-Ireland, Ethnicity, Eigse: A Jnl of Irish Studies, Tulsa Studies in Women's Literature, James Joyce Qtly, Canadian Jnl of Irish Studies, Ireland of the Welcomes, Jnl of American Culture, Studies in the Novel. Ed, American Com for Irish Studies News Letter, 1971-78; consulting ed., Transations of the Wis. Acad, 1976-78; editorial consultant to scholarly jnls. BA, Hunter Coll of the City Univ of N.Y., 1951; MA, New York Univ, 1962, Ph. D., 1966; post doctoral study, Dublin Inst for Advanced Studies, 1978, 1981, and Tel Aviv Univ, 1986. Lectr. in English, Hunter Coll of the City Univ of N.Y., 1964-66; asst. prof. of English, State Univ. of N.Y. at Stony Brook, 1966-70; asst. prof., Univ of Wis-Milwaukee, 1970-71, assoc. prof., 1971-76, prof. of English, 1976—. Visiting prof., Univ of Illinois at Urbana-Champaign, fall, 1978; Fulbright prof., Tel-Aviv Univ., 1986. Member: Intl. Assn. for the Study of Anglo-Irish Lit (mem. exec. com., 1970-76), MLA, American Com for Irish Studies (secy. 1972-75), James Joyce Fdn, Wis. Acad of Sci, Arts and Letters (v.p. for Letters, 1977), Wis. Coordinating Council of Women in Higher Education, English Graduate Assn of New York Univ. Summer research grantee, State Univ. of N.Y., 1967, 69, Grad Schl faculty grantee for fummer research, 1968; summer research grantee, Univ. of Wis.-Milwaukee, 1970, 72, 77, 82; ACLS grantee, 1971; American Irish Fndn grantee, 1973, 74; Fromkin Meml lectr and grantee, 1976; elected to Hunter College Hall of Fame, 1978; American Philosophical Soc grantee, 1980; Guggenheim fellow, 1983-84; Camargo Meml Fndn fellow, 1984; Fulbright scholar, 1986. Office: Dept Eng Univ Wis Milwaukee WI 53201

DUNLEVY, BRIDGET, see Dunlevy, Marion B.

DUNLEVY, MARION B., (Bridget Dunlevy), b. Jamaica, NY, Aug. 11, 1930, d. Joseph and Marion (Boyle) Dunlevy; div.; 1 son, Joseph. Author: Virago: The Story of Anne Newport Royall (with Alice Maxwell), 1985; "Mythomania" columnist Greater Red Bank Voice, Red Bank, N.J. Wrkg. on feminist biography. Actress various prodns. N.Y. and N.J. Home: 27 Monroe St Red Bank NJ 07701

DUNN, HAMPTON, b. Floral City, FL, Dec. 14, 1916; s. William Harvey and Nancy (Hemrick) D.; m. Charlotte Rawls, Aug. 16, 1941; children: Janice Kay Dunn Oldroyd, Henry Hampton Jr., Dennis Harvey. Author: Rediscover Florida, 1969, WDAE, Florida's Pioneer Radio Station, 1972, Yesterday's Tampa, 1972, Yesterday's St. Petersburg, 1973, Yesterday's Clearwater, 1973, Florida Sketches, 1973, Yesterday's Tallahassee, 1975, Accent Florida, 1975, Yesterday's Lakeland, 1976, Back Home, A History of Citrus County, Florida, 1976, Wish You Were Here—A Grand Tour of Early Florida Via Old Postcards, 1981, Tampa—A Pictorial History, 1985, Florida—A Pictorial History, 1987; editor Sunland Tribune, Tampa Hist. Soc. Staff, Tampa Daily Times, Fla., 1936-58, mng. editor, 1949-58; poli. commentator, news analyst Sta. WCKT-TV, Miami, 1958-59; editor Fla. Explorer, Pensinula Motor Club, Tampa, 1959-87; consl. Peninsula Motor Club, 1987—. Served to major USAF, 1942—. 46, MTO, Bronze Star medal, 5 battle stars. Recipient Award of Merit, Fla. Hist. Soc., 1970, Fla. Patriot award Fla. Bicentennial Commn., 1976, D.B. McKay award Tampa Hist. Soc., 1978, Outstanding Citizen award Fla. Library Assn., 1983, Best Spot News award AP of Fla., 1946, others. Mem. Fla. Mag. Assn., Fla. Public Relations Assn., Sigma Delta Chi (past pres.). Home: 10610 Carrollwood Dr Tampa FL 33618

DUNN, JONAH MARSHALL, b. near Morgantown, WV, Nov. 9, 1913; s. Howard Marshall and Olive Pearl (McMillen) D.; m. Elizabeth Theresa Rice, Dec. 3, 1955; children: Theresa Marie, John Michael, Mary Michele, Ann Monica Dunn Harrell. Author: articles, short stories, poems in magazines and newspapers such as Target, Grit, Poultry Tribune; during 1930s in mail order pubns. such as Progressive Mail Dealer, Mailbox, Mail Order Money Magazine, Swapper's Friend, Verity Syndicate Magazine; syndicated monthly column, "I See by the Mails" till 1940s; technical, quasi-legal policy and prodedural manuals for fedl. govt. from mid-40s to 1980, as well as items to Baltimore News-American, Baltimore Sun, others. Attended Morgantown Business Coll., 1941-42, Geo. Washington Univ., 1961-65; Univ. of Md., Baltimore, 1965-67. Administrative asst., Manhattan Project, 1945; Social Security Administration, 1946-80 (mgmt. analyst, wrtr., 1967-80); owner/operator, books by mail, Baltimore, 1980-85; freelance wrtr. and direct mktg. consultant, 1986—. Social Security Employee Scholar of the Year, George Washington Univ., 1963-64. Mem. Natl. Wrtrs. Club, Am. Entrepeneurs Assn. Office: 353 So Betalou St Baltimore Md 21223

DUNN, JULIA, b. Fort Benning, GA, Dec. 10, 1953; d. Billy James and Mildred Jean (Coffee) Dunn. Mng. editor: Take Five mag., 1985-86. Contrbr. articles to popular mags. Wrkg. on screenplay, advt., pub. relations writing. BA with honors in film studies, U. Calif.-Santa Barbara, 1980. Acct. exec. Dennis Davidson Assocs., Beverly Hills, Calif., 1981-84; supr. pub. info. KNME-TV, Albuquerque, 1985—; prtnr. The Writes Assocs., Albuquerque, 1985—; Mem. Southwest Wrtrs. Workshop, Delta Zeta (chmn. pub. relations 1972-73). Home: Box 27639 Albuquerque NM 87102

DUNN, STEPHEN ELLIOTT, b. Forest Hills, NY, June 24, 1939, s. Charles Francis and Ellen Dorothy (Fleischman) D.; m. Lois Ann Kelly, Sept. 24, 1964; children—Andrea Ellen, Susanne Rebecca. Author: Looking for Holes in the Ceiling, 1974, Full of Lust and Good Usage, 1976, A Circus of Needs, 1978, Work and Love, 1981, Not Dancing, 1984, Local Time, 1986. BA in History, Hofstra U., 1962; MA in Creative Writing, Syracuse U., 1970. Asst. prof. Southwestern State U., Marshall, Minn., 1970-73;

prof. creative writing Stockton State Coll., Pomona, N.J., 1974—; vis. lectr. Syracuse U., 1973-74; adj. prof. writing Columbia U., N.Y.C., 1983—. NEA fellow, 1974, 83, Guggenheim Fdn. fellow, 1984-85. Mem. PEN, AWP. Home: 445 Chestnut Neck Rd Port Republic NJ 08241

DUNNE, JOHN GREGORY, b. Hartford, CT, May 25, 1932; s. Richard Edwin and Dorothy (Burns) D.; m. Joan Didion, Jan. 30, 1964; 1 adopted dau., Quintana Roo. Author: books, including Delano "The Story of the California Grape Strike", 1967, The Studio, 1969, Vegas: A Memoir of a Dark Season, 1974, True Confessions, 1977, Quintana and Friends, 1978, Dutch Shea, Jr., 1982; (with Joan Didion) screenplay Panic in Needle Park, 1971, Play It As It Lays, 1972, True Confessions, 1981; contbr. articles to mags., including Natl. Rvw, New Republic, New York, Atlantic Monthly, BA, Princeton U., 1954. Writer, editor Time mag., NYC. Columnist: (with Joan Didion) Points West, Saturday Evening Post, 1967-69, The Coast, Esquire mag., 1976-77. Served with AUS. Address: ICM 40 W 57th St New York NY 10019

DUNNIHOO, DALE RUSSELL, b. Dayton, OH, June 8, 1928; s. John R. and Hazel Nora (Roth) D.; m. Betty Lu, Sept. 1, 1950; children—Diana, John, Dale, Bryan, Janet. B.S., Gannon Coll., 1949; M.S., U. Mich., 1950; M.D. cum laude Washington U. Schl. Med., 1956; Ph.D., U. Southern Calif., 1972. Chmn. dept. of obstetrics/gynecology Keesler U.S. Air Force Med. Center, Biloxi, MS, 1972-78; prof., dir. dept. obstetrics/gynecology La. State U. Schl. Medicine, Monroe, 1980—. Contrbr. articles to profl. jnls., monographs; poems to anthols. Home: 107 Dupont Circle West Monroe LA 71291

DUNNING, ETHEL FLO, (Flo Austin Dunning), b. Eddyville, IL, Jan. 22, 1935; d. Edwin Ira and Lottie Jane (Wells) Austin; m. David James Dunning, Jan. 23, 1953 (div. June 1, 1970); children—Steven (dec.), Bonita, Ronnie, Gregory. Contrbr. poems to newspapers, mags.; short stories to Springhouse Mag. Wrkg. on novel, Backwater. Home health aide Tip of Ill. health Services, Carterville, IL, 1980-83; cook, home health aide Visiting Nurse Assn., Evansville, IN, 1984—. Home: Box 565 Golconda IL 62938

DUNNING, LAWRENCE, b. Kansas City, MO, Aug. 8, 1931, s. Lawrence M. and V. Elizabeth (Morisey); m. Barbara Lee Adams, Apr. 11, 1958; children—Melissa, Tracey, Jennifer. Author fiction: Neutron Two Is Critical, 1977, Keller's Bomb, 1978, Taking Liberty, 1981. BA, So. Meth. U., 1952. Wrtr., ed. Petroleum Info., Denver, 1957-62; ed. AF Acctg. and Fin. Center, Denver, 1962-84, publs. mgr., 1984—. Served as sgt. USAF, 1952-56. Mem. AG, Colo. Authors League, Mensa. Home: 1211 S Quebec Way 15-205 Denver CO 80231

DUNWOODY, KENNETH REED, b. Washington, IA, Oct. 1, 1953; s. Kenneth W. and Marilyn Jane (Green) D. Ed., contrbr., game & fish pubns., 1986—.BS in Jnlsm., U. IL, 1976. Sports announcer, WPGU Radio, Champaign, IL, 1973-75; sports ed. Free Press Nwsprs., Carpentersville, IL, 1976-79, Daily Crystal Lake Herald (IL), 1979-82; ed. Fur-Fish-Game Mag., Columbus, OH, 1982-86. Mem. OWAA. UPI awards Best Sports Columns, 1978, 79, 80, 81, Best Sports Writing, 1980, Best Sports Section, 1979, 80, 81. Home: 1550 Terrell Mill Rd 4K Marietta GA 30067

DUPES, MARTHA GAIL, (Martha Taylor), b. Hobart, IN, May 5, 1940; d. Lowell Edgar and Mary Louise (Cherrington) D. Contrbr. articles to mags. including Parents Mag., others. B.S. in Physical Edn., Ind. U., 1966, M.S. in Health and Safety Edn., 1969. Substitute tchr. The Spa Emporium, Clearwater and Largo, FL, 1983—. Fellow St. Petersburg Wrtrs. Club. Home: 1415 Main St 419 Dunedin FL 34698

DU PRIEST, TRAVIS TALMADGE, b. Richmond, VA, Aug. 15, 1944; s. Travis T. and Mildred (Abbitt) Du P.; m. Mabel Benson, Sept. 1, 1972; children—Travis Edgerton, Benson Hunter. Author: Soapstone Wall (poetry), 1981, Jeremy Taylor's Discourse on Friendship (intro.), 1985; contrbr. poems, essays, articles to jnls and mags. BA, U. Richmond, 1966; PhD,U. Ky., 1972; MTheol. Studies, Harvard, 1974. Prof. English Carthage Coll., Kenosha, Wis., 1974—; asst. to rector St. Luke's Chapbook., Racine, Wis., 1979—, chaplain De Koven Fdn., 1980—; editorial asst. The Living Church, Milw., 1983—. Co-founder Episcopal Peace Fellowship of St. Luke's Chapbook., 1980. Clark Library fellowship UCLA, 1982. Mem. Christianity and Lit, Natl. Huguenot Soc. (gen. Chaplain, 1985-87). Home: 508 De Koven Ave Racine WI 53403

DURAN, NATIVIDAD PEREZ, b. Chamberino, NM, Oct. 4, 1946; s. Natividad M. Duran and Maria P. (Porras) Perez; m. Judy Gardner, Aug. 29, 1963 (div. June 1972), children—Frank, Denise; m. 2d, Shannon M. Anderson, Apr. 25, 1980; 1 child, Michelle. Author: The Navajo, The Forgotten American, 1975, El Paso, Tex., Gateway to Crime, 1977, A Leak in the Protection Program, 1980, The English Way, 1981, The Punishment of Michael, 1981, The Notary Along the Border, 1984, The Valley After Billy the Kid, 1985. Wrkg. on The Illegal Alien, Why? BA, U. Pacific, 1966. Mgr., Seaboard Fin., Los Angeles, 1964-66; asst. mgr., South Ariz. Bank, Phoenix, 1970-72; free-lance writer, Berino, N. Mex., 1980—. Served to 1st lt., U.S. Army, 1966-70. Home: Star Rt Box 160 Mesilla Park NM 88047

DURANT, PENNY LYNNE RAIFE, b. Albuquerque, May 22, 1951; d. John Carl and Patricia Fay (Bremermann) Raife; m. Omar Duane Durant, Jan. 2, 1971; children—Geoffrey Alan, Adam Omar. Author: Cinnamon Smoke: Science Activities for Young Children, 1986. Contrbr. articles to mags. Wrkg. on novels for juveniles. BA, U. N.Mex., 1973, MA, 1980. Tchr. Albuquerque pub. schls., 1973-76; tchr. Calcio Butterfly Preschool, Albuquerque, 1980-81, 84—, dir., 1984—. Mem. Soc. Children's Book Writers. Home 305 Quincy NE Albuquerque NM 87108

DURHAM, KENNETH M., b. Bakersfield, CA, Jan. 14, 1953; s. Morgan Durham and Cora Estelle (Lane) Wolf; m. Mary Good Honor; children—Dallas, Kala, Denver, Austin. Ed.: Kindred Spirit, 1985—, Searcher, 1985-86; motorsports columnist Dallas Morning News, 1986—; mng. ed. Dallas/Ft. Worth Living, 1980-81; dep. sports ed., Bakersfield Californian, 1981-82; assoc. ed. Texas Business, 1980-82; contrbr. to numerous pbns. including Christian Athlete, Worldwide Challenge, Athletes in Action, Twin Cities Christian, Bakersfield Californian Newspaper, Racing Wheels, FORE Mag.; author Study Guide to Words and Works of Jesus Christ (video), 1986. BA, Cal. State/Long Beach, 1975; postgrad. Dallas Theological Seminary. Mem. Evangelical Press Assn. Office: Dallas Sem 3909 Swiss Ave Dallas TX 75204

DURHAM, MARILYN JEAN (WALL), b. Evansville, IN, Sept. 8, 1930; d. Russel Reams Wall and Stacy Frances (Birdsall) Alldredge; m. Kilburn Homer Durham, Nov. 24, 1950; children: Joyce Elaine, Mary Jennifer. author: (novels) The Man Who Loved Cat Dancing, 1972; Dutch Uncle, 1973; Flambard's Confession, 1982. Student U. Evansville, 1949-50. Recipient fiction award Soc. Midland Authors, 1973. Home: 1508 Howard St Evansville IN 47713

DUTTA, PRABHAT KUMAR II, (Sriranjan), b. Calcutta, India, Apr. 13, 1940, came to U.S., 1973, permanent resident since 1973; s. Prakash C. and Rani Bala (Basu) D.; m. Tanushree Bhattacharya, July 18, 1970; children—Prabal, Malini. Author: (stories) Stories of the Evening Circle, 1966, Krouncho Mithun, 1966, And Arindam, 1986; (poems) Dwaita Bhavana, 1967, Asamanya Churi, 1986; (children's recreational) The Card Tricks, 1967; (drama) Svet Kapot, 1968; (recreational) The Beauty and Charm of Puzzling Numbers, 1986, Mathmagic, 1988. Contrbr. numerous articles to mags. Assoc. ed.: Maya Mancha, 1965-66; ed.: Atalantik, 1979—. Wrkg. on novel, Ranjana, Amar Ranjana. B.S. in Electrical Engineering, Jadavpur Univ., Calculta, India, 1963; M.S. in Electrical Engineering, Polytechnic Inst. N.Y., 1977, M.S. in Econ. Systems, 1980. Mgr. pump dept. Blue Star Ltd., Calcutta, 1970-72; sales officer Premier Irrigation Equipment Ltd., Calcutta, 1972-73; engineer Am. Elec. Power Svc. Corp., Columbus, OH, 1974—. Life mem. Children Lit. Council. Home: 7630 Deer Creek Dr Worthington OH 43085

DUVAL, JOHN TABB, b. Phila., Oct. 19, 1940, s. Thaddeus Ernest DuVal and Helene Cau; m. Mary Katherine Niell; children—Kathleen Anne, John Niell. Author: Cuckolds, Clerics and Countrymen, 1982, The Fabliaux: The B.N. 837 Manuscript, vol. 1, 1984, vol. 2, 1986; translation ed. The Poetry Miscellany, 1983—; contrbr. to Intro, Ralph, Poetry Miscellany, Lazarus, Translation Rvw, New Eng. Rvw and Bread Loaf Qtly, Mundus Artium, Poetry World. AB in English, Franklin and Marshall U., 1962; MA in English, U. Pa., 1965; MA in French, U. Ark., 1974, PhD in Comparative Lit., 1977, MFA in Transl., 1979. Instr. S.W. Mo. State U., Springfield, 1965-68, Ark. State U., Josesboro, 1969-70; asst. prof. Albany Jr. Coll., Ga., 1978-82; asst. prof. English, U. Ark., Fayetteville, 1982—, also dir. transl. program. Served with U.S. Army, 1963-65. Recipient award for an outstanding acad. book Choice, 1983. Mem. ALTA. Office: 333 Kimpel Hall U Ark Fayetteville AR 72701

DWIGHT, OLIVIA, see Hazzard, Mary Dwight

DWYER, NANCY JEAN, b. Milw., Aug. 30, 1945; d. Burney Alex and Theresa Catherine (Keller) Peters; m. David J. Dwyer; children—Michael, Susan. Columnist: Sport Flyer Mag., 1985-87. Contrbr. articles to outdoors, sports mags. Sci. ed.: Sagamore, 1986-87. B.A., Bradley U., 1967; M.S., Med. Coll. Wis., 1969. Research scientist Lakeside Labs., Milw., 1969-71; free-lance wrtr., 1982—. Recipient Best Issues Article award Sigma Delta Chi, Indpls., 1985. Home: 143 W 88th St Indianapolis IN 46260

DYBECK, DENNIS JOSEPH, (Art Beck), b. Chgo., Oct. 18, 1940, s. Rudolph W. and Marie (Olchawa) D.; m. Kathleen Phelan, July 3, 1963; children—Danelle, Julianne, Michael. Author: Enlightenment, 1977, The Discovery of Music, 1977, North Country (New Works), 1981, Art Beck Translates Luxorius, 1982, Rilke, 1983;

contrbr. to Sequoia, Invisible City, Vagabond, Pinchpenny. Home: 2528 25th Ave San Francisco CA 94116

DYBEK, STUART JOHN, b. Chgo, Apr. 10, 1942; s. Stanley and Adeline (Sala) D.; m. Caren Bassett; children: Anne, Nicholas. Author: Brass Knuckle, 1979, Childhood and Other Neighborhoods, 1980. MA, Loyola U.-Chgo., 1967; MFA, U. Ia., 1973. Caseworker Cook County Pub. Aid, Chgo., 1964-66; tchr. St. Martha Schl., Morton Grove, Ill., 1966-67, Wayne Aspinal Schl., Virgin Islands, 1968-70; tchg. fellow Univ. Ia., Iowa City, 1970-73; prof. Engish W. Mich. Univ., Kalamazoo, 1973—. Guggenheim fellow, 1981, NEA fellow, 1982; recipient Writers award Whiting Fdn., 1985, O. Henry award, 1985, Nelson Algren award, 1985. Mem. PEN, AWP, NBCC. Address: 320 Monroe Kalamazoo MI 49007

DYKES, IVA REE, b. McKenzie, AL, Jan. 28, 1942; d. Ira James and Una Vay (Hudson) Holt; m. Robert Dykes, Dec. 31, 1971. Contrbr. to Primary Treasure, Prattville Progress News Paper, Good News Broadcaster, By Line, Anthols., Hi Call. Graduated Massey Draughon Bus. Coll., 1963; student U. Ala., 1985—. Administrative sec. Prison Management Systems, Montgomery, AL, 1980-82; stenographer Public Health Dental, Montogomery, 1982-83, State Health Plan Agy., Montgomery, 1983—. Chpt. sec. Muscular Distrophy Assn., Montgomery, 1969. Home: 3645 Gaylord Pl Montogomery AL 36105

EADY, CORNELIUS ROBERT, b. Rochester, NY, Jan. 7, 1954; s. Cornelius and Alveeta (Hayes) Eady; m. Sarah Gordon Micklem, May 31, 1978. Author poetry: Kartunes, 1980, Victims of the Latest Dance Craze, 1986. Wrtr.-in-res., Sweet Briar College, Sweet Briar, VA, 1982-84; poet-in-res., Poets-in-the-schls., Richmond, VA, 1982-85; master poet, Young Writers Workshop, Charlottesville, VA, 1984-85, wrtr.-in-res. Coll. of William and Mary, 1987-1988, vis. wrtr. Sarah Lawrence Coll, 1987-88. Awards: 1985 Lamont Prize, Academy of American Poets, NEA Fellowship, 1984-85. Mem. PSA, VA Commission for the Arts, VA Center for the Creative Arts. Home: 27 Bethune St New York NY 10014

EAKINS, PATRICIA, (Patty Ann Briggs), b. Phila., Nov. 16, 1942; d. Jesse Walter and Stina Marie (Osbeck) Eakins; m. Peter Martin, Apr. 17, 1982. Contrbr. chapbook Oono, 1982; story in A Reader of New Am. Fiction; mags. inclg. Black Warrior Rvw, Chgo Rvw, Colo State Rvw, Epoch, Open Places, Mass. Rvw, Bus Stop (serial fiction), Worcester Rvw, Exquisite Corpse. BA, Wellesley Coll., 1964, MFA, Goddard Coll., 1977. Freelance writer, editor, NYC, 1974—; instr. NY Inst. Tech.-Metro campus, NYC, 1979—. Project dir. Catskill Reading Soc., Claryville, NY, 1985-86. NEA fellow, 1982; fiction fellow, CAPS, 1979. Mem. P&W, NWU. Address: 1200 Broadway 4C New York NY 10001

EAST, CHARLES, b. Shelby, MS, Dec. 11, 1924; s. Elmo Montan and Mabel (Gradolph) E.; m. Sarah Simmons, Sept. 30, 1948; 1 child, Charles. Author: (short stories) Where the Music Was, 1965; The Face of Louisiana, 1969; Baton Rouge: A Civil War Album, 1977; contrbr. chpt. to Touched by Fire: A Photog. Portrait of the Civil War, vol. 1, 1985, New Writers of the South, 1987. BA, La. State U., 1948, MA, 1962. Editorial asst. Collier's mag., NYC, 1948-49; reporter Morning Adv., Baton Rouge, 1949-52, Sunday Mag. ed., 1952-55; asst. city ed. State-Times, Baton Rouge, 1955-62; ed., assoc. dir. La. State U. Press, Baton Rouge, 1962-70, dir., 1970-75; ed., asst. dir. U. Ga. Press, Athens, 1980-83, ed. Flannery O'Connor award for short fiction, since 1981—; freelance ed., 1984—. Home: 1455 Knollwood Dr BatonRouge LA 70808

EASTBY, ALLEN GERHARD, b. Bklyn., Oct. 6, 1946; s. Gerhard Shervington and Alice Mildred (Krogstad) E.; m. Clara Ann Wetzel, Aug. 14, 1971. Author: The Tenth Man, 1986. Contrbr. articles to outdoor and sports mags. including Sports Afield, Outdoor Life, Field and Stream. BA, Wagner College, 1968; AM, NYU, 1970, PhD, 1973. Asst. prof. U. Ala., Huntsville, 1973-74, N.Y.U., NYC, 1974; free-lance writer, 1975—. Mem. Trout Unltd., Sierra Club, Isaac Walton League, Fedn. Flyfishers, OWAA. Home: Rt 1 Box 223 Branchville NJ 07826

EASTLAKE, WILLIAM DERRY, b. NYC, July 14, 1917; s. Gordon and Charlotte (Bradley) E. Author: novels Go in Beauty, 1955, The Bronc People, 1958, Portrait of an Artist with Twenty-Six Horses, 1963, Castle Keep, 1965, The Bamboo Bed, 1969, Dancers in the Scalp House, 1975, The Long Naked Descent Into Boston, 1977; poems and essays A Child's Garden of Verses for the Revolution, 1970, short stories Jack Armstrong in Tangier, 1984; corr. in Vietnam for The Nation mag.; author stories pub. in 40 anthologies and textbooks, 1 screen play, 13 fgn. lang. editions; Contrbr. stories to Harper's, Atlantic Monthly, Ms. Student, Alliance Francaise, Paris, 1948-50; LLD, U. Albuquerque, 1970. Lectr. U. N.Mex., 1967-68, U. So. Calif., 1968-69, U. Ariz., 1969-71, U.S. Mil. Acad., 1975. Writer-in-residence, Knox Coll., Galesburg, Ill., 1967. Served with inf. AUS, World War II; ETO. Decorated Bronze Star; recipient Les Lettres Nouvelles award for best fgn. novel pub. in France, 1972; Ford Fdn. grantee, 1963; Rockefeller Fdn. grantee, 1966, 67. Mem. AG, WG, PEN, AAUP. Address: 15 Coy Rd Bisbee AZ 85603

EATON, CHARLES EDWARD, b. Winston-Salem, NC, June 25, 1916; s. Oscar Benjamin and Mary Gaston (Hough) E.; m. Isabel Patterson, Aug. 16, 1950. Author poems: The Bright Plain, 1942, The Shadow of the Swimmer, 1951, The Greenhouse In the Garden, 1956, Countermoves, 1963, On The Edge of the Knife, 1970, The Man in the Green Chair, 1977, Colophon of the Rover, 1980, The Thing King, 1983, The Work of the Wrench, 1985, New and Selected Poems 1942-1987; short stories: Write Me From Rio, 1959, The Girl From Ipanema, 1972, The Case of the Missing Photographs, 1978; art criticism/biography: Karl Knaths: Five Decades of Painting, 1973. AB, U. of NC, 1936; MA, Harvard, 1940. Instr., Ruiz Gandia Schl., PR, 1937-38; instr., U. of Missouri, Columbia, 1940-42; vice consul, American Embassy, Brazil, 1942-46; asst. prof., U. of NC, Chapel Hill, 1946-51. Mem. PSA, AAP, New England Poetry Club. Home: 808 Greenwood Rd Chapel Hill NC 27514

EATON, ROBERT CHARLES, b. Los Angeles, Aug. 14, 1946; s. Charles Hardman Eaton and Ruth Irene (Cook) Christopher; 1 son, Christopher Charles. Author: (with M.C. Grant) Biological Science in the Laboratory, 1984. Contrbr. articles to profl. jnls. Ed.: Neural Mechanisms of Startle Behavior, 1984. B.A., U. Calif.-Riverside, 1968, Ph.D., 1974; M.S., U. Oreg., 1970. Research neuroscientist U. Calif., San Diego, 1974-78; asst. prof. U. Colo., Boulder, 1978-83, assoc. prof., 1983—. Home: 1390 Fairfield Dr Boulder CO 80303

EBEL, CHARLES WILLIAM, b. Washington, June 24, 1951; s. Francis Gustav and Bernadine Patricia (O'Donoghue) E; m. Lise Meryam Uyanik, May 14, 1978. Contrbr. articles to The Progressive, Seven Days, BBC, Pacific News Serv., Colliers Yearbook. AB in Anthropology, Duke U. Copy ed. Africa News Service, Durham, NC, 1973-75, mng. ed., 1975—, pubs. cons. Organizer, Triangle Friends of the Farm Workers, Durham, 1973. Address: 115 E Maynard Ave Durham NC 27704

EBEN, LOIS ELLEN, b. Kearny, NJ, Mar. 10, 1922; d. Louis and Ellen Reid (Laird) Eben. Author: 129 Art Lessons in 26 Media, 1977, Getting Kids Started in Arts and Crafts, 1982. Contrbr. articles to profl. jnls. including NJEA Rvw, Instructor, Grade Tchr., School Arts. BS magna cum laude, NYU, 1956, MA 1959, EdD, 1973. Supr. art Shrewsbury Boro Schl., N.J., 1956-83; tchr. art Monmouth County Ednl. Services Commn., Long Branch, N.J., 1984; freelance wrtr., 1954—; tchr. art workshops, courses Kean Coll, Rutgers Coll., Symposium for the Arts, Monmouth Coll. Lois Ellen Eben Art award named in honor by Shrewsbury Boro PTA. Mem. N.J. Ed. Assn. (assoc.), Natl. Edn. Assn., Monmouth County Edn. Assn., NWC. Home: 1006 Florence Ave Union Beach NJ 07735

EBERHART, RICHARD, b. Austin, MN, Apr. 5, 1904; s. Alpha LaRue and Lena (Lowenstein) E.; m. Helen Elizabeth Butcher, Aug. 29, 1941; children:Richard Butcher, Margaret Ghormley. Author: A Bravery of Earth, 1930, Reading the Spirit, 1936-37, Song and Idea, 1940, 42, Poems New and Selected, 1944, Burr Oaks, 1947, Brotherhood of Men, 1949, An Herb Basket, 1950, Selected Poems, 1951, Undercliff: Poems, 1946-1953, 1953, Great Praises, 1957, Collected Poems, 1930-60, 1960, Collected Verse Plays, 1962, The Quarry, 1964, Selected Poems, 1930-65, 1965, Thirty One Sonnets, 1967, Shifts of Being, 1968, Fields of Grace, 1972, Poems to Poets, 1976, Collected Poems, 1930-1976, 1976, co-author: To Eberhart from Ginsberg, 1976; Of Poetry and Poets, (criticism), 1979; poems Survivors, 1979, Ways of Light, 1980, Four Poems, New Hampshire/Nine Poems, 1980, Festschrift Richard Eberhart: A Celebration, 1980; Richard Eberhart Symposium, Negative Capabilities, 1986; Chocorua, Florida Poems, 1981, The Long Reach, 1984; Collected Poems 1930-1986, 1986; verse drama The Visionary Farms, publ. with others in Collected Verse Plays, 1962; editor: (with Seldon Rodman) War and the Poet, 1945. Student, U. Minn., 1922-23; AB, Dartmouth Coll., 1926, BA, Cambridge U., 1929, MA, 1933; student grad. schl. arts and sci., Harvard U., 1932-33. Tutor son of King Prajadhipok of Siam, 1930-31; master English, St. Mark's Schl., Southborough, Mass., 1933-41; tchr. English, Cambridge Schl. Kendal Green, Mass., 1941-42; vis. prof. English, U. Conn., 1953-54; Wheaton vis. prof. English, poet in residence Wheaton Coll., 1954-55; resident fellow (prof.) in creative writing and Christian Gauss lectr. Princeton U., 1955-56; prof. English, poet in residence Dartmouth Coll., 1956—, Class of 1925 prof., 1968-71, emeritus 1970—, disting. vis. prof. U. Fla., Gainesville, spring, 1974, vis. prof., 1975—; with Butcher Polich Co., Boston, 1946—, v.p., 1952, hon. 1958, also dir.; mem. Yaddo Corp., 1955—, dir., 1964—; cons. in poetry Library of Congress, 1959-61, hon. cons. in Am. Letters, 1963-69; founder, first pres. The Poets' Theater, Inc., Cambridge, Mass., 1951; hon.

pres. 3d World Congress Poets, Balt., 1976; mem. adv. com. on arts Natl. Cultural Center, 1959—. Served from lt. to lt. comdr USNR, 1942-46. Recipient Guarantors price Poetry mag., 1946, Harriet Monroe Meml. prize, 1950; The Golden Rose, N.E. Poetry Soc., 1950; Shelley Meml. prize Poetry Soc. Am., 1951; 1000 grant Natl. Inst. Arts and Letters, 1955; Bollingen prize, 1962; Pulitzer prize, 1966; Natl. Book award, 1977; President's medallion U. Fla., 1977, Fla. Ambassador of the Arts, 1984; Natl. Poetry Day award N.Y. Qtly, 1980; Sarah Josepha Hale award Newport (N.H.) Library, 1982; Robert Frost Medal, PSA, 1986; named poet laureate of N.H., 1979; AAP fellow, 1969; Richard Eberhart Day proclaimed by Gov. R.I., 1982, Dartmouth Coll., 1982. Mem. Natl. Acad. Arts and Scis., PSA, AAIAL, American Academy of Arts and Letters. Home: 5 Webster Terr Hanover NH 03755

EBERT, ROGER JOSEPH, b. Urbana, IL, June 18, 1942, s. Walter H. and Annabel (Stumm) E. Author: An Illini Century, 1967, Beyond the Valley of the Dolls, 1970, Beyond Narrative: The Future of the Feature Film, 1978. BS, U. of Ill., 1964; grad. student, U. Cape Town, South Africa, U. Ill., U. Chgo. Editor Daily Illini, 1963-64; staff writer News-Gazette, Champaign-Urbana, Ill., 1958-66; film critic Chgo. Sun-Times, 1967—, US mag., 1978-79, NBC TV News, Chgo., 1980-83. Recipient award Overseas Press Club, 1963, Chgo. Headline Club, 1963, Chgo. Newspaper Guild, 1973, Pulitzer price, 1975, Emmy award, 1979. Mem. Am. Newspaper Guild, WG Am. West, Natl. Soc. Film Critics. Office: S-T 401 N Wabash Ave Chicago IL 60611

EBERTS, MICHAEL ALBERT, b. Hollywood, CA, Nov. 2, 1955; s. Albert Francis and Shirley Jeane (Moore) Eberts. Author numerous feature and opinion articles in daily newspapers, including Los Angeles Times, Los Angeles Herald-Examiner. BA, Cal State U., Los Angeles, 1979-82, MA, 1982, postgrad, U. of So. Calif., 1982-85. Asst. edit., Specialist Publications, Encino, CA, 1979; research asst., Citizens Research Fdn., 1981—; instr., Long Beach City College, CA, 1985—. Home: 1853 N Highland Ave Hollywood CA 90028

EBY, CECIL DEGROTTE, b. Charles Town, WV, Aug. 1, 1927; s. Cecil and Ellen (Turner) E.; children: Clare Virginia, Lillian Turner. Author: Porte Crayon: The Life of David H. Strother, 1960, The Siege of the Alcazar, 1965, (translations in Italian, German, Finnish, Dutch, Portuguese) Between the Bullet and the Lie: American Volunteers in the Spanish Civil War, 1969, That Disgraceful Affair: The Black Hawk War, 1973; Editor: The Old South Illustated, 1959, A Virginia Yankee in the Civil War, 1961. AB, Shepherd Coll., 1950; MA, Northwestern U., 11951; PhD, U. Pa., 1958. Served with USNR, 1945-46. Rackham Research grantee, 1967, 71, 77, 79. Office: Haven Hall U Mich Ann Arbor MI 48104

ECONOMOU, GEORGE, (Farmer Fitzsteward), b. Great Falls, MT, Sept. 24, 1934; s. Demetrios George and Amelia (Ananiadis) E.; m. Rochelle Owens, June 17, 1962. Author: The Georgics, 1968, Landed Natures, 1969, The Goddess Natura in Medieval Literature, 1972, Poems for Self Therapy, 1972, AMERIKI: Book One and Selected Earlier Poems, 1977, Voluntaries, 1984, harmonies & fits, 1987; ed., contrbr.: In Pursuit of Perfection, 1975, Geoffrey Chaucer, 1975; ed.: Proensa, 1978; translator: Philodemos, 1983. AB, Colgate U., 1956; MA, Columbia U., 1957, PhD, 1967. Mem. faculty L.I. U., Bklyn., 1961-83; prof., chmn. dept. English, U. Okla., Norman, 1983—. ACLS fellow, 1975, Com. Artists in Public Service fellow N.Y. Council on Arts, 1976. Mem. Medieval Acad. Am., MLA, Dante Soc. Office: Dept Engl Univ Okla 760 Van Vleet Oval Norman OK 73019

EDEL, (JOSEPH) LEON, b. Pitts., Sept. 9, 1907; s. Simon and Fannie (Malamud) E.; m. Roberta Roberts, Dec. 2, 1950 (div. 1979); m. Marjorie P. Sinclair, May 30, 1980. Author: Henry James: Les annees dramatiques, 1932, The Prefaces of Henry James, 1932, James Joyce: The Last Journey, 1947, Life of Henry James, 5 vols. (Untried Years, 1953, Conquest of London, Middle Years, 1962, Treacherous Years, 1969, The Master, 1972), Henry James: A Life, 1985, The Psychological Novel, 1955, Literary Biography, 1957, (with E.K. Brown) Willa Cather, 1953, (with Dan H. Laurence) Bibliography of Henry James, 1957, H. D. Thoreau, 1970, Bloomsbury: A House of Lions, 1979, Stuff of Sleep and Dreams, 1982, Writing Lives, 1984; editor: The Ghostly Tales of Henry James, 1949, Stories of the Supernatural, 1970, The Complete Tales of Henry James, 12 vols., 1963-65, The Complete Plays of Henry James, 1949, (with Lyall H. Powers) The Complete Notebooks of Henry James, 1986, Selected Fiction of Henry James, 1953, Selected Letters of Henry James, 1955, The Future of the Novel, 1956, The American Essays of Henry James, 1956, (with Gordon N. Ray) Henry James and H.G. Wells, 1958, The Bodley Head Henry James, 11 vols., 1967-74, The Diary of Alice James, 1964, Letters of Henry James, 4 vols., 1974-84, Edmuns Wilson Papers: The Devils and Canon Barham, 1974, The Twenties, 1975, The Thirties, 1980, The Forties, 1982, The Fifties, 1986. MA, McGill U., LittD, U. Paris, Sorbonne, 1932. Writer, journalist, 1932-43. Served as lt. AUS, World War II; dir. Press Agy., 1945-47; U.S. zone Germany. Decorated Bronze Star; recipient Pulitzer price in biography, 1963; Natl. Book award for nonfiction, 1963; Natl. Book Critics award, biography, 1986; medal of lit. Natl. Arts Club, 1981; Bollingen Fdn. fellow, 1958-61; Natl. Inst. Arts and Letters grantee, 1959; Gold medal for biography Acad.-Inst., 1976; Hawaii Writers award, 1977; Guggenheim fellow, 1936-38, 65-66; NEH grantee, 1974-77. Fellow Am. Acad. Arts and Scis., Royal Soc. Lit. (Eng.); mem. Am. Acad. Arts and Letters, Natl. Inst. Arts and Letters, Soc. Authors (Eng.), AG, PEN. Address: 3817 Lurline Dr Honalulu HI 96816

EDELMAN, ELAINE, b. Mpls., d. B. P. and Rhae (Rubenstein) E. Author: Boom-de-Boom, 1980, I Love My Baby Sister (Most of the Time), 1984; Noeva: Three Women Poets, 1975; contrbr. poems to over 30 mags. including Am. Poetry Rvw, Open Places, Confrontation, Prairie Schooner; contrbr. essays and articles to N.Y. Times Book Rvw, McCall's, Playbill, Pubs. Weekly, Esquire, Connoisseur, Vanity Fair, Town & Country; appeared in anthologies 8 Young North American Poets, 1974, I Hear My Sisters Say'g, 1976, A Change in the Weather, 1978. BA, Sarah Lawrence Coll. Assoc. producer pub. affairs dept. CBS-TV, 1963-65; writer-producer NBC-TV, 1965; editor Am Heritage Pubs., N.Y.C., 1966-68; sr. editor McGraw-Hill Pub. Co., 1969-71, sr. editor, Harper & Row, 1971-81; featured poet-reader Spoleto USA Festival, Charleston, S.C., 1982. Va. Ctr. for Creative Arts fellow, 1984; grantee Dramatists Guild, 1975. Fellow New Dramatists; mem. PEN, AG. Home: 415 E 85th St New York NY 10028

EDELSON, JUDITH WHITE, (Judie White), b. Wedowee, AL, Feb. 15, 1949; d. Paskal Charley Wesley and Margaret Elizabeth (Day) White; m. Barry Edelson, May 12, 1984; 1 dau., Kate Elizabeth. Author poetry: Moods & Mysteries, 1978, Quiet Thoughts, 1985; screenwriter TV pilot The Four Seasons, 1983. Media Coordinator Forward Advtg. Agey. St. Petersburg, Fla., 1969-71; dir. purchasing C-Ran Corp., Largo, Fla., 1972-77; freelance wrtr., Miami, Fla., 1978-87; owner, operator CompuFast, North Miami Beah, Fla. Mem. Fla. Freelance Wrtrs. & Graphic Artists Guild. Assn. Office: CompuFast 14500 W Dixie Hwy North Miami Beach FL 33161

EDELSON, MORRIS, b. Los Angeles, Apr. 25, 1937; s. Louis Terrell and Leah Verona (Gard) E.; m. Betsy Booth, 1966 (div. 1970); m. 2d, Melissa Lynn Bondy, 1981. Ed.: A Charles Bukwoski Sampler—preface, 1967, The Madison Collages of d.a. levy, 1968; transl.: A Communist Manifesto Comic Book, 1968, 71, 84; contrbr. articles to numerous mags. Ed., transl., Letters to Mrs. Z., by Kazimierz Brandys, 1987; wrkg. on The Great Homestead Steel Strike, by Richard Krooth (ed.). PhD, U. Wis., 1974. Ed. Houston Digest (Tex.), 1982—. Pub. Quixote Magazine, 1968—. Fulbright prof. Am. Lit., U. of Lodz, Poland, 1969-71; prof. U. of Houston-Downtown, 1983—. Mem. SPJ. Home: 1810 Marshall Houston TX 77098

EDELSTEIN, SCOTT SAMUEL, b. Pitts., Oct. 17, 1954, s. Morris and Estelle (Rellis) E. Author: College: A User's Manual, 1985, The Indispensable Writer's Guide, 1988, No-Experience-Necessary Writer's Course, 1987, How to survive Freshman Composition, 1988; ed.: Future Pastimes, 1977; columnist Wrtr.'s Digest, 1985—, The Artist's Mag., 1985—; contrbr. to Glamour, Essence, Ellery Queen's Mystery Mag., Artlines, Writer's Yearbook, other publs. BA in Creative Writing, Oberlin (Ohio) Coll., 1978; MA in English, U. Wis.-Milw., 1984. Ed. Aurora Pubs., Nashville, 1974-76; adj. instr. U. Minn., Mpls., 1979-83, Met. State U., Mpls., 1982-83; mng. ed. Artlines Mag., Taos, N.Mex., 1983-84; wrtr.-in-res. Ohio Arts Council, 1985—. Edward Albee Fdn. fellow, 1978. Mem. AWP. Home: 179 Berkeley Rochester NY 14607

EDEN, KATE, see Paradisco, K. L.

EDLOSI, MARIO, see Leih, Grace Janet

EDMONDS, DAVID CARSON, b. Ellisville, MS, Dec. 19, 1937; s. David Stephen and Roselle (Garrison) E.; m. Lucinda Louise Sibille, Sept. 9, 1967; children—Christopher, Julie, Alex, Davy. Author: Yankee Autumn in Acadiana (Lit. award La. Library Assn., 1980), 1979, Vigilante Committees of the Attakapas, 1981, Guns of Port Hudson: The River Campaign, 1983, Guns of Port Hudson: The Investment, Siege and Reduction, 1985. B.A. Econ., Univ. of Southern Miss., 1962; M.A., La. State U., 1967; Ph.D., Am. U., 1971. Economist, U.S. Treasury Dept., Washington, 1967-71; Fulbright prof. U.S. State Dept., Monterrey, Mexico, 1972-73; prof. econ. U. Southwestern La., Lafayette, 1973—. Served to sgt. U.S. Marine Corps, 1955-59. Office: Dept Econ USLA Box 44570 Lafayette LA 70504

EDWARDS, CLAUDIA JANE, b. Monterey, CA, July 13, 1943; d. Alfred Claude and Jane Isabel (McKinley) E. Author: Taming the Forest King, 1986, A Horsewoman in Godsland, 1987. Wrkg. on Bright and Shining Tiger and a fantasy trilogy. B.A., U. Tex., 1965. Vol. Peace Corps, Palau, Micronesia, 1966-68; elem. tchr. Joseph City Public Sch., AZ, 1969-70, Sierra Vista Public Schs., AZ, 1970—. Mem. NEA, Ariz. Edn. Assn. Home: Rt 1 Box 100C Hereford AZ 85615

EDWARDS, HELEN JEAN, b. Terre Haute, IN, Jan. 26, 1937; d. Charles Edwards Adams and Emily (Mann) Adams-Bean; m. Larry A. Edwards, July 6, 1957; children—Kelly, Kerry, Jeff, Dana, Brandi. Author: Stormy, 1983, May I Have This Dance, 1984, Go With Love, 1985. Columnist: Merrillville Connection, A Woman's Touch, 1987. Contrbr. articles, commls., publicity info. A.A., Terre Haute Bus. Coll., 1957. Co-owner, v.p. Pioneer Pest Control Inc., Terra Haute, 1980-87; free-lance wrtr., 1960—; secy, program copywrtr. sta. WEAT-TV, 1956-60. Mem. NWC, Terra Haute Fee Lance Wrtrs. Group. Home: 3401 Linn Ave Terre Haute IN 47805

EDWARDS, J.M.B., b. Sidcup, Kent, U.K., May 21, 1935, came to U.S., 1958, s. Horace Ernest and Agnes Mary (White) E.; m. Patricia Louise Remolif, May 28, 1965; children—Livia, Kieron. Ed.: Passing Farms, Enduring Values (by Yvonne Jacobson), 1984, The Saga of Dazai Osamu (by Phyllis I. Lyons), 1985, Chez Panisse Desserts (by Lindsey Shere), 1985, 1985, The Mother of Dreams (by Makato Veda), 1986, Coevolution (by Wm. H. Durham), 1988; ed. books, reports by U.S. Office Edn., numerous pub. cos.; co-author: Greece and Rome (with A.R. Burn), 1970, Human Environments and Natural Systems (with Ned Greenwood), 1973; contrbr. to: Intl. Encyc. of Social Scis., 1968. Wrkg. on non-fiction on Am. women and mass media. BA, Oxford (Eng.) U., 1958. Freelance ed., wrtr., Berkeley, Calif., 1971—. Mem. NWC, Wrtrs. Connection. Address: 2432 California St Berkeley CA 94703

EDWARDS, JANE ELIZABETH, (Jane Campbell), b. Miles City, MT, Mar. 31, 1932; d. Christopher Martin and Josephine Cecelia (Gast) Campbell; m. Richard Byron Edwards, Sept. 26, 1953; children—Linda, Richard, Andrew, Sheila, Patrick. Author: What Happened to Amy?, 1961, 2d. ed., 1965, Carol Stevens, Newspaper Girl (as Jane Campbell), 1964, The Houseboat Mystery, 1965, reprinted as The Affair of the Albatross, Believe no Evil (as Jane Campbell), 1969, Island Interlude, 1969, Listen with Your Heart, 1986; co-author: The Mexican-American, His Life Across 4 Centuries (with Martinez), 1973; contrbr. short stories, novelettes, articles to profl. publs.; contrbr. to ednl. texts, The Favorites anthology, 1976. Educated: Catholic schls., San Francisco. Home: 2525 Rocky Pt Bremerton WA 98312

EDWARDS, JOHN CHARLES, see Parkhurst, Louis Gifford, Jr.

EDWARDS, KEVIN DALE, b. Christoper, IL, Setp. 18, 1957; s. Beverly Dale and Bernice Loretta (Medley) E.; m. Sonia A. Net Prieto, Dec. 17, 1986. Contrbr. poetry to lit. mag. Ed.: (lit. mag.) Page One, 1972-74. B.S. in Electrical Engrng., Southern Ill. U., 1980. Dir. quality control Dowzer Electric, Mt. Vernon, IL. 1980—. Home: Rt 2 Box 300 Mulkeytown IL 62865

EDWARDS, LINDA ANN, (Linda Wallace Edwards), b. Lawrenceburg, TN, July 3, 1944; d. Edward Henry and Ruth Kathlene (Faires) Wallace; m. Robert Gary Edwards, July 31, 1966; children—Troy Lynn, Eric Gwyn, Robert Scott. Author: The Diary of Angelita, 1986, Shalem's Revenge, 1986. Wrkg. on The Legend of White Sky. Grad. public schls., Brimfield, IL. Home: Box 94 Yates City IL 61572

EDWARDS, LYNN, see Beetler, Dianne Lynn

EDWARDS, P. E., see Clyne, Patricia Edwards

EDWYNEL, REV., see Ver Becke, W. Edwin

EFRON, ARTHUR, b. Chgo., Nov. 2, 1931; s. Miles J. and Molly (Manosevitz) E.; m. Ruth G. Kirstein, 1981; 1 dau. (previous marriage) Sonia. Author: Don Quixote and the Dulcineated World, 1971, ed (with Dennis Hoerner) David Boadella, The Spiral Flame: A Study in the Meaning of D.H. Lawrence, 1977, ed (with John Herold) Root Metaphor: The Live Thought of Stephen C. Pepper, 1980, The Sexual Body: An Interdisciplinary Perspective, 1985. Contrbr to jnls, including Intl Rev of Psychoanalysis, Minnesota Review, Dissent, Energy and Character, and Catalyst. BA, Univ of Wash., 1958, Ph. D., 1964; grad study at Univ. of Calif., Los Angeles, 1958-60. Instr, State Univ. of N.Y. at Buffalo, 1963-64, asst prof, 1964-68 assoc prof, 1968-76, prof of English, 1976—. Pub. and ed of Paunch (small press) and Paunch (mag), 1963—. Cervantes lectr at Fordham Univ., 1973. Chmn. of exec. com. of Independent Schl of Buffalo, 1967-68. Member: MLA, American Soc. for Aesthetics, D.H. Lawrence Soc., Virginia Woolf Soc., Niagara-Erie Writers. State Univ. of N.Y. faculty research awards, Summers, 1965, 68, 71; Dewey Fndn senior research fellow, 1983. Military service: U.S. Army, 1952-54; served in Japan and Korea; became sergeant; received Bronze Star. Home: 123 Woodward Ave Buffalo NY 14214

EGAN, FEROL, b. Sonora, CA, July 25, 1923; s. Ferol Ruoff and Verna Mae (Maffox) E.; m. Martha Toki Oshima, Mar. 6, 1965. Author: (novel) The Taste of Time (Merit award WWA, 1978), 1977; The El Dorado Trail: The Story of the Gold Rush Routes across Mexico (Silver medal Commonwealth Club of Calif., 1971), 1970, Sand in the Whirlwind: The Paiute Indian War of 1860 (Silver medal Commonwealth Club of Calif., 1973), 1972, Fremont: Explorer for a Restless Nation (Gold medal Commonwealth Club of Calif., 1978), 1977. Ed.: Incidents of Travel in New Mexico (George D. Brewerton), 1969, A Sailor's Sketch of the Sacramento Valley in 1842 (John Yates), 1971, California, Land of Gold or Stay at Home and Work Hard (J. Muller), 1971, A Dangerous Journey (J. Ross Browne), 1972, Overland Journey to Carson Valley and California (Hozial H. Baker), 1973, With Fremont to California and the Southwest 1845-1849 (Thomas S. Martin), 1975. B.A. Univ. of Pacific, 1946, postgrad., 1949-50; M.A. in English, U. Calif., Berkeley, 1959, postgrad, 1960. Sci. wrtr. U. Calif., Berkeley, 1961-65; assoc. prof. humanities San Francisco State U., 1984-85; prof. humanities Fromm Inst., San Francisco, 1984—. Active Friends of the Bancfoft Library. Home: 1199 Grizzly Peak Blvd Berkeley CA 94708

EGERTON, JOHN WALDEN, b. Atlanta, June 14, 1935; s. William Graham and Rebecca Crenshaw (White) E.; m. Ann Elizabeth Bleidt, June 6, 1957; children: Brooks Bleidt, March White. Author: A Mind to Stay Here, 1970, The Americanization of Dixie, 1974, Visions of Utopia, 1977, Nashville: The Faces of Two Centuries, 1979, Generations, 1983, Southern Food, 1987; contbr. articles to mags. Student, Western Ky. State Coll., 1953-54; BA, U. Ky., 1958, MA, 1960. Staff writer, So. Edn. Report mag., 1965-69, Race Relations Reporter mag., 1969-71; contrbg. editor, 1973-74; free-lance writer, Nashville, 1971—; journalist-in-residence, Va. Poly. Inst. and State U., Blacksburg, 1977-78; contrbg. editor: Saturday Rvw of Edn., 1972-73, So. Voices, 1974-75. Served with AUS, 1954-56. Address: 4014 Copeland Dr Nashville TN 37215

EGGLESTON, ALAN EARL, b. Hastings, MI, Oct. 20, 1949; s. Earl Boyd and Ellen Suzanne (Johnson) E.; m. Katherine T. Tomaszczyk, Oct. 23, 1976; 1 dau., Hilary Katherine. Contrbr. articles to mags.; author corporate product brochures. Ed.: Intl. Newsline, 1981-84, Newsgram, 1983-84, Pacesetter Report radio program, 1984-85, Amway comml. News, 1985—, ProMotions, 1987—. B.S. in Broadcast and Cinematic Arts, Central Mich. U., 1972; M.A. in Communications, Western Mich. U., 1985. Wrtr., producer Sta. WZZM-TV, Grand Rapids, MI, 1973-80; sr. wrtr. Amway Corp., Ada, MI, 1980-87; editor, 1987—. Home: 6464 Wahlfield NW Comstock Park MI 49321

EGNOR-BROWN, ROSE MARIE, b. Cartwright, NY. Author: A Parent Who Reads—A Child Who Learns, 1979, Reading Diagnosis and Remediation—A Handbook, 1986. B.S. Ed., Univ. of Dayton, 1975; M.S. in Edn., U. Dayton, 1977; Ph.D., Ind. U., 1987. Reading specialist Centerville Schls., OH, 1975-80; assoc. instr. Ind. U., Bloomington, IN, 1980-83; asst. prof. U. Dayton, OH, 1983—. Mem. Intl. Reading Assn., Am. Ednl. Research Assn. Office: U of Dayton 300 College Park Dayton OH 45469

EHLE, JOHN, b. Asheville, NC, Dec. 13, 1925; s. John Marsden and Gladys (Starnes) E.; m. Rosemary Harris, Oct. 21, 1967; 1 child, Jennifer Anne. Author: (novels) Move Over, Mountain, 1957; Kingstree Island, 1959; Lion on the Hearth, 1961; The Land Breakers, 1964; The Road, 1967; Time of Drums, 1970; The Journey of August King, 1971; The Changing of the Guard, 1975; The Winter People, 1982; Last One Home, 1983. AB, U. N.C., 1949, MA, 1952. Served with inf., AUS, 1944-46; ETO. Recipient Sir Walter Raleighprize N.C. Lit. and Hist. Soc., 1964, 67, 70, 75, 83; N.C. award State of N.C., 1972; Lillian Smith award So. Regional Council, 1982; Thomas Wolfe award Western N.C. Hist. Assn., 1984. Home: 125 Westview Dr NW Winston-Salem NC 27104

EHRHART, WILLIAM DANIEL, b. Roaring Spring, PA, Sept. 30, 1948; s. John Harry and Evelyn Marie (Conti) E.; m. Anne Senter Gulick, June 27, 1981. Author: A Generation of Peace, 1975/77, Rootless, 1977, Empire, 1978, The Awkward Silence, 1980, The Samisdat Poems, 1980, Matters of the Heart, 1981, Channel Fever, 1982, To Those Who Have Gone Home Tired, 1984, The Outer Banks, 1984, Vietnam-Perkasie, 1983/85, Marking Time, 1986; Going Back, 1987; contrbr. Winning Hearts and Minds, 1972; co-editor: Demilitarized Zones, 1976; contrbg. editor: Those Who Were There, 1984; editor: Carrying the Darkness, 1985. BA, Swarthmore Coll., Pa., 1973; MA, U. Ill., Chgo., 1978. Served as sgt. USMC, 1966-69. Grantee Mary Roberts Rinehart Fdn., 1980; Pa. Council of Arts fellow, 1981; Poet Laureate, Bucks County Council on Arts, 1983; winner 1st Prize, Lehigh Valley Poets, 1985. Mem. PSA, P&W, Soc. Profl. Journalists. Address: 6845 Anderson St Philadelphia PA 19119

EHRLICHMAN, JOHN DANIEL, b. Tacoma, Mar. 20, 1925; s. Rudolph I. and Lillian C. (Danielson) E.; m. Christy McLaurine, Nov. 3, 1978; children: Peter, Jan, Thomas, Jody, Robert, Michael. Author: The Company, 1976, The Whole Truth, 1979, Witness to Power, 1982, The China Card, 1986, Sketches and Notes, 1987. Numerous periodicals. BA, UCLA, 1948; JD, Stanford U., 1951. Bar: Calif. 1951-75, Wash. State 1952-75. Partner firm Hullin, Ehrlichman, Roberts & Hodge, Seattle, 1952-68; dir. conv. activities, tour dir. Nixon for President campaign, 1968; counsel to Pres. Nixon, 1969; asst. to Pres. for domestic affairs, also exec. dir. staff Domestic Council, Washington, 1969-73; mem. Fed. Property Rvw. Bd., 1970-73, Pres.'s Council Intl. Econ. Policy, 1971-73. Radio and TV commentator, MBS, 1978-80. Served with AUS, 1943-45, ETO. Decorated Air medal with clusters D.F.C. Mem. Kappa Sigma. Office: Box 5559 Santa Fe NM 87502

EIFERMAN, SHARON REES, b. Philadelphia, April 26, 1948; d. Arthur and Betty (Schuster) Rees; m. Barry Lee Eiferman, Dec. 23, 1972; 1 son, Kenneth Rees. Author: (poetry chapbook) Statements from the Crystal, 1986; (children's book) The Golden Brush of Zayda, 1987. Poetry in lit mags and anthols. BA, Temple U., 1969, MA, 1972. Tching. asst., Temple U., Phil. Pa., 1971-72; instr. Rutgers U., Camden, NJ, 1973-74; instr. Burlington County College, Pemberton, NJ, 1974-76; instr. Phila. Commun. College, 1974-85. Mem. NJ Poetry Soc. Home: 30 Efland Ln Willingboro NJ 08046

EIKENBERRY, ARTHUR RAYMOND, b. Sebrin, Fl, June 5, 1920; s. Leroy Albertus Eikenberry and Vernie Cordelia (Griffin) Eikenberry Bell; m. Carol Jean Parrott, June 10, 1955; children—Robin René, Shari LaVon, Jan Rochelle, Karyn LaRae, Kelli Yevette. Author: Investment Strategies for the Clever Investor, 1988. Student Pasadena Jr. Coll., 1939, Kunming U., China, 1944. Served with USAF, 1941-45, 47-73, ret.; adminstrv. officer U. Colo. Health Scis. Center, Denver, 1975—; owner, mgr. Strategic and Precious Metals Researcher, Aurora, Colo. Address: Box 31509 Aurora CO 80041

EILTS, KARIN LYNN, b. Pomona, CA, Aug. 3, 1956; d. Jean Leonard McGriff and Gladys Alvina (Johnson) Thomas; m. Bobby Ray Eilts, June 10, 1975; children—Jehremy Alan, Mariah Anne. Contrbr.: The Poet's Hand, Many Voices/Many Lands, Once Upon a Poet, Hearts on Fire Vol. IV, numerous others. Mem. staff Christianity Today, Inc., Carol Stream, Ill., 1982-84; asst. mgr. Edens Motel, Chgo., 1984—. Home: 3244 S Rocky Hill Rd Box 35 Galena Il 61036

EINBOND, BERNARD LIONEL, b. NYC, May 19, 1937; s. Hyman and Julia (Parsont) E.; m. Linda Sara Saxe, Feb. 20, 1977; children—Aaron, Julia. Author: The Coming Indoors and Other Poems, 1979; contrbr. anthologies: Live Poetry, 1971, The Haiku Anthology, 1974; contrbr. poems to Sunbury, Bogg, Modern Haiku, Frogpond, numerous others. AB, Columbia Coll., 1958; PhD in English, Columbia U., 1966. Mem. faculty Lehman Coll., CUNY, Bronx, 1968—, assoc. prof. dept. English, 1973—, chmn. dept., 1976-79. Recipient Keats Poetry prize, U.K., 1975. Mem. Haiku Soc. Am. (Merit Book award 1981). Home: Box 307 Fort George Sta NYC 10040

EINZIG, BARBARA ELLEN, b. Ann Arbor, May 31, 1951, d. Robert Stanley and Mary (Kinitzer) Einzig; m. David M. Guss, Mar. 20, 1985; 1 dau., Chloe Indigo. Author: Color, 1976, Disappearing Work, 1979, Robinson Crusoe: A New Fiction, 1983, Life Moves Outside, 1981, Life Moves Outside, 1987. One and All; translator works from Russian for numerous publs.; contrbr. to A Big Jewish Book, Language of the Birds, A Book of Women Poets from Antiquity to Now, other anthologies; ed.: New Wilderness Letter No. 10: Special Dream-work Issue, 1981, Read All About It, 1982; assoc. ed. New Wilderness Letter. BA with highest honors, U. Calif.-San Diego, 1972; postgrad., U. Wis.-Milw., 1974-75. Freelance ed., Los Angeles, 1977-81; staff ed. Los Angeles County Mus. Art, 1981-83; vis. scholar NYU, 1985-87; wrtr.-in-res. Rockland County Center for Arts, N.Y., 1987. MacDowell Colony fellow, 1985. Mem. P&W, St. Mark's Poetry Project. Home: 21 Bay St Piermont NY 10968

EISENHAUER, GALE ANN, b. Newcastle, WY, Nov. 3, 1955; d. Henry Curtis and Carol (Moore) Vickers; m. Patrick Maurice Eisenhauer, July 7, 1979. Assoc. ed.: Wy. Wool Grower Mag., Casper, 1978-81; ed.: Wy. Rural Electric News, Casper, 1981-86. Student Casper Coll., 1979-80. Mem. Casper Bus. Profl. Orgn., Wy. Press Assn., Wy. Press Women. Home: Box 3805 Casper WY 82602

EISENSTEIN, PAUL ALLAN, b. Chgo., May 6, 1953; s. Philip Pierre and Pauline (Kitay) E.; m. Chrisitne Marie Anderson, Sept. 20, 1986. Contrbr. articles: Investor's Daily Christian Sci. Monitor, Time, Newsweek, US Banker, Mfg. Week, USA Today, Heritage Mag., numerous other natl. publs. and broadcast syndications. BS cum laude, U. Mich., 1978. reporter, newswrtr. WXYZ radio-TV, Southfield, Mich., 1978-79; corr. Nat. Public Radio, Pleasant Ridge, Mich., 1979-84; bur. chief, owner The Detroit Bur., Pleasant Ridge, MIch., 1979—. Mem. Soc. Profl. Journalists, Labor Wrtrs. League N.Am. (co-organizer Detroit chptr.). Home: 22 Cambridge Blvd Pleasant Ridge MI 48069

EKLUND, GORDON STEWART, b. Seattle, July 24, 1945; s. Alfred James and DeLois (Stewart) E.; m. Dianna Jean Mylarski, Mar. 12, 1969; 1 son, Jeremy Clark. Author: novels include, The Eclipse of Dawn, 1971, Beyond the Resurrection, 1973, All Times Possible, 1974, The Grayspace Beast, 1976, If the Stars Are Gods, 1977; contrbr. short stories to Analog, Fantasy and Sci. Fiction and Galaxy mags. Student, Contra Costa Coll., 1973-75. Free-lance writer, El Cerrito, Calif. 1969—. Served with USAF, 1963-67. Mem. Sci. Fiction Writers Am. (Nebula award 1975). Home: 6305 East D St Tacoma WA 98403

EKSTROM, MOLLY ANNE, b. Benton Harbor, MI, May 30, 1929; m. Jonathan Oliver Ekstrom, Sept. 11, 1954; children—Elizabeth Lee, Kenneth Franklin. Contrbr. articles to newspapers, mags., radio, including The Ariz. Republic, Ariz. Daity Sun, others. B.A. in Interdisciplinary Studies, Western Ill. U., 1988. Linguist-translator Wycliffe Bible Translators, AZ, 1954-75, wrtr., assoc. ed., Huntington Beach, CA, 1975-83, communications coord., Thornton, CO, 1983-85; free-lance wrtr., 1985—. Address: 2631 N Chrysler Dr Tucson AZ 85716

EL, YUSUF ALI, b. Chgo., Mar. 8, 1948, s. Frank Mitchell and Bonnie (Randall) E.; 3 dau.—Quenna Ali, Giovanna, Laverne. Author poetry collections: One Room Shack, O Woman, Lovin' You, Nature's Child, Vignettes, Blacklash Blues, Odyssey, Tapestry; poetry and short stories: The Book of Joe; children's books: Ryme Tyme for Growing Minds, My Father Knows, Thank You & Please,When I Grow Up; ed.: Chicago Renaissance 1, 2, 3, 4, 5. Ba magna cum laude, U. N.H., 1972; MA in Lit., Governor State U., Park Forest South, Ill., 1974. Founder, pub. NRU Pubs., Markham, Ill., 1972—; v.p. Moorish Temple, Chgo., 1979—, Moorish Inst., Chgo., 1984—. Recipient Noble Drew Ali award Moorish Sci. Temple, Chgo., 1982. Mem. Phi Beta Kappa, Pi Gamma Mu. Home: 3531 Roesner Dr Markham IL 60426

ELDER, GARY MICHAEL, b. Pendleton, OR, Apr. 16, 1939; s. Wanita May Binder, Harvey Keith Elder; m. Audrey Albrecht, 1958 (div. 1963); m. 2d, Tommye Jeanne Noble, Apr. 6, 1963. Author: Arnulfsaga, 1970 (new ed. 1979); Making Touch, 1971; Grosser Fagott Fugit, 1973; A Vulgar Elegance, 1974; Eyes on the Land, 1980; Hold Fire, 1986; ed. The Far Side of the Storm, 1975. Student Whitman Coll., 1957-59; U. Calif.-Berkeley, 1960-61. Co-dir. youth drama program Neighborhood House, Richmond, Calif., 1967-68; arts critic Livermore Ind., Livermore, Calif., 1974-81; west coast ed. Snowy Egret mag., Williamsburg, Ky, 1975-80; ed./pub. Holmangers Press, Shelter Cove, Calif, 1974—; poet-in-the-schls., San Francisco, 1980-81. NEA grantee 1976, 78, 80. Publicity dir. Eugene O'Neil/Tao House Fdn., Danville, Calif, 1975. Mem NWU. Address: 95 Carson Ct Shelter Cove Whitethorn CA 95489

ELDER, KARL CURTIS, b. Beloit, WI, July 7, 1948; s. Amos Leutellus (Ted) and Anna Mae (Greife) E.; m. Brenda Kay Olson, Aug. 23, 1969; children—Seth Wade, Wade Alexander. Author: (poems) Can't Dance an' It's Too Wet to Plow, 1975, The Celibate, 1983, Phobia, 1987. Editor: (essays) What Is the Future of Poetry?, 1981; (lit. mag.) Seems, 1973—. BS in edn., Northern Ill. U., 1971, MS in edn., 1975; MFA, Wichita State U., 1977. Instr., Southwestern Mo. State U., Springfield, 1977-79; assoc. prof. Lakeland Coll., Sheboygan, Wis., 1979—. Recipient Lucien Stryk award for poetry, 1974, Poetry award Ill. Arts Council, 1975; grantee Ill. Arts Council, 1978-78. Home: 432 Madison Howards Grove WI 53082

ELDER, LEON, see Young, Noel B.

ELEVITCH, MORTON D., (M.D.), b. Duluth, MN., July 23, 1925; s. Herman and Evelyn (Blehart) E.; legally sep.; children—Nikolas, Ilena, Kathrin. Author novels: Grips, or Efforts to Revive the Host, 1972, Americans at Home, 1976; contrbr. to anthologies: Breakthrough Fictioneers, New Departures in Fiction, New Voices, Statements, New Directions in Prose and Poetry, Self-Portrait; contrbr. to Audience, Chelsea, Chgo. Rvw, Small Press Rvw, Trace, TriQuarterly, Transatlantic Rvw, others; NY Times, LA Free Press. BA, U. Minn, 1949, MA, 1950. Fiction ed. Audience Mag, Cambridge, Mass., 1959-60; founder and ed. First Person Mag, Boston, 1960-61; co-founder and dir. info. Assoc. Lit. Mags. Am., 1961-64; co-founder and dir. Wrtrs. Round Table, Rockland Ctr. for the Arts, W. Nyack, NY, 1978-80; editorial staff the Pushcart Prize, NYC,1976—. Served to Pfc USArmy Infantry, 1944-45, ETO. Yaddo fellow, 1975, 76; fellow, Virginia Center for the Creative Arts, 1986. Mem. PEN, AG, AL, AWP. Address: Box 604 Palisades NY 10964

ELIASEN, REINE, see Reynolds, Lorraine Phyllis

ELICK, CATHERINE LILLY, b. Waynesboro, VA, Feb. 22, 1953; d. Winston Newton and Fannie Lou (Dickerson) Elick; m. David Dickerson May 23, 1987. BA, James Madison Univ., 1975, MA, 1977; PhD, English, Vanderbilt Univ., 1986. Tchg. fellow, Vanderbilt Univ., 1977-82; Instructor, Fisk Univ., 1982; editor and bus. mgr., The Tennessee Conservationist, 1983—. Recipient Harold Stirling Vanderbilt scholarship, Vanderbilt Univ., 1977-80; Outstanding Young Women of America, 1984. Mem. Assn. for Conservation Information. Home: 2101 Belmont Blvd E-3 Nashville TN 37212

ELITZIK, PAUL, b. NYC, May 11, 1945; s. Harold and Mary (Bunin) E.; m. Peggy Wiedmann, June 29, 1974; 1 dau., Laurie. Contrbr. to Chicago Jnl, Cineaste, Political Companion to Film, 1987. BA summa cum laude, honors in linguistics, City College of CUNY, 1966; MA, Harvard Univ., 1971. Lectr. in classics, Boston Univ., 1968-71, Loyola Univ. (Chgo.), 1980—; lectr., School of Art Inst. (Chgo.), 1984—. Mng. ed., Harvard Grad. News, 1967; The Mole (Cambridge, MA), 1971; freelance wrtg., poetry, 1978—; pub., pres., Lake View Press, Chgo., 1983—. Recipient Woodrow Wilson Fellowship, 1966-67, Claflin Awards in Greek & Latin, City College of CUNY, 1984, 85, Drabkin Award in Classics, City College of CUNY, 1986. Mem. Phi Beta Kappa. Office: Box 578279 Chicago IL 60657

ELIZABETH, ANN, see Kirchner, Elizabeth Ann

ELKIN, STANLEY LAWRENCE, b. NYC, May 11, 1930; s. Philip and Zelda (Feldman) E.; m. Joan Marion Jacobson, Feb. 1, 1953; children: Philip Aaron, Bernard Edward, Molly Ann. Author: Boswell, 1964, Criers and Kibitzers, Kibitzers and Criers, 1966, A Bad Man, 1967, The Dick Gibson Show, 1971; editor: Stories from the Sixties, 1971, The Making of Ashenden, 1972, Searches and Seizures, 1973, The Franchiser, 1976, The Living End, 1979, Best American Short Stories of 1980, 1980, Stanley, Elkin's Greatest Hits, 1980, George Mills, 1982, The Magic Kingdom, 1985. AB, U. Ill., 1952, MA, 1953, PhD, 1961. Served with AUS, 1955-57. Recipient Humor prize Paris Rvw, 1965; Longview Fdn. award, 11962; Guggenheim fellow, 1966-67; Rockefeller grantee, 1968-69; NEH grantee, 1972; Am. Acad. and Natl. Inst. Arts and Letters award, 1974; So. Rvw award for short fiction, 1981; Natl. Book Critics Circle award, 1982. Mem. Am. Acad. Arts and Letters, Natl. Inst. Arts and Letters. Home: 225 Westgate University City MO 63130

ELKINS, MERRY CATHERINE, b. Los Angeles, May 5, 1948, d. Bertram and Mona Dorothy (Brinig) Elkins. Contrbr. articles to People, Tennis Illustrated, Am. Cinematographer, airlines mags., numerous other publs. Student Northwestern U.; AB in Photojournalism, U. So. Calif., 1971. Dancer Dean Martin Presents: The Golddiggers; actress commls., television programs; now television interviewer Entertainment Tonight, local television stations; freelance public relations wrtr.; cons. comml.-advt. industry. Mem. SPJ. Home: 8735 Dorrington Ave Los Angeles CA 90048

ELLEDGE, SCOTT BOWEN, b. Pitts., Jan. 7, 1914; s. Harvey Gerald and Eva (Bowen) E.; m. Liane von Krolikiewicz, Feb. 15, 1950. Editor: Eighteenth Century Critical Essays, 1961, The Continental Model, 1960, Lycidas (Milton), 1966, Paradise Lost (Milton), 1975. Author: E.B. White: A Biography, 1984; contbr. articles to ednl. jnls. AB, Oberlin Coll., 1935; AM, Cornell U., 1936, PhD, 1941. Mem. MLA. Home: 107 Overlook Rd Ithaca NY 14850

ELLENBOGEN, MILTON JOSEPH, b. NYC, Mar. 18, 1935; s. Jacob and Edith (Horowitz) E.; m. Linda Letich, Mar. 11, 1973; children, Michael Joseph, Eve Ruth. Tech. writer Coastal Publs., NYC, 1960-65; assoc. editor Elec. Equipment Mag., White Plains, N.Y., 1969-71, editor, 1971-82; mng. editor Indsl. Distbn. Mag., NYC, 1982—. Contrbr. short stories to popular mags. BA in English Lit., Queens Coll., 1974, MA, 1977. Served with USN, 1952-56; Korea. Mem. Am. Bus. Press, MWA, Natl. Writers Club. Home: 20 Daniels Pl White Plains NY 10604

ELLER, DAWN-MARIE, b. Cloquet, MN, Oct. 11, 1951; d. Wilfred John and Lorraine-Eddie (LaTourniou) Allen; m. Steven Dale Eller, Oct. 5, 1974; children—Aaron-Christopher, Luke Steven. Contrbr. poetry to anthols., newspapers. Lic. practical nurse, St. Lukes Hosp., Duluth, Minn., 1970-73, Moose Lake Regional Treatment Ctr., Minn., 1973-86; journalist/humorist Star Gazette, Moose Lake, 1985-86. Chmn. pub. Barnum PTA, Minn., 1985-86, Community Theater Players, Barnum, 1985-86; mem. planning, evaluation and reporting com. Barnum Schl. Dist. Home: Box 221 Barnum MN 55707

ELLER, SCOTT, see Holinger, William

ELLERMAN, GENE, see Wells, Basil E.

ELLIOT, BRUCE, see Field, Edward

ELLIOT, JEFFREY M., b. Los Angeles, June 14, 1947; s. Gene and Harriet (Sobsey) E. Author: Keys to Economic Understanding, 1977, Literary Voices, 1980, Political Ideals, Policy Dilemmas, 1981, Fantasy Voices, 1981, Deathman Pass Me By, 1983, Tempest in a Teapot: The Falkland Islands War, 1983, Kindred Spirits, 1984, The Presidential-Congressional Political Dictionary, 1984, Black Voices in American Politics, 1985, Urban Society, 1985, Fidel Castro: Nothing Can Stop the Course of History, 1985, The Work of R. Reginald: An Annotated Bibliography and Guide, 1985, The Analytical Congressional Directory, 1986, Discrimination in America: An Annotated Resource Guide, 1986, Fidel Castro: Resources on Contemporary Persons, 1986, others. Contrbr. articles, rvws., interviews to profl. mags. Editor: Jnl. Black Poli. Studies, 1985—, Jnl. Caribbean-Am. Studies, 1985—, Jnl. Congressional Studies, 1985—. Wrkg. on books, articles, rvws., interviews. BA, U. Southern Calif., 1969, MA, 1970; DArts, Claremont Grad. Schl., 1978; LHD (hon.), Shaw U., Raleigh, N.C., 1985, City Univ. of Los Angeles, 1986. Asst. prof. history and poli. sci. U. Alaska-Anchorage, 1972-74; asst. dean acad. affairs Miami-Dade Community Coll., 1974-76; asst. prof. poli. sci. Va. Wesleyan Coll., Norfolk, 1978-79; sr. curriculum specialist Edn. Devel. Ctr., Newton, Mass., 1979-81; prof. poli. sci. N.C. Central U., Durham, 1981—; disting. adv. on fgn. affairs U.S. Hs. Reps., Washington, 1985—. Speechwrtr. U.S. Senator Howard W. Cannon, Washington, 1969-82; adv. urban affairs Mayor Samuel W. Yorty, Los Angeles, 1971-72; chmn. Fla. Com. for Ednl. Stability, Miami, 1975. Recipient Disting. Service through Community Effort award Fla. Assn. Community Colls., 1976, Balrog award for outstanding nonfiction achievement, 1981, Best Wrtr. award Small Press Wrtrs. and Artists Orgn., 1982, Outstanding Acad. Achievement award N.C. Central U., 1986; named Outstanding Educator of Am., U.S. Senator Mike Gravel, Washington, 1973. Home: 1419 Barliff Pl Durham NC 27712

ELLIOT, ROBERT, see Boris, Robert Elliot

ELLIOTT, JOHN GIBSON, b. Chgo., June 16, 1908; s. John Adair and Mary (Gibson) E.; m. Sylvia Hiller, June 10, 1950. Author: Matter, Life, Evolution, 1977, rev. ed., 1982, Attributes of Universal Consciousness, 1987. BA, U. Okla., 1968, MA, 1970; MS, Wright State U., 1974. Mgr. William Bannerman Co., Chgo., 1925-36, Gibson-Hiller Co., Dayton, Ohio, 1975—; rep. NASA and U.S. Air Force, Dayton, 1958-64. Served as sgt. USAF, 1941-44, Asia. Home: 1254 Canfield Ave Dayton OH 45406

ELLIOTT, JOYCE WHITEHEAD, b. Muncie, IN, Aug. 3, 1931; d. Ernest Lynn and Lora Mabel (Fisher) Whitehead; m. John Norris Elliott, Aug. 2, 1953; children—Donald Lynn, Stephen Paul. Contrbr. adult self-help articles, features on children and music, songs to mags., books. B.A., DePauw U., 1953; M.A. in Edn., Ball State U., 1979. Home: 327 W Tabe St Fort Wayne IN 46807

ELLIOTT, MARGARET (PEG) JOHNSON, b. Muncie, IN, May 20, 1913; d. Fenton Doyle and Lora Arizona (Harty) Johnson; m. Ernest Richard Elliott, Dec. 23, 1933 (dec. 1983); children—Michael Francis, Timothy Doyle. Columnist, wrtr. Muncie (Ind.) Star, 1979—. Wrkg. on collection of columns, Ed., Ball State U. Mem. Nat. League Am. Pen Women, Women's Press Club Ind., Nat. Fedn. Press Women. Home: 4501 N Wheeling Ave BA-102 Muncie IN 47304

ELLIOTT, SUMNER LOCKE, (Sumner Locke-Elliot), b. Sydney, Australia, Oct. 17, 1917; s. Henry Logan and Sumner (Locke) E. Came to the U.S., 1948 became citizen in 1955. Author: under name Sumner Locke-Elliott (novels) Careful, He Might Hear You, 1963, Some Doves and Pythons, 1966, Rusty Bugles, 1968, Edens Lost, 1969, The Man Who Got Away, 1972, Going, 1975, Water Under the Bridge, 1977, Signs of Life, 1980, About Tilly Beamis, 1983, Waiting for Children, 1987; (plays) Buy Me Blue Ribboms, prod. on Broadway, 1951, John Murray Anderson's Almanac, prod. on Broadway, 1953; (televison plays) Wish on the Moon, U.S Steel Hour, 1959, Water Under the Bridge (based on novel of same title), Australia, 1980. Also au of more than thirty other television plays, including The King and Mrs. Candle, starring Cyril Ritchard, Mrs. Gilling and the Skyscraper, starring Angela Lansbury, Playhouse 90. Also adapter of works by other authors for television. Education: Attended elementary and high schools in Australia. Actor, novelist, and playwright. Appeared in productions of The Little Foxes, The Corn Is Green, You Can't Take It With You, Interval, The Seagull, Sweetest and Lowest, Street Scene, Hassan, Lady Precious Stream, Housemaster, Call It a Day, and Winterset. Member: WG of America, DG, Natl. Acad. of Television Arts and Scis. Miles Franklyn Prize, for best novel, 1964, Careful, He Might Hear You: Patrick White Award, 1978. Military service: Australian Army, served five years during World War II. Home: 211 E. 70th St New York NY 10021

ELLIOTT, THOMAS MORROW, b. Malden, MA, Mar. 12, 1939; s. Thomas Henry and Margaret Isabelle (Morrow) E.; m. Margarete Anne Koch, July 30, 1960 (div. 1984); children—Thomas Christian, Lisa Ruth, Dawn Michelle. Ed.: Intro. to Programming, 1968; author: Compendium on Arrhythmia Monitoring, 1975, Clowns, Clients, & Chaos, 1985; contrbr. to profl. jnls. incl. Cybernetics '70, Medical Electronics & Data, 1979, Distributors' Link, 1980, Control Engineering, 1983. Telemarketing, 1985; prodr. & scriptwriter Boston Showcase, Jane Harmon Show, Personal Perspectives, SexStyles (wkly. TV series). Student, Bentley Coll., 1957-59, Suffolk U., 1960-61. Asst. pubs. mgr. Digital Equip. Corp., Maynard, MA, 1967-69; mkt. pubs. mgr. Telefile Corp., Waltham, MA, 1969-71; sr. writer Mohawk Data Sciences, Utica, NY, 1971-73; sr. mktg. writer Hewlett-Packard, Waltham, 1973-81; pubs. mgr. AI Corp., Waltham, 1981—. Assoc. ed./book rvwr.: MENSA Bulletin, 1987—.Home: 276 Cambridge St Suite 4 Boston MA 02114

ELLIS CRAWFORD TAYLOR, EMILY, b. Melrose, MA, Sept. 25, 1898, d. James and Annie (Stewart) Crawford; m. Herbert Taylor, June 20, 1931 (dec. 1965); children—Herbert A., John E.; m. 2d, William Ellis, Aug. 21, 1965 (dec. 1985). Contrbr. poetry to numerous publs.; author tech. papers. Wrkg. on novel. BA, Wellesley Coll., 1921; postgrad., MIT, Harvard. Physicist, meteorologist, Ft. Monmouth, N.J., 1952-68. Home: 33 Jensen Ln Union NJ 07083

ELLIS, BARBARA WILLIAMS, b. Morristown, NJ, May 19, 1953; d. William Warren, Jr., and Jane Ann (Wells) Ellis; m. Peter Thomas Evans, Oct. 19, 1985. Contrbr. articles to mags. including Family Circle Mag. Editor, author: Endangered Wildflowers Calendar, 1985, 86, 87; editor: North American Horticulture: A Reference Guide, 1982, American Horticultural Society's Garden Diary, 1983, Am. Horticulturist mag. and News Edition, 1986—. BA, Kenyon Coll., 1975; BS in hort., Ohio State U. 1978. Administr., exec. asst. Fred C. Gloeckner Co., NYC, 1978-80; assoc. ed., Am. Hort. Soc., Mt. Vernon, Va., 1980-83, dir. pubs., ed., 1983—. Home: 18 Sunset Dr Alexandria VA 22301

ELLIS, ELLA THORP, b. Los Angeles, July 14, 1928; d. William Dunham and Marion Cornelia (Yates) Thorp; m. Leo H. Ellis; children: Steven, David, Patrick. Author: (novels) Roam the Wild Country, 1967 (ALA notable book award 1967); Riptide, 1969; Celebrate the Morning, 1972 (ALA notable book award 1972, Jr. Lit. Guild award 1972); Where the Road Ends, 1974; Hallelujah, 1976; Sleepwalker's Moon, 1980; Hugo and the Princess Nena, 1983. BA in English, UCLA, 1966; MA in English, San Francisco State U., 1976. Lectr. Calif. Adult Schl., 1970-75, San Francisco State U., 1976-80; extension lectr. U. Calif., Berkeley, 1975-80; condr. pvt. seminars, Buenos Aires, Argentina, 1981-85. Mem. AG, Soc. Childrens Book Wrtrs., Calif. Wrtrs. Club. Home: 1438 Grizzly Peak Berkeley CA 94708

ELLIS, JERRY L., b. Fort Payne, AL, Nov. 28, 1947; s. Jesse Paul and Viva (Buckles) E. Author: (screenplay) Reach for the Sky, 1985, No Regrets, 1986, Wild Rodeo Rose, 1987, Boy's Town, 1987; trilogy one-act plays, Watermelon Hearts, 1987. Contrbr. short stories to Penthouse, Gallery. B.A. in English, U. Ala., 1970. Artist-in-residence Ala. Arts Council, Birmingham, 1985-86; free-lance wrtr., 1985—. Recipient 1st prize for playwriin U. Southwest La., 1984. Fellow Ala. Arts Council, 1986-87. Home: Rt 2 Box 114 Valley Head AL 35989

ELLIS, JOYCE K., b. St. Louis, Aug. 31, 1950; d. Edward William Krohne, Jr. and Eunice Ann (Harrison) K.; m. Steven Wayne Ellis, Nov. 29, 1969; children—Gregory, Sharie, Maryanne. Author: Wee Pause, 1977, The Big Split, 1979, 83, Overnight Mountain and other Missionary Stories, 1980, Tell Me A Story, Lord Jesus, 1981, Snowmobile Trap, 1981, Plug into God's Rainbow, 1984, Tiffany, 1986; contrbr. anthols.: The Christian Family Bedtime Reading Book, 1982, Wondrous Power, Wondrous Love, 1983, Saved by A Broken Pole. Student pub. schls., Maplewood, MO, 1964-68. Clerk-typist MN Dept. of Transp., St. Paul, 1970; craft tchr./sales Artcraft Concepts, Mpls., 1979; freelance writer/ed., Mpls., 1972—. Mem. NLAPW, MN Christian Writers Guild. Home: 17372 Evener Way Eden Prairie MN 55344

ELLIS, MARGARET BOLAND, (Marty Boland), b. Meridian, MS, Dec. 30, 1925; d. Leo Paul and Ethel (Nelson) Boland; m. Wesley Crosby Ellis, May 12, 1957; children—Leslie, Margaret N., John H. Author: Be Good Sweet Maid, 1984. Contrbr. articles to mags., newspapers including Womens Sports Mag., N.Y. Times, others. Ed.: Mobile Opera Guild newsletter, 1960-68, Mobile Tennis Club newsletter, 1960-64. Student Miss. U. Women, 1943-45; B.A., U. Miss., 1946. Dir. public relations Deep South Girl Scouts, Mobile, 1965-69, St. Paul's Episcopal Sch., Mobile, 1969—. Recipient M.O. Beale Scroll of Merit award Mobile Press-Register, 1974. Mem. Public Relations Council Ala. Home: 4661 Pinewood Dr Mobile AL 36618

ELLISON, GLENN, (Tiger), b. Pittsboro, MS, Feb. 7, 1911; s. Samuel Arthur Ellison and Beatrice Madonna Payne; m. Elsie Mae Campbell, June 6, 1938 (dec. Aug. 25, 1986); children—Nita Mata, Barbara A. Hartsook, Carolyn Buckley; m. Dawn McClain, July 16, 1987. Author: Run and Shoot Football, 1965, Persuasive Speaking, 1967, Power Speaking, 1970, Lincoln Library of Sports Champions, 1975, Football's Now Attack, 1984, Atchi & Tiger, 1987. A.B., Denison Coll., 1933; M.S., Xavier Coll., 1957. Tchr., coach public schs., Middletown, OH, 1933-63; asst. football coach Ohio State U., Columbus, 1963-69. Home: 317 Grayston Pl Sun City Center FL 33570

ELLISON, HARLAN JAY, b. Cleve., May 27, 1934; s. Louis Laverne and Serita (Rosenthal) E.; m. Charlotte Stein, 1956 (div. 1959); m. Billie Joyce Sanders, 1961 (div. 1962); m. Lory Patrick, 1965 (div. 1965); m. Lori Horwitz, 1976 (div. 1977); m. Susan Toth, 1986. Author: 42 books including Web of the City, 1958; The Sound of a Scythe, 1960, Gentleman Junkie, 1961, Memos from Purgatory, 1961, Spider Kiss, 1961, Ellison Wonderland, 1962, Paingod (transl. into French, Japanese, German, Spanish), 1965, I Have No Mouth & I Must Scream (transl. into Japanese, French, Italian, Spanish, German), 1967, From the Land of Fear, 1967, Love Ain't Nothing But Sex Misspelled, 1968, The Beast that Shouted Love at the Heart of the World, 1969, Over the Edge, 1970, Alone Against Tomorrow, 1971, Partners in Wonder, 1971, Approaching Oblivion, 1974, Deathbird Stories, 1975, No Doors, No Windows, 1976, Strange Wine, 1978, All the Lies That Are My Life, 1980, Shatterday, 1980, Stalking the Nightmare, 1982, Sleepless Nights in the Procrustean Bed, 1984, An Edge in My Voice, 1985, The Essential Ellison, 1987; editor, compiler: anthology Dangerous Visions, 1967, Again, Dangerous Visions, 1972; editor: Medea: Harlan's World, 1985; author 4 books on juvenile delinquency; writer: weekly television column The Glass Teat, Los Angeles Free Press, 1968-71, pub. in 2 vols., 1970, 75; weekly column Harlan Ellison Hornbook, Los Angeles Free Press, 1972-73, An Edge in My Voice, Future Life, 1980-81, Los Angeles Weekly, 1982-83, pub. in 1 vol., 1985; Creator (with Larry Brody) weekly series The Dark Forces, CBS-TV, 1986; (with Ben Bova) series Brillo, ABC-TV, 1974; creative consultant, director, The Twilight Zone, CBS-TV, 1984-85; creator, editor: Harlan Ellison Discovery Series of 1st novels for Pyramid Books, 1973-77. Student, Ohio State U., 1953-55. A founder Cleve. Sci-Fiction Soc., 1950; pub. mag. Sci.-Fantasy Bulln. (later retitled Dimensions); editor Rogue Mag., Chgo., 1959-60, Regency Books, 1960-61; lectr. colls. and univs.; book critic Los Angeles Times, 1969-82; editorial commentator Canadian Broadcasting Co., 1972-78; pres. Kilimanjaro Corp., 1979—; instr. Clarion Writers Workshop, Mich. State U., 1969-77, 84. Actor, Cleve. Playhouse, part time 1944-49; script writer: television series Logan's Run; others, 1962-77; writer 7 scripts for Burke's Law; creator (under pseudonym Cordwainer Bird): The Starlost, NBC TV series; scenarist: 2-hour NBC spcl. The Tigers are Loose, 1974-75; writer: motion pictures The Dream Merchants, The Oscar, Nick the Greek, Best by Far, Harlan Ellison's Movie; adaptations I, Robot, 1978; scenarist: Bug Jack Barron, 1982-83; writer: Nebula-winning novella-into-film A Boy and His Dog, 1975 (Hugo award for film adaptation 1976). Served with AUS, 1957-59. Recipient Hugo awards World Sci.-Fiction Conv., 1965 (2) 67, 68, 73, 74, 75, 77, 86; Special Achievement awards, 1968, 72; Certificate of Merit Trieste Film Festival, 1970; Edgar Allan Poe award MWA, 1974; George Melies awards for cinematic achievement, 1972, 73; Jupiter award Instrs. Sci. Fiction in Higher Edn., 1974, 77; award for journalism PEN Intl., 1982. Mem. WG Am. (Most Outstanding Script awards 1965, 67, 74, 86, screen bd., mem. West council 1971-72), Sci. Fiction Writers Am. (cofounder, Nebula awards, 1965, 69, 77, v.p. 1965-66). Host: HOUR 25, KPFK-FM, 1986-87. Address: 3484 Coy Dr Sherman Oaks CA 91423

ELMAN, RICHARD, (Eric Pearl, Michael Lasher, Michael Parnell), b. Bklyn., Apr. 23, 1934; s. Edward and Pearl (Bekerman) E.; divorced 1971; 1 dau., Margaret; m. Alice Gorde, Apr. 9, 1978; 1 dau., Lila. Author numerous novels, poetry including (novel) An Education in Blood, 1970, Fredi & Skirl & the Kids, 1971, The Breadfruit Lotteries, 1979; (poetry) Homage to Fats Navano, 1975; (jnlsm.) odetails at Somuza's, 1981, The Menu Cypher, 1982. Contrbr. articles to mags., newspapers. B.A., Syrause U., 1955; M.A., Stanford U., 1957. Served with U.S. Army, 1957-58. Mem. PEN (Short Fiction prize 1983), AG. Home: Box 216 Stoneybrook NY 11790

ELMORE, JAMES BERNARD, b. Buffalo, Apr. 13, 1949, s. Bernard Levere and Adeline (Wolowiec) E.; m. Lorraine Joyce Corbin, Apr. 1, 1978; children—Jason, David, Kristen. Contrbr. to Contemporary Poets, Personnel Administrator, P.S. I Love You, Rochester Art Scene Qtly, numerous other publs. Wrkg. on poetry, articles, marketing songs. BA, MS, Niagara U., 1971-72. School counselor/adminstr., Nicagara County, NY. Recipient Spcl. Achievement award Niagara Falls C. of C., 1981. Address: 1200 Doebler Dr North Tonawanda NY 14120

ELSBERG, JOHN WILLIAM, b. NYC,Aug. 4, 1945; s. John Christian and Paula (Hutter) E.;

m. Connie Waeber, June 17, 1967; 1 son, Stephen John. Author: Cornwall and Other Poems, 1972, The Price of Reindeer, 1979, Walking As a Controlled Fall, 1980, The Limey and the Yank, 1981, Homestyle Cooking on Third Avenue, 1982, Torn Nylon Comes with the Night, 1987; U.S. ed. Bogg mag., 1975-80, pub., 1980—; fiction ed.: Gargoyle mag., 1976-78. BA, Columbia U., 1967; MA, U. Cambridge (Eng.), 1973. Lectr. history European program, U. Md., United Kingdom, 1970-73; ed., prodn. mgr. Center Mil. History, Washington, DC, 1974—. Mem. Wrtrs.' Ctr., PSA, Va. Ctr. for Creative Arts. Home: 422 N Cleveland St Arlington VA 22201

ELSON, R. N., see Nelson, Radell Faraday

ELYSE, JOY, see Ashcroft, Shelley Alane

EMERSON, KATHY LYNN, (Kaitlyn Gorton), b. Liberty, NY, Oct. 25, 1947; d. William Russell and Theresa Marie (Coburg) Gorton; m. Sanford Merritt Emerson, May 10, 1969. Author: Wives and Daughters: The Women of Sixteenth Century England, 1984, The Mystery of Hilliard's Castle, 1985, Julia's Mending, 1987, The Missing Bagpipe, 1988, Someday, 1988. Contrbr. to anthol. Wrkg. on biography of Nellie Bly. A.B., Bates Coll., 1969; M.A., Old Dominion U., 1972. Free-lance wrtr., 1976—. Mem. SCBW, MWA. Home: Box 156 Wilton ME 04294

EMERSON, MARK, see Hester, Martin Luther

EMMONS, MARGUERITE ATTEBERRY, b. Frankfort, KY, May 13, 1949; d. James S. Atteberry and Joan Timmons (Moss) Case; m. James W. Emmons, Aug. 7, 1971; children—Helen Kathryn, Stephen Christopher. Contrbr. poems to anthols; assoc. ed. Pandora, 1985—. B.A. cum laude, Georgetown Coll., 1971; M.A. in English, U. Ky., 1973. Substitute tchr. public schs., Lexington and Georgetown, KY, 1973—. Home: 2210 Burton Pike Georgetown KY 40324

EMORY, ROBERT, see Anstett, Robert Emory

EMRY, DOUGLAS KRISS, b. Topeka, KS, Sept. 19, 1938; s. Paul Laverne and Elizabeth Louise (Johnson) E.; m. Juanita Pearl Blackwood, 1955 (div. 1960); children: Jesse Lynn, Cassandra Michelle. Pub. and Mng. ed. Writers West Mag., San Diego, Calif. 1982—, San Diego's Little Literary Magazine, 1986—. Served in USN, 1956-64, PTO. Address: Box 16097 San Diego CA 92116

EMSHWILLER, CAROL FRIES, b. Ann Arbor, MI, Apr. 12, 1921; d. Charles Carpenter and Agnes (Carswell) Fries; m. Ed Emshwiller, Aug. 31, 1949; children—Eve, Susan, Peter. Author short story collection Joy in Our Cause, 1974; contrbr. short stories to TriQtly, 13th Moon, Croton Rvw, Epoch, other lit mags; author TV narrations. BA in Music, U. Mich., 1945, B Design, 1949. Tchr. Clarion Summer Sci. Fiction Workshop, Lansing, Mich., 1972, 73; adj. asst. prof. continuing edn., NYU, 1974—; guest faculty Sarah Lawrence Coll., Bronxville, N.Y., 1982. MacDowell Colony fellow, 1973, grantee N.Y. State Creative Artist Public Service, 1975, NEA, 1980. Home: 260 E 10th St Apt10 NYC 10009

ENDEMANN, CARL T., b. Goettingen, Germany, Aug. 20, 1902; m. Agnes Stewart, 1927; m. Ranie Maya Franzmann, 1951; children—Donald, Astra, Gerda, Frederick. Author: The Ring of Alta Napa, 1977, Forks in the Road, 1977, La Dorada, the Romance of San Francisco, 1978, Voyage to Gondwana, 1978, Voyage into the Past, 1981, The Wandering Poet (biography of Carl Heinz Kurz), 1985; ed. Voices of the Wineland, 1978; fgn. ed. and columnist "Easing the Writer's Life" in monthly mag. Published, 1985-86; contrbr. articles and poems to various mags. and anthologies in Can., France, Germany, Korea, China, India, Austria, U.S.; translator, ed. 2 books from German by C.H. Kurz, 1982, 83. Wrkg. on The Supreme Court of Eternal Justice, The Road to La Serenidad (sequel to voyage into the Past), non-fiction transls. from French and German. Home: 1969 Mora Ave Calistoga CA 94515

ENDERLIN, LEE, (Gene Berto), b. San Antonio, Oct. 25, 1951; s. Leon William and Rena (Berto) E.; m. Marie Antoinette Accetta, Sept. 19, 1987. Author: Day of the Mayfly, 1986; columnist: Jnl. Inquirer Newspaper, 1981. Contrbr. articles to mags., newspapers including Military History Mag., Sports History Mag., others. Contrbg. ed: Sports History Mag., 1987—. B.A., U. Notre Dame, 1973. Disc jockey Sta. WWF, Manchester, CT, 1974-77, Sta. WMNB AM-FM, North Adams, MA, 1977-78; account exec. Manchester Herald, Manchester, 1978-81, Jnl. Inquirer, Manchester, 1981-84; pres. MLC Advt., Manchester, 1984-87; Acctg. Data Systems operator Ask Mr. Foster Travel Agy., East Hartford, CT, 1987—. Home: 93 Island Pond Rd Springfield MA 01118

ENDORE, GITA, b. Los Angeles, Oct. 16, 1944; d. Guy and Henrietta (Portugal) E.; 1 son, Guy Endore-Kaiser. Ghost ed. fiction books. B.A., U. Calif.-Berkeley, 1966. Mem. Phoenix Soc. Communicating Artists, Jewish Bus. Profl. Women. Home: 6902 E Pasadena Ave Scottsdale AZ 85253

ENGEL, MONROE, b. NYC, Apr. 22, 1921, s. Henry Joshua and Henrietta (Birnbaum) E.; m. Brenda Sartorius, Nov. 22, 1946; children—Robin, Winslow, Stephanie, Matthew. Novelist: A Length of Rope, 1952, The Visions of Nicholas Solon, 1959, Voyager Belsky, 1962, Fish, 1981, Statutes of Limitations, 1988; author: The Maturity of Dickens, 1959; ed.: The Uses of Literature, 1973. AB, Harvard U., 1942; PhD, Princeton U., 1954. Ed. Reynal & Hitchcock, NYC, 1946-47, Viking Press, NYC, 1947-51; lectr. Princeton (N.J.) U., 1954-55; asst. prof., lectr., sr. lectr. Harvard U., Cambridge, Mass., 1955—. Served to capt. U.S. Army, 1942-45, ETO. NEH fellow, 1973-74. Mem. PEN, AG, AAUP. Home: 17 Hilliard St Cambridge MA 02138

ENGLE, PAUL HAMILTON, b. Cedar Rapids, IA, Oct. 12, 1908; s. Hamilton Allen and Evelyn (Reinheimer) E.; m. Mary Nomine Nissen, July 3, 1936; children—Mary Engle Burge, sara; m. Hualing Nieh, May 14, 1971. Author: (poetry) American Child, 1945, The Word of Love, 1951, Poems in Praise, 1959, A Prairie Christmas, 1960 (non-fiction), Embrace: Poems, 1969, Images of China, 1981, A Woman Unashamed, 1965, novel Golden Child, 1960; Women in the American Revolution, 1976, Images of China, Poems, 1982; editor: anthology Midland, 1961, (with Joseph Langland) Poet's Choice, 1962; editor: On Creative Writing, 1964, An Old Fashioned Christmas, 1964, Portrait of Iowa, 1974; co-editor: Reading Modern Poetry, 1955, 1968; translator: (with Hualing Nieh Engle) Poems of Mao Tse-Tung, 1972; contbr. to popular mags., N.Y. Times. AB, Coe Coll., 1931; AM, State U. Iowa, 1932; postgrad., Columbia U. 1932-33; AB, Merton Coll., Oxford (Eng.) U., 1936, AM, 1939. Writer, prof. English, 1946—, dir. program in creative writing U. Iowa, Iowa City, 1937-65; cons., co-founder Intl. Writing Programs, 1966—. Librettist Opera: produced TV Golden Child, 1960. Recipient award for West of Midnight, Friends Am. Writers, Chgo, 1941, (with Hualing Nieh Engle) Iowa award for disting. service to arts. Mem. adv. com. John F. Kennedy Cultural Center, Washington; mem. Natl. Council on Arts White House; judge Natl. Book Award, 1955, 70. Lamont award AAP, 1958-61; Guggenheim Fdn. fellow, 1953-54. Mem. Phi Kappa Phi, Phi Gamma Delta. Home: 1104 N Dubuque St Iowa City IA 52240

ENGMAN, JOHN ROBERT, b. Mpls., Mar. 26, 1949; s. Robert Sheldon and Evelyn Louise (Olsen) E. Author: Alcatraz, 1980; Keeping Still, Mountain, 1984. BA, Augsburg Coll., Mpls., 1971; MFA, U. Iowa, 1975. Lectr. U. Minn., Mpls., 1985—. Recipient Loft-McKnight award Loft and McKnight Fdn., 1983; Midwest Voices award P&W, 1984; Minn. Arts Bd. poetry grantee, 1977, creative writing fellow, 1985. Home: 1916 Colfax Ave S Minneapolis MN 55403

ENNIS, LAMAR WALLACE, b. Macon, GA, June 29, 1954; s. Jack Wallace and Audrey Etta (Cater) E.; m. Terre Angela Kite, Aug. 12, 1984; 1 son, Dylan Wallace. Contrbr. poems to anthols., lit. jnls. Wrkg. on collection of poetry, poems, novel. A.S., Macon Jr. Coll., 1975; B.A., Mercer U., 1981. Tchr. English, Perry Middle Schl., GA, 1981-84, Northside Jr. High Schl., Warner Robins, GA, 1984—. Mem. Profl. Assn. Ga. Educators. Home: 3987 Guyton St Macon GA 31206

ENROTH, THERESA LOUISE, (Tess), b. Mpls., Aug. 20, 1925; d. Francis Daniel and Theresa Marie (Low) McElwee; m. Clyde Adolph Enroth, Sept. 27, 1947 (div. 1976); children—Daniel, Kate, Sarah. Contrbr. essays, stories, poems to Wide Open, Athena, Pinchpenny, Cottonwood, numerous other lit. publs. BA, U. Minn., 1947; MA, Calif. State U., Sacramento, 1967; DA, SUNY-Albany, 1981. Tchr. Sacramento County Schls., 1961-63, Am. River Coll., Sacramento, 1967, Student Assn., Sao Paulo, Brazil, 1972-73. Mem. summer poetry workshop Radcliffe Coll., 1974; NEH fellow, 1976-77. Mem. Sacramento Poetry Center. Home: 7048 La Costa Ln Citrus Heights CA 95621

ENSLIN, THEODORE VERNON, b. Chester, PA, March 25, 1925; s. Morton Scott and Ruth May (Tuttle) E.; m. Mildred Marie Stout Aug. 1, 1945 (div.); children: Deirdre, Jonathan Morton; m. 2d, Allison Jane Jose Sept. 14, 1969; 1 son, Jacob Hezekiah. Author: The Work Proposed, 1958, New Sharon's Prospect, 1966, To Come To Have Become, 1966, Forms (5 vols.), 1970-73; Synthesis, 1975, The Median Flow—Poems 1943-73, 1975, Carmina, 1976, Ranger (2 vols.), 1978, 80, Songs Without Notes, 1984, Meeting at JAL (with Keith Wilson), 1985, Music for Several Occasions, 1986. Studied music privately with Nadia Boulanger and others, Boston & Cambridge, 1942-46. Niemann award, 1955; NEA fellowship, 1976-77. Wrkg. on antiphonal and serial poems. Home: RFD Box 289 Kansas Rd Milbridge ME 04658

ENTREKIN, CHARLES EDWARD, JR., b. Birmingham, AL, Aug. 15, 1941; s. Charles Edward and Betty Ruth (Allison) E.; m. Karen Marie Keena, Jan. 17, 1969 (div. 1984); children—Demian, Caleb, Benjamin, Nathan; m. V. Gail Rudd, Feb. 1986. Author: All Pieces of a Legacy, 1975, Casting for the Cutthroat, 1977, Casting for the Cutthroat and Other Poems, 1980; contrbr.: Anthology of Mag. Verse and Yearbook of Am. Poetry, 1984, lit mags. BA, Birmingham So. Coll., 1964; MFA, U. Mont., 1974. Pres., mng. ed. Berkeley Poets Workshop and Press, Calif., 1969—; assoc. dir. creative writing program John F. Kennedy U., Orinda, Calif., 1979, 80. Yaddo Colony fellow, 1980. Office: Berkeley Poets Co-op Box 459 Berkeley CA 94701

EPLEY-SHUCK, BARBARA JEANNE, b. Fairfield, NB, Nov. 28, 1936, d. Elden Claude and Clara Joan (Cornelius) Epley; m. Elmer Eugene Shuck, June 8, 1958; children—Douglas, Bruce, Michael. Ed. newspaper for Synod of Northeast Presbyn. Ch.; contrbr. articles to Utica (N.Y.) Observer Dispatch. BA, Hastings (Nebr.) Coll., 1957; profl. cert. in journalism, U. Nebr., 1961. Reporter, photographer Lincoln (Nebr.) Evening Jnl., 1960-61; mkt. researcher U. Nebr., Lincoln, 1961, freelance, Utica, N.Y., 1961-63; pub. relations dir. Utica YWCA, 1970-80. Mem. Theta Kappa Tau, Theta Sigma Phi. Home: 20 Vine Circle Whitesboro NY 13492

EPPES, WILLIAM DAVID, b. Goodwater, AL; s. Talmadge de Witt and Annie Lou (McCord) E.; Works: The Empire Theatre 1893-1957, 1978, Gertrude Michael—A Star of the Golden Age of Hollywood, 1984; contrbr. to various jnls. AB, Coll. of William & Mary, 1939; BS, Vanderbilt U., 1940; MA, NY U., N.Y.C., 1959. Reference librarian George Washington U., 1943-45, CA State U., San Francisco, 1945-46; head stack personnel Butler Library, Columbia U., 1954-58; assoc. prof. Kean State Coll., Union, NJ, 1958-61; asst. librarian Cooper Union, N.Y.C., 1961-70. Mem: Author and Writers Guild, Theatre Library Assoc., American League of Historic American Theatres, Theatre Historical Soc. Home: 34 Almeria Ave Coral Gables FL 33134

EPPS, WILLIAM DAVID, b. Kingsport, TN, Jan. 15, 1951; s. William Elmer and Kathleen (Luster) E.; m. Cynthia Scott Douglas, Sept. 6, 1971; children—Jason, John, James. Author: (songs) Worship the Lord, A Prayer for Guidance, My Heart Yearns. Contrbr. articles to mags., newspapers including Good News, Pentecostal Evangel, others. B.Social Work, East Tenn. State U., 1975; D.Ministry, Berean Coll., 1981. Dir. WACARCA, Johnson City, TN, 1979-81; assoc. minister The Fayette Fellowship, Peachtree City, GA, 1983—. Served with U.S. Marine Corps, 1970-73. Named Instr. of Yr., Christian Martial Arts Fedn., 1986. Mem. Fayette County Ministerial Assn. (pres. 1985-86). Home: 113 Azalea Dr Peachtree City GA 30269

EPSTEIN, DANIEL MARK, b. Washington, Oct. 25, 1948; s. Donald David and Louise (Tilman) E.; m. Wendy Roberts, May 29, 1976; children: Johanna, Benjamin. author: (poetry) No Vacancies in Hell, 1973; The Follies, 1977; Young Men's Gold, 1978; The Book of Fortune, 1982; Spirits, 1987; (stories and essays) Star of Wonder, 1986; (textbooks) The Heath Guide to Poetry, 1983; The Heath Guide to Literature, 1984. AB magna cum laude with highest honors in English, Kenyon Coll., 1970. Poet-in-residence Md. Arts Council, Balt., 1972-86; vis. asst. prof. Johns Hopkins U., Balt., 1979-82; disting. wrtr.-in-res. Randolph-Macon Coll., Lynchburg, Va., 1983; wrtr.-in-res. Towson State U., Balt., 1983—. Recipient Prix de Rome, Am. Acad. Arts and Letters, 1978; Emily Clark Balch award Va. Qtly, 1981; Danforth Fdn. and Woodrow Wilson fellow U. Va., 1971; NEA grantee, 1974; Guggenheim fellow, 1984. Mem. PEN, PSA, AWP. Home: 401 Wingate Rd Baltimore MD 21210

EPSTEIN, JOSEPH, b. Chgo., Jan. 9, 1937; s. Maurice and Belle (Abrams) E.; m. Barbara Maher, Feb. 27, 1976; children: Mark, Burton. Author: Divorced in America, 1975, Familiar Territory, 1980, Ambition, 1981, The Middle of My Tether, 1983, Plausible Prejudices, 1985, Once More Around the Block, 1987; editor: Masters, 1981. AB, U. Chgo., 1959. Editor Am. Scholar, Washington, 1975—; vis. lectr., Northwestern U., Evanston, Ill., 1974—. Served with U.S. Army, 1958-60. Office: Am Schlr 1811 Q St Nw Washington DC 20009

EPSTEIN, LESLIE DONALD, b. Los Angeles, May 4, 1938; s. Philip G. and Lillian Ella (Targan) E.; m. Ilene Gradman, Nov. 1, 1969; children—Anya, Theo, Paul. Novelist: P.D. Kimerakov, 1975, King of the Jews, 1979, Regina, 1982; author: Steinway Quintet Plus Four (stories), 1976, Goldkorn Tales (novellas), 1985. BA, Yale U., 1960, DFA, 1967. Prof. English Queens Coll., N.Y.C., 1965-78; dir. grad. creative writing program Boston U., 1978—. Rhodes scholar, 1960-62; Guggenheim fellow, 1978, NEA fellow, 1980; recipient Distinction in Lit., AAIAL, 1976. Mem. PEN, AG, Assn. Am. Rhodes Scholars. Home: 23 Parkman St Brookline MA 02146

EPSTEIN, SEYMOUR, b. NYC, Dec. 2, 1917, s. Joseph and Jenny (Pomerantz) E.; m. Miriam Kligman, May 2, 1956; children—Alan, Paul. Novelist: Pillar of Salt, 1960, The Successor, 1961, Leah, 1964, Caught in That Music, 1967, The Dream Museum, 1971, Looking for Fred Schmidt, 1973, A Special Destiny, 1986, September Faces, 1987; author: A Penny for Charity (short stories), 1965. Student CCNY and NYU. Prof., then prof. emeritus U. Denver, 1968—. Served with USAF, 1942-45; ETO. Recipient Edward Lewis Wallant Meml. Book award, 1964; Guggenheim fellow, 1965. Mem. PEN, AG Amer Diabetes Assn. Home: 3205 S St Paul St Denver CO 80210

ERBE, JACK RUDOLPH, b. Phila., Jan. 9, 1926; s. John R. and Lucy (Peebalg) E.; m. Bonnie Marie Porter (div. 1985). Author: The Fifty Billion Dollar Directory, 1984, How to Promote and Sell Small Products, 1985, How to Get Your Product Selling in Millions of Mail Order Catalogs, 1985, How to Make Money Running Your Own Weekend Workshops, 1985, How to Start Your Own Mail Order Bus., 1985, How to Set Yourself Up in Bus. as a Printing Broker, 1985, Directory of Calif. Sales Cos., 1986, Directory of Arts & Crafts Publs., 1986, How to Find a Product, 1986, How to Be More Successful in your Own Bus., 1986, and others. Student Temple U., 1946-48. Self-employed as sales agent, 1946-58; pres. and CEO Roman Fountains, Inc., Albuquerque, NM, 1958-78. Address: 6318 Vesper Ave Van Nuys CA 91411

ERICK, MIRIAM A., b. Norwich, CT, Apr. 1, 1948; d. Eugene and Toini (Lampi) E. Author: Pregnancy & Nutrition: The Complete D.I.E.T. Guide, 1986, D.I.E.T. During Pregnancy: The Complete Guide & Calendar; contrbr. to Frankly Speaking, wrtr Nutrition Continuum column for Intl Jrnl Childbirth Ed; BS, U.Conn., 1970; postgrad. U. Rhode Is., 1978. Regist. Dietitian, Brigham/Women's Hosp., Boston, MA, 1979-86; pres. Grinnen-Barrett Pub. Co., Brookline, MA, 1984—. Mem. COSMEP, Women's Natl. Bk. Assn., AMWA, American Dietetic Assn, Massachusetts Dietetic Assn. Home: 36 Winchester St 8 Brookline MA 02146

ERICKSON, DAVID BURDETTE, b. Balt., June 7, 1950. Markets ed.: Purchasing, Newton, MA, 1979-81; ed.: CPI Purchasing, Newton, MA, 1986—. Acct. exec. Adams & Rinehart, NYC, 1983-84; cons., Technomic, Inc., Cambridge, MA, 1984-85. Recipient Poetry prize Wrtrs. Digest, 1978. Mem chemical Mktg. Research Assn. Home: 83 Orchard St Cambridge MA 02140

ERICKSON, D. H., see Erickson, Donna Mary

ERICKSON, DONNA MARY, (Rebecca Nolan, D. H. Erickson), b. Tremonton, UT; d. Clarence Marion and LaVerne (Liljenquist) Hacking; m. Royle Dee Erickson, Aug. 21, 1958; children—Deonn, Renee, Annette, Janine, Teresa, Melinda, Laura, Nathan, Seth, Mariann, Don. Contrbr. articles to jnls., mags. Recipient Golden Poet award World of Poetry, 1985, 86, 87, Idaho rep. Cowboy Poetry Gathering, Idaho Writer's League honors. Mem. Idaho Writer's League. Home: 533 E 9000 S Rexburg ID 83440

ERICKSON, NEIL LE ROY, II, b. Muskegon, MI, July 14, 1951; s. Neil LeRoy and Gloria Ann (Schroeder) E.; m. Virginia Beth Noble, May 7, 1983. Author: The Whole New and Vital Permanent Weight Loss Program, 1985. AA, Muskegon Bus. Coll., 1971. Payroll supr. Bank Bldg. Corp., Muskegon, 1972-75; asst. secy. West Mich. Dock and Market Corp., Muskegon, 1975—; author, pub. Algonquin Enterprises, Muskegon, 1984—. Office: Algonquin Enterprises Box 1410 Muskegon MI 49443

ERPENBECK, MARY-LOU BROCKETT, b. New London, CT, Nov. 18, 1961; d. Paul Vincent and Priscilla Gail (Schiller) Brockett; m. Russ Alan Erpenbeck, Jan. 7, 1984. Contrbr. poetry and short story to Aldebaran and Calliope; ed. Calliope, 1981, 83, Aldebaran, 1983. BFA, Roger Williams Coll., 1979-83. Substitute tchr. Roger Williams Coll., Bristol, RI, 1983, New London public schls., Conn, 1984-85; public relations Sportsman's Boating Co, Waterford, Conn, 1985—. Address: Box 447 Niantic CT 06357

ERSKINE, FRANCES ELAINE, b. Kalamazoo, MI, Oct. 2, 1947; d. Herbert Frank Sr. and Agnes Dorothy (Kolhoff) Stevens; m. Maxwell John Ersking (div.); children: Maxwell John III, Mara Elaine. Poetry in antohlogies. Wrkg. on short stories, poetry. Ed. Kellogg Community Coll. Home: 4133 McKibbin Rd Delton MI 49046

ESAREY, MELVIN M., b. Beechwood, IN., Nov. 11, 1910; s. Calvin M. and Millie (Merrilees) E.; m. Mignon Hope Froman, June 4, 1950; 1 dau., Sharman Sue. Co-author: Drive Right, 7th ed. 1982, Drive Right Workbook, 1960, 2d ed., 1965, Drive Right Individual Learning Book, 1973, 2d ed., 1977. BS, Central Normal Coll.; MS, U. Ill. Tchr. public schls. throughout Ill., 1934-75, dept. head New Trier High Sch. West, Northfield, 1965-75. Served to capt. arty. U.S. Army, 1941-45; ETO. Mem. ednl. orgns. Home: 375 Woodlawn Ave Glencoe IL 60022

ESBENSEN, BARBARA JUSTER, b. Madison, WI, April 28, 1925; d. Eugene Meyer and Isabel Sinaiko Juster; m. Thorwald S. Esbensen, June 24, 1953; children—Julie, Peter, Daniel, Jane, George, Kai. Author: Who Shrank My

Grandmother's House? 1989, Ladder to the Sky, 1988, Words with Wrinkled Knees: Animal Poems, 1986; The Star Maiden, 1988, Cold Stars and Fireflies, 1984, A Celebration of Bees, 1975, Swing Around the Sun, 1965; poetry in numerous jnls and anthols including Poetry Now, Milkweed Chronicles, Great River Rvw. BA, U. of Wisc., 1947. Tchr., Madison, Wisc. pub. schls., 1947-51; consultant, South Shore, Wisc. pub. schls., 1953-55, cons., Pacific Is. Central School., 1956-58; tchr., Eureka, Calif. pub. schls., 1961-63; cons., College of St. Scholastica, Duluth, MN, 1970-72; freelance wrtr., 1973—. Mem. Soc. of Children's Book Writers, AAP, PSA. Home: 5602 Dalrymple Rd Edina MN 55424

ESCANDELL, NOEMI, b. Havana, Cuba, Sept. 27, 1936, came to U.S., 1957; d. Luis Escandell and Ada (Santana) Paz; children—Marta, Alice, Peter, Andrew Knapp. Author: Ciclos, 1981, Cuadros, 1981, Palabras/Words (with English translations by Joan Dargan), 1986. Wrkg. on short story collection. BA magna cum laude, Queens Coll., 1968; MA, Harvard U., 1971, PhD, 1976. Asst. prof. Bard Coll., Annandale-on-Hudson, N.Y., 1976-83, acad. dir. experiment in intl. living, Granada, Spain, spring 1983; prof. dept. modern fgn. langs. Westfield (Mass.) State Coll., 1983—; resident Millay Colony for Arts, Austerlitz, N.Y., 1983. Grantee Radcliffe Inst., Cambridge, Mass., 1970-73. Mem. MLA, Feministas Unidas. Home: 7 Holland Ave Westfield MA 01085

ESHE, AISHA, see Carmen, Marilyn Elaine

ESHLEMAN, CLAYTON, b. Indpls., June 1, 1935; s. Ira Clayton and Gladys Maine (Spencer) E.; m. Caryl Reiter, May 21, 1969; 1 son by previous marriage, Matthew. Author numerous books, including Walks, 1967, Indiana, 1969, Bearings, 1971, Altars, 1971, The Sanjo Bridge, 1972, Coils, 1973, The Gull Wall, 1975, Grotesca, 1977, What She Means, 1978, Nights We Put The Rock Together, 1980, Hades In Manganese, 1981, Fracture, 1983, The Name Encanyoned River: Selected Poems 1960-85, 1986; contrbg. author: Erotic Poetry, 1963, Contemporary Latin American Literature, 1970, The Voice that is Great within Us, 1970, Doors and Mirrors, 1972, Messages, 1973, Open Poetry, 1973, America A Prophecy, 1973, Giant Talk, 1975; translator: Residence on Earth (Pablo Neruda), 1962, (with Denis Kelly) (Aime Cesaire), 1966, Human Poems (Cesar Vallejo), 1968, Artaud The Momo (Antonin Artaud), 1972, Letter to Andre Breton (Antonin Artaud), 1974, (with Jose Rubia Barcia) Take This Cup From Me (Cesar Vallejo), 1974, (with Norman Glass) To Have Done with the Judgment of God (Antonin Artaud), 1975, (with Jose Rubia Barcia) Cesar Vallejo: The Complete Posthumous Poetry, 1978; translator: (with Annette Smith) Aime Cesaire: The Collected Poetry, 1983, Given Giving: Selected Poems of Michael Deguy, 1984; editor: Folio, 1959-60; editor, pub.: Caterpillar mag., 1966-73; Caterpillar Books series, 1966-67; editor, A Caterpillar Anthology, 1971; ed., pub, Sulfur Mag, 1981—. BA in Philosophy, Ind. U., 1958, MAT in English Lit., 1961. Instr. in English U. Md. Far Eastern Div., Taiwan, Korea and Japan, 1961-62; tchr. English lang. program Matsushita Electric Corp., Osaka, Japan, 1962-64; instr. Am. Lang. Inst., N.Y. U., 1966-68, Schl. Critical Studies, Calif. Inst. Arts, 1970-72; tchr. 20th century world poetry and creative writing pvt. workshop, Sherman Oaks, Calif., 1973; instr. contemporary Am. poetry Am. Coll. in Paris, 1974; lectr. advanced poetry workshop extension UCLA, 1975—; Dreyfuss lectr. in creative writing Calif. Inst. Tech., Pasadena, 1979-83; prof. Eng. Dept., Eastern Michigan Univ., 1986—; participant poetry in the schls. program, NYC, 1967, Los Angeles, 1974-75; cons., bd. dirs. CCLM, 1968-71; co-organizer N.Am. Poetry Circuit, 1969. Recipient award for translating Vallejo Natl. Transl. Ctr., 1967, Fels award for non-fiction prose CCLM, 1975, PEN Transl. award, 1976, Natl. Book award for Cesar Vallejo: The Complete Posthumous Poetry, 1979; Natl. Transl. Center grantee, 1967, 68; Center Inter-Am. Relations grantee, 1968; CCLM grantee, 1968, 70, 73; Guggenheim fellow, 1978; NEH grantee, 1980, 81. Address: 210 Washtenaw Ave Ypsilanti MI 48197

ESKESEN, BENNET HALLUM (HAL) JR., b. Stanford, CT, Nov. 18, 1947; s. Bennet Hallum and Elaine Mary (Dunning) E. Author: Sebastian Le Fou: Prelude to the Poet's 19th Nervous Breakdown, 1972, Virtue Can Take Shape, 1977. BA, Harvard, 1969. Reporter and copy ed. Fairfield County newspapers, Stanford, Conn, 1971—. Served to Cpl., USMC, 1965-69. Address: 82 East Ave New Canaan CT 06840

ESLER, ANTHONY JAMES, b. New London, CT, Feb. 20, 1934, s. James Arthur and Helen Wilhelmina (Kreamer) E.; m. Carol Eaton Clemeau, June 17, 1961; children—Kenneth Campbell, David Douglas. Author history: Aspiring Mind of Elizabethan Younger Generation, 1966, Bombs Beards and Barricades, 1971, Youth Revolution, 1974, Generations in History: The Concept, 1982, Generation Gap in Society and History, 1984, Human Venture: Great Enterprise, 1985, Human Venture: Globe Encompassed, 1986; author fiction: Castlemayne, 1974, Hellbane, 1975, Lord Libertine, 1976, Forbidden City, 1977, Freebooters, 1979, Bastion, 1980, Babylon, 1980. BA, U. Ariz., 1956; MA, Duke U., 1958, PhD in History, 1961. Asst. prof. history Coll. William and Mary, Williamsburg, Va., 1962-67, assoc. prof., 1967-72, prof. history, 1972—; vis. assoc. prof. Northwestern U., Evanston, Ill., 1968-69. Fulbright fellow, 1961-62, grantee, 1984; Am. Council Learned Socs. fellow, 1969-70. Mem. AG, World History Assn. Office: Dept History William and Mary Williamsburg VA 23185

ESLER, WILLIAM CHRISTOPHER, b. Chgo., Nov. 18, 1951; s. Walter James Esler, Sr., and Marion Katherine (Fogarty) E. Author research rpts.: Direct Mail Printing, 1981, On-Demand Printing, 1982, The Printing Plant of 1995, 1984, Fibre Market News, 1980. BA in Engl. lit., Knox Coll., 1983. Pressman, Monarch Matrix, Chgo., 1974-75; typographer, Spiegel Catalog, Chgo., 1975; print ad. mgr. Ace Hardware Corp., Oakbrook, IL, 1976; print prodn. mgr. Professional Press, Chgo., 1977-78; features ed. Am. Printer Mag., Chgo., 1979-80; editorial dir. Innes Publishing, Chgo., 1981-87; pub. Print Mergers & Acquisitions newsletter, 1986. Mem. Tech. Assn. Graphic Arts. Judge, PIA Natl. Print Conf., 1985, 86, 87, A.B. Dick Natl. Print Conf., 1985. Home: 1234 West Elmdale Chicago IL 60660

ESPAILLAT, RHINA POLONIA, b. Santo Domingo, Dominican Republic, Jan. 20, 1932 (arrvd. USA 1939), d. Homero and Dulce Maria (Batista) E.; m. Alfred Moskowitz, June 28, 1952; children—Philip Elias, Warren Paul; 1 foster child, Gaston W. Dubois. Contrbr. to Amelia, Black Washed and Ghost Bright, Blue Unicorn, Commonweal, Encore, Golden Year, Home Chat, Hymns for Children and Grown-ups, Ladies' Home Jnl, Lyric, Modern Lyrics, Muse Anthology, N.Am. Mentor Mag., Parthenon Anthology, Plains Poetry Jnl, Poet Lore, Poetry Rvw, others. BA, Hunter Coll., 1953; MSE, Queens Coll., 1964. Tchr. pub. schls., NYC, 1953-54, Jamaica High Schl., N.Y., 1965-80; cons. NYC Bd. Edn., 1984—. Mem. PSA, AAP, Women Poets N.Y., Shelley Soc., P&W. Home: 72-04 162d St Flushing NY 11365

ESPOSITO, DONNA J., b. Camden, NJ, July 21, 1954; d. John and Anne (Henderson) E. BA in Art, Rutgers Coll., 1976. Ed.-in-chief Printed Circuit Fabrication, Alpharetta, GA, 1979—. Office: PMS Ind 1790 Hembree Rd Alpharetta GA 30201

ESPY, WILLARD R., b. Olympia, WA, Dec. 11, 1910; s. Harry Albert and Helen Medora (Richardson) E.; m. Hilda S. Cole, 1940; m. Louise J. Manheim, 1962. Author: Bold New Program, 1951, The Game of Words, 1972, An Almanac of Words at Play, 1975, Oysterville: Roads to Grandpa's Village, 1977, The Life and Works of Mr. Anonymous, 1977, O Thou Improper, Thou Uncommon Noun, 1978, Say It My Way, 1980, Another Almanac of Words at Play, 1980, Have a Word on Me, 1981, Espygrams, 1982, A Children's Almanac of Words at Play, 1982, Word Puzzles, 1983, The Garden of Eloquence, 1983, Words to Rhyme With, 1986; contrbr. articles to periodicals. BA, U. Redlands, 1930; student, U. Paris, Sorbonne, 1930-31. Reporter Tulare (Calif.) Times, 1932, Brawley (Calif.) News, 1932; asst. editor World Tomorrow, NYC, 1933-35; copy editor L'Agence Havas, 1937-40; mng. promotion and pub. relations Reader's Digest, 1941-57; producer, interviewer radio program "Personalities in Print," 1957-58; creative advt. dir. Famous Artists Schls., 1958-63; publisher Charter Books, 1963-66. Contrbg. editor: Harvard Mag., 1978—, Writer's Digest, 1985—. Mem. PEN, Natl. Book Critics' Circle, AG. Home: 529 W 42nd St New York NY 10036

ESSOCK, CYD PAULINE, b. Fort Atkinson, WI, Dec. 1, 1956; d. Theodore Sidney and Jeanne Margaret (Travis) E. Contrbr. articles, ednl. booklets, advt./promotional materials to mags., newspapers, jnls. including Milw. Sentinel, Balt. Sun, numerous others. B.S. cum laude in Jnlsm., U. Wis., Whitewater, 1980, postgrad., 1980—. Campus representative Am. Passage Media Corp., Chgo., 1978—; market researcher Gulf Coast Research, St. Petersburg, FL, 1986—; market representative Act Now, Bay area, 1987—. Mem. Soc. Creative Anachronism, Natl., Fla. Assn. Parliamentarians, Fla. Herb Soc., NLAPW (chmn. art & ode contest). Home: 5376 106th St N Saint Petersburg FL 33708

ESTERBROOK, ELIZABETH, see Hill, Millicent Elizabeth

ESTRIN, HERMAN A., b. North Plainfield, NJ, June 2, 1915, s. Morris I. and Ida Ruth (Bender) E.; children—Robert Keith, Karen Ruth. Author: The New Scientist: Essays on the Methods and Values of Science, 1962, Higher Education in Engineering and Science, 1963, Technical and Professional Writing: A Practical Anthology, 1963, College and University Teaching (with Delmer Good), 1966, Freedom and Censorship of the College Press (with Arthur Sanderson), 1966, The American Student and His College (with Esther Lloyd-Jones), 1967, How Many Roads? The 70's (with Lloyd-Jones), 1970, The American Language in the 1970's (with Donald Mehus), 1974, The Teaching of Technical Writing, 1975; ed.: The Best Student Poetry in New Jersey, 1978, 79, 80, 81, 82, 83, 84, 85, Poetic Engineers (with Bruce Bennett), 1983, 86. Wrkg. on non-fiction. BA, Drew U., 1937; AM, Columbia U., 1942, EdD, 1954. Mem. faculty N.J. Inst. Tech., Newark, 1950—, prof. emeritus of English, 1981—; dir. N.J. Wrtrs. Conf., N.J. Author Awards, N.J. dir. N.J. Literary Hall of Fame, 1976. Poetry Contest, 1959-86. Recipient award, N.J. Literary Hall of Fame, 1976, listee, 86, disting. service award Natl. Council Media Advisers, 1984. Home: 315 Henry St Scotch Plains NJ 07076

ETTER, DAVE, b. Huntington Park, Calif., Mar. 18, 1928, s. Harold Pearson and Judith Ann (Goodenow) E.; m. Margaret Ann Cochran, Aug. 8, 1959; children—Emily Louise, George Goodenow. Author poetry: Go Read the River, 1966, The Last Train to Prophetstown, 1968, Strawberries, 1970, Voyages to the Inland Sea, 1971, Crabtree's Woman, 1972, Well You Needn't, 1975, Bright Mississippi, 1975, Central Standard Time, 1978, Alliance, Illinois, 1978, Open to the Wind, 1978, Riding the Rock Island Through Kansas, 1979, Cornfields, 1980, West of Chicago, 1981, Boondocks, 1982, Alliance, Illinois (complete ed.), 1983, Home State, 1985, Live at the Silver Dollar, 1986, Selected Poems, 1987; contrbr. over 60 anthologies and textbooks. Wrkg. on poetry vols. BA, U. Iowa, 1953. Ed. Northwestern U. Press, Evanston, Ill., 1962-63, Encyc. Britannica, Chgo., 1964-73, No. Ill. U. Press, DeKalb, 1974-80; freelance wrtr., tchr., Elburn, Ill., 1980—. Served with U.S. Army, 1953-55. Recipient Midland Authors Poetry Prize, 1967, Poetry Prize, Ill. Sesquicentennial, 1968, Theodore Roethke prize Poetry Northwest mag., 1971, Carl Sandburg prize Chgo. Public Library, 1982. Home: Box 413 Elburn IL 60119

EUBANKS, JACKIE KAREN, b. Chgo., d. Albert and Helen Meta (Post) Peldzus; m. Lloyd Webster Eubanks, Dec. 31, 1968 (div. 1979). Sr. ed. Alternatives In Print, 1970—; contrbr. A Short Course in Writing, 1985. AB, U. Chgo., 1959, MA, 1963, MA, Columbia U. Tchrs. Coll., 1969. Librarian U.S. Dept. Army Spcl. Services, Baumholder, Germany, 1963-65; asst. librarian Am. Assn. Advt. Agys., N.Y.C., 1965-66; assoc. prof. Bklyn. Coll., CUNY, 1966—, exhibits mgr., 1974—. Office: CUNY Bklyn Coll Library Brooklyn NY 11210

EVANBAR, B. H., see Steinberg, Bernhard Evanbar

EVANS, ALICE MC DONALD, b. Plainfield, NJ, Dec. 11, 1940; d. Henry Clay Jones and Evelyn McDonald (Myers) Evans. Contrbr. poems mags., anthols. Wrkg. on poems. B.A., Colby Coll., Waterville, Maine, 1962; M.A., Seton Hall U., 1979; postgrad. NYU, 1980-83. Secretarial asst. Roosevelt Hosp., Edison, N.J., 1970-84; med. typist NYU Med. Ctr., 1984-85; typesetter L & B Typo, NYC, 1985—. Telephone worker Contact We Care, 1985—. Recipient Solomon Gallert English prize for short story Colby Coll., 1960, 2 cert. of merit, N.Am. Mentor Mag., 1985. Home: 716 Field Ave Apt 3 Plainfield NJ 07060

EVANS, DAVID ALLAN, b. Sioux City, IA, Apr. 11, 1940, s. Arthur Clarence and Ruth (Lyle) E.; m. Janice Kaye Johnson, July 4, 1958; children—Shelly, David, Karlin. Author: Among Athletes (poems), 1971, Train Windows (poems), 1976, Real and False Alarms (poems), 1985, Remembering the Soos, 1986; ed.: What the Tallgrass Says, 1981, New Voices in American Poetry, 1976, (with others) The Sport of Poetry/The Poetry of Sport, 1979; contrbr. poetry to anthologies: Heartland: Poets of the Midwest, Best Poems of 1969 (Borestone awards), Baseball Diamonds, Poetspeak, Pocket Poems, Strings, others. BA, Morningside Coll., Sioux City, Iowa, 1962, MA, U. Iowa, 1964; MFA, U. Ark., 1976. Asst. prof. English Adams State Coll., Alamosa, Colo., 1966-68; assoc. prof. English S.D. State U., Brookings, 1978—. Breadloaf scholar, Breadloaf Wrtrs. Schl., 1971; grantee NEA, 1976, S.D. Arts Council, 1982. Mem. PSA, Sports Lit. Assn. Home: 1222 3rd St Brookings SD 57006

EVANS, HAROLD MATTHEW, b. Manchester, Eng., June 28, 1928; s. Frederick Albert and Mary Hannah (Haselum) E.; m. Enid Parker, Apr. 15, 1953 (div. 1978); children: Ruth, Katherine, Michael; m. Tina Brown, Aug. 19, 1981. Editor The Sunday Times, London, 1967-81, The Times, London, 1981-82; dir. editorial bd. Goldcrest Films & TV, London, 1982-85; editor-in-chief Atlantic Monthly Press, N.Y.C., 1984; editorial dir. U.S. News & World Report, Washington, 1984—; sr. journalist in residence Duke U., N.c., 1983. B.A. with honors, Durham U., London, 1952; M.A., Durham U., 1966; Ph.D. (hon.), Sterling U., 1982. Harkness fellow U. Chgo., 1956-57. Recipient Intl. Editor of Yr. award World Press Review, 1974; Editor of Yr. award Granada Press Awards, 1982. Fellow Soc. Indsl. Designers, Inst. Journalists (European Gold medal, 1978). Mem. Intl. Press Inst. (Journalist of Yr. award 1973). Office: U.S. News & World Report 2400 N St NW Washington DC 20037

EVANS, JOHN WAYNE, b. Los Angeles, Dec. 18, 1943, s. Jess Everett and Nellie May (Jeffress) E. Author, ed., pub.: The Poets I, 1974, I Soul a Poem, 1977, Desires Road, 1982, Seeking Wisdom—Finding Love, 1986. Student San Jose City Coll., 1964-66. Freelance poet, Aptos, Calif., 1971—. Address: 9011 Soquel Dr Aptos CA 95003

EVANS, KAROLYN E., b. Detroit, Jan. 16, 1953; d. Theodore E. Harris and Shirley A. Evans; 1 son, Ebon DeVon. Contrbr. poems to anthols. Wrkg. on poetry manuscript, Phases of Love. Student Wayne State U. Clerical, Detroit, 1974—. Recipient Merit cert. Talent & Associated Cos., 1984; award of Merit, World of Poetry, 1986, Silver Poet Award, 1986, Golden Poet award, 1987. Home: 3880 Gladwin Detroit MI 48214

EVANS, LARRY FREDRIC, b. Balt., July 13, 1947; s. Vincent Jeffery and Dorothy S. Evans; m. Leslie Byrd, May 20, 1980; 1 child, Ducky. BA, Loyola Coll., Balt., 1970. Steelworker U.S. Steel Corp., Pitts., 1976-81; ed. Mill Hunk Herald Mag., Pitts., 1979—. Mem. NWU. Office: Mill Hunk 916 Middle St Pittsburgh PA 15212

EVANS, MARI, b. Toledo. Author: (poems)Where Is All the Music, 1968, I Am A Black Woman, 1970, Nightstar, 1980; (juveniles) J.D., 1973; (playwright, dir.) River of My Song, 1977, Boochie, 1985, Portrait of a Man, 1985; (playwright) Eyes, 1982; editor: (non-fiction) Black Woman Writers 1950-80: A Critical Evaluation, 1984; Contrbr. poetry to textbooks, anthologies, periodicals. Student, U. Toledo. Instr. Black lit., writer-in-res. Ind. U.-Purdue U. at Indpls., 1969-70; asst. prof. Black lit., writer-in-residence Ind. U., Bloomington, 1970-78; cons. ethnic studies Bobbs-Merrill Co., 1970-73. Producer, dir., writer: TV program "The Black Experience," WTTW, Indpls., 1968-73. Recipient Ind. U. Writers Conf. award, 1970, 1st Annl. Poetry award Black Acad. Arts and Letters, 1971; John Hay Whitney fellow, 1965-66. MacDowell fellow, 1975; Copeland fellow Amherst Coll., 1980; NEA grantee, 1981-82. Mem. AG, AL Am. Home: Box 483 Indianapolis IN 47206

EVANS, NORENE RUSSELL (RUSTI), b. Deming, NM, June 30, 1935; d. Theodore Hoy and Dorothy Gertrude (Baker) Russell; m. Robert Hill Evans, Oct. 7, 1955; children: Lauralyn Lee, Robert Hill Jr., Dana Shawn. Contrbr. of articles to profl. jnls. Ledger and Clergy Jnl., also Chaplain Rvw; author handbooks Going Public, 1980, Publicity Patterns, 1983, A New Ministry, 1985. AS, SUNY, 1978. Pvt. practice cons. and trng., freelance wrtr. Fort Huachuca, Ariz., 1977-79, Springfield, Va., 1979—; founder, exec. dir. Milcom & Chapel Publicity and Sharing Assoc. and Publicity Press, Springfield, 1986—. Mem. Natl. Religious Pub. Relations Council Inc., Washington Religious Pub. Relations Council Inc., Intl. Assn. Bus. Communicators, Am. Soc. Trng. and Devel. Home: 8611 Burling Wood Dr Springfield VA 22152

EVANS, ROSE MARY, b. San Francisco, Jan. 30, 1928; d. John Gillespie and Hazel Elenor (Tait) MacPhee; widowed; children—Anne, John, David, Valeria. Author: Friends of All Creatures, 1984. BA, Stanford U., 1947; MA, San Francisco State U., 1979. Instr., Aid Retarded Citizens, San Francisco, 1976-80; tchr., ednl. dir. Susan Snyden Center, San Francisco, 1980-82; pub. Sea Fog Press, Inc., San Francisco, 1984—. Home: 447 20th Ave San Francisco CA 94121

EVELETH, E. ELIZABETH, see Farrington, Esther Elizabeth

EVELETH, JANET STIDMAN, b. Balt., Sept. 6, 1950; d. John Charles and Edith (Scales) Stidman; m. Donald Peter Eveleth, May 11, 1974. Ed. & pub.: Food Industry Skirmisher, 1981, MAFDA News, Mid-Atlantic Food Dealers Annual Rpt., Mid-Atlantic Region Buyers' Guide, 1984, Maryland Builder, News Update, HBAM Annual Directory, HMAM Annual Rpt., 1984—. BA in Amer. Studies, Washington Coll., 1972; MS in Cslg./Commun., Johns Hopkins U., 1973. Cslr., Mayor's Office, Balt., 1973-76; asst. dir. Children Commn., Balt., 1976-79; communic. spclst., Medical Assn., Balt., 1980-81; public affairs dir. Food Dealers Assn., Balt., 1981-84; sr. dir. commun. Home Builders Assn. of MD, Balt., 1984—. Mem. PRSA. Home: 525 Piccadilly Rd Towson MD 21204

EVERETT, GRAHAM, b. Oceanside, NY, Dec. 23, 1947; s. James H. and Jacqueline (Vaughan) E.; m. Elyse Arnow, Dec. 27, 1981; 1 child, Logan James. Books of poetry: The Trees, 1977, Strange Coast, 1979, The Sunlit Sidewalk, 1985. Novel: Nothing Left to Fake, 1976. Co-ed.: Paumanok Rising, 1981. BA, Canisius Coll., 1970. Pub. Street Press, Port Jefferson, NY, 1972—; secy.-treas. Backstreet Edits. Inc., Port Jefferson, 1982—; ed. Byrne Lithographers, Setauket, NY, 1985—. Mem. Am. Printers History Assn. Office: Box 555 Port Jefferson NY 11777

EVERETT, JOANN MARIE, b. Phila., Nov. 26, 1950; d. Wilbur Charles and Constance Patricia (Shimkus) Koch; m. Dale W. Everett, Aug. 12, 1972; 1 son, Jonathan Samuel Koch Everett. Author: The Wandering Song, 1980, Whispered Beginnings, 1984, Seasons in Thunder Valley,

1986; editor: Scintillations I, 1984, II, 1984, III, 1985, IV, V, 1986, VI, 1987 (newsletter) Calliope, 1985—, ABPA Poetry Award, 1985, Calliope Fiction Award, 1987; contrbrg. editor: Icicle Carnival, 1984, Book of the Living Dead, 1985, She Is Me, 1986. BS in Edn., Kutztown U., 1972, MS in Edn., Temple U., 1976. Tchr., St. Anselm's, Phila., 1980-81; pub. Jasmine Press, Croydon, Pa., 1983—; dir. Bensalem Assn. of Women Wrtrs., Croydon, 1983—; Speaker and dir. Poetry, Fiction and Women's Isssues; freelance wrtr., 1983—. Recipient Poetry award Submit, 1985, 1st prize Odessa Poetry Rvw, 1986. Mem. AAUW, 1987. Fellow Intl. Women's WG, P&W, World Poetry Assn. Office: Box 236 Croydon PA 19020

EVERETT, S. W., see Stillman, William Everett

EVERHART, ROBERT PHILLIP, b. St. Edward, NB, June 16, 1936; s. Philip McClelland and Martha Matilda (Meyers) E. Author poetry: Mountains of Nebr., 1970, Silver Bullets, 1977, Prairie Sunset, 1978, Savage Trumpet, 1982; hist. novels: Clara Bell, 1976, Hart's Bluff, 1976; travel: Snoopy Goes to Mex., 1980; Everhart's Music, 1983; screenscripts: Jimmie Rodgers, 1982, Matecombe Treasure, 1983. Student, U. Nebr., 1961-63, London Schl. of Jnlsm., Iowa W. Univ., 1973. Announcer WOW Radio, Omaha, 1960-61; gen. mgr. KJNO Radio, Juneau, Nebr., 1973-75; recipient. artist Folkways Records, NYC,1976—; ed. Tradition Mag., Council Bluffs, Iowa, 1976—, contrbr. Prairie News, 1977—. Mem. Citizens for Community Improvement, Council Bluffs, 1982—. Served to RM2, USN, 1954-59; PTO. Recipient Country Performer of Year award Holland Country Music Assn., Helmond, Holland, 1984, Men of Achievement award Cambridge Univ., Eng., 1985. Mem. BMI, Natl. Traditional Country Music Assn. (pres. 1976 —), Natl. Old Time Fiddlers Assn., Western States Country Music Assn., Natl. Journalism Assn. Home: 106 Navajo Council Bluffs IA 51501

EVERNDEN, MARGERY ELIZABETH, b. Okeechobee, FL, June 6, 1916, d. Hans Foord and Rose (Wagner) E.; m. Earl A. Gulbransen, July 2, 1938; children—Karen, Kristin, David. Author: (juveniles) The Secret of the Porcelain Fish, 1947, Wilderness Boy, 1955, Simon's Way, 1972, Kite Song, 1984, The Dream Keeper, 1985, others; contrbr. poetry, articles, short stories, plays, rvws. to natl. publs. AB, U. Calif., Berkeley, 1938; MA, U. Pitts., 1968. Prof. emerita English, U. Pitts., since 1986; freelance wrtr., since 1934. Recipient various spcl. recognitions for children's books and plays; Atlantic Monthly recognition for teaching univ. writing students. Home: 63 Hathaway Ct Pittsburgh PA 15235

EWALD, HEATHER H., b. Oak Park, IL, Sept. 15, 1948; d. Ernest and Erma K; m. Roger Ewald, Aug. 12, 1972; 2 daus., Mary Kathryn, Christina Frances. Author: My Dad, Ernie Klassen—Evangelizing the World, One Person At A Time, 1985. BA in Math, Taylor U., 1966-69. Home: 160 W Altgeld Glendale Hts IL 60139

EWING, JACK, (Jasper Wing, Dirk Saxon), b. Chgo., Jan. 21, 1945; s. John C. and Irene R. (Roeder) E. Author: (novel) A Freshman's Confessions, 1962, Soft, More, 1963. BA Parsons Coll., Fairfield, Ia., 1966; MA SUNY-Oswego, 1970. Copy chief Paul, John & Lee Advtg., Syracuse, N.Y., 1977-80, Williamson & Reinhard/Cline, Boise, Idaho, 1986; creative dir. Belcher, Bagley & Wehren Advtg., Boise, 1980-82; free-lance writer Mr. E Enterprises, Syracuse, 1970-80, Wizard of Words, Boise, 1982—; tchr. Boise Community Edn., 1982-85. Recipient Andy N.Y. Advt. Club., NYC, 1978, Silver award Advt. Club of NYC, 1977, Essay award Syracuse Newspapers. Mem. Boise Advt. Fedn. (numerous silver and gold Rockies 1980-86). Home: 1303 Manitou Ave Boise ID 83706

EWING, JEANNE BUNDERSON, b. Rural, NE, May 6, 1933; d. Oscar Bunderson and Charlotte D. Lester; children—Sydne, Barbara Lindsey, Mary Elizabeth. Author: A Rural Village in a Changing World, Coping with Chronic Illness, Societal Factors in Education; contrbr. articles to newspapers, profl. jnls., mags. including Women's Health Issues, The Owl Newsletter. Contrbg. ed. France Today Mag., 1985-86. A.B. history, U. Calif. Berkeley, 1977; M.A., 1978, Ph.D., 1980, Dir., The Owl Ed. Service, Berkeley, 1978-86, Applied Research Assocs., Berkeley, 1982-85. Fellow Community Services Admin., Washington, DC, 1980. Mem. Natl. Assn. Female Execs., Am. Assn. Higher Edn., Am. Edn. Research Assn., Conservatory Am. Letters, NWC, Clin. Sociology Assn., Am. Hist. Assn., Assn. State & Local History, NAACP, Adult Edn. Assn., Assn. Eds. Pubs. Address: Box 89 Berkeley CA 94701

EWING, SONDRA DARLENE, b. Santa Cruz, CA, Feb. 13, 1948; d. Milo Richard Boyles and Arveda Eldona (Buffington) Brown; m. Stphen William Wissbaum, Oct. 12, 1967 (div. Nov. 21, 1974); hildren—Michael William, Gregory Milo; m. Donnie Steward Ewing, Sept. 22, 1978. Wrtr., prs. Ewing Co., Shreveport, LA, 1984—; freelance wrtr., 1974—. Mem. Golden Triangle WG, RWA. Home: 6142 Pebble Beach Shreveport LA 71129

EWING, TESS, see Smiley, Virginia Kester

EXETASTES, see Harakas, Stanley Samuel

EXLER, ANDREW ROSS, (Dr. Drew), b. Encino, CA, Mar. 23, 1961, s. Robert Allan and Marilyn Ruth (Grant) E. Contrbr. to mags., newspapers; ed., pub. Civil Rights Report, 1985—; political ed. Edge Mag, 1986—.Asst. to med. dir. Careunit Hosp. of Orange, Calif., 1982-83; adminstrv. asst. Cedars-Sinai Med. Ctr., Los Angeles, 1983—. Office: 6000 Sunset Blvd Los Angeles CA 90028

EYESTONE, see Oisteanu, Valery,

EYSMAN, HARVEY A., b. NYC, Nov. 16, 1939; s. Mouritz and Etta M. (Schwartz) Eysman; m. Donna O'Hara, Sept. 28, 1969; 1 dau.—Regan Tara. Novel: Courier's First, 1981; contrbr. to various periodicals. LLB, (JD), LLM Brooklyn Law School, 1966. Self-emplyd. attorney (NY), 1965—. District deputy grand master, Masons, NY. Home: 15 Stonehenge Rd Great Neck NY 11026

EZELL, CAROLYN WOLTZ, b. NYC, Nov. 5, 1949. Author: (hist. novel) The Marble Tear, 1980; Alabama Visions: Whispering of a Southern Land, 1988. Contrbr. articles to Highlights for Children, Creative Ideas for Living. Recipient award Ala. Alumni Mag., 1981. Mem. Guild Profl. Wrtrs. for Children (pres. 1986-87, 87-88), Chi Delta Phi, Alpha Kappa Delta. Home: 1426 Queen City Ave Tuscaloosa AL 35401

FABER, INEZ MC ALISTER, (Elizabeth Beresford), b. Monroe County, IA, Feb. 9, 1897; d. Robert Bruce and Margaret Elizabeth (Robinson) McAlister; m. Richard Andrew Faber, Aug. 30, 1922 (dec. 1974); children—Vaughn Bernard, Charles Franklin, Richard Bruce, Irvin Earl. Author: Out Here on Soap Creek, 1982. Columnist, Centerville (IA) Iowegian, Moravia (IA) Union, Moulton (IA) Tribune; short stories pubd. Student Chadron State Coll. Historian, IA City Branch, NPWJ, 1984-86. Mem. NPW, Ottumwa (IA) Writers' Club. Home: Benton Place Albia IA 52531

FABIAN, R. GERRY, b. Doylestown, PA; s. Robert Gerald and Elaine (Usilton) F.; m. Sally Donchez (div.); 1 child, Jesse. Author: (poetry chapbooks) Long Distances, 1980, Murmurings and Palpitations, 1982, Doubleheader, 1983, A Fallen Woman, 1981, Last Call, 1978. BS in English, Mansfield State U., 1971; MS in English, Trenton State U., 1975. English instr. Central Bucks West High Schl., Doylestown, 1972—; poetry lectr. Lambertville Swan Poets, N.J., 1979; guest poet The Kindred Spirit, St. John, Kans., 1986; editor Raw Dog Press, 1975—. Named Poet of Yr., Am. Soc. Poemists, 1984. Home: 2-34 Aspen Doylestown PA 18901

FABILLI, MARY, b. Gardiner, NM, Feb. 16, 1914; d. Vincenzo and Giacinta (Pone) Fabilli. Author: The Old Ones, 1966, Aurora Bligh & Early Poems, 1968, The Animal Kingdom, 1975, Ray Boynton & the Mother Lode, 1976, Poems 1976-1981, 1982, Winter Poems, 1983, Pilgrimage, 1985. AB, U. Calif., Berkeley, 1941. Assoc. curator Oakland (Calif.) Mus., 1949-77. Mem. Delta Epsilon. Home: 2445 Ashby Ave Berkeley CA 94705

FACKLAM, MARGERY (METZ), b. Buffalo, NY, Sept. 6, 1927; d. Eduard Frederic, and Ruth (Schauss) Metz; v. Howard F. Facklam, Jr., July 9, 1949; children: Thomas, David, Jogn, Paul, Margaret. Author: Whistle for Danger, 1962, Behind These Doors: Science Museum Makers, 1968, (with Patricia Phibbs) Corn Husk Crafts, 1973, Froz4n Snakes and Dinosaur Boes (Junior Literary Guild selection), 1976, Wild Animals, Gentlewomen (Junior Literary Guild Selection), 1978, (with Howard Facklam) From Cell to Clone: The Story of Genetic Engineering (Book-of-the-Month Club selection), 1979, The Brain, Magnificent Mind Machine, 1982, (with H. Facklam) Changes in the Wind, 1986, Spare Parts for People, 1987, So Can I, 1987, But Not Like Mine, 1987. Contrbr to periodicals, including Ranger Rick and Cricket. BA, Univ. of Buffalo, 1947; MS, Buffalo State Coll., 1976. High school teacher of sci. in Snyder, N.Y., 1949-50; asst admin. of educ., Buffalo Museum of Sci., 1970-74; curator of educ., Aquarium of Niagra Falls, Niagara Falls, N.Y., 1974-77; dir. of educ., Buffalo Zoo, 1977-79; freelance writer and instructor for Institute of Children's Literature, Member: American Soc. of Journalists and Authors, Soc. of Children's Book Writers, Natl League of American Pen Women, AG. Home: 9690 Clarence Center Rd Clarence Center NY 14032

FACOS, JAMES, b. Lawrence, MA, July 28, 1924; s. Chris and Theresa (McAdam) F.; m. Cleo Chigos, Dec. 1, 1956; children: Tina, Joy, Tony. Author: (novel) The Silver Lady, 1972; (plays) The Piper O'The May, 1962, The Legacy, 1967, A Day of Genesis, 1969, Silver Wood, 1976, One Daring Fling, 1978; (poetry) Morning's Come Singing, 1981; contrbr. short stories and novella to Stories, Negative Capbility. AB, Bates U., 1949; MA, Fla State U., 1958. Prof. English, Norwich Univ., Northfield, Vt., 1959—. Recipient Alden award, Dramatists Alliance, Calif., 1956; Arthur Wallace Peach award Vt.

Poetry Soc., 1962, Corinne Davis award, 1970. Mem. New England Poetry Club, NCTE. Address: 333 Elm Montpelier VT 05602

FACULAK, MARY HELEN, (Fac), b. Charlevoix, MI, May 3, 1960; d. Anthony William and Shirley Magdeline (Lund) F. Ed.: Northern Mich. Weekend, 1984. Wrkg. on poetry, jnl., short stories, novel. A.A., North Central Mich. Coll., 1980. Home: Rt1 Lake Viiew Ranch 01936 US 31 S Charlevoix MI 49720

FAEDER, GUSTAV S., b. NYC, Mar. 30, 1921; s. Nathaniel and Adah May (Quadland) F.; M. Marjorie E. Fairfield, June 16, 1944; children—Sara Lee, David William, Andrea Louise. Condtrbr. articles to mags. including Civil War Times Illustrated, Va. Country's Civil War Quarterly. B.S.E., U. Mass., 1942; M.A., Columbia U., 1947. Cryptanalyst, Natl. Security Agcy., Washington, 1949-54; adminstrv. officer Central Intelligence Agy., Washington, 1955-70; tng. officer U.S. Postal Service, Bethesda, MD, 1970-71; free-lance wrtr. Home: 2424 N Federal Boynton Beach FL 33435

FAIRBROTHER, ANNE ELMORE, (A La Lansun), b. Richmond, VA, July 24, 1922; d. Richard Edgar and Florence CoyKendall (Rex) Elmore; m. Paul Wiswall Fairbrother, June 19, 1947 (div. Dec. 5, 1955); 1 dau., Linda Anne Fairbrother Tyler. Author: What Are Your Dreams Telling You?, 1986. Wrkg. on Patterns of Awareness. Student Wayne State U., 1941-43; Diploma, Am. Acad. Dramatic Art, 1944, Famous Wrtrs. Schl., diploma 1968. Free-lance actress Sta. WXYZ, Detroit, 1936-39, Sta. WWJ-TV, Detroit, 1947-55, Jam Handy Orgn., Detroit, 1947-55, Wilding Pictures, Detroit, 1947-55; sr. ed. technical pubs. Sperry Corp., Phoenix, 1973-85, retired. Recipient 1st place for short story Harmonious Pub. Co., 1983, Honorable Mention, World of Poetry, 1986. Mem. SAG, AFTRA. Home: Sedona Shadows MHC 136 Sedona AZ 86336

FAIRFIELD, JOHN, see Livingstone, Harrison Edward

FALCO, EDWARD, b. Los Angeles, Nov. 25, 1948; s. Joseph and Edith (Catapano) F. Author: As A Falling Leaf, 1973, Evocations, 1979, Concert in the Park of Culture, 1984; contrbr. fiction to Ga. Rvw, Sou'wester, Permafrost, Crop Dust, numerous other publs.; contrbr. poetry to Tendril, Mid-Am. Rvw, Chowder Rvw, over 50 mags. BA, SUNY-New Paltz, 1970, MA, Syracuse U., 1979. Part-time instr. Syracuse (N.Y.) U., 1979-84, Lemoyne Coll., Syracuse, 1982-84; instr. Va. Poly. Inst. and State U., Blacksburg, 1984—. Mem. AWP. Office: Va Poly Dept English Blacksburg VA 24061

FALK, DIANE M., b. NYC, May 22, 1947; d. Leon Harrison Falk and Jessie Constance (Lilienthal) Hilton. Editor: World Student Times, NYC, 1979, Focus, NYC and Washington, 1979-80, (cultural) Home and Church, NYC, 1983—. BA in English and writing, Columbia U., 1973; MLS, 1979. Reporter, Newsworld Communications NYC, 1977-78. Mem. Editorial Freelancers, Poetry Project. Home: 4306 17th St NW Washington DC 20011

FALK, PETER HASTINGS, b. New Haven, CT, Oct. 27, 1950; s. Wilbur Nelson and Patricia (Hastings) Falk; m. Margaret Lake, May 28, 1977; children—Kristen, Kerrin. Author: Who Was Who in American Art, 1985, Milton J. Burns, Marine Artist, 1984, Lester G. Hornby, Painter-Etcher, 1984, Ellen Day Hale, 1982. Student Rhode Island School of Design, 1976. Prop. Hastings Falk, Inc. (Madison, CT), 1977—. Mem. Intl. Soc. Independent Publishers.Home: Madison CT 06443

FALLIER, JEANNE HANWAY, b. Indpls., Sept. 28, 1920; d. Paul Scott H. and M. Louise (Seward) Hanway; m. Charles N. Fallier, June 12, 1943; children—Robert Seward, Forrest Ewing. Author, pub.: JF Manual for Traditional Rug Hooking, 1983, Little Critters Book of Story and Patterns, 1984, Handling Public Relations, a Guide Book, 1985, History and Art of Traditional Rug and Tapestry Hooking, 1986; contrbr. poetry: The Harbinger; contrbr. articles numerous spl. interest periodicals and local publs. Wrkg. on poetry, history of rug and tapestry hooking. Mem. editiorial staff Doubleday and Co., 1944-46; ed. spl. events, feature wrtr. Centre Island News, Hicksville, N.Y., 1952-56; owner, operator The Rugging Room, Westford, Mass., 1975—; ed. newsletter Assn. Traditional Hooking Artists, 1983-87; freelance wrtr., 1975—. Mem. Nashoba Area Wrtrs.' Guild, numerous art orgns. Home: 10 Sawmill Dr Westford MA 01886

FALLON, TOM, b. Winchester, MA, Feb. 17, 1936; m. Jacqueline F. Thibodeau, 1960; seven children. Contrbr. poetry, non-poetry and prose to Red Dust New Writing 3, Through a Stranger's Eyes, Atlanta's Children, Uncensored Paper Mill. Wrkg. on The Man on The Moon. Mem. Maine Writers and Publishers Alliance. Address: 226 Linden St Rumford ME 04276

FALLOWS, JAMES MACKENZIE, b. Phila., Aug. 2, 1949; s. James Albert and Jean (Mackenzie) F.; m. Deborah Jean Zerad, June 22, 1971; children—Thomas Mackenzie, Tad Andrew. Staff editor Washington Monthly, 1972-74; freelance mag. writer, 1972-76; assoc. editor Tex. Monthly, 1974-76; chief speechwriter Pres. U.S., Washington, 1977-79; Washington editor Atlantic Monthly, 1979—. Author: National Defense, 1981; contrbr. articles to numerous mags. and jnls. BA magna cum laude, Harvard U., 1970; diploma in econ. devel. (Rhodes scholar), Oxford U., 1972. Address: Atlantic 8 Arlington St Boston MA 02116

FANTON, ROLAND BENJAMIN, (Ben Fanton), b. Wellsville, NY, March 25, 1943; s. Roland Arthur and Dorotha Emma (Sadler) F.; m. Barrie Ruth Brown, Nov. 2, 1963; children—Lorraine, Ian, Molly. Articles in mags. and newspapers including TV Guide, Northwest Orient Magazine, Ford Times, Baseball Digest, New York Alive, Buffalo News Magazine, Newsday. BA, Alfred U., 1968; MS, State U. of NY, Geneseo, 1970. Freelance wrtr. Home: RD 4 Box 15 Wellsville NY 14895

FARAH, MADELAIN, b. Portland, OR, Dec. 20, 1934, d. Salim Khalil and Laurice (Nasrallah) Farah; m. John Habib, Mar. 3, 1962 (div. 1966); 1 dau., Leila. Author: Lebanese Cuisine, 1972, 7th ed., 1985, Pocket Breat Potpourri: Meals in Minutes, 1984, Marriage and Sexuality in Islam, 1984. BA, Portland State U., 1960, MAT, 1967; PhD, U. Utah, 1976. Cooking instr. Portland (Oreg.) Community Coll., 1976-77; pres. Farah's Lebanese Cuisine, Inc., Portland, 1983—; tchr. French, Portland public schls., 1972—. Home: 3427 E Burnside St Portland OR 97214

FARLEY, JOSEPH, b. Phila., Dec. 28, 1961; s. Francis William and Joanne (Hafer) F. Author: (chapbook) January, 1985. Contrbr. poems, stories, articles to lit. mags., anthols., profl. jnls. Ed.: Implosion mag., 1983; ed., pub.: Axe Factory Rvw., 1985—. B.A., St. Joseph's U., 1983; postgrad. Temple U., 1986—. Library asst. Free Library of Phila., 1983-85; social worker Phila. Dept. of Human Services, 1985; administr. Phila. Commn. on Human Relations, 1987—.Home: 8619 Colony Dr Philadelphia PA 19152

FARLEY, MYRON FOSTER, (Luigi Renaldi), b. Dyersburg, TN, June 30, 1921; s. Myron A. and Mary Hamilton) F.; m. Ethel N. Nifong, Dec. 28, 1957; children—Mary A., Marc Steven. Author: Newberry County in American Revolution, 1976, Indian Summer, An Account of a Visit to India, 1976, History of Stranger's Fever in Charleston 1699-1876, 1978, The Flight of the Four Hundred, 1986. BA, Furman U., 1947; MA, U. S.C.-Columbia, 1952. Instr., U. Tampa, Fla., 1951, Columbia Coll., 1952; prof. history Newberry Coll., S.C., 1954-56, 58—. Named Prof. of Yr., Newberry Coll., 1984-85. Served to sgt., U.S. Army Air Corps, 1942-46. Mem. Sons of Confederate Vets., Sons of Am. Revolution, Gen. Soc. of War of 1812, Bonnie Blue Soc., Am. Hist. Assn., S.C. Hist. Assn., Southern Hist. Assn. Home: Box 364 Newberry SC 29108

FARLEY, STACEY JEANNE, b. NYC, Jan. 21; d. James Thomas and Lynn Ann (Cyphert) F. Contrbr. articles and short stories: Chronicle of the Horse, Secrets, Tiger Beat, other publs. Wrkg. on novel. Home: 4061 SW 82d Terrace Davie FL 33328

FARLEY, WALTER LORIMER, b. NYC, June 26, 1925; s. Walter Patrick and Isabelle (Vermilyea) F.; m. Rosemary Lutz, May 26, 1945; children—Pamela, Alice, Walter Steven, Timothy. Author: The Black Stallion, 1941, plus 16 more Black Stallion books, including The Black Stallion Picture Book, 1979, The Black Stallion Returns Picture Book, 1983, The Black Stallion Comic Book, 1983; Blood Bay Colt, 1950, Great Dane Thor, 1968, Horse Tamer, 1958, Horse that Swam Away, 1965, Island Stallion, 1948, Big Black Horse, 1953, Island Stallion Races, 1955, Island Stallion's Fury, 1951, Little Black, a Pony; Little Black Goes to the Circus, 1963, Man O'War, 1962, Little Black Pony Races, 1968. Grad., Mercersburg (Pa.) Acad., 1936; edn. Columbia U., 1941. Served with AUS, 1941-46. Address: Random Hs 201 E 50th St New York NY 10022

FARMER, PHILIP JOSE, b. North Terre Haute, IN, Jan. 26, 1918; s. George and Lucile Theodora (Jackson) F.; m. Elizabeth Andre, May 10, 1941; children—Philip Laird, Kristen. Author: 65 books including Strange Relations, 1960, The Lovers, 1961, The Alley God, 1962, Riverworld Series: To Your Scattered Bodies Go, 1971, The Fabulous Riverboat, 1971, The Dark Design, 1977, The Magic Labyrinth, 1980, Riverworld and other Stories, 1979, Tarzan Alive, 1972, Venus on the Half-Shell (as Kilgore Trout), Gods of Riverworld, 1984, Dayworld, 1985, The Adventure of the Peerless Peer by John H. Watson, M.D., 1974, The Cache, 1981, A Barnstormer in Oz, 1982; Dayworld Rebel, 1987; short stories Riverworld, 1980. BA, Bradley U., 1950. Tech. writer, various cos., 1956-69. Recipient Hugo award, 1953, 68, 72. Address: 5911 N Isabell Ave Peoria IL 61614

FARNAGLE, ALPHAED E., see Smith, William Hovey

FARNSWORTH, SHORTY, see Humphrey, Edwin Lowell

FARQUHAR, PAUL GEORGE, b. Boston, Apr. 16, 1949; s. Henry Alexander and Alice (Grant) F. Columnist: Boston Herald, 1981-82. Student Northeastern U, Boston, 1975-82. Sales clrk. Jordan Marsh, Boston, 1967; financial clrk. U.S. Postal Service, Boston, 1967—. Served with U.S. Navy, 1968-70. Home: 28 S Main St Winthrop MA 02152

FARRANT, ELIZABETH, (Reardon, Janet Mauk, legal name), b. Toledo, OH, June 26, 1914; d. Jay George and Mary Jane (Little) Mauk; m. Albert Francis Reardon, April 23, 1937; 1 dau., Ann Reardon Crowley. Poetry in America, Poet Lore, Poet and Critic, Poetry View, Poem, Bitterroot, other mags. AB cum laude, Mary Manse College, Toledo, 1936; Library asst., Arlington Va. Dept. of Libraries, 1961-75. Mem. PSA, P&W. Home: 8273 Anderson Dr Fairfax VA 22031

FARRE, THOMAS R., b. Bronx, NY, July 26, 1946. Ed.: HiFi Buyer's Review, 1978, Tape Deck, 1978, Car Stereo Buyer's Guide, 1979, CES Daily News, 1979, Video Buyer's Review, 1979, Buyer's Guide to Small Computers, 1982, Guide to Pre-Recorded Video, 1982, Audiophile Buyer's Guide, 1982, Buyer's Guide to Telephones, 1982, Computer Show Daily, 1983, Semicon Show Daily, 1984, Fiberoptic Product News, 1985, Laser Pioneer Interviews, 1985; contrbr. to The Green World, 1972, Long Island Fisherman, 73; ed.-in-chief Lasers & Applications, 1985—. BA in Eng. lit., New Paltz State U., 1968, MA, 1970. Ed., CES Daily News, NYC, 1978-83; Vp/editorial dir. Hampton Intl. Communics., NYC, 1983-85; ed.-in-chief High-Tech Pubns., Torrance, CA, 1985—. Mem. Laser Industry Assn. Home: 1 E Forwood Morris Plains NJ 07950

FARRELL, EDMUND JAMES, b. Butte, Mont., May 17, 1927; s. Bartholomew J. and Lavinia H. (Collins) F.; m. Jo Ann Hayes, Dec. 19, 1964; children—David, Kevin, Sean. Author: (with others) Exploring Life Through Literature, 1964, Counterpoint in Literature, 1967, Projection in Literature, 1967, Outlooks in Literature, 1973, Fantasy: Forms of Things Unknown, 1974, Science Fact/Fiction, 1974, Comment, 1976, Myth, Mind and Moment, 1976, I/You, We/They, 1976, Traits and Topics, 1976, Up Stage/Down Stage, 1976, To Be, 1976, Conflict in Reality, 1976, Arrangement in Literature, 1979, Album U.S.A., 1983, Discoveries in Literature, 1985, Patterns in Literature, 1985. AB, Stanford U., 1950, MA, 1951; PhD, U. Calif., Berkeley, 1969. Served with USN, 1945-46. Home: 6500 Sumac St Austin TX 78731

FARRELL, JAMES JOSEPH, b. Washington, May 22, 1949; s. Lee James and Eileen Frances (Egger) F.; m. Barbara Jean Bednard, Dec. 21, 1970; 2 sons, John Francis Bednard, Paul Gabriel Bednard. Author: Inventing the American Way of Death 1830-1920, 1980, The Nuclear Devil's Dictionary, 1985. Wrkg. on The Bomb That Fell on America: A Cultural History. AB in Poli. Sci., Loyola U.-Chgo., 1971; PhD in Am. Culture, U. Ill.-Urbana, 1980. Prof. St. Olaf Coll., Northfield, Minn., 1977—. Mem. ASA, Orgn. Am. Historians, Educators for Social Responsibility. Home: 4700 Pleasant Ave South Minneapolis MN 55409

FARRELL, PAMELA BARNARD, b. Mount Holly, NJ, Oct. 11, d. George Wimmel and Audrey (Clerihue) Barnard; m. Joseph Donald Farrell, Sept. 1, 1968. Contrbr. poetry to Voices, Prickly Pears, Am. Poetry Anthology, Earth Scenes, Reflections, others; contrbr. articles to profl. publs. Wrkg. on poetry, education books. BA in English, Radford (Va.) Coll., 1965, MS in English, 1975; Cert. of Grad. Study in Wrtg., Northeastern U., 1986. Tchr. English and creative writing, dir. writing center Red Bank Regional High Schl., Little Silver, N.J., 1966—; writing cons., poet, 1982—. Woodrow Wilson fellow, 1985. Mem. NCTE (judge lit. mags., 1984—, judge for writing awards 1986), MLA, Columbia Press Assn. Home: 12 Essex Dr Little Silver NJ 07739

FARREN, PAT, b. Rochester, NY, July 15, 1944, s. Arthur and Mary (Bigham) F.; m. Glenda Alderman, Sept. 21, 1974; children—Jesse, Caitlin, Gabriel. Ed.: Peacework: A New England Peace and Social Justice Newsletter, 1973-86, What Will it Take to Prevent Nuclear War?, 1983. BA, St. Bonaventure U., Olean, N.Y., 1966. Vol. Peace Corps, West Africa, 1966-68; peace organizer, ed. Am. Friends Service Comm., Cambridge, Mass., 1973—. Mem. Consortium on Peace Research, Edn. and Devel. Address: Am Friends Service Comm 2161 Massachusetts Ave Cambridge MA 02140

FARRINGTON, ESTHER ELIZABETH, (E. Elizabeth Eveleth), b. Auburn, ME, Aug. 18, 1938; d. Charles Henry and Grace Lillian (Hodgkins) Eveleth; divorced; children— Kimberly, Sherri, Janet, Larry John. Contrbr. articles to mags., poems to anthols. Wrkg. on young adult novel, poems, articles, short stories. Grad. public schls., Auburn. Home: 57 Main St Mexico ME 04257

FARWELL, BYRON EDGAR, b. Manchester, IA, June 20, 1921; m. Ruth Saxby; children—Joyce, Byron John, Lesley. Author: the Man Who Presumed: A Biography of Henry Morton Stanley, 1953, 57, Burton: A Biography of Sir Richard Francis Burton, 1963, 75, Prisoners of the Mahdi, 1967, 71, Queen Victoria's Little Wars, 1972, The Great Anglo-Boer War, 1976, For Queen and Country, 1981, The Gurkhas, 1984, Eminent Victorian Soldiers, 1985, The Great War in Africa, 1914-18, 1986; lectr. in field; contrbr. numerous articles to newspapers, rvws. mags.; editorial bd.: Small Towns Inst. Fellow Royal Soc. Lit. (U.K.). Student, Ohio State U., 1939-40; AM, U. Chgo., 1968. Address: Box 81 Hillsboro VA 22132

FASEL, IDA, b. Portland, ME, May 9, 1909; m. Dr. Oskar A. Fasel, Dec. 24, 1946 (dec. 1973). Works include: On the Meanings of Cleave, 1979, Thanking the Flowers, 1981, West of Whitecaps, 1982, All of Us, Dancers, 1984, Amphora Full of Light, 1985. Contrbr. to The Study of Writing of Poetry: American Poets Discuss Their Craft, 1983. BA, MA, Boston U., PhD,U. of Denver. Prof. of Eng. Emer., U. of Colorado at Denver, 1962-77. Mem. PSA, Poetry Soc. of TX, Natl. League of Am. PEN Women, Phi Beta Kappa, Intl. Poetry Soc., Walt Whitman Assoc., Milton Soc. of Am., Friends of Milton's Cottage, Conf. on Christianity and Lit. Home: 165 Ivy St Denver CO 80220

FASS, SUSAN R., (Susan Ross), b. NYC, Feb. 27, 1941; d. Sylvia Finkelstein; m. Jerome Birnbaum, Aug. 28, 1958 (div. July 4, 1968); m. Fred Fass; children—Paul Birnbaum, Jason Fass. Contrbr. articles to Bowling Beat, The Herald, Village Voice. Wrkg. on novel, mag. articles. Cert., NYU., 1972. Administr. Western Union Corp., NYC., 1968-72. Home: 2225 Bombay Dr Lake Havasu City AZ 86403

FAST, HOWARD, b. NYC, Nov. 11, 1914; s. Barney and Ida (Miller) F.; m. Betty Cohen, June 6, 1937; children—Rachel Ann, Jonathan. Author: Two Valleys, 1932, Strange Yesterday, 1933, The Children, 1936, Place in the City, 1937, Conceived in Liberty, 1939; (biography) Haym Salomon, 1941; The Last Frontier, 1941; (biography) Baden Powell, 1941; Tail Hunter, 1942, The Unvanquished, 1942; (biography) Goethals and the Panama Canal, 1942; Citizen Tom Paine, 1943, Freedom Road, 1944, The American (biography of Peter Altgeld), 1946, Peekskill, U.S.A., 1951, Spartacus, 1952, The Naked God, 1957, Moses, Prince of Egypt, 1958, Tony and the Wonderful Door, 1968, The Crossing, 1971; General Zapped an Angel, 1971, Last Frontier, 1971, The Hessian, 1972; My Glorious Brothers, 1972, A Touch of Infinity, 1973, Selected Works of Paine (ed.), 1945, Patrick Henry and the Frigate's Keel (short stories), 1945, Carkton, 1947, My Glorious Brothers, 1948, Departure, 1949, Literature and Reality, 1949, The Proud and the Free, 1950, The Passion of Sacco and Vanzetti, 1953, 72, Silas Timberman, 1954, The Story of Lola Gregg: The Winston Affair, 1959, April Morning, 1961, Power, 1962, The Crossing (play), 1962, Agrippa's Daughter, 1964, The Hill (drama), 1963, Torquemada, 1966, The Hunter and the Trap, 1967, The Jews, 1968, The Hessians, 1970, The Immigrants, 1977, Second Generation, 1978, The Establishment, 1979, The Legacy, 1981, Max, 1982, The Outsider, 1984, The Immigrant's Daughter, 1985, The Dinner Party, 1987; as E.V. Cunningham: Sylvia, 1960, Phyllis, 1962, Alice, 1963, Helen, 1966, Margie, 1966, Sally, 1967, Samantha, 1967, Cynthia, 1968, Millie, 1973, Case of the Angry Actress, 1974, Case of One Penny Orange, 1975, Case of the Poisoned Eclairs, 1976, Case of the Russian Diplomat, 1977, Case of the Sliding Pool, 1980, Case of the Kidnapped Angel, 1981, Case of the Murdered MacKenzie, 1982, Case of the Angry Actress, 1983. Edn. George Washington High Schl., NYC, N.A.D. Began writing, 1932; European corr. for Esquire and Coronet mags., 1945; mem. overseas staff OWI, 1942-43; Army film project, 1944, Newspaper Guild Equality Award, 1944, Emmy award for The Ambassador, Benjamin Franklin, 1974. Office: Houghton Mifflin 2 Pk St Boston MA 02107

FATELEY, WILLIAM GENE, b. Franklin, IN, May 17, 1929; s. Nolan William and Georgia (Scott) F.; m. Wanda Lee Glover, Sept. 1, 1953; children: Leslie Kaye, W. Scott, Kevin L., Jonathan H., Robin L. Author: (co-author) Infrared and Raman Selection Rules, 1973, Characteristic Raman Frequencies, 1974. AB, Franklin Coll., 1951, DSc (hon.), 1965; postgrad., Northwestern U., 1951-53, U. Minn. 1956-57; PhD, Kansas State U., 1955. Head phys. measurement Dow Chem. Co., Williamsburg, Va., 1958-60; fellow Mellon Inst., Pitts., 1960-62, head sci. relations, 1962-64, asst. to pres., 1964-67, sr. fellow in ind. research, 1965-72; asst. to v.p. for research, 1967-72; prof. chemistry Carnegie-Mellon U., 1970-72; prof., head dept. chemistry, Kansas State U., 1972-79; vis. prof. chem. dept. U. Tokyo, 1973, 1981; pres. D.O.M. Assocs., Intl., 1979—; dir. Pitts. Conf. on Analytical Chemistry and Applied Spectroscopy, 1964-65, pres., 1970-71; editor Jnl Applied Spectroscopy, Raman Newsletter. Recipient Coblenz award for outstanding contrbn. to molecular spectroscopy, 1965; Spectroscopy award Pitts. Conf. Analytical Chemistry and Applied Spectroscopy, 1976; named 1st outstanding grad. chemistry Kansas State U., 1964; H. H. King award, 1979. Fellow Optical Soc. Am.; mem. Am. Chem. Soc. Sigma Xi, Sigma Alpha Epsilon Pi Mu Epsilon. Home: 1928 Leavenworth Manhattan KS 66502

FAUBION, ANNE, see Wolf, Virginia Simmons

FAULKNER, RONNIE WAYNE, b. Erwin, NC, Sept. 15, 1952; s. Silas Salmon and Mary Etheline (Carroll) F. Contrbr. chap. The Smaller Academic Library, A Mosaic of Memories; articles in Polity, NC Hist. Rvw, Tenn. Librarian, Tenn. Hist. Qtly, W.Va. Libraries, Library Software Rvw, Tching. Poli. Sci., Library Acquisitions, Standing Stone Press, Southeastern Librarian, ERIC Collection on Microfiche; compiler and editor The Glenville Democrat Subject Index, 1935-50, Obituaries Index, 1980-85; editor The Rotary Record, 1985—. BA in History, Campbell Coll., 1974; MA in History, East Carolina U., 1976; MSLS, U.NC, 1978, PhD, U.SC-Columbia, 1983. Reference librarian Tenn. Tech. Univ., Cookeville, 1979-81, coordinator of Public Service, 1981-84; library director Glenville State Coll., W.Va., 1984—. Recipient Wilson award Southeastern Library Assn., 1984. Mem. W.Va. Library Assn., ALA, Orgn. Am. Historians, Southeastern Library Assn., So. Hist. Assn., Natl. Trust for Historic Preservation, Library Adminstrn. and Mgmt. Assn., W.Va. Poli. Sci. Assn., W.Va. Hist. Soc., W.Va. Hist. Assn., Phi Alpha Theta. Address: Robert F Kidd Lib Glenville WV 26351

FAUST, IRVIN, b. NYC, June 11, 1924; s. Morris and Pauline (Henschel) F.; m. Jean S. Faust, Aug. 29, 1959. Author: (non-fiction) Entering Angel's World, 1963; (fiction) Roar Lion Roar And Other Stories, 1965; (novels) The Steagle, 1966 (made into film 1971), The File on Stanley Patton Buchta, 1970, Willy Remembers, 1971, Foreign Devils, 1973, A Star in the Family, 1975, Newsreel, 1980; contrbr. stories to Paris Rvw, Sewanee Rvw, Esquire, Atlantic, Northwest Rvw, Carleton Miscellany, Saturday Evening Post, Transatlantic Rvw; included in Prize Stories, O. Henry Awards, 1982, contrbr. to Voice of Am. Series: American Writing Today. BS, CCNY, 1949; MA, Columbia U. Tchrs. Coll., 1952, EdD, 1960. Lectr. fiction and creative writing U. Rochester. Served with AUS, 1943-46; Philippines, ETO. Mem. PEN. Home: 417 Riverside Dr New York NY 10025

FAUST, NAOMI FLOWE, b. Salisbury, NC, d. Christopher Leroy and Ada Luella (Graham) Flowe; m. Roy Malcolm Faust. Author: Speaking in Verse (A Book of Poems), 1974, Discipline and the Classroom Teacher, 1977, All Beautiful Things (poetry), 1983. Wrkg. on poetry book. AB, Bennett Coll., Greensboro, N.C.; MA, U. Mich.; PhD, NYU. Tchr. English, numerous schl. systems; prof. English edn. Queens Coll., CUNY, Flushing. Mem. N.Y. Poetry Forum, World Poetry Soc. Intercontinental, NCTE, AAUP. Home: 112-01 175th St Jamaica NY 11433

FAX, ELTON CLAY, b. Balt., Oct. 9, 1909; s. Mark Oakl and Willie Estelle (Smith) F.; m. Grace Elizabeth Turner, Mar. 12, 1929 (dec.); children: Betty Louise (Mrs. James Evans), Virginia Mae (dec.), Leon. Author: Contemporary Black Leader's 1970, Seventeen Black Artists, 1971, Garvey, 1972, Through Black Eyes, 1974, Black Artists of the New Generation, 1977, Hashar, 1980, Elyuchin, 1984; Soviet People as I Knew Them, 1988. 1984, BFA, U. Syracuse, 1931. Free lance writer, 1940—; participant Union Bulgarian Writers Conf., Sofia, 1977. MacDowell Colony fellow, 1967; Coretta Scott King Authors award, 1972. Mem. AG Am., PEN Am. Home: 51-28 30th Ave Woodside NY 11377

FAY, JULIE, b. Balt., Dec. 5, 1951, d. Dudley Holland Jr. and Jean Isabel (Preston) Fay. Author: In Every Mirror, 1985; contrbr. poetry: Shenandoah, Tar River Poetry, Poetry, Am. Poetry Rvw, River Styx, 13th Moon, other lit mags. BA cum laude, U. Conn., 1974; MA, Ariz. State U., 1977, MFA, U. Ariz., 1979. Poet-in-schls., Ariz. Commn. on Arts, 1976-80; vis. poet N.C. Arts Council, 1980-81; asst. prof. poetry writing, lit., composition, East Carolina U., 1981—. Grantee East Carolina U., 1982, 83; Michael Karolyi Meml. Fdn. fellow, France, 1982, 85; MacDowell Colony fellow, 1983, Va. Center for Creative Arts fellow, 1983, Millay Colony fellow, 1984; recipient Poetry prize Primavera Mag., U. Chgo., 1984. Home: Rt 2 Box 372 Winterville NC 28590

FEATHER, LEONARD GEOFFREY, b. London, Sept. 13, 1914; U.S., 1935, naturalized, 1948; s. Nathan and Felicia (Zelinski) F.; m. Jane Larrabee, May 18, 1945; 1 dau., Lorraine. Author: Inside Jazz, 1949, Encyclopedia of Jazz, 1955, Book of Jazz, 1960, New Yearbook of Jazz, 1958, New Encyclopedia of Jazz, 1960, Laughter From the Hip, 1964, The Encyclopedia of Jazz in the '60s, 1966, From Satchmo to Miles, 1972, The Pleasures of Jazz, 1976, The Encyclopedia of Jazz in the '70s, 1977, The Passion for Jazz, 1981, The Jazz Years, 1986; contrbr. to World Book Ency. and yearbooks, 1955-85. Student, Univ. Coll. Schl., London, 1920-26, St. Paul's Schl., London, 1926-31. Writer, London Melody Maker, 1933—, Esquire mag., 1943-56, Down Beat, 1951—, Playboy, 1956-62, Intl. Musician, 1961—, Show Mag., 1962-66, Rolling Stone, 1975-77, Contemporary Keyboard, 1976—; also for mags. in London, Paris, Stockholm, Berlin; arranger, Count Basie, other orchs.; composer lyrics and music, various popular singers; composer: music The Weary Blues for record album of Langston Hughes poems, 1958; script writer: TV series Jazz Scene U.S.A., 1962-63. Mem. Acad. Rec. Arts and Scis. (bd. govs. 1968-69), ASCAP. Home: 13833 Riverside Dr Sherman Oaks CA 91423

FEDCHAK, GREGG GEORGE, b. Waverly, NY, Dec. 17, 1956, s. Philip and Jeane (Arnts) F.; m. M. Elaine Robinson, Aug. 11, 1979. Author: Yammering Away: The Best of Letters Home, 1985; contrbr. to Am. Poetry Anthology, Country Poet, Another Place to Publish, North of Upstate, Earthwise, The Small-Towner. BA in Govt., St. Lawrence U., 1979. Procurement specialist Dept. Energy, Washington, 1980; Korean linguist Dept. Def., Ft. Meade, Md., 1980-83; freelance wrtr./pub. Night Tree Press, Boonville, NY., 1983—; corr., columnist Park Newspapers of St. Lawrence, Inc., 1984—. First place, Best Feature Columnist, wkly., NY Press Assn., 19896. Mem. COSMEP, Wrtrs. Assn. State N.Y., Phi Beta Kappa. Home: RD 2 140G The Gorge Road Boonville NY 13309

FEIFFER, JULES, b. NYC, Jan. 26, 1929; s. David and Rhoda (Davis) F.; m. Judith Sheftel, Sept. 17, 1961 (div. 1983); 1 dau., Kate.; m. Jennifer Allen, Sept. 11, 1983; 1 dau., Halley. Author: Sick, Sick, Sick, 1959; Passionella and other stories, 1960, The Explainers, 1961, Boy, Girl, Boy, Girl, 1962, Hold Me, 1962; (musical revue) The Explainers, 1961; (one-act play) Crawling Arnold, 1961; (novels) Harry, The Rat with Women, 1963, Ackroyd, 1977; Feiffer's Album, 1963, The Unexpurgated Memoirs of Bernard Mergendeiler, 1965, The Great Comic Book Heroes, 1965, Feiffer's Marriage Manual, 1967; (plays) Little Murders (voted best fgn. play of yr. by London critics; Obie award), 1967, Grownups, 1981; Feiffer on Civil Rights, 1967, God Bless, 1968, The White House Murder Case, 1970; (screenplays) Little Murders, 1971, Carnal Knowledge, 1971, Popeye, 1980; Pictures at a Prosecution, 1971, Feiffer on Nixon: The Cartoon Presidency, 1974; (play) Knock-Knock, 1976; (revue) Hold Me!, 1977; cartoon novel Tantrum, 1979; A Think Piece, 1982; Jules Feiffer's America: From Eisenhower to Reagan, 1982, Marriage Is an Invasion of Privacy, 1984, Feiffer's Children, 1986. Student, Art Students League, NYC, 1946, Pratt Inst., 1947-48, 49-51. Asst. to syndicated cartoonist Will Eisner, 1946-51. Cartoonist, author: syndicated Sunday page Clifford; engaged in var. art jobs, 1953-56; contrbg. cartoonist: Village Voice, 1956—; cartoons pub. weekly in London (Eng.) Observer, 1958-66, 72-82; in Playboy mag., 1959—; nationally syndicated U.S., 1959—. Recipient Acad. award for animated cartoon, Munro, 1961, spcl. George Polk Meml. award 1962, Outer Circle Drama Critics award 1969, 70, Pulitzer Prize editorial cartooning, 1986. Served with AUS, 1951-53. Mem. AG, DG (council, pres. found. 1982-83), PEN, Am. Assn. Editorial Cartoonists. Office: UP Synd 4900 Main St Kansas City MO 64112

FEIN, CHERI, b. Phila., Mar. 10, 1950, d. Leonard and Charlotte Vera (Bregman) Fein; m. George T. Gilbert, Sept. 11, 1983. Author: How to Get Your Child into Modeling and Commercials, 1986, New York: Open to the Public. A Guide to Museums, Exhibitions Spaces, Historic Houses, Botanical Gardens and Zoos, 1982; contrbr. poetry, fiction to Ploughshares, Mudfish, Nimrod, Pequod, other lit mags; contrbr. articles, book rvws. to Village Voice, NY Times Bk Rvw, Glamour, Cosmopolitan, others. BS, Oberlin (Ohio) Coll., 1972. Research dir. P&W, Inc., NYC, 1972-75, publs. dir., 1975-76, mng. dir., 1976-78, cons., 1978-80; dir. Alliance Lit. Orgns., NYC, 1979-80; N.Y. devel. coordinator Va. Center for Creative Arts, 1980-81; poetry series publicist Grove Press, NYC, 1982; freelance wrtr., 1978—; cons., guest panelist, presenter workshops for numerous orgns. Wrtr.-in-res. grantee N.Y. State Council on Arts, 1982-83, 83-84; NEA creative writing fellow, 1982-83. Mem. AG, PSA (Mary Carolyn Davies Meml. award 1978), ASCAP, NBCC, ASJA. Address: 156 Waverly Pl New York NY 10014

FEIN, LEONARD, b. Bklyn., July 1, 1934; s. Isaac M. and Clara (Wertheim) F.; m. Zelda Kleiman, 1955 (div.); children—Rachel, Naomi, Jessica. Author: Politics in Israel, 1967, Israel: Politics and People, 1968, The Ecology of the Public Schools: An Inquiry Into Community Control, 1971; editor: American Democracy: Essays on Image and Realities, 1965; Jewish Possibilities, 1987; editor- in-chief: Moment Mag., 1974-87. Home: 189 Marlborough St Boston MA 02116

FEINBERG, BEA, see Freeman, Cynthia

FEINE, PAUL MONEY, b. Springfield, MA, Feb. 27, 1942; s. Hazelden Almon Money and Mary Virginia (Burns) F.; m. Leslie Elizabeth Morginson-Eitzen, Apr. 30, 1966 (div. Apr. 30, 1973); m. Gail Frederica Zwirner, Oct. 25, 1986. Washington Bureau Chief & contrbr. arts. & columns: World Gas Rpt., 1980-86, European Offshore Petroleum Nwsltr., 1980-86, Noroil Mag., 1980-86, Utility Spotlight, 1983-86, Coal

Industry News, 1980-83; contrbr. The Energy Daily, 1980-86, Platt's Oilgram News, 1982-84, The Oil Daily, 1982-84, Energy Economist, 1984; writer, broadcaster Assoc. Press Radio Network, 1983-84; synd. columnist News-Post News Svc., 1986-87. BS, Georgetown U., 1965. Writer/ed., U.S. Dept. Commerce, Washington, 1965-69; mgr. media relns. Amer. Gas Assn., Arlington, VA, 1970-74; dir. public affairs natural Gas Supply Assn., Washington, 1974; speechwriter Fedl. Energy Admin., Washington, 1974-76, Fedl. Energy Regulatory Commn., 1976-80; freelance writer Feine Communics., Washington, 1980-86; exec. wrtr., Dominion Resources, Inc., Richmond, VA, 1986—. Mem. NPC. Mem. Presdl. Transition Team, Office of the President-Elect of the U.S., 1980-81; Natl. Press Club Bd. of Govs., 1983-86. Home: 2308 Park Ave Richmond VA 23220

FEINSTEIN, ROBERT N (ORMAN), b. Milw., Aug 10, 1915; s. Jacob I. and Jennie (Cohen) F.; m. Betty J. Greenbaum, May 15, 1941; children—Ann Elizabeth Feinstein-Levis, Jean Louise Feinstein-Lyon. Author: Oysters in Love, 1984. Contrbr. articles to profl. jnls., light verse to mags. Ed.: Chemical Bulltn., 1949-50. wrkg. on light verse. B.S. in chemistry, U. Wis., 1937, M.S. in Biochemistry, 1938, Ph.D. in Biochemistry, 1940. Instr. biochemistry to assoc. prof. U. Chgo., 1945-55; assoc. scientist to sr. scientist Argonne Natl. Lab., IL, 1955-80, retired. Guggenheim fellow, 1959-60. Mem. Fedn. Am. Scientists. Home: 4624 Highland Ave Downers Grove IL 60515

FEIRSTEIN, FREDERICK, b. NYC, Jan. 2, 1940: s. Arnold and Nettie (Schechter) F.; m. Linda Bergton, June 9, 1963; 1 son, David Ben. Author: poetry Survivors, 1974 (Outstanding Book award Choice), Manhattan Carnival, 1981, Fathering, 1982, Family History, 1986; plays The Family Circle, 1973, Carnival, 1981, Fathering, 1982. BA, U. Buffalo, 1960; MA, NYU, 1961. Guggenheim fellow in poetry, 1979-80; recipient award in playwriting OADR, 1976, award in poetry CAPS, 1977, John Masefield award PSA, 1977. Mem. PEN, DG, WG East, PSA. Address: Dumler 575 Madison Ave New York NY 10022

FEIWEL, JEAN LESLIE, b. NYC, Feb. 5, 1953; d. Henry and Maria (Weschler) F. Asst. to mng. editor Avon Books, NYC, 1976-77, asst. to children's book editor, 1977, sr. editor, children's books, 1977-81, editorial dir. books for young readers, 1981-83; editorial dir., div. v.p. Secondary Book Group, Scholastic, Inc., NYC, 1983—. Mem. Children's Book Council (dir. 1982—), Am. Assn. Pubs. (dir. intellectual freedom com. 1983—). BA, Sarah Lawrence Coll., 1976. Office: Scholastic 730 Broadway New York NY 10003

FELDMAN, IRVING, b. Bklyn., Sept. 22, 1928; m. Carmen Alvarez del Olmo, 1955; 1 son, Fernando R. Author: Works and Days, 1961, The Pripet Marshes, 1965, Magic Papers, 1970, Lost Originals, 1972, Leaping Clear, 1976, New and Selected Poems, 1979, Teach Me, Dear Sister, 1983; contrbr. to periodicals. Edn. CCNY, Columbia U. Recipient Poetry prize Jewish Book Council Am., 1962; Ingram Merrill Fdn. grantee, 1963; Natl. Inst. and Am. Acad. Arts and Letters award, 1973; Guggenheim fellow, 1973; N.Y. State CAPS grantee, 1980. Home: 349 Berryman Dr Buffalo NY 14226

FELDMAN, JOSEPH DAVID, b. Hartford, CT, Dec. 13, 1916; s. Max and Rebecca (Hurewitz) F.; m. Nomi Granott, Oct. 27, 1926; children—Orna FeldmanHall, Danah, Ruth. Author 151 scientific articles in refereed jnls., chapters in 9 books. BA, Yale U., 1937; MD, Long Island Coll. Med., 1941. USPHS Research Fellow, NIH, 1948-50; instr. then lectr. Hebrew U./Hadassah Med. Schl., Jerusalem, 1950-54; assoc. prof. pathology, Pitts. U. Schl. Med. (PA), 1954-56, prof. pathology 1956-61; mem. Scripps Clinic & Res. Fdn., La Jolla, CA, 1961-83 (now Emeritus); ed.-in-chief Jnl of Immunology, San Diego, CA, 1971-87. Served to Major, Med. Corps, 1941-45, S.W. Pacific. Home: 13030 Via Grimaldi Del Mar CA 92014

FELDMAN, LAWRENCE HERBERT, b. NYC, Nov. 27, 1942; s. Jack and Ruth (Menzer) F. Author: Papers of Eschintla & Guanacapan, 1974, Riverine Maya, 1975, A Fragment of an Early K'tkchi Vocabulary, 1975, Indexing Early Central Mexican Documents, 1979, A Tumpline Economy, 1985, History of the Foundation of the Town of Chamiquin, 1987. Contrbr. numerous articles to profl. jnls. Wrkg. on When the Earth Shock, the Story of the 1917 Quake in Guatemala; Those Who Dared, Officers Who Won the War for the Nationalists. B.A., San Diego State Univ., 1964; M.A., U. Calif.-Los Angeles, 1966; Ph.D., Penn. State U., 1971. Museum dir., curator U. Mo., Columbia, 1973-84; free-lance wrtr., 1984—; Fulbright researcher, Guatemala, 1987. Grantee NEH, 1975-77, 83, Am. Philosophical Soc., 1979; Woodrow Wilson fellow, 1984-85. Home: 13 Calle 0-43 Guatemala City Guatemala Zone 10 01010 Guatemala-Ciudad

FELDMAN, RUTH DUSKIN, b. Chgo., June 13, 1934; d. Boris and Rita (Schayer) Duskin; m. Gilbert Feldman, June 14, 1953; children—Steven Jeffrey, Laurie Nadine, Heidi Carolyn. Author: Chemi the Magician, 1947, Whatever Happened to the Quiz Kids, 1982. Contrbr. articles to popular Mags., newspapers including Chgo. Tribune, N.Y. Daily News, Discovery, Woman's Day, others. Guest ed. Mademoiselle, 1952; creative ed. Humanistic Judaism, Farmington Hills, MI, 1983—. Wrkg. on 4th ed. of Human Development. B.S., Northwestern U., 1954. Tchr., Nichols Sch., Evanston, IL, 19d54-55, U.S. Army, Fort Sheridan, IL, 1964; tchr., curriculum coord. Congregation Beth Or, Deerfield, IL, 1970-80; corr., staff wrtr. Lerner Newspapers, Highland Park, IL, 1973-81. Coord. Jr. Great Books reading program, Highland Park, 1962-73. Recipient Best column award Lerner Newspapers, 1978, 79, Hon. Mention for features, 1979, 80, Benjamin Fine award Natl. Assn. Secondary Sch. Principals, 1983, Lowell Thomas award runnerup SATW, 1986. Mem. AG, AL, ASJA, SPJ, SMA, Ind. Wrtrs. Chgo., NWU. Home: 935 Fairview Rd Highland Park IL 60035

FELDMAN, RUTH (WASBY), b. May 21, 1911; m. Moses D. Feldman (dec.). Author: The Ambition of Ghosts, 1979, Poesie di Ruth Feldman, 1981, To Whom It May Concern, 1986; transls: Moments of Reprieve, 1986, Liber Fulguralis, 1986; co-ed., transl., Collected Poems of Lucio Piccolo, 1973, Selected Poetry of Andrea Zansotto, 1975, Shema, 1976, Italian Poetry Today, 1979, The Dawn Is Always New, 1980, The Hands of the South, 1980, The Dry Air of the Fire, 1981. Contrbr. to numerous lit mags, revw, anthologies. BA, Wellesley Coll, 1931, workshops, Boston Univ., Radcliffe Inst. Devil's Advocate Award, 1972, monthly awards Poetry Society of Am., Duncan Lawrie Award, Sotheby's Intl. Poetry Prize Competition, 1982. Mem. PSA, New Eng. Poetry Club, Am. Lit. Transl. Assn. Co-winner John Florio, 1976, Circe-Sabaudia, 1983. Home: 221 Mt. Auburn St Cambridge MA 02138

FELDSTEIN, ALBERT B., b. Bklyn., Oct. 24, 1925; s. Max and Beatrice (Segal) F.; m. Claire Szep, Sept. 2, 1944 (div. Jan. 13, 1967); m. Natalie (Lee) Sigler, Jan. 27, 1967 (dec. Sept. 7, 1986;) children: Leslie, Susan (dec.), Jamie, Alan Weiss, Mark. Free-lance artist-writer comic book industry, NYC., 1945-47; freelance artist-writer, editor, E.C. publs. Inc., NYC., 1947-55; editor MAD Mag., 1955-85; supr.: MAD TV Spcl, 1974; Author TV scripts; illustrator children's record album covers. Student, Bklyn. Coll., 1942-43; League scholar, Art Students League, 1943-43. Served with USAAF, 1943-45. Home: Wellers Bridge Rd Roxbury CT 06783

FELL, FREDERICK VICTOR, b. Bklyn., May 21, 1910; s. Samuel and Victoria (Greenhut) F.; m. Selma Shampain, May 18, 1975; children—Linda Fell Firetein, Nancy. Author: (pseudonym Vic Fredericks) Crackers in Bed, 1953, More For Doctors Only, 1953, Jest Married, 1958, For Golfers Only, 1964, Wit and Wisdom of Presidents, 1966, others. Student, NYU, 1928-31; LLB, Bklyn. Law Schl., 1935. Pres. Frederick Fell Pubs., Inc., NYC, 1943-81; prin. Frederick Fell & Assocs., Inc., Literary Agts., Hollywood, Fla., 1981—. Mem. Assn. Am. Pubs., Am. Booksellers Assn., Book Group South Fla. Home: 3800 Hillcrest Dr 1120 Hollywood FL 33021

FELL, MARY ELIZABETH, b. Worcester, MA, Sept. 22, 1947, d. Paul Henry and Elizabeth Adrena (Delong) F. Author: The Triangle Fire, 1983, The Persistence of Memory, 1984. BA, Worcester State Coll., 1969; MFA, U. Mass., 1981. Info. and referral specialist Office Human Services, Worcester, 1976-77; teaching assoc. U. Mass., Amherst, 1978-81; asst. prof. Ind. U. East, Richmond, 1981—. Mem. lit. panel Ind. Arts Commn., 1984—. Recipient award Natl. Poetry Series, 1983; Ind. Arts Commn. master artist fellow, 1985. Mem. AWP, MLA, NCTE. Home: 1118 Ridge St Richmond IN 47374

FELLOWES, PETER, b. Washington, Oct. 26, 1944. Contrbr. poetry to Karomu, Poetry Now, Yale Rvw, Tri Qtly, other lit. mags. BA, Colgate U., 1966; MA, Johns Hopkins U., 1967; PhD, U. Va., 1973. Instr. English, Mary Washington Coll., Fredericksburg, Va., 1967-72; lectr. English, U. Va., Charlottesville, 1972-74, Hampden-Sydney Coll., Va., 1972-73; prof. English, North Park Coll., Chgo., 1974—. Gilman fellow, 1966. Office: N Park Coll 5125 N Spaulding Chicago IL 60625

FELSEN, KARL EDWIN, b. Hornell, NY, July 29, 1948; s. Irwin and Nell (Shaffer) F.; m. Carol Ann Terko; children—Kristen Elizabeth, Alexander Karl. Contrbr. wrtr. various mags. including Cosmopolitan and Shakespeare Quarterly. BA, U. Santa Clara, CA, 1969; MA, State U. NY, Albany, 1972, PhD,1975. Teaching fellow, State U. NY, 1972-74, instr., 1975; correspondence dir., NY State Assembly, 1976-81; project dir., media specialist NY State Council on Children & Youth, 1981-82; public relations dir. NY State Civil Service Dept., 1982-84; public info. dir. NY State Dept. of Taxation & Finance, 1984—. Home: 26 Pinewood Rd Guilderland NY 12084

FENADY, ANDREW JOHN, b. Toledo, OH, Oct. 4, 1928; s. John Andrew and Mary (Beneta) Fenady; m. Mary Frances Dolan, June 30, 1956;

children—Gena, Duke, Sean, Shannon, Andy Frank, Thomas. Novels: The Man With Bogart's Face, 1977, The Secret of Sam Marlow, 1980, Claws of the Eagle, 1984, The Summer of Jack London, 1985. BA, U. of Toledo. Film and TV wrtr. and producer, songwriter. pres., Fenady Assoc., Los Angeles, 1959—. Awards: Edgar Allen Poe Award, Emmy awards, 1954, 55, 56, MWA. Home: 126 N Rossmore Los Angeles CA 90004

FENICK, BARBARA JEAN, b. St. Paul, Jan. 19, 1951, d. Harvey H. and Leah S. (Pogoler) Fenick; m. Rick A. Kolodziej, Nov. 14, 1981; children—Nicholas Sean, Jessica Lynne. Ed.: Collecting the Beatles, vol. 1, 1982, vol. 2, 1985. BA, U. Minn., 1976. Ed. The Write Thing, Mpls., 1974—. Office: Box 18807 Minneapolis MN 55418

FENNELLY, TONY, b. Orange, NJ, Nov. 25, 1945; d. Thomas Richard and Mary Virginia (Lynch) Fennelly; m. Richard Catoire, Dec. 24, 1972. Author: The Glory Hole Murders, 1985, The Closet Hanging, 1987. Wrkg. on Kiss Yourself Goodbye. B.A. in Drama, U. New Orleans, 1976. Mem. AG, MWA, NWC. Home: 921 Clouet New Orleans LA 70117

FERACA, JEAN STEPHANIE, b. NYC, Dec. 20, 1943, d. Steven Edward and Rose Marguerite (Sinisgalli) Feraca; m. Frank Louis Casale, Nov. 30, 1968 (div. 1975); 1 son, Giancarlo; m. 2d, Thomas Leroy Fernow, Sept. 21, 1978; 1 son, Dominick. Author: South From Rome: Il Mezzogiorno, 1975; contrbr. to anthologies: Kentucky Renaissance, 1976, Two Decades of New Poets, 1983, The Dream Book, 1985. BA cum laude Manhattanville, Coll., 1965; MA, U. Mich., 1971. Poet-in-schls., Ohio Arts Council, 1975-76, Ky. Arts Commn., 1977-79; poet-in-res. Transylvania U., Lexington, Ky., 1976-77; arts producer, reporter sta. WGUC, Cin., 1980-81; humanities producer Wis. Public Radio, Madison, 1984—. Recipient Hopwood award for poetry, for essay, U. Mich., 1971, Discovery award 1st prize, NYC, 1975. Mem. P&W. Home: 1418 Winslow Lane Madison WI 53711

FEREBEE, GIDEON, JR., b. NYC, Oct. 29, 1950; s. Gideon and Alesia (Foreman) F. Contrbr. poems to lit. mags. Wrkg. on performance collaboration with Chasen Gaver. BA, Valparaiso U., 1972. Theater Reviewer City Paper, Washington, 1984-85. Leader poetry workshop Shilo Bapt. Ch., Washington, 1985-86. Grantee Painted Bride Arts Ctr., Phila., 1986. Mem. Wrtr.'s Ctr., Am. Fedn. TV Radio Artists. Home: 1224 C St NE Washington DC 20003

FERGUSON, DOROTHY MARGUERITTE, b. Dorchester, MA; d. John Robert and Josephine (Friel) Hughes; m. Daniel John M. Ferguson, Feb. 12, 1938; children—Gail Ferguson Washburn, Diane Ferguson Donaldson. Poetry in anthologies. Wrkg. on novel. Student U. Pa., 1929-31, U. Md., 1950-51. Tng. program adminstr. Community Devel. Fdn., Norwalk, Conn., 1962-67, wrtr., ed., 1962-67; cons. Save the Children, Westport, Conn., 1968—; ed., sec.-treas. Intl. Soc. Community Devel., N.Y.C., 1968—. Home: 43 East Ave Norwalk CT 06851

FERGUSON, JOAN M., b. Long Island, NY, Feb. 15, 1930, d. William Adolph and Helen Celia (Closson) Metzger; m. Henry Ferguson, July 18, 1953; children—Jean Ferguson Gerbini, Cynthia Ferguson Waldman, Henry C., Margaret S. Author: Village Life Study Kit (with others), 1971, The Fabric of India, 1974, Discovering the Prehistoric Iroquois, 1982, Tracking Down the Past, 1983, Curriculum Guides to N.Y. State Museum Films, 1984; ed.: Red Dust on the Green Leaves (novel by Johy Gay), 1973, The Africa Sketches, 1974. Wrkg. on suspense novel, novel of India. BA, Wellesley Coll., 1951. Vice pres., pub. InterCulture Assn., Thompson, Conn., 1969-80; ednl. kit designer N.Y. State Mus., Albany, 1981-84; freelance wrtr., Albany, 1984—. Home: 5 Chestnut Hill N Loudonville NY 12211

FERGUSON, WILLIAM R., b. Fall River, MA, Feb. 14, 1943; s. William and Helen (Rotch) F.; m. Raquel Halty, June 22, 1968 (div. Dec., 1980); m. 2d, Nancy King, Nov. 28, 1983. Author: La Versificacion Imitativa En Fernando de Herrera (monograph), 1981, Freedom and Other Fictions (short stories), 1984. BA, Harvard, 1965, PhD, 1975. Asst. prof. Spanish, Boston U., Boston, 1971-77; assoc. prof. Spanish, Clark U., Worcester, Mass., 1977—. Home: 1 Tahanto Rd Worcester MA 01602

FERLINGHETTI, LAWRENCE, b. Yonkers, NY, 1920; s. Charles and Clemence (Mendes-Monsanto) F.; m. 1951; children—Julie, Lorenzo. Author: (poetry) Pictures of the Gone World, 1955, A Coney Island of the Mind, 1958, Starting from San Francisco, 1961, After the Cries of the Birds, The Secret Meaning of Things, Open Eye Open Heart, 1973, Who Are We Now?, 1976, Landscapes of Living and Dying, 1979, Endless Life: Selected Poems, 1981; (novel) Her, 1960; (plays) Back Roads to Far Places; (poetry and prose jnl) Northwest Ecolog, 1978, (with Nancy J. Peters) Literary San Francisco: A Pictorial History, 1980; editor: City Lights Books, Anarchist Resistance Press. AB, U. N.C.; MA, Columbia, Doctorat De L'Universite, Sorbonne, 1950. Founder (with Peter D. Martin) first all paperbound bookstore in U.S., City Lights Books, San Francisco, firm also publishes works of modern poets and writers; widely traveled poetry reader; participant, One World Poetry Festival, Amsterdam, 1981. Served with USNR, World War II. Address: City Lts 261 Columbus Ave San Francisco CA 94133

FEROE, PAUL JAMES, b. Duluth, MN, May 16, 1951; s. Arthur M. and Lucille (Johnson) F.; m. Julie Nelson, Aug. 18, 1980; 2 daus., Kirsten, Rebecca. Ed. Sucking-Stones mag. (with Neil Klotz), 1973, Silent Voices: Recent American Poems On Nature, 1979. Wrkg. on a series of cassette tapes by Robert Bly. BA, St. Olaf Coll., 1973. Ed. College Press Svc., Denver, 1973-79; ed. and pub. Ally Press, St. Paul, 1973—. Bd. dirs. Vegetarian Soc. Colo., Denver, 1973-79, Food Co-op, St. Paul, 1984. Address: Ally Press 524 Orleans St St Paul MN 55107

FERRARO, BERNADETTE A., b. Newark, Apr. 19, 1952; d. Dominic A. and Josephine C. (Massucco) F. Contrbr. poetry to Il Lettere Mag., 1972, 1973, Our World's Most Cherished Poems, 1986; contrbr. articles to Respiration, 1981, Intl. Synopses Periodical/Div. Thoracic Diseases, 1982. BA in Zoology, Rutgers U., 1974; cytology degree, U. Med. & Dent. of NJ, 1977, magna cum laude. Clinical cytologist U. Med. & Dent. of NJ, Newark, 1978-80, biomed. writer assist., 1980-82, cytology prog. & edn. coord., lectr. in cytology, Dept. of Pathology, 1982; biomed. writing instr., Nutley, NJ, 1982—. Mem. AAAS, NY Acad. Scis., Am. Film. Inst., profl. orgns. Golden Poet Award, 1986. Home: 77 Povershon Rd Nutley NJ 07110

FERRELL, NANCY WARREN, b. Appleton, WI, Aug. 23, 1932; d. Harry Warren and Carolyn Burg; m. C. Edgar Ferrell, Mar. 3, 1955; children—Patricia, William. Author: (young readers) The Fishing Industry, 1984, Passports to Peace, 1986, The New World of Amateur Radio, 1986. Contrbr. short stories to mags. including Jack and Jill, Highlights for Children, Humpty Dumpty, others. B.A., Lawrence Coll., 1954. Tchr. Bureau of Indian Affairs Schls., Sitka, AK, 1958-62; liason head Bur. Labor Statistics, Juneau, AK, 1963-66; children's library worker Juneau Libraries, 1980—. Recipient Outstanding Achievement award City and Boro of Juneau, 1986. Mem. SCBW, NLAPW (1st place for non-fiction 1986), Alaska Library Assn. Home: 512 5th St Juneau AK 99801

FERRELL, ROBERT HUGH, b. Cleve., May 8, 1921; s. Ernest Henry and Edna Lulu (Rentsch) F.; m. Lila Esther Sprout, Sept. 8, 1956; 1 dau., Carolyn Irene. Author: Peace in Their Time, 1952, American Diplomacy in the Great Depression, 1957, American Diplomacy: A History, 1959, 2d rev. ed., 1969, 3d ed., 1975, 4th ed., 1987, Frank B. Kellogg and Henry L. Stimson, 1963 (with M.G. Baxter and J.E. Wiltz) Teaching of American History in High Schools, 1964, George C. Marshall, 1966, (with R.B. Morris and W. Greenleaf) America: A History of the People, 1971, (with others) Unfinished Century, 1973, Harry S. Truman and the Modern American Presidency, 1983, Truman: A Centenary Remembrance, 1984, Woodrow Wilson and World War I, 1985; editor: Off the Record: The Private Papers of Harry S. Truman, 1980, The Autobiography of Harry S. Truman, 1980, The Eisenhower Diaries, 1981, Dear Bess: The Letters from Harry to Bess Truman, 1984, Joseph Douglas Lawrence, Fighting Soldier, 1985, (with Samuel Flagg Bemis) The American Secretaries of State and Their Diplomacy, new series 10 vols., 1963-85. BS in Edn., Bowling Green State U., 1946, BA, 1947, LLD (hon.), 1971; MA, Yale U., 1948, PhD, 1951. Served with USAAF, 1942-45. Home: 512 S Hawthorne St Bloomington IN 47401

FERRELL, SKIP, see Mynatt, Cecil F.

FERRINI, VINCENT, b. Saugus, MA, June 24, 1913, s. Giovanni and Rena (DeCarlo) F.; children—Sheila, Owen. Author 30 books of poetry and plays including: Selected Poems, 1976; author: Know Fish, books 1, 2, 1979, book 3, 1984, books 4, 5, 1986. Wrkg. on books 6, 7 of Know Fish. Recipient Playwriting award Mass. Council on Arts, Boston, 1976. Mem. Dramatist Guild, Poet of Gloucester. Home: 126 E Main Gloucester MA 01603

FERRIS, KIMBERLEE ROBIN, b. Peoria, IL, July 21, 1955; d. William Dale and Juanita Evelyn (Stout) Ferris. Poetry in anthologies. Wrkg. on poetry, novel. Diploma Bronson Meth. Hosp. Sch. Nursing; student U. Mich.-Flint. Nurse Oakdale Regional Center, Lapeer, Mich., 1978—, asst. ed., reporter Oakdale Happenings, 1987—. Home 110 Crestview Dr Lapeer MI 48446

FERRIS, ABBOTT LAMOYNE, b. Jonestown, MS, Jan. 31, 1915; s. Alfred William O. and Grace Chiles (Mitchell) F.; m. Ruth E. Sparks, Dec. 21, 1940; children—John Abbott, William Thomas. Contrbr. numerous chpts. to books, articles to profl. jnls. (Books) Attitudes of Far Eastern Air Force Personnel Toward Natives, 1954, The Allocation of Material-Control Functions in Six Armament—Electronics Maintenance Squadrons, 1956, Reducing Traffic Accidents by Use of Group Discussion-Decision, ed. 1957, The National Recreation Survey, 1962,

Indicators of Trends in American Education, 1969, Indicators of Change in the American Family, 1970, Indicators of Trends in the Status of American Women, 1971, Research and the 1970 Census, ed. 1971, A Career in Demography, 1974, The Federal Effort, 1979; (jnls.) Editor: The Sociologist, 1965-68, PAA Affairs, 1968-71, Social Indicators Research, April 1979, The Southern Sociologist, 1981-84, Dinet, 1984—. B.J., U. Mo, 1937; M.A. in Sociology, U.N.C., 1943, Ph.D. in Sociology, 1950. Assoc. study dir. office of econ. & manpower studies Natl. Sci. Fdn., 1962-67; research sociologist Russell Sage Fdn., 1967-70; chmn. sociology & anthropology dept. Emory U. Atlanta, 1970-76, prof., 1970-82, emeritus prof., 1982—. Served with U.S. Army, 1943-46. Mem. Sociological Research Assn., Am. Sociology Assn., D.C. Sociology Soc. (pres. 1969-70; Stuart A. Rice award 1984), Southern Sociological Soc. (pres. 1986-87). Home: 1273 Oxford Rd NE Atlanta GA 30306

FERTIG, HOWARD, b. NYC, s. Benjamin and Rose (Mallman) F.; m. Ellen C. Bandler; children—Paul, Daniel. Book reviewer Village Voice, 1956-57; editor Queens Post, NYC, 1957-60; asst. editor Commentary mag., 1960; editor Alfred A. Knopf, Inc., NYC, 1961-62; chief editor Univ. Library Paperbacks, Grosset & Dunlap, NYC, 1962-65; pres., editor-in-chief Howard Fertig, Inc., Pub., NYC, 1966—. BA, NYU, Mem. MLA, PEN. Home: 315 E 68th St New York NY 10021

FETLER, ANDREW, b. Riga, Latvia, July 24, 1925, came to U.S., 1939, s. Basil Andreyevitch and Barbara (Kovaleski) Fetler-Malof. Author: The Travelers, 1965, To Byzantium, 1976. BA, Loyola U., Chgo., 1959; MFA, U. Iowa, 1964. Prof. dept English U. Mass., Amherst, 1964—. Recipient Fiction award NEA, 1976, 83, O. Henry award, Doubleday, 1977, 84; Guggenheim Fdn. fiction fellowship, 1978. Mem. PEN, AG. Home: 125 Amity St Amherst MA 01002

FEUERSTEIN, GEORG, b. Wurzburg, WGer, May 27, 1947; came to U.S., 1981; s. Erwin and Dorothea (Gimperlein) F.; m. Patricia Lamb, Feb. 14, 1985; children—David, Daniel. Author: Yoga—Sein Wesen und Werden (in German), 1969, The Essence of Yoga: A Contribution to the Psychohistory of Indian Civilization, 1974, Introduction to the Bhagavad-Gita: Its Philosophy and Cultural Setting, 1974, 2d edit., 1983, Textbook of Yoga, 1975, Yoga-Sutra: An Exercise in the Methodology of Textual Analysis, 1979, The Bhagavad-Gita: A Critical Rendering, 1980, The Yoga-Sutra of Patanjali: A New Translation and Commentary, 1980, The Philosophy of Classical Yoga, 1980. Structures of Consciousness: The Genius of Jean Gebser—An Introduction and Critique, 1987; ed. 13 books; co-author 2 books. Wrkg. on book on creativity in relation to self-transcendence. M Letters U. Durham, Eng., 1976. Editorial dir. Dawn Horse Press, San Rafael, Calif., 1981-86; dir. Integral Pub., Lower Lake, Calif., 1986—; co-dir. Calif. Center for Jean Gebser Studies, Felton, 1986—; ed. Spectrum Rvw., 1987—. Mem. AG. Home: Box 1386 Lower Lake CA 95457

FEUERWERKER, ALBERT, b. Cleve., Nov. 6, 1927; s. Martin and Gizella (Feuerwerker) F.; m. Yi-tsi Mei, June 11, 1955; children—Alison, Paul. Author: China's Early Industrialization, 1958, History in Communist China, 1968, The Chinese Economy 1870-1911, 1969, Rebellion in 19th Century China, 1975, The Foreign Establishment in China, 1976, Economic Trends in the Republic of China, 1977, Chinese Social and Economic History from the Song to 1900, 1982; bd. editors: Am. Hist. Review, 1970-75, The China Qtly, 1967—, Comparative Studies in Soc. and History, 1964—. AB, Harvard U., 1950, PhD, 1957. Served with AUS, 1946-47. NEH fellow, 1971-72, Guggenheim fellow, 19878-88; Social Sci. Research Council-ACLS fellow, 1962-63. Fellow AAAS. Home: 1224 Ardmoor Ave Ann Arbor MI 48103

FEYNMAN, RICHARD PHILLIPS, b. MYC, May 11, 1918; s. Melville Arthur and Lucille (Phillips) F. Author: Quantum Electrodynamics, Theory of Fundamental Processes, Character of Physical Law, Statistical Mechanics; contbr. theory of quantum electrodynamics, beta decay and liquid helium. B.S. MIT, 1939; Ph.D., Princeton, 1942. Address: Physics Dept Calif Inst Technology Pasadena CA 91125

FICKLING, AMY LEIGH, b. Raleigh, NC, June 17, 1957, d. Dwight Russell and Frances Maxine (Kerley) Fickling. BA in English and History, Wake Forest U., 1979; MA in journalism, Am. U., 1985. Wire ed., arts critic The Dispatch, Lexington, N.C., 1979-83; copy ed., reviewer Times-Daily, Florence, Ala., 1984; mng. ed. Olney (Md.) Courier-Gazette, 1985—. Mem. Soc. Profl. Journalists, Kappa Tau Alpha. Home: 510 Palmtree Dr Gaithersburg MD 20878

FIEDLER, LESLIE AARON, b. Newark, Mar. 8, 1917; s. Jacob J. and Lillian (Rosenstrauch) F.; m. Margaret Ann Shipley, Oct. 7, 1939 (div. 1972); children—Kurt, Eric, Michael, Deborah, Jenny, Miriam; m. 2d, Sally Andersen, 1973; stepchildren: Soren and Eric Charles Andersen. Author: (with others) Leaves of Grass: 100 Years After, 1955, An End to Innocence, 1955, The Art of the Essay, 1959, rev. ed. 1969, The Image of the Jew in American Fiction, 1959, Love and Death in the American Novel, 1960, rev. ed. 1966, No, In Thunder, 1960, Pull Down Vanity (stories), 1962, The Second Stone (novel), 1963, (with J. Vinocur) The Continuing Debate, 1964, Waiting for the End, 1964, Back to China, 1965, (with others) The Girl in the Black Raincoat, 1966, The Last Jew in America, 1966, The Return of the Vanishing American, 1967, Nude Croquet and Other Stories, 1969, Being Busted, 1970, Collected Essays, 1971, The Stranger in Shakespeare, 1972, The Messengers Will Come No More, 1974, In Dreams Awake, 1975, Freaks, 1977, A Fiedler Reader, 1977, The Inadvertent Epic, 1979, Olaf Stapledon, 1982, What Was Literature, 1982; editor: Master of Ballantrae, 1951, Waiting for God (S. Weil), 1952, Poems of Whitman, 1959, (with Arthur Zeiger) O Brave New World, 1967; assoc. editor: Ramparts, 1959-65; contrbg. editor: Am. Judaism; lit. editor: Running Man, 1967-69; contrbr. short stories, poems, articles to jnls. U.S. and abroad. BA, N.Y. U., 1938; MA, U. Wis., 1939, PhD, 1941; postdoctoral student, Harvard, 1946-47. Served from ensign to lt. (j.g.) USNR, 1942-46. Rockefeller fellow humanities, 1946-47; recipient Furioso prize for Poetry, 1951; Fulbright fellow, 1951-53; Kenyon Rvw fellow in criticism, 1956-57; award natl. Inst. Arts and Letters, 1957; Guggenheim fellow, 1970-71. Mem. MLA, PEN. Home: 154 Morris Ave Buffalo NY 14214

FIEDLER, SALLY A., b. Joliet, IL, Nov. 13, 1939, d. Terry Patillo and Blanche (Wright) Smith; m. Sayre D. Andersen, 1960 (div. 1966); children—Soren M. Eric C.; m. 2d, Leslie A. Fiedler, Feb. 1, 1973; 6 stepchildren. Author: Timepieces, 1971, Skin and Bones, 1972, To Illinois, With Love, 1975. BA, U. Ill., Urbana, 1961, MA, 1962, PhD in English, 1967. Asst. prof. English U. Ill., Urbana, 1967-73; tchr. poet-in-the-schls. program, N.Y. State, 1974-76; tchr. Nichols Schl., Buffalo, 1979-84, Buffalo Sem., 1984-86. Mem. N.Y. State P&W, Niagara-Erie Wrtrs. Home: 154 Morris Ave Buffalo NY 14214

FIELD, EDWARD, (Bruce Elliot), b. Bklyn., June 7, 1924, s. Louis and Hilda (Taubman) F. Author: Stand Up, Friend, With Me, 1963, Variety Photoplays, 1967, Eskimo Songs and Stories, 1973, A Full Heart, 1977, Stars in My Eyes, 1978, (under name Bruce Elliot) Village, 1982; ed. A Geography of Poets, 1979. Student NYU, 1942, 46-48, 50. Served to 1st lt. USAAF, 1942-46, ETO. Recipient Lamont award AAP, 1962, Shelley Meml. award PSA, Prix de Rome, Natl. Inst. Arts and Letters, 1982-83; Guggenheim fellow, 1963. Home: 463 West St Apt D610 NYC 10014

FIELD, HARRY RUSH, see Schlert, Mary Esther

FIELD, STANLEY, b. Ukraine, Russia, s. Henry and Nina (Cibulski) F.; m. Joyce Stillman, Dec. 7, 1935; children—Jeffrey Michael, Constance Elyse. Author: Television and Radio Writing, 1958, Bible Stories, 1968, Guide to Opportunities in the Sciences, 1967, Professional Broadcast Writer's Handbook, 1974, The Mini-Documentary, 1975, The Freelancer, 1984; contrbr. to Va. Country Mag., Home Life Mag., Jnl of Broadcasting, The Disciple Mag., numerous others. BA, Bklyn. Coll., 1934. Info. specialist Dept of Army, Washington, 1942-75; adj. prof. Am. Univ., Washington, 1955-78; dir. creative writing workshops, 1979-85; freelance wrtr., San Diego, 1985—. Media dir. Arlingtonians for Better Community, Va., 1949. Mem. AG, P&W. Home: 5196 Middleton Rd San Diego CA 92109

FIELDING, PEGGY LOU MOSS, (P.M. Fielding), b. Davenport, OK, Oct. 28, d. John Richard and Hazel (Matlock) Moss. Author: New Day for Love, 1984, Summer Job, Winter Love, 1984, Season of One Night, 1984, A National Directory of Four Year Colleges, Two Year Colleges and Post High School Training Programs for Young People with Learning Disabilities; contrbr. articles to Computer Bookbase, Family Computing, Nation's Business, others; contrbr. poetry, cartoons to Broomstick Mag.; contrbr. stories to Union Gospel Press, Crusader, Sun Press anthology. BS, Central State U.; MA, U. Santo Tomas. Wrtr., ed. Prtnrs. in Pub., Tulsa, 1976—. Children's lit. fellow U. Ga., 1970. Mem. Okla. Wrtrs. Fedn., Soc. Scholarly Pub., Tulsa Night Wrtrs., Romance Wrtrs. Am., WWA, Northeastern Okla. Romance Authors. Address: Prtnrs in Pub 1419 W 1st St Tulsa OK 74127

FIELDS, RICK D., b. NYC, May 16, 1942, s. Allen D. and Reva (Fried) F. Author: How the Swans Came to the Lake, A Narrative History of Buddhism in America, 1980, rev. ed., 1986, Chop Wood, Carry Water, A Guide to Finding Spiritual Fulfillment in Everyday Life (with others), 1985; ed.: Loka, A Journal from Naropa Institute, 1975/76. Student Harvard U., 1960-62, 63. Contrbg. ed. New Age Jnl, Boston, 1980—; ed.-in-chief Vajradhatu Sun, Boulder, Colo., 1983—. Artist-in-residence Briarcombe Fdn., Bolinas, Calif., 1979; Time, Inc. fellow in non-fiction Bread Loaf Wrtrs. Conf., Middlebury, Vt., 1982. Office: Vajradhatu Sun 1345 Spruce St Boulder CO 80302

FIELDS, SUSAN LOUISE, (S.S. James), b. Fremont, OH, Dec. 2, 1952; d. Darwin Arthur and Jean Louise (Swedersky) Reichert; m. Jerry Allen Fields, Nov. 6, 1970; children—Tonya Sue, Terra Michelle. Poetry in anthologies. Wrkg. on poetry. Student Vanguard Vocatl. Center, 1969-71, Terra Teh. Coll., 1978-81. Quality Control analyst, inspector Heinz U.S.A., Fremont, Ohio, 1978—. Recipient awards, letters of commendation. Home: 130 N Columbus Ave Fremont OH 43420

FIFIELD, WILLIAM, b. Chgo., Apr. 5, 1916, s. Lawrence Wendell and Juanita (Sloan) F.; m. Mercedes McCambridge, Donna Hamilton, then Aaltje Guyt; children—John Lawrence, Donnali, Brian Robert, Edwina. Author: The Devil's Marchioness (novel), 1957, The Sign of Taurus (novel), 1959, Matadora (novel), 1960, The Sherry Royalty, 1978, Entretiens avec Jean Cocteau (in French) 1973, Modigliani (biography), 1976, In Search of Genius, 1982; contrbr. to: Story Mag., Penthouse, Paris Rvw, Gentlemen's Qtly, numerous other publs. AB magna cum laude, Whitman Coll., 1937. Announcer, CBS, Chgo., 1937-40, wrtr., Hollywood, Calif., 1941-42, announcer, dir., NYC, 1944-45; freelance wrtr., Europe, 1946-85, Rancho Palos Verdes, Calif., 1985—. Recipient O. Henry Meml. award for short stories, 1944. Home: 5700 Ravenspur Dr 307 Rancho Palos Verdes CA 90274

FILCHOCK, E., Contrbr. poetry: Am. Poetry Showcase, Yes Press, Cambridge Collection, numerous other publs. and anthologies; lyricist for reord albums: Nashco Records, Brea Music, Inc., Columbine Records, Rainbow Records, others; contrbr. children's stories: Little People's Press. Wrkg. on poetry, lyrics, short stories. BS in Edn., Kent State U. Tchr. public schs., Cleve. Mem. Akron Manuscript Club. Home: 32447 Hamilton St Solon OH 44139

FILLINGHAM, PATRICIA, b. Bklyn., May 4, 1924; d. William G. Parmelee and Eva (Sanderson) Child; m. Peter J. Fillingham, June 29, 1951; children—Michael, David, Lydia. Author: Progress Notes on a State of Mind, 1980, John Calvin, 1982, Anna's Elephant, 1983. Ed.: Kartunes (Cornelius Eady), 1980, From a Distance (Marta Fenyves), 1981, Breathe! An Antismoking Anthology (Shel Horowitz, ed.), 1981, Running Backwards (Barbara A. Holland), 1983, Hiking the Crevasse, Poems on the Way to Divorce (Penny Harter), 1983, Rising and Falling (Margot Farrington), 1985, Candles in the Daytime (Kathryn Nocerino), 1985. BEE, Cornell U., 1946; BA, Rutgers U., 1970, MA in Sociology, 1971. Prof. Stevens Inst., Rutgers U., Seton Hall, NJ, 1970-78; ed., pub. Warthog Press, West Orange, NJ, 1979—. Home: 29 S Valley Rd West Orange NJ 07052

FINALE, FRANK LOUIS, b. Bklyn., Mar. 10, 1942, s. Ralph and Mary (Guidone) F.; m. Barbara Ann Allegro, Oct. 20, 1973; children—Michael Long, Alan Long, Steven Long. Contrbr. poetry to natl. and intl. mags.: Ga. Rvw, Kans. Qtly, Blue Unicorn, Poet Lore, Plains Poetry Jnl, New York Qtly, new renaissance, Negative Capability, Poetry Now; Poem; contrbr. poetry to anthologies: A Celebration of Cats, 1974, Peace Is Our Profession, 1981, Dear Winter, 1984, Anthology of Magazine Verse and Yearbook of American Poetry, 1985, Blood to Remember: American Poets on the Holocaust, Dan River Anthology, 1985, Dan River Anthology, 1986, Blood to Remember. BS in Edn., Ohio State U., 1964; MA in Human Devel., Fairleigh Dickinson U., 1976. Tchr. Toms River (N.J.) Regional Schl. System, 1964—; founding ed. Without Halos, 1983, ed.-in-chief, 1985—; tchr. poetry workshops throughout N.J., 1984—. Mem. Ocean County Poets Collective (founder, 1983). Home: 921 Riverside Dr Pine Beach NJ 08741

FINCH, ANNIE RIDLEY CRANE, b. New Rochelle, NY, Oct. 31, 1956; d. Henry Leroy and Margaret Evelyn (Rockwell) Finch; m. Glen Brand, Dec. 6, 1985. Contrbr. poems and critical essays to lit. mags., profl. jnls., anthols. Wrkg. on book, Poetess' Poetics; epic feminist verse drama, Pandora. B.A., Yale U., 1979; M.A., U. Houston, 1986; postgrad. Stanford U., 1986—. Editorial asst. Natural History Mag., N.Y.C., 1981-83; poetry bd. reader Sequoia Mag., Palo Alto, CA, 1987—. Recipient Tinker prize Yale U., 1979. Mem. MLA, PSA. Home: 1076 College Ave Palo Alto CA 94306

FINCHER, JAMIE, see Fincher, Wanda Faye

FINCHER, WANDA FAYE, (Jamie Fincher), b. Swifton, AR, Oct. 16, 1946; d. Andrew Jackson Hardin and Maxine (Moore) Adams; m. James Curtis Fincher, Jr., Kec. 10, 1977; stepchildren—Kim, Erik. Author: (how-to for divorcees) On Your Own Again, 1977; (autobiography) Go For the Rose, 1982; (novel) Revenge is Mine, 1987. Wrkg. on screen play, video script, articles, books. Nursing degree, Ark. State U., 1973. Served as VISTA vol. BRAD Law Co., AR, 1971-74; 1st Lt. USAF Nurse Corps, 1974-76. Member D.A.V. Freelance wrtr., production nurse. Chmn. Lawrence county Am. Cancer Soc., 1973; secy. bd. dirs. United Farm Workers, 1972, State Bd. of Food Nutrition and Health, Ark., 1971-73. Mrs. South Carolina and runnerup to Mrs. America, 1982. Recipient Feature Wrtr. award Ark. Wrtrs. Conf., 1986, 2d place Oxbow Western Wrtrs. award Eureka Ark. Conf., 1986. Clairol Take Charge Award winner, 1987. Mem. Ozark Creative Wrtrs., (charter) Natl. Assn. Unknown Players, Ark. Lit. Soc. WORDS. Home: Rt 1 Box 375 Austin AR 72007

FINCKE, GARY W., b. Pitts., July 7, 1945, s. William A. and Ruth (Lang) F.; m. Elizabeth Locker, Aug. 17, 1968; children—Derek, Shannon, Aaron. Author poetry collections: Breath, 1984, The Coat in the Heart, 1985, The Days of Uncertain Health, 1986, Thiel, 1987. Contrbr. poetry to Paris Rvw, Prairie Schooner, Pequod, Cimarron Rvw, others; contrbr. fiction to: FLA. Rvw, Newsday, Beloit Fiction Jnl, Louisville Rvw, others. BA, Theil Coll., Greenville, Pa., 1967; MA, Miami U., Oxford, Ohio, 1969; PhD,Kent (Ohio) State U., 1974. Educator, 1968—, dir. writing program Susquehanna U., Selinsgrove, Pa., 1980—; mem. faculty Pa. Gov.'s Schl. for Arts, 1984-85. Poetry fellow Pa. Council on Arts, 1982, 85; recipient Syndicated Fiction award PEN-NEA, 1984, Fiction prize The Gamut, Cleve. State U., 1984. Mem. P&W. Home: 3 Melody Ln Selinsgrove PA 17870

FINE, ELSA HONIG, b. Bayonne, NJ, May 24, 1930; d. Samuel Morris and Yetta Edith (Susskind) Honig; m. Harold J. Fine, Dec. 23, 1951; 2 daus., Erika Susan, Amy Minna. Author: The Afro-Am. Artist: A Search for Identity, 1973, Women and Art: A History of Women Painters and Sculptors from the Renaissance to the 20th Century, 1978. M.Ed. in Art, Temple U., 1967; Ed.D., U. Tenn., 1970. Ed. and pub. Woman's Art Jnl, Knoxville, 1980—. Mem. Coll. Art Assn., Women's Caucus for Art. Home: 7008 Sherwood Dr Knoxville TN 37919

FINIFTER, ADA W(EINTRAUB), b. NYC, June 6, 1938; d. Isaac and Stella (Colchamiro) Weintraub; m. Bernard M. Finifter, 1960 (div. 1984). Author: Alienation and the Social System, 1972, ed, Political Science: The State of the Discipline, 1983, Using Your IBM Personal Computer: Easywriter, 1984. Contrbr and mem of editorial be, American Jnl of Poli. Sci., 1971-75, Sex Roles: A Jnl of Research, 1975-79, American Poli. Sci Rvw, 1976-81, American Politics Qtly, 1978-81, and Political Behavior, 1979-82. BA (cum laude), Brooklyn Coll,. 1959; MA, Univ of Mich., 1961; Ph. D., Univ. of Wis. (now Univ of Wis.-Madison), 1967. Asst study dir of pol. behavior prog at Survey Research Center, Univ of Mich, 1961-62; prof of soc sci, Catholic Univ, Caracas, Venezuela, 1963-64; asst prof, Mich. State Univ, 1967-72, assoc prof, 1972-81, prof of poli sci, 1981—. Congressional fellow, 1973-74; vis. fellow, Australian Natl Univ, 1978. Mem: Intl Pol Sci Assn (mem prog com, 1986-88), American Pol Sci Assn (mem of concl, 1973-75, chairperson of Woodrow Wilson award com, 1977; prog chmn, 1982; vp, 1983; Midwest Poli Sci Assn (mem exec cncl, 1971-74; pres, 1986-87; chmn of adv com on American politics). Natl Sci Fndn grantee, 1973, 77-78, 78-79; senior Fulbright scholar in Australia, 1978; grants from Russell Sage Fndn, 1979-84. Home: 341 Rampart Way East Lansing MI 48823

FINK, BARBARA (BOBBIE) ARLENE, (Barbara Gilbert, Zelda McNee, Diane Amery), b. Mpls., Aug. 27, 1949; d. Victor Lewis and Eva (Nadler) Fink. BA, U. Calif.-San Diego, 1972; MS, San Jose State U., 1974. Overnight news ed. radio sta. KSDO, San Diego, 1974-77, News-West news sevice, San Diego, 1977-79; wrtr., reporter Globe Communications Corp., Boca Raton, Fla., 1983-86; now freelance wrtr., Palm Beach and Miami Fla., tchr. coll. and high sch. journalism, writing and English. Mem. Fla. Freelance Wrtrs.' Assn. Home: 15276 SW 104th St Miami FL 33465

FINK, R. CULLEN, b. Newark, May 6, 1955; s. Halsey Cullen and Dorothy (Clark) F.; m. Leanne Metz, Sept. 30, 1984. Humor columnist On the Scene Mag., 1984; theater critic Premiere Mag., 1983. Contrbr. fitness articles Aquarian Arts Weekly, 1984-85. Wrkg. on book on pubg. Editor: Spray Dust Mfg., Rahway, N.J., 1984—; creative dir. Indelible Images, Inc., Irvington, N.J., 1983—. Mem. Dramatists Guild. Home: 401 W Meadow Ave Rahway NJ 07065

FINKEL, DONALD, b. NYC, Oct. 21, 1929; s. Saul A. and Meta (Rosenthal) F.; m. Constance Urdang, Aug. 14, 1956; children—Elizabeth Antonia, Thomas Noah, Amy Maria. Author: The Clothing's New Emperor, 1959, Simeon, 1964, A Joyful Noise, 1966, Answer Back, 1968, The Garbage Wars, 1970, Adequate Earth, 1972, A Mote in Heaven's Eye, 1975, Endurance and Going Under, 1978, What Manner of Beast, 1981, The Detachable Man, 1984, The Wake of the Electron, 1986, Selected Shorter Poems, 1986. BS, Columbia U., 1952, MA, 1953. Poet-in-residence Washington U., St. Louis, 1965—; cons. prosody Random House Dictionary. Guggenheim fellow, 1966; grantee Ingram Merrill Fdn., 1972, NEA, 1973. Address: 6943 Columbia Pl Saint Louis MO 63130

FINKELSTEIN, CAROLINE, b. NYC,Apr. 22, 1941, d. Louis and Rasha (Remin) Shapiro; children—Adam, Gabriel, Nicholas. Author: (poetry) Windows Facing East, 1986. MFA, Goddard Coll., 1978. Fellow Vt. Council on Arts, 1980, NEA, 1984. Home: 575 New Bedford Rd Rochester MA 02770

FINKELSTEIN, MIRIAM, b. Worcester, MA, June 14, 1928; d. Jacob and Anita (Asher) Ginsburg; m. James Finkelstein, June 16, 1952; children: Anne, David. Author: (novel) Domestic Affairs, 1982; contrbr. short stories to Moving Out, Kayak, Room, Letters, Ascent, Ariz. Qtly, Spectrum. BA, Radcliffe Coll., 1950; postgrad. Bank Street Coll. Edn., NYC, 1968. Asst. ed. news bulltn. Inst. Intl. Edn., NYC, 1952-57; learning specialist Bank Street Schl. for Children, 1968-85; self-employed learning specialist, 1985—. Mem. AG, P&W, Wrtrs. Community. Home: 680 West End Ave New York NY 10025

FINLEY, GLENNA, b. Puyallup, WA, June 12, 1925; d. John Ford and Gladys De Ferris (Winters) F.; m. Donald MacLeod Witte, May 19, 1951; 1 son, Duncan MacLeod. Author: numerous books—latest, Master of Love, 1978, Beware My Heart, 1978, The Marriage Merger, 1978, Wildfire of Love, 1979, Timed for Love, 1979, Love's Temptation, 1979, Stateroom for Two, 1980, Affairs of Love, 1980, Midnight Encounter, 1981, Return Engagement, 1981, One Way to Love, 1982. BA cum laude, Stanford U., 1945. With news bur. Life Mag., 1950; publicity and radio writer, Seattle, 1950-51, freelance writer, 1951-57; contract writer New Am. Library, NYC, 1970—. Mem. Free-lances, MWA, Romance Writers Am. Home: Box 866182 Plano TX 75086

FINN, BOBBY, see Kaufman, Stuart J.

FINNEGAN, ROSE, see Hamilton, Rosemary Ann

FIORI, PAMELA ANNE, b. Newark, Feb. 26, 1944; d. Edward A. and Rita Marie (Rascati) F.; m. Colton Givner. Assoc. editor Holiday Mag., 1968-71, Travel and Leisure Mag., 1971-74, sr. editor, 1974-75, editor-in-chief, 1975-80; editor-in-chief, exec. v.p. Am. Express Pub. Corp. (Travel and Leisure/Food and Wine), 1980—. Contbr. articles to periodicals; columnist: Window Seat, 1976—. BA cum laude, Jersey City State Coll., 1966. Mem. Am. Soc. Mag. Editors (exec. com.), N.Y. Travel Writers. Home: 345 E 57 St New York NY 10022

FIRCHOW, PETER EDGERLY, b. Needham, MA, Dec. 16, 1937; s. Paul Karl August and Marta Loria (Montenegro) F.; m. Evelyn Maria Scherabon Coleman, Sept. 18, 1969; 1 dau., Pamina Maria Scherabon. Author: Friedrich Schlegel's Lucinde and the Fragments, 1971, Aldous Huxley, Satirist and Novelist, 1972, The Writer's Place: Interviews on the Literary Situation in Contemporary Britain, 1974, (with E.S. Firchow) East German Short Stories: An Introductory Anthology, 1979, The End of Utopia: A Study of Aldous Huxley's "Brave New World," 1984, The Death of the German Cousin: Variations on a Literary Stereotype, 1890-1920, 1986; contrbr. articles on modern lit. to profl. jnls. BA, Harvard U., 1959; postgrad., U. Vienna, Austria, 1959-60; MA, Harvard U., 1961; PhD, U. Wis., 1965. Fellow Inst. for Advanced Studies in Humanities, Edinburgh, 1977, vis. prof, Natl. Cheng Kung U. (Taiwan), Vis. prof, Jilin Univ., 1987 (Peoples Republic of China). Mem. MLA, Midwest Modern Lang. Assn. (v.p. 1977, pres. 1978), Am. Comparative Lit. Assn. Home: 135 Birnamwood Dr Burnsville MN 55337

FISCHER, LYNN HENRY, b. Red Wing, MN, June 2, 1943, s. Reinhart Henry and Marie Katherine (Olson) F. Author: The 1, 2, 4 Theory: A Synthesis, 1971, Human Sexual Evolution, 1971, Sexual Equations of Electricity, Magnetism, and Gravitation, 1971, A Revised Meaning of Paradox, 1972, Middle Concept Theory, 1972, Unitary Theory, 1973, An Introduction to Circular or Fischerian Geometry, 1976, Two, Four Eight Theory, 1976, Fischer's Brief Dictionary of Sound Meanings, 1977, Introducing the Magnetic Sleeve: A Novel Sexual Organ, 1983, The Expansion of Duality, 1984, The Inger Poems, 1985. Cassettes: Country Wit, 1985, The Inger Poems and Early Poems, 1985, Letters of the Poet Lynn, 1987. Address: 1415 E 22d St 1108 Minneapolis MN 55404

FISH, LILIAN MANN, b. Methuen, Mass., Sept. 6, 1901, d. Samuel Eleazer and Ella Agnes (Hobbs) Mann; m. Charles Melvin Fish, Dec. 25, 1923 (div. 1933). Ed. Ancestors West mag., 1978—; contrbr. articles to Phi Delta Delta mag., DAR mag. JD magna cum laude, Southwestern U., 1932. Practice law, Los Angeles and Santa Barbara, Calif., 1932—. Mem. legal and genealogical socs. Address: 2546 Murrell Rd Santa Barbara CA 93109

FISH, STANLEY EUGENE, b. Providence, Apr. 19, 1938; s. Max and Ida Dorothy (Weinberg) F.; m. Adrienne A. Aaron, Aug. 23, 1959 (div. 1980); 1 dau., Susan; m. Jane Parry Tompkins, Aug. 7, 1982. Author: John Skelton's Poetry, 1965, Surprised by Sin: The Reader in Paradise Lost, 1967, Seventeenth Century Prose: Modern Essays in Criticism, 1971, Self-Consuming Artifacts, 1972, The Living Temple: George Herbert and Catechizing, 1978, Is there a Text in This Class?, 1980; editorial bd.: Milton Studies, Milton Qtly. BA, U. Pa., 1959; MA, Yale U., 1960, PhD, 1962. Fellow ACLS, 1966; Guggenheim fellow, 1969. Mem. MLA. Office: Dept Eng Duke U Durham NC 27706

FISHER, ARTHUR, b. NYC, Mar. 10, 1931; s. Abraham G. and Sadie (Gold) F.; m. Liliane E. Kowarsky, Aug. 18, 1951; 1 son, Anthony E. Author: (with Ernest V. Heyn) Century of Wonders, 1972, Fire of Genius, 1976, The Healthy Heart, 1981; contrbr. articles to mags. BA, NYU, 1951. Mng. editor Dodge Books, 1957-62, Sci. World & Sr. Sci., 1962-68; group editor sci. and engring. Popular Sci., NYC, 1969—. Recipient citations for excellence in sci. writing Deadline Club, 1973, 74; Claude Bernard Sci. Journalism award Natl. Soc. Med. Research; Sci. Writing award Am. Heart Assn., 1981; winner 1985 Am. Inst. of Physics, science writing award in physics and astronomy; winner 1986 AAAS-Westinghouse Sci. Journalism award for distinguished science writing in magazines. Mem. Natl. Assn. Sci. Writers. Home: 120 Cabrini Blvd New York NY 10033

FISHER, GEORGE WILLIAM, b. Sept. 18, 1946. Contrbr. Second Coming, Samisdat, Xanadu, other lit mags, On Turtle's Back, 1981, Paumanok Rising, 1983, other anthologies; ed.: Xanadu mag., 1974-77, Sanctuary mag., 1983-84, books for Pleasure Dome Press, 1976-77. Bd. dirs. L.I. Poetry Collective, 1974-79; L.I. Baroque Ensemble, Roslyn Harbor, 1979-82, L.I. Greenbelt Trail Conf., 1984—; ed. L.I. Nature Conservancy, Cold Spring Harbor, 1983-85. Home: 105 Laux Pl North Bellmore NY 11710

FISHER, HAL DENNIS, b. Milford, UT, Nov. 2, 1948; s. Hal Joseph and Norma Donna (Goudie) F.; m. Roberta Esther Griffith, Mar. 16, 1974; children—Sarah Lynn, Deborah Sue. Contrbr. religious articles to mags., jnls, including Moody Monthly, Discipleship Jnl., The Standard, The Twin Cities Christian. BA in humanities, Biola Coll., 1972; M.Div, Conservative Bapt. Theol. Sem., Denver, 1976; post-grad. Fuller Theol. Sem. With Campus Crusade for Christ, Berkeley, Calif., Colo., 1976-80; assoc. pastor Wooddale Ch., Eden Prairie, Minn., 1980-86; faculty Decision Sch. Christian Writing, Roseville, Minn., 1985; adj. prof. Bethel Theol. Sem., St. Paul, 1986; asst. prof. Moody Bible Inst., Chicago, 1986—. Mem. Minn. Christian Writer's Guild, Optimists. Home: 2407 Oak Ln Rolling Meadows IL 60008

FISHER, JAMES ABNER, JR., b. Phila., May 15, 1933; s. James Abner and Beanie (Norwood) F.; m. Chunqja Park, Apr. 9, 1963 (dec. Dec. 1973); children: Theresa B. Janrary, Myonqsoon Park, InSoon Park, Darrel Tempson, James A., Jr.; m. Darlene Maria Jackson, Mar. 25, 1985. Author: The Virtue of the Black Female Sex, 1983, (play) Self-Deception, 1986, The Plan of the Snake, 1979, Of Love, Life, and Childhood Days (poetry), 1986. Grad. Benjamin Franklin High Schl., Phila., 1952. Mem. DAV (life), Dramatists Guild Inc. of NYC. Served to cpl. U.S. Army, 1955-57. Named Prospect of Month, Ring Mag., 1952. Home: 2339 N Fairhill St Philadelphia PA 19133

FISHER, JERRY SAUL, b. Bronx, NY, Mar. 24, 1931; s. Abraham Samuel and Rose (Richard) F.; m. Sue Chidakel, Apr. 7, 1957; children—Stevan, Jody, David. Author numerous arts. on small business, franchising, gen. bus., 1958—. BBA, Clark U., 1952; JD, Boston U., 1955. Staff atty. S.E.C., Washington, 1956-58; var. posits. to deputy admin., S.B.A., Washington, 1958-67; v.p. Internat. Industries, Los Angeles, 1967-72; atty., bus. consultant, Los Angeles, 1972—; ed./pub. Tile & Decorative Surfaces, 1979—, Contemporary Dialysis, Worldwide Meetings and Incentives, 1980—, Dimensional Stone, 1985—. Mem. ASJA. Office: Tile & Dec 17901 Ventura Blvd Encino CA 91316

FISHER, MARY ANN, b. Savannah, Ga., Oct. 21, 1926, d. Herbert Rich and Edna Reine (Johnson) Holt; m. H. Roger Hotchkin, Feb. 14, 1987; children—Robert, Geoffrey, Gina. Ed. Tex. Christian U., U. Hawaii. Mem. public relations staff Time, Inc., Los Angeles, 1955-62, wrtr. various Time publs., 1962-78; ed. Westways mag., Los Angeles, 1980-86; dir. pub. rel. Auto Club So. Calif., 1986—; press adviser Republican party, Honolulu, 1968-74. Mem. Public Relations Soc. Am., Time-Life Alumni Assn., Western Publs. Assn. Office: Auto Club 2601 S Figueroa St Los Angeles CA 90007

FISHER, THOMAS MICHAEL, b. Kansas City, KS, Aug. 25, 1951; s. Solon D. and Faye Ella (Hatcher) F. Author: Selections from Pontiac, 1972; Untitled Book of Indian Poems, 1974; Night Dreams, 1974; contrbr. over 500 poems, also book rvws, letters, articles, prose and jnl excerpts to over 200 jnls throughout world. Wrkg. on representative manuscript of 15 yrs.' work. BA in English, St. Andrews Coll., Laurinburg, N.C., 1974; MA in English, N.Mex. State U., 1980. Asst. counselor Peace Corps, Las Cruces, N.Mex., 1976-77; vol. VISTA, San Miguel, N.Mex., 1977-78; instr. English, N.Mex. State U., Las Cruces, 1981-85; San Francisco City Coll., 1985-87; pub., ed. Star-Web Paper, lit. and arts jnl, since 1971—; consulsting ed. various jrnls, 1971-87. Mem. Rio Grande Wrtrs. Assn., Berkeley Poets Collective. Home: Box 40029 Berkeley CA 94704

FISHKIN, HOWARD S., b. Flint, MI, Feb. 27, 1946; s. Hyman M. and Bessie Fleisher Fishkin; m. Ilene Marsha Benson, Nov. 3, 1975; 1 son—Nathan. Author: Taxpayer's Survival Manual, 1979; editor: The Leaves Still Talk, and other books by David Kalugin, 1980, Tomorrow is So Far From Now, 1980. BA, U. of MI, 1968. Editor Book Promotion Press (Flushing, MI), 1968—. Office: Box 122 105 E Main St Flushing MI 48433

FISHMAN, CHARLES, b. Oceanside, NY, July 10, 1942; s. Morris (Murray) and Naomi (Toby) Fishman; m. Ellen Marcie Haselkorn, June 25, 1967; children—Jillana, Tamara. Author: Aurora, 1974, Mortal Companions, 1977, Warm-Blooded Animals, 1977, An Index to Women's Magazines and Presses, 1977, The Death Mazurka, 1987; editor: Blood to Remember: American Poets on the Holocaust, 1988. BA, Hofstra U., 1964, MA, 1965; DA, SUNY at Albany, 1982. Tchr., Long Island pub. schls., 1965-70; prof., SUNY at Farmingdale, 1970-87; dir. of programs in the arts, SUNY at Farmingdale, 1987—(Chancellor's Award for excellence in tchg., 1985). Gertrude B. Clayton Mem. award, 1986. Address: SUNY Rt 110 & Melville RD Farmingdale NY 11735

FISHWICK, NINA MARIE, (Marie Stewart), b. Chgo., Mar. 5, 1961; d. George Gile F. and Judith Lynn (Stewart) F. Author: (With Ed Stewart) Group Talk, 1985; (leader's guide) Liberated for Life (John Mac Arthur), 1985; ed. courses Bible Commentary for Laymen series, 1984-85; contrbr. articles to Hardcopy Mag., Focus, Light Force Youth Curriculum. BA in Communication, Azusa Pacific U., Calif., 1983; adult curriculum ed. Gospel Light Publs., Ventura, Calif., 1984-85; asst. publicity dir. Bethel Coll., St. Paul, 1985—. Home: 4134 N Lexington 2112 Shoreview MN 55126

FISK, MARGARET CRONIN, b. Detroit, Oct. 7, 1946, d. John Raymond and Margaret Jean (MacLennan) Cronin; m. Alan Fisk, Sept. 25, 1971; 1 dau., Elizabeth Ann. Author: The Gambler's Bible, 1976; (with A. Fisk) The Paradise Rehearsal Club, 1982. Contrbr. articles to popular mags., newspapers including Reader's Digest, Woman's Day, Newsday, Phila. Inquirer. Editor: (Newspaper) The Metro, Detroit, 1969-72; assoc. editor: Ed. & Pub. mag., NYC., 1972-74. Wrkg. on non-fiction book on child sexual abuse. Student, Wayne State U., 1964-69. Freelance wrtr., ed., 1974—. Home: 141 Columbia Heights 4C Brooklyn NY 11201

FITCH, CHARLES MARDEN, b. NYC, July 30, 1937, s. W.P. and Murrie (Marden) F. Author: Television Educativa (in Spanish), 1968, The Complete Book of Houseplants, 1972, The Complete Book of Terrariums, 1974, The Complete Book of Houseplants Under Lights, 1975, The Complete Book of Miniature Roses, 1977, All About Orchids, 1981, Rodale Book of Garden Photography, 1981, Handbook on Orchids, 1986. BS, NYU, 1960, MA, 1962, PhD, CPU, 1982. Editor, Indoor Gardening, 1987; Media Specialist "Exotic Plants" laser videodisc), 1986. Performer, producer WNET-TV, NYC, 1960-63; dir., producer Peace Corps, Colombia, South Am., 1963-65; media specialist Larchmont-Mamaroneck Schls., N.Y., 1965-66, 1968; exec. dir., producer U.S. Dept. State, El Salvador, 1966-67; communications cons. OAS, South America, 1968. Fellow Royal Horticultural Soc., Garden Wrtr.'s Assn. Am.; mem. Am. Orchid Soc. (awards photographer). Address: Talisman 1120 Cove Rd Mamaroneck NY 10543

FITZALLAN-HOWARD, R. F., see Margo Chanler Howard-Howard

FITZGERALD, FRANCES, b. 1940; d. Desmond and Marietta Peabody Fitzgerald Tree. Author: Fire in the Lake: The Vietnamese and the Americans in Vietnam, 1972, America Revised, 1979; contrbr. articles to mags. Grad. magna cum laude, Radcliffe Coll., 1962. Writer: series of profiles Herald Tribune mag.; freelance writer, Vietnam, 1966. Recipient Overseas Press Club award for interpretative reporting, 1967; Natl. Inst. Arts and Letters award, 1973; Pulitzer prize, 1973; Natl. Book award, 1973; numerous others. Address: Random Hs 201 E 50th St New York NY 10022

FITZGERALD, ROBERT, (Stuart Fitzgerald), b. Geneva, N.Y., Oct. 12, 1910; s. Robert Emmet and Anne Montague (Stuart) F.; m. Sarah Morgan, Apr. 19, 1947 (div. 1982); children—Hugh Linane, Benedict Robert Campion, Maria Juliana, Peter Michael Augustine, Barnaby John Francis, Caterina Maria Teresa; m. 2d, Penelope Laurans, May 16, 1982. Author: Poems, 1935, A Wreath for the Sea, 1943, In the Rose of Time, 1956, Spring Shade, 1971; translator: Oedipus at Colonus (Sophocles), 1951, Odyssey (Homer), 1961, Chronique, Birds (St. John Perse), 1961-66, Iliad (Homer), 1974, Aeneid (Virgil), 1983, (with Dudley Fitts) Alcestis (Euripides), 1935, Antigone (Sophocles), 1949. Grad., Choate Schl., Wallingford, Conn., 1929; AB, Harvard U., 1933; student, Trinity Coll., Cambridge (Eng.) U., 1931-31. Reporter N.Y. Herald Tribune, 1933-35; writer Time mag., 1936-49. Guggenheim fellow, 1953, 71; recipient Shelley award PSA, 1955; grantee creative writing Ford Fdn., 1959; Ingram Merrill Lit. award, 1978; others. Fellow AIAL (award 1957), Am. Acad. Arts and Scis., AAP (chancellor 1968). Address: 15 Giles St Hamden CT 06517

FITZGERALD, ROGER J., b. Boston, Nov. 24, 1937, s. James Bernard and Lucy (Donnelly) F.; m. Mary Frances Dupuis, Sept. 10, 1962 (div. 1975); children—Michael, Mary. BA in English, U. Portland, 1961; MA, Reed Coll., 1970; EdM, Harvard U., 1971. Tchr., 1962-77; comml. fisherman, Alaska, 1977-78; sr. ed. Waterfront Press, Seattle, Wash., 1978—, publs. include Alaska Fisherman's Jnl., Seafood Leader, Pacific Northwest Mag., Fishing News Intl. Home: 6540 7th St NW Seattle WA 98117

FITZGERALD, STUART, see Fitzgerald, Robert

FITZPATRICK, KEVIN JOHN, b. St. Paul, Oct. 3, 1949. Contrbr. poetry Down on the Corner, 1987. BA in English and Sociology, U. Minn., 1971; MA in Edn., Coll. St. Thomas, 1977. Editor Lake St. Rvw, Mpls., 1977—. Bd. dirs. Minn. Lit. Newsletter. Address: Box 7188 Powderhorn Sta Minneapolis MN 55407

FITZSIMMONS, THOMAS, b. Lowell, MA, Oct. 21, 1926. Author: With the Water (poetry), 1972, Rocking Mirror Daybreak (bilingual, with Ooka Makoto), 1982, The Sound of Chrysanthemums (in Japanese), 1986; (poetry chapbooks) This Time This Place, 1969, Meditation Seeds, 1971, Mooning, 1971, Playseeds, 1973, The Big Huge, 1975, The Nine Seas & the Eight Mountains, 1981; contrbr. poetry, prose to Antioch Rvw, Ikebana Sogetsu, Trace, Wormwood, many other lit mags. in U.S., Japan. Student, Fresno (Calif.) State Coll., 1947-49, Sorbonne and Institut de Science Politique, Paris, 1949-50; BA, Stanford U., 1951; MA, Columbia U., 1952. Fulbright lectr. Tokyo U. Edn., 1962-64, Tsuda U., Tokyo, 1962-64, U. Nice, France, 1968, U. Bucharest, 1967-68; vis. lectr. Keio U., Tokyo, 1973-75; vis. prof. Tokyo U. Edn., 1973-75; prof. English Oakland U., Rochester, Mich., 1966—, also dir. Japanese poets-in-residence, ed. Asian Poetry in Translation and Perspectives on the Arts of Asia book series. Editor, pub., Katydid Books. NEA fellowship, 1967, 82. Address: Oakland Univ Rochester MI 48063

FITZSTEWARD, FARMER, see Economou, George

FLACK, DORA D(UTSON), b. Kimberly, ID, July 9, 1919; d. Alonzo Edmund and Iona (James) Dutson; m. A. LeGrand Flack, Jan. 7, 1946; children: Marc Douglas, Lane LeGrand, Kent Kutson, Marlane (Mrs. Alan T. Smith), Karen (Mrs. Ronald B. Hall), Marie (Mrs. Leonard Hardle). Author: (with Vernice G. Rosenvall and Mabel H. Miller) Wheat for Man: Why and How, 1952, rev ed, 1975, (with Ida Watt Stringsham), England's First Mormon Convert, 1956, (with Louise Nielsen) The Dutson Family History, 1957, What About Christmas?, 1971, contrbr, Duane S. Crowther and Jean D. Crowther, eds, The Joy of Being a Woman, 1972, Fun with Fruit Preservation, 1973, rev ed, 1980, (with Lula Parker Betenson) Butch Cassidy, My Brother, 1975, Dry and Save, 1976, (with Janice T. Dixon) Preserving Your Past, 1977, Christmas Magic, 1977, Testimony in Bronze, 1980, (with Karla C. Erickson) Gifts Only You Can Give, 1984, Bread Making Made Easy, 1984, contrbr, Flood Fighters of 1983-84, 1985. Contrbr of articles and short stories to periodicals, including Utah Historical Qtly, American West, Organic Gardening, Guideposts, Friend, Ensign, and New Era. Attended Univ of Utah, Brigham Young Univ, Utah State Univ, and Latterday Saints Business College. Sec. to bank executive, Salt Lake City, 1938-46. Writer; lectr on the dying, preservation and storage of food; also on personal and family history, Mem: Natl League of American Pen Women, League of Utah Writers (bd mem; chpt pres, 1972-74, state pres, 1975-76). Writing awards from Utah Arts Cncl, League of Utah Writers, and Natl League of American Pen Women; Dry and Save selected by the U.S. Information Agency for showcase of American books at Intl Book Fair, Cairo, Egypt, 1978; named Writer of the Year by League of Utah Writers, 1982. Address: 448 East 775 North Bountiful UT 84010

FLAHERTY, DOUG, b. Lowell, MA, Apr. 25, 1939; s. Douglas Ernest and Hazel G. (Shinkwin) F. Author: (poems) Near the Bone, 1975, To Keep the Blood from Drowning, 1976, Love-Tangle of Roots, 1977. Contrbr. poems to anthols., lit. mags., newspapers. Wrkg. on novel, Carry Water from the Moon, poems. B.S., Merrimack Coll. (Mass.), 1961; M.A., U. Mass., 1963; M.F.A., U. Iowa, 1965./ Asst. porof. U. Wis., Oshkosh, 1966—. Grantee NEA for Road Apple Rvw., 1969-71; recipient 1st prize for poetry, Kansas City, KS, 1966. Home: 3263 Shorewood Dr Oshkosh WI 54901

FLAMMONDE, PARIS, (M. M. Delfano), b. Richmond, VA, May 25. Author: The Grey Man, 1965, The Age of Flying Saucers, 1971, The Kennedy Conspiracy, 1969, The Mystic Healers, 1974, UFO Exist! 1976, The Living Prophets, The Modern Psychics. Co-founder and board member, Committee to Investigate Assassinations, 1969-80. Mem. AG, PSA. Home: RD 6 Box 6199 Stroudsburg PA 18360

FLANAGAN, NEIL, see Schmidt, George Neil

FLECK, RICHARD FRANCIS, b. Phila., Aug. 24, 1937, s. J. Keene and Anne Myrtle (DeLeon) F.; m. Maura Bridget McMahon, June 29, 1963; children—Richard Sean, Michelle Marie, Ann Maureen. Author: Palms, Peaks and Prairies (poetry), 1967, Clearing of The Mist (novel), 1979, Cottonwood Moon (poetry), 1979, Bamboo in The Sun (poetry), 1983, Henry Thoreau and John Muir Among The Indians, 1986; ed.: The Indians of Thoreau, 1974, Henry Thoreau's Maine Woods, 1983, John Muir's Our National Parks, 1981, John Muir's Mountaineering Essays, 1984. Henry Thoreau's The Maine Woods, 1987. BA, Rutgers U., 1959; PhD,U. N. Mex., 1970. Instr. North Adams (Mass.) State Coll., 1963-65; asst. prof. to prof. English, U. Wyo., Laramie, 1965—; exchange prof. Osaka (Japan) U., 1981-82, SUNY-Cortland, 1986-87. Recipient John Van der Poel prize Rutgers U., 1959; grantee Wyo. U., 1967, 71, Wyo. Humanities Council, 1977, 79. Mem. P&W, Thoreau Soc., Sierra Club. Office: Dept English Univ Wyo Laramie WY 82071

FLEER, MARILYN JUNE, b. Laredo, TX, July 17, 1931; d. Cecil Howard and Bernice Elizabeth (Mars) F. Contrbr. articles to newspapers, poems to anthols. Wrkg. on articles, non-fiction books, hist. novels, fantasy and sci. fiction short fiction and novels, cookbooks, poems. B.A. in Jnlsm., U. Okla., 1954, M.A., 1971. Tehnical wrtr. Okla. Center for Continuing Edn., Norman, OK, 1972; office asst. Harlow Pubs., Norman, 1975; circulation asst. Blue Chip Mag., Norman, 1980; free-lance ed., 1984—. Mem. Okla. Wrtrs. Fedn. (5th place for rhymed poetry 1981, 2d place for feature article 1982, Honorable Mention for feature article 1983), U. Okla. Jnlsm. and Mass Communication Alumni Assn. Home: 1406 George Ave Norman OK 73072

FLEGLER, JOEL B., b. NYC, Jan. 9, 1941; s. Edward and Mildred (Jacobs) F. BA, Bucknell U., 1962; MA, U. PA, 1963, Columbia U. Tchrs. Coll., 1964. Rptr., The Record, Hackensack, NJ, 1963; tchr. Tenafly (NJ) Bd. Edn., 1964-82; ed./pub. Fanfare, Tenafly, 1977—. Office: Fanfare 273 Woodland St Tenafly NJ 07670

FLEISCHER, DENISE M., b. Chgo., Aug. 11, 1958; d. Irving Phillip and Sandra Ester (Lubeck) Miller; m. Ernest Jack Fleischer, May 29, 1977; 1 dau., Jennifer Lynne. Contrbr.: Nutshell News. Wrkg. on short fiction, sci. fiction book. Student Oakton Community Coll., With Jrnl. and topics Newspapers, Des Plaines, Ill. 1982—, food ed., columnist, 1986—. Home: 612 Cobblestone Circle Glenview IL 60025

FLEISCHER, LESLIE, b. NYC,Aug. 13, 1934, d. Hyman Frank and Edith (Landau) F.; m. Fonda Rothblatt, June 2, 1963 (div. 1984); children—Randall, Steven. Author poetry collections: Renewal: In the Forest of My Mind, 1983, Renewal II, 1985; contrbr. to anthology Ashes to Ashes, 1984, Reflections. . . BA, NYU, 1955; Music Edn., Manhattan Schl. Music, 1961. Tchr. music pub. schls. N.Y.C., 1959-69, Smithtown, N.Y., 1970-72, New Paltz, N.Y., 1974-76; freelance wrtr., 1976—. Mem. Stone Ridge Poetry Soc. Address: Box 1353 Kingston NY 12401

FLEISCHMAN, ALBERT SIDNEY, b. Bklyn., Mar. 16, 1920; s. Reuben and Sadie (Solomon) F.; m. Beth Elaine Taylor, Jan. 25, 1942; children—Jane, Paul, Anne. Author: children's books including Mr. Mysterious & Company, 1962, The Ghost in the Noonday Sun, 1965, Jingo Django, 1971, The Hey Hey Man, 1979, McBroom and the Great Race, 1980, The Whipping Boy, 1986. BA, San Diego State Coll., 1949. Newspaper reporter San Diego Daily Jnl, 1949-50; freelance screenwriter; lectr. fiction writing UCLA. Served with USNR, 1941-45. Recipient Spur award WWA, Commonwealth Club award, Lewis Carroll Shelf award, Mark Twain award, Newberry award, 1987. Mem. WG Am., AG, Soc. Children's Book Writers. Home: 305 10th St Santa Monica CA 90402

FLEMING, BERRY, b. Augusta, GA, Mar. 19, 1899; s. Porter and Daisy (Berry) F.; m. Anne Molloy, Aug. 12, 1925 (dec. 1972); 1 dau., Shirley Moragne. Works include: The Conqueror's Stone, 1926, The Square Root of Valentine, 1931, Siesta, 1935, Colonel Effingham's Raid, 1943, The Lightwood Tree, 1947, Carnival, 1953, The Winter Rider, 1960, Lucinderella, 1967, The Make-Believers, 1973, Two Tales for Autumn, 1979, Country Wedding, 1982, Once There was a Fisherman, 1984, The Bookman's Tale, and Others, 1986. Student, Middlesex, 1918; BS, Harvard, 1922. Home: 3050 Walton Way Augusta GA 30909

FLEMING, JAMES KLEIN, b. Mason City, Iowa, Oct. 11, 1949; s. Charles Edward and Josephine Rosa (Klein) F. Instr Hunter Coll, 1981—. Editor: Semiotext(e), 1979—, Simulations, 1983, In the Shadow of the Silent Majorities, 1983, On the Line, 1983, Pure War, 1984, Driftworks, 1984, Rethinking Marxism, 1985, Metatron, 1985, Bolo' bolo, 1985, Scandal: Studies in Islamic Heresy, 1986, Forget Foucault, 1986, Speed and Politics, 1986, New Lines of Alliance, 1986, Nomadology, 1986, Marx Beyond Marx, 1987, Trotskyism and Maoism, 1987, Film and Politics in the Third World, 1987, Compact, 1987, Fatal Strategies, 1987, Semiotexte USA, 1987. Wrkg. on Arcane of Reproduction, also Horsexe: Essay on Transexuality. BA, U. Iowa, PhD. Editor, Autonomedia, Bklyn. Office: Box 568 Brooklyn NY 11211

FLEMING, THOMAS JAMES, b. Jersey City, July 5, 1927; s. Thomas James and Katherine (Dolan) F.; m. Alice Mulcahey, Jan. 19, 1951; children—Alice, Thomas, David, Richard. Author: Now We Are Enemies, 1960, All Good Men, 1961, The God of Love, 1963, Beat the Last Drum, 1963, One Small Candle, 1964, King of the Hill, 1966, A Cry of Whiteness, 1967, West Point, The Men and Times of the U.S. Military Academy, 1969, The Man from Monticello, 1969, Romans Countrymen Lovers, 1969, The Sandbox Tree, 1970, The Man Who Dared the Lightning, 1971, The Forgotten Victory, 1973, The Good Shepherd, 1974, 1776: Year of Illusions, 1975, Liberty Tavern, 1976, Rulers of the City, 1977, New Jersey, 1977, Promises To Keep, 1978, A Passionate Girl, 1979, The Officers' Wives, 1981, Dreams of Glory, 1983, The Spoils of War, 1985, Time and Tide, 1987; also TV scripts, articles, short stories; editor: Affectionately Yours, George Washington, 1967, Benjamin Franklin, A Biography in His Own Words, 1972, The Living Land of Lincoln, 1980. AB, Fordham U., 1950; postgrad., Schl. Social Work, 1950-51. Reporter Yonkers (N.Y.) Herald Statesman, 1951; asst. to Fulton Oursler, 1951-52, lit. executor estate, 1953; assoc. editor Cosmopolitan mag., 1954-58, exec. editor, 1959-61; writer, 1961—. Recipient Achievement award in communications arts Fordham U., 1961, Mass Media award NCCJ, 1963; Fiction award natl. Cath. Press Assn., 1974; Best Book award Am. Revolution Round Table, 1975; others. Fellow N.J. Hist. Soc., Soc. Am. Historians; mem. PEN (pres. 1971-73). Home: 315 E 72d St New York NY 10023

FLEMMING, KAY ESTELLE, b. Seivierville, TN, June 4, 1905, d. Lovella and Mary Emma (Burden Pate; m. James Phillip Allen (dec. 1962); m. 2d, Herbert Flemming (dec. 1976); 1 dau., Doris A. Kelly. Contrbr. award-winning poetry to Clover Intl. Showcase Collection, Poetry of the Americas, New Voices in American Poetry, other publs.; contrbr.: Yesterday's Magazet mag., Wrtrs. Newsletter for Sr. Group, other publs. BA, Knoxville Coll., 1931. Past reporter Louisville Defender; past corr. Jet and Ebony mags., Chgo.; now columnist Westchester County Press, N.Y. Mem. Soc. Lit. Designates. Home: 289 Nepperhan Ave Apt 4C-B Yonkers NY 10701

FLESHER, DALE LEE, b. Albany, IN, June 27, 1945; s. Myron Lee and Deloris Rachel (Wright) F.; m. Tonya Kay Maloney, June 6, 1970; 1 son, Flyn Lee. Author: Operations Auditing in Hospitals, 1976, Accounting for Advertising Assets, 1978, Accounting for Mid-Management, 1980, Accounting for Middle Management, 1980, Tax Tactics for Small Business, 1980, Independent Auditors Guide to Operational Auditing, 1982, Operational Auditing Study Guide, 1982, CMA Examination Review, 2 vols., 1984, 1987, The New-Product Decision, 1984, Test Bank to Accompany Intermediate Accounting, 1984, CPE Using CMA Examination Review, 1985, Operational Audit of the Purchasing Function, 1985, Introduction to Financial Accounting, 1987. BS, Ball State U., 1967, MA, 1968; PhD U. Cin., 1975. Asst. mgr. Price's Food Mkt., Albany, 1960-66; asst. prof. Ball State U., Muncie, Ind., 1968-71; instr. acctg. U. Cin., 1971-73; assoc. prof. Appalachian State U., Boone, N.C., 1973-77; staff acct. Arthur Andersen & Co., New Orleans, 1978; prof. accountacy U. Miss., Oxford, 1977—. Recipient Disting. Performance cert. Inst. Cert. Mgmt. Accts., 1974; named Outstanding Tchr. of Yr., Appalachian State U., 1976, Outstanding Researcher of Yr., U. Miss., 1979, 83, 87. Mem. Acad. Acctg. Hist. (v.p., ed., pres.), Natl. Assn. Accts. (natl. dir.), Am. Inst. CPAs, Inst. Internal Auditors (Outstanding Contributor award 1984; mem. natl. history com.), Am. Acctg. Assn. Home: 130 Lakeway Dr Oxford MS 38655

FLETCHER, AARON, b. Middlesboro, KY, Jan. 20, 1934; m. Jean; 1 dau.—Cheryl Ann. Author: Bronson, 1974, Ice Pick, 1975, Ryker, 1975, Treasure of the Lost City, 1976, The Master Planner, 1976, Bloody Sunday, 1976, Mommy's Gone, 1976, Microwave Factor, 1977, Cowboy, 1977, The Surrogate, 1977, Bounty Hunter, 1977, The Labyrinth, 1977, Love's Gentle Agony, 1978, Render Unto Caesar, 1978, The Gypsy Moths, 1978, Outback, 1978, Mountain Breed, 1979, Flames of Chandrapore, 1979, The Card Game, 1980, Frontier Fires, 1980, The Reckoning, 1981, Frontier Healers, 1981, Rawhide Country, 1982, Lone Star Legacy, 1982, The Capricorn People, 1983, The Castaway, 1984, The Founders, 1984, Project Jael, 1985, series of historical novels published under pen names by the book producer Book Creations Incorporated; nonfiction in numerous magazines and periodicals. Mem. Authors Guild. Home: Box 652 Fair Oaks CA 95628

FLETCHER, BARBARA RAINBOW, b. San Francisco, Oct. 15, 1935; d. Merrill Dale Jones and Mary Elizabeth (Scyster) Jacobs; m. Patrick Ledray, May 27, 1954 (div. 1974); children—Michael Ledray, Sandra Ledray, Charles Ledray; m. 2d, Donald Dean Fletcher, May 28, 1977. Don't Blame the Stork!—The Cyclopedia of Unusual Names, 1981 (prod. in Braille for Visually Impaired by Lib. of Cong., 1984). Working on: Down in the Dumps(ters)!—Gifts From the Garbage (recycling guide). AA, Sea Central Commun. Coll., 1976. Home: 9520 NE 120th A2 Kirkland WA 98033

FLETCHER, HARRY GEORGE, III, b. Bklyn., Mar. 25, 1941; s. Harry G. and Helen T. (Dawson) F.; m. Toni A. Owen, 1966; children—Alexandra, Thomas More. Author: Aldus Manutius and the Aldine Press, 1987; editor: The Heritage of New York, 1970, A Miscellany for Bibliophiles, 1979; co-editor: Paradosis, 1976; contrbr. articles to profl. jnls. AB, Fordham Coll., 1962, MA, 1970; postgrad., U. Munich, 1962-63. Asst. editor Fordham U. Press, Bronx, N.Y., 1966-69, editor, 1969-81, dir., 1972—. Served with AUS, 1963-66. Office: Fordham U Press Bronx NY 10458

FLETCHER, KAY, see Wilson, Patricia Ann

FLETCHER, PAULINE CHARLOTTE, b. Salisbury, Zimbabwe, Oct. 6, 1938; arr. U.S. Sept., 1975; d. Charles Henry and Olga (Foulger) Mitchell; m. David John Fletcher, Mar. 2, 1959. Author: Gardens and Grim Ravines, 1983; contrbr. articles to Victorian Poetry, UNISA English Studies, Studies in Romanticism, Univ. of Cape Town Studies in English, English Studies in Africa, Theoria, Crux, Encyclopedia on Victorian England; edited CEA Critic, 1985. MA, Natal U., South Africa, 1964; PhD, U. Rochester, 1980. Asst. prof. Univ. Natal, South Africa, 1966-75, Univ. So. Africa, Pretoria, 1977-78, Bucknell Univ., Lewisburg, Pa., 1981-85, assoc. prof., 1985—. Mem. Victorians Inst., Coll. Eng. Assn. Address: RD 2 Box 738 New Columbia PA 17856

FLORA, PHILIP CRAIG, b. Roanoke, VA, June 2, 1950; s. Kenneth Van and Betty Louellen (Crum) F. Pub. Robotics Age Mag., Robotics Pub., La Canada, CA, 1979-81; pub. AI Mag., Amer. Assn. for Artificial Intell., Menlo Park, CA, 1980-81; ed./pub. Computerized Mfg., Conroe, TX, 1983—. Publns. include Computerized mfg., 1983—, Computer Aided Design/Computer Aided Mfg. (CAD/CAM) Industry Directory, 1983, Industrial Sensor Dir., 1983, Intl. Robotics Industry Dir., 1984, Intl. CAD/CAM Software Dir., 1985, Intl. Engring./Scientific Software Dir., 1985, Intl. Programmable Controllers Dir., 1985, Intl. Computer Vision Dir., 1985, Intl. Industrial Sensor Dir., 1986, Intl. CAD Dir., 1986, Intl. CAM Dir., 1986. Office: Box 720 Conroe TX 77305

FLORES, JOSE OBED, (Robert Wells, Lee Hamada) b. Havana, Cuba, May 23, 1954; came to U.S., 1966. Author: 9mm SMG, 1980, Mac Items, 1981, Full Auto, 1981, Free World—Rifles, 1982, Free World—Pistols, 1982, Free World—SMG, 1983, Disposable Silencers, 1984, Disposable Silencers Vol. II, 1985, The Anarchist Handbook, 1985. Wrkg. on how to train security dogs, ninja stick and knife fighting, and the complete self-defense manual. Editor: Modern-day Ninjutsu, 1986. AA, Pasadena City Coll., 1975. Home: 4247 N Arica Ave Rosemead CA 91770

FLORIAN, JOHN S., b. Hartford, CT, Apr. 27, 1947; s. Sherwood Lester and Shirley (Moeller) F.; m. Julie Montello, May 31, 1985. BS in Broadcasting & Film, Boston U., 1969. City ed. Winsted (CT) Evening Citizen, 1973-74; ed. Northeast Outdoors, Waterbury, CT, 1974-82, Drycleaners News, Waterbury, 1974-82, Puerto Rico Living, 1978-85, Alternative Energy Retailer, 1980-86; editorial dir. Zackin Pubns., Waterbury, 1974—; ed. dir. Secondary Marketing Executive, Waterbury, 1986; ed. Northeast Van; ed./pub. Editors Only, 1982—. Served to Capt., USAF, 1969-73. Mem. ASBPE, NYBPE. Office: Box 2180 Waterbury CT 06722

FLORSHEIM, STEWART JAY, b. NYC,Nov. 14, 1952, s. Max and Flora (Falk) F. Contrbr. to: Berkeley Poet's Coop., Blue Unicorn, Men Talk, Yoga Jnl, other lit. publs. BA, Syracuse U., 1974; MA, San Francisco State U., 1978. Ed. Excerpta Medica, Amsterdam, Holland, 1974-76; dir. communications ASK Computers, Los Altos, Calif., 1978. Active Amnesty Intl., San Francisco. Home: 319 Lexington St San Francisco CA 94110

FLORY, JOYCE V., b. Chgo., Sept. 3, 1947; d. Charles Verbik and Sylvia Pechman; m. Keith Flory, 1971 (div. 1973). Pubns. incl.: Consumer Alert, 1979-83, Dental Assistant, 1979-80, Dimensions, 1980-82, Healthcall, 1980-82, Hospital & Health Svcs. Admin., 1982-86, Healthcare in the 1990's: Trends and Strategies, 1984, Healthcare Executive, 1985-86. BA, U. IL, 1968; PhD, IN U., 1972. Asst. prof. U. MN, Duluth, 1972-79, Northeastern IL U., Chgo., 1975-79; dir. profl. relns. Amer. Dental Assts. Assn., Chgo., 1979-80; mgr. pub. relns. MacNeal Hosp., Berwyn, IL, 1980-82; dir. communics. Amer. Coll. of Healthcare Execs., Chgo., 1982-86. Home: 1340 N Dearborn Pkwy Chicago IL 60610

FLOWERS, BETTY SUE, b. Waco, TX., Feb. 2, 1947, d. Paul Davis and Betty Lou (Lewis) Marable; m. John Garland Flowers III, July 14, 1967; 1 son, John Michael. Author: Browning and the Modern Tradition, 1976; contrbr. articles, poems to profl. jnls, lit mags: Rocky Mountain Rvw, Thicket, The Arnoldian, others. BA, U. Tex.-Austin, 1969, MA, 1970; PhD, U. London, 1973. Asst prof. English U. Tex.-Austin, 1973-79, assoc. dean grad. studies, 1979-82, assoc. prof., 1979—; chmn. spl. projects Tex. Com. for Humanities, 1983—; bd. dirs. Salado Inst. for Humanities, Tex., 1979—. Mellon fellow Aspen Inst. for Humanities, 1976. Mem. MLA, Omicron Delta Kappa, Phi Beta Kappa. Office: Dept Eng U Tex Austin TX 78712

FLOYD, CAMILLE MAXINE, b. Corning, NY, Jan. 17, 1940; d. Edward C. and Rose C. (Mackey) Morris; m. Richard Allen Floyd, June 29, 1968; children—Edward, Robert. Contrbr. articles to mags., newspapers including Children's Digest, Catholic Digest, others. B.A., Nazareth Coll., 1961; M.S., Elmira Coll., 1969. Staff wrtr. Maintenance & Modernization Supvr., Olney, MD, 1986—, Building & Grounds Maintenance, Olney, 1986—; ed. Petroleum Marketing Management Mag., Rockville, MD, 1986—. Home: 17613 Wheat Fall Dr Rockville MD 20855

FLOYD, WAYNE, b. Cedartown, GA, Apr. 24, 1930; s. Clarence and Edith (Smith) F.; m. Jo Robinson, Jan. 6, 1978. Author: Floyd's Photo Tips, 1960, How to Retouch and Spot Negatives and Prints, 1961, Decorating with Photographs, 1965, ABCs of Developing, Printing and Enlarging, 1965, Jason's Dictionary of CB Slang, 1975, The Double Exposure Book, 1984. Served to sgt. USAF, 1948-52. Home: 1407 Darlene Arlington TX 76010

FLUCK, SANDRA SQUIRE, b. Phila., Feb. 6, 1944; d. Grant Robert and Leta Jean (McDevitt) Squire; m. Tadeusz M. Bugaj, Mar. 10, 1967 (div. 1969); children: Justine Fluck; m. Richard Allen Fluck, June 23, 1970; children: Jason, Jesse. Author: Experiential English, 1973; (poetic dramas) Festival of the Knock, 1980, Blood Spirit, 1980; Forgiving the Beasts, 1982, Newspiece, 1982; Language Play: A Children's Writing Program for Human Betterment, 1987; How To Organize a Peace Essay Contest in Your Community, 1982; poetry in various mags. and anthologies. MA, UCLA, 1966; MA in Religion magna cum laude, Lancaster Theol. Sem., Pa., 1980. Prof. Westlake Schl. for Girls, Beverly Hills, Calif., 1968-69, Moorpark Coll., Calif., 1969-70, Harrisburg Area Community Coll., Pa., 1976-77, Franklin and Marshall Coll., Lancaster, 1978-85; freelance writer, 1986—. Co-founder Lancaster Writers Guild, 1980; co-founder Poets on Stage, Lancaster, 1982; founder Lancaster Ctr. Peace and Justice, 1979-80; founder, editor Lancaster Writers Mag., 1982-84. editor Feminist Voice, 1986-87. Mem. NCTE, Assn. Transarmament Studies, Natl. Women's Studies Assn., Educators for Social Responsibility, International Women's Writing Guild. Home: 746 N Pine St Lancaster PA 17603

FLUTY, STEVEN JAY, b. Troy, OH, Aug. 29, 1957; s. Francis Jay and Lilla Lee (Jones) F. BS Communics., Ohio U., 1980; MA Jnlsm., Amer. U., 1983. Contrbr. Delaware Gazette, 1978; production techn. Warner/Amex Cable TV, Columbus, OH, 1980-82; teaching asst. Amer. U., Washington, 1982-83; news asst. Satellite News Channel, Washington, 1983; ed./wrtr. Phillips Pub., ed. Digital Bypass Report, 1984-86, Viewtext, 1984-86; contrbr. to Cable News, 1984, DBS News, 1985, Satellite News, 1985; contrbr. to Washington Technology, 1986; editor, Jnl of Information and Image Management, 1986—. Mem. RTNDA. Home: 8560 Freyman Dr 101 Chevy Chase MD 20815

FLYNN, JOHN DAVID, b. Jackson, TN, Apr. 4, 1948, s. John Aloysius and Mary Evelyn (Groom) F.; m. Deborah Ann Coleman, Jan. 28, 1978; 1 dau., Caitlin Rose. Contrbr. fiction to Real Fiction, Mont. Rvw, CottonBall, Atlanta Rvw, Story Quarterly; ; contrbr. poetry to Kansas Qtly, Just Pulp, Foothills, Confrontation Poems for the Dead (anthology), Through a Glass Darkly (anthology), numerous other publs.; contrbr. articles to Constrn. Bull., U.S.A. Report, Nashville Business Jnl, others. BA, BJ, U. Mo., Columbia, 1971, MA, U. Denver, 1972; MA, Boston U., 1980, PhD, U. Nebr., 1984. Reporter Memphis Press-Scimitar, 1973-74; ed. Chapin Pub. Co., Mpls., 1976-77; mem. faculty Tenn. State U., Nashville, 1978-79, Suffolk U., Boston, 1980-81, Boston U., 1980-81, U. Nebr., Lincoln, 1984-85; adj. asst. prof. Middle Tenn. State U., Murfreesboro, 1985—; publs. cons. Japan Ctr., Murfreesboro. Home: 3934 Keeley Dr Nashville TN 37211

FLYNN, RICHARD MC DONNELL, b. Evanston, IL, Jan. 17, 1955; s. Richard James and Joanne Elizabeth (Resseguie) F.; m. Evangeline Areti Pappas, Jan. 4, 1979; 1 son, Richard Nicholas. Contrbr. poetry, essays and reviews to Gargoyle, Wash. Rvw, The Reaper, The Laurel Rvw, Whose Woods These Are, G W Rvw, Skyline, The New Laurel Rvw, Ariel, Carousel. BA, George Washington Univ., 1977, M Philosophy Am. Lit., 1984; MA in Lit., Am. U., 1980; PhD in Am. Lit., Geo. Wash. Univ., 1987. Law libn. Fedl. Bar Fdn., Washington, 1977—, lectr. in English, George Washington Univ., 1983—; editor SOS Books, 1982—. Lit. ed., Washington Rvw, 1987—. Mem. MLA, The Writer's Ctr,

Washington Area Comm. Poetry, P&W, Am. Assn. Law Libraries, Law Libns.' Soc. Washington. Address: 1710 15th St NW Washington DC 20009

FLYNT, CANDACE, b. Greensboro, NC, Mar. 12, 1947, d. Ralph MacAulay Lambeth and Dorothea Elaine (Patterson) Bray; m. John Christopher Johnson, Apr. 4, 1969 (div. 1972); m. 2d, Charles Homer Flynt, Jr., Apr. 13, 1974; 1 son, David MacAulay; stepchildren—Charles III, Elizabeth. Novelist: Chasing Dad, 1980, Sins of Omission, 1984, Mother Love, 1987; contrbr. stories to Carolina Qtly, Greensboro Rvw, Redbook mag., Atlantic. BA, Greensboro Coll., 1969; MFA, U. N.C.-G., 1974. Reporter Greensboro News Co., 1969-74. Home: 2005 Madison Ave Greensboro NC 27403

FOELL, EARL WILLIAM, b. Houston, Sept. 21, 1929; s. Ernest W. and Margaret (Kane) F.; m. Cordelia Treanor, Sept. 20, 1962; children—David, Jonathan, Hayden. Reporter, editorial writer, fgn. corr. Christian Sci. Monitor, Boston, 1953-68; UN corr. Los Angeles Times, 1968-70; mng. editor Christian Sci. Monitor, 1970-79, editor, 1979-83, editor-in-chief, 1983—. BA, Principia Coll., 1949. Hon. Dr. of Humane Ltrs., Monterey Inst. of International Studies, 1986. Home: 43 Black Horse Ln Cohasset MA 02025

FOERSTER, RICHARD A., b. NYC, Oct. 29, 1949; s. Alfons and Elizabeth (Zakrzewicz) Foerster; m. Valerie Elizabeth Malinowski, Oct. 28, 1972, (div. 1985). Author: Two Nocturnes (with Dana Gioia), 1985; contrbr. poetry to The Nation, Poetry, Tar River Poetry, and many other mags. and anthologies. BA, Fordham U., 1971; MA, U. of Va., 1972; edit. asst., C.L. Barnhart, Inc., Bronxville, NY, 1973-76; editor, Prentice-Hall, Englewood Cliffs, NJ, 1976-79; assoc. editor, Chelsea Rev., NYC,1978—; pres., Blue-Pencil, Inc., Mt. Kisco, NY, 1979-86; free-lance wrtr. of language arts text books, 1979—. Awards Discovery/The Nation Prize, 1985; MacDowell Fellow, 1985; Virginia Center for the Creative Arts Fellow, 1987. Mem. PSA, P&W, AAP. Home: Box 1040 York Beach ME 03910

FOGEL, DANIEL MARK, b. Columbus, OH, Jan. 21, 1948; s. Ephim Gregory and Charlotte Edith (Finkelstein) F.; m. Rachel Kahn, June 23, 1973; children—Nicholas, Rosemary. Author: A Trick of Resilience, 1975, Henry James and the Structure of the Romatic Imagination, 1981. Editor: Henry James Rvw, 1979—. BA, Cornell U., 1969, MFA., 1974, PhD, 1976. Asst. prof., 1976-80, assoc. prof., 1980-84, prof., 1984—. Mem. MLA, Henry James Soc. Home: 741 Rue Crozat Baton Rouge LA 70810

FOLDVARY, FRED E., b. Haifa, Palestine, May 11, 1946; s. Otto and Tina F.; came to U.S., 1952. Author: The Soul of Liberty, 1980, Natural Rights, 1985. BA, U. CA, 1969. Ed., Topical Time Mag., San Francisco, 1981—, Libertarian Digest, Berkeley, CA, 1981—. Home: 1920 Cedar St Berkeley CA 94709

FOLKMAN, GEORGIA, see Reed, Delpha Mae

FOLLETT, KENNETH MARTIN, (Symon Myles), b. Cardiff, Wales, June 5, 1949; s. Martin D. and Lavinia C. (Evans) F.; m. Mary Emma Ruth Elson, Jan. 5, 1968 (div. 1985); children: Emanuele, Marie-Claire; m. Barbara Broer, Nov. 8, 1985. Author: The Secret of Kellerman's Studio, 1976, The Bear Raid, 1976, The Shakeout, 1976, Eye of the Needle, 1978, Triple, 1979, The Key to Rebecca, 1980, The Man from St. Petersburg, 1981, On Wings of Eagles, 1983, Lie Down with Lions, 1986; as Symon Myles: The Big Needle, 1973; as Zachary Stone: The Modigliani Scandal, 1976, Paper Money, 1977; author screenplays: Fringe Banking, 1978, A Football Star, 1979, Lie Down with Lions, 1968. B.A., Univ. Coll., London, 1970. Reporter South Wales Eho, 1970-73; reporter Evening News, London, 1973-74; editorial dir. Everest Books Ltd., London, 1974-76, dep. mng. dir., 1976-77. Office: Writers House 21 W 26th St New York NY 10010

FOLLETT, ROBERT JOHN RICHARD, b. Oak Park, IL., July 4, 1928; s. Dwight W. and Mildred (Johnson) F.; m. Nancy L. Crouthamel, Dec. 30, 1950; children: Brian L., Kathryn R., Jean A., Lisa W. Author: Your Wonderful Body, 1961, What to Take Backpacking and Why, 1977, How to Keep Score in Business, 1978, The Financial Side of Book Publishing, 1982, rev. ed., 1987. A.B., Brown U., 1950; postgrad., Columbia u., 1950-51. Editor Follett Pub. Co., Chgo., 1951-55, sales mgr., 1955-58. gen. mgr. ednl. div., 1958-68, pres., 1968-78; chmn. Follett Internat., 1972—; chmn., dir. Follett Corp., 1979—; dir. Maxton Pub. Corp., Follett Coll. Stores Corp., United Coll. Bookstores Co.; v.p. United Learning Corp.; chmn. School Pubs., 1971-73; pub. Alpine Guild, 1977—; chmn. Book Distbn. Task Force of Book Industry, 1978-81. Bd. dirs. Ctr. Book Research, 1985—. Served in AUS, 1951-53. Mem. Assn. Am. Pubs. (dir. 1972-79); Chgo. Pubs. Assn. (pres. 1976—); vp. & dir. Am. Book Council, 1986—; founding dir., Mid-Am. Pubs. Assn., 1987—. Home: 300 S Euclid Ave Oak Park IL 60302

FONDA, JANE, b. NYC, Dec. 21, 1937; d. Henry and Frances (Seymour) F.; m. Rober Vadim (div.); 1 child, Vanessa; m. Tom Hayden, Jan. 20, 1973; 1 child, Troy. Author: Jane Fonda's Workout Book, 1981, (with Mignon McCarthy) Women Coming of Age, 1984, Jane Fonda's New Workout & Weight-Loss Program, 1986. Student, Vassar Coll. Address: Box 491355 Los Angeles CA 90049

FONDREN, KERVIN, b. Bessemer, AL, May 3, 1963; s. Fred and Gertrude (Houston) F. Contrbr. poems, articles to newspapers, lit. mags., anthols. Student U. Ala., 1987—. Nursing asst. U. Ala. Diabetes Hosp., Birmingham, 1986. Served with U.S. Army, 1981-85. Recipient Cert. of Merit, World of Poetry, 1987, Golden Poet award, 1987. Home: 216 Ave T Pratt City Birmingham AL 35214

FONER, ERIC, b. NYC, Feb. 7, 1943; s. Jack D. and Liza F.; m. Lynn Garafola, May 1, 1980. Author: Free Soil, Free Labor, Free Men, 1970, Tom Paine and Revolutionary America, 1976, Politics and Ideology in the Age of the Civil War, 1980, Nothing But Freedom, 1983. BA, Columbia U., 1963, Oxford (Eng.) U., 1965; PhD, Columbia U., 1969. ACLS fellow, 1972-73; Guggenheim fellow, 1975-76, NEH fellow, 1982-83. Home: 606 W 116th St New York NY 10027

FONT, DAVID JAMES, SR., b. Bklyn., May 7, 1955; s. Victor Manuel and Louise (Bogert) F.; m. Denise Elizabeth McGovern, May 5, 1984; 1 son, David James. Contrbr. children's fiction to Jack and Jill. Wrkg. on children's fiction and poems. Student Jersey City State Coll., 1975-77., Inst. Children's Lit., Redding Ridge, Conn., 1986. Tchr.'s aide Secaucus Day Trng., N.J., 1978-82; recreation house parent Harrison Group Home, N.J., 1984; activity therapist North Bergen Adult Activities, N.J., 1982-86; pres. Home Buyer Counseling Services, Inc., Bayonne, N.J., 1986—. Prog. svpvr. Springfield Supportive Employment, N.J., 1986—. Scoutmaster Hudson Hamilton council Boy Scouts Am., Jersey City, N.J., 197-73. Mem. Am. Soc. Notary Pubs. Home: 80 W 51st St Bayonne NJ 07002

FOOTE, HORTON, b. Wharton, TX, Mar. 14, 1916; s. Albert Horton and Hallie (Brooks) F.; m. Lillian Vallish, June 4, 1945; children: Barbarie Hallie, Albert Horton, Walter Vallish, Daisy Brooks. Author: (novel) The Chase, 1956, Three Plays, 1987; writer numerous screenplays including: Storm Fear, 1956; To Kill a Mockingbird (Acad. award, Writers Guild Am. award), 1962, Baby, The Rain Must Fall, 1964, Hurry Sundown, 1967, Tomorrow, 1972, Tender Mercies (Acad. award), 1983, 1918, 1985, Valentine's Day, 1985; writer, co-producer: The Trip to Bountiful, 1985; plays include: Texas Town, 1942, Only The Heart, 1944, Celebration, 1948, The Chase, 1952, The Trip to Bountiful, 1953, The Traveling Lady, 1954, The Dancers, 1963, Gone with the Wind, 1971, The Roads to Home, 1982, The Road to the Graveyard, 1985, Blind Date, 1986, Lily Dale, 1986, The Widow Claire, 1986. TV scripwriter, works include: Only The Heart, NBC, 1947, Ludie Brooks, CBS, 1951, The Travelers, NBC, 1952, The Old Beginning, NBC, 1953, The Trip to Bountiful, NBC, 1953, Young Lady Of Property, NBC, 1953, The Oil Well, NBC, 1953, Rocking Chair, NBC, 1953, Expectant Relations, NBC, 1953, Death of the Old Man, NBC, 1953, Tears of My Sister, NBC, 1953, John Turner Davis, NBC, 1953, The Midnight Caller, NBC, 1953, The Dancers, NBC, 1954, The Shadow of Wilie Geer, NBC, 1954, The Roads to Home, ABC, 1955, Flight, NBC, 1956, Drugstore: Sunday Noon, ABC, 1955, Member of the Family, CBS, 1957, Traveling Lady, CBS, 1957, Old Man, CBS, 1959, Tomorrow, CBS, 1960, 71, The Shape of the River, CBS, 1960, Nights of the Storm, CBS, 1961, Gambling Heart, NBC, 1964, The Displaced Person, PBS, 1977, Barn Burning, PBS, 1980. Student, Pasadena Playhouse Sch. Theatre, Calif., 1933-35, Tamara Daykahanova Schl. Theatre, NYC, 1937-39; tchr. of playwriting. Address: Dramatists Play Svc 440 Park Ave S New York NY 10016

FOOTE, SHELBY, b. Greenville, MS, Nov. 17, 1916; s. Shelby Dade and Lillian (Rosenstock) F.; m. Gwyn Rainer, Sept. 5, 1956; children—Margaret Shelby, Huger Lee. Author: novels Tournament, 1949, Follow Me Down, 1950, Love in a Dry Season, 1951, Shiloh, 1952, Jordan County, 1954, September September, 1978; history The Civil War, A Narrative: Vol. 1, Fort Sumter to Perryville, 1958, Vol. II, Fredericksburg to Meridian, 1963, Vol. III, Red River to Appomattox, 1974; play Jordan County: A Landscape in the Round, 1964. Student, U. N.C., 1935-37; disting. alumnus award, U. N.C., 1975; DLitt (hon.), U. of the South, 1981, Southwestern U., 1982. Novelist lectr., U. Va., 1963; playwright in residence, Arena Stage, Washington, 1963-64; writer-in-res. Hollins Coll., Va., 1968. Guggenheim fellow, 1955-57; Ford Fdn. fellow, 1963-64. Address: 542 E Parkway S Memphis TN 38104

FORD, ELAINE, b. White Plains, NY, Dec. 12, 1938, d. John H. and Ruth (Palmer) Ford; m. Gerald Bunker, Oct. 18, 1958 (div. 1976); children—Mark, Geoffrey, Lisa, Andrew, Anne-Elizabeth; m. 2d, Arthur Boatin, Dec. 27, 1977. Author: The Playhouse, 1980, Missed Connections, 1983, Ivory Bright, 1986. AB, Radcliffe, 1960. Asst. prof. dept English U. Me., Orono,

1986—. NEA fiction grantee, 1982, 86. Home: RFD 1 Box 340B Milbridge ME 04658

FORD, GERTRUDE, b. NYC., Apr. 6; d. Sam and Lean (Gewirtz) Unger; m. Abraham Ford, Nov. 16, 1938; children: Barbara F., Elizabeth R. Author: 1181 Sheriff Street, 1981. BSS, Bklyn. Coll. Supervising mgr. NYC Housing Authority, 1948—. Home: 568 Grand St New York NY 10002

FORD, JESSE HILL, b. Troy, AL, Dec. 28, 1928; s. Jesse Hill and Lucille (Musgrove) F.; m. Lillian Pellettieri, Nov. 15, 1975; children—Charles Davis, Sarah Ann, Elizabeth. Author: Mountains of Gilead, 1961, The Liberation of Lord Byron Jones, 1965, (with Stirling Silliphant) screenplay, 1969, The Feast of St. Barnabas, 1969, The Raider, 1975; short story collection Fishes, Birds and Sons of Men, 1967; play The Conversion of Buster Drumsright, 1963; musical Drumwright, 1982. BA, Vanderbilt U., 1951; MA, U. Fla., 1955; postgrad. (Fulbright scholar), U. Oslo, Norway, 1961-62; LittD (hon.), Lambuth Coll., 1968. Reporter The Nashville Tennessean, 1950-51; news writer U. Fla., 1953-55. Served with USNR, 1951-53. Atlantic grantee, 1959; Guggenheim fellow, 1966; included O. Henry Prize Collection Short Stories, 1961, 66, 67; Best Detective Stories, 1972-76; recipient Edgar award for short story "The Jail," MWA, 1976; guest columnist, USA Today, 1986—. Address: 500 Plantation Ct Nashville TN 37221

FORD, KATHLEEN, b. Orange, NJ, Mar. 21, 1945, d. Edward Roderick and Catharine Clare (Gibney) Ford; m. Richard J. Bonnie, June 15, 1967; children—Joshua, Zachary, Jessica. Author: Jeffrey County, 1986; contrbr. short stories to Redbook, So Humanities Rvw, Antietam Rvw, Yankee, numerous other mags. BA, Notre Dame of Md., Balt., 1966; MA, Columbia U., 1967. Recipient 2 PEN Syndicated Fiction awards, 1984-85. Home: 917 Rugby Rd Charlottesville VA 22903

FORD, PHYLLIS, see Choyke, Phyllis May

FORD, RICHARD C., b. Jackson, MS, Feb. 16, 1944, s. Parker Carroll and Edna Lavon (Akin) F.; m. Kristina Hensley, Mar. 22, 1968. Novelist/storywriter: A Piece of My Heart, 1976, The Ultimate Good Luck, 1981, The Sportswriter, 1986, Rock Springs: Stories, 1987; contrbr. stories, essays to Esquire, Antaeus, TriQtly, Harpers, New Yorker, other publs. BA, Mich. State U., 1966, MFA, U. Calif., Irvine, 1970. Asst. prof. U. Mich., Ann Arbor, 1974-76; lectr. Williams Coll., Williamstown, Mass., 1978-79, 81, Princeton (N.J.) U., 1979-80. Recipient fellowships Guggenheim Fdn., 1977, NEA, 1979, 86, Mich. Soc. Fellows, 1971-74. Mem. PEN. Address: Urban ICM 40 W 57th St NYC 10019

FORD, SARAH LITSEY, b. Springfield, KY, June 23, 1901, d. Edwin Carlile and Carrie Rachel (Selecman) Litsey; m. Frank Wilson Nye, June 17, 1933 (dec. July 3, 1963); 1 son, Christopher; m. 2d, William Wallace Ford, Dec. 1, 1979. Author: There Was a Lady, 1945, The Intimate Illusion, 1955, A Path to the Water, 1962 (novels), Legend, 1936, For the Lonely, 1937, The Oldest April, 1957, Toward Mystery, 1974 (poetry); contrbr. to poetry and fiction anthols. Condr. wrtrs. workshops, Conn. and N.J., 1955-63; instr. Famous Writers Schl., Westport, Conn., 1961-84; condr. writers workshops, Conn., 1975—. First prize, PSA, 1940, N.Y. Women Poets, 1958, 59, 74, 83, 84; quarterly prize, The Lyric, Va., 1983, memorial prize, 1984. Mem. N.Y. Women Poets, PEN, PSA. Home: 248 Newtown Tnpk W Redding CT 06896

FORD-CHOYKE, PHYLLIS, see Choyke, Phyllis May

FORDE, JOYCE P., b. Paterson, NJ, Feb. 19, 1950; d. Joseph R. and Alice S. (Schmidt) Forde. Author: advertising copy; contrbr. National Poetry Anthology, 1986. Wrkg. on two novels, short stories, poetry collection, screen play. AB, Upsala Coll.; MA, Montclair State Coll. Tchr. NJ public shls., 1972-78; acct. exec., Executive Search, 1980-81; reading spclst. Madison (NJ) public schls., 1981-82; secy., 1983-86; restaurant mgr., 1986—. Home: 14 Watchung Ave Chatham NJ 07928

FORE, ROBERT CLIFFORD, b. Jacksonville, FL, Feb. 23, 1948; s. Clifford Roy and Annie Laurie (Wiltshire) F.; m. Rorie Elizabeth Smith, Aug. 8, 1970; children—Dorian Brooke, Jessica Allison. BA, U. So. Fla., 1969, M.Ed., 1972; Ed.D, U. GA, 1976. Tchr./co-ord. Duval Co. Schl. Bd., Jacksonville, FL, 1969-73; U.S. Off. Edn. doctoral fellow, U.GA, 1973-76; asst. prof. edn., Jacksonville U., 1975-77; edn. supr. GA Acad. for Blind, Macon, 1977-79; assoc. exec. dir., Fla. Medical Assn., & exec. ed. Jnl. Fla. Med. Assn., Jacksonville, 1982—. First place Best State Med. Jnl. in nation, Sandoz Pharmaceutical Co., 1983. Mem. Am. Assn. Med. Soc. Execs., Alliance for Continuing Med. Edn. Home: 4216 Rapallo Rd Jacksonville FL 32244

FORELLE, HELEN, see Leih, Grace Janet

FORER, ANNE RUTH, (Anne U) b. NYC, Apr. 4, 1945; d. Leon and Marion (Kessler) Forer. Pub./ed. and contrbr. Vague, 1981, The Stories & Letters of Anne & Basha, 1977; contrbr. Nimrod,Exquisite Corpse, Heresies, Green Mt. Qtly, A Room of One's Own, Avenue E, Do Da, Meeting Ground. BA, Antioch Coll., 1962-63, CCNY, 1963-67. Recipient CAPS award for fiction, NY State fellowship, NYC, 1980; Katherine Anne Porter award, Nimrod Mag., Tulsa, Okla, 1983. Mem P & W, St. Marks Ch. Poetry Project. Address: 87 First Ave 3B New York NY 10003

FORER, BERNARD, b. Trenton, NJ, Mar. 30, 1907; s. Hyman and Hannah (Kaplan) F.; m. Rose E. Forer, Aug. 19, 1934; children—Arthur H., Helen F. Author: A New Practical Tennis Book, 1974, The A-B-C-D of Successful College Writing (with others), 1971; contrbr. poetry: Black Bear Rev., San Fernando Poetry chapbooks, 1985, 86. Wrkg. on poetry collection. AB, Rutgers U., 1927; MA, NYU, 1930. Tchr. public schs., Trenton, N.J., 1927-64; mem. faculty West Chester (Pa.) Coll., 1964-66, Bucks County Community Coll., Newtown, Pa., 1966-72; adj. prof. Rutgers U., New Brunswick, N.J. Mem. AAP, Conservatory Am. Letters. Home: 4568 Narraganset Trail Sarasota FL 34233

FORESTER, BRUCE MICHAEL, b. NYC., May 25, 1939, s. Bernard and Ruth F.; m. Erica Simms, Dec. 21, 1962; children—Brent, Robin, Russell. Author: In Strict Confidence, 1982, Signs and Omens, 1987; Fatal Memory. BA, Dartmouth Coll., 1961; MD, Columbia U., 1965. Practice medicine specializing in psychiatry; asst. clin. prof. psychiatry Columbia U., N.Y.C., 1971—. Mem. MWA, med. orgns. Home: 55 Northway St Bronxville NY 10708

FORRESTER, SUSAN ANNETTE, B. Gulfport, MS, Nov. 9, 1962; m. Steven Robert Forrester, June 5, 1982. Contrbr. articles to Golden Yrs. mag., newspapers. B.A. in Jnlsm., Brevard Commun. Coll., 1986. Tutor, Lit. Council, Melbourne, FL, 1986-87. Home: 683 Young St Melbourne FL 32935

FORSTER, ARNOLD, bNYC, June 25, 1912; s. Hyman Lawrence and Dorothy (Turits) Fastenberg; m. May Kasner, Sept. 29, 1940; children—Stuart William, Jane E. Author: Anti-semitism in the United States, 1947, A Measure of Freedom, 1950, (with B.R. Epstein) The Troublemakers, 1952, Cross-Currents, 1956, Some of My Best Friends, 1962, Danger on the Right, 1964, (with Epstein) Report on the Ku Klux Klan, 1965, Report on the John Birch Society, 1966, Radical Right: Report on the John Birch Society and Its Allies, 1967, Report from Israel, 1969, The New Anti-Semitism, 1974. LLB, St. John's Coll., 1935. Author, corr. (TV and radio program series) Dateline Israel, 1967-83. Recipient Emmy award for film Avenue of the Just, 1980, Zubin and the I.P.O., 1983. Home: 79 Wykagyl Terr New Rochelle NY 10804

FORTSON, SANNA, b. Newton, MS, July 8, 1944; d. Warren Dee and Velma Lee (Royals) Fortson. Contrbr. articles to newpapers, popular and trade mags. including Gurney's Gardening News, MIss. Mag., Nat. Fisherman. Ed.: Clinton-Times, Clinton, MS, 1976. Wrkg. on juvenile books, novel, articles. Student U. Southern Miss., 1965-67, 72-73. Broadcast journalist Sta. WJDX-WZZQ, Jackson, MS, 1973-74, Sta. WOKJ-WJMI, Jackson, 1976-77, MS News Network, Jackson, 1979-80; program dir. Sta. WBKH, Hattiesburg, MS, 1981-84. Mem. Natl. Wrtr.'s Club. Home: 213 Patton Ave Hattiesburg MS 39401

FORTUNÉ, MONIQUE JOAN, b. Brooklyn, NY, Jan. 24, 1961; d. Gontran Petrus and Joan Altima Tyson-Fortuné. Contrbr. to various publs. of Syracuse U.; poetry readings: New Media Studio, NYC,1977-79, WAER Radio, Syracuse, 1978-82, Salt City Center for Perf. Arts, Syracuse, 1981. BS in Brdcst. Jnlsm., Syracuse U., 1982. Admin. Asst. Personnel Pool of NY City, Inc., 1983-84; promotions coord. WWRL Radio (Woodside, NY), 1984—. Mem. AUDELCO, Am. Women in Radio and Television, Coalition of 100 Black Women, NY. Address: 790 Concourse Village West Bronx NY 10451

FOSTER, BARBARA, b. Phila., June 27, 1938; d. Emanuel and Lillian (Dolfman) Farbman. Author: (biography) Forbidden Journey; contrbr. lit mags U.S., England, Ireland, and Can. MLS, Columbia U., 1960; postgrad Hunter Coll., Tulane U. Asst. prof. in library sci., Hunter Coll., NYC, 1967—. Recipient Shuster grant, Hunter Coll., 1982, 85. Mem. CODA. Address: 62 Barrow St New York NY 10014

FOSTER, GRACE ELIZABETH, b. Lewisville, AR, Oct. 15, 1928; d. Benjamin Franklin and Era Letha (Mayfield) Carroll; m. John Kilby Foster, Sept. 6, 1949; children—John K., Lindsey Ann Hinshaw, Steven C., David N. Author: History of Woman's Club of Southern Maryland, 1979, Carroll Frontiersmen: From North Carolina to Arkansas, 1805- 1987, 1987. Contrbr. features, articles to mags., newspapers. Wrkg. on novel, Winds Blew from the South. A.A., Prince George's Commun. Coll., 1972; B.S. in Jnlsm., U. Md., 1974. Feature wrtr. Times/Crescent News, LaPlata, MD, 1976-78; sect. ed. Md. Ind.-News, Waldorf, MD, 1979-84; free-lance wrtr., 1984—. Recipient 1st place for front page design Md.-Del.-DC Press Assn., 1982. Home:

Trinity Dr Rt 1 Box 337 Charlotte Hall MD 20622

FOSTER, LINDA NEMEC, b. Garfield Heights, OH, May 29, 1950; d. John Joseph and Helen Agnes (Kumor) Nemec; m. Anthony Jesse Foster, Oct. 26, 1974; children—Brian Jesse, Ellen Kathleen. Author: A History of the Body, 1986; poetry to Another Chicago Mag, Croton Rvw, Laurel Rvw, Manhattan Poetry Rvw, Midwest Poetry Rvw, Negative Capability, Nimrod, The Pennsylvania Rvw, Univ. of Windsor Rvw, Worcester Rvw, Poetry Now, other lit mags; poetry to numerous anthologies. BA, Aquinas Coll., 1972; MFA, Goddard Coll., 1979. Social analyst Center for Environmental Study (Grand Rapids, MI), 1971-74; instr. Ferris State Coll. (Big Rapids, MI), 1983-84; wrtg. tchr. Michigan Council for the Arts, 1980—. Creative Artist Grant, Michigan Council for Arts, 1983-84. recipoient: Grand prize, APA, 1986; Emerging Wrtrs, 1987. Mem. PSA. Home: 427 W Pere Marquette Big Rapids MI 49307

FOSTER, LIZ, see Lystra, Helen Perey

FOSTER, R(OBERT) J(AMES), b. Oak Park, IL., Feb. 13, 1929, s. George Peter and Helen (McLaughlin) F.; m. Marilyn Joan Cronin, May 29, 1954; children—Mark Cronin, Matthew McLaughlin. Author: Tuyere Am I and Other Poems, 1962, The Pregnant Mule, 1968, The Sun Is a Sugar Cookie, 1977, Three Cheers for Me, 1978; Nipping Leaves, 1987; contrbr. poetry, essays to Concept, The Prairie Poet, N.Am. Mentor, other publs. BA in English, Culver-Stockton Coll., 1955; MA in English, No. Ill. U., 1971. Tchr. English, now at Elgin (Ill.) High Schl. Served with USMC, 1951-53. Mem. Modern Poetry Assn., NCTE, profl. orgns. Home: 491 Hubbard Ave Elgin IL 60120

FOSTER, VICKIE LYNN, b. Dayton, July 28, 1952; d. Eugene Earl and Virginia Winifred (Childers) F. Editor: DCS reference manuals Buick, Cadillac, Chevrolet, Oldsmobile, Mercedes-Benz, Pontiac, GMC Truck, Ford, genl. interest articles to newspapers, mags., newsletters. Wrkg. on short fiction pieces. B.A., U. Dayton, 1975, M.A., 1981. Documentation specialist Reynolds and Reynolds Co., Dayton, 1984—. Recipient Fiction Writing award Dayton Daily News, 1984. Mem. IABC. Home: 1617 Lindsey Ave Miamisburg OH 45342

FOURNIER, CARLOS, b. Habana, Cuba, May 9, 1953, came to U.S., 1962, naturalized 1977; s. Carlos Secundino and Antonia (Pegueiras) F.; m. Marta Maria Cordova, Aug. 27, 1977; children—Carlos Marcel, Denise Marie. Contrbr. sports articles to mags., newspapers including Boxing Digest, The Miami Herald, others. B.B.A., Fla. Intl., U., 1976; M.B.A., Nova U., 1983. Accounting mgr. Southeast Bank, Miami, 1982-84; asst. controller Broward Fed. Savings & Loan, Ft. Lauderdale, FL, 1984-86; bus. mgr. Post-Newsweek Fla., Miami, 1986—. Voting mem. Law Vegas Boxing Hall of Fame, 1987. Mem. Broadcast Financial Management Assn. Home: 18000 NW 68 Ave 211 Hialeah FL 33015

FOUTZ, DELL R., b. Ogden, UT, Nov. 15, 1932; s. Leslie and Veva (Riggs) Foutz; m. Sherry Bradfield, Dec. 22, 1953; children—Vicki, Janice, Tracy, Paul, Connie. Author: Where Is the Gold on the Colorado River, 1982; co-author: Annotated Bibl. Uranium of World, 1981; contrbr. to Outlook Mag, Colorado Field Trip Guide, 1985. BS, Brigham Young U., 1955, MA, 1960; PhD, Washington State U., 1965. Exploration & Production Geologist Exxon (TX), 1965-72; geology prof. Mesa College (Grand Junction, CO), 1972—; technical wrtr. US Bureau Reclam.-damsites, 1976, Paraho Corp., 1981-83. First Lt, USAF, 1956-59, Korea. Home: 221 Mesa Ave Grand Junction CO 81501

FOWLER, ANNE CARROLL, b. Portland, ME, May 5, 1946; d. Aleander Robert and Sally (Holt) Fowler; 1 dau., Elizabeth Holt Fowler. Contrbr. numerous poems to lit. mags., anthols. B.A., Radcliffe Coll., 1968; M.A., Boston U., 1971, Ph.D., 1979; M.Div., Episcopal Divinity Schl., 1984. Asst. prof. humanities Wentworth Inst., Boston, 1979—; asst. rector St. Dunstan's Episcopal Ch., Dover, MA, 1985—. Recipient prize Brigham Young U., 1984; featured poet Pudding Mag., 1987. Mem. PSA, Soc. Values in Higher Edn. Home: 50 Gilbert Rd Belmont MA 02178

FOWLER, DOUGLAS R., b. Springfield, IL, Oct. 12, 1940, s. Russel Henry and Sarah Nadina (Boardman) F.; m. Marilyn Stachenfeld, Feb. 27, 1965 (div. 1983); 1 son, Nicholas. Author: Reading Nabokov, 1974, A Reader's Guide to Gravity's Rainbow, 1980, S.J. Perelman, 1983, Ira Levin, 1987; ed.: The Kingdom of Dreams, 1986; contrbr. to The Poetry and Plays of T.S. Eliot Intro 3, 1987; contrbr. to Epoch, Extrapolation, Encyc. Am. Humorists, numerous other publs. BA, Cornell U., 1962, MFA, 1970, PhD, 1972. Prof. English Fla. State U., Tallahassee, 1972—. Served as sgt. U.S. Army, 1966-68. Recipient numerous lit. awards Cornell U. Home: Apt E 1815 Nicklaus Dr Tallahassee FL 32301

FOWLER, GENE, b. Oakland, CA., Oct. 5, 1931; s. Jack Fowler and Janice Nadine (Campbell) LaFrance; m. April Corioso, May 6, 1981. Author: Field Studies, 1965, Shaman Songs, 1966, Her Majesty's Ship, 1969, Fires, 1971, Felon's Journal, 1975, Fires: Selected Poems 1963-1976, 1976, Return of the Shaman, 1981, Waking the Poet, 1982, The Quiet Poems, 1982. Contrbr. poems to numerous anthols. Ed. publ schls. Recipient Dymaxion award Buckminster Fuller Inst., 1967; achievement award grantee NEA, 1970. Home: 1432 Spruce St Berkeley CA 94709

FOWLER, WILLIAM MORGAN, JR., b. Clearwater, FL, July 25, 1944; s. William Morgan and Eleanor Louise (Brennan) F.; m. Marilyn Louise Noble, Aug. 11, 1968; children—Alison Louise, Nathaniel Morgan. Author: William Ellery: A Rhode Island Politico and Lord of Admiralty, 1973, Rebels Under Sail, 1976, The Baron of Beacon Hill: A Biography of John Hancock, 1980, Jack Tars and Commodores, 1985; contrbr. numerous articles to nwsprs., jnls, books. BA, Northeastern U., 1967; MA, U. Notre Dame, 1969, PhD, 1971. Asst. Prof. hist., Northeastern U., Boston, 1971-77, assoc. prof., 1977-80, prof. and managing ed., New England Quarterly, 1981—. Home: 323 Franklin St Reading MA 01867

FOX, CONNIE T., b. Chgo., Feb. 12, 1932, d. Hugh Bernard and Helen Marie (Mangan) Fox; m. Nono W. Grimes, Sept. 15, 1971 (div. Nov. 23, 1986); children: Margaret, Alexandra, Christopher; m. 2d, Dr. M. B. Costa, Dec. 1, 1986. Author: Blood Cocoon, 1980, The Dream of the Black Topaze Chamber, 1981, 10 to the 170th Power, 1986, Babicka, 1986, Schreckliche Engel, 1986, Nachthymnen, 1986; The Schoenbrunn Monologues (play) published as spcl. issue of Dramatika, 1981. Wrkg. on Noria, long poem about The Mind as Cosmic Stage, using Buddhistic principles interwoven with contemporary Blitzkrieg psychology. Doctorate, French lit., 1956. Freelance writer, editor, 1957—. Address: Box 703 San Francisco CA 90045

FOX, EDWARD INMAN, b. Nashville, Aug. 22, 1933; s. Herbert Franklin and Ladye (Inman) F. Author: Azorin as a Literary Critic, 1962, La Crisis Intelectual del 98, 1976, Liberalismo y socialismo, 1984; articles, translations, poetry; editor: La voluntad, 1969, 2d edit., 1973, 3d edit., 1981, Antonio Azorin, 1970, Articulos desconocidos de R. de Maeztu, 1977, Ensayos sobre el arte y la literatura de Ortega y Gasset, 1986; co-editor: Spanish Thought and Letters in the Twentieth Century, 1966. BA, Vanderbilt U., 1954, MA, 1958; student, U. Montpellier, France, 1956-57; AM Princeton U., 1959, PhD, 1961; LHD, Knox Coll., 1982, Monmouth Coll., 1982. Served to lt. (j.g.) USNR, 1954-56; capt. Res. Woodrow Wilson fellow, 1956-57; Fulbright scholar, France, 1956-57; Herbert Montgomery Bergen fellow, 1958-59; grantee Am. Philo. Soc., 1963, 68; Fulbright research scholar, Spain, 1965-66; Guggenheim fellow, 1970-71; NEH fellow, 1983. Mem. MLA, consultant NEH. Address: 1508 Hinman Apt 4B Evanston IL 60201

FOX, ELEANOR MAE COHEN, b. Trenton, NJ, Jan. 18, 1936; d. Harman and Elizabeth (Stein) Cohen; m. Byron E. Fox, Mar. 31, 1957; children—Douglas Anthony, Margot Alison, Randall Matthew. Author: (novel) W.L., Esquire, 1977; (with Byron E. Fox) Corporate Acquisitions and Mergers, Vol. 1, 1968, Vol. 2, 1970, Vol. 3, 1973; bd. editors: N.Y. Law Jnl, 1976—. BA, Vassar Coll., 1956; LLB, N.Y. U., 1961. Editor high schl. textbooks Cambridge Book Co., NYC, 1956-57; editor labor service publ. Bur. Natl. Affairs, Washington, 1957-58. Fellow Am. Bar Fdn., N.Y. Bar Fdn. Home: 69 W 89th St New York NY 10024

FOX, GEORGE H., b. Madanapalle, Madras, India, Jan. 4, 1933, came to U.S., 1963, s. Silas F. and Emma (Grau) F.; m. Jean M. Bond, Apr. 21, 1954 (div. 1984); children—David P., Alice M., Ruth E., Richard S., George H. Jr., Joyce A. Author: Reel Christianity, 1978, So Big my World (with Dorothy Haskin), 1979; contrbr. to Christian Life Mag. MA, Columbia Pacific U., 1984, PhD, 1985. Ed., pub. Herald in Hindi, 1959-61; wrtr., ed. Worldwide Pictures, Burbank, Calif., 1964-65; prodn. mgr. Associated Film Services, Burbank, 1966-69; pres., producer Master Media, Burbank, 1969-78; wrtr., producer Moody Inst. Sci., Whittier, Calif., 1976-77; v.p. Joy Prodns., North Hollywood Calif., 1982-85; cons., Somis, Calif., 1985-86; regl. dir. Christian Challenge Ministries, 1986—. Home: 328 Capitol Vill Circle San Jose CA 95136

FOX, HUGH BERNARD, b. Chgo., Feb. 12, 1932, s. Hugh Bernard and Helen Marie (Mangan) F.; m. Lucia Ungaro de Zevallos, June 12, 1956 (div. 1970); children—Hugh, Cecilia, Marcella; m. 2d, Nona Woodyne Grimes, Oct. 3, 1970; children—Margaret, Alexandra, Christopher. Author: Problemas de Nuestro Tiempo, 1965, America Hoy: Un Cursillo En Estudios Norteamericanos, 1965, 40 Poems, 1966, Teatro-Theater—A Night with Hugh Fox, 1966, Eye into Now, 1967, Soul-Catcher Songs, 1968, Henry James, A Critical Introduction, 1968, The Headless Centaurs, 1968, Glyphs, 1969, The Permeable Man, 1969, Ghost Dance Portfolio No. 1 (with S. Schott), 1969, The Angel of the Chairs, 1969, Son of Camelot Meets the Wolfman, 1969, Capabilities, 1969, Open Letter to a Closed System, 1969, Charles Bukowski: A Critical and Bibliographical Study, 1969, Omega Rising, 1969,

The Living Underground: A Critical Overview, 1970, The Ecological Suicide Bus, 1970, The Kansas City Westport Mantras, 1971, The Paralytic Grandpa Dream Secretions (poetry), 1971, Handbook Against Gorgons (with E.A. Vigo), 1971, The Industrial Ablution (with G. Deisler), 1971, Just (novel), 1972, The Angel, The Mago and Mama Glinka (novel), 1972, Survival Handbook (poetry), 1972, Peeple, 1973, Huaca, 1975, The Face of Guy Lombardo, 1976, The Gods of the Cataclysm, 1976, The Invisibles: A Dialectic (novel), 1976, Yo Yo Poems, 1977, Papa Funk, 1977, Honeymoon & Mom (2 novels in one volume), 1978, The Poetry of Charles Potts, 1979, Leviathan: An Indian Ocean Whale Herd Journal (novel), 1980, Almazora 42, 1982, Quarter-Jerk and Wiggle, 1985, Lyn Lifshin: A Critical Study, 1985, The Guernica Cycle—The Year Franco Died, 1986 The Dream of the Black Topaze Chamber, 1988, The Voyage to the House of the Sun—The Bolivian Episode, 1988; ed.: The Living Underground: An Anthology of Contemporary American Poetry, 1973, First Fire: Central and South American Indian Poetry, 1978; contrbr. to Vagabond Anthology, Aspect Anthology, First-Person Intense Anthology, Second Coming Anthology, other anthologies, periodicals; contrbg. ed.: Choice, 1968—, Newsart, 1968—, The Smith, 1968—, Pulpsmith, 1968—; ed.: Ghost Dance, 1968—; Latin-Am. ed. N.Am. Rvw, 1960s; S.Am. ed. Western World Rvw, 1960s. Wrkg. on novel, myth. MA, Loyola U., Chgo., 1955; PhD, U. Ill., 1958. Fulbright prof. Am. Studies, U. Sonora, Mex., 1961, Instituto Pedagogico-U. Catolico, Caracas, Venezuela, 1964-66; Fulbright prof. Am. Lit., U. Santa Catarina, Brazil, 1978-80. Grantee CCLM; Pan Am. Union fellow, Argentina, 1970. Mem. COSMEP (bd. dirs. San Francisco chpt. 1968-78, chmn. 1983). Home: 526 Forest St East Lansing MI 48823

FOX, JOHN, b. Bronx, NY, May 26, 1952, s. John George Sr. and Joan Marie (Manz) F. Novelist: The Boys on the Rock, 1984; contrbr. short stories to: Christopher Street mag., First Love/Last Love anthology, Men on Men anthology, Central Park mag., NER/BLQ mag. BA, Lehman Coll., 1975; MFA, Columbia U., 1984. Yaddo Fdn. fellow, 1985. Home: 426 W 46th St New York NY 10036

FOX, KARL AUGUST, b. Salt Lake City, July 14, 1917; s. Feramorz Young and Anna Teresa (Wilcken) F.; m. Sylvia Olive cate, July 29, 1940; children: Karl Richard, Karen Frances Anne. Author: Econometeric Analysis for Public Policy, 1958, (with others) The Theory of Quantitative Economic Policy, 1966, rev. edit., 1973, Intermediate Economic Statistics, 1968, rev. edit., (with T.K. Kaul) Intermediate Economic Statistics, 1980, (with J.K. Sengupta) Economic Analysis and Operations Research, 1969, (with W.C. Merrill) Introduction to Economic Statistics, 1970, Social Indicators and Social Theory, 1974; author-editor: Economic Analysis for Educational Planning, 1972; Co-editor: Readings in the Economics of Agriculture, 1969, Economic Models Estimation and Risk Programming (essays in nonor of Gerhard Tinter), 1969, Systems Economics, 1986. Home: 234 Parkridge CR Ames IA 50010

FOX, MICHAEL WILSON, b. Bolton, Eng., Aug. 13, 1937; came to U.S., 1962; s. Geoffrey and Elizabeth (Wilson) F.; m. Deborah Johnson, Aug. 1974; 1 dau., Mara; children by previous marriage: Michael Wilson, Camilla. Author: Canine Behavior, 1965, Canine Pediatrics, 1966, Integrative Development of Brain and Behavior in the Dog, 1971, Behavior of Wolves, Dogs and related Canids, 1971, Understanding Your Dog, 1972, Understanding Your Cat, 1974, Concepts in Ethology: Animal and Human Behavior, 1974, Between Animal and Man: The Key to The Kingdom, 1976, The Dog, Domestication and Behavior, 1977, Understanding Your Pet, 1978, The Soul of the Wolf, 1980, One Earth One Mind, 1980, Returning to Eden: Animal Rights and Human Responsibility, 1980, How to be Your Pet's Best Friend, 1981, What Is Your Cat Saying?, 1981, The Healing Touch, 1982, Love is a Happy Cat, 1982, Farm Husbandry, Behavior and Veterinary Practice, 1983, The Whistling Hunters: Field Studies of the Asiatic Wild Dog (Cuon alpinus), 1984, The Animal Doctor's Answer Book, 1984, Agricide: The Hidden Crisis that Affects Us All, 1986, Laboratory Animal Husbandry, 1986; (juveniles) The Wolf, 1973 (Christopher award), Vixie, The Story of a Fox, 1973, Sundance Coyote, 1974, Ramu and Chennai, 1975 (Sci. Tchrs.' award), Wild Dogs Three, 1977; co- author: What Is Your Dog Saying?, 1977, Whitepaws: A Coyote-Dog, 1979, Dr. Fox's Fables, 1980, The Touchlings, 1981, The Way of the Dolphin, 1981. Editor: Abnormal Behavior in Animals, 1968, Readings in Ethology and Comparative Psychology, 1973, The Wild Canids, 1975, On the Fifth Day: Animal Rights and Human Ethics, 1978, Intl. Jnl for Study of Animal Problems, Advances in Animal Welfare Sci. B.Vet. Med., Royal Vet. Coll., London, 1962; PhD, U. London, 1967, DSc, 1975. Contrbg. editor: McCall's mag.; author: syndicated newspaper column "Ask Your Animal Doctor." Mem. WG, AFTRA. Office: 2100 L St NW Washington DC 20037

FOX, R. MURDO, see Kimball, Richard Wilson

FOX, ROBERT R., b. Bklyn., Feb. 2, 1943, s. Charles and Mary (Wilkes) Fox; m. Susan H. Goldstein, Aug. 20, 1967; children—Joshua Wilkes, Jessica Sara. Author: Destiny News (stories), 1976, TLAR/CODPOL: The Last American Revolution, and Confessions of a Dead Politician (two novels), 1987; contrbr. to From the Hudson to the World, 1978, 73 Ohio Poets, 1978, Night House Anthology, 1983, Poetry Ohio: The Art of the State, 1984, Green Isle in the Sea, 1986, Sudden Fiction: American Short Short Stories, 1986, Epiphanies, 1987, Best Ohio Fiction, 1987, numerous other books and anthologies; ed.: They Came to School Dressed Like Flowers, 1977, Good Old Poems/I Love Them, 1979, Goodbye Cartoons/Hello Park, 1981, Something i wrote myself, 1983, Poems, 1978-82, 1983, The World is Flippied and Damzled Out, 1986. BA, Bklyn. Coll., 1967; MA, Ohio U., 1969. Wrtr.-in-residence Rider Coll., Lawrenceville, N.J., 1971-72; asst. ed. Ohio U. Publs., Athens, 1973-77; wrtr-in-res. Ohio Arts Council, Columbus, 1977—; adv. panelist NEA, 1984-87; trustee Ohioana Library Assn., 1986—. Recipient Citation in Lit., Ohioana Library Assn., 1982, PEN Syndicated Fiction Award, 1988. Home: 264 Richards Rd Columbus OH 43214

FOX, SUSAN CHRISTINE, b. Akron, OH, Dec. 5, 1943, d. Charles Isadore and Midge Adele (Weinstein) Fox. Author: Poetic Form in Blake's Milton, 1976; contrbr. articles to Critical Inquiry, In Britain; contrbr. poetry to Paris Rvw, Marxist Perspectives, Salome, Poetry Now, other publs. AB, Cornell U., 1965; PhD, Yale U., 1970. Assoc. prof. Queens Coll., CUNY, Flushing. Home: 7 E 14th St No 701 New York NY 10003

FOX, VERNON BRITTAIN, b. Boyne Falls, MI, Apr. 25, 1916; s. John Lorenzo and Ethel (Hamilton) F.; m. Laura Grace Ellerby, Mar. 22, 1941; children: Karen, Vernon, Loraine. Author: Violence Behind bars, 1956, Guidelines for Corrections Programs in Community and Junior Colleges, 1969, Crime and Law Enforcement, 1971, Introduction to Corrections, 1972, 2d ed., 1977, 3d ed., 1985, A Handbook for Volunteers in Juvenile Court, 1973; co-author, editor: Crime and Law Enforcement, 1971; co-author: Introduction to Criminal Justice, 1975, 1975, 2d ed., 1979, Introduction to Criminology, 1975, 2d ed., 1985, Russian ed., 1980, 85, 2d ed., 1985, Community-Based Corrections, 1977 (with Burton Wright) Criminal Justice and the Social Sciences, 1978, Correctional Institutions, 1983; internat. bd. editors: Abstracts in Criminology, 1959-71; assoc. editor: Criminal Justice, 1971—, Jour. Humanics, 1973—; mem. adv. bd. dirs.: Criminal Justice Rvw., 1975—; bd. advisors: Intl. Jnl. Comparative and Applied Criminal Justice, 1976—; abstractor: Abstracts for Social Workers, Fed. Probation. AB, Mich. State U., 1940, MA, 1943, PhD, 1949. Served with AUS, 1945-46. Home: 644 Voncile Ave Tallahassee FL 32303

FOXHALL, KATHRYN, b. Selma, AL, Feb. 6, 1950; d. Willard and Isabelle (Cadle) F. BS, Birmingham-Southern, 1972. Ed., Selma (AL) Free Press, 1972; asst. ed. Southern Living Books, Birmingham, AL, 1973-74; editorial asst. Air Force Mag., Washington, 1974-75, Am. Pub. Health Assn., Washington, 1975-78; ed. The Nation's Health, Washington, 1978—. Home: 2501 Q St. N W Washington DC 20007

FOY, CATHERINE ANTHONY, (Cat Foy, C. A. Bethel), b. Harrisburg, PA, Apr. 19, 1957; d. John Anastasios and Catherine Burgess (Simmons) Anthony; m. Clifton David Bethel (div. Feb. 1983); children—Mary Ellen, Sarah Nicole; m. Robert E. Foy, June 22, 1984. Contrbr. articles to newspapers, mags. including The Entertainer's Rvw., Images, others. Corr. Daily Dispatch, Moline, IL, 1981-82, Prairie Sun, Peoria, IL, 1981-82; ed., pub. River-Cities Rvw., Moline, 1982. Student Black Hawk Coll., 1976, 78-81, U. Houston, 1985-86. Chief wrtr. Am. Resume Service, Houston, 1984-86. Chief wrtr. Am. Resume Service, Houston, 1984-86; columnist Katy Kalender, Houston, 1985; ed. Community Hs. Newsletter, 1984-85; free-lance wrtr., Phoenix, 1986—. Home: 6708 E Moreland Scottsdale AZ 85257

FRADY, MARSHALL BOLTON, b. Augusta, GA., Jan. 11, 1940; s. Joseph Yates and Jean Marshall (Bolton) F.; m. Susanne Barker, Jan. 20, 1961 (div. Oct. 1966); m. Gloria Mochel, Nov. 10, 1966 (div. 1975); children: Katrina, Carson, Shannon; m. Gudrun Barbara Schunk, May 14, 1975. Author: Wallace, 1968, Across A Darkling Plain, 1971, Billy Graham, 1979, Southerners, 1980. B.A., Furman U., 1963; postgrad., U. Iowa, 1965-66. Corr. Newsweek mag., Atlanta and Los Angeles, 1966-67; staff writer Saturday Evening Post, Atlanta, 1968-69; contrbg. editor Harper's mag., Atlanta, 1969-71; writer Life mag., Atlanta, 1971-73; chief corr. ABC News "Closeup," NYC., 1979—. Recipient Golden Eagle Council Intl. Non-Theatrical Events, 1980, 83, Emmy Natl. Acad. TV Arts and Scis., 1981-82. Office: ABC News 7 W 66th St New York NY 10023

FRAGOLA, ANTHONY NICHOLAS, b. Syracuse, June 22, 1943, s. Vito James and Mary Rose (Cavallaro) F.; m. Anne Heywood, June 6, 1969; children—Marian, Nicholas, Ellen. Chief ed. The Artful Dodger lit mag, 1969, The Brown Bag lit mag, 1969; assoc. ed. Intl. Poetry Rvw, 1976-80; asst. ed. So. Calif. Anthology, 1985; contrbr. to Chariton Rvw, Dreamworks, St. Andrews Rvw, Swallow's Tale, Il Caffe, numerous other publs. Filmaker, wrtr: adaptation of "The Secret Miracle," 1987. Wrkg. on novel, short stories, screenplay, play. BA, Columbia U., 1966; MA, U. N.C.-Chapel Hill, 1973; MProfl. Wrtg., U. So. Calif.-Los Angeles, 1985. Freelance wrtr.-ed., Asolo, Italy, 1969-71; instr. U. N.C., Greensboro, 1975-83, spcl. lectr., 1985-86, asst. prof., 1986—. Recipient Fiction award Coraddi, 1968, Unico Natl. award for fiction, 1975, Greensboro Rvw Fiction award, 1976, others. Mem. AWP. Home: 301 Woodlawn Ave Greensboro NC 27401

FRANCIS, BETTY JOE, (Jane Johnson), b. Wichita, KS., Feb. 16, 1930; d. Elmer Floyd Morgan and Flossie Ferm (Miller) Ricks; divorced; children—Gaye D. Hanlan, Teddi A. Gunter, Kevin M. Francis, Kerin L. Francis, Robert B. Francis. Contrbr. nursing articles, fiction, inspirational articles to profl. jnls, popular mags. Columnist Jnl of Nursing Care, 1981-82, contrbg. editor, 1980-82. Mem. adv. bd. Nursing, 1984—. L.P.N., Wichita Practical Nursing Schl., 1973. L.P.N. surgical intensive care St. Francis Regional Med. Ctr., Wichita, 1973—. Recipient "Fifteen Nurses of Distinction," Nursing mag., 1986, First prize in prose, Nat'l. Soc. Daughters Amer. Revolution, 1987. Mem. Am. Assn. Critical Care Nurses, Natl. Fedn. L.P.N.s, Pub. Fellowship Wrtr.'s Group. Home: 531 S Elizabeth Wichita KS 67213

FRANCIS, EDWARD, see Beetler, Dianne Lynn

FRANK, COURTENAY, see Bourdin, Thomas Francis

FRANK, DARLENE, b. Doylestown, PA, July 2, 1946, d. Clarence and Sara (Bergey) Nyce. Author: Silicon English: Business Writing Tools for the Computer Age, 1985; contrbr. to Performance and Instrn. Jnl. BA in English, SUNY-Buffalo, 1971. Exec. dir. Southwest Regional Trng. Center, Los Angeles, 1977-78; tech. wrtr., ed. Operants, Inc., San Rafael, Calif., 1978-80; bus. writing cons. Darlene Frank & Assocs., San Francisco, 1980—. Mem. Natl. Soc. for Performance and Instruction, Soc. Tech. Communication, Nat'l Assoc. Women Bus. Owners. Home: 3836A Sacramento St San Francisco CA 94118

FRANK, GEROLD, b. Cleve., Aug. 2, 1907; s. Samuel and Lillian (Frank) Lefkowitz; m. Lillian Cogen, Sept. 1, 1932; children—Amy (Mrs. William Rosenblum), John Lewis. Author: Out in the Boondocks, 1943, (with James D. Horan) U.S.S. Seawolf, 1945, (with Lillian Roth and Mike Connolly) I'll Cry Tomorrow, 1954 (Christophers award), (with Diana Barrymore) Too Much Too Soon, 1957, (with Sheilah Graham) Beloved Infidel, 1958, Zsa Zsa Gabor: My Story, 1960, The Deed, 1963 (Edgar Allan Poe award), The Boston Strangler, 1966 (Edgar Allan Poe award), An American Death: The True Story of the Assassination of Dr. Martin Luther King Jr., 1972, Judy (biography of Judy Garland), 1975; panelist: Harper's Dictionary of Contemporary Usage, 1975, 83; contrbr. to Grolier Encyc., articles to popular mags. BA, Ohio State U., 1929; MA, Western Res. U., 1933. With Cleve. News, 1933-37; with N.Y. Jnl Am., 1937-43; U.S. war corr. Overseas News Agcy., Middle East, 1943-44, Europe and Middle East corr., 1946-50; sr. editor Coronet mag., 1952-58; screen writer Warner Bros., 1960; bd. dir. Copyright Clearance Ctr.; juror Am. Book Awards, 1981. Mem. AG, PEN, AL, Overseas Press, ASJA. Home: 930 Fifth Ave New York NY 10021

FRANK, JOHN PAUL, b. Appleton, Wis., Nov. 10, 1917; s. Julius Paul and Beatrice (Ullman) F.; m. Lorraine Weiss, May 11, 1944; children—John Peter, Gretchen, Karen, Andrew, Nancy Jo. Author: Mr. Justice Black, 1949, Cases on Constitutional Law, 1950, Cases on the Constitution, 1951, My Son's Story, 1952, Marble Palace, 1958, Lincoln as a Lawyer, 1961, Justice Daniel Dissenting, 1964, The Warren Court, 1964, American Law: The Case for Radical Reform, 1969, also articles. BA, U. Wis., 1938, MA, LLB, 1940; JSD, Yale U., 1946; LLD, Lawrence U., 1981. Fellow Am. Bar Fdn. Home: 5829 E Arcadia Ln Phoenix AZ 85010

FRANK, JOSEPH NATHANIEL, b. NYC, Oct. 6, 1918; s. William and Jennie (Garlick) F.; m. Marguerite J. Straus, May 11, 1953; children—Claudine, Isabelle. Author: The Widening Gyre, 1963, F.M. Dostoevsky: Seeds of Revolt, 1976; editor: A Primer of Ignorance, 1967. Student, NYU, 1937-38, U. Chgo., 1960. Grantee ACLS, 1970-71, Rockefeller Fdn., 1979-80. Mem. MLA (James Russell Lowell prize 1977), Natl. Acad. Arts and Scis. Office: Princeton U 326 E Pyne Princeton NJ 08544

FRANK, PETER (SOLOMON), b. NYC, July 3, 1950; s. Reuven and Bernice (Kaplow) F.; m. Janet Milstein, Oct. 21, 1979. Author: The Travelogues, 1982; Something Else Press: An Annotated Bibliography, 1983; Co-author: New Used & Improved, 1987; contrbr. to Breaking the Sound Barrier, Performance by Artists, Correspondence Art, Younger Critics of North America, Video Art. BA, Columbia U., 1972, MA, 1974. Art critic Soho Weekly News, NYC., 1973-76, Village Voice, NYC., 1977-79, Diversion Planner, NYC., 1983—; assoc. ed. Natl. Arts Guide, Chgo., 1979-81, Art Express, NYC., 1980-81; ed. Re.Dact, NYC, 1983—. NEA fellow, 1978, 81. Mem. Intl. Assn. Art Critics, Coll. Art Assn. Am Home: 712 Broadway No 5 New York NY 10003

FRANK, REUVEN, b. Montreal, Que., Can., Dec. 7, 1920; came to U.S., 1940, naturalized, 1943; s. Moses Zebi Reichenstein and Anna (Rivenovich) F.; m. Bernice Kaplow, June 9, 1946; children: Peter Solomon, James Aaron. Writer-producer: Berlin-Window on Fear, 1953, The Road to Spandau, 1954, Outlook; series, 1956-59, Time Present, 1959-60, Chet Huntley Reporting, 1960-63, Israel The Next Ten Years, 1958, The S-Bahn Stops at Freedom, 1958, The American Stranger, 1958, The Requiem for Mary Jo, 1959, The Big Ear, 1959, Our Man in Hong Kong, 1961, The Land, 1961, The Many Faces of Spain, 1962, Our Man In Vienna, 1962, Clear and Present Danger, 1962, The Tunnel, 1962, A Country Called Europe, 1963, The Problem with Water is People, 1963; exec. producer: Weekend, 1974-79; exec. producer, co-writer: If Japan Can. . . .Why Can't We? Works, 1981, The Biggest Lump of Money in the World, 1985, The Japan They Don't Talk About, 1985. Student, Univ. Coll., U. Toronto, 1937-40; BS in Social Scis., Coll City N.Y., 1942, MS in Journalism, Columbia, 1947. Reporter Newark Evening News, 1947-49, night city editor, 1949-50; mem. staff NBC News, 1950-67, exec. v.p., 1967-68, pres., 1968-72, exec. producer, 1972-82, pres., 1982-84, editorial advisor, 1984—; news editor Camel News Caravan, 1951-54. Recipient Sigma Delta Chi award news writing for TV, 1955; Columbia Journalism Alumni award distinguished service, 1961; others.; Poynter fellow Yale, 1970. Mem. WG Am. (organizing com. 1954-56), Am. Newspaper Guild (Newark News organizing com. 1948-50). Office: 30 Rockefeller Plaza New York NY 10020

FRANK, ROBERT JOSEPH, b. Dickinson, ND, 1939, s. Ralph and Rose (Schoch) F.; m. Arva Marie Utter, Aug. 15, 1964; children—Kirsten, Andrew. Author: Don't Call Me Gentle Charles: A Reading of Lamb's Essays of Elia, 1976; contrbr. to Fifty Western Writers, 1983; co-ed.: The Pacific Northwest: A Region in Myth and Reality, 1983, The Grains or Passages in the Life of Ruth Rover, With Occasional Pictures of Oregon, Natural and Moral, 1986. BA, St. John's U., 1962; MA, U. Minn., PhD, 1969. Asst. prof. English, Oreg. State U., Corvallis, 1969-70, 71-75, assoc. prof., 1975-83, prof., 1983—, chmn. dept., 1978—, acting dean Coll. Liberal Arts, 1985-87; institutional rep. NCAA, 1987—; asst. prof. Eastern Mich. U., Ypsilanti, 1970-71. Mem. MLA, Assn. Depts. English. Home: 403 NW 13th St Corvallis OR 97330

FRANK, THAISA, b. NYC, Aug. 25, 1943, d. Robert Worth and Gladys (Loeb) Frank; m. William Rodarmor, May 11, 1980; 1 son, Casey Alexander. Author: Desire (short fiction), 1982); contrbr. short stories to Epoch, Primavera, N.Am. Rvw, Miss. Rvw, other lit mags. BA in Philosophy, Oberlin Coll. (Ohio) Psychotherapist, NYC,1969-76, Berkeley, Calif., 1976—; lectr. creative writing U. Calif., Berkeley, 1979—. Squaw Valley Wrtr.'s Conf. fellow, 1982; listed in Best Books 1982, San Francisco Rvw, Best Small-Press Books 1982, Natl. Library Jnl, 1983. Home: 459 66th St Oakland CA 94609

FRANK, TRACY STEVEN SCOTT, b. Springville, NY, June 7, 1965; s. Kenneth Glen and Gail (Pearson) Frank. Student pub. schls., Ellicotville, NY. Editor and staff writer, ARCANS Periodicals, Ellicottville, NY, 1982-83; freelance wrtr., 1983—; wrkg. on short stories, science fiction, and children's books. Mem. International Press Associates. Home: Rt 219 Box 235 Ellicottville NY 14731

FRANKEL, ELLEN, b. Boston, Mar. 26, 1938; d. Archie and Frances (Tocman) Sudhalter; m. Hyman Frankel; children—Elizabeth Gennis, Shepherd Gelber, Dylan Yarne. Account exec. The Siesel Co., NYC, 1977-79; design ed. 1001 Decorating Ideas, NYC, 1979-81; assoc. home furn. ed. Woman's Day, NYC, 1981-83; home design ed. McCall's, NYC, 1983-86; ed. 1001 Home Ideas, NYC, 1986—. Mem. Natl. Home Fashions League. Writers Hall of Fame, Southern Furniture Mkt., 1985. Office: 1,001 Home Ideas 3 Park Ave New York NY 10016

FRANKEL, MAX, b. Gera, Germany, Apr. 3, 1930; came to U.S., 1940, naturalized, 1948; s. Jacob A. and Mary (Katz) F.; m. Tobia Brown, June 19, 1956; children: David M., Margot S., Jonathan M. Mem. staff N.Y. Times, 1952—, chief Washington corr., 1968-73, Sunday editor, 1973-76, editorial pages editor, 1977—. A.B., Columbia, 1952, M.A. in Polit. Sci, 1953. Served with AUS, 1953-55. Recipient Pulitzer prize for intl. reporting, 1973. Office: 229 W 43d St New York NY 10036

FRANKEN, DARRELL, b. Eddyville, IA, Oct. 28, 1930; s. Henry E. and Harriet J. (Dykshorn) F.; m. Marilyn J. Tanis, June 5, 1959; children: Kent, Julie, Todd. Author: Health Through

Stress Reduction, 1985, Healing through Stress Management, 1985, Marital Transactional Analysis, 1985, Life Stress and Coping Strength Inventory (computer program), 1985, Christian Stress Management, 1986, Stress Control, 1986, Personality Profile, 1986. BA, Central Coll., Pella, Iowa, 1952,; MDiv. Western Sem., Holland, Mich., 1955; MA, U. Chgo., 1963. Pastor, Hope Reformed Ch., Chgo., 1957-59, Everglade Ref. Ch., Grand Rapids, Mich., 1959-61, Bahrain Community Ch., Arabian Gulf, 1961-68; chaplain M.D. Anderson Hosp., Tex. Med. Ctr., Houston, 1969-71; counselor Christian Counseling Service, Holland, 1971—. Mem. Am. Assn. Pastoral Counselors, Christian Assn. Psychol. Studies. Lic. marriage and family counselor, Mich. Home: Box 2397 Holland MI 49423

FRANKLIN, J. MANNING, see Franklin, Miriam

FRANKLIN, JOHN HOPE, b. Rentiesville, OK, Jan. 2, 1915; s. Buck Colbert and Mollie (Parker) F.; m. Aurelia E. Whittington, June 11, 1940; 1 son, John Whittington. Author: Free Negro in North Carolina, 1943, From Slavery to Freedom: A History of Negro Americans, 5th ed., 1980, Militant South, 1956, Reconstruction After the Civil War, 1961, The Emancipation Proclamation, 1963, A Southern Odyssey, 1976, Racial Equality in America, 1976, (with others) Land of the Free, 1966, Illustrated History of Black Americans, 1970, George Washington Williams, 1985. Editor: Civil War Diary of James T. Ayers, 1947, A Fool's Errand by Albion Tourgee, 1961, Army Life in a Black Regiment by Thomas Higginson, 1962, Color and Race, 1968, Reminiscences of an Active Life by John R. Lynch, 1970, (with August Meier) Black Leaders in the Twentieth Century, 1982; mem. editorial bd. Am. Scholar, 1972-76. AB, Fisk U., 1935; AM, Harvard, 1936, PhD, 1941; numerous hon. degrees. Edward Austin fellow, 1937-38; Rosenwald fellow, 1937-39; Guggenheim fellow, 1950-51, 73-74; Pres. fellow Brown U., 1952-53, Center for Advanced Study in Behavioral Sci., 1973-74; Sr. Mellon fellow Natl. Humanities Center, 1980-82; Fulbright prof., Australia, 1960. Fellow Am. Acad. Arts and Scis.Home: 208 Pineview Rd Durham NC 27707

FRANKLIN, MIRIAM ANNA, (J. Manning Franklin), b. Rossville, KS., Oct. 3, 1894; d. Joseph Manning and Luch (Kunkel) Franklin. Author: Rehearsal, 1938, 6th ed., 1983, Demons Dive from the Sky, Tornadoes, Hurricanes, Typhoons, 1982, Famous Men Speak, 1970, Trilby's Fate, 1975. Contrbr. articles to mags. BA, Washburn U., 1919; MA, Northwestern U., Evanston, Ill., 1938. Actor, entertainer Circuit Chautauquas, 1918-29; prof. Grove Cit Coll., Pa., 1929-46, Washburn U., Topeka, 1946-53, Guam Coll., 1958-59. Recipient Lit. Achievement award for writing Kans. Authors' Club, 1985, 1st State Honors, 1985. Home: 1208 W 29th Terr S-22 Topeka KS 66611

FRANKLIN, ROBERT McFARLAND, b. Memphis, Mar. 13, 1943; s. Robert Dumont and Mary McFarland (Wilson) F.; m. Cheryl Jane Roberts, Jan. 18, 1975; 2 sons, Charles McRee, Nicholas Roberts. A.B., Yale, 1965; postgrad. Columbia, 1965-66. Cataloger Columbia Univ., NYC,1965-66; ed. Scarecrow Press, Metuchen, N.J., 1969-73, exec. ed., 1973-79; pres. McFarland & Co. Inc. Pubs., Jefferson, N.C., 1979—. Actor, Ashe County Little Theatre, Jefferson, 1979—. Served to E6 US Army, 1966-68. Recipient Gov.'s award Gov.'s Bus. Council on Arts and Humanities, N.C., 1985. Mem.Soc. for Scholarly Publishing, Am. Soc. Psychical Res., ALA, Parapsycholog. Assn. (hon.) Home: Box 611 Jefferson NC 28640

FRANKLIN, WALT, b. Schwabach, W.Ger., June 19, 1950; arrd. U.S. 1954; s. Walter D. and Ilse F.; m. Leighanne Parkins, Sept. 4, 1982; 1 son, Brent. Author: EKOS, 1987, Talking to the Owls, 1984, Topographies, 1985, The Glass Also Rises, 1985, Little Water Company, 1985, Earthstars, Chanterelles, Destroying Angels, 1986; ed. Susquehannock (with Mike Czarnecki), 1986; contrbr. to more than 140 small mags, jnls and anthologies. BS in psychology, Alfred U., 1974, tchg. cert., 1975. Counselor Grafton Schl., Berryville, Va, 1976-80; adv./mgmt. ARC, Alfred, NY, 1981-85; ed./writer/poet Great Elm Press, Rexville, NY, 1980-86. Mem. Appalachian Writers Assn., P & W. Address: Rd 2 Box 37 Rexville NY 14877

FRANZ, JEFFREY BRIAN, b. Balt., June 14, 1947; s. Robert Elihu and Phyllis (Moran) F.; m. Kathryn Runde, Jan. 11, 1986. Ed: (poetry anthol.) On the Threshold of a Dream, 1988; (biography) Who's Who in Am. Nursing, 1984, 86, Who's Who Among Human Service Profls., 1984, 86. Wrkg. on Who's Who in Am. Edn. B.S., U. Md., 1970. Speech wrtr. U.S. Dept. of Health and Human Services, Washington, 1983-85; ed.-in-chief Natl. Reference Press, Owings Mills, MD, 1982—. Recipient Md. Print Quality award Printing Industries of Md., 1986, 87. Home: 431 Church Rd Reisterstown MD 21136

FRANZEN, RICHARD B., b. Chgo., Nov. 11, 1946; s. Norman Harry and Leona Elizabeth F.; m. Judy Ann Loos, Aug. 16, 1969 (div. 1985); children: Richard Jr., Carrie, Shelley. Contrbr. stories: Atlanta Singles, The Mastodon, Agincourt Irregular, other publs.; weekly drama critic The Worth-Palos (Ill.) Reporter, 1986-87. Wrkg. on novels. Student Mont. State U., 1968-71. Home: 16601 Clover St Tinley Park IL 60477

FRASER, BRUCE WICKERSHAM, b. Syracuse, NY, Oct. 10, 1941, s. Henry Solomon F. Contrbr. articles on personal fin. mgmt. to: Christian Sci. Monitor, Fin. World, Amex Jnl, numerous others. BA, Nasson Coll., Springvale, Me., 1965; MS, Syracuse U., 1972. Wrtr. Gannett Newspapers, Upstate N.Y., 1967-76, Fairchild Publs., NYC, 1976-78, Gannett Co., Rochester, N.Y., 1978-81, Whitney Publs., NYC, 1981; freelance fin. wrtr., NYC, 1981—. Mem. ASJA, NWU, N.Y. Fin. Wrtrs. Assn., Publicity Club N.Y. (Disting. Service award 1975, 85). Address: 460 E 79th St 14G New York NY 10021

FRASER, RUSSELL ALFRED, b. Elizabeth, NJ, May 31, 1927; s. Roger John and Mary Louise (Narden) F.; m. Eleanor Jane Phillips, May 31, 1947 (div. 1979); children—Karen Mildred, Alexander Varennes; m. Mary Nelva Zwiep, July 5, 1980. Author: Shakespeare's Poetics, 1962, The War Against Poetry, 1970, An Essential Shakespeare, 1972, The Dark Ages and the Age of Gold, 1973, The Language of Adam, 1977, A Mingled Yarn: The Life of R.P. Blackmur, 1982, The Three Romes, 1984. Editor: The Court of Venus, 1955, The Court of Virtue, 1961, King Lear, 1963, Oscar Wilde, 1969, (with others) Drama of the English Renaissance, 2 vols., 1976, All's Well That Ends Well, 1986. AB, Dartmouth Coll., 1947; MA, Harvard U., 1949, PhD, 1950. Guggenheim fellow, Rome, 1973-74; Rockefeller resident scholar, Bellagio, 1975; sr. Fulbright-Hays scholar, 1975; NEH fellow, 1978-79. Mem. AG. Office: Dept Eng U Mich Ann Arbor MI 48109

FRASIER, THOMAS DANIEL, b. Munishing, MI, Aug. 22, 1938; s. Roy Andrew and Otilya Libuse (Trefil) F. Columnist: Balt. Gay Paper, 1980-85. Contrbr. art rvws. to newspapers including Balt. Chronicle, others. Wrkg. on anthol., biography of Winslow Homer. B.S. in Design U. Mich., 1960, M.A. in Art, 1962. Instr. art, Piedmont Coll., 1967-72, U. of the South, Sewanee, TN, 1972-77; real estate salesman Frasier Assocs., Balt., 1977-85; free-lance wrtr., 1986—. Home: Box 5638 Baltimore MD 21210

FRATZ, DONALD DOUGALS, b. Oakland, MD, Nov. 18, 1952; s. Donald Henry and Anna Mary (Savage) F.; m. Naomi Richfield, Feb. 3, 1979; 1 son, Alexander Paul. Contrbr. book rvws to Thrust, Washington Post, Stardate mag, Fantasy Rvw. BS in Chemistry, U. Md, 1970-74; MS in environ sci., Geo Washington U., 1981-83. Res. asst. NIH, Bethesda, 1972-74; ed. and pub. Thrust Pubs, Gaithersburg, Md, 1973—; chemist FDA, Wshington, 1974-80; dir. sci. affairs Chemical Specialties Mfrs. Assn., Washington, 1980—. Mem SFWA. Address: 8217 Langport Terr Gaithersburg MD 20877

FRAUENGLAS, ROBERT ALAN, b. Bklyn, Apr. 25, 1950; s. Seymour Maurice and Miriam (Levy) Frauenglas. Contrbr. to Adventure Travel, Backpack, Midstream, Blue Plate Special, New Pages, Image, Judaica Book News, Outposts, Kirkus Rvw, Jerusalem Post, New Brooklyn, many more; editor: Brooklyn Prospects, 1984, Festina Lente, 1982, Samples . . . Fables from the Slope, 1983, others; author: The Eclectic Musings of a Brooklyn Bum (poet./prose), 1980; wrkg. on Down the Road, a Mile or So (full- length non-fict.), When a Miracle's Long Overdue (novel). BA in History, State U. of NY at Binghamton, 1973; JD St. Louis U. School of Law, 1981. Bouncer, Castle Pub (London), 1973; Cowboy, kibbutz (Matsuva, Israel), 1971-72; freelance wrtr., pres. Bklyn. Pub. Co., Ltd., 1984—; wrtr., 1979—; pub. Somrie Press (Brooklyn), 1979—; asst. natl. coord. Student Struggle for Soviet Jewry (Bklyn.), 1984-85 exec. dir. Com for Absorption of Soviet Emigres, 1986, co-dir. Brooklyn Book Fair. Office: Ryder Street Sta Box 328 Brooklyn NY 11234

FRAUSTINO, DANIEL VICTOR, b. Buffalo, NY., Aug. 22, 1945, s. Daniel Victor and Helena Daisy (Asserti) F.; m. Lisa Ann Rowe, Oct. 30, 1982; children—Julia Daisy, Daniel Sebastian. Contrbr. to Ariz. Qtly, Studies in Short Fiction, Jnl Evolutionary Psychology, other publs. AB, SUNY-Buffalo, 1967; Phd, SUNY-Binghamton, 1977. Adj. instr. SUNY-Binghamton, 1976-77; asst. prof. U. Me., Orono, 1977-82; assoc. prof. U. Scranton, Pa., 1982—; wrtr.-in-residence NEA, Orono, 1979. Grantee U. Me., 1978. Home: 303 Maine Ave Clarks Summit PA 18411

FRAZIER, APRIL, see Cooke, Audry

FRAZIER, KENDRICK CROSBY, b. Windsor, CO, Mar. 19, 1942; s. Francis Elliott and Sidney Lenore (Crosby) F.; m. Ruth Toelle, Sept. 10, 1964; children—Christopher, Michele. Author: The Violent Face of Nature, 1979, Our Turbulent Sun, 1982, Solar System, 1985, People of Chaco, 1986. Editor: Paranormal Borderlands of Science, 1981, Science Confronts the Paranormal, 1986. BA in Journalism, U. Colo., 1964; MS, Columbia U., 1966. Reporter Greeley (Colo.) Daily Tribune, 1962; news editor Golden (Colo.) Transcript, 1963-64; newsman Denver bur. UPI, 1964-65; editor News Report, Natl. Acad. Scis., Washington, 1966-69; earth scis. editor Sci. News mag., Washington, 1969-70, mng. editor, 1970-71, editor, 1971-77, contrbg. editor, 1977-82; sci. writer Sandia Natl. Labs., Albuquerque, 1983—; editor The Skeptical Inquirer, 1977—; freelance sci. writer, 1977—; adj. instr. U. Mo. Schl. Journalism, 1975-77. Boettcher Fdn. scholar, 1960-64; Pulitzer traveling fellow, 1966; Robert E. Sherwood scholar, 1966. Mem. Natl. Assn. Sci. Writers, Com. for Sci. Investigation of Claims of the Paranormal (editor 1977—). Home: 3025 Palo Alto Dr NE Albuquerque NM 87111

FREDERICK, DAWN HILDRED RUTH, b. NYC, Oct. 18, 1956, d. LeRoy Nathaniel and Yvonne (Brady) Frederick. Contrbr. to Rock 'n' Soul, other publs. Ed., Windham Coll., Putney, Vt., CUNY. Arts ed., wrtr. The Free Press, Putney, 1977-78; wrkg. on novel Animascopes (with Esther Plaut), now prin. Frederick's Lyrics, Inc., NYC Office: Box 5252 FDR Sta New York NY 10150

FREDERICK, LINDA LENORE, (Linda Little Frederick), b. Pontiac, MI, Oct. 20, 1949; d. Lawrence Francis and Sybil Lenore (Brown) Carey; m. Lowell Vincent Little, Sept. 1, 1966 (dec. Nov. 4, 1971); 1 son, Jeffrey David; m. Robert E. Frederick, Sept. 16, 1972; children—Carrie Lenore, Alyson Burdette. Contrbr. articles to Christian and secular mags. Grad. public schls., Waterford, MI. Norton corr. Sun Banner Pride, OH, 1987, Akron Beacon Jnl., OH, 1987; free-lance wrtr., 1985—. Active Friends of the Library, Norton, 1987—. Mem. NWC, Akron Manuscript Club. Home: 3491 Middlehurst Norton OH 44203

FREDERICKS, VIC, see Fell, Frederick Victor

FREDETTE, JEAN MARIE, b. Long Beach, CA, Mar. 11, 1940; d. Wilfred B. and Elizabeth (Steen) Goulett; m. Alan Lee Fredette, June 20, 1964; children—Michelle, Andy, Scott. Contrbr. articles to Writers Digest, Writers Yearbook, Cin. Mag. BA in French, U. Ky.-Lexington, 1961; grad. cert. in profl. writing, Fairfield U., 1977-78. Asst. ed. (fiction) Market Writer's Digest Books, Cin., 1980-81, fiction ed., 1981-86, acquisitions ed., 1986—, ed. Fiction Writer's Market, 1981-1986, acquisitions ed., 1986—. Address: F&W 1507 Dana Ave Cincinnati OH 45207

FREED, LYNN RUTH, b. Durban, South Africa; came to U.S., 1967; d. Harold Derrick and Anne (Moshal) F.; 1 child, Jessica Gamsu. Author: Heart Change, 1982; Home Ground, 1986. Wrkg. on new novel. BA, U. Witwatersrand, 1966; MA, Columbia U., 1968, PhD, 1972. University Wit fellow Columbia U., 1969; fellow Yaddo, 1984, 85, 87, fellow MacDowall Colony, 1986, 87. Home: 57 Ashbury Terr San Francisco CA 94117

FREED, RAY FORREST, b. Los Angeles, Feb. 1, 1939, s. Matthew James Freed and Viola Beth (Atwood) Whitten; m. Joann Elaine Bishop, Apr. 7, 1977; children—Phillip Forrest, Christopher Michael. Author: Morgan's Choice, 1968, Sea Animal on Land, 1970, Necessary Lies, 1975, Shinnecock Bay, 1977, Moom, 1979, Hualalai, 1986; ed.: Dr. Generosity's Almanac: 17 Poets, 1970, On Good Ground, Poems & Photographs of Eastern Long Island (with Jim Tyack), 1981, Turtle Dance, Poems (by Aelbert Aehegma), 1984; contrbr. poetry: Clare Market Rvw, Descant, Fiddlehead, On Turtle's Back, other lit mags. Student U. Hawaii, 1959-61. Pub., ed. Dr. Generosity Press, N.Y.C., 1969-73; ed. Street Press and Street Mag., Port Jefferson, N.Y., 1973-80; freelance wrtr., ed., 1980—. Home: Box 2883 Kailua Kona HI 96745

FREEDMAN, ERIC, b. Brookline, MA, Nov. 6, 1949; s. Morris and Charlotte (Nadler) F.; m. Mary Ann Sipher, May 24, 1974; children—Ian Sipher, Cara Sipher. Contrbr. articles to law jnls., newspapers, popular mags. including Boston Herald, PC Mag., others. Contrbg. ed.: PCjr Mag., 1984. B.A., Cornell U., 1971; J.D., N.Y. U., 1975. Legal/political reporter Knickerbocker News, Albany, NY, 1976-84; legal reporter Detroit News, Lansing, MI, 1984—. Recipient Scripps award Evening News Assn., 1986. Mem. Investigative Reporters & Eds., N.Y. Bar Assn. (Annual Media award 1977, 79, 80, 81, 82), State Bar of Mich. Home: 2698 Linden Dr East Lansing MI 48823

FREEDMAN, HELEN ROSENGREN, b. Melbourne, Australia, Oct. 24, 1952 (arrvd. USA Dec. 1975), d. James Francis and Mary Elizabeth (Hogan) Rosengren; m. Howard Samuel Freedman, Apr. 12, 1980; 1 child, Lauren Charlotte. Author: The Writer's Guide to Magazine Markets: Fiction, 1983, The Writer's Guide to Magazine Markets: Non-Fiction, 1983, Big Apple Baby: A Resource Guide to New York for Expectant and New Parents, 1985; contrbr. articles to New Idea, Woman's Day, Women's Weekly, Cleo, Savvy, Woman's World, Woman, Fair Lady. Reporter/feature wrtr. Melbourne Herald, 1970-75, corr. N.Y. Bur., 1976-78; assoc. editor Accent mag., 1978-80; author/freelance wrtr., 1980-85; pres. Laurel-Howard, Inc., pub. co., NYC,1985—. Home: 201 E 21st St New York NY 10010

FREEHLING, WILLIAM WILHARTZ, b. Chgo., Dec. 26, 1935; s. Norman and Edna (Wilhartz) F.; m. Natalie Paperno, Jan. 27, 1961 (div. Apr. 1970); children—Alan Jeffrey, Deborah Ann; m. Alison Goodyear, June 19, 1971; children—Alison Harrison, William Goodyear. Author: Prelude to Civil War: The Nullification Controversy in South Carolina, 1816-1836, 1966. AB, Harvard, 1958; MA, U. Calif. at Berkeley, 1959, PhD, 1964. Woodrow Wilson fellow U. Calif. at Berkeley, 1961-63. Natl. Humanities Fdn. fellow, 1968; Guggenheim fellow, 1970. Home: 1808 Belfast Rd Sparks MD 21152

FREEMAN, ANNE HOBSON, b. Richmond, VA, Mar. 19, 1934, d. Joseph Reid Anderson and Mary Douthat (Marshall) Hobson; m. George Clemon Freeman, Jr., Dec. 6, 1958; children—Anne Colston, George Clemon III, Joseph Reid Anderson. Contrbr. to Va. Qtly Rvw, Commonwealth, Mademoiselle, A Green Place, 1982, The Best American Short Stories, 1982, From Mount San Angelo: Stories Poems & Essays, 1985. AB, Bryn Mawr Coll., 1956; MA, U. Va., 1973. Reporter Intl. News Service, USSR and Eastern Europe, 1957; public relations asst., instr. Bryn Mawr (Pa.) Coll., 1958; ed. mem.'s bulln. Va. Mus., Richmond, 1960-63; lectr. English, U. Va., Charlottesville, 1972—; oral historian, wrtr. Hunton & Williams, Richmond, 1983—. Recipient Emily Clark Balch prize for fiction Va. Qtly Rvw, 1985. Fellow Va. Center Creative Arts; mem. Va. Wrtrs. Club, Ellen Glasgow Soc. Home: 10 Paxton Rd Richmond VA 23226

FREEMAN, CYNTHIA, (Bea Feinberg), b. NYC, d. Albert C. and Sylvia Jeannette (Hack) F.; married; 2 children. Author: A World Full of Strangers, 1974, Fairytales, 1978, Days of Winter, 1977, Portraits, 1979, Come Pour the Wine, 1980, No Time for Tears, 1981, Catch the Gentle Dawn, 1983. Student public schls. Office: Arbor Hs 235 E 45th St New York NY 10017

FREEMAN, MARCUS A., JR., b. Smithville, TX, Sept. 14, 1934; s. Marcus Antonio Freeman, Sr. and Willie B. (Jones) F.; m. Jacquelyn Faye Freeman, June 30, 1974; children—Mark III, Carol Marie, Vijay Anton. Ed. Black Tennis Mag., 1977—. AB, Prairie View U., 1955, MA, 1956; EdD, East Texas State U., 1975. Tchr., Dallas Ind. Schl. Dist., 1959-70, asst. principal, 1970—. Served to Cpl., U.S. Army, 1957-59. Mem. Dallas, U.S., and Texas Tennis Assns. Home: Box 210767 Dallas TX 75211

FREEMAN, MARK, see Dawson, George Amos

FREEMAN, PAT S.,, b. Wauchula, FL, Feb. 24, 1943; d. F. Lamar and Elizabeth (Kirby) Freeman. Contrbr. poetry, short stories: Argus, Sundry Scopes, other lit. mags.; ed. profl. orgn. newsletters. MA, Fla. State U. Tchr. high sch. English, Wauchula, Fla., 1965-71, Tutusville, Fla., 1971—; tchr. Coll. Humanities, Titusville, 1987—; minister New Testament Fellowship, Titusville, 1981—; pres. Pegasus Unlimited, Titusville, 1985—; cons., public speaker. Mem. profl. orgns. Home: 80 Sky Ln Titusville FL 32796

FREEMAN, PETER J., see Calvert, Patricia

FREERICKS, MARY AVAKIAN, b. Tabrtiz, Iran, Mar. 26, 1935; came to U.S., 1945; d. Paul Pokhos and Sonia Sophia (Lievschitzov) Avakian; m. Charles Knox Freericks, May 2, 1959; children: Charles John, James Knox. Author: Creative Puppetry in the Classroom, 1979; contrbr. poetry to Cosmopolitan, N.Y. Qtly., Christian Sci. Monitor, Passaic Rvw, Breadloaf Crumb, Bitterroot, also anthologies including The Feathered Violin. BA, Beaver Coll., 1957; postgrad. Northwestern U., summers 1957-58. In-service instr. Bergen County Edn. Assn., 1974-86; cons. in poetry and puppetry, 1975—; tchr. grant workshops in poetry, writing courses. Recipient disting. achievement award for photog. journalism Ednl. Press Assn. Am., 1981; N.J. Council on Arts fellow, 1985. Mem. P&W of N.Y., Bergen Poets. Home: 450 Vera Pl Paramus NJ 07652

FREIBERT, LUCY M., b. Louisville, KY, Oct. 19, 1922, d. Joseph Anthony and Amelia Josephine (Stich) Freibert. Contrbg. author: American Women Writers vols. II and III, 1980, Women and Utopia, 1983; ed.: Hidden Hands: An Anthology of American Women Writers, 1790-1870 (with Barbara A. White), 1985; contrbr. to Melville Soc. Extracts, Ariz. Qtly, Can. Lit., Jnl. of Popular Culture, other publs. BA, Spalding Coll., 1957; MA, St. Louis U., 1962, PhD, U. Wis.-Madison, 1970. Assoc. prof. English Spalding Coll., Louisville, Ky., 1960-71; prof. English U. Louisville, 1971—. Mem. MLA, Natl. Women's Studies Assn., Melville Soc. Home: 1507 Hepburn Ave Louisville KY 40204

FREIBURGER, BETSEY, b. Balt., Feb. 15; nee Huss; m. Leo H. Freiburger, June 24; children—Betsey Sally, Richard H.; 1 dau. by previous marriage, Nancy Vardi. Author: The Bread You Spread to Get Rid of Rolls, 1986. Contrbr. articles, features to mags., newspapers including N.Y. Times, WSJ, others. Wrkg. on Dining in the Dark Hides Wrinkles; TV program syndicated nationally. B.A., Goucher Coll. Chmn. Palm Beach Festival of Performing Arts, FL,

1986-87. Mem. NALPW (bd dirs.). Home: 2999 Date Palm Rd Boca Raton FL 33432

FREILICHER, MELVYN S., b. NYC,Nov. 8, 1946, s. Jack and Frances (Altman) F. Ed. Crawl Out Your Window mag., 1974—; mem. editorial staff PsychoSources, 1973; pres. Fdn. for New Literature, 1981—; contrbr. to numerous lit and art mags., periodicals, anthologies including Contemporary Am. Fiction, Performance Anthology, Soho Weekly News, Jnl Los Angeles Inst. Contemporary Art, Flue, Central Park. BA, Brandeis U., 1968; postgrad. U. Calif., San Diego, 1972. Vis. lectr. lit. dept. writing program U. Calif., San Diego, 1978—; lectr. lit. dept. San Diego State U., 1979—. Home: 4641 Park Blvd San Diego CA 92116

FREILINGER, IDA M. W., b. Wilkinsburg, Pa., Apr. 30, 1943; d. Huttson A. Watson and Ruth (Campbell) Watson Diamond; m. Michael J. Freiliner, Jan. 11, 1969; children—Steven M., Suzanne M. Contrbr. poetry: Dragonfly, Voices of Auraria, other lit. mags.; ed.: Voices fo Auraruia, 1982-85, Windmills and Wishing Wells, 1983; ed. Metrosphere, 1983-84, mng. ed., 1984-85. BA, Met. State coll., Denver. Wrtr., Shuttle, Spindle & Dyepot, West Hartford, Conn., 1979—. Mem. NWC, Poetry Soc. Colo. Home: 7365 S Washington St Littleton CO 80122

FREIVALDS, JOHN, b. Skujene, Latvia, Mar. 12, 1944, came to U.S., 1951, s. Evalds and Margarita (Dzenis) F.; m. Susan Alexander, Jan. 21, 1967; children—Karla, Maija, Jill. Author: Grain Trade, 1976, Fumini Plot, 1979, Agribusiness Worldwide, 1979, Successful Agribusiness Management, 1984, Foreign Trade, 1984. BS, Georgetown U., 1966; MA, George Washington U., 1967. Economist Devel. and Resources, Sacramento, 1970-73; exec. I.S. Joseph, Mpls., 1973-76, 80-82; v.p. Experience, Inc., 1976-80; Euramerica, 1986—. Home: 8208 W Franklin St Minneapolis MN 55426

FRELL, ELLEN FRANCES, b. Bloomington, IL, Sept. 29, 1950; d. Albert Calabria and Irene (Burbank) Frell; m. Richard Frankel Levy, May 4, 1980; children—James Daniel, Alexandra. Contrbr.: McCalls, Arizona Highways, Working Mother, Christian Science Monitor, numerous other publs. BS, Northwestern U., 1970. Winner Emmy award Nat. Assn. TV Arts and Scis., 1975. Home: 1040 N Lake Shore Dr 5A Chicago IL 60611

FRENCH, E(MMA) YULEE, b. Key West, FL, Jan. 20, 1926; d. Clement Henry and La Dora Maria (Sanchez) Hudson; m. Arthur Warren French, Nov. 18, 1948; 1 son, Keith. Contrbr. features, articles, profiles to newspapers including The Orlando Sentinel, The Fla. Horseman, LaFemme. Wrkg. on novel. Student Newspaper Inst. Am., 1956-58. Asst. purchasing agent Orange County, Orlando, FL, 1964-68; free-lance wrtr., 1974—. Mem. NLAPW (past pres. Winter Park branch, reording sec. for Fla.). Home: 6215 Forest Grove Blvd Orlando FL 32808

FRENCH, MARILYN, b. NYC, Nov. 21, 1929; d. E.C. and Isabel (Hazz) Edwards; married; children—Jamie, Robert. Author: (criticism): The Book as World—James Joyce's "Ulysses," 1976; author: (novels) The Women's Room, 1977, The Bleeding Heart, 1980; (criticism): Shakespeare's Division of Experience, 1981, introductions to Edith Wharton's Summer and The House of Mirth, 1981; (social and moral thought) Beyond Power: On Women, Men, and Morals, 1985. BA, Hofstra Coll., 1951, MA, 1964; PhD, Harvard U., 1972. Mellon fellow Harvard U., 1976-77; writer, lectr., 1967—. Mem. MLA, James Joyce Soc., Virginia Woolf Soc. Office: Summit Bks 1230 Ave of Americas New York NY 10020

FRENCH, MICHAEL HARVEY, b. Denver, Oct. 5, 1949; s. Harvey Francis French and Dolores Marie (San Giacomo) Bigelow. Contrbr. poems to anthols.; articles to Creightoneer newsletter. Ed.: Creightoneer, 1986-87. Wrkg. on collection of poems, Mudholes and Kite Strings Sometimes Sing. B.A., U. Wyo., 1972. Tchr. Lebanon R-3 Schls. (Mo.), 1974-76, Creighton Schls. (Phoenix, Ariz.), 1976-79 Gilbert public schls. (Ariz.), 1979-80; sales assoc. Russ Lyon Realty and Bradley Realty, Tempe, AZ, 1980-82; outside sales assoc. Hinkleys Lighting, Phoenix and Scottsdale, AZ, 1982-84; tchr. Creighton Schs., Phoenix, 1984—. Served with U.S. Army, 1972-74. Recipient Golden Poet award World of Poetry, 1985, 86. Mem. Natl., Ariz., Creighton (pres.) edn. assns. Home: 7729 E 6th St Scottsdale AZ 85251

FRENKEL, KAREN A., b. NYC, Sept. 7, 1955, d. David Allen and Irene Georgina (Goldberger) Frenkel. Author: Robots: Machines in Man's Image (with Isaac Asimov), 1985; contrbr. articles to Forbes, Med. World News, Technology Rvw, other publs. BA, Hampshire Coll.; MS in Sci. Communication, Boston U. Freelance sci. wrtr., NYC, 1982-84; features wrtr. Communications of the ACM, NYC, 1984—. Mem. SPJ, Deadline Club, NASW. Home: 240 W 98th St New York NY 10025

FRESE, MILLIE KAY, b. Manchester, IA, Dec. 24, 1963; d. Clifford Albert and Susan Elaine (Albright) Kehrli; m. Jeffrey Robert Frese, Aug. 11, 1984. Contrbr. feature articles to newspapers, magazines. Wrkg. on feature articles. B.A., U. Iowa, 1985. Reporter, photographer Manchester Pub. co., 1981-82, Jessamine Jnl., Nicholasville, KY, 1985-86; reporter, librarian Press Citizen, Iowa City, IA, 1984; research asst. U. Iowa, Iowa City, 1984; pubs. asst. Asbury Theol. Seminary, Wilmore, KY, 1986—. Named Outstanding Jnlsm. Student, U. Iowa, 1983, 84. Mem. Kappa Tau Alpha (Top Scholar award 1985). Home: 338 Epworth Ave Wilmore KY 40390

FRETTER, T. W., see Andre, Michael

FRICKERT, E.M., see Bell, Victor L.

FRIDAY, NANCY, b. Pitts., Aug. 27, 1937; d. Walter and Jane Colbert F.; m. W.H. Manville, Oct. 20, 1967. Author: My Secret Garden, 1973; Forbidden Flowers, 1975, My Mother, My Self, 1977, Men in Love: Men's Sexual Fantasies, 1980. Student, Wellesley Coll. Reporter, San Juan Island Times, 1960-61; editor Islands in the Sun, 1961-63. Office: S&S 1230 Ave of Americas New York NY 10020

FRIED, ELLIOT, b. St. Louis, Jan. 22, 1944; s. Meyer and Fanny F.; m. Helen Enriquez, Aug. 2, 1979. Author: Picking Up the Pieces, 1973, Single Life, 1974, Poem City, 1975, Strip Tease, 1979, The Man Who Owned Cars, 1984; ed. Amorotica, 1981, Men Talk (with Barry Singer), 1985. MFA, U. Calif.-Irvine, 1969. Prof. English Calif. State Univ., Long Beach, 1970—. Address: Dept Eng Calif State Univ Long Beach CA 90840

FRIED, PHILIP HENRY, b. Atlanta, Ga., Jan. 8, 1945; s. Seymour and Mollie Ellen (Green) Fried; m. Lynn Adele Saville, Oct. 5, 1985. Poetry and articles in Partisan Rvw, Paris Rvw, Poetry Northwest, Hollins Critic, Abraxas, others. BA, Antioch College, 1966; MFA, U. of Ia., 1968; PhD, UNY at Stony Brook, 1978. Admin. asst., Gloria Stern Lit. Agent, NYC, 1978-1979; ed, Mitchell/Titus, 1979-1984; editor, Holt, Rinehart, & Winston, 1984-86; ed, Prentice-Hall, 1986—; founder and editor, Manhattan Review, NYC,1980—. Mem. NWU, P&W, PSA, CCLM. Home: 304 Third Ave 4A New York NY 10010

FRIEDAN, BETTY, b. Peoria, IL, Feb. 4, 1921; d. Harry and Miriam (Horwitz) Goldstein; m. Carl Friedan, June 1947 (div. May 1969); children—Daniel, Jonathan, Emily. Author: The Feminine Mystique, 1963, It Changed My Life: Writings on the Women's Movement, 1976; contrbg. editor: McCall's, 1971—. BA summa cum laude, Smith Coll., 1942, LHD, 1975. Mem. PEN, Soc. Mag. Writers. Address: 31 W 93d St New York NY 10025

FRIEDBERG, MARTHA A., b. Chgo., May 7, 1916; d. Louis and Alice (Wormser) Asher; m. Stanton Friedberg, July 8, 1939; children: Ann, Cass, Jonathan, Laura. Contrbr. poems to lit mags; guest ed. Woman Poet; chapbooks Finally, 1981, The Water Poem and Others, 1985. BA, Vassar, 1938; postgrad, U. Chgo, 1939. Mem. Vis. comm. on Music, U. Chgo, 1979, Music of the Baroque, 1979, Radcliffe Selection Comm., 1982, Mem. Poetry Center, 1974, Modern Poetry Assn. Address: 5730 Kenwood Chicago IL 60637

FRIEDLAND, SUSAN HELEN, b. Brklyn., Apr. 18, 1947; d. Rudolph Albert and Leatrice Renee (Bernstein) Schuman; m. Louis Allen Friedland, Mar. 2, 1969; children—Cheryl, Mark. Contrbr. poems to anthols. Wrkg. on book of poems. Grad. public schls., Brklyn. Dental asst. H. Gaulkin, D.D.S., Miami Beach, FL, 1971-73; bookkeeper Layne Insurance, Inc., North Miami Beach, FL, 1985—. Recipient Golden Poet award World of Poetry, 1985, 86. Home: 8529 Southampton Dr Miramar FL 33025

FRIEDMAN, ALAN, see Horowitz, Shel Alan

FRIEDMAN, B(ERNARD) H(ARPER), b. NYC,July 27, 1926, s. Leonard and Madeline (Uris) F.; m. Abby Noselson, Mar. 6, 1948; children—Jackson, Daisy. Author: Circles (novel), 1962, Yarborough (novel), 1964, Whispers (novel), 1972, Museum (novel), 1974, Almost a Life (novel), 1975, The Polygamist (novel), 1981, Coming Close (stories), 1982, Jackson Pollock: Energy Made Visible (biography), 1972, Gertrude Vanderbilt Whitney (biography), 1978. BA, Cornell U., 1948. Trustee Whitney Mus., 1961—, Broida Mus., 1983—; dir. Fine Arts Work Center, Provincetown, Mass., 1968-82. Served with USN, 1944-46, PTO. Recipient Fels award CCLM, 1975, Nelson Algren award Chgo. Mag., 1983. Mem. Fiction Collective (founding mem.), AG, PEN, DG. Home: 439 E 51st St New York NY 10022

FRIEDMAN, BETTY, b. Peoria, IL, Feb. 4, 1921; d. Harry and Miriam (Horwitz) Goldstein; m. Carl Friedan, June 1947 (div. May 1969); children: Daniel, Jonathan, Emily. Author: The FEminine Mystique, 1963, It Changed My Life: Writings on the Women's Movement, 1976, The Second Stage, 1982; contrbg. editor: McCall's mg., 1971—; contbr. to Atlantic Monthly. BA summa cum laude, Smith Coll., 1942. Mem.

PEN, Soc. Mag. Writers. Address: Summit 1230 Ave Ams New York NY 10020

FRIEDMAN, DOROTHY, b. NYC, Mar 10; d. Harry and Annie (VanGlish) Kaplan; m. Leo Friedman, Feb. 1 (dec. May 18, 1969); children: Ruth Michele, Mark, David. Author: The Ethnic Am. Woman; contrbr Calif. Mag., New Age Jnl., Guideposts, Mod. Maturity, Pioneer Women, Inside Mag., Jewish Press, Aim Mag., Agada, Lake Superior Rvw, LA Rvw, LA Times, LA Herald Examiner, NY Daily NEws, Christian Sci. Monitor, Balt. Jewish Times, Crosscurrents, Atlanta Rvw, The Haven, Newsday, others. AA, Valley Jr. Coll.; postgrad, Northridge State Coll. Social worker, NYC, 1963-82; freelance writer, 1982—. Mem. CODA, Women Writers West. Address: 1825 N Edgemont St Los Angeles CA 90027

FRIEDMAN, JEFFREY H., b. Chgo., June 14, 1950; m. Colleen Randall. Author: The Record-Breaking Heat Wave, 1986; contrbr. to MSS, Ironwood, Quarry West, other publs.; co-founder, ed.: Pavement, 1980; poetry ed. Iowa Jnl Lit. Studies, 1980. BA, Macalester Coll., 1975; MFA, U. Iowa, 1980. Vis. wrtr.-in-res. N.C. Arts Council, Forest City, N.C., 1980-81; ed. Am. Book Co., NYC, 1981-82; instr. U. Mo., St. Louis, 1983-84; freelance ed., NYC, 1984. Winner Mahon Poetry Contest, U. Mo., 1977; tchr. poetry wrtg. fellow U. Iowa, 1978-80. Mem. AWP. Home: 229 Jackson St Brooklyn NY 11211

FRIEDMAN, NORMAN, b. Boston, Apr. 10, 1925, s. Samuel and Eva (Nathanson) F.; m. Zelda Nathanson, June 7, 1945; children—Michael, Janet. Author: E.E. Cummings: The Art of His Poetry, 1960, Poetry: An Introduction to Its Form and Art (with C. A. McLaughlin), 1963, E.E. Cummings: The Growth of a Writer, 1964, Form and Meaning in Fiction, 1975, The Magic Badge: Poems 1953-1984, 1984; ed.: E.E. Cummings: A Collection of Critical Essays, 1972. AB, Harvard U., 1948, AM, 1949, PhD,1952; MSW, Adelphi U., 1978. Mem. faculty U. Conn., Storrs, 1952-63; prof. Queens Coll., CUNY, Flushing, 1963—. Grantee ACLS, 1959, 60; recipient Northwest Rvw Poetry Prize, 1963, Borestone Mountain Poetry Awards, 1964, 67; Fulbright lectr., France, 1966-67; winner All Nations Poetry Contest, Triton Coll., Ill., 1977. Mem. MLA, NWU, AAUP, Phi Beta Kappa. Home: 33-54 164th St Flushing NY 11358

FRIEDMAN, PAUL ALAN, b. Bklyn., Apr. 21, 1937, s. Jack and Eva (Punia) F.; m. Mary Lynn Seidel, Mar. 27, 1960, children—Mysti, Joseph, Molly. Author short story collections: And If Defeated Allege Fraud, 1971, Serious Trouble, 1986. BS, U. Ill., 1961; MFA, U. Iowa, 1963. Tchr. Wis. State U., Stevens Point, 1964-68, U. Ill., Urbana, 1968—. Recipient Sherwood Anderson award Mid Am. Rvw, 1983, Fiction fellowship, Ill. Arts Council, 1986. Home: 310 W Illinois St Urbana IL 61801

FRIEDMAN, ROY BENNIS, b. NYC,Mar. 25, 1934, s. Ralph J. and Miriam (Bennis) F.; m. Louise Elizabeth Shapiro, Oct. 17, 1968; 1 dau.—Rebecca Jane. Novelist: The Insurrection of Hippolytus Brandenberg (alt. selection Lit. Guild), 1968; contrbr. short stories to Wis. Rvw, St. Andrews Rvw, Phoebe; contrbr. nonfiction to Shantih, Holiday, Punta Europa. Wrkg. on quantum mechanics for laymen, short stories, play. BA, Dartmouth Coll., 1956; PhD,CUNY, 1982. Instr. English Baruch Coll., N.Y.C., 1971-76, U. South Fla., Tampa., 1983-85. Served with U.S. Army, 1959-61. Fla. Cultural Affairs Div. fellow, 1985; winner PEN-NEA Syndicated Fiction competition, 1985. Home: 23 Waters Edge Old Farm Lake Chappaqua NY 10514

FRIEDMAN, STANLEY P., b. Seattle, Feb. 3, 1925, s. Jacob S. F. Author: Kennedy Women, Kennedy Family, True Quotes, Ronald Reagan; His Life Story in Pictures; contrbr. to Esquire, New York, Village Voice, Cosmopolitan, People Parade, N.Y. Times, American Photographer, Popular Photography, Harpers, Ms Mag., Oui, Natl. Lampoon., others. BA, U. Wash. MA, 1952. Served to 2d lt. USAAF, 1943-45: ETO. Address: RFD 1 Route 129 Yorktown Heights NY 10598

FRIEDRICH, OTTO ALVA, b. Boston, Feb. 3, 1929; s. Carl Joachim and Lenore (Pelham) F.; m. Priscilla Boughton, Apr. 13, 1950; children—Elizabeth Charlotte, Margaret Emily, Nicholas Max, Amelia Anne, Charles Anthony. Author: (novels) The Poor in Spirit, 1952, The Loner, 1964; (non-fiction) Decline and Fall, 1970 (George Polk Meml. award); Before the Deluge, 1972, The Rose Garden, 1972, Going Crazy, 1976, Clover, 1979, The End of the World, 1982, City of Nets, 1986; (juveniles with wife) The Easter Bunny That Overslept, 1957, Clean Clarence, 1959, Sir Alva and the Wicked Wizard, 1960, The Marshmallow Ghosts, 1960, The Wishing Well in the Woods, 1961, Noah Shark's Ark, 1961, The Christmas Star, 1962, The April Umbrella, 1963, The League of Unusual Animals, 1965. AB magna cum laude, Harvard, 1948. Mem. copy desk Stars & Stripes, 1950-52; with United Press in Paris and London, 1952-54; with telegraph desk N.Y. Daily News, 1954-57; mem. fgn. dept. Newsweek, 1957-62, asst. fgn. editor, 1959-62; fgn. editor Sat. Eve. Post, 1962-63, asst. mng. editor, 1963-65, mng. editor, 1965-69; freelance writer, 1969-71; sr. editor TIME, 1971-80, sr. writer, 1980—. Home: 569 Bayville Rd Locust Valley NY 11560

FRIEDRICH, PAUL WILLIAM, b. Cambridge, MA., Oct. 22, 1927; s. Carl Joachim and Lenore Louise (Pelham) F.; m. Lore Bucher, Jan. 6, 1950 (div. Feb. 1966); children—Maria Elizabeth, Susan Guadalupe, Peter Roland; m. 2d, Margaret Hardin, Jan. 26, 1966 (div. June 28, 1974); m. 3rd Deborah Joanna Gordon, Aug. 9, 1975; children—Kanya Ann, Joan Lenore. Author: Agrarian Revolt in a Mexican Village, 1970, 77, Proto-Indo-European Trees, 1970, The Tarascan Suffixes of Locative Space, 1971, Proto-Indo-European Syntax, 1975, The Meaning of Aphrodite, 1978, 1982, Bastard Moons, 1979, Language, Context and the Imagination, 1979, The Language Parallax, 1986, The Princes of Naranja, 1986. Wrkg. on new problems in anthropology and linguistics, new poems. BA, Harvard, 1950; PhD,Yale, 1957. Instr. U. Conn., Stamford, 1956-57, Harvard, Cambridge, 1957-58; jr. linguistic scholar Deccan Coll., Poona, India, 1958-59; asst. prof. Univ. Pa., Phila., 1959–62; asst. prof. Univ. Chgo., 1962-67, prof., 1967—. Mem. Linguistic Soc. Am., Am. Anthropolog Assn., Am. Assn. Tchrs. Slavic and East European Langs. Address: 5550 S Dorchester Chicago IL 60637

FRIESE, HELEN MARIE, b. Chgo., May 16, 1925; d. George Adolph Miller and Marie Augusta Wilhelmia (Vetter) Borkenhagen Miller; m. John Clark Friese, June 12, 1948; children—Diane, David. Columnist: Creative Loafing, 1982—, Go Mag., 1987—. contrbr. articles to newspapers, anthol. Wrkg. on book, Dear Mom—The Lost Art of Writing Home or Anywhere Else. Cert., Bryant & Stratton Bus. Coll., 1945; student DeKalb Coll., 1983-87, Ga. State U., 1987—. Secy., Superintendent of Schls., Hudson, NH, 1976-78; pres., founder Village Wrtrs. Group, Atlanta, 1979-83. Bd. dirs. DeKalb Council for the Arts, Atlanta, 1983-85; mem. newsletter advisory bd. Am. Heart Assn., Atlanta, 1981-87. Mem. SPJ, Atlanta Press Club. Address: 548 Susan Creek Dr Stone Mountain GA 30083

FRIESEKE, FRANCES, (Mrs. Kenton Kilmer), b. Paris, Aug. 2, 1914 (arrived USA 1937), d. Frederick Carl and Sarah Anne (O'Bryan) F.; m. Kenton Kilmer, June 2, 1937; children—Hugh, Anne, Noelie, Nicholas, Martin, Rosamond, Matthew, Miriam, Deborah, Jonathan. Co-ed. (with K. Kilmer) The Tidings Poets, Vol. 2. Contrbr. to Poetry in Am., Commonweal, Spirit, Catholic World, Carillon, Washington Post, Poetry, Horn Book. Founder-prin. Green Hedges Schl., Arlington, Va., 1942-55, Vienna, Va., 1955-68. Mem. PSA, Poetry Soc. Va. Home: 411 Windover Ave NW Vienna VA 22180

FRIMAN, ALICE, b. NYC,Oct. 20, 1933; d. Joseph and Helen (Friedman) Pesner; m. Elmer Friman, July 3, 1955 (div. 1975); children—Richard, Paul, Lillian. Author: A Question of Innocence, 1978, Song to My Sister, 1979, Reporting From Corinth, 1984; editor: Loaves and Fishes: A Collection of Indiana Women Poets, 1982; poetry in Georgia Rvw, Southwest Rvw, Indiana Rvw, and many other lit mags. BA, Brooklyn Coll., 1954; MA, Butler U., 1971. Teacher, NYC pub. schls., 1954-56; assoc. prof., IN Central U., Indpls, 1971—. Mem. MLA, PSA. Home: 6312 Central Ave Indianapolis IN 46220

FRIO, KAZE UTADA, see Frio, Mary Oliver Brown

FRITCHIE, HAZEL M., (Marge Hamilton), b. Bridgeport, Ill., May 19, 1926; d. Harry Edward and Nettie Lee (Mason) Hamilton; m. Walter T. Fritchie, Sept. 19, 1945; children—Walter, Barbara, Becky. Contrbr. articles: Farm Wife News, Sunshine Mag., Grit, other jnls. and gen. interest publs. Home: 202 N Pike St Palestine IL 62451

FROHMAN, HOWARD LOEB, b. New Haven, CT, Oct. 15, 1916; s. Elias and Rhea (Flaks) F.; m. Ruth Beer, July 2, 1954; 1 child: Gene Hillery. Author: articles, stories and poems in New Haven Historical Soc., Opinion Mag., Life Today, Woman's Day, New Haven Register Section. B.A., Yale Univ., 1948; Columbia Grad. Schl. of Jnlsm., 1950-51; M.A. Southern Conn. State Univ., 1985. Staff mem., New Haven Redevelopment Agcy., 1956-76; freelance wrtr., 1951—. Pvt. 1st class, U.S. Army, 1936-39, First Lieutenant, U.S. Army, Airborne, 82nd Div. N. Africa, Europe, 1942-44. Mem. Conn. Acad. of Arts and Sciences, New Haven Historical Soc., Retired Officer Assn. Wrkg. on WWII fiction. Home: 530 Summit Dr Orange CT 06477

FROMMER, SARA HOSKINSON, b. Chgo., June 6, 1938; d. Charles C. and Isabel (Saulmon) Hoskinson; m. Gabriel Paul Frommer, June 14, 1958; children—Charles, Joseph. Author: Murder in C Major, 1986. Wrkg. on sequel. B.A. in German, Oberlin Coll., 1958; A.M. in German, Brown U., 1961. Sr. ed. Agcy. for Instructional Technology, Bloomington, IN, 1978—. Mem. MWA. Home: 828 S Fess Ave Bloomington IN 47401

FROST, DAVID DUANE, b. NYC, June 30, 1925; s. Rev. Edward Lawrence and Helen-

Mary (Goodenough) F.; m. Dorothy Ruth Jacobson, Dec. 27, 1979 (div. June 1983); children (by previous wives): Stephanie L., Amy. Author: Broadsides, 1980, Boxcars, 1986; editor: Your Runic Zodiac, 1986, The Night Line, 1986, Boxcars, 1986. AB in poli. sci., Syracuse U., 1948. Store mgr. various mid-Atlantic states, 1948-72; owner Periodical Distbr., L.I., N.Y., 1973-79; acct. The Game Keeper, Santa Barbara, Calif., 1980—; owner, editor Summer Stream Press, Santa Barbara, 1980—. Served with USNR, 1943-46, PTO. Mem. Calif. State Poetry Soc., Calif. Fedn. Chaparral Poets, N.Y. Poetry Forum. Home: 3755 San Remo Dr 166 Santa Barbara CA 93105

FROST, FAYE JUANITA, b. Texarkana, TX, Feb. 15, 1927; d. Morris Mineard Wood and Mabel Louise (Erskine) Wood Mackinnon; m. Sam A. Rizzo, Sept. 14, 1946 (div. 1970); children—Donna Lynne, Steven Mark, Ronald Michael; m. 2d, John Ernest Frost, Jan. 17, 1972. Author, pub.: The Instant Article Writer, 1983, The Educator's Guide to Self-Publishing, 1986; contrbr. over 900 articles to: American Mag., Denver Post, Chgo. Tribune, Good News, numerous other newspapers and mags. Student SUNY-Buffalo, 1943-46. Freelance wrtr., 1958—; advt. coordinator Walter Drake & Sons, Colorado Springs, Colo., 1971-72; dir. public relations Marco Distributors, Arvada, Colo, Colo., 1972-79; pres. Faye Frost & Assocs., Denver, 1979—. Mem. CAL. Office: 1333 W 120th Ave Suite 110 Denver CO 80234

FROST, JASON, see Obstfeld, Raymond

FROST, RICHARD GEORGE, b. Palo Alto, CA, April 8, 1929; s. Willis George and Ruth (Kettlewell) Frost; m. Frances Edna Atkins, Sept. 2, 1951 (div. 1969); children—Robert Willis, Diana Ruth, Catherine Patricia; m. 2d, Carol Kristin Kydd, Aug. 23, 1969; children—Daniel Adam, Joel Richard. Author: The Circus Villains, 1965, Getting Drunk With The Birds, 1971. AB, San Jose State U., 1951, MA, 1957. Tchr., San Jose publ. schls., 1952-56; instr., Towson State Coll., Towson, Md., 1957-59; prof., State Univ. College, Oneonta, NY, 1959—. Mem. PSA, PEN. Home: RD 2 Box 73 Otego NY 13825

FROULA, JAMES, b. Oak Park, IL, May 17, 945, s. James C. and Helen B. (Tanana) F.; m. Barbara Leftwich, June 8, 1968; children—Matt, Anna. BSME, U. Tenn., 1967, MME, 1968. Devel. engr. IBM, Boulder, Colo., 1970-82; secy.-treas. Tau Beta Pi, Knoxville, Tenn., 1982—, ed. The Bent of Tau Beta Pi, 1982—, dir., Assoc. Coll. Honor Soc., 1987-1989. Served to 1st lt. U.S. Army, 1968-70, Vietnam. Decorated Bronze Star. Mem. AAAS, ASME, NSPE. Office: Box 8840 Univ Sta Knoxville TN 37996

FRUMKES, LEWIS BURKE, b. NYC. May 10, 1939; s. Harry and Beatrice (Burke) Frumkes; m. Alana June Martin; children—Timothy, Amber. Author: Wall Street Laid Bear, 1970, How to Raise Your I.Q. By Eating Gifted Children, 1983. The Mensa Think-Smart Book, 1986, Name Crazy, 1987. BA, Trinity College, NYU, 1962. Faculty, Marymount-Manhattan College, 1985—. Mem. ASJA, NASW, AG, P&W, PEN. Home: 1 Gracie Terrace New York NY 10028

FRYE, JOHN, b. Montreal, Que., Can., Jan. 22, 1930, s. J. Stevenson and Beatrice (Pratt) F.; m. Ann Lyons (div. 1957); children—Leslie, William; m. 2d, Marlies Strillinger, June 14, 1957; 1 dau., Nicole. Author: No Hill Too Fast (with Phil and Steve Mahre), 1985; contrbr. articles various ski and sport mags. BA, McGill U., Montreal. Wrtr., Forster, McGuier Co., Montreal, 1952-57; mng. ed. Am. Metal Market, NYC, 1958-64; ed.-in-chief Ski mag., NYC, 1964-72; editorial dir. Ski mag., Golf mag., Outdoor Life mag., NYC, 1969-80; pub. cons., Katonah, N.Y., 1982—. Mem. Overseas Press Club Am. Home: 23 E Lake Dr Katonah NY 10536

FRYE, DELLA MAE, b. Roanoke, VA, Feb. 16, 1926; d. Henry Vetchel and Lavina Theradosia (Eardley) Pearcy-Pierce; m. James Frederick Frye, 1944; children—Linda Jeanne Frye-Chaikin, James Marvin, David Scott. Contrbr. poems, articles to newspapers; author songs. Student Hope Coll., 1968, Grand Valley State Coll., 1969-71, N.Y. Schl. Interior Design, 1978. Tchr. private art classes, 1964-74; realtor, 1978-80; with Diversified Financing, 1979-82; portrait artist, 1967—; cons. World Traders, Grand Rapids, MI, 1986—. Home: 7677 Steele Ave Jenson MI 49428

FRYE HOFFMAN, LOIS, b. Battle Creek, MI., May 10, 1955; d. Otis Franklin and Marian Frances (Brueck) Frye; m. James Glenn Hoffman, Apr. 25, 1987. Columnist, contrbr. to local newspapers; contrbr. articles to periodicals; poetry in anthologies. AA in Electronic Data Processing, Kellogg Community Coll., 1981. Freelance wrtr. Mem. NWC, Tri-State Wrtrs. Club, Soc. Tech. Communication. Home: 3010 W Drive S Apt 11 Athens MI 49011

FRYM, GLORIA LYNN, b. Bklyn., Feb. 28, 1947; d. Bernard and Claire (Perlstein) F.; m. David Theodore Benedetti, III (div. Aug. 1976). Author: Impossible Affection, 1979; Second Stories, 1979; Back to Forth, 1982; contrbr. rvws. and articles to San Francisco Rvw. Books, San Francisco Chronicle, San Jose Mercury, Balt. Sun, San Francisco Camerawork Qtly BA, U. N.Mex., 1968, MA, 1973. Freelance wrtr.-ed., San Francisco, 1976—; artist, instr. San Francisco County Jail, 1982-83, 85—; ed. Northstar Computers, San Leandro, Calif., 1984-85; lectr. dept. creative writing San Francisco State U., 1984—. Recipient book award San Francisco State U. Poetry Ctr., 1982. Mem. P&W, Media Alliance. Home: 2112 Essex St Berkeley CA 94705

FRYM, GLORIA LYNN, b. Bklyn., Feb. 28, 1947; d. Bernard and Claire (Perlstein) F.; m. David Theodore Benedetti, III (div. Aug. 1976). Author: Impossible Affection, 1979; Second Stories, 1979; Back to Forth, 1982; contrbr. rvws. and articles to San Francisco Rvw. Books, San Francisco Chronicle, San Jose Mercury, Balt. Sun, San Francisco Camerawork Qtly BA, U. N.Mex., 1968, MA, 1973. Freelance wrtr.-ed., San Francisco, 1976—; artist, instr. San Francisco County Jail, 1982-83, 85—; ed. Northstar Computers, San Leandro, Calif., 1984-85; lectr. dept. creative writing San Francisco State U., 1984—. Recipient book award San Francisco State U. Poetry Ctr., 1982. Mem. P&W, Media Alliance. Home: 2112 Essex St Berkeley CA 94705

FUCHS, LAUREL BERNICE, b. Leland, IL, Feb. 14, 1935; d. George William and Edna Winifred (Mcgee) F. Contrbr. poems to anthols., newspapers. Wrkg. on poems, article, songs. Grad. public schls., Leland. Seamstress, Century Manufacturing Corp., Sandwich, IL, 1955-81; genl. factory assembly Domar Industries, Sandwich, 1981—. Recipient (3) awards of Merit, World of Poetry, 1986, Golden Poet award, 1986, Silver Poet award, 1987. Home: 325 W Grant Box 93 Sheridan IL 60551

FUENTES, MARTHA AYERS, (Scat Lorimer), b. Ashland, Ala., Dec. 21, 1923; d. William Henry and Elizabeth (Dye) Ayers; m. Manuel Solomon Fuentes, Apr. 11, 1943. Playwright: Go Stare at the Moon, 1969, Two Characters in Search of an Agreement (one-act play), 1970, others; contrbr. articles to numerous nat. mags. BA, U. South Fla. Freelance wrtr., 1953—. Recipient George Seigel Drama award U. Chgo., 1969 (for Go Stare at the Moon). Mem. Dramatists Guild, AG, Soc. Children's Book Wrtrs., Southeastern Theatre Assn., Alliance of Resident Theatres N.Y. Home: 102 3d St Belleair Beach FL 34635

FUKUYAMA, BETTY M., b. Heppner, OR, Feb. 25, 1922, d. Jesse Albert and Miriam (Brown) Adkins; m. Tsutomu Tom Fukuyama, Aug. 10, 1945; children—David, Mary, Peter, James, Timothy. Author: (chapbook) 25 Poems, 1975; ed. Pierce County Poetry, 1975; contrbr. poems to Alaska Rvw, Bitterroot, Christian Century, Christian Sci. Monitor, Crosscurrents Rvw, West Coast Poetry Rvw, others. BA, Boston U., 1947; MA, U. Wash., 1972; MA psychology, Antioch U., Seattle, 1986. Freelance feature article wrtr. Surburban Times, Tacoma, 1967-68; tchr. poetry workshop Ft. Steilacoom Community Coll., Tacoma, 1969-74; poet-in-res. Western State Hosp., Ft. Steilacoom, Wash., 1973-75; CETA wrtr. Tacoma-Pierce County Civic Arts Commn., 1975; adminstrv. sec. 1st Congl. Ch., Tacoma, 1978-80. Mem. PSA, Wash. Poets Assn. (co-founder; sec. 1971-75, pres. 1975-78, pres. emeritus), Oreg. State Poetry Assn., Tacoma Wrtrs. Club (pres. 1964-66). Home: 112 Regents Blvd Apt 1 Tacoma WA 98466

FULLER, BLAIR FAIRCHILD, (Blair Fuller), b. NYC, Jan. 18, 1927; d. Charles Fairchild Fuller and Jane Sage (White) Canfield; m. Diana Burgess (div. Dec. 1985); children: Maria Gubina, Anthony Blair, Diana Whitney. Author: A Far Place, 1957; A Butterfly Net and a Kingdom (part of Three Short Novels), 1961; Zebina's Mountain, 1976. AB, Harvard U., 1951. Paris ed. Paris Rvw, 1960-61; lectr. Stanford U., 1961-67; prof. English, Calif. State U., Hayward, 1967-69; Fulbright prof. U. Oran, Algeria, 1969-70; gen. dir. Squaw Valley Community Wrtrs., Olympic Valley, Calif., 1970-85; freelance wrtr. Served with USNR, 1944-46; PTO. Recipient O'Henry award Doubleday & Co., 1973, 78. Mem. PEN. Address: 725 2d St San Francisco CA 94107

FULLER, MARGARET CATHCART, b. Palo Alto,CA, Mar. 22, 1935; d. Wallace Daniel and Eleanor Shepard (Hanford) Cathcart; m. Wayne P. Fuller, Aug. 31, 1954; children—Douglas, Leslie, Neal, Hilary, Stuart. Author: Trails of the Sawtooth and White Cloud Mountains, 1979, Trails of Western Idaho, 1982, Trails of the Frank Church—River of No Return Wilderness, 1987. Contrbr. articles to mags., newspapers including Idaho Wildlife, Sun Valley Mag., Cascade New. Wrkg. on revision of Trails of the Sawtooth and White Cloud Mountains. AB, Stanford, U., 1956. Free-lance wrtr., 1975—; instr. backpacking community edn. dept. Coll. Id., Caldwell, 1983-85; lectr. Trek leader Id. Lung Assn., Boise, 1981-85. Mem. Id. Wrtr.'s League (named Wrtr. of Yr. 1982), AAUW. Home: Box 148 Weiser ID 83672

FULLER, MARY MARGARET STIEHM, b. Lincoln, NE, Apr. 23, 1914; d. Ewald Ortwin and Marie Daisy (Douglass) Stiehm; m.

Curtis Gross Fuller, Sept. 24, 1938; children: Nancy Abigail Fuller Abraham, Michael Curtis. Free-lance writer, 1940-52; asst. editor FATE mag., 1952-54, exec. editor, 1954-56, editor, 1956-77, editor, assoc. pub., 1977—; pres. Clark Pub. Co., Highland Park, Ill., 1949—; v.p., secy. Woodhall Pub. Co., Highland Park, 1965-85. BA, U. Wis., 1938. Home: 815 Deerpath Rd Lake Forest IL 60045

FULLER, MIKE ANDREW, (Nona Dextrose Plume), b. Jackson, MS, Mar. 11, 1964; s. Jack Norris and Emily Cordelia Wilmaut (Livingston) F. Contrbr. poems to anthols. Wrkg. on book, Just a Little Mad Cap Ferocity, poems. Grad. public schs., Jackson. Designer, painter Gaddliss' Screen Printing & Signs, Jackson, 1983; genl. merchandise mgr. Jitney Jangle Stores, Jackson, 1984-86. Home: 113 Brantley Dr Terry MS 39170

FULMER, SANDRA LEE, b. Shelby, OH, May 19, 1953; d. Olen C. and Bette Jane (Garner) F. Contrbr. articles to rodeo mags. including The (Horsemans) Corral, Rodeo News, others. Student West Tex. State U., 1971-74. With media dept. Intl. Pro Rodeo Assn., Pauls Valley, OK, 1985; telemarketer Hutch-N-Sons, Pauls Valley, 1986; advt. designer Wynnewood Gazette, OK, 1987—. Home: Rt 2 Box 21 Wynnewood OK 73098

FULTON, ALICE, b. Troy, NY, Jan 25, 1952; d. John R. and Mary Agnes (Callahan) Fulton; m. Hank De Leo, June 27, 1980. Author: Anchors of Light, 1979, Dance Script with Electric Ballerina (winner AWP Poetry award), 1983, Palladium (winner 1985 Poetry Series Competition), 1986; contrbr anthologies: Ecstatic Occasions, Expedient Forms; New Am. Poets of the 80s, New Voices/1979-83, Sotheby's Poetry Competition 1982, Strings: A Gathering of Family Poems, Leaving the Bough: 50 Am. Poets of the 80s, The Poet Dreaming in the Artist's House, The Wings the Vines, Rapunzel, Rapunzel; contrbr poems The New Yorker, Poetry, Parnassus, Am. Scholar, Ploughshares, Epoch, Boston Rvw, others. BA in Creative Writing, Empire State Coll., 1978; MFA in Creative Writing, Cornell U., 1982. Asst. prof. Univ Mich., Ann Arbor, 1983—; Wm. Wilhartz Prof., 1986—. Fellow Mich. Soc., Ann Arbor, 1983—, recipient lit. grant, Mich. Council for the Arts, Detroit, 1986, Guggenheim fellowship, 1987, winner open competition, Natl. Poetry Series, NYC, 1985, Rainer Maria Rilke Prize, Consuelo Ford award, PSA, 1984, AWP Poetry prize, 1982, AAP prize, 1982, Emily Dickinson award, PSA, 1980. Mem. PSA, P&W. Address: 2370 LeForge Rd RR2 Ypsilanti MI 48198

FULTON, LEN, b. Lowell, MA, May 15, 1934; s. Claude E. and Louise E. (Vaillant) F.; son, Timothy. B.A., U. Wyo., 1961, postgrad., U. Calif., Berkeley. Pub. Tourist Topic, Kennebunkport, Maine, also Weekly News, Freeport, Maine, 1957-59; biostatistician Calif. Dept. Public Health, 1962-68; editor, pub. Dustbooks, 1963—; chmn. COSMEP, 1968-71, 73; cons. small presses ALA. Author: novels, The Grassman, 1974, Dark Other Adam Dreaming, 1975; co-author: non-fiction, American Odyssey, 1975, with Ellen Ferber. Panelist Calif. Arts Commn., 1975. Served with AUS, 1953-55. Grantee NEA, 1959-61, CCLM, 1970-73, NEA, 1974, 75. Mem. PEN. Address: Box 100 Paradise CA 95969

FUNGE, ROBERT, b. San Francisco, Sept. 13, 1931, s. Frank and Edna (Trouin) F.; children—Pamela Marie, Christopher. Author: The Lie the Lamb Knows, 1979; contrbr. poems to Centennial, Chariton, Cottonwood, Great River, Greenfield, Madison Rvw, Ohio Rvw, Aura, Kans. Qtly, New Letters, Spoon River Qtly, Ezra Pound Anthology, others. Served with USN, 1950-54. Mem. PSA. Home: 782 Elm St Box 1225 San Carlos CA 94070

FUNK, VIRGINIA B., (Ginny Funke), b. Rockaway Beach, NY, Feb. 10, 1923, d. Harry August and Bertha Ella (Renke) Hirt; m. Martin William Funk, Dec. 14, 1944; children—Michael Dana, Shelley Ann Neuss, George Bernard. Author: The Complete Akita (with Joan Linderman), 1983, local history and lore booklet, 1984; beauty ed.: Senior Life Mag.; columnist: Tri-Valley Herald and News, 1967-70, Dog Lovers' Digest, 1970-74, self-syndicated to regional papers, 1978-83; contrbr. to People on Parade, Dog Fancy, Ideals, Modern Maturity, other publs.; ed.: Kanine Knews, 1971, beauty ed. Gemco/ Memco Courier, 1979-80. Student Columbia U. Freelance wrtr.; approved judge Am. Kennel Club, 1969—; dist. chmn. creative writing and lit. Palomar dist. Calif. Fedn. Women's Clubs, 1984—. Mem. Dog Wrtrs. Assn. Am. (newspaper writing awards 1969, 70, 81), director, Fallbrook Wrtrs.' Workshop. Home: 697 Sleeping Indian Rd San Luis Rey CA 92068

FUNKE, GINNY, see Funk, Virginia B.

FUNKHOUSER, EILEEN, b. Takoma Park, Md., July 17, 1957; d. Robert Earl and Colleen Marie (Ryan) Funkhouser. Typesetter Times Pub. Co., St. Petersburg, Fla., 1975-76; copy ed. Suncoast Beacon, Largo, Fla., 1978-79; reporter, photographer, ed. Largo Leader, Seminole Beacon, 1979—. Home: 1005 10th St SW Largo FL 34640

FURLONG, MARCELLA LEE, b. Bryn Mawr, PA, Nov. 30, 1964; d. Alfred William and Nancy Anne (Joiner) F. Contrbr. poems to anthols. Wrkg. on short stories, book. Sandwich maker, waitress Piccolo's Pizza-Deli, Bradenton, FL, 1987—. Recipient Golden Poet award World of Poetry, 1985, Silver Poet award, 1986. Home: 6633 53d Ave E Bradenton FL 34203

FURLONG, MAURICE B., b. Buffalo, Nov. 14, 1909, s. James C. and Frances R. (Bennett) F.; m. Helen Carey, Apr. 30, 1938; children—Mary D., Maureen E., Maurice B.Jr., Frances R. Contrbr. articles on poliomyelitis epidemic, clubfoot correction and evaluation and treatment of foot deformities to profl. jnls. Wrkg. on pediatric care book. BA, Canisius Coll., Buffalo, 1931; MD, U. Buffalo, 1935. Practice medicine specializing in pediatrics, Buffalo, 1935-38, Jamestown, N.Y., 1946—. Served as flight surgeon USAF, 1942-46. Home: 649 Fairmount AVE NE Jamestown NY 14701

FURLOTTE, NICOLAS, b. NYC, Mar. 13, 1952; s. Robert and Dorothy (Ohlandt) F. BA in English, U. NH, 1975. News writer Cablevision News, Jericho, NY, 1976-77; ed. Atlantic Cable Publishing, Jericho, 1977-78; news producer & dir. Cablevision, Woodbury, NY, 1978-80; ed. Cable Mktg. Mag., NYC, 1981-84; editorial dir./exec. ed. Jobson Pub. Liquor Group, NYC, 1984—. Home: 160 West 77th St New York NY 10024

FURMAN, LAURA, b. NYC, Nov. 19, 1945; d. Sylvan Seymour and Minnie (Airov) F.; m. Joel Warren Barna, Jan. 3, 1981. Pub. works: The Glass House, 1981, The Shadow Line, 1982, Watch Time Fly, 1983, Tuxedo Park, 1986. BA, Bennington Coll., 1968. Vis. asst. prof. U. Houston, 1979-80; lectr. So. Meth. U., Dallas, 1981-82; asst. prof. U. Tex., Austin, 1983—. Mem. Tex. Inst. Letters (Council), PEN, AG. Recipient short story prize Tex. Inst. Letters, 1980; Best Book of Fiction, Jesse Jones Award, Texas Inst. Letters, 1981; CAPS award in fiction, NY State Council on Arts, 1976; Dobie Paisano fellow Tex. Inst. Letters and U. Tex., 1981-82; Guggenheim fellow, 1982-83. Office: Dept. Eng U Tex Austin TX 78712

FURNAS, JOSEPH CHAMBERLAIN, b. Indpls., Nov. 24, 1905; s. Isaiah George and Elizabeth (Chamberlain) F.. Author: The Prophet's Chamber, 1937, Many People Prize It, 1938, Anatomy of Paradise, 1948 (Anisfield-Wolff non-fiction award), Voyage to Windward; The Life of Robert Louis Stevenson, 1951; Collaborator: (with Ernest M. Smith) Sudden Death and How to Avoid It, 1935, How America Lives, (with editorial staff of Ladies' Home Jour.), 1941; author: Goodbye to Uncle Tom, 1956, The Road to Harpers Ferry, 1959, The Devil's Rainbow, 1962, The Life and Times of the Late Demon Rum, 1955, Lightfoot Island, 1968, The Americans, 1969, Great Times, 1974, Stormy Weather, 1977, Fanny Kemble, 1981 (George Freedley award 1982). AB., Harvard, 1927. Mem. Phi Beta Kappa. Address: Brandt & Brandt 1501 Broadway New York NY 10036

FUSON, ROBERT HENDERSON, b. Bloomington, IN, July 7, 1927; s. Raymond and Daisy Sanders (Henderson) F.; m. Amelia Carmen Fernandez, Feb. 16, 1952; children—Robin, Karen. Author: Sabana Central de Panama, 1960, The Origin and Nature of American Savanas, 1963, Fundamental Place-Name Geography, 1966, 6th ed., 1988, A Geography of Geography, 1969, Introduction to World Geography, 1977, The Log of Christopher Columbus, 1987; (with others) Laboratory Exercises in Physical Geography, 1959, 3d ed., 1974, Problems in World Cultural Geography, 1960, 2d ed., 1967, Resource Conservation in the United States, 1961. Ed. numerous books including A Geography of Regions, 1972, Spatial Foundations of Urbanism, 1972, A Geography of Politics, 1973, A Geography of Energy, 1974, Modern Political Geography, 1975. Contrbr. chpts. to books, articles to mags., jnls. Wrkg. on book on Christopher Columbus. A.B., Ind. U., 1949; M.A., Fla. State U., 1951; Ph.D., La. State U., 1958. Asst. prof. U. New Orleans, 1958-60; asst. prof. U. South Fla., Tampa, 1960-61, assoc. prof., 1961-66, prof., 1966-86, prof. emeritus, 1986—.Served U.S. Army, 1944-45, USN, 1945-46. Recipient Outstanding Achievement award Fla. Soc. Geography, Orlando, 1966, Outstanding Contribution award State of Fla., Tallahassee, 1976, Merit award Miami Expo 500, 1982, Webb-Smith Essay award U. Tex.-Arlington, 1986. Mem. AG, Assn. Am. Geographers, Soc. for History of Discoveries, Intl. Platform Assn. Home: 11405 Gibraltar Pl Temple Terrace FL 33617

GABBARD, DANA CHESTER, b. San Diego, Apr. 28, 1962; s. Dana Ray and Patricia Ann (Corbin) G. Edit., Duckburg Times, Selah, WA, 1980. BA, U. of Southern California, 1987—. Home: 2635 Portland St No. 5 Los Angeles CA 90007

GABBARD, GREGORY N., b. Ft. Smith, AR, Oct. 4, 1941. Author: Runes from an Infant Edda, 1980, Tiger Webs, 1982, Dragon Raid, 1986. Wrkg. on verse trans. of Beowulf; also Dillinger Analects. BS, MIT, 1962; MA, U. Tex., 1964,

PhD, 1968. Instr. Old Dominion Coll., Norfolk, Va., 1967-68; asst. prof. N.Mex. Highland U., Las Vegas, 1968-69, U. Nev., Reno, 1969-74; typist Dept. Def., Texarkana, Tex., 1981—. Recipient John Masefield award, PSA, 1978. Home: Box 781 New Boston TX 75570

GABOR, GEORGIA MIRIAM, b. Budapest, Hungary, Aug. 30, 1930, came to U.S., 1947; children—Roberta Golub, Donald Glunts. Author: My Destiny: Survivor of the Holocaust (autobiography), 1981, Your Growing Years, 1986; contrbg. author: Profiles in Survival (by Mendel), 1978; contrbr. research studies Calif. Jnl Ednl. Research. BA, UCLA, 1965, MA, 1968. Tchr. math., 1969—. Address: Box 3612 Arcadia CA 91006

GABRIEL, MARK A., b. NYC, Jan. 26, 1954, s. John A. and Laura (Oakes) G.; m. Melissa Ann Cafiero, Aug. 29, 1982; 1 dau., Paula Mare. BA, Fordham U., 1976. Reporter Paramus (N.J.) Post, 1976; reporter, asst. bur. chief Paterson (N.J.) News, 1976-77; mng. ed. Ski Mag., NYC, 1977-78, Ski Racing, Inc., Poultney, Vt., 1978-82; ed., pub. Sports Ink Mags., Fair Haven, Vt., 1982—. Mem. Boating Wrtrs. Intl., U.S. Ski Wrtrs. Assn. Office: Sports Ink 2 S Pk Pl Fair Haven VT 05743

GACH, GARY GREGORY, b. Hollywood, CA, Nov. 30, 1947; s. Eugene Hugh and Carla (Pfeiffer) G. Author: Preparing the Ground, 1974, Offices, 1984; contrbr. Coyote's Jnl, City/Country Miner, A Code of Signals, Hambone, Technicians of the Sacred, A Brotherhood in Song. BA, San Francisco State U., 1970; typographer-ed.-writer, San Francisco, 1971—. Mem. AAP. Address: 1243 Broadway San Francisco CA 94109

GADDIS, WILLIAM, b. NYC, 1922. Author: (novels) The Recognitions, 1955, J R, 1975 (Natl. Book Award for fiction 1976), Carpenter's Gothic, 1985. Student, Harvard U. Natl. Inst. Arts and Letters grantee, 1963; NEA grantee, 1967; Guggenheim fellow, 1981; MacArthur Prize fellow, 1982. Mem. AAIAL. Address: Donadio 231 W 22 St New York NY 10011

GAEL, J. S., see Moran, John Charles

GAERTNER, KENNETH CLARK, b. Saginaw, MI, Jan. 18, 1933; s. Frederick Carl and Helen May (Miller) G.; m. Mary Ann Vega, Aug. 15, 1972. Author: Koan Bread, 1978; (plays) Blood Money, The Old Man's Death, 1975, The Lady and God, 1975, Moon on Snow, 1978, Dog's Tooth, 1985 (all produced); contrbr. poetry to Anthology of American Poetry, Commonweal, New Oxford Rvw., America, Christian Century, Am. Poet, Poet Lore, Midwest Qtly, Generation, Tampa Poetry Jnl, Discourse, others, short stories to Voices, Four Quarters; (libretto) Haiku for chamber orch. and soprano, 1977. Youth specialist State of Mich., Whitmore Lake, Mich., 1971—. Served with USMC, 1951-54. Mem. DG. Home: 11447 Weiman Dr Hell MI 48169

GAFFORD, CHARLOTTE KELLY, b. St. Louis; d. Walter Joseph and Charlotte (d'Ailly) Kelly; m. Franklin H. Gafford (dec.); children—Frank, Charlotte Gafford Mabry, Mary K. Contrbr. prose and poetry to New England Rvw, Iowa Rvw, Esquire, Country Jnl, Southern Poetry Rvw, Prairie Schooner, others; ed. Messages, 1976; Bethel: The Early Years, 1975; film scripts. BA, Birmingham-So Coll., 1949, MA, 1962; MFA, U. Iowa, 1971. Assoc. prof. English and Communications Norwich Univ., Northfield, Vt., 1976—. Mem. MLA, AWP, P&W, AAUP. Address: 221 Lauderdale Rd Nashville TN 37205

GAGLIARDI, ANNETTE JANE, b. Mpls., Jan 24, 1950; d. Oscar William and Anna-Grace (Williamson) Stabnow; m. Timothy-Michael Gagliardi, July 3, 1971; children—Richael, Erica, Marian. Author: Reflections of Sunshine, 1982. Contrbr. poems to anthols, articles, short stories to newsletters, jnls, including Totline News, Tex. Childcare Quarterly, La Leche League News. BApplied Sci., U. Minn., 1982. Tchr., St. Paul Soc. for the Blind, Minn., 1970-73; family day care provider, Mpls., 1973-84; day care trainer Hennepin County, Mpls., 1979—; parenting educator South West Community Schl., Mpls., 1979—, Early Childhood and Family Edn., Mpls., 1986—. Recipient 3d Place award Poetic Moods Quarterly, 1985. Mem. Natl., Minn. assns. edn. of young children, Minn. Christian Writer's Guild. Home: 4643 Pillsbury Ave S Minneapolis MN 55409

GAICH, SHARON DENISE, b. Oregon, OH, July 27, 1961; d. Sam and Ora Katherine (Lawson) G. Contrbr. articles to newspapers. B.A. in Communications, U. Toledo, 1983. News corr. News Herald, Port Clinton, OH, 1983-84; reporter, photographer Suburban Press/Metro Press, Millbury, OH, 1984—; free-lance scriptwrtr., 1986, 87, WBGU-TV, Bowling Green, OH. Recipient 1st place for original reporting Ind. Free Papers of Am., 1987. Mem. Northwest Ohio Wrtrs. Forum. Home: 24203 Reservation Rd Curtice OH 43412

GAINES, ERNEST J., Author: Catherine Carmier, 1964, Of Love and Dust, 1967, Bloodline, 1968, The Autobiography of Miss Jane Pittman, 1971, A Long Day in November, 1971, In My Father's House, 1978, A Gathering of Old Men, 1983. DLitt (hon.), Denison U., 1980. Prof. and wrtr.-in-res. U. Southwestern La., Lafayette. La. Library Assn. award, 1972; Black Acad. Arts and Letters award, 1972; award for excellence of achievement in field of lit. San Francisco Arts commn., 1983. Address: Oppenheimer 435 E 79th St New York NY 10021

GALASSI, JONATHAN, b. Seattle, WA, Nov. 4, 1949; s. Gerard Goodwin and Dorothea Johnston (White) Galassi; m. Susan Grace, June 21, 1975; 2 daus., Isabel Grace, Beatrice Grace. Editor: Understand the Weapon, Understand the Wound: Selected Writings of John Cornford, 1976, The Second Life of Art: Selected Essays of Eugenio Montale, 1982, The Random Review (with others), 1982; translator: Otherwise: Last and First Poems of Eugenio Montale, 1984. AB, Harvard, 1971; MA, Cambridge U., 1973. Editor, Houghton Mifflin, Boston, 1973-75; editor, Houghton Mifflin, NYC,1975-81; sr. editor, Random House, NYC,1981–86; poetry editor, Paris Rvw, 1978—; exec. ed., vp, Farrar, Straus and Giroux, 1986—; NY correspond., Nuovi Argomenti, Rome Italy, 1985—. Mem. PEN, PSA. Address: Farrar, Straus & Giroux 19 Union Sq W NYC 10003

GALBRAITH, JOHN KENNETH, b. Iona Station, Ont., Can., Oct. 15, 1908; s. William Archibald and Catherine (Kendall) G.; m. Catherine Atwater, Sept. 17, 1937; children—Alan, Peter, James. Author: numerous books including American Capitalism, 1952, A Theory of Price Control, 1952, The Great Crash, 1955, The Affluent Society, 1958, The Liberal Hour, 1960, Economic Development, 1963, The Scotch, 1964, The New Industrial State, 1967, Indian Painting, 1968, The Triumph, 1968, Ambassador's Journal, 1969, Economics, Peace and Laughter, 1971, A China Passage, 1973, The Age of Uncertainty, 1977, Economics and the Public Purpose, 1973, Money: Whence It Came, Where It Went, 1975, (with Nicole Salinger) Almost Everyone's Guide to Economics, 1978, Annals of an Abiding Liberal, 1979, The Nature of Mass Poverty, 1979, A Life in Our Times, 1981, The Anatomy of Power, 1983. BS, U. Toronto, 1931; MS, U. Calif., 1933, PhD, 1934; postgrad., Cambridge (Eng.) U., 1937-38. Mem. bd. of editors Fortune Mag., 1943-48. Fellow Am. Acad. Arts and Scis.; mem. Natl. Inst. of Arts and Letters. Home: 30 Francis Ave Cambridge MA 02138

GALE, WILLIAM A., b. Houston, June 23, 1939; s. Arthur Sullivan and Harriet-MacaFee (Cross) G.; children—Marion Ethelyn, Rebekah Elizabeth. Author: Life in the Universe: The Ultimate Limits to Growth, 1979, Inflation: Causes, Consequents, and Cures, 1982, Artificial Intelligence and Statistics, 1986, College: Choice: Maximize Your Lifetime Income, 1987. PhD, Rice U., 1968. Mem. tech. staff AT&T Bell Labs, Murray Hill, NJ, 1968-86. Mem. Am. Assn. Artif. Intell., Am. Statist. Assn., Intl. Statist. Inst. Home: 439 S Orange Ave South Orange NJ 07079

GALL, SALLY MOORE, b. NYC,July 28, 1941, d. John Alexander and Anna Betty (Clark) Moore; m. John K. Marshall, 1961 (div. 1965); m. 2d, W. Einar Gall, Dec. 8, 1967. Author: The Modern Poetic Sequence: The Genius of Modern Poetry (with M.L. Rosenthal), 1983; Ramon Guthrie's Maximum Security Ward: An American Classic, 1984; ed.: Maximum Security Ward and Other Poems (by Ramon Guthrie), 1984; contrbr.: Great Writers of the English Language, 1979, Dictionary of Literary Biography, 1980, Contemporary Poets, 1980, Funk & Wagnalls New Encyclopedia, 1983, Good Reading, 1985; contrbr. Am. Poetry Rvw, Shenandoah, Present Tense, other lit mags. BA, Harvard-Radcliffe U., 1963; MA, NYU, 1971, PhD,1976. Vis. prof. Drew U., Madison, N.J., 1978; adj. asst. prof. NYU, 1978-81; founding ed. Eidos/ The Intl. Prosody Bull., 1984—. Winner (with M.L. Rosenthal) Explicator Lit. Fdn. Award, 1984. Mem. AG, Conf. Eds. Learned Jnls., P&W, Natl. Poetry Fdn., MLA. Home: 29 Bayard Ln Suffern NY 10901

GALLAGHER, KAREN, b. Charleston, WV, Nov. 8, 1948, d. Jess James and Elizabeth-Virginia (Lyon) Fisher; 1 dau., Stephanie Wilson. BA, U. Charleston. Asst., AP, Charleston, 1971-74; mng. ed. Jnl. Coal Quality, Charleston, 1981-85, cons., 1985, advt. rep., 1985—; pres. Kg Inc. editorial services, South Charleston, W.Va., 1985—. Mem. Soc. Tech. Communications. Office: Kg Inc 1001 Overlook Way South Charleston WV 25309

GALLAGHER, MARY BETH, b. New Haven, Nov. 7, 1946; d. Arthur R. and Mary (Whalen) Gallagher. Contrbr.: Jnl. Bus. Edn., Bus. Edn. Forum, New Eng. Bus. Educators Assn. Bulltn., Profl. Med. Asst. BS, Quinnipiac Coll., 1970; MS, U. Bridgeport, 1973; postgrad., So. Conn. State U., 1984. Tchr. City of New Haven, 1971-73; asst. prof. Sacred Heart U., Bridgeport, Conn., 1973-80, Quinnipiac Coll., Hamden, Conn., 1980—. Mem. AAUW (v.p. New Haven br.). Home: 72 Blue Hills Ave Hamden CT 06514

GALLAGHER, PATRICIA CECILIA, b. Lockhart, TX; d. Frank Joseph and Martha

Leona (Rhody) Bienek; 1 son, James Craig. Author: The Sons and the Daughters, 1961, Answer To Heaven, 1964, The Fires of Brimstone, 1966, Shannon, 1967, Shadows of Passion, 1971, Summer of Sighs, 1971, The Ticket, 1974, Castles in the Air, 1976, Mystic Rose, 1977, No Greater Love, 1979, All For Love, 1981, Echoes and Embers, 1983, On Wings of Dreams, 1985, A Perfect Love, 1987. Student, Trinity U., 1951. Former mem. San Antonio Mag. Council. Mem. AG. Address: Scott Meredith 845 3d Ave New York NY 10019

GALLAGHER, TESS, b. Pt. Angeles, WA, July 21, 1943; d. Leslie Orphis and Georgia Marie (Morris) Bond; m. Lawrence Gallagher, June 1963 (dec. 1969); m. Michael Burkard, June 1973 (div. 1977); companion, Raymond Carver. Author: (poetry) Instructions to the Double, 1976, Portable Kisses, 1978, Under Stars, 1978, On Your Own, 1983, Willingly, 1984, Amplitude: New and Selected Poems, 1987; (short stories) The Lover of Horses, 1986; (essays) A Concert of Tenses, 1986; film scripts, The Life of Dostoevsky (with Raymond Carver), 1985; appearances in numerous poetry, essay and story anthologies, including The Generation of 2000, The Morrow Anthology of Younger Poets, American Short Stories 1985, American Short Story Masterpieces, Praise of What Persists, Graywolf Annual II; ed. with Madeline DeFrees lit mag Ploughshares, Jan. 1987 issue. BA, U. Wash., 1968, MA, 1970; MFA, U. Iowa Writers Workshop, 1974. Asst. prof., St. Lawrence U., 1975-76, Hamilton Coll., 1976-78; vis. lectr., U. Montana, Missoula, 1977-78; asst. prof., U. Arizona, 1979-80; prof., Syracuse Univ., 1980—, resides in Pt. Angeles, WA, when not teaching. NEA grants in poetry, 1976, 81; Guggenheim fellowship, 1978. Mem. NOW, AAP, Am Poetry Soc. Office (falls only, when teaching at Syracuse): Eng Dept Syracuse U Syracuse NY 13210

GALLAHER, CYNTHIA, b. Chgo., Jan. 16, 1953; d. Gilbert Patrick Gallaher and Evelyn Maria (Bryg) Hamm; m. Carlos Cumpian, Sept. 8, 1984; 1 child. Ed: Before the Rapture: Poetry of Spiritual Liberation mag, 1980-84, Amphora Full of Light (chapbook), 1985; contrbr. articles to Letter Ex, Chgo. Poetry Letter News, Small Press Rvw, Poetry — ampersand; contrbr. poetry to Calif. Qtly, Oyez Rvw, Lucky Star, As Is, Syncline, Mati, Salome, others. BA in history of art, U. Ill.-Chgo. Stock supvr. book dept. Marshall Field & Co, Chgo, 1974-76, copywriter adv. dept., 1976-78; broadcast copywriter Sears, Roebuck, Chgo., 1978-80; acct. exec. Marvin Frank Adv., Chgo., 1980-82, adv. dir. Natl. Pride, Melrose Pk, Ill., 1982—. Creative writing workshop leader, PACE Inst., Cook County Jail, 1982-83. Recipient Judges prize, Nethers Farm Poetry award, 1981. Address: 5327 W Giddings Ave Chicago IL 60630

GALLANT, JAMES T., b. Delaware, OH, Oct. 2, 1937, s. James Morgan and Juanita (Tucker) G.; m. Christine Condit, Aug. 19, 1961; 1 child, Sarah. Contrbr. to Kans. Qtly, Transatlantic, Great Lakes, N.Am., Miss., Ga., Mass. rvws, Story Qtly, Best Am. Short Stories of 1978, Puerto del Sol, Epoch. BA, Denison U., 1960; MA, U. Minn., 1965. Instr. Mt. Union Coll., Alliance, Ohio, 1965-67; asst. prof. U. Evansville, Inc., 1967-72; janitor, 1972-77, 80-84; salesman Eureka Co., Atlanta, 1985—. Woodrow Wilson fellow, 1960. Home: 642 Atlanta Ave SE Atlanta GA 30312

GALLANT, PAMELA L., b. Malden, MA, Sept. 15, 1942; d. Richard H. Sheldon and Jane M. (Cotten) Sheldon Killoran; m. Terrence J. Gallant, Aug. 21, 1966; 1 son, Paul J. Contrbr. poetry: The Little Wanderer. Wrkg. on short stories, articles. BA, Rivier Coll. Tchr. Billerica (Mass.) public schs., 1965-70, Salem (Mass.) public shs., 1974-79; head clk Mass. Dept. Social Services, Lynn, 1983—. Home: 9 Abbott St Salem MA 01970

GALLASSERO, HILDA KILMER, b. Crowley, LA, Sept. 7, 1928; d. George William and Lacy (Fruge) Killmer; m. William A. du Bois (div. 1960); children—Regina, Renee, Henri; m. Charles Gallassero, Feb. 17, 1968. Contrbr. numerous articles to newspapers, and magazines. Wrkg. on Who Exactly Was Marie Laveau-Louisiana's Voodoo Queen?, hist. and genealogical connections of La. people. Home: 117 Meche Rd Carencro LA 70520

GALLIGAN, EDWARD L., b. Taunton, MA, Jan 14, 1926; s. Joseph E. and Monica L. (Lawlor) G.; m. Isabel M. Brown, Jan. 1, 1949; 2 sons, Joseph E, James M. Ed: A Choice of Days (H. L. Mencken), 1980, The Comic Vision in Lit., 1984; contrbr. fiction, articles, essays, and rvws. to Sewannee Rvw, Midwest Qtly, South Atlantic Qtly, Greensboro News & Record, Encyc. of World Lit. in the 20th Century, The Mass. Rvw, Texas Studies in Lang. and Lit., AAUP Bulln., Ramparts, Ellery Queen's Mystery Mag., The Realist, Satire Newsletter, The Jnl of Higher Edn. BA, Swarthmore Coll., 1948; PhD, U. Pa., 1958. Instr. to asst. prof., De Pauw Univ., Greencastle, Ind, 1949-58; asst. prof to prof. Western Mich Univ., Kalamazoo, 1958—. Mem. Mark Twain Soc. (hon.), P.G. Wodehouse Soc. Address: 152 Millview Ave Kalamazoo MI 49001

GALLO, DONALD ROBERT, b. Paterson, NJ, June 1, 1938; s. Sergio and Thelma Mae (Lowe) G.; divorced; 1 son, Brian Keith. Author: Reading Rate and Comprehension, 1972, Recipes, Wrappers, Reasoning and Rate, 1974, Bookmark Reading Program, 1979; author, ed.: Novel Ideas, 1980. Ed.: Conn. English Jnl, 1976-81, Sixteen: Short Stories by Outstanding Writers for Young Adults (Best Book for young adults Am. Library Assn. 1984, Best Book of Yr., Schl. Library Jnl. 1984), 1984, Books for You: A Booklist for Senior High Students, 1985, Visions: Nineteen Short Stories by Outstanding Writers for Young Adults, 1987. Contrbr. chpts. in profl. Books, articles on reading, writing, lit. to profl. jnls. B.A. in English, Hope Coll., 1960; M.A.T. in English Edn., Oberlin Coll., 1961; Ph.D. in English Edn., Syracuse U., 1968. Asst. prof. to assoc. prof. edn. U. Colo., Denver, 1968-72; reading specialist Golden Jr. High Sch., Jefferson County, CO, 1972-73; prof. English, Central Conn. State U., New Britain, CT, 1973—. Mem NCTE (pres. assembly on lit. for adolescents 1986—, v.p. 1985-86 dir. 1979-82; mem. editorial bd. 1985—; chmn. com. to revise Books for You 1982-85, trustee research fdn. 1975-78), Conf. English Edn. (vice chmn. 1982-84, exec. com. 1981-85), Intl. Reading Assn. Home: 857 Mountain Rd West Hartford CT 06117

GALLO, LOUIS JACOB, b. New Orleans, Sept. 6, 1945, s. Liberato Louis and Grace (Surbeck) G.; m. Rebecca Ida, Sept. 10, 1966 (div. 1975); 1 dau., Rebekah Rachael; m. 2d, Pamela Buddington, Sept. 17, 1978; 1 dau., Sophie Wells. Ed.: A New Orleans Review, 1973, Barataria Review, 1973-74, New Orleans Courier (contrbg. ed.), 1970-75, Pushcart Press (contrbg. ed.), 1978—; contrbr. poetry to numerous lit mags. PhD, U. Mo., 1973. Instr. U. Mo., Columbia, 1969-73, U. New Orleans, 1973-78; assoc. prof. Columbia (S.C.) Coll., 1978-85, Radford (Va.) U., 1985—; mem. task force S.C. Arts Commn., Columbia, 1985. S.C. Arts Commn. fellow, 1980. Mem. Pop Culture Assn. of the South. Office: Dept English Radford Univ Radford VA 24142

GALLUP, DICK, b. Greenfield, MA, July 3, 1941, s. Harry K. and Edna Hattie (White) G.; m. Carol Jean Clifford, Dec. 6, 1964 (div. 1976); children—Christina Danielle, Samuel Sabine. Author: Hinges, 1965, The Bingo, 1966, Where I Hang My Hat, 1969, Above the Tree Line, 1976, Plumbing the Depths of Folly, 1982. BA, Columbia U., 1968. Tchr., adminstr. St. Marks Poetry Project, NYC, 1969-73; poet-in-res. W.Va. Arts Commn., 1973, S.C. Arts Commn., 1975-76; head dept. poetics Naropa Inst., Boulder, Colo., 1978-79 Grantee Poets Fdn., NYC, 1970, NEA, 1980. Home: 1450 Castro St San Francisco CA 94114

GALLUP, GRANT MORRIS, b. Stambaugh, MI, Jan. 28, 1932; s. Allan Murray and Eleanor Else Wilhelmina (Daumitz) G. Asst. ed. Am. Church Quarterly, 1961-70; ed. The Integer, 1975-85, Integrity Forum, 1980-83, Anglican Clarion & Tattler, 1982. Wrkg. on homilies, anthol. of lesbian/gay clergy biographies. B.A., Alma Coll., 1954; M.Div., Seabury-Western Theol. Seminary, 1959. Curate, Ch. of the Atonement, Chgo., 1959-61; vicar St. Andrew's Ch., Chgo., 1961—. Served with U.S. Army, 1954-56. Fellow Coll. Preachers. Home: 1619 W Warren Chicago IL 60612

GALLUP, STEPHEN EDMONDS, b. Louisville, KY, Oct. 15, 1950; s. Braxton and Janie (Stephenson) Gallup; m. Judy Mercedes Bell, Aug. 22, 1976; 1 son—Joseph. Author: Get the Job You Deserve, 1984, technical reports and proposals within govt. agencies; ed. Space Leader Mag. BS, NC State U., 1973; MA, U. of Virginia, 1977, Human Developmentalist, Institutes for the Achievement of Human Potential, 1986. Technical Wrtr. Atlantic Research Corp. (Gainesville, VA), 1977-83; publications/proposals ed. General Dynamics (San Diego), 1983—. Home: 1222 River Glen Row San Diego CA 92111

GALPHIN, BRUCE MAXWELL, b. Tallahassee, Aug. 11, 1932; s. Lawrence Tatum and Helen (Hoskins) G. Author: The Riddle of Lester Maddox, 1968, Atlanta: A Celebration, 1978, 500 Things To Do in Atlanta for Free, 1981; co-author: Atlanta: Triumph of a People, 1982; author: also articles. AB, Fla. State U., 1954. Atlanta Constitution, 1954-63, edl. assoc., 1963-69; Atlanta bur. Chief, Washington Post, 1969-70; mng. editor Atlanta Mag., 1971-77, exec. editor, 1977-78; pub. WINEWS, 1980—; syndicated wine columnist, 1970-75; wine columnist, Atlanta Jnl & Constitution, 1981—; writer, editorial cons. Neiman fellow Harvard, 1962-63. Address: 217 Westminster Dr NE Atlanta GA 30309

GALT, THOMAS F. JR, (Tom); b. Wequetonsing, MI, Jul. 29, 1908. Author: Volcano, 1946, How the UN Works, 1947, Peter Zenger, Fighter for Freedom, 1951, The World has a Familiar Face, 1981. Translator The Little Treasury (from Japanese), 1982. BA, Harvard U., 1932. Home: Box 417 Wellfleet MA 02667

GALVAN, ROBERT A., (Roberto), b. San Antonio, Feb. 25, 1923; s. Eulalio and Gregoria (Arispe) G.; m. Eva Ruiz, Aug. 11, 1957; children—Robert, Rosalinda, Nancy Louise, Marie Yvette, Nora Noel, Sylvia Dee, Albert Gregory.

Author: Student Study Guide for Contrastive Analysis of Regional and Standard Spanish (with Damon Miller), 1949, Poemas English enespanol por un mexiamericano, 1977, El diccionario espanol de Tejas, 1975, El diccionario del espanol chicano (with Richard V. Techner), 1977. Wrkg. on 3d edition of El diccionario del espanol chicano, 2d anthology of poems in Spanish. Instr. Spanish and French Trinity Univ., San Antonio, 1954-55, Southwest Tex. State Jr. Coll., Uvalde, 1956-64; prof. of Spanish Southwest Tex. State Univ., San Marcos, 1964—. Asst. Cub Master, Boy Scouts Am., San Marcos, 1967-69; mem., Lions, San Marcos, 1985—. Mem. Academia Norteamerica de la Lengua Espanola, Am. Assn. Tchrs. Spanish and Portuguese (emeritus), (So. Central) MLA. Recipient Piper Professor award, Minnie Stevens Piper Fdn., San Antonio, 1968, Cervantes award Am. Assn. Tchrs. Spanish and Portuguese, 1974, Disting. Tchr. award Alumni Assn. Southwest Tex. State Univ., San Marcos, 1976. Address: 704 Franklin Dr San Marcos TX 78666

GALVIN, BRENDAN JAMES, b. Everett, Mass., Oct. 20, 1938; s. James Russell and Rose Marie (McLaughlin) G.; m. Ellen Emily Baer, Aug. 1, 1968; 2 children: Peter, Anne. Author poetry books: No Time for Good Reasons, 1974, The Minutes No One Owns, 1977, Atlantic Flyway, 1980, Winter Oysters, 1983, Seals in the Inner Harbor, 1986; chapbooks: The Narrow Land, 1971, The Salt Farm, 1972, A Birder's Dozen, 1984; contrbr. articles to Northwest Rvw, Concerning Poetry, Ploughshares; poetry in The New Yorker, Atlantic, Harper's, Paris Rvw, others; fiction in Crazy Horse, Laurel Rvw, The Falcon. BS, Boston Coll., 1960; MA, Northeastern U., 1964; MFA, U. Mass.-Amherst, 1968, PhD, 1970. Tchg. fellow to instr. Northeastern U., Boston, 1963-65; asst. prof. in English Slippery Rock State Coll., Pa., 1968-69; vis. writer Conn. Coll., New London, 1975-76; prof. of English Central Conn. SU, New Britain, 1969—. Recipient creative writing grants, NEA, Washington, 1974, Writer's Fdn., Boston, 1978, Conn. Commn. for Arts, Hartford, 1981, 84. Mem. AWP, AAUP, Boston Authors' Club. Address: Box 54 Durham CT 06422

GALVIN, MARYANNE, b. Worcester, MA, Mar. 6, 1954; d. Stephen Frances and Bernadette Marie (McGuinn) G. Author: Handbook of Social Skills Training and Research, 1984, Interpersonal Communication: A Social Skills Analysis, 1985. Contrbr. chpts., articles to profl. books, jnls. B.S. in Child Psychology, Wheelock Coll., 1976; Ed.D. in Counseling Psychology, U. Mass., Amherst, 1980. Private practice psychologist, 1980—; consulting psychologist McBer Co., Boston, 1985-86; lit. cons. Tufts Med. Schl., Boston, 1986—. Home: 228 Newbury St 41 Boston MA 02116

GAMBOA, REYMUNDO , b. Anthony, NM, Feb. 2, 1948; s. Jose L. and Concha (Torres) G.; m. Josefina R. Ramos, Aug. 23, 1969; children: Adrian, Alejandro, Michael. Contrbr. poetry to El Grito, Denver Qtly, Cafe Solo, La Luz, other lit mags. BA, Calif. State U.-Fresno, 1970; MEd, Pepperdine U., 1978. Instr. Hancock Coll., Santa Maria, Calif., evenings 1972-80; asst. prof. Calif.State U., San Luis Obispo, 1975-76; translator City of Santa Maria, 1980-85; tchr. Righetti High Schl., Santa Maria, 1980-84. Recipient annl. Chicano lit. prize, 1974 (poetry), 1979 (short story). Scwrip fellow U. Santa Barbara, Calif., 1983. Home: 408 Chaparral Santa Maria CA 93454

GAMMILL, WILLIAM, b. Silaom Springs, AR, Apr. 28, 1949, Author: Seattle, First Avenue, 1973, 13 Stones & The River Poem, 1974, Souvenir Music Box (chapbook), 1975, Prune (chapbook), 1981, the perfect poem (chapbook), 1985. BS, Central State U., Edmond, Okla., 1975, MFA in Creative Studies, 1976. Poet-in-residence State Arts Council, Oklahoma City, 1971-76, Central State U., 1977-78, Oklahoma City U., 1978-79, Mont. Arts Council, Missoula, 1981-82, Central State U., 1983—. HEW master poet grantee NEA, 1975; wrtg. fellow Centrum Fdn., Port Townsend, Wash., 1976, Macdowell Art Colony, Peterborough, N.H., 1977, 82; cultural exchange participant Rotary Intl., India, 1981. Mem. AWP. Home: 3734 N Shartel St Oklahoma City OK 73118

GANAS, JANE ANDREW, b. Sparta, Greece, Oct. 15, 1942; came to U.S., 1962; naturalized, 1967; d. Soteros and Demetra (Halulos) Gana; m. Ted Andrew, May 6, 1962 (div. 1985); children—Stamy Andrew Gunderson, Thea, Andrew. Contrbr. numerous poems, short story to lit. mags., anthols. Wrkg. on novel. B.A. in English/Psychology, Metro State Coll., 1974. Recipient Best Poem award Dragonfly, 1975, 81, Best Story award Reflect, 1987. Home: 1250 Washington 4 Des Plaines IL 60016

GANDER, FORREST, b. Barstow, CA, Jan. 21, 1956. Contrbr. poems Tyuonyi; Poetry Now, Five Fingers Rvw, Raccoon, others. BS/BA, Coll. William and Mary, 1978; MA, San Francisco State U., 1981. Co-ed. Lost Roads Pub., Providence, R.I., 1981—; adj. prof. Providence Coll., 1986—. Address: Lost Rds Box 5848 Providence RI 02903

GANGEMI, KENNETH, b. Bronxville, NY, Nov. 23, 1937, s. Frank Paul and Marjorie Vivian (Wesstrom) G.; m. Jana Fisher, Mar. 1961 (div. 1974). Author: Olt (novel, translated into German, French), 1969, Lydia (poetry collection), 1970, Pilote de Chasse (novel), 1975, Corroboree (humor and satire), 1977, The Volcanoes from Puebla (nonfiction), 1979, The Interceptor Pilot (English version of Pilote de Chasse), 1980; contrbr. poetry, fiction, nonfiction to mags, anthologies in U.S., Europe. BS in Mgmt. Engring., Rensselaer Poly. Inst., 1959. Stegner fellow Stanford U., 1968-69; CAPS fellow N.Y. State, 1976; recipient Pushcart prize, 1985. Mem. PEN, AG, PSA. Home: 211 E 5th St New York NY 10003

GANN, ERNEST KELLOGG, b. Lincoln, Nebr., Oct. 13, 1910; s. George Kellogg and Caroline (Kupper) G.; m. Eleanor Michaud, Sept. 18, 1933 (div.); children—George Kellogg (dec.), Steven Anthony, Polly Wing; m. Dodie Post, May 20, 1966. Author: Island in the Sky, Blaze of Noon, Fiddler's Green, Benjamin Lawless, The High and the Mighty, Soldier of Fortune, Twilight for the Gods, Trouble with Lazy Ethel, Fate is the Hunter, Of Good and Evil, In the Company of Eagles, Song of the Sirens, The Antagonists, Band of Brothers, Flying Circus, Hostage to Fortune, Gentlemen of Adventure, The Magistrate, The Aviator, and The Triumph. Student, Culver Mil. Acad., Yale U. Schl. Fine Arts. Served as capt. Air Transport Command AUS, 1942-46. Home: Red Mill Farm San Juan Island WA 98250

GANNELLO, ALFREDA MAVIS, (Mavis Gannello), b. London, Nov. 17, 1926; m. Carmelo Charles Gannello, Jan. 2, 1954. Contrbr. poems, articles to mags., newspapers, anthols.; poem readings, Lion's Club of Illinois, 1986. Graduate Christian Wrtrs. Ins., Wheaton, Ill., 1971-72. Ins. Clrk. Oak Park Hosp., Ill., 1974-75; clrk. info. and referral Suburban Area of Aging, Oak Park, 1975-76; free-lance wrtr., 1965—. Recipient Honorable Mention, Carlisle Poets, 1973, Poetry Press, 1986; cert. of Outstanding Lit. Achievement, Major Poets, 1974. Book in progress: Meet Carmelo, 1987. Home: 621 S Maple Ave Oak Park IL 60304

GANNELLO, MAVIS, see Gannello, Alfreda Mavis

GANNON, DEE, b. Charleston, WV, Sept. 11, 1953; d. Edward L. and Betty J. (Bailes) O'Hara; m. Thomas F. Gannon, III, Feb. 14, 1976 (div. Apr. 19, 1984). Author: Rare Breed Review, 1983, Rare Breed Review II, 1984, Rare Breed Handbook, 1987. Contrbr. dog stories to mags., bulln. Editor: Sam Talk, 1979-81, Rarities, 1980-86, Eskie-Pades, 1982-84. BA, BA, W.Va. U.-Morgantown, 1985; postgrad. in law, Rutgers U., 1986—. Property mgr. Goodwin Homes, Mt. Laurel, N.J., 1976-80; mgr. Sambo's Corp., Canton, Ohio, 1980-81; sales rep. Hanes DSD, King of Prussia, Pa., 1981-85, Mark I, Chgo., 1985; mgr., wrtr. The Resume Dr., Phila., 1986—. Mem. Hudson Valley Rare Breed Dog Club (pres.), Peruvian Inca Orchid Club of Am. (pres.), Tri-State Oriental Breed Dog Club (dir.), Akbash Dog Assn. Am. (dir.). Home: 1160 Cattel Rd Wenonah NJ 08090

GANNON, ROBERT HAINES, b. White Plains, NY, Mar. 5, 1931; s. John Arthur and Dorothy Bell (Merric) G. Author: Complete Book of Archery, 1964, Time is Short and the Water Rises, 1967, What's Under a Rock?, 1971, Pennsylvania Burning, 1976, Half Mile Up Without an Engine, 1982; (with Alfred Zamm) Why Your House May Endanger Your Health, 1980. Columnist, Family Circle, 1962-1963, Metronome 1959-1960. Contrbr. numerous articles to popular mags. including Reader's Digest, Saturday Evening Post, True, Sci. Digest, others. Editor: Great Survival Adventures, 1973, Natural Life Styles, Popular Sci., 1967—. Student Miami U., Oxford, Ohio, 1949-1953, Columbia U., 1955-1960. Publicist, Leo Burnett, NYC, 1956-57; acct. exec. Daniel J. Edelmann Assocs., NYC, 1957-59; assoc. prof. Pa. State U., University Park, Pa., 1974—; free-lance wrtr., 1957—. Bd. dir. Bellefonte Historical and Cultural Assn, 1985—. Mem. D&H Canal Hist. Soc., ASJA, NASW, AAAS. Home: 334 E Howard St Bellefonte PA 16823

GANS, BRUCE MICHAEL, b. Chgo., Aug. 23, 1951; s. Benjamin J. and Dorothy (Marcus) G.; m. Christine Perri. Contrbr. short stories to Mademoiselle Mag., Modine Gunch, Memphis State Rvw, ND Rvw, Wind Mag, Widener Rvw, Chgo. Reader, Heatherstone Press, Lakeview Mag., Expresso, Midland Rvw, Madison Rvw, Spirit That Moves Us, Kingfisher, others. BA in English, U Wis.-Madison, 1969-73; MFA in Fiction, U. Iowa, 1973-75. Freelance writer, Chgo., 1975-80; reporter Fairchild Publs., Chgo, 1980; asst. prof. English, Chgo. City Colleges, 1981—. Recipient Mademoiselle fiction prize, NYC, 1972, NEA fellow, 1974, Best Nonfiction of 1978 prize, Soc. Midland Authors, 1980, Heatherstone Fiction Award, 1981. Mem. Soc. Midland Authors (bd.dirs.), AG, AWP. Address: 1123 W Columbia Chgo IL 60626

GANZ, ALICE, b. Bronx, NY, Nov. 24, 1943, d. Sidney and Sari (Arnstein) Klein; m. Michael H. Ganz, Aug. 29, 1964; children—David Ian, Douglas Spencer. Contrbr. to Lang. Arts, Early

Years, The English Record. BA, Queens Coll., 1965, MS, 1968. Elem. tchr. Ridge Schl., N.Y., 1974—; speaker on writing edn. to local and natl. profl. confs.; fellow, cons. L.I. Writing Project; asst. dir. Project WRITE, Longwood Schl. Dist., 1985. NCTE tchr.-researcher grantee, 1984. Mem. NCTE, N.Y. State English Council (cons.), Middle Island Tchrs. Assn. (trustee). Home: 18 Brandley Dr Shoreham NY 11786

GARAND, PIERRE ARTHUR, b. Amesbury, MA, Apr. 25, 1954; s. Maurice Henry and Cecile Lillian (Nicol) G. Contrbr. poems to anthols., lit. mag.; play rvws. to newspapers. Ed.: Parnassus lit. mag., 1974-75. Grad. public schls., Amesbury. Screen printer ABC Plastics, Inc., Boston, 1984-85; handyman, gardener Arctic Windows, Inc., Ipswich, MA, 1985-86; free-lance factotum, 1986—. Address: Hickory Ln Box 1344 East Kingston NH 03827

GARBO, NORMAN, b. NYC, Feb. 15, 1919; s. Max W. and Fannie (Deitz) G.; m. Rhoda Ivy, Apr. 15, 1942; 1 son, Mickey. Author: Pull Up An Easel, 1955, (with H. Goodkind) Confrontation, 1966, The Movement, 1969, To Love Again, 1977, The Artist, 1978, Cabal, 1979, Spy, 1980, Turner's Wife, 1983, Gaynor's Passion, 1985; also short stories. Student, CCNY, 1935-36; BFA, Acad. Fine Art, NYC, 1940. Author syndicated art column, Chgo.-Tribune-N.Y. News Syndicate, 1954-61. Address: 161 Sands Point Rd Sands Point NY

GARCIA, IGNACIO MOLINA, b. Nuevo Laredo, Mexico, Oct. 28, 1950; came to U.S., 1956; naturalized, 1972; s. Virgilio Rendon and Amada (Molina) G.; m. Alejandra Aguirre, Mar. 10, 1973; children—Roman Gabriel, Veronica Alejandra, Ignacio, Valeria Annahi. Contrbr. articles to mags., newspapers including Chgo. Tribune, Quest, others. Ed.: Renato Rosaldo Lecture Series, 1983-87, Saguaro 1984-87, De la Vida y del Folclore de la Frontera (Miguel Mendez), 1986. Wrkg. on La Raza Unida Party B.A., Tex. A&I U., 1976; postgrad. U. Ariz., 1984—. Sports ed. Laredo News, TX, 1978; regional ed. Nuestro Mag., San Antonio, 1979-83; reporter Tucson Citizen, 1983-84; pubs. ed. U. Ariz., Tucson, 1984—. Served with U.S. Army, 1969-73. Recipient 2d place for newspaper series Tex. Press Assn., 1978, 1st place for newspaper series on El Salvador, Ariz. Press Assn., 1984; selected as jnlst. to attend Am. Assembly at Columbia U., 1979. Mem. SSP, Assn. Documentary Editing. Office: Mexican Am Studies Modern Langs Rm 209 U Ariz Tucson AZ 85721

GARCIA, JULIAN S., b. San Antonio, Mar. 16, 1950; s. Antonio F. and Ventura (Flores) G.; m. Dolores Melendes, Aug. 8, 1976. Contrbr. articles to newspapers, jnls. including San Antonio Express News, San Antonio Light; fiction to anthols. including Southwest Tales, Saguaro Review. Non-fiction editor: Centro Cultural Aztlan, San Antonio, 1981-85, fiction editor, 1985—. BA, Our Lady of Lake U., San Antonio, 1975; MA, U. Tex.-San Antonio, 1979. Tchr., Harlandale Ind. Schl. Dist., 1975-77, San Antonio Ind. Schl. Dist., 1977—. Recipient Fiction prize Caracol Jnl, 1978. Mem. NCTE, AAUP, San Antonio Council Tchrs. English, Natl. Hispanic WG, Tex. State Tchrs. Assn., Am. Fedn. Tchrs. Home: 13727 Wilderness Creek San Antonio TX 78231

GARDINER, HARRY WALTER, b. Worcester, MA, Sept. 17, 1938; s. Harry Miller and Dorothy (Francis) G.; m. Ormsin Sornmoonpin, Mar. 9, 1968; children—Alisa Jarin, Alan Verason, Alexina Tippa, Aldric Harin. Author: Newspapers as Personalities: A Psychological Study of the British Natl. Daily Press, 1966, Instructor's Manual for Essentials of Psychology, 1977, Contemp. Issues and Strategies for Change in Nursing, 1977, Child and Adolescent Devel., 1981; contrbr. chapters to profl. pubns.: Applied Cross-Cultural Psychology, 1975, Women and Men: Research and Experience, 1984, Measurement and Personality Assessment, 1985, The World's Women in Cross-Cultural Perspect., 1986. MA, U. Hawaii, 1963; PhD, U. Manchester (England), 1966. Psych. consult., speechwriter U.S. Senator Daniel K. Inouye, Hawaii, 1961-62; media dir. Jack Benson Co., Honolulu, 1962-63; visiting lect. Chulalongkorn U., Bangkok, Thailand, 1966-68; prof./chmn. psych. Coll. St. Teresa, Winona, MN, 1969-74; prof. psych. U. WI, LaCrosse, WI, 1974—; freelance wrtr., 1982—. Mem. AG, profl. orgns. Office: Psych Dept Univ Wis 1725 State St LaCrosse WI 54601

GARDINER, LINDA, b. Edinburgh, Scotland, Oct. 20, 1947; arrd. U.S., Sept. 1968. BA, U. Sussex-England, 1968; MA, Brandeis U., 1969, PhD, 1973. Asst. prof. Wellesley Coll, 1975-83; ed. and pub. Women's Rvw of Books, Wellesley, 1983—. Address: 20 Leach Ln Natick MA 01760

GARDINER, WAYNE JAY, b. Valentine, NB, Mar. 1, 1943; s. L. Jay and Evelyn B. (DeFrance) G.; m. Kathleen R. Poloway, Dec. 28, 1968; children—Heather M., Thomas J. Author: The Man on the Left, 1981. B.S. in Edn., Chadron State Coll., 1965. Advt. sales Chgo. Tribune, 1968-77, mgr. mktg. services, 1978-81; dir. Midwest sales Food & Wine Mag., 1981—. Mem. Chgo. Advt. Club. Home: 910 Harper Dr Algonquin IL 60102

GARDNER, GEOFFREY, b. Chgo., Mar. 23, 1943; s. Alan and Marion (Rittenbrug) G.; m. Isabel Leff, Aug. 1, 1965 (div. Apr., 1966); m. 2d, Frieda H. Brunings, Sept. 15, 1966 (div. June, 1986); 1 dau., Kate. Contrbr. poems, translations and essays to many periodicals; ed. For Rexroth (intro. Gardner); translated The Horses of Time (Jules Supervielle), intro. Gardner). BA, NYU, 1964; MA., philo., New Schl. Social research, 1970. Poet, writer translator NYC, 1965-70, Mpls., 1970-81, Milton, Vt., 1981-82, Monkton, Vt., 1982-83, Cambridge, Mass., 1983—; ed. and pub. The Ark, Cambridge, 1977—. Awarded fellowship for literary translation by Literature Program, NEA, 1987. Chmn. bd. dirs., Southside Fam. Schl.., Mpls., 1979-81; bd. dirs. Minn. Tenants Union, Mpls., 1979-81; co-chmn, Cambridge Tenants Union—1987. Address: 35 Highland Ave Cambridge MA 02139

GARDNER, GERALD FAYE, b. Mound Bayou, MS, Sept. 18, 1950; d. John Robert and Annie Lee (Pace) Gardner. Contrbr.: Am. Poetry Anthology, The Art of Poetry: A Treasury of Contemporary Poetry, other anthologies. Wrkg. on hist. book and poetry. Past student Kennedy King Coll., Loop Coll., Am. Acad. Art Sch. Se.-transcriber U. Ill. Hosp., Chgo., 1980—. Home: Box 198313 Chicago IL 60619

GARDNER, JOSEPH LAWRENCE, b. Willmar, MN, Jan. 26, 1933; s. Elmer Joseph and Margaret Eleanor (Archer) G.; m. Sadako Miyasaka, Feb. 25, 1967; children—Miya Elise, Justin Lawrence. Author: Labor on the March, 1969, Departing Glory, Theodore Roosevelt as ex-President, 1973; editor: series Newsweek Condensed Books, 1971-76, The World's Last Mysteries, 1978, Reader's Digest Wide World Atlas, 1979, Reader's Digest Atlas of the Bible, 1981; Eat Better, Live Better, 1982. Researcher, writer, asst. editor, mng. editor Am. Heritage Books div. Am. Heritage Pub. Co., Inc., NYC, 1959-65; editor Am. Heritage Jr. Library and Horizon Caravel Books, 1965-68; mng. editor Newsweek Books div. Newsweek Inc., NYC, 1968-70, editor, 1971-76; sr. staff editor Reader's Digest Genl. Books, NYC, 1976-81, group editor genl. reference, 1982—. Student, U. Portland, Oreg., 1951-52; BA summa cum laude, U. Oreg., 1955; MA (Woodrow Wilson fellow), U. Wis., 1956. Home: 17 Cohawney Rd Scarsdale NY 10583

GARDNER, JOYCE D., b. Holbrook, NE, Jan. 17, 1915; d. Samuel F. and Eva H. (Frazier) Davis; m. William A. Gardner, Jan. 2, 1942; children—Harriet, Cherrille. Contrbr. to Oral Language Continuum Checklist, 1975, A Written Language Continuum Checklist, 1976, Psychomotor Continuum Checklist, 1977, Handbook of 35 Basic Wrtg. Skills, 1978, Living in Hell: An Agoraphobic Experience, 1980, California Citrus Fruit Cookbook, 1983. BA, U. of Cal., 1960, MA, 1965. Teacher Compton Unified Schools (CA), 1953-65, curriculum consult., 1965-74; special consult. Calif. state dept. of ed. (Sacramento), 1975-81. Fulbright-Hayes awd., 1968. Mem. Calif. Press Women, Inc., Westminister/ Fountain Valley Branch, AAUW of Calif. Home: 16707 Glass Mountain Fountain Valley CA 92708

GARDNER, NANCY BRUFF, b. Fairfield County, CT, Nov. 15, 1909; d. Austin Jenkins Bruff and Alice Hastings (Birdsall) Weekes; m. Thurston Clarke; children—Thurston Bruff, Penelope; m. 2d, Esmond Brown Gardner, July 20, 1963. Works include: The Manatee, 1945, The Beloved Woman, 1949, Cider From Eden, 1947, The Fig Tree, 1965, My Talon in Your Heart, 1946, The Country Club, 1969, Mist Maiden, 1975 (re-issued as Desire on the Dunes, 1984), Walk Lightly on the Planet, 1985, Five Great Healers Speak Here, (with Esmond Gardner), 1982. Student, Sorbonne, Paris, 1927-30. Mem. AG, PSA. Home: 200 East 66th St New York NY 10021

GARDNER, PAUL ALLEN, b. Philipsburg, PA, Nov. 28, 1950; s. Roscoe Bert and Vera Rose (Biddle) G.; m. Ann Hales, Apr. 23, 1975; children—Charity Ann, Catherine Shirley. Contrbr. non-fiction articles to Western Outdoors, Ariz. Hunter and Angler, Ariz. Daily Sun. BS, Penn. State Univ., 1974; M.S., Brigham Young U., 1977; Ph.D., Northern Ariz. U., 1987. Wildlife biologist U.S. Forest Service, Salt Lake City, 1977; research specialist U. Utah, Salt Lake City, 1977-79; surgical technologist Flagstaff Med. Center, AZ, 1979—. Served with U.S. Army, 1968-71. Mem NWC. Home: 81 Shoshone Flagstaff AZ 86001

GARDNER, RICHARD ALAN, b. Bronx, NY, Apr. 28, 1931; s. Irving and Amelia (Weingarten) G.; m. Lee Robbins, Apr. 14, 1957; children—Andrew Kevin, Nancy Tara, Julie Anne. Author: The Child's Book about Brain Injury, 1966, The Boys and Girls Book about Divorce, 1970, Therapeutic Communication with Children: The Mutual Storytelling Technique, 1971, Dr. Gardner's Stories about the Real World, Vol. I, 1972, Vol. II, 1983, MBD: The Family Book about Minimal Brain Dysfunction, 1973, The Talking, Feeling, and Doing Game, 1973, Understanding Children—A Parents Guide to Child Rearing, 1973, Dr. Gardner's Fairy Tales for Today's Children, 1974, Psychotherapeutic Approaches to the Resistant Child, 1975, Psychotherapy with Children of Divorce, 1976, Dr. Gardner's Modern Fairy Tales, 1977, The Parents Book About Divorce, 1977, Gardner Steadiness Tester, 1978, The Boys and Girls Book About One-Parent Families, 1978, Reversals Frequency Test, 1978, Adoption Storytelling Cards, 1978, The Objective Diagnosis of Minimal Brain Dysfunction, 1979, Dorothy and the Lizard of Oz, 1980, Dr. Gardner's Fables for Our Times, 1981, Family Evaluation in Child Custody Litigation, 1982; editor-in-chief Intl. Jnl Child Psychotherapy, 1972-73. AB, Columbia U., 1952; MD, State U. N.Y. Downstate Med. Center, 1956. Served to capt. M.C. U.S. Army Res., 1960-62. Home: 54 Forest Rd Tenafly NJ 07670

GARDNER, STEPHEN LEROY, b. Columbia, SC, Apr. 8, 1948; s. Stephen Leroy and Sara Ida (Roberts) G.; m. Nancy Sarah Rawlinson, 1969 (div. 1977); m. 2d, Mignon Pendleton Whittinghill Derrick, July 14, 1977. Contrbr. poems to lit. mags. Editor: Kudzu: A Poetry Mag, 1978-83. BA, U. S.C., 1970, MA, 1972; PhD, Okla. State U.-Stillwater, 1979. Instr. English to assoc. prof. U. S.C., Aiken, 1972-83, prof. English, chmn. div. arts & letters, 1983—, coordinator English dept., 1971-81, dean coll. humanities, 1986—. Active Aiken Environmental Coalition, Palmetto Alliance. Recipient Borestone Mt. Poetry award, 1977, 1st prize AAP, 1978, Faculty Exchange Research award, U. S.C., 1982. Mem. Caribbean Studies Assn., Coll. English Assn., Council Colls. Arts & Scis., Natl. Audubon Soc. Home: Rt 2 Box 129 Coogler Rd Irmo SC 29063

GAREY, TERRY A., b. Berkeley, CA, Aug. 7, 1948; d. Phil Donald and Donna Mae (Scearcy) G.; m. Dennis K. Lien, July 2, 1984. Contrbr. poetry anthologies: Contemp. Women Poets, 1977, The Rysling Anthol, 1981, Aliens and Lovers, 1983, Burning with a Vision, 1984; contrbr. poetry to Aurora, Starline, Uranus 4, Mag. of Speculative Poetry, Woman Spirit, Princeton Spectrum, Contact II, La Confluencia, The Blatant Image, Paradox, others; contrbr. articles to Mainstream, Pretentious Sci. Fiction Qtly, Janus, Aurora, Star Line, Genre Plat; short stories in Weird Tales—1986, Tales of the Unanticipated; ed: Tales of the Unanticipated. AA, Contra Costa Coll., 1970. Secy. and temp. clrk., San Francisco Bay Area; library asst. Univ. of Minnesota. Mem. Minn Fantasy Writers Assn., Sci Fiction Poetry Assn, P&W. Address: 2528 15th Ave S Minneapolis MN 55404

GARFIELD, BRIAN WYNNE, b. NYC., Jan. 26, 1939; s. George and Frances (O'Brien) G.: M. Virve Sein, 1962 (div. 1965); m. Shan Willson Botley, 1969. Author: Range Justice, 1960, The Arizonans, 1961, (under name Frank Wynne) Massacre Basin, 1961, Justice at Spanish Flat, 1961, (under name F. Wynne) The Big Snow, 1962, (under name Frank O'Brian) The Rimfire Murders, 1962, Act of Piracy, 1975, (under name Bennett Garland) Seven Brave Men, 1962, The Lawbringers, 1962, Trail Drive, 1962, (under name F. Wynne) Arizona Rider, 1962, Rio Concho, 1963, Lynch-Law Canyon, 1964, Call Me Hazard, 1964, The Lusty Breed, 1966, The Wolf Pack, 1967, Dragoon Pass, 1963, (under name Brian Wynne) Mr. Sixgun, 1965, The Night It Rained Bullets, 1966, The Bravos, 1967, The Proud Riders, 1967, Brand Of The Gun, 1968, A Badge For A Badman, 1969, Gundown, 1969, Big Country, Big Men, 1970, The Thousand-Mile War, 1969, Sliphammer, 1970, Valley of the Shadow, 1970, The Hit, 1970, The Villiers Touch, 1970, Sweeny's Honor, 1971, Gun Down (also titled The Last Hard Men), 1971, What of Terry Conniston?, 1971, Deep Cover, 1971, Relentless, 1972, Line of Succession, 1972, Death Wish, 1972, Tripwire, 1973, (in collaboration with Donald E. Westlake) Gangway!, 1973, Kolchak's Gold, 1974, The Threepersons Hunt, 1974, The Romanov Succession, 1974, Hopscotch, 1975 (Edgar Allen Poe best novel award Mystery Writers Am.), Death Sentence, 1975, Recoil, 1977, Wild Times, 1979, The Paladin, 1980, Checkpoint Charlie, 1981, The Vanquished, 1982, Valley of the Shadow, 1983, Necessity, 1984, Tripwire, 1985, Fear in a Handful of Dust, 1985. Screen stories for films Death Wish, 1974, The Last Hard Men, 1974, The Last Hard Men, 1976, Relentless, 1977, Wild Times, 1980; story and screenplay for Hopscotch, 1979. B.A., U. Ariz., 1959, M.A., 1963. Served with AUS, 1957-65. Mem. WWA (pres. 1967-68), AG, AL, DG, WG Am. (East), Crime Writers Assn. (U.K.), MWA. (dir. 1974—). Home: Myst Press 129 W 56 St New York NY 10019

GARFINKEL, ALAN, b. Chgo., Sept. 6, 1941; s. Bernard D. and Tillie (Schaffner) G.; m. Sonya Pickus, July 10, 1965; children: two. Author: (with Isabel M. Sirgado and Miguel Angel Sirgado) Modismos al momento ("Idioms at your Fingertips"), 1977, (with Guillermo Latorre) Trabajo y vida ("Work and Life"), 1983, (with Thomas Alsop) Spanish Emergency Lesson Plan, 1986; ed (with Stanley Hamilton) and contrbr, Designs for Foreign Language Teacher Education, 1976, ed (with Sharyl L. Mitchell and Loranna M. Moody) and contrbr, ESL and the Foreign Language Teacher, 1982, (with Mitchell and Moody) The FL Class-room: New Techniques, 1983; contrbr: Dale L. Lange, ed., The Britannica Review of Foreign Language Education, vol. 3, 1971, P.B. Westphal, ed, Strategies for Foreign Language Teaching: Communication, Technology, Culture, 1984, Thirty Days Hath September and a Bunch of Other Things You Can Teach with the World Calendar: A Teacher's Guide, 1985, Westphal, ed, Meeting the Call for Excellence, 1985, B. Snyder, ed, Second Language Acquisition, 1986. Contrbr to N.Y. State Assn of Foreign Language Tchrs Yearbook, 1986, ed by Anthony Papalia. Contrbr of articles and book rvws to language jnls, including American Foreign Lang Tchr, Foreign Lang Annals, Hispania, and Modern Lang Jnl. Ed, Notes and News in Modern Lang Jnl, 1974—. BA, Univ of Ill., 1963, MA, 1964; Ph. D., Ohio State Univ., 1969. High School Spanish tchr, Waukegan, Ill, 1964-66; asst prof of foreign lang. educ., Okla. State Univ, 1969-72; asst prof, Purdue Univ, W. Lafayette, Ind., 1972-74, assoc prof of foreign lang educ, 1974—, coord. of Educational Professions Extension, 1978-80, asst dir of Div of Sponsored Progs of Purdue Research Fndn, 1981-85. Eulbright lecturer in Bogota, Colombia, at Univ. of Los Andes. Mem: Teachers of English Speakers of Other Langs Intl (exec sec, Indiana chpt, 1979-81), American Cncl on the Teahing of Fgn Langs (bibliographer, 1973-75), MLA, Natl Soc for the Study of Educ, American Assn of Tchrs of Spanish and Portuguese, Indiana Fgn Lang Techrs Assn, Phi Delta Kappa (chpt pres, 1982-83), U.S. Information Agcy Specialist's award, Buenos Aires, Arg., 1985; Organization of American States onsultant award, Rep. of Trinidad and Tobago, 1986. Office: Purdue Univ Coulter Hall West Lafayette IN 47907

GARFUNKEL, JOSEPH M., b. Miami, FL, Jan. 1, 1926; s. Joseph and Kathryn C. (Boyle) G.; m. Geraldine M. Ohrin, Apr. 16, 1949; children—Joseph, Michael, Kathryn, Barbara, Thomas, Elizabeth. Asst. ed., assoc. ed., ed. Jnl Pediatrics, 1965—; author numerous articles in profl. jnls. MD, Temple U., 1948, MS, 1953. Pediatrician, Phila., 1954-62; dir. outpatients, St. Christopher's Hosp., Phila., 1962-67; chief of pediatrics, Polyclinic Hosp., Harrisburg, PA, 1967-72; chairman dept. pediatrics, So. Ill. U. Schl. Med., Springfield, 1972-83; prof. pediatrics, UNC Schl. Med., Chapel Hill, 1984—; ed. Jnl Pediatrics, 1977—. Named Pediatrician of Year, Ill. Chapter Amer. Acad. Pediatrics, 1981. Office: UNC Schl of Med Chapel Hill NC 27514

GARGAN, WILLIAM MICHAEL, b. Bklyn., Apr. 18, 1950, s. John Francis and Agnes H. (Duffy) G.; m. Sharon Ann Goodstine, June 8, 1980; children—Amy, Catherine. Author: Find That Tune: An Index to Rock, Folk Rock, Disco & Soul in Collections, 1984; contrbr. to Mags. for Libraries, 4th ed., 1982, Catching Up with Kerouac, 1984, Serials for Libraries, 2d ed., 1985. BA in English, SUNY-Stony Brook, 1972; MA, Columbia U., 1973, MS, 1976. Adult services librarian Bklyn. Public Library, 1974-79; assoc. prof. library dept. Bklyn. Coll., 1979—. Mem. ALA, MLA, James Joyce Soc., Ernest Hemingway Soc., other profl. orgns. Office: Bklyn Coll Library Brooklyn NY 11210

GARIEPY, HENRY, b. Meriden, CT, Jan. 17, 1930; s. Elizabeth (Moore) G.; m. Marjorie Ramsdell, Jan. 28, 1952; 4 children. Author: Portraits of Christ, 1974, Footsteps to Calvary, 1977, The Advent, 1979, 100 Portraits of Christ, 1987. Contrbr. articles to popular mags. Wrkg. on book on Salvation Army. BA, Cleveland State U., 1972, MS, 1974. Editor-in-chief The Salvation Army, Verona, N.J., 1980—. Club: Kiwanis (pres. 1972). Home: 435 Essex Ave Bloomfield NJ 07003

GARLAND, BENNETT, see Garfield, Brian Wynne

GARLAND, JOANNE MARIE, b. Utica, NY, Jan. 3, 1947; d. Roy John and Marie (Stark) Garland, Co-author: Ruth Montgomery: Herald of the New Age, 1986; contrbr.: Strangers Among Us (by Ruth Montgomery), 1979. BA, U. Mass., 1969. Thr., 1969-73; paralegal, 1973-80. Mem. Assn. for Past-Life Research and Therapy. Address: Box 104 Deerfield MA 01301

GARLINGTON, JACK O'BRIEN, b. Vaughn, NM, Aug. 30, 1917; m. Dorothy Jane Nugent, Jan. 28, 1947 (dec. Jul. 29, 1967); children—Joseph O'Brien, Jane Ann Garlington Berlin, Robert Nugent; 2nd m. Margaret Hewins Waldo, Apr. 14, 1972. Editor: Western Humanities Review, 1962—. PhD, U. of Wisconsin, 1953. Teacher Dept. of English U. of Utah (Salt Lake City), 1953—; asst. dir. Econ. Institute U. of Colorado (Boulder), summers 1958-66; Fulbright instructor U. of Madrid, 1960-61, Cuttington Coll. (Liberia), 1969-71. 1st Lt. CWS, 1941-49, Pacific, Japan. Editors' Award, CCLM, 1975, 76. Mem. MLA. Home: 1779 Oakridge Dr Salt Lake City UT 84106

GARNER, STANTON BERRY, b. Corning, NY, Sept. 1, 1925; s. Edward Samuel and Helen (Berry) G.; m. Lydia Magalhaes Nunes, Mar. 28, 1969; 1 son, Edward Charles; children by previous marriage: Stanton Berry, George Francis. Author: Harold Frederic, 1969; editor: The Captain's Best Mate—The Journal of Mary Chipman Lawrence on the Whaler Addison, 1856-1860, 1966, 1986, A Bibliography of Writings by and about Harold Frederic, 1975, The Correspondence of Harold Frederic, 1977, The

Market Place by Harold Frederic, 1981, The Damnation of Theron Ware by Harold Frederic, 1985; genl. editor: Works of Harold Frederic; contrbr. articles to profl. jnls. Grad., Manlius Schl., 1943; BS, U.S. Naval Acad., 1948; AM, Brown U., 1960, PhD, 1963. Served with AUS, 1943-44; Served with USN, 1948-58; comdr. Res. (ret.). Mem. MLA, Melville Soc., Poe Studies Assn., Nathaniel Hawthorne Soc., Thoreau Soc. Home: 1016 Live Oak Ln Arlington TX 76012

GARNER-LIPMAN, KAREN LEE, (Karen Lee Garner), b. Elizabeth, NJ, Dec. 7, 1947, d. Louis Theodore and Hilda (Loebel) Gittleman; m. David Theodore Lipman, Dec. 9, 1978. Wrtr. newsletter items, social sci. research results. Wrkg. on novels. BA magna cum laude in Communications and English, Hunter Coll., N.Y.C., 1979. Freelance wrtr., 1970—; fundraiser, asst. ed. William A. White Inst., N.Y.C., 1972-74; asst. ed. and program aide Social Sci. Research Council, N.Y.C., 1974-83; researcher, asst. ed. NYU, N.Y.C., 1983—; v.p. K&D Assocs., Bklyn., 1980—. Home: 2380 Ocean Ave Brooklyn NY 11229

GARRARD, CHRISTOPHER, see Milton, John R.

GARRETT, BEATRICE, b. Freeport, NY, Dec. 13, 1929, d. Roosevelt and Loretta (Commodore) Glasco; children—Crystal, Shawn, Kenya, Omar. Author: Welfare on Skid Row (novel), 1974; contrbr. to Black Hollywood, 1978-80; contrbr. poetry to Dawn Mag., Pure Pleasure, Los Angeles Sentinel. Wrkg on poetry book. AA in nursing, Trade Tech. Coll., 1982, postgrad., 1983—. RN, Calif. Staff nurse U. So. Calif. Med. Ctr., Los Angeles, 1983—. Home: 1322 W 60th St Los Angeles CA 90044

GARRETT, EDWARD CORTEZ, b. Quezon City, Philippines, Sept. 25, 1948; came to U.S., 1972; s. Edward Flagg and Leonor Cristobal (Cortez) G. Contrbr. to Fennel Stalk, Negative Capability, South Fla. Rvw, Third Wind, Nightsun; assoc. ed. First Inago Anthology of Poetry. BA in English, De la Salle Coll., Manila, 1971; MA in Speech Communication, U. Ariz., 1974. contract ed. Hecker & Philips, Tucson, 1981-83; pvt. tutor 1-2-1 Tutoring, Tucson, 1986—. Recipient 1st place award AAP, 1976. Mem. Tucson Pub. Library Poetry Workshop. Home: 455 S Irving Ave Apt 101 Tucson AZ 85711

GARRETT, GEORGE PALMER, JR., b. Orlando, FL, June 11, 1929; s. George Palmer and Rosalie (Toomer) G.; m. Susan Parrish Jackson, June 14, 1952; children—William, George, Rosalie. Author: The Reverend Ghost: Poems (Poets of Today IV), 1957, King of the Mountain (short fiction), 1958, The Sleeping Gypsy and Other Poems, 1958, The Finished Man (novel), 1959, Which Ones Are the Enemy? (novel), 1961; Abraham's Knife (poetry), 1961, In the Briar Patch (short fiction), 1961; Sir Slob and the Princess (play), 1962, Gold Ground Was My Bed Last Night (short fiction), 1964; The Young Lovers (screenplay), 1964, Do, Lord, Remember Me (novel), 1965, For a Bitter Season (poetry), 1967, A Wreath for Garibaldi (short fiction), 1969, Death of the Fox (novel), 1971, The Magic Striptease (short fiction), 1973, Welcome to the Medicine Show, Postcards/Flashcards/Snapshots (poetry), 1978, To Recollect a Cloud of Ghosts: Christmas in England 1602-03 (short fiction), 1979, Luck's Shining Child: Poems, 1981, The Succession: A Novel of Elizabeth and James, 1984, The Collected Poems of George Garrett, 1984, James Jones (biography), 1984, An Evening Performance (short fiction), 1985, Poison Pen, 1986. Editor: The Girl in the Black Raincoat, 1966, The Sounder Few, 1971, The Writer's Voice, 1973, Botteghe Obscure Reader, 1975, Intro 8: The Liar's Craft, 1977, Intro 9: Close to Home, 1978. AB, Princeton U., 1952, MA, 1956, PhD, 1985. Writer-in-residence, resident fellow in creative writing Princeton U., 1964-65; Hoyns prof. creative writing U. Va., Charlottesville, 1984—. Served in occupation of Trieste, Austria, and Germany. Recipient Rome prize Am. Acad. Arts and Letters, 1958-59, Sewanee Rvw fellow poetry, 1958-59; Ford Fdn. grantee in drama, 1960; NEA grantee, 1966; Guggenheim fellow, 1974, AAIAL award. Fellow Am. Acad. in Rome; mem. MLA, AL. Home: 1845 Wayside Pl Charlottesville VA 22903

GARRETT, LESLIE, b. Phila., July 5, 1932, s. Herbert Henry and Thelma Florence (Bradley) G.; m. Jean Deloras Collier, June 6, 1951 (div. 1956); 1 dau., Dawne Deloras; m. Linda Kerby, Mar. 18, 1973. Novelist: The Beasts (Maxwell E. Perkins Commemorative Novel award), 1966; contrbr. short stories to Four Quarters, Nuggett, Karamu, other lit mags. Freelance wrtr.; dir. Fiction Wrtrs. Workshop, Knoxville, Tenn., 1984-85. Grantee PEN, 1978, Authors League Fund, 1978, Carnegie Fund for Authors, 1978. Home: 1409 Clinch Ave Knoxville TN 37916

GARRETT, SUSAN MARY, b. Bklyn., Aug. 11, 1961; d. John Steven and Arlene G. Ed./contrbr. Vampire Quarterly, 1985; contrbr. to Daredevil Mag., 1983, Fantasy Empire, 1983. BA, U. Dallas, 1983. Home: 142 Sunvalley Dr Toms River NJ 08753

GARRETT, WILBUR EUGENE (BILL GARRETT), b. Kansas City, MO, Sept. 4, 1930; s. Clay D. Garrett and Cecil Z. Melton; m. Lucille Hall, Dec. 26, 1950; children—Michael, Kenneth. Writer, photog., ed. National Geographic Magazine, 1954—; contrbr. to N.G. book pubns.; co-prod. N.G. TV spcl., Alaska. Assoc. of Engring., Kansas City Jr. Coll.; BJ, U. MO, 1954. Photographer, Hallmark Cards, Kansas City, MO, 1948-50, U.S. Navy, Korea, 1950-52; picture ed., assoc. illus. ed., sr. asst. ed., assoc. ed./illus., National Geog. Soc., Washington, 1954-80, ed., 1980—. Mem. NPC, Natl. Press Photog. Assn., White House News Photog. Assn., Overseas Writers. National Magazine Award for General Excellence, 1984. Office: Natl Geo 1145 17th St NW Washington DC 20036

GARRIGAN, SEAN, see Bennett, John Frederic

GARRIGUS, TRISH, see Lowry, Betty

GARRISON, MAHALA, see Daniels, Gladys Roberta Steinman

GARRISON, THOMAS S., b. Bakersfield, CA, Jan. 18, 1952; s. Thomas S and Nell Louise (Chinnis) G.; m. Lorraine Denise Irwin, June 24, 1974 (div. 1980); m. 2d, Deborah Ann Looker, Mar 8, 1982. BA magna cum laude, Calif. State Coll., Bakersfield, 1974, MA, U. Cal.-Davis, 1976. Instr Allan Hancock Community Coll., Santa Maria, Cal, 1977; tchg. assoc. U. Calif., Santa Barbara, 1979-80, tchg. fellow, 1980; coordinator The Gathering Place, 1981; mng. ed. Current World Leaders, 1981—. Mem. Socialist Party, Santa Barbara and Calif chpts., 1982—, var. offices; mem. Natl. Orgn. of the Socialist Party; mem. ACLU, bd. dirs. South Coast Info. Project, 1984—; vice, chairperson, Rental Housing Mediation Task Force, all Santa Barbara, 1986. Mem. APSA, Acad. Poli. Sci. Address: 1013 Niel Park St Santa Barbara CA 93103

GARRISON-KILBOURNE, CLARA ANNE, see Kilbourne, Clara Anne

GARTH, MATHEW, see Mathews, Keith Rowland

GARY, MADELEINE SOPHIE, b. Chgo., 1923; d. George Philip and Panola (Rice) Gary. Author: Vignettes of the Beam in a Nigger's Eye, 1970, 82; contrbr. wrtr. American Women, C.J. Racette, 1985, J'ai Pense, 1941, Whispers in the Wind, 1985. BA, summa cum laude, Windsor U., Los Angeles, 1976. MasterFood Preserver, University of California, Cooperative Extension, 1985. Founded New Writers Guild, 1960, Director, 1965-85, member of New Watts Writers Workshops, 1974-80; publisher New Writers Guild Press, 1980-85. Asst. syndicated columnist Bill Mahan, 1972-86. Poet Laureate Intl. Chili Soc., 1978, Las Vegas. Home: 6323 Rimpau Blvd Los Angeles CA 90043

GASNER, ANNE, b. Berlin, Germany, Oct. 17, 1927, came to U.S., 1938, d. Hirsch and Leia (Korn) Adler; m. Akiva Gasner, Dec. 21, 1946; children—Steven, Deborah Gasner Rund. Contrbr. short story to Jewish Life mag. BA, CCNY, 1963; MSW, Columbia U., 1967. Social worker N.Y.C. Div. Sr. Centers, 1963—. Winner prizes short story contests, 1962, 64, 83, 85. Mem. MWA. Home: 120 Cabrini Blvd New York NY 10033

GASS, WILLIAM H., b. 1924. Author: Omensetter's Luck, 1966, In the Heart of the Heart of the country and Other Stories, 1968, Willie Masters' Lonesome Wife, 1968, Fiction and the Figures of Life, 1970, On Being Blue, 1976, The World Within the Word, 1978, Habitations of the Word, 1985. AB, Kenyon Coll., 1947, LHD (hon.), 1973, 82; PhD, Cornell U., 1953. Address: Washington U Saint Louis MO 63130

GASSMAN, JAYNE DANA, (Jayne Dana), b. Rawalpindi, Pakistan, Sept. 12, 1957, d. Jay H. and Beatrice (Carlin) Gassman. Author: About Us booklet series, 1984—. BA in poli. sci., Albany U., 1978; MA in Public Adminstrn., LI U., 1982. Wrtr. Penthouse Mag., NYC and Los Angeles, 1979-82; asst. ed Omni Mag., NYC, 1979-82, Forum mag., Variations mag., NYC, 1979-82; freelance wrtr., NYC, 1984-85; wrtr. Office of Comptroller, City of N.Y., 1985—. Mem. N.Y. Non-Fiction Wrtrs.' Group. Home: 17-85 215th St Bay Terrace NY 11360

GATES, NANCY GOTTER, b. Columbus, OH, Jul. 21, 1931; d. Robert James and Alice (Jennings) Gotter; m. George Henry Gates, Jr., Sept. 21, 1952; children—Karen, George, Robert. Contrbr. to Army Times, Ladycom, Working Woman, Farm Wife News, Greensboro Daily News, Columbus Dispatch, other mags. and nwsprs.; fiction in O'Henry Festival Stories (1985), Colonades, Senior American News, Pipeline. BS in Ed., Ohio State U., 1952. PR direct. Seal of Ohio Girl Scout Counc. (Columbus), 1972-75; commun. direct. pub. libr. of Columbus & Franklin Co. (Columbus), 1975-76. Mem. NC Wrtrs. Network, NC Poet. Soc., Greensboro Wrtrs. Club. Home: Box 9731 Greensboro NC 27429

GATES, REGINALD D., b. 1942; s. Reginald S. and Zethyl M. (Crosby) Gates. Contrbr. to Coaching Review of Canada, BYTE, Infoworld, Interface Age, Dance Teacher, Car Collector/

Car Classics, Creative Computing, Personal Computing, Player. BA in Math, U. of Colo., 1964. Manager McDonnell Douglas (Cypress, CA), 1982. Home: 4244 Carfax Ave Lakewood CA 90713

GATHERIDGE, R. EDWARD, see Wilson, Robert Edward

GATOS, STEPHANIE, see Kath, Steve Robert

GAUCH, PATRICIA LEE, b. Detroit, Jan. 3, 1934; d. Melbourne William and Muriel (Streng) Lee; m. Ronald Raymond Gauch, Aug. 27, 1986; children—Sarah, Christine, John. Author: Christina Katerina and The Box, 1969, Aaron and the Green Mountain Boys, 1974, This Time, Tempe Wick?, 1975, Fridays, 1979, The Green of Me, 1978, Thunder of Gettysburg, 1975, Kate Alone, 1980, Morelli's Game (Dragons on the Road), 1982, The Year the Summer Died, 1986, Night Talks, 1984, Christina Katerina and the Time She Quit the Family, 1987. Contrbr. articles to newspapers including Louisville Courier Jnl. Editor: Philomel Books, 1985—. BA, Miami U., Oxford, Ohio, 1956; MATchg, Manhattanville Coll., 1968; MPhil, Drew U., 1985. Reporter, Louisville Courier Jnl, 1957-79; tchr. Gill-St. Berhards Schl., Gladstone, N.J., 1972-83; part-time prof. Drew Univ., Madison, N.J., 1984, 85, Rutgers U., New Brunswick, N.J., 1984, 85; cons. "let's read about it" program Am. Library Assn., 1986. Chmn. Rutgers Adv. Council on Children's Lit., New Brunswick, 1984-86. Mem. Soc. Children's Book Wrtrs., AG. Home: 43 Manor Dr Busking Ridge NJ 07920

GAULT, SETH R., b. St. Louis, Mar. 18, 1935; s. George E. and Rissie I. (Duncan) G.; m. Juanita L. Vance, Mar. 16, 1953 (div. June, 1980); children—Charles J., Laura K., Kenneth R., Tracy L.; m. 2d, Barbara L. Thomas, Dec. 3, 1983. BSME, Washington U., 1957; MBA, Indiana U., 1961. Mechanical engr. Westinghouse Elec., Bloomington, IN, 1956-61; prodn. mgr. Ingersoll-Rand Co., Painted Post, NY, 1961-67; dir. prodn. Lindsay-Schaub Nwsprs., Decatur, IL, 1967-80; ed. Full Cry mag., Boody, IL, 1980—. Office: Box 10 Boody IL 62514

GAUSTAD, EDWIN SCOTT, b. Rowley, IA, Nov. 14, 1923; s. Sverre and Norma (McEachron) G.; m. Helen Virginia Morgan, Dec. 19, 1946; children—Susan, Glen Scott, Peggy Lynn. Author: The Great Awakening in New England, 1957, Historical Atlas of Religion in America, 2d ed., 1976, A Religious History of America, rev. ed., 1974, Dissent in American Religion, 1973, Baptist Piety: The Last Will and Testimony of Obadiah Holmes, 1978, George Berkeley in America, 1979; editor books, most recent being: Documentary History of Religion in America, 2 vols., 1982, 83; editor: Arno Press, 1970-79; editorial bd.: Jnl Ch. and State, 1970—. BA, Baylor U., 1947; MA, Brown U., 1948, PhD, 1951. Served to 1st lt. USAAC, 1943-45. Decorated Air medal; ACLS grantee, 1952-53, 72-73; Am. Philo. Soc. grantee, 1972-73. Office: Dept Hist Univ Calif Riverside CA 92521

GAUTREAUX, TIM MARTIN, b. Morgan City, LA, Oct. 19, 1947; m. Winborne Howell; children—Robert, Tom. Contrbr. poetry to Poet Lore, Voices Intl., Greensboro Rvw, others; contrbr. to Lit. Mag. Rvw, Kans. Qtly, Mass. Rvw. BA, Nicholls State U., 1969; PhD, U. S.C.-Columbia, 1972. Assoc. prof. English Southeastern La. U., Hammond, 1972—; ed. Louisiana Literature. Home: 231 SW Railroad Ave Ponchatoula LA 70454

GAVAC, DONNA BRODERICK, b. Portland, OR, Sept. 16, 1926; d. W. Morris and Lulu Grace (Youngs) Heacock; m. Stanley Savage; children—Bill, Mike Broderick; m. 2d, Stanley Gavac, June 8, 1979; stepchildren—Tim, Mark, Gavac, Jan La Valley. Author: Choir Arrangements for Teenagers, 1949; Teaching of High School Social Studies (with others), 1963; research studies for sch. accreditation, planning; assoc. ed., Northwest Sundial, 1956-58; abstractor, Hist. Abstracts, 1960-65, America: History and Life, 1960-65; author numerous papers, lectures. Wrkg. on hist. research, ednl. writing, short stories. MA, U. Mich., 1952; PhD, U. Portland, 1960. Asst. prof., Portland State U., 1960-65; assoc. prof. & dean, U. of Alaska, 1971-80. Pres., Donley Prodns., Inc., Anchorage, 1980-85; Western Wordcraft, Anchorage, 1985—. Mem. NWC, Am. Hist. Assn., Medieval Acad. Am. Home: 7315 Crawford Dr Anchorage AK 99502

GAVIN, THOMAS MICHAEL, b. Newport News, VA, Feb. 1, 1941, s. Donald James and Virginia•Marie (Michael) G.; m. Claire Ellen Campbell, Apr. 15, 1967; children—Wendy Marie, Emily Sandra. Author: Kingkill (novel), 1977, The Last Film of Emile Vico (novel), 1986. BA in English, U. Toledo, 1969, MA in English, 1971. Lectr. in English Delta Coll., University Center, Mich., 1972-75; asst. prof. Middlebury (Vt.) Coll., 1975-80; assoc. prof. English U. Rochester, N.Y., 1980—. NEA fellow, 1980, Andrew W. Mellon Fdn. fellow, 1980-81, 84. Office: Dept Eng River Campus Univ Rochester Rochester NY 14627

GAWRYN, MARVIN, b. Montreal, Quebec, Canada, July 22, 1951; s. Leon and Pearl (Bokor) G.; m. Francyl Streano, May 15, 1976; children—Mikaila, Jessica. Author: Reaching High: The Psychology of Spiritual Living, 1980. BA in psych., Antioch Coll., 1974; MA in psych., U.S. Intl. U., 1975. Psychotherapist in priv. pract., Berkeley, CA. Home: Box 9085 Berkeley CA 94709

GAY, PETER, b. Berlin, Germany, June 20, 1923; came to U.S., 1941, naturalized, 1946; s. Morris Peter and Helga (Kohnke) G.; m. Ruth Slotkin, May 30, 1959; stepchildren: Sarah Khedouri, Sophie Glazer Cohen, Elizabeth Glazer. Author: The Dilemma of Democratic Socialism: Eduard Bernstein's Challenge to Marx, 1952, Voltaire's Politics: The Poet as Realist, 1959, The Party of Humanity: Essays in the French Enlightenment, 1964, A Loss of Mastery: Puritan Historians in Colonial America, 1966, The Enlightenment: An Interpretation, vol. 1, The Rise of Modern Paganism, 1966 (Nat. Book award 1967), (Melcher Book award 1967), Weimar Culture: The Outsider as Insider, 1968 (Ralph Waldo Emerson award Phi Beta Kappa 1969), The Enlightenment, Vol. II, The Science of Freedom, 1969, The Bridge of Criticism: Dialogues on the Enlightenment, 1970, (with R.K. Webb) Modern Europe, 1973, Style in History, 1974, Art and Act, 1976, Freud, Jews, and Other Germans, 1978, Education of the Senses, 1984, Freud for Historians, 1985, The Tender Passion, 1986, A Godless Jew: Frevd, Atheism and the Making of Psychoanaalysis, 1987. B.A., U. Denver, 1946; M.A., Columbia, 1947, Ph.D., 1951. Fellow ACLS, 1959-60; fellow Center Advanced Study Behavioral Scis., 1963-64; Guggenheim fellow, 1967-68, 77-78; Overseas fellow Churchill Coll., Cambridge, 1970-71; Rockefeller Fdn. fellow, 1979-80. Home: 105 Blue Trail Hamden CT 06518

GEANNOPULOS, NICK GEORGE, b. Chgo., Mar. 12, 1930; s. George Nick and Alice E. (Doulogeris) G.; m. Maryann E. Satterlee, Sept. 4, 1954; children—Kerry, Tim, Lisa, Sara, Lindsey. Asst. editor Popular Mechanics, 1952-55; editorial dir. Golf Course Supts. Assn. Am., Chgo., 1970-73; dir. commun., Kiwanis Intl., 1973-83; exec. vp, Dartnell Corp., 1983—. Contrbr., editor: Picture History of American Transportation, 1955, World Book Encyc., Brit. Jr. Encyc. BS, Northwestern U., 1951. Served with CIC AUS, 1955-57. Home: 572 Hawthorne St Elmhurst IL 60126

GEBELEIN, ROBERT SEAVER, b. New Bedford, MA, May 7, 1934; s. Ernest George and Roberta (Seaver) Gebelein. Author: Re-Educating Myself: An Introduction to a New Civilization, 1985. AB Harvard U., 1956. Programmer Computer Usage Co. (Palo Alto, CA), 1964, Philip Hankins Inc. (Arlington, MA), 1967-69, 1970, Wang Laboratories (Lowell, MA), 1973-78. PFC, US Army, 1956-58, Us. Home: 438 Commercial St Provincetown MA 02657

GEBMAN, EVA URLISH, b. NYC, Oct. 29, 1948; children: Eva, Jacqueline, Francis. Contrbr. poetry anthologies. Edn. h.s., Brooklyn. Professional dancer, 1975-77; pub. & ed., Eva's Ad Sheet, 1980-83; manuscript typist, 1983—. Golden Poet Award, World of Poetry, 1985. Address: Box 428 Camillus NY 13031

GECKLE, GEORGE LEO, III, b. Danbury, CT, Dec. 2, 1939; s. George Leo and Dorothy Marian (Hill) G.; m. Justine Virginia Carroll, Aug. 19, 1961; children—George, Richard. Author: John Marston's Drama, 1980; editor: Twentieth Interpretations of Measure for Measure, 1970. AB, Middlebury Coll., 1961; MA, U. Va., 1962, PhD, 1965. Mem. MLA, South Atlantic MLA. Home: 303 Southwood Dr Columbia SC 29205

GEE, F. DENISE, b. Houston, May 28, 1965, d. John Stuart and Freddie Lee (Bailey) Gee. BS, La. State U., 1986. Wrtr. Natchez (Miss.) Democrat, 1985; feature wrtr. The Gazette antiques mag., Bon Temps mag., Baton Rouge, La., 1986—. Mem. Sigma Delta Chi, Women in Journalism. Home: 816 State St Natchez MS 39120

GEER, GALEN LEE, b. Blackwell, OK, Mar. 9, 1949; s. Fredrick Allen and Dora Ellen (Salla) G.; m. Patricia Ann Carroll, July 26, 1968 (div. May 1979); children—James Marie, Christopher Lee; m. Diana Gail Kimbrel, Nov. 29, 1980. Author: The Crossbow as a Modern Weapon, 1985, Canteen Cup Cookery, 1985, Meat on the Table, 1985. Contrbr. numerous articles to mags. including Colo. Outdoors, V.F.W. mag., Guns & Action. Ed.: U.S. Veteran Mag., Sunnyvale, CA, 1976-77, The Indianhead, 1977-78; assoc. ed. Colo. Springs Mag., 1979; exec. ed. Colo. Outdoor Jnl., 1986—; contrbr. ed. S.W.A.T., Firepower. Student De Anza Coll., 1974-76. Served to sgt. USMC, 1966-74, U.S. Army, 1977-79. Decorated Commendation medal, 1978, Korean Service medal, 1978; recipient Honorable Mention for story Korean-Am. Friendship Assn., 1978, Best News Story, U.S. Army, 1977, 78, 2d place for best journalist, 1977, 78. Mem. USMC Combat Corr. Assn., OWAA. Home: Box 175 Florence CO 81226

GEHMAN, CHRISTIAN, b. NYC, Nov. 11, 1948; s. Richard Boyd Gehman and Katherine Susan (Wiman) Bair; m. Caroline Coles, Oct. 30, 1982 (div.); 1 son, Francis Meriwether. Author: Beloved Gravely, 1984, A Southern Celebration: Charleston and Savannah Proclaimed, 1985. Student Iowa Wrtrs. Workshop, U. Va., Hamilton Coll. Restaurant reviewer Style Weekly, Richmond, Va., 1985; br. mgr. Aesop Services, Richmond, 1985—. Pres. Woodstock Youth Ctr., N.Y., 1965. Recipient Maxwell Perkins prize Charles Scribner's Sons, 1984. Mem. AWP, NWU, AG. Home: 300 N Lombardy Richmond VA 23220

GEIGER, HELENE R., b. June 26, 1950, Lewistown, PA, d. Samuel L. and Lillian Hurwitz. Author tng. materials: ASTD Handbook, 1986, Information Age Technology, 1986. Wrkg. on video scripts. BA in Edn., Rider Coll., 1972; MS in Instrn. Technology, Rochester Inst. Technology, 1981. Pres. Prometheus Trng. Corp., Rochester, N.Y., 1982—. Mem. profl. orgns. Office: Prom Trng 3000 Winton Rd S Rochester NY 14623

GEIST, MAGGIE ANN, b. Shreveport, LA, Apr. 30, 1939; d. Howard W. Greenwood and Lorene (Stewart) Greenwood Watson; m. Jack Barney Doss, Apr. 20, 1957 (div. 1967); children—David, Shelley, Jennifer; m. 2d, Ellis ivan Geist, Dec. 10, 1972. Author: The History of Northport: A Native Son's Story (children's history book), 1984. BS in Edn., U. Ala., 1971. Tchr. elem. sch., Tuscaloosa, Ala., 1971-86. Mem. ednl. organs. Home: 1704 Dearing Pl Tuscaloosa AL 35401

GELB, ARTHUR, b. NYC, Feb. 3, 1924; s. Daniel and Fanny G.; m. Barbara Stone, June 2, 1946; children—Michael, Peter. Mem. staff NY Times, 1944—, asst. drama critic, 1958-61, chief cultural corr., 1961-63, met. editor, 1967-76, dep. mng. editor, 1976-86, mng. editor, 1986—; lectr. on theatre, also Eugene O'Neill, 1961—. Author: (with Mrs. Gelb) O'Neill, 1962; (with Dr. Salvatore Cotolo) Bellevue Is My Home, 1956; (with A.M. Rosenthal) One More Victim, 1967; editor: The Pope's Journey to the United States, 1965, The Night the Lights Went Out, 1965, The World of New York, 1986; a series of books under the general title "The Sophisticated Traveler," 1983-1986. Mem. Am. Soc. Newspaper Editors, A.P. Mng. Editors; Century Club; Commandeur, France's Order of Arts and Letters; Pulitzer Prize Juror. Address: NY Times 229 W 43rd St New York NY 10036

GELBER, JACK, b. Chgo., Apr. 12, 1932; s. Harold and Molly (Singer) G.; m. Carol Westenberg, Dec. 23, 1957; children—Jed, Amy. Author: plays The Connection, 1959, The Apple, 1961, Square in the Eye, 1965, The Cuban Thing, 1968, Sleep, 1972, Rehearsal, 1976; novel On Ice, 1964, Barbary Shore, 1974, Rehearsal, 1976. BS in Journalism, U. Ill., 1953. Recipient Best Play award for The Connection, Village Voice, 1959-60; Vernon Rice award for outstanding contrbn. to off-Broadway, 1959-60; Directing award, Village Voice, 1972-73; Guggenheim fellow, 1963-64, 66-67; Rockefeller grantee, 1972; NEA fellow, 1974; CBS fellow Yale U., 1974-75. Office: Grove 196 W Houston New York NY 10014

GELLIS, BARRIE FABIAN, b. NYC,June 5, 1950; s. Ira and Esther G.; m. Deborah Sue Clearfield, June 1, 1986; 1 child, Dande (previous marriage). Contrbr. Magical Blend, Long Shot, Yellow Silk, Rolling Stone, Aero Sun-Times, Aquarian Weekly, Conversations with Seth (vols. 1, 2), Source, The Archer, Jean's Jnl, WBAI-FM Folio. BA in Creative Writing and Photography, Empire State Coll., 1982. Creator and dir. Renegade Poetry Readings, Flushing, NY, 1976-80; ed. and writer WBAI-FM Folio, NYC,1982-83; shorts writer AP, NYC,1985—. Ed. Queens Council on the Arts, Jamaica, NY, 1977-80. Mem. P&W, AAP, NWU. Address: 43-06 159 St Flushing NY 11358

GENADER, ANN MARIE, b. West Milford, NJ, May 28, 1932; d. Arthur J. and Verina A. (Mathews) Genader. BS, Jersey City State (NJ), 1954; MA, William Paterson Coll., 1969. Tchr., reporter, West Milford Bd. Ed. Matzner Pubs., 1954—; correspondent, Morning Call (Paterson, NJ), 1951-70; correspondent, Paterson News, 1953-71; correspondent, Herald News (Passaic, NJ), 1955-83; tchr., 1954—; freelance newspaper photographer, North Jersy, 1954—; literary media rvwr., Modern Liturgy magazine (San Jose, CA), 1979—, reporter, Greenwood Lake, NY, News, 1986—. Home: 1681 Union Valley Rd West Milford NJ 07480

GENTZ, WILLIAM HOWARD, b. Cokato, MN, May 10, 1918; s. William Herman and Adelia Florence (Peterson) G.; children—Gracia, Brian, Deborah, Emily, Linnea. Author: World of Philip Potter, 1974, Career Opportunities in Religion, 1979, Religious Writer's Marketplace, 1980, 85; Writing to Inspire, 1983, 1987; ed., Christian Writer's Newsletter, 1980-1987, Dictionary of Bible and Religion, 1986. BA, U. MN, 1939; MDiv, Luther Seminary, St. Paul, 1945. Parish ministry, Lutheran Church, 1945-67; book ed., 1967-80; freelance wrtr., ed., 1980-87. Home: 300 E 34th St 9C NYC 10016

GEORGAKAS, DAN, b. Detroit, Mar. 1, 1938; s. Frank and Sophia G. Author: numerous bks., inclg. Ombre Rosse, 1968, Red Shadows, 1973, The Broken Hoop, 1973, Detroit: I Do Mind Dying, 1975. In Focus, 1980, The Methuselah Factors, 1980, Solidarity Forever: An Oral History of the IWW, 1985; ed. numerous pubs., inclg. Selected Poems of Yannis Ritsos, 1969, Prison Poetry, 1973, The Cineaste Interviews, 1983; contrbr.: poetry & prose to numerous bks., mags, & nwsprs.; film crit. to numerous pubs. inclg. Cineaste, Sightlines, Film Qtly, political arts. to numerous mags. BA, Wayne State U., 1960; MA, U. MI, 1961. Mentor, Empire State Coll., NYC, 1978—; ed. staff Jnl of the Hellenic Diaspora, NYC, 1977-82; edl. bd. Cineaste, NYC, 1969—. Recipient Fulbright, 1963, NEH grant, 1985. Mem. AL. Home: Box 1803-GPO Brooklyn NY 11202

GEORGE, BARBARA, b. Upper Darby, PA, Nov. 15, 1942; d. John Adams and Betty Jean (Higgins) Wallace; m. Robert F. George, June 21, 1965; 1 dau., Anna. Author: Bicycle Road Racing, 1977, Bicycle Track Racing, 1977, Winning Bicycle Racing (with Jack Simes), 1976, The Complete Book of Long-Distance and Competitive Cycling (with Tom Doughty and Ed Pavelka), 1983; ed.: Velo-news, 1972-77, 1981-86, N.E. Running, 1982-83. BA, Ind. U.-Bloomington, 1964; M.A.T, Antioch Coll., 1968. Tchr. Putney Reading, Vt., 1964-72; ed. and pub. Velo-news, Brattleboro, Vt., 1972-77, 81-87; pub. N.E. Running, Brattleboro, 1984-87. Mem. Phi Beta Kappa. Home: 12 Cherry St Brattleboro VT 05301

GEORGE, JEAN CRAIGHEAD, b. Washington, July 2, 1919; d. Frank Cooper and Carolyn (Johnson) Craighead; m. John L. George, Jan. 28, 1944 (div. Jan. 1964); children—Twig Craighead, John Craighead, Thomas Lothar. Author: My Side of the Mountain, 1959, Summer of the Falcon, 1962, Gull Number 737, 1964, The Thirteen Moons, 1967-69, Coyote in Manhattan, 1968, River Rats, Inc., 1968, Who Really Killed Cock Robin?, 1971, Julie of the Wolves, 1972, American Walk Book, 1978, Cry of the Crow, 1980, Journey Inward, 1982, The Talking Earth, 1983, One Day on an Alpine Tundra, 1984, How to Talk to Your Animals, 1985, Water Sky, 1987; Survival Filmstrips, 1984, film My Side of the Mountain, 1959, Nature Filmstrips, 1978-80. BA, Pa. State U., 1941. Reporter Washington Post, 1943-44; United Features, 1945-46; roving editor Reader's Digest, 1973-82. Recipient Newbery Honor Book award, 1961; medal, 1973; Hans Christian Andersen Honor List award, 1964; World Book Award, 1971; others. Address: 20 William St Chappaqua NY 10514

GERALD, CAROLYN, b. Hattiesburg, MS, Oct. 26, 1943, d. Robert Wheeler Thomas and Harriet (Bodie) Jones; m. Paul E. Gerald, June 16, 1962; children—Kimberly, Kelly, Matt, Luke. Contrbr. articles to Medica, Geriatric Cons., Med. Econs., numerous other med. publs. AS in Nursing, Perkinston Jr. Coll., 1964; BS in Biology, U. So. Miss., 1976; MD, U. Miss., 1980. Practice medicine specializing in family medicine, Hattiesburg, Miss., 1982—; chief of staff Methodist Hosp. Stone County, Wiggins, Miss., 1985-86. Served as sr. asst surgeon USPHS, 1980-81. Mem. profl. med. orgns. Home: Rt 1 Box 317 Brooklyn MS 39425

GERALD, JOHN BART, b. NYC, Sept. 25, 1940; s. John and Elizabeth; m. Julie Maas. Author: A Thousand Thousand Mornings, 1964, Conventional Wisdom, 1972, Applegather, 1978, Soul Game, 1980, Conscience, 1984, novels; Dissident Accounts, 1980, Lectures for Nonconformists, 1983, essays; Jonsongs, 1981, Plainsongs, 1985, poems; On Resistance, a pamphlet, 1982; contrbr. short stories var. publs. inclg. Ararat, Harper's Atlantic, Fiction Intl., Fiction, Shankpainter, Tex. Qtly, Portsmouth Mag, Confrontation, Ploughshares, Maine Folkpaper, others. AB, Harvard, 1962. Tchr. var. colls. inclg. CCNY, Harvard, L.I.U. Brooklyn, Bennington, 1960s-80s; writer, 1963—. Mem. PEN, AG NWU, Me Writers and Pubs Alliance, PEN francais. Address: Box 252 Moody ME 04054

GERARDINO, WILLIAM ERNEST, b. NYC, Apr. 27, 1933; s. William E. Gerardino and Jean (Goyco) Schiavello; m. Virginia Alice DeBrunner, Jan. 24, 1968; children—Sebrina Marie, Nikki Ann, Traci Celeste. Ed.: Mid-Nite Sun, Fort Lauderdale, FL, 1966-68, Ohio V.F.W. News, 1985—. Student Broward Coll., 1967-68. Sportswrtr., feature wrtr. Hollywood Sun Tattler, FL, 1968-69; stringer AP, Miami, 1968-69; photo asst. Cinematronics-Jaf Fletcher, Fort Lauderdale, 1969-70; ed. Veterans Fgn. Wars, Columbus, OH, 1985-87, dir. public relations, 1985-87, mem. natl. public relations com., 1985, 86, 87—, mem. natl. legislative com., 1985-87. Mem. NPA (2d place 1986, 87). Home: 560 Nashoba Columbus OH 43223

GERBER, DANIEL FRANK, (Dan), b. Fremont, MI, Aug. 12, 1940; s. Daniel Frank and Dorothy (Scott) G.; m. Virginia Elizabeth Hartjen, Aug. 12, 1961; children: Wendie, Frank, Tamara. Author: The Revenant, 1971, Am. Atlas, 1973, Departure, 1973, Out of Control, 1974, Indy, The World's Fastest Carnival Ride, 1977, The Chinese Poems, 1978, Snow on the Backs of Animals, 1986, Grass Fires, 1987; contrbr to The Nation, New Yorker, Playboy, Sports Illus., Partisan Rvw, Ga. Rvw, New Letters, Ohio Rvw, Chariton Rvw, Poetry Now. BA, Mich State U,

1962. Poet-in-residence, Grand Valley State Coll., Allendale, Mich., 1969, Mich. State Univ., East Lansing, 1970. Mem PEN, PSA, AG. Address: Box 39 Fremont MI 49412

GERBER, JOHN CHRISTIAN, b. New Waterford, OH, Jan. 31, 1908; s. Christian G. and Leonora (Hauptmann) G.; m. Margaret E. Wilbourn, Sept. 3, 1941; children: Barbara Page Barrett, Ann Wilbourn Gerber Sakaguchi. Author: (with Walter Blair) Factual Prose, 1945, Literature, 1948, Writers Resource Book, 1953, (with Fleece and Wylder) Toward Better Writing, 1958, (with Arnold and Ehninger) Repertory, 1960, Twentieth Century Interpretations of the Scarlet Letter, 1968, Studies in Huckleberry Finn, 1971; also chpts. in Toward General Education, 1948. A.B., U. Pitts., 1929, M.A., 1932; Ph.D., U. Chgo., 1941; D.Letters (hon.), Morningside Coll., 1979. Editorial bd.: Coll English, 1947-48, 65-71, Am. Qtly, 1963-68; editorial adviser: Philol. Qtly, 1951-57; editorial adv. bd.: Resources for American Literary Study, 1971—; chmn. editorial bd.: Windhover Press, 1968-72; mem. editorial bd.: U. Iowa Press, 1963-67; chmn. editorial bd.: Iowa-California Ed. of the Works of Mark Twain, 1965-83; hist. editor: Tom Sawyer vol., 1980; editor: Teaching Coll. English, 1965, Scott-Foresman Key Editions: contbr. articles to profl jnls.; author intros. several books. Mem. MLA (chmn. Am. lit. sect. 1969, mem. seec. council 1972-75, mem. nominating com. 1981-83), Midwest MLA (pres., 1966), N.E. MLA, Address: U Iowa Eng Dept Iowa City IA 52240

GERGELY, ARPAD JOZSEF, b. Nema, Hungary, July 24, 1938; came to U.S., 1957; naturalized, 1972; s. Arpad Gergely and Margit Lapikas; m. Ilona Nagy Kazinczy, Feb. 11, 1957; children—Zsuzsanna, Tenzi. Author: (musical comedy) Opening Night, 1973, Here Come Da Judge, 1974; (slide/sound presentation) Inside Scandinavia, 1976; Publicity Notebook, 1977. Contrbr. short story to Harvest Mag. Ed., Sharing & Caring, 1987. Assoc. degree, U. Agrl., Hungary, 1956. Reporter, Hartford Times, CT, 1972-76. Recipient Bronze medal Intl. Film & TV Festival, NYC, 1976, Senatorship award Jaycees Intl., 1977; named 20th Century Pilgrim, Conn. Bicentenial Commn., 1976. Mem. Conn. Wrtrs.' League. Home: 26 D'Annunzio Ave Enfield CT 06082

GERHARDT, LILLIAN NOREEN, b. New Haven, Sept. 28, 1932; d. Victor Herbert and Lillian (Beecher) G. Assoc. editor Kirkus Service, Inc., 1962-66; exec. editor Schl. Library Jnl Book Rvw, R.R. Bowker Co., Juvenile Projects, NYC, 1966-71; editor-in-chief Schl. Library Jnl, 1971—. Sr. editor: Best Books for Children, 1967-70; sr. editor, project coordinator: SLJ Book Review Cumulative, 1969, Children's Books in Print, 1969, Subject Guide to Children's Books in Print, 1970. Judge Juvenile Natl. Book Award. Mem. ALA (mem.-at-large council 1976-80, Mildred Batchelder award com. 1970, Newberry-Caldecott award com. 1970), Woman's Natl. Book Assn., Assn. Library Services to Children (pres. 1978-79). BS, So. Conn. State Coll., 1954; postgrd., U. Chgo., 1961-62. Home: 39 Gramercy Park N New York NY 10010

GERMAN, NORMAN, b. Lake Charles, LA, May 25, 1955; s. Bobby Leon and Eveline Irene (Martin) G. Author: Anthony Hecht, 1988; contrbr. lit. criticism, fiction and poetry rvws., poems, fiction to anthols., lit. mags. Wrkg. on novel. B.A. in history, McNeese State, 1977; M.A. in English, U. Tex., 1979; Ph.D. in English, U. Southwestern La., 1982. Instr. English, Lamar U., Beaumont, TX, 1982-85; asst. prof. Northwestern State U. La., Natchitoches, 1985—. Recipient 1st prize for poetry U. Southwestern La., 1982, 5th prize for poetry, 1984, 3d prize for poetry, 1985. Mem. Coll. English Assn., Coll. Lang. Assn., AAP. Home: 108 McVay St Lake Charles LA 70605

GERNES, SONIA GRACE, b. Winona, MN, Nov. 15, 1942, d. Albert Jerome and Sophia Marie (Boerboom) Gernes. Author: The Mutes of Sleepy Eye (Best Poetry Book of 1981, Soc. Midland Authors), 1981, Brief Lives (poetry), 1981, The Way to St. Ives (novel, Notable Book of 1981, ALA), 1982. BA, Coll. St. Teresa, 1966; MA, U. Wash., 1971, PhD,1975. Asst. prof. dept. English U. Notre Dame, South Bend, Ind., 1975-81, assoc. prof., 1981—. Mem. WG, P&W. Home: 936 Twyckenham St South Bend IN 46615

GERSDORF, ANTOINETTE GRAHAM, b. Detroit, Dec. 11, 1952; d. Robert G. and Elaine (Snider) Graham; m. Gregory Wayne Gersdorf, May 14, 1976; children—Rene Geneva, Randall Graham. Author: (young adult novels) The Bird, 1986, Eden's Daughters, 1986, Claw the Cold, Cold Earth, 1987, Trouble at Catskill Creek, 1987; Selling Used Books by Mail, 1984. Contrbr. articles, short stories to lit. mags., popular mags. Ed.: Profile, 1984-87. B.A., Grand Valley State Coll., 1973. Owner, The Scribbling Bookmonger, 1977—. Mem. Cape Coral Wrtrs. Club (pres.), NWC, Fla. Freelance Wrtrs. Assn., Fla. Antiquarian Bksellers. Assn. Home: 1613 Silverwood Ct North Fort Myers FL 33903

GERSHATOR, DAVID, b. Haifa, British-mandated Palestine—Israel; Dec. 2, 1937; s. Abraham and Mary (Fisher) Gershator; m. Phillis Manuela, Oct. 19, 1963; children—Yonah, Daniel. Author: Play Mas: West Indies Poems, 1981; editor and trans.: The Selected Letters of Federico Garcia Lorca; assoc. ed. Home Planet News. MA, Columbia U., 1960; PhD, NY U., 1967. Assoc. prof., Brooklyn College, NY, 1973-75; adj. prof., Long Island U., NY, 1979-82; prof., College of The Virgin Islands, St. Thomas, 1985—. Awards: NEH Grant, 1971, NY Creative Artists Public Svc. Grant, 1979. Mem. PSA. Home: Box 3353 St Thomas Virgin Islands 00801

GERSHMAN, ELIZABETH GIBSON, b. Mansfield, Ohio, Oct. 16, 1927; d. Edward Douglas and Daisie Marie (Taylor) Gibson; div; m. 2d, James David Gershman, June 29, 1957; two children: Katherine Anne, Taylor James. Contrbr. articles to Stamford Past and Present (anthology), 1976; Stamford Advocate; performing arts rvw. wkly. col., Stamford Mail. AA in Theater, Stephens Coll, 1947; BGS in Am Studies, U Conn, 1978. Owner/pub. Knights Press, Stamford, Conn, 1983-84. Mem Conn. Press Club, Entrepreneurial Women, GLPA, AFTRA. Address: 88 Saddle Hill Rd Stamford CT 06903

GERSON, NOEL BERTRAM, b. Chgo., Nov. 6, 1914; s. Samuel Philip and Rosa Anna (Noel) G.; children—Noel Anne (Mrs. Brennan), Michele (Mrs. Schechter), Margot (Mrs. Burgett), Paul; m. Marilyn A. Hammond. Author: The Golden Lyre, 1961, The Land is Bright, 1961, The Naked Maja, 1962, Queen of Caprice, 1963, The Slender Reed, 1964, Old Hickory, 1963, Sex and the Mature Man, 1964, Kit Carson, 1964, Lady of France, 1965, Yankee Doodle Dandy, 1965, Give Me Liberty, 1966, Sex and the Adult Woman, 1965, Light-Horse Harry Lee, 1966, The Swamp Fox, The Anthem, 1967, Sam Houston, 1968, Jefferson Square, 1968, The Golden Ghetto, 1969, P.J., My Friend, 1969, TR, 1969, Mirror, Mirror, 1970, Warhead, 1970, The Divine Mistress, 1970, Because I Loved Him, 1971, Island in the Wind, 1971, Victor Hugo, 1971, Double Vision, 1972, The Prodigal Genius, 1972, George Sand, 1972, Daughter of Earth and Water, 1973, State Trooper, 1973, Peter Paul Rubens, 1973, Rebel-Thomas Paine, 1974, The Exploiters, 1974, All That Glitters, 1975, The Caves of Guernica, 1975, Special Agent, 1976, Harriet Beecher Stowe, 1976, Liner, 1977, The Vidocq Dossier, 1977, The Smugglers, 1977, Trelawny's World, 1977, Wagons West, 1979, White Indian, 1980; also other fiction and non-fiction books and articles under own name and various pseudonyms. AB, U. Chgo., 1934, MA, 1935. Reporter, rewriteman Chgo. Herald-Examiner, 1931-36; exec. WGN, Chgo., 1936-41. Radio and TV scriptwriter over 10,000 scripts for natl. networks, 1936-51. Fellow Intl. Inst. Arts and Letters; mem. AG Am., WWA, MWA. Home: 7946 Palacio del Mar Dr Boca Raton FL 33433

GERSTLER, AMY, b. San Diego, Oct. 24, 1956. Author: Yonder, 1981, Christy's Alpine Inn, 1982, White Marriage/Recovery, 1984, Early Heaven, 1984, Martine's Mouth, 1985, The True Bride, 1986. Contrbr. articles to mags. BA, Pitzer Coll., Claremont, Calif. Library asst. Beyond Baroque Lit./Arts Ctr., Venice, Calif., asst. dir. Home: 1173 N Ardmore 6 Los Angeles CA 90029

GERSTNER, JOHN J., b. Frankfort, KS, Sept. 19, 1946; s. Lloyd E. and Rita (Flaherty) G.; children—Shawna, Alisha. Contrbr. to Inside Organizational Communication, 1983, Pictures for Organizations, 1982, Getting Your Message Across: A Practical Guide to Business Communication, 1981. BS, KS State U., 1968; MA, U. IA, 1985. Regional ed. The Furrow, Deere & Co., Moline, IL, 1968-72, ed. JD Jnl, 72—. Gold Quill award, IABC, 1977-79, 81-83; Best Internal Pub. & Best of Show, Natl. Agri-Mktg. Assn., 1982 and 1986; Communication of the Month, Maranto Memo, June 1987; Clarion award, WIC. Mem. IABC, Friends of Photography, Visual Studies Wkshop. Home: 3510-70th St, No. 102 Moline IL 61265

GERSTNER, LILLIAN POLUS, b. Nashville, Oct. 10, 1951; d. Moses and Ursula (Husarzewski) Polus; m. Alan Ira Gerstner, Dec. 12, 1976; children—Michael, Lisa. Contrbr. articles to mags. including Redbook Mag., others. collection of dramatic adaptions of Yiddish folk tales. B.S. in Speech, Northwestern U., 1973. Office mgr. Blau/Bishop & Assoc., Chgo., 1973-79, bookkeeper, 1981-83. Mem. Ill. Theatre Assn. Home: 10018 LaCrosse Skokie IL 60077

GERTZ, ELMER, b. Chgo., Sept. 14, 1906; s. Morris and Grace (Grossman) G.; m. Ceretta Samuels, Aug. 16, 1931 (dec.); children—Theodore, Margery Ann Hechtman; m. Mamie L. Friedman, June 21, 1959; 1 son, Jack M. Friedman. Author: (with A.I. Tobin) Frank Harris: A Study in Black and White, 1931, The People vs. The Chicago Tribune, 1942; play Mrs. Bixby Gets a Letter, 1942; Joe Medill's War, 1946, American Ghettos, 1946, A Handful of Clients, 1965, Moment of Madness: The People vs. Jack Ruby, 1968; foreword The Tropic of Cancer On Trial, 1968; To Life, 1974 (Friends of Lit. award), Short Stories of Frank Harris, 1975, Henry Miller and Elmer Gertz, 1978, German edit., 1980, Odyssey of a Barbarian, 1979, (with Joseph Posciotte) Charter for a New Age, 1980, others; contrbr. to: Henry Miller and the Critics, 1963, Mass Media and the Law, 1969, For the First

Hours of Tomorrow, 1971; author articles in various periodicals and encys. PhB, U. Chgo., 1928, JD, 1930. Mem. Soc. Midland Authors (award 1969, secy. 1976, award for body of work, 1984), AG. Home: 6249 N Albany Ave Chicago IL 60659

GERY, JOHN ROY OCTAVIUS, b. Reading, PA, June 2, 1953, s. Addison Harbster Jr. and Eugenie Gunesh (Guran) G. Author: Charlemagne: A Song of Gestures (poetry), 1983; co-ed.: Little Mag., 1975, La. English Jnl, 1983-85; poetry ed.: Nassau Lit. Mag., 1974-75; contrbg. ed.: Swallow's Tale mag., 1984—; contrbr. poetry to Intro 7, Nebo, Poet Lore, Pig Iron, other lit mags; contrbr. articles to Modern Poetry Studies, Poesis, Threepenny Rvw, Wind, other jnls. AB with honors in English, Princeton U., 1975; MA in English, U. Chgo., 1976; MA in Creative Wrtg., Stanford U., 1978. Lectr. in English Stanford (Calif.) U., 1977-79, San Jose (Calif.) State U., 1977-79; instr. English, U. New Orleans, 1979-84, asst. prof., 1984—, faculty adviser Ellipsis mag., 1981-84; assoc. dir. New Orleans Poetry Festival, 1981. Mirrielees fellow Stanford U., 1976-77; recipient Plumbers Ink Poetry award, Cerrillos, N.Mex., 1982; grantee U. New Orleans, 1984. Mem. AAP (poetry award 1975), P&W, Dir. Philol. Assn. La., SCMLA, ACA/PCA. Office: Dept Eng U New Orleans New Orleans LA 70148

GESNER, ELSIE MILLER, b. Guilford, CT, Dec. 8; d. William and Katherine (Hart) Miller; m. Rev. Lewis G. Gesner, Jr., July 5, 1947; children—Joy, Lewis, III. Author children's books: The Lumber Camp Kids, 1957, In the Stillness of the Storm, 1963. Contrbr. short stories, articles, profiles to religious mags. Wrkg. on young adult book, adult Christian hist. novel, young adult Christian novel. Student Barrington Bible Coll., RI, 1937-38, 1945-47. Statistician Am. Univ. Ins. Co., 1948-51, asst. cashier U. Maine, Orono, 1966-67; paralegal, Rockland, ME, 1972-82. Home: 65 Longfellow St Portland ME 04103

GESTON, MARK SYMINGTON, b. Atlantic City, NJ, June 20, 1946; s. John Charles and Mary T. (Symington) G.; m. Gayle Francis Howard, June 12, 1971 (div. 1972); m. 2d, Marijke Havinga, Aug. 14, 1976; children—Camille LaCroix, Robert LaCroix, Emily S. Author: Lords of the Starship, 1967, Out of the Mouth of the Dragon, 1969, The Day Star, 1972, The Seige of Wonder, 1976. BA in History, Kenyon Coll., 1968, JD, NUY, 1971. Atty. Eberly & Berlin, Boise, Idaho, 1971—. Me. Idaho State Bar, ABA. Address: 1829 Edgecliff Terr Boise ID 83702

GETZ, MIKE, b. Bklyn., Dec. 29, 1938; s. Joseph A. and Rose (Palter) G; m. Virginia Lee Pellegrini, May 21, 1966; 1 son, Vincent Michael. Author: Baseball's 3,000 Hit Men, 1982; The Mets Trivia Book, 1984, New York Yankees Trivia, 1987, St. Louis Cardinals Trivia, 1987, New York Mets Trivia—The Silver Anniversary Book, 1987; contrbr. Diamond Report mag; Baseball Bulletin. Student NYU, 1957. Recreation wrkr. OMRDD, Brooklyn,NY, 1965—. Served to cpl, US Army, 1962-64, USA. Mem. Soc. for Am. Baseball Research. Address: 2067 58th St Brooklyn NY 11204

GEYER, GEORGIE ANNE, b. Chgo., Apr. 2, 1935; d. Robert George and Georgie Hazel (Gervens) G. Author: The New Latins, 1970, The New 100 Years War, 1972, The Young Russians, 1976; (autobiography) Buying the Night Flight, 1983. B.S., Northwestern U., 1956; postgrad. (Fulbright scholar), U. Vienna, Austria, 1956-57; Litt. D. (hon.), Lake Forest Coll., (Ill.), 1980. Reporter Southtown Economist, Chgo., 1958; soc. reporter Chgo. Daily News, 1959-60, gen. assignment reporter, 1960-64, Latin Am. corr., 1964-67, roving fgn. corr. and columnist, 1967-75; syndicated columnist Los Angeles Times Syndicate, 1975-80; columniist Universal Press Syndicate, 1980—āle M. Spencer prof. journalism Syrause U., 1976. Recipient 1st prize Am. Newspaper Guild, 1962; 2d prize Ill. Press Editors Assn., 1962; award for best writing on Latin Am., Overseas Press Club, 1966; numerous others. Mem. Women in Communications, Midland Authors. Address: 800 25th St NW Washington DC 20037

GHIGNA, CHARLES, b. L.I., NY, Aug. 25, 1946, s. Charles V. and Patricia (Pelletier) G.; m. Debra Holmes, Aug. 2, 1975. Author: Plastic Tears, 1973, Stables, 1974, Cockroach, 1977, Divers and Other Poems, 1978, Circus Poems, 1979, Howard Be Thy Name, 1987, Returning to Earth, 1988; contrbr.to Harper's, McCall's, Good Housekeeping, Sat. Evening Post, Rolling Stone, Writer's Digest, Humpty Dumpty, Jack and Jill, Children's Digest, other publs.; former poetry ed. English Jnl. BA, Fla. Atlantic U., 1967, MA, 1970. Poet-in-residence Ala. Schl. Fine Arts, Birmingham. Recipient grants, fellowship John F. Kennedy Center for Performing Arts, Rockefeller Bros. Fund, Mary Roberts Rinehart Fdn. Home: 204 W Linwood Dr Homewood AL 35209

GHISELIN, BREWSTER, b. Webster Groves, MO, June 13, 1903; s. Horace and Eleanor (Weeks) G.; m. Olive F. Franks, June 7, 1929; children: Jon Brewster, Michael Tenant. Author: (poetry) Against the Circle, 1946, The Nets, 1955, Country of the Minotaur, 1970, Light, 1978, Windrose: Poems 1929-1979, 1980; Writing, 1959; ed. The Creative Process, 1952, pb ed. with Foreword, 1985; contrbr. poetry, fiction, essays to numerous mags., including Poetry, Story, Am. Scholar, Sewanee, Kenyon, Hudson rvws. AB, UCLA, 1927; MA, U. Calif., Berkeley, 1928. Mem. faculty dept. English, U. Utah, Salt Lake City, 1929-31, 34—, assoc. prof., 1946-50, prof., 1950-71, prof. emeritus, 1971—, disting. research prof., 1967-68, dir. Wrtrs.' Conf., 1947-66. Recipient award Nat. Inst. Arts and Letters, 1970; Blumenthal-Leviton-Blonder prize Poetry, 1973, Levinson prize, 1978; William Carlos Williams award PSA, 1981; Gov.'s award for arts Utah Arts Council-State of Utah, 1982; Ford Fdn. fellow, 1952-53. Mem. MLA, Utah Acad. Scis., Arts and Letters. Home: 1747 Princeton Ave Salt Lake City UT 84108

GIANNINI, DAVID, b. NYC, Mar. 19, 1948; s. Walter Giannini. Author: (poetry) Opens, 1971; Stories, 1974; Fourfield, 1976; Close Packet, 1978; (with Bob Arnold and John Levy) 3, 1978; Stem, 1982; contrbr. poetry to numerous anthologies and mags.; ed. poetry and prose collections by children. Ed./co-founder Genesis: Grasp Publs., 1968-71. Osa and Lee Mays Award Morris Harvey Coll., 1969; grantee No. Berkshire Community Arts Council, 1984, Inst. for Arts, Boston, 1985, 86, New Eng. Fdn. for Arts, 1986. Mem. Berkshire Wrtrs.' Guild. Home: Box 98 Pittsfield MA 01202

GIANOLI, PAUL LOUIS, b. New Britain, CT, April 11, 1943; s. Louis Paul and Anna Alice (Rozkowski) G.; m. Christy Guinnette Saxon, Aug. 27, 1979; children: Mark, Anna. Author: (poetry) Blueprint, 1980; ed. Midlands, 1976-77; mem. editorial staff Mo. Rvw, 1978-79; contrbr. poetry to Wis. Rvw, Focus Midwest, Huerfano, So. Dak. Rvw, Webster Rvw, other lit mags. AB, St. Michael's Coll., Winooski, Vt., 1965; PhD, U. Mo., 1979. Instr. U. Mo., Columbia, 1970-79; asst. prof. Schl. of the Ozarks, Point Lookout, Mo., 1980-86. Served with U.S. Army, 1965-67. Home: HCR7 Bronson MO 65616

GIBB, ROBERT, b. Pitts., Sept. 5, 1946, s. Robert James and Helen Catherine (Freinstein) G.; m. Margaret Marie Lewis; 1 son, Matthew Robert. Author: Whale Songs, 1976, The Margins, 1979, Whalesongs, 1979, The Names of the Earth in Summer, 1983, The Winter House, 1984, Entering Time, 1986, A Geography of Common Names, 1987, Momentary Days, 1988; contrbr. to A Celebration of Cats, From A to Z: 200 Contemporary Am. Poets, Tide Turning, Bird Verse Portfolio, other anthologies. BFA, Kutztown (Pa.) U., 1971; MFA, U. Mass., 1974; MA, Lehigh U., 1978, PhD, 1986. Winner, 10th Anniversary Award Vol., Stone Country, 1983; grantee Pa. Council on Arts, 1984, Camden Poetry Award, 1987, The Devil's Millhopper Press Chapbook Contest, 1987. Mem. P&W, AWP. Home: RD 2 Box 181 Zionsville PA 18092

GIBBONS, (WILLIAM) REGINALD, (JR.), b. Houston, TX, Jan. 7, 1947; s. William Reginald and Elizabeth (Lubowski) G.; m. Virginia Margaret Harris, June 8, 1968 (div. July 1982); m. Cornelia Maude Spelman, Aug. 18, 1983. Author: (poems) Roofs, Voices, Roads, 1979, The Ruined Motel, 1981, Saints, 1986; Selected Poems of Luis Cernuda (trans.), 1977, Guillen on Guillen (trans. with Anthony L. Geist), 1979; edited The Poet's Work, 1979, TQ20 (with Susan Hahn), 1985, Criticism in the University (with Gerald Graff), 1985, The Writer in Our World, 1986. Editor, TriQuarterly, 1981—. AB, Princeton Univ., 1969; MA, Stanford Univ., 1971, PhD, 1974. Instr. Spanish, Rutgers Univ., 1975-76; lectr. creative wrtg., Princeton, 1976-80, Columbia Univ., 1980-81; lectr. Eng., Northwestern Univ., 1981-87; prof., 1987—. Guggenheim Fellowship, 1984, NEA Poetry Fellowship, 1984. Mem. PEN, PSA, Texas Inst. of Letters. Home: 1428 Crain St Evanston IL 60202

GIBBS, BARBARA FRANCESCA, b. Los Angeles, Sept. 23, 1912, d. Walter Sylvester and Marjorie (Loftus) G.; m. James V. Cunningham, June 1937 (div. 1942); 1 dau.—Marjorie Lupien; m. 2d, Frances Golffing, Feb. 1, 1942. Contrbr. to Twelve Poets of the Pacific, 1937, The Well, 1941, A Little Treasury of World Poetry, 1952, Flowers of Evil, 1955, The Green Chapel, 1958, An Anthology of French Poetry from Nerval to Valery, 1958, Poems Written in Berlin, 1959, The New Yorker Book of Poems, 1969, People in Poetry, 1969, Translations by American Poets, 1970, The Meeting Place of the Colors, 1972; contrbr. to New Republic, Partisan Rvw, New Yorker, Village Voice, other periodicals. BA, Stanford U., 1934; MA, UCLA, 1935. Recipient James Phelan fellowship, 1942, Partisan Rvw prize, 1945, Oscar Blumenthal prize, Poetry, Chgo., 1949, Guggenheim fellowship, N.Y.C., 1955, 56. Home: 272 Middle Hancock Rd Peterborough NH 03458

GIBBS, JAMIE, b. Indpls., Aug. 24, 1955, s. Irvin and Glenna (Reid) G. Author: Landscape Maintenance Manual for the State Parks of Indiana, 1978, Handicap Access to the State Parks, Indiana, 1978, John Jay Park-Reborn, 1983, Landscape it Yourself, Tips from a Landscape Architect, 1987, other books; contrbr. to numerous trade and consumer publs, nwsprs, and video scripts. Lectures nationwide on gardening, landscape design and construciton methods. Wrkg. on landscaping history book. BS in

Hort. and Landscape Architecture, Purdue U., 1977; M in Historic Preservation, Columbia U., 1982; ed.-in-chief Landscaping Homes and Gardens, Garden Projects, Pools and Patios, Green Guerillas Report, Mem. numerous hort. and garden orgns. Office: 340 E 93d St 14C New York NY 10128

GIBSON, BARRY JOSEPH, b. Boston, Feb. 6, 1951; s. Joseph W. and Marjorie (Jacobs) G.; m. Jean Harley Reese-Gibson, Oct. 11, 1980. Contrbr. articles and photos to major outdoor mags. inclg. Outdoor Life, Field & Stream, Fishing Facts. BA, U. Miami (FL), 1973. Assoc. ed. Salt Water Sportsman, Boston, MA, 1977-81; assoc. boating ed. Outdoor Life, NYC, 1980-81; ed.-in-chief Salt Water Sportsman, Boston, 1981—. Mako Outdoor Writer of the Year, 1982. Mem. OWAA, NEOWA. Office: SW Sportsman 186 Lincoln St Boston MA 02111

GIBSON, DE MARCHIA, b. West Palm Beach, FL, Jan. 15, 1956; d. Eugene and Christen Gibson. Contrbr.: The Art of Poetry-A Treasury of Contemporary Verse, Am. Poetry Anthology. Wrkg. on poetry collection. BA in English, Bethune-Cookman Coll., 1978. Editorial assoc. South-Western Pub. Co., Cin., 1978-80; tchr. Northboro Sch., West Palm Beach, Fla., 1980—. Home: 3617 N Dixie Hwy West Palm Beach FL 33407

GIBSON, JAMES RILEY, JR., b. Sioux City, IA, Sept. 17, 1944, s. James Riley and Ella (Hudson) G.; m. Sandra Underwood, Dec. 16, 1967; children—Christopher James, Laura Elizabeth. Author: How to Make More in Music, 1985, How You Can Make $30,000 a Year as A Musician, 1986. BA, Mercer U., 1967; MA, Ga. State U., 1972. Tchr. Fulton County Schls., Atlanta, 1972-74; public relations wrtr. Ga. Dept. Edn., Atlanta, 1974-76; freelance musician, wrtr., Atlanta, 1976—. Home: 1663 Homestead Ave Atlanta GA 30306

GIBSON, KEIKO MATSUI, b. Kyoto, Japan, Sept. 4, 1953, came to U.S. as permanent res. alien, 1979; d. Yoshinobu and Masako (Katayama) Matsui; m. Morgan Gibson, Sept. 14, 1978; 1 son: Christopher So, b. Oct. 6, 1986. Author: (poems) Tremble of Morning, 1979, Stir Up the Precipitable World, 1983; (poems and prose) (with Morgan Gibson) Kokoro: Heart-Mind, 1981. Contrbr. poems, translations, rvws. to anthols, lit mags, articles to profl. mags. BA in English, Kwansei Gakuin U., Nichinomiya, Japan, 1976; MA in comparative lit., U. Ill.-Champaign-Urbana, 1983; doctoral student, Ind. U.-Bloomington, 1983—. Instr. English, ECC Lang. Ins., Osaka, Japan, 1973-79; instr. Japanese, Northwestern Mich. Coll., Traverse City, 1980, Adult Edn. Program, Frankfort, Mich., 1979-81; research asst. to curator Krannert art mus. U. Ill., Champaign-Urbana, Ill., 1981-83; assoc. instr. comparative lit. Ind. U., Bloomington, 1984-85. Recipient Kenneth Rexroth Spl. award for poetry in English and Japanese, Kyoto Am. Ctr., 1982. Mem. Am. Comparative Lit. Assn., Intl. Comparative Lit. Assn., Phi Kappa Phi. Home: 251 Standish Rd Box 212 Frankfort MI 49635

GIBSON, MARGARET FERGUSON, b. Phila., Feb. 17, 1944; d. John Spears and Mattie Leigh (Doyle) Ferguson; m. Ross S. Gibson, Aug. 27, 1966 (div., 1973); m. 2d, David Wilbur McKain, Dec. 27, 1975; step-children—Joshua, Megan. Author: The Duel, 1966, Lunes, 1973, On the Cutting Edge, 1975, Signs, 1979, Long Walks in the Afternoon, 1982, Memories of the Future, 1986; co-editor: Landscape and Distance: Poets from Virginia, 1975. BA, Hollins College, 1966; MA, U. of Va., 1967. Instr., Madison College, Harrisburg, Va., 1967-68; instr., Va. Commonwealth U., Richmond, 1968-70; asst. prof., George Mason U., Fairfax, Va., 1970-75; lectr. U. of Conn., Groton, CT, 1977-84; wrtr.-in-res., Phillips Academy, Andover, Mass., 1984-87. Awards: Woodrow Wilson Fellowship, 1966-67; AAP Lamont Selection, 1982 (Long Walks in the Afternoon); NEA Fellowship, 1985. Home: RFD 1 Watson Rd Preston CT 06360

GIBSON, MARY ELIZABETH G., b. Springfield, MA, Jan. 9, 1924, d. Francis Clarence Gagnier and Beatrice Grace (Tait) Henrich; m. Francis Charles Davis, July 18, 1942 (div. Aug. 1964); children: Beverley Tait Davis Clarke, Susan Olds Davis English, Maralee Ruth Dana Davis Chris; m. David Joel Thibault, Nov. 9, 1964 (div. Oct. 1967); m. William Carter Gibson, Jan. 21, 1970, Author: (poetry) Soliloquy's Virgin, 1965, The Valley of Self, 1970; contrbr. to Poems from the Hills, Poetry Rvw, Stone Country, Green Age Lit. Rvw, various anthologies. Student Bay Path Jr. Coll., Springfield, 1941-42, Greenfield Community Coll., Mass., 1984—. Wrtr. Amherst Jnl, Mass., 1952-54; reporter Greenfield Recorder Gazette, Mass., 1958-62; asst. ed. Sportsmen's News, Northampton, Mass., 1963-64; freelance writer, 1963—; treas. Hillcrest Park Cemetery Marker Service, Springfield, 1972—. Recipient citation Natl. Fedn. Poetry Socs., 1970, World Poetry Soc., 1970, Shenandoah Valley Acad. Lit., 1978, 79. Mem. PSA. Address: Box 301 North Amherst MA 01059

GIBSON, MORGAN, b. Cleveland, June 6, 1929, s. George Miles Jr. and Mary Elizabeth (Leeper) G.; m. Barbara Ann Browne, Sept. 1, 1950 (div. 1972); children—Julia Mary, Lucy Alice; m. 2d, Keiko Matsui, Sept. 14, 1978. Author: Our Bedroom's Underground, 1964 (with Barbara Gibson), Mayors of Marble, 1966, Stones Glow Like Lovers' Eyes, 1970, Kenneth Rexroth, 1972, Dark Summer, 1977, Speaking of Light, 1979, Kokoro: Heart-Mind, 1980 (with Keiko Matsui Gibson), The Great Brook Book, 1981, Tantric Poetry of Kukai (Kobo Daishi) Japan's Buddhist Saint, 1982 (with Hiroshi Murakami), Revolutionary Rexroth: Poet of East-West Wisdom, 1986; editor, publisher: Prelude to International Velvet Debutante (Gerard Malanga), 1967, The Blossom or Billy the Kid (Michael McClure), 1967, The Thief of Kisses (James Hazard), 1968; poetry ed, Arts in Society, 1965-72, editor of spcl. issue, The Arts of Activism, 1969. BA in English, Oberlin Coll., Ohio, 1950; MA in Eng. Lit. and Creative Wrtg., U. Iowa, 1952, PhD,1959. Tchg. asst. English, U. Iowa, 1952-53; instr. English and humanities Shimer Coll., Mt. Carroll, Ill., 1953-54; instr. English and humanities Wayne State U., Detroit, 1954-58, tchg. asst. history, 1958-59; asst. prof. English, American International Coll., Springfield, Mass., 1959-61; asst. prof., assoc. prof. U. Wis., Milwaukee, 1961-72; chmn. graduate faculty Goddard Coll., Plainfield, Vt., 1972-75; prof. English lang. and culture Osaka U., Japan, 1975-79; visiting faculty Ehime U. and Matsuyama U., Japan, Michigan State U. Ext., U. Illinois, research assoc., Indiana U.; prof. English, Chukyo U., Nagoya, Japan, 1987—. Writers Workshop Fiction Award, Gage Prize for Poetry, Oberlin Coll., 1950; Fiction First, Mutiny mag., 1961; Uhrig Award for Excellent Teaching, U. Wis. at Milwaukee, 1965; grants for writing and research, U. Wis., 1966-67. Mem. PEN, AAP, PSA, Buddhist Peace Fellowship. Home: 251 Standish Rd Frankfort MI 49635

GIDDINGS, LAUREN, see Gideon, Nancy A.

GIDEON, NANCY ANN, (Dana Ransom, Lauren Giddings), b. Kalamazoo, MI, May 27, 1955; d. Floyd L. and Helen L. (Ransom) Crumb; m. Richard E. Gideon, July 11, 1981; children—Travis, Andrew. Author: Sweet Tempest, 1987, Pirate's Captive, 1987, Rebel Vixen, 1987. B.A. cum laude, Western Mich. U., 1977. Saleswoman Farm Bur. Insuarance, Kalamazoo, 1982; clrk. Ind. Group Services, Kalamazoo, 1985. Mem. RWA. Home: 4102 Truman Kalamazoo MI 49007

GIFFIN, MARY ELIZABETH, b. Rochester, MN, Mar. 30, 1919; d. Herbert Ziegler and Mary Elizabeth (Nace) Giffin. Author: Her Doctor, Will Mayo, A Cry for Help, BA, Smith Coll., 1939; MD, Johns Hopkins U., 1943. Cons. Mayo Clinic, Rochester, Minn., 1948-58; med. dir. Joselyn Clinic, Northfield, Ill., 1958—. Mem. med. orgns. Home: 1190 Hamptondale Rd Winnetka IL 60093

GILBAUGH, NO JUNE, b. Sherrodsville, OH, June 27, 1923; d. Walter Brice and Jennie Marie (Hagey) Boyd; m. Ward E. Gilbaugh, June 16, 1961. Author poetry: Heart Treasures, 1983, (with companion musical tape) Heavenly Thoughts with Heavenly Music, 1984. Contrbr. numerous poems to lit. mags., anthols. B.A. summa cum laude, Malone Coll., 1965; post-grad. Wright State U., 1975. English instr. Carrollton High Schl., OH, 1965-80, retired. Home: 5275 Antigua Rd SW Sherrodsville OH 44675

GILBERT, BARBARA, see Fink, Barbara Arlene

GILBERT, CELIA, b. Phila., Sept. 9, 1932; d. I. F. and Esther (Roisman) Stone; m. Walter Gilbert, Dec. 29, 1953; children—John, Kate. Author: Queen of Darkness, 1976, Bonfire, 1983; contrbr.: Working it Out, 1976, Making for the Open, 1984, Mother to Daughter, Daughter to Mother, 1984. BA, Smith College, 1954; MA, Boston U., 1973. Awards: Emily Dickinson Award, PSA, Discovery Award, 92nd St. YM-YWHA, Pushcart Prize IX. Mem. PEN, AG. Home: 107 Upland Rd Cambridge MA 02140

GILBERT, CHRISTINA IDA, b. South Bend, IN, July 2, 11950; d. Herbert Hugo and Dolores Ann (Wagner) Swanson; m. Larry A.C. Gilbert, Aug. 5, 1972; 1 dau., Nicole Marie. Contrbr. poetry, short stories to lit. mags., anthols. Student Ind. U., 1968-72. Asst. librarian Ind. U. Library, South Bend, 1970-72, 84—; free-lance wrtr., 1969—; antique dealer, Elkhart, IN, 1987—. Actress, Elkhart Civic Theatre, Bristol, IN, 1976-84, asst. dir., 1983; actress Napanee Civic Theatre, 1985. Home: 59674 Garver Elkhart IN 46517

GILBERT, CHRISTOPHER, b. Birmingham, AL, Aug. 1, 1949; s. Floyd and Rosie Mae (Walker) Gilbert. Author: Across the Mutual Landscape, 1983 (winner of 1983 Walt Whitman Award, PSA); editor: Something Else: A Sample of Third World Writing, 1981. BA, U. of Michigan, 1972; MA, Clark U., 1975. Staff psychologist, Judge Baker Guidance Center, Boston, Mass., 1978-84; staff psychologist, Univ. of Mass. Medical School Counseling Center, Worcester, 1978-83; poet-in-residence, University of Pittsburgh, 1986 Winter; poet-in-residence, The Robert Frost Place, Franconia, New Hampshire, Summer 1986. Home: 588 Pleasant St Worcester MA 01602

GILBERT, HERMAN CROMWELL, b. Marianna, AR, Feb. 23, 1923; s. Van Luther and Cora (Allen) G.; m. Ivy McAlpine, July 19, 1949; children—Dorothea Gilbert Lassiter, Vincent Newton Gilbert. Author: The Uncertain Sound, 1969, The Negotiations, 1983. Wrkg. on The Campaign (fiction); This Needs Saying (non-fiction), Sharp Blades in Tender Grass (play). Student, LaSalle Ext.U., 1942-44. Feat. ed. Chgo. Globe Nwspr. (IL), 1950-51; asst. intl. program coord., United Packinghouse Wrkrs. of Am., AFL-CIO, 1955-57; mng. ed., Chicago Westside Booster Newspaper, 1959-60; mng. ed., Chicago Citizen newspapers, 1965-70; asst. admin. IL Dept. Labor, Chgo., 1958-80; chief of staff Cong. Gus Savage, Washington, 1981-82; ed. dir. Path Press, Chgo., 1983—. Mem. SMA, IBWC. Home: 11539 S Justine St Chicago IL 60643

GILBERT, ILSA, b. Bklyn. Apr. 27, 1933, d. Saul and Isabelle (Segall) Gilbert. Author: Survivors and Other New York Poems, 1985; playwright, librettist and lyricist; over 30 productions and staged readings including The Bundle Man (one-act verse play filmed for Cable-TV), 1974, The Dead Dentist, 1974, Pardon the Prisoner, (published), 1976, Travellers, 1977, Berlin Blues, 1985; contrbr. poetry: Waterways, Poet Lore, Voices, St. Clement's Quarterly, numerous other lit mags; contrbr. stories, articles to various nationwide magazines. BA in English, Bklyn. Coll., 1955. Asst. ed. Screen Stories mag., Dell Pub. Co., NYC, 1956; assoc. ed., mng. ed. True Experience mag., Macfadden Publs., NYC, 1956-65; copywrtr., Creative Dir. Murray Leff & Co. 1962; asst. to creative dir. Mogel, Williams & Saylor NYC, 1959-60; assoc. ed. Movie TV Secrets, ed. Ladies Home Companion, staff wrtr. Countrywide Publs., Inc., NYC, 1962-63; freelance wrtr., poet, playwright, 1965—. Poetry awards-Honorable Mention, the Atlantic, 1955, Poet Lore, 1968. Dorset (Vt.) Wrtrs. Colony resident, 1982, 1986, 1987. Nominated for NEA Grant by the Classic Theatre (Playwright-in-Residence), 1981-82. Playwright in Residence, Eccentric Circles Theatre 1983-85. Mem. PEN, P&W, AL of Am., DG. Home: 203 Bleecker St New York NY 10012

GILBERT, JACK, b. Pitts. Author poetry collections: Views of Jeopardy, 1962, Monolithos, 1982, Kochan, 1984. Recipient Yale Younger Poets award, Yale U., 1962; Guggenheim fellow, 1964, NEA fellow, 1974. Home: 919 Oak St New Port Richey FL 33552

GILBERT, MARIE ROGERS, b. Florence, SC, Jan. 27, 1924; d. Frank Mandeville and Marie Louise (Barringer) Rogers; m. Richard Austin Gilbert, Apr. 24, 1946; children—Richard Austin, Laurie Gilbert Sanford. Author poems: From Comfort, 1981, The Song And The Seed, 1983; contrbr. poetry to numerous mags. BA, Rollins Coll., Winter Park, FL, 1945. 2d. place, Oscar Arnold Young Book Award, NC Poetry Council, 1982, 2d. place Zoe Kincaid Brockman Book Award, NC Poetry Soc., 1984. Mem. NC Poetry Soc., NC Wrtrs. Conf., Greensboro Wrtrs. Club. Home: 2 St Simons Sq Greensboro NC 27408

GILBERT, VIRGINIA LEE, b. Elgin, IL, Dec. 19, 1946; d. Blair Edward and Florence Amelia (Swailes) G. Author: (chapbook) To Keep at Bay the Hounds, 1985. Contrbr. articles and numerous poems to lit. mags., anthols. including Prairie Schooner, The North Am. Rvw., NY Quarterly. B.A., Iowa Wesleyan Coll., 1969; M.F.A., U. Iowa, 1971. Instr. English, Peace Corps, 1971-73, Iran, 1976-79, Coll. Lake County, IL, 1979; tchg. fellow creative writing and composition U. Utah, 1974-75; adminstrv. asst. AAP and Wrtrs.' Commun., NYC, 1976; dir. program in creative writing and visiting reading series Ala. A&M U., Normal, 1980—, asst. prof. English, 1980—. Fellow NEA, 1976. Mem. AWP, P&W, PSA. Home: 136 Stone Meadow Ln Madison AL 35758

GILBERTSON, B(ERNICE) CHARLOTTE, b. Boston, Nov. 11; d. Elmer Nordin and Otelia Sigurd (Peterson) G. Columnist: Palm Beach Mirror, 1982-84. B.A., Boston Univ., 1944. Staff wrtr. Palm Beach Post Times, West Palm Beach, FL, 1981-82, asst. to pub. and ed., 1982-84; wrtr. Palm Beach Mirror, FL, 1982-84. Home: 18 Schl House Rd Harwich Port MA 02646

GILBO, ANNA-CAROLYN, b. Hickory, NC, Aug. 25, 1940; d. Martin Luther and Frances Louise (Miller) Stirewalt; m. Jay Gilbo, May 28, 1972; children—Lisa Catherine Yost, Theodore Yost. Author: I Hate You! Love, Don—The Autobiography of a Teacher, 1985; contrbr. to various mags and anthols. inclg. Hyperion, St. Andrews Review, Soundings, Award Winning Poems, 400 Years Along the Way; ed., cookbook, The Best of Priscilla's Tea Room, 1984. BS, Wittenberg U., Springfield, OH, 1962. Mem. P&W, NC Poetry Soc., NC Writers' Conf., Burlington Writers Club, Chapel Hill Friday Noon Poets. Home: 900 W King St Hillsborough NC 27278

GILDEMEISTER, JERRY, b. Highland Pk, MI, June 24, 1934; s. Edwin E. and Florence V. (Kuhn) G.; m. Cathy L. Nelson, Aug. 14, 1978. Author: Rendezvous, 1978, Traces, 1980, Where Rolls the Oregon, 1985, A Letter Home, 1987. BS in Forestry, Mich. State U., 1951-55. Forester US Forest Service, Union, Ore., 1955-57, mgr., 1959-72; photographer Gildemeister Design, Union, 1960—; ed. and designer Bear Wallow Pub, Union, 1978—. U.S. Army, 1957-59. Address: High Valley Foothill Rd Union OR 97883

GILDNER, GARY, b. W. Branch, MI, Aug. 22, 1938; s. Theodore Edward and Jean Helen (Szostak) G.; 1 dau., Gretchen. Author: First Practice, 1969, Digging for Indians, 1971, Eight Poems, 1973, Nail, 1975, Out of This World (ed), 1975, Letters From Vicksburg, 1976, The Runner, 1978, Jabon, 1981, The Crush (stories), 1983, Blue Like The Heavens, 1984, A Week In South Dakota, 1987 (stories), The Second Bridge, 1987 (novel); contrbr. to more than 40 anthologies and textbooks, including Treasury of Am. Poetry, A Geography of Poets, 1978, Am. Poetry Anthology, 1974, Blasters: Am. Shorts, 1986, 9 New Am. Writers, 1986. BA, Mich. State U., 1960, MA, 1961. Writer/univ. relations Wayne State Univ., Detroit, 1962, interviewer WDET-FM; instr. No. Mich. Univ., Marquette, 1963-66; instr. to prof. Drake Univ., Des Moines, Ia, 1966—; writer-in-res. Reed Coll., Portland, Oreg., 1983-85; vis. wrtr. Mich. State Univ., 1987. NEA fellow, 1971, 76; recipient Robert Frost fellowship, Breadloaf, 1970, William Carlos Williams prize, New Letters Mag, 1977, Theodore Roethke prize, Poetry Northwest, 1976, Helen Bullis prize, Poetry Northwest, 1979, Yaddo fellow, 1972, 73, 75, 76, 78, Pushcart Prize, 1986, Natl. Mag. Award for Fiction, 1986. Address: 2915 School St Des Moines IA 50311

GILES, MOLLY, b. San Francisco, Mar. 12, 1942, d. John D. and Doris (McConnell) Murphy; m. Daniel R. Giles, Sept. 29, 1996 (div. 1974); children—Gretchen, Rachel; m. 2d, John Richard King, July 22, 1976; 1 dau., Devon. Author: Rough Translations (Flannery O'Connor award for short fiction U. Ga. Press), 1985. BA, San Francisco State U., 1978, MA, 1980. Lectr. San Francisco State U., 1980—. Home: Box 137 Woodacre CA 94973

GILGUN, JOHN FRANCIS, b. Malden, MA, Oct. 1, 1935; s. Francis Augustus and Beatrice Irene (Burke) G. Author: Everything That Has Been Shall Be Again: The Reincarnation Fables of John Gilgun, 1981. BA, Boston U., 1953-57; MA, U. Ia., 1959, MFA, 1970, PhD, 1972. Prof. Miss Western Coll., St. Joseph, 1972. Recipient Am. Inst. Graphic Arts award, NYC, 1981, Chgo. Book Clinic award, 1981, Midwestern Book award, Univ. Ky., Lexington, 1981, Bumbershoot award, Seattle, 1981 all for Everything That Has Been. . . Mem. MLA, NCTE, P&W, AWP. Address: Box 1638 St Joseph MO 64507

GILL, BRENDAN, b. Hartford, CT, Oct. 4, 1914; s. Michael Henry Richard and Elizabeth (Duffy) G.; m. Anne Barnard, June 20, 1936; children: Brenda, Michael, Holly, Madelaine, Rosemary, Kate, Charles. Author: Death in April and Other Poems, 1935, The Trouble of One House, 1950, The Day The Money Stopped, (adapted play with Maxwell Anderson, 1958), La Belle, 1962, Fat Girl, 1971, Tallulah, 1972, (with Robert Kimball) Cole, 1971, (with Jerome Zerbe) Happy Times, 1973, Ways of Loving, 1974, Here at the New Yorker, 1975, Lindbergh Alone, 1977, (with Dudley Witney) Summer Places, 1978, (with Derry Moore) The Dream Come True, 1980, Wooings, 1980, A Fair Land to Build In: The Architecture of the Empire State, 1984; editor: States of Grace; Eight Plays by Philip Barry, 1975. A.B., Yale U., 1936. Contbr. to New Yorker, 1936—, film critic, 1961-67, drama critic, 1958—. Address: The New Yorker 25 W 43d St New York NY 10036

GILLAN, MARIA MAZZIOTTI, b. Paterson, NJ, Mar. 12, 1940; d. Arturo and Angelina (Schiavo) Mazziotti; m. Dennis P. Gillan, June 28, 1964; children: John Arthur, Jennifer Lisa. Author poetry: Flowers From the Tree of Night, 1981, Winter Light, 1985; ed. Footwork Mag.; The NJ Poetry Resource Book; Passaic County Coll. Poetry Center Anthology; contrbr. to anthology: The Dreambook, 1981; articles to ND Qtly; book rvws. to Choice, Home Planet News, Small Press Rvw. BA, Seton Hall U, 1961; MA in English, NYU, 1963. Instr. Burgen County Coll., Paramus, NJ, 1973-81, Bloomfield Coll., 1975-82, Drew Univ., Madison, NJ, 1981-82; affairs coordinator, poetry ctr. dir, Passaic County Community Coll., Paterson, 1980—. Steering Comm., Essex Phoenix Mills, Paterson, 1984-85. Recipient NJ State Council grant, 1981-85; Sri Chimnoy award, NYC, 1981, 82, 83, 84; William Carlos William award, 1972, 76. American Book Award, 1986, American Literary Translator's Award, Crosscurrents '87 Award. Mem. PSA, P&W, MLA. Address: 40 Post Ave Hawthorne NJ 07506

GILLETTE, BOB, see Shaw, Bynum Gillette

GILLETTE, ETHEL PERRY, b. Plainfield, NJ; m. John H. Gillette, 1943; children—Susan Lynn (dec.), John III. Contrbr. nursing jnls., mags. including Video Action, Let's Live, Suncoast Mag., Golden Yrs., Sunday Women. Columnist, 1980-83; contrbg. ed. nursing jnls. Assoc. degree St. Pete Jr. Coll., 1975; B.A. magna cum laude, St. Leo's Coll., 1985. Consumer advocate nursing homes, 1978; chairwoman Ombudsman Com., 1979. Recipient Albert Young award for book that best exemplifies the spirit of human giving and optimism, 1987. Fellow, Fine Arts Com., 1978; mem. Am. Nurses Fdn. Century Club. Home: 4409 58th Ave Saint Petersburg FL 33714

GILLETTE, PAUL, b. Carbondale, PA, Oct. 1, 1938; Author: How Did a Nice Girl Like You Get into this Business?, 1963 (made into film), (with Eugene Tillinger) Ku Klux Klan, The Invisible Empire, 1964, paperback issued as Inside the Ku Klux Klan, 1965, An Uncensored History of Pornography, 1965, transl. and ed., Petronius Arbiter, Satyricon: Memoirs of a Lusty Roman, 1965, Psychodynamics of Unconventional Sex Behavior and Unusual Practices, 1966, transl. and ed., The Complete Marquis de Sade, 1966, The Lopinson Case, 1967, Paul Gillette's Ribald Classics, 1968, The Complete Sex Dictionary, 1969, Encyclopedia of Erotica, 1969, Where Do I Come From?, 1969, ed. (with Mrie Hornbeck) The Complete Medical Encyclopedia, 1969, What Every Woman Wants to Know about the Pill, 1969, transl., Pierre Louys, Trois Filles, 1969, ed., The Layman's Explanation of Human Sexual Inadequeacy, 1970, ed, New Facts About the Pill, 1970, The Big Answer Book about Sex, 1970, ed., U.S. Government Directory of Prescription Drugs and Over-the-Counter Drugs, 1971, ed., The Complete Guide to Student Financial Aid, 1971, Cat o' Nine Tails (novel), 1971, Carmela (novel, Pulitzer Prize nom.), 1972, Play Misty for Me (novel; made into film), 1972, The Vasectomy Information Manual, 1972, Vasectomy: The Male Sterilization Operation, 1972, (with Marie Hornbeck) Depression: A Layman's Guide, 1973, (with Robert L. Rowan) Your Prostate Gland, 1973, (with Marie Hornbeck) Psychochemistry, 1974, Superstar (novel), 1974, (with Peter Gillette) Playboy's Book of Wine, 1974, Unusual Sex Behavior and Practices, 1974, Enjoying Wine, 1976, 305 East (novel), 1977, (with Robert L. Rowan) The Gay Health Guide, 1978, The Chinese Godfather (novel), 1980, One of the Crowd (novel), 1980, California Red Wine Book (wine Library, vol. 1), 1984, California White Wine Book (Wine Library, vol. 2), 1984, (with Fred E. Jandt) Win-Win Negotiating: Turning Conflict into Agreement, 1985, Wine Tasting Handbook, 1986. Contrbr. of articles, short stories, humorous essays, and commentaries to most American mags and newspapers, including Newsweek, Sports Illustrated, N.Y. Times Sunday Mag, Esquire, Cosmopolitan, True, Ladies' Home Journal, and Forbes. Founder, The Wine Newsletter, for the trade. Founder, ed., publ, Popular Psychology, 1967—. Adjunct prof., Profl. Wrtg. Program, Univ of Southern Calif., and private workshop. Ph. D., psychology. General assignment reporter and photograoher, Scranton (Pa.) Tribune, 1951-53. Campaign aide to John F. Kennedy, 1960. Writer and editor, 1963—. Radio and television: writer and host, Camera Three, CBS-TV; producer, writer, host, Enjoying Wine with Paul Gillette, PBS. Office: 6515 West Sunset Blvd Los Angeles CA 90028

GILLIAM, ELIZABETH M., b. Kansas City, MO, Mar. 1, 1930; d. Urcil Wilford and Ruth Elizabeth (Williams) Smoot; m. Ronald R. Gilliam, Mar. 28, 1956; children—Ursula M., Alessandra T., Pamela C. Contrbr. poems, cover illustrations to lit mags, anthols. Editor: (poems) South of San Francisco, 1976. Diploma, Kansas City Art Inst. Artist, U.S. Army Engrs., Kansas City, Mo., 1952-53, Rand Corp., Santa Monica, Calif., 1955-56; free-lance artist, poet, 1953-55, 1957—. Active Palos Verdes Art Ctr., 1983—. Mem. Calif. Fedn. Chaparral Poets (pres. Palos Verdes chpt. 1984-86), Intl. Poetry Soc. Home: 208-D S Broadway Redondo Beach CA 90277

GILLIGAN, ROY, b. Covington, KY, Apr. 23, 1923, s. Leo F. and Alice M. (Atzenhofer) G.; m. Jane Gilligan, Jan. 22, 1949; 1 dau., Robin. Author: Chinese Restaurants Never Serve Breakfast (mystery); contrbr. book rvws., articles to San Francisco Chronicle, San Jose Mercury-News, Monterey Peninsula Herald. BA, U. Cin., 1947. Copywrtr. various radio and TV stas., Cin., 1947-56, sta. KSBW-TV, Salinas, Calif., 1956-57; wrtr. San Francisco Chronicle, 1957-63; tchr. James Lick High Schl., San Jose, Calif., 1968—. Served with inf. U.S. Army, 1943-45. Mem. Mensa, ednl. orgns. Home: 5193 Rhonda Dr San Jose CA 95129

GILLILAND, HAP, b. Willard, CO, Aug. 26, 1918; s. Samuel S. and Esther Julia (Sandstedt) Gilliland; m. Erma Louise Rodrieck, Apr. 21, 1946; children—Lori Sargent, Diane Bakun, Dwight. Author of many books including A Practical Guide to Remedial Reading, 1978, Chant of the Red Man, 1976, 13 children's books. 1965-85; editor: many books in Indian Culture Series, Council for Indian Education, 1969—, Montana Journal of Reading, 1964-70; contrbr. to The Reading Teacher, Reading Horizons, Reading Process & Success, Journal—Reading Association of Ireland; wrkg. on A Relevant Education for the Native American (college text). BA, Western State Coll., 1949, MA, 1950; Ed.D. U. of Northern Colorado, 1958. Prof. of Education Eastern Montana Coll. (Billings), 1960-80; reading special. Lake & Peninsula Schools (King Salmon, Alaska), 1980-84; wrtr./ed. Council for Indian Ed. (Billings), 1970—. Cpl. US Air Force, 1941-45, South Pacific. Merit Award for Research and Creative Endeavor, Eastern Montana College, 1977. Home: 517 Rimrock Rd Billings MT 59101

GILMAN, JULIA M., (Maggie Buchanan), b. Logansport, IN, July 21, 1942; d. Franklin Veryl and Ruth Amelia (Davidson) Snoke; m. Ronald K. Gilman, Aug. 16, 1964; children—Tamara S., Marc L. Author: William Wells and Maconaquah, White Rose of the Miamis, 1985. BS in Home Ec. & Biol. Ed., Purdue, 1964; MA in Home Ec., Ball State U., 1970. 4H agent Extension Svc., Milw., 1964-65; subst. tchr., Pitts., 1966-77; tech. writer Dravilis Assocs., Monroeville, PA, 1977; writer Wyoming Living Mag. (OH), 1984-85. Mem. COSMEP. Home: 165 Congress Run Rd Cincinnati OH 45215

GILMAN, RICHARD, b. NYC, Apr. 30, 1925; s. Jacob and Marion Wolinsky) G.; 1 son, Nicholas; m. Lynn Nesbit; children—Priscilla, Claire. Author: The Confusion of Realms, 1970, Common and Uncommon Masks, 1971, The Making of Modern Drama, 1974, Decadence, 1979, Faith, Sex, Mystery: A Memoir, 1987; contrbg. editor: Partisan Rvw, 1972—. BA, U. Wis., 1947; LHD, Grinnell Coll., 1967. Free-lance writer, 1950-54; assoc. editor Jubilee mag., 1954-57; drama critic, lit. editor Commonwealth, 1961-64; assoc. editor, drama critic Newsweek mag., 1964-67; lit. editor New Republic, 1968-70; pres. PEN Am. Center, 1981-83, v.p., 1983—. Served with USMCR, 1943-46. Recipient George Jean Nathan award for drama criticism, 1971; Morton Dauwen Zabel award AAIAL, 1979; fellow N.Y. Inst. for Humanities, 1977-80. Office: Yale Schl Drama New Haven CT 06520

GILMER, MARY ELIZABETH, b. Foster, IN, Mar. 23, 1911; d. Ludwig Rollin and Mary Luella (Siddens) Reiff; m. James Garfield Walden, Apr. 27, 1935 (dec. July 10, 1945); 1 son, Ernest Leroy; m. Ralph Emerson Gilmer, May 14, 1955. Ed., contrbr. inspirational articles: Okla. Ch. Woman, 1973-85. Contrbr. article to mags. A.B., Lincoln Christian Coll., 1956. Missionary, Mexican Bible Seminary, Nogales, AZ, 1951-54, Spanish Printing, Eagle Pass, TX, 1956-59. Pres. Shortgrass Art League, Mangum, OK, 1973-74. Mem. Am. Assn. Retired Persons (publicity and reporter). Home: Box 357 409 N Harden Mangum OK 73554

GILMORE, CLARENCE PERCY, b. Baton Rouge, Feb. 8, 1926; s. Clarence Percy and Clara (Cobb) G.; m. 2d, V. Elaine Gilmore, Oct. 5, 1985; children—Robert Dillard, Patricia Anne. Reporter various radio, TV stas., 1948-56, free-lance mag. writer, 1956—; sci. editor Metromedia TV, 1967-85; editor-in-chief Times Mirror Mags., NYC, 1971—; cons. in field. Student, La. State U., 1942-44, 46-48. Served with USNR, 1944-46. Recipient Claude Bernard sci. journalism award Natl. Soc. Med. Research, 1969; spcl. commendation med. journalism AMA, 1969, 70; Sci. Writing award physics and astronomy Am. Inst. Physics, 1970; Albert Lasker award for med. wrtg., 1969; Natl. Assn. for Advancement of Sci. award, 1980. Mem. NASW. Home: 201 W 70th St New York NY 10023

GILMORE, MICHAEL, b. Port Royal, SC, Dec. 1, 1952; s. Jimmy Grey and Betty Jean (Oliver) G.; m. Kate Pilgrim, Apr. 8, 1974 (div. Aug. 10, 1976); m. Peggy Creelman, Apr. 9, 1979 (div. Aug. 9, 1986); 1 child, Noya Isolda. Author: (books of poetry) Lyrika, 1981, Celtica, 1982; editor Aileron Mag., 1979—; Editor, Aileron Press, Austin, Tex., 1979—. librarian's asst. Humanities Research Ctr., Austin, 1982—. Served with U.S. Army, 1972-74. Home: 1403 Kinney Ave Austin TX 78704

GILROY, WILLIAM GERARD, b. Scranton, PA, June 19, 1954; s. Joseph Richard and Helen Frances (Durkin) G.; m. Janet Noll, Apr. 23, 1983. Ed., The Scranton Jnl, 1980-83, Catholic Golden Age World, 1984—; contrbr. articles to num. nwsprs. & mags. BS, U. Scranton, 1976; MA, Notre Dame, 1979. Mem. Catholic Press Assn. Home: 1306 Marion St Dunmore PA 18509

GILSTAD, JUNE RUSSELL, b. La Jolla, CA, June 6, 1928; d. Earl Wilson and E. Duetta (Esse) Russell; m. Roger L. Gilstad (div.). Author: Thinking and Reading in High School, 1981; ed.: Source Book of Evaluation Techniques for Reading, 3d ed., 1972; co-ed.: Topics in Reading newsletter, 1971, Decisions in Reading newsletter, 1971-72; contrbr. articles to numerous ednl. periodicals. ALA, Univ. of Minn., 1948, BA, Bapt. Missionary Tng. Sch., Chgo., 1950; MDiv, Princeton Theol. Sem., 1956; MS, Ind. U., 1960, PhD in Reading Edn. and Am. History, 1974. Spl. cons. Reading Clinic Devel. Project, Ala. Luth. Coll., Selma, 1977-78; ednl. cons., Kokomo, Ind., 1978—. Home: 5900 Dartmouth Ct Kokomo IN 46901

GINSBERG, ALLEN, b. Newark, June 3, 1926; s. Louis and Naomi (Levy) G. Author: Howl and Other Poems, 1955, Empty Mirror, 1960, Kaddish and Other Poems, 1960, Reality Sandwiches, 1963, Planet News, Poems, 1961-67, 1968, Indian Journals, 1970, The Fall of America: Poems of these States, 1973 (Natl. Book award 1974), The Gates of Wrath: Early Rhymed Poems 1948-51, 1973, Allen Verbatim, 1974, First Blues, 1975, Journals Early 50's Early 60's, 1977, Contest of Bards, 1977, Mind Breaths, Poems 1972-77, 1978, As Ever: Correspondence A.G.

and Neal Cassady 1948-68, 1978, Poems All Over the Place, 1978, Mostly Sitting Haiku, 1978, Composed on the Tongue, Literary Conversations, 1967-77, 1980, Straight Hearts Delight: Love Poems and Selected Letters, 1980, Plutonium Ode, Poems 1977-80, 1982, Collected Poems, 1947-80, 1984, White Shroud Poems 1980-85, 1986, Howl Annotated, 1986. Recordings include Songs of Innocence and of Experience by William Blake Tuned by Allen Ginsberg, 1970, Two Evenings with Allen Ginsberg, 1980, First Blues: Songs, 1982, Birdbrain, 1981, Allen Ginsberg First Blues, 1981. AB, Columbia U., 1948. Dir. Com. on Poetry Fdn., 1971—, Kerouac Schl. Poetics, Naropa Inst., Boulder, Colo. Assoc. with early Beat Generation prose-poets, 1945—; poetry readings, Columbia U., Harvard U., Yale U., numerous other univs. and assembly halls abroad. Guggenheim fellow in poetry, 1965-66; Golden Wreath of Struga Poetry Festival, Yugoslavia, 1986. Mem. AAIAL. Home: Box 582 Stuyvesant Sta New York NY 10009

GINSBURG, CARL S., b. NYC, July 13, 1936; s. Benjamin and Cora (Kling) G.; m. Phyllis Pianin, June 15, 1958; children—John J., Sarah B. Contrbr. articles, poems to mags., lit. mags., jnls. Editor: The Master Moves (Moshe Feldenkrais), 1984. BS, Rensselaer Polytech. Inst., 1957; PhD, Ohio U.-Athens, 1962. Asst. prof. Utica Coll., N.Y., 1962-70; assoc. prof. SUNY, Syracuse, 1970-74. Mem. Feldenkrais Guild (v.p. 1981, pres. 1982-83, chmn. profl. trng. bd. 1985—), Rio Grande Wrtrs. Assn., Assn. Humanistic Psychology. Home: 57 Juniper Hill Ct NE Albuquerque NM 87122

GINZBURG, RALPH, b. Bklyn., Oct. 28, 1929; s. Raymond and Rachel G. (Lipkin) G.; m. Shoshana Brown, Dec. 16, 1958; children—Bonnie, Shepherd, Lark. Author: 100 Years of Lynching, 1961, An Unhurried View of Erotica, 1956, Eros on Trial, 1964, Castrated: My Eight Months in Prison, 1973. BBA, CCNY, 1949; postgrad., Bklyn. Coll., 1950; diploma, Henry George Schl. Econs., 1951. Copyboy N.Y. Daily Compass, 1949-50; rewrite man Washington Times-Herald, 1950-51. Free-lance writer for: mags. including Parade; others, 1951-53; staff writer, NBC, 1954-55; mng. bd.: Look mag, 1955-56; articles editor Esquire, 1956-58; editor: Eros, 1962-63, Fact, 1964-68, Avant-Garde, 1969—, Moneysworth, 1971—, Am. Business, 1976—, EXTRA!, 1977—, Better Living, 1980—, Uncle Sam, 1981—. Served with AUS, 1950-51. Office: 251 W 57th St New York NY 10019

GIOIA, (MICHAEL) DANA, b. Los Angeles, Dec. 24, 1959; s. Michael and Dorothy Grace (Ortez) G.; m. Mary Elizabeth Hiecke, Feb. 23, 1980. Ed. The Ceremony & Other Stories, 1984, Two Prose Sketches, 1984, Daily Horoscope, 1986; co-ed., Poems from Italy, 1986. BA, Stanford U., 1973, MBA, 1977; MA, Harvard U., 1975. Poetry ed. Inquiry Mag., Washington, DC, 1977-83; various positions General Foods Corp., White Plains, NY, 1977-85, Manager of New Business Development, 1985—. One of Esquire's best Am. wrtrs. under 40, 1984. Mem: PEN, Wesleyan Wrtrs. Conf. Home: 22 Hastings Landing Hasting-on-Hudson NY 10706

GIOSEFFI, DANIELA, b. Orange, NJ, Feb. 12, 1941, d. Donato and Josephine (Buzeska) G.; m. Richard J. Kearney, Sept. 7, 1964 (div. Nov. 1984); 1 child, Thea D.; m. Dr. Lionel B. Luttinger, June 6, 1986. Author: Eggs in the Lake, 1977 (satiric novel pub. Eng. and U.S.), The Great American Belly, 1977 (transl. into Serbo-Croatian; made into screenplay), Eggs in the Lake, 1979 (poems), Earth Dancing; Mother Nature's Oldest Rite, 1981; contrbr. to anthols: An Introduction of Lit., Structure and Meaning, Seasons of Women, Living Lit.; Am. Voices, Rising Tides; Contemporary Am. Poets, Contemporaries, The Dream Book; contrbr. criticism, rvws. articles, poems and fiction to numerous publs. in U.S. and fgn. countries. BA in English and Speech, Montclair State Coll., 1963; MFA in Drama, Catholic U. Am., 1966. Profl. stock and repertory actress, 1965-69; poet/cons. N.Y. State Poets-in-Schls., Inc., N.Y.C., 1970-87; prof. speech and communication arts St. Francis Coll., N.Y.C., 1971—. Mem. Writers and Pubs. Alliance for Nuclear Disarmament (exec. bd. 1980—), PEN Am. Ctr., PSA. Office: Earth Celebrations GPO Box 197 Brooklyn Heights NY 11202

GIOVANNI, NIKKI, b. Knoxville, TN, June 7, 1943; d. Jones and Yolande Cornelia (Watson) G.; 1 son, Thomas Watson. Author: Black Feeling, Black Talk, 1968, Black Judgement, 1969, Re- Creation, 1970, Broadside Poem of Angela Yvonne Davis, 1970, Night Comes Softly, 1970, Spin a Soft Black Song, 1971, Gemini, 1971, My House, 1972, A Dialogue: James Baldwin and Nikki Giovanni, 1973, Ego Tripping and Other Poems for Young Readers, 1973, A Poetic Equation: Conversations Between Nikki Giovanni and Margaret Walker, 1974, The Women and the Men, 1975; recordings: Truth Is On Its Way, 1972, Like A Ripple on a Pond, 1973. BA with honors in history, Fisk U., 1967; postgrad., U. Pa. Schl. Fine Arts, 1968; LHD (hon.), Wilberforce U., 1972, Worcester U., 1972, DLitt, Ripon U., 1974, Smith Coll., 1975. Founder pub. firm TomNik Ltd., 1970. Ford Fdn. grantee, 1967. Address: Morrow 105 Madison Ave New York NY 10016

GIOVANNINI, GIOVANNI, see Kleinhans, Theodore John

GIPSON, ANGELA CHRISTINA, b. Phila., Aug. 10, 1954; d. Joseph Michael and Catherine (DiGiambattista) DiAdamo; m. Joe Wayne Gipson, Oct. 13, 1979; stepchildren: Dawn Marie Gipson Norton, Jeffrey Wayne. Contrbr. articles, short stories: Young & Alive, Single Parent, Aztec Peak, Alive! For Young Teens, numerous other publs. BA in Eng. Lit., Lehigh U., 1976; grad. Inst. Children's Lit., 1983. Singer, songwrtr., recording artist, 1980—; reporter, feature wrtr. Youth Today Publs., Flint, Mich., 1985-86; freelance wrtr., 1983—. Home: 816 Tacken St Flint MI 48532

GIPSON, GORDON, b. Caldwell, ID, Oct. 26, 1914; s. James Herrick and Esther (Sterling) G.; m. Tryntje Heeling, Dec. 27, 1961; children—Craig, Amy. Student, Coll. of Idaho, 1933-34. Edit./pub., Caxton, Caldwell, ID, 1935—. Home: 2211 S 10th St Caldwell ID 83605

GIRARD, JAMES PRESTON, b. Tillamook, OR, July 6, 1944; s. Preston Leroy G. and Inez Elizabeth (May) Pierce; m. Barbara Joyce Scott, June 1, 1966; children—Virginia Amanda, Preston John Amos. Author: Changing All Those Changes, 1976; contrbr. poetry and fiction Kans. Qtly, short stories Penthouse, Mag. of Fantasy and Sci Fi, Cottonwood Rvw, New Dimensions. BA, U Kans., 1966; MA, Johns Hopkins, 1967. Instr. Coll. of Emporia, 1967-68; reporter Topeka Daily Capital, 1969-73; ed. Univ. Kans., Lawrence, 1973-76, instr., 1976-78; copy ed. Wichita Eagle-Beacon, 1978-82, systems ed., 1982—. Mem. Kans. Writers Assn., AWP, P&W. Address: 1215 Berry Newton KS 67114

GIRARD, SALLI, see West, Salli Lou

GITLIN, TODD, b. NYC,Jan. 6, 1943. Co-author: Uptown: Poor Whites in Chicago, 1970; author: Busy Being Born, 1974, The Whole World Is Watching: Mass Media in the Making and Unmaking of the New Left, 1980, Inside Prime Time, 1983. The Sixties: Years of Hope, Days of Rage, 1987; ed., Watching Television, 1987. BA, Harvard U., 1963; MA, U. Mich., 1966; PhD, U. Calif.-Berkeley, 1977. Asst. prof. sociology U. Calif.-Berkeley, 1978-83, assoc. prof., 1983—. Recipient Non-Fiction award Bay Area Book Reviewers Assn., 1984. Mem. PEN, NBCC, Am. Sociol. Assn. Office: Dept Sociology Univ Calif Berkeley CA 94720

GITTELSON, NATALIE LEAVY, b. NYC, Jan. 22, 1929; d. Abraham Harris and Celia (Siegel) Leavy; m. Mark R. Gittelson (div.); children—Celia, Eve, Anthony. Author: The Erotic Life of the American Wife, 1970; Dominus: A Woman Looks at Men's Lives, 1978. Formerly editor and/or writer with, Vogue mag., Glamour mag., Seventeen mag., Harper's Bazaar mag.; editor, N.Y. Times Sunday Mag.; now editorial director McCall's mag., NYC. BA, N.Y. U. Home: 1 Lincoln Plz New York NY 10023

GLAEFKE, DEBORAH S., (Deb Baldanza, Olwen Leigh Gray, Leigh Morgan), b. Cleve., Apr. 11, 1956; d. John W. and Angela (Oliver-Perez) Glaefke; m. Lawrence James Baldanza, May 12, 1979; children—Hester Rose, Dylan Halley. Featured poet Metrosphere Lit. Jnl., 1986, 87; contrbr. poetry: Whiskey Island, Black River Rev., othes; poetry in anthologies. Wrkg. on poetry collection, novel. BA, Coll. Wooster, 1978. Corr. The Cleve. Press, 1981-82; founder, dir. Lakewood Freelancers, Ohio, 1982-83; creative writing instr. Westlake Adult Edn., Ohio, 1984-85, Rocky River Adult Edn., Ohio, 1984—; founder, dir. Northcoast Wrtrs.' Group, Lakewood, 1984—; lit. critic Black River Rev., Lorain, Ohio, 1987—, judge poetry contest, 1987—, staff ed., 1987, talk show host for radio program, 1987, assoc. ed., 1988—. Winner 1st prize Akron Area Poetry Soc., 1983, Iconoclast Poetry Competition, Reynoldsburg, Ohio, 1987; recipient numerous other writing awards. Mem. AAP, Black River Poets, Lorain Freelancers, other orgns. Home: 1436 Elmwood Ave Lakewood OH 44107

GLANCY, DIANE, b. March 18, 1941, Kansas City, MO; d. Lewis Hershel and Edith (Wood) Hall; m. Dwane Glancy, May 2, 1964 (div. March 31, 1983); children—David, Jennifer. Author: Traveling On, What Do People Do West of the Mississippi, Drystalks of the Moon, The Woolslayer, Amiel Haymaker, Brown Wolf Leaves the Reservation (poems), 1984; biography in Two Dresses, 1986; contrbr. lit mags, poems and short stories, including Prairie Schooner, Florida Rvw, Black Ice, En Passant, Snowy Egret. BA, Univ. of Missouri, 1959-64; MA, Central State Univ., 1983. Wrtr.-in-Res., Heller Theater (Tulsa), 1983—; Poet-in-Schls., Arts and Hum. Council Tulsa, 1981—; Artist-in-Res., Oklahoma, 1984—, Arkansas, 1985—. Mem. PSA, Poetry Soc. Oklahoma, Natl. Fed. of State Poetry Socs. Laureate of Five Civilized Tribes, 1984-86. Home: 1508 S Elwood Tulsa OK 74119

GLANG, GABRIELE, b. Arlington, VA, July 18, 1959; d. Reinhard and Heidi (Friedrich) Glang; m. John Christopher Doyle, July 18, 1983. Author: Roundelay, 1981. Contrbr. poems to anthols. BA, George Mason U., 1979; Cert. in Pubs. Specialist Program, George Washington

U., 1981. Editorial asst. Natl. Jogging Assn., Washington, DC, 1979-80; copy ed. Am. Chem. Assn., Washington, 1980-82; free-lance ed., designer, wrtr., Washington, and Dublin, Ireland, 1982-83; ed. Natl. Telephone Coop. Assn., Washington, 1983-84, D.C. Budget Office, Washington, 1984-85; dir. pubs. Am. Assn. Dental Schls., Washington, 1985—. Recipient Antonio J. Waring Jr. Meml. prize Poetry Soc. of Ga., 1978. Finalist, Nat'l Soc Arts and Letters John Ciardi Meml. Prize, 1987. Home: 3900 Conn Ave NW 304F Washington DC 20008

GLANN,, ELIZABETH JANE,, b. Des Moines, May 26, 1934; d. Harry H. and Jane (Ramsay) Dilley; m. Kenneth Warren Glann, July 18, 1956; children—Sheryl, Shawn, Brent, Bradley. Contrbr.: Wee Wisdom, Turtle, Children's Playmate, Humpty Dumpty, Child Life, Jack & Jill, other children's publs. AA, William Woods Coll., 1954; BS, Drake U., 1956. Tchr. elem. and pre-schs., Colo., 1956-58, 72-78; curriculum wrtr. R-1 Schls., Lakewood, Colo., 1973-78; librarian Arvada Public Library, Colo., 1978—. Mem. Soc. Children's Book Wrtrs., NWC. Home: 6571 Marshall St Arvada CO 80003

GLASER, ISABEL JOSHLIN, b. Birmingham, AL, June 7, 1929, d. Notreab and Ethel Kathleen (Sigler) Joshlin; m. Melvin W. Glaser, Nov. 7, 1954 (dec. 1966); children—Susan Elaine, Stephen Philip. Author: Old Visions . . . New Dreams, 1977. Represented in anthols: More Surprises, 1987, Dinosaurs, 1987, Good Books, Good Times, 1988, Bear in Mind, 1988; contrbr.: Wind Lit. Jnl, Old Hickory Rvw, Child Life, Humpty Dumpty's Mag., numerous others. Student Randolph-Macon Coll., 1947-49; BA, George Peabody Coll., Nashville, 1951; post-grad. Baldwin Wallace Coll., Memphis State U., Kent State U., Ohio U. Tchr. pub. schls. Tenn., 1951-53, Cleve., 1953-66, Memphis, 1978—. Mem. Nat. League Am. PEN Women (letters chmn. Chickasaw br.), Poetry Soc. TN (dir). Home: 5383 Mason Rd Memphis TN 38119

GLASER, MICHAEL S., b. Chgo., Mar. 20, 1943, s. Milton A. and Rona (Schmidt) G.; m. Kathleen Webbert, May 8, 1976; children—Brian, Joshua, Daniel, Amira, Eva. Contrbr. poetry, stories to Christian Sci. Monitor, Milkweed Chronicle, The Smith, other jnls; represented in 1981 and 1987 Anthology of Magazine Verse, others, ed. The Cooke Book: A Seasoning of Poets (anthol), 1987. BA, Denison U., Granville, Ohio, 1965; PhD,Kent (Ohio) State U., 1971. Mem. faculty St. Mary's Coll. Md., 1970—, prof., 1982—, co-dir. Annl. Festival Poets and Poetry. Danforth Fdn. assoc., Maryland Poets-in-the Schools poet in res, 1987—. 1980-85. Mem. AWP, Wrtr.'s Center, Inst. Human Excellence. Home: Box 1 Saint Mary's City MD 20686

GLASS, AMANDA, see Leaf, Mindy Glass

GLASER, WILLIAM A(RNOLD), b. NYC, Dec. 4, 1925; s. Lewis and Evelyn (Wiener) G.; m. Mary Todd Daniels, 1958; m. Gilberte Vansintejan, 1981; children: James Todd, Andrew Rollins, Gillian Elisabeth. Author: Three Papers on the Intgrated Bar, 1960, Public Opinion and Congressional Eletions, 1962, The Government of Associations, 1966, An International Survey of Sheltered Employment, 1966, Pretrial Discovery and the Adversary System, 1968, Social Settings and Medical Organization, 1970, Paying the Doctor, 1970, The Brain Drain, 1978, Health Insurance Bargaining, 1978, Paying the Hospital, 1987. BA, N.Y. Univ., 1948; MA, Harvard Univ, 1949, Ph. D., 1952. Instr, Mich. State Univ. of Agriculture and Applied Sciene (now Mich. State Univ), East Lansing, Mich., 1952-55, asst prof of soc sci, 1955-56; research asst, Columbia Univ, NYC, 1956-58, sen. research assoc in sociology and pol. sci, 1958-82; prof of health services administration, New School for Social Research, Grad. Schl of Management, NYC., 1982—. Cons to the U.S. govt and to various health and rehabilitation orgns. Mem: Intl Fedn of Voluntary Health Services Funds, Intl Pol Sci Assn, Soc. for Intl. Development, Intl. Studies Assn, American Sociological Assn, American Poli Sci Assn, American Public Health Assn. Military service: U.S. Army Med Corps, 1944-46; became staff sergeant. Home: 54 Morningside Dr New York, NY 10025

GLASSER, PERRY, b. Bklyn., July 7, 1948. Author: Suspicious Origins, 1983, Singing on the Titanic, 1987; contrbr. short fiction to N.Am. Rvw, MS., Twilight Zone Mag., TriQtly, numerous other lit mags; contrbr. rvws. to N.Y. Times Book Rvw, N.Am. Rvw, others. BA, Bklyn. Coll., 1969; MFA, U. Ariz., 1982. Tchr. NYC Public Schls., 1969-79; asst. prof. Drake U., Des Moines, 1982-85, Bradford (Mass.) Coll., 1985—. Grantee Iowa Council on Arts, 1984; Pushcart Prize, 1984, PEN Syndication Fiction award, 1985, 86. Office: Bradford Coll Bradford MA 01830

GLEASNER, DIANA COTTLE, b. New Brunswick, NJ, Apr. 26, 1936; d. Delmer LeRoy and Elizabeth (Stanton) Cottle; m. G. William Gleasner, July 12, 1958; children: Stephen William, Suzanne Lynn. Author: The Plaid Mouse, 1966; Pete Polar Bear's Trip down the Erie Canal, 1970; Women in Swimming, 1975; Women in Track and Field, 1977; Hawaiian Gardens, 1978; Kauai Traveler's Guide, 1978; Oahu Traveler's Guide, 1978; Big Island Traveler's Guide, 1978; Maui Traveler's Guide, 1978; Break Through: Women in Writing, 1980; Sea Islands of the South, 1980; Rock Climbing, 1980; Callaway Gardens, 1981; Inventions that Changed our Lives: Dynamite, 1982; Charlotte: A Touch of Gold, 1983; Breakthrough: Women in Science, 1983; Inventions that Changed our Lives: The Movies, 1983; Windsurfing, 1985; Florida off the Beaten Path, 1986, Lake Norman, Our Inland Sea, 1986. BA, Ohio Wesleyan U., 1958; MA, SUNY-Buffalo, 1965. Free-lance wrtr. Mem. ASJA, SATW, OWAA, Women in Communications. Home: 132 Holly Ct Denver NC 28037

GLEE, GLENNA, see Jenkins, Glenna Glee

GLEN, EMILIE, b. Fredonia, NY, Mar. 13, 1937, d. Willard Alonson and Carolyn (Johnson) G.; m. Charles Reuben Dash, Nov. 25, 1952; children—Glenda Leigh, John Charles. Author poetry bks., chapbooks: Roast Swan, Dark of Earth, A Hero Somewhat, 77 Barrow Street, Up to us Chickens, Twat Shot, Late to the Kitchen; contrbr. poetry to New Directions, New Voices, Poems from the Hills, other anthols; contrbr. poetry to Antaeus, Confrontation, Taurus, Blue Unicorn, numerous lit mags in U.S., France, Eng., Can., Switzerland, Germany, Italy, Sweden, India. Edn., Columbia U., Juilliard Schl. Music. Past mem. editorial staff New Yorker. Recipient Stephen Vincent Benet award, medal for excellence in poetry, Third World Congress Poets. Mem. PSA, United Poets Laureate Intl. Home: 77 Barrow St New York NY 10014

GLENN, NANCY NOYES, b. Boston, Oct. 6, 1953; d. Donald Partelow and Edith Jane (Colegrove) Noyes; m. Ronald Christopher Russo, July 3, 1975 (div. 1982); 1 son, Christopher Todd; m. 2d, John Arthur Glenn, June 12, 1983; 1 son, Gregory John. Contrbr.: Little, Brown Book of Anecdotes, 1987. Wrkg. on children's fiction, adult suspense story, Student Garlan Jr. Coll., 1971-72. Tech. publs. asst. Environ. Research and Technology, Lexington, Mass., 1973-74; asst. ed. Redeeming Features ch. newsletter, 1985-87, ed., 1987—; freelance researcher, wrtr. Based on Fact, Lexington, 1987—. Home: 5 Essex St Lexington MA 02173

GLENN, PEGGY, b. Haverhill, MA, July 12, 1944; d. Joseph Flinn and Mildred (Leary) Mooradian; m. James Allison, Apr. 12, 1963 (div. 1969); children—Jane Marie, Michael James; m. Gary A. Glenn, Sept. 27, 1975. Author: How to Start and Run a Successful Home Typing Business, 1980, Word Processing Profits at Home, 1983, Kerosene Heaters: A Consumer's Review, 1984, Publicity for Books and Authors, 1984; (with Gary A. Glenn) Don't Get Burned!, 1982. Grad. public schls., Haverhill. Owner, Aames-Allen Pub., Huntington Beach, CA, 1980—. Mem. Southern Calif. Public Fire Edn. Assn. (staff wrtr. 1982—), Pubs. Marketing Assn. (founder 1983—, chmn. member services com.). Home: 1106 Main St Huntington Beach CA 92648

GLIMM, ADELE, b. NYC, Aug. 27, 1937, d. Sidney and Belle (Sobel) Strauss; m. James Gilbert Glimm, June 30, 1957; 1 dau., Alison Glimm Pearson. Novelist: Richard's Wife, 1968; contrbr. short stories to Redbook, Cosmopolitan, Aphra, Epoch, other mags and lit jnls; short stories reprinted in Gt. Britain, Australia, S. Africa, Norway, Netherlands, Germany, Denmark. AB, Barnard Coll., 1958; AM, Columbia U., 1962. Asst. ed. Harvard U., Cambridge, Mass., 1961-63; sr. wrtr. Rockwell & Newell Public Relations, NYC,1982—; instr. Ed.'s Desk Wrtrs. Conf., Mays Landing, N.J., 1984—; freelance wrtr., 1963—. Mem. Wrtrs. Community. Home: 530 E 72d St New York NY 10021

GLIXON, DAVID M(ORRIS), b. Bklyn., Sept. 23, 1908; s. Montague and Bertha Helen (Simons) G.; m. Helen Bertha Marx, Feb. 5, 1938; children—Jonathan E., Judith Glixon Kutt. Author: The Bird Watchers Guyed, 1986; co-author: Allusions, 2d ed., 1986. Editor Book Prodn. Mag., 1934-43; with various pubs., NYC, 1945-47; mgr. Story Classics, Emmaus, Pa., 1948-53; asst. editor, asst. art dir., Ltd. Editions Club and Heritage Club, NYC, 1954-58, editor, art dir., 1958-76; editor Lit. I.Q., reference book reviewer Saturday Rvw, 1962-72; editor Tchrs. Quiz, Lit. Cavalcade, Scholastic Mags., 1973-82; book reviewer Hartford Courant, 1981—; wrtr. Heritage Club, Easton Press, Norwalk, Conn., 1977—, Ltd. Editions Club, NYC, 1979-85, Lawrence Urdang, Inc., 1982—. Translator: La Fontaine's Adonis, 1954, Hugo's The Sea and the Wind, 1961. Chmn. Trade Book Clinic, Am. Inst. Graphic Arts, 1941. BA magna cum laude, Washington Sq. Coll., NYU, 1934. Home: 108 Montclair Dr West Hartford CT 06107

GLOVER, LYNDIA RUTH, b. Frederick, OK, Oct. 11, 1945; d. Walter Edward and Celia Moline (Snow) Haldaman; m. John William Glover, Nov. 24, 1970; 1 dau., Stephanie Gale. Contrbr. poems to numerous anthols., lit. mags. Diploma in Cosmetology, Peggy's Beauty Coll., (year graduated please?) 19 . Secy. Natl. Life an Accident, Oklahoma City, OK, 1965-67; cosmetologist, Jerry's Coiffures, Oklahoma City, 1967-70. Mem. North Shore Women Wrtr.'s Alliance, Oreg. State Poetry Assn., Bensalem Assn. Women Wrtrs., Poet's Study Club. Home: 2631

Spencer Ln Choctaw OK 73020

GLUCK, LOUISE ELISABETH, bNYC, Apr. 22, 1943; d. Daniel and Beatrice (Grosby) G.; m. Charles Hertz (div.); 1 son, Noah Benjamin; m. John Dranow, 1977. Author: Firstborn, 1968, The House On Marshland, 1975, Descending Figure, 1980, The Triumph of Achilles, 1985. Student, Sarah Lawrence Coll., 1962, Columbia U., 1963-65. Vis. poet Goddard Coll., U. N.C., U. Va.; vis. poet U. Iowa; Scott prof. poetry Williams Coll., 1983; vis. prof. UCLA, 1985, 86, 87. Rockefeller Fdn. grantee; NEA grantee, 1979-80; Guggenheim Fdn. grantee. Recipient AAIAL, Award in Lit., 1981; Natl. Bk. Critics' Circle Award, 1985; Melville Cane Award, PSA, 1986; Sara Teasdale Meml. Prize, Wellesley Coll., 1986. Address: Creamery Rd Plainfield VT 05667

GLUCKSON, JAMES ANDREW, b. White Plains, NY, April 6, 1956; s. Herbert Julian Robert and Dorothy Irene (Sosinsky) Gluckson. BA, Skidmore College, 1978. Correspondent, Track and Field News, 1983; contributing editor, NY Running News, 1983—. Mem. NY Track Writers Assoc. Address: New York Running News 9 E 89th St NYC 10028

GOBLE, PAUL, b. Haslemere, Eng., Sept. 27, 1933; s. Robert John and Elizabeth Marian (Brown) G.; m. Janet A. Tiller, June 2, 1978; 1 son, Robert George; children by previous marriage: Richard, Julia. Author, illustrator numerous children's books including: The Fetterman Fight, 1972, Custer's Last Battle, 1969, Lone Bull's Horse Raid, 1973, The Friendly Wolf, 1974, The Girl Who Loved Wild Horses, 1978 (Caldecott medal), The Gift of the Sacred Dog, 1980, Star Boy, 1983, Buffalo Woman (ALA Notable Children's Bk.), 1984, The Great Race, 1985, Death of the Iron Horse, 1986. Diploma in Design with distinction, Central Schl. Art and Design, London, 1959. Fellow Royal Soc. Arts, Soc. Indsl. Artists and Designers. Address: Nemo Route 1749 Deadwood SD 57732

GOCEK, MATILDA ARKENSOUT, b. Hoboken, NJ, Feb. 18, 1923; m. John A. Gocek, Nov. 18, 1956; children: Ruth Ann, Dianne Karen, John Jacob. Author: Library Service for Commuting Students: A 4-County Study, 1974, Tuxedo Park Library: Social Aspects of Growth 1900-1941, 1978, Benedict Arnold: Readers Guide and Bibliography, 1980, Orange County, N.Y. Readers Guide and Bibliography, 1981, Love Is a Challenge: A Philosophy, 1982. BA, SUNY-New Paltz, 1963; MLS, SUNY-Albany, 1967; PhD (hon.), Colo. State Chr. Coll., 1973. Dir. Monroe Free Library, N.Y., 1958-62, Tuxedo Park Library, N.Y., 1963-77, Suffern Free Library, N.Y., 1977—; pres. Library Research Assocs. Inc., Monroe, 1984—. Columnist, Times Herald Record, Middletown, N.Y., 1977-80; historian Town of Tuxedo, N.Y., 1974-77; pres. Mus. Village Orange County, Monroe, 1980-83. Recipient Poetry Award of Yr., Idiom, 1965. Mem. Living History Assn., Pub. Librarians of N.Y. State. Club: Woman's (Suffern). Office: RD 5 Box 41 Monroe NY 10950

GODBOUT, PAMELA SUE, b. Chgo., Nov. 12, 1948; d. Robert S. Benjamin and Margaret Frances (Gurganus) Benjamin Scaglione; m. Charles Norman Godbout, Oct. 5, 1968; children—Heather, Christopher. Mng. ed. Loquitur lit. mag., Coll. St. Francis, Joliet, Ill., 1987, columnist coll. newspaper, 1987. BA, Coll. St. Francis, 1987. Home: 4145 Poplar Ave Richton Park IL 60471

GODIN, H. RICHARD, b. Stratford, CT, Jan. 10, 1931; s. Joseph E. and Augusta C. (Bertram) G.; m. Norma C. Holvik, May 1, 1965; children—Scott R., Jon C. BA, Syracuse U., 1953; postgrad. U. Minn., 1956. Mgr. direct mail Brown & Bigelow, St. Paul, 1957-61; mgr. editorial services Airco, NYC, 1961-69; dir. communications Union Pacific Corp., NYC, 1969-79; v.p. Dudley-Anderson, NYC, 1979-80; v.p., mgr. acct. group Keyes Martin, Springfield, N.J., 1981—. Mem. Landmark Commn., Hanover Twp., N.J., 1984—. Recipient Photography award Bausch & Lomb, 1957; fellow U. Minn., 1956. Mem. Nat. Investor Relations Inst., Sigma Delta Chi. Office: Keyes Martin 841 Mt. Ave Springfield NJ 07081

GODWIN, GAIL KATHLEEN, b. Birmingham, AL, June 18, 1937; d. Mose Winston and Kathleen (Krahenbuhl) G. Author: novels including The Perfectionists, 1970, Glass People, 1972, The Odd Woman, 1974, Violet Clay, 1978, A Mother and Two Daughters, 1982, The Finishing School, 1985, A Southern Family, 1987; short stories Dream Children, 1976, Mr. Bedford and The Muses, 1983; (with Robert Starer) librettos The Last Lover, 1975, Apollonia, 1979, Anna Margarita's Will, 1981, Remembering Felix, 1987. Student, Peace Jr. Coll., Raleigh, N.C., 1955-57; B.A. in Journalism, U. N.C., 1959; M.A. in English, U. Iowa, 1968, Ph.D., 1971. News reporter Miami Herald, 1959-60; rep., cons. U.S. Travel Service, London, 1961-65ðitorial asst. Saturday Evening Post, 1966; lectr. Iowa Writers Workshop, 1972-73, Vassar Coll., 1977, Columbia U. Writing Program, 1978-81. Fellow Center for Advanced Study, U. Ill., Urbana, 1971-72; Nat. Endowment Arts grantee, 1974-75; Guggenheim fellow, 1975-76; recipient award in lit. Am. Acad. and Inst. of Arts and Letters, 1981. Mem. Pen, AG, AL, Natl. Bk. Critics Circle, ASCAP. Home: Box 946 Woodstock NY 12498

GOEDICKE, PATRICIA, b. Boston, MA, June 21, 1931; d. John Bernard and Helen Victoria (Mulvey) McKenna; m. Victor Goedicke, 1956 (div. 1968); m. Leonard Wallace Robinson, June 3, 1971. Author: Between Oceans, 1968, For the Four Corners, 1976, The Trail That Turns on Itself, 1978, The Dog That Was Barking Yesterday, 1980, Crossing the Same River, 1980, The King of Childhood, 1984, The Wind of Our Going, 1985, Listen, Love, 1986; poems and articles in The New Yorker, Harper's, New Letters, The Nation, and many others. BA, Middlebury College, 1953; MA, Ohio U., 1965. Lectr. Hunter College, NYC,1969-71; assoc. prof., Instituto Allende, Mexico, 1972-79; guest faculty, poetry, Sarah Lawrence Coll., 1980-81; assoc. prof., U. of Montana, Missoula, 1983—. Mem. AAP, AWP, PEN, PSA. Home: 310 McLeod Missoula MT 59812

GOENNER, JUDITH MARY, b. St. Paul, July 28, 1948; d. Roy John and Rita Catherine (Zawacki) Bielejeski; m. Bruce Gilbert Goenner, Aug. 2, 1968; children—Jessica, Molly. Contrbr. nonfiction to Escape mag., BusinessWoman, author bi-wkly. column "It's A Woman's World," Minnesota Direct Mailer. AA in Nursing, St. Mary's Jr. Coll. RN, St. Cloud (MN) Hosp., 1968-79; personnel admin. Woodcraft, St. Cloud, 1979-82; mkt. rep. Central MN Group Health Plan, St. Cloud, 1982—. Mem. Central MN Writers' Wkshp. Home: 1620 9th Ave SE St Cloud MN 56301

GOETZ, JOHN BULLOCK, b. Natchez, MS, July 8, 1920; s. Charles Clifton and Katie G. (Meath) G.; m. Lorette Graves McClatchy, Feb. 17, 1945 (div. May 1980); children—Charles, Christopher, Karen, Stephen. Reporter Mobile (Ala.) Press-Register, 1941-42; prodn. editor Henry Holt & Co., NYC, 1946-48; book designer Am. Book Co., NYC, 1948-49; mgr. design and prodn. U. Calif. Press, 1950-58; mgr. design and prodn. U. Chgo. Press, 1958-62, asst. dir., 1963-65; mng. editor Am. Dental Assn., Chgo., 1966-84; pres. Design & Prodn. Svcs. Co., Chgo., 1984—. Lectr. publ. design U. Chgo. Downtown Center, 1959-60; lectr. dental editors seminar Ohio State U., 1967-73, Mich. State U., 1974-81. AB, Spring Hill (Ala.) Coll., 1941; postgrad., Pratt Inst., 1946-48. Served to lt. USNR, 1942-46; PTO. Decorated Bronze Star; recipient Bronze medal for book design Leipzig (Germany) Book Fair, 1963; Gold medal for book design Sao Paulo (Brazil) Biennial, 1964; Distinguished Service award for journalism Am. Coll. Dentists, 1974; Disting. Service award Am. Assn. Dental Editors, 1978; Disting. Service award Intl. Coll. of Dentists, 1984. Mem. Am. Inst. Graphic Arts, Chgo. Book Clinic (pres. 1965). Home: 33 E Cedar St Chicago IL 60611

GOETZ, MAXWELL, see Maxwell, Alice S.

GOGISGI, see Arnett, Carroll,

GOGOL, JOHN MICHAEL, b. Westfield, MA, Aug. 15, 1938; s. Michael and Jennie (Petros) Gogol. Contrbr. to American Indian Basketry and Other native Arts Mag., Revue Des Langues Vivantes, Germano-Slavica, Malahat Rvw, Qtly Rvw of Literature; book of poems: Native American Words, 1973. BA, Clark U., 1960; MA, U. of Washington, 1965, ABD, 1970. Asst. prof. Pacific U. (Forest Gove, OR), 1970-74, ed. & publ. Mr. Cogito, 1973-86; pub. American Indian Basketry and Other Native Arts Mag., 1979-85. Fulbright Fellow U. of Heidelberg and Munich, 1965-66. Mem. CCLM, Oregon Historical Soc., Inst. for Study of Traditional American Indian Arts. Office: Am Indian Basketry Box 66124 Portland OR 97266

GOJMERAC-LEINER, GEORGIA, b. Croatia, Yugoslavia, July 5, 1949, came to U.S., 1965, d. Ivan and Ljubica (Crnic) Gojmerac; m. Craig T. Leiner, July 26, ,75 children—Gabriel, Tobias. Author: A House in Pravutina (poetry), 1984; contrbr. to Visions, Poet Lore, Va. Qtly Rvw, Whose Woods These Are; co-ed.: The Year of Dog anthology, 1972. MA in English, U. Va., 1980. Grantee Mid-Atlantic States Arts Consortium P&W, Fairfax, Va., 1984; recipient Reading prize Folger Shakespeare Library, Washington, 1985. Home: 46 Mansfield Ave Essex Junction VT 05452

GOLD, DORIS BAUMAN, b. NYC, Nov. 21, 1919, d. Saul and Gertrude (Reiss) Bauman; m. Bernard G. Gold, Oct. 1953; children—Albert, Michael. Author: Stories for Jewish Juniors, 1967, Honey in the Lion (poetry), 1979, Opposition to Volunteerism (annotated bibliography), 1979, Yesterday and Today: An American Jewish Teen Life (Japan), 1985; essay in Woman in Sexist Society, 1971; ed. Young Judaean Mag., NYC, 1963-72; sr. ed. Pharaohs of the Seas vol. IX (Jacques Cousteau), 1976. Editor/publisher Biblio Press, 1979—. BA, Bklyn. Coll., 1946; MA, Washington U., 1955. Public relations assoc. Associated YM-YWHAs of N.Y., NYC, 1978-83; researcher Gale Research Co., NYC, 1978-83; public relations wrtr. Paul Kresh Communications, NYC, 1983-85; free-lance wrtr./ed. Grantee N.Y. State Council on Arts, 1969-71. Mem. Assn. Jewish Book Pubs. Office: Biblio

Press PO Box 22 Fresh Meadows NY 11365

GOLD, HERBERT, b. Cleve., Mar. 9, 1924; s. Samuel and Frieda (Frankel) G.; m. Edith Zubrin, Apr. 1, 1948 (div. 1956); children: Ann, Judy; m. Melissa Dilworth, Jan. 26, 1968 (div. 1975); children: Nina, Ari, Ethan. Author: novels Birth of a Hero, 1951, The Prospect Before Us, 1954, The Man Who Was Not With It, 1956, The Optimist, 1958, Therefore Be Bold, 1961, Salt, 1963, Fathers, 1967, The Great American Jackpot, 1970, Swiftie the Magician, 1974, Waiting for Cordelia, 1977, Slave Trade, 1978, He/She, 1980, Family, 1981, True Love, 1982; short stories Love and Like, 1960, The Magic Will, 1971; essays The Age of Happy Problems, 1962, My Last Two Thousand Years, 1973, A Walk on the West Side: California on the Brink, 1981. BA, Columbia, 1948, MA, 1949; postgrad., U. Paris, France, 1949-51. Recipient award for best novel Commonwealth Club, 1982; Fulbright fellow, 1950-51; Hudson Rvw fellow, 1956; Guggenheim fellow, 1957; Ford Fdn. grantee, 1960, award Am. Inst. Arts and Letters, 1957; Longview award, 1959. Address: 1051-A Broadway San Francisco CA 94133

GOLD, IVAN, b. NYC, May 12, 1932, s. Murray Arthur and Syd (Hartman) G.; m. Vera Cochran, Oct. 22, 1968; 1 child, Ian Matthew. Author: (stories) Nickel Miseries, 1963, (novel) Sick Friends, 1969; contrbr. to New World Writing, Esquire, Noble Savage, Playboy, Genesis West, Woodstock Times, Boston Globe, Boston Review, N.Y. Times Book Rvw, Village Voice, The Nation, Harper's, Commonweal, Newsday, others; represented in numerous anthologies including Sex Roles in Lit., Myth of Am. Manhood, Travelers, The Shape of Fiction, Open and Closed, 50 Years of Am. Short Story, The World of Modern Fiction, Breakthrough, Best Am. Short Stories, Prize Stories, O. Henry Awards. BA, Columbia U., 1953; MA, U. London, 1959. Instr. writing Boston U., 1974-88, staff writer, 1977-79; instr. writing MIT, 1980, Holy Cross Coll., 1982-86; vis. wrtr. U. Mass., Boston, 1986-87. Guggenheim fellow, 1963; recipient Natl. Inst. Arts and Letters, Rosenthal Fdn. award, 1964; grantee Ingram-Merrill Fdn., 1964, NEA, 1966, N.Y. State Council on Arts, 1972. Served with U.S. Army, 1953-55. Mem. PEN, AL, AG, AWP. Home: 96 Bay State Rd Boston MA 02215

GOLD, JOE, b. Gary, IN, June 5, 1950; s. Lea Gold; m. Phyllis Susan Levin, Jan. 2, 1972; children—Russell Morris, Rebecca Emily. Contrbr. features to Arizona Daily Star, Phila. Evening Bulltn. B.A. in Jnlsm., U. Ariz., 1972. Creative dir. Trustman Advt., Tucson, 1973-77; dir. production Perlin Advt., Tucson, 1977-79; pres. Gold Images Inc., Tucson, 1979-84; instr. advt./marketing Pima Commu. Coll., Tucson, 1980—. Chmn. Ariz. Center for Experiments in Television, Tucson, 1976; bd. dirs. Commun. Orgn. for Drug Abuse Control, Tucson, 1981-84; dir. production Neighbors for Safe & Efficient Transportation, Tucson, 1986. Recipient 1st prize for series writing Ariz. Press Club, 1973. Assoc. mem. SFWA. Home: 2818 Calle Glorietta Tucson AZ 85716

GOLD, PATRICIA MC MANUS, b. Raleigh, NC, Aug. 7, 1934, d. Jehu deWitt and Grayce (Caudell) Paulson; m. Jason McManus, 1959 (div. 1964); 1 son, J. Alan; m. 2d, Fritz Gold, May 14, 1985. Contrbr. articles to: New York, Parade, Christian Sci. Monitor, Savvy, others. BA, U. N.C., 1956. Reporter Womens Wear Daily, NYC, 1965-68; pub. relations account exec. Bass & Co., NYC, 1969-70, Allied Chem. Corp., NYC, 1970-72, R.S. Taplinger Co., NYC, 1972-74. Home: 233 E 69th St New York NY 10021

GOLD, SEYMOUR MA(URRAY), b. Detroit, Oct. 20, 1933; s. Max and Betty (Smith) G.; m. Susan Williams, Sept. 2, 1962 (div. 1981); children: Daniel, David, Robert. Author: Urban Recreation Planning, 1973, Urban Planning and Leisure Service, 1974, Recreation Planning and Design, 1980, Impat of Fees and Charges on Urban Recreational Facilities, 1980. Ed, Man and the Environment Information Guide series. Contrbr: Richard Harris, ed, Planning and Design of the Recreation Environment, 1970, and Leisure, Society and Politics, 1972, William B. Stapp, ed, Environment and the Citizen, 1973, Robert McNally, ed, Biology: An Uncommon Introduction, 1974, Frank S. So, Israel Stollman and Frank Beal, eds, The Practice of Local Government Planning, 1979, Special Report on Human Services, 1981, James A Fawcett, Andres T. Manus, and Jens C. Sornesen, eds, Recreation Acess to the Coastal Zone, 1981, Thomas L. Goodale and Peter H. Witt, eds, Recreation and Leisure: Issues in an Era of Change, 1985, Clayne R. Jensen and Clark T. Thorstenson, eds, Issues in Outdoor Recreation, 1986. Coauthor of city planning reports; contrbr of articles to prfl jnls; rvwr, Jnl of the American Planning Assn, 1971-84, Jnl of Leisure Research, 1972-81, Jnl of Leisure Sci, 1977-81, Parks and Recreation. Assoc ed, Jnl of Leisure Research, 1974-77, and Jnl of Leisure Research and Management, 1981-85. Mem editorial bd, Intl Jnl of Environmental Studies, 1971-83, Jnl of the American Inst of Planners, 1972-76, Jnl of Leisure Studies, 1983-85, Society and Leisure Jnl, and Calif. Parks and Recreation. BS, Mich. State Univ., 1957, MS, 1958; M.U.P., Wayne State Univ., Detroit, 1962; Ph. D., Univ. of Mich., 1969. Landscape asst, Parks Dept, Detroit, Mich, 1951-53, jr city planner, City Planning Commn, Detrot, 1959-60, intermed. city planner, 1960-63; senior planner, Vilican—Leman & Assocs, Southfield, Mich., 1963-64; state recreation planner, Ill. Dept. Of Conservation, Springfield, 1964-66; principal planner, City Planning Dept., Ann Arbor, Mich., 1966-67; assoc prof of environmental planning, Univ. of Calif., Davis, 1969-79, prof of environmental planning, 1980—. Research assoc., School of Natural Resources, Univ of Mich., 1967-68; fellow, Natl Acd of Leisure Scis, 1980. Editorial consultant, William Kaufman, Inc. Publishers, 1972-76, and McGraw-HIll, 1977-81. U.S. Army Signal Corps, post landsape officer, 1958-59, active duty, 1959-60; reserve, 1960-66; became captain. Home: 2422 Bucklebury Rd., Davis, CA 95616

GOLDBERG, ALAN (HOWARD), b. Chgo., Apr. 4, 1942, s. Joseph and Frances Dunn (Hornstein) G. Author: Solar Flames, being the first radius of the Poem, 1984. BBA, U. Ga., 1963; LLB, U. Va., 1966. Atty., Washington, 1969-72; researcher in Jungian psychology, San Francisco, 1973-81; pub. Red Leopard Press, Berkeley, Calif., 1983—. Home: 1602 Lincoln St Berkeley CA 94703

GOLDBERG, BARBARA JUNE, b. Wilmington, DE, Apr. 26, 1943; d. Eric Heymann and Emily (Briess) Glauber; m. J. Peter Kiers, June 7, 1963 (div. Jan. 1971); m. Charles Ellis Goldberg, May 11, 1972; children—Benjamin, Jesse. Author: Berta Broadfoot and Pepin the Short: A Merovingian Romance, 1986. Contrbr. poetry to Chronicle of Higher Edn., Ohio Jnl., Washington Rvw., others. B.A., Mt. Holyoke Coll., 1963; M.Edn., Columbia U., 1971; M.F.A., Am. U., 1985. Wrtr., researcher CBS News, NYC, 1965-69; adj. prof. Am. U., Washington, 1982—; workshop leader The Wrtr.'s Ctr., Bethesda, MD, 1985—, The Jewish Commun. Ctr., Rockville, MD, 1986—. Fellow Md. State Arts Council, 1987, Corp. of YADDO, 1987, NEA, 1986; recipient Fiction Project award PEN, 1985, 86. Mem. PSA, AWP, Wrtr.'s Ctr. (readings com. 1984—). Home: 6100 Lenox Rd Bethesda MD 20817

GOLDBERG, HILARY THAM, (Hilary Tham), b. Klang, Selangor, Malaysia, Aug. 20, 1946, came to U.S., 1971, d. Sun Hong Tham and Lin Tei Au; m. Joseph Ray Goldberg, Feb. 16, 1971; children—Ilana, Shoshana, Rebecca. Author: Paper Boats (Malaysian poetry anthology), 1987, No Gods Today (Malaysian anthology), 1969; contrbr. Snow Summits in the Sun, 1985, Poet Lore, Waterways, Apogee-Microcosm, Antietam Review, Sombra, Lip Service, other lit mags. BA with honors, U. Malaya, 1971. Tutor Royal House of Selangor, Malaysia, 1965-66; teaching asst. dept. English U. Malaya, Kuala Lumpur, 1971; instr. claims corr. Blue Cross and Blue Shield Health Ins., Washington, 1973-77; Chmn. No. Va. Coalition for Relief of Boat People, 1978-80. Fellow Jenny McKean Moore Poetry Workshop; mem. Wrtrs.' Center. Home: 2600 N Upshur St Arlington VA 22207

GOLDEMBERG, ISAAC, b. Chepen, La Libertad, Peru, Nov. 15, 1945; arr. U.S. 1964; s. Isaac and Eva (Bay) G. Author: The Fragmented Life of Don Jacobo Lerner, 1976, La Vida a plazos de don Jacobo Lerner, 1978, Tiempo al Tiempo, 1984, Play by Play, 1985; poetry: Tiempo de Silencio, 1970, De Chepen a La Habana, 1973, Just Passing Through, 1981. Mem. Phi Beta Kappa. Instr. NYU, NYC,1970—; coordinator New York's Latin Am. Book Fair, NYC,1985—. Address: 515 West 110 St Apt 6A NYC 10025

GOLDENSOHN, BARRY NATHAN, b. NYC, Apr. 26, 1937, s. Joseph Benjamin and Shirley (Friedberg) G.; m. Lorrie Sanchez Myer, Aug. 5, 1956; children—Matthew, Rachel. Author: St. Venus Eve (poetry), 1972, Uncarving the Block (poetry), 1978, The Marrano (poetry), 1987; contrbr. articles to Yale Rvw, October, Iowa Rvw; contrbr. poetry to Ploughshares, Poetry, The New Republic, Pushcart X (anthology), Salmagundi, Antioch Rvw, other publs. BA, Oberlin (Ohio) Coll., 1957; MA in English, U. Wis.-Madison, 1959. Tchr. Goddard Coll., Plainfield, Vt., 1965-77; dean Humanities and Arts, Hampshire Coll., Amherst, Mass., 1977-82; assoc. prof. English Skidmore Coll., Saratoga Springs, N.Y., 1982—; vis. assoc. prof. wrtrs.' workshop U. Iowa, Iowa City, 1970-72. Grantee Vt. Council of Arts, 1977, N.Y. Fdn. for Arts, 1986. Home: 11 Seward St Saratoga Springs NY 12866

GOLD FRANKE, PAULA CHRISTINE, b. Ft. Campbell, KY, June 24, 1952; d. John Thomas Gold and Marlyn Maria (Pastor) Hawkins; m. Wallace Henry Franke, Mar. 26, 1977. Scriptwrtr. children's TV program Magic Door, 1986-87; columnist Radiosporting mag., 1986-87; reporter, relief ed. Beecher Herald newspaper, 1984-87. BA, Governors State U., 1982, MA in Media Communications, 1986. Freelance wrtr., 1984—. Mem. NWC. Home: Box 873 Beecher IL 60401

GOLDHURST, WILLIAM, b. NYC, Aug. 8, 1929; s. Harry Golden and Genevieve (Gallagher) G.; m. Ellen Eiseman; children—Barney, Rex. Author: F. Scott Fitzgerald and His Contemporaries, 1963, Our Own Confidence Man, 1979, also articles, photo-stories in mags.; book reviewer lit. jnls; editor: Contours of Experience, 1967. BA, Kenyon Coll., 1953; MA, Columbia, 1956; PhD, Tulane U., 1962. Recipient Broome Lit. Agt. award for short fiction, 1979. Assoc. prof. English, Univ. Puerto-Rico, 1960-63, assoc. prof. and full prof. English and humanities, Univ. of Florida, 1964—, Fulbright Prof. Am. lit., Univ. of Buenos Aires, 1969. Mem. South Atlantic MLA, Poe Soc. (Balt., Richmond). Home: 3927 NW 21st St Gainesville FL 32605

GOLDLEAF, STEVEN, b. Bklyn., June 18, 1953; m. Carolyn Yalkut, Aug. 23, 1981, 1 dau., Elizabeth Lee. Contrbr. The Brand-X Anthology of Fiction, 1983, Contemporary American Stories, 1986; several pages to 1986 Bill James Baseball Abstract, peom in The Dreamlife of Johnny Baseball, 1987. BA, Columbia U., 1976; MA, Johns Hopkins U., 1980; PhD,U. Denver, 1985. Asst. prof. LeMoyne Coll., Syracuse, NY, 1985-87. Recipient Cornell Woollrich Fellowship, 1975-76, Gerald Warner Brace award Boston U., 1980, AAP prize, Denver, 1983; MacDowell fellow, Peterborough, N.H., 1985, fellow at Virginia Ctr. for the Creative Arts, 1986. Mem. MLA. Home: 119 Alpine Dr Apt 9 Syracuse NY 13214

GOLDMAN, MARTIN RAYMOND RUBIN, b. NYC, Oct. 3, 1920; s. David and Rose (Arkin) Rubin; m. Marian Beatrice Gordon, Mar. 30, 1947; 1 dau., Susanna Linda. Assoc. editor Encyc. Intl., NYC, 1961-62; sr. copy editor Look mag., NYC, 1962-67, asst. mng. editor, 1967-68, mng. editor, 1968-71; editor Intellectual Digest, NYC, 1971-74; sr. editor Time mag., 1974-77; editor, pub. New Harvest mag., 1977—; cons. editor Am. Health mag., 1971—, Mother Earth News mag., 1986—. Cons. Modern Lang. Assn.-NEH. Mem. adv. bd. Johns Hopkins Mag., N.Y. U. Alumni News. Contrbg. author: The Army Air Forces in World War II, 1958. Served with USAAF, 1942-45. Decorated Air medal with oak leaf cluster, Purple Heart. Mem. ASME. Home: 1 Captains Walk The Springs East Hampton NY 11937

GOLDOWSKY, BARBARA, b. Dachau, Germany, Nov. 11, 1936; arrd. U.S. 1950; m. Noah Goldowsky, June 9, 1961 (dec. 1978); children—Alexander, Boris; m. 2d, Norman C. Pickering, Sept. 11, 1979. Contrbr. poetry Natl. Writers Press, St. Andrews Rvw, Midstream, Zephyr, Midwest Poetry Rvw, Astronomy Mag, anthols; prose to Jnl of the Violin, Hamptons Mag, NY Times, Byline Mag, Southampton Press. BA in Poli. Sci., U. Chgo., 1958. Self- employed writer and art dealer since 1961. Mem. Sane, Amnesty Intl., Nature Conservancy, NWC, P&W. Address: Box 663 Southampton NY 11968

GOLDSBERRY, STEVEN., Author: The Craft of Hawaiian Lauhala Weaving (with others), 1982, Maui: The Demigod. An Epic Novel of Mythical Hawaii, 1984; ed.: Haku Mele o Hawaii, 1979; contrbr. to Aloha: The Mag. of Hawaii and the Pacific, Am. Poetry Rvw, The New Yorker, Iowa Review, GEO (Germany), Honolulu, Hawaii Rvw, Bamboo Ridge: The Hawaii Wrtrs.' Qtly, Loon, other lit mags. BA, Ch. Coll. Hawaii, 1971; MA, U. Hawaii, 1973; MFA, U. Iowa, 1978, PhD, 1979. Recipient William O. Douglas prize poetry competition, 1976, City and County of Honolulu award for excellence in writing, 1978, Lorin Tarr Gill writing award Natl. League Am. Pen Women, 1982; Michener fellow, 1981. Freelance copywrtr., ed.; lit. ed., contrbg. ed. Aloha, 1981—; assoc. prof. dept. English, U. Hawaii, Honolulu. Mem. Screen Actors Guild, Hawaii Lit. Arts Council, Film Actors Workshop. Office: Dept Eng U Hawaii Honolulu HI 96822

GOLDSMITH, ARTHUR AUSTIN, b. Merrimac, MA, July 7, 1926; s. Arthur Austin and Daisy (Bishop) G.; m. Carolyn Milford, Sept. 2, 1948; children—Arthur, James, Susan, Amy. Author: How To Take Better Pictures, 1956, (with Alfred Eisenstadt) The Eye of Eisenstadt, 1969, The Photography Game, 1971, The Nude in Photography, 1975, The Camera and Its Images, 1979; editor: Photojournalism: The World Gallery of Photography, 1983. Student, U. N.H., 1946-47; BS in Journalism, Northwestern U., 1951, MS, 1951. Asst. editor to exec. editor Popular Photography, NYC, 1951-60; picture editor This Week, NYC, 1960-62; editor, head of instrn. Famous Photographers Schl., Westport, Conn., 1962-69, pres., dir., 1969-72; editorial dir. Popular Photography, NYC, 1972-85, ed.-at-large, 1986—. Contrbr. photography to Encyc. Brit. Yearbook, 1974—; columnist: PTN Newsletter, 1981-85; studio photography, 1986—. Served with USN, 1944-46. Recipient Harrington award Medill Schl. Journalism, Northwestern U., 1951, Editor of Yr. award United Jewish Appeal, 1982. Office: Pop Photog 1 Park Ave New York NY 10016

GOLDSMITH, BARBARA, b. NYC, May 18, 1931; d. Joseph J. and Evelyn (Cronson) Lubin; m. Frank Perry; children—Andrew, John Goldsmith and Alice Elgart. Author: (novel) The Straw Man, 1975; (non-fiction) Little Gloria...Happy at Last, 1980; contributor, Johnson v Johnson, 1987, The New Journalism, 1980. BA, Wellesley Coll., 1953; DLitt (hon.), Syracuse U., LHD, Pace U., 1980. Entertainment editor Woman's Home Companion, NYC, 1954-57; contrbr. NY Herald Tribune, NY Times Bk. Rvw, NY Times Mag., Esquire Mag., New Yorker, 1957-64; founder, contrbg. editor New York Mag., 1968-73; sr. editor Harpers Bazaar Mag., NYC, 1970-74. Spcl. writer TV documentaries and entertainments. Recipient Brandeis Library Trust award, 1982. Trustee New York Public Library, Libraries Research Committee, dir. Ntl. Dance Inst. Mem. PEN (exec. bd., 1983-86), P&W. Address: Janklow 598 Madison Ave New York NY 10022

GOLDSMITH, HOWARD, (Ward Smith, Dayle Courtney), b. NYC, Aug. 24, 1943, s. Philip and Sophie (Feldman) G. Author: Turvy, The Horse that Ran Backwards, 1973, The Whispering Sea (novel), 1976, What Makes a Grumble Smile?, 1977, The Shadow and Other Strange Tales, 1977, Terror by Night, 1977, Spine-Chillers (with Roger Elwood), 1978, Sooner Round the Corner (novel), 1979, The Plastic Age, 1979, Invasion:2200 A.D. (novel), 1979, Toto the Timid Turtle, 1980, The Ivy Plot (novel), 1981, Three-Ring Inferno (novel), 1982, The Tooth Chicken, 1982, Mireille L'Abeille, 1982, Ninon, Miss Vison, 1982, Toufou Le Hibou, 1982, Fourtou Le Kangourou, 1982, Plaf Le Paresseux, 1982, The Sinister Circle (novel), 1983, Shadow of Fear (novel), 1983, Welcome, Makoto!, 1983, Treasure Hunt, 1983, The Contest, 1983, Little Dog Lost, 1983, Stormy Day Together, 1983, The Circle, 1983, The Square, 1983, Maggie the Mink, 1984, Sammy the Sloth, 1984, Helpful Julio, 1984, The Secret of Success, 1984, A Day of Fun, 1984, Pedro's Puzzling Birthday, 1984, Rosa's Prank, 1984, The Rectangle, 1984, Ollie the Owl, 1985, Kirby the Kangaroo, 1985, The Twiddle Twins' Haunted House, 1985, The Flying Kitten, 1987; contrbr. anthologies, textbooks; contrbr. to Scholastic, Short Story Intl., Outlook, Opinion, Comet, Ideals, Wings, Chillers, Void, Crux, London Mystery, numerous children's mags.; ed. textbook series: When I Grow Up, 1985, Thanks To..., 1985. BA, CUNY, 1965; MA, U. Mich., 1966. Editorial cons. Mountain View Center for Environ. Edn., U. Colo., Boulder, 1970—; free-lance wrtr., ed., 1970—; sr. ed. Santillana Pub. Co., Northvale, N.J., 1982-84. Mem. P&W, SFWA, Soc. Children's Book Wrtrs., Phi Beta Kappa, Sigma Xi, Psi Chi, Phi Kappa Phi. Home: 41-07 Bowne St 6B Flushing NY 11355

GOLDSMITH, LARRY DEAN, b. Coffeyville, KS, Oct. 19, 1952; s. Willis Graves and Bessie Alzada (Tullis) G.; m. Ramona Kay Kantack, Jan. 14, 1979. Pubns. include: Golf Course Superintendents Assn. of Amer. ForeFront, 1979-82, GCSAA Newsline, 1979-82, Proceedings of Intl. Turfgrass Conf., 1980, 81, 82, Golf Course Mgt. Mag., 1979-82, The Piano Technicians Jnl, 1983—, Pain, Body & Equipment Assn. Nwsltr., 1985—. BS in Jnlsm., U. KS, 1974. Wire ed. Iola (KS) Daily Register, 1974-75; photog. Pitts. (KS) Morning Sun, 1975-77; free-lance writer, Lawrence, KS, 1978-79; mgr. info. svcs. GCSAA, Lawrence, 1979-82; ed. The Noon News, Hallmark Cards, Inc., Kansas City, MO, 1982-83; client communic. dir. Martin Fromm & Assoc., Kansas City, MO, 1983—. Mem. Kansas City/Intl. IABC, COSMEP. Home: 34 East 55th Terr Kansas City MO 64113

GOLDSTEIN, ALAN, bNYC, Oct. 1, 1953; s. Alex and Nellie Marie (Gray) G.; m. Cynthia Lesley Elson, Oct. 21, 1978; children—Timothy Oliver, Annadare Lesley. Ed.: Interservice Mag., 1981—, ALA Worldwide Directory & Fact Book, 1981—, ALA Exec. Briefing Nwsltr., 1981—. BA, New England Coll., 1978. Acct. exec. Russell-Greer Assocs., London, 1979-80; research assoc. Lloyd-Hughes Assocs., London, 1980-81; dir. info. & res. American Logistics Assn., Washington, 1981—. Served to Sgt., E/5, USMC, 1973-77. Mem. NPC, SNAP, Washington Edn. Press Assn. Office: Amer Log Assn 1133 15th St NW Washington DC 20005

GOLDSTEIN, LAURENCE ALAN, b. Los Angeles, Jan. 5, 1943; s. Cecil and Helen (Soltot) G.; m. Nancy Jo Copeland, April 28, 1968; children: Andrew, Jonathan. Author: Ruins and Empire, 1977; Altamira, 1978; The Flying Machine and Modern Lit, 1986; The Three Gardens, 1987; ed. The Automobile and Am. Culture (with David L. Lewis), 1983; ed. Mich. Qtly Rvw, 1977—. BA, UCLA, 1965; PhD, Brown U., 1970. Asst. prof. English, Univ. Mich., Ann Arbor, 1970-77, assoc. prof., 1977-84, prof., 1984—. Andrew Mellon fellow Univ. Pittsburgh, 1975-76. Address: 408 Second St Ann Arbor MI 48103

GOLDWASSER, JUDITH WAX, b. Detroit, June 29, 1944; d. Reuben D. and Rena (Krause) Wax; m. James Stephen Goldwasser, Sept. 15, 1968; children: Amy, Lawrene. Contrbr.: LHJ, The Cranbrook Jnl, Family Circle, Gifted Children's Newsletter, Edn. U.S.A., Sci., numerous other publs. BA in English, U. Mich., 1966. Reporter Detroit Free Press, 1966-70; (part of staff awarded Pulitzer for genl. local reporting, 1968); freelance wrtr, 1970-81; prin. JG Edit. Services, Birmingham Mich., 1981—. Mem. Wrtrs. Info. Network. Office: JG Edit Svcs 1776 Maryland Blvd Birmingham MI 48009

GOLDWITZ, SUSAN, b. NYC,Oct. 17, 1949; d. Samuel Joseph and Selma (Goldstein) G. Author: Dreams of the Hand, 1985; contrbr. poems Selections, Five in One, The Bellingham Rvw, Dalmo'ma, Eleven, Gargoyle, Half the Sky, Hanging Loose, Kalliope, Northeast Jnl, Stone Country, Tendril, The Wascana Rvw, Works in Progress, others. BA, Northeastern U., MA, Brown U., 1978. Lectr. in English Northeastern Univ., Boston, 1978-87; curator of education, Danforth Museum of Art, 1986—. Mem. AAP (poetry award), PSA, PW. Address: 9 Mendum St Roslindale MA 02131

GOLDWYN, CRAIG D., b. Chgo., June 4, 1949; s. Jerome H. and Norma J. (Smollett) G.; m. M.L. Tortorello, Sept. 14, 1974. Weekly columnist Chicago Tribune, 1978-81; monthly columnist Washington Post, 1986—; contrbr. numerous photography and wine books. BS in Jnlsm., U. FL, 1971; MFA, Art Inst. of Chgo., 1975. Publisher, International Wine Review, Ithaca, NY, 1981—. Office: 227 Enfield Falls Rd Ithaca NY 14850

GOLDWYN, ROBERT M., b. Worcester, MA, Sept. 17, 1930, s. Jacob and Pauline (Altman) G.; m. Aug. 3, 1958; children—Linda, Laura. Author: The Unfavorable Result in Plastic Surgery: Avoidance and Treatment, 1972, 2d edit., 1984, Plastic and Reconstructive Surgery of the Breast, 1976, Long-term Results in Plastic and Reconstructive Surgery, 1980, The Patient and the Plastic Surgeon, 1981, Beyond Appearance: Reflections of a Plastic Surgeon, 1986. Wrkg. on essays about medicine and plastic surgery. AB, Harvard U., 1952, MD, 1956. Practice medicine specializing in plastic surgery, Boston; clin. prof. surgery Med. Schl., Harvard U.; ed. Plastic and Reconstructive Surgery, 1979—. Recipient Book award AMA, 1977. Mem. Council Biology Eds. Home: 54 Willow Crescent Brookline MA 02146

GOLIN, MILTON, b. Oak Park, IL, Apr. 2, 1921; m. Irene Frances Golin, Sept. 4, 1946 (dec. Apr. 1972); children—Lawrence, Jeffery, James; m. 2d, Carol Brierly Golin, Dec. 12, 1975; children—Amy, John. Author: Business Side of Medical Practice, 1958; contrbr. articles to natl. mags., including Coronet, Reader's Digest, Saturday Evening Post, Changing Times, Sci. Digest, Mademoiselle, Seventeen, Mechanix Illust., Natl. Observer, Catholic Digest. Student Wright City Coll., 1939-41, Central YMCA Coll., Chgo., 1941-42. Fndg. radio-TV ed. City News Bur., Chgo., 1951-56; asst. ed. Jnl of AMA, Chgo., 1956-60; asst. to pres. Pharmaceut. Mfrs. Assn., Washington, 1960-68; fndg. ed. 6 medical pubns., Washington & Chgo., 1968-73; mng. ed. Med. Liability Monitor, Chgo., 1973—; ed./pub. Med. Group News, Computers & Med., Chgo., 1968—. Served to 1st Lt., USAF, 1942-46. Mem. ASJA, NASW. Office: Box 36 Glencoe IL 60022

GOLSON, GEORGE BARRY, b. Lynn, MA, Dec. 12, 1944; s. George Albert and Beverly Margaret G.; m. Thia Anne MacKenzie, Aug. 24, 1968. Columnist, mng. editor Atlas World Press Rvw, 1969-71; asst. articles editor Playboy mag., NYC, 1972-74, sr. editor, 1974-76, exec. editor, 1976—. Free-lance writer, 1971-72; editor: The Playboy Interview, 1981; contrbr. articles on politics, satire and travel to various publs. BA, Yale U., 1967; postgrad., Stanford U., 1967-68. Recipient 1st place Writer's award Playboy Mag., 1972; Ford fellow, 1968. Mem. ASME, ASJA, PEN. Office: Playboy 747 3d Ave New York NY 10017

GOLUB, MARCIA HELENE, b. Bklyn., Apr. 8, 1953, d. Jack and Lilly (Gutterman) Golub; m. Robert Steven Rosen, June 25, 1978. Contrbr. to Introduction to Cultural Anthropology, 1979, Sci. Digest, 1980, The Volume Library, 1980, 82, Student Handbook, Vol. II, 1983, Macmillan Dictionary for Students, 1984, Earthwise Poetry Jnl; ed. books, articles for numerous pub. cos. BA, SUNY, New Paltz, 1974. Editorial asst. Mag. Mgmt., N.Y.C, 1975, mng. ed., 1975-77; wrtr., ed., N.Y.C., 1977—. Address: 119 E 84 St New York NY 10028

GOMERY, DOUGLAS, (John Montgomery), b. N.Y.C., Apr. 5, 1945; s. John Edgar Jr. and Julia (Halsted) G.; m. Marilyn L. Moon, Jan. 13, 1973. Author: High Sierra, 1979, Film History (with Robert C. Allen), 1985, The Hollywood Studio System, 1986, The Will Hays Papers, 1987; contrbr. articles: Mediapourvoirs, Marquee, Cinema Jnl., The Velvet Light Trap, numerous other publs. Wrkg. on bus. history of Am. film industry. BS, Lehigh U., 1967; MA, U. Wis., 1970, PhD, 1975. Mem. faulty U. Wis.-Milw., Northwestern U., Evanston, U. Iowa, Iowa City, 1974-82; assoc. prof. U. Md., College Park, 1981-86, prof., 1987—. Mem. editorial bd. Cinema Jnl., Jnl. of Film and Video. Recipient grants, fellowships. Mem. Am. Film Inst. (trustee), Theatre Hist. Soc. Home: 4817 Drummond Ave Chevy Chase MD 20815

GOMEZ, ROGELIO ROBERTO, b. Castano, Coahuila, Mex., June 7, 1950, came to U.S., 1956; s. Ireneo and Elvira (Mondragon) G; m. Deborah H. Ramon, Mar. 25, 1971; children—Laban, Eli, Mariel. Contrbr. short stories to lit. mags. Fiction editor: Cactus Alley Jnl; mng. editor: ViAztlan Mag. BA, U. Tex.-San Antonio. Telephone operator Southwestern Bell, San Antonio, 1981—. Recipient 2d place for short story U. Ariz., Tucson, 1985. Home: 117 Ripford San Antonio TX 78204

GOMPERTZ, ROLF, b. Krefeld, Rhineland, W.Germany, Dec. 29, 1927; s. Oscar and Selma (Herrmann) G.; came to U.S. June 11, 1939; m. Carol B. Brown, Apr. 28, 1957; children—Ron, Philip, Nancy. Author: My Jewish Brother Jesus, 1977, Promotion & Publicity Handbook for Broadcasters, 1977, Sparks of Spirit, 1983, A Celebration of Life, 1983, The Messiah of Midtown Park, 1983. BA, UCLA, 1951, MA, 1953. Ed., Torrance Press (CA), 1953-57; publicist NBC, Burbank, CA, 1957-83; dir., Gen. Progs. Press, NBC, Burbank, 198387; freelance wrtr, public relations consultant, 1987. POub. WorDoctor Pubs., No. Hollywood, CA, 1974—. Co-winner, NBC Employee Writing Compet., 1985. Mem. WG. Home: 6516 Ben Ave No Hollywood CA 91606

GONDER, BUDD ELI, b. Long Beach, CA, June 23, 1930; s. Walter Lemuel Gonder and Minta (Duggins) Bolitho; m. Margaret Jean, Aug. 22, 1953; children—Thomas Wade, Douglas Wayne, Linda Elizabeth. Author: The Coast Guard License-Six Pac to Ocean Operator, 9 eds. since 1978, The Rules of the Road, 3 eds. since 1978, mag. articles on marine science subjs. BA in Hist.,U. Calif., secondary creds., UCLA. Tchr., Santa Barbara H.S. Dist., CA, 1963—. Address: Box 675 Goleta CA 93116

GONDOSCH, LINDA ANN, b. Hinton, WV, Ot. 25, 1944; d. Edgar Vernon and Mary Pauline (Ellison) Wicker; m. Werner Klalus Gondosch, Sept. 4, 1965; children—Lisa, Stephen, Amy, Kathy. Author: The Strawberryland Choo-Choo, 1984, Who Needs a Bratty Brother?, 1985, The Witches of Hopper Street, 1986, Who's Afraid of Haggerty House?, 1987, The Monsters of Marble Avenue, 1988. Contrbr. short stories to mags. B.S. in Edn., Ohioo U., 1966; M.A. in Edn., Northern Ky. U., 1986. Tchr., South Dearborn High Sch., Aurora, IN, 1982-83. Mem. SCBW, Nat. Assn. Young Wrtrs. Home: 1020 Fairview Dr Lawrenceburg IN 47025

GONZALEZ-MENA, JANET, b. Loma Linda, CA, Dec. 10, 1937, d. Richard Lawrence and Mary Evelyn (Davis) Waldron; m. Paul Wallach, Aug. 2, 1959 (div. 1970); children—Bruce, Bret, Adam, Robin; m. 2d, Frank Gonzalez-Mena, Aug. 2, 1971; 1 son, David. Author: English Experiences, A Program of English as a Second Language for Preschool and Kindergarten, 1975, Experiencias En Espanol, A Spanish Language Development Program for Preschool and Kindergarten, 1976, The Big E., An English Language Development Program for First and Second Grade, 1976, Infancy and Caregiving, 1980; contrbr. articles to profl. publs.; columnist Twins mag., 1984—. BA, U. Calif.-Davis, 1959, MA, Pacific Oaks Coll., 1977. Instr. early childhood edn. Canada Community Coll., Redwood City, Calif., 1972-79, Solano Community Coll., Suisun, Calif., 1975-78, 80-83, now Napa (Calif.) Valley Coll. Mem. profl. orgns. Home: 5348 Suisun Valley Rd Suisun CA 94585

GOODBODY, SLIM, see Burtein, John

GOODELL, LARRY, b. Roswell, NM, June 20, 1935, s. Lawrence and Dorothy (Brown) G.; m. Lenore Schwartz Dec. 2, 1968; 1 son, Joel. Author: Cycles, 1965, Pecos Bill, 1981, The Mad New Mexican, 1986, Songs 1981-1986, a casette tape. BA, U. So. Calif., 1957. Performance poet, musician; program dir. Living Batch Bookstore, Albuquerque, 1980—. Ed., pub., duende Press, 1964—. Grantee NEA, 1983. Mem. Rio Grande Wrtrs. Assn. Home: Box 571 Placitas NM 87043

GOODENOUGH, JUDITH B., b. Berea, KY, Oct. 25, 1942, d. Robert Fullerton and Eva (Ripley) Beach; m. John Byer Goodenough, Apr. 23, 1966; children—Anne, Elizabeth. Author: Dower Land, 1984, Homeplace, 1987; contrbr. 650 poems to lit jnls, 1979—. BA, Harvard U., 1964. Home: 300 Wildberry Rd Fox Chapel PA 15238

GOODIN, MICHAEL ANTHONY, b. Detroit, Feb. 9, 1951; s. Stanley Ivan and Mary Elizabeth (Adams) G.; m. Willa Dean Roberts, Dec. 1, 1981. Contrbr. photographs, stories, features to mags., newspapers including Jet Mag., Dtroit Free Press, others. B.A. in Political Sci., Wayne State U., 1986. Ed., Am. Postal Workers Union, Detroit, 1971-77; sign artist J. L. Hudsons, Detroit, 1977; keyliner, graphic artist Artex Printing, Detroit, 1978; mng. ed. South End Press, Detroit, 1978-79; reporter Mich. Chronicle, Detroit, 1979—. Recipient 2d prize for best news story Natl. Newspaper Pubs. Assn., 1986. Mem. Natl. Assn. Black Jnlsts. (v.p. Detroit chpt. 1985-87); Home: 20020 Lahser Detroit MI 48219

GOODINE, FRANCENA WHITE, b. Burlington, VT, Aug. 10, 1940; d. Leon Frank and Anna Katherine (Bayley) White; m. Carroll Edward Goodine, Ot. 18, 1959; children—Julie, Joelle, Jonathan. Author book rvws.: Livermore Falls Advertiser, 1979-82. Contrbr. recipes, needlework and knitting patterns, short stories, poems to mags., newsletters, anthols. needlework designs and patterns, play. Cert. in Fiction Writing, Famous Writers Shl., 1969. Clothing cons. Queensway, Niles, IL, 1975-77; asst. libraian

Treat Meml. Library, Livermore Falls, ME, 1977—. Home: RFD Box 617 Canton ME 04221

GOODING, JUDSON, b. Rochester, MN, Oct. 12, 1926; s. Arthur Faitoute and Frances (Judson) G.; m. Francoise Ridoux, June 21, 1952; children—Anthony, Amelie, Timothy. Author: The Job Revolution, 1972; contrbr. to American Dreams, The Environment, The Hippies, The Survival Equation, The Failure of Success; contrbr. articles to popular mags. and profl. jnls. Grad. with honors, Yale U., 1948; diplome d'Etudes Francaises, U. Paris, 1950. Staff writer Dept. Army, Hdqrs. EUCOM. Germany, 1950-52; script writer Affiliated Film Producers, NYC, 1952-53; news writer WCCO-CBS, Mpls., 1953; reporter Mpls. Tribune, 1953-57, Life mag., NYC, 1957-60, fgn. corr., Paris, 1960-62, Time mag., 1962-65; chief of bur. Time-Life News Service, San Francisco, 1966-68; edn. editor Time mag., NYC, 1968-69; assoc. editor Fortune mag., 1969-73; editor Trend Report, Chgo., 1973-75; exec. editor Next Mag., NYC, 1979-81, contrbg. editor, 1981-82; counselor, U.S. Perm. Del. to UNESCO, Paris, 1982-84; writing cons. UN, Ford Fdn., Am. Assembly, also corps. Served with USNR, 1944-46. Recipient 1st place award U. Mo. Schl. Journalism Penney-Mo., 1980—. Mem. ASJA. Office: Box 745 Walpole NH 03608

GOODMAN, JOEL BARRY, b. Hampton, VA, Dec. 31, 1948; s. Alex and Paula (Cohen) Goodman; m. Marjorie Jean Ingram, Oct. 7, 1979; 1 dau.—Alyssa Jaye, 1 son—Adam Seth Ingram. Ed: Laughing Matters Mag., 1981—, Turning Points, vol. I, 1978, vol. II, 1979; co-author: Health Education: The Search for New Values, 1977, Playfair: Everybody's Guide to Noncompetitive Play, 1980, Magic and the Educated Rabbit, 1981, Humanizing Environmental Education, 1981, Let the Buyer Be Aware, 1981; contrbr. to Learning, Today's Education, Handbook of Humor and Research, American Humor, other mags, profl. jnls, txtbks. BA, U. of Pennsylvania, 1970; MEd, U. of Mass., 1971; EdD, U. of Mass, 1975. Dir. The Humor Project Saratoga Inst. (Saratoga Springs, NY), 1977—; project dir. Sagamore Inst. (Saratoga Springs), 1976-84, assoc. dir., 1975-76; adjunct faculty U. of Mass. Hampshire Coll (Amherst, MA), 1973-75, faculty, Russell Sage College, 1977—. Work as dir. of Humor Project featured on PM Mag., PBS' Latenight Am., other tv, radio, mags. Home: 179 Spring St Saratoga Springs NY 12886

GOODMAN, WALTER, b. NYC, Aug. 22, 1927; s. Hyman and Sadie (Rybakof) G.; m. Elaine Egan, Feb. 10, 1951; children—Hal, Bennet. Author: The Committee, 1968, All Honorable Men, 1963, The Clowns of Commerce, 1957, Black Bondage, 1969, A Percentage of the Take, 1971; also numerous articles. BA magna cum laude, Syracuse U., 1949; MA, Reading (Eng.) U., 1953. Editor, N.Y. Times, NYC, 1974—, mem. editorial bd., 1977—, critic, 1983—; exec. editor WNET, 1979—; lectr. Breadloaf Writers Conf., Columbia U. Schl. Journalism. Guggenheim fellow, 1974. Mem. PEN. Home: 4 Crest Dr White Plains NY 10607

GOODMAN, WILLIAM BEEHLER, b. Bklyn., July 1, 1923; s. Philip Howard and Anne Louise (Landersman) G.; m. Lorraine Rappaport, Nov. 24, 1948; children—Jonas Robert, Sara Emily. Editor coll. and trade Harcourt Brace Jovanovich Inc., NYC, 1956-76; genl. editor Harvard Univ. Press, Cambridge, Mass., 1976-79; editorial dir. David R. Godine Pub. Inc., Boston, 1979—. BA, Washington Sq. Coll., NYU, 1948; MA, U. Mich., 1952. Served with AUS, 1943-44. History and lit. tuotr, Harvard U., 1953-54, lectr. in English, 1982-83, 84-85. Mem. PEN Am. Ctr. Home: 240 Brattle St Cambridge MA 02138

GOODNER, JOHN ROSS, JR., b. Beaver, OK, Apr. 13, 1927; s. John Ross and Vesta (Carter) G.; m. Charlotte Gustafson, Aug. 19, 1950; 1 son, Charles; m. Sue Lummus, Feb. 11, 1962; 1 dau., Mary. Sports writer Daily Oklahoman, Oklahoma City, 1953-62, N.Y. Times, 1962-66; mng. editor Golf mag., NYC, 1966-67, editor, 1967-71, exec. editor, 1974-77; assoc. editor Golf Digest mag., Norwalk, Conn., 1977—; sr. writer Grand Bahama Devel. Co., Freeport, Bahamas, 1971-72; mgr. N.Y. News Bur., Bermuda Dept. Tourism, 1973. Author: Golf's Greatest, 1978; editor: Tips From the Teaching Pros, 1969, America's Golf Book, 1970; contrbr. to Encyc. of Golf, 1975. Student, Panhandle A&M Coll., Goodwell, Okla., 1947-49; BA, U. Okla., 1954. Served with AUS, 1945-46. Mem. Golf Writers Assn. Am. (Best mag. Story of Year award 1974). Office: 495 Westport Ave Norwalk CTJ 06856

GOODRIDGE, GEORGIA ESTHER, b. Columbia, MO, Jan. 29, 1950; d. George Stanley and Esther Joanne (Krigbaum) Little; m. Kaylon Davis; children—Jennifer, Heather; m. 2d, Jim Goodridge, Sept. 19, 1977. Editor, Fair Times Newspaper, Dealers Desk Reference, Great Amer. Flea Mkt. Directory. Student, South Oklahoma City Jr. Coll., 1971-72. Salesman, Buffalo Nickel Trading Co., Arnold, MO, 1975-80; ed. Fair Times Newspaper, Arnold, 1980—. Mem. MO Press Assn. Office: ID Assn 3630 Jeffco Blvd Arnold MO 63010

GOODWIN, BILL, JR., b. Windsor, NC, Oct. 20, 1942; s. Willie Parker and Annie (Cobb) G. Author: Frommer's Dollarwise Guide to the South Pacific, 1987. Contrbr. articles to mags., newspapers including Washington Post, Miami Herald, Cosmopolitan, others. Ed. U.S. Senate com. reports, 1970-83. B.A. in Jnlsm., U. N.C., 1965; J.D., George Washington U., 1973. Bar: N.C., 1973, D.C., 1981, Hawaii, 1983. Staff wrtr. The News & Observer, Raleigh, NC, 1963-65; staff wrtr. Atlanta Jnl., 1967-69, Washington, 1970-74, Senator Sam Nunn, Washington, 1975-83; free-lance wrtr., 1984—. Recipient Spot News award N.C. Press Assn., 1964, Newswriting award Hearst Fdn., (2) 1965, Spl. Series award Theta Sigma Phi, 1968. Mem. Washington Ind. Wrtrs. Home: 4204 Fordham Rd Baltimore MD 21229

GOODWIN, FRANCIS MAURICE, b. Charleston, SC, Mar. 22, 1956; s. Francis Maurice and Joan Elaine (Diefendorf) G. Contrbr. articles to Monthly Deroit, Auto Week. B.A. in Mass Communication, Wayne State U., 1984. Newsman, UPI, Detroit, 1982-85, UPI-Natl. Broadcast, Chgo., 1985—. Home: 2312 W Iowa 2-R Chicago IL 60622

GOODWIN, STEPHEN, b. East Stroudsburg, PA, Oct. 20, 1943; s. Claudius Lee and Jeannette Frances (Levy) G.; m. Lucia Stanton, June 14, 1964 (div. 1977); 1 child, Eliza Keeler; m. Karen Walter, May 31, 1986. Author: Kin, 1975; The Blood of Paradise, 1979. AB, Harvard U., 1964; MA, U. Va., 1969. Instr. Washington and Lee U., Lexington, Va., 1969-73; asst. prof. Bryn Mawr Coll., Pa., 1973-77; assoc. prof. George Mason U., Fairfax, Va., 1979—. Served with U.S. Army, 1966-68. NEA fellow, 1973, 83; Guggenheim fellow, 1985. Mem. PEN South (chmn. 1983), PEN Am. Ctr. (exec. bd.). Home: 706 Nutley St Vienna VA 22180

GOOTNICK-BRUCE, STEPHANIE, b. Bklyn., July 21, 1954; d. Seymour Isaac and Doris (Glaser) Gootnick; m. Douglas Christian Bruce, June 27, 1987. Wrkg. on screenplays, corp. writing. Student SUNY-Potsdam, 1972-74, George Peabody Coll., 1974-76. Sr. ed. Capitol Records, Nashville and Los Angeles, 1977-79; assoc. ed. Avenews Mag., Los Angeles, 1979-80; staff wrtr. Broadcast Music, Inc., N.Y.C., 1981; corr. Miami (Fla.) News, 1985-86; mng. ed. Voice of Agr., Dade County (Fla.) Farm Bur., 1986-87; freelance wrtr., 1976—. Mem. Fla. Freelance Wrtrs.' Assn., Miami Press Club, Fla. Farm Bur. Home: 15845 SW 90th Ct Apt C Miami FL 33157

GORDEN, NANCY D., b. Traverse City, MI, Apr. 30, 1937; d. Harry Lester and Vera Velma (Donner) Doty; m. Jerry Lee Gorden, June 1, 1958; children—Steven, Shelly, Sherry. Ed., MGCA Nwsltr., news ed., The Gardener mag. AA, Graceland Coll. Secy., Men's Garden Clubs of America, Johnston, IA, 1973-78, Natl. Catholic Rural Life Conf., Des Moines, 1980-81; exec. secy. Men's Garden Clubs of Am., Johnston, 1981—. Mem. Profl. Secys. Intl., Am. Soc. Assn. Execs. Office: Box 241 Johnston IA 50131

GORDETT, MAREA BETH, b. Cambridge, MA, Apr. 5, 1949, d. Louis and Lillian Sarah (Kramer) G.; m. Thomas Joseph Morrissey, Sept. 22, 1985. Author: (poems) Freeze Tag, 1984; contrbr. to Ga., Antioch, Chgo., Partisan, Mass., Miss., Cin. Poetry rvws, The Nation, Prairie Schooner, MSS, Poetry Now, Poetry N.W., Denver Qtly. BA, U. Pa., 1971; MFA, U. Mass., 1979. Lectr. English, Boston U., 1979-82, Tufts U., Medford, Mass., 1985-86; artist- in-residence N. Mex. Arts Div., Taos, 1983-84. Recipient Pushcart prize, 1980. Home: 16 Joyce Rd Medford MA 02155

GORDON, FRITZ, see Jarvis, Frederick Gordon

GORDON, GUANETTA STEWART, b. Kansas City, MO, Oct. 4, d. Samuel Lewis and Minnie Anna (Brown) Stewart; m. Lynell F. Gordon (dec. 1979); children: Stewart, Krista Sharon, Gordon Morris. Author: Songs of the Wind, 1953, Under the Rainbow Arch, 1965, Petals from the Moon, 1971, Shadow Within the Flame, 1973, Above Rubies (Women of the Bible), 1976, Red are the Embers, 1980. Student Baker U., Baldwin City, Kans., 1922-24, U. Kans., Lawrence, 1935-37. Poetry contest judge, public speaker. Mem. Intl. Acad. Poets, Natl. League Am. Penwomen (mem. exec. bd.). Home: 11847 Hacienda Dr Sun City AZ 85351

GORDON, HARRIS A., b. Bklyn., Mar. 15, 1907, s. Henry and Ida (Siegel) G.; m. Ethel Gordon, June 29, 1948; 1 son, Robert M. Playwright: Shelter, 1985, The Dumbwaiter, 1986. BCS, NYU, 1928. Exec. dir. Woodstock (N.Y.) Playhouse Assn., 1974—; mem. Woodstock Arts Festival Com. Mem. Albany League of Arts, Intl. Soc. Performing Arts Adminstrs. Address: Box 396 Woodstock NY 12498

GORDON, JACK MARSHALL, b. Detroit, Nov. 29, 1949; s. Jack Marshall and Pauline J. (Blake) G.; m. Beth A. Lundholm, Feb. 17, 1979; children—Megan E., Erica L. Contrbr. to Twin Cities Mag., St. Paul Dispatch & Pioneer Press, Corporate Report Mag. BA, U. Colo., 1971. Rptr., KWBZ Radio, Denver, 1976; news dir. KGOS/KERM Radio, Torrington, WY, 1977;

sports ed./ gen. assign. rptr. Sentinel Nwsprs., Denver, 1977-79; mng. ed. Airport Services. Mgt. Mag., Mpls., 1980-82; ed. Training Mag., Mpls., 1983—. Mem. ASBPE, Am. Soc. for Trng. & Dev. Office: Lakewood Pub 50 S Ninth St Minneapolis MN 55402

GORDON, JAIMY, b. Balt., July 4, 1944, s. David P. and Sonia (Cohen) G. Author: Shamp of the City-Solo (novel), 1974, 80, The Rose of the West (text for a masque), 1976, The Bend, The Lip, The Kid, Reallife Stories (poetry), 1978, Circumspections from an Equestrian Statue (novella), 1979, The Adventuress (novel), 1987. BA, Antioch Coll., 1966; MA, Brown U., 1972, DArts, 1975. Wrtr.-in-residence R.I. State Council on Arts, Providence, 1975-77; dir. creative writing Stephens Coll., Columbia, Mo., 1980-81; asst. prof. English Western Mich. U., Kalamazoo, 1981—; mem. lit. adv. panel R.I. State Council on Arts, 1978, lit. grants screening panel NEA, 1979, adv. panel Ohio Arts Council Aid to Individual Artists Grants Program, 1983. NEA creative writing fellow, 1978, 83, Fine Arts Work Center fellow, Provincetown, Mass., 1979-80, Bunting Inst. fellow Radcliffe Coll., 1984-85; grantee Mich. Council for Arts, 1983. Office: Dept English Western Mich Univ Kalamazoo MI 49008

GORDON, PAUL PERRY, b. Frederick, MD, May 23. 1927's. Dave and Minnie (Griedlander) G.; m. Rita Simon, July 2, 1948; children—Stuart Yael, Hugh Ellis, Myla Gordon Roberson. Author: The Jews Beneath the Clustered Spires, 1971; A Textbook History of Frederick County, 1975. Wrkg. on hist. novel. BBA, U. Md., 1950. Treas. Frederick Gas Co., 1950-66; sr. v.p. Kettler Bros., Inc., Gaithersburg, Md., 1966—; feature wrtr. Mount Airy Courier Gazette, 1985—. Home: 202 Meadowdale Ln Frederick MD 21701

GORE, JEANNE GUERRERO, b. Dallas, June 4, 1945, d. Joaquin Eugene and Sara (Erwin) Guerrero; m. Charles Smith Gore, Mar. 25, 1973; children—Jesse Laurence, Blythe Elizabeth. Founder, mem. editorial bd. Cumberland Poetry Rvw, 1981—; contrbr. to Homewords: A Book of Tennessee Wrtrs., 1986, The Tennesseans: Old Hickory Rvw, Allen Tate: In Memoriam, other lit. publs. In progress: Bridging the Gap (poetry collection). BA, Emory U., 1967; MA, Ga. State U., 1970; PhD, Vanderbilt-Peabody U., 1981. Tchr. Atlanta Public Schls., 1967-73, Nashville Public Schls., 1976-79, 81—. Mem. Poetics, Inc. (treas. 1981—), Tenn. Lit. Arts Assn. Home: 6013 Kenwood Dr Nashville TN 37215

GOREAU, ANGELINE W., b. Wilmington, DE, Sept. 12, 1951; d. Theodore Nelson and Eloise (Keaton) Goreau; m. Stephen J. McGruder. Author: Reconstructing Aphra: A Social Biography of Aphra Behn, 1980, The Whole Duty of a Woman, 1985; contrbr. articles to Sexualites Occidentales, 1982, Feminist Theorists, 1983, elsewhere. BA, Barnard Coll., 1973. Wrkg. on a book about Anne Bronte and a novel. Fellow, NEH, Washington, 1975, NEA, 1981; Hodder Fellow, Council of Humanities, Princeton Univ., 1982-83; grantee, Belgian Council of the Arts, Brussels, 1978. Mem. AG, Natl. Arts Club. Address: 420 E 72 St New York NY 10021

GORES, JOSEPH NICHOLAS, b. Rochester, MN, Dec. 25, 1931; s. Joseph Mathias and Mildred Dorothy (Duncanson) G.; m. Dori Jane Corfitzen, May 16, 1976; children—Timothy, Gillian. Author: A Time of Predators, 1969, Marine Salvage, 1971, Dead Skip, 1972, Final Notice, 1973, Interface, 1974, Hammett, 1975, Gone, No Forwarding, 1978, Come Morning, 1986; screenplays Hammett, 1977, Deadfall, 1977, Paper Crimes, 1978, Paradise Road, 1978, A Wayward Angel, 1981, Cover Story, 1985, Come Morning, 1986, Run Cunning, 1987,; teleplays Kojak, 1975-77, Golden Gate Memorial, 1978, Eischied, 1979, Kate Columbo, 1979, The Gangster Chronicles, 1981, Magnum, P.I., 1983 High Risk, 1985 (with Brian Garfield), Remington Steele, 1984, Scene of the Crime, 1984, Helltown, 1985, T.J. Hooker, 1985, Mike Hammer, 1983-86; editor: Honolulu: Port of Call, 1974; (with Bill Pronzini) Teleplays Tricks and Treats, 1976. BA, U. Notre Dame, 1953; MA, Stanford, 1961. Recipient Edgar Allan Poe award for A Time for Predators as best first novel MWA, 1969, for "Goodbye, Pops" as best short story in Am. mags, 1969, for best teleplay in a dramatic series (Kojak) 1976. Falcon Award, Maltese Falcon Society of Japan (Hammet) 1986.Served with AUS, 1958-59. Mem. MWA, Crime Writers Assn., president MWA, 1986. WG Am. Address: 401 Oak Crest Rd San Anselmo CA 94960

GOREY, EDWARD ST. JOHN, b. Chgo., Feb. 22, 1925; s. Edward Leo and Helen Dunham (Garvey) G. Author: The Unstrung Harp, 1953, The Doubtful Guest, 1957, The Hapless Child, 1961, The Willowdale Handcar, 1962, The Wuggly Ump, 1963, The Remembered Visit, 1965, The Gilded Bat, 1966, The Blue Aspic, 1968, The Other Statue, 1968, The Epileptic Bicycle, 1969, The Awdrey-Gore Legacy, 1972, Amphigorey, 1972, Category, 1973, Amphigorey Too, 1975, The Broken Spoke, 1976, The Loathsome Couple, 1977, The Gilded Bat, 1979, Gorey Endings, 1979; numerous other works. BA, Harvard U., 1950. Served with AUS, 1943-46. Address: Congdon & Weed 298 5th Ave New York NY 10001

GORKIN, JESS, b. Rochester, NY, Oct. 23, 1913; s. Barnett and Bessie (Berk) G.; m. Dorothy Kleinberg, June 23, 1940; children: Michael, Brett, Scott. Editor-in-chief Daily Iowan, Iowa City, 1936-37; assoc. editor Look Mag., NYC, 1937-41; originated and edited picture mag. for distrbn. in friendly and occupied countries Photo Review, OWI, 1942-46; mng. editor Parade, NYC, 1947-49, editor, 1949-79, cons. editor, 1983—; editor 50 Plus, NYC, 1979—. BA, U. Iowa, 1936. Recipient Christopher Award, 1956, citation Overseas Press Club, 1955, editorial award Natl. Comdr. Am. Legion. Home: 4320 Falmouth Dr Longboat Key FL 33548

GORMAN, JOHN ANDREW, b. Hoboken, NJ, Aug. 28, 1938; s. Thomas Francis and Edith (Ward) G. Author: The Reception of Federico Garcia Lorez in Germany, 1973. Translator Heinrich Mann and his Public, 1969. Contrbr. to book, numerous articles to mags., newspapers. B.A., Manhattan Coll., 1960; M.A., John Hopkins U., 1961, Ph.D., 1967. Asst. prof. German, U. Miami, Coral Gables, FL, 1967-74; purser on cruise ships, Miami, 1976-81; freelance jnlst., 1981—. Recipient Honorable Mention, WD, 1971, 74, 78, 83, 87. Mem. NWU, FFWA. Home: 4713 NW 7 St 305 Miami FL 33126

GORMAN, JUDY, b. Hartford, CT, Nov. 8, 1942; d. Buel Clark and Emmily (Brown) Grant; m. Edmund Joseph Gorman, Sept. 8, 1962; 1 dau., Sara Grant Gorman Bryce. Author: The Culinary Craft, 1984, Judy Gorman's Vegetable Cookbook, 1986. Contrbr. articles to mags. including Yankee Mag., Working Mother, MCall's, others. Wrkg. on Judy Gorman's Book of New England Breads. B.A. in Edn., St. Joseph Coll., 1978. Recipient Tastemaker's award R. T. French, 1985. Home: 69 Dale Rd Manhester CT 06040

GORRELL, DENA RUTH, b. Loyal, OK, June 8, 1932; d. John James and Viola Ruth (Ogle) Groenewold; m. John Sterling Gorrll, Nov. 14, 1953; children—James Everton, Deanne Marie Gorrell-Steinmetz. Author: (poems) Truths, Tenderness, and Trifles, 1986. Contrbr. poems to anthols, Ed. poetry column: Edmond Sunday newspaper. A. Commerce, Oklahoma State U., 1952. Clrk.-stenographer Social Seurity Administration, Enid, OK, 1958-61. Mem. Poetry Soc. Okla. (asst. publicity dir.), Natl. Fedn. State Poetry Socs., AAP, Poets at Work (1st prize 1987, runner-up 1987), Okla. Wrtrs. Fedn. Home: 14024 Gateway Dr Edmond OK 73013

GORTON, KAITLYN, see Emerson, Kathy Lynn

GORMEZANO, KEITH STEPHEN, (Shabetai Ben-Israel), b. Madison, WI, Nov. 22, 1955; s. Isadore G. and Mirium (Fox) G.; m. Emma Lee Rogers, Aug. 17, 1986. Contrbr. U.S. Law News, Attorney Eagle Eye Service Newsletter, Columnist: Iowa City Life and Times newspaper, 1970. Contrbr. articles to newsletters, trade and bus. mags. Ed.: M'Godolim: A Jewish Lit. Mag., 1980-82, Beacon Rvw., 1980-84. B.Genl. Studies, U. Iowa, 1977; postgrad. U. Puget Sound, Schl. of Law, 1984-86. Ed., 31 Flavours Mag., Iowa City, IA, 1972-73; co-pub. Iowa City Life & Times, Iowa City, 1979; public info. officer Operation Improvement Fdn., Seattle, 1980-81; pub. Le Beacon Presse, Seattle, 1980—; mgr. Washington Park Properties, Seattle, 1982-87. Recipient Outstanding Small Press Mag. award Pushcart Prize/Press, 1983, 86. Mem. Small Press Rvw. Home: Box 15945 Seattle WA 98115

GORTSEMA, JANET PHILLIPS, b. Cin., d. Elwood Hudson and Edna Mae (Johnson) Phillips; m. Frank P. Gortsema, Oct. 17, 1959; 1 son, Grant. Author: Second Chance for Ruth, 1984. BA, Anderson Coll., 1957; MS, Purdue U., 1960. Tchr., Markleville High Schl., Madison County, Ind., 1957-58, pub. schls., Parma, Ohio, 1959-63, Tarrytown pub. schls., N.Y., 1965—; adj. prof. Marymount Coll., Tarrytown, 1982—. Recipient Syford Poetry award Anderson Coll., 1956. Mem. N.Y. State Tchr.'s Assn. Home: 7 Briarwood Ln Pleasantville NY 10570

GOSSMAN, LIONEL, b. Glasgow, Scotland, May 31, 1929; came to U.S., 1958; s. Norman and Sarah (Gold) G.; m. Eva R. Reinitz, Mar. 7, 1963; 1 dau., Janice Naomi. Author: Men and Masks: A Study of Moliere, 1963, Medievalism and the Ideologies of Enlightenment, 1968, French Society and Culture, 1972, Augustin Thierry and Liberal Historiography, 1976, The Empire Unpossessed: An Essay on Gibbon, 1981, Orpheus Philologus: Bachofen Versus Mommsen, 1982; editorial bd.: MLN, 1959-76, Comparative Lit., Eighteenth Century Studies, French Forum. MA, Glasgow U., 1951; D Phil., Oxford U., 1958. NEH fellow, 1978-79; Pro Helvetia Fdn. fellow, 1983; ACLS fellow, 1969-70. Mem. Acad. Lit. Home: 54 Maclean Cr Princeton NJ 08540

GOTTFRIED, LEON ALBERT, b. Ames, IA, Nov. 6, 1925; s. Samuel and Louise G.; children—Laura, Ann. Author: Matthew Arnold and the Romantics, 1963. AB, U. Ill., 1948, MA, 1951, PhD, 1958. Served with USNR, 1944-46, PTO. Mem. MLA. Office: Dept Eng Purdue U

West Lafayette IN 47907

GOTTSCHALK, ASHER M., b. Zion, IL, s. Joseph R. and Ida King (Means) G.; m. Elizabeth Kathryn Shaub, June 19, 1937; children—James, Jerome, Thomas, Miriam. Author: Growing Up in Blooming Glen, 1984. Contrbr. articles on stained glass to religious mags. AB, Albright Coll., Reading, Pa., 1934, BD, 1937; MST, Luth. Theol. Sem., Phila., 1957. Ordained to ministry. Pastor, United Meth. Ch., 1937-74. Mem. Am. Assn. Retired Persons (chaplain). Club: Rotary (v.p. 1958). Home: 608 S Granite St Deming NM 88030

GOTTSCHALL, EDWARD MAURICE, b. NYC, Dec. 28, 1915; s. Mayer and Stephanie (Krauss) G.; m. Lee Beatrice Natale, Feb. 6, 1943 (dec. 1984); 1 son, Robert; m. 2d, Alice J., Jan. 20, 1985. Author: Typography Today, 1987. Ed., Graphic Arts Production Yearbook, 1937-51, Art Direction, Rush mags., 1952-67, Typographic i, 1969-79; co-ed. Advtg. Directions, vols. 1-4, 1960-64; co-author Commercial Art as a Business, 3d ed., 1972; cons. ed. Graphic Arts Manual, 1980; author/ed. Graphic Communication 80's, 1981. BSS, CCNY, 1937; MS, Columbia Schl. Jnlsm., 1938. Ed., Colton Press, NYC, 1937-51; sr. ed. Popular Merchandising, Passaic, NJ, 1964-67; ed./co-pub. Art Direction, NYC, 1952-67; exec. dir. Amer. Inst. Graphic Arts, NYC, 1969-75; exec. v.p./ed. International Typeface Corp., NYC, 1975—. Served to T/5, USAAF, 1943-45, ETO. Founder annl. exhib. typographic excellence, Type Directors Club. Mem. Type Dirs. Club, Amer. Printing Hist. Assn. Home: 63 Highland Ave Eastchester NY 10707

GOTTSTEIN, KAREN, b. San Francisco, Nov. 18, 1946; d. Howard R. and Ruth (Zakeim) G. Contrbr. articles to mags. including The Volcano Rvw, The Blatant Image, Small Press, H & N Albuquerque News. Editor: H & N Albuquerque News. BA in visual communication, Antioch Coll. West, San Francisco, 1978. Mkgt. mgr. Ind. Pubs. Services, Volcano, Calif., 1978-82, Molzen-Corbin, Albuquerque, 1984; mkgt. coordinator Holmes & Narver, Inc., Albuquerque, 1985—; award-winning free-lance photographer, Volcano, 1972-78. Active Volcano Community Assn., 1972-82; vol. Land Commnr. Campaign, Albuquerque, 1986. Recipient numerous awards N. Mex. Soc. Profl. Photographers, 1983. Mem. Soc. Mkgt. Profl. Services. Home: Box J Corrales NM 87048

GOUGEON, LEN GIRARD, b. Northampton, MA, Aug. 8, 1947; s. William Louis and Helen Ann (Murphy) G.; m. Deborah Jean Zagorsky, Feb. 22, 1980; children—Elliott, Nadia, Wesley. Contrbr. to New England Qtly, Am. Lit., Studies in the Am. Renaissance, Am. Transcendental Qtly, Walt Whitman Qtly Rvw, Negro History Bulltn., Thoreau Soc. Bulltn., Jnl Evolutionary Psychology. BA, St. Mary's U., 1969; MA, U. Mass.-Amherst, 1972, PhD, 1974. Grad. instr. Univ. Mass., Amherst, 1970-74; asst. prof., Univ. Scranton, Pa., 1974-78, assoc. prof., 1978-82, prof., 1982—. NEH fellow, 1982. Mem. MLA, Thoreau Soc., Am. Studies Assn. Address: Box 147 Glendale Avoca PA 18641

GOULART, RON(ALD JOSEPH), b. Berkeley, CA, Jan. 13, 1933; s. Joseph Silveira and Josephine (Macri) G.; m. Frances Ann Sheridan, June 13, 1964; children—Sean, Steffan. Author: sci. fiction Brinkman; Galaxy Jane; sci. fiction story collections Odd Job 101; mystery novels Ghosting; novel The Tremendous Adventures of Bernie Wine; sci. fiction The Robot in the Closet, After Things Fell Apart, Big Bang; non-fiction The Great Comic Book Artists; from films Capricorn One; from comics Snakegod; editor: The Great British Detective. BA, U. Calif., Berkeley, 1955. Copywriter Guild, Bascom & Bonfigli, San Francisco, 1955-57, 58-60, free-lance writer, 1968—. Recipient Edgar Allan Poe award, MWA, 1971. Mem. SFWA (past v.p.), MWA (dir. 1979-83, 1984-87). Address: 30 Farrell Rd Weston CT 06883

GOULD, JEAN ROSALIND, b. Greenville, OH, May 25, 1919; d. Aaron J. and Elsie E. (Elgutter) G. Author: Miss Emily, 1946, Robert Frost, The Aim Was Song, 1964, The Poet and Her Book: A Biography of Edna St. Vincent Millay, 1969, Amy—The World of Amy Lowell and the Imagist Movement, 1975, American Women Poets, Pioneers of Modern Poetry, 1980, Modern American Women Poets, 1985, others; works include short stories, biographies. AB, U. Toledo, 1939. Free-lance writer, editorial rewriter, radio-script writer, 1941—. Fellow Va. Center Creative Arts (adv. bd.), MacDowell Colony, Huntington Hartford Fdn., Wurlitzer Fdn. Mem. PEN, AL Am. Address: Dodd Mead 71 Fifth Ave New York NY 10003

GOULD, LOIS, m. Philip Benjamin, 1959 (dec.); children—Anthony, Roger; m. Robert E. Gould. Author: novels Such Good Friends, 1970, Necessary Objects, 1972, Final Analysis, 1974, A Sea-Change, 1976, La Presidenta, 1981; essays Not Responsible for Personal Articles, 1978; story X: A Fabulous Child's Story, 1978. BA, Wellesley Coll. Former police reporter, feature writer L.I. Star Jnl; former exec. editor, Ladies Home Jnl; contrbr.: articles to N.Y. Times, McCalls, Ms.; columnist: N.Y. Times, 1977. Address: Rembar & Curtis 19 W 44 St New York NY 10036

GOULD, ROBERTA, b. Bklyn., July 16, 1941; d. Michael and Leah Gould. Author: Dream Yourself Flying, 1979; Writing Air, Written Water, 1980; Only Rock & Other Poems, 1985. Student Bklyn. Coll., 1959; MA, U. Calif., Berkeley, 1965. CCLM grantee, 1979. Mem. PEN, PSA, N.Y. Poets Co-op. Home: Van Aiken Farm Box 126 Stone Ridge NY 12484

GOULDEN, JOSEPH CHESLEY, b. Marshall, TX, May 23, 1934; s. Joe C. and Lecta M. (Everitt) G.; m. Leslie Cantrell Smith, 1979; children by previous marriage: Joseph C., Jim Craig. Author: The Curtis Caper, 1965, Monopoly, 1968, Truth is the First Casualty, 1969, The Money Givers, 1971, Meany, 1972, The Superlawyers, 1972, The Benchwarmers, 1974, The Best Years, 1976, The Million Dollar Lawyers, 1978, Korea: The Untold Story of the War, 1982, Jerry Wurf: Labor's Last Angry Man, 1982, The Death Merchant, 1984, The Dictionary of Espionage (as Henry S.A. Beckett), 1986; co-author: (with Paul Dickson) There Are Alligators in Our Sewers, 1983; editor: Mencken's Last Campaign, 1976. Student, U. Tex., 1952-56. Reporter Marshall News Messenger, 1956, Dallas News, 1958-61, Phila. Inquirer, 1961-68. Served with AUS, 1956-58. Mem. Tex. Inst. Letters, Washington Ind. Writers, Assn of Former Intelligence Officers. Home: 2500 Q St NW Washington DC 20007

GOVIG, VALERIE COWLS, b. Portland, OR, Sept. 4, 1934; d. Thomas John Ewart and Charlene Alma (Endecott) Cowls; m. Melvin Emerson Govig, Sept. 4, 1954; children—Dana Hope, Kari Joy. Contrbr. articles to World Book Encyc. Editor: (newsletter) The Windy Notice, 1969-74, Chesapeake council Camp Fire Girls, 1971-73; publisher-editor Kite Lines (magazine), 1977—. BA, U. Oreg.-Eugene, 1956. Advt. copywriter Hutzler's Dept. Store, Balt., 1969-71; free-lance wrtr., Balt., 1972-76. Founder, Md. Kite Festival, Balt., 1967, chmn. pub. Liberty Rd. Recreation & Parks Council, Baltimore County, Md., 1971-73. Mem. Md. Kite Soc. (founder), Am. Kitefliers Assn. (founder). Home: 7106 Campfield Rd Baltimore MD 21207

GOW, ELLEN B., b. Holyoke, MA, May 2, 1950; d. James Dunlop and Gladys Winifred (Wilson) G. Author: Go To the Head of the Class, 25th ed., 1986, Extra! Extra!, 1982, Introduction to Word Processing, 1982. Author activity sheets for classroom computer software; contrbr. articles to teaching mags. B.S. in Edn., Framingham State Coll., 1972. Tchr., Hodgkins Sch., East Brookfield, MA, 1979-80, Leverett Schl., MA, 1980—. Home: 219 Amity St Amherst MA 01002

GRABER, DORIS APPEL, b. St. Louis, Nov. 11, 1923; d. Ernest and Martha (Insel) Appel; m. Thomas M. Graber, June 15, 1941; children—Lee Winston, Thomas Woodrow, Jack Douglas, Jim Murray, Susan Doris. Author: The Development of the Law of Belligerent Occupation, 1949, 68, Crisis Diplomacy: A History of U.S. Intervention Policies and Practices, 1959, Public Opinion, The President, and Foreign Policy, 1968, Verbal Behavior and Politics, 1976, Mass Media and American Politics, 1980, 2d ed., 1984, 3rd ed., 1988, Crime News and the Public, 1980, (with others) Media Agenda Setting in a Presidential Election, 1981, Processing the News: How People Tame the Information Tide, 1984, 2nd ed. 1988; editor, contrbr.: The President and the Public, 1982; editor: Media Power in Politics, 1984. AB, Washington U., St. Louis, 1941, MA, 1942; PhD, Columbia U., 1947. Feature writer St. Louis County Observer, Univ. City Tribune, St. Louis, 1939-41; editor textbooks Harper & Row, Evanston, 1956-63; prof. poli. sci., U. of Ill. at Chgo., 1964—. Home: 2895 Sheridan Pl Evanston IL 60201

GRABILL, JAMES ROSCOE, JR., b. Bowling Green, Ohio, Nov. 29, 1949, s. James Roscoe and Bette Lou (Baker) G. Author: One River, 1975, Clouds Blowing Away, 1976, To Other Beings, 1981, In the Coiled Light, 1985; contrbr. poetry to: Kayak, Poetry Northwest, New Letters, NRG, Bluefish, numerous other mags. and anthologies. BFA, Bowling Green (Ohio) State U., 1974; MA, Colo. State U., 1984. Colo. State U., Ft. Collins, adjunct instr. dept English, 1985—; co-producer Transmissions: Poetry Mag.-of-the-Air, sta. KBOO, Portland, Oreg., 1979-80; coord. reading series Power Plant Visual Arts Center, 1985-86; co-ed. Leaping Mountain Press, Ft. Collins, 1985—. Mem. AWP, AAP. Home: 508 Edwards St Fort Collins CO 80524

GRABO, NORMAN STANLEY, b. Chgo., Apr. 21, 1930; s. Stanley Valentine and Effie Louise (Nelson) G.; children—Carolyn Deane, Scott David. Author: Edward Taylor, 1961, American Thought and Writing, 1965, American Poetry and Prose, 1970, The Coincidental Art of Charles Brockden Brown, 1981; editor: Arthur Mervyn, 1980. BA, Elmhurst Coll., 1952; MA, UCLA, 1955, PhD, 1958. Folger Shakespeare Library fellow, 1959; Guggenheim fellow, 1970-71; NEH fellow, 1980; Soc. Religion in Higher Edn. fellow, 1966-67. Mem. MLA, Mich. Acad. Sci., Arts and Letters, South Central MLA. Office: Eng Dept U Tulsa Tulsa OK 74104

GRABOWSKI, WILLIAM J(OHN), (William John Pillips), b. Cleve., May 8, 1958; s. Stanley Anthony and Muriel Elizabeth (Fry) G. Contrbr. rvws., interviews, poems, short stories to sci. fiction & horror mags., Newspapers. Book reviewer, interviewer: The Horror Show, 1984—. Wrkg. on Escorts into Darkness: The Creators of Horror Fiction; Toxic Shadows (collection of short stories); Black Roses (novel). Student Kent State U., 1976. Lab asst. schl. of dentistry Case Western Reserve U., Cleve., 1978-82; free-lance wrtr., 1983—. Home: 6970 SOM Center Rd Solon OH 44139

GRACE, EUGENE VERNON, b. Jackson, TN, Dec. 12, 1927. Ed.: Essentials of Ophthalmology (Roland I. Pritikin, M.D.), 1969; author: The Most Beautiful Love Poetry in the English Language, 1984, MASH, Central America, 1985, From These Stones, 1986; fndr. and publish. of Moore Publ. Co. (1968-81). MD, U. of Michigan, 1956. Private practice in ophthalmology, 1963—. Mem. NC Assoc. for Blind, NC Heart Assoc. Home: 911 Broad St Durham NC 27705

GRADDICK, RICHARD ADOLPH, b. Phila., Nov. 2, 1918; m. Norma Hipoloto, Apr. 29, 1981; children: Riccardo, Alvin. Author: U.S. Navy's Project Handclasp: A Grasp on Journalist Writing, 1985. Wrkg. on novel, articles. BS, U. of State of NY; MA, PhD in public relations, Columbia Pacific U., 1984. Reporter Phila. Tribune, 1932-43; prin. public relations firm Graddick & Graddick, Phila., 1936-44; chief journalist U.S. Navy, 1944-76 (1st race member to be selected by USN jnlst.); staff wrtr. Chronicle Newspaper, Charleston, S.C., 1981-82; freelance wrtr., Charleston, 1985—. Recipient numerous awards includng 4 Annl. Gold Medal awards, Freedoms Fdn. Home: 1385 Ashley River Rd 55D Charleston SC 29407

GRAF, GARY R., b. Columbus, OH, Mar. 6, 1947; s. Campbell Roger Gr an Edna Louise (Lasure)) Graf Drake; m. Lynn D., May 19, 1979. Contrr. articles: Darkroom Photography mag., Air & Space Mag., Space World mag., numerous others. BA in Journalism, Ohio Stat U., 1973. Copy boy N.Y. Times, 1967; wrtr., photographer Buffalo (Wyo.) Bulltn., 1973-77; account exec., v.p. William Katka & Assocs. Public Relations, Denver, 1978-85; freelance wrtr., Denver, 1985—. Mem. Aviation-Space Wrtrs. Assn. (Space Journalism award 1986), Am. Soc. Mag. Photographers, NWC. Home: 1870 S Ogden St Denver CO 80210

GRAF, JESS D., b. Columbus, NB, Nov. 11, 1935, s. John Derleth and Lydia Lucille (Schliegert) G.; m. Ilene Graf, Jan. 9, 1959 (div. 1970); children—Dawn, Joans, Heather, Jesse S. Author:: Rap a Poem Round Yer Beer, 1977, The Mountain Cat, 1980, 2d ed., 1982, Preaching at the Cemetery, 1986; ed. Mountain Cat Rvw, 1984—; contrbr. to Pikestaff Forum, San Fernando Poetry Jnl, Arulo/Vega, Moraginine, Amputated Fingers, Spree, New York Smith, also others. AA, Lamar Jr. Coll., 1957; BA, Adams State Coll., 1962. Poet, ed. Mountain Cat Press, Denver, 1976—; tchr., substitute tchr. pub. schls., Farmington, N.Mex., 1973-74, Casper, Wyo., 1978-79, Boulder, Colo., 1980-82, Denver, 1982—. Served with USMC, 1954-57. Recipient D'Anunzio award J. Fish Studios, 1980, Dr. Marie C. Pohndorf poetry award Spree mag., 1980, 7th annl. poetry book award Realities Library, 1980. Mem. P&W, Soc. for Advancement Poetics. Home: 14 Washington St Denver CO 80203

GRAFF, J. WILLIAM, b. Camden, NJ, Sept. 13, 1930; s. C. James and Mae G. (Nuss) G.; m. Betty Jean Hite, June 27, 1964; children—John E., Sandra L., Joseph A. BS in Engring. Physics, Drexel U., 1961; MS in Math., Stevens Inst. of Tech., 1966. Pub./ed. The Business Review, Vienna, VA, 1978—. Home: 12847 Tewksbury Dr Herndon VA 22071

GRAGASIN, JOSE VALLIENTE, b. Gerona, Philippines, Feb. 28, 1900, came to U.S., 1919, s. Laureano Tabago and Rosa (Valliente) G.; m. Socorro Patricio, Oct. 5, 1930; children—Joseph, Joscorro, Altagracia, Lilia, Raul, Evelyn, Digna, Walter. Author: Introduction to Sociology, 1940, Business Psychology, 1948, Methodology of Research, 1949, Comparative Education, 1953, Introduction to Economic Analysis, 1960, Business Cycles, 1961, Price Theory, 1961, The Preparation and Writing of Research Papers, 1961, Principles of Economics in Philippine Setting, 1961, The Philippine Agrarian Reform Code and Program Under the New Society, 1972, The Philippine Economic Problems and Their Solutions, 1964, Philippine Cooperatives: Organization and Management, 1965, Philippine Cooperatives and Agrarian Reform Program, 1972, The Attributes to the Greatness of the American People (poetry), 1980, What Makes the Filipinos a Great People (poetry), 1984; contrbr. poetry to Our World's Best Loved Poems, Today's Greatest Poems, other publs. AB, Kansas City U., 1922, BCS, 1923; BD, Garrett Theol. Sem., 1926, PhD, Chgo. Law Schl., 1927, DH (hon.), Kansas City U., 1928. Ednl. cons., econ. cons. U.S. and Philippines; v.p. acad. affairs, dean Grad. Schl., Northeastern Coll, Philippines, 1972-74, acting pres., 1974-75; now ret. Recipient numerous plaques, certs. of appreciation. Mem. PSA, AAP, Md. Poetry Soc., World Lit. Acad. Home: 104 S Collins Ave Baltimore MD 21229

GRAHAM, JOE MICHAEL, b. Denver, July 22, 1952; s. Leo Harding and June Ellenor (Cannon) G.; m. Judy Elizabeth Welch, June 25, 1982; 1 dau., Katherine Elizabeth, 1 son, Trent Michael. BJ, U. MO, 1974. Ed., American Bee Jnl, Hamilton, IL, 1974—. Home: RR 1 Box 409 Hamilton IL 62341

GRAHAM, LOLA AMANDA BEALL, b. Bremen, GA, Nov. 12, 1896, d. John Gainer and Nancy Caroline Idella (Reid) Beall; m. John Jackson, Aug. 13, 1917; children—Billy Duane, John Thomas, Helen Marie, Donald Jackson, Beverly Ann. Poet, photographer, work published in Readers Digest, Encyc. Britannica, Audubon's Nature Encyc., numerous others. Recipient over 100 natl. awards in photography contests, poetry awards. Mem. Chaparral Poets (pres.). Home: 225-93 Mt Hermon Rd Scotts Valley CA 95066

GRAHAM-HENRY, DIANE MICHELLE, b. Fresno, CA, Jan. 25, 1946; d. William Graham and Darleen Roberta (Sullenger) Malette; m. John Raymond Henry, Jan. 27, 1967 (div. Feb. 1, 1977). Contrbr. articles to mags. including Chicagoland Monthly, British Jnl. Photography, Screen; columnist, contrbr.: N.Y. Photo Dist. News, 1983—. B.A., U. Ill., 1971; M.F.A., Sch. Art Inst., Chgo., 1977. Pres., Diane Graham-Henry Photo, hgo., 1977—. Printmaking fellow NEA, 1974. Mem. Am. Soc. Mag. Photographers (membership chair 1981-82, secy., 1st v.p., 1982-83, pres. 1983-85). Home: 613 W Belden Chicago IL 60614

GRANAT, ROBERT, see Grant, Robert L.

GRANGER, BILL, b. Chgo., June 1, 1941; s. William Cecil and Ruth Elizabeth (Griffith) G.; m. Lori Meschke, June 27, 1967; 1 son, Alec. Author: The November Man, 1979, Sweeps, 1980, Public Murders, 1980, Schism, 1981, Queen's Crossing, 1981, Time for Frankie Coolin, 1981, The Shattered Eye, 1982, The British Cross, 1983, (with Lori Granger) Fighting Jane, 1980, Chicago Pieces, 1983. Student, DePaul U., 1959-63. Reporter UPI, Chgo., 1963, Chgo. Tribune, 1966-69, freelance columnist, 1980—; reporter, columnist Chgo. Sun-Times, Chgo. Tribune, 1969—. Served with AUS, 1963-65. Office: Trib 435 N Michigan Ave Chicago IL 60011

GRANGER, DENNIS LEE, b. Lake Mills, WI, July 24, 1938; s. James William Granger and Cynthia Jane (Fisher) Casterton; m. Mildred Helen Raine, Dec. 6, 1958; children—Cheryl Jane, Teri Lynn, Robin Leigh. Contrbr. articles to mags., jnls. including Eastern Psychologies, Jnl. Humanistic Psychology, others. B.A., Governors Stat U., 1981; Ph.D., Saybrook Inst., 1986. Served to capt. USAF, 1956-68. Mem. Am. Assn. Advancement Sci., N.Y. Acad. Scis., Assn. Transpersonal Psychology, Assn. Humanistic Psychology. Office: 687 Tamarisk Terr Crystal Lake IL 60014

GRANT, CLAUDE DE WITT, (C.D. Grant), b. NYC, Dec. 20, 1944; s. Claude Allen Grant and Rose Levonia (Nelson) Chenault; m. Margarette Louise White, June 16, 1973 (div. 1978); 2 children, Damian Allen, Tahra Lore; m. Gloriana Beatrice Waters, Aug. 7, 1983. Author: (poetry) Keeping Time, 1981, Images in a Shaded Light, 1986; ed. New Rain anthology, Vols. I-VII; contrbr. articles and poetry to Essence, West End, Quindaro, Black in Vogue, Umesika, other lit mags, profl. jnls. BA, Hunter Coll., 1974; MA, Mercy Coll., Dobbs Ferry, N.Y., 1979. Music ed. Essence, 1970-75; co-founder, chief ed. Blind Beggar Press, Inc., Bronx, N.Y., 1977—. Served with U.S. Army, 1962-65. Mem. P&W, Bronx Council on the Arts, Community College Journalism Assn, Natl. Assn of Black Journalists.Home: 1783 Bussing Ave Bronx NY 10466

GRANT, J. B., (John Barnard, Jack) b. Hartford, CT, Mar. 23, 1940; s. Ellsworth S. and Marion H. G.; m. Ann H. Grant, May 28, 1965; 2 children, Jason, Schuyler. Author: Two Beastly Tales (with Katharine Houghton), 1975; Skateboarding, 1976; The World of Women's Gymnastics (with Jim Gault), 1976; Soccer: A Personal Guide, 1978; Ins & Outs of Soccer, 1983; Companions in Spirit (Leah Garfield), 1985; ed. The Geocentric Experience, 1972; Learning & Tchg., 1974; Your Body Speaks Its Mind, 1975; contrbr. essays to San Francisco Rvw of Books, stories and poems in 50 anthologies, lit. mags. BA, U. Cal.-Berkeley, 1965. Tchr. phys. ed. and outdoor skills Green Valley Schl., Orange City, Fla., 1966-68, math and English Deerborne Schl., Coral Gables, 1969-70; self-emp. charter sailboat capt, Bradenton Beach, Fla., 1968-69; dir. devel. Calif. Outward Bound, Palo Alto, 1970-71; writer, ed. and pub., Los Gatos and Sebastopol, Calif, 1971—. Coach, youth soccer and Analy High Schl., Sebastopol, 1976—. Mem. Mus. Local No. 292. Address: 1162 West Sexton Rd Sebastopol CA 95472

GRANT, ROBERT L., (Robert Granat), b. Havana, Cuba, Feb. 7, 1925, s. David E. and Pauline (Greenberg) G.; m. Carolyn McMullan; children—Theo, Beata, Paul, Seth, Anna, John. Author novels: The Important Thing, 1961, Re-genesis, 1972; contrbr. short stories, essays to Studia Mystica, Parabola, Am. Rvw, Tex. Qtly, various anthologies, schl. texts. Editor AMIGO, pubn. of Natl. Alliance for the Mentally Ill, NM. BA, Yale U., 1947. Recipient O.Henry award, 1958, 61. Home: Box 99 Dixon NM 87527

GRAPES, MARCUS JACK, b. New Orleans, Sept. 11, 1942; s. Samuel Joshua and Regina (Schreiber) G.; m. Susan Eva Schwarz, July 8, 1968 (div. 1978). Wrks. include: Trees, Coffee, and the Eyes of Deer, 1986, Breaking on Camera, 1978, Termination Journal, 1974, Perchance, In All Your Travels, Have You Ever Been To Pittsburgh?, 1969, Seven is a Frozen Number, 1967, A Savage Peace, 1965. BA, Tulane U., 1966, MFA, 1968. Profl. actor, 1967—; wrtr./ed., Virtus Prods., Los Angeles, 1983-84; ed./pub., Bombshelter Press, Hermosa Beach, CA, 1976—. Cons. Coord., CA Poets-in-the-Schls., 1979—; poetry tchr., UCLA Extension; Beyond Baroque; CA Poets-in-the-Schls., 1977—; poetry ed. South Bay Magazine. Awards: NEA Fellowship, 1984, CA Arts Council Artist-in-Res. Grants, 1981-84, 1985-86. Home: 6421-1/2 Orange St Los Angeles CA 90048

GRAVEL, CLIFFORD RICHARD HILAIRE, b. Passaic, NJ, Mar. 5, 1939; 1 dau., Genevieve. Contrbr. articles and poetry to mags., including Natl. Billiard News, Am. Billiard Rvw, Vidya, Albuquerque Jnl., NM Daily Lobo, others. Ed.: Touch-Ups, 1977-79, Menzie, 1981-82, Turning Point, 1985-86, Brush Strokes, 1987—. B.S., U. NM, 1986. Mgmt. cons. Benjamin Moore Co., Montvale, NJ, 1973-81; sales agt. Tronics Co., Albuquerque, 1981-83; student tchr. Cleveland Midschool, Albuquerque, 1986-87. Grantee NM Sci. Tchrs. Assn., 1985-86; mem. Returning Students Assn. (grantee 1985-86, dir. 1985-86), Mensa, Intl. Platform Assn., Phi Lambda Theta. Home: 5800 Osuna NE 307 Albuquerque NM 87109

GRAVES, JOHN ALEXANDER, b. Fort Worth, Aug. 6, 1920; s. John Alexander and Nancy Mary Kay) G.; m. Bryan Huthison, 1946 (div. 1951); m. Jane Marshall Cole, Dec. 27, 1958; children—Helen, Sally. Author: Goodbye to a River, 1960, The Nation's River, 1968, Hard Scrabble, 1974, From a Limestone Ledge, 1980; (with others) The Water Hustlers, 1971; (with Scott Gentling and Stuart Gentling) Of Birds and Texas, 1987. B.A., Rice U., 1942; M.A., Columbia U., 1948 Instr. U. of Tex., 1948-51; adj. prof. Tex. Christian U., Fort Worth, 1956-65; cons.-wrtr. U.S. Dept. of Interior, Washington, 1965-68; free-lance wrtr., 1946—. Fellow Tex. Inst. Letters (past pres., Car P. Collins Non-Fiction award 1960, 74); mem. PEN. Home: Box 667 Glen Rose TX 76043

GRAVES, ROY NEIL, b. Medina, TN, Feb. 2, 1939; s. Roy Neil and Georgia Mae (Reed) G.; m. Sue Lain Hunt, June 5, 1965 (div. July 1982); children: Anna Hunt, Benjamin Lain, Molly Brett. Author books and monographs: Emily Dickinson and Imagism, 1964, A Picture History of Hall-Moody, 1976, Medina and Other Poems, 1976, Out of Tenn., 1977, Hugh John Massey of the Royal Hall, 1977, John Massey Un-hyd, 1977, The Runic Beowulf and Other Lost Anglo-Saxon Poems, Reconstructed and Annotated, 1979, Shakespeare's Lost Sonnets, 1979; ed. River Region Monographs, 1975; contrbr. poetry to Appalachian Jnl, Mountain Rvw, Goddard Jnl, Old Hickory Rvw, Miss. Rvw, Jnl of the Jackson Purchase Hist Soc, Duke Archive, NY Mag, Vanderbilt Poetry Rvw, Homewords: A Book of Tenn. Writers, Christian Sci. Monitor; contrbr. articles and rvws. to The Princeton Tiger, TenneScene, Upstart Crow, Phylon. BA, Princeton U., 1961; MA, Duke U., 1964; DA, U. Miss., 1977. Tchg. asst. Duke Univ., Durham, NC, 1963-64; asst. prof. English Univ. Va., Lynchburg, 1965-69, coordinator of humanities, 1968-69; asst/assoc/prof Univ. of Tenn., Martin, 1969—. Recipient first place for Poetry, The Miscellany: A Davidson Rvw, 1976. Mem. Tenn. Philol Assn. Address: R2 Box 473 Martin TN 38237

GRAVLEE, GRACE DOWNING, b. Covin, AL, May 6, 1913; d. Thomas Shelton and Minerva Elizabeth (Hankins) Lollar; m. Fred M. Downing, Oct. 19, 1940 (dec. 1969); children—Edward F., LeMoyen Downing Hunter; m. 2d Levert G.Gravlee, Sept. 16, 1972. Contrbr. poetry: Atlantic mag. Wrkg. on hist. novel. BA, Auburn U., 1936-47; freelance wrtr., lectr., 1947—. Mem. Ala. Wrtrs.' Conclave (pres. 1983-85), Ala. Poetry Soc. (program chmn. 1986-87). Home: 2221 Gay Way Birmingham AL 35216

GRAVLEY, ERNESTINE HUDLOW, b. Russellville, AR, Feb. 4; d. Joseph Ernest and Mary Consuela (Mullins) Hudlow; m. Loupe H. Gravley, Jan. 12, 1940; children—Almalou Gravley Cowan, Carol Ann Gravley Fugit. Author biographies: Hang onto the Willows, 1967, Judges of the Place of Fire, 1980. Contrbr. numerous articles, short stories, children's stories, hist. works, poems to mags., newspapers, jnls. including Cosmopolitan, Capper's Weekly, others. Audiologist, bookkeeper Beltone Electronics, Shawnee, OK, 1963; legal secy. District Judge Office, Shawnee, 1976; free-lance wrtr. (1945-76.) Recipient Diana Sherwood Hist. award Arkansas Wrtrs. Conf., 1950, Margaret Moore Jacobs award for inspirational writing Ark. Wrtrs. Conf., 1952; holds largest number of state conf. writing prizes in the nation. Mem. NLAPW (Juvenile Writing award 1950), Natl. Fedn. State Poetry Socs., Okla. Wrts. Fedn. (past pres., bd. dis.), Ark. Wrtrs. Conf. (advisory bd.), Shawnee WG (pres.-dir.), Authors Composers Artists Soc., Poetry Soc. Okla., Poet's Roundtable Ark. Home: 1225 Sherry Ln Shawnee OK 74801

GRAY, ALICE WIRTH, b. Chgo., Apr. 29, 1934, d. Louis and Mary (Bolton) Wirth; m. Ralph Gareth Gray, July 16, 1954; children—Mary Louise, Elizabeth Katherine. Contrbr. poetry Am. Scholar, Poetry, The Atlantic, other publs.; contrbr. short fiction Helicon Nine, Primavera, others; contrbr. book rvws., San Francisco Chronicle. BA, U. Calif.-Berkeley, 1958, MA, 1960. Recipient Conrad Aiken award Poetry Soc. Ga., 1974, Lit. award Ill. Arts Council, 1980, Duncan Lawrie prize Arvon Fdn., Kilnhurst, Eng., 1985. Mem. PSA (Gordon Barber prize 1981), Berkeley Wrtrs.' Club. Home: 1001 Merced St Berkeley CA 94707

GRAY, CAROL LIPPERT, b. NYC, Mar. 31, 1950; d. Michael and Lenore Lippert; m. Lewis Gray, Sept. 5, 1970; children—Holly, Meredith. Author: Weight Watchers' 365-Day Menu Cookbook, 1982. Editor: Crochet Fantasy Mag., 1984—. BA in history, Douglass Coll., New Brunswick, N.J., 1970; MS in broadcast journalism, Boston U., 1976. Mng. editor Carstens Pubs., Newton, N.J., 1981-82, All Am. Crafts, Sparta, N.J., 1983—; free-lance writer, 1976—. Active Sussex County Med. Soc. Aux., Newton, 1978—; secy., trustee Sussex County Arts Council, Newton, 1981—. Mem. N.J. Press Women. Home: 65 Brookside Dr Sparta NJ 07871

GRAY, FRANCINE DU PLESSIX, b. Warsaw, Poland, Sept. 25, 1930; came to U.S., 1941; naturalized, 1952; d. Bertrand Jochaud and Tatiana Liberman (Iacovleff) du Plessix; m. Cleve Gray, Apr. 23, 1957; children—Thaddeus Ives, Luke Alexander. Author: Divine Disobedience: Profiles in Catholic Radicalism, 1970 (Natl. Cath. Book award), Hawaii: The Sugar-Coated Fortress, 1972 (Newswomen's Club NYC award), Lovers and Tyrants, 1976, World Without End, 1981, October Blood, 1985, Adam & Eve and the City, 1987. BA, Barnard Coll., 1952; LittD (hon.), CUNY, 1981, Oberlin Coll., 1985; Univ. of Santa Clara, 1985. Reporter UP, 1952-54; book editor Art in Am., 1964-66. Mem. Am. PEN, AG, Natl. Book Critics Circle. Address: Borchardt Agcy 136 E 57 St New York NY 10022

GRAY, HOWARD, see Arlen, Gary O'Hara

GRAY, LIZ, see Toomey, Jeanne Elizabeth

GRAY, OLWEN LEIGH, see Glaefke, Deborah S.

GRAY, PATRICK WORTH, b. Oak Park, IL, Dec. 1, 1937; s. Worth and Lousie Emma (Trainor) G.; m. Jocelynn Joy Hamre, Sept. 1, 1962; 1 dau., Emma Lynn. Author: Poems, 1975, Five Poems, 1979, Disappearances, 1979, Spring Comes Again to Arnett, 1986; ed. Periodical of Art in Nebr., 1974-76, Annex 21, 1978, 82; contrbr. to anthologies: Macmillan Gateway English, Anthology of Mag. Verse, Columbus Names the Flowers, Elements of Literature, 70 on the 70s, Traveling Am. with Today's Poets, Vietnam Flashbacks, 1984; contrbr. to Ariel, Calif Qtly, Carolina Qtly, Coll. English, Concerning Poetry, Denver Qtly, Ga. Rvw, Hanging Loose, Saturday Rvw, So. Poetry Rvw, others. BA, Phillips U., 1963; MFA, U. Ia., 1968. Served to Capt, US Army, 1968-71, Vietnam. Recipient Pushcart Prize, 1976, Yaddo fellow, 1978, MacDowell fellow, 1980. Address: 1109 Kingston Ave Bellevue NE 68005

GRAY, SPALDING, b. Barrington, RI, 1941, s. Rockwell and Elizabeth G. Author: In Search of the Monkey Girl (tet for photos), 1982, Swimming to Cambodia, 1985, Sex and Death to the Age 14, 1986. Gra. Emerson College, Boston, 1965. Summer Stock, Cape Cod, theater in Saratoga, NY, NYC, Performance Group, leading role in Sam Shepard's Tooth of Crime, 1973-75; formed Wooster Group, 1979, trilogy Three Places in Rhode Island. Monologues: Sex and Death to the Age 14, 1979, Booze, Cars, and College Girls, India and After, Interviewing the Audiene, 1980, In Search of the Monkey Girl, 1982. Acting in the film The Killing Field, 1983-84. Monologues: Swimming to Cambodia, Terrors of Pleasure, 1986. Artist-in-residence, Mark Toper Forum, Los Angeles, 1986-87. Address:

Program Dev 136 E. 65th St New York NY 10021

GRAYSON, RICHARD, b. Bklyn., June 4, 1951; s. Daniel and Marilyn (Sarrett) G. Author: With Hitler in New York, 1979, Disjointed Fictions, 1981, Eating at Arby's, 1982, Lincoln's Doctor's Dog, 1982, I Brake for Delmore Schartz, 1983. BA, Bklyn Coll, CUNY, 1973, MFA, 1976; MA, CUNY Staten Island, 1975. Asst. ed. Fiction Collective, Bklyn., 1974-77; lectr. LI Univ., Bklyn., 1975-78, CUNY, NYC, 1978-81, 84-86; instr. Broward Community Coll., Ft. Lauderdale, Fla., 1981-84; dir. trng. Computer Learning Systems, Davie, Fla, 1986—. Bd. dirs., Bklyn Coll. Alumni Assn., 1973-81; treas., Floridians for Interstate Banking, Davie, 1983—;

vice-chmn., Comm. for Fla. Income Tax, Davie, 1985—. Fellow, Natl. Arts Club, NYC, 1978, Fla. Arts Council, Tallahassee, 1981-82, Va. Center for Creative Arts, Sweet Briar, 1981-82. Mem. PEN, AG, AWP. Address: 2732 S University Dr 8A Davie Fl 33328

GREBNER, BERNICE MAY PRILL, b. Peoria, IL, May 23; d. John Elmer and Emma Lena (Dubs) Prill; m. Arthur Conrad Grebner (div.); children—Marjorie Grebner Welsch, David Arthur. Author: Luna Nodes—New Concepts, 1967, Decanates—A Full View, 1976, Everything Has a Phase, 1982, Mercury—The Open Door, Part I, 1987; poetry in APA vols. Composer and performer of music. Wrkg. on astrology books. Freelance astrologer. Address: 5137 N Montclair St Peoria Heights IL 61614

GRECO, JOANN, b. NYC, Sept. 6, 1960; d. Joseph John and Joan Frances (Campanella) Greco. Contrbr. to The New York Post, Fodor's Travel Guides, Video Store Magazine, The Electronic Mailbox, New York Review, Metro Foodservice, West Side Spirit, The Business of Fur, Enter, Smart Living, Romantic Times, other newsletters, consumer pbls. BA in Journalism, NYU, 1981. Editor N. Y. Review, NYC, 1982-83; writer/researcher Presentation Cons., Inc., NYC, 1984-85; freelance writer. Home: 1724 Putnam Ave Ridgewood NY 11385

GREELEY, ANDREW MORAN, b. Oak Park, IL, Feb. 5, 1928; s. Andrew T. and Grace (McNichols) G. Author: The Church and the Suburbs, 1959, Strangers in the House, 1961, Religion and Career, 1963, (with Peter H. Rossi) Education of Catholic Americans, 1966, Come Blow Your Mind With Me, 1971, Friendship Game, 1971, Life for a Wanderer: A New Look at Christian Spirituality, 1971, The Denominational Society: A Sociological Approach to Religion in America, 1972, Priests in the United States: Reflections on A Survey, 1972, The Sinai Myth, 1972, That Most Distressful Nation, 1972, New Agenda, 1973, Jesus Myth, 1971, The Denominational Society: A Sociological Approach to Religion in America, 1973, Unsecular Man, 1974, Ethnicity in the United States: A Preliminary Reconnaissance, 1974, Ecstasy: A Way of Knowing, 1974, The Devil, You Say!, 1974, Building Coalitions: American Politics in the 1970's, 1974, Sexual Intimacy, 1975, The Great Mysteries: An Essential Catechism, 1976, The Communal Catholic: A Personal Manifesto, 1976, Death and Beyond, 1976, The American Catholic: A Social Portrait, 1977, The Mary Myth: On the Feminity of God, 1977, The Making of the Popes, 1978, 79, The Cardinal Sins, 1981, Thy Brother's Wife, 1982, Ascent Into Hell, 1983. AB, St. Mary of Lake Sem., 1950, STL, 1954; MA, U. Chgo., 1961, PhD, 1961. Syndicated columnist: People and Values. Recipient Cath. Press Assn. award for best book for young people, 1965, others. Office: 6030 S Ellis Ave Chicago IL 60637

GREEN, ASHBEL, bNYC, Mar. 15, 1928; s. Ashbel and Katherine McKenzie (Murchison) G.; m. Anna Welsh McCagg, June 17, 1960; children—Ashbel Stockton, Alison McKenzie. Sr. editor Prentice- Hall, Inc., 1960-64; mng. editor Alfred A. Knopf, Inc., NYC, 1964-73, v.p., sr. editor, 1973—. Co-author: Get the Most From Your Money in New York, 1970. Grad., Kent (Conn.) Schl., 1945; BA, Columbia, 1950, MA in History, 1952. Served with USNR, 1946-48. Home: 70 E 96th St New York NY 10128

GREEN, COPPIE, b. Henderson, NC, Dec. 28, 1946, d. John Felix and Lucy Evelyn (Newell) G.; 1 child, Elizabeth Ann Green Taylor. Poetry ed. Greensboro Rvw, 1982; contrbr. poems to TriQtly, Blue Pitcher, Shite Poke, Permafrost, Heartland, Greensboro Rvw. MA, U. N.C., Greensboro, 1975, MFA, 1985. Instr. Carteret Community Coll., Morehead City, N.C., 1976-77, Rockingham Community Coll., Westworth, N.C., 1977-78; wrtr. Greensboro Housing Authority, N.C., 1978-82; instr. U. Alaska, Fairbanks, 1984, wrtr., 1984—. Recipient prize AAP, 1984. Mem. AWP. Home: Box 80393 Fairbanks AK 99708

GREEN, ELIZABETH ADINE HERKIMER, b. Mobile, AL, Aug. 21, 1906; d. Albert Wingate and Mary Elizabeth (Timmerman) G. Author: Teaching Stringed Instrument in Classes, 1966, The Modern Conductor, 1961, 4th ed., 1987, The Dynamic Orchestra, 1987; (with Nicolai Malko) The Conductor and His Score, 1975, 2d ed., 1985. Contrbr. numerous articles to mags. Ed.: A Certain Art, 1966. Music B., B.S., Wheaton Coll., 1928; M.Music, Northwestern U., 1939. Asst. prof. to prof. U. Mich., Ann Arbor, 1955-75, prof. emeritus, 1975—. Home: 1225 Ferdon Rd Ann Arbor MI 48104

GREEN, GERALD, b. Bklyn., 1922; married; 3 children. Author: Sword and the Sun, 1954, The Last Angry Man, 1957, The Lotus Eaters, 1959, The Heartless Light, 1961, The Portofino PTA, 1962, The Legion of Noble Christians, 1965, (with Lawrence Klingman) His Majesty O'Keefe, 1948, To Brooklyn With Love, 1968, The Artist of Terezin, 1968, Faking It, 1971, The Stones of Zion, 1971, Blockbuster, 1973, Tourist, 1973, My Son the Jock, 1975, An American Prophet, 1977, Girl, 1977, Holocaust (Emmy award for best screenplay, NCCJ Media award 1979), 1978 (Prix Internatl. Dag Hammarskjold award 1979), The Healers, 1979, Cactus Pie, 1979, The Hostage Heart, 1976, The Chains, 1980, Murfy's Men, 1981. Screenplay, Wallenberg: A Hero's Story, 1984, Karpov's Brain, 1983, Not in Vain, 1985, East and West, 1986. Grad., Columbia Schl. Journalism. Writer various TV documentaries. Mem. WG Am., AL, PEN. Address: Scott Meredith 845 3d Ave New York NY 10022

GREEN, JEAN SUSANNE, b. Balt., Mar. 8, 1949; d. Albert Wilson and Mary Elizabeth (Wise) House; m. Joseph William Green, Sept. 21, 1968; children—Christine, Jennifer, Katherine. Contrbr. poems, games, crafts to children's mags. including Highlights, Jack and Jill, others. Grad. public schls., Balt. Free-lance wrtr., 1984—. Home: 4354 Roberton Ave Baltimore MD 21206

GREEN, LARRY ALLEN, b. Waukegan, IL, Sept. 2, 1947; s. Lawrence Allen and Laura Anna (Barrack) G.; m. Pamela Lou Reynolds, Sept. 2, 1972 (div. Mar. 30, 1983). Assoc. ed. Woodall's RV Travel, 1977-80; ed. Camping Hotline, 1980-83; sr. ed. Specifying Engr., 1984-87; ed., Equipment Management, 1987—; ed., contrbr. numerous pubns., incl.: Better Homes & Gardens, 1982, 84, Carguide, 1983, Consumers Digest, 1982-86, Dairy Record, 1983-84, Freelance Art Monthly, 1978-80, New Driver, 1981-86, The Rotarian, 1974-77, Science Challenge, 1983-85, Tent and Trail, 1982-83. BA, So. Ill. U., 1969. Asst. dir. Coll. Adm. Ctr., National ACAC, Evanston, IL, 1970, admin. asst., Skokie, IL, 1972-74; special svcs. Rotarian Mag., Evanston, 1974-77. Served to E/4, U.S. Army, 1970-71. Address: 379 N Lake St Grayslake IL 60030

GREEN, LEWIS, b. Amesbury, MA, Jun. 3, 1946; s. Herman Wilcox and Cecile Dolly (Tiadore) Green; m. Kay Ellen Keuchenmeister, Aug. 29, 1974. Author: Classic Resorts & Romantic Retreats, 1986; Fairs & Festivals of the Pacific Northwest, 1985, Bed and Breakfast Washington, 1984; co-ed./contrbr. to Rough and Ready (textbook); contrbr. to Washington Mag., Oregon Mag., Northwest Mag., The Los Angeles Times, The National Law Journal, others. BS in Journalism U. of Florida, 1975. Teacher Lake Villa pub. schls. (IL), 1978-82; ed. Scott, Foresman (Glenview, IL), 1982-83; freelance wrtr. (Seattle, WA), 1983—. Home: 737 Tenth Ave E Seattle WA 98102

GREEN, RALEIGH E., II, b. Youngstown, OH, Oct. 6, 1951, s. Raleigh E. and Mary Lou (Heck) G.; m. Kim Marie Goddard, Nov. 3, 1969 (div. 1972); 1 dau., Tiffiney Lynn. Contrbr. poetry to Flyin' High, Our World's Best Loved Poems, Celebration, Am. Poetry Anthology, other publs. Wrkg. on Songwrtg., volume of poetry. Shipping mgr. Kimstock, Inc., Santa Ana, Calif., 1973—. Recipient Golden Poet award World of Poetry, 1985. Mem. AAP, Natl. Acad. Songwrtrs. Home: 10232 Kamuela Dr Huntington Beach CA 92646

GREEN, SAMUEL LEONARD, b. Sedro Woolley, WA, Dec. 2, 1948; s. Andrew Westley and Vera Jean (Todd) G.; m. Sally K. Purdy, Dec. 18, 1971; 1 son: Lonnie Robert. Author: (poetry) Gillnets, 1977; (poetry chapbooks) Wind: Four Letters to Melinda Mueller, 1980, Hands Learning to Work, 1984; editor Jeopardy Mag., 1973-74. BA in English with honors, Western Wash. State Coll., 1973; MA in English, Western Wash. U., 1982. Editor, co-pub. Jawbone Press, 1976-82, Brooding Heron Press, 1982—; poet-in-res. Wash. State Poetry-in-the-Schls. Program, 1977, 78-79, 80, 83-84, 85-86, King County Arts Commn., 1977-78; vis. prof. So. Utah State Coll., 1986. Home: New Mountain Rd Waldron Island WA 98297

GREEN, THEO, (Seamus O'Rourke), b. Oakland, Calif., Jan. 15, 1956. Author: Fragmented Ink, 1980, Piano Key Transparency, 1982, Sharp Calligraphy, 1986; ed.: Stories (by Brion Gysin), 1984, Out of Step & Out of Detroit (by Una Zero), 1986, Inkblot Mag., 1983—. Wrkg. on novel, oil paintings, ink drawings. Dir., artist Inkblot, Oakland, Calif., 1980—. Home: 439 49th St Oakland CA 94609

GREENBERG, ALFRED HENRY, b. NYC, Apr. 13, 1924; s. Edward and Sadie C. (Selwyn) G.; m. Adele Z. Rodbard, July 10, 1960; children—Danielle, Michele, Suzanne. Asst. mng. editor Cotton Trade Jnl, Memphis, 1951-54; mng. editor Hosiery and Underwear Rvw, 1954-55; sect. editor Women's Wear Daily, 1955-56; editor Chronicle of the UN, 1957-58, McCall Corp., 1958-64; exec. editor Skiing mag., NYC, 1964-70, editor, 1971-74, editor-in-chief, 1974-85, ed.-at-large, 1986—. Co-author: Comeback, 1974; Translator: Sartre on Cuba, 1961; contrbr. articles to profl. jnls. AB, Columbia, 1947; post-grad., U. Paris, 1947-49; MS, Yeshiva U., 1958. Served with AUS, 1942-45. Home: 55 Chatsworth Ave Larchmont NY 10538

GREENBERG, ALVIN DAVID, b. Cin., May 10, 1932; children—Matthew, Nicholas, Ann. Author: Going Nowhere (novel), 1971, The House of the Would-Be Gardener (poetry), 1972, Park Lands (poetry), 1973, Metaform (poetry), 1975, The Invention of the West (novel), 1976, In/Direction (poetry), 1978, The Discovery of

America & Other Tales of Terror (short stories), 1980, And Yet (poetry), 1981, Delta Q (short stories), 1983, The Man in the Cardboard Mask (short stories), 1985. BA, U. Cin., 1959, MA, 1960; PhD, U. Wash., 1969. Instr. U. Ky., Lexington, 1963-65; prof. English Macalester Coll., St. Paul, 1965—. Fulbright lectr., India, 1966-67; Bush Fdn. fellow, 1976, 81; grantee Witter Bynner Fdn., 1985. Mem. AWP (Short Fiction award 1982), MLA. Office: Macalester 1600 Grand Ave Saint Paul MN 55105

GREENBERG, BARBARA LEVENSON, b. Boston, Aug. 27, 1932; m. Harold L. Greenberg; 2 sons, David, Russell. Author: (poems) The Spoils of August, 1974, (stories) Fire Drills, 1982; wrkg. on a novel and a collection of poetry. BA, Wellesley Coll., 1953; MA, Simmons Coll., 1973. Address: 47 Dolphin Rd Newton Centre MA 02159

GREENBERG, JOANNE, b. Bklyn., Sept. 24, 1932; d. Julius Lester and Rosalie (Bernstein) Goldenberg; m. Albert Greenberg, Sept. 4, 1955; children—David, Alan. Author: The King's Persons, 1963 (Daroff Meml. award fiction 1963), I Never Promised You a Rose Garden, 1964 (Fromm-Reichmann award Am. Acad. Psychoanalysis 1967), The Monday Voices, 1965, Summering, 1966, In This Sign, 1970 (Kenner and Christopher awards 1971), Rites of Passage, 1972, Founder's Praise, 1976, High Crimes and Misdemeanors, 1979, Season of Delight, 1981 (Rocky Mountain Woman's Inst. award 1983), The Far Side of Victory, 1983, Simple Gifts, 1986, Age of Consent, 1987. BA, Am. U., 1955. Address: 29221 Rainbow Hills Rd Golden CO 80401

GREENBERG, MARGARET H., b. NYC, Jan. 29, 1935; d. Charles Jarvis and Ruth Elizabeth (Hillyar) Hill; m. Louis Morris Greenberg, May 28, 1968 (div. 1979); 1 dau., Alison Rachel. Author: The Sanibel Shell Guide, 1982, A Child's Guide to Sanibel and Captiva, 1982, Simple Sanibel Seafood, 1982, Scenes from Sanibel in Season, 1984, Nature on Sanibel, 1985; contrbr. articles: Yankee, Hampshire Life, Fla. Mag., other publs. BA, Smith Coll., 1956; MA, U. Md., 1968; diploma in French, Alliance Francaise, Paris, 1970. Tchr. in coll. preparatory schs., 1957-77; freelance wrtr., 1977—. Mem. Fla. Freelance Wrtrs. Assn. Home: Box 170 Sanibel FL 33957

GREEENBERG, MARILYN WERSTEIN, b. Bklyn., Oct. 29, 1937; d. Louis Eli and Charlotte (Jaffe) W.; m. Eugene Greenberg, Jan. 29, 1956; children—Leigh Elliot, Matthew. Co-author, Ethnic Svcs. Task Force: Collection Evalution Project Rpt., 1982; contrbr. to Libraries and Young Adults: Media Svcs. and Librarianship, Media and the Young Adult, Supplement, Library Quarterly, Calif. Librarian, School Libraries, School Lib. Jnl, CMLEA Jnl; ed. School Library Media Quarterly, 1985-88. BA, Bklyn. Coll., 1960; MA, U. Chgo., 1969, PhD, 1981. Librarian, Joyce Kilmer Schl., Chgo., 1965-67; instr. U. So. Cal., Los Angeles, 1970-74; prof. Cal. State U., Los Angeles, 1974—. Mem. Am., Cal. Lib. assns.; Calif. Media & Lib. Educators Assn.; So. Calif. Council on Lit. for Child. & Young Pple. Office: Cal State U 5151 State Univ Dr Los Angeles CA 90032

GREENBERG, NANCY JEAN, b. Chgo., July 25, 1947; d. Robert Louis and Nancy (Robertson) Rosberg; m. Larry P. Greenberg, June 7, 1980; 1 dau., Kimberly. Contrbr. articles to newspapers, mags. including Chgo. Tribune, others. Student Triton Coll., 1976-78, DePaul U., 1978-80. Financial analyst 1st Natl. Bank Chgo., 1967-82; real estate saleswoman B.Q.S. Realty, Chgo., 1982—. Recipient 2d prize for draft of novel Triton Coll., 1978. Home: 5887 N Central Ave Chicago IL 60646

GREENBERG, MARTIN MRS., see Fox, Paula

GREENBERG, PAUL, b. Shreveport, LA, Jan. 21, 1937; s. Ben and Sara (Ackerman) G.; m. Carolyn Levy, Dec. 6, 1964; children—Daniel, Ruth Elizabeth. Editorial page editor Pine Bluff (Ark.) Comml., 1962-66, 67—; syndicated columnist, 1970—; editorial writer Chgo. Daily News, 1966-67. B. Journalism, U. Mo., 1958, MA in History, 1959; student, Columbia Grad. Schl., 1960-62. Served to capt. AUS, 1969. Recipient Grenville Clark award for best editorial, 1964, Pulitzer prize editorial writing, 1969, award Natl. Newspaper Assn., 1968, U. Mo. Schl. Journalism award, 1983. Office: 300 Beech St Pine Bluff AR 71601

GREENBURG, DAN, b. Chgo., June 20, 1936; s. Samuel and Leah (Rozalsky) G.; m. Nora Ephron, Apr. 9, 1967 (div.); m. Suzanne O'Malley, June 28, 1980. Author: How to Be a Jewish Mother, 1964, Kiss My Firm But Pliant Lips, 1965, How to Make Yourself Miserable, 1966, Chewsday: A Sex Novel, 1968, Jumbo the Boy and Arnold the Elephant, 1969, Philly, 1969, Porno-Graphics, 1969, Scoring: A Sexual Memoir, 1973, Something's There: My Adventures in the Occult, 1976, Love Kills, 1978, What Do Women Want?, 1982, (with Suzanne O'Malley) How to Avoid Love and Marriage, 1983, True Adventures, 1985, Confessions of a Pregnant Father, 1986, How to Make Yourself Miserable for the Rest of the Century, 1987, The Nanny, 1987; films I Could Never Have Sex with any Man Who Has So Little Regard for My Husband, 1973, Private Lessons, 1981, (with Suzanne O'Malley) Private School, 1983; plays Arf, 1969; The Great Airplane Snatch, 1969, also articles; contrbr. to: Broadway rev. Oh, Calcutta, 1969. BFA, U. Ill., 1958; MA, UCLA, 1960. Copywriter Lansdale Co., Los Angeles, 1960-61, Carson Roberts Advt., 1961-62; mng. editor Eros mag., NYC, 1962-63; copywriter Papert, Koenig, Lois (advt.), NYC, 1963-65; free- lance writer, NYC, 1965—. Recipient Silver Key award Advt. Writers Assn., NYC, 1964, Playboy Humor award, 1964, 72, 76. Mem. DG, AG Am., AFTRA, Screen Actors Guild, WG Am., MWA. Home: 323 E 50th St New York NY 10022

GREENE, BETTE, b. Memphis, June 28, 1934; d. Arthur and Sadie (Steinberg) Evensky; m. Donald Sumner Greene, June 14, 1959; children—Carla, Jordan Joshua. Author: novels Summer of My German Soldier, 1973, Philip Hall Likes Me I Reckon Maybe, 1974, Morning Is A Long Time Coming, 1978, Get On Out Of Here, Philip Hall!, 1981, Them That Glitter and Them That Don't, 1983, I've Already Forgotten Your Name, Philip Hall, 1984. Student, U. Ala., 1952, Memphis State U., 1953, Columbia U., 1955. Address: 338 Clinton Rd Brookline MA 02146

GREENE, CARLA, b. Mpls., Dec. 18, 1916; d. William L. and Charlotte (Wunderman) G. Author: numerous children's books including How to Know Dinosaurs, 1966, Animal Doctors, 1967, Lighthouses, 1969, Los Camioneros, 1969, Before the Dinosaurs, 1970, How Man Began, 1972 (named Best Book of Year, Jr. Sci. Tchrs. Am. 1972), Cowboys, 1972, Our Living Earth, 1974, Man and Ancient Civilizations, 1977; contrbr. adult articles and stories to mags. Mem. AL Am., PEN Intl. Office: 8300 Sunset Blvd Los Angeles CA 90069

GREENE, CHARLES E. III., see Cooper, John Charles

GREENE, DEBORAH, b. Rutherfordton, NC, Dec. 19, 1951, d. William Eugene and Meredith (Roberson) Greene. Contrbr. to Variations: An Anthology of Contemporary Poetry. Wrkg. on grammar text for high school students at elementary level, poetry collection. BA, U. S.C., 1974, MEd, U.S.C., 1978. Tchr. Union County (S.C.) Schls., 1976—; instr. English, U. S.C., Union, 1980—. Mem. NCTE, Assembly on Lit. for Adolescents, Natl. Writing Centers Assn. Folger Shakespeare Library Museum Foundation. Home: 202 Gregory St Union SC 29379

GREENE, DONALD JOHNSON, b. Moose Jaw, Sask., Can., Nov. 21, 1916; s. Waldron Joseph and Katharine Annie (Beaton) G. Author: The Politics of Samuel Johnson, 1960, The Age of Exuberance, 1970, (with James L. Clifford) Samuel Johnson: A Survey and Bibliography of Critical Studies, 1970; Editor: Samuel Johnson: A Collection of Critical Essays, 1965, Samuel Johnson, Political Writings, 1977. BA, U. Sask., 1941; MA, U. London, 1948, D Lit., 1973; PhD, Columbia U., 1954. Served with Can. Army, 1941-45. Guggenheim fellow, 1957-58, 79-80; Can. Council sr. fellow, 1965-66. Fellow Royal Soc. Can., mem. MLA, The Johnson Soc. (Eng.; pres., 1985). Office: Dept Eng U So Calif Los Angeles CA 90007

GREENE, PAT RYAN, b. Chgo., Oct. 14, 1930; d. Lawrence Donat and Marie (Dahm) R.; m. Raymond, Jan. 26, 1952 (div. 1979); children—Larry, Mary Catherine, Peggy, Michael, Tom, Chris. Writer/ed. var. corp. pubns., 1979—; ed. Urban Voices, Intermedia; contrbr. articles and book reviews to: Natl. Catholic Rptr., America, Commonweal, The Way: Catholic Viewpoints, Catholic World, Cross and Crown. BS, U. Rochester, 1952; MA, U. MN, 1983. Parish co-ord. St. Joan of Arc Church, Mpls., 1972-76; p.r. mgr. MSI Insur., Arden Hills, MN, 1979—. Chairman's award, MN Press Club, 1981, 83. Co-founder, Communicators for Peace; mem. MN Press Club, MENSA, Am. Lg. PEN Women. Home: 300 W 50th St Minneapolis MN 55419

GREENE, ROBERT BERNARD, JR., (Bob Greene), b. Columbus, Ohio, Mar. 10, 1947; s. Robert Bernard and Phylis Ann (Harmon) G.; m. Susan Bonnet Koebel, Feb. 13, 1971; 1 dau., Amanda Sue. Author: We Didn't Have None of Them Fat Funky Angels on the Wall of Heartbreak Hotel and Other Reports from America, 1971; Running: A Nixon-McGovern Campaign Journal, 1973, Billion Dollar Baby, 1974, Johnny Deadline, Reporter: The Best of Bob Greene, 1976, (with Paul Galloway) Bagtime, 1977, American Beat, 1983. BS, Northwestern U., 1969. Reporter Chgo. Sun-Times, 1969-71, columnist, 1971-78; syndicated columnist Field Newspaper Syndicate, Irvine, Calif., 1976-81, Tribune Co. Syndicate, 1981—; contrbg. corr. ABC news Nightline, 1981—; columnist Chgo. Tribune, 1978—. Contrbg. editor: Esquire Mag., 1980—. Recipient Natl. Headliner award for best newspaper column in U.S., 1977, Peter Lisagor award, 1981. Office: Tribune 435 N. Mich Ave Chicago IL 60611

GREENE, LORNA, b. Newark, July 23; m. Murray Greenwald; 1 child, Anton Greene; m. 2d, William Hellinger, Sept. 9, 1955. Author: Pictures and Poetry, 1978, Go, from Head to

Toe, 1980, L.A. Light Forum, 1980, Citizen News, 1981; contrbr. poetry, articles, photographs to various publs., anthologies. Grad. James Monroe High Schl.; student of photography and sculpture; tchr.'s cert. in Yoga. Actress in various shows and films N.Y. and Calif., 1950—; Yoga tchr. Beverly Hills Health Club, Calif., 1960-75; tchr. YWCA and YMCA clubs, also homes, 1976-86; freelance photographer, 1975—; freelance author, 1977—; freelance artist/sculptor, 1983-85. Recipient Golden Poet award World of Poetry, 1985, 86. Mem. Actor's Equity, Screen Actor's Guild, AFTRA, Publicists of So. Calif., Los Angeles Photography Ctr., Beyond Baroque. Home: 1728 Laurel Canyon Blvd Los Angeles CA 90046

GREENFIELD, ELOISE LITTLE, b. Parmele, NC, May 17, 1929; d. Weston Wilbur Sr. and Lessie Blanche (Jones) Little; m. Robert Joseph Greenfield, Apr. 29, 1950; children: Steven Robert, Monica Joyce. Author: (juveniles) Bubbles, 1972, Rosa Parks, 1973 (Carter G. Woodson award 1974), Sister, 1974, She Come Bringing Me That Little Baby Girl, 1974 (Irma Simonton Black Book award 1974), Paul Robeson, 1975 (Jane Addams Children's Book award 1976), Me and Neesie, 1975, First Pink Light, 1976, Mary McLeod Bethune, 1977, Good News, 1977, Africa Dream, 1977 (Coretta Scott King award 1978), Honey, I Love, 1978, Talk About a Family, 1978, (with Lessie Jones Little) I Can Do It By Myself, 1978, (with Lessie Jones Little and Pattie Ridley Jones) Childtimes: A Three Generation Memoir, 1979, Grandmama's Joy, 1980, Darlene, 1980, Daydreamers, 1981, Alesia, 1981; also short stories, articles. (Recipient citation Council Interracial Books for Children 1975): producer: children's rec. Honey, I Love 1982. Student, Miner Tchrs. Coll., Washington, 1946-49. Freelance writer, 1958—; writer-in-res. D.C. Commn. Arts, 1973; mem. staff D.C. Black Writers Workshop, 1971-74. Mem. AG. Office: Box 29077 Washington DC 20017

GREENWAY, WILLIAM HENRY, JR., b. Atlanta, Feb. 19, 1947, s. William Henry and Mary Faye (Sheridan) G.; m. Betty Lee Tootle, July 28, 1978. Author: (poems) Pressure under Grace, 1982, Where We've Been, 1987; asst. ed. Miss. Rvw; contrbr. poems to Poetry, New Letters, So. Poetry, Seattle, Greenfield, New Va, Lit., Laurel, Miss., Fla. rvws, Plainsong, Cape Rock, Arete, Blue Unicorn, others. BA, Ga. State U., 1970; MA, Tulane U., PhD, 1984. Instr. Tulane U., New Orleans, 1982-83, U. So. Miss., Hattiesburg, 1983-85; asst. prof. Youngstown State U., 1986. Served with USN, 1970-75. Recipient prize AAP, 1975. Home: Dept Eng Youngstown State U Youngstown OH 44555

GREENWOOD, JOHN EDSON, b. Warren, OH, Nov. 8, 1927; s. John Eugene and Ruth (Norton) G.; m. Margaret Anne Barnes, June 7, 1950; children—J. Eric, Thomas C., Paul E., Alan M., Daniel Q. Contrbr. numerous articles to profl. military jnls. Ed.: Marine Corps Gazette, 1980—. B.S., U.S. Naval Acad., 1950; postgrad. Natl. WAr Coll., 1972. Enlisted Marine Corps 1945; commissioned 1950; advanced to Col.; retired 1980. Mem. U.S. Naval Inst., Marine Corps Hist. Fdn., Marine Corps Assn., Naval Maritime Correspondents Circle. Home: 4006 Nelly Custis Dr Arlington VA 22207

GREER, GERMAINE, b. near Melbourne, Australia, Jan. 29, 1939; d. Eric Reginald and Margaret May Mary (Lafrank) G. Author: The Female Eunuch, 1970, The Obstacle Race, 1979, Sex and Destiny: The Politics of Human Fertility, 1984, others. Columnist Sunday Times, London, 1971-73. B.A. with honors in English and French Lit, U. Melbourne, 1959; M.A. with honors in English, U. Sydney, Australia, 1961; Ph.D. (Commonwealth scholar), Newham Coll. of Cambridge U., Eng., 1964. Instr. poetry, dir. Center for Study of Women's Lit., U. Tulsa, 1979—. Office: Dept Eng U Tulsa 600 S College Ave Tulsa OK 74104

GREGOR, ARTHUR, b. Vienna, Austria, Nov. 18, 1923, s. Benjamin and Regine (Reiss) G.; came to U.S., 1939. Author: Octavian Shooting Targets, 1954, Declensions of a Refrain, 1957, Basic Movements, 1966, Figure in the Door, 1968, A Bed by the Sea, 1970, Selected Poems, 1971, The Past Now, 1975, Embodiment & Other Poems, 1982, A Longing in the Land, 1983; (for children) The Little Elephant, 1956, 1 2 3 4 5, 1956, Animal Babies, 1959; (for young adults) Bell Laboratories, 1972; contrbr. poems to numerous mags and anthols. BS, N.J. Inst. of Tech., Newark, 1945. Electronics engr. Electronic Transformer Co., NYC,1947-54; tech. ed. Industrial Design, NYC,1956-61; senior ed., trade dept., Macmillan Pub., NYC,1962-70; visiting prof., Calif. State U., Hayward, 1972-73; prof. English, Hofstra U., Hempstead, N.Y., 1974—. First Appearance Prize, Poetry Mag., 1948; First Prize for New Play, U. Ill., 1952; Palmer Award, PSA, 1962. Mem. PSA, Transl. Center, PEN, AG. Home: 250 W 94th St New York NY 10025

GREGORY, CAROLYN HOLMES, b. Rochester, NY, Jan. 27, 1950; d. Harry Palmer and Anna Gertrud (Holmes) Miller. Author: The Wait: A Chapbook of Poetry, 1983, For Lovers and Other Losses, 1981, The Rope Singers: A Chapbook, 1983; ed.: Claysheet, 1983, Herself mag., 1976-79. B.A., U. Mich., 1972, M.A., 1980. Poetry coordinator Guild House, Ann Arbor, MI, 1977-81; adminstrv. asst. Dana-Farber Cancer Inst., Boston, 1984—. Active Fenway Arts Council, Boston, 1982—, Red Bookstore Poetry Council, Jamaica Plain, MA, 1985-87; exec. bd. Women's Intl. Leage for Peace and Freedom, Boston, 1982-84. Mem. APS. Home: 4 Camelot Ct Brighton MA 02135

GREGORY, JOSEPHINE LANE, (Jo Lane Gregory), b. Balt., July 6, 1955; d. David Lawson and Josephine Lane (Doughton) G. Contrbr. articles to mags. including Baby Talk Mag., others. B.A. in Political Sci., George Washington U., 1976; M.F.A. with honors in Creative Writing, Am. U., 1986. Asst. ed. Kiosk, Balt. County Government, Towson, MD, 1977-79; public relations wrtr. Kaiser Permanente, Washington, 1984-85, ASPO/Lamaze, Arlington, VA, 1985; mgr. member benefits American Occupational Therapy Assn., Rockville, MD, 1986-87; ed. Memo, newsletter Providence Hospital, Wash. D.C. Mem. Bethesda Wrtrs. Center, Soc. Creative Profls. Home: 15891 Dorset Rd Laurel MD 20707

GREGORY, MICHAEL, b. Toledo, OH, Dec. 19, 1940; s. Elmer Wilhoyte and Cleta Almeda (Kehle) Gregory. Author: The Valley Floor, 1978, Hunger Weather—1959-75, 1979, 82; co-author: Song of the Beast (with Christ Dietz), 1983, What's in the Smoke, 1982, The Path From Here, 1986; co-editor: The Second Bisbee Anthology, 1984; poetry contrbr. to Massachusetts Rvw., Meanjin Qtly., N. Dakota Qtly., Poetry Northwest, Antioch Rvw, other poetry mags. BA, U. of Toledo, 1962; MA, Pennsylvania State U., 1965. Self-employed Mother Duck Press (McNeal, AZ), 1975—; assoc. faculty Cochise Coll. (Douglas, AZ), 1982-86; founding mem. Bisbee Press Collective, 1975; co-dir. Bisbee Poetry Festival, 1984. Home: Rt 1 Box 25A McNeal AZ 85617

GREGORY, PATRICIA DIANE, b. Columbus, GA, Dec. 16, 1952; d. Garrett Ray Gregory and Betty Jean (Hobgood) Wolbert. Contrbr. poems to anthols.; author songs. Grad. public schls., Tampa. Waitress, Steak n' Shake, Tampa, 1973-85; machine operator Tampa Maid Seafood, 1985—. Recipient Honorable Mention, World of Poetry, (4) 1984-85, Golden Poet award, 1985, 86. Mem. Songwriters Am. Home: 308 S Albany Ave Tampa FL 33606

GRENDA-LUKAS, JOHN MICHAEL, b. Lawrence, MA, Mar. 25, 1945; s. John and Julia Elizabeth Theresa (Grenda) (Luksevicius-Lukzewez). Editorial advisor schl. pubs. poetry. B.A. in English, History, B.Edn., U. Mass., Amherst, 1966; M.A. in Guidance, Syracuse U., 1967. English tchr. public schls., Pi sfield, MA, Copenhagen, NY, Lawrence, MA. Mem. NCTE, Mass., New England Councils Tchrs. English, CCCC, Jnlsm. Ed. Soc. Home: 361 Hamsphire St Lawrence MA 01841

GRENFELL, CLARINE COFFIN, b. Bangor, ME, Dec. 31, 1910; d. Millard Fillmore and Clara Beatrice Kelley Coffin; m. Rev. Jack Grenfell, June 28, 1938 (dec. July 2, 1980); children—John Millard, Lornagrace Bowron Stuart, Pamela Smith. Author: Novely Grammar Tests, 1936; editor: English for the Academically Talented, 1957, English Can be Fun, 1947, Oral English Can be Fun, 1958, Upgrade, 1960, Adult Lea Flets, 1972; author: the Caress and the Hurt, 1982, Women My Husband Married, 1983, Roses in December, 1984, A Backward Look, 1985. Wrkg. on Jeb and the Clowns, The Scent of Water. Reading cons. Westport Public Schls., CT, 1964-76; ed. ednl. div. Reader's Digest, Pleasantville, NY, 1970-71; dir. Grenfell Reading Center, Orland, ME, 1976—. Home: Box 98 Orland ME 04472

GREY, LESLIE, b. Providence, RI; widowed; children—William, Lisa. Contrbr. articles to video mags. B.A., Brown U. Exec. ed. Knowledge Ind. Pubs. Inc., White Plains, NY, 1979—. Home: 76 Pinesbridge Rd Ossining NY 10562

GRIER, BARBARA G., b. Cin., Nov. 4, 1933; d. Phillip Strang and Dorothy Vernon (Black) Grier. Author: The Lesbian in Literature, 3rd ed., 1983; Lesbiana, 1976, Lesbian Home Journal, 1976, Lesbian Lives, 1976, Lavender Herring, 1976, 29 other novels. Student pub. schls., Kansas City, Kansas. Asst. ed., The Ladder, San Francisco, CA, 1957-65, fict. and poetry ed., 1965-67, ed., 1968-70; ed. and pub. The Ladder, Reno, Nev., 1970-72; vp. and gen. mgr. The Naiad Press, Tallahassee, Fla., 1973—. Mem. SECLAG, NGTF, Women in Print, Amer. Bookseller Assoc. Home: Rt One Box 3319 Havana FL 32333

GRIFF, BERNARD MATTHEW, b. Newark, NJ, Oct. 5, 1935; s. Harry and Frances (DeGruttola) Griff; m. Carol Ann Stewart, Aug. 12, 1961 (div. July 1968); children—Matthew, Francis, Elizabeth, Laura. Contrbr. articles, poems to profl. jnls., periodicals; songwrtr. Wrkg. on The Computer Cat (juv.). Elementary schl. tchr., 1960—, Foxfire Learning model tchr.; traveling folksinger, 1973-74, pub. children's record, The Ecology Sea in Song and Ballad, 1973, song arranger for record A Shepherd Sings by Basque Shepherd Louis Irigary. Mem. Computer Using

Educators, Educators for Social Responsibility. Home: 408 Meadow Way San Geronimo CA 94963

GRIFFIN, EMILIE RUSSELL DIETRICH, b. New Orleans, LA, July 22, 1936; d. Norman Edward and Helen (Russell) Dietrich; m. Henry William Griffin, Aug. 31, 1963; children: Luch Adelaide, Henry Francis, Sarah Jeannette. Author: contrbr, Herbert S. Dordick, ed, Proc. of the Sixth Annual Telecommunications Policy Research Conf, 1978, contrbr, Palmer and Dorr, eds, Children and the Faces of Television, 1980, Turning: Reflections and the Experience of Conversion, 1980, Clinging: The Experience of Prayer, 1984. Contrbr to American Catholic Catalog. Columnist, Praying, 1985—. Contrbr to jnls and mags, including Cross Currents, Jnl of Advt, Publishers Weekly, and CSL: the Bulletin of the NYC C.S. Lewis Soc. BA, Tulane Univ, 1957. Reporter, New Orleans Item, 1957-58; advt copywriter-producer, Swigart and Evans, Inc., New Orleans, 1958-59; advt copywriter, Fuller & Smith & Ross, Inc., N.Y.C., 1959-62; advt copywriter and copy group head, Norman, Craig & Kummel, N.Y.C., 1962-64; copywriter and copy group head, Compton's Advt Inc, N.Y.C., 1964-70, v.p. 1968-70; creative marketing cons and freelance writer, 1970-74; dir. Children's Advertising Review Unit, Council of Better Business Bureaus, Natl Advt. Division, N.Y.C., 1974-77; v.p. and creative supervisor, Compton Advt., Inc., 1977-80; exec. v.p. and dir of marketing, Helen R. Dietrich, Inc., New Orleans, 1980-82; copy chief, Bauerlein Advt, New Orleans, 1982-84; v.p. and creative dir, Montgomery & Stire, New Orleans, 1984-86; marketing cons and freelance writer, 1986—. Copywriter and cons for Gen Foods Corp, Proctor & Gamble Co., and others, 1970—. Film rvwr for Natl Catholic Office for Pictures, 1963-69; panel cochmn at Airlie House Conf on Telecommunications Policy, 1978. Seven awards from American Television Commercials Festivals, and one from Venice Film Festival, 1962, for Alcoa advertisements; American Television Commercials Festival named "Ivory Bar" ad among the one hundred best-read ads of 1968; first prize from Louisiana Cncl for Music and the Performing Arts, 1971, for playscript, The Only Begotten Son; named Advertising Copywriter of the Year by Advt Club of New Orleans. Office: 5120 Prytania St New Orleans LA 70115

GRIFFIN, RACHEL, b. Springfield, IL, May 16, 1917; d. Albert and Alice Eleen (Slater) Ennis; m Wilbert Harold Griffin, June 23, 1933 (div. 1963); children—Rose Marie Griffin Cooper, Garold Wayne, Bonnie Jean Griffin Mitchelson, William, Albert Leroy, Michael, Margie Griffin Hurst, Glen Ray. Author: Something Humorous, Something Sad (poetry), 1963; poetry in anthologies. Wrkg. on poetry book, mystery novel, autobiography. Student public schls., Taylorville, Ill. Home: 630 N Webster St Taylorville IL 62568

GRIFFIN, WALTER, b. Wilmington, DE, Aug. 1, 1937, s. William Samuel and Nina Opal (Blalock) G.; 1 son, Paul Anthony. Author: Port Authority, 1976, Nightmusic (Intl. Small Press Book award 1974), Skulldreamer, 1977, The Poet's Guide and Handbook, 1986, others; contrbr. to anthologies: The Male Muse, Southern Poetry; contrbr. poetry to Harper's, Prairie Schooner, Evergreen Rvw, London Mag., other lit mags. BA in Engish, Ohio State U., 1961. Former dir. Poetry-in-Schls. program, Tenn. and Ga.; served 110 residencies in secondary and elem. schls., colls. and prisons, Tenn., S.C. and Ga., 1971-81. Recipient 1st Prize Poetry, The Miscellany, Davidson (N.C.) Coll., 1976. Home: 2518 Maple St East Point GA 30344

GRIFFITH, GERALINE MOELLER, b. Kinde, MI, Jan. 3, 1916; d. Edward George and Matilda E. (Pochert) Moeller; m. Richard Francis Griffith, Aug. 18, 1947; children—Fleur, Chorrellis. Contrbr. poems to anthol., newspapers; articles on drama, piano to local newspaper. Wrkg. on novel, The Race Set Before Me; completed ednl. music book, Teaching Piano on T.V.; book of family chronicles; collection of poetry; recipe book, book of ch. horuses. B.S., Wayne State U. 1942; M.A., Columbia U., 1942; Music tchr. Holmes Schl., Phila., 1944-45; tchr. Am. English, Am. Embassy, Trieste, Italy, 1961; vocal tchr. Norwood High Schl., N.Y., 1968-69. Producer, dir., coord. Potsdam Commun. Theatre, N.Y., 1960-68; tchr. creative writing Newcomers in Tucson, AZ, 1984—. Recipient Golden Poet award World of Poetry, 1987. Mem. IL-APW, PEN Women. Home: 8886 Lakeshore Rd Jeddo MI 48032

GRIFFITH, PATRICIA BROWNING, b. Fort Worth; d. Robert James Browning and Alonza Lee (Johnston) Browning; m. William Byron Griffith, June 16, 1960; 1 dau., Ellen Flannery. Author: The Future Is Not What it Used to Be, 1970, Tenn Blue, 1981; contrbr. short stories Paris Rvw, Harper's, Colorado Qtly, others; play Outside Waco, Theatre Three, Dallas, 1984, Hudson Guild, 1985. A play, Safety, opened July 1987, Theatre Three, Dallas. BA, Baylor U., 1958. Recipient O. Henry prize stories awards, 1970, 76. Mem. PEN, Dramatists Guild, AG, Writer's Ctr. Address: 1215 Geranium St NW Washington DC 20012

GRIFFITHS, IRIS C., see Johnston, Iris C.

GRIFFO, LYNN JENNIFER, b. Bronxville, NY, Dec. 3, 1957; d. Henry Philip and Betty Ann (Olson) G. Mng. ed. Securities Week, 1986. BS, Cornell U., 1980. Assoc. ed. Institutional Investor's Newsletter Div., NYC, 1981-82; staff rptr. Pensions & Investment Age, NYC, 1982-83; assoc. ed. Securities Week, NYC, 1983-86, mng. ed., 1986—. Office: McGraw Hill 1221 Ave of Americas New York NY 10020

GRIGG, WILLIAM, b. Washington, Mar. 22, 1934; s. Robert Dinwiddie Jr. and Lillian Hunter (Maurice) G.; m. Martha Whitfield Livdahl, Apr. 18, 1970. Contrbr. to books: Save the Mustang, 1974, The Cat Almanack, 1973, Congressional Humor, 1975, 1976 Guide to Organizing a Congressional Office; contrbr.: Washington Post, Christian Sci Monitor, specialized jnls. Wrkg. on novel. BA, Washington and Lee U., 1956. Sci. wrtr. Richmond (Va.) Times-Dispatch, 1959-60; med. wrtr. Washington Star, 1961-71; press asst. U.S. Congress, Washington, 1971-79; public affairs specialist FDA, Rockville, Md., 1979-84, dir. press relations, 1984—. Recipient press awards numerous govt. orgns. Mem. Natl.Assn. Govt. Communicators (1st prize for feature writing 1987, Spl. award 1986). Home: 4607 Merivale Rd Chevy Chase MD 20815

GRIGSBY, DARYL RUSSELL, b. Washington, Jan. 12, 1955; s. Russell Dean and Jaqueline Helen (Bate) G.; m. Leslie Robinson, Mar. 14, 1981. Author: Reflections on Liberation, 1985, Black Art!, 1986, For the People: Black Socialists in the United States, the Caribbean, and Africa; contrbr. articles to Christian Herald, Voice & Viewpoint, National Drum, Newsline, The Student, Etcetera, National Leader, Describing Ourselves, Unity newspaper, Creative Expressions. BA in Hist., Chgo. State U., 1977. Workshop mgr. North Shores Center, San Diego, 1978-81; mgt. asst. City of San Diego, 1981—. Recipient Black Achievement Award, Jnlsm., and NAACP Role Model award, 1986, for article "Reflections on Liberation." Mem. San Diego Writers & Editors, (founder) Black Writers & Artists, Multicultural Art Coalition. Home: 3445 Herman Ave San Diego CA 92104

GRIGSBY, GORDON, b. Washington, May 22, 1927, s. Louis Sinclair and Suzanne (Kay) G.; children—Michael, Susan, Ann, Andrew. Author: Tornado Watch, 1978, Mid-Ohio Elegies, 1985; contrbr. poems, essays, reviews to Prairie Schooner, Antioch Rvw, numerous other lit mags; poetry ed. The Ohio Journal, 1977-79, Gambit, 1985-86; anthol. of Chinese poems and pictures (with R. Wang). BA, Gettysburg Coll., Pa., 1950; MA, U. Wis., Madison, 1954, PhD,1960. Tchg. asst., Pa. State U., 1950-51, U. Wis., Madison, 1953-57; instr. to prof. Ohio State U., Columbus, 1957—. Served to 1st lt. with U.S. Army, 1951-53. Fulbright Award, Council of Intl. Exchange of Scholars, Iran, 1961-62; Dist. Tchg. Award, Ohio State U., 1966; Dasher Award for Poetry, Coll. English Assoc. of Ohio, 1978-80. Mem. P&W, PSA. Office: English Dept OSU 164 W 17th Ave Columbus OH 43210

GRILLI, CHLOE LENORE, b. Tallant, OK, Feb. 5; d. James Conrad and Rosalie (Spencer) Ifland; m. Eugene F. Grilli, June 12, 1943 (div. 1952); children—Michael, Robert, Nancy Esther. Author: I Grande'-I-Love-You, 1987. Wrkg. on Deep Red Star. A.A., Coffeyville Coll., 1939. Profl. pianist Am. Fedn. Musicians Worcester, MA, 1956-87; playwright Theatre Now, Worcester, 1986—. Mem. Dramatist Guild. Home: 27 Mt Vernon St 3704 Worcester MA 01605

GRIMES, NIKKI, (Naomi Grimes), b. NYC, Oct. 20, 1950; d. James and Bernice (McMillan) G. Author: Growin', 1977 (best book of yr. award Child Study Assn. 1977); Something on My Mind, 1978 (Notable Book of Yr. award ALA 1978,/ Best Book of Season award Saturday Rvw 1978); In Touch with Life Abroad, 1980; Songs for All Seasons, 1985; contrbr. to Pacific Qtly, Moana, N.Z., Essence Mag., Today's Christian Woman, Sunday Woman, Callaloo, Greenfield Rvw, Cricket, Obsidian, Jnl Black Poetry, others. BA in English, Rutgers U., 1974. Researcher Ford Fdn., Tanzania, 1974-75; theatre/arts critic Amsterdam News, NYC, 1976-77; lit. cons. Cultural Council Fdn., NYC, 1978-79; freelance wrtr./producer Swedish Ednl. Radio, 1979-80; freelance wrtr., 1985—. Mem. AG, P&W, NWU. Home: Box 441 San Pedro CA 90733

GRIMES, NIKKI, see Grimes, Naomi

GRIMM-RICHARDSON, ANNA LOUISE, (A. Grimm-Richardson), b. Menlo, WA, Mar. 2, 1927; d. George J. and Anna Marie (Richter) Grimm; m. Alfred Joseph Richardson, Mar. 9, 1951; children: Alfred Charles, Allan George, Anne Marie. Contrbr. to various publs. including Travelin' Vans, Van World, Panama Am., La Republica, Star & Herald, Tico Times, others. Student Clark Coll., 1966, Fla. State U. (Panama extension), 1972-75. Freelance writer, 1952-67; freelance writer/photographer, Gatun, Republic of Panama, 1967-83; cons. Star & Herald, Panama, 1980-81; editor Gatun Key, Panama, 1981-82; pub. Tiptoe Pub., Naselle, Wash., 1986—. Mem. Gatun Residents Adv. Council, 1972-84. Winner 1st place essay contest IAM Aux., 1959, poetry contest Writer's Digest, 1977. Mem. Crossroads Writers Panama (secy./pub. relations dir. 1978-83), Wahkiakum-Pacific Writers Assn. (advisor), Support Services Alliance, COSMEP. Home: 101 Wildwood Dr Box 206-H Naselle WA 98638

GRIMMETT, GERALD GLEN, (Jack Crandal), b. Idaho Falls, ID, Aug. 15, 1942; s. Glen H. and Rama Jean (Buxton) G.; m. Cynthia Ann Herron, June 23, 1984; children—Pilar Christina, Gerard Glen. Author: The Hours, 1970, Last Entries: Poems from the Ice, 1984. Editor: Reason, 1966-68, The News Examiner, 1983. Contrbr. articles, poems to numerous books, anthols. BA, Idaho State U.-Pocatello, 1974. Served to ensign, U.S. Navy, 1960-65. Recipient Best Spot News award Idaho Press Assn., 1985. Home: Cold Hill Run Box 353 Idaho City ID 83631

GRIMSHAW, THOMAS DRYSDALE, b. Detroit, Feb. 14, 1933; s. Thomas Drysdale Grimshaw and Eleanor Eunice (Jester) Lewellyn; m. Karen Jeanenne Glendinning, May 25, 1982; children—Thomas D., Caryn D., Amy L. Contrbr. articles to auto, racing mags. Wrkg. on fiction novel, book on history of U.S. profl. rallying, North Am. Rally Annual. B.A., Walsh Inst., 1958. Mng. ed. Rallye Mag., Dallas, 1978-79; pro rally co-driver Audi Am., Troy, MI, 1985-86; freelance jnlst., 1980—. Named Outstanding Columnist, Sports Car Club of Am. and Sports Car Mag., 1984. Mem. NWC. Home: 12100 Perry Overland Park KS 66213

GRIMSLEY, WILL HENRY, b. Monterey, IN, Jan. 27, 1914; s. Alvis Chilton and Bertie Eliza (Elrod) G.; m. Nellie Blanchard Harris, Feb. 12, 1937; children—Aleena Gayle, William Kelly, Nellie Blanchard. Author: Golf—Its History, People and Events, 1966, Tennis—Its History, People and Events, 1971, Football—Greatest Moments of the Southwest Conference, 1968; supervising editor: A Century of Sports, 1971, Sports Immortals, 1971. Student pub. schls., Nashville. Sports writer then sports editor Eve. Tennessean, Nashville, 1933-39; sports writer Nashville Tennessean, 1940-42; corr. AP, Memphis, 1943-47, sports writer, NYC, 1947—, spcl. corr., 1969, natl. sports columnist, 1977—. Named Natl. Sportswriter of Yr., Natl. Sportscasters and Sportswriters Assn. Am., 1978, 80, 81, 83. Mem. Golf Writers Assn. Am. (pres. 1977-78), Natl. Sportscasters and Sportswriters Assn. (pres. 1986-87), Baseball Writers Assn. Am. Home: 2 Prescott St Garden City NY 11530

GRINKER, MORTON, b. Paterson, NJ, May 19, 1928, s. Joseph and Betty (Sobel) G.; m. Lynn Murphy, June 28, 1963. Author: Meditation, Hegyohn Leebee, Ch'an, 1966, To the Straying Aramaean, 1972, The Gran Phenician Rover (books One, Two and Three); contrbr. poetry: Shig's Rvw, Perspectives, Amphora, Hyperion, other publs. BA in English, U. Idaho, 1952. Served with U.S. Army, 1946-48; Japan. Home: 1367 Noe St San Francisco CA 94131

GRISEZ, GERMAIN G., b. University Heights, OH, Sept. 30, 1929; s. of William J. and Mary C (Lindesmith) G.; m. Jeannette Eunice Selby, June 9, 1951; children: Thomas, James, Joseph (deceased), Paul. Author: Contraception and the Natural Law, 1965, Abortion: The Myths, the Realities, and the Arguments, 1971, (with Russell Shaw) Beyond the New Morality: The Responsibilities of Freedom, 1974, 2d ed, 1981, Beyond the New Theism: A Philosophy of Religion, 1975, (with Joseph M. Boyle, Jr. and Olaf Tollefsen) Free Choice: A Self-Referential Argument, 1976, (with Boyle) Life and Death with Liberty and Justice: A Contribution to the Euthanasia Debate, 1979, The Way of the Lord Jesus, vol. 1: Christian Moral Principles, 1983, (with Boyle and John Finnis) Nuclear Deterrence, Morality and Realism, 1987. Contrbr to philo and theol jnls, including Natural Law Forum. BA (magna cum laude), John Carroll Univ., 1951; MA and P.L. (summa cum laude), Dominican Coll of St. Thomas Aquinas, 1951; Ph.D., Univ. of Chicago, 1959. Clerical worker, Fed. Reserve Bank, Chicago, 1951-56; asst prof to prof of philo, Gerogetown Univ., 1957-72; prof of philo, Univ. of Regina, Campion Coll, Regina, Sask., 1972-79; Rev. Harry J. Flynn Prof of Christian Ethics, Mount St. Mary's Coll, Emmitsburg, Md., 1979—. Lectr at Univ. of Va., 1961-62. Spcl asst, Archdiocese of Washington, D.C., 1968-69, cons., 1969-72. Member: American Philo Assn, Metaphysical Soc of America, American Catholic Philo Assn (mem of exec cncl, 1968-70; v.p., 1982-83; pres., 1983-84), Fellowship of Catholic Scholars (fnding mem), Catholic Theol. Soc of America. Fellowship of Catholic Scholars, spcl award, 1981, for scholarly work, and Cardinal Wright award, 1983. Office: Mount St. Mary's College Emmitsburg MD 21727

GRISSOM, STEVEN EDWARD, b. Waco, TX, Oct. 10, 1949; s. Ted Loyd Grissom and Lynn Larver; m. Sandra Kay Mason, Dec. 15, 1973; children—Lori, Tamara, Tara, Steven. B.A., U. Ark., 1983. Contrbr. articles to mags., newspapers including Western Flyer, Air Alaska, others. Ed., contrbr.: Eaglewood News, 1987—. Technician, technical wrtr. Sohio Alaska Petroleum Corp., Anchorage, AK, 1978-84; project adminsitr. Architects GDM, Anchorage, 1984-85; free-lance wrtr, photographer, 1985—. Served U.S. Army, 1970-78. Mem. Aviation/Space Wrtrs. Assn. Home: 18756 S Lowrie Loop Eagle River AK 99577

GROGAN, EARLEAN STANLEY, b. Pensacola, FL, Mar. 4, 1922; d. Ervin Stanley and Mamie (Hayes) Stanley Ash; m. William Joseph Grogan, July 22, 1942; children—William Joseph Jr., Bradley I., Desirē P., Amyvonne. Author: Inspired Writings of Earlean S. Grogan, 1964; contrbr. poetry: The Worker, Impressions, numerous ch. publs.; poetry in anthologies. Wrkg. on book of poems. Student public schs. Monessen, Pa. Reipient certs. of tng. George Washington U., U.S. Dept. Agr. Grad. Sch., others. Clerical staff and editorial asst. various U.S. Govt. agys., Washington, 1948-82; wrtr., ed. The Worker, Nannie Helen Burroughs Sch., Inc., Washington, 1986—. mem. Soc. Tech. Communications, profl. orgns. Home: 6413 White Oak Ave Temple Hills MD 20748

GROHSKOPF, BERNICE, b. Troy, NY; 1 dau., Peggy. Author: Seeds of Time, 1963, From Age to Age, 1968, The Treasure of Sutton Hoo, 1970, 73, Shadow in the Sun, 1975, Notes on the Hauter Experiment, 1975, Children in the Wind, 1977, Blood and Roses, 1979, Tell me Your Dream, 1981, End of Summer, 1982; contrbr. Random House Encyclopedia, 1976; text for photo book on Saratoga, 1986. BA, Columbia U., 1948, MA, 1954. Wrtr.-in-residence Sweet Briar (Va.) Coll., 1980-82; mem. editorial staff William James Edition, 1984—; tutor Literacy Vols. of Am., Charlottesville, Va., 1983—. Resident fellow MacDowell Colony, Peterborough, N.H., 1976, 78, 80, Va. Center Creative Arts, 1977, 79, 83, Karolyi Fdn., France, 1979, 80; N.J. State Council on Arts fellow, 1980; grantee Andrew Mellon Fdn., 1981; recipient Syndication Fiction award PEN-NEA, 1984, 86. Mem. AG, PEN. Home: 116 Turtle Creek Rd Charlottesville VA 22901

GROPPA, CARLOS G., b. Buenos Aires, May 9, 1931; s. Martin and Josefina Groppa. Author: Humor Para Melancolicos, 1977, Desnudese Madame, 1975, La Mujer Que Queria Asesinar a Hitchcock, 1983, El Hombre Que No Hablaba Ingles, 1986. University of Buenos Aires, Architecture Mayor, Buenos Aires, Argentina. Wrtr., director, movie prod., scriptwriter, Argentina and Mexico, 1949-77; ed., La Prensa Newspaper, Los Angeles, Los Angeles, 1978-86. Home: 1261 N Laurel Ave West Hollywood CA 90046

GROSS, CAROL COTT, b. NYC, Oct. 9, 1942, d. Nathan and Estelle (Jacobson) Cott; m. Herbert E. Gross, Aug. 25, 1962; children—David, Saul, Terri. Contrbr. articles to N.Y. Times, Family Jnl, The Exceptional Parent, numerous other publs. BA in English Lit., SUNY-Stony Brook, 1978. Co-founder, since dir. Fly Without Fear, N.Y.C., 1969—. Mem. Phobia Soc. Am. Office: Fly Without Fear 310 Madison Ave NYC 11731

GROSS, MARILYN AGNES, b. Rolla, MO, Jan. 23, 1937; d. John Andrew and Florence M. (White) Robertson; m. James Dehnert Gross, Jan. 9, 1960; children—Kathleen Ann, Terrence Michael, Brian Andrew, Kevin Matthew. Author: The President's Book, 1971, Making It Happen—Creative Systems for Creative People, 1988. Wrkg. on series of books on bus. management for artists. B.S., St. Louis U., 1958. Pvt. practice of speech therapy, Milligton, TN, 1959-60; owner, dir. Marilyn's Studio, Streator, IL, 1983—; bus. mgr. Pathology Services, Streator, 1984—. Representative to White House Conf. on Library and Info. Services, 1978, visual arts representative to Curriculum Devel. Subcom, for Ill. Public Sch. System on Improvement of Fine Arts Curriculum in schs., 1986. Recipient poetry award Peter Herring Natl. Poetry Competition, 1975. Mem. Intl. Soc. Artists, Assoc. Photographers Intl., Am., Natl., Midwest, Ky., Ill. watercolor socs., North Coast Collage Soc., Ill. Arts League, Chgo. Artists Coalition, Pictoralists Club. Home: 54 Sunset Dr Streator IL 61364

GROSS, THEODORE LAWRENCE, b. Bklyn., Dec. 4, 1930; s. David and Anna (Weisbrod) G.; m. Selma Bell, Aug. 27, 1955; children—Donna, Jonathan. Author: Albion W. Tourgee, 1964, Thomas Nelson Page, 1967, Hawthorne, Melville, Crane: A Critical Bibliography, 1971, The Heroic Ideal in American Literature, 1971, Academic Turmoil: The Reality and Promise of Open Education, 1980; also essays, rvws; editor: Fiction, 1967, Dark Symphony: Negro Literature in America, 1968, Representative Men, 1969, A Nation of Nations, 1971, The Literature of American Jews, 1973; genl. editor: Studies in Language and Literature, 1974, America in Literature, 1978, Academic Turmoil: The Reality and Promise of Open Education, 1986. BA, U. Maine, 1952; MA, Columbia U., 1957, PhD, 1960. Served with AUS, 1952-54. Grantee Rockefeller Fdn., 1976-77, ACLS. Mem. MLA, PEN, Salzburg Seminar in American Studies, 1982. Home: 113 Old Mill Rd Great Neck NY 11023

GROSSMAN, ANDREW JOSEPH, (A. J. Toos), b. Coatesville, PA, Apr. 24, 1958, s. Richard Levi and Doris Jeanette (Genn) G.; m. Anita

Louise Randall, Nov. 3, 1983. Contrbr. to Am. Collegiate Poets, Coll. Poetry, New Laurel, Altadena, Laurel, Connecticut River, Piedmont Lit., Crab Creek rvws, Young Am. Poets, Poetry Newsletter, Magazine, Apalachee Qtly, others; cartoon writer (under pseudonym A.J. Toos) New Yorker, Sat. Eve. Post, Penthouse, Field & Stream, Inside Sports, Washingtonian, others. BA in English, Pa. State U., 1981. Freelance cartoon and greeting card wrtr. since 1983. Mem. NWC, Wrtrs. Ctr. Home: 3912 Ingomar St NW Washington DC 20015

GROSSMAN, MARTIN ALLEN, b. Chgo., June 15, 1943; s. Leon and Esther Belle (Immerman) G.; m. Julia Lynn Becker, June 14, 1970; children: Sarah Esther, Jessica Leah. Author: The Arable Mind, 1977, Seeing Double, 1981; ed. Skywriting, 1970-83; contrbr. to Voices Within the Art: The Modern Jewish Poets, 1983. BA cum laude Mich. State U., 1969; MFA, U. Oreg., 1972. Instr. W. Mich. Univ., Kalamazoo, 1974-79; prtnr. Words, Etc., Kalamazoo, Mich, 1979—. Mem. lit. panel, Mich. Council for the Arts, Detroit, 1981-87; bd. dirs. Cong. of Moses, Kalamazoo, 1984—; pres., Kalamazoo Jewish Fedn., 1985—. Recipient Creative Artist fellowship, Mich. Council for the Arts, 1983, 85. Address: 2005 Academy St Kalamazoo MI 49007

GROTH, BRIAN JOSEPH, b. NYC,June 29, 1960, s. Charles Richard and Dorothy Margaret (Emigholz) G. Contrbr. poetry to Manna, Prose Poetry, Poets & Peace International Anthology, Poets Eleven/Audible, Wide Open Magazine, numerous other lit publs. Student public schls., NYC. Mem. staff N.Y. Public Library, 1978-79, N.Y. Telephone Co., 1979—. Mem. Fla. State Poets Assn, P&W, NYC. Home: 139-40 Caney Ln New York NY 11422

GROTH, PATRICIA CELLEY, b. White Plains, NY, May 22, 1932; d. Albert Myrle and Helen Elizabeth (Davis) Celley; m. William Charles Groth, June 10, 1951; children—William, Barbara, Daniel, John, Susan. Author: (poems) Before the Beginning, 1985, Bedtime Stories for Job's Children, 1987; contrbr. poems to anthols, lit mags. Editor, contrbr. Stones and Poets, 1980. BA, Trenton State Coll., 1974, MA, 1981; MA, Rutgers U., 1985. Tchg. asst. Rutgers U., New Brunswick, N.J., 1983—; wrtr. Russian-Am. Friendship Project, Pennington, N.J., 1985. Trustee, Unitarian-Universalist Ch., Washington Crossing, N.J., 1986. Mem. Delaware Valley Poets, MLA, P&S, N.J. Council on Arts. Home: 423 S Main St Pennington NJ 08534

GROVES, CATHERINE, b. NYC, Nov. 21, 1952; d. Andrew and Catherine (Parkinson) Vervueren; m. Thomas P. Groves III, Mar. 12, 1983. Editor: That Which Is, 1983. BA in religious studies and social studies summa cum laude, Wagner Coll., 1975. Pub. Bethsheva's Concern, Clifton, N.J., 1983—. Office: Box 276 Clifton NJ 07011

GRUE, LEE MEITZEN, b. Plaquemine, LA; d. LeRoy Robert and Bernice Catherine (McCullar) Meitzen; m. Ronald David Grue, Oct. 28, 1963; children: Celeste, Ian, Teal. Author: Poems: Trains and Other Intrusions, 1976; The French Quarter Poems, 1978; ed. Going Downtown New Orleans, 1975; The New Laurel Rvw, 1982—. BA, U. New Orleans, 1964; MFA in creative writing, Warren Wilson Coll., Swannanoa, N.C., 1982. Dir. New Orleans Poetry Forum, 1972—. Recipient book award for poetry Acme Bookstore, Baton Rouge, 1982; NEA grantee, 1984. Home: 828 Lesseps St New Orleans LA 70117

GRUENWALD, GEORGE HENRY, b. Chgo., Apr. 23, 1922; s. Arthur Frank and Helen Marie (Duke) Gruenwald; m. Corrine Rae Linn, Aug. 16, 1947; children—Helen Marie Orlando, Paul Arthur. Author: New Product Development—What Really Works, 1985, Generation of Choice, 1982. BA, Medill Schl. Jnlsm., Northwestern U., 1947. Asst. to pres. UARCO, Inc., Chgo., 1947-49; crtv. dir., merchdg. mng. Willys-Overland Motors, Toledo, 1949-51; brand. & advt. mng. Toni Co., Chgo., 1951-53; exec. vp, mgmt. Supvr North Advertising, Chgo., 1955-71. Editor-in-chief, Oldsmobile Rocket Circle Mag., 1956-64; editor, Hudson Family Magazine, 1955-56. Pres., CEO, Advance Brands, Inc., Chgo., 1963-71; pres., CEO, Pilot Prod. Inc., 1964-71; pres. Campbell-Mithun, Inc., 1972-80, chmn. bd., 1980-81, CEO, 1981-83, chief creative officer, 1983-84; vice-chairman, Ted Bates WorldWide, NYC, 1979-80; consultant on new product devl., Rancho Santa Fe, Ca., 1984—; dir. Am. Inst. Wine & Food, San Francisco, 1985—; PBS, Washington, DC, 1978-86; trustee Linus Pauling Inst. Sci. & Med., 1985—, Community Advisory Bd., KPBS, San Diego, 1986—. Mem. Sigma Delta Chi. Home: Box 1696 5012 El Acebo Rancho Santa Fe CA 92067

GRUMBACH, DORIS, b. NYC, July 12, 1918; d. Leonard and Helen Isaac; divorced; children: Barbara Wheeler, Jane Emerson, Elizabeth Cale, Kathryn. Author: The Spoil of the Flowers, 1962, The Short Throat; The Tender Mouth, 1964, The Company She Kept, 1967, Chamber Music, 1979, The Missing Person, 1982, The Ladies, 1984, (intro.) Writer's Choice, 1983, The Magician's Girl, 1987; contrbr. to Book Reviewing, 1978. AB, NYU, 1939; MA, Cornell U., 1940. Served to lt. USN (WAVES), 1942-44. Prof. English, Coll. of Saint Rose, Albany, NY, 1952-72; lit. ed. New Republic, Washington, 1972-74; prof. English, Am. U., Washington, 1974-84; vis. prof. Johns Hopkins U., Balt., vis. prof., Writers' Workshop, Univ. of Iowa, 1979, 1981, 1984, 1986; book reviewer, Natl. Public Radio, 1985—. Office: 909 N. Carolina Ave SE Washington DC 20003

GRUNER, CHARLES RALPH, b. Nov. 6, 1931; s. Henry Phillip and Opal Mae (Helvey) G.; m. Marsha Fay Wiehn Sept. 6, 1958; children—Mark Harriss, Valery Jo. Author: (with Logue, Freshley Huseman) Speech Communiation in Society, 1972, 2d ed., 1977; (with Logue, Freshley, Huseman) Speaking: Back to Fundamentals, 1976, 3d ed., 1982; Understanding Laughter: The Workings of Wit and Humor, (Golden Anniversary award for best book by mem. Speech Communication Assn., 1979) 1978, Plain Public Speaking, 1983. Contrbr. articles to profl. jnls. Wrkg. on satire as persuasion. B.S., Southern Ill. U., 1955, M.S., 1956; Ph.D., Ohio State U., 1963. Asst. prof. St. Lawrence U., Canton, NY, 1957-64; asst. prof. to assoc. prof. U. Nebr., Lincoln, 1964-69; assoc. prof. to prof. U. Ga., Athens, 1969—. Served with USAF, 1952-54. Mem. Speech Communication Assn., Intl. Soc. Genl. Semantics, Southern Speech Communication Assn. Home: 395 Brookwood Dr Athens GA 30605

GRZANKA, LEONARD, b. Ludlow, MA, Dec. 11, 1947, s. Stanley Simon and Claire (Rozkuszka) G.; m. Jannette Donnenwirth, Sept. 3, 1984 (div. 1987). Author: Neither Heaven Nor Hell, 1978; ed.: Masterpieces of Contemporary Japanese Crafts, 1977; contrbr.: Kokinshu: A Collection of Poems Ancient & Modern (winner Lit. Transl. award Japan-U.S. Friendship Commn.), 1984; columnist: Calif. Farmer mag., 1986, PC Companion Mag., 1986; West Coast ed. VAR mag., 1986; contrbg. ed.: Silicon Valley Mag., 1982-85. BA, U. Mass., 1972; MA, Harvard U., 1974. Mng. ed. Miller-Freeman Publs., San Francisco,1982-84, mng. ed. Portable Computer mag.; prin. Grzanka Assocs., San Francisco, 1984—; lectr. Golden State U., San Francisco, 1985-86; San Francisco bur. chief, Digital News newspaper, 1986—. Mem. Press Club San Francisco. Home: 1324 Jackson St 5 San Francisco CA 94109

GUENTHER, CHARLES (JOHN), b. St. Louis, Apr. 29, 1920, s. Charles Richard and Hulda Clara (Schuessler) G.; m. Esther Laura Klund, Apr. 11, 1942; children—Charles John, Cecile Anne, Christine Marie. Author: Modern Italian Poets, 1961, Phrase/Paraphrase, 1970, Paul Valery in English, 1970, Voices in the Dark, 1974, High Sundowns, 1974, Jules Laforgue: Selected Poems, 1984, Selected Translations, 1986; co-translator Alain Bosquet: Selected Poems, 1963; contrbr. to over 300 U.S. and fgn. mags. including Poetry, Kenyon, Lit., Partisan rvws, Qtly Rvw Lit., The Nation, The Critic, Perspective, Webster Rvw, Edge. AA, Harris Tchrs. Coll., 1940; BA, Webster U., 1973, MA, 1974; postgrad. St. Louis U., 1979. With Def. Mapping Agcy., Aerospace Ctr., St. Louis, 1943-75, chief tech. library, 1957-75; adj. prof. St. Louis U., Met. Coll., Harris Stowe State Coll., Maryville Coll., McKendree Coll., U. Mo., St. Louis, 1976-84; free-lance writer, translator; book reviewer St. Louis Post-Dispatch, 1953—, Globe-Democrat, 1972-82. Decorated comdr. Order of Merit of Italian Republic; recipient lit. award Mo. Library Assn., 1974; St. Louis Arts and Humanities fellow, 1981. Mem. PSA (Midwest regional v.p. 1977—, James Joyce award 1974, Witter Bynner poetry transl. grantee 1979), Mo. Wrtrs. Guild (pres. 1973-74), St. Louis Wrtrs. Guild (pres. 1959, 1976-77), St. Louis Poetry Ctr. (pres. 1974-76), McKendree Wrtrs. Assn. (hon. life), ALTA, Academi d'Alsacs, Sigma Delta Pi. Home: 2935 Russell Blvd St Louis MO 63104

GUERARD, ALBERT JOSEPH, b. Houston, Nov. 2, 1914; s. Albert Leon and Wilhelmina (Macartney) G.; m. Mary Maclin Bocock, July 11, 1941; children—Catherine Collot, Mary Maclin, Lucy Lundie. Author: The Past Must Alter, 1937, Robert Bridges, 1942, The Hunted, 1944, Maquisard, 1945, Joseph Conrad, 1947, Thomas Hardy, 1949, Night Journey, 1950, Andre Gide, 1951, Conrad the Novelist, 1958, The Bystander, 1958, The Exiles, 1963, The Triumph of the Novel: Dickens, Dostoevsky, Faulkner, 1976, The Touch of Time: Myth, Memory and the Self, 1980, Christine/Annette, 1985; co-editor: The Personal Voice, 1964. AB, Stanford U., 1934, PhD, 1938; AM, harvard U., 1936. Served as tech. sgt. psychol. warfare br. AUS, World War II. Rockefeller fellow, 1946-47; Fulbright fellow, 1950-51; Guggenheim fellow, 1956-57; Ford fellow, 1959-60; NEA fellow, 1967-68; NEH fellow, 1974-75; recipient Paris Review Fiction prize, 1963. Mem. Am. Acad. Arts and Scis. Home: 635 Gerona Rd Stanford CA 94305

GUERNSEY, NANCY PATRICIA, (Red Guernsey), b. Newark, Oct. 12, 1955, d. Orville Wendell and Dorothy Elizabeth (Maccia) Guernsey. Contrbr. articles to Aircraft Owners and Pilots Assn. Pilot, 99 News, other aviation publs. BE in Mech. Engring., Manhattan Coll., 1977; MS in Nuclear Engring, Bklyn. Poly. Inst., 1986. Systems engr. Grumann Aerospace Co.,

Bethpage, N.Y., 1977-83; product support engr. Harris Corp., Syosset, N.Y., 1983-86; public health eng., Nassau County, NY, 1987—. Mem. AIAA, numerous engring. and aviation orgns. Home: 14 3d St Ronkonkoma NY 11779

GUEST, BARBARA, b. Wilmington, NC, d. James Harvey and Ann (Hetzel) Pinson; m. Lord Stephen Haden-Guest; 1 dau—Hadley; m. 2d, Prof. Trumbull Higgins; 1 son—Jonathan. Author poetry vols.: The Location of Things, 1960, Poems, 1962, The Blue Stairs, 1968, Moscow Mansions, 1973, The Countess from Minneapolis, 1976, The Turler Losses, 1978, Biography, 1982, An Emphasis Falls on Reality, 1987; author: Seeking Air (novel), 1977, Herself Defined, The Poet H.D. and Her World (biography), 1984. BA, U. Calif., Berkeley, 1943. Mem. PEN, PSA. Address: 49 W 16 St New York NY 10011

GUEST, JUDITH ANN, b. Detroit, Mar. 29, 1936; d. Harry Reginald and Marion Aline (Nesbit) G.; married, Aug. 22, 1958; children: Larry, John, Richard. Author: Ordinary People, 1976 (Janet Heidinger Kafka prize), Second Heaven, 1982. BA in Edn., U. Mich., 1958. Mem. Detroit Women Writers, AG, PEN Am. Center. Office: Viking 40 W 23d St New York NY 10010

GUIDO, JO ANN, b. Bridgeport, CT, July 17, 1952; d. Franklin Benjamin and Ann Clara (Mihalovic) Spodnick; m. William Joseph Guido, Jr., Oct. 31, 1971. Contrbr. articles to mags. Student Cameron U., 1987. Hairstylist, Beautiful People, Duncan, OK, 1981-86, Shear Experience, Duncan, 1986—; contrbg. wrtr. Jazziz Mag., Gainesville, FL, 1986—. Recipient 2d place for writing/critic Jazziz Mag., 1986. Home: Rt 3 Box 247G Duncan OK 73533

GUINN, GARY MARK, b. Siloam Springs, AR, Jan. 27, 1948; m. Mary Ann Huskins, July 16, 1976; children—Mark Jason, Michael Daniel. Contrbr. poems to lit. mags., anthols. B.A. in English Edn., John Brown U., 1974; M.A. in English, U. Ark., 1978. Asst. prof. English, John Brown U., Siloam Springs, 1980—. Bd. dirs. Sager Creek Arts Assn., Soloam Springs, 1985—. Mem. NCTE, Conf. Christianity and Lit. Home: Rt 2 Box 154a Siloam Springs AR 72761

GUION-SHIPLEY, JOYCE, b. Cleve., June 26, 1946; d. Harry Edward and Catherine (Evans) Guion; m. John Joseph Rakauskas, Jan. 13, 1968 (div. Aug. 26, 1977); 1 dau., Mandala Jane; m. Kenneth L. Shipley, Dec. 18, 1978. Author: Little Words, 1981, In Other Words, 1982, Ideas of their Own, 1984. Contrbr. poems to anthols. Grad. public schls., Cleve. Mem. Poets' League. Home: 15965 York Rd North Royalton OH 44133

GULBRANSEN, MARGERY ELIZABETH, see Evernden, Margery Elizabeth

GULDNER, MARY ELLEN, (Pifer Guldner), b. Orange, NJ, d. Lewis A. and Mary Pifer; m. Donald L. Guldner Jr., May 8, 1976; children—Heather, Donny. BA, Hope Coll., Holland, Mich., 1975. Mem. editorial staff South Bergenite, Rutherford, N.J., 1984—; freelance wrtr; contrbr. poetry to Am. Poetry Anthology, vol. VI, no. 4, Words of Praise, Vol. III. Home: 222 Woodward Ave Rutherford NJ 07070

GULDNER, PIFER, see Guldner, Mary Ellen

GULLANS, CHARLES (BENNETT), b. Mpls., May 5, 1929, s. Charles Sophus and Ethel (Bennett) G. Author: Moral Poems, 1957, The English and Latin Poems of Sir Robert Ayton, 1963, A Checklist of Trade Bindings Designed by Margaret Armstrong, 1968, A Bibliography of . . . J.V. Cunningham, 1973, Imperfect Correspondences, 1978, Many Houses, 1981, A Diatribe to Dr. Steele, 1982, Under Red Skies, 1983, The Bright Universe, 1983, Local Winds, 1985, The Wrong Side of the Rug, 1986; translator Last Letters from Stalingrad, 1962. BA, U. Minn., 1948; PhD, Stanford U. 1956. Instr. U. Wash., Seattle, 1955-61, UCLA, 1961—. Fulbright fellow King's Coll., Durham U., Eng., 1953-55; Inst. Creative Arts, U. Calif. fellow, 1965-66. Pub., The Symposium Press. Mem. Scottish Text Soc. (v.p.). Home: 1620 Greenfield Ave Los Angeles CA 90025

GULLY, CHESTER, see Baizer, Eric

GUMA, GREG, b. NYC, Mar. 4, 1947; s. F. William and Olga (Lupia) G.; m. Jo Harte Schneiderman, June 5, 1976 (div. 1980); 1 son, Jesse Lloyd. Author: Dawn of the People, 1984, Where Do We Go From Here?, 1985, Burlington's Progressive Past, 1986. Ed.: Quadrille, 1970, Public Occurrences, 1975-76, Inroads, 1982-83, Bread & Puppet: Stories of Struggle & Faith, 1985. B.S., Syracuse U., 1968; M.Ed., U. Vt., 1975. Reporter, Bennington Banner, VT, 1968-70; pubs. dir. Bennington Coll., 1970-71, faculty mem. Burlington, Coll. 1974-77; project dir. Dept. of Labor, Bulington, VT, 1971-74; ed. Vanguard Press, Burlington, 1978-83, Toward Freedom, Burlington, 1986—. Fellow NEH, 1980; recipient 1st prize Chittenden Hist. Soc., VT, 1984. Home: 300 Maple St Burlington VT 05401

GUNDERSON, JOANNA, (Anna Holmes, Anne de Viri), b. NYC, May 14, 1932, d. Earle and Margaret (Henderson) Bailie; m. Warren Gunderson, May 2, 1970; children—Lucy, Thomas. Author: Shanta, 1957, Indrani and I, 1967, Sights: Three Novellas, 1963. BS, Columbia U., 1954. Freelance wrtr., N.Y.C., 1955—; pub. Red Dust, NYC,1961—. Grantee NEA, N.Y. State Council on Arts, numerous others. Home: 1148 Fifth Ave New York NY 10128

GUNN, JAMES EDWIN, (James Edwin), b. Kansas City, MO, July 12, 1923, s. Jesse Wayne and Elsie Mae (Hutchison) G.; m. Jane Frances Anderson, Feb. 6, 1947; children—Christopher Wayne, Kevin Robert. Author: This Fortress World, 1955, (with Jack Williamson) Star Bridge, 1955, Station in Space, 1958, The Joy Makers, 1961, The Immortals, 1962, Future Imperfect, 1964, The Witching Hour, 1970, The Immortal, 1970, The Burning, 1972, Breaking Point, 1972, The Listeners, 1972, Some Dreams Are Nightmares, 1974, The End of the Dreams, 1975, Alternate Worlds: The Illustrated History of Science Fiction, 1975, The Magicians, 1976, Kampus, 1977, Isaac Asimov: The Foundations of Science Fiction, 1982, Crisis!, 1986; ed. Man and Future, 1968, Nebula Award Stories Ten, 1975, The Road to Science Fiction: From Gilgamesh to Wells, 1977, From Wells to Heinlein, 1979, From Heinlein to Here, 1979, From Here to Forever, 1982. BS, U. Kans., 1947, MA, 1951. Ed. Western Printing Co., Racine, Wis, 1951-52; asst. instr. English, U. Kans., Lawrence, 1955-56, instr., 1958-70, lectr., 1970-74, prof., 1974—, alumni ed., 1956-58, dir. pub. relations, 1958-70. Served to lt. (j.g.) USN, 1943-46, PTO. Recipient Byron Caldwell Smith prize, 1971; spl. award World Sci. Fiction Conv., 1976, Hugo award, 1983. Mem. SFWA (pres. 1971-72), Sci. Fiction Research Assn. (Pilgrim award 1976, pres. 1980-82), WG. Home: 2215 Orchard Ln Lawrence KS 66044

GUNN, THOM, (Thomson William Gunn), b. Gravesend, Eng., Aug. 29, 1929; came to U.S., 1954; s. Herbert Smith and Ann Charlotte (Thomson) G. Author: Fighting Terms, 1954, The Sense of Movement, 1957, My Sad Captains, 1961, Touch, 1967, Moly, 1971, Jack Straw's Castle and Other Poems, 1976, Selected Poems, 1979, The Passages of Joy, 1982, The Occasions of Poetry, 1982. BA, Trinity Coll., Cambridge (Eng.) U., 1953. Address: 1216 Cole St San Francisco CA 94117

GUNNELL, JOHN A., (Gunnner), b. Staten Island, NY, Nov. 14, 1947; s. Albert A. and Ceceilia (Morrison) G.; m. Catherine "Kitch", May 13, 1967; children—Suzanne, John, Thomas, Jesse. Author: How-to Convert Old Cars into RVs, 1981, 75 Years of Pontiac-Oakland, 1983, How-To-Dress-Up Your Car with Factory Accessories, 1983, How-to Convert Old Cars into Four-Wheel-Drives, 1983, Pontiac Trans Am Photo Facts, 1984, Chrysler 300 Photo Facts, 1985, Complete Convertible Story, 1985, Illus. Firebird Buyer's Guide, 1986; contrbr./ed.: Standard Catalog of Amer. Cars, 1946-75, 1983, SCAC, 1805-1942, 1985; contrbr. articles to For Vettes Only, High-Perform, Pontiac, Calif. Hwy. Patrolman, EJAG Mag., Vette Mag, others. AA, Staten Island Comm. Coll., 1971; BS, Richmond Coll., 1975. Traffic clk. Ingersoll-Rand, NYC, 1967-68; sales mgr. Beechnut-Lifesavers, Canojoharie, NY, 1968-73; dept. mgr. Supermkts. Genl., Woodbridge, NJ, 1973-78; ed. Krause Pubns., Iola, WI, 1978—. Mem. Soc. Automotive Historians, IMPA. Home: 120 Mill St Iola WI 54945

GURIAN, MICHAEL W., b. Honolulu, Apr. 11, 1958. Author: As the Swans Gather (poetry), 1984; contrbr. to: Reflection, Charter, Artpaper, Pegasus, numerous others; fiction ed. Willow Springs, 1983-85, contrbg. ed., 1985—. BA, Gonzaga U., Spokane, Wash., 1980; MFA in Fiction Wrtg., Eastern Wash. U., Cheney, 1985. Adj. faculty Eastern Wash. U., 1983-86, Whitworth Coll., Spokane, 1985-86. Recipient Costello Poetry award Gonzaga U., 1980. Home: E. 9708 Maringo Dr Spokane WA 99206

GURKIN, KATHRYN BRIGHT, b. Whiteville, NC, Nov. 23, 1934; d. Henry Bern and Ruby Mae (Prease) Bright; m. Worth Wicker Gurkin, July 9, 1955; children—Worth Wicker, Richard Sean, David Bern. Author books: Rorschach, 1977, Terra Amata, 1980. Student Meredith College, Raleigh, NC, 1953-55. Executive Dir. Sampson Arts Council, Clinton, NC, 1975-76. St. Andrews Review Poetry Prize, Laurinburg, NC, 1977, Zoe Kincaid Brockman Book Award, NC Poetry Soc., 1980. Mem. NC Writers Conf. Home: 112 Barrus Ave Clinton NC 28328

GURNEY, ALBERT RAMSDELL, JR., b. Buffalo, Nov, 1, 1930; s. Albert Ramsdell and Marion (Spaulding) G.; m. Mary Forman Goodyear, June 8, 1957; children—George, Amy, Evelyn, Benjamin. Author: Best Short Plays, 1955-56, 57-58, 69, 70, The Golden Fleece, 1969, Scenes From American Life, 1971, Children, 1974, The Gospel According to Joe, 1974, Who Killed Richard Cory, 1976, The Middle Ages, 1977, Entertaining Strangers, 1977, The Wayside Motor Inn, 1977, O Youth and Beauty, TV adaptation of story by John Cheever, 1979, The Golden Age, 1980, The Dining Room, 1981, What I Did Last Summer, 1982, The Snow Ball, 1985, The Perfect Party, 1986, Sweet Sue, 1986, Another Antigone, 1987. BA, Williams Coll., 1952; MFA, Yale, 1958, DDL, 1984. Served with USNR, 1952-55. Recipient N.Y. Drama Desk award, 1971; Rockefeller Playwrights award, 1977, America Academy and Institute of the Arts Award, 1980, Playwriting award NEA, 1981-82. Mem. council DG, AL Am., WG. Home: 74 Wellers Bridge Rd Roxbury CT 06783

GURVIS, SANDRA JANE, b. Dayton, OH, Jan. 23, 1951; d. Isadore Reuben and Regina (Rosenfeld) Goldberg; m. Ronald Alan Gurvis, July 20, 1975; children—Amy, Alex. Contrbr. articles, short stories to mags., newspapers including USA Weekend, Country Living, others. B.A. in Psychology, Miami U., 1973; postgrad. Ohio State U., 1975-76. Job analyzer, technical wrtr. Defense Construction Supply Center, Columbus, Oh, 1973-78; ed. Merrill Pub., Columbus, 1983-84; free-lance wrtr., ed., 1979-83, 84—. Mem. NLAP, WR. Home: 10095 Hounsdale Dr Pickerington OH 43147

GUSEWELLE, C. W., b. Kansas City, KS, July 22, 1933; s. Hugh L. and Dorothy A. (Middleton) G.; m. Katie J. Ingels, Apr. 16, 1966; children: Anne Elizabeth, Jennifer Sue. Author: A Paris Notebook, 1985; contrbr. to Va. Qtly Rvw, Tex Qtly, Antioch Rvw, Transatlantic Rvw, Audience, Am. Heritage, Paris Rvw, Harper's, Blair & Ketchum's Country Jnl, Harrowsmith, Pushcart. BA, Westminster Coll., 1955. Reporter Kans. City Star, 1955-66, edl. writer, 1966-76, foreign ed., 1976-79, assoc. ed. and columnist, 1979—. Served to 1st lt, US Army Infantry, 1956-58, US. Recipient Aga Khan prize, Paris Rvw, 1977, film profile, NEH, 1979, included Audio Prose Library, 1983, Best Daily columnist, Mo. Press Assn., 1984, 85, Clarion award, Women in Communications, 1985. Address: 1245 Stratford Rd Kansas City MO 64113

GUSTAV, KARL, see Anderson, Paul Dale

GUSTON, DAVID H., b. Livingston, NJ, July 9, 1965, s. Herbert Martin and Sheila (Eckhaus) BA Yale, 1987, cum laude; student at M.I.T. in Political Science PhD program. G. Contrbr. Yale Daily News. Student Yale U. Staff wrtr., asst. ed. Yale Sci. Mag., New Haven, 1985, ed.-in-chief, 1986 Honeywell Futurist Award winner. Home: 7 Wichita Path Oakland NJ 07436

GUTHRIE, SALLY RECORD, b. Elmira, NY, Jan. 10, 1929; d. Harry Evans and Marian (Looney) Record; m. Donald L. Guthrie, Aug. 19, 1950; children—Jessica, J. Ben, Daniel M., Donald L., Mary Scott. Editor: Probable Cause, 1980. BA, Elmira Coll., MS. Ed. Homelite div. Textron, Port Chester, N.Y., 1970-72; ed., dir. pubs. Jonathan Club, Los Angeles, 1973—. Mem. Town Hall, Los Angeles, 1980—. Recipient Mark of Excellence award Kimberly Clark Corp., 1974. Mem. IABC(Merit award 1975-76, Bronze Quill award 1983; past dir., past secy.). Home: 902 A Calif Ave Santa Monica CA 90403

GUTTMAN, DENA ANN, b. Passaic, NJ, May 27, 1934; d. Jack and Elsie (Berlin) Guttman. Author: Teacher's Arts & Crafts Almanack, 1978. BA, Paterson State Coll., 1956; MA, Montclair State Coll., 1968. Tchr. art Passaic pub. schls. 1956—; freelance writer. Mem. AG, NEA, IWGG. Home: 123 Allwood Rd Clifton NJ 07014

GUY, CAROL ANN, (Joan Clayton), b. Dayton, OH, Setp. 17, 1943; d. Paul Caleb and Mary Elizabeth (Mitchell) Mumma; m. Richard Dee Guy, Mar. 3, 1964 (div. 1983); children—David Mitchell, Sally Ann. Contrbr. articles to profl. jnl., mag. including Ladies' Home Jnl. Cert. in Secretarial Sci., Miami Jacobs Coll., 1963. Pharmacy technician Fiedlity Prescriptions, Dayton, 1983-84; customer service representative Outdoor Sports Headquarters Inc., Dayton, 1984-86; telemarketing mgr. Micor-Base Corp., Dayton, 1986-87. Home: 6510 Wildwood Trail 8 Myrtle Beach SC 29577

GWYNN, R(OBERT) S(AMUEL), b. Eden, NC, May 13, 1948, s. Dallas Edmund and Thelma (Howe) G.; m. Faye LaPrade, June 15, 1969 (div. 1977); m. 2d Donna Skaggs, June 1, 1977; 1 son, William Tyree; stepsons—Jason Blair Simon, Dustin Brant Simon. Author: Bearing & Distance (poetry), 1977, The Narcissiad (poem), 1981, The Drive-In (poetry), 1986; poetry critic Tex. Rvw; contrbr. rvws. to Prairie Schooner, Sewanee Rvw; contrbr. poetry to Poetry, Sewanee Rvw; contrbr. translations to Playboy, Pulpsmith. AB, Davidson (N.C.) Coll., 1969; MA, U. Ark., 1972, MFA, 1973. Instr. Southwest Tex. State U., San Marcos, 1973-76; assoc. prof. Lamar U., Beaumont, Tex., 1976—. Mem. Tex. Assn. Creative Wrtg. Tchrs., South Central MLA, Conf. Coll. Tchrs. English, Tex. Joint Council Tchrs. English. Home: 225 Canterbury Ln Beaumont TX 77707

GYSI, CHARLES L., III, b. Phila., Dec. 21, 1957; s. Charles L., Jr., and Virginia Ethel (Eglof) G.; m. Janet Lynn Lammers, Oct. 5, 1985. Author: Scanner Master Greater Philadelphia/South Jersey Guide, 1983, 2d ed., 1985, Pocket Guide, 1987, Scanning Hunterdon County, 1985. Contrbg. ed.: Popular Communications, mag., 1983—; ed., reporter: Today's Spirit, Hatboro, PA, 1974-80; ed.: The Courier-News, Bridgewater, NJ, 1980—. B.A. in Jnlsm., Temple U., 1979. Home: Rt 2 Stockton NJ 08559

HABERMAN, DANIEL, b. NYC, July 15, 1933; s. Benjamin and Daisee (Balen) Haberman; children—Ray, Thomas. Author: Poems, 1977, Erinna to Baucis, With Antipater of Sidon's Epigram (trans. with Marilyn B. Arthur), 1978, The Furtive Wall, 1982. BS, Carnegie Mellon U., 1954; postgrad., New York U., 1956-57. Poet-in-res., Cathedral of St. John the Divine, NYC, 1983-86; elector to The Poet's Corner, 1983-88; graphic arts consultant, NYC, 1957—. 1st Lt. with USMC, 1954-56. Mem. PEN, PSA. Home: 433 East 51st St New York NY 10022

HACHEY, THOMAS EUGENE, b. Lewiston, ME, June 8, 1938; s. Leo Joseph and Margaret Mary (Johnson) H.; m. Jane Beverly Whitman, June 9, 1962. Author: Problem of Partition: Peril to World Peace, 1972, Britain and Irish Separatism, 1977; editor: Voices of Revolution, 1972, Confidential Despatches, 1974. BA, St. Francis Coll., 1960; MA, Niagara U., 1961; PhD, St. John's U., 1965. Chmn. of History, Marquette Univ., 1979—. Pres. Amer. Conf. on Irish Studies, 1984-86, Pres. Mid-West Conf. on Irish Studies, 1987-89. Fellow Anglo-Am. Assocs. Home: 663 N 75th St Wauwatosa WI 53213

HACKETT, SUZANNE FRANCES, b. Burbank, CA, Apr. 12, 1961; d. David Woolan and Krystyna Barbara (Skalmowski) Hackett; m. Dr. Vernon Orrin Tyler, Mar. 28, 1980 (div. 1982). Contrbr. Montana Magazine, Hot Springs Gazette, Cutbank 21,22, Jeopardy. BA, W. Wash. U., 1979-82; postgrad., U. Mont., 1983-84. Ed. Jeopardy mag., Bellingham, Wash., 1981-82, Cutbank mag., Missoula, Mont., 1983-85, Mountain Bell, Helena, 1985; artist Angelo Pizzo, Inc., Culver City, Calif, 1985-88; ed. Hot Springs Gazette, Helena, Mont., 1985—; sports ed. Richland County Leader, Sidney, Mont., 1986—, newswitr. Glendive Ranger. Review, Glendive, Mont. Address: 415 E. Hughes Glendive MT 59330

HACTHOUN, AUGUSTO, b. Havana, Cuba, Dec. 17, 1945, came to U.S., 1961, naturalized, 1979. Contrbr. articles, fiction, poems to Spanish mags., jnls. B.A., U. South Fla., 1967; Ph.D., U. Fla., 1978. Asst. prof. U. Ala., Birmingham, 1972-77, Wheaton Coll., Norton, MA, 1977-84; asst. dean U. Penn., Phila., 1984—. Mem. MLA. Office: U Penn 100 Logan Hall Philadelphia PA 19104

HADAS, PAMELA WHITE, b. Holland, MI, Oct. 31, 1946; d. James Floyd and Phyllis Elizabeth (Pelgrim) White; m. David Elkus Hadas, Dec. 31, 1970. Author: Marianne Moore: Poet of Affection, 1977, Designing Women, 1979, In Light of Genesis, 1980, Beside Herself: Pocahontas to Patty Hearst, 1983. Student, Interlochen Acad. Arts, 1962-64; BA, Washington U., St. Louis, 1968, MA, 1970, PhD, 1973. Staff assoc. Bread Loaf Writer's Conf., 1980-83. Poetry editor: Webster Rvw, 1978-83. Recipient Witter Bynner award AAIAL, 1980, Oscar Blumenthal award Poetry; Robert Frost fellow Bread Loaf Writers Conf., 1979. Mem. PSA, PEN, P&W. Home: 6628 Pershing Ave St Louis MO 63130

HADAS, RACHEL, b. NYC, Nov. 8, 1948; d. Moses and Elizabeth (Chamberlayne) Hadas; m. Stavros Kondilis, Nov. 6, 1970 (div. 1978); m. 2d, George Edwards, July 22, 1978. Author: Starting From Troy, 1975, Slow Transparency, 1983, Form, Cycle, Infinity: Landscape Imagery in the Poetry of Robert Frost, 1985. BA, Radcliffe, 1969; PhD, Princeton U., 1982. Assoc. prof., Rutgers U., Newark, NJ, 1981—. Mem. PEN, PSA, Modern Greek Studies Assn. Home: 838 West End Ave 3A New York NY 10025

HADDIE, see Nowak, Edward, Jr.

HAGAN, MARTY, b. Jersey City, NJ, Apr. 28, 1965; s. Martin Joseph and Anna Marie (DiRenzi) H. Contrbr. poems to Come Get High With Me, 1987, and to mags. Workg. on novel. AA, NYU, 1984; BA, New Schl., 1986. Laborer, Local 325, Jersey City, 1982—. Recipient N.J. Writing Achievement award William Paterson Coll., 1982, 2d Best Poem award Odessa Poetry Rvw, 1986. Home: 575A Jersey Ave Jersey City NJ 07302

HAGER, JIMMY NELSON, b. Gastonia, NC, March 5, 1947; s. Robert Carl and Thelma (Nelson) H.; m. Melodie Ruth Benford, June 7, 1974; children: Elizabeth, Arlyne, Jonathan. BA, College of Charleston, 1987. Owner Freeway rock band, Columbia, SC, 1967-71; owner Contract Colors, Summerville, 1983—. Awards: first prize fiction, News & Courier (Charleston), 1982; first prize fiction, College of Charleston, 1985, 86. Wrkg. on short stories about Charleston lower and middle class. Home: 704 W Old Orangeburg Rd Summerville SC 29483

HAILE, H. G., b. Brownwood, TX, July 31, 1931; s. Frank and Nell (Goodson) H.; m. Mary Elizabeth Huff, Sept. 1, 1952; children: Jonathan, Christian, Constance. Author: Das Faustbuch nach der Wolfenbuttler Handschrift, 1963, The History of Doctor Johann Faustus, 1965, Artist in chrysalis: A Biographical Study of Goeth in Italy, 1973, Invitation to Goethe's Gaust, 1978, Luther: An Experiment in Biography, 1980, 1983, From Humanism to Humanity: A History of Germany in the Early Modern, 1986; contrbr. articles on German lit. and highr edn. in Am. to profl. and popular jnls. BA, U. Ark., 1952, M.A., 1954; student, U. Cologne, Germany, 1955-56; PhD, U. Ill., 1957. Fulbright fellow, 1955; Fellow ACLS(1961-62. Office: For Lang Bldg Univ Ill Urbana IL 61801

HAINES, JOHN M., b. Norfolk, VA, June 29, 1924; s. John Meade and Helen M. (Donaldson) Haines; m. Jo Ella Hussey, Oct. 1960 (div. 1970). Works include: Winter News, 1966, The Stone Harp, 1971, Leaves and Ashes, 1974, In Five Years' Time, 1976, In a Dusty Light, 1977, Living Off the Country (essays), 1981, Other Days, 1982, News from the Glacier, Selected Poems, 1982, Of Traps and Snares, 1983, Stories We Listened To, 1986. Student, American U., 1948-49; student, Hans Hofmann, New York, 1950-52. Lectr., U. of Montana, 1974-75; vis. prof., U. of Wash., 1974; wrtr.-in-res., U. of Alaska, 1972-73; freelance wrtr./lectr., 1975—. Awards: Guggenheim Fellowship, 1965, 1984; NEA, 1967. Hon. Doct., U. of AL, 1983. Mem. PSA. Home: Mile 68 Richardson Hwy SR 10 Fairbanks AK 99701

HAINING, JAMES HOWARD, b. Dallas, Feb. t, 1950; s. James H. and Gladine (Watson) H.; m. Michalea Moore, Nov. 26, 1976; children: Morgan Whitney, Emma. Author: A Quincy History, 1981. Wrkg. on variations on A Child's Garden. B.A., Antioch U., 1973. Dir. reprographics Southwest Tex. State U., San Marcos, 1987—. Home: 1804 E 38 1/2 St Austin TX 78722

HAIRS, HUGH MICHAEL, b. London, Sept. 8, 1940, came to U.S., 1964; s. Bernard William and Irene (Daniel) H.; m. Sharon Ann Cranen, Feb. 7, 1970 (div. Apr 25, 1973); 1 son, Bernard William. Author: Hugh's Review, 1984—. Wrkg. on And Yet Another, Delti-Loafology. With Deltec Intl., Chgo., Coral Gables, FL, 1967-76, Sears & Roebuck, Enid, OK, 1978—. Mem. Enid Wrtrs., Okla. Wrtrs. Fedn., Don Blanding Poetry Circle. Home: 207 E King St Waukomis OK 73773

HALBERSTAM, DAVID, b. NYC, Apr. 10, 1934; s. Charles A. and Blanche (Levy) H.; m. Elzbieta Tchizevska, June 13, 1965 (div.1977); m. Jean Sandness Butler, June 29, 1979; 1 dau., Julia Sandness. Author: The Noblest Roman, 1961, The Making of a Quagmire, 1965, One Very Hot Day, 1968, The Unfinished Odyssey of Robert Kennedy, 1969, Ho (Ho Chi Minh), 1971, The Best and the Brightest, 1972, The Powers That Be, 1979, The Breaks of the Game, 1981. AB, Harvard U., 1955. Reporter West Point (Miss.) Daily Times Leader, 1955-56, Nashville Tennessean, 1956-60; mem. staff N.Y. Times, 1960-67, corr., Congo, 1961-62, Vietnam, 1962-63, NYC, 1964-65, Warsaw, Poland, 1965-66, NYC, 1966-67; contrbg. editor Harper's mag., 1967-71. Recipient Pulitzer prize for intl. reporting, 1964, Page One award for Congo reporting, 1962; Overseas Press Club award, 1973. Address: Knopf 201 E 50th St New York NY 10022

HALCOLM, , see Patton, Michael Quinn

HALDEMAN, JOE WILLIAM, b. Oklahoma City, June 9, 1943; s. Jack Carroll and Lorena (Spivey) H.; m. Mary Gay Potter, Aug. 21, 1965. Author: War Year, 1972, Cosmic Laughter, 1974, The Forever War, 1975, Mindbridge, 1976, Planet of Judgement, 1977, All My Sins Remembered, 1977, Study War No More, 1977, Infinite Dreams, 1978, World Without End, 1979, Worlds, 1981, (with Jack C. Haldeman, II) There is No Darkness, 1983, Worlds Apart, 1983; editor: Nebula Awards 17, 1983, Dealing in Futures, 1985, Tool of the Trade, 1987. BS in Physics and Astronomy, U. Md., 1967; MFA in English, U. Iowa, 1975. Assoc. prof. writing program MIT, 1983-87. Served with AUS, 1967-69. Decorated Purple Heart; Recipient Hugo award, 1976, 77, Nebula award, 1975. Mem. SFWA, AG, P&W. Home: 5412 NW 14th Ave Gainesville FL 32605

HALE, A. DEAN, b. Blackwell, OK, Aug. 28, 1929, s. Herbert Atkins and Dorothea Wilhelmina (Alberts) H.; m. Barbara Dean Chambers, Oct. 12, 1952; 1 son, Steven Edward. Ed., pub. Iron Horses of the Sante Fe Trail, 1965; contrbr. tech. articles, bus. reports and hist. articles on transp. to numerous publs. Wrkg. on railway and public transportation histories. BS in indusl. engring. and mgmt., Okla. State U., 1953. Reporter, bur. chief Daily Oklahoman, Stillwater, 1950-53; ed. Petroleum Engineer Pub. Co., Dallas, 1953-56, Am. Gas Jnl, Dallas, 1956-70, Pipeline & Gas Jnl, Dallas, 1970-87. Editorial and publishing consultant, 1987—. Pres. (1970-82) and dir. (1970—) Kachina Press; chmn. Station Press (1983—). Served with US Army, 1946-48; PTO. Recipient Jesse H. Neal award Am. Bus. Publs., 1980, numerous awards from Dallas Press Club, Western Publs. Assn. Home: 3412 High Bluff Dallas TX 75234

HALE, ALLEAN LEMMON, b. Lincoln, NE, July 13, 1914; d. Clarence Eugene and constance (Harlan) Lemmon; m. Mark Pendleton Hale, Dec. 31, 1936 (dec. Nov. 4, 1977); children—Susanna Hale Day, Mark Pendleton. Author: Petticoat Pioneer, 1957, rev., 1968; (plays) Last Flight Over, 1935, Remind Me to Live, 1960, Two in a Trap, 1966, The Second Coming of Mrs. C, 1971; columnist: Christian Coll. Mag., 1951-56. Contrbr. poems, critical article, articles on Tennessee Williams, fiction to lit. mags., popular mags. including Saturday Evening Post, Parents' Mag., Mo. Rvw., others. Ed.: Alumni Mag. of hrisian Coll., 1951-56, A Death in the Sanchez Family (Oscar Lewis), 1969; asso. ed.: Tom: The Young Years of Tennessee Williams (Lyle Leverich), 1988. Wrkg. on book of late plays of Tennessee Williams. B.A., U. Mo., 1935; M.A., U. Iowa, 1963. Instr. writing U. Iowa, Iowa City, 1960-62; editorial asst. to Oscar Lewis, Urbana, IL, 1966-69. Recipient 1st prize for playwriting Samuel French & Zeta Phi Eta, 1933, Midwestern Intercollegiat Contest, 1934; 1st prize for story U. Mo., 1936; 1st honors Mo. Women's Press Club, 1953; Disting. Alumna award Christian Coll., 1964. Mem. Ill. Wrtrs., Red Herring Fiction Workshop. Home: 22 G H Baker Dr Urbana IL 61801

HALE, HOPE, see Davis, Hope Hale

HALE, JUDSON DRAKE, b. Boston, Mar. 16, 1933; s. Roger Drake and Marian (Sagendorph) H.; m. Sara Huberlie, Sept. 6, 1958; children: Judson Drake, Daniel, Christopher. Author: Inside New England, 1982. Asst. editor Yankee, Inc., Dublin, N.H., 1958-61, assoc. editor, 1961-63, mng. editor, 1963-69, editor, v.p., 1969—, also dir.; editor, v.p. Old Farmers Almanac, dir. Solar Environ. Scis., Inc. Editor: That New England, 1968. BA, Dartmouth Coll., 1958. Served with AUS, 1955-57. Home: Valley Rd Dublin NH 03444

HALE, NANCY, b. Boston, May 6, 1908; d. Philip L. and Lilian (Westcott) H.; m. Fredson Bowers, Mar. 16, 1942; children (by former marriages)—Mark Hardin, William Wertenbaker. Author: (novels) The Young Die Good, 1932, Never Any More, 1934, The Prodigal Women, 1942, The Sign of Jonah, 1950, Dear Beast, 1959, Black Summer, 1963, Secrets, 1971; (short stories) The Earliest Dreams, 1936, Between the Dark and the Daylight, 1943, The Empress's Ring, 1955, Heaven and Hardpan Farm, 1957, The Pattern of Perfection: Thirteen Stories, 1960; A New England Girlhood (memoir), 1958, The Realities of Fiction: A Book About Writing, 1962, The Life in the Studio (memoir), 1969, Mary Cassatt (biog.), 1975, The Night of the Hurricane (juvenile) 1977; editor: New England Discovery: A Personal View, 1963, Daughter of Abolitionists (Ellen Wright), 1964; short stories in more than 40 anthologies. Grad. Winsor Schl., Boston, 1926; student, Schl. of Boston Mus. Fine Arts, 1927-28; studied in father's studio several years. Asst. ed., 1928-32, Vanity Fair, 1933-34; news reporter N.Y. Times, 1935; adv. to advt. agy., 1930-35; lectr. short story Bread Loaf Writers Conf., 1957-65. Recipient O. Henry short-short story prize, 1933, Benjamin Franklin special citation for short story 1958, Henry H. Bellaman award for lit., 1969, Sarah Joseph Hale award, 1974; Phi Beta Kappa vis. scholar, 1971-72. Home: Rt 14 Box 7 Charlottesville VA 22901

HALE, RICHARD LEE, (Dick) b. Formoso, KS, Jan. 3, 1930; s. Glenn Becton andRuby T. (Johnson) H.; m. Nancy J. Craig, Feb. 22, 1953; children—Steven C., Kristin L. Hale Schurtz, Michael J., Sarah J. Author: PGA Book of Golf, 1976, 77, 78, 79; PGA Championship Annual, 1976-79; USGA Championships of 1981, 1981. BS in Jnlsm., U. KS, 1952. Ed., Bird City (KS) Times, 1955-58; ed./pub. St. Francis (KS) Herald, 1958-74; ed. Golf Course Mgt., Lawrence, KS, 1974-76, PGA Mag., Palm Beach Gardens, FL, 1976-80; dir. communics. Golf Course Supts. Assn Am., Lawrence, KS, 1980-82; ed. Dental Economics, Tulsa, 1982—. Served to Spcl. Agent/CIC, U.S. Army, 1952-54. Mem. Amer. Assn. Dental Eds. Home: 6436 E 95th St Tulsa OK 75137

HALEY, ALEX PALMER, b. Ithaca, NY, Aug. 11, 1921, reared in Henning, TN; s. Simon Alexander and Bertha George (Palmer) H.; m. Nannie Branch, 1941 (div. 1964); children—Lydia Ann, William Alexander; m. Juliette Collins, 1964 (div. 1972); 1 dau., Cynthia Gertrude. Author: The Autobiography of Malcolm X, 1965, Roots, 1976 (now in 37 lang. transl., 6,000,000 hardcover copies sold; 12-hr. TV miniseries, 1977, based on bk.; viewed by 130 million), Roots: The Saga of an American Family, 1979; Freelance wrtr., 1960—. Student, Elizabeth City (N.C.) Tchrs. Coll., 1937-79; 17 honorary academic doctorates. Enlisted USCG, 1939; advanced to chief journalist, 1949; ret., 1959. Recipient Spcl. Pulitzer prize, Natl. Bk. Award, 1977. Mem. AG, Soc. Mag. Writers. Address: Kinte Corp Box 3338 Beverly Hills CA 90212

HALEY, VANESSA LEIGH, b. Wilmington, DE, Jan. 19, 1954. Author chapbook: Horse Latitudes, 1980; contrbr. to So. Poetry Rvw, Alaska Qtly Rvw, Tar River Poetry, Poetry, Greensboro Rvw, other lit mags; contrbr. to Anthology of Mag. Verse and Yearbook of Am. Poetry, 1981, 84. BS, U. Del., 1976; MFA, U. N.C., Greensboro, 1979. Instr. Jamestown Community Coll., Olean, N.Y., 1983, Va. Commonwealth U., Richmond, 1983-87, visiting sr. lctr. Mary Washington Coll., 1987-88. Recipient AAP prize, 1979; Individual Artist fellow Del. Arts Council, 1983, Virginia Ctr. for the Creative Arts fellowship, 1986.. Mem. AWP. Home: 2325A Grove Ave Richmond VA 23220

HALL, AILEEN, b. Banner, KY, Dec. 9, 1926; d. Jack and Nancy (Akers) Sellards; m. Walter Hall, June 5, 1946; children—Nancy H. Spradlin, Rhonda H. Blackburn. Author: (poems) Candlelight, 1982. Contrbr. short stories to newspapers, mags. Wrkg. on collection of short stories. Postmaster, U.S. Postal Service, Stanville, Ky., 1949-63, Betsy Layne, Ky., 1963-86. Named to Order of Vest, Air Transport Assn. Am., 1981. Mem. Natl. Assn. Postmasters (pres. Ky. chpt. 1972, Postmaster of Yr. 1984), Ky. State Poetry Soc. Home: Rt 23 Box 188 Betsy Layne KY 41605

HALL, ANN LOUISE, b. Hartford, CT, June 17, 1946; d. Frank and Katharine (Birner) Eichinger; m. Daniel Waldron Hall, Jan. 17, 1970; children—Christopher Wagner, Jonathan Lyman. Contrbr. article to encyc. Devel. ed.: Managing Effective Organizations, 1984, Principles of Management, 1987. B.A., Syracuse U., 1968. Reporter, The Hartford Courant, 1968-73, book rvwr., 1974-78; free-lance wrtr., 1978—; free lance ed., 1983—. Recipient Faculty award for service to schl. jnlsm. Syracuse U., 1968. Mem. WIC. Home: 10 Lavender Hill Ln Andover MA 01810

HALL, BETTY KATHLEEN, b. Auburn, Ky, Apr. 7, 1908, d. Thomas Jefferson and Ella (Rolland (McElwain) Hall. Author: Inspiration and Recall (poetry), 1976, A Prelude to Christmas (poetry), 1976, For the Glory of God (poetry), 1980, Jewels for God (poetry), 1987, Miss Liberty Waltz (song), in Hollywood Gold Album, 1987; contrbr. poetry to World of Poetry Press. Grad. Palmer Wrtrs.' Schl. Recipient Golden Poet award, World of Poetry, 1985, 86, 87. Numerous awards of merit. Address: 803 Hillcrest Dr Bowling Green KY 42101

HALL, CHRISTIE LEA, b. Pasadena, CA, Dec. 30, 1958; d. James Wendell and M. Gayle (Jones) Hall-Christensen; m. Ed Prather, Oct. 21, 1983. BA in Intl. Relations, Pomona Coll.; MS in Jnlsm. (NBC/RCA fellow), Northwestern U. Asst. ed. Daily News, Whittier, Calif., 1982-84; vis. lectr. Univ. Calif., Riverside, 1983-85; copy ed. Press-Enterprise, Riverside, 1984-87. Asst. city ed. San Bernardino County Sun, 1987—.Press aide, Return George Brown to Congress Comm., San Bernardino, Calif., 1982. Address: 608 Lincoln St Redlands CA 92374

HALL, DONALD, b. New Haven, Sept. 20, 1928; s. Donald Andrew and Lucy (Wells) H.; m. Kirby Thompson, Sept. 13, 1952 (div. Feb. 1969); children—Andrew, Philippa; m. Jane Kenyon, Apr. 17, 1972. Author: poems Exiles and Marriages, 1955, The Dark Houses, 1958, A Roof of Tiger Lilies, 1963, The Alligator Bride, 1969, The Yellow Room, 1971, The Town of Hill, 1975, A Blue Wing Tilts at the Edge of the Sea, 1975, Kicking the Leaves, 1978, The Toy Bone, 1979, The Happy Man, 1986; criticism Marianne Moore: The Cage and the Animal, 1970, Goatfoot, Milktongue, Twinbird, 1978, To Keep Moving, 1980, The Weather for Poetry, 1982; juvenile Andrew the Lion Farmer, 1959, Riddle Rat, 1977; Ox Cart Man, 1979, The Man Who Lived Alone, 1984; memoir String Too Short to be Saved, 1961, 79, Remembering Poets, 1978; biography Henry Moore, 1966, Dock Ellis in the Country of Baseball, 1976, (with David Finn) As the Eye Moves, 1970; limericks The Gentleman's Alphabet Book, 1972; prose Writing Well, 1973, 5th ed., 1985, Playing Around, 1974, Fathers Playing Catch with Sons, 1985; editor: Harvard Adv. Anthology, 1950, (with L. Simpson and R. Pack) The New Poets of England and America, 1957, (with R. Pack) New Poets of England and America, Second Selection, 1962, A Poetry Sampler, 1962, Contemporary American Poetry, 1962, 2d edit., 1971, (with W. Taylor) Poetry in English, 1963, 2d edit., 1970, (with S. Spender) A Concise Ency. of English and American Poets and Poetry, 1963, 2d edit., 1970, Faber Book of Modern Verse, 1966, The Modern Stylists, 1968, A Choice of Whitman's Verse, 1968, Man and Boy, 1968; Anthology American Poetry, 1969, Pleasures of Poetry, 1971, (with D. Emblen) A Writer's Reader, 1976, 4th ed., 1985, To Read Literature, 1981, rev. ed. 1983, 3d ed., 1986, To Read Poetry, 1982, Oxford Book American Literary Anecdotes, 1981, Claims for Poetry, 1982, Oxford Book of Children's Verse in America, 1985. BA, Harvard U., 1951; B Litt (Henry fellow), Oxford U., 1953; postgrad., Stanford U., 1953-54; LHD (hon.), Plymouth State Coll., D Litt, Presbyn. Coll., D.Letters, Colby-Sawyer Coll., 1984. Creative writing fellow Stanford U., 1953; jr. fellow Soc. Fellows, Harvard U., 1954-57; poetry editor Paris Review, 1953-61; mem. poetry bd. Wesleyan U. Press, 1958-64; cons. Harper & Row, 1964-81; judge Bollingen Prize for Poetry, 1958, 59, Lamont Poetry Competition, 1967-69, Natl. Book Awards, 1968, Edgar Allen Poe and Copernicus awards Acad. Am. Poets, 1975, Natl. Poetry Series, 1979; Lamont Poetry Selection AAP, 1955; Edna St. Vincent Millay Meml. award Poetry Soc. Am., 1955; Longview Fdn. award, 1960; Sarah Joseph Hale award, 1983; Guggenheim fellow, 1963, 72. Mem. MLA, AG, PEN. Home: Eagle Pond Farm Danbury NH 03230

HALL, D. ELAINE, (Shauna Robins, Wade Douglas), b. Hot Springs, Ark., July 30, 1949; Robert O. and Warrene (Sorrells) Allbritton; m. Wade D. Hall, June 14, 1968; children—V. Robin, Shauna Lynne. Author: Aware, 1986. Home: 105 Fernwood St Hot Springs AR 71901

HALL, GRACE, b. Calumet City, IL, May 7, 1941; d. Adelbert and Clara (Deering) Grzelak; m. Clifford D. Hall, July 1, 1961; Children: Shawn, Vincent, Michael. Poetry in Am. Poetry Anthology, 1986. Wrkg. on mystery novel, short stories. Student Newspaper Inst. Am. Corr. The Daily News, Iron Mountain and Kingsford, Mich., 1987, feature wrtr., 1987—. Home: 431 Tobin Alpha Rd Crystal Falls MI 49920

HALL, JAMES BYRON, b. Midland, OH, July 21, 1918; s. Harry and Florence (Moon) H.; m. Elizabeth Cushman, Feb. 14, 1946; children—Elinor, Prudence, Kathryn, Millicent, James M. M. Author: Not by the Door, 1954, The Short Story, 1955, 15X3 (with R.V. Cassill and Herbert Gold), 1957, Racers to the Sun, 1960, Us He Devours, 1964, Realm of Fiction, 1965-77, Modern Culture and the Arts, 1967-75, Mayo Sergeant, 1967, The Hunt Within, 1973, The Short Hall, 1981; contrbr. stories, poetry to anthols. Student, Miami Univ., Oxford, OH, 1938-39; Univ. Hawaii, 1938-40; BA, State Univ. Iowa, 1947; MA, 1948; PhD,1953; postgrad., Kenyon College, 1949. Wrtr.-in-res. Miami Univ., 1948-49; Univ. of NC, Greenville, 1954, Univ. B.C., 1955, Univ. Colo., 1963; instr. Cornell Univ., 1952-53; asst. prof. Eng. Univ. Oregon, 1954-57, assoc. prof., 1958-60, prof., 1960-65; prof. Eng., dir. The Writing Center, Univ. Calif. at Irvine, 1965-68; provost Univ. Calif. at Santa Cruz, 1968-75, prof. and wrtr.-in-res. 1976-83, emeritus 1984—; freelance wrtr. and consultant, 1983. James B. Hall Art Gallery named by Univ. Calif. regents, 1985. Consulting ed. Doubleday & Co., 1960-65. Founder Summer Acad. Contemporary Arts, 1959; cultural spclst. U. S. State Dept., 1964. Served with AUS, 1940-46. Octave Thanet prize, 1950, Oreg. Poetry prize, 1958, Emily Clark Balch Fiction prize, 1967. Rockefeller grantee, 1955. Mem. AAUP. Literary Archive Materials, Miami Univ., Ohio; regents named James B. Hall Art Gallery, 1986. West Coast grievance officer, Natl. Wrtrs. Union, 1985—. Home: 31 Hollins Dr Santa Cruz CA 95060

HALL, JEANNINE D., b. New Haven, Apr. 30, 1973; d. Ernest L. and Bettie C. Hall. Contrbr. poetry: Hearts on Fire, Seven Hills Rvw, Best New Poets of 1986, Am. Poetry Anthol. Student Cincinnati Covntry Day Schl. Home: 9256 Village Green Dr Cincinnati OH 45221

HALL, JEROME, b. Chgo., Feb. 4, 1901; s. Herbert and Sarah (Rush) H.; m. Marianne Cowan, July 2, 1941; 1 dau., Heather Adele. Author: Readings in Jurisprudence, 1938, General Principles of Criminal Law, 2d ed., 1960, Cases and Readings on Criminal Law and Procedure, 4th ed., 1983, Living Law of Democratic Society, 1949, Theft, Law and Society, 2d ed., 1952, Studies in Jurisprudence and Criminal Theory, 1958, Comparative Law and Social Theory, 1963, Foundations of Jurisprudence, 1973, Law, Social Science and Criminal Theory, 1982; editor: 20th Century Legal Philosophy Series, 8 vols.; contrbr. articles profl. jnls. PhB, U. Chgo., 1922, JD, 1923; JurScD, Columbia, 1935; SJD, Harvard U., 1935; LLD, U. N.D., 1958, U. Tubingen (W.Ger.), 1978. Bar: Ill. 1923. Spcl. fellow Columbia Law Schl., 1932-34; Benjamin research fellow Harvard Law Schl., 1934-35. Home: 1390 Market St San Francisco CA 94102

HALL, JOAN JOFFE, b. NYC, Feb. 16, 1936, d. Louis and Leah Mildred (Edelstein) Joffe; m. James Baker Hall, June 8, 1959 (div. 1978); children—Matthew, Michael; m. 2d, David Morse, Jan. 10, 1981. Author: Cutting the Plant, 1977, The Rift Zone, 1978, The Aerialist's Fall, 1981, Romance & Capitalism at the Movies, 1985; contrbr. to Anthology of Magazine Verse & Yearbook of American Poetry, Mass. Rvw, Modern Lang. Qtly, Fiction Intl., other lit publs. BA, Vassar Coll., 1956; MA, Stanford U., 1957, PhD,1961. Prof. U. Conn., Storrs, 1963—. Mem. MLA, New Eng. Women's Studies Assn., Natl. Women's Studies Assn. Home: 64 Birchwood Heights Storrs CT 06268

HALL, PHIL, b. Bronx, NY, Oct. 12, 1964. Contrbr. articles: N.Y. Daily News, Jerusalem Post, Sunrise (London), numerous other publs. Wrkg. on novel. BA in Journalism, Pace U., White Plains, N.Y., 1986. UN corr., Fairchild Broadcast News, NYC, 1984-86, assoc. ed. Whitney Communications, NYC, 1986—. Home: 3215 Arlington Ave Bronx NY 10463

HALL, SANDRA JEAN, b. Hannibal, MO, Mar. 6, 1958; d. Roy Arthur and Betty Jean (Olson) Cookson; m. John Robert Hall, Aug. 12, 1979; children—Amanda Jean, Crystal Marie. Author: A Christmas Wish, 1986, After-effects, 1987, Perchance to Dream, 1987, Pox on Both Your Houses, 1987, Atonement, 1987, Salt in the Wound, 1987. Ed.: A Shoe to Walk On (Jim Boltinghouse), 1987. A.D. in Nursing, Hannibal LaGrange Hosp., 1983; B.S. in Biology, Southwest Baptist U., 1979. Grad. nurse St. Elizabeth Hosp., Hannibal, 1983; staff nurse Wake County Med. Center, Raleigh, N.C., 1984-86. Recipient 1st place for short story Hannibal Wrtr.'s Club,

1986. Home: Box 63 Plainville IL 62365

HALL, THEODORE DANA, b. Greenwich, CT, July 23, 1943; s. Theodora Dana and Lillian (Hansen) H.; m. Roberta Morris, Mar. 23, 1968 (div. 1976); 1 son, Theodore D. Hall Jr. Writer/ ed. ICPI Rpt., 1980—; author: ICPI Handbook for Insur. Personnel, 1985, Other Stages, 1980, To Rule The World (screenplay), 1986, poems, critical articles in lit mags. BA, U. MI, 1966; MA, PhD, Syracuse U., 1970. Asst. prof. Engl., Muskingum Coll., 1970-80; writer/ed. Insur. Crime Prevention Inst., Westport, CT, 1980—. AAP Award, Syracuse U., 1967. Mem. DG, Screenwriters Guild. Home: 409 Saw Mill Rd West Haven CTJ 06516

HALLA, ROBERT CHRISTIAN, (Chris), b. Oshkosh, WI, Feb. 16, 1949; s. Floyd Earl (born Hanson) and Laura Blanche (Roberts) H.; m. Janet Lee Gramoll nee Williams, Aug. 23, 1969; children: Joshua Aaron, Rachel Anne. Author: River Bottom, 1973, Adventures of a Freelance Farmer, 1974, Dreamboats and Milestones, 1981, River Boy, River Town, River, 1981, The Harley-Davidson Story, 1982, Cougar, 1984; ed. River Bottom Mag and Press, 1974-78, Wolfsong, 1978-81, Old Cars Newspaper, 1977-81, Car Exchange Mag, 1979-81, Wis. Weekend, 1981-82, Wis. Trails, 1981-82; contrbr. to Road Apple Rvw, Pembroke, Wis. Acad. Rvw, Poetry Now, Cream City Rvw, Northeast, Writer's Digest, Small Press, Automobile Qtly, Ab Intra, View, etc. BS, U Wis-Oshkosh, 1973. Ed/Illus Oshkosh Truck Corp, Wis., 1973-75; writer/ed. Harley-Davidson Motor Co., Milw., 1977; ed. Krause Publs., Iola, Wis. 1977-81; mng. ed. Wis Tales & Trails, 1981-82; devel. mgr. J.J. Keller & Assocs., Neenah, Wis., 1983—; freelance writer/ed., Wis, 1973—. CCLM grantee, 1975. Address: 1455 W Prospect Appleton WI 54914

HALLER, AMELIA JANE, b. Tood County, MN, Oct. 25, 1927; d. Ervin Swan and Zoa May (McGowan) Anderson; m. Max Ray Haller, June 25, 1945; children—Pamela, Larry, Richy, Daniel, Catherine, Christine, Patrick, Randal. Author: (chapbook) Now Time is Blending, 1980, Plowing Time, 1982. Contrbr. poems, short stories, articles to mags., anthols. A.Liberal Arts, Tacoma Commun. Coll., 1987. Instr. creative writing workshops, Buckley and Tacoma, WA, 1979, 80, 83, 85, 87. Recipient 1st place for poetry Poetry Day, Spokane, WA, 1965, Calif. State, 1981, Bellingham Rvw., WA, 1987. Mem. NLAPW, Wash. Poets Assn. (past pres.; 1st place for poetry 1984), Northwest Renaissance Poets Pubs., Tacoma Wrtrs. Club (past pres., 1st place for poetry 1986, 87), Pacific Northwest Wrtrs. Conf. (info. asst.). Home: 6002 S Fife Tacoma WA 98409

HALLER, TERRY, b. Kitchener, Ont., Can., Sept. 1, 1934; s. Alfred and Myrtle (Hinnegan) H.; m. Anna, Nov. 5, 1965; children—Colin, Aaron, Gregory. Author: Secrets of the Master Business Strategist, 1983; Danger: Marketing Researcher at Work, 1983; The Successful Strategist, 1984. BA, U. Western Ontario, MBA, U. Toronto. Brand mgr. Procter & Gamble, Cin., 1957-65; mktg. exec. R.J. Reynolds, Winston-Salem, NC, 1965-73; intl. mktg. exec. Quaker Oats Co., Chgo., 1973-76; pres./CEO Chgo. Research Co. (IL), 1976-85; ed. Renews Mag., KONA Communications, Deerfield, IL, 1985—. Dir. PR, Citizens for Reagan, Chgo., 1980. Listed Amer. Mktg. Assn. National Speakers List. Office: KONA Comm 707 Lake Cook Rd Deerfield IL 60015

HALLETT, LEWELLYN, b. Atlanta, Sept. 20, 1953; d. James harrison and LewEllyn Grace (Lundeen) Finch; m. Christopher Mark Hallett, July 5, 1987. Contrbr. poems, articles to mags.; author ads. Ed.: The Way Mag., 1987—, Heart, 1987—. Student Emory U., 1971-73; B.A. in Creative Writing, U. N.M., 1975-77. Advt. copywriter Lucky Stores, Inc., Milan, IL, 1978-81, Federated Stores, Atlanta, 1981-84; wrtr. The Way Intl., New Knoxville, OH, 1985-87, asst. mng. ed., 1987—. Office: Box 328 New Knoxville OH 45871

HALL-MEIER, CHARLOTTE, see Plucker, Charlotte Ann

HALLORAN, DANIEL F., b. Cohoes, NY, Oct. 14, 1926, s. Francis D. and Georgianna (Cole) H.; m. Dorothy Kahl, Apr. 11, 1959; children—Daniel, Eileen, Maynel, Timothy, Jonathon, David. Columnist: The Evangelist, Catholic New York; contrbr. articles to: America, Management World, Reader's Digest, Personnel Jnl, other publs. Wrkg. on biography of Charlotte Bronte. BA, Siena Coll., 1951, MS, 1954; MPA, Syracuse U., 1962. Dir. manpower N.Y. State Tax Dept., Albany, 1970-83; lectr. Albany Bus. Coll., 1983-86, Coll. St. Rose, Albany, 1984-85, Siena Coll., Loudonville, N.Y., 1985—. Mem. Bronte Soc. Home: 970 New Scotland Rd Albany NY 12208

HALLSTEAD, WILLIAM FINN III, (William Beechcroft), b. Scranton, Pa., April 20, 1924; s. William F. II and Winifred (Mott) H; m. Jean Little, Oct. 9, 1948; children: William F. IV, Alyssa Jean. Author: juveniles: The Secret of Wildcat Swamp (31st book in the Hardy Boys series), 1952, Ev Kris: Aviation Detective, 1961, Dirigible Scout, 1967, Sky Carnival (Jr. Literary Guild selection), 1969, The Missiles of Zajecar, 1969. Ghost Plane of Blackwater, 1974, The Man Downstairs (Young Adult Literary Guild selection), 1980, Conqueror of the Clouds (Young Adult Literary Guild selection), 1980, The Launching of Linda Bell, 1981, Tundra, 1984. Adult nonfiction: How to Make Money Writing Articles for the Free Lance Market, 1976, Broadcasting Careers for You, 1983. Under pseudonym William Beechcroft, adult fiction: Position of Ultimate Trust, 1981, Image of Evil, 1985, Chain of Vengeance, 1986, The Rebuilt Man, 1987, Secret Kills, 1988, Youth stories anthologized in junior high school readers and textbooks. Contrbr. short stories to Boy's Life and other juvenile mags and articles to engineering trade jnls and other periodicals. Mng ed, Architects' Report, 1960-64 and Md. Engineer, 1963-64. Ed, Baltimore Scene (bimonthly mag), 1963-64, and Jnl of the Md Center for Public Broadcasting, 1969-84. Educated at The Hill School, Pottstown, Pa. Flight instructor, Scranton, Pa., Municipal Airport Corp., 1947-49; draftsman, Penn. Dept of Highways, 1950-52; sr highway designer, Whitman, Requardt & Assocs (consulting engineers), Baltimore, Md., 1952-58; pres, Colony Publishing Corp., Baltimore, 1958-64; dir of info services, The Rouse Co. (real estate developers), 1965-68; dir of development and info services, Md. Center for Public Broadcasting, Owings Mills, Md., 1969-84. Member: American Aviation Hist Soc, AG, Authors League of Amererica, MWA, Book of the Year awards from Child Study Assn, 1980, for Conqueror of the Clouds, and 1985, for Tundra. U.S. Army Air Forces, 1942-45; radio operator-gunner on B-24 with 15th Air Force in Italy; became sergeant. Home: 1077 S Yachtsman Dr Sanibel Island FL 33597

HALLSTEN MC GARRY, SUSAN JOAN, (M. Hal Sussman), b. Mpls., June 27, 1948; d. Clarence Albert and Evelyn Mildred (Nelson) Hallsten; m. Stephen Joseph McGarry, Aug. 11, 1978. Co-author with G . Harvey Jones, Taking Stock: Paintings and Sculpture by G. Harvey. BA, U. MN, 1973, MA, 1978. Instr. U. MN, Mpls., 1973-78; proposals writer, CRS, Houston, 1978; ed.-in-chief Southwest Art, Houston, 1979—. Award of Excellence, Art Directors, NYC, 1985. Mem. Toastmasters Int. Home: 3718 Grennoch Lane Houston TX 77025

HALPERIN, MARK WARREN, b. NYC, Feb. 19, 1940; s. George Waldo and Minna (Scherzer) H.; m. Barbara Scott, June 15, 1966, 1 son, Noah Corey. Author: Backroads, 1976, The White Coverlet, 1979, Gomer, 1979, A Place Made Fast, 1982. Wrkg. on a new book of poems. BA in Physics, Bard Coll., 1960; MFA in Poetry, U. Iowa, 1966. Instr. English Central Washington Univ., Ellensburg, 1966-83, prof., 1984—. Recipient US award Intl. Poetry Forum, 1975. Address: Rt 4 Box 279A Ellensburg WA 98926

HALPERN, DANIEL, b. Syracuse, NY, Sept. 11, 1945; s. Irving and Rosemary (Glueck) Halpern; m. Jeanne Carter. Author poetry: Seasonal Rights, 1982, Life Among Others, 1978, Street Fire, 1975, Traveling On Credit, 1972, The Lady Knife-Thrower, 1975; books: The Good Food: Soups, Stews, and Pastas, 1985; contrbr. var. poetry and short fiction anthologies. MFA, Columbia U. Edit.-in-chief, The Ecco Press, NYC,1971—; edit.-in-chief, Antaeus, NYC,1969—. Awards: NEA Fellowship, 1973, 1975; YMHA Discovery Award, 1971. Address: c/o Ecco Press 18 West 30th St NYC 10001

HALSEY, WILLIAM DARRACH, b. Washington, Sept. 17, 1918; s. William D. and Mary Flagg (Price) H.; m. Frances Murlin, June 27, 1942; m. Elizabeth Darby, Apr. 11, 1966. Mng. editor Thorndike-Barnhart Comprehensive Desk Dictionary, 1951—, Thorndike-Barnhart Beginning Dictionary, 1952—, Thorndike-Barnhart Jr. Dictionary, 1952—, High Schl. Dictionary, 1952—, Thorndike-Barnhart Advanced Jr. Dictionary, 1957—; editorial dir. Collier's Encyc., 1960, Merit Students Encyc., 1965, Macmillan Dictionary, 1973, Macmillan Schl. Dictionary, 1974, Macmillan Dictionary for Children, 1975; v.p. Crowell-Collier Pub. Co., 1962-65, Crowell Collier and Macmillan, Inc., 1965—; pres. Crowell-Collier Ednl. Corp., 1964—; sr. v.p. Macmillan, Inc., 1968—. Co-author: New Century Cyclopedia of Names, 1954, New Century Handbook of English Literature, 1956. Grad., Loomis Schl., 1936; BS, Haverford Coll., 1940. Home: 40 E 9th St New York NY 10028

HAMARNEH, SAMI KHALAF, b. Madaba, Jordan, Feb. 2, 1925; came to U.S., 1952, naturalized, 1957; s. Khalaf and Nura A. (Zumut) H.; m. Nazha T. Ajaj, July 4, 1948; 1 son, Faris. Author: Bibliography of Medicine and Pharmacy in Medieval Islam, 1964, Index of Arabic Manuscripts on Medicine and Pharmacy at the National Library of Cairo, 1967, Index of Manuscripts on Medicine and Pharmacy in the Zahiriyah Library, 1969, Temples of the Muses and a History of Pharmacy Museums, 1972, Pharmacy Museums USA, 1972, Origins of Pharmacy and Therapy in the Near East, 1973, The Physician, Therapist and Surgeon Ibn al-Quff, 1974, Catalogue of Arabic Manuscripts on Medicine and Pharmacy at Brit. Library, 1975, Directory of Historians of Arabic- Islamic Science, 1980, also articles; editor: Jnl. History Arabic

Sci., 1976—. BSc in Pharmacy, Syrian U., Damascus, 1948; MSc in Pharm. Chemistry, N.D. State U., Fargo, 1956; PhD in History of Pharmacy and Medicine, U. Wis., 1959. E. Kremers award for distinguished pharmaco-hist writings, 1966. Home: 4631 Massachusetts Ave NW Washington DC 20016

HAMBY, JAMES A., b. Oakland, CA, May 16, 1943; s. Walter B. Hamby and Jane E. (Harvey) Petrie; children—Jean Marie, Deborah Suzanne, Tracey Gail. Collaborator: A Critical Guide to Herman Melville, 1971, Drama: A Critical Collection, 1971, Classic Short Fiction, 1972; co-author: Principles and Issues in Nutrition, 1985; author: Instructor's Manual to Principles and Issues in Nutrition, 1985. BA in humanities, Southern Oreg. State Coll., 1965, MA in English, 1969. Faculty Medford High Schl., Oreg., 1967-70, Utah State U., Logan, 1970-71, Coll. of the Redwoods, Eureka, Calif., 1971-76; genl. mgr. Humboldt State U. Fdn., Arcata, Calif., 1971—. Recipient Creative award for poetry Utah Inst. Fine Arts, 1971. Mem. P&W, AWP, Council for Advancement Support of Edn. Home: Box 1124 Arcata CA 95521

HAMILL, PAUL J., b. Quincy, MA, July 11, 1943; s. Paul J. and Margaret (Shea) H.; m. Monica H., June 17, 1967; children—Paul, Stephen, Katherine. Poetry in Poetry, Midwest Qtly, Kudzu, The Smith, Lyric and various other lit mags. BA, Boston College, 1964; PhD,Stanford, 1971; asst. prof., Morehouse College, Atlanta, Ga., 1968-69; asst. prof., Temple U., Phila., Pa., 1970-76; asst. prof., Indiana State U., Terre Haute, 1969-70; asst. vice pres., College of Charleston, SC, 1976-82; asst. provost and assoc. prof., College of Charleston, 1982—. Mem. PSA, Amer. Assn. of Higher Ed., Poetry Soc. of South Carolina. Address: Coll of Charleston 66 George St Charleston SC 29424

HAMILL, PETE, (William Pete Hamill), b. Bklyn., June 24, 1935; s. William and Anne (Devlin) H.; m. Ramona Negron, Feb. 3, 1962 (div. 1970); children: Adriene, Deirdre. Author: novels A Killing for Christ, 1968, The Gift, 1973, Flesh and Blood, 1977; non-fiction Irrational Ravings, 1972, The Invisible City: A New York Sketchbook, 1980; screenplays Doc, 1971, Badge 373, 1973; contrbr. articles to numerous mags. Student, Pratt Inst., 1952, Mexico City (Mexico) Coll., 1956-57. Reporter N.Y. Post, later columnist, 1960-74; columnist N.Y. Daily News, 1965-67, 69-79; contrbg. editor Saturday Evening Post, 1963-64; contrbr. Village Voice, 1974—. Served with USNR, 1952-54. Recipient Meyer Berger award Columbia Schl. Journalism, 1962, award Newspaper Reporters Assn., 1962. Mem. WG Am., AG, Soc. Mag. Writers. Address Random Hs 201 E 50th St New York NY 10022

HAMILL, WILLIAM PETE, see Hamill, Pete

HAMILTON, CAROL JEAN, b. Enid, OK, Aug. 23, 1935; d. Clarence DeWitt and Ruby Raye (Settles) Barber; m. Joseph Jefferson Hamilton, Aug. 25, 1956; children: Debra Susan Hamilton Havenar, Christopher David, Stephen Anthony. Author: (chapbook) Daring the Wind, 1984; (juvenile) The Dawn Seekers, 1986; contrbr. over 1,000 poems, short stories and articles to newspapers, lit mags. BA, Phillips U., 1957; MA, Central State U., Edmond, Okla., 1978. Tchr. pub. schls., North Haven, Conn., 1957-59, Indpls., 1970-71, Tinker AFB, Okla., 1971-82, Acad. Ctr. for Enrichment Mid-Del, Oklahoma City, 1982—. Mem. Natl. League Am. Pen Women, AAP, Poetry Soc. Okla. (pres. 1984), Mid-Okla. Wrtrs.(pres. 1982), Okla. Wrtrs. Fedn. (bd. dirs. 1983), Individual Artists Okla. (bd. dirs. 1975-85). Home: 9608 Sonata Ct Midwest City OK 73130

HAMILTON, DONALD BENGTSSON, b. Uppsala, Sweden, Mar. 24, 1916; s. Bengt L.K. and Elise (Neovius) H.; m. Kathleen Stick, 1941; children—Hugo, Elise, Gordon, Victoria. Creator Matt Helm series: Death of a Citizen, 1960, The Wrecking Crew, 1960, The Removers, 1961, The Silencers, 1962, Murderer's Row, 1962, The Ambushers, 1963, The Ravagers, 1963, The Shadowers, 1964, The Devastators, 1965, The Betrayers, 1966, The Menacers, 1968, The Interlopers, 1969, The Poisoners, 1971, The Intriguers, 1972, The Intimidators, 1974, The Terminators, 1975, The Retaliators, 1976, The Terrorizers, 1977, The Revengers, 1982, The Annihilators, 1983, The Infiltrators, 1984, The Detonators, 1985, The Vanishers, 1986; as well as Date with Darkness, 1947, The Steel Mirror, 1948, Murder Twice Told, 1950, Night Walker, 1954, Smoky Valley, 1955, Assignment: Murder, 1956, The Big Country, 1958, Texas Fever, 1960, Donald Hamilton on Guns and Hunting, 1970, Cruises with "Kathleen," 1980, The Mona Intercept, 1980; editor, Iron Men and Silver Stars, 1967; contrbr. articles on hunting, yachting and photography to mags. BS, U. Chgo., 1938. Mem. MWA, WWA, assoc. mem. OWAA. Office: 984 Acequia Madre Box 1045 Santa Fe NM 87501

HAMILTON, DORIS JEAN, b. Frankfort, KY; adopted d. William Van Buren and Carrie B. Osborne; m. Roy Lee Hamilton, Mar. 11, 1950; 1 dau., Ginger Lee Renaker. Contrbr. poems to anthols.; author songs to cos. including Capitol Records, others. Student Cin. U., Eastern Ky. U., Somerset Community Coll., LaSalle Extension U. Security guard U.S. Army Corps of Engrs., Somerset, Ky., 1972-75; consumer protection agt. Continental Protective Agcy., Lake Success, N.Y., 1973-75. Recipient 3 hon. mention awards World of Poetry, 1984, 86, spcl. mention award, 1984, 3 Golden Poet awards, 1985, 86, 87. Mem. Broadcast Music. Home: Box 210 Rt 3 Cedar Hill Waynesburg KY 40489

HAMILTON, ELISSA LYNN ALKOFF, (Elissa Malcohn), b. Bklyn., Oct. 18, 1958; d. Sylvia (Farber) and Bernard Alkoff. Contrbr. poetry to Aurora, Beacon, Portland, Harvard Bus. rvws, Earth's Daus., Round Table, Planetarian, San Fernando Poetry Jnl, Isaac Asimov's Sci. Fiction Mag., Uranus, Velocities, Black Maria, others; contrbr. fiction to Karmic Runes, Black Maria, Yellow Silk, Isaac Asimov's Sci. Fiction Mag., River Reader. BA, Wagner Coll., 1979; MS, Stevens Inst. Tech., 1982. Teaching/research asst. Stevens Inst. Tech., Hoboken, N.J., 1979-81; adminstrv. asst. Women's Peace Edn. Project, NYC, 1981-82; staff asst. Harvard U. Bus. Schl., Boston, 1983—. Mem. FWG, FSWA, Sci. Fiction Poetry Assn. (ed.), P&W. Home: Box 1764 Cambridge MA 02238

HAMILTON, JAMES, b. Chester, SC, Dec. 4, 1938; s. Herman Prioleau and Edith Muriel (Gilchrist) H.; m. Siri Kristina Hagglund, July 14, 1979; children—William James, Erik Gilchrist, Kathryn Heyward. Author: The Power to Probe: A Study of Congressional Investigations, 1976; ed., contrbr. Congressional Investigations: Legal Issues and Practical Approaches, 1987. contrbr. articles to profl. jnls., major newspapers. AB, Davidson Coll., 1960; LL.B., Yale U., 1963; LL.M., U. London, 1966. Bar: D.C. 1967. Served at 1st lt. AUS, 1963-65. Decorated Army Commendation medal; Ford Fdn. Travel and study grantee, 1974-75. Home: 3321 Rowland Pl NW Washington DC 20008

HAMILTON, LEONA, b. Kansas City, MO, Jan. 3, 1915; d. Charles and Allene (Goodyear) Trahern; adopted d. Abram and Jessie Piper; m. Homer Hamilton (dec.); 1 dau., Martha Hamilton Fultz. Author: Duel Before Dawn, 1960, poetry in numerous mags and anthols inclg. Spring Anthology, Diamond Anthology, Good Housekeeping; Poetry Digest, Voices International. Student, Shawnee Mission, Kansas. Sub. tchr., Brownsville, TX pub. schls., 1964-72; secretary, National Council on Aging, Brownsville, TX, 1972-78. Mem. PSA, Tyler Creative Writer's Club. Home: 503 Copperfield Village Dr Victoria TX 77904

HAMILTON, LINDA KAY, b. Waukegan, IL, May 13, 1945; d. Lloyd Henry and Vida May (Harms) Fruth; 1 dau., Arwen Elizabeth. Sect. head Mich. State U. Libraries, Detroit, 1973-75, network coordinator, 1975-76; asst. dir. Mich. Library Consortium, 1976-77; mgr. bibliographic services Univ. Microfilms Intl., Ann Arbor, Mich., 1977-79; mgr. collections ops., 1979-82; v.p. acad. micropublishing, dir. Research Publs. Inc., Woodbridge, Conn., 1982—. Editor: MLA Intellectual Freedom Newsletter, 1974-75, Cort Cat News, 1974-77; contrbr. articles to profl. jnls. Mem. ALA. Office: Research Pubs 12 Lunar Dr Woodbridge CT 06525

HAMILTON, MARCELLA DENISE, (Lee Hendrix), b. NYC, Mar. 5, 1954; d. George Hamilton and Cleo Lipkins. Author: Prisoner of Business, 1986; (pamphlet) Cut the Maze of Computer Costs, 1986. Contrbr. articles to mags. Wrkg. on humor novel. Grad. public schls., NYC. Accounts mgr. Ztech, Denver, 1987—. Mem. NWC (v.p. membership Denver chpt. 1986). Home: 3816 Zuni Box 12326 Denver CO 80212

HAMILTON, PATRICIA WARDLEY, b. Chgo., Sept. 15, 1930; d. Charles Anson and Anna (Critchfield) Wardley; m. Lloyd Alexander Hamilton, Jr., MD, Aug. 23, 1952; children—Diana Hope, Lloyd Alexander III, Andrea Marguerite. Ed., Dun & Bradstreet Reports, 1979—; contrbr. to New York Times. AB in English Lit., Connecticut Coll., 1952; MA in English Lit., Columbia U., 1972. Writer adv. copy Houghton Mifflin, Boston, 1952-54, William Morrow Co., NYC, 1954-58; freelance writer, 1960-69; tchr. Eng., Pearl River HS (NY), 1972-74; writer/ed. Editors Unlimited, Greenwich, CT, 1974-79; ed. D & B Reports, Dun & Bradstreet, NYC, 1979—. Mem. ASME. Home: 180 River Rd Grand View-on- Hudson NY 10960

HAMILTON, ROSEMARY ANN, (Rosemary Dean, Rose Finnegan), b. Delphi, IN, July 10; d. Mark Victor O'Malia and Dorothy Mae (Popejoy) O'Malia Eaton; m. James Thomas Finnegan, July 11, 1942 (div. 1957); children—Melissa Lee Finnegan Axton, Miranda Ann Finnegan Mannis, Thomas Clark (nee Finnegan) Hamilton, Elizabeth Jane Finnegan Roy. m. 2d, M.E. Hamilton, July 3, 1959, Contrbr. short stories: Ellery Queen Mystery Mag., Cosmopolitan, Chatelaine, McCall's, other publs. Wrkg. on novel. Student public schs., Mishawaka, Ind. News ed. Delphi (Ind.) Jnl., 1957-59; jr. ed. Meyer-Both Advt. Agy., N.Y.C., 1944; guest lectr. in creative writing, Purdue U. Home: Lafayette IN

HAMILTON, VIRGINIA, b. Yellow Springs, OH, Mar.12, 1936; d. Kenneth James and Etta Belle (Perry) H.; m. Arnold Adoff, Mar. 29, 1960; children: Leigh Hamilton, Jaime Levi. Author: children's novels Zeely, 1967 (Nancy Block Meml. award Downtown Community schl. Awards Com.), The House of Dies Drear, 1968 (Edgar Allan Poe award for best juvenile mystery 1969), The Time-Ago Tales of Jadhu, 1969, Planet of Junior Brown, 1971; W.E.B. Dubois: A Biography, 1972; children's novels Time-Ago Lost: More Tales of Jahdu, 1973, M.C. Higgins the Great (John Newbery medal 1974), 1974, (Nat. Bood award 1975), Paul Robeson: The Life and Times of a Free Black Man, 1974, Arilla Sund Down, 197; Illusion and Reality, 1976, The Justice Cycle: Justice and Her Brothers, 1978, Dustland, 1980, Gathering, 1980, Jahdu, 1980, Sweet Whispers, Brother Rush, 1982, The Magical Adventures of Pretty Pearl, 1984, A Little Love, 1984, Junius Over Far, 1985, The People Could Fly, 1985. Editor: Writings of W.E.B. Dubois, 1975. Student, Antioch Col., 1952-58, New Sch. for Social Research. Recipient Ohioana Lit. award, 1969. Office: Box 293 Yellow Springs OH 45387

HAMILTON, WILLIAM ROGER, b. Patrick AFB, FL, May 25, 1955, s. D.rwin Roger and Ruth (Smith) H.; m. Lauren Froelich, Dec. 21, 1975 (div. 1982). Contrbr. poetry to N.Am. Mentor. Wrkg. on novel, poetry collection. BS in Mech. Engring., U. Houston, 1977, MBA in Finance, 1982. Engring. mgr. Hughes Tool Co., Houston, 1977—. Home: 5402 Alamosa Ln Spring TX 77379

HAMMER, LOUIS ZELIG, b. New Britain, CT, Sept. 27, 1931, s. Isadore and Grace Lillian (Gans) H. Books of poetry: Bone Planet, 1967, To Burn California, 1974, Lying on the Earth, 1975, Birth Sores/Bands, 1980, The Book of Games, 1985, The Mirror Dances, 1986; author textbook: Value and Man, 1966. BA, Yale U., 1953, PhD,1960. Philosophy educator 1960—, U. So. Calif., Los Angeles, Hebrew U., Jerusalem, Wellesley Coll., Mass., Brandeis U., Waltham Mass., Rensselaer Poly. Inst., Troy, N.Y.; editor Sachem Press, Old Chatham, NY, since 1980. Served with U.S. Army, 1956-58. Mem. Am. Philos. Assn., Am. Soc. Aesthetics, Hudson Valley Wrtrs.' Guild. Home: Box 9 Old Chatham NY 12136

HAMMER, ROGER A., b. San Francisco, CA, Nov. 11, 1934; s. Paul A. and Margaret J. (Lilly) H. Author: The People (Native Americans), 1975, Black America, 1978, American Woman, 1980, Hispanic America, 1984, My Own Book!, 1987; publisher: Read America! (newsletter), quarterly since 1984. BA, U. of Minnesota, 1973. Asst. news ed., Mobile (AL) Press Register, 1959-66; asst. bureau chief, UPI (Montgomery, AL), 1966-69; PR mgr., Carl Byoir & Assoc. Honeywell (Minneapolis, MN), 1969-80; exec. ed., Hammer News Service (Golden Valley, MN), 1980—. Writer of Year AL Mental Health Assn., 1966. Mem. Soc. Prof. Jnlsts. Office: Hammer News Service 3900 Glenwood Ave Golden Valley MN 55422

HAMMON, ARTHUR CHRISTOPHER, b. Farmer City, IL, Feb. 20, 1951; s. Mary Helen (Bates) Hunt; m. Ann Elizabeth Bellinger, Oct. 26, 1975. Author: (script) What Happens to All that Blood Anyway?, 1983, Foundation for the Future, 1984, The Long Run Baptist Family, 1985, Life is Here, 1986; (book) Heritage for Tomorrow, 1986. Editor: The Colloquy, 1984—. BA in philo., Southern Ill. U., 1977; MDiv, Southern Bapt. Theol. Sem., 1978-81, Kentuckiana Metroversity, Louisville, 1981-82. Prin. Christopher Hammon Prodns., Louisville, 1982—. Recipient Etherton Essay award Bapt. Student Union, 1974, Louie award Advt. Club of Louisville, 1985. Mem. Bapt. Pub. Relations Assn., Assn. Ind. Video and Filmmakers, IABC. Home: 150 Pennsylvania Louisville KY 40206

HAMMOND, RUTH ELIZABETH, b. Kenosha, WI, Nov. 2, 1954, d. Eugene Raymond and Patricia Verda (Lawler) Hammond. Contrbr. short stories to Kans. Qtly, Lake St. Rvw, Newsday Mag., Village Advocate, numerous other publs. BA, U. Wis., Madison, 1975. Reporter Kenosha (Wis.) News, 1971-75, Duluth (Minn.) News-Tribune, 1976-77, Mpls. Tribune, 1977-82; freelance wrtr., ed., regional mags., U. Minn., Mpls., 1982—. Grantee Minn. State Arts Bd., 1985; recipient PEN Syndicated Fiction award, 1985, The Loft Mentor Series award, 1984, Loft McKnight Wrtrs. award, 1984. Home: 909 Summit Ave Minneapolis MN 55403

HAMPL, PATRICIA, b. St. Paul, MN, March 12, 1946; d. Stanley R. and Mary (Marum) H. Author: Contrbr, Martha Foley, ed, Best American Short Stories 1977, 1977, Woman before an Aquarium (poetry), 1978, A Romantic Education (prose memoir), 1981, Resort and Other Poems, 1983, (with Steven Sorman) Pillville, 1987. Contrbr to mags, including American Poetry Review, New Yorker, Paris Review, Iowa Rvw. Co-editor, Lamp in the Spine, 1971-74. BA, Univ. of Minn., 1968; MFA, Univ. of Iowa, 1970. Salesclerk; telephone operator; ᵏJN-Radio, St. Paul, ed. Minn. Monthly, 1973-75; free-lance ed and wrtr, 1975-79; vis asst prof, Univ. of Minn., 1979-84, assoc prof of English, 1984—. Founding mem Loft (for literature and the arts); lectr; presents workshops; gives readings of her own poetry. NEH grantee, 1976; Bush Fdn grantee, 1979; Houghton Mifflin literary fellow, 1981, for A Romantic Education; Ingram-Merrill fellow, 1986. Office: Univ of Minn 207 Lind Hall Minneapolis MN 55455

HANCOCK, ALEXANDER DiGIULIO, b. Chgo., June 26, 1952, s. John Kemp and Lisa (DiGiulio) H.; m Marcia Aldrich, Nov. 25, 1977 (div. 1982); m. 2d, A. Kim Barovic, July 5, 1985; 1 son, Nicholas Earl. Novelist: Into the Light, 1985. BA, Haverford (Pa.) Coll., 1973; MA, U. Wash., Seattle, 1982. Ed., wrtr., public speaker Com. for Children, Seattle, 1983—. Home: 1710 E Denny St Apt 6 Seattle WA 98122

HANCOCK, NIEL ANDERSON, b. New Mexico, Jan. 8, 1941. Author: Circle of Light, vol. 1, Greyfax Grimwald, 1977; vol. 2, Faragon Fairingay, 1977; vol. 3, Calix Stay, 1977; vol. 4, Squaring the Circle, 1977, Dragon Winter, 1978, The Wilderness of Fire, vol. 1, Across the Far Mountain, 1980; vol. 2, On the Boundaries of Bleakness, 1981; vol. 3, The Plains of the Sea, 1981; vol. 4, The Road to the Middle Islands, 1981, The Fires of Windameir (first novel in quartet), 1985, The Sea of Silence (second), 1987, A Wanderer's Return (third), 1987, The Bridge of Dawn (fourth), 1988. U.S. Army, 1966-68; served in Vietnam. Address: Collier Assoc 875 Avenue of Americas 1003 New York NY 10001

HAND, SUSAN, see Robinson, Susan Hand

HANDY, MARY NIXEON CIVILLE, (Nixeon Civille Handy), b. March 5, 1909, Ocean Park, CA; d. Leroy Harvey and Lorena Frances (Casey) Civille; m. Lawrence A. Handy, Feb. 14, 1932; children—William Leroy, Lorena Catherine Handy Pollock, David Lawrence (dec.), Nixon Jay. Author: (poems) Do Not Disturb the Dance: Enter It, 1973, Earth House, 1978, Grandma Casey, 1982, poems in lit mags, anthols. Contrbtg. ed. Fellowship in Prayer, 1978-83. Student Pomona Jr. Coll., 1927; BE, Univ. Calif., LA, 1930; ME Central Wash. State Coll., 1958; postgrad. Univ. Wash., 1963, 72; Claremont Schl. Theology, 1969, 71. Tchr. elem. schls., Placentia, CA, 1931, Wenatchee, WA, 1954-55; instr. Eng. and jnlsm. Wenatchee Valley Coll., 1956-63, dean of women, 1961-66, poetry Workshop, 1961-66; dir. Released Time Ed., Visalia, CA, 1945, Dir. Girls Camp, YMCA, Lake Wenatchee, 1953-59; dir. girls' and women's program YMCA, Wenatchee, 1954-55; dir. adult ed. United Meth. Ch., Sandpoint, Seattle, 1967-69; supt. Ruth Schl. for Girls, Burien, WA, 1970; dir. relig. ed., Des Moines, Seattle, 1970-71; poetry staff Pacific NW Writers Conf., 1975-81; poetry staff Christian Writers Conf. Warner Pacific Coll., Portland, OR, 1975-80. Home: 19240 10th NE Seattle WA 98155

HANES, FRANK BORDEN, b. Winston-Salem, NC, Jan. 21, 1920, s. Robert March and Mildred (Borden) H.; m. Barbara Lasater; children—Frank Borden, Nancy Hanes White, Robin. Author: Abel Anders, 1951, The Bat Brothers, 1953, Journey's Journal, 1957, The Fleet Rabble, 1961, Jackknife John, 1964, The Seeds of Ares, 1977, The Garden of Nonentities, 1983; contrbr. to N.C. Poets, N.C. Hist. Rvw. AB, U. N.C., 1942. Reporter, copy ed., columnist Twin City Sentinel, Winston-Salem Jnl. & Sentinel, 1946-49. Served to lt. USNR, 1942-45, PTO. Recipient Ragan award for contrbns. to fine arts St. Andrews Coll. Mem. PEN, N.C. Lit. and Hist. Assn. (past pres.), Roanoke-Chowan award for poetry 1953, Sir Walter Raleigh award for fiction 1961, N.C. Wrtrs. Assn. (past chmn.). Home: 1057 W Kent Rd Winston-Salem NC 27104

HANEY, DAVID P., b. Dayton, oH, Jan. 11, 1938; s. George G. and Lucille (Bales) H.; m. Aileen Faulkner, Nov. 9, 1957; children: Karen, Steven, Philip. Author: Renew My Church, 1972, The Idea of the Laity, 1973, Breakthrough into Renewal, 1974, Journey into Life, 1974, Renewed Reminders, 1976, The Lord and His Laity, 1978, Couples on Mission, 1979, Boild New Laity, 1980, Traveling Together: Love Letter for Couples, 1982. Attended Harrison-Chilhouse Baptist Acad, 1955-57; BA, Georgetown Coll, 1961; grad study, Southeastern Baptist Theol. Sem; MA, Earlham School of Religion, 1966; Th. D., Luther Rice Sem, 1969. Ordained to Baptist ministry, 1958; pastor of Baptist churches in Sadieville, Ky., 1958-61, New Lebanon, Ohio, 1961-67, and Annapolis, Md, 1967-74; dir of lay ministries, Southern Baptist Convention, Memphis, Tenn., 1974-80, dir of Men's Div, 1980-81; dir-counselor, The Counseling Center, Memphis, 1982—. Office: 5705 Stage Suite 222 Memphis TN 38134

HANEY, SHARON, b. Santa Monica, CA, Feb. 8, 1950. Collab. with R.S. McCombe on: Alaska On The Cover, 1983; contrbr. to: Orca Poetry Anthol., 1981, Tides of Morning, 1985. Student UCLA, 1968-72. Legal sec'y. Hughes, Thorsness, et.al., Anchorage, 1972-74, Ely, Guess & Rudd, Anchorage, 1974-76; admin. sec'y. Delta/Greeley School Dist., Delta Jct., AK, 1979-83; freelance writer & ed., Delta Jct., 1983—. 3rd place Best News Release, AK Press Club, 1981. Mem. AK Press Club, AK Assn. Small Presses. Office: Box 644 Delta Junction AK 99737

HANFF, HELENE, b. Phila., Apr. 15, 1916; d. Arthur and Miriam (Levy) Hanff. Author: 84, Charing Cross Road, 1971, London, 1971, Duchess of Bloomsbury St., 1973, London, 1974, Apple of My Eye, 1977, London, 1977, Underfoot in Show Business, 1980, London, 1980, Q's Legacy, 1985, London, 1985; children's history books and articles for juvenile encyc., 1960s; dramatic scripts for live TV, 1950s. Vice. pres. and pres., Lenox Hill Democratic Club, NYC, 1966-71. Address: 305 E 72 St 8G New York NY 10021

HANGER, CLIFFORD, see Rusk, Nance J.

HANKLA, CATHRYN, b. Richlands, VA, Mar. 20, 1958, d. Alden Staley and Joyce Saunders (Burnette) Hankla; m. Richard H.W. Dillard, Mar. 24, 1979. Author: Phenomena (poems), 1983, Learning the Mother Tongue (stories), 1987, A Blue Moon in Poorwater (novel) 1988; contrbr. poems to Anthology of magazine Verse and Yearbook of American Poetry, 1984, 85, Woman Poet: The South, The Best of Intro.; contrbr. to Tex. Rvw, Denver Qtly, New Va. Rvw, Ploughshares, others. BA summa cum laude, Hollins Coll., Roanoke, Va., 1980, MA, 1982. Tchr. English North Cross Schl., Roanoke, 1982-83; lectr. in film, Hollins Coll., 1982-83, lectr. in English, 1983, asst. prof., 1986—. Lectr. creative wrtg. U. Va., Charlottesville, spring 1985, wrtr. in res. Randolph-Macon Women's College, Lynchburg, Spring 1987. Recipient AAP prize, 1978, 79, Hollins Fiction prize, 1980, Andrew James Purdy Fiction prize, 1982. Mem. Ibsen Soc. Am., Phi Beta Kappa, Omicron Delta Kappa. Home: 6915 Ardmore Dr NW Roanoke VA 24019

HANLON, EMILY, b. NYC, Apr. 26, 1945; m. Ned Tarasov, June 25, 1966; children—Natasha, Nicholas. Author: What If A Lion Eats Me and I Fall into a Hippopotamus' Mud Hole?, 1975, How A Horse Grew Hoarse on the Site Where He Sighted a Bare Bear, 1976, It's Too Late for Sorry, 1978, The Swing (Children's Choice award), 1979, The Wing and the Flame, 1980, Circle Home, 1981, Love is No Excuse, 1982. BA, Barnard Coll., 1967. Mem. NWU (founder member), AG. Address: Chapman Rd RD Yorktown NY 10598

HANNA, THOMAS LOUIS, b. Waco, TX, Nov. 21; s. John Dwight and Winifred (Beaumier) H.; m. Susan Taff, May 12, 1950; children—Mary Alice, Michael John, Wendell France; m. Eleanor Camp Criswell, June 25, 1974. Author: The Thought and Art of Albert Camus, 1958, The Bergsonian Heritage, 1963, The Lyrical Existentialists, 1963, Bodies in Revolt: A Primer in Somatic Thinking, 1970, The End of Tyranny: An Essay on the Possibility of America, 1975, Explorers of Humankind, 1979, The Body of Life, 1980; Founder, editor: Somatics, 1976—. BA, Tex. Christian U., 1949; BD, U. Chgo., 1954, PhD, 1958. Writer-in-res. Duke, 1964-65. Fellow ACLS, 1968-69. Office: 1516 Grant Ave 220 Novato CA 94947

HANNAY, MARGARET PATTERSON, b. Rochester, NH, Dec. 20, 1944; d. Ralph E. and Lois Patterson; m. David Hannay, Aug. 14, 1965; children: Deborah, Catharine. Author: Contrbr, Peter Schakel, ed., Longing for a Form, 1977; ed and contbr. As Her Wimsey Took Her: Critical Essays on Dorothy L. Sayers; 1979, C.S. Lewis, 1981; Contrbr., Ronald G. Shafer, ed., Ringing the Bell Backward: The Proceedings of the First International Milton Symposium, 1982; ed. and contrbr., Silent but for the Word: Tudor Women as Patrons; Translators, and Writers of Religious Works, 1985; contrbr., Paul Schleuter and June Schleuter, eds., British Women Writers, 1987, contrbr., Katharine Wilson, ed., Renaissance Women Writers, 1987. Contrbr of articles and rvws to jnls, including Spenser Newsletter, Sidney Newsletter, Christianity & Literature, Sayers Rvw, Christian Scholars Rvw, Tolkien Jnl, ELR, Spenser Studies, Seven, Vox Benedicitna, and Daughters of Sarah. Adv. ed., Christianity and Literature; mem. ed. bd., Sidney Newsletter. BA (summa cum laude), Wheaton (Ill.) Coll., 1966; MA, Coll of St. Rose, 1970; Ph. D., State Univ of N.Y. at Albany, 1976. Lectr in English, State Univ of N.Y. at Albany, 1975-80; asst prof of English, Siena Coll, Loudonville, N.Y., 1985 assoc. prof., 1986—; mem. or chmn. of numerous coms and bds. Rvwr for Fairleigh Dickinson Press; participant in preparing an index to the works of C.S. Lewis, 1965-68. Member: Conf. on Christianity and Literature (mem. bd. dirs., 1976-79; natl. v.p., 1980-83, pres., 1985—), Milton Soc. of America, MLA (chair of special sessions, 1977, 78, 79, 83, 85), chair, program comm., Spenser at Kalamazoo, 1987-89, Spenser Soc., Northeast MLA. Office: Dept of Eng Siena College Loudonville NY 12211

HANNIBAL, EDWARD L., b. Manchester, MA, Aug. 24, 1936, s. Joseph Leary and Loretta Louise (McCarthy) H.; m. Margaret Twomey, June 14, 1958; children—Mary Ellen, Edward J., Eleanor, John, Julia. Author: Chocolate Days, Popsicle Weeks, 1970, Dancing Man, 1973, Liberty Square Station, 1975, Blood Feud (with Robert Boris), 1979, A Trace of Red, 1982. BA in English, Boston Coll., 1958. Vice-pres., copywrtr. Grey Advt., NYC, 1975-79, v.p. creative supr., 1985—; prin. Hannibal Figliola Advt., NYC, 1979-82. Served to 1st lt. U.S. Army, 1958-62. Recipient Houghton Mifflin Lit. Fellowship award, 1970. Mem. PEN. Office: Grey Advt 777 3d Ave NYC 10017

HANNON, BRIAN OWENS, b. Tallahassee, Apr. 20, 1959; s. Jack Owens Hannon and Vicki (Brown) Fuqua. Author: (stories) The Deep End of Dogtown, 1986. Wrkg. on short stories. BA, Fla. State U., 1982; MA, U. So. Miss., 1984. Instr. U. So. Miss., Hattiesburg, 1982-84; freelance wrtr., 1984—. Mem. AWP. Home: 7919 Oak St New Orleans LA 70118

HANNON, THOMAS MICHAEL, (Michael Hannon), b. Los Angeles, Jan. 9, 1939; s. Thomas Martin and Janet Amelia (Kilbourn) H.; m. Linda Pennell Fowler, 1958 (div. 1960); 1 child, Dylan Patrick; m. 2d, Nancy Carol Dahl, Dec. 22, 1979; 1 child, Colin Dahl. Author: Solar Fur, 1972; A Door in the Water, 1975; My Mother Walked Out, 1976; Ship without Paper, 1977; Venerations & Fables, 1982; Slender Means, 1983; Poems & Days, 1986; The Autumn Poet, 1986; Clouds & Rivers, 1986; contrbr. to City Lights Jnl No. 3, New Directions No. 44, Arvon Fdn. 1980 Anthology, Language of the Birds. Wrkg. on poems from the Mumonkan, collaborations with artist William T. Wiley. Student pub. schls., San Luis Obispo, Calif. Home: 611 Mar Vista Dr. Los Osos CA 93402

HANNUM, SUSAN MICHELLE, b. Passaic, NJ, Apr. 25, 1956; d. Arthur Donald and Dorothy (Reynics) H. BA, Montclair State, 1978, MA, 1983. Proofreader, Coopers & Lybrand, NYC, 1978-80, ed., 80-82; assoc. ed. Modern Drummer Pub., Cedar Grove, NJ, 1980—, mng. ed. Modern Percussionist, 1983-87. Home: 565 Grove St Apt D7 Clifton NJ 07013

HANSEN, ANN NATALIE, b. Newark, OH, Sept. 15, 1927; d. Albert and Mary Elizabeth (Schaus) Hansen. Author: Ohio: 1954, Ohio, 1955, Westward the Winds: Being Some of the Main Currents of Life in Ohio, 1788-1873, 1974, So You're Going Abroad: How To Do It, 1984, The English Origins of the "Mary & John" Passengers, 1985, The Dorchester Group: Puritanism and Revolution, 1987. BA, Coll. of St. Mary of the Springs, 1948, MA, Ohio State Univ., 1950; B.Litt., Somerville Coll., Oxford U., 1963. Instr. Coll. of St. Mary of the Springs (Columbus), 1953, 1961-63, Berea Coll. (KY), 1964, U. of Dayton (OH), 1966. Mem. Natl. League of Am. Pen Women. Home: 2341 Brixton Rd Columbus OH 43221

HANSEN, ELIZABETH J., b. Redwood City, CA, Sept. 14, 1930, d. Conrad and Macil (Gibbens) Hansen. Author: Silverplate Directory, 1972, Book of Marks, 1984 The Jewelry Manual, 1986, The Furniture Manual, Vols. 1 and 2, 1987; contrbr. articles to West Coast Peddler, Art & Antiques Collector, Antiques Today, Antique Dealers, Antique Dealer Mag., Hobbies Mag., other antique publs. Owner, operator Hansen's Acad., Freedom, Calif., 1980—. Home: 161 Harkin Slough Rd Watsonville CA 95076

HANSEN, GARY B(ARKER), b. Ogden, UT, Oct. 4, 1935; s. Clarence James and Lena (Barker) H.; m. Helen Ure, Sept. 7, 1962; children: Mark Gary, Ann Marie, Janet Kay Karen Alice. Author: (with Leonard J. Arrington) The Richest Hole on Earth: The History of the Bingham Copper Mine, 1963, Britain's Industrial Training Act: Its History, Development and Implications for America, 1967, (with Mark Randle) Drop-outs and Completers in the Utah Apprenticeship System, 1969-1974: Causes and Consequences, 1975, (with M.T. Bentley and others) Manpower Advisory Services in the Workplace: A Missing Link in National Manpower Policy, 2 vol, 1976, (with Bentley and T.G. Fritts) Shutdown: A Case Study of Displaced Rural Workers, 1978, (with Bentley and C.D. Jorgensen) Problems and Solutions in a Plant Shutdown: A Handbook for a Community Action Team, 1979, (with Bentley and R. Davidson) Hard Rock Miners in a Shutdown: A Case Study in the Post-Layoff Experiences of Displaced Lead-Zinc-Silver Miners, 1980, (with Bentley and M. Skidmore), Plant Closings, People, and Communities: A Selected Bibliography, 1981, 2d ed, 1982, (with Bentley Skidmore, and R. Pond) A selected Annotated Bibliography on Plant Shutdowns and Related Topics, 1981, 2d ed, 1983, (with Bentley, Skidmore, and J.H. Gould) Life after Layoff: A Handbook for Workers in a Plant Shutdown, 1981, (with Bentley) Problems and Solutions in a Plant Shutdown: A Handbook for Community Involvement, 1981, (with Bentley) Mobilizing Community Resources to Cope with Plant Shutdowns: A Demonstration Projet—Final Report, 1981, contrbr (with Bentley) Quality of Work Life: A Book of Readings, 1982, contrbr, Proc. of the 10th Intl Cont on Training and Development, 1982, ed, The Role of Productivity and Quality of Working Life Centers in Natl Development: An Intl Perspective, 1982, Cooperative Approaches for Dealing with Plant Closings: A Resource Guide for Employers and Communities, 1984, contrbr, Rick Sweigart, ed, Managing Plant Closings and Occupational Readjustment: An Employers Guidebook, 1984, (with R.C. Richardson and A.C. Wendt), Instructor's Guide to Collective Bargaining by Objectives, 2d ed, 1985. Also co-au with Frank T. Adams, Putting Democracy to Work: A Practical Guide for Starting Worker-Owned Businesses. Contrbr to

Labor Law Jnl, Personnel Management (England),Training and Development Jnl, Industrial Relations Research Assn Proc, Comparative Educ Rvw, Utah Hist Qtly, Jnl of European Training, Personnel Administration, Employee Relations Law Jnl. BS, Utah State Univ, 1957, MS, 1963; Ph. D., Cornell Univ, 1971; grad study, London School of Economics. Fulbright scholar, London School of Economics, 1965-66; asst prof, Utah State Univ, Logan, 1967-73, assoc prof, 1973-77, prof of econ, 1977—, dir, Utah Center for Productivity and Quality of Working life, 1976—. Chmn, U.S. Natl Productivity Network, 1982. Mem: Secy. of Labor's Task Force on Plant Closings and Worker Dislocation, 1985-86. Mem: Indstl Rel Res Assn (former pres Utah chpt), Am Econ Assn, Soc of Profls in Dispute Resolution. Outstanding Educator's Award, 1974. Military service: U.S. Army, 1957-59; became first lieutenant. Home: 1950 North 1050 East Logan UT 84321

HANSEN, GUNNAR, b. Reykjavik, Iceland, Mar. 4, 1947; arrd. U.S., 1952; s. Skuli Eggert and Sigrid Eva (Satersmoen) H. Author: Bear Dancing on the Hill, 1979, Not A Common House, 1981; contrbr. to Me. Mag., Down East, Main Sunday Telegram, Yankee, Trade, Wash. County Mag., Island Jnl, Chic, The Yacht, Sailor, Habitat, Yachting Monthly, WoodenBoat. BA, U Tex.-Austin. Assoc. ed. Me. Mag., Ellsworth, 1976-78; freelance writer, 1977—; ed./pub. LoonBooks, Northeast Harbor, Me., 1979—; contrbr. ed. Island Jnl, Vinalhaven, Me., 1985—, The Yacht, Newport, RI, 1986—. Mem. Me. Writers and Pubs. Alliance (grantee 1982, 85). Address: Summit Road Northeast Harbor ME 04662

HANSON, DICK VINCENT, b. Bode, IA, Sept. 15, 1925; s. Lawrence Herman and Pearl (Watnem) H.; m. Marilyn Louise Taylor, Apr. 23, 1949; children: Dirk Taylor, Kimberly Ann, Richard Elliott. Mem. editorial staff Successful Farming mag., Des Moines, 1949—, exec. editor, 1955-57, editor, 1957—, agrl. editorial dir., 1981—; mem. journalism curriculum com. U. Ill. at Urbana, 1969—. Mem. Am. Agrl. Editors Assn. (past pres.), Am. Assn. Agrl. Coll. Editors, OWAA. Home: RR 1 Winterset IA 50273

HANZLICEK, CHARLES GEORGE, b. Owatonna, MN, Aug. 23, 1942; s. George John and Freda Martha (Schuenke) H.; m. Dianne Staley, May 11, 1968; 1 child, Leah Rose. Author: (books of poetry) Living In It, 1971, A Bird's Companion (trans. of Am. Indian songs), 1974, Stars, 1977, Calling the Dead, 1982, A Dozen for Leah, 1982, Mirroring: Selected Poems of Vladimir Holan (trans. from the Czech with Dana Habova), 1985, When There Are No Secrets, 1986. BA, U. Minn., 1964; MFA, U. Iowa, 1966. Prof. English, Calif. State U., Fresno, 1966—. NEA fellow, 1976; recipient Devins award for poetry U. Mo. Press, 1977. Home: 738 E Lansing Way Fresno CA 93704

HARAKAS, STANLEY SAMUEL, (Exetastes), b. Pitts., Jan. 13, 1932; s. Samuel and Katherine (Moraitis) H.; m. Emily Georgia Maniates, Aug. 28, 1955; children—Spyridon, Katherine Mary, Demetrius, Angelica, George. Author: Living the Liturgy, 1974, Contemporary Issues: Orthodox Christian Perspectives, 1976, Contemporary Moral Issues Facing the Orthodox Christian, 1982, Let Mercy Abound: A Chronicle of Greek Orthodox Social Concerns, 1983, The Orthodox Church: 455 Questions and Answers, 1988, Health and Medicine in the Eastern Orthodox Tradition, 1988. Translator: Partakers of Divine Nature (George Stavropoulos), 1976. Author Booklets. Mem. editorial bd. Jnl. Ch. & State, 1985—, Second Opinion, 1986-87; assoc. ed. Greek Orthodox Theol. Rvw., 1986—. Wrkg. on Living the Truth: The praxis of Orthodox Christian Ethics. B.A., holy Cross Greek Orthodox Schl. Theol., 1957, B.Div., 1959; Th.D., Boston U., 1965. With faculty Holy Cross Greek Orthodox Schl. Theol., Brookline, MA, 1966—, prof., 1972-86, Arch. Iakovox prof. orthodox theol., 1986—. Office: Holy Cross Schl Theol 50 Goddard Ave Brookline MA 02146

HARALSON, CAROL LOUISE, b. Miami, OK, Dec. 9, 1948; d. John Goolsby and Mary Louise (Goheen) H.; m. William Thomas Fullerton, May 6, 1972 (div.). Ed., designer Painters of the Humble Truth (William Gerdts), 1981, Magic Images (Wade and Strickland), 1982, Cleora's Kitchens: Memoir of a Cook (Butler), 1985; ed., designer, co-author: As in a Vision, 1984; designer: Prairie City (Debo), 1985; coordinating ed.: Arts of the North American Indian, 1986. BFA, U. Tulsa, 1972; MAT, Oklahoma City U., 1974. Graphic designer/chief publs./dir. interpretive programs Philbrook Art Ctr., Tulsa, 1977—; designer/cons. Council Oak Books Ltd., pubs., Tulsa, 1985—. Recipient Pablo Neruda prize for poetry Nimrod, 1979; design excellence awards Print mag., 1986, also numerous awards for book designs. Home: 271 W Victoria St Tulsa OK 74106

HARDAWAY, BILLIE TOUCHSTONE, see Signer, Billie Touchstone

HARDEN, MICHELE LOUISE, b. Bklyn., Mar. 18, 1958, d. Ernst Josef and Margaret Theresa (Lo Vetere) Tegeler; m. David Guy Harden, July 23, 1977; children—Laura, Christopher. Ed.: The Twig that Became an Umbrella Tree: The Growth of Mormonism in the Anaheim Area, 1980, Biography of William S. Harden, 1983; contrbr. to The Citizen, Coast Dispatch, San Diego Seagull. Co-ed. The Eye of Harmony, Santa Ana, Calif., 1979-80; dir. public communications Anaheim 1st Ward Ch. Jesus Christ of the Latterday Saints, 1983, Cardiff Ward, 1984-85; ed. Cardiff Chronicles, Encinitas, Calif., 1984-85, columnist, 1985—. Tech ed. The Marine Review Committee of the California Coastal Commission. Mem. Am. Film Inst. Home: 276 Aspenwood Ln Encinitas CA 92024

HARDENBROOK, YVONNE IMOGENE, (Leigh Britt), b. Hot Springs, VA, Feb. 15, 1928; d. Raymond Ledbetter Moore and Gladys Lee (Britt); m. Donald E. Anthony, Aug. 29, 1948 (div.1972); children: Donald Britt (dec.), Michael Bryant, Mark David; m. Carl Nathaniel Hardenbrook, Feb. 9, 1980. Author: (poetry chapbooks) 37 Poems, 1984, Whalebone and Royal Blood, 1985, one of 12 in anthol. A Wider Giving: Women Writing After a Long Silence, 1987; contrbr. poetry to Pudding, Encore, Centered on Columbus, Dragonfly, Modern Haiku, Red Pagoda, Amelia, Pig Iron, The Poet's Job: To Go Too Far (anthol), Cicada, Midwest Poetry Rvw., The Pen Woman, Poetry in the Park. BS, W.Va. Wesleyan Coll., 1949; postgrad. Ohio State U., 1951, 56-59, 66. Tchr. pub. schls., Logan County, WV, 1950-52, 55, Columbus, Ohio, 1956-68; ed. Columbus Edn. Assn. Bulln., 1965-67; freelance wrtr., 1981—. Recipient prizes Ohio Poetry Day Assn., 1983, Poets at Work, 1986, Amelia, 1986, Ntl. Fed. of State Poetry Societies, 1987, Westmoreland Arts and Heritage Festival, 1987; commendation Ohio Genl. Assembly, 1983. Mem. AAP, AAUW, Verse Wrtrs. Guild Ohio (past pres.), Natl. Fedn. State Poetry Socs. (3d place award of merit 1982), Natl. League Am. Pen Women (lit. chmn. Central Ohio br.). Home: 3573 Meadowgate Dr Murrysville PA 15668

HARDIN, HELEN, see Hoots, Helen H.

HARDIN, KENNETH LEE, b. Clinton, IL, Mar. 18, 1916; s. Merritt Lee and Bessie Pearl Hardin; m. Thelma Mae Hargis, Mar. 31, 1937; 1 dau., Cheryl Le. Ed.: Creative Hodgepodge, 1985—; author: Bluebells Forever, 1984, Tomorrow's Joy, 1986, Ezekiel, A Pentecostal Perspective, 1986; contrbr: Bell's Letters, Parnassus, other lit. mags. and anthologies. ThB and ThM, Ridgedale Theol. Sem.; DMin, Berean Christian Coll. Ordained minister Assemblies of God Ch., 1937—; dean, v.p. Ridgedale Theol. Sem., Chattanooga, 1972-77. Home: 441 Washington Rd Farwell MI 48622

HARDING, WALTER, b. Bridgewater, MA, Apr. 20, 1917; s. Roy Valentine and Mary Alice (MacDonald) H.; m. Marjorie Brook, June 7, 1947; children—David, Allen, Lawrence, Susan. Author: Days of Henry Thoreau, 1965, The Thoreau Handbook, 1959, Variorum Walden, 1963; editor: (with others) The Thoreau Correspondence, 1958; editor-in-chief: Writings of Thoreau, 1965-73. BS in Edn., Bridgewater (Mass.) State Coll., 1939; MA, U. N.C., 1947; PhD, Rutgers U., 1950; DLit, SUNY, 1984. Dir. SUNY Research Fdn., 1970-84. Fellow Am. Council Learned Socs., 1965. Mem. MLA, Thoreau Soc. (pres. 1963). Home: 19 Oak St Geneseo NY 14454

HARDISON, OSBORNE BENNETT, JR., (H. O. Bennett), b. San Diego, Oct. 22, 1928; s. Osborne Bennett and Ruth (Morgan) H.; m. Marifrances Fitzgibbon, Dec. 23, 1950; children—Charity Ruth, Sarah Frances, Laura Fitzgibbon, Agnes Margaret, Osborne Bennett, Matthew Fitzgibbon. Author: Lyrics and Elegies, 1958, The Enduring Momument: The Idea of Praise in Renaissance Literary Theory and Practice, 1962, 1973, Christian Rite and Christian Drama in the Middle Ages, 1965, 1983, Practical Rhetoric, 1966, (with Leon Golden) Aristotle's Poetics: A Translation and Commentary, 1968, 1981, Toward Freedom and Dignity: The Humanities and the Idea of Humanity, 1972, (poetry) Pro Musica Antiqua, 1977, Entering the Maze: Change and Identity in Modern Culture, 1951; editor: Modern Continental Literary Criticism, 1962, English Literary Criticism, The Renaissance, 1963, (with others) The Encyclopedia of Poetry and Poetics, 1965, enlgd. 1975, Medieval and Renaissance Studies, Nos. 1-4, 1966-71, The Quest for Imagination, 1971, (with others) Film Scripts I-IV, 1971-72, (with Leo Golden) Classical and Medieval Criticism, 1974, ed. and transl., Medieval Literary Criticism, 1985, (with others) The Princeton Handbook of Poetry and Poetics, adv. editor: Jnl Medieval and Renaissance Studies, 1986; BA, U. N.C., 1949, MA in English Lit., 1950; PhD, U. Wis., 1956. Teaching asst. U. Wis., 1950-53; instr. English. U. Tenn., 1954-56, Princeton U., 1956-57; mem. faculty U. N.C. at Chapel Hill, 1957-69, prof. English and comparative lit., 1967-69; dir. Folger Shakespeare Library, Washington, 1969-84; Univ. prof. English Georgetown U., 1985—. Trustee U. Detroit, 1969-79. Decorated Cavaliere della Republica Italiana, Order Brit. Empire; Fulbright fellow, Rome, 1953-54; Folger Library fellow, summer, 1958; Guggenheim fellow, 1963-64; recipient Haskins medal Medieval Acad. Am.,1967. Mem. MLA (exec. council 1968-71), Renaissance Soc. Am., Am.

Assn. Higher Edn. (dir. 1980—), Phi Beta Kappa. Home: 1708 21st St NW Washington DC 20009

HARDWICK, ELIZABETH, b. Lexington, KY, July 27, 1916; d. Eugene Allen and Mary (Ramsey) H.; m. Robert Lowell, July 28, 1949 (div. Oct. 1972); 1 dau., Harriet. Author: novels The Ghostly Lover, 1945, The Simple Truth, 1955, Sleepless Nights, 1979; essays A View of My Own, 1962; Seduction and Betrayal, 1974; editor: The Selected Letters of William James, 1960; adv. editor: N.Y. Rvw Books: contrbr. to New Yorker. AB, U. Ky., 1938, MA, 1939; postgrad., Columbia U., 1939-41. Guggenheim fellow, 1947; recipient George Jean Nathan award, dramatic criticism, 1966. Mem. AAIAL. Home: 15 W 67th St New York NY 10023

HARDY, C. COLBURN, (Jonas Blake, Hart Munn, Leonard Peck), b. Boston, Mass., Jan. 13, 1910; s. Charles A. and Gladys M. (Blake) H.; m. Ruth E. Hart, June 27, 1942; children: Dorcas Ruth. Author: Personal Money Management, 1976, ABC'S of Investing Your Retirement Funds, 1978, 2d ed, 1982, Investor's Guide to Technical Analysis, 1978, Your Money and Your Life, 1979, 2d ed, 1982, Safe in Retirement, 1980, Financing Retirement, 1982, Guide to Financially Secure Retirement, 1982, Facts of Life, 1984, Blue Chip Investing, 1987, Blue Chip Investment Strategy, 1987. Ed, Dun & Bradstreet's annl publ, Guide to Your Investments, 1974-84. Contrbr, sometimes under pseuds., to periodicals, including Physician's Management, Dental Management, Banking, and Money. AB, Yale Univ, 1931; additional study, Columbia Univ, 1934. Republican representative in N.J. Assembly, 1943; staffer to v.p., Carl Byoir & Assocs (pub rels firm), 1948-59; exec. v.p., Jones Brakeley & Rockwell (pub rels firm), 1960-64; dir of publ rels, Federal Pacific Electric Co., Newark, N.J., 1965-67; dir of publ rels, General Dynamics Co., N.Y.C., 1967-76; pres, C. Colburn Hardy & Assocs (pub rels firm), 1972—. Pres, Social Welfare Cncl and Community Service Cncl (both N.J.), 1967-69; mem bd dirs, United Way, 1967-70, JET Corp, 1981-85, Fla Cncl on Aging/Adult Services, and Fla AARP State Legislativ Com. Member: Public Relations Soc of America, Phi Beta Kappa. Military service: U.S. Naval Reserve, 1943-46; became lieutenant-commander; received seven battle stars. Office: 2542 Canterbury Dr S West Palm Beach FL 33407

HARDY, JOHN EDWARD, b. Baton Rouge, Apr. 3, 1922; s. Roger Barlow and Mary (McCoy) H.; m. Marie Elam, Dec. 30, 1942 (div.); children: Margot (Mrs. Timm Ferguson), Leonore (Mrs. David Dvorkin), Catherine (Mrs. Didier Pouligny), Laura, Anne (Mrs. George Biswell), Eve; m. Willene Schaefer, June 25, 1969. Author: (with Cleanth Brooks) Poems of Mr. John Milton, 1951, The Curious Frame, 1962, Man in the Modern Novel, 1964, Katherine Anne Porter, 1973, Certain Poems, 1958; Editor: The Modern Talent, 1964, (with Seymour L. Gross) Images of the Negro in American literature, 1966. B.A., La. State U., 1944; M.A., State U. Iowa, 1946; Ph.D., Johns Hopkins U., 1956. Fulbright prof. Am. lit. U. Munich, Germany, 1959-61; Ford Faculty Study fellow, 1952-53; Rockefeller fellow poetry, 1954. Mem. MLA. Home: 1115 N Ridgeland Oak Park IL 60302

HARJO, JOY, b. Tulsa, OK, May 9, 1951; d. Allen William Foster and Wynema Jewell (Baker) Pickett; children—Phil Dayn and Rainy Dawn. Author: The Last Song, 1975, What Moon Drove Me To This, 1980, She Had Some Horses, 1983; contrbr. poetry to That's What She Said, The Third Woman, Words in the Blood, The Woman Poet, The Face of Poetry, and numerous mags. BA, U.NM, 1976; MFA, U. Ia., 1978. Instr. Inst. Am. Indian Arts, Santa Fe, 1978-79, 83-84; asst. prof. Univ. Colo., Boulder, 1985—. NEA fellow, 1978; recipient first place award AAP, 1976, Writers Forum, U. Colo., 1977. Lit. Panel NM Arts Commn., Santa Fe, 1979, 80, 84, Natl. Third World Writers Assn., NYC,1980-81, dir. Phoenix Indian Ctr., 1980-81; policy panel lit., NEA, Washington, 1980-83. Mem. PEN Intl., NWU, Rio Grande Writers Assn. Address: Dept Eng Box 226 U of CO Boulder CO 80309

HARKNESS, DONALD RAY, b. St. Paul, Sept. 26, 1921, s. Alfred Ray and Gertrude Marie (Swanson) H.; m. Mary Lou Barker, Sept. 2, 1967; children—Judith Louise, Kristine Southwick. Author: Crosscurrents: American Anti-Democracy from Jackson to the Civil War, 1955; ed.: Sports in American Culture, 1980, Humanistic Issues in Child Abuse, 1981, numerous publs. of Southeastern Am. Studies Assn., 1979-87. BA, Hamline U., 1942; MA, U. Minn., 1947; PhD, U. Minn., 1955. Asst. prof. social sci. U. Fla., Gainesville, 1950-60; assoc. prof. social sci. U. So. Fla., Tampa, 1960-72, prof. Am. Studies, 1972—; ed., pub., pres. Am. Studies Press, Inc., since 1977. Home: 13511 Palmwood Ln Tampa FL 33624

HARLAN, ROSS, b. Poteau, OK, July 11, 1919; s. E. L. and Leola (Carter) H.; m. Margaret Burns, Jan. 28, 1920; childrn—Raymond, Rosemary, Marvin, Scott. Contrbr. articles to mags. including Reader's Digest, poems to anthols. B.A. in Bus., Okla. State U., 1941; postgrad. Harvard U., 1942. Mgr. rate dept. Okla. Gas and Electric Co., Oklahoma City, OK, 1953-63, v.p., 1963-80, r. v.p., 1980-84. Served to lt. col. U.S. Air Force, 1940-45. Recipient George Washington Honor Medal Freedom Fdn., 1975. Office Box 781 Bethany OK 73008

HARLEMAN, ANN, (Ann Harleman Stewart), b. Youngstown, OH, Oct. 28, 1945; d. Samuel Thomas and Mary (Hagan) Harleman; m. Russell K. Stewart, Dec. 26, 1965 (div. June 10, 1975; 1 dau., Sarah; m. Bruce Allan Rosenberg, June 20, 1981. Author: Graphic Representation of Models in Linguistic Theory, 1976; (with Bruce A. Rosenberg) Ian Fleming: A Critical Biography, 1988. Contrbr. numerous articles, fiction, poems to profl. jnls., lit. mags., anthols., newspapers; chpts. to books. B.A., Rutgers U., 1967; Ph.D., Princeton U., 1972, MFA Brown U., 1988. Assoc. prof. English, U. Washington, Seattle, 1974-84; visiting assoc. prof., research affiliate MIT, 1984-86; visiting scholar Brown U., Providence, 1986—. Guggenheim fellow, 1976-77, fellow Huntington Library, 1979, 80, Fulbright fellow, 1980-81; I.R.E.X. Sr. Scholar ACLS, 1976-77; recipient 1st prize for short story Raymond Carver Contest, 1986, runnerup Nelson Algren competition, 1987. 1986, Mem. MLA (chair exec. com.), Linguistic Soc. Am., P&W. Home: 55 Summit Ave Providence RI 02906

HARLLEE, JOHN THOMAS, b. Florence, SC, Feb. 20, 1935; s. John McSween and Fay (Turner) Harllee. Editor Southern Libertarian Messenger, 1973—. BA, U. of South Carolina, 1955, M.Ed., 1958. Self-employed CPA (Florence, SC), 1968—. Secretary SC Libertarian Party, 1976-86. Home: Rt 10 Box 52A Florence SC 29501

HARMET, A(RNOLD) RICHARD, b. Chgo., Nov. 13, 1932; s. Alfred Aloysius and Evelyn Amelia (Riesche) H.; m. Joan Harriet Morris, Dec. 28, 1957; children: Lynn Anne, Andrew Morris. Mng. editor Popular Mechanics Press, Chgo., 1958-61; dir. publs. Ill. Inst. Tech., Chgo., 1961-63; dir. lit. counseling Am. Med. Assn., Chgo., 1963-65; mng. editor Sci. Yr., 1965; v.p., exec. editor World Book Yr. Book and Sci. Yr., 1966-69, World Book Ency., Chgo., 1969—. BA., Ripon Coll., 1954; MSJ., Northwestern U., 1958. Served as lt., inf. AUS, 1954-56. Home: 1530 N Dearborn Chicago IL 60610

HARMONY, TERRENCE, see Ameen, Mark Joseph

HARMS, VALERIE, b. Chgo., July 17, 1940; d. Gunther William and Virginia (Jensen) Harms; m. Laurence Sheehan, Dec. 1, 1962 (div. Apr. 1982); children—Aurelie, Alex. Author: Unmasking, 1972, Celebration with Anais Nin, 1973, Stars In My Sky, 1976, Tryin' To Get To You, 1978, Beezus and Ramona Diary, 1986. BA, Smith Coll., 1962. Freelance author and photog., Norwalk, Conn., 1965-70, Weston, 1972—; instr. Inst. Children's Lit, Weston, 1979—; intensive jnl. cons., Weston, 1977—. Pres. bd., Norwalk Montessori Assn., 1965-70. Mem. NOW, AG, PEN, Soc. Children's Book Writers. Address: 10 Hyde Ridge Rd Weston CT 06883

HARNACK, CURTIS, b. Le Mars, IA, June 27, 1927, s. Henry and Caroline (Lang) H.; m. Janie Slicher, Aug. 31, 1951 (div. 1957); m. Hortense Calisher, Mar. 23, 1959. Author: (novels) The Work of An Ancient Hand, 1960, Love and Be Silent, 1962, Limits of the Land, 1979, (memoir) Persian Lions, Persian Lambs, 1965, 1981, We Have All Gone Away, 1973, 81, (short stories) Under My Wings Everything Prospers, 1977, (history) Gentlemen on the Prairie, 1985. BA, Grinnell Coll., 1949, L.H.D., 1985; MA, Columbia U., 1950; hon. degree Westmar Coll., Le Mars, 1976; Grinnell Coll., 1986. Instr. English, Grinnell Coll., 1952-56; instr. Wrtrs. Workshop, U. Iowa, Iowa City, 1957-58, lectr., 1959-60; Fulbright prof. U. Tabriz, Iran, 1958-59; mem. lit. faculty Sarah Lawrence Coll., Bronxville, N.Y., 1960-71; exec. dir. Corp. of Yaddo, Saratoga Springs, N.Y., 1971-86. Served with USN, 1945-56. Recipient Johnston Brigham award Iowa Library Assn., 1974; Guggenheim fellow, 1961. Mem. PEN, AG, Dramatists Guild. Home: 205 W 57th St Apt 10 CB NYC 10019

HARNEY, KENNETH ROBERT, b. Jersey City, NJ., Mar. 25, 1944; s. Carroll John and Agnes Theresa (Flanagan) H.; m. Lynne Andrea Leon, Aug. 26, 1967; children: Alexandra Erin, Brendan Leon, Timothy Andrew. Author: Beating Inflation with Real Estate, 1979, Guide to Federal Housing Programs, 1982, AB, cum laude, Princeton U., 1966; postgrad. (grad. fellow), U. Pa., 1966-67. Exec. editor, partner The Housing & Devel. Reporter, Washington, 1972—; columnist Washington Post, 1974—; pub., editor Real Estate Rehab. Investor, 1983—. Recipient First prize Natl. Journalism Achievement Competition Nat. Assn. Realtors, 1979. Mem. Natl. Assn. Real Estate Editors, AFTRA. Home: 3801 Bradley Ln Chevy Chase MD 20815

HARPER, DOUGLAS C., b. Glen Ridge, NJ, Oct. 12, 1934, s. Alfred Florio and Mable Katherine H.; m. Carol Sue Passi, Aug. 17, 1962 (div. 1971); 1 dau.—Alexandra. Author: Another World—Book 1, 1985; contrbr. TV Dawn to Dusk, 1983, 84, Afternoon TV, 1984, Soap Opera World, 1982-85, Grace Log, 1983, American Hairdresser, 1983-84, Society and Association Manager, 1983, 84, Incentive Travel Manager,

1982-84, Successful Meetings, 1983, 84, Industrial Distribution, 1984. BA Jnlsm., Kent (Ohio) State U., 1959; MFA in Cinematography, NYU, 1970. Exec. wrtr. Babcock & Wilcox, NYC, 1968-74; exec. v.p. A.J. Lazarus Assocs., NYC, 1974-78; ptnr. Harper/Starkey Assocs., NYC,1978-82; prin. Harper Communications, NYC,1982-84; sr. editor Tech. Pub. Co., NYC,1984—. Served to 1st lt. U.S. Army, 1954-57. Mem. Acad. TV Arts and Scis., Editorial Freelancers Assn. (dir. 1980—), Publicity Club N.Y. Home: 144 E 22d St New York NY 10010

HARPER, LINDA, see Linda Marie Lloyd

HARRELL, IRENE BURK, (Mildred Waylan), b. Montcalm County, MI, Mar. 10, 1927; d. Howard Lofton and Marguerite Luella (Weatherby) Burk; m. Allen Waylan Harrell, June 22, 1952; children—Tommy, Alice, James ("Dino"), Susan, Marguerite, Maria. Author, co-author of more than 40 books; contrbr. articles, stories, poems to natl. mags. BA, Ohio State U. summa cum laude, 1948; BS in Lib. Sci., U.N.C., 1949. Var. lib. positions incl. Head Librarian, Atlantic Christian Coll., Wilson, NC, 1958-64; ed. Logos Internatl., 1969-77; writer & ed., 1966—; pres. Star Books, Wilson, NC, 1982—. Home: 408 Pearson St Wilson NC 27893

HARRELL, LORI O'MEL, (Lori O'Mel), b. Jacksonville, FL, Feb. 26, 1964; d. David Edwin Harrell and Barbara O'Mel (Walker) Johnson. Contrbr. fiction to Cairn. B.A. in Psychology, Stetson U., 1986. Dir. youth Ortega Methodist, Jacksonville, 1987—. Recipient Ed.'s Choice award for short story St. Andrews Press, 1985. Home: 2407 Castellon Dr Jacksonville FL 32217

HARRINGTON, GERI, b. New Haven, CT, d. Frederick A. and Evelyn (Richey) Spolane; m. Don Harrington, children: Peter Tyrus, John Jeffrey. Author: The College Cookbook, 1975, rev ed, 1977, Summer Garden, Winter Kitchen, 1976, The Salad Book, 1977, The Wood-Burning Stove Book (Better Homes and Gardens Book Club and Popular Mehanics Book Club selection), 1977, rev ed, 1979, Grow Your Own Chinese Vegetables, 1978, rev ed, 1984, Fireplace Stoves, Hearths and Inserts, 1980, Never Too Old: A Complete Guide for the Over-Fifty Adult, 1981, Total Warmth: The Complete Guide to Winter Well—being, 1981, The New College Cookbook, 1982, The Medicare Answer Book, 1982, Cash Crops for Thrifty Gardeners, 1984, The Health Insurance Answer Book, 1985, Real Food, Fake Food, 1987. Contrbr of articles and poems to mags. BA, Smith College. Market research analyst, Good Housekeeping mag., N.Y.C., 1949-50; writer/analyst, U.S. Dept of Commerce, Washington, D.C., 1950-52; writer and analyst, Columbia Univ., Bur of Applied Social Research, NYC., 1953-55; copywriter, Ted Bates, Inc., NYC, 1955-57; copywriter, Grey Advt., NYC, 1957-59; partner, Don Harrington Assocs (advt firm), contract writer, Natl. Inst. of Health. Wilton, Conn., 1960—, Member: Northeast Archeological Researchers, Inst. of Food Tehnologists, Huxley Inst.Home: Merwin Lane W Wilton CT 06897

HARRINGTON, MICHAEL, b. St. Louis, Feb. 24, 1928; s. Edward Michael and Catherine (Fitzgibbon) H.; m. Stephanie Gervis, May 30, 1963. Author: The Other America, 1963, The Retail Clerks, 1963, The Accidental Century, 1965, Toward a Democratic Left, 1968, Socialism, 1972, Fragments of The Century, 1974, Twilight of Capitalism, 1976, The Vast Majority: A Journey to the World's Poor, 1977, Decade of Decision: The Crisis of the American System, 1980, The Next America: The Decline and Rise of the U.S., 1981, The Politics at God's Funeral, 1983, The New American Poverty, 1984, Taking Sides: The Education of a Militant Mind, 1986, The Next Left, 1987; editor: (with Paul Jacobs) Labor in a Free Society, 1959; editor: Newsletter Democratic Left, 1973—; editorial bd. Dissent. AB, Holy Cross Coll., 1947; postgrad., Yale Law Schl., 1947-48; MA, U. Chgo., 1949; DHL, Bard Coll., 1966. Assoc. editor Catholic Worker, 1951-52; editor New Am., 1961-62. Riordan award D.C. Newspaper Guild, 1964; others. Office: 15 Dutch St 500 New York NY 10038

HARRINGTON-CONNORS, ERIN, b. Huntington, NY, Sept. 3, 1959, d. Dennis Joseph and Bridgid Elizabeth (Toolan) Harrington. Contrbr. to Film News, Nightlife Mag, Innerview, Pro Sound News, Artist's Mag, Soap Opera World, Studio Photography, Video Age Intl., Single Times, Poetry Press. BA cum laude, Adelphi U., 1981. Reporter Charlottesville (Va.) Observer, 1981-82; ed. Synergy Corp., Farmingdale, N.Y., 1982-83; assoc. ed. Nightlife Mag., Deer Park, N.Y., 1983-84; pub. relations wrtr. Harriett Ruderman P.R., Port Washington, N.Y., 1984-85; contrbg. ed. PTN Pub. Co., Woodbury, N.Y., 1984—; contrbg. wrtr. Artist's Mag., Cin., 1984—, editorial mgr., Dunhill, Babylon, NY, 1986-87. Address: 5 Kenilworth Dr East Northport NY 11731

HARRINGTON-HUGHES, KATHRYN, b. Washington, Mar. 6, 1955, d. James Michael and Mary Louise (Shea) Harrington; m. Gary David Hughes, June 4, 1977. BS, U. Md., 1977. Asst. prodn. ed. Water Pollution Control Fedn., Washington, 1977-79; prodn. ed. Assn. for Advancement of Med. Instrumentation, Arlington, Va., 1979-84; publs. mgr. Am. Coll. Health Care Adminstrs., Bethesda, Md., 1984-85; dir. publs. Inst. Transp. Engrs., Washington, 1985—. Mem. Soc. Scholarly Publishing. Office: Trans Eng 525 School St SW Washington DC 20024

HARRIS, BEULAH MAE, see Harris, Edna Mae

HARRIS, EDNA MAE, (Beulah Mae Harris), b. Lincoln, DE, Feb. 28, 1950; d. William T. and Golden (Moore) Warren; m. Oscar Anthony Harris, Feb. 7, 1970; children—Leonard, Tammy, Eric. Contrbr. poems to anthols. Wrkg. on novel, In the Cool of the Night. B.S., American North U., 1982, M.A., 1982. Wrtr., Vantage Press, N.Y.C., 1986—. Recipient award of Merit, World of Poetry, 1984, 85, 86, 87, Golden Poet award, 1985, 86, 87. Mem. Songwriters Club Am. Home: Rt 1 Box 272 Lincoln DE 1960

HARRIS, EMILY KATHARINE, see Hill, Emily Katharine

HARRIS, FRANK, III, b.Waukegan, IL, Sept. 28, 1956; s. Frank and Kate Marian (Davidson) H.; m. Teresa A. Johnson, May 4, 1985. Contrbr. essays, short stories to newspapers, mags., anthols. including The N.Y. Times, Newsday, Essence Mag., others. Wrkg. on novel, The Reign of Sunev, essays, short fiction. B.S., Southern Ill. U., 1978; M.A., U. Tex., 1980. Press relations specialist Genl. Electric Co., Albany, NY, 1980-81; marketing specialist, Plainville, CT, 1981-83; assoc. ed.: Almanac Golf Digest/Tennis, Inc., Norwalk, CT, 1983-84, marketing mgr., analyst Golf Digest/Tennis, Inc., NYC, 1984—. Home: 70 Coleman Rd West Haven CT 06516

HARRIS, JANA N., b. San Francisco, Sept. 21, 1947, d. Richard Harmon and Cicely Ann (Herman) H.; m. Mark Allen Bothwell, Aug. 19, 1977. Author: (poems) This House That Rocks with Every Truck on the Road, 1976, Pin Money, 1977, The Book of Common People, 1978, The Clackamas, 1980, Who's That Pushy Bitch?, 1981, Manhattan as a Second Language, 1982, (novel) Alaska, 1980. BS, U. Oreg., 1969; MFA, San Francisco State U., 1972. Dir., wrtrs.-in-performance Manhattan Theatre Club, NYC,1980-85; co-founder, Poetry Flash, Berkeley, Calif., 1972. N.J. State Council on Arts poetry fellow, 1981-82. Mem. PEN, AWP, PSA, Women's Salon NYC (bd. dirs.). Home: 32814 120th St SE Sultan WA 98294

HARRIS, JOSEPH HERBERT, b. Birmingham, AL, Aug. 18, 1918; s. Herbert Hamill and Nannetta Maud (Ellis) H.; m. Rosa Mary Stewart, Apr. 19, 1946; children—Theresa Lynne, Stewart Hamill. Contrbr. poems and short stories to numerous lit. mags., jnls., newspapers, rvws., including Saturday Evening Post, Notable Am. Poets, Intl. Poetry Rvw, Am. Poetry Anthol., Literary Rvw. Wrkg. on novel, poems. AB, Birmingham-Southern Coll., 1941; postgrad. U. Ala., 1951-1952, Fairleigh-Dickinson U., 1962-1963. Indsl. engr. U.S. Steel, Birmingham, 1941-42; tchr. Birmingham Univ. Schl., 1946-52, headmaster, 1952-57; headmaster Mead Hall Episc. Schl., Aiken, S.C., 1957-84; freelance wrtr., 1946—. Bd. dirs. Aiken Community Playhouse. Served to sgt. U.S. Army, 1942-46. Mem. Natl. Assn. Episcopal Schls., Episcopal Schl. Assn. (chmn. 1965—), P&W, AAP. Home: 194 Dogwood Rd Aiken SC 29801

HARRIS, KEVIN J., b. Sewickley, PA, Sept. 18, 1953; s. Leonard and Doris Jeannette (Higgens) H. Author: (short fiction biography) Kevin in Wunderland I, 1982, II, 1986, III, 1984, IV, 1986; I Wish I Could, 1985; Guys Shooting Craps, 1983; Judybright Starlight, 1984; Twilight Dreams, 1983; Complete Diana, 19878; High Lonesome Sounds, 1987. BA in English and psychology, Duquesne U., 1981, MA, 1982. Mem. P&W. Address: 2045 University Ave Berkeley CA 94707

HARRIS, MAC DONALD, b. South Pasadena, CA, Sept. 7, 1921; m. Ann Julia Borgman, June 13, 1947; children—Paul Adrian, Conrad James. Novelist: Private Demons, 1961, Mortal Leap, 1964, Trepleff, 1969, Bull Fire, 1973, The Balloonist, 1976, Yukiko, 1977, Pandora's Galley, 1979, The Treasure of Sainte Foy, 1980, Herma, 1981, Screenplay, 1982, Tenth, 1984, The Little People, 1986; author: The Sailed Alone (juvenile non-fiction), 1972. PhD, U. So. Calif., 1952. Prof. U. Utah, Salt Lake City, 1953-65, U. Calif.-Irvine, 1965—. Served to lt. USNR, 1943-46. Recipient prize in lit. AAIAL, 1982, Spcl. Achievement award PEN, 1985. Mem. AG, PEN (London and Los Angeles). Home: 1743 Bonaire Way Newport Beach CA 92660

HARRIS, MADALENE RUTH, b. Portland, OR, Oct. 6, 1925; d. Arnold Emil and Madalene Martha (Anderson) Krafft; m. Harlan L. Harris, June 7, 1946; children—Lenee Schroeder, Harlan, Jr., Christine Pinello, David. Author: The Moon Is Not Enough, 1978, Lonely, But Never Alone, 1981, Dreaming and Achieving the Impossible, 1984, Becoming Who I Am, 1988. Contrbr. articles to Ladies' Home Jnl., Today's Christian Woman. Student Wheaton Coll., 1943-44, 45-46, Multnomah Coll., 1944-45. Home: 810 Crystal Park Rd Manitou Springs CO 80829

HARRIS, MARIE, b. NYC,Nov. 7, 1943; d. Basil and Marie (Murray) Harris; m. Charter Weeks, Nov. 4, 1977; children—William P. Matthews, Sebastian Matthews, Manny Weeks. Author: Raw Honey, 1975, Interstate, 1980. Editor: Dear Winter, 1984, A Gift of Tongues, 1987; contrbr. to Mountain Moving Day, Blacksmith Anthology, and Ardis Anthology of New Am. Poetry. BA, Goddard College. Poet, NH Commission on the Arts, 1972—; partner, Isinglass Studio, Barrington, NH, 1979—; freelance wrtr. and editor, Barrington, NH, 1977—. Awards: NEA Fellowship, 1976-77. Mem. PSA. Home: RFD 2 Scruton Pond Rd Barrington NH 03825

HARRIS, MARIE-THERESE, b. NYC, May 20, 1939, d. Desmond (dec.) and Clarita (Rosey) Hassell; m. Roland Harris, Dec. 6, 1958 (div. 1973); children—Michael, Gisele, Andrea, Roland. Contrbr. short story to Lenox Inst. Homeless Search Project, 1983; contrbr. article N.Y. Times, 1983. Selected to submit 3 short stories to Marymount Manhattan Coll. Literary and Art Rvw., Spring 88 edition. Student Marymount Manhattan Coll. Adminstrv. sec. Mt. Sinai Hosp., NYC, 1971-83, adminstrv. asst., 1983—. Home: 766 E 228th St New York NY 10466

HARRIS, MARK, b. Mt. Vernon, NY, Nov. 19, 1922; s. Carlyle and Ruth (Klausner) Finkelstein; m. Josephine Horen, Mar. 17, 1949; children: Hester Jill, Anthony Wynn, Henry Adam. Author: Trumpet to the World, 1946, City of Discontent, 1952, The Southpaw, 1953, Bang the Drum Slowly, 1956, Something About a Soldier, 1957, A Ticket for a Seamstitch, 1957, Wake Up, Stupid, 1959; play Friedman & Son, 1963, Mark the Glove Boy, 1964, Twentyone Twice: A Journal, 1966, The Goy, 1970, Killing Everybody, 1973, Best Father Ever Invented: Autobiography, 1976, It Looked Like For Ever, 1979, Saul Bellow: Drumlin Woodchuck, 1980; also essays, articles, stories. BA, U. Denver, 1950, MA, 1951; PhD, U. Minn., 1956. Rptr. Port Chester (N.Y.) Item, 1944, PM, NYC, 1945, I.N.S., St. Louis, 1945-46. Served with AUS, 1943-44. Recipient award Natl. Inst. Arts and Letters, 1961; Ford grantee, 1960; Guggenheim Fdn. fellow, 1965, 74. Home: 5801 Northumberland St Pittsburgh PA 15217

HARRIS, MARK JONATHAN, b. Scranton, PA, Oct. 28, 1941; s. Norman and Ruth (Bialosky) H.; m. Susan Popky, June 9, 1963; children: Laura, Jordan. Author: With a Wave of the Wand (juvenile; Intl. Reading Assn children's choice selection), 1980, The Last Run (juvenile), 1981, (with Franklin D. Mitchell and Stevem J. Schechter) The Homefront: America During World War II, 1984, Confessions of a Prime-Time Kid, 1985. Screenplays: The Rainbow Boys, 1971, The Magician, 1972; also au, Birds of a Feather, 1974; co-author with Trevor Greenwood, The Mustangers, 1975, and Black Tide, 1976, and with Joanne Bario, The Main Act, 1986. Documentary films: The Golden Calf, 1965, (also producer) Hulega!, 1967 and The Foreigners, 1969, (also co-producer), The Redwoods, 1968; also au, Speak for Myself, 1966. Educational films and film strips: (also dir.) The Dayn Grandpa Died, 1969, Wheels, Wheels, Wheels, 1969, Almost Anyone Can Build a House, 1970, The Story of a Pair of Blue Jeans, 1970, The Story of a Peanut Butter Sandwich, 1970; co-au, History of Tehnology (twelve film strips), 1972; also prod, dir, How Many Ways Do I Grow, 1974; Communications Panorama (Twelve filmstrips), 1975. Alao writer-prod of two sixty-second public service television spot for Natl Lutheran Cncl of the U.S. to commemorate the 450th anniversary of the Protestant Reformation, 1967. Cntrbr to mags and newspapers, including Prime Time, TV Guide, Washington Post, New york Times, and Newsday. Past contrbtng ed, New West. Ba. (magna cum laude), Harvard Univ, 1963. Reporter, Associate Press, Chicago, Ill., 1963-64; documentary and educational filmmaker, 1964-75; prof of film-video, Calif. Inst. of the Arts, Valencia, 1976-83; asoc. prof of cinema- television, Univ of Southern Calif, Los Angeles, 1983—. Assoc. prod of film As They Like It, 1965, and co-producer, The Homefront, 1984. Member: Writers Guild of America, Soc. of Children's Book Writers, Southern Calif. Concl on Lit for Children and Young People. Regional Emmy awards from Acad of TV Arts and Scis, 1965, for The Golden Calf and As They Like It; first prize from Intl Film and TV Festival for public service spots, 1967; Acad. Award for short doc film from Motion Picture Acad of Arts and Scis, and Golden Eagle from Cncl. on Intl. Non-theatrical Events, both 1968, for The Redwoods. Award of Merit from Vancounver Intl. Film Festival and special award from Leipzig Intl. Film Fetival, both 1968, for Huelga!; Gold Medal from NY Intl Film and TV Festival, 1969, for The Day Grandpa Died; Merit Award from Athens Intl Scriptwriting competition, 1975, for The Mustanges; Andrew Mellon grant, 1981; Golden Spur award for best western juvenile fiction from Western Writers of America, 1981, Dorothy Canfield Fisher Award nomination, 1982-83; Mark Twain Award nomination, 1983 84, all for The Last Run; Mary Louise-Kennedy—Weekly Reader fellowship in writing for children, Bread Loaf Writers' Conference, 1982. Blue Ribbon from American Film Festival, Special Jury Award from Houston Film Fetival, and Golden Eagle from Cncl on Intl Nontheatrical Events, 1985, all for The Homefornt. Address: 1043 Point View St Los Angeles CA 90035

HARRIS, MARVIN, b. Bklyn., Aug. 18, 1927; s. Irving and Sadie (Newman) H.; m. Madeline Grove, Jan. 25, 1953; children: Robert Eric (dec.), Susan Lynn. Author: Town and Country in Brazil, 1956, (with Charles Wagley) Minorities in the New World, 1958, Patterns of Race in the Americas, 1964, The Nature of Cultural Things, 1964, The Rise of Anthropological Theory, 1968, Culture, Man and Nature, 1971, Cows, Pigs, Wars and Witches: The Riddles of Culture, 1974, Culture, People, Nature, 1975, Cannibals and Kings: The Origin of Cultures, 1977, Cultural Materialism: The Struggle for a Science of Culture, 1979, Culture, People, Nature, 1980, America Now: Why Nothing Works, 1981, Cultural Anthropology, 1983. AB, Columbia U., 1949, PhD, 1953. Served with AUS, 1945-47. Home: 1511 NW 38th St Gainesville FL 32605

HARRIS, MELANIE GAUSE, b. Florence, SC, Mar. 4, 1949; d. Rufus Marvin and Kathryn (Epps) Gause; m. Burton Jay Harris, July 15, 1978; 1 dau., Kathryn Eliza. Contrbr. articles fiction and poems to lit. mags. Story and poem in chapbook to be pub. by Francis Marion Coll., 1987; 3 poems to be pub. in anthol. From the Green Horseshoe: The Poetry of James Dickey's Students, 1988. BA, Columbia Coll, 1970; MA, U. S.C.-Columbia, 1972, PhD in Am. Lit., 1978. Prof. Trident Tech. Coll., Charleston, S.C., 1975-81; part-time prof. Bapt. Coll. at Charleston, 1981-82. Recipient Poetry prize AAP, 1970, 1st place prize for poetry, 1971, 1st runner-up for poetry, 1972, hon. mention for poetry, 1973; 1st runner-up for poetry S.C. Rvw, 1973; Frank Durham Creative Writing award U. S.C., 1972; S.C. Fiction Project winner State Mag. and S.C. Arts Commn., 1986, finalist Santa Cruz/Monterey Ntl. Writer's Union Poetry Competition, 1986. Home: 315 Mayfield St Summerville SC 29483

HARRIS, MERRY, b. Chattanooga, TN; d. William Lee and Kansas (Ridge) Buchanan; m. John Banks Harris, Jr., Sept. 13, 1971. Author of 5 books of poetry; poems in approx. 80 anthols. Publisher of Desert Diamonds, 1984, Laughter: A Revelry of Joy, 1985. Student, Ventura College, CA, 1957-60; San Diego State U., 1973. Freelance photojournalist, 1940-71; publisher, Insight Press, 1982—. Mem. UAP, BAPA, Tennessee Poetry Society, American Academy of Poets, Women in the Arts. Address: Drawer 949 Ocotillo CA 92259

HARRIS, T. GEORGE, b. Simpson County, KY, Oct. 4, 1924, s. Garland and Luna (Byrum) H.; m. Sheila Hawkins, Oct. 31, 1953 (dec. 1977); children—Amos, Anne, Crane, Gardiner; m. 2d, Ann Rockefeller, Mar. 3, 1979; stepchildren—Clare, Joseph, Mary Louise, Rachel Pierson. Student Oxford (Eng.) U., 1948; BA, Yale U., 1949. Reporter Time-Life-Fortune, Time, Inc., NYC, 1949-62, bur. chief, Chgo., Atlanta, San Francisco, sr. ed. Look, 1962-68; ed.-in-chief Psychology Today, 1969-77; founder, ed.-in-chief, chmn. Am. Health, NYC, 1981—. Recipient ASME Genl. Excellence award for Psychology Today, 1973, for Am. Health, 1985, numerous awards for reporting. Home: 1125 Fifth Ave New York NY 10128

HARRIS, WILLIAM J., b. Fairborn, OH, Mar. 12, 1942, s. William Lee and Camilla (Hunter) H.; m. Susan H. Kumin, Aug. 25, 1968. Author: Hey Fella Would You Mind Holding This Piano a Moment, 1974, In My Own Dark Way, 1977, The Poetry and Poetics of Amiri Baraka: The Jazz Aesthetic, 1985. BA, Central Ohio State U., 1968; PhD,Stanford U., 1974. Asst. prof. Cornell U., Ithaca, N.Y., 1972-77, U. Calif., Riverside, 1977-78; assoc. prof. SUNY- Stony Brook, 1978—. Andrew W. Mellon fellow Harvard U., 1982-83, W.E.B. DuBois fellow, Harvard U., summer, 1985. Mem. MLA. Home: 152 Baltic St Brooklyn NY 11201

HARRISON, CHARLES EDWARD, (C.E.D. Harrison), b. Wilkes-Barre, PA, Jan. 31, 1923, s. George Edmund and Iona May (Gollus) H.; children—Charlene, June, Donald, Diane, Nichole. Author: POL of/GA-The American Way, 1985, Life Think's, 1983, When Presidents Cried, 1985, The History of Gordon Ashland, Mt Carmel 2nd Frack, 1952, Now is the Time to Find Rest, 1986. Wrkg. on poetry, songwriting. AB, Dickinson Coll., 1950; BD, Temple U., 1953. Nat. mktg. mgr. L.O.C. Industries, Nashville, 1969-71; owner, mgr. auto VAP Corp., Dallas, 1974; now prin. Charlie Records, Hopewell Junction, N.Y. Served as staff sgt. U.S. Army, 1952-56; PTO. Recipient cert. of recognition Music Songwrtrs., 1982. Mem. ASCAP, Songwrtrs. World. Home: 178 Riley Rd New Windsor NY 12550

HARRISON, EDNA (LUCELLA) BRIGHAM, b. Beaumont, KS, Oct. 23, 1902; d. Leo Jennings and Carrie Belle (Simmons) Brigham; m. Wayne James Harrison, Sr., Oct. 10, 1923; children—Marian Marvonne Thiessen, Wayne james, Ronald Jean. Contrbr. poems, articles, short stories to newspapers, lit. mags., anthols., profl. jnls. Wrkg. on collection of poetry, short stories, articles. B.A. in Edn. and Psychology, Wichita State U., 1951; M.A. in Counseling and Psychology, Columbia U., 1959. Tchr. public schs. Marion, KS, 1920-23, 33-34, Wichita, 1946-56; counselor/psychologist public schs., Wichita, 1957-66; schl psychologist West Diagnostic Ctr., Wichita, 1966-71; free-lance wrtr., 1926—. Mem. Kans. Assn. Schl. Psychologists (life), Natl Assn. Schl. Psychologists (life cert.), NEA, Kans. Author's Club, Kappa Delta Pi. Home: 3441 Country Club Pl Wichita KS 67208

HARRISON, HARRY (MAX), original name Henry Dempsey; name legally changed; b. Stamford, Conn, March 12, 1925; s. Leo and Ria (Kirjassof) H.; m. Joan Merkler, 1954; children: Todd, Moira. Author: novels: Deathworld (first book of trilogy), 1960, Planet of the Damned (published in England as Sense of Obligation, 1967, 1962, Death-world 2: A Sequel to Deathworld (second book in trilogy), 1964 (published in England as The Ethical Engineer, 1964), Bill, The Galactic Hero, 1965, Plague from Space, 1965 (published as The Jupiter Legacy, 1970), Make Room!, 1966, The Tehnicolor Time Machine, 1967, Deathworld 3 (third book of trilogy), 1968, Captive Universe, 1969, The Daleth Effect: A Science Fiction Novel, 1970 (published in England as In Our Hands, the Stars, 1970), The Deathworld Trilogy: Three Novels (contains Deathworld, Deathworld 2, and Deathworld 3), 1970, Montezuma's Revenge, 1972, Tunnel Throug the Deeps, 1972), (with Leon E. Stover), Stonehenge, 1972, Star Smashers of the Galaxy Rangers, 1973, Queen Victoria's Revenge, 1974, Skyfall, 1976, 1977, (with Gordon R. Dickson), The Lifeship, 1976 (published in England asLifeboat, 1977), Planet Story, 1979, The QE2 Is Missing, 1980, Planet of No Return, 1980, Invasion Earth, 1982, The Jupiter Plague, 1982, A Rebel in Time, 1983, (with Stover) Stonehenge: Where Atlantis Died, 1983, West of Eden, 1984, Winter in Eden, 1986. The Stainless Steel Rat series: The Stainless Steel Rat: A Science Fiction Novel, 1961, The Stainless Steel Rat's Revenge, 1970, The Stainless Steel Rat Saves the World, 1972, The Stainless Steel Rat Wants You!, 1978, 1979, The Stainless Steel Rat for President, 1982, The Stainless Steel Rat (interactive game book), 1985. Also au of the interactive game book You Can Be the Stainless Steel Rat. To the Stars series: Homeworld, 1980, Wheelworld, 1981, Starworld, 1981. Short story collections: War with the Robots: Sciene Fiction Stories, 1962, Two Tales and Eight Tomorrows, 1965, 1968, Prime Number, 1970, One Step from Earth, 1970, The Best of Harry Harrison, 1976. Juveniles: The Man from P.I.G., 1968, published as The Men from P.I.G. and R.O.B.O.T., 1974, 1978, Spaceship Medic, 1970, The California Iceberg, 1975. Nonfiction: Great Balls of Fire: History of Sex in Sciene Fiction, 1977, Mehanismo: An Illustrated Manual of Science Fiction, 1977, Mehanismo: An Illustrated Manual of Science Fiction Hardware, 1978, (with Malcolm Edwards) Spacecraft in Fact and Fiction, 1979. Editor or compiler: John W. Campbell, Jr., Collected Editorials from Analog, 1966, (with Nebula Award Stories, vol. 2, 1967, pub. in Enplandas Nebula Award Staries 1967, 1967 on Aldiss) Best SF: 1967, 1968; 1968-76 annual editions published by various publishers and in England under varying titles; (with Stover) Apeman, Spaceman: Anthropological Sciene Fiction, 1968, SF: Authors' Choice, vol. 1, 1968 (published in England as Blast Off: SF for Boys, 1969), Four for the Future: An Anthology on the Theme of Sacrifice and Redemption, 1969, Nova I: An Anthology of Original Science Fiction Stories, 1970, The year 2000: An Anthology, 1970, The Light Fantastic: Science Fiction Clasmics from the Mainstream, 1971, Nova 2, 1972, (with Theodore J. Gordon) Ahead of Time, 1972, (with Aldiss) The Astounding-Analog Reader, vol. 1, 1972, vol. 2, 1973; A Science Fiction Reader, 197 Astounding: The John W. Campbell Memorial Anthology of Science Fiction, 1973; Nova 3, 1973, Nova 4, 1974, (with Aldiss) Hell's Cartographers: Some Personal Histories of Science Fiction Writes, 1975, (with Willis E. McNelly) Science Fiction Novellas, 1975, (with Aldiss and contrbr) SF Horizons, 1975, (with Aldiss) Decade, the 1940s, 1975, 1978, Decade, The 1950s, 1976, 1978, Decade, the 1960s, 1977. Editor of SF Impulse, 1966—, and at various times for Science Fiction Adventures, Fantasy Fiion, Amazing Stories, and Fantastic; co-ed and publ, SF Horizons, 1966—. Freelance commercial artist, 1946-55; freelance writer, living in Mexico, England, Italy, Spain, Denmark, California, and Ireland, 1956—. Member: Universal Espeanto Assn (hon. patron), Science Fiction Writers of America (v.p., 1968-69). Military service: U.S. Army Air Forces, 1943-46; became sergeant. Address: Sobel Assocs 146 E 19th St New York NY 10003

HARRISON, JAMES THOMAS, b. Grayling, MI, Dec. 11, 1937; s. Winfield Sprague and Norma (Walgren) Harrison; m. Linda May King, Oct. 10, 1960; children—Jamie Louise, Anna Severin. Author novels: Wolf: A False Memoir, 1971, A Good Day to Die, 1973, Farmer, 1976, Legends of the Fall, 1979, Warlock, 1981, Sundog, 1984; poetry: Plain Song, 1965, Walking, 1967, Locations, 1968, Oulyer and Ghazals, 1971, Letters to Yesenin, 1973, Selected and New Poems, 1961-81, 1982. BA, Michigan State U., 1960, MA, 1964. Awards: NEA Fellowship, 1968-69; Guggenheim Fellowship, 1969-70. Home: RR 1 Lake Leelanau MI 49653

HARRISON, JEFFREY WOODS, b. Cincinnati, Oct. 10, 1957; s. Robert Sattler and Anne Landon (Woods) H.; m. Julia Ann Wells, Nov. 28, 1981. Author: The Singing Underneath, chosen for Natl. Poetry Servies, 1988. Poetry in Missouri Rvw, Poetry, The New Republic, The Hudson Rvw, Anthology of Magazine Verse and Yearbook of American Poetry, The Antioch Rvw., Boulevard, Crazy Horse, The Quarterly, The Yale Review, and other lit mags and anthols. BA, Columbia U., 1980; MFA, U. of Ia., 1984. Tchr., Berlitz School, Sapporo, Japan, 1980-81; researcher/wrtr., H.W. Wilson Pub., Bronx, NY, 1981-82. Mem. PSA. Awards: Stegner Fellowship, Stanford U., 1985-86, Ohio Arts Council Grant, 1986-87. Home: 4040 Mount Carmel Rd Cincinnati OH 45244

HARRISON, JOHN DEVEREUX, JR., (Phillip Capice, John Rich), b. Oklahoma City, OK, Oct. 16, 1955. Author TV commls.: Wendy's Where's the Beef?; television scripts and characters: Dallas, Miami Vice, Murder She Wrote, Hill St. Blues, L.A. Law, Max Headroom, others; movie concepts, characters, bits of script, oneliners: Poltergist, Star Wars, Superman. Wrkg. on scripts for stage and screen, short stories, novels. Radio news reporter-anchor, disc jockey, 1975—. Recipient Presidental medallion Prs. Johnson, 1968. Home: 1110 Sherwood Ln 221 Oklahoma City OK 73116

HARRISON, PHILIP LEWIS, b. Lynn, MA, Nov. 30, 1945; s. Michael and Florence (Moline) H.; m. Margaret Ann Taylor, Aug. 19, 1977; children—Michael, Jennifer. Contrbr. articles to mags., jnls. including Ariz. Living, Phoenix Home & Garden, Electronics West, others. Assoc. ed.: ASHRAE Jnl., 1968-69, Railway Age, 1969-70; asst. ed.: Reader's Diget, 1970-71. Coauthor: The Official Evan Mecham Jokebook, 1987. B.Sc., Brklyn. Coll., 1969. Asst. planetarium dir. Worcester Sci. Center, MA, 1975-77; assoc. engineer Goodyear Aerospace, AZ, 1977-78; free-lance wrtr., 1979—. Recipient Golden Pen award Phoenix Gazette, 1986, Copper Quill award IABC, 1986. Home: 3370 W Grandview Rd Phoenix AZ 85023

HARRISON, WILLIAM NEAL, b. Dallas, Oct. 29, 1933; m. Merlee Portman, Feb. 1, 1959; children: Laurie, Wean, Quentin. Author: The Theologian, 1965, In a Wild Sanctuary, 1969, Lessons in Paradise, 1971, Roller Ball Murder and Other Stories, 1975, Africana, 1976, Savannah Blue, 1981, Burton and Speke, 1982. BA, Tex. Christian U., 1955; MA, Vanderbilt U., 1960; postgrad., U. Ia., 1961-62. Guggenheim fellow, 1973-74. Office: Morris Agcy 1350 Ave of Ams New York NY 10019

HARROLD, WILLIAM EUGENE, b. Winston-Salem, NC, June 24, 1936, s. William Benton and Helen Russia (Mason) H. Author: (poems) Beyond the Dream, 1972, The Variance and the Unity: A Study of the Complementary Poems of Robert Browning, 1973; contrbr. to Paris, Antioch, S.C., Cream City rvws, Modern Lang. Qtly, Shakespeare Jahrbuch West, Midwest Qtly, Second Coming, Sparrow Mag., Poetry Now, Calif. Qtly, Abraxas; represented in anthologies Heartland II: Poets of the Midwest, Ten Years in Retrospect, Gathering Place of the Waters, also others. BA, Wake Forest U., 1959; MA, U.N.C., 1962, PhD, U.N.C., 1967. Teaching asst. U.N.C., Chapel Hill, 1962-65; from instr. to prof. English, U. Wis., Milw., 1965—; lectr. Lees-McRae Coll., Banner Elk, N.C., 1962. Recipient Oscar Arnold Young Meml. award N.C. Poetry Soc., 1973, All Nations Poetry award Triton Coll., 1979. Mem. MLA, Midwest MLA, Wis. Fellowship Poets (dist. dir.), Browning Inst. Home: 1982 N Prospect Ave 2A Milwaukee WI 53202

HARSEN, EDWARD CHARLES, (Jesse D'Argnac), b. Bklyn., Dec. 30, 1958, s. Edward James and Joan Marie (Collins) H. Author poetry collections: Rent, 1978, Surf Club, 1982; contrbr. to Zephyr Mag., Street Mag., On Good Ground anthology, other lit. mags. Poet Evolution, Bayshore, N.Y., 1972-76, Street Mag., Smithtown, N.Y., 1976-83; poet S&R Andrews, Bohemia, N.Y., 1983-84, St. James, N.Y., 1984-86, safety officer, Ronkonkoma, N.Y., 1983—; ed., bus. mgr. Street Press, Port Jefferson, N.Y., 1977-83; printer Shad Alliance, Smithtown, N.Y., 1977-83, War Resisters' League, Smithtown, 1977-83, Indsl. Workers of the World, Smithtown, 1977-83. Winner 1st prize, poetry, NYU System, Albany, 1978, Golden Poet award World of Poetry, 1985. Home: 7 Astor Ave Saint James NY 11780

HART, BOBBY SIDNA, b. Pulaski, VA, Aug. 27, 1954. Author: Escape from Witchcraft, 1972; contrbr. to The Unicorn, Pegasus, World of Poetry Anthology, NC Signs Along the Way. Senior computer operator Wachovia Corp. (Winston-Salem, NC), 1979—. Mem. AAP, NC Poet. Soc., NC Wrtrs. Netwrk. Home: 1951 Hinshaw Ave Winston-Salem NC 27104

HART, EDWARD LEROY, b. Bloomington, ID, Dec. 28, 1916; s. Alfred Augustus and Sarah Cecilia (Patterson) H.; m. Eleanor May Coleman, Dec. 15, 1944; children: Edward Richard, Paul LeRoy, Barbara Dixon, Patricia Hellebrandt. Author: Minor Lives, 1971; Instruction and Delight, 1976; (biography) Mormon in Motion, 1978; (poems) To Utah, 1979; (essays) More than Nature Needs, 1982; (lectures) God's Spies, 1983; ed. Poems of Praise, 1980. BS, U. Utah, 1939; MA, U. Mich., 1941; DPhil, Oxford U., 1950. Asst. prof. U. Wash., Seattle, 1949-52; asst. prof. to prof. Brigham Young U., Provo, Utah, 1952-82, prof. emeritus, 1982—; vis. prob. U. Calif., Berkeley, 1959-60, Ariz. State U., Tempe, 1968; sr. Fulbright lectr., 1973-74. Served to lt. USNR, 1942-46; PTO. Rhodes scholar, 1939; fellow ACLS, 1941, Am. Philo. Soc., 1964. Fellow Utah Acad. Scis., Arts and Letters (Redd award in humanities 1977); mem. MLA, Rocky Mountain MLA, Am. Soc. 18th Century Studies. Home: 1401 Cherry Ln Provo UT 84604

HART, HENRY WALKER, b. Torrington, CT, July 6, 1954; s. Henry Warren and Virginia (Walker). Author: The Poetry of Geoffrey Hill, 1985; ed. Verse (lit. jnl). BA, Dartmouth Coll., 1976; DPhil, Oxford (England), 1983. Asst. prof. The Citadel, Charleston, SC, 184-86; Coll. of William and Mary, Williamsburg, Va., 1986—. Address: Engl Dept William and Mary Williamsburg VA 23185

HART, JEANNE, (Jeanne McGahey, Jeanne McGahey Hart), b. Empire, OR, Jan. 21, 1906; d. Louis Elmer and Viola May (Davis) Brown; m. David McGahey, Mar. 27, 1930 (div. 1944); m. Lawrence Hart, July 7, 1944; 1 child, John. Author: Gloomy Erasmus, 1957; Scareboy, 1957; Oregon Winter, 1973; contrbr. poems, criticism to Poetry, Qtly Rvw, Accent, East and West, Works Qtly, New Republic, numerous others, also represented in numerous anthologies including Notes on a Gift of Watermelon Pickle. Student Oreg. State U., 1923-26, U. Calif., Berkeley, 1931-32. Former copywrtr. for advt. agys. Bender Fdn. grantee, 1943. Home: Box 4181 San Rafael CA 94913

HART, (JILL) ALISON, (Jennifer Greene, Jeanne Grant, Jessica Massey), b. Detroit, Dec. 9, 1948; d. Frank Michael Hart and Lorraine Newkirk; m. Larry James Culby, June 20, 1970; children: Ryan, Jennifer. Romance novelist: (as Jeanne Grant) Man from Tennessee, 1981, A Daring Proposition, 1981, Kisses from Heaven, 1982, Sunburst, 1983, Wintergreen, 1983, Trouble in Paradise, 1983, Silver and Spice, 1984, Cupid's Confederates, 1984, Conquer the Memories, 1984, Ain't Misbehaving, 1985, Can't Say No, 1985, Sweets to the Sweet, 1986, No More Mr. Nice Guy, 1986, Tender Loving Care, 1987; (as Jessica Massey) Stormy Surrender, 1982; (as Jennifer Greene) Body an Soul, 1986, Foolish Pleasures, 1986, Madam's Room, 1987, Dear Reader, 1987, Minx, 1987, Lady be Good, 1987, Secrets, 1988, Love Potion, 1988. BA, Mich. State U., 1970. Mem. Romance Wrtrs. Am. Named Best Sensual Series Author, Romantic Times, 1985. Home: 1280 Hillandale St Benton Harbor MI 49022

HART, JOAN, b. London, Dec. 5, 1939, came to U.S., 1953, d. Alexander Konopla and Katie (Gordon) Vein; m. Bruce Edward Hart, Oct. 12, 1966 (div.); children—John Alexander, Darren Douglas. Personnel mgr. Armorlite, Inc., Burbank, Calif., 1967-76; assoc. pub., ed. Creative Age Publs., Van Nuys, Calif., 1976—. Home: 21340 Parthenia Ave 209 Canoga Park CA 91304

HART, JOHN, b. Berkeley, CA, June 18, 1948, s. Lawrence Hart and Jeanne (Brown) McGahey. Author: Hiking the Bigfoot Country, 1975, Walking Softly in the Wilderness, 1977, rvw. edit., 1984, The Climbers (poetry), 1978, San Francisco's Wilderness Next Door, 1979, Hiking the Great Basin, 1981; ed. The New Book of California Tomorrow, 1984; contrbr. poetry and rvws. to Western Am. Lit., Interim, Works, Southern Poetry Rvw, others; contrbr. articles to Outside, Sierra, Calif. Living, Family Weekly, others. AB, Princeton U., 1970. Freelance wrtr., 1970—; tchr. Lawrence Hart Seminars, San Rafael, Calif., 1981—; assoc. ed. the poetry LETTER, San Rafael, 1983—. Recipient James D. Phelan award San Francisco Fdn., 1970. Mem. P&W, Marin Arts Council. Address: Box 556 San Anselmo CA 94960

HART, LOIS BORLAND, b. Syracuse, May 15, 1941; d. Leslie R. and Laura S. (Styn) Borland; m. Arnold L. Hart, July 4, 1969; children—Christopher, Richard. Author: A Conference and Workshop Planners' Manual, 1979, Moving Up! Women and Leadership, 1980, Are You Stuck?, 1980, Learning from Conflict, 1980, Sexes at Work, 1982, Saying Hello, 1983, Saying Goodbye, 1983, Computer Quest Series, 1985, Taming Your Junk Jungle, 1986, Survivors of Successful Sales, 1986. B.S., Univ. of Rochester, 1966; M.S., Syracuse U., 1972; Ed.D., U. Mass., 1974. Field service coordinator U. Mich., Ann Arbor, 1975-77; trainer Mt. States Employers Council, Denver, 1979-80; prs. Organizational Leadership, Inc., Lansing, MI, 1977-79, Leadership Dynamics, Boulder, CO, 1980—. Mem. Rocky Mountain Pubs. Assn., AAUW, Am. Soc. Tng. Development, Toast-masters, Pi Lambda Theta, Phi Delta Kappa. Home: 119 Longs Peak Dr Lyons CO 80540

HART, PATRICK JOSEPH, b. Green Bay, WI, June 14, 1925; s. Michael Joseph and Frances Marie (Fox) H. Editor: Thomas Merton/Monk: A Monastic Tribute, 1974 (Religious Book award Cath. Press Assn. 1975), (Thomas Merton) The Monastic Journey, 1977, The Literary Essays of Thomas Merton, 1981, The Message of Thomas Merton, 1981, The Legacy of Thomas Merton, 1986; co-editor: The Asian Journal of Thomas Merton, 1973, (Thomas Merton) Love and Living, 1979, Thomas Merton: First and Last Memories, 1986; editor-in-chief: Cistercian Studies, 1981—. BA in Philosophy, U. Notre Dame, 1966. Bd. dirs. Cistercian Publs., 1975—; Monastery Archivist, 1986—. Address: Abbey of Gethsemani Trappist KY 40051

HART, ROSANA L., b. Washington, Sept. 24, 1942; d. Paul Myron Anthony Linebarger and Margaret (Snow) Roberts; m. Kelly Hart, 1972; 1 stepdau., Ajila Hart. Author: Living with Llamas: Adventures, Photos and a Practical Guide, 1985. Wrkg. on another llama book and one on prosperity consciousness. BA, Stanford U., 1964; MLS, U.C. Berkeley, 1967. Librarian, Sonoma County Lib., Santa Rosa, CA, 1969-81; hypnotherapist, time mgt. cons., wkshop ldr., Hartworks, Forestville, CA & Ashland, OR, 1980—; writer/pub. Juniper Ridge Press, Ashland, 1983—. Home: Box 338 Ashland OR 97520

HART, WILLIAM, b. Wichita, KS, Jan. 27, 1945; s. W. J. and Louise Loy H.; m. Jayasri Majumdar; 1 dau., Lynda. Contrbr. poems, short stories to lit mags, anthols. BA, U. Ks., 1967; MProfl. Writing, U. Southern Calif., 1985, PhD in English, 1985. Tchg. asst. Wichita State U., 1977-79; lectr. U. Southern Calif., Los Angeles, 1979-85; instr. Calif. State U., Los Angeles, 1984—. Home: 502 S Occidental 17 Los Angeles CA 90057

HARTER, PENNY, b. NYC, Apr. 9, 1940, d. George H. and Barbara (Kingsley) Harter; m. William J. Higginson, May 31, 1980; children by previous marriage—Charles Harter Bihler, Nancy Condit Bihler. Author: House by the Sea (poems), 1975, The Orange Balloon (poems), 1980, Lovepoems, 1981, White Flowers in the Snow (poems, stories), 1981, Hiking the Crevasse: Poems on the Way to Divorce, 1983, From the Willow, 1983, In the Broken Curve (poems), 1984, The Price of Admission, 1986, The Monkey's Face, 1987; co-ed., contrbr.: Advance Token to Boardwalk, 1977, Between Two Rivers (with William J. Higginson), 1980, 81, The Haiku Handbook: How to Write, Share, and Teach Haiku (with William J. Higginson), 1985; contrbr. to The Haiku Anthology: English Language Haiku, 1986, The Mother Poet, other anthols. BA, Douglass Coll., 1961. Cons. poets-in-schls. program N.J. State Council on Arts, Trenton, 1973-79; tchr. writing public schls., Woodbridge, N.J., 1978-83; tchr. Madison (N.J.) public schls., 1983—. Poetry fellow N.J. State Council on Arts, 1978-79, 85-86. Mem. PSA, PEN Am. Ctr., Haiku Soc. Am. (v.p. 1985-86, pres. 1986—). Home: 2364 Mountain Ave Scotch Plains NJ 07076

HARTJE, JUDY ANN, (Tory Ferguson), b. Rockford, IL, May 9, 1964; d. Earl John and Merita Mae (Weeden) Hartje. Contrbr. Red Cedar Rev. Wrkg. on local h. hitory. BA in English Lit., Mich. State U. Sr. Ed. Red Cedar Rev., East Lansing, Mich., 1984-86; freelance ed., Rockford, 1986—; sr. ed. 1st Assembly of God Ch., Rockford, 1987—. Home: 2750 N Mulford Rd A206 Rockford IL 61111

HARTLEY, JEAN AYRES, b. San Leandro, CA, Dec. 21, 1914, d. Milton Trevor and Meribel (Shaeffer) Ayres; m. William Stewart Hartley, July 24, 1942; children—Jeanine Sue, Roger Stewart. Contrbr. nearly 400 articles to Modern Maturity, Family Weekly, Bon Appetit, People on Parade, numerous other mags., newspaper travel sects. AB, Stanford U., 1938. Mem. ASJA Calif. Wrtrs. Club, Intl. Travel Wrtrs. Home: 5020 Winding Way Sacramento CA 95841

HARTMAN, ELIZABETH ANN, (Liz Ann), b. Buffalo, NY, Feb. 3, 1959; d. Kenneth Walter and June Marie (Hillman) Hartman. Author poems: The World's Great Contemporary Poets, 1981, Eternal Echoes, 1982, Poetry Press Anthology, 1983. Student Erie Community Coll., Williamsville, NY. Home: 221 Palmdale Dr Williamsville NY 14221

HARVEY, DOROTHY MAY, b. Bartlesville, OK, Apr. 3, 1922; d. Paul and Vila May (Ray) H. AA, Bartlesville Jr. Coll., 1942; BS in Commerce, Okla. A & M, 1950. Tech. asst. Phillips Petroleum Co., Bartlesville, 1942-48; asst. prog. dir, 1950-53, off. mgr. & p.r., 1953-55, YWCA, Topeka; assoc. ed. Capper's Weekly, Topeka, 1955-73, ed., 1974—. Mem. WIC. Home: 2311 Hazelton Court Topeka KS 66606

HARVEY, EDMUND HUXLEY, JR., b. Wilmington, Del., Oct. 27, 1934; s. Edmund Huxley and Margaret Howland Silliman H.; m. Nancy Day Brill, June 11, 1955 (div. 1970); children: Christopher LeRoy, Edmund Fenn, Abigail Day, Jonathan Easton; m. Gail Stephenson Dravneek, Oct. 10, 1970; children: Hannah Stephenson, Caroline Fletcher. Author: Quest of Michael Faraday, 1961, Quest of Archimedes, 1962, Exploring Biology, 1963, Television, 1968, Mission to the Moon, 1969. AB in English, Harvard, 1956. Writer, Street & Smith, NYC., 1956-58; assoc. J.F. McCrindle Lit. Agy., NYC., 1958-59; writer Doubleday & Co., NYC., 1959-61; assoc. editor 1972-76; assoc. editorial dir. social studies and sci. Scholastic Mags., 1976-77, editorial dir., 1977—; acting editor Update, 1983—; freelance writer, NYC., 1965-67; sr. editor Reader's Digest Gen. Books, NYC., 1967-71. Mem. Natl. Assn. Sci. Writers.Home: 438 7th St Brooklyn NY 11215

HARVEY, JULIA, (Juley) b. Gary, IN; d. Dale Leland and Alice Julia (Dels) Harvey. Poetry in Cosmopolitan, McCall's Sciene Fiction Poetry Anthology, 1985, Shorelines Poetry Yearbook 1986, 1987, other mags and anthologies; articles in Napa Valley Times, Baltimore Sun, Tri-Valley Herald, The Poway News Chieftain. B.A., Indiana University, 1970. News editor, Poway News Chieftain, Poway, CA, 1976-1978; youth page editor, Tri-Valley Herald, Livermore, CA, 1978-80; teh editor, ANSER, Arlington, VA, 1983-85; reporter, Napa Valey Times, Napa, CA, 1987—; poet, 1983—. Home: 1159 Marina Dr Napa CA 94559

HARVEY, KENNETH RICARDO, b. Little Rock, Jan. 19, 1956; s. Boss Esau and Ella Jean (Thompson) H.; m. Kathi Ann Northrup, Mar. 24, 1979; 1 son, Kenneth Jared. Editor: (newsletters) Footnotes, 1983-85, PR Tips, 1985, The Bond Report, 1985, The Trend Monitor, 1986, The Communicator, 1986, The Winner's Edge, 1986. AA in Liberal Arts, Spokane Falls Community Coll., 1976; BA in Radio/TV Mgmt., Eastern Wash. U., 1981. Mgr. promotion and merchandising KGA & KDRK-FM, Spokane, 1981-83; community relations officer Tacoma Pub. Library, Wash., 1983-86; pub. Write Pubs., Federal Way, Wash., 1986—. Dir. pub. Citizens for Tacoma Library Bond Issue, 1984. Mem. Wash. Library Assn. Home: 2805 11th St SE Puyallup WA 98374

HARVEY, TAD, see Harvey, Edmund Huxley, Jr.

HASLAM, GERALD WILLIAM, b. Bakersfield, CA, Mar. 18, 1937; s. Frederick Martin and Lorraine Hope (Johnson) H.; m. Janice Eileen Pettichord, July, 1961; children—Frederick, Alexandra, Garth, Simone Carlos. Contrbr. to Forgotten Pages of Am. Lit., 1970, William Eastlake, The Language of the Oilfields, Okies Selected Stories, Western Writing, Afro-Am. Oral Lit., Jack Schaefer, Masks, Calif. Heartland (ed. with James Houston), 1978, The Wages of Sin, Hawk Flights, Snapshots, The Man Who Cultivated Fire, 1987, Voices of a Place, 1987, (co-ed.) Literary History of the American West, 1987. BA, San Francisco State U., 1963, MA, 1965; PhD,Union Grand Schl., 1980. Instr. San Francisco State U., 1966-67; prof. Sonoma State Univ., Rehnert Pk, Calif., 1967—. Served to Pfc, US Army, 1958-60. Recipient Ariz. Qtly award, 1969, Joseph Henry Jackson award, 1971, Bernara Asaton Raborg award, 1985, Meritorius Perf. award, Sonoma State Univ., 1985, 1987. Mem. The Sierra Club, 1961—, Comm. of Two Million, 1976—, E. Clampus Vitas, 1979—, Greenpeace, 1980—, Western Lit. Assn. (pres.), Coll. Lang. Assn., MELUS (founding). Address: Box 115 Penngrove CA 94951

HASSAN, IHAB HABIB, b. Cairo, Egypt, Oct. 17, 1925; came to U.S., 1946, naturalized, 1956; s. Habib and Faika (Hamdi) H.; m. Sarah Margaret Greene, 1966; 1 son, by previous marriage, Geoffrey. Author: Radical Innocence: Studies in Contemporary Affairs, Novel, 1961, Crise du Heros Americain Contemporain, 1963, The Literature of Silence: Henry Miller and Samuel Beckett, 1967, The Dismemberment of Orpheus: Toward a Post- modern Literature, 1971, 82, Contemporary American Literature: 1945-72, 1973, Paracriticisms, 1975, The Right Promethean Fire, 1980, Out of Egypt: Scenes and Fragments of an Autobiography, 1986, The Postmodern Turn: Essays in Postmodern Theory and Culture, 1978; editor: Liberations: New Essays on the Humanities in Revolution, 1971; co-editor: Innovation/Renovation: New Perspectives on the Humanities, 1983. BSc with highest honors, U. Cairo, 1946; MS, U. Pa., 1948, MA, 1950, PhD, 1953. Mem. editorial bd. Am. Qtly, 1965-67, Wesleyan U. Press, 1963-66. Dir. NEH Summer Seminars for Coll. Tchrs., 1982, 84. Guggenheim fellow, 1958-59, 62-63; fellow Ind. U. Schl. Letters, 1964; Sr. Fulbright lectr., 1966, 75; sr. fellow Camargo Fdn., 1974-75; fellow, Bellagio Study and Conference Ctr., 1978; Japan Fdn. grantee, 1979, lctr., USIA Cultural Programs in Europe, Africa, and Asia, 1966—. Home: 2137 N Terrace Ave Milwaukee WI 53202

HASSELSTROM, LINDA M., b. Houston, July 14, 1943; d. John and Mildred H.; m. George Randolph Snell, Mar. 10, 1979. Author: Caught by One Wing (poetry), 1984, Windbreak: A Woman Rancher on the Northern Plains, 1987; Going Over East: Reflections of a Woman Rancher, 1987; Roadkill, 1987. Journal of a Mountain Man: James Clyman, 1984. BA, U. SD, 1965; MA in English, U. MO, 1970. Grad. instr. in English, U. MO, Columbia, 1969-71; instr., commun., Black Hills State Coll., Spearfish, SD, 1972-73; owner/pub. Lame Johnny Press, Hermosa, SD, 1971-85; ed., multi-media, U. of Mid- Amer., Lincoln, NE, 1976; free-lance writer, rancher. NEA fellowship 1984. Mem. WWA. Home: HCR83 Box 9A Hermosa SD 57744

HASSETT, JOSEPH MALK, b. Buffalo, May 1, 1943; s. Paul Michael and Dorothy (Meegan) H.; m. Carol A. Melton, June 23, 1984; 1 son, Matthew. Author: Yeats and the Poetics of Hate, 1986. Contrbr. articles to books on Shaw, Yeats. AB, Canisius Coll., 1964; LLB, Harvard U., 1967; PhD, U. Coll. Dublin, 1985. Prtnr. firm of Hogan & Hartson, Washington, 1975—. Home: 1940 35th St NW Washington DC 20007

HASSLER, DONALD M., b. Akron, OH, Jan. 3, 1937, s. Donald M. and Frances E. (Parsons) H.; m. Diana Cain, Oct. 8, 1960 (dec. 1976); children—Donald, David; m. 2d Sue Strong, Sept. 13, 1977; children—Shelly, Heather. Author: On Weighing a Pound of Flesh (poems), 1973, Erasmus Darwin, 1973, The Comedian as the Letter D: Erasmus Darwin's Comic Materialism, 1973, Comic Tones in Science Fiction, 1982, Hal Clement, 1982; ed.: Patterns of the Fantastic, 1983, Patterns of the Fantastic II, 1984, Death and the Serpent, 1985; co-ed. Extrapolation, 1987. Wrkg. on book of poems, critical book on Isaac Asimov. BA, Williams Coll., 1959; PhD, Columbia U., 1967. Wrtr. Crowell-Collier, NYC, 1960; tchr. U. Montreal, 1961-65, Kent (Ohio) State U., 1965—, coordinator, wrtg. cert. prog., Kent State, 1986—. Woodrow Wilson Nat. Fdn. fellow, 1959. Mem. Sci. Fiction Research Assn. (pres.). Home: 1226 Woodhill Dr Kent OH 44240

HASSLER, JON (FRANCIS), b. Minneapolis, March 30, 1933; s. Leo Blaise and Ellen (Callinan) H.; m. Marie Schmitt, Aug. 18, 1956; children: Michael, Elizabeth, David. Author: novels: Four Miles o Pinecone (young adult), 1977, Staggerford, 1977, Simon's Night, 1979 (also au of play adaptation prod. in drama workshop in Minn.), Jemmy (young adult), 1980, The Love Hunter, 1981, A Green Journey, 1985, Grand Opening, 1987. Contrbr of short stories to lit. jnls, including Prairie Schooner and Blue Cloud Qtly. BA, St. John's Univ., Collegeville, Minn., 1955; MA, Univ. of North Dakota, 1960. high School English teacher, Melrose, Minn., 1955-56, Fosston, Minn., 1956-59, and Park Rapids, Minn., 1959-65; instructor in English, Bemidji State University, Bemidji, Minn., 1965-68; Brainerd Community Coll., Brainerd, Minn, 1968-80; St. John's Univ., Collegeville, Minn., writer-in-res., 1980—. Guggenheim Foundation fellow, 1980. Office: Dept of Eng St. John's U Collegeville MN 56321

HASTINGS, JOEL PRESCOTT, b. NY, Sept. 18, 1948; s. Robert Haven and Helen (Prescott) H.; m. Elizabeth Ann Lomber, 1967; 1 son, Jonathan Prescott Hastings. Asst. ed., N.Y. Holstein News, 1969-70, Penn. Holstein News, 1970; assoc. ed. Holstein World, 1970, mng. ed., 78, ed., 80, ed./pub. 84—; contrbr. Progress of the Breed—Holstein Hist. for 100 Years, 1985. BA, cum laude, Oberlin Coll. corporate sec'y, 1975, corp. v.p., 1977, corp. pres., 1984—. Home: 8967 S Main St Sandy Creek NY 13145

HATCH, DOROTHY L., b. Los Angeles, April 6, 1920; d. Edwin Harrison and Estelle Saff LeBaker; m. William Edward Hatch (dec.), June 22, 1941; children—Dorothea Lee, William Edward, Jr. Works include: Waking to the Day, 1985, Dear Elizabeth: (Letters of Walter de la Mare), 1988. BA, Stanford U., 1943. Features wrtr., Pasadena Star News, CA, 1936-38; instr., Garden City Library Poetry Workshops, NY, 1976-77; edit. consultant, The Stonehouse Press, Long Island, NY, 1982—. Mem. PSA, LI Poetry Collective, Grolier Club of NY, Actors' Equity, SAG, AFTRA, The Pen and Brush, Inc. Home: 153 Kensington Rd Garden City NY 11530

HATCH, PATRICIA M., b. Melrose, MA, Feb. 26, 1953, d. William Ernest Hatch; Myrtle Christina (Johnson) Hatch. Author: Motifs for a Major Design, 1986. AA, Cape Cod Community College, 1975; BA, University of Massachusetts, 1977; MFA, Brooklyn College, 1983. Teacher high schools, Mass. and New York. Contributing editor Spectrum. Contributor to Pegasus, Broadsheet, Ariel, Passage VI. Recipient All Nations Poetry Award, Triton College Press, and Salute to The Arts Award. Managing editor, New Sea of Amethyst Press, 1986—. Address: PO Box 410 Chatham MA 02633

HATCHER, ROBIN LEE, b. Payette, ID, May 10, 1951; d. Ralph E. and Lucille B. (Johnson) Adams; m. Michael D. Hatcher, Sept. 3, 1968 (div. Sept. 15, 1981); children—Michaelyn Jo, Jennifer Lee; m. 2d, Gene L. Peterson, Sept. 14, 1983. Author: Stormy Surrender, 1984, Heart's Landing, 1984, Thorn of Love, 1985, Heart Storm, 1986, Passion's Gamble, 1986, Pirate's Lady, 1987. Contrbg. editor: Blazer Tales, 1979-81. Student pub. schls., Boise, Id. Freelance novelist, Boise, 1981—; instr. Boise Schls. Community Edn., 1982-84, Coll. Id. Continuing Edn., Caldwell, 1984-85. Mem. Id. Wrtrs. League (named Wrtr. of Yr. 1983; pres. Boise chpt., 1985, 86), Romance Wrtrs. Am. (v.p. Southern Id. chpt., 1986). Home: 2125 Mohican Pl Boise ID 83709

HATHAWAY, KATHY R. MOORE, b. Sioux City, IA, Oct. 9, 1953; d. Harold Wayne and Marie E. (Karrer) Moore; m. Bruce A. Hathaway, Dec. 27, 1975 (div. Nov. 17, 1982); 1 son, Tyler Daniel Hathaway. BA in Communics., U. SD, 1975. Copywriter, public affairs, KEZT Radio, Ames, IA, 1976-79; pub. relns./sales mgr. Hot Line Inc., Ft. Dodge, IA, 1979-81; exec. mgr. Intl. Assn. Milk, Food & Environmental San., Ames, 1981—. Office: Milk Food 502 E Lincoln Way Ames IA 50010

HATHAWAY, MICHAEL JERRY, b. El Paso, TX, Sept. 20, 1961; s. Jerry Robert and Elsie Jane (Smith) Hathaway. Contrbr. to New Voices, Calliopes Corner, Forum for Universal Spokesmen, Waterways, RFD, Daring Poetry Qrtly., Clock Radio, Psychopoetica, other periodicals; ed.: The Kindred Spirit, 1982—. Student St. John, KS pub. schls. Typist/typesetter Great Bend Tribune (KS), 1981-87. Home: Rt 2 Box 111 St John KS 67576

HATHAWAY, WILLIAM KITCHEN, b. Madison, WI, Dec. 18, 1944, s. Baxter Levering and Sherry (Kitchen) H.; m. Dixie Ann Blaszek, Feb. 26, 1966; children—Jesse, Nathaniel, Susanne. Author: True Confessions and False Romances, 1971, A Wilderness of Monkeys, 1975, The Gymnast of Inertia, 1982, Fish, Flesh & Fowl, 1985, The Heart of Light, 1988. BA, U. Mont., 1967; MFA, U. Iowa, 1969. Instr. Cornell U., Ithaca, N.Y., 1969-70; instr. La. State U., Baton Rouge, 1970-73, asst. prof., 1973-81, assoc. prof., 1981-83; vis. assoc. prof. Cornell U., 1983-84, Union Coll., Schenectady, 1984—. Bread Loaf Wrtrs. Conf. fellow, 1983. Mem. AWP. Home: Box 5 Porter Corners NY 12859

HATTON, ROBERT WAYLAND, b. Columbus, OH, Feb. 5, 1934; s. Wayland Charles and Ida Catherine (Eblin) H.; m. Marlene Ruth Tuller, June 25, 1954; children—Marc, Heidi, Kevin. B.A., Capital U., 1957; M.A., Middlebury Coll., 1959. Author: La Gloria de Don Ramiro, 1966, Hombre Hispanico, 1970, Los Clarines del Miedo, 1971, The Bullfight: A Teaching and Study Guide, 1974, Global Insights: People and Culture, 1987. Instr. Ohio Wesleyan U., Delaware, 1962-63; prof. Capital U., Columbus, 1963—. Mem. MLA (Coll. Fgn. Lang. Tchr. of Yr. 1986-87), Am. Assn. Tchrs. Spanish Portuguese, Am Council Tchrs. Fgn. Langs. Home: 6565 Calgary Ct Columbus OH 43229

HATVARY, GEORGE EGON, b. Budapest, Hungary, Apr. 2, 1921, came to U.S., 1935, s. Carlo E. and Magda M. (Kovacs) H.; m. Bertha M. Humez, June 16, 1952 (div. 1960); m. 2d, Laurel T. Trencher, Sept. 30, 1961; 1 dau., Maura. Author: Horace Binney Wallace, 1977, The Suitor (novel), 1981; co-ed. Poe's Prose Romances, 1968. BA, New Schl. Social Research, 1947; MA, NYU, 1948, PhD,1957. Prof. St. John's U., NYC,1963—. Served with U.S. Army, 1943-46. Mem. MLA. Home: 61 Jane St New York NY 10014

HAUGER, LESLIE STARR, b. Indpls., Sept. 23, 1904; s. C.D. and Hattie Mildred (Starr) H.; m. Mary Eva Burnett, Sept. 12, 1929; children—Leslie S., George Burnett. Contrbr. articles in popular and trade mags. including Advt. Age; editorials to Tulsa Tribune. Student U. Louisville, 1924-27. Advt. mgr. Everts Jewelry, Tulsa, 1934-42; account exec. Watts, Payne Advt. Inc., Tulsa, 1942-65, pres., 1965-70; cons. Intl. Exec. Service Corps, 1970-77. Mem. Tulsa Advt. Fedn. (honorary, pres. 1960), Southwestern Assn. Advt. Agys. (honorary), Advt. Fedn. Am. (governor 10th district 1961; Sterling Service award 1962; named Most Valuable Member 1960). Home: 1955 E 34th St Tulsa OK 74105

HAUGH, BARBARA ANN, (Barbina Haugh), b. Findlay, OH, Sept. 4, 1950; d. Raymond LeRoy and Martha Wilma (Dela Hamaide) H. Author poetry: Prism Poems, 1985, Comic Curios, 1987. B.A. in English, Ohio State U., 1980. Supply clrk. Rickenbacker Air Natl. Guard Base, Columbus, OH, 1981-86, Newark Air Force Base, Heath, OH, 1986—. Served with U.S. Air Force, 1972-74, Ohio Air Natl. Guard, 1974-79, 81-86. Home: Box 488 Hebron OH 43025

HAUKENESS, HELEN LIZA, b. N.D., Mar. 7, 1938, d. O.J. and Ella (Norum) H.; m. James B. Ranck, Jr., June 9, 1961; 1 child, Mary. Contrbr. short stories to Mich. Qtly, Yale, Cimarron, S.D., N. Am. rvws, Four Quarters, Cardinal, N. Am. Mentor, Providence Jnl, Milw. Jnl Sunday Mag. BA, Augsburg Coll., Mpls. Freelance ed. Avon Books, NYC, 1976-80, Charles Scribner's Sons, NYC, 1981—. Recipient Hopwood award U. Mich., 1970; fellow MacDowell Colony, 1971-73, 75, 78, 82, Va. Ctr. for Creative Arts, 1983, 84, Yaddo, 1984. Mem. AG, P&W. Home: 100 Bank St New York NY 10014

HAUSEMAN, CASS, see Caporale, Patricia Jeane

HAUSMAN, GERALD ANDREWS, b. Balt., Oct. 13, 1945, s. Sidney and Dorothy Emma (Little) H.; m. Loretta Ruth Wright, June 21, 1968; children—Mariah Fox, Hannah. Author: The Shivurrus Plant of Mopant, 1968, Eight Poems (with David Kherdian), 1968, New marlboro Stage, 1969, Circle Meadow, 1972, Beth, The Little Girl of Pine Knoll, 1973, Sitting on the Blue-Eyed Bear: Navajo Myths and Legends, 1975, The Pancake Book, 1976, The Yogurt Book, 1977, Night Herding Song, 1978, The Day the White Whales Came to Bangor, 1979, No Witness, 1980, Runners, 1984, Meditations with Animals, 1986. AA, Union Coll., Cranford, N.J., 1965; BA, Highlands U., Las Vegas, N.Mex., 1968. Poet-in- residence Pittsfield (Mass.) Public schls., 1970-76, Conn. State Coll. (New Britain), 1973-74; vis. poet State of Conn., 1969-76; v.p., mng. ed. Sunstone Press, Santa Fe, 1978-82; tchr. Santa Fe Prep. Schl., 1982-86. Ed.-In-chief N.Mex. Craft Mag., 1977-78; ed. Lotus Press, Santa Fe and Albuquerque, 1985-86. Home: Box 517 Tesuque NM 87574

HAUSRATH, RALPH ALLAN, b. Copiague, NY, Jan. 9, 1918; s. Allan Charles and Ethel May (Austin) H.; m. Matte Elizabeth Prince, Feb. 20, 1942; children—Richard William, Stephen Guy. Contrbr. wrtr. to various newspapers and mags. BA, Washington & Lee U., Lexington, VA, 1940; MS, Hofstra Coll., 1960; grad study, linguistics, U. NC, Chapel Hill, 1965-66. Reporter, Newsday, Hempstead, NY, 1940-42; ed. 1946-57; tchr. Bay Shores (NY) Schools, 1957-73; retired, 1973—. Served USN, 1942-46. Mahan Creative Writing Award, Washington & Lee U., 1939. Home: Box 96 South New Berlin NY 13843

HAUSS, DEBORAH, b. Elizabeth, NJ, Sept. 5, 1955; d. Henry and Beatrice (Manasse) H. Ed./assoc. pub. Premium/Incentive Bus., 1984—. BA, U. Delaware, 1977. Assoc. ed. Premium/Incentive Bus., Gralla Pubns., NYC, mng. ed. Kitchen & Bath Bus., Gralla Pubs., NYC, 1980-84. Office: Gralla Pub 1515 Broadway New York NY 10036

HAVEY, ELIZABETH A., b. Evergreen Park, IL, Feb. 19, 1947; d. Albert George and Virginia Marie (Rausch) Pfordresher; m. John Maurice Havey, Aug. 29, 1970; children—Caroline Anne, Christine Elizabeth. Contrbr.: Creative Woman, Greens Mag., Hobnob, Chgo. Tribune, numerous other publs.; wrtr., ed., chap. contrbr. various publs. of McDougal Littell. BA in English, Mundelein Coll., 1969. Freelance wrtr., 1974—; book reviewer Flossmoor Public Library, Flossmoor Book Club. Mem. Flossmoor Wrtrs. Group. Home: 18544 Dundee Ave Homewood IL 60430

HAVIARAS, STRATIS, b. Nea Kios, Greece, June 28, 1935; arr. U.S. Sept. 2, 1967; s. Christos and Georgia (Hadzikyriakos) H.; m. Gail Flynn, June 3, 1967 (div. 1973); living with Heather E. Cole; 1 dau., Elektra. Author: Crossing the River Twice (poetry), 1976; novels: When the Tree Sings, 1979, The Heroic Age, 1984 (trans. and pub. in Europe and S. Am.); ed. The Poet's Voice, Arion's Dolphin, Ploughshares. BA, Goddard Coll., 1973, MFA, 1978. Orders and Receipts Spclst. Harvard Coll. Library, Cambridge, Mass., 1968-73, head gifts and exchange div., 1973-74, curator poetry and Farnsworth rooms, 1974—. Mem. Signet Soc., Modern Greek Studies Assn., Phi Beta Kappa, PEN. Address: 19 Clinton St Cambridge MA 02139

HAWKE, ROSE LAGMAN, b. Mobile, AL, June 12, 1931; d. John Henry and Rosa Belle (Hyndman) Lagman; m. Wilmer Malcolm Hawke, Aug. 25, 1950; children—Malcolm Daniel, John David, Cecilia Marie. Poetry in anthologies. Wrkg. on collection of religious an inspirational poetry. BA, U. South Ala.; postgrad. Racelia Frye Sch. Ballet, Madeline McDonald Sch. Ballet and Dance. Recipient poetry awards. Mem. Am. Poetry Assn. Home: 5624 Vista Bonita Dr N Mobile AL 36609

HAWKES, JOHN, b. Stamford, CT, Aug. 17, 1925; s. John C.B. and Helen (Ziefle) H.; m. Sophie Goode Tazewell, Sept. 5, 1947; children—John Clendennin Burne III, Sophie Tazewell, Calvert Tazewell, Richard Urquhart. Author: novels The Cannibal, 1949, The Beetle Leg, 1951, The Goose on the Grave and The Owl (one vol.), 1954, The Lime Twig, 1961, Second Skin, 1964, The Blood Oranges, 1971, Death, Sleep and the Traveler, 1974, Travesty, 1976, The Passion Artist, 1979, Virginie: Her Two Lives, 1981, Adventures in the Alaskan Skin Trade, 1985, Innocence in Extremis, 1985; 4 short plays The Innocent Party, 1966; shorter fiction Lunar Landscapes, 1969, Humors of Blood and Skin: A John Hawkes Reader, 1984. AB, Harvard, 1949; AM (hon.), Brown U., 1962. Served with Am. Field Service, 1944-45; Italy and Germany. Recipient Prix du Meilleur Livre Etranger, 1973, Prix Medicis Estranger, 1986; Grantee in lit. Natl. Inst. Arts and Letters, 1962; Guggenheim fellow, 1962-63; Ford Fdn. fellow poets and fiction writers, 1964; Rockefeller Fdn. grantee, 1966. Mem. Am. Acad. Arts and Sci., Am. Acad. and Inst. of Arts and Letters. Home: 18 Everett Ave Providence RI 02906

HAWKINS, HUNT, b. Washington, DC, Dec. 23, 1943, s. Edward Russell and Hermione Helen (Hunt) H.; m. Elaine Yvonne Smith, Sept. 4, 1976; 1 child, Samuel Hunt. Contrbr. to Conrad Revisited: Essays for the Eighties, Writing: How and Why, AAP Prize Anthology, Place, New Eng. Qtly, PMLA, Conradiana, Joseph Conrad Today, Jnl Modern Lit, South Atlantic Rvw, Polish Rvw, CLA Jnl, Beloit Poetry Jnl, Kayak, Wormwood, Bellingham, Ga., Fla, So. rvws, others. BA, Williams Coll., 1965; PhD, Stanford U., 1976. Tchr. Kurasini Coll., Dar es Salaam, Tanzania, 1966-67; instr. Tex. So. U., Houston, 1968-70; teaching asst. Stanford U.,

1972-73; asst. prof. U. Minn., 1977-78; asst. prof. English, Fla. State U., Tallahassee, 1978-83, assoc. prof., 1983—. Recipient prize AAP, 1963, 65, 73; Woodrow Wilson fellow, 1965; NEH grantee, 1982. Mem. MLA, South Atlantic MLA, Joseph Conrad Soc., Phi Beta Kappa. Home: 1918 Sharon Rd Tallahassee FL 32303

HAWLEY, DONALD SPRINGER, b. Ft. Huachuca, AZ, Sept. 25, 1928; s. Donald Coe and Marion (Springer) H; m. Barbara Anne Key, June 1956 (div. 1957); m. 2d, Simin Bahi, Oct. 7, 1961; 3 sons, Shiidon, Shervin, Shahrom. Author: The Nature of Things, 1959. Contrbr. articles, short stories to mags. BArchitecture, U. Mich., 1954; MS in Engring., U. N.Mex., 1965. Pres. United Gen. Corp., Orlando, Fla., 1972-74; natl. architect, engr. Bahai Natl. Ctr., Wilmette, Ill., 1974-78; sr. engr. Brown & Root, Houston, 1978-83; chief engr. design Holloman AFB, N.Mex., 1983-85; chief engr. Bergstrom AFB, Tex., 1985—. Recipient 3d prize for novel Okla. Fedn. Wrtrs., 1982. Home: 8000 Wykeham Dr Austin TX 78749

HAWTRE, AUSTELLE ARRIAYNNE, see Canfield, Joan Giltner

HAY, (GEORGE) AUSTIN, b. Johnstown, PA, Dec. 25, 1915, s. Dr. George and Mary (Austin) H. Author, illustrator: Seven Hops to Australia, 1945, The Performing Arts Experience, 1972, Life About the Earth (television program), 1965; ed., illus., The Arts Scene, 1986; wrtr., ed. World Painting in the Museum of Modern Art (film), 1971. Wrkg. on novel, travel book, poetry collection, biography, film script, book on sculpture. BS, U. Pitts., 1938, MLitt, 1948; MA, Columbia U., 1948. Promotion wrtr. Metropolitan Group, NYC, 1950-53; motion picture prodn. specialist, Army Pictorial Center, Astoria Studios, U.S. Dept. Def., N.Y., 1955-70; motion picture wrtr., dir. U.S. Dept. Transp., Washington, 1973—. Served as ed. U.S. Army, 1942-46; PTO. Recipient St. Bartholomew Silver Achievement Trophy, NYC, 1966, Intl. Film Festival Cert. of Merit for documentary, Zagreb, Yugoslavia, 1975. Mem. Natl. Press Club, Washington Area Wrtrs., AMWA, NWC, ALA, Soc. Scribes, Shakespeare Oxford Soc., Natl. Arts Club, Players, Natl. Acad. Television Arts and Scis. Home: 2022 Columbia Rd NW Washington DC 20009

HAYASHI, TETSUMARO, b. Sakaide City, Japan, Mar. 22, 1929; came to U.S., 1954, naturalized, 1969; s. Tetsuro and Shieko (Honjyo) H.; m. Akiko Sakuratani, Apr. 14, 1960; 1 son, Richard Hideki. Author: Sketches of American Culture, 1960, John Steinbeck—A Concise Bibliography, 1967, Arthur Miller Criticism, 1969, Robert Greene Criticism, 1971, Shakespeare's Sonnets: A Record of 20th Century Criticism, 1972, Index to Arthur Miller—Criticism, 1976; editor: A Looking Glass for London and England (Thomas Lodge, Robert Greene), An Elizabethan Text, 1970, (with Richard Astro) Steinbeck—The Man and His Work, 1971, Steinbeck's Literary Dimension, 1973, A Study Guide to Steinbeck: A Handbook of His Major Works, 1974, (with Richard Astro) John Steinbeck: A Dictionary of His Fictional Characters, 1976; also 7 monographs; founder, editor-in-chief: Steinbeck Qtly, 1968—; gen. editor: Steinbeck Monograph Series, 1970—. BA, Okayama (Japan) U., 1953; MA, U. Fla., 1957, Kent State U., 1959, PhD, 1968. Editorial research grantee, 1970; Folger fellow, 1972; Am. Philo. Soc. fellow, 1975, 81; ACLS fellow, 1976. Mem. MLA Am., Midwest MLA, Shakespeare Assn. Am., Intl. John Steinbeck Soc. (founder, pres.). Home: 1405 N Kimberly Ln Muncie IN 47304

HAYDEN, DOLORES, b. NYC, March 15, 1945; d. J. Francis and Katharine (McCabe) Hayden; m. Peter Horsey Marris, May 18, 1975. Author: Redesigning the American Dream, 1984, The Grand Domestic Revolution, 1981, Seven American Utopias, 1976. Poetry in Manhattan Poetry Rvw., Stone Country, Poets On, other lit. mags. BA, Mount Holyoke College, 1966, M Arch., Harvard Graduate School of Design, 1972. Assoc. prof., MIT, Mass., 1973-78; prof., UCLA, Cal., 1978—. Awards: NEA fellowship; 1976-77 and 1986-87; Rockefeller Hum. fellowship, 1980; Guggenheim fellowship, 1981, ACLS/Ford fellowship, 1988. Home: 8313 Ridpath Dr Los Angeles CA 90046

HAYDEN, TOM, b. Royal Oak, Mich., Dec. 11, 1939; m. Jane Fonda; children: Troy, Vanessa. Author: Port Huron Statement, 1962, Rebellion in Newark, 1967, Rebellion and Repression, 1969, Trial, 1970, The Love of Possession is a Disease with Them, 1972, The American Future, 1980; co-author: The Other Side, 1967; contrbr.: articles to periodicals including Washington Post, Los Angeles Times, N.Y. Times. Grad., U. Mich. Office: 1337 Santa Monica Mall 313 Santa Monica CA 90401

HAYES, ANN LOUISE, b. Los Angeles, May 13, 1924, d. George Henry and Bernice (Derby) Bowman; m. Frank Ambrose Hayes, Oct. 29, 1943 (dec. Oct. 1968). Author: (poems) The Dancer's Step, 1973, The Living and the Dead, 1975, Witness: How All Occasions, 1977, Progress Dancing, 1986; co-author: A Model for an Advanced Placement English Course, 1967; A New Model for an Advanced Placement English Course, 1986; ed., mem. editorial com. Carnegie Series in English, various vols.; contrbg. ed. Three Rivers Poetry Jnl; contrbg. wrtr. Academic Preparation in English, 1985; contrbr. poems to So. Rvw, N.Mex. Qtly Rvw, Am. Scholar, City Lights, Hudson Rvw, also essays. BA summa cum laude, Stanford U., 1950. Instr. English, Stanford U., 1950; teaching assoc. Ind. U., 1953-55; instr. Coe Coll., 1955-57; instr. English, Carnegie Mellon U., Pitts., 1957-60, asst. prof., 1960-65, assoc. prof., 1965-74, prof., 1974—. Recipient poetry award Borestone Mountain, 1969. Mem. NCTE, PSA. Home: 5722 Melvin St Pittsburgh PA 15217

HAYES, EDWIN KEITH, b. Norman, OK, Nov. 18, 1956; s. James Edwin and Chessie Mae (Smith) H. Student Snead State Jr. Coll., 1974-77, Athens State Coll., 1977-78. Contrbr. numerous poems to anthols. Wrkg. on book of poetry, Hand Sown, Home Grown. Handicapped asst. Lake Guntersville State Park, AL, 1982; genl. duty McElrath Farms, Albertville, AL, 1983—. Recipient Honorable Mention, World of Poetry, 1986, (2) 87, Golden Poet award, 1986. Home: Rt 3 Box 476 Grant AL 35747

HAYES, CHARLES LEONARD, b. Lake Worth, FL, June 10, 1940; s. Otis Leo and Dorothy Mae (Williams) H. Ed.: Va. Film Notes; fiction ed. New River Rvw; cons. ed. Film Jnl; contrbr. short stories and poetry to St Andrews Rvw, Sou'wester, Carian, Samisdat, Telephone, other lit mags. BS, Troy State Coll., Ala., 1963; MA, Ind. U., 1968. Assoc. prof. Radford U., Va., 1967—. Home: PO Box 5741 Radford VA 24142

HAYES, JAMES RUSSELL, (Bear, Rusty), b. Penscola, FL, Nov. 25, 1953; s. James Ray Hayes and Lilly Mae Johnson; m. Francoise Dominique Christina, Aug. 27, 1977; children—Jennifer Marie, Laurene Ann. Contrbr. poems to anthols. U.S. Navy, 1972-81. Home: 40 Webber Ave Bath ME 04530

HAYES, JOSEPH, b. Indpls., Aug. 2, 1918; s. Harold J. and Pearl (Arnold) H.; m. Marrijane Johnston, Feb. 18, 1938; children—Gregory J., Jason H., Daniel D. Author: Leaf and Bough, 1949; book, play, motion picture The Desperate Hours (Lit. Guild, Readers Digest book clubs selection), 1954 (Antoinette Perry award 1954-55); play The Midnight Sun, 1959; novel The Hours After Midnight, 1959; play Calculated Risk, 1962; novel Don't Go Away Mad, 1963, The Third Day, 1964, The Deep End, 1967, Like Any Other Fugitive, 1971, The Long Dark Night, 1974, Island on Fire, 1979, Winner's Circle, 1980, No Escape, 1982, The Ways of Darkness, 1985; numerous screen plays; co-author (with wife) 18 pub. plays; also (novel) Bon Voyage, 1956; novel Missing and Presumed Dead, 1977; play Impolite Comedy, 1976; contrbr. short stories to natl. mags. Student, Ind. U., 1951, DHL, 1970. Asst. editor: Samuel French Plays, 1941-43; free-lance writer, 1943—. Home: 1168 Westway Dr Sarasota FL 34326

HAYES, RICHARD ALAN, b. Escondido, CA, Sept. 3, 1957; s. Guy Herman and Edna Lela (Beck) Hayes, m. Ruth Ellen Hayes, July 1, 1987. Author: Cross Cultural Education in the local Church, 1983, Youth and the Sunday Morning Worship Service, 1984, How D. W. Love the Ghetto?, 1984. BS, Biola U., 1983; M of Divinity Talbot Seminary, 1986. Fire dispatcher Fallbrook fire dept. (CA), 1979-80; Manager Westland Found. (Temecula, CA), 1980-81; assoc. pastor Bell Gardens Bap. Ch. (CA), 1985-86; asst. pastor, Calvary Baptist Ch. (La Puente, CA). Home: 15824 San Jose Ave La Puente CA 91744

HAYES, SARAH HALL, b. Anderson, SC., Dec. 3, 1934; d. Wilton Earle and Mary Elizabeth (Lightsey) Hall; m. John Haralson Hayes, Sept. 6, 1958; children: Heather Ruth, John Alexander, Megan Elizabeth. Sr. book editor Droke House Publs., Anderson, S.C., 1968-69; assoc. editor Quote mag., Anderson and Atlanta, 1971-73, editor, 1973—. Editor: The Quotable Lyndon Johnson, 1968. BA, Agnes Scott Coll., 1956; postgrad., Candler Schl. Theology, Emory U., 1957, So. Baptist Sem., 1958, Princeton Sem., 1959-60. Address: 976 Swathmore Dr NW Atlanta GA 30327

HAYNES, LINCOLN MURRAY, (Liveson Hidalgo), b. Los Angeles, CA, Aug. 10, 1924; s. Gerald Sylvester and Florence Theresa (Murray) Haynes; m. Matilde Consuelo Castro, Dec. 16, 1950 (div. 1962); 1 dau.—Linda. Co-founder/managing ed.: LA Magazine; co-author: Begatting of a President, 1969, 1972; Begatting of a Ronald Reagan, 1982; contrbr. to TV Guide, Sat. Evening Post, Saturday Review, The Nation, other mags. BA, U. of Calif., LA, 1947; MA, Calif. State U., 1975. Copy ed. LA Times, 1963-65; publicist CBS TV Network (LA), 1965-71; copy ed., feature wrtr. Press-Telegram (Long Beach, CA), 1974—. Mem. Newspaper Guild. Home: 2821 Calle Aventura Rancho Palos Verdes CA 90274

HAYTON, RICHARD NEIL, (Thomas Starling), b. Pine Bluff, AR, Nov. 25, 1916, s. Raymond Richard and Ruth Naomi (Owens) H.; m. Virginia Ann Ridenour, Apr. 18, 1943; children—Richard Neil Jr., Stephen Brian. Novelist: The King and the Cat, 1975, The Garlic Kid, 1978, Jethrow's Cabin, 1982; newsletter ed.: Writers on Writing, 1982—. BS, U. Md., 1955; MA in Govt., George Washington U., 1956. Public Relations specialist, intelligence specialist, mil. historian, asst. prof. air sci. various Air Force bases, U.S., Europe and Japan, 1940-60; freelance wrtr., pub., ed. Spindrift Press, Cocoa, Fla., 1960—. Served to maj. USAF, 1940-60. Office: Spindrift Press Box 2222 Cocoa FL 32923

HAZARD, JAMES ARTHUR, b. Hammond, IN, Apr. 12, 1935, s. Arthur Henry and Lois Elizabeth (James) Hazard; m. Susan Firer, July 10, 1971; children—Erin, Caitlin; children by previous marriage—Jennifer, Carl, Dylan. Author: The Day the War Ended, 1964, The Outlaw Museum Guide, 1968, The Thief of Kisses, 1971, A Hive of Souls (Selected Poems, 1964-1976), 1976, Voyage of the Inland Sea No. VIII, 1978, Fire in Waiting, 1981, New Year's Eve in Whiting, Indiana, 1986. AB, Northwestern U., 1958; MA, U. Conn., 1960. Instr. English, St. Joseph's Coll., East Chicago, Ind., 1960-62, U. Wis.-Oshkosh, 1963-68; prof. English U. Wis.-Milw., 1968—. Wis. Arts Bd. poetry fellow, 1983. Home: 1514 E Kensington St Milwaukee WI 53211

HAZZARD, MARY DWIGHT, (Olivia Dwight), b. Ithaca, NY, May 3, 1928, d. Albert Sidney and Florence Bernice (Woolsey) H.; m. Peter Swiggart, Aug. 11, 1952 (div. June 1981); children—William Field, Katherine Anne. Author: (mystery) Close His Eyes, 1961, (children's book) The Cat with Five names, 1970, (novels) Sheltered Lives, 1980, Idle and Disorderly Persons, 1981; ed. fiction and drama Intro 15, 1987; author (plays) Little Girls, Diary of the Seducer, Coming Apart, Telephone Play. BS, Skidmore Coll., 1949; MFA in Drama, Yale U., 1982. Fellow Mass. Arts and Humanities Fdn., 1977, MacDowell Colony, 1985, 87, Yaddo, 1986, NEA Playwright Grant, 1987. Mem. AG, DG, PEN. Home: 452 Woodward St Waban MA 02168

HAZZARD, SHIRLEY, b. Sydney, Australia, Jan. 30, 1931; d. Reginald and Catherine (Stein) H.; m. Francis Steegmuller, Dec. 22, 1963. Author: Cliffs of Fall and Other Stories, 1963; novel The Evening of the Holiday, 1966; fiction People in Glass Houses, 1967; novel The Bay of Noon, 1970; social history Defeat of an Ideal: A Study of the Self-Destruction of the United Nations, 1973; novel The Transit of Venus, 1980; contrbr. short stories to New Yorker mag. Ed., Queenwood Schl., Sydney, to 1946. Recipient 1st prize O. Henry Short Story awards, 1976; grantee in lit. Natl. Inst. Arts and Letters, 1966; Guggenheim fellow, 1974; Natl. Book Critics Circle award for Fiction, 1981; Mem. Natl. Inst. Arts and Letters. Address: 200 E 66th St New York NY 10021

HEAD, EVELYN HARRIS-SHIELDS, b. Memphis, Jan. 12, 1944; d. John Lewis an Alzie Lee (Harris) Fletcher; m. Ernest Alexander, June 23, 1980; children—Le'Sha'Renee, Eric. BS, Mich. State U., 1975, BS Ferris State Coll., 1983; MS, PhD, Columbia Pacific U., 1987. Columnist, Pioneer Press, Big Rapids, Mich., 1983-87, Lake County Star, Baldwin, Mich., 1983-87, Osceola County Herald, Reed City, Mich., 1983-87; pres. Head & Assocs., Inc., Arlington Heights, Ill., 1985—. Office: 2290 W Nichols Rd Arlington Heights IL 60004

HEAD, MATTHEW, see Canaday, John Edwin

HEAD, ROBERT, b. Memphis, Jan. 7, 1942; s. Robert Grady and Nell (Langham) H.; m. Darlene Fife. Author: (poetry) I Once Was Alive, 1982, Enriched Uranium Poems, 1983, Blue Valley, 1985; (prose) Longing for Peace in the Heart of the Lion, 1973. Editor, Nola Express, New Orleans, 1968-73; owner bookstore, Lewisburg, W.Va., 1977—. Home: Rt 2 Box 206 Alderson WV 24910

HEAD, YVONNE, b. CA., May 11, 1948; d. John H., Sr. and Marguerite Elizabeth (Hopper) Rose; m. Michael T. Head; 2 daus. Author: Probate Procedure Manual: Los Angeles Superior Court, 1975; E.E.I. Chronical (4 vol.) 1976-87. Ed.: Backbone 3, 1986. Editing the political poems of Emily Dickinson. B.A., U. Wash.; 5th year, UCLA; M.A. in Creative Writing, U. Wash., 1986; M.A. in American Lit., U. Wash., 1986; PhD expected 1988, Ohio State U. Mem. AWP. Mem. MMLA. Office: 421 Denney Hall 164 W 17th Ave OSU Columbus OH 43210

HEALD, JANE DEWEY, b. Evergreen Park, IL, Mar. 19, 1931; d. Kirk Martin and Grace Gray (Thomas) D.; m. Mark Aiken Heald, June 9, 1952; children—Kathryn Grace, John Stanton, Charles Kirk. Co-author (with Carol Pierskalla) seminar Help for Families of the Aging, 1982, manual, 1983; compiler survey of support services Help for Families of the Aging, 1984; contrbg. editor Photophile, 1976-78; editor bulletin Change, 1982-86. BA, Oberlin Coll., 1952; BS, New Haven State Tchrs. Coll., 1953; MLS, Drexel U., 1970. Reference librarian J. Lewis Crozer Library, Chester, Pa., 1971-78; assoc. dir. Natl. Support Ctr. Families of Aging, Swarthmore, Pa., 1981-83, exec. dir., 1983-86. Mem. Am. Assn. Counseling and Devel., Phi Beta Kappa, Beta Phi Mu. Home: 420 Rutgers Ave Swarthmore PA 19081

HEAPHY, JAMES CULLEN, III, b. Detroit, Mar. 28, 1952; s. James Cullen, Jr., and Elizabeth Jane (Davidson) H.; m. Debra sue Klebanoff, Sept. 6, 1981; 1 child, James Cullen IV. Ed.: Space for All People, 1980—. Contrbr. articles on space policy in Space Age Rvw, Science for the People, In These Times, Frontline. BS, U. San Francisco, 1983. Communications supvr. Kaiser Hosps., San Francisco, 1975-82; project mgr. J. di Cristina & Son, San Francisco, 1982-84; genl. mgr. Western Plastics Co., San Francisco, 1984—. Home: 77 Bosque Ave Fairfax CA 94930

HEARON, SHELBY, b. Marion, KY, Jan. 18, 1931; d. Charles B. and Evelyn (Roberts) Reed; m. Robert Hearon, Jr., June 15, 1953 (div.); children—Anne Shelby and Robert Reed; m. 2d, Bill J. Lucas, Apr. 19, 1981. Author: Armadillo in the Grass, 1968, The Second Dune, 1973, Hannah's House, 1975, Now and Another Time, 1976, A Prince of a Fellow, 1978, Painted Dresses, 1981, Afternoon of a Faun, 1983, Group Therapy, 1984, A Small Town, 1985, Five Hundred Scorpions, 1987; contrbr. short stories to Cosmopolitan, Redbook, SW Rvw, others; book rvws. NY Times, LA Times, Dallas Morning News, Houston Post; articles in Tex. Monthly, Redbook, Goodlife, Washington Post, The Writer. BA, U. Tex., 1949-53. Taught U. of Tex., Houston, Clark, U. Calif., Irvine. Fellow, Guggenheim Fdn., 1982, NEA, Washington, 1983; recipient NEA/PEN syndication short story prize, Washington, 1983, 84, 85; best novel award Tex. Inst. Letters, 1973, 78. Mem. Tex. Inst. Letters (pres., 1980), PEN, Women in Communications, AWP, P&W. Address: 5 Church St North White Plains NY 10603

HEATH, LYN BARRETT, (Lyn Barrett), b. Fairmont WV, Nov. 8, 1934; d. James Franklin and Helen Verne (Smith) Barrett; divorced; 1 dau., Tamara Shannon Lyrica Heath. Fiction ed., Minnesota Rvw, 1965-67; West Coast fictioned., December mag., 1968-71. Poems to lit. mags, anthols.Wrkg. on poems, comedy monologue, short story. Student Ohio State U., 1959-62. Recipient Robert Frost Poetry award Ethos Mag., 1963. Home: Box 2462 Mpls MN 55402

HEBALD, CAROL, b. NYC, July 6, 1934; d. Henry Hebald and Ethel (Miller) Lifland. Contrbr. poetry and fiction to Kansas Women Writers, Yearbook of Modern Poetry, Ararat, New Letters, DeKalb Lit. Arts Jnl, Confrontation, Cottonwood, others. BA magna cum laude, CUNY, 1969; MFA, U. Iowa, 1971. Stage actress, NYC, 1952-64; instr. NYU, 1975-76; vis. lectr. U. Wis., 1976-77; assoc. prof. U. Kans., Lawrence, 1977-84. Grantee Wis. Arts Bd., 1976-77, U. Kans., 1978, N.Y. State Council on Arts, 1985; fellow MacDowell Colony, 1976, 77, 78, Millay Colony, 1978, 85, Va. Ctr. for Creative Arts, 1981, 83, 84, 85, Edward Albee Fdn., 1984, also others. Mem. PSA, NWU, P&W. Home: 1375 E 18th St Apt B5 Brooklyn NY 11230

HEBBARD, NEYSA STANLEY, b. NYC; d. Stuart M. and Ethel (Seymour) Stanley, Holly Elizabeth. Contrbr. articles to books, cookbooks, mags. including Yankee Mag. Ed.: The Snowshoe Book, 1971, A Walk on the Crust of Hell, 1973, Famous Horses and Their People, 1975, Orienteering, 1977, Italian provincial Cookery, 1986; contrbr., ed.: More Great New England Recipes, 1985. Wrkg. on letters collection, two novels. Student Vassar Coll., New Schl. Social Work, (years Columbia U. Assoc. ed. Current History Mag., Norwalk, CT, 1963-67, The Stephen Greene Press, Brattleboro, VT, 1971-79; free-lance wrtr., ed., 1979—. Mem. Women's Natl. Book Assn., Pilot Book Assn. (representative 1985—). Home: 137 Pembroke St Boston MA 02118

HECHT, ANTHONY EVAN, b. NYC, Jan. 16, 1923; s. Melvyn Hahlo and Dorothea (Holzman) H.; m. Patricia Harris, Feb. 27, 1954 (div. 1961); children—Jason, Adam; m. Helen D'Alessandro, June 12, 1971; 1 son, Evan Alexander. Author: A Summoning of Sontes, 1954, The Seven Deadly Sins, 1958, A Bestiary, 1960, The Hard Hours (Brit. Poetry Book Soc. choice 1967, Miles Poetry award Wayne U., Pulitzer Prize, 1968), 1968 (Russell Loines award Natl. Inst. Arts and Letters), Millions of Strange Shadows, 1977, The Venetian Vespers, 1979, Obbigati: Essays in Criticism, 1986; co-author, co-editor: Jiggery Pokery, 1967; translator: (with Helen Bacon) Seven Against Thebes (Aeschylus), 1973. BA, Bard Coll., 1944, D.Litt. (hon.), 1970; MA, Columbia U., 1950; LHD (hon.), Georgetown U., 1981, Towson State U., 1983. Recipient Prix de Rome, 1950, Brandeis U. Creative Arts award, 1965; Guggenheim fellow, 1954, 59; Hudson Rvw fellow, 1958; Ford Fdn. fellow, 1960; Rockefeller Fdn. fellow, 1967; Fulbright prof., Brazil, 1971; recipient Bollingen prize, 1983. Fellow AAP (chancellor 1971); mem. Natl. Inst. Arts and Letters, Am. Acad. Arts and Scis. Univ. prof. at the Graduate Schl. of Georgetown Univ. Home: 4256 Nebraska Ave NW Washington DC 20016

HECHT, HARVEY E., b. Excelsior Springs, MO, Aug. 15, 1939; s. Harry J. and Wanda (Pare) H.; m. Lea Jarrett, Aug. 4, 1962; children: Mathew, Laura. Assoc. editor: The Cape Rock, 1971-83; editor: The Cape Rock, 1983—. BA,

William Jewell Coll., 1961; PhD, U. Tenn., 1972. Prof. English, Southeast Mo. State U., Cape Girardeau, 1969—. Mo. Arts Council grantee, 1984, 85, 86. Home: 834 Merriwether Cape Girardeau MO 63701

HECKELMANN, CHARLES NEWMAN, (Charles Lawton), b. Bklyn., Oct. 24, 1913; s. Edward and Sophia (Hodum) H.; m. Anna M. Auer, Apr. 17, 1937; children—Lorraine Heckelmann Kane, Thomas Edward. Author: Vengeance Trail, 1944, Lawless Range, 1945, Six-Gun Outcast, 1946, Deputy Marshal, 1947, Guns of Arizona, 1949, Let The Guns Roar, 1950, Two-Bit Rancher, 1950, Outlaw Valley, 1950, Danger Rides the Range, 1950, Fighting Ramrod, 1951, Hell In His Holsters, 1952, The Rawhider, 1952, Hard Man With A Gun, 1954, Bullet Law, 1955, Trumpets in the Dawn, 1958, The Big Valley, 1966, The Glory Riders, 1967, Writing Fiction for Profit, 1968, Stranger from Durango, 1971, Return to Arapahoe, 1980, Wagons to Wind River, 1982; books and stories adapted for motion pictures Deputy Marshall, 1949; Stranger from Santa Fe, 1947, Frontier Feud, 1948; author (pen name Charles Lawton): Clarkvill's Battery, 1937, Ros. Hackney, Halfback, 1937, The Winning Forward Pass, 1940, Home Run Hennessey, 1951, Touchdown to Victory, 1942, Jungle Menace, 1937. BA maxima cum laude, U. Notre Dame, 1934. Sports feature writer Bklyn. Eagle, 1934-37; editor-in-chief Cupples & Leon, NYC, 1937-41, Popular Library, 1941-58, v.p., 1953-58; pres., editor-in-chief Monarch Books, Inc., NYC, 1958-65; mng. editor, rights dir. David McKay, NYC, 1965-68; sr. editor Cowles Book Co., NYC, 1968-71; sr. editor, rights dir. Hawthorn Books, NYC, 1971-72, editor-in-chief, 1972-75, v.p., 1972-75; book editor Natl. Enquirer, 1975-78. Mem. Cath. Writers Guild of Am. (pres. 1949-52), WWA (v.p. 1955-57, pres. 1964-65). Home: 10634 Green Trail Dr S Boynton Beach FL 33436

HECKER, HELEN JEAN, Author: Travel for the Disabled: A Handbook of Travel Resources and 500 Worldwide Access Guides, 1985, Directory of Travel Agencies for the Disabled, 1986, writes monthly travel column for Paraplegia News. Pres. Northwest Assn. Book Pubs., COSMEP, Am. Bk. Council, Pub. Marketing Assn. (bd. dirs.). Office: Box 8097 Portland OR 97207

HECKLER, JONELLEN BETH, b. Pitts., Oct. 28, 1943; d. John Edward and Florence Elizabeth (Milliken) Munn; m. Louis Roy Heckler, Aug. 17, 1968; 1 son, Steven Louis. Author: Safekeeping, 1983, A Fragile Peace, 1986. BA, U Pitts, 1965. Secy. United Fund, Pitts., 1965-67; pub. relations dir. United Fund, Ft. Lauderdale, 1967-68; program planner NC Heart Assn., Chapel Hill, 1968-69; copywriter, Charlotte, NC, 1969-70, Hillman Pub. Relations, Indpls., 1970-72; freelance writer, Charlotte and Ft. Myers, Fla, 1972—. Mem. AG. Address: 5562 Pernod Dr SW Fort Myers FL 33919

HEDGES, DAN, b. NYC, July 13, 1951. Author: Rock Guitarists: Vol. II, 1977, British Rock Guitar, 1977, Yes: The Authorized Biography, 1981, Eddie Van Halen, 1986; contrbr. to Los Angeles Times Syndicate, San Francisco Chronicle, Detroit News, Rolling Stone, Record, Internat. Musician, Guitar Player, Sounds, Melody Maker, Circus, Hit Parader, Player, also others. BFA in Film, NYU, 1973. Home: 211 E 17th St New York NY 10003

HEDGES, JAMES, b. Iowa City, May 10, 1938; s. Robert M. and Mary Margaret (Ayres) H.; m. Ardis Hughes, June 26, 1975; 1 dau., Karen. Editor, printer, pub.: (chapbook series on autobiography) Dust (from the ego trip), 1985—; editor Natl. Speleological Soc. Bulletin, 1973-83; tech. and copy editor: Cave Minerals of the World, 1986, editor the Journal of Spelean History, 1987—; also contrbr. articles to sci. jnls. BA in music, U. Iowa, 1960; MA in geography, U. Md., 1972. Tuba player U.S. Marine Band, Washington, 1960-80. Mem. exec. com. Natl. Temperance and Prohibition Council, Washington, 1974-78; 4-H Club leader, Fulton County, Pa., 1981—; secy. Friends of Library, Fulton County, 1985-86. Served with USMC, 1960-80. Fellow Natl. Speleological Soc. (Citation of Merit 1985), fellow Iowa Acad. Sci., Am. Amateur Press Assn, Amal. Printers Assn. Home: Big Cove Tannery PA 17212

HEDLEY, LESLIE WOOLF, b. Newark, Mar. 23, 1921; m. Koky Olson Hedley. Author poetry vols.: The Edge of Insanity, 1948, Death of A World, 1951, Selected Poems, 1953, Zero Hour, 1957, Abraxas & Other Poems, 1960, On My Way to The Cemetery, 1981; author: Motions & Notions, 1961, Confessions, 1984, The Day Japan Bombed Pearl Harbor & Other Stories, 1984, XYZ & Other Stories, 1985; co-ed.: Fiction 1983, Fiction 1985, Fiction 1986, over 30 books; producer record album Pacifica, 1954. Ed. NYU, Oxford (Eng.) U., Ohio State U.; PhD. Ed., cons. Inferno Press Edits., Calif., 1949-60, The Minority of One mag., N.J., 1964-70; pub. Exile Press, Novato, Calif., 1983—. Served to sgt. maj. U.S. Army, 1942-46; PTO, North Africa, Asia. Recipient Rosenthal award for fiction, Berne, Switzerland, 1977, Prix de Satire, Amsterdam, Holland, 1979, Ampersand Poetry prize, Calif.-Can., 1981. Home: 765 Sunset Pkwy Novato CA 94947

HEFFERNAN, MICHAEL JOSEPH, b. Detroit, Dec. 20, 1942, s. Joseph William and Susan Gertrude (Schneider) H.; m. Anne Miller, Aug. 14, 1968 (div. 1975); m. Kathleen Spigarelli, Aug. 9, 1975; children—Joseph Rinaldo, James Brendan, Michael Eamon. Author poetry books: Booking Passage, 1973, A Figure of Plain Force, 1978, The Cry of Oliver Hardy, 1979, To the Wreakers of Havoc; contrbr. to Heartland II: Poets of the Midwest, 1975, Strong Measures, 1986, Patterns of Poetry, 1986, Writing Poems, 1987; poetry ed. Midwest Qtly, 1970-84. AB, U. Detroit, 1964; MA, U. Mass., 1967, PhD, 1970. Prof. English Pittsburg (Kans.) State U., 1969—; vis. prof. U. Ark., Fayetteville, 1986-87. Woodrow Wilson Fdn. fellow, 1964, NEA wrtg. fellow, 1978-79; Bread Loaf Wrtrs.' Conf. scholar, 1977; grantee NEH, 1980. Mem. PSA, AWP, Kans. Wrtrs. Assn. Home: 510 W Euclid St Pittsburg KS 66762

HEFFERNAN, THOMAS (CARROLL, JR.), b. Hyannis, MA, Aug. 19, 1939; s. Thomas Carroll and Mary Elizabeth (Sullivan) H.; m. Nancy Elizabeth Iler, July 15, 1972 (div. 1977). Author: (poetry) Mobiles and Other Poems, 1974, A Narrative of Jeremy Bentham, 1978, The Liam Poems, 1981, City Renewing Itself, 1983; editor: A Poem Is a Smile You Can Hear, 1976, Celtic issue, Intl. Poetry Rvw, spring, 1977; contrbr. to various lit. jnls. AB in English, Boston Coll., 1961; MA in English, U. Manchester, Eng., 1963. Asst. lectr. U. Manchester, 1964-65, U. Bristol, Eng., 1965-66; instr. English. U. Hartford, West Hartford, Conn., 1967-70; poet-in-the-schls. N.C. Dept. Pub. Instrn., Raleigh, 1973-77; vis. artist-in-poetry Central Piedmont Community Coll., Charlotte, N.C., 1977-78, Guilford Tech. Community Coll., Jamestown, N.C., 1978-80, Davidson Community Coll., Lexington, N.C., 1980-81; PACE prof. Fla. Jr. Coll., Jacksonville and Norfolk, Va., 1981-84, City Colls. of Chgo. and San Diego, 1984; lectr. English and philosophy U. Md. Asian Div., Tokyo, 1984—. Recipient Crucible mag. award, 1977, Roanoke-Chowan award, 1982, Mainichi Award for Haiku (Tokyo), 1985, JAL/Mainichi Award for Haiku (Tokyo), 1986; NEA lit. fellow, 1977. Mem. AAP, PSA, Intl. Assn. Study of Anglo-Irish Literature (Japan), Am. Comm. for Irish Studies, N.C. Writers Conf. Clubs: Yokota Officers. Office: U Md Box 100 APO San Francisco CA 96328

HEGI, URSULA JOHANNA, b. Buederich, W. Ger, May 23, 1946; arr. US 1965; d. Heinz and Johanna (Maas) Koch; div.; children—Eric, Adam. Author: Intrusions, 1981; contrbr. fiction poetry and book rvws. to MS, Louisville Rvw, NY Times Book Rvw, LA Times, Feminist Studies, Poetry Northwest, Boston Globe, Blue Buildings, Prairie Schooner, others. BA, U. NH, 1978, MA, 1979. Lectr. Univ. NH, Durham, 1979–84; asst. prof. EW Univ., Cheney, Wash, 1984—, dir. MFA program in Creative Wrtg., EW Univ., 1986—. Mem. Amnesty Intl., 1985—. Bread Loaf fellow, 1983, PEN/NEA fiction award 1984, 1986 fellowship from Washington State Arts Commission. Mem. AWP. Address: 708 W 14th Spokane WA 99204

HEGYELI, RUTH INGEBORG ELISABETH JOHNSSON, (John Andrews), b. Stockholm, Aug. 14, 1931; came to U.S., 1963; d. John Alfred and Elsa Ingeborg (Sjögren) Johnsson; m. Andrew Francis Hegyeli, July 2, 1966 (dec. 1982). Ed.: Proceedings of the Artificial Heart Program Conference, 1970, Report by the National Heart and Lung Institute Task Force on Arteriosclerosis (vols. I and II), 1971, Proceedings, USA-USSR Exchange in Cardiovascula Area 1972-1977, 1977, Measurement and Control of Cardiovascular Risk Factors, 1980, Prostaglandins and Caardiovascular Diseases, 1981, Nutrition and Cardiovascular Disease, 1979-85; contrbr. chap.: Biomaterials, Bioengineering Applied to Materials and Soft Tissue Implants, 1971, Antitumor Compounds of Natural Origin: Chemistry and Biochemistry (vol. II), 1981; 40 poems pub. in natl. anthologies. BA, U. Toronto, 1958, MD, 1962. Med. officer Nat. Heart and Lung Inst., Bethesda, Md., 1969-73, chief program devel. br., 1973-75, acting dir. office of program planning and evaluation, 1975-76; asst. dir. intl. programs Nat. Heart, Lung and Blood Inst., Bethesda, 1976-86, assoc. dir. intl. programs, 1986—. Recipient profl. awards. Mem. med. and sci. orgns. Home: 7063 Wolftree Ln Rockville MD 20852

HEIDRICK, VIRGINIA LOUISE, b. Los Angeles, Feb. 9, 1951; d. John Robert and E. Louise (Peevey) Rhodes. Contrbr. poems. to anthols., organizational paperss. B.F.A., U. Ariz., 1981. Drama tchr. Aqua Fria U. High Schl., Avondale, AZ, 1981-82; GED instr. Fedl. Correctional Inst., Phoenix, 1985—. SErved with U.S. Navy, 1974-78. Home: 1902 E Grandview Dr Phoenix AZ 85022

HEILBRUN, CAROLYN GOLD, b. East Orange, NJ, Jan. 13, 1926; d. Archibald and Estelle (Roemer) Gold; m. James Heilbrun, Feb. 20, 1945; children: Emily, Margaret, Robert. Author: The Garnett Family, 1961, Towards Androgyny, 1973, Reinventing Womanhood, 1979; 7 novels as Amanda Cross, 1964— (recipient Nero Wolfe award 1981). BA, Wellesley Coll.,

1947; MA, Columbia U., 1951, PhD, 1959. Guggenheim fellow, 1966; Rockefeller fellow, 1976. Mem. MLA, Mystery Writers Am. Office: Columbia U 613 Philo Hall New York NY 10027

HEILMAN, JOAN RATTNER, d. Louis and Erna (Schneider) Rattner; m. Morton Heilman, Aug. 12, 1956; children: Katherine, Julia, David. Author: (with Jean Nidetch) The Story of Weight Watchers, 1970, Growing Up Thin, 1975, The Complete Book of Midwifery, 1977, Having a Cesarean Baby, 1978, Diabetes: Controlling It the Easy Way, 1982, rev ed, 1985, The Complete University Medical Diet, 1984, (with Eileen Ford) The Ford Models' Crash Course in Looking Great, 1985, (with Lila Nachtigall) Estrogen: The Facts Can Change Your Life, 1986; Unbelievably Good Deals & Great Adventures That You Absolutely Can't Get Unless You're Over 50, 1988. Contrbr of nonfiction articles to numerous periodicals, including Ladies' Home Journal, Family Circle, Parade, Travel & Leisure, and Suburbia Today. BA, Smith ollege. Women's ed., This Week (mag), New York, N.Y., 1954-69; freelance writer, 1969—. Member: ASJA, AG. Address: 812 Stuart Ave Mamaroneck NY 10543

HEILMAN, M. GRANT, b. Tarentum, PA, Sept. 29, 1919; s. Marlin W. and Martha (Grant) H.; m. Marjorie Mapel, May 21, 1946 (dec.); 1 son, Hans; m. 2d, Barbara Whipple, July 14, 1961. Author: The Psalms Around Us, 1970, Farm Town, 1974, Wheat Country, 1977, Wildflowers of Lancaster Country, 1980. Wrkg. on book on Am. agr. BA in Econs., Swarthmore Coll. Prin. Grant Heilman Photography, Lititz, Pa., 1946-87, chmn., 1987—. Served to capt. US Army, 1941-45; ETO, NATOUSA. Mem. Natl. Agri-Mktg. Assn., Picture Profls. Am. Home: Box 609 Buena Vista CO 81211

HEIMBURGER, DONALD JAMES, b. Urbana, IL, Apr. 24, 1947; s. Raymond William and Agnes Marie (Ruhnow) H.; m. Marilyn Martha Zoellick, Dec. 30, 1972; children—Amy, Allison. Author/ed.: D&RGW Narrow Gauge Plan Book, 1976, Rio Grande Steam Locomotives, 1981, Wabash, 1984, Along the East Broad Top, 1987. BS in Communics., U. IL, 1969. Rptr./ed. Champaign-Urbana (IL) News Gazette, 1965-69, radio anncr., WPGU, Urbana; stringer Louisville Courier-Jnl, 1971; ed. U.S. Army Nwspr., Ft. Knox, KY, 1971; asst. pub. Chicagotown newspaper, 1969-70; press rep. IL Central Gulf RR, Chgo., 1969-76; press mgr. Citicorp, Chgo., 1976-80; pub. County Star, Tolono, IL, 1980-84; pub. Heimburger House Pub. Co., River Forest, Ill. Ed. and pub. S Gaugian & Sn3 Modeler mags, 1980—. Served to Spclst./4, U.S. Army, 1970-72. Bd. of dir., U.IL Communications Alumni-Chicago area, 1984—, adv. bd. of dir., DuPage mag., 1986—. Home: 310 Lathrop Ave River Forest IL 60305

HEINLEIN, ROBERT ANSON, b. Butler, MO, July 7, 1907; s. Rex Ivar and Bam (Lyle) H.; m. Virginia Doris Gerstenfeld, Oct. 21, 1948. Author: 45 books including Beyond This Horizon, 1948, The Green Hills of Earth, 1951, Puppet Masters, 1951, Double Star, 1956 (Hugo award), The Door Into Summer, 1957, Citizen of the Galaxy, 1957, Methuselah's Children, 1958, Have Space Suit-Will Travel, 1958, Starship Troopers, 1959 (Hugo award), Stranger in a Strange Land, 1961 (Hugo award), Glory Road, 1963, The Moon is a Harsh Mistress, 1966 (Hugo award), I Will Fear No Evil, 1970, Time Enough for Love, 1973, others; films Destination Moon, 1950, Project Moonbase, 1954; tech. books including Test Procedures for Plastic Materials Intended for Structural and Semi-Structural Aircraft Uses, 1944; also tech. and popular novels. Grad., U.S. Naval Acad., 1929; postgrad. physics and math., UCLA, 1934. Served to lt. (j.g.) USN, 1929-34. Recipient Best Sci. Fiction Novel award World Sci. Fiction Conv., 1956, 59, 61, 66; Sequoyah award, 1961; Best Liked Book award Boys Clubs Am., 1959; Nebula award SFWA, 1975. Mem. AG, Am. Address: Spectrum lit 432 Park S 1205 New York NY 10016

HEINRICH, PEGGY, b. NYC, Feb. 20, 1929, d. Max S. and Norma (Kraus) Herrman; m. Martin R. Heinrich, Apr. 4, 1952 (dec. 1976); children—Ellen Nicole, Jean Michelle. Author: Haiga Haiku (with artist Barbara Gray), 1983, A Patch of Grass, 1984, co-author (with John Uhlmann): The Soul of Fire: How Charcoal Changed the World, 1987; contrbr. poems: Blue Unicorn, Calliope, Conn. Artists, other lit mags; articles: Conn. Today, County, Americana, Smithsonian. Ed. of Conn. River Rvw, 1985-87. BA, Hunter Coll., NYC,1949. Asst. pub. dir. Doherty Clifford Steers & Shenfield, 1950-59. Awards: Western World Haiku Soc., 1974, 79, 80; fiction prize, Trumbull Arts Festival, 1980; Sri Chimmoy Awd., Comm. for Spiritual Poetry, 1980; 2d prize, N.C. Haiku Soc., 1984; Medal for Lit. Achievement, State of Conn., 1985. Mem. PSA, Haiku Soc. of Am., Western World Haiku Soc., AAP. Home: 30 Burr Farms Rd Westport CT 06880

HEINZ, BRIAN JAMES, b. Bklyn., Nov. 1, 1946, s. Howard Charles and Kathleen (Geraghty) H. Author: Beachcraft Bonanza, 1986; contrbr. articles to Instructor mag., Science and Children Mag. Wrkg. on juvenile fiction. AA, Suffolk Community Coll., 1966; BA, SUNY-Stony Brook, 1974, MA, 1976. Tchr. elem. schls. various locations, N.Y., 1975—; instr. SUNY-Stony Brook, 1986. Recipient teaching awards. Home: RR 1 Box 447C Sylvan Dr Wading River NY 11792

HELBERG, BARBARA ANNE, b. Holgate, OH, Jan. 28, 1946; d. Robert and Bonita Jean (Knapp) Helberg; m. Neil Ellis Burns, Mar. 30, 1973 (div. Dec. 24, 1981); children—Abigail, Tyler Neil. Student Defiance Coll., 1980-81. Reporter Northwest-Signal, Napoleon, OH, 1965-66; mgn. ed. Connections, Holgate, OH, 1983—; reporter Henry City Messenger, Leipsic, OH, 1985, ed., 1985—; free-lance wrtr., 1987—. Home: 209 S Brayer St Holgate OH 43527

HELDRETH, LEONARD GUY, b. Shinnston, WV, Apr. 8, 1939; s. Orie Guy and Grace Louise (Myers) H.; m. Lillian Ruth Marks, June 18, 1964; children—Randall, Terrence. Contrbr. numerous chpts. to books. Wrkg. on Reader's Guide to Fred Saberhagen; editing The Blood Is the Life Critical Essays on the Vampire in Literature. B.S., W.V.U., 1962; Ph.D., U. Ill., 1973. Abstractor, ed. NCTE, Champaign, IL, 1968—70; prof. English, Northern Mich. U., Marquette, 1970—, head English dept., 1987—. Mem. Intl. Assn. Fantastic in Arts (div. head), Sci. Fiction Research Assn., Popular Culture Assn. Home: 367 E Hewitt Ave Marquette MI 49855

HELLBUSCH, JAY JAY, b. Boulder, CO, Nov. 10, 1939, d. Robert Edgar and Janet Fae (Andrew) Johnson; m. Donald Edwin Hellbusch, Jan. 2, 1962 (div. 1974); children—Heidi Lynn, Danon Troy. Author: Cowrie: Biography of a Snail, 1981, Cowrie Magic, 1983; contrbr. articles to mags. and newspapers; free-lance ed. BA magna cum laude, Calif. State U.-Northridge, 1974, MA summa cum laude, 1976. Art prodn. dir., mng. ed., ed.-in-chief Phoenix Pub. Co., Bloomington, Inc., 1981-83; art dir., then creative dir. Cardinal Graphics and Advt. Co., Bloomington, 1979-81; mktg. and advt. dir. Topaz Industries, Bloomington, 1979-85; lectr. College of Canyons, 1976-78, Citrus Community Coll., Azusa, Calif., 1985-86. Mem. NWC, Women in Communications. Home: 230 Crestglen Rd Glendora CA 91740

HELLER, JANET RUTH, b. Milw., July 8, 1949; d. William C. and Joan (Pereles) Heller; m. Michael A. Krischer, June 13, 1982. Ed. and founder Primavera, 1974—; contrbg. ed. Lilith, 1979—; contrbr short story to Agada; articles in Charles Lamb Bulletin, Poetics, Lang. and Style, PBSA, Concerning Poetry, Revista de Estudios Hispanicos, Theatre Jnl, Shakespeare Bulletin; poetry in Light Year '85, Poets' Voices 1984, Great Lakes Rvw, The Writer, Cottonwood Rvw, others. BA, U. Wis.-Madison, 1971, MA, 1973, PhD, U. of Chicago, 1987. Coordinator writing program Univ. Chgo., 1976-81, lectr. ext. div., 1981-82; instr. N. Ill. Univ., DeKalb, 1982—. Mem MLA, Ill. Writers. Address: 701 N Eddy St Sandwich IL 60548

HELLER, JOSEPH, b. Bklyn, May 1, 1923; m. Shirley Held, Sept. 3, 1945; children—Erica Jill, Theodore Michael. Author: Catch-22, 1961 (novel); We Bombed in New Haven, 1968 (play); Something Happened, 1974 (novel), Clevinger's Trial, 1974, Good as Gold, 1979 (novel); No Laughing Matter (with Speed Vogel), 1986. BA, NYU, 1948; MA, Columbia, 1949, Oxford Univ., 1949-59. Instr. Pa. State Univ., 1950-52; advtg. wrtr., Time, 1952-56, Look, 1956-58; promotion mgr. McCall's, 1958-61. Served to lt. USAAF, WW II. Address: S&S 630 Fifth Ave New York NY 10020

HELLER, MARC, see Siegel, Martin

HELLER, MARLENE ANN, b. Bklyn., NY, Aug. 31, 1953; d. Theodore and Gertrude (Kaplan) Greenman; m. Gary Robert Heller, July 27, 1975; children—Robyn Rose, Jeffrey Samuel. Contrbg. ed. Model Retailer, 1981-83; articles in Home Fashions-Textiles, 1980, Retail Week, 1981, Flowers+, 1984. BA, Monmouth Coll., 1975. Assoc. ed. Craft Model & Hobby Ind. Mag., NYC, 1975-76; prod. ed. Bell Labs, 1976; mkt. ed. Gifts & Decorative Accessories Mag., NYC, 1977-80, bus. correspondent North Brunswick News, 1987—; freelance writer, 1980—. Mem. NWC. Home: 1249 Huron Rd North Brunswick NJ 08902

HELLEW, JOYCE VIRGINIA, b. Bklyn., Dec. 17, 1949; d.Wade Hellew and Rose Genevieve (Meshelany) Weener. Ed., co-pub., Straight Ahead: New Young Wrtrs. from River East; contrbr. poetry to Portland Rvw, The Little Mag., The Archer, Avenue, Newsletter Inago, Maat, 2d Inago Anthology of Poetry, Encore, Poetry Today, Voices Intl., Women's Record, Wide Open mag, other lit mags. BA magna cum laude, Pace U., 1983. Exec. v.p. Devon, Ltd., NYC, 1979-83. Recipient Curtis Owens award for poetry, 1982, 83; Sarah Willis scholar, 1979, 81, 82. Mem. MLA, NWU, IWWG, AAP. Home: 318 W 100th St Apt 7A New York NY 10025

HELLIE, RICHARD, b. Waterloo, IA, May 8, 1937; s. Ole Ingeman and Mary Elizabeth (Larsen) H.; m. Jean Laves, Dec. 23, 1961; 1 son, Benjamin. Author: Muscovite Society, 1967, Enserfment and Military Change in Muscovy, 1971, Slavery in Russia 1450-1725, 1982. BA, U. Chgo., 1958, MA, 1960, PhD, 1965; postgrad.,

U. Moscow, 1963-64. Ford Fdn. Fgn. Area Trng. fellow, 1962-65; Guggenheim fellow, 1973-74; NEH fellow, 1978-79; NEH grantee, 1982-83. Mem. PEN. Home: 4917 S Greenwood Ave Chicago IL 60615

HELLINGER, DOUGLAS A(LAN), b. NYC March 11, 1948; s. James L. and Eleanor (De Young) H. Author: (with brother, Stephen H. Hellinger) Unemployment and the Multinationals: A Strategy for Tehnological Change in Latin America, 1976, (with Fred O'Regan and S.H. Hellinger) U.S. Foreign Assistance to Africa: A New Institutional Approah, 1977, (with S.H. Hellinger, Eric G. Walker, and others) Alternative Programs of Credit and Integrated Services in Latin America, 1979, (with S.H. Hellinger, Supporting Central American and Caribbean Development: A Critique (with S.H. Hellinger) Mainsteaming Major Donor Support for Third World NGOS: Guidelines for Construtive Collaboraration, 1986 (with S.H. hellinger and F.O'Regan) Aid for Just Development: Proposals for a New Development Assistance Structure, 1987. Contrbr World Development. BA, Queens College of the City Univ of N.Y., 1969; MBA, Columbia Univ, 1973. Volunteer worker in Northeast Brazil, Peace Corps, Washington, D.C., 1970-72; cons, Inter-American Fdn, Washington, D.C., 1973-74; assoc, Developing World Indutry and Tehnology, Inc., Washington, D.C., 1975-76; co-dir, Development Corp for Alternative Policies, Inc., Washington, D.C., 1977—. Office: 1010 Vermont Ave NW Suite 521 Washington DC 20005

HELLINGER, STEPHEN H(ENRY), b. New York City, March 11, 1948; s. James L. and Eleanor (De Young) H. Author: (with brother, Douglas A. Hellinger) Unemployment and the Multinationals: A Strategy for Technological Change in Latin America, 1976, (with Fred O. Regan and Douglas Hellinger) U.S. Foreign Assistance to Africa: A New Insiutional Approach, 1977, (with Douglas Hellinger, Eric G. Walker, and others) Alternative Programs of Credit and Integrated Services in Latin America, 1979, Supporting Contral American and Caribbean Development. A Critique of the Caribbean as in Initiative (with Douglas Hellinger) Mainstreaming Major Donor Support for Third World NGO: Guidelines for Contructive Collaboration, 1986, (with Douglas Hellinger and Fred O'Regan) Aid for Just Development; Proposals for a New Development Assistance Structure, 1985. Consultant to UNESCO and the World Bank. BA, Queens College of the City Univ. of N.Y., 1969; MBA, Columbia Univ., 1973. Volunteer worker inNicargua and Venezuela, Peace Corps, Washington, D.C., 1970-72; cons, Inter-American Fdn, Washington, D.C., 1973; assoc fellow, Overseas Development Cncl, Washington, D.C., 1975-76; cons, Developing World Industrial and Technology, Inc., Washington, D.C., 1976, co-dir., Development Group for Alternative Policies, Inc., Washington, D.C., 1977—. Office: 1010 Vermont Ave NW Suite 521 Washington DC 20005

HELLMAN, DONNA LEE, b. Livermore, CA, Jan. 29, 1958, d. Louis Wilson and Margaret Celia (Hicks) Hellman. Author: Songs for All Seasons, 1985, In Quiet Places, 1985; contrbr. to Amer. Poetry Anthol. 1986, Impressions 1986, World of Poetry Anthol. 1987, Chasing Rainbows 1987. Awards: hon. mention, Golden Poet 1986. Student public schls., Manteca, Calif. Employed by Memorial Hosp. Assn., 1986—. Home: 21011 S Airport Way Manteca CA 95336

HELLMAN, HAL, b. NYC, Sept. 15, 1927; s. Louis B. and Anna (Rosman) H.; m. Sheila Almer, Feb. 11, 1951; children: Jillana, Jennifer. Author: Navigation: Land, Sea and Sky, 1966, The Art and Science of Color, 1967, Controlled Guidance Systems (Aerospace), 1967, Light and Electricity in the Atmosphere, 1968, The Right Size, 1968, High Energy Physics, 1968, Defense Mechanisms, from Virus to Man, 1969, The City in the World of the Future, 1970, Helicopters and Other Vtols, 1970, Energy and Inertia, 1970, Biology in the World of the Future, 1971, The Lever and the Pulley, 1971, The Kinds of Mankind, An Introduction to the Study of Race and Racism (with Morton Klass), 1971, Feeding the World of the Future, 1972, Population, 1972, Energy in the World of the Future, 1973, Transportation in the World of the Future, 1968, 2d ed. 1974, Communications in the World of the Future, 1969, 2d ed. 1975, Epidemiological Aspects of Carcinogenesis (editor), 1974, Technophobia: Getting Out of the Technology Trap, 1976, (with Ludwik Kowalski) Understanding Physics, 1978, Deadly Bugs and Killer Insects, 1978, Computer Basics, 1983; editor Psychosocial and Cultural Determinants of Population Policies, 1974, Migration, Urbanization, and Fertility, 1976; also numerous articles pub. in sci. publs. MS in Physics, Stevens Inst. Tech., 1961; MBA, CCNY, 1955. Tech. info. mgr. Gen. Precision Inc., Wayne, N.J., 1956-66; freelance writer, 1966—. Served with M.C., U.S. Army, 1947. Sci. writer-in-residence Council for Advancement of Sci. Writing, Marine Biol. Lab., Woods Hole, Mass., 1980. Mem. ASJA, Natl. Assn. Sci. Writers. Home: 100 High St Leonia NJ 07605

HELLMAN, SHEILA ALMER, b. NYC, July 8, 1928; d. Julius Robley and Kate (Goodman) Almer; m. Hal Hellman, Feb. 11, 1951; children: Jillana, Jennifer. Contrbr. poetry and articles to lit. mags., N.Y. Times, anthologies. BA, Marietta Coll., Ohio, 1949; MA, NYU, 1951. Freelance dancer, poet, 1952-76; cultural arts dir. YM-YWHA of New Jersey, Wayne, N.J.,1976—. Mem. AAP, P&W. Home: 100 High St Leonia NJ 07605

HELM, MIKE, b. Seattle, May 21, 1942, s. Robert Stanfield and Mary Patricia (Hamley) H.; m. Christine Elizabeth Cooper, Dec. 14, 1968; children—Benjamin Tuan, Malindi Jane, Polly Ann, Luke Nathaniel. Author: Eugene, Oregon—A Guide, 1979, Conversations with Pioneer Women, 1981, Conversations with Bullwhackers, Muleskinners, etc., 1982, Visionaries, Mountain Men & Empire Builders, 1983, A Bit of Verse, 1983, Oregon's Ghosts and Monsters, 1984. BS in Social Sci., Oreg. State U., 1966; MS in English, U. Oreg., 1969, MS in Edn., 1973. Vol. U.S. Peace Corps, Mbale, Uganda, 1967-68, Machakos, Kenya, 1969; tchr. public schls. Coos Bay, Oreg., 1970-72, Eugene, Oreg., 1973—; tchr. Yukon-Kuskokwim Schl. Dist., Tununak, Alaska, winter 1980. Recipient Pacific Northwest Booksellers award for Lit. Excellence, Seattle, 1981. Home: 1147 E 26th St Eugene OR 97403

HELMES, L. SCOTT, b. Ft Snelling, MN, Oct. 27, 1945; s. Leslie Charles and Marilyn (Tomlinson) H.; m. Julie H. Williams, Sept. 15, 1967 (div. Dec. 4, 1973). Author: OPUS Plus-Minus, 1985, Great Poets, 1985, Visual Poems, 1986; contrbr. Paris Rvw, Avant-Garde Today, (co-compiler) 10th Assembling, White Walls, Lake St Rvw, Xerolog 3, 10-5155-20, Interstate, Against Infinity Anthology, Kaldron. BArch, U. Minn., 1968. Dir. physical planning and design Park Nicollet Med. Fdn., Mpls, 1983-86; Helmes Architects, 1986—. Recipient 1st prize concrete poetry, Gamut Mag, Ohio, 1982. Mem. Natl. C Slow Assn., AIA, Profl. Ski Instr. Am., ILYA. Address: 862 Tuscarora St St Paul MN 55102

HELMINSKI, EDMUND RICHARD, b. Jersey City, NJ, July 1, 1947; s. Edmund F. and Mary (Orlowski) H.; children—Mathew, Shams, Cara. Translator: Ruins of the Heart (Jelaluddin Rumi), 1982. Wrkg. on translation of poetry of Yunus Emre: The Drop that Became the Sea. BA, Wesleyan U., 1968. Pub., ed. Threshold Books, Putney, Vt., 1981—. Home: RD 3 Box 1350 Putney VT 05346

HEMMES, MICHAEL, b. Merrillville, IN, Nov. 9, 1958. Contrbr. over 600 pieces to numerous publs., including Wrtrs. Digest, Ford Motor Co. publs. BS in Bus, and Journalism, Butler U., 1981. Chief copywriter Stephen M. Dickhaus & Assocs., Inc., Indpls., 1981-82; spcl. events reporter UPI, Indpls., 1982, broadcast ed., Chgo., 1982-83; editorial coordinator Acad. Gen. Dentistry, Chgo., 1983-84, mng. ed., 1984-85; asst. ed. Am. Hosp. Pub., Inc., Chgo., 1985-86, sr. ed., 1986—. Mem. Natl. Soc. Newspaper Columnists. Home: 3930 N Pine Grove Ave 1503 Chicago IL 60613

HEMMING, GEORGE FRED, b. Middleburgh, NY, Jul. 17, 1937; s. Fred Eugene Hemming and Eleanor (Stanndard) Deukmejian; m. Eileen Helen Murray, Feb. 3, 1962; children—Dawn, Doreen Kimberly, Kelly, Helen, Gregory, Jason. Publ./ed. Home Waters newsltr., 1985; contrbr. to Fly Tyer Mag., Clearwater Currents, Times Record, Northeast Woods & Waters, Army Logistician mag. Assoc. in Applied Science Hudson Valley CC, 1957. Admin. tech. Dept. of Army (Troy, NY), 1962-76, Admin. special., 1977-80 (ret.); Custom fly tyer, 1980—; fly tying and fishing instr. Brittonkill schls. (Troy), 1984— and Hudson Valley CC, 1986—. SGM ARNG, 1954-80, NY. Office: 1032 Cloverlawn Rd Center Brunswick (Troy) NY 12180

HEMSCHEMEYER, JUDITH, b. Sheboygan, WI, Aug. 7, 1935; d. Bernard Andrew and Aurelia Ann (Miller) Hemschemeyer; m. Morton Shelly Rosenfeld, Aug. 12, 1958 (dec. May 19, 1979); children: Stephanie, David. Author juvenile fiction: Trudie and the Milch Cow, 1967; poetry: I Remember The Room was Filled with Light, 1973, Very Close and Very Slow, 1975, The Ride Home, 1987. BA, U. Wis.-Madison, 1957, MA, 1959. Asst. prof. Univ Utah, Salt Lake City, 1976-77, Sarah Lawrence Coll., Bronxville, NY, 1977-78, Douglass Coll., New Brunswick, NJ, 1978-80, Univ. Central Fla., Orlando, 1982—. Recipient Hodder fellowship, Princeton Univ., 1981-2. Mem. PEN, ALTA. Address: Engl Dept U Central Fla Orlando FL 32816

HEMSING, ALBERT E., b. Barmen, Germany, Feb. 27, 1921; s. Paul and Josephine (Ferder) H.; m. Esther Davidson, Dec. 27, 1944; 1 dau., Josephine Claudia. author: (with Esther Hemsing) documentary The Yellow Star, 1981; writer: Top Secret—The July 20, 1944, Revolt Against Hitler, 1980. BSS, CCNY, 1942; MA, NYU, 1947. Home: 215 E 79th St New York NY 10021

HENDERSON, ARCHIBALD, b. Chapel Hill, NC, Dec. 20, 1916; s. Archibald and Barbara Curtis Bynum (Minna) H.; m. Helen Claire White, June, 1954 (div. June, 1974); children—

Archibald, Russell Van. Author: Omphale's Wheel, 1966, The Puzzled Picture, 1971, Where You Are Now, 1984, A Guide to "Much Ado About Nothing," 1966; co-translator: Introduction to the Psychoanalysis of Mallarme (Charles Mauron), 1963. AB, U. NC, 1937, MA, 1941; PhD,Columbia U., 1954. Instr. English Auburn U., 1948-49; Sophie Newcomb College, New Orleans, 1949-54; prof. English, U. Houston, 1954-82. Capt. USAF, 1941-45. Mem. PSA. Home: 2615 Marilee Houston TX 77057

HENDERSON, BRUCE RAYMOND, b. Verona, NJ, Mar. 17, 1948, s. Frank Irvin and Amy Jean (Lampenfeld) H.; m. Linda Foster, July 1, 1971 (div. July 1976). Author: Oakland Organic, 1982. Contrbr. to Student Voices/One, Tunnel Road, Agapae, Albany Rvw, Yoga Jnl. BA in English, Oberlin Coll., 1972; MA in English, U. Wash., 1973; DA, SUNY, Albany, 1986. Instr. Antioch Coll./West, San Francisco, 1973-74, Russell Sage Coll., Troy, N.Y., 1984-86, Hudson Valley Community Coll., Troy, 1986—; tchg. asst. SUNY, Albany, 1983-86; tchg. fellow, Rollins College, 1986—, instr. SUNY, Farmingdale, 1987—. Home: 7 Clover Lane Verona NJ 07044

HENDERSON, ERSKINE D., b. Aurora, CO, Apr. 11, 1949, s. Dale Theodore and Anna (Darden) H. Playwright: Blessed Are the Meek; contrbr. poetry: New Voices in American Poetry, American Poetry Anthology, poetry mags. Wrkg. on collection of short stories, poetry, collection of one-act plays. BA cum laude, Wesleyan U., 1971; JD, Columbia U., 1976. Assoc. firm Rein, Mound & Cotton, NYC, 1976-77, firm Skadden, Arps, Slate, Meagher & Flom, NYC, 1977—; cons. Hughes Investments, Denver, 1983—; prtnr., counsel P.H. Enterprises, NYC, 1984—; pres. The PH Fund, 1986. Parker Prize, 1971; Outstanding Young Men of America, 1985. Office: 919 Third Ave New York NY 10022

HENDERSON, HARRY BRINTON, JR., b. Kittanning, PA, Sept. 9, 1914; s. Harry Brinton and Sallie Campbell (Findley) H.; m. Beatrice Conford, 1937; children: Albert K., Harry Brinton III (dec.), Joseph P. Author: (with Sam Shaw and H.C. Morris) War in Our Time, 1942, (with Romare Bearden) Six Black Masters of American Art, 1972, History of America's Black Artists, 1987. BC., Pa. State Coll., 1936. Reporter various Pa. newspapers, 1936-40; contbr. to Argosy, Collier's, Cosmopolitan, Redbook, Harper's, Readers Digest, others, 1956—; with World Wide Med. Press, also Med. Tribune and Hosp. Tribune, N.Y.C., 1956—, editor-in-chief, 1971-79. Mem. AG. Home: 18 Franklin Ave Croton-on-Hudson NY 10520

HENDERSON, JULIE K., b. Ada, MN, May 30, 1950; d. Ernest Byron and Myrtle (Norum) H. Contrbr. 300+ articles to local & regional nwsprs. & mags.; freelance writer num. brochures, convention bklets, nwsltrs. BS, Moorhead State U., 1968-73; MS, ND State U., 1973-77. Info. officer ND Water Inst., Fargo, 1980-82; media coordin. St. Luke's Hosps., Fargo, 1982-84; mkting. writer Great Plains Software, Fargo, 1984-85; instr. ND State U., Fargo, 1985—; freelance writer/ed., 1973—. Num. natl., state, & local awards. Mem. ND Press Women, Fargo-Moorhead Media Club, Fargo-Moorhead Adv. Fedn. Home: 912 Ninth Ave N Moorhead MN 56560

HENDERSON, KATHLEEN HAYDEN, (Kakie, Housewife Hannah, Sage of Monkey's Eyebrow), b. Paducah, KY, April 30, 1919; d. William Gross and Stella Carmen (Rickman) Hayden; m. Carlos Payne Henderson, Sept. 28, 1935; children: Don, Dr. Kenneth, Pamella Lawrence, William, Sam, Kerry, Lori Wiggins and Debbie (twins). Editor Livingston Ledger, Smithland, Ky.; jnlst., columnist ("Kakie" and "Housewife Hannah"); feature wrtr., local history, underworld characters, Indian lore. Author: Watchtower on the Waters, Chickasaw Country, History of Ballard County, Steamboat Days on the Cumberland, others. Wrkg. on book on Welch tradition in Kentucky. First poem published at age 12. Created lyrics to "Double-Crossing Momma" for Ernest Tubbs. Member Kentucky Historical Society. Home: Rt 2 Box 405 Cairo Rd Paducah KY 42001

HENDERSON, KATHLEEN SUSAN, b. Detroit, July 15, 1952; d. Vernon Eugene Davidson and Peggy Ann (Bauman) Tucker; m. Keith Thoma Henderson, Sept. 19, 1970; children—Eric, Amy. Author: Market Guide for Young Writers, 1986, 88; former assoc. ed.: Thumb Farm News; family living ed. Sanilac County News; contrbr. articles to trade publs. Gra. Inst. Children's Lit., Redding Ridge, Conn., 1986. Freelance wrtr., 1971—. Recipient Best Books for Teens award N.Y. Public Library, 1987. Mem. Okla. Wrtrs. Fedn. (Cherubim award 1987), Natl. Assn. Young Wrtrs. (bd. trustees), Soc. Children's Book Wrtrs. (Mich. adviser), Children's Reading Round Table, Thumb Area Wrtrs. Club (founder). Home: 2151 Hale Rd Sandusky MI 48471

HENDERSON, MAURICE BRIAN, b. Phila., Jan. 1, 1961; s. Frances E. Henderson. Author: (poetry and short stories) When I Stopped To Think, 1983; (monologues and poems) Images: Behind Closed Doors & Open Minds, 1984; ed.: When the Walls Come Tumbling Down, 1986. BBA, Adelphi U., 1983; postgrad. N.Y. Inst., 1984. Prof. Temple U., Phila., 1984—, Phila. Community Coll., 1985—. Recipient Black Arts award Langston Hughes Inst., 1985; lit. award Alpha Phi Alpha, 1986. Mem. Theatre Assn. Pa. Home: 2340 Tasker St Philadelphia PA 19145

HENDERSON, MICHAEL DOUGLAS, b. London, England, Mar. 15, 1932; s. Arthur Douglas and Erina Doreen (Tilly) H.; m. Erica Mildred Hallowes, Apr. 16, 1966; 1 dau., Juliet Rachel Erina. Author: From India with Hope, 1972, Experiment with Untruth, 1977, 3d edit., 1979, A Different Accent, 1985. Contrbr. articles to popular and profl. mags., newspapers. Columnist: Lake Oswego Rvw, Oreg., 1984—, Union Jack, 1985—, Ctr. Island Penny Saver, 1985-86; commentator: KBOO-radio sta., Portland, 1983—, KOAP, KOAC-radio sta., 1985. Editor: New World News, London 1961-65, 71-77. Bd. dirs., past pres., World Affairs Council of Oreg., Portland, English-Speaking Union, Williamette Wrtrs. Awards: George Washington Honor Medal, 1986, ARBY for radio commentary by Acad. of Religious Broadcasting, 1987. Mem. Inst. Journalists (U.K.), Oreg. Christian Wrtrs., Oregon Wrtrs. Colony. Home: 10605 SW Terwilliger Pl Portland OR 97219

HENDERSON, MILDRED K., (M. K.), b. Phila., May 7, 1931; d. Valdemar John and Mildred (Buckley) Klammer; m. William G. Henderson, Mar. 31, 1951; children: Valerie, William Jr., Robert, James, Richard, Janet, Virginia, Thomas. Pub. MOMs Club Mail Call, HOB-NOB mag, Meanderings; contrbr. articles to Harper's Weekly, Puzzles and quizzes Dell Puzzle Pubs.; composed four pieces church music. BA in English and art (cum laude) Millersville State U., 1980. Secy. Franklin and Marshall Coll., Lancaster, Pa., 1951-52; info. speclst. and resource asst. Millersville State Univ., Penna., 1980-81. Recipient readers choice awards for prose and poetry, Amateur Writers Jnl., Bellaire, Ohio, 1970s. Mem. Donegal chpt. DAR, Lancaster, treas., 1983-86, United Methodist Women, vice pres., 1986-87. Address: 994 Nissley Rd Lancaster PA 17601

HENDERSON, SAFIYA (SHARON), b. NYC, Dec. 30, 1950; d. Chet Otis Lee Henderson and Esther Vera Richardson; m. Preston Leon Holmes, Jan. 1, 1978; 1 child, Naimah Lateefah. Contrbr. poetry to Black Creations, Jnl New African Lit. and Art, Continuities, Black Scholar, Womanwise, Essence, Arts Against Apartheid; play, I'll be home soon. Wrkg. on novel, collection of poems and short stories, play. BS in Physiotherapy, NYU, 1972; MA in Creative Writing, CCNY, 1982. Staff therapist Mt. Sinai Hosp., NYC, 1972-74, Brookdale Hosp., Bklyn., 1974-75; sr. therapist Harlem Hosp., NYC, 1975-80, supr. therapy, 1980—; prof. English, Touro Coll., Bklyn. Br., 1985—. U.S. Cultural Delegate, World Peace Congress, Copenhagen, 1986. Recipient award for poetry Creative Artist Program, 1983, NY Fdn. Arts Grant for poetry, 1986. Mem. P&W, DG. Home: 409 Edgecombe Ave Apt 9B New York NY 10032

HENDERSON, VICTOR MAURICE, b. Groesbeck, TX, Aug. 23, 1924; s. Robert Lee and Augusta (Cox) G. Author: Man and Providence, vol. 1. Wrkg on vols. 2, 3, 4 of Man and Providence. BS, Tri-State Coll. (Angola, IN), 1948. Engineer, Fairchild Camera (Hicksville, NY), 1948-56; project engineer, Vanguard Instruments, 1956-61; self-employed wrtr., 1961—. Cpl., US Army, 1942-45, Panama. Home: 14033 Mayport Ave Norwalk CA 90650

HENDERSON, WILLIAM CHARLES, b. Phila., Apr. 5, 1941; s. Francis Louis and Dorothy Price (Galloway) H. Author: The Galapagos Kid, 1971, His Son: A Child of the Fifties, 1981; editor, pub.: The Publish It Yourself Handbook, 1973, The Pushcart Prize: Best of the Small Presses, 1976—; editor: The Art of Literary Publishing, 1980. BA, Hamilton Coll., 1963; postgrad., Harvard U., 1963, U. Pa., 1965-66. Assoc. editor Doubleday & Co., NYC, 1972-73; pub. Pushcart Press, Yonkers, N.Y., 1972—; sr. editor Coward, McCann & Geohagan, Inc., NYC, 1973-75; cons. editor Harper & Row Inc., 1976—; Recipient Author award N.J. English Tchrs. Assn., 1972; Newsboy award Horatio Alger Soc., 1973, Carey Thomas award, PW, 1978. Mem. PEN, COSMEP. Home: Box 380 Wainscott NY 11975

HENDRICKS, KATHLEEN, b. Salem, VA, July 28, 1939; d. Russell D. and Thelma Lucille (Palmer) Mountcastle; m. Robert Fulton Hendricks, Sr., Apr. 26, 1958; children—Robert Fulton, Jr., Kelly Kathleen. Trivia columnist, Solon, IA; orgn. rptr. Iowa City nwspr.; contrbr. articles to Salem, VA, nwspr., Writers' Inst. Am. nwspr.; contrbr. poetry to Am. Poetry Assn., 1985, 1986. Stud. Natl. Bus. Coll., 1957-58, Writers' Inst. Am., 1968-70. Exec. secy., New York 1958-60; priv. secy., Dean of Students, Mary Washington Coll., Fredericksburg, VA, 1960-61; med. asst., Iowa City, IA, 1968-71; tchr. typing, Solon, IA Schl., 1972; member, chairperson in community and national charities in VA, Michigan and Iowa, 1960—; owner suprmkt. chain, Iowa, 1976—; writer/jnlst./poet, 1958—. Home: 261 Hillcrest Ct Central City IA 52214

HENDRICKS, THOMAS MANLEY, b. Twin Falls, Idaho, Sept. 15, 1949, s. Manley W. and Esther Roseman (Stoeve) H. Author: Some Collected Writings, vol. 1, 1983, vol. 2, 1984, vol. 3, 1986 vol. 4, 1987, Grey Stone/Yellow Brick and Other Stories, 1984, Short Poems, Long Thought, 1984, Essays, 1984, Players (A Game of Twelves), 1980, Cendrillon (The True Story of Cinderella) (radio play), 1984, The Workbook, 1976, 6th edit., 1987. Student Tyler (Tex.) Jr. Coll., 1967-69, N.Tex. State U., 1969-72. Pub., T.M.H. Pub. Co., Dallas. Home: 4000 Hawthorne St 5 Dallas TX 75219

HENDRICKSON, CAROL FOLLMUTH, b. Carpenter, IA, Sept. 8, 1920; d. George and Maud (Tollefsrud) F.; m. Allen Silas Hendrickson, Dec. 7, 1940; children—Joanne, Karen, Mark. Author poetry: Bent Grass, 1967, One Hand Clapping, 1973; contrbr. poetry to anthols: Kennedy Commemorative Anthol, Avalon Anthol, Feelings, 1979, Anthol of World Brotherhood and Peace, 1981, APA Spring Anthol, 1987, Odessa Poetry Rvw., 1987; A New Day, 1987, others; songwriter: "Look Up Weary World," 1968, From Sea to Sea In Song Anthol., others; contrbr. to Candor, American Bard, Am. Courier, Midwest Federated Chaparral Poets, IA Poetry Assn. & IA Poetry Day Assn. pubns., nwsprs., radio progs., church periodicals. Tchg. degree, Mason City Jr. Coll., 1940; postgrad. U. No. IA, 1941, 1965. Appreciation award, No. Am. Mentor mag., 1965; spcl. mention Writer's Digest poetry contest, 1975. Mem. Midwest Fedn. Chaparral Poets, IA Poetry Assn. Home: 118-21st St SE Mason City IA 50401

HENDRICKSON, JO ANN ELIZABETH, b. Phoenix, June 14, 1944, d. Joseph and Anne McCormick; m. Arnold Hayden Hendrickson, Dec. 27, 1969 (div. 1978). Ed.: I Love Radio, 1975, Survey of California Indian Tribes, 1985; wrtr., ed. publs. on employee benefits, retirement, investments, health and child devel. BA in English, Santa Clara U., 1966; MA with honors in English, San Francisco State U.,1974. Ed. Devel. Assocs., San Francisco, 1976-78; tech. publs. supr. GTE Sylvania, Mountain View, Calif., 1978-79; med. wrtr. W.H. Freeman Pub., San Francisco, 1979-81; sr. ed. U. Calif., San Francisco, 1981-84; sr. adminstrv. analyst, benefits U. Calif. Office of the Pres., 1984-85, mgr. tech. communications, benefits, 1985-86; benefits comm. spclst., Stanford Univ., 1986—. Photographer Young Artists Ballet Assn., Tucson, Ariz., 1984. Mem. IABC, San Francisco Press Club, Natl. Assn. Press Women. Office: Stanford U Benefits Old Pavilion Stanford CA 94305

HENDRIX, LEE, see Hamilton, Marcella Denise

HENES, DONNA, b. Cleve., Sept. 19, 1945; d. Nathan and Adelaide (Ross) Trugman. Author: Noting the Process of Noting the Process, 1977, Dressing Our Wounds in Warm Clothes, 1982; contrbr. to The Politics of Female Spirituality, Heresies, High Performance, Earth Rites, Fireweed, Feminist Studies, Lady-Unique, Book Art, Artist as Writer, TRA. BS, CCNY, 1970, MS, 1971. Self-employed as a ritual artist and writer, NY. Co-founder, Stand Together for Affirmative Neighborhood Development, Bklyn, 1983—, Ctr. for Celebration; judge for book awards, Jane Addams Peace Assn., UN at NYC,1983—. NEA fellow, 1982, grantee, 1984; grantee Beards' fund, Jerome Fdn., Money for Women, 1985, NY Fdn. for the Arts, 1986. Address: 351 Jay St Brooklyn NY 11201

HENN, SISTER MARY ANN, b. Frazee, MN, June 17, 1930; d. George B. and Ella Margaret (Rudolph) H. Entered convent, 1950. Chapbooks: Just Beyond Sigt, 1985, Jigsaw Solver, 1986, Light Through Stained Glass, 1986, Contrbr. poetry to numerous lit. mags. BA, St. Benedict's Coll., St. Joseph, Minn., 1964. Teacher grade schl. and high schl. English, Spanish, art, and lit. for 13 yrs. Address: St Benedict's Convent Saint Joseph MN 56374

HENNE, NANCY DIANE, b. Hammonton, NJ, Aug. 21, 1955; d. Thomas and Elizabeth Keith (Story) Sherman; m. Jack F. Henne, Jr., Dec. 27, 1976. Contrbr. poems to books, jnls., newspapers including Atlantic City Press, Rhyme Time, The Sandpaper, Hearts of Fire, vol. II, Pine Barrens Banner; also essays, articles. BA, Stockton State Coll., 1980. Operator N.J. Bell Telephone, Manahawkin, 1973-76; CRT operator Western Union, Moorestown, N.J., 1977-80, mgr.-sr. supvr., 1980-83; free-lance model, Medford, N.J., 1985—; free-lance writer, 1984—. Mem. Library Assn., NWC. Home: Box 102 Prospect St Parkertown NJ 08087

HENNESSY, , see Smolinski, Madeleine Joyce

HENNESSY, MADELEINE JOYCE, (Smolinski), b. Syracuse, NY, Sept. 18, 1948, d. Richard Clarence and Doris Muriel (Howe) Hennessy; m. Thomas Joseph Smolinski, Dec. 22, 1973; 2 daus., Caitlin Anne, Julia Grace. Author: Pavor Nocturnus and Other Poems (chapbook), 1979; contrbr. poetry: Ploughshares, 13th Moon, Yankee, Washout Rvw, Groundswell, numerous other lit. publs.; contrbg. ed. Washout Rvw, vol. 1, number 1, 1975, vol. 3, number 1, 1978. BA, SUNY- Plattsburgh, 1970. Supr. Schenectady County Dept. Social Services, N.Y., 1970-84. Mem. P&W. Home: 35 Batchelder Rd Boxford MA 01921

HENNING, BARBARA J., b. Detroit, Oct. 26, 1948, d. Robert Henry and Ferne Elizabeth (Hostetter) Henning; m. Allen Lee Saperstein, Dec. 27, 1972; children—Linnee, Michah. Contrbr. poetry, short fiction to Straits, Mich. Qtly Rvw, Labyris, Mockersatz, other publs. Short fiction coll. Smoking in the Twilight Bar, 1988. BA, Wayne State U., 1981, MA, 1983. Instr. Wayne State U., Detroit, 1981-83; adj. instr. Queens (N.Y.) Coll., 1984-85; English specialist L.I. U., Bklyn., 1985—. Recipient Tompkins Award for Fiction and Poetry, Wayne State U., 1982, 83. Mem. P&W. Home: 1912 8th Ave Apt. 3L Brooklyn NY 11215

HENRICKSEN, BRUCE CONLEY, b. Wanamingo, MN, Feb. 26, 1941, s. Donald and Janet Helen (Engstrom) H.; m. Carolyn Henricksen; children—Jessica, Teag. Author: Murray Krieger and Contemporary Critical Theory, 1986. BA, U. Minn., 1963; PhD, U. So. Calif., Los Angeles, 1970. Assoc. prof. dept. English Loyola U. New Orleans, 1970—, chmn. dept., 1978-82; ed. New Orleans Rvw, 1980—. NEH fellow, 1977, Mellon Fdn. fellow, 1980, 83. Mem. MLA. Office: Dept Eng Loyola U 6363 St Charles Ave New Orleans LA 70118

HENRIKSEN, MARY JO, b. Audubon, IA, June 23, 1954; d. Norman Leroy and Dorothy Marie (Schwartz) Henriksen; m. Alan Kent Hanson, Apr. 17, 1976; children—Maren Kjestine Henriksen Hanson, Kirstine Marie Henriksen Hanson. Author: (devotions) Christ in Our Home, 1986. Editor: VOICES Newsletter, 1985—. BA, Dana Coll., Blair, Nebr., 1976. Social worker various agcys., Minn., 1976-80; dir. Mary's Day Care, Cottage Grove, Minn., 1981—dfree-lance writer, 1984—. Mem. Danish Genealogy Group (charter, steering com. 1980), Danish Immigrant Mus. Home: 8630 81st St S Cottage Grove MN 55016

HENRY, DE WITT P., b. Wayne, PA, June 30, 1941; s. John and Kathryn (Thralls) H.; m. Constance Sherbill, Aug. 25, 1973; children: Ruth Kathryn, David Jung Min. Contrbr. fiction and essays to Ploughshares, Transatlantic Rvw, Antioch Rvw, Aspect, Agni Rvw, Wilson Lib. Bulletin, Am. Book Rvw, others; ed. The Ploughshare Reader: New Fiction for the 80s. AB, Amherst Coll., 1963; AM, Harvard U., 1964, PhD, 1971. Dir. Ploughshares, Inc., Watertown, Mass, 1971—, Book Affair, Inc., 1975-83; asst. prof. English, Emerson Coll., Boston, 1983—. Lit. panelist, NEA, Washington, 1982-85; adv. panelist, NE Fdn. for Arts, Cambridge, Mass, 1983—. Edl. Fellowship award, CCLM, NYC, 1979; NEA fellow, Washington, 1979; short-listed by Sinclair prize for fiction, Natl. Book League, London, 1983. Mem. CCLM, AWP. Address: 33 Buick St Watertown MA 02172

HENRY, MARGUERITE, b. Milw.; d. Louis and Anna (Kaurup) Breithaupt; m. Sidney Crocker Henry. Author: Auno and Tauno, 1940, Dilly Dally Sally, 1940, Eight Pictured Geographies, Mexico, Canada, Alaska, Brazil, Argentina, Chile, West Indies, Panama, 1941, Geraldine Belinda, 1942, Birds at Home, 1942, rev. edit., 1972, Their First Igloo (with Barbara True), 1943, A Boy and A Dog, 1944, Justin Morgan Had a Horse, 1945, rev. edit., 1954, film 1971; Robert Fulton, Boy Craftsman, 1945, The Little Fellow, 1945, rev. edit., 1975, Eight Pictured Geographies, Australia, New Zealand, Bahama Islands, Bermuda, Brit. Honduras, Dominican Republic, Hawaii, Virgin Islands, 1946, Benjamin West and His Cat Grimalkin, 1947, Always Reddy, 1947, Misty of Chincoteague, 1947, King of the Wind, 1948 (John Newbery award), Little or Nothing from Nottingham, 1949, Sea Star: Orphan of Chincoteague, 1949, Born to Trot, 1950, Album of Horses, 1951, Portfolio of Horses, 1952, Brighty of the Grand Canyon, 1953, Wagging Tails, 1955, Cinnabar, the One O'Clock Fox, 1956, Black Gold, 1957 (Sequoyah Children's Book award 1959), Muley-Ears, Nobody's Dog, 1959, Gaudenzia, Pride of the Palio, 1960 (Clara Ingram Judson award Soc. Midland Authors 1961), Misty, 1961, Five O'Clock Charlie, 1962, All About Horses, 1962, rev. edit., 1967, Stormy, Misty's Foal, 1963, White Stallion of Lipizza, 1964, Mustang, Wild Spirit of the West, 1966 (Sequoyah children's Book award 1970), Brighty; film, 1967, Dear Readers and Riders, 1969, Album of Dogs, 1970, San Domingo, the Medicine Hat Stallion, 1972 (Soc. Midland Authors award 1973), Stories from Around the World, 1974, Peter Lundy and the Medicine Hat Stallion; film, 1977; One Man's Horse, 1977, The Illustrated Marguerite Henry, 1980 (Recipient So. Calif. Council Lit. for Children award 1973), A Pictorial Life Story of Misty, 1976, The Story of a Book; 19-minute documentary, 1979; Marguerite Henry's Treasury, 1982, Our First Pony, 1984. Office: R-McNally 8255 Central Pk Ave Skokie IL 60076

HENSLEIGH, SARAH ESTHER, b. Blanchard, IA, Mar. 7, 1911, d. Lawrence Mortimer and Margaret (Jeffrey) Hensleigh. Contrbr. to Our Western World's Most Beautiful Poems, Our Twentieth Century's Greatest Poems, 1982, Page County Iowa History, 1984; ed. Iowa Poetry Day Assn. Brochure of Poems, 1975-83. BS,

Northwest Mo. State U., 1937; MA, State U. Iowa, 1941. Tchr. elementary schl., Iowa, 1930, 1933-36, secondary schl., Iowa, 1937-46; Page Cty. Supt. Schls., Clarinda, Iowa, 1946-75. Recipient Golden Poetry award, 1985. Home: 410 Linden Ave Shenandoah IA 51601

HENSLEY, JOE L., b. Bloomington, IN, Mar. 19, 1926; s. Ralph Ramon and Frances Mae (Wilson) H.; m. Charlotte Bettinger, June 18, 1950; 1 son, Michael Joseph. Author: The Color of Hate, 1960, Deliver Us To Evil, 1970, Legis. Body, 1972, The Poison Summer, 1974 (NY Times Best of the Year listing, 1974), Song of Corpus Juris, 1975, The Black Roads, 1976, Rivertown Risk, 1976, A Killing in Gold, 1978 (NY Times summer Best listing, 1978), Minor Murders, 1980, Outcasts, 1981, Final Doors (short stories), 1981, Robak's Cross, 1985, Robak's Fire, 1986, The Color of Hate (updated version), 1987; contrbr. more than 60 short stories to Ellery Queen Mag, Alfred Hitchcock Mag, Mag of Fantasy and Sci. Fiction. BA, Ind. U., 1950, LLB, 1955. Prtnr. Metford & Hensley, Madison, Ind., 1955-72, Ford, Hensley, Todd, 1972-75; judge pro tem 40th Circuit, Versailles, Ind., 1975-76, 5th Judicial Circuit, Madison, 1977—. State rep., Ind. Genl. Assembly, 1961-62; prosecutor, 5th Judicial Circuit, Madison, 1963-66. Served USN, 1944-46 and 1951-52 Korean War. Mem. Ind. Judges Assn. (pres. 1983-84), MWA (bd. dirs.). Address: 2315 Blackmore Madison IN 47250

HENTOFF, MARGOT, b. NYC, July 5, 1930; d. David B. and Theresa (Lazarus) Goodman: M. Devi Wolynski (div. July 1959); children: Mara Wolynski, Lisa Wolynski; m. Nat Hentoff, Aug. 15, 1959; children: Nicholas, Thomas. Columnist: Village Voice, 1966-69, 74—; contrbr. movie and book rvws. to Vogue, 1969-70; TV and book rvws. N.Y. Rvw of Books, 1968—; contrbg. editor: Am. Jnl, 1972—; author: essays and short stories. Student, Syracuse U., 1947-50, New Schl. for Social Research, 1950-53. Address: 25 Fifth Ave New York NY 10003

HENTOFF, NATHAN IRVING, b. Boston, June 10, 1925; s. Simon and Lena (Katzenberg) H.; m. Miriam Sargent, 1950 (div. 1950); m. Trudi Bernstein, Sept. 2, 1954 (div. Aug. 1959); children: Jessica, Miranda; m. Margot Goodman, Aug. 15, 1959; children: Nicholas, Thomas. Author: The Jazz Life, 1961, Peace Agitator: The Story of A.J. Muste, 1963, The New Equality, 1964, Jazz Country, 1965, Call the Keeper, 1966, Our Children Are Dying, 1966, Onwards, 1967, A Doctor Among the Addicts, 1967, I'm Really Dragged but Nothing Gets Me Down, 1967, Journey into Jazz, 1968, A Political Life: The Education of John V. Lindsay, 1969, In The Country of Ourselves, 1971, State Secrets: Police Surveillance in America, 1973, This School Is Driving Me Crazy, 1975, Jazz Is, 1976, Does Anybody Give a Damn? Nat Hentoff on Education, 1977, The First Freedom: The Tumultuous History of Free Speech in America, 1980, Does This School Have Capital Punishment?, Blues for Charles Darwin, 1982, The Day They Came to Arrest the Book, 1982; contrbr. with others. BA with highest honors, Northeastern U., 1945; postgrad., Harvard U., 1946; Fulbright fellow, Sorbonne, Paris, 1950. Writer radio sta. WMEX, 1944-53; assoc. editor Down Beat mag., 1953-57; co-founder, co-editor The Jazz Review, 1958-60; staff writer Village Voice, 1957—; staff writer The New Yorker, 1960—. Editor: (with Nat Shapiro) Hear Me Talkin' to Ya, 1955, The Jazz Makers, 1957, (with Albert McCarthy) Jazz, 1959, The Collected Essays of A.J. Muste, 1966. Mem. steering com. Reporters Com. for Freedom of Press. Mem. AL Am., AFTRA. Address: 25 Fifth Ave New York NY 10003

HERBERT, MICHAEL KINZLY, b. Battle Creek, MI, Dec. 1, 1942; s. Walter N. and Elaine F. (Hamblet) H.; m. Lana Ann Viereg Stanton, May 7, 1966; children—Nancy Ann, Susan Elaine. Author: The Riddell Guide to Physical Fitness, 1977, Mike Schmidt, The Human Vacuum, 1983. Student, Kenyon Coll., 1961-62; Kellogg Community Coll., 1962-63; BA, Western Mich. U., 1966. Sports reporter Chgo. Tribune, 1968-71; mng. editor Letterman Mag., Wheaton, Ill., 1971-72; editor Century Pub. Co. (publishing Inside Sports, Auto Racing Digest, Baseball Digest, Basketball Digest, Bowling Digest, Football Digest, Hockey Digest, Soccer Digest), Evanston, Ill., 1972—. Mem. Profl. Football Writers Am., Football Writers Assn. Am., Profl. Basketball Writers Assn. Am., U.S. Basketball Writers Assn., Profl. Soccer Reporters Assn. Am., Am. Auto Racing Writers and Broadcasters Assn., Midwest Bowling Writers, Bowling Writers Assn. Am. Office: 1020 Church St Evanston IL 60201

HERD, SHIRLEY, see Deal, Shirley Mae Herd

HERMAN, GRACE G., b. Lawrence, NY, May 12, 1926, d. Samuel Gales and Frances (Gleberman) Roberts; m. Roland B. Herman, July 22, 1945 (div. 1981); children—Gail Ellen, Joan Elizabeth. Contrbr. poetry: Yet Another Small Mag., Pembroke Mag., Purchase Poetry Rvw, numerous other periodicals; contrbr. articles to med. publs. Wrkg. on poetry manuscript. BA, Cornell U., 1945; MD, Columbia U., 1949. Examining physician employee health Met. Life Ins. Co., NYC, 1969—. Mem. PSA (mem. peer workshop group 1984, 85). Home: 370 First Ave New York NY 10010

HERMAN, MICHELLE, b. Bklyn., Mar. 9, 1955; d. Morton and Sheila Marcia (Weiss) H. Contrbr. short stories to No. Am. Rvw, Story Qtly, Plainswoman, other lit. mags. BS, Bklyn. Coll., 1976; MFA, U. Iowa, 1986. Freelance ed. various book pubs., NYC, 1976-84; instr. fiction writing Coll. Medicine, U. Iowa, Iowa City, 1984-86, dept. English, 1985-86, teaching-writing fellow, 1985-86. Recipient syndicated fiction award PEN, 1985; NEA grantee, 1986. Mem. AG. Home: 4112 Calif St Omaha NE 68131

HERNADI, PAUL, b. Budapest, Hungary, Nov. 9, 1936; s. Lajos and Zsuzsanna (Furedi) H.; m. Virginia Tucker, Aug. 18, 1964; children—Charles, Christopher. Author: Beyond Genre—New Directions in Literary Classification, 1972, Interpreting Events: Tragicomedies of History on the Modern Stage, 1985; editor: What is Literature?, 1978, What is Criticism?, 1981, The Horizon of Literature, 1982. PhD, U. Vienna, 1963, Yale U., 1967. Resident fellow Wesleyan U., Middletown, Conn., 1974. NEH fellow for ind. study and research, 1982-83. Mem. MLA, Am. Comparative Lit. Assn. Office: Dept Eng U Calif Santa Barbara CA 93106

HERNTON, CALVIN C., b. Chattanooga, Apr. 28, 1934; s. Magnolia (Tigner) Jackson; m. Mildred Webster, 1959 (dec. 1982); 1 child, Antone. Author: (poetry) The Coming of Chronos to The House of Nightsong, 1963; Sex and Racism in America, 1965; (essays) White Papers for White Americans, 1966, 80, Coming Together: Black Power, White Hate and Sexual Hangups, 1971; (sci. study) (with Joseph Berke) The Cannabis Experience, 1974; (novel) Scarecrow, 1974; (collected poetry) Medicine Man, 1976, The Sexual Mountain and Black Women Writers: Adventures in Sex, Literature, and Real Life, 1987. BA in sociology, Talledega Coll., 1954; MA in sociology, Fisk U., 1956. Wrtr.-in-residence Oberlin Coll., Ohio, 1970-72, assoc. prof. black studies, 1972-80, prof., 1980—. Mem. AG. Home: 35 N Prospect St Oberlin OH 44074

HERON, JACQUELINE BRENDA, b. Jackson, MI., Aug. 10, 1949; d. Samuel Jackson Horton and Vera Lucille (McKnight) Horton Boudrie; m.Ross Francis Heron, Oct. 3, 1980; 1 son, Eric Ross. Author: Exploring Careers in Nursing, 1986, Exploring Careers in Health and Fitness, 1987; author pamphle series for juvenile epilepsy victims. Wrkg. on fantasy novel. Assoc. in Nursing, Oakland Community Coll. Hosp. nurse, nursing adminstr., 1971-83; cons., freelance wrtr., 1984—. Mem. Soc. Tech. Communicators. Home: 30590 Helmandale St Franklin MI 48025

HERRICK, WILLIAM, b. Trenton, NJ, Jan. 10, 1915, s. Nathan and Mary (Saperstein) Horvitz; m. Jeannette E. Wellin, Aug. 31, 1948; children—Jonathan, Michael, Lisa. Novelist: The Itinerant, 1967, Strayhorn, 1968, Hermanos!, 1969, The Last to Die, 1971, Golcz, 1976, Shadows and Wolves, 1980, Love and Terror, 1981, Kill Memory, 1983, That's Life (Present Tense-Joel H. Cavior Lit. award), 1985. Mem. PEN, AG. Home: Riders Mills Rd Old Chatham NY 12136

HERRING, ROBERT H(ERSCHEL), b. Charleston, MS, March 26, 1938; s. Percy Floyd and Maureen (Davidson) H.; m. Joan Burns, Feb. 8, 1958; children: Lisa Lynn, Geoffrey. Author: Hub (novel), 1981, contrbr, Dorothy Abbott, ed, Mississippi Writers: Reflections of Youth, 1985, McCampbell's War (novel), 1986, contrbr, Douglas Pascholl and Alice Swanson, eds, Homewords: A Book of Tennessee Writers, 1986. Contrbr of sories to mags, including Colorado Qly, Laurel Review, Mountain Review, and Epoch. Attended Baylor Univ., 1955-56, and Memphis State Univ., 1958-59; BA, Mississippi Coll, 1960, MA, 1961; attended Univ. of Tenn, 1964-66. Instructor in English, Mississippi State Univ, Starkville 1962-63; instructor in English, Univ of Tenn, Knoxville, 1964-66; asst prof to prof of English, Middle Tennessee State Univ., Murfreesboro, 1966—. Vis lectr, Univ of the South, Univ. of Tenn. at Knoxville, Southwestern at Memphis, and Austin Peay State Univ. Bes novel for young adults citation from ALA, 1982, for Hub; Individual Artists fellowship from Tenn. Arts Commn, 1982; Touring Writer award from Tenn. Lit. Arts Assn, 1982-83. Home: 1918 Greenland Dr Murfreesboro TN 37132

HERRINGTON, TERRI, (Tracy Hughes), b. Belleville, IL, Dec. 7, 1957; d. Omer L. Ward and Jo Ann (Rogers) Weathersby; m. George Donald Herrington, Jan. 7, 1978; 1 dau., Michelle Denise. Author: Blue Fire, 1984, Quiet Lightning, 1986, Lovers' Reunion, 1986, A Secret Stirring, 1986, Tender Betrayer, 1986, Impressions, 1986, Head Over Heels, 1986, Stolen Moments, 1987, Ticket to a Fantasy, 1987, Tangled Triumphs, 1987, Wife Wanted, 1988, Broken Wings, 1988; novelization of Dallas TV series, All My Children TV soap opera. B.A. in English, Northeast La. U., 1981. Mem. RWA. Home: 143 Turtledove Dr Monroe LA 71203

HERRMANN, DUANE LAWRENCE, b. Topeka, Nov. 30, 1951, s. Lawrence Carl and Sylvia Juanita (Boaz) H.; m. Susan Marie Roth; children—Hilari, Justin, Trosten. Contrbg. author: Once to Every Man and Nation, 1985, Circle of Spirit, 1986, Studies in Babi and Baha'i History, 1987; ed.: Inscape of Washburn, 1986; contrbg. ed.: Spiritual Mothering Jnl, Baha'i Encyc.; contrbr. poetry, stories: Child's Way mag., New Horizons, Farm Woman News, The Passionate Few, other publs. Wrkg. on Baha'i history, juvenile novel, poetry, Houses as Perfect as. BS in edn., Ft. Hays State Coll., 1974; BA in history, Ft. Hays State U., 1985. Freelance wrtr., 1978—; lit. agt. Baranski Lit. Agcy. Ed. Kansas Baha'i, 1977-79; dir. Kansas Baha'i History Project. Pres. Headwaters Lit. Soc., Washburn U., 1985-87. Home: 9126 S.E. Shadden Rd Berryton KS 66409

HERRMANN, JOHN, ,b. Berkeley, CA, May 17, 1931; s. John Phillip Herrmann and Roberta Louise (Neuwohner) Liberto; m. Andrea Bess Watson, May 25, 1968; children by previous marriage—Deborah Autsen, Linda West, Kathryn Anne Topper. Author: (story colletion) Summer Will Rise, 1975; Office Automation, 1984. Contrbr. fiction and articles on politics, health care, info. systems/computer issues to numerous mags. including Northwest Rvw., S.D. Rvw., Management Tech. Mag. Ed., founder Chrysalis mag., 1960-64; articles ed. Hearst Mag., 1981-82; assoc. ed. trade pubs., 1982-86; ed.: Rvw. Mag., 1986—. S.F. State U., B.A., 1960, M.A., 1961; M.F.A., U. Iowa, 1964. Program founder, dir. creative wrtg. U. Mont., Missoula, 1963-66; asst. prof. State U. of N.Y., Oswego, 1966-69, Lock Haven U., PA, 1980-81; visiting prof. English, Pahlavi U., Shiraz, Iran, 1969-70; instr. English, U. Md., 1970-71; wrtr.-in-residence Cedar Crest Coll., Allentown, PA, 1971-78. Recipient Hart Crane award in poetry Am. Weave Press, 1970. Home: 12 Echo Point Little Rock AR 72210

HERRON, ROBERT LANE, b. San Francisco, Dec. 14; s. Charles Lewis and Alice Julia (Dies) H. Author: Much Ado About Dolls, 1979, Price Guide to Dolls & Paperdolls, 1981, Complete Book of Dolls, 1977, Collectible Dolls, 1976. Contrbr. articles on antiques, antique and modern dolls and toys to mags. Wrkg. on children's book, novels. Home: 709 Madison Ave NE Albuquerque NM 87110

HERSCHLER, DALE C., b. Columbus, OH, Mar. 4, 1911; children—Betty, Max, Carol. Author: (writes under pen name C. W. Dalton) The World of the Weird, 1979, The Liberated Senior Citizen, 1981, You're OK—The World's All Wrong, 1985. How to Raise a Winner, 1986. Mgr., Big Blue Books, Lakeside, CA, 1984—. Home: 13239 Vanguard Way Lakeside CA 92040

HERSEY, JOHN, b. Tientsin, China, June 17, 1914; s. Roscoe Monroe and Grace (Baird) H.; m. Frances Ann Cannon, Apr. 27, 1940 (div. Feb. 1958); children—Martin, John, Ann, Baird; m. Barbara Day Kaufman, June 2, 1958; 1 dau., Brook. Author: Men on Bataan, 1942, Into the Valley, 1943, A Bell for Adano, 1944, Hiroshima, 1946, The Wall, 1950, The Marmot Drive, 1953, A Single Pebble, 1956, The War Lover, 1959, The Child Buyer, 1960, Here To Stay, 1963, White Lotus, 1965, Too Far To Walk, 1966, Under the Eye of the Storm, 1967, The Algiers Motel Incident, 1968, Letter to the Alumni, 1970, The Conspiracy, 1972, The Writer's Craft, 1974, My Petition for More Space, 1974, The President, 1975, The Walnut Door, 1977, Aspects of the Presidency, 1980, The Call, 1985, Blues, 1987. Student, Hotchkiss Schl., 1927-32, Clare Coll., Cambridge (Eng.) U., 1936-37; BA, Yale U., 1936. Pvt. secy. to Sinclair Lewis, summer 1937; writer for Time mag., editor, 1937-44; sr. editor Life Mag., 1944-45; war and fgn. corr. Time, Life, New Yorker, 1942-46; fellow Berkeley Coll., Yale U., 1950-65, Pierson Coll., Yale, 1965—; writer-in-res. Am. Acad. in Rome, 1970-71. Recipient Pulitzer prize for fiction, 1945; others. Mem. AL Am., Am. Acad. and Inst. Arts and Letters, Am. Acad. Arts and Scis., AG. Home: 719 Windsor Lane Key West FL 33040

HERSHEY, DANIEL, b. NYC, Feb. 12, 1931; s. Frank and Anna (Scharf) H.; m. Barbara Drury, Sept. 5, 1965; children—Michael, Andrea. Author: Chem. Engring. in Medicine and Biology, 1967, My University My God, 1970, Blood Oxygenation, 1970, Everyday Science, 1971, Transport Analysis, 1973, Lifespan and Factors Affecting It, 1974, A New Age-Scale For Humans, 1980, Must We Grow Old, 1984. BS Cooper Union, 1953; PhD, U. Tenn., 1961. Asst. prof. to prof., chem. eng., Univ. Cin., 1962—, asst. to pres., 1973-75; vice-pres. BasalTech., Inc., Cin., 1983—. Served to pfc. US Army, 1956-57. Recipient Outstanding Tchr. awards, Tau Beta Pi, Cin., 1970, 72, Fulbright fellow, Wash., 1975, 1st place, Cin. Eds. Assn., 1977; received patent: Whole Body Calormeter, 1983. Mem. AAUP (pres. 1971-72), Sigma Xi (pres. 1973-75). Home: 726 Lafayette Ave Cincinnati OH 45220

HERSHEY, JONATHAN RICHARD, b. Bon Secour, AL, Apr. 14, 1956; s. Richard Charles and Patricia McGauly) H.; m. Paula Ann Blalock, Nov. 23, 1985. Editor: Old Red Kimono, 1983-87; fiction ed. The Black Warrior Review, 1979-81; contrbr. to Intro 12, Indiana Review, Beloit Fiction Jnl, Vanderbilt Street Rvw, Black Warrior Rvw. BA in English U. of Alabama, MFA in Writing. English instructor U. of Alabama (Tuscaloosa, AL) 1978-83, Floyd Jr. Coll. (Rome, GA), 1983-86; dir. of public info. Floyd Jr. Coll., 1985-87. Indiana Review Fiction Award, 1985. Home: Box 5785 Rome GA 30162

HERSHON, ROBERT MYLES, b. Bklyn., May 28, 1936; s. Mark and Barbara (Pernick) H.; m. Donna Brook, Oct. 10, 1982; children by previous marriage: Elizabeth, Jed. Author: Swans Loving-Bears Burning The Melting Deer, 1967, Atlantic Avenue, 1970, 4-Telling (with others),1971, Little Red Wagon Painted Blue, 1972, Grocery Lists, 1972, Rocks and Chairs, 1975, A Blue Shovel, 1979, The Public Hug: New and Selected Poems, 1980, How to Ride on the Woodlawn Express, 1985; contrbr. to mags. and anthologies. BS, NYU, 1957. Co-editor Hanging Loose Press, Bklyn., 1966—; exec. dir. Print Ctr., Inc., NYC, 1976—. Fellow NEA, 1980, N.Y. State Council on Arts, 1976. Home: 231 Wyckoff St Brooklyn NY 11217

HERTZ, URI L., b. Culver City, CA, Sept. 23, 1949; s. Morris Hertz and Miriam (Wasserman) Moorman. Author: (poems) Occupied Territory, 1978. Contrbr. articles to lit. mags., newspapers. Ed., pub.: Third Rail, Los Angeles, 1975—. B.A. in Comparative Lit., Immaculate Heart Coll., 1978; M.A. in Comparative Lit., U. Oreg., 1983. Home: Box 46127 Los Angeles CA 90046

HERZOG, ARTHUR, III, b. NYC, Apr. 6, 1927; s. Arthur, Jr. and Elizabeth Lindsay (Dayton) H.; 1 son by previous marriage. Author: (with others) Smoking and the Public Interest, 1963, The War-Peace Establishment, 1965, The Church Trap, 1968, McCarthy for President, 1969, The B.S. FActor, 1973, The Swarm, 1974, Earthsound, 1975, Orca, 1977, Heat, 1977, IQ 83, 1978, Make Us Happy, 1978, Glad To Be Here, 1979, Aries Rising, 1980, The Craving, 1982, L.S.I.T.T., 1983, Student, U. Ariz., 1945-46; BA, Stanford U., 1950; MA, Columbia U., 1956. Editor Fawcett Publs., 1957-59. SErved with USNR, 1944-45. Mem. AG, AL, PEN. Address: 484 W 43d ST Suite 44H New York NY 10036

HESS, KAREN JO MATISON, b. Austin, MN, Apr. 11, 1939; d. George Wilbur and Marie Regina (Barnitz) Matison; m. Sheldon Thomas Hess, 1962; children—Christine Marie, Timothy Sheldon. Author: (with Shafer and Morreau) Success in Reading, 1967, Developing Reading Efficiency, 1975; Basic Writing Skills, 1976, Appreciating Literature: As You Read It, 1978; (with Baldwin) Programmed Review for the Engineer in Training, 1978; (with Bell and Matison) Art: As You See It, 1979; (with Nelson) God's Joy in my Heart, 1980; (with Halverson) The Wedded Unmother, 1980; (with Quie) In the Potter's Hand, 1981; (with Wrobleski) Introduction to Private Security, 2d ed., 1987, Introduction to Law Enforcement and Criminal Justice, 2d ed., 1986, For the Record. Report Writing in Law Enforcement, 2d ed., 1986; (with Bennett) Investigating Arson, 1984, Criminal Investigating, 2d ed., 1986; (with Bentley) A Programmed Review for Electrical Engineering, 2d ed., 1985; (with Stallard and Scales) Dental Marketing: Ideas that Work, 1986. Editor: The Positive Manager, 1984, Creating the High Performance Team, 1987. BA, BS, U. Minn., 1961, MA, 1965, PhD, 1968. Instr., Hopkins High Schl., Minn., 1961-66, Normandale Community Coll., Bloomington, Minn., 1972—; project dir. Central Midwest Regional Ed. Lab., Mpls., 1969-71; dir. Innovative Programming Systems, Bloomington, 1971—. Active NCTE, 1961—. Mem. Bloomington C. of C. (edn. council 1978—) Assn. for Supvn. and Curriculum Dvlpmt., 1987—, Bloomington Community Education and Services Council Advisory Council and Exec. Bd., 1986—, Phi Beta Kappa. Pres, Inst. for Professional Communications, 1987—, v. pres., Milestone Pub. Co., 1987—. Home: 9001 Poplar Bridge Rd Bloomington MN 55437

HESS, LORETTA ROONEY, Editor: Business Communications: A Guide To Effective Writing, 1985, The Reference Manual For Office Workers, 1984, The Cancer Risk No One Talks About, 1984; contrbr. to various health care pubs. including Hospitals, RX Home Care, and Applied Radiology. BA, Adelphi U., 1978. Editor, Careers for Women, Los Angeles, 1978-80; editor, California Bride, Los Angeles, 1982-83; The Bride Guide, 1982; freelance editor and writer, 1980—. Mem. Women in Communications, Indep. Wrtrs. of So. Calif., Women's Natl. Book Assn., Editorial Freelancers Assn., National Federation of Press Women. Home: 5539 Village Green Los Angeles CA 90016

HESS, MARIE ELIZABETH, b. Duluth, MN, Jan. 29, 1954; d. Albert Guenther and Gisela Elisabeth (Oppens) H. Contrbr. articles to newspapers, mags. Wrkg. on novel. B.S., Duquesne U., 1976; M.S., Ohio U., 1983. Human services counselor Dept. Health and Rehabilitative Services, Orlando, FL, 1984-86, med. disability spclst., 1986—; free-lance wrtr., 1980—. Home: 312 San Rafael CT Winter Springs FL 32708

HESS, MARY BARBARA, b. Toledo, Mar. 25, 1953; d. Samuel Andrew and Annabel (Danhof) Hess. Contrbr. poetry to Poetry Enclave, Midway Rvw, Overtures, The Third Eye, San Fernando Poetry Jnl, others. BA, Kalamazoo Coll., 1975, MS in Mktg. Communications, Roosevelt U., 1982. Address: 509 Wapella Ave Mt Prospect IL 60056

HESSELBACH, BRUCE WILLIAM, b. Queens, NY, Sept. 29, 1950, s. William Bruce and Margaret Loretta (Walsh) H.; m. Carol Louise Streeter, June 3, 1972; children—Erica Nancy, Brian Jeffrey. Contrbr. poetry to Waterways, 1985, 1986, 1987, Poetic Justice, 1985, The Lyric, 1986, Reflect, 1986. BA, Yale U., 1972; J.D., Villanova U., Pa., 1975. Atty. firm Easton & Echtman, P.C., NYC,1976—. Recipient James Ashmun Veech prize Yale U., 1971. Mem. LI Poetry Collective. Home: 145-14 33rd Ave Flushing NY 11354

HESSION, EILEEN MELIA, b. Rockaway, NY, d. John and Marguerite (Rourke) Melia; m. Peter Hession, Apr. 14, 1973; 1 dau.—Amanda. Author: A History of New Hyde Park, 1983; contrbr. to Family Circle, Catholic Digest, Baby Talk, Readers' Digest, Saturday Evening Post, Instructor, Big Idea, True Story, National Enquirer, Long Island Fisherman, NY Times, Newsday. BS, SUNY, Plattsburgh, 1971; MA, Hofstra U., Hempstead, N.Y., 1976. Tchr. New Hyde Park (N.Y.) schls., 1971-85. Mem. adv. bd. Newsday, 1982—; ed. cons. Harcourt, Brace, Jovanovich, 1985—. Mem. Long Beach Wrtrs.' Assn. (pres. 1983-85). Home: 516 W Beech St Long Beach NY 11561

HESSION, JOSEPH MICHAEL, b. San Francisco, May 2, 1955, s. Joseph Michael and Dianne (Hopkins) H.; m. Vicki K. Morgan, Nov. 24, 1984. Author: Forty Niners: Looking Back, 1985, The Rams: From Cleveland to Los Angeles, 1986. BA in English Lit., U. Calif., Santa Cruz, 1984. Staff wrtr. City on a Hill Press, Santa Cruz, 1979-81, The Citizen, Solana Beach, Calif., 1981-83; ed. Caveat, San Francisco, 1983-84; wrtr., ed. Foghorn Press, San Francisco, 1984—. Served as sgt. USMC, 1973-77. Recipient Spcl. Merit award Calif. Newspaper Pub. Assn., 1981. Mem. Soc. Profl. Journalists, COSMEP, Assn. Ind. Pubs., Media Alliance, Profl. Football Researchers Am. Home: 2687 45th Ave San Francisco CA 94116

HESTER, MARTIN LUTHER, (Mark Emerson), b. Greensboro, NC, Aug. 18, 1947; s. Martin Luther and Avis Marie (Emerson) H.; m. Marsha Anne Hutchins, July 1, 1966 (div. 1978), 1 dau., Leigh Anne. Author: Penny Progressions (poetry), 1973, Looking at You (novel), 1984; contrbr. poetry, fiction, criticism to many publs. inclg. Am. Scholar, Confrontation, Minn. Rvw, Chariton Rvw, So. Humanities Rvw, Denver Qtly. Student Guilford Coll., 1966-67, U. NC-Greensboro, 1967-71. Cons. ed. Tudor Pubs., Greensboro, 1986—. Recipient St. Andrews prize, St. Andrews Rvw, 1976, Kans. Qtly fiction award, 1985. Mem. AWP, Soc. Children's Book Writers. Address: 3007 Taliaferro Rd Greensboro NC 27408

HESTER-MITICH, LOUIS JOHN, (del Chivo Viejo), b. Chgo., Jan. 19, 1929; s. Jack Mitich and Margaret (quinn) Hester; m. Maria Angelina Perez, Nov. 5, 1962 (div. 1985); children-Frederick, Ana Maria, Dawn, Wendy, David, Daniel. Contrbr. poems to numerous anthols.; author: Blossom Fell/Merida, my Merida (Mexico)/Lady by the Sea; musical lyrics. Merchant marine; Airborne soldier. B.A., Roosevelt U., graduated 1947. Sales manager, stock exchange computers Teleregister, 1960-65; commodity/stock broker rep. Merrill-Lynch, South Florida, 1965-1970, retired. Mem. FFWA, N.Y. Poetry Assn., Walt Whitman Soc. Office: Box 144635 Coral Gables FL 33114

HETTICH, MICHAEL, b. Bklyn., Sept. 25, 1953, s. Arthur M. and Mary Elizabeth H.; m. Colleen Hettich, Aug. 2, 1980; 1 son, Matthew. Author: Habitat (poems), 1986, Lathe (poems), 1987; ed.: Moonsquilt Press Poetry Chapbook Series, 1978—; contrbr. poetry: How to Read A Poem (by Burton Rafel), 1984, Pulpsmith, Longhouse, New Letters, other lit mags. BA, Hobart Coll., 1975; MA, U. Denver, 1979. Tchr. public schls. North Miami Beach, Fla., 1982—; mem. faculty Univ. Without Walls, North Miami Beach, 1985—; tchr. writing Broward Community Coll., Ft. Lauderdale, Fla., 1985—. Home: 16401 NE 4th Ave North Miami Beach FL 33162

HEWITT, JERENE CLINE, b. Chinook, MT, Dec. 25, 1917; d. Charles G. and Dorothy Elizabeth (Strother) Grobee; m. Ronald A. Cline, Oct. 28, 1938 (div. 1960); children—Alan, Scott, Mike; m. 2d, William F. Hewitt, June 25, 1977. Author: Selected Poems, 1968, Essentials for English Papers, 1972 (2d ed. 1974, five printings), The Epigram in English, 1982; editor: Tempo, 1969-70, cons. Houghton Mifflin, 1972-73; Buzza Cardoza, 1968-70; contrbr. anthologies Lights and Shadows, A Celebration of Cats, Poetry Ventured, Pegasus, America Sings, Poetry Mensa (London); contrbr. prose to Reader's Digest, McCall's, Ladies Home Jnl, Family Circle, Bridge World; contrbr. poetry to Today's Poets, Chgo. Tribune, Poet Lore, Yankee, Christian Sci. Monitor, LA Times, Dun's Bulltn., Poet, Galley Sail Rvw, Westways, Interim, Reader's Digest. BA, U. Calif.-Irvine, 1966, MFA, 1968, PhD, 1981. Free-lance writer and ed., 1948—; tchg. asst. to assoc. Univ. Calif., Irvine, 1966-68; asst. prof. Calif. State Univ., Los Angeles, 1968-71; asst. prof., assoc. prof., prof., dir. creative writing program, Pasadena City Coll., Calif., 1971-83, prof. emerita, 1983—; prtnr. Words Inc., Whittier, Calif., 1977—. Mem. AAP, AAUP, MLA, AWP, Mensa, Whittier Writer's Club (pres. 1962-64; workshop leader, poetry workshop, 1984-86), 25th annual Writers Conf. (dir. 1979). Address: 13713 Philadelphia Whittier CA 90601

HEYEN, WILLIAM H., b. Bklyn, Nov. 1, 1940; m. Hannelore Greiner, 1962; 2 children. Author: Depth of Field, 1970, A Profile of Theodore Roethke (ed.), 1971, Noise in the Trees: Poems and a Memoir, 1974, American Poets in 1976, 1976, The Swastika Poems, 1977, Long Island Light: Poems and a Memoir, 1979, The City Parables, 1980, Lord Dragonfly: Five Sequences, 1981, Erika: Poems of the Holocaust, 1984, The Generation of 2000: Contemporary American Poets (ed.), 1984, The Chestnut Rain, 1986, Vic Holyfield and the Class of 1957, 1986; contrbr. poems, prose to periodicals and lit mags, including The New Yorker, Harper's, The Nation, Poetry, Iowa Rvw, TriQtly. BS, Ed., SUNY Coll. at Brockport, 1961; MA, Eng., Ohio Univ., 1963; PhD, Eng., Ohio Univ., 1967. Fulbright lectureship (Germany), 1971, NEA fellowship, 1973, 84, Guggenheim fellowship, 1977, NY Fdn. for the Arts fellowship, 1985. Prof. English, SUNY Coll. at Brockport, 1967—. Home: 142 Frazier St Brockport NY 14420

HEYMANN, C. DAVID, see Heymann, Clemens Claude

HEYMANN, CLEMENS CLAUDE, (C. David Heymann), b. NYC, Jan. 14, 1945, s. Ernest Frederick and Renee Kitty (Vago) H.; m. Jeanne Ann Lunin, Nov. 10, 1974; 1 dau., Chloe Colette. Author: The Quiet Hours (poetry), 1968, Ezra Pound: The Last Rower, 1976, American Aristocracy: The Lives and Times of James Russell, Amy and Robert Lowell, 1980, Poor Little Rich Girl: The Life and Legend of Barbara Hutton, 1984; contrbr. numerous articles, rvws. to mags. and newspapers. Wrkg. on biography of Jacqueline Kennedy Onassis. BS, Cornell U., 1966; MFA, U. Mass., 1969. Lectr. dept. English SUNY-Stony Brook, 1969-76, Antioch Coll., NYC, 1979-80. Recipient Borestone Mountain poetry award, 1979, ALA citation, 1980. Mem. NWU, PEN. Home: 360 Central Park W New York NY 10025

HEYMONT, GEORGE, (Bob Cartland, Tessi Tura), b. Bklyn., July 8, 1947, s. Joseph and Rose Hilda (Schreibman) H. Contrbr. articles to Westways, Executive, Opera News, Stallion, other mags. and newspapers. BA, Bklyn. Coll., 1969. Fine arts ed. Bay Area Reporter, San Francisco, 1977—; contrbg. ed. Amtrak Express, Huntington, N.Y., 1985—, People Expressions, Miami, Fla., 1985-87. Recipient Cable Car award, 1979, 82, 83. Mem. Gay Press Assn. (Journalism award 1983), Music Critics Assn. Home: 487 B Dolores St San Francisco CA 94110

HIAT, ELCHIK, see Katz, Menke

HICKMAN, IRENE, b. IA, d. Urban and Effie Jane (Ray) Hill; m. Robert Giles, June 27, 1937 (div. 1951); children—Shelley Emerson, Sherwood Nelson; m. 2d, Jack Hickman, Dec. 3, 1951; 1 son, Alan Jack. Author: Mind Probe-Hypnosis, 1983; ed pub., Free Spirit (by Antoinette May), 1985; ed. Regression Therapy, 1986. BA, Simpson Coll., Indianola, Iowa; DO, Coll. Osteopathic Physicians and Surgeons, Los Angeles. Sole practice medicine, Los Angeles and Sacramento, 1949—66; county assessor, Sacramento County, 1966—71; ed., mgr. Hickman Systems, Kirksville, MO, 1983—; jnl. ed. Assn. for Past Life Research and Therapy, Riverside, Calif., 1985—; lectr., workshop leader. Home: 4 Woodland Ln Kirksville MD 63501

HICKMAN, JEANNINE FRANCES, b. East St. Louis, IL, Feb. 12, 1944; d. James Franklin South and Jeanne Frances (Wahl) Walter; m. George Ezra Hickman, Aug. 8, 1968; children—Steven, Kevin, Dwayne, Lisa, Scott. Contrbr. poems to anthols, Student Muskingun Area Technical Coll., 1981. Ednl. aide Mid-East Ohio Vocational Schl., Cambridge, 1986—. Recipient Silver Poet award World of Poetry, 1986, Golden Poet award, 1987; 1st place for essay Heart of Ohio Girl Scouts, Zanesville, 1986. Mem. Cambridge Wrtrs. Workshop (pres.). Home: 6007 Bloomfield Rd Cambridge OH 43725

HICKOK, FLOYD A., b. Defiance, OH, Sept. 22, 1907; m. Mary M. Hickok, Sept. 3, 1985. Author: numerous technical manuals for electronic eqpt., 1946-72; Handbook of Solar and Wind Energy, 1973, Buywise Guide to Solar Energy, 1974, Home Improvement for Conservation and Solar Energy, 1976, Your Energy Efficient Home, 1979; (plays) An Office Romance, 1930, The Trumpet Song, 1984, General Store on Hog Wallow Creek, 1986. AB, Defiance Coll., 1930; MA, Ohio State Univ., 1945. Dept. mgr., Laboratory for Electronics, 1946-68; tech. wrtr., Raytheon, 1968-72. USN, 1942-62, Lt. Cdr. Mem. Soc. Tech. Wrtrs. (pres. 1960).

Home: 6400 46th Ave N Kenneth City FL 33709

HICKS, CLIFFORD BYRON, b. Marshalltown, IA, Aug. 10, 1920; s. Nathan LeRoy and Kathryn Marie (Carson) H.; m. Rachel G. Reimer, May 12, 1945; children: David P., Douglas L., Gary R. Author: Do-It-Yourself Materials Guide, 1955, First Boy on the Moon, 1958, The Marvelous Inventions of Alvin Fernald, 1960, Alvin's Secret Code, 1963, The World Above, 1965, Alvin Fernald, Foreign Trader, 1966, Alvin Fernald, Mayor for a Day, 1969, Peter Potts, 1972, Alvin Fernald, Superweasel, 1974, Alvin's Swap Shop, 1976, Alvin Fernald, TV Anchorman, 1980, The Wacky World of Alvin Fernald, 1981; also author fiction and non-fiction in mags.; editor: Popular Mechanics Do-It-Yourself Encyc. BS cum laude, Northwestern U., 1942. With Popular Mechanics mag., Chgo., 1945—, editor, 1960-63, spcl. publs. editor, 1963—. Served to maj. USMCR, 1942-45. Decorated Silver Star. Mem. Soc. Midland Authors. Home: Rt 1 Box 171 Brevard NC 28712

HIDALGO, LIVERSON, see Haynes, Lincoln Murray

HIGDON, DAVID LEON, b. Oklahoma City, OK, March 22, 1939; s. E. Ray and Gertrude Vernoyce (Petricek) H.; m. Mary Ann Johnston, Aug. 29, 1958; children—David Lynn, Liana Claire, Andrew Ray. Author: Time and English Fiction, 1977, Shadows of the Past in Contemporary British Fiction, 1984, A Concordance to Joseph Conrad's "Under Western Eyes," 1983, other lit studies. BA, Oklahoma City U., 1962; MA, U. of Kansas, 1964, PhD, 1968. Assoc. prof. Texas Tech U. (Lubbock), 1974-78, prof., 1978-83, Paul Whitfield Horn prof., 1983—. Editing/research grant NEH, 1974-77, research/travel, 1982. Mem. MLA, Rocky Mountain MLA; assoc. ed. South-Central MLA. Home: 3309 61st Lubbock TX 79413

HIGGINS, BETTY, b. Oshkosh, WI, May 25, 1925; m. Sam L. Higgins, 1946; children—Stephan Daniel, David, Patricia, Douglas. Author: The Jellybean Collection (for children 4-12), vol. 1, 1986, vol. 2, 1986, vol. 3, 1987; poetry in anthologies; contrbr. book revs., articles to newspapers in Ariz., Calif. Student Otis Art Inst., Los Angeles, 1943-45, Inst. of Children's Lit. Presenter writing workshop, Scottsdale (Ariz.) Public Schs., 1987; lectr. in children's lit. Address: Sun Star Publs Box 519 Phoenix AZ 85016

HIGGINS, GEORGE VINCENT, b. Brockton, MA., Nov. 13, 1939; s. John Thompson and Doris (Montgomery) H.; m. Elizabeth Mulkerin, Sept. 4, 1965 (div. Jan. 1979); children: Susan, John; m. Loretta Lucas Cubberley, Aug. 23, 1979. Author: The Friends of Eddie Coyle, 1972, The Digger's Game, 1973, Cogan's Trade, 1974, A City on a Hill, 1975, The Friends of Richard Nixon, 1975, The Judgment of Deke Hunter, 1976, Dreamland, 1977, A Year of So With Edgar, 1979, Kennedy for the Defense, 1980, The Rat On Fire, 1981, The Patriot Game, 1982, A Choice of Enemies, 1984, Penance for Jerry Kennedy, 1985, Impostors, 1986; columnist: Boston Herald Am., 1977-79, Boston Globe, 1979-85, Wall Street Jour., 1984. A.B., Boston Coll., 1961, J.D., 1967; M.A., Stanford U., 1965; D.H.L. (hon.), Westfield State Coll., Mass., 1986. Reporter Providence Jnl., 1962-63; corr. A.P., Springfield, Mass., 1963-64, Boston, 1964-66. Mem. WG Am. Home: 15 Brush Hill Ln Milton MA 02186

HIGGINS, PAULA ELIZABETH, b. White Plains, NY, Jan. 17, 1954; d. Joseph Roland and Lillian (Krueger) Belarge; m. Jeffrey John Higgins, Oct. 2, 1976; children—Christopher, Daniel. Contrbr. features, news stories, investigative pieces Herald Statesman, 1981, Enterprise, 1981—, NYTimes Westchester Opinion Page, 1984—, Greenburgh Inquirer, 1985, Scarsdale Inquirer, 1987, Spotlight Mag., feature art., Jan. 1987. BA, soc. & psychology, Mercy Coll., 1975. Personnel admin., Polychrome Corp., 1975-79; investigative reptr., Enterprise (Hastings, NY), 1981—, assoc. ed., 1983—. Mem. Hastings Creative Arts Council, Natl. Wrtrs. Club, Soc. of Profl. Jnlsts. Home: 64 Prince St Hastings-on-Hudson NY 10706

HIGGINS, RICHARD CARTER, (Dick Higgins), b. Jesus Pieces, Cambridge, England, March 15, 1938; s. Carter Chapin and Katharine (Bigelow) H.; m. Alison Knowles, May 31, 1960 (div. 1970); children: Hannah and Jessica (twins). Active in Happenings (theater) movement, 1958-60; co-founder Fluxus movement, 1961—; U.S. editor De-Collage Mag., Germany, 1962—; founder Something Else Press, NYC, 1964, pub., 1964-74; prof. publishing Calif. Inst. Arts, 1970-71; founder Unpub. Edits. (defunct in 1986), West Glover, Vt., 1973—; fellow Center for 20th Century Studies, U. Wis., Milw., 1977. Author (with Richard Maxfield); first electronic opera Stacked Deck, 1958-59; What Are Legends, 1960, Jefferson's Birthday/Postface, 1964, FOEW & OMBWHNW, 1968, Die Fabelhafte Getraume von Taifun-Willi, 1969, Computers for the Arts, 1970, Amigo, 1972, A Book about Love & War & Death, 1972, The Ladder to the Moon, 1973, For Eugene in Germany, 1973, Modular Poems, 1975, Classic Plays, 1976, Legends and Fishnets, 1976, George Herbert's Pattern Poems: In Their Tradition, 1977, Everyone Has Sher Favorite (His or Hers), 1977, A Dialectic of Centuries: Notes Towards a Theory of The New Arts, 1978, The Epickall Quest of the Brothers Dichtung, 1978, Hymns to the Night, 1978, some recent snowflakes (and other things), 1979, A Dialectic of Centuries, 1979, Piano Album, 1980, Of Celebration of Morning, 1980, Ten Ways of Looking at a Bird, 1981, 26 Mountains for Viewing the Sunset From, 1981, Sonata for Prepared Piano, 1982, Variations on a Natural Theme, 1982, Selected Early Works, 1982; Horizons: The Poetics and Theory of the Intermedia, 1983, Poems, Plain and Fancy, 1985, Fluxus: Theory and Reception, 1987, Pattern Poems: Guide to an Unknown Literature, 1987, Happytime the Medicine Man, 1988; also numerous plays, movies; transl.: Novalisi Hymns to the Night, 1978; editor: (with Wolf Vostell) Pop Architektur, 1969, Fantastic Architecture, 1971. Student, Yale, 1957; BS, Columbia, 1960; postgrad., Manhattan Schl. Printing, 1960-61; AM in English, NYU, 1977. Mem. N.Y. Audiovisual Soc. (v.p.), N.Y. Mycol. Soc., Am. Mongolian Soc. Home: Box 27 Barrytown NY 12507

HIGGINSON, WILLIAM J., b. NYC, Dec. 17, 1938, s. William J. and Nellie May (Roby) H.; m. Penny Harter, May 31, 1980; 1 dau., Elizabeth Ann. Author: Itadakimasu: Essays on Haiku and Senryu in English, 1971, Death Is & Approaches to the Edge (poems and essay), 1981, Paterson Pieces: Poems 1969-1979, 1981, The Haiku Handbook: How to Write, Share, and Teach Haiku, 1985, The Healing and Other Poems, 1986, Ten Years' Collected Haiku, vol. 1, 1987; co-ed. with Penny Harter: Union County Literature Today, 1980, Ten North Jersey Poets, 1981; ed., translator: Twenty-Five Pieces of Now: Classical Japanese Haiku with English Translations by Hian, 1968, thistle brilliant morning, 1973; contrbr. poetry, essays to anthologies. BA, So. Conn. State Coll.; cert. in Japanese studies, Yale U. Ed. Haiku Mag., Paterson, N.J., 1971-76; cons. N.J. State Council on Arts, Trenton, 1973-83; pub. From Here Press, Paterson and Fanwood, N.J., 1975—; adminstr. Office Cultural and Heritage Affairs, Union County, N.J., 1983—; leader writing workshops, speaker in field. Served with USAF, 1959-63. N.J. State Council on Arts poetry fellow, 1977-78. Mem. PEN, PSA, Haiku Soc. Am. (past pres.). Office: Box 219 Fanwood NJ 07023

HIGH, MONIQUE RAPHEL, b. NYC, May 3, 1949; d. David and Dina (Cornfield) Raphel; m. (1) Robert Duncan High, June 6, 1969 (div. March 7, 1981), (2) Gregory Raiport, Nov. 8, 1985 (div. Oct. 22, 1987), (3) Ben Walter Pesta II, 1988; children: (first marriage) Nahalie Danielle. Author: novels, The Four Winds of Heaven, 1980, Encore, 1981, The Eleventh Year, 1983, The Keeper of the Walls, 1985, Thy Father's House, 1987.AB, Barnard College, 1969. Asst pub. rels dir, Thomas More College, Fort Mithell, Ky., 1969-70; writer, 1970—. Mem bd dirs, Los Angeles Commn on Assaults Against Women. Member: AL of America, AG, Alliance Francaise of Pasadena, League of Women Voters of Pasadena. Home: 431 South Rexford Dr Beverly Hills CA 90212

HIGHAM, ROBIN, b. London, June 20, 1925; arrd. U.S., 1940, naturalized, 1954; s. Frank David and Margaret Anne (Stewart) H.; m. Barbara Davies, Aug. 5, 1950; children—Susan Elizabeth, Martha Anne, Carol Lee. Author: Britain's Imperial Air Routes, 1918-39, 1960, The British Rigid Airship, 1908-31, 1961, Armed Forces in Peacetime: Britain 1918-39, 1963, The Military Intellectuals in Britain: 1918-39, 1966, (with David H. Zook) A Short History of Warfare, 1966, The Compleat Academic, 1975, Air Power: A Concise History 1973, 84, (with Mary Cisper and Guy Dresser) A Brief Guide to Scholarly Editing, 1982; Diary of a Disaster, 1986; editor: Bayonets in the Streets, 1969, Civil Wars in the Twentieth Century, 1972, A Guide to the Sources of British Military History, 1971, A Guide to the Sources of U.S. Military History, 1975, supplements, 1981, 85, The U.S. Army in Peacetime, 1975, Intervention or Abstention, 1975, (with Jacob W. Kipp) Soviet Aviation and Air Power, 1977, Flying Combat Aircraft, vol. 1, 1975, vol. 2, 1978, vol. 3, 1981; cons. and author of 23 entries, Dictionary of Business Biography, 1980-85. AB cum laude, Harvard U., 1950, PhD, 1957; MA, Claremont Grad. Schl., 1953. Instr. Webb Schl. Calif., 1950-52; grad. asst. in oceanic history Harvard U., 1952-54; instr. U. Mass., 1954-57; asst. prof. U. N.C., Chapel Hill, 1957-63; assoc. prof. Kansas State U., 1963-66, prof., 1966—; historian Brit. Overseas Airways Corp., 1960-66, 76-78; editor Mil. Affairs, 1968-88, emeritus 1989, Aerospace Historian, 1970—; editor, co-pub. Jnl of West, 1977—; adv. editor Tech and Culture, 1967—; founder, pres. Sunflower Univ. Press, 1977—; mil. adv. editor Univ. Press Ky., 1970-75; cons. Epic of Flight, Time/Life Books, 1980-82; mem. publs. com. Conf. Brit. Studies, 1965—; adviser Core Collection for Coll. Libraries, 1971-72; pres. cons. com. Revue Intl. d'Histoire Militaire, 1976-85. Organizer Gov.'s Conf. on Future of Rural Kans., 1975. Served with RAF, 1943-46. Soc. Sci. Research Council natl. security policy research fellow, 1960-61. Mem. Org. Am. Hist. (permanent liaison officer with Soc. History Tech.), Am. Aviation Hist Soc., Aviation and Space Writers Assn., Soc. Hist. Tech. (liaison officer with Am. Hist. Assn.), Friends of RAF Mus. (life mem.), trustee of the Air Force Hist. Fdn., U.S. Naval Inst., Soc. Army History Research (corr. mem. council 1980—), Am. Mil. Inst., AIAA (standing com. history 1973—), Am. Com. History Second World War (dir. 1973-75, 79-82, archivist 1977—), U.S. Commn. on Mil. History (chmn pubs. com), Soc. Scholarly Pub. (natl. publs. com. 1980-82). Home: 2961 Nevada St Manhattan KS 60502

HIGHBERGER, CRAIG BENDER, b. Pitts., Oct. 24, 1953; s. Frank McMaster and Martha Jean (Bender) Highberger. Ed., NYU. Wrtr., producer KTTC-TV, Rochester, Minn., 1977-80; freelance wrtr., 1980-84; wrtr., producer Kemper Group, Long Grove, Ill., 1984-86, Bell & Howell Co., Chgo., 1986—. Recipient cert. of merit Chgo. Internat. Film & Video Festival, 1985, 86. Mem. Intl. Television Assn. (Gold Reel award 1982). Home: 913 W Van Buren St Chicago IL 60607

HIGHWATER, JAMAKE, b. MT, Feb. 14, 1942; s. Jamie and Amana (Bonneville) H. Author: Indian America: A Cultural and Travel Guide, 1975, Song From the Earth: American Indian Painting, 1976 (Anisfield-Wolf Award, Cleveland Foundation), Ritual of the Wind: No. American Indian Ceremonies, Music and Dances, 1977, Many Smokes, Many Moons, 1978 (Jane Addams Peace Book award), Dance: Rituals of Experience, 1978; novel Journey to the Sky: Stephens and Catherwood's Rediscovery of the Maya World, 1978; The Sweet Grass Lives On: 50 Contemporary North American Indian Artists, 1980, Masterpieces of American Indian Painting, 2 vols., 1978-80, The Primal Mind: Vision and Reality in Indian America, 1981 (Virginia McCormick Scully Lit. award 1982); novels Anpao: An American Indian Odyssey, 1977 (Newbery Honor award and named Best Book for Young Adults, ALA, 1978), The Sun, He Dies: The End of the Aztec World, 1980 (named Best Book for Young Adults, Schl. Library Jnl 1980); Legend Days, 1984, The Ceremony of Innocence, 1985, I Wear the Morning Star, 1986, Eyes of Darkness, 1986; On Popular Music Rock and Other Four Letter Words, 1968, Mick Jagger: The Singer Not the Song, 1973; contrbr. critiques to various lit. jnls; classical music editor: Soho Weekly News, 1975-79; sr. editor Fodor Travel Guides, 1970-75; contrbg. editor: N.Y. Arts Jnls, 1978-86, Indian Trader, 1977-80, Stereo Rvw, 1972-79, Native Arts/West, 1980-81. Writer of TV series Native Land and The Primal Mind, PBS Network, 1983-86. Mem. AFTRA, Authors Guild, Dramatists Guild, Authors League, PEN (exec. bd. Am. Ctr. 1983-84). Office: Box 2026 Canal St Sta New York NY 10013

HILBERRY, CONRAD ARTHUR, b. Melrose Park, IL, Mar. 1, 1928; s. Clarence Beverley and Leah Ruth (Haase) H.; m. Marion Bailey, Apr. 21, 1951; children: Marilyn, Jane, Ann. Author: (poems) Encounter on Burrows Hill, 1968, Rust, 1974, Man in the Attic, 1980, Housemarks, 1980, The Moon Seen as a Slice of Pineapple, 1984; (children's story) Jacob's Dancing Tune, 1986, (case study) Luke Karamazov, 1987; (with M. Keeton and others) Struggle & Promise: A Future for Colleges, 1969; ed. (with others) The Third Coast: Contemporary Michigan Poetry, 1976. BA, Oberlin Coll., 1949; PhD, U. Wis., 1954. Instr., asst. prof. DePauw U., Greencastle, Ind., 1954-61; program assoc. Assoc. Colls. Midwest, Chgo., 1961-62; assoc. prof., prof. English, Kalamazoo Coll., 1962—. Recipient Mich. Arts award Mich. Fnd. for Arts, 1983; NEA fellow, 1974, 84; MacDowell Colony fellow, 1977, 83; Florence J. Lucasse fellow, 1979. Home: 1601 Grand Ave Kalamazoo MI 49007

HILL, BILL, see Lipton, W. Lawrence

HILL, CARLENE BAY, b. Brunswick, ME, Oct. 7, 1957; d. George David and Edith Mae (Larrabee) H. Contrbr. articles to mags., newspapers. including Christian Life, Commonweal, Boston Phoenix, others. Wrkg. on tourist's guide to religious history in New England. B.A., U. Mass., 1981; posgrad. Gordon-Conwell Theol. Seminary, 1984-86. Reporter The Sun, Lowell, MA, 1981-83, copy ed., 1983-85; asst. ed. New England Church Life, Boston, 1986-87, ed., 1987—. Mem. Evangelical Press Assn. Home: 9 Hudson St Malden MA 02148

HILL, CATHERINE, see Prance, June E.

HILL, CHERRY LYNN, b. Warren, MI, Nov. 5, 1947; d. Bennie F. Swider and Sally M. (Bawol) George; m. Richard P. Klimesh, Mar. 25, 1975. Author: The Formative Years: Raising & Training the Young Horse from Birth to two Years, 1987, From th Center of the Ring: A Guide to Horse Competitions from a Judge's Perspective, 1988. Contrbr. articles to trade mags. including Horseman, Quarter Horse Jnl., Chronicle of the Horse. B.S. in Animal Sci., Iowa State U., 1973. Instr. equine sci. Olds Coll., Alberta, Canada, 1976-77; instr., adminstr. equine Highland Coll., Freeport, IL, 1979-83; instr., head equestrian dept. Colo. State U., Fort Collins, 1983-85; freelance wrtr., 1985—. Mem. NWC, Wrtrs. of Round (1st place for fiction 1985), Appaloosa Horse Club (judge), Palomino Horse Breeders (judge), Intl. Bukskin Horse Assn. (judge), Natl. Cutting Horse Assn., U.S. Dressage Fedn. Recipient 1st place for fiction Sentinel Mag., 1980. Home: Box 140 Livermore CO 80536

HILL, CRAG A., b. Ithaca, NY, Aug. 25, 1957; s. Charles Stanley and Doris Rae (Manypenny) Hill; m. Beth Schneider, Jan. 1, 1983. Author: Sixixsix, 1983, I Chings and Prototypes, 1982, Dict, 1987; editor: Score, a mag. of visual poetry, twice yearly since 1983; contrbr. to Atticus Rvw, Chimera, Abacus Plus, After the End, Inkblot, other lit mags. Student U. of Wisconsin, 1977-79. Asst. photo manager Graphic Reproduction (San Francisco), 1980—; editor/publisher Score Publications (Oakland, CA), 1983—. Home: 491 Mandana Blvd No. 3 Oakland CA 94610

HILL, DOROTHY J., b. Chico, CA, May 6, 1922, d. James Franklin and Margaret Ellen (Cabaniss) Morehead; m. Mack Wier Hill, July 16, 1944; children—Kathryn, Carol, Margaret. Author: Maidu Use of Native Flora and Fauna, 1972, The Indians of Chico Rancheria, 1978; ed.: Rancho Chico Indians, 1980; ed., Concow-Maidu Indians of Round Valley—1926, 1980. BA, U. Calif.-Berkeley, 1943; MA in Anthropology, Calif. State U.-Chico, 1970. Instr. anthropology Butte Community Coll., Chico, 1969-75; lectr. Calif. State U.-Chico, 1972-75; cons. Indian history, No. Calif., 1975—. Mem. natl. League Am. Pen Women. Home: Box 3278 Chico CA 95927

HILL, EMILY KATHARINE, (Emily Katharine Harris), b. Ithaca, NY, Oct. 30, 1921, d. Cyril Beverly and Emily Linnard (Loman) Harris; m. Richard William Hill, Nov. 29, 1969. Author: The Drum Concerto (stories), 1979, Saintly Milk to Better Wine (poems), 1968, A Gypsy Sold Me Heather (poems), 1974, Walk Chant (poems), 1976. Student Phila. Mus. Schl. Art., 1949-53; BA in English Lit., Radcliffe U., 1943. Home: 451 Guinnip Ave Elmira NY 14905

HILL, HYACINTHE, (Virginia Rose Kain), b. NYC, May 24, 1920, d. Joseph Thomas and Angela Virginia (Bradley-Bruen) Cronin; m. Johan Jonas Anderson, July 15, 1940 (dec.); children: John Luke, Matthew Mark (dec.); m. 2d, John Henry Kain, Dec. 28, 1978. Author: Shoots of a Vagrant Vine (Price Book award Avalon Books), 1950, Promethea (Cameo Press award), 1957, Squaw, No More, 1975, Poetry and the Stars, 1986; ed.: Different and Flame mags., 1952-63; co-ed. The Diamond Year poetry anthology, 1971; N.Atlantic ed. Great Am. World Poets, 1973. Wrkg. on poetry collection. BA cum laude, Bklyn. Coll., 1961; MA with honors in English, Hunter Coll., 1965; ABD, PhD, Fordham U., 1969; PhD (hon.) No. Pontifical Acad., Sweden, 1969; DArts and Letters (hon.), Gt. China Arts Coll., 1969; DHumanities (hon.), Coll. Alfred the Great, Eng., 1970, LHD (hon.) L'Universite Libre d, Asie, Pakistan, 1974. Tchr. pub. schls., NYC, 1962-82. Recipient numerous awards including: York (Eng.) Poetry award, 1974, Keats Poetry prize, London, 1975; named poet laureate, Manila, Philippines, 1973, 74, 75. Mem. AAP, PSA (exec. bd. 1969-71), United Poet Laureates Intl., N.Y. Poetry Forum (recipient Eleanor Otto award 1969, 70), Natl. Soc. Lit. and the Arts. Address: Scop and Gleemam 876 Las Ovejas Terra Linda San Rafael CA 94903

HILL, ISAAC WILLIAM, b. Opelika, AL, Aug. 8, 1908; s. Isaac William and Laura Texas (Jones) H.; m. Catherine Humbird Dawson, June 25, 1932 (dec. Sept. 1974); children: Catherine Roxane Hill Hughes, Joyce Elizabeth Hill Stoner; m. Louise B. Andrews, June 22, 1979. Co-author: Mirror of War, 1961; author: (novels) Hue and Cry, 1985, Flip Side, 1986; contrbr. short fiction to Cosmopolitan, other mags., also numerous articles to mags. and newspapers. AB, Washington and Lee U., 1929. Rptr. Mobile, Ala. Press, 1929-30; copy-city ed. Washington Star, 1930-48, news. ed., 1948-62, mag. ed., 1962-68, assoc. ed., 1968-73; Washington corr. Ed. & Pub., NYC, 1974-81; book ed. Island Packet, Hilton Head, S.C., 1983—; ed.-in-residence DePauw U., 1970. Recipient Jester award Newspaper Comics Council, 1960. Mem. Am. Soc. Newspaper Eds., AP Mng. Eds. Assn. (pres. 1966-67), Natl. Press Club, Sigma Delta Chi. Home: 30 Gloucester Rd Hilton Head Island SC 29928

HILL, JUDITH, b. Gulfport, MS, Mar. 19, 1945; d. Charles Clayton and Marian Ruth (Rockwell) Tennant; m. Michael James Hill, Feb. 1, 1969. Editor: Michel Guerard's Cuisine for Home Cooks, 1983, The Cuisine of Fredy Girardet, 1984. MA, U. of MO, 1969; PhB, Wayne St. U., 1966. Dir. of publs. Ecole de Cuisine La-Varenne, Paris, 1979-84; ed.-in-chief Cook's Magazine, Bridgeport, CT, 1984—. Office: Cook's Mag 2710 North Ave Bridgeport CT 06604

HILL, MILLICENT ELIZABETH, (Elizabeth Esterbrook), b. Nashville, d. Mildred (Wharton) Moore; m. Ezekiel H. Hill, 1962 (div. 1969); children—Carroll E., David E. Contrbr. poetry to various publs.; ed. The Media, 1981, Pillar of Salt, 1983, Selected Black American/African & Caribbean Authors, 1984. BA, Fisk U., Nashville, 1962. Tchr., counselor, journalism adv. pub. schls., Los Angeles, 1966—; lectr. wrtg. project U. So. Calif., Los Angeles, 1984. Poet laureate Black Women's Bus. Coalition, Los Angeles,

1980. Home: 5402 Sanchez Dr Los Angeles CA 90008

HILL, PATRICIA, b. Delta, LA, Aug. 17, 1932, d. John Richard Hill and Bessie Alice (Robinson) Sanders; m. Paul Hill, Sept. 10, 1949 (dec. 1985); children: Dennis, Paula Hill Pogue. Author: Fix Life in the Eye (poetry), 1976, How to Help Your Child in School, 1983, A Handbook for Parents, 1979; contrbr. poetry to Pegasus. Wrkg. on novel, children's book, greeting cards. AA, Itawamba Jr. Coll.; BA, MEd, U. Miss. Tchr. Pontotoc County (Miss.) Schls., 1976—. Home: Rt 3 Box 54 Houlka MS 38850

HILL, PATRICIA SUSAN, (Patrice Hill), b. Taipei, Republic of China, Ot. 27, 1954; d. Robert John, Jr. and Gladys (Evers) H. Contrbr. to Help: The Indispensible Almana of Consumer Info., 1980, 81, Consumer Newsweekly, Washington Credit Letter, Fedl. Reserve Week, Inside E.P.A. Weekly Report, Inside the Administration, other financial mags. and newsletters. Syndicated columnist: Help-Mate, 1979-82. B.A., Oberlin Coll., 1976. Reporter, Consumer News, Washington, 1979-82, Capitol Reports, Washington, 1982-83, Inside Washington, Washington, 1983-85, Am. Banker/Bond Buyer, Washington, 1986—. Mem. Natl. Press Club. Home: 1661 Grant Pl NW 507 Washington DC 20009

HILLERMAN, TONY, b. May 27, 1925; s. August Alfre and Lucy (Grove) H.; m. Marie Unzner, Aug. 16, 1948; children: Anne, Janet, Anthony, Monica, Stephen, Daniel. Author: The Blessing Way, 1970, The Fly on the Wall, 1971, The Boy Who Made Dragonfly, 1972, Dance Hall of the Dead, 1973, The Great Taos Bank Robbery, 1973, New Mexico, 1975, Rio Grande, 1975, ed., The Spell of New Mexico, 1976, Listening Woman, 1977, The People of Darkness, 1978, The Dark Wind, 1981, Ghostway, 1984, Skinwalkers, 1986, Indian Country, 1987. Contrbr to True, New Mexico Qtly, national Geographic, Popular Psychology, Reader's Digest, and others. Attended Oklahoma State Univ., 1943; BA, Univ. of Okla., 1946; MA, Univ. of New Mexico, 1966. Reporter, Borger (Texas) News Herald, 1948-50; political reporter in Oklahoma City, Okla., United Press, 1950-52, bur. mgr, Santa Fe, N.M., 1952-54; political reporter, later ed, New Mexican, Santa Fe, 1954-63; asst to the pres, Univ. of New Mexico, Albuquerque, 1963-66, 1976-81, chmn., dept. of journalism, 1966-73, prof. of journalism, 1981-85; writer. Member: Sigma Delta Chi, Phi Kappa Phi, Albuquerque Press Club. Edgar Allan Poe award, Mystery Writers of America, 1974, for Dane Hall of the Dea, Le Gran Prix de Literature Policiere, 1987 (best foreign mystery novelist published in French). Military service: U.S. Army, 1943-45; received Silver Star, Bronze Star, Purple Heart. Home: 2729 Texas NE Albuquerque NM 87110

HILLERT, MARGARET, b. Saginaw, MI, Jan. 22, 1920; d. Edward Carl and Ilva Lee (Sproull) H. Author 67 children's books, most rent include The Ball Book, 1982, Pinocchio, 1982, Tom Thumb, 1982, Little Red Riding Hood, 1982, The Boy and the Goats, 1982, Why We Have Thanksgiving, 1982, The Witch Who Went for a Walk, 1982, Let's Have a Play, 1982, The Funny Ride, 1982, Fun Days, 1982, The Cow that Got Her Wish, 1982, Go to Sleep, Dear Dragon, 1985, A Friend for Dear Dragon, 1985, I Need You, Dear Dragon, 1985, Come to School, Dear Dragon, 1985, Help for Dear Dragon, 1985, It's Cirus Time, Dear Dragon, 1985, Rabbits and Rainbows, 1985, Dandelions and Daydreams, 1987; Seasons, Holidays, Anytime, 1987. Contrbr. numerous poems, chapt. to mags., anthols., book. Wrkg. on 4 easy-read books on Bible themes. A.B., Wayne U., 1948; B.S. in Nursing, U. Mich., 1944. Primary tchr. public schls., Royal Oak, MI, 1948-82, retired. Recipient awards Poetry Soc. Mich., 1956, 66, 69, 70, 71, 73, 75, 79, 80. Mem. SCBW, Detroit Women Wrtrs., Emily Dickinson Soc., CRRT (awards, 1982, 83, 84, 85), Children's Lit. Assn. Home: 31262 Huntley Sq E 1224 Birmingham MI 48009

HILLIARD, GARRISON LEE, b. Cin., July 26, 1960; s. Walter Raymond, Jr. and Jeanette (MaIntosh) H. Contrbr. poems to lit. mags. Wrkg. on novel concerning Africa, short fiction. RA in English, U. Cin., 1983, M.A. in English Lit., 1986. English instr. U. Cin. Erotica wrtr., scripter for Warner Cable TV. Mem. Cin. Commn. on Arts., Contemporary Arts Center. Mem. Cin. Playwriter's Project, Arts. Consortium, Queen City Balladeers. Home: Box 25102 Cincinatti OH 45225

HILLMAN, AARON WADDELL, b. Chaffee, MO, Sept. 29, 1926, s. Basil Emory and Erthel Dora (Pearman) H.; m. Rosemary Theresa Witherow, Aug. 6, 1953; 1 son, David Emory. Contrbr. chaps.: Human Teaching for Human Learning, 1972, The Live Classroom, 1974, Educational Change, 1976; ed.: The Confluent Education Jnl, 1972-86, The Confluent Edn. Tchrs. Handbook, 1982-86, Santa Barbara Book Rvw, 1983-86; contrbr. poetry to Am. Poetry: Old and New: 1965, Am. Poets 1968, numerous others; playwright: The Swagger Stick, 1980. Wrkg. on play, poetry book. PhD, U. Calif.-Santa Barbara. Tchr. Dos Pueblos High Schl., Goleta, Calif., 1968—; pres. CEDARC, Santa Barbara, 1972-85; ed., pub. Bibliotherapy, Inc., Santa Barbara, 1974-86. Served as tchr., U.S. Army, 1944-65. Home: 833 Via Granada Santa Barbara CA 93103

HILLMAN, BRENDA LYNN, b. Tucson, AZ, Mar. 27, 1951, d. Jimmye Standard and Helen Frances (Smith) Hillman; m. Leonard Michaels, Aug. 8, 1976; 1 dau., Louisa Alice. Author: Coffee, 3 A.M., 1983, White Dress, 1985. BA magna cum laude, Pomona Coll., 1973; MFA, U. Iowa, 1976. Mem. sales staff Univ. Press Books, Berkeley, Calif., 1976-80; vis. faculty Warren Wilson Coll., Ashville, N.C., 1984; lectr. St. Mary's Coll., Moraga, Calif., 1985—. NEA writing fellow, 1984; recipient Jerome Shestach prize Am. Poetry Rvw, 1985. Mem. PSA. Home: 438 Beloit Ave Kensington CA 94708

HILLYER, CARTER SINCLAIR, b. New Orleans, Sept. 24, 1948; s. Haywood Hansel and Ellen Blair (Sinclair) H.; m. Patricia Jones, Dec. 27, 1969; children—Charles Carter, William Sinclair. Contrbr. articles to mags., newspapers including Miss. mag., Miss. Bus. Jnl, USA Today, Southern Boating, Popular Mechanics. Editor, reporter: Daily Iberian, New Iberia, La., 1973. BA, La. State U.-Baton Rouge, 1971; MA in English, U. Central Fla., 1976. Tchr., Cayman Islands High Schl., 1976-80, St. Stanislaus High Schl., Bay St. Louis, Miss., 1981-84; free-lance wrtr., Pass Christian, Miss., 1984—. Home: Box 564 Pass Christian MS 39571

HILTON, LINDA ANN, b. Chgo., Oct. 13, 1948; d. Donald Joel and E. Elaine (Mueller) Wheeler; m. R. Douglas Hilton, June 7, 1969; childen—Rachel Suzanne, Kevin James. Author: (novel) Legacy of Honor, 1985, Firefly, 1988. ontrbr. to Rave Rvws., Final Draft. Assoc. ed.: The Final Draft, 1987—. Wrkg. on novels Illuminations and Sinagua. Editorial asst. FarWestern Cons., Phoenix, 1987—; free-lance wrtr., lectr., 1984—. Mem. RWA, Wrtr.'s Refinery. Home: 2000 S Apache Rd Buckeye AZ 85326

HILTON, RONALD JAMES, b. Geneva, NY, March 28, 1932; s. Leslie Edmund Hilton and Helen Margaret (Radcliffe) Milliman; m. Norma J. Shipman Aug. 11, 1962; m. 2d, Brenda J. Vogt, Nov. 25, 1970 (div., 1985); m. 3d, Sharon G. Scott, Feb. 28, 1987; children—Jessica, Lynnette, Wendy, Paul. Author: Who We Are: What Some Educators of Adults Say About Their Characteristics, Competencies and Roles (with Alexander N. Charters), 1978. Chairman, English Dept., College of Continuing Education, Rochester Institute of Tech., 1964-70, dir., city center, 1970-76, dir. of res. and profl. dev., 1976-84, chairman, lib. arts, 1984-87. BS SUNY Geneseo, 1954, MA, U. of Ark., 1959, PhD, Syracuse U., 1981. Mem. NCTE. Home: 378 Roxborough Rd Rochester NY 14619

HILTON-REGAN, JUDITH ANN, b. St. James, MN, Sept. 21, 1938; d. Raymond Rosco and Marcielle Janette (Swensen) Teter; m. Donald Ray Regan, Nov. 1, 1959 (div. June 14, 1971); m. Donald Owen Hilton, Mar. 11, 1972; stepchildren—Melodie Lou, Harmonie Jean. Contrbr. articles to Stars & Stripes, Overseas Weekly, Lions Mag. Ed.: Chickasaw News-Herald, AK, 1974-77; assoc. ed.: Ace Newspaper, Mobile, AL, 1977. Student U. South Ala., 1974, Falkner State Coll., 1974-75. Photo-jnlst. Adutzer, Fort Walton Beach, FL, 1969, Playground Daily News, Fort Walton Beach, 1970-73; free-lance photo-jnlst., 1977—. Home: 31 Ryan St Box 11033 Chickasaw AL 36611

HIMES, GEOFFREY, b. Hanover, PA, Apr. 17, 1952, s. George Null and Rose Marie (Wagner) H.; 1 stepson, David Sobel. Contrbr. poetry, songs: december, Salt Lick, Unicorn Times, other publs., produced, wrote lyrics for record album Nightwaves, 1987; contrbr. criticism to Washington Post, Rolling Stone, Columbia Flier, others. BA in English, Antioch Coll., 1972, MA in Edn., 1975. Poet-in-schls. Md. Arts Council, Balt., 1976-81; music critic Washington Post, 1977—, Nat. Public Radio, Washington, 1985; arts ed. Patuxent Pub., Columbia, Md., 1980—; freelance journalist; liner note wrtr. for Rounder Records and Time-Life Records, 1982—. Natl. Critics Inst. fellow, 1977. Mem. NWU. Home: 3720 Greenmount Ave Baltimore MD 21218

HIMMELFARB, GERTRUDE, (Mrs. Irving Kristol), b. NYC, Aug. 8, 1922; d. Max and Bertha (Lerner) H.; m. Irving Kristol, Jan. 18, 1942; children—William, Elizabeth. Author: Lord Acton: A Study in Conscience and Politics, 1952, Darwin and the Darwinian Revolution, 1959, Victorian Minds, 1968, On Liberty and Liberalism—The Case of John Stuart Mill, 1974, The Idea of Poverty: England in the Early Industrial Age, 1984, Marriage and Morals Among the Victorians, 1985, The New History and the Old, 1987; editorial bd.: Am. Hist. Rvw, Am. Scholar, This World, Albion. BA, Bklyn. Coll., 1942; MA, U. Chgo., 1944, PhD, 1950. Guggenheim fellow, 1955-56, 57-58; Rockefeller Fdn. fellow, 1955-56, 1957-58, 1980-81; sr. fellow NEH, 1968-69; ACLS fellow, 1972-73; Woodrow Wilson Center fellow, 1976-77. Fellow British Academy Royal Hist. Soc., Am. Philo. Soc., Am. Acad. Arts and Scis., Soc. Am. Historians. Office: CUNY 33 W 42d St New York NY 10036

HINDS, SALLIE ANN, b. Saginaw, MI, June 8, 1930; d. Alex W. and Elsie E. (Letourneau) Chriscaden; m. James Frederick Hinds, Aug. 25, 1951; children—Amy-Lynn McLean, Jennifer L. Wanner. Author poems: Bits & Pieces of Nature's Seasons, 1986. Contrbr. poems to anthols., mags.; articles to newspaper. Wrkg. on book of poems. Student MacMurray Coll., 1948-49, Mich. State U., 1980, 81, 85. Township treas. Sims Township, Arenac County, MI, 1980—. Recipient award for logo Saginaw Township, 1976, Omer Sucker Fetival, MI, 1984, Omer Chamber of Commerce, 1985, Mich. Airways, Inc., 1987; Silver Poet award World of Poetry, 1986, Golden Poet award, 1987. Mem. Northeastern Mich. Arts Council (award for logo 1983). Home: 767 Crescent Dr Point Lookout AuGres MI 48703

HINKLE, RICHARD PAUL, b. San Jose, CA, Apr. 6, 1946, s. George William and Josephine (Barboza) H.; m. Beverly Jean Harris. Author: The Napa Valley Wine Book, 1979, The Central Coast Wine Book, 1980, screenplay, Wines of a Place. BA, U. San Francisco, 1969. Columnist Santa Rosa Press Democrat; wrtr., consulting ed. Wine & Spirits Buying Guide, Berkeley, Calif., 1982—; feature wrtr. Liquor Store Mag., NYC, 1985—; freelance wrtr., 1976—. Named Wine Wrtr. of Yr., Riverbank Wine Festival, 1981. Address: Box V Boyes Hot Springs CA 95416

HINSLEY-LOEBER, CHARLES ERNEST, b. Ridgewood, NJ, Feb. 10, 1962; s. Robert G. and Patricia A. (Wolf) L.; m. Mary C. Hinsley, Oct. 15, 1986; 1 dau., Erica Terese Hinsley-Loeber. Author: The Golden Pen, 1984. Contrbr. article to lit. mag. Recipient Rank and File award En Passant Pubs., Inc., 1987. B.A. in Psychology and Philosophy, Boston Coll., 1984. Resource ons. Walker Home & Schl., Inc., Needham, MA, 1985—.Mem. NWC. Home: 21 Claybrook Rd Dover MA 02030

HINSON, JERRY LEE, b. Topeka, Feb. 17, 1951; s. Dan W. and Sarah F. (Whiteside) H.; m. Deborah S. Sewing, July 26, 1975; children—Kristoffer, Ulrika. Columnist, asst. editor: Mensa Bulltn., 1982-83; contrbg. editor: Isolated M, 1985-86. Contrbr. articles to mags. BA, Emporia State U., 1973, MS, 1975. Patrolman, Civil Service, Emporia, Kans., 1973-75; schl. psychologist Sedgwick County Ednl. Services, Goddard, Kans., 1975-82; schl. counselor Goddard Pub. Schls., 1982-83; free-lance wrtr., ed., psychol. cons., Goddard, 1983—. Home: 19945 W 13th Ct Goddard KS 67052

HIRSCH, EDWARD, b. Chgo., Jan. 20, 1950; s. Kurt and Irma (Ginsburg) H.; m. Janet Landay. Author: For the Sleepwalkers, 1981, Wild Gratitude, 1986. BA, Grinnell College, 1972; PhD,U. of Penn., 1979. Asst. prof., Wayne State U., Detroit, MI, 1979-85; assoc. prof., U. of Houston, 1985—. Awards: NEA fellowship, 1982; Guggenheim fellowship, 1985; Natl. Book Critics Circle Award, 1987; Tex. Inst. of Arts and Letters Award, 1987. Home: 2304 Addison Rd Houston TX 77030

HIRSCH, GEORGE AARON, b. NYC, June 21, 1934; s. George J. and Sylvia (Epstein) H.; m. Brenda Baldwin Walker (div.); children—David Aaron, William George. AB magna cum laude, Princeton U., 1956; MBA, Harvard U., 1962. With Time-Life Intl., 1962-67; founder, pres., dir. New York Mag. Co., 1967-71, pub. New York mag; chmn., pres., chief exec. officer New Times Communications Corp. (founder, pub. New Times Mag.), 1973-79; founder, pub. The Runner mag., 1978-87, pub. Runner's World mag., 1987—. TV sports commentator, 1979—. Mem. Publ. bd. Princeton Alumni Weekly, 1979—. Served as officer USNR, 1957-60. Home: 246 32d St New York NY 10016

HIRSCH, MARY TONE, b. Waterloo, IA, Oct. 22, 1944, d. George Guy and Jane (Snyder) Hutchison; m. John Myers, June 1965 (div. 1972); children—Melissa, Lindsay; m. Michael Hirsch, May 2, 1986. Business columnist Des Moines Business Record; contrbr. articles: Wall St. Jnl, Ebony Jr., Black Collegian, Am. Craft, numerous other mags., newspapers. BS in English and Journalism, Fla. State U., 1966; MS in Mass Communications, Iowa State U., 1987. Instr. journalism Iowa State U., Ames, 1982-84; asst. ed. Iowan Mag., Des Moines, 1982-84; corr. Wall St. Jnl, 1983—; mng. ed. Des Moines Bus. Record, 1984-86. Recipient Carl Johnson Feature Writing award Iowa State U., 1982, Best Mag. Feature award, Best Mag. Interview award Iowa Press Women, 1983; winner awards Iowa Newspaper Assn., 1984, 85. Mem. Women In Communications, Iowa Press Women. Home: 325 45th St Des Moines IA 50312

HIRSCHEL, LIESELOTTE ANNE, (Alice Richard), b. Apr. 17, 1926, came to U.S., 1949, naturalized, 1952; d. Richard F. and Alice Engel; m. John U. Hirshel, Dec. 16, 1948; children—Anthony G., Alison E. Contrbr. articles to encyclopedias, popular mags. including Travel Holiday, Dazzle, Am. Baby, numerous others. Licentiate Dental Surgery, Royal Coll. Surgeons, U. London, 1948, B. Dental, Surgery, 1949; D.D.S., U. Mich., 1952. Pvt. practice in dentistry, Detroit, 1952-67, Southfield, MI, 1967-86; free-lance wrtr., 1972—. Fellow, Royal Soc. of Health. Mem. AMWA. Home: 20120 Ledgestone Southfield MI 48076

HIRSHFIELD, JANE, b. NYC, Feb. 24, 1953; d. Robert L. and Harriet (Miller) Hirshfield. Author: Alaya, 1982, Of Gravity and Angels, 1988; co-transl. The Ink Dark Moon, 1988; contrbr. to The Nation, The New Yorker, Atlantic Monthly, Am. Poetry Rvw, Ironwood, Antioch Rvw, others. AB magna cum laude and Phi Beta Kappa, Princeton, 1973. Poet-tchr. Calif. Poet-in-the-Schls. project, 1980-85, coordinator for Marin County, 1982-85. Bd. dirs. Marin Arts Council, 1982-85, Marin Poetry Ctr., 1982—. Guggenheim fellow, 1985-86; Columbia U. Translation Ctr. Award, 1987; Joseph Henry Jackson Award, 1986; recipient QRL Poetry Prize, Quarterly Rvw Lit., 1982. Mem. PSA, AWP, PEN. Address: 367 Molino Ave Mill Valley CA 94941

HITCHCOCK, GEORGE PARKS, b. Hood River, OR, June 2, 1914. Author: Another Shore (novel), 1971, Notes of the Seige Year: Eight Entertainments (stories), 1974; author poetry: Poems and Prints, 1962, Tactics of Survival and Other Poems, 1964, The Dolphin with the Revolver in Its Teeth, 1967, Two Poems, 1967, A Ship of Bells, 1968, Twelve Stanzas in Praise of the Holy Chariot, 1969, The Rococo Eye, 1971, Lessons in Alchemy, 1976, The Piano Beneath the Skin, 1978, Mirror on Horseback, 1979, The Collected Poems, Stories, and Collages: George Hitchcock, 1981, The Wounded Alphabet: Poems Collected and New, 1953-1983, 1983, Cloud Taxis, 1984; playwright: The Counterfeit Rose, 1967, The Devil Comes to Wittenberg: A Tragicomedy, 1980, Five Plays, 1981, numerous produced plays; contrbr. to anthologies: Modern Short Story in the Making, Where Is Vietnam?: American Poets Respond, Surrealism in English, numerous others; contrbr. to Chelsea, Hudson Rvw, Malahat Rvw, others. BA, U. Oreg., 1935. Assoc. ed. San Francisco Rvw, 1958-63; ed., pub. Kayak mag., Kayak Books, Inc., Santa Cruz, Calif., 1964—; former lectr. San Francisco State Coll., now U. Calif.-Santa Cruz; actor San Francisco area theater groups. Recipient NEA Book Pub. award, 1967, 68, 69. Mem. PEN. Address: 325 Ocean View Ave Santa Cruz CA 95062

HITE, SHERE D., b. St. Joseph, MO. Author: Sexual Honesty: By Women For Women, 1974, The Hite Report: A Nationwide Study of Female Sexuality, 1976, The Hite Report on Male Sexuality, 1981; cons. editor: Women and Therapy; Jnl Sex Edn. and Therapy; Jnl Sexuality and Disability. BA cum laude, U. Fla., 1964; MA, 1968; postgrad., Columbia U., 1968-69. Recipient disting. svc. award Am. Assn. Sex Educators, Counselors and Therapists, 1985. Office: PO Box 5282 FDR Sta New York NY 10022

HOAGLAND, EDWARD, b. NYC, Dec. 21, 1932; s. Warren Eugene and Helen Kelley (Morley) H.; m. Amy J. Ferrara, 1960 (div. 1964); m. 2d, Marion Magid, Mar. 28, 1968; 1 dau., Molly. Author: Cat Man, 1956, The Circle Home, 1960, The Peacock's Tail, 1965, Notes from the Century Before: A Journal from British Columbia, 1969, The Courage of Turtles, 1971, Walking the Dead Diamond River, 1973, The Moose on the Wall: Field Notes from the Vermont Wilderness, 1974, Red Wolves and Black Bears, 1976, African Calliope: A Journey to the Sudan, 1979, The Edward Hoagland Reader, 1979, The Tugman's Passage, 1982, City Tales, 1986, Seven Rivers West, 1986; gen. ed. Penguin Nature Library, a new paperback series, 1987—; essays and stories for publs. including New York Times, Village Voice, New Yorker, Atlantic, Nation, Vanity Fair, Am. Heritage, Sat. Rvw, Harper's; contrbr. nature editorials, N.Y. Times, editorial page, N.Y. Times, 1979—. AB cum laude, Harvard U., 1954. Served with AUS, 1955-57. Houghton Mifflin Lit fellow, 1954; AAAL traveling fellow, 1964; Guggenheim fellow, 1964, 75; recipient Longview Fdn. award, 1961, O. Henry award, 1971, NEA award, 1982; others. Mem. AAAL. Office: Random Hs 201 E 50 St New York NY 10022

HOAGLAND, GUY WHITNEY, b. Brooklyn Heights, NY, May 16, 1920; s. Guy and Florence (Stickles) H.; m. Mardell Nedley (div. Aug. 1963); children—Barbara Ann, Susan Marie, Janet Karen; m. Eva-Rita Aarnivirta, Feb. 4, 1968; children—Maria Tuli, Tanja Susannah. Author (poetic script) 4-D Mexican Epic Oem, 1986. Contrbr. articles to trade jnls. Ed.: Brimming Over, 1978, Suncoast Poems, 1981-83, numerous public sch. anthols., 1974-83. B.A. in English, U. Minn., 1974. Technical wrtr. Oy Wartsila Ab, Jarvenpa, Finland, 1977-79; poet-in-the-schls. Pinellas and Hillsborough Counties, FL, 1980-83; indsl. sales profiles wrtr. Tampa Bay Industry, FL, 1984-87. Tchr., Performing Arts Devel. Ctr., St. Petersburg, FL, 1986-87. Served to lt. col., USAF, 1941-62. Recipient Grant prize for Gala Laughing, Americana Festival, St. Petersburg, 1982. Mem. Konglomerati (tchr.). Home: 12788 81 Ave N Seminole FL 33542

HOCH, EDWARD D., b. Rochester, NY, Feb. 22, 1930, s. Earl George and Alice Mary (Dentinger) H.; m. Patricia McMahon, June 5, 1957. Author: The Shattered Raven, 1969, The Transvection Machine, 1971, The Fellowship of the

Hand, 1973, The Frankenstein Factory, 1975, The Thefts of Nick Velvet, 1978, All But Impossible, 1981, The Quests of Simon Ark, 1984, Leopold's Way, 1985; ed. Dear Dead Days, 1972, Best Detective Stories of the Year, 1976-81, Year's Best Mystery & Suspense Stories, 1982-87. Student U. Rochester, 1947-49. Publicity wrtr. Hutchins Advt. Co., Rochester, 1954-68; freelance wrtr., 1968—. Served with U.S. Army, 1950-52. Mem. MWA (Edgar award 1968, pres. 1982-83), AG, SFWA. Home: 2941 Lake Ave Rochester NY 14612

HOCKS, PAULA JEANNE, b. Muskogee, OK; d. Malcolm and Eileen (Magruder) Neathery. Poems pub. in mags. inclg. The Nation; 30 artist's books in major libs. and museums inclg. Newberry Lib., Chgo., Tate Gallery Special Collects., London, NY Pub. Lib., Smithsonian Mus. Design. Lit. grant, NEA, 1979. Address: Box 9607 Santa Fe NM 87504

HODGELL, PATRICIA CHRISTINE, b. Des Moines, Mar. 16, 1951; d. Robert Overman and Lois Adele (Partridge) Hodgell. Author: God Stalk, 1982, Dark of the Moon, 1985. Contrbr. short stories to anthols. BA, Eckerd Coll., 1973; MA, U. Minn.-Mpls., 1976, PhD, 1987. Lectr., U. Wis., Oshkosh, 1981-85. Mem. SFWA. Home: 1237 Liberty St Oshkosh WI 54901

HOEFLING, JOHN ERWIN, b. Washburn, WI, May 29, 1927; s. Fred Henry and Grace Elizabeth (Swanby) H.; m. June Louise Holmes, June 22, 1949; 1 dau., Vicki Linn Hoefling Andersen. Ed./pub., Along the Ski Trails, 1968-75, Northwest Skiing, 1985—; corresp.: Ski Mag., 1962-84, Ski Racing, 1970-80, Ski Industry Letter, 1984-85, Ski Business, 1965-80, Ski Area Mgt., 1970-82. Student, Lewis & Clark Coll. Owner/dir. Western Ski Pros, Mt. Hood, OR, 1962—; free lance writer, Portland, OR, 1950—; var. bus. & data processing posits., 1950-78; Admin. Svcs. Mgr., Fred Meyer S & L, Portland, 1979-82; owner/pres. Fast Print, Inc., Portland, 1982—. Mem. U.S. Ski Writers Assn., Profl. Ski Instrs. Am., Natl. Ski Patrol. Served to EM3/C, USN, 1944-45, PTO. Dir., Northwest Wintersports Hall of Fame, 1984—. Home: 2039 S E 103rd Dr Portland OR 97216

HOEPPNER, IONA RUTH, (Jovak Von Hess, Edgar S. Cooper, Ruth Snider, C. C. Arndt), b. Denver, Aug. 17, 1939; d. Edgar Hamlet and Thelma Marie (Arndt) Snider; m. Floyd W. Bills, May 13, 1950 (div. 1969); children—Norman, Stephanie, William Scott, David, Richard E., Kim, Tami, Athena, Crystal; m. Richard Allen Hoeppner, Dec. 14, 1975. Author: The Gypo's Guide to Making It on 18 Wheels, 1984, Incorporate Yourself for Under $20!, 1985, Highway to Nowhere, 1986, Just Me, 1985, Water!, 1986, How to REALLY Get Started in Business, 1986, The Complete Guide to RVs, 1987, The Executive Syndrome, 1987, Private Stock Issues Can Make You Rich, 1987, The Complete RV Handbook, 1988, The Teacher's Guide to Rural Education, 1988, The Administrator's Guide to Rural Education, 1988. Ed.: The Best of CROSSROADS, 1976, Facts, Figures and Folklore on Colorado License Plates, 1985. B.A., U. Southern Colo., 1978; postgrad. Western State Coll., 1983. Proprietor, Hoeppner Transport, Fleming, CO, 1958—; tchr. Brigdale Schls., CO, 1978-81, St. Patricks Acad., Sidney, NE, 1983-84; chmn. of the bd. High Lighter, Inc., Fleming and Haxtun, CO, 1986—; free-lance wrtr., 1960—. Mem. NWC, NEA, Natl. Assn. Computing Machinery, Colo. Press Assn., Am. Trucking Assn. Home: 20027 County Rd 85 Fleming CO 80728

HOEY, ALLEN S., b. Kingston, NY, Oct. 21, 1952; s. Allen P. and Hazel E. (Metcalf) H.; m. Cynthia E. Pitts, May 26, 1973; 2 sons, Owen Fergus, Stephen James. Author: First Light in February, 1975, Evening in the Antipodes, 1977, Cedar Light, 1980, Hymns to a Tree, 1983, Listening for Bear, 1982, New Year, 1986, A Fire in the Cold House of Being, 1986, Work the Tongue Could Understand, 1986; transl. Transfigured Autumn (Georg Trakl), 1985; ed. Wetting Our Lines Together, 1982. BA, SUNY, 1974; MA, Syracuse U., 1980, DA, 1984. Adj. instr. Le Moyne Coll., Syracuse, N.Y., 1984-85, instr. Syracuse Univ., 1984-85; asst. prof. Ithaca Coll., N.Y., 1985—. Mem. MLA (Northeast), AWP. Recipient AAP prize, 1984, Camden Poetry Award, 1985. Home: 131 Fellows Ave Syracuse NY 13210

HOFF, B. J., Barbour County, WV, June 1, 1940; d. William M. and Reta (Phillips) Simon; m. James Jacob Hoff, July 1, 1966; children—Dana Noel, Jessica Lea. Author: To Love and Honor, 1986, Mists of Danger, 1986, Meetings with the Master, 1986, A Whisper in the Wind, 1987, Storm at Daybreak, 1987, The Domino Image, 1987. Contrbr. articles to lit. mags. Mem. AG, Ohio Press Women, NWC, Christiam Wrtrs. League, Christian Wrtrs. Fellowship. Home: 2015 Coldspring Dr Lancaster OH 43130

HOFF, DONNAFRED MARY, (Donnafred), B. Decorah, IA, June 12, 1903; d. Fred Davis Baker and Mary (Helen) Carter. Author: Daughter of Eve, 1952, Pocket Piece, 1971, Hold Me, Earth, 1977, Love Runs Naked, 1977, Mountain Magic, 1985. Contrbr. poems, quips to Chgo. Tribune, natl. mags., lit. mags. Student Upper Iowa U., 1922-26, Art Inst. Chgo., 1937-38. Tchr. creative writing and oil painting Gila Pueblo Coll., Globe, AZ, 1971-73. Recipient numerous poetry awards NLAPW, N.M. State Poetry Soc., Natl. Fedn. State Poetry Socs., 1960's—. MEm. Downers Grove AG (pres. 1957), Gila Country Fine Arts Assn. (pres. 1972), Ariz. State Poetry Soc. (treas.), Cobre Valley Fine Arts Guild (bd. dirs., exhibitor). Home: 760 Agave Dr Globe AZ 85501

HOFFBERG, JUDITH A., b. Hartford, CT, May 19, 1934; d. George and Miriam (Goldenberg) Hoffberg. Contrbr. art exhbn. rvws., art articles, artist interviews, essays to books, art mags; columnist: High Performance mag., 1984—; editor: (newsletter) Umbrella, 1978—; Artists' Publications in Print, 1980-83; Directory of Art Libraries & Visual Resource Collections in North America, 1978. BA cum laude, UCLA, 1956, MA, 1960, MLS, 1964. Librarian Brand art ctr. Glendale Pub. Library, Calif., 1971-73; exec. sec. Art Libraries Soc. N.Am., Glendale, 1973-77; ed., pub. Umbrella Assocs., Pasadena, Calif., 1978—. Mem. ALA, Intl. Assn. Art Critics (Am. sect.), Coll. Art Assn. Am., Intl. Council Mus., Phi Beta Kappa. Home: Box 40100 Pasadena CA 91104

HOFFMAN, CINDY JANE, b. Manhattan, KS, Feb. 14, 1946; d. Edward Keith and Juanita Madge (Cooper) Beard; m. Alan Richard Hoffman, June 7, 1967; children—Colter Keith, Alain Cie. Author: North Spring Lake, 1983; contrbr. Ideals Mag., Denver Parent, Midwest Motorist, Farm Woman, Baby Talk, numerous other publs. BS, U. Kans., 1968. Tchr. English high schs. in Kans., Colo., 1968—. Mem. NCTE. Home: 5242 W Fair Dr Littleton CO 80123

HOFFMAN, DANIEL, b. NYC, Apr. 3, 1923; s. Daniel and Frances (Beck) H.; m. Elizabeth McFarland, May 22, 1948; children: Kate, Macfarlane. Author: (poetry) An Armada of Thirty Whales, 1954, A Little Geste, 1960, The City of Satisfactions, 1963, Striking the Stones, 1968, Broken Laws, 1970, The Center of Attention, 1974, Able Was I Ere I Saw Elba, 1977, Brotherly Love, 1981; (prose) Paul Bunyan, Last of the Frontier Demigods, 1952; The Poetry of Stephen Crane, 1957; Form and Fable in American Fiction, 1961; Barbarous Knowledge: Myth in the Poetry of Yeats, Graces, and Muir, 1967; Poe Poe Poe Poe Poe Poe Poe, 1972; ed. The Red Badge of Courage and Other Stories, 1957; American Poetry and Poetics, 1962; ed., contrbr. Harvard Guide to Contemporary American Writing, 1979; ed., Ezra Pound and William Carlos Williams, 1983. BA, Columbia U., 1947, MA, 1949, PhD, 1956. Instr. English, Columbia U., 1952-56; asst. prof. to prof. Swarthmore Coll., 1957-66; prof. English, U. Pa., Phila., 1966—, poet-in-residence, 1978—, Schelling prof. English, 1983—; cons. in poetry to Library of Congress, 1973-74, Served to 1st lt. USAAF, 1943-46. Recipient Meml. medal Hungarian PEN, 1980; Hazlett Meml. award for lit. Pa. Arts Council, 1983; research fellow ACLS, 1961-62, 66-67, NEH, 1979-80; fellow Guggenheim Fdn., 1983-84. Mem. AAP (chancellor), AG (council). Office: Dept Eng U Pa Philadelphia PA 19104

HOFFMAN, DANIEL PAUL, b. Cascade, WI, Jan. 13, 1912; s. John E. and Adella (Habighorst) H.; m. Marie E. Thomas, Sept. 3, 1938; children—Dana Joan, Susan Ann, Paul W., Nancy Rachel. Author: India's Social Miracle, 1961, The Coming Culture, 1963, An American Saravodya Pilgramage, 1966, Essays on Primitive Christianity, 1987. contrbr. numerous articles to natl. and intl. mags. B.A., U. Wis., 1933; J.D., Georgetown U., 1938. Part-time prof. Chabot Coll., Hayward, CA, 1960-70; prof. genl. and technical studies Ind. U. NW, Gary, IN, 1970-75, retired. Home: Box 173 Brook IN 47922

HOFFMAN, DEAN ALLEN, b. Cin., Sept. 9, 1949, s. Robert Thomas and Ruth Alice (Logsdon) H.; m. Linda Sue Patton, Mar. 30, 1974. BS in Journalism, 1971. Vice-pres. Adams, Gaffney & Assocs., Cin., 1973-79; dir. public info. Ohio Electric Utility Inst., Columbus, 1979-81; exec. ed. Hoof Beats mag., Columbus, 1981—, assoc. ed. Hub Rail, Columbus, 1973-81; spcl. contrbr. The Standard-bred, Acton, Ont., Can., 1975-81. Named Wrtr. of Yr., Calif. Harness Horse Breeders Assn., 1984. Mem. U.S. Harness Wrtrs. Assn., Harness Publicists Assn. Office: Hoof Beats 750 Michigan Ave Columbus OH 43215

HOFFMAN, ERCELL H., b. Cotton Valley, LA, Aug. 16, 1941, d. Adell and Rosie (Flowers) Harris; m. Charles L. Hoffman, July 26, 1965 (div. 1970); children—Bonnie, Cynthia, Lisa. Novelist: The Acknowledgment; contrbr. poetry: A Time to be Free, Earthshine, Eternal Echoes, other anthologies; contrbr. articles to numerous gen. interest publs. Wrkg. on book of poetry, novel. BA, Calif. State U.-Long Beach, 1977, MPA, 1980. Freelance wrtr. Home: 4034 Elizabeth St Compton CA 90221

HOFFMAN, GLORIA L., b. Norfolk, VA, Feb. 8, 1933; d. Maxwell L. and Jessie (Mashbitz) Levy; m. Frank Katz Hoffman, Sept. 18, 1954 (dec. Oct. 24, 1982); children—Daniel L., L. Stephen, Victoria Anne, Jonathan M. (dec.). Creator: I Belong To Me!, 1984, graphically expanded 2d ed., I Belong To Me!—Each Person's

Right To Be A Somebody, 1984, rev. ed., I Belong To Me—Each Person's Right To Be A Somebody Special...And To Feel Our Own Feelings, 1985. BA in Speech & Radio, U.WI, 1954. Actress, Resident Theatre, Kansas City, MO, 1963-68, U.MO Playhouse, 1964-76; p.r. Menorah Med. Ctr., Kansas City, 1965-83, ed. Scope 1977-82; free-lance writer 1960—. Home: 1250 W 63rd St Kansas City MO 64113

HOFFMAN, HENRY WILLIAM, b. Charleston, WV, May 16, 1925; s. Henry William and Margaret Julia (Beckley) H.; m. Alice Richardson, Apr. 17, 1957; children—Ruth Beckley, Margaret Kay. Novels: The Trumpet Unblown, 1955, Days in the Yellow Leaf, 1958, A Place for My Head, 1960, The Dark Mountains, 1963, Yancey's War, 1966, A Walk to the River, 1970, A Death of Dreams, 1973, The Land That Drank the Rain, 1982, Godfires, 1985. Collected stories: Virginia Reels, 1978. Over 50 stories pub. in various mags. BA, Hampden-Sydney Coll., 1949; postgrad. Washington and Lee U., 1949-50. Served to pfc. U.S. Army, 1943-46; ETO. Journalist, Evening Star, Washington, 1950-51; banker Chase Natl. Bank, NTC, 1951-52; assoc. prof. Hampden-Sydney Coll., Va., 1952-57, writer-in-res., 1964-71. Mem. AG. NEA fellow, 1980. Home and Office: Box 382 Charlotte Courthouse VA 23923

HOFMANN, HANS, b. Basel, Switzerland, Aug. 12, 1923; came to U.S., 1951, naturalized, 1956; s. Oscar and Henriette (Burbiel) H.; m. Emilie Scott Welles, Oct. 15, 1955; children—Elizabeth Scott, Mark Lawrence, David Hans, Scott Cluett. Author: The Theology of Reinhold Niebuhr, 1955, Religion and Mental Health, 1961, Incorporating Sex, 1967, Breakthrough to Life, 1969, Discovering Freedom, 1969; Editor: Making the Ministry Relevant, 1960, The Ministry and Mental Health, 1960, Sex Incorporated, 1967. AB, Thurg. Kantonsschule, 1943; BD, U. Basel, 1948; ThD, U. Zurich, 1953. Mem. Intl. Platform Assn., Natl. Inst. Arts and Letters. Home: 110 Evening Glow Pl Sedona AZ 86336

HOGAN, JUDY FORDHAM, b. Hutchinson, KS, May 27, 1937; d. William Robert and Margaret Elizabeth (Roys) Stevenson; m. Thomas J. Fordham, 1960 (div. 1964); children—Amy Fordham; m. 2d, Terry Michael Hogan, May 12, 1967 (div. 1977); children—Timothy Michael, Virginia Lynn. Author (poetry): Cassandra Speaking, 1977, Sun-Blazoned, 1983, Susannah, Teach Me to Love/Grace, Sing to Me, 1986; contrbr. poetry Eat Your Natchos (anthol.) Black Sun, New Moon, Hyperion. Wrkg. on poetry collections and diary novel. BA cum laude, U. Okla., 1959; postgrad. in Classics, U. Calif.-Berkeley, 1964-68. Tching. asst., reader and typist, U. Calif., Berkeley, 1964-68; cons. COSMEP, Chapel Hill, N.C., 1974-78; coord. Home Grown Book Rvw. Service, Chapel Hill, 1978-81; ed., pub., tchr., Carolina Wren Press, Chapel Hill, 1976—. Vol. Fellowship to Reverse Arms Race, Chapel Hill, 1984. Woodrow Wilson fellow, 1959-60. Mem. P&W, NC Writers' Network (pres. 1985-86, bd. dirs., chmn. steering comm., 1984-86), Works in Progress, COSMEP, 1970-80 (chmn. bd., San Francisco, 1975-78). Address: Box 277 Carrboro NC 27510

HOGAN, LINDA K., b. Denver, July 16, 1947, d. Charles Colbert and Cleona Florine (Bower) Henderson; children—Sandra, Tanya. Author: Calling Myself Home, 1979, Daughters, I Love You, 1981, Eclipse, 1984, That Horse, 1985, Seeing through the Sun, 1985 (winner Am. Bk. Award from Before Columbus Fdn., 1986); co-ed. The Stories We Hold Secret, 1986; contrbr. to over 25 anthologies, 60 lit mags. MA, U. Colo., 1978. Wrtr.-in-residence state arts councils, Okla., Colo., 1980-84; asst. prof. Colo. Coll., 1982-84; assoc. prof. Am. studies/Am. Indian studies U. Minn., Mpls., 1984—. Recipient Five Tribes playwriting award, 1980; D'Arcy McNickle fellow Newberry Library, 1981; U. Minn. faculty fellow, 1985, Minn. State Arts Bd. grant; ind. writing fellow State of Colo., 1984, NEA grant, 1986, Pushcart Prize, 1986. Home: Box 141 Idledale CO 80453

HOGGARD, JAMES MARTIN, b. Wichita Falls, TX, June 21, 1941; s. Earl Reid and Helen Marie (Christensen) H.; m. Bonnie Hubly, Jan. 28, 1964 (div. May 25, 1975); m. 2d, Lynn Taylor, May 23, 1976; children—James Jordan, Bryn Marie. Author: (novel) Trotter Ross, 1981; (nonfiction) Elevator Man, 1983; (poetry) Eyesigns: Poems on Letters & Numbers, 1977, The Shaper Poems, 1983, Two Gulls, One Hawk, 1983, Breaking an Indelicate Statue, 1986; ed. Mensa Alta Anthol., 1983, Mammals of North Central Tex., 1984. BA, SMU, 1963; MA, U. Kans., 1965. Reporter Wichita Falls Record News, Tex., 1965-66; instr. Midwestern State Univ., Wichita Falls, 1966-69, asst. prof., 1969-72, assoc. prof., 1972-77, prof. English, 1977—. Bd. dirs., Wesley Fdn., Wichita Falls, 1967—, Wichita Falls Symphony Orchestra, 1977—. NEA fellow, 1979. Mem. Tex. Inst. Letters, Tex. Assn. Creative Writing Tchrs. (pres.), ALTA. Address: 2414 Leighton Circle N Wichita Falls TX 76309

HOHEISEL, PETER F., b. Detroit, Nov. 5, 1938. Contrbr. poetry to Seven Lake Superior Poets, 1979, Shaping the Word: A Guide for Teaching Poetry Writing, 1986. Wrtr.-in-residence Mich. Council for Arts, Houghton, 1983-86. Home: Rt 1 Box 244AJ Lake Linden MI 49945

HOLADAY, SUSAN MIRLES, b. Batavia, NY, Nov. 2, 1938; d. Norman and Sada Jule (Jacobson) Goldberg; m. William Campbell Holaday, Dec. 25, 1968 (dec. Feb. 28, 1977). BA, Syracuse U., 1960; MA, U. Chgo., 1963. Equipment ed. Institutions Mag., Chgo., 1964-65; company ed. Wyman-Gordon Co., Worcester, MA, 1967-68; ed. Profile Communics., Maynard, MA, 1968-69; assoc. ed., ed. Food-Service East (formerly Lodging & Food Svc. News), Boston, 1972—. Office: Food-Svc E 755 Boylston St Boston MA 02116

HOLBROOK, JAMES J., see Johnson, James Holbrook

HOLDEN, JONATHAN, b. Morristown, NJ, July 18, 1941; s. Alan Nordby and Cornelia Jaynet (Conselyea) H.; m. Gretchen Weltzheimer, Nov. 16, 1963; children—Alanna Kim, Zachary. Author poetry and critical books, 1972—, latest being The Names of the Rapids (poems), 1985, and Style and Authenticity in Postmodern Poetry, 1986. BA, Oberlin College, 1963; MA, San Francisco St. College, 1970; PhD, U. Colorado, 1974. English instr., Stephens Coll., Columbia, MO, 1974-77; prof., KS State U., 1977—. Devins Award, U. MO Press, 1972, AWP Award Series for poetry, 1982; Juniper Prize, U. MA Press, 1985; Creative Writing Fellowship, NEA, 1975, 85. Home: 1731 Fairview Manhattan KS 66502

HOLDITCH, W. KENNETH, b. Ecru, MS, Sept. 18, 1933, s. Sidney Williamson and Dora Faye (Dickerson) H. Contrbr. to Explorations of Literature, 1967, The Grandissimes: Centennial Essays, 1981; editor: In Old New Orleans, 1983; contrbr. to Reflections of Childhood and Youth, Vol. 1, Vol. 2, Vol. 3, Borges the Poet, 1986, The Pineywoods, 1986, Gale Contemporary Authors, 1988. BA with honors, Southwestern in Memphis, 1955; MA, U. Miss., 1957, PhD, 1961. Asst. prof. English, U. New Orleans, 1964-67, assoc. prof., 1967-74, prof., 1974—. Named La. Tchr. of Yr., Amoco Fdn., 1974; So Fellowships Commn. fellow, Duke U., 1958-60. Mem. MLA, PMLA, AWP, Phi Kappa Phi. Home: 732 Frenchmen St New Orleans LA 70116

HOLDRIDGE, BARBARA, b. NYC, July 26, 1929; d. Herbert L. and Bertha T. (Gold) Cohen; m. Lawrence B. Holdridge, Oct. 9, 1959; children—Eleanor, Diana. Author: Ammi Phillips, Portrait Painter, 1968, Aubrey Beardsley Designs from the Age of Chivalry, 1983; contrbr. to: Art in Amer., 1960, Antiques, 1961; ed.: I'm Nobody! Who Are You?—Poems of Emily Dickinson for Young People, 1978, A Swinger of Birches—Poems of Robert Frost for Young People, 1982, Under the Greenwood Tree—Shakespeare for Young People, 1986. Asst. ed. Liveright Pub. Corp., NYC, 1950-52; co-fdr. Caedmon Pub., NYC, 1952-54; co-fdr./pres. Caedmon Records, NYC, 1954-75; fdr./pres. Stemmer House Pub., Owings Mills, MD, 1975—. Mem. Child.'s Bk. Council. Home: 2627 Caves Rd Owings Mills MD 21117

HOLDT, DAVID M., b. Cleve., May 12, 1941, s. Jacob S. and Henrietta (Stewart) H.; m. Sandra B. Wood, June 26, 1976; 1 child, Brooke Stewart. Author poetry chapbooks: Sun Through Trees, 1973, River's Edge, 1985; contrbr. poetry to Chelsea, Embers, Stone Country, Poets On, numerous other lit mags. BA, Wesleyan U., 1963; MA, Duke U., 1967. Tchr., adminstr. schls. Conn. and Pa., 1963-77; Dean Watkinson Schl., Hartford, Conn., 1978—. Home: 3 Orchard Hill Rd Canton CT 06019

HOLEMAN, MARILYN BATEY, b. Gainesville, FL, Feb. 20, 1938; d. Hal Crockett, Jr. and Marguerite (Smith) Batey; m. James Lynn Holeman, June 6, 1957; children—Marilyn Gay, James Lynn. Student U. Ala., Huntsville, 1986—. Contrbr. articles to mags., newspapers. Wrkg. on short stories. Staff wrtr. The Exponent newspaper, U. Ala., Huntsville, 1981. Technical wrtr. Center for High Technology Management and Econ. Reasearch, 1987. Mem. Writing Group. Home: 8018 Tea Garden Rd Huntsville AL 35802

HOLENDER, BARBARA D., b. Buffalo, Mar. 15, 1927, d. Israel W. and Mildred (Ehrenreich) Dautch; m. H. William Holender, May 8, 1949 (widowed 1982); children—Fred, Judith. Author: Shivah Poems, 1986, Ladies of Genesis (poetry), 1986; contrbr. poetry to anthologies, mags. and newspapers. Student, Cornell U., Ithaca, N.Y., 1944-46; BA, U. Buffalo, 1948. Instr. English, SUNY, Buffalo, 1973-77; poet-in-schl., N.Y. State, Buffalo, 1976. Mem. PSA, P&W. Home: 263 Brantwood Rd Snyder NY 14226

HOLINGER, RICHARD, b. Chgo., March 20, 1949, s. Paul Henry and Julia (Drake) Holinger; m. Cecilia Rush June 15, 1979. Poetry, fiction and nonfiction in numerous mags. including Calliope, North Dakota Qtly, The Poetry Rvw, Cottonwood Rvw, Modern Images, The Southern Rvw., The Ohio Rvw., and The English Jnl. BA, Hartwick College, 1971, MA, Washington U., 1975. English instr. Marmion Acad, Aurora, IL,

1979—. Mem. PSA, AAP, P&W, AWP. Home: 304 Gray St St. Charles IL 60174

HOLINGER, WILLIAM, (Scott Eller), b. Chgo., June 12, 1944; s. Paul Henry and Julia (Drake) H.; m. Dorothy Powe, Aug. 18, 1978; stepchildren—Gordon Ondis, Jr., Aleta Ondis. Author: The Fence-walker, 1985; co-author Short Season, 1985. BA in English, Wesleyan U., 1966, MA in Creative Writing, Brown U., 1977. Lectr. Univ. Mich., Ann Arbor, 1978-80, adj. asst. prof., 1983—, fellow Mich. Soc. of Fellows, Ann Arbor, 1980-83. Recipient AWP award in the novel, 1984. Address: 502 W Davis St Ann Arbor MI 48103

HOLLABAUGH, MARK, (Mark Potter), b. Toledo, May 22, 1949; s. George Washington and Elaine (Potter) H. Author: Storage Master Model 409 Maintenance Training Manual, 1984, Increasing Rigid Removeable Disk Market Share, 1984, Expanding Flexible Disk Sales, 1985. Contrbr. articles, book rvws. to mags., jnls including The Lutheran Standard, Astronomy, Astrophysical Letters, others. BA, St. Olaf Coll., 1971; MS, U. Denver, 1973; MDivinity, Luther Theol. Sem., St. Paul, 1977. Instr. physics and religion St. Olaf Coll., Northfield, Minn., 1977-80; instr. Breck Schl., Mpls., 1979-80; instr. astronomy Normandale Community Coll., Bloomington, Minn., 1981-85; trng. cons. Control Data Corp., Bloomington, 1980-85; instr. physics Augsburg Coll., Mpls., 1985-86; tchg. asst., Schl. Physics and Astronomy, U. Minn., 1986—. Bd. Dirs. Wingspan Ministry, St. Paul, 1980-82. Mem. Am. Astronomical Soc., Minn. Area Assn. Physics Tchrs. Home: 91 North Kent St. Apt 1 Saint Paul MN 55102

HOLLAND, BARBARA, b. Portland, ME, July 12, 1925, d. Leicester Bodine and Louise Elizabeth Whetenhall (Adams) H. Author: Running Backwards, 1983, From the Shadows, 1984. Student U. Pa., 1950-51. Clrk. Carl Marx, NYC,1964-73. Address: 14 Morton St Apt 9 NYC 10014

HOLLAND, JOYCE, see Morice, David Jennings

HOLLAND, STEPHEN THOMAS, b. Iowa City, Jan. 20, 1952. Author: Talkin' Dan Cable, 1983; ed.: Mental Training for Peak Performance, 1984. BA, U. Iowa, 1974, MA, 1983. Instr. writing Kirkwood Community Coll., Cedar Rapids, Iowa, 1986—; pub. Bingo Bugle newspaper, Iowa City, 1986. Recipient state honors, AP, NYC,1980, 81, Gannett award, Rochester, N.Y., 1981. Mem. ACLU, Am. Soc. Profl. Journalists. Home: Box 2104 Iowa City IA 52244

HOLLAND, SUSAN PALMIERI, b. NYC, July 31, 1956; d. Francis Anthony and Patricia Katherine (McGuinness) Palmieri; m. Mark Andrew Holland, July 16, 1977. Author: (children's play) Daisy's Reward, 1978. Contrbr. poems, short stories to lit. mags., anthols. Ed.: Chimes, 1977-78. B.A., St. Mary's Coll., 1978. Mem. Local Wrtr.'s Exchange. Home: 34 Angela Circle Hazlet NJ 07730

HOLLANDER, ELLA H., b. Trappe, MD, May 29, 1908; d. Percy L., Sr. and Ida May (Haddaway) Dawson; m. J. Edwin Hollander, Nov. 20, 1943 (dec. June 6, 1976); 1 son, George A. Contrbr. poems to anthols. Recipient Golden Poet award, World of Poetry, 1987, award of Merit, 1987. Home: 4832 S 4th Louisville KY 40214

HOLLANDER, JEAN, b. Vienna, Austria; m. Robert Hollander; children—Cornelia, Buzz. Author: Crushed into Honey (poetry), 1986; contrbr. poetry to various lit mags. MA, Columbia U., postgrad. Tchr. Trenton (N.J.) State Coll., 1970—; poetry ed. The Princeton Packet, 1980-87; lectr. Princeton (N.J.) U., 1983—, dir. Trenton State Coll. Annual Wrtrs. Conf. N.J. State Council on Arts fellow, 1980, 84; recipient Billie Murray Denny award, 1981, Barnes award Saturday Press, 1986. Mem. PSA. Home: RR 2 Box 177 Hopewell NJ 08525

HOLLANDER, JOHN, b. NYC, Oct. 28, 1929, s. Franklin and Muriel (Kornfeld) H.; m. Anne Hellen Loesser, June 15, 1953 (div.); children—Martha, Elizabeth; m. 2d, Natalie Charkow, Dec. 15, 1981. Author poetry: A Crackling of Thorns, 1958, Movie-Going and Other Poems, 1962, Visions from the Ramble, 1965, Types of Shape, 1968, The Night Mirror, 1971, The Head of the Bed, 1974, Tales Told of the Fathers, 1975, Reflections on Espionage, 1976, Spectral Emanations, 1978, In Place, 1978, Blue Wine, 1979, Looking Ahead, 1982, Powers of Thirteen, 1983, Dal Vero (with Saul Steinberg), 1983, In Time and Place, 1986; The Untuning of the Sky, 1961, Images of Voice, 1970, Vision and Resonance, 1975, The Figure of Echo, 1981, Rhyme's Reason, 1981; ed.: The Wind and the Rain (with Harold Bloom), 1961, Poems of Ben Jonson, 1961, Jiggery-Pokery (with Anthony Hecht), 1966, Poems of Our Moment, 1968, Modern Poetry: Essays in Criticism, 1968, American Short Stories Since 1945, 1968, The Oxford Anthology of English Literature (with Frank Kermode, Harold Bloom, J.B. Trapp, Martin Price, Lionel Trilling), 1973, I.A. Richards: Essays in His Honor (with R.A. Brower, Helen Vendler), 1973, Literature as Experience (with David Bromwich, Irving Howe), 1979. BA, Columbia U., 1950, MA, 1952; PhD, Ind. U., 1959. Prof. English, CUNY, NYC, 1966-77, Yale U., New Haven, 1977—. Recipient Levinson Prize, Poetry Mag., 1974, Bollingen Prize, Beinecke Library, Yale U., 1983; recipient LittD, Marietta (Ohio) Coll., 1982. Mem. AAP, AAIAL, Am. Acad. Arts and Scis. Home: 95 Beecher Rd Woodbridge CT 06525

HOLLENSWORTH, MAYME STEVENS, b. Leola, AR, Nov. 3, 1910; d. Charles and Ida (Harrison) Stevens; widowed; children—Joe, Judith Hope. Author: Eat Thy Bread with Joy, 1960. Contrbr. numerous articles to newspapers, mags. including Glamour Mag., Farm Wife, others. L.I., Cottey Coll., 1929, student Yale U., 1962. Home: 5506 A St Little Rock AR 72205

HOLLINGSWORTH, KENT, b. St. Louis, Aug. 21, 1929; s. Denzil M. and Thelma (Parrott) H.; m. Mary Warfield, Aug. 26, 1981; children—Val, Randolph, Amery, Letitia, Wright, Charles. Works incl.: Of The World's Great Stallions, 1956, John E. Madden, 1965, Quarter-Century American Racing and Breeding, 1967, The Great Ones, 1970, The Kentucky Thoroughbred, 1976, rev. ed., 1985. AB, UKY, 1950; LLB, JD, U. KY, 1959. Rptr. Lexington (KY) Leader, 1954-63; correspondent Sports Illustrated, Lexington, 1957-63; attorney, Lexington, 1959-64; ed./pub. The Blood-Horse, Lexington, 1963—. Served to Capt., US Army, 1952-54. Chmn., Racing Hall of Fame, 1981—. Wrkg. on Archjockey of Canterbury and Other Tales. Office: Box 4038 Lexington KY 40544

HOLLIS, JOCELYN, b. NYC, June 3, 1927; d. William Holroyd and Marian Phyllis (Thomas) Topham; m. Raymond Erwin Hollis, May 2, 1948 (div. Apr.1970); children—Karen Elli Hollis Peters, Constance Jane Hollis Fusilier, Kurt Thomas. Author: Chopin and Other Poems, 1972, Vietnam Poems: The War Poems of Today, 1979, Poems of the Vietnam War, 1980, Peace Poems, 1983, Vietnam Poems II: A New Collection, 1983, Beirut and Other Poems, 1985, The Foundations of Paradise, 1985, Collected Vietnam Poems and Other Poems, 1986; editor (Jocelyn Topham), Morning's Come Singing, 1981, DiVersity Poems (anthology), 1979, Vietnam Heroes: A Tribute, 1982, Paradise Lost . . . A Continuation, 1983, Modern Metaphysical Lyrics, 1983, (with M. Stefan Sikora) Talisman, 1983, Vietnam Heroes III: That We Have Peace, 1983, 1985, Religious Poems for Today's World, 1984, Twentieth Century Sonnets, 1984, Vietnam Heroes II: The Tears of a Generation, 1984, Vietnam Heroes IV, The Long Ascending Cry, 1985, Vietnam Literature Anthology: A Balanced Perspective, 1985. BA, U. Del., 1973, MA, 1979. Asst. editor PS Mag. U.S. Army, Aberdeen Proving Ground, Md., 1953-54; pub. and editor, Am. Poetry and Literature Press, Upper Darby, 1978—. Recipient 1st prize Calif. Olympiad of the Arts, 1964; 1st prize DeKalb Literary Arts Jnl Contest, Ga., 1969; 1st prize First State Writers' Poetry Contest, Del., 1976; Modern Poetry Contest, Phila. Writers Conf., 1978. Office: Box 2013 Upper Darby PA 19082

HOLLOMAN, HUGH JERRY, b. Staten Island, NY, Dec. 2, 1947, s. Hubert Jerry and Laverne Phyllis (Robb) H.; m. Janet Beverley Holloman, Nov. 16, 1968; children—Jennifer, James. Ed. Mobility Mag., 1980—. BS in Journalism, U. Md., 1973. Bus. ed. Alexandria (Va.) Gazette, 1974; asst. v.p. Alexandria C. of C., 1974-76; public affairs officer OPIC, Washington, 1976-77; ed. Natl. Savs. & Loan League, Washington, 1977-79; dir. publs. Employee Relocation Council, Washington, 1979—. Recipient Investigative Reporting award Va. Press Assn., 1974. Home: 8139 Mary Jane Dr Manassas VA 22111

HOLLON, WILLIAM EUGENE, b. Commerce, TX, May 28, 1913; s. Samuel Horace and Myrtle (Payne) H.; m. Francis Elizabeth Cross, May 10, 1941; 1 dau., Susan Jean. Author: The Lost Pathfinder: Zebulon Montgomery Pike, 1949, History of Pre-Flight Training in the USAAF, 1917-52, 1953, Beyond the Cross Timbers: The Travels of Randolph B. Marcy, 1955, William Bolaert's Texas, 1956, (with Berthrong and Owings) Outline Histoy of the United States, 2 vols., 1957, The Southwest Old and New, 1961, The Great American Desert, 1966 (with LeRoy Hafen) Western America, 1970, Violence on the American Frontier, Another Look, 1974, The Movie Cowboy, 1981. BA, E. Tex. State Coll., Commerce, 1934; MA, U. Tex., 1937, PhD, 1942. Fellow Newberry Library, 1953, Am. Philo. Soc., 1947, 50, 64, Huntington Library, 1969, 72, 77; Fulbright and Smith-Mundt fellow, 1958, 1966-67. Editorial bd., Great Plains Hist. Assn. Home: Rt 7 Box 109WH Santa Fe NM 87501

HOLLOWAY, GLENNA PRESTON, b. Nashville, Feb. 7, 1938, d. Rollin Yeargin and Evelyn (Johnson) Preston; m. Robert Wesley Holloway. Contrbr. poems, articles, photography, book reviews to Georgia Rvw, N.Y. Times, Orbis, Ideals, McCall's, Poet Lore, Manhattan Poetry Rvw, Chgo. Tribune, Saturday Rvw, Western Humanities Rvw, Light Year '87, numerous other mags., newspapers, anthols. Student, Ward Belmont Coll., Nashville. Self-employed, int. designer, multi-media artist. Awards: Dellbrook-

Shenandoah, Shenandoah Acad. of Lit., Va., 1979; Alice Moser Claudell Meml., La. State Poetry Soc. & Natl. League Am. PEN Women, 1985; Daniel Whitehead Hicky, Ga. State Poetry Soc., 1982; Best of Best, NLAPW Biennial, 1984, 1st Pl. Grand Ntl Award, NFSPS, 1986, (3) 1st Pl. Ntl League of Amer. Pen Women Mid-Ad, 1987, Hart Crane Memorial Award, Kent State, 1987, 1st, Poet's Pen, 1987. Mem. NLAPW, PSA, Chgo. Poets Club. Home: 913 E Bailey Rd Naperville IL 60565

HOLLOWAY, JUDY A., b. Herington, KS, Dec. 3, 1950; d. Harvey Lee and Alta Mae (Aldridge) Fleming; m. Gary C. Holloway, Aug. 9, 1969; children—Barry, Chris. Author, illustrator: Aunt Amanda: Speech Helper Stories & Activities, 1986, Aunt Amanda: On Cloud Nine, 1987, Luck to Be Me, 1988. Student Hutchinson Commun. Jr. Coll. Asst., sec. LTL/USD 418 McPherson, KS, 1985-86. Home: 612 Manchester Ct McPherson KS 67460

HOLLOWAY, MARCELLA MARIE, CSJ, b. St. Louis, MO, Dec. 1, 1913; d. John James and Mary Maude (Kopp) Holloway. Works: Prosodic Theory of G.M. Hopkins, 1947, Should You Become A Sister?, 1978; author plays, 1958—, latest being Talitha, 1976; contrbr. wrtr. and poet to various mags. and jnls. MA, U. MO, 1943; PhD, Catholic U., Washington, DC, 1947. Chmm. English dept. Avila College, Kansas City, MO, 1947-63; tchr. summer sessions Catholic U., 1948-70; English dept. Fontbonne College, St. Louis, 1963-85. NEH, 1973, 76, 80; First prize poetry and feature article, Natl. League of Penwomen, St. Louis Branch, 1985. Mem. MLA. St. Louis Writers Guild, St. Louis Poetry Center, Natl. League of Am. Penwomen. Home: 6321 Clemens St Louis MO 63130

HOLMAN, BOB, b. LaFollette, TN, Mar. 10, 1948, s. Benjamin Geller and Sally Ruth (Lewis) H.; m. Elizabeth Murray; children—Sophia, Daisy. Author: Tear to Open, 1980, 8 Chinese Poems, 1982, Sweat & Sex & Politics, 1984, Panic*DJ, 1987; contrbr. to anthologies: Fresh Paint, 1977, The Big House, 1978, Poets Theatre, 1979 Out of This World, 1987, Up Late, 1987; poetry videos: Poets in Performance, 1979, Rapp it Up!, 1984; poetry records: Rock 'n' Roll Mythology, 1982, (The New) Death Valley Days, 1986. AB, Columbia U., 1970. Dir. Woods Hole (Mass.) Theater Co., 1973-75; poet-in-residence CETA Artists Project, NYC,1977-80; coordinator St. Marks Poetry Project, 1978-84; dir. Eye & Ear Theater, NYC,1980-83; tchr. poetry-video learning project, NYC,1986-87. Organizer, Poets Encounter for Peace, Managua, Nicaragua, 1986. Creative Artists in Public Service fellow, 1980; poet-in-performance Polyphonix, Paris, 1982. Home: 17 White St New York NY 10013

HOLMES, ANNA, see Gunderson, Joanna

HOLMES, BARBARA WARE, b. Roanoke, VA, Sept. 2, 1945; d. Robert Hoxie (stepfather) and Dorris Mae (Vest) Savoy; m. David Jeffrey Holmes, Nov. 30, 1968; 1 dau., Sarah Anne. Author: Charlotte Cheetham: Master of Disaster, 1985, Charlotte the Starlet, 1988. Contrbr. short stories (fiction) to mags. including Redbook, Samisdat, Moving Out, Pig Iron Mag. BA in English edn., Springfield Coll., Mass., 1967; MA in English, Northeastern U., Boston, 1969. Reference librarian, clerk Springfield City Library, 1968; schl. librarian Montville Schl. system, Conn., 1969-70, Ketchikan pub. schls., Alaska, 1970-72; advt. mgr., asst. to editor ind. schl. bulltn. Natl. Assn. Ind. Schls., Boston, 1973-74; free-lance writer, 1975—. Mem. pub. relations com. Zane North Schl. PTA, Collingswood, N.J., 1981-84. Mem. AG. Home: 322 Collings Ave Collingswood NJ 08108

HOLMES, HELEN JUANITA, d. Garland Woodrow and Verdie Inez (Turnage) Holmes; children—Sara Kimberly Holmes, Jason Woodrow Holmes, Jennifer Lynne Holmes. Author Echoes of Broadslab (poetry), 1977. Wrkg. on novel. Edn. Campbell Coll., Buies Creek, N.C. Mem. N.C. Poetry Soc., Am. Poet. Home: Rt 4 Box 199 Benson NC 27504

HOLMES, JANET ALICE, b. Libertyville, IL, Mar. 15, 1956; d. Paul Allen and Miriam (O'May) Holmes. Author: Paperback Romance, 1984 (as Janet Holmes Stewart); poetry and criticism in lit mags. BA, Duke U., 1973-76; MFA, Warren Wilson Coll., 1983-85. Address: Rt 1 Box 147 Santa Fe NM 87501

HOLMES, JOHN CLELLON, b. Holyoke, MA, Mar. 12, 1926; s. John McClellan and Elizabeth Franklin (Emmons) H.; m. Marian Miliambro Holmes, July, 1944 (div. 1952); m. 2d, Shirley Anise Allen, Sept. 11, 1953. Author: Go, 1952, The Horn, 1958, Get Home Free, 1964, Nothing More To Declare (memoirs), 1967, The Bowling Green Poems, 1977, Death Drag Poems, 1979, Visitor: Jack Kerouac in Old Saybrook, 1980, Interior Geographies, 1981, Gone in October, 1985, Displaced Person, 1987, Dire Coasts (poems), 1987; contrbr. articles, poems, short stories and criticism to Atlantic, Harper's, NY Times Mag, Holiday, Saturday Rvw, Poetry Mag, Partisan Rvw, So Rvw, Playboy, Poetry NOW, Nugget, Contact, Esquire, Penthouse, New Letters, Audience, Les Lettres Nouvelles, Glamour, Venture, Neurotica, Dict. of Lit. Bio., many more. Student, Columbia U., 1943, 45-46, New Schl. Social Research, 1949-50. Vis. lectr. Univ. Iowa, Iowa City, 1963-64; writer-in-res. Univ. Ark., Fayetteville, 1966, assoc. prof., 1975-79, prof., 1980-87; vis. prof. Brown Univ., Providence, RI, 1971-72; vis. prof. Bowling Green Univ., Ohio, 1968, 1975. Served to AB, USN, 1944-45, USA. Recipient best non- fiction award, Playboy Mag., 1964, 70, 71, 72, 73; Alex Cappon prize, New Letters Mag., 1978, Guggenheim fellow, NYC, 1976-77; Pulitzer prize fiction jury, NYC, 1982. Mem. PEN, AWP (bd. dirs.). Address: Box 75 Old Saybrook CT 06475

HOLMES, MARILYN ADAMS, b. Des Moines, Nov. 1, 1930, d. Everett Victor and Vivian Gudren (Jorgensen) Adams; m. Hardin Glenn Holmes, Dec. 30, 1954 (div. 1978); children—Geoffrey Hardin (dec.), Vivian Talbot, Whitney Adams. Ed., photographer The Automobile and the Future of Denver; contrbr. numerous articles to newspapers, mags. Wrkg. on non-fiction book. BA with honors, State U. Iowa, 1954. Editorial asst. Films in Rvw, NYC; asst. ed. Bus. Week, NYC; dir. public relations Colo. Counties, Denver; pres. Capitol News Service, Denver, 1975—; exec. ed. Woman's View, Denver, 1985—; press aide U.S. Senatorial cand., Denver, 1975. Mem. Public Relations Soc. Am. (accredited), ASJA, Natl. Fedn. Press Women, Colo. Press Women (1st place in public relations, promotion, publicity 1982). Home: 511 S Gilpin St Denver CO 80209

HOLMES, MARJORIE ROSE, b. Storm Lake, IA; d. Samuel Arthur and Rosa (Griffith) H.; m. Lynn Mighell, Apr. 9, 1932; children—Marjorie Mighell Croner, Mark, Mallory, Melanie Mighell Dimopoulos; m. Dr. George Schmieler, July 4, 1981. Author: World By the Tail, 1943, Ten O'Clock Scholar, 1946, Saturday Night, 1959, Cherry Blossom Princess, 1960, Follow Your Dream, 1961, Love is a Hopscotch Thing, 1963, Senior Trip, 1962, Love and Laughter, 1967, I've Got to Talk to Somebody, God, 1969, Writing the Creative Article, 1969, Who Am I, God?, 1971, To Treasure Our Days, 1971, Two from Galilee, 1972, Nobody Else Will Listen, 1973, You and I and Yesterday, 1973, As Tall as My Heart, 1974, How Can I Find You God?, 1975, Beauty in Your Own Back Yard, 1976, Hold Me Up a Little Longer, Lord, 1977, Lord, Let Me Love, 1978, God and Vitamins, 1980, To Help You Through the Hurting, 1983, Three from Galilee: The Young Man from Nazareth, 1985, Writing the Creative Article Today, 1985, The Messiah, 1987, Marjorie Holmes' Secrets of Health, Energy and Staying Young, 1987; contrbg. editor: Guideposts, 1977—. Student, Buena Vista Coll., 1927-29, DLitt (hon.), 1976; BA, Cornell Coll., 1931. Tchr. writing Cath. U., 1964-65, U. Md., 1967-68; mem. staff Georgetown Writers Conf., 1959-81. Free-lance writer: short stories, articles, verse for mags. including Reader's Digest; weekly columnist "Love and Laughter," Washington Evening Star, 1959-75; monthly columnist, Woman's Day, 1971-77; bd. dirs., The Writer, 1975—. Recipient Woman of Achievement award natl. Fedn. Press Women, 1972. Mem. Am. Newspaper Women's Club, Va. Press Women, Washington Natl. Press Club, Children's Book Guild. Home: 637 E McMurray Rd McMurray PA 15317

HOLMSTEN, VICTORIA LYNN, b. Hinsdale, IL, Nov. 27, 1953; d. Victor Theodore and Marion Gunhild (Barkstrom) Holmsten; m. Donald Glen Allen, Aug. 18, 1984. Contrbr. articles to newspapers, mags. including Chgo. Tribune, N.Mex. Tchr., others. Contrbr., editor: Western N.Mex. Lunatic Fringe Newsletter, 1982—. Wrkg. on short non-fiction stories, hist. romance, teacher book. BA, Macalester Coll., 1975; MA, Middlebury Coll., 1985. Office aide, wrtr. Albuquerque Civic Light Opera, 1979-81; tchr. English, Laguna-Acoma High Schl., New Laguna, N.Mex., 1981-85; tchr. lang. arts Bur. of Indian Affairs Wingate High Schl., Ft. Wingate, N.Mex., 1985-87. Mem. Wingate Area Wrtrs. Assn., AAUW, N.Mex. Council Tchrs. English (pres. 86-87), NCTE. NCTE. Home: Box 3219 Shiprock NM 87420

HOLNICK, CATHERINE SIGMUND, b. Neptune, NJ, Jan. 8, 1959; d. John Stuart and Catherine Coyne (Brasch) Sigmund; m. Stephen Richard Holnick, June 6, 1981. Assoc. ed., ed. Bowling Proprietor Mag., 1982—. BA, Shippensburg U., 1981. Assoc. ed. Bowling Proprietors' Assn., Arlington, TX, 1982-83. Mem. SPJ, Bowling Writers Assn. Am. Home: 3004 Oxford Court Flower Mound TX 75028

HOLP, CAROLYN ELAINE, b. Thornton, WV, June 8, 1947; d. James William Skiles and Helen Poling Nelson; m. John Alex Babics III, May 23, 1968 div. 1976); children—Richard, Carol Dawn Allen, John; m. Andrew Jon Holp, Sept. 15, 1984. Contrbr. poems to anthols. Wrkg. on novel, articles, children's story. Grad. public schls., Vermilion, OH. Compositor, The Jnl., Lorain, OH, 1979-80; free-lance wrtr., 1983—. Recipient Golden Poet award World of Poetry, 1986, Honorable Mention, 1986. Home: 1937 Tait Ave Lorain OH 44053

HOLSAERT, FAITH S., b. NYC, Jan. 8, 1943, d. James and Eunice (Spellman) H.; children—Jonah Liebert, Carmela Liebert. Contrbr. to

Redbook, Intro, Phoebe. BA, Barnard Coll., 1966; MFA, Warren Wilson Coll., Swannanoa, N.C., 1982. Various teaching and cons. positions; freelance wrtr. Finalist Algren award PEN, 1984, Flannery O'Connor award U. Ga., 1985. Mem. AWP. Home: 1622 Kenwood Rd Charleston WV 25314

HOLSTON, JAMES EUGENE, b. Terre Haute, IN, Jan. 4, 1951; s. James W. and Marie A. (Kern) H.; m. Kathleen Karr, Aug. 6, 1977; children—James Steven, Marianne. Book rvwr., Bible Truth; contrbr. articles to Firm Fdn., Restoration Quarterly, The Iowan. BA, Harding U., 1974; MTh, Harding U. Grad. Schl. Relig., 1980. Part-time minister, Ch. of Christ, Aubrey, AR, 1974-75, Snowden Circle Ch. of Christ, Memphis, 1976-77; tchr. Union Ave. Ch. of Christ Day Schl., Memphis, 1979; minister Ch. of Christ, Ames, IA, 1979-86; Eastside Ch. of Christ, Eastside, NY, 1986—. Home: Box 74 East Syracuse NY 13057

HOLT, ROCHELLE LYNN, b. Chgo., Mar. 17, 1946, d. Russell Thomas and Olga Genevieve (Kochick) Holt; m. D.H. Stafanson, Aug. 7, 1970 (div. 1978). Author: (poetry) From One Bird, 1978, Train in the Rain, 1982, Timelapse, 1983, The Blue Guitar, 1984, Mendsongs & Soulspace (with Linda Zeizer), 1984, Haiku of Desire (with Linda Zeizer), 1985, Extended Family, 1985; (prose) The Invisible Dog, 1981, Legend in His Time, 1981, Pangs, 1982, Letters of Human Nature (with Virginia Love Long, nominated for Pulitzer prize small press prose div.), 1985, Shared Journey: Journal of Two Sister Souls (with Virginia Love Long), 1986, Poetry: Prescriptions for Psyche, 1986, numerous others. BA, U. Ill., Chgo., 1967; MFA in English, U. Iowa, 1970; PhD, Columbia Pacific U., 1980. Wrtr.-in-residence Miss. Indsl. Coll., Holly Springs, 1974-75, Miles Coll., Birmingham, Ala., 1976, Vail Dean Acad., Mountainside, N.J., 1985, Kean Coll., Elizabeth, N.J., 1985; instr. English, Union Coll., Cranford, N.J., 1984-85; judge children's lit. W.Va. Wrtrs. Soc. contest, 1983, 84; judge poetry Telewoman, Berkeley, Calif., 1985; freelance wrtr., poetry evaluator. Grantee U. Minn. Office Advanced Drama Research, 1975, Dodge Fdn. N.J., 1979, NEA, 1976, 77. Mem. Women's Inst. Freedom of Press (founding mem.), Feminist Wrtrs. Guild (chair natl. steering com. mems.-at-large 1981-83), IWWG, AWP, AAP, PSA, P&W, Natl. Assn. Poetry Therapists. Address: 3101 Lake Pine Way Tarpon Springs FL 33589

HOLTZ, VICTORIA, Author: Mistress of Mellyn, 1960, Kirkland Revels, 1962, Bride of Pendorric, 1963, Legend of the Seventh Virgin, 1965, Menfreya In the Morning, 1966, The King of the Castle, 1967, The Queen's Confession, 1968, Shivering Sands, 1969, The Secret Woman, 1970, Shadow of the Lynx, 1971, On the Night of the Seventh Moon, 1972, The Curse of the Kings, 1973, The House of a Thousand Lanterns, 1974, Lord of the Far Island, 1975, Pride of the Peacock, 1976, The Devil on Horseback, 1977, My Enemy the Queen, 1978, The Spring of the Tiger, 1979, The Mask of the Enchantress, 1980, The Judas Kiss, 1981, The Demon Lover, 1982, The Time of the Hunters Moon, 1983, The Landower Legacy, 1984, The Road to the Paradise Island, 1985, Secret For a Nightingale, 1986, The Silk Vendetta, 1987. Address: Doubleday Garden City NY 11530

HOTZ, HERMAN, b. Phila., June 26, 1919; s. David Leon and Anna Miriam (Hanken) H.; m. Sharon Goldberg, Mar. 4, 1974; children—Arlene, Donna, Debbie, Alan. Author: Government Contracts, 1979, The $100 Billion Market: How to Do Business with the Government, 1980, Profit from Your Money-Making Ideas, 1980, Profit-Line Management, 1981, The Winning Proposal: How to Write It, 1981, Directory of Federal Purchasing Offices, 1982, The Secrets of Practical Marketing for Small Business, 1982, How to Succeed as an Independent Consultant, 1983, 2d ed., 1987, 2001 Sources of Financing for Small Business, 1983, Successful Newsletter Publishing for the Consultant, 1983, Mail Order Magic, 1983, Persuasive Writing, 1983, Beyond the Resume, 1984, How to Buy the Right Peronal Computer, 1984, How to Make Money with Your Microcomputer, 1984, Word Processing for Office Publications, 1984, Computer Work Stations, 1985, The Business of Public Speaking, 1985, The Consultant's Edge, 1985, How to Sell Computer Services to Government Agencies, 1985, How to Become a More Successful Consultant with your Personal Computer, 1985, Utilizing Consultants Successfully, 1985, Marketing with Seminars and Newsletters, 1986, Advice, A High Profit Business, 1986, The Consultant's Guide to Proposal Writing, 1986, The Direct Marketer's Workbook, 1986, The Business Writer's Problem Solver, 1986, The Consultant's Guide to Newsletter Profits, 1987, Expanding Your Practice with Seminars, 1987. Mgr. Volt Info. Scis., Lanham, MD, 1967-74; owner HRH Communications, Wheaton, MD, 1975—. Served to sgt. U.S. Army, 1941-45. Address: II 1131 Univ Blvd W 319 Wheaton MD 20902

HOLYER, ERNA MARIA, (Ernie Holyer) b. Weilheim, Bavaria, Ger., Mar. 15, 1925; d. Mathias and Anna Maria (Goldhofer) Schretter; came to U.S., 1956; m. Friedrich Rupp, May 27, 1943 (div. 1949); m. 2d, Gene Wallace Holyer, Aug. 24, 1957. Author children's books, 1965—, latest being Reservoir Road Adventure, 1982; contrbr. to various anthols. AA, San Jose Evening College, D. Lit., World Univ., Tuscon, 1984. Freelance wrtr., 1960—; writing tchr., San Jose Metropolitan Adult Ed. Program, 1968. Mem. CA Writer's Club. Home: 1314 Rimrock Dr San Jose CA 95120

HOLYER, ERNIE, see Holyer, Erna

HOLZBERGER, WILLIAM GEORGE, b. Chgo., Jan. 6, 1932; s. William Alexander and Mary Frances (Ward) H.; m. Annegret Meseke, Apr. 24, 1965; children—Stefan, Rebecca. Editor: Perspectives on Hamlet (with Peter B. Waldeck), 1973; The Complete Poems of George Santayana, 1979. PhB in Philosophy, Northwestern U., 1960, MA in Philosophy, 1965, MA in English, 1966, PhD in English, 1969. English tchr. Tuley public high schl., Chgo., 1961-65; prof. English Bucknell Univ., Lewisburg, Pa., 1969—. Editing The Works of George Santayana. Recipient grant-in-aid, Am. Philo. Soc., Phila., 1970, ACLS, 1972, 73; sr. research fellow, NEH, Washington, 1975-76. Mem. AAUP, MLA, Soc. for the Advancement of Am. Philosophy, Intl. Santayana Soc., NCTE. Address: Eng Dept Bucknell Univ Lewisburg PA 17837

HOMBURGER, FREDDY, b. Saint Gall, Switzerland, Feb. 8, 1916, came to U.S., 1941, naturalized, 1952; s. Ludwig and Cecile (Gaille) H.; m. Regina Thurlimann, Nov. 8, 1939. Author: The Medical Care of the Aged and Chronically Ill, 1955, 2d ed., 1964, The Biologic Basis of Cancer Management, 1957. Contrbr. numerous articles to profl. jnls. Ed.: The Physiopathology of Cancer (Karger), 1953, 3d ed., 1974, Progress in Experimental Tumor Research, 1960, 85, Concepts in Toxicology, 1984—. Wrkg. on memoirs, novel, collection of poems. U. Med. Schl., Vienna, 1937; M.D., U. Geneva, 1940. Reserach prof. medicine Tufts U. Med. Schl., Boston, 1948-57; pres., dir. Bio-research Inst., Cambridge, MA, 1957—; research prof. pathology Boston U., 1977—. Home: 759 High St Dedham MA 02026

HOMESLEY, HORACE EDWARD, (Nicholas Sokolnikoff, Louis Tenkiller, Whitecloud), b. Jacksonville, AL, July 9, 1928; s. Horace Edward and Ethel Euphene (Couch) H.; m. Sara Grace Walker, Dec. 16, 1945; chidren—Katrina D. Harrell, Angela B. Matthews, Dennis E., Michael W., Timothy P. Author: Sturm-Liouville Oscillation Theorems, 1957, Nuclear Physics, 1958, Basic Mathematics, 1959, A History of U.S. Army Squads and Platoons, 1965, Small Unit Combat Experience in Vietnam, 1966, Pitfalls and Pratfalls in Practical Pursuits of Systems Analysts Are OK But I Wouldn't Want My Sister to Marry One, 1970, The Decline and Collapse of American Civilization, 1976, Operations Research—Scientific Management, 1982, Administrative Systems, 1984. Measuring Program Output, 1984, Army Readiness as a Function of Budgets, 1984. B.S., U. Fla., 1951, M.S., 1957; Ph.D. in Public Administration, Nova U., 1984. Exec. Asst. Secy. of Commerce, Washington, 1977; spcl. asst. Chief of Staff, U.S. Army, Washington, 1978; chief systems analyses U.S. Army TROSCOM, St. Louis, 1973-77, 78-87. Served to major U.S. Army, 1951-54, Korea. Home: 1106 E Washington St Thomasville GA 31792

HOMSTAD, GARY DUANE, b. Paris, TX, Aug. 30, 1945; s. Clyde Arthur and June (White) H. Contrbr. articles, photographs to mags., jnls. including Port Cities Mag., Draft Horse Jnl, Wild Am., Colo. Outdoor Guide Mag. Editor, author (articles, photographs) The Black Hills Sentinel, 1966-69. Ed. Black Hills Sentinel, Ellsworth AFB, S.D., 1966-69; asst. editor Am. Wilderness Alliance, Denver, 1978-79; assoc. editor Colo. Outdoor Guide, Denver, 1978-79; copywriter KGDS radio sta., Duluth, Minn., 1985-86; ed. Consortium Report, Northern Lakes Health Consortium, 1986—. Served to ensign-4 U.S. Air Force, 1966-69. Mem. Duluth C. of C. Home: 101 Mesaba Ave A-2 Duluth MN 55806

HONGO, GARRETT KAORU, b. Volcano, HI, May 30, 1951; s. Albert Kazuyoshi and Louise Tomiko (Kubota) H.; m. Cynthia Anne Thiessen, May 15, 1982: 2 sons, Alexander Kazuyoshi, Hudson Hideo. Author: The Buddha Bandits Down Highway 99, 1978, Yellow Light, 1982, The River of Heaven, 1988. Poetry editor: The Mo. Rvw, 1984—. Contrbr. poems to anthols. BA cum laude, Pomona Coll., 1973; MFA, U. Calif.-Irvine, 1980. Dir., Asian Multi Media, Seattle, 1976-77; poet-in-residence Seattle Arts Commn., 1977-78; tchg. asst. U. Calif., Irvine, 1980-82, vis. poet, 1983-84; vis. asst. prof. U. Southern Calif., Los Angeles, 1982-83; asst. prof. U. Mo., Columbia, 1984—. Recipient Hopwood Poetry prize U. Mich., 1975, NEA fellowship, 1982, Pushcart selection, 1987, Lamont Poetry Prize, 1987. Mem. AWP. Home: 18 Clinton Dr Columbia MO 65203

HONIG, EDWIN B., b. NYC,Sept. 3, 1919; s. Abraham David and Jane (Freundlich) H.; m. Charlotte Gilchrist, April 1, 1940 (dec. 1963); m. Margot S. Dennes, Dec. 15, 1963 (div. 1978); children—Daniel D., Jeremy D. Author: poems, The Moral Circus, 1955, The Gazabos, 1960, Survivals, 1964, Spring Journal, 1968, Four

Springs, 1972, Shake a Spear with Me, John Berryman, 1974, At Sixes, 1974, The Affinities of Orpheus, 1976, Selected Poems (1955-1976), 1979, Interrupted Praise, 1983; criticism, Garcia Lorca, 1944, Dark Conceit: The Making of Allegory, 1959, Calderon and the Seizures of Honor, 1972, The Poet's Other Voice, 1985; stories Foibles and Fables of an Abstract Man, 1979; trans. Calderon: 4 Plays, 1961, Cervantes' Interludes, 1964, Calderon's Life Is a Dream, 1970, Pessoa's Selected Poems, 1971, Garcia Lorca's Divan and other Writings, 1974, La Dorotea (with A. S. Trueblood), 1985, Pessoa's Keeper of Sheep, 1986, Poems of Fernando Pessoa, 1986; plays and play production, Ends of the World and Other Plays, 1981; (with Oscar Williams) anthols. The Mentor Book of Major American Poets, 1961, The Major Metaphysical Poets, 1968, Spenser, 1968. AB, Univ. of Wis., 1941, AM, 1947. Prof. Eng., Brown Univ., 1957-85 (chairman, 1967-68; dir. creative wrtg. program, 1958-75). AUS, 1943-46, ETO. Guggenheim fellow, 1948, 62; NEH fellow, 1975, grantee, 1977-80; NEA fellow, 1977, 81. Home: 78 Barnes St Providence RI 02906

HOOD, GWENYTH ELISE, b. White Plains, NY, Dec. 10, 1955; d. Thomas Arthur and Marion Louise (Snee) H. Author: The Coming of the Demons, 1982; (jnl. on seven authors) Seven, vol. VIII, 1987. Wrkg. on fantasy trilogy, articles on J. R. R. Tolkien and C.S. Lewis, short stories. B.A., Wellesley Coll., 1977; A.M., U. Mich., 1978, Ph.D., 1984. Lectr., Purdue U., West Lafayette, IN, 1982-84; asst. prof. English, Marshall U., Huntington, WV, 1985-86, Mansfield, PA, 1986—. Recipient Major Hopwood prize U. Mich., 1979. Mem. MLA, Mythopoeic Soc. Home: 214 N Main St Mansfield PA 16933

HOOD, JAMES BYRON, b. Tallassee, AL, July 27, 1951; s. James Jackson and Margie Ruth (Mann) H. Exec. ed. and v.p., Shelby Report of the Southwest, 1981—, Shelby Report of the Southeast, 1981—, Shelby's Southwest Foodservice, 1984—. BS in Poli. Sci., Auburn U., 1974. Editorial asst. Arone Pub., Arlington, Va., 1978-79; asst. editor Body Forum (mag.), Atlanta, 1979-81; editor-in-chief Shelby Pub., Gainesville, Ga., 1981—. Recipient Williams award Kappa Sigma, 1974; named Trendsetter of Yr., North Tex. Foodservice Brokers Assn., 1986. Home: 3458 Rockhaven Circle NE Atlanta GA 30324

HOOD, PHILIP BOYCE, b. Burlington, NC, June 28, 1951; s. William Boyce and Ruth (Waters) H.; m. Merrill Hobar, Mar. 9, 1974 (div.1978); m. 2d, Connie Jean Ford, Jan. 19, 1979. Contrbr. to Things Chinese, 1980; writer/ed. Encyc. of Kit Cars, 1983; ed. Amer. Folk Artists, 1986. BA in Econ./Jnlsm., Penn. State U., 1974. Dist. mgr. McGraw-Hill Book Co., Novato, CA, 1975-78; national media liaison Arcosanti Festival, Phoenix, AZ, 1978-79; ed. Auto Logic Pub., San Jose, CA, 1979-84, GPI Pubns., Cupertino, CA, 1984—. Mem. West. Pubns. Assn. Home: 1021 Ramona Avenue San Jose CA 95125

HOOD, ROBERT ERIC, b. Mildred, PA, Apr. 15, 1926, s. Charles Dunbar and Alice Victoria (Johnson) H.; m. Ann Margaret King, Oct. 15, 1955; children—Carol Ann, Eric Charles. Author: Find a Career in Photography, 1959, 12 at War, Great Photographers Under Fire, 1967, The Gashouse Gang, 1976, Let's Go to a Baseball Game, 1973, Let's Go to a Football Game, 1975, Let's Go to a Basketball Game, 1976, Let's Go to a Stockcar Race, 1974; ed. numerous juvenile sport books for G.P. Putnam's Sons, Coward-McCann. BA in English, SUNY-Binghamton; postgrad., NYU. Mem. staff Boys' Life Mag., Irving, Tex., 1953-86, now free-lance wrtr.; children's book reviewer N.Y. Times, 1958-78. Mem. ASME, Overseas Press Club, AG. Home: 67 Witch Tree Rd Woodstock NY 12498

HOOF, DAVID LORNE, (David Lorne), b. Washington, Dec. 2, 1945; s. Wayne and Mary Elinor (English) Hoof; m. Bethea Leigh Gledhill, Dec. 18, 1976 (div. Aug. 10, 1987); children—Laura Louise, Emily Joy. Author novels: Appointment with Lazarus, 1982, Apocalypse Vector, 1983, Hacker, 1984, Movie Rights, 1984, Mutants, 1985, Curtain Call, 1986, Killer, 1987. Contrbr. to mags., anthols. A.B., Cornell U., 1969; Ph.D., Purdue U., 1974. Energy analyst City of Rockville, MD, 1978-79; mgr. technology develop. U.S. Dept. of Energy, Washington, 1977—. Recipient award for best humerous article Realtor Mag., 1985, Honorable Mention for fiction San Jose State U., 1986. Mem. Washington Ind. Wrtrs. Home: 20200 Thunderhead Way Germantown MD 20874

HOOPER, PATRICIA, b. Saginaw, MI, May 4, 1941, d. John Phillip and Edythe Margaret (Sharpe) Hooper; m. John A. Everhardus, June 22, 1963; children: John Christian, Katherine Marie. Author: Other Lives, 1984, A Bundle of Beasts, 1987. Contrbr. to anthologies: Anthology of Magazine Verse and Yearbook of American Poetry, New Directions Anthology; contrbr. to Am. Scholar, Am. Poetry Rvw, Poetry, Chgo. Rvw, Mich. Qtly Rvw, Carolina Qtly, others. BA, U. Mich., 1963, MA, 1964. Recipient Hopwood award U. Mich., 1960, 61, 62, 63. Mem. Detroit Women Writers, PSA (Bernice W. Ames award 1981, Norma Farber First Book award 1984). Address: 616 Yarmouth Rd Birmingham MI 48009

HOOPLE, SALLY CROSBY, b. Dansville, NY, Oct. 23, 1930; d. Thomas Joseph and Lucille Esther (Rex) Crosby; m. Donald Graham Hoople, June 3, 1951; children—Nancy, Anne Ralte, Douglas, David. Contrbr. articles to jnls. B.A., Syracuse U., 1952, M.A., 1953; M.A., N.Y. U., 1971; Ph.D., Fordham U., 1984. English tchr. public high schl., White Plains, NY, 1963-86; asst. prof. humanities and communication Maine Maritime Acad., Castine, 1986—. Mem. MLA, Northeast MLA. Home: Box 184 Castine ME 04421

HOOSE QUINCEY, SHELLEY, b. Los Angelse, Nov. 20, 1955; d. Harned Pettus and Georgia Faye (Johnston) Hoose; m. Martain Karl Quincey, July 12, 1981; children—Ramona, Ayla. Contrbr. articles to mags. including Am. History Illustrated, Working Parents, Talk Story, others. Asst. ed.: Soaring Mag., 1977-79. B.A. in Jnlsm., U. Southern Calif., 1977. Free-lance wrtr., 1984—. Mem. West Hawaii Wrtr.'s Group. Home: Box 695 Captain Cook HI 96704

HOOT, PATRICIA LYNCH, b. Honolulu, Aug. 31, 1921, d. Lindon Lamar and Genevieve (Springstun) Lynch; m. Willard D. Hoot, Dec. 14, 1946 (div. 1960); 1 son, Willard D. II. Contrbr. articles to Dude Ranchers' mag. Wrkg. on short stories, articles. BS, U. Oreg., 1943; postgrad., Boise State U., 1963—. Tchr. elem. schls., Calif., Oreg. and Idaho, 1960—. Home: 2625 Woody Dr Boise ID 83703

HOOTS, HELEN HARDIN, (Helen Hardin), b. Hannibal, MO, Jan. 3; d. Walter Raleigh and Mary (Andris) Hardin; m. Harold Wayne Hoots, June 24, 1939. Author: Ourline of Folklore and Folk Custom, 1940, Illinois, 1942, History of Jefferson County, CO, 1979, History of Pueblo West, CO, 1979; (play) Little Red Riding Hood, 1937; columns in Pens and Brushes, 1982. Contrbr. articles, features, to mags., newspapers, newsletters; radio programs, WGN Chicago, 1937-42. Ed.: Christian Advocate, 1950. B.A., Culver-Stockton Coll., 1929; postgrad. Decatur Sch. Speech, 1932-34. Creative head W.E. Nunn & Assoc., Chgo., 1946-48; assoc. ed., contrbg. ed. Telephony Pub. Corp., Chgo., 1958-81; communications cons., Pueblo West, CO, and Chgo., 1972—. Recipient medal of Distinction, Culver-Stockton Coll., 1961. Mem. Women's Advtg. Club (Silver Service cert. 1978), NFPW (bd. dirs.), Colo. Press Women (counselor), WICI, NLAPW (Colo. pres., 1986-88). Home: Box 7297 Pueblo West CO 81007

HOOVER, CAROL FAITH, b. Eagle Grove, IA, Jan 24, 1921, d. Calvin Bryce and Faith Miriam (Sprole) H.; m. Henry Madison Oliver, Jr., Sept. 14, 1940 (div. 1957); 1 dau., Sheila Faith Hoover Shelton. Contrbr. to The American Family, 1979; short fiction to Story, Denver Qtly, Tex. Qtly; articles to psychol. and psychiatric jnls. BA, Duke U., 1940; MSW, U. N.C., 1947; DSW, Catholic U., 1973. Social worker VA Hosp., Murfreesboro, Tenn., 1957-58, St. Elizabeth's Hosp., Washington, 1958-61, NIMH, Bethesda, Md., 1961-84; pres. Ariadne Press, Rockville, Md., 1976—. Mem. Washington Ind. Wrtrs., Wrtrs. Center, Bethesda. Home: 4817 Tallahassee Ave Rockville MD 20853

HOOVER, JESSE WILBERT, b. West Milton, OH, July 7, 1908; s. Elmer Benjamin and Lydia Ellen (Hoke) H.; m. Esther Naomi Stump, Aug. 24, 1932; 1 son, Vernon Ezra. Co-author ed.: A Manual for Christian Youth, 1945; A History of the Hokes, 1953. Wrkg. on A New History of the Hokes, A History of the Hoovers. B.A., Wheaton Coll., 1932. Pastor Brethren in Christ Ch., Phila., 1939-43; ed. E.V. Pub., Nappanee, IN, 1943-47; onwer, mgr. Hoover Homecraft, Nappanee, 1948-60. Home: 520 N 200 W Greenfield IN 46140

HOOVER, MAE MORGAN, b. Brady, TX, Jan. 4, 1940; d. Joseph Ray and LaVita (Smith) Morgan; m. Alex K. Hoover, June 21, 1958; children—Thomas Len, Teri Ruth, Andrew Weldon. Contrbr. articles, fillers to mags., newsletters including Reader's Digest, Partnership, others. Ed.: Tex. District Voice of Evangelical Mehtodism, 1967-68, Mexico Missions Newsletter, 1983. B.S. cum laude, North Tex. State U., 1971; Diploma, Sch. Spanish, Guadalajara, Mexico, 1979. Owner, operator Gift Shop, Ft. Worth, 1976-77; missionary Evangelical Methodist Church, Chihuahua, Mexico, 1977-84; free-lance wrtr., 1984—. Recipient Honorable Mention for fiction Brite Schl. Christian Wrtrs., 1984, Top Ten award for non-fiction Christian Wrtrs. Inst., 1987, Two Heads Are Better than One award U. Toledo, 1987. Mem. Christian Wrtrs. Fellowship (organizer, leader), Natl. Evangelical Wrtrs. Fellowship (organizer, leader), Natl. Evangelical Wrtrs. Soc. Home: 27354 Evergreen Rd Lathrup Village MI 48076

HOOVER, SUSAN FRANTZ, b. Montreal, Que., Can., Feb. 10, 1939, d. Walter Scott Hoover and Suzanne (Young) Walsh. Contrbr. poetry to EPT, Isinglass Rvw, Ppress, As If the World Had Not Known Sorrow, Ear Mag., Cover, Arts New York, other lit mags; contrbr. to book Taxi Dancer, 1977; collaborator on screenplay: Do Us Part, 1983; co-ed.: Insight lit mag., 1965. AA, Colby Jr. Coll., New London, N.H., 1958; BA, U. Colo., Boulder, 1960. Poet, songwriter, musician, guitar tchr., freelance copywrtr., NYC. Mem. P&W, ASCAP (assoc.). Home: 211 W 10th St New York NY 10014

HOPE, AKUA LEZLI, b. NYC,June 1, 1957, d. Albert Howe and Hope Edwina White. Contrbr. poetry to Obsidian, 1986, Ikon Art Against Apartheid, 1986, Isaac Asimov's Sci. Fiction Mag., Hambone No. 4 1984, lit mags; works included in anthologies inclg. Confirmation, 1983, Extended Outlooks, 1983, Black and in Brooklyn, 1983. MS in Journalism, Columbia U., 1977, MBA, 1978. Mem. Tchrs. & Wrtrs., Sci. Fiction Poetry Assn., New Renaissance Wrtrs. Guild, Soc. Black Profls., P&W. Home: Box 33 Corning NY 14830

HOPES, DAVID BRENDAN, (C.D. Cormac), b. Akron, OH, Sept. 1, 1953, s. Eugene David and Marion Elizabeth (Summers) H. Author: The Glacier's Daughters, 1981. MA, Syracuse U., 1980, PhD,1980. Postdoctoral fellow Syracuse (N.Y.) U., 1979-81; George Bennett fellow Phillips Exeter (N.H.) Acad., 1981-82; vis. asst. prof. English Hiram (Ohio) Coll., 1982-83; asst. prof. lit. U. N.C., Asheville, 1983—. Recipient Juniper prize U. Mass. Press, 1981, Saxifrage prize, Chapel Hill, N.C., 1982, So. Playwrights; prize, N.C. Playwrights Fund, Greenville, 1986. Mem. MLA, PW, Phi Beta Kappa. Office: Dept Lit U NC Asheville One University Heights Asheville NC 28804

HOPKINS, HARRISON, see Plaut, Martin Edward

HOPKINS, JAMES D., b. Elgin, IL, Nov. 25, 1961; s. Raymond E. and Marguerite L. (Beyer) H. Poetry in anthologies. Wrkg. on play-ballet, musical play, poetry. Student public schs., Carperntersville, Ill. Fireman, paramedic Carpentersville and Countryside Fire Dept., Ill., 1981—; CPR instr. ARC, Carpentersville, 1982; active Elgin Community Theatre, Ill. Home: 727 Jackson St Carpentersville IL 60110

HOPP, JAMES LEE, b. Rogers City, MI, Sept. 5, 1949; s. Carroll Paul and Helen Kathryn (Mulka) H. Author: M'Aidez!, 1981. A.A., Alpena Commun. Coll., 1970; B.S., Central Mich. U., 1974. Tchr., Rogers city Schls., MI, 1974—. Home: 273 S Lake St Rogers City MI 49779

HOPPER, JEANNETTE M., (Jay Byrd), b. Oakland, CA, Mar. 17, 1959, d. Jack William and Hazel Marie (Langley) Rogers; m. Melvin Henry Hopper, Jr., Oct. 7, 1978; children—Mark Henry, Jaclyn Corwin-Langley. Contrbr. to: Punnable Horror Stories, Portents, New Blood, (Not) One of US, Footsteps, Grim Graphix, Byline Mag., Dark Regions No. 1, other publs, Horror Columnist Scavenger's Newsletter, 2d. GAS Mag. Diploma Inst. Children's Lit., 1983, Wrtr.'s Digest Schl., 1985. Mem. Small Press Wrtrs. and Artists Orgn. Home: 3049 A Zanetta Dr Marina CA 93933

HOPPER, VIRGINIA SHEARER, b. Newport News, VA, Sept. 15, 1940, d. Louis Cabe and Daisie Virginia (Bell) Shearer; m. Edward William Hopper, Apr. 29, 1933. Author poetry book: A Closed Garden, 1966; contrbr. articles and poems to N.Y. Times, Christian Sci. Monitor, Poet Lore, Hearthstone, other publs. BA, Randolph-Macon Women's Coll., 1925. Mem. N.C. Poetry Soc., Va. Poetry Soc., Pitts. Poetry Soc., AAP, Natl. League Am. Pen Women. Home: 19 Oxford Apts Chapel Hill NC 27514

HORBERT, JANET L. H., see Tabin, Janet Hale

HORNIG, DOUGLAS, b. NYC,Nov. 19, 1943; s. Douglas C. and Yvonne F.H. Author: Foul Shot, 1984, Hardball, 1985, The Dark Side, 1986, Waterman, 1987. BA, Geo. Washington U., 1965. Full-time writer. Edgar nominee, MWA, 1984. Mem. PW, AWP, Writers in Va. Address: Rt 2 Box 816 Afton VA 22920

HORNSTEIN, HAROLD, b. Brklyn., Sept. 10, 1920; s. William and Frances (Heller) H.; m. Patricia Ann Hubbell; children—Jeffrey, Deborah. Author: New Haven Celebrates the Bicentennial, 1976. B.J., Mo. U. Sch. Jnls., 1947; B.A., Brklyn. coll., 1942. Reporter, Columbus Enquirer, GA, 1947-52; news ed. Town Crier, Westport, CT, 1952-53; ed. Post-Telegram, Bridgeport, CT, 1954-68; editorialist, columnist The Register, New Haven, 1968-86. Recipient Best Editorial award for interest of youth Conn. Am. Legion Auxiliary, 1981; 2d place for New England editorial writing AP, 1983, 3d place, 1985. Mem. New Haven Colony Hist. Soc. (bd. dirs. 1975-78), Easton Swimming Assn. (pres. 1964), Sigma Delta Chi (1st prize for editorial writing Conn. chpt. 1981, Honorable Mention for editorial writing Conn. chpt. 1984, 85). Home: 90 Norton Rd Easton CT 06612

HOROWITZ, DAVID JOEL, b. NYC, Jan. 10, 1939; s. Philip and Blanche (Brown) H.; m. Elissa Krauthamer, June 14, 1959; children Jonathan, Sarah, Benjamin, Anne, Author: Student, 1962, Free World Colossus, 1965, Empire and Rekvolution, 1969, Shakespeare-An Existential View, 1965, Fate of Midas, 1973; co-author: The Rockefellers: An American Dynasty, 1976, The First Frontier, 1979, The Kennedys: An American Drama, 1984; contrbg. editor: Calif. Mag. AB, Columbia U., 1959; MA, U. Calif.-Berkeley, 1961. Editor Ramparts mag., Berkeley, 1969-74. Address: Borchadt 136 E 57th St New York NY 10022

HOROWITZ, IRVING LOUIS, b. NYC, Sept. 25, 1929; s. Louis Esther (Tepper) H.; m. Ruth Lenore Horowitz, 1950 (div. 1964); children—Carl Frederick, David Dennis. Author: Idea of War and Peace in Contemporary Philosophy, 1957, Philosophy, Science and the Sociology of Knowledge, 1960, Radicalism and the Revolt Against Reason: The Social Theories of Georges Sorel, 2d edit., 1968, The War Games: Studies of the New Civilian Militarists, 1963, Historia Elementos de la Sociologia del Connocimento, 1963, The New Sociology: Essays in Social Science and Social Values in Honor of C. Wright Mills, 1964, Revolution in Brazil: Politics and Society in a Developing Nation, 1964, The Rise and Fall of Project Camelot, 1967, rev. ed., 1976, Three Worlds of Development: The Theory and Practice of International Stratification, 1966, rev. ed., 1972, Professing Sociology: The Life Cycle of a Social Science, 1963, Latin American Radicalism: A Documentary Report on Nationalist and Left Movements, 1969, Sociological Self-Images, 1969, The Knowledge Factory: Student Power and Academic Politics in America, 1970, Masses in Latin America, 1970, Cuban Communism, 1970, 4th ed., 1979, Foundations of Political Sociology, 1972, Social Science and Public Policy in the United States, 1975, Ideology and Utopia in the United States, 1977, Dialogues on American Politics, 1979, Taking Lives: Genocide and State Power, 1979, Beyond Empire and Revolution, 1982, C. Wright Mills: An American Utopian, 1983, Communicating Ideas: The Crisis of Scholarly Publishing, 1986, Cuban Communism (6th edition). BSS, CCNY, 1951; MA, Columbia U., 1952; PhD, Buenos Aires (Argentina) U., 1957; postgrad. fellow, Brandeis U., 1958-59. Asst. prof. sociology Bard Coll., 1960; assoc. prof. social theory Buenos Aires U., 1955-58; chmn. dept. sociology Hobart and William Smith Colls., 1960-63; assoc. prof., then prof. sociology Washington U., St. Louis, 1963-69; chmn. dept. sociology Livingston Coll., Rutgers U., 1969-73, prof. sociology grad. faculty Rutgers U., 1969—, Hannah Arendt prof. social and polit. theory, 1979—. Editor-in-chief, Transaction/SOCIETY, 1963—. Fellow AAAS; Mem. AAUP, Am. Poli. Sci. Assn., Am. Sociol. Assn., AG, Centre Intl. pour le Devel. (founder), Center for Study The Presidency, Council Fgn. Relations, Intl. Studies Assn., Latin Am. Studies Assn., Intl. Soc. Poli. Psychology (founder). Home: Rt 206 1247 St Rd Blawenburg Rd Princeton NJ 08540

HOROWITZ, LENORE WISNEY, b. Dumont, NJ, Jan. 6, 1946; d. Leonard Gustave and Rosemary (McCann) Wisnyi; m. Lawrence Carl Horowitz, 1970; children—Mirah, Jeremy, Michael, Lauren. Author: Underground Guide to Kauai, Hawaii, annually, 1980—, Red and Purple—A Language Skill Development Program, 1982. AB, Brown U., 1967; PhD, Cornell U., 1971. Prog. asst. NEH, 1970-71; instr. Madeira School, McLean, VA, 1971-73; lect. U. of Santa Clara, Santa Clara, CA, 1974-77; lect. Amer. U., Washington, 1977-86. Home: 362 Selby Ln Atherton CA 94025

HOROWITZ, SHEL ALAN, (Alan Friedman, Alan Kaye), b. N.Y.C., Dec. 24, 1956; s. Norman A. Horowitz and Gloria (Gleich) Yoshida; m. Deborah Friedman, Oct. 9, 1983. Author: Keep Your Money: How to Save Thousands in Advertising, 1985; (with Curtis and Hogan) Nuclear Lessons, 1980. Contrbr. articles on arts, politics, travel, small bus., people, food, ethnicity/culture to mags., newspapers including Vegetarian Times, Boston Globe, numerous others. Columnist: Western Mass. Bus. & Exon. Rvw., 1987—. Ed.: Breathe!, 1981. B.A., Antioch Coll., 1977. Reporter, ed. Atlanta Co-op News Project, 1976; reader Meredith Lit. Agy., N.Y.C., 1977-78; info. specialist NYPIRG/VISTA, N.Y.C., 1979-80; dir. Accurate Writing & More, Northampton, MA, 1981—. Mem. NWU. Home: Box 1164 Northampton MA 01061

HOROWITZ, SHEL A., b. NYC,Dec. 24, 1956, s. Norman Aaron Horowitz and Gloria (Gleich) Yoshida; m. Deborah Friedman, Oct. 9, 1983. Contrbr. over 400 articles to numerous publs. including East Side, Folio/WBAI, Peace Is Our Profession, In These Times, Walking Jnl., Vegetarian Times, The Wrtr., MacWorld, Dayton Daily News, Providence Evening Bulltn., Boston Herald, Boston Globe; author: Keep Your Money: How To Save Thousands in Advertising, 1985; co-author: Nuclear Lessons, 1980; ed. poetry anthology Breathe!, 1980. BA, Antioch Coll., 1977. Manuscript reader Curtis Lit. Agcy., NYC,1978-79; vol. outreach specialist VISTA, Bklyn., 1979-80; dir. Accurate Writing & More, Northampton, Mass., 1981—. Mem. NWU, P&W. Home: Box 1164 Northampton MA 01061

HORRIGAN, PATRICIA ANN, (Olivia McCormack, Patricia Austin), b. Billings, Mont., Jan. 19, 1934; d. George Charles and Helen Viola (McCormick) Austin; m. Jack Allen Horrigan, June 8, 1963; children—Marianne Michael, Aileen Elizabeth, William George. Contrbr. as Olivia McCormack: New Voices in American Poetry, New World Lit. Jnl., San Fernando Poetry Jnl., Am. Poetry Assn. Anthologies, Odessa Poetry Rvw, others; contrbr. as Patricia Austin: Creative with Words Publs. BS in Edn., Oreg. State U., 1957; diploma, Assn. Montessori Internationale, 1968. Tchr. elem. grades Idaho Springs (Colo.) Schs., 1958-63, Denver Mus. Natural History, 1985-86; directress Montessori Schl. Denver, 1969-70, Carrousel Acad., Aurora, Colo., 1971-73. Recipient poetry awards. Home: Box 06436 Denver CO 80206

HORVAT, MARTIN MICHAEL, b. Watsonville, CA, Jan. 16, 1946; s. Martin Thomas Horvat and Edna Mae (Steinfelt) Hill; m. Susan Rae Wampler, Jan. 20, 1973; children: Jennifer Emily, Matthew Christopher, Rebecca Elizabeth. Author: Civil Rights in Amateur Journalism; editor: Library Journal of American Private Press Association, 1982—; editor: Golden Argosy, 1982, The Winter Rhythm, 1986. BS in math, U. Calif.-Davis, 1967; MA in history of sci., Oreg. State U., 1971. Instr. Linn-Benton Community Coll., Albany, Oreg., 1972-74; wilderness homesteading in No. Calif., 1974-76; vocatl. math. co-ordinator Linn-Benton Community Coll., Albany, 1976-77; proprietor Liberty Press, Stayton, Oreg., 1978—; graphic arts chmn. Stayton High Schl., 1985—. Mem. Printing Industries of Pacific, Natl. Amateur Press Assn. (editor 1983, pres. 1986-87), Am. Pvt. Press Assn. (librarian), Fossils (librarian), Stayton C. of C. (pres. 1982-83), Lions Club (pres. 1986). Served with U.S. Army, 1968-71, Vietnam. Home: 112 E Burnett Stayton OR 97383

HORVATH, ELEMER (GEORGE), b. Csorna, Hungary, Apr. 15, 1933; s. John and Margaret (Nagy) H.; came to U.S., 1962; m. Marjorie Dawes, May 29, 1968. Author poems: The Face of Everyday, 1962, From the Diary of a White Negro, 1976, Mayan Mirror, 1982, The Neck of the Hourglass, 1980. Student, U. Budapest, 1955-56, U. Florence, Italy, 1957-60; librarian, Hungary, 1956. Mem. PSA, PEN. Home: Bullet Hole Rd Mahopac NY 10541

HORVATH, JOHN, b. East Chicago, IN, Mar. 12, 1948; s. Janos and Alois Elizabeth (Metro-Csoka) H.; m. Cherylynn Knott, Aug. 12, 1982; children: Kana Lin, Elijah John, Anisa Maxine, Bronco Dennis. Contrbr. poetry to numerous jnls. & lit mags in Am., Can. and Great Britain, 1968—. BA, Peabody Tchrs. Coll., Vanderbilt U., 1975; MA, Fla. State U., 1979. Vis. instr. Fla. A&M U., Tallahassee, 1979-80; writing cons., 1980—; research fellow Purdue U., Lafayette, Ind., 1984-85. Served with USAF, 1966-69. Address: Eng Dept Fl State U Tallahassee FL 32304

HOSTETLER, SHERI ANN, b. Millersburg, OH, May 24, 1962; d. Lyman and Beverly Ann (Hostetler) H. Contrbr. articles to Seeds. B.A., Bluffton Coll., 1984. Reporter, Holmes co. Farmer-Hob, Millersburg, OH, 1984, ed., 1984-85; communications mgr. St. Mary's Food Bank, Phoenix, 1985-87. Recipient Excellence in Jnlsm. award Reader's Digest Fdn., 1987. Home: 1308 Rosemary 5 Columbia MO 65201

HOSTROP, RICHARD WINFRED, b. Waterloo, IA, Oct. 8, 1925; s. Winfred Ditlev and Frances Lucille (Walton) Elkins; m. LeeOna Selland, Dec. 27, 1950; 2 daus., Holly Lee, Kristin Ingrid. Author: Teaching and the Community College Library, 1975, Handbook for Achieving Academic Success, 1977, Library Centered Approach to Learning, 1978, Managing Education for Results, 1983. Ed.D., UCLA, 1968. Pres. Prairie State Coll., Chgo. Hts., Ill., 1967-70; ed. Shoe String Press, Homewood, Ill., 1970-72; pub. ETC Publs., Palm Springs, Calif., 1972—. Served to sgt. USAF, 1943-46; Philippines, Japan. Office: ETC Publications Box ETC Palm Springs CA 92262

HOTCHKISS, BILL, b. New London, CT, Oct. 17, 1936, s. William Henry and Merle Bertha (Stambaugh) H.; m. Judith Shears, Apr. 10, 1976; children—Steve, Jennifer; 1 stepdau., Anne Renier. Author: Steephollow Poems, 1966, To Christ, Dionysus, Odin (poems), 1969, The Graces of Fire (poems), 1974, Jeffers: The Sivaistic Vision, 1975, Fever in the Earth (narrative poetry), 1977, Climb to the High Country (poems), 1978, Middle Fork Canyon (poems), 1979, The Medicine Calf (novel), 1981, Crow Warriors (novel), 1981, Soldier Wolf (novel), 1982, Ammahabas (novel), 1983, Spirit Mountain (novel), 1984, Mountain Lamb (novel), 1985, Seasons of Witness (poems), 1985, Acorn Girl (novel), 1985, Fire Woman (novel), 1986; co-author: Tilting at Windmills, 1968, Poet from the San Joaquin (criticism), 1978, Shoshone Thunder (novel), 1983, Pawnee Medicine, 1983; contrbr. poetry to Green Fuse, Nitty Gritty, other lit mags. BA, U. Calif.-Berkeley, 1959; MA, San Francisco State U., 1960; MFA, U. Oreg., 1964, DA, 1971, PhD, 1974. Ed. Sierra Jnl, 1965-78; ed., pub. Blue Oak Press, Castle Peak Eds., 1966—; tchr. English, presenter poetry readings; speaker at acad. confs. Home: Box 1299 Cedar Ridge CA 95924

HOUGHTON, TIMOTHY DANE, b. Dayton, OH, Mar. 1, 1955; s. William Ivan and Mary Augusta (Logan) H.; m. Barbara Anne Bolz, Aug. 17, 1985. Poetry has appeared in over 40 mags. and anthologies, including Poet Lore, Ariz. Qtly, Denver Qtly, Descant, Intro, Tar River Poetry; also rvws. and 1 short story; ed. Panoply, a poetry mag. BA, U. Pa., 1977; MA, San Francisco State U., 1979; PhD, U. Denver, 1984. Teaching asst. San Francisco State U., spring 1979; teaching fellow U. Denver, 1979-83; lectr. U. Colo., Boulder and Denver, 1983-85; asst. prof. William Jewell Coll., Liberty, Mo., 1985—. Mem. NCTE. Recipient award in poetry contest AAP, 1976, 77, 79, hon. mention Browning Soc., 1978. Home: 117 N Leonard St Liberty MO 64068

HOULIHAN, BRIAN T., b. Chgo., Feb. 4, 1944, s. William Leo and Catherine (Cusack) H.; m. Linda Baldassini, Aug. 12, 1977. Playwright: Surprise!, 1977, Nosy Neighbors, 1978, Wired (screenplay), 1979, Why, Judy, Why? (screenplay), 1985; Temporary Tommy (novel), 1986. Wrtr.. industrial films for IBM, Natl. Recreational Vehicle Inst., Wernecke Studios, Chgo. BS in Speech, Northwestern U., Evanston, Ill., 1966. Actor television commls., NYC,1968-70; copywriter J.C. Penney Co., NYC,1971-72; wrtr. Allied News Co., Chgo., 1972-74; resident humorist WABC-TV Eyewitness News, NYC,1981-82. Mem. Screen Actors Guild, Actors Equity Assn., AFTRA. Home: 5609 Colfax 167 North Hollywood CA 91601

HOUSE, RICHARD CALVIN, (Beau Jacques), b. Ashtabula, OH, Feb. 22, 1927; s. Harold Cushman and Lillian Marie (Poore) H.; m. Doris Elaine Beckwith, Dec. 21, 1950; children—Laura Jane House Lopez, Jonathan Daniel House. Author novels: So The Loud Torrent, 1977, Vengeance Mountain, 1981; wking. on nonfict. ms. on 1862 Sioux uprising in Minnesota. BA, Kent State U., 1951. Rptr./ed. Evening Record, Ravenna, OH, 1950-53; tech. ed. Goodyear Aircraft, Akron, OH, 1953-54; employee communics. spclst. Ford Motor Co., Cleve., OH, Dearborn, MI, 1954-62; ed. employee mag. Occidental Life of CA, Los Angeles, 1963-69; ed. employee communics. Jet Propulsion Lab., Pasadena, CA, 1969—. Ford Ed. of Year, 1959. Served to PFC, U.S. Army, 1945-47. Mem. WWA. Home: 466 Alpine St Pasadena CA 91106

HOUSEN, SEVRIN, b. Bremerton, WA, Nov. 6, 1948, s. Bernard Albert and Hildur Ann (Wilson) H. Ed.: Feathers & Bones—Ten Poets of the Irish Earth, 1981, numerous other books; contrbr. poetry to newspapers, mags. and anthologies. BA in English, Western Wash. U., 1972; Secondary Teaching Credential, Calif. State U., Sacramento, 1984. Ed.-in-chief Naturegraph Pubs., Happy Camp, Calif., 1976-79; tchr. Sacramento City Unified Schl. Dist., 1985—. Recipient Dominic F. Bazzanella award Calif. State U., Sacramento, 1983. Mem. Sacramento Poetry Center. Home: 1700 49th St Sacramento CA 95819

HOUSTON, JAMES D, b. San Francisco, Nov. 10, 1933, s. Albert D. and Alice L. (Wilson) H.; m. Jeanne Wakatsuki, Mar. 27, 1957; children—Corinne, Joshua, Gabrielle. Novelist: Between Battles, 1968, Gig, 1969, A Native Son of the Golden West, 1971, Continental Drift, 1978, Love Life, 1985; author: Gasoline (satirical stories), 1980, Farewell to Manzanar (with Jeanne Wakatsuki Houston), 1973, Open Field (with John R. Brodie), 1974, Three Songs for my Father, 1974, Californians: Searching for The Golden State, 1982, One Can Think about Life after the Fish is in the Canoe and Other Coastal Sketches, 1985, The Men in My Life (non-fiction stories), 1987; ed.: Writing from the Inside, 1973, California Heartland: Writing from the Great Central Valley (with Gerald Haslam), 1978, West Coast Fiction: Modern Writing from California, Oregon and Washington, 1979; contrbr. stories, articles, essays, rvws to Rolling Stone, N.Y. Times, Los Angeles mag., Solidaridad, numerous other publs. BA in Drama, San Jose State U., 1956; MA in Lit., Stanford U., 1962. Wrtr., tchr. Stanford (Calif.) U., 1968-69; lectr. writing U. Calif.-Santa Cruz, 1969—; mem. Calif. Council for Humanities, San Francisco, 1983—; mem. adv. bd. San Jose Poetry Center, Tandy Beal Dance Co., Santa Cruz. Recipient Joseph Henry Jackson award for fiction, San Francisco Fdn., 1967, Wallace Stegner Wrtg. fellow, 1966-67, Amer. Book Award, from Before Columbus Foundation, 1983; creative writing grantee NEA, 1976-77, Gilliland Chair in Telecommunications, San Jose State Univ., 1985. Mem. PEN, AG, WGA, Western Am. Lit. Assn. Home: 2-1130 E Cliff Dr Santa Cruz CA 95062

HOWARD, BENJAMIN W., b. Iowa City, June 22, 1944; s. Marion Curtis and Johanne Elizabeth (Nehrkorn) Howard; m. Susan Hepner, July 26, 1969 (div.); 1 son, Alexander Benjamin. Author: Northern Interior, 1986, Father of Waters, 1979, Lenten Anniversaries, 1988; poems, essays, reviews in Poetry, Parnassus, Midwest Qtly, Kenyon Rvw., other lit qtlys. BA, Drake U., 1966; MA, PhD, Syracuse U., 1971. Prof., Alfred U., Alfred, NY, 1969—. Mem. AWP. Home: 17 S Main Street Alfred NY 14802

HOWARD, BETTY RUTH, b. Walnut Ridge, AR, Nov. 2, 1946; d. Jarreld Brance Arnold and Thelma Vernell (Tyson) Mooney; m. Gerald Attison Howard, Mar. 25, 1967; children—Kevin Taylor, Robert Lee, Ginger Diana. Contrbr. poem to anthol. Diploma, Inst. Children's Lit., 1985. Secy., Farm Service Inc., Hoxie, AR, 1982-4; owner Howard & Huskey, Lynn, AR, 1985—;

feature wrtr. Ozark Jnl., Imboden, AR, 1987—. Home: Box 381 Lynn AR 72440

HOWARD, DAVID H., b. Albany, OR, July 21, 1944, s. Hal H. and Vera L. (Bond) H.; m. Veronica S. Kind, Sept. 4, 1966 (div. 1971); 1 son—Daniel; m. 2d, Georgetta L. Cooper, Aug. 3, 1973; children—Richard, David, Jr. Author: News Handbook for Granges, 1984. BA in Journalism, Whitworth Coll., 1966; postgrad., San Diego State U., 1966-67. Social worker, State of Washington, Spokane, 1969-70, 72-76; ed. The Universal Message, 1973-77; editor: Grange News, Seattle, 1982—. Mem. Wash. Press Assn., Coop. Communicators Assn. Home: 38281 Mt Home Dr Lebanon OR 97355

HOWARD, JANE TEMPLE, b. Springfield, IL, May 4, 1935; d. Robert Pickrell and Eleanor Grace (Nee) H. Author: Please Touch: A Guided Tour of the Human Potential Movement, 1970, A Different Woman, 1973, Margaret Mead: A Life, 1984, Families, 1978; contrbr. articles to popular mags. AB, U. Mich., 1956. Editorial trainee Time, Inc., 1956-58; reporter Life mag., 1959-61, asst. editor, 1962-68, staff writer, 1969-72, contract writer, 1972-73; vis. lectr. U. Iowa Writers Workshop, 1974, U. Ga. Schl. Journalism, 1975, Yale U., 1976, SUNY-Albany, 1978. Recipient Non-Fiction award Chgo. Fdn. for Lit., 1974; fellow Mac Dowell Colony, 1973, 76, 80. Address 54 Riverside Dr New York NY 10024

HOWARD, JOSEPH, see Howard, Richard

HOWARD, RICHARD, (Joseph Howard), b. Cleve., Oct. 13, 1929. Author: poetry Quantities, 1962, The Damages, 1967, Untitled Subjects, 1969, Findings, 1971, Two-Part Inventions, 1974, Fellow Feeling, 1976, Misgivings, 1979, Lining Up, 1984; criticism Alone With America, 1969, Preferences, 1974; lit reviewer various mags.; poetry editor: New Republic; translator works from French. BA, Columbia U., 1951; postgrad., Sorbonne, Paris, 1952-53. Recipient Pulitzer prize, 1970; Guggenheim fellow, 1966-67; fellow Morse Coll., Yale U.; Natl. Inst. Arts grantee, 1970, Am. Book Award, 1984. Mem. PEN-Am. Center (pres. 1977-79). Address: 23 Waverly Pl New York NY 10003

HOWARD-HOWARD, MARGO CHANLER, (R. F. Fitzallan-Howard); b. Republic of Singapore, July 15, 1935; arrd. U.S., 1943; d. Lord John Fitzallan and Alida Beekman (Chanler) Howard; m. Giles P. Howard, June 7, 1956 (div. July 2, 1960); 1 dau., Alida Howard Wrigley. Author: A Bar Harbor Jnl., 1960; contrbr poetry to Tangerine, United Artists, Telephone. BA in history, Cambridge U.-Christ Ch. Coll. (England), 1952-56, MA, 1959. Libn./archivist IM Pei, NYC, 1959-65; art history instr. Vassar Coll., Poughkeepsie, NY, 1966-76. Founder, The Mary Stuart Soc (affil. Royal Stuart Soc., London), NYC, 1982. Mem. English Speaking Union, Poetry Soc. Great Britain, Byron Soc. Address: Mary Stuart Soc 6 St Lukes Pl New York NY 10014

HOWE, IRVING, b. NYC, June 11, 1920; s. David and Nettie (Goldman) H.; m. Ilana Wiener; 2 children. Author: Politics and the Novel: A World More Attractive, 1963, Steady Work, 1966, Thomas Hardy, 1967, The Decline of the New, 1969, The Critical Point, 1973, World of Our Fathers, 1976 (Nat. Book award); co-author: The Radical Papers, 1966; editor: periodical Essential Works of Socialism, 1971; co-editor: A Treasury of Yiddish Poetry, 1971. Grad. CCNY. Served with AUS, World War II. Recipient Longview Fdn. prize for lit. criticism; Natl. Inst. Arts and Letters award; Kenyon Rvw fellow for lit. criticism, 1953; Bollingen Fdn. fellow; Guggenheim fellow, 1971. Address: Dept Eng Hunter Coll New York NY 10021

HOWELL, BARBARA MILES, b. Chgo., Jan. 26, 1937, d. William H. and Margaret (Miles) H.; m. Alain LeRoy, Nov. 22, 1958 (div. 1963); 1 child, William LeRoy; m. Alan Edward Woltz, Oct. 30, 1977. Author: (nonfiction) Don't Bother to Come in on Monday, 1973, (novels) A Mere Formality, 1982, 1984, Balancing Act, 1985. BA, Barat Coll., Lake Forest, Ill., 1957; postgrad. Columbia U., 1960. Copywrtr. Benton & Bowles, Marschalk Co., BBDO, NYC,1962-71. Fulbright grantee U. Lille, 1957-58. Mem. PEN, AG, Women Wrtrs. Network, P&W. Home: 220 E 67th St New York NY 10021

HOWELL, DEAN MYRAL, b. Brush, CO, Sept. 10, 1932; s. Joe C. and Florence M. (Joppa) H.; m. Shirley A. O'Brien, Sept. 3, 1954; children—Randy, Lori, Author: How to Sell Tax Free Bonds, 1986, How to Buy Tax Free Bonds (The Inside Story), 1987. Wrkg. on investment oriented books. B.S., B.A., Denver U., 1954. Exec. v.p. Gerwin & Co., Denver, 1970-81; sr. v.p. Denver Nat. Bank, 1982-86; free-lance wrtr., 1986—; owner DH Pub., Denver, Colo., 1986—. Mem. NWC. Home: 1551 Larimer St 2405 Denver CO 80202

HOWER, EDWARD, b. NYC, Jan. 10, 1941. Author: (short fiction) Kikuyu Woman, 1979, (novels) The New Life Hotel, 1980, Wolf Tickets, 1986. BA, Cornell U., 1963; diploma in ed. Makerere U., Kampala, Uganda, 1964; MA, anthropology, UCLA, 1971. Instr. Ithaca Coll., N.Y., 1975—; asst. prof. Cornell U., Ithaca, summers 1980—. Grantee NEA, 1977, N.Y. State Council on Arts, 1982, Ingram Merrill Fdn., 1986, Fulbright fellowship to India, 1986-87. Mem. PEN. Home: 1409 Hanshaw Rd Ithaca NY 14850

HOWES, BARBARA, b. NYC, May 1, 1914; d. Osborne and Mildred (Cox) H.; m. William Jay Smith, Oct. 1, 1947 (div. June 1965); children—David E., Gregory Jay. Author: poetry The Undersea Farmer, 1948, In the Cold Country, 1954, Light and Dark, 1959, Looking up at Leaves, 1966, The Blue Garden, 1972, A Private Signal: Poems New and Selected, 1977, Moving, 1980; editor: 23 Modern Stories, 1963, From the Green Antilles: writings of the Caribbean, 1966, The Sea-Green Horse: short stories for young people, (with G.J. Smith), 1970, The Eye of the Heart: Stories from Latin America, 1973 (Christopher award); author: short stories The Road Commissioner and Other Stories, 1980. BA, Bennington Coll., 1937. Editor: Chimera Qtly, NYC, 1943-47. Guggenheim fellow, 1955; recipient Brandeis U. Creative Arts poetry grant, 1958, Natl. Inst. Arts and Letters lit. award, 1971, Golden Rose award New Eng. Poetry Soc., 1973; Christopher award, 1974; Bennington award for outstanding contrbns. to poetry, 1980. Home: Brook House N Pownal VT 05260

HOWLETT, JOAN GAIL, (Joan Agostino), b. Bay Shore, NY, Jan. 20, 1943, d. John Edward and Christine Mary (Neet) Howlett. Ed.: Gypsy Table I, 1972, Kansas City Rejects: A Women's Anthology, 1974; contrbr. to 25 East, The Doberman Qtly, Peace & Pieces: An Anthology of Contemporary American Poetry, 1973, Variations in White, 1986, numerous other lit publs. BA cum laude, St. John's U., 1964; MA, Boston Coll., 1967; MSW, SUNY-Stony Brook, 1987. Tchr. San Francisco public schls., 1966-69; instr. English as 2d lang. San Francisco Community Coll. Dist., 1969-75, Rogne Community Coll., Grants Pass, Ore., 1976-77; freelance wrtr., 1975—; clinical social worker, 1987—. Received spcl. mention W.E. Houck & Co. 1st Annl. Poetry Contest, Tex., 1974; grantee Ore. Com. for Humanities, 1977. Mem. P&W. Home: Box 351 Homer NY 13077

HOWSE, HAROLD D., b. Poplarville, MS, Nov. 8, 1928, s. William Jefferson and Artie Mittie (Smith) H.; m. Mittie Hazel Gibson, Dec. 18, 1960; children—Trijetta Lynn Gibson Cropp, Claude Demetris Gibson. Ed.: Marine Briefs (founding), 1972-74, Gulf Research Reports, 1974—; contrbr. articles to Aquaculture, Tissue & Cell, Jnl Submicroscopic Cytology, numerous other profl. publs. BS, U. So. Miss., 1959, MS, 1960; PhD, Tulane U., 1967. Mem. staff Gulf Coast Research Lab., Ocean Springs, Miss., 1967—, prof. microscopic anatomy, dir., 1972—. Served with USN, 1950-54; Korea. Mem. sci. orgns. Home: 703 E Beach Blvd Ocean Springs MS 39564

HRASCINSKI, JO ANNE VICTORIA, (JoAnne Raz), b. Chgo., Apr. 10, 1967; d. Frank Edward and Constance JoAnne (Holsman) H. Contrbr. poemss to anthols. Grad. Public schls., Carol Stream, IL. Teller, Glen Ellyn Savings, IL, 1985-86; accountant Berlin Industries, Addison, IL, 1986—. Recipient cert. of Merit, World of Poetry, 1983, 84, Golden Poet award, 1985, 86. Home: 1363 Glen Ellyn Rd Glendale Heights IL 60139

HRUSKA, ELIAS NICOLAS, (Tizoc), b. San Francisco, July 7, 1943, s. Nicholas Emanuel Hruska and Silvia Maria (Cortes) Warren; m. Maria De Simone, Jan. 29, 1966; children—Sonia Katrina, Shala Marien, Karim Marti. Ed., contrbr. Investment Briefs. MA, U. Calif.-Berkeley, 1968. Prin. Eli Hruska & Assocs., San Jose, Calif., 1978—; ed. Investment Briefs, San Jose, 1983—; br. mgr. Fin. Network Investments Corp., Torrance, Calif., 1985—. Mem. Intl. Assn. Fin. Planners. Office: Eli Hruska & Assocs 4010 Moorpark Ave San Jose CA 95117

HUBBELL, PATRICIA ANN, b. Bridgeport, CT, July 10, 1928; d. Franklin H. and Helen Eugenie (Osborn) Hubbell; m. Harold Hornstein, Mar. 10, 1954; children—Jeffrey Hornstein, Deborah Alexander. Author: (poetry) The Apple Vendor's Fair, 1963, 8 a.m. Shadows, 1965, Catch Me a Wind, 1968. Contrbr. poems to numerous anthols., textbooks; articles to popular mags., newspapers including The N.Y. Times, Christian Sci. Monitor, Conn. Mag. Women's ed. The Wetport Town Crier, CT, 1952-54. B.S., U. Conn., 1950. Mem. AG, SCBW. Home: 90 Norton Rd Easton CT 06612

HUBBLE, BEVERLY, see Tauke, Beverly Hubble

HUBBS, GALEN JAY, b. Ellsworth, KS, June 18, 1941; s. Ralph and Marie Elizabeth (Biesterfeld) H.; m. Priscilla Jo Denton, Jan. 5, 1981; 1 stepdau., Amy Lynn. BS in Agriculture, Fort Hays State U., 1965; BS in Jnlsm., KS State U., 1970. Info. spclst. USAF, var. locations, 1966-69; writer-sports ed. Goodland Daily News (KS), 1971-73; assoc. ed. High Plains Jnl, Dodge City, KS, 1973-82, ed., 1983—. Served to SSgt., USAF, 1965-69. Office: 1500 East Wyatt Earp Dodge City KS 67801

HUBER, ROBERT EDGER, b. Denver, June 27, 1931; s. Ralph and Essie May (Reed) H.; m.

Marilyn Louise Wheeler, June 21, 1952; children—Tracy Lecocq, Glen, Holly. Contrbr. articles to mags. including Newsweek, Field & Stream, Empire Mag. Political and statehouse columnist Inside N.Mex., 1976-79; reporter Daily Record, Roswell, N.Mex., 1961-63, Denver Post, 1968-69; bur. chief UPI, Sante Fe, 1963-68. Editor, pub.: N.Mex. Capitol Observer, 1972-81. BA, U. Colo.-Boulder, 1956. Served with USCG, 1948-51. Home: Box 2488 Sante Fe NM 87501

HUBLER, DAVID ELLIOT, b. NYC, Sept. 3, 1941, s. Nathaniel and Gladys (Somers) H.; m. Rebecca Summer, Sept. 4, 1966; children—Robert Nathaniel, Geoffrey Alan. Author: You Gotta Believe!, 1983, The Politicians' Health, Diet and Sex Guide, 1984; contrbr. articles to travel mags. BA, NYU, 1963; MS, U. N.H., 1965. Ed. Fgn. Broadcast Info. Service, Washington, 1966-77; sr. wrtr. Voice of Am., Washington, 1977—; freelance travel wrtr. Mem. Washington Indep. Wrtrs. Home: 4109 Breezewood Ln Annandale VA 22003

HUBLER, H. CLARK, b. Portland, July 26, 1910; s. W. Herbert and Elsie Rowena (Clark) H.; m. Retal Frances Allinson, June 12, 1934; children—Keith, Bonnie, Thomas, Rowena, Craig. Student: Working with Children in Science, 1957, Science for Children, 1974, Overpopulation, 1985, Nuclear Energy: Nightmere or Salvation, 1987. Wrkg. on Magnificant Mountains, trade books involving sci. in social affairs. B.A., Western Washington U., 1937; M.A., Columbia U., 1947, Ed.D., 1949. Prof., Wheelock Coll., Boston, 1949-64, Fulbright Lectr. Philippines, 1964-65, Ohio U., 1966-76, retired. Home: 2101 Timlin Hill Portsmouth OH 45662

HUBSCHER, WILLIAM DONALD, b. Irvington, NJ, Nov. 9, 1956; s. Alfred Otto and Natalia (Izidro) H. Author, Cadavear Here, Cadavear There, 1984, Operations, Training—Let's Get Serious, 1987. Model, William Schuler Agency, NYC, 1968-73; procedure & documentation writer & tchr. Bell Communications Research, Piscataway, NJ, 1977—. First prize—annual poetry, The Beachcomber, 1984. Home: 11 Huckleberry Ct Bricktown NJ 08723

HUDDLE, DAVID, b. Ivanhoe, VA, July 11, 1942, s. Charles Richard Jr. and Mary Frances (Akers) H.; m. Marie Lindsey Massie, Aug. 31, 1968; children—Elizabeth Ross, Mary Massie. Author: A Dream with No Stump Roots In It (short stories), 1975, Paper Boy (poems), 1979, Only the Little Bone (short stories), 1986. BA, U. Va., 1968; MFA, Columbia U., 1971. Instr., asst. prof., assoc. prof. U. Vt., Burlington, 1971-81, prof. dept English, 1982—; vis. prof. Middlebury (Vt.) Coll., 1981-82. NEA fellow, 1978, 87. Home: 34 N Williams St Burlington VT 05401

HUDGINS, ANDREW, b. Killeen, TX, Apr. 22, 1951; s. Col. A. L. and Roberta (Rodgers) H. Author: Saints and Strangers, 1985. AM, U. Ala., 1976-78; MFA, U. Ia., 1981-83. Instr. Auburn Univ., Montgomery, Ala., 1978-81; lectr. Baylor Univ., Waco, Tex., 1984-85; asst. prof. Univ. Cin., 1985—. Recipient Wallace Stegner fellowship, Stanford Univ., 1983-84, AAP award, 1984. Mem. AWP. Address: Dept Eng U Cin Cincinnati OH 45220

HUDGINS, BARBARA, b. NYC, Nov. 16, 1932; d. Max and Rose (Rooten) Mencher; m. Webster Ransone Hudgins, June 16, 1966. Author: New Jersey Day Trips, 1986, Trips and Treks: A Guide to Outings in N.J. and Beyond!, 1983; nwspr. travel writer; contrbr. articles to Signature, N.Y. Times. BA in English, Bklyn. Coll., 1954; MLS, Pratt Inst., 1960. Reference librarian, NY Pub. Lib., NYC, 1960-62, Hunter Coll., NYC, 1962-65, U. Hawaii Lib., Honolulu, 1966; freelance writer, travel columnist, 1966—. Mem. NJ Press Women. Office: Box 108 Green Village NJ 07935

HUDGINS, WILLIAM FREEMAN, JR., b. Somers Point, NJ, Oct. 6, 1953; s. William F. and Genevieve Alice (Truman) H.; m. Elizabeth Ann Billington, June 21, 1985. Author: Doing it on the Lawn. Contrbr. articles to Am. Turf Monthly, Racing Star Weekly. Wrkg. on (novel) The Upper Crust. Student U. Md.-Eastern Shore, 1971-73. Designer English Greenhouses Inc., Camden, N.J., 1978-86. Employed by Avalon Commercial Corp., Pleasantville, NJ. Home: 119-110 Erial/New Brooklyn Rd Sicklerville NJ 08081

HUDSON, ELLEN MATILDA, b. Atlanta, Oct. 3, 1915; d. Charles Clifford and Lillian Beryl (Hardage) Hudson. Author, illustrator: Secrets (poetry), 1988; poetry in anthologies. AB, Tift Coll.; MA in Organ and Music Ed., Columbia U. Elem. sch. tchr. Nelson (Ga.) Public Schs., 1937-38, Atlanta Public Schs., 1938-80. Active ednl. and organ music orgns., church organist 14 yrs. Recipient numerous awards. Home: 268 Mt Vernon Dr Decatur GA 30030

HUDSON, MARCUS ALLAN, (Marc), b. Berkeley, CA, Feb. 3, 1947; s. George Afton and Edith Gertrude (Goldsmith) H.; m. Helen Ilene Mundy, May 13, 1980; 1 son, Ian Geoffrey. Author poetry: Island, 1978, Afterlight, 1983, Journal for an Injured Son, 1985; contrbr. poetry to The Anglo-Welsh Rvw, CutBank, Fine Madness, Kenyon Rvw, Mass Rvw, NER/BLQ, Poetry, others; contrbr. articles to Audubon, Environmental Action, Iceland Rvw, Pacific Northwest. BA, Georgetown Un, 1968; MA, U Wash, 1973, PhD, 1983. Ed. Harold F. Wise Inc., Washington, DC, 1974-75; tchg. fellow Univ. Washington, 1977-80, 81-82, ed., 1982-84, vis. lectr., U. of Wisconsin, Green Bay, 1985—. NEA fellow, 1984; recipient Juniper Prize, Univ. Mass. Press, 1983, Heilman Prize Univ. Washington, 1983, Strousse Award, Prairie Schooner, 1984. Address: 518 S Baird Green Bay WI 54301

HUEMER, JOSEPH WILSON, b. Newark, Mar. 4, 1913; s. Ludwig and Josefine (Zamazal) H.; m. Kathleen Watt, Aug. 15, 1941; children—John L., Christina G., Lisa E. (dec.), Francesca, David R. Author: The United States in a World of Neighbors, 1965, Gifts and Wings for Tomorrow's Leaders, 1984; ed. Diagramming—An Aid to Correct Usage; contrbr. articles to N.Y. Times. BA, Montclair State, 1940; MA in reading, NYU, 1946. Tchr., Pleasantville (NJ) H.S., 1940-42, East Orange (NJ), 46-48; tchr./principal Mendham Twnshp., Brookside, NJ, 1948-51; principal Alexander Hamilton, Morristown, NJ, 1951-61, Lake Parsippany, Par-Troy, NJ, 61-67; asst. supt. schls., Parsippany Schl., Par-Troy, 1967-72. Served to Lt. Cmdr., USNR, 1942-46. George Washington medal, Freedoms Fdn., 1952, 53, 54; dist. svc. prof., Newark State Coll., 1972; author's award, NJ Assn. Tchrs. of Engl.; others. Home: 14 Park Ave Mendham NJ 07945

HUETTEMAN, SUSAN ANN BICE, (Ann Marscot), b. Crossville, IL, Jan 24, 1934; d. Francis Joseph and LaVern (Brown) Bice; m. Albert George Huetteman, June 12, 1956; children—Scott Christopher, Mark Bice. Author: (with Albert Huetteman) Basic Music Theory, 1986, 2d ed., 1987. Contrbr. articles, cartoonist gags to mags., newspapers. Ed.: Iowa Music Tchr., 1966-67. A.A. in Music, Colby-Sawyer Coll., 1953; B.Music in Voice, New England Conservatory, 1956; M.A. in Communications, Goddard Coll., 1979. Owner, Huetteman Studio, Pelham, MA, 1958—; dir. Performing Arts Div. U. Mass., Amherst, 1977—. Poem selected for arhives Ohio State Archives, 1970. Home: 19 Arnold Rd Pelham MA 01002

HUGHES, HELEN RUTH, b. Antlers, OK, Sept. 5, 1914; d. Jewel J. and Maggie Mayoma (Messer) Almond; m. Royal William Sargent, Nov., 1935 (dec. Aug. 1950); 1 dau., Shirley Ruth; m. 2d, Hubert J. Hughes, April 19, 1951; 1 dau., Margaret Anne. Technical editor Radio Notams for biweekly Airman's Guide (GPO), 1954-62. First tchr. to teach a unit on space in a public schl. (Bowie, Md.), 1963. Civil Svc. employee, 1941-62. Student 4 years Southeastern State Univ., Durant, Okla. Mem. Business and Profl. Women's Club, Wash. D.C., 1957, Natl. Assn. Retired Federal Employees. Address: 4301 Orange Grove Blvd North Ft Myers FL 33903

HUGHES, JON CHRISTOPHER, b. Elkhart, IN, Jan. 30, 1945, s. David Wesley and Katharyn (DeWees) H.; m. Susan Elaine Zavodny, Jan. 15, 1968; children—Sean Christopher, Caitlin Amanda. Author: The Tanyard Murder, 1982, Ye Giglampz, 1983, The Jolly Book, 1984, numerous screenplays, teleplay treatments; contrbr. American Humor Mags. and Comic Newspapers, N.Am. Union List of Victorian Serials; AdWeek, Working Woman, Horizons, numerous other publs. Wrkg. on books, screenplays. BS, Ball State U., 1967, MA in Journalism, 1972. Reporter Kalamazoo (Mich.) Gazette, 1967; copy ed. Bay City (Mich.) Times, 1968; reporter, columnist Jackson (Mich.) Citizen Patriot, 1970-72; ed. Cincinnati Reporter, 1977; prof. U. Cin., 1972—, journalism program coordinator, 1975—; freelance wrtr., 1972—. Mem. AAUP, NWU. Home: 578 McAlpin Ave Cincinnati OH 45220

HUGHES, KIM KNOX, b. Princeton, NJ, Aug. 1, 1953; d. Francis T. and Roselle Lempriere (Toland) Chambers; m. Simon Henry Cadman Hughes, Oct. 27, 1981. Contrbr. to Moonscape, Fantasy Book, Fantasy & Sci. Fiction, Space Grits, SPWAO Showcase V. BA in Music cum laude, Middlebury Coll., 1975; PhD in Scottish Studies, Edinburgh U., 1980. Mem. SFWA (affiliate), Small Press Wrtrs. and Artists Orgn. Home: 36135 N Grand Oaks Ct Gurnee IL 60031

HUGHES, LENORE HARRIS, b. Shubert, NB, Mar. 30, 1914, d. Charles Grover Cleveland and Jennie Virginia Jemima (Brown) Harris; m. Delbert Littrell Hughes, Jan. 1, 1950 (dec. Dec. 27, 1970). Author: Give Me Room, 1971, Seasons of Our Lives, 1977-78 (poetry), How to Write and Publish a Book, 1977, The Emir, 1980, Holy Adobe, 1981, Addicted to Symphonies, 1985 (poetry), Adobe Abodes, 1985; co-editor of The Woman's Pulpit, 1965-72; contrbr. articles and poems to newspapers and mags. BA, Omaha U., 1937; MA, Phillips U., Enid, Okla., 1947. Tchr. rural schls., high schls., Nebr., Ky., 1932-34, 1938-40; instr. Walker Jr. Coll., Jasper, Ala., 1940-45; relig. ed. dir. Christian Church (Disciples), Calif., Ark., Okla., Kan., 1947-50; journalism adviser El Paso Public Schls., 1958-78; self-publisher, 1978—. Grant: WSJ Newspaper Fund, 1964. Awards: Golden Key, Columbia U., 1973; Golden Quill, Tex. Interscholastic League, 1977. Mem. El Paso Art Assn., El Paso Color Camera Club, Pencrafters.

Home: 453 De Soto Dr El Paso TX 79912

HUGHES, PATRICIA SADDLER, b. Louisville, Dec. 16, 1931; d. Olaf Shircliffe and Hilda Madonna (Raley) Saddler; m. Henry Arch Hughes, Apr. 22, 1950; children—Michael, Madonna, Joe (dec.), Henry Arch, Patrick John, 4 grandchildren. Contrbr. poems to anthols. Student Jefferson Community Coll., 1977-83. Recipient Hon. Mention, Ky. State Poetry Soc., 1980, Silver Poet award World of Poetry, 1986; named to Dean's List, Jefferson Community Coll, 1980. Home: 2220 Blvd Napoleon Louisville KY 40205

HUGHES, RICHARD GLYNNE, b. Utica, NY, Jun. 19, 1955; s. Richard and Gwenfron (Parry) Hughes. Author: Palm Beach: The Novel, 1984, Educating the Whole Brain of the Young Child, 1983, Walrus Tales (TV series), 1979, other books on child ed. M Ed. Florida Atlantic U., 1979; PhD, Nova U., 1983. Wrtr./ed. Beachcomber Nwspprs. (Lake Worth, FL), 1973-75; wrtr./pub. Creative Concern Publications (Lake Worth), 1978—; educator Palm Beach Country Schools (FL), 1977. PFC, USAR, 1979-85. Mem. NWC, FL Freelance Wrtrs. Assoc. Home: 3208 E Mayaguana Ln Lantana FL 33462

HUGHES, TRACY, see Herrington, Terri

HUGHES, WALTER JAY SR., (Joseph Allen Oneal, A. David Venture, J. D. Montanna), b. St. Louis, July 30, 1942; divorced; children—Katherine Jolene, Theresa Marie, Michael J. (dec.); m. Katherine Elaine Hewes, July 1971; children—John Richard, Michael Joseph, Steven Walter. Author: (essays) Innermost Being of I, 1984, About Human Love, 1984; (novels) The Long Bloody Run, 1987, Colombian Guns, 1987, Just Thoughts, 1987, Point Blank, 1988. Contrbr. poems to anthols. Post judge advocate Amvets of Am., 1984, 85, 86, 87, post commander, 1986; judge advocate Veterans of Fgn. Wars, 1984, 85, 86, 87. Served with U.S. Navy, 1959-61. Address: Box 337 Waldo FL 32694

HUGHES-CALERO, HEATHER, b. Detroit, Mar. 18, 1938; d. John Michael and Viola Ann (McGowan) Maticic; m. Henry H. Calero, June 26, 1981. Author: The Sedona Trilogy: Book One, Through the Crystal, 1985, Book Two, Doorways between the Worlds, 1985, Book Three, Land of Nome, 1985, The Golden Dream, 1987. Wrkg. on a biographical novel. Mem. Intl. Women's Writing Guild, Author's Guild of Amer. WG. Home: Box 486 Carmel CA 93921

HUHTA, RICHARD S., b. Chgo., Nov. 4, 1931, s. Arthur Oscar and Taublee Ruth (Ziegmund) H.; m. Martha MacDougall, Apr. 24, 1954; children—Julia Martha, Carter Richard. Ed: Science Milestones, 1955, Lawn & Garden Guide, 1956, Land Reclamation—A Fresh Look, 1983. Wrkg. on waste material utilization study. BS in Journalism, Bradley U., 1953. Ed., wrtr. Popular Mechanics Press, 1953-56; mng. ed. Rock Products Mag., 1956-61, ed., 1980—; ed. Concrete Products Mag., 1961-63, Concrete Constrn. Mag., 1963-68; public relations wrtr. Portland Cement Assn., 1968-69; account exec., group v.p. Burson-Marsteller Public Relations, 1969-80. Recipient Jesse H. Neal award Associated Bus. Publs., 1957, 84, Golden Trumpet award Publicity Club Chgo., 1969, 76, 79. Home: 8 Court of Island Pt Northbrook IL 60062

HUMMER, PAUL JACOB, JR., b. Danville, PA, Aug. 12, 1932; s. Paul Jacob and Helen Phylliss (Pursel) H.; m. Janice Elizabeth Routzahn, Mar. 31, 1956; childrn—Sarah, Anne, Karl, Andrew. Author: (with Al Kaskel) Probing Levels of Life, 1973, 5th ed., 1986; (with Kaskel) Investigating Living Systems, 1973, 5th ed., 1986; (with Kaskel and Lucielle Daniel Biology—An Everyday Experience, 1981, 3d ed., 1988; (with Kaskel and Daniel) Biology—Laboratory Experiences, 1981, 3d., 1988. Contrbr. articles to sci. edn. mags. Contrbg. ed.: Idea Bank, 1985, 86, 87. B.S. in Edn., Lock Haven U., 1958; M.A. in Sci. Teaching, Union Coll., 1968. Biology tchr. Middletown High Schl., MD, 1982-86; adj. instr. sci. ed. Hood Coll., Frederick, MD, 1972-86, asst. prof. biology, 1986—. Home: 1798 Amber Ct Frederick MD 21701

HUMPERT, JOHN E., b. Evansville, IN, Aug. 10, 1962; s. Norman E. and Carolyn Sue (Biggerstaff) H. Contrb. poetry: Tintentaucher, other Ger. publs. BA in Communications, U. So. Ind., 1984. Translator, U. Hamburg, W. Germany, 1984-86; tchr. English inlingua Hamburg, 1985-86; tchr. German, Reitz Meml. High Sch., Evansville, 1986—. Home: 1625 Reiter Dr Evansville IN 47712

HUMPHREY, EDWIN LOWELL, (Shorty Farnsworth), b. Memphis, May 19, 1920; s. Mervyn G. and Mary Elizabeth (Kemp) H.; m. Rolene Louise Koehler, Oct. 23, 1943; children—Reginald Leigh, Kenneth Allan, Lawrence Douglas. Ed.: Englewood Eagle, Joliet News, Kansas City Flyer, Detroit Monthly; contrbr. articles: San Juan Horseshoe, Muscadine, Heartland Jnl. Wrkg. on short-story collection. BS, Purdue U., 1943; postgrad., U. Mo., 1954. Human resources cons., N.Y.C., 1963-70; personnel dir., Detroit, 1970-76. Recipient regional writing awards. Mem. Ariz. Authors' Assn. Home: 11601 Coggins Dr N Sun City AZ 85351

HUMPHREY, PAUL, b. NYC, Jan. 14, 1915; s. Joseph Lee and Winifred (Ball) H.; m. Eleanor Nicholson, Feb. 22, 1941; children—Paul, Paul, Joel. Author: Burnt Toast, or Slices at Life, 1977, Suburban Briefs, 1987, How to Run Your Own Employment Agency, 1983, Inside Track to the Editor's Desk, 1984. Author travel brochures, public addresses, biographies, schl. bd. policy manuals. Contrbr. poems to lit. mags., anthols., articles to newspapers. B.A., U. Rochester, 1940, M.A., 1941. Advt. wrtr. F. E. Compton Co., Chgo., 1948-61; free-lance wrtr., 1961—. Mem. P&W, AG, Rochester Poets (pres. 1984-87). Home: 2329 S Union St Spencerport NY 14559

HUMPHREYS, JOHN RICHARD ADAMS, (J. R. Humphreys), b. Mancelona, MI, June 7, 1918, s. John C. Adams and Blanche Belle (Beam) Adams Humphreys, adopted by Harold Llewellyn Humphreys; m. June K. Tolton, Apr. 11, 1942 (div. 1954); 1 dau., Catherine Anne; m. 2d, Joan Aucourt, Apr. 10, 1955 (div. 1958); m. 3d Peggy Frink, June 20, 1959. Author: Vandameer's Road, 1946, The Dirty Shame, 1955, The Lost Towns and Roads of America, 1961, rev. edit., 1967, The Last of the Middle West, 1966, Subway to Samarkand, 1977; contrbr. short stories, articles to Collier's, Cosmopolitan, Argosy, Perspectives, other mags. AB, U. Mich., 1940; Grad. N.Y. Inst. Photography, 1956. Feature wrtr. Detroit Free Press, 1940-41; articles ed. Beachcomber Mag., NYC,1960-61; sr. lectr. in English, Columbia U., 1946—, dir. creative writing program, 1962—. Recipient fellowships Guggenheim Fdn., 1947, Huntington Hartford Fdn., 1953, McDowell Colony, Peterborough, N.H., 1950, 55, Wurlitzer Fdn., Taos, N.Mex., 1968, NEA, 1979; recipient Best Amer. Short Stories, Martha Foley, 1947. Two Avery Hopwood awards, 1939., Ann Arbor, Mich., 1947. Mem. PEN, AG. Service in World War II, 1941-46, lst Lt., Sig. Corps. Home: 70 LaSalle St New York NY 10027

HUMPHRY, DEREK JOHN, b. Bath, U.K., Apr. 29, 1930, came to U.S., 1978; m. Jean Crane, May 10, 1953 (dec. 1975); m. Ann Wickett, Feb. 16, 1976. Author: Because They're Black, 1971, Police Power and Black People, 1972, Passports and Politics, 1974, False Messiah, 1977, The Cricket Conspiracy, 1976, Jean's Way, 1978, Let Me Die Before I Wake, 1982, The Right to Die: Understanding Euthanasia, 1986. Reporter Daily Mail, U.K., 1955-61; dep. ed. The Luton News, U.K., 1961-63; ed. Havering Recorder, U.K., 1963-67; home affairs corr. The Sunday Times, London, 1967-78, roving corr. in N.Am., 1979-81; spl. wrtr. Los Angeles Times, 1978-79; now joint ed. Hemlock Qtly. and The Euthanasia Rvw. Recipient Martin Luther King Meml. prize, 1972. Office: Box 66218 Los Angeles CA 90066

HUND, ROBERT ARTHUR, b. Detroit, Apr. 12, 1927; s. Arthur Alexander and Ruth Rose (Thomas) H.; m. Carole Kathleen Olson, July 9, 1950; childrn—Kathie Ayres, June, Cynthia, Jonathan. Contrbr. articles on use and maintenance of dimensional stone and ceramic tile to trade and consumer mags. Ed.: (mag.) Through the Ages, 1984—; (manual) Dimensional Stone, Vol. III, 1985. B.S. in Edn., Wayne State U., 1951. Mgr., Henry I Christal Co., Detroit, 1957-63; v.p. Roy Clark, Inc., Detroit, 1963-67; pres. Robert Hund Inc., Farmington, MI, 1967—; mng. dir. Marble Inst. of Am., Farmington, 1980—. Served to sgt. U.S. Army, 1945-47. Deorated Comendation ribbon, 1946; recipient Presidental citation Am. Soc. Interior Designers, 1981. Mem. Adcraft Club of Detroit, Mich. Advt. Agency Council, ASTM, ANSI. Home: 34219 Cortland Farmington MI 48024

HUNDMAN, ROBERT LOUIS, b. Bloomington, IL, May 23, 1935; s. John Clem and Rena Mae (Wiles) H.; m. Nancy Jeanne Watts, Sept. 27, 1957; children—Amie, Cathy, Debby, Cindy; m. Ann Crowell, Jan. 4, 1978. Ed./pub. Mainline Modeler Mag., 1980—; The Allegheny—Lima's Finest, 1984, Lima—The History, 1986. BS in Engring., Purdue U. Project engr. CDI, Peoria, IL, 1965-69, Alstate Design, Cin., 69-70; project mgr. Jeffrey Mining, Columbus, OH, 1970-75; v.p. mfg. Mat Industries, W. Frankfort, IL, 1975-77; with PFM, Edmonds, WA, 1977-79; ed./pub./ owner Hundman Pub., Edmonds, 1979—. Home: 5115 Monticello Dr Edmonds WA 98020

HUNKER, T(RACY) ALLEN, b. Tiffin, OH, April 4, 1957, s. Laurel L. and Wilma E. (Miller) H. BFA, Ohio State U., 1986. Pub., ed. Testube mag., Columbus, Ohio, 1979-85; ed. Wind Power Digest, Bascom, Ohio, 1984—, Solar Energy Info. Service, Bascom, 1984-85, Testube DataBase, Columbus, 1985—; pub., ed. High St. Art, Columbus, 1985—. Office: Box 8421 Columbus OH 43201

HUNT, ANNICE ELIZABETH, b. Palmetto, FL, Mar. 30, 1934; s. William Alva and Doris Elizabeth (Mann) Hunt. Author of seven nature booklets, 1976-79; editor: Calli's Tales, quarterly since 1981. BS, Abilene Christian U., 1961; postgrad. Florida State U., 1962-63. Librarian Defense Doc. Centr. (Alexandria, VA), 1965-67; freelance wrtr., 1969—. Office: Calli's Tales Box 1224 Palmetto FL 34220

HUNT, BERNICE (KOHN), (Bernice Kohn), b. Philadelphia, PA, June 15, 1920; d. Joseph B. and Sarah (Freedman) Herstein; m. (1) David Kohn (div. 1964), (2) G. David Weinich (dec. 1970), (3) Morton Hunt, Sept. 10, 1971; children: Barbara Adler, Judith Wolman, Eugene Kohn. Author: adult nonfiction: (with Morton Hunt) Prime Time: A Guide to the Pleasures and Opportunities of the New Middle Age, 1975, (with M. Hunt) The Divorce Experience, 1977, (with Clifford J. Sager) Intimate Partners: Hidden Patterns in Love Relationships, 1981. Juveniles: Pigeons, 1973, Skunks, 1973, Marriage, 1976, Apples, 1976, The Whatchamacallit Book, 1976, Your Ant Is a Which: Fun with Homophones, 1976, Dams: Water Tamers of the World, 1977, Great Bread! The Easiest Way Possible to Make Almost 100 Kinds, 1977; juveniles under name Bernice Kohn: Our Tiny Servants: Molds and Yeasts, 1962, Computers at Your Service, 1962, The Peaceful Atom, 1963, Everything Has A Shape, 1964, Everything Has a Size, 1964, Marvellous Mammals: Monotremes and Marsupials, 1964, The Scientific Method, 1964, Light, 1965, repr., 1979, Echoes, 1965, repr, 1979, One Day It Rained Cats and Dogs, 1965, Koalas, 1965, Light You Cannot See, 1965, Fireflies, 1966, Telephones, 1967, repr 1979, Levers, 1967, The Bat Book, 1967, repr, 1979, Raccoons, 1968, Secret Codes and Ciphers, 1968, All Kinds Seals, 1968, The Look-It-Up Book of Transportation, 1968, Ferns: Plants without Flowers, 1968, Ramps, 1969, (with G. David Weinick) A First Look at Psychology, 1969, Talking Leaves: The Story of Sequoyah, 1969, The Beachcomber's Book, 1970 (reissved 1987), Chipmunks, 1970, The Armistad Mutiny, 1971, How High Is Up?, 1971, Out of the Cauldron: A Short History of Witchcraft, 1972, The Busy Honeybee, 1972, One Sad Day: A Story, 1972, The Organic Living Book, 1972, The Gypsies, 1972, What a Funny Ting to Say!, 1973, Easy Gourmet Cooking, 1973, The Spirit and the Letter: The Struggle for Rights in America, 1974, Communications Satellites: Message Centers in Space, 1975, Contrbr of numerous articles to periodicals, including Reader's Digest, Ladies' Home Journal, Woman's Day, Red Book, and Family Circle. Attended Univ of Wis-Madison, Columbia Univ., and Empire State Coll of the State Univ. of N.Y; MS, Long Island Univ. Freelance writer. Editor, children's sci. books, Coward-McCann, 1964-66; adj prof of creative writing, Southampton Coll of Long Island Univ., 1977-78; ed-in chief, Dandelion Press, 1978-81; psychotherapist in private practice, 1982—. Mem: AG, AL of America, ASJA. Address: 8 Ledgewood Commons Millwood NY 10546

HUNT, DEBORAH LEE, b. Norwalk, OH, July 5, 1960; d. Lloyd Robert and Elaine Belle (Little) Hunt; m. Gilbert Glen Pate, Apr. 6, 1979 (div. 1984). Contrbr. short stories: Mythic Circle, Space and Time; poetry in anthologies. Wrkg. on sci. fiction, fantasy short stories. Student Oakland Community Coll. Supr. KJ Law Engrs., Farmington Hills, Mich., 1980—. Home: 22600 Middlebelt Rd E29 Farmington Hills MI 48024

HUNT, MAURICE ARTHUR, b. Lansing, MI, Oct. 30, 1942, s. Elmore Clare and Irene Elizabeth (Moran) H.; m. Gloria Lee Bowles, Sept. 26, 1967 (div. 1972); m. 2d, Pamela Helene Coyle, June 24, 1978; children—Alison, Jeffrey, Andrew, Thomas. Contrbr. scholarly articles to Shakespeare Qtly, Modern Lang. Studies, Explorations in Renaissance Culture, Essays in Lit., numerous other publs. BA, U. Mich., 1964; PhD, U. Calif.-Berkeley, 1970. Instr. Coll. of Marin, Kentfield, Calif., 1970-73, 74, 76; lectr. Dominican Coll., San Rafael, Calif., 1974-75; assoc. prof., dir. freshman composition Baylor U., Waco, Tex., 1981—; vis. asst. prof. Ariz. State U., Tempe, 1980-81. Mem. MLA, South-Central Renaissance Conf., Phi Beta Kappa. Office: Dept Eng Baylor Waco TX 76798

HUNT, MORTON M(AGILL), b. Phila., Feb. 20, 1920; s. Alfred R. and Hattie (Magill) Greenstein; m. (1) Lois Marcus (a singer under the name Lois Hunt), Aug. 10, 1946 (div. 1965), (2) Eveline Portnoy, 1968 (div. 1971), (3) Bernice Kohn, Sept. 10, 1971; children (first marriage) Jeffrey. Author: nonfiction: The Natural History of Love, 1959, Mental Hospital, 1962, Her Infinite Variety: The American Woman as Lover, Mate, and Rival, 1962, (with Rena Corman and Louis Ormont) The Talking Cure: A Practical Guide to Psychoanalysis, 1964, Thinking Animal, 1964, The Inland Sea, 1965, The World of the Formerly Married, 1966, The Affair: A Portrait of Extramarital Love in Contemporary America, 1969, The Mugging, 1972, Sexual Behavior in the 1970s, 1974, (with Bernice Hunt), Prime Time: A Guide to the Pleasures and Opportunities of the New Middle Age, 1975, The Young Person's Guide to Love, 1975, Gay: What You Should Know about Homosexuality (young adult book), 1977, (with B. Hunt; rev. ed. 1987), The Divorce Experience, 1977, What Is a Man? What Is a Woman? (young adult book), 1979, The Universe Within: A New Science Explores the Human Mind, 1982, Profilessss of Social Research: The Scientific Study of Human Interactions, 1985. Contributor of about 400 articles, primarily in behavior al science to various magazines, including New Yorker, Harper's, New York Times Magazine McCall's and Playboy. AB, Temple Univ, 1941; grad. study, Univ. of Penn., 1941, 1946. Researcher, staff writer, Look, New York, N.Y., 1946-47; assoc ed, Science Illustrated, New York, N.Y., 1947-49; freelance writer, 1949. New Yorker, contract writer, mainly profiles, 1958-73; lectr, Univ. of Denver, summer, 1958. Mem: ASJA (formerly Soc. of Magazine Writers; v.p., 1954; pres., 1955) Military service: U.S. Army Air Forces, pilot, 1942-46; became first lieutenant; awarded Air Medal with two Oak Leaf clusters. Addresses: 8 Ledgewood Commons Millwood NY 10546

HUNT, TIMOTHY A., b. Calistoga, CA, Dec. 22, 1949, s. Arthur Lee and Nancy May (Rouke) H.; m. Merrill Elizabeth Vargo, Aug. 1971 (div. Oct. 1982); m. Susan D. Spurlock, Nov. 1982; 1 child, John Howard. Author: Kerouac's Crooked Road, 1981, Lake County Diamond, 1986; contrbr. rvws., articles and poems to Rvw Contemporary Fiction, Quarterly West, Westigan Rvw, Notes, Ironwood, Epoch, So. Poetry Rvw, others. AB cum laude, Cornell U., 1970, MA, 1974, PhD, 1975. Asst. prof. English, U. Utah, 19674-76; lectr. honors program U. Del., 1976-80; vis. asst. prof. English, Colby Coll., 1980-81; dir. communications and humanities Nova Coll., 1982-84; adj. instr. English, U. Wash., 1984-85; asst. prof. English, Ind. U.-Purdue U., Ft. Wayne, 1985-87, acad. dean, Deep Springs Coll., Deep Springs, CA, 1987—. Recipient 1st prize for poetry competition Chester H. Jones Soc., 1983. Mem. MLA, Western Am. Lit. Assn. Address: Deep Springs Coll Dyer NV 89010

HUNT, WILLIAM, b. Chgo., May 21, 1934; s. William W. and Verna (Robinson) Hunt; m. Elizabeth Yeomans, April 1976; children—Phillip, Katherine, Damon, Julia. Author: Oceans and Corridors of Orpheus, 1979, Of the Map That Changes, 1974. BA, U. of Chgo., 1964. Admin., Esperanza School, Chgo., 1972-82; asst. prof., N.E. Illinois U., Chgo., 1979-81; lectr., Northwestern U., Evanston, 1981; asst. prof., Loyola U., Chgo., 1981-82; lectr., Simons Rock College, Gt. Barrington, Mass., 1985; reporter, Springfield (MA) Union-News, 1987—. Awards: NEA Fellowship, 1968-69. Home: RD 1 Box 100 Christian Hill Rd Great Barrington MA 01230

HUNTER, DONNELL WALKER, b. Rigby, Idaho, June 5, 1930; s. William Wallace and Bertha (O'Donnell) H.; m. Nita Kearsley, Oct. 15, 1952; children—Donita, Michael, Kerry, Sally, Edward, Alan, Kim, Nathan. Author: The Frog in Our Basement, 1984, Children of Owl, 1985, At Fort Worden, 1986; contrbr. poetry to more than 70 mags. BA, Ricks Coll., 1954; MFA, U. Mont., 1982. Tchr. high schl., Rexburg, Idaho, 1954-55; asst. librn. Ricks Coll., Rexburg, 1955-60, instr. English, 1960-64, 1966—; asst. prof. English Ch. Coll. of Hawaii, Laie, 1964-66, prop., Honeybrook Press. Bd. dirs., Schl. District No. 251, Rigby, 1974-77. Mem. AWP, Pacific NW Regional Council of English in the Two-Year Colleges (ed. newsletter). Address: Box 883 Rexburg ID 83440

HUNTER, EVAN, (Ed McBain), b. NYC, Oct. 15, 1926; s. Charles F. and Marie (Coppola) Lombino; m. Anita Melnick, Oct. 17, 1949 (div.); children: Ted, Mark, Richard; m. Mary Vann Finley, June 1973; 1 stepdau., Amanda Eve Finley. Author: The Blackboard Jungle, 1954, Second Ending, 1956, Strangers When We Meet, 1958, A Matter of Conviction, 1959, The Remarkable Harry, 1960, The Wonderful Button, 1961, Mothers and Daughters, 1961, Happy New Year, Herbie, 1963, Buddwing, 1964, The Paper Dragon, 1966, A Horse's Head, 1967, Last Summer, 1968, Sons, 1969, Nobody Knew They Were There, 1971, Every Little Crook and Nanny, The Easter Man, 1972, Come Winter, 1973, Streets of Gold, 1974, The Chisholms, 1976, Me and Mr. Stenner, 1977, Walk Proud, 1979, Love, Dad, 1981, Far from the Sea, 1983, Lizzie, 1984; also mystery novels under pseudonym Ed Mc Bain: The Pusher, Cop Hater, The Mugger, 1956; The Con Man, 1957, Killer's Choice, Killer's Payoff, Lady Killer, 1958, Killer's Wedge, 'Til Death, King's Ransom, 1959, Give the Boys a Great Big Hand, The Heckler, See Them Die, 1960, Lady, Lady, I Did It, 1961, The Empty Hours, Like Love, 1962, Ten Plus One, 1963, Ax, 1964, The Sentries, 1965, He Who Hesitates, Doll, 1965, Eighty Million Eyes, 1966, Fuzz, 1968, Shotgun, 1969, Jigsaw, 1970, Hail, Hail, the Gang's All Here, 1971, Sadie When She Died, Let's Hear It for the Deaf Man, 1972, Hail to the Chief, 1973, Bread, 1974, Where There's Smoke, 1975, Blood Relatives, 1975, So Long As You Both Shall Live, 1976, Long Time No See, 1977, Goldilocks, 1978, Calypso, 1979, Ghosts, 1980, Rumpelstiltskin, 1981, Heat, 1981; Beauty and the Beast, Ice, 1983, Jack and the Beanstalk, 1984, Lightning, 1984; Snow White and Rose Red, 1985, Eight Black Horses, 1985, Cinderella, 1986, Poison, 1987, Puss in Boots, 1987, Tricks, 1987. writer screenplays: Strangers When We Meet, 1960; The Birds, 1962, Fuzz, 1972, Walk Proud, 1979. Dream West, 1986; stage plays: The Easter Man, 1964; The Conjuror, 1969. BA, Hunter Coll., 1950. Served with USNR, 1944-46. Address: Farquharson Ltd 250 W 57th St New York NY 10019

HUNTER, KATHY, b. Portland, OR, Mar. 11, 1944; d. Harold Wayne and Ruthann McKenzie; m. Duncan Bert Hunter, July 13, 1963; children—Mindy, Brad. Contrbr. to mags., newspapers including Alaska Mag., Natl. Fisherman, Woman's Day, others. Ed.: Alaska Mag., Natl. Fisherman, Woman's Day, others. Ed.: Alaska Today Mag., 1984-85. Wrkg. on book, Alaska Nicknames. B.A., U. Alaska-Fairbanks, 1984. Recipient Joe and Clare Fejes Bookwriting award, U. Alaska, 1982, James Gordon Bennett award, 1984; Honorable Mention for editing NFPW, 1986, 3d place for book, 1987. Mem. Alaska Press Women (1st place for editing 1986, 1st place for book 1987). Home: HC04 9356 Palmer AK 99645

HUNTER, KRISTIN, see Lattany, Kristin Eggleston

HUNTER, SHERYL LYNN, b. Greenfield, MA, Jan. 23, 1958; d. Gilbert Stanley and Dorothy Mae (Wright) H. Contrbr. articles to mags. including Seventeen, others. A.A. in Liberal Arts, Greenfield Commun. Coll., 1978; B.A. in Psychology, U. Mass., Amherst, 1980. Spcl. needs instr. First Ten Steps, Greenfield, 1981; vocational instr. Incentive Commun. Enterprises, Greenfield, 1981-85, employment coord., 1985—. Mem. SCBW. Home: 25 Harrison Ave Greenfield MA 01301

HUNTER-GAULT, CHARLAYNE, b. Due West, SC., Feb. 27, 1942; d. Charles S.H, Jr. and Althea Brown Hunter; m. (1) Walter Stovall, div., d. Susan, (2) Ronald Gault, 1971, s. Chuma. Wayne State Univ., Detrott), 1959-61; BA in jounalism, U. of Ga. (Athens), 1963. Editorial asst., New Yorker, 1963, staff writer and shortstories, 1964-67; investigative reporter and anhorwoman, WRC-TV (NBC), Washington, D.C., 1967; reporter, metro. staff, N.Y. Times, 1968-77; natl. correspondent and swing anchor, MacNeil/Lehrer News (PBS), 1978—. Also published in Vogue, Ms, Life, Essence, Saturday Review, Coronet, New Leader, Change, NYT Magazine, NYT BK Rvw. N.Y. Times Publisher's award with Joseph Lelyveld), 1970, 1974 (2); Emmy award, Grnada invasion, 1983, profile of Elmo Zumwalt III, 1985; Peabody award, effects of racial separatism in S. Africa, 1986. Office: MacNeil/Lehrer 356 W 58th St New York NY 10019

HUNTINGTON, CYNTHIA, b. Meadville, PA, Feb. 6, 1951; d. Richard Edward and M. Roberta (Hulings) Dickson; m. James Albert Yarborough, May 28, 1980; 1 son, Samuel John. Author: (poems) The Fish-Wife, 1986. Contrbr. poems, articles, essays to lit. mags., newspapers, mags. BA, Mich. State U., 1973; MA, Middlebury Coll., 1983. Asst. prof. English, U. Calif., Irvine, 1985—. Recipient Poetry award AWP, 1985, Pacific Poetry Series award U. Hawaii Press, 1985; fellow Fine Arts Work Ctr., Provincetown, Mass., 1979, 83, NEA, 1984. Home: 311 Oswego Ave Huntington Beach CA 92648

HURLEY, LUCILLE SHAPSON, b. Riga, Latvia, May 8, 1922, came to U.S., 1925, naturalized, 1929; m. Kenneth Thompson, 1967; children by previous marriage, Barbara Hurley, Michael Hurley; step-children: Tamara Thompson, Marcus Thompson, Nicholas Thompson. Ed. Jnl. Nutrition, 1984—; mem. editorial bd.: Teratology, 1967-75, Am. Jnl Clin. Nutrition, 1977-80, Jnl Inorganic Biochemistry, 1978—, Biol. Trace Element Research, 1978—, Magnesium Bulltn., 1980-84, Nutrition Research, 1981-84, Magnesium, 1983—, Annales de Recherches Veterinaires, 1983—, Issues and Rvws. in Teratology, 1985—. BS in Nutrition, U. Wis.-Madison, 1943; PhD in Nutrition, U. Calif.-Berkeley, 1950. Mem. faculty U. Calif.-Davis, 1955—, prof. nutrition, 1966—; vis. prof. and scientist numerous ednl. and research orgns. U.S. and Europe; mem. subcoms. and adv. councils to numerous fed. agcys. and sci. orgns. Recipient numerous research and teaching awards. Mem. profl. orgns. Address: Dept Nutrition U Calif Davis CA 95616

HURLEY, MAUREEN VIOLA, b. San Francisco, Nov. 24, 1952, d. Joseph Edward Hurley and Maureen Helen (Reilly) Panis. Contrbr. poetry to Marin Poetry Rvw, Magabark, Ridge Rvw, Women's Voices: Of Ways of Weaving, Poets of the Vineyard; chapbook Falling to Sea Level; contrbr. to numerous newspapers, newsletters; ed. Tracks in the Widest Orbit (J.H. Montrose), 1985; ed., contrbr. Forgotten Languages, 1986, Sonoma Mandala, 1979-81, Seeds Deep in the Earth, 1982, The Program, 1979-81, Open Hand, 1979-80, The Poem Is the Person's Life, 1985, Someone Inside Me, 1986. AA in Art, Coll. of Marin, 1973; BA in Art, Sonoma State U., Cotati, Calif., 1976. Mgr. Western Star Press, Kentfield, Calif., 1973-75; lectr. arts and ednl. orgns.; ed., cons. ed. trade books, newsletters; graphic artist; mem. faculty Napa Poetry Conf., 1983, 84; freelance photojournalist; artist-in-residence numerous sites, Calif. Arts Council, 1980—; poet-in-residence, Bahamian Poetry Soc., Nassau, 1985. Mem. Artists in the Schls. Sonoma County (founding mem.), Russian River Wrtrs. Guild (coordinator 1979—), Pub. Poetry Ctr. (founder, program dir. 1979-82), Marin Poetry Ctr. Address: 7491 Mirabel Rd Forestville CA 95434

HURWITZ, JOHANNA, b. NYC, Oct. 9, 1937; d. Nelson and Tillie (Miller) Frank; m. Uri Hurwitz, Feb. 19, 1962; children—Nomi, Beni. Author children's books, 1976—, latest being Adventures of Ali Baba Bernstein, 1985, Russell Rides Again, 1985. BA, Queens College, Flushing, NY, 1958; MLS, Columbia U., 1959. Librarian, NY Public Library, 1959-64; Calhoun School, NYC,1968-75; New Hyde Park School Dist., NY, 1975-77; Great Neck Library, NY, 1978—; lecturer Queens College, 1965-68. Notable Book Award, Am. Library Assoc., 1979, 82, 83, Parents' Choice Magazine Award, 1982, 84, Children's Choice Award, Intl. Reading Assoc., 1980, 82. Mem. AG, Soc. of Children's Writers, PEN. Home: 10 Spruce Pl Great Neck NY 11021

HUTCHESON, CAROLYN PIRTLE, b. Melbourne, FL, Jan. 1, 1930; d. Clyde Robert and Diantha (Edenfield) Pirtle; m. Edgar David Wenger, July 11, 1955 (div. Apr. 16, 1973); children—David Eugene, Kimberley, Edgar David, Sean Wright; m. Donnie Dee Hutcheson, July 13, 1975; 1 dau., Caroline Deanna. Contrbr. to Hardeman County Tenn. History, PURRRR Newsletter, Women's Circle Home Cooking; artwork to The Nightingale, 1972-73. Cert. in Licensed Practical Nursing, Franklin County Vocational-Technical Coll., 1973. Nurse, Dr. Abelardo Lacano, Merritt Island, FL, 1978-79, Dr. Joseph Rojas, Titusville, FL, 1984; semi-profl. artist Central Brevard Art Assn., Rockledge, FL, 1972—; free-lance wrtr., 1979—. Home: 994 Alsup Dr Rockledge FL 32955

HUTCHERSON, HARMON HARDING, (A.H. Keeley, Rhesa Todd), b. Hartford, Ky., Sept. 15, 1929; d. William Knox and Constance Genora (McKinley) Harding; m. Estill Creech Lee, Jan. 12, 1945 (dec. 1946); 1 son, W. Keith; m. 2d, W. Powell Hutcherson, Feb. 19, 1966 (div.). Contbrb.: Western Reorder, True Story, Fireside. Wrkg. on mystery novel. Ed., Evansville Coll., U. Ky., U. Chgo. Assoc. dir. admissions U. Chattanooga, 1961-66; freelance wrtr. Home: Box 232B DeSota Pkwy Mentone AL 35984

HUTCHINS, JEANE M., b. Roanoke, VA, Oct. 22, 1947, d. Jacque Lee and June Kathleen (Kane) Hutchins; m. Robert C. McQueen, May 25, 1985. Ed.: The Fiberarts Design Book II, 1983. BA, U. Tenn., 1969. Advt. dir. Lark Communications, Asheville, N.C., 1980-82; ed. Yarn Market News, Atlanta, 1982—. Office: YM News 588 St Charles Ave NE Atlanta GA 30308

HUTCHINS, SHIRLEY M., (Lee), b. Center Moriches, NY, Apr. 9, 1933; d. Richard I. and Gertrude M. (Carter) Bernstein. Poetry to Maine Life, East End Arts Council Newsletter, Puzzle Pieces (booklet). BA in English Adelphi Coll., 1962. Tchr. East Moriches Schl. (NY), 1962-69, Wm. Floyd Schl. (Shirley, NY), 1969-71. Mem. Poetry Fellowship of Maine. Home: 57 Chichester Ave Center Moriches NY 11934

HUTCHISON, DAVID A., b. Newark, NJ, Oct. 18, 1946; s. James Duward and Erma Dorothea (Koethe) H. Author: Special Effects, Vols. 1-4, 1979, 80, 81, 84, Fantastic 3-D, 1982, Film Magic, 1987. Student U. FL, 1964-66, FL State U., 1966-69. Sci. ed. Future Life, NYC, 1979-81, Starlog, NYC, 78—; ed.-in-chief Cinemagic, NYC, 1979—. Office: Starlog 475 Park Ave So New York NY 10016

HUTCHISON, JOSEPH G., JR., b. Denver, June 26, 1950, s. Joseph G. and Helen F. (Hill) H.; m. Jill A. Reynolds, Aug. 29, 1970; children—Susannah Bryn, Brian Christopher. Author: Weathers, Vistas, Houses, Dust, 1980, Shadow-Light, 1982, Thirst, 1984, The Undersides of Leaves, 1985; contrbr. poetry to Amer. Poetry Rvw, Denver Qtrly, The Nation, Ohio Rvw, Tendril, numerous other lit. mags and anthols; ed. Pendragon mag., 1981-84 pres. and co-founder Wayland Press, 1985—. BA summa cum laude, U. No. Colo., 1972; MFA, U. B.C., 1974. Poet-in-schls., Colo. Council on Arts, 1975-77, 78-79, Oreg. Fdn. for Arts, 1977-78; book buyer Auraria Book Center, Denver, 1978-81; staff wrtr. United Bank Denver, 1981—; freelance wrtr., 1975—; mem. grants panel Colo. Council on Arts, 1982-85. Recipient Macmillan award for poetry, Macmillan Co. Can., 1974. Mem. Rocky Mountain Wrtrs. Guild (bd. dirs. 1984—), NWU, Intl. TV Assn. Home: 25 N Cody Ct Lakewood CO 80226

HUTCHISON, MICHAEL S., b. Pitts. Author: Central America, 1980, rev. ed., 1982, The Book of Floating, 1984, Megabrain, 1985; contrbr. short stories, articles to Chgo. Rvw, Changes, Crawdaddy, Esquire, Outside, New Age Jnl, Village Voice, N.Y. Press, Woodstock Poetry Rvw, L.A. Times Mag., Chgo. Tribune, Chgo. Sun-Times, Fusion, Travel & Leisure, others; contrbr. poetry to Partisan Rvw, Woodstock Poetry Rvw, Fried Shoes, others. BA, Coll. of Wooster, Ohio; MFA, U. Iowa, Iowa City. Recipient James Michener prize for fiction, Copernicus Fdn., 1982. Address: 207 E 5th St Apt 11 NYC 10003

HUTT, JOANNA CRAVEY, b. Montgomery, AL, Aug. 11, 1943; d. John Thomas and Anna Rebecca (Coine) Cravey; Joe Lee Hutt, Apr. 18, 1970; children—John Cravey, Mary Maxwell. Contrbr. articles to mags., newsletter inluding Ala. Mag., Ala. Monthly, others; brochures, press/media kits, features to trade pubs. Asst. ed., researcher The Gray Letter, 1979-80;

contrbg. wrtr., ed. Ala. Monthly, 1983-84, Ala. Mag., 1983—. Ed., Am. Assn. Univ. Adminstrs. newsletter. B.S., U. Ala., 1965, postgrad., 1967-72. Part-time English instr. U. Ala., Tuscaloosa, 1978-79, part-time instr. composition and lit., 1980—; owner The Write Stuff, Tuscaloosa, 1980—. Office: Box 3127 Tuscaloosa AL 35404

HUTTER, DONALD STEPHEN, b. London, Dec. 30, 1932; s. Stefan Severin and Catherine (Hutter) Fraenkel; m. Martha Corbett, Aug. 17, 1957; children—Anne Victoria, Stephanie Grace, Sarah Catherine. Author: Abraham, 1947, Upright Hilda, 1967; contrbr. short stories to Best American Short Stories, 1965; also mags., including Esquire. Editor Charles Scribner's Sons, NYC, 1957-67; sr. editor Dial Press, NYC, 1967-69, editor-in-chief, 1969-72; exec. editor Holt, Rinehart & Winston, NYC, 1972-81, editor-in-chief, 1981-82; v.p., sr. editor Simon & Schuster, 1982-85; ed. Donald Hutter Books (with Henry Holt and Co.), 1987—. Served with F.A. AUS, 1955-57. Home: 154 White Oak Shade Rd New Canaan CT 06840

HUTTON, LINDA JO, b. Kalispell, MT, Oct. 4, 1947; d. Joseph John and Selma (Gilder) Leaf; m. Gordon Andrew Hutton, Mar. 30, 1971; stepchildren—Jeffrey, Deborah, Gregory, David. Contrbr. fiction, non-fiction, plays, poems to mags. Contrbg. markets ed.: Byline, 1985—, The Freelancer's Report, 1987—, Wrtr.'s Nook news, 1987—, Published!, 1986—δ., pub. Rhyme Time Poetry Newsletter, 1981—, Mystery Time Anthol., 1982—, The Best of Rhyme Time, 1981—, Wrtr.'s Info., 1985—. Student U. Mont., 1965. Ed., Hutton Pubs., Coeur d'Alene, ID, 1980—. Recipient 3d prize for poetry Woman's Day Mag., 1985, 2d prize for poetry Byline Mag., 1985, 2d prize for fiction Kaleidoscope Mag., 1986, 1st prize for essay NBC Radio Talknet, 1987. Mem. League Minn. Poets, World Soc. Poets. Address: Box 2377 Coeur d' Alene ID 83814

HUTTON, PAUL ANDREW, b. Frankfurt, Fed. Republic Germany, Oct. 23, 1949; s. Paul Andrew and Louise (Johnson) H.; m. Vicki Bauer, July 25, 1972 (div. Aug. 1984); 1 dau., Laura Bauer. Author: Custer and His Times, 1981, Ten Days on the Plains, 1985, Phil Sheridan and His Army, 1985, Soldiers West: Biographies from the Military Frontier, 1987. Wrkg. on study of Alamo as Am. icon. BA, Ind. U., Bloomington, 1972, PhD, 1981. Assoc. ed. Western Hist. Quarterly, Logan, Utah, 1977-84; ed. N. Mex. Hist. Rvw, Albuquerque, 1985—; assoc. prof. U. N.Mex., Albuquerque, 1985—. Recipient Evans Biography award Brigham Young U., 1986, Ray Allen Billilngton Award, 1987. Mem. Western History Assn., Orgn. Am. Hists., WWA (Golder Spur award 1986). Office: U NM History Dept Albuquerque NM 87131

HUZVAR, BARBARA JO, b. Grafton, WV, Apr. 29, 1950; d. Dorsey Clyde and Emma Jean (Henderson) Lake; m. John William Huzvar, Sept. 28, 1968; children—Jean, John. Contrbr. poems to anthols. Grad. public schls., Diamond, OH. Recipient Golden Poet award World of Poetry, 1985, 86, 87, award of Merit, 1985, 86, 87. Home: 1606 Manchester Ave Lake Milton OH 44429

HYAMS, JOE, b. Cambridge, MA, June 6, 1923; s. Joseph Irving and Charlotte (Strauss) H.; m. Elke Sommer, Nov. 18, 1964. Author: (with Walter Wanger) My Life With Cleopatra, 1963, (with Maj. Riddle) A Weekend Gamblers Handbook, 1963, (with Edith Head) How To Dress for Success, 1966, (with Peter Sellers) Seller's Market, 1964, Bogie, 1966, A Field of Buttercups, 1968, (with Thomas Merton) Accomplices to the Crime, 1969, (with Tony Trabert) Winning Tactics for Weekend Tennis, 1972, Mislaid in Hollywood, 1973, (with Pancho Gonzales) Winning Tactics for Singles, 1973, (with Billie Jean King) Billie Jean King's Secrets of Winning Tennis, 1974, Bogart and Bacall: A Love Story, 1966, The Pool, 1978, Zen in the Martial Arts, 1979, The Last Award, 1981, Playboy Guide to Self-Defense, 1981, Murder at the Academy Awards, 1983 (with Chuck Norris) Inner Strength, 1986. BS, N.Y.U., 1948, MA, 1949. Editor Reporter Publs., 1947-50; columnist N.Y. Herald Tribune, 1950-64. Mem. AG, Am. Newspaper Guild. Address: St Martin's 175 Fifth Ave New York NY 10010

HYDE, LEWIS, b. Boston, Oct. 16, 1945, s. Walter Lewis and Elizabeth (Sanford) H.; m. Patricia Vigderman, Nov. 27, 1981; 1 son, Matthew. Author: This Error Is the Sign of Love, 1988; The Gift: Imagination and the Erotic Life of Property, 1983; ed. with introduction: A Longing for the Light: Selected Poems of Vincente Aleixandre, 1979, On the Work of Allen Ginsberg, 1984; translator: Vincente Aleixandre World Alone (with David Unger), 1982; ed., translator: Twenty Poems of Vincente Aleixandre (with Robert Bly), 1977; contrbr. essays to Am. Poetry Rvw, Kenyon Rvw, Lamp in the Spine, other periodicals. BA, U. Minn., 1967; MA, U. Iowa, 1972. Ast. prof. ofs English, Harvard U., Cambridge, Mass., 1985—; v.p. The Artists Fdn., Boston, 1985. Recipient AAP prize, U. Minn., 1966, Columbia U. Translation Center award, 1979, Completion award Mass. Council on Arts and Humanities; poetry writing fellow NEA, 1977, NEH fellow, 1979, poetry fellow Mass. Council on Arts and Humanities, 1980, NEA creative non-fiction fellow, 1982, 86; wrtr.-in-residence Centrum Fdn., Port Townsend, Wash., 1984. Home: 8 Donnell St Cambridge MA 02138

IBUR, JANE ELLEN, b. St. Louis, Oct. 21, 1950; d. Leslie Louis and Betty (Harris) I. Contrbr. poems, short stories to lit. mags., anthols. B.A., Webster U., 1972. Recipient Honorable Mention award St. Louis Poetry Ctr., 1981. Home: 3536 Victor Saint Louis MO 63104

ICE, RUTH, (Claire Pomeroy), b. Buffalo, Nov. 24, 1928; d. Francis Worthington and Grace Berdine (Ernisse) Ice; m. E. V. Walter; six children. Author: Fight it Out, Work it Out, Love it Out, 1977 (paper 1979); contrbr. short stories Epoch, Lit Rvw, Kans Qtly. BA, Ohio Wesleyan, 1951; MA, Ohio State, 1959. Writer, Brookline, Mass. Address: 204 Aspinwall Ave Brookline MA 02146

IDDINGS, KATHLEEN ANN, b. West Milton, OH, d. Ralph Myers and Ruth Amelia (Kinneson) Wolfe; m. Kent Nolan Iddings (div.); children—Angela Iddings Klein, Pamela Iddings Hanover, Sherrie Iddings Manson, Stan David Iddings. Author poetry books: The Way of Things, 1984, Invincible Summer, 1985, Promises to Keep, 1986; ed. five poetry anthologies forSan Diego Poets Press which she helped originate in 1981. Started La Jolla Poets Press, 1984, published: Survival, Evasion & Escape (by Hank Malone), 1985, To Face the Inscription (by Natalie Safir, 1987, What She Could Not Name (by Nancy Shiffrin), 1987, The Blessed Ordinary (by Gwen Jansma), 1987contrbr. numerous poems to anthologies, rvws. and lit mags. BS, Miami U., Oxford, Ohio, 1966; postgrad. U. Calif.-San Diego, other univs. Ed., dir. San Diego Poets Press, 1981—; ed., pub. La Jolla (Calif.) Poets Press, 1984—; freelance wrtr., 1979—; mem. selection bd. COMBO, San Diego, 1985. Recipient COMBO fellowship, 1986 and other honors. Fellow Calif. Poetry Soc., World Poetry Soc., Sea Coast Poets; mem. PSA, AAP (assoc.). Office: Box 8638 La Jolla CA 92038

IDE, PATRICIA LOUISE, b. Kansas City, MO, Aug. 2, 1935; d. Robert Riley and Myrtle Magdeline (Hartman) Nash; m. Joseph Dean Ide, Dec. 29, 1955; children—Gregory Dean, James Matthew, Linda Sue, Paul Andrew. Contrbr. poetry to Editors Desk, Profl. Poet, Fine Arts Press, World of Poetry, Poetry Press, Byline Mag., Tarragon Publs., Am. Poetry Assn. Secy./tchr. Emmanuel Bapt. Ch., Ocean Springs, Miss., 1962-64; treas. Chandler Rd. Bapt. Ch., Omaha, 1965-67; tchr. aide, San Jose, CA, 1973-75; vol. McKee Med. Ctr., Loveland, Colo., 1985—. Recipient Poet of the Year award Eds. Desk, Ocala, Fla., 1983-84. Home: 6407 West 23d St Loveland CO 80537

IGNATOW, DAVID, b. Bklyn., Feb. 7, 1914; s. Max and Henrietta (Reinbach) I.; m. Rose Graubart, July 20, 1940; children—David, Yaedi. Author: Poems, 1948, The Gentle Weight Lifter, 1955, Say Pardon, 1962, Figures of the Human, 1964, Rescue the Dead, 1968, Earth Hard, Selected Poems, 1968, Facing the Tree, 1973, Tread the Dark, 1975, Whisper to the Earth, 1981, Leaving the Door Open, 1984, Poems: 1934-1969, New and Collected Poems; 1970-1985; prose The Notebooks of David Ignatow, 1973, Open Between Us, 1980. Academic grad., New Utrecht H.S. (Bklyn.), 1932. Assoc. ed. Am. Scene, 1935-37; lit. arts ed. NY Analytic, 1937; ed. Beloit Poetry Jnl, 1949-59; poetry ed. The Nation, 1962-63; ed.-at-large Am. Poetry Rvw., 1973-76; instr. New Schl. for Social Research, 1963-65; lectr. Univ. of Ky., 1965-66; lectr., Univ. of Kansas, 1966-67; Poet-in-res. Vassar Coll., 1967-68; prof. York Coll. CUNY, 1968-84; visiting prof. NYU and Columbia, 1985—. Natl. Inst. of Arts and Letters award, 1964; Shelley Meml. award, 1964; Guggenheim fellowship, 1964, 73; NEA grant, 1970, Bollingen Prize, 1977, Wallace Stevens Fellowship, Yale Univ., 1977, Poet-in-Residence, Walt Whitman Birthplace Assoc., 1987. Mem. PSA (pres. 1981-85), PEN. Address: Box 1458 East Hampton NY 11937

ILG, RUTH MERKLE, b. Konstanz, W.Ger., July 29, 1945, came to U.S., 1967, d. Eugen Friedrich and Erna Helena (Frommelt) Merkle; m. Otto Manfred Ilg; 1 son, Boris Alexander Patrick. Author: Reflections (poetry), 1978; contrbr. poetry to New Beginnings, Better Days & Happy Endings, 1986, Suwanee Poetry Anthology, N.Am. Poetry Rvw, other publs. Wrkg. on poetry book, novel. Ed. W.Ger., France, Eng. Guest columnist Anderson (S.C.) Ind. Daily Mail, Catholic Banner; pres. Anderson County Arts Council, 1974-76; dir. Palmetto Wrtrs. Conf., Anderson, 1976-77. Mem. Anderson Wrtrs. Guild (pres. 1975-76), S.C. Poetry Soc. (dir. 1976-77), Foothills Authors Guild, Anderson Art Assn. Home: 2800 Rambling Path Anderson SC 29621

IMMEL, MARY BLAIR, b. Wichita, KS, Dec. 8, 1930; d. Virgil Ashenfelter; adopted d. Clint and Hope (deVore) Blair; m. Daniel M. Immel, Sept. 7, 1950; children—Daniel C., Michael Vernon, Douglas Blake. Author: Men of God, 1960, Two Way Street (Hoosier Authors award Ind. U. 1966), 1965, Call Up the Thunder, 1969, River of Wind, 1977, No Longer Sings the Brown Thrush, 1988; (with Bertie Layne) Keys to Many Doors, 1964. Contrbr. poems, short stories, articles, ch. schl. curriculum to secular and religious pubs. B.A. in Edn., Religion, Chapman Coll., 1952; M.A. in History, Political Sci., Purdue U., 1967. Asst. dir. Tipecanoe Co. Hist./ Museums, Lafayette, IN, 1967-71; instr. Butte Commun. Coll., CA, 1972-80. Recipient Creative Writing award Knights of Pythias, 1948. Home: 215 N Newlin St Veedersburg IN 47987

IMPERATO, PASCAL JAMES, b. NYC, Jan. 13, 1937, s. James Anthony and Madalynne Marguerite (Insante) I.; m. Eleanor Anne Maiella, June 4, 1977; children—Alison Madalynne, Gavin Humbert, Austin Clement. Author: Doctor in the Land of the Lion, 1964, Bwana Doctor, 1967, The Treatment and Control of Infectious Diseases in Man, 1974, The Cultural Heritage of Africa, 1974, A Wind in Africa: A Story of Modern Medicine in Mali, 1975, What to do About the Flu, 1976, African Folk Medicine: Practices and Beliefs of the Bambara and Other Peoples, 1977, Historical Dictionary of Mali, 1977, 2d edit., 1986, Dogon Cliff Dwellers: The Art of Mali's Mountain People, 1978, Medical Detective, 1979, Mali: A Handbook of Historical Statistics (with Eleanor M. Imperato), 1982, Buffoons,, Queens and Wooden Horseman, 1983, Acceptable Risks (with Greg Mitchell), 1985, Arthur Donaldson Smith and the Exploration of Lake Rudolf, 1987, Boli, 1988; ed.: Last Adventure: The Martin Johnsons in Borneo (by Osa Johnson), 1966. BS magna cum laude, St. John's U., 1958, DSc (hon.), 1977; MD, SUNY, 1962; MPH & TM, Tulane U., 1966. Med. epidemiologist USPHS-Center for Disease Control, Mali, West Africa, 1966-72; dir. Bur. Infectious Disease Control, NYC Dept. Health, 1972-74, 1st dep. commr., 1974-77; commr. health, chmn. bd. dirs. NYC Health and Hosps. Corp., 1977-78; prof., chmn. dept. preventive medicine and community health SUNY Downstate Med. Center, Bklyn., 1978—; ed. Jnl Community Health, 1985—, N.Y. State Jnl Medicine, 1986—. Fulbright sr. scholar North Yemen, 1985. Mem. AG, numerous med. orgns. Office: NY St Jnl Med 420 Lakeville Rd Lake Success NY 11042

INDIANA, BOB, see Novak, Robert Lee

INEZ, COLETTE, b. Brussels, Belgium, June 23, 1931; arrd. USA, 1937 (naturalized, 1952); m. Saul A. Stadtmauer, July 26, 1964. Author: The Woman Who Loved Worms, 1972, Alive and Taking Names, 1977, Eight Minutes from the Sun, 1983, Family Life, 1988; poetry in anthologies and lit. mags. BA, Hunter Coll., 1961. Instr., SUNY-Stony Brook, 1975, vis. prof., Hunter Coll., 1978, mem. faculty, The New School, 1973-84, poet-in-res., Kalamazoo Coll., 1975, 76, 78, 81, 85, lectr., Columbia Univ., 1981—. Recipient Guggenheim fellowship, 1985-86, Hunter College Hall of Fame, 1987, Rockefeller Fdn. fellowship, 1980, NEA fellowship, 1974, Great Lakes Colleges Assn. natl. 1st book book prize, 1973. Mem. PSA, PEN. Home: 5 W 86th St New York NY 10024

INFANTE, CHRISTINE MARIE, b. Pitts., May 3, 1952, d. Umberto Rocco and Elizabeth Ann (Aiello) Infante; m. Paul Henri Levy, June 9, 1980; children—Aaron Paul Infante-Levy, Alexia P. Infante-Levy. Contrbr. articles to newspapers, trade publs. BA, Carnegie-Mellon U., Pitts., 1974. Supr., J&L Steel Co., Pitts., 1974-76, mgr. 1976-79; communications cons., C.M. Infante, San Diego and San Francisco, 1979-83; ed. Pacific, Pacific Bell-Pacific Telesis Group, San Francisco, 1984-86; commns. cons., Mercer-Meidinger, Boston, 1986—. Recipient Arnold's Admirables award Ragan Report, 1984, Best Cover award, 1985; Internal Publ. award Pub. Relations Soc. Am., San Francisco, 1985; Design Ann. award PRINT mag., NYC, 1985; named in Outstanding Corp. Publs., 1985. Home: 19 Manemet Rd Boston MA 02159

INGALLS, JEREMY, b. Gloucester, MA, Apr. 2, 1911, d. Charles Augustine and May Estelle (Dodge) I. Author: A Book of Legends, 1941, The Metaphysical Sword, 1941, Tahl, 1945, The Galilean Way, 1953, The Woman from the Island, 1958, These Islands Also, 1959, The Epic Tradition, 1964, This Stubborn Quantum, 1983, Summer Liturgy, 1985; translator: A Political History of China, 1840-1928 (with S.Y. Teng), 1956, The Malice of Empire (from Yao Hsinnung's Ching-Kung Yuan), 1970, Nakagawa's Tenno Yugao, 1975; contrbr. articles: Classical Jnl, Kobe Jogakiun Studies, Ariz. Qtly, numerous other publs.; contrbr. poetry: Studia Mystica, Blue Unicorn, Beloit Poetry Jnl, Today's Japan, numerous other lit. publs. Wrkg. on narrative poetry, translation. AB, Tufts U., 1932, AM, 1933, LittD, 1965; fellow in classical Chinese, U. Chgo., 1945-47. Guest poet at 25 colls. and univs., 1940-64; Yale Series Yngr. Poets award, 1941; Guggenheim fellowship, 1943; Am. Acad. Arts and Ltrs. grant, 1944; Ford Fdn. fellow in Asian studies, 1952-53; Fulbright prof. Am. lit., Japan, 1957-58; Rockefeller Fdn. lectr. in Am. poetry, Japan, 1958, Steinman Fdn. lectr. poetry, 1960. Life Mem. PSA (Shelley Meml. award 1950, Lola Ridge Meml. award 1951, 52), Dante Soc., AG, Assn. Asian Studies, New Eng. Poetry Club, MLA. Asst. prof. Am. lit., Western Coll., 1941-43; resident poet, assoc. prof., Rockford Coll., 1946-52; sr. prof., Eng. dept. chmn., dir. Asian Studies, Rockford Coll., 1953-60; honorary LHD and prof. emerita, Rockford Coll., 1960. Mem. Phi Beta Kappa, Authors Guild. Home: 6269 E Rosewood St Tucson AZ 85711

INGAMELLS, JULIA IRENE, b. Independence, IA, Apr. 11, 1945; d. Alva Jr. and Dora Ella (McLaughlin) McCalley; m. Brian Eugene Fanton, Jan. 10. 1965 (div. Dec. 1974); children—Kim Noelle, Kandi Rene, Kara Kaye. m. Lynn Russell Ingamells, Aug. 7, 1976; 1 son Eric John. Contrbr. poems to anthols., articles to mags. Columnist: Rural, 1982—, The Evener, 1983-84. Student Luther Coll., 1963-64; B.A in Art, Edn., Upper Iowa U., 1976. Recipient cert. of Merit, Scholastic Mags., 1963, Honorable Mention, Iowa Poetry Day Assn., 1963. Mem. Northeast Iowa Art Assn. Home: Rt 1 Box 56 Stanley IA 50671

INGERSOLL, ROY, see Safford, Dan Scott

INGRAM, ALYCE M., b. St. Paul, Jan. 30, 1914, d. Alexander and Elizabeth (Maser) Meisner; m. Paul Thomas Ingram, Aug. 31, 1941. Contrbr. short stories to lit mags and anthols., including Small Pond, Greensboro, Mediterranean, N.Am., Cream City rvws, Event, Eureka, New Renaissance, Room, Vagabond Anthology, Moving to Antarctica, 25 Minn. Wrtrs. Freelance wrtr. Recipient short fiction award McKnight Found., 1964. Home: 401 Sibley St Mears Park Pl St Paul MN 55101

INMAN, PETER T., b. Bronxville, NY, Mar. 31, 1948, s. John R. and Ellen Nice (Thomas) I.; m. Tina Darragh, June 12, 1977; 1 son, Jack. Author: Platin, 1979, Ocker, 1982, Uneven Development, 1984; contrbr. to anthologies: None of the Above, 1976, L-A-N-G-U-A-G-E Book, 1984, In The American Tree, 1986; contrbr. to Abacus, Ironwood, Oink, Dog City, numerous other lit mags; co-ed. (with Doug Lang) EEL, 1974-78. BA, Georgetown U., 1969. Library technician Library of Congress, Washington, 1979—.Home: 3324 Buchanan St Mount Rainier MD 20822

INMAN, WILL, b. Wilmington, NC, May 4, 1923, s. William Archibald and Delia Ellen (Inman) McGirt. Author poetry vols.: 108 Prayers for J Edgar, 1965, A Generation of Heights, 1969, Voice of the Beech Oracle, 1977, A Way Through for the Damned, 1983; author: A Trek of Waking, 1985; Brother Word (with Charles Taylor); contrbr. poems, short stories and articles to various publs.; ed. Kauri poetry newsletter, 1964-71, New Kauri poetry mag., 1980-84. BA, Duke U., 1943. Instr. English Am. U., Washington, 1967-70, Montgomery Coll., Rockville, Md., 1969-73; mem. staff Ariz. State Trng. Program, Tucson, 1977-86, tchr Arizona State Prisons System, 1985-86. Poet-in-residence Am. U., Washington, 1967. Home: 2551 W Mossman Rd Tucson AZ 85746

INNES, RUTH, b. Warren, PA, May 1, 1929; d. Siegfried William and Rose May (Hefren) Okerberg; m. George James Innes, May 18, 1954 (div. Sept. 1986); children—Bridget, Brenda, George James, Steven. Contrbr. short stories, poems to mags., anthols. including Mature Living, others. B.S., Indiana U. of PA, 1950. Sec. Deloitte Haskins & Sells, Miami, 1970-85; legal sec. Sparber, Shevin, it al., Miami, 1985—. Mem. ALPW. Home: 525 Allendale Rd Miami FL 33149

INNESS-BROWN, ELIZABETH ANN, b. Rochester, NY, May 1, 1954. Author: (short story collection) Satin Palms, 1981. Stories and rvws. in N. Am. Rvw, Ascent, fiction intl., Chelsea, Boulevard, Lo Spazio Umano, The New Yorker, St. Petersburg Times, N.Y. Arts Jnl, So. Qtly. BA, St. Lawrence U., 1976; MFA, Columbia U., 1978. Asst. prof. English, U. So. Miss., Hattiesburg, 1979-84, assoc. prof., 1985—; vis. prof. St. Lawrence U., Canton, NY, 1984-85. Recipient AWP award series, 1981, award for fiction St. Lawrence U., 1982, Pushcart prize, 1982; NEA grantee, 1982. Mem. AWP, P&W. Office: U So Miss S Station Box 5144 Hattiesburg MS 39406

IODICE, RUTH GENEVIEVE WORK, b. Crystal Lake, IL, Aug. 16, 1925, d. John Mason and Irene Christine Marie (Heinlin) Work; m. Cosimo Leo Iodice, June 20, 1953; 1 son, John Kay. Contrbr. poetry to Poet Lore, Modern Haiku. Cedar Rock, other lit mags. Editor: Blue Unicorn, a triqtly. of poetry, 1977—; ed.-in-chief Calif. State Poetry Qtly, 1976-77. BA, Ind. State U., 1948; postgrad. U. Chgo., 1951-54, U. Calif.-Berkeley, 1963-65. Tchr. public schls. throughout Mich., Ind., Ill., 1949-63; wrtr., poet, ed., toy creator, Kensington, Calif., 1963-80; tutor Regional Occupational Program, Richmond, Calif., 1980—. Mem. PSA, P&W. Home: 22 Avon Rd Kensington CA 94707

IRION, MARY JEAN, b. Newport, KY, Nov. 6, 1922; d. Verd Anderson and Mary Della (McNeil) McElfresh; m. Paul Ernst Irion, Aug. 29, 1944; children—Mark, Lisa. Author: From the Ashes of Christianity, 1968 (non-fiction), Yes, World, 1970 (essays), Holding On, 1984 (poetry). BA, Millersville U., 1966. Tchr. English lit. Lancaster Country Day Schl., Pa., 1968-74, 80-81; instr. poetry Chautauqua Inst., NY, 1982-86. Recipient Unicorn award, Natl. Fedn. State Poetry Socs., 1976, Chautauqua poetry award, 1976, 77, 78, PSA honorable mention, 1983.

Mem. Soc. of Arts, Religion in Contemp. Culture, P&W, PSA. Address: 149 Kready Ave Millersville PA 17551

IRSFELD, JOHN HENRY, b. Bemidji, MN, Dec. 2, 1937; s. Hubert Louis and Mary Lillian (McKee) I.; m. 1st Margaret Elizabeth Drushel, Aug. 29, 1965 (div. Feb. 22, 1978), 1 dau., Hannah Christine; m. 2d, Janet Elizabeth Jones, May 5, 1984. Author: Coming Through, 1975, Little Kingdoms, 1976, Rats Alley, 1987; ed. Las Vegan mag., 1976-85, LV: The Mag. of Las Vegas, 1985—. BA, U. Tex. 1959, MA, 1966, PhD,1969. Asst. prof. English Univ. Nev., Las Vegas, 1969-73, assoc. prof., 1973-77, prof., 1977—, chmn. English dept., 1977-84, asst. to academic vice-pres., 1984-87; deputy to the pres., 1987—. Served as Sgt. E5 US Army Infantry, 1961-64, US. Address: 3605 Briarglen Ln Las Vegas NV 89108

IRVING, JOHN WINSLOW, b. Exeter, NH, Mar. 2, 1942; s. Colin F.N. and Frances (Winslow) I.; m. Shyla Leary, Aug. 20, 1964; children: Colin, Brendan. Author: novels including Setting Free the Bears, 1969, The Water-Method Man, 1972, The 158-Pound Marriage, 1974, The World According to Garp, 1978, The Hotel New Hampshire, 1981. Student, U. Pitts., 1961-62, U. Vienna, 1963-64; BA, U. N.H., 1965; MFA, U. Iowa, 1967. Writer-in-residence U. Iowa, 1972-75. Rockefeller Fdn. grantee, 1971-72; NEA fellow, 1974-75. Address: Random Hs 201 E 50th St New York NY 10022

IRWIN, DEBBI, see Newton, Debra Irwin

IRWIN, FAY, see Briggs, Charlie I.

IRWIN, MARK, b. Faribault, MN, Apr. 9, 1953, s. William Thomas and Mary Lou (Milliron) I. Author: (poetry) the Halo of Desire, 1987, Against the Meanwhile (three elegies), 1988, Umbrellas in the Snow, 1985; translator: Notebook of Shadows (by Philippe Denis), 1982, Ask the Circle to Forgive You (by Nichita Stanescu), 1983; contrbr. poetry to Antaeus, Malahat Rvw, Poetry Now, Shenandoah, other lit mags; long poems published in Kenyon Rvw, 1984, 85. MFA, U. Iowa, 1980; PhD, Case Western Res. U., 1981. Lectr. Case Western Res. U., Cleve., 1974-76, U. Akron (Ohio), 1981—; asst. prof. Cleve. Inst. Art, 1984—. Fulbright scholar, Romania, 1981; Ohio Arts Council poetry fellow, 1985. Mem. AWP. Office: Cleve Inst Art University Circle Cleveland OH 44106

IRWIN, MIRIAM OWEN, b. Columbus, OH, June 14, 1930; d. John Milton and Faith (Studebaker) Owen; m. Kenneth J. Irwin, June 5, 1960; 1 son, Christopher Owen Irwin. Author: Lute and Lyre, 1977, Miriam Mouse's Survival Manual, 1977, Miriam Mouse's Costume Collection, 1977, Miriam Mouse's Marriage Contract, 1977, Miriam Mouse, Rock Hound, 1977, Silver Bindings, 1983; ed. Tribute to the Arts, 1984. BS in Home Econ., Ohio State U., 1952, postgrad. in Bus. Adminstrn., 1961-62. Editorial asst. The Am. Home Mag., NYC, 1953-56; salesman Owen Realty, Dayton, Ohio, 1957-58, Clevenger Realty, Phoenix, 1958-59; home economist Columbus & Southern Electric Co., Ohio, 1959-60; pub. Mosaic Press, Cin., 1977—. Mem. Am. Philol. Assn., 1975—, Miniature Book Soc. (bd. dirs.), 1983—, Intl. Guild Miniature Artisans, 1980—. Home: 358 Oliver Rd Cincinnati OH 45215

ISAACS, FLORENCE, b. Bklyn., July 2, 1937; d. Joseph and Sylvia (Tanklow) Satow; m. Harvey A. Isaacs, Sept. 1, 1962; children—Jonathan, Andrew. Contrbr. to various mags. including Reader's Digest, Good Housekeeping, Family Circle, Savvy, Mademoiselle. BBA, Baruch School of CCNY, 1957. Advertising promotion manager, Dell Pub. Co., mag. div., 1960-70; freelance wrtr., 1975—. Mem. ASJA. Home: 175 W 13th St New York NY 10011

IAACS, MARK D., b. Mpls., Sept. 16, 1955; s. Elwood M. and Linda (Halverson) I.; divorced; children—Haley R., Venna E. Contrbr. numerous articles to newspapers, mags. including Freeman, Libertarian Rvw., Washington Inquirer, others. Columnist, feature ed.: The New Am., 1985—; managing ed.: On Principle newsletter, West Springfield, MA, 1982-84; ed.: The Bus. Times, 1986—. B.A. in Econ., Westfield State Coll., 1980; postgrad. in English, Trinity Coll., Hartford, CT. Mem. NWC. Home: 544 Tolland St East Hartford CT 06108 Office: Bus Times 8 Glastonbury Ave Rocky Hill CT 06067

ISRAELOFF, ROBERTA, b. NYC, Mar. 1, 1952, d. Jack Eli and Rae (Engelberg) Israeloff; m. Bruce David Fleisher, Sept. 11, 1977; 1 son, Benjamin. Author: Coming to Terms, 1984; contrbr. articles, columns and essays to Glamour, McCall's, Parenting, Self, Women's Day; contrbr. short stories to North Am. Rvw, Pig Iron. BA, Barnard Coll., 1973; MA, Johns Hopkins U., 1975. Public relations asst. Jewish Theol. Sem., NYC, 1975-77; adj. lectr. N.Y. Inst. Technology, 1975-77, NYU, 1978-86; adj. instr. C.W. Post Coll., Greenvale, N.Y., 1978-79, Hunter Coll., 1980—. Mem. AG, Phi Beta Kappa. Home: East Northport NY 11731

ITZIN, CHARLES FRANCIS, b. Des Moines, Nov. 14, 1946; s. Francis Henry and Neva Lenore (Smith-Mahley) I. Contrbr. poetry to anthologies and lit mags including New letters, Nimrod, Greenfield Rvw, Sou'wester. BA with honors in English, U. Iowa, 1970; MFA in Creative Writing, U. Oreg., 1974. Peace Corps vol., Salvador, Bahia, Brazil, 1970-72; dir. Centro Colombo Americano, Cali, Colombia, 1974-76; poet in schls. Arts Council, Pinellas, Fla., 1976-77; owner, operator Am. Study Tours, Santa Monica, Calif., 1977—. Mem. PSA, P&W. Home: 45 1/2 Ozone Ave Venice CA 90291

IVERSON, LUCILLE KARIN, b. Detroit, Aug. 3, 1925, d. Carnot Francis and Esther (Piercey) Iverson; m. Pierre Romaine deVise, Dec. 21, 1946 (div. 1959); 1 son, Peter Charles Iverson deVise. Co-editor: We Become New, 1975; author: Outrage, Poems, 1971-1974, 1974; contrbr. to Libera, Amazon Qtly, Off Our Backs, Broomstick, The Villager, other lit mags; contrbr. articles to Women & Film, The Militant, Manhattan Tribune; columnist Soho Weekly News, 1975-77; film critic for Cable TV, 1973-75. BA, Wayne State U., 1948; postgrad., U. Chgo., 1957-60; MA, NYU, 1972. Tchr. of English, Chgo., 1955-60, NYC, 1960-65; copy ed., Bobbs-Merrill Co., Inc., 1967-69; poet-in-schls., NYC, 1974. Mem. PEN, P&W, PSA, Maine P&W. Home: 93 Mercer St New York NY 10012

IVES, KENNETH HOLBROOK, b. Phila., Oct. 10, 1916; s. Herbert Eugene and Mabel Agnes (Lorenz) I.; m. Renee R. Wagshal, July 13, 1957 (dec. May 1, 1984). Author: Which Friends Groups Are Growing, N Why?, 1977, rev. 1983, Written Dialects: History N Alternatives, 1979, New Friends Speak: How and Why They Join Friends (Quakers) in the Mid-1970's, 1980, Bookkeeping for Small Organizations, 1981, Nurturing Spiritual Development: Stages, Structure, Style; A Quaker Viewpoint, 1982, Black Quakers: Brief Biographies, 1986; editor jnls. Case Analysis, 1977—, Sociological Practice, 1983-87. BA, Earlham Coll., 1938; MA, New Schl. Social Research, 1950, MSW, Wayne State U., 1957. Research social worker Ill. State Psychiat. Inst., Chgo., 1967-71; Dir. Statistics and Research United Charities, Chgo., 1972-82. Mem. Soc. Sci. Study of Religion, Soc. Study of Social Problems, Am. Sociol. Assn., Natl. Assn. Social Workers. Home: 401 E 32d Apt 1002 Chicago IL 60616

IVES, RICH LEE, b. Aberdeen, SD, Feb. 8, 1951; s. Lyle Dean and Jean E. (Pratt) I. Contrbr. poems to anthols. Translator: Vagrant Embers (Peter Huchel), 1987. Editor: Rain in the Forest, Light in the Trees; The Other Image, 1984; From Timberline to Tidepool; CutBank, 1975-76, Owl Creek Press, 1979—, The Montana Rvw, 1979—; assoc. editor: Crosscurrents, 1986—. BA in English, Eastern Wash. U., 1973; MFA in writing, U. Mont.-Missoula, 1977. Interlibrary loans dir. U. Mont. Library, Missoula, 1979-85; faculty Everett Community Coll., Wash., 1985—. Creative writing fellow NEA, 1986. Home: 1620 N 45th St No 205 Seattle WA 98103

JABEN, JAN ELAINE, b. Kansas City, MO, May 12, 1952; d. Ed and Rae Frances (Horovitz) Jaben; m. Jerry Weiner (div. 1984). Contrbr.: N.Y. Times, Consumer Reports, Washington Journalism Rev., Nat. Real Estate Investor, numerous other nat. and regional trade and spl. interest publs. Wrkg. on self-help book. BA, U. Conn., 1974. Staff reporter North Fulton Today, Roswell, Ga., 1976-78; sr. staff wrtr. Atlanta Bus. Chronicle, 1978-84; now assoc. ed. U.S. Banker; freelance wrtr, 1984—. Mem. Atlanta Press Club (pres. 1984-86), Sigma Delta Chi, Phi Beta Kappa. Home: 38 Hillsbury Ln Stamford CT 06903

JACK, ALEX, b. Chgo., Aug. 21, 1945; s. Homer A. and Esther (Williams) J. Works include: The Cancer-Prevention Diet, 1983, Diet for a Strong Heart, 1985, Macrobiotic Diet, 1985, One Peaceful World, 1987. BA, Oberlin Coll., 1967. Ed., East West Journal, Brookline, MA, 1979-82; dir., Kanthaka Press, Brookline, 1973—; author, 1982—. Home: 4 Fairbanks St Brookline MA 02146

JACKANIN, ALBINA VERONICA, b. NYC, Dec. 22, 1924, d. Edward and Felicia Thelma (Bukowski) Boblinski; m. Joseph Michael Jackanin, Nov. 6, 1948; children—Michael, Joanne, Diane, Juliana, Gerard. Student public schls., NYC. Community service rep., ed. People's Firehouse Bulletin, Bklyn., 1978—. Home: 93 N 8th St Brooklyn NY 11211

JACKER, CORINNE LITVIN, b. Chgo., June 29, 1933; d. Thomas Henry and Theresa (Bellak) Litvin. Author: Man, Memory and Machines, 1964, Window on the Unknown, 1966, A Little History of Cocoa, 1966, The Black Flag of Anarchy, 1968, The Biological Revolution, 1971; playwright: The Scientific Method, 1970, Seditious Acts, 1970, Travellers, 1973, Breakfast, Lunch, & Dinner, 1975, Bits and Pieces, 1975 (Obie award 1975), Harry Outside, 1975 (Obie award 1975), Night Thoughts & Terminal, 1976, Other People's Tables, 1976, My Life, 1977, After the Season, 1978, Later, 1979, Domestic Issues, 1981, In Place, 1982, Let's Dance, 1986; TV writer, including: 3 episodes Actors' Choice, NET, 1970; Virginia Woolf: The Moment Whole, NET, 1972 (CINE Golden Eagle award 1972); story editor: 4 episodes series Benjamin Franklin, CBS, 1974, The Adams Chronicles, 1975, Loose Change, NBC, 1978, Best of Families, NET, 1978, The Jilting of Granny Weatherall, NET, 1980; radio play Night Thoughts and Terminal, BBBC, 1978; Overdrawn at the Memory Bank, NET, 1983. Student, Stanford U., 1950-52; BS, Northwestern U., 1954, MA, 1955, postgrad., 1955-56. Editor Liberal Arts Press, 1959-60, MacMillan Co., 1960-63; story editor Sta. WNET-TV, 1969-71, CBS-TV, 1972-74; instr. playwriting NYU., 1976-78; vis. prof. playwriting Yale U., 1979-81, Princeton Univ., 1986. Assoc. Prof. Adjunct, Columbia Univ., 1986—. Head writer: Another World (TV daytime serial), 1981-82. Rockefeller Fdn. grantee, 1979-80; Rockefeller Fdn., Bellagio Center, 1987. Mem. DG, WG Am. East, PEN. Home: 110 W 86th St New York NY 10024

JACKO, DIANE NEWELL, b. NYC; d. Andrew F. and Margaret Mary (Golden) Newell; m. Joel E. Jacko, Jun. 22, 1968; children—Bradley, Craig, Shawn (dau). Author: Jock Momma, 1985; contrbr. to NY Times, Newsday, Los Angeles Herald Examiner. BA, Trinity Coll. Freelance wrtr. Home: 17 Torlen Court Hauppauge NY 11788

JACKSON, FLEDA BROWN, b. Columbia, MO, July 20, 1944, d. Phillips Hamlin and Mable Frances (Simpich) Brown; m. Harry Gale Gray, III, Jan. 27, 1962 (div. 1973); children—Kelly Margaret, Scott Christopher; m. 2d, M. Dennis Jackson, Sept. 6, 1975. Contrbr. poetry, articles to Kenyon Rvw, Iowa Rvw, So. Humanities Rvw, numerous other lit mags; ed.: Caesura (U. Del.'s lit mag), 1983—; Current: The Jnl of Marine Education, 1982-86; Delaware: A Celebration of Its Maritime Heritage, 1982. PhD,U. Ark., 1983. Tchr. Springdale (Ark.) Public Schls., 1970-75; asst. prof., U. Del., Newark, 1985—; ed. newsletter D. H. Lawrence Soc. N. Am., 1981—. Recipient Joseph P. Slomovich award Cedar Rock poetry jnl, 1981, Pres.'s award Natl. Marine Edn., Assn., 1985. Mem P&W, MLA, D.H. Lawrence Soc. N.Am., Phi Beta Kappa. Office: Dept Eng Univ Del Newark DE 19711

JACKSON, JOSEPH, see Challem, Jack Joseph

JACKSON, MARK, see Kurz, Ron

JACKSON, RICHARD PAUL, b. Lawrence, MA, Nov. 17, 1946; d. Richard Paul and Mary (Morrissey) Jackson; m. Margaret Louise McCarthy, June 28, 1970; 1 dau., Amy. Author: Part of the Story, 1983, Acts of Mind: Conversations with Contemporary Poets, 1983, (cited by Choice as one of best academic bks. of yr.), Worlds Apart, 1987, Dismantling the Time: Studies in Contemporary Poetry, 1987; MA, Middlebury College, 1972; PhD Yale U., 1976. Asst. prof., U. of Tenn. Chattanooga, 1976-79, U.C. Fdn. assoc. prof., 1979-87, professor, 1987—; ed., The Poetry Miscellany, 1971—. Awards: NEA Fellowship, 1983; Pushcart Prize, 1987; Fulbright Fellowship, 1986; NEH Fellowship, 1979; Robert Frost Fellowship, (Bread Loaf Writers Conf.), 1983; tchg. awards, 1983, 84, 85, 87. Mem. PSA, SAMLA, CCLM, MLA. Home: 3413 Alta Vista Dr Chattanooga TN 37411

JACKSON, ROSA CATHERINE, b. Dayton, OH, Jan. 6, 1948; d. William Andrew and Helen (Iannantuoni) Jackson. Contrbr. poems to anthols. A.A., Miami-Dade Commun. Coll., 1979; B.S. in Spl. Edn., Fla. Intl. Univ. 1984. Private learning disabilities tutor, Miami, 1984—. Recipient Golden Poet award World of Poetry, 1985, 86, 87. Home: 10700 SW 109 Ct 410 Miami FL 33176

JACKSON, THOMAS H., b. Detroit, Aug. 19, 1930; s. Herbert Williamson and Annie Swift (Peers) J.; m. Julie Kiedrowski (div. 1961); m. 2d, Gabriele Johanna Bernhard; 2 daus., Olivia Kate, Emily Anne. Author: The Early Poetry of Ezra Pound, 1968, Twentieth-Century Interpretations of Miss Lonelyhearts, 1971; ed. and pub. Poesis, 1977—. BA, Wayne State U., 1954; PhD, Yale U., 1960. Instr. English Yale Univ., 1959-63; asst. prof. MIT, Cambridge, Mass., 1963-67; asst. prof. Brandeis Univ., 1967-68; assoc. prof. and prof. Bryn Mawr Coll., Pa., 1968—. Woodrow Wilson fellow, 1954; Robert R. McCormick fellow, Yale, 1957, Ingram-Merrill Fdn. grantee, 1982. Mem. MLA (pres. northeast div., 1979). Address: 521 Greystone Rd Merion PA 19066

JACOB, JOHN C., b. Chgo., Aug. 27, 1950; s. Bertram Frank and Eleanor (Addy) J.; m. Martha Ann Devore, Aug. 22, 1970; children—Lucas John, Kathleen Rebecca. Author: Razor & Cut, 1971, Parfleche for Captain Jack, 1972, Ward of the State, 1975, Making Play, 1976, Knee: Whip of Occasions, 1977, Scatter: Selected Poems 1968-78, 1979, Ninja, 1981, Hawk Spin, 1983, Summerbook, 1983 Wooden Indian, 1987, Long Ride Back, 1988. Editor: Mojo Navigator(e), 1969-77, Focus: Young Chicago Poets, 1974, The Michael McClure Symposium, 1976. Publisher: Cat's Pajamas Press, 1968—. Wrkg. on novel, novella, collection of poems. AB, U. Mich., 1972; MA, U. Ill., 1973. Chief wrtr. Legislative Investigative Com., Chgo., 1979-82; dir. devel. Family Inst., Chgo., 1983-85; tchg. asst. U. Ill., Chgo., 1985—; freelance wrtr., 1972—. Bd. dirs. Sarah's Inn, Oak Park, Ill., 1985. Recipient Carl Sandburg award Chgo. Pub. Library, 1980, lit award Ill. Arts Council, 1985; grantee IAC, 1979, 84. Mem. MLA, AWP, Multi-Ethnic Lit. U.S. Home: 527 Lyman St Oak Park IL 60304

JACOB, MARY ELLEN L., (Nell Duvall), b. Dearborn, MI, Feb. 9, 1939; d. James Herbert and Verna Rhoda (Fletcher) DuVall; m. Robert M. Jacob, Oct. 1965 (dec. Jan. 1981); children: Judith, Elizabeth, Brian, Tenaya. Author: Telecommunications Networks: Issues and Trends (ed.), 1986, Domestic Technology, 1988; contrbr. articles to Cataloging & Classification Qtly, Library Hi Tech, Library Trends, Bulltn. Am. Soc. for Information Science, Information Tech. and Libraries, other profl. jnls. Masters, Lib. Sci., U. of Mich., 1963; Masters, Engr. Sci., U. of New South Wales, Australia, 1979. Staff member, Sandia Corp., Albuquerque and Livermore, Calif., 1963-67; systems officer, U. of Sydney, Australia, 1968-77; director, OCLC, Columbus, OH, 1977-84, vice pres., Dublin, OH, 1984—. Wrkg. on novels. Mem. ALA, Am. Assn. for the Advancement of Science, Am. Soc. of Mechanical Engineers. Office: OCLC 6565 Framtz Rd Dublin OH 43017

JACOBI, PETER PAUL, b. Berlin, Mar. 15, 1930, came to U.S., 1938, naturalized, 1944; s. Paul A. and Liesbeth (Krom) J.; m. Harriet Ackley, Dec. 8, 1956 (div. 1981); children—Keith Peter, John Wyn. Author: Writing with Style, The News Story and the Feature, 1982: The Messiah Book—The Life and Times of G.F. Handel's Greatest Hit. 1982; (with Jack Hilton) Straight Talk about Videoconferencing, 1986; music columnist: Chicagoan Mag., 1973-74, Bloomington (IN) Herald-Telephone, 1985—. Contrbr. articles on writing to mags., enyc. Ed.: Chgo. Lyric Opera News. 1958-61, Music Mag., Mus. Courier, Chgo., 1961-62. B.S., Northwestern U. Medill Schl. Jnlsm., 1952, M.S., 1953. Profl. lectr. to assoc. prof., Northwestern U., Evanston, IL, 1955-69, prof. jnlsm., 1969-81, assoc. dean, 1966-74; communications cons., NYC, 1980-84; prof. jnlsm. Ind. U., Bloomington, 1985—; news assignment ed., newscaster, theatre-music reporter NBC, Chgo., 1955-61; news ed. ABC, Chgo, 1952-53; arts corr. Christion Sci. Monitor, 1956-81; radio commentator music and opera, 1958-65; theatre, film critic Sta. WMAQ-TV, Chgo., 1964-74, Hollister Newspapers of Suburban Chgo., 1963-70; arts critic Sta. WTTW, Chgo, 1975-77; script cons. Goodman Theater, Chgo., 1973-75; syndicated commentator on arts and media N. Am. Radio Alliance, 1978-81; mem. Ind. Arts Comm., Soc. Profl. Jnlsts. Served to corporal U.S. Army, 1953-55. Recipient Disting. Achievement award EPAA, 1985. Mem. Natl. Acad. TV Arts and Scis., Assn. Edn. Jnlsm. Home: 3003 Browncliff Bloomington IN 47401

JACOBOWITZ, JUDAH L., b. NYC, s. Jacob and Ida Miriam (Appelbaum) J.; m. Celia D. Goldstein, Aug. 17, 1947; children—Elliott, Diane. Contrbr. poetry: Cape Rock, Anthology of Mag. Verse, 1985, Cream City Rvw, Mass. Rvw, Crab Creek Rvw, other lit mags; contrbr. ed. Del. Valley Poets Anthology. BCE, CCNY, 1945. Sr. assoc. engr. Mobil Research and Devel. Corp., Princeton, N.J.; presenter poetry readings. First place, NJ Statewide Poetry Competition, 1985. Mem. P&W. Home: 6 Cleveland Ln-RD4 Princeton NJ 08540

JACOBS, HORACE, b. Chatham, Ont., Can., Sept. 23, 1911; came to U.S., 1945; s. Jesse Robert and Laura (France) J.; m. Charlotte E. Zahn, July 12, 1949; children: Lilo C., Fred S., Jeannette M., Robert H. Co-author: Missiles and Space Projects Guide, 1962; series ed. Advances in Astronautical Scis., also ed. selected vols., Vols. 1-63, 1957-87; AAS Microfiche Series, Vols. 1-53, 1968-86; Sci. and Tech. Series, Vols. 21-66, 1970-87; also articles in AAS History Series. BA, U. Alta., 1935, MA, 1942; PhD, U. So. Calif., 1952. Chief ed., Librascope, Glendale, 1949-51; staff scientist Lockheed Aircraft Co., Burbank, Calif., 1955-63, mgr. info. services, 1963-76; pres., pub. Univelt Inc., San Diego, 1970—. Served with U.S. Army, 1945-46. Mem. Soc. for Tech. Communication (sr.), Spcl. Libraries Assn. Fellow: Am. Astronautical Soc., British Interplanetary Soc. Home: Box 28130 San Diego CA 92128

JACOBSEN, LAURA BETH, b. Aurora, IL, Sept. 14, 1951; d. David Lee and Barbara Maxine (Messinger) Sperry; m. Dennis Guy Jacobsen, Sept. 21, 1972. Contrbr. short stories, poems to mags. including Ouboboros, Late Knocking, Grue Mag, Authors & Artists mag. Grad. public schls., Flossmoor, IL. Recipient 3d prize for poetry Bell Telephone Co., 1965, 66. Home: 128 Dogwood St Park Forest IL 60466

JACOBSEN, MICHAEL A., b. Pequannock, NJ, Aug. 26, 1957; m. Brenda Merrill, Feb. 14, 1981; 2 sons, Keith, Kevin. Ed., Happi Mag., 1980-83, Nonwovens Industry Mag., 1983—. BA in Jnlsm., Moravian Coll., 1979. Rptr. Ridgewood Nwsprs. (NJ), 1979-80; ed. Rodman Publishing, Ramsey, NJ, 1980—. Mem. NYBPE, Tech. Assn., Pulp & Paper Industry, INDA, Assn. of Nonwoven Fabrics Industry. Office: Rodman Pub 26 Lake St Ramsey NJ 07446

JACOBSEN, NORMAN HOWARD, b. Worcester, MA, Dec. 2, 1947; s. Andrew Howard and Alice Louise (Rydberg) J.; m. Deborah Ann Spencer, Apr. 6, 1968 (dec. Oct. 6, 1980); m. Judith Dides, Oct. 30, 1982 (div. Feb. 10, 1984). Author: Oil Field Diving: The Diver's Story, 1983. Wrkg. on short fiction. Comml. diver Sub Sea Intl., New Orleans, 1974—. Served to captain U.S. Army, 1966-70. Home: 1441 Verna St New Orleans LA 70119

JACOBSON, SID, b. Chgo., May 30, 1952; s. Joseph and Joanne (Levy) J. Author: Meta-Cation: Prescriptions for Some Ailing Educational Processes, 1983, Meta-Cation, Vol. II: New Improved Formulas for Thinking about Thinking, 1986, Meta-Cation, Vol. III: Powerful Applications for Strong Relief, 1986. BS, Tulane U., 1974, MSW, 1977; PhD, Profl. Sch. Psychol. Studies, San Diego, 1987. Owner, dir. South Central Inst. Neuro-Linguistic Programming, New Orleans, 1982—. Address: Box 15757 New Orleans LA 70175

JACQUES, BEAU, see House, Richard Calvin

JAEGER, BRENDA KAY, b. Fairbanks, AK, July 20, 1950; d. Clarence Paul Jae and Catherine M. (Simon) Jaeger; m. James Thomas Hanlen; children—Bent Omar, Shishaldin Simone Augustina. Author: Karasuyama Poems, 1988. BA, Eastern Wash. U., 1972; MAT, Whitworth Coll., 1975. Instr. art U. Alaska, Anchorage, 1978; owner Brenda Jaeger Art Studio, 1979—. Mem. Natl., Am., Alaska watercolor socs. Office: Box 2152 Longview WA 98632

JAEGER, SHARON ANN, b. Douglas, AZ, Jan. 15, 1945, d. Paul and Catherine (Simon) J. Author: (poems) Keeping the Lowest of Profiles, 1982, Filaments of Affinity, 1988; contrbr. articles to Dictionary Am. Book Pub., Am. Lit. Mags., Revista das Letras; contrbr. poems to numerous periodicals and anthologies including Intro 13, Cimarron Rvw, Plains Poetry Jnl, Poet and Critic, Calyx, Stone Country, Spoon River, Western Poetry, Midwest qtlys; co-translator: Duineser Elegien. BA summa cum laude, U. Dayton, 1966; MA in English, Boston Coll., 1971; DA in English, SUNY-Albany, 1982. Freelance writer, ed., translator, 1980—; co-ed. Sachem Press, Old Chatham, NY, 1980—; ed./pub. INTERTEXT, Anchorage, 1982—; Fulbright lectr. U. Nova de Lisbon, U. Aveiro, Portugal, 1983-84; adj. asst. prof. Drexel U., Phila., 1985. Austrian Govt. scholar, summer 1966; Presdl. fellow SUNY, Albany, 1979-82; Fulbright grantee, Portugal, 1983-84. Mem. PSA, AAP, ALTA, MLA, Alaskan Assn. Small Presses, COSMEP. Home: Box 100014 DT Anchorage AK 99510

JAFFE, DAVID, b. Slonim, Poland, Jan. 20, 1911; came to U.S., 1912, naturalized, 1921; s. Louis and Sadie (Arner) J.; m. Sylvia S. Turner, Nov. 8, 1942. Author: The Stormy Petrel and the Whale: Some Origins of Moby-Dick, 1976, Bartleby the Scrivener and Bleak House: Melville's Debt to Dickens, 1981; contrbr. articles to newspapers, profl. lit. jnls. BA, Duke U., 1933, MA, 1937. State editor Durham Morning Herald, (N.C.), 1938-41; mem. editorial staff U. N.C. Press, 1942-44; freelance editor NYC, 1946-47; mem. editorial staff Ctr. for Mil. History, Washington, 1948-76, sr. editor, 1961-76; pub. Mardi Press, Arlington, Va., 1976—. Mem. Melville Soc. Home: 1913 S Quincy St Arlington VA 22204

JAFFE, HAROLD, b. NYC,July 8, 1940, s. Lester and Blanche (Weber) J.; m. Maggie Aronoff, Aug. 1980. Author: (novels) Mole's Pity, 1979, Dos Indios, 1983, (fiction) Mourning Crazy Horse, 1982, Beasts, 1986; ed. The Am. Experience: A Radical Reader, 1970, (short story anthology) Affinities, 1976; contrbr. fiction to Boundary 2, Fiction Intl., Exquisite Corpse, New Directions Annl., Minn. Rvw, Fiction, others. BA, Grinnell Coll.; PhD, NYU, 1967. Prof. English, L.I. U., 1965-76; prof. creative writing and lit. San Diego State U., 1982—; ed. Fiction Intl., San Diego, 1983—. Fulbright grantee, 1971-72; NEA grantee, 1983. Mem. P&W, PEN, Fiction Collective (past dir.). Home: 3551 Granada Ave San Diego CA 92104

JAFFE, MAGGIE, b. NYC, June 21, 1948; d. Harry and Miriam (Weiner) Aronoff; m. Harold Jaffe, Aug. 25, 1979. Contrbr. poetry to Minn Rvw, Negative Capability, Passion for Industry, ACM, Confrontation, Creeping Bent, Blueline, Helicon Nine, other lit mags. BA, New School, 1976, MA, San Diego State U., 1982. Lectr. in English, Southhampton Coll., NY, 1977-82, in creative writing San Diego State Univ., CA, 1982—. Mem. P&W. Address: 3551 Granada Ave San Diego CA 92104

JAFFE, RONA, b. NYC, June 12, 1932; d. Samuel and Diana (Ginsberg) J. Author: The Best of Everything, 1958, Away From Home, 1960, The Last of the Wizards, 1961, Mr. Right is Dead, 1965, The Cherry in the Martini, 1966, The Fame Game, 1969, The Other Woman, 1972, Family Secrets, 1974, The Last Chance, 1976, Class Reunion, 1979, Mazes and Monsters, 1981. BA, Radcliffe Coll., 1951. Assoc. editor Fawcett Publs., NYC, 1952-56. Address: E. London 875 3d Ave New York NY 10022

JAFFEE, ANNETTE WILLIAMS, b. Abilene, TX, Jan. 10, 1945, d. Jules Henry and Evelyn June (Witensky) Williams; m. Dwight M. Jaffee, Aug. 16, 1964; children—Jonathan Williams, Elizabeth Evelyn. Author: Adult Education (novel), 1981, adapted to screenplay, 1985; contrbr. short fiction to Missouri Rvw, Ontario Rvw, others. BS, Boston U., 1966. Panelist N.J. Arts Council, Trenton, 1986. Office: 37 Hodge Rd Princeton NJ 08540

JAFFER, FRANCES E., b. Hartford, CT, Mar. 13, 1921; d. Louis Jaffer and Celia Pauline (Bassevitch) Greenburg; m. Rodney Pain, Mar. 22, 1942 (div. 1954); children—Lincoln, Duncan, Louis; m. Mark Linenthal, Nov. 5, 1959. Author: (chapbook) Any Time Now, 1977, She talks to herself in the language of an educated woman, 1980, Alternate Endings, 1985. Contrbr. poems, articles to anthols. Assoc. ed.: (mag) How(ever), 1984-86. A.B., Stanford U., 1943. Mem. Wrtrs. Union, NOW. Home: 871 Corbett Ave San Francisco CA 94131

JAGGERS, ANNIELAURA MIXON, b. Cypert, AR., Dec. 22, 1918; d. Frederick Franklin and Laura Ozella (Walker) Mixon; m. Carl Jasper Jaggers, Mar. 3, 1940; children—Carl Frederick, Christiana Jaggers Rollans. Contrbr. poetry: South & West, Arkansia, 5¢ Cigar, Nebo, numerous other publs. Wrkg. on fiction, research, travel articles. MA in Humanities, U. Ark., 1966, MA in Philosophy, 1977. Mem. faculty dept. philosophy, Ark. Tech. U., Russellville, 1965—. Grantee Ark. Endowment for Humanities, Little Rock, 1980-81. Home: 102 Walnut St Dardanelle AR 72834

JAKES, JEAN ANN, b. Ft. Belvoir, VA, Aug. 25, 1956; d. Frank Robert Jakes and Ann Donaldson Davis. Contrbr. short stories to popular mags. including True Story, Modern Romances, True Confessions, others. Home: 10665 58th St N Pinellas Park FL 34666

JAKES, JOHN WILLIAM, b. Chgo., Mar. 31, 1932; s. John Adrian and Bertha (Retz) J.; M. Rachel Ann Payne, June 15, 1951; children: Andrea, Ellen, John Michael, Victoria. Author: The Texans Ride North, 1952, A Night for Treason, 1956, Murder He Says, 1958, When the Star Kings Die, 1967, Master of the Dock Gate, 1970, Am. Bicentennial Series: The Bastard, 1974, The Rebels, 1975, The Seekers, 1975, The Furies, 1976, The Titans, 1976, The Warriors, 1977, The Lawless, 1978, The Americans, 1980, North and South, 1982, Love and War, 1984. A.B., De Pauw U., 1953, Litt.D. (hon.), Wright State U., 1976. With creative dept. various advt. agencies, 1960-69; creative dir. Dancer Fitzgerald Sample Co., Dayton, Ohio, 1969-70. Mem. SFWA, DG, AG, PEN. Address: HBJ 1250 6th Ave San Diego CA 92101

JAKUBOWSKI, DONNA MARIE, (Donna Oreka), b. New Brunswick, NJ, Jan. 5, 1957; d. Anthony Bernard and Margaret Agnes (Mazza) Oreka; m. Donald Jakubowski, Sept. 26, 1981. Editor: Squibb Sales Bulltn., 1984–87, Studio Technik, 1985—, Synapse, 1986–87. Contrbr. articles to photography mags. BA, Douglass Coll., New Brunswick, 1979. Copywriter WCTC/WMGQ radio sta., New Brunswick, 1979; traffic coord. Wells, Rich, Greene, NYC, 1979-81; copywrtr., Panasonic Co., Secaucus, N.J., 1981-84; editor E.R. Squibb & Sons, Princeton, N.J., 1984–87. Public affairs mgr, E. R. Squibb & Sons, New Brunswick, NJ, 1987—. Home: 63 Townsend St Milltown NJ 08850

JAKUBOWSKY, FRANK R., b. Belfield, ND, Oct. 11, 1931, s. William and Catherine (Obach) J. Author: Creation, 1978, Jesus Was a Leo, 1979, Psychological Patterns of Jesus Christ, 1982, Creative Theory of the Universe, 1983, Caldecott, 1985. Student, U. N.D. Lab. tech. Sherwin-Williams, Emeryville, Calif., 1958–86; president, Jesus Books, 1987. Served with U.S. Army, 1952-54. Home: 1565 Madison St Oakland CA 94612

JAMES, DAVID L., b. Detroit, Sept. 1, 1955; s. Lindon Donald and Sharon Rose (Kyle) J.; m. Debra Marie Ketterer, Dec. 30, 1977; children—Collin, Nathan, Leah. Author: A Heart Out of This World, 1984. BA, Western Mich U., 1977; MA, Central Mich. U., 1979. Counselor Youth Service Bur., Port Huron, Mich., 1979-80; coordinator program promotion Siena Hts. Coll., Southfield, Mich., 1980-82, assoc. dir. admissions, 1982-84, dir. admissions, Adrian, Mich. campus, 1984-86; dir. admissions, U. of Mich.-Flint, 1986—. Recipient creative writers' grant, Mich. Council Arts, 1984. Mem. Mich. Council for the Arts. Address: 211 Lindenwood Linden MI 48451

JAMES, DIANE LOUISE, b. Skokie, IL, Aug. 7, 1965; d. Paul Douglas and Charlotte Jean (Reith) J. Editorial asst. Triquarterly mag., Evanston, IL, 1986-87; mng. ed. Extension mag., Evanston, 1986-87, poetry ed., 1986-87. Wrkg. on collection of poetry. B.S., Northwestern U., 1987. Market info. specialist Recycled Paper Products, Chgo., 1987—; mng. ed. Purple Swordsmen. Recipient J. Hirshfield Meml. Poetry award Evanston Public Library, 1986; Spectra award of merit IABC, Chgo., 1987. Home: 911 S Harrison Park Ridge IL 60068

JAMES, EDWIN, see Gunn, James Edwin

JAMES, EMLYN, see Tribble, Robert James

JAMES, FRANK WILLIAM, b. Rensselear, IN, Apr. 24, 1946; s. Harold and Ruth Irene (Wurzbacher) J.; m. Cathy Ann Gudeman, Jan. 27, 1977; children—Valerie Victoria, Michael Thomas. Contrbr. articles to mags. including Guns mag., Am. Handgunner mag., Fur, Fish & Game, Ind. Prairie Farmer, others. Author: Sub-Guns and Full Auto Games, 1987. B.A. in Agricultural Econ., Purdue U., 1969; postgrad. Louisville U., Valparaiso U., 1969-70. Courier Brinks Armored, Lafayette, IN, 1984-87; pvt. investigator Banks Detective Agy., Ft. Wayne, IN, 1984—; grain farmer, Wolcott, IN, 1975—. Mem. Natl. Rifle Assn., Fraternal Order of Police. Natl. Firearms Assn. Home: Rt 2 Box 129 Wolcott IN 47995

JAMES, JAMES YOUNGER, see Craig, James Duhadway

JAMES, MARK, see Kibler, Wallace Edward

JAMES, S.S., see Fields, Susan Louise

JAMES, THEODORE JR., b. NJ, Aug. 10, 1934, s. Theodore and Marian Sophia J. Author: The Waldorf-Astoria Cookbook, 1969, Backgammon, The Action Game, 1969, The Colony Cookbook, 1970, Europe: The Second Time Around, 1971, Fifth Avenue, 1972, The Empire State Building, 1975, Flower Gardening, 1976, The Gourmet Garden, 1984, How to Select and Grow African Violets and Other Gesneriads, 1984, How to Select and Grow Fruits, Berries and Nuts, 1984. Wrkg. on landscaping book. BA, Princeton U., 1957. Columnist Women's Wear Daily, NYC,1963-66. Home: RR 3 1415 Indian Neck Ln Peconic NY 11958

JAMES, WILLIAM N., see Senti, R. Richard

JANES, JUDY, see Mayer, Jane S.

JANES, STEVEN M., b. Idaho Falls, ID, June 26, 1954; s. Edward V. and Golda Ethel (Moss) J.; m. Kim Sharon Roy, Jan. 21, 1977; children—Kimber Lee, Jade Lyn, Drew Ann. BA in Jnlsm., U. Utah. Sports ed. Standard-Jnl, Rexburg, ID, 1979; outdoors ed. The Post-Register, Idaho Falls, ID, 1979-81; ed. Harris Publishing, Idaho Falls, 1981—. Home: 4665 E 49th N Idaho Falls ID 83401

JANEWAY, ELIZABETH HALL, b. Bklyn., Oct. 7, 1913; d. Charles H. and Jeannette F. (Searle) Hall; m. Eliot Janeway; children: Michael, William. Author: The Walsh Girls, 1943, Daisy Kenyon, 1945, The Question of Gregory, 1949, The Vikings, 1951, Leaving Home, 1953, Early Days of the Automobile, 1956, The Third Choice, 1959, Angry Kate, 1963, Accident, 1964, Ivanov Seven, 1967, Man's World, Woman's Place, 1971, Between Myth and Morning: Women Awakening, 1974, Powers of the Weak, 1980, Cross Sections: From a Decade of Change, 1982, Improper Behavior, 1987; contrbr. to: Comprehensive Textbook of Psychiatry, 2d ed., 1980, Harvard Guide to Contemporary American Writing, 1979, also short stories and critical writing in periodicals and newspapers. Student, Swarthmore Coll.; AB, Barnard Coll. Assoc. fellow Yale. Mem. AG, AL Am., PEN. Home: 15 E 80th St New York NY 10021

JANEWAY, MICHAEL CHARLES, b. NYC, May 31, 1940; s. Eliot and Elizabeth Ames (Hall) J.; m. Mary Struthers Pinkham, Dec. 18, 1965; children: Samuel Struthers, Mary Warwick. Reporter Newsday, Garden City, N.Y., 1963; writer, editor Newsweek, NYC, 1964; assoc. editor The New Leader, 1965; editor The Atlantic, Boston, 1966-70, mng. editor, 1970-76, exec. editor, 1976-77; editor Sunday mag. Boston Globe, 1978-81, asst. mng. editor, 1981-82, mng. editor, 1982—. Co-editor: Who We Are: An Atlantic Chronicle of the United States and Vietnam, 1969; contrbr. numerous articles, rvws. to publs. BA, Harvard, 1962. Served with AUS, 1963-64. Shaw Travelling fellow Harvard, 1962-63. Home: 21 Buckingham St Cambridge MA 02138

JANNICELLI, MATTEO, b. Newark, NJ, Aug. 26, 1935; s. Vito and Maria Sue (Zarro) J. Founder, ed., Evening Literary Review, Newark, 1974-76; contrbr. poetry to lit mags and anthols. BFA, Kean Coll., Union, NJ, 1976. Sculpture, photography, fine art, and crafts exhibited nationally. Tchr. fine arts, School of Fine and Indsl. Arts, Newark, 1970-75. Served to SP/4, U.S. Army, 1958-60. Mem. Ocean County Poets Collective, Point Pleasant Beach, NJ. Recipient numerous awards for poetry, art; Golden Poet Award, 1987. Home: 529 Pennsylvania Ave Bricktown NJ 08724

JANNIS, DOROTHY, see Worth, Dorothy Janis

JANOWITZ, ABRAHAM, b. Bklyn, Jan. 1, 1908, s. Barnett and Anna J.; m. Rose Carmel, Aug. 11, 1935; 2 sons, Robert James, Kenneth Jordan. Contrbr. to The Archer, Attention Please!, Bardic Echoes, Expanding Horizons, Gong, Huerfano, Jewish Spectator, New Voices, Published!, Seven Stars, World Over; play, Taking My Turn, performed Entermedia Theater, NYC, 1983. BSoc Sci, CCNY, 1930. Tchr, Bd. Edn; NYC, 1931-49, asst. prin., 1949-54, prin., 1953-73; adj. prof. edn., CCNY, 1956-66, Bklyn. Coll., 1966-70. Mem. Madison Democratic Club, Bklyn., 1950-65; Common Cause, Washington, 1972—. Mem. Ret. Schl. Supervisors Assn., Hunter Coll. Address: 2500 Johnson Ave Riverdale NY 10463

JANOWITZ, PHYLLIS, b. NYC, d. Morris and Lilliam (Reiner) Winer; m. Julian Janowitz (div. 1968); children—Tama, David. Author: Rites of Strangers (poems), 1978 (Va. Commonwealth Series 1st selection), Visiting Rites (NBCC nominee), 1982. BA, Queens Coll., MFA, U. Mass., 1970. Asst. prof. English Cornell U., Ithaca, NY, 1980—. Bunting Inst. fellow Radcliffe Coll., 1971-73, Hodder fellow Princeton U., 1979-80; grantee NEA, 1974-75. Mem. PSA (Emily Dickinson award 1983), PEN, AWP. Home: 1 Lodge Way Ithaca NY 14850

JANOWITZ, TAMA, b. San Francisco, Apr. 12, 1957; d. Julian and Phyllis (Winer) J. Author: (novel) American Dad, 1981, (short fiction) Slaves of New York, June 1986. Short fiction pub. in The New Yorker, Interview, Mississippi Rvw, Social Text, Spin, Bomb, Paris Rvw, New York Talk, Lo Spazio Umano, other publs. BA, Barnard Coll., 1977; MFA, Columbia U., 1985. Humor/fiction columnist Interview mag., NYC, 1984—; columnist New York Talk, NYC, 1986—. Mem. PEN, AWP, P&W. Fellow, Fine Arts Work Ctr. in Provincetown, 1981; recipient NEA award in fiction, 1982, CAPS award in fiction, 1984, award CCLM/Gen. Electric Fdn., 1984, Ludwig Vogelstein Fdn. award in fiction, 1985, NEA award in fiction, 1986. Home: 92 Horatio St 5E New York NY 10014

JANUZ, LAUREN ROBERT, b. Highland Park, IL, Jan. 1, 1930; s. Cipron Peter and Elsie (Nelson) J.; m. Dorothy A. Apr.4, 1964. Author: Time Management for Executive, 1971. Pub.: (newsletters) Creative Selling, 1976-82, Telephone Marketing Report, 1980-85, Execu*Time, 1980-87, Januz Direct Marketing Letter, 1974-87. Wrkg. on 2d ed. of Time Management for Executives. B.A., Nat. Coll. Edn., 1960; M.B.A., Keller Graduate Schl. Management, 1982. Pres. Januz Marketing Communications Inc., Chgo., 1971-83, Crown Calendar and Pen, Chgo., 1984-86, Timlet Corp., Chgo., 1987—; acting chief exec. officer FPC Assoc., Chgo., 1982-84; regional v.p. Golnick Advt., Ft. Lauderdale, FL, 1986-87. Served capt. U.S. Coast Guard, 1958-84. Mem. Am. Management Assn., Am. Marketing Assn., Specialty Advt. Assn., Profl. Photographers Am. Office: Timlet Corp 26940 N Longwood Rd Lake Forest IL 60045

JARVIS, FREDERICK GORDON, (Fritz Gordon), b. Hartford, CT, July 25, 1930, s. Frederick Gordon and Ruth (Bisbee) J.; m. Helen Norris Smith, Sept. 2, 1967; 1 dau., Emily Ruth. Author: The Flight of the Bamboo Saucer (as Fritz Gordon), 1967, Tonight They Die to Mendelssohn (as Fritz Gordon), 1968, The First Hundred Years (with Bob Considine), 1969, Murder at the Met, 1970, The Divas (with Robert Merrill), 1971. BA, Yale U., 1952. Restaurant critic Met. Host, NYC, 1956-61; ed. Winged Foot Mag., NYC, 1961—, D.A.C. Jnl, NYC, 1972-78; prodn. mgr. Westchester Country Club News, Rye, N.Y., 1961—. Home: 190 Riverside Dr New York NY 10024

JASON, PHILIP KENNETH, b. NYC, Dec. 25, 1941; s. Leon Abraham and Esther (Bookbinder) J.; m. Ruth Epstein, Jan. 28, 1962; children: Hope, Daniel. Author: (poems) Thawing Out, 1979, Near the Fire, 1983; ed.: Anais Nin Reader, 1973; Shaping: New Poems in Traditional Prosodies, 1978. BA, New Schl. for Social Research, 1963; PhD, U. Md., 1971. Instr., asst. prof., Georgetown U., Washington, 1966-73; asst. prof., assoc. prof., prof. U.S. Naval Acad., Annapolis, Md., 1973—; chmn. lit. panel Md. Arts Coucil, 1986. Mem. MLA, AWP, NCTE. Home: 11500 Patriot Ln Potomac MD 20854

JAUSS, DAVID RUSSELL, b. Windom, MN, Feb. 25, 1951. Author: (short stories) Crimes of Passion; contrbr. short story to Prize Stories 1983: The O. Henry Awards; ed. Strong Measures: Contemporary Am. Poetry in Traditional Forms (with Philip Dacey), 1986. MA, Syracuse U., 1974; PhD, U. Iowa, 1980. Asst. prof. Univ. Ark.-Little Rock, 1980-82, assoc. prof., 1982—, mng. ed. Crazyhorse mag., 1981-82, asst. poetry ed., 1981-84, fiction ed., 1981—. Recipient Ark. Arts Council fellowship, Little Rock, 1986. Address: English Dept U Ark 33rd and Univ Little Rock AR 72204

JAVERS, RON, m. Eileen; children—Eamon, Quinn. Author: The Suicide Cult: The Inside Story of the Peoples Temple Sect & the Massacre in Guyana (with M. Kilduff), 1978; contrbr. articles and reviews to numerous pubns. inclg. The Washington Post, Commonweal, Boston Globe, Phila. Inquirer, Los Angeles Times. Assoc. ed., editorial page ed., Phila. Daily News, 1969-75; special projects ed. San Francisco Chronicle, 1976-80; assoc. ed. Phila. Mag., 1980-81, ed., 1982—; v.p. and ed.-in-chief Metrocorp. (Phila., Boston, Atlanta, & Manhattan, inc. mags.). Office: Metrocorp 1500 Walnut St Philadelphia PA 19102

JAY, RALPH, see Blauvelt, Ralph

JAY, THELMA GERTRUDE ALLEN, b. Paonia, CO, May 13, 1923, d. F. Ernest and T. Blanche (Knight) Allen; m. Robert Arthur Jay, Dec. 27, 1942; children—Carol, David, Rebecca, Katherine, Connie. Contrbr. to Farmland Mag., The Good Deeder, Fruit of the Vine, Harper's Weekly, Reader's Digest, Highlights for Children, other publs.; author drug abuse and religious education materials; contrbr. articles to local newspapers. Wrkg. on drug abuse book to be translated for use in Africa. Student Friends U., 1941-42; diploma, Christian Wrtrs.' Inst., 1965. Wrtr., photographer, 1955—. Mem. Kans. Authors Club (recipient numerous state and regional awards), NWC. Home: Box 351 Haviland KS 67059

JAYCOX, ELBERT RALPH, b. Miami, AZ, Oct. 13, 1923; m. Barbara B. Gravink, Sept. 5, 1947; children—Susan, John, Julia, Holly. Author: Beekeeping in the Midwest, 1976, Beekeeping Tips & Topics, 1982; columnist Am. Fruit Grower, 1979-80, Gleanings in Bee Culture, 1986—; ed.: Info. on Beekeeping, 1985—, Newsletter on Beekeeping, 1984—, Bees & Honey, 1975-81; contrbr. articles in field to agrl. and entomological jnls. MS, U. Calif.-Davis, 1951, PhD,1956. Supr. apiary inspection Calif. Dept. Agr., Sacramento, 1953-58; entomologist U.S. Dept. Agr., Logan, Utah, 1958-63; assoc. prof. entomology U. Ill., Urbana, 1963-69, prof., 1969-81; adj. prof. entomology N. Mex. State U., Las Cruces, 1981—. Home: 5775 Jornada Rd N Las Cruces NM 88001

JEBB, ROBERT DUDLEY, b. Waterbury, CT, Feb. 1, 1944; s. William Thomas and Marion (Harper) J.; m. Jeanne Frances Elliott, Dec. 23, 1973. Novel: Mirages My Father Left Me, 1983; contrbr. to Publisher's Weekly. BA in International Relations U. of the Pacific, 1966; MS in Journalism U. of Utah, 1972. Commun. Bureau Chair New Mexico Energy Dept. (Santa Fe), 1977-78; owner Solo Wrtg. & Edit. (Santa Fe), 1978-82; publisher Teal Press (Portsmouth, NH), 1983—. Office: Teal Press Box 5326 Portsmouth NH 03801

JEFFERS, AVANELLA CARMEN, b. Vermillion County, IN, Mar. 10, 1922; d. Arthur Carmen and Dorthea (Daly) Shew; m. Dale Jeffers, July 8, 1946 (div. July 12, 1984) 1 dau., Sherri Michele. Author: History of Edgar County Illinois 1809-1865, 1953; Problems of Teaching Social Studies in the Intermediate Grades, 1955. Contrbr. poems to Prairie Light Rvw. Wrkg. on children's joke book, children's sci. fiction, childhood country adventure. B.S., Eastern Ill. State U., 1949, M.S., 1956. Tchr. elem. schls., Paris, IL, 1942-44, 46-47, Roswell, MN, 1949-50, Sullivan, IL, 1950-51, Bethany, IL, 1951-55, Mooseheart, IL, 1955-63, Aurora, IL, 1966-84, retired. U.S. Army, 1945-46. Mem. NEA. Home: 1412 Surrey Rd Batavia IL 60510

JEFFRIES, BETTY, see Demby, Betty

JEKEL, PAMELA L., b. Santa Monica, CA, June 28, 1948, d. William Dale and Delorse Patricia (Roth) Jekel; m. William Easton Koons, Dec. 31, 1977. Author: The Perfect Crime and How to Commit It, 1980, Seastar, 1983, Columbia, 1986, Thomas Hardy: A Chorus of Heroines, 1986. Wrkg. on fiction. BA, UCLA, 1975; PhD, U. Va., 1981. Ed. NASA, Langley, Va., 1977-79; tchr. U. Va., Charlottesville, 1981; tchr., lectr. Calif. Wrtrs.' Club, Wrtrs.' Connection. Mem. AG, Natl. League Am. Penwomen, Calif. Wrtrs.' Club, P&W. Address: Targ 105 W 13th St New York NY 10011

JELLEMA, ROD(ERICK) HARTIGH, b. Holland, MI, Aug. 11, 1927, s. John Frank and Elizabeth Marion (den Hartigh) J.; m. Mary Travis Todd, Dec. 18, 1971; children by previous marriage—John Frank II (dec.), David M., Michael R. Author: Peter De Vries (critical book), 1966, Something Tugging the Line (poetry), 1974, The Lost Faces (poetry), 1979, The Eighth Day: New and Selected Poems, 1984, Country Fair (poems translated from the Frisian), 1985; ed.: Christian Letters to a Post-Christian World (Dorothy Sayers), 1969, Contemporary Writers in Christian Perspective (critical monographs), 1965-71; contrbr. poetry to Field, Beloit Poetry Jnl, Three Rivers Poetry Jnl, Poet Lore, other lit mags. BA, Calvin Coll., 1951; PhD, U. Edinburgh, Scotland, 1962. Mem. faculty U. Md., College Park, 1955—, dir. creative wrtg., 1968-85, prof., 1985—. Served with USN, 1945-47. Recipient Hart Crane award, 1969, NEA prize, 1969; grantee NEA, 1970, Fdn. for Translation of Dutch Lit. Works, 1983, Columbia U. Transl. Ctr. Award, 1986; NEA fellow, 1980. Mem. Wrtrs. Center (dir. 1981—), AAP, AWP, Conf. on Christianity and Lit. Home: 4527 Avondale St Bethesda MD 20814

JELLINEK, ROGER, b. Mexico City, Mexico, Jan. 16, 1938; s. Frank Louis Mark and Marguerite Lilla Donne (Lewis) J.; m. Margherita Dicenzo, Dec. 22, 1963; (div. 1984), m. Eden-Lee Murray, June 30, 1984; children: Andrew Mark, Claire. Assoc. editor Random House, 1963-64; editor Walker & Co., 1964-65, N.Y. Times Book Rvw, 1966-70, depy. editor, 1970-73; editor-in-chief Times Books, Quadrangle/The N.Y. Times Book Co., 1974-78, sr. editor, 1978-81; pres. Clairemark, Ltd., Palisades, N.Y., 1981—; exec. vp, Bd. Trustees, Rockland Ctr. for the Arts, 1986—. Student, Bryanston Schl., Dorset, Eng., 1951-56; MA, Clare Coll., Cambridge (Eng.) U., 1961. Served with Royal Marines, 1956-57; as 2d lt. Brit. Intelligence Corps, 1957-58. Mellon fellow Yale, 1961-63. Office: Washington Springs Rd Palisades NY 10964

JENKINS, GLENNA GLEE, (Glenna Glee), b. Anderson, IN, Feb. 1, 1918; d. Adalaska and Lou Eva (Weir) Ellsworth); m. Robert Paul Williamson, Dec. 24, 1939 (dec. July 13, 1969); children—James A., Rex A.; m. 2d, Alvin R. Jenkins, Apr. 20, 1973 (dec. 1977). Author: Kerosene Lamp, 1978, Mindwind, 1983. Contrbr. poems to lit. mags. Student pub. schls., Anderson. Laborer, Gen. Motors Corp., Anderson, 1936-74. Named Poet Laureate, Indiana State Fedn. of Poetry Clubs, 1980-81. Mem. Intl. Graphoanalyst Soc. (master, pres, Ind. chpt. 1984-85), Ind. Poetry Soc. (contest dir. 1982—), ISFPC (pres. 1986), Midwest Wrtrs. Workshop (sec. 1980—), Natl. Fedn. State Poetry Socs., AAP. Home: 808 E 32d St Anderson IN 46014

JENKINS, JERRY BRUCE, b. Kalamazoo, MI, Sept. 23, 1949; s. Harry Phillip and Bonita Grace (Thompson) J.; m. Dianna Louise Whiteford, Jan. 23, 1971; children—Dallas Lawrence, Chadwick Whiteford, Michael Bruce. Author: numerous books, 1973—, including (with Robert Flood) Teaching the Word, Reaching the World, 1986; (with Pat and Jill Williams) Rekindled, 1986, Keep the Fire Glowing, 1987; (with Meadowlark Lemon) Meadowlark, 1987; fiction including The Operative, 1987, Meaghan (Angel award 1983), 1982, Margo's Reunion (Angel award 1984), 1983, Margo Mysteries Vol. 1, 1985, Vol. 2, 1986, Too Late to Tell, 1984, Gateway, 1984, The Calling, 1985, Veiled Threat, 1985, The Jennifer Grey Mysteries, 1986; children's books including Mystery at Raider Staduim, 1986, Daniel's Big Decision, 1986, Before the Judge, 1986, The Strange Swimming Coach, 1986, The Angry Gymnast, 1986. Ed.: Moody Monthly, 1974-78. Wrkg. on sequel to The Operative. Student Moody Bible Inst., 1967-68, Loop Coll., 1968, Wm. R. Harper Coll., 1968-70. Ed., Scripture Press Pub., Wheaton, IL, 1971-73; dir. Moody Monthly, Moody Bible Inst., Chgo., 1978-81, dir. Moody press, 1981-83, mgr. pub. div., 1983-85, v.p. for pub., 1985—. Bd. dirs. North Area Youth for Christ, Arlington Heights, IL, 1981—, Christian Action Council, Washington, 1983—, Waukegan Christian Sch., Zion, IL, 1984—, Sammy Tippit Ministries, San Antonio, 1987—, Grace Missionary Church, Zion, 1987—. Mem. Evangelical Press Assn. Home: Three-Son Acres 40542 Cornell St N Zion IL 60099

JENKINS, JOHN TIERCE, b. Ashville, AL, Apr. 11, 1920; s. James Everett and Helen Corry (Maxwell) J.; M. Liddy Kersey, Mar. 8, 1945; 1 dau., Jennifer Jean. BA in Jnlsm., U. FL, 1947. Staff Florida Cattleman, Kissimmee, FL, 1947-48; ed./pub. Southern Livestock Jnl, Macon, GA, 1948—, Livestock Breeder Jnl, Macon, 1948—, Beefweek, Macon, 1948—. Served to Sgt., USAF, 1942-45. Mem. Livestock Pubns. Council, GA Printers Assn. Office: Box 4264-567, 4001 Vineville Ave Macon GA 31210

JENKINS, MARJORIE C., (Catherine Brown), b. Beaufort, SC, Jan 1, 1911; d. Tecumseh and Elizabeth (Jones) Brown; m. Wilson H. Jenkins (dec. 1968); 1 son—Roland H. Contrbr. poetry to church publications, song lyrics; personal performances. Wrkg on book of poems, short stories. Edn. Penn Normal and Indsl. Schl., Beaufort, SC; fiction wrtg. with Pauline Bloom, NYC. Fashion designer, dressmaker, Brooklyn, 23 years, health care and adult rehab, Brooklyn and Atlantic City, 10 years. Home: 10 Somerset Ave Pleasantville NJ 08232

JENKINS, PAUL R., b. Waterloo, IA, Apr. 9, 1942; s. Richard Thomas and Rachael M. (Holmes) J.; m. Ellen K. Watson; 1 dau., Eve Benda. Author: Forget the Sky, 1979, A House and a Vein of Water, 1987; contrbr. poetry Paris Rvw, Kenyon Rvw, NY Qtly, Poetry Northwest, others; fiction ed. The Mass. Rvw, 1971-75, poetry ed. 1975—, assoc. ed., 1984—. BA, Grinnell Coll., 1964; MA, U. Washington, PhD,1969. Asst. prof. English Univ. Mass. Amherst, 1969-76; archivist town of Greenfield, ess., 1977-80; assoc. prof. English Elms Coll., Chicopee, Mass., 1982—. Fulbright lectr. Brazil, 1980-82. Address: Manning Rd Conway MA 01341

JENKS, CAROLYN BOYD, (Carla Clad), b. Evanston, IL, June 4, 1935; d. Kenneth Urban and Sarah Elizabeth (Boyd) Jenks; 1 son, Christopher. B.A., U. Wis., 1959; M.A. in Theology, Emmanuel Coll., 1976; M.S.W., U. Conn., 1982. Reporter, Bus. Week, Chgo., 1959-60; mng. ed. Universal, N.Y.C., 1966-68, Ballantine Books, NYC 1961-66; dir. Carolyn Jenks Literary Agcy., Cambridge, MA, 1966—; private practice in clinical social work, Cambridge, 1982—. Mem. PEN. Office: Jenks Lit Agcy 205 Walden St Cambridge MA 02140

JENNINGS, JENNIFER ANGELENE, (Kayla Whitney), b. Pitts., Sept. 26, 1968; d. Samuel Jr. and Marilyn Ann (Stark) Jennings. Contrbr, poetry: Manna, Green Feathers, Alive!, Suwanee Poetry. Wrkg. on poetry collection. Ed. public schs., Oscoda, Mich. Home: 8212 C Florida St Wurtsmith AFB MI 48753

JENNISON, PETER SAXE, b. Swanton, VT, July 2, 1922; s. Clark Saxe and Louise (Warren) J.; m. Jane Dryden Lowe, May 11, 1946; 1 son, Andrew Clark. Contrbr. The Mimosa Smokers, The Governor; ed. The Official Vt. 1976-77 Bicentennial Guide, Vt: An Explorer's Guide (with Christina Tree), 1983, 85, The History of Woodstock, Vt. 1890-83, 1985 Vermont on $500 a Day, 1987. BA Middlebury Coll. Asst ed. Pubs. Weekly, NYC, 1947-52; asst. mng. dir. Am Book Pubs. Council, NYC, 1952-64; exec. dir. Natl. Book Comm., NYC, 1964-71; founder, bd. chmn. The Countryman Press, Woodstock, Vt, 1973—. Served to t/sgt US Army, 1943-46, ETO. Trustee Norman Williams Pub. Library, Woodstock, 1983—, Vt. Hist Soc, Montpelier, 1984—. Mem. PEN. Address: Happy Valley Rd Taftsville VT 05073

JENSEN, DALE ALAN, (Jens Alfredsen), b. Oakland, CA, Aug. 1, 1949; s. Alfred William and Ruth Mildred (Peterson) J. Contrbr. to various mags including Inkblot, Star * Line, Industrial Sabotage, Random Weirdness, and Metier. BA, U. of Calif., Berkeley, 1971; MA, U. of Toronto, 1973. Various positions with Social Security Administration, California, 1973—. Editor: Malthus. Mem. Science Fiction Poetry Assoc. Home: 2317B Carleton St Berkeley CA 94704

JENSEN, DWIGHT WILLIAM, b. Malad, ID, Sept. 4, 1934; s. Glenden Jacob and Lola Ethel (Nutting) J.; m. Claudia Davison, Apr. 16, 1955; children—Leonard, Julia. Author: Discovering Idaho, 1977, There Will Be a Road, 1978, Visiting Boise, 1981; contrbr. to Encyclopedia of the States, 1982, Biographical Dictionary of Am. Journalism, 1987. BA, Idaho State U., 1955; MA, Central Missouri State U., 1983. Reporter Daily Times (Chester, PA), 1960-61; reporter/anchor KBOI (Boise, ID), 1961-74; assist. prof. Syracuse U. (NY), 1982—. Candidate for U. S. Senate (ID), 1978. Office: Newhouse II Syracuse Univ Syracuse NY 13210

JENSEN, GERALD RANDOLPH, (Jerry), b. Kalispell, MT, Aug. 12, 1924, s. Hans Clemen and Mabel Jensen; m. Helen Jeanne Levine, Dec. 11, 1943; 1 dau., Marjorie Jeanne Jensen Perez. Author: The Amazing Shakaram Storm, 1964, Steps to the Upper Room, 1965, Pictorial Images of Mexico Today, 1975, Voice of Hope, 1982, A Crack in the Wall, 1984; contrbr. to Total Health Mag., World Map Digest, Between Friends, Praise mag., other publs.; editorial and graphics mgr.: Sacred Records, Inc. Bible Voice Pubs., 1970-80, Supreme/Cornerstone Records, 1967-81, Uplift Books, 1981-85. GTh, Life Coll.; PhD, Union U. Ed., dir. publs. Full Gospel Bus. Men's Fellowship, Intl., Los Angeles, 1962-69, ed., dir. publs., 1965—; pres. Claiborne-Jensen advt., Arcadia, Calif., 1962-65. Office: Full Gospel 3150 Bear St Costa Mesa CA 92626

JENSEN, LAURA LINNEA, b. Tacoma, WA, Nov. 16, 1948, d. Theodore Jonas and Linnea Serena (Gord) Jensen. Author: After I Have Voted (chapbook), 1972, Anxiety and Ashes, 1976, Bad Boats (poetry), 1977, Tapwater (chapbook), 1978, The Story Makes Them Whole (poetry), 1979, Memory, 1982, A Sky Empty of Orion (chapbook), 1985, Shelter, 1985. Contrbr. to anthologies: Am. Poetry Anthology, 1975, The Poets Choice, 1980, Open Places Retrospective, 1982, Iowa Rvw Women's Issue Anthology, 1982, Field-Longman Anthology, 1983, Rain in the Forest, Light in the Trees, 1983, 45 Contemporary Poems, 1985. BA, U. Wash., 1972; MFA, U. Iowa, 1974. Recipient Honors award Wash. State Arts Commn., 1978-79; NEA poetry fellow, 1980-81; grantee Ingram Merrill Fdn., 1982. Mem. AWP, P&W. Home: 302 N Yakima C3 Tacoma WA 98403

JENSEN, MAXINE ELIZABETH, (Maxine Dowd Jensen), b. Sedalia, MO, Apr. 7, 1919; d. Luther Clare and I. Emmaline (Taylor) Dowd; m. Clifford Berger Jensen, Sept. 26, 1959 (dec. Dec. 12, 1972); stepchildren—Joyce Jensen Williams, Lorraine Jensen Swanson. Author: The Warming of Winter, 1977, Your Aging Parent, 1985, Beginning Again, 1985. Contrbr. articles to anthols., popular mags., newspapers. Cert., Wright Jr. Coll,. 1938. Div. staff asst. Ill. Bell Telephone Co., Chgo., 1946-72; free-lance wrtr., 1928—. Recipient 3d prize for short story St. Davids Wrtrs. Conf., 1970's. Mem. Ozark Wrtr.'s League (Honorable Mention for short story 1986), WG. Home: Rt 7 Box 390 Mountain Home AR 72653

JENSON, MAXINE DOWD, see Jensen, Maxine Elizabeth

JERME, MARIAH, see Rusk, Nance J.

JEROME, JUDSON, b. Tulsa, Feb. 8, 1927; s. Ralph and Gwen (Stewart) Luer; m. Martha-Jane Pierce, June 20, 1948; children: Michelle, Beth, Polly, Christopher. Author: (poems) Light in the West, 1962; The Poet and the Poem, 1963, 74, 79; (novel) The Fell of Dark, 1966; Poetry: Premeditated Art, 1968; (verse drama and autobiography) Plays for an Imaginary Theater, 1970; Culture out of Anarchy: The Reconstruction of American Higher Learning, 1971; Families of Eden: Communes and the New Anarchism, 1975; (poems for children) I Never Saw . . ., 1974; Thirty Years of Poetry: 1949-79, 1979; The Poet's Handbook, 1980; On Being a Poet . . ., 1984; The Village: New and Selected Poems, 1987; Poet's Market, 1985, 86, 87, contrbr. poems, stories, articles, essays to numerous publs. Wrkg. on new collection of poems, novel. Columnist (poetry) Wrtrs Digest, 1960—; ed., Poetry Markets, Small Press Review, 1984—. MA, U. Chgo., 1950; PhD, Ohio State U., 1955. Prof. lit. Antioch Coll., Yellow Springs, Ohio, 1953-73; freelance wrtr./ed., 1973—; assoc. ed. Kettering Rvw, Kettering Fdn., Dayton, Ohio, 1985—. Served with USAAF, 1945-47. Huntington Hartford Fdn. fellow, 1957; Amy Lowell travelling poetry scholar, Eng., Spain, 1960-61. Home: 917 Xenia Ave Yellow Springs OH 45387

JERRETT, CATHY LOUISE, b. Tampa, FL, Nov. 13, 1953; d. Morris McCann and Catharine (Rader) J. Contrbr. poems to anthols.; author God is Asking, 1985. Student pub. schls., Jersey City, NJ, Chgo., IL. Home: 144 Bowers St Jersey City NJ 07307

JERSILD, ARTHUR T(HOMAS), b. Elk Horn, IA, Nov. 12, 1902; s. Thomas Nielson and Anna (Bille) J; m. Catherine Livingstone Thomas, Feb. 22, 1930; children: Catherine (dec.). Author: Mental Set and Shift, 1927, Training and Growth in the Development of Children, 1932, Child Psychology, 1933, 7th ed, 1974, In Search of Self, 1952, When Teachers Face Themselves, 1955, Psychology of Adolescence, 1957, 3d, 1978, (with F.V. Markey and C.L. Jersild), Children's Fears, Dreams, Wishes, Daydreams, Likes, Dislikes, Pleasant and Unpleasant Memories, 1933, (with F.B. Holmes), Children's Fears, 1933, (with Markey) Conflicts between Preschool Children, 1935, (with S.F. Bienstock), Development of Rhythm in Young Children, 1935, (with M.D. Fite), The Influence of Nursery School Experience on Children's Social Adjustments, 1939, (with others) Educational Psychology, 1942, rev. ed, 1950, (with others) Child Development and the Curriculum, 1946, (with E.S. Woodyard C. del Solar) Joys and Problems of Child Rearing, 1949, (with R.J. Tasch) Children's Interests, 1949, (with K. Helfant), Education for Self-Understanding, 1953, (with E. Allina Lazar and A. Brodkin) The Meaning of Psychotheraphy in the Teacher's Life and Works, 1962. Contrbr., W. Dennis, ed, Readings in Child Psychology, 1951, Manual of Child Psychology, 1954, P.H. Phenix, ed, Philosophies of Education, 1961. Also contrbr to more than 100 other books. Contrbr to profl jnls. Assoc ed, Journal of Genetic Psychology and Genetic Psychology Monographs. AB, Univ of Nebraska, 1924; Ph. D., Columbia Univ, 1927. Instrctr, Barnard Coll, N.Y.C., 1927-29; asst prof, Univ of Wis.-Madison, 1929-30; asst prof to prof of psych and educ and professor emeritus, Columbia Univ, Teacher's College. N.Y.C., 1930—, 1967—. Consulting psychologist, CBS, 1935-48. Mem: American Psychological Assn (pres., div. of childhood and adolescence, 1951), Soc. for Research in Child Development, Phi Beta Kappa, Sigma Xi, Century Club (N.Y.). LL. D., Univ. of Nebraska, 1962. Home: 1800 Highway 35 King's Row, Apt. 263 Middletown NJ 07748

JESSOP, DOROTHY EMMA, b. Williams, AZ, June 8, 1929; d. Edward Morris and Emma Fredericka (Salomon) Norvell; m. Dan Calvin Jessop, Aug. 27, 1946; children—Dan, Karen, Melissa, Alveda, Alvera, Doran, Alvin, Lehi, Melody, Enid, Martha, Pauline, Marylyn. Contrbr. articles to Good Old Days, Grit Newspaper. Wrkg. on Pleasant Journey. A.A., Mohave Commun. Coll., 1980; B.A., Loretto heights Coll., 1981. Tchr. Colorado City Schs., AZ, 1981-85, speech pathologist, 1985—. Recipient prize Council on Aging, Provo, UT, 1985. Home: 220 Jessop Ave Hildale UT 84784

JEWELL, RICHARD, b. Monmouth, IL, Jan. 21, 1949; s. Louis C. and Helen S. Jewell; divorced; children: Jessica, Gabriel, Marian. Author: Writing for Publication, 1983; The Creative Writing Workbook, 1985; contrbr. mag. articles and stories to Lutheran Standard, My Weekly, Gallery, Home & Away, Genesis, Fair Lady, Annabel, Cavalier, Gnostica, numerous others. MA in Theology, San Francisco Theol. Sem., 1972, MDiv, 1973; MA in English, St. Cloud State U., 1985. Freelance mag. wrtr. to natl. and fgn. mags., 1976—; writing-seminar tchr. community edn. programs, Minn., 1981—; tchr.-seminar trainer Minn. pub. schl. systems, 1985—; instr. English, St. Cloud State U., Minn., 1985—; instr. composition and humanities, St. Cloud Bus. Coll. Mem. The Loft, Minneapolis Wrtrs Wrkshp. Mem. Central Minn. Wrtrs. Workshop. Home: 305 NE 3d St Little Falls MN 56345

JHABVALA, RUTH PRAWER, b. Cologne, Germany, May 7, 1927, came to U.S., 1975, naturalized, 1986; d. Marcus and Eleonora (Cohn) Prawer; m. Cyrus Jhabvala, June 16, 1951; children—Renana, Ava, Firoza. Author: (novels) Amrita, 1956, The Nature of Passion, 1957, Esmond in India, 1959, The Householder, 1960, Get Ready for Battle, 1964, A Backward Place, 1954, Travelers, 1971, Heat & Dust, 1975, In Search of Love and Beauty, 1983, Three Continents, 1987; (short story collections) Like Birds, Like Fishes, 1963, A Stronger Climate, 1968, An Experience of India, 1970, How I Became a Holy Mother, 1976, Out of India: Selected

Stories, 1986. MA, London U., 1951, D Litt (hon.), 1974. Recipient Booker prize, 1975, MacArthur Fdn. award, 1984-89; Guggenheim fellow, 1976, Neil Gunn Intl. fellow, 1979. Fellow Royal Soc. Lit.; mem. AG, WG. Home: 400 E 52d St New York NY 10022

JIMENEZ, FRANCISCO, b. San Pedro, Mex., June 29, 1943, came to U.S., 1946, naturalized, 1965; s. Francisco and Joaquina (Rico) J.; m. Laura Catherine Facchini, Aug. 17, 1968; children—Francisco Andres, Miguel Antonio, Tomas Roberto. Author: Los Episodios Nacionales de Victoriano Salado Alvarez, 1974, Mosaico de la Vida: Prosa Chicana, Cubana y Puertorriquena, 1981; (with others) Viva la Lengua, 1975, Spanish Here and Now, 1978. Editor: The Identification and Analysis of Chicano Literature, 1979; (with others) Hispanics in the United States: An Anthology of Creative Literature, 1980, vol. II, 1982. BA, Santa Clara U., 1966; MA, Columbia U., 1969, PhD, 1972. Asst. prof. Santa Clara U., Calif., 1973-77, assoc. prof., 1977-81, prof., 1981—, dir. arts & humanities, 1981—, trustee, 1980—. Recipient Best Short Story award, Ariz. Quarterly, 1973. Mem. MLA, Nat. Chicano Council on Higher Edn., Pacific Coast Council Latin Am. Studies, Natl. Assn. Chicano Studies. Home: 624 Enos Ct Santa Clara CA 95051

JOAN, , see Chopp-Scheuermann, Joan Janet

JOAN, ANNA, see Tarantino, Alice M. Bagley

JOB, DONALD D., b. Portland, OR, July 8, 1942; s. Dexter B. and Mary A. (Haley) J.; divorced; children—Lisa J., Alyson Ann. Author: Guide to Developing a Marketing Plan, 2d ed., 1985, Guide to Developing a Business Plan, 2d ed., 1985, The Inventors Guide, 1986. Contrbr. articles to technical pubs., bus. mags. Wkrg. on 2d ed. of The Inventors Guide. B.A., Linfield Coll., 1964; Ph.D., U. of Ill., Urbana, 1968. Mgr. life Sci GTE Labs., Waltham, MA, 1973-77; mgr. bus. devel. GTE Lighting Products, Salem, MA, 1977-79; pres. Enbede Co., Lexington, MA, 1979—, Haley Pubs., Lexington, 1986—. Mem. Christian WG. Home: 24 Oxbow Rd Lexington MA 02173

JOHN, DONAS, b. Orofino, Idaho, d. Arthur and Florence (Foster) Tyer. Contrbr. poetry to Vega, Lean Frog, Valhalla, Now Times, others. Wrkg. on novel. AA, Trade-Tech-LA, 1973. Free- lance wrtr., since 1970. Mem. Feminist Wrtrs. Guild. Home: 1629 Cimarron St Los Angeles CA 90019

JOHNEE, see Bennett, John M.

JOHN, BETTY, b. Cin., Oct. 25, 1907; d. Charles Worcester and Laura Zoe (Bogue) Beaman; m. Henry Jaroslav John, Oct. 9, 1928 (dec. Mar. 28, 1970). Author: Flak Bait, 1948, Seloe, 1955, Hummingbirds, 1960, Medical Milestones, 1965, El Capitano Pelicano Cafe, 1975, Ruth, 1980, Feathermaiden of Tzintizuntzan, 1982, Libby, 1987; columnist Medical Memo, 1965-70. Contrbr. articles to popular mags. including Today's Health, Nature, NM Mag. Ed.: Acad. Med. Bulltn., 1965-68. Student U. Cin., 1925-28, Cleve. Inst. Art, 1946-48. Recipient Walnut Enamel Dossal Cross award Coventry Craft Council, England, 1950, Top 100 award for feature article Wrtr.'s Digest, 1985. Mem. Natl. League Am. PEN Women (prs. 3 times, 2nd prize 1986), Western Enamel Soc., Women's Overseas Service League pres. Cleve. unit 1948-52). Home: 10501 Lagrima de Ord 338 Albuquerque NM 87111

JOHNS, ROY, (Bud), b. Detroit, July 9, 1929, s. Roy Clinton and Isabel (Horton) J.; m. Ann Barbour Greve, 1957 (div. 1967); m. 2d, Judith Spector Clancy, Mar. 28, 1971. Author: The Ombibulous Mr. Mencken, 1968, What Is This Madness?, 1985; co-ed.: Bastard in the Ragged Suit, 1977; Let's Look at the Old Met (intro.), 1969; contrbr. numerous articles to newspapers, mags. BA, Albion (Mich.) Coll., 1951. Reporter Flint (Mich.) Jnl, San Diego Union, 1942-60; bur. chief Fairchild Publs., San Diego and San Francisco, 1960-69; dir. corp. communications, v.p. Levi Strauss & Co., San Francisco, 1969-81; pres. Synergistic Press, San Francisco, 1968—. Mem. WWA. Office: Synergistic Press 3965 Sacramento St San Francisco CA 94118

JOHNSEN, GRETCHEN LYNNE, b. Tacoma, WA, Dec. 22, 1952; d. Earl Meidel and Janet Marilyn (Williams) Johnsen. Contrbr. Cumberland Jnl, Gargoyle Mag, Tightrope, Cream City Rvw, Poet & Critic, Frank, X-A Jnl Arts, Exquisite Corpse, Menu, Bogg, Abbey. Student Antioch Coll., 1970-71, Portland State Univ., 1971-73. Salad chef L'Auberge restaurant, Portland, 1971-73, kitchen staff Mother Courage, NYC,1973-75, chef of W. Averill Harriman, Washington, DC, 1975-86; co-ed. Gargoyle Mag and Paycock Press, Washington, 1978—. Address: 3038 N Street NW Washington DC 20007

JOHNSON, A. PAUL, b. Indpls., Jan. 27, 1955; m. Minda April Stephens, Feb. 14, 1981. Ed. periodicals: New Art Rev., 1974-77, The Lively Arts, 1987—; composer, lyricist, book wrtr. for musical theatre and opera: A Magic Mirage, 1974, Kamar, 1978, Anzollo & Valeria, 1984, The Road to Viznar (with Don Musselman), 1986, Dream Child, 1987. Diploma, Brebeuf Inst., Indpls., 1973. Artist-in-residence Pinellas Artsss Council, Clearwater, Fla., 1979-81; tchr., St. Petersburg, Fla., 1980-85; artistic dir. Royal Palm Theatre, Redington Beach, Fla., 1986—; producer Fla. Performing Arts, St. Petersburg, 1987—. Grantee Ind. Arts Council, 1978, 82; recipient music fellowships. Home: 554 63rd Ave So St Petersburg FL 33705

JOHNSON, CHRISTOPHER RALPH, b. Cleve., Sept. 13, 1947; s. Charles Luthi and Jacqueline Jane (Zeile) J.; m. Barbara Anne Melle, Dec. 4, 1971; children—Matthew, Emily. Contrbr. articles to mags. including Phi Delta Kappan, Wis. Rvw., others. Wrkg.on mag. articles. B.A., U. Notre Dame, 1969; M.A., Northwestern U., 1973. Asst. ed. Scott, Foresman & Co., Glenview, IL, 1977-79; ed. Houghton Mifflin, Boston, 1981-85; program mgr. Silver Burdett & Ginn, Needham, MA, 1985—. Reipient Disting. Achievement award EPAA, 1982. Home: 207 Bishop Dr Framingham MA 01701

JOHNSON, CURTIS LEE, (Curt Johnson), b. Mpls., May 26, 1928; s. Hjalmar N. and Gladys M. (Goring) J.; m. Jo Ann Lekwa, June 30, 1950 (div. 1974); children—Mark Alan, Paula Catherine; m. Rochelle Miller Hickey, Jan. 11, 1975 (div. 1980); m. Betty Axelrod Fox, Aug. 28, 1982. Author: How to Restore Antique and Classic Cars (with George Uskali), 1954; short fiction, articles, rvws. in periodicals, lit mags; novels Hobbledehoy's Hero, 1959, Nobody's Perfect, 1973, Lace and a Bobbitt (novella), 1976, The Morning Light, 1977, Song for Three Voices, 1984. Editor: Stories from the Literary Magazines (with Jarvis Thurston), 1970, Best Little Magazine Fiction, 1970, 1971 (latter with Alvin Greenberg), Writers in Revolt: The "Anvil" Anthology (with Jack Conroy), 1973, Green Isle in the Sea: An Informal History of the Small Press 1960-85 (with Diane Kruchkow), 1986; essays The Forbidden Writings of Lee Wallek, 1978. BA, U. of Iowa, 1951, MA, Am. Civ., 1952. How-to mag. and encyc. editing and wrtg., 1953-60, textbook and ednl. editing and wrtg., 1960-66, freelance editing, wrtg., copywriting, and prodn., 1966—. Editor, pub. December mag. and Press, 1962—; mng. ed. Aldine Pub. Co., 1972-73; mng. ed. & vp St. Clair Press, 1973-77; sr. copywriter Bradford Exchange, 1978-81; mng. ed. Regnery Gateway, 1981-82; ed. American Bar Association, 1983-84; copywriter Marquis Who's Who, 1984-85. Consulting ed. Panache mag., 1967-76; consulting ed. The Motion Picture Guide, 1984-85; (vols. 1 & 2) pub., ed., Who's Who in U.S. Writers, Editors & Poets, 1985—. Served with USN, 1946-48. NEA writing grants, 1973, 81; O. Henry Prize Stories, 1973, and Best American Short Stories, 1980. Mem. Phi Beta Kappa, NWU, Club d'Ronde. Address: 940 Waukegan Rd 2AN Deerfield IL 60015

JOHNSON, DIANE, b. Moline, IL, Apr. 28, 1934, d. Dolph and Frances (Elder) Lain; m. B. Lamar Johnson, Jr., July 1953; children—Kevin, Darcy, Amanda, Simon; m. 2d, John Frederic Murray, May 31, 1968. Author: Fair Game, 1965, Loving Hands at Home, 1968, Burning, 1971, Lesser Lives, 1973, The Shadow Knows, 1974, Lying Low, 1978, Terrorists & Novelists, 1983, Dashiell Hammett, 1984, Persian Nights, 1987. BA, U. Utah, 1957; MA, U. Calif., 1966, PhD, 1968. Mem. faculty U. Calif.-Davis, 1968—, now prof. English. Guggenheim fellow, 1977-78; recipient Mildred and Harold Strauss Livings ($50,000 annually for 5 years), 1987. Mem. PEN, MLA. Home: 26 Edith St San Francisco CA 94133

JOHNSON, DONNA M., b. Yankton, SD, May 23, 1939, d. William E. and Martha E. (Westra) Johnson; 1 dau., Joyel. Contrbr. to Chgo. Sun Times, Chgo. Tribune, N.Y. Times, numerous daily and weekly newspapers in Tex., N. Mex. and S.D.; contrbr.: Variations of White poetry anthology, Your Host-New Mexico. Wrkg. on newspaper articles, one-act plays, poetry series, children's history books, fables. Student Augustana Coll., Sioux Falls, S.D., 1957-59, Northwestern U., 1961-63. Freelance wrtr., publicist, 1968—. Home: Box 2246 Deming NM 88031

JOHNSON, DOROTHY STRATHMAN GULLEN, b. San Gabriel, CA., Sept. 19, 1931; d. Orin Clark Strathman and Frances (Cosman) Strathman Patrick; m. J. A. Gullen, Jr., May 22, 1952; m. 2d, Richard Guerrier Johnson, Jan. 6, 1979 (dec. 1985); children—Joseph A. Gullen III, Carrol A. Gullen, Jocelyn E. Gullen-Pinder. Author non-fiction and video trng. program. BA, U. Miami, 1972; MA in Social Psychology, U. No. Colo., 1974; Orgnl. Devel. and Trng. Cert., Fla. InH. U., 1987; Doctorate in Bus. Adminstrn., Nova U., 1988. Trng. dir. T.A. Assocs., 1972-76; pres. Process Consultants Intl., Inc., 1976—; mem. faculty Nova U., Miami Dade Community Coll., 1983-87. Address: 17171 SW 87 Ct Miami FL 33157

JOHNSON, DOUGLAS W(AYNE), b. Clinton Co., IL, Aug. 21, 1934; s. Noel Douglas and Laura Margaret (Crocker) J.; m. Phyllis A. Heinzmann, June 8, 1956; children: Kirk Wayne, heather Renee, Kristen Joy, Tara Carlynne. Author: ed, Information and Research Needs of the Churches in the 1970s, 1970, (with Paul Pi-card and Bernard Quinn) Churches and Church Membership in the United States: 1971, 1971, (with George W. Cornell) Punctured Preconceptions: What North American Christians Think About the Church, 1972, Managing Change in the Church, 1974, contrbr Jackson W. Carroll, ed, Small Churches Are Beautiful, 1977, The Care and Feeding of Volunteers, 1978, (with Carroll and Martin Marty), Religion in America, 1978, The Challenge of Single Adult Ministry, 1982, Reaching Out to the Unchurched, 1982, Let's Be Realistic About Your Church Budget, 1983, Growing Up Christian in the Twenty-Firt Century, 1984, Computer Ethics, 1984, The Tithe, 1984, Ministry with Young Couples, 1985, The Secretary's Guide to Church Office Management, 1985, Finance in the Church, 1987, (with Alan K. Waltz) Facts and Possibilities: An Agenda for the United Methodist Church, 1988. Contrbr to relig. jnls. BA, McKendree Coll, 1956; S.T.B., 1959, MA 1963, Boston Univ; Ph. D., Northwestern Univ., 1968. Ordained Methodist minister, 1959; pastor in Chicago, Ill., 1960-64; dir. of research for Chicago Home Missionary and Church Extension Soc, Rock River Conf. of the Methodist Church, 1964-66; research asst, Bureau of Social and Religious Research, Garrett Theological Sem, Evanston, Ill., 1966-68, teaching fellow, 1967-68; dir of research services in Office of Planning and Program, Natl Cncl of Churches, N.Y.C., 1968-73, assoc in Office of Research, Evaluation and Plannning, 1973-75; exec. dir, Inst. for Church Development, Ridgewood, N.J., 1975-85; research dir., National Program Div., Gen. Bd of Ministry, United Methodist Church N.Y.C., 1986—. Teacher at Western Conn. State Coll, 1969-73. Mem: American Sociological Assn, Religious Research Assn (mem bd dirs, 1970-76), Soc for the Scientific Study of Religion. Home: 420 Cambridge Rd Ridgewood NJ 07450

JOHNSON, EARL, JR., b. Watertown, SD, June 10, 1933; s. Earl Jerome and Doris Melissa (Schwartz) J.; m. Barbara Claire Yanow, Oct. 11, 1970; children: Kelly Ann, Earl Eric, Agaarn Yanovitch. Author: Justice and Reform: The Formative Years of the American Legal Services Program, 1974, 2d ed., 1978, Toward Equal Justice: A Comparative Study of Legal Aid in Modern Societies, (with Mauro Cappelletti; and James Gordley), 1975, Outside the Courts: A Survey of Diversion Alternatives in Civil Cases, (with Valerie Kantor and Elizabeth Schwartz), 1977, Dispute Processing Strategies, 1978, Dispute Resolution in America (with Jonathan Marks and Peter Szanton), 1984, California Trial Guide, 1986; editor: U. Chgo Law Rvw, 1960; contrbr. articles to books and periodicals. BA in Econ., Northwestern U., 1955, LLM, 1961; JD, U. Chgo., 1960. Ford Fdn. fellow, 1960 grantee Ford Fdn. Russell Sage Fdn., Natl. Sci. Fdn. Home: 852 Fifteenth Santa Monica CA 90403

JOHNSON, ELLWOOD G., b. McCall, ID, Nov. 4, 1924; s. Orlando Bennet and Hilkea J.; m. Barbara Schear, July 7, 1953; children—Wendy, Hilkea, Karen; m. 2d, Diane Ostrom, Aug. 25, 1983; 1 son, Michael. Contrbr. to Jnl of Aesthetics and Art Criticism, Markham Rvw, Wallace Stevens Jnl; ed. Concerning Poetry, 1978—. Wrkg. on history of Am. lit. and thought. PhD, U. Wash., Seattle, 1969. Prof. Western Wash. U., Bellingham, 1963—. Mem. MLA. Home: 1125 Sudden Valley Bellingham WA 98226

JOHNSON, EVELYNE, b. NYC, Jan. 20, 1922; d. David and Rose (Geiger) Levow; m. Frank A. Johnson, Jr., Oct. 10, 1942; children: Barry. Author: juveniles, The Elephant's Ball, 1977, The Cookie Cookbook, 1979, My Animal Friends, 1979, My Favorite Toys, 1979, Baby's Farm, 1979, Beddybye Baby, 1979, Peek-a-Boo Baby, 1979, Fun in the Tub, 1979, I Am A Baby, 1979, A First Cookbook for Childrn, 1983, The Cow in the Kitchen: A Folk Tale, 1983, (with Frank Daniels) The Sharon Picture Word Book, 1983, (with Daniels) The Sharon First Picture Dictionary, 1983. Attended New York Univ., Natl. Acad. of Design, New School for Social Research. Freelance artist and copywritr. Proprietor, Evelyne Johnson Associates, NYC, 1965—. Mem. Soc of Illustrators, Soc. of Photographers and Artists Representatives, Natl. Arts Club, Graphic Artists Guild. Address: 201 East 28th St New York NY 10016

JOHNSON, FREDERICK WILLIAM, b. Sturgeon Bay, WI, Jul. 19, 1947; s. William Mancel and Delphine Anna (McArdle) Johnson. Author: Exultations for the Diefiers of the Empyreal Antelope Queen, 1973, How I Became Popular Overnight, 1975, The Fable of Fast Finger Freddie, 1976; editor: Dead Reckoning (G. Bailin), 1984, The Door County Almanak, 1982, 85, 86, 87. BS, U. Wisconsin-LaCrosse, 1970; MA, U. Wis., Madison, 1973, MFA, 1975. Artist/framer Pint Box Gallery (Sister Bay, WI), 1971—; manager/projectionist Lake Cinema (Bailey's Harbor, WI), 1976—; PTF clerk US Postal Service (Sister Bay), 1985—. Home: 10905 BayShore Dr Sister Bay WI 54234

JOHNSON, GREG, b. San Francisco, s. Raymond F. and JoAnn (Untersee) J. Author: Emily Dickinson: Perception and the Poet's Quest, 1985, Understanding Joyce Carol Oates, 1987; contrbr. fiction: Va. Qtly Rvw, Ontario Rvw, Prairie Schooner, Ascent, other lit mags. BA, So. Meth. U., 1973, MA, 1975; PhD, Emory U., 1979. Asst. prof. English, Emory U., Atlanta. Recipient O. Henry award, 1986. Home: 564 Emory Oaks Way Decatur GA 30033

JOHNSON, JAMES BLAIR, b. Chgo., Sept. 16, 1944; s. James Benjamin and Elouise (Letson) J.; m. Beverly Ann Williams, Sept. 1, 1967; 1 son, Blair William. Novels: Daystar and Shadow, 1981, Trekmaster, 1987, Mindhopper, 1988. Contrbr. short stories to Swallow's Tale Mag., Analog, Mag. of Fantasy and Sci. Fiction. Tambay Legacy. B.A., Fla. State U., 1965., 1965, M.A., 1983. Served to capt. U.S. Air Force, 1966-77. Mem. SFWA. Home: 4134 Palau Dr Sarasota FL 34241

JOHNSON, JAMES HOLBROOK, (James J. Holbrook), b. Bronxville, NY, Sept. 8, 1955, s. James Wiley and Barbara Helen (Nelson) Johnson; m. Katherine Lee Harp, Sept. 1, 1985. Contrbr. to Am. Forests, Science 86, Mpls./St. Paul Mag., Minn. Law Jnl, other publs. Wrkg. on book about Mayans. BS in Oceanography, Fla. Inst. Tech., 1980. Sales engr. Mogul Corp., Mpls., 1980-85; freelance wrtr., Mpls., 1985—. Home: 2937 41st Ave So Minneapolis MN 55406

JOHNSON, JANE, see Francis, Betty Joe

JOHNSON, JEAN V., b. Pine Bluff, AR, Feb. 18, 1952; d. Sidney and Versie Lee (Jordan) J. B.A., U. Wis., Madison. Public relations asst. Atlanta Hawks, 1974-78; asst. program researcher ABC-TV, Century City, CA, 1978-79; asst. to dir. of devel. Paramount Studios, Hollywood, CA, 1979-80; asst. to pres., Unlimited Gold Records, Studio City, CA, 1981-84; staff wrtr. universal Studios, Universal City, CA, 1985—. Home: 1113 S Cloverdale Ave 3 Los Angeles CA 90019

JOHNSON, JOAN E. STOUT, b. Springfield, IL, Jan. 3, 1944; widowed; Contrbr. news and feature articles to gen. interest, travel, edn. and antique publs. BS in Edn., Western Ill. U., 1966. Tchr., Lewistown, Ill., 1966-72, 83-85; feature wrtr. Port 30 News, Havana, Ill., 1975-85, River Valley News, Havana, Ill., 1975-85; publicity and public relations dir. Spoon River Scenic Drive, Fulton County, Ill., 1982—, ed. cookbooks, 1986, 87; freelance wrtr. Home: Box 308 Lewistown IL 61542

JOHNSON, JUDITH EVELYN, b. NYC, Oct. 3, 1936; d. Edgar and Eleanor (Kraus) Johnson; m. James T. Sherwin, June 21, 1955 (div. 1985); children—Miranda, Alison Dale, Galen Leigh. Works published before 1986 published under the name Judith Johnson Sherwin. Author: Uranium Poems, 1968; short stories The Life of Riot, 1970; poems Impossible Buildings, 1973, The Town Scold, 1977, How the Dead Count, 1978, Transparencies, 1978, Dead's Good Company, 1978, contrbr. poetry and fiction to numerous publs., readings, lectr. workshops univs., cultural instns., radio and TV. Student, Radcliffe Coll., 1954-55; BA cum laude, Barnard Coll., 1958; postgrad. (Woodrow Wilson fellow), Columbia U., 1958-59. Cons. NY State Council on Arts, 1976, P&W, Inc., 1976-77; instr. poetry workshop Poetry Center, 92nd St YMCA (NYC), 1976, 78, 81; poet-in-residence Wake Forest U., 1980, SUNY-Albany, 1980-81, asst. prof. English and women's studies, 1981—. Recipient AAP prize, 1958, Amy Loveman prize, 1958, Van Rensselaer prize, 1957, Yale Series Younger Poets prize, 1968, poetry prize St. Andrews Rvw, 1975, Playboy fiction prize, 1977. Mem. PSA (exec. bd. 1973-75, pres. 1975-78, chair exec. com. 1979-80, pres. emeritus, 1980-84), PEN, AG. Address: Eng Dept 1400 Washington Ave Albany NY 12222

JOHNSON, MARKHAM P. III, b. Norman, OK, Nov. 25, 1953, s. Markham P. Johnson, Jr. and Marilyn (Rush) Wright; m. Dawn Marie White, July 10, 1979; children, Laurel Bay, Gabriel. Contrbr. poems to Nimrod, Louisville Rvw, Kansas Qtly, others. BA, Eckerd Coll., 1982; MFA, Vt. Coll., 1984. Poetry ed. Nimrod, Tulsa, 1982-85; exec. dir. Mich. Festival, 1986—. Mem. P&W, AWP, Natl. Assembly Local Arts Agcys. Home: 451 Glenmoor 11 E Lansing MI 48823

JOHNSON, MARTY JO, b. Salisbury, NC, June 3, 1947; d. Joseph Wayne and Martha (Deibert) Johnson; m. Philip Duke Stukey, Dec. 20, 1969 (div. June 1976); 1 son, Peter Duke. Contrbr. articles NYT, Newsday, others, numerous real estate pvbns., columnist Metal, Blds. Rvw.,, 1982-84, B.S. in Jnlsm., U. Fla., 1970. Recipient Addy award Am. Advt. Fdn., 1986. Mem. Fla. Free-lance Wrtrs. Assn. Office: Box 247 Indian Rocks Beach FL 34635

JOHNSON, MARY LOU, b. Cin., Oct. 28, 1953; d. John Jackson and Dorothy Mae (Decker) Howard. ontrbr. poems to anthols. Grad. public schls., Nancy, KY. Reipient Honorable Mention, World of Poetry, 1985, 86, Golden Poet award, 1985, 86. Home: HC 66 Box 965 Faubush KY 42532

JOHNSON, NICHOLAS, b. Iowa City, Sept. 23, 1934; s. Wendell A.L. and Edna (Bockwoldt) J.; m. Karen Mary Chapman, 1952 (div. 1972); children: Julie, Sherman, Gregory. Author: Cases and Materials on Oil and Gas Law, 1962, How to Talk Back to Your Television Set, 1970, Life Before Death in the Corporate State, 1971, Test Pattern for Living, 1972, Broadcasting in America, 1973, Cases and Materials on Communications Law and Policy, 1981-86. Law clk. to U.S. Supreme Ct. Justice Hugo L. Black, 1959-60; acting assoc. prof. law U. Calif., Berkeley, 1960-63; practice DC, 1963-64; adminstr. Maritime Admin., U.S. Dept. of Commerce, 1964-66; Commissioner FCC, 1966-73; prof. law various schls. 1971—; syndicated columnist: Gannett News Service, 1982-84, Register and Tribune Syndicate, 1984; Cowles Syndicate, 1985-86; King Features Syndicate, 1986—; contrbg. editor, host: PBS The New Tech Times, 1983-84. BA, U. Tex., 1956, LLB, 1958; LHD, Windham Coll., 1971. Mem. DC, Iowa bar assns., State Bar Tex. Mem. Phi Beta Kappa. Home: Box 1876 Iowa City IA 52244

JOHNSON, NORMA ALICE, b. Bemidji, MN, July 18, 1932; d. Nels Herbert and Alice (Aune) Nordstrom; m. Leonard Arthur Johnson, May 27, 1953; children—James LeRoy, Suzanne Arlene Gordon. Author: Wagon Wheels, 5 vols., 1981-86; co-author: Ehanna Woyakapi, 1972; hist. coloring book, 1984. History columnist Sisseton Courier, 1979—. BS in Elem. Edn., Northern State Coll., Aberdeen, S.D., 1977. Tchr. elem. pub. schls., S.D., 1950-67, Sisseton Elem. Schl., S.D., 1967—. Mem. local, state, and natl. Cow Belles, S.D., 1973—. Recipient award for Disting. Contrbn. to Preservation of History of S.D. and Dakota Territory, Dakota State Coll, S.D., 1984. Mem. Marshall Hist. Soc., S.D. Edn. Assn., Annie D. Tallent Club. Home: RD 1 Box 62 Eden SD 57232

JOHNSON, ORA MAE, b. Indpls., Dec. 28, 1944; d. Leroy and Ruth (Wilson) Lewis; m. Marion Tinsley, May 14, 1961 (div. 1972); children—Tanya I., Damon, Antwan; m. Elroy Johnson, Oct. 12, 1975. Diploma Inst. Children's Lit., 1987. Contrbr. poems to anthols. Wrkg. on poems. Clrk. U.S. Postal Service, Indpls., 1964-69, Ind. Natl. Bank, Indpls., 1971-72, Ind. Bell & ATTIS, Indpls., 1972-83. Recipient Golden Poet award World of Poetry, 1987. Home: 6124 Georgetown Rd F Indianapolis IN 46254

JOHNSON, PETER CHRISTOPHER, b. Denver, Jan. 18, 1954, s. Roger Lundeen and Jacqueline Ruth (O'Neill) J.; m. Deanne Lee Garrett, Nov. 23, 1985; children—Kristen, Scott. Contrbr. articles: Jnl Am. Chiropractic Assn., Woodenboat, Romantic Dining & Travel News, other publs. BA, Calif. State U., 1979. Wrtr., ed. Orange County Illustrated, Irvine, Calif., 1979-81; ed. Prep Mag., Anaheim, Calif., 1981-82, Leisureguide, Inc., Agoura, Calif., 1982-84; public info. officer Los Angeles Coll. of Chiropractic, Whittier, Calif., 1984—; contrbg. ed., dining critic Orange Coast Mag. Recipient Maggie award Western Book Pubs. Assn., 1983. Mem. AG, Ind. Wrtrs. So. Calif. Home: 15214 E Cullen St Whittier CA 90603

JOHNSON, ROBERT THOMAS, b. Louisville; s. Jesse Lewis and Hatha Ezma (Dunagan) J.; m. Patricia Brown Bennett, Mar. 1, 1951 (div. 1975); children—Lisa, Peter, Joseph, Robert Cole; m. 2d, Betty Ann Tichenor, Apr. 30, 1975; children—Melody, Douglas. Author: Stay Well!, 1985. Contrbr. articles to mags. including Woman's World, Outdoor Life, Health, Sports Parade, Total Fitness, others. Syndicated columnist Your Family Doctor, Harris & Assocs. BS, Ky. Wesleyan U., 1959; MD, U. Lousiville, 1963. Diplomate Am. Acad. Family Practice. Practice medicine specializing in family medicine, Hartford, Ky., 1964—; free-lance writer, Hartford, 1979—. Pres. Citizen's Alcohol and Drug Action Com., 1986—; chmn. pub. relations com. Ky Acad. Family Practice, 1986—; bd. dirs. Northwest Haiti Christian Mission. Mem. AMWA. Home: 312 B Main St Hartford KY 42347

JOHNSON, ROGER N., b. Dayton, OH, Apr. 22, 1939. Author: Aggression in Man & Animals, 1972; contrbr. arts. to profl. jnls., op-ed. features to N.Y. Times, other pubns. inclg. N.J. Monthly, Garden State Rpt. BA, Swarthmore Coll., 1961; MA, U. CT, 1962, PhD, 1966. Asst. prof., Amherst (MA) Coll., 1965-68, Tufts U., Boston, 68-71; prof. Ramapo Coll., Mahwah, NJ, 1971—. Fulbright scholar, Jyvaskyla, Finland, 1979. Mem. profl. orgns. Home: 100 Deerhaven Rd Mahwah NJ 07430

JOHNSON, RONALD LEROY, b. Vancouver, WA, July 16, 1943; s. Roy and Helen Elizabeth (Olmstead) J.; m. Sheila Marie MacLure, May 25, 1967; children: Jonathan, Ann Marie. Contrbr. to Magill's Lit. Ann., Masterplots II, Studies in Short Fiction, Western Humanities, Lit. Mag., Westigan rvws, Dow Jones/Magill's Book Rvws, Western Am. Lit. Fiction Monthly, Qtly West, Edge. MFA, U. Calif., Irvine, 1971; PhD, U. Utah, 1980. Instr. Shasta Coll., Redding, Calif., 1976-77; mng. ed. Western Humanities Rvw, Salt Lake City, 1979-80; prof. McNeese State U., Lake Charles, La., 1981-84, No. Mich. U., Marquette, 1984—. Recipient Bicentennial award for fiction U. Utah, 1976; 1st place for novel Utah Arts Council, 1981; grantee McNeese State U., 1982. Home: 1240 Norwood Apt 1 Marquette MI 49855

JOHNSON, RONALD, b. Ashland, KS, Nov. 25, 1935; s. Albert Theodore and Helen (Mayse) J. Author: A Line of Poetry, A Row of Trees, 1964, Sports & Divertissements, 1965, The Book of the Green Man, 1967, Valley of the Many-Colored Grasses, 1969, Balloons for Moonless Nights, 1969, The Spirit Walks, The Rocks Will Talk, 1969, Songs of the Earth, 1970, Eyes & Objects, 1976, RADI OS I-IV, 1977, ARK: The Foundations, 1980, ARK 50, 1984; cookbooks: The Aficionado's Southwestern Cooking, 1968, The American Table, 1983, Southwestern Cooking: New & Old, 1985. BA, Columbia, 1960. Served to PFC, US Army, 1956-58. Recipient Boar's Head prize, Columbia Univ., 1960, Inez Boulton Award Poetry, Chgo., 1965, NEA grantee, 1970, 72, Natl. Poetry Series. Address: 73 Elgin Pk San Francisco CA 94103

JOHNSON, SAMMYE LA RUE, b. Dallas, Oct. 8, 1946, d. Sam S. and Poppy LaRue (Hammond) Malosky; m. William H. Johnson, Aug. 1, 1970 (div. 1983). Contrbr. articles: Journalism Educator, Studies in Journalism and Mass Communication Jnl, Journalism Qtly, Public Relations Rvw, other profl. publs.; contrbr. to Ladies' Home Jnl, Ultra, Off Duty, VIVA, other genl. interest publs. BS in Journalism, Northwestern U., 1968, MS in Journalism, 1969. Feature wrtr. Chgo. Today newspaper, 1969-71, Sunday mag. ed., 1971-73; dir. public relations U.S. Armed Forces Library System, Nurnberg, W.Ger., 1974-75; ed.-in-chief San Antonio Mag. 1976-79; asst. prof. U. Kans., Lawrence, 1979-80; assoc. prof. Trinity U., San Antonio, 1980—; communications cons. Target '90 Growth Plan, San Antonio, 1983—, numerous non-profit orgns. Mem. Women in Communications (past pres. San Antonio chap.), Assn. Edn. in Journalism and Mass Communications (vice chmn, mag. div., newsletter ed.), SPJ. Home: 2906 Spring Bend San Antonio TX 78209

JOHNSON, SHIRLEY JEANNE, b. Trenton, MO, Oct. 18, 1928; d. James Albert and Florence Hazel (Callicotte) Walsh; m. Jerry E. Johnson, 1962 (div. 1966). Author: The Siamese Cat Handbook, 1986. Contrbr. articles to pet mags. Ed. U.C.F.-Forts, 1979-81, Siamese News Quarterly, 1986—; contrbg. ed. numerous newsletters, pet jnls. B.A. in Jnlsm., U. Mo., 1952. Adminstrv. supvr. Tumpane Co., Ankara, Turkey, 1963-66; research asst. U.S. Civil Service, Tucson, 1966—. Mem. Am. Cat Fanciers Assn. (all-breed judge, breed council exec. com.), Siamese Cat So. Am. (pres.). Home: Box 1149 Green Valley AZ 85622

JOHNSON, TREBBE, b. Indianapolis, March 10, 1948; d. U. Cone and June Signa (Trebbe) J.; m. Andrew Gardner, May 3, 1986. Contrbr. essays, articles, poetry numerous mags, including The Nation, North American Rvw, Ladies Home Journal, Massachusetts Rvw, Imprints Qtly, Amicus Jnl, Prism. BA cum laude, Stephens College, 1970. Secy./researcher, Erich Segal, New Haven, 1970-73; wrtr./prod., Spotlight Presents, NY, 1975-77; freelance wrtr./scriptwrtr., New York, 1977—. Awards: Intl. Film & TV Festival, gold medal, 1982, silver medal, 1980; John Masefield Award, PSA, 1975, non-fiction award, Prism, 1985; recipient of SPDF grant, Natl. Pub. Radio, to write and produce "A Mountain Split in Two: The Story of the Navajo-Hopi Land Dispute," 1986. Mem. Assn. for Multi-Image, Amnesty Intl, Urgent Action Comm. Home: 363 W 19th St New York NY 10011

JOHNSON, WALTER, b. Nahant, MA, June 27, 1915; s. Alfred and Annie (Hogan) J.; m. Bette Gifford, Sept .13, 1955; 1 son, Gifford; children by previous marriage: Deborah, Richard. Author: The Battle Against Isolation, 1944, William Allen White's America, 1947, (with Avery Craven) The United States: Experiment in Democracy, 1947, How We Drafted Adlai Stevenson, 1955, American Studies Abroad, 1963; coauthor: The Fulbright Program: A History, 1965; editor: Selected Letters of William Allen White, 1947, Roosevelt and The Russians, The Yalta Conference (Edward R. Stettinius, Jr.), 1949, Turbulent Era: A Diplomatic Record of Forty Years (Ambassador Joseph C. Grew), 1952, 1600 Pennsylvania Avenue: Presidents and the People, 1929-59, 1960, The Papers of Adlai E. Stevenson, 8 vols AB, Dartmouth Coll., 1937; MA, U. Chgo., 1938, PhD, 1941. Newberry Library fellow, 1945. Home: Bass Lk Rt 1 Pentwater MI 49449

JOHNSTON, CAROLE ANNE, b. Knoxville, TN, Aug. 6, 1944, d. Theodore Roosevelt and Opal Louise (Laugherty) Turner; m. Terrence Tyler Johnston, July 7, 1978, children—Robert, Marty, Elizabeth. Contrbr. poetry to Lyrical Iowa, Home Life, Women's Image, Am. Muse, Christian Herald, English Jnl, other publs. BA, U. Tenn., 1968; MSS, Univ. South Dakota. Tchr. pub. schls., Knoxville, Tenn., 1967-70, Jackson, Neb., 1971-73, 75-76, Sioux City, Iowa, 1978-80, 83—; dir. transp. community action Sioux City, 1976-78. Mem. Iowa Poetry Assn. Home: 2519 Canterbury St Sergeant Bluff IA 51054

JOHNSTON, CICELY ANNE, b. San Francisco, Oct. 7, 1912; d. Stanislaus Maximilian Skurtun an Nicia Marie (Kolasa) Catharin; m. James Lawrence Riordan, July 3, 1936 (div. 1946); m. Eugene Carlyle Johnston, Mar. 20, 1976; children—Gordon James, Sandra Jeannette. Contrbr. prose, poetry to anthols. Office mgr. Coast Apparatus, Martinez, CA, 1948-58,

L. N. Curtis & Sons, Oakland, CA, 1959-79. Recipient award of Merit, World of Poetry, 1984, 85, Golden Poet award, 1985. Home: 2815 Roosevelt Ave Richmond CA 94804

JOHNSTON, GARY, b. Bronx, NY, Dec. 4, 1946, s. Ralph and Ruth J. Co-founder, ed.: Blind Beggar Press, Bronx, since 1977; author: Sunbury Number 5, 1974, Black Nation, 1983, Presstime, 1984, Long Journey Home, 1985, Making Eyes Thru Morning, 1979; ed. New Rain: Anthology Vol. I-VII, 1987; published in Practice Mag. AA, Bronx Community Coll., 1974; BA, Herbert Lehman Coll., 1976. Mem. Bronx Council on Arts, 1977—. Recipient Bronx Council on Arts award, 1973. Mem. P&W, Black Wrtrs. Union, Am. Wrtrs. Congress. Office: Box 37 Williamsbridge Sta NY 10467

JOHNSTON, HUGH BUCKNER, b. Wilson County, NC, Apr. 11, 1913; s. Hugh Bolden and Ruth (Thomas) Johnston; m. Elizabeth Briggs, Nov. 8, 1941 (div. Dec., 1952); 1 son, Thomas Owen Drakeford; m. 2d, Edna Elizabeth Long, Oct. 23, 1953; 1 son, Hugh Bolden. Author genealogical volumes, 1958—, latest being The Johnsons and Johnstons of Corrowaugh, 1979; contrbr. to various quarterlies and newspapers. Wrkg. on four genealogical volumes. BA, Davidson (NC) Coll., 1933, MA, George Washington U., 1946. Tchr., public schls., NC, 1935-37, 1953-55; prof. of languages Atlantic Christian College, Wilson, NC, 1955-78; archivist, 1978-84; retired, 1984—. Home: Rt 4 Box 160 Wilson NC 27893

JOHNSTON, MARIE E., see Peck, Marie Johnston

JOHNSTON, WILLIAM ARNOLD, (Arnie Johnston) b. Cambuslang, Lanarkshire, Scotland, May 31, 1942; came to U.S., 1951; s. James Reid and Eliza (Arnold) J.; m. June Eve LaValley, June 23, 1963 (div. Sept. 1969); m. Kristin Lucille Tyrrell, Sept. 16, 1972. Author: (play) The Witching Voice, 1973 (produced in Kalamazoo, Grand Rapids, Alma, Mich., Colorado Springs, Colo); Of Earth and Darkness: The Novels of William Golding, 1980; script ed. radio series Voices from Michigan's Past, 1975; plays produced Scrimshaw, The Edge of Running Water, Suitors. PhB, Wayne State U., 1963; MA, U. Del, 1966, PhD, 1970. Asst. prof. English, Western Mich. U., Kalamazoo, 1966-73, assoc. prof., 1973-80, prof., 1980—. Fellow NDEA, 1963-66, Western Mich. U., 1974, 80; grantee Mich. Arts Council, 1981-83. Mem. Am. Theater Assn., Mich. Theater Assn. Home: 1012 N. Fletcher Kalamazoo MI 49007

JOHNSTONE, DAVID MOORE, (Grig Moore), b. New Haven, Mar. 21, 1926, s. Charles Henry and Augusta (Bantle) J.; m. Marion Joanne Davis, Aug. 4, 1947 (dec. 1966); children—Melanie Davis (Stinson), Heather Anne (Marcinak); m. 2d, Marjorie Louise Douglas, Sept. 21, 1971 (div. 1976). Author: American Law as an Instrument for Man's Survival, 1951, Metastasis (poetry), 1959, People and Places (with Gordon G. Dupee), 1967; poetry ed. U. Chgo. Maroon, 1945, December mag., 1963; promotion, Britannica Schools Systems for Education, Chgo., 1963-64, Quadrangle Books, 1967, Crain Books, 1971-80; contrbr. to Rental Management, 1975-81. Student U. Chgo., Temple U. Freelance wrtr., 1967-83, ret. Mem. ACLU, 1944-65; AFSC/FCL, 1960-66; WRL (staff, 1944), 1944-54. Home: 2525 N Richmond St Chicago IL 60647

JONAS, ANN, b. Joplin, MO, July 15, 1919; d. Morris and Leah (Marov) Moskovitz; m. Walter H. Jonas, Mar. 30, 1942; 1 dau., Wendy Jan Jonas Bischof. Contrbr. to anthologies and lit mags including the So. Rvw, So. Humanities Rvw, Prism Intl., Poetry Rvw, Orbis (Eng. awards issue), Midwestern Univ. Qtly, Colo. Qtly, Carolina Qtly, others; also Am. Haiku, Haiku (Can.), Haiku West, others. Grad. Goodman Theatre, Chgo., 1939. Commentator, sta. WMBH, Joplin, 1939-40; writer, actress sta. WJJD, Chgo., 1940-41; commentator, actress, wrtr sta. WHAS, Louisville, 1942-47; commentator, actress, wrtr, sta. WAVE, Louisville, 1947-54; freelance poet, 1960—. Yaddo fellow, 1968, Henry Rago Meml. award, 1972, Edwin Markham Poetry Prize, 1977 (co-winner), Cecil Hemley Meml. award, 1972, Caddo Wrtg. Ctr. poetry prize, 1985. Mem. Ky. CLU, Louisville, 1985. Fellow Intl. Poetry Soc. (Eng.); mem. PSA, Centro Studi E Scambi Internazionali Italy (hon. v.p. 1975). Home: 2425 Ashwood Dr Louisville KY 40205

JONES, ALAN HEDRICK, b. Ann Arbor, MI, April, 18, 1937; s. Volney Hurt and Joyce (Hedrick) J.; m. Susan Holtzer, June 2, 1960; 1 son, Mason T. Jones. Ed, Teacher Education Quarterly, 1987—, co-ed., Foundations mag., 1986—; mng. ed. The Edn. Digest, 1981—, School Shop, 1983—; co-ed. (with Erskine S. Dottin) The CASA Handbook, 1984; editor Civic Learning for Teachers, 1985; contrbr. articles to ednl. mags. BS, U. MI, 1959, MA, 1961, PhD, 1971. Instr. & researcher, U. MI, Ann Arbor, 1959-62, 65-68, 73-74; asst. prof. Eastern MI U., Ypsilanti, 1968-72; chairman dept. edn. Sacred Heart U., Bridgeport, CT, 1972-73; chief, planning & eval. Comm. for Tchr. Prepn., Sacramento, CA, 1974-76, 78-81; exec. secy. MI Conf. of AAUP, Lansing, 1976-78; pub. & exec. ed. Prakken Pubns., Ann Arbor, MI, 1981—. Pres.-elect, American Educational Studies Assn., Vice-pres., EPAA, Council Learned Socs. in Edn. Office: Box 8623 Ann Arbor MI 48107

JONES, ANN (MARET), b. Eau Claire, WI, Sept. 3, 1937, d. Oscar Trygve and Bernice (Rufsvold) Slagsvol. Author: Uncle Tom's Campus, 1973, Women Who Kill, 1980, Everyday Death: The Case of Bernadette Powell, 1985; contrbr. to Take Back the Night: Women on Pornography, 1980, Women's Worlds: From the New Scholarship, 1985; contrbr. articles, rvws. to Vogue, Harper's Bazaar, The Nation, MS, NY Times, Newsday, other publs. BS, U. Wis.-Madison, 1960, PhD, 1970; MA, U. Mich., 1961. Asst. prof. CCNY, 1970-73; coordinator women's studies U. Mass., Amherst, 1973-75; freelance wrtr., NYC, 1975—; vis. prof. U. So. Me., Portland, 1985; wrtr.-in-residence Lake George (N.Y.) Arts Council, 1986; wrtr. Mt. Holyoke Coll., South Hadley, Mass., 1986—; lit. panelist N.Y. State Council on Arts, 1982-86; bd. dirs. Millay Colony for Arts, Austerlitz, N.Y., 1984—. Mem. AG, PEN, NWU, New York Book Critics Circle. Home: 229 Sullivan St New York NY 10012

JONES, BAILEY ARMSTRONG, b. Birmingham, AL, Oct. 19, 1961; s. William Bailey and Polly Anne (Armstrong) J. Contrbr. features, articles to Auburn Plainsman, Opelika-Auburn News, Birmingham News, Sports Afield. Wrkg. on collection of personal essays, short stories and anecdotes. Student Sumford U., 1979-81, Auburn U., 1981-87. Home: Box 13 Alexander City AL 35010

JONES, DI ANNA LYNN, b. Orlando, FL, July 20, 1949, d. Ocillor and Ethel Gwendolyn (Richardson) Jones. Contrbr. poetry, articles to The Strawberry Saxifrage, Our Town, Park Avenue Peat, East Side Express, other publs. Student NYU, 1985-86, CCNY, 1986—. Word processing operator Exxon Corp., NYC,1979-80, Peat, Marwick, Mitchell & Co., NYC,1980-82; freelance wrtr., word processor, NYC,1982—. Mem. NWC, Am. Film Inst. Home: 346 W 47th St New York NY 10036

JONES, DON, b. Kimball, NE, Feb. 11, 1938, s. Lawrence Roswell and Hazel M. (Stemen) Jones. Author: Medical Aid and Other Poems, 1967, 9 Postal Poems, 1971, Miss Liberty, Meet Crazy Horse, 1972. Contrbr. poetry to Prairie Schooner, Salt Creek Reader, Crow Call, Phantasm, other publs. BA, U. No. Colo., 1960; MA, Johns Hopkins U., 1961. Instr. English, wrtr.-in-residence U. Nebr., Hastings Coll., Carleton Coll., St. Olaf Coll., 1962-72. Recipient AAP prize, 1963, Vreeland award U. Nebr., 1965, Star award Kansas City (Mo.) Poetry Contests, 1965; Wurlitzer Fdn. fellow, Taos, N.Mex., 1976-78; grantee Carnegie Fund Authors, 1977, PEN Am. Center, 1977. Home: 1423 8th St Greeley CO 80631

JONES, DOUGLAS CLYDE, b. Winslow, AR, Dec. 6, 1924; s. Marvin Clyde and Bethel Mae (Stockburger) J.; m. Mary Arnold, Jan. 1, 1949; children: Mary Glenn, Martha Claire, Kathryn Greer, Douglas Eben. Author: Treaty of Medicine Lodge, 1966, Court Martial of G. A. Custer, 1976 (Spur award WWA), Arrest Sitting Bull, 1977, Creek Called Wounded Knee, 1978, Winding Stair, 1979, Elkhorn Tavern, 1980 (Friends of Am. Writers award 1980), Weedy Rough, 1981, The Barefoot Brigade, 1982, Season of Yellow Leaf, 1983, Gone the Dreams and Dancing, 1984, Roman, 1986 (won Spur WWA), Hickory Coved, 1987. BA in journalism, U. Ark., 1949; MS in mass communications, U. Wis., Madison, 1962. Prof. U. Wis. Schl. Journalism, Madison, 1968-74; chief armed forces news br. Dept. Def., 1966-68, ret., 1968; novelist, 1976—. Served with AUS, World War II; Commd. AUS, 1949, advanced through grades to lt. col., 1968; served in W. Ger. and Korea; PTO. Decorated Commendation medal (3) Legion of Merit. Address: 1987 Greenview Dr Fayetteville AR 72701

JONES, EDNAH, see Buthmann, Ednah Jones

JONES, ETHELENE DYER, b. Blairsville, GA, May 13, 1930; d. Marion Jewel and Fannie Azie (Collins) Dyer; m. Grover Duffie JOnes, Dec. 23, 1949; children—Elton Keith, Cynthia Denise Joness Berenguer. Author: (poems) The Singing in the Wood, 1984. Ed., author: Faith through Flood and Fire, 1983, The Hi-Line, 1984—; ed: The Media News Leader, 1983-86, The Newsletter of Ga. State Poetry Soc., 1985—. B.A., Mercer U., 1953; M.A. in Edn., Western Carolina U., 1968; Spealist in Edn., u. Ga., 1971. Tchr. public shs., Blue Ridge, GA, 1961-68; librarian, media specialist Fannin County High Shl., Blue Ridge, 1968—; adj. prof. Brenau and Truett McConnell Coll., 1972—. Mem. Ga. Library/Media Dept. (pres. 1981-82; William E. Patterson award 1985, Media Specialist of Yr. Award, 1986), Ga. State Poetry Soc. (v.p. 1984-87), Fannin County History Book Projet Assn. (co-dir.). Home: Box 120 Epworth GA 30541

JONES, JEAN R., b. Modesto, CA, Nov. 29, 1919, d. Frank Huntington and Allene Simmons (Kelley) Russell; m. Troy Frank Jones, July 1, 1942 (dec.); children—Troy Russell, Keith Robert, Bruce Allen, Kenneth Humphrey. Pub.: Jelm Mt. Publs., 1979—; author chapbooks. BA, San Jose State U., 1942; MEd, U. Wyo., 1969. Tchr. elem. schls. Va., Calif., 1942-46; wrtr. for Sunday Schl. Bd., So. Bapt. Conv. Publs., 1953-65; tchr. Harmony Schl. Dist., Laramie, Wyo., 1969-72; guidance counselor Carbon Cty. (Wyo.) Schl. Dist. Encampment, 1972-73. Mem. Wyo. Presswomen. Address: Jelm Mt Pubs Jelm WY 82063

JONES, J. NICHOLAS, b. Tulsa, OK, Nov. 24, 1944; s. Howard Cleo and Berble (Jones) Hanley; m. Else Ortrud Neurohr, Mar. 22, 1979. Contrbr. poetry: Poetic Symphony-Music from the Heart, numerous anthologies. Wrkg. on fiction and non-fiction novels, surrealistic poetry. PhD in Psychology, U. ky., 1977; MSW, Chapel Hill State Coll., 1985. 1st Sp. Ops. Comm. Army, 1963, advanced through grades to col., 1984; case officer CIA, 1963-78; commdr. spcl. forces, Washington, 1965-85; chief investigator Internat. Criminology Entrprise, Chgo., 1979—. Awarded Black Lit. Letters, Am. Black Book Wrtrs. Assn., 1984. Home: 3239 W Lemoyne St Chicago IL 60651

JONES, JACK PAYNE, b. Timmonsville, SC, Nov. 20, 1928; s. Ed McDuffie and Laura Leola (Payne) J.; m. Ernestine Julia Ryals, Oct. 15, 1955; children—Gregory, Kenneth, Ronald, Laura. Author: Wagons in the Wind, 1953, Manual of Professional Remodeling, 1982, Spec Builder's Guide, 1984, Three Across Texas, 1984, Three Across Kansas, 1986, Handbook of Construction Contracting, Vol. 1, 1986, Vol. 2, 1986. Wrkg. on two novels and technical construction book. B. Law, LaSalle Extension U., 1948. Investigator Robins Air Force Base, Warner Robins, GA, 1956-58, chief of investigation, 1958-61, chief of police, 1961-63, industrial security specialist, 1963-69; genl. contractor Jones Builders, Middle GA, 1969-82. Mem. AG, WWA, Nat. Assn. Home Workshop Wrtrs. Home: Rt 2 Double J Farm Eastman GA 31023

JONES, MARGARET BRIDWELL, (Margaret Bridwell), b. Richmond, VA, Feb. 11, 1939, d. James Broadus Bridwell and Ada (Moss) Robson; m. Robert Drake Jones; children—Timothy, Chad, Amy. Contrbr. short stories to Bravara Lit Mag, Northwoods Jnl, Calliope, Colo. North Rvw, Hob Nob, Green's Mag, other lit publs. Student Mira Costa Coll., Palomar Coll., Sherwood Oaks Exptl. Coll., U.S.C. Advt. copywrtr. numerous TV and radio stas., advt. agcys., 1958—; free-lance public relations wrtr.. Mem. AWP, P&W, NWC, Ventura Wrtrs Club. Home: 275 Swan Retreat Bigfork MT 59911

JONES, MARY HOLMES, b. Independence, WV, Apr. 8, 1921; d. Clarence Lee and Maude May (Hill) Holmes; m. James Victor Jones, May 3, 1940; 1 son, James Victor. Author: (poetry) Life's Tapestry, 1979. Contrbr. short stories, articles, poems to mags., newspapers, anthols. Salesclerk, bookkeeper Eleanor Shops, Inc., Morgantown, W.Va., 1971-75; salesclerk House of Cards, Morgantown, 1975-78; head infant's dept. Murphy Mart, Morgantown, 1978-81, retired. Recipient Modern Poetry award Morgantown Poetry Soc., 1985. Mem. W. Va. Poetry Soc. (George M. Nolte award 1983, Gladys Iker award for best poem 1985; treas. 1982-83, treas. Morgantown chpt. 1983—), W.Va. Writers. Home: Rt 1 Box 44 Morgantown WV 26505

JONES, NANCY JOY, (Sara Blacksmith), b. Butte, MT, Apr. 1, 1939; d. Alfred Ralph and Mary Lorraine (McClain) Hedval; m. Roger Lee Jones, Aug. 27, 1960; children—Douglas S., Jana Lynne, Roger Kristian, Audrianna. Weekly food and genl. comment columnist Times-News, Twin Falls, Id., 1984—. Wrkg. on 2 cookbooks. AA, Boise Jr. Coll., 1959; BA U. Id.-Moscow, 1961. Tchr. journalism Minico High Schl., Rupert, Id., 1962-64; with pub. relations dept. Pomerelle Ski Area, 1965-73; mgr. Village Sport Den, Burley, Id., 1976-82. Chmn. library bd. DeMary Meml. Library, Rupert, 1975-84; mem. regional library bd. South Central Library Dist., Id.; guardian Job's Daus. Bethel, 1984-85. Mem. Id. Press Club. Home: 1020 I Rupert ID 83350

JONES, PAMELA LORRAINE, b. Oak Ridge, TN, Jan 2, 1956; d. Pershing Whitney Jones and Jane (Albrecht) Duguay. BA, U. AZ, 1977; MA, U. CA, 1979. Assoc. ed. Biarritz Mag., Costa Mesa, CA, 1980-81, Mountain News, Lake Arrowhead, CA, 81-83; assoc. & mng. ed., Technological Horizons in Education (T.H.E.) Journal, Irvine, CA, 1985—. Mem. Western Pubns. Assn., Orange County Press Club. Office: Box 17239 Irvine CA 92713

JONES, PAUL M., b. Hickory, NC, Feb. 5, 1950, s. John Paul and Mary (Silvester) J.; m. Janet Jones, June 29, 1985. Poetry ed.: Cardinal (An Anthology of N.C. Wrtrs.), 1986; contrbr. poetry: Ironwood, Carolina Qtly (1st place poetry 1980), Loblolly, Plainsong, other lit mags; contrbr. Anthology of Mag. Verse and Yearbook of Am. Poetry, 1980, 85, New N.C. Poetry—The Eighties. BS in Computer Sci. N.C. State U., Raleigh, 1972. Dir. ArtSchool Poets' Exchange. N.C. Arts Council fellow, 1981. Vice pres. N.C. Wrtrs.' Network. Home: 200 Barclay Rd Chapel Hill NC 27514

JONES, PETER D'ALROY, b. Hull, Eng., June 9, 1931; came to U.S., 1959, naturalized, 1968; s. Alfred and Margery (Rutter) J.; m. Beau Fly, June 10, 1961 (div. Dec. 22, 1980); children: Kathryn Beauchamp, Barbara Collier; m. Johanna Maria Hartinger, Feb. 20, 1987; 1 dau., Heather Marie. Author: Economic History of U.S.A. since 1783, 2d ed., 1965, The Story of the Saw, 1961, Acerica's Wealth, 1963, The Consumer Society, 2d ed., 1967, The Christian Socialists Revival, 1968, The Robber Barons Revisited, 1968, Robert Hunter's Poverty; Social Conscience in the Progressive Era, 1965, La Sociedad Consumidora, 1968, Since Columbus: Poverty and Pluralism in the History of the Americas, 1975, The U.S.A.: A History of Its People and Society, 2 vols., 1976; editor: Pegasus, 1966-68; (with M. G. Holli) The Ethnic Frontier: Group Survival in Chicago and the Midwest, 1977, Ethnic Chicago, 1981, rev. and enlarged ed., 1984, Biographical Dictionary of American Mayors, 1820-1980, 1981. BA, Manchester (Eng.) U., 1952, MA, 1953; PhD, London U., 1963; postgrad., U. Brussels, 1954. Freelance editor, London, 1953-56. Adviser pubs. Served with RAF, 1956-57. Office: Dept His U Ill at Chgo Chicago IL 60680

JONES, RICHARD ANDREW, b. London, Aug. 8, 1953; arrd. USA, 1954; s. Richard Andrew, Jr., and Flora (Watson) Jones. Author poetry: Windows and Walls, 1982, Innocent Things, 1985, Walk On, 1986, Country of Air, 1986, ed. Poetry and Politics, 1984, Of Solitude and Silence: Writing of Robert Bly, 1982. BA, U.Va., 1975, MA, 1976. Lectr. in writing, Univ. Va., Charlottesville, 1981-86; asst. prof. Ripon Coll., Wis., 1986-87; asst. prof. DePaul Univ, 1987—. Recipient editor's award CCLM, 1985, winner 1986 Posner Award. Address: Dept Eng DePaul 802 Belden Ave Chicago IL 60614

JONES, R(ICHARD) P(RESTON), b. NYC, July 25, 1942, s. Richard III and Margaret (Peffer) J.; m. Mary Katherine Chandler, June 13, 1964 (div. 1977); children—Amanda, Alexandra, Ian; m. 2d, Julia Bramlett, Oct. 5, 1985. Author: Waiting for Spring, 1978, The Rest is Silence, 1984, Scapegoat, 1987. AB, Harvard U., 1964; MA, U. Mass., 1969, MFA, 1969. Mem. faculty Pacific Luth. U., Tacoma, Wash., 1969—, assoc. prof. dept. English, 1984—. Recipient William Stafford award Wash. Poets Assn., 1979, Regency Award, Pacific Lutheran Univ., 1984. Home: 12524 Aqueduct Dr E Tacoma WA 98445

JONES, ROCKY, see Stewart, June

JONES, ROGER WALTON, b. Morristown, NJ, Nov. 22, 1953, s. Chastine W. and Gloria (Gamble) J. Contrbr. stories to Nostoc mag., Hob Nob Annl., Time to Pause; contrbr. rvw. to Lamar Jnl. of Humanities. Wrkg. on fiction. AB, Kenyon Coll., Gambier, Ohio, 1976; MA, So. Ill. U., Carbondale, 1979. Adj. prof. Kean Coll., Union, N.J., 1979-80; instr. Lamar U., Beaumont, Tex., 1981-84; teaching asst. Tex. A&M U., College Station, 1984—. Mem. P&W. Home: 1401 FM St 2818 67 College Station TX 77840

JONES, RUSSELL EUGENE, b. El Dorado, KS, Dec. 1, 1928; s. Roy C. and Mattie M. (Allen) J.; m. Mary M. Allen, May 19, 1951; children—Reginald, Susan, Terrance, Kent, Steven Jones. Contrbr. articles to newspapers, club mags.; poems to Am. Poetry Anthol. Life underwriter, 1977. Insurance agent Metropolitan, Winfield, KS, 1957-60, agcy. mgr., St. Joseph, MO, 1960-66; asst. mgr. N.Y. Life, Chillicothe, MO, 1966-72, genl. mgr., Amarillo, TX, 1972-80; agent Genl. Am., Belleville, IL, 1980—. Recipient Golden Poet award World of Poetry, 1985, 86, 87, Natl. Management award Genl. Agents and Mgrs., 1976, 77, 78, 79. Home: 17 Lake Forest Dr Belleville IL 62220

JONES, SEABORN GUSTAVUS, JR., b. Macon, GA, Oct. 10, 1942, s. Seaborn Gustavus and Anne (Reynolds) J.; m. Betty Aberlin; 1 dau., Bronwyn Price. Author: Drowning From the Inside Out (poetry), 1982; contrbr. N.Y. Qtly, Amelia, Xanadu, other publs. Student Mercer U., Macon, 1961-63. Mem. prodn. staff WQED-TV, Pitts., 1972-73; location mgr. Cinema Nova Ltd., San Francisco, 1973-79; prin. Clean Hands, Macon. Home: 949 Magnolia St Macon GA 31201

JONES, TIMOTHY DALE, b. Saginaw, MI, Dec. 13, 1949; s. Richard Isham and Melba Esther (Guy) J. Author: Fandom Directory, 1981. Ed. public schls., Saginaw. Owner, mgr. Painted Pony Book Store, Saginaw, 1978—. Home: 1027 N Harrison St Saginaw MI 48602

JONES, VICKI SUE, b. Pontiac, MI, Sept. 4, 1957; d. James E. and Deanna (Bradley) J. Contrbr. poems to anthols. Med. Asst. Diploma, Ferndale Medical Careers, 1978. Direct care worker Macomb Oakland Regional Center, Sterling Heights, MI, 1980—. Recipient Golden Poet award World of Poetry, 1985, 86. Home: 46 Brookside Pl Northville MI 48167

JONG, ERICA MANN, b. NYC, Mar. 26, 1942; d. Seymour and Eda (Mirsky) Mann; m. Allan Jong (div. Sept. 1975); m. Jonathan Fast, Dec. 1977 (div. Jan. 1983); 1 dau., Molly. Author: (poems) Fruits & Vegetables, 1971, Half-Lives, 1973, Loveroot, 1975, At The Edge of the Body, 1979, Ordinary Miracles, 1983; (novels) Fear of Flying, 1973, Loveroot, 1975, How to Save Your

Own Life, 1977, Fanny, 1980 Parachutes and Kisses, 1984, Serenissima, 1987; (poetry and nonficton) Witches, 1981; (juvenile) Megan's Book of Divorce, 1984. BA, Barnard Coll., 1963; MA, Columbia U., 1965. Recipient Bess Hokin prize Poetry mag., 1971, Alice Faye di Castagnola award PSA, 1972; NEA grantee, 1973. Mem. AG, (dir. 1975), P&W, WG Am.-West, PEN. Address: Janklow 598 Madison Ave New York NY 10022

JONSSON, RICHARD EUGENE THOMAS, b. Cleveland Heights, OH, Feb. 10, 1935; s. John Eric Walter and Anna Patricia (McGrath) Johnson; m. Betty Lasap Calado, Aug. 14, 1984; 1 dau., Brenda Anne. Author: Full sails, 1971; contrbr. poetry, criticism, rvws. Contest ed.: Dragonfly mag., 1974-75. B.A. in Social Studies, Mexico City Coll., 1960; M.A. in English, Northeastern U., Boston, 1973. Library asst. San Diego Public Library, 1974-76; announcer Sta. WDCS-FM, Portland, ME, 1979-80; bilingual tutor Anchorage School Dist., 1980—. Recipient Marjorie Bertram Smith award, 1970, Bronze medal Centro Studi Scambi Internazionali, Rome, 1972, Harold G. Henderson award Haiku Soc. Am., 1975. Home: 223 Fawn Ct Anchorage AK 99515

JORDAN, BARBARA LESLIE, b. NYC, Sept. 30, 1915; d. William Methren and Maud (Prendergast) Leslie; m. Philip V.R. Schuyler, Jr., May 18, 1934 (div. May, 1935); 1 son, Philip V.R. III (dec. March 29, 1987); m. 2d, Richard Hanford Jordan, Sept. 26, 1936 (div. Nov. 1950); 1 son, Richard H.; m. 3d, John Ingle Yellott, June 2, 1951 (dec. Dec. 27, 1986); stepchildren—John I., Ann. Author (poems): Web of Days (3 bks.), 1949, Comfort the Dreamer, 1955, Silver Song, 1980; contrbr. poet and wrtr. to various periodicals and newspapers. Student pvt. schls., NYC and Farmington, CT. Editor, NY Jr. League magazine, 1933-34; Treasurer, John Yellott Engineering, Phoenix, AZ, 1958—. Recipient Bronze Medal For Achievement in Poetry, Natl Soc. of Arts and Letters, 1987 Mem. PSA, NY Women Poets, Natl. Soc. of Arts & Letters (Valley of the Sun). Home: 901 W El Caminito Dr Phoenix AZ 85021

JORDAN, PAUL RICHARD, b. Wayland, KY, Apr. 1, 1926; s. Paul Jackson Jordan and Versa (Hall) Moore; m. Dorothy Ruth Wright, Apr. 20, 1954; 1 son, Paul R. Author: Water Crisis in Kentucky?, 1966. Reporter Herald Dispatch, Huntington, W.Va., 1951-52. Contrbr. fiction and non-fiction to mags. including Reader's Digest, Sci. Tchr., Green's mag., others. News editor: Paintsville Herald, Ky., 1950-51. BA in Journalism, U. Ky., Lexington, 1950. Newsman, corr. AP, Louisville-Frankfort, Ky., 1952-62; mag. ed. Ky. State Govt., Frankfort, 1962-67; officer pub. info. U.S. Govt., Washington, 1968-81; free-lance wrtr., 1981—. Home: 663 Maple St Lebanon KY 40033

JORDAN, ROBERT, see Rigney, James Oliver, Jr.

JORDEN, DORIS MARIE, b. Sikeston, MO, Feb. 18, 1943; d. Moree Hunt and Cora Mae (Sturdivant) Barron; m. John Jorden, June 20, 1970; 1 son, Larry Hunt. Author: Sister Katie, The Prayer, 1984, The Restaurant, 1984, The Confrontation, 1984, Thunderstorms, 1985. AA, Malcolm X Coll., 1975-78; B in Writing, Columbia Coll., 1983, postgrad., 1983—. Med. transcriber Mt. Sinai Hosp., Chgo., 1978-82; tchr. Columbia Coll., Chgo., 1983—. Address: 5035 W Washington Chicago IL 60644

JORGENSEN, RICHARD EDWARD, (Jorg), b. Nanchang, China, May 1, 1948; s. Charles William, Jr., and Dorothy J. Author: The Fire Above, The Lake Below, 1971; Revolution Fruit Pie, 1978; ed. The Stone mag. 1975—. BA in English, Franklin and Marshall Coll., 1969; MFA in Creative Writing, Cornell U., 1971. Canvasser, crew chief Greenpeace, San Francisco, 1979-80, canvass coordinator, Santa Cruz, Calif., 1980—; owner, pub. The Stone Press, 1975—. Grantee PEN, 1975-77, NEA, 1978, CCLM. Home: 116 2d St Santa Cruz CA 95060

JOSEPH, FRED, JR., b. Thibodaux, LA, Aug. 9, 1942; s. Fred and Adele (Jabour) J.; m. Patricia Ann Stallone, Apr. 7, 1973; 1 son, J. Brent. Bus. columnist: Counselor, 1981. Contrbr. sci. and bus. articles to jnls. and mags. B.S. in Biological Scis./Chemistry, U. Southwestern La., 1965; postgrad. La. State U., 1963-64, 68-69. Med. Research specialist La. State U. Med. Schl., New Orleans, 1971—; owner, pres. Imprintas Co., New Orleans, 1973—; bus. and sci. wrtr., 1981—. Address: Box 50265 New Orleans LA 70150

JOSEPH, FRANK SAMUEL, b. Chgo., Jan. 17, 1940, s. Irwin S. and Marjorie Lee (Baum) J.; m. Carol Anna Jason, Jan. 20, 1979; 1 son, Samuel Jason. BA, Northwestern U., 1962. Author XX Century Fund, Washington, 1970-71; ed. Washington Post, 1971-75, Observer Pub. Co., Washington, 1975-77; ed., prtnr. United Communications Group, Bethesda, Md., 1979-82; pub., propr. Key Communications Group, Bethesda, 1982—. Mem. Newsletter Assn. (pres. Washington chpt. 1985). Office: Key Comm 4715 Cordell Ave Bethesda MD 20814

JOSEPH, JACK, see Challem, Jack Joseph

JOSEPH, JENNIFER, b. NYC, Apr. 10, 1961; s. Mark Richard and Ruth (Edelman) Joseph-Long. Author: The Future Isn't What It Used To Be, 1984; ed. The Manic D Sampler, 1987; contrbr to Lobster Tendencies, Beef, 1/2 Beat, The Closest Penguins. BA, Oberlin Coll, 1982. Freelance writer Epics to Epitaphs, San Francisco, 1982-84, ed. and pub. Manic D Press, 1983—, ed. San Francisco Poetry Qtly, 1985—. Staff mem., San Francisco Arts Fest '85. Address: Manic D Press 1853 Stockton San Francisco CA 94133

JOSEPH, RONALD K., b. Ft. Wayne, IN, Aug. 10, 1962, s. Ronald K. and Elizabeth M. (Gordon) J. Ed. Breathless mag., 1985—. Wrkg. on novel, short-story collection. BA in English Lit., SUNY-Binghamton. Graduate NYU summer inst. mag. and book pubg., 1986. Home: 910 Broad St Endicott NY 13760

JOVANOVICH, WILLIAM, b. Louisville, CO, Feb. 6, 1920; s. Iliya M. and Hedviga (Garbatz) J.; m. Martha Evelyn Davis, Aug. 21, 1943. AB, U. Colo., 1941; grad. study, Harvard, 1941-42, Columbia, 1946-47. With Harcourt Brace Jovanovich, Inc. (formerly Harcourt, Brace & Co.), NYC, 1947—; assoc. editor Harcourt Brace Jovanovich, Inc., 1947-53, vp, dir., 1953-54, pres., chief exec. officer, dir., 1955-70, chmn., chief exec. officer, dir., 1970—; Regent prof. U. Calif.-Berkeley, 1967; lectr. Adelphi U., 1973. Author: Now Barabbas, 1964, Madmen Must, 1978; also essays. Regent State of N.Y., 1974-77. Life Fellow Morgan Library, NYC. William Jovanovich lectrs. in pub. affairs named in his honor, Colo. Coll., 1976. Office: HBJ 1250 Sixth Ave San Diego CA 92101

JOWERS, LAWRENCE VICTOR, b. Jacksonville, FL, Aug. 26, 1921; s. Verdyree Victor and Minnie Jowers; m. Lula Mae Sutton, Dec. 18, 1942; children: Lawrence Victor, Gerald Drayton, Ronald Gregory, Barbara Eileen Jowers Burt. Ed.: The Recorder, 1949—. BS, U.S.C., 1942; MD, Emory U. 1944. Diplomate Am. Bd. Family Practice, Am. Bd. Law and Medicine; genl. practice medicine, Columbia, S.C., 1945—. Served to lt. (j.g.) USN, 1945-48; PTO. Home: 231 Lanewood Rd Columbia SC 29210

JOY, PERIHAN DURSUN, b. Istanbul, Turkey, Nov. 26, came to U.S., 1976. Contrbr. poems to anthols. Wrkg. on collection of different interest areas. Diploma in Fine Arts and Art History, Gazi Egitim Enstitusu, Ankara, Turkey, 1967. Recipient award for poetry Cagdas Yayinevi, Istanbul, 1963. Home: Box 5381 Takoma Park MD 20912

JOZWIK, FRANCIS XAVIER, b. El Paso, TX, Jul. 4, 1940; s. Andrew and Dagmar Elizabeth (Wettermark) Jozwik; m. Phyllis Anne Angevine, Dec. 27, 1974; children—Melissa, John, Monika. Author: Plants for Profit, 1984; editor: national Greenhouse Industry, 1985-86; wrkg. on Gypsy Gardens—A Complete Guide to Growing and Enjoying Potted Flowers and Plants. PhD,U. of Wyoming, 1966. Research Scientist Commonwealth Scientific Organization (Canberra, Australia), 1967-69; owner Johnny Appleseed, Inc. (Casper, WY), 1969—, Andmar Press (Mills, WY), 1984-86. National Science Foundation Fellow, 1963. Mem. Garden Wrtrs. Soc. of Amer. Office: Box 217 Mills WY 82644

JUBA, ROBERT DAVID, (Dr. Juba), b. Chgo., Oct. 15, 1948, s. Robert L. and Ophelia Marie (Outlaw) D. Author: Flights into Time, 1979; contrbr. poetry to Haight Ashbury Lit. Jnl, World of Poetry, other lit. mags. and publs. Student U. Wis., Madison, 1967-70, San Francisco Art Inst., 1971-72. Multi-cultural arts adminstr Meary Gallery, Santa Cruz, Calif., 1977-78, Evidence Music Co., Oakland, Calif., 1979-81; drama critic Lorraine Hansberry Theatre, San Francisco, 1982—; mgr. Dr. Juba's Cafe, San Francisco, 1986—. Grantee Deep Stream Fdn., Santa Cruz, 1978, Rhapsody Intl., San Francisco, 1982, Lewis Fdn., 1983-84. Mem. AAP, West Oakland Wrtrs.' Workshop, Western Addition Cultural Center. Office: Metaphor 109 Minna St San Francisco CA 94105

JUDD, RALPH WAVERLY, b. Zillah, WA, Apr. 22, 1930, s. Van Evrie and Theona Ruth (Stanhope) J. Contrbr. to Reader's Digest, Natl Lampoon, numerous U.S. Coast Guard publs. Wrkg. on non-fiction books, articles. BS, U.S. Coast Guard Acad., 1954; MBA, George Washington U., 1964, Phd (candidate) Clayton Univ., 1957. Served with U.S. Coast Guard, 1949-72, commanding officer Loran Sta., Con Son, Vietnam, 1966-67, ret. commdr., 1972. Mem. NWC, Am. Film Inst., ACLU, Media Alliance, Wrtrs Connection. Home: 1330 Bush St Apt 4H San Francisco CA 94109

JUDYWHITE, , see White, Judith Ann

JULIAN, ALFRED, see Menkus, Belden

JURCZYK, IRENE DONOHUE, (Irene Michaels, Irene Mary Donohue), b. Columbus, OH, Aug. 20, 1949; d. James Francis and rosalie Frances (Ryan) Donohue: m. Glenn Joseph Jurczyk, Dec. 27, 1969; children—Michael Glenn, Kathryn Ryan, James Patrick. Author novel:

Frenchman's Mistress (B. Dalton best seller list 1981), 1980. Wrkg. on novels: Tomorrow, Rosalie and Alias Mae; screenplay with Richard Noone, The Eye of Horus. Student in Jnlsm. U. Ga., 1967-70. Ed.-in-chief The Sr. Tribune, Atlanta, 1974-78; technical ed. Kurt Salmon Assoc., Atlanta, 1978-81; cons., lit. agent, Atlanta, 1981-87; marketing dir. News/Sun Newspapers, Decatur, GA, 1987—. Mem. RWA, Dixie Council Authors & Jnlsts., Atlanta Writing Resource Center. Home: 3904 Longview Dr Atlanta GA 30341

JUST, WARD SWIFT, b. Michigan City, IN, Sept. 5, 1935, s. Franklin Ward and Elizabeth (Swift) J. Author: To What End, 1968, A Soldier of the Revolution, 1970, Military Men, 1970, The Congressman Who Loved Flaubert, 1973, Stringer, 1974, Nicholson At Large, 1975, A Family Trust, 1978, Honor, Power, Riches, Fame and the Love of Women, 1979, In The City of Fear, 1982, The American Blues, 1984, The American Ambassador, 1987; short stories included in Best American Short Stories, 1972, 73, 76, O. Henry Collection, 1985, 86; contrbr. short fiction to The Atlantic, Harper's, Esquire, Gentleman's Qtly, other publs. Wrtr. Newsweek, Chgo. and Washington, 1959-62, London, 1963; wrtr. The Reporter, Washington, 1962-63, The Washington Post, 1965-70; wrtr.-in-residence Philips Acad., Andover, Mass., 1982-84. Home: Box 342 RFD Vineyard Haven MA 02568

JUSTICE, DONALD RODNEY, b. Miami, FL, Aug. 12, 1925; s. Vascoe J. and Mary Ethel (Cook) J.; m. Jean Catherine Ross, Aug. 22, 1947; 1 son: Nathaniel Ross. Author: The Summer Anniversaries, 1960, Night Light, 1967, Departures, 1973, Selected Poems, 1979, Platonic Scripts, 1984, The Sunset Maker, 1987; ed., The Collected Poems of Weldon Kees, 1960. BA, Univ. of Miami, 1945; MA, Univ. of N.C., 1947; PhD, Univ. of Iowa, 1954. Professor, Univ. of Iowa, 1957-65, 71-82; Syracuse Univ., 1965-70; Univ. of Florida, Gainesville, 1982—. Recipient Lamont Award in Poetry, 1959, Guggenheim fellowship, 1976, Pulitzer Prize (poetry), 1980, Harriet Monroe prize, 1984, NEA grants, 1967, 73, 80. Home: 2717 SW 5th Pl Gainesville FL 32607

JUSTICE, JACK RONALD, b. Middlesboro, KY, July 2, 1940; s. Scott A. and Ethel M. (Hodge) Justice; m. Judy A. Cappel, May 15, 1965; children—Thomas, Laura, Nancy. Author: Country Birthday; contrbr. poems to lit. mags., anthols, including Hampden-Sydney, WIND, Hiram Poetry Rvw. B.S., U. Cin., 1963. Pharmacist, SuperX, Cin., 1966—. Teaches U. of Cin., Med. Ctr., Coll. of Pharmacy. Mem. PSA, AAP, Mensa. Home: 9023 Shadetree Dr Cincinati OH 45242

KACHMAR, JESSIE K., b. Portland, OR, Mar. 28, 1913; d. Charles and Fanny (Mida) Kalmans; m. John F. Kachmar, Dec. 26, 1946; 1 child, Carlajean. Author: Snow Quiet, 1976, Apertures to Anywhere, 1979; editor and contbr. Chicago Choice, 1959-60; contrbr. (anthologies): Port Chicago Poets, 1966, Twigs, 1976, Our Only Hope Is Humor, 1972, The Women Poet, 1985; contbr., cons. editor Gallery Series; contrbr. poetry to various jnls including Poetry Northwest, Chicago Dial a Poem, others. BA, U. Wash. Tchr., Chgo. area, 1962-85. Recipient Women Writers Hon., U. Minn., 1953; Triton Intl. Poetry Contest winner, 1980, 85. Home: 9300 Home Ct Des Plaines IL 60016

KACOHA, MARGIE, b. Hammond, IN, Oct. 29, 1955; d. Joseph and Sophie (Bojda) K. Contrbr. articles to mags. including Vegetarian Times, Cat Fancy, Wrtr.'s Digest, others. B.A. in Communications, Ind. U., 1978, M.A. in Jnlsm., 1982. News wrtr. Sta. WFIU, Bloomington, IN, 1977; reporter Sta. WJOB, Hammond, IN, 1977-78, Sta. WLNR, Lansing, IL, 1978-80; fgn. lang. proofreader Techno-Graphics, Lansing, 1982-86; free-lance corr. The Times, Hammond, 1987—. Home: 4245 Henry Ave Hammond IN 46327

KAEL, PAULINE, b. Petaluma, CA., June 19, 1919; d. Isaac Paul and Judith (Friedman) K.; 1 dau., Gina James. Author: I Lost it at the Movies, 1965, Kiss Kiss Bang Bang, 1968, Going Steady, 1970, Deeper into Movies, 1973, Reeling, 1976, When the Lights Go Down, 1980, 5001 Nights at the Movies, 1982, Taking It All In, 1984, State of the Art, 1985; contrbr. to The Citizen Kane Book, 1971, Student, U. Calif. at Berkeley, 1936-40. Movie critic New Republic mag., 1966-67, New Yorker mag., 1968—. Recipient Polk award in criticism, 1970, Natl. Book award for Deeper into Movies, 1974, Front Page award Newswomen's Club N.Y., 1974, 83; Guggenheim fellow, 1964. Address: New Yorker 25 W 43d St New York NY 10036

KAETER, MARGARET, b. St. Cloud, MN, Dec. 21, 1957; d. James Louis and Dorothy (Kuchera) K.; m. Michael John Olesen, Aug. 18, 1979; 1 dau., Gretchen Hulda Kaeter Olesen. Ed., Farm Store Merchandising Mag., 1984—. BA, U. MN, 1980; postgrad. in Agriculture, U. MN, 1983—. Free-lance ed., Mpls., 1979-81; ed. Commonwealth Terrace Corp., St. Paul, 1980-81; ed. internal pubs., Super Valu, Mpls., 1981-82; mng. ed. Miller Pub. Co., Mpls., 1982-84, ed. Farm Store Mag., 1984—. Mem. AAEA. Home: 2292 Long Ave St Paul MN 55114

KAHN, HANNAH, b. NYC, June 30, 1911; d. David and Sarah (Seigelbaum) Abrahams; m. Frank M. Kahn, Mar. 5, 1941 (dec. Jan. 1975); children—Melvin, Daniel, Vivial Dale. Author: Eve's Daughter, 1963, Time, Wait, 1983; poetry to American Scholar, Harper's, Saturday Review, Ladies Home Journal, others. BA, Fla. Atlantic U. in Boca Raton, 1974. Ed. Miami Herald, 1958-73. Mem. PSA, AAP, Women in Communications. Home: 3301 NE 5th Ave No. 318 Miami FL 33137

KAHN, PAUL, b. Queens, NY, Sept. 20, 1949. Author: A Kansas Cycle, 1973, January, 1976, The Secret History of the Mongols, 1985. Coeditor Bezoar, 1975-80. BA, Kenyon Coll., 1971. Computer researcher Brown U., Providence, 1985—. Mem. Mongolia Soc. NEA poetry fellow, 1979-80. Office IRIS Brown U. Box 1946 Providence RI 02912

KAHN, ROGER, b. Bklyn., Oct. 31, 1927; s. Gordon Jacques and Olga K. K.; m. Joan Rappapert, July 14, 1950 (div. Oct. 1963); 1 son, Gordon Jacques II; m. Alice Lippincott Russell, Sept. 22, 1963 (div. Apr. 1974); children: Roger Lawrence, Alissa Avril; m. Wendy Meeker, Sept. 27, 1974. Author: The Passionate People, 1968, The Battle for Morningside Height, 1970, The Boys of Summer, 1972, But Not to Keep, 1978, The Seventh Game, 1982, Good Enough to Dream, 1985. Student, Univ. Coll., NYU, 1944-47. Sports reporter N.Y. Herald Tribune, NYC, 1948-55; sports editor Newsweek, NYC, 1956-60; editor-at-large Saturday Evening Post, NYC, 1963-69; asst. prof. journalism L.I.U., 1967; adj. prof. creative writing Colo. Coll., 1972; dir. nonfiction writers workshop U. Rochester, 1974, 75, 77. Recipient Best Mag. Sports Article of Yr. award E.P. Dutton Pubs., 1960, 69, 70, 80, 82. Mem. AG, U.S., Soc. Authors and Journalists. Home: 231 Hessian Hills Rd Croton-on-Hudson NY 10520

KAHN, SY MYRON, b. NYC, Sept. 15, 1924, s. Max and Sophie (Wagner) K.; 1 son, David M. Author poetry books: Our Separate Darkness, 1963, Triptych, 1964, A Later Sun, 1966, The Fight is with Phantoms, 1966, Another Time, 1968, Facing Mirrors, 1980; ed., contrbr.: Interculture: A Collection of Essays (with Martha Raetz), 1975, Devour the Fire: Selected Poems of Harry Crosby, 1984; contrbr.: Essays in Modern American Literature, 1963, The Twenties: Poetry and Prose, 1966, The Thirties: Fiction, Poetry, Drama, 1967, Modern American Drama: Essays in Criticism, 1968, The Forties: F, P, D, 1969, The Fifties: F, P, D, 1970, Survey of Contemporary Literature, 1971, Tennessee Williams: A Collection of Critical Essays, 1977, Tennessee Williams: A Tribute, 1977, Dictionary of Literary Biography (vol. 4), 1980, A Bibliographical Guide to Midwestern Literature, 1981, Modern American Dramatists (vol. I), 1984, other books. BA in English, U. Pa., 1948; MA in English, U. Conn., 1951; PhD in English, U. Wis.-Madison, 1957. Asst. prof. English Beloit (Wis.) Coll., 1955-60, U. South Fla., Tampa, 1960-63; prof. English and drama U. of the Pacific, Stockton, Calif., 1963-86, chmn. dept. drama, 1970-81; exec. dir. Fallon House Theatre, Columbia, Calif., 1969-84; ret. U. of the Pacific, Prof. Emeritus, 1986, vis. prof. American Studies U of Wisles, Wales, Jan.-July 1987, vis. prof. Theater, Justus Liebig U., West Germany, Oct.-Dec. 1987; Fulbright prof. Am. lit. Conf. for Intl. Exchange of Scholars, Greece, 1958-59, Poland, 1966-67, Austria, 1970-71, Portugal, 1985-86; recipient Borestone poetry award, 1964, Promethean Lamp prize, 1966, Grand Prize in poetry, U. of the Pacific, 1985; Salzbourg Seminar fellow Salzbourg Inst., Austria, 1972. Mem. MLA, AAUP, Am. Theatre Assn., Phi Kappa Phi. Address: Box 4322 Stockton CA 95204

KAIL, ROBERT LEE, b. Spencer, IA, s. Konrad and Mabel (Pedersen) K.; m. Josephine Sperrazza; children—Mary Ellen, John, Andrea. Author novels: Dealer's Choice, 1979, Swastika, 1981, Wind Nor Rain, 1983, Seekers of the Sky, 1983. BM, Morningside Coll., Sioux City, IA; Lic. Phil, U. of Zurich, Switzerland. Freelance wrtr., ed., musician, U.S.M.A. Band, West Point, NY. Home: 18 Stuyvesant Oval New York NY 10009

KAIN, VIRGINIA ROSE, see Hill, Hyacinthe

KAISER, ERNEST DANIEL, b. Petersburg, VA, Dec. 5, 1915; s. Ernest Bascom and Elnora Blanche (Ellis) K.; m. Mary Gertrude Orford, 1949; children: Eric, Joan. Author: In Defense of the People's Black and White History and Culture, 1970; co-author: Harlem: A History of Broken Dreams, 1974; editor: A Freedomways Reader, 1978; co-founder, assoc. editor: Freedomways mag., 1961-85; contrbg. editor: Science and Society; co-editor: The Negro Almanac, 1971, Black Titan: W.E.B. DuBois, 1970 Paul Robeson: The Great Forerunner, 1978, 2d ed., 1985; contrbr. essays, book reviews, introductions, bibliographies to numerous books, mags., newspapers. Student, CCNY, 1935-38. Adminstrv. assoc. Schomburg Center for Research in Black Culture, N.Y. Pub. Library, 1945-86; ret. 1986; cons., reviewer, editor manuscripts about blacks for McGraw-Hill Pub. Co., R.R. Bowker Co., W.E.B. Du Bois papers U. Mass. Press, Chelsea House Pubs. Adviser and 10 introductions for Arno Press series The American Negro: His History and Literature, 145 vols. Home: 31-37 95th St East Elmhurst NY 11369

KALASKI, ROBERT JOHN, b. Scranton, PA, Feb. 1, 1941, s. Victor Walter and Sophie (Andrukaitus) K.; m. Christine Pauline Janesko, June 22, 1963; children—Robert Jr., Barbara Lynn, Kenneth John. BS in Public Relations, Boston U. Public info. officer U.S. Air Force, Kansas City, Mo., 1962-66; assoc. ed. Intl. Assn. Machinists and Aerospace Workers, Washington, 1966-77, ed. The Machinist, 1977—, dir. communications, 1979—. Mem. Intl. Labor Press Assn. (v.p. 1977-83), Intl. Labor Communications Assn. (pres. 1983-85), Aviation and Space Wrtrs. Assn., Am. Auto Racing Wrtrs and Broadcasters Assn. Office: Intl Assn Mach 1300 Connecticut Ave NW Washington DC 20036

KALECHOFSKY, ROBERTA, b. NYC, May 11, 1931; d. Julius Joseph Kirchik and Naomi Jacobs; m. Robert Kalechofsky, June 7, 1953; 2 sons, Hal, Neal. Author: (fiction) Solomon's Wisdom; Justice, My Brother; Orestes in Progress, Stephen's Passion, La Hoya; (essays) Rejected Essays, and Other Matters; (prose poem) The 6th Day of Creation; monograph on George Orwell; contrbr. to jnls and lit mags, anthologies, including The Best Am. Short Stories (1972); ed. and intros: The Echad Series, 1979, South African Jewish Voices, 1981, Phoenix Rising, 1982, Jewish Writing From Down Under, 1984, The Text of the Holocaust, 1985, Haggadah for the Liberated Lamb, 1985, poetry of Israel Eliraz; intro. James Parkes: End of Exile, 1983, Kaputt, by Curzio Malaparte, 1984, The Jewish Cat Book, 1984; ed. and pub: Encounters with Israeli Authors, 1983, Echad 5: Intl. Anthology Jewish Women Writers. BA, Bklyn. Coll., 1952; PhD, NYU, 1970. Instr. dept. English, Bklyn. Coll., 1956-59, 62-63; ed. and pub. Micah Pubs., Marblehead, Mass., 1975—. Vol., Comms. for Soviet Jewry and Ethiopian Jewry Rescue Missions, 1974—. NEA grantee, 1979, 82, 83. Mem. COSMEP, Assn. Jewish Pubs, Assn. Jewish Studies, Israel Bibliophile Soc.; Animal Rights activist. Address: 255 Humphrey St Marblehead MA 01945

KALIAN, ROBERT P., b. NYC, July 1, 1939; s. Frank and Irene K.; m. Linda J. Siviglia, Feb. 11, 1967; 2 sons, Christopher, Dennis. Author: A Few Thousand of the Best FREE Things in Am., 1979 (ed. and revd. each year). BS, NYU, 1961. Pres. Roblin Enterprises, Yonkers, NY, 1973—. Served to cpl, US Army Artillery, 1959-60, CK. Address: 23 Rosedale Rd Yonkers NY 10710

KALLAS, PHILLIP G, b. Beaver Dam, WI, Aug 31, 1946; s. John J. and Angeline J. (Jaspers) K.; m. Priscilla L. Lake, June 1, 1974; 2 daus.: Rachel, Rebekah. Contrbr. articles to Wis. Academy Rvw, The Pinery, Markers, Inscriptions, A Place Called Plover Portage, The Eve of Revolution. BS, Wis. State U.-Stevens Point, 1969, MAT, 1974. Bookseller Chpt. 1 Book Shoppe, Stevens Point, Wis., 1975-77. Vice-pres., Portage County Hist. Soc., Stevens Point, Wis., 1976—, ed. Wis State Old Cemetery Soc. 1981—, hist. comm. chmn., 125 Comm., 1982-83, bd. dirs. Portage Co. Vets Serv. Comm., 1983—. Served to spcl. 4, US Army 1969-71, Vietnam; retired, Stevens Point, 1971—; recipient many medals. Mem. Vietnam Vets Am., 1982-85, TKE Alumni Assn, 1979-. Address: 308 Acorn St Whiting Stevens Point WI 54481

KALPAKIAN, LAURA ANNE, b. Long Beach, CA, June 28, 1945, d. William J. and Peggy Johnson; m. Julian P. McCreary, Jr., Mar. 18, 1977 (div. 1984); children: Bear, Brendan. Novelist: Tiger Hill (as Carenna Jane Grey), 1985, Beggars and Choosers, 1978, These Latter Days (selected by Brit. Good Books Book Club, New South Wales Book Club Assocs.), 1985, Ftirtugueto, 1986, Fair Augusto and Other Stories, 1986, Jerusalem's Road, 1987, Crescendo, 1987; contrbr. stories to Ararat, Woman's Own, Hawaii Rvw, Mickle St. Rvw., other publs.; contrbr. essays, interviews to Los Angeles Times, Ararat, Miami Herald, other publs. AB in History, U. Calif.-Riverside, 1967; MA in History, U. Del., 1971; postgrad. U. Calif.-San Diego, 1973-77. Mem. faculty Lincoln U., Oxford, Pa., 1970-72, Muir Writing Program, U. Calif.-San Diego, 1973-77; freelance book critic, 1979—; vis. wrtr. Redlands (Calif.) U., 1980; vis. prof. English Western Wash. U., Bellingham, 1984—. Recipient 1st prize Intl. Short Story Competition, Stand Mag., 1983, PEN Los Angeles Center Award for Best Short Fiction, 1986. Mem. P&W, PEN, AG, Soc. Authors. Office: Dept Eng Wash Univ Bellingham WA 98225

KALUSE, KATHRYN ANN, (Kate Montgomery), b. Rochester, MN, Nov. 29, 1954; d. William Arnold and Willanna (Veit) Klause; m. Robert Lee Montgomery, Apr. 7, 1983. Author: Standard Alaska Prodution Company's Hazard Communication Program, 1986. Contrbr. articles to popular mags., profl. jnls. including Minn. Veterinarian, Pacific Fishing, others. B.S. in Veterinary Sci., U. Minn., 1977, D. Vetrinary Medicine, 1979.. Veterinarian, Mt. McKinley Animal Hosp., Fairbanks, AK, 1979-80, 82-84; clinic mgr., staff veterinarian Sand Lake Animal Hosp., Anchorage, 1982-82; rlief veterinarian Kenai Veterinary Clinic, AK, 1985; environmental cons. Standard Alaska Production Co., Anchorage, 1986—. Mem. Am. Veterinary Med. Assn., Interior Alaska Vetrinary Med. Assn. (prs. 1982-84). Home: 3224 LaTouche F-2 Anchorage AK 99508

KAMENETZ, RODGER LEE, b. Balt., Jan. 20, 1950; s. Irvin and Miriam (Kierr) K.; m. Moira Liane Crone, Oct. 14, 1979; 1 child, Anya. Author: (poems) The Missing Jew, 1979, Nympholepsy, 1985; (essays) Terra Infirma, 1985. BA, Yale U., 1970; MA, Johns Hopkins U., 1972. Assoc. prof. English, La. State U., Baton Rouge, 1981—. Home: 3175 Hundred Oaks Ave Baton Rouge LA 70808

KAMINSKY, ALICE R., b. NYC; d. Morris and Ida (Spivak) Richkin; m. Jack Kaminsky; 1 son, Eric (dec.). Author: George Henry Lewes as Critic, 1968, Logic: A Philosophical Introduction, 1974; editor: Literary Criticism of George Henry Lewes, 1964, Chaucer's Troilus and Criseyde and the Critics, 1980, The Victim's Song, 1985. BA, NYU, 1946, MA, 1947, PhD, 1952. Mem. MLA, AG, Chaucer Soc., Office: Dept Eng SUNY Cortland Cortland NY 13045

KAMINSKY, MARC, b. NYC, Oct. 8, 1943; s. Peretz and Mildred (Schwartzman) K.; m. Madelaine Santner; 1 dau., Julia Suzanne. Author: (poetry) Birthday Poems, 1972, A New House, 1974, A Table with People, 1982, Daily Bread, 1982, The Road from Hiroshima, 1984; (prose) What's Inside You It Shines Out of You, 1974; (chapbook) The Rime of Patch McFinn, 1963; contrbr. prose and poetry to New York Qtly., Denver Qtly., New York Times, Socialist Rvw., Sun, others; represented in anthologies such as Blood to Remember: American Poets on the Holocaust and Ten Jewish American Poets; also writer of theatre and radio pieces. BA, Columbia U., 1964, MA, 1967. Dir. artists and elders project Teachers and Writers Inc., NYC, 1978-81; dir. Inst. on Humanities, Arts and Aging, Brookdale Ctr. on Aging at Hunter Coll., NYC, 1981-85; dir. program devel. Associated YM-YWHAs of Greater New York, 1985—. Active Mobilization for Survival, NYC. Recipient Art of Peace Fdn. award, 1984; grantee Santvoord Fdr., 1978, Emet Fdn./Liebovitz Fund, 1985. Mem. Gerontol. Soc. Am. (chmn. com. humanities and arts 1985), PSA, AAP. Home: 291 Eleventh St Brooklyn NY 11215

KAN, KAN, see Chapman, Constance Ann

KANABUS, HENRY, b. Amberg, Bavaria, W. Ger., Feb. 25,1949; arrd. U.S., 1950; s. Henryk and Maria (Drozdowski) K.; children: Sarah, David. Author poetry: Floodlights, 1975, Carapace, 1978, Chesterfield, 1979, Rain in the Shelter, 1982, The War Magician, 1984, Reptiles in Confinement, 1987, Harmonia's Necklace, 1987; prose: Battle Figurines, The Jeffie Papers, The October Killings, The Fires of Cygni and Other Stories, Roadkill; contrbr anthologies: 15 Chgo. Poets, Banyan Anthology 2, The Hat Issue; contrbr to Oyez Rvw, B-City, UP LATE: American Poetry Since 1970; ed. Stone Wind Mag., 1973-75. BA in English lit., Northeastern Ill. U., 1972, MA in anthropology, 1976. Poet-in-the-schls. Ill. Arts Council, Chgo., 1976-77; pub. relations spclst pub. Library System, Chgo., 1977-81; freelance poet/writer/reader, Chgo., 1982— founder, Analytic Design and Consultation, 1986. Recipient Ill. Arts Council award for poetry. Address: 2925 N Kenneth Ave Chicago IL 60641

KANANOWITZ, ANNA GILSON, b. Perth Amboy, NJ, July 16, 1924; d. Stephen and Anna (Kokus) DoBo; m. Maurice Robert Gilson, July 13, 1942 (div. Dec. 26, 1958); children: Joan, Dolores, Robert, Louis, Richard, Laura; m. 2d Edward Kananowitz, Feb. 17, 1962 (div. Oct. 6, 1966); 1 son: Daniel. Contrbr. National poetry Anthology, 1986. Ed. Perth Amboy public schls. Nurse's aide in Perth Amboy General Hospital, 1964-80. Home: 149 Madison Ave Perth Amboy NJ 08861

KANE, PATRICIA, b. Cin., May 9, 1955; m. Edward Kane, Oct. 16, 1983; 1 son, Shawn. Author: Mommy, I'm Hungry, 1982, Food Makes the Difference, 1985. PhD, Columbia Pacific U., 1983. Chief of nutrition, Carl C. Markwood, Sacramento, CA, 1980-82. Mem. NY Acad. Scis., British Soc. Nutritional Med. Home: 5 Osprey Dr Millville NJ 08332

KANE, WILLIAM L., b. Hot Springs, SD, Aug. 6, 1938; s. Joe A. and Marie (Marking) K.; m. Mary Virginia Widtfeldt, June 3, 1961; children—Nick, David, Todd. Contrbr. poems to anthols. Grad. public schls., Edgemont, SD, and Colby, KS. Sheriff, Rawlins County, Atwood, KS, 1973-81; self-employed truck driver, 1981—. Served to 1st class seaman U.S. Navy, 1954-55. Recipient Golden Poets award World of Poetry, 1985, 86, 6th place, 1986. Home: Rt 2 Atwood KS 67730

KANGAS, JAMES RICHARD, b. Chgo., June 22, 1944, s. Ernest Arvid and Helmi Mary (Kohtala) K. Contrbr. poetry to: New Letters, Poet Lore, Cottonwood Rvw, Pteranodon, numerous other lit mags. BA, No. Mich. U., 1966;

AM, U. Mich., 1967, AMLS, 1968. Librarian Chgo. Public Library, 1968-72; librarian Flint (Mich.) Public Library, 1973—; violist Flint Symphony Orchestra, 1975—. Home: 1506 Indiana Ave Flint MI 48506

KANIGEL, ROBERT, b. Bklyn., May 28, 1946; s. Charles and Beatrice (Wolshine) Kanigel; m. Judith Schiff, June 28, 1981; 1 son, David Saul. Author: Apprentice to Genius: The Making of a Scientific Dynasty, 1986. Contrbr. articles, essays, book rvws. to mags., newspapers, including N.Y. Times Mag., Science 85, Washington Post, Hippocrates, The Sciences, Psychology Today, others. Columnist: Balt. Evening Sun, 1982—. Contrbg. ed.: Johns Hopkins Mag., 1977—. B.S., Rensselaer Polytehnic Inst., 1966. Recipient A.D. Emmart award for writing in the humanities, 1979; Smolar award for excellence in Am. Jewish jnlsm., Council of Jewish Fdns., 1978, 80; citation for best articles of yr. Council for Advancement and Support of Edn., 1982, Silver medal for best articles of yr, 1985; Simon Rockower, 2nd place award for excellence in Jewish jnlsm., Am. Jewish Press Assn., 1983. Mem. NASW, EWA, Natl. BK. Critics Circle, Balt. Wrtrs. Alliance. Address: 2643 N Calvert St Baltimore MD 21218

KANO, SUSAN LESLIE, b. Boston, MA, Sept. 28, 1959; d. Cyrus H. and Dorothy (Weinz) Kano. Author: Making Peace with Food: A Step-by-Step Guide to Freedom from Diet/Weight Conflict, 1985. BA in Psychology and Sociology, Wesleyan U., 1982. Speaker for schools and hospitals, 1984—; workshop leader Simmons Coll. Health Center (Boston), 1983—. Home: 229 Highland Ave Somerville MA 02143

KAONIS, DONNA CHRISTINE, b. San Francisco, Nov. 2, 1949; d. Donald Templin and Dorothy I. (Tronnes) Rush; m. Charles Chapman, Sept. 2, 1972 (div. Oct. 1976); m. 2d, Donald Keith, Dec. 17, 1977. BA, Muskingum Coll., 1971. Acct. exec./writer Accent Studios, San Diego, 1976—; ed./pub. & feature wrtr. Collectors' Showcase, 1981—. Office: Accent Studios 1018 Rosecrans San Diego CA 92106

KAPLAN, DAVID MICHAEL, b. NYC, Apr. 9, 1946; s. Sidney and Minnie Marie (Henson) K.; m. Elizabeth Hope Crighton, Aug. 16, 1976 (div.). Author: Comfort (short stories), 1987; contrbr.: The Atlantic, Ohio Rvw, Newsday, Miss. Rvw, N.Mex. Humanities Rvw, The Wooster Rvw, Shankpainter, Yellow Silk. BA, Yale U., 1967; postgrad. Univ. Iowa, 1985—. Instr. English NC Advancement Schl., Winston-Salem, 1965-66; curriculum cons. Learning Inst., Durham, NC, 1968-71, creative dir. Shadowstone Films, Durham, 1971-76; prdn. dir. Natl. TV News, Los Angeles, 1976-84; free-lance writer, Los Angeles, 1984-85; instr. English Univ. Iowa, 1985—. Recipient film awards CINE, NY Intl. Film and TV Fest., PRSA, Am. Me. Writers Assn.; fellow Fine Arts Work Ctr., Provincetown, Mass., 1984-85, Yaddo, 1985, Millay Ctr., Austerlitz, NY, 1985. Mem. AWP. Address: 2645 Thorntree Dr Pittsburgh PA 15241

KAPLAN, JUSTIN, b. NYC, Sept. 5, 1925; s. Tobias D. and Anna (Rudman) K.; m. Anne F. Bernays, July 29, 1954; children: Susanna Bernays, Hester Margaret, Polly Anne. Author: Mr. Clemens and Mark Twain, 1966, Lincoln Steffens, A Biography, 1974, Mark Twain and His World, 1974, Walt Whitman: A Life, 1980; Editor: Dialogues of Plato, 1948, With Malice Toward Women, 1949, The Pocket Aristotle, 1956, the Gilded Age, 1964, Great Short Works of Mark Twain, 1967, Mark Twain, A Profile, 1967, Walt Whitman: Complete Poetry and Collected Prose, 1982; Contrbr. to N.Y. Times, New Republic, Am. Scholar, others. BS, Harvard U., 1944, postgrad., 1944-46,. Free-lance editing, writing, NYC, 1946-54; sr. editor Simon & Schuster, NYC, 1954-59; prose writer-in-residence Emerson Coll., Boston, 1977-78, Recipient Pulitzer prize for biography, 1967, Natl. Book award in arts and letters, 1967, Am. Book award for biography, 1981; Guggenheim fellow, 1975-76. Fellow Am. Acad. Arts and Scis. Mem. AAIAL, Massachusetts Hist. Soc. Home: 16 Francis Ave Cambridge MA 02138

KAPLAN, MILTON, b. NYC, Mar. 6, 1910; s. Israel and Rebecca Kaplan; m. Marion Wall, Aug. 24, 1939 (dec. 1967); children: Joan, Jonathan; m. Marie Grimaldi, July 29, 1973; 1 step-child, Maria. Author: Radio and Poetry, 1949; In a Time between Wars, 1973; co-ed. The World of Poetry, 1965; contrbr. poetry and prose to Harper's, New Yorker, Harper's Bazaar, Am. Scholar, Redbook, Poetry: A Mag. of Verse, Partisan Rvw., New Republic, Nation, Saturday Rvw, others. PhD, Columbia U., 1946. Prof. English, Tchrs. Coll., Columbia U., NYC, 1964-75; ret., 1975. Mem. PSA. Home: 554 Summit Ave Oradell NJ 07649

KAPLAN, STUART R(ONALD), b. NYC, April 1, 1932; s. William and Nettie (Weiss) K.; m. Marilyn Reck, Nov. 16, 1957; children: Mark Stuart, Petr John, Michael Louis, Christopher Ned, Jennifer Anne. Author: Mining, Minerals, and Geoscience, 1965, Tarot Cards for Fun and Fortune Telling, 1970, Official Rules of the Tarotrump Card Game, 1972, Tarot lassic, 1972, James Bond 007 Tarot Book, 1973, The American Historical Playing Card Deck: Portraits in American History, 1974, Devil's Tarot, 1974, Tarot of the Witches, 1974, Royal Fez Moroccan Tarot, 1975, Spanish Tarot, 1975, Viscontisforza Tarochi, 1975, Oswald Wirth Tarot, 1976, Starter Tarot, 1977, The Encyclopedia of Tarot, vol. 1, 1978, vol. 2, 1985, vol. 3, 1986, Angel Tarot, 1980, Egyptian Tarot, 1980, (with Godfrey Dowson) Hermetic Tarot, 1980, Minchiate of Florence, 1980, (with Giorgia Tavaglione) Oracle of the Sibyl, 1980, Prager Tarot, 1980, Cagliostro Tarot, 1981, Heron's Tarot of Marseilles, 1981, (with Dirk Dykstra) Ravenswood Eastern Tarot, 1984, Sicilian Tarot, 1981, Tarocchi of Mantagna, 1981, Papus Tarot, 1982, Emoil Gavat Taro, 1983, Solleone Tarot, 1983, Ukiyoe Tarot, 1983, Tarocco Egiziano, 1983, Cary-Yale Visconti Tarocchi, 1984, Hanson-Roberts Tarot, 1984. Certificate, Sorbonne, Univ. of Paris, 1951; BS, Univ. of Penn., 1955. Employed by Standard Industries, Inc. (conglomerate holding co.), 1958-73, v.p., 1960-73; founder and pres., U.S. Games System, Inc., 1968—. Military service: U.S. Army, 1956-58. Office: 38 East 32nd St New York NY 10016

KARAGIANIS, MARIA ELIZABETH, b. Winthrop, MA, May 24, 1948; d. Fred S. amd Latjerome Taschioglou Karagianis; m. Timothy Patrick O'Neill, May 19, 1982; children—Katherine, Elizabeth. Contrbr. articles to mags., newspapers including Boston Globe Mag., Chgo. Tribune, Redbook, others. A.B. in English Lit., Simmons Coll., 1970. Staff wrtr. Rand Daily Mail, Johannesburg, South Africa, 1977-78, Boston Globe, 1973-85; free-lance wrtr., 1985-86; sr. policy advisor Mayor Raymond Flynn, Boston, 1986—. Mem. Boston Women Pub. (named Best Mag. Jnlst. 1982). Home: 18 Barrington Rd Boston MA 02124

KARBOWIAK, CAROL JEAN, (Ford Matthews), b. St. Marys, OH, July 3, 1966; d. Raymond John and Evelyn Ann (Fleck) K. Contrbr. articles to newspapers, yearbooks; author news for radio. Student Bowling Green State U., 1984—. Staff wrtr. Wapakoneta Daily News, OH, 1986, Fremont News-Messenger, OH, 1987; copy ed. Bowling Green News, OH, 1987. Mem. SPJ (secy.). Home: 131 State St B-7 Bowling Green OH 43402

KARL, JEAN EDNA, b. Chgo., July 29, 1927; d. William A. and Ruth (Anderson) K. Author: From Childhood to Childhood, 1970, The Turning Place, 1976, Beloved Benjamin Is Waiting, 1978, But We Are Not of Earth, 1981, Strange Tomorrow, 1985. Editor children's books Abingdon Press, 1956-61; dir. children's book dept. Atheneum Pubs., NYC, 1961-85, v.p., 1964-85, also dir.; field ed., 1985—. BA, Mt. Union Coll., 1949, hon. doctor of letters, Mt. Union Coll., 1969. With Scott, Foresman & Co., Chgo., 1949-56; Mem. joint com. ALA-Children's Book Council, 1961-66; chmn., 1961-63; bd. dirs. Children's Book Council, 1963-66, 74-77, pres., 1965; bd. dirs. Children's Services div. ALA, 1971-74. Mem. Freedom to Read Com.Assn. Am. Pubs., 1974-79, Vice-pres. and pres, elect, U.S. sect. Intl. Bd. on Book for Young People, 1986-87, pres., 1987-88; administrator Don Freeman Grant in Aid of the Soc. of Children's Book Wrtrs., 1986—; trustee Mt. Union Coll., 1970-73, 1986—. Home: 20 Rockford Rd Wilmington DE 19806

KARL, MICHAEL, see Ritchie, Michael Karl

KARNI, MICHAELA JORDAN, (Karin Berne, Diana Burke), b. Danville, IL, Apr. 25, 1941; d. Charles Stanley and Evelyn Lucille (Williams) Jordan; m. Shlomo Karni, Feb. 7, 1961; children—Gideon, Sarah. Author: (as Diana Burke) The Heart of the Matter, 1980, The Impoverished Heiress, 1981; (as Karin Berne) Bare Acquaintances, 1985, Shock Value, 1985; False Impressions, 1986. BA, summa cum laude, U. N.Mex., 1964, MA, 1968. Recipient M-3 program award Ford Fdn., 1962-64, Telfair Hendon Meml. prize U. N.Mex. English Dept., 1963; James scholarship U. Ill.-Urbana, 1959-61. Mem. Phi Kappa Phi. Home; 2313 Ada Pl NE Albuquerque NM 87106

KARPACS, JOANNE MARY, b. Phila., Feb. 2, 1945; d. Joseph Raymond and Mae Lucile (Jackson) Murtaugh; m. George Michael Karpacs, Mar. 26, 1983; 1 dau., Theresa Marie. Contrbr. articles to Living with Preschoolers, 1985, Creative Years, 1986, The Messenger of the Sacred Heart, Our Family, Woman's Touch. Free-lance wrtr., 1983—. Recipient hon. mention World of Poetry, 1983, Silver Poet Award, 1986. Home: 523 Buckingham Dr Sewell NJ 08080

KARR, JAY MILES, b. Des Moines, IA, Aug. 17, 1926; s. Jay Arthur and Ferne Cleo (Gordon) K.; m. Phyllis Elaine Hammer, Dec. 21, 1952; children—Jay Matthew, Juliet Alison, April Celeste. Contrbr. Janus Lit., December, Missouri Life mags; fiction, criticism. Pub., Kingdom House (novel revivals): King's Row, 1981, Paris Mitchell of King's Row, 1986. BA, Drake U., 1944-50; MFA, U. Iowa, 1952-56. Asst. ed. books Meredith Pub. Co., Des Moines, 1950-52; asst. prof. English Univ. Idaho, Lewiston, 1958-61, Humboldt State Coll., Arcata, Calif., 1961-65; prof. Westminster Coll., Fulton, Mo., 1965—. US Army, 1944-46, 11th A/B Div., Philippines/ Japan. Campaign worker Adlai Stevenson, John

Kennedy, Jerry Brown. Mem. AAUP, AWP. Address: 309 W 7th Fulton MO 65251

KARSHNER, ROGER KAY, b. Columbus, OH, Nov. 10, 1928; s. Noble Porter and Edith Bookwalter (Maag) K.; m. Mary Kathryn Rockfield, Sept. 5, 1948; children—Julie, David, Sally, Molly. Author stageplays: Hot Turkey at Midnight, 1975, Monkey's Uncle, 1975, Love on the Cusp, 1976, The Man with the Plastic Sandwich, 1979, The Dream Crust, 1981; author drama books: 30 Modern Monologues, 1980, 30 Modern Scenes, 1980, Monologues They Haven't Heard, 1982, Scenes They Haven't Seen, 1982, More Monologues They Haven't Heard, 1983. Student pub. schls., Springfield, OH. Mem. WGA, DG. Song writer, Broadcast Music, Inc. Home: 10470 Riverside Dr 201 Toluca Lake CA 91602

KASH, WYATT KEITH, b. Chgo., Mar. 26, 1955; s. Edward Ellery and Doris (Glenn) K.; m. Ellen Raymond, Oct. 11, 1986. Contrbr. numerous articles to mags. & nwsprs.; contrbr./ed. numerous consumer attitude & research projects. BS, Syracuse U., 1979. Free-lance writer/photog., 1975-80; material control supr. Parsons Corp., Prudhoe Bay, AK, 1975-77; field, then assoc. ed. National Home Ctr. News, NYC, 1980-82, exec. ed., 1982-83, ed.-in-chief, 1983—. Mem. SPJ. Office: Home Ctr News 425 Park Ave New York NY 10022

KASPER, MICHAEL, b. NYC, Jan. 7, 1947; s. Philip and Rachel (Goldsmith) K.; m. Mary Luce, Sept. 7, 1970; 1 son, Tobias. Author, illustrator: Chinese English Sentence Cards, 1979, Odds 'n' Ends from the Lost 'n' Found, 1980, 20 Trial Briefs, 1981, Billy! Turn Down That TV!, 1983, All-Cotton Briefs, 1985, Verbo-Visuals, 1985, Plans for the Night, 1987. Contrbr. articles to mags. Ed.: The Northampton Herald, 1980-83. B.A., Harpur Coll., 1967; M.L.S., U. British Columbia, Vancouver, Canada, 1973. Librarian Lilly Public Library, Florence, MA, 1978—79, Amherst Coll., MA, 1978—. Grantee Line II, 1986; recipient award Wormwood Rvw., 1980. Home: 106 High St Florence MA 01060

KATZENBACH, JOHN STRONG MINER, b. Princeton, NJ, June 23, 1950; s. Nicholas deB. and Lydia Phelps (Stokes) K.; m. Madeleine H. Blais, May 10, 1980; children—Nicholas, Justine. Author: (novel) In the Heat of the Summer, 1982, 4th ed., 1987, The Traveler, 1987; (non-fiction) First Born: The Death of Arnold Zeleznik, Age Nine: Murder Madness, and What Came After, 1984. Reporter: The Trenton Times, NJ, 1973-76, The Miami News, 1976-79, The Miami Herald, 1981-84. Wrkg. on novel. B.A., Bard Coll., 1972. Mem. WG, MWA, PEN. Home: 186 ShutesburyRd Amherst MA 01002

KASTNER, CHRISTINE KRIHA, b. Cleve., Aug. 27, 1951; d. Joseph Calvin and Grace Margaret (Weber) Kriha; m. Donald William Kastner, June 30, 1979; 1 son, Paul Donald. Contrbr. articles: The Plain Dealer, New Cleve. Woman Jnl., other publs. Assoc. degree Lakeland Community Coll., 1976; BA, Cleve. State U., 1983. Sec. dept. public relations TRW Inc., Cleve., 1978-83, asst. ed., 1983-85; ed. Kaiser Permanente, Cleve., 1985—. Recipient gold ADDY award Am. Advt. Fedn., 1986, award of Excellence Women in Communications, 1987. Mem. Internat. Assn. Bus. Communicators (recipient Bronze Quill 1987). Home: 1383 Gordon Rd Lyndhurst OH 44124

KATOPES, PETER JAMES, b. NYC, June 29, 1947, s. James Peter and Evelyn (Pappas) K.; m. Norah Anne Nikolis, Jan. 16, 1971; children—Andrew, Jamie. Author: The Child-Killer, 1985; contrbr. to Confrontation, 1985, Source, 1984, Dictionary of Literary Biography, 1979, Black American Writers, 1978, numerous lit mags and publs. BA, St. John's Univ., 1973; MA, SUNY-Stony Brook, 1974, PhD,1978. Freelance ed. CBS Publs., NYC,1973-76; teaching asst. SUNY-Stony Brook, 1974-78; prof. Adelphi U., Garden City, N.Y., 1978—, asst. dean, 1984-85. Mem. lit. div. Queens Council on Arts, 1973. Served to 1st lt. U.S. Army, 1966-69; Vietnam. Mem. PSA, AG, P&W. Office: Univ Coll Adelphi Univ Levermore 217 Garden City NY 11530

KATSONOV, FLORENCE JEAN, see Kosoff, Flora May

KATZ, AMNON, b. Krakow, Poland, July 17, 1935, came to U.S., 1961, s. Benzion and Klara (Goldstoff) K.; m. Ora Minkovich, Nov. 4, 1959; children—Aya, Nets Hawk. Author: Classical Mechanics, Quantum Mechanics, Field Theory, 1965, Principles of Statistical Mechanics, 1967; translator classical English poetry to Hebrew for Gazit, Israel; contrbr. to Aleph, other Canaanite publs., Israel; ed.: Inverted-A, Inc. MSc, Hebrew U., Jerusalem, 1958; PhD, Weizmann Inst., Rehovot, Israel, 1961. Assoc. prof. Weizmann Inst., 1961-71; engring. specialist LTV Aerospace, Dallas, 1971-83; founder, since pres. Inverted-A, Inc., Grand Prairie, Tex., 1976—. Mem. Elder Canaanite Movement, Israel, 1968-70. Office: Inverted-A Inc 401 Forrest Hill Grand Prairie TX 75051

KATZ, COLLEEN BURKE, b. Newark, May 5, 1936; d. John Joseph and Marion Agnes (Dull) Burke; m. Robert A. Katz, Jan. 29, 1956; children—Warren, Howard, Judy. Works incl.: Craft Horizons, 1978, Women Today, 1978, Compass, 1979, Encyc. of Textiles, 1979, How to Collect Fine Crafts, 1980; contrbr.: Recorder Nwsprs., 1971-74, Worrell Newsprs., 1973. BA, Montclair State Coll., 1957. Ed., Woman's Day special intl. pubs., NYC, 1972-76; ed.-in-chief Butterick Fashion Mktg. Co., NYC, 1976-77, New Jersey Monthly, Morristown, 1982-85; ed. Insurance Rev., NYC, 1985—. Mem. SPJ, Amer. Soc. Mag. Eds., IABC. Office: Ins Info Inst 110 William St New York NY 10038

KATZ, ELIOT, b. Orange, NJ, Jan. 4, 1957; s. Harry S. and Toby K. Contrbr. poetry New Blood, Bombay Gin, Big Screen, Friction, NY Qtly, Passaic Rvw; co-ed. Long Shot. BA, Rutgers Coll., 1979, MA in English, 1981. Tching. asst. Douglass Coll., New Brunswick, NJ, 1980; printer Downtown Printing Ctr., New Brunswick, 1981—. Mem. P&W. Address: Box 456 New Brunswick NJ 08903

KATZ, MENKE, (Elchik Hiat, Menke Badanes), b. Michaleshik, Lithuania, June 7, 1906, came to U.S., 1920, s. Heershe Dovid and Badane (Gubersky) K.; m. Chaske Blacker, 1926 (div.); children—Troim Katz Handler, Noah (dec.); m. 2d, Ruth Rivke Feldman, July 30, 1950. Author poetry in Yiddish: Three Sisters, 1932, Dawning Man, 1935, Brenedik Shtetl (2 vols.), 1938, My Grandmother Myrna Speaks, 1939, A Story to be Told in Happier Days, 1941, The Simple Dream, 1947, Midday, 1954, Safad, 1979; in English: Land of Manna, 1965, Rockrose, 1970, Burning Village, 1972, Forever and Ever and a Wednesday (short stories), 1980, Two Friends (with Harry Smith), 1981, A Chair for Elijah, 1985; ed.: Anthology of Yiddish Poets (English translation), 1986, This Little Land, 1987. Ed., Columbia U., 1924-26, U. So. Calif. 1926-27, SUNY-Bklyn., 1946-48. Tchr. Jewish studies U.S. and Israel, 1936-74; lectr. on poetry, Kabala Jewish history numerous univs., 1920s—; ed.-in-chief Bitterroot Poetry Mag., NYC, 1962—. Recipient Stephen Vincent Benet award Poet Lore, 1969, 73, 74. Mem. PEN, PSA, World Poetry Soc. (Disting. Service citation 1972), United Poets Laureate Intl. (hon. poet laureate). Home: Mountaindale Rd Spring Glen NY 12483

KATZ, STEVE ROBERT, (Stephanie Gatos), b. NYC, May 14, 1935; s. Alexander and Sally (Goldstein) K.; m. Patricia Oliver Bell, June 5, 1956 (div. Apr. 1980); children: Avrum, Nikolai, Rafael. Author: The Lestriad, 1962; The Weight of Antony, 1965; The Exagggerations of Peter Prince, 1968; Creamy and Delicious, 1970; Posh, 1971; Saw, 1972; Cheyenne River Wild Track, 1972; Moving Parts, 1976; Stolen Stories, 1984; Wier & Pouce, 1984, Florry of Washington Heights, 1986. Asst. prof. Cornell U., 1962-67; lectr. fiction U. Iowa, 1969-70; adj. asst. prof. Queens Coll., CUNY, 1971-75; assoc. prof. U. Notre Dame, 1976-78; prof. English, U. Colo., Boulder, 1978—. Grantee N.Y. State Council, 1979, NEA, 1979, 82. Mem. WG, PEN. Home: 3060 8th St Boulder CO 80302

KATZ, SUSAN A., b. NYC, Dec. 3, 1939; d. Edward Maurice and Selma (Stark) Arons; m. Donald Ira Katz, M.D., June 20, 1961; children—David Lawrence, Elizabeth Cheryl. Author: Two Halves of the Same Silence, 1985, The Separate Sides of Need, 1984; poems in Lyrical Treasures: Classic and Modern, 1982, Anthology of Magazine Verse and Yearbook of Am. Poetry, other anthols; poetry in American Scholar, Arts Journal, Carleton Miscellany, other lit mags. BFA, Ohio U., 1961. Poet/tchr., NY Poets in the Schools, NYC,1977-85; book rvw. editor, Bitterroot Magazine, Spring Glen, NY, 1985—. Mem. PSA, AAP, Intl. Acad. of Poets. Home: 12 Timothy Ct Monsey NY 10952

KATZ, WILLIAM LOREN, b. Bklyn., June 2, 1927; s. Bernard and Madeline (Simon) K. Author: Eyewitness: The Negro in American History, 1967 (Gold Medal award for non-fiction NCCJ), Teacher's Guide to American Negro History, 1968, (with Warren J. Halliburton) American Majorities and Minorities: A Syllabus of United States History for Secondary Schools, 1970, The Black West: A Documentary and Pictorial History, 1971, (with Halliburton) A History of Black Americans, 1973, The Constitutional Amendments, 1974, Making Our Way: America at the Turn of the Century, 1975, Black People Who Made the Old West, 1977, Teaching Approaches to Black History in the Classroom, 1973, An Album of the Civil War, 1974, An Album of Reconstruction, 1974, Minorities in American History, Vols. I-VI, 1974-75, An Album of the Great Depression, 1978, An Album of Nazism, 1979, Black Indians: A Hidden Heritage, 1986, The Invisible Empire: The Ku Klux Klan Impact on History, 1986; editor, The American Negro: His History and Literature, 147 vols., 1968-71, (with James M. McPherson) The Anti-Slavery Crusade in America, 69 vols., 1969, Minorities in America: Picture Histories, 1972—, Pamphlets in American History, 1977-82; editorial bd. jnl: Black Studies, 1970-73; editorial dir.: (with Henry Steele Commager and Arthur Schlesinger, Jr.) Vital Sources in American History for High School Students, 168 vols., 1980; curator, The Black

West Exhibition, Schomburg, Br., NY Pub. Library, 1985-86. Contrbr. articles to Sat Rvw, Jnl Negro History, N.Y. Times, Jnl Negro Edn., Jnl Black Studies, Reader's Digest, others. BA, Syracuse Y., 1950; MA, NYU, 1952. Served with USNR, 1945-46. Home: 231 W 13th St New York NY 10011

KATZENBACH, JOHN STRONG MINER, b. Princeton, NJ, June 23, 1950; s. Nicholas deB. and Lydia Phelps (Stokes) K.; m. Madeleine H. Blairs, May 10, 1980; children—Nicholas, Justine. Author: (novel) In the Heat of the Summer, 1982, 4th ed., 1987, The Traveler, 1987; (nonfiction) First Born: The Death of Arnold Zeleznik, Age Nine: Murder Madness, and What Came After, 1984. Reporter: The Trenton Times, NJ, 1973-76, The Miami News, 1976-79, The Miami Herald, 1981-84. Wrkg. on novel. B.A., Bard Coll., 1972. Mem. WG, MWA, PEN. Home: 186 Shutesbury Rd Amherst MA 01002

KAU, LAWRIE ELIZABETH, b. Pioneer Mine, BC, Canada, Nov. 25, 1942; arrd. U.S.A., 1983; d. John and Patricia (Mooney) Peters; m. Vernon Tomlin Simpson, Aug. 22, 1962 (div. 1969); m. 2d Howard Bernard Kau, Jan. 22, 1962 (div. 1969); m. 2d Howard Bernard Kau, Jan. 29, 1983; 1 dau.: Aimee Nalani Oi Yung. Contrbr. poetry to anthols. B. Edn., Univ. of B.C., Vancouver, Canada, 1967; MFA, Instituto Allende, San Miguel de Allende, Mexico, 1968. Preschl. teacher, Christ United Methodist, Honolulu, Hawaii, 1985-86; tchr., Dept. of Ed., Honolulu, 1986—; freelance artist (as Erin Alway), poet, 1969—. Home:1539 Liholiho St Apt 204 Honolulu HI 96822

KAUFELT, DAVID A., b. NJ; m. Lynn Kaufelt; 1 son, Jackson. Novelist: Six Months with an Older Woman (made into TV movie), 1973, The Bradley Beach Rumba, 1974, Spare Parts, 1978, Late Bloomer, 1979, Midnight Movies, 1980, The Wine and the Music, 1981, Silver Rose (Lit. Guild and Doubleday Book Club main selection), 1982, Souvenir, 1983, American Tropic, 1987. BS in Econ., U. Pa.; MA, NYU. Former advt. exec.; past dir. public interest Henry St. Settlement, NYC; tchr. creative writing Upsala Coll. Sits on Fla. Endowment for the Hum. bd.; past pres. Founders Soc. Tennessee Williams Fine Arts Ctr., Key West; co-founder Key West Literary Seminar & Festival. Served with U.S. Army. Home: Box 153 Sugarloaf Shores FL 33044

KAUFFMAN, JANET, b. Lancaster, PA, June 10, 1945. Author: Writing Home (with Jerome J. McGann), 1978, The Weather Book, 1981, Places in the World a Woman Could Walk, 1984, Collaborators, 1986. BA, Juniata Coll., 1967, MA, PhD,U. Chgo., 1968, 1972. Recipient Pushcart prize V, 1980; Rosenthal award AAIAL for fiction, 1985; Mich. Council for Arts creative artist's grantee, 1984; NEA fellow, 1984. Home: 1321 Beecher Rt 3 Hudson MI 49247

KAUFFMANN, LANE, b. Washington, July 24, 1921; s. Philip Christopher and Nancy (Lane) K.; m. Faith Diana Lilien, Oct. 17, 1959; children—Christopher Lane, Jill Suzanne. Author: The Perfectionist, 1954, Six Weeks in March, 1956, A Lesser Lion, 1958, Waldo, 1960, An Honorable Estate, 1964, Another Helen, 1968, A Plot of Grass, 1970, The Villain of the Piece, 1973; trans. Vicente Silva & His 40 Bandits, 1947. Address: 5 Wagon Wheel Ct Glen Arm MD 21057

KAUFFMANN, STANLEY JULES, b. NYC, Apr. 24, 1916; s. Joseph H. and Jeannette (Steiner) K.; m. Laura Cohen, Feb. 5, 1943. Author: The Hidden Hero, 1949, The Tightrope, 1952. A Change of Climate, 1954, Man of the World, 1956, A World on Film, 1966, Figures of Light, 1971; editor: (with Bruce Henstell) American Film Criticism: From the Beginnings to Citizen Kane, 1973, Living Images, 1975, Persons of The Drama, 1976, Before My Eyes, 1980, Albums of Early Life, 1980, Theater Criticisms, 1983, Field of View, 1986. BFA, NYU, 1935. Assoc. editor Bantam Books, 1949-52; editor-in-chief Ballantine Books, 1952-56; editor Alfred A. Knopf, 1959-60; film critic New Republic. NYC, 1958-65, 67—, assoc. lit. editor, 1966-67, theater critic, 1969-79, Saturday Rvw, 1979-85; drama critic N.Y. Times, 1966. Recipient George Jean Nathan award for dramatic criticism, 1972-73, George Polk award for criticism, 1982, Edwin Booth award for contribution to New York theater, 1986; Ford Fdn. fellow for study abroad, 1964, 71; hon. fellow Morse Coll., Yale U., 1964; Guggenheim fellow, 1979-80. Address: 10 W 15th St New York NY 10011

KAUFMAN, AMY REBECCA, b. Long Beach, CA, Oct. 8, 1951, d. Dr. Albert Abraham and Betty (Rubinstein) Kaufman. Founder, pub. STORIES mag., 1982— (selections reprinted in Best Am. Short Stories 1984, and in Prize Stories 1985: The O. Henry Awards). BA, U. Calif.-Berkeley, 1972. Office: STORIES 14 Beacon St Boston MA 02108

KAUFMAN, BEL, b. Berlin, May 10, d. Michael J. and Lyala Kaufman; children—Jonathan and Thea Goldstine. Novelist: Up the Down Staircase (natl. best seller 65 weeks), 1965, Love, etc., 1979; contrbr. chap. on grandfather Sholom Aleichem to Abroad in America, 1976; author TV plays, lyrics for musicals; transl. Russian poetry in Poems of One World, 1943; contrbr. short stories, articles to numerous natl. mags. BA magna cum laude, Hunter Coll., NYC,1934; MA with first honors, Columbia U., 1936; LittD, Nasson Coll., 1965. Author, lectr., presenter fiction workshops for many colls. and univs. Winner short story contest NEA and PEN, 1983; recipient Paperback of Yr. Fiction award, 1966, Screenwriters Annl. award, 1966, Edl. Assn. of America awards for best articles on education, 1976 and 1979, Hunter Coll. Hall of Fame, 1972. Numerous plaques and awards from humanitarian orgns. Mem. AL, AG, PEN. Home: 1020 Park Ave New York NY 10028

KAUFMAN, DEBRA JANE, b. Bloomington, IL, Oct. 14, 1951; d. Rogers L. and Kathleen M. (Grusy) K.; m. Barrie W. Oblinger, July 16, 1978; children: Bryce, Darcy. Contrbr. poetry to Primavera, Sing Heavenly Muse, Penumbra, Pig Iron, Sunrust, Arts Jnl, Helicon Nine, other lit mags and anthology Cardinal. BA in English, U. Iowa, 1974. Ed. The Maine Issue, Portland, 1976-78; news corr. Portland Press Herald, Maine, 1978-80; copy ed. Law Library Jnl., Duke U. Law Library, Durham, N.C., 1984—. Recipient New Voices award N.C. Arts Council, 1984; artist-in-schls. award Durham Arts Council, 1986; Poets Broadcast System award N.C. Arts Council, Sta. WUNC, N.C. Wrtr.'s Network, 1986. Pres. N.C. Wrtr.'s Network. Home: Box 17002 Durham NC 27705

KAUFMAN, MARTIN, b. Boston, Dec. 6, 1940; s. Irving and Rose (Langbort) K.; m. Henrietta Flax, Dec. 22, 1968; children—Edward, Linda. Author: Homeopathy in America, 1971, American Medical Education: Formative Years, 1976, University of Vermont College of Medicine, 1979. Ed.-in-chief: Dictionary of Am. Med. Biography, 1984, Guide to Mass. History, 1988, Dictionary of Am. Nursing Biography, 1988; ed.: (with Loretta Higgins, Joellen Hawkins, Alice Friedman) Springfield, 1636-1986, 1986; editorial dir. Hist. Jnl. of Western Mass., 1972-79, Hist. Jnl. of Mass., 1980—. Wrkg. on historiographical guide to the history of Am. medicine, history of Am. schl. health. A.B., Boston U., 1962; M.A., U. Pitts., 1963; Ph.D., Tulane U., 1969. Asst. prof. Westfield State Coll., MA, 1969-72, assoc. prof., 1972-75, prof. history, 1975—, chairperson dept. of history, 1984—. Mem. Orgn. Am. Hisorians. Home: 666 Western Ave Westfield MA 01085

KAUFMAN, STUART J., (Sandy Stuart, Bobby Finn), b. Bklyn., Apr. 8, 1950, s. Martin Harris and Edith (Plonsker) K.; m. Debra Kaufman, Dec. 12, 1971; children—Jonathan, Maxwell. Author: Return to Black and White, 1976, Four Fingers Showing: A Chapbook, 1975, The Ultimate Cigar and Other Poems, 1985. BA, Bklyn. Coll., 1971, MFA, 1976. Assoc. prof. Bennington (Vt.) Coll., 1980-83; adj. prof. Adelphi U., Garden City, N.Y., 1984—. Mem. P&W, Natl. Testing Network in Writing, PSA. Home: 82 S Hewlett Ave Merrick NY 11566

KAUFMANN, JOSEPH GREGORY, JR., b. Phila., Feb. 23, 1953; s. Joseph Gregory and Mary Agnes (O'Donnell) K.; m. Kendra Sue Schell, July 29, 1978; 1 dau., Kathleen. Contrbr. articles to Army Aviation, 1984, U.S. Army Aviation Digest, 1985. BA in Engl., Niagara U., 1975; MA in Am. and Brit. Lit., U. Penn., 1987. Major, U.S. Army, var. U.S. locats., 1975—. Monthly writing award, U.S. Army Aviat. Dig., 1985. Mem. MLA, NCTE, Army Aviat. Assn. Am. Instr. dept of Engl. at U.S. Milit. Acad., West Point, NY. Home: 578-A Benedict Rd West Point NY 10996

KAUFMANN, S. MARIE, see Kaufmann, Sherri Marie

KAVALER, REBECCA, b. Atlanta, d. Emanuel and Mary (Yawitz) Boorstein; m. Frederic Kavaler; children—Ethan Matthias, Peter Joshua. Author: Further Adventures of Brunhild, 1978, Doubting Castle, 1984, Tigers in the Wood, 1986. BA, U. Ga. NEA fellow, 1979, 85, N.Y. State Creative Artists in Public Service program fellow, 1984. Home: 425 Riverside Dr New York NY 10025

KAVERMAN, DONALD LEE, b. Grand Rapids, MI, Sept. 27, 1952; s. Henry Louis and Wava Pauline (Kurtz) K.; m. Suzanne Marie Ketelaar, June 27, 1981. Book rvw. ed., Athletic Training, 1976-80, ed., 1985—. BA, MI State U., 1975, MA, 1977. Asst. athletic trainer, Northwestern U., Evanston, IL, 1976-77, The Detroit Lions, Pontiac, MI, 1977-80; co-ordinator sports med., Ferris State Coll., Big Rapids, MI, 1980—. Home: 17291 Outer Dr Big Rapids MI 49307

KAYE, ALAN, see Horowitz, Shel Alan

KAYE, EVELYN, b. London, Oct. 1, 1937; came to U.S. June, 1963; m. Christopher J. Sarson, Mar. 1963; children—Katrina, David. Author: Crosscurrents: Children, Families and Religion, 1981, (with Ann Loring) Write and Sell Your TV Drama!, 1985, (with Janet Gardner) The Parents Going Away Planner, 1986, The Hole in the Sheet: A Modern Woman Looks at Orthodox and Hasidic Judaism, 1987; contrbr. to N.Y. Times, Ladies Home Jnl, Parents, Glamour,

Writers Digest, Pub. Wkly., other mags. and nwsprs. Staffmember, Reuters News Agency, Paris, 1961-62, The Guardian, Manchester, Engl., 1962-63; indep. jnlst. and author, 1974—. Mem. AG, ASJA, SPJ. Office: 147 Sylvan Ave Leonia NJ 07605

KAYE, RASA, see Brittain, Rasa

KAZIN, ALFRED, b. Bklyn., June 5, 1915; s. Charles and Gita (Fagelman) K.; m. Caroline Bookman, May 23, 1947 (div.); 1 son, Michael; m. Ann Birstein, June 26, 1952 (div.); 1 dau., Cathrael; m. Judith Dunford, May 21, 1983. Author: On Native Grounds, 1942, A Walker in the City, 1951, The inmost Leaf, 1955, Contemporaries, 1962, Starting Out in the Thirties, 1965, Bright Book of Life, 1973, New York Jew, 1978, An American Procession, 1984, A Writer's America, 1987; co-author: Introduction to the Works of Anne Frank, 1959; General Introduction to Dell Edition of the Novels of Theodore Dreiser, 1960; others.; editor: The Viking Portable William Blake, 1946; Editor:F.Scott Fitzgerald, The Man and His Work, 1951, Moby-Dick, 1956, Introduction to Selected Stories of Sholem Aleichem, 1956, The Open Form: Essays For Our Time, 1961, The Selected Short Stories of Nathaniel Hawthorne, 1966; Co-editor: The Stature of Theodore Dreiser, 1955; co-editor: Emerson: A Modern Anthology, 1958; The Ambassadors (James), 1969; contrbr. articles to newspapers, mags. BSS, CCNY, 1935; AM, Columbia U., 1938; LittD, Adelphi U., 1965, Y. New Haven, 1976, Hebrew Union Coll., 1982. Lit. editor New Republic, 1942-43, contrbg. editor, 1943-45, Fortune Mag., 1943-44. Writer-in-residence, Am. Acad. in Rome, 1975. Guggenheim fellow, 1940, 1947; Rockefeller fellow, 1945; NEH sr. fellow, Stanford, 1977-78; Recipient George Polk Meml. award for criticism, 1966; Brandeis U. Creative Arts award, 1973; Hubbell medal MLA, 1982. Mem. Natl. Inst. Arts and Letters, Am. Acad. Arts and Scis. Office: Eng Dept CUNY 33 W 42d St New York NY 10036

KEARNEY, LAWRENCE MICHAEL, b. Oxford, England, Feb. 18, 1948; s. James and Margaret Mary (Brindley) Kearney. Author: Kingdom Come, 1980; poetry in Atlantic Monthly, Massachusetts Rvw, Paris Rvw, Chicago Rvw, Pushcart Prize VI, Poets West, other lit mags and anthologies. BA, SUNY at Buffalo, 1970; MFA, U. of AZ, 1975. Tchr., U. of AZ, Tucson, 1972-75; instr., Wayne State U., Detroit, MI, 1978-79. Awards: Guggenheim Fellowship, 1984-85, NEA Fellowship, 1981-82; Pushcart Prize, 1981. Home: 3 Arlington St Cambridge MA 02140

KEARNS, JOSEPHINE ANNA, (Josie), b. Flint, MI, Oct. 21, 1954; d. James V. and Gladys Hilda (Randall) Luchinbell; m. Joseph Matthew Matuzak, July 18, 1981. Author: Life After the Line, 1988; contrbr. poetry to many mags and anthologies. BA, U. of Michigan, Flint, 1983. Director, Visiting Writers Program, U. of Michigan, Flint, 1983-86; contrbr. edit., BRIX Magazine, 1985-86. Creative Artist Award from Michigan Council for the Arts, 1986. Mem. Poetry Resource Center, Flint Institute of Arts, (pres.) Genesee Writers, dir. of Visisting Wrtr. series/Young Wrtrs Academy, Univ. of Michigan-Flint. Home: 431 Thomson Flint MI 48503

KEATING, JOHN RODERICK, (Claudio mbu) b. Buenos Aires, Argentina, Jan. 5, 1941; s. Laurence Freeman K. and Margaret Joan (Henzell) de Ley. Author: Guidelines (text), 1984, Assemblage, 1985; contrbr. articles on Argentina to N.Y. Times. BA, Columbia, 1962; MA, NYU, 1964. Instr., C.W. Post Coll., Greenvale, NY, 1967-70; adj. lectr. Bklyn. Coll., 1970-74, Lehman Coll., Bronz, NY, 74-80; adj. assoc. prof. Bklyn.Ctr. L.I.U., 1985; writing coach Birch Wathen 1986—. Mem. NCTE, WPA. Home: 80 Wooster St New York NY 10012

KEATS, JOE, see McCarty, Jessie Louis Henry

KEEBLE, JOHN ROBERT, b. Winnipeg, Man., Can., Nov. 24, 1944, s. Raymond Charles William and Olivia Mae (Wallace) K.; m. Claire Sheldon, Sept. 4, 1964; children—Jonathan, Zeke, Carson. Author: Crab Canon, 1971, Mine (with Ransom Jeffery), 1974, Yellowfish, 1980, Broken Ground, 1987. BA magna cum laude, U. Redlands, 1966; MFA, U. Iowa, 1969. Wrtr.-in-residence Grinnell (Iowa) Coll., 1969-72; assoc. prof. eastern Wash. U., Cheney, 1973—. Guggenheim fellow, 1982-83. Mem. PEN. Home: RR 2 Box 142-7 Medical Lake WA 99022

KEEL-WILLIAMS, MILDRED YVONNE, b. Chadbourn, NC, Sept. 20, 1954, d. Clarence and Alice Katy (Suggs) Keel; m. Michael Gavin Williams, Sept. 12, 1982. Author: Legacies of a Shopping Bag Lady (poetry), 1984; ed.: Gifts (with Lasana K. Harewood), 1981, Waterfalls (with Zakee Nadir), 1986; contrbr. poetry to Freshtones, 1978, Afro-Realism/A New Era in Third World Literature, 1979, Gifts, 1981, Black and in Brooklyn: Creators and Creations, 1983. AAS, Fashion Inst. Tech., NYC, 1974. Assoc. dir., project mgr. Erasmus Neighborhood Fedn., Bklyn., 1985—; co-founder, ed. Muse Fedn. Ink, Jamaica, N.Y., since 1980. Mem. P&W, Collective of African Am. Pubs., Cross-Section African Am. and Caribbean Fine Arts Assn. Office: Box 642 Saint Albans Sta Jamaica NY 11412

KEELEY, A.H., see Hutcherson, Harmon Harding

KEELEY, EDMUND, b. Damascus, Syria, Feb. 5, 1928; came to U.S., 1939; s. James Hugh and Mathilde (Vossler) K.; m. Mary Kyris, Mar. 18, 1951. Author: The Libation, 1958; Six Poets of Modern Greece, 1960; The Gold-Hatted Lover, 1961; George Seferis: Collected Poems, 1967; The Impostor, 1970; C.P. Cavafy: Passions and Ancient Days, 1971; Voyage to a Dark Island, 1972; C.P. Cavafy: Selected Poems, 1972, C.P. Cavaty: Collected Poems, 1975; Odysseus Elytis: The Axion Esti, 1974; Cavafy's Alexandria, 1976; Ritsos in Parentheses, 1979; Angelos Sikelianos: Selected Poems, 1979; Odysseus Elytis: Selected Poems, 1979; A Conversation with Seferis, 1982; Modern Greek Poetry: Voice and Myth, 1983; A Wilderness Called Peace, 1985; Yannis Ritsos: Exile and Return, 1985; ed. Modern Greek Writers, 1972; The Legacy of R. P. Blackmur: Essays, Memoirs, Texts; 1987. BA, Princeton U., 1949; DPhil., Oxford U., 1952. Instr. Brown U., 1952-53; prof. Salonika Univ., Greece, 1953-54, Princeton U., N.J., 1954—. Served with USN, 1945-46; mem. USAFR. Recipient Rome prize Acad. Arts and Letters, 1959; Landon transl. award AAP, 1980; Behrman award Princeton U., 1982; Guggenheim fellow, 1960, 72; NEA grantee, 1980, 81, 83, Fulbright grantee, 1985-87. Mem. ALTA (exec. bd.), PEN Am. Ctr. (exec. bd.), Modern Greek Studies Assn. (exec. com.). Home: 140 Littlebrook Rd Princeton NJ 08540

KEENAN, GERARD PATRICK, b. Paterson, NJ, Sept. 19, 1945, s. Leo James and Gloria Virginia (Cordisco) K.; m. Ellen Geraldine Murray, Sept. 10, 1966 (div. 1977); children—Paul Marius, Karen Christine Lee, Duane Raymond; m. 2d, Kathryn Marie Delahanty, May 14, 1977; children—Lindsay Renee, Kimberly Alexandra. Contrbr. articles: Brit. Heritage Mag., Sports Parade Mag., "The American" newspaper for Americans living in U.K., other publs.; columnist Darts World mag., Y.K., 1984—; wrtr., ed. Leisure London, USN publ. for personnel stationed in London, 1985. Student U. Md., London Campus, 2 yrs. Enlisted U.S. Navy, 1963, communications specialist U.S. Naval Communication Unit, London, 1980-83, ret.; editorial asst. Hdqrs. U.S. Naval Activities U.K., London, 1985; top secret control officer, security asst. comdr.-in-chief U.S. Naval Forces Europe, London, 1986—. Mem. Bur. Freelance Photographers. Address: Box 2 Cincusnaveur FPO New York NY 09510

KEENE, IRENE, b. Chgo., Aug. 3, 1953; d. William Henry and Imogene (Farr) K. Contrbr. poems to anthols. Wrkg. on short stories, collections of poetry. A.Applied Sci., Central YMCA Coll., 1979. Radiologic Tehnician U. Chgo. Hops., 1979—. Recipient Golden Poet award World of Poetry, 1986, 87, award of Merit, (6) 1986-87; award of Merit, Creative Enterprise, 1987, award of Appreciation, 1987. Home: 6127 S Greenwood Chicago IL 60637

KEER, KATHLEEN, see McGowan, Kathleen Keer

KEHRER, DANIEL M., b. Watertown, WI, Aug. 10, 1953; s. Paul Conrad and Margaret (Hoefs) K.; m. Kaye Kittrell, Oct. 27, 1979. Author: Pills & Potions: New Discoveries in Prescription and Over-The-Counter Drugs, 1983, Strategies For the Successful Internat. Investor, 1985, The Cautious Investor's Guide To Profits in Precious Metals, 1985, Making Risk in America: The Essence of Enterprise, 1987; contrbr. mags. & nwsprs. inclg.: Changing Times, Sci. Digest, Am. Health, Parade, McCall's, NY Times, Washington Post, L.A. Times, Chgo. Tribune. BA, Marquette U., 1975; postgrad., Amer. U., 1980-81. Bureau chief Washington Financial News Bureau, 1979-81; ed.-in-chief FACT Mag., NYC, 1981-87; Pres. Financial Press Alliance, NYC, 1985—; free-lance writer, Washington, NYC, 1979—; nationally syndicated columnist, "To Your Wealth," 1986; ed., Investment Monthly, 1987—. Mem. AG, Amer. Soc. Mag. Eds. Office: Box 4350 Grand Central Sta New York NY 10163

KEIM, KATHIE MARIE, b. Orlando, FL, Nov. 22, 1947; d. Frank Frederick and Althea Detweiler (Leidy) K. B.S. in Jnlsm., U. Fla., 1969. Reporter, Boca Raton News, FL, 1969-70; feature wrtr. Broward Times, Fort Lauderdale, FL, 1970-71; courthouse reporter Hollywood Sun-Tattler, FL, 1971-73; courthouse and bur. reporter Fort Lauderdale News, 1973-74; sports newsdesk copy ed. Morning Sentinel, Waterville, ME, 1974—. Mem. WIC. Home: Box 454 Waterville ME 04901

KEITHLEY, GEORGE, b. Chgo., July 18, 1935, s. James Balliet and Helen Catherine (Stuart) K.; children—Elizabeth, Clare, Christopher. Author: The Donner Party, 1972 (BOM Club selection), Song in a Strange Land, 1974, Scenes from Childhood, 1987, To Bring Spring, 1987; co-ed.: Themes in American Literature, 1974; contrbr.: 19 New American Poets of the Golden Gate, 1984; contrbr.: Writers' Forum, The Reaper, Studia Mystica, other lit publs. BA, Duke U., 1957; postgrad. Stanford U., 1957-58; MFA, U. Iowa, 1960. Prof. Calif. State U., Chico,

1962—; disting. vis. wrtr. U. Calif., Santa Barbara, 1984, 85. Recipient Duke Players Playwright award Duke U., 1977, DramaRama 1st prize Playwrights' Center San Francisco, 1982. Mem. PSA (Alice Fay DiCastagnola award 1973), New Eng. Poetry Club (Leighton Rollins award 1977, Rosalie Boyle award 1980, Daniel Varoujan award 1984), DG, AWP. Home: 1302 Sunset Ave Chico CA 95926

KELLEHER, JAMES P., b. Clondrohid, County Cork, Ireland, May 24, 1914, came to U.S., 1920, s. Jeremiah Michael and Ellen (Ring) K. Author: Call Me Monsignor, 1965, On Being a Catholic, 1976, Patriotism Is a Virtue, 1982, One More Time (poems), 1985. Wrkg. on collection of sermons. MA, Boston U., 1948, PhD, 1965; Ed.M. Harvard U., 1949. Prof. lit. St. Ambrose Coll., Davenport, Iowa, 1954-73, asst. to pres., 1973-74, v.p. research, 1974-79, prof. emeritus, 1981—. Home: 4028 Hillandale Rd Davenport IA 52806

KELLER, DAVID M., b. Berkeley, CA, May 26, 1941, s. Joseph Michaels and Kathleen (Clear) K.; m. Diana Ward Coe, Sept. 1, 1981. Author New Room (Quarterly Rvw of Lit poetry series), 1987; contrbr. poetry to over 45 jnls. and anthologies. AB, Harvard U., 1964; PhD, U. Wis., Madison, 1974. Recipient Annex 21 prize U. Nebr., 1981; grantee N.J. State Council on Arts, 1979, 82, recipient NJ State Council on Arts Artistic Merit award, 1985. Mem. US1 Poets' Coop., MLA, PSA, Eldridge Park Artists. Home: 14 N Valley Rd Roosevelt NJ 08555

KELLER, ROBIN KUYKENDALL, b. Great Lakes, IL, may 30, 1953; m. Karlton K. Keller; 2 children. Author: Choral Warmups. 1983, Voice Exercise System: High and Low Edition, 1986, Scorecard, 1985. B.Music, Millikin U., 1975; M.Music, Andrews U., 1978. Choir dir. Zion United Ch. of Christ, Baroda, MI, 1978—; instr. Lake Mich. Coll., Benton Harbor, MI, 1987—. Home: 9268 Amy Dr Baroda MI 49101

KELLEY, JAMES J., JR., b. Tuskegee, AL, July 7, 1949; s. James and Thelma (Chamblis) K.; m. Sharon E. Glanton, Dec. 27, 1975; children—Derek, Scott. Author: Positive Reinforces Can Decrease Childhood Fears, 1975, Have a Safe Halloween, 1977, Exceptional Children in Regular Education, 1980. B.S., Elizabeth City State Univ., 1971; M.Ed., Western Ga. Coll., 1977, Ed. S., Troy State U., 1981. Emotional conflict specialist Dothan City Schl., AL, 1976-84, parent involvement dir., 1984-86, principal, 1986—. Mem. NEA, Ala. Edn. Assn. Home: 1105 W Powell St Dothan AL 36303

KELLEY, KATE, b. Tulsa, May 2, 1955, d. John Lee and Ruth Mitchell (Olesen) Kelley; m. John Lewis Shobe, July 25, 1979; 1 dau., Rosalie Margaret. Author: Diver's Guide to Underwater America, 1980, rev. ed., 1982. BA in English, U. Tex., 1979. Mem. Austin Wrtrs.' League. Home: 2206 Lindell St Austin TX 78704

KELLMAN, JEROLD L., b. Chgo., Mar. 3, 1945; s. Bernard and Bertha (Goldberg) K.; m. Nancy L. Holleb, May 28, 1967; children—Gabriel, Gayle. AB, U. Mich.-Ann Arbor, 1967; MA, U. Calif.-Berkeley, PhD,1972. Ed. Consumer Guide, Skokie, Ill., 1972-80; pres. Gabriel House, Inc., Skokie, 1980—. Office: Gabriel House Inc 5045 W Oakton Skokie IL 60077

KELLY, ARMANDINE FRANCES, b. Barnegat, N.J., Oct. 22, 1947; d. John Joseph Kelly, Jr. and Armandine Clara (Kaupp). Author: Seasonal Stories for Family Festivals, 1987; contrbr. read-aloud stories Festivals Mag., 1981—; workshop columnist Modern Liturgy Mag., 1981—; contrbr. articles to Cath. mags. Tchr. 3d and 6th grades Camden Diocese Cath. schls., Lindenwold and Gloucester, N.J., 1969-71; tchr. reading Camden pub. schls., 1971—. Recipient Klein award, hon. mention Newspaper Inst. of Am., 1977. Mem. NWC, N.J. Ednl. Assn. Home: 1879 S 4th St Camben NJ 08104

KELLY, DAVID MICHAEL, (Dave Kelly), b. Grand Rapids, MI, June 23, 1938; s. Earl Peter and Margaret (Weisel) K.; m. Sylvia Hayden Neahr, Aug. 12, 1960; children: Jordu, Colette, Willow. Author: The Night of the Terrible Ladders, 1966; All Here Together, 1969; Summer Study, 1969; Dear Nate, 1969; Instructions for Viewing a Solar Eclipse, 1972; At a Time: A Dance for Voices, 1972; Did You Know They're Beheading Bill Johnson Today?, 1974; The Flesh-Eating Horse and Other Sagas, 1976; In These Rooms, 1976; Poems in Season, 1977; Filming Assassinations, 1979; Northern Letter, 1980; Great Lakes Cycle, 1980; contrbr. over 300 poems and short stories to lit. mags. and anthologies. BA, Mich. State U., 1961, MA, 1962; MFA, U. Iowa, 1966. Instr. English, U. Wis., Stout, 1962-65, East Iowa Community Coll., Muscatine, 1966-67; teaching asst. U. Iowa, Iowa City, 1965-66; assoc. prof. English, SUNY, Geneseo, 1967—. Recipient Discovery award NEA, 1969; spl. distinction award Elliston Fnd., 1980; lit. fellow N.Y. State Council Arts, 1974, 79, NEA, 1976. Mem. PSA, AWP. Home: Box 53 Geneseo NY 14454

KELLY, GEORGE ANTHONY, b. NYC, Sept. 17 1916; s. Charles W. and Bridget (Fitzgerald) K. Author: Who Should Run the Catholic Church?, 1976, The Battle for the American Church, 1979, The Crisis of Authority: John Paul II and the American Bishops, 1981, The New Biblical Theorists: Raymond E. Brown and Beyond, 1983. MA in Social Sci., Catholic U Am., 1943, PhD, 1946. Ordained priest Roman Catholic Ch., 1942, elevate to msgr., 1960; pastor St. Monica's Parish, NYC, 1945-56; dir Family Life Bur., 1955-65; dir. dept. edn. Archdiocese NYC, 1966-70; dir. Inst. Advance Studies in Cath. doctrine, St. John's U., Jamaica, NY, 1975—; exec. secy. Fellowship of Cath. Scholars, 1976, prs., 1986—. Address: Saint John's U Jamaica NY 11439

KELLY, JOSEPH JOHN, b. Phila., Jan. 16, 1948, s. Joseph John and Lillian Marie (Gallagher) K.; m. Maureen Frances Connelly, Sept. 6, 1979; 1 son, Brendan Joseph. Ed.: The Poet's Marketplace, 1984, The Year of the Pennsylvania Writer, 1985; contrbr. poetry to Plains Poetry Jnl, Kans. Qtly, Chariton Rvw, Poet Lore; contrbr. articles, rvws. to Renaissance and Reformation, Irish Lit. Supplement, Eire/Ireland; contrbr. to Phila. Inquirer, Camden (N.J.) Courier-Post. BA, Pa. State U., 1969; MA, Temple U., 1973, PhD in English, 1980. Instr. English, Temple U., Phila., 1974-80, Pa. State U., Abington, 1974-80; asst. prof. humanities Drexel U., Phil., 1980-81; freelance wrtr., 1981-83; spcl. programs officer Pa. Humanities Council, Phila., 1983—. Grantee N.J. Hist. Commn., 1983. Mem. P&W, MLA, Am. Com. Irish Studies. Home: 130 Peyton Ave Haddonfield NJ 08033

KELLY, MARY JO, (Jo Kelly), b. Baton Rouge, LA, Nov. 25, 1947; d. Theodore McKowen and Patricia Marilyn (Faul) Wilkes; m. John Richard Kelly, Jan. 20, 1967 (div. 1973); 1 dau., Patricia Lynn. Contrbr. articles to newspapers; author brochure. Contrbr., ed.: The Tchr.'s Voice, 1979-85, Now...EBRPAE, 1983-87, Straight Talk, 1983-87, Stateside Cajunland, 1985-87, The Bridge, 1984-87; contrbr., mem. editorial bd.: Instructional Resources, 1983-84; ed.: Action Line, 1978-79. B.S., La. State u., 1970, M.Edn., 1973, Ed.D., 1980. Tchr. Easton Baton Rouge Parish Schl., Baton Rouge, 1979-80; free-lance wrtr., producer The Video Co., Baton Rouge, 1984—. Home: 4442 Arrowhead St Baton Rouge LA 70808

KELLY, MARY LEE, b. Fargo, ND, Feb. 17, 1949; d. Warren E. and Leona M. (Ulven) K.; contrbr. to various mags and jnls; ed., Communique 1984-85; Repertoire, 1984. BA, U. MN, 1972; MA, Vanderbilt U., 1978. Managing ed. Soundings: An Interdisciplinary Jnl, Nashville, 1977-80; freelance wrtr., ed., 1980—; wrtr., ed. Combined Arts & Edn. Council of San Diego County, 1984-86. Mem. Seacoast Poets. Home: 15851 Highland Ct Solana Beach CA 92075

KELLY, RICHARD, b. NYC, Mar. 16, 1937; s. Bernard and Anna K.; m. Barbara Hunter, June 12, 1961. Books: The Night of Noah, 1968, The Best of Mr. Punch: The Humorous Writing of Douglas Jerrold, 1970, Douglas Jerrold, 1972, Lewis Carroll, 1977, The Andy Griffith Show, 1981 (rev. ed., 1984), George du Maurier, 1983, Graham Greene, 1984, Daphne du Maurier, 1987. BA, CCNY, 1959; MA, Duke U., 1960, PhD, 1965. Instr. English, U. N.C., Chapel Hill, 1964-65; asst. prof. English, U. Tenn., Knoxville, 1965-69, assoc. prof., 1969-75, prof., 1975—. Mem. South Atlantic MLA, Lewis Carroll Soc. of North Am., Phi Beta Kappa. Woodrow Wilson fellow, 1960; NDEA fellow, 1963. Office: Dept of Eng U Tenn Knoxville TN 37996

KELLY, ROBERT, b. Bklyn., Sept. 24, 1934; s. Samuel Jason and Margaret Rose (Kane) K.; Author (poetry): Armed Descent, 1961, Her Body Against Time, 1963, Round Dances, 1964, Words in Service, 1966, Devotions, 1967, Axon Dendron Tree, 1967 (video, 1985), Sonnets, 1968, Songs I-XXX, 1969, The Common Shore, 1969, Kali Yuga, 1970, Flesh Dream Book, 1971, Ralegh, 1972, The Pastorals, 1972, Reading Her Notes, 1972, The Tears of Edmund Burke, 1973, The Mill of Particulars, 1973, The Loom, 1975, Sixteen Odes, 1976, The Lady Of, 1977, The Convections, 1977, The Book of Persephone, 1978, Kill the Messenger, 1979, Sentence, 1980, The Alchemist to Mercury, 1981, Spiritual Exercises, 1981, Mulberry Women, 1982, Under Words, 1983, Thor's Thrush, 1985, Not This Island Music, 1987; (fiction) The Scorpions, 1967 (2d ed. rev., 1986), Cities, 1972, A Line of Sight, 1974, Wheres, 1978, The Cruise of the Pnyx, 1979, A Transparent Tree, 1986; (essays) In Time, 1971; editor: (with Paris Leary) A Controversy of Poets (anthol.), 1965; co-founder, editor, Chelsea Rvw, 1957-60; co-ed., Trobar mag. and Trobar Books, 1960-65; ed., Matter, 1963—; contrbg. ed., Caterpillar, 1968-72, Alcheringa, 1977-80, Sulfur, 1980-81. AB, CCNY, 1955; postgrad., Columbia U., 1955-58. Translator, treas. Continental Transl. Service, NYC, 1955-58; lectr. English Wagner Coll., 1960-61; prof. English Bard Coll., 1961—; dir. wrtg. program Milton Avery Grad. Schl. Arts, 1980—; vis. prof. SUNY, Buffalo, 1964; vis. prof. Tufts U., 1966-67; dir. Fedl. Writers Project, NY., 1967—; participant NY Writer's Conf., 1967; poet-in-res. CA Inst. Tech., 1971-72, U. KS., 1975, Dickinson Coll., 1976. NEA fellowship, 1976; CAPS fellowship, 1978; LA Times award for Best Book of Poetry of Year, 1980; colonel, Honorable Order of Ky. Colonels, 1986—; award for distinction, AAIAL, 1986. Address: Lindenwood Hs Annandale-on-Hudson NY 12504

KELLY, ROBERT E., b. Melrose, MA, Mar. 7, 1926; s. James Joseph and Mildred Rose (Burns) K.; m. Margaret Mary Rodden, Apr. 28, 1976; children: Robert, Steven, Karen, Kristen. Contrbr.: Inc mag., Natl. Pastime, Baseball Research Jnl., Lighthouse Mag. BBA, Boston Coll. Pres. CEO Consulting, Peabody, Mass., 1979—. Served with USN, 1943-46. Mem. MWA, NWC. Home: 17 Country Club Rd Peabody MA 01960

KELLY, SYLVIA HAYDEN NEAHR, b. Grand Rapids, MI, Nov. 13, 1938; d. William Richard and Frances June (Hayden) Neahr; m. David Michael Kelly, Aug. 12, 1960; children—Jurdu Annette, Colette Susan, Willow Loren. Author: Yours, 1980, Haitian Passages, 1984, Colorado Migrant Health, 1985; cartoon strip: Juan and Cool, 1981-85; contrbr. poetry and fiction to Transpacific, La Huerta, Ragged Oaks anthology; ed. In-Camp Guide Book, 1978. BA, U. Iowa, 1967; postgrad. SUNY-Geneseo. Tchr. Central Schl., Honeoye, NY, 1968-76; dir. tchrs. Geneseo Migrant Ctr., NY, 1975-77, writer and cons., 1977-79, coord. BOCES, NY, 1979—. Bd. dirs. Am. Cancer Soc., Geneseo, 1974-77; Geneseo Valley Council on the Arts, 1983-85, Literacy Vols. of Livingston County, 1980-86, Soc. Advancement Gifted Edn. Recipient Nelson Algren short fiction contest, Chgo., 1984; Tchr. of Excellence award NY State English Council, 1985. Mem. P&W, Literacy Vols. Am. Address: Box 53 Geneseo NY 14454

KELSON, ALLEN HOWARD, b. Chgo., May 4, 1940; s. Ben and Esther Mae (Ashkin) K.; m. Carla S. Lipson, Aug. 18, 1966; children—David Lauren, Melina Elisabeth. Author: Guide to Chicago, 1983, 100 Menus, 1984, 86. Student, U. IL, Chgo., 1957, 1958; BA in English, Roosevelt U., Chgo., 1965. Catalog copywriter Sears, Roebuck & Co., Chgo., 1962-64, sales promotion writer, 1964-67, spcl. projects dir., catalog advt. div., 1967-68; editor-in-chief WFMT Guide, Chgo. Guide, Chgo. mag. WFMT, Inc., Chgo., 1968-85; publ relations and advt. mgr. WFMT, Inc. 1968-70, v.p., dir., 1974-86; assoc. pub. Chgo. mag., 1977-85; Prin. Kelson Kapuler Advt., 1962-68; editor Chgo. GuideBook, 1972-73; dining critic, Chicago mag., 1969—; pub. Chicago mag., Chicago Scene mag., 1985-87. Address: Box 2022 Highland Park IL 60035

KEMELMAN, HARRY, b. Boston, Nov. 24, 1908; s. Isaac and Dora (Prizer) K.; m. Anne Kessin, Mar. 29, 1936; children—Ruth (Mrs. George Rooks), Arthur Frederick, Diane (Mrs. Murry Rossant). Author: Friday the Rabbi Slept Late, 1964, Saturday the Rabbi Went Hungry, 1966, The Nine Mile Walk, 1967, Sunday the Rabbi Stayed Home, 1969, Commonsense in Education, 1970, Monday the Rabbi Took Off, 1972, Tuesday, the Rabbi Saw Red, 1973, Wednesday, the Rabbi Got Wet, 1976, Thursday, the Rabbi Walked Out, 1978, Conversations with Rabbi Small, 1981 Someday, the Rabbi Will Leave, 1985, One Fine Day, the Rabbi Bought a Cross, 1987. AB, Boston U., 1930; MA, Harvard, 1931. Tchr. Boston pub. schls., 1935-41; chief job analyst and wage adminstr. Boston Port Embarkation, 1942-49; free-lance writer, 1949-63; tchr. Franklin Inst., Boston, 1963-64, St. Coll., 1964—. Recipient Edgar award for best first novel, 1965; Faith and Freedom Communications award, 1967. Mem. AL, MWA. Address: Box 674 Marblehead MA 01945

KEMMETT, WILLIAM J., b. Boston, s. William J. and Mildred (Bouve) Farese K.; m. Jacqueline B. Tompkins, Aug. 2, 1957; children—William, Kimberly, Christopher, John, Gerald. Author: Riverbank Moss, 1978, The Presence, 1980, Faith of Stone, 1983; contrbr. to Gargoyle, Stone Country, Hanging Loose, Dragonfly, Yankee mag., others. MFA, Vt. Coll., 1986. Recipient Haiku of Yr. award Dragonfly mag., 1978. Mem. PSA, New Eng. Poetry Club. Home: 53 Samoset Dr Hanover MA 02339

KEMP, NETTIE EMMERINE, b. Scott City, KS, Mar. 26, 1908; d. Arthur Lincoln and Nettie May (Colyer) Sisam; m. Elkan V. Kemp, Jan. 3, 1941; children–Paul James, Everett Alan, Earl David. Contrbr. children's songs, stories, articles to children's periodicals. B.A., Coe Coll., 1935; postgrad. U. Calif.-Berkeley, 1950, U. Calif.-San Francisco, 1951. Tchr. public schs., Novato, CA, 1950-52, Fife,Scotland, 1956-58, DEs Moines, IA. 1959-62; spl. edn. instr. public schl., Lyons, NE, 1970-73, retired. Recipient prize and blue ribbon Grand Prairie Festival of Arts, Stuttgart, AK, 1977, prize for creative writing, 1979; blue ribbon for creative writing Festival of Arts, Little Rock, 1978; 1st place blue ribbon for poem Fla. Fedn. Women's Clubs, 1983. Home: 184 Annapolis Ln Rotonda West FL 33947

KEMPER, STEVEN EDWARD, b. Louisville, KY, Nov. 25, 1951; s. Edward John and Ann (Peterson) K.; m. Judith Ann Kaufman, June 15, 1986. B.A., U. Detroit, 1973; Ph.D., U. Conn., 1980. Free-lance wrtr., 1980—. Recipient 1st prize for news feature, weekly supplement Conn. SPJ, 1987. Home: 146 Brookside Rd Newington CT 06111

KEMPER, TROXEY, b. Granite, OK, Apr. 29, 1915, s. William Charles and Ona Lee (Dawson) K.; m. Eloise Jeanne Doty, July 31, 1954 (div. 1962); children—Karen Lynn Kemper Woolf, Ann Patricia. Author poetry collections: Mainly on the Plain, 1983, Whence and Whither, 1983, Folio and Signature, 1985; contrbr. numerous articles to newspapers, mags., fiction and poetry to mags. BA, Jnlsm., U. N.Mex., 1951. Clrk., reporter Univ. News Bur., U. N.Mex., Albuquerque, 1947-51; reporter, copy ed. Albuquerque Jnl, 1951-70. Mem. P&W, NWU, NWC, Calif. Wrtrs. Roundtable. Home: 3108 W Bellevue Ave Los Angeles CA 90026

KEMPTON, KARL, b. Chgo., July 1, 1943, s. Edmund W. and Kathryn E. (Hogan) K.; m. Sylvia Wilburn, Dec. 6, 1969 (div. 1981); m. Ruth Ann Searcy, June 21, 1983. Author: Lost Alfabet Found, 1979, Rune, 1980, Rune 2: 26 Voices, 1980, Black Strokes White Spaces, 1984, Ko (with Loris Essary), 1984, The Light We Are, 1985, Alignment, 1985, 4 Plus 3, 1987, Deep Square Wave, 1987, An Ensemble, 1987; ed.: The Trubador Anthology (with Charles Potts), 1973, The Uinta Gargoyl, 1974-75, Kaldron intl. jnl. visual poetry and lang. art, 1976—; guest contrbg. ed. Cafe Solo, 1978, 79; guest ed. (with Dick Higgins) 10-5155-20, 1983. BS in Econ., U. Utah, 1968. Labor economist State of Utah, Salt Lake City, 1968-70; cabinet maker, Salt Lake City, 1973-74; archeological tech., San Luis Obispo, Calif, 1979-83; house painter, 1983—; currently poetry ed. Cafe Solo. Co-winner concrete poetry prize The Gamut mag., 1983. Home: Box 7036 Halcyon CA 93420

KEMSKE, FLOYD STEVEN, b. Wilmington, DE, Mar. 11, 1947; s. Robert Paul and Marybeth (Parks) K.; m. Alice Geraldine Morse, Dec. 21, 1968. Contrbg. author Starry Messenger: The Best of Galileo, 1978. BA in Hist., U. of DE, 1970; MA in Hist., MI State U., 1971. Asst. dean stud. affairs, BU Schl. Md., Boston, 1975-78; review ed. Galileo Mag., Boston, 1976-78; mng. ed., 1978-80; ed. Galaxy Mag., Boston, 1980, Data Trng. & Trng. News, Boston, 1980-84, Info. Ctr. Mag., 1985—. Mem. ASBPE. Excellence in writing award, ASBPE. Home: 46 Ferdinand St Melrose MA 02176

KENDIG, DIANE LYN, b. Canton, OH, May 8, 1950; d. Russell George and Gladys (Young) Kendig. Author: A Tunnel of Flute Song, 1980, A Pencil to Write Your Name: Poems from the Nicaraguan Poetry Workshop Movement (Nicaraguan folk poetry in transl. with photos by Steve Cagan), 1986. BA, Otterbein Coll., 1972; MA, Cleve. State U., 1977. Lectr. Cleve. State Univ., 1976-84; asst. prof. Findlay Coll., Ohio, 1984—. Ed. NOW, Cleve-E, 1982; mem. faculty and staff for Social Change, Cleve., 1984; poetry ed., College Composition and Communication. Recipient Poetry award, MW Writers Conf., Canton, Ohio, 1984; Yaddo Fellow, 1986. Mem. Poets League of Cleve (bd. trustees), Ohio Arts Council Artists in Edn. Address: 130 Howard St Findlay OH 45840

KENDLER, BERNHARD, b. Cin., Jan. 28, 1934; s. Harry Harlan and Mildred (Black) K.; m. Jill Ferguson, Dec. 12, 1975. BA in English, NYU, 1955; MA in Comparative Lit., U. MI, 1956. Research asst. Calif. Tchrs. Assn., 1958-60; editor A.S. Barnes & Co., Inc., NYC, 1960-62; copy editor J.B. Lippincott Co., PA, 1962-63; mng. editor, editor (classics and lit.) Cornell U. Press, Ithaca, NY, 1963—. Mem. Am. Studies Assn., Phi Beta Kappa. Address: 47 Sheraton Dr Ithaca NY 14850

KENDRICK, NONA CAROLINE, b. Summerville, GA, Jan. 7, 1932; d. Allmon Kellett and Cynthia Minerva (Tudor) K. Contrbr. poems to anthols. Grad. public schls., Lyerly, GA. Hairdresser Jordanlane Beauty Shop, Huntsville, AL, 1959-81; owner, operator Nona's Hair Designs, Huntsville, 1981—. Recipient award of Merit, World of Poetry, 1983, Silver Poet award, 1986. Home: 2103 Hill St Huntsville AL 35810

KENEALY, PATRICK, b. Boston, Oct. 31, 1959; s. William P. and M. Carol (Barry) K. Ed., writer num. pubns. inclg.: Computerworld, Infoworld, Computer Design, Computer Review, Minicomputer Review, others. BA, Harvard Y., 1980. Mng. ed. GML Info. Svcs., Lexington, MA, 1977-81; sr. ed. Cahners Pub., Boston, 1981-83; ed.-in-chief Digital Rvw, Ziff-Davis Publishing, Boston & NYC, 1983-86. Pub. Digital News, CW Commns., Framingham, MA, 1986—. Mem. ASME, ABP. Home: 7 Hancock Ave Lexington MA 02173

KENNEDY, ADELE PATTIN, b. NYC, Dec. 10, 1936, d. Louis and Lena S. Pattin; m. John M. Kennedy, 1955; children—Jo Emily, Edward Charles. Author: Touching for Pleasure, 1986. Wrkg. on self-help book, training manual. Cert. Symonds Sensory Awareness Center, San Bernardino, Calif., 1974, Lowry Center for Counselling Skills, Kentfield, Calif., 1974. Sex surrogate prtnr., West Hollywood, Calif., 1972—; sr. staff assoc. Center for Social and Sensory Learning, Encino, Calif., 1974-84; dir. Sexual Enrichment Center, Human Process Inst., Encino, 1978-79; staff assoc. A Creative Change Place, Encino, 1979—; lectr. in field. Mem. profl. orgns. Home: 1119-1/2 Hacienda Place West Hollywood CA 90069

KENNEDY, BARTON, see McLanathan, Richard

KENNEDY, BULA BERNICE, b. Kenvir, KY, Sept. 9, 1941; d. Caleb and Nellie (Williams) Cox; m. Robert Daniel Hair, July 24, 1968 (div. June 6, 1975); children—Kim P. Aair, Robert D. Hair, Jris m. Charles Ray Kennedy, Mar. 10, 1979 (div. Feb. 1987). Contrbr. poems to anthols. Cert. in Cosmetology, La French Beauty Schl., 1968; student Bible Baptist Acad., 1981-85. Genl. mgr. House of Kim Beauty & Wig Salons, Miami, 1962-69; Accelerated Christian Education monitor Bible Baptist Acad., Woodbine, GA, 1981-85. Recipient award of Merit, World of Poetry, (2) 1987, Golden Poet award, 1987. Home: 100 Mary Powell Dr C20 Saint Marys GA 31558

KENNEDY, JAMES HARRINGTON, b. Lawrence, MA, Feb. 20, 1924, s. James Harrington and Margaret Helen (Hyde) K.; m. Sheila Conway, July 1, 1950; children—Kathleen, Brian, Kevin, Gail, Patricia, Maureen, Constance. Author: The Handbook of Executive Search, 1974, Public Relations for Management Consultants, 1980, The Future of Management Consulting, profl. directories. BS, Lowell Textile Inst., 1948; SM, MIT, 1950. Mng. ed. Textile World, Greenville, S.C., 1951-54; dir. communications Bruce Payne & Assocs., Westport, Conn., 1954-58; pres. James H. Kennedy & Co., Westport, 1958-70, Kennedy & Kennedy, Fitzwilliam, N.H., 1970—; ed. Consultants News, 1970—, Exec. Recruiter News, 1980—. Mem. N.Y. Bus. Press Eds., Newsletter Assn. Am. Home: Mt Common Farm Fitzwilliam NH 03447

KENNEDY, JOHN M., b. NYC, Sept. 13, 1921, s. Edward and Annette (Chevalier) K.; m. Adele Pattin, Nov. 26, 1952; children—Jo Emily, Edward. Author, illustrator: Making Electricity Work, 1959, sci. kit manuals for Intl. Rectifier, Inc., 1963; contrbr. Am. Poetry Anthology, 1983. Wrkg. on novel, nutrition book, BSEE, Lehigh Univ., 1944; cert. in comml. photography Schl. Modern Photography, N.Y.C., 1947; postgrad. New Schl. Social Research, UCLA, U. So. Calif., others. Tech. ed., engr.Edo Aircraft Co., N.Y.C., 1950-52, The Austin Co. Spcl. Devices Div., N.Y.C., 1955-56; design engr. Nemos Corp., Bronx, N.Y., 1956; engring. section head Mergenthaler Linotype Co., Bedford-Stuyvesant, N.Y., 1957-62; sr. staff engr. Hughes Aircraft Co., Los Angeles, 1962—. Served to 1st lt. parachute inf., U.S. Army, 1943-46; Greenland. Mem. NWC, Acad. Sci. Fiction, Fantasy and Horror Films. Home: 11676 Chenault Brentwood Los Angeles CA 90049

KENNEDY, JON REID, b. Vintondale, PA, May 31, 1942; s. Harry Fickes and Cleota Viola (Smiley) K.; m. Beth Ann Leithmann, May 25, 1968 (div. 1982); children: Christy An, Michael Ian, Kevin Scott. Author: A Scenic Guide to 33 Pennsylvania Counties, 1962, The Youth Revolution, 1968, The Reformation of Journalism, 1972, Biblical Dynamics, 1978, The Whole Body Catalog, 1976, others; contrbr. newspapers, mags., jnls, rvws; feature editor Sedloff Publs. newspapers, 1961-63. Editor Nancy Glo Jnl., Pa., 1961-63; dir. pub. relations mgr. Christian Beacon, Collingswood, N.J., 1963-68; dir. Kuyper Inst., Stanford, Calif., 1969-83; dir., editor Writers Connection, Cupertino, Calif., 1983-86; editor Almaden Times, San Jose, Calif., 1985—, Christian Wkly., San Ramon, Calif., 1986—. Bd. dirs. Intl. Christian Youth USA, Collingswood, 1963-69, Vine Assocs., San Jose, 1984-86. DuMont fellow UCLA, 1970; recipient Keystone Press award Pa. State Press Assn., 1963, Pres.'s award Shelton Coll., 1967. Home: 411 Lewis Rd 432 San Jose CA 95111

KENNEDY, JOSEPHA MARIE, b. Elmira, NY, Mar. 21, 1928, d. Clarence Henry and Rose (Cosgrove) K. Author: Paraliturgical Music in Italy, 1600-1650, 1969; contrbr. articles to Grove's Dictionary of Music and Musicians, Clavier, Musical Qtly, Music Jnl, Musart, Renascence, Rvw for Religious, Sisters Today, poems to Sat. Rvw, The Bedside Phoenix Nest (anthol.), 1965. BA, Nazareth Coll., Rochester, N.Y., 1950, BS, 1954, MS, 1958; MA, Columbia U., 1966, PhD,1969. Joined Sisters of St. Joseph of Rochester, NY, 1946; tchr. Rochester Diocese, 1950-60; instr. Nazareth Coll., Rochester, 1960—. Clarence Barker fellow Columbia U., 1966-69. Mem. Am. Musicological Soc. Home: 4245 East Ave Rochester NY 14610

KENNEDY, MARGARET SWIERZ, b. Milford, MA, Oct. 19, 1941; d. Mitchell Martin and Jennie (Novack) Swierz; m. Eugene Martin Kennedy Jr., Nov. 7, 1964; 1 son, Eugene Martin. AB, Clark U., 1963. Secy. Conde Nast Publs., NYC, 1963—; also asst. editor House and Garden Mag., NYC, editor furniture and design projects; exec. editor House Beautiful Mag., NYC, 1981—; guest editor Mademoiselle Mag., 1962. Mem. NY Home Fashions League, Decorators Club, Inc., Decorative Arts Trust, Phi Beta Kappa. Address: 46 East 91st St New York NY 10128

KENNEDY, RICHARD JEROME, b. Jefferson City, MO, Dec. 23, 1932; s. Donald and Mary Louise (O'Keefe) K.; m. Lillian Elsie Nance, Aug. 3, 1960; children—Joseph Troy, Matthew Cook. Author: Amy's Eyes, 1985, 17 children's books,; included in Collected Stories, 1987.BS, Portland State U., 1958. Address: 415 W Olive Newport OR 97365

KENNEDY, SANDRA HAYS, b. Atlanta, Sept. 23, 1945; d. Loyd Urben and Marion Clyde (Andrews) Hays; m. Robert Hall Kennedy, Aug. 27, 1966; children—Christopher and Andrew (twins). Contrbr. articles, reports to sailing mags. including Sailors Gazette, Sailing World, Soundings. Ed. The Mainsheet. Diploma in Nursing, Ga. Baptist Sch. Nursing, 1966. Supvr. nursing service Ga. Baptist Med. Center, Atlanta, 1971-74, nurse epidemiologist, 1975-80; dir. nurses Med. Personnel Pool, Atlanta, 1974-75; clinical specialist Centers for Disease Control, Atlanta, 1975-80; free-lance wrtr., photographer, 1984—. Mem. Boating Wrtrs. Intl. Home: 615 Sailwind Dr Roswell GA 30076

KENNEDY, TERRY, b. Bellows Falls, VT, Nov. 28, 1941; s. Jack Reis and Blanch (Szysko) K.; div. 1981; children: Lee, Shaila, Eugene; m. Mark James Miller, June 7, 1987. Author: Durango, 1979, Ludlow Fugue, 1980, Heart, Organ, Part of the Body, 1981, Blood of Their Blood, 1980; wrkg. on Impure Thoughts, a novel. BA, Regis Coll., 1963; MA, Goddard Coll., 1976. Freelance writer, 1976—. Address: 375 Broadway 227 Laguna Beach CA 92651

KENNEDY, THOMAS EUGENE, b. NYC, Mar. 9, 1944; s. George Ryan and Ethel May (Paris) K.; m. Monique M. Brun, Dec. 28, 1974; children—Daniel F., Isabel A. Author: The Short Stories of Andre Dubus, 1988. Contrbr. fiction, lit. criticism, poetry, translations to lit. mags., newspapers, profl. jnls. Ed.: Nordic Literary Dossier, 1987. B.A. summa cum Laude, Fordham U., 1974; M.F.A. in Writing, Vermont Coll., 1985; postgrad. Copenhagen U., Denmark, 1985—. Ed., WMA Intl. News, N.Y.C., 1967-74; news ed. World Med. Jnl., Ferney-Voltaire, France, 1974-76; mng. ed. Danish Med. Bulltn., Copenhagen, Denmark, 1976—; lectr. English, U. Md., Europe and Copenhagen, 1986—; fiction faculty, Vermont Coll. MFA writing Program, 1987—. Bd. dirs. This World Poetry Fdn., 1984—. Grantee Goodman Fund, 1970, 71, 72. Mem. Danish Wrtrs. Union, MLA, AWP, ASCAP. Address: Dept Eng VT Coll Montpelier VT 05602

KENNEDY, WILLIAM , b. Albany, NY, Jan. 16, 1928, s. William Joseph, Sr. and Mary Elizabeth (McDonald) K.; m. Ana Daisy (Dana) Sosa, Jan. 31, 1957; children—Dana, Katherine, Brendan. Author: (novels) The Ink Truk, 1969 (repr. td. 1984), Legs, 1975, Billy Phelan's Greatest Game, 1978, Ironweed, 1983 (Natl. Bk. Critis Circle Award, Pulitzer Prize, 1984), (essays) O Albany! 1983; (screenplay with Francis Ford Coppola) The Cotton Club, 1984; (screenplay) Ironweed, 1986; (children's book with Brendan Kennedy) Charlie Malarkey and the Belly-Button Mahine, 1986; (novel) Quinn's Book, 1988; short fiction: San Juan Review, Epoch, Harper's; articles, interviews, and reviews: New York Times Magazine, New York Times Book Review, Washington Post Book World, National Observer, New Republic, Look. BA, Siena College (Albany), 1949, Asst. sports ed. and col., Pst Star. Glen Falls, N.Y., 1949-50, reporter, 1952-56; asst. mng. ed. and col., Puerto Rico World Journal, San Juan, 1956; reporter, Miami Herald (Fla.), 1957; corr. for Time-Life Publns. in Puerto Rico and reporter for Dorvillier (Bus.) newsletter and Knight Newspapers, 1957-59; founding mg. ed., Star, San Juan, 1959-61; full-time fiction writer, 1961-63; spcl. writer, Albany Time Union, 1963-70, film critic, 1968-70 book editor, 1971. Lectr., State Univ. of NY at Albany, 1974-82, prof. of English, 1983—, Cornell U., 1982-83. U.S. Army, 1950-52, sports ed. and col. for Army newspapers NEA fellow, 1981, MacArthur Fdn. fellow, 1983; Founder, NY State Writers Inst., Albany, 1983-84. Creative Arts Award, Brandeis Univ., 1986; NYS Governor's Arts Award, 1984. Address:NYS Wrtrs Inst 1400 Washington Ave Albany NY 12222

KENNEDY, WILLIAM S., b. South Norfolk, VA, Jan. 23, 1926, s. William Sidney and Alice Washburn (Coggins) K. Author: Paranormal Writing, Music Writing; founder, 1979, since pub., ed. Reflect poetry lit. mag. Student Coll. of William and Mary, Norfolk, 1947, Hartnett Music Studios, NYC, 1949-53. Founder spiral movement in poetry, fiction. Served with USN, 1944-46; PTO. Home: 3306 Argonne Ave Norfolk VA 23509

KENNEDY-VERBEL, JEANNE MARIE, b. Queens, NY, June 22, 1965; d. George Richard and Marjorie Jeanne (Morgan) K., M. Eric H. Verbel. Contrbr. poems, short fiction to anthols., lit. mags. B.A., Coll. St. Elizabeth, 1987. Ed., The Sector, 1986-87. Recipient 8 cert. of Merit, World of Poetry, 1984-85, Golden Poet award, 1985, 86; 1st prize for poetry Coll. St. Elizabeth, 1985. Home: M14 E Garden Way Dayton NJ 08810

KENNEDY, X.J., (Joseph Kennedy), b. Dover, NJ, Aug. 21, 1929; s. Joseph Francis and Agnes (Rauter) K.; m. Dorothy Mintzlaff, 1962; children—Kathleen, David, Matthew, Daniel, Joshua. Author: Nude Descending a Staircase, 1961, Introduction To Poetry, 1966, 6th edit., 1985, Growing into Love, 1969, Breaking and Entering, 1971, Emily Dickinson in Southern California, 1974, Celebrations After the Death of John Brennan, 1974, (with J.E. Camp, Keith

Waldrop) Three Tenors, One Vehicle, 1975, One Winter Night in August, 1975, Literature, 1976, 4th ed., 1986, Introduction to Fiction, 1976, 4th ed., 1986, The Phantom Ice Cream Man, 1979 (with Dorothy M. Kennedy) The Bedford Reader, 1982, 2nd ed., 1985, Did Adam Name the Vinegarroon?, 1982, (with Dorothy M. Kennedy) Knock at a Star: a Child's Introduction to Poetry, 1982, The Owlstone Crown, 1983, The Forgetful Wishing-Well, 1985, Cross Ties: Selected Poems, 1985, Brats, 1986, (with Dorothy M. Kennedy) The Bedford Guide for College Writers, 1987; Poetry Editor: Paris Rvw, 1961-64; editor: (with J.E. Camp) Mark Twain's Frontier, 1963, (with J.E. Camp, Keith Waldrop) Pegasus Descending, 1971, Messages, 1973, Tygers of Wrath: poems of hate, anger and invective, 1981; editor, pub.: (with Dorothy M. Kennedy) Counter/Measures mag., 1971-74. BSc, Seton Hall U., 1950; MA, Columbia U., 1951; certificate, U. Paris, France, 1956. Teaching fellow U. MI, Ann Arbor, 1956-60, instr. English, 1960-62; lectr. English dept. Woman's Coll., U. NC, Greensboro, 1962-63; asst. prof. English Tufts U., Medford, MA, 1963-67, assoc. prof., 1967-73, prof., 1973-79; vis. lectr. Wellesley Coll., 1964, U. CA at Irvine, 1966-67. Served with USN, 1951-55. Recipient Lamont Poetry award AAP, Bess Hokin prize Poetry Mag., 1961; grant National Council Arts and Humanities, 1967-68; Shelley Meml. award, 1970; Guggenheim fellow, 1973-74; Los Angeles Times Book Award for poetry, 1985. Mem. PEN, MLA, NCTE, Children's Lit. Assn., AG, Phi Beta Kappa. Home: 4 Fern Way Bedford MA 01730

KENNER, WILLIAM HUGH, b. Peterborough, Ont., Can., Jan. 7, 1923; s. Henry Rowe Hocking and Mary I. (Williams) K.; m. Mary Josephine Waite, Aug. 30, 1947 (dec. Dec. 1964); children—Catherine, Julia, Margaret, John, Michael; m. Mary Anne Bittner, Aug. 13, 1965; children—Robert, Elizabeth. Author: Poetry of Ezra Pound, 1951, Dublin's Joyce, 1956, The Invisible Poet, T.S. Eliot, 1958, Samuel Beckett, 1961, The Stoic Comedians, 1963, The Counterfeiters, 1968, The Pound Era, 1971, Bucky: A Guided Tour of Buckminster Fuller, 1973, A Readers Guide to Samuel Beckett, 1973, A Homemade World, 1975, Geodesic Math and How to Use It, 1976, Joyce's Voices, 1978, Ulysses, 1980, A Colder Eye, 1983. BA, U. Toronto, 1945, MA, 1946; PhD, Yale U., 1950. Asst. prof. Assumption Coll., Windsor, Ont., 1946-48; instr. U. CA at Santa Barbara, 1950-51, asst. prof., 1951-56, assoc. prof., 1956-58, prof. English, 1958-73, chmn. dept. English, 1956-62; prof. English, Johns Hopkins, 1973-75, Andrew W. Mellon prof. in humanities, 1975—, chmn. dept. English, 1980—. Guggenheim fellow, 1956, 64. Address: 103 Edgevale Rd Baltimore MD 21210

KENNETT, JIYU, b. St. Leonards-on-Sea, Sussex, Eng., Jan. 1, 1924, d. Walter James Carthew and Sarah Annie (Miles) Kennett. Author: Selling Water by the River, 1972, rev. ed. published as Zen is Eternal Life, 1976, How to Grow a Lotus Blossom, 1977, The Wild, White Goose, vol. I, 1977, vol. II, 1978, The Book of Life (with Daizui MacPhillamy), 1979, The Liturgy of the Order of Buddhist Contemplatives (inclg. The Shasta Abbey Book of Ceremonies and The Shasta Abbey Psalter), 1987Rligion corr. Japan Times, 1967-69; contrbr. to religious mags. BMus, U. Durham, Eng., 1960; FTCL, Trinity Coll. Music, London, 1960; Sei degree, teaching diploma, Dai Hon Zan Soji-ji, Yokohama, Japan, 1967. Ordained Buddhist priest, 1962; abbess, Shasta Abbey, Mt. Shasta, Calif., 1970—, pres., 1970-76, chair bd. dirs., 1976—; lectr. U. Calif. Extension, 1971—. Address: Shasta Abbey Box 199 Mount Shasta CA 96067

KENNISH, KATHARINE, see Wright, Katharine Miranda

KENNY, ADELE M., b. Perth Amboy, NJ, Nov. 28, 1948, d. William John and Adele (Petro) Kenny; m. Raymond James Richards, Oct. 31, 1985. Author: A Creative Writing Companion, 1981, Notes from the Nursing Home, 1982, An Archaeology of Ruins, 1982, Refusing the Frog, 1983, The Roses Open, 1984, Illegal Entries, 1984, Promise and Prayer, 1985, Between Hail Marys, 1986, Migrating Geese, 1987, An Arts Activities Approach to Counseling the Gifted, serialized in G/C/T magazine. ed.: Dust Behind the Door, 1982; poetry ed. NJARTFORM Magazine, 1981-83; contrbr. poetry, rvws. and nonfiction to over 250 publs. BA, Kean Coll., 1970; MS, Coll. New Rochelle, 1982. Tchr. Rahway (N.J.) Pub. Schls., 1970—, creative writing specialist, 1978-81, resource tchr. for gifted program, 1981-86; artist-in-res. & poetry cons. various arts councils and agcys., 1979—; adj. prof. Coll. New Rochelle (graduate school), N.Y., 1981-85. Poetry fellow N.J. State Council on Arts, 1982 and 1987; grants review panelist, NJ State Council on Arts, 1985; recipient Merit Book award Haiku Soc. Am., 1983-84, Henderson Award, 1984; Author's Citations for Illegal Entries, 1985 and An Archaeology of Ruins, 1982, NJ Writers Conference, Writers Digest Magazine Writing Competition Award, 1981, NJ Poetry Monthly Award, 1977, Teacher innovation Grant, 1973, NJ State Department of Education. Mem. Haiku Soc. Am., Pres. Home: 207 Coriell Ave Fanwood NJ 07023

KENNY, HERBERT A., b. Boston, Dec. 22, 1912; s. Herbert A. and Mary (Conroy) Kenny; m. Teresa F. Flaherry; children—Ann Gonzalez, Herbert A, III, Susan Carroll. Author: Catholic Quiz Book, 1937, Suburban Man, 1974, The Secret of the Rocks, 1980, A Boston Picture Book, 1974, Suburban Man (poetry), 1959, Sonnets to the Virgin Mary, 1949, Literary Dublin: A History, 1970, Cape Ann, Cape America, 1960. AB, Boston College, 1934. Night city editor, Boston Post, 1933-56, arts and books ed., Boston Globe, 1956-74; freelance wrtr., 1974—. Mem. PEN, PSA, National Book Critics Circle, N.E. Poetry Club. Home: 804 Summer St Manchester MA 01944

KENNY, KATHRYN, see Sanderlin, Owenita Harrah

KENNY, MAURICE F., b. Watertown, NY, Aug. 16, 1929, s. Andrew Anthony and Doris Marie Parker Herrick Kenny Welch. Author: (poems) The Smell of Slaughter, 1982, The Mama Poems, 1984, Is Summer This Bear, 1985, Rain & Other Fictions, 1985, Blackrobe: Isaac Jogues, 1986, Between Two Rivers: Selected Poems, 1986, Greyhounding This America, 1986, (prose history) Roman Nose & Other Essays, 1986; ed. Wounds Beneath the Flesh, 1984; contrbr. to Earth Power Coming, Coyote Was Here, Words in the Blood, Harper's Book of 20th Century Native Am. Poetry, The North Country, Blue Smoke, Open Places, Another Chgo. Mag., Ikon, Saturday, Greenfield rvws, Abraxas, Steppingstones, Mirage, Contact/11, numerous others. Recipient Am. Book award Before Columbus Fdn., 1984, natl. award Corp. for Pub. Broadcasting, 1984. Mem. PEN, CCLM (bd. dirs. 1980-86). Home: Box 1029 Saranac Lake NY 12983

KENT, CAROL, b. Portland, OR, Nov. 23, 1944; m. David L. Kent, Dec. 19, 1974; children—Robert Lloyd, Susannah Mary, Zachary Miller, David Clark. Editor: John, 1983, The Medical Say What? 1984, Strong-In-Right-Is-Ra, 1984, The White Goddess, 1985, To Cairo Came a Certain Man, 1985, Ward Ritchie, 1986, Milk Like Wine, 1987, A Garland of Bookbinders, 1987. BA, U. of North Carolina, 1966. Founder Press at the Humanities Research Center (Univ. of Texas-Austin), 1986—; founder Erespin Press (Arlington, VA), 1980—; freelance researcher (Washington, DC), 1974-80. Mem. Amalgamated Printers' Assn. (Pres., 1984-88), Miniature Book Society, Citizens for the Classics. Home: 929 E 50th Austin TX 78751

KENT, RICHARD VINCENT, b. NYC, Dec. 3, 1949; s. Ben M. and Ann (Mateo) K. Author: Tales of the Alimentary Canal, 1986. contrbr. articles to popular mags. B.S., New Paltz Coll., 1971; postgrad. Rutgers U., 1972-73. Reporter, The Bradenton Herald, FL, 1975-78; free-lance wrtr., 1986—. Recipient 1st place for public service Fla. Soc. Newspaper Eds. Mem. Nat. Wrtrs. Club, Fla. Freelance Wrtrs. Assn., Bay Area Profl. WG (v.p.). Home: 404 S Fremont Ave Apt A Tampa FL 33606

KENT, ROLLY, b. Summit, NJ, June 8, 1946. Author: The Wreck in Post Office Canyon, 1977, Southside: 21 Poems by Children, 1981, Spirit, Hurry, 1985; ed. Willa & Marie: Poems from a Nursing Home, 1982. BA, Middlebury Coll., 1968; MFA, U.Ariz., 1974. Dir. Tucson Public Library Wrtrs. Project, 1980—, and Tucson Wrtrs. Conf., 1983—. Bd. dirs., Cultural Alliance of Tucson, 1982. Address: 10 N Congress Terr Tucson AZ 85745

KENYON, BRUCE GUY, (Daisy Vivian, David Reynolds), b. Cadillac, MI, Aug. 16, 1929; s. Guy Chauncy and Daisy Vivian (Dobyn) K.; m. Marian Long, Mar. 1950 (div. 1954). Author: Rose White, Rose Red, 1983, The Forrester Inheritance, 1985, Fair Game, 1986, Wild Rose, 1986, A Marriage of Inconvenience, 1986, The Counterfeit Lady, 1987. Contrbr. articles, poems, short stories to mags. Student Marion Coll., Inc., 1949-1951, Columbia U., 1952. Actor 1954-59; mgr. merchandising Doubleday Book Shop, NYC, 1959-85; radio producer WBAI-Pacifica radio sta., NYC, 1975-76. Mem. AG. Address: Walker Pub. 720 5th Ave New York NY 10019

KENYON, KAREN BETH, b. Oklahoma City, Sept. 4, 1938; d. Claude Emory Smith and Evelyn Grace (Brown) Bass; m. Richard B. Kenyon, Feb. 14, 1963 (dec. Nov. 1978); children: Richard Laurence, Johanna Leigh (dec.). Author: Many Faces, 1971 (creativity award San Diego Creativity Assn. 1974); Sunshower, 1981; The Way of Writing; contrbr. essays to Newsweek, articles to Redbook, Ladies' Home Jnl. BA in English with honors, San Diego State U., 1977, MA in English, San Diego State Univ. 1987. Mem. faculty U. Calif. at San Diego Extension, La Jolla, 1981—, San Diego State U. Extension, 1983—; instr. Mira Costa Coll., Del Mar, Calif., 1981—; freelance journalist Los Angeles Times, San Diego, 1984—. Recipient achievement award for poetry Atlantic Monthly, 1975. Mem. PEN, P&W. Address: Box 12604 La Jolla CA 92037

KEREMES, CONSTANCE ANDREA, b. NYC,Apr. 22, 1958, d. George and Winifred (Marquette) Keremes. Contrbr. poetry, prose to Harper & Row English, 1983, Poetry in Motion (by Lee Bennett Hopkins), 1984, Munching (by

Hopkins), 1985, Scribner Reading Series, 1987. BS summa cum laude in Edn., Adelphi U., 1980. Asst. ed. Harper & Row Publs., NYC, 1980–85; assoc. ed. Macmillan Pub. Co., NYC, 1985—. Home: 23 7th Ave S Huntington Sta NY 11746

KERFOOT, GLENN WARREN, b. McKeesport, PA, July 30, 1921; s. Julius Cannon and Ruth Elizabeth (McWhinney) K.; m. Nadine McKnight, Dec. 20, 1960; 1 son, Warren Kevin. Contrbr. articles to numerous mags., newspapers. Student Orange County Community Coll., Middletown, N.Y., 1954-56. Wrtr. IBM Co., Lexington, Ky., 1956-63, ed., 1963-66, mgr. communications, 1966-82; owner The Letter Doctor, Lexington, 1982—. Served with U.S. Army, 1943-46. Active Friends of Lexington Library, 1968—. Recipient Versatility in Writing award N.Y. WG, 1956, 3 Bonds Promotion awards U.S. Treasury Dept., 1973, 75, 76; named Ky. Col., State of Ky., 1956. Mem. Intl. Assn. Bus. Communicators (Editorial Writing award 1985 ,86; dir. 1966—), Central Ky. Wrtrs., Am. Soc. Trng. Devel., Ky. Aviation History Roundtable (dir. 1979—). Home: 1754 Harrogate Rd Lexington KY 40505

KERLEY, GARY LEE, b. Newport News, VA, Aug. 28, 1949; s. Royd Steve and Doris Jeanne (Darnell) K.; m. Edna Patricia Amos, Mar. 12, 1977; children—James B. French Jr., Patricia Milette Langston. Contrbr. to anthologies inclg. Ga. Poets, Internal Weather, The Reach of Song; ed.: The Impression, 1971, The Crucible, 1977; pub.: Sorrows of the Inner Ear, 1976. BS Edn., U.Ga., 1971, MA, 1973; PhD, U.SC, 1980. Prof. English, Truett-McConnell Coll., Cleve., 1977-78, adj. prof., 1979-82; assoc. prof. humanities Brenau Coll., Gainesville, Ga., 1978—, instr. English, Brenau Acad., 1978—. Mem. NCTE, MLA (Am. Lit section). Address: 1315 Vine St Gainesville GA 30501

KERMAN, JUDITH BERNA, b. Bayside, NY, Oct. 5, 1945, d. Harry and Betty (Zeltsman) K. Author: (poems) Obsessions, 1974, The Jakoba Poems, 1976, Mothering, 1978, Driving for Yellow Cab, 1985, (scholarly) Merwin's Journey: The Poems of W.S. Merwin as a Hero-Journey, 1977, (opera libretto) To Catch a Comet, 1980, also other works. BA with honors, U. Rochester, 1967; MA in English, SUNY, Buffalo, 1973, PhD in English, 1977. Grad. asst. SUNY, Buffalo, 1970-75, program coordinator continuing edn., 1973-78; regional dir. U. Mich. Extension, 1978-81; ed., founder Mayapple Press, 1979—; founder, mem. editorial bd. Earth's Daughters Mag., 1971—; asst. dir. mgmt. devel. Henry Ford Community Coll., Dearborn, Mich., 1981-82; dir 2-yr. tech. programs Kent State U., Ohio, 1982—. Arts and Letters fellow SUNY, Buffalo, 1970. Mem. PEN, Sci. Fiction Research Assn., Niagara Erie Wrtrs., Poets League Greater Cleve., Am. Folklore Soc. Home: Box 3185 Kent OH 44240

KERN, CANYON, see Raborg, Frederick Ashton Jr.

KERN, EDITH, b. Dusseldorf, Germany, Feb. 7, 1912; d. L.G. Berg and J. Bison. Author: Sartre, 1962, Existential Thought and Fictional Technique, 1970, The Absolute Comic, 1980; contrbg. author: Disciplines of Criticism, 1968, Boccaccio, 1974, Beckett, 1978, Literary Theory and Criticism, 1984; mem. editorial bd.: Twentieth Century Lit. 1972—; founding editor: DadaSurrealism; contrbr. articles profl. jnls. BA, Bridgewater Coll., 1942; MA, 1944, PhD in Romance Lang. and Lit, Johns Hopkins U., 1946. Instr. to asst. prof. modern langs. U. MD, U. KS; dir. TV project U. PA, 1946-60; prof. French Grad. Schl., St. Johns U., NYC, 1960-65; prof. Romance lit. and comparative lit. U. WA, Seattle, 1965-72; D. Silbert prof. humanities, chmn. comparative lit. Smith Coll., Northampton, MA, 1972-77; John Cranford Adams prof. Hofstra U., 1977-80; O'Connor Prof., Colgate U., 1981-82; Dist. Prof., Purdue U., 1984. faculty New School for Social Research. Yaddo, 1964, 65; Bollingen Fdn. fellow, 1967, 75, 76; NEH fellow, 1972; Harvard Radcliffe fellow, 1975.; Guggenheim fellow, 1976; Rockefeller fellow, 1982. Appointed to Cncl. of Scholars for Library of Congress, 1982. Mem. MLA (pres. 1977), Comparative Lit. Assn., Natl. Soc. Lit. and Arts, Intl., Am. Comparative Lit Assn., PEN.. Address: 1025 Fifth Ave New York NY 10028

KERN, ELLYN R., b. Mar. 19, 1938; d. Gilbert J. and Helen B. (Krueger) Rutenschroer; m. Kenneth C. Kern, June, 1958 (div. 1973); children: Deborah Kern Wildrick, Douglas, Lincoln, Bennett; m. 2d, Gerald F. Brown; stepchildren: Brian, Andrea. Author: Where the Am. Presidents Lived, 1982; ed. newsletter: The Presidents' Jnl; contrbr. articles; wrkg on hist. romance and book on presidential facts. BA in sociol., U. Cin., 1959. Pres., Story a Month, Indpls., 1970; secy.-treas., Am. Sunbathing Assn. 1984-86. Mem. NWC, COSMEP, Mensa. Address: R1 Bennington IN 47011

KERNER, DEBORAH ANN, b. Melrose Park, IL, Sept. 11, 1961; d. Hadyn H. and Helen (Mattes) K. Contrbr. poems, short stories tolit. mags., anthols. Assoc. ed. Examiner Pubs., Winfield, IL, 1987. B. Gen. Studies, Northern Ill. U. Served with U.S. Army, 1984-87. Deocrated Army Achievement medal, 1986; recipient Honorable Mention award World of Poetry, 1987. Home: 102 Oxford Ln Glendale Heights IL 60139

KERR, JEAN, b. Scranton, PA, July 1923; d. Thomas J. and Kitty (O'Neill) Collins; m. Walter Kerr, Aug. 16, 1943; children: Christopher, John and Colin (twins), Gilbert, Gregory, Katharine. Author: play Jenny Kissed Me, 1949, Touch and Go, 1950, (with Eleanor Brooke) King of Hearts, 1954, Please Don't Eat the Daisies, 1957, The Snake Has All the Lines, 1960, Mary, Mary, 1961, Poor Richard, 1964, Penny Candy, 1970, Finishing Touches, 1973, How I Got to Be Perfect, 1978, Lunch Hour, 1980. MFA, Cath. U. Am., 1945; LHD, Northwestern U., 1962, Fordham U., 1965. Mem. Natl. Inst. Arts and Scis. Home: 1 Beach Ave Larchmont NY 10538

KERR, KATHRYN ANN, (Leona Fisher, Willi Red Bear), b. St. Louis, Aug 15, 1946; d. Harry Milton and Joan (Crawford) Kerr. Author: Conewer, 1977, Equinox, 1979, First Frost, 1985; ed. Matrix 7, 8, 9, 10, Red Herring chapbooks Nos. 12 & 14; contrbr. Ascent. Another Chgo. Mag., Spoon River Qtly, Miss. Valley Rvw, Great River Rvw, Karamu. BA, SIU, 1971; MS, EIU, 1984. Tchr. Sparta High Schl, Ill., 1971-72; library asst. SIU, Carbondale, Ill., 1973-76; biologist Ill. Natural Areas Inventory, Urbana, Ill. 1976-78; freelance biol. cons. 1978—. Mem. Audubon Soc., Champaign, 1986. Recipient Pushcart Critics Choice for First Frost, 1986, poetry award EIU Fine Arts Fest, 1978, Ill. Wesleyan Writers Conf., 1979, Ill. Arts Council, 1982; fellowship, Ill. Arts Council, 1985. Mem. Ill. Writers, Inc. (chmn.), Ill. Arts Council, Midwest Natural Areas Assn. Address: Box 431 Sidney IL 61877

KERR, LESLIE ANN, b. Pitts., Sept. 25, 1949; d. Richard David and Lorna Deane (Grant) Kerr; m. C.K. Pfalfi; Mar. 6, 1974 (dec.); 1 son, J. Grant; m. J. B. Vera Martinez, Mar. 28, 1987. Contrbr. articles to mags., profl. jnls. inluding Bride's Mag., Karate Illustrated, others. B.A. in Jnlsm., Calif. State U., 1977; Cert. in Corp. Communications, U. Southern Calif., 1986. Asst. mng. ed. Calif. State Bar Legal Jnl., Los Angeles, 1974-76; exec. ed. Rainbow Pubs., Burbank, CA, 1978-80, Transworld Exhibits, Chgo., 1980-82; mgr. communications Everest & Jennings, Inc., Camarillo, CA, 1984-87. Named Outstanding Young Woman in Jnlsm., Calif. Press Assn., 1971, Tchr. of yr., Univ. Without Walls, Los Angeles, 1986. Mem. IABC, WIC. Home: 164 Shamrock Court Newbury Park CA 91320

KERR, WALTER F., b. Evanston, IL, July 8, 1913; s. Walter Sylvester and Esther (Daugherty) K.; m. Jean Collins, Aug. 16, 1943; children—Christopher, Colin, John, Gilbert, Gregory, Katharine. Author: (plays) Touch and Go, Sing Out Sweet Land; (books) How Not to Write a Play, 1955; Criticism and Censorship, 1957, Pieces at Eight, 1958, The Decline of Pleasure, 1962, The Theatre in Spite of Itself, 1963, Tragedy and Comdey, 1967, Thirty Plays Hath November, 1969, God on the Gymnasium Floor, 1971, The Silent Clowns, 1975, Journey to the Center of the Theater, 1979; also articles. BS in Speech, Northwestern U., 1937, MA, 1938, LHD, 1962; LL.D., St. Mary's Notre Dame; DLitt, LaSalle, 1956, Fordham U., 1965, Notre Dame U., 1968, U. MI, 1972. Instr. speech and drama Cath. U., Washington, 1938-45, assoc. prof. drama, 1945-49; drama critic Commonweal, 1950-52, NY Herald Tribune, 1951-66, NY Times, 1966-83; specialist drama theory, criticism. Address: 1 Beach Ave Larchmont Manor NY 10538

KERR, WALTER H., b. Indpls., June 21, 1914; s. Ezra Levin and Ada Muriel (Eskew) K.; m. Lelia M. Funkhouser, Dec. 31, 1950; 1 son, William Arthur. Author: Populations of the Heart, 1961, Countdown in Bedlam, 1978; co-ed.: Rye Bread: Women Poets Rising, 1977, American Classic: Car Poems for Collectors, 1985; contrbr. poetry: Southern Poery Rev., Red Clay Reader, Borestone Mountain Poetry Awards, Fire, Sleet and Candlelight, numerous other periodicals. Wrkg. on poetry. Printer U.S. Govt. Printing Office, Washington, 1931-69. Home: 6602 Wells Pkwy Hyattsville MD 20782

KERRIGAN, (THOMAS) ANTHONY, b. Winchester, MA, Mar. 14, 1918; s. Thomas Aloysius and Madeline (Flood) K.; m. Elaine Gurevitch, Sept. 11, 1951; children—Michael, Antonia, Camilo Jose, Patrick, Elie, Malachy. Editor, translator: 50 books including 7 vols. the Selected Works of Miguel de Unamuno; author 3 books poetry. Licenciado ed filosofia y letras, U. Habana, Cuba, 1945, U. Paris, 1952, U. Barcelona, Spain, 1951. Mem. faculty U. FL, Gainesville, 1950-51; grantee Bollingen Fdn., 1961-75; editor, translator Princeton U. Press, 1969-75; vis. prof. English State U. NY, Buffalo, 1974; vis. prof. Spanish U. IL, 1977-78; faculty fellow Center Study Man in Contemporary Soc., Sr. Guest Scholar, Kellogg Institute, U. Notre Dame, 1979—. Served with Mil. Intelligence US Army, World War II. Winner Natl. Book award, 1975; finalist, 1974; Translation Center Columbia U. fellow, 1977-78; NEA grant, 1982; NEH fellowships, 1981, 84; MacArthor Foundation President's Grant, 1981; Fellow Am. Acad. Learned Socs.; mem. Intl. Council of the Translation Center. Address: Kellogg Institute U Notre

Dame IN 46556

KESEY, KEN ELTON, b. La Junta, CO, Sept. 17, 1935, s. Fred A. Kesey and Geneva (Smith) Kesey Jolley; m. (Norma) Faye Haxby, May 20, 1956; children—Shannon A., Zane C., Jed M., Sunshine M. Author: One Flew Over the Cuckoo's Nest, 1962, Sometimes a Great Notion, 1964, Garage Sale, 1972, Demon Box, 1986; contrbr. stories to Esquire, Rolling Stone, Oui, Spit in the Ocean, other mags. BS, U. Oreg., 1957; postgrad. Stanford U., 1958-60. Home: 85829 Ridgeway Rd Pleasant Hill OR 97455

KESSEL, JEFFREY BRIAN, b. Bradford, PA, July 31, 1960; s. Marvin Blain and Edythe Lorraine (Pfouts) K. Contrbr. articles on rel. AA with high honors, Jamestown Community Coll., 1980; BA in Social Sci. cum laude, Pitt U., 1982. Substitute tchr. and coach Limestone high schl., N.Y., 1983; research asst. Orkand Corp., Silver Spring, Md., 1984; library tech. Library of Congress, Wash., 1985—. Home: 3526 Peartree Ct 24 Silver Spring MD 20906

KESSLER, JASCHA FREDERICK, b. NYC, Nov. 27, 1929; s. Hyman and Rose (Bronsweig) K.; m. Julia Braun, July 17, 1950; children: Margot Lucia, Adam Theodore, William Allessandro. Author: An Egyptian Bondage and Other Stories, 1967; (poems) Whatever Love Declares, 1969, After the Armies Have Passed, 1970, In Memory of the Future, 1976; Bearing Gifts: Two Mythologems, 1979, (trans. from Hungarian with Charlotte Rogers) The Magician's Garden: 24 Stories by Geza Csath, 1978 (Trans. award Columbia U. 1978), Lee Mullican, 1980, (trans. from Persian with Amin Banani) Bride of Acacias: The Selected Poems of Forugh Farrokhzad, 1982, Death Comes for the Behaviorist: A Novella and Three Long Stories, 1983, (trans. from Hungarian with Charlotte Rogers) Opium and Other Stories, 1983, (trans. from Serbo-Croatian with G. Olujic) Rose of Mother-Of-Pearl: A Fairytale, 1983, (trans. from Bulgarian with Alexander Shurbanov) Time As Seen from Above and Other Poems (Nicolai Kantchev), 1984, (trans. from Hungarian) Under Gemini: The Selected Poems of Miklos Radnoti, 1985, Transmigrations: Eighteen Stories, 1985, Classical Illusions: Twenty-Eight Stories, 1985, (trans. from Bulgarian with Alexander Shurbanov) Medusa: The Selected Poetry of Nicolai Kantchev, 1985, (trans.) The Face of Creation: Twenty-Six Hungarian Poets, 1987; Lo! The Guiding Dawn: Selected Poems of Táheréh, 1987, (trans. from Persian with Amin Banani). BA, NYU, 1950; MA, U. Mich., 1951, PhD, 1955. Faculty, U. Mich., Ann Arbor, 1951-54, NYU, NYC, 1954-55, Hunter Coll., NYC, 1955-56, Hamilton Coll., Clinton, N.Y., 1957-61, UCLA, 1961—. Fellow in writing Yaddo, 1958, Danforth Fdn., 1960, Helene Wurlitzer Fdn., 1961; D.H. Lawrence fellow in writing U. N.Mex., 1961; Fulbright research fellow in Italy, 1963-64; Fulbright sr. prof., Rome, 1970, NEA fellow, 1974-75, Inst. Creative Arts fellow U. Calif., 1974, Regents fellow in humanities U. Calif., 1977, Rockefeller Fdn. fellow, Italy, 1979, Intl. Research and Exchanges fellow, 1983-84. Mem. PSA, PEN (Los Angeles Ctr.), Natl. Book Critics Circle, ASCAP, ALTA. Home: 218 16th St Santa Monica CA 90402

KESSLER, MILTON, b. Bklyn., May 9, 1930; s. Arthur and Elizabeth (Racow) K.; m. Sonia Berer, Aug. 24, 1952; children—David Lawrence, Paula Nan, Daniel Solomon. Author: A Road Came Once, 1963, Called Home, 1967, Woodlawn North, 1970, Sailing Too Far, 1973, Everyone Loves Children: A Long Poem, 1982; translator: (with Gerald E. Kadish) Love Songs and Tomb Songs of Ancient Egypt in Alcheringa, 5, 1973, (with Tateo Imamura) Random Talks of Deibutsu (Kosho Shimizu), 1979; co-editor: (with John Logan) Choice: A Mag. of Poetry and Graphics, 1972—. BA magna cum laude, U. Buffalo, 1957; MA, U. WA, 1962; postgrad. OH St. U., 1959-63. Lectr. in English Queens Coll., City U. NY, 1963-65; mem. faculty St. U. NY at Binghamton, 1965—, prof. English, 1974—, dir. creative writing program, 1973-75, 78-79, 85; vis. prof. English U. Negev, Beersheva, Israel, 1971-72; vis. lectr., U. Haifa, Israel, 1973, vis. prof., 1981, U HI, 1975; vis. lectr. Keio U., Tokyo, 1978—, U. Antwerp, 1985; vis. poet Black colls. MS, and pub. schls., Pitts., Ann Arbor, MI, Tacoma, also NY, 1967-82. NEA grantee, 1967. Robert Frost fellow, Bread Loaf, 1961; Yaddo, Macdowall fellowship, 1966-69; Millay Fdn. fellow, 1979; Va. Ctr for the Arts fellow, 1982-83. Mem. PEN, Phi Beta Kappa. Address: 25 Lincoln Ave Binghamton NY 13905

KESSLER, ROD, b. NYC, Sept. 15, 1949; s. Irving and Deidre (Rosenfeld) K. Author: Off in Zimbabwe, 1985;, contrbr. stories Apalachee Qtly, Black Ice, Crosscurrents, Boston Lit Rvw, Cottonwood, Painted Bride Qtly, Pig Iron, NM 0umanities Rvw, North American Rvw, Greensboro Rvw, Intro 13; contrbr. poetry Interim, Odessa Poetry Rvw, Anima, Balcones Rvw, The Pink Chameleon, Ploughshares. AB, Harvard, 1971; MFA, U. Ariz., 1981. Asst. prof. English Salem State Coll., Mass., 1983—. Fiction faculty Vt. Coll. MFA Program, 1985-87. Phillips Exeter Acad. fellow 1982-83, AWP short fiction award, 1985. Mem. AWP, MLA, Massachusetts Assn of Teachers of English, Natl. Council Tchrs, New England Assa of Teachers of English. English. Address: 190 Lafayette St Salem MA 01970

KETTER, PAM, see Browning, Pamela

KETTERER, DAVID (ANTHONY THEODOR), b. Leigh-on-Sea, Essex, England, June 13, 1942; s. Joseph Theodor and Eileen (Philp) K.; m. Jacqueline Ruth Langsner, March 17, 1972 (div. Feb. 1980). Author: New Worlds for Old: The Apocalyptic Imagination, Science Fiction, an American Literature, 1974, Frankenstein's Creation: The Book, the Monster, and Human Reality, 1979, The Rationale of Deception in Poe, 1979, The Science Fiction of Mark Twain, 1984, Imprisoned in a Tesseract: The Life and Work of James Blish, 1987. Contrbr, R.G. Collins, ed., The Novel and Its Changing Form, 1972, Mark Rose, ed., Science Fiction, 1976, Sarah Blaher Cohen, ed., Comic Relief: Humor in Contemporary American Literature, 1978, Peter Nicholls and John Clute, eds, The Encyclopedia of Sciene Fiction, 1979, John Robert Colombo, ed, Other Canadas: An Anthology of Siene Fiction and Fantasy, 1979, Kirpahl Singh and Michael Tolley, eds, The Stellar Gauge, 1980, E. Slusser and others, eds, Bridges to Fantasy, 1981, Allison R. Ensor, ed, A Conneticut Yankee in King Arthur's Court (Norton critical ed.), 1982, William Toye, ed., The Oxford companion to Canadian Literature, 1983, Robert A. Collins and Howard D. Peare, eds, The Scope of the Fantastic, 1985. Contrbr to literature jnls, including PMLA, Jnl of American Studies, American Transcendental Qtly, Extrapolation, Foundation, Science Fiction Studies, Mosaic, Criticism, and Missouri Rvw. BA (with honors), Univ. of Wales, 1964; MA, Carleton Univ., Ottawa, Ont., 1965; D. Phil., Univ. of Sussex, 1969. Lectr in English, McGill Univ., Montreal, Que., 1965-66; to prof of English, Concordia Univ., Sir George Williams Campus, Montreal, Que., 1967—. Canada Cncl Fellow, 1973-74, 1976-77, research grantee, Soc. Scis. and Humanities Research Concl. of Canada, 1982-83, 87-88. Religion: Roman Catholic. Home: 4231 Wilson Ave Montreal Que Canada H4A 2V1

KEUNING, PATRICIA DUBRAVA, (Pat L. Urioste), b. NYC, March 9, 1944; d. Albert Anno and Wanda Louise (Day) Keuning; m. Robert Lee Urioste, Feb., 1971; m. 2d, Philip Joseph Normand, March 15, 1983. Author poetry: Choosing the Moon, 1981; author play: Volver, Volver, 1982; numerous poems, short stories, articles in var. mags 1966—. BA, U. of Florida, 1966. Asst. dir., Chicano Humanities & Arts Council, Denver, 1981-85; admin. asst., Denver Regional Council of Governments, 1985—. Home: 2732 Williams Denver CO 80205

KEY, DONALD, b. Iowa City, Jan. 30, 1923; s. Philip R. and Lola (Diehl) K.; m. Patricia Anne Miller, May 11, 1947; 1 son. Theodore Allen. Author: Future Unknown; contrbr. articles to profl. jnls. BA in journalism, U. IA, 1950, asst. to editor, fine arts columnist Cedar Rapids (IA) Gazette, 1950-59; art editor Milw. Jnl, 1959-72. Served with AUS, 1942-46; ETO. Mem. Theta Xi, Sigma Delta Chi. Club: Milwaukee Press. Address: 7519 N Crossway Rd Milwaukee WI 53217

KEYES, DANIEL, b. NYC, Aug. 9, 1927; s. William and Betty (Alicke) K.; m. Aurea Georgina Vazquez, Oct. 14, 1952; children—Hillary Ann, Leslie Joan. Author: Flowers for Algernon, 1966, The Touch, 1968, The Fifth Sally, 1980; (non-fiction) The minds of Billy Milligan, 1981, Unveiling Claudia, 1986. Wrkg. on novel. B.A., Brklyn. Coll., 1950, M.A., 1961. Ed., Stadium Pub., N.Y.C. 1950-52; co-owner Fenko & Keyes Photography, N.Y.C., 1952-53; tchr. English, Thomas Jefferson High Schl., N.Y.C., 1954-61; instr. English, Wayne State U., Detroit, 1962-66; lectr. English, Ohio State U., Athens, then prof. MacDowell Colony fellow, 1967, fellow Ohio Arts Council, 1986-87; recipient Hugo award World Sci. Fiction Convention, Pitts., 1959, Nebula award SFWA, 1966. Mem. PEN, DG, AWP, Author's League Am. Home: 306 E State St Athens OH 45701 Office: Morris Agcy 1350 Ave of Americas New York NY 10019

KEYES, DANIEL, b. NYC, Aug. 9, 1927, s. William and Betty (Alicke) K.; m. Aurea Georgina Vazquez, Oct. 15, 1952; children—Hillary Ann, Leslie Joan. Author: Flowers for Algernon (novel), 1966, The Touch (novel), 1968, The Fifth Sally (novel), 1980, The Minds of Billy Milligan (nonfiction), 1981, Unveiling Claudia (nonfiction), 1986. BA, Bklyn. Coll., 1950, MA, 1961. Lectr. English Wayne State U., Detroit, 1962-66; prof. English Ohio U., Athens, 1966—. Recipient Hugo award 19th World Sci. Fiction Conv., 1959, Nebula award SFWA, 1966, Spcl. award MWA, 1981. Mem. PEN, DG, Authors League of Am., AWP. C/O Morris Agency 1350 Avenue of the Americas New York NY 10019

KEYES, RALPH JEFFRY, b. Cin., Jan. 12, 1945, s. Scott and Charlotte Esther (Shachmann) K.; m. Muriel Lee Gordon; 1 child, David Gordon. Author: We, the Lonely People, 1973, Is There Life After High School?, 1976, The Height of Your Life, 1980, Chancing It, 1985; contrbr. articles to Esquire, Harper's, Antioch Rvw, Inside Sports, McCall's, Mademoiselle, Newsweek, The Nation, other periodicals. BA in History, Antioch Coll., 1967; postgrad. London Schl. Econs. and Polit. Sci., 1967-68. Asst. to pub., feature wrtr. Newsday, Garden City, N.Y., 1968-70. Recipient Headliner of Yr. award in lit. San Diego Press Club, 1975. Mem. AG, Phila. Wrtr.'s Orgn. (adv. bd.). Home: 537 Westdale Ave Swarthmore PA 19081

KEYISHIAN, M. DEITER, b. NYC; d. Maurice and Rose (Teverofsky) Deiter; m. Harry Keyishian, July 30, 1966; children: Sarah, Elizabeth, Amy, Emily. Contrbr. poetry and fiction Lit Rvw, NY Qtly, Fiction, Ararat, Graham House Rvw, Outerbridge, articles in Arts Mag. BFA, Columbia, MA in English. Instr. Fairleigh Dickinson Univ., Madison, NJ, 1965—. Address: 110 Burnham Pkwy Morristown NJ 07960

KEYS, KERRY SHAWN, b. Harrisburg, PA, June 25, 1946, s. Elmer Richard and Helen Kirk K.; m. Ann Fletcher James, June 2, 1972 (div. 1985), m. ZiZa Almeida, June 7, 1986 (separated May 1987). Author: Swallowtails Gather These Stones, 1973, Jade Water, 1974, O Pintor E O Poeta, The Painter and the Poet, Jose Paulo Moreira Da Fonseca, 1976, Loose Leaves Fall, 1977, Seams, 1985, A Gathering of Smoke Gopian's South Indian Prose-Poem Jnl, 1986; ed. bilingual anthology Quingumbo, Nova Poesia Norte-Americana, 1980; translator A Knife All Blade (Uma Faca So Lamina by Joao Cabral de Melo Neto), 1980. BA in English Lit., U. Pa., 1970; MA in English Lit., Ind. U., 1973. Instr. Pa. State U., Mont Alto, 1973, Brasas, Rio de Janeiro, Brazil, 1975-77, Mid-Susquehanna Arts Council, 1977-78, Dickinson Coll., Carlisle, Pa., 1980, Harrisburg (Pa.) Area Community Coll., 1979-84; poet, prin. English Lang. Escort, Landisburg, Pa., 1986—. Fulbright grantee, 1983-84; Pa. Council on Arts fellow, 1983. Mem. P&W. Home: Box 530 RD 1 Landisburg PA 17040

KIBLER, WALLACE EDWARD, (Mark James), b. S.I., NY, Jan. 28, 1936, s. Jennings Franklin and Ruby Marie (Pitcock) K.; m. Faith Angellica Bernard, Dec. 17, 1960 (div. 1982); children—Mark, Jeffrey. Contrbr. poetry to Odessa Poetry Rvw., Yes Press, New York Poetry Society, Am. Poetry Assn., Hieroglyphics Press, Green Valley Pub. Co., others. Wrkg. on historical poetry, song lyrics. Freelance wrtr., poet, songwrtr., N.Y.C., 1985—. Recipient Golden Poet award World of Poetry, 1986. Mem. Songwrtrs. Club Am., Country Music Soc. Am. (charter). Home: Box 842 Staten Island NY 10314

KICKNOSWAY, FAYE, b. Detroit, Dec. 16, 1936, d. Walter and Mable Louise (Standish) Blair; m. Leonard Kicknosway, Dec. 11, 1959 (div. 1967); children—Kevin Leo, Lauren Beth. Author: O. You Can Walk on the Sky? Good., 1972, Poem Tree, 1973, A. Man Is a Hook. Trouble., 1974, The Cat Approaches, 1978, Nothing Wakes Her, 1979, Asparagus, Asparagus, Ah Sweet Asparagus, 1981, Butcher Scraps, 1982, She Wears Him Fancy in Her Night Braid, 1983, Who Shall Know Them?, 1985, A Calendar (prose and drawings), 1985, Collected Poems, Vol. One, 1986. BA, Wayne State U., Detroit, 1967; MA, San Francisco State Coll., 1969. Instr., Wayne State U., 1970-76; visiting lectr. S.F. State U., 1975, 77; on faculty, MFA Prog., Goddard Coll., Plainfield, Vt., 1977, 78-79; visiting instr. Oakland U., Rochester, Mich., 1978-79; visiting prof. U. Hawaii, Honolulu, 1986. AAP Poets Prize, 1969; Mich. Fdn. for the Arts Award, 1980; Indiv. Artist Grant, Mich. Council for the Arts, 1981, 85; NEA Fellowship, 1985. Mem. PSA. Office: Eng Dept. 1733 Dmaghho Rd U Hawaii Honolulu HI 96815

KIENINGER, RICHARD GEORGE, (Eklal Kueshana) b. Chgo., Aug. 15, 1927; s. Rudolph and Melba Ruth (Wallden) K.; m. Gail, 1960 (div. 1976); 1 dau., Dawn. Author: The Ultimate Frontier, 1963; (collected essays) Observations, 1971, Observations II, 1974, Observations III, 1974, Observations IV, 1979, Spiritual Seekers' Guidebook, 1986. Student Northwestern U. Office: Box 75 Quinlan TX 75474

KIERULFF, CHARLES TAYLOR, b. Los Angeles, Mar. 5, 1919, s. Charles Rogers and Barbara (Taylor) K.; m. Barbara Phillips Smith, Sept. 21, 1940; children—Stephen Charles, William Douglas, Nancy Christine. Author: Twentieth Century Kjaerulfs, 1986. BEE, U. Calif.-Berkeley, 1941; postgrad., Harvard U., MIT, 1942-43. With Kierulff Electronics, Inc. (merged with K-Tronics into Ducommun, Inc., 1961) and Kierulff Sound Corp., Los Angeles, 1946-65, pres. K-Tronics, Los Angeles, 1961-65, div. mgr. Ducommun, Inc., Los Angeles, 1961-65. Served with AUS, 1942-46. Mem. engring. assns. Home: 358 S Bentley Ave Los Angeles CA 90049

KIERULFF, STEPHEN, b. Los Angeles, June 17, 1942; s. Charles Taylor and Barbara (Smith) Kierulff; m. Carol Jean Winter, June 14, 1970 (div. 1982); son—Benjamin Ernest. Author: How to Play Professional Rock 'n' Roll, 1968; contrbr. articles to Journal of Holistic Medicine. BA, U. of Calif., Berkeley; PhD, U.S. Intl. U., San Diego, CA. Freelance wrtr., NYC and San Diego, 1967-81. Prof., U.S. Intl. U., Glendale, 1984—; clinical psych., CA 1983—. Mem. Amer. Psych. Assoc. Home: 358 S Bentley Ave Los Angeles CA 90049

KIKEL, RUDY JOHN, b. Bklyn., Feb. 23, 1942; s. Rudolph and Pauline (Staudacher) K. Author: Shaping Possibilities, 1980, Lasting Relations, 1984; contrbr. A True Likeness: Gay & Lesbian Writing Today, 1980, Gay Community News, Gay Sunshine, The Advocate, Boston Gay Rvw, Stony Hills, Boston Sunday Globe, Bay Windows, Am Book Rvw; contrbr. poetry Shenandoah, Mass Rvw, Ploughshares, Christopher St., Mouth of the Dragon, Cumberland Poetry Rvw, Small Moon. BA, St. Johns U., 1963; MA in English, Pa. State U., 1965; PhD in English, Harvard, 1975. Instr. Suffolk Univ., Boston, 1970-75, freelance writer, 1975—, poetry ed. Bay Windows, Boston, 1983—, arts and entertainment ed., 1985—. Coord. First Night gay and lesbian poetry readings, Boston, 1979-81, vis. Glad Day Bookshop gay and lesbian writers reading series, 1980-81. Recipient Grolier Books poetry prize, Cambridge, Mass., 1977. Address: 112 Revere St Boston MA 02114

KILBOURNE, CLARA ANNE, (Claire Anne) b. Port Jervis, NY, Aug. 3, 1939; d. Eston Arthur and Anna Elizabeth (Coss) Garrison; m. Charles Warren, June 17, 1961; children—Caroline Anne, Kevin Charles. Works include: America Sings, 1960, Chimes, 1961, Best Loved Contemp. Poems, 1979, Gifted/Talented Prog. Guide, Grades 6, 7, & 8, 1984, articles on gifted edn. BA, Engl. ed., Trenton State Coll., 1961; postgrad. in gifted edn., Rider Coll. Engl. tchr. Hopewell (NJ) Schl., 1961-62; supplemental instr. Grice Middle Schl., Trenton, NJ, 1974-77, tchr. of gifted, 77-88. Home: 200 Carlisle Ave Yardville NJ 08620

KILGUS, EDWARD JOHN, b. Flushing, NY, Jan. 18, 1947. B.S. in English, Adelphi U., 1970. Contrbr. poems to lit. mags., numerous anthols.; author song lyrics. Recipient Golden Poet award World of Poetry, 1986, 87, (7) Honorable Mentions, 1986, 87. Mem. FFWA, Brockway Meml. Library for Authors. Home: Arthur Apts 417 NE 17 Ave Ft Lauderdale FL 33301

KILLOREN, ROBERT, b. St Louis, July 20, 1950; s.R.A. and L.A. (Rodenbaugh) K.; m. Patricia S. Preckel, Aug. 5, 1972; children: Michael, Sarah, Emily. Author: Rising Out of the Flinthills, 1972, Windmills, Coyotes, and Other Night Sounds, 1979; poetry in Smithsonian Exhibit on the Prairie; Emily Dickenson's Poetic Consciousness, 1976, Late Harvest: Plains and Prairie Poets, 1976; contrbr. to Sou'Wester, Focus/Midwest, Eads Bridge Rvw. AB, St. Louis U, 1972, MA, U. Mo., 1976. Lit. program dir. Mo. Arts Council, St Louis, 1970-72, writer McDonnell Douglas, St Louis, 1972-74; instr./adminstr. Univ. Mo., St Louis, 1974-80, dir. research Columbia br., 1980—. Dir./actor, CAST Theater Group, St Louis, 1968-72; host, ARS Poetica show/ Mo. Arts Council, 1978-80. Mem. Natl. Council Research Adminstrs., Soc. Research Adminstrs. Address: 1516 Killian Ct Columbia MO 65203

KILMER, KENTON, b. Morristown, NJ, Mar. 21, 1909; s. (Alfred) Joyce and Aline (Murray) K.; m. Frances Edith Frieseke, June 2, 1937; children—Hugh, Anne, Noelie, Nicholas, Martin, Rosamond, Matthew, Miriam, Deborah, Jonathan. Author: (with Donald Sweig) The Fairfax Family in Fairfax County, 1975; ed. (with Frances Kilmer) The Tidings Poets, Vol. II, 1944, This Is My America, Poems from The Washington Post, 1946, (with Ernest S. Griffith) The Congressional Anthology, 1955, 58; translator, A Man in Three Worlds Midstream, New Oxford RVW; contrbr to America, Catholic World, NY Times, Commonweal, Contemporary Poetry, Ladies Home Jnl. (Andre Chouraqui), 1984. BA, St. Mary's Coll., St. Marys, KS, 1930; MA, Georgetown U., 1931. Poetry ed. Washington Post, 1940-47; various positions, Library of Congress, 1939-67. Mem. PSA, Poetry Soc. of VA, Am. Forestry Assoc. Home: 411 Windover Ave NW Vienna VA 22180

KIM, RICHARD E., b. Hamhung City, Korea, Mar. 13, 1932; naturalized, ,64; s. Chan-Doh and Ok-Hyun (Rhee) K.; m. Penelope Ann Groll, 1960; children—David, Melissa. Author: The Martyred, 1964, The Innocent, 1968, Lost Names, 1970, In Search of Lost Years, 1985. Student, Middlebury (VT) Coll., 1955-59; MA, Johns Hopkins U., 1960; MFA, State U. IA, 1962; MA, Harvard, 1963. Instr. English Long Beach (CA) St. Coll., 1963-64; asst. prof. English U. MA at Amherst, 1964-68, assoc. prof., 1968-69, adj. assoc. prof., 1969-70; vis. prof. Syracuse U., 1970-71, San Diego St. U., 1975-77. Served to 1st Lt. Republic of Korea Army, 1950-54. Guggenheim fellow, 1965; NEA fellow, 1978; Fulbright scholar Seoul Natl. U., 1981-83. Address: Leverett Rd Shutesbury MA 01072

KIMBALL, CHARLES ARTHUR, b. Boston, MA, June 4, 1939; s. Stanley and Alice (Worthington) Kimball; m. Liselotte Isler, Jan. 25, 1964; children—Jessica, Sophia, John. Novels: The Monster from the Middle Class, 1971, The Monster From the Middle Class and Other Books, 1984; contrbr. to Sandscript mag, 1977, 78, 79. BS, Trinity Coll., 1961. Teacher pub. schls. (Easthampton, Sharon, MA), 1964-67, Scottsdale pub. schls. (AZ), 1967-69; carpenter's helper Don Taylor (West Yarmouth, MA), 1971-72, Rogers & Marney (Osterville, MA), 1972-73; self- employed odd jobs, painter, landscaper (Centerville, MA), 1973—. Home: 151 Captain Lijah's Rd Centerville MA 02632

KIMBALL, CONNIE E, see Ark, Connie Eileen

KIMBALL, RICHARD WILSON, (R. Murdo Fox, Simon K. Ashley), b. Nashua, N.H., Aug. 14, 1938; s. Rowe Wilson and Helen Louise (Thompson) K.; m. Barbara Helen Adams, Sept. 22, 1960 (div. Nov. 1975); children: R. Michael, Daniel W. Author: The Book of Quetzalcoatl, 1978; ed. The Loran-C Newsletter, 1978-79; Salty Subjects newsletter, 1982-83; Distant Drums mag., 1984—. Wrkg. on book about Hawaiians in early west. BA, U. N.Mex., 1975. Freelance wrtr., 1976—; sr. VDT ed. Westinghouse Electric Co., 1980-83; copy ed. Lawton Constn., Okla., 1984-85; jr. publs. analyst SciSo, Inc., Albuquerque, 1985-86; comm. coord., Yavapai Coll., Prescott, Ariz., 1986; reporter, Lake Powell Chronicle, Page, Ariz. Served with USCG, 1977-79. Recipient Mark Bilich award for journalism La. Indian Heritage Assn., 1980. Mem. Soc. Profl. Journalists. Home: 142 9th Ave Bx 3163 Page AZ 86040

KIMBALL, ROBERT ERIC, b. NYC, Aug. 23, 1939; s. Morris Harold and Eve (Schulman) K.; m. Abigail Leon Kuflik, May 23, 1972; children: Philip Zachary, Miranda Erica. Author: Cole, 1971, (with William Bolcom) Reminiscing With Sissle and Blake, 1973, (with Alfred Simon) the Gershwins, 1973, The Unpublished Cole Porter, 1975, The Complete Lyrics of Cole Porter, 1983: (with Alfred Simon) liner notes for recs. Grov's Dictionary of Music. BA, Yale U., 1961, LL.B., 1967. Carnegie teaching fellow Am. history Yale, 1961-62; legis. asst. to Rep. John V. Lindsay, 17th Congl. Dist. NY, 1962-63; dir. Republican Legis. Research Assn., 1963-64; curator Yale Collection of Lit Am. Mus. Theatre, 1967-71; lectr. Am. Studies Yale, 1970, 74; music, dance reviewer NY Post, 1973—, NBC, 1975-77; sr. research fellow, vis. prof. music Inst. for Studies in Am. Music, Bklyn, Coll., City U. NY, 1974-75; lectr. drama NYU 1979-80; lectr. music Yale U., 1980-81; cons. Goodspeed Opera House, 1974-75, 82—. Co-producer: Black Broadway, NYC, 1979, 80. Address: 180 W 58th St New York NY 10019

KIMBRELL, GRADY NED, b. Tallant, OK, Apr. 6, 1933, s. Virgil Leroy and Lavera Dee (Underwood) K.; m. Marilyn Louise King, May 30, 1953 (div. 1970); children—Mark Leroy, Joni Lynne; m. 2d, Mary Ellen Cunningham, Apr. 11, 1973; 1 dau., Lisa Christine. Author: Introduction to Business and Office Careers, 1974, Strategies for Implementing Work Experience Programs, 1975, Activities for Entering the World of Work, 2d ed., 1983, Entering the World of Work, 2d ed., 1983, The Savvy Consumer (and activities book), 1984, Independent Study for the World of Work, 3d ed., 1984, The Testmaker, 1986, World of Work Career Interest Survey, 1986, Succeeding in the World of Work (and activities book), 4th ed., 1986. BA, Southwestern Coll., 1956; MA in Edn., Colo. State Coll., 1958. Coordinator work edn. Santa Barbara (Calif.) Schls., 1960-74, dir. research, 1974—. Home: 4379 Via Esperanza Santa Barbara CA 93110

KIMM, LUANA LEE, see Seagull, Samantha Singer

KIMMELMAN, BURT JOSEPH, (L.V. Mack), b. Bklyn., May 6, 1947, s. David Brown and Sylvia (Levin) K.; m. LaVonne Lee Marie Mack, June 6, 1970 (div. 1973). Participating author: Natural Process, 1971; ed. Regement of Princes (Thomas Hoccleve), Transition mag., 1967-70, Poetry New York, 1986; contrbr. to Biog. Dictionary of Contemporary Catholic Am. Writing. BA in English, SUNY, Cortland, 1982; post-grad. in English, CUNY, 1983—. Dir. creative writing program Lower East Side Service Ctr., NYC, 1981-84; instr. English, Hunter Coll., NYC, 1984—; dir. Grad. Ctr. Poetry Workshop, NYC, 1984—. CUNY fellow, 1983, teaching fellow, 1984-87. Mem. P&W, Dictionary Soc. N.Am., EIDOS: Intl. Prosody Assn., Early English Text Soc., MLA, Mid Hudson MLA (chmn. Old and Middle English panel 1986). Home: 33-41 71st St Jackson Heights NY 11372

KINDER, CHARLES ALFONSO, II, b. Montgomery, WV, Oct. 8, 1946, s. Charles Alfonso and Eileen Reba (Parsons) K.; m. Diane Cecily, Mar. 22, 1975. Author: (novels) Snakehunter, 1973, The Silver Ghost, 1979, Also chaps. of books pub. in TriQuarterly, Tendril. Wrkg. on novel. BA, W.Va. U., 1967, MA in Lit., 1968; MA in Writing, Stanford U., 1973. Jones lectr. fiction Stanford U., 1973-76; wrtr.-in-residence U. Calif., Davis, fall 1979, U. Ala., Tuscaloosa, winter 1980; assoc. prof. English, U. Pitts., 1980—. Edith Mirrelees fellow Stanford U., 1971-73; Yaddo fellow, 1984-86; NEA grantee, 1979. Mem. AWP, MLA. Home: 5629 Darlington Rd Pittsburgh PA 15217

KINDEL, ROBERT JAMES, b. Wadsworth, OH, June 3, 1947; s. Michael Peter and Alice Lucille (Geisler) K.; m. Caren Diane Crom, Jan. 31, 1970; 1 son, Ian Christopher. Contrbr. articles to mags. B.S. in Nursing, Kent State U., 1975. Instr. St. Thomas Schl. of Nursing, Akron, OH, 1976-77; staff nurse Veterans Administration, Brecksville, OH, 1977—; ed. Jnl. of the Ohio Gaming Assn., Cuyahoga Falls, OH, 1983—. Served with U.S. Army, 1967-70. Fellow Am. Acad. Action Arts Design. Home: 1559 2d St Cuyahoga Falls OH 44221

KING, ALVIN THOMAS, b. Emporia, KS, Oct. 3, 1944; s. Leicester Thomas and Frieda Pauline (Hartzler) K.; m. Jill Anne Gordon, June 10, 1968. Author: Property Taxes, Amenities, and Residential Land Values, 1973, Household Production and Consumption, 1975, Microeconomic Simulation Models, 1980, Discrimination in Mortgage Lending, 1981, Do Housing Allowances Work, 1984; ed. Housing Finance Review, 1982—, Secondary Mortgage Markets, 1983-86. AB, Stanford U., 1966; PhD, Yale U., 1972. Research assoc. & asst. prof. U. MD, College Park, 1970-78; financial economist Federal Home Loan Bank Board, Washington, 1978-83; sr. economist and ed. Freddie Mac, Washington, 1983—; trustee, Catgut Acoustical Soc., 1987—;. Office: Box 37248 Washington DC 20013

KING, CAROL SOUCEK, b. Whittier, CA, Sept. 8, 1943; d. Romus and Anne Rachel Soucek; m. Richard King, Jan. 31, 1976. BA, U. So. CA, 1966; MFA, Yale U., 1967; PhD, U. So. CA, 1976. Lifestyle staff writer, then ed. Los Angeles Herald Examiner, 1973-77; ed.-in-chief Designers West Mag., Los Angeles, 1978—. Press mem.: Natl. Home Fashions Lg., Am. Soc. Interior Designers, Inst. Bus. Designers. Dallas Mkt. Ctr. Award for editorial excell., 1983. Office: Designers West 8770 Beverly Blvd Los Angeles CA 90048

KING, CYNTHIA BREGMAN, b. NYC, Aug. 27, 1925, d. Adolph and Elsie (Oschrin) Bregman; m. Jonathan King, July 26, 1944; children—Gordon B., Austin A., Nathaniel B. Author: In the Morning of Time, The Story of the Norse God Balder, 1970, The Year of Mr. Nobody, 1978, Beggers And Choosers, 1980, Sailing Home, 1982; contrbr. short stories, articles to Quartet, Tex. Stories & Poems, Met. Detroit Mag. Good Housekeeping; contrbr. book rvws. to Los Angeles Daily News, NY Times Book Rvw, Detroit News. Student Bryn Mawr Coll., 1943-44, U. Chgo., 1944-46. Mng. ed. Hillman Periodicals, NYC, 1946-50, Fawcett Publs., NYC, 1950-55; tchr. creative wrtg. Awty Schl., Houston, 1973-75; freelance wrtr., 1968—. Grantee Mich. Council for Arts, 1985-86. Mem. Detroit Women Wrtrs. (past pres., dir. seminars 1981-82, dir. Short Story Symposium 1985), AG, P&W. Home: 4 Marsh Hen Cove Fripp Island SC 29920

KING, ELIZABETH CHIU, (Lun-Lun), b. Shanghai, China, July 25, 1935; came to U.S., 1955; d. Frank T.P. and Rowena (Luk) Chiu; m. Albert I. King, June 18, 1960; children—Albert I. Jr., Thomas I. Author: Eating the Chinese Way in Detroit, 1980, The Chinese Zodiac, 1982, The 15-Minute Chinese Gourmet, 1986; contrbr.: Mich. Living, Detroit Monthly. Wrkg. on cookbooks, novel, jnl. BSc, U. San Francisco, 1957; MA in English, U. Calif.-Berkeley, 1960; MLS, U. Mich., 1966. Librarian Henry Ford Community Coll., Dearborn, Mich., 1967—. Ed., bd. dirs Assn. Chinese Ams., Detroit, 1972-78; pres. Chinese Am. Edn. and Cultural Center Mich., Ann Arbor, 1977—. Mem. Am. Inst. Wine and Food, AG. Home: 1000 Bretton Ln Bloomfield Hills MI 48013

KING, KAREN JEANNE, b. Washington, December 6, 1953; d. Jack H. and Dorothy L. (Boyd) Pippin; m. Barry M. King, June 1, 1974 (div. Sept. 1987); children—Jason Matthew, Kelly Anne. Contrbr. articles to dentistry jnls. Student Salisbury State Coll., 1984-86, Old Dominion U., 1987—. Mng., marketing dir. Family Dental Assocs., Salisbury, MD, 1978-86; marketing dir. Gary L. Newell, D.D.S., Virginia Beach, VA, 1987—; founder, cons. Profl. Practice Innovations, Virginia Beach, 1987—. Recipient 1st place for radio advt. Natl. Conf. on Dental Advt. and Public Relations, 1985, 2d place for public relations programs. Address: Profl Prac Innov 5319 Maize Dr Virginia Beach VA 23464

KING, KATHRYN ELIZABETH, b. NYC, Jan. 26, 1926; d. Richard A. and Helen Eugenia (King) Hayes. Ed.: "Joint" Conference, 1974-81; Columbia Road Review, 1980-85; pub. numerous poetry chapbooks, two poetry books. Student, U. VT, 1945-47. Typesetter, own firm, Washington, DC, 1964-74; ed., pub. King Publications, Washington, DC, 1974—. Served as sgt., USA-WAC, 1951-54. Fels Ed. Fellowship Award, CCLM, 1976; Ed. Grant Fellowship, CCLM, 1980. Office: King Publications Box 19332 Washington DC 20036

KING, MARCIA LOUISE, b. Toledo, Nov. 13, 1950; d. Raymond Arthur Gruenwald and Dorothy June (Greenwalt) Streib; m. Michael Jay Friemark, June 26, 1970 (div. Nov. 1973); 1 dau., Lisa Marie Friemark-King; m. Gene Nelson King, June 10, 1976. Contrbr. articles to numerous mags., newspapers including Christian Sci. Monitor, others Student U. Toledo, 1983-86. Secy. Children Services Bd., Maumee, OH, 1973-77; real estate agent Ned Smith Realty, Toledo, 1977-80; free-lance wrtr., 1980—. Arts reporter Sta. WGTE-TV, Toledo, 1986. Mem. Northwest Ohio Wrtrs. Forum (program chairperson). Home: 2972 115th St Toledo OH 43611

KING, PHIL JOHN, b. Erie, PA, Sept. 28, 1940; s. John McCarthy and Eleanor Ann (Niebauer) K.; m. Janice Ellen Graig, 1965 (div. 1968); 1

dau., Selene Yvette Graif; m. 2d, Pearl Grzybowsky 1983 (div. 1984). Author: A Collection of Works by Phil King, 1978, Another Collection of Works by Phil King, 1979, And Another Collection of Works by Phil King, 1979, And Yet Another Collection of Works by Phil King, 1982, And Of Course Another Collection of Works by Phil King, 1985, Wild Wines, Colas and Whiskeys, 1985. Wrkg. on Wild Foods What's Worth Eating? Student Gannon U. Utility man Hammermill Paper Co., Erie, 1970—. Served with USNR, 1957-65. Home: Carter's Beach Erie PA 16511

KING, REY REGINALD, b. Berkeley, CA, Oct. 5, 1954, s. Daniel Barlow and Artee M. (Allen) K. Pub., ed., wrtr., illustrator: I Am Mag., 1973, Cosmic Circus art and lit. mag., 1974-84; illustrator, ed.: Basic Media in Education, 1975; pub., ed., illustrator The Last American Novel, 1985. Student L.A. Pierce Coll., Los Angeles, 1972-74. Pub., ed. Cosmicircus Prodns., Berkeley, Calif., 1974-84, 86—; tech. illustrator Stanford Telecommunications, Mountain View, Calif., 1980-82. NEA, CCLM grantee, 1980. Mem. East Bay Artist Network (founder). Home: 414 S 41st St Richmond CA 94804

KING, STEPHEN EDWIN, b. Portland, ME, Sept. 21, 1947; s. Donald and Nellie Ruth (Pillsbury) K.; m. Tabitha Jane Spruce, Jan. 2, 1971; children: Naomi, Joe Hill, Gwen. Novels include Carrie, 1974, Salem's Lot, 1975, The Shining, 1976, The Stand, 1978, Firestarter, 1980, Danse Macabre, 1981, Cujo, 1981, Different Seasons, 1982, The Dark Tower: The Gunslinger, 1982, Christine, 1983, Pet Sematary, 1983, Cycle of the Werewolf, 1985, Skeleton Crew, 1986; short story collection Night Shift, 1978. BS U. ME, 1970. Tchr. English, Hampden (ME) Acad., 1971-73; writer-in-res, U. ME at Orono, 1978-79. Mem. AG Am., SAG, Screen Writers of Am., WG. Address: Viking Press 625 Madison Ave New York NY 10022

KINGERY, LIONEL BRUCE, b. New Albany, IN, June 13, 1921; s. Glenda and Frances Emma (Foster) K.; m. Mary Margaret DeShon; children—Mary Frances, David Bruce, Deborah Rose, Melody Ellen. Author: educational seminars, workbooks for labor workshops, manuscripts of poetry about labor and social justice, philosophy, & WWII. BA, MA and Ed.D., Wayne State University. International Representative, Education Department, UAW International Union, 1964-85. Education and Training Consultant to UAW-Ford NDTP Center, Dearborn, Michigan; UAW-Chrysler National Joint Training Committee, Detroit, Michigan. U.S. Army, 1952-46, PTO. U.S. Army Captain-Infantry, Retired. Member, Board of Control, Ferris State College, Michigan. Home: 947 Francis Rochester Hills MI 48063

KINGSTON, CECELIA M., b. Hastings, NY. Contrbr. to NYSED Jnl, Impact, Critical Issues in Writing, Education Digest, Instructor Mag., othr. prof. jnls. AB, SUNY at Albany, 1951; MA, Hunter Coll., 1969. Pres. Cecelia Kingston & Assoc., Inc (Hastings, NY), 1981—; English tchr. Tarrytown pub. schls. (NY), 1963-72, Fremont High Schl. (Sunnyside, CA), 1960-63; adjunct prof. Fordham U. (NY), 1981-84. Outstanding tchr. of Bay Area, San Jose State Coll., 1961. Mem. NY State English Council, Assn. of Supervisors & Curriculum Developers. Office: 52 Columbia Ave Hastings on Hudson NY 10706

KINNELL, GALWAY, b. Providence, Feb. 1, 1927; s. James Scot and Elizabeth (Mills) K.; m. Ines Delgado de Torres; children—Maud Natasha, Fergus. Author: poems What a Kingdom It Was, 1960, Flower Herding on Mount Monadnock, 1964; translation The Poems of Francois Villon, 1965; novel Black Light, 1966; poems Body Rags, 1968; translation On The Motion and Immobility of Douve, 1968, The Lackawanna Elegy, 1970; poems First Poems, 1971, The Book of Nightmares, 1971, The Avenue Bearing the Initial of Christ into the New World, 1974, interviews Walking Down the Stairs, 1978; rev. translation The Poems of Francois Villon, 1977; poems Mortal Acts, Mortal Words, 1980, Selected Poems, 1982, The Past, 1985. AB, Princeton U., 1948; MA, U. Rochester, 1949. Guggenheim fellow, 1963-64, 74-75. Mem. Natl. Acad. and Inst. Arts and Letters. Address: Sheffield VT 05866

KINNEY HANSON, SHARON D., b. East St. Louis, IL, Sept. 29, 1942; m. Richard Hanson. Contrbr.: Show Me Libraries, Sheba Rvw—Lit. Mag. for the Arts, Unterrified Democrat, other publs.; contrbr. poetry: Sou'Wester, The We Collective, River Styx, other lit mags; author: Directory of Art Museums and Galleries in Missouri, 1983; sr. ed. The First Anthology of Missouri Women Writers, 1987. BA, So. Ill. U., 1967; MEd, U. Mo., 1977. Curator edn. Mo. State Mus., Jefferson City, 1979-80; ed. Elegance mag., Lakeland, Fla., 1981; project dir. book discussion program Mo. Com. Humanities, 1984-86, Southwest Mo. regional coordinator, 1985—; ed. Midwest Arts & Lit., Jefferson City, 1978—. Mem. Mo. Wrtrs. Guild (state pres., 1986-87; Best Non-Fiction award 1985), Mo. Com. Lit. (coordinator 1982-84), PSA. Office: PO Box 1623 Jefferson City MO 65102

KINSELLA, W(ILLIAM) P(ATRICK), b. Edmonton, Alta., Canada, May 25, 1935; s. John Matthew and Olive (Elliot) K.; m. (1) Mildred Clay, Sept. 10, 1965 (div., 1978), (2) Ann Knight, Dec. 30, 1978; children: Shannon, Erin. Author: Dance Me Outside (stories), 1977, Scars (stories), 1978, Shoeless Joe Jackson Comes to Iowa (stories), 1980, Born Indian, 1981, Shoeless Joe (novel; based on title story in Shoeless Joe Jackson Comes to Iowa), 1982, The Ballad of the Public Trustee (chapbook), 1982, The Moccasin Telegraph (stories), 1983, 1984, The Thrill of the Grass (chapbook), 1984, The Thrill of the Grass (stories; includes chapbook story), 1984, The Alligator Report (stories), 1985, The Iowa Baseball Confederacy (novel), 1986, Five Stories (chapbook), 1986, The Fencepost Chronicles (stories), 1986, 1987, Red Wolf, Red Wolf, 1987, The Further Adventures of Slugger McBatt, 1988. Contrbr to anthologies, including Best Canadian Stories: 1977, 81, 85, Aurora: New Canadian Writing, 1979, More Stories from Western Canada, Oxford Anthology of Canadian Literature, Pushcart Prize Anthology 5, The Spirit That Moves Us Reader, Introduction to Fiction, The Temple of Baseball, Penguin Book of Modern Canadian Short Stories, The Armchair Book of Baseball, Small Wonders, Illusion Two, West of Fiction, Anthology of Canadian Literature in English, vol. 2, Contexts: Anthology 3, Aquarius, New Worlds, The Process of Writing, A Sense of Place, The Anthology Anthology, New Voices 2, 3, Rainshadow, Here's the Story. Also contrbr of more than 200 stories to American and Canadian mags, including Sports Illustrated, Arete: Jnl of sports Literature, Story Qtly, Matrix, Canadian Fiction Mag. BA, Univ. of Victoria, 1974; MFA, Univ. of Iowa, 1978. Clerk, Govt. of Alberta, Edmonton, 1954-56; mgr, Retail Credit Co., Edmonton, Alta., 1956-61; acct. exec., City of Edmonton, Alta., 1961-67; owner, Caesar's Italian Village (restaurant), Victoria, B.C., 1967-72; student and taxicab driver, Victoria, 1974-76; instr, Univ. of Iowa, Iowa City, 1976-78; asst prof of English and creative writing, 1978-83; writer, 1983—. Member: Writers' Union of Canada, American Amateur Press Assn, Soc. of American Baseball Researchers, American Atheists, Enoch Emery Soc. Houghton Mifflin Literary Fellowship, 1982, Books in Canada First Novel award, 1983, and Canadian Authors Assn prize, 1983, all for Shoeless Joe; Writers Guild of Alberta, O'Hagan novel medal, 1984, for The Moccasin Telegraph; Alberta Achievement Award for Excellence in Literature; winner Stephen Leacock Award for Humor, 1987, for The Fencepost Chronicles. Address: Box 400 White Rock British Columbia Canada V4B 5G3

KINSMAN, LAWRENCE CHARLES, b. NYC, Jan. 7, 1953, s. Edward Lawrence and Concetta (Spaziani) K. Contrbr. poems, stories to Foxtail '85, Pacific Rvw, Touchstone, Conn. River Rvw, numerous other lit mags. BA in English, SUNY-Oneonta, 1975; D Arts, SUNY- Albany, 1983. Instr. English N.H. Coll., Manchester, 1984—, Fulbright Jr. Lectr. in American Lit at Univ. of Oporto, Portugal, 1986-87. Mem. AWP. Home: 8 Worcester Sq Boston MA 02118

KINZIE, MARY, b. Montgomery, AL, Sept. 30, 1944, d. Harry Ernst and Mary Louise (Huey) Kinzie; m. Jon Arvid Larson, May 30, 1972; 1 child, Phoebe Kinzie-Larson. Author: (verse) The Threshold of the Year, 1982; ed. Prose for Borges, 1972; co-ed. The Little Magazine in America, 1979; ed. Elpenor (contemporary poetry series). PhD, Johns Hopkins U., 1980. Instr. English, Northwestern U., 1975-78, lectr., 1978-85, assoc. prof., 1985—, dir. English major in writing, 1978—; exec. ed. TriQtly, 1975-78. Recipient awards for poetry Ill. Arts Council, 1977, 80, 84, awards for essay, 1978, 82; Devins award for 1st vol. of verse U. Mo. Press, 1982; DeWitt Wallace fellow MacDowell Colony, summer 1979; Ill. Arts Council artist grantee, summer 1983; Guggenheim fellow in poetry, 1986. Mem. PEN, PSA, Soc. Midland Authors. Office: Dept Eng Univ Hall 102 Northwestern U Evanston IL 60201

KIPLINGER, AUSTIN HUNTINGTON, b. Washington, Sept. 19, 1918, s. Willard Monroe and Irene (Austin) K.; m. Mary Louise Cobb, Dec. 11, 1944; children—Todd Lawrence, Knight Austin. Co-author: Boom and Inflation Ahead, 1958, Washington Now, 1975, The Exciting '80s, 1979. AB, Cornell U., 1939; LLD (hon.), Union Coll., 1977; DAM (hon.), Embry-Riddle Aeronautical U., 1980; DH (hon.), Bryant Coll., 1982, DHL, St. Mary's Coll. of Md., 1986. Reporter Kiplinger Washington Letter, 1939, San Francisco Chronicle, 1940-41; mng. ed. Changing Times Mag., Washington, 1945-48; bus. columnist Chgo. Jnl Commerce, 1948-50; news commentator ABD and NBC, Chgo., 1950-56; ed. Kiplinger Washington Letter, Washington, 1961—; editorial chmn. Changing Times mag., 1961—. Office: 1729 H St NW Washington DC 20006

KIPLINGER, CHRISTINA LOUISE, b. L.I., NY, May 7, 1957; d. Frank Edward Havlatko and Margaret Louise (Golden) Richards; m. Richard Stewart, July 17, 1973 (div. Aug. 1977); 1 child, Karen Anne; m. Douglas Hugh Kiplinger, Sept. 24, 1977. Author: Blood Red Pens, 1987; contrbr. to Undinal Songs, Fantasy Rvw.,

Ohioana Qtly, Tri-State Trader, Horror Show, Bleeding Virgin, Bloodrake, Footsteps. Freelance wrtr., 1980—. Mem. P&W, SFWA, Cambridge Wrtrs. Workshop, Small Press Wrtrs. Home: Box 612 Cambridge OH 43725

KIRBY, TOM, see Bowart, Walter Howard

KIRCHER, JOYCE MEGGINSON, b. Cin., June 5, 1928; d. William Conrad and Theresa Philomena (Keller) Kircher; m. George Maurice Megginson, June 1, 1957; children—Amy, Barbara Ann, Christopher George. Contrbr. articles, verses, greeting card copy, employee motivation pieces. A.B., Miami U., 1950; M.B.A., Stetson U., 1976. Public relations dir. Shillito's, Cin., 1950-57; corr. Fairchild Pubs., NYC, 1960-65; owner Glad Tidings, Merritt Island, FL, 1960—; free-lance wrtr., 1960—. Mem. AAUW (public info. officer 1980's), Space Coast Public Relations Assn. (secy. 1980's), NWC, Fla. Free-Lance Wrtrs. Assn., Mensa, Phi Beta Kappa. Home: 545 Patrick Ave Merritt Island FL 32953

KIRCHNER, ELIZABETH ANN, (Elizabeth Ann), b. Long Beach, CA, Jul. 19, 1952; d. Emmett Wm. Augustine Kirchner and Betty Elizabeth (Butner) Bortles; m. David Michael Giorgi, Jul. 17, 1982; children—Daniel, Christian. Contrbr. to Our 20th Century's Greatest Poems, 1982, The World's Best Loved Poems, 1983. Student Westmont Coll. Technical special. Mr. Natural's Electric classroom (San Francisco), 1985—; computer operator SETA (Sacramento), 1980-85. Golden Poet Award, World of Poetry, 1985. Home: 1943 Hayes San Francisco CA 94117

KIRK, NORMAN ANDREW, b. NYC, May 22, 1937, s. Justin Norman and Vagner Amanda (Vorland) K.; m. Carolina Marie Olson, Apr. 18, 1970. Author: Some Poems, My Friends, 1981, Panda Zoo, 1983. AA, Boston U., 1957, postgrad., 1957-59. Ed. The Kirk Syndicate, Wayland, Mass., 1961—, West of Boston, Wayland, 1983—; assoc. ed. Bitterroot, Bklyn., 1977—; freelance poet, 1955—; chmn. Wayland Arts Council, 1980. Founder, pres. Mass. Assn. Paraplegics, 1963; mem. Vocat. Rehab. Planning Commn., Boston, 1965, Mass. Rehab. Planning Council, Worcester. Office: Box 2 Cochituate Sta Wayland MA 01778

KIRK, PEARL LOUISE, (Mayette Trails), b. Houston, ID, Feb 8, 1930; d. Pearl Ruel and Norma Ida (Wallace) Renz; m. Merit Ruby Kirk, Sept 6, 1949. Author: Timy Boy, 1963, Branches, 1963, Velvet Branches, 1966, Alone With God, 1966, Golden Moments, 1967, Pearl's Pen, 1970, Dear Americans, 1970, Labor of Love, 1970; contrbr. Grit, True Romance, others. Ed./pub. Inky Trails Publs. Mem. Id. Writer's League, Genl. State Writers Guild, Id. press Women, United Amateur Press, Toastmistress-E Dah How. Address: Box 345 Middleton ID 83644

KIRK, RUSSELL AMOS, b. Plymouth, MI, Oct. 19, 1918; s. Russell Andrew and Majorie (Pierce) K.; m. Annette Yvonne Courtemanche, Sept. 19, 1964; 4 daus. Author: John Randolph of Roanoke, 1951, 64, 78, The Conservative Mind, 1953, St. Andrews, 1954, A Program for Conservatives, 1954, Academic Freedom, 1955, Beyond the Dreams of Avarice, 1956, The Intelligent Woman's Guide to Conservatism, 1957, The American Cause, 1957, Old House of Fear, 1961, The Surly Sullen Bell, 1962, Confessions of a Bohemian Troy, 1963, The Intemperate Professor, 1965, A Creature of the Twilight, 1966, Edmund Burke, 1967, Political Principles of Robert A. Taft, 1967, Enemies of the Permanent Things, 1969, Eliot and His Age, 1972, Roots of American Order, 1974, The Princess of All Lands, 1979, Decadence and Renewal in Higher Learning, 1979, Lord of the Hollow Dark, 1979, Portable Conservative Reader, 1982, Reclaiming a Patrimony, 1983, Watchers at the Strait Gate, 1984, The Wise Men Know What Wicked Things Are Written on the Sky, 1987; also critical intros. and prefaces to reprints standard scholarly works. BA, MI St. U., 1940; MA, Duke U., 1951; DLitt., St. Andrews U., Scotland, 1952. Contrbr. to scholarly and popular publs., including Sewanee Rvw, Fortnightly Rvw, Dublin Rvw, Yale Rvw, Jnl History of Ideas, Annals of Am. Acad., NY Times Mag., Fortune, Wall St. Jnl, History Today, Gen. Edn., The Critic, Kenyon Rvw, Natl. Rvw, Commonweal, Christianity Today, Queen's Qtly, America, Contemporary Rvw, Analysis, Center mag.; founder qtly. jnl, Modern Age; ed. qtly., Univ. Bookman. Constitutional fellowship NEH; Guggenheim fellow; Sr. fellow ACLS; awarded Weaver Prize of Ingersoll Awards, 1984; Fulbright Lecturer, St. Andrews Univ., Scottland, Address: Piety Hill Mecosta MI 49332

KIRKPATRICK, JEANE DUANE JORDAN, b. Duncan, OK., Nov. 19, 1926; d. Welcher F. and Leona (Kile) Jordan; m. Evron M. Kirkpatrick, Feb. 20, 1955; children: Douglas Jordan, John Evron, Stuart Alan. Author: Foreign Students in the United States: A National Survey, 1966, Mass Behavior in Battle and Captivity, 1968, Leader and Vanguard in Mass Society: The Peronist Movement in Argentina, 1971, Political Woman, 1973, The Presidential Elite, 1976, Dismantling the Parties: Reflections on Party Reform and Party Decomposition, 1978, The Reagan Phenomenon, 1982, Dictatorships and Doublestandards, 1981; Editor, contbr.: Elections USA, 1956, Strategy of Deception, 1963, The New Class, 1978, The New American Political System, 1978. A.A. Stephens Coll., 1946; A.B., Barnard Coll., 1948; M.A., Columbia U., 1950, Ph.D., 1967; postgrad (French govt. fellow), U. Paris Inst. de Sci. Politique, 1952-53, Earhart fellow, 1956-57. Office: Am Ent Inst 1150 17th St. NW Washington DC 20036

KIRSCHT, JUDITH MARY (KENYON), b. Chgo., Sept. 21, 1933; d. Allan T. and Lois E. (Gardner) Kenyon; m. John Patrick Kirscht, Sept. 19, 1953 (div. Jan. 1975); children: Miriam Louise, Paula Clarice (dec. July, 1962). Contrbr. to Ann Arbor League of Women Voters Bull., Good Morning Mich., The Main-Sheet, Notes on Tchg. English, Ariadne's Thread, Mss, Jnl. Adv. Composition No. IV, Blue Ox Rvw. BA, U. Chgo., 1953; MA, MFA, U. Mich., 1971, 74, 83-85. Instr. Washtenaw Community Coll., Ann Arbor, Mich., 1977-79, Henry Ford Community Coll., Dearborn, Mich., 1978-79, Eastern Mich. Univ., Ypsilanti, 1978-79, Schoolcraft Coll., Livonia, 1978; lectr. Univ Mich., Ann Arbor, 1979-86. Campaign mgr., publicity writer, Democratic Party, Ann Arbor, 1963-75; bd. dirs., League of Womens Voters, Ann Arbor, 1961-65 lecturer, Univ. of Calif., Santa Barbara, 1986—. Mem. NCTE. Address: 7084 Marymount Way Goleta CA 93117

KIRTLEY, PHYLLIS, see Thompson, Phyllis Hoge

KISSICK, GARY RICHARD, b. Iowa City, IA, Feb. 6, 1946, s. William Dean and Mary Helena (Mauke) K.; m. Yukiko Shinozaki, Nov. 30, 1979; 1 son, Dean Nobutomo. Author: Outer Islands (winner 1983 Pacific Poetry Series competition), 1984; ed.: Hawaii Rvw, 1975-77; contrbr. poetry: Esquire, Hawaii Rvw, Prairie Schooner, Rolling Stone, numerous other mags and lit jnls; contrbr. fiction: Bamboo Ridge, San Francisco Chronicle, Village Advocate, Cin. Enquirer; contrbr. anthologies: Manna-Mana, 1975, Poetry East-West, 1975, Poetry Hawaii, 1979, The Best of Bamboo Ridge, 1987. BA in English, Miami U., Oxford, Ohio, 1967; MFA in Creative Wrtg., U. Iowa, 1969. Instr. English U. Hawaii, Honolulu, 1969-72, 75-80, La. State U., Baton Rouge, 1980-81, European div. U. Md., Heidelberg, Germany, 1981—. Winner poetry competitions Honolulu Commn. on Culture and the Arts, 1975, Hawaii Lit. Arts Council-U. Hawaii Press, 1983; recipient PEN Syndication Fiction award, 1984; grantee NEA, 1982. Mem. P&W. Address: Box 2616 APO New York NY 09009

KITCHIN, ROSEMARIE A., b. Springfield, IL, June 6, 1939, d. Bernard and L. Lucille (McCarty) Atkin; m. Kenneth Thomas Kitchin Jr., Dec. 17, 1960 (div. 1974); children—Kraig Thomas, Kevin Thomas. BS in Journalism, Northwestern U., 1961. Free-lance wrtr., publicist, Detroit, 1967-72; dir. public relations Jewish Welfare Fedn. of Detroit, 1972-76; owner, pres. Rm. Communications, Detroit and Kansas City, 1974-84; mgr. public relations Chrysler Corp., Detroit, 1976-79; mgr., then v.p. communications Martin Fromm & Assocs., Kansas City, Mo., 1979-84; regional mgr. Chilton Corp., Atlanta, 1984-86; chief ed. Automotive Mktg., Chilton Corp., Radnor, Pa., 1986—. Mem. Women in Communications. Home: 49 Iroquois Ct Wayne PA 19087

KITE, L. PATRICIA (PAT), b. NYC, Feb. 2, 1940; d. Oscar and Sarah (Evenchick) Padams; m. 1962 (div. 1975); children—Rachel, Karen, Laura, Sally. Novel: (romance), 1984, Controlling Lawn and Garden Insects, 1987. Other books self-pub.: How to Self-Promote Your Book, Freeland Interview Tips and Tricks, How to Be Successfully Interviewed by the Press, How to Write Fast, Fun Money Fillers, 1985/86, Syndicating Your Column, 1987. Also over 700 mag./newspaper articles, short stories in print. BS, U. Calif. Med. Ctr., San Francisco, 1961; MS in Mass Communication, San Jose State U., 1982. Phys. therapist, 1975—; free-lance writer P.K. Writing Services, Newark, Calif., 1975—; instr. journalism Ohlone Coll., Fremont, Calif., 1982—; TV producer/host The Writing Life, Newark and San Francisco, 1983—; newspaper columnist P.K. Writing Services, Syndicate, 1983—. Active in pub. relations for community polit. candidates, Newark, 1976-85; vol. Calif. Schl. for Deaf, Fremont, 1983-84; TV producer/host The Writing Life, Newark, Fremont and San Francisco. Mem. Natl. Soc. Newspaper Columnists (dir. pub. relations), Garden Wrtrs Assn of America,No. Calif. Sci. Writers Assn., Sigma Delta Chi. Recipient short fiction award Calif. Writers Stanford Conf., 1977, newspaper column genl. interest award natl. Soc. Newspaper Columnists, 1984, Best of Berkley/Jove Romance Line, Romance Writers Assn., 1984. Home: 5318 Stirling Ct Newark CA 94560

KIZER, CAROLYN ASHLEY, b. Spokane, WA, Dec. 10, 1925; d. Benjamin Hamilton and M. (Ashley) K.; m. Stimson Bullitt, Jan. 1948 (div.); children—Ashley Ann (Mrs. Wilham Schwartzman) Scott, Jill Hamilton; m. 2d, John Marshall Woodbridge, Apr. 11, 1975. Author: The Ungrateful Garden, 1961, Knock Upon Silence, 1965, Midnight Was My Cry, 1971, Yin, 1984 (Pulitzer Prize, 1985), Mermaids in the

Basement, 1984, The Nearness of You, 1986; Carrying Over (translations), 1987. Founder, editor: Poetry N.W. 1959-65; contrbr. poems, articles to Am., Brit. jnls. BA, Sarah Lawrence Coll., 1945; postgrad., Columbia, 1946-47; studied poetry with Theodore Roethke U. WA, 1953-54. Specialist in lit. US Dept. St., Pakistan, 1964-65; first dir. lit programs NEA, 1966-70; poet-in-residence U. NC at Chapel Hill, 1970-74; Hurst Prof. Lit. WA U., St. Louis, 1971; lectr. Spring Lecture Series Barnard Coll., 1972; acting dir. grad. writing program Columbia, 1972; McGuffey Lectr., poet-in-residence, Ohio U., 1974; vis. poet IA Writer's Workshop, 1975; vis. poet Stanford, 1986; sr. fellow in the hum., Princeton, 1986. Mem. ACLU, Amnesty Intl., PEN, PSA, AWP. Award, natl. Acad. & Inst. Arts & Ltrs., 1985. Address: 19772 8th St East Sonoma CA 95476

KIZER, KATHRYN W., b. Greenville, SC, Nov. 2, 1924; d. Basil Cowan and Kathryn (Russell) Willingham; m. Rev. Lawton E. Kizer, Jr., June 12, 1948; children—Lawton E., Russell. Contrbr. chapters to: Reaching Preschoolers, 1980, The Ministry of Childhood Edn., 1985; author: Circus Tent Summer, 1976, The Harley Shields: Alaskan Missionaries, 1982, The Preschool Challenge: Sunday School Outreach, 1986, 200+ Ideas for Teaching Preschoolers, 1986, Things to Remember About My First Year. AB, Winthrop Coll., 1945; postgrad., U. South Carolina, 1948, 50, Union Theol. Sem., 1968. Ed. Start/Shave/Mission Friends products, Woman's Missionary Union, Birmingham, Ala.Mem. NAEYC, SACUS. Office: Box C-10 Birmingham AL 35283

KLAASSEN, CAROL S., b. Two Rivers, WI, Dec. 10, 1951, d. Richard William and Elizabeth Ann (O'Connell) Dawson; m. Michael John Klaassen, Oct. 1, 1977; children—Trevor John, Mitchell Ryan. Contrbr. children's stories, articles to Turtle Mag., Out Little Friend, On The Line mag.. Wrkg. on juvenile fiction, novel. BS in Edn., Kans. U., 1974; grad. Inst. Children's Lit. course; tchr. Westford Acad., Coral Springs, Fla., 1974-75, St. Francis of Assisi Schl., Wichita, Kans, 1975-76; freelance wrtr., 1983—. Mem. NWC. Home: 2054 Flynn St Wichita KS 67207

KLAHR, MYRA BLOSSOM, b. NYC,Apr. 16, 1933, d. David and Sophie (Margolis) Cohen; children—Marc, Ellen, Susan, Shari. Author: The Waiting Room, 1972; ed. The Eagle Soars, 1980; contrbr. poetry to Hanging Loose, Sesheta, Small Pond, Unicorn; contrbr. articles to newspapers, mags. BS in Edn., Queens Coll., 1954, MA, 1960. Tchr., various schls. in N.Y., 1954-57, 60-70; founder, exec. dir. N.Y. State Poets in the Schls., Inc., N.Y.C., 1973—; exec. dir. Poets in Public Service, N.Y.C., since 1973. Winner Dylan Thomas prize New Schl. for Social Research, N.Y.C., 1972. Office: Poets in Public Service One Union Sq New York NY 10003

KLAIBER, TERESA LYNN MARTIN, b. Portsmouth, OH, Aug. 15, 1949; d. John G. and Mary Helen (Feyler) Martin; m. James David Klaiber, Apr. 28, 1968; children—John Ian, David Martin, Matthew. Author: Klaiber Cousins, 1981, Clayton Connections, a New Jersey Research Guide, 1984, New Conord, Ohio 1833-1902, 1984, W. I. Potter's Travels 1868, 1986; (with Sharon Irby) Guide to Cemetery Preservation, 1987. Wrkg. on Medicine nd the Railroad in Southeastern Ohio. Student Eastern Ky. U., 1968; cert. in Secretarial Sci., U. Ky., 1970. Civil service secy. U. Ky., Lexington, 1967-70; owner, researcher Family Lineage Investigations, New concord, OH, 1971—. Home: 160 Fairfield Dr New Concord OH 43762

KLAPPERT, PETER, b. Rockville Center, NY, Nov. 14, 1942; s. Herman Emil and Grace Barbara (Rupp) Klappert. Author: Lugging Vegetables to Nantucket, 1971, Circular Stairs, Distress in Mirrors, 1975, Non Sequitur O'Connor, 1977, The Idiot Princess of the Last Dynasty, 1984, '52 Pick-Up: Scenes from the Conspiracy, 1984, Internal Foreigner, 1984; contrbr. poetry to 50 Contemporary Poets: The Creative Process, 1976, The American Poetry Anthology, 1975, The Heath Guide to Poetry, 1982, others. BA, Cornell U., 1964; MA, U. of Ia., 1967, MFA, 1968. Instr., Rollins Coll., Winter Park, Fla., 1968-71; lectr. Harvard, Cambridge, Mass., 1971-74; wrtr.-in-res., College of William and Mary, Williamsburg, Va., 1976-77, asst. prof., 1977-78; asst. prof., 1978-81, assoc. prof., 1981—, and dir. of wrtg. program, 1979–80, 85—. George Mason U., Fairfax, Va., 1978—. Awards: Yale Series of Younger Poets, 1970, NEA fellowship, 1973, 1979; Ingram Merrill Fdn. Grant, 1983. Mem. PSA, AWP, AAP, PEN. Address: Dept of Eng George Mason Univ Fairfax VA 22030

KLASKIN, RONNIE, see Klaskin, Ruth Laura

KLASS, SHEILA SOLOMON, b. Bklyn., Nov. 6, 1927; d. Abraham Louis and Virginia (Glatter) Solomon; m. Morton Klass, May 2, 1953; children—Perri Elizabeth, David Arnold, Judith Alexandra. Author: Come Back on Monday, 1960, Everyone in This House Makes Babies, 1964, Bahadur Means Hero, 1969, A Perpetual Surprise, 1981, Nobody Knows Me in Miami, 1981, To See My Mother Dance, 1981, Alive and Starting Over, 1983, The Bennington Stitch, 1985, Page Four, 1986, Credit-Card Carole, 1987. BA, Bklyn. Coll., 1949; MA, U. Ia., 1951, MFA, 1953. Tchr. jr. high schl. Julia Ward Howe Schl., NYC,1951-57; lectr. to prof. English Manhattan Comm. Coll., NYC,1965—. Mem. NOW, SANE. Recipient Bicentennial playwriting award, Players Guild, 1976. Mem. PEN. Address: 330 Sylvan Ave Leonia NJ 07605

KLEIN, KENNETH D., b. Bklyn., 1954. Author scripts for T.V. including Love Am. Style, Kate & Allie. Student Jordan Coll. Music, Indpls., 1972-76; BS in Communications, Butler U., Indpls., 1976. Licensed marine, radio telephone-telegraph FCC, 1971, 72. News reporter WLWI-TV and WAJC-FM, Indpls., 1974-75; producer WTHR-TV, Indpls., 1975-76; freelance wrtr., 1976—, U.S. Copyright for screenplay "Jersey Milk." Mem. Soc. For Technical Communication, Wash. D.C. Home: 37 Hillcrest Ave Morristown NJ 07960

KLEIN, NORMA, b. NYC, May 13, 1938, d. Emanuel and Sadie (Frankel) Klein; m. Erwin Fleissner, July 27, 1963; children—Jennifer Luise, Katherine Nicole. Author: Wives and Other Women, 1982, Give and Take, 1985, 12 other adult novels, 17 for young adults, 7 picture books for younger children. BA, Barnard Coll., 1960; MA, Columbia U., 1963. Home: 27 W 96th St New York NY 10025

KLEIN, VIRGINIA S., b. Liberty, NY, Dec. 30, 1936; d. Abraham and Lillian (Malin) Levine; m. Andrew Klein, July 21, 1961; children—Earl Saul, Holly Jo. Author: How to Get Free!, 1985, Hairy Fairy Tales. BS, Rutgers U., 1972, MSW, 1974, PhD, 1978. Mem. adjunct faculty, GSSW, Rutgers U., New Brunswick, NJ, 1974-80; social wkr. II, NJ Corr. Inst. for Women, Clinton, NJ, 1972-75; psychotherapist, priv. pract., Somerville, NJ, 1977—. Mem. profl. orgns; Co-chair 1st Intl. Conf. on Incest & Related Problems, Zurich, Switzerland, 1986. Home: 18 S Cadillac Dr Somerville NJ 08876

KLEIN, WILLIAM HARRY, b. NYC, Oct. 17, 1951; s. Stanley William and Roslyn (Specht) K. Author: The Shadow is Color Still, 1983; contrbr. poetry to Slant, The Blue Unicorn, Pivot, Voices Intl., Earthwise, The Eras Rvw. BA, Stony Brook, 1972; MA, Vanderbilt, 1985. Ed. Human Sci Press, NYC, 1976-77, Alan L. Liss Inc., NYC, 1979-82, Doubleday & Co., NYC, 1982-84, Pfizer Pharmaceutical, NYC, 1985—. Mem. Mensa, DG, WG, P&W. Address: 126 E 27 St NYC NY 10016

KLEINBERG, FREDRIC LAUFER, b. NYC, Oct. 13, 1949; s. Joseph and Sylvia (Laufer) K.; m. Kelly Ann Breene, May 31, 1972; children—Joseph, Peter, Robert. Author: The Aladdin Network, 1986. B.A. in Economics, Mich. State U., 1970. Pres., F. L. Kleinberg & Co., Boulder, 1979-86; computer cons. Wrtr.'s Partnership, Boulder, 1986—; free-lance wrtr., 1986—. Served to Lt. USN Mem. Naval Inst., Rocky Mountain Wrtrs. Guild (bd. dirs.). Home: 3882 Wonderland Hill Ave Boulder CO 80302

KLEINER, RICHARD ARTHUR, b. NYC, Mar. 9, 1921; s. Israel Simon and Alma (Kempner) K.; m. Hortensia Rivas, Aug. 7, 1954; children—Katherine Evert, Cynthia Smetana, Peter. Author: E.S.P. And The Stars, 1970, Index of Initials and Acronyms, 1971, Take One, 1974, The Two Of Us, 1976, Hollywood's Greatest Love Stories, 1976, Please Don't Shoot My Dog, 1981; contrbr. articles to mags. LittB, Rutgers U., 1942. With Newspaper Enterprise Assn., Clev., 1947-49, NYC, 1949-64, Los Angeles, 1964-85, sr. editor, 1977-85, West Coast dir. United Media Prodns., 1982-85; mem. journalism faculty CA St. Coll., Long Beach, 1975-77, UCLA, 1977-82; Book Editor, Desert Sun, Palm Springs, CA, 1985—. Served with US Army, 1942-46. Address: Box 2978 Palm Desert CA 92261

KLEINHANS, THEODORE JOHN, (Jon Littlejon, Jean Petitjean, Giovanni Giovannin), b. Oswego, KS, Mar. 29, 1924; s. Theodore and Marie (Hellwig) K.; m. Leona E., Dec. 22, 1956; children—Christopher A., Kathryn A. Author: Marin Luther: Saint and Sinner, 1956, The Music Master: Johann Sebastian Bach, 1962, The Year of the Lord, 1967, 10 other books, 1,000 mag. articles; co-ed. several movie scripts. Student Concordia Coll., 1939-44; MA, U. MI, 1949. Instr., U. MI, Ann Arbor, 1947-49; pub. reins. Lutheran World Fedn., Geneva, Switzerland, 1950-52; chaplain, USAF, worldwide, 1953-73; ed. Aid Assn. for Lutherans, Appleton, WI, 1973—. Mem. AG, AL. Home: 1710 S. Bluemound Dr Appleton WI 54914

KLEINSCHMIDT, EDWARD JOSEPH, b. Winona, MN, Oct. 29, 1951; s. Edward Joseph and Altrude Marion (Kulas) Kleinschmidt. Author: Magnetism, 1987; contrbr. to Poetry, MSS, Poetry Northwest, Stand, Calif. Qtly, many other lit mags. BA, St. Mary's College, 1974; MA, Hollins College, 1976. Poet, tchr., Calif. Poets in The Schools, SF, 1979-82; lectr., DeAnza College, Cupertino, CA., 1980-82; lectr., Stanford U., 1981-82; lectr., Santa Clara U., CA., 1981—. Mem. PSA, MLA. Home: 2022 Broderick St San Francisco CA 94115

KLEINSCHROD, WALTER ANDREW, b. Long Island City, NY, Jan. 1, 1928; s. Max Joseph and Martha (Forst) K.; m. Patricia Rita Corbett, Sept. 22, 1951; children—Kathy, Linda, Mary, Jeanne, Carol. Author: (with Harry Yeates) Selling Gifts and Decorative Accessories, 1965; Word Processing, 1974, Management's Guide to Word Processing, 1975; (with Kruk and Turner) Word Processing: Operations, Applications, and Administration, 1983; Critical Issues in Office Automation, 1986. Editor: Gifts & Decorative Accessories, 1953-61, Administrv. Mgmt, 1961-84. Wrkg. on novel. BA, NYU, 1951. Prin. Walter A. Kleinschrod Editorial Services, Clifton Park, N.Y., 1984—. Recipient Disting. Journalism award Indsl. Mkgt., 1962, 64, Jesse Neal award Assn. Bus. Pubs., 1966. Mem. Overseas Press Club Am., Soc. Profl. Journalists, N.Y. Bus. Press Eds. Home: 13 Mountain Way Clifton Park NY 12065

KLIEBHAN, JEROME L., b. Milw., Sept. 21, 1932, s. Adolph Ernest and Eleanor (Blask) K.; m. Margaret Mary Grogan, May 7, 1960; children—Thomas, Daniel, Lawrence, Robert, John, Ted, Virginia. BS, Marquette U., 1955. Circulation mgr. Nelson R. Crow Publs., Anaheim, Calif., 1965-69, Clissold Pub. Co., Chgo., 1969-71, Ofcl. Airline Guides, Oak Brook, Ill., 1971-74; pub. Bus. News, County Bus. Publs., Inc., Winfield, Ill., 1975—. Office: Box 193 Winfield IL 60190

KLIEWER, WARREN, b. Mountain Lake, MN, Sept. 20, 1931, s. John G. and Elizabeth (Kroeker) K.; m. Darleen Alseike, June 4, 1960 (div. 1969); m. 2d, Michele LaRue, May 23, 1971. Author: Moralities and Miracles (poems and short plays), 1961, A Bird in the Bush (opera libretto), 1962, The Prodigal Son (play), 1962, The Violators (short stories), 1964, A Trial Can Be Fun if You're the Judge (play), 1965, Liturgies, Games, Farewells (poems), 1974, How Can You Tell the Good Guys from the Bad Guys?, 1975; contrbr.: What Are We Going to Do with All These Rotting Fish? and Seven Other Short Plays, 1970, Playwrights for Tomorrow, 1975; playwright numerous produced works published in periodicals. Editor: Religious Theatre, 1964-71. BA magna cum laude, U. Minn., 1953, MFA, 1967; MA, U. Kans., 1959. Assoc. prof. English and theatre Wichita (Kans.) State U., 1966-69; prodn. dir. Natl. Humanities Series, Woodrow Wilson Natl. Fellowship Fdn., Princeton, N.J., 1970-73; free-lance wrtr., dir., actor, 1973—; artistic dir. The East Lynne Co., 1980—; actor, dir. off-Broadway, regional theatres, numerous nationwide company tours, univ. theatre prodns. Grantee Danforth Fdn., 1965-66. Mem. Actors' Equity, Screen Actors Guild, Soc. Stage Dirs. and Choreographers, New Dramatists, Dramatists Guild, Phi Beta Kappa. Home: 281 Lincoln Ave Secaucus NJ 07094

KLINE, LLOYD WARFEL, b. Lancaster, PA, Sept. 26, 1931; s. Lloyd and Daisy M. (Warfel) K. Author: Silverbrook Methodist Church 1880-1965, 1965, Education and the Personal Quest, 1971 translated as Busqueda Personal y Educacion (by Ramon Alcade, 1973), Learning to Read, Teaching to Read, 1985, They That See the Sun, 1985, 1973. Contrbr. chpt. to The Teachers Handbook, 1970; articles, newsletters, spcl. reports, poems, brochures. A.B., Franklin & Marshall Coll., 1953; M.A., Middlebury Coll., 1962; Ed.D., U. Mass., 1970. Jnls. ed. Intl. Reaing Assocs., Newark, 1970-75, dir. pubs., 1974-84; prin. Words and Services, Newark, 1984—. Mem. EPAA (awards of Excellence 1972-76), IABC. Home: 81 Kells Ave Newark DE 19711

KLINKOWITZ, JEROME, b. Milw., Dec. 24, 1943; s. Jerome Francis and Lucille Ann (McNamara) K.; m. Elaine Ann Ptaszynski, Jan. 29, 1962 (div. Jan. 16, 1978); children—Jonathan, Nina; m. 2d, Julie Ann Huffman, May 27, 1978. Author: Literary Disruptions, 1975, 2d. ed., 1980, The Life of Fiction, 1977, The Practice of Fiction in America, 1980, The American 1960s, 1980, Kurt Vonnegut, 1982, Peter Handke and the Postmodern Transformation, 1983, The Self-Apparent Word, 1984, Literary Subversions, 1985, The New American Novel of Manners, 1986; (compiler) Kurt Vonnegut, Jr.: A Descriptive Bibliography, 1974, Donald Barthelme: A Comprehensive Bibliography, 1977. Editor: Innovative Fiction, 1972, The Vonnegut Statement, 1973, 2d. ed., 1975, Writing Under Fire: Stories of the Vietnam War, 1978, Vonnegut in America, 1977, The Diaries of Willard Motley, 1979, Crosscurrents/Modern Critiques series, 1983—. Wrkg. on book on Rosenberg/Barthes/Hassan, baseball novel, World War II narratives, jazz study. BA, Marquette U., 1966, MA, 1967; PhD, U. Wis.-Madison, 1970. Asst. prof. Northern Ill. U., DeKalb, 1969-72; assoc. prof. U. Northern Iowa, Cedar Falls, 1972-76, prof. 1976—, Univ. disting. scholar, 1985—. Exec. dir. Waterloo Prof. Baseball, Inc., Waterloo, Iowa, 1978—. Recipient Syndicated Fiction award PEN, 1984, 85. Mem. PEN Home: 1904 Clay St Cedar Falls IA 50613

KLOTZER, CHARLES LOTHAR, b. Berlin, Nov. 1, 1925; came to US, 1947; naturalized 1953; s. Salo and Meta (Mayer) K.; m. Rose Finn, June 7, 1953; children—Miriam, Daniel, Ruth. BA, Washington U., 1954, postgrad studies in Poli. Sci. Mng. ed. Troy Tribune, Troy, Ill., 1948-51; founding ed. and pub. Jewish Star, St. Louis, 1954, ed. Jewish Light, 1955; p.r. and advt. dir. Fruin-Colnon, St. Louis, 1955-60; founding ed. and pub. Focus/Midwest, St. Louis, 1961-83, founding ed. and pub. St. Louis Journalism Rvw, 1970—. Served to Cpl. US Army, 1951-53. Recipient awards from Greater St. Louis Assn. of Black Jnlsts., 1977, 81, Lowell Mellet award for Investigative Journalism, 1978, 83, SIU Citation, 1981. Mem. SPJ, St. Louis Press Club, Investigative Reporters and Editors. Home: 884 Berick Dr St Louis MO 63132

KLOUDA, NAOMI GLADYS, b. Weiser, ID, Dec. 17, 1960; d. James H. and Arleen Eleanor (Ward) Warren; married; children—Nolan, Rosanne. Contrbr. articles to mags., newspapers including Outside mag., Women's Sports & Fitness, Alaska Mag., Anchorage Daily News. Ed.: Articulation—Alaska Press Women Newsletter 1987—. B.A. in Jnlsm., Gonzaga U., 1983. Jnlst., The Anchorage Times, 1983—. Home: 6324 Air Guard Rd Anchorage AK 99502

KLUFF, BARRY, see Stein, Joseph A.

KLUG, RONALD ALLAN, b. Milw., June 26, 1939, s. Harold Alfred and Linda (Kavemeier) K.; m. Lynda Rae Hosler, Feb. 20, 1971; children—Rebecca, Paul, Hans. Author: Strange Young Man in the Desert, 1970, Lord, I've Been Thinking, 1978, Psalms: A Guide to Prayer and Praise, 1978, Philippians: God's Guide to Joy, 1981, Job: God's Answer to Suffering, 1982, My Prayer Journal, 1982, How to Keep a Spiritual Journal, 1982, Growing in Joy, 1982, You Promised, Lord, 1983, Philippians: Living Joyfully, 1983, Psalms: Folk Songs of Faith, 1984, Mark: A Daily Dialogue with God, 1984, Bible Readings on Prayer, 1986; co-author: New Life for Men (with Joe Vaughn), 1984, numerous other religious books with Lyn Klug. BS in Edn., Dr. Martin Luther Coll., 1962; postgrad. U. Wis.-Milw., 1965-68. Copywrtr. Concordia Publ. House, St. Louis, 1968-69; ed. Augsburg Publ. House, Mpls., 1970-76; tchr. Am. Schl., Ft. Dauphin, Madagascar, 1976-80; free-lance wrtr., ed., 1980—. Mem. Soc. Children's Book Wrtrs. Home: 1115 S Division St Northfield MN 55057

KLYMAN, ANNE GRIFFITHS, (Reve Tamayo), b. Guantánamo, Cuba, Aug. 27, 1936; came to U.S., 1951. Author bi-lingual textbooks: El Mas Alla de Don Miguel, 1985, El Mundo de Garcia Lorca, 1985, El Mundo de Ana María Matute, 1985, El Mundo de Pablo Neruda, 1986, El Mundo Imaginario de Jorge Luis Borges, 1986; author: Los Espanoles, 1987, Los Latinoameicanos, 1987. Wrkg. on transl. of Jorge Luis Borges' works. BS in Edn., U. Vt., 1957; MEd, Towson State U., 1979. Tchr. Spanish, lan. and lit. various schls. in Md., 1965—; lectr. Am. Sch. in London, 1984-85; researcher, presenter curriculum plans, reading programs, other ednl. programs. Mem. numerous ednl. orgns. Home: 1605 Carlyle Dr Crofton MD 21114

KNAUTH, STEPHEN CRAIG, b. Milw., Dec. 5, 1950; s. Henry Martin and Dorothy Ruth (Theurer) K.; m. Sara Elizabeth Cox, Feb. 5, 1975; 1 dau., Elizabeth Reed. Author: The Flying People, 1980, Night-Fishing on Irish Buffalo Creek, 1982, The Pine Figures, 1986; contrbr to Ironwood, Prairie Schooner, Pacific Rvw, Sierra Madre Rvw, Miss. Rvw, So. Poetry Rvw, Colo. State Rvw, Carolina Qtly, others. BA, Ohio U., 1972. Writer/producer Cardinal Assocs., Charlotte, NC, 1973-75; head writer Phoenix Enterprises, Charlotte, 1976—. Recipient award New Writer's Contest, Carolina Qtly, 1978; Brockman Meml. Award, NC Poetry Soc., 1982, NEA grantee, 1984; AWP anniversary awards for Poetry, 1985. Address: 805 E Worthington Ave Charlotte NC 28203

KNEITEL, THOMAS STEPHEN, b. Bklyn., Jan. 28, 1933, s. Seymour Holtzer and Ruth Florence (Fleischer) K.; m. Sara M. Jarlien, Sept. 8, 1952 (div. 1960); m. 2d, Judy Gibson, Apr. 26, 1961; children—Robin, Kerry, Kathleen, David, Karin, Terri, Skip (dec.), Sandy. Author: Top Secret Registry, 1978, 79, 80, 81, 83, 87, Air-Scan, 1979, 80, 81, 84, Radio Station Treasury, 1986; contrbr. to Encyc. Americana, TV Guide, Electronics Illustrated, Communications World, numerous other publs. MA, NYU; PhD, Columbia U. Ed. Ziff-Davis Pub. Co., NYC, 1960-61, Horizons Publs., Modesto, Calif., 1961-62, Hobby Radio Mag., Port Washington, N.Y., 1962-82; v.p., ed. Popular Communications Mag., Hicksville, N.Y., 1982—. Home: Box 908 Smithtown NY 11787

KNIGHT, ARTHUR WINFIELD, b. San Francisco, Dec. 29, 1937; s. Walter Arthur and Irja (Blomquist) K.; m. Veronica Joyce, 1960 (annulled 1961); m. 2d, Carole Gail Smith, Aug. 10, 1963 (div. Sept. 26, 1966); m. 3d, Glee Marquardt, Sept. 27, 1966 (dec. Oct. 30, 1975); m. 4th, Kit Marie Duell, Aug. 25, 1976; 1 dau., Tiffany. Author: Interior Geographies (with Kit Knight), 1981, The First Time, 1982, The Golden Land, 1985, King of the Beatniks, 1986; ed. The Beat Book (with Glee Knight), 1974, The Beat Diary (with Kit Knight), 1977, Dear Carolyn, Jack Kerouac's Letters to Carolyn Cassady (with Kit Knight), 1983, The Beat Vision (with Kit Knight), 1987. Wrkg. on The End of the Rainbow. BA in English, San Francisco State U., 1960, MA in Creative Writing, 1962. Jnlsm. instr.

Riverside City Coll., Calif., 1964-65; Eng. instr. Delta Coll., Univ. Ctr., Mich., 1965-66; prof. English Calif. Univ. of Pa., 1966—. Recipient award Joycean Lively Arts Guild, 1982. Address: Box 439 California PA 15419

KNIGHT, BECKY, b. Oberlin, OH, Aug. 8, 1941; d. John Robert and Ruth (Westbrook) Hartley; divorced; children—Andrew John, Thomas Arthur. Contrbr. numeous poems, short stories, poetry. Grad. public schls., Savannah, OH. Linotype operaor Enterprise Rvw., Greenwich, OH, 1962-69; free-lance wrtr. Recipient Golden Poet award World of Poetry, 1985, 86, 87, numerous other awards. Mem. Firelands Writing Group. Home: 102 S Main St Trailer 32 North Fairfield OH 44855

KNIGHT, JUNE ELIZABETH, b. Weld County, CO, June 26, 1920; d. Ellis Howard and Nellie Bird (Mullikin) Curtis; m. Herman Jasper Knight, June 26, 1940; children—Herman James, Sonia Lee and Sandra Dee (twins) Contrbr. numerous articles, poems to lit. mags., popular mags., anthols. including Idaho Farmer, Homelife, The Christian, Hyacinths & Biscuits, Poetry Today. Grad. high sch., Caldwell, ID, 1940. Home: RR 2 Box 111 Caldwell ID 83605

KNIGHT, NANCY CAROL, (Jenna Darey), b. Spartanburg, S.C., Jan. 10, 1947; d. Harold David and Bessie (Steadman) Christopher; m. Larry Sproles, Aug. 14, 1965 (div.); 1 son, Michael; m. 2d, Robert R. Knight, June 3, 1978. Novelist: The Very Best, 1987; contrbr. story, articles: Romance Wrtrs. Report, Modern Romance. Student Ga. State U., 1984-86. Mem. Ga. Romance Wrtrs. (past pres.), Southeastern Wrtrs. Assn. (dir.), Romance Wrtrs. Am. (bd. dirs.). Home: 4021 Gladesworth Ln Decatur GA 30035

KNIGHT, REBECCA R., b. Oberlin, OH, Aug. 8, 1941, d. J.R. and Ruth (Westbrook) Hartley; m. Richard Allison Knight, June 1969 (div.); children—Andrew John, Thomas Ar thur. Author: For the Glory of Jesus (as Becky Hartley), 1964; columnist: Creative Urge mag.; contrbr.: The Plough, over 150 other mags. and anthologies. Wrkg. on short stories, poetry. Student public schls., Savannah, Ohio. Freelance wrtr., 1980—. Named Golden Poet of Yr. 3 consecutive years World of Poetry, 1985, 86, 87. Mem. Firelands Writing Center, NWC, Intl. Women Wrtrs. Guild, Wrtrs. World 1000 Club, New Horizons Poetry Club. Home: Trlr 32 102 S. Main St North Fairfield OH 44855

KNIGHT-WEILER, RENE MARGARET, b. Bethesda, MD, Oct. 1, 1953; d. James Lee and Violet (Boldogh) Knight; m. William John Weiler, Aug. 5, 1978; children—Denali Reed Knight Weiler, Hayden Allen Knight Weiler. Contrbr. articles to Home Edn. Mag. Ed.: Spiritual Mothering Jnl., 1984—. Student Oreg. State U., 1973-76; B.S., U. Md., 1978. Physical therapist Ketchikan Hosp., AK, 1978-79, Eastmoreland Hosp., Portland, OR, 1979-81, Mt. Hood Med. Center, Gresham, OR, 1986—. Home: 18350 Ross Ave Sandy OR 97055

KNOBLER, PETER STEPHEN, b. NYC, Dec. 4, 1946; s. Alfred E. and Selma (Frankel) K.; m. Jane Dissin, May 16, 1982. Co-author: Giant Steps: The Autobiography of Kareem Abdul-Jabbar, 1983, Out of Control (with Thomas "Hollywood" Henderson), 1987; screenwriter, Pride and Passion (NBA championship film, 1984), That Championship Feeling (NBA championship film, 1983), "NBA Magazine" video program, 1984, U.S. Tennis Assn. U.S. Open championship films, 1982, 83, 84; USTA U.S. Open clay court championship films, 1982, 83; songs recorded by Chris Hillman, The Oak Ridge Boys, The Desert Rose Band. BA, Middlebury (VT) Coll., 1968; postgrad. creative writing, Columbia U. Reporter Liberation News Service, NYC, 1969; editor Zygote mag., NYC, 1970; assoc. editor Crawdaddy mag., NYC, 1971-72; editor, 1972-79; pres. Knobler Mgmt. Inc., NYC, 1983—. Home: 67 Greene St New York NY 10012

KNOEPFLE, JOHN, b. Cin., 1923; m. Margaret Sower, 1956; children—John, Molly, David, Christopher. Author: (poems) 16 books including most recently Thinking of Offerings, 1975, A Gathering of Voices, 1978, A Box of Sandalwood: Love Poems, 1979, Poems for the Hours, 1979, Selected Poems, 1985, Poems from the Sangamon, 1985. Translator: (with Wang Shouyi) Tang Dynasty Poems, 1985, Sung Dynasty Poems, 1985. Contrbr. poems to anthols. PhB, Xavier U., 1947, MA, 1949, PhD, Saint Louis U., 1967. Asst. prof. U. Coll. of Washington U., 1963-66, Saint Louis U., 1966-70, SUNY, Buffalo, 1969; assoc. prof. Saint Louis U., 1970-72; prof. lit. Sangamon State U., Springfield, Ill., 1972—. Served with U.S. Navy, 1943-46. Rockefeller fellow, 1967, fellow NEA, 1980. Home: 1008 W Adams Auburn IL 62615

KNOLL, ERWIN, b. Vienna, Austria, July 17, 1931; came to US, 1940, naturalized, 1946; s. Carl and Ida (Schaechter) K.; m. Doris Elsa Ricksteen, Mar. 1, 1954; children—David Samuel, Jonathan Robert. Author: (with William McGaffin) Anything But the Truth, 1968, Scandal in the Pentagon, 1969, No Comment, 1984; editor: (with Judith Nies McFadden) American Militarism, 1970, 1969, War Crimes and the American Conscience, 1970. BA, NYU, 1953. Reporter, editor, Editor and Publisher mag., NYC, 1948-53; assoc. editor Better Schools, NYC, 1956-57; reporter, editor Washington Post, 1957-62; Washington editor Los Angeles Times-Washington Post News Service, 1962-63; Washington corr. Newhouse Natl. News Service, 1963-68; Washington editor The Progressive, 1968-73, editor, Madison, WI, 1973—; commentator NPR, 1980-82; Cons. Natl. Commn. on Urban Problems, 1968. Home: 6123 Johnson St McFarland WI 53558

KNORR, JUDITH R., b. Marietta, OH, June 15, 1941, d. Lyell Frederick and Ruth Eloise (Schimmel) Roush; m. David J. Knorr, June 24, 1967; children—Paul David, Kent Michael. Contrbr. articles to: Newsday Mag., Woman's Day, Decorating and Crafts Mag., other publs. Wrkg. on microwave cookbooks. BS in Home Econ., Ohio U., 1963. Tchr. home econ. in Ohio and Ill., 1963-69; coop. extension agent Adams County, Quincy, Ill., 1967-68; home economist Microwave Kitchen, Huntington, N.Y., 1971—. Home: 852 Park Ave Huntington NY 11743

KNOWLES, JOHN, b. Fairmont, WV, Sept. 16, 1926; s. James Myron and Mary Beatrice (Shea) K. Author: (novels) A Separate Peace (Rosenthal award Natl. Inst. Arts and Letters, William Faulkner Fdn. award, 1960), Morning in Antibes, 1962, A Vein of Riches, 1978, Peace Breaks Out, 1980, A Stolen Past, 1983, The Private Life of Axie Reed, 1986; travel, Double Vision, 1964, Indian Summer, 1966; short stories, Phineas, 1968, The Paragon, 1970, Spreading Fires, 1974; also articles, short stories. Grad., Phillips Exeter Acad., 1945; BA, Yale U., 1949. Reporter Hartford (CT) Courant, 1950-52; free-lance writer, 1952-56; assoc. editor Holiday mag., 1956-60; writer-in-res. U. NC, 1963-64, Princeton U., 1968-69. Home: Box 939 Southampton NY 11968

KNOWLTON, EDGAR COLBY, JR., b. Delaware, OH, Sept. 14, 1921; s. Edgar Colby and Mildred (Hunt) K. Author: Esteban Echeverria, 1986; co-author: V. Blasco Ibanez, 1972; translator: Francisco de Sa de Meneses, The Conquest of Malacca, 1970, Almeida Garrett, Camoens, 1972, Casimiro de Abreu, Camoens and the Man of Java, 1972, Machado de Assis, You, Love, and Love Alone, 1972, Almeida Garrett, Afonso de Albuquerque, 1977; contrbr. articles to profl. jnls. AB, Harvard U., 1941, AM, 1942; PhD, Stanford U., 1959. Instr., U. HI, Honolulu, 1948-53, asst. prof. European langs., 1954-59, assoc. prof., 1959-65, prof., 1965—, acting chmn. dept., 1984-86; vis. prof. linguistics U. Malaya, Kuala Lumpur, 1962-64; vis. prof. linguistics, Fulbright awardee Universidad Central de Venezuela, Caracas, 1975; music reviewer Honolulu Advertiser, 1957-61. Served with USNR, 1944-46, 51-52. Recipient Transl. prize, Lisbon, 1973. Mem. American Assn of Teachers of Spanish and Portuguese, MLA., Phi Beta Kappa, Sigma Delta Pi. Home: 1026 Kalo Pl Honolulu HI 96826

KNOX, ANN BREWER, b. Buffalo, NY, Jan. 31, 1926; d. George E., Jr. and Ann (Fraser) Brewer; m. Gordon Knox, Dec. 6, 1947; children—Ann K. Velletri, Marion, Gordon, Andrew. Contrbr. short stories, poems to numerous lit. mags. B.A., Vassar Coll., 1946; M.A., Catholic U., 1970; M.F.A., Warren Wilson Coll., 1980. Tchr., Karachi-Am. Schl., Pakistan, 1964-66, Georgetown Day Schl., Washington, 1970-78; ed. Antietam Rvw., Hagerstown, MD, 1984—. Secy., Washington County Arts Council, Hagerstown, 1984—; panelist Md. State Arts Council, Balt., 1984—; mem. poetry com. Folger Shakespeare Library, Washington, 1986—. Mem. P&W, AAP, PSA. Home: Box 65 Hancock MD 21750

KNUDSLIEN, DEWEY VICTOR, b. Harmony, MN, Feb. 17, 1929, s. Helmer Roy and Lillian Myrtle (Bendickson) K. Contrbr.: Contemporary American Thought, Today's Greatest Poems, Our Western World's Most Beautiful Poems, others. Wrkg. on Western novel, poetry book. Student public schls., Harmony. Military Service, U.S. Army 1951-53. Recipient cert. of merit Am. Song Festival, 1978, Golden Poet award World of Poetry, 1985, 86, 87, 4 Cert. of Merit Awards, 1984, 85, two in 1986. Home: PO Box 214 Raymond IA 50667

KO, SUNG-WON, b. Haksan-myon, Korea, Dec. 8, 1925, came to U.S., 1964, s. Myong-chol Ko and Yong-sun Kwon; m. Hesun Kim (div. 1972); children—Yu Bong, Yu Jin; m. 2d, Young-Ah Lee, June 22, 1974; children—Walter HyongJin, Elaine Yunju. Contrbr.: Kalmaegi, South Korean Poets of Resistance, With Birds of Paradise, Mulnoul, numerous other poetry vols. MFA, U. Iowa, 1965; PhD, NYU, 1974. Mem. faculty Bklyn. Coll., 1970-77, Sacred Heart U., Fairfield, Conn., 1983-84, Calif. State U., Los Angeles, 1984-85, Los Angeles City Coll., 1985-86, UCLA, 1986—. Creative writing grantee Asia Fdn., 1963, 64-65; translation grantee John D. Rockefeller III Fdn., 1966; recipient poetry award Kans. City Star, 1966. Mem. MLA, PEN, Transl. Center. Home: 11820 Paso Robles Ave Granada Hills CA 91344

KOBELSKI, IRENE CATHERINE, b. Hartford, CT, Nov. 2, 1960; d. Zigmund Peter and Louise Rose Marie (Miller) Olszewski; m. Robert Bruce Kobelski, Aug. 13, 1983. Contrbr. to

United Polka Boosters (UPB) Mag. Wrkg. on history of Polish-Am. polka music ion U.S., humor pieces, non-fiction articles, polka-related research. Student Manchester Commun. Coll., 1979-80, U. Hartford, 1980-83. Ed., United Polka Boosters Newsletter, Glastonbury, CT, 1984-86; mng. ed. UPB Mag., Glatonbury, 1986—. Mem. Conn. Wrtrs. Group (organizer). Address: 607 Balaban Rd Colchester CT 06415

KOCH, JAMES VERCH, b. Springfield, IL, Oct. 7, 1942; s. Elmer O. and Wilma L. K.; m. Donna L. Stickling, Aug. 20, 1967; children—Elizabeth, Mark. Author: Industrialization Organization and Prices, 2d ed., 1980, Microeconomic Theory and Applications, 1976, The Economics of Affirmative Action, 1976, Introduction to Mathematical Economics, 1979. BA, IL State U., 1964; PhD, Northwestern U., 1968. Research economist Harris Trust Bank, Chgo., 1966; from asst. prof. to prof. econ. IL State U., 1967-78, chmn. dept., 1972-78; dean Faculty Arts and Scis., RI Coll., Providence, 1978-80; prof. econ., provost, v.p. acad. affairs Ball State U., Muncie, IN, 1980-86; pres. U. Montana, 1986—. Home: 1325 Gerald Missoula MT 59801

KOCH, KAREN JEAN, b. Cleve., Mar. 7, 1945, d. Frank and Mary (Orehovec) Zajec; m. Brian J. Koch, May 2, 1969; 1 child, Kevin. Author: Save the Broker's Commission, 1978; monthly columnist Techniscribe, 1984-86. BS, Case Western Res. U., 1967; MS, Pa. State U., 1972. Tech. wrtr., 1972—, including ATV Systems, CIE Systems, Hughes Co, Western Digital. Mem. Soc. for Tech. Communication (v.p. 1984-86, award for newsletter 1985), Women in Communications. Home: 35 Carson St Irvine CA 92720

KOCH, KENNETH, b. Cin., Feb. 27, 1925; s. Stuart J. and Lillian Amy (Loth) K.; m. Mary Janice Elwood, June 12, 1954; 1 dau., Katherine. Author: Poems, 1953; Ko, of A Season on Earth, 1959, Permanently, 1961, Thank You and other Poems, 1962, When the Sun Tries to Go On, 1969, The Pleasures of Peace, 1969, The Art of Love, 1975, The Duplications, 1977, The Burning Mystery of Anna in 1951, 1979, Days and Nights, 1982, Selected Poems, 1985, On the Edge, 1986, Seasons on Earth, 1987; (fiction) The Red Robins, 1975; (plays) Bertha and Others Plays, 1966, A Change of Hearts, 1973, The Red Robins, 1980; plays produced Little Red Riding Hood, 1953, Bertha, 1959, The Election, 1960, Pericles, 1960, George Washington Crossing The Delaware, 1962, Guinevere or the Death of the Kangaroo, 1964, The Love Suicides at Kaluka, 1965, The Moon Balloon, 1969, The Artist (opera), The Red Robins, 1978, Bertha (opera), The gold Standard, 1975, The Art of Love, 1976, The New Diana, 1984; A Change of Hearts (opera), 1985; Popeye Among the Polar Bears, 1986; edn. Wishes, Lies and Dreams: Teaching Children to Write Poetry, 1970; Rose Where Did You Get That Red? Teaching Great Poetry to Children, 1973, I Never Told Anybody: Teaching Poetry Writing in a Nursing Home, 1977, Les Couleurs des voyelles—pour faire ecrire de la poesie aux enfants, 1978, Sleeping on the Wing (with Kate Farrell), 1981. AB, Harvard U., 1948; MA, columbia U., 1953; PhD, 1959. Mem. faculty Columbia U., 1959, asst. prof. English and comparative lit., 1966-71, prof. English and comparative lit., 1971—. Bd. editors, Locus Solus, 1960-62. Fulbright fellow, 1950-51, 78, 82; Guggenheim fellow, 1961-62. Home: 25 Claremont Ave New York NY 10027

KOCIN, SIDNEY, b. Bronx, NY, Nov. 23, 1914; s. Moses and Pauline (Zuckerman) K.; m. Iola B. Grimm, Feb. 22, 1941; 1 dau., Ann K. Flam. BS in Chem., CCNY, 1934; JD, NYU, 1940. Editor, American Grocer, Bay Harbor Islands, FL, 1950—. Address: 9111 E Bay Harbor Dr Bay Harbor Isles FL 33154

KOCO, LINDA GALE, b. Chgo., Sept. 3, 1945; d. Peter Robert and Laura Sylvia (Albert) Young; divorced; 1 son, Charles Adam Kocolowski. Author trade textbook: Property Insurance Training Course, 1972. Contrbr. hundreds of articles to newspapers, trade and bus. pubs.; poems to lit. mags, anthols. Acting ed. trade newspaper: The Ind. Underwiter, 1986; contrbr., ed.: (newsletter) Assurex Bi-Monthly Bulltn., 1975-77, Directory of Greater Cleve.'s Enterprising Women Newsletter, 1987; (book) How to Repair Your Credit, 1986; ed. computer language textbook: SPSS Prime, 1972. Wrkg. on articles. B.A. with special honors, Lake Forest Coll., 1967. Tchr. writing and English, Lake Forest High Schl., IL, 1967-69; wrtr. training div. Allstate Insurance Co., Northbrook, IL, 1969-70; asst ed. The Natl. Underwriter, Cin., 1970-78; owner Koco Freelance Writing, Lakewood, OH, 1978—. Co-Founder, moderator Cin. Poets' Workshop, 1978-85; mem. young author's com. Lakewood Bd. Edn., 1986—. Recipient Gale DeHerder prize for excellence in writing Lake Forest Coll., 1967, numerous poetry awards Ohio Poetry Day Assn., 1978, 79. Mem. Am. Soc. Profl. Exec. Women, Poets League of Greater Cleve., Phi Beta Kappa. Home: 1351 Ethel Ave Lakewood OH 44107

KOEHLER, JO ANN M., b. Cleve., Mar. 9, 1951; d. Fred and Lillian Ann (Conway) Kuglin; m. Jeffrey William Koehler, Sept. 22, 1973; children—Jeff, Bryan F., Kristin M. Contrbr. articles to mags. newspapers including Living Mag., Fla. Bus. Tampa Bay, others. Asst. ed., contrbr.: The Marion Advocate newsletter. Wrkg. on local directory, Choices for Children. B.S., U. Dayton, 1973; M.S., U. South Fla., 1983. Owner, Creative Corner Inc., Tampa, FL, 1983-86; audiologist Tampa Speech & Hearing, 1985-86; freelance wrtr., 1984-87; co-owner JBK Pubs., Tampa, 1987—. Mem. Bay Area Profl. WG (dir.), Natl. Assn. Bus. Pofl. Women, FFWA, Small Bus. Network. Home: 708 Foggy Ridge Parkway Lutz FL 33549

KOEHLER, RONALD E., b. St. Louis, Aug. 8, 1953; s. Robert Ernest and Violet Louise (Upton) K.; children—Wynn Louis, Alex Robert; m. Jeanne Roberta Sherman, May 16, 1987; BS, So. Ill. U., MA, Sangamon State U. Legislative corresp., UPI, Springfield, IL, 1979-80, overnight ed., Chgo., 80-81, bur. mgr., Grand Rapids, MI, 81-84; assignment ed. WOTV-NBC, Grand Rapids, 1984-85; ed. Grand Rapids Mag. & Grand Rapids Bus. Jnl., 1985—. Mem. SPJ vicepres., Press Club or Grand Rapids, panelist, West Michigan Week, WGVC-TV. Office: Gemini Comm 40 Pearl NW Grand Rapids MI 49503

KOEHN, ILSE CHARLOTTE, b. Berlin, West Germany, Aug. 6, 1929; came to U.S., 1958; naturalized, 1976; d. Fritz Wilhelm and Charlotte Martha (Sckrabe) Koehn; m. John H. Van Zwienen, May 24, 1969 (div. June 19, 1987). Author: Mischling, Second Degree, Tilla, 1981. Student Art Acad., Berlin, 1953-59. Assoc. art dir. J. Walter Thompson, NYC., 1959-64; art dir. Campbell Downe Ad Agy., NYC., 1965-68; freelance wrtr., 1968—. Recipient Hornbook award for best non-fiction Boston Globe, 1978, Hon. award Jane Addams Peace Assn., 1978, Lewis Carroll Shelf award, 1978. Mem. AG, Graphic AG. Home: 322 Riverside Ave Riverside CT 06878

KOELSCH, WILLIAM ALVIN, (A. Nolder Gay), b. Morristown, NJ, May 16, 1933; s. Alvin Charles and Alice Boniface (Smith) K. Author: View From the Closet, 1978, Incredible Day-Dream:, 1985, Clark Univ.: A Narrative History, 1987; ed: Lectures Hist. Geog. of US, 1962, co-ed Am Habitat, 1973; contrbr. Dictionary Am. Biog., Geographies of the Mind, Origins of Am. Academic Geog., Soundings, Annals, Va. Qtly Rvw, Jnl of Geography, Bulln. Am. Meteorol. Soc., Jnl Hist. Geography, Proc. Am. Antiquarian Soc., NE Qtly, others; columnist (pseudonym) Gay Community News, Esplanade, Integrity Forum, Bay Windows. ScB, Bucknell U., 1955; AM, Clark U., 1959; PhD, U. Chgo., 1966. Instr. to asst. prof. Eckerd Coll., St. Petersburg, Fla., 1963-67; asst. prof. to prof. Clark Univ., Worcester, Mass, 1967—, univ. archivist, 1972-82, univ. historian, 1982—. Commr., Mass. Archives Adv. Comm., Boston, 1974—; bd. dirs. Archives and Library Bd. Episcopal Diocese of Mass., Boston, 1981-86; bd. dirs. Bostonian Soc., 1984—; fin. comm., Anderson Campaign, Washington, 1980; mem. Gay Book Award Comm. ALA Soc. Res. Round Table, Phila, 1982-87. Recipient Danforth fellow, 1957-63; NSF grantee, 1970, 72; Penrose Fund grantee, Am. Philo. Soc., 1971; vis. prof. Univ. Trier, W. Ger., 1984. Mem. Soc. for Values in Higher Edn., Orgn. Am. Historians, Am. Geog. Soc., Intl. Geog. Union Comm. on History of Geog. Thought, others. Address: 34 Reed St Worcester MA 01602

KOENINGER, KAY, b. Austin, TX, Apr. 16, 1951; d. Charles Edwin and Betty (Berry) Koeninger; m. Scott A. Warren, June 16, 1974. Contrbr. to The Marer Collection of Contemporary Ceramics, 1984; ed., contrbr., Native American Art From the Permanent Collection, 1979, American Reflections: Paintings 1830-1940 from the Collections of Pomona Coll. and Scripps Coll. (Am. Assn. of Museums Award of Merit), 1985. BA, Kenyon Coll., Gambier, OH, 1973; MA, E. Washington U., Cheny, WA, 1975. Grad. teaching fellow E. Washington U., 1973-74; registrar Claremont (CA) U. Center Art Collection, 1975-77, Galleries of the Claremont Colls., 1977-81, curator, 1981—. Home: 1251 N College Ave Claremont CA 91711

KOEPF, MICHAEL, b. San Mateo, CA, Mar. 14, 1940; s. Ernest and Ursula (Kane) K.; div.; children: Michelle, Ehren. Author: Save the Whale, 1978. BA, San Francisco State U., 1964, MA, 1968. Soldier, fisherman, novelist and columnist, Calif, 1958—. Served to Cpl, US Army, SE Asia. Cong. candidate of the Dem Party, Mendocino, Calif, 1986. Mem. NWU. Address: Box 1055 Elk CA 95432

KOERTGE, RONALD BOYD, b. Olney, IL, Apr. 22, 1940, s. William Henry and Bulis Olive (Fiscus) K. Author: (poems) The Father Poems, 1973, Men under Fire, 1976, 12 Photographs of Yellowstone, 1976, Sex Object, 1980, The Jockey Poems, 1980, Dairy Cows, 1981, Life on the Edge of the Continent: The Selected Poems, 1982, (fiction) The Boogeyman, 1982, Where The Kissing Never Stops, 1987. BA, U. Ill., 1962; MA, U. Ariz., 1965. Instr. Pasadena City Coll., Calif., 1965—. Recipient poetry prize Jazz Press, 1985. Home: 1115 Oxley St South Pasadena CA 91030

KOLAR, JOHN JOSEPH, b. St. Louis, Aug. 19, 1927; s. John and Helen (Jacko) K.; m. Billie Lee Smith, Dec. 26, 1953. Ed./contrbr. Introduction to Diecasting; ed. Custom Die Caster, 1975-82, Die Casting Mgt. Mag., 1982—. BSBA, Washington U., 1954, MBA, 1964. Adv. & sales promo spclst., General Electric, Schenectady, NY & Fort Wayne, Ind., 1954-59; asst. adv. mgr. Metal Goods Corp., St. Louis, 1959-65; mgr.—adv. & sales promo. Crane Co., Chgo., 1965-69; v.p. adv. Norm Ulrich Studios, Oak Park, IL, 1969-70; mgr.—adv. & sales promo. Allis-Chalmers, Matteson, IL, 1970-73; corp. adv. mgr. Symons Corp., Des Plaines, IL, 1973-75; mktg. dir. & ed.American Die Casting Inst., Des Plaines, 1975—. Served to MM2, USN 1945-49, 2nd Lt., U.S.Army, 1952-54. Home: 827 S Jackson Hinsdale IL 60521

KOLB, GWIN JACKSON, b. Aberdeen, MS, Nov. 2, 1919; s. Roy Rolly and Nola Undine (Jackson) K.; m. Ruth Alma Godbold, Oct. 11, 1943; children: Gwin Jackson II, Alma Dean. Editorial asst. Modern Philology, 1946-56; co-author: Dr. Johnson's Dictionary, 1955, Reading Literature: A Workbook, 1955; editor: (Samuel Johnson) Rasselas, 1962; co-editor: A Bibliography of Modern Studies Compiled for Philological Quarterly, 1951-65, 3 vols., 1962-72, Modern Philology, 1973—. BA, Millsaps Coll., 1941; MA, U. Chgo., 1946, PhD, 1949. Served with USNR, 1942-45. Guggenheim fellow, 1956-57; grantee ACLS, 1961-62. Mem. MLA. Home: 5819 Blackstone Ave Chicago IL 60637

KOLB, KENNETH LLOYD, b. Portland, OR, July 14, 1926; s. Frederick and Ella May (Bay) K.; m. Emma LaVada Sanford, June 7, 1952; children: Kevin, Lauren, Kimrie. Author: Getting Straight, 1967, The Couch Trip, 1970, Night Crossing, 1974; prize teleplay in A Variety of Short Plays, 1966, contrbr. short stories and humor to natl. mags, 1953-67; screenwriter with more than 100 solo credits on prime time TV drama shows; feature films: Seventh Voyage of Sinbad, 1967, Snow Job, 1972. BA, U Calif-Berkeley, 1950; MA, San Francisco State U., 1953. Freelance writer, 1953—. Foreman, Grand Jury, Plumas County, Calif., 1970; chmn., Criminal Justice Planning Commn., Region C, Calif, 1975-77. Served as ET 2/C, USN, 1944-46, USS Sicily. Recipient Best Half-Hour Drama award, WGA, 1956. Mem. Phi Beta Kappa, WG, AG. Address: Box 22 Cromberg CA 96103

KOLLER, JAMES ANTHONY, b. Oak Park, IL, May 30, 1936, s. James Anthony and Elsie Loreen (Clark) K.; m. Leslie Ann Burhoe (div.); children—Bertie, Ida Rose; children by previous marriage—Deirdre, Jessie, Jedediah, Theadora. Author: Brainard & Washington St. Poems, 1965, Two Hands, 1965, The Dogs and Other Darkwoods, 1966, Some Cows, 1966, I Went to See My True Love, 1967, California Poems, 1971, Messages, 1972, If You Don't Like Me You Can Leave Me Alone, 1974, Shannon Who Was Lost Before, 1975, Bureau Creek, 1975, Poems for the Blue Sky, 1976, Messages/Botschaften, 1977, Andiamo, 1978, O Didn't He Ramble/O Ware Er Nicht Umhergezogen, 1980, Back River, 1981, One Day At A Time, 1981, Great Things are Happening, 1984, Working Notes, 1985, Gebt Dem Alten Hund Nen Knochen, 1986 Give the Dog A Bone, 1986, Openings, 1987. BA, North Central Coll., Naperville, Ill., 1958. NEA fellow, 1973. Home: Box 629 Brunswick ME 04011

KOLODZIEJ, KRYSIA, b. Hartford, CT, Oct. 6, 1948; d. Michael and Pamela May (Woodford) K.; m. Peter Rudolf Jaffe, July 15, 1983. Contrbr. to San Francisco Free Critic, Sojourner, Red Cedar Rvw., Moving Out: Feminist Lit. & Arts Jnl, Qtly Rvw Lit., Acad. Am. Encyc., Philosophy & Pub. Affairs, Milkweed Chronicle, others. BS, Eastern Mich. U., 1970; MA, Wayne State U., 1977. Contrbg. ed. Moving Out, Detroit, 1974-76; ed., bd. dirs. Sojourner, Boston, 1976-77; asst. to eds.Qtly Rvw Lit., Princeton, N.J., 1977-79; asst. to mng. ed., editorial coordinator Arete Pub. Co., Princeton, 1979-80; asst. to sci. acq. ed., copy ed., Princeton Univ. Press, 1980-81; mng. ed. Philosophy & Pub. Affairs, Princeton U. Press, 1981-83; freelance wrtr./ed., translator, 1983—. Mem. Editorial Freelancers Assn. AWP. Home: 9 Laurel Ave Box 628 Kingston NJ 08528

KOLUMBAN, NICHOLAS, b. Budapest, Hungary, June 17, 1940; s. Dr. Karoly and Martha (Yoo) Kolumban. Author: In Memory of My Third Decade, 1981, Reception at the Monoglian Embassy, 1987; translator: Sandor Csoori's Selected Poems: Memory of Snow, 1983, Turmoil in Hungary, 1982; poetry and translations in American Poetry Rvw, Chicago Rvw, Epoch, New Letters, other lit mags. BA, Penn State U., 1962, MA, 1966. Instr., Virginia Polytechnic Inst., Blacksburg, VA, 1965-68; tchr., Bridgewater-Raritan Schl. Dist., Raritan, NJ, 1971-86. Mem. PEN, PSA. Home: 150 West Summit St Somerville NJ 08876

KONING, HANS, (Hans Koningsberger), b. Amsterdam, Holland, July 12, 1924, came to U.S., 1951, s. David and Elizabeth (Van Collem) K.; m. Kathleen Scanlon, 1964; children—Christina, Andrew; children by previous marriage—Lynne, Tessa. Author: The Affair, 1958, An American Romance, 1960, A Walk with Love and Death, 1961, I Know What I'm Doing, 1964, Love and Hate in China, 1966, The Revolutionary, 1967, Along the Roads of Russia, 1968, Future of Che Guevara, 1971, The Almost World, 1971, Death of a Schoolboy, 1974, Petersburg-Cannes Express, 1975, Columbus, His Enterprise, 1976, A New Yorker in Egypt, 1976, The Kleber Flight, 1981, America Made Me, 1983, DeWitt's War, 1983, Nineteen Sixty-Eight, 1987. Acts of Faith, 1988. Ed. Holland, Switzerland, France. Served as sgt. British Army, 1944-46. Recipient NEA award, 1978, 85. Mem. ASCAP, WG East. Office: Lantz Agcy 888 7th Ave NYC 10106

KONINGSBERGER, HANS, see Koning, Hans

KONKLE, JANET MARIE EVEREST, b. Grand Rapids, MI, Nov. 5, 1917; d. Charles Arthur and Minnie (Koegler) Everest; m. Arthur J. Konkle, Feb. 14, 1941, (dec. 1983); children—Kraig, Jil-Marie Konkle Gahsman, Dan. Author, photog. illustrator children's books: Once there was a Kitten, 1951, Kitten and the Parakeet, 1952, Christmas Kitten, 1953, 64, Easter Kitten, 1955, Tabb's Kittens, 1956, J. Hamilton Hamster (named Ambassador Book, English Speaking Union), 1957, Sea Cart, 1961, Schoolroom Bunny, 1965, The Raccoon Twins, 1972; contrbr. children's stories: Jack & Jill Mag., Childcraft Encyc.; contrbr. poetry: Parnassus Lit. Jnl., Jean's Jnl., Red Pagoda; work represented in de Grummond Children's Collection, U. So. Miss. AA, Grand Rapids Jr. Coll., 1937; U. Mich., 1938; postgrad., BS Western Mich. U., 1938-39. Elem. sch. tchr., Grand Rapids, Mich., 1939-41, 52-79; columnist Ocala (Fla.) Star-Banner, 1987—. Mem. fla. Freelance Wrtrs. Assn., Citrus County Wrtrs., Fla. State Poets Assn., Gingerbread Poets (treas.). Home: Box 1660 Dunnellon FL 32630

KONO, TOSHIHIKO, (Toshio Kohno), b. Ashiya, Japan, Nov. 8, 1930; came to U.S., 1966; s. Zenshiro and Miyo (Mitsumori) K.; m. Edna Libby, June 20, 1968; childrn—Miyo, Kaori. Contrbr. musical essays, articles, rvws. to mags. including Japan/NY Mag., OCS News. L.L.B., Kyoto U., Japan, 1953; postgrad. Mannes Coll. Music, 1966, Stanford U., 1967. Cellist, Am. Symphony Orchestra, NYC, 1968—. Recipient Disting. Service award and Silver medal(IBA), 1974, Contemporary Achievement award, 1975. Home: 400 W 43d St New York NY 10036

KONRAD, G. GREGORY, b. Denver, Sept. 13, 1951, s. George and Mary Beverly (Kissell) K. Author: Keys to Freedom and Harmony—Through Your Astrological Aspects, 1985. Student Met. State Coll., Denver, 1969-72. Host radio program sta. KOA, Denver, 1982; pub. Ivory Pub. Co., Denver, 1985—. Office: Box 4595 Denver CO 80204

KOOB, RAYMOND JOSEPH, b. Upper Darby, PA, Nov. 2, 1947; s. Robert R. and Dorothy (Crosby) K.; m. Peggy Ann Frank, Aug. 31, 1985; children—Jamie, Bobby, Alex, Amy. Author: (poems) KOOBOOK, vol. I, 1985. BS in Commerce, Rider Coll., 1970. Real estate broker Berger Realty, Ocean City, M.J., 1970—. Home: 9 Bay Rd Ocean City NJ 08226

KOONTZ, THOMAS WAYNE, b. Ft. Wayne, IN, July 9, 1939, s. Wayne Francis and Dorothy Ruth (Price) K.; m. Phyllis Hart, Sept. 7, 1959 (div. 1984); children—Wren, Kenyatta, Soren, Vienna, Nicole. Author poetry collections: To begin with, 1983, Charms, 1983; ed. poetry anthology: The View from the Top of the Mountain, 1981. BA, Miami U., Oxford, Ohio, 1961; MA, Ind. U., 1965, PhD,1970. Instr. George Washington U., 1965-67; prof. Ball State U., Muncie, Inc., 1967—; ed.-in-chief Barnwood Press, Daleville, Inc., 1978—. Woodrow Wilson fellow, 1961; Eli Lilly Endowment fellow, 1985. Mem. AWP. Home: RR 2 Box 11C Daleville IN 47334

KOPERWAS, SAM EARL, b. Roanoke Rapids, VA, June 11, 1948; s. Nicholas George and Crystal (Wilson) K.; m. Suzette Henry, June 25, 1968 (div. 1973) 1 dau., Betty; m. 2d, Ernestine Bellamy (div. 1986); children: Roy, Warren, Charlotte. Author: Hot Stuff, 1978, Easy Money, 1983, Westchester Bull, 1985. BA in philosophy, Brkyn. Coll., 1966-70; MFA, Bowling Green State U., 1971-73. Guggeheim fellow, 1980. Mem. Gemolog. Inst. Am. Address: 2701 NE 35th Dr Ft Lauderdale FL 33308

KOPPEL, SHEREE POWERS, b. Brockton, MA, Feb. 3, 1951; d. F. Randall and Marjorie Mae (Hanback) Powers; m. Arthur John Koppel, Sept. 2, 1978. Contrbr. articles to profl. jnls. B.A. in English, U. Louisville, 1972, M.A. in Reading Instruction, 1977, Ed.D. in Supervision, 1986. Asst. principal Mercy Acad., Louisville, KY, 1985—. Home: 2907 Livingston Ave Jeffersontown KY 40299

KORAN, CONNIE JEAN, (Jean M. Constantine), b. Cleve., June 15, 1953; d. Donald Edwin Sniff and Nancy Jean (Hisrich) Kunes; m. W.A. McSweeney, Aug. 28, 1976 (div. Feb. 15, 1985); 1 son, Patrick; m. Matthew Huseyin Koran, June 13, 1986. Contrbr. article to Sunshine Mag. Cons. ed. Neonatal-Perinatal Medicine, 2d ed., 1977, Nelson Textbook of Pediatrics, 11th ed., 1979, Care of the High Risk Neonate, 1979, The Diabetic Pregnancy, 1979, Clinical Rheumatology, 1982, Neonatal-Perinatal Medicine, 3d ed., 1983,

Nelson Tetbook of Pediatrics, 12th ed., 1983, Osteoarthritis: Diagnosis and Management, 1984; mng. ed.: Med. Care, 1983—. Wrkg. on novels: Ashes to Ashes, Dust to Dust; children's books. Freelance ed., 1979—, editorial asst. Univ. Hosps., Cleve., 1977-79; editorial asst. Med. Care, Cleve., 1982-83, mng. ed., 1983—, Mem. Council Biology Eds., Women Business Owners Assn., Am. Pub. Health Assn. Home: 26911 Westwood Ln Olmsted Township OH 44138

KORBAR, MARCIA MARIE, b. Gowanda, NY, Nov. 20, 1955; d. Ralph James and Annamae (Ball) Korbar. Poetry in various lit mags inclg. Young American Poet and Young Collegiate Poet. Student Jamestown Comm. College, NY, 1975-77. Mental hygiene therapist, Gowanda Psych. Center, NY, 1981—. Home: 106 Chestnut St Gowanda NY 14070

KORDA, MICHAEL VINCENT, b. London, Eng., Oct. 8, 1933; s. Vincent and Gertrude (Musgrove) K.; m. Carolyn Keese, Apr. 16, 1958; 1 son, Christopher Vincent. Author: Male Chauvinism: How It Works, 1973, Power: How to Get It, How To Use It, 1975, Success!, 1977, Charmed Lives, 1979, Worldly Goods, 1982. B.A., Magdalen Coll., 1958. With Simon and Schuster, N.Y.C., 1958—, successively editor, sr. editor, mng. editor, exec. editor, now sr. v.p., editor-in-chief. Served with RAF, 1952-54. Office: S&S 1230 Ave of Americas New York NY 10020

KORN, HENRY, b. NYC, Sept. 19, 1945, s. Samuel Henry and Ruth (Beck) K.; m. Joan Willner, Dec. 22, 1968 (div. 1977); m. 2d, Donna Stein, Feb. 14, 1982. Author: Exact Change, 1974, Pontoon Manifesto, 1975, Proceedings of the National Academy of the Avant Garde, 1976, Muhammad Ali Retrospective, 1977, Inside Thirteen Flags, 1981, A Difficult Act to Follow: Stories & Essays 1969-79, 1982, Marc Chagall, 1985; ed.: Assembling Nos. 1-9; contrbr. to: US No. 3, 1970, In Youth, 1972, Art Work, No Commercial Value, 1972, Human Connection & the New Media, 1973, Breakthrough Fictioneers, 1973, Voices of Brooklyn, 1973, Poets Encyclopedia, 1978. BA, Johns Hopkins U., 1968; cert. mgmt. Columbia U., 1978. Asst. admin. public relations Bklyn. Mus., 1969-71; admin. coord. Staten Island Inst., N.Y.C., 1971-74; adminstr. Jewish Mus., N.Y.C., 1975-78; exec. dir. Lower Manhattan Cultural Council, 1978-80; exec. dir. Santa Monica Art Commn. Fdn., 1986—. NEA fiction fellow, 1977. Home: 918 S Wooster St Los Angeles CA 90035

KORNEGAY, ROBERT MADRID, b. Dothan, FL, Sept. 24, 1952; s. Robert B. and Dorothy (Hickman) K.; m. Vicki Fryer, June 10, 1977; 1 son, Richard Kyle. Contrbr. articles to numerous outdoors mags. including Fins and Feathers, Great Am. Outdoors, La. Sportsman, others. Columnist: Fins and Feathers, 1986—, Wildlife Magazine, 1986—. B.S. in Edn., Troy State U., 1974. Tchr., Early County Schs., Blakely, GA, 1974—. Excellence in Craft Award, 1986-87, Ga. Outdoor Wrtrs. Assn. Mem. OWAA, Southeastern Outdoor Press Assn., Ga. Outdoor Wrtrs. Assn. Home: 618 Meadowbrook Dr Blakely GA 31723

KORTEPETER, CARL MAX, b. Indpls., May 27, 1928; s. Carl and Olive (Derbyshire) K.; m. Cynthia A. King, Apr. 7, 1957; six children. Author: Ottoman Imperialism During the Reformation, Europe and the Caucasus, 1972, (with M. Farah and A. Karls) The Human Experience, 1984, (with G. Renda) The Transformation of Turkish Culture, 1986; ed. The Modern Middle East, Lit. and Soc., 1972, Ali of Turkey, 1969, All Color Series in Sci. and History, 32 vols, 1968-72, Middle East Series: Leaders, Politics and Social Change in the Islamic World; AB, Harvard U., 1950; MA, McGill U.-Montreal, Can., 1954; PhD, U. London, 1962. Lectr. to assoc. prof. Univ. Toronto, Ont., Can., 1961-67; assoc. prof. M.E. history NY Univ., NYC, 1967—; secy.-treas. Kingston Press, Princeton, NJ, 1981—. Mem. Yorkville Civic Council, Toronto, 1964-66. Recipient fellow Am Research Inst. in Turkey, Istanbul, 1966-67. Intl. Research and Exchanges Bd., NYC, 1973-74, Am. Research Center in Egypt, Cairo, 1979. Mem. Middle East Studies Assn., Middle East Inst., Turkish Studies Assn., Princeton Middle East Soc. Address: 32 Oxford Circle Skillman NJ 08558

KOSBAB, F(REDERIC) PAUL, b. Berlin, Germany, Mar. 29, 1922, came to U.S., 1956, naturalized, 1961; Paul August W. and Elisabeth C. (Schulze) K.; m. Marianne E. Bodmann, May 2, 1951 (dec. June 13, 1986). Author: Neurologie fuer Studierende (Neurology for Medical Students), 1948. Contrbr. numerous articles to profl. jnls., popular mags. Wrkg. on imagery techniques, psychology of wrtrs. and witing, applied linguistics, phonetics and phonology, learning theory, functions and potentials of the right and left cerebral hemispheres. M.D., Cert. Grad., Berlinisches Gymnasium zum Grauen Kloster, 1939; Cand. Med., Leopold-Franzens-Univ. Innsbruck Med. Schl., 1942; Friedrich-Wilhelms U. Med. Schl., Berlin, 1945. Asst. prof. to prof. psychiatry Med. Coll. Va., Richmond, 1964-69; prof., acting chmn. psyciatry Med. Coll. Va., Va. Commonwealth U., Richmond, 1969-70, prof., assoc. chmn., 1970-73; prof. psychiatry Eastern Va. Med. Schl., Norfolk, 1977-82; prof., chmn. psychiatry Oral Roberts U. Schl. Medicine, Tulsa, OK, 1982-86, prof., chmn. emeritus, 1987—. Home: Box 700747 Tulsa OK 74170

KOSINSKY, BARBARA TIMM, b. St. Louis, July 4, 1942; d. Paul Edwin and Virginia Louise (Borcherding) Timm; m. John Paul Kosinsky, July 25, 1964; children—James, Bethany. Contrbr. articles to mags., newsletters, children's religious mags., profl. jnls. Ed.: LIBRAS Line Newsletter, 1985-87. Wrkg. on children's books, library articles. B.S. in Edn., Concordia Coll., 1964; M.L.S., SUNY, Buffalo, 1971; B.A. in Computer Sci., North Central Coll., 1986. Library trainee Niagara Falls Public Libray, NY, 1969-70; systems librarian North Central Coll., Naperville, IL, 1981—; free-lance wrtr., 1976—. mem. ALA, NWC, Am. Assn. Univ. Profs., Am. Soc. Info. Sci. Home: 2721 Rolling Meadows Dr Naperville IL 60565

KOSINSKI, DENNIS STEVEN, b. Chgo., Dec. 20, 1946; s. Stephen V. and Florence S. (Galesinski) K.; m. Elizabeth Ferrans, Aug. 26, 1973 (div. May 7, 1977). Author: The Alexandria Letters—the Final Prophecies of the 20th Cy., 1985. BA in Sociol., So. Ill. U., 1971; MA in Communications, Gov. State U., 1976. Community Ser. Splst. City of Chgo., Chgo., 1972-76; admin. State of Ill. Dept. Corrections, Chgo., 1976-84; writer and ed. Devonshire Pub. Co., Batavia, Ill., 1984—. Address: Devonshire Pub 11 N Batavia Rd Batavia IL 60510

KOSINSKI, JERZY NIKODEM, b. Lodz, Poland, June 14, 1933; U.S., 1957, naturalized, 1965; s. Mieczyslaw and Elzbieta (Liniecka) K.; m. Mary H. Weir, Jan. 11, 1962 (dec. 1968). Author: (nonfiction pseudonym Joseph Novak): The Future is Ours, Comrade, 1960, No Third Path, 1962, (novels) The Painted Bird, 1965, Steps, 1968, Being There, 1971, screenplay, 1978; The Devil Tree, 1st ed., 1973, rev. ed., 1981, Cockpit, 1975, Blind Date, 1977, Passion Play, 1979, screenplay, 1982/86; Pinball, 1982, The Working Papers of Norbert Kosky, 1987. MA in poli. sci., U. Lodz, 1953, in history, 1955; assoc. prof. Inst. Sociology E Cultural History, Polish Acad. Scis., Warsaw, 1955-57; postgrad., Columbia U., 1958-65. Recipient Natl. Book award fiction for Steps, 1969; Award in Lit. Am. Acad. Arts and Letters and Natl. Inst. Arts & Ltrs., 1970; Best Screenplay award for Being There WG Am., 1979; Brit. Acad. Film and TV Arts award, 1981; Polonia Media Perspectives award, 1980; Ford Fdn. fellow, 1958-60, Guggenheim Lit. fellow, 1967; fellow Center Advanced Studies, Wesleyan U., 1968-69; sr. fellow Council Humanities. Mem. PEN (exec. bd., pres. 1973-75). Natl. Writers Club (exec. bd.). AG, WG Am. Address: 18-K Hemisphere HS 60 W 57th St New York NY 10019

KOSKENMAKI, ROSALIE M., b. Victoria, TX, Nov. 8, 1943, d. Paul Joseph and Irene C. (Nash) Maggio; m. David C. Koskenmaki, Dec. 28, 1968; children—Elizabeth, Catherine, Matthew. Author: Travels of Soc, 1985, The Nonsexist Word Finder: A Dictionary of Gender-Free Usage, 1987; contrbg. author: Writers and Editors at Work, 1980, Real Food Places, 1981, Aging: A New Look, 1982, Bookfinder III, 1984; contrbr. to Women's Sports & Fitness, Cricket, Jack and Jill, Parish Teacher, McCalls, Am. Guidance Service, other mags and newspapers; ed.: Intl. Surgery Bulltn., numerous books on parenting, edn. and religious topics. Wrkg. on biography, juvenile mysteries. BA, Coll. St. Catherine, 1965; cert., Universite de Nancy, France, 1966. Dir. public relations French Consulate Gen., Chgo., 1966; ed. Am. Jnl Ophthalmology, Chgo., 1967, Intl. Coll. Surgeons, Chgo., 1967-70; free-lance wrtr., ed., St. Paul, 1970—. Home: 1297 Summit Ave St Paul MN 55105

KOSOFF, FLORA MAY, (Florence Jean Katsonov), b. Portland, OR, Oct. 13, 1926; d. Vladimir Vasily Katsonov (Mike V. Kosoff) and Geneva May (Adamson) Kiele; 1 dau., Linda Alayne Wemus. Contrbr. poems, short stories to lit mags, anthols. Diploma in Nursing, St. Joseph's Hosp., Lewiston, Idaho, 1950. Recipient Honorable Mention awards World of Poetry, 1985, Poetry Press, 1986, 2 First Prizes, 1986. Mem. Idaho Wrtr.'s League. Home: Rogue Auto Travel Park Sp 33 Gold Beach OR 97444

KOSTAR, RONALD EDWARD, b. Trenton, NJ, Mar. 7, 1950; s. William Peter and Leona (Howard) K.; m. Deirdre Sheean, July 3, 1984; 1 son, Nathaniel Avery. Author: (poetry) Light Bulbs from Wilkes Barre, 1981; editor In the Mail mag., 1981; contrbr. numerous poems, articles, essays, rvws. to mags., other publs. BA, Bucknell U., 1974; MA, CCNY, 1979; PhD in progress, Rutgers U., 1984—. Comml. fisherman, 1975-77, 84-86 (summers); freelance writer Princeton-based newspapers, 1981-83; English instr. Rutgers U., New Brunswick, N.J., 1983-86. Bucknell U. scholar, 1969-74; Russell fellow Rutgers U., 1984. Home: 24 Witherspoon Ln Princeton NJ 08540

KOSTELANETZ, RICHARD, b. NYC, May 14, 1940; s. Boris and Ethel (Cory) K. Author: The Theatre of Mixed Means, 1968; Master Minds, 1969, Spanish transl., 1972; The End of

Intelligent Writing 1974, reprinted as Literary Politics in America, 1977; I Articulations/Short Fictions, 1974; "The End" Appendix/"The End" Essentials, 1979; Twenties in the Sixties, 1979; The Old Poetries and the New, 1981; Autobiographies, 1981; Arenas/Fields/Pitches/Turfs, 1982; American Imaginations (in German), 1983; Epipanies (in German), 1983; Recyclings, 1984; Autobiographlien New York-Berlin (in German), 1986; Prose Pieces/Aftertexts, 1987; The Old Fiction and the New, 1987; Texts and Proposals for Radio, 1988; The Grants-Fix, 1987; On Music and Musicians, 1988; edited & co-authored: The New American Arts, 1965 (Spanish transl., 1967, Portuguese transl, 1968); anthologies edited: On Contemporary Literature, 1964; enlarged & revised ed., 1969. Twelve from the Sixties, 1967; The Young American Writers, 1967; Possibilities of Poetry, 1970; Imaged Words & Worded Images, 1970; Moholy-Nagy, 1970; John Cage, 1970 (German transl., 1973, abridged Spanish transl., 1974); Social Speculations, 1971; Human Alternatives, 1971; Essaying Essays, 1975; Esthetics Contemporary, 1978, enlarged, rev. ed., 1988; Visual Literature Criticism, 1979; Text-Sound Texts, 1980; The Yale Gertrude Stein, 1980; American Writing Today, 2 vols., 1981; The Avant-Garde Tradition in Literature, 1982; Conversing with John Cage, 1987; theatricral texts: Epiphanies (performed Univ. of North Dakota, 1980, Vassar College, 1981), Seductions (unperformed); advisory editor Contemporary Dramatists, 1973, 76, 81, 87, Performing Arts Jnl, 1976-81, Literature in Performance, 1980—; contrbg. editor: Lotta Poetica, 1970-71, Arts in Soc., 1970-75, The Humanist, 1970-78, N.Y. Arts Jnl, 1980-82, The Pushcart Prize, 1977—. AB with honors, Brown U., 1962; MA in Am. History, Columbia U., 1966. Co-founder, pub. Assembling & Assembling Press, NYC, 1970-82; lit. dir. Future Press of the Cultural Council Fdn., NYC., 1976—; freelance wrtr., artist, 1965—. Mem. Phi Beta Kappa, PEN, Audio Ind., Fdn. Ind. Video Film, Intl. Assn. Arts Critics, Libertarian Party, Soc. Origination of Horspiel Am. (founding mem.). Home: Box 444 Prince St New York NY 10012

KOSTINER, EILEEN T., b. Waterbury, CT, June 9, 1938; d. Fred F. and Camille (Labuz) Tirella; m. Edward Kostiner, Aug. 25, 1960; 2 sons, Jonathan, David. Author: Loves Other Face, 1982; contrbr. poetry to So. Rvw, Hollow Springs Rvw of Poetry, Red Fox Rvw, Woman Spirit, Blue Unicorn. BA, Tufts U., 1960; cert. Bus. Adminstrn., Harvard, 1961. Address: 19 Thompson Rd Storrs CT 06268

KOTELLY, GEORGE VINCENT, b. Boston, MA, Aug. 27, 1931; s. James and Pauline (Plaha) K.; m. Shirley Elizabeth Mullo, June 14, 1959; children—Kenneth James, William John, Douglas George, Joanne Elizabeth. Author numerous tech. manuals & papers, 1960-77; tech. ed. Computer Design mag., 1977-79; ed. & contrbr. EDN Mag., 1979-83; Mini-Micro Systs. Mag., 1983—. BSEE, Tufts U., 1953. Engring. writer Raytheon Corp., Burlington, MA, 1970-73; sr. tech. writer USM Corp., Beverly, MA, 1973-75, Analogic Corp., Wakefield, MA, 1975-77; tech. ed. Computer Design, Littleton, MA, 1977-79; sr. ed. EDN, Boston, 1979-83; ed.-in-chief Mini-Micro Systs., Newton, MA, 1983—. Served to Cpl, US Army, 1954-56. Home: 48 Vaille Ave Lexington MA 02173

KOTKER, NORMAN RICHARD, b. Chelsea, MA, Nov. 16, 1931; s. Harry Aaron and Betty (Kaplan) K.; m. Zane Hickcox, June 7, 1965; children—David, Ariel. Author: (fiction) Herzl the King, 1972, Miss Rhode Island, 1978; (history) The Holy Land in the Time of Jesus, 1967, The Earthly Jerusalem, 1969, Massachusetts, A Pictorial History, 1976, New England Past, 1980. Editor: The Horizon Book of the Elizabethan World, 1967, The Horizon Book of the Middle Ages, 1968, The Horizon History of China, 1969. AB, Harvard U., 1952. Researcher, Look Mag., NYC, 1953-56; reporter Bus. Week mag., NYC, 1956-57; ed. Horizon Books, Horizon Mag., NYC, 1960-69, Charles Scribners Sons, NYC, 1969-78; freelance wrtr., Northampton, Mass., 1978—. Fiction grantee NEA, Mass. Artists' Fdn. Mem. PEN, Bay State Wrtr.'s Assn. (co-chair). Home: 45 Lyman Rd Northampton MA 01060

KOTKER, ZANE, b. Waterbury, CT, Jan. 2, 1934, d. Edward Scovill and Jean (Cadwallader) Hickcox; m. Norman Kotker, June 7, 1965; children—David, Ariel. Novelist: Bodies in Motion, 1972, A Certain Man, 1976, White Rising, 1981; contrbr. to Mademoiselle, Savvy, Cimarron Rvw, other publs. BA, Middlebury (Vt.) Coll., 1956; MA, Columbia U., 1960. Co-pub. A New Eng. Rvw, New Haven, 1960-63; vis. prof. Mt. Holyoke Coll., South Hadley, Mass., spring 1983, U. Mass., Amherst, fall 1983. NEA fiction grantee 1974; MacDowell Colony resident, Peterborough, N.H., 1979, 82, 84, 87; work transcribed to cassettes Am. Audio Prose Library, 1984. Mem. PEN, Bay State Wrtrs. (founding mem.). Office: 160 Main St Northampton MA 01060

KOTTICK, GLORIA, b. Bronx, NY, Aug. 7, 1930; d. Joseph and Rose (Lerman) Astor; m. Edward Leon Kottick, May 10, 1953; children—Judith, Janet. Contrbr. essays, editorials, articles to numerous mags, newspapers, including Kansas City Star, Newsday, Des Moines Register, L.A. Times, Chgo. Tribune, Cat Fancy, Farm Wife News, Woman's Day, others; "Outlooks" columnist Cedar Rapids Gazette. BA, NYU, 1952. Head interlibrary loan U. Mo., St. Louis, 1966-68; library asst. State Hist. Soc., Iowa City, 1968-70; dept. secy. U. Ia., Iowa City, 1972-86. Mem. Natl. League Am. PEN Women (1st place in non-fiction 1985, 2nd place non-fiction, 1986), Phi Beta Kappa. Home: 2001 Muscatine Ave Iowa City IA 52240

KOUBA, SANDRA LOUISE, b. Birmingham, AL, Dec. 22, 1941; d. James William and Nellie Louise (Morgan) Sisk; divorced; children—Kimberly Frank, Michelle, Marcus; m. David Edward Kouba, Sept. 22, 1984. Contrbr. poems to anthols. Diploma, Ind. Vocational and Technical Schl., 1980. Med. aide Continental Convalescent Center, Indpls., 1979-82; home health care worker Hospitality Home Health Services, Montgomery, AL, 1984—. Recipient Golden Poet award World of Poetry, 1985, 86, 87. Home: 106 Happy Hollow Rd Odenville AL 35120

KOVAR, MILO, b. Pisek, Czechoslovakia, Feb. 8, 1926; arrived in U.S., 1952; s. Vaclav and Josefa K. Author: Five Keys to Inner Wisdom and Aura, Your Vital Essence, 1979, Astrology, the Star Science from A to Z and Astro-Rhythms, 1982, New Age Astrology Guide (annl. 1st pub. 1970). MA, Charles U., Prague, 1942; BS, U. San Francisco, 1957. Pvt. import/export bus., Lima, Peru, 1947-49; import/export Hardie Ltd., Sydney, Australia, 1949-52; claims examiner Grace Lines, San Francisco, 1954-62, Am. Pres. Lines, San Francisco, 1969—. Mem. Astro-Psychology Inst. (pres, founder 1979—), Am. Fedn. Astrologers (faculty mem.). Home: 2640 Greenwich #403 San Francisco CA 94123

KOVEL, RALPH M., b. Milw.; s. Lester and Dorothy (Bernstein) K.; m. Terry Horvitz; children: Lee, Karen. Author: (with Terry Kovel) Dictionary of Marks Pottery and Porcelain, 1953, Directory of American Silver, Pewter and Silver Plate, 1958, American Country Furniture, 1780-1875, 1963, Know Your Antiques, rev. ed., 1981, Kovels' Antiques + Collectible Price List, (annually since 1968), Kovels' Book of Antique Labels, 1982, Kovels' Price Guide for Collectors Plates, Figurines, Paperweight and Other Ltd. Editions, 1974 and 1978, Kovels' Collector's Guide to American Art Pottery, 1974, Kovels' Know Your Collectibles, 1981, Kovels' Illustrated Price Guide to Depression Glass and American Dinnerware, 2d ed., 1983, Kovels' Illustrated Price Guide to Royal Doulton, 2d ed., 1984, Kovels' Collectors Source Book, 1983, Kovels' New Dictionary of Marks, Pottery and Porcelain, 1850-Present, 1985. Kovels' Advertising Collectibles Price List, 1986, Kovels' Guide to Selling Your Antiques & Collectibles, 1987. Student, Ohio State U. Writer: (with Terry Kovel) syndicated column Kovels Antiques and Collecting. 1955—, Your Collectibles, House Beautiful, 1979—; editor: monthly newsletter Kovels on Antiques and Collectibles. 1974—. Address: Box 22200 Beachwood OH 44122

KOVEL, TERRY HORVITZ, (Mrs. Ralph Kovel), b. Cleve., 1928; d. Isadore and Ris (Osteryoung) Horvitz; m. Ralph Kovel; children: Lee R., Karen. Author: (with Ralph Kovel) Kovels' guides to collectibles and antiques, 1953—(see Ralph Kovel entry). Address: Box 22200 Beachwood OH 44122

KOWACIC, JOSEPH PETER, b. Calumet, MI., Aug. 1, 1919; s. Joseph and Victoria (Gemeiner) K. Author: Embers (poetry), 1987; poetry in anthologies. Wrkg. on poetry vols. BA, Duns Scotus Coll., 1944; MA, Catholic U. Am., 1952; PhD, Bryn Mawr Coll., 1958. Tchr. St. Francis Preparatory Sch., Spring Grove, Pa., 1947-51, Wilson's Tchrs.' Coll. and Am. U., Washington, 1951-53; prof. St. Joseph's U., Phila., 1954-85. Fulbright scholar U. Freiburg, W.Germany, 1953-54. Home: 1187 Calumet Ave Calumet MI 49913

KOWACIC, JOSEPH PETER, b. Calumet, MI, Aug. 1, 1919; s. Joseph and Victoria (Gemeiner) K. Author: Embers (poetry), 1987; poetry in anthologies. Wrkg. on poetry vols. BA, Duns Scotus Coll., 1944; MA, Catholic U. Am., 1952; PhD, Bryn Mawr Coll., 1958. Tchr. St. Francis Preparatory Sch., Spring Grove, Pa., 1947-51, Wilson's Tchrs.' Coll. and Am. U., Washington, 1951-53; prof. St. Joseph's U., Phila., 1954-85. Fulbright scholar U. Freiburg, W. Germany, 1953-54. Home: 1187 Calument Ave Calumet MI 49913

KOWALSKI, JOHN, b. Worcester, MA., Oct. 8, 1928; s. John Joseph and Marion Caroline (Mosevech) K.; m. Fayne McMaster, Apr. 18, 1959; children: Tricia, Kathryn, Joan. Contrbr. articles, poems: Jnl. Irish Lit., Pipe Dream, Salome: A Lit. Dance Mag., Chgo. Tribune, The Clearing House, Denver Post, numerous other publs. AB, Emerson Coll.; EdM, Worcester State U.; postgrad., So. Conn. State U. Tchr. English, Lyman Hall High Sch., Wallingford, Conn., 1960—. Mem. NCTE, other profl. orgns. Home: 118 Algonquin Dr Wallingford CT 06492

KOWIT, STEVE MARK, b. NYC, June 30, 1938; s. Michael and Billie (Ginsburg) K.; m. Mary Leigh Petrangelo, Aug. 11, 1967. Author: (poetry) Cutting Our Losses, 1982, Heart in Utter Confusion, 1982, Lurid Confessions, 1983,

Passionate Journey, 1984 (also cassette rec. 1985), Everything Is Okay, 1985; translator: Incitement to Nixonicide and Praise for the Chilean Revolution (Pablo Neruda), 1979; poetry ed. Canard Anthology, 1984; ed. Gorilla Extract, Nos. 1-10, 1981-85; ed., pub. View from the End of the Pier (LoVerne Brown), 1984. Wrkg. on anthology of contemporary anti-acad. poetry. BA, Bklyn. Coll., 1965; MA, San Francisco State Coll., 1967. Instr. Coll. of South Idaho, 1970-71, San Diego City Coll., 1979—; vis. prof. Garrett Community Coll., McHenry, Md., 1974-75, U. Calif., San Diego, 1982-83; prof. U.S. Intl. U., San Diego, Calif., 1979-80, lectr. San Diego State U., 1978—; founder, coordinator Animal Rights Coalition Calif., San Diego, 1982—; pub. Gorilla Press, 1981—. Served with U.S. Army, 1963-64. Recipient Joseph Slomovitch Meml. award Cedar Rock Press, Tex., 1983; NEA fellow, 1985; NEA/Combo grant, 1986. Home: 1868 Ebers St San Diego CA 92107

KOZER, JOSE, b. Havana, Cuba, Mar. 28, 1940, came to U.S., 1960, s. David and Ana (Deutsch) Kozer; m. Sheila Isaac, Sept. 1, 1962 (div. 1973); 1 dau., Mia; m. Guadalupe Barrenechea, Dec. 20, ,74; 1 dau., Susana. Author poetry books: Padres y otras profesiones, 1972, Este judio de numeros y letras, 1975, Y asi tomaron posesion en las ciudades, 1978, La rueca de los semblantes, 1980, Jarron de las abreviaturas, 1980, Antologia breve, 1981, Bajo este cien, 1983, La garza sin sombras, 1985, El carillon de los muertos, 1987; work translated into English, Portuguese, French, Greek; contrbr. poetry, essays, short stories to numerous lit. mags. MA, Queens Coll., 1971, PhD, 1983. Assoc. prof. Queens Coll., NYC, 1965—. Recipient Julio Tovar Poetry Prize, Nuestro Arte, Canary Island, Spain, 1974. Home: 65-06 110th St Forest Hills NY 11375

KOZOL, JONATHAN, b. Boston, Sept. 5, 1936; s. Harry Leo and Ruth (Massell) K. Author: Death At An Early Age (Natl. Book award 1967), Free Schools, 1972, The Night is Dark and I Am Far From Home, 1975, Children of the Revolution, 1978, Prisoners of Silence, 1980, On Being A Teacher, 1981, People of the Book, 1982, Alternative Schools, 1983, Illiterate America, 1986; corr.: Los Angeles Times, USA Today, 1982-83. B.A., Harvard U., 1958; Rhodes scholar, Magdalen Coll., Oxford, 1958-59. Saxton fellow in creative writing from Harper & Row, 1964; Guggenheim fellow, 1970, 84; Field Fdn. fellow, 1972; Ford Fdn. fellow, 1974; Rockefeller Fdn. sr. fellow, 1978, 82. Mem. PEN. Address: Nesbit 40 W. 57 St New York NY 10019

KRAMAN, CYNTHIA, b. NYC, June 3, 1950; d. Eli and Esther (Weinstock) Kraman; m. Abbot Genser, June 1, 1969. Author: The Mexican Murals, 1986, Club 82, 1979, Taking on the Local Color, 1974. ontrbr. poetry to anthologies, including Rain in the Forest, 1983; New York: Poems, 1980. BA, U. of Mass., Amherst, 1972. Mem. PSA, P&W. Home: 16-18 Charles St New York NY 10014

KRAMER, AARON, b. Bklyn., Dec. 13, 1921; s. Hyman and Mary (Click) K.; m. Katherine Kolodny, Mar. 10, 1942; children: Carol, Laura. Author: Another Fountain, 1940; Till the Grass Is Ripe for Dancing, 1943; Thru Our Guns, 1945; The Glass Mountain, 1946; The Thunder of the Grass, 1948; The Golden Trumpet, 1949; Thru Every Window, 1950; Denmark Vesey, 1952; Roll the Forbidden Drums, 1954; The Tune of the Calliope, 1958; Moses, 1962; Rumshinsky's Hat, 1964; Henry at the Grating, 1968; The Prophetic Tradition in American Poetry, 1835-1900, 1968; On Freedom's Side: American Poems of Protest, 1972; Melville's Poetry: Toward the Enlarged Heart, 1972; On the Way to Palermo, 1973; O Golden Land, 1976; Carousel Parkway, 1980; In Wicked Times, 1983; The Burning Bush, 1983; In the Suburbs, 1986; translator: The Poetry and Prose of Heinrich Heine, 1948; Rosenfeld: The Teardrop Millionaire, 1955; Goethe, Schiller, Heine: Songs and Ballads, 1963; Rilke: Visions of Christ, 1967; Poems by Abraham Reisen, 1971; co-ed. West Hills Rvw, 1978-85; Whitman ed. Paumanok Rising, 1980, Jnl of Poetry Therapy, 1987; contrbr. numerous poems to lit mags and profl. jnls; poems transl. into numerous langs. BA, Bklyn. Coll., 1941, MA, 1951; PhD, NYU, 1966. Prof. English, Dowling Coll., Adelphi U., Oakdale, N.Y., 1961—. Recipient Reynolds lyric award Lyric mag., 1961; 1st prize (with Feldman) Los Altos Film Makers Festival, 1965; Hart Crane Meml. award Hart Crane and Alice Crane Williams Meml. Fund, 1969; 6 gold prizes All Nations Poetry Contest, 1975-78; 1st prize (with Cherry) young composers contest Natl. Fedn. Music Clubs, 1976; 2d prize (with Black) Professional Theatre Program Award, U. of Mich., 1978; ASCAP awards; Meml. Fdn. for Jewish Culture fellow, 1978. Mem. PEN, ASCAP, N.E. MLA, Edna St. Vincent Millay Soc., Intl. Acad. Poets, DG, OG. Office: Eng Dept Dowling Coll Oakdale NY 11769

KRAMER, JANE, b. Providence, Aug. 7, 1938; d. Louis Irving and Jessie (Shore) K.; m. Vincent Crapanzano, Apr. 30, 1967; 1 dau., Aleksandra. Author: Off Washington Square, 1963, Aleksandra. Author: Off Washington Square, 1963, Allen Ginsberg In America, 1969, Honor to the Bride, 1970, The Last Cowboy, 1978, Unsettling Europe, 1980; writer: The Morningsider, 1962, The Village Voice, 1963, New Yorker Mag., 1963—. BA, Vassar Coll., 1959; MA, Columbia U., 1961. Recipient Am. Book Award for nonfiction, 1981; Overseas Press Club Am. award, 1979; Front Page award, 1977. Mem. Phi Beta Kappa PEN (bd.) AG, AL, WG, Comm. to Protect Jnlsts. (bd.), Comm. on Central and East European Pubg. (bd.) Natl. Book Critics Circle. Office: New Yorker 25 W 43d St New York NY 10036

KRAMER, KEITH, b. Chgo., Mar. 22, 1959; s. G. Lionel and Myra L. K. m. Stacey Kramer, Sept. 3, 1984. Contrbr. articles, photographs: New York Times, AAA-Home & Away, American Hockey mag., Steamboat mag., American Clean Car, Service Reporter mag., numerous other trade and spl. interest mags. Degree in Tech. Journalism, Colo. State U. Assoc. ed. Crain Communications, Chgo., 1983-84; mng. ed. Tech. Reporting, Wheeling, Ill., 1984-85; reporter Steamboat Pilot newspaper, Steamboat Springs, Colo., 1985-86; founder, pres. Mountain Media writing and photography service, Steamboat Springs, 1986—. Recipient news reporting award Colo. Press Assn., 1986. Address: Box 880524 Steamboat Springs CO 80488

KRAMER, PHILIP EARL, (Dr. George Simmons), b. Hammond, Ind., Apr. 9, 1940; s. Helen Clara (Curtis) Kramer. Author: Religious Mind Therapy, 1987, How to Build Memory Skills, 1986, Psychological Aspects in Management, 1985; contrbr. articles: The Leaves, The Capuchians, Knights of Columbus, Catholic Crosswinds. Wrkg. on testing research. NS, U. Houston, 1965; MA, U. Colo., 1978. Indsl. cons., prin. Kramer's Inc., Denver, 1977—; assoc. prof. psychology U. So. Colo., Pueblo, 1985—. Home: 1020 E 7th St Pueblo CO 81001

KRANER, MADELINE R., b. Bklyn., d. Meyer J. and Adele I. (Grassgreen) Yeaker; m. Thomas J. Kraner; children—Michael, Lisa. Contrbr. to Prayer Book of Michelino da BeSozza (facsimile), Photo- Graphics, others. BA, Bklyn. Coll. MA in Art History, CUNY. Sr. ed. Pubs. Weekly, NYC; art administr Bristol-Myers Co., NYC; prodn. ed. Girl Scouts U.S.A., NYC; copy and prodn. ed. Scholastic mags., NYC; prod. ed., McGraw-Hill, NYC; free-lance line ed., numerous pubs., spclties: 20th-century art and computer use. Home: 1330 E 24th St Brooklyn NY 11210

KRAPF, NORBERT, b. Jasper, IN, Nov. 14, 1943, s. Clarence A. and Dorothy E. (Schmitt) K.; m. Katherine Anne Trahan, June 12, 1970; children—Elizabeth, Daniel. Author: The Playfair Book of Hours, 1976, Arriving on Paumanok, 1979, Lines Drawn from Durer, 1981, Heartwood, 1983, Circus Songs, 1984, A Dream of Plum Blossoms, 1985, East of New York City, 1986; ed.: Finding the Grain: Pioneer Journals, Franconian Folktales, Ancestral Poems, 1977, Under Open Sky: Poets on William Cullen Bryant, 1986; translator: Shadows on the Sundial: Selected Early Poems of Rainer Maria Rilke, 1987. BA in English, St. Joseph's Coll., 1965; MA, U. Notre Dame, 1966, PhD in English, 1971. Mem. faculty L.I. U., 1970—, prof. English C.W. Post Campus, Greenvale, N.Y., 1984—. Sr. Fulbright lectr. Am. Lit., Council Internat. Exchange of Scholars, Germany, 1980-81. Mem. MLA, Walt Whitman Birthplace Assn., Ind. German Heritage Soc. Home: 219 Main St Roslyn NY 11576

KRAUS, HELEN ANTOINETTE, b. Bklyn., Aug. 25, 1909, d. Christian William M.D. and Clara Helen (Langenburg) Janson; m. Harold George Kraus, June 27, 1934; children—Harold Christian, George Robert, Phyllis Ann. BS, Boston U., 1929; postgrad. Cornell U., Adelphi U., Columbia U., SUNY-New Paltz. Tchr. public schls. various locations in N.Y., 1929-71; adviser student magazine/newspaper,Nassau Tb Assn., Mineola, N.Y., 1934-36; ed. Servicemen's Newsletter, 1942-45; ed. Pi Lambda Theta Women in the News, 1960-65; ed. Pi State News Pi Lights, Delta Kappa Gamma, 1971-83; public relations ed. Rockville Centre Guild for the Arts. Mem. AAUW. Home: 25 Norcross St Rockville Centre NY 11570

KRAUS, JOANNA HALPERT, b. Portland, ME., Dec. 7, 1937; d. Harold and Florence Halpert; m. Ted M. Kraus, 1966; children: Timothy Yang Kun. Author: The Ice Wolf (three-act play; prod., NYC, 1964), 1967, Mean to Be Free (two-act play, prod., NYC, 1968), 1968, Vasalisa (three-act play; prod. Davidson, NC, College Theatre, 1972), 1973, Two Plays from the Far East (The Dragon Hammer and The Tale of Oniroku), 1977, Circus Home (two-act play; prod. Poncho Theatre, Seattle, Wash., 1977), 1979, The Last Baron of Arizona (two-act play; prod. Arizona State Univ., Tempe, 1984), 1986, Kimchi Kid (two-act play; prod. at Rutgers Univ., New Brunswick, N.Y., 1986, The Devil's Orphan (two-act play; prod. Calif. Theatre Ctr.), 1987. Also one act play The Shaggy Dog Murder Trial, prod. Rochester, N.Y.; co-author Tenure Track (prod. Omaha Magic Theatre, 1987. Seven Sound and Motion Stories (fiction), 1971, rev. ed., 1980, The Great American Train Ride, Using Creative Dramatics for Multi-Disciplinary Classroom Project (nonfiction), 1975; contrbr,

Honor Moore, ed, New Women's Theatre, 1977, contrbr of essay, Nellie McCaslin, ed, Children and Drama, 2d ed, 1980. Contrbr of rvws and articles to periodicals, including Times Herald Reord, Children and Drama, Children's Theatre Rvw, and Critical Digest. Attended Westfield College, London, 1957-58; AB, Sarah Lawrence Coll, 1959; MA, Univ. Of Calif., Los Angeles, 1963, Ed. D., 1972. Assoc dir and creative drama tchr, Children's Theatre Assn, Baltimore, Md., 1960-61; drama dir, Strathmore School of the Arts, North Gower, Ont., Can., summers, 1961-63; dir of drama program, New Rochelle, (N.Y.) Acad., 1962-63; asst dir and supervisor of performance program, 1963-65; creative drama teacher, Young Men's and Young Women's Hebrew Assn, N.Y.C., 1965-70; instr in public speaking and oral interpretation, N.Y.C. Community Coll, 1966-69; supervisor of student teachers in speech and theatre, Columbia Univ., Teacher's College, N.Y.C., 1970-71; instructor in theatre and drama, State Univ. of New York College at Purhase, 1970-72; lectr, State Univ. of N.Y. College at New Palz, 1972-75, asst prof of theatre and educ, 1973-79; assoc prof, State Univ. of N.Y. College at Brockport, 1979-85, prof of children's drama, 1986—, coordinator of interdisciplinary arts for children, 1981—. Chairperson of Children's Theatre Showcase, 1963-65. Guest storyteller on WEVD-Radio show Let's Tell Tales, 1973-75. Guest lectr at Western Washington Univ. Inst. for Drama and the Child, Summer, 1978. Director of plays, including The Indian Captive, 1973, A Christmas Carol, 1979, Tom Sawyer, 1980, and A Wrinkle in Time, 1984. Co-ordinator of Arts for Children program, 1980, and children's theatre mini-tours, 1980, 81, 84, 85. Member: Intl Assn of Theatre for Young People, American Alliance of Theatre for Youth and Edn., ASSITES, DG, United University Professions. Charlotte B. Chorpenning Cup from American Theatre Assn, 1971, for achievement in playwrighting. Creative Artists Public Servie fellow in playwrighting, 1976-77. Home: 395 Alexander St. R12 Rochester NY 14607

KRAUSE, NINA, b. Delta, OH, Aug. 11, 1932, d. Robert Allen and Bertha Fiser (Hays) Younkin; m. William W. Krause, Mar. 5, 1955; children—Carrol, James. Contrbr. poems to Connecticut River Rvw, Ky. Poetry Rvw, Contemporary Ky. Poetry, Natl. Cattery Directory, Ten, The Ky. Book, Modern Lyrics Anthology, The Dream Shop, Stratford '85, others. BA, Bowling Green State U., 1954. Mem. PSA, AAP, Conn. Poetry Soc. (v.p. 1985-86, treasurer, 1986-88). Home: 587 Woodlawn Ave Stratford CT 06497

KRAUSS, JANET, b. Cambridge, MA, July 17, 1935, d. Simon and Lena (Katzenberg) Hentoff; m. Bert Krauss, June 16, 1957; children—David, Simon. Contrbr. essays to N.Y. Times, poetry to Yarrow, Wind, Coll. English, Negative Capability, Tar River Poetry, Seattle Rev, others; co-ed.: Connecticut River Rvw, 1985-87. People of the Shell, 1986; poetry ed. Westport News, 1976-80, Norwalk News, 1980-84. BA, Brandeis U., Waltham, Mass., 1957; MA in Am. Studies, Fairfield U., Conn., 1973. Asst. prof. English St. Basil Coll., Stamford, Conn., 1973—; adjunct prof. English Fairfield (Conn.) U., 1978—. Mem. P&W. Home: 17 Loren Ln Westport CT 06880

KREADER, BARBARA BARLOW, b. Sidney, NE, Aug. 17, 1946; d. Robert Andrew and Margaret Virginia (Bailey) B.; m. J. Lee Kreader, Nov. 24, 1967; children—Benjamin Colman, Eleanor Alice. BA, Loretto Heights Coll., 1967; MM, Northwestern U., 1974. Tchr., Phila. pub. schls., 1967-68, Applecreek (OH) Elem. Schl., 1968-69; tchg. assoc. Northwestern U., Evanston, IL, 1974-86; ed. Clavier mag., The Instrumentalist, Northfield, IL, 1982—. Mem. profl. orgns. Office: 200 Northfield Rd Northfield IL 60093

KREMENTZ, JILL, b. NYC, Feb. 19, 1940; d. Walter and Virginia (Hyde K.; m. Kurt Vonnegut, Jr., Nov., 1979; 1 dau., Lily. Author: Sweet Pea—A Black Girl Growing Up in the Rural South (foreword by Margaret Mead), 1969, A Very Young Dancer, 1976, A Very Young Rider, 1977, A Very Young Gymnast, 1978, A Very Young Circus Flyer, 1979, A Very Young Skater, 1979, The Writer's Image, 1980, How It Feels When a Parent Dies, 1981, How It Feels to be Adopted, 1982, How It Feels When Parents Divorce, 1984. Student, Drew U., 1958-59. Reporter Show mag., 1962-64; assoc. editor Status Diplomat mag., 1966-67; contrbg. editor N.Y. mag., 1967-68; corr. Time-Life Inc., 1969-70; Mem. PEN. Address: Knopf 21 E 50 St New York NY 10022

KREMER, JOHN FREDERICK, b. Perham, NJ, Jan. 16, 1949; s. Frank Matthew and Lucille Ernee (Nester) K. Author: FormAides for Successful Book Publishing, 1983, Directory of Short-Run Book Printers, 1983 (3d edit. 1985), Self-Publishing Book Review, 1983 (3d edit. 1986), Kinetic Optical Illusions, 1984, Book Mktg. Made Easier, 1986, 101 Ways to Market Your Books, 1986, Book Mktg. Opportunities, 1986, Specialty Booksellers Directory, 1987. BA, Macalester Coll., 1971; MA, Maharishi Internat. U., 1975. Freelance writer, St. Paul, 1971-73, 77-79; instr. Maharishi Internatl. Univ., Fairfield, Iowa, 1975-77; research and devel. First Impressions, Fairfield, 1980-83; publisher Ad-Lib Publs., Fairfield, 1983—. Mem. COSMEP (bd. dirs, 1985—), Pubs. Assn. S. Calif., Am. Booksellers Assn., Upper Midwest Booksellers Assn. Home: 51 N Fifth St Fairfield IA 52556

KRESS, AGNES IRENE, b. Balt., Nov. 8, 1947; d. Joseph Ellwood and Agnes Irene (Hahn) Federline; m. Leo Monroe Kress, Apr. 18, 1970; children—Joell Lee, Angela Irene. Author: The War Virus, 1988. Contrbr. poems to lit . mags., anthols. A.A. in Laboratory Technology, Commun. Coll. Balt., 1968; B.S. in Microbiology, U. Md., 1980, postgrad., 1980-81. Med. technologist U. Md. Med. Schl., Balt., 1969-72; ind. researcher, 1979-81; owner, pres. Creative Topiary-Designs, Ellicott City, MD, 1984—. Recipient Honorable Mention for script writing WD, 1984, 85. Mem. AAP, Am. Film Inst. Home: 4576 Roundhill Rd Ellicott City MD 21043

KRIEGEL, LEONARD, b. NYC, May 25, 1933, s. Fred and Sylvia (Breittholz) K.; m. Harriet May Bernzweig, Aug. 24, 1957; children—Mark Benjamin, Eric Bruce. Author: The Long Walk Home (autobiography), 1964, Edmund Wilson (criticism), 1971, Working Through (autobiography), 1971, Notes for the Two-Dollar Window (memoir), 1976, On Men and Manhood (polemic), 1978, Quitting Time (novel), 1982; ed. The Essential Works of the Founding Fathers, 1964. PhD, NYU, 1960. Guggenheim fellow in writing, 1973, McDowell fellow in writing, 1976, Rockefeller fellow in humanities, 1976. Mem. PEN, AG. Home: 355 8th Ave New York NY 10001

KRIEGER, MURRAY, b. Newark, Nov. 27, 1923; s. Isidore and Jennie (Glinn) K.; m. Joan Alice Stone, June 15, 1947; children: Catherine Leona, Eliot Franklin,. Author: The New Apologists for Poetry, 1956, The Tragic Vision, 1960, A Window to Criticism: Shakespeare's Sonnets and Modern Poetics, 1964, The Play and Place of Criticism, 1967, The Classic Vision, 1971, Theory of Criticism: A Tradition and Its System, 1976, Poetic Presence and Illusion, 1979, Arts on the Level, 1981, The Aims of Representation: Subject/Text/History, 1987; editor: (with Eliseo Vivas) The Problems of Aesthetics, 1953, Northrop Frye in Modern Criticism, 1966, (with L.S. Dembo) Directions for Criticism: Structuralism and its Alternatives, 1977. Student, Rutgers U., 1940-42; MA, U. Chgo., 1948; PhD (Univ. fellow), Ohio State U., 1952. Instr. Kenyon Coll., 1948-49, Instr. Ohio State U., 1951-52, Asst. Prof., U. of Minn., 1952-55, Assoc. Prof., 1955-58, Profl, U. of Ill., 1958-63, Carpenter Prof., U. of Iowa, 1963-66, Prof., U. of Cal., Irvine, 1967—, UCLA, 1973-82, U. Prof., U. of Cal., 1974—;. Served with AUS, 1942-46. Guggenheim fellow, 1956-57, 61, 62; ACLS, postdoctoral fellow, 1966-67; grantee NEH, 1971-72; Rockefeller Fdn. humanities fellow, 1978, Humboldt Fdn. Research Prize, 1985-86. Fellow Am. Acad. Arts and Scis. Mem. MLA, Acad. Lit. Studies. Home: 407 Pinecrest Dr Laguna Beach CA 92651

KRIEGER, THEODORE KENT, (Ted), b. Charles City, IA, Sept. 26, 1950; s. Dale Theodore and Beverly Jean (Clapp) K., m. Elaine Dorwin, Aug. 3, 1974 (div. June 1979). Author: Imperfection of the Fields, 1978, Bearing It Alone, 1979; contrbr. to more than 50 jnls, including Poetry Now, Sou'Wester, Western Poetry, Webster Rvw, Cape Rock. BA in English, Northwest Mo. State U., 1977. News reporter Charles City Press, Ia., 1977-80; agt. Travel Aid Safety, Osceola, Mo., 1980-83; security guard Guard Systems Ltd., Charles City, 1985—. Recipient Voices Intl. award in poetry, Ark. Poetry Soc., Little Rock, 1980. Mem. Ia. Arts Council. Address: 403 8th Ave Charles City IA 50616

KRIM, SEYMOUR, b. NYC, May 11, 1922; s. Abraham and Ida (Goldberg) K.; m. Eleanor Goff, 1947 (div. 1951). Author: Views of a Nearsighted Cannoneer, 1961, Shake it for the World, Smartass, 1970, You and Me, 1974; Editor; Manhattan, An Anthology, 1954, The Beats, An Anthology, 1960; Contrbr. rvws. and articles to newspapers and mags. Student U. N.C., 1939-40. Reporter, New Yorker mag., 1941-42; writer, OWI, 1943-45; publicity writer, Paramount Pictures, 1952-54; script-reader, United Artists, 1955-61; editor, Nugget mag., 1961-65; reporter, N.Y. Herald Tribune, 1965-66; cons. editor, Evergreen rvw, 1967. Tchr. non-fiction writing St. Marks in the Bowery Writing Workshop, 1967-69, U. Iowa Writers Workshop, 1970-72, NYU, 1972-73, U. P.R., 1973-74, 78-79, Pa. State U., 1973-74, Columbia U., 1964, 1978—. Home: 120 E 10th St New York NY 10003

KRISTWALD-KALLEFELZ, ELFRIEDE HILDEGARDE, (Elfriede Wald), b. Bydgoszcz, Poland, May 22, 1938; came to U.S., 1960; naturalized, 1970; d. Walter and Frieda Helene (Abrams) Kicjiak; m. John M. Kallfelz, Feb. 12, 1959 (div. Oct. 1987); children—William M., Catherine E., Carol F. Contrbr. articles to mags., newspapers inluding Atlanta Mag., Atlanta Bvs. Chronicle, Southline, Creative Loafing, others. B.A. in History, Oglethorpe U., 1977; Lang. Cert., Georgia State U., 1984; grad. student comm. Ga. State Univ. Recipient 1st prize Natl. Christmas Poetry Contest, AAP, 1986, 2d prize for poetry, 1986; Honorary Mention, Ga. State Poetry Assn., 1986, 87. Mem. Village

Wrtrs. Group (social sec. 1986—). Dixie Council Authors Jnlsts. (1st prize for non-fiction book proposal 1987), So. Atlantic Lit. Assn., Ga. State Poetry Soc., Feminist Wrtrs. Guild, Assn. Translators Interpretors. Home: 3454 Hallcrst Dr NE Atlanta GA 30319

KROEKEL, JULIETTE ANN, b. Chgo., Apr. 27, 1947; d. Neil Iverson and Emma Pauline (Mihalovich) Skau; m. Wulf Kroekel, Feb. 10, 1968; children—Andrea, Valerie. Columnist: Western Sportsman's Assn., 1983—. Contrbr. short stories to mags. including Family Circle, Grit, Am. Hospice Jnl., Arabian Horse Mag., others. Ed.: Brighton Standard, CO, 1986—. Diploma, Palmer Wrtrs. Schl. Wrtr., reporter Brighton Blade, 1976-85; feature wrtr. Brighton Standard, 1985-86. Active Brighton Centennial Coms., 1986-87, fdn. mem. Platte Valley Med. Ctr., Brighton, 1987. Reipient 1st place for feature writing Daus. Am. Revolution, 1984. Mem. Brighton Bus. Profl. Women Assn. Home: 2765 Appaloosa Ave Brighton CO 80601

KROESEN, JILL ANNE, b. Berkeley, CA, May 12, 1949, d. Joseph Bernard and Jeanne B. (Saidiner) Kroesen. Author: Disposable Art, 1975, Dramatika, 1977, High Performance, 1984. BA, Mills Coll., Oakland, Calif., 1972, MFA, 1974. Creative Artists in Public Service fellow, 1979, N.Y. Fdn. fellow, 1985, NEA fellow, 1983, 84. Mem. Media Alliance. Home: 15 E 17th St Apt 5 NYC 10003

KRONENBERG, MINDY H., b. Bklyn., Oct. 26, 1954. Contrbr. numerous articles and essays for: Sunstorm, Writer's Connection, Writer's Lifeline, Author's Guild Bulletin, Writer's Jnl; contrbr. numerous poems to anthologies, lit mags, including Cumberland Poetry Rvw, Centennial Rvw, Centennial Rvw, Crosscurrents Quarterly, Prospice, Manhattan Poetry Rvw, Blue Unicorn; BA in English, SUNY-Stony Brook, 1977. Freelance ed., Miller Place, N.Y., 1979—; book reviewer Wrtrs. Alliance, N.Y.C., 1982—; script wrtr. PEM, Inc., N.Y.C., 1984—; workshop instr. Medford-Miller Place Adult Edn., 1982—. First prize winner, Chester H. Jones Fdn national poetry Competition, 1986. Mem. Wrtrs. Alliance, P&W, AAP, NWU. Home: 9 Garden Ave Miller Place NY 11764

KRONENBERG, SUSAN L., b. NYC, July 19, 1948, d. William Leo and Dorothy (Freedman) K. Contrbr. to Poetry Now, Helicon Nine, Crab Creek Rvw, Slipstream, Dark Horse, Four Zoas Night House Anthology, Manhattan Poetry Rvw, The ARTS, Home Planet News, Conditions Telephone, Earth's Daughters, City. BA, Queens Coll., 1969. N.Y. State tchg. grants: Council on Arts, 1980-83; tchr. Seattle pub. schls., 1983-85; Capitol Hill Arts Commn grant for poetry performance, April 1987. Poetry performance: Channel 29TV "In the Round" and "Cactus Poets Series," July and Oct. 1987. Winner contest King County Arts Commn., 1984; writing fellow for poetry Yaddo, 1981, Millay Colony, 1981, Va. Ctr. for Creative Arts, 1982. Mem. P&W, PSA. Home: 5519 6th Ave NW Seattle WA 98107

KRUCHKOW, DIANE, b. Stamford, CT, June 10, 1947; d. Norman and Shirley Kruchkow; 1 dau., Hannah Malina Gay. Author: (poetry) Odd Jobs, 1975. Editor: (with Curt Johnson) Green Isle in the Sea: An Informal History of the Alternative Press, 1960-85, 1986; Zahir, 1970-79 Stony Hills: News & Rvws. of the Small Press, 1977—, Small Press News, 1981; editor, contrbr. (anthol.) Changes of the Day, 1975, Contrbr. poems to antholos., rvws., mags. Wrkg. on collection of short stories, commentaries, rvws. BA, U. N.H., Durham, 1969, postgrad., 1969-70. Proofreader Knowlton & McLeary Co., Farmington, Me., 1985-87; lectr. in English, U. Me., Farmington, 1983—. Mem. Lit. panel Me. State Commn. on Arts & Humanities, Augusta, 1980-82. Fellow Ford Fdn., 1969-70. Mem. COSMEP (bd. dirs. 1973-75, chair, 1974-75) Me. Wrtrs. Pubs. Assn., CCLM (grants com. 1977, 85), New Eng. Small Press Assn. (coordinator 1972-79), Judge for Austin (Texas) Book Award, 1987, Phi Beta Kappa, Phi Kappa Phi. Home: Weeks Mills New Sharon ME 04955

KRUEGER, CARYL WALLER, b. Chgo., Apr. 1, 1929; d. Thomas Floyd and Astrid Alvina (Johnson) Waller; m. Cliff Walter Krueger, Aug. 11, 1951; children—Chris W., Carrrie W., Cameron W. Author: Six Weeks to Better Parenting, 1981, numerous articles in Parade, Weekend, Parents, Christian Science Monitor, 1951—. BS, Northwestern U., 1950; student U. Chgo., 1950-51, U. Calif., 1971-73. Writer, WGN-TV, Chgo., 1950-51, The Toni Co., Chgo., 1951-52; acct. exec. Advert. Div., Inc., Chgo., 1952-60, W.S. Meyers Co., Honolulu, 1961-70, Caryl Krueger Assoc., Honolulu, 1963-68; currently author/lectr. on parent/child relats. and time mgmt. Ad. writer of year, Chgo. Ad. Club, 1959. Mem. Wom. in Communics., NPW. Address: Box 970 Rancho Santa Fe CA 92067

KRUGER, MOLLEE (COPPEL), b. Bel Air, MD, March 28, 1929; d. Benjamin and Mary (Hoffman) Coppel; m. Jerome Kruger, Feb. 20, 1955; children: Lennard Gideon, Joseph Avrum. Author: The Putty Bungalow Come (one-at play), prod. in Washington (D.C.) Dept. of Recreation One Act Tournament, 1959, Unholy Writ: Jewish Poems for the Non-neurotic, 1970, More Unholy Writ: Jewish Verses and Vices, 1973, Yankee Shoes: A Light Verse Saunter through Our Second Hundred Years, 1975, Daughters of Chutzpah: Humorous Verse on the Jewish Woman, 1983. Also au of A Complete Guide to the College Girl, 1968. Au of Tv scripts for loal organizations. Au of Unholy Writ, a column of light verse syndicated by Maryben Books, 1969—. Au of several dozen TV scripts on Jewish themes, such as Mr. Lincoln and the Peddler, Samson Benderly, A Maccabean and a Hellenist Woman, prod. on Washington, D.C., TV stations, 1960-67. Pulpit dramas for presentation by temples and synagogues during religious services: The Muted Note, Poetry of the Bible, Poetry of the Golden Age in Spain, Poetry of the Apocrypha, and The Dowry. Rearched, wrote, and produced commemorative musical play "Prithee Happy Birthday Maryland, 1984. Light verse and feature articles in various jnls, including Baltimore Evening Sun, Mizrahi Woman, Modern Maturity, Washington Post, Woman's Home Companion, and Writer's Digest. BA, Univ of Maryland, 1950; grad study at Catholic University of America, Washington, D.C., 1966. Advertising copywrtr., Joseph Katz Agcy., Baltimore, Md., 1951-55; TV scriptwriter, Jewish Community Center of Greater Washington, D.C., 1960-67; columnist, Jewish Week, Washington, D.C., 1967-75, feature writer, 1968-72; editor, The Standard, 1978—. Freelance writer, 1967-78; owner-publisher, Maryben Books (publishing co.), 1969-79; teacher of creative writing to senior adults, Jewish Community Centr of Greater Washington, D.C., 1975—; speaker, Jewish Welfare Bd leture bureau; apptd mem Montgomery Co. (md.) Commission on the Humanities, 1984-87. Member: Natl League of American Pen Women, Mortar Board Alumni Assn (prs, 1977-78). College Bd. Award from Mademoiselle, 1948; Family Tree Award from Women's League for Conservative Judaism, 1976; Gold Ribbon from Women's League of America, 1976, for Bicentennial project; Award of Excellence from Soc. for Technical Publishing, 1978; Natl League of American Pen Women short story award, 1984; first prize for serious poetry and first prize for light verse, 1985. Home: 619 Warfield Dr Rockville MD 20850

KRULIK, STEPHANIE MIRIAM, b. Bklyn., Aug. 18, 1943; d. Harry Benjamin and Miriam (Karten) Spring; m. Gary Martin Krulik, June 24, 1966; children—Douglas, Tracy. Contrbr. articles to mags., newspapers including Backstretch Mag., Fla. Horse Mag., Atlantic Sun Newspaper, others. Feature wrtr., ed. The Forum Newspaper, Coral Springs, FL, 1986—. B.A., C.W. Post Coll., 1965. Spl. edn. tchr. public schs., Hicksville, NY, 1965-68. Mem. Fla. Freelance Wrtrs. Assn., WIC. Home: 2700 NW 107th Ave Coral Springs FL 33065

KRUMHANSL, BERNICE ROSEMARY, b. Cleve., Apr. 17, 1922; d. Frank Ralph and Anne (Pren) K. Author: Opportunities in Physical Theraphy, 1968, 4th ed., 1987. Contrbr. chpt. to med. text, articles to profl. jnls., travel articles, fiction to mags. Wrkg. on 3 novels, med. articles, short story fiction. B.A., Notre Dame Coll. Ohio, 1943. dir. physical therapy St. Luke's Hosp., Cleve., 1952-86; asst. prof. Ohio Coll. Podiatric Medicine, Cleve., 1986—; private practice physical therapist, 1986—. Home: 1167 Addison Rd Cleveland OH 44103

KRUPINSKY, JACQUELYN STOWELL, b. Springfield, VT, July 2, 1932; d. Lewis Henry and Ethel Nellie (Warren) Stowell; m. Marvin Joseph Krupinsky, June 15, 1954; children—Lisa Ann Krupinsky Paul, Steven Scott Krupinsky. Author: Look Out for Loons. BA, U. Vt.-Burlington, 1954. Library asst., MSAD, Hallowell-Farmingdale, Maine, 1980-85; freelance wrtr., pub., 1978—; pub. Woodbury Press, 1983—. Mem. Soc. Children's Book Wrtrs., Maine Wrtrs. Pub.'s Alliance, Maine Media Women. Home: Whipporwill Rd RFD No. 1 Box 700 Litchfield ME 04350

KRUTENAT, RICHARD CARROLL, (Rich Carr), b. Buffalo, Feb. 25, 1934; s. Carl Alfred and Doris Elouise (Baldeck) K.; m. Ann Littlefield Cowles, Aug. 18, 1956 (div. Dec. 1968); m. 2d, Donna Jean Spurling, Dec. 27, 1968; children—Richard Lyle, Gretchen Elizabeth. Contrbr. articles to profl. jnls., encyclopedias. Editor proceedings of profl. confs; assoc. ed. Jnl of Vacuum Sci. & Tech. BS, Eastern Nazarene Coll., 1956; MS, Tufts U., 1958; PhD, M.I.T., 1965. Research assoc. United Techs., East Hartford, Conn., 1964-73, Exxon Corp., Florham Park, N.J., 1973-86; prin. scientist, AVCO TEXTRON, Lowell, Mass., 1986—. Contrbr. Art Inst. Chgo. Mem. Am. Chem. Soc., Am. Soc. Metals, Am. Vacuum Soc. (Best Tech. Paper 1971). Home: 3 Skyview Dr Nashua NH 03062

KRYSL, MARILYN, b. Anthony, KS, Feb. 26, 1942; d. Richard R. and Evelyn P. (Peterson) Krysl; m. Pepter Michelson, Feb. 14, 1975; 1 child. Author: Saying Things, 1975, More Palomino, Please, More Fuchsia, 1980, Diana Lucifera, 1981, Honey, You've Been Dealt a Winning Hand, 1980, Mozart, Westmoreland, and Me, 1985; Contrbr. to Best Little Magazine Fiction, 1971, The Uses of Poetry, 1975, To Make A Poem, 1982, other anthologies. BA, U. of

Oregon, 1964, MFA, 1968. Asst. prof., U. of Colorado, Boulder, 1973-80, assoc. prof., 1981—. Awards: NEA grant, 1974. MEM. RMMLA. Home: 1070 Grant Place Boulder CO 80302

KUBLER-ROSS, ELISABETH, b. Zurich, Switzerland, July 8, 1926; came to U.S., 1958, naturalized, 1961; d. Ernst and Emma (Villiger) K.; children: Kenneth Lawrence, Barbara Lee. Author: On Death and Dying, 1969, Questions and Answers on Death and Dying, 1974, Death-The Final Stages of Growth, 1975, To Live Until We Say Goodbye, 1978, Working It Through, 1981, Living With Death and Dying, 1981, Remember The Secret, 1981, On Children an Death, 1985; contbr. chpts. to books, articles to profl. jnls. M.D., U. Zurich, 1957; D.Sc. (hon.), Albany (N.Y.) Med. Coll., 1974, Smith Coll., 1975, Molloy Coll., Rockville Centre, N.Y., 1976, Regis Coll., Weston, Mass., 1977, Fairleigh Dickinson U., 1979; LL.D., U. Notre Dame, 1974, Hamline U., 1975; hon. degree, Med. Coll. Pa., 1975, Anna Maria oll., Paxton, Mass., 1978; Litt. D. (hon.), St. Mary's Coll., Notre Dame, In., 1975, Hood Coll., 1976; L.H.D. (hon.), Amherst Coll., 1975, Loyola U., Chgo., 1975. Bard Coll., Annandale-on-Hudson, N.Y., 1977, Union Coll., Schenectady, 1978, D'Youville Coll., Buffalo, 1979, U. Miami, Fla., 1976; D.Pedagogy, Keuka Coll., Keuka Park, N.Y., 1976; Litt.D. (hon.), Rosary Coll., River Forest, Ill., 1976. Address: Box 2396 Escondido CA 92025

KUBLY, HERBERT OSWALD, b. New Glarus, WI, April 26, 1915; s. Nicholas Heinrich and Alda Sabina (Ott) K.; 1 son (adopted), Alexander. Author: American in Italy (travel memoir), 1956 (Natl. Bk. Award), Easter in Sicily (travel memoir), !956, Varieties of Love (short stories), 1958, Italy, 1961, The Whistling Zone (novel), 1963, Switzerland, 1964, At Large (essays), 1964, Gods and Heroes, 1969 (non-fiction 1st award, Council for Wis. Wrtrs.), The Duchess of Glover, 1975 (novel; fiction 1st award, Council for Wis. Wrtrs.), Native's Return, 1981, The Parkside Stories, 1985; plays: Men to the Sea, 1944, The Cocoon, 1948, The Virus, 1973, Perpetual Care, 1975. BA, Univ. of Wis., 1937. Reporter, Sun-Telegraph, Pittsburgh, 1937-42, Herald Tribune, NYC, 1942-44; music critic, Time, 1945-47; writer, Holiday & Life, 1955-64; assoc. prof, Univ. of Ill., 1949-54; prof. San Francisco State Coll., 1964-68; Univ. of Wis., Parkside, Kenosha, 1968-84; prof. emeritus, 1984—. Home: W4970 Kubly Rd New Glarus WI 53574

KUBY, LOLETTE BETH, b. Cleve., July 6, 1943, d. Sally Miller; m. Donald Kuby, 1962 (div. 1981); m. 2d, Stanley Goldhamer; children—Lauren, David. Author: An Uncommon Poet for the Common Man: A Study of Philip Larkin's Poetry, 1972, In Enormous Water, 1981; ed.: Forum: Ten Poets of the Western Reserve, 1977; contrbr. articles, poems, short stories to Clev. Mag., Prairie Schooner, Appalachee Rvw., Light Year '84 & '85, lit mags. PhD, Case Western Res. U., 1970. Asst. prof. Cleve. State U., 1970-72; assoc. dir. Whiting Coll. Bus., Cleve., 1972-74; pres. Cleve. Wrtg. Studios, 1979—; presenter seminars; tchr. bus. wrtg., creative wrtg. Mem. Poets' League Greater Cleve. (trustee 1980-82). Home: 3341 Warrensville Ctr Rd Shaker Heights OH 44122

KUEHL, JOHN RICHARD, b. Davenport, IA, Mar. 19, 1928, s. Hans Henry and Genevieve Vivian (Mills) K.; m. Joan Sidman, Sept. 8, 1953 (div. 1963); m. 2d, Linda Lipnack, Oct. 10, 1967 (div. 1971); m. 3d, Linda Kandel, Jan. 31, 1974. Author: The Apprentice Fiction of F. Scott Fitzgerald, 1909-1917, 1965, Thoughtbook of Francis Scott Key Fitzgerald, 1965, Write and Rewrite: A Study of the Creative Process, 1967 (published as Creative Writing and Rewriting: Contemporary American Novelists at Work 1967), Dear Scott/Dear Max: The Fitzgerald-Perkins Correspondence (with Jackson R. Bryer), 1971, The Fool-Spy (novel), 1967, The Basil and Josephine Stories (with Bryer), 1973, John Hawkes and the Craft of Conflict, 1975, Adventures in American Literature (with Kenneth Silverman), 1980, In Recognition of William Gaddis (with Steven Moore), 1984; contrbr. articles, interviews, rvws. to scholarly publs.; contrbr. stories to Queen's Qtly, Motive, Forum. AB, U. Iowa, 1952; MA, UCLA, 1955; PhD, Columbia U., 1958. Mem. faculty Princeton (N.J.) U., 1958-66, NYU, 1966—; prof. Am. lit. and modern drama. Served USMCR 1946-48. Lydia C. Roberts grad. fellow Columbia U., 1954-56, sr. Fulbright scholar, 1976. Mem. Phi Beta Kappa. Address: Dept Eng NYU 19 University Place New York NY 10003

KUEHN, AARON S., b. Paw Paw, MI, Feb. 27, 1967· Leonard Earnest and Charlene Ruth (Fisk) K. Contrbr. articles to mags. short story. Student Westrn Mich. U., 1984—. Typesetter Kalamazoo Gazette-Newhouse Newspapers, MI, 1986—. Home: 45801 CR 653 Paw Paw MI 49079

KUENSTER, JOHN JOSEPH, b. Chgo., June 18, 1924; s. Roy Jacob and Katheryn (Holechek) K.; m. Mary Virginia Maher, Feb. 15, 1947 (dec. Feb. 1983); children—Kathy, Jim, Lois, Virginia, Peggy. Kevin, Mary Frances, Bob. Ed., Baseball Digest, 1969—; exec. ed. Football Digest, Hockey Digest, Basketball Digest, Inside Sports, ed./contrbr. Cobb to Catfish, 1975; booklets: Mexicans in Am., Honesty: Is It the Best Policy, Money, Mission in Guatemala, The Police. Ed., The Columbian, Chgo., 1948-57; staff writer Chgo. Daily News, 1957-65; ed. Baseball Digest, Evanston, IL, 1969—. Mem. Baseball Writers Assn of Am. Home: 9546 S Ridgeway Ave Evergreen Park IL 60642

KUETHE, PEGGY SUE, b. Litchfield, IL., Sept. 3, 1958, d. Marion Andrew and Ruth Mae (Beckwith) Pinkerton; m. Kevin Reed Kuethe, May 1, 1982; 1 dau., Kendra Leigh (born May 24, 1985). Ed. bus. and instn. newsletters, 1980-84; contrbr. Inst. Children's Lit. textbook: First Time Authors, 1986. Wrkg. on local history. BS, Ill. State U., 1980. Ed. Heinrichs Publs., Inc., Litchfield, Ill., 1980—, ed. Sunshine Mag., Good Reading Mag., Illinois Mag. Mem. McKendree Wrtrs. Assn. (guest panelist, conf. 1986). Home: 605 E Olive St Staunton IL 62088

KUHNE, SHARON ANGLIN, b. Berea, KY, Mar. 12, 1951; d. Henry Calvin and Geraldine (Clifford) Anglin; m. A Keith Kuhne, June 19, 1971; 1 child, Jody Carson. Ed./illus./pub. Intervisions: Poems and Photographs (with James Dickey), 1983. BA, U. NC, 1979; MFA, East. Tenn. State U., 1984. Mus. asst. Berea Coll., Ky., 1969-71; photographer NC dept. Archives and History, Raleigh, 1971-72, NC State Univ., 1972-74; graphic designer Asheville Tech. Coll., NC, 1977-80; lectr. in graphic arts McDowell Tech. Coll., Marion, NC, 1984—; owner Visual alternatives, Penland, NC, 1983—. Mem, NC Peacelinks, Asheville, 1985-86. Recipient Outstanding Achievement in Photography award Design Intl., 1984, 85. Mem. Blue Mountain Art Gallery, SE Center for Contemp. Art, Design Intl. Address: 109 Wing Rd Bakersville NC 28705

KULIK, BOLES, see Costley, Bill

KULVINSKAS, VICTOR P., b. Vilkaviskis, Lithuania, USSR, May 3, 1950, s. Kazimieras and Stase (Grazina Kairys) K. Author: Love Your Body, 1973, Survival Into 21st Century, 1976, Sprout For Love of Everybody, 1978, Life in 21st Century, 1983, Wheatgrass Magic Gardens, 1984, Live Food Longevity Recipes, 1984, Jesus Diet for your Culinary Sins, 1986, From Longevity to Immortality, 1986, Holistic Vegetarian Directory, 1986; pub., ed. 21st Century Journey, 1984, 85, 86. BS, U. Conn., 1963, MS, 1966; PhD, Am. Holistic Co-1 Nutrition, 1986. Dir. research Hippocrates Health Inst., Boston, 1969-75; owner, pub. 21st Century Publs., Fairfield, Iowa, 1974-86; dir., founder Survival Fdn., Wethersfield, Conn., 1981—. Co-director, lectr., Dick Gregory Intl. Health Resort, Nassau, Bahamas, 1986. Home: 79 Buckland Rd Wethersfield CT 06109

KUMIN, MAXINE, b. Phila., June 6, 1925, d. Peter and Doll (Simon) Winokur; m. Victor Kumin, June 29, 1946; children—Jane, Judith, Daniel. Author: (poems) Halfway, 1961, The Privilege, 1965, The Nightmare Factory, 1970, Up Country, 1972, House, Bridge, Fountain, Gate, 1975, The Retrieval System, 1978, Our Ground Time Here Will Be Brief, 1982, The Long Approach, 1985, (novels) Through Dooms of Love, 1965 (pub. in Eng. as A Daughter and Her Loves), The Passions of Uxport, 1968, The Abduction, 1971, The Designated Heir, 1974, (essays) To Make a Prairie, 1980, In Deep, 1987, (short stories) Why Can't We Live Together Like Civilized Human Beings?, 1982. AB, Radcliffe Coll., 1946, AM, 1948. Hurst prof. Brandeis U., 1975, Washington U., St. Louis, 1977; vis. lectr. Princeton U., 1977, 79, 81-82; cons. in poetry Library of Congress, 1981-82; vis. prof. MIT, 1984. Vis. Wrtr. MIT, 1986-87. Recipient Tietjens Meml. prize Poetry mag., 1972; Pulitzer prize for poetry, 1973; award AAIAL, 1980; AAP fellow, 1985; Levinson prize Poetry Mag., 1986. Mem. PEN, AG, PSA, NWU. Home: Joppa Rd Warner NH 03278

KURTZ, PATTI JOAN, b. Albany, GA, June 20, 1957; d. Theodore Thomas and Helen Elizabeth Kurtz; m. Gary T. Schroeder, Oct. 13, 1984. Contrbr. poems, articles to newspapers, lit. mags. Wrkg. on young adult novels, romances and mysteries. B.A. in English, Waynesburg Coll., 1979; postgrad. Clarion U., 1980-84. Dir., WTOV-TV, Steubenville, OH, 1981-86, WVIT-TV, Hartford, CT, 1986—. Recipient Garvin award Waynesburg Coll. English Dept., 1978. Home: 418 Farmington Ave G-10 New Britain CT 06053

KURZ, RON, (Mark Jackson), b. Balt., Nov. 27, 1940, s. Gordon L. and Dorothy (Driver) K.; m. Shelley Nelkens; children—Scott, Daniel. Novelist: Lethal Gas, 1974, Black Rococo, 1976; author screenplays: King Frat, 1979, Eyes of a Stranger (with others), 1981, Friday the 13th, Part II, 1981, Off The Wall (with others), 1983. Student Balt. Jr. Coll., 1965-67. Correctional officer Md. Dept. Correction, Balt., 1961-69; mgr. JF Theatres, Balt., 1970-72, Schwaber Theaters, Balt., 1973-74. Mem. WG Am. East. Home: Box 164 Antrim NH 03440

KUSLER, REX ERNEST, b. Maryville, Mo., Feb. 5, 1952, s. Ernest and Julaine (Olson) K; m. Elizabeth Irene Sprague, Nov. 22, 1986. Contrbr. humorous fiction to The Meridian, Alma, Mark, Uncle, numerous others. Wrkg. on novel. Designer Stanford U., Palo Alto, Calif.,

1985—. Home: 1055 Tuers Ct San Jose CA 95121

KUTTNER, PAUL, b. Berlin, Sept. 20, 1931 (arrvd. USA 1947), s. Paul and Margarete (Fraenkel) K.; m. Ursula Timmermann, Dec. 1963 (div. 1970); 1 child, Stephen. Author: (novels) The Man Who Lost Everything, 1977, Condemned, 1983, Absolute Proof, 1984, The Iron Virgin, 1987; translator from German Creative Enamelling & Jewelry Making, 1965, Make Your Own Mobiles, 1965, Karate: Basic Principles, 1967, Coloring Papers, 1968, Potato Printing, 1968, Candle Making, 1968, Nail Sculpture, 1968, Flower Pressing, 1972, Eye Teasers: Optical Illusions & Puzzles, 1976. Student schls., Berlin, Dorset, Eng. Fgn. corr. Switzerland's Der Weg, London, 1946-47; journalist London News Chronicle Hollywood, Calif., 1948; columnist What's on in London-The London Week, Hollywood and NYC, 1948-56; salesman Watson-Guptill Pubs., NYC, 1956-62; publicity dir. Guinness Book of World Records, NYC, 1962—. Home: 37-26 87th St Jackson Heights NY 11372

KUTZ, MYER PAUL, b. Mar. 31, 1939; s. Samuel Sol and Dorothy (Beritz) K.; m. Cynthia Jean Van Hazinga, June 25, 1965 (div. 1978); m. 2d, Mary Enid Dorrance, Oct. 6, 1979. Author: Temperature Control, 1968, Rockefeller Power, 1974, Midtown North, 1976; editor-in-chief: Kent's Mechanical Engineer's Handbook, 13th ed., 1976. B.S., MIT, 1959; MS Rensselaer Poly. Inst., 1961. Freelance writer, NYC, 1971-76; editor John Wiley & Sons Inc., NYC, 1976-81, pub., 1981—. Served to 1st lt. AUS, 1962-64. Mem. Assn. Am. Pubs. Home: 270 11th St Brooklyn NY 11215

KUYPER, VICKI JEAN, b. Oakland, CA, Dec. 30, 1956; d. Frank Anthony and Jean Eileen (Mulaskey) Miller; m. Mark William Kuyper, June 7, 1981; children—Ryan Michael, Katrina Noelle. Contrbr. articles, rvws. to Bookstore Jnl., Am. Baby, Aspen Leaves. B.S., Calif. Polytehnic U., 1982. Office mgr. Campus Life, San Luis Obispo, CA, 1981-83; free-lance ed., 1986—. Home: 3865 Beltana Dr Colorado Springs CO 80920

KWIATKOWSKI, DIANA J., b. NYC, Dec. 30, 1958, d. Leo Richard and Gladys Ellen (Dempsey) K. Author: Panorama, 1979, The Poet Pope, 1980, View from This Side of Heaven, 1982; contrbr. poetry, short stories, lit. criticism to numerous mags. BA, Marymount Manhattan Coll. With Random House, Inc., 1979—; spcl. features ed. Gusto Press. Recipient numerous poetry awards. Mem. AAP, P&W, Wrtrs. Community. Home: 53-92 62nd St Maspeth NY 11378

KWOCK, LAUREEN C., (Clarice Peters, Laureen Ching), b. Honolulu, Sept. 11, 1951; d. Thomas E.C. and Annabelle (Ching) Ching; m. Adrian P. Kwock, June 13, 1976; 1 child, Jeremy. Contrbr. (under name Laureen Ching or Laureen Kwock) to Travel and Leisure, Coronet, Wrtrs. Digest, Hawaii, Pawn, S.D., Mississippi Valley rvws., Bitterroot, Dacotah Ter., Cat's Eye, Wind, Bridge; author: (under pseudonym Clarice Peters) Samantha, 1983, The False Betrothal, 1984, Thea, 1985, Rosalind, 1985; contrbg. ed. San Francisco Rvw. of Books, 1978. BA, U. Hawaii, 1973. Mem. AG, Phi Betta Kappa. Home: 2930 Varsity CR Apt 4 Honolulu HI 96826

KYLE, MARY J., b. St. Paul, Oct. 27, d. Ernest Beverly and Edith May (Burnette) James; m. Earle F. Kyle, Nov. 12, 1927 (dec.); children—Shirley Kyle Heaton, Robert C., Earlene Kyle Walker, Earl F., Jr. Contrbr. short stories to Crisis mag., juvenile publs.; contrbr. articles to Ladies Home Jnl, Dog World, Catholic Digest, genl. interest publs.; contrbr. poetry trade to publs., juvenile mags. Wrkg. on short stories, non-fiction. Ed., U. Minn. Columnist Observer-Sun Newspapers, Mpls., 1948-52, ed., bus. mgr., 1952-66; ed. Twin Cities Courier, Mpls., 1967-86, pub., 1968—; pres. Minn. Sentinel Pub., Co., Mpls., 1968-86; freelance wrtr. Recipient numerous journalistic and civic awards. Me. Sigma Delta Chi, Minn. Press Club, Press Women Minn., Nalt. Newspaper Assn., Natl. Newspaper Pubs. Assn., Natl. Press Women, Minn. Newspaper Assn., Twin City Black Journalists. Home: 3637 4th Ave S Minneapolis MN 55409

LABONTE, JOHN JOSEPH, b. Buffalo, Jan. 22, 1939; s. James Lennon and Mary Agnes (Coffey) LaB.; m. Sandra Lee Vass, May 23, 1970; children—Mary Elisabeth, Jennifer Ann, James Paul. Author: (with John Manear, Tim White) Advanced Placement English II: Challenging Approaces for Honors, Gifted, and AP English Classes, 1986, 2d ed., 1987. Contrbr. poems., essays, translations, articles, rvws. to lit. mags., profl. jnls. Wrkg. on literary criticism of 20th century novel. B.A. in Classics, Fordham U., 1962, M.A. in Humanities, 1965; Ed.S. in English, Fla. Atlantic U., 1973. Inst. humanities Regis High Schl., Loyola Coll., NYC and Balt., 1962-67; asst. prof. English, Marymount Coll. and Miami Commun. Coll., Boca Raton, FL and Miami, 1967-72; sales dir. Ind. Bus. Cons., Italy, Sweden, Argentina, 1972-80; chmn. English dept. Brophy Coll. Preparatory Schl., Phoenix, 1981—. Vice pres. N.Y. Forensic League, NYC., 1965-66. Named Coach of Yr., N.Y. Forensic League, 1965; recipient Humanities award Colegio San Salvadore, Buenos Aires, Argentina, 1968; natl. writing fellow Center for Learning, John Carroll U., 1985. Home: 5401 E Wethersfield Rd Scottsdale AZ 85254

LACEY, JOAN MARY, b. Manchester, England, Sept. 8, 1920 (arrd. USA, Dec. 24,1958); d. George and Lilee Vivian (Hume) Wainwright; m. Edward George Lacey May 15, 1943; children: Karen Margaret, Edward Michael. News columns Islip Press, Bay Short Sentinel, Brentwood News, Babylon Eagle (Long Island, NY), 1947-71; travel columns, Brentwood News, 1966-67, Vanguard, East Islip, 1967-68, New Mexico Flying Review mag, 1973, Roadrunner (Rio Rancho, NM), 1972-75, The Observer (Rio Rancho), 1975-82; travel column, Travel-Age West, 1975; contrbr. poetry to Wide Open Magazine, The Observer, anthologies; included in Best Poets of 1986, Reflections, Earth Scenes Poetry, Chasing Rainbows. Cert., Burleigh Sectl. Coll. (Manchester), BA, Victoria Univ. (Manchester), Royal Coll. of Technology (Manchester), cert. counsellor, ASTA Travel (Washington, DC). Travel agcy. owner, Long Island, 1956-81; columnist Islip Press/Syndicate, 1962-71; radio travel show, KZIA (Albuquerque), 1978. Founder, pres., Profl. Women in Travel, Long Island and NM, 1971-81. Completing bk of poetry and autobiography. Home: 4610 Los Reyes Rd SE Rio Rancho NM 87124

LACH, ALMA, b. Petersburg, IL; d. John H. and Clara E. (Boeker) Satorius; m. Donald F. Lach, Mar. 18, 1939; 1 dau., Sandra Judith. Author: A Child's First Cookbook, 1950, The Campbell Kids Have a Party, 1953, The Campbell Kids at Home, 1953, Let's Cook, 1956, Candlelight Cookbook, 1959, Cooking ala Cordon Bleu, 1970, Alma's Almanac, 1972, Hows and Whys of French Cooking, 1975; contrbr. to World Book Yearbook, 1962-75, Grolier Soc. Yearbook, 1962, Bon Appetit Mag.; feature writer, children's Activities mag., 1954-55; creator, performer: TV program Let's Cook, children's cooking show, 1955; food ed.: Chgo. Daily Sun-Times, 1957-66, CBS-TV Food Show, 1962-66; columnist Modern Packaging, 1967-68; food cons., Food Bus. Mag.; cons., Lettuce Entertain You Enterprises, The Pump Room, Bitter End Yacht Club, V.I., Midway Airlines, Piedmont Airlines, Flying Food Fare, The Berghoff; Diplome de Cordon Bleu, Paris, 1956. Pres. Alma Lach Kitchens, Inc., 1966—, Alma Lach Cooking Schl., 1976-86; lectr. numerous schls., 1962-82. Pillsbury award 1958, Grocery Mfrs. Am. trophy award and Certificate of Honor award, 1959, 61. Mem. Chevalier du Tastevin, Confrerie de la Chaine Des Rotisseurs, Les Dames d'Escoffier. Home: 5750 Kenwood Ave Chicago IL 60637

LACHENBRUCH, DAVID, b. New Rochelle, NY, Feb. 11, 1921; s. Milton Clevel and Leah Judith (Herold) L.; m. Gladys Kidwell, Dec. 12, 1941; 1 dau., Ann Leah (Mrs. Daniel J. Zulawski). Author: Videocassette Recorders—The Complete Home Guide, 1978; co-author: Adult Toys, 1982, The Complete Book of Adult Toys, 1983; columnist: Radio-Electronics, TV Guide mags.; contrbg. ed. N.Y. Times Encyc. of TV. BA, U. MI, 1942. Corr. Variety, also Detroit Times, 1940-42; rptr., asst. city ed., then wire ed. TV Digest with Consumer Electronics, Washington, 1950-58; mng. ed., 59-68, editorial dir., NYC, 1968—; v.p. TV Digest, Inc., Washington, 1962—; editorial adv. bd. Channels Mag. Served with AUS, Radiotechnique et Electronique. Home: 77 Seventh Ave New York NY 10011

LADD, EVERETT CARLL, JR., b. Saco, ME, Sept. 24, 1937; s. Everett Carll and Agnes Mary (McMillan) L.; m. Cynthia Louise Northway, June 13, 1959; children—Everett Carll, III, Corina Ruth, Melissa Ann, Benjamin Elliot. Author: Negro Political Leadership in the South, 1966, Ideology in America: Change and Response in a City, a Suburb, and a Small Town, 1969, rev. ed., 1986, American Political Parties: Social Change and Political Response, 1970, (with S.M. Lipset) Professors, Unions, and American Education, 1973, Academics, Politics, and the 1972 Election, 1973, The Divided Academy: Professors and Politics, 1975, (with C.D. Hadley) Political Parties and Political Issues: Patterns in Differentiation Since the New Deal, 1973, Transformations of the American Party System: Political Coalitions from the New Deal to the 1970's, 2d ed., 1978, Where Have All the Voters Gone?, 1978, 2d ed., 1982, The American Polity, 1985; editorial bd.: Public Opinion Qtly, 1976—, Political Behavior, 1978—, Politics and Behavior, 1980, Polity, Micro Politics, Political Sci. Qtly, 1982—; cons. ed., mem. editorial bd., Public Opinion Mag., 1977—, sr. ed., 1983—. AB magna cum laude, Bates Coll., 1959; PhD, Cornell U., 1964. Asst. dean students for public affairs Cornell U., 1963-64; asst. prof. U. CT, Storrs, 1964-67, assoc. prof., 1967-69, prof. poli. sci., 1969—; dir. Inst. for Social Inquiry, 1968—; co-exec. dir. Roper Ctr. for Pub. Opinion Research, 1977-79, exec. dir., pres., 1979—. Ford fellow, 1969-70; Guggenheim fellow, 1971-72; Rockefeller fellow, 1976-77. Mem. Am. Assn. Public Opinion Research, Phi Beta Kappa. Home: 86 Ball Hill Rd Storrs CT 06268

LADENHEIM, KALA EVELYN, b. Ithaca, NY, May 13, 1950; d. Herman Charles and Martha Oettinger (Rosenthal) L.; m. Robert Wesley

Saunders, Apr. 12, 1985. Author: Brotherly and Other Loves, 1980; Not Far from the Mountains of the Mora, 1983; co-wrtr., ed., pub. The Night Robin Came to Town, 1973; contrbr. poems and short stories to lit mags. BA, Harvard U., 1972; MS in Pub. Health, U. N.C., 1985. Area rep. Maine CETA, 1975-78; self-employed wrtr., 1972—; ed./pub. Woman's Free Express, 1974—; research asst. U. N.C., 1983-85; policy analyst Project Hope, Millwood, Va., 1985—. Maine Council for Arts and Humanities, 1979. Mem. P&W, Maine Wrtrs. and Pubs. Alliance (ed./ pub. newsletter 1980-81). Home: 8515 Greenwood Avenue 5 Takoma Park MD 20912

LADER, LAWRENCE, b. NYC, Aug. 6, 1919; s. Ludwig and Myrtle (Powell) L.; m. Jean McInnis, Aug. 24, 1942 (div. Jan. 1946); m. 2d, Joan Summers, Sept. 27, 1961; 1 dau., Wendy Summers. Author: Margaret Sanger, 1955, The Bold Brahmins, New England's War Against Slavery, 1961, Abortion, 1966, Margaret Sanger, 1969 (juvenile), Breeding Ourselves to Death, 1971, Foolproof Birth Control, 1972, Abortion II: Making the Revolution, 1973, Power on the Left: American Radical Movements since 1946, 1979, Politics, Power and the Church, 1987. AB, Harvard U., 1941. With press dept. ABC, 1941-42; contrbg. ed. Coronet Mag., 1946; feature ed. Glamour mag., 1953; lectr. NYU, 1957-59, Philips Brooks Assn., Harvard, 1962—; regular contrbr. Am. Heritage, Reader's Digest, McCall's, other mags, 1941—; fgn. corr. Arab-Israeli War, 1948; adj. assoc. prof. jnlsm. NYU, 1967-72. Served to lt. AUS, 1942-46; officer-in-charge N.Y. Troop Info., Armed Forces Radio Svc. Mem. ADJA. Home: 51 Fifth Ave New York NY 10003

LAFFAL, FLORENCE, b. Newark, Jan. 3, 1921; d. Jacob and Sarah (Berman) Schultz; m. Julius Laffal, Aug. 23, 1943; 2 sons, Paul and Kenneth. Author: Breads of Many Lands, 1975; ed./pub. Vivolo & His Wooden Children, 1976; ed./pub. Folk Art Finder, 1980—. BS, South CT State, MA, Columbia Tchrs. Coll. Art tchr. & artist; book ed. Gallery Press, Essex, CT, 1970-80; ed. Folk Art Finder, Gallery Press, 1980—. Home: 117 N Main Essex CT 06426

LAFFERTY, SUSAN LEE, b. Midland, MI, June 22, 1948; d. Wilbur Richard and Betty Lou (Hekerthorne) Stephenson; m. John Michael Lafferty, July 11, 1970; children—John Michael Jr., James Colin. Contrbr. articles to newspapers. Student Ferris State U., 1966-68. Copy person The Courier, Findlay, OH, 1980-81; feature wrtr. The Advance, Findlay, 1984—; resident wrtr. D. L. Dorney and Ohio Arts Council, 1986-87, 87-88. Public speaker Findlay Area Arts Council, 1986-87. Home: 2632 Eton Pl Findlay OH 45840

LAGAN, CONSTANCE HALLINAN, b. Jamaica, NY, Feb. 18, 1947, d. John Francis and Muriel Helen (Mylett) Hallinan; m. Patrick Andrew Lagan, June 17, 1967; children—Colleen, Kelly, Erin Dawn, Kerry. Wrtr., ed., pub. Mktg. Options Reports for Craftspeople, 1983—; contrbr. to Cottage Crafts & Fibers; past contrbg. ed.: Entrepreneur mag.; past crafts ed.: The Homemaker; contrbg.ed., Homeworking Mothers; co-author: Mothers' Money Making Manual. AS, Nassau Community Coll., 1966; student Hofstra U., 1981-83. Prin. Creations by Connie, North Babylon, N.Y., 1980—. Home: 35 Claremont Ave North Babylon NY 11703

LAGO, MARY MCCLELLAND, b. Pitts., Nov. 4, 1919; d. Clark Russell and Olive Arabella (Malone) McClelland; m. Gladwyn Vaile Lago, Mar. 4, 1944; children—Jane Hazel, Donald Russell. Editor: Imperfect Encounter, 1972, (with W.K. Beckson) Max and Will, 1975, Rothenstein, Men and Memories, 1978, Burne-Jones Talking, 1981, (with P.N. Furbank) Selected Letters of E.M. Forster, 2 vols., 1983, 84; comp. Calendar of the Letters of E. M. Forster, 1985thor Rabindranath Tagore, 1976; mem. editorial bd. Twentieth Century Lit., 1979—. BA, Bucknell U., 1940; MA, U.MO, 1965, PhD, 1969; D.Litt. (hon.) Bucknell U., 1981. Editorial asst. Friendship Press, NYC, 1941-43, Congl. Ch. Natl. Hdqrs., 1944-47; tchg. asst. U. MO, Columbia, 1964-70, lectr. English, 1971-77, assoc. prof., 1977-79, prof. English, 1979—; Hon. Vis. Prof. of English, Univ. of Manchester, 1985-86. Research grantee NEH, 1980-83. Mem. MLA, Soc. Authors, Phi Beta Kappa. Home: 834 Greenwood Ct Columbia MO 65211

LAGOWSKI, BARBARA JEAN, b. Adams, MA, Nov. 9, 1955; d. Frank Louis and Jeanette (Wanat) L.; m. Richard Dietrich Mumma III, Oct. 11, 1980. BA, U. So. FL, 1977; MA, Johns Hopkins U., 1978. Co-author: Good Spirits: Alcohol-free Drinks for All Occasions. Poet-in-the schls. Hillsborougho County Arts Council, Tampa, FL, 1976-77; poet-in-residence Cloisters Childrens Mus., Balt., 1977-78; asst. ed. Fred Jordan Books Grossett and Dunlap Pubs., NYC, 1978-80; mng. ed. Methuen Inc., NYC, 1980-81; mng., assoc., sr. ed. Bobbs-Merrill Co. Inc., NYC, 1981-84; NAL, 1984-85; free-lance wrtr./ed., 1986—. Home: 442 Dewey St Long Branch NJ 07740

LAHR, JOHN, b. Los Angeles, July 12, 1941; s. Bert and Mildred (Schroeder) L.; m. Anthea Mander, Aug. 12, 1965; 1 son, Christopher David. Author: Notes on a Cowardly Lion: The Biography of Bert Lahr, 1969, Up Against the Fourth Wall, 1970, The Autograph Hound, 1973, Astonish Me, 1973, (with Jonathan Price) Life-Show, 1973, Hot to Trot, 1974, Prick Up Your Ears: The Biography of Joe Orton, 1978 (Gay News lit. prize 1979; film, 1987), Coward: The Playwright, 1983, Automatic Vaudeville, 1984; ed.: (with Anthea Lahr) Casebook on Harold Pinter's The Homecoming, 1969, The Complete Plays of Joe Orton, 1976, The Orton Diaries. BA, Yale, 1963; MA, Worcester Coll., Oxford, 1965. Drama critic Manhattan East, 1966-68, New York Free Press, 1968-70, Evergreen Rev., 1968-71, Village Voice, 1969-72, The Nation, 1981-82; contrbg. ed. Harper's, 1979-83; lit. adviser Tyrone Guthrie Theatre, Mpls., 1968; lit. mgr. Repertory Theatre of Lincoln Ctr., 1969-71. George Jean Nathan award for drama criticism, 1969. Address: Knopf 201 E 50th St New York NY 10022

LAIR, JESSE K., b. Bricelyn, MN, Oct. 11, 1926; s. Merle Thomas and Bertha Christina (Eggen) L.; m. Jacqueline Patricia Carey, July 7, 1949; children—Janet Mary, Barbara Ann, Jesse Howard, Joseph Thomas, Michael Thaddeus. Author: I Ain't Much Baby—But I'm All I've Got, 1972, (with Jacqueline C. Lair) Hey God, What Should I do Now?, 1973, I Ain't Well, But I Sure Am Better, 1975, Ain't I a Wonder, And Ain't You a Wonder Too, 1977, Sex—If I Didn't Laugh, I'd Cry, 1979, I Don't Know Where I'm Going—But I Sure Ain't Lost, 1981, How to Have a Perfect Marriage with Your Present Mate, 1985. BA, U. MN, 1948, MA, 1964, PhD, 1965. Copywriter Bruce B. Brewer, Mpls., 1952-56, Leo Burnett Advt., Chgo., 1956-57; mktg. cons. Jesse Lair Co., Mpls., 1957-62; assoc. prof. U. MN, Mpls., 1963-67; assoc. prof. ednl. psych., Montana State U., Bozeman, 1967-77. Served with USAAF, 1944-45. Home: Box 249 Bozeman MT 59715

LAIRD, ELIZABETH W., b. Galveston, TX, Apr. 19, 1936; d. Stanford Edwin and Helen Benita (Clark) Wilmore; m. Wilfredo Hernandez, Oct. 29, 1966 (div. 1976); m. 2d, Elwood Laird, Mar. 9, 1979. Poetry in anthologies. Wrkg on poetry collections. BA, Marillac Coll., 1962; MEd, Xavier U., 1977. Tchr. parochial schls. Salt Lake City, Dallas, Mayaguez, P.R., and various locations in La., 1956-77; tchr. Jefferson Parish Sch. Bd., Marrero, La., 1977—. Recipient teaching and youth leadership awards. Mem. PSA. Home: 188 June Dr Avondale LA 70094

LA JOIE, RAYMOND ALBERT, b. Central Falls, RI, May 25, 1920; s. Joseph Romulus and Josephine (Provost) LaJ. Author: (western novelettes, 1957-61) Trail of Vengeanance, Blood in the Dust, Legend of Billy the Kid, The Eagle and the Ghost, Give a Man Enough Rope, Kill the Violent Men, The Kid Who Knew No Fear Contrbr. numerous articles, stories, features to mags., newspapers. B. Bvs. Sci., Rider Coll., 1946. Free-lance wrtr., 1953—. Served to sgt. major U.S. Army, 1942-45; awarded 5 medals. Recipient award Radio Free Europe, 1953, Wrtr.'s Digest, 1958, 60, 76. Honorary Lifetime Mem. U.S. Capítol Soc. Mem. Worchester County Eds. Council (ed., pres., 1971), WG, PRSA. Home: 143 Pleasant St Worcester MA 01609

LALLY, GARVIN E., b. W. Hartford, CT, May 18, 1962; s. Hugh Garvin and Carol Joan (Kelley) L. Author: num. poems. BA in written communic., Ramapo Coll. of NJ, 1984. Freelance ed./writer Lang Mktg., Midland Park, NJ, 1983-84, Sika Corp., Lyndhurst, NJ, 1983-84, Paulist Press Pubg., Ramsey, NJ, 1983-84, Design-a-Shirt, Wayne, NJ, 1983-84, Videonet Inc., Oakland, NJ, 1983-84; ed. The New Paper, 1983-84; ed. Dorm Mag., Saddle River, NJ, 1984—. Ginsberg Meml. Poetry Award, Chaucer Guild, 1984; Am. Poetry Award, APA, 1985. Office: Dorm Mag 90 Knollwood Rd Upper Saddle River NJ 07456

LALLY, MARGARET M., b. Cleve.; m. Thomas Robert Lally, Oct. 21, 1961 (div. 1976); 2 sons, Patrick John, Michael James. Contrbr. Ohio Rvw, Lit Rvw, Writing Poems, Bits 7, Bits 1. MA in English, Case Western Res. U., 1974, PhD in English, 1982. Lectr. in English Case Western Res. Univ., Cleve., 1975—, Univ. Akron, 1982—. Wrkg. on poetry about one of Barnum's human oddities. Recipient Individual Artist's award Ohio Arts Council, 1984. Mem. MLA, AWP. Address: Dept Eng U Akron Akron OH 44325

LALLY, MICHAEL DAVID, b. Orange, NJ., May 25, 1942; s. James A. and Irene I. (Dempsey) L.; children: Caitlin Maeve, Miles Aaron. Author: 20 books, including Rocky Dies Yellow, 1974, German edit., 1982, Dues, 1974, Catch My Breath, 1976, Just Le Me Do It, 1978, Attitude, 1982, Hollywood Magic, Los Angeles, 1983; contbr. articles and poetry to profl. jnls., newspapers, mags. B.A., U. Iowa, 1968, M.F.A., 1969. Book reviewer Washington Post, 1974-77; editor Franklin Library div. Franklin Mint, 1976-79; editor, pub. various newspapersand presses including Iowa Defender, Some of Us Press, The Washington Review of the Arts, 1966-80; bd. dirs. The Print Center, Bklyn., 1972-75, Washington Film Classroom, 1970-72; freelance writer, reviewer, actor, N.Y.C., 1975-82, screenwriter, 1982—. Served with USAF, 1962-66. Recipient Discovery award N.Y. Poetry Center, 1972, award Poets Fdn., 1974, NEA fellow, 1974, 81. Mem. WG Am., PEN. Address: 711 10th St Santa Monica CA 94114

LAMB, ELIZABETH SEARLE, b. Topeka, KS, Jan. 22, 1917; d. Howard Sanford and Helen Baker (Shaver) Searle; m. F. Bruce Lamb, Dec. 1941; 1 dau., Carolyn. Author: Today and Every Day, 1970, Inside Me, Outside Me, 1974, In This Blaze of Sun, 1975, Picasso's Bust of Sylvette, 1977, 39 Blossoms, 1982, Casting into a Cloud: Southwest Haiku, 1985; co-author, The Pelican Tree and Other Panama Adventures, 1953. BA, U. of Kansas, 1939, BM, 1940. Editor, Frogpond, Haiku Soc. of America, Santa Fe, 1984—; freelance wrtr., 1942—. Mem. Haiku Soc. of America, Rio Grande Writers Assn., PSA. Home: 970 Acequia Madre Santa Fe NM 87501

LAMBERG, WALTER JEROME, b. St. Louis, Nov. 2, 1942; s. Ben and Julia (Bleiweiss) L.; divorced; 1 son, Alan B. Author: (with Charles E. Lamb) Reading Instruction in the Content Areas, 1980; (with Elaine Fowler) Banner English, 1980; (with others) Gateway, 1984, Skills for Reading, 1984; Essential Written Expression, 1982. B.A., U. Houston, 1964, M.A., 1966; Ph.D., U. Mich., 1974. Asst. lprof. U. Tex., Austin, 1974-80; technical wrtr. U.S. Fidelity and Guaranty, Balt., 1982-84, mgr., 1984—; freelance wrtr., 1980-82. Mem. STC. Home: 1151 B Charles View Way Baltimore MD 21204

LAMBERT, GEORGIA LYNN, b. Ventura, CA, Sept. 25, 1948; d. Harry Morris Paul and Myrtle Estelle (Pettay) Imhoof; m. Danny Lee Ruffin, Jun. 15, 1968 (div. Sept., 1979); 2nd m. James Russell Lambert, Apr. 18, 1981; children—Elizabeth Lacy, Harry Hartsell. Contrbr. to Atlantic (UK), Lady's Circle, Intl. Living, Am. Soc. in London Newsltrs., Focus Information Referral Centre Newsltrs., Dict. of Lit. Biography, 1983. BA, Old Dominion U., 1973. Freelance wrtr. (London, England), 1980-85, (Danville, CA), 1985—. First VP Hampstead Wms. Club, 1982-83. Home:4355 Quail Run Ln Danville CA 94526

LAMBERT, JANE K., b. Bangor, ME, Dec. 15, 1924, d. Guy Lord and Elen (Frye) Knapton; m. William B. Lambert, Nov. 25, 1945; children—Susan Lambert Peacock, Mark K. Contrbr. to: Wind Chimes, Jean's Jnl., Dragonfly, other newspapers and mags. BS, Longwood Coll. Freelance wrtr., Grifton, N.C., 1978-85. Mem. Dixie Council Authors and Journalists, N.C. Poetry Soc., N.C. Haiku Soc., Western World Haiku Soc. Home: 205 Charles St Grifton NC 28530

LAMM, MICHAEL, b. London, Feb. 11, 1936, came to U.S., 1937, s. Heinrich and Annie Thea (Hirschel) L.; m. Joanne Carol Sills, Aug. 15, 1959; children—Robert, Charles, John. Author, ed., pub.: The Camaro Book, 1978, The Fabulous Firebird, 1979, Camaro, the Third Generation, 1982, The Newest Corvette, 1983. Wrkg. on car books. BS, Columbia U., 1959. Ed. Fgn. Car Guide mag., 1959-60; mng. ed. Motor Life mag., 1960-62, Motor Trend mag., 1962-65; columnist AP Newsfeatures, 1965-76, independent, 1976-81; founder, co-owner, ed. Special-Interest Autos mag., 1970-74, 76-78; West-Coast ed. Popular Mechanics mag., 1969-85; owner, pub. Lamm-Morada Pub. Co., Inc., Stockton, Calif., 1978—. Recipient Cugnot award Soc. Automotive Historians, 1974, Moto award Imperial Palace, 1984. Office: Box 7607 Stockton CA 95207

LAMONT, CORLISS, b. Englewood, NJ, Mar. 28, 1902, s. Thomas W. and Florence Haskell (Corliss) L.; m. Margaret Hayes Irish, June 8, 1928 (div. 1962); children—Margaret, Florence, Hayes, Anne; m. 2d, Helen Boyden Lamb, 1962 (dec); m. 3d, Beth Fennell, 1986. Author: The Illusion of Immorality, 1935, Freedom Is As Freedom Does: Civil Liberties in America, 1956, 2d ed., 1981, The Philosophy of Humanism, 1957, 6th ed., 1962, Freedom of Choice Affirmed, 1967, 2d ed., 1981, Remembering John Masefield, 1971, Yes to Life: Memoirs of Corliss Lamont, 1981; ed.: The Thomas Lamonts in America, 1971, Dialogue on John Dewey, 1981, Dialogue on George Santayana, 1981, Collected Poems of John Reed, 1985; Co-ed. with Lansing Lamont, Letters of John Masefield to Florence Lamont, 1979. AB, Harvard U., 1924; PhD, Columbia U., 1932. Instr. philosophy Columbia U., NYC, 1928-32, lectr. Schl. Genl. Studies, 1947-59, seminar assoc., 1971—. Home: 315 W 106th St New York NY 10025

L'AMOUR, LOUIS DEARBORN, b. Jamestown, ND; s. Louis Charles and Emily (Dearborn) LaMoore; m. Katherine Elizabeth Aams, Feb. 19, 1956; children—Beau Dearborn, Angelique Gabrielle. Author numerous works incl.: Smoke From This Altar, 1939, Hondo, 1953, Sitka, 1957, The Daybreakers, 1960, The Sky-Liners, 1967, Matagorda, 1967, Down the Long Hills, 1968 (Golden Spur award WWA), Conagher, 1969, A Man Called Noon, 1970, North to the Rails, 1971, Under the Sweet-Water Rim, 1971, Treasure Mountain, 1972, The Ferguson Rifle, 1973, The Quick and the Dead, 1973, Sackett's Land, 1974, War Party, 1975, Rider of Lost Creek, 1976, To the Far Blue Mountains, 1976, Borden Chantry, 1977, Showdown at Yellow Butte, 1978, The Mountain Valley War, 1978, Bendigo Shafter, 1979, The Iron Marshal, 1979 (Golden Plate award), Shalako, 1980, Yondering, 1980, The Comstock Lode, 1981, Buckskin Run, 1981, The Shadow Riders, 1982, The Lonesome Gods, 1983, The Walking Drum, 1984, Son of a Wanted Man, 1984, Louis L'Amour's Frontier, 1984, others. Self ed.; LLD (hon.), Jamestown Coll., 1973. Lectr. numerous colls. Served to 1st lt. AUS, 1942-46. Congl. Medal of Honor, 1983, Presdl. Medal for Freedom, 1984. Mem. AMPAS. Address: Bantam 666 5th Ave New York NY 10019

LAMPARSKI, RICHARD, b. Grosse Pointe Farms MI, Oct. 5; s. Benjamin Walter and Virginia (Downey) Lynch. Author: Whatever Became of...?, Vols. I-X, 1967-86, Lamparski's Hidden Hollywood, 1981; producer, host radio series Whatever Became of...?, WBAI, NYC, 1965-73. Clk. CBS Radio, 1952-54; press agt. Ice Capades, 1954-57; asst. promotion dir. KTLA Channel 5, Los Angeles, 1957-60; press agt. Allen, Foster, Ingersoll, NYC, 1964; pres. Lamparski's Hello from Hollywood. Home: 3289 Carse Dr Hollywood CA 90068

LANCE, JEANNE LOUISE, b. Morristown, NJ, May 21, 1945; d. Leroy Hildebrant and Helen Glenda (Hoffman) L.; m. Peter John Holland, Nov. 18, 1975. Author: (poetry) Nothing, 1979; (short stories) Mass Psychosis, 1983; (poetry and short prose) Loose Arrangement, 1983; (short prose) Water Burial, 1985. Ed.: Worth Pubs., NYC, 1968-73, Far West Lab. for Ednl. Research and Devel., San Francisco, 1974-80, Natl. Assn. Social Workers, Silver Spring, MD, 1981-87. A.B., Bryn Mawr Coll., 1967; M.A., U. Toronto, 1971. Mem. P&W. Home: 25 Carlin St Norwalk CT 06851

LANDAU, ANNETTE HENKIN, b. Bronx, NY, Apr. 7, 1921, d. Bernard and Bessie (Diamond) Henkin; m. Philip Landau, Aug. 16, 1942; children—Harriette, Robert, Jessica. Contrbr. short stories to Commentary, Confrontation, Moment, Other Voices, articles to N.Y. Times. BA, Queens Coll., 1941; MA, Columbia U., 1943, MPhil, 1973; MS, L.I. U., 1969. Instr. Queens Coll., Flushing, N.Y., 1943-48; research librarian East Meadow Pub. Library, N.Y., 1969-81; freelance wrtr., 1977—. Recipient PEN syndication fiction award 1985, 1986. Mem. P&W, IWWG. Home: 301 E 66th St New York NY 10021

LANDAU, PETER EDWARD, b. NYC, July 16, 1933; s. Edward and Charlotte (Schmidt) L. AB, Duke, 1955; MS in Econs., Columbia, 1959. Editorial asst. Newsweek Mag., NYC, 1955-57, asst. ed., 1958-61, assoc. ed., 1962-67; v.p. Tiderock Corp., 1967; sr. ed. Instl. Investor, NYC, 1968, mng. ed., 1968-70, ed., 1971—. Home: 300 E 51st St New York NY 10022

LANDES, WILLIAM-ALAN, b. Bronx, NY, Apr. 27, 1945, s. Sidney Harold and June Dorothy (Heal-Gordon) L.; 1 dau., Wendy Alyn. Author: Wondrawhoppers (young audience musicals of classical fairy tales), 1979-81, Grandpa's Bedtime Story (with Mark Lasky), 1979, Pyramus and Thisbe, 1979; playwright: Diary of a Madman, 1980, A Pair of Uses, 1981, Lunatics, 1982; author: Survival (An Entertainment Career), 1986; screenwrtr.: Aces and Eights, 1972, Cracked Sidewalk, 1974, The Baby Maker, 1979. Wrkg. on children's musical plays. BS, Hunter-Lehman Coll., 1970; MA, Calif. State U.-Los Angeles, 1971. Artistic dir. Players USA, Los Angeles, 1975—; talent mgr., producer Empire Mgmt., Los Angeles, 1977—; chmn. bd. dirs. Players Press, Inc., Studio City, Calif., 1978—. Named Best New Playwright, Players USA, 1972; cited for best new play Showcase Mag., 1972. Mem. AFTRA, Screen Actors Guild, Actors Equity, Soc. Stage Dirs. and Choreographers. Home: Box 1344 Studio City CA 91604

LANDIS, BRENDA REINHART, b. Covington, KY, June 9, 1960; d. Rodney Reinhart and Jewell Rita Reinhart; m. christopher Mark Landis. Editor: The Ohio Banker, 1986—. BA, Ohio State University, 1982. Sales Coordinator, Pony-X-Press, Columbus, Ohio, 1983-86; Diretor of Communications, Ohio Bankers Association, Columbuss, Ohio, 1986—. Member WICI Office: OBA 51 North High St Suite 401 Columbus 43215

LANDIS, ELWOOD WINTON, b. Wichita, KS, June 14, 1928; s. Jacob Harrison and Christina (Fry) L.; m. Nancy Gauss, Nov. 22, 1961; children—Frederic, Laura. BA, Friends U., Wichita, 1950; MS in Jnlsm., Northwester U., 1953. Rptr. Wichita Eagle, 1953; copy ed. Omaha World Herald, 1955-57; publicity dir. Bethany (KS) Coll., 1957-61; publs. dir. tchr. edn. project Central MI U., 1961-64; mng. ed. Voice newspaper, E. Lansing, MI, 1965—. Served with AUS, 1953-55. Home: 308 S Circle Dr Williamston MI 48895

LANDSMAN, JOSEPH K., b. NYC, Oct. 3, 1934; s. Harry Lewis and Sonia (Vogel) L.; m. Susan Tucker (div. 1970); 1 dau., Serena; m. 2d, Jan Koster, Aug. 6, 1982. Student Coe Coll., 1952-1955, NYU 1956-1958. Dir. prodn. Derujinsky Studios, NYC, 1967-70; wrtr., ed. Mutual of N.Y. Ins. Co., NYC, 1970-72, Playhouse

Prodns., NYC and Calif., 1972-74, Woofenill Works, Inc., NYC, 1980-82. Recipient Gold medal N.Y. Intl. TV & Film Festival, 1969, San Francisco Intl. TV & Film Festival, 1969; Disting. Service award Urban League, NYC, 1970. Home: 516 E 81st St New York NY 10028

LANDSMAN, SAMUEL N.B., (Sandy Landsman), b. New Rochelle, NY, Oct. 22, 1950; s. Benjamin M. Bienstock and Shirley E. (Kripke) Landsman; m. Wendie Ruth Paisner, July 16, 1978. Author: The Gadget Factor, 1984, Castaways on Chimp Island, 1986; (musical) Rake's Alley: A Musical for Cat-Lovers of All Ages, 1977. Contrbr. articles to mags. BA, Columbia U., 1972; postgraduate St. John's U., Jamaica, N.Y., 1985—. Asst. ed. Jason Aronson, Inc., NYC, 1972-73; children's entertainer Sandy Landsman, the Music Clown, NYC, 1971—; freelance ed. Univ. Mktg. Corp., NYC, 1973-75; freelance wrtr., dir., The Knowledge Tree Group, NYC, 1979-81, Grantee N.Y. State Fdn. for Arts, 1980. Home: 43-57 Union St 6C Flushing NY 11355

LANDSMANN, LEANNA, b. Ithaca, NY, May 26, 1946; d. George and Katherine (Mehlenbacher) Abraham; m. Guy Landsmann, July 14, 1968. BA, St. Lawrence U., 1968. Tchr. pub. schls., Ivory Coast, West Africa, 1968-69, Prattsburg, NY, 69-70; assoc. ed. Instr. Publs., Inc., NYC, 1971-76, ed.—in-chief, 76—, pub., 78—, also pres.; v.p. Harcourt Brace Jovanovich Inc.; mem. faulty Stanford U. Pub. Course, 1980, 81. Mem. EDPRESS, NAEYC, Intl. Reading Assn., ACEI, MPA, ASCD. Address: 545 Fifth Ave New York NY 10017

LANE, CAROLYN BLOCKER, b. Providence, June 4, 1926; d. Harry T. and Margaret (Creitenfeld) Blocker; m. M. Donald Lane, Jr., Apr. 28, 1951; 1 son, Jay Donald. Author: (children's books) Uncle Max and the Sea Lion, 1970, Turnabout Night at the Zoo, 1971, The Voices of Greenwillow Pond, 1972, The Winnemah Spirit, 1975, Princess, 1979, 3d., 1986, Echoes in an Empty Room, 1981, Princess and Minerva, 1981, 2d. ed., 1986, Ghost Island, 1985; (children's plays) Turnabout Night at the Zoo (Annual Merit award Commun. Children's Theater of Kansas City, MO, 1963), 1967, The Wayward Clocks (Best Children's Play, Pioneer Drama Service, 1969), 1969, The Runaway Merry-Go-Ground, 1978, Tales of Hans Christian Anderson, 1978, The World of the Brothers Grimm, 1979, The Ransom of Emily Jane, 1980; (adult plays) The Last Grad (1st prize Theatre Guild of Webster Groves, MO, 1969), 1970, Child of Air, 1972, The Scheme of the Driftless Shifter (2d prize Theatre Guild of Webster Grove, 1980), 1981. Contrbr. articles, short stories, book rvws. to mags. including Wrtrs. Digest, N.Y. Times Book Rvw. B.A., Conn. Coll., 1948. Mem. AG, DG, SCBW, Mystic Art Assn. Home: 40 Skyline Dr Mumford Cove Groton CT 06340

LANE, LOIS M. WHITE, b. Baldwin County, GA, Dec. 27, 1914; d. Alfonza and Leila (Hogans) White; m. David Julian Lane, Aug. 2, 1956 (dec. 1973). Author: A History of Flagg Chapel, 1978, The Last of the Thirteen Growing Up in Georgia, 1987. Wrkg. on novel. BS, Ft. Valley State Coll., 1946; MA, Atlanta U., 1953. Tchr. Baldwin County Bd. Edn., Milledgeville, Ga., 1932-54, 66-74; supr. Negro edn. Hancock County Bd. Edn., Sparta, Ga., 1954-66. Mem. ednl. orgns. Address: Box 383 Milledgeville GA 31061

LANE, MALIA, see Thornton, Mary Jane

LANE, MARC J(AY), b. Chicago, IL, Aug. 30, 1946; s. Sam and Evelyn (Light) L; m. Rohelle Nudelman, Dec. 21, 1971: children: Allison, Amanda, Jennifer. Author: The Doctor's Lawyer: A Legal Handbook for Doctors, 1974, (with Alvin G. Becker), Review of Tax Reduction Act of 1975 and Tax Planning Opportunities, 1975, Legal Handbook for Small Business, 1978, The Professional Corporation, 1979, The Doctor's Law Guide: Essentials of Practice. Management, 1979, Corporations: Pre-Organization Planning, 1980, Taxation for the Computer Industry, 1980 A Taxation for Small Business, 1980, 2d ed, 1982, Taxation for Engineering and Technical Consultants, 1980, Taxation for Small Manufacturers, 1980, (with Becker) Twenty-Third Annual Federal Tax Course, 1980, Legal Handbook for Nonprofit Organizations, 1981, Amortization of Intangibles, 1983, Purchase and Sale of Small Businesses: Tax and Legal Aspects., 1985, Impact of 1986 Tax Code on Closely Held Businesses, 1986, Representing Corporate Officers and Directors, 1987. Also au The Professional Corporation in 1978, 1977. Au of cassettes, suh as Keeping What's Yours, for Yourself and Your Family, 1982, Financing Growth in Today's Economy, 1982, Tax Planning for the Smaller Business, 1982. Contrbr to law jnls. BA (with honors), Univ. of Illinois; JD, Northwester Univ., 1971. Admitted to Bar of Illinois, 1971, and the Bar of U.S. Tax Court 1974. Law offices of Marc J. Lane, Chicago, Ill., president, 1971—. Pres. of Medico-Legal Inst., Chicago, 1976—. Letr for various profl assns; coordinator of optometric jurisprudence curriculum, Ill. Coll of Optometry, 1973—. Member: ABA, Ill. State Bar Assn, Chicago Bar Assn, Chicago Counil of Lawyers (past chairperson of com on corporate responsibility). Lincoln Award from Ill. Bar Assn, 1973, for Discrimination in Corporate Pensions and Profit-Sharing Plans and 1977 for Foreign Transfers Under the Tax Reform Act of 1986. Home: 6715 North Longmeadow Lincolnwood IL 60646

LANE, MARK, b. NYC, Feb. 24, 1927; s. Harry Arnold and Elizabeth (Brown) L.; m. Patricia Erdner, Feb. 7; children—Anne-Marie, Christina, Vita. Author: Rush to Judgment, 1966, A Citizens Dissent, 1968, Chicago Eye-Witness, 1969, Arcadia, 1970, Conversations with Americans, 1970, Executive Action, 1973, (with Dick Gregory) Code Name Zorro, 1977, The Strongest Poison, 1980; film producer (with Emile de Antonio) Rush to Judgment, 1967; producer of film, Two Men in Dallas, 1987; fdr. publns.: Citizens Qtly, 1975, Helping Hand, 1971. LLB, Bklyn. Law Schl., 1951. Lawyer, NYC, 1952-62; prof. law Catholic U., Washington, 1975—; mem. firm Lane & Associates, 1979—. Served with AUS, 1945-47. Mem. N.Y. State Assembly, 1960-62. Office: 105 2nd St NE Washington DC 20002

LANE, NANCY, b. NYC, Dec. 20, 1938; d. Morton and Lillian (Gelb) L. AB in Am. Civ., Barnard Coll., 1960. Mem. staff N.Y. Times, 1959-61; asst. to mng. ed. Poli. Sci. Qtly, Columbia U., NYC, 1962-64, asst. ed., 1965-66, assoc. ed., 1967-70; asst. to mng. ed. Procs. Acad. Poli. Sci., 1962-64, asst. ed., 1965-66, assoc. ed., 1967; assoc. ed. Am. Hist. Rvw, Am. Hist. Assn., Washington, 1970-72, mng. ed., 1973-74; sr. ed. Oxford U. Press, NYC, 1974—. Mem. Am. Hist. Assn., Orgn. Am. Historians. Home: 45 W 10th St New York NY 10011

LANE, PINKIE GORDON, b. Phila., d. William Alexander and Inez Addie (West) G.; m. Ulysses S. Lane, 1948 (dec. 1970); 1 son, Gordon Edward. Author: Wind Thoughts, 1972, The Mystic Female, 1978, I Never Scream, 1985; ed.: Poems by Blacks, 1975, Discourses on Poetry: Prose and Poetry by Blacks, Vol. IV, 1972. BA, Spelman Coll., 1949; MA, Atlanta U., 1956; mem. faculty So. U., Baton Rouge, La., 1959—, chmn. dept. English, 1974—. Mem. PSA, AAC, MLA. Home: 2738 77th Ave Baton Rouge LA 70807

LANG, CECIL YELVERTON, b. Walstonburg, NC, Sept. 18, 1920; s. Wilton Earl and Lillie (Yelverton) L.; m. Violette Noelle Guerin-Lese, Apr. 2, 1952; 1 son, Francois-Michel. Ed.: The Swinburne Letters, 6 vols., 1959-62, New Writings of Swinburne, 1964, The Pre-Raphaelites and Their Circle, 1968; co-ed. The Tennyson Letters, vol. I, 1982, vol. II, 1987. AB, Duke U., 1951, AM, 1942; MA, Harvard U., 1947, PhD, 1949. Instr., then asst. prof. English, Yale, 1949-57; assoc. prof. English Claremont Grad. Schl., 1957-59; prof. English, Syracuse U., 1959-65, U. Chgo., 1965-67; prof. Ctr. for Adv. Studies, U. VA, 1967-70, 82-83, Commonwealth prof. English, 1970-85; John Stewart Bryant prof. English, 1985—. Served to 1st lt. USAAF, 1942-46. Guggenheim fellow, 1951-52, Fulbright fellow, 1951-52, Morse fellow, 1956-57. Home: 1820 Edgewood Ln Charlottesville VA 22903

LANG, MIRIAM, (Margot Leslie), b. Chgo., Apr. 30, 1915; d. Barnet S. and Rose (Smoleroff) Milman; m. Theodore Lang, Aug. 18, 1940; children—Rosemary, Patricia, Jonathan. Author: (with Elaine Mardus) Doctors to the Great, 1962; Lovestruck, 1983. BA, Wellesley (MA) Coll., 1936; MA, Columbia U., 1938. English tchr. Lafeyette High School, Bklyn., 1940-42, Port Chester (NY) High School, 1966-80; English instr. Westchester Community Coll., Valhalla, NY, 1956-62; works in progress An Emmy for Love; New Girl in Town. Home: 18 Sammis Ln White Plains NY 10605

LANGBAUM, ROBERT WOODROW, b. NYC, Feb. 23, 1924; s. Murray and Nettie (Moskowitz) L.; m. Francesca Levi Vidale, Nov. 5, 1950; 1 dau., Donata Emily. Author: The Poetry of Experience: The Dramatic Monologue in Mod. Lit. Trad., 1957, The Gayety of Vision: A Study of Isak Dinesen's Art, 1964, The Modern Spirit: Essays on the Continuity of Nineteenth and Twentieth Century Lit., 1970, The Mysteries of Identity: A Theme in Mod. Lit., 1977; ed.: The Tempest (Shakespeare), 1964, The Victorian Age: Essays in Hist. and in Soc. and Lit. Crit., 1967; editorial bd.: Victorian Poetry, 1963—, New Lit. Hist., 1969—, Bull. Research in Humanities, 1977, Studies in Eng. Lit., 1978, So. Humanities Rvw., 1979. AB, Cornell U., 1947; MA, Columbia U., 1949, PhD, 1954. Instr. English, Cornell U., 1950-55, asst. prof., 1955-60; assoc. prof. U.VA, Charlottesville, 1960-63, prof. English, 1963-67, James Branch Cabell prof. English and Am. Lit., 1967—. Served to 1st lt. M.I. AUS, 1942-46. Ctr. for Advanced Study, Stanford, Ford Fdn. fellow, 1961-62; ACLS grantee, 1961, 75-76; Guggenheim fellow, 1969-70; sr. fellow NEH, 1972-73; fellow Clare Hall Cambridge U., Eng., 1978; fellow U. Va. Ctr. for Advanced Study, 1982. Mem. MLA, AAUP, Acad. Lit. Studies, PEN, Phi Beta Kappa. Home: 223 Montvue Dr Charlottesville VA 22901

LANGDON, LARRY, (Lawrence E.), b. Evanston, IL, Aug. 31, 1940; s. Lawrence E. and Edna T. (Shouba) Langdon; m. Nancy (Russell) Langdon Jones (div.); children—Laura Kimberley, Elizabeth Ann; 2nd m. Genie. Author:

Can Colleges Be Saved?, 1969, Creating Peace: A Positive Handbook, 1982; editor: The Words of Jesus on Peace, 1985; contrbr. of articles on peace to numerous publications including **XX** Century and Peace (Soviet peace jnl), Holyearth Jnl, In Context. BA, Psychology, U. of Redlands; MA, Psychology, Cal. State L.A.; postgrad. Claremont Graduate School. Employed in various positions applying experimental psychology to industry problems, 1964-74; investor/writer/entrepreneur, 1975—. Home:5155 Nectar Way Eugene OR 97405

LANGE, AUGUSTA ANN (Ann Lewis), b. Bellaire, OH, Jan. 14, 1934; d. Russell and Augusta Mildred (Brandau) Butt; m. Edgar William Lange, Jr., Oct. 11, 1959; 1 dau., Tamara Ann. columnist: Signal, 1977—. Contrbr. articles to newspapers. B. Biblical Studies, Trinity Bible Coll., 1985. Pastor, United Methodist Ch., Massillon, OH, 1976—; corr. Daily Reord, Woostr, Oh, 1977—. Home: 3914 Alabama NW North Lawrene OH 44666

LANGE, GERALD WILLIAM, b. Green Bay, WI, June 30, 1946, s. Carl Frederick and Harriet May (Miller) L. Author: Starless & Bible Black, 1975; contrbr. to Three Rivers Poetry Jnl, Agni Rvw, Rolling Stone, also others. Ed./pub. The Bieler Press, Mpls., 1975—, Master Printer, USC Fine Arts Press, Bieler Press, Los Angeles, 1975-. Mem. Ampersand Club, Am. Printing History Assn. (Charter), Pacific Center for Book Arts, Minn. Ctr. for Book Arts (charter). Home: 615 South Detroit Los Angeles CA 90036

LANGFORD, RICK C., b. Santa Monica, CA, July 31, 1953, s. Nathan Bee and Ann Louise (Ross) L.; m. Linda Lee Chamberlain, Aug. 30, 1979; children—Jason James Berry, Janiene Marie. Contrbg. ed.: The Hungry Years, 1978-80; contrbr. articles to City Escort, Triathlon, Tahoe Daily Tribune, fiction, Women's World, Loosepress. Diploma in Fiction Wrtg., Writer's Digest Schl., 1983. Cert. of Achievement, fiction, Writer's Digest Competition, Ill., 1984. Mem. Lake Tahoe Wrtrs. Assn. Address: 1084 Margaret St South Lake Tahoe CA 95731

LANGGUTH, A.J., b. Mpls., July 11, 1933, s. Arthur John and Doris Elizabeth (Turnquist) L. Author: Jesus Christs, 1968, Wedlock, 1972, Marksman, 1974, Macumba, 1975, Hidden Terrors, 1978, Saki, 1981. Wrkg. on history of Am. Revolution. AB, Harvard U., 1955. Corr. N.Y. Times, 1963-65, bur. chief, Saigon, 1965; prof. U. So. Calif., Los Angeles, 1978—. Served with U.S. Army, 1956-58. John S. Guggenheim Fdn. fellow, 1976. Mem. AG, Home: 1922 Whitley Ave Los Angeles CA 90068

LANGHAM, BARBARA DEE, b. Chireno, TX, June 6, 1938; d. Robert Bruce and Helen Celeste (Hicklin) L.; m. Harmon Charles Beyer, Dec. 21, 1959 (div. Dec. 1981); children: Craig Kendall, Bruce Walter, Jill Rene. Contrbr. short stories to N.Am. Rvw, Descant, Fiction Texas, poetry to Pig Iron, Poetry Now, Nightsun, other lit mags and anthols, articles to periodicals. Student So. Meth. U., 1956-59; BA, Furman U., 1968; MA, Carnegie Mellon U., 1971, D.A., 1977. Tchr. pub. schls., Pitts., 1968-69, Bethel Park, Pa., 1969-80; asst. prof. English, So. Ill. U., Carbondale, 1980-82; asst. to provost Am. Ednl. Complex, Killeen, Tex., 1982, dir. Pacific Far East Campus, Korea/Japan, Seoul, 1982-83, assoc. dean, Pacific Far East Campus, Japan/Okinawa, Yokota AFB, Japan, 1983-84; v.p. adminstrn. and mktg. Langham Energy, Inc., Houston,1984-86; pres. BD Langham Public Relations, Houston,1986—. Ill. Arts Council grantee, 1981. Mem. Intl. Poetry Forum, P&W. Home: 2526 McClendon Houston TX 77030

LANGHAM, JOAN, see Coe, Joe Ann

LANGHAM-COE, JOAN, see Coe, Joe Ann

LANGILLE-MATTEI, SUZANNE YVONNE, b. Chehalis, WA, Oct. 10, 1954, d. Blanche MacFarlane (Dunkin) Langille; m. Loren Neal Mattei, Sept. 27, 1985. Author: Kids, Cats, & Puppydogs I, 1985, Dreams and Wishes I, 1985, Bittersweet, 1985; contrbr. poems to Raindrops Haiku Anthol, 1985, Ursus New Poets/Four Anthol, 1985, WomanSpirit, Wide Open, Scintillations, other mags; contrbr. songs to People's Songletter, Broadside, nonfiction to WomanSpirit. BA, English, Washington State U., 1977; JD, Yale, 1981. Staff atty. Conn. Fund for the Environment, New Haven, 1981—, dir., 1985—. Mem. IWWG, P&W, AAP. Home: 64 Nash St New Haven CT 16511

LANGLAIS, PATRICIA ANN, b. Kentfield, CA, Sept. 8, 1949; d. William Arthur Langlais and Mary Jane (Smith) Packard. Contrbr. articles to newspapers, lit. mag. B.A., Dominican Coll., 1972; M.A., U. Tulsa, 1984. Reporter Cleburne County Times, Heber Springs, AR, 1977-78; coed. U. Central Ark. Echo, Conway, 1978-79; news ed. Grove Leader, OK, 1980; reporter Sapulpa Daily Herald, OK, 1981. Recipient 1st place for news writing Ark. Collegiate Pubs. Assn., 1978, 2d place for intrview, 1979. Home: 2830 E 90 St S 1708 Tulsa OK 74137

LANGLAND, JOSEPH THOMAS, b. Spring Grove, MN, Feb. 16, 1917; s. Charles M. and Clara Elizabeth (Hille) L.; m. Judith Gail Wood, June 26, 1943; children—Joseph Thomas, Elizabeth Langland, Paul. Author poetry: For Harold, 1945, The Green Town, 1956, The Wheel of Summer, 1963, 2d edit., 1966, An Interview and Fourteen Poems, 1973, The Sacrifice Poems, 1975, Any Body's Song, 1980, A Dream of Love, 1986; co-ed.: Poet's Choice, 1962, 83, The Short Story, 1956; co-transl. Poetry From the Russian Underground, 1973. BA, U. IA, 1940, MA, 1941. Instr. in English, Dana Coll., Blair, NB, 1941-42; asst., then assoc., prof., U. WY, 1948-59; mem. faculty U. MA, Amherst, 1959-79, prof. English, 1964-79, prof. emeritus, 1979—, dir. prog. for MFA in writing 1964-70, 78-79; poetry reader, lectr., U.S. and Europe. Served to capt., inf. AUS, 1942-46; ETO. Melville Cane prize poetry, PSA, 1964. Home: 16 Morgan Circle Amherst MA 01002

LANGSETH, MURIEL AVONNE, b. Faribault, MN, June 13, 1939; d. Thosten Andrew and Myrtle Josephine (Dalbotten) Quam; m. Boyd Wayne Langseth, Aug. 6, 1960; children—Mark, Brenda, Steven. Author: Outlooks From Outstate, 1983; co-author (with William H. Frey II, M.D.) Crying, The Mystery of Tears, 1985. Degree in dental hygiene, U. MN; student MN State Metro. U., 1986. Ed., Pine County Courier, Sandstone, MN, 1980-81, columnist, 1981—. Home: Rt 1 Box 260 Sandstone MN 55072

LANGTON, DANIEL J., b. Paterson, NJ, Sept. 6, 1927; s. Daniel P. and Martha Langton; m. Eva Heymann, Feb. 1, 1949; 1 son, Mark. Author: Querencia, 1976, The Hogarth-Selkirk Letters (with Robert Stock), 1985, The Inheritance, 1987; poetry and nonfiction in numerous anthologies. PhD, U. of Cal., Berkeley, 1970. Tchr., San Rafael public schls., Cal., 1963-67; prof., San Francisco State U., 1967—. With USAF, 1945-47. Mem. PSA, AAP. Home: 1673 Oak St San Francisco CA 94117

LANHAM, RICHARD ALAN, b. Washington, Apr. 26, 1936; s. Roy Benjamin and Leolia Elizabeth (Reid) L.; m. Carol Dana, Sept. 7, 1957. Author: Sidney's Old Arcadia, 1965, A Handlist of Rhetorical Terms, 1968, Tristram Shandy: The Games of Pleasure, 1973, Style: An Anti-Textbook, 1974, The Motives of Eloquence: Literary Rhetoric in the Renaissance, 1976, Revising Prose, 1979, Revising Business Prose, 1981, Analyzing Prose, 1983, Literacy and the Survival of Humanism, 1983. AB, Yale U., 1956, MA, 1960, PhD, 1963. Instr., Dartmouth Coll., 1962-64, asst. prof. English, 1964-65; asst. prof. UCLA, 1965-69, assoc. prof., 1969-72, prof., 1972—, dir. writing progs., 1979—. Served with AUS, 1956-58. NEH sr. fellow, 1972-74. Mem. MLA. Home: 10792 Ashton Ave Los Angeles CA 90024

LANIER, GERALDINE FE, b. San Francisco, CA, Aug. 1, 1951; d. Primo and Clara (Fajardo) Arellano; m. Francis Xavier Lanier; children—Christopher, Xavier. Author: six short stories for Positive Action curriculum program; book rvws., San Fran. Chronicle. Mem. of year Society of Children's Book Wrtrs., 1982-83; Bd. dir. Soc. of Children's Book Wrtrs., 1985-89; MWA. Home: 22 Whitney St San Francisco CA 94131

LANIUS, GLORIA HELENE, b. NYC., Nov. 23, 1917; d. Philipp and Erna (Rottmann) Marx; m. Victor Lanius, Nov. 14, 1944; children—Lorraine, Victor Philipp. Novelist: Violet Are Blue, 1971; poetry in anthologies. Wrkg. on hist. novel, short-story collection. BA, Duke U., 1939. Tchr. public schs. Cranford, N.J., 1942-45, River Edge, N.J., 1947-53, Ft. Walton Beach, Fla., 1955-61, Pensacola, Fla., 1965-67; instr. Okaloosa Walton Jr. Coll., Niceville, Fla., 1967-70. Home: 769 Indian Trail Destin FL 32541

LANNIGAN, JULIE BETH, b. Poteau, OK, May 30, 1953; d. Thomas George Lannigan and Dorris Addiville (Dugan, Lannigan) Midgley; m. Tommy Carl Breshears, Jr., Feb. 3, 1973 (div. Sept. 18, 1973); m. 2d, Robert Dean Reid, II, Aug. 17, 1974 (div. Nov. 25, 1977); 1 son, Branndon Keith Reid; m. 3d, David Compton Edwards, May 16, 1981 (div. Sept. 26, 1985). Contrbr. articles to numerous newspapers, poetry mags., training manual. City news ed.: Moore Times, 1968; ed.: Amphibian, 1974-75, Patrol, 1978. Wrkg. on novel, articles. B.A. in Jnlsm., U. Okla., 1985. Jnlst., U.S. Navy, San Diego, CA and Honolulu, 1973-78; public info. specialist Westark Commun. Coll., Fort Smith, AK, 1986-87; ed. Poteau News & Sun, 1987; free-lance technical wrtr., prop., Victory Press (div. of Victory Enterprises, J.B. Lannián, owner), Oklahoma City, OK and Poteau, 1984—. Mem. Okla. Wrtr.'s Fedn., Inc., Bus. Profl. Women, Green County Ruff Riters (reporter). Home: Rt 1 Box 141-A Poteau OK 74953

LANSKY, VICKI LEE, b. Louisville, KY, Jan. 6, 1942; d. Arthur and Mary (Kaplan) Rogosin. Author: Feed Me I'm Yours, 1974, Dear Babysitter, 1980, Toilet Training, 1984, Practical Parenting Tips for the School Age Years, 1985, other books on child rearing; "Koko Bear" children's books. BA, Conn. Coll., 1973. Buyer Mercantile Stores (NYC), 1969; owner Meadowbrook Press (Minneapolis, MN), 1975-83; owner Practical Parenting (Minneapolis), 1983—. Owner, The Book Peddlers lit. agcy., 1984—. Home: 3342 Robinson Bay Rd Deephaven MN

55391

LANSUN, A LA, see Fairbrother, Anne Elmore

LANT, JEFFREY LADD, b., Maywood, IL, Feb. 16, 1947; s. Donald Marshall and Shirley Mae (Lauing) Lant. Author: Insubstantial Pageant: Ceremony and Confusion at Queen Victoria's Court, 1979, The Consultant's Kit, 1983, The Unabashed Self-Promoter's Guide, 1984, Tricks of the Trade: The Complete Guide to Succeeding in the Advice Business, 1986, other non-fiction. BA U. of Calif., 1969; MA Harvard, 1970, PhD, 1975. Coordinator, Student Services Boston Coll. evening Coll., 1976-78; asst. to pres. Radcliffe Coll., 1978-79; pres. treas. dir. Jeffrey Lant Assoc., 1979—. Office: 50 Follen St 507 Cambridge MA 02138

LA PALMA, MARINA de BELLAGENTE, b. Varese, Italy, Jan. 10, 1949, d. Edoardo de Bellagente and Theresa Luisa (Pinardi) de-Bellagente; m. William Raymond Bostedt, May 1970 (div. 1978); m. 2d, Richard James Goldstein, Dec. 19, 1979. Author: Poems from Neurosuite, 1975, Casablanca Carousel, 1977, Grammars for Jess & Twenty-Two Cropped Sets, 1981, Facial Index, 1983; contrbr. poetry, fiction: Reality Studios (London), ZETA (Turin, Italy), Waves, Rampike, numerous other lit. mags.; contrbg. ed.: Artweek, Option, EAR; columnist High Performance; contrbr. anthologies: Bilingual Anthology Italo-American Poets, 1985, Stealing the Language—The Emergence of Women's Poetry in America, 1986, others. BA, Mills Coll., 1980; MFA, U. Calif.-San Diego, 1984. Free-lance wrtr., ed., 1977—; mem. faculty U. Calif.-San Diego, 1982-84, Otis Art Inst. of Parsons Schl. Design, Los Angeles, 1984—. NEA creative writing fellow, 1984. Mem. P&W., So. Calif. Art Wrtrs. Home: 815 N Gardner St Los Angeles CA 90046

LAPHAM, CONSTANCE SUMNER, (Connie), b. Pasadena, CA, Nov. 16, 1921; d. Chester B. and Nelle Martha (Wells) Sumner; m. Dudley Nelson Lapham, April 19, 1943; children—Rosemary Lapham Murphy, Roger Sumner Lapham. Ed. Rose Soc. Bulletin; contrbr. to Monterey Peninsula Herald. BA, Reed Coll., 1943. Ed. Monterey Bay Rose Soc. (Watsonville, CA), 1983—; columnst. Monterey Peninsula Herald (CA), 1985—. Home: 1061 Lorenzo Ct Seaside CA 93955

LAPHAM, LEWIS HENRY, b. San Francisco, Jan. 8, 1935; s. Lewis Abbot and Jane (Foster L.; m. Joan Brooke Reeves, Aug. 10, 1972; children—Lewis Andrew, Elizabeth Delphine, Winston Peale. Author Fortune's Child, 1980, High Technology and Human Freedom, 1985, Money and Class in America, 1988. BA, Yale, 1956; postgrad., Cambridge U., 1956-57. Rptr. San Francisco Examiner, 1957-60, N.Y. Herald Tribune, 60-62; author, ed. USA-1, NYC, 1962, Saturday Evening Post, 63-67; writer Life Mag., Harper's, NYC, 1968-70; mng. ed. Harper's NYC, 1971-75, ed., 1975-83. Address: Harper's 666 Broadway New York NY 10012

LAPIDUS, JACQUELINE, b. NYC, Sept. 6, 1941; d. Joseph and Edith Judith (Friedman) L. Author: (books of poems) Ready to Survive, 1975, Starting Over, 1977, (with photos by Tee Corinne) Yantras of Womanlove, 1982. Trans. novels: (by Aris Fakinos) The Marked Men, 1971, and The Restricted Zone, unpub., 1972. Author unpub. book of poems: Ultimate Conspiracy, 1980. Poetry has appeared in Calyx, Conditions, Hanging Loose, Heresies, Sinister Wisdom, Sojourner, others. BA, Swarthmore Coll., 1962. Letters. Corr. Life mag., NYC, 1962-64; tchr. English, Greek-Am. Cultural Inst., Iraklion, Crete, 1964-67; freelance trans., Paris, 1967-72; asst. Martonplay Agy., Paris, 1972-77; instr. English, U. Paris, CESTI, 1977-80; assoc. ed. Selection du Reader's Digest, Paris, 1981-85; asst. ed. Womantide, Provincetown, 1984-87, ed., The Walking Magazine, Boston, 1986. Mem. P&W, Phi Beta Kappa. Home: Box 963 Provincetown MA 02657

LA PLANTE, J. DUNCAN, b. Washington, Jan. 6, 1956; s. John H. and Anne (Machita) LaP. Assoc. ed.: Handbook of Futures Markets, 1984; contrbr.: We The People-Poetry, Secrets and Mysteries, Awakenings, numerous others. BA, Am. U., 1980; postgrad., Folger Inst., 1981. Prin. J. Duncan LaPlante Adviser-Cons., Princeton and NYC., 1984—. Home: 506 Rt 601 Belle Mead NJ 08502

LAPPE, FRANCES MOORE, b. Pendleton, OR, Feb. 10, 1944; d. John and Ina (Skrifvars) Moore; m. Marc Lappe, Nov. 11, 1967 (div. 1977); children—Anthony, Anna; m. 2d, J. Baird Callicott, 1985. Author: Diet for A Small Planet, 1971, 75, 82, World Hunger: 10 Myths, 1982, Now We Can Speak, 1982; co-author: (with Joseph Collins) Aid as Obstacle, 1980, Food and Farming in the New Nicaragua, 1982, (with Joseph Collins and D. Kinley) What Can We Do?, 1980, (with William Valentine) Mozambique and Tanzania: Asking the Big Questions, 1980, (with Adele Beccar-Varela) Casting New Molds: First Steps Toward Worker Control in a Mozambique Factory, 1980, (with Peter Sketchley) Food First: Beyond the Myth of Scarcity, 1977, rev. (with Joseph Collins), 1979, World Hunger: 12 Myths, 1986, What to do After You Turn off the TV, 1985. BA in history, Earlham Coll., 1966; PhD (hon.), St. Mary's Coll., 1983, Lewis and Clark Coll., 1983, Macalester Coll., 1986, PhD (hon), Hamline Univ., 1987. Co-fdr., mem. staff Inst. for Food and Devel. Policy, San Francisco, 1975—. Named to Nutrition Hall of Fame Ctr. for Sci. and Pub. Interest, 1981. Office: Inst Food 1885 Mission St San Francisco CA 94103

LARDAS, KONSTANTINOS N., b. Steubenville, OH, Aug. 3, 1927, s. Nicholas Demetrios and Constantina (Moraitis) L.; m. Sofia G. Lardas; children—Nicholas Orestes, George Alexander, Stephan Jason. Author: And in Him, Too: In Us, 1964, A Tree of Man, 1968; contrbr. poetry, short stories, translations from Greek to over 100 lit. rvws. Wrkg. on Greek folk song translations. MA, Columbia U., 1951; PhD, U. Mich., 1966. Mem. faculty CCNY, NYC, 1967—, prof. English, 1976—. Served with U.S. Army, 1946-47. Grantee Fulbright Fdn., 1962, 82, Rockefeller Fdn., 1964. Home: 68 Wakefield Ave Yonkers NY 10704

LARDNER, RING WILMER, JR., b. Chgo., Aug. 19, 1915; s. Ring Wilmer and Ellis (Abbott) L.; m. Silvia Schulman, Feb. 19, 1937 (div. 1945); children: Peter, Ann (Dr. Waswo); m. Frances Chaney, Sept. 28, 1946; children: Katharine, Joseph, James. Author: novels, The Ecstasy of Owen Muir, 1955, 72, All for Love, 1985; The Lardners: My Family Remembered, 1985. Student, Princeton U., 1932-34. Reporter N.Y. Daily Mirror, 1935; publicity asst., Selznick Intl. Pictures, Culver City, Calif., 1936-37. Screenwriter various film companies, 1937-82, including: (with Michael Kanin) Woman of the Year, 1942 (Oscar for best original screenplay, 1942), (with Leopold Atlas) Tomorrow the World, 1944, (with Albert Maltz) Cloak and Dagger, 1946, (with Philip Dunne) Forever Amber, 1947, (with Terry Southern) The Cincinnati Kit, 1965, M*A*S*H, 1970 (Oscar for best screenplay adapted from another medium 1970), The Greatest, 1977; also mag. and TV pieces. Mem. WG of Am., AG, PEN, Acad. of Motion Picture Arts and Scis. Home: 4 Hilltop Rd Weston CT 06883

LARKIN, EMMET, b. NYC, May 19, 1927; s. Emmet and Annabell (Ryder) L.; m. Dianne Willey, Aug. 13, 1966; children—Heather, Siobhan. Author: James Larkin, Irish Labour Leader, 1876-1947, 1965, The Roman Catholic Church and the Creation of the Modern Irish State, 1878-1886, 1975, The Historical Dimensions of Irish Catholicism, 1976, The Roman Catholic Church and the Plan of Campaign in Ireland, 1886-1888, 1978, The Roman Catholic Church in Ireland and The Fall of Parnell, 1888-1891, 1979, The Making of the Roman Catholic Church in Ireland, 1850-1860, 1980, The Consolidation of the Roman Catholic Church in Ireland, 1860-1870, 1987. BA, NYU, 1950; MA, Columbia U., 1951, PhD, 1957, D. Litt (honoris causa), National University of Ireland. Instr. history Bklyn. Coll., 1954-60; asst. prof. M.I.T., 1960-66; mem. faculty U. Chgo., 1966-71, prof. history, 1971—. Served with AUS, 1944-46. Fulbright scholar, 1955-56, Newberry Library fellow, 1976-77, NEH sr. fellow, 1984-85. Home: 5021 S Woodlawn Ave Chicago IL 60615

LARKIN, MARY ANN, b. Pitts., d. James Grant and Marie (Larkin) Connors; m. Daniel Cronin, July 23, 1960 (div. 1977); children—Patrick, Andrew, Molly. Contrbr. poetry to: Bits, Milkweed Chronicle, Tinderbox, other lit. mags.; contrbr. to The Poet Upstairs, 1979, The Ear's Chamber, 1981, Harbor Lights, 1985, other anthologies; author: The Coil of the skin, 1982 (poetry). BA in Sociology, Duquesne U.; MA in English, St. Louis U. Tchr., 1964-82; publs. devel. cons., wrtr., ed. McGraw Hill, Info. World, Watershed Fdn., Natl. Geographic, Natl. Public Radio, NIH, other orgns.; ed. Fdn. Giving Watch, Corp. Giving Watch, 1985—. Mem. Big Mama Poetry Troupe (founding), Capitol Hill Poetry Group. Address: 6413 Marjory Ln Bethesda MD 20817

LARRABEE, ERIC, b. Melrose, MA, Mar. 6, 1922; s. Harold Atkins and Doris (Kennard) L.; m. Eleanor Barrows Doermann, Apr. 4, 1944. Author: The Self-Conscious Society, 1960, The Benefolent and Necessary Institution, 1971, (with Massimo Vignelli) Knoll Design, 1981, Commander in Chief, 1987; ed.: Am. Panorama, 1957, (with Rolf Myersohn) Mass Leisure, 1958, Museums and Edn., 1968; co-ed. (with Robert E. Spiller) Am. Perspectives, 1961; contrbr. arts. to natl. mags. AB cum laude, Harvard U., 1943; LLD, Keuka Coll., 1961. Assoc. ed. Harper's Mag., 1946-58; exec. ed. Am. Heritage, 1958-61, mng. ed., 1961-62; mng. ed. Horizon, 1962-63; editorial cons. Doubleday & Co., NYC, 1963-69; provost arts and letters SUNY-Buffalo, 1967-70, prof. 1967-72; exec. dir. N.Y. State Council on Arts, NYC, 1970-75; pres. Natl. Research Ctr. Arts, NYC, 1976-78; adj. prof. Schl. Arts Columbia U., NYC, 1980—; Noble Fdn. prof. art & cultural history, Sarah Lawrence Coll., 1986; Pratt Institute, 1987–. Served to 1st lt. AUS, World War II. Decorated Bronze Star medal. Guggenheim fellow, 1982-83. Mem. ACLS, Phi Beta Kappa. Home: 448 W 20th St New York NY 10011

LARRIMORE, GLORIA DEAN, b. Conway, SC, De. 24, 1949; d. Harry Lee Taylor and Jettie (Sanders) Benton; m. Oscar Levone Larrimore,

May 19, 1970; children—Larry, James, Angelia. Contrbr. poems to anthols. Grad. public schls., Conway. Sewing mahine operator Factory, Conway, 1969; tower operator Forestry Co., Marion, SC, 1974—. Reipient Golden Poet award World of Poetry, 1985, 86. Home: Rt 3 Box 2870 Marion SC 29571

LARSEN, JEANNE LOUISE, b. Washington, Aug. 9, 1950; d. George Edward and Hope (Harrin) Larsen; m. Thomas Hugh Mesner, Aug. 13, 1977; stepchildren—Scot Tanner, Kili Jean. Author: Brocade River Poems: Selected Works of the Tang Dynasty Courtesan Xue Tao, 1987, James Cook in Search of Terra Incognita: A Book of Poems, 1979; contrbr. various journals and anthologies. BA, Oberlin College, 1971; MA, Hollins Coll., 1972; PhD, U. of Iowa, 1983. Lectr., Tunghai Univ., Taiwan, 1972-74; asst. prof., Hollins College, 1980-86, assoc. prof., 1986—; edit., Artemis magazine, 1980—. Mem. PSA. Home: Box 9542 Hollins College VA 24020

LARSEN, KENNETH MARSHALL, b. San Francisco, June 5, 1946; s. Frank and Klara Margaret (Ashman) L. Pub.: Cultural Democracy, 1982-83; guest ed.: Ridge Rvw, 1983. BA, Antioch Coll., 1968. PhD, U. Calif., Davis, 1986. Ed., pub. ARC/ Rural Arts Newsletter, Mendocino, Calif., 1980—, RADIUS/Calif. Community Arts, Mendocino, 1985—; book rvw. ed. Ridge Rvw, Mendocino, 1985—; grants rvw. panelist Calif. Arts Council, 1980-84; co-chmn. publs. comm. Alliance for Cultural Democracy, Washington, 1981-83. Grantee Calif. Arts Council, 1980-83, 85—, NEA, 1985. Vice-pres. Mem. Calif. Confedn. for Arts. Office: Box 1547 Mendocino CA 95460

LARSEN, WENDY WILDER, b. Boston, July 29, 1940, d. David Wilder and Katharine (Metcalf) Perkins; m. Jonathan Larsen (div.). Author: (with Translator Thi Nga) Shallow Graves: Two Women and Vietnam, 1986; contrbr. poetry to Dark Horse, Tendril, 13th Moon, Manhattan Poetry Rvw, other lit mags. BA in English, Wheaton Coll., Norton, Mass., 1962; MAT, Harvard U., 1963. Mem. intl. council Mus. Modern Art; bd. dirs. Open Space Inst. Mem. P&W (bd. dirs.). Home: 439 E 51st St New York NY 10022

LARSON, DANIEL WILLIAM, b. Chgo., Oct. 24, 1954; s. William R. and Patrica E. (Keogh) L. Contrbr. articles to mags., newspapers including So. Ill. Univ. Daily Egyptian, Logansport Pharos-Tribune, UP Intl., Lafayette Jnl.-Courier, Super Service Sta., Nat. Petroleum News. Assoc. ed.: Super Service Sta., Lincolnwood, IL, 1981-84; news ed.: Natl. Petroleum News, Des Plaines, IL, 1985-86, ed., Service Sta. Mgr., 1987—. Mem. Assn. Petroleum Wrtrs. (v.p.) ASBPE. Home: 8530 W Catalpa Chicago IL 60656

LARSON, MARJORIE MARIE, b. Kansas City, MO, Aug. 26, 1922; d. Frank T. and Rose H. (Christina) Summers; m. Arthur G. Larson, Feb. 6, 1944 (dec. Aug. 29, 1987); children—Janice Baker, Gloria Elijah, Rebecca Pohle. Author: The Gift of His Heart, 1961, Trainex Medical Training Programs, 1966, Communication Principles & Film Evangelism, 1970. Contrbr. article to mags., newspapers; radio scripts; film strip scripts including Luxembourg, 1972 and Japan, 1972. M.A. in Jnlsm. Edn., Calif. State U.-Fullerton, 1971. Home: 1816 Kennedy Ave Loveland CO 80538

LARSON, RANDALL D., b. San Francisco, July 13, 1954, s. John Arthur and Eleanore (Gitschel) L. Author: Musique Fantastique: A Survey of Film Music in the Fantastic Cinema, 1985, The Complete Robert Bloch (bibliography), 1986, The Reader's Guide to Robert Bloch, 1986; contrbg. author: Discovering Stephen King, 1985, Discovering Modern Horror II, 1986; contrbr. to Eldritch Tales mag., CineFantastique mag., Soundtrack: The Collector's Qtly, Crypt of Cthulhu mag., numerous others. Ed., pub. Cinemascore: The Film Music Jnl, 1981—, Threshold of Fantasy mag., 1982—, others. AS, De Anza Jr. Coll., Cupertino, Calif., 1979. Ed., pub. Fandom Unlimited Enterprises, Sunnyvale, Calif., 1971—; freelance wrtr., 1976—. Office: Fandom Unlimited Box 70868 Sunnyvale CA 94086

LARSON, RANDY, see Bartkowech, R.

LA RUE, ARLENE CATHERINE, b. Syracuse, May 5, 1912, d. John Coughlin and Barbara (Reichert) La Rue. Author: All Out Yesterdays (Friends of Reading award 1978), 1977. Wrkg. on book. BS in Journalism, Syracuse U., 1934. Reporter The Herald, Syracuse, 1934; reporter Daily Sentinel, Rome, N.Y., 1935-41, city ed., 1941-47; women's ed., lifestyle ed., Syracuse Herald-Am., 1947-77, columnist, 1975—; tchr. journalism Syracuse U., 1969-70; ed. ch. and civic newsletters. Winner 1st prize playwriting contest N.Y. State Fair, 1954; named Outstanding Communicator, Women in Communications, Inc., Syracuse, 1983. Mem. Nat. League Am. Pen Women, Women in Communications, Inc. Home: 770 James St Syracuse NY 13203

LA SALLE, PETER, b. Providence, May 27, 1947, s. A. Norman and Hope (Conroy) LaS. Author: (short stories) The Graves of Famous Writers, 1980, (novel) Strange Sunlight, 1984; contrbr. stories, poems and lit. journalism to N.Am., Antioch, Ga., Iowa, Mass. rvws, Fiction Intl., Epoch, Esquire, The Nation, New Republic, The Progressive, Worldview, Los Angeles Times, also anthologies including The Best Am. Short Stories. BA, Harvard U., 1969; MA, U. Chgo., 1972. Lectr. creative writing Johnson State Coll., Vt., 1974-76; vis. asst. prof. creative writing U. Tex., Odessa, 1976-77, asst. prof. English, Iowa State U., Ames, 1977-80, asst. prof. English, U. Tex., Austin, 1980-86; assoc. prof. U. Tex., Austin, 1986—; wrtr.-in-residence Green Mountains Workshop, Johnson, summers 1980-84; vis. asst. prof. creative wrtg. Harvard U., summers 1985-87. Recipient short story award Kans. Qtly, 1980; NEA creative writing fellow, 1982. Office: Dept Eng U Tex Austin TX 78712

LASCH, CHRISTOPHER, b. Omaha, June 1, 1932; s. Robert and Zora (Schaupp) L.; m. Nell Commager, June 30, 1956; children—Robert, Elisabeth, Catherine, Christopher. Author: The American Liberals and The Russian Revolution, 1962, The New Radicalism in America, 1965, The Agony of the American Left, 1969, The World of Nations, 1973, Haven in a Heartless World, 1977, The Culture of Narcissism, 1979, The Minimal Self, 1984. BA, Harvard U., 1954; MA, Columbia U., 1955, PhD, 1961; LHD (hon.), Bard Coll., 1977, Hobart Coll., 1981. Mem. history faculty Williams Coll., 1957-59, Roosevelt U., Chgo., 1960-61, U. IA, 1961-66, Northwestern U., 1966-70; mem. faculty U. Rochester, N.Y., 1970—, Don Alonzo Watson prof. history, 1979—; dept. chmn., 1985—; Freud lectr. Univ. Coll., London. Fellow Ford Fdn., 1974, Guggenheim Fdn., 1975. Mem. Orgn. Am. Historians, Am. Hist. Assn. Office: Dept Hist U Rochester Rochester NY 14627

LASHER, MICHAEL, Elman, Richard

LASHNITS, THOMAS PETER, b. Pelham, NY, July 14, 1948, s. George R. and Marie (Kiernan) L.; m. Judi Wright, July 25, 1973; children—Erin Wright, John Kiernan. Contrbr. to: N.Y. Times, Reader's Digest, numerous other newspapers and mags. BA, Franklin & Marshall Coll., 1971; MBA, NYU, 1982. Asst. ed., publicity assoc. Harper & Row, NYC, 1971-73; asst. ed. Putnam's, NYC, 1973; researcher, wrtr. Time-Life Books, NYC, 1973-76; assoc. ed. Reader's Digest, Pleasantville, N.Y., 1976-81, sr. ed., 1983—; assoc. ed. Families Mag., Pleasantville, 1981-82. Mem. Overseas Press Club. Office: Reader's Digest Pleasantville NY 10570

LASKY, JANET LOUISE, b. Washington, Oct. 17, 1955; d. Raymond and Barbara Lamar (Coplan) Lasky; m. Paul Lewis Thompson, June 6, 1980 (div. 1982). Author: The Stages & Pages of Life (poetry), 1983, DayBreak, 1984; poetry in anthologies. Paralegal cert. George Washington U., 1987. Mem. data entry staff Immigration andd Naturalization Service, Washington 1978-82, U.S. Atty.'s Office, Dept. Justice, Washington, 1982—. Home: 1220 East West Hwy Apt 1609 Silver Spring MD 20910

LASONDE, MARILYNN JOY, b. Springfield, MA, Nov. 4, 1956; d. Edward Henry and Celestine May (Chevalier) Miller; m. Robert William Lasonde, June 1982 (div. Jan. 1984). Author: Reach for the Stars; contrbr. poems to anthols. Grad. public schs., Springfield. craftsperson Needles & Wood, Springfield, MA, 1985—; freelance wrtr., 1986—. Recipient Honorable Mention, World Poetry Assn., 1986. Home: 94 Upland St Springfield MA 01104

LASSITER, ISAAC STEELE, b. Johnston County, NC, July 4, 1941; s. David Bruce and Mabel Colon (Byrd) Lassiter; m. Elsie Langston Bugg, June 13, 1970; 1 dau., Laura Louise. Author: The Owl's Nest Betrayal (poetry), 1971; contrbr. poetry to various mags and anthols. BS, Campbell U., 1970. Tchr., Johnston Co. pub. schls., 1966-71; submissions writer, Brotherhood of Maintenance Way Employees, Chgo., 1979—. Home: 412 E Bryn Mawr Ave Roselle IL 60172

LATEINER, BONNIE, b. New Rochelle, NY, July 29, 1949; d. Alfred Roger Lateiner and Mary Elizabeth (Klein) Schaffer. Contrbr. to Outskirts, Networks, Luna Tack, Potrero Lit. Supplement; author: ACCUPANCY, 1986. Student Russell Sage Coll., Boston U., Pub. Vortex Eds. and ed. Volition mag. Recipient Am Book Award, Before Columbus Fdn., San Francisco, 1985. Mem. CCLM. Address: Box 42698 San Francisco CA 94101

LATTA, JOHN ALEX, b. Ypsilanti, MI, Feb. 6, 1954, s. William Carl and Harriet (Mabon) L. Author poetry collection: Rubbing Torsos, 1979; ed., pub.: Ithaca House Poetry Series, 1981-86, Chiaroscuro: A Poetry Mag., 1976-86; contrbr. poetry to Ohio Rvw, Bluefish, Ubu, Moosehead Rvw, numerous other lit mags. AB in English, Cornell U., 1976. Ed., pub. Ithaca House, N.Y., NEA creative writing fellow, 1979-80, Henry Hoyne Fellowship, 1987-88, Univ. of Virginia. Home: 1718 Jefferson Park Ave 4 Charlottesville VA 22903

LATTANY, KRISTIN EGGLESTON, (Kristin Hunter), b. Phila., Sept. 12, 1931, d. George Lorenzo and Mabel Lucretia (Manigault) Eggleston; m. Joseph Edgar Hunter, Feb. 29, 1952 (div. 1962); m. 2d, John Irving Lattany, Sr., June 22, 1968. Author novels: God Bless the Child, 1964, The Landlord, New York, 1966, The Soul Brothers and Sister Lou, 1968, The Survivors, 1975, The Lakestown Rebellion, 1978, Lou in the Limelight, 1981; author: Boss Cat (juvenile fiction), 1970, Guests in the Promised Land (short stories), 1973. BS, U. Pa., 1951. Info. officer City of Phila., 1964-65, 65-66; sr. lectr. dept. English, U. Pa., Phila., 1972—. John Hay Whitney Fdn. fellow, 1959-60; winner 1st prize Council Interracial Books for Children, 1968, Book World prize Chgo. Tribune, 1973; N.J. State Council on Arts prose fellow, 1981-82, 85-86. Mem. PEN, NCTE, MLA. Home: 721 Warwick Rd Magnolia NJ 08049

LAUBER, PEG CARLSON, b. Detroit, Apr. 8, 1938; d. Grant William and Margaret Elizabeth (John) Carlson; m. Jack M. Lauber, Aug. 7, 1964; children—Chad William, Megan Margaret. Author: Locked in Wayne County Courthouse, 1977-82; ed.: A Change in Weather: Midwest Women Poets, 1978, and var. poetry chapbooks; contrbr. poems to numerous lit and poetry mags. and jnls. MA, U. Mich., 1960; MFA, U. Iowa, 1964. Instr., Ohio State U., Columbus, OH, 1964-67, U. Wis., Eau Claire, WI, 1969-71, 77-85; asst. prof. U. Wis., Eau Claire, WI, 1985—. Hopwood Award of Poetry, U. Mich., 1960; AAP Prize, U. Iowa, 1964. Mem. P&W. Home: 1105 Bradley Ave Eau Claire WI 54701

LAURA, JUDITH, see Willis, Judith Laura Levine

LAUREN, LINDA, b. Newark, Apr. 16, 1952, d. Jerry and Frances (Monica) Gialanella. Auther: One of Grandma's Photographs, 1984, Video Romance, 1984, Profile: Romantic Times, 1986. Wrkg. on novels, collected works of fiction. Student Montclair State Coll, 1973-77. Wrtr. press releases The Cherenson Group, Livingston, N.J., 1977-80; ed., mgr. Jon-Kachell, Inc., Malibu, Calif., 1978-79; wrtr., ed. Rexnord, Inc., Union, N.J., 1984; v.p. Banana Sound Prodns., West Orange, N.J., 1981-86. Home: 45 Pillot Pl West Orange NJ 07052

LAURIE, MARGARET SANDERS, b. Phila., Oct. 11, 1926, d. Joseph A. and Elizabeth E. (Simmons) Sanders; m. Dominic Laurie, Jan. 31, 1945; children—Lucille M., Donald J. Author: Centering Your Guide to Inner Growth, 1978, 82, 83, 86. BA, Syracuse U. and Alfred U., 1948; MA in English, Niagara U., 1967. Engr. Remington Arms, Ilion, N.Y., 1943-47; tchr. English Lewiston-Porter High Schl., Youngstown, N.Y., 1961-63; prof. English, Niagara County Community Coll., Sanborn, N.Y., 1966—. Recipient award for short story, Weight Watchers mag., 1970. Mem. Assn. Profl. Women Writers (pres. Niagara Falls 1972-74), Natl. League Am. Pen Women, Coll. English Assn. Home: 310 N 4th St Lewiston NY 14092

LAURITSEN, JOHN P., b. Grand Island, NE, s. Walter P and Sarah Marie (Grosshans) L. Coauthor: The Early Homosexual Rights Movement, 1974; ed: John Addington Symonds: Male Love: A Problem in Greek Ethics and Other Writings, 1983; co-author: Death Rush: Poppers & AIDS, 1986; contrbr. to The Freethinker, NY Native, Civil Liberties Rev, GLC Voice, Gay News. AB, Harvard U., 1963. Mkt. research, 1968—; pres. and dir. Pagan Press, NYC, 1982—. Address: 26 St Mark's Place New York NY 10003

LA VEE, KATIE, see Staff, LaVada Falkner

LA VEGLIA, GERI, b. Bronz, NY, Nov. 5, 1943, d. John and Geraldine (Pepe) Machin; m. Michael L. LaVeglia, Apr. 19, 1969 (div. 1986); children—Keli Robin, Cindy Lynn. Contrbr. poetry to World of Poetry. Wrkg. on poetry collection, fiction. Student public schls., Bronx. Instr., coordinator N.Y. State Art and Lit. Workshop, 1964-86. Recipient Golden Poet award World of Poetry, Reno, 1985, Silver Post award, 1986; three honorable mentions, World of Poetry, 1985-87; honorable mention, Tin Penny, 1987. Home: 18 Appel Dr E Shirley NY 11967

LAVERRIERE, LORRAINE MOREAU, b. Roxbury, MA, Jan. 8, 1938, d. Louis Eugene and Beatrice (Pothier) Moreau; children—Rebecca and Philip (twins), Toby James. Ed., pub. New Voices mag., 1979—, Rebirth of Artemis poetry mag., 1981—, Write Now Books, 1985—; author poetry chapbook Birth of Astra, 1980. BA, Lowell (Mass.) U., 1979, MA, 1985. Office: 24 Edgewood Terr Methuen MA 01844

LAVERS, NORMAN, b. Albany, Calif., Apr. 21, 1935; s. Cecil Norman and Mary (Parker) L.; m. Cheryl Lynne Dicks, July 20, 1967; 1 child, Gawain. Author: Mark Harris, 1978; Selected Short Stories, 1979; Jerzy Kosinski, 1982; (novel) The Northwest Passage, 1984; ed. newsletter Ark. Audubon Soc., 1976—; contrbg. ed. Bird Watchers Digest. BA, San Francisco State U., 1960, MA, 1963; Ph.D. U. Iowa, 1969. Instr. English, No. Ill. U., 1963-65; instr. fiction writing U. Iowa, 1967-69; asst. prof. English, Western Wash. U., 1970-76; prof. English, Ark. State U., Jonesboro, 1976—, Srinakharinewirot U., Bangkok, 1985-86. Served with U.S. Army, 1956-59; Korea. Fellow Wrtrs. Workshop, Iowa City, 1967-69, NEA, 1982-83. Mem. P&W, Fiction Collective. Home: Rt 5 Box 203 Jonesboro AR 72401

LAVINE, HAROLD, b. NYC, Feb. 19, 1915; s. Elias and Pauline (Bershadsky) L.; m. Violet Edwards, Dec. 25, 1936; 1 dau., Cammie Caroline Edwards. Author: Fifth Column in America, 1940, (with James A. Wechsler) War Propaganda and the United States, 1940, Central America, 1964, Smoke-Filled Rooms, 1970. Student, Townsend Harris Hall, 1927-30. Rptr. N.Y. Am., 1932-33, N.Y. Evening Jnl., 33-34, N.Y. Evening Post, 34-36; asst. mng. ed. PM, 1941-44; with U.S. Army News Sv., 1944-46; sr. ed. Newsweek Mag., 1946-63, Forbes Mag., 63-74; editorial writer, columnist Ariz. Republic, 1974—. Page One award, 1961; Ariz. Press Club award, 1979, 81, 83. Home: 6505 N 12th Way Phoenix AZ 85014

LAW, JANICE, see Trecker, Janice Law

LAWBAUGH, PENELOPE, b. Evanston, IL, Jan. 6, 1945; d. Albert C. and Eva E. (Holmhansen) Williamson; m. Edward Nelson (dec., 1972); children—Kimberly Nelson, Corinne Nelson; m. 2d, Michael J. Lawbaugh, Aug. 1, 1981. Writer/ed.: Threshold mag., 1981-84, View Nwsltr., 1981-84, Focus Nwsltr., 1984—, People mag., 1984—, Aqueduct mag., 1984—. BA, New Mexico State U., 1974. Sr. writer New Mexico State U., Las Cruces, NM, 1970-81; ed. St. Vincent Med. Ctr., Los Angeles, 1981-84; publ.dir. Metropolitan Water Dist., Los Angeles, 1984—. Mem. IABC, PRSA, NASW, SPJ. Gold Quill award, IABC,1984, Prism award, PRSA, 1982, 83, 84, 85, 86. Office: Metro Water Dist 1111 Sunset Los Angeles CA 90054

LAWDER, DOUGLAS WARD, JR., b. NYC, June 12, 1934, s. Douglas Ward and Janice (Chapman) L.; m. Elizabeth Glidden Carvel (div.); children—Leland Gregory, Douglas Ward III. Author: (poetry) Trolling, 1977; included in Three Northwest Poets, 1969. BA, Kenyon Coll., 1957; MFA, U. Oreg., 1967. Head Spanish dept. Wayland Acad., Beaver Dam, Wis., 1962-64; instr. U. Oreg., Eugene, 1964-67; head creative writing dept. Earlham Coll., Richmond, Ind., 1967-69; assoc. prof. English, Mich. State U., East Lansing, 1969—. Grantee NEA, 1967, Danforth Fdn., 1968. Mem. PSA. Home: 6373 E Reynolds St Haslett MI 48840

LAWLESS, GARY CAMERON, b. Belfast, ME, Apr. 30, 1951, s. Richard and Ruth (Dow) L. Author: Full Flower Moon, 1974, Wintering, 1976, Two Owls, 1976, Dark Moon/White Pine, 1977, Gulf of Maine Reader, 1977, Wolf Driving Sled, 1980, Ice Tattoo, 1981, Bear Magic, 1986. BA in East Asian Studies, Colby Coll., Waterville, Me., 1973. Asst. mgr. Bookland of Maine, Brunswick, 1973-79; owner, mgr. Gulf of Maine Books, Brunswick, 1979—. Recipient Cabot Trust award, 1979; grantee Que./Labrador Fdn., 1980. Home: Chimney Farm RR1-Box 228 Nobleboro ME 04555

LAWRENCE, ARTHUR PETER, b. Durham, NC, July 15, 1937; s. George Harold and Addie Grace (Waterman) L. Ed. The Diapason, 1976-82; assoc. ed. The Am. Organist, 1982—. DMA, Stanford U., 1968; AMLS, U. MI, 1974. Music instr. Centre Coll., Danville, KY, 1968-69; assoc. music prof. St. Mary's College, Notre Dame, IN, 1969-80. Home: 234 E 14th St No 6C NYC 10003

LAWRENCE, E. A., see Abel, Ernest Lawrence

LAWRENCE, JEAN HOPE, b. Waukegan, IL, Mar. 5, 1944; d. George Herbert and Hope Delinda (Warren) L.; 1 child, Kelsey Lawrene, Creator: GET IT DONE! newsletter; contrbr. articles to popular mags., trade jnls., newspapers including Communication Exec., Chamber Exec., Washington Post, Travel & Leisure, Washingtonian. Contrbg. ed.: Communications concepts, 1984-86; Southern Exec., 1986-87; Director Smithsonian seminars on creativity, direct mail. B.A. in Asian Studies, George Washington U., 1966. Ed., wrtr. Am. Chem. Soc., Washington, 1966; proposal wrtr. Krohn-Rhodes Inst., Washington, 1966-67; asst. legislative counsel Aerospace Industries Assn., Washington, 1967-82; ed. cons., Washington, 1982—. Mem. Washington Edn. Press Assn., Washington Ind. Wrtrs. Home: 3217 Connecticut Ave NW 71 Washington DC 20008

LAWTON, CHARLES, see Heckelmann, Charles Newman

LAWTON, THOMAS GERARD SAMUEL, b. Mineola, NY, Sept. 1, 1962; s. George William and Jacqueline Agnes (Maguire) Lawton. Contrbr. to Omnivore, Berkeley Beacon, Gangsters in Concrete; ed. Berkeley Beacon, 1983, 1984. BFA, Emerson Coll., 1984. Acct. exec. AT&T Info. Systems (NYC), 1984—. Home: Box 163 Cornish Flat NH 03746

LAY, NANCY DUKE S., b.in the Philippines, Jan. 26, 1938; d. Duke S. and (Cheong) Choy Ping Lay. Author: (with Doris Fassler) Encounter with a New World, 1979, Say It in Chinese, 1980, Making the Most of English, 1983, Developing Language Skills for Science and Technology, 1987. Contrbr to academic jnls. Mem ed bd, Jnl of Basic Writing, 1972-83. Ed. D., Columbia Univ, 1971. Instr in fgn langs, New School for Social Research, 1967; instr in English as a fgn lang, Japan-America Inst, N.Y.C., 1967-70; asst prof, City Coll of the City Univ of N.Y., 1970-80, assoc. prof of English, 1980—, coordinator of English as a Second Language (ESL) program, 1973-78, ESL program dir, 1980-86, ESL dept chmn, 1986—. Coordinator of English as a second language at Cooperative Coll Center of the State Univ. of N.Y. and initiator of Chinatown Planning Cncl's English lang Center, both 1970; del to World Congress on Reading, Singapore, 1976; mem of natl advisory cncl of Asian Ameican Assembly for Policy Research, 1978. Mem: Tchrs of English to Speakers of Other Languages, MLA, Natl Assn of Fgn Student Affairs, Chinese Lang Tchrs Assn, NCTE, N.Y. State English to Speakers of Other Langs and Bilingual Educators Assn (chairperson of spcl interest grp on English a second language in higher education, 1979-80). Scholar of Altrusa Intl Fndn, 1968. Home: 100 La Salle St No. 12B New York NY 10027

LAYMON, HAROLD JAMES, b. Kalamazoo, MI, June 30, 1951; s. Glen Eugene and Joan (Price) L.; m. Suzanne Beverly Hulbert, Aug. 10, 1973; children: Harold James Jr., Stacy Sue. Poetry in anthologies. Home: Box 45 Schoolcraft MI 49087

LAYNE, DONNA, see Sager, Donna Layne

LAYTON, THOMAS RALPH, b. Johnstown, PA, Mar. 17, 1947; s. David Elmer and Esther Hazel (Buterbaugh) L.; m. Peggy Brandy, June 9, 1973; children—Roslyn, Thomas, Anthony, Charles. ontrbr. articles on burns and trauma to med. jnls. including Surgery, Gynecology, and Obstetrics, Jnl. Trauma, Jnl. Toxicology, others. B.S., Grove City coll., 1969; M.D., Jefferson Med. Coll., 1973. Dir. burn ctr. Mercy Hosp., Pitts., 1979-84, dir. trauma ctr., 1979-84; mem. emergency dept. Naples Hosp., FL, 1985—. Fellow Am. Coll. Surgeons; mem. AMWA, Am. Burn Assn., Am. Soc. Burns Recovered (treas. 1979-84). Office: Box 2507 350 Seventh ST N Naples FL 33940

LAZAR, PAUL, b. Ellenville, NY, Dec. 31, 1922; s. Ephriam B. and Fannie (Springfield) L.; m. Miriam Nierman, June 25, 1948; children—Andrew, Jon. Contrbr. articles to profl. jnls. Editor: (with others) Cutaneous Toxicity, 1983; Assoc. ed. Jrnl of Cutaneous and Occular Toxicology. BA, Northwestern U., Evanston, Ill., 1941-43; MD, N.Y. Med. Coll., 1947. Practice of medicine specializing in dermatology Northwestern U. Med. Ctr., Chgo., 1953—, instr. to prof. clinical dermatology, 1969—; pres. bd. dirs. Dermatology Fdn., Evanston, 1978-84. Bd. dirs. The Lambs, Inc., Libertyville, Ill., 1961-86, pres. bd. dirs., 1972-76, bd. dirs. American Academy of Dermatology. Served to capt. U.S. Army, 1951-53. Fellow Am. Acad. Dermatology (bd. dirs.), Soc. Investigative Medicine; mem. Am. Med. Assn., Northwestern Dermatol. Soc. Home: 855 Walden Ln Lake Forest IL 60045

LAZARUS, A(RNOLD) L(ESLIE), (A.L. Leslie), b. Revere, MA, Feb. 20, 1914; s. Benjamin Alfred and Bessie (Winston) Lazarus; m. Keo Smith Felker July 24, 1938; children—Karie, Dianne, David, Peter. Author: Your English Helper (handbook), 1950, 51, 53; The Grosset and Dunlop Glossary of Lit. & Lang., 1970, 71, 73; Harbrace English Lang. Series, 1963; Selected Objectives in the Lang. Arts, 1967; (with Victor Jones) Beyond Graustark, 1981; The NCTE Gloss of Lit. & Comp., 1983 (with Wendell Smith); ed.: Harbrace Adventures in Modern Literature, 1956, 62, 70; The Indiana Experience, 1977; The Best of George Ade, 1985; poetry: Entertainments & Valedictions, 1970; A Suit of Four, 1973; contrbr. (poems, rvws.) to APR, New Republic, Sat. Rvw, Lit. Rvw, other lit jnls; ed. (with others) Quartet mag., 1962–68; poetry ed. Quartet, 1968-73; BA, U. of Mich., 1935; MA, UCLA, 1941, PhD, 1957. Assoc. prof. Engl. U. of TX (Austin), 1959-62; prof., Engl. & Am. lit. Purdue U. (Lafayette, IN), 1962-79. Private, Special Serv., Camp Cooke. Ford Fdn. Fellow, 1954; Best Tchr. Award, Purdue U., 1974, Phi Beta Kappa. Mem. PSA, MLA, NCTE, Screenwrtrs. Assn. of Santa Barbara. Home: 945 Ward Dr Santa Barbara CA 93111

LAZARUS, KEO FELKER, b. Calloway, NE, Oct. 22, 1913, d. John Edwin and Penola Joyce (Smith) Felker; m. Arnold Leslie Lazarus, July 1938; children—Karie (Mrs. J. Friedman), Dianne (Mrs. J. Runnels), David, Peter. Author juvenile fiction: Rattlesnake Run, 1968, The Gismo, 1970, Tadpole Taylor, 1970, The Billy Goat in the Chili Patch, 1972, The Shark in the Window, 1972, A Totem for Ti-Jacques, 1979, The Gismonauts, 1981, A Message from Monaal, 1981; contrbr. numerous stories and poems to Cricket, Jack & Jill, Highlights for Children. BS, UCLA, 1938; postgrad., Purdue U., 1960-68. Tchr. Los Angeles pub. schls., 1939-41, 50-55. Archaeologist on Ft. Ouiatenon dig, Tippecanoe County Hist. Soc., Lafayette, Ind., 1970-76. Mem. Soc. Children's Book Wrtrs., Chgo. Children's Reading Roundtable. Home: 945 Ward Dr Santa Barbara CA 93111

LEACH, JOSEPH LEE, b. Weatherford, TX, May 2, 1921; s. Austin Felix and Eula Lee (Gose) L.; m. Dorothy Ann Stuart, June 5, 1958; children—Joseph Lee, Jonathan Stuart, Anne Stuart, Christopher Bryan, Timothy Peter, Hilary, Melinda. Author: The Typical Texan, 1952, Bright Particular Star, 1970; ed. A Treasury of American Folklore, 1981; co-ed. World Lit. Written in English, 1969; contrbr. to scholarly pubs., pop. mags. BA, So. Methodist U., 1942; PhD, Yale U., 1948. Prof. English, U. TX, El Paso, 1947—. Served with inf. AUS, 1946-47. Mem. MLA, NCTE. Home: 735 DeLeon St El Paso TX 79912

LEADER, CARL, see Taylor, Conciere Marlana

LEAF, MINDY GLASS, (Amanda Glass), b. Gottenburg, Sweden, Jan. 11, 1952; came to U.S., 1952; naturalized, 1957; d. Chaim and Hilda (Neuger) Glass; m. Arthur Weinberger, July 31, 1972 (div. Oct. 6, 1982); m. Jesse J. Leaf, Sept. 8, 1983. Contrr. poems, poetry rvws., short story to lit. mags, articles to consumer mags. Ed: The Invaluable Pearl (by Dr. H.E. Yedidian Ghatan), 1986. B.A., Brklyn. Coll., 1973; postgrad. Ephrata Coll., Jerusalem, Israel, 1972-73. Ed., subscription mgr. Advt. Research Fdn., NYC., 1983-85; free-lance wrtr., 1981—. Home: 312 Northlake Dr 301 North Palm Beach FL 33408

LEAF, PAUL, b. NYC, May 2, 1929; s. Manuel and Anna (Dardick) L.; m. Nydia Ellis, Oct. 22, 1955; children—Jonathan, Alexandra, Ellen. Dir., proucer var. Broadway shows, most recent being The Subject Was Roses, 1964; prod., dir. films incl.: Judge Horton and the Scottsboro Boys, 1976 (Peabody award), Desperate haracter, 1972, Hail to the Chief, 1973, Sister Aimee, 1977, Every Man a King, 1977; prod., dir. TV prodns. incl. Sgt. Matlovich vs. the U.S. Air Fore, 1978; author Tender Comrades (novel), 1984, Red, Right Returning (novel), 1987. BA in Drama with honors, CCNY, 1952. Served with U.S. Army, 1952-54. Decorated Meritorious Svc. medal. Twenty internat. festival and profl. awards incl. Venice, 1967, London, 1967, 68, 69, N.Y., 1967, 68, 69, Berlin, 1972. Mem. Dirs. Guild Am., WG. Home: 2800 Neilson Way Santa Monica CA 90405

LEAHY, WILLIAM JOSEPH, b. Chgo., Nov. 16, 1933, s. William Joseph and Adeline Lillian (Leo) L. More than 200 North American publications inclg. radio play, poetry, short stories, satirical pieces, feature articles, literary criticism, reviews, news stories in periodicals and newspapers; contrbr. short stories, features, news stories to numerous Irish magazines and newspapers; wrtr., interviewer, on-air reporter Radio Eireann-Irish Natl. Radio. Wrkg. on radio plays, novel. BA, DePaul U., 1955; MA, U. Chgo., 1957-59. Served with USN, 1955-57. Mem. AG, NWU, Natl. Union Journalists (Dublin Free-lance br.). Home: 1929 W Waveland Ave Chicago IL 60613

LEAPER, ERIC JOHN, b. San Pedro, CA, June 14, 1953; s. John Milburn and Anne Faye (Faries) Leeper; m. Ximena Chacon, Aug. 29, 1981; 1 son, Adam. Ed. Currents mag., 1979—. BA, U. Utah, 1972. Exec. secy. Am. Canoe Assn., Denver, 1978-79; exec. dir. Natl. Orgn. for River Sports, Colorado Springs, Colo., 1979—, ed. Voice, 1979—. Office: 314 N 20th st 200 Colorado Springs CO 80904

LEARY, EDWARD ANDREW, b. Bridgeport, CT, May 3, 1913; s. Edward J. and Edna Currence (Hill) L.; divorced; children—Tim, Karen Anders, Jeannie Cherwin, Andrew. Author: (books) Indianapolis, Story of a City, 1970, The Nineteenth State, Indianapolis, Story of a City, 1970, The Nineteenth State, Indiana, 4th ed., 1968, Pictorial History of Indianapolis, 1970 Compassionate Mission, 1986; (documentary) At Home in Indiana, 1966; (plays) Wonderful World of Number One, 1970, What Next, Mr. Ralston?, 1976, Bonanza, 1962, Spangles, 1951; (radio drama series) House of Mystery, 1983; columnist Indpls. Star, 1970-76. Wrkg. on How to Write for Broadcast; a novel, Fragments.. Creative dir. Format, Indpls., 1960-64; pres. Ed Leary & Assoc., Indpls., 1964-82; instr. Ball State U., Muncie, IN, 1982—. Home: 7314 Manchester Dr Apt A Indianapolis IN 46260

LEASURE, JANET LYNN, b. Chgo., Jan. 26, 1949; d. Samuel Richard Nuccio and Evelyn F. (Boettge) Fields; m. Jon R. Leasure; children—Jordan Lynn, Jade Ashley. Author: Jan's Consumer Savings, 1981, Big Bucks for Kids, 1983; wrtr., ed.: Jan Leasure's Inflation-Proof Reipes, 1980, The New Coupon/Refund Encyclopedia, 1986, The Contest/Sweepstakes Encyclopedia, 1987. BA, No. Ill. U., 1971, MA, 1973. Freelance wrtr., 1970—; tchr. Waukegan (Ill.) Public Shs., 1971-81; prof. writing, English, Columbia Coll., Mo., 1973-82; nationally sydicated columnist, $uper $aver, 1980—, Contest Fever, 1987—, both with Universal Press Syndicate. Mem. Newspaper Features Guild, AG, AFTRA/ Sreen Actors Guild, WG. Home: 1430 Greenbrier Dr Libertyville IL 60048

LEAVITT, CAROLINE SUSAN, b. Quincy, MA, Jan. 9, 1952, d. Henry and Helen (Sandlovitz) L. Author: (novels) Meeting Rozzy Halfway, 1980, Lifelines, 1982, Jealousies, 1983; contrbr. story to Redbook, Mich. Qtly Rvw, articles to The Wrtr., also included in anthology. BA in English with honors, U. Mich., 1974. Tchr. English, Three Rivers Acad., Pitts., 1978-81; copywrtr. Bamberger's Dept. Store, N.J., 1983—. Recipient 1st prize Redbook Young Wrtr.'s Contest, 1978. Mem. P&W, AG, NWU. Home: 409 W 24th St Apt 12 NYC 10011

LEAVITT, WILLIAM D., b. East Chgo., IN, Apr. 4, 1941; s. Joseph A. and Violet Irene (Johnson) L.; m. Ann Marie Olszewski, Apr. 26, 1980; 1 dau., Kimberly Marie. Writer/ed.: Canadian Bldg. News mag., 1968—, Form and Function mag., 1968—, Rebldg. Am. (brochure), 1979, 85; writer: textbk. series on flame-cutting machs., Chemetron, 1964-66, series Tech Briefs & a tech. compilation, NASA, 1966-67, misc. tech. & other arts. Purdue Exponent & Purdue Engr., 1961-64, num. artticles & pubns. for Soc. Tech. Communic., other mags. & Nwsprs., 1968—; contrbr. Audience Analysis & Response, 1983, Proceedings Internatl. Tech. Communics. Conf., 1978, 79, 83, 85. BA, Purdue U., 1964; postgrad. IL Inst. Tech., 1966-67. Asst. tech. ed. Chemetron Corp., Chgo., 1964-66; staff writer Corplan/div. IITRI, Chgo., 1966-67; assoc. ed. U.S.Gypsum, Chgo., 1968-74, ed. ext. pubs., 1974—. Num. awards for editing, design, mag. mgt., writing. Assoc. fellow STC. Office: U S Gypsum 101 S Wacker Dr Chicago IL 60606

LE BLANC, CATHERINE ANNE, b. Northampton, MA, Apr. 24, 1955; d. Clayton and Dorarhea (Martin) Merhand; m. Daniel Alan LeBlanc, Dec. 13, 1975 (div. Oct. 1985); 1 son, Michael S. Contrbr. poems to anthols. short story. A.S., Holyoke Commun. Coll., 1975. Keypuncher, Baystate Med. Center, Springfield, MA, 1985—. Recipient award of Merit, World of Poetry, 1983, Golden Poet award, 1985, Silver Poet award, 1986. Home: 17 Salem St 2 Springfield MA 01105

LE BLANC, JOY COMEAUX, b. Lockport, LA, De. 9, 1937; d. Clarence Marie and Laura Lee Comeaux; m. Gillis Joseph LeBlanc, Jr., Nov. 9, 1959; children—Rodney John, Lori Ann, Andre Rene. Contrbr. poems to lit. mags., anthols. B.A. in Edn., Francis J. Nicholls Coll., 1959. Tchr. public schls., LA, 1959-63. Recipient Merit award Mentor Mag., 1975, 85. Home: 912 Main St Lockport LA 70374

LEBOVITZ, DONNA RUDNICK, b. Manchester, NH, Mar. 13, 1943; d. Harry and Josephine M. (Carp) Rudnick; m. Phil Lebovitz, June 20, 1964; children—Miriam Dara, Aaron Joshua. AB, cum laude, Barnard Coll., 1964. Career counselor, U. of Houston, 1964-67; orig. and wrtr., Book Chat, Kol Am Shalom, Chgo., 1978-82; co-class corresp., Barnard Alumnae Mag., 1984—; asst./ed., Who's Who in U.S. Writers, Editors & Poets, 1986—. Co-coord., No. Shore Friends Ch. 11, 1978-80; chmn. Lib. Bd., Cong. Am. Shalom, 1978-82; Barnard Coll. Area Rep., 1984—. Home: 1128 Green Bay Rd Glencoe IL 60022

LEBOW, JEANNE, see Lebow-Shepard, Jeanne Swift Gregory

LEBOW-SHEPARD, JEANNE SWIFT GREGORY, (Jeanne Lebow), b. Richmond, VA, Jan. 29, 1951; d. Eugene Swift and Beatrice Lawson (Harmon) Gregory; m. Howard Marc Lebow (div.); m. 2d, Steven Louis Shepard. Contrbr. poems in mags., rvws., including Sun Dog, Dickinson Rvw, Jnl. Sport Lit., Memphis State Rvw, New Va. Rvw, South Fla. Poetry Rvw; contrbr. articles in books. AB, Coll. of William & Mary, 1973; MA, Hollins Coll., 1982; postgrad. in Creative Writing, U. Southern Miss., 1984—. Tchr. English, Park View Jr. High Schl., South Hill, Va., 1973-75; tchr. English/drama Falling Creek Jr. High Schl., Richmond, 1975-77; asst. mgr. sales Barn Dinner Theatre, Roanoke, Va., 1977-78; service rep. Photo Div. Kroger, Roanoke, 1978-81; instr. English, Memphis State U., 1982-84; tchg. asst. U. Southern Miss., Hattiesburg, 1984-87; asst. dir., So Miss. Writing Project, 1986-87. Fulbright grant to lecture in Am. lit., Univ. of Ouagadougou, Burkina Faso, West Africa, 1987-88. Asst. coord. River City Contemporary Writers Series, Memphis, 1983-84. Recipient Natl. award Ga. State Poetry Soc., 1983. Mem. South Central MLA, SAMLA, MLA, NCTE, CCCC. Address: Box 290 Gautier MS 39553.

LEBOWITZ, ALBERT, b. St. Louis, June 18, 1922; s. Jacob and Lena (Zemmel) L.; m. Naomi Gordon, Nov. 26, 1953; children—Joel Aaron, Judith Leah. Author: Laban's Will, 1966, The Man Who Wouldn't Say No, 1969, also short stories; ed. Perspective (lit mag), 1961-80. AB, Washington U., St. Louis, 1945; LLB, Harvard, 1948. Lawyer, assoc. Frank E. Morris, St. Louis, 1948-55; partner firm Morris, Schneider & Lebowitz, St. Louis, 1955-58, Crowe, Schneider, Shanahan & Lebowitz, 1958-66; counsel firm Murphy & Roche, St. Louis, 1966-67, Murphy & Schlapprizzi, 1967-81; partner firm Murphy, Schlapprizzi & Lebowitz, 1981—. Served as combat navigator USAAF, 1943-45; ETO. Mem. Am., Mo., St. Louis bar assns., Phi Beta Kappa. Home: 743 Yale Ave St Louis MO 63130

LECKENBY, NANCY L., b. Washtucna, WA, Sept. 13, 1936; d. James Chester and Josephine Marguerite (Phillippay) Gordon; children—Erin, Laura, Lisa, Charlie. Ed.: As I Remember (by Minola Phillippay), 1971, Kahlotus Is Home (by Minola Phillippay), 1973; author biographies: Philippay 100th Salute, 1981, Gordon Golden Salute, 1982. BA, U. Idaho. Columnist The Steamboat Pilot, Steamboat, Colo., 1967-87, polit. reporter, 1974-87; columnist Colo. Statesman, Denver, 1982-87, polit. reporter, 1982—; columnist, reporter The Villager, Englewood, Colo., 1987—. Mem. Natl. Newspaper Assn. (Newspaper Writing Excellence awards 1981, 83, 87), Colo. Press Assn. (Newspaper Writing Excellence awards 1980, 86). Home: 202 Madison St Denver CO 80206

LE COMTE, EDWARD SEMPLE, b. NYC, May 28, 1916; s. John Radway and Mary (Semple) Le C.; m. Marie Munzer, Jan. 19, 1945; 1 son, Douglas Munzer. Author: Endymion in England: The Literary History of a Greek Myth, 1944, Yet Once More: Verbal and Psychol. Pattern in Milton, 1953, A Dict. of Last Words, 1955, The Long Road Back, 1957, He and She, 1960, A Milton Dict., 1961, Grace to a Witty Sinner: A Life of Donne, 1965, The Notorious Lady Essex, 1969, The Man Who Was Afraid, 1969, Milton's Unchanging Mind, 1973, Poets' Riddles: Essays in Seventeenth-Century Explication, 1975, Sly Milton: The Meaning Lurking in the Contexts of His Quotations, 1976, Milton and Sex, 1978, The Professor and the Coed, 1979, A Dict. of Puns in Milton's English Poetry, 1981; contrbr. on 17th-century lit. to scholarly jnls; ed.: Paradise Lost and Other Poems, 1961, Justa Edovardo King, 1978. AB, Columbia U., 1939, AM, 1940, PhD, 1943. Instr. English Columbia, 1943-45; asst. prof. English, U. CA-Berkeley, 1945-48, Columbia U., 1948-56, assoc. prof., 1956-64; prof. English SUNY-Albany, 1964-81, prof. emeritus, 1981—. Mem. Milton Soc. (Honored Scholar, 1985), MLA, PEN, Phi Beta Kappa. Home: Box 113 North Egremont MA 01252

LEDERER, KATHERINE GAY, b. Trinity, TX, Mar. 19, 1932, d. Leon McRae and Katherine (Lipscomb) Gay; children—Susan, Geoffrey. Author: Lillian Hellman, 1979; contrbr. to Springfield! mag. Wrkg. on book on black history, book on growing up in segregated east Texas. BA, Sam Houston State U., 1952; MA, U. Ark., 1958, PhD, 1967. Grad. asst./instr. U. Ark., Fayetteville, 1956-60; prof. English, S.W. Mo. State U., 1960—, head dept., 1985—. Mo. Com. for Humanities-NEH grantee, 1982-84. Mem. SFWA, Mo. Folklore Soc. (bd. dirs.), Popular culture Assn. Home: 733 S McCann St Springfield MO 65804

LEDERER, WILLIAM JULIUS, b. NYC, Mar. 31, 1912; s. William J. and Paula (Franken) L.; m. Ethel Hackett, Apr. 21, 1940 (div. Jan. 1965); children—Brian, Jonathan, Bruce; m. 2d, Corinne Edwards Lewis, July 1965 (div. May 1976). Author: All the Ships at Sea, 1950, The Last Cruise, 1950, Spare Time Article Writing for Money, 1953, Ensign O'Toole and Me, 1957, (with Eugene Burdick) The Ugly American, 1958, A Nation of Sheep, 1961, Timothy's Song, 1965, Sarkhan, 1965, Pink Jade, 1966, Our Own Worst Enemy, 1967, (with Don D. Jackson) The Mirages of Marriage, 1968, (with Joe Pete Wilson) Complete Cross-Country Skiing and Ski Touring, 1970, (with others) Marriage For and Against, Marital Choices, 1981, A Happy Book of Happy Choices, 1981, I, Giorghos, 1984, Creating a Good Relationship, 1984. BS, U.S. Naval Acad., 1936; assoc. Nieman fellow, Harvard U., 1950-51. Enlisted USN, 1930, commd. ensign, 1936, advanced through grades to capt., 1952, ret., 1958; Far East corr. Reader's Digest, 1958-63; lectr. colls. and univs., 1949—; author-in-residence, Harvard U., 1966-67. Mem. Signet Soc., AG. Address: East Hill Farm Peacham VT 05862

LEE, ANTHONY ASA (Tony Lee), b. Truskegee Institute, AL, Aug. 5, 1947; s. Asa Penn and Manila Hudlin (Smith) L.; m. Flor Geola, Apr. 29, 1979; children—Faizi Geola, Taraz Geola, Corinne Geola. Author children's books: The Cornerstone, 1979, The Black Rose, 1979, The Proud Helper, 1980, The Unfriendly Governor, 1980, The Scottish Visitors, 1980. Contrbr. articles, rvws. to profl. jnls. Ed.: Circle of Unity: Baha'i Approahes to Current Social Issues, 1985, Circle of Peace: ReflecZ Vtions on the Baha'i Teachings, 1986. B.A. in Political Sci.-Intl. Relations, U. Calif., Los Angeles, 1968. B.A. in Political Sci.-Intl. Relations, U. Calif., Los Angeles, 1968, M.A. in African Studies, 1974, C.Phil. in African History, 1976; student U. Mich., 1968-69. Office mgr. Los Angeles Baha'i Center, 1973-76; mng. ed., owner Kalimat Press, Los Angeles, 1978—. Home: 826826 Dianthus St Manhattan Beach CA 90266

LEE, AUDREY (M.), b. Phila. Author: Clarion People, 1968, The Workers, 1969; contrbr. short stories, poems, nonfiction Essence Mag, Black World, Negro Digest, Sat. Evening Post, Hartford Courant, and anthols. Winning poem in Triton College Salute to the Arts competition, 1986. Mary Roberts Reinhart grantee, 1966. Mem. P&W. Address: Box 16622 Philadelphia PA 19139

LEE, HAMILTON HANGTAO, b. Chohsien, Shandong, China, Oct. 10, 1921; s. Peiyuen and

Huaiying Lee; m. Jeam Chang, Aug. 24, 1945; children—Wei, Clarence, Karen, Kate. Contrbr. poetry to Poets at Work, Lyrical Fiesta, Threshold, 1980 national Poetry Anthology, The Honey Creek Anthology of Contemporary Poetry, and other anthologies and mags; contrbr. Education Tomorrow, 1977-79; editor and contrbr.: Readings in Instructional Technology, 1970. BA, National Peiping Teachers U., China, 1948; MA, U. of Minn., 1958; EdD, Wayne State U., 1964. Tchr., Taiwan publ. schools, China, 1948-56; res. assoc., Wayne State U., Detroit, 1958-64; asst. prof., Moorhead State U., Moorhead, Minn., 1964-65; assoc. prof., U. of Wisc., LaCrosse, 1965-66; prof., East Stroudsburg U., Pa., 1966-84, prof. emer., 1984—. Mem. PSA, Pennsylvania Poetry Society. Home: 961 Long Woods Dr Stroudsburg PA 18360

LEE, LANCE, b. NYC, Aug. 25, 1942, s. David Levy and Lucile (Wilds) Levy; m. Jeanne Barbara Hutchings, Aug. 30, 1962; children—Heather, Alyssa. Playwright: Time's Up, 1979, Fox, Hound & Huntress, 1973; contrbr. poetry to Glass Onion, Poet Lore, Revista del Universidad de Chile, Whiskey Island Qtly, Poetry Northwest, The Smith, others; contrbr. short stories to Riverside Qtly, Lit. Rvw; contrbr. articles to Chgo. Rvw, Coast mag., others; ed.: Not Dying and Keeping Hope Alive (by F. Robert Rodman), 1977, 86, Youth Rebellion: Patterns of Interaction (by Marianne Marchak), 1980. BA, Brandeis U., 1964; MFA, Yale U., 1967. Educator, Conn. and Calif., 1967—; freelance wrtr., ed. Grantee, U. So. Calif., 1970—71, Rockefeller Fdn., 1971, Theatre Devel. Fund, 1976; NEA fellow, 1976; poetry scholar Squaw Valley, 1982, 83, Port Townsend Wrtrs. Conf., 1985. Mem. PSA, AAP, Dramatists Guild, Authors Lg. of Am. Home: 1127 Galloway St Pacific Palisades CA 90272

LEE, LINDA, see Stirn, Linda L.

LEE, MAURICE (DU PONT) JR., b. Buffalo, NY, Sept. 4, 1925; s. Maurice du Pont and Geraldine (Shaw) L.; m. Helen Cotton, July 8, 1948; children: Maurice, Blair. Author: ed (with E. A. Beller) Selections from Bayle's Dictionary, 1952, James Stewart, Earl of Moray: A Political Study of the Reformation in Scotland, 1953, reprtd. 1971, John Maitland of Thirlestane and the Foundation of the Stewart Despotism in Scotland, 1959, The Cabal, 1965, James I and Henry IV: An Essay in English Foreign Policy, 1970, ed, Dudley Carleton to John Chamberlain, 1603-24: Jacobean Letters, 1972, Government by Pen: Scotland under James VI and I, 1980, The Road to Revolution: Scotland under Charles I, 1625-1637, 1985. Contrbr of articles and rvws to scholarly jnls. AB, Princeton Univ., 1945, MA, 1948, Ph. D., 1950. Instr, Princeton, Univ., 1945, MA, 1948, Ph. D., 1950. Instr, Princeton, N.J., Princeton, N.J., 1949-53, asst prof of history, 1953-59; assoc prof, Univ of Ill. at Urbana-Champagne, 1959-62, prof of history, 1962-66; prof of history, Rutgers Univ, Douglass Coll, New Brunswick, N.J., 1966—. Mem: Conf on British Studies, American Historical Assn, Royal Historical Soc, Scottish Historical Soc. David Berry Prize of Royal Historical Soc, 1958, for MS of John Maitland of Thirlestane and the Foundation of Stewart Despotism in Scotland. Guggenheim fellow, 1961-62, 1966. Military service: U.S. Navy, 1945-46. Home: 10 Symmes C Cranbury NJ 08512

LEE, ROBERT E. A., b. Spring Grove, MN, Nov. 9, 1921, s. Knute and Mathilda Clara (Glasrud) L.; m. Elaine Elizabeth Naeseth, July 29, 1944; children—Margaret Lee Barth, Barbara Lee Greenfeldt, Sigrid Lee Biggi, Richard, Sylvia Lee Thompson, Paul. BA, Luther Coll., 1942; DFA (hon.), Susquehanna U., 1979. Novelist: Question 7, 1962, Behind the Wall, 1964; author: Martin Luther: The Reformation Years, 1947, Popcorn and Parable (with Roger Kahle), 1971, The Joy of Bach, 1979; producer numerous films and video prodns. Exec. dir. Lutheran Film Assn., NYC,1954-88; exec. dir. communications Luth. Council USA, NYC, 1969-88. Pres. Real-World Communications, 1988–. Served to lt. USNR, 1942-45; PTO. Recipient Faith and Freedom award Religious Heritage Found., 1980. Mem. Religious Pub. Relations Council. Home: 766 Lakeside Dr Baldwin NY 11510

LEE, WILLIAM DAVID, b. Matador, TX, Aug. 13, 1944; s. Chant D. and Ruth (Rushing) Lee; m. Jan Marie Miller, Aug. 13, 1971; children—Jon Dee, Jodee Duree. Author: The Porcine Legacy, 1978, Driving and Drinking, 1979, Shadow Weaver, 1984, The Porcine Canticles, 1984. MA, Idaho State U., 1970; PhD, U. of Utah, 1973. Prof., So. Utah State College, Cedar City, 1971—. NEA fellowship, 1986. Served with US Army, 1967-69. Mem. PSA, AWP, MLA. Home: Box 62 Paragonah UT 84760

LEECE, WILLIAM JOSEPH, b. Regina, Sask., Canada, Oct. 19; s. William G. and Irene M. (Boisvert) L.; m. Carolyn Jean Leptich, July 24, 1971; children—Bill, John. Author: Those Who Can Teach, 1985, 86. BA, Loyola U., Montreal, Que., Canada, 1964; MEd, Loyola U., Chgo., 1971. Tchr. High Sch. Dist. 214, Mount Prospect, Ill., 1971—. Mem. No. Ill. Scholastic Press Assn. (bd. dirs.), NCTE. Office: Rolling Meadows HS 2901 Central Rd Rolling Meadows IL 60008

LEEDOM-ACKERMAN, JOANNE, b. Dallas, Feb. 7, 1947, d. John Nesbit and Joanne (Shriver) Leedom; m. Peter Ackerman, June 3, 1972; children—Nate Leedom Ackerman, Elliot Leedom Ackerman. Author: The Dark Path to the River (novel), 1988, No Marble Angeles (short stories), 1985; contrbr. to What You Can Do: Pratical Suggestions on Major Problems of the Seventies, 1971, The Bicentennial Collection of Texas Short Stories, 1974, Fiction and Poetry by Texas Women, 1975; 2 novels under contract. BA, Principia Coll., 1968; MA, Johns Hopkins U., 1969, Brown U., 1974. Reporter Christian Sci. Monitor, Boston, 1969-72; mem. faculty CUNY, 1974-76, NYU, 1976-78, Occidental Coll., Los Angeles, 1978-80, UCLA, 1985—. Mem. PEN, AG. Home: 858 Manning Ave Los Angeles CA 90024

LEEDS, ROBERT X., b. Detroit, Feb. 24, 1927; s. Harry A. and Beatrice (Burnette) L.; m. Peggy Baran, July 4, 1948; children—Leslie Arlyne, Marc Baron, Gail Lenore. Author: How Santa's Best Friend Saved Christmas, 1978, Build a Better You—Starting Now, 1981, All the Comforts of Home, 1987; contrbr. articles to mags. Wrkg. on How to Almost Make A Million Dollars. BS, MBA, Wayne State U. Gen. supr., methods engr. Gen. Motors Corp., Livonia, Mich., 1954-72; pres. Am. Pet Motels, Inc., Prairie View, Ill., 1972—. Served as comdr. Israeli Airborne, 1947-48. Awarded medals, govt. of Israel. Home: 1122 Coffin Rd Long Grove IL 60047

LEEPER, PATTI, see Wilson, Patricia Ann

LEFCOWITZ, BARBARA F., b. NYC, Jan. 15, 1935; m. Allan Lefcowitz; children—Marjorie, Eric. Books, poetry: A Risk of Green, 1978, The Wild Piano, 1981, The Queen of Lost Baggage, 1986; contrbr. poetry, fiction, reviews to over 100 journals and anthologies. BA, Smith College; PhD, Univ. of Maryland. Prof. of English, Anne Arundel Comm. College, Arnold, MD, 1971—. Awards: NEA fellowship, 1984, fellowship, Rockefeller Fdn., 1984. Mem. of Bd. of Directors, The Writer's Center, Bethesda, MD. Home: 7803 Custer Rd Bethesda MD 20814

LEFEVERE, PATRICIA ANN, b. St. Cloud, MN, Aug. 1, 1943, d. Clarence Edward and Mary Helen (Murray) Scharber; m. Andre Lefevere, Aug. 22, 1970; 1 dau., Katelijne Angelique. Contrbr. fiction to MSS, Marquette Jnl Qtly; contrbr. articles to Asia Week, Bus. Europe, Bus. Intl., Middlesex Advertiser & Gazette (U.K.), Sabena Mag. (Brussels), Sydney Maining Herald (Australia), numerous newspapers and periodicals U.S. and abroad. BA in Journalism, Marquette U.; MA in Lit., U. Essex, U.K. Staff wrtr. Cath. Bulltn., St. Paul, 1965-67; sr. ed. Middlesex Advertiser-Gazette, Uxbridge, U.K., 1969-70; dir. mktg. and promotions Bus. Intl., Hong Kong, 1971-73; desk ed., staff wrtr. To The Point Intl., Antwerp, Belgium, 1974-77; free- lance wrtr., journalist, 1977—; tchr. creative writing St. Edwards U., Austin, Tex., 1985. Recipient journalistic awards. Mem. Austin Wrtrs.; League (wrtr. of month 1986), Phi Beta Kappa. Home: 24 MacKay Dr Tenafly NJ 07670

LEGENDRE, PAULA, see Strauge, Cathy Lee

LEGGETT, JOHN WARD, b. NYC, Nov. 11, 1917, s. Bleecker Noel and Dorothy Arlene (Mahar) L.; children—Timothy, John B., Anthony. Author: Wilder Stone, 1960, The Gloucester Branch, 1964, Who Took the Gold Away, 1969, Ross and Tom, 1974, Gulliver House, 1979, Making Believe, 1986. AB, Yale U., 1942. Ed. Houghton Mifflin Co., Boston, 1950-60; ed. Harper & Row, NYC, 1960-67; dir. wrtrs. workshop U. Iowa, Iowa City, 1969-87. Home: 1781 Patrick Rd Napa CA 94558

LEGGETT, STEPHEN CHARLES, b. Big Rapids, MI, July 9, 1949; s. Charles William and Helen Jeanette (Schroeder) L.; 1 child, Japhy McMillan. Author: Wild Apples, 1973; Monk Poems, 1975; The Gift of Water, The Gift of Fire, 1978; The All-Forest, 1980. B. Individualized Studies, Central Mich. U., 1978. Recipient poetry award Louisville Rvw, 1978. Home: Box 254 Manistee MI 49660

LEGLER, PHILIP, b. Dayton, OH, March 7, 1928; s. Ellis Peter and Mary (Ferguson) Legler; m. Martha Prater, Aug. 26, 1950; children—David, Barbara, Amy. Author: A Change of View, 1964, The Intruder, 1972; co-editor: Listen to Me, 1976. BA, Denison U., Granville, OH; MFA, U. of Iowa. Instr., Ohio U., Athens, OH, 1953-56; asst. prof., Central Missouri, Warrensburg, MO, 1956-59; asst. prof., IL Wesleyan, Bloomington, IL, 1960-63; asst. prof., Sweet Briar College, Sweet Briar, Va., 1963-66; prof., Northern Michigan U., Marquette, MI, 1968—. With USMC, 1946-47. Mem. PSA. Home: 128 E Magnetic Marquette MI 49855

LE GUIN, URSULA KROEBER, b. Berkeley, CA, Oct. 21, 1929, d. Alfred Louis and Theodora Covel (Kracaw) Kroeber; m. Charles Alfred Le Guin, Dec. 22, 1953; children—Elisabeth, Caroline, Theodore. Novelist: Rocannon's World, 1966, Planet of Exile, 1966, City of Illusions, 1966, The Left Hand of Darkness, 1969, A Wizard of Earthsea, 1968, The Tombs of

Atuan, 1970, The Farthest Shore, 1972, The Lathe of Heaven, 1971, The Dispossessed, 1974, The Word for World is Forest, 1976, Very Far Away from Anywhere Else (A Very Long Way...), 1976, Malafrena, 1979, Three Hainish Novels, 1978, The Beginning Place (Threshold), 1980, The Eye of The Heron, 1983, Always Coming Home, 1986; author: Wild Angels (poetry), 1974, The Wind's Twelve Quarters (short stories), 1975, Orsinian Tales (short stories), 1976, Hard Words (poetry), 1981, The Compass Rose (short stories), 1982, In the Red Zone (poetry), 1983. BA, Radcliffe Coll., 1951; MA, Columbia U., 1952. Educator, resident wrtr. numerous colls. and univs., 1971—. Mem. SFWA (Nebula award 1969, 74, 75), Intl. Sci. Fiction Assn. (Hugo award), AL of Am., WG, PEN. Home: Box 10541 Portland OR 97210

LEHAN, RICHARD D'AUBIN, b. Brockton, MA, Dec. 23, 1930; s. Ralph A. and Mildred L.; m. Ann Evans, June 11, 1960; 1 son, Edward Scott. Author: F. Scott Fitzgerald, 1966, Theodore Dreiser, 1969, Literary Existentialism, 1973. BA, Stonehill Coll., 1952; MA, Boston Coll., 1953; PhD, U. WI, 1958. Mem. faculty U. WI-Madison, 1953-57, U. TX-Austin, 1958-62; mem. faculty dept. English UCLA, 1962—, prof. English, 1969—, chmn. dept. English, 1971-73. Award for disting. tchg. U. TX, 1962, UCLA, 1970, Fulbright award to Soviet Union, 1975, Guggenheim Fellowship, 1978-790 Home: 333 Oakhurst Dr Beverly Hills CA 90212

LEHMAN, DAVID, b. NYC, June 11, 1948, s. Joseph and Anne (Lusthaus) L.; m. Stefanie T. Green, Dec. 2, 1978; 1 child, Joseph. Author: (poems) An Alternative to Speech, 1986; ed. Beyond Amazement: New Essays on John Ashbery, 1980, (with Charles Berger) James Merrill: Essays in Criticism, 1983, Ecstatic Occasions, Expedient Forms, 1987; contrbr. articles, essays and rvws. to Newsweek, N.Y. Times Mag., Washington Post Book World, TLS, poems to Paris Rvw, Poetry, Partisan Rvw, TLS; contrbg. ed. Partisan Review, 1987—. BA, Columbia U., 1970, PhD in English, 1978; MA, Cambridge U., 1972. Preceptor in English, Columbia U., 1974-75; instr. Bklyn. Coll., 1975-76; asst. prof. Hamilton Coll., Clinton, N.Y., 1976-80; fellow Soc. for Humanities, Cornell U., Ithaca, N.Y., 1980-81; lectr. Wells Coll., Aurora, N.Y., 1981-82; wrtr., book critic Newsweek, 1983—. Kellett fellow, 1970-72; Book of Month Club creative writing fellow, 1970; Woodrow Wilson fellow, 1970; Ingram Merrill Found. fellow, 1976, 82, 84; NEH grantee, 1979. NEA grantee in poetry, 1987; bd. dirs. Natl. Bk. Critics Circle, 1987—. Mem. PEN, Phi Beta Kappa, Natl. Bk. Critics Circle. Home: 159 Ludlowville Rd Lansing NY 14882

LEHMANN, RUTH PRESTON MILLER, b. Ithaca, NY, Feb. 18, 1912; d. Ernest Allen and Lillian Allen (Phillips) Miller; m. Winfred P. Lehmann, Oct. 12, 1940; children—Terry Jon, Sandra Lehmann Hargis. Ed.: Fled Duin na nGed, 1964, (with W.P. Lehmann) Introduction to Old Irish, 1975, Early Irish Verse, 1982. BA, Cornell U., 1932, MA, 1934; postgrad., Bryn Mawr Coll., 1935-36; PhD, U. WI-Madison, 1942. Tchg. asst. U. WI-Madison, 1938-43; ed. lang. texts U.S. Armed Forces Inst., Washington, 1943-44; instr. George Washington U., Washington, 1944-46; lectr. Washington U., St. Louis, 1946-47; instr. Georgetown U. English Lang. Program, Ankara, Turkey, 1955-56; assoc. prof. English Huston Tillotson Coll., Austin, TX, 1956-58; lectr. English, U. Tex., Austin, 1960-67, assoc. prof., 1967-72, prof. 1972-80, prof. emeritus, 1980—. Mem. MLA, Medieval Acad. Am., Early English Texts Soc., Phi Beta Kappa. Home: 3800 Eck Ln Austin TX 78734

LEHMANN-HAUPT, CHRISTOPHER CHARLES HERBERT, b. Edinburgh, Scotland, June 14, 1934; s. Hellmut Otto Emil and Letitia Jane H. (Grierson) Lehmann-H.; came to U.S., 1934; m. Natalie Robins, Oct. 3, 1965; children—Rachel Louise, Noah Christopher. Author: Me and Dimaggio: A Baseball Fan Goes in Search of His Gods, 1986. BA, Swarthmore Coll., 1956; MFA, Yale U., 1959. Ed. A.S. Barnes & Co., Inc., NYC1961-62, Holt, Rinehart & Winston, 1962-63; sr. ed. Dial Press, 1963-65; mem. staff N.Y. Times Book Review, 1965-69; sr. daily book reviewer N.Y. Times, 1969—; asst. prof. lit. CUNY, 1973-75. Office: NY Times 229 W 43d St New York NY 10036

LEHNER, CHRISTINE REINE, b. Boston, May 15, 1952; d. Philip and Monique (Brancart) L.; m. Jeffrey Richardson Hewitt, Sept. 11, 1976; children: Reine Wing, Tristram Jeffrey. Author: (novel) Expecting, 1982. Wrkg. on new novel. BA,U. Calif., Santa Barbara, 1973; MA, Brown U., 1977. Home: 618 Broadway Hastings-on-Hudson NY 10706

LEHRER, JAMES CHARLES, b. Wichita, KS., May 19, 1934; s. Harry Frederick and Lois Catherine (Chapman) L.; m. Kate Staples, June 4, 1960; children: Jamie, Lucy, Amanda. Reporter Dallas Morning News, 1959-61; reporter, columnist, city editor Dallas Times Herald, 1961-70; exec. producer, corr. Sta. KERA-TV, Dallas, 1970-72; corr. NPACT-WETA-TV, Washington, 1973—; now assoc. editor-co-anchor Mac-Neil/Lehrer Newshour; instr. creative writing Dallas Coll., So. Meth. U., 1967-68. Author: (fiction) Viva Max, 1966, We Were Dreamers, 1975, Kick the Can, 1987; (play) Chili Queen, 1987. A.A., Victoria Coll., 1954; B.J., U. Mo., 1956. Served with USMC, 1956-59. Recipient George Polk award; Peabody award; Emmy award; Columbia-Dupont award. Mem. Tex. Inst. Letters. Office: WETA-TV Box 2626 Washington DC 20013

LEHRER, STANLEY, b. Bklyn., Mar. 18, 1929; s. Martin and Rose L.; m. Laurel Francine Zang, June 8, 1952; children—Merrill Clark, Randee Hope. Author: John Dewey: Master Educator, 1959, Countdown on Segregated Edn., 1960, Religion, Govt., and Edn., 1961, A Century of Higher Edn.: Classical Citadel to Collegiate Colossus, 1962, Automation, Edn. and Human Values, 1966, Conflict and Change on the Campus: The Response to Student Hyperactivism, 1970, Leaders, Teachers, and Learners in Academe: Partners in the Ednl. Process, 1970, Edn. and the Many Faces of the Disadvantaged: Cultural and Histl. Perspectives, 1972; contrbr. to natl. mags., nwsprs. and profl. jnls.; producer: Report on Edn., WBAI-FM, NYC, 1960-61. BS in Jnlsm., N.Y.U., 1950; postgrad. in edn., San Antonio Coll., 1952. Ed. and pub. Crossroads mag., Valley Stream, NY, 1949-50; youth svc. ed. Open Road Mag., NYC, 1950-51; mng. ed. School & Society, NYC, 1953-68, v.p., 1956-68; pub. School & Society Books, NYC, 1963-86, School & Society Mag., 1968-72, Intellect Mag., NYC, 1972-78, editorial dir., 1974-78; pub., editorial dir. USA Today mag., 1978—, Newsview, 1979—, Your Health, 1980—, The World of Sci.., 1980—. Served with Signal Corps U.S. Army, 1951-53. Non-fiction award Midwestern writers Conf., Chgo., 1948. Mem. Soc. Advancement of Edn. Mem. natl. jr. book awards com. Boys' Clubs Am., 1954. Home: 82 Shelbourne Ln New Hyde Park NY 11040

LEHRER, WARREN I., b. NYC, July 22, 1955, s. Arthur and Ruth (Waldman) L.; m. Jan Baker, Jan. 4, 1980. Author: Willow Weep Don't, 1980, Versations, 1981, Social Security, 1983, I Mean You Know, 1984, French Fries, 1985; GRRRHHHH: A study of Social Patterns, 1987. BA, Queens Coll., 1977; MFA, Yale U., 1980. Asst. prof. Southeastern Mass. U., North Dartmouth, 1980-82, SUNY-Purchase, 1982—. Grantee N.Y. State Council on Arts, 1979, Ford Fdn., 1983; recipient Whole Book award Am. Inst. for Graphic Arts, NYC, 1981, 83, 85; NEA art fellow, 1985. Address: Main PO Box 299 Purchase NY 10577

LEHRMAN, NAT, b. Bklyn., Aug. 5, 1929; s. Louis and Lena (Goldfarb) L.; m. Kazuko Miyajima, Nov. 13, 1956; children—Jerome M., Cynthia H. Author: Masters and Johnson Explained, 1970. BA, Bklyn. Coll., 1953; MA, NYU, 1961. Travel ed. intl. travel dept. AAA, 1955-57; ed. Relax Mag., 1958; mng. ed. Dude Mag., Gent Mag., 1959-61; ed., then assoc. to asst. mng. ed. Playboy Mag., 1976—, dir. mag. div., 1980-82, pres. pub. div., 1982-85; chmn., Journalism Dept., Columbia College, Chicago 1987—; dir. Essence mag.; adv. bd. Guitarra mag. Served with U.S. Army, 1953-55. Spcl. adv. bd. Masters and Johnson Inst. Office: 919 N Michigan Ave Chicago IL 60611

LEIBER, FRITZ, b. Chgo., Dec. 25, 1910; s. Fritz and Virginia (Bronson) L.; m. Jonquil Stephens, 1936 (dec. 1969); 1 son, Justin. Author: numerous novels inclg.: Conjure Wife, 1953, Gather Darkness!, 1956, Destiny Times Three, 1957, The Big Time, 1961, The Wanderer, 1964, A Specter is Haunting Texas, 1969, Our Lady of Darkness, 1977, The Best of Fritz Leiber, 1974, The Worlds of Fritz Leiber, 1976, The Ghost Light, 1983. BPh, U. Chgo., 1932; postgrad. Gen. Theol. Sem., NYC. Formerly staff writer Standard Am. Ency., Chgo., instr. speech and drama Occidental Coll., Los Angeles; mem. editorial staff Sci. Digest, 1945-56. Gandalf award, 1975, August Derleth Fantasy award, 1976. Office: Ace Books 200 Madison Ave New York NY 10016

LEIBOWITZ, HERBERT AKIBA, b. Staten Island, NY, Apr. 26, 1935; s. Morris and Rose (Rabinowitz) L.; m. Susan Yankowitz, May 3, 1978; 1 son, Gabriel. Author: Hart Crane: An Introduction to the Poetry; ed.: Musical Impressions, 1968, Selected Music Criticism of Paul Rosenfeld, 1970, Parnassus: Poetry in Review, 1972—. BA, Bklyn. Coll., 1956; MA, Brown U., 1958; PhD, Columbia U., 1966. Asst. prof. English Columbia U., 1967-70; asst. prof. humanities Richmond Coll., Staten Island, NY, 1971-73, assoc. prof., 1973-76; assoc. prof. English, Coll. Staten Island, CUNY, 1976-81, prof. English, 1981—; prof. English CUNY Grad. Ctr., 1986—. Fels award for editorial distinction, CCLM, 1975. Mem. PEN. Home: 205 W 89th St New York NY 10024

LEIGHTON, FRANCES SPATZ, b. Geauga County, OH, Sept. 4. Author numerous books inclg.: (with Frank S. Caprio) How to Avoid a Nervous Breakdown, 1969, (with Mary B. Gallagher) My Life with Jacqueline Kennedy, 1969, (with William "Fishbait" Miller)—The Memoirs of the Congressional Doorkeeper, 1977, (with Lillian Rogers Parks) My 30 Years Backstairs at the White House, 1979 (made into TV miniseries), (with Hugh Carter) My Life with the Carter Family of Plains, Georgia, 1978, (with

Jerry Cammarata) The Fun Book of Fatherhood—or How the Animal Kingdom is Helping to Raise the Wild Kids at Our House, 1978, (with Natalie Golos) Coping with Your Allergies, 1979, (with Ken Hoyt) Drunk Before Noon—The Behind the Scenes Story of the Washington Press Corps, 1979, (with Louis Hurst) Memoirs of the Senate Restaurateur, 1980, (with John M. Szostak) In the Footsteps of Pope John Paul II, 1980, (with Lillian Rogers Parks) The Roosevelts, a Family in Turmoil, 1981, (with June Allyson) June Allyson, 1982, (with Beverly Slater) Stranger in My Bed, 1984, (with Oscar Collier) How to Write and Sell Your First Novel, 1986, The Search for the Real Nancy Reagan, 1987. Student Ohio State U. Washington corr. Am. Weekly; corr. and Washington ed. This Week Mag.; Washington corr. Met. Group Sunday Mags.; contrbg. ed. Family Weekly; free-lance jnlst. Metro Sunday Group, Washington. Mem. Senate Periodical Corr. Assn., WHCA, ANWC, NWC, NPC, pres. Wrtrs. Lg. of Washington. Office: 1035 National Press Bldg Washington DC 20045

LEIH, GRACE JANET, (Helen Forelle, Mario Edlosi), b. Canton, SD, Dec. 2, 1936; d. Geurt and Ruth Victoria (Hall) L.; m. John Maxwell Jeffords, Dec. 2, 1956 (div. 1968); children: Ruth Ann Rose Jeffords, John Maxwell Jeffords III, Pamela Leah Jeffords Meder. Author: (under pseudonym Mario Edlosi) Which Way the Wind Blows, 1978; (under pseudonym Helen Forelle) Conversations in a Clinic, 1981, The Adventures of Mortimer Troll, 1981, If Men Got Pregnant, Abortion Would Be a Sacrament, 1982; ed. Pasque Petals, 1983—; ed. A Sixty Year Comprehensive Index of Pasque Petals (1926-1986), 1987; ed. staff Serendipity Newsletter, 1985-87; contrbr. to Broomstick, Candle, Pasque Petals, Lincoln Logs, Celibate Woman, Voices of S.D., Homestones, Lyrical Treasures, Bird Verse Portfolio. BA, Memphis State U., 1967. Typist State of S.D., Sioux Falls, 1985—. Served with USN, 1954-56. Recipient various awards. Mem. S.D. Poetry Soc. (past pres.), Sioux Falls Bardic Round Table, Feminist Wrtrs. Guild. Home: 3001 W 57th St Sioux Falls SD 57106

LEINSTER, COLIN RONALD, b. Tynemouth, Eng., Dec. 19, 1939; s. Ronald Styan and Sheila Mary (Wright) L.; came to U.S., 1964; m. Emily Banks, July 18, 1972. Author: The Heritage of Michael Flaherty (novel); contrbg. ed. Hearst Corp. Books; editorial cons. Manpower Devel. Research Corp., NYC; text ed. Tree Communics.; staff ed. Bus. Week, 1982. Student, London Poly. Schl. Jnlsm., 1961-64. Rptr. West London Press, 1961-64, Cleve. Plain Dealer, 1964-65, New Orleans States-Item, 1965-66; Vietnam corr. Life Mag., 1967-69, Midwest Bur. chief, 1970-71, assoc. ed., 1971-72; free-lance writer, 1972-75; staff writer Free Enterprise Mag., NYC, 1975-77. Home: 600 West End Ave New York NY 10024

LEIPER, ESTHER M., b. West Chester, PA, Nov. 18, 1946; d. John Ashhurst and Hannah Mather (Shelly) L.; m. Peter Hall Estabrooks, Dec. 23, 1972; children: Hannah Margaret, Thomas Leiper. Author: (poems) Christmas Colt, 1974; How To Enter Poetry Contests To Win, 1984; Tamari's Son and Other Christmas Sonnets, 1987; 1987; contrbr. to numerous mags; author: The Wars of the Faery, 12-part epic romance pub. Amelia, Jan. 1987—, book pubn: 1989. BA in English, Va. Commonwealth U., 1970; BS in Education, St. Joseph's Coll., Phila., 1972. Co-owner Jefferson Hill Enterprises, 1976-86; freelance wrtr., 1963—; humor columnist North Country Weekly, 1982—; poetry columnist, ed. The Inkling, Alexandria, Minn., since 1983. Recipient over 500 writing awards. Mem. Poetry Soc. N.H., Poetry Soc. Pa., Poetry Soc. Ga., Poets Study Club. Home: Box 96 Jefferson NH 03583

LEISTER, MARY MCFARLAND, b. Brackenridge, PA, Oct. 4, 1917; d. William Clare and Martha C. (Nolf) McFarland. Author: The Silent Concert, 1970, Wildlings, 1976, Flying Fur, Fin, and Scale, 1977, Wee Green Witch, 1978, Seasons of Heron Pond, 1981. Contrbr. numerous nature articles to Balt. Sunday Sun, Humpty Dumpty's Mag., other articles, short stories, verse to mags. including Natl. Wildlife, Boy's Life, Jack and Jill, many others. Student Johns Hopkins McCoy Coll., 1949-51. Address: 13940 Old Frederick Rd Sykesville MD 21784

LEITMEYER, WALTER JAMES JR., b. Phila., Nov. 27, 1954, s. Walter James and Dorothea Anna (McQuiggan) L.; m. Rosemary C. Emmerich, June 24, 1978; children—Walter James, Melissa. Contrbr. poetry to Dreams, Vol. II, 1980, Eternal Echoes, Vol. III, 1982, Our Twentieth Century's Greatest Poems, 1982, Earthsine, Vol. II, 1983, Gung-Ho mag. BA, U. Ariz., 1976. Capt., U.S. Army, 1976-81, U.S. Marine Corps, 1981—. Home: 5427 Lariat Way Oceanside CA 92056

LELAND, CHRISTOPHER TOWNE, b. Tulsa, Oct. 17, 1951, s. Benjamin Bowne and Julia Elizabeth (Sanford) L. Author: Mean Time, 1982, The Last Happy Men: The Generation of 1922, Fiction and the Argentine Reality, 1986, Mrs. Randall, 1987. BA, Pomona Coll., Claremont, Calif., 1973; PhD, U. Calif., San Diego, 1982. Lectr. Pomona Coll., 1982, U. Calif., San Diego, 1983; Briggs-Copeland asst. prof. Harvard U., Cambridge, Mass., 1983—. Fulbright fellow, Buenos Aires, Argentina, 1979, 84; wrtr.-in-residence Montalvo (Calif.) Center for Arts, 1978. Mem. MLA. Office: Dept. Eng Harvard 34 Kirkland St Cambridge MA 02138

LELCHUK, ALAN, b. Bklyn., Sept. 15, 1938, s. Harry and Belle (Simon) L.; m. Barbara Kreiger; 1 son, Saul. Novelist: American Mischief, 1973, Miriam at Thirty-Four, 1974, Shrinking, 1978, Miriam in Her Forties, 1985, On Home Ground, 1987; co-ed. 8 Great Hebrew short novels, 1983. BA, Bklyn. Coll., 1960; MA, Stanford U., 1962, PhD,1965. Asst. prof., wrtr.-in-residence Brandeis U., Waltham, Mass., 1966-81; vis. wrtr., prof. Amherst (Mass.) Coll., 1982-84; adj. prof. Dartmouth Coll., Hanover, N.H., 1985—; assoc. ed. Modern Occasions mag., Cambridge, Mass., 1970-72. Guggenheim fellow, 1976-77; Mishkenot Sha'ananim residency, Jerusalem Fdn., 1976-77; recipient Wrtr.-in-Residence award Fulbright Fdn., U. Haifa, Israel, 1986-87. Mem. PEN. Home: RFD 2 Canaan NH 03741

LEMASTER, JIMMIE RAY, b. Pike County, OH, Mar. 29, 1934, s. Dennis LeMaster and Helen Smith; m. Wanda LeMaster, 1966; children—Lisa Lou, Lynn DeNae, Lon Keith. Author: Children of Adam, 1971, Weeds & Wildflowers, 1975, Jesse Stuart: A Reference Guide, 1979, Jesse Stuart: Kentucky's Chronicler-Poet, 1980, The New Mark Twain Handbook, 1985; ed. The World of Jesse Stuart: Selected Poems, 1975, Jesse Stuart: Selected Criticism, 1977, Making Sense of Grammar, 1980. BS in English, Defiance Coll., 1959, MA in English, 1962; PhD in English, Bowling Green State U., 1970. Tchr. pub. schls., 1959-62; prof., chmn. dept. lang. and lit. Defiance Coll., Ohio, 1962-77; prof. English, Baylor U., Waco, Tex., 1977—, dir. Am. studies, 1977—. Served with USN, 1951-55. Named Ohio Poet of Yr., 1976; Dean of Coll. award for acad. excellence Defiance Coll., 1977. Mem. South Central MLA, Conf. on Christianity and Lit., Conf. Coll. Tchrs. English, Tex. Assn. Creative Writing Tchrs., Am. Studies Assn. Home: 201 Harrington Ave Waco TX 76706

LEMAY, HARDING, b. North Bangor, NY., March 16, 1922; s. Henry James and Eva (Gorrow) L.; m. (1) Priscilla Amidon, Sept. 1947 (marriage dissolved, 1953), (2) Dorothy Shaw, Sept. 19, 1953; children: (second marriage) Stephen, Susan. Author: Inside, Looking Out (autobiography), 1971; au of introd., Arthur H. Bremer, An Assassin's Diary, 1973, Eight Years in Another World, 1981. Plays (first produced at New Dranatists Work-shop, N.Y.C.): Look at Any Man, 1963, The Little Birds Fly, 1965, From a Dark Land, 1967, Return Upriver, 1968, The Death of Eagles, 1970, The Joslyn Circle, 1971, also prod. at Dublin Theatre Festival, 1973, The Off Season, 1973, Escape Route, 1979. Author of TV scripts, including They (with Marya Mannes), prod. by WNDT-TV, NYC., 1970, and Whose Life?, produced by NBC-TV, 1970. Contrbr to Life, Washington Post, New Yorker, and N.Y. Hearld Tribune Books. Studied at Neighborhood Playhouse School of the Theatre, NYC., 1946-48. Member special assignment staff, N.Y. Public Library, 1952-56; member TV liaison staff, American Book Publishers Concl, NYC., 1956-58; publicity mgr, Alfred A. Knopf, Inc., NYC, 1958-61, asst to chairman and to pres, 1961-63, v.p., 1963-67; freelance writer, 1967—; head writer for Another World TV series, NBC-TV, N.Y.C., 1971-79. Also worked as script writer for The Guiding Light TV series. Lectr, Hunter Coll of the City Univ of N.Y., 1968-72. Mem: DG, PEN. American Center (v.p., 1960-70), New Dramatists Com. (mem exec bd, 1965-71), The Players (mem bd dirs). Natl. Book Award nomination, 1972, for Inside, Looking Out; Emmy awards from Natl. Acad. of TV Arts and Scis, 1975, for Another World TV series, and 1980 for The Guiding Light TV series, Military service: U.S. Army; became corporal. Address: 143 West 13th St New York NY 10001

LEMBKE, JANET, b. Cleve., Mar. 2, 1933. Author: Duo (with M. Felix), 1966, Bronze and Iron, 1973, Aeschylus' Suppliants, 1975, Aeschylus' Persians (with C.J. Herington), 1981, Euripides' Hecuba (with K.J. Reckford), 1986, Euripides' Hecuba, Electra (both with K.J. Reckford), 1988. BA, Middlebury Coll., 1953. Self-employed writing and tching., 1972—. Natl. Translation Ctr. fellow, Austin, Tex., 1968-69. Founder and leader Creative Righters Workshop, Va. Dept. Corrections, Staunton, 1978-84. Mem. PEN (Am.). Address: 210 N Madison St Staunton VA 24401

LEMKE, CARLTON EDWARD, b. Buffalo, Oct. 11, 1920; s. Carl and Estelle (Yuhnke) L.; m. Martha C. Harris, Feb. 5, 1948 (dec. Feb. 1976); children—Paul S., Susan M. Assoc. ed.: Jnl. Inst. Mgmt. Scis., 1967—, Jnl Computer and Systems Scis., 1967—, Jnl Math. Programming, Jnl Math. Operations Research. BA magna cum laude, U. Buffalo, 1959; MS, Carnegie Inst. Tech., 1951, PhD, 1953. With Gen. Electric Co., 1954-55, RCA, 1955-56; mem faculty Rensselaer Poly. Inst., 1956—, prof. math., 1963-m, now Ford Fdn. prof. math.; cons. to industry, 1963-70. Served with AUS, 1940-45. Co-recipient John von Neumann Theory prize Inst. Mgmt. Scis.-Ops. Research Soc. Am. 1978. Home: 10 Burke

Dr Troy NY 12180

LEMON, GEORGE EDWARD, (J.C. Brainbeau), b. Youngstown, Ohio, June 23, 1907; s. John and Eliza Ann (Hamilton) L. Columnist in Daily Mail Order Advertiser, 1977—. Student Ohio State U., 1929. Steel worker Youngstown Sheet & Tube Co., Ohio, 1930-72, now ret. Served to lst lt. CE, U.S. Army, 1941-44; NATOUSA. Home: 286 Lora Ave Youngstown OH 44504

LEMOND, ALAN ROY, b. Evansville, IN, Feb. 27, 1938; s. Jesse R. and Dorothy E. (Taylor) LeM.; m. Mary A. Hirsch, July 19, 1969; children—Lisa Anne, Nicole Christina. Works include: Mug Shots, 1972, Ralph Nader: A Man and a Movement, 1972, No Place to Hide, 1975, The Mark Spitz Complete Book of Swimming, 1976, Men's Hair: The Long and Short of It, 1979, Bravo Baryshnikov, 1978; co-fdr., ed. Your Land mag., 1972; ed. Nostalgia Illustrated mag., 1974-75. BA in English, Oakland City (IN) U., 1965. Copywriter Esquire Mag., 1965-67; assoc. ed., ed. Cavalier mag., 1967-70; pres. New Earth, Inc., NYC, 1970—, Sweet Sulphur Springs, Inc., Velpen, IN, 1978—; exec. ed. Celebrity Mag., 1975—; genl. partner, pub., ed. The Patoka Valley Citizen, Jasper, IN; adj. scholar Am. Enterprise Inst., 1980—. Served with AUS, 1961-63. Address: Box 65 Velpen IN 47590

LEMPERLE, VIRGINIA MAXINE, b. Sault Ste. Marie, MI, Dec. 25, 1921, d. Grant Arthur and Madelyn (Charles) Crowell; m. Richard H. Lemperle, May 19, 1945; children—Madelyn L. Griffin, Myron, Carol L. VanderKamp, Lydia. Contrbr. to Our Western World's Greatest Poems, Am. Poetry Anthology, Today's Greatest Poems, Our World's Best Loved Poems, Am. Poetry Showcase, Hearts on Fire, Eastern Gate. Recipient hon. mention World of Poetry Press, 1983, spcl. mention, 1984, Golden Poet award, 1985, 86. Home: 8 Episcopal Ave Honeoye Falls NY 14472

LENAHAN, MEA LORRAINE, b. Lebanon, NH, Feb. 29, 1932; d. Errol Ralston and Ruth Leete (Whitcher); m. Robert Lawrence Carran, Dec. 17, 1957 (div. Sept. 1959); 1 son, Stephen Michael Carran; m. Shelby Ward Lenahan, May 27, 1960 (dec. Apr. 27, 1970); children—Shelby Stuart, Dale Gordon, John Daniel. Author: What Father Left Behind, 1975. Contrbr. feature articles, editorials to Jnl.-Record, Progress. A.S., Brewer State Jr. Coll., 1977; B.S., U. Ala., 1980. Reporter, The Jnl.-Record, Winfield, AL, 1982-85; insurance agent United Insurance Co., Russellville, AL, 1986; part-time reporter The Progress, Hamilton, AL, 1986—; payroll clrk. Health-Tex, Inc., Guin, AL, 1986—. Recipient Honorable Mention for short story New England Homestead, 1948, I Dare You award Danforth, 1949. Home: Rt 2 Box 498 Winfield AL 35594

L'ENGLE, MADELEINE, b. NYC, Nov. 29, 1918; d. Charles Wadsworth and Madeleine (Barnett) Camp; m. Hugh Franklin, Jan. 26, 1946; children—Josephine Franklin Jones, Maria Franklin Bion. Author: The Small Rain, 1945, Ilsa, 1946, Camilla Dickinson, 1951, A Winter's Love, 1957, And Both Were Young, 1949, Meet the Austins, 1960, A Wrinkle in Time, 1962, The Moon by Night, 1963, The 24 Days Before Christmas, 1964, The Arm of the Starfish, 1965, The Love Letters, 1966, The Journey with Jonah, 1967, The Young Unicorns, 1968, Dance in The Desert, 1969, Lines Scribbled on an Envelope, 1969, The Other Side of the Sun, 1971, A Circle of Quiet, 1972, A Wind in the Door, 1973, The Summer of the Great-grandmother, 1974, Dragons in the Waters, 1976, The Irrational Season, 1977, A Swiftly Tilting Planet, 1978, The Weather of the Heart, 1978, Ladder of Angels, 1979, A Ring of Engles Light, 1980, Walking on Water, 1981, A Severed Wasp, 1982, And it was Good, 1983, A House Like a Lotus, 1984, A Stone for a Pillow, 1985, Many Waters, 1986 AB, Smith Coll., 1951; postgrad., New Schl., 1941-42, Columbia U., 1960-61. Tchr. St. Hilda's and St. Hugh's Schl., 1960—; mem. faculty U. IN, 1965-66, 71; writer-in-res. Ohio State U., 1970, U. Rochester, 1972, Wheaton Coll., 1976—, Cathedral St. John the Divine, NYC, 1965—. Newbery medal 1963, Sequoyah award 1965, Lewis Carroll Shelf award 1965, Austrian State Lit. award 1969. Mem. AG (pres., 1987), AL (council member), WG. Home: Crosswicks Goshen CT 06756

LENGYEL, CORNEL ADAM, b. Fairfield, CT, Jan. 1, 1915; s. Elmer Alexander and Mary Elizabeth (Bismarck) L.; m. Theresa Delaney Murphy, July 10, 1933; children—Jerome Benedict, Paul Joel, Michael Sebastian, Cornelia (Mrs. Charles Burke). Author: Thirty Pieces, 1933, The World's My Village, 1936, Jonah Fugitive, 1937, The Shadow Trap, 1939, The Atom Clock, 1950, The Last Shelter, 1954, American Testament, 1956, Four Days in July, 1958, Benedict Arnold, 1969, Presidents of the United States, 1961, Ethan Allen, 1962, Will of Stratford, 1983, Jesus the Galilean, 1966, The Declaration of Independence, 1968, Four Dozen Songs, 1970, The Lookout's Letter, 1971, The Creative Self, 1971, Late News From Adam's Acres, 1983; author plays: The Case of Benedict Arnold, 1975, Doctor Franklin, 1976, The Master Plan, 1978; contrbr. anthols.: The Golden Year, 1960, The Britannica Lib. of Great Am. Writing, 1961, The Menorah Treasury, 1964, Interp. for Our Time, 1966. Student pub. schls. Ed., supr. Fedl. Research Project, San Francisco, 1938-41; music critic The Coast, San Francisco, 1937-41; mgr. Forty-Nine Theatre, Georgetown, CA, 1946-50; ed. W.H. Freeman Co., San Francisco, 1952-54; guest lectr. M.I.T., 1969; founder, exec. ed. Dragon's Teeth Press, Georgetown, 1969—. Served with U.S. Merchant marine, 1944-45. 1st prize Maritime Poetry awards, 1945, Maxwell Anderson award drama, 1950, Di Castagnola award, PSA, 1971, NEA fellow, 1976-77. Mem. MLA, AAUP, PEN, PSA, Poetry Soc. Eng. Address: Adam's Acres Georgetown CA 95634

LENSE, EDWARD LOUIS, b. Dayton, OH, Sept. 9, 1945; s. Norman Edward and Esther Louise (Korte) L.; m. Deborah Diane Fleming, Oct. 15, 1978. Author chapbook Buried Voices, 1982; articles The Explicator, Green River Rvw, Mod Poetry Studies, Abraxas, Agni Rvw, Aspen Anthology, Aura, Big Moon, Combinations, Cornfield Rvw, Dark Tower, others. BA, NYU, 1969, PhD, Ohio State U, 1976. Mem. MLA. Address: 337 E Kelso Rd Columbus OH 43202

LENSON, DAVID, b. Kearny, NJ, June 28, 1945, s. Michael and June (Rollar) L.; m. Pamela Glaven, Dec. 21, 1982. Author: Achilles Choice: Examples of Modern Tragedy, 1975, The Gambler (poems), 1977, Ride the Shadow (poems), 1979, The Birth of Tragedy: A Commentary, 1987; contrbr. fiction: Pulpsmith; contrbr. poetry: lit mags; contrbr. articles to newspapers, periodicals, lit. mags. AB summa cum laude, Princeton U., 1967, PhD, 1971. Pub., ed., pres. Panache, Inc., Sunderland, Mass., 1974-80; pub., ed. Oh No! Oh No!, Northampton, Mass., 1984-86. Home: Whatley Rd South Deerfield MA 01373

LENT, JOHN ANTHONY, b. East Millsboro, PA, Sept. 8, 1936; s. John and Rose (Marano) L.; children—Laura, Andrea, John, Lisa, Shahnon. Author: Asian Nwsprs. Reluctant Revoln., 1971, Asian Mass Communics.: A Compreh. Bibliog., 1975, 78, Third World Mass Media and Their Search for Modernity, 1977, Broadcasting in Asia and the Pacific, 1978, Topics in Third World Mass Media, 1979, Caribbean Mass Communics., 1981, Asian Nwspr.: Contemp. Trends and Problems, 1982, Malaysian Studies, 1985, others; ed. books in field; mem. editorial bd. Crossroads, Human Rights Qtly, Communics. Booknotes Gazette, Asian Thought and Society, Indian Jnl of Comm., Media Hist. Digest, Studies in Latin Am. Pop. Culture, others; contrbr. to profl. jnls; mng. ed. Witty World; ed., Berita. BS, OH U., 1958, MS, 1960; PhD, U. IA, 1972. Var. tchg. positions, 1960-70; asst. ed. Internatl. Communic. Bull., Iowa City, 1970-72; assoc. prof. communics. Temple U., Phila., 1974-76, prof., 1976—; asst. dir. Ctr. for Communic. and Public Policy; founding ed. Berita, 1975—. Fulbright scholar, Philippines, 1964-65. Mem. Assn. for Asian Studies, Intl. Assn. Mass Communics. Research, Caribbean Stud. Assn., Latin Am. Stud. Assn. Home: 669 Ferne Blvd Drexel Hill PA 19026

LEON, JUDENE MARIE, b. Rochester, NY, June 11, 1931; d. John Vincent and Jennie (Ingrassia) Leon. Author: (text and jnl.) Jesus, Lord and Savior, 1982; Bible Games for Teams and Groups, 1984; This Is Our Faith, grade 1, 1986. Contrbr. articles to booklet, religious jnls. Ed. William H. Sadlier Co., N.Y. BA in Edn., Duquesne U., 1964; MA in Techology, St. Mary's Ecumenical Inst., Balt., 1975. Tchr. various religious edn. orgns., Pa., N.Y., Washington, Va., Md., N.C., S.C., P.R., Venezuela, 1952-86. Mem. NWC, Oakdale Ladies Golf Assn., Natl. Wrtrs. Club, Am. Cemetery Assn. Home: 2069 Union Blvd 2C Bayshore NY 11706

LEON, STEVE, b. Fresno, CA, Sept. 4, 1948; s. Salvador Hernandez and Carmen (Almaraz) L.; m. Anna Gonzales, Oct. 5, 1974. Contrbr. articles to trade mags. A.A. in Graphic Arts, Clark County Commun. Coll., 1980, A.A. in Management, 1981. Pubs. ed. Reynolds Electrical & Engineering Co., Las Vegas, 1972-79, public info. officer, 1979—. Mem. Graphic art advisory bd. Clark County Commun. Coll., Las Vegas, 1985. Mem. IABC (Bronze Quill award 1984, award of Ecellence 1985). Office: Reynolds Elec 2501 Wyandotte Las Vegas NV 89114

LEONARD, ELMORE JOHN, b. New Orleans, Oct. 11, 1925; s. Elmore John and Flora Amelia (Rive) L.; m. Beverly Claire Cline, Aug. 30, 1949 (div. 1977); children—Jane, Peter, Christopher, William, Katherine; m. 2d, Joan Leanne Lancaster, Sept. 15, 1979. Author: 25 novels inclg. Hombre, 1961, Stick, Cat Chaser, 1982, LaBrava, 1983, Glitz, 1985, Bandits, Touch, 1987, Freaky Deaky, 1988; feature-film screenplays. PhB, U. Detroit, 1950. Served with USN, 1943-46. Mem. WG, AG, MWA, WWA. Office: Swanson Inc 8523 Sunset Blvd Los Angeles CA 90069

LEONARD, PHYLLIS G(RUBBS), (Isabel Ortega) b. Westerville, OH, Oct. 4, 1924; d. Maynard Lee and Lura McEwen (Steele) Grubbs; m. Walter M. Leonard, Jan. 31, 1948. Author: (fiction) Prey of the Eagle (1st prize Ariz. Press Women, 1974, 2d prize NFPW, 1974) (German ed.), 1974, Phantom of the Sacred Well (French ed.), 1976, Warrior's Woman, 1977, Tarnished Angel, 1980 (Italian ed.), Mariposa, 1983

(French ed.), Beloved Stranger, 1985, Street of the Madwoman, 1978 (Spanish & English eds.). Contrbr. fiction to anthol.; non-fiction to mags. including Christian Sci. Monitor, Highlights for Children, Pacific Discovery, Am. Horseman, others. Wrkg. on novels, TV script, story ideas. Cert., U. San Carlos, Guatemala City, Guatemala, 1948, Am. Grad. Sch. Intl. Management, 1949. Ptnr., Leonard Insurance Co., Phoenix, 1952-63, pres., 1963-71; pres., treas. Leonard Corp., Phoenix, 1971-81; free-lance wrtr., 1971—. Pres. bd. trustees Library, Tombstone, AZ, 1983-88; sec. advisory bd. Cochise County Library, AZ, 1986-87; founder Friends of the Reading Sta., Tombstone, 1986, sec., 1987—88. Mem. Soc. Southwestern Authors (1st prize for fiction 1976). Home: Box 400 215 West Allen Tombstone AZ 85638

LEONE, NORMA LEONARDI, b. Ithaca, NY, Nov. 23, 1935; d. Salvatore Anthony and Mary Baldini Leonardi; m. Anthony James Leone, Jr., Jun. 15, 1957; 1 dau.: Christina—1 son: Anthony III. Author: A Mother's Guide to Computers, 1986. Contrbr. to Upstate Mag., Road Rider, Auburn Citizen-Advertiser, Skating, Rochester Times Union. BA, St. John Fisher, 1982. Home: 19 Greentree Pittsford NY 14534

LEPORE, DOMINICK JAMES, b. Enfield, CT, July 1, 1911; s. John and Anna (Porcello) Lepore; m. Agatha Katherine Maggio, Jan. 15, 1949; 1 dau., Anna Lepore Kasabian. Author: The Praise and the Praised, 1955, Within His Walls, 1968; poetry in Blue Unicorn, English Jnl, Christian Science Monitor, PSA Diamond Anthology, and many other lit mags and anthologies. BA, College of the Holy Cross, 1933; MA, U. of CT, 1959. IRS agent, U.S. Govt., Hartford, CT, 1950-55; educator, Enfield, CT Board of Ed., 1955-75. Mem. PSA, New England Poetry Club, NCTE, New Eng. Council of Tchrs. of Eng. Home: 4 Mitchell Dr Enfield CT 06082

LERCH, SHARON, b. Chgo., Dec. 31, 1940, d. Samuel and Anne (Leiferman) Primack; m. Irving A. Lerch, Feb. 24, 1963. Contrbr. articles to: N.Y. Times, N.Y. Post, other mags; contrbr. fiction to: Confrontation, Washington Sq. Writes, Kansas Quarterly, The Literary Review, N.D. Qtly, others. Working on novels. BS, U. Ill., 1963. Promotional wrtr., advt. copywrtr. Sears, Roebuck & Co., Chgo., 1963-73; fgn. corr. Chgo. Mag., 1970-75; dir. writing workshop Source Network, New York Institute of Technology, Old Westbury, N.Y., 1984—; instructor, graduate level fiction workshop, The New School for Social Research, NYC, 1986—; free-lance wrtr., 1970—. Recipient Aaron H. Rubenfeld award in fiction New Schl., NYC, 1977; National Arts Club Scholar Bread Loaf Writers Conf., 1981, fiction teaching fellow Wesleyan Wrtrs. Conf., Middletown, Conn., 1985; fiction fellow Bennington Writing Workshops, 1986; Fiction resident fellow Yaddo, 1985, 1987. Mem. P&W, Wrtrs. Community. Home: 146 W 74th St New York NY 10023

LERMAN, ALBERT, b. Chgo., June 24, 1936; s. David and Mary (Oseas) L.; m. Phyllis Carpenter, June 28, 1959; children—Dawn, April. Creator numerous advt. campaigns incl. Fly The Friendly Skies of United & The Happy Cooker; writer popular songs. BJ, Northwestern U., 1958. Sr. writer Playboy Mag., Chgo., 1958-59; promotion mgr. Helene Curtis Co., Chgo., 1959-61; pres. Lerman Assocs., Chgo., 1961-63; creative dir. Leo Burnett Co., Chgo., 1964-72; exec. v.p., creative dir. McCann-Erickson & Marschalk Co., NYC, 1972-77; sr. v.p., creative adv. to pres. Foote Cone & Belding, NYC, 1978-80; exec. creative dir. Foote Cone & Belding Intl., Chgo., 1980—. Golden Lion award Cannes Film Festival, 1970. Office: FC & B Intl 401 N Michigan Ave Chicago IL 60611

LERMAN, RHODA, b. NYC, Jan. 18, 1936; m. Robert Lerman, Sept. 15, 1957; children—Jill, Julia, Matthew. Author: Call Me Ishtar, 1973, Girl that He Marries, 1976, Eleanor, a novel, 1979, Book of the Night, 1984; contrbr. to jnls and mags; wrtr. TV drama (CBS) First Lady of the World, film, Soul of Iron. BA, U. Miami, Coral Gables, Fla., 1958. Vis. prof. creative writing Syracuse (NY) U., 1985, U. Colo., 1982-84; NEH disting. prof. in Humanities, Hartwick Coll., Oneonta, NY, 1985. Mem. PEN, WG. Home: Shore Acres Cazenovia NY 13035

LERNER, GERDA, b. Vienna, Austria, Apr. 30, 1920; d. Robert and Ilona (Neumann) Kronstein; came to U.S., 1939, naturalized, 1943; m. Carl Lerner, Oct. 6, 1941 (dec.); children—Stephanie, Daniel. Author: No Farewell, 1955, Black Like Me, 1964 (screenplay), The Grimke Sisters from South Carolina: Rebels Against Slavery, 1967, The Woman in American History, 1971, Black Women in White America: A Documentary History, 1972, The Female Experience: An American Documentary, 1976, A Death of One's Own, 1978, The Majority Finds Its Past: Placing Women in History, 1979, Teaching Women's History, 1981, Women and History, vol. 1, The Creation of Patriarchy, 1986. BA, New Schl. Soc. Research, 1963; MA, Columbia U., 1965, PhD, 1966. Lectr., New Schl. Soc. Research, NYC, 1963-65; asst. prof. L.I.U., 1965-67, assoc. prof., 1967-68; mem. faculty Sarah Lawrence Coll., Bronxville, NY, 1968-80; dir. Master's Program in Women's History, 1972-76, 78-79; Robinson-Edwards prof. hist., U. WI, Madison, 1980—, Wis. Alumni Research Fdn. Research Prof., 1984—. Ford grantee, 1978-79; Guggenheim fellow, 1980-81. Mem. AAUP, AL, PEN. Office: Dept Hist 455 N Park St Univ WI Madison WI 53706

LERNER, LINDA, b. Sept. 27; d. Philip and Frieda Lerner. Author: (chapbook) Target Practice, 1978; contrbr. poems to The Wrtr., Christian Sci. Monitor, Croton Rvw, Coll. English, Confrontation, Wis. Rvw, Poetry Now, San Jose Studies, Crosscurrents, others. BA, Bklyn. Coll., 1964, MA, 1969. Lectr. Bklyn Coll., 1970-84, Poly. U. N.Y., 1976—. Mem. P&W. Home: 98 State St Brooklyn NY 11201

LESCHAK, PETER MAX, b. Chisholm, MN, May 11, 1951; s. Peter and Agnes Marie (Pavelich) L.; m. Pamela Dianne Cope, May 4, 1974. Contrbg. editor: Twin Cities Mag., 1984-86; contrbg. editor, columnist TWA Ambassador Mag., 1985-86. Author: Letters from Side Lake (essays), 1987; contrbr. articles to mags. including Minn. Monthly Mag., Mpls./St. Paul Mag., New Age Jnl., Fdn. Commentator, Astronomy Mag, Children's Magic Window. Photo District News, Boundary Waters Jrnl. BA, Ambassador Coll., Big Sandy, Tex., 1974. Free-lance wrtr., 1983—. Firefighter Town of French Vol. Fire Dept., Side Lake, Minn., 1981—. Mem. Side Lake Civic Assn., 1982—. Home: Box 51 Side Lake MN 55781

LE SHAN, EDA J(OAN), b. NYC, June 6, 1922; d. Max and Jean (Schick) Grossman; m. Lawrence Le Shan, Aug. 19, 1944; 1 dau.: Wendy Jean. Author: How to Suvive Parenthood, 1965, The Conspiracy Against Childhood, 1967, Sex and Your Teen-ager: A Guide for Parents, 1969, Natural Parenthood: Raising Your Child without a Script, 1970, How Do Your Children Grow?, 1971, On "How Do Your Children Grow?, 1971, On "How Do Your Children Grow?": A Dialogue with Parents, 1972, What Makes Me Feel This Way?: Growing up with Human Emotions, 1972, The Wonderful Crisis of Middle Age: Some Personal Reflections, 1973, You and Your Feelings, 1974, In Search of Myself and Other Children, 1976, (with Lee Polk) The Incredible Television Machine, 1977, What's Going to Happen to Me?: When Parents Separate and Divorce, 1978, rev. ed., 1986, Winning the Losing Battle: Why I Will Never Be Fat Again, 1979, The Roots of Crime: What You Need to Know about Crime and What You Can Do about It, 1981, Eda Le Shan on Living Your Life, 1982, Grandparents: A Special Kind of Love, 1984, When Your Child Drives You Crazy, 1985, Oh, to Be Fifty Again: Too Late for a Midlife Crisis, 1986, When A Parent Is Very Sick, 1986, When Growups Drive You Crazy, 1988. Also au. of Public Affairs pamphlets. Contrbr to Parents' Magazine, National Parent-Teacher Magazine, New York Times Magazine, Redbook, McCall's Reader's Digest, and many other publications. Cntrbg ed, Woman's Day, 1967—, columnist, 1981—. BS, Columbia Univ., 1944; MA, Clark Univ, 1947. Diagnostician and play therapist, Worcester Child Guidance Clinic, Worcester, Mass., 1947-48; parent educ. discussion leader, Assn for Family Living, Chicago, Ill., 1949-51; dir. of educ., Guidance Center, New Rochelle, N.Y., 1955-60; educ. dir., Manhattan Soc. for Mental Health, N.Y.C., 1960-62, consultant, 1962—. Advisory cncl mem of Adult Learning Services div. of N.Y. State Dept. of Educ.; mem N.Y. State Regents' Com on Parent Educ, 1963-66. Moderator of How Do Your Children Grow? for Public Broadcasting System (PBS), 1970-72; co-host of In-TUN for WCBS-TV, 1976; consultant to children's prog Alex and Annie for American Broadcasting Co. (ABC), 1979-81. Also commentator on locally broadcast programs Newsfront, 1968-70, and Daytime, 1976. Commentator for Getting Along on the Columbia Broadcasting System (CBS) Radio Network, 1981—. Has made guet appearances on TV talk shows, including The Today Show, Good Morning, America, and the Phil Donahue Show. Member: Natl Acad of TV Arts and Scis (mem bd govs, 1980—), American Psychological Assn, Authors League, American Fedn of TV and Radio Artists. Emmy Award nominee, 1971, for TV program How Do Your Children Grow?; Quality of Life Award from B'nai B'rith Women District One, 1972; named Outstanding Woman of the Year by the N.J. Chapter of Brandeis Univ. alummi, 1973; annual award for consistently superior contrbtn toward public understanding of homosexual men and women, from Homosexual Community Counseling Center, 1974. Address: 263 West End Ave New York NY 10023

LE SHAN, LAWRENCE L(EE), (Edward Grendon), NYC, Sept. 8, 1920; s. Julius and Rose (Adelson) L.; m. Eda Grossman, Aug. 19, 1944; 1 dau.: Wendy Jean. Author: (with Margaretta K. Bowers, Jackson, and Knight) Counselling the Dying, 1964, ed (with David Morris Kissen) Psychosomatic Aspects of Neoplastic Disease, 1964, Toward a General Theory of the Paranormal: A Report of Work in Progress, 1969, 3d ed, 1973, How to Meditate: A Guide to Self-Discovery, 1974, The Medium, the Mystic, and the Physicist: Toward a General Theory of the Paranormal, 1974 (publ in England as Clairvoyant Reality: Toward a General Theory of the Paranormal, 1981), Alternate Realities: The

Search for the Full Human Being, 1976, You Can Fight for Your Life: Emotional Factors in the Causation of Cancer, 1977, (with Henry Margenau) Einstein's Space and Van Gogh's Sky: Physical Reality and Beyond, 1982, The Mechanic and the Gardener: Making the Most of the Holistic Revolution in Medicine, 1982 (publ. in England as Holistic Health, 1984), From Newton to ESP: Another Apple is Falling, 1985 (publ. in England as The Science of the Paranormal: The Final Frontier, 1987). Sound recordings: Toward a General Theory of the Paranormal, 1969, (with Frank Haronian, Sanford Unger, and Florence Miale) Psychotherapy: A Synthesis and a Model, 1971. (with Edward Newman Jackson), Experiences in Psychic Healing, 1972. Contrbr of numerous articles to psychological and psychiatric jnls. Also contrbr of short stories to sci. fiction mags. BA, Coll of William and Mary, 1942; MS, Univ of Neb., 1943; Ph.D., Univ of Chicago, 1954. Instr, later asst prof of psychology, Roosevelt College, 1948-51; assoc. psychologist, Worthington Assocs, Inc., 1950-51; research assoc, Fndn for Human Research, 1952-54; research assoc, Ayer Fnd, Inc., New York City, 1954-70; chief of dept of psychology, Trafalgar Hospital and Institute of Applied Biology, New York City, 1954-64, chief investigator in parapsychology project, 1964—. Research psychologist, Union Theol. Sem. Program in Psychiatry and Religion. Member: Assn for Humanistic Psychology (pres, 1985), Parapsychology Assn, American Psychological Assn, Fed of American Scientists, American Soc. for Psychical Reearch. Christopher award, 1975, for How to Meditate. Office: 29 West 75th St New York NY 10023

LESHINSKI, LINDA, b. Pitts., Feb. 25, 1952; d. Edmund Adam and Helen (Castelli) Leshinski. Contrbr. Our Roots Grow Deeper Than We Know, 1985; Pa. Rvw, 1985. BA, U. Pitts., 1973; MFA, U. Ariz., 1977. Lectr. Univ. Ariz., Tucson, 1977-78; dir. writing program, Univ. Pitts., Bradford, 1978-85, chmn. humanities, 1985—. Coordinator, Bradford Writers' Collective, 1985—. Recipient Pa. Rvw award in nonfiction, 1985. Address: 122 Congress No 2 Bradford PA 16701

LESLIE, LOTTIE LYLE, b. Huntsville, AL., Aug. 5, 1930; d. James Peter Jr. and Amanda Elizabeth (Lacy) Burns; m. Thomas E. Lyle; 1 son, Thomas Ervin, Jr.; m. 2d, Theodore Leslie; 1 son, Chris. Poetry in anthologies. BS, Ala. A&M U., 1953. Tchr. Madison County (Ala.) Schs., 1955-75. Home: 3207 Farriss Dr NW Huntsville AL 35810

LESNIAK, ROSE, b. Chgo., Feb. 26, 1955, d. Joseph R. and Mary (Rotolo) Lesniak. Author: Young Anger, 1979, Throwing Spitballs at Nuns, 1980; producer Manhattan Poetry Video Project (1st place Blue Ribbon Am. Film Festival, NYC, 1985). BA, Northeastern Univ., 1979, BS in Psychology, Northeastern Ill. Univ., 1979. Pres. Out There Prodns., Inc., NYC,1979—; freelance poet, producer, pub. Mem. Media Alliance, ASCAP, Mary Stewart Soc., P&W. Address: 156 W 27th St New York NY 10001

LESSER, RIKA ELLEN, b. Bklyn., July 21, 1953; d. Milton Sidney and Celia (Fogelhut) L. Author: (poems) Etruscan Things, 1983; (picture book) Hansel and Gretel, 1984; Rilke: Between Roots, Poems Rendered from the German, 1986; translator: Hours in the Garden and Other Poems by Hermann Hesse, 1979; Guide to the Underworld by Gunnar Ekelof, 1980; Pictor's Metamorphoses and Other Fantasies by Hermann Hesse, 1982; contrbr. poems, transl., rvws. and essays to New Republic, Am. Poetry, Kenyon, N.Y. Times Book, Partisan rvws, New Directions, New Yorker, Poetry, The Nation. BA, Yale U., 1974; MFA, Columbia U., 1977. Vis. lectr. English, Yale U., fall 1976, 78, spring, 1987; adj. lectr. English, Baruch Coll., N.Y.C., fall 1979; instr. poetry workshop 92d Street YMCA, N.Y.C., 1982-85; Jenny McKean Moore vis. lectr. creative writing George Washington U., 1985-86. Recipient Harold Morton Landon transl. prize for poetry AAP, 1982; John Courtney Murray fellow, 1974-75; Amy Lowell poetry traveling scholar, 1974-75; Ingram Merrill Fdn. grantee, 1978-79. Mem. PEN, AWP, ASCAP, ALTA, bd. of Columbia Univ. Translation Center. Home: 133 Henry St Apt 5 Brooklyn NY 11201

LESSER, WENDY CELIA, b. Santa Monica, CA, Mar. 20, 1952; d. Murray Leon Lesser and Millicent (Gerson) Dillon; m. A. Richard Rizzo, Jan. 18, 1985; 1 son, Nicholas. BA, Harvard U., 1969-73; MA, Cambridge U.-England, 1973-75; PhD, U. Cal.-Berkeley, 1975-82. Prtnr. Lesser & Ogden, Berkeley, 1977-81; founding ed. The Threepenny Rvw, Berkeley, 1979—. NEH fellow, 1983; recipient Bellagio residency, Rockefeller Fdn., Italy, 1984. Mem. Bay Area Book Reviewers, Natl. Book Critics Circle. Address: 1614 Grant St Berkeley CA 94703

LESSITER, FRANK DONALD, b. Pontiac, MI, Oct. 5, 1939; s. Milon John and Donalda Belle (Taylor) L.; m. Pamela Ann Fuzak, Nov. 23, 1963; children—Deborah, Susan, Michael, Kelly. Author: (with Pamela Lessiter) Agricultural Travel Guide, 1971, Horsepower, 1977, 100 Most Common No-Tillage Questions, 1981; contrbr. Commodity Yearbook, 1972, 75. BS in Dairy Sci., MI State U., 1961, postgrad. in Advt., 1962-65. Info. specialist MI Coop. Extension Svc., East Lansing, 1962-65; exec. ed. Agrl. Pubs., Milw., 1965-68; ed. Natl. Livestock Producer, 1974-78; ed. Farm Bldg. News, 1977—; exec. v.p. Reiman Assocs., 1977-81; pres. Am. Farm Bldg. Svcs., Inc., 1981—, No-Till Farmer, Inc., 1981—. Best Farm Mktg. Writer CIBA-Geigy, 1976; Farm mag. Writer of Yr., 1977. Mem. Agrl. Eds. Assn. Home: 16000 Choctaw Trail Brookfield WI 53005

LESTER, JULIUS B., b. St. Louis, Jan. 27, 1939; s. W.D. and Julia (Smith) L.; m. Alida Carolyn Fechner; children—Jody Simone, Malcolm Coltrane, Elena, David Julius. Author: (with Pete Seeger) The 12-String Guitar as Played by Leadbelly, 1965, Look Out, Whitey, Black Power's Gon' Get Your Mama, 1968, To Be a Slave, 1968 (Newberry Honor Book 1968), Black Folktales, 1969, Revolutionary Notes, 1969, Search for the New Land, 1969, The Knee-High Man and Other Tales, 1972, Long Journey Home: Stories from Black History, 1972, Two Love Stories, 1972, Who I Am, 1974, All is Well, 1976, This Strange New Feeling, 1982, Do Lord Remember Me, 1985; ed. The Tales of Uncle Remus: The Adventures of Brer Rabbit, 1987, Seventh Son: The Thought and Writings of W.E.B. DuBois, vols. 1 & 2, 1971; assoc. ed. Sing Out, 1964-69; contrbg. ed. Broadside of New York, 1964-70; contrbr. others. BA, fisk U., 1960. Profl. musician & singer, recording for Vanguard Records; folklorist and writer; prof. Afro-Am. studies & Judaic Studies, U. MA, Amherst; dir. Newport Folk Festival, 1966-68. Address: 600 Station Rd Amherst MA 01002

LESTI, MARY LYNN, see Dinardo, Marilynn

LETCHER, TINA H, b. Rochester, NY, May 11, 1938; d. James D. Havens and Gladys (Colcord) Havens; m. Stephen V. Letcher, July 11, 1959; children: Ben, Abby. Articles and poems in var lit mags; ed: Northeast Jnl. 1972—. BA, Mt Holyoke, 1959; MA, Brown U, 1963. Creative writing instr. Adult Corr. Inst., Providence, 1980-85. Active Kingston Congl. Ch., Kingston, 1965—; anti-nuclear adv., Women for non-Nuclear Future, 1980—. Peace emissary to USSR, Bridges for Peace, 1986. Address: 41 Stonehenge Kingston RI 02881

LEVENDOSKY, CHARLES LEONARD, b. Bronx, NY, July 4, 1936, s. Charles Leonard and Laura (Gregorio) L.; m. Charlotte Anne, July 15, 1960; children—Alytia Akiko, Ixchel Nicole. Author poetry books and chapbooks: perimeters, 1970, Small Town America, 1974, Words & Fonts, 1975, Aspects of the Vertical, 1978, Distances, 1980, Wyoming Fragments, 1981, Nocturnes, 1982, Hands and Other Poems, 1986; contrbr. poetry to anthologies: Breakthrough Fictioneers, 1972, Traveling America with Today's Poets, 1977, Point Riders Press Anthology of Great Plains Poetry, 1981, 48 Younger American Poets, 1982; contrbr. poetry: N.Y. Qtly, Poetry Now, Am. Poetry Rvw, numerous other lit mags. BS in Physics, U. Okla., 1958, BA in Math, 1960; MA in Edn., NYU, 1963. Mem. faculty NYU, NYC, 1967-72; poet-in-residence Wyo. Council on Arts, Casper, 1972-82; ed. editorial page Casper (Wyo.) Star-Tribune, 1982—. Founder, dir. Poetry Programs Wyo., 1973-78; mem. selection comm. Gov.'s Award for Arts, Cheyenne, 1985-86; mem. Gov.'s Comm. on Children's Services, Cheyenne, 1985-86. Librettist fellow NEA, 1974; recipient commn. Ga. Council for Arts, 1975, Silver medal for book design Internationale Buchkunst-Austellung, Leipzig, 1977, Award for Arts, Gov. of Wyo., 1983, Column Writing award Wyo. Press Assn., 1986, Friend of Education Awards, Wyoming Education Assoc., 1987, Wyoming Governor's Award for the Arts, 1987, John Phillip Immroth Memorial Award for Intellectual Freedom, Intellectual Freedom Round Table of the American Library Assn., 1987. Mem. PEN, P&W, AWP, Nat. Soc. Columnists. Home: Box 3033 Casper WY 82602

LEVENSON, FRED BARRY, b. Buffalo, Nov. 12, 1955. Asst. ed., contrbr. Blatherskite, 1981; ed. Western New York Printed Matter Catalog, 1985; contrbr. to ARTicles, The Grin, Swift Kick, pure light, Tempus Fugit. Wrkg. on poems. Student Niagara County Community Coll., 1973-74. Recording sec. Niagara-Erie Wrtrs., Buffalo, 1983, asst. ed., 1984-85, mem. bd., 1986—. Mem. P&W. Home: 385 DeWitt St Buffalo NY 14213

LEVENSON, JORDAN, b. Los Angeles, s. Max and Hilda Judith (Rothstein) L. Author, pub.: Retail Fruit Species: Your Shopper's Guide to their Best Varieties, 1972, 2d ed., 1979, The Back Lot: Motion Picture Studio Laborer's Craft Described by a Hollywood Laborer, 1972, Abilities of Refracting Telescope Optics: A "Nonmathematical" Understanding for Buyers and Users, 1973, Vitamins: A Systems Analysis Solution to the Doctor vs. Health Faddist Controversy, 1974, Underlying Concepts of Room Lighting for the Intelligent Layman, 1974, Underlying Concepts of Room Acoustical Control for the Intelligent Layman, 1976, rev. ed., 1979, Poor Man's Route to Rich Man's Stock Market Wealth, 1980, How to Buy and Understand Refracting Telescopes, 1981, Irish in Memoriam Poetry: The Book of Tears (ed. "Jordan O'Levenson"), 1983, Your

First Trip to Europe, 1985. BS, Calif. State U.-Los Angeles, 1966; MBA, U. So. Calif., 1970. Pub., ed., author Levenson Press, Los Angeles, 1972—; prin. Levenson Importing and Exporting, Los Angeles, 1977—. Mem. Book Publicists So. Calif. Address: Box 19606 Los Angeles CA 90019

LEVENTHAL, ANN Z., b. NYC, Jan. 28, 1936; d. Samuel and Sadie (Krellenstein) Zinman; m. H. David Leventhal, Aug. 28, 1955; children—Amy, Adam, Max, Seth. Author: Life Lines (novel), 1986, All By Herself (children's book), 1986; contrbr. articles, rvws., poems to Publishers Weekly, The Writer Pacific Rvw, Rubicon, The Fiddlehead, Vanderbilt Rvw, Crow Call, R.I. Rvw, Maenad, Radcliffe Qtly, Hartford Courant, Saturday's Women, Vietnam Flashbacks, New Women's Times, others. BS, St. Joseph Coll., 1957; MFA, Goddard Coll., 1980. Columnist and ed. The Westender, Hartfoed, Conn., 1975-78; coordinator Trinity Coll. Women's Ctr., Hartford, 1976-77; investigative reporter WTIC-TV, Hartford, 1979; aerobic dance instr., YMCA, Hartford, 1985—. Mem. Intl. Women's Writing Guild, AAP, Writers and Pubs. Against Nuclear Arms, Friends of P&W. Address: 19 Woodside Cr Hartford CT 06105

LEVERING, DONALD WARREN, b. Kansas City, KS, June 19, 1949. Author: (poetry) The Jack of Spring, 1980; Carpool, 1983; Outcroppings from Navajoland, 1985. BA, Baker U., 1971; MFA, Bowling Green State U., 1978. Various blue collar and teaching positions, Portland, Oreg., Kansas City, Mo., Safford, Ariz., Crownpoint, N.Mex., 1971-83; computer operator State of N.Mex., Sante Fe, 1985. Pamphlet wrtr. Crownpoint Citizens' Alliance, N.Mex., 1980-82. Devine Meml. fellow Bowling Green State U., 1977; NEA fellow, 1984. Home: 2503 Alamosa Dr Santa Fe NM 87505

LEVERTOV, DENISE, b. Ilford, Eng., Oct. 24, 1923; came to U.S., 1949; m. Mitchell Goodman, 1947; 1 son. Author: (poetry) The Double Image, 1946, Here and Now, 1957, Overland to the Islands, 1958, With Eyes at the Back of Our Heads, 1959, The Jacob's Ladder, 1961, O Taste and See: New Poems, 1964, The Sorrow Dance, 1967, Penguin Modern Poets 9 (with Kenneth Rexroth and William Carlos Williams), 1967, Relearning the Alphabet, 1970, To Stay Alive, 1971, Footprints, 1972, The Freeing of the Dust, 1975, Life in the Forest, 1978, Collected Earlier Poems, 1940-1960, 1979, Candles in Babylon, 1982, Oblique Prayers, 1984, Breathing the Water, 1987, other ltd. editions; (essays) The Poet in the World, 1973, Light Up the Cave, 1981; editor: Out of the War Shadow: An Anthology of Current Poetry, 1967; editor and trans. (with Edward C. Dimock, Jr.) In Praise of Krishna: Songs from the Bengali, 1967; trans. Selected Poems of Guillevic, 1969. Vis. Lectr. Drew U., 1965, U. Calif.-Berkeley, 1969; tchr. CCNY, 1965, Vassar Coll., 1966-67; vis. prof. MIT, Cambridge, 1969-70; U. Cin., 1973; prof. Tufts U., Medford, Mass., 1973-79; poet-in-residence Brandeis U., Waltham, Mass., 1981-83; prof. Stanford U., Calif., 1981—. Guggenheim fellow, 1962; Natl. Inst. Arts and Letters grantee, 1966; Elmer Holmes Bobst award, 1983. Mem. AAIAL, Academie Mallarme (corr.). Office: New Directions 80 8th Ave New York NY 10011

LEVI, JAN HELLER, b. NYC, May 9, 1954; d. J. Elliot and Marjory (Weinberg) Levi; m. Ken Sofer. Contrbr. poetry to Pequod, Socialist Rvw, Iowa Rvw, Beloit Poetry Jnl, Sojourner, Ploughshares, 13th Moon; contrbr. to anthologies: Extended Outlooks, 1982, Secret Destinations, 1985; contrbr. fiction to Redbook; founder and ed. Flamingo Press. BA, Sarah Lawrence Coll., 1977. Asst. ed. Dell Pub., NYC, 1977-78; personal asst. poet Muriel Rukeyser, NYC, 1978-80; dir. pub. relations Sarah Lawrence Coll., Bronxville, NY, 1981-83; freelance writer, NYC, 1983—. Address: 25 Tudor City Pl Apt 615 New York NY 10017

LEVI, STEVEN C., (Warren Sitka), b. Chgo., Dec. 9, 1948; s. Mario and Janice (Houghton) L. Author: Committee of Vigilance, The San Francisco Chamber of Commerce Law and Order Committee 1916-1919 1984, The Pacific Rim (textbook), 1987, Sourdough Journalist (as Warren Sitka), 1984; author poetry books: Alaskan Phantasmagoria, 1978, The Last Raven, 1979, The Phantom Bowhead, 1979, We Alaskans, 1980, Fish-Fed Maize, 1981, Our National Tapestry (natl. chapbook competition winner), 1986; contrbr. numerous articles: Alaska Jnl. Commerce, Pacific Historian, Take Me Away, Pacific Flyer, other publs. BA in History, U. Calif.-Davis, 1970; MA in History, San Jose State Coll., 1973. Feature wrtr. Alaska Bus. and Industry, Horizons Monthly, Travelhost, numerous other publs., 1981—; co-ed. Harpoon, 1978-81; ed. Alaska Host, 1980-81; columnist Horizons Mag., 1980—. Home: 8512 E 4th ST Anchorage AK 99504

LEVI, TONI MERGENTIME, b. NYC, July 29, 1941; d. Lloyd and Charlotte (Lief) Mergentime; m. Paul Alan Levi, Oct. 29, 1967; 1 child, Rebecca A. Contrbr. poems to Anthol. of Mag. Verse and Yrbk. of American Poetry, 1986-87, Kans., Apalachee qtlys, Electrum, Tex., S.D. rvws, Swallow's Tale, Blueline, Xanadu, small Pond 1986-87, Sing Heavenly Muse, Blind Alleys, Thirteen, Wind, Poem, others; prize-winning opera librettist, Thanksgiving. AB, Cornell U., 1963, MA, Syracuse U. Schl. of Journalism, 1966; Moblzn. for Youth, NYC, 1965-68; freelance wrtr./ed., 1968-76; dir. devel. NYC Schl. Vol. Program, 1976—. Mem. Natl. Soc. Fund Raising Execs, Women in Communications, Phi Beta Kappa. Home: 105 W 73d St New York NY 10023

LEVIN, AMY BETH, b. Bklyn., Jan. 11, 1942; d. Herbert Daniel Suesholtz and Shirley (Burrows) Alter; m. Robert J. Levin, May 10, 1967 (dec. May 1976); m. 2d, Arthur M. Cooper, June 9, 1979. BA, Syracuse U., 1963. Asst. ed. Redbook Mag., NYC, 1964-65, assoc. ed., 1966-70, sr. ed., 1971-76, assoc. arts. ed., 1976-78; arts. ed. Ladies Home Jnl, NYC, 1978-80; ed.-in-chief Mademoiselle Mag., NYC, 1978—. Citation for genl. excellence, ASJA, 1982. Office: Mademoiselle 350 Madison Ave New York NY 10017

LEVIN, DAN, b. Simferopol, Russia (now USSR), Mar. 7, 1914, came to U.S., 1921, Author: Mask of Glory, 1949, 3d ed., 1985, The Dream in the Flesh, 1953, Son of Judah (transl. to Spanish and German), 1961, Stormy Petrel: The Life and Work of Maxim Gorky, 1964, (Brit. ed., 1965), 3d ed., 1985, Spinoza, 1970. Address: Box 540 North Bellmore NY 11710

LEVIN, DAVID, b. York, PA, Nov. 21, 1924; s. Louis and Rose (Braufman) L.; m. Patricia Marker, July 12, 1945; children—David, Rebecca. Author: What Happened in Salem?, 1952, History as Romantic Art, 1959, In Defense of Historical Literature, 1967, Cotton Mather, 1978; ed. France and England in North America (Francis Parkman), 1983; mem. editorial bd.: Am. Qtly, 1969-72, Am. Literature, 1970-73, Clio, 1971—. AB, Harvard U., 1947, AM, 1949, PhD, 1955. Instr. to prof. English, Stanford U., 1952-71; Commonwealth prof. English, U. VA, Charlottesville, 1971—; Charles Warren research fellow, Harvard, 1976-77. Served with USAAF, 1943-46. Fulbright Exchange lectr., 1956-57; sr. fellow NEH, 1968-69. Mem. MLA, AAUP. Home: Rt 2 Box 311 Charlottesville VA 22901

LEVIN, IRA, b. NYC, Aug. 27, 1929; s. Charles and Beatrice (Schlansky) L.; m. Gabrielle Aronsohn, Aug. 20, 1960 (div. 1968); children—Adam, Jared, Nicholas; m. 2d, Phyllis Finkel, Aug. 26, 1979 (div. 1982). Author novels: A Kiss Before Dying, 1953, Rosemary's Baby, 1967, This Perfect Day, 1970, The Stepford Wives, 1972, The Boys from Brazil, 1976; author plays: No Time for Sergeants, 1955, Interlock, 1958, Critic's Choice, 1960, General Seeger, 1962, Drat! The Cat, 1965, Dr. Cook's Garden, 1967, Veronica's Room, 1973, Deathtrap, 1978, Break a Leg, 1979. AB, NYU, 1950. Free-lance writer, 1950—. Served with U.S. Army, 1953-55. Edgar Allan Poe award, 1954, 80. Office: Ober Assocs 40 E 49th St New York NY 10017

LEVIN, STEVE, see Rafalsky, Stephen Mark

LEVINE, HERBERT MALCOLM, b. NYC, Sept. 11, 1933; s. Jacob and Bella (Wilensky) L. Author: Challenge of Controversy, 1985. Ed.: Point-Counterpoint, 1981, 2d. ed., 1983, The Politics of State and Local Government Debated, 1985, World Politics Debated, 1983, 2d ed., 1986, Political Issues Debated, 1982, 2d ed., 1987, Public Administration Debated, 1988; (with David Carlton) The Nuclear Arms Race Debated, 1986, The Cold War Debatd, 1988; (with Jean Edward Smith) Civil Liberties and Civil Rights Debated, 1988. Wrkg. on editing 3d ed. of World Politics Debated and 3d ed. of Point-Counterpoint. A.B., Columbia Coll., 1955; Ph.D. in Political Sci., Columbia U., 1969. Asst. prof. political sci. U. Southwestern La., Lafayete, 1965-69, assoc. prof., 1969-74, prof. 1974-85; freelance wrtr., 1985—. Mem. AG. Address: 5500 Friendship Blvd N1608 Chevy Chase MD 20815

LEVINE, JANET, b. Johannesburg, S.Africa, Dec. 16, 1945; d. Solly and Eileen (Rosenberg) Berman; m. Franklin S. Levine, July 26, 1971; children—Roger S., Anthony J. Contrbr.: Strategic Investment, 1986; contrbr. articles: New York Times Magazine, Yale Rvw, Milton Mag., Boston Phoenix, Boston Globe, numerous jnls. and newspapers in S. Africa; columnist The Post, Soweto, S.Africa, 1978-79. Wrkg. on, hist. novel; political memoir to be published fall 1988. BA with honors in English, U. Witwatersrand, 1968. Freelance wrtr., tchr., S. Africa, 1964-84; freelance wrtr., Mass., 1984-86; tchr., wrtr. Milton Acad. (Mass.), 1986—; elected city councillor Johannesburg, S.Africa, 1977-84; cons. 2-hr. documentary of S.Africa, PBS, 1986; lectr. in field. Home: 230 Atherton St Milton MA 02186

LEVINE, JUDITH L., see Wallis, Judith Laura Levine

LEVINE, MARK LEONARD, b. Bath, ME, Mar. 6, 1945; s. Saul and Sophie (Greenblatt) L. Co-editor: The Tales of Hoffman, 1970, The Complete Book of Bible Quotations, 1986; contrbg. editor: Small Press (R.R. Bowker); contrbr. articles to Writers Digest and Small Press. AB, Columbia Coll., 1966; JD, NYU, 1969; MS, Columbia U., Schl. of Jnlsm., 1979. Lawyer, NYC, 1969—; pub. Scarf Press NYC, 1979—. Mem. Am. Book Producers Assn. (bd.

dirs. 1984—), AG. Home: 58 E 83d St New York NY 10028

LEVINE, PHILIP, b. Detroit, Jan. 10, 1928; s. A. Harry and Esther Gertrude (Priscol) L.; m. Frances Artley, July 14, 1954; children—Mark, John, Teddy. Author: On the Edge, 1963, Not This Pig, 1968, Pili's Wall, 1971, Red Dust, 1971, They Feed The Lion, 1972, On The Edge & Over, 1976, The Names of the Lost, 1976, 7 Years from Somewhere, 1979 (Natl. Book Critics Circle award), Ashes, 1979 (Natl. Book Critics Circle award, Am. Book award), One for the Rose, 1981, Selected Poems, 1984, Sweet Will, 1985; ed.: (with W. Trejo) The Selected Poems of Jaime Sabines, (with Ada Long) Off the Map, The Selected Poems of Gloria Fuertes. BA, Wayne State U., 1950, AM, 1955; MFA, U. IA, 1957. Instr. U. IA, 1955-57; from instr. to prof. English, CA State U., Fresno, 1958—; prof. English, Tufts U., 1981—. Chmn. lit. bd., NEA, 1984-85. Guggenheim fellow, 1973-74, 80; AAAL award, 1973; Lenore marshall award best Am. book of poems, 1976; NEA grantee. Named outstanding prof. CA State U. System, 1972. Home: 4549 N Van Ness Fresno CA 93704

LEVINE, SAMUEL PAUL, b. NYC, June 10, 1911; m. Florence Fern, Oct. 20, 1941 (dec. 1964); m. 2d, Lucy Snapp, Feb. 22, 1977. Author: Soft Cell in a Discount House, 1965, Ham—Kosher Style!, 1979; feature columns: Consumers Dilemma, USA, The Consumer Wants to Know. Cert., Acad. Adv. Traffic, NYC, 1933; registered practitioner, ICC, Wash., 1932. Traffic mgr. H.L. Green Co., NYC,1929-41; appliance mgr. White Front stores, Canoga Pk., Calif., 1957-74; freelance writer Temecula, Calif., 1974—. Address: 42367 Cosmic Dr Rancho Temecula CA 92390

LEVINE, VICKI LUCILLE, b. Bournemouth, Eng., Apr. 17, 1927, came to U.S.A., 1946; d. Charles Henry and Elsie Rose (Samuels) Charles; m. Nathan Levine, Sept. 13, 1953; children—Toby Matlee Levine Bersak, Karen Rachel Levine Bartels. Contrbr. to Pegasus, Monmouth Rvw, other lit, publs. Wrkg. on book of poetry. BA summa cum laude, Monmouth Coll., 1985. Home: 105 Townsend Dr Middletown NJ 07748

LEVINSOHN, FLORENCE HAMLISH, b. Chgo.; d. Emil and Ethel (Finklestein) Hamlish; m. David Levinsohn, Sept. 9, 1955 (div. June, 1965); children—Julie Moore, Ann Porter. Author: Harold Washington: A Political Biography, 1983, What Teenagers Want to Know, 1960, The Art of Aging, 1961; editor: School Desegregation: Shadow and Substance, 1974, Financing the Learning Society, 1975, Changing Women in a Changing Society, 1968. Managing ed., Am. Journal of Sociology, Chgo., 1968-78; managing ed., In These Times, Chgo., 1978-79; edit./publ., Lincoln Park Spectator, Chgo., 1984-85; freelance wrtr./edit., Chgo., 1978—, articles, reviews, essays mainly in Chicago pubns., fiction and poetry in lit mags. BA, Roosevelt U.; MA; U. of IL. Mem. NWU. Home: 1321 W Sunnyside Chicago IL 60640

LEVITAS, GLORIA B(ARACH), b. NYC, March 2, 1931; d. Albert Samuel and Sylvia (Schnall) Barach; m. Mitchel Levitas, Dec. 24, 1950; children: Anthony, Daniel. Author: ed, The World of Psychology, 1962, ed, The World of Psychoanalysis, 1965, ed, Culture and Consciousness: Perspectives in the Social Sciences, 1967, ed (with Frank and Jacqueline Vivelo) American Indian Prose and Poetry: We Wait in Darkness, 1974, ed (with Helen Icken Sofa) Social Problems in Corporate America, 1975, Economic Transformation and Steady-State Values, 1976. Contrbr of articles and book rvws to Playboy, New York Times, New York Times Mag, N.Y. Times Book Rvw, New York Tribune, Washington Post, Change, and Man/Environment Systems. BA, Brooklyn Coll (now Brooklyn Coll of the City Univ of N.Y.), 1950; Ph.D., Rutgers Univ, 1980. Asst ed, Mercury Pubs, NYC., 1952-58; editorial cons, George Braziller, NYC., 1960-66; asst. prof. in anthropology, Queens Coll of the City Univ of N.Y., Flushing, N.Y., 1972—. Publs dir of Ethical Education for N.Y. Soc for Ethical Culture, 1970-71. Member: American Anthropological Assn, N.Y. Acad of Scis. Home: 229 West 78th St New York NY 10024

LEVITT, PETER, b. NYC, Sept. 2, 1946; s. Jesse and Tilia (Hoffman); m. Joan Iten Sutherland; 1 dau., Sheba. Author: Homage: Leda as Virgin, A Book of Light, 1982, Running Grass (Poems 1970-77), Two Bodies Dark/Velvet, 1975; contrbr. poems, short stories and trans. (Chinese and Spanish) to many lit mags; co-ed. Choice, 1972-73. BA in English, SUNY-Buffalo, 1970, MA, 1971. Peace activist. Mem. P&W. Address: 3134 Los Flores Canyon Rd Malibu CA 90265

LEVITT, SUSAN B., b. Bklyn., June 27, 1953; d. Irving and Charlotte (Moldauer) Baker; m. Steven R. Levitt, Apr. 11, 1976; 1 son, Robert. Guide ed., contrbr. to Parentguide Mag. BS, tchr. handicapped, Trenton State Coll., 1975; MA, reading spclst., Kean Coll., 1980. Tchr., Woodbridge (NJ) Bd. Edn., 1975-82. Home: 1283 Madison Hill Rd Rahway NJ 07065

LEVY, CAROL, b. Lynn, MA, Apr. 13, 1931; d. Samuel and Helen (Alpers) L. BA, Syracuse U., 1952. Mem. staff The Reporter mag., 1952-53, True mag., 1953-54; with spcl. svcs. U.S. Army, 1954-56; mem. staff Forbes mag., 1957-61; research ed. Dun's Rvw, NYC, 1961-62, sr. ed., 1963-69, asst. mng. ed., 1969-71, mng. ed., 1971—. Home: 10 Downing St New York NY 10014

LEVY, LARRY, b. Rochester, NY, Sept. 23, 1947; s. Leo and Evelyn (Rivenson) L.; m. Cheryl Kern, Aug. 23, 1969; children—Matthew Dale, Kathryn Cynthia. Contrbr. poems, articles on edn. to mags., anthol.; contrbr. chpt. to What Makes Writing Good, 1984. Wrkg. on essays, articles on teaching, ed., Writing Across the Curriculum. B.A., Ohio Weleyan U., 1969; M.A., U. Wyo., 1974. Instr. Muscatine Commun. Coll., IA, 1974-77; assoc. Prof. English, Delta Coll., University Center, MI, 1977—. Pres. Grace Dow Library Friends of Library, Midland, MI, 1979-80. Recipient Poetry prize Ohio Weleyan U., 1969, U. Wy., 1974; Issue award Poet & Critic, 1976. Mem. NCTE, Mich. Council Tchrs. English. Home: 18 Brown CT Midland MI 48640

LEVY, LEONARD WILLIAMS, b. Toronto, Ont., Can., Apr. 9, 1923; s. Albert and Rae (Williams) L.; m. Elyse Gitlow, Oct. 21, 1944; children—Wendy Ellen, Leslie Anne. Author: The Law of the Commonwealth and Chief Justice Shaw, 1957, Legacy of Suppression: Freedom of Speech and Press in Early Am. Hist., 1960, Jefferson and Civil Liberties: The Darker Side, 1963, Origins of the Fifth Amendment, 1968 (Pulitzer prize in hist. 1969, 2d. ed., 1987), Judgments: Essays on Am. Constl. Hist., 1972, Against The Law: The Nixon Court and Criminal Justice, 1974, Treason Against God: Hist. of the Offense of Blasphemy, 1981, Emergence of a Free Press, 1985 Sigma Delta Chi prize for best journalism history; Obeler Award, Am. Library Assn, best book in intellectual history), Constitutional Opinions, 1986, The Establishment Clause: Religion and the First Amendment, 1986; ed.: Major Crises in Am. Hist., 1962, The Am. Polit. Process, 1963, The Presidency, 1964, The Congress, 1964, The Judiciary, 1964, Parties and Pressure Groups, 1964, Freedom of the Press from Zenger to Jefferson, 1966, Am. Constl. Law, 1966, Judicial Rvw. and the Supreme Ct., 1967, Freedom and Reform, 1967, Essays on The Making of the Constn., 1969, The Fourteenth Amendment and the Bill of Rights, 1970, The Supreme Court Under Earl Warren, 1972, Jim Crow in Boston, 1974, Essays on the Early Republic, 1974, Blasphemy in Mass., 1974; ed.-in-chief, Encyclopedia of the American Constitution, 4 vols., 1986; genl. ed.: Am. Heritage Series, 60 vols., Harper Documentary Hist. of West. Civiln., 40 vols.; editorial bd. John Marshall Papers, Rvws. in Am. Hist.; contrbr. to profl. jnls. BS, Columbia U., 1947, MA, 1948, PhD, 1951. Research asst. Columbia U., 1950-51; from instr. to prof. Brandeis U., 1951-70, first incumbent Earl Warren chair constl. hist., 1957-70, dean Grad. Schl. Arts and Scis., 1958-63, dean faculty Arts and Scis., 1963-66; Andrew W. Mellon prof. humanities, hist., chmn. grad. faculty hist. Claremont (CA) Grad. Schl., 1970—. Served with AUS, 1943-46. Guggenheim fellow, 1957-58; NEH sr. fellow, 1974. Mem. Am. Soc. Legal Hist. Am. Hist. Assn., Org. of Am. Historians, Soc. of Am. Historians, Am. Antiquarian Soc. Pulitzer prize juror, chmn. biog. jury 1974, hist. jury 1976. Home: 1630 Tulane Rd Claremont CA 91711

LEVY, ROBERT, b. NYC, Oct. 1, 1926; s. Mack and Reggy (Steinbrecher) L.; m. Corinne Schlissel, Apr. 26, 1953; children—Randall Mark, Meredith Robin. BS, CCNY, 1949. Sr. ed. Tide mag., NYC, 1950-53; contrbg. ed. Time mag., NYC, 1953-55; sr. ed. Forbes mag., NYC, 1955-59; v.p. Manning Pub. Relations Firm, NYC, 1960-63; dir. pub. relations Elgin Watch Co., NYC, 1963-64; sr. assoc. Ruder & Finn, NYC, 1965; sr. ed. Dun's Review, NYC, 1966-86; sr. ed. Business Month, NYC, 1987—;. Served with USAAF, World War II. Mem. N.Y. Financial Writers Assn. Home: 42 Wedgewood Dr Westbury NY 11590

LEVY, ROBERT JEFFREY, b. NYC, Jan. 31, 1956, s. Stanley Donald Levy and Joan Doris (Goldberg) Phillips; m. Kari Elizabeth Jenson, Oct. 18, 1980. Poetry in Confrontations, Georgia, Pequod, Rvw, Hollins Critic, Quarterly West, Michigan Qtly Rvw, Yankee, Poetry Now, Prairie Schooner, others. Author: Whistle Maker 1987, The Glitter Bait, 1986. BA, St. John's College, Annapolis, MD, 1978; MA, Oxford U., Oxford, England, 1980. Proofreader, Woman's Day Magazine, NYC, 1980-82; editor/wrtr., House Beautiful Magazine, 1982-85; assoc. ed. United Media, 1986—. Awards: Celia B. Wagner Award, PSA, 1984; Gordon Barber Award, PSA, 1983, Open Voice Award, West Side YMCA, 1987. Mem. PSA, P&W. Home: 785 West End Ave New York NY 10025

LEVY, STEPHEN, b. Bklyn., May 11, 1947; s. Morris and Bessie (Barouch) L; m. Ellen Bettina Eichel, Mar. 16, 1975; 1 son, Mordechai Salomon Levy-Eichel. Contrbr. to anthology: Voices Within the Ark: The Modern Jewish Poets, 1980. Author: Many Hands: A Gathering of Sephardic Songs and Proverbs with a Poem, in Judezmo and English, 1982. Translator: A Guide to Reading and Writing Judezmo, 1975. Co-ed., co-pub., Adelantre! The Judezmo Soc.,

1975—. Grantee: Change, Inc., 1975, Meml. Fdn. for Jewish Culture, 1979. Home: 106 W 13th St New York NY 10011

LEWIN, LEONARD C., (L.L. Case), b. NYC, Oct. 2, 1916, s. M.G. and Eva (Case) L.; children—Michael Z., Julie E. Author: A Treasury of American Political Humor, 1964, Report from Iron Mountain, 1967, Triage, 1972; contrbr. to various periodicals. Wrkg. on fiction. BA, Harvard U., 1936. Freelance wrtr., 1963—. Mem. AG, PEN, ASJA. Home: 6 Long Hill Farm Guilford CT 06437

LEWIN, REBECCA, b. Dover, NJ, May 5, 1954, d. Leo and Joyce (Cohen) Lewin. Contrbr. to: Newsday, Womanews, Samisdat, New York Native, numerous other publs. BA, Syracuse U., 1977; MA, CCNY, 1981. Editorial assoc. Fiction mag., 1982; book ed. New Directions for Women, 1986. Recipient Woolrich Award fellowship Columbia U., 1980, Bennett Cerf award, 1980, Goodman Fund Prize for Extended Fiction, CCNY, 1981, PEN Syndication Fiction award, NEA-PEN, 1985. Mem. P&W, NWU, Feminist Wrtrs. Guild (steering com. 1979-81). Home: 203 W 107th St New York NY 10025

LEWIS, ANN, see Lange, Augusta Ann

LEWIS, ANNA, see Wilbert, Felicia Fibo

LEWIS, CECIL PAUL, see Lewis, Jack

LEWIS, DAVID LANIER, b. Bethalto, IL, Apr. 5, 1927, s. Donald F. and Edith (Jinkinson) L.; m. Florence Yuri Tanaka, Apr. 5, 1953; children—Kim, Leilani, Sumiko, Lance. Author: The Public Image of Henry Ford: An American Folk Hero and His Company, 1976, The Automobile and American Culture, 1983, Ford: 1903 to 1984, 1984; assoc. ed., columnist Cars & Parts; contrbg. ed. Model T. Times. BS, U. IL, 1948, MS, Boston U., 1955; MA, U.MI, 1956, PhD, 1959; Fulbright scholar London Schl. Econs., 1956-57. Rptr. Edwardsville (IL) Intelligencer, 1948; bur. chief, state ed. Alton (IL) Telegraph, 1948-50; ed. employee publs. St. Louis Lincoln-Mercury Plant, 1950-51; press relations rep. Borden Co., NYC, 1952, Ford Motor Co., Dearborn, MI, 1952-55; pub. rels. exec. Gen. Mtrs. Corp., Detroit, 1959-65; assoc. prof. bus. hist. U. MI, Ann Arbor, 1965-68, prof., 1968—; mem. exec. com. U. MI Press, 1979-82. Served with USNR, 1945-46. Mem. Soc. Automotive Historians. Trustee Natl. Automotive Hist. Collectn. Home: 2588 Hawthorn St Ann Arbor MI 48104

LEWIS, DOUGLAS, b. Centreville, MS, Apr. 30, 1938. s. Charles Douglas and Beatrice Fenwick (Stewart) L. Author: The Late Baroque Churches of Venice, 1979, The Drawings of Andrea Palladio, 1981. BA in Art History, Yale U., 1960, MA, 1963, PhD, 1967; BA in Fine Arts, Clare Coll., Cambridge (Eng.) U., 1962, MA, 1966. Asst. instr. Yale U., 1962-64; asst. prof. art Bryn Mawr Coll., 1967-68; adj. prof. Johns Hopkins U., 1973-77; vis. lectr. with rank of prof., Georgetown Univ., 1980—curator sculpture Natl. Gallery Art, Washington, 1968—. Copley medal Natl. Portrait Gallery, 1981. Mem. Am. Soc. Archtl. Historians, Natl. Trust Historic Preservation. Mem. natl. citizens stamp adv. com. U.S. Postal Svc. Office: Natl Gallery of Art Washington DC 20565

LEWIS, GREGG ALLAN, b. Ann Arbor, MI, Apr. 30, 1951; s. Ralph Loren and Margie Alma (Miller) L.; m. Deborah Ruth Shaw, Mar. 9, 1973; children—Andrew, Matthew, Lisette, Benjamine. Ed., Campus Life Mag., 1977—; contrbr. articles to num. relig. & secular mags.; author: Telegarbage, 1977, The Hurting Parent, 1980, Inductive Preaching, 1984, Am I Alive?, 1986. BA, Asbury Coll., 1973; MA, Wheaton Coll, 1977. Assoc. ed. Jr. High Pubns., David C. Cook Pub., Elgin, IL, 1973-76; assoc. ed.Campus Life Mag., Carol Stream, IL, 1977-79, ed., 79-84, sr. ed., 1984—. Mem. Evangelical Press Assn. Office: Campus Life 465 Gundersen Carol Stream IL 60188

LEWIS, HARRIET (HATTIE), b. Greenwood, SC, May 18, 1905; d. John Harklin and Daphne G. (Moore) Griffin; m. W. Bernard Lewis, Jan. 25, 1921; children: Bernard, Frederick, Earl, Victoria, Rosalie. Author: The Night of Joseph's Lamentation and Joy, 1974, The Tempter, 1976; contrbr. anthologies, 1979-85. Wrkg. on novels. Founder, Jamaica Excelsior Club, Inc., 1948. Mem. New York State Community Theatre, Negro Actors Guild of America (life member). Home: Springfield Gardens NY

LEWIS, HARRY, b. Bklyn., Nov. 10, 1942, s. Sol and Sylvia (Pincus) L.; m. Barbara Berman, Dec. 26, 1966 (div. 1969); m. 2d, Estelle Rae Press, June 8, 1983. Author: Crab Cantos, 1969, Before and After Abraham, 1971, Spring, 1975, Home Cooking, 1976, The Candy Store, 1978, Babies, 1979, Hudson (1-16), 1980, The Well springs, 1982; ed. mags.: Mulch, 1970-76, Number, 1976-80, Jnl. Mind and Behavior, 1985—. MA, PhD-ABD, NYU, 1969; MSW, Fordham U., 1980. Pvt. practice character analyst-psychoanalyst, NYC, 1980—; mem. social sci. faculty New Sch. Social Research, NYC, 1982—; mem. psychology faculty Coll. Human Services, NYC, 1982—. Home: 115 Morton St New York NY 10014

LEWIS, JACK (CECIL PAUL LEWIS), b. N. English, IA, Nov. 13, 1924; s. Cecil Howell and Winifred (Warner) L.; children—Dana Claudia, Brandon Paul. Author 8 novels, 15 other books, 11 TV shows, 7 motion pictures; contrbr. articles to mags. BA, State U. IA, 1949. Rptr. Santa Ana (CA) Register, 1949-50; motion picture writer Monogram Pictures, 1950; rptr. Daily Pilot, Costa Mesa, CA, 1956-57; ed. Challenge Pub., N. Hollywood, CA, 1957-60; pres. Gallant/Charger Pub., Inc., 1960—. Ed. Gun World, 1960—ð., pub., Horse and Horseman, Bow and Arrow, Fishing and Boating, Fishing and Boating Illus. Decorated Bronze Star, Air Medal (3), Meritorious Svc. Medal. Mem. WG, U.S. Marine Corps Combat Corrs. Assn. Home: 405 Avenida Teresa San Clemente CA 92672

LEWIS, JANET, see Winters, Janet Lewis

LEWIS, JOHN (EARL), b. Provo, UT, Dec. 23, 1931; s. Walter E. and Marie (Burt) L.; m. Carolyn Coles, Sept. 24, 1953; children: Lynn Anne, John R., Jeannine. Author: novels: Vengeance Is Mine, 1975, The Man Called Sam, 1975, The Silver Mine Trail, 1979, Escape to Fort Bridge 1980, The Guns of Tombstone, 1980, Utah Vengeance, 1981, The Valiant Die but Once, 1981, The Fallen Badge, 1982, Six-Gun Mission, 1983, Railroad Guns, 1983, The Lost Mine, 1983, Guns in the Sand, 1983, The Angry Marshal, 1984, The Evil Brothers, 1984, Along the Overland Trail, 1986, Guns Across the Border, 1987. Contrbr of more than fifty articles to National Guardsman, Christian Science Monitor, and Supervision. BS, Brigham Young Univ, 1953; grad study at Brigham Young Univ, 1957-59, and at Univ of Utah, 1960-61. Utah State Dept. of Employment Security, 1954—, began as asst personnel dir in Salt Lake City, currently asst personnel dir and lead interviewer in Provo. Member: Intl Assn of Personnel in Employment Security (v.p. Utah chapter, 1965), Reserve Officers Assn (pres of central Utah chapter, 1975—). Freedoms Fndn essay awards, 1970, 1972. Military service: U.S. Army Reserve, 1950-84; ret as colonel. Home: 682 West 40 North Orem UT 84057

LEWIS, JUDY JONES, b. Middlesboro, KY, Nov. 12, 1956; d. Carl John and Myrle Jean (Kelly) Jones; m. Joe Rogers Lewis, May 18, 1985. Contrbr. articles to newspapers. Wrkg. on reporting in Eastern Ky.'s mountain region. Studen U. Ky., 1974-79. Recipient Best Investigative Story award Ky. Press Assn., 1984, Best News Story award, 1984. Home: HC 61 Box 2010 Hyden KY 41749

LEWIS, LINDA WARD, b. River, KY, Aug. 20, 1945; d. Carl and Sarah Jane (Preston) Ward; m. W. Lavon Lewis, July 8, 1968; 1 child, Stacey A. Ed. Intl. Jnl. Gynecology and Obstetrics, 1974-76, Cat Fancy, Dog Fancy, Horse Illustrated, Bird Talk, Pet Health News. BA, Eastern Ky. U., 1966, MA in English, 1967. Sr. ed. Intl. Fertility Research Program, Chapel Hill, N.C., 1972-76; editorial dir. Fancy Publs., San Juan Capistrano, Calif., 1977—. Home: 27022 Peciados Mission Viejo CA 92691

LEWIS, LOIS FULLER, b. Lancaster, OH, May 4, 1930; d. Roland Andrew and Judith Edith (Kelman) Fuller; m. William Braley Lewis, Aug. 12, 1951; children—Clifford Fuller, Robin Ann. Contrbr. short stories to children's mags. B.Sc. in Elem. Edn., Ohio State U., 1951; M.Edn. in Reading, Kent State U., 1972. Elem. tchr. Wooster Schls., Oh, 1954-55; reading tchr. Ravenna Schls., OH, 1969-86, retired. Coord. Bill Delaney Workshop for Wrtrs., Ravenna, 1986-87. Home: 515 E Main St Ravenna OH 44266

LEWIS, MARJORIE, b. NYC, May 3, 1929; d. Leon and Julie (Rudomin) Schwartz. M. Philip Lewis, Sept. 12, 1954; children—Victoria, Laura, David, James. Author: The Boy Who Would Be a Hero, 1982, Ernie and The Mile Long Muffler, 1982, Wrongway Applebaum, 1984; stories, reviews in School Library Jnl, MS Magazine. BA, Russell Sage Coll., 1949; MLS, Rutgers U., 1970. Film prod. and researcher, CBS TV, NYC, 1951-55; film prod., Compton Adv., NYC, 1955-58; librn., Brookside School, Montclair, NJ, 1965-71, children's librn., Scarsdale Pub. Lib., 1974-76; librn., Scarsdale Jr. High, NY, 1976—. Mem. ALA, Schl. Library Assn., Southeastern NY Authors Guild, NOW, Natl Wrtrs Union, Soc. of Children's Book Wrtrs, Amnesty Intl. Home: 13 Hubbard Dr White Plains NY 10605

LEWIS, MONTE ROSS, (Ludwig von Bogenstadt), b. Archer City, TX, Aug. 20, 1937; s. William Herman and Ruby Lillian (Ellis) L.; m. Susan Marie Brown, May 25, 1974; children—Christy, Ross, Lillian, Ellisa. Ed.-in-chief Cross Timbers Rvw, 1983—. Wrkg. on books on Chickasaw Indian Removal and James Hamilton Jr. MA, Midwestern U., 1966; PhD, N. Texas State U., 1981. Instr. Cisco Jr. Coll., Cisco, Tex., 1980—, ed., 1983—. Vice pres. W. Tex. Hist. Assn., Abilene, 1982—; v.p. Texas Oral Hist. Assn., 1986; dir. Ft. Belknap Archives Assn., Graham, Tex., 1983—; pres. Fort Belknap Soc., 1985—; curator Cisco Hist. Soc., 1986—; mem. Panhandle-Plains Hist. Soc., Tex. State Hist. Assn. Served to P.F.C. USNG, 1954-57. Home: 1412 Park Dr Cisco TX 76437

LEWIS, RICHARD STANLEY, b. Pitts., Jan. 8, 1916; s. S. Morton and Mary L. (Lefstein) L.; m. Louise G. Silberstein, June 8, 1938; children—Jonathan, David. Author: The Other Child, rev. ed., 1960, A Continent for Science, 1965, Appointment on The Moon, 1968, rev. ed., 1969, The Nuclear Power Rebellion, 1972, The Voyages of Apollo, 1964, From Vinland to Mars: 1000 Years of Exploration, 1976, The Other Child Grows Up, 1977; prin. author The New Illustrated Ency. of Space Exploration; ed.: Man on the Moon, 1969, Alamagordo Plus 25 Years, 1970, Frozen Future, 1972, The Energy Crisis, 1972, The Environmental Revolution, 1973. BA, PA State U., 1937. Rptr. Cleve. Press, 1937-38; rewrite man, drama critic Indpls. Times, 1938-43, rptr., city ed., 1946-49; rptr. St. Louis Star-Times, 1949-51; mem. staff Chgo. Sun-Times, 1951-68, sci. ed., 1967-68; mng. ed. Bull. Atomic Scientists, Chgo., 1968-70, ed., 1971-74. Served with AUS, 1943-46; ETO. Fellow Brit. Interplanetary Soc.; mem. AG, AL. Home: 1401 S Magnolia Dr Indialantic FL 32903

LEWIS, RICHARD WARRINGTON BALDWIN, b. Chgo., Nov. 1, 1917; s. Leicester Crosby and Beatrix Elizabeth (Baldwin) L.; m. Nancy Lindau, June 29, 1950; children—Nathaniel Lindau, Sophia Baldwin. Author: The American Adam, 1955, The Picaresque Saint, 1959, Trials of the World, 1965, Edith Wharton: A Biography, 1975 (Pulitzer prize 1976); ed.: Herman Melville (A Reader), 1962, The Presence of Walt Whitman, 1962, Malraux: A Collection of Critical Essays, 1964, Short Stories of Edith Wharton, 1910-1937; contrbg. ed. Major Writers of America, 1962. AB, Harvard U., 1939; MA, U. Chgo., 1941, PhD, 1953; Litt.D., Wesleyan U., Middletown, CT, 1961. Tchr. Bennington Coll., 1948-50; dean Salzburg Seminar Am. Studies, 1950-51; assoc. then full prof. English, Rutgers U., 1954-59; prof. English and Am. studies, Yale U., 1960—; lit. cons. Universal Pictures, 1966—. Office: Am Studies Yale U New Haven CT 06520

LEWIS, RICKI, b. Brooklyn, NY, Oct. 29, 1954; m. Larry Lewis, Aug. 3, 1975; children—Heather, Sarah. Author textbook: Biology and Human Concerns, 1987; assoc. ed.: The New Biology of Mood; contrbr. to High Technology, Health, Biology Digest, Women's Sports, Inside Running, other mags. Columnist Schenectady Gazette. MA in Zoology Indiana U., 1978, PhD in Genetics, 1980. Author Worth Publishers (NYC), 1982—; genetic counsel. (Scotia, NY), 1975—; lecturer SUNY (Albany), 1984—; vis. asst. prof. Empire State Coll. (Fulton-Montgomery), 1986—. Mem. NASW. Home: 7 Harvest Dr Scotia NY 12302

LEWIS, ROGER, (Siwel Regor), b. NYC, Sept. 9, 1945; s. Thomas John and Dorothy (Boulanger) Lewis. Novel: Numin's Curse, 1976; poetry: The Carbon Gang, 1983; contrbr. to New Essays on The Great Gatsby, 1985. AB, Middlebury Coll., 1967; AM, India U., 1968. Asst. prof. of English George Mason U. (Fairfax, VA), 1973—; editor Orchises Press (Summit, NJ), 1983—. First Lt. US Army, 1969-71, USA. Office: Dept Eng George Mason U 4400 Univ Fairfax VA 22030

LEWIS, STEVEN RICHARD, b. Pickens, SC, Aug. 15, 1953, s. E.R. and Hazel Lorraine (Seaborn) L. Ed., contrbr.: Ind. Spirit, 1981-82; contrbr. to State Mag., Columbia, S.C., Charlotte Observer, So. Living; columnist Artifacts mag., S.C. Arts Commn. publ., 1985—. BA in English, Coll. Charleston, 1977. Assoc. ed. Ports South mag., Beaufort, S.C., 1979; asst. media arts coordinator S.C. Arts Commn., Columbia, 1980-81, dir. lit. arts, 1982—. Mem. AWP, COSMEP, CCLM (bd. dirs. 1986), S.C. Acad. Authors (bd. govs. 1986—). Home: Box 50213 Columbia SC 29250

LEWIS, SYLVIA, b. NYC, Apr. 8, 1945. Contrbr. articles to The New York Times, Ms., Chgo. Tribune, Chgo. Sun-Times, Seattle Times, Seattle Post-Intelligencer, Inland Architect, Planning. BA, Cornell U., 1967; MS in Jnlsm., Northwestern U., 1974. Rptr., Seattle Post-Intelligencer, 1968-69; news ed., Planning, Am. Planning Assn., Chgo., 1974-75, mng. ed., 1975-77, dir. of pubns., 1979—. Harrington award, Medill Schl. Jnlsm., 1974. Mem. SPJ, Phi Beta Kappa. Office: Am Plan Assn 1313 E 60th St Chicago IL 60637

LEWIS, THOMASINE ELIZABETH, b. Manila, Philippines, Sept. 20, 1958; d. Thomas Donald and Elizabeth Jane (Munson) L.; came to U.S., 1973. Copy ed., feature news writer, The News Nwspr., Mexico City, 1977-78; prodn. ed., feat. news writer, The Independent Alligator, Gainesville, FL, 1979; mng. ed. Gentleman's Companion, Los Angeles, 1979-82; mng. ed., then ed.-in-chief Playgirl Mag., 1983-85; creative consultant Playgirl On the Air (video); ed.-in-chief Slimmer Mag., Santa Monica, CA, 1986—. Mem. Hollywood Press and Entert. Club, San Francisco Press Club. Office: 3420 Ocean Park Blvd Santa Monica CA 90405

LEWY, GUENTER, b. Breslau, Germany (now Wroclaw, Poland), Aug. 22, 1923; s. Henry and Rosel (Leipziger) L.; m. Ilse Nussbaum, Dec. 29, 1950; children: Barbara Jean, Peter Ralph. Author: Constitutionalism and Statecraft during the Golden Age of Spain: A Study of the Political Philosophy of Juan de Mariana, S.J., 1960, The Catholic Church and Nazi Germany, 1964, Religion and Revolution, 1974, America in Vietnam, 1978, False Consciousness: an Essay on Mystification, 1982, The Federal Loyalty-Security Program: The Need for Reform, 1983. Contrbr: Nils Petter Gleditsch, ed, Kamp und Vapen, 1965, D.B. Schmidt and E.R. Schmidt, eds, The Deputy Reader: Studies in Moral Responsibility, 1965, David Spitz, ed, Political Theory and Social Change, 1967, Richard A. Wasserstrom, ed, War and Morality, 1970, Encyclopedia Judaica, 1971, Michael P. Smith and Kenneh L. Deutsch, eds, Political Obligation and Civil Disobediance: Readings, 1972, Allen Mitchell, ed, The Nazi Revolution, 1973, Donald E. Smith, ed, Religion and Political Modernization, 1974, Charles F. Delzell, ed, The Papacy and Totalitarianism between the Two World Wars, 1974, Harold D. Lasswell and others, eds, Propaganda and Communication in in World History, vol. 2: Emergence of Public Opinion in the West, 1980, Sam C. Sarkisian, ed, Combat Effectiveness, Cohesion, Stress and the Volunteer Military, 1980, Horst Neumann and Heinz Scheer, eds, Plus Minus 1984: George Orwells Vision in heutiger Sicht, 1983. Also au of several technical reports pub by Dept. of Govt, Univ of Mass. Contrbr of articles and bk rvws to American Political Science Rvw, Parameters, and other jnls. BSS, City Coll (now City Coll of the City Univ of N.Y), 1951; MA, Columbia Univ, 1952, Ph. D., 1957. Instr in govt, Columbia Univ, 1953-56; asst prof of govt, Smith Coll, Northampton, Mass., 1957-63; assoc. prof, Univ of Mass-Amherst, 1964-66, prof of pol sci, 1966-85. Dir, NEH Inst.: War and Morality, 1979. Vis scholar, American Enterprise Inst, 1981-82. Member: Phi Beta Kappa. Social Sci. Research Council fellow, 1956-57, 1961-62; Rockefeller Fdn fellow, 1963-64, 1976-77; Natl Book Award nomination, 1974, for Religion åd Revolution. Military service: British Army, 1942-46; became sergeant; received Africa Star and Italy Star. Home: 4101 Cathedral Ave NW Washington DC 20016

LEXAU, HENRY, b. St. Paul, Feb. 8, 1928; s. Ole Hendrijk an Anne (Haas) L.; m. Eileen O'Hara, Oct, 18, 1952; children—Catherine, Margaret, Daniel, John, Elizabeth, Benjamin. BA, Coll. St. Thomas, 1949. Asst. editor Catholic Digest, St. Paul, 1949-72, mng. editor, 1972-75, editor, 1975—. Served with U.S. Army, 1950-52. Decorated Bronze Star. Home: 1941 Selby Ave St Paul MN 55104

LEY, JAMES M., b. Balt., July 21, 1958, s. Norman W. and Mildred M. (Morton) L. Author: Computers are Useless: 100 Uses for a Dead Computer, 1983. BEE, Cornell U., Ithaca, N.Y., 1980. Product engr. Nat. Semiconductor, Santa Clara, Calif., 1980-81; mktg. engr. Hewlett Packard Corp., Cupertino, Calif., 1981-83; project mgr. Elecon System, Sunnyvale, Calif., 1983-84; pub. Thunderbolt Publs., Sunnyvale, 1983—; system trng. engr. Daisy Systems, Mountain View, Calif., 1984—. Address: Box 70427 Sunnyvale CA 94086

LEYDEN, JOAN MARIE, b. Storm Lake, IA, Nov. 7, 1944; d. Leo Joseph and Florence Olivia (Korgman) Schumacher; m. J. Kim Leyden, Mar. 30, 1964; children—John Gregory, Christopher David, Joel Andrew, Nicholas Joseph. Contrbr. poems to anthols. Wrkg. on novel.Secy. U. Ia., 1962-1964. Librarian, Washington Pub. Library, Ia., 1974-76; secy. Washington High Schl., Ia., 1978-80. Home: 1402 E Main Washington IA 52353

L'HEUREUX, JOHN CLARKE, b. S. Hadley, MA, Oct. 26, 1934; s. Wilfred Joseph and Mildred (Clarke) L'H.; m. Joan Ann Polston, June 26, 1971. Author: Quick as Dandelions, 1964, Rubrics for a Revolution, 1967, Picnic in Babylon, 1967, One Eye and a Measuring Rod, 1968, No Place for Hiding, 1971, Tight White Collar, 1972, The Clang Birds, 1972, Family Affairs, 1974, Jessica Fayer, 1976, Desires, 1981. AB, Weston Coll., 1959, PhL, 1960; MA, Boston Coll., 1963; STL, Woodstock Coll., 1967; postgrad., Harvard U., 1967-68. Writer-in-res. Georgetown U., 1964-65, Regis Coll., 1968-69; staff ed. The Atlantic, 1968-69, contrbg. ed., 1969—; assoc. prof. Stanford U., 1973-79, prof., 1981—, dir. creative writing prog., 1976—. Ordained priest Roman Catholic Ch., 1966, laicized, 1971. Office: Eng Dept Stanford U Stanford CA 94305

LIBERMAN, ALEXANDER, b. Kiev, Russia, Sept. 4, 1912; came to U.S., 1941, naturalized, 1946; s. Simon and Henriette (Pascar) L.; m. Tatiana Yacovleff Du Plessix, Nov. 4, 1942; 1 stepdau., Francine Du Plessix Gray. Author: The Artist in His Studio, Greece, Gods and Art, 1968. Student in Architecture, Ecoles des Beaux Arts, Paris, 1930; D.F.A. (hon.), R.I Schl. Design, 1980. Art dir., mng. editor Vu Paris, 1931-36; art dir. Voque mag., Conde Nast Publs., NYC., 1941-43, art dir. Conde Nast Publs., 1943—, editorial dir., 1962—. Subject of book Alexander Liberman (Barbara Rose). Office: Conde Nast 350 Madison Ave New York NY 10017

LIBHART, BONNI, b. Paragould, AR, Feb. 11, 1935; d. William Moses and Meriam Gladys (Gardner) Taylor; m. Hubert Dean Baird, Jan. 9, 1952 (div. 1956); 1 dau., Deana Lyn; m. Anthony Canova Libhart III, July 12, 1958; children—Emily Dawn, Anthony Canova. Author: (series) It's Possible, 1973-83; Born-Again Managers, 1978, Build a Better You Starting Now, 1981. Contrbr. articles to mags. including Guidepost, Christian Life. Wrkg. on The Dream Makers: How the New Kid on the Block Can Compete with Big Boys, How to Find Your God Given Gifts (and What to Do With Them). A.A., Crowleys Ridge Coll., 1966; B.S. in Radio/TV, 1976-77; broadcaster, Sta. WACO, Waco, 1977-82; chief exec. officer AAPLEX, Inc., Little Rock, 1982—. Mem SPJ, Natl. Speakers Assn. Home: 11260 Rivercreast Dr Little Rock AR 72212

LICHT, LILLA GILES MCKNIGHT, b. Flushing, NY, d. John Oakey and Kathryn (Brassil) McKnight; m. Frederic John Licht, Feb. 22, 1957; children—Randolph Stewart, Frederic John Jr., Robert Salladin. Author, pub.: My Irish Ancestry—The Brassil Family, 1973, Our Dutch Ancestry—Stymets, Gerrits, Van Wagenen Families, 1977, The English-American Ancestry of Dorothy M.S. Licht, 1979, The Scotch-Irish Ancestors of Kathryn B. McKnight, 1980, McKnight Genealogy, 1754-1981, 1981, Ancestry of Some of the Descendants of Hugh Maxwell, 1983, Daniel Leab and His Family, 1985, A Family Album: William McClelland and Alexander Pirnie Families, 1985, Allen Family, 1986; author: A History of St. James the Apostle Church, 1972; ed., pub. McKnight Newsletter, 1981—; genealogy columnist newspapers. Wrkg. on genealogy textbook. Student U. London, 1956-57; BCP, U. Penn., 1956, M.City Planning, 1957. Prof. genealogy Tompkins Cortland Community Coll., Dryden, NY., 1973-79; reporter, columnist, wrtr., pub., 1963—. Mem. numerous hist. and genealogical orgns. Address: 490 M St SW Box 604 Washington DC 20024

LICHTI, ALLAN, see Cline, Richard Allan

LIDDLE, CATHERINE DIANE, (Samatha Crea) b. Mansfied, OH, May 11, 1952; d. Bernard Lee and Joyce Ann (Bryant) Elrod; m. Maurice F. Liddle, Apr. 7, 1973 (div. Oct. 27, 1981); children—Dewran Jacob, Michael Maurice. Contrbr. articles to mags., newspapers. Student Marshall U., 1983—. Proof operator Portsmouth Bank, OH, 1971-76. Mem. Phi Theta Kappa, Sigma Tau Delta, Phoenix Wrtrs. Home: Rt 1 Box 499-B1 Portsmouth OH 45662

LIDDY, JAMES, b. Dublin, Ireland, July 1, 1934, s. James and Clare (Reeves) L. Novelist: Young Men Go Out Walking, 1986; author poetry books: In a Blue Smoke, 1964, Blue Mountain, 1968, A Life of Stephen Dedalus, 1968, A Monster Song of Love and War, 1969, Orpheus in the Ice Cream Parlour, 1975, Baudelaire's Bar Flowers, 1975, Corca Bascinn, 1977,351omyn's Lay, 1979, Chamber Pot Music, 1982, Moon and Star Moments, 1982, A White Thought in a White Shade: New and Selected Poems, 1987; contrbr. poetry, fiction: Tuatara, Cream City Rvw, Strange Fruit, Icarus, numerous other lit mags, anthologies and collections; contrbr. articles to scholarly publs.; author monographs; ed.: Nine Queen Bees, 1970, Gorey Art Festival, 1973—, The Gorey Detail, 1977—, The Big Potato, 1982—. BA, Natl. Univ. Ireland, 1956, MA, 1958; Barrister-at-Law, King's Inns, Dublin, 1961, Practice law, Ireland, 1961-66; educator, 1967—; mem. faculty U. Wis.-Milw., 1976—, assoc. prof. dept. English, 1982—. Grantee NEH, 1977. Mem. AWP, AESDANA. Office: Dept Eng Univ WI Milwaukee WI 53201

LIEBER, FAITH, see Rehns, Marsha Lee

LIEBER, TOOD MICHAEL, b. Phila., Nov. 30, 1944; s. Sylvan and Sally (Wiser) L.; div. 1982; 1 dau., Terry Lynn. Contrbr. Endless Experiments: The Heroic Experience in Am. Romanticism, 1973; Am. Qtly, Am. Lit., Western Humanities Rvw, Piedmont Lit. Rvw, Nebr. Rvw, Kans. Qtly, Yale Review, Mss, Colo. Rvw, Sun Dog, Missouri Review. MFA, U. Ariz., 1981-83; PhD, Case Western Res. U., 1966-69. Prof. English Simpson coll., Indianola, Iowa, 1969-86.; NEA Fellowship Grant, 1987. Address: RR2 Box 150 Indianola IA 50125

LIEBERMAN, HERBERT H., b. New Rochelle, NY, Sept. 22, 1933, s. Arthur Charles and Silvia (Kissel) L.; m. Judith Betsy Barsky, Sept. 9, 1963; 1 dau., Zoe. Author: Matty and the Moron and Madonna, 1964, The Adventures of Dolphin Green, 1967, Crawlspace, 1971, The Eighth Square, 1973, Brilliant Kids, 1975, City of the Dead, 1976, The Climate of Hell, 1978, Nightcall from a Distant Time Zone, 1982, Nightbloom, 1984, The Green Train, 1986. AB, CCNY, 1955; AM, Columbia U., 1957. Wrtr. N.Y. Times, 1960-61; asst. ed. Macmillan Pub. Co., NYC, 1961-64; sr. ed. Am. Book Co., NYC, 1964-67; exec. ed. Reader's Digest Condensed Books, 1967—. Served with U.S. Army, 1957-60. Recipient First Prize Charles Sergel award for playwriting U. Chgo., 1963, Grand Prix de Litterature Policiere, French govt., 1978; Guggenheim Meml. Fdn. grantee, 1964. Home: 14 Haights Cross Chappaqua NY 10514

LIEBERMAN, LAURENCE, b. Detroit, Feb. 16, 1935; s. Nathan and Anita Helen (Cohen) L.; m. Bernice Braun, June 17, 1956; children—Carla, Deborah, Isaac. Author: The Achievement of James Dickey, 1968; author poems, 1968—, latest being Eros At The World Kite Pageant, 1983; The Mural Of Wakeful Sleep, 1985. BA, U. MI., 1956, MA, 1958. Asst. English prof. Coll. of Virgin Islands, 1964-68; English prof. U. IL, 1968—. Poetry ed. U. IL Press, 1971—. Yaddo Fellowships, Saratoga Springs, NY, 1963, 67, 71; Center for Advanced Study, U. IL, 1981-82; Creative Writing Fellowship, IL Arts Council, Chgo., 1982; Humanities Research Board, U. IL, spring, 1985, NEA fellowship, 1986-87. Mem. AWP, MLA, PSA. Home: 1304 Eliot Dr Urbana IL 61801

LIEBERSON, STANLEY, b. Montreal, Que., Can., Apr. 20, 1933; s. Jack and Ida (Cohen) L.; m. Patricia Ellen Beard, 1960; children—Rebecca, David, Miriam, Rachel. Author: (with others) Metropolis and Region, 1960, Ethnic Patterns in American Cities, 1963; ed.: Explorations in Sociolinguistics, 1967, (with Beverly Duncan) Metropolis and Region in Transition, 1970, Language and Ethnic Relations in Canada, 1970, A Piece of the Pie, 1980, Language Diversity and Lang. Contact, 1981, Making It Count, 1985 (paperback edition, 1987); assoc. ed.: Social Problems, 1965-67, Sociol. Methods and Research, 1971—; editorial cons. Sociol. Inquiry, 1965-67; adv. ed. Am. Jnl Sociology, 1969-74; editorial bd.: Lang. in Society, 1972-74, Intl. Jnl Sociol. of Lang., 1974—, Canadian Jnl Sociol., 1975—, Social Forces, 1980-83; advisory council: Sociol. Abstracts, 1972-73, Lang. Problems and Lang. Planning, 1977—. Student, Bklyn. Coll., 1950-52; MA, U. Chgo., 1958, PhD, 1960. Assoc. dir. IA Urban Community Research Ctr., U. IA, 1959-61, instr., asst. prof. sociology, 1959-61; asst. prof. sociol. U. WI, 1961-63, assoc. prof., 1963-66, prof., 1966-67; prof. sociol. U. WA, 1967-71, dir. Ctr. Studies Demography and Ecology, 1968-71; prof. sociol. U. Chgo., 1971-74, assoc. dir. Populn. Research Ctr., 1971-74; prof. sociol. U. AZ, Tucson, 1974-83, head dept., 1976-79; prof. sociol. U. CA-Berkeley, 1983—. Guggenheim fellow, 1972-73. Fellow AAAS. Home: 560 Valle Vista Ave Oakland CA 94610

LIFSHIN, LYN DIANE, b. Burlington, VT, July 12, 1949, d. Ben and Frieda May (Lazarus) Lipman. Author: Black Apples, 1970, Upstate Madonna, 1975, Glass, 1980, Lady Lyn, 1974, Shaker House Poems, 1979, North, 1978, offered by owner, 1979, Blue Horses Nuzzle Thursday, 1983, Naked Charm, 1984, The Radio Psychic is Shaving Her Legs, 1984, Black Cellophane, Carnation Thighs, 1984, Matinee, 1984, Kiss the Skin Off, 1985, Want Ads, 1985, Mad Girl Poems, 1985, Reading Lips, 1985, Remember the Ladies, 1985, Doctors, 1985, Hotel Lifshin, 1985, Dobermans in my Wrist, 1985, Madonna Who Shifts for Herself, and over 50 other books and chapbooks; ed.: Tangled Vines, 1978, Ariasdne's Thread, 1982, Raw Opals, 1987, Red Hair and the Jesuit, 1987, Matinee, 1987, The Doctor May be Let Go, 1987, Rubbed Silk, 1988, contrbr. poetry, prose to Epoch, Ploughshares, Unmuzzled Ox, Cutbank, other lig mags, Ms. mag., Rolling Stone. BA, Syracuse U.; MA, U. Vt.; postgrad., Brandeis U. Wrtr., ed., tchr. Yaddo fellow, 1970, 71, 75, 79, 80, MacDowell Colony fellow, 1973, Millay Colony fellow, 1975, 79. Jack Kerovac award, Centennial Review award, 1986. Address: 2142 Appletree Ln Niskayuna NY 12309

LIFSHITZ, LEATRICE H., b. Bklyn., Aug. 15, 1933, d. Irving and Bertha (Rosenberg) Heilizer; m. Kenneth Lifshitz, Dec. 28, 1952; children—Rhona, Lawrence, Edward. Contrbr. poetry to: Modern Haiku, Epos, Parnasus Lit Jnl, Am. Rvw, other lit jnls; contrbr. to anthologies: I Name Myself Daughter and It Is Good, 1981, Peace or Perish: A Crisis Anthology, 1983, Reflections on the Sacred Gift of Life, 1985, others. Wrkg. on narrative poems about John Brown's wives. BA, Hunter Coll., 1954; MS, CUNY, 1969. Reader Jane Addams Children's Book Award Comm., 1984, 85. Recipient Award in Arts, Rockland County Women's Network, 1985, first place Hans S. Bodenheimer Award, 1986. Mem. Rockland Poets (founder), Rockland County Haiku Society (founder), 1986, Bergen Poets, N.Y. P&W. Home: 3 Hollow Tree Ct Pomona NY 10970

LIFTON, ROBERT JAY, b. NYC, May 16, 1926; s. Harold A. and Ciel (Roth) L.; m. Betty Jean Kirschner, Mar. 1, 1952; children—Kenneth Jay, Natasha Karen. Author: Thought Reform and the Psychology of Totalism: A Study of Brainwashing in China, 1961, Revolutionary Immorality: Mao Tse-Tung and the Chinese Cultural Revolution, 1968, Death in Life: Survivors of Hiroshima, 1969 (Natl. Book award, Van Wyck Brooks award), History and Human Survival, 1970, Boundaries: Psychological Man in Revolution, 1970, Home from the War: Vietnam Veterans—Neither Victims nor Executioners, 1973, (with Eric Olson) Living and Dying, 1974, The Life of the Self, 1976, (with Shuichi Kato and Michael Reich) Six Lives/Six Deaths: Portraits from Modern Japan, ,79, The Broken Connection: On Death and the Continuity of Life, 1979, Indefensible Weapons: The Political and Psychological Case Against Nuclearism (with Richard Falk), 1982; The Nazi Doctors: Medical Killing and the Psychology of Genocide (Natl Jewish Book award, 1987); The Future of Immortality and Other Essays For a Nuclear Age,

1987; creator humorous cartoons: Birds, 1969, PsychoBirds, 1979; ed.: Woman in America, 1965, America and the Asian Revolutions, 1970, (with R.A. Falk & G. Kolko) Crimes of War, 1971, (with Eric Olson) Explorations in Psychohistory: The Wellfleet Papers, 1975, Last Aid: Medical Dimensions of Nuclear War, 1982 (with Eric and Susanna Chivian, John E. Mack), In a Dark Time, 1984 (with Nicholas Humphrey). Student Cornell U., 1942-44; MD, N.Y. Med. Coll., 1948, DHL, 1977; DSc (hon.), Lawrence U., 1971, Merrimack Coll., 1973 Univ. Vermont, 1984; DHL, Wilmington Coll., 1975, Marlboro Coll., 1983, Maryville Coll., 1983 Univ. New Haven, 1986; Doc. of Law (hon.) Iona College, 1984. Faculty Washington Schl. Psychiatry, 1954-55; research assoc. psychiatry, assoc. East Asian studies Harvard U., 1956-61; assoc. prof. Yale Med. Schl., 1961-67, research prof., 1967-85; The Center on Violence and Human Survival, 1985—. Served to capt. USAF, 1951-53. Fellow AAAS, Group Study Psychohist. Process. Office: John Jay Coll CUNY 444 West 56th St New York NY 10019

LIGHT, WILL, Author: Uni-Verse (poetry), 1978, Opening Your Creative Flow! The Magic Keys (how-to manual), 1984. Producer, dir., performer, musical prodns.; pub. Golden Glow Press, Mt. Shasta, Calif., 1978—. Office: Box 36 Mt Shasta CA 96067

LIGHTBURN, JEFFREY CALDWELL, b. Columbus, OH, June 17, 1947, s. Willis Caldwell and Nancy Ellen (Snyder) L.; m. Jeanne Kay McGraw, June 13, 1970; children—Nicole Ann, Benjamin Caldwell. BS, So. Ill. U., 1970. Reporter Capital Cities Communication-Belleville (Ill.) News Democrat, 1973–76; ed. Ralston Purina Co., St. Louis, 1976–78; sr. communications specialist, ed. Bandwagon mag., Main-stream mag., Frito-Lay, Inc., Dallas, 1978–81; mgr. public relations Curtis Mathes Corp., Dallas, 1981-83; mgr. employee communications, ed. employee publs. Pizza Hut, Inc., Wichita, Kans., 1983-85, dir corp. communications, 1985—. Recipient newswriting awards UPI, AP, 1973, 76. Mem. Intl. Assn. Bus. Communicators (Gold Quill award 1976, 77, 78), Soc. Profl. Journalists. Office: Box 428 Wichita KS 67201

LILLY, DORIS, b. Los Angeles, Dec. 26, 1930; d. Otto William and Edith Marie (Humphries) L. Author: How to Marry a Millionaire, 1951, How to Make Love in Five Languages, 1964, Those Fabulous Greeks: Onassis, Niarchos and Livanos, 1970, Glamour Girl, 1977, How to Meet a Billionaire, 1984. contrbr. to maj. natl. mags. inclg. Photoplay. Student pub. schls. Soc. columnist N.Y. Post, 1958-68; gossip columnist WPIX, NYC, 1974-77; syndicated gossip columnist, McNaught Syndicate, 1977—. Office: Manor Books 45 E 30th St New York NY 10016

LIMA, ROBERT, b. Havana, Cuba, Nov. 7, 1935 (arrived in US, 1945); s. Robert F. and Joan (Millares) Lima; m. Sally A. Murphy, June 27, 1964; children—Mark X., Keith E., Michele B., Debra C. Author: The Theatre of Garcia Lorca, 1963, An Annotated Bibliography of Ramon del Valle-Inclan, 1972, Dos ensayos sobre teatro espanol de los 20, 1984; poetry: Fathoms, 1981, The Olde Ground, 1985; translations include The Lamp of Marvels (Ramon del Valle-Inclan), 1986; contrbr. to Theatre Annual, Modern Drama, Latin American Literary Rvw, Images, Saturday Rvw, other jnls, mags, nwspprs. Wrkg. on variety of projects including a biography of Valle-Inclan, Valle-Inclān-The Theatre of His Life, 1987. BA, Villanova U., 1957, MA, 1961; PhD, New York U., 1968. Poet-in-Residence U. Nacional San Marcos (Lima, Peru), 1976-77; visit. prof. C. Litera U. Catolica del Peru (Lima), 1976-77; prof. of Spanish/Comparative lit. Penn State U. (University Park, PA), 1965—, fellow, Institute for the Arts and Humanistic Studies. Mem. AATSP, AIA, PSA, Intl. PEN-American Center. Office: N 346 Burrowes Bldg University Park PA 16802

LINCOLN, C(HARLES) ERIC, b. Athens, AL, June 23, 1924; s. Less and Mattie (Sowell) L.; m. Lucy Cook, July 1, 1961; children—Hilary Anne, Less Charles II; children by prev. marriage—Cecil Eric, Joyce Elaine. Author: The Black Muslims in America, 1971, 2d edit., 1973, My Face is Black, 1964, The Negro Pilgrimage in America, 1967, Sounds of the Struggle, 1967, Is Anybody Listening?, 1968, The Black Americans, 1969, A Profile of Martin Luther King, 1969, The Black Experience in Religion, 1974, The Black Church since Frazier, 1974, Race, Religion and the Continuing American Dilemma, 1984; gen. ed. C. Eric Lincoln Series in Black Religion; contrbr. arts. to N.Y. Times, books, periodicals. AB, Lemoyne Coll., 1947; AM, Fisk U., 1954; postgrad. law U. Chgo., 1948-49, BD, 1956; MEd, Boston U., 1960, PhD, 1960; LLD, Carleton Coll., 1968; LHD, St. Michael's, 1970, Lana Coll., 1982, Clark Coll., 1983. Pastor John Calvin Presby. Ch., Nashville, 1953-54; asst. personnel dean Fisk U., Nashville, 1953-54; asst. prof. religion and philos. Clark Coll., 1954-60, assoc. prof. soc. philos., 1960-61, prof. soc. relats., 1961-65, asst. to pres., 1960-63; prof. sociol. Portland (OR) State U., 1965-67; prof. sociol. and relig. Union Theol. Sem., NYC, 1965-73; adj. prof. sociol. Vassar Coll., 1969-70; adj. prof. religion Columbia U., 1965-73, Vanderbilt U., 1973-76; prof. sociol. and relig., chmn. dept. relig. studies Fisk U., Nashville, 1973-76; prof. relig. Duke U., Durham, NC, 1976—. Fellow AAAS; mem. AAUP, NEA. Founding Pres. Black Acad. Arts & Letters. Home: Kumasi Hill Rt 1 Box 1010 Hillsborough NC 27278

LINDAHL, HELEN GERTRUDE, b. Superior, WI, Nov. 15, 1917, d. James Edward and Gladys Irene (Schofield) McDonald; m. Howard Louis Lindahl, Mar. 16, 1942 (dec. 1984); 1 son, David Gordon. Contrbr. articles to Hub Rail, Horses & Hoofbeats, Dogs Mag., Organic Gardening & Farming, numerous other publs. Wrkg. on autobiography, juvenile fiction. Student U. Wis.-Madison, 1959, 60. Freelance wrtr., 1959—. Recipient awards Wrtr.'s Digest mag., 1964, 65. Mem. Superior Wrtrs.' Club (publicity chair 1960-65), Wis. Regional Wrtrs.' Assn. Home: 2346 Western Ave N Saint Paul MN 55113

LINDAHL, ROGER MATHEWS, b. Orange, NJ, July 22, 1955; s. Melvin August and Barbara (Davenport) L.; m. Po-Yee Au, June 12, 1979; 1 dau., Patricia Si-Ling Lindahl. Ed., National Commercial News, 1984-85, Daily Commercial News, 84-85, Commercial News Intl., 85—. BA, Franklin & Marshall Coll., 1977; MBA, U. MI, 1982. Research assoc. business InH. Asia/Pacific, Hong Kong, 1982-83; ed. Commercial Publishing, San Francisco, 1984—. Mem. Phi Beta Kappa, Office: Comm News 99 S Van Ness Ave San Francisco CA 94103

LINDBERG, STANLEY WILLIAM, b. Warren, PA, Nov. 18, 1939; s. Carl Leander and Leah Lucille (Henderson) L.; m. Jeanne Grace Heller, June 26, 1965; children—Kristin Anne, Eric Heller, Carl Muir. Co-ed.: Ohio Rvw, Athens, 1971-77, Indland Boat Poetry Series (10 vols.), 1980; author The Annotated McGuffey, 1976; co- author Van Nostrand's Plain English Handbook, 1980; ed. The Plays of Frederic Reynolds (3 vols.), 1983. AB, 1961; MA, U.PA, 1967, PhD, 1969. Asst. prof. English Ohio U., Athens, 1969-75, assoc. prof., 1975-77; prof. humanities U. GA, Athens, 1977-83, prof. English, 1983—; cons. ed. Pushcart Prize Anthology, NYC, 1978—; ed. GA Rvw, Athens, 1977—. Served to 1st lt. U.S. Army, 1962-64. Mem. MLA, Conf. Eds. of Learned Jnls, Phi Beta Kappa. Home: 195 Maple Cr Athens GA 30606

LINDEMANN, JO ANN, b. Llano, TX, Nov. 20, 1960; d. James William and Viola Ann L. Author: (chapbook) Skyward, 1982. Contrbr. poems to anthols. Wrkg. on collection of poems, poetry. Grad. public schs., Mason, TX. Recipient Golden Poet award World of Poetry, 1985, 86. Home: Box 48 Art TX 76820

LINDENAU, JUDITH WOOD, b. Janesville, OH, May 22, 1941; d. Vernon Earl and Jean Elizabeth (Hogan) Wood; children: Jonathan, Sarah. Contrbr to Novea, Wheatfield, SD Rvw, The Exec. Officer, Mich. Exec. Officer, Grand Traverse Bus. BA, Baldwin Wallace Coll., MA, U.SD. Instr. English Univ. SD, Vermillion, 1963–67, Interlochen Arts Acad., Mich., 1967-72, Ferris State Coll., Traverse City, Mich., 1972-77; writer-in-residence pub schls., Traverse City, 1977-79; exec. vp Bd. Realtors, Traverse City, 1978—; dir. Schl. of Real Estate, Traverse City, 1985—. Chmn bd., Data Research Center, Traverse City, 1985—. Mem. Am. Soc. Assn. Execs., Address: 1610 Indian Woods Dr Traverse City MI 49684

LINDENBERG, ARTHUR JAY, b. NYC, Mar. 16, 1942; s. Samuel and Sylvia (Taubin) L.; m. Karen E. Metzger, Aug. 28, 1963; children—Haidee, Marc. Author: (novel) Fragments, 1970, (fiction collection) Elaine and Other Stories, 1967. Contrbr. short stories, poems to mags. Ed.: One Summer, 1977, Second Summer, 1978, 79, The Macguffin, 1983—. A.B., U. Calif.-Berkeley, 1963; M.F.A., U. Oreg., 1967. Prof. English, Schoolcraft Coll., Livonia, MI, 1967—. Mem. NCTE, Midwest Regional Conf. English (regional coordinator). Home: 1327 Culver Rd Ann Arbor MI 48103

LINDENBERGER, HERBERT SAMUEL, b. Los Angeles, Apr. 4, 1929; s. Hermann and Celia (Weinkrantz) L.; m. Claire Flaherty, June 14, 1961; children—Michael James, Elizabeth Celia. Author: On Wordsworth's Prelude, 1963, Gerog Buechner, 1964, Lear and Cordelia at Home, Cordelia at Home (play), 1968, Georg Trakl, 1971, Historical Drama: The Relation of Literature and Reality, 1975, Saul's Fall: A Critical Fiction, 1979, Opera: The Extravagant Art, 1984. BA, Antioch Coll., 1951; PhD, U. WA, 1955. From instr. to prof. English and comp. lit. U. CA Riverside, 1954-66; prof. German and English, chmn. prog. comp. lit. Washington U., 1966-69; Avalon prof. humanities Stanford U., 1969—, chmn. prog. comp. lit., 1969-82. Fulbright scholar, Austria, 1952-53; Guggenheim fellow, 1968-69; NEH fellow, 1975-76, 82-83; Stanford U. Humanities Ctr. Fellow, 1982-83. Mem. MLA, Am. Comp. Lit. Assn. Home: 901 Wing Pl Stanford CA 94305

LINDFORS, VIVECA, b. Uppsala, Sweden, Dec. 29, 1920, came to U.S., 1945, d. Thorsten and Karin Lindfors; m. George Tabori (div.); children—John, Lena, Kristoffer. Author: Anna, the Gypsy Swede, I Am A Woman, Viveka...Viveca: A Woman, An Actress, A Life (autobiog.), 1981. Ed. Royal Dramatic Theatre, Sweden. Film and stage performer; films include Night unto Night and Unfinished Business; plays, Anastasia, Brecht on Brecht, Mother Courage, Dance of Death, I Am A Woman, Anna, the Gypsy Swede. Artistic dir., founder, Berkshire Theatre Festival. Recipient Vasaorden from King of Sweden, Berlin Film Festival award, N.Y. Drama League award. Mem. Am. Film Inst. Home: 172 E 95th St New York NY 10128

LINDGREN, CHARLOTTE HOLT, b. Ipswich, MA, Jan. 5, 1924, d. Hilmer Harold and Edith Grace (Whittier) Lindgren; m. Donald James Winslow, Aug. 11, 1978. Author: The Love Poems and Letters of William Barnes and Julia Miles, 1986, co-author: William Barnes, The Dorset Engravings (winner of Mansel-Pleydell prize), 1986; contrbr. articles to History Today, PHP (Japan), Antigonish Rvw (Can.), Dorset Mag., other publs. Prof. wrtg., lit. and publishing Emerson Coll., Boston, 1960—. AB, Boston U., 1945, MA, 1947, PhD, 1961. Mem. Thomas Hardy Soc., Herman Melville Soc., Phi Beta Kappa. Home: 23 Maple St Auburndale MA 02166

LINDO, DAVID KENNETH, b. Mpls., Sept. 24, 1936, s. Kenneth H. and Grace (Knoblauch) L. Contrbr. articles to New Orleans Bus., Career World, Supervision, The Toastmaster, numerous other publs. BBA, U. Minn., 1958; MA, Calif. Coast U., 1983, PhD, 1985. Mem. Institute of Management Accounting, Administrative Mgt. Society, other profl. orgns. Home: 2601 London Ct Burnsville MN 55337

LINDQUIST, BARBARA LOUISE, b. Chgo., May 25, 1930; d. Clarence Everett and Oma Agnes (Coleman) Holmes; m. Jack Rudolph Lindquist, Jan. 25, 1955 (div. Mar. 1975); children: Kurt, Klindt, Kim, Keith. Editor and illustrator: Something Happened to Me (Phyllis Sweet), 1981; editor: Why Me? Help for Victims of Child Sexual Abuse (Even If They Are Adults Now) (Lynn B. Daugherty), 1984, Fear or Freedom: A Woman's Options in Social Survival and Physical Defense (Susan E. Smith), 1986, NEWS (Heather Conrad), 1987; contbr. poetry to Means Mag., Primipara mag.; author: 1 book of poetry. BA in English lit. and edn., U. Wis.-Parkside, 1972. Mgr. Mother Courage Bookstore, Racine, Wis., 1978-83; chief exec. officer, mng. editor Mother Courage Press, Racine, 1981—. Mem. Wis. Regional Writers Assn., Wis. Women in Arts. Home: 1533 Illinois St Racine WI 53405

LINDSEY, JOHANNA, b. Frankfort, Germany, Mar. 10, 1952; came to U.S., 1954; d. Edwin Denis Howard and Wanda E. (Donaldson) Boston; m. Ralph Bruce Lindsey, Nov. 28, 1970; children: Alfred, Joseph, Garret. Author: Captive Bride, 1977, A Pirate's Love, 1978, Fires of Winter, 1980, Paradise Wild, 1981, Glorious Angel, 1982, So Speaks the Heart, 1983, Heart of Thunder, 1983, A Gentle Feuding, 1984, Brave the Wild Wind, 1984, Tender is the Storm, 1985, Love Only Once, 1985, When Love Awaits, 1986, A Heart so Wild, 1986, Hearts Aflame, 1987, Secret Fire, 1987, Beloved Rogue, 1988. Wrkg. on romance novels. Mem. AG. Recipient awards for romance novels. Home: 47-598 Puapoo Pl Kaneohe HI 96744

LINDSEY, WILLIAM FUSELLE (BILLY), b. Rocky Mount, NC, Mar. 22, 1923; s. Robert Penn and Willolha (Fuselle) L.; m. Gwendolyn Ruth Caverly, Dec. 28, 1948; children—Charles Penn, Rebecca Ruth. Pub./ed. Colorado Editor Magazine, 1964—; author The Westerners, 1971. BA, Westminster Coll., 1948; BS, U. CO, 1951. Sales dir. Colorado Press Svc., Denver, 1952-64; secy. dir. Colorado Press Assn., Denver, 1964—. Served to T/Sgt., AAF, 1942-45. Mem. Newspr. Assn. Mgrs., Inc., Natl. Nwspr. Assn., Denver Press Club. Home: 405 Baseline Rd Boulder CO 80302

LINDSTROM, JOYCE LEAH EVANS, b. Rigby, ID, Jan. 8, 1931; d. Sheridan Stewart and Leah Emma (Ripplinger) Evans; m. Virgil Harold Lindstrom, Nov. 6, 1951; children—John Nils, Launa Joyce, Kurt Terry, Joni Marie, Todd Evan, Cecelia Ann, Janae Eleanor. Author: History of Lewisville, Idaho 1882-82, 1982, Idaho's Vigilantes, 1984. Contrbr. articles to mags. Wrkg. on 2 hist. novels. Student Ricks Coll., 1949-51. Secy., Idaho Wrtr.'s League, Idaho Falls, 1972-74, v.p., 1980-82, pres., 1982-84, secy.-treas., 1984—. Named wrtr. of Yr., Idaho Wrtr.'s League, 1984. Home: Rt 1 Box 40 Roberts ID 83444

LINEBARGER, JAMES MORRIS, b. Abilene, TX, July 6, 1934, s. James Elmo and Mamie Estelle (Gaines) L.; children—Terry Glyn, Steven Randall. Author: John Berryman, 1974, Five Faces (poetry), 1976, Arthur Sampley, 1978; contrbr. articles to schl. jnls, poems to lit mags. AB, Columbia U., 1956, MA, 1957; PhD, Emory U., Atlanta, 1963. Instr., asst. prof., Georgia Tech, 1957-62; asst. prof., assoc. prof., N. Texas S.U., 1963-70, prof., 1970—. Mem. PSA: fellow AAP. Home: 1911 Whippoorwill St Denton TX 76205

LINETT, DEENA, b. Boston, Aug. 30, 1938; d. M. Henry and Esta (Markowitz) Schiff; children: 2 sons, 1 dau. Author: (novels) On Common Ground (co-winner AWP Award Series 1982), 1983, The Translator's Wife (winner Sweeny-Cox prize San Jose State U.), 1986; contbr. poetry to Harvard Mag., Stone Country, Calliope, others; contbr. short stories to MSS, Croton Rvw.; contbr. essays to Contemporary Poetry, Ms., others. AB in English, boston U., 1961; EdM, Rutgers U., 1977. Ed.D., 1982. Fellow, Corp. of Yaddo, 1981, 85. Mem. MLA, NCTE, AWP. Prof. Montclair State Coll., Upper Montclair, N.J., 1983—. Home: 318 N Fullerton Ave Montclair NJ 07042

LING, EDWIN RODGER, b. Wichita, KS., Nov. 17, 1931; s. Frank Edwin and Lila M. (Smith) L.; m. Ingrid June Hilke, June 2, 1956; children: Lorelei, Rodger, Kristin, Clifford. Author: The National Space Technology Laboratories, 1983; The Space Crescent: The Untold Story, 1984, One Family, Many Animals, 1987. BA, Grinnell Coll., 1954; JD, NYU, 1957. Dep. chief counsel NASA, Huntsville, Ala., 1963-77, chief counsel Natl. Space Tech. Labs., Miss., 1977-86; pvt. practice law, Waveland, Miss., 1978—; exec. dir. Gov.'s Office Adminstrv. Services, Jackson, 1984-86. Fellow Phi Beta Kappa. Home Friendship Oaks 107-A Coleman Ave Waveland MS 39576

LINN, EDWARD ALLEN, b. Boston, Nov. 14, 1922; s. Hyman and Gertrude (Ober) L.; m. Ruth Goldberg, June 12, 1949; children—Michael, David, Hildy. Author: Veeck—as in Wreck, 1962, The Last Loud Roar, 1964, The Hustler's Handbook, 1965, Koufax, 1966, Masque of Honor, 1969, Thirty Tons a Day, 1972, The Adversaries, 1973, Big Julie of Vegas, 1974, Out of the Fire, 1975, Nice Guys Finish Last, 1975, Where The Money Was, 1976, Inside the Yankees, The Championship Season, 1978, Steinbrenner's Yankees, 198_. BS in Jnlsm., Boston U., 1950. With USIS, Washington, 1951-52; asst. ed. Macfadden Publs., 1952-53; freelance writer, 1953-63; contrbg. ed. Sat. Eve. Post, 1964-68. Named Mag. Sportswriter of Year, Natl. Sportscasters and Sportswriters Assn., 1963. Address: 46 Marilyn Blvd Plainview NY 11803

LINNEY, ROMULUS, b. Phila., Sept. 21, 1930; s. Romulus Zachariah and Maitland (Thompson) L.; m. Ann Leggett Sims, Apr. 14, 1963 (div. 1966), 1 dau., Laura; m. 2d, Margaret Jane Andrews, Sept. 14, 1967, 1 dau., Susan. Author novels: Heathen Valley, 1962, Slowly, By Thy Hand Unfurled, 1965, Jesus Tales, 1980; plays: The Sorrows of Frederick, 1968, Democracy & Esther, 1973, The Love Suicide at Schofield Barracks, 1973, Holy Ghosts, 1976, Old Man Joseph and His Family, 1978, Tennessee, 1980, El Hermano, 1982, Childe Byron, 1982, The Captivity of Pixie Shedman, 1982, The Death of King Philip, 1984, Laughing Stock, 1984, Sand Mountain, 1985. Wrkg. on plays and novels. BA, Oberlin Coll., 1953; MFA, Yale U., 1958. Faculty Manhattan Schl. Music, NYC, 1964-72; vis. prof. Columbia Univ., NYC, 1972-74, Conn. Coll., New London, 1979, Princeton Univ., NJ, 1983-85, Univ. Pa., 1979-86. Fellow, NEA, 1974, Guggenheim Fdn., 1980, Rockefeller Fdn., 1986; recipient AAIAL award in lit, 1984; selected for OBY award, Village Voice, NYC, 1980. Mem. DG, AG, PEN (Am). Address: 235 W 76 St 14A NYC 10023

LINOMARL, , see Beilke, Marlan

LINSER, PAUL WILLIAM, (Wilhelm Milton)b. Menominee, MI, Nov. 2, 1939, s. Milton William and Ruth Estelle (Dunham) L.; m. Shirley Ann Bawyn, Mar. 26, 1960; children—Cynthia, Kimberley, Beverley. Author poetry books: The Deserted Railroad Depot, 1983, Menekaunee Train Bridge, 1984, Pulp Writing, 1984, Forsaken Patriot, 1984, Chicago Northwestern Christmas 1957, 1984. Student U. Md., 1966-67, 76, Monterey Penninsula Coll., 1980-84. Served with U.S. Army, 1957-78; instr. electronics Bay Valley Inst., San Jose, Calif., 1979-80; sr. electronics technician COMSAT Corp., Jamesburg, Calif., 1980— Home: 1765 Mescal St Seaside CA 93955

LINZNER, GORDON, b. NYC, Apr. 9, 1949, s. Charles and Harriett (Woodworth) L.; m. Jani Anderson, Oct. 1, 1976. Novelist: The Spy who Drank Blood, 1984, The Oni, 1986; contrbr. to: Mag. of Fantasy and Sci. Fiction, Rod Serling's The Twilight Zone Mag., Swords Against Darkness, vols. IV and V, others. Wrkg. on novel. Student Queens Coll., 1968-70. Ed., pub. small press Space and Time, NYC, 1966—. Mem. Horror & Occult Wrtrs, Horror Wrtrs of America (HWA), Science Fiction Wrtrs of America (SFWA) Small Press Wrtrs. & Artists Orgn. (SPWAO) (Best Ed. award 1980-84). Home: 138 W 70th St New York NY 10023

LIOTTA, PETER HEARNS, b. Burlington, VT, Sept. 16, 1956, s. Robert Gaspar and Barbara Anne (Hearns) L.; m. Donna Lee Jarosak, Oct. 20, 1979. Ed. Epoch, 1985-87, Icarus, 1977-78; contrbr. poetry to Poetry Australia, N.D. Qtly, Dakota Arts Qtly, Plains Poetry Jnl, Great River, Wascana, Coll. Poetry rvws, Pegasus, Anthology of Mag. Verse and Yearbook of Am. Poetry, others; fiction to Vermilion Lit. Project, Icarus, No. Plains Writing Project. BS, U.S. Air Force Acad., 1978; MA in Communications, U. Okla., 1984; postgrad. in English, Cornell U. Humanities scholar N.D. Humanities Council, 1983-85 MA in English, Cornell U, 1987, MFA in Writing

Cornell U, 1987; artist-in-residence N.D. Arts Council, 1983-85. Served as pilot USAF, 1978—. NEA grantee, 1983-85. Mem. AAP, P&W, Simon Johnson Lit. Guild (charter). Home: QTRS 4310D USAF Academy CO 80840

LIPKING, LAWRENCE, b NYC, Apr. 28, 1934; m. Joanna Brizdle, 1965. Author: The Ordering of the Arts in Eighteenth-Century England, 1970, The Life of the Poet, 1981; contrbr. arts. to scholarly jnls, poems and book rvws. to lit. jnls; co-ed. Norton Anthol. of Eng. Lit., 1974, 79, 86. BA, Western Res. U., 1955; MA, Cornell U., 1956, PhD, 1962. Mem. faculty dept. English, Princeton U., 1960-79, prof. comp. lit., 1975-79; Chester Tripp prof. humanities Northwestern U., Evanston, IL, 1979—, dir. program in comp. lit. & theory, 1982-84; guest lectr. colls. and univs. in U.S., 1965—. AAP award, 1956; Guggenheim fellow, 1980-81; Christian Gauss award, 1982, trustee, Newberry Library. Mem. Schl. of Criticism and Theory, MLA, ACLA, Phi Beta Kappa. Home: 425 Hamilton St Evanston IL 60202

LIPMAN, BURTON E., b. San Francisco, Feb. 19, 1931; m. Diane H. Lipman, June 21, 1953; children—Michele Lipman Fusillo, Rhonda Lipman Slaff, Joanne. Author: How to Control and Reduce Inventory, 1974, rev. ed., 1982, Successful Cost Reduction and Control, 1977, The Executive Job Search Program, 1982, The Professional Job Search Program, 1983, How to Become a Vice President in Two Weeks (More or Less), 1983, Uplaws—The Laws of Career Success, 1986. BA, Columbia Coll., 1953. Long Range Planning mgr. Johnson & Johnson, New Brunswick, N.J., 1953-62, Engring. mgr., Mobil Chem. Co., NYC, 1962-67; v.p. operations Glamorene Products, Clifton, N.J., 1967-79, v.p. operations Am. Home Products, NYC, 1980-82; pres., chief exec. officer Lehman Bros., Jersey City, 1979-80; pres., ed.-in-chief Bell Publishing, East Brunswick, N.J., since 1982. Office: Bell Pub 15 Surrey Ln East Brunswick NJ 08816

LIPMAN, DAVID, b. Springfield, MO, Feb. 13, 1931; s. Benjamin and Rose (Mack) L.; m. Marilyn Lee Vittert, Dec. 10, 1961; children—Gay Ilene, Benjamin Alan. Author: Maybe I'll Pitch Forever, 1962, Mr. Baseball, The Story of Branch Rickey, 1966, Ken Boyer, 1967, Joe Namath, 1968; co-author: The Speed King, The Story of Bob Hayes, 1971, Bob Gibson, Pitching Ace, 1975, Jim Hart, Underrated Quarterback, 1977. BJ, U. MO, 1953. Sports ed. Jefferson City (MO) Post-Tribune, 1953, Springfield Daily News, 1953-54; gen. assignment rptr. Springfield Leader and Press, 1956-57; rptr., copy ed. Kansas City (MO) Star, 1957-60; sports rptr. St. Louis Post-Dispatch, 1960-66, asst. sports ed., 1966-68, news ed., 1968-71, asst. mng. ed., 1971-78, mng. ed., 1979—; v.p., dir. Pulitzer Prodns. Inc., 1981—; guest lectr. Am. Press Inst., Columbia Jnlsm. Schl., 1967-70. Served to 1st lt. USAF, 1954-56. Mem. Football Writers Assn. Am., Am. Soc. Newspaper Eds., Soc. of Profl. Jnlsts. Office: 900 N Tucker Blvd Saint Louis MO 63101

LIPMAN, JOEL ABELMAN, b. Washington, Mar. 18, 1942, s. Norman Stanley Abelman and Anna Lee (Goldstein) Lipman; m. Pauline Melcher, 1964; m. 2d, Cynthia Lou Landrum, Dec. 18, 1982; children—Jesse Melcher, Samantha Lea. Author: Mercury Vapor Lamp, 1980, Chicago You Got a Wide Stance, 1981, 83, Reprint Original Reprint, 1983, Glass Will: An Anthology of Toledo Poetry, 1986; contrbr. poems and rvws. to Exquisite Corpse, Lost & Found Times, photoSTATIC, Am. Poetry, Berkeley Poetry, Cream City, Minn., Wis., Mid-Am., Lit. Mag. rvws, Quixote, Paunch, Poetry Ohio, Poetry Australia, Gravida, Bloody Twin Press Broadside, others. Wrkg. on translitics, artist's books, research on Bareiss collection of illustrated books. BS, U. Wis., 1964, JD, 1968; MA, U. Buffalo, 1973. Mem. faculty Columbia Coll., Chgo., 1969-73, U. Toledo, 1975—; mem. vis. faculty U. Ill., Chgo. 1976-77. Individual artist fellow Ohio Arts Council, 1977, 80, 85, Gov.'s award, 1985. Mem. P&W, Toledo Poets Ctr. (dir., 1975—). Home: 2720 Winsted Toledo OH 43606

LIPPARD, LUCY ROWLAND, b. NYC, Apr. 14, 1937; d. Vernon William and Margaret Isham (Cross) L.; m. Robert Tracy Ryman, Aug. 19, 1961 (div.); 1 son, Ethan Isham. Author: 13 books, including: From the Center: Feminist Essays on Women's Art, 1976, Eva Hesse, 1976, I See-You Mean, 1979, Ad Reinhardt, 1981, Overlay: Contemporary Art and the art of Prehistory, 1983, Get the Message? A Decade of art for Social Change, 1984; contrbg. ed. Art in Am., NYC, 1972—; art columnist Village Voice, NYC, 1981—85; art columnist, In These Times, Chicago, 1985—; co-fdr.: Heresies: A Feminist Pubn. on Art and Politics, 1976, Politl. Art Documen.-Distn., 1979; co-ed.: Upfront, 1981, Cultural Democ., 1983. BA, Smith Coll., 1958; MA, NYU, 1962; DFA (hon.), Moore Coll. Arts, Phila., 1972, San Francisco Art Institute, 1985. Free-lance writer, curator, lectr., 1960—. Guggenheim fellow, 1968, NEA fellow, 1972, 76. Home: 138 Prince St New York NY 10012

LIPPERT, RONALD STEVEN, b., NYC., May 13, 1949. Ed.: Methods: Jnl. Animal Health Technology, 1978-80, San Francisco Animal Health Technician Assn. Newsletter, 1979-81, San Francisco Ind., 1982—, San Francisco Style, 1985—, Near Escapes, 1985—, Grocery Express, 1985—, Bay Area Advt. News, 1986—; ed., pub. New Methods: Jnl. Animal Health Technology, San Francisco, 1981—. AS, Cosumnes River Coll., Sacramento, 1979. Pub. relations coordinator Cosumnes River Coll., 1978-79; pub. relations Staff Calif. Animal Health Technician Assn., San Leandro, 1982-84. Office: Box 22605 San Francisco CA 94122

LIPSET, SEYMOUR MARTIN, b. NYC, Mar. 18, 1922; s. Max and Lena (Lippman) L.; m. Elsie Braun, Dec. 26, 1944 (dec., Feb. 27, 1987); children—David, Daniel, Carola. Author: Agrarian Socialism, 1950, (with others) Union Democ., 1956, (with R. Bendix) Social Mobility in Industl. Society, 1959, Politl. Man, 1960, rev. ed. 1981, The First New Nation, 1963, rev. ed 1979, Revoln. and Counter Revoln., 1968, (with Earl Raab) The Politics of Unreason, rev. ed. 1978, Rebellion in the University, 1972, (with Everett Ladd) Academics and the 1972 Elect., 1973, Professors, Unions and Am. Higher Edn., 1973, The Divided Academy, 1975, (with David Riesman) Edn. and Politics at Harvard, 1975, (with I.L. Horowitz) Dialogues on Am. Politics, 1978, (with William Schneider) The Confidence Gap, 1983, Consensus and Conflict, 1985; co-ed.: Class, Status and Power, 1953, Labor and Trade Unionism, 1969, Sociology: The Progress of a Decade, 1961, Culture and Social Char., 1971, The Berkeley Student Revolt, 1965, Class, Status and Power in Comparative Perspect., 1966, Soc. Struct., Mobility and Econ. Devel., 1966, Elites in Latin Am., 1967, Party Systems and Voter Alignments, 1967, Students in Revolt, 1969, Issues in Polit. and Covt., 1970, Failure of a Dream? Essays in the Hist. of Am. Socialism, 1974, Pub. Opin. mag.; ed.: Students and Pol., 1967, Pol. and Soc. Sci., 1969, Emerging Coalitions in Am. Pol., 1978, The Third Century, 1979, Party Coalitions in the Eighties, 1981, Unions in Transition: Entering the Second Century, 1986. BS, CCNY, 1943; PhD, Columbia U., 1949; MA (hon.), Harvard U., 1966; LLD, Villanova U., 1973, Hebrew U., 1981. Lectr. U. Toronto, 1946-48; asst. prof. U.CA-Berkeley, 1948-50; asst., then assoc., prof. grad. faculty Columbia U., 1950-56, asst. dir. Bur. Applied Soc. Research, 1954-56; prof. sociol. U.CA-Berkeley, 1956-66, dir. Inst. Intl. Studies, 1962-66; prof. govt. and sociol., Harvard U., 1966—, George Markham prof., 1974-75; prof. poli. sci. and sociol., sr. fellow Hoover Instn., Stanford U., 1975—, Caroline S.G. Munro prof., 1981—. Gunnar Myrdal prize, 1970; Townsend Harris medal, 1971; Guggenheim fellow, 1971-72; Margaret Byrd Dawson award, 1986, Northern Telecom Intl. Prize in Canadian Studies, 1987. Fellow AAAS, numerous profl. orgns. Office: Hoover Meml Bldg. Stanford U Stanford CA 94305

LIPTON, WILLIAM LAWRENCE, (Bill Hill), b. Queens, NY, Oct. 8, 1944; s. Bernard and Florence (Simon) L.; m. June Ann Schilowsky, Jan. 20, 1966 (dec. Sept. 5, 1968); children—Seth Alexander, Samantha Bryl. Author: (non-fiction) Prophecy Notebook, 1978, Beyond the Seventh Seal, 1978; (novel) Chinese Sabbatical, 1986, Chopped Liver, 1987; (film short) The Meeting, 1966. Wrkg. on spy mystery, sequel to mystery. B.S. in Edn., N.Y. U., 1968; B.A. in Real Estate, Pace U., 1972, M.B.A. in Accounting, 1974. Film maker, artist, 1964-70; real estate broker, N.Y.C., 1966—; free-lance wrtr., 1978—. Home: Wilson District Rd Harrington ME 04643

LISH, GORDON JAY, b. Hewlett, NY, Feb. 11, 1934; s. Philip and Regina (Deutsch) L.; m. Loretta Frances Fokes, Nov. 7, 1956 (div. May 1967); children: Jennifer, Rebecca, Ethan; m. Barbara Works, May 30, 1969; 1 son, Atticus. Author: English Grammar, 1964, The Gabbernot, 1965, Why Work, 1966, A Man's Work, 1967, New Sounds in American Fiction, 1969, Secrets High and Low, 1979; What I Know So Far (short stories), 1981; Dear Mr. Capote (novel), 1983, Peru (novel), 1986. BA cum laude, U. Ariz., 1959; postgrad., San Francisco State Coll., 1960. Broadcaster stations KPDN, Tex., WELI, New Haven, WVNJ, NYC, 1960-63; instr. English, Mills High Schl. and Coll., San Mateo, CA, 1961-63; editorial dir. Genesis West lit mag, 1961-65; ed.-in-chief, dir. linguistic studies Behavioral Research Labs, Menlo Park, CA, 1963-66; with Ed. Devel. Corp., Palo Alto, 1966-69; fiction ed., Esquire, 1969-77; with Alfred A. Knopf, 1977—; tchr. fiction wrtg. Columbia U., 1980—. Address: Knopf 201 E 50 St New York NY 10022

LISOWSKI, JOSEPH ANTHONY, b. Pitts., Sept. 17, 1944; s. Anthony Francis and Harriet Antoinette (Kruszewska) L.; m. Eileen Geneive Connors, May 28, 1966 (div. 1976); children—Julia, David, Christa; m. 2d, Linda Rose Tucker, Dec. 6, 1980; 1 dau., Christina. Author: The Brushwood Gate (trans. T'ang Dynasty poet Wang Wei), 1984, Three Islands, a collection of poetry by Trevor Parris and Joseph Lisowski, 1987, Spring Street Blues (winner of Black Bear Press intl. competition) 1987. Contrbr. poetry to Negative Capability, Amelia, The Lit Rvw, Forum, Boundary 2, Buckle, Poetry Today, Earthwise Jnl, The Yellow Butterfly, Mid South Writer, Visions, Mozart Park, Salome, Blue Unicorn, White Rock Reunion, Crosscurrents, Goblets, Pacific Poetry and Fiction Rvw, Sun

Dog, Am Lit Rvw, Princeton Spectrum, others. Wrkg. on mystery novel and a rewriting of Dante's Divine Comedy. MA, Duquesne U., 1968; PhD, SUNY-Binghamton, 1974., assoc. prof. of English, Univ. of the Virgin Islands, 1986-, NEH fellow, 1980-81. Mem. P&W, Writers in Va. Address: 12 Faculty East U Virgin Islands St Thomas USUI 00802

LISTER, MARILYN J., b. Los Angeles, Nov. 24, 1930; d. Walter H. and Juanita E. (Hughes) L. Ed. & contrbr., Physical Therapy, 1979—; author Chapter 6, The Physical Therapist, in Orthopedic Rehabilitation, 1982. BS, UCLA, 1953. Staff/sr. physical therapist, L.A. County/ USC Med. Ctr., Los Angeles, 1953-59; instr./ supr. Rancho Los Amigos Hosp., Downey, CA, 1959-74; dir. of Phys. Ther., Helen Hayes Hosp., W. Haverstraw, NY, 1974-76; asst. ed. Physical Therapy, Washington, 1977-79, ed. 1979—. Mem. AMWA. Home: 4126 Bruning Ct Fairfax VA 22032

LITCHFIELD, ADA BASSETT, b. Harwich, MA, Apr. 1, 1916; d. Ernest Irving and Elizabeth Jane (Taylor) Bassett; m. Paul Ordello Litchfield, July 17, 1959. Author: A Button in Her Ear, 1976, A Cane in Her Hand, 1977, Words in Our Hands, 1980, It's Going to Rain, 1980, Cap'n Hook—That's Me!, 1982, Making Room for Uncle Joe, 1983; ednl. TV scripts. B.S. in Ed., Hyannis Tchrs. Coll., 1937. Wrtr., ed. Rust Craft Pubs., Boston, Dedham, MA, 1953-59; ed. Ginn & Co., Boston, 1959-62, Houghton Mifflin, Boston, 1962-72, retired; free-lance wrtr., 1973—. Mem. SCBW. Home: 72 Bassick Circle Stoughton MA 02072

LITEWKA, JACK, b. NYC, Oct. 23, 1945, s. Julko and Leja (Segal) L. Author: Software Packages: An Encyclopedic Guide (3 vols.), 1970, The Socialized Penis, 1973, How the Conversation Begins (poems), 1980, The Dolphin and the Piano (poems), 1980, The Bicycle Bus, 1981, How to Conduct Market Research, 1981, A Training Manual for a Digital Reflection Densitometer (with cassette), 1982, A Training Manual for Computer Typesetting for Financial Printers, 1984; co-author: Pesticide Application and Safety Training (with M.W. Stimmann), 1977, Pesticide Toxicities (with Stimmann), 1979, Skills Analysts Look at the Ergonomics of Keyboarding (with Lillian G. Malt), 1984. BA, U. Calif.-Berkeley, 1967; MFA, Columbia U., 1969. Ed.-in-chief System Interaction, NYC, 1969-70; exec. dir. NECTI, New Haven, 1980-83; ed. Spectrum mag., NYC, 1983-84; mng. dir. Aris Books, Berkeley, Calif., 1985—. Recipient Ida Coolbrith Meml. Poetry award U. Calif., 1967—; Woodrow Wilson fellow, 1967. Home: Box 22585 Seattle WA 98122

LITMAN, ROBERT BARRY, b. Phila., Nov. 17, 1947, s. Benjamin N. and Bette E. (Saunders) L.; m. Androniki Thomas, Apr. 21, 1985; 2 daus., Riva Belle and Nadya Beth. Author: Wynnefield and Limer (novel), 1983. BS, Yale U., 1967, MD, 1970, MS, 1972, MPhil, 1972. Practice medicine, New Haven, 1971-77, Ogdensburg, N.Y., 1977—; med. commentator radio, TV stas., Ogdensburg, Watertown, N.Y., 1978—. Mem. med. orgns, charter member, National Assn. of Physician Broadcasters. Home: Box 29 Ogdensburg NY 13669

LITSEY, SARAH, see Ford, Sarah Litsey

LITT, IRIS, b. NYC., Mar. 18, 1928, d. Arthur Oren and Belle (Zanditon) Litt; m. Gilbert Burris, July 11, 1948 (dec. 1954); children—Jonathan, Dean. Contrbr. poetry: Poetry Now, Poet Lore, Icarus, Bitterroot, numerous other lit. publs.; contrbr. articles: Wrtr.'s Digest, Miss America, Calling All Girls, others. BA, Ohio State U. Copywrtr. Benton & Bowles Advt., N.Y.C., 1962-64; copy supvr. Clinton Frank Advt., NYC., 1964-70, AC&R Advt., NYC, 1971-84; prin. The Village Wordsmith, NYC., 1984—; guest ed. Mademoiselle mag., 1947; assoc. ed. Mag. Mgmt. Co., 1948, 49. Me. PSA. Home: 252 W 11th St New York NY 10014

LITTLE, GERALDINE CLINTON, b. Portstewart, N. Ireland, Sept. 20, 1923; arrd. U.S.A., 1925; d. James Robert and Louisa Margaret (Corr) Clinton; m. Robert Knox Little, Sept. 26, 1953; children: Rory Knox, Timothy Howard, Rodney Clinton. Author: Hakugai: Poem From A Concentration Camp, Contrast in Keenings: Ireland, Endless Waves, Stilled Wind, Seasons in Space, Beyond the Boxwood Comb, The Spinalonga Poems; contrbr. poems to more than 150 jnls including Shenandoah, Cal. Qtly, Seneca Rvw, Poetry NW, Commonweal, Yankee, Confrontations. BA in lit., Goddard Coll., 1971; MA in English lit., Trenton State Coll., 1976. Exec. secy. Max Levy & Co, Phila, 1945-55; prof. English Burlington County Coll., Pemberton, NJ, 1978—; prof. Rutgers Univ., 1979; prof. creative writing Trenton State Coll., NJ, 1985. Pres. Treble & Bass Clef Chorus, Mt. Holly, NJ, 1960; pres. Friends of the Library, Mt. Holly, 1970-71. Mem PSA (recipient Gordon Barber award, Alfred Kreymborg award, Cecil Hemley award, Gustave Davidson award). Address: 519 Jacksonville Rd Mt Holly NJ 08060

LITTLE, KERRY, see Sheftel, Beatrice K.

LITTLE, LOYD HARRY, JR., b. Hickory, NC, Sept. 12, 1940; s. Loyd Harry and Rebecca Lillian (Bailey) L.; m. Drena Edwards, Dec. 23, 1963. Author: Parthian Shot, 1975 (Ernest Hemingway award), In the Village of the man, 1978. BA in Journalism, U. NC, 1962, postgrad., 1967-68. Editor Lumbee weekly nwspr., Pembroke, NC, 1966; med. rptr. Winston-Salem (NC) Jnl, 1967-69; bus. ed. Raleigh (NC) News and Observer, 1969; ed. Carolina Fin. Times, Raleigh, 1970-75; spcl. projects ed. Durham (NC) Morning Herald, 1976-79; tchr. creative writing courses U. NC, 1979—. Served with Green Berets U.S. Army, 1962-65. Decorated Commendation medal, Combat Inf. badge, Combat Med. badge, Vietnamese Bronze Star medal. Mem. PEN. Home: Rt 3 Box 660 Hillsborough NC 27278

LITTLEDALE, FREYA LOTA, b. NYC, d. David Milton and Dorothy Ida (Passloff) Brown; 1 son, Glenn David. Writer, editor: The Magic Fish, 1967, Timothy's Forest (with others), 1969, King Fox and Other Old Tales, 1971, The Magic Tablecloth, 1972, The Boy Who Cried Wolf, The Elves and the Shoemaker (Scholastic Blue Ribbon Book), 1975, Seven at One Blow, 1976, The Snow Child, 1978, Snow White and the Seven Dwarfs, 1981, Pinocchio, 1979, I Was Thinking (poetry), 1979, The Magic Plum Tree, 1981, The Farmer in the Soup, 1987, The Wizard of Oz, 1982, Frankenstein, 1983, The Sleeping Beauty, 1984, The Little Mermaid, 1986; ed.: A Treasure Chest of Poetry, 1964, Thirteen Ghostly Tales, 1966, Andersen's Fairy Tales, 1966, Ghosts, Witches and Demons, 1971, Ghosts and Spirits of Many Lands, 1970, Strange Tales from Many Lands, 1975; plays: Stop That Pancake, 1975, The King and Queen Who Wouldn't Speak, 1975, The Giant's Garden, 1975, The Big Race, 1976; contrbr.: Scribner Anthology for Young People, 1976, This Way to Books, 1983, New Treasury of Children's Poetry, 1984, Conn. River Rvw, 1985, Stories and Poems for a Rainy Day, 1986 On This Crust of Earth, 1986; writings included in Laidlaw Reading Program, Scott Foresman Reading Systems, Silver Burdett Social Studies Program, Sci. Research Assocs. Rading Lab. BS, Ithaca Coll.; postgrad., NYU. Assoc. ed. Maco Mag. Corp., NYC, 1960-62; juvenile book ed. Parents' Mag. Press, NYC, 1962-65; free-lance wrtr., ed., 1965—; instr. juvenile writing course Fairfield (Conn.) U., 1984, 86, 87. Mem. PEN, AG, Soc. Children's Book Wrtrs. Office: c/o Curtis Brown 10 Astor Pl New York NY 10003

LITTLEFIELD, BILL, b. Montclair, NJ, July 13, 1948; m. Mary Atlee, Jan. 16, 1982. Contrbr. poetry to numerous jnls. BA, Yale U., 1970; EdM, Harvard U., 1973. Asst. prof. Curry Coll., Milton, Mass., 1977—; commentator WBUR-FM, Boston, 1984—, Natl. Public Radio, Washington, 1984—. Winner 2 AP Broadcast awards, 1985. Mem. AAUP. Home: 51 Lawton Rd Needham MA 02192

LITTLEJON, JON, see Kleinhans, Theodore John

LITWACK, LEON FRANK, b. Santa Barbara, CA, Dec. 2, 1929; s. Julius and Minnie (Nitkin) L.; m. Rhoda Lee Goldberg, July 5, 1952; children—John Michael, Ann Katherine. Author: North of Slavery: The Negro in the Free States, 1790-1860, 1961, Too Look for America (film), 1971, Been in the Storm So Long: The Aftermath of Slavery, 1979, The United States, 1981; ed. Am. Labor Movement, 1962; co-ed. Reconstruction, 1969. BA, U. CA- Berkeley, 1951, MA, 1952, PhD, 1958. Asst. prof., then assoc. prof. history U. WI, Madison, 1958-65; mem. faculty U.CA- Berkeley, 1965—, prof. history, 1971-, Alexander F. and May T. Morrison Prof. of History, 1987; Fulbright prof. Am. history Moscow (USSR) State U., 1980. Served with AUS, 1953-55. Pulitzer prize history, 1980; Am. book award in history, 1980; Guggenheim fellow, 1967-68, Rockefeller fellow, 1983; grantee NEH, 1971, NIMH, 1972-73. Mem. Orgn. Am. Historians, Am. Hist. Assn., Southern Historical Assn., Society of American Historians, Orgn. of American Historians, 1986-87. Home: 801 Cragmont Ave Berkeley CA 94708

LITWEILER, JOHN BERKEY, b. South Bend, IN, Feb. 21, 1940; s. Ernest John and Lucile (Yoder) L. Author: The Freedom Principle, 1984 (also U.K. and Fed. Republic Germany editions). Articles, rvws: Chicago, Reader, Tribune, Sun Times, NY Times Book Rvw, Jazz Monthly, and others. BA, North Central Coll., Naperville, Ill., 1962. Staff ed. Downbeat, Downbeat Books, Chgo., 1974-75, 79-81. Fellow Music Critics Assn., 1974, NEH, 1981. Mem. NWU. Home: 5633 S Kenwood Ave Chicago IL 60637

LITZ, ARTHUR WALTON, JR., b. Nashville, Oct. 31, 1929; s. Arthur Walton and Lucile (Courtney) L.; m. Marian Ann Weller, Feb. 2, 1958; children—Katharine, Andrew, Victoria, Emily. Author: The Art of James Joyce, 1961, Modern Am. Fiction: Essays in Criticism, 1963, Jane Austen, 1965, James Joyce, 1966, James Joyce's Dubliners, 1969, The Poetic Development of Wallace Stevens, 1972, Eliot in His Time, 1973, Scribner Quarto of Mod. Lit., 1977, Major Am. Short Stories, 1980, Ezra Pound and Dorothy Shakespear: Their Letters 1909-14, 1984. AB, Princeton U., 1951; D.Phil., Oxford (Eng.) U., 1954. Instr. Princeton U., 1956-58; lectr. Columbia U., 1957-58; mem. faculty Princeton U., 1958—, prof. English lit., 1968—, chmn. English dept., 1974-81; mem. editorial bd. Princeton U. Press, 1967-71. Sr. fellow NEH, 1974-75; Guggenheim fellow, 1982-83. Home: 187 Prospect St Princeton NJ 08540

LIU, STEPHEN SHU-NING, b. Fu-Ling, Sichuan, China, Mar. 16, 1930; m. Shirley S.N. Yu, Dec. 23, 1966; 2 daus., Miranda, April Liu. Author: Dream Journeys to China, 1982; contrbr. poetry to textbooks: An Introduction to Fiction, Poetry and Drama, An Introduction to Poetry; contrbr. poems and short stories to more than 200 lit mags in US, China, Can., England and Australia, inclg. Am. Poetry Rvw, Western Humanities Rvw, Colo. Qtly, Calif. Qtly, Malahat Rvw. PhD in English, U.ND, 1973. Asst. prof. No. Mont. Coll., Harve, 1965-70; tchg. asst. U. ND, Grand Forks, 1970-73; prof. Eng. Clark County Comm. Coll., Las Vegas, Nev., 1973—. Recipient NEA award, 1981-82, PEN fiction contest, 1983. Address: 4024 Deerfield Ave Las Vegas NV 89117

LIU, TANYA FU-CHIANG, see Seagull, Samantha Singer

LIVINGSTON, J.A., b. NYC, Feb. 10, 1905; s. Solomon Joseph and Maud (Stern) L.; m. Rosalie L. Frenger, Sept. 16, 1927; 1 dau., Patricia Livingston Herban. Author: Reconversion—The Job Ahead, 1944, The American Stockholder, 1958, rev. edit., 1963; nwspr. series: America's Stake in the British Crisis, 1959, The Soviet Challenge, 1956, The Kennedy Crash, 1962, The Common Market, 1962, The Powerful Pull of the Dollar, 1964, Gold and the Dollar, 1966, The Great Society and the Stock Market, 1966, Economic Consequences of Vietnam, 1968, Gold vs. the Dollar, 1968, Money—A New Epoch, 1969, The British Economy—Human Race Against Ruin, 1974, The Second Battle of Britain, 1975, Great Britain in Adversity, 1977, The Decline of the Dollar: An American Tragedy, 1978, South Africa: In the Throes of Change, 1978, English Lessons for America, 1981, The '80s: The Dangerous Decade, 1983; contrbr. to natl. publs. and learned jnls & Compton's Ency. AB, U;. MI, 1925; Litt.D., Temple U., 1966. Nwspr. rptr., 1925-30; exec. ed. N.Y. Daily Investment News, 1931-34; pub. utility ed. Financial World, 1935; economist Bus. Week, 1935-42, W.P.B. and Office War Moblzn. and Reconversion, 1942-45; column "Bus. Outlook" (now syndicated), 1945—; fin. ed. Phila. Record, 1946; bus. columnist Washington Post, 1947; fin. ed. Phila. Bull., 1948-67, econ. columnist, 1968-72, Phila. Inquirer, 1972—; broadcaster WCAU, Phila., 1962-64; prof. econs. Temple U., 1971-72. Recipient numerous awards. Home: 2110 Delancey Pl Philadelphia PA 19103

LIVINGSTON, JAY CARL, (Edwards, Livingston), b. Milw. Author: The Fount of Dreams, 1977, The Romantic Muse, 1978, Poetics, Prosody & Passion, 1979. Editor: Portai of Peace, 1978, Seasons of Love, 1978, The Seventh Pillar, 1981; contrbr. to Fuse, Bugle Am., Milw. Rvw, St. Louis Concert News; ed.: De Profundis; multi-media: Water Torture, American Bicentennial, Readings from the Fount. Plays: A Hero's Death, 1982, We Are Only Human, 1984. MA, D.Litt., Rozenkreuz Inst. Arts, Upper Knebworth, UK. Founder Gen. Literatum; scout, Inner Earth Soc.; steward, Arq Turus Astralis; branch dir. Fraternite Querir Balai. Office: Metatron Agcy Box 10333 Milwaukee WI 53210

LIVINGSTON, MYRA COHN, b. Omaha, NE, Aug. 17, 1926; d. Mayer L. and Gertrude (Marks) Cohn; m. Richard Roland Livingston, Apr. 14, 1952; children—Joshua, Jonas Cohn, Jennie Marks. Author: Whispers and Other Poems, 1958, Wide Awake and Other Poems, 1959, I'm Hiding, 1961, See What I Found, 1962, I Talk to Elephants, 1962, I'm Not Me, 1963, Happy Birthday, 1964, The Moon and a Star and Other Poems, 1965, I'm Waiting, 1966, Old Mrs. Twindlytart and Other Rhymes, 1967, A Crazy Flight and Other Poems, 1968, The Malibu and Other Poems, 1972, When You Are Alone/It Keeps You Capone: An Approach to Creative Writing with Children, 1973, Come Away, 1974, The Way Things Are and Other Poems, 1974, 4-Way Stop and Other Poems, 1976, A Lollygag of Limericks, 1978, O Sliver of Liver and Other Poems, 1979, No Way of Knowing: Dallas Poems, 1980, A Circle of Seasons, 1982, How Pleasant to Know Mr. Lear!, 1982, Sky Songs, 1984, A Song I Sang To You, 1984, Monkey Puzzle and Other Poems, 1984, The Child as Poet: Myth or Reality?, Celebrations, 1985, Worlds I Knew and Other Poems, 1985. Sea Songs, 1986, Earth Songs, 1986. The Writing of Poetry; co-ed. The Scott-Foresman Anthology, 1984, ed. 20 poetry anthologies; creator film strips; contrbr. arts. on children's lit. to ednl. publs., essays on lit. and reading in edn. to var. books. BA, Sarah Lawrence Coll., 1948. Profl. horn player, 1941-48; asst. ed. Campus mag., 1949-50; var. pub. rels. positions and pvt. sec. to Hollywood (CA) personalities, 1950-52; tchr. creative writing Dallas (TX) public lib. and schls., 1958-63; poet-in-residence, Beverly Hills (CA) Unified Schl. Dist., 1966-84;, sr. instr. UCLA Extension, 1973—; cons. to var. schl. dists., 1966—, cons. poetry to publishers children's lit., 1975—. Excellence in poetry award NCTE, 1980. Mem. AG, SCBW, So. Calif. Council on Lit. for Children and Young People (Notable Book award 1972), PEN., Texas Inst. of Letters Award, 1961 and 1980. Address: 9308 Readcrest Dr Beverly Hills CA 90210

LIVINGSTON, PATRICK MURRAY, b. Pitts., Oct. 16, 1920; s. John and Sarah Ann (Malloy) L.; m. Eileen Hamilton, Nov. 24, 1962; children—Linda Maureen, Patricia Michele; 1 stepson, James L. Hamilton III. Author: Pro Football Handbook, 1961, The Pittsburgh Steelers, an Illustrated History, 1980, BA, St. Francis Coll., Loretto, PA, 1941; LLB, JD, Duquesne U. Publicity dir. Pitts. Steelers, 1942-48; sports writer, sports ed. Pitts. Press Co., 1949-84; elector Profl. Football Hall of Fame. Dick McCann award Pro Football Writers Assn. Am.; Pitts. Man of Year in Communications, 1983. Mem. Pitts. Press Club. Home: 4920 Brightwood Rd C-212 Bethel Park PA 15102

LIVINGSTONE, HARRISON EDWARD, (John Fairfield), b. Urbana, IL., May 23, 1937. Author: Poems, 1967; (novel under name John Fairfield) David Johnson Passed Through Here, 1972; (novel) The Wild Rose, 1985. JD U. Balt., 1964; BA, Harvard U., 1970. Home: Siple 1609 Park Grove Ave Baltimore MD 21228

LIVINGSTON-WHITE, DEBORAH JOYCE HALEMAH, (Debi Starr-White), b. DeQuoin, IL, Nov. 21, 1947; d. Jetson Edgar and Tressie Mae (Gaston) Livingston; m. William Tyrone White, Jan. 31, 1971. Author: In Love & In Business, 1986; (screenplay) The Best of Simple, 1980. Contrbr. articles, poems to popular and lit. mags., profl. & research jnls. B.S., Southern Ill. U., 1968, M.S. in Edn., 1971; Ed.D., Northern Ill. U., 1975. Entrepreneur, lectr., wrtr. Intl. Cons., 1980—; dir. spcl. ed. Oak Park Schl. District, MI, 1987—; spcl. ed. cons. Dept. Edn., Lansing, MI, 1978—. Recipient 3d place Am. Printers Assn., 1965, Fresh Start Award Chrysler Corp. and SELF Mag., 1986. Mem. Council Exceptional Children, Natl. Assn. Songwriters, Studio on Washington-Poetry Resource Center. Office: Intl Consultants 24041 Geneva Oak Park MI 48237

LLEDIAITH, RHIANNON MARIE, b. Lake Charles, LA, Mar. 23, 1962; d. Milton August Fontenot and Judith Kay (New) Jewett. Contrbr. articles to book, newspapers, including Washington Post, USA Today, others. Ed.: Overseas Tribune, 1985-87, Suburban Record, 1985-87, India News, 1985-87, Indian Cultural Coordination Com., 1987. B.A., Gallandet U., 1987. Comml. artist Suburban Record, Silver Spring, MD, 1984-87; artistic dir. Prout Univ., 1987—. Home: 10121 Greeley Ave Silver Spring MD 20902

LLOYD, DAVID HUBERT, (DH), b. Marietta, OH, June 16, 1948; s. Hubert Fenwick and Mary Agnes (Smith) L.; m. Shelley V. Hellen, Sept. 6, 1980; 1 son, Jesse. Author: Mog & Glog & Other Stories, 1978, If Gravity Wasn't Discovered, 1979, Dream, Myths & Other Realities, 1984, Bible Bob Meets a Jesus Honker, 1986; contrbr. short stories to Nitty Gritty, Slick Press, Italia Am., Truely Fine Press, Kindred Spirit, The Fantastic; contrbr. poetry to Wormwood Rvw, Blind Alley, Etc., Impulse Press, Visions of Peace, Crawl Space, Pinchpenny, others. BS, Calif. State U-Long Beach, 1978. Quality control tech. Johns-Manville, Denison Tex., 1966; data processing Humble Oil Co., Houston, 1967; elec. tech. Krayco, Long Beach, Calif., 1974, Calif. State Univ., 1978—, math instr., 1985—. Served to E5, USN, 1967-73. Address: 1239 E 10th Long Beach CA 90804

LLOYD, LINDA MARIE, (Linda Harper), b. Saginaw, MI, July 29, 1941; d. John Lloyd and Dorothy (Dabbert) Jones; m. James R. Nette, Aug. 1, 1964 (div. 1976); 1 son, David Lloyd Nette. Author: Classroom Magic, 1982, Computers in Education, 1985. Wrkg. on 2d edit. Classroom Magic. AB in Edn., U. Mich.-Ann Arbor, 1963; MAT Spcl. Ed., Oakland U., Rochester, MN, 1978. Tchr. elementary schls. Southfield, Mich., 1963-67, 75—. Home: 5366 Breeze Hill Troy MI 48098

LO, QUINN, see Tausch, Susan Diane

LOBEL, ARNOLD STARK, b. Los Angeles, May 22, 1933; s. Joseph and Lucille Harriet (Stark) L.; m. Anita, Apr. 16, 1955; children—Adrianne, Adam. Author, illustrator children's books: Zoo for Mister Muster, 1962, Prince Bertram the Red, 1963, Holiday for Mister Muster, 1963, Giant John, 1964, Lucille, 1964, Martha the Movie Mouse, 1966, Great Blueness and Other Predicaments, 1968, Small Pig, 1969, Frog and Toad Are Friends, 1970, Ice-Cream Cone Coot and Other Rare Birds, 1971, On the Day Peter Stuyvesant Sailed into Town, 1971, Mouse Tales, 1972, Frog and Toad Together, 1972, The Man Who Took the Indoors Out, 1977, How the Rooster Saved the Day, 1977, Gregory Griggs and the Nursery Rhyme People, 1978, Days with Frog and Toad, 1979, Fables, 1980 (Caldecott award 1970-71, Newberry award 1972, Christopher award 1971-76), On Market Street, 1981, Uncle Elephant, 1981, Ming Lo Moves the Mountain, 1982, The Book of Pigericks, 1983. BFA, Pratt Inst., 1955. Mem. AG. Address: Harper & Row 10 E 53d St New York NY 10022

LOCKE, EDWARD, b. NYC, Nov. 9, 1928, s. Morris Ralph and Celia (Zimmerman) L.; m. Elisabeth Hildesheimer, Feb. 4, 1956 (dec. 1970); 1 son, David; m. 2d, Janet Schillinger, Jan. 3, 1976. Author: Pause and Other Poems, 1954, Harlequin Ade, 1981; contrbr. anthols. Riverside Poetry 2, 1956, American Poetry Old and New, 1965. MA, NYU, 1950; MS, Columbia U., 1956. Mem. New Eng. Poetry Club (treas., recipient Rosalie Boyle award 1983), PSA. Home: 12 Flagstaff Hill Terr Canton MA 02021

LOCKETT, REGINALD FRANKLIN, b. Berkeley, CA, Nov. 5, 1947; s. Jewell and Alyce Irene (Matthis) L.; m. Faye Arvis West, Jan. 23, 1983 (div. Sept. 1, 1987); children—Maya Lomasi Lauren Aimee. Author: Good Times & No Bread, 1978. Contrbr. numerous poems to lit. mags., anthols. Ed.: Folio, 1977. B.A., San Francisco State U., 1971, M.A., 1972. English instr. North Peralta Commun. Coll., Oakland, CA, 1973-75, Laney Coll., Oakland, 1975-76; lectr. creative writing San Francisco State U., 1976-78; reading lab instr. City Coll. San Francisco, 1982—. Home: 3717 Market St Oakland CA 94608

LOCKHART, ANITA MAY, b. Rome, NY, Feb. 10, 1934, d. Albert Leslie and Sarah Elizabeth (Wilkinson) Phelps; m. Frank Paul Lockhart, Aug. 23, 1952; children—Paul Anthony, Margo June. Author: Sense and Sentiment (poetry), 1977; ed.: Yesterday's Blacksmith (by Charles Nolan), 1985. Wrkg. on poetry, poetry anthology. Student public schl., Camden, N.Y. With Rome (N.Y.) Air Devel. Center, 1966—, adminstrv. officer, 1979—. Home: Box 527 RR 2 Blossvale NY 13308

LOCKRIDGE, ERNEST HUGH, b. Bloomington, IN, Nov. 28, 1938, s. Ross Franklin and Vernice (Baker) L.; m. Rebecca Bryant, Aug. 26, 1960 (div. 1980); children—Laurel, Ellen, Sara; m. 2d, Laurel Richardson, Jan. 12, 1982. Author: Hartspring Blows His Mind (novel), 1968, Prince Elmo's Fire (novel, Book-of-the-Month Club alt.), 1974, Twentieth-Century Interpretations of The Great Gatsby, 1968, Flying Elbows (novel), 1975. AB, Ind. U., 1960; PhD, Yale U., 1964. Mem. faculty Yale U., New Haven, 1963-71; assoc. prof. Ohio State U., Columbus, 1971-76, prof., 1976—. Center for Advanced Study fellow, U. Ill., 1969-70. Mem. Phi Beta Kappa, Phi Gamma Delta. Home: 143 W South St Worthington OH 43085

LOCKSMITH, JOSEPH LOUIS, b. NYC, Nov. 17, 1926; s. Joseph L. and Rita (Barnenoble) L.; m. Maria Bart, Mar. 16, 1946; children—Thomas, Rebecca. Author: Ruins of a River, 1956, Men Against Birds, 1966, Siege, 1976, Order from Entropy, 1979. BS, U. of Iowa, 1950. Served as pvt. AUS, 1944-45. Home: 3093 Dato Highland Park IL 60035

LODWICK, TERESA JANE, (Elizabeth Michaels), b. Portsmouth, OH, May 12, 1959; d. Kenneth Douglas and Janie Lou (Dunlap) Cooper; divorced; children—Michael Blaine Cooper, Kevin Dale. Author poetry: A Woman's Heart, 1985, Empty Eyes, 1986. Contrbr. poems to anthols., newspapers, lit. mags. Poetry ed.: Shawnee Silhouette, 1984-87. Wrkg. on collection of poetry: Heroes. A.A., Shawnee State U., 1985; B.A. in English, Ohio U., 1988. Recipient Golden Poet award World of Poetry, 1985, 87. Mem. Shawnee Poetry Circle (past pres.), Phoenis Wrtrs. (fellow). Home: 1532 Third St Portsmouth OH 45662

LOEB, TIMOTHY ALLAN, b. Chgo., Nov. 30, 1950; s. Thomas Henry and Joan (DeHaven) L. AB, U. Pa., 1974; MBA, Thomas Coll., 1987. Mgr. New Eng. Music Co., Waterville, Maine, 1974-77; editor Thorndike Press, Maine, 1977-80, sr. editor, 1980-86, Controller, 1986, Pres. T.A. Loeb & Assocs, 1986—. Office: Box 91 Thorndike ME 04986

LOEFFLER, CARL EUGENE, b. Cleve., Nov. 14, 1946. Editor: Performance Anthology: Source Book for California Performance Art, Art Com mag.; series ed., Contemporary Documents. Exec. dir. Contemporary Arts Press, San Francisco, 1975—; exec. dir. Art Com Electronic Network, San Francisco, 1975—. Critics Fellowship, NEA, 1979. Address: Box 3123 Rincon Annex San Francisco CA 94119

LOENING, SARAH (ELIZABETH) LARKIN, (Sarah Larkin), b. Nutley, NJ, Dec. 9, 1896, d. of Adrian Hoffmann and Katherine (Satterthwaite) Lakin; m. Albert Palmer, Nov. 28, 1922; children: Albert Palmer, Jr. Author: (under name Sarah Larkin), Three Rivers: A Tale of New France (poem), 1934, The Trevals: A Tale of Quebec (poem), 1936, Radisson (poem), 1938, Dimo (prose in French), 1940, 2d ed, 1978, transl publ under same title, 1979, Joan of Arc (poem), 1951, The Old Master and Other Tails, 1967, Mountain in the Field (prose), 1971, The Gift of Life, 1978, Vignettes of a Life, 1983. Educated at private schools in New York and Paris. Author. Member: National Soc. of Colonial Dames, Huguenot Soc. of America, Colony Club, Hroswitha Club, Southampton Garden Club (past pres.). La Medaille de la Reconnaissance from the government of France, 1920; assoc. dame, Order of St. John of Jerusalem. Home: Box 905 38 Harvest Lane Southampton NY 11968

LOGAN, JOHN BURTON, b. Red Oak, IA, Jan. 23, 1923; s. James Borland and Agnes (Remmers) L.; m. Guenevere Minor, July 9, 1945; children—John, Theresa, Christina, Peter, Alice, Mark, David, Stephen, Paul. Author: Ghosts of the Heart, 1960, Spring of the Thief, 1963, Zig Zag Walk, 1969, Anonymous Lover, 1973, Only The Dreamer Can Change the Dream, 1981, Bridge of Change, 1981. BA, Coe Coll., Cedar Rapids, IA, 1943; MA, State U. IA, 1949. Tutor St. John's Coll., Annapolis, MD, 1947-51; assoc. prof. English Notre Dame U., 1951-63; prof. English San Francisco State U., 1965-66, SUNY, Buffalo, 1966—. Rockefeller fellow, 1969; Guggenheim fellow, 1979; NEA fellow, 1980. Mem. PEN, PSA. Home: 808 Key Rt Albany CA 94808

LOGSDON, THOMAS S(TANLEY), (Tom Logsdon), b. Springfield, Ky., Sept. 27, 1937; s of George Stanley and Margaret (Buckman) L.; m. Fae Shobe, Aug. 21, 1960 (div., 1977); children: Donna Lorraine. Author: The Rush toward the Stars, 1969, (under name Tom Logsdon): An Introduction to Computer Science and Technology, 1974, (with Fae Logsdon), The Computers in Our Society, 1974, workbook, 1975, Programming in BASIC: With Applications, 1977, (with F. Logsdon), Our Computerized Society with BASIC Programming, 1978; Computers and Social Controversy, 1980, How To Cope with Computers, 1981; The Robot Revolution (Book-of-the-Month Club selection), 1984, Computers Today and Tomorrow: The Microcomputer Explosion, 1985; BASIC Programming with Structure and Style, 1985, rev ed. 1987, Space, Inc.: Your Guide to Investing in Space Exploration, 1988, The Robots in Your Future: Survival Guide to the Coming Age of Automation, 1988. of cols., Grouches by Groucho and The Spice of Life in Eastern Progress. Regular contrbr to Technology Illustrated and High Technology. BS, Eastern Kentucky Univ., 1959; MS, Univ. of Ky, 1961; grad. study at Univ of Calif., 1961-81. Student trainee, Naval Ordinance Lab, Silver Spring, Md, 1958; sr. engineer, Douglas Aircraft, Santa Monica, Calif, 1959-63; flight mechanics engineer, Rockwell International, Seal Beach, Calif, 1963—; adj prof, Univ. of Southern Calif, Los Angeles, 1978—. Lectr for Technology Transfer Society, Los Angeles, 1980—, and Leigh Bureau, Los Angeles, 1984—; local, network, cable TV appearances. Mem: North American Mathematical and Statistical Community, American Inst of Aeronautics and Astronautics, American Astronautical Soc., American Mathematical Soc., Natl Aerospace Educ Cncl, American Inst for the Advancement of Sci, American Platform Speakers Assn, Inst of Navigation, Thursday Exchange Club. Radio Corp. of America sci. scholarship, 1957-58; National Defense fellow, 1959; Sustained Superior Performance Award, National Aeronautics and Space Admin., 1968; Rockwell Presidential Award, 1973 Sustained Superior Performance Award, 1978, Pride Award, 1979. Home: 235 Clipper Way Seal Beach CA 90740

LOHAN, WILLIAM DENIS (BILL), b. Bklyn., July 31, 1931; s. Frank James and Adele Victoria (Chrysler) L.; m. Iris Hariette Drawdy, Apr. 10, 1954; children: William Dennis, Suzan Adele, Timothy Francis, Julie Ann. Author: Quackers, 1984, Bastards in Leggins, 1986; also articles and cartoons pub. in mags. & newspapers. Degree in Criminal Justice, Orangeburg-Calhoun Tech. Coll., 1975. Writer, woodworker, Waubay, S.D., 1972—. Served as sgt. USMC, 1948-72; decorated Purple Heart, 1951. Home: Rt 1 Box 866 Waubay SD 57273

LOHMANN, JEANNE RUTH ACKLEY, b. Arcanum, Ohio, May 9, 1923, d. Harry Whitehouse and Lillian Edna (Albright) Ackley; m. Henry George W. Lohmann, Sept. 7, 1947 (dec. 1985); children—Stephen, David, Karen, Brian. Author: Bonnie Jeanne (with Harry A. Ackley), 1971, Where the Field Goes, 1976, Steadying the Landscape, 1982; contrbr. poetry to Friends Bull., Yankee, Studia Mystica, Oconee Rvw, numerous other publs. BA, Ohio State U., 1945; MA, San Francisco State U., 1979. Assoc. ed. Friends Bull., San Francisco, since 1978. Danforth Fdn. fellow, 1945-46; winner 1st place Napa Valley Poetry Conf., Calif., 1981. Mem. PSA. Home: 722 10th Ave San Francisco CA 94118

LOLLAR, COLEMAN AUBREY, b. Birmingham, AL, Feb. 22, 1946; s. Coleman A. and Vera (Wingard) L. Works incl.: Islands of the Mediterranean, Tunisia. BA in Jnlsm., U. AL, 1968. Tchr., Peace Corps, Sierra Leone, 1968-70; ed. Metropolitan Life, NYC, 1970-71, ASTA Travel News, NYC, 71-79, Frequent Flyer Mag., NYC, 1979—. Mem. SATW, NY Travel Writers Assn., Amer. Soc. Mag. Eds. Honored by Japanese govt. for best U.S. coverage of Japan, 1976. Home: 79 Charles St New York NY 10014

LOMASK, MILTON NACHMAN, b. Fairmont, WV, June 26, 1909; s. Samuel Josiah and Clara Regina (Reinheimer) L. Author: The Man in the Iron Lung, 1956, Odd Destiny: A Life of Alexander Hamilton, 1958, Andrew Johnson: President on Trial, 1960, Seed Money: the Guggenheim Story, 1964, This Slender Reed: A Life of James K. Polk, 1966, (with Constance McL. Green) Vanguard: A History, The First

Am. Revoln., 1974 (ALA Notable Book), A Minor Miracle: An Informal Hist. of the Natl. Sci. Fdn., 1976, Aaron Burr: The Years from Princeton to Vice Pres., 1979, The Conspiracy and Years of Exile, 1982;, The Biographer's Craft, 1986; contrbr. to Dict. Am. Biog., 3d supplement, Ency. Am., 1974; contrbr. to pop. mags. BA, U. IA, 1930; MA, Northwestern U., 1941. Sunday mag. ed. Des Moines Register, 1930-37; copy ed. N.Y. Jnl.-Am., 1937-40; advt. mgr. Nedicks, Inc., NYC, 1945-50; free-lance writer, 1950—; lectr. Washington Sq. Writing Ctr., NYU, 1950-60; lectr. on writing, adult div. Cath. U. Am., 1964-84; editorial cons. NSF, 1971-72; hist. cons. NPACT-BBC TV prodn. The Impeachment Trial of Andrew Johnson, 1974. Served with CWS AUS, 1942-45. Mem. Children's Book Guild of Washington, AG. Office: 212 Lawton St Falls Church VA 22046

LOMBARDO, IRENE E., b. Astoria, NY, Jan. 13, 1944; d. John L. and Elizabeth (Ricov) Francin; m. Joseph L. Lombardo, Oct. 8, 1966; children—Carolyn, Donna. Contrbr. articles to newspapers, trade mags., bulltn. Ed., contrbr.: CDC News, 1980-82; ed.: Compass, 1984—. B.A., Queens Coll., 1980. Public relations wrtr. Continental Corp., NYC, 1980-84, mgr. editorial services, 1985-87, asst. vp edl. sres., 1987—. Home: 1850 Blossom Ct Yorktown Heights NY 10598

LOMMATZSCH, RUTH MYRTLE, b. Chgo., Sept. 14, 1913; d. Karl Herman and Amanda Minnie (Huck) Klemm; m. Reinhold Hans Lommatzsch, Sept. 19, 1936; 1 son, Richard Louis. Poetry in anthologies; contrbr. stories, articles, poems: Chgo. Tribune, various juvenile mags. Wrkg. on novel. Grad. Ill. Bus. Coll., 1929. Prodn. ed. Laidlaw Bros. Pub. Co., River Forest, Ill., 1960-62; ed. Benefit Press, Chgo., 1968-70, art dir., 1970-72; freelance wrtr., 1973—. Mem. NWC. Home: 229 Oakridge Ave Hillside IL 60162

LOND, HARLEY WELDON, b. Chgo., Feb. 5, 1946; s. Henry Sidney and Dorothy (Shaps) L.; m. Marilyn Ann Moss, Aug. 20, 1981. Ed.: Intermedia Mag., 1974-81, Boxoffice Mag., 1981—; contrbr. to: Photography and Language (book), 1976, Art Communic. Ed. 9, 1978, Assembling, 1977, Momentum, 1978, The New Commercialist, 1978, The Dumb Ox, 1979, Edition Shimizu, 1979, Critical Assembling (book), 1980, Studio Internat., 1980, Cahiers du Cinema, 1984.; sydicated film and home video columnist for the McNaught Syndicate. BA in Jnlsm., Cal. State U., 1972. Ed. Intermedia Mag., Los Angeles, 1974-81; prodn. mngr. FilmRow Pubns., Los Angeles, 1981; assoc. ed. Boxoffice Mag., Hollywood, CA, 1981-82, mng. ed., 1982-84, ed., 1984-85, ed./assoc. pub., 1986—. Mem. SPJ, AEJMC. NEA Grant, 1976-77. Home: 2027 Hollyvista Box 27670 Los Angeles CA 90027

LONDON, JACK, b. Duluth, MN, Oct. 10, 1915; s. Hyman and Dora (Sanders) L.; m. Ethel Robbins, Nov. 22, 1947; children—Jack Murray, Daniel Gary; 1 stepdau., Robin Gail. Author: (with Joel Seidman, others) A Worker Views His Union, 1958, (with Robert Wenkert) Adult Education and Social Class, 1964; also chpts. in other books, monographs, articles on Sociol., adult ed., Africa. AB, Central YMCA Coll., 1939; PhD, U. Chgo., 1952. Lithographer, Chgo., 1931-41; trng. specialist on-the-job trng. VA, 1946-48; asst. prof., research sociologist U. Chgo., 1948-53; tchr. in workers edn. Roosevelt U., Chgo., 1949-53; asst. prof. U. CA, 1953-57, assoc. prof., 1957-64, prof., 1964—; vis. prof. in Nigeria, Tanzania, Kenya, Hong Kong, Vancouver, Toronto. Served with U.S. Army, 1942-45. Home: 1 Captain Dr 158 Emeryville CA 94608

LONDON, JONATHAN PAUL, b. NYC, March 11, 1947; s. Harry Sherwood and Anne (Sittenreich) London; m. Maureen Mary Weisenberger, March 21, 1976; 1 son, Aaron. Author: All My Roads, 1983, In a Season of Birds, 1979, Between the Sun and the Moon, 1979. Contrbr. poems and short stories to numerous mags. and anthologies. BA, San Jose State U., 1969; MA, San Jose State U., 1970. Poet-tchr., Poetry in the Schools, Forestville, CA, 1985—. Home: Box 537 Graton CA 95444

LONDRE, FELICIA HARDISON, b. Fort Lewis, WA., April 1, 1941; d. Felix M. and Priscilla (Graham) Hardison; m. Venne-Richard Londre, Dec. 16, 1967; children: Tristan Graham, Georgianna Rose. Author: Tennessee Williams, 1979, (contrbr) Lina Mainiero and Langdon Lynne Faust, eds, American Women Writers, 4 vols., 1979-81, Tom Stoppard, 1981, Federico Garcia Lorca, 1984, (assoc ed and contrbr), Samuel L. Leiter, ed, Shakespeare around the Globe: A Guide to Notable Postwar Revivals, 1986. Plays: Worth a Thousand Words (one-act, prod Masquer Theatre, May 10, 1962, Missoula, Mont.) published in Venture, 1962, Belonging (two-act; prod Unicorn Theatre, May 24, 1981), The Fourth Generation (prod Univ of Mo-Kansas City Academic Theatre, 1981), Miss Millay Was Right (one-act; prod in Kansas City for Avila Coll Alternate Theate Series, 1983), Play "Melancholy Baby" (one-act; prod Kansas City for Missouri Repertory Theatre Showcase Series, 1983), Duse and D'Annunzio (prod Kansas City for Mo. Repertory Theatre Showcase Series, 1984). Also au of Gangs, consisting of two related one-act plays, Slumber Party and Stag Party. Translations of plays: The Snowmaiden from Alexander Ostrovsky's Snegurochka (perf. by U-Rock Players, 1973, Two Maples from Evgeny Shwarts, Dva Klyona, (perf by U.Rock Players, 1975), Little Humpbacked Horse from P.G. Malyarevsky, Konyok-Gorbunok (prod Univ of Texas at Dallas Theatre, 1976), Andree Chedid, The Show-Man, 1984, Trio from Kado costzer, Tres Voces (prod by Mo. Repertory Theatre in Kansas City, 1984), Stairway to Happiness from Victoria Therame (prod by New Directions Theatre Co., Kansas City, 1985. Also transl, The Audience from Federico Garcia Lorca, El Publico, and The Winter Place from Serge Rezvani, Le palais d'hiver. Contrbr articles and rvws to theatre jnls, including theatre Research International, Theatre Journal, Theatre History Studies; bk rvw ed Theatre Jnl, 1984-86. Mem edtl bds for various jnls, such as Theatre History Studies, 1981-87, Theatre Jnl, 1984-86, Studies in American Drama, 1945—, Nineteenth Century Theatre Research, 1984—, Tennessee Williams Rvw, 1985—, and Jnl of Dramatic Theory and Criticism, 1986—. BA (with high honors), Univ. of Montana, 1962; attended Univ. of Caen, 1962-63; MA, Univ of Wash., Seattle, 1964; Ph. D., Univ of Wis., 1969. Publicity dir for Wisconsin Players, Univ of Wis. (now Univ of Wis-Madison), 1964-69; asst prof, Univ. of Wis, Rock County campus, Janesville, 1969-75, assoc prof of drama and film, 1975; asst prof of theatre and head of theatre prog, Univ of Texas at Dallas, Richardson, 1975-78; assoc prof, Univ of Mo.-Kansas City, 1978-82, prof of theatre 1982-87, Curators prof of theatre, 1987—; dramaturg for Mo. Repertory Theatre, 1978—. Actress, set designer and technical dir, costume and lighting designer, dir of drama workshops. Mem of Wis. Art Bd theatre and films advisory panel, 1974-75; mem advisory bd Bookmark Press, 1981; consultant to Dallas Children's Theatre. Member: Intl Fedn for Theatre Research, American Theatre Assn (chmn comm. on theatre research 1984-86), American Soc for Theatre Research (mem exec com), Literary Managers and Dramaturgs of America, Mid-America Theatre Conference, MLA, Midwest MLA, Dramatists Guild, Theatre Library Assn. Fulbright grant for France, 1962-63; younger humanist from NEH, 1971, grant, 1979, senior humanist grant, 1980; semifinalist, Unicorn Theatre Natl. Playwriting Competition, 1981 for The Fourth Generation; winner second prize in John Gassner Memorial Playwrighting Award Competition, 1982, for Miss Millay Was Right; Weldon Springs Endowment Fund Grant, 1984-85, for creation of an original opera based on Duse and D'Annunzio; winner of Actors Theatre of Louisville National Classics in Context Competition for Dramaturgs, 1986. Home: 528 East 56th St Kansas City MO 64110

LONG, CHARLES FRANKLIN, b. Norman, OK, Jan. 19, 1938; s. James Franklin and Mary Katherine (Nemecek) L.; m. Joan Hampton, Sept. 16, 1961; children—Charles Franklin, David Hampton, Stephen Andrew. Author: With Optimism for the Morrow, 1965. BA, U. OK, 1961. Sports writer San Angelo (TX) Standard-Times, 1961-62; news rptr., Norman Transcript, 1962-63; assoc. ed. Sooner Mag., U. OK, 1963-66; news ed. Quill Mag., Chgo., 1967-71, ed., 1971-80; sr. ed. Cahners Pub. Co., Des Plaines, IL, 1981-83; mgr. commns., Beatrice Cos., Inc., 1983-86; dir. corporate communications, BCI Holdings Corp., 1986-. Named to Okla. Jnlsm. Hall of Fame, 1979. Mem. Am. Soc. Bus. Press Editors, SPJ-Sigma Delta Chi, Beta Theta Pi. Home: 1106 N Washington St Wheaton IL 60187

LONG, EUGENE HUDSON, b. Waco, TX, Nov. 4, 1908; s. Eugene Hugh and Cora Lee (Hudson) L.; m. Martha Stephenson Crawford, July 3, 1936 (Dec. 1983); 1 son, Eugene Crawford. Author: O. Henry, the Man and His Work, 1949, Mark Twain Handbook, 1958; ed. (with E.S. Bradley, R.C. Beatty) The American Tradition in Literature, 1956, Mark Twain's A Connecticut Yankee, 1960, Short Novels of Henry James, 1961, Twain's Huckleberry Finn, 1962, Hawthorne's The Scarlet Letter, 1962, Crane's The Red Badge of Courage, 1962, Twain's Pudd'nhead Wilson, 1964, Tolstoy's Anna Karenina, 1966, (with others) Essays on American Literature, 1967, O. Henry—American Regionalist, 1969, American Drama—A Bibliography, 1970, Southwestern Amer. Lit., 1980. AB, Baylor U., 1931, MA, 1931; PhD, U. PA, 1942; postgrad. U.VA, 1933-34, Oxford, 1935. Instr. in English AL Poly. Inst., 1937-41, U. DE, 1941-42, U. PA, 1945-46; asst. prof. OH State U., 1946-47, Vanderbilt U., 1947-49; Prof. Am. Lit. Baylor U., co-chmn. Am. Civ. Prog., 1949—, acting chmn. dept. English, 1952-54, chmn., 1955-73, dist. prof. English, 1973-76, emeritus, 1976—. Mem. Am. Studies Assn., TX Folklore Soc.; adv. ed. Am. Realism, Southwestern Am. Lit. Asst. historian Combined Chiefs Staff, Washington, 1943-45. Home: 5029 Lake Highlands Waco TX 76710

LONG, FRANK WEATHERS, b. Knoxville, TN, May 7, 1906; s. Clifton J. and Leora May (Weathers) L.; m. Laura Mae Whitis, Sept. 19, 1942; 1 dau., Angela Elaine Whitacre. Author: Heracles, The Twelve Labors, 1930, The Creative Lapidary, 1976, Lapidary Carving, 1982. Contrbr. articles to jnls., mags. including Outdoor Life. Student Chgo. Art Inst., Pa. Acad. Fine Arts, Academie Julien, Paris. Field rep. Indian arts & crafts bd. U.S. Dept. Interior, Alaska, Fla., U.S. Southwest, 1951-69. Mem. Albuquerque Designer Craftsmen (pres. 1964), N. Mex. Designer Craftsmen (pres. 1965), Common Cause. Home: 1836 Florida NE Albuquerque NM 87110

LONG, G. GORDON, b. Westfield, NJ, Nov. 6, 1953; s. Earl William and Doris Mary (Lamoreaux) L. Contrbg. ed., columnist, Office Systems Mag., 1984-86; feature writer The Lobby, 1986; contrbr.: Travel Holiday, 1985, Office Mag., 1982-86, Pulpsmith, 1980, Coffee Break Mag., 1979, Antique Dealer, 1983-84, Between Two Rivers (anthol.), 1979, Tri-State Antique Almanac, 1983. AS in acctg., Union Coll., 1980; AS in comp. sci., U.C.T.I., 1982, Masters, Communications Technology Certificate, American Inst., 1987. Corp. mgr. Rhone-Poulenc Inc., Monmouth Jnct., NJ, 1975—. Mem. NWC, P & W. Home: RD 3 Box 193 W Woodschurch Rd Readington NJ 08822

LONG, HELEN HALTER, b. St. Louis, Nov. 19, 1906; d. Charles C. and Ida (May) Halter; m. Forrest E. Long, June 22, 1944. Author: Society in Action, 1936, National Safety Council Lesson Units, 1944-52, (with Forrest E. Long) Social Studies Skills, 8th ed., 1976. AB, Washington U., 1927, AM, 1928; PhD, NYU, 1937. Grad. fellow Washington U., 1927-28; tchr. social studies, Venice, IL, 1928-30; asst. prof. social sci. N.Y. State Coll. for Tchrs., Albany, 1930-38; assoc. ed. Clearing House, 1935-55; tchg. fellow NYU Schl. Edn., 1936-37; div. gen. edn. NYU, 1938-39, instr., 39-43; tchr. pub. schls. Mamaroneck, NY, 1938-42, elementary and jr. high schls. prin., 42-54, asst. supt. schls., 54-61; dir. curriculum studies Inst. Instructional Improvement, NYC, 1962—; pres. Books of World, Sweet Springs, MO, 1962—. Diamond Jubilee Outstanding Women award 1968. Mem. Phi Beta Kappa, Alpha Xi Delta. Home: 107 Medallion Dr Sweet Springs MO 65351

LONG, MARILYN, see Dufour, Darlane

LONG, ROBERT, b. NYC., Oct. 15, 1954, s. Robert T. Sr. and Mary J. (Gillick) L. Author: Getting Out of Town (chapbook), 1978, What It Is (chapbook), 1981, What Happens (poetry), 1988; ed. Long Island: Poets (anthology), 1986, Bird Effort mag., 1975-77; contrbr. to: New Yorker, Poetry, Kayak, Crazyhorse, other mags., New American Poets of the 80s (anthology). BA, L.I.U., 1977; MFA, Vt. Coll., 1984. Adj. assoc. prof. English L.I.U., Southampton, N.Y., 1979-83, 86—; freelance art critic, various publs., 1983—, East Hampton (N.Y.) Stary, 1984—85. Yeats fellow L.I.U., Sligo, Ireland, 1976. Mem. PSA. Home: 25 Mudford Ave Easthampton NY 11937

LONG, ROBERT HILL, b. Raleigh, NC, Nov. 23, 1952, s. McKendree Robbins and Mildred Eastwood (Page) L.; m. Sandra Lynn Morgen, Mar. 22, 1980; 1 child, Seth Morgen. Author: The Power to Die (poems), 1986. Contrbr. poetry, essays and book rvws. to periodicals and anthologies including Bloomsbury, Kenyon Crescent, Seneca rvws, Poetry East, The Archive, Passages North, Puerto del Sol, Intro 15, Arts Jnl, Pig Iron, Durham: A Living Anthology, Cardinal, Aspen Anthology, Davidson Miscellany. BA, Davidson Coll., 1975; MFA, Waren Wilson Coll., Swannanoa, N.C., 1983. Poetry co-ed. Aspen Anthology, Colo., 1980-81; dir. Poets' Co-op, Carrboro, N.C., 1983-85; ed. Duke Policy News, Durham, N.C., 1984-85; exec. dir. N.C. Wrtrs. Network, Durham, 1984—. Recipient NC lit. fellowship, 1986 emerging artist award Durham Arts Council, 1986; Aspen Leaves Lit. Fdn. fellow, 1981. Mem. AAP, NWU, N.C. Poetry Soc. Home: 25 Corticelli St Northampton MA 01060

LONG-TIMS, MARILYN VIRGINIA, b. Greenville, SC, May 28, 1940; d. Lewis Virginia Long and Mary Kathleen (Miller) Boyter; m. James Albert Tims, Jan. 5, 1956 (dec. June 19, 1975); children—Jamie, Dale, Danny, Kirstan. Contrbr. poems to lit. mags., anthols. Student Greenville Tech. Schl., 1978-1982. Recipient 6 Merit awards World of Poetry, 1983-86, 3 Golden Poet awards, 1985-86. Home: 125 Glenwood Rd Greenville SC 29615

LONGETEIG, IVER J., b. Potlatch, ID, Apr. 7, 1941; s. Iver J., Jr. and Margaret Nell (Waters) L.; m. Jody Kay Wiegand, July 25, 1964 (div. Apr. 20, 1978); children—Halle J., Andrew W. Contrbr. articles to profl. jnls., Mensa. Ed.: Advocate, 1975-80. B.A., U. Id., 1962, J.D., 1965. Ptnr. Runft & Longeteig, Boise, ID, 1974-81; attorney Renaissance Devel., Las Vegas, 1981-83; sole practice Longeteig Law Offices, Boise, 1983—. Recipient cert. of Merit for newsletter Natl. Mensa, 1985. Office: 1312 Eastman Boise ID 83702

LONGHURST, SUZANNE ELIZABETH, b. Denver, Aug. 7, 1958; d. Philip and Joy Elaine (Pullium) L. Ed., contrbr.: Practice Life, Atlanta, 1985—; ed.: Times of Mineral County, Hawthorne, NV, 1984. Wrkg. on novel. Student U. Colo.-Boulder, 1976-77, 81, Ft. Lewis Coll., 1983. Traffi mgr. Sound 74, Inc., Cortez, CO, 1977-82; mgr. Sears Catalog Store, Cortez, 1978-82; personal banker First Atlanta Bank, Atlanta, 1985. Home: 875 Bresslyn Rd Nashville TN 37205

LONGIN, TOM, see Longinovic, Tomislav Z.

LONGINOVIC, TOMISLAV Z., b. Belgrade, Yugoslavia, June 12, 1955 (arrvd. USA 1982), s. Zoran T. and Danica M. (Stojadinovic) L.; m. Ksenija Bilbija, May 27, 1983. Author: The Boy and the Cut on His Knee, 1984, It's Only Blues, 1985, Pain Sales, 1985, Shaping, 1986. Wrkg. on psychoanalysis and lit., history of Russian avantgarde, novel. BA, U. Beograd, Yugoslavia, 1980; MFA, U. Iowa, 1984. Ed. Vidici, Beograd, 1980-81; translator Prosveta/CCD, Zagreb, Yugoslavia, 1980-82; free-lance wrtr., 1980—; teaching asst. U. Iowa, Iowa City, 1984—. USIA hon. fellow in writing 1982. Fellow Intl. Writing Program; mem. ALTA, AWP, Am. Comparative Lit. Assn. Home: 305 S Lucas St Iowa City IA 52240

LONGLAND, JEAN ROGERS, b. Boston, Jan. 11, 1913; d. John Alan and Grace Lucie (Lamb) L. Translator from the Portuguese, chiefly poetry, for books and lit mags and profnl. jnls., including Mundus Artium, Poet Lore, CHICAGO Rvw, Lit Rvw. AB, Wheaton College (Mass.), 1935; SB, Simmons College, 1936. Entire professional career at Hispanic Society of America, NY: first cataloguer, curator of Portuguese books, curator of the library, curator of the library, emeritus. Mem. PEN, AG, PSA, Am. Lit. Translators Assn., Am. Portuguese Society, ATA. Poet Lore 1970 translation award; Portugal Prize, 1973, of Intl. Poetry Assn. Home: 490 West End Ave New York NY 10024

LONGLEY, DIANE GENE, b. Bath, ME, Nov. 16, 1937; d. Cyrus William and Annie Elizabeth (Chandler) L. Author: Steel Over Kennebec Building a Maine Bridge, 1978, Fort Popham, Maine, 1864, History of a Civil War Fort, 1986. Contrbr. articles to mags. Ed.: Edna Maine Lobster Activity Book for Children (Arlene Whitney), 1986, Edna Maine Lobster Cookbook (Arlene Whitney), 1987. USAF, 1958-59; Central Tech. Inst., 1957, B.S., U. Maine, 1972. Mem. Maine Wrtrs. Pubs. Alliance. Home: Box 13 Bath Me 04530

LONGLEY, LAURA ANN, b. Aurora, IL, Sept. 27, 1948; d. Donald Halliwell and Therese Mae (Ruddy) L.; m. Andrew B. Babb, Jr., Nov. 27, 1970; 2 sons, Paul Longley, Andrew Donald Longley. Asst. editor Playboy mag., Chgo., 1970-72; assoc. editor Washingtonian mag., 1972-73; assoc. editor, book cons. Washington Post Writers Group, 1973-77; editor Washington Post mag., 1977-81; text editor Time-Life Books, Alexandria, Va., 1981-82; dir. of communications John F. Kennedy Center for the Performing Arts, 1982—. Editor: The Washington Post Guide to Washington, 1976, 2d edit., 1978, Of the Press, 1974, Writing in Style, 1975, The Editorial Page, 1976, Keeping Posted: One Hundred Years of News From the Washington Post, 1977. B.J., U. Mo., 1970. Office: Kennedy Ctr Washington DC 20566

LONIGAN, PAUL RAYMOND, b. NYC, May 27, 1935; s. William Raymond Maloy and Irene Rita (Hickman) Lonigan; m. Cynthia Ann Hartley, June 5, 1965; children: Rebecca, Jennifer, Cynthia, Paul. Author: Gormont et Isembart: Problems and Interpretation of an Old French Epic, 1976, Chretien's Yvain: A Study of Meaning through Style, 1978, The Early Irish Church: From the Beginnings to the Two Doves, 1985, Twenty-three Poems, 1970; founding mem., advisor Circulo de Cultura Panamericana; advisor Circulo, 1963-77; lit. advisor, contrbr. Circulo poetico, 1970—; also contrbr. articles on medieval, Renaissance and modern lit., mythology. BA, Queens Coll., 1960; PhD, Johns Hopkins U., 1967. Instr. Russell Sage Coll., Troy, N.Y., 1963-65; assoc. prof. SUNY-Oswego, 1965-67; prof. Queens Coll. and CUNY Grad. Ctr., NYC, 1967—.Mem. Irish-Am. Cultural Inst., Irish Texts Soc. (life), Phi Beta Kappa, Delta Phi Alpha. Served with USMC, 1954-62, Korean War. Home: Box 243 Montgomery NY 12549

LOOMIS, JAN, b. Houston, July 21, 1944, d. Richard William and Mary Evelyn (Richards) Roby; m. Robert L. Loomis, Feb. 10, 1965; children—Robert Duncan, Richard Roby. BA, Scripps Coll., 1966. Pres. Santa Monica (Calif.) Bay Print and Publishing, 1983—; ed.-in-chief L.A. West Mag., Santa Monica, 1985—. Mem. Western Pubs. Assn., Mag. Pubs. Assn., Prodn. Club Los Angeles. Office: Bay Prtg 919 Santa Monica Blvd Santa Monica CA 90401

LOOMIS, SABRA, b. Cin., Dec. 5, 1937, d. Alfred L. and Virginia (Davis) Loomis. Contrbr. poetry: Dark Horse, Milkweed Chronicle, Raspberry Press, Negative Capability, other lit. mags. BA, Radcliffe Coll., 1960; postgrad. in creative writing, NYU. Concert singer performing in U.S. and Europe, 1970—. MacDowell Colony fellow, 1985. Mem.AAP. Home: 465 W. 23d St New York NY 10011

LOPATIN, JUDY, b. Detroit, Oct. 5, 1954; d. Irving and Dorothy Ruth (Simon) Lopatin. Author: Modern Romances, 1986; contrbr. fiction to mags Miss Rvw, Benzene, Zone and Diana's Almanac. AB, U. Mich., 1976; MFA, Columbia U., 1979. Mem. P&W. Address: 601 W 110 St New York NY 10025

LOPEZ, BARRY HOLSTUN, b. Port Chester, NY., Jan. 6, 1945; s. Adrian Bernard and Mary Frances (Holstun) L.; m. Sandra Jean Landers, June 10, 1967. Author: Desert Notes, 1976; Giving Birth to Thunder, 1978; Of Wolves and Men, 1978; River Notes, 1979; Winter Count, 1981; Arctic Dream, 1986; contrbr. newspapers, periodicals, including NY Times, Wash. Post, Natl. Geographic, North Am. Rvw, Antaeus; contrbg. ed., North Am. Rvw, 1977—, Harper's Mag., 1981—. John Burroughs Medal, 1979, disting. recognition award in fiction Friends Am. Wrtrs., 1982, BA, U. Notre Dame, 1966, MAT, 1968. Wrtr., 1970—. Recipient award in literature AAIAL, 1986. Mem. PEN, AG. Address: Matson 264 5th Ave New York NY 10001

LOPEZ, RAYMOND MICHAEL, b. Bklyn., Sept. 1, 1959; s. Alfred Raymond and Mary Carmen (Roqueni) Lopez; m. Paula Margarett Gill, dec. 25, 1981. Author poetry published in var. mags. and anthologies. Student Calif. State U., Fullerton; student, Saddleback Community College, Mission Viejo, CA., BA Calif. State U., Hayward, enrolled in MA program in English at U.C. Berkeley. Counselor, St. Mary's of the Angels Home, Syosset, NY, 1979-80; dept. probation couns., Orange County Prob., Lake Elsinore, CA, 1980-87, Contra Costa Probation Dept., Martinez, CA. Mem. Orange County Literary Foundation. Home: 933 9th St Bldg 56 Albany CA 94710

LOPEZ, SHARON YOLANDA, b. Jersey City, NJ, Oct. 30, d. George Adolph and Mary (Gardner) Lopez. Contrbr. to Essence, Encore, Response, Crisis, other publs. BA, Howard U., 1975; MA, Syracuse U., 1984. Feature wrtr. New World Outlook, 1982—, Black Enterprise, 1985—; adj. prof. SUNY-Old Westbury, 1984. Mem. N.Y. Assn. Black Journalists. Home: 409 Edgecombe Ave 3B New York NY 11369

LORAN, JASON D., see Certo, Dominic Nicholas

LORCEE, PETER, see Cole, E(ugene) R(oger)

LORD, ROBERT WILDER, b. Keene, NH, May 14, 1917, s. Edward Brown and Alice (Buffum) L.; m. Barbara Lillian Joanni, June 24, 1967; children by previous marriage: Rowena Burgess Lord Soteros, Robert Wilder Jr., Richard Edward Bradley. Author: Running Conventions, Conferences, and Meetings, 1981; ed., contrbr. numerous trade publs. Wrkg. on novels, newspaper articles. AB with honors, Middlebury Coll., 1939; MA, NYU, 1964. Ed. Flitcraft, Inc., Oak Park, Ill., 1944-48, A.M. Best Co., NYC., 1948-65; ed., v.p. Communication Channels, Inc., NYC., 1966-74; freelance wrtr., NYC, 1974—. Mem. Soc. Profl. Journalists., NY Business Press Eds. Home: 61 Jane St New York NY 10014

LORD, WALTER, b. Balt., Oct. 8, 1917; s. John Walter and Henrietta Mactier (Hoffman) L. Author: A Night to Remember, 1955, Day of Infamy, 1957, The Good Years, 1960, A Time to Stand, 1961, Peary at the Pole, 1963, The Past That Would Not Die, 1965, Incredible Victory, 1967, The Dawn's Early Light, 1972, Lonely Vigil, 1977, The Miracle of Dunkirk, 1982, The Night Lives On, 1986. Editor: The Fremantle Diary, 1954. B.A., Princeton, 1939; LL.B., Yale, 1946. Editor bus. information services, 1946-53. Trustee Soc. Am. Historians, 1972, pres., 1981-84; trustee Council Authors Guild, Inc., 1966-72; Council Authors League, 1972-83, secy., 1975-80. Mem. AG, ASCAP. Address: 14 W Hamilton St Baltimore MD 21201

LORDE, AUDRE GERALDIN, b. NYC, Feb. 18, 1934; d. Frederic Byron and Linda Gertrude (Belmar) L.; m. Edwin Rollins, Mar. 31, 1962 (div. Jan. 1970); children—Beth, Jonathan. Author: The First Cities, 1969, Cables to Rage, 1970, From a Land Where Other People Live, 1973, NY Head Stop and Museum, 1974, Coal, 1976, Between Our Selves, 1976, The Black Unicorn, 1978, The Cancer Journals, 1980, Chosen Poems—Old and New, 1982, Zami, A New Spelling of My Name, 1982; poetry editor: Chrysalis; adv. editor: Black Box Mag; contrbg. editor: Black Scholar Mag. BA, Hunter Coll., NYC, 1959; MLS, Columbia U., 1961. Grantee CAPS, 1972, 76; NEA, 1968, 80; recipient award Broadside Poets, 1975. Mem. PEN, AG, AL Am. Home: 207 St Pauls Ave Staten Island NY 10304

LORENZ, SARAH E., see Winston, Sarah

LORIMER, SCAT, see Fuente, Martha Ayers

LORNE, DAVID, see Hoof, David Lorne

LORRAH, JEAN, b. Canton, OH, Nov. 28; d. Walter W. and Marie A. (Unger) Lorrah. Author: First Channel, 1980, Savage Empire, 1981, Dragon Lord of the Savage Empire, 1982, Channel's Destiny, 1983, Captives of the Savage Empire, 1984, The Vulcan Academy Murders, 1984, Ambrov Keon, 1986, Flight to the Savage Empire, 1986, Sorcerers of the Frozen Isles, 1986; ed. Pandora Mag., 1983-86, Zelerod's Doom, 1986, Wulfston's Odyssey, 1987. PhD, Fla. State U., 1968. Ed. Banks/Baldwin, Cleve., 1963, writer Am. Greetings, 1962; tchr. Monteverde Acad., Fla., 1963-66; grad. asst. Fla. State U., Tallahassee, 1966-68; prof. English Murray State U., Ky., 1968—. Mem. NWC, SFWA, Internatl. Assn. for the Fantastic in the Arts. Home: 301 S 15th St Murray KY 42071

LORRANCE, ARLEEN, b. NYC., Feb. 26, 1939; d. Irving and Rose Udoff; m. Richard Lorrance. Author: The Love Project, 1972; (with Pike) Channeling Love Energy, 1973; Buddha from Brooklyn, 1974; Musings for Mediation, 1975; Why Me? How to Heal What's Hurting You, 1978; (with Pike) The Love Project Way, 1979; Born of Love, 1980; India through Eyes of Love, 1981; Images, 1985. MFA, Bklyn. Coll., 1971. Exec. dir. The Love Project, San Diego, 1972—; facilitator creative/consciousness workshops. Home: Box 7601 San Diego CA 92107

LORTS, JACK E., b. Wichita, KS, Sept. 4, 1940; s. Kenneth Warren and Doris Maxine (Hedberg) L.; m. Cecilia Ann Kennedy, Nov. 9, 1960; children—Jackie, Geri, Virginia. Contrbr. poems publs inc Ariz. Quarterly, Kans. Quarterly, English Jnl, Ore. English, Vis-a-Vis, Cafe Solo, Nomad, White Dove Rvw; articles on Freemasonry and occult in Fate, Ore. Freemason, Ore. Masonic News. Wrkg. on The Tao of Trivia. BA, Calif. State U., 1962; M.Ed., U. Ore., 1978. Lang. Arts Tchr. LA County Pub. Schls., El Monte, Calif., 1962-74; English tchr. So. Umpqua High schl., Myrtle Creek, Ore., 1974—. Past master Masons Maple Lodge No. 127, Myrtle Creek, 1981, 83; NEH fellow, 1984. Mem. Natl. Council Tchrs. English. Address: 991 Mason St Myrtle Creek OR 97457

LOSEY, JEANNE K., b. Shelbyville, IN, July 4, 1925; d. Harry N. and Ruth Franklin (Greene) Knowlton; m. Glen . Losey, July 25, 1943 (dec. 1980); children-Brenda, Linda, Judith, David, Michael, James, Denise, Daniel. Author: Star Spangled Pride, 1986; contrbr. poetry to Electric Consumer; poem Challenger read into Congressional Record. Wrkg. on book of poems. Named poet laureate World of Poetry conv., 1986. Home: 109 E South St Shelbyville IN 46176

LOSURE, JOYCE NELMA, b. Batavia, NY, Sept. 21, 1928, d. Asa Conrad and Nellie Maude (Gillett) Popp; m. Robert Francis Losure, Dec. 24, 1947; children—David Robert, Donald Charles, Walter Wayne. Editor: Rural Education: Yesterday, Today and Tomorrow, 1978, Rural Education on the Move, 1979, Survival in the 80s, 1980, Creativity Growing Out of Austerity, 1982, Perfecting and Understanding Roles in Education, 1983, Quality Education the Rural Way, 1984; contrbr. to Small Schl. Forum, 1981. BA in English, Iowa State U., 1971; MA in Edn., U. No. Iowa, 1984. Instr. Fort Doge Center, Iowa, 1985—; mem. adj. faculty Buena Vista Coll., Storm Lake, Iowa. Mem. People United for Rural Edn. (contrbr. to newsletter, lobbyist, officer; recipient Spl. Recognition award 1982). Home: RR Box 35 Kamrar IA 50132

LOTT, BRET, b. Hawthorne, CA., Oct. 8, 1958; s. Wilman Sequoia and Barbara Joan (Holmes) L.; m. Melanie Kai Swank, June 28, 1980; children: Zebulun Holmes, Jacob Daynes. Author: (novel) The Man Who Owned Vermont, 1987; contrbr. to Writers Forum 9, Yankee Mag., Iowa Rvw., Yale Rvw., Seattle Rvw., other lit mags; co-editor Writers Forum, 1985—, Ohio Jnl., 1985-86. BA in English, Calif. State U., Long Beach, 1981; MFA in English, U. Mass., 1984. Asst. prof. English, writer-in-residence Coll. of Charleston, S.C. Ohio Arts Council fellow in lit., 1986-87; Syndicated Fiction Project, PEN, NEA, 1985. Mem. P&W, AWP. Home: 1215A Meadow Park Ln Mount Pleasant SC 29464

LOTT, CLARINDA HARRISS, b. Balt., Mar. 9, 1939; d. Robert Preston and Margery Willis Harriss; children—Lisa Harriss Lott, Andrew Tyler Lott. Author: The Pearl, 1970, The Bone Tree, 1971, Forms of Verse, British and Amer., 1971, The Night Parrot, 1988; bi-wkly. Op Ed columns in sev. Balt. nwsprs., over 300 poems. BA, Goucher, 1960; MA, Johns Hopkins, 1962. Tchr., Balt. Schls., MD, 1960-67; instr. Goucher, Towson, MD, 1967-70; spec. cons. MD Public TV, Owings Mills, MD, 1982—; asst. prof. Towson State U. (MD), 1971—; ed./dir. New Poets Series, Inc., Balt., 1973—. Recipient 5 NEA and numerous local grants. Mem. MLA, AAUP, MD Writer's Council. Spcl. advisor to Writer's Club at MD House of Correct. for Men. Home: 541 Piccadilly Rd Towson MD 21204

LOTT, RICK, b. Beaverton, AL, Nov. 13, 1950; s. Henry Thomas and Maxine (Cantrell) L.; m. Janet Denise, June 14, 1980; 1 son, Lee Alexander. Author: Digging for Shark Teeth, 1985; recent publs.: Poetry, Kenyon RVW; The Patience of Horses, 1987; contrbr. Dictionary Lit. Bio., 1983; poetry in Poetry Australia, Intro 16, Cimarron Rvw, Western Humanities Rvw, Tex Rvw, Centennial Rvw, others. BS, Livingston U., 1979; PhD, Fla. State U., 1986. Poetry ed. Sun Dog mag., Tallahassee, Fla., 1981-84; instr. English Fla. State Univ., 1985-86., asst. prof. of English, Arkansas State Univ. Recipient AAP prize, Fla. State Univ., 1984, Hackney lit. award, Birmingham-So. Coll., 1985. Mem. MLA, AWP. Address: 1503 Sally Ln Jonesboro AR 72401

LOUGHLIN, RICHARD L(AWRENCE), b. Brooklyn, Oct. 29, 1907; s. Richard Lawrence and Annie (Cannon) L.; m. Laura Brennan, July 15, 1950; 1 dau.: Laurie Bernadette. Author:

(with T.C. Pollock) Thought and Expression, with Teacher's manual, 1954, 7th ed, pub as Macmillan English Series 8, 1978, ed, James Michener, The Bridges of Toko-Ri (school ed), 1960, ed (with L.M. Popp) Journeys in Science Fiction, 1961, ed (with Popp) Four Complete World Novels, with teacher's manual, 1961, (with M. Meister, A. Tauber, and M. Mullin) Higher Education and You (pamphlet), 1961, Spotnotes: Moby Dick (study guide), 1967, Laugh and Grow Wise with Oliver Goldsmith, 1972, Verses Vice Verses, 1981. Au of Let Me Give Thanks, radio play, broadcast by WNYC-Radio, November, 1937; also au of songs and brochures. Contrbr to yearbooks, procs, and honorary volumes. Contrbr of more than 225 articles, poems, plays and rvws to profl jnls, including College English, English Jnl, English Rvw, Costerus, English Record, Univ. Coll Qtly, and Educational Forum. Mem editorial com Faculty Facts, 1960-62; co-editor, English Review, 1962-66. BS, St. John's Univ, Jamaica, N.Y., 1929; MA, Columbia Univ, 1931; Ph.D., N.Y. Univ, 1947. English and history teacher in private school, 1929-31; high school teacher of English and speech, 1931-43, 1946-54, dept chmn, 1954-60; assoc prof, Bronx Community Coll of the City Univ of N.Y., 1960-61, prof of English, 1961-73, prof emeritus, 1973—, head of dept of English and speech, 1960-64, coordinator of liberal arts and scis, 1961-70. Teacher at Brooklyn Inst of Industrial Relations, spring, 1948; lectr, Brooklyn Coll (now Brooklyn Coll of the City Univ of N.Y.), 1948-50. Guest poet, Centenary coll, 1969 and 1976, George Peabody Coll for Teachers (now of Vanderbilt Univ), 1971, Bakersfield Coll, 1972, St. Johns Univ, 1974-75, 77, Ouachita Baptist Univ, 1977, and Manatee Jr. Coll, 1977, 78, 79. Camp Counsellor, 1929-43; dir of workshops; public speaker. Mem: College English Assn, Doctorate Asn of N.Y. Educators (pres, 1952-53), N.Y. Acad of Public Educ, N.Y. State English Council, N.Y. City Assn of Teachers of English (mem exec bd, 1962; v.p. for colleges, 1962-66), Kappa Delta Pi (pres of Beta Pi Chpt, 1942-43). harian Creative Books Poetry Award, 1981, 1983. Military service: U.S. Army, instructor, chaplain's assistant, and medical historian 1943-46; became first lt; received Army Commendation Ribbon and New York State Conspicuous Service Cross. U.S. Army Reserve, 1946-62. Home: 83-57 118th St Kew Gardens NY 11415

LOUIS, WILLIAM ROGER, b. Detroit, May 8, 1936; s. Henry Edward and Bena May (Flood) L.; m. Dagmar Cecilia Friedrich; children by prev. marriage: Antony Andrew, Catherine Ann. Author: Ruanda-Urundi, 1963, Germany's Lost Colonies, 1967, (with Jean Stengers) E.D. Morel's History of the Congo Reform Movement, 1968, British Strategy in the Far East, 1919-1939, 1971, Imperialism at Bay, 1977, British Empire in the Middle East, 1984; editor: (with P. Gifford) Britain and Germany in Africa, 1967, France and Britain in Africa, 1971, The Origins of the Second World War: A.J.P. Taylor and his Critics, 1972, National Security and International Trusteeship in the Pacific, 1972, Imperialism: The Robinson and Gallagher Controversy, 1976, (with William S. Livingston), Australia, New Zealand and the Pacific Islands since the First World War, 1979, (with P. Gifford) The Transfer of Power in Africa, 1982; (with R. Stookey) End of the Palestine Mandate, 1986. BA, U. Okla., 1959; MA, Harvard U., 1960; DPhil, Oxford U., 1962, DLitt, 1979. Asst. then assoc. prof. history, Yale U., 1962-70; prof. history U. Tex., Austin, 1970—. Woodrow Wilson fellow; Am. Inst. Indian Studies fellow; Marshall scholar; Nat. Endowment Humanities fellow; Guggenheim fellow. Office: Dept History Univ Texas Austin TX 78712

LOURIE, DICK, b. Hackensack, NJ, Dec. 31, 1937, s. Norman Victor Lourie and Doris (Kaplan) Rosenberg; m. Abby Jean Freedman, Sept. 19, 1981. Author: The Dream Telephone, 1968, Letter for You to Answer, 1970, Stumbling, 1973, Anima, 1978; ed. Come to Power, 1970. AB, Princeton U., 1959; MA, Columbia U., 1960; MA, Harvard U., 1986. Cons. N.Y. State Poets-in-Schls. program, 1972-78, Artists Fdn. Boston, 1980-81; ed. Hanging Loose Press, NYC, 1966—, U. Mass. at Boston, 1984—. Office: Publs Univ Mass Boston Harbor Campus Boston MA 02125

LOURIE, IVEN B., b. LI, NY, Dec. 13, 1946, s. Norman Victor and Betty (Pokrassa) L.; m. Moira Ann Dougherty, May 25, 1975; children—Bethany, Taramin. Ed.: The Human Biological Machine as a Transformational Apparatus, 1985, The Real World Catalog, 1985; contrbr. poetry to Joyous Childbirth, 1977; contrbr. poetry to Hanging Loose, The Spirit that Moves Us, Prickly Pear, Wings mag., other lit jnls. BA, U. Chgo., 1969; MFA in English, U. Ariz., Tucson, 1978. Poetry ed. Chgo. Rvw, 1968-69; instr. English North Country Community Coll., Saranac Lake, N.Y., 1970-71; program planner Center Employment Tng., Tucson, 1979-81; project evaluator Tucson Unified Schls., 1982-83; sr. ed. Gateways Books, Nevada City, Calif., 1984—; publs. asst. Inst. for Devel. of Harmonious Human Being, Inc., Crestline, Calif., 1976-77; bd. dirs. Arts for All, Inc., Tucson, 1978-79; co-tchr. Furnished Rooms Wrtrs. workshop, Tucson, 1980-81; sponsor, founder Central Arts Collective Readings, Tucson, 1980-81. Home: 315 Main St Roseville CA 95678

LOVE, NANCY, b. Phila., Nov. 1, 1927; d. Isadore H. and Ann (Zeitlyn) Krekstein; children—Steven A., Judith Ann. Author: Philadelphia Magazine's Guide to Philadelphia, 1964; contrbr. articles to others. BA, U. Pa., 1949. Successively asst. editor, sr. editor, mng. editor Phila. mag., 1964-71; editor Boston mag., 1971-74, Washingtonian Books, Washington, 1974-76, American Home Mag., NYC, 1976-77, Cue New York, 1977-80, NYC Access, Access Press, 1983—; mag. cons., 1980-83; freelance wrtr., ed., 1980—; literary agent, 1984—. Address: 250 E 65th St New York NY 10021

LOVELACE, CAREY, b. Los Angeles, Aug. 21, 1952, d. Jon B. and Lillian Lovelace. Contrbr. articles to Art Com, Harpers, El Diario (Barcelona), Los Angeles Times, Boston Globe, Millenium Film Jnl., New Art Examiner, NJ Arts, New Manhattan Rvw., Art News, High Performance, Flash Art. BFA, Calif. Inst. of Arts, Los Angeles, 1975; MA, NYU, NYC, 1984 instr. N.Y.U., New School, 1986-; N.Y. Ed., New Art Examiner, 1986, freelance ed., Abrams, 1987—. Composer contemporary music, 1974-80; mem. pub. relations staff Hudson Inst., Croton-on-Hudson, N.Y., 1980-81, Intl. Assn. of Art Critics; freelance journalist, arts critic, 1982—. Address: 480 Broome St New York NY 10013

LOVELESS, WILLIAM EDWARD, b. Providence, Nov. 3, 1951; s. Cornelius Edwin and Emma Yolanda (Zannini) L.; m. Denise Frances Benoit, July 19, 1980. BA in Journalism, U.R.I., 1973. Reporter Evening Times, Pawtucket, R.I., 1973-80; reporter McGraw-Hill Publs., Washington, 1980-81, ed., 1981—, mng. ed. Inside F.E.R.C. weekly newsletter, 1981, mng. ed., chief ed. Inside Energy/with Fed. Lands weekly newsletter, 1981—. Mem. Natl. Press Club. Home: 901 Little St Alexandria VA 22301

LOW, ANTHONY, b. San Francisco, May 31, 1935; s. Emerson and Clio (Caroli) L.; m. Pauline Iselin Mills, Dec. 28, 1961; children—Louise, Christopher, Georgianna, Elizabeth, Peter, Catherine, Nicholas, Alexandra, Michael, Frances, Jessica. Author: Augustine Baker, 1970, The Blaze of Noon, 1974, Love's Architecture, 1978, The Georgic Revolution, 1985; editor: Urbane Milton, 1984. AB, Harvard U., 1957, MA, 1959, PhD,1965. Mem. Milton Soc. MLA. Home: 18 Greenacres Ave Scarsdale NY 10583

LOW, DENISE LEA, b. Emporia, KS, May 9, 1949; d. William Francis and Dorothy Lea (Bruner) Dotson; m. Donald Andrew Low; children: David Andrew, Daniel Lee; m. 2d, Anthony Thomas Allard, Dec. 18, 1983. Author: Dragon Kite, 1981. Quilting, 1984, Spring Geese and Other Poems, 1984, Learning the Language of Rivers, 1987; ed.: 30 Kans. Poets, 1979, Confluence, 1983, A Confluence of Poems (co-ed. David Low), 1984; contrbr. to Heartwomen, The Art of Reading. BA, U. Kans., 1971, MA, 1974; MFA, Wichita State U., 1984. Instr. Kans. State. Univ., Manhattan, 1975-77; lectr. Univ. Kans., Lawrence, 1978-84, Washburn Univ., Topeka, 1982-84; prof. Haskell Indian Jr. Coll., Lawrence, 1984—; ed. Cottonwood Press, Lawrence, 1979-82. Recipient grant Kans. Arts Commn., Topka, 1979, 83, CCLM, 1980; Lichtor Poetry Prize, Kansas City Jewish Center, 1980. Mem. Woodley Meml. Press, Kans. Writers Assn., Kans. Assn. Tchrs. English, NATE. Address: 1916 Stratford Rd Lawrence KS 66044

LOW, MARY, see Machado, Mary

LOWE, DOUGLAS HAYSE, b. Pikeville, KY, Mar. 9, 1952; s. Hayse and Ethel (Hanners) L. Author: poetry pub. in Rainbow Over the Mountains, 1983. Student U. Ky-Prestonsburg, 1984-85. Clrk., salesperson Montgomery Ward, Ann Arbor, Mich., 1970-73; real estate salesman Ogden & Elmer. Ypsilanti, Mich., 1973-75; route sales rep. Mean Services, Haroldy, Ky., 1976-79; owner, mgr. Lowes Cleaning Services, Prestonsburg, 1979—; free-lance wrtr., 1981—. Mem. NWC. Home: 3941 W Mtn Pkwy Prestonsburg KY 41653

LOWE, JONATHAN F., b. Mpls., Sept. 29, 1953; s. Ebon I and Genie L. (Bostrum) L. Contrbr. fiction and poetry Phoebe, Dekalb Arts Jnl., Buffalo Spree, Wind, Rampike, Singlelife, Writer's West, Contemporary Drama Service, Adventure Travel, Atlanta Weekly, Grays Sporting Jnl., ND Horizon. BBA, Bob Jones U., 1975. Ed. Criterion RVW, Greenville, S.C., 1985— Campus Cards, 1985—. Recipient 3d Prize in Fiction, Writers' Digest mag., Cin., 1982, 1st Prize in Poetry, Roger C. Peace Competition, Greenville, 1982, Best in Sci. Fiction, 1984, '86 SC Fiction Project Winner. Address: Box16315 Greenville SC 29606

LOWE, KENNETH STEPHEN, b. St. Paul, July 18, 1921, s. Malcolm and Erma Alta (Henderson) L.; m. Marie Elizabeth Contway, June 18, 1949; children—Stephen (dec.), Scott, Stuart. Editor: Westwind Woods, 1978, Hunters' Heritage: A History of Hunting in Michigan, 1979, Michigan's 50 Best Fishing Lakes, 1982, Bass and How To Catch 'Em, 1983, Hunt Michigan, 1984, Trout Streams of Michigan, 1985. BA, U. Mich., 1948. Telegraph ed. Daily Mining Jnl,

Marquette, Mich., 1948-51, assoc. ed., 1951-55, ed., 1955-72; free-lance public relations rep., 1972-75; ed. Mich. Out-of-Doors, Lansing, 1975—. Mem. Outdoor Wrtrs. Assn. Am., Mich. Outdoor Wrtrs. Assn. (pres. 1969-71), Natl. Audubon Soc. Office: Box 30235 Lansing MI 48909

LOWENKAMP, WILLIAM CHARLES JR., b. NYC., Oct. 9, 1941, s. William Charles and Margaret Louise (Poll) L.; m. Martha Maria Engle, Aug. 1964 (div. 1968); 1 dau., Christina Monika Lowenkamp-Jergen; m. 2d, Camille Jones, June 7, 1979. Author: Of Life and Love, 1982, The Country Poet on the Road Again, 1983; contrbr. poetry: Glowing Embers, P.S. the Universe Sings, Rhinestone Rooster, Reach for the Stars, numerous other lit. publs. Wrkg. on nonfiction. BA in Bus., Sussex (Engl.) Coll., 1977; postgrad. numerous instns. throughout U.S. and Europe. Quality engr. Royal Maid Assn. for the Blind, Hazlehurst, Miss., 1980—. Mem. Am. Soc. for Quality Control, Am. Inst. of Ind. Engrs., Country Music Assn., Am. Soc. Artists, Jackson (Miss.) Arts Alliance. Home: Box 878 Hazlehurst MS 39083

LU, DAVID JOHN, b. Keelung, Taiwan, Sept. 28, 1928; came to U.S., 1950, naturalized, 1960; s. Ming and Yeh (Lai) L.; m. Annabelle Compton, May 29, 1954; children—David John, Daniel Mark, Cynthia Ellen, Stephen Paul. Author: From the Marco Polo Bridge to Pearl Harbor, 1961 (Japanese edit.) Taiheiyo Senso e no Dotei, 1967, Sources of Japanese History, 2 vols, 1974, Bicentennial History of the United States (in Japanese), 1976, The Life and Times of Matsuoka Yosuke, 1880-1946, 1981, (co-trans.) The China Quagmire, 1983, (trans.) What Is Total Quality Control? The Japanese Way, 1985, Kanban: Just-in-Time at Toyota, 1986. Contrbr.: Sekai to Nippon, weekly, Tokyo, Japan. BA in Econs, Nat. Taiwan U., 1950; postgrad., Westminster Theol. Sem., Phila., 1950-52; M. Internat. Affairs, Columbia, 1954; certificate, East Asian Inst., 1954, PhD,1960. Editor Prentice-Hall, Inc., 1956-60. Fulbright-Hays scholar, Japan, 1966-67. Home: 635 Broadway Milton PA 17847

LUBAR, ROBERT, b. NYC, Oct. 10, 1920; s. George H. and Helen (Gang) L.; m. Patricia Raney, Aug. 2, 1947; children—John, Nicholas, Stephen, Andrew. Writer N.Y. Times, 1942-43; contrbg. editor, then fgn. corr. Time mag., 1946-58; assoc. editor Fortune mag., 1958-60, bd. editors, 1960-64, 80—, asst. mng. editor, 1964-70, mng. editor, 1970-80. AB, Columbia, 1940, MS in Journalism, 1941. Home: 60 Sutton Pl S New York NY 10022

LUBER, ELLIOT B., b. Camden, NJ., July 20, 1959. BA in Journalism, Northeastern U. Sr. ed. Pro Sound News, Carle Place, N.Y., 1983-86; ed. The Music and Sound Retailer, Carle Place, 1983-87; news ed. Post Mag., Carle Place, 1986-87; Managing ed. Auto sound & Communications, Ny, N.Y., 1987-; Home: 2514 S Seamans Neck Rd Seaford NY 11783

LUBEROFF, BENJAMIN J., b. Phila., Apr. 17, 1925; s. Louis and Bertha (Adelman) L.; m. Renee Barbara Pines, Aug. 1, 1944; children—Neil, Nancy, David. BChE, The Cooper Union, 1949; MA, PhD, Columbia U., 1955. Varied scientific, tech., & exec. positions in chemical industries, 1953-71; founding ed. CHEMTECH, 1971—; pres. The ConcepTeam, Inc., Summit, NJ, 1975—; pub. Innovators Digest, 1982—. Home: 19 Brantwood Dr Summit NJ 07901

LUBETSKY, ELSIE, (Elsen Lubetsky), b. NYC., Mar. 12, 1917; m. Alfred Lubetsky; children: Susan, Lawrence. Author: (chapbooks) A Double Mix, 1984, Freely Connected, 1985; contrbr. to Voices for Peace, other anthologies, Sing Heavenly Muse, Broomstick, Prophetic Voices, Day Tonight/Night Today, Calliopes Corner, Left Curve, Thirteen, Poetic Justice, Parnassus Lit. Rvw, other lit mags. BA, Hunter Coll., 1940. Supvr., counselor, interviewer N.Y. State Employment Service, N.Y.C., 1961-76. Recipient 1st prize for poetry Calliopes Corner, 1985. Mem. Feminist Wrtrs. Guild, Hudson Valley Poetry Group (pres. 1982-83). Home: 613 Queen St Boone NC 28607

LUCAS, OUIDA LA FORREST, b. Patterson, GA, Sept. 30, 1915; d. Roma Eli and Ella Saphronia (Smith) Griner; m. Guy Lucas, Sept. 14, 1935 (dec. 1974). Poetry in 13 anthologies. Wrkg. on poetry. Student public schls., Patterson. City clk. Brunswick, GA., 1960-76. Home: Rt 2 Box 18 Patteson GA 31557

LUCKETT, KAREN BETH, b. Canton, MS; d. Gus and Georgia L. Contrbr. fiction to mags. including Highlights for Children, Wee Wisdom, others. Grad. public schs., Columbus, GA. Recipient 1st place for juvenile fiction South Eastern Wrtrs., Emory U., 1971, 3d place for nonficiton, 1971. Mem. South Eastern Wrtrs. Assn. (3d place for juvenile fiction 1969), SCBW. Home: 864 Peachtree Dr Columbus GA 31906

LUCZUN, MARY ELLEN TERESA, b. Bklyn., Sept. 23, 1951; d. John Francis and Florence Elizabeth (Vander Drift) Luczun. Author: PostAnesthesia Nursing: A Comprehensive Guide, 1984. Contrbr. research articles to profl. jnls, chapter to the PostAnesthesia Nursing Review for Certification. Assoc. editor Jnl. PostAnesthesia Nursing, 1986—; ed., Handbook of PostAnesthesia Nursing, 1987. BS with distinction in nursing, Cornell U., 1976; MS, Hunter Coll., 1982. Sr. staff nurse recovery rm. N.Y. Hosp.-Cornell Med. Ctr., N.Y.C., 1971-82; clin. instr. Hunter Coll. Sch. Nursing, N.Y.C., 1985—. Recipeint Genl. Excellence award St. Vincent's Med. Ctr., Staten Island, N.Y., 1971. Mem. Am. Soc. PostAnesthesia Nurses, N.Y. State Recovery Rm. Nurses' Assn., Sigma Theta Tau. Home: 9601 Shore Rd Brooklyn NY 11209

LUDDIE, WALTER JOSEPH(Pen Oak), b. New Britain, Jan. 24, 1917; s. Frank and Sophie L.; m. Carol Murphy (dec.); children: Julie, Caryn, Robert, Joel. Author: America, We Can Do It Together, 1983. Student Georgetown U., 1936-38; BS in Econ., U. Conn., 1940. Pres. Stanley Motor Sales, New Britain, 1948—; mgr. Co Burn & Middlebrook, Hartford,Conn., 1961—. Active in civic fundraising. Recipient spcl. recognition for book as inspirational by chmn. Pres.'s Comm. on Govt. Waste. Home: 1009 E Lake Rd Oakdale CT 06370

LUDLUM, ROBERT, b. NYC, May 25, 1927; s. George Hartford and Margaret (Wadsworth) L.; m. Mary Ryducha, Mar. 31, 1951; children—Michael R., Jonathan C., Glynis J. Author: The Scarlatti Inheritance, 1971, The Osterman Weekend, 1972, The Matlock Paper, 1973 (BOMC alt. selection), The Rhinemann Exchange, 1974, The Gemini Contenders, 1976 (dual selection Lit. Guild), The Chancellor manuscript, 1977 (dual selection Lit. Guilt), The Holcroft Covenant, 1978 (Lit. Guild selection), The Matarese Circle, 1979 (Book of Month selection), The Bourne Identity, 1980 (Lit. Guild Selection), The Parsifal Mosaic, 1982, The Aquitaine Progression, 1983 (BOMC selection). BA with distinction, Wesleyan U., 1951. Novelist, 1969—. Served with USMC, World War II. Mem. AG. Office: Morrison 58 W 10th New York NY 10011

LUDVIGSON, SUSAN GAYLE, b. Rice Lake, WI, Feb. 13, 1942; d. Howard Charles and Mabel B. (Helgeland) Ludvigson; 1 son, Joel David Bartels. Author: Step Carefully in Night Grass, 1974, Northern Lights, 1981, The Wisconsin Women, 1980, The Swimmer, 1984, Defining the Holy, 1986; editor: Intro 13, 1982. Poetry in Atlantic Monthly, Poetry, The Nation, others. BS, U. of Wisc., 1965; MA, U. of NC, 1973. Tchr., River Falls publ. schls., Wis., 1964-68; tchr., Ann Arbor publ. schls., MI, 1968-71; prof., Winthrop College, Rock Hill, SC, 1975—. Awards: Guggenheim Fel., 1983, Fulbright Fel., 1984; NEA Fel., 1984-85. Mem. AWP, MLA, P&W. Home: 224-22 N Poplar St Charlotte NC 28202

LUDY, ANDREW WILLIAM, b. Paterson, NJ, Oct. 31, 1947; s. Ralph William and Alice Ruth (Beatty) Ludy. Author: Condominium Ownership: A Buyer's Guide, 1982, Diet Diary, 1984. BSME Fairleigh Dickinson U., 1978. Home: 17 Sherwood Way Landing NJ 07850

LUECKE, JANEMARIE, O.S.B., b. Okeene, OK, April 24, 1924; d. William and Gertrude (Boeckman) Luecke. Author: A Prosody Manual, 1971, Measuring Old English Rhythm, 1978, The Rape of the Sabine Women, 1978, Wild Birds Eggs, 1984; articles in Modern Philogy, PMLA, Modern Fiction Studies, other scholarly jnls; poetry and non-fiction in numerous jnls. and mags. MA, Marquette U., 1956, PhD, Notre Dame U., 1964. Tchr., parochial schls., Oklahoma, 1945-56; acad. dean and tchr., Benedictine Heights Coll., Tulsa, Ok., 1957-61; research proj. dir., St. Joseph's Convent, Tulsa, 1964-66; asst. then assoc. prof., Okla. State U., Stillwater, 1966-73, prof., 1973—. Mem. MLA, NCTE, AAP, PSA, MPS, Med. Academy, New Chaucer Soc., Natl. Women's Studies Assoc., Natl. Coalition of Am. Nuns. Home: 2117 Erin Pl Oklahoma City OK 73120

LUEDERS, EDWARD GEORGE, b. Chgo., Feb. 14, 1923; s. Carl G. and Vera (Simpson) L.; m. Julia Demaree, June 5, 1946; children—Kurt D., Joel E., Julia Anne. Author: Carl Van Vechten and the Twenties, 1955, Carl Van Vechten, 1965, Images and Impressions: Poems by Brewster Ghiselin, Edward Lueders and Clarice Short, 1969, The Gang from Percy's Hotel and Other Poems, 1971, The Clam Lake Papers, A Winter in the North Woods, 1977; editor: (with others) Reflections on a Gift of Watermelon Pickle and Other Modern Verse, 1966, Some Haystacks Don't Even Have Any Needle and Other Complete Modern Poems, 1969, (with Primus St. John) Zero Makes Me Hungry, 1976, Western Humanities Rvw, 1969-72. AB, Hanover Coll., 1947; MA, Northwestern U., 1948; PhD, U. N. Mex., 1952. Served with USAAF, 1943-46; CBI. Recipient Poetry prize Utah Inst. Fine Arts Creative Writing Competition, 1969; NEA fellow, 1983. Wrtr.-in-res., School of the Ozarks, 1971, Penn State U., 1972, U. of Wisc., Madison School of the Arts, 1986. Mem. AG. Home: 3840 San Rafael Ave Salt Lake City UT 84109

LUKACS, JOHN ADALBERT, b. Budapest, Hungary, Jan. 31, 1924; came to U.S., 1946, naturalized, 1953; s. Paul and Magdalena Maria L.; m. Helen Schofield, May 29, 1953 (dec. 1970); children—Paul, Annemarie; m. 2d, Stephanie

Harvey, May 18, 1974. Author: The Great Powers and Eastern Europe, 1953, A History of the Cold War, 1961, Decline and Rise of Europe, 1965, The Passing of the Modern Age, 1970, Historical Consciousness, 1968, 2d enlarged ed., 1985, The Last European War, 1939-41, 1976; 1945, Year Zero, 1978, Philadelphia: Patricians and Philistines, 1900-1950, 1981, Outgrowing Democracy: A historical interpretation of the U.S. in the last 100 years, 1984; contrbr. numerous articles, essays, revs. to hist. and lit. jnls. PhD, Palatine Joseph U., Budapest, 1946. Chmn. dept. history, Chestnut Hill Coll., 1947—. Home: Valley Park Rd Phoenixville PA 19460

LUKAS, SUSAN, b. Chgo., Oct. 9, 1940; d. Hugo and Rose (Stern) Ries; m. Christopher Lukas, July 1, 1962; 2 daus., Megan, Gabriela. Author: Fat Emily, 1974, Stereopticon, 1975, Morgana's Fault, 1981. BA, UCLA, 1962. Film critic KCOS-FM, San Francisco, 1978-79; ombudsman Westchester County, White Plains, NY, 1980-83. Mem. PIN, DG. Address: Rockland Rd Sparkill NY 10976

LUKE, DOROTHY RAWLS, b. Charleston, SC, July 15, 1907; d. Edward Heber and Julia Anna (Fincken) Rawls; widowed, 1935; children—John Guthrie, Daniel Rawls. Author: A Window to the Child's Mind, 1955, The Lion and the Dove (play), 1976, From Time to Time (play), 1983, Disarming Affinities (novelette), 1986, Champion of Children, A Biography of Helen Parkhurst 1975-1987, 1987; ed. works of Helen Parkhurst: Growing Pains (recipient McCall's Gold Mide award, Am. Med. Women's Assn. award), 1959, Undertow—The Story of a Boy Called Tony, 1961, Autobiography, 1969-72. Wrkg. on autobiography. Graduate Sarah Lawrence College first class 1930, BA, New Schl. Social Research, 1954; MS, Western Conn. Coll., 1966. Tchr. various schls., Conn., 1962-75; ednl. asst. Westinghouse Broadcasting Co., NYC., 1957-59, 60. Home: 8 Habersham Pl Rt 4 Clarkesville GA 30523

LUM, DARRELL H.Y., b. Honolulu, Apr. 2, 1950; s. Edward B. K. and Florence Y. C. (Lee) L.; m. Mae Amy Miyamoto, Aug. 14, 1976; 1 dau., Lisa. Author: Sun, Short Stories & Drama, 1980. Contrbr. scripts, articles to books, mags. Contrbr., editor: Talk Story, an Anthology of Hawaii's Local Writers, 1978; editor: (with others) Bamboo Ridge, the Hawaii Wrtr.'s Quarterly, 1978-86. B.A., U. Hawaii-Manoa, 1972, M. Edn., 1976. Co-ed. Bamboo Ridge Press, Honolulu, 1978—. Recipient Playwriting contest winner U. Hawaii, 1986. Mem. P&W, Hawaii Lit. Arts Council. Home: 990 Hahaione St Honolulu HI 96825

LUMMUS, MARION MORRIS, b. Atlanta, May 19, 1934; d. Samuel Leslie and Marion (Hull) Morris; m. Harold Campbell, Jr., June 18, 1953 (div. 1978); children—Jeanette Bragg, Harold Campbell Lummus, III, Leslie McDaniel. Author: Good Reading for Everyone, 1986. Student U. Ga., 1953; Diploma Inst. of Children's Lit., 1984. Home: 1306 Wilwood Ave B2 Columbus GA

LUMPKIN, KENNETH CHARLES, b. Queens, NY, July 18, 1951; s. Charles Curtis and Grace June (Nunno) L.; m. Ilene Frances Greenfield, June 21, 1981. Ed., Alternative Foundations, 1978-81; story ed. Talking Wood, 1979-80; ed./contrbr. Oikos, 1981—; contrbr. poetry to High Rock Review, San Fernando Poetry Review; author poetry: Gather the Ashes, 1984. BA in Envir. Studies, Ramapo Coll., 1984; MA in Anthro., Montclair State, 1985. Tchr., Barnstable School, Glen Rock, NJ, 1982-83, Yeshiva of Telshe, Westwood, NJ, 83-84, New Milford Jewish School (NJ), 1984; med. records clrk. AT&T Info. Syst., Parsippany, NJ, 1985—. Mem. AAP. Home: 42 Greenwood Ave Peqaunnock NJ 07440

LUMSDAINE, ARTHUR ALLEN, b. Seattle, Nov. 23, 1913; s. Arthur H.V. and Gladys (Strayer) L.; m. Marion Rebecca Harper, Apr. 7, 1945; children—John, David, Peter. Co-author and/or editor: Experiments on Mass Communication, 1949, The American Soldier, vol. II, 1949, Learning From Films, 1958, Teaching Machines and Programmed Learning, 1960, Student Response in Programmed Instruction, 1961, Brain Function and Learning, 1967, Fertility Control Techniques, 1973, Evaluation and Experiment, 1975. BS, U. Wash., 1937; PhD, Stanford, 1949. Sr. Fellow East-West Center, 1973. Fellow AAAS, Am. Psychol. Assn. (pres. div. ednl. psychology 1968-69). Home: 8022 Ridge Dr NE Seattle WA 98115

LUND, ORVAL A., JR., b. Fargo, ND, May 11, 1940, s. Orval A. and Katherine A. (Petersen) L.; m. Michele Lynn Grier, Aug. 5, 1967; children—John Christopher, Matthew Michael. Fiction ed. Great River Rvw, 1984; ed. GRR, 1985—; contrbr. poems to Milkweed Chronicle, Minn. Monthly, Rag Mag, Loonfeather, Lucky Star, Anti-War Poets II. BA, Moorhead State U., 1966; MA, U. Ariz., 1968, MFA, Vermont Coll., 1987. Asst. prof. English, Winona State U., Minn., 1968—. Served with U.S. Army, 1962-63. Mem. AWP, NCTE. Home: 917 Evergreen Ln Winona MN 55987

LUNDBERG, FERDINAND EDGAR, b. Chgo., Apr. 30, 1902; s. Otto Ferdin. and Hannah (Svendsen) L.; m. Elizabeth Young, Sept. 19, 1944; children—Randolph Horner, Laurence Young. Author: Imperial Hearst, 1936, America's Sixty Families, 1937, Modern Woman: The Lost Sex, 1947, The Treason of the People, 1953, The Coming World Transformation, 1963, The Rich and the Super-Rich, 1968, Scoundrels All, 1968, The Rockefeller Syndrome, 1975, Cracks in the Constitution, 1980; editor: Medical studies in Merchant Seaman, 1943. BS, Columbia, 1948, MA, 1952. Journalist Chgo. Daily Jnl, 1924-26, U.P.I., 1926-27; financial writer N.Y. Herald Tribune, 1927-34; editor Twentieth Century Fund, NYC, 1946-51. Home: 598 Quaker Rd Chappaqua NY 10514

LUNDE, DAVID ERIC, b. Berkeley, CA, Oct. 14, 1941; s. John Peer and Alice Ann (Leslie) L; m. Mary Lee Brannock, Dec. 18, 1966 (div. Sept. 4, 1981); 1 dau., China Fontaine Lee; m. 2d, Marilyn Catherine Masiker, Aug. 28, 1983; 1 son, Eric Otto. Author: Ironic Holidays, 1965, Les Papillons, 1967, Sludge Gulper, 1971, Calibrations, 1981, Critical Mass: Poems & Parables. BA, Knox Coll, 1963; MFA, U.Ia., 1967. Prof. English SUNY, Fredonia, NY, 1967—; ed./pub. The Basilisk Press, Fredonia, 1970—. Mem. SFWA, SFPA. Address: 252 King Rd Forestville NY 14062

LUNDE, DIANE S., b. Chgo., July 4, 1942; Contrbr. poems to lit. mags., anthols. B.A., U. Calif.-Berkeley, 1965; M.A., U. London, 1976. Tutor in English, Jr. Coll. of Albany, NY, 1983-85; free-lance copy ed. SUNY Press, Albany, 1983-86; tchr. N.Y. Correctional Facilities, 1985-86; teaching asst. State U. N.Y., Albany, 1986—. Recipient award for public service announcement script Inst. for Mental Health Initiatives, 1984. Mem. Hudson Valley WG. Home: 6 S Lake Ave Apt S-25 Albany NY 12203

LUNDQUIST, CARL, b. Kansas City, KS, Oct. 24, 1913, s. David Axel and Elsie Elizabeth (Larm) Lundquist; m. Marjorie Esther Mattson, Sept. 1, 1940; children—Susan Carol Schwadron, Richard David. Author: The Almost Official Fan's Guide to the New York Yankees, 1983, 70 Nights in a Ball Park, 1958, United We Stood, 1985. Student, Kansas City pub. schls., 1928-31. Sports wrtr., United Press, Kansas City, St. Louis, Detroit, NYC, 1937-56, promotions dir., Professional Baseball, Columbus, OH, 1957-62, edit.-Eastern mgr., The Sporting News, NYC, 1963-65, assignment wrtr., 1966-; columnist, Coll. & Pro Football Newsweekly, 1982—, Publicity Dir. N.Y. State Games for the Physically Challenged, 1985—. Mem. Baseball Writers of America. Home: 848 Leonard Drive Westbury NY 11590

LUNDQUIST, RICHARD D., b. Lindsborg, KS, July 8, 1947; s. Verner Emanuel and Mildred Irene (Ahlstedt) L.; m. Henriette Adriana Pruyser, Sept. 6, 1968 (div. 1975); m. 2d, Sandra Kathlene Lee, July 21, 1978; children—Gabriel, Maiya, Amanda. Contrbr. stories to Kans. Qtly, Cold-Drill, Colorado North Rvw, Pendragon; contrbr. non-fiction to local mags., newspapers. BA, U. Kans., 1970; MA, Calif. State U.-San Francisco, 1973. Broadcast ed. AP, Kansas City, Mo., 1968-69; campus corr. Time, Lawrence, Kans., 1969-70; informational wrtr. U. Kans., Lawrence, 1969-70; free-lance wrtr., Boise, Idaho, 1979—; instr. English Boise State U., 1980—. Recipient Distinctive Short Story award Houghton-Mifflin, 1977. Mem. AWP. Office: Dept Eng BSU 1910 Univ Dr Boise ID 83725

LUNG, CHANG, see Rigney, James Oliver, Jr.

LUNN, JEAN, b. Boston, Sept. 9, 1933, d. John Aleck and Susan Elizabeth (Williams) Lunn. Contrbr. poetry to: Radcliffe Quar., Stone Country, Christian Sci. Monitor, Yankee, Manhattan Poetry Rvw, numerous other publs.; transl. vocal and choral works of Bach, Brahms, Handel, Mendelssohn, many other composers; poetry ed. Sandscript, 1981—. AB, Radcliffe Coll., 1955; Teaching Cert. Acad. Jewish Studies, Boston, 1970. Vocal soloist concerts, opera, religious orgns., 1958-78; freelance translator, ed., 1959—. Recipient Bicentennial Poetry prize Barnstable Libraries, Mass., 1976, Rosalie Boyle award New Eng. Poetry Club, 1985. Mem. Am. Guild Organists, New Eng. Poetry Club. Home: 25 Harvard St Hyannis MA 02601

LUNSFORD, M. ROSSER, b. Hogansville, GA, Mar. 1, 1922, s. Roy B. and Mary Elizabeth (Rosser) L.; m. Vera Jenkins, Feb. 22, 1955; children—Ralph Rosser, Danny Ross, Mary Elizabeth. Author: Folkway, 1962, I Am, 1962, Eye of Memory, 1986, After Thoughts, 1986; contrbr. over 400 poems to numerous lit mags and periodicals. Student, South Ga. Coll., 1939-40. Foreman Lockheed Aircraft Co., Marietta, Ga., 1951-54, Douglas Aircraft Co., Santa Monica, Calif., 1954-62; mgr. recreation, LaGrange and Tucker, Ga., 1962-67; dept. head Grady Meml. Hosp., Atlanta, 1967-84. Served with USAAC, 1940-45, ETO. Recipient Little Brs. award Inky Trails mag., 1983, Freedom award, 1982; Poet of Yr. award Rhyme Time mag., 1983, twice best of issue award Tiotis mag., 1983; 1st place award Explorer mag., 1984, 85, Fine Lines MAG *$: CERT OF MERIT GA Poetry Soc., 1983, numerous others. Mem. P&W, Poets Council, Heritage Soc. Authors and Writers Am., Dr. Stella Woodall Poets Intl. (hon.). Home: 5458

Mill Valley Dr Douglasville GA 30135

LUNTZ, PERRY, b. Bklyn., Mar. 9, 1927; s. Edward and Jean (Simon) L.; m. Edith Lieberman, Apr. 21, 1947 (div. 1974); children—Ira, Lloyd, Russell; m. Carol Ann Rinzler, Oct. 20, 1978. Author sales promotion materials, indsl. films. Ed.: Beverage Alcohol Market Report, 1982—, N.Y. Mag. On the Town, 1982-85. B.S., NYU., Supvr. copy group Young & Rubicam, NYC, 1972-74; ed., pub. Beverage Alcohol Market Report, NYC, 1982—. Recipient Silver medal N.Y. Intl. Film/TV Festival, 1966. Home: 160 E 48th St New York NY 10017

LURIE, ALISON, b. Chgo., Sept. 3, 1926; children—John, Jeremy, Joshua. Author: V.R. Lang: a Memoir, 1959, Love and Friendship, 1962, The Nowhere City, 1965, Imaginary Friends, 1967, Real People, 1969, The War Between the Tates, 1974, Only Children, 1979, The Language of Clothes, 1981, Foreign Affairs, 1984. AB, Radcliffe Coll., 1947. Recipient award in lit. Am. Acad. Arts and Letters, 1978; Yaddo Found. fellow, 1963, 64, 66; Guggenheim fellow, 1965; Rockefeller Found. fellow, 1967; Pulitzer Prize in fiction, 1985. Address: Dept Engl Cornell U Ithaca NY 14850

LURIE, TOBY, b. Seattle, May 12, 1925, s. Myer and Edith L.; m. Janis Lurie, Sept. 24, 1950 (div. 1977); children—Mark, Drew, Lisa. Author: The Last Rondo in Paris, 1984, The Beach at Cleone, 1983, Word Music, 1983, A Leaf of Voices, 1980, Serial Poems, 1979, Conversations and Constructions, 1978, Conversation with the Past, 1976, Mirror Images, 1974, Handbook on Vocal Poetry, 1969, New Forms New Spaces, 1971, Measured Spaces, 1977. Wrkg. on performance paintings. BA in Music Theory, U. Calif.-Santa Barbara, 1975. Home: 1429 Page St Apt F San Francisco CA 94117

LUTHER, SUSAN MILITZER, b. Lincoln, NE, May 28, 1946, d. Walter Ernest and Sarah Clementine (Newman) Militzer; m. Robert Norman Luther, July 18, 1971. Co-ed.: The Scribbler, 1975, 76; asst. ed. Poem, 1985—; contrbr. poetry to Bloodroot, Malahat RVW, Small Pond, Kalliope, numerous other lit. mags.; contrbr. articles to scholarly publs. BA in English, La. State U., 1969; MA in English, U. Ala., 1976; PhD in English, Vanderbilt U., 1986. Tchr. various public schls. and colls; lectr. in English, U. Ala., Hunstville, 1986—. Mem. P&W, Modern Poetry Assn. (assoc.), Alabama State Poetry Soc., bd. mem. Huntsville Literary Assn., MLA, SAMLA, NCTE. Home: 2115 Buckingham Dr SW Hunstville AL 35803

LUTHOLTZ, M WILLIAM, b. Indpls., Apr. 2, 1954; s. Myron E. and Blossie E. (Moore) L.; m. Catherine Hanley, Dec. 30, 1976; children—Ann Marie, Thomas. Ed.: The Indac Mag., 1978-79, The Fifth Wheel Mag., 1976-78, The AULnews, 1979—, City Lights of Indpls., 1975; contrbr. to The Sagamore, IUPUI, Indpls. Mag., Indpls. Monthly, Indiana Bus. Mag., Indpls. Bus. Jnl, TheCarmel News Jnl., the Hamiltonian Mag. AB in Poli. Sci., IUPUI, 1976. Rptr./photog. News Jnl., Carmel, IN, 1974-76; ed. City Light, Indpls., 1975, The Fifth Wheel, Indpls., 76-78, The Indac Mag., Indpls., 78-79, The AULnews, Indpls., 79—; freelance writer, Indpls. Mag., 1973—. Communicator of Year & President's award, IABC, 1983. Mem. IABC. Home: 615 N Riley Indianapolis IN 46201

LUXNER, MORTON BENNETT, b. Newark, NJ, June 2, 1917; s. Abraham and Lillian Dorothy (Salov) L.; m. Trudy Wolfe, Dec. 2, 1945; Children-Marilyn Lashmore, Adrienne Armstrong, Lawrence David; Ed.-in-Chief: The Craftsman, 1957-65; contrbg. ed., The New Age, 1958-66; Natl. Dep. Ed., Jewish War Vetrans, 1965-79; columnist: Adv. Rev., 1977—, The Mirror newspaper group, So. Fla., 1979-86; The Jewish Journal, 1987—. Compltd MS on The Selling Game (non-fiction) and wrkg on novel of suspense/intrigue. Ed., Bklyn Coll., Washington & Lee U. and S.M.I. Tchr. Mpls. Sch. System, 1968-70; Tchr. creative writing, Broward Schl. Board, 1970—; pres., Miami Brands, Ltd. 1970-87. Served as sgt. USArmy, 1941-45; ETO, EAME. Named Soldier-Poet of WWII for lyrics to Song of the Army Engineers, USArmy CE, 1943. Mem. Fla. Freelance Wrtrs Assn. Address: Box 25487 Ft. Lauderdale FL 33320

LUZADER, S. D., see Prust, Susan Luzader

LYCAN, KELLY G., b. Wooster, OH, Dec. 3, 1958; d. Raymond G. and Floris C. (Schuefler) Zimmerman. BFA, Bowling Green State U., 1981. Asst. op. Water Pollution Control plant, Wooster, Ohio, 1978-81; football and track coach Wooster High Schl., 1982-83, sub. tchr., 1982-83, carpenter, 1982-85; grad. asst. in Eng. Univ. Ark., Fayetteville, 1983-85, women's track coach, Univ. of Arkansas, Fayetteville, 1985—. Recipient Lily Peter fiction award, Univ. Ark., 1985. Address: Barnhill Arena Fayetteville AR 72701

LYFORD, JOSEPH PHILIP, b. Chgo., Aug. 4, 1918; s. Philip and Ruth (Pray) L.; m. Margaretta Jean Thomas, Feb. 16, 1963; children—Amy Jean, Joseph Philip. Author: Candidate, The Agreeable Autocracies, 1961, The Talk in Vandalia, 1963, The Airtight Cage, 1966, The Berkeley Archipelago, 1981. Grad., Phillips Acad., Andover, Mass., 1937; AB with honors, Harvard, 1941. Reporter Boston Post, 1938-41, Intl. News Service, 1946-47; asst. editor New Republic, 1947-48; European corr. Hartford (Conn.) Times, 1951; prof. journalism U. Calif. at Berkeley, 1966—. Served to lt. USNR, 1941-46. Decorated for outstanding performance of duty during Okinawa invasion, ,67; recipient Sidney Hillman Fdn. award in lit., 1967. Home: 216 Crestview Dr Orinda CA 94563

LYLE, IDALEE MARTIN, b. Ashland, AL, Dec. 17, 1907; d. John Simeoon and Leila Ophelia (Strong) Martin; m. Albert Homer Lyle, June 14, 1930 (dec. 1985); 1 dau., Jean Jacqueline. Novelist: Before Sunset, 1961; contrbr. fiction to numerous publs. AB, (now) Univ. of North Alabama, 1925; earned teaching cert. (was) Florence State Tchr.'s Coll., 1944. Tchr., Decatur, Ala., 1926-48. Home: 210 Wilson St Apt A3 Decatur AL 35601

LYLE, WILLIAM DAVID, b. Kalamazoo, MI, Mar. 16, 1950; s. Jack and Mary Jane (Bradfield) L.; m. Cynthia Cline, Aug. 8, 1983. Author poetry: I Care, 1976, Carry On, 1978, Sometimes I Never Think So Clear, 1981. BS, Mich. State U., 1975. Merchant seaman US Merchant Marine, Duluth, Minn., 1972-74, 75-77; insp. US Customs Service, Detroit, 1977-79, sta. dir., Dutch Harbor, Alaska, 1979-81; sales mgr. Walstrom marine, Harbor Springs, Mich., 1981—. Home: 4600 Cottontail Ln Harbor Springs MI 49740

LYNDON, AMY, see Radford, Richard Francis Jr.

LYNDS, DENNIS, (Michael Collins, Mark Sadler, John Crowe, William Arden, Carl Dekker), b. St. Louis, Jan. 15, 1924, s. Archibald John Douglas and Gertrude (Hyem) L.; m. Doris Flood, Dec. 17, 1949 (div. 1956); m. 2d, Sheila McErlean, Oct. 27, 1961 (div. 1985); children—Katherine Harold, Deirdre Anne; m. 3d, Gayle Hallenbeck Stone, Feb. 14, 1986. Author: Combat Soldier, 1962, Uptown Downtown, 1963, Charlie Chan Returns, 1974, S.W.A.T.—Crossfire, 1975, Why Girls Ride Sidesaddle (short stories), 1980; (as Michael Collins): Act of Fear, 1967, The Brass Rainbow, 1969, Lukan War (sci.-fiction), 1969, Night of the Toads, 1970, The Planets of Death (sci.-fiction), 1970, Walk a Black Wind, 1971, Shadow of a Tiger, 1972, The Silent Scream, 1973, Blue Death, 1975, The Blood-Red Dream, 1976, The Nightrunners, 1978, The Slasher, 1980, Freak, 1983, Minnesota Strip, 1987; Red Rosa, 1988 (as Mark Sadler): The Falling Man, 1970, Here to Die, 1971, Mirror Image, 1972, Circle of Fire, 1973, Deadly Innocents, 1986; (as John Crowe): Another Way to Die, 1972, A Touch of Darkness, 1972, Bloodwater, 1974, Crooked Shadows, 1975, When They Kill Your Wife, 1977, Close to Death, 1979; (as William Arden): A Dark Power, 1968, Deal in Violence, 1969, The Goliath Scheme, 1971, Die to a Distant Drum, 1972, Deadly Legacy, 1973: (as Carl Dekker): Woman in Marble, 1973; contrbr. stories to December mag., Mike Shayne Mystery Mag., Alfred Hitchock's Mystery Mag., Masters of Mystery, Argosy, numerous other publs. BA, Hofstra Coll., 1949; MA, Syracuse U., 1951. Asst. ed. Chem Week, NYC., 1951-52; editorial dir. Am. Inst. Mgmt., NYC, 1952-54; assoc. ed. then mng. ed. Chem. Engring. Progress, NYC., 1955-61; ed. Chem. Equipment mag., Lab. Equipment mag., NYC., 1962-66; freelance wrtr. Served. with AUS, 1943-46; decorated Bronze Star, Purple Heart. Recipient Arbeitsgemeinschaft Kriminalliteratur spcl. commendation for entire body of work, 1981; guest of honor 8th Festival du Roman et du Film Policiers, Reims, France, 1986. Mem. MWA (Edgar Allan Poe award 1968, Spcl. award 1969), Pvt. Eye Wrtrs. Am. (pres. 1985; Shamus nominee 1984), AG, Crime Wrtrs. Assn. Gt. Britain. Home: 12 St Anne Dr Santa Barbara CA 93109

LYNES, (JOSEPH) RUSSELL, (JR.), b. Great Barrington, MA, Dec. 2, 1910; s. Joseph Russell and Adelaide (Sparkman) L.; m. Mildred Akin, May 30, 1934; children—George Platt II, Elizabeth Russell. Author: Highbrow, Lowbrow, Middlebrow, 1949, Snobs, 1950, Guests, 1951, The Tastemakers, 1954, A Surfeit of Honey, 1957, Cadwallader, 1959, The Domesticated Americans, 1963, Confessions of a Dilettante, 1966, The Art-Makers of 19th Century America, 1970, Good Old Modern, 1973, More Than Meets the Eye, 1981, The Lively Audience, 1985; contrbg. editor: Harper's, Art in Am., 1969-71; contrbr. articles, stories, essays to mags. Student, Cathedral Choir Schl., N.Y., 1920-25, Berkshire Schl., Sheffield, Mass., 1925-28; B.A., Yale U., 1932; D.F.A. (hon.), Union Coll., Schenectady; L.H.D., Md. Inst., 1973, City U. N.Y., 1980; Litt.D., North Adam State Coll., 1977. With Harper & Bros. (pubs.), 1932-36; dir. publs. Vassar Coll., Poughkeeepsie, N.Y., 1936-37; asst. editor Harper's , 1944-47, mng. editor, 1947-67, contrbg. editor, 1967—. Mem. AL. Office: 427 E 84th St New York NY 10028

LYNN, SANDRA DYKES, b. Longview, TX, Sept. 16, 1944; d. James DeLesley and Inez (Sumner) Dykes; m. Hervey Stuart Hutchins IV; 1 child, DeLesley Stuart; m. Richard Earl Brown, Mar. 20, 1982. Author: I Must Hold

These Strangers, 1980; Three Texas Poets, 1986; contrbr. to anthologies. BA, U. Tex., Austin, 1967; MA, U. Calif., Berkeley, 1968. Instr. Austin Community Coll., 1973-76, St. Edward's U., Austin, 1978-80, S.W. Tex. State U., San Marcos, 1983—; tech. wrtr./ed. Applied Research Labs., Austin, 1980-82; fgn. expert Harbin Inst. Tech., China, 1985-86. Woodrow Wilson fellow, 1967-68; Dobie Paisano fellow Tex. Inst. Letters, 1982. Mem. Austin Wrtrs. League. Home: 3305 Westhill Dr Austin TX 78704

LYNN, THOMAS EDWARD, b. St. Louis, May 19, 1930; s. Thomas U. and Mary Frances (Greer) L.; m. Trudy Pearl White, June 15, 1966; children—Frances Ruth, Kenneth Thomas, Joseph Edward, Timothy Eugene, Tammy, Sherry Laverne. Contrbr. articles, poems to lit. mags., anthols. including Rhyme Time, Odessa Poetry Rvw., numerous others. Enforcement officer U.S. Customs Dept., Tampa, 1960-67; spcl. agent office of Inspector General. U.S. Dept. Agrl., Atlanta, 1967-82, retired. Recipient Exellence in Lit. award Pinewood Poetry, 1987; named Poet of Yr., Ed.'s Desk, Ocala, FL, 1987. Mem. WV Poetry Soc. (Betty Grugin Ballad awar 1983), Ga. Poetry Soc. Home: 545 Birch Ln Lawrenceville GA 30245

LYNSKEY, EDWARD C., b. Arlington, VA, June 20, 1956; s. Edward E. and Gail (Roberts) Ritchie L.; m. Heather Tervo, June 9, 1982. Author poetry Wrought Iron, 1980 (Manassas Prize), Teeth of the Hydra, 1986; ed. Home Planet News, 1981-85, Rockingchair, 1982-84; contrbr. Atlantic Monthly, Am. Poetry Rvw, Coll. English, So. Poetry Rvw, Georgia Rvw; rvws. Kans. City Star, Columbus Dispatch, NY Times. BA in Latin Am. History, George mason U., 1979, MA in English, 1984. Sr. tech writer Atlantic Research Corp, Alexandria, Va., 1979—; founder and pub. Crop Dust Press, 1980—. Address: Rt 5 Box 75 Warrenton VA 22186

LYON, DAVID WILLIAM, b. Ashland, KY, June 24, 1949; s. Lionel Olus and Marie Little Bear (Perkins) L. Author poetry: The Waters, 1975, Coyote's Wife, 1980, The Sound of Horns, 1984; criticism, Philosophical Dualism in the Works of James Branch Cabell and the Unpublished Works of Mark Twain, 1970; contrbr. fiction Boston Globe Mag, Fantasy and Sci Fi, Kalki, Venture, Imagination; contrbr. poetry 50 mags inclg. Beloit Poetry Jnl, No. Am. Rvw, Mass. Rvw, New Rivers, others; contrbr. criticism Boston Globe, NY Times, San Francisco Rvw Books, LA Times, Washington Post, Paeduma; contrbr. jnlsm. major publs. BA, U. Me., 1970; MFA, U. Mass., 1973. Ed. Lynx House Press, Amherst, Mass., 1971-82; jnlst. Foster's Daily Dem., Dover, NH, 1976-77, Greenfield Recorder, Mass., 1977-78; ed. academic news U. Mass. and Boston Univ., Amherst and Boston, 1978-84; freelance jnlst., Cambridge, 1969—. Panelist, Mass. Council Arts & Humanities, Boston, 1980-82; lit spclst., New England Fdn. for the Arts, Cambridge, 1984-85. Mem. New England Poetry Club. Address: 6 Crawford St Cambridge MA 02139

LYON, GEORGE ELLA, b. Harlan, KY, Apr. 25, 1949; d. Robert Vernon and Gladys Marion (Fowler) Hoskins Jr.; m. Stephen Craig Lyon, June 3, 1972; 2 sons, Benjamin Gerard and Joseph Fowler. Author: (chapbook) Mountain, 1983, (children's book) Father Time and the Day Boxes, 1985; Braids, a play, 1985. BA, Centre Coll., 1971; MA, U. Ark., 1972, PhD, Ind. U.-Bloomington, 1978. Part-time instr. var. univs., 1971—; free-lance writer and editor, 1971—; writer-in- res. Centre Coll., Danville, Ky., 1985, tchr. Ky. Dept. Libs. and Archives, Frankfort, 1985. Mem. Bluegrass Nuclear Freeze campaign, Lexington, 1984—. Mem. Virginia Woolf Soc., DG, Soc. for Children's Book Writers, Phi Beta Kappa. Address: 913 Maywick Dr. Lexington KY 40504

LYON, TED, b. Salt Lake City, UT, May 13, 1939; s. T. Edgar and Hermana (Forsberg) Lyon; m. Cheryl Larsen, June 12, 1962; children—Thomas, Ann Marie, Jennifer, Gregory, Peter. Editor: Chasqui-Revista de Litertura Latinamericana, 1971-72, 1981—, Juan Godoy (Twayne), 1972. BA, U. of Utah, 1963; PhD, UCLA, 1967. Asst. prof., U. of Wisconsin (Madison), 1969-72; senior research fellow U. of Glasgow (Scotland), 1980; prof. BYU, Provo, UT, 1972—. Professor of Year, BYU, 1985. Pres. Rocky Mountain MLA. Office: Dept Spanish 4050 JKHB BYU Provo UT 84604

LYONS, CHOPETA C., b. Tucson, Dec. 22, 1949; d. Talbot Truxtun and Leslie Fern (Collie) Smith; m. Peter Lyons, Sept. 6, 1975 (div. June 8, 1985). Author: Discover Writing, 1984. Contrbr. short stories to mags., newspapers, anthols. Editor, contrbr.: CP:M Adam Home Computer, 1984. AA, Stephens Coll., BA, U. Ariz.-Tucson; M.A. Faculty, Jefferson Jr. Coll., 1975-79, adj. faculty, dir. basic skills Greater Hartford Community Coll., Conn., 1980-82; senior tech. wrtr. Coleco Industries, Hartford, 1982-85; CBT trng. author Data Base Mgmt. Inc., Hartford, 1985—. Recipient 1st prize Hackney awards for short fiction Birmingham Festival of Arts, 1976, 77, 79, 3d prize Hackney award for short fiction, 1978; 1st prize Natl. award Primavera Mag., 1985. Mem. Soc. Tech. Communications (Disting. Tech. Communication award 1986), P&W, AWP, Sierra Club. Home: 26 Pinney St 20 Ellington CT 06039

LYONS, EDWARD TIMOTHY, b. Jersey City, NJ, May 9, 1946; s. Timothy and Mary (Tooher) L. Author: The Program of the Good, 1983. Two yrs. accumulated credit in Bus. Administrn., Rutgers Coll.-Jersey City Br., 1965-71. Cons. conservation, Jersey City, 1982—. Committeeman Republican Party, Jersey City, 1982. Served as yeoman U.S. Navy, 1971-81. Recipient Good Conduct medal, 1975. Mem. Am. Legion. Home: 84 Carlton Ave Jersey City NJ 07306

LYONS, RICHARD E., b. Detroit, June 9, 1920, s. Frank C. and Daisy L. (Sweeny) L.; children—Christopher D., Cressida D. Author: Men and Tin Kettles, 1956, One Squeaking Straw, 1958, Paintings in Taxicabs, 1965, Above Time, 1966, John, Where Are You?, 1967, Walking Wide, 1970, Public Journal, 1972, Racer and Lame, 1975, The Quest and the Questions, 1976, The Facts and the Fantasies, 1976, A Cast of (Nameless) Characters, 1978, Scanning the Land, 1980, A Wilderness of Faith and Love (stories); stories in Virginia Qtly Rvw, Northwest Rvw, Chelsea; ed. Poetry North, 1970. AB, Miami U., Oxford, Ohio, 1942, MA, 1946; postgrad. Ind. U., 1948-50, U. Minn., 1959-60. Mem. faculty N.D. State U., Fargo, 1950-82. Mem. PEN. Home: 9 Deane St Gardiner ME 04345

LYONS, RICHARD M., b. Bklyn., May 8, 1935. Author: Amara (children's book). Contrbr. fiction, articles to Discourse, Colo. State Rvw, Assembling, Greenfield Rvw, Permafrost, Ohio Rvw, El Urogallo, other lit mags, prof. jnls. BA, Brooklyn Coll., 1957; MFA, Univ. of Iowa, 1962. Asst. prof., Univ. of Wis., Oshkosh, 1963-69; prof., Univ. of Oregon, 1969—. Emily Clark Balch Short Story Award, 1977, NEA Fellowship, 1981, PEN Syndication Fiction Project Award, 1985. Office: Eng Dept U Oregon Eugene OR 97403

LYSTAD, MARY HANEMANN, (Mrs. Robert Lystad) b. New Orleans, Apr. 11, 1928; d. James and Mary (Douglass) Hanemann; m. Robert Lystad, June 20, 1953; children—Lisa Douglass, Anne Hanemann, Mary Lunde, Robert Douglass, James Hanemann. Author: Millicent the Monster, 1968, Social Aspects of Alienation, 1969, Jennifer Takes Over P.S. 94, 1972, James the Jaguar, 1972, As They See It: Changing Values of College Youth, 1973, That New Boy, 1973, Halloween Parade, 1973, Violence at Home, 1974, A Child's World as Seen in His Stories and Drawings, 1974, From Dr. Mather to Dr. Seuss: 200 Years of American Books for Children, 1980, At Home in America, 1984; ed.: Innovations in Mental Health Services to Disaster Victims, 1985, Violence in the Home, 1986. AB cum laude, Newcomb Coll., 1949; MA, Columbia U., 1951; PhD, Tulane U., 1955. Postdoctoral fellow social psychology S.E. La. Hosp., Mandeville, 1955-57; feature writer African div. Voice Am., Washington, 1964-73, sociologist, Natl. Inst. of Mental Health, Wash., 1969—. Home: 4900 Scarsdale Rd Bethesda MD 20816

LYSTRA, HELEN PERCY, (Liz Foster), b. Detroit, Mar. 13, 1939; d. Charles Browning and Dora-Marie (Foster) Percy Jr.; m. Edward Harry Lystra, May 22, 1976; 1 son, Marshall Foster. Author: Historical Cookbook, 1985; ed.: Historical Tour of Downtown Grand Haven, MI, 1982, Kitchen Sampler Cookbook, 1983. Workg. on a historical novel. Student Hillsdale Coll., 1957-58; BA, Grand Valley State, 1980. Chmn. Hist. Commn., Grand Haven, Mich., 1980-87; chmn. Sesquicentennial Steering Com., Grand Haven, 1982-83, mem. com., 1984-85. Mem. Internat. Assn. Bus. Communicators (v.p., 1985-86). Home: 943 Lake Ave Grand Haven MI 49417

MAAS, PETER, b. NYC, June 27, 1929; s. Carl and Madeleine (Fellheimer) M.; m. Audrey Gellen, Apr. 4, 1962 (dec. July 1975); 1 son, John Michael. Author: The Rescuer, 1967, The Valachi Papers, 1969, Serpico, 1973, King of the Gypsies, 1975, Made in America, 1979, Marie: A True Story, 1983, Manhunt, 1986. BA, Duke U., 1949;; postgrad., The Sorbonne, Paris, 1950. Assoc. editor Collier's mag., 1954-56; sr. editor Look mag., 1959-61; contrbg. editor New York mag., 1968-71. Free-lance contrbr. natl. mags., newspapers, 1954—; spcl. cons. David Brinkley's Jnl, NBC-TV, 1961-62. Served with USNR, 1952-54. Mem. PEN Am. Ctr. Office: Intl Crtv 40 W 57th St New York NY 10019

MABE, CHAUNCEY, b. Wytheville, VA, Nov. 3, 1955; s.George Eugene and Mary Charlotte (McAllister) M.; m. Monica Marie Strand, July 1, 1978; children—Alexis, Rachel, Karla. Contrbr. feature articles: Echelon Mag., Delta Sky Mag., various newspapers. Wrkg. on articles, novel, non-fiction book. Reporter Cleveland (Tenn.) Banner, 1977-79, Palm Beach Post, West Palm Beah, Fla., 1979-84; ed. mags. halsey Pub. o., Miami, Fla., 1984-87; book ed. Ft. Lauderdale (Fla.) Sun Sentinel, 1987—. Mem. Fla. Mag. Assn. (recipient numerous awards). Office: Sun-Sentinel 101 N New River Dr East Fort Lauderdale FL 33302

MABEE, CARLETON, b. Shanghai, China, Dec. 25, 1914; s. Fred Carleton and Miriam (Bentley) M.; m. Norma Dierking, Dec. 20, 1945;

children—Timothy I., Susan (Mrs. Paul Newhouse). Author: The American Leonardo, A Life of Samuel F.B. Morse, 1943, The Seaway Story, 1961, Black Freedom: The Nonviolent Abolitionists from 1830 through the Civil War, 1970, Black Education in New York State: From Colonial to Modern Times, 1979; also articles; editor: (with James A. Fletcher) A Quaker Speaks from the Black Experience: The Life and Selected Writings of Barrington Dunbar, 1979. AB, Bates Coll., 1936; MA (Perkins scholar), Columbia U., 1938, PhD, 1942. Recipient Pulitzer prize, 1944; others. Home: Rt 1 Gardiner NY 12525

MACADO, MARY STANLEY, (Mary Low), b. London, May 14, 1912, came to U.S., 1965; d. Vernon Forster and Hilda Lunn (Blandford-Wright) Stanley-Low; m. Juan Ramon Brea, Sept. 25, 1937 (dec. April 17, 1941); m. 2d, Armando Machado, Nov. 9, 1944 (dec. Jan. 19, 1982); children—Helga Silva, Yara Guzman, Maria-Julia Bermudez. Author: (with J. Brea) Red Spanish Notebook, 1937, La Saison des Flutes, 1939, La Verdad Contemporanea, 1943; Alquimia del Recuerdo, 1946, 2d ed., 1986, Three Voices, 1957, (textbook) English Is Easy, 1958; In Caesar's Shadow, 1975, 2d ed., 1984, Alive in Spite of, 1981, A Voice in Three Mirrors, 1984. Art editor: Classics Chronicle, 1978-84, dir. 1985—. Secy.-treas., The Concerned Classicists, 1978—. BA, U. Havana, Cuba, 1956. Prof. English, English Tchrs.' Coll., Havana, 1956-70, U. Havana, 1960-64; tchr. Latin, Gulliver Acad., Miami, 1968-78; Recipient tchr. Classics, Holy Cross Acad., Miami, 1986—. Recipient Spanish Poetry prize U. Havana, 1954, history and history of art prizes, 1956. Mem. Am. Classical League, Classical Assn. Fla., Am. Inst. Archaeology, Assn. Ancient Hists. (assoc.), Vergilian Soc., Ermine St. Guard (assoc.). Home: 8951 SW 10th Terr Miami FL 33174

MAC AFEE, NORMAN, b. Phila., Mar. 18, 1943. Author: A New Requiem (poetry), 1987; contrbr. poetry Little Mag., Gandhabba, Nuovi Argomenti, numerous other lit mags; co-translator: Pier Paolo Pasolini: Poems, 1982, Les Miserables (by Victor Hugo), 1987, Atlas of the West (by Daniele del Giudice), 1988; ed., Sartre: A Life (by Annie Cohan-Solal), 1987; contrbr. translations to: Paris Rvw, Unmuzzled Ox, Christopher St. Freelance copy-ed., 1971—; New Theatre critic, Cover mag., 1986—. Mem. PEN (Renato Poggioli award 1980), P&W. Home: 542 E 79th St New York NY 10021

MACARTHUR, GLORIA, b. Washington, May 14, 1924; d. Emmet Carlyle and Genevieve (Walsh) Gudger; m. Colin Macarthur, Mar. 17, 1949; 1 son, Glen Cameron. Poetry included in anthologies: Avalon Anthologies, 1957, 58, Poets of American Anthology, 1957, Epos Anthology, 1958, 75, The Poetry Society America Anthologies, The Golden Year, 1960, The Diamond Anthology, 1971; also numerous lit mags. Student, Vassar Coll., 1942-43; BA cum laude, U. Minn., 1946. Columnist Mpls. Daily Times, 1946-48; reporter, page editor Palm Springs (Calif.) News, 1948-49. Mem. PSA, Poetry Soc. Ga. Address: 9901 SW 67th Ave Miami FL 33156

MAC ARTHUR, LOREN, b. San Francisco, CA, Oct. 15, 1935; d. Henry Crawford and W. Adele (Roos) MacArthur; m. Alton Shaul Bock, Jun. 17, 1961 (dec. Jun. 15, 1980); 1 son—Duncan. Author: LA Bike Rides; contrbr. to East-West Network, City Sports Mag., Automation News. AB, Stanford U., 1957. Mem. NWU. Home: 328 Market St Venice CA 90291

MACAULEY, ROBIE MAYHEW, b. Grand Rapids, MI, May 31, 1919; s. George William and Emma (Hobart) M.; m. Anne Draper, June 19, 1948; m. 2d, Pamela Painter, Aug. 9, 1979; 1 son, Cameron. Author: novel The Disguises of Love, 1952; short stories The End of Pity, 1957; criticism Technique in Fiction, 1964, rev. ed., 1987; novel A Secret History of Time to Come, 1979. AB, Kenyon Coll., 1941; MFA, State U. Iowa, 1950; postgrad. U. London, 1964-65; DLitt, Kenyon Coll., 1986. Editor Kenyon Rvw, 1959-66; sr. editor Playboy mag., Chgo., 1966-77, exec. editor Houghton Mifflin Co., Boston, 1977—. Served with AUS, 1942-46. Guggenheim fellow, 1964; Fulbright research fellow, 1964-65; O'Henry Short Story winner, 1967. Mem. PEN. Office: Houghton Mifflin 2 Park St Boston MA 02108

MACCHIA, DONALD DEAN, b. Gary, IN, May 17, 1948; d. Mike Dominick and Elizabeth (Pilla) M.; m. Gloria Jean Sicuro, Jan. 1969 (div. Mar. 1980); children—Anthony, Marianne. Author: Weight Training in Sports: A Reference Guide, 1985, The Weightlifters Handbook, 1986. Contrbr. articles to popular mags. including Muscle Digest, Ironman, Muscular Devel., articles on physiology and anatomy to profl. jnls; assoc. ed. Dean Aster Publ., 1984-86. AB Ind. U.-Bloomington, 1970; MA, Ball State U., 1973; MSA, U. Ill.-Urbana, 1974, PhD, 1977. Asst. prof. U. Chgo, 1979-80; asst. prof. Ind. U., Bloomington, 1980-85, assoc. prof. and chmn. pharmacol., 1985—. Home: 7434 Grand Blvd Hobart IN 46432

MACDONALD, CYNTHIA, b. NYC, Feb. 2, 1928; d. Leonard and Dorothy (Kiam) Lee; m. E.C. Macdonald, 1954 (div. 1975); children—Jennifer Tim, Scott Thurston. Author: (poems) Amputations, 1972, Transplants, 1976,; (chapbook) Pruning the Annuals, 1976, (W)holes, 1980, The Rehearsal Copera Libretto), Alternate Means of Transport, 1985. Contrbr. poems, essays, rvws., articles to anthols., popular mags., lit. mags. including The New Republic, Washington Post Book World, New Yorker. B.A., Bennington Coll., 1950; postgrad. Mannes Coll. Music, 1951-52; M.A., Sarah Lawrence Coll., 1970; academic grad. Houston-Galveston Psychoanalytic Inst., 1987 pvt. practice, specializing in writer's block. Opera and concert singer, 1953-66; asst. prof. Sarah Lawrence Coll., Bronxville, NY, 1970-74, assoc. prof., acting dean of studies, 1974-75; prof. Johns Hopkins U., Balt., 1975-79; co-dir. writing programs U. Houston, 1979—. Fellow NEA, 1973, 79, Yaddo Fnd., 1974, 76, 79, Rock-feller Fnd., 1978; recipient award Natl Acad. and Inst. of Arts and Letters, 1977; Guggenheim fellowship, 1983. Mem. PEN (bd. dirs.), Critics Circle, Am. So. Composers, Authors and Pubs. Office: Creative Wrtg Dept Eng U Houston TX 77004

MACDONALD, KATHRYN ELIZABETH, b. Seattle, Jan. 16, 1948; d. Albert Roger and Ann Carolyn (Christensen) Church; m. James M. Snydal, July 25, 1970, and May 1, 1986. Contrbr. poetry to Madrona, Tar River Poetry, Matrix, Bitterroot, GA Rvw, Poetry NW, Lit. & Belief, other mags. BA, U. Wash., MA. Seattle, 1981-83; ed. Fine Madness Mag, Seattle, 1982—; vice pres. Had We But, Inc., Seattle, 1984—. Mem. AAP. Address: 11034 Old Creosote Hill Rd NE Baínbrdge Island WA 98110

MACDONALD, MALCOLM MURDOCH, b. Uniontown, PA, June 15, 1935; s. Morgan Bowman and Ruth (Newcomb) Greene MacD.; m. Constance Emily Marsh, June 13, 1959; children—Randall Malcolm, Alison Margaret, Ellen Marsh. Author: (with Cecil E. Johnson) Society and the Environment, 1971, (wth Robert E. Davis) Chemistry and Society, 1972. BA, Trinity Coll., Conn., 1957. Assoc. sci. editor, 1962, sci. editor, 1963-68, Van Nostrand Reinhold Co., NYC, 1968-70; editor Pa. State U. Press, State College, Pa., 1970-72; chief editor U. N.C. Press, Chapel Hill, 1972—, asst. dir., 1975-76; asst. dir., editor U. Ga. Press, Athens, 1976-78; dir. U. Ala. Press, 1978—; co-prin. (with Constance M. MacDonald) Editorial Assocs., cons. in field. Office: Box 2877 University AL 35486

MACDONALD, WILLIAM LLOYD, b. Putnam, CT, July 12, 1921; s. William Lloyd and Susan (Elrod) MacD.; children—Noel, Nicholas. Author: Early Christian and Byzantine Architecture, 1962, The Architecture of the Roman Empire, I, 1965, rev. ed., 1982, II, 1986. Northampton Massachusetts Architecture and Buildings, 1975, The Pantheon-Design, Meaning and Progeny, 1976, Piranesi's Carceri, 1979; assoc. editor: Princeton Encyc. of Classical Sites, 1976. Student, Gov. Dummer Acad., 1938; AB, Harvard U., 1949, AM, 1953, PhD, 1956. Served with USAAF, 1942-45. Morse fellow Yale U., 1962-63; recipient award Am. Council Learned Soc., 1959, 68; Rome prize fellow Am. Acad. Rome, 1954-56; Getty Scholar, 1985-86. Home: 3911 38th St NW Washington DC 20016

MACDOUGALL, WILLIAM LOWELL, b. Des Moines, July 24, 1931; s. David Gregory and Elizabeth Jeanette (Dugan) MacD. Author: American Revolutionary: A Biography of General Alexander McDougall, 1977. AB, Willamette U., Salem, Oreg., 1952; MJ (Pulitzer scholar 1953-54), Columbia U., 1953. Reporter Washington Star, 1958-62; corr. Los Angeles Times, 1962-63; assoc. editor, London corr. U.S. News & World Report, 1964-68, asst. mng. editor, Washington, 1978—. Served with USAF, 1954-57. Office: 2400 N St NW Washington DC 20037

MACEBUH, SANDY, Contrbr. poetry Yes Press, Ezra Pound Anthology, Am. Poetry Soc., Green Valley Publs., VOA, NY Anthology, Galaxy of Verse, Poetry Press, others. Terminal, NYU; BA, U. Minn.; MA, Wayne State U. Communications faculty Adelphi Bus. Coll., Santa Ana, Calif., 1985—; communications asst. Business Strategy Inst., Tustin, Calif., 1984-85; free-lance writer. Poet laureate Univ. Mont. Dept. Communications, Bozeman. Mem. Women in Communications, Women in Mgmt., Writers and Artists Alliance, LA Press Club. Address: Box 852 Saddlebrook NJ 07662

MACESICH, GEORGE, b. Cleve., May 27, 1927; s. Walter (Vaso) and Milka (Tepavac) M.; m. Susana Sonia Svorkovich, Feb. 16, 1955; children—Maja Susana Radmila, Milka Milena Milica, George Milan Peter. Author: Commercial Banking and Regional Development, 1965; Yugoslavia: Theory and Practice of Development Planning, 1964; Statistical Abstracts for Florida, 1963; Money and the Canadian Economy, 1967; Economic Stability: A Comparative Analysis, 1973; Money in a European Common Market Setting, 1972; Monetary Theory and Policy: Theoretical and Empirical Issues, 1973; Financing Industrial and Regional Development: American Experience with the Small Business Administration, 1955-65, 1972; Monetary and Financial Organization for Growth and Stability: The U.S. and Yugoslavia, 1972; (with D. Dimitrijevic) Money and Finance in Contemporary Yugoslavia, 1973; International Monetary Economy and the Third World, 1981; (with H. Tsai) Money in ECONOMIC Systems, 1982; Monetarism: Theory and Policy, 1983; (with D. Dimitrijevic) Money and Finance in Yugoslavia: A Comparative Analysis, 1983; Politics of Monetarism: Its Historical and Institutional Development, 1984; World Crises and Developing Countries, 1984; World Banking and Finance: Cooperation Versus Conflict, 1984; Banking and The Third World Debt: In Search of Solutions, 1985; Economic Nationalism and Stability, 1985, Monetary Policy and Rational Expectations, 1987; contrbr. articles to profl. jnls. AA, George Washington U., 1951, BA, 1953, MA, 1954; PhD, U. Chgo., 1958. Mng. editor Slavic Papers, 1967-74, Procs. and Reports, 1974—. Served with USN, 1944-53. Econ. Assn. (editorial bd. Jour. 1961-63). Home: 2401 Delgado Dr Tallahassee FL 32304

MACHLIN, MILTON ROBERT, b. NYC, June 26, 1924; s. Morris Lewis and Lillie (Manevetz) M.; m. Barbara Scadron Sheckley, June 11, 1959; 1 foster son, Jason Sheckley. Author: Ninth Life, 1961, Private Hell of Hemingway, 1962, MacArthur—A Fighting Man, 1965, The Search for Michael Rockefeller, 1972, The Family Man, 1974, French Connection II, 1975, The Setup, 1975, Pipeline, 1976, Atlanta, 1979, The Complete UFO Book, 1979, Libby, 1980, Complete UFO Catalogue, 1980, The Gossip Wars, 1980, The Worldshakers, 1984, Strangers in the Land, 1985, Minsky's Burlesque, 1986. AB, Brown U., 1948; Degre Avance, Sorbonne, Paris, France, 1949. Reporter, columnist Clifton (N.J.) Morning Leader, 1950-52; editor Service American AFP (news wire service), 1952, Magazine House, 1953-55, Hillman Periodicals, 1955-57; mng. editor Argosy mag., 1960—, editor, 1969—. Served with AUS, 1942-45. Recipient Mystery Writers spl. award, 1976, Porgie award, 1977. Mem. Mystery Writers Am. Home: 27 Washington Sq New York NY 10011

MAC INNES, MAIRI, b. Norton-on-Tees, County Durham, U.K., Jan. 5, 1925, came to U.S. 1959, d. John and Mabel (Wood) MacInnes; m. John Owen McCormick, Feb. 4, 1954; children—Peter, Antoinette, Fergus. Author: Splinters (poems), 1955, Admit One (novel), 1956, Herring, Oatmeal, Milk & Salt (Qtly Rvw Lit poetry prizewinning series) 1981; co-ed.: Versions of Censorship (anthology with commentary), 1962, 63, Dictionary of Words About Alcohol, 1968, 82; contrbr. New Yorker, Lit. Rvw, Ont. Rvw, Qtly Rvw Lit, TriQtly, Prairie Schooner, Canto, 13th Moon, others. MA, U. Oxford (Eng.), 1952. Served with Royal navy, 1944-46. N.J. State Council on Arts fellow, 1983; grantee NEA, 1984, Ingram-Merrill Found., 1985-86; winner Arvon-Faber competition, London, 1985. Mem. PSA, Princeton Research Forum. Address: 158 Terhune Rd Princeton NJ 08540

MAC INTYRE, REGINA, see Noah, Hope E.

MACK, JAMES MELVIN, b. Des Plaines, IL, Oct. 24, 1947; s. Charles Melvin and Eleanor Julia (Nichols) M.; m. Linda Lee Carter, Mar. 15, 1969; children—Jenifer Erin, Joshua Charles. Ed., Mobile/Manufactured Home Merchandiser, 1972—, Real Estate Today, 1977, Savings & Loan News, 1980. BS, So. Ill. U., 1969. Ed., Material Svc. Corp., Chgo., 1971-72; asst. ed., then ed. Vance Pub., Chgo., 1972-75; ed. & asst. pub. RLD Group, Inc., Chgo., 1975—. Office: Mobile Home 203 N Wabash Chicago IL 60601

MACK, L. V., see Kimmelman, Burt Joseph

MACK, WAYNE, see Mackey, Vaino Ilmar

MACKENZIE, CLARA CHILDS, b. Biltmore, NC, May 28, 1931; d. William W. and Mildred (Stevens) Childs; m. Allen H. Mackenzie, June 15, 1957; children—David, Sarah, Clara, William. Author: (with Clara Childs Puckette) Edisto, A Sea Island Principality, 1978; Sarah Barnwell Elliott, 1980, Wolfmeller (Zhoh Gwatsan), 1985. Ed.: Some Data (and Other Stories of Southern Life) (Sarah Barnwell Elliott), 1981; Learning Notes, 1974-76. Wrkg. on editing four-part novel of southern Piedmont region. B.A., Converse Coll., 1951; M.A., Duke U., 1954; Ph.D., Case Western Reserve U., 1971. Tchr. English, Bratenahl High Schl., OH, 1971-74; Asst. Dir. Center for Effective Learning, Cleve. State U., 1974-76; free-lance wrtr., ed., 1976—. Home: 12211 Coit Rd Cleveland OH 44108

MACKENZIE, DONALD, b. Toronto, Ont., Canada, Aug. 11, 1918; s. Harrington and Marie (de Tellier) M. Divorced; children: a daughter. Author: mystery novels: Nowhere to Go, 1956, repr, 1976 (publ in U.S. as Manhunt, 1957), The Juryman, 1957, repr, 1974, Scent of Danger, 1958 (publ in England as Moment of Danger, 1959), Dangerous Silence, 1960, Knife Edge, 1961, The Genial Stranger, 1962, Double Exposure, 1963 (publ as I, Spy, 1964), Cool Sleeps, Balaban, 1964, The Lonely Side of the River, 1965, Salute from a Dead Man, 1966, Death Is A Friend, 1967, The Quiet Killer, 1968, (publ in Eng. as Three Minus Two, 1968) Dead Straight, 1969, Night Boat from Puerta Vedra, 1970, The Kyle Contract, 1970, Sleep Is for the Rich, 1971 (publ. in Eng as The Chalice Caper, 1974), Postscript to a Dead Letter, 1973, Zaleski's Percentage, 1974, The Spreewald Collection, 1975, Deep, Dark and Dead, 1978, The Last of the Boatriders, 1981, Harrier!, 1983. Raven series: Raven in Flight, 1976, Raven and the Ratcatcher, 1977, Raven and the Kamikaze, 1977, Raven Settles a Score, 1978, Raven After Dark, 1979, Raven Feathers His Nest, 1979, Raven and the Paperhangers, 1980, Raven's Revenge, 1982, Raven's Longest Night, 1983, Raven's Shadow, 1985, Nobody Here by That Name, 1986, A Savage State of Grace, 1988. Other: Occupation: Thief (autobiography), 1955 (also publ in Eng as Fugitives, 1955), Gentleman at Crime, 1956, repr, 1974. Also au of play The Bailie, 1970. Contrbr to Esquire, Collier's, Cosmopolitan, and other publs. Atended several preparatory schools in England and France and Schloss Mayenfels in Switzerland. Author. Professional thief, burglar, and confidence man, 1930-48. Address: Heath 79 St. Martin's Lane London WC2 England

MACKENZIE, GINNY LEE, b. Clearfield, PA, Sept. 20, 1945; d. Eugene LeGrande and Dorothy (Beish) MacKenzie; m. John Alex Berthot, July 13, 1962; 1 son, John Rene. Author: By Morning, 1984; poetry and fiction in The Nation, Iowa Rvw, Shenandoah, The Little Magazine, Carleton Miscellany, Ploughshares, other lit mags and anthols. MFA, Goddard College, 1981. Director, Warren Benedak Gallery, NYC, 1975-80; prof., City U., NYC, 1984—; prof., School of Visual Arts, NYC, 1981—. Mem. PSA, AAP, P&W, Art without Walls. Home: 66 Grand Street New York NY 10013

MACKEY, HOWARD HAMILTON JR., b. Washington, May 10, 1926; s. Howard Hamilton and Matilda Eleanor (Kendricks) M.; m. Anna Catharine Thompson, Feb. 15, 1947 (dec. 1982); children—Howard Hamilton III, Stanford, Karen, Adrienne; m. 2d, Ernestine Amelia Carter, Sept. 10, 1982. Author: The Black Nymph and Other Poems of Passion, 1986; poetry in anthologies. Wrkg. on book of poetry. BArch, Howard U., 1953. Architect pvt. firms, Washington, 1953-57, fed. govt., Washington, 1957-81; architect, owner M & M Enterprises, Annapolis, Md., 1981—. Served as sgt. U.S. Army, 1945-47; ETO. Mem. NWC, Internat. Clover Poetry Assn. Home: 4721 Colorado Ave NW Washington DC 20011

MACKEY, MARY, b. Indpls., Jan. 21, 1945; d. John Edward and Jean (McGinness) Mackey. Author: (novel) Immersion, 1974, McCarthy's List, 1979, The Last Warrior Queen, 1984, A Grand Passion, 1986; (poems) Split Ends, 1973, One Night Stand, 1976, Skin Deep, 1978, The Dear Dance of Eros, 1986; (screenplay) Silence, 1974. Contrbr. poems, articles to newspapers, popular mags. including MS Mag., Saturday Evening Post, others. BA, Harvard Coll., 1966; PhD, U. Mich., 1970. Prof. English, wrtr.-in-residence, Calif. State U., Sacramento, 1972—.Mem. Media Alliance, WG, West. Home: Box 8524 Berkeley CA 94707

MACKEY, VAINO ILMAR, (Wayne Mack), b. Ashtabula, OH, Jan. 9, 1911; s. Onni Einar and Emma Sophia (Huntus) Mackey; m. Rosena Turnbull, June 27, 1933; children—Donna Fishbaugh, Jean Kumler, Lynn Mack, David. Author radio programs: Profiles to Respective Months, 1966-75, Hometown Park Band Concerts, 1950-57, Waltz Palace, 1950-57, Cleveland, 2001, 1983, Perchance to Dream, 1936, Master Minds Attention, 1941. Student Cleve. Inst. Music, 1941-43. Program dir. (1950-54), producer Sta. WDOK, Cleve., 1950-80, Sta. WZAK, Cleve., 1980-81; producer, announcer Sta. WCLV, Cleve., 1981—. Citations for radio broadcasting State of Ohio, 1986, City of Cleve., 1986, City of Lakewood, OH, 1986, City of Ashtabula, OH, 1987; named to Jnlsm. Hall of Fame, Cleve. Press Club, 1986; named lifelong mem. Am. Fedn. TV/Radio Artists, 1981. Home: 12595 Lake Ave Lakewood OH 44107

MACKIN, JEANNE A., b. Waterloo, NY, June 9, 1948, d. Richard F. and Helen (Campfield) Mackin; m. Stephen F. Poleskie, 1979. Ed.: Energy and Technology-The Design Connection, 1979; contrbr.: King Features Syndicate, Upstate Mag., Home Mag., AP, UPI, Consumer's Research, other maj. newspapers and publs. BA in Lit., Ithaca Coll., 1970; MFA in Creative Writing, Bennington Coll., 1985. Columnist Ithaca (N.Y.) Jnl., 1977-82, Ithaca Times, 1978-80; ed., staff wrtr. Cornell News Service, Ithaca, 1978—; instr. journalism Tompkins Cortland (N.Y.) Community Coll., 1985-86; auditor N.Y. State Council on Arts, N.Y.C., 1983—. Recipient Excellence in Newswriting, CASE, 1983, 86. Grantee Time-Life, Inc., 1985. Mem. P&W, AWP. Home: 306 Stone Quarry Rd Ithaca NY 14850

MACLAINE, SHIRLEY, b. Richmond, VA, Apr. 24, 1934; d. Ira O. and Kathlyn (MacLean) Beatty; m. Steve Parker, Sept. 17, 1954; 1 dau., Stephanie Sachiko. Author: Don't Fall off the Mountain, 1970, The New Celebrity Cookbook, 1973, You Can Get There from Here, 1975, Out on a Limb, 1983, Dancing in the Light, 1985; ed. McGovern: The Man and His Beliefs, 1972. Ed. high schl. Actress on Broadway (Me and Juliet, 1953, Pajama Game, 1954); in movies, including The Trouble with Harry, 1954, Some Came Running, 1958 (Fgn. Press Award, 1959), Ask Any Girl (Silver Bear Award as Best Actress Intl. Berlin Film Festival), The Apartment, 1959 (Best Actress Prize Venice Film Festival),

Irma La Douce, 1963, The Turning Point, 1977, Terms of Endearment, 1983 (Academy Award, 1984); TV shows; producer, co-dir. documentary on China: The Other Half of the Sky. Office: C-P-R Agcy 9255 Sunset Blvd Los Angeles CA 90069

MACMANUS, YVONNE CRISTINA, b. Los Angeles, Mar. 18, 1931; d. Daniel S. and Josefina Lydia (Pina) MacM. Author: With Fate Conspire, 1974, Bequeath Them No Tumbled House, 1977, Better Luck Elsewhere, 1976, Deadly Legacy, 1981, The Presence, 1982, 87, You Can Write a Romance, 1983; contrbr. articles profl. publs. Student, NYU, U. London, U. So. Calif. Assoc. editor Bobbs-Merrill, NYC, 1960-63; editor-in-chief Leisure Books, Los Angeles, 1970-72; sr. editor Major Books, 1975-77; co-pub., editor-in-chief Timely Books, New Milford, Conn., 1977—; co-owner MS./smiths-Editorial Consultants, New Haven, Conn., 1978—. Address: 1043 Townsend Ave New Haven CT 06512

MAC NAMARA, DONAL E. J., b. NYC, Aug. 13, 1916; s. Daniel Patrick and Rita (Chambers) MacN.; m. Margaret Scott, June 30, 1953; 1 son, Brian Scott. Co-author: (with E. Sagarin) Sex, Crime, and The Law, 1977, 78, (with L.W. McCorkle) Crime, Criminals, and Corrections, 1982, (with P.J. Stead) New Dimensions of Trans-National Criminality, 1982, (with Andrew Karmen) Deviants: Victims or Victimizers?, 1983, Felons Before Puberty, 1986; author other books. BS, Columbia, 1939, M.Phil., 1948; M. Pub. Adm., NYU, 1946. Asst. prof. pub. adm., USC, Los Angeles, 1948-50; Dean, NY Inst. Criminology, NYC, 1950-63; dist. prof. Criminal Justice, Grad. Sch. CUNY, NYC, 1966-86. Presidential citation, Hon. Ronald Reagan, Gubernatorial Proclamation, Hon. Hugh Carey, NY, others. Mem. Am. Soc. Criminology, Am. Sociological Assn., Inter-Am. Congress Criminology, Societe Internationale de Criminologie. Home: 206 Christie Hts Leonia NJ 07605

MAC NAUGHTON, ANNE L., b. Little Rock, June 16, 1945; d. William A. and Anne Charlene (O'Hair) MacNaughton; m. Peter L. Douthit (Rabbit); children: Daphne Julep, Brendan Daniel Raphael. Author: Calendar of Claude Elliott Collection, 1970; ed. Wordworks, vols. 1-4, 1976-80; illustrator, Ornithology, Peter Rabbit, 1983; contrbr. poetry to Spree, ARTlines, Wordworks, Muse, other lit mags. BA, U. Tex.-Austin, 1967. Archivist State Archives, Austin, 1967-69; asst. librarian Mich. Municipal League, Ann Arbor, Mich., 1969-70; dir. and tchr. Libre Schl., Farisita, Colo., 1975-79, Lama Mountain Schl., Questa, N.Mex., 1980-82; tutor municipal schls., Taos, N.Mex., 1979—; exec. dir. SOMOS, Taos, 1983—. Treas and sec, Libre Schl., Farisita, 1972-79; mem. League Women Voters, Taos, 1981-83; bd. dirs. Taos Local TV, 1985—. Mem. Rio Grande Writers Assn., Soc. Muse SW (treas., 1982—). Address: Box 2615 Taos NM 87571

MAC RANE, BUICK, see Mitchell, Robert Wayne

MACY, MARK H., b. Windsor, CO, Nov. 15, 1949, s. R.B. and Genevieve (Shaltis) M.; m. Regina Elizabeth Hoys, July 4, 1985. Ed.: World Model—Paths to Peace, 1985, Last Chance for Peace, 1985, Solutions for a Troubled World, 1987. BA in Journalism, U. No. Colo., 1976. Reporter, ed. Town & Country News, Greeley, Colo., 1975-78; tech. wrtr., writing cons. computer and telecommunication cos., Colo., 1978—; mng. ed. Earthview Press, Boulder, Colo., 1984—. Mem. Assn. World Edn., Consortium on Peace Research, Edn. and Devel. Office: Box 11036 Boulder CO 80301

MADDEN, DAVID, b. Knoxville, TN, July 25, 1933; s. James Helvy and Emile (Merritt) M.; m. Roberta Margaret Young, Sept. 6, 1956; 1 son, Blake Dana. Author: novels Cassandra Singing, 1969, Bijou, 1974, The Suicide's Wife, 1978, Pleasure Dome, 1979, On the Big Wind, 1980; stories The Shadow Knows (Natl. Council on Arts selection), 1970, The New Orleans of Possibilities; (lit. criticism) Wright Morris, 1964; Poetic Image in Six Genres, 1969, James M. Cain, 1970, A Primer of the Novel, 1980, Writers' Revisions, 1981, Revising Fiction, 1988; asst. editor: Kenyon Rvw, 1964-66; editor: Remembering James Agee, 1974. BS, U. Tenn., 1957; MA, San Francisco State Coll., 1958; postgrad., Yale Drama Schl., 1959-60. Writer-in-res. La. State U., Baton Rouge, 1968—. Served with AUS, 1953-55. Recipient Rockefeller grant, 1969, John Golden fellow in playwriting, 1959. Mem. AL, AWP. Home: 614 Park Blvd Baton Rouge LA 70806

MADGETT, NAOMI LONG, b. Norfolk, VA, July 5, 1923; d. Clarence Marcellus and Maude Selena (Hilton) Long. m. Julian Fields Witherspoon, Mar. 31, 1946 (div. 1949); 1 dau., Jill Witherspoon Boyer; m. 2d, William Harold Madgett, Nov., 1954 (div. 1960); m. 3d, Leonard P. Andrews, Mar. 31, 1972. Author poetry: Songs to a Phantom Nightingale, 1941, One and the Many, 1956, Star by Star, 1965, 1970, Pink Ladies in the Afternoon, 1972, Exits and Entrances, 1978, Phantom Nightingale: Juvenilia, 1981; textbooks: Success in Language and Lit, 1967, A Student's Guide to Creative Writing, 1980. BA, Va. State U., 1945; MEd, Wayne State U., 1956; PhD, Intl. Inst. Advanced Studies, 1980. Ed./pub. Lotus Press, Inc., Detroit 1974—; lectr. Univ. Mich., Ann Arbor, 1970; tchr. pub. schls., Detroit, 1955-65, 66-68; research assoc. Oakland Univ., Rochester, Mich., 1965-66; prof. Eastern Mich. Univ., Ypsilanti, 1968-84, prof. emeritus, 1984—. Historian, Plymouth United Ch. of Christ, Detroit, 1969—; recorded reading Library of Congress, 1978; recipient Mott fellowship, 1965; Robert Hayden Runagate award, Your Heritage House, Detroit, 1985; Arts Achievement award in lit., Wayne State Univ., 1985; creative artist award, Mich. Council for the Arts, 1987. Mem. Detroit Women Writers, Coll. Lang. Assn., Alpha Kappa Alpha. Address: 16886 Inverness Ave Detroit MI 48221

MADIGAN, GRACE EVELYN, (Grace Patrick Madigan), b. Alton, IL, Oct. 18, 1902; d. Lewis Clarence Moore and Edith Arhusa (Lively) Moore; m. Charles Dale Patrick, Oct. 10, 1936 (dec. Dec. 7, 1963); m. James Patrick Madigan, July 4, 1969 (dec. Sept. 14, 1980). Contrbr. poems to anthols., lit. mags.; articles to mags. A.B., Millikin U., 1927; postgrad. U. Ill., Northwestern U., 1928-35. Home: 4440 Ironwood Circle 109D Bradenton FL 34209

MAD MIKE, see Marine, Michael R.

MADRI, ALBERTA MARIA, (Bobbi Ray), b. Murphysboro, IL, June 14, 1924; d. Charles Thomas and Lucy Maria (Sarguias) Stelle; m. Daniel Angelo Madri, Mar. 27, 1974; stepchildren: Judith, Donna, Gail, Daniel, Todd. Author: Teen Profile, 1973, The Milady Illustrated Cosmetology Dictionary, 1985, Human Relations for Success in Business, 1986, The Job Seeker's Guide, 1987; wrtr. & researcher, Standard Textbook for Professional Estheticians, 1979, rev. ed., 1985; ed. Woman's Guide, 1967, rev. ed., 1982, The Model's Handbook, 1988, The Art and Science of Professional Makeup, 1988. Student, New Schl. Social Research, 1969; BA, Mount Mercy Univ., Dobbs Ferry, NY, 1969; assoc. speech & drama, Vance Professional Schl., Chgo. (now Bryant & Stratton), 1952. Asst. Dir., Durbin Theatrical Agcy., Ft. Wayne, Ind., 1945-50; Founder, owner, dir., Schl. Theatrical Arts, Ft. Wayne Finishing Schl., 1952-65; instructor, Cleveland Jr. Coll., 1966-69; dir. Human relations, author, ed., MPC Edl. Pub. (div. John Wiley & Sons), 1969—. Home: 91 B. Heitman Dr Spring Valley NY 10977

MADSON, JERRY, b. Roseau, MN, Oct. 25, 1948, s. Clayton and Ruby (Johnson) M. Author: (poetry) Race Horse Station, 1974, (fiction) Letters to F.A., 1974, (novel) A Summer of Blues, 1975, (poetry) In the Bag, 1975, (fiction) Paperbag Novel, 1976, (mixed-media) Dadavision, 1976, Xebec, 1981, American Wolf, 1984, Alpha Pour, 1987; ed. Truly Fine, poetry, fiction, mixed-media collection, 1973—; contrbr. to MATI, NRG, Press Me Close, Rag Mag, North Country Anvil, Northwoods, also others. BA, Bemidji State Coll., 1970. Wire/layout ed. The Pioneer, Bemidji, Minn., 1975—. Home: Box 891 Bemidji MN 56601

MAGARRELL, ELAINE, b. Clinton, IA, June 2, 1928; d. Samuel Philip and Ida (Seidelman) Reisler; m. Jack S. Magarrell, Feb. 25, 1950; children—Debra, Lisa, Daniel. Author: On Hogback Mountain, 1985. Contrbr. poems to lit. mags., anthols. B.A., U. Iowa, 1950. Tchr. public schs., West Des Moines, IA, Iowa City, IA, 1963-72; researcher, clrk. N.Y. Times, Washington, 1974-80; free-lance wrtr., 1980—. Fellow, Va. Ctr. for Creative Arts, 1987; recipient Edgar Allen Poe Meml. prize Poetry Soc. Va., 1987. Mem. Washington Wrtrs. Pub. House (prize 1985, v.p.), Wrtrs.' Ctr. Home: 2131 Tunlaw Rd NW Washington DC 20007

MAGER, DONALD NORTHROP, (Don), b. Santa Rita, NM, Aug. 24, 1942; s. Winthrop Melvin and Eleanor (Miller) Hyde m; m. Barbara Feldman, 1967 (div. 1973): children: Marlowe, Rainer; m. 2d, William A. McDowell, Nov. 13, 1981. Contrbr. transl. to East European Poets, Chgo Rvw, New Orleans Rvw, Pebble, The Wayne Rvw, The Lamp in the Spire; poetry to West Coast Rvw, Greenfield Rvw, Mouth of the Dragon, Pebble, Tex Qtly, Quartet, Corridors, others. BA, Drake U., 1960-64; MA, Syracuse U., 1964-67, PhD, Wayne State U., 1981-86. Instr. Syracuse Univ., NY, 1964-67; dir CALLL Day Care Center, Detroit, 1973-76, 78-80; exec. dir. Mich. Orgn. Human Rights, Detroit, 1976-78; instr. Wayne State Univ., Detroit, 1981—; asst. prof. Johnson C. Smith Univ., 1986—. Recipient Hallmark Card Co. prize, Kansas City, 1966. Mem. MLA (co-chmn. Gay and Lesbian Caucus), Mich. Council for the Arts. Address: 718 N Poplar 2A Chrlotte NC 28202

MAGIDA, PHYLLIS ROSE, b. Chgo., Nov. 18, 1936; d. Herbert Norell Magida and Brina Kritz; m. Arnold Goldberg, Aug. 4, 1963 (div. Apr. 1970); 1 son, Andrew. Author: Eating Drinking & Thinking, 1973, Cake Decorating, 1980, Fish on the Grill, 1985, Southwestern Sampler, 1987. Wrkg. on books: Shellfish on Grill, Entertaining with Fish on Grill, Pandora Experiment, File It Under Love. B.A., Roosevelt U., 1959. Reporter, Chgo. Tribune, 1978—. Home: 5757 N Sheridan Rd Chicago IL 60660

MAGGIO, LOIDA WEBER, b. June 14, 1919, d. John Raymond and Rose (Garcia) Weber; widowed; children—Julia, Ralph F. Contrbr. poetry: Sweet Seventies Anthology, Poetry Coast to Coast, Earth Shine, World of Poetry, numerous other anthologies. BA with honors, Coll. New Rochelle. Rent examiner, supvr. HDA Rent Control, NYC, 1959-76. Recipient "Danae," Clover Intl. Poetry Assn., 1974, Golden Poet award World of Poetry, 1985-86. Home: 607 Windmill Ave Babylon NY 11704

MAGNER, JAMES EDMUND JR., b. NYC, Mar. 16, 1928, s. James Edmund and Lillian Elizabeth (Campbell) M.; m. Mary Ann Dick, July 13, 1957 (dec. 1971); children—James E. III, Maureen M., Gregory A., David B. Author: Toiler of the Sea, 1965, Although There is The Night, 1968, Gethsemane, 1969, John Crowe Ransom: Critical Principles and Preoccupations, 1971, The Dark Is Closest to the Moon, 1973, The Women of the Golden Horn, 1976, To Whom You Shall Go, 1978, Till No Light Leaps, 1981, Rose of My Flowering Night, 1985. BA, Duquesne Univ., 1957, MA in English, U. Pitts., 1961, PhD in English, 1966. Seminarian Roman Catholic Passionist Order, N.Y., Pa. and Conn., 1951-56; tchr. South Hill Catholic High Schl., Mt. Lebannon, Pa., 1957-61; prof. English John Carroll U., Cleve., 1962-86. George E. Grauel Meml. fellow John Carroll U., 1968, 81, 87; work preserved in James E. Magner Jr. Spcl. Collection, Spcl. Collections and Archives, Ohio U., Athens, 1980; named Ohio Poet of Yr., Ohio Verse Wrtrs. Guild, 1981; recipient Spcl. Commendation for Poetic Achievement Ohio Ho. of Reps., 1981, Hart Crane Meml. Award Kent State U., 1984. Home: 3307 Chadbourne Rd Shaker Heights OH 44120

MAGORIAN, JAMES IRVIN, b. Palisade, NE, Apr. 24, 1942, s. Maurice John and Dorothy Mae (Gorthey) M. Author: Almost Noon, 1969, Ambushes and Apologies, 1970, The Garden of Epicurus, 1971, The Last Reel of the Late Movie, 1972, Distances, 1972, Mandrake Root Beer, 1973, The Red, White, and Blue Bus, 1975, Bosnia and Herzegovina, 1976, Alphabetical Order, 1976, Two Hundred Push-Ups at the YMCA, 1977, The Ghost of Hamlet's Father, 1977, Safe Passage, 1977, Notes to the Milkman, 1978, Phases of the Moon, 1978, Piano Tuning at Midnight, 1979, Revenge, 1979, The Night Shift at the Poetry Factory, 1979, Ideas for a Bridal Shower, 1980, The Edge of the Forest, 1980, Spiritual Rodeo, 1980, Tap Tancing on a Tightrope, 1981, Training at Home to Be A Locksmith, 1981, The Great Injun Carnival, 1982, Taxidermy Lessons, 1982, The Walden Pond Caper, 1983, Travel Expenses, 1984, The Emily Dickinson Jogging Book, 1984, Weighing the Sun's Light, 1985, Charles Darwin and the Theory of Evolution, 1985, Summer Snow, 1985, The Magician's Handbook, 1986, Karl Marx and International Communism, 1986, Squall Line, 1986; author children's stories: School Daze, 1978, 17%, 1978, The Magic Pretzel, 1979, Ketchup Bottles, 1979, Imaginary Radishes, 1980, Plucked Chickens, 1980, Fimperings and Torples, 1981, Floyd, 1982, The Three Diminutive Pigs, 1982, Kumquats, 1983, Fouled Spark Plugs, 1983, Griddlemort and the Questionists, 1983, The Witches' Olympics, 1983, Piffle, 1983, Cucumber Cake, 1984, The Lion and the Mouse, 1984, Keeper of Fire, 1984, Bad Report Cards, 1985. BS, U. Nebr.-Lincoln., 1965; MS, Ill. State U., 1969; postgrad. Oxford (Eng.) U., 1972, Harvard U., 1973. Home: 1225 N 46th St Lincoln NE 68503

MAGOTEAUX, CHERYL ANN, b. Cocoa Beach, FL, Jan. 13, 1955; d. Neal L. McDonald and Margaret Anjou (Murray) Watterson; m. Jeffrey Thomas Magoteaux, Dec. 8, 1984; 1 dau., Savannah Ann. Contrbr. articles to rodeo and horse mags. including Appaloosa World, Horseman, others. ontrbr., ed.: Rodeo News, 1983-87. BA, U. Ala., Birmingham, 1977. Pub. Southeast Rodeo Sports Reporter, Rainsville, AL, 1980-83; natl. media dir. Intl. Pro Rodeo Assn., Pauls Valley, OK, 1983—; bus. ed. Rodeo News, Pauls Valley, 1984—; co-owner Promotion Management Services, Pauls Valley, 1985—. Office: Box 1123 Pauls Valley OK 73075

MAGOVENY, DIANNE JEANNE, b. New Haven, Mar. 23, 1948; d. John Salvatore and Emelda Blanche (St. Arnault) Lion; m. Glenn Scott Magoveny; children—Amy, Eric, Jonathan. Contrbr. poems to anthols. Diploma, Acad. Bus Careers, 1984. Head teller Amity Bank orp., Woodbridge, CT, 1980-84; receptionist NICO, Hamden, CT, 1985-86; secy. Quinnipack Valley Health District, Hamden, 1986—. Home: 91 Fourth St Hamden CT 06514

MAGUIRE, CECILIA GERTRUDE, (Susan Mallon) b. Phila., Oct. 3, 1917, d. Francis Thomas Maguire II and Mary Loretta (Farrell) Maguire O'Connell. Author: Excelling/Nutritional Way to Good Health, 1985; contrbr. poetry to Am. Poetry Anthology, 1983. AB, Coll. Mt. St. Vincent, NYC. Wrtr., ed. Lincoln Center, NYC, 1964; account exec. Doremus & Co., NYC, 1964-71; med. wrtr. for cardiovascular surgeon, NYC, 1974-76; free-lance wrtr. on health for young adults, Yonkers, N.Y., 1972—. Home: 2 Sunnyside Dr Yonkers NY 10705

MAHANAIM, ANNA, see Young, Carol Ann Morizot

MAHLER-SUSSMAN, LEONA JULIA, b. Middletown, OH, Oct. 12, 1926; d. Eli and Jeannette Belle (Kaplan) Mahler; m. Morris Ralph Sussman, Dec. 1, 1950; children—Rebecca Jo, Steven Aaron, Stacey Eve, Deborah Adrienne. Contrbr. poems to anthols., jnls, book-art. AB, U. Cin., 1948. Asst. ed. McGraw Hill Pub., NYC, 1950-54; freelance artist, wrtr., 1965—. Mem. Women's Caucus Art, P&W. Home: 50 Beverly Rd Cedar Grove NJ 07009

MAHONEY, EUGENE FREDERICK, b. San Pedro, CA, May 19, 1923; m. Nathalie Dolores Mahoney, Apr. 14, 1946 (dec. 1973); children—Mike, Jeanne Mahoney Juncal; 1 stepdau.—Lana Hansen; m. 2d, Ethel Marie Arrowood, July 21, 1976; stepchildren—Jeri Stapp, Cathi Glassman. Author: Anatomy of an Arsonist (novel), 1978, Fire Department Hydraulics (textbook), 1980, Introduction to Fire Apparatus and Equipment (textbook), 1981, training manuals, articles. BS, U. So. Calif., Los Angeles, 1956, MS, 1959. Firefighter, various cities in Calif., 1947-75; assoc. prof. Rio Hondo Coll., Whittier, Calif., 1976—. Home: 1121 Indian Springs Rd Glendora CA 91740

MAHONEY, JOHN MARQUIS, b. Newport, VT, Oct. 26, 1935; s. Jeremiah Patrick and Gertrude Emma (Marquis) M.; m. Jane Theresa Goyette, Aug. 29, 1959; children: Sean Patrick, Kevin Gene, Keith Michael, Denis Kirk. Author, editor: (photographs) Open Only in Total Darkness, 1970, Soul of Vermont, 1971; contrbr. Photographs, 1969; author: Vermont's Best-Kept Secret, 1983; author intro to reprint: Beautiful Waters (William Bullock), vol. I, 1985, vol. II, 1985; author: Horatio, The Duck Who Thought He Was a Dog, 1986.; contrbr., ed., Voices on the Border, 1987; ed., Beautiful Memphremagos, 1987. Diploma, Country Schl. of Photography, South Woodstock, Vt., 1957; BA, Goddard Coll., 1971. Photographer, NYC, Boston, Vt., 1957-62; journalist various Vt. publs., 1962-68; faculty Goddard Coll., Plainfield, Vt., 1968-72; freelance writer and photographer, Can. and U.S., 1972—; editor, pub. Pigwidgeon Press, Derby Line, Vt., 1985—. Served to cpl. U.S. Army, 1953-56. Recipient hon. mention for food writing Natl. Mag. Awards Fdn., Can., 1982. Mem. COSMEP. Office: Box 706 Derby Line VT 05830

MAHONEY, JOHN THOMAS FITZSIMMONS, b. Elizabeth, NJ, Dec. 5, 1941; s. John Thomas and Catherine Elizabeth (Fitzsimmons) M.; m. Anna Lenore English, Dec. 8, 1950. Translator: Nirvana Tao (Daniel Odier), 1986, The Interior Realization (Hubert Benoit), 1986. Cons. Journey into the Light (Isha Schwaller de Lubicz). BS, U.S. Naval Acad. 1964. Research assoc. George Washington U., Washington, 1969-70; tchr. Newark pub. schl., 1970-74; dir. West Orange Community Schl., N.J., 1974-76, Cummins Metropower, Newark, 1977-85. Mem. Natl. Wrtrs. Club. Home: 612 Summer Ave Newark NJ 07104

MAHONEY, WILLIAM FRANCIS, b. Joliet, IL, Jan. 24, 1935; s. Cletus George and Mildred M. (Ochs) M.; m. Carroll Francis Johnson, June 28, 1958; children—Erin, Kevin, Megan, Sheila, Nora. Ed.: Investor Relations Update, New York Soc. of Security Analysts News. BS in Jnlsm., Marquette U., 1957. Mgr. communics. Motorola, Chgo., 1959-65; ed. Young & Rubicam, Chgo., 1966-68; mgr. communics. Chemetron Corp., Chgo., 1970-76; dir. communics. Scott Paper Co., Phila., 1976-80; partner Mahoney & Mitchell, Inc., Phila., 1981—; ed. Update, Natl. Investor Relns. Inst., Washington, 1981—. Home: RR 2 Box 66A Chadds Ford PA 19317

MAHONY, ELIZABETH ALSOP, (Elizabeth Winthrop), b. Washington, d. Stewart J.O. and Patricia (Hankey) Alsop; m. Walter B. Mahony III. Author juvenile fiction: Bunk Beds, 1972, Walking Away, 1973, A Little Demonstration of Affection (awards Schl. Library Jnl, ALA), 1975, Potbellied Possums, 1977, That's Mine!, 1977, Knock, Knock, Who's There? (ALA award), 1978, Are You Sad, Mama?, 1979, Journey to the Bright Kingdom, 1979, I Think He Likes Me, 1980, Marathon Miranda, 1979, Miranda in the Middle, 1980, Sloppy Kisses, 1980, Katharine's Doll, 1983, A Child is Born, The Christmas Story, 1983, Tough Eddie, 1984, Lizzie and Harold, 1986, The Shoelace Box, 1984, Happy Easter, Mother Duck, 1984, Belinda's Hurricane, 1984, The Christmas Pageant, 1985, Shoes, 1986, He is Risen, The Easter Story, 1985, The Castle in the Attic, 1985, Maggie and the Monster, 1987, In My Mother's House (adult novel), 1988. BA, Sarah Lawrence Coll., 1970. Mem. AG, PEN, Soc. Children's Book Wrtrs. Home: 160 Riverside Dr 7A New York NY 10024

MA HOOD, JAMES HERBERT, b. Mineola, NY, Mar. 22, 1937; s. Cecil Heber and Mayme Revere (Cudd) MaH. Co-editor: Mosher Survey: Sexual Attitudes of 45 Victorian Women, 1980; contrbr. to The Engineer, 1966, The Physician, 1967, Wheels, 1967, Early Islam, 1967, Food and Nutrition, 1967, The World of Durer, 1967, The World of Picasso, 1967, The World of Cezanne, 1968, The World of Bruegel, 1968, The World of Manet, 1968, The World of Rembrandt, 1968, Wines and Spirits, 1968, Our Amazing

World of Nature, 1969; contbr. to books, mags, jnls, tech. publs. BA in Eng. Lit., U. Mass., 1961; MA in East-West Psychology, Calif. Inst. Integral Studies, 1984. Staff writer Time Inc., NYC, 1963-68; reporter Evening Record, Hackensack, N.J., 1969; assoc. editor Newsweek Books, NYC, 1969-70; writing instr. Calif. Inst. Integral Studies, San Francisco, 1984—; English, Coll. of San Mateo, Calif., 1986—; English, De Anza Coll., CA, 1987—; freelance writer and editor, Redwood City, Calif., 1971—. M. U.S. Army, 1957-63. Kern Found. scholar, 1983-84. Mem. Writers Connection, TESOL, Calif. Assn. TESOL., NCTE, AWP. Home: Box 5213 Redwood City CA 94063

MAHR, DOUGLAS JAMES, b. St. Paul, Aug. 20, 1946; s. Burnley Upton and Lorraine (Hafiz) M. Author: Real Estate Investments, 1967, The Easter Hippopotamus, 1980; co-author: The Ominous Dragoon, 1985, (with Ramtha) Voyage to the New World, 1985, (with Ramtha) Destination Freedom, 1987, (with Ramtha) Did You Know, Genies Are Usually Green, 1987. editor: Island Ebb and Flow, 1985. AA in Bus., Fullerton Jr. Coll., Calif., 1967. Address: Genl Deliv Lopez Isle WA 98261

MAILER, NORMAN, b. Long Branch, NJ, Jan. 31, 1923; s. Issac B. and Fanny (Schneider) M.; m. Beatrice Silverman, 1944 (div. 1952); 1 dau., Susan; m. Adele Morales, 1954 (div.); children—Danielle, Elizabeth; m. Jean Campbell (div.); 1 dau., Kate; m. Beverly Bentley, 1963 (div.); children—Michael, Steven; m. Carol Stevens (div.); 1 dau., Maggie; m. Norris Church; 1 son, John Buffalo. Author: war novel The Naked and the Dead, 1948, Barbary Shore, 1951, The Deer Park (dramatized 1967), 1955, Advertisements for Myself, 1959; poetry Deaths for the Ladies and Other Disasters, 1962; The Presidential Papers, 1963; poetry An American Dream, 1965; Cannibals and Christians, 1966; poetry Why are We in Viet Nam? 1967; The Armies of the Night (Nat. Book award), 1968 (co-winner Pulitzer prize), Miami and the Siege of Chicago, 1968 (Nat. Book award), Of A Fire On The Moon, 1971, The Prisoner of Sex, 1971, Existential Errands, 1972, St. George and the Godfather, 1972, Marilyn, 1973, The Faith of Graffiti, 1974, The Fight, 1975, Some Honorable Men, 1975, Genius and Lust, 1976, A Transit to Narcissus, 1978, The Executioner's Song, 1979 (Pulitzer Prize for Fiction 1980), Of Women and Their Elegance, 1980, Pieces and Pontifications, 1982, Ancient Evenings, 1983, Tough Guys Don't Dance, 1984. Editor: Dissent, 1953-69; co-founder: Village Voice, 1955; pres. PEN Am. Ctr., 1984-86. S.B., Harvard U., 1943; postgrad., Sorbonne, Paris, France. Served with AUS, 1944-46. Office: 40 Rembar 19 W 44th St New York NY 10036

MAINONE, ROBERT FRANKLIN, b. Flint, MI, Feb. 11, 1929, s. Robert Henry and Nell Claudine (Phillips) Mainone; m. Carolyn Beryl Bothwell, Aug. 12, 1972. Haiku poetry: An American Naturalist's Haiku, 1964, Where Waves Were, 1966, Shadows, 1971, Moonlight, 1979, The Journey North, 1984, others. BS, Michigan State U., 1951, BSF, 1952, MS, 1959. Jr. curator Detroit Zoological Park (MI), 1959-60; interpretive naturalist Kalamazoo nature Center (MI), 1961-66; interpretive ecologist MSU Kellogg Biological Station/Bird Sanctuary (Augusta, MI), 1967—. Life Fellow Intl. Acad. of Poets, 1980, Harold G. Henderson Award Haiku Soc. of Amer., 1977, 80. Home: 7431 Pine Lake Rd Delton MI 49046

MAINSTER, DONNA MARIE, (Donna M. Burton), b. Kent County, RI, June 16, 1954; d. James Warren Burton and Hope Evelyn (Rosskam) Minor; m. Jeffery Clark Wedge, Mar. 15, 1980 (div. Oct. 3, 1984); 1 dau., Elizabeth Coday; m. Kenneth Harold Mainster, Oct. 20, 1984. Contrbr. articles to Mags., newspapers including Mature Years, Am. Coin Op Mag., others. Wrkg. on children's book on divorced parents, adoption book for prospective families. A.A., Broward Commun. Coll., 1974. Clrk. outpatient admitting Coral Reef Hosp., Miami, 1982-83, head cashier, 1983-84; free-lance wrtr., 1985—. Mem. NWC. Home: Box 8372 West Palm Beach FL 33407

MAINWARING, WILLIAM LEWIS, b. Portland, Oreg., Jan. 17, 1935; s. Bernard and Jennie (Lewis) M.; m. Mary E. Bell, Aug. 18, 1962; children—Anne Marie, Julia Kathleen, Douglas Bernard. Author: Exploring the Oregon Coast, 1977, Exploring Oregon's Central and Southern Cascades, 1979. BS, U. Oreg., 1957; postgrad., Stanford, 1957-58. With Salem (Oreg.) Capital Jnl, 1958-76, editor, pub., 1962-76; pub. Oreg. Statesman, 1974-76; pres. Statesman-Jnl. Co., Inc., Salem, 1974-76, Westridge Press, Ltd., 1976—, MEDIA America, Inc. (pub. Oreg. Bus. Mag.). Served as 2d lt. AUS, 1958; capt. Res. Ret. Mem. Oreg. Newspaper Pubs. Assn. (pres. 1969-70), Pacific Northwest Newspaper Assn. (v.p. 1971). Home: 1090 Southridge Pl S Salem OR 97302

MAIOLO, JOSEPH, b. Hinton, WV, Oct. 20, 1938, s. James Vincent Maiolo and Mary Josephine (Voni) Cherry; m. Julie Ann Violet Brown, July 18, 1964; children—Joshua Joseph, Ann Elise, Lotti Sun. Author: Elverno: A Tale from a Boyhood (novella), 1972; contrbr. stories: Ploughshares, Tex. Rvw, Greensboro Rvw, Carry Me Back: An Anthology of Virginia Fiction, numerous other publs.; ed.: From Three Sides: Reading-; for Writers, 1976. MA, U. Va., 1968; MFA, U. N.C., Greensboro, 1974. Assoc. prof. English No. Va. Community Coll., Annandale, 1968-76; prof. U. Minn., Duluth, 1976—. Recipient Houghton Mifflin Fiction award, 1970; grantee Minn. State Arts Bd., 1977, 80; NEA fellow, 1978, 83. Office: Dept Engl Univ Minn Duluth MN 55812

MAIORANA, RONALD, b. NYC, Mar. 19, 1930, s. Victor and Catherine (Alfieri) M.; m. Phyllis Virginia Fixel Momballou, Nov. 14, 1955; children—Ronald Peter, Linda Catherine Janice Virginia. BA, NYU, 1960. Reporter N.Y. Times, 1955-67; press. secy. Gov. Nelson Rockefeller, N.Y., 1968-73; commr. wagering systems State of N.Y., 1974-75; dir. Specl. State Prosecutor, N.Y., 1976; pres. Garth Group, Inc., N.Y., 1977-85, Maiorana Connelly Communications, Inc., N.Y.C.,1985—; poli. cons. numerous candidates U.S. and abroad, 1976-85. Home: 10 Chatfield Rd Bronxville NY 10708

MAIRS, NANCY PEDRICK, b. Long Beach, CA, July 23, 1943, d. John Eldredge Smith and Anne (Pedrick) Cutler; m. George Anthony Mairs, May 18, 1963; children—Anne Eldredge, Matthew Anthony. Author: Instead It Is Winter (poetry), 1977, In All the Rooms of the Yellow House (poetry), 1984, Plaintext (essays), 1986; contrbr. poetry, short stories, articles, essays to MSS, Anima, Intro 13, other jnls. Wrkg. on feminist memoir, House Bound: An Erotics of Place and Space. AB in English Lit., Wheaton Coll., Norton, Mass., 1964; MFA in Creative Writing, U. Ariz., 1975, PhD in English Lit., 1984. Jr. ed. Smithsonian Astrophys. Obs., Cambridge, Mass., 1966-69; editorial asst. Harvard Law Sch., Cambridge, 1970-72; tchr. pvt. schls., Tucson, 1975-77; asst. dir. Southwest Inst. Research on Women, Tucson, 1983-85; teaching asst. U. Ariz., Tucson, 1972-75, 77-83, 85—; vis. lectr. UCLA wrtg. progs., 1986-87. Named Wm. P. Sloan Fellow in nonfiction, 1984; recipient Western States Book award, Western States Arts Fdn., 1984. Mem. MLA, P&W, Nat. Women's Studies Assn. Home: 1527 E Mabel St Tucson AZ 85719

MAISEL, ERIC RICHARD, b. Bronx, NY, Jan. 14, 1947; s. Esther Shapiro; m. Leanne Clarke, 1970 (div. 1978); 1 son, David; m. 2d, Ann Louise Mathesius, July 7, 1980; children: Natalya, Kira. Author novels: Dismay, 1983, The Blackbirds of Mulhouse, 1984, The Fretful Dancer, 1987; ghostwriter: Biorythm, 1976, The Kingston Papers, 1977, The Black Narc, 1978; contrbr. to Inflation Fighting Handbook, 1975. BS in philosophy, U. Ore.,1970; MA in Creative Writing San Francisco State U., 1980, BA in Psychology, 1984, MS in Counseling Psychology, 1987. Dir. drama and lit. programming Edn. Media Assocs., Kensington, Calif., 1975-83; intern/therapist First Offender program, San Francisco, 1984, Marina Counseling Center, 1986. Served to E-5. US Army, 1965-68 Korea. Address: 216 Cardenas Ave San Francisco CA 94132

MAIVALD, JAMES JOHN, b. Oakbrook, IL, May 19, 1956; s. William James and Clara (Swanson) M. Contrbr. to Art Post. BA in English, U. IL/Chgo., 1985. Ed., Casting Central, Maywood, IL, 1982-85, Design Graphics World, Atlanta, 1985—. Served to E5, U.S. Navy, 1974-78. Home: 3371F Peachtree CC Norcross GA 30092

MAJOR, CLARENCE LEE, b. Atlanta, Dec. 31, 1936; s. Clarence and Inez (Huff) M.; m. Pamela Jane Ritter, May 8, 1981. Author: (novels) All Night Visitors, 1969, No, 1973, Reflex and Bone Structure, 1975, Emergency Exit, 1979, My Amputations, 1986, Such Was the Season, 1987; (non-fiction) Dictionary of Afro-American Slang, 1970, The Dark and Feeling: Black American Writers and Their Work, 1974, (poetry) Swallow the Lake, 1970, Symptoms and Madness, 1971, Private Line, 1971, The Cotton Club, 1972, The Syncopated Cakewalk, 1974, Inside Diameter: The France poems, 1985; (anthology) The New Black Poetry, 1969. BS, SUNY-Albany; PhD, Union Grad. Schl. Recipient Natl. Council on Arts award, 1970, Pushcart prize, 1976, Book award for fiction, Western States Arts Fdn., 1986; Fulbright fellow, 1981-83. Address: Dept Eng Univ Colo Boulder CO 80309

MAJOR, JAMES RUSSELL RICHARDS, b. Riverton, VA, Jan. 7, 1921; s. Julian Neville and Jean (Richards) M.; m. Blair Louise Rogers, June 9, 1945; children—Blair Louise, Randon Leigh, Clara Jean, James Russell Richards. Author: The Estates General of 1560, 1951, Representative Instns. in Renaissance France, 1421-1559, 1960, The Deputies to the Estates General of Renaissance France, 1960, The Western World: Renaissance to the Present, 2d edit., 1971, The Age of the Renaissance and Reformation, 1970, Bellievre, Sully and The Assembly of Notables of 1596, 1974, Representative Government in Early Modern France, 1980; also articles. AB, Va. Mil. Inst., 1942; MA, Princeton, 1948, PhD, 1949. Bd. editors: Jnl Modern History, 1966-69. Served to capt. UAS, 1942-46. Decorated Silver Star, Bronze Star, Purple Heart with 2 clusters; Fulbright fellow, France, 1952-53; Guggenheim fellow, 1953-54, 67-68; Faculty Research fellow Soc. Sci. Research Council, 1955-58; fellow, 1961-62; member Inst. Advanced Study, Princeton, 1967-68, 1979-80; sr. fellow NEH, 1973-74. Home: 2223 Hill Park Ct Decatur GA 30033

MAKUCK, PETER, b. New London, CT, Oct. 26, 1940; s. Peter and Helen Cecelia (Landers) M.; m. Phyllis Zerella, Dec. 22, 1968; 1 son, Keith. Author: (short stories) Breaking and Entering, 1981, (poems) Where We Live, 1982; editor (with Kirkland and Sanders) Poetry: Sight and Insight, 1982; founder, editor Tar River Poetry Jnl, 1978—; contrbr. poems and short stories to The Nation, American Scholar, Southern Rvw, Yankee, New Eng. Rvw, Crosscurrents, others. BA, St. Francis Coll., Biddeford, Maine, 1963; PhD, Kent State U., 1971. Instr. French, Norwich Free Acad., Conn., 1964-66; fellow in English, Kent State U., Ohio, 1966-71; asst.prof. West Liberty State Coll., W.Va., 1971-74; maitre asst. Universite de Savoie, France, 1974-75; prof. East Carolina U., Greenville, N.C., 1976—, also dir. Poetry Forum, 1979—. Fulbright exchange prof. in France, 1974-75. Home: 406 Maple St Greenville NC 27834

MALANGA, GERARD JOSEPH, b. NYC, March 20, 1943; s. Gerardo and Emma (Rocco) M. Author: numerous bks., including 3 Poems for Benedetta Barzini, 1967, Prelude to International Velvet Debutante, 1967, Screen Tests/ A Diary (with Andy Warhol), 1967, The Last Benedetta Poems, 1969, Cristinas World, 1970, 10 Poems for 10 Poets, 1970, The Blue Book, 1970, Chic Death, 1970, Beatle Calendar, 1970, Poetry on Film, 1972, Wheels of Light, 1972, 7 Poems for Pilar Crespi, 1973, Incarnations, 1974, Rosebud, 1975, Leaping over Gravestones, 1976, Ten Years After, 1977, 100 Years Have Passed, 1978, This Will Kill That, 1983, Autobiography of a Sex Thief, 1984, Uptight: The Velvet Underground Story (with Victor Bockris). Student Coll. Applied Arts, Univ. of Cincinnati, 1960-61; New Schl. for Social Research, 1961; BA, Wagner Coll., 1964. Associate Andy Warhol, 1963-70; co-founder, co-ed., INTERVIEW, 1969; ed. The Anthology's Forefoot, 1971, Transatlantic Review 52, Little Caesar 9, 1979, Coldspring Jnl 12, 1979. Film-making fellowship, Am. Film Inst., 1969. Mem. PSA, Natl. Park Svc., Jamaica Bay Unit. Photo Archivist, NYC Dept. Parks, 1985—. Home: 203 E 14 St New York NY 10003

MALASCHAK, DOLORES BOYER, b. Illmo, MO, Mar. 19, 1923; d. John Stanley and Ida Jane (Garison) Boyer; m. Anthony Michael Malachak, May 17, 1941; children—Gary Gene, Susan Marie, Anthony M., David Lee, Kimberley Ann. Author: (poetry) Run in the Morning, 1968, Rainbow in my Hand, 1984; (play) The Prodical, 1987. Contrbr. to lit. mags., newspapers, anthol. Co-ed.: Lincoln Log Poetry Mag., 1984-87. B.S. in Edn., Southern Ill. U., 1972. Tchr. public schs., Cahokia, IL, 1972-75, substitute tchr., Gilman City, MO, 1984—. Recipient Gold medal, cert. Centro E. Scambi Internazionale, Rome, 1968. Mem. NLAPW (past pres., co-founder Metro East branch). Home: Box 13 Gilman City MO 64642

MALBROUGH, RAY THOMAS, b. New Orleans, Mar. 12, 1952; s. Lawney Mark and Jeanne Odette (Babin) M. Author: Charms, Spells and Formulas (a written record of Hoodoo magic of So. Louisiana), 1986. Wrkg. on French Louisiana, a basic dictionary of the dialect showing the possibility of writing it. Grad. Terrebonne High Schl., Houma, La., Chef, Houma, to present. Recipient 1st place ribbon Terrebonne Fine Arts Guild, 1967, 2d place, 1966. Home: 413 Harding Dr Houma LA 70363

MALCOHN, ELISSA, see Hamilton, Elissa L. Alkoff

MALE, ROY RAYMOND, b. Bklyn., Mar. 15, 1919; s. Roy Raymond and Mary Edwards (Brooks) M.; m. Carolyn Kate Conlisk, Aug. 19, 1944; children—Marilyn, Frank. Author: Hawthorne's Tragic Vision, 1957, Enter, Mysterious Stranger, 1979; editor: Types of Short Fiction, 2d edit., 1970, Money Talks, 1981; co-editor: Am. Literary Masters, 1974. BS, Hamilton Coll., 1939; MA, Columbia U., 1940; PhD, U. Tex., 1950. Served with AUS, 1940-45. Ford Found. fellow, 1954-55. Mem. MLA, South Central MLA (pres. 1968). Home: 40 Field Sparrow Rd Hilton Head Island SC 29925

MALEFAKIS, EDWARD E., b. Springfield, MA, Jan. 2, 1932; s. Emmanuel A. and Despina (Sophoulakis) M.; m. Mary Anne Wilson, June 15, 1960; children—Michael, Laura. Author: Agrarian Reform and Peasant Revolution in Spain, 1970; editor: Indalecio Prieto, 1975, La Guerra de Espana: 1936-39, 1986. AB, Bates Coll., Lewiston, Maine, 1953; MA, Johns Hopkins U., 1955; PhD, Columbia U., 1965. NEH grantee, 1977; Guggenheim fellow, 1974. Home: 25 Claremont Ave New York NY 10027

MALIN, IRVING, b. NYC, March 18, 1934; s. Morris and Bertha (Silverman) M.; m. Ruth Lief, Dec. 18, 1955; 1 son, Mark. Author: William Faulkner: An Interpretation, 1957; New American Gothic, 1962, Jews and Americans, 1965, Saul Bellow's Fiction, 1969, Nathanael West's Novels, 1972, Isaac Bashevis Singer, 1972; co-ed.: Breakthrough: A Treasury of Contemporary American Jewish Literature, 1964, William Styron's The Confessions of Nat Turner: A Critical Handbook, 1970, The Achievement of William Styron, 1975; ed.: Psychoanalysis and American Fiction, 1965, Saul Bellow and the Critics, 1967, Truman Capote's In Cold Blood: A Critical Handbook, 1968, Critical Views of Isaac Bashevis Singer, 1969, Contemporary American-Jewish Literature: Critical Essays, 1973, Conrad Aiken's Prose, 1982; co-ed., Paul Bowles, 1987. BA, Queens Coll., 1955; PhD, Stanford Univ., 1958. Acting instr. Eng. Stanford Univ., 1955-58; instr. Eng., Ind. Univ., 1958-60, Coll. City NY, 1960-63, asst. prof., 1964-68, assoc. prof. Eng., 1969-72, prof. 1972—. Mem. MLA, PEN, Am. Studies Assn., AAAS, PSA, Pop. Culture Assn., Natl. Bk. Critics Circle, Sherwood Anderson Soc., Kafka Soc., Multi-Ethnic Lit. U.S. Soc., Am. Jewish Congress, Phi Beta Kappa. Home: 96-13 68th Ave Forest Hills NY 11375

MALING, GEORGE C. JR., b. Boston, Feb. 24, 1931, s. George C. and Marjory (Bell) M.; m. Norah J. Horsfield, Dec. 29, 1960; children—Ellen P., Barbara J., Jeffrey C. AB, Bowdoin Coll., 1954; SB, MIT, 1954, SM in Elec. Engring., 1958, PhD, 1963. Sr. physicist IBM Corp., Poughkeepsie, N.Y., 1965—; ed. Noise/News, 1972—; assoc. ed. Jnl of Acoustical Soc. Am., 1977-83; ed. conf. proceedings for engineering orgns. Office: Box 390 Poughkeepsie NY 12602

MALLEN, RONALD EDWARD, b. NYC, July 9, 1942; s. Charles and Mildred M.; m. Penelope L. Below, June 20, 1969; children—Justin M., Seth J. Author: Legal Malpractice, 3d ed., 1987, A Manual of Legal Malpractice, 1981, Legal Malpractice: How To Recognize and Avoid It, 1979. BS in Chem. Engring, Stanford U., 1964; JD, U. Calif., San Francisco, 1967. Bar: Calif. 1967. Office: 101 California St San Francisco CA 94111

MALLON, SUSAN, see Maguire, Cecilia Gertrude

MALLORY, AILEEN LUCILE, b. Jamestown, KS, Feb. 26, 1917; d. Walter Albert and Clara Mabel (Moe) Carlile; m. Raymond A. Williams, Mar. 1937 (div. 1940); 1 dau., Shirley Rae Williams Wilson; m. 2d, Paul Edward Mallory, Aug. 12, 1946; 1 step-dau., Norma Mallory Rutledge. Author: Paving for Clubs, Prize Game and Party Book. Editor: Community Health; contrbg. editor: Topeka Mag. Student Kans. State Coll. Assoc. ed. Capper's Farmer, Topeka, 1951-60; teenage dir. YWCA, Topeka, 1960-61; chief pub. info. Kans. State Dept. Health, Topeka, 1961-72; free-lance wrtr., 1972—. Mem. Kans. Pub. Health Assn. (Spcl. Svc. Award, 1973), Kans. Press Women (awards for wrtg., 1951-87), Natl. Fedn. Press Women, Women in Communications, Natl. League Am. PEN Women. Home: 9640 SW 10th St Topeka KS 66615

MALLORY, LEE W., III, b. San Mateo, CA, Mar. 16, 1946; s. Lee W. Mallory and Mary Ann (Gadd) Rector; m. Adell Josephine Patterson, June 27, 1969; children—Misty Ann, Natalee Adell. Author: Beach House Poems, 1969, 91739, 1970, Oatmeal Candy, 1970. Contrbr. poems to lit. mags. Editor: Malpelo Press, 1970. BA in French, U. Calif.-Santa Barbara, 1969; MA, Calif. State U.-Long Beach, 1978. Instr. Rancho Santiago Community Coll., Santa Ana, CA, 1980—. Pres. Central Newport Beach Community Assn., Calif., 1984-86. Pres. Acad. Senate (1986-87). Phi Beta Kappa. Home: 413 38th St Newport Beach CA 92663

MALLORY, LIN, see Riker, Leigh Bartley

MALOFF, SAUL, b. NYC, Sept. 6, 1922; s. David and Yetta (Friedman) M.;)married); 1 dau., Jadis Karla Lorca Norman. Author: novel Happy Families, 1968, Heartland, 1973; also editor poetry and prose anthologies; author short stories, rvws, articles, essays in lit. criticism. BA, Coll. City N.Y., 1939-42; MA, U. Iowa, 1947, PhD, 1952. Books editor Newsweek mag., 1964-68; cons. Guggenheim Fdn. Exec. bd. Am. Center PEN. Served with US, 1943-46. Guggenheim fellow; recipient George Polk Meml. award lit. criticism. Home: Second Hill Rd Bridgewater CT 06752 Address: 659-B Heritage Vill Southbury CT 06488

MALONE,, ELMER TAYLOR II JR., b. Wilson, NC, Dec. 18, 1943; s. E. T. and Mildred B. (Winborne) M.; m. Lynda A. Cyrus, June 15, 1969; children—Anna Richmond, Edward Winborne. Author: (poems), The Cleared Place of Tara, 1970, The Tapestry Maker, 1972, The View from Wrightsville Beach, 1987; (with Richard Walser) Litrary North Carolina, 1986; columnist (syndicated book column): The Literary Lantern; reporter: The Raleigh Times, NC, 1969. Contrbr. articles to books, lit. jnls. Ed.: The Dunn Dispatch, Dunn, NC, 1969-70 Harnett County News, Lillington, NC, 1972-74; asst. news ed.: The Durham Sun, NC, 1974-77. B.S. in English, Campbell Coll., 1967; M.A. in English, U. NC, 1975. Lectr. English, N.C. Central U., Durham, 1977-84; editor. hist. pubs. sect. N.C. Div. of Arhives & History, Raleigh, NC, 1984—. Served with U.S. Army, 1967-78. Recipient Jnlsm. award ampbell Coll., 1966; Smith-wick award N.C. Soc. County & Local Hist., 1977. Mem. N. C. Folklore Soc. (pres. 1984, 85, Cratis Williams award 1979), N.C. Lit. Hist. Soc., N.C. Wrtrs.' Conf., N.C. Wrtrs.' Network. Home: 103 Carl Dr Rt 4 Chapel Hill NC 27514

MALONE,, MICHAEL CHRISTOPHER,, b. NC, 1942; s. Thomas Patrick and Faylene Jones M.; m. Maureen Quilligan, May 17, 1975; 1 dau., Margaret Elizabeth. Author: (novels) Painting the Roses Red, 1974, The Delectable Mountains, 1976, Dingley Falls, 1980, Uncivil Seasons, 1984, Handling Sin, 1986, Times Witness, 1988; (non-fiction) Psychetypes, 1975, Heroes of Eros, 1979; (play) Defender of the Faith; (musical) City of Angels. Contrbr. short stories, essays to popular mags. including Harpers, The Nation, Playboy; rvws. to N.Y. Times Book Rvw., Newsday, Phila. Inquirer, others. B.A., U. NC, 1964, M.A., 1967; M.A., Harvard U., 1970, postgrad., 1967—. Bd. trustees Conn. Opera Co. Recipient O. Henry award, 1982. Mem. PEN, WG, East DG, MWA, Authors Guild & League, NBCC. Home: 32 Commerce St Clinton CT 06413

MALONE, MICHAEL PATRICK, b. Chgo., Apr. 17, 1951; s. Robert John and June (Hasenbank) M.; m. Anne Celeste Frisbie, Sept. 3, 1977; children: Honor, Clare. Contrbr. to PEN Short Story Collection, Chgo. Tribune, San Francisco Chronicle, Chgo. Sun-Times, Ascent, U.S. Catholic, New Letters, Cimarron, Miss., Mississippi Valley, Mid-Am. rvws. BA, U. Ill., 1973; MFA, Bowling Green State U., 1975. Lectr. U. Ill., Chgo., 1977-80, asst. prof., Urbana, 1980; dir. publs. Coll. of Du Page, Glen Ellyn, Ill., 1981-82, Moraine Valley Coll., Palos Hills, Ill., 1982-84, No. Ill. U., De Kalb, 1984—. Ill. Arts Council grantee, 1977; NEA fellow, 1981. Mem. P&W. Home: 342 Lorraine Glen Flyn IL 60137

MALONE, PAMELA ALTFELD, b. Buffalo, Dec. 13, 1943, d. Merwin Richard and Mildred Frances (Kirschbaum) Altfeld; m. Joseph Lawrence Malone, Jan. 31, 1964; children—Joseph Timothy, Otis Taig. Contrbr. to Gates to the New City (transl.), A Treasury of Modern Jewish Tales, 1983, Yellow Silk, Poet's Pride, Against the Wall, Mother, Fire, numerous other lit mags. BA, U. Calif.-Berkeley, 1965; MA, NYU, 1976. Head tchr. Temple Judea, Bronx, N.Y., 1972-76; adj. prof. Paterson State Coll., Wayne, N.J., 1976-80. Mem. P&W, Assn. Jewish Studies. Home: 169 Prospect St Leonia NJ 07605

MALONEY, DENNIS MICHAEL, b. Buffalo, May 11, 1951; s. Thomas Joseph and Luciele (Booth) M.; m. Anita Schnell, May 21, 1973 (div. Jan. 1978); 1 child, Timothy Joseph; m. 2d, Elaine Susan Taddio, Aug. 17, 1985. Author: Rimrock, 1978; I Learn Only To Be Contented, 1981; Pine Hut Poems, 1984; translator: Naked Music, Poems of Juan Ramon Jimenez, 1976; Dusk Lingers—Haiku of Issa, 1981; (with others) Windows That Open Inward: Images of Chile (Pablo Neruda), 1985; The Landscape of Soria: Antonio Machado, 1985; The Stones of Chile (Neruda), 1986; Tangled Hair—Poems of Yosano Akiko, 1986; contrbr. poems and transls. to lit mags. BS in Landscape Architecture, SUNY, Syracuse, 1973. Landscape architect City of Buffalo, 1973—; ed./pub. White Pine Press, Buffalo, 1973—. Witter Bynner Fdn. translation and editing grantee, 1985-86. Mem. P&W, Niagara-Erie Wrtrs. (exec. officer 1979-82, chmn. bd. 1983-85). Home: 76 Center St Fredonia NY 14063

MALOTT, ADELE RENEE, (Amanda Rhoades)b. St. Paul, July 19, 1935; d. Clarence R. and Julia A. (Christiansen) Lindgren; m. Gene E., Oct. 25, 1957. Editor num. mags and newspapers, including Hillsborough Boutique & Villager, 1967-76, Consumer Life, 1978, Cat's Pride, 1978-80, Energy Horizons, 1978, Living Trends, 1979, Going Slim, 1982-83, Friendly Exchange, 1981—, Wing Elite, 1984, HealthScenes, 1983-84. BS, Northwestern U., 1957. News co-ord. KGB Radio, San Diego, 1958-60; asst. p.r. dir. Chamber of Commerce, St. Paul, 1960-63; night ed. Daily Local News, West Chester, PA, 1963-66; ed. Boutique & Villager, Burlingame, CA, 1966-76; sr. ed. The Webb Co., St. Paul, 1978-85; exec. ed. GEM Pub. Co., Reno, NV, 1985—. Num. awards Press Women of MN, CA, NV. Mem. IABC, NFPW. 250 E Riverview Cr Reno NV 89509

MAMET, DAVID ALAN, b. Chgo., Nov. 30, 1947; s. Bernard Morris and Lenore June (Silver) M.; m. Lindsay Crouse, Dec., 1977. Author: (books) Writing in Restarunts (essays), 1986, The Owl (with Lindsay Crouse), 1987; (plays) The Duck Variations, 1971, Sexual Perversity in Chicago, 1973, (Village Voice Obie award 1976), Reunion, 1973, Squirrels, 1974, American Buffalo (Village Voice Obie award 1976), 1976 (N.Y. Drama Critics Circle award 1977), A Life in The Theatre, 1976, The Water Engine, 1976, The Woods, 1977, Lone Canoe, 1978, Prairie du Chien, 1978, Lakeboat, 1980, Donny March, 1981, Edmond, 1982 (Village Voice Obie award 1983), The Disappearance of the Jews, 1983, Glengarry Glen Ross, 1984 (Pulitzer price for drama, N.Y. Drama Critics Circle award), Speed the Plow, 1987; (screen plays) The Postman Always Rings Twice, 1979, The Verdict, 1980, House of Games, 1987, The Untouchables, 1987, Things Change (with Shel Silverstein), 1988, We're No Angels, 1988. BA, Goddard Coll., Plainfield, Vt., 1969. Acad. award nominee for best screen adaptation, 1983; Rockefeller grantee, 1977; CBS Creative Writing fellow Yale U. Drama Schl., 1976-77. Home: New York New York

MANCHESTER, WILLIAM, b. Attleboro, MA, Apr. 1, 1922; s. William Raymond and Sallie E.R. (Thompson) M.; m. Julia Brown Marshall, Mar. 27, 1948; children—John Kennerly, Julie Thompson, Laurie. Author: Disturber of the Peace, 1951, The City of Anger, 1953, Shadow of the Monsoon, 1956, Beard the Lion, 1958, A Rockefeller Family Portrait, 1959, The Long Gainer, 1961, Portrait of a President, 1962, The Death of a President, 1967 (BOMC selection), The Arms of Krupp, 1968 (LG selection), The Glory and the Dream, 1974 (LG selection), Controversy and Other Essays in Journalism, 1976, American Caesar—Douglas MacArthur, 1880-1964, 1978 (BOMC selection), Goodbye, Darkness, 1980 (BOMC selection), The Last Lion: Visions of Glory, 1983 (BOMC selection), One Brief Shining Moment, 1983 (BOMC selection); contrbr. to: Ency. Brit., various publs. BA, U. Mass., 1946, LHD, 1965; A.M., U. Mo., 1947; LHD, U. New Haven, 1979, Lit. D. Skidmore Coll., 1987. Reporter Daily Oklahoman, 1945-56; reporter, fgn. corr., war corr. Balt. Sun, 1947-55; mng. editor Wesleyan U. Publs., 1955-65; fellow Wesleyan U. Center for Advanced Studies, 1959-60; writer-in-residence, Wesleyan U., 1975—; adj. prof. of history, 1979—. Served with USMC, 1942-45. Decorated Purple Heart; recipient Dag Hammarskjold prize, 1966; citation for best book on fgn. affairs Overseas Press Club, 1968; U. Mo. honor award for distinguished service in journalism, 1969; Conn. Bar Assn. Distinguished Svc. Award, 1986; others. Guggenheim fellow, 1959-60. Mem. AG. Address: Olin Meml Lib Middletown CT 06457

MANCUSO, JAMES VINCENT, b. Batavia, NY, June 16, 1918; s. Benjamin J. and Laura (Russo) M.; m. Clarissa Pope, 1945; children—Richard, Robert, Linda, Laura. Authoe: (book and audio-cassette) Successful Automobile Selling—The Professional Way, 1986. Contrbr. articles on automobile topics, patriotism to mags. including Auto Age, Ward's Auto Dealer, Dealership Management Rvw., Am. Legion Mag. Wrkg. on articles for mags., book on experiences as an auto dealer. Cert. in Advanced Dealer Management, Genl. Motors Technical Inst., 1949. Pres., Service Suvey Systems, Winnetka, 1984—, The Mancuso co., Winnetka, 1984—; pres., Chmn Mancusco Cadillac, Barrington, IL, 1974-82, Mancuso Chevrolet, Skokie, IL, 1953-84. Home: 17 Longmeadow Rd Winnetka IL 60093

MANDEL, CHARLOTTE, b. Bklyn. Author: poetry—A Disc of Clear Water, 1981, Doll, 1986; editor: Saturday's Women, 1982; poetry, fiction, essays in Iowa Rvw, Women's Studies, Literature/Film Qtly, other lit mags. BA, Brooklyn College; MA, Montclair State College. Mem. PSA, MLA. Home: 60 Pine Dr Cedar Grove NJ 07009

MANDEL, OSCAR, b. Antwerp, Belgium, Aug. 24, 1926; came to U.S., 1940. Author: A Definition of Tragedy, 1961, The Theater of Don Juan, 1963, Chi Po and the Sorcerer: A Chinese Tale for Children and Philosophers, 1964, The Fatal French Dentist: A Farce, 1967, The Gobble-Up Stories, 1967; (trans.) Seven Comedies by Marivaux, 1968, Five Comedies of Medieval France, 1970; The Collected Plays (2 vols.), 1970-72; (trans.) Three Classic Don Juan Plays, 1971; (poems) Simplicities, 1974; The Patriots of Nantucket: A Romantic Comedy of the American Revolution, 1976, Amphitryon: Licentiously Translated from Moliere, 1977; (trans.) The Land of Upside Down (Ludwig Tieck), 1978; Annotations to Vanity Fair, 1981, Philoctetes and the Fall of Troy: Plays, Documents, Iconography, Interpretations, 1981, Collected Lyrics and Epigrams, 1981, The Ariadne of Thomas Corneille, 1982; (essays) The Book of Elaborations, 1985. Office: Calif Inst Tech Pasadena CA 91125

MANDEL, SIEGFRIED, b. Berlin, Germany, Dec. 20, 1922; came to U.S., 1933, naturalized, 1938; s. Nathan and Pauline (Scheinman) M.; m. Dorothy Isaacs, Feb. 3, 1946; children—Elise Judith, Theodore Scott. Editor, contbg. author: Writing in Industry, 1959 (with D.L. Caldwell) Proposal and Inquiry Writing, 1962, Modern Journalism, 1962, (Rainer Maria Rilke) The Poetic Instinct, 1965, (with Aaron Kramer) Rainer Maria Rilke: Visions of Christ, 1967, Contemporary European Novelists, 1968, Dictionary of Science, 1969, Writing for Science and Technology, 1970, Group 47: The Reflected Intellect, 1973; editor, translator: Lou Andreas-Salome: Ibsen's Heroines, 1985; Lou Salome: Friedrich Nietzsche in His Works; contrbr. articles and book rvws. to profl. jnls. BA, Bklyn. Coll., 1946; MA, Columbia U., 1947; PhD, U. Denver, 1967. Sr. editor Inst. Econ. Affairs, NYC, 1952-53; writer, editor Asso. Transp., Inc., 1954-55; book rvw. columnist Newsday, 1954-55; indsl. lectr. writing workshops Internat. Tel. & Tel. Corp., 1959-60. Served with AUS, 1943-46. Faculty fellow lit. research U. Colo., 1968-69, 75-76; Eugene M. Kayden Natl. prize in the humanities for translation, 1984. Mem. MLA, Nat. Book

Critics Circle; others. Home: 355 Balsam Ln Pine Brook Hills Boulder CO 80302

MANDELL, MEL, b. Boston, Mar. 19, 1926, s. Maurice Sylvester Mandell and Sylvia (Burg) Ainsberg; div.; 1 son, Matthew I. Author: Being Safe (alt. selection Lit. Guild, serialized in N.Y. Post), 1972, The Handbook of Business and Industrial Security, 1972, 1001 Ways to Operate Your Business More Profitably, 1975, Keep Your Customers and Keep Them Happy (with Stanley Fenvessy), 1976, The Handbook of Home Security, 1978; contrbr. chap. to Miniaturization, 1961, Handbook of Modern Office Management and Administrative Services, 1972, The Encyclopedia of Management, 1973, 82. BS, Columbia U., 1945, MA, 1950. Assoc. ed. Electronic Design, N.Y.C., 1954-55; ed. Research & Engring., Stamford, Conn., 1955-57; sr. ed. Dun's Rev., NYC, 1957-61; editorial dir. United Tech. Publs, Garden City, N.Y., 1964-69; ed. Computer Decisions, Hasbrouck Heights, N.J., 1978-87. Served as lt. USN, 1944-46, 50-52. Recipient Neal Award, Associated Bus. Pubns., 1986. Mem. N.Y. Bus. Press Eds. Home: 3206 Fairfield Ave New York NY 10463

MANDELL,, PATRICIA ATHENA,, b. New London, CT, June 5, 1952; d. Donald Burt and Thalia Irene (Callichy) Mandell; m. Eliot Jay Lees, Oct. 16, 1982. Contrbr. essays to Microcomputer Applications: A Hands-On Approah to Problem Solving (Larry Joel Goldstein), 1987. B.A., U. Conn., 1974. Feature wrtr. New London Day, 1975-78; bus. ed. Prentice-Hall, Waterford, CT, 1978-79; photo ed. New Britain Herald, CT, 1979; copy ed. Ptriot Ledger, Quincy, MA, 1980-84, PC week, Boston, 1984-85; freelance jnlst., 1985—. Home: 40 Ireland Rd Marshfield MA 02050

MANDELL, RICHARD S., b. Chgo., Feb. 3, 1953, s. Seymour Irving and Florence Roslyn (Landsman) M.; m. Martha Ellen Gray, Sept. 5, 1982. Author: (novel) The Bats, 1981; ed. Kairos, 1982—, Encyc. of Psychoactive Drugs, 1984—; contrbr. fiction and book rvw. to Hambone, novella to The Long Story. BA in Psychobiology, Oberlin Coll., 1975; MA in Creative Writing, Brown U., 1979. Pub./ed. Hermes House Press, Northampton, Mass., 1980—; asst. to printer Faculty Press, NYC, 1983-84; assoc. ed. Chelsea House Pubs., NYC, 1984—. Dorland Mountain Colony resident, Temecula, Calif., 1982. Mem. PEN, AAP, COSMEP. Home: 39 Adare Pl Northampton MA 01060

MANDINO, OG, b. Boston, Dec. 12, 1923; s. Silvio and Margaret T. (Lee) M.; m. Bette L. Lang, Dec. 9, 1957; children—Dana, Matthew. Author: A Treasury of Success Unlimited, 1967, The Greatest Salesman in the World, 1968, (with Edward R. Dewey) Cycles, The Mysterious Forces That Trigger Events, 1970, U.S. in a Nutshell, 1971, The Greatest Secret in the World, 1972, The Greatest Miracle in the World, 1975, (with Buddy Kaye) The Gift of Acabar, 1978, The Christ Commission, 1980, The Greatest Success in the World, 1981, Og Mandino's University of Success, 1982. Student, Bucknell Jr. Coll., 1941. Exec. editor Success Unlimited mag., Chgo., 1965-72; pres. Success Unltd., Inc., Chgo., 1972-76. Served to 1st lt. USAAF, 1942-45. Decorated D.F.C., Air medal with 5 Oak leaf clusters. Mem. AL, AG. Home: 6130 E Via Estrella Ave Scottsdale AZ 85253

MANEJIAS,, SERGIO,, b. Remedios, Cuba, Sept. 14, 1909; came to U.S., 1963; s. Jose and Adela (Romero) M.; m. Maria Veliz, June 1, 1936; children: Renaldo, Roland Author poetry books: Susie (poems for children), 1983, Por los Caminos de la Fe (religious), 1984, Poemas Infantiles, 1985. Blitt, Coll. La Progresiva, Cuba: Theology, Evangel. Sem. Rio Piedras, Puerto Rico. Pastor Prsbyn. Ch., Cuba, 1936-63, Bklyn., 1963-72. Recipient numerous awards. Home: 56 46th St Weehawken NJ 07087

MANESSE, DANIEL ARTHUR, b. NYC, Apr. 19, 1921, s. Louis and Frances Beatrice (Spunt) M.; m. Margaret Novins, Jan. 28, 1976. Novelist: The Mammon Madness, 1970, Gotham College, 1973; playwright: Morgan Le Fay, 1962, Nature's Grandeur, 1966, The Myth of Verbio, 1967; contrbr. poetry, art criticisms to Comparisons; contrbr. articles to: Geyer's Dealer Topics, The Paper and Twine Jnl; ed.: Philosophy and the Arts lit. and philos. jnl, 1975—. Home: Box 431 Jerome Ave Sta Bronx NY 10468

MANFRED, FREDERICK FEIKEMA, (Feike Feikema), b. Doon, Iowa, Jan. 6, 1912; s. Feike Feikes, VI and Aaltje (Van Engen) Feikema; m. Maryanna Shorba, Oct. 31, 1942 (div. Oct. 1978); children—Freya, Marya, Frederick Feikema. Author: The Golden Bowl, 1944, Boy Almighty, 1945, This Is The Year, 1947, The Chokecherry Tree, 1948, Lord Grizzly, 1954, Morning Red, 1956, Riders of Judgment, 1957, Conquering Horse, 1959, Arrows of Love (stories), 1961, Wanderlust trilogy (The Primitive, The Brother, The Giant), 1962, Scarlet Plume, 1964, The Man Who Looked Like the Prince of Wales, 1965, Winter Count (poems), 1966, King of Spades, 1966; Apples of Paradise (stories), 1968, Eden Prairie, 1968, Conversations, 1974, Milk of Wolves, 1976, The Manly-Hearted Woman, 1976, Green Earth, 1977; The Wind Blows Free (reminiscence), 1979, Sons of Adam, 1980, Winter Count II (poems), 1987, Prime Fathers (portraits), 1987; contrbr. articles and stories mags. AB, Calvin Coll., Grand Rapids, Mich., 1934; student, Nettleton Comml. Coll., Sioux Falls, S.D., 1937, U. Minn., 1941-42. Reporter Mpls. Jnl, 1937-39; editor Modern Medicine, 1942-43; writer-in-residence Macalester Coll., 1949-52, U. S.D., 1968-82, consultant in the humanities, Augustana Coll., 1983—. Fiction grant-in-aid Am. Acad. Arts and Letters, 1945; U. Minn. Rockefeller Found.; Regional Writing fellowship, 1944-46; Field Found. fellowship, 1948-49; Andreas Found. fellowship, 1949-52; McKnight Found. fellow, 1958-59; Huntington Hartford Found. fellow, 1963-64; Avon Found. fellow, 1958-59. Recipient Mark Twain Literary Award, 1981. Mem. PEN, Author's League Am., Soc. Midland Writers, The Players. Home: Roundwind RR 3 Luverne MN 56156

MANGAN, JEAN, b. Widnes, England, May 30, 1934, came to U.S., 1963, naturalized, 1988; d. Thomas James and Eileen (Hughes) McCafferty; m. Daniel Mangan, Dec. 12, 1961 (div. Sept. 17, 1981); children—Paul, Allyson. Editor: Colorado Professional's Resource Guide & Directory, 1987. Student Widnes Coll. Commerce, 1949-51. Home: 8555 Fairmount Dr E-203 Denver CO 80231

MANGIONE, JERRE GERLANDO, b. Rochester, NY, Mar. 20, 1909; s. Gaspare and Giuseppina (Polizzi) M.; m. Patricia Anthony, Feb. 18, 1957. Author: Mount Allegro: A Memoir of Italian American Life, 1943, new ed. 81, Ship and the Flame, 1948, Reunion in Sicily, 1950, 2d edit., 1984, Night Search, 1965, Life Sentences for Everybody, 1966, A Passion for Sicilians: The World Around Danilo Dolci, 1968, 72, new ed. 85, America is Also Italian, 1969, The Dream and the Deal: Federal Writers Project (1935-43), 1972, 2d edit., 1983, An Ethnic at Large: A Memoir of America in the Thirties and Forties, 1978, 2d ed., 1983; contrbr. to newspapers and mags. BA, Syracuse U., 1931; MA (hon.), U. Pa., 1971, Litt.D. (hon.), 1980, U. Pa.; Doctor of Humane Letters (hon.), State Univ. of NY, 1987. Writer, Time mag., 1931; book editor Robert M. McBride & Co., NYC, 1934-37; nat. coordinating editor Fedl. Writers's Project, 1937-39; advt. writer, pub. relations dir., 1948-61; dir. writing program, U. Pa., 1965—; editor WFLN Phila. guide, 1960-61; book reviewer, 1931—; adv. editor The Humanist, 1979—; judge nat. Book Award in Fiction, 1968; adv. editor Italian Americana, 1974—; mem. lit. panel NEA, 1980-81. Chmn. lit. arts com. Phila. Art Alliance, 1958-61; mem. adv. bd. U. Pa. Press 1983-84. Guggenheim fellow, 1945; Fulbright research fellow, 1965; MacDowell Colony fellow, Yaddo fellow; Va. Center Arts fellow; Rockefeller grantee, 1968; Am. Philos. Soc. grantee, 1971; Earhart Fdn. grantee, 1975; NEH grantee, 1980-83; recipient 10th ann. Lit award Friends Rochester Pub. Library, 1966; numerous other awards. Mem. PEN, AG. Home: 1901 Kennedy Blvd Philadelphia PA 19103

MANHEIM, JAROL B(RUCE), b. Cleveland, OH, April 17, 1946; s. Harvey and Norma (Blaugrund) M.; m. Amy Lowen, Sept. 6, 1969. Author: The Politics Within: A Primer in Political Attitudes and Behavior, 1975, 2d ed, 1982, (with Melanie Wallace) Political Violence in the United States, 1875-1974: A Bibliography, 1975, Deja Vu: American Political Problems in Historical Perspective, 1976, (with Richard C. Rich) Empirical Political Analysis: Research Methods in Political Science, 1981, 2d ed, 1986, American Politics Yearbook, 1982, contrbr, Stuart S. Nagel, ed, Encyclopedia of Policy Studies, 1983, (with Allison Ondraik) Data Map: Index of Published Tables of Statistical Data, 1983, contrbr, Doris A. Graber, ed, Media Power in Politics, 1984, 84, 86, contrbr with Ondrasik, Nagel, ed, Basic Literature in Policy Studies: A Comprehensive Bibliography, 1984, contrbr, Margaret L. McLaughlin, ed, Communication Yearbook 10, 1986. Also contrbr to Robert L. Savage and Michael W. Mansfield, eds, Political Communication, Political Culture, and Democratic Community. Ed, Annual Editions: Readings in American Government serie, 1974-76; ed, Professional Studies in Political Communication and Policy series (monographs), 1979-85. Contrbr to Periodicals, including Journalism Qtly, Jnl of Communication, Public Relations Rvw, American Political Sci Rvw, Annals, Policy Studies Jnl, and N.Y. Time. Advisory ed, Longman, Inc., 1979-86; editorial advisor, Irving Rochwood & Assocs, Inc., 1985—; MS consultant, Prentice-Hall, Harpers & Row, Free Press, Longman, and Univ of Wis Press. Asoc ed, Jnl of Politics, 1978-79; literature rvws ed and mem edit bd, Policy Studies Jnl, 1985. BA, Rice Univ, 1968; MA, Northwetern Univ., 1969, Ph.D., 1971. Asst prof of political sci, City College of the City University of N.Y., 1971-75; asst prof, Virginia Polytechnic Inst and State University, Blacksburg, 1975-77, assoc prof of political sci, 1977-87; prof. poli. ci, & communication and dir. program in poli. communication, The Goerge Wshington Univ., 1987—. Presented numerous papers and paticipated in workshops and panel discussions at annual meetings and conferences in the U.S. and Canada. Oiginator, program coordinator, and participant, Virginia Digest, public affairs radio and television series, 1975-78. Mem: Assn for Politics and the Life Sciences, American Political ci Assn, Omicron Delta

Kappa. Woodrow Wilson fellow, 1970-71; awarded numerous grants, 1978-85; awarded Certificate of Teaching Excellence, Va. Polytechnic Inst and State University, 1980, 1981; Data Map designated Outstanding Reference Source of 1984 by ALA, 1985; elected to Acad of Faculty Service, Virginia Polytechnic Inst and State Univ, 1985, 1986; A Model of Agenda Dynamics selected as one of three best papers in political communication at annual meeting of Intl. Communication Assn, 1986. Home: 5309 Waneta Rd Bethesda MD 20816

MANN, ARTHUR, b. Bklyn., Jan. 3, 1922; s. Karl and Mary (Koch) Finkelman; m. Sylvia Blut, Nov. 6, 1943; children—Carol Ruth, Emily Betsy. Author: Yankee Reformers in the Urban Age, 1954, Growth and Achievement, Temple Israel, 1854-1954, 1954, La Guardia, A Fighter Against His Times, 1882-1933, 1959, Immigrants in American Life, 1968, rev. ed., 1974, The One and the Many: Reflections on the American Identity, 1979, others. Editor: The University of Chicago Press Documents in American History series; adv. editor Am. History series, U. Chgo. Press; mem. editorial bd. Ethnicity; editorial cons.: Social Service Rvw. BA summa cum laude, Bklyn. Coll., 1944; MA, Harvard U., 1947, PhD1952. Served with AUS, 1943-46. Fellow ACLS, 1962-63; Fulbright-Hays sr. scholar, Australia, 1974. Home: 4919 S Woodlawn Ave Chicago IL 60615

MANN, DICK, see Mann, Richard Dale

MANN, JIM, b. Cambridge, MA, Dec. 9, 1919; s. Demetrios Peter and Germaine (Lambertz) Manousos; m. Mary Dimitrakis, July 21, 1962. Author: Solving Publishing's Toughest Problems, 1982, Magazine Editing: Its Art and Practice, 1985, Ad Sales: Interviews with 23 Top Magazine Executives, 1987; contrbr. Handbook of Mag. Publishing, 1977; ed. Media Mgt. Monographs, 1978—. MFA, Fordham U., 1956. Exec. asst. World Wide Pubs., NYC, 1958-60; managing ed. The Gallagher Report, NYC, 1960-68, v.p. & exec. ed., 1969, v.p. & editorial dir., 1970-71, pres. & ed., 1972-74; pres. & founder Jim Mann & Assoc., Gales Ferry, CT, 1974—. Home: 9 Mount Vernon Dr Gales Ferry CT 06335

MANN, NED, b. Hartford, CT, Jan. 29, 1955, s. Edward Guild and Martha Jane (McCloy) M.; m. Mary Art, Nov. 18, 1980. Author: The Speakers Manual, 1982, The Target Marketing Reader, 1983, The Book of Business, 1983, Great Recruiting Ideas, 1984, The Planner's Sourcebook, 1985. BS in Acctg., Bentley Coll., 1977, BS in Bus. Communications, 1978. Stringer The Jnls., Windsor, Conn., 1977-79; research ed. LIMRA, Hartford, Conn., 1978-79, ed., Farmington, Conn., 1979-84, sr. ed., Farmington, 1984—; ed., Managers Magazine. Mem. Conn. Intl. Assn. Bus. Communicators. Office: LIMRA 8 Farm Springs Rd Farmington CT 06032

MANN, RICHARD DALE, (Dick Mann), b. Topeka, Nov. 24, 1931; s. John Graham and Mollie Lou (Packard) M.; m. Lydia Flores Cruz, Sept. 14, 1956; children—Iris Darlene Mann McKay, Cheryl Louise Mann Carr. Contrbr. articles to Worldwide News. BA in History and Poli. Sci., Washburn U., 1962. Asst. mgr. advt. dept. Wal Thompson Hardware, Topeka, 1963-65; contract officer job trng. Kans. Dept. Human Resources, Kansas City, 1971-74, mgr. suboffice, 1974-75, dir. apprenticeship info., 1976-77, asst. mgr., vet. rep., Olathe, Kans., 1977-86; Overland Park, KS, Job Svc, 1987-. Served as aviation electronics technician, USN, 1951-55. Recipient Achievement in Vet. Employment award Kans. Dept. Human Resources, 1985. Mem. Kansas City Spokesman Club (pres. 1984-85), Intl. Assn. Personnel in Employment Security, Kans. Assn. Pub. Employees, Am. Legion. Home: 3715 Matney Kansas City KS 66106

MANNING, LILLIAN O'NEAL, b. Urbana, IL, July 23, 1956; d. Richard Eugene and Dorothy Ann (schlegel) O'Neal; m. John Patrick Manning V, Dec. 4, 1982. Contrbr. papers to profl. jnls.; ed., author (with others): Research and Creative Activities, 1986; Graduate Schl. Catalog, 1987-89, 1987; news ed.: Alestle, Edwardsville, IL, 1975-77; bus. ed., reporter News-Democrat, Belleville, IL, 1978-79; ed.: Sou'wester, 1977-78, Papers on Lang. and Lit., 1981. B.A. in Mass Communication/Jnlsm., English, Southern Ill. U., Edwardsville, 1978, M.A. in English, 1983. Part time music criti Alton Telegraph, IL, 1976-78; product mgr., copywrtr. C.V. Mosby Co., St. Louis, 1979-82; copywrtr. Wausau Insurane Co., St. Louis, 1982-83; devel. officer, staff asst. graduate schl. Recipient cert. of Achievement, Wrtr.'s Digest, 1986, 87. Southern Ill. U., Edwardsville, 1983—. /Mem. Southern Ill. Network of Women (v.p. 1987), Natl. Council Univ. Research Administrs., Musicians Local. Home: 725 Yale Ave Edwardsville IL 62025

MANO, D. KEITH, b. NYC, Feb. 12, 1942; s. William F. and Marion Elizabeth (Minor) M.; m. Laurie E. Kennedy, July 18, 1980; children—Roderick Keith, Christopher Carey. Author: Bishop's Progress, 1968, Horn, 1969, War is Heaven!, 1970, The Death and Life of Harry Goth, 1971, The Proselytizer, 1972, The Bridge, 1973, Take Five, 1982; contrbr. articles to profl. jnls. BA summa cum laude, Columbia U., 1963; postgrad. (Kellett fellow), Clare Coll., Cambridge (Eng.) U., 1964-65. Contrbg. editor, columnist: Nat. Rvw. mag., 1972—; contrbg. editor: Oui mag., 1972—. Woodrow Wilson fellow Columbia U., 1965-66; recipient Best Religious Book award Publs. of MLA, 1969, Best Non-Fiction award Playboy mag., 1977. Address: 392 Central Pk W New York NY 10025

MANTELL, SUZANNE, b. West Orange, NJ, Nov. 26, 1944; d. Milton A. and Florence B. M.; m. Peter Gray Friedman, 1985; 1 child—Erica Mantell Friedman. Assoc. editor Harper's mag., NYC, exec. editor; 1977-80; editor Harper's Bookletter, 1974-77; editor Learning Mag., 1980-81; ed. Calif. Living Mag., 1983-84; freelance wrtr., 1984—; rdr. for BOMC, 1985—; ed. Banana Republic, Travel Bookstore catalog, 1985-87; assoc. ed., The New York Observer, 1987-; also lectr. mag. writing Stanford U., U. Calif. at Santa Cruz. Student, U. Chgo., 1962; BFA, Pratt Inst., 1967. Mem. PEN, Nat. Book Critics Circle. Home: 302 W 12th St New York NY 10014

MANUEL, FRANK EDWARD, b. Boston, Sept. 12, 1910; s. Morris and Jessica (Fredson) M.; m. Fritzie Prigohzy, Oct. 6, 1936. Author: Politics of Modern Spain, 1938, American-Palestine Relations, 1949, Age of Reason, 1951, The New World of Henri Saint-Simon, 1956, The Eighteenth Century Confronts the Gods, 1959, The Prophets of Paris, 1962, Isaac Newton, Historian, 1963, Shapes of Philosophical History, 1965, A Portrait of Isaac Newton, 1968, Freedom From History, 1971, The Religion of Isaac Newton, 1974, The Changing of the Gods, 1983; editor: The Enlightenment, 1965, Utopias and Utopian Thought, 1966, Herder's Reflections on the Philosophy of the History of Mankind, 1968; co-author: Utopian Thought in the Western World, 1979 (Melcher prize, Phi Beta Kappa Emerson award, Am. Book award); co-editor: French Utopias: An Anthology of Ideal Societies, 1966; cons. editor: Psychoanalysis and Contemporary Sci; adv. editor: Clio. AB, Harvard, 1930, AM, 1931, PhD, 1933; postgrad., Ecole des Hautes Etudes Politiques et Sociales, Paris, 1933; LittD (hon.), Jewish Theol. Sem. Am., 1979; Doctor of Humane Letters (hon.), Brandeis U., 1986. Served with AUS, 1943-45. Rogers Traveling fellow, 1932-33; Guggenheim fellow, 1957-58; fellow Center for Advanced Study in Behavioral Scis., 1962-63; vis. member Inst. for Advanced Study, 1976-77; fellow Am. Acad. Arts and Scis. (mem. com. on publs. 1969-71). Home: 10 Emerson Pl Boston MA 02114

MANULKIN, DENA, b. New Brunswick, NJ, Apr. 23, 1947; d. Herbert Spencer and Jean (Guth) Rogin; m. Steven M. Manulkin, Jan. 2, 1982. BA, Temple U., 1968. Test dev. ed. Natl. Bd. Mdl. Examiners, Phila., 1969-72; mng. ed. A.S. Barnes & Co., Cranbury, NJ, 1972-78; assoc. ed. Arete Pub. Co., Princeton, NJ, 1978-80; ed. Geriatric Medicine Today, Plainsboro, NJ, 1981—. Office: 1000 Off Ctr 666 Plainsboro Rd Plainsboro NJ 08536

MAPP, ALF JOHNSON, JR., b. Portsmouth, VA, Feb. 17, 1925; s. Alf Johnson and Lorraine (Carney) M.; m. Hartley Lockhart, Mar. 28, 1953; 1 son, Alf Johnson III; m. 2d, Ramona Hartley Hamby, Aug. 1, 1971. Author: The Virginia Experiment, 1957, 2d edit., 1974, Frock Coats and Epaulets, 1963, 71, America Creates Its Own Literature, 1965, Just One Man, 1968, The Golden Dragon: Alfred the Great and His Times, 1974, 75, 80, Thomas Jefferson: A Strange Case of Mistaken Identity; co-author: Chesapeake Bay in the American Revolution, 1981; also film and TV scripts; co-editor: Place names of Early Portsmouth, 1973, 74; non-fiction editor: New Va. Rvw, 1982-84; contrbr.: articles to N.Y. Times, other newspapers, mags. AA, Coll. William and Mary, 1945, AB, 1961. Editorial writer Portsmouth Star, 1945-46, asso. editor, 1946-48, editorial chief, 1948-54; news editor, editorial writer Virginian-Pilot, Norfolk, 1954-58; freelance writer, 1958—; lectr. thru prof. English, history, journalism, creative writing Old Dominion U., 1961-82; eminent prof. 1982—. Mem. editorial bd. Jamestown Fdn., 1967—; Laureate award Commonwealth of Va., 1981; Liberty Bell Award, 1985. Mem. AG, Poetry Soc. Va. (pres. 1974-75, adv. com. 1976—), Va. Writers Club. Home: Willow Oaks 2901 Tanbark Ln Portsmouth VA 23703

MARAVELAS, PAUL, b. Mpls., Sept. 25, 1956; m. Joni Scheftel, Sept. 3, 1979. Ed. texts pertaining to the invention of the balloon in 1782, 1985. Established pvt. press, 1981. BA, U. Minn., 1981. Curator Univ. Minn., Mpls., 1982-83; curator of printing Murphy's Landing, Shakopee, Mn., 1985; asst. libn., Mpls. Inst. of Arts, 1986-. Mem. Am. Assn. Museums, Am. Printing History Assn., Minn. Hist. Soc. Home: Box 637 Watertown MN 55388

MARCHAND, CECELIA GLORIA, b. Chiefland, FL, Nov. 10, 1933; d. Joe Bryant and Lora Elizabeth (Wynn) Davis; m. Robert Joe Marchand, Sept. 15, 1951 (dec. 1987); children—Yvonne, Beverly, Teresa, Kathleen, Bruce. Author: Once Upon a Rainbow, 1987; contrbr poetry: Hearts on Fire, I Love you, Prickly Pears, Heart Songs, numerous other lit. publs. BA in English, Livingston U., 1974, MA in English, 1975, MLS, 1977. Librarian Demopolis (Ala.)

City Schs., 1982-87. Home: Rt 2 Box 206 Coatopa AL 35470

MARCHITTI, ELIZABETH VAN HOUTEN, b. NJ, Mar. 16, 1931; d. Krine and Anna (Johnson) Van H.; m. John Edward Marchitti, Sept. 8, 1951; children—Jo-Ann, Diane Betty Lynn, Edward. Author poetry pubd. in Quarterly, the lit. mag. of Montclair State Coll., other small pubns. Student Montclair State Coll. Secy. ins. agency, Paterson, NJ, 1948-52; poet, 1981—. Home: 165 Dewey Ave Totowa NJ 07512

MARCUS, ADRIANNE MARIS, b. Everett, MA, March 7, 1935; d. George Z. and Edith Delores (Cohen) Stuhl; m. Warren Marcus, June 13, 1954 (div. Dec. 1981); children—Stacey Ann, Shelby Alice, Sarah Naomi. Author poetry: Lying, Cheating and Stealing, 1984, Child of Earthquake Country, 1980, Faced With Love, 1978, The Moon Is a Marrying Eye, 1969; author books: The Photojournalist, 1975, The Chocolate Bible, 1978. AB, San Francisco State U., 1955, MA, 1963. Awards: NEA Fellowship, 1968. Mem. PEN, PSA, Overseas Press Club. Home: 165 Alpine Terr San Francisco CA 94117

MARCUS, MORTON JAY, b. NYC, Sept. 10, 1936, s. Max Pincus and Rae (Babchek) M.; m. Wilma Kantrowich, Apr. 17, 1958 (div. 1971); children—Jana Lin, Valerie Anna; m. 2d, Donna Mekis, Aug. 17, 1986. Author: Origins (poems), 1969, The Santa Cruz Mountain Poems, 1972, Where the Oceans Cover Us (poems), 1972, The Armies Encamped in the Fields Beyond the Unfinished Avenues: Prose Poems, 1977, Big Winds, Glass Mornings, Shadows Cast by Stars: Poems, 1972-1980, 1981, Pages from a Scrapbook of Immigrants, Poems, 1988, Movie Milestones: A Personal History of Film, 1988. The Brezhnev Memo (novel), 1980. BA, State U. Iowa, 1961; MA, Stanford U., 1967. Mem. faculty Cabrillo Coll., Aptos, Calif., 1968—. Resident fellow MacDowell Colony, Peterboro, N.H., 1975. Mem. PEN. Home: 1325 Laurel St Santa Cruz CA 95060

MARCUS, STANLEY, b. Dallas, April 20, 1905; s. Herbert and Minnie (Lichtenstein) M.; m. Mary Cantrell, Nov. 7, 1932 (dec. 1978); children—Jerrie, Richard and Wendy (twins); m. 2d, Linda Cumber, Mar. 30, 1979. Author: Minding the Store, 1974, My Fashion Business, 1976, Quest for the Best, 1979, His and Hers, 1982; contrbr. articles to Atlantic Monthly, Rdrs. Digest, Pageant, Glamour, Architectural Digest, other periodicals. Publisher Somesuch Press, Inc. (miniature bk. editions). BA, Harvard Univ., 1925, Harvard Bus. Schl., 1926; D. Humanities, So. Meth. Univ., 1965; D. Arts and Ltrs, North Texas State Univ., 1982. With Neiman-Marcus, Dallas, 1926—, exec. VP, 1935-50, pres., 1950-72, chmn. bd., 1972-75, chmn. exec. com., 1975-77, chmn. emeritus, 1977—. Mem. exec. com. Center for the Book, Library of Congress; mem. exec. com. Natl. Council for Arts and Edn.; mem. bd. publs., trustee So. Methodist Univ., also past chmn. library advancement program; past mem. Texas Fine Arts Commission; past pres. Dallas Art Assoc.; chmn. Texas Com. Selection Rhodes scholarship. Named Headliner of Year Dallas Press Club, 1958; Library of Fashion So. Methodist Univ. established in his honor, 1976; Texas Business Hall of Fame, 1984; James K. Wilson Award for Performing Arts, 1985; Natl. Urban League trustee. Home: One Nonesuch Rd Dallas TX 75214

MARCUS, STEVEN, b. NYC, Dec. 13, 1928; s. Nathan and Adeline Muriel (Gordon) M.; m. Gertrud Lenzer, Jan. 20, 1966; 1 son, John Nathaniel. Author: Dickens: From Pickwick to Dombey, 1965, The Other Victorians, 1966, Engels, Manchester and the Working Class, 1974, Representations, 1976, Doing Good, 1978, Freud and The Culture of Psychoanalysis, 1984; assoc. editor: Partisan Rvw. PhD, Columbia U., 1961. Served with AUS, 1954-56. Guggenheim Fdn. fellow, 1967, Rockefeller Fdn. fellow in humanities, 1980-81. Fellow Am. Acad. Arts and Scis., Acad. Lit. Studies. Home: 39 Claremont Ave New York NY 10027

MARDER, DANIEL, b. Chgo., July 10, 1923, s. Hart Samuel and Bertha (Isler) M.; m. Barbara Humphrey, Aug. 7, 1954 (div. 1978); children—Kathleen, Mary, Danya; m. 2d, Roberta Ellison, Aug. 12, 1983; stepchildren—Julie Bird, Lisa Bird. Author: Exiles at Home: A Story of Literature in Nineteenth-Century America, 1985, The Spectrum of Rhetoric, 1986, Safe on Earth and Above, 1964, The Craft of Technical Writing, 1961, 76, Hugh Henry Brackenridge, 1967; ed.: Brackenridge's Incidents of the Insurrection, 1972, A Hugh Henry Brackenridge Reader, 1969, Who Goes to Graduate School, 1961; contrbr. essays to Rhetorical Rvw, Am. Wrtrs. Before 1800, Nature of Identity, other books, publs.; contrbr. stories to Nimrod, December, New Letters, Accent, other lit. mags. Wrkg. on novel. MFA, U. Iowa, 1950; PhD, U. Pitts., 1961. Ed., wrtr. Maxson Corp., NYC, 1951-52; ed.-in-chief Spanish Am. Courier, Madrid, 1953-54; corr. Time-Life, Madrid, 1953-54; prof., head English, U. Tulsa, 1970—; program dir. Tulsa Arts and Humanities Council, 1971-85. Recipient Fulbright award, Skopje, Yugoslavia, 1966-67, Disting. Tech. Communications award Soc. Tech. Wrtrs., 1979. Mem. NASW, MLA, CCCC. Home: 2773 E 56th Pl Tulsa OK 74105

MARG, CAROLINE CATHERINE, b. Watervliet, MI, May 25, 1962; d. Fred. C. and Rita Caroline (Kibler) Woodward; m. Stanley John Marg, Aug. 8, 1981. Contrbr. poem to anthol. Diploma in Occupational Proficiency, Winona Area Vocat. Tech. Inst., Minn., 1981. Office asst. U. Minn. Heart Study, Winona, 1983-84; paper processing tech. Camera Arts, Winona, 1984-86. Sec.-treas. Wilson Vol. Fire Dept. Aux., Wilson, Minn., 1983-84. Mem. Distributive Edn. Clubs Am., C. of C., Downtown Bus. Assn. Home: Rt 1 Box 28 Winona MN 55987

MARGESON, HECTOR, b. New Bedford, MA, Oct. 16, 1924; s. William and Maria (Smith) M.; m. Florence Evelyn Osbourne; children: Eva Louise, George, Hector, Jr. Author: genl interest column, weekly newspaper. Student Cape Cod Community Coll./Mass. Maritime Academy, 1 yr. Constuction inspector, U.S. Army Corps of Engineers, 18 years. Recipient ltrs. of commendation, U.S. Army Corps of Engineers, testimonial Commonwealth of Mass., svs. WWII. Address: 30 Maple St Buzzards Bay MA 02532

MARGIE, JOYCE DALY, b. Washington, May 29, 1940; d. Harry John and Maryhelen (Dillon) D.; m. Robert Paul Margie, May 18, 1968; children—Paul, Andrew. Ed., Dialogues in Nutrition (nwsltr.), 1974-79, The Clinical Viewpoint, 1981-83; author: (with others) The Mayo Clinic Renal Diet Cookbook, 1975, (with J.C. Hunt) The Hypertension Diet Cookbook, 1978, (with others) Living Better: Recipes for a Healthy Heart, 1980, (with T.B. Van Itallie) Finding Your Thin Self, 1982, (with A. Block) Nutrition and The Cancer Patient, 1983, (with P.J. Palumbo) The Complete Diabetic Cookbook, TBP 1987; contrbr.: Present Knowledge in Nutrition, 1977, Proceedings—First Intl. Cong. on Nutrition and Renal Disease, 1977, Hypertension Update: Mechanisms, Epidemiology, Evaln. and Mgt., 1980, Chronic Renal Disease, 1985. BS, Coll. of St. Elizabeth, 1962; MS, U. MD, 1972. Dietitian, Wash. Hosp. Ctr., 1962-63, 65-66, D.C. Genl. Hosp., 67-68; research nutritionist, Mayo Clinic, Rochester, MN, 1968-72; ed. Dialogues in Nutrition, Health Learning Syst., Linhurst, NJ, 1974-79, The Clinical Viewpoint, McGraw-Hill, NYC, 1981-83; consultant govt. & industry on devel. health & med. edn. progs., 1973—. Mem. AG, profl. orgns. Home: 135 Rotary Dr Summit NJ 07901

MARGOLIES, LUISE, b. NYC., Sept. 7, 1947; d. Albert and June (Ackerman) M.; m. Graziano Gasparini, July 7, 1970; 1 son, Graziano Andrey. Author: Princes of the Earth: Subcult Diversity in a Mexican Municipality, 1979, The Venezuelan Peasant in Country & City, 1983; (with G. Gasparini) Inca Archiecture (Best Academic Book of Yr., Choice, 1983), 1984, Paraguanna, 1986, Arquitectura Popular de Venezuela, 1987. Wrkg. on guidebook to social sci. research in Latin Am. B.A., Barnard Coll.; B.Li., Oxford U.; M.A., Columbia U., 1969, Ph.D., 1972. Prof. anthropology Central U. Venezuela, Caracas, 1979—; dir. Ediciones Venezuela de Antropologia, Caracas, 1979—. Office: Apartado 3305 Caracas 1010 Venezuela

MARGOLIS, GARY FRANCIS, b. Great Falls, MT, May 24, 1945, s. Edward Howard and Pearl (Binen) M.; m. Wendy Dorothea Lynch, May 24, 1975; children—Samuel, Ariana. Author: The Day We Still Stand Here, 1983, Falling Awake, 1986. BA, Middlebury (Vt.) Coll., 1967; PhD, SUNY-Buffalo, 1971. Dir. counseling and human relations Middlebury Coll., 1972—. Millay Colony for Arts resident, 1976; grantee Vt. Council on Arts, 1980; Robert Frost fellow Bread Loaf Wrtrs.' Conf., 1982. Home: RD 2 Box 1500 Middlebury VT 05753

MARGOLIS, JOSEPH, b. Newark, May 16, 1924; s. Harry J. and Bluma (Goldfarb) M.; m. Clorinda Goltra Hunter, Aug. 24, 1968; children—Ann, Paul, Michael, Jennifer, Ellen. Author: Philosophy Looks at the Arts, 1962, rev. ed., 1978, The Language of Art and Art Criticism, 1965, Psychotherapy and Morality, 1966, Contemporary Ethical Theory, 1966, An Introduction to Philosophical Inquiry, 1968, 2d ed., 1978, Fact and Existence, 1969, Values and Conduct, 1971, Knowledge and Existance, 1973, Negativities: The Limits of Life, 1975, Art and Philosophy, 1980; Persons and Minds, 1978, Culture and Cultural Entities, 1983, Philosophy of Psychology, 1984; mem. adv. bd.: Intl. Studies in Philosophy and Medicine, 1982—; editor: Philos. Monographs, 1975-80, Aesthetics and the Arts, 1980—, Mt. Adams Rvw, 1970-71; cons. editor: Jnl Theory of Social Behavior, 1976—; contrbg. editor: Book Forum, 1972—; cons.: Jnl Critical Analysis, 1973—; cons. editor: Behaviorism, 1976—; mem. adv. bd.: Intl. Studies in Philosophy and Medicine, 1982—; adv. editor: Applied Philosophy, 1982—; editorial bd.: Philosophy and Tech. Ann., 1976—, Speculative Letters, 1978—, The Monist, 1982—, New Ideas in Philosophy, 1982—. BA, Drew U., 1947; MA, Columbia, 1950, PhD, 1953. Served with AUS, 1943-45. Decorated Purple Heart. Home: 500 Catharine St Philadelphia PA 19147

MARGOT, LESLIE, see Lang, Miriam

MARGULIS, JERRY, b. Newark, Dec. 7, 1929; s. James and Elly (Orshefsky) M.; m. Barbara Sue Jelling, Feb. 18, 1961; children—Jeffrey, Stuart. Contrbr. to Phila. Inquirer Daily News, Round Table, Orben's Current Comedy, The Jokesmith, Contemp. Comedy; writer comedy material: Off the Wall, NJ Cable TV, 1982, scripts for comedienne Hilda Vincent, 1983—. AB, Rutgers U., 1952; MA, Montclair State Coll., 1961. Sales admin. Plextone Corp. Am., Newark, 1955-58; Engl. tchr. Irvington (NJ) H.S., 1959-65, Columbia H.S., Maplewood, NJ, 1965—. River City Pubns. award, 1984. Mem. ednl. orgns. Home: 7 Concord Dr Livingston NJ 07039

MARIANI, PAUL LOUIS, b. NYC, Feb. 29, 1940; s. Paul Patrick and Harriet (Green) Mariani; m. Eileen Mary Spinosa, Aug. 24, 1963; children—Paul Philip, Mark Thomas, John Matthew. Author: A Commentary on the Complete Poems of Gerard Manley Hopkins, 1970, William Carlos Williams: The Poet and His Critics, 1975, William Carlos Williams: A New World Naked, 1981; Timing Devices: Poems, 1979, Crossing Cocytus, 1982, Prime Mover, 1985, A Usable Past: Essays on Modern & Contemporary Poetry, 1984. BA, Manh. College, 1962; MA, Colgate U., 1964, PhD, CUNY, 1968. Lectr. Colgate U., Hamilton, NY, 1963-64; asst. prof., John Jay Coll., NYC, 1967-68; asst. prof., U. of Mass., Amherst, 1968-71, assoc. prof., 1971-75, prof., 1975—. Awards: Guggenheim fellow, 1985-86; NEH fellow, 1974-75, 1981-82 NEA fellow, 1983-84. Mem. PSA, MLA. Home: 24 Main St Montague MA 01351

MARIE, JANET, see Roberts, Janet Marie

MARINE, GENE, b. San Francisco, Dec. 31, 1926; s. Fred and Gloria (Rodrigues) M.; children—April, Craig, Sheila, Kevin. Author: America the Raped, 1969, The Black Panthers, 1969, A Male Guide to Women's Liberation, 1972; co-author: Food Pollution, 1972, also numerous articles; columnist: East Bay Express, 1983—. Student, San Francisco State Coll., 1948-49. News analyst radio sta. KPFA, Berkeley, Calif., 1951-57; West coast corr. The Nation, 1954-64; assoc. editor Frontier mag., 1957-59; pub. affairs and program dir. radio sta. KPFK, Los Angeles, 1959-60; news dir. radio sta. KPFA, 1960-62; contrbg. editor Pacific Scene, 1964-65; with CBS News, 1964; sr. editor Ramparts mag., 1966-69. Served with USMCR, 1943-46. Recipient Radio-TV Newswriting award (Sigma Delta Chi, 1960). Mem. AG, Bay Area Jazz Soc. Address: 1740 Rose St Berkeley CA 94703

MARINE, MICHAEL RAY, (Mad Mike), b. Washington, Mar. 12, 1954; s. Melvin Irving Marine and Elaine (Bresler) Tanenbaum; m. Louise Ann Kadish, Apr. 6, 1979; children—Lenny, Kaen, Rachel. Author: 101 Ways to Get Rid of a Lettuce Head Doll, 1984. Wrkg. on diet book, Just Say No to Food. B.S., Cornell U., 1976; M. Public Health, Tulane U., 1978. Accounting mgr. Georgetown U., Washington, 1983-85; dir. fiscal affair Washington Home, 1985-87; controller Decorating Den Systems, Bethesda, MD, 1987—. Home: 4905 Falstone Ave Chevy Chase MD 20815

MARION, DOUGLAS WELCH, b. Des Moines, May 9, 1944, s. Francis Orville and Alice Virginia (Welch) M.; m. Patricia Fisher, Sept. 2, 1967; children—Douglas Welch Jr., Ann Welch. Contrbr. stories Friends mag. BA, Parsons Coll., 1980; postgrad., Fresno State U. With Argus Pub. Co., Los Angeles, 1976—, ed. Super Chevy mag., 1980—. Office: Argus 12301 Wilshire Blvd Los Angeles CA 90025

MARION, JOHN FRANCIS, b. Norfolk, VA, Feb. 23, 1922; s. Everett Edward and Aileen (McCarthy) M. Author: Lucrezia Bori of the Metropolitan Opera, 1962, Bicentennial City, 1974, Philadelphia Medica, 1976, Famous and Curious Cemeteries, 1977, The Charleston Story, 1978, The Fine Old House, 1980, Within These Walls, 1984, Walking Tours of Historic Philadelphia, 1984,. BA, Pa. State U., 1948. Editor Commercial America mag., Phila., 1948-49, Philadelphia mag., 1949-50; dir. publicity J.B. Lippincott Co., Phila., 1952-53; editor Graphic Arts Rvw, Phila., 1953-55; head John F. Marion Lit. Agcy., Phila., 1958-62; editor-in-chief Chilton Book co., Phila., 1962-72. Served with AUS, 1943-46. Home: 1836 Delancey Pl Philadelphia PA 19103

MARK, ANGELA S., b. Astoria, NY, Oct. 23, 1960, d. Louis K. and Edith M. (Fierro) Mark; m. Michael W. Shores, Sept. 14, 1985. Author: Jungle Warrior, 1984, After the Rockets Have Fallen, 1985, Established Patterns of Living, 1985; contrbr. to: Cracker Chronicles, Zontar mag., Bag of Wire Expose; ed., pub. Am. Living mag. (with Michael Shores); Allston, Mass., 1982—. Student New Eng. Schl. Art and Design, Boston, 1979-80, Schl. of Mus. of Fine Art, Boston, 1980-82. Gallery asst. Gallery In the Sq., Boston, 1981-82; graphic asst. Garber Travel, Boston, 1982—. Office: American Living Box 901 Allston MA 02134

MARKFORT, ANNE MARIE, b. Norfolk, VA, Aug. 16, 1950; d. Francis Sylvester and Joan Marie (Witschen) Markfort; m. Larry Edward Nelson; children—Leo Francis Markfort, Edward Jon Markfort, Matthew August Markfort. Contrbr. articles to newsletters including Lower Minn. River Valley Geneological Newsletter, Greater Twin Cities Sumac Cairn Terrier Newsletter. Wrkg. on family history, non-fiction. BA in Biology, St. Cloud State U., 1978. Mem. LWV. Home: 8250 Old Hwy 169 Blvd Jordan MN 55352

MARKHAM, MARION M., b. Chgo., June 12, 1929; d. William Joseph and Marion (Dammann) Bork; m. Robert Bailey Markham, Dec. 26, 1955; children: Susan Markham Andersen, Jane Markham Madden. Author: Escape from Velos, 1981, The Halloween Candy Mystery, 1982, The Christmas Present Mystery, 1984, The Thanksgiving Day Parade Mystery, 1986; contrbr. to The Ocean Almanac, Miniature Mysteries. BS in Speech, Northwestern U., 1953. Continuity dir. WTVP-TV, Decatur, Ill., 1953-54; TV bus. mgr. Earle Ludgin Adv., Chgo., 1955-58. Pres., Pub. Library, Northbrook, Ill., 1981-83, bd. dirs. 1976-86. Mem. MWA, AG, Soc. Children's Book Writers. Address: 2415 Newport Rd Northbrook IL 60062

MARKOWSKI,, BENEDICT STEPHEN,, b. Hamtramck, MI, Mar. 5, 1932; s. Lawrence J. and Gladys Joanna (Jaskowiak) M. Author: Carissima (lyric drama), 1980—; ed.: Behold! The Polish Americans (by Joseph Wytrwal), 1977, Polish-Black Encounter: A History of Polish and Black Relations in America Since 1619 (by Wytrwal), 1982; founding ed.: The Eaglet (tri-annual organ of Polish Genealogical Soc. Mich.), 1980—. BA, Central Mich. U., 1954—; MLS, George Peabody Coll. Tchrs., 1956. With Detroit Public Library, 1957—, archivist Burton hist. collection, 1974—. Home: 19311 Orleans Ave Detroit MI 48203

MARKOWSKI, MICHAEL A., b. Harrisburg, PA, May 23, 1947; s. Anton Edmond and Catherine (Sasa) M.; m. Roberta Ann Telford, May 26, 1974. Author: The Hang Gliders Bible, 1976, The Ency. of Homebuilt Aircraft, 1979, Ultralight Aircraft, 1981, 82, 83, Ultralight Flight, 1982, Ultralight Technique, 1983, ARV—The Ency. of Aircraft Recreatl. Vehicles, 1984;; contrbr. articles to: Scientific Am., Popular Science, & other profl. & genl. int. mags. BS in Aerospace Engr., Penn. State, 1968. Engr./scientist Douglas Aircraft, Long Beach, CA, 1968; research engr. Sikorsky Aircraft, Stratford, CT, 1968-70; design engr. Atkins & Merrill, Maynard, MA, 1970-72; pres./chf. engr. two hang glider mfrs., MA, 1973-75; sales engr. Saxton Air Systems, Harrisburg, PA, 1976-81; pub./ed. Ultralight Pubs., Hummelstown, PA, 1981—. Home: One Oakglade Cr Hummelstown PA 17036

MARKS, ADA GREINER, b. Hawarden, IA, Aug. 19, 1896, d. Theodore Augustus and Emma Jane (Mason) Greiner; m. Raymond Teeple, May 30, 1920 (dec. 1983); children—Margaret, Barbara. Author: These are my Hills, 1971, Scent of Lilacs, 1985; contrbr. to Ted Malone's Scrapbook, From Sea to Sea in Song, Am. Mosaic, Quaderni di Poesia, Centri studi e Scambi Internationali, numerous other anthologies, poetry to newspapers. BS, teaching cert. in music, Partsons Coll., 1918. Recipient numerous state and local poetry awards. Mem. Natl. Fedn. State Poetry Socs., League Minn. Poets, Mpls. Poetry Soc., Chaparral Poets. Home: 3520 12th Ave S 21 Minneapolis MN 55407

MARKS, FRANK HENRY, b. Washington, Jan. 25, 1898; s. Henry and Etta (Goldstein) M. Weekly columnist: Chgo. Tribune, 1969-70. Contrbr. short stories, poems, non-fiction articles to mags., law jnls. newspapers. Wkg. on non-fiction articles. B.S., Swarthmore Coll., 1922; M.S., George Washington U., 1923, LL.B., 1926. Commissioned U.S. Army Res., 1925, advanced through ranks to lt. col., retired, 1960; free-lance wrtr., 1969—. Mem. NWC, Sigma Delta Xi. Home: 4940 E End Ave Chicago IL 60615

MARKS, RUTH ANTOINETTE, b. Slater, WY, Dec. 6, 1920; d. Arthur Frederick and Myrtle Catherine (Houlehan) M. Contrbr. numerous short stories, non-fiction articles to mags. B.A., Northwest Nazarene Coll., 1952; M.Edn., Coll. Id., 1959; Ed.D., Northern Colo. U., 1969. State elem. supvr. Dept. Edn., Boise, ID, 1963-70; prof. edn. Boise State U., 1970-83, retired; free-lance wrtr., 1983—. Home: 4517 Shirley St Boise ID 83703

MARKSON, DAVID M., b. Albany, NY, Dec. 20, 1927; s. Samuel A. and Florence (Stone) M.; m. Elaine Kretchmar, Sept. 30, 1956 (sep. 1982); children—Johanna, Jed. Author: The Ballad of Dingus Magee, 1966; Going Down, 1970; Springer's Progress, 1977; Malcolm Lowry's Volcano: Myth, Symbol, Meaning, 1978. BA, Union Coll., 1950; MA, Columbia U., 1952. Editor Dell Books, NYC, 1953-54; asst. prof. LI Univ., Bklyn., 1964-66; lectr. Columbia Univ., NYC, 1979-84, 1986. Served to s/sgt., US Army, 1946-48. Fellow Centro Mexicano de Escritores, Mex., DF, 1960-61. Mem. PEN. Address: 215 W 10th St New York NY 10014

MARKUN, PATRICIA MALONEY, (Mrs. David Joseph Markun), b. Chisholm, MN, Aug. 24, 1924; d. Andrew Michael and Helen Edith (Ryan) Maloney; m. David Joseph Markun, June

14, 1948; children—Sybil, Meredith, David Joseph, Paul. Author: The First Book of the Panama Canal, 1957, 62, rev. ed., 1979, The Secret of El Baru, 1958, The First Book of Mining, 1960, The First Book of Central America and Panama, 1963, 72, 82, The First Book of Politics, 1969; editor: The Future of American Oil, 1976, Witnesses for Oil, 1976. BA magna cum laude, jnlsm., Univ. Minn., 1945. News wrtr., announcer, WMFG (Hibbing, MN), KSTP (St. Paul), WCCO (Mpls.), 1942-45; ed. employees mag., Elec. Machinery Mfg. Co., 1945-46; pub. relations Mpls. Inst. Arts, 1946-48; exec. ed. Funk & Wagnalls Yng. Students Encyc., 1971-72; ed. assoc. Assn. for Childhood Intl., 1973-75; exec. ed. Petroleum Today mag., 1975-78; mgr. corp. spkr. activities, Fed. Home Loan Mort. Corp., 1979-85. Freelance wrtr. 1948—. Mem. Wash. Children's Book Guild. Home: 4405 W St NW Washington DC 20007

MARKUS, JULIA, b. Jersey City; divorced. Author: (novels) La Mora, 1976; Uncle, 1978; American Rose, 1981; Friends along the Way, 1985; ed.: Casa Guidi Windows (Elizabeth Barrett Browning), 1978. Wrkg. on novel. BA in Comparative Lit., Boston U., MA in Comparative Lit.; PhD in English, U. Md., 1976. Assoc. prof. English and Creative writing Hofstra U., Hempstead, N.Y., 1981—. Recipient Houghton Mifflin lit. award, 1977; NEA fellow, 1979. Mem. PEN, AG. Home: Box A434 Madison Sq Sta New York NY 10159

MARLOWE, JEANNE, b. Huntington, WV, Jan. 10, 1942; d. Wilbur Winston and Della Mae (Noble) Thacker; m. Byron Henry Marlowe, Feb. 12, 1961 (div. Sept. 1971); children—Craig, Julie, Terri. Author: Directory of Singles Groups in Central Ohio, 7 eds., 1979-86. Wrkg. on: Meeting People Without Hanging Out Where You'd Rather Not Be. BA, Bowling Green State U., 1967, MA, 1969; postgrad. Ohio State U., 1968-70. Contrb. ed. Living Single Mag., Columbus, OH, 1982-85; pub./ed. Columbus Single Scene Mag. (OH), 1985—. Home: 92 Orchard Hill Ct Gahanna OH 43230

MARSCOT, ANN, see Huetteman, Susan Ann Bice

MARSH, CAROLE, b. Atlanta, Dec. 22, 1946; d. Mason S. and Dorothy (Byrd) Spence; m. Robert Longmeyer, Dec. 26, 1980; children—Michele Marsh, Michael Marsh. Author: history mystery books (12 titles), 1979-86, Crosstaff: A Fictional Journal of Eleanor Dare, 1982 (nominee Am. Bk. Awards), Thistleworth: Poetry to Read Aloud, 400!, A Mystery Musical for America's 400th Anniv. of the First Colony, 250 other titles; contrbr. numerous mags., newspapers. Pres., Marsh Media Methods, Rocky Mount, NC, 1972-79; pres. Gallopade: Pub. Group, Bath, NC, 1979—. Office: Gallopade Bath NC 27808

MARSH, FLORENCE GERTRUDE, b. Rochester, NY., Sept. 15, 1916; d. Charles D. and Ruth (Galloway) M. Author: Wordsworth's Imagery: A Study in Poetic Vision, 1952; contbr. article to profl. jnls. AB, Mt. Holyoke Coll., 1937; MA, U. Tenn., 1943; PhD, Yale, 1951. Mem. MLA. Home: 4883 Country side Rd Lyndhurst OH 44124

MARSH, JUDITH ANN, b. Detoit, July 2, 1941; d. James Herbert and Verna Rhoda (Fletcher) DuVall; m. Lowell D. Marsh, Ma. 10, 1964; children—Barbara, Michael, Jeffery, Timothy. Poetry in anthologies. Wrkg. on poery, short story. Grad. Newspaper Inst. Am., 1984. Owner, mgr. The Choice Shoppe, Evart, Mich., 1980-81. Home: 2690 E Three Mile Rd Evart MI 49631

MARSH, RICHARD PHILIP, b. Detroit, Aug. 17, 1961; s. Edward Roman and Josephine Agnes (Darmofial) M. Author play: Death for Dessert, 1985. Contrbr. articles to mags., newsletters. Wrkg. on short stories, novel. B.Genl. Sci., U. Mich. Dearborn. Staff wrtr. Dearborn Press & Guide, 1982-84; entertainment ed., 1984-87, mng. ed., 1985-87, features ed., 1987—. Home: 3541 Academy Dearborn MI 48124

MARSHALL, JOHN, b. Berkeley, CA, July 23, 1913; s. John and Hazel (Knowles) M.; divorced; children—Jackie Lou, John Gary. Author fiction: The Fatal Triangle, 1981, 2d ed., 1988. Wrkg. on new novel, The Fatal Triangle Book II. Grad. public schls., Oakland, CA. Municipal mgr. City of McAlester, OK, 1978-81; engineer North Am. Aviation Co., Calif., 1958-71. Served with U.S. Marine Corps, 1935-38. Home: 505 S 15th McAlester OK 74501

MARSHALL, LOREN DEAN, b. Lewistown, MT, Apr. 30, 1953, s. Donald R. and Ellen Dean (Brown) M.; m. Rebecca J. Brocies, Sept. 21, 1980. Author: (with Stephen LaFevers) Prehospital Care for the EMT Intermediate, 1984. Contrbr. articles to profl. jnls., newspapers. Ed. (with others): Aeromedical Evacuations in Alaska, 1985. Wrkg. on Introduction to Paramedic Practice. B.A. in English, Harvard U., 1975; A.A.S. in Paramedical Technology, Anchorage Commun. oll., 1987. Emergency med. technician Salvation Army, Anchorage, 1978-79; emergency med. technician instr. Southern Region Emergency Med. Services, Anchorage, 1981; paramedic Anchorage Fire Dept., 1981—. Recipient Maggie, Western Pubs. Assn., 1987. Mem. Alaska Paramedical Assn., Intl. Assn. Fire Fighters. Home: 1705 Bartlett Dr Anchorage AK 99507

MARSHALL, MURIEL, b. Nara Visa, NM; d. Eber Robert and Leta Inez (Chamberlain) Edwards; children—Hal, Linda, Crystal. Author: (novel) Lovely Rebel, 1950; (regional history) Uncompahgre, 1981, Red Hole in Time, 1988. Contrbr. fiction and non-fiction to mags. including Reader's Digest, Sunset, Woman's Day, others. Feature ed.: Delta County Ind., Delta, CO, 1962-77. Wrkg. on novels, Stranger in the Mirror and Chief Yes. Home: 2004 I-50 Rd Austin CO 81410

MARSHALL, MYRNA ESTEY, b. Syracuse, NY, Oct. 27, 1938; d. Elmer Erwin and Emily Adele (Rowley) Estey; m. James D. Marshall, June 24, 1957; children-Diana, Denise, Joe, Sarah. Author: Something Worth Saving, 1987; columnist: Assn. Surplus Dealers Trade News, 1986-87. Contrbr. articles to mags. Wrkg on book on the care and feeding of a WWACA (women who attend church alone). Grad. public schls., Cazenovia, NY. Sales mgr. Peacock-Southwest Cordage, Tulsa, OK, 1982-84, v.p., 1984-87. Coord. Professionalism in Writing Schl., Tulsa, 1988. Mem. Tulsa Christian Wrtrs. (pres. 1985-87). Home: 1320 N 157th E Ave Tulsa OK 74116

MARSHALL, SALLY ANN, b. Detroit, Nov. 19, 1942; d. Edward Lloyd and Dorothy May (Thomas) Banks; m. Kenneth Lewis Decker, Aug. 15, 1964 (div. 1975); children: Jennifer Lee, James Leroy; m. 2d, Earl Allen (Jack) Marshall, Apr. 1982 (sep.). Contrbr. poetry to Wellspring, Poetry Today, Pudding, Byline, Up Against the Wall, Mother, Manna, Starline, Spring Harvest, others. BA, Calif. State-Long Beach, 1965, MA, Cal Poly, Pomona, 1987; tchr. Arcadia Schl. Dist., Calif, 1965-66, 67-68; Azusa Unified Schl. Dist., Calif, 1968—. Mem. Sigma Tau Delta, Calif. Tchrs. Assn., NEA. Address: 167 Lowell Ave Glendora CA 91740

MARSHALL-NADEL, NATHALIE, b. Pitts., Nov. 10, 1932, d. Clifford Benjamin and Clarice (Stille) Marshall; m. Robert Alfred Van Buren, May 1, 1952 (div. 1965); children—Christine Van Buren Popovic, Clifford Marshall, Jennifer Katheryn Van Buren Lake. Poet, designer, chapbook: Vibrations on Revelations, 1973; The Firebird, 1982; author: Be Organized for College, 1980; ed., designer: Court Theaters of Europe, 1982; contrbr. articles, poetry to numerous publs.; illustrator: The Desert: What Lives There, 1972. AFA, Silvermine Coll. Art, 1967; BFA, U. Miami, 1977, MA, 1982, PhD, 1982. Chief artist Rockefeller U., NYC, 1973-75; mem. faculty Barry U., Miami Shores, Fla., 1979-81, U. Miami, Coral Gables, Fla., 1977-81, Nova U., Ft. Lauderdale, Fla., 1981-86; prof. art, Arts Div., Old College, Reno, NV, 1986—. Mem. MLA. Home: 2754 Powder Dr Reno NV 89503

MARTEKA, VINCENT JAMES, JR., b. Uxbridge, MA, Jan. 29, 1936; s. Vincent James and Genevieve (Ramian) M.; m. Janet Littler, May 26, 1962; children—Andrew, Peter, Katherine. Author: Bionics, 1965, Mushrooms: Wild and Edible, 1980. BS, geol., Univ. Mass., 1958; MS, Rennsselaer Poly. Inst., 1959. Editor U.S. Geol. Survey, 1959-60; sci. wrtr., news ed. Sci. Service, 1961-63; sci. ed. My Weekly Rdr., 1964-65; ed. Current Sci., 1966—. Served with AUS, 1960. Mem. Natl. Assoc. Sci. Writers, Mycological Soc. Am., Natl. Audubon Soc. Home: Jobs Pond Rd Portland CT 06480

MARTH, ELMER HERMAN, b. Jackson, WI, Sept. 11, 1927; s. William Frederick and Irma Alvina (Bublitz) M.; m. Phyllis Eileen Menge, Aug. 10, 1957. Ed., Jnl. of Food Protection, 1967—, Standard Methods for the Exam. of Dairy Products, 14th ed., 1978; co-author: Low-Temp. Preserv. of Foods and Living Matter, 1973, Staphylococci and Their Significance in Foods, 1976 (Russian ed., 1980), Microbial Survival in the Environment: Bacteria and Rickettsiae Important in Human and Animal Health, 1984; author, co-author over 450 articles in domestic & foreign sci. jnls. BS, U. WI, 1950, MS, 1952, PhD, 1954. Instr., U. WI, Madison, 1954-57; research microbiol., Kraft, Inc., Glenview, IL, 1957-66; assoc. prof. U. WI, Madison, 1966-71, prof., 1971—. Meritorious svc. award, Amer. Public Health Assn., 1977, 83, num. others. Mem. num. profl. orgns. inclg. Council of Biology Editors. Office: Food Sci 1605 Linden Dr Madison WI 53706

MARTIN, ALEJANDRO, see Martin, Alexander Stella

MARTIN, ALEXANDER STELLA, (Alejandro Martin), b. Zapotlanejo, Jalisco, Mexico, Dec. 12, 1929, s. Alessandro Sciabola and Nora Margret (Davis) Martini; m. Dolores Velazquez y Gonzalez, Aug. 15, 1962 (div. 1971); 1 dau., Maria Consuelo Martin y Velazquez. Author: Civismo Comparativo de los Gobiernos de los Estados Unidos y Mexico. Wrkg. on history of Mexico. MA, U. Conn., 1958; PhD, Sussex (Eng.) Technol. U., 1984. Bilingual tchr. San Ysidro (Calif.) Schl. Dist., 1968—; poet-in-residence San Ysidro Fedn. Tchrs., 1985. Mem. AAP. Home: 181 Willow Rd Apt 27 San Ysidro CA 92073

MARTIN, ANN MATTHEWS, b. Princeton, NJ, Aug. 12, 1955; d. Henry Read and Edith Aiken (Matthews) M. Author children's bks.: Bummer Summer, 1983, Just You and Me, 1983, Inside Out, 1984, Stage Fright, 1984, Me and Katie (The Pest), 1985, With You and Without You, 1986, Missing Since Monday, 1986, Just a Summer Romance, 1987, The Baby-sitters Clubs, bks. 1, 2, 3, 1986, 4, 5, 6, 1987. AB, Smith Coll., 1977. Tchr., Plumfield Schl., Noroton, CT, 1977-78; editorial asst. Archway Paperbacks, NYC, 1978-80; copywriter TAB Bk. Club, Scholastic, Inc., NYC, 1980-82, ed., 1982-83; sr. ed. bks. for yg. rdrs. Bantam Bks., NYC, 1983-85; freelance writer, ed., NYC, 1985—. Children's Choice Award, 1984. Mem. AG, SCBW. Address: 425 Park Ave So 4D New York NY 10016

MARTIN, DEAN FREDERICK, b. Woodburn, IA, Apr. 6, 1933; s. Herman A. and Frances M. (Rausis) M.; m. Barbara Bursa, Dec. 22, 1956; children—Diane, Bruce, John, Paul, Biran, Eric. Author: (with Barbara B. Martin) Coordination Compounds, 1964, (with Therald Moeller) Laboratory Chemistry, 1965, Marine Chemistry, 2 vols., 1968, 70; editor: (with George M. Padilla) Marine Parmacognosy, 1973. AB, Grinnell Coll., 1955; PhD, Pa. State U., 1958. NSF postdoctoral fellow Univ. Coll., London, 1958-59. Home: 3402 Valencia Rd Tampa FL 33618

MARTIN, DENISE BELISLE, b. West Springfield, MA, Sept. 15, 1940; d. Paul E. and Grace A. (St. Onge) Belisle; m. Roger H. Martin, Jr., Aug. 18, 1962 (div.); daughter—Sara B. BA magna cum laude, Smith Coll., 1961; MA, Radcliffe Coll., 1962; postgrad., Univ. Minnesota, 1968-70. Volunteer Peace Corps, Colombia, 1966-68; Soho Wkly. News, 1976-77, assoc. ed., 1977-78, mng. ed., 1978, arts ed., 1979; assoc. ed. Portfolio, 1979-80, exec. dir., 1980. Mem. Art Table, Phi Beta Kappa. Home: 35 Bond St New York NY 10012

MARTIN, DIANE D., b. Cin., d. Christian Herman Paul Emil and Cornelia Josephine (Van Schouwen) Dettmer; m. Richard C. Martin, 1957 (div. 1980); children—Katherine Elizabeth, Kristyne Suzanne Van Schouwen. Author: Be Your Own Astrologer, 1984, Bring to the Boil and Simmer Gently, 1985; ed. Zodiac Pattern Book, 1985, Of Tarragon, Thyme, and Tauving, 1985. Wrkg. on astrology book, herb book, art book. BA, Vassar Coll., Poughkeepsie, NY, 1957. Pub., wrtr., ed. Scriptorium Press, Alfred, NY, since 1983. Pres. Alfred Community Theatre Orgn. of Renovators, 1980—. Mem. Herb Soc. Am. (dir. 1977-79). Home: 71 S Main St Alfred NY 14802

MARTIN, DON ROGER, b. Barre, VT, Oct. 22, 1945; s. Lester Guy and Shirley Mae (Blanchard) M.; m. Marilyn Carol Blanchard, Dec. 1970 (div. Feb. 1986); children: Stacy Scott, Tina Mae; m. Joan Marie Marie Nuopponen, Feb. 20, 1986; children: Robin Rosanne, Dana Marie, Wendy Denise. Author: (poetry) May Tend To Incriminate Me, 1980, A Friend among Strangers, 1981, Specimens, 1981, Classic Summer, 1982, No Dreams for Sale, 1983, Minor League Veteran, 1986; contrbr. to Samisdat, Yellow Butterfly, Prophetic Voices, Fire!, Salome, Fate, Rolling Stone, Taurus, Jump River, Small Press rvws, Gypsy, The Pub, Kindred Spirit. Home: 5 Pleasant St Randolph VT 05060

MARTIN, GEORGE (WHITNEY), b. NYC, Jan. 25, 1926; s. George Whitney and Agnes Wharton (Hutchinson) M. Author: The Opera Companion, A Guide for the Casual Operagoer, 1961, 3d edit., 1982, The Battle of the Frogs and Mice, An Homeric Fable, 1962, 2d edit., 1987, Verdi, His Music, Life and Times, 1963, 3d edit., 1983, Spanish edit., 1984, The Red Shirt and The Cross of Savoy, The Story of Italy's Risorgimento, 1748-1871, 1969, Causes and Conflicts, The Centennial History of the Association of the Bar of the City of New York, 1870-1970, 1970, Madam Secretary: Frances Perkins, 1976, The Companion to Twentieth Century Opera, 1979, 2d edit., 1984, The Damrosch Dynasty, America's First Family of Music, 1983, Aspects of Verdi, 1987; contrbr. articles to profl. jnls., mags. BA, Harvard, 1948; student, Trinity Coll., Cambridge (Eng.) U., 1950; LL.B., U. Va., 1953. Engaged in writing, 1959—. Address: 333 E 68th St New York NY 10021

MARTIN, GEORGE RAYMOND RICHARD, b. Bayonne, NJ, Sept. 20, 1948; s. Raymond and Margaret (Brady) M.; m. Gale Burnick, Nov. 15, 1975 (div. Dec. 1979). Author sci. fiction: A Song for Lya, 1976, Songs of Stars and Shadows, 1977, Sandkings, 1981, Dying of the Light, 1977, Windhaven, 1981, Fevre Dream, 1982, The Armageddon Rag, 1983, Songs the Deadmen Sing, 1983; editor: New Voices I, 1977, NV II, 1979, NV III, 1980, NV IV, 1981; contrbr. short stories to mags. BS summa cum laude, Northwestern U., 1970; MS cum laude, 1971. Journalism intern Medill News Service, Washington, 1971; sportswriter, pub. relations officer N.J. Dept. Parks, Bayonne, 1971; instr. journalism Clarke Coll., Dubuque, Iowa, 1976-78, writer-in-res., 1978-79; founder, chmn. Windy City Sci. Fiction Writers' Workshop, Chgo., 1972-76. Mem. SFWA. Home: 102 San Salvador Santa Fe NM 87501

MARTIN, HAROLD HARBER, b. Commerce, GA, Sept. 17, 1910; s. Gabriel Pierce and Mary Edna Augusta (Harber) M.; m. Boyce Lokey, Apr. 23, 1935; children—Marian Hamilton, Harold Harber, John P., Nancy Boyce. Author: (with Gen. M.B. Ridgeway) Soldier, 1956, Father's Day Comes Once a Year and Then it Always Rains, 1960, Starlifter, 1972, Ralph McGill, Reporter, 1973, Three Strong Pillars, 1974, History of Georgia, 1977, Atlanta Mayor William B. Hartsfield, 1978, This Happy Isle, 1978, Harold Martin Remembers a Place in the Mountains, 1979; humor Cats, Dogs, Children and Other Small Creatures, 1980; A Good Man, A Great Dream: D.W. Brooks of Gold Kist, 1982; History of Columbus, GA, Bank and Trust Co., 1984. AB in Journalism, U. Ga., 1933. Sports and feature writer, Atlanta Georgian and Sunday Am., 1932-39; feature writer, columnist Atlanta Constn., 1939-74; contrbr. to Harper's, Collier's, Liberty, Sat. Eve. Post, 1944-50; assoc. editor Sat. Eve. Post, 1951-53, contrbg. editor, 1958-63, editor-at-large, 1964-69; lectr. journalism Ga. State U., Atlanta, 1972—. Served to captain USMCR, 1943-45. Decorated Bronze Star; recipient award for non-fiction Southeastern Writers Assn., 1979. Address: 2895 Normandy Dr NW Atlanta GA 30305

MARTIN, HERBERT WOODWARD, b. Birmingham, AL, Oct. 4, 1933; s. David Nathaniel and Willie Mae (Woodward) Martin; m. Elizabeth Susan McAfee Altman, June 9, 1979; children—Sarah Elizabeth Altman, Julia Johanna Martin. Author: New York The Nine Million and Other Poems, 1969, The Shit-Storm Poems, 1973, The Persistence of the Flesh, 1976, Paul Laurence Dunbar: A Singer of Songs, 1979, The Forms of Silence, 1980; wrkg. on Courting the Muse (poetry text). Ed. (with R.P.E. Stetson) Der Rabe (Swiss-German jnl of new Afro-Am. lit.). BA, U. of Toledo; MLitt, Middlebury College; DA, Carnegie-Mellon. Prof., U. of Dayton, 1970—. Mem. MLA, PSA. Address: U Dayton 300 College Prk Dr Dayton OH 45469

MARTIN, JANETTE GOULD, b. Jamestown, NY, Mar. 25, 1957, d. Frank Jesse and Mina Jane (Gould) G.; m. Rick A. Martin, Aug. 12, 1978; 1 child, Dustin G. Contrbr. to Seek, People in Action, Superintendent Profile, The Volunteer Fireman, Aevum, The Poet, Hob-Nob Ann., Encore. Wrkg. on romance novel, mag. stories, chapbook-length poem, mag. articles. BA in English summa cum laude, NY State Univ. Coll., 1980, MA in Brit. Lit. summa cum laude, 1982. Adj. faculty, Jamestown Comm. Coll. Recipient various wrtg. awards, Ky. State Poetry Soc., 1983, Natl. Fedn. State Poetry Socs., 1983, The Humanist, 1983, 85. Mem. Intl. Women's Wrtg. Guild, Soc. of Children's BK. wrtrs., AG. Home: RD 3 Box 173 Forest Ave Ext Jamestown NY 14701

MARTIN, JAY (HERBERT), b. Newark, NJ., Oct. 30, 1935; s. Sylvester K. and Ada (Smith) M.; m. Helen Benadette Saldini, June 9, 1956; children: Helen Elizabeth, Laura Ann, Jay Herbert. Author: biography: Conrad Aiken: The Life of His Art, 1962, Nathanael West: The Art of His Life, 1970, Robert Lowell (monograph), 1970, Always Merry and Bright: The Life of Henry Miller—An Unauthorized Biography, 1978. Editor: (and au of introduction) Winfield Townley Scott, 1961, A Collection of Critical Essays on The Waste Land, 1968, Nathanael West: A Collection of Critical Essays, 1971, A Singer in the Dawn: Reinterpretaions of Paul Laurence Dunbar, 1975, A Dunbar Reader, 1975. Contrbr: John G. Kirk, ed, America Now, 1968, Centenay Essays on Edwin Alington Robinson, 1969, John Harrison and Henry Stein, eds, Muckraking in the United States, 1973, Louis Rubin, Jr., ed, The Comic Imagination in America, 1973, Robert C. Elliot, ed, In Search of the American Dream, 1974, The Spoils of Poynton: A Film Guide, 1976, Luther S. Luedtke, ed, The Study of American Culture: Contemporary Conflicts, 1977, Rudolf Haas, ed, Theater und Drama in Amerika, 1978, Marta Sienicka, ed, Proc of a Symposium on American Lit, 1979, Richard Koselanetz, ed, American Writing Today, vol. 1, 1982, Howard Kerr and others, eds, The Haunted Dusk: American Super-natural Fiction, 1820-1920, 1983, Robert Satelmeyer and J. Donald Crowley, eds, Centenary Essays on Huckleberry Finn, 1985, Justin Call and others, eds, Frontiers of Infant Psychiatry, vol 2, 1986, Steven Gould Axelrod and Helen Deese, eds, New Perspectives on Robert Lowell, 1986. Other: Harvests of Change: American Lit 1865-1914, 1967, rev. ed., 1988, (au of introduction) Dennis P. Vannatta, Nathanael West: A Guide to the Scholarship, 1976, (au of introduction) Anthony J. Campos, Mexican Folk Tales, 1977, Winter Dreams: An American in Moscow, 1979, Who Am I This Time: Uncovering the Fictive Personality, 1988. Also au of Circles, a novel, and Psychoanalysis and the Life of Literature; au of William Faulkner, a one-hour radio drama prod by National Public Radio, 1980. Contrbr to Los Angeles Times Book Review and other periodicals. Mem of edit bd, American Lit, 1978-81 and Humanities in Society, 1979-83; ed-in-chief, Psychoanalytic Education, 1984-88. AB, Columbia Univ, 1956; MA, Ohio State Univ, 1957, Ph. D., 1960; Ph. D. in psychoanalysis, Southern Calif Psychoanalytic Inst, 1983. Instr in English, Penn State Univ, State Coll, 1957-58, instr in English and American Studies, Yale

Univ, New Haven, Conn., 1960-64; fellow, Sillman Coll, 1964-68, asst prof and undergraduate dir of American studies, 1964-67, assoc prof, 1967-68; prof of English, American studies, and comparative culture, Univ of Calif., Irvine, 1968-79, lectr in psychiatry in School of Medicine, 1978—, chmn American studies dept., 1968-69, dir of program in comparative culture, 1969-71, and of Education Abroad program, 1971-75; Leo S. Bing Prof of English and American Lit, Univ of Southern Calif, Los Angeles, 1979—, dir of English dep grad studies program, 1980-83. Mem of faculty, Southern Calif Psychoanalysis Inst, 1985—. Bicentennial Prof of American Lit and Culture, Moscow State Univ, 1976. Univ of Calif Regents fellow in humanities, 1971; fellow of Rockefeller Study Center (Bellagio, Italy), 1983. Yale Univ faculty club lectr, 1963; lectr abroad, including visit to Leningrad, Woclaw (Poland), San Jose (Costa Rica), Berlin, Pais, Montreal, Cannes (France), and Bergen (Norway). Mem membership panel of NFH, 1974-79. Consultant to Guggenheim Fndn, NEH, NEA, Calif Council for the Humanities and Public Policy, and to numerous publishing firms. Member: Intl Psychoanalytic Assn, Assn Internationale d'Histoire de la Psychoanayse, Intl Assn of Univ Profs of English, American Psychoanalysis Assn (coordinator of com on deviations, 1984), MLA, Authors Guild, P.E.N., Aurelian Honor Soc (research clinical fellow, 1977-81), Southern Calif American Studies Assn (pres, 1969-71), Phi Beta Kappa. Morse research fellow, Yale Univ, 1963-64; American Philosophical Soc fellow, 1966; Guggeheim fellow, 1966-67; Univ of Calif, Irvine, Friends of Library award, 1971, for Nathanael West: The Art of His Life, and, 1978, for Always Merry and Bright: The Life of Henry Miller-An Unauthorized Autobiography; Rockefeller fdn. sr. fellow in humanities, 1975-76; Univ of Southern Calif Phi Kappa Phi award, 1981, for bes faculty publication; Marie H. Biehl Prize for Research in Child Psychoanalysis, Calif Psychoanalytic Soc, 1981; Fritz Schmidl Memorial Prize for Research in Applied Psychoanalysis, Seattle Assn for Psychoanalysis, 1982; NEH sr research grantee, 1983-84; Franz Alexander Prize for Psychoanalytic Research. Home: 18651 Via Palatino Irvine CA 92715

MARTIN, JEAN, see McArthur, Barbara Jean

MARTIN, JIM, b. San Mateo, CA, Dec. 19, 1939, d. Harry Tracy and Subina Elizabeth (Prior) M.; m. Joyce Elaine Schreiter, Dec. 31, 1966; children—JoAnna Marie, Christina Lynne. Contrbr. numerous poems to lit. jnls; contrbr. articles to mags. BA, U. Santa Clara, 1962, MBA, 1975. Asst. ed. IMPACT mag., 1976-80; assoc. ed. Def. Sci. Mag., 1984—, ed. Def. Sci. and Electronics Mag., 1984—, both with Rush Franklin Pub. Co., Campbell, Calif. Office: Franklin Pub 300 Orchard City Dr Campbell CA 95008

MARTIN, JOHN RUPERT, b. Hamilton, Ont., Can., Sept. 27, 1916; came to U.S., 1941, naturalized, 1959; s. John Smith and Elizabeth (Hutchinson) M.; m. Barbara Janet Malolm, Aug. 23, 1941; 1 dau., Hilary Jane. Author: The Illustration of the Heavenly Ladder of Joh Climaus, 1954, The Portrait of John Milton at Princeton and Its Place in Milton Iconography, 1961, The Ceiling Painting by Rubens for the Jesuit Church in Antwerp, 1968, Rubens: the Antwerp Altarpieces, 1969, The Decorations for the Pompa Introitus Ferdinandi, 1972, Baroque, Style and Civilization, 1977, (with G. Feigenbaum) Van Dyck as Religious Artist, 1979; also articles; Editor: Rubens before 1620, 1972; editor-in-chief: Art Bull., 1971-74. B.A., McMaster U., 1938, D. Litt., 1976; M.F.A., Princeton, 1941, Ph.D., 1947. Served to maj. Canadian Army, 1942-46. Reipient Charles Rufus Morey book award Coll. Art Assn., 1974; ACLS fellow, 1956-66. Home: 107 Mercer St Princeton NJ 08540

MARTIN, JUDITH, (Miss Manners), b. Washington, DC, Sept. 13, 1938; d. Jacobina and Helen (Aronson) Perlman; m. Robert Martin, Jan. 30, 1960; children—Nicholas Ivor, Jaobina Helen. Author: The Name on the White House Floor, 1972, Miss Manners' Guide to Excrutiatingly Correct Behavior, 1982; novel, Gilbert: A Comedy of Manners, 1982; Miss Manners' Guide to Rearing Perfect Children, 1984, Common Courtesy: In Which Miss Manners Solves the Problem That Baffled Mr. Jefferson, 1985; (novel) Style and Substance: A Comedy of Manners, 1986. BA in English, Wellesley (Mass.) College,/ 1960. Washington Post: copy girl summers while in college; reporter, feature writer, and critic, 1960-84; syndicated columnist from 1978. Critic at large, Vanity Fair, 1983-84. Home: 1651 Harvard St NW Washington DC 20009

MARTIN, JULIAN S. S., (Julian Sienkiewicz), b. Bklyn. NY, June 27, 1929; s. Paul and Lucy (Glowacki) Sienkiewicz; m. Gladys Kaplan, Aug. 4, 1951; children: Kathi (Mrs. Jay Handt), Paul. Author: 50 Vacuum Tube Ciruits for the Eletronics Experimenter, 1960, How to Read Schematic Diagrams, 1965; contbr. to articles to profl. jnls., consumer mags. Publs. dir. Belock Instrument Corp., College Point, N.Y., 1956-58; mng. editor Ziff-Davis Pub. Co., N.Y.C., 1958-63; editor-in-hief, coordinator eletronics group, assoc. pub. Davis Publs., Inc., N.Y.C., 1963-81; pres. Sci. Commentary Co., 1980—; ed. Gernsback Pubs., 1982—. Served with USNR, 1948-51; Served with AUS, 1951-53. Fellow Radio Club Am. Home: 2480 E 7th St Brooklyn NY 11235

MARTIN, (MARGERY) LEE, b. near Harris, CA, d. Kidrick Francis and Josephine Katherine (Phillips) Martin; div. Contrbr. short mystery and romance stories: Ranch Romances, Zane Grey Mag., Woman's World, Yarnspinner, other publs. Wrkg. on short stories, novel. BSL, Peninsula U., 1977, JD, 1979. Practice law, Calif., 1983—. Mem. NWC. Home: Box 278 Mountain View CA 94042

MARTIN, PATRICIA STONE, b. Ft. Wayne, IN, Jan. 18, 1931; d. Charles Fleming and Nira (Knell) Stone; m. Robert Charles Martin, Jr., Mar. 28, 1953; children—Mary, Robert, Laurie, Daniel. Author: (children's books) The Christmas Gift, 1986, A Special Friend for Valentine's Day, 1986, Timid Timothy and the Halloween Ghost, 1986, The Most Special Mommy in the Whole World, 1986, May I Have a Bunny for Easter?, 1986, I Hunt Tigers at Thanksgiving, 1986. Contrbr short stories, poems, articles to mags. including Jack and Jill, Highlights for Children, others. B.S. in Elem. Edn., Ind. U., 1955. Tchr. public schs., Wadsworth, OH, 1955-56, Elkhart, IN, 1967, Evansville, IN, 1967-72, Vero Beach, FL, 1982-83; free-lance wrtr., artist, 1972—. Mem. Vero Beach Art Club, SCBW. Home: 1336 45th Ave Vero Beach FL 32966

MARTIN, R. WILLIAM, b. Hastings, NE, Oct. 9, 1943, s. Robert William and Mary Ardelle (Watson) M.; m. Mary Margaret Thibodeau, Oct. 19, 1966; children—Mary Agnes, Virginia Anne. Wrtr., ed. producer multi image shows, multimedia shows, videotape prodns., films. Wrkg. on scriptwriting, short stories, novel. Broadcaster various radio stations, Nebraska, 1960-69; audiovisual wrtr., producer, Omaha, 1969-79, NYC, 1979-83; exec. producer, Marsden, NYC, 1983-86; freelance mag. wrtr., 1986-. Recipient Bronze and Silver medals for wrtg. and prodn., N.Y. Intl. Film and TV Festival, 1983, 84, 85. Home: 26 Winthrop St Brooklyn NY 11225

MARTIN, RALPH GUY, b. Chgo., Mar. 4, 1920; s. Herman and Tillie (Charno) M.; m. Marjorie Jean Pastel, June 17, 1944; children—Maurice Joseph, Elizabeth, Tina. Author: Boy From Nebraska, 1946, The Best is None Too Good, 1948, Ballots and Bandwagons: Five Key Conventions since 1900, 1964, Skin Deep, 1964, Wizard of Wall Street, 1965, Jennie: The Life of Lady Randolph Churchill, The Romantic Years, 1969, vol. II, The Dramatic Years, 1971, World War II, 1966, The GI War, 1967, A Man for All People, 1968, Lincoln Center, 1971, The Woman He Loved: The Story of the Duke and Duchess of Windsor, 1974, Cissy, The Extraordinary Life of Eleanor Medill Patterson, 1979; author: A Hero For Our Time, An Intimate Study of the Kennedy Years, 1983, Charles and Diana, 1985; co-author: Eleanor Roosevelt: Her Life in Pictures, 1958, The Human Side of FDR, 1960, Man of Destiny: Charles DeGaulle, 1961, Man of the Century: Winston Churchill, 1961, Front Runner, Dark Horse, 1960, Money, Money, Money, 1960, Three Lives of Helen Keller, 1962. World War II: From D-Day to VE-Day, 1962, World War II: War in the Pacific, 1965. Contrbr. to: Yank, The GI History of The War: Stevenson Speeches, 1952, Social Problems in America, 1955, Democracy in Action, 1962, others. B.J., U. Mo., 1941. Reporter, mng. editor Box Elder News Jnl, Brigham, Utah, 1940-41; contrbr. mags. including Sunday N.Y. Times, Look, Harpers, 1945-53; assoc. editor New Republic mag., 1945-48; assoc. editor charge spcl. reports Newsweek mag., 1953-55; exec. editor House Beautiful mag., 1955-57; pub., pres. Bandwagon, Inc. Mem. AL, AG. Home: 135 Harbor Rd Westport CT 06880

MARTIN, ROBERT BERNARD, b. La Harpe, IL, Sept. 11, 1918, s. Morris Carl and Margaret Ethel Martin. Author: A Companion to Victorian Literature, 1955, Charles Kingsley's American Notes, 1958, The Dust of Combat: A Life of Charles Kingsley, 1959, Enter Rumour: Four Early Victorian Scandals, 1962, Victorian Poetry: Ten Major Poets, 1964, The Triumph of Wit: A Study of Victorian Comic Theory, 1974, Tennyson, The Unquiet Heart, 1980, With Friends Possessed: A Life of Edward Fitzgerald, 1985, (under name Robert Bernard) Death Takes a Sabbatical, 1967, Death Takes the Last Train, 1967, Deadly Meeting, 1970, Illegal Entry, 1971. Wrkg. on biography of G.M. Hopkins. AB, State U. Iowa, 1943; AM, Harvard U., 1947; BLitt, Oxford U., 1950. From instr. to prof. Princeton U., N.J., 1951-75, prof. emeritus, 1975—; free-lance writer, Oxford, Eng., 1975-81; Citizens' prof. U. Hawaii, Honolulu, 1981-82, 84—. Served to 1st lt. USAAF, 1943-46, ETO. Recipient Duff Cooper award for biography, 1981; James Tait Black award for biography U. Edinburgh, 1981; Christian Gauss award for lit. scholarship and criticism, 1981; fellow ACLS, 1966-67, Guggenheim Fdn., 1971-72, 83-84; NEH sr. fellow, 1976-77. Fellow Royal Soc. Lit. (W.H. Heinemann award 1981). Office: Dept Eng U HI 1733 Donaghho Rd Honolulu HI 96822

MARTIN, SCOTT D., b. NYC, Feb. 19, 1952; s. Donald Neil and Beatrice Mary (Sullivan) M. Clrk. Dunlap Advt., Los Angeles, 1970-75; driver

L.O.D., L.I., N.Y., 1975; guard Burns Security, Phila., 1976; editor The New Press, NYC, 1984—. Mem. Fountain House, NYC, 1986—. Wrkg. on a New York novel. Mem. CCLM. Home: 127 Ludlow St 4C New York NY 10002

MARTIN, STEPHEN-PAUL, b. Chgo., Sept. 19, 1949, s. Norman H. and Katherine (Fitzgerald) M. Author: Edges (poetry collection), 1978; co-ed. Central Park jnl. of arts and social theory, NYC, 1979—; contrbr. poetry, fiction, essays, articles, rvws. to Fiction Intl., Kans. Qtly, Asylum, other periodicals; contrbr.: Best of Poets series (Third Eye Press), 1983. MA, NYU, 1975, PhD, 1984. Asst. prof. NYU, N.Y.C., 1979—, Pace U., 1980—, CUNY, 1980—. Recipient AAP prize, 1975, CCLM ed.'s award, 1987. Home: 50 W 72d St Apt 1514 New York NY 10023

MARTIN, VALERIE METCALF, b. Sedalia, MO, Mar. 14, 1948, d. John Roger and Valerie Haydel (Fleisher) Metcalf; m. Robert M. Martin, Dec. 10, 1970 (div. 1984); 1 dau., Adrienne Metcalf; m. 2d, James Elsworth Watson, Mar. 30, 1985. Author: Set in Motion, 1979, Alexandra, 1980, A Recent Martyr, 1987. BA, U. New Orleans, 1970; MFA, U. Mass., 1974. Asst. prof. U. New Orleans, 1980-84, 85-86; assoc. prof. U. Ala., Tuscaloosa, 1984-85; lectr. creative writing Mt. Holyoke Coll., South Hadley, Mass., 1986—. Judge awards series in novels, AWP, 1981; admissions panelist Cummington Arts Community, Mass., 1983—. Grantee La. Div. of Arts, 1982. Home: 4 Stanton Ave So Hadley MA 01075

MARTINEAU, FRANCIS (FRANK) EDWARD, b. Attleboro, MA, Jan. 15, 1921, s. Edward Francis and Yvonne Marie (Langlois) M.; m. Dorothy May Clanfield, May 26, 1945; children—Jane E. Martineau Mandeville, Jill F. Martineau Cornish, Gail K. Martineau Parker, Paul F. Reporter, photographer Woonsocket (R.I.) Daily Call, 1940-46; pres. Frank Martineau, Inc. advt. and public relations, Providence, R.I., 1946-66; mem. future study group U.S. Air Natl. Guard, Washington, 1966-67; exec. dir. Aircraft Owners and Pilots Assn. Fdn., Washington, 1967-70; dir. public relations Air Line Pilots Assn., Washington, 1970-72; genl. mgr. Natl. Assn. Counties, Washington, 1972-73; ed., pub. Assn. Trends Newsweekly, 1973-85 pres., chmn. Martineau Corp., Washington, 1973—. Served with RCAF & USAF as pilot, World War II. Mem. Public Relations Soc. Am., Am. Soc. Assn. Execs., Aviation-Space Wrtrs. Assn., Natl. Newspaper Assn. Home: 7204 Clarendon Rd Bethesda MD 20814

MARTINES, LAURO RENE, b. Chgo., Ill., Nov. 22, 1927; m. Julia O'Faolain, Nov. 20, 1957; 1 son, Lucien. Author: The Social World of the Florentine Humanists, 1963, Lawyers and Statecraft in Renaissance Florence, 1968, Power and Imagination: City-States in Renaissance Italy, 1979, Society and History in English Renaissance Verse, 1985; co-author: Not in God's Image: Women in Western Civilization, 1973; editor: Violence and Civil Disorder in Italian Cities 1200-1500, 1972. AB, Drake U., 1950; PhD. Harvard, 1960; fellow Villa I Tatti, Harvard Center for Italian Renaissance Studies, Florence, Italy, 1962-65; fellow ACLS, 1962-63; fellow Guggenheim Meml. Fdn., 1964-65; sr. fellow NEH, 1971, 78-79. Served with AUS, 1945-47. Vis. prof., Warburg Inst., London, 1985. Office: Dept Hist U Calif Los Angeles CA 90024

MARTINEZ, GEORGINA V. (Percie Blue), b. Havana, Cuba, Dec. 23, 1953, came to U.S., 1966; d. Eduardo and Caridad E. (Rodriguez) M. Contrbr. poems to anthols., lit. mags. A.A., La Valley Coll., 1980; B.A., St. Thomas U., 1986. Budget asst. Veterans Administration Hosp., Miami, 1985—; substitute tchr. New World Inst., Miami, 1987—. Mem. Dickinson Studies, Fla. State Poets Assn., Natl. Fedn. State Poetry Societies. Studies, Home: 61 E 52d Pl Hialeah FL 33013

MARTINO, MARIA LINDA, b. Phila., Aug. 19, 1962, d. Albert A. and Marie L. (Midiri) Martino. BA in Journalism, Polit. Sci., Pa. State U., 1984; postgrad., Drexel U. Feature wrtr. Bucks County Courier Times, Levittown, Pa., 1983; asst. to ed. Phila. Bus. Jnl, 1984; feature wrtr. The Reporter, Lansdale, Pa., 1984-85; asst. ed. Bus. Forms and Systems, N.Am. Pub. Co., Phila., 1985; ed. In-Plant Reproductions and Electronic Pub., Phila., 1985—. Home: 11 Taylor Way Washington Crossing PA 18977

MARTINSON, A. DENISE, b. Detroit, Apr. 14, 1947; d. Daniel Michael and Florence Helena (Tuson) Gallik; m. Michael R. Martinson, Apr. 28, 1973; children—Danielle Suzanne, Michael Daniel. Contrbr. poetry: Wide Open mag., N.Am. Poetry Rev., Poetic Symphony, Odessa Poetry Rev., numerous others; contrbr. children's stories, articles: Living with Children mag., Shining Star mag., Pathways mag., Primary Treasure, Our Litle Friend mag. Wrkg. on children's book. Freelance wrtr.; illustrator Friend mag. Mem. Soc. Children's Book Wrtrs., NWC. Home: 29050 Shirley St Madison Heights MI 48071

MARTINSON, DAVID KEITH, b. San Diego, May 13, 1946, s. Henry Melvin and Rosella Georgine (Olson) M. Author poetry: Rough Music, 1986, Strips and Shavings, 1978, A Cedar Grew From His Forehead, 1976, Bleeding the Radiator, 1974; author children's books: Cheer Up, Old Man, 1976, Manobozo and the Bullrushes, 1976, Shemay: The Bird in the Sugarbush, 1975, Real Wild Rice, 1975; author: A Long Time Ago Is Just Like Today, 1976; ed.: Angwamas Minosewag Adisokan: Time of the Indian (vol. 9), 1979, Aseban, 1978; contrbr. anthologies. BA, Moorhead State U., 1968. Poet-in-schls. Minn. Arts Council, N.D. Arts Council, 1971-80; wrtr.-in-res. Minn. Arts Council, Stillwater, 1972-73, Minn. Chippewa Tribe, Cass Lake, 1979-80; lectr. N.D. State U., Fargo, 1981—. Grantee Minn. Arts Council, 1973, fellowship recipient, 1978. Home: 404 18th Ave S Moorhead MN 56560

MARTONE, MICHAEL, b. Ft. Wayne, IN, Aug. 22, 1955, s. Anthony Samuel and Patricia (Payne) M.; m. Theresa Pappas, Apr. 3, 1984. Author: At A Loss, 1977, Alive and Dead in Indiana, 1984, Return to Powers, 1985; contrbr. articles to N.Am. Rvw, Lit Mag Rvw, Life, other publs.; contrbr. prose to Windless Orchard, Ind. Writes; contrbr. fiction to Available Press/PEN Short Story Collection, 1985, Stories About How Things Fall Apart and What's Left When They Do, 1985, others; contrbr. to Antaeus, Pig Iron, Ascent, Aura, other lit mags. AB, Ind. U., 1977; MA, Johns Hopkins U., 1979. Fellow in Writing Seminars Johns Hopkins U., Balt., 1979-80; asst. prof. Iowa State U., Ames, 1980-83, assoc. prof., 1983—; ed. Poet & Critic mag.; contrbg. ed. Denver Qtly, 1986—, N.Am. Rvw, 1986. NEA fellow, 1983; recipient PEN Syndicated Fiction award, 1983-84. Home: 1116 N 2d St Ames IA 50010

MARTTIN, PAUL, see Plaut, Martin Edward

MASARIK, ALBERT E., b. Wilmington, DE, Feb. 24, 1943, s. Albert and Pearl (Dougherty) M.; m. Jill Andrea Masarik, May 13, 1966. Contrbr. poetry to Wormwood Rvw, Litmus, Nola Express, other lit mags. BA, LaSalle U., 1965. Poet-in-schls. Calif. Poe9s in Schls. program, San Francisco, 1984—; artist-in-res. Calif.-Nev. Arts Council, 1985-86. Served with U.S. Army, 1966-68; Korea. Home: 1037 Minna St San Francisco CA 94103

MASON, BOBBIE ANN, b. Mayfield, KY, May 1, 1940. Author: The Girl Sleuth, 1976, Shiloh and Other Stories, 1982, In Country (novel), 1985; Nabokov's Garden (criticism), 1974. BA, U. Ky., 1962; PhD, U. Conn., 1972. Recipient PEN Hemingway Award for First Fiction, 1982. Office: c/o Amanda Urban 40 W 57th St New York NY 10019

MASON, CHARLES ELLIS III, b. Boston, Oct. 31, 1938; s. Charles Ellis, Jr. and Ada Brooks (Trafford) M. Author: (with Buddy Melges) Sailing Smart, 1983; editor: Best of Sail Trim, 1976, Best of SAIL Navigation, 1981. BA, Yale U., 1960. Assoc. editor Sail mag., Boston, 1968-74, exec. editor, 1974—. Served with USNR, 1960-62. Home: 16 Joy St Boston MA 02114

MASON, DAVID STEWART, b. Washinton, Nov. 23, 1947; s. Richard Stewart and Sheila (Farquharson) M.; m. Sharon Ann Wood, June 17, 1970; children—Dana Kathryn, Melanie Elizabeth. Author: Public Opinion and Political Change in Poland, 1980-82 (Quincy Wright Book award Intl. Studies Assn., 1986), 1985. Contrbr. chpts. to books, articles in profl. jnls. B.A., Cornell U., 1969; M.A., Johns Hopkins U., 1971; Ph.D., Ind. U., 1978. Asst. prof. political sci. Butler U., Indpls., 1976-82, assoc. prof., 1982—. Mem. Intl. Studies Assn. (pres. Midwest chpt.), Am. Political Sci. Assn., Am. Assn. Advancement Slavic Studies. Home: 4835 N Illinois Indianapolis IN 46208

MASON, JERRY, b. Balt., MD., Apr. 6, 1913; s. Daniel A. and Esther (Schapira) Myerberg; m. Clarise Finger, Nov. 26, 1936; children—Michael Maury, Judy Ann Mason Underhill. Author: I Find Treason, 1939; editor, pub.: Family of Man, 1955, Private World of Pablo Picasso, 1958, The World's Family, 1983. AB, Johns Hopkins U., 1933; MS in Journalism, Columbia U., 1934. Writer for magazines, also engaged in pub. relations, 1934-41; mem. staff This Week mag., NYC, 1941-49, assoc. editor, 1945-59; editor-in-chief Argosy mag., 1949-53; also editorial dir. Popular Publs. Co.; pres., founder Maco Mag. Corp., NYC, 1953-57; founder Ridge Press, NYC, 1957, Pound Press, 1981; pub. VBI, NYC,1979. Home: Barnegat Rd Pound Ridge NY 10576

MASSÉ, MARK HENRY, b. White Plains, NY, Oct. 24, 1952; s. Donald Merton and Margaret Louise (Hart) M.; m. Eleanora Elizabeth Estok, May 31, 1986. Contrbr. non-fiction articles to newspapers, mags. including N.Y. Times, Plain Dealer, Cleveland Mag., others. Contrbg. ed.: Cities within a City (Burt W. Griffin), 1980, Marketing your Schools, 1987. B.A., Miami U., 1974. Dir., LFS Communications, Cleve., 1982-86; dir. marketing Polaris Caree Center, Middleburg Heights, OH, 1986-87; instr. Polaris Adult Edn. Writing Program, 1986-87; freelance wrtr., consultant, 1987—. Recipient Best of Cleve. award Cleve. Ad Club, 1984. Mem. NWC, Press Club of Cleve., PRSA (Silver Anvil regional award

1983), IABC (Gold Quill award of Merit 1983). Home: 2816 Lakeview Ave Rocky River OH 44116

MASSE, PEGGY HART, b. Johnstown, PA, Aug. 7, 1925; d. Herbert Henry and Margaret Mary (Bradley) Hart; m. Donald M. Masse, Oct. 31, 1947; children—D. Michael, Mark H., Peter Paul, Marguerite Clair, Andrew. Contrbr. feature articles to Club Management Mag.; poems to anthol. Ed., contrbr. Harrison Republican, 1962-67. Student N.Y.U., 1962-63. Public relations dir., asst. mgr. Polo Clubs, Inc., Palm Beach, Fla., Blind Brook, NY, 1951-67; pres., owner PDM Assocs., Inc., pub. rel., Cleveland, 1972—; tchr. creative writing Kent State U., OH, 1976-77, Cuyohoga Commun. Coll., Cleveland, 1985, 86, 87. Recipient 1st prize Akron Manuscript Club, OH, 1978. Mem. NFPW, WG. Home: 20550 Detroit Rd Rocky River OH 44116

MASTERMAN-SMITH, VIRGINIA, b. NYC, Nov. 18, 1937, d. Walter Randall and Elizabeth (Hoff) LoPinto; m. Kenneth Masterman-Smith, Nov. 24, 1966; children—Stephen Kenneth, Michael David. Author: The Treasure Trap, 1979, The Great Egyptian Heist, 1982; contrbg. ed. Monmouth Bus. Mag., 1985-86. Wrkg. on novel, musical play, children's nature stories. AB, Georgian Ct. Coll., 1969. Tchr. pub. schls. various cities in N.J., 1958—; freelance wrtr., 1983—; instr. bus. communications Katharine Gibbs Schl., Piscataway, N.J., 1985-86; instr. reading, Long Branch Middle Schl., 1986—. Mem. AG, Soc. Children's Book Wrtrs. Home: 1237 Eatontown Blvd Oceanport NJ 07759

MASTERS, HILARY THOMAS, b. Kansas City, MO, Feb. 3, 1928; s. Edgar Lee and Ellen Francis (Coyne) M.; m. Polly Jo McCulloch, Mar. 14, 1955; children—Joellen, Catherine, John. Author: (novels) The Common Pasture, 1967, An American Marriage, 1969, Palace of Strangers, 1971, Clemmons, 1985, Cooper, 1987, (biography) Last Stands: Notes from Memory, 1982, (stories) Hammertown Tales, 1986. AB, Brown U., 1952. Writer-in-res. Ohio Univ., Athens, 1979; vis. writer Univ. NC, Greensboro, 1980-81, Univ. Denver, 1982; lectr. Univ. Jyvaskyla, Finland, 1983; assoc. prof. Carnegie-Mellon Univ., Pitts., 1983—. Served to PO 3/C, USN, 1946-47, Washington. Adv. to speaker, NY Assembly, Albany, 1967-68, candidate to NY Assembly, 1965-66. Recipient Yaddo fellowship, 1980; Fulbright lects. in Am. Lit., Finland, 1983. Mem. AG, PEN, AWP. Address: 1213 Monterey St Pittsburgh PA 15212

MASTERSON, PATRICIA O'MALLEY, b. Worcester, MA, May 15, 1952; d. Paul Francis and Dorothy Madelaine (O'Malley) M. contrbr. articles to mags., newspapers. Wrkg. on newsletters. B.F.A., Emerson Coll. 1974; M.A., Goddard Coll., 1980. Reporter, photographer Patroit Newspaper, Webster, MA, 1976-78; dir. public relations Mount Pleasant Hosp., Lynn, MA, 1980-84; ed. pubs. Ocean Spray Cranberries, Inc., Plymouth, MA, 1984—. Recipient Best Overall Newsletter Aaward Ed.'s Forum, 1986, 2d place for employee pub. Cooperative Info. Fair, Anaheim, CA, 1987. Mem. WIC, Cooperative Communicators Assn. (2d plae for employee news-letter 1986, 1st place 1987), South Shore Ad Club (publicity com.). Home: 132 Union St Rockland MA 02370

MASUMOTO, DAVID MAS, b. Selma, CA, Jan. 20, 1954; m. Marcia Rose Thieleke, May 7, 1983; 1 dau., Nikiko Rose. Author: Distant Voices, A Sansei's Journey to Gila River Relocation Center, 1982, Silent Strength, Stories from the Japanese-American Experience, 1985, The History of Fresno County, Part II, 1986, Country Voices, The Oral History of A Japanese American Family Farm Community, 1987. BA, U. Calif.-Berkeley, 1972-76, MA, -Davis, 1980-82. Farmer, Del Rey, Calif., 1976—; writer Sanger Herald, Calif., 1978-79; researcher, Univ. Calif., Davis, 1980-81. Bd. dirs. Asian Pacific Advocates of Calif., Sacramento, 1981-82, Calif. Assn. Family Farmers, Davis, 1982-85. Recipient James Clavell Natl. Literary award, 1981, 86; Regents fellow, U. Calif., Davis, 1981. Home: 9336 E Lincoln Del Rey CA 93616

MATCHA, JACK, (John Tanner), b. NYC, Feb. 28, 1919, s. Frank and Matilda (Azar) M.; m. Margaret Hudgins, 1946 (div. 1950); m. 2d, Shirley Paron, Mar. 6, 1960; children—Franklin Scott, Nicole Liane. Author: Prowler in the Night (novel), 1959, A Rogue's Guide to Europe, 1965; playwright: 24 Hrs. (Aerobics Segment), 1983. BS, CCNY, 1941; MS, Columbia U., 1942. Reporter Balt. Sun, 1942-45; assoc. prof. U. So. Calif., Los Angeles, Los Angeles Southwest Coll. Winner Norman Corwin playwrtg. contest, Los Angeles, 1967, Jewish Community Ctr. playwrtg. contest, NYC, 1980. Mem. DG, WGA. Home: 7716 Teesdale Ave Los Angeles CA 91605

MATHEWS, BEVERLY, b. Long Beach, CA, Oct. 25, 1928; d. Henry John and Cornelia (Bruce) Schafer; m. Walter Mathews, Apr. 30, 1954; children—William, Timothy, Karen, Lauren. Author: Start Your Own Bed & Breakfast Business, 1985, Bed & Breakfast: How to Put Your House to Work, 1984; editor/publisher: Bed & Breakfast Update, bi-monthly nwsltr., 1984—. Assoc. Arts, UCLA, 1949. Actress/TV spokeswoman-freelance, fashion commentator (NY and LA), 1952-80; freelance production coordinator (LA), 1980-85; author/publisher (North Hollywood), 1984—. Founder/1st president, LA Chapters of Natl. Alliance of Homebased Businesswomen, mem. COSMEP. Home: 4326 Bellaire Ave Studio City CA 91604

MATHEWS, KEITH ROWLAND, (Mathew Garth), b. Santa Barbara, CA, Dec. 27, 1934; s. Benjamin Albert and Mary Edith M.; m. Catherine Lou Olds, June 3, 1980 (div.); children—Sherry, Kelvin, Natasha, Charlie. Author: (with Gregory C. Knapp) Stranglehold, 1973; Assembly Language Primer for the Macintosh, 1985, Encyclopedia, Macintosh ROM, 1987. Dir., Walden House, San Francisco, 1971-75, Awareness House, Inc., Oakland, CA, 1976-80; freelance wrtr./hacker, 1981—. Served USAF, 1954-68. Home: Box 142 Inverness CA 94937

MATHIS, SHARON BELL, b. Atlantic City, NJ, Feb. 26, 1937; d. John Willie and Alice Mary (Frazier) Bell; m. Leroy F. Mathis, July 11, 1957 (div. Jan. 1979); children—Sherie, Stacy, Stephanie. Author: Brooklyn Story, 1970, Sidewalk Story, 1971 (award Council on Interracial Books for Children), Teacup Full of Roses, 1972, Ray Charles, 1973, Listen for the Fig Tree, 1974, The Hundred Penny Box, 1975 (Boston Globe-Horn Book Honor book 1975, Newbery Honor Book 1976), Cartwheels, 1977. BA, Morgan State Coll., 1958; MSc, Catholic U. Am., 1975. Interviewer Children's Hosp. of D.C., 1958-59. Recipient Outstanding Book of Yr. award N.Y. Times, 1972. Address: c/o Brown 10 Astor Pl New York NY 10022

MATHIS-EDDY, DARLENE FERN, b. Elkhart, IN, Mar. 19, 1937, d. William Eugene and Fern Roose (Paulmer) Mathis; m. Spencer Livingston Eddy, Jr., May 23, 1964 (dec. 1971). Author: The Worlds of King Lear, 1970, Leaf Threads, Wind Rhymes: A Collection of Lyric Poetry, 1985, Weathering: A Collection of Lyric Poetry, 1988; contrbr. articles to: Am. Lit., English Lang. Notes, Green River Rvw, others; contrbr. poetry to Calyx, Pebble, Bitterroot Intl. Poetry Jnl., others; poetry ed., BSU Forum. BA summa cum laude, Goshen (Ind.) Coll., 1959; PhD, Rutgers U., 1966. Mem. faculty Ball State U., Muncie, Ind., 1967—, prof. English, 1975—. Woodrow Wilson fellow, 1959-62; recipient numerous grants, Ball State U. Mem. MLA, Shakespeare Assn., AAUP. Home: 1409 W Cardinal St Muncie IN 47303

MATLAGA, JOAN, b. Elizabeth, NJ, Jan. 26, 1942. Contrbr. poetry to Hearts on Fire, Offshoots of Orgonomy, Writer's Info, Beyond the Horizon. Address: 2180 Mt Hood Ln Toms River NJ 08753

MATRANGA, FRANCES CARFI, b. Tarrytown, NY, May 18, 1922; d. Joseph and Nellie (Corallo) Carfi; m. Philip Matranga, Sr., Nov. 2, 1941; children—Philip, Paul, Peter, Francine. Author: (adult novels) Land of Shadows, 1977, Summer Magic, 1979, Destiny in Rome, 1979; (children's books) Secret Behind the Blue Door, 1981, Follow the Leader, 1982, Happy Time Bible Activities, 1983, Good Times Bible Activities, 1983, The Mysterious Prowler, 1984, The Perfect Friend, 1985, My Book of Prayers, 1985, The Contest, 1986, The Forgotten Treasure, 1986, The Mystery of the Missing Will, 1986, One Step at a Time, 1987, The Big Top Mystery, 1987. Contrbr. numerous fiction, features to adult an children's mags. including Highlights for Children, Instrutor, Jack and Jill, Woman's World, many others. Wrkg. on mystery novel. Cert. in Comml. Art, Famous Artists Schs., 1964. Recipient 6 prizes, honor cert. Wrtr.'s Digest, 1960, 61, 69, 75, 80, 82, Honorable Mention, NWC, 1975, 1st prize N.Y. WG, 1960. Mem. SCBW. Home: 1600 Harmony Dr Port Charlotte FL 33952

MATRAZZO, DONNA J., b. Braddock, PA, Oct. 7, 1948; d. Frank James and Gertrude (Puhala) Matrazzo. Author: The Corporate Scriptwriting Book, 1980, rev. ed., 1985; contrbg. author: Fiber Structures, 1976, Video Handbook, 1983. BA, Duquesne U., 1970. Silver and Bronze Awards, Intl. Film & TV Festival of New York, 1977, 79, 82, 85; Gold Award, Information Film Producers of Am., 1981. Mem. Intl. Television Assn., NW Assoc. of Book Publishers. Office: Scripts and Concepts/Communicom 548 NE 43rd Ave Portland OR 97213

MATSON, JOHN WILLIAM II, b. Nashville, Sept. 15, 1944, s. John William and Janet (Reese) M. Ed.: How to Make Gasohol on Your Kitchen Counter, 1981, consumer reports. Wrkg. on nonfiction, acrostic poetry. AB with honors, William Penn. Coll., 1968; AM with honors, Creighton U., 1971. Prin. John William Matson II A.M. Publisher, Beverly Hills, Calif., 1980—. Address: 22319 Burton St Canoga Park CA 91304

MATT, LINDA ANN, b. Eunice, LA, Aug. 5, 1952; d. Joseph C.A. Matt and Betty Jean Aucoin. Author: Lyrical Fiesta, 1985; contbr. poetry to numerous lit. publs. and poetry rvws. Grad. Eunice High Schl. Clrk. West Bros., Eunice, 1973-74, Pet Boutique, Eunice, 1972-73; tchr. Tender Care, Eunice, 1980-83. Recipient Award of Merit, World of Poetry, 1985, Golden Poet award, 1985, 87, Silver Poet award, 1986. Home: Box 442 Eunice LA 70539

MATTE, JAMES ALLAN, b. Bklyn., Mar. 10, 1931, s. James Matte and Noela (Potvin) Natiello; m. Ann Smith, Jan. 19, 1964 (div. 1977); 1 child, Garreth. Author: The Art and Science of the Polygraph Technique, 1980; playwright: The Polygraphist, 1983, The Defector, 1983; contrbr. numerous articles to sci. and profl. publs. Wrkg. on textbook. BS in Criminalistics, Empire State Coll., SUNY-Buffalo, 1976. Spcl. agt. U.S. Air Force, 1962-68, U.S. Army, 1968-72; v.p. Hammer Security, Buffalo, 1973-76; pres. Matte Polygraph Service, Inc., Buffalo, 1976—, Psychophysiological Inst., Buffalo, 1985—. Mem. Niagara-Erie Wrtrs., numerous profl. orgns. Office: 321 Statler Towers Buffalo NY 14202

MATTEI, LOREN NEAL, b. New Haven, Oct. 22, 1949; s. Joseph Bernard and Mary Ann (Spinnato) Mazzacane; m. Suzanne Yvonne Mattei, Sept. 27, 1987; 1 son, Jamie Macfarlane. Contrbr. poems, articles to jnls., mags. Pub, Cardboard Boxes (Purcell Press). B.A., Southern Conn. State U., 1971; postgrad. U. Cin., 1974-75. Winner Lafcadio Hearn Haiku Contest, 1987. Mem. Haiku Soc. Am., NWC (Honorable Mention 1986), P&W. Home: 88A Edwards St New Haven CT 06511

MATTHEWS, ALLAN FREEMAN, b. Wakefield, MA, May 27, 1916, s. Ralph Freeman and Mary Adeline Morrill (Hill) M.; m. Shirley Jean Spencer, Dec. 23, 1937 (div. 1955); children—David, Kim (Melinda) Matthews; m. 2d, Doris Olive Haignere, June 26, 1962. Contrbr. Encyc. Britannica, 1954, 57, Bull. Atomic Scientists, 1957, Intl. Devel. Rvw, 1967, The Global 2000 Report to the President, 1980, Revolution in Earth Sciences, 1983; author: Reshaping the 1974 Budget, 1973. BA, Carleton Coll., 1937; MS, Antioch Coll., 1939. Tech. ed. Indsl. Publs., Inc., Chgo., 1940-41; ed. U.S. Bur. Mines, Washington, 1941-51; asst. dir. Pres.'s materials Policy Commn., Washington, 1951; program officer U.S. AID, Washington, 1954-75; del. to Global Modelling Conf., UN, Paris, 1982. Served to lt. (j.g.) USN, 1944-46; PTO. Home: 11500 Fairway Dr 503 Reston VA 22090

MATTHEWS, ELLEN, see Bache, Ellyn

MATTHEWS, FORD, see Karbowiak, Carol Jean

MATTHEWS, JACK, (John Harold), b. Columbus, OH, July 22, 1925; s. John Harold and Lulu Emma (Grover) M.; m. Barbara Jane Reese, Sept. 16, 1947; children: Cynthia Ann Matthews Warnock, Barbara Ellen Matthews Platt, John Harold. Author: Bitter Knowledge, 1964 (Ohiana Award), Hanger Stout, Awake!, 1967, The Charisma Campaigns, 1972, Sassafras, 1983, Crazy Women, 1986, Booking in the Heartland, 1986, Ghostly Populations, 1986. BA, Ohio State Univ., 1949, MA, 1954. Clrk., U.S. Post Office, Columbus, 1950-59; prof. English Urbana Coll., Ohio, 1959-64, Ohio Univ., Athens, 1964-77, disting. prof., 1977—. Served with USCG, 1943-45. Guggenheim fellow, 1974-75. Mem. Phi Beta Kappa. Home: 24 Briarwood Dr Athens OH 45701

MATTHEWS, JOHN FLOYD, b. Cin., OH, Apr. 8, 1919; s. Floyd L. and Helen (Orth) M.; m. Maurine Zollman, Mar. 4, 1945 (dec. 1959); children—Lauralee Alice, Caroline Elaine (dec.); m. Brenda Martin, Aug. 27, 1966. Author: plays, including The Scapegoat, 1950, Michael and Lavinia, 1956, Barnum, 1962; books: The Old Vic In America, 1946, El Greco, 1952, Shaw's Dramatic Criticism, 1959, George Bernard Shaw, 1969, Reflections on Abortion, 1976; contrbr.: fiction to lit mags, Reflections on Abortion; cons., play doctor for script and prodn. problems of numerous Broadway and off-Broadway plays and musicals; TV scriptwriter for maj. networks, 1955-64; screenwriter, MGM, United Artists, Asso. Screen Prodns., Toronto, Ont., Can., 1958-64; contbg. editor: Library of Living Painters, 1949-51, Dictionary of the Arts, 1946, Ency. World Biography, 1970. Student, Wooster Coll., 1935-37, Northwestern U., 1937; BA, U. Cin., 1940, postgrad., 1940-41, Columbia U., 1943, New Schl. for Social Research, 1944-45. Lectr. in playwriting CCNY, 1947-63; Schulman Prof. dramatic lit. and history, Richter Prof. Am. Studies, Brandeis U., 1952-84, vis. critic Yale Schl. of Drama, 1963, network radio writer, 1939-45; screenwriter, Warner Bros., 1945. Home: 162 Pine Ridge Rd Waban MA 02168

MATTHEWS, JOSEPH RONALD, b. Los Angeles, Apr. 15, 1942; s. Ronald Oliver and Jeanne (Dooly) M.; m. Martha Moore, Aug. 3, 1968; children: Paul, Matthew, Erin. Author: Choosing an Automated Library System, 1980, A Reader on Choosing an Automated Library System, 1983, Using Outline Catalogs: A Nationwide Survey, 1983, Public Access to Outline Catalogs, 2d ed. 1985, The Directory of Automated Library Systems, 1985. BBA, Calif. State U.-Long Beach; MS in Adminstrn., U. Calif.-Irvine. Programmer, Douglas Aircraft, Long Beach; research assoc. Pub. Policy Research Orgn., U. Calif., Irvine, seminar instr. Univ. Extension and Continuing Edn.; pres. J. Matthews & Assocs., Inc., Grass Valley, Calif., 1976—. Peace corps vol. in Nepal, 1966-68. Mem. ALA, Am. Soc. Info., Soc. Mgmt. Info. Systems. Office: 256 Buena Vista 100 Grass Valley CA 95945

MATTHEWS, MIKE, see Schaaf, Richard Edmund

MATTHEWS, PEARL PARKERSON, b. Chgo., Feb. 26, 1941; d. Finis Eugene and Gertie Catherine (Williams) Parkerson; m. Arthur William Green, Sept. 22, 1984; children by previous marriage—Crystal R. Latimer-Murray, Kelly R. Latimer. Contrbr. articles to mags., newspapers including Essence Mag., Observer Newspaper, Ebony Jr! Mag., others; contrbr., ed.: First Edition Newsletter, 1978-1980. Wrkg. on novel. Student Roosevelt U., 1980-1981. Legal sec. McDermott, Will & Emery, Chgo., 1969-84, Katten Muchin & Zavis, Chgo., 1984—. Recipient 3d prize for fiction Phila. Wrtr.'s Conf., 1977, 1st place for dramatic reading Toastmasters Intl., 1986. Mem. Intl. Black Wrtrs. Conf. (Best Performing Artist 1987, 3d prize for fiction 1987), First Ed. Wrting Workshop (founder), League of Black Women. Home: 9151 S Marshfield Ave Chicago IL 60620

MATTHEWS, WILLIAM, b. Cincinnati, OH, Nov. 11, 1942; m. Maria Harris, May 5, 1963; children—William, Sebastian; m. 2d, Arlene Modica, Sept. 23, 1985. Author: Ruining the New Road, 1970, Sleek for the Long Flight, 1972, Sticks & Stones, 1975, Rising and Falling, 1979, Flood, 1982, A Happy Childhood, 1984, Foreseeable Futures, 1987. BA, Yale, 1965; MA, U. of North Carolina, 1966. Instr. Wells College, 1968-69; asst. prof., Cornell U., 1969-73; wrtr.-in- res., Emerson College, 1973-74; prof. U. of Col., 1974-78; prof., U. of Wash., 1979-83; wrtr.-in-res., City College, NYC, 1985—. Awards: NEA Fellowship, 1974, 1983-84; Ingram Merrill Fdn. Fellowship, 1983. Mem. PSA (pres., 1984-88); PEN. Home: 523 W 121 St New York NY 10027

MATTHIESSEN, PETER, b. NYC, May 22, 1927; s. Erard A. and Elizabeth (Carey) M.; m. Patricia Southgate, Feb. 8, 1951 (div.); m. 2d, Deborah Love, May 8, 1963 (dec. Jan. 1972); children—Lucas C., Sara C., Rue, Alexander F.L.; m. 3d, Maria Eckhart, Nov. 28, 1980. Author: Race Rock, 1954, Partisans, 1955, Raditzer, 1960, Wildlife in America, 1959, The Cloud Forest, 1961, Under the Mountain Wall, 1963, At Play in the Fields of the Lord, 1965, Sal si Puedes, 1969, Blue Meridian, 1971, The Tree Where Man Was Born, 1972, The Wind Birds, 1973, Far Tortuga, 1975, The Snow Leopard, 1978 (Nat. Book award), Sand Rivers, 1981, In the Spirit of Crazy Horse, 1983, Indian Country, 1984, Nine-Headed Dragon River, 1986, Men's Lives, 1986. Student, The Sorbonne, Paris, France, 1948-49; BA, Yale, 1950. AAAL grantee, 1963. Mem. Nat. Inst. Arts and Letters, 1974. Home: Bridge Ln Sagaponack NY 11062

MATTILL, JOHN ISHAM, b. Rochester, NY, Sept. 12, 1921; s. Henry Albright and Helen (Isham) M.; m. Anne Waterman, Oct. 14, 1947. Ed., Technology Review, 1965—. BA, Carleton Coll., 1943; MA, U. IA, 1947. Asst. dir. news off. Mass. Inst. Tech., Cambridge, 1948-53, dir. pubns., 53-64; ed. Technology Review, Cambridge, 1965—. Served to 1st Lt., Sig. Corps, 1943-45. Mem. NASW, AAAS, Council Advancement & Support Edn. Office: MIT 77 Massachusetts Ave Cambridge MA 02139

MATTINGLY, RICHARD E. (RICK), b. Louisville, Feb. 20, 1950. Ed.: Modern Percussionist mag., 1984—, Master Studies (Joe Morello), 1983, Drum Wisdom (Bob Moses), 1984, New Breed (Gary Chester), 1985, The Spirit of Percussion (Airto), 1985. Ed., Modern Drummer Publications, Inc., Cedar Grove, NJ, 1981—. Office: Drummer 870 Pompton Ave Cedar Grove NJ 07009

MATTOX, LEWIS E., b. Bethesda, MD, June 12, 1949. Author: training matls. for U.S. Army Reserves, tech. matls. for Inst. of Profl. Bowling Instruction; articles for ORBUS mag., Orlando Bus. Jnl., Orange County Sun and Orlando Sentinel, Tournament Bowler, Bowler's Jnl; ed. 3HUNDRED Magazine (monthly sports pubn.); brochures and newsletters for Crime Commission, Inc. BS, Western Ill. Univ., Macomb, 1971; attended Lake Forest Grad. Schl. of Management, Ill., 1978-80. Flight attendant/mktg. coordinator, United Airlines, 1973-84; supvsr., Orange County Library System, Fla., 1986—; freelance wrtr., researcher, 1982—. Mem. Florida Freelance Wrtrs. Assn. Home: 6326 Shenandoah Way Orlando FL 32807

MATUZAK, JOSEPH MATTHEW, b. Flint, MI, Dec. 12, 1955; s. David and Mary (Amersdorfer) M.; m. Josie Kearns, July 18, 1980. Contrbr. poems to Kansas Qtly, Corridors, Cedar Rock, Fedora, other lit mags; asst. ed. New Pages, ed. Kwasind, Artifact, BRIX. BA, Eng. and Psychology, Univ. of Mich., 1984. Mgr. IO Software, 1984-85; coord. American Red Cross (Flint, Mich.), 1979-85; revwr./reporter, Flint Jnl, 1984-85. Mem. Genesee Writers, Poetry Resource Ctr. Hopwood Award for Poetry, 1983, 84. Home: 431 Thomson St Flint MI 48503

MAU, ERNEST EUGENE, b.NYC, Feb. 18, 1945; s. Ernest and Constance Gertrude (Kluger) M.; m. Barbara Mew, July 22, 1972. Author: The Free-Lance Writers Survival Manual, 1981,

Create Word Puzzles with your Microcomputer, 1982, Secrets of Better BASIC, 1982, Getting the Most from your Microcomputer, 1983. Contrbr. numerous articles to computer mags.; word games and word puzzles to puzzle mags. Author numerous tehnical manuals, brochures. Product rvws. ed.: Online Today Mag., 1984—. Student U. Rochester, 1963-65, U. Colo., 1965-67. Technical wrtr. Data Products Corp., Englewood, CO, 1969, Stanley Aviation, Inc., Aurora, CO, 1970-71; mgr. technical communications Electronic Processors, Inc., Englewood, CO, 1971-73; technical/marketing wrtr. Lear Siegler, Inc., Englewood, 1973-75; free-lance wrtr., ed., 1975—. Recipient awards Soc. Technical Communicators, 1978—84. Mem. Colo. Authors League (Top Hand awards 1982-86), NWC, Computer Press Assn. Address: 3108 S Granby Way Aurora CO 80014

MAULE, HAMILTON BEE, b. Ojus, FL, Mar. 19, 1915; s. Claude Wendell and Zelita (Bee) M.; m. Ann Moore (div. Feb. 1958); children: Hamilton Bee, Halsey Coykendall, Robin Hamilton, Frederica (Mrs. James Rosenfield); m. Dorothy Levins, Apr. 25, 1959. Author: Jeremy Todd, 1958, The Pros, (with Robert Riger), 1959, Footsteps, 1960, The Rookie, 1961, The Quarterback, 1962, The Shortstop, 1962, The Game, 1963, 65, 68, Championship Quarterback, 1963, Beatty of the Yankees, 1963, Rub-a-Dub-Dub, 1964, The Running Back, 1964, The Last Out, 1965, The Linebacker, 1965, The Corner Back, 1966, The Receiver, 1967, The Players, 1968, The Pro Season, 1970, Running Scarred, 1972, Bart Starr, Quarterback, 1973, The Professionals, 1980, The Front Four, 1981. Student, St. Mary's U., 1934-37; BJ, U. Tex. at Austin, 1947. Pub. dir. Los Angeles Rams Football Club, 1949-52, Dallas Football Club, 1952. Sports Writer: Austin (Tex.) Am.-Statesman, 1946, Dallas Morning News, 1947-48; sports writer: Dallas News, 1953-56; sr. editor: Sports Illus., 1957-75; sr. writer: Classic Mag., 1975-79; columnist, contrb. editor: Pro Mag., The Runner, from 1980. Served with U.S. Merchant Marine, 1939-45. Mem. AG, WG Am. Home: 25 Sutton Pl S New York NY 10022

MAXFIELD, MARIA URSULA, b. Bad Heilbrunn, Fed. Republic Germany, June 8, 1932; came to U.S., 1956, naturalized, 1980; d. Johann and Maria (Steinberger) Weber; m. D. Bruce Maxfield, Sept. 11, 1954 (div. 1961); children—Sylvia, Solveig. Contrbr. poems to anthols., nonfiction articles to jnls., book rvws. and abstracts to profl. jnls. Author newsletters, operations and user manuals for computers, 1979—. BA, Coll. Poli. Sci., Munich, 1952; Cert. in Lab. Relations, Cornell U., 1953; post-grad. Union Grad. Schl., Yellow Springs, Ohio, 1972-76. Editorial researcher Time Mag., NYC, 1957-58; chief abstractor Sociol. Abstracts Inc., San Diego, 1964-72; copy ed. NYT Info. Bank, Parsippany, N.J., 1974-76; asst. editor Jnl Alcohol Studies, Rutgers U., Piscataway, N.J., 1976-79; tech. writer Am. Cyanamid Co., Clifton, N.J., 1979-82, Warner-Lambert Co., Morris Plains, N.J., 1982—. Mem. Am. Sociol. Assn., Tech. Communication. Home: 11 Westcrest Trail Kinnelon NJ 07405

MAXSON, NOEL TOPE, b. Oak Park, IL, Apr. 2, 1926; s. Noel Millar and Mary Louise (Cook) M.; m. Nancy Bishop, July 1, 1950; children—William Noel, Robert Alan, Judith Lynn. AB, U. Rochester; DDS, Northwestern U. Self-employed dentist, Oak Park, IL, 1951—; ed. CDS Review, Chgo. Dental Soc., 1983—. Office: 840 S Oak Park Ave Oak Park IL 60304

MAXWELL, ALICE S. (Maxwell Goetz), b. Mt. Vernon, NY, d. Robert Guy and Mary Louisa Lawrence (Frank) Stubing; m. Robert W. Maxwell, Sept. 8, 1945; children—Laura Barton Maxwell Wheeler, David Lawrence, Robert Stevenson. Author: Asia Revisited, 1952, Virago: The Story of Anne Newport Royall (with Marion Dunlevy), 1985; contrbr. articles to Holiday mag., Travel mag. Natl. Geographic mag. BA, Barnard Coll. Editorial asst. N.Y. Times, 1945-46; freelance corr. UPI and AP, Philippines and Indonesia, 1950-52; chmn. public relations N.J. Fedn. Republican Women, 1962-68; columnist Advisor, Middletown, N.J., 1964-74. Office: 27 Monroe St Red Bank NJ 07701

MAXWELL, BRUCE DAVID, b. Los Angeles, Dec. 27, 1949; s. Morris James and Ruth Vera (Anderson) Maxwell; m. Janice Marie Funk, Nov. 7, 1980; children—Dionne (Campbell), Sharome (Campbell). Contrbr. to The Ensign, and Utah Historical Qtly. BA, Calif. State U., 1980. Freelance music wrtr. Mem. Associated Latter Day Media Artists. Home: 19142 Bryant St Northridge CA 91324

MAXWELL, JANE, see Smith, Jane Davis

MAXWELL, OTIS ALLEN, b. Waco, TX, Nov. 24, 1915; s. Otis Allen and Myra (Vesey) M.; m. Emma Vee Dunlap, Aug. 31, 1940; children—Otis Allen III, Mary Susanna, Rebecca Agnes. Asst. book editor Dallas Morning News, 1937-42, 48-58, book editor, 1958-81; asst. dir. So. Meth. U. Press, 1939-42, dir., 1946-82; mng. editor Southwest Rvw, 1939-42, editor, 1946-63; adj. prof. English, SMU, 1973-82; vice pres. Assn. Am. Univ. Presses, 1955. Editor: The Present Danger: Four Essays on American Freedom, 1953, (with Mody C. Boatright and Wilson M. Hudson) Folk Travelers: Ballads, Tales and Talk, 1953, Texas Folk and Folklore, 1954, Mesquite and Willow, 1957, Madstones and Twisters, 1958, And Horns on the Toads, 1959, Singers and Storytellers, 1961, The Golden Log, 1962, (with Lon Tinkle) The Cowboy Reader, 1959, (with Boatright and Hudson) A Good Tale and a Bonnie Tune, 1964 (with Hudson) The Sunny Slopes of Long Ago, 1966. BA, So. Methodist U., 1937, BS in Commerce, 1937, MA, 1940. Served from ensign to lt. comdr. Supply Corps, USNR, 1942-46. Mem. Phi Beta Kappa, Tex. Inst. Letters, Tex. Folklore Soc. Home: 6610 Northwood Rd Dallas TX 75225

MAXWELL, WILLIAM, b. Lincoln, IL, Aug. 16, 1908; s. William Keepers and Eva Blossom (Blinn) M.; m. Emily Gilman Noyes, May 17, 1945; children—Katharine Farrington, Emily Brooke. Author: Bright Center of Heaven, 1934, They Came Like Swallows, 1937, The Folded Leaf, 1945, The Heavenly Tenants, 1946, Time will Darken It, 1948, 83, (with Jean Stafford, John Cheever, Daniel Fuchs) Stories, 1956, The Chateau, 1961, The Old Man at the Railroad Crossing, 1966, Ancestors, 1971, Over by the River, 1977, So Long, See You Tomorrow, 1979. Student, U. Ill., 1926-30, 31-33, Harvard U., 1930-31. Editorial staff New Yorker mag., 1936-76; also stories, book reviews; editor: Letters of Sylvia Townsend Warner. Mem. Natl. Inst. Arts and Letters. Home: 544 E 86th St New York NY 10028

MAY, BARBARA L., b. Chgo., Nov. 1, 1937, d. Ralph Stayart and Lorraine (Miecke) Lightbody; m. W. Marshall May, Apr. 25, 1958; children—Abigail, Fred, Peter. Newsletter ed.: Consuming Passions, Caregivers. Student U. Chgo. Pres. May Services, Inc., Norwood, N.J., 1981-85, Fulfillment Etc., Inc., Norwood, 1985—. Office: Box 802 Georgetown CT 06829

MAY, ERNEST RICHARD, b. Ft. Worth, TX, Nov. 19, 1928; s. Ernest and Rachel (Garza) M.; m. Nancy Caughey, Dec. 15, 1950; children—John Ernest, Susan Rachel, Donna LaRee. Author: The World War and American Isolation, 1914-17, 1959, The Ultimate Decision, The President as Commander in Chief, 1960, Imperial Democracy, The Emergence of America as a Great Power, 1961, The American Image, 4 vols., 1963, (with John W. Caughey) A History of the United States, 1964, (with the editors of Life) The Progressive Era, 1964, War, Boom and Bust, 1964, From Isolation to Imperialism, 1898-1919, 1964, (with John W. Caughey and John Hope Franklin) Land of the Free, 1966, American Imperialism: A Speculative Essay, 1968, Lessons of the Past: The Use and Misuse of History in American Foreign Policy, 1973, The Making of The Monroe Doctrine, 1975, (with Dorothy G. Blaney) Careers for Humanists, 1981; author: A Proud Nation, 1983, Knowing One's Enemies: Intelligence Assessment before the Two World Wars, 1984. AB, UCLA, 1948, MA, 1949, PhD, 1951. Served as lt. (j.g.) USNR, 1951-54. Guggenheim fellow, 1958-59; faculty research fellow Social Sci. Research Council, 1959-61; fellow Center for Advanced Study Behavioral Scis., 1963-64, Woodrow Wilson Intl. Center, 1983. Office: Hist Dept Harvard U Cambridge MA 02138

MAYER, IRA, b. NYC, June 10, 1952; s. Ludwig and Trude (Seligmann) M.; m. Riva Bennett, Mar. 13, 1983. Contrbr.: Sunday N.Y. Times, N.Y. Post, High Fidelity, American Way, Channels, Video Store, Village Voice, Stereo Review, Rolling Stone; Good Time Guide to Montreal, 1983, Fun In London, 1984, The Electronic Mailbox, 1985. BA, Hunter Coll., 1974; MA, NYU, 1979. Ed., Record World, NYC, 1974-77, N.Y. Law Jnl. Pub., NYC, 78-79; pres. Presentation Consultants, NYC, 1981—. Mem. NYBPE, Computer Press Assn. Address: 488 E 18 St Brooklyn NY 11226

MAYER, JANE S., b. NYC, Mar. 5, 1929, d. Michael Sommerfield and Nettie Needle; m. Perry Mayer, Apr. 6, 1950; 1 child, Kerry. Contrbg. ed. Chocolate News; contrbr. articles to Boston Globe, Calif. Good Life, Los Angeles Daily News, Los Angeles Times, Los Angeles Herald Examiner, Newsday, Washington Post. BA, Bklyn. Coll. Mem. West Valley Writer's Group (pres. 1982-85), So. Calif. Book Publicists. Home: 19471 Oxnard St Tarzana CA 91356

MAYER, MARTIN PRAGER, b. NYC, Jan. 14, 1928; s. Henry and Ruby (Prager) M.; m. Ellen Moers, June 23, 1949 (dec. Aug. 1979); children—Thomas, James; m. 2d, Karin Lissakers, Oct. 25, 1980; children—Fredrica, Henry. Author: (novel) The Experts, 1955; Wall Street, Men and Money, 2d edit., 1960, Madison Avenue, USA, 1958; (novel) A Voice That Fills the House, 1959; The Schools, 1961, Where, When & Why, Social Studies in American Schools, 1963, The Lawyers, 1967, Emory Buckner, 1968, Diploma, 1968, (with Cornell Capa) New Breed on Wall Street, 1969, Bricks, Mortar and the Performing Arts, 1970, All You Know Is Facts, 1970, The Teachers Strike, 1970, About Television, 1972, The Bankers, 1975, Conflicts of Interest: Broker-Dealer Firms, 1975, Today and Tomorrow in America, 1976, The Builders, 1978; (novel) Trigger Points, 1979; The Fate of the Dollar, 1980, The Met: One Hundred Years of Grand Opera, 1983, The Diplomats, 1983, The

Money Bazaars, 1984, Grandissimo Pavarotti, 1986, Making News, 1987. AB, Harvard U., 1947; DLitt (hon.), Wake Forest U., 1977, Adelphi U., 1981. Reporter, N.Y. Jnl Commerce, 1947-48; asst. editor Labor and Nation, 1948-49; editor Hillman Periodicals, 1949-51; assoc. editor Esquire mag., 1951-54, freelance writer, 1954—. Office: Curtis Brown 10 Astor Pl New York NY 10003

MAYER, SANDRA LEE, see Seagull, Samantha Singer

MAYER, SUSAN M., b. Troy, NY, Feb. 10, 195g; d. Joseph and Eileen (Davin) M. Ed./wrtr. & contrbr.: Water Technology Mag., Ground Water Age Convention Daily, 1984—; contrbr.: Professional Carwashing Mag., Ground Water Age Mag., Water Technology Mag., 1982—. AA in Theatre Arts, Jr. Coll. of Albany, 1979; BA in English & Pub. Communics., The Coll. of Saint Rose, 1982. Editorial asst. National Trade Pubns., Latham, NY, 1982-83, mng. ed. 1983-84, ed., 1984-86; exec. ed., Water Technology, Ground Water Age, Professional Car Washing, GAS RETAILER, 1986-. Mem. NAFE. Home: 386 3rd Ave Troy NY 12182

MAYERSON, PHILIP, b. NYC, May 20, 1918; s. Theodore and Clara (Fader) M.; m. Joy Gottesman Ungerleider, Nov. 25, 1976; children—Miriam Mayerson, Clare Mayerson, Peter Ungerleider, Steven Ungerleider, Jeanne Ungerleider, Andrew Ungerleider. Author: The Ancient Agricultural Regime of Nessana and the Central Negeb, 1961, Classical Mythology in Literature, Art and Music, 1971; contrbr. articles in field to profl. jnls. AB, NYU, 1947, PhD, 1956. Served with USN, 1942-45. Rockefeller Fdn. grantee, 1956-57; ACLS fellow, 1961-62. Home: 4 Oak Ln Larchmont NY 10538

MAYES, HERBERT RAYMOND, b. NYC., Aug. 11, 1900; s. Herman and Matilda (Hutter) M.; m. Grace Taub, Dec. 6, 1930; children: Victoria, Alexandra. Author: Alger, A Biography Without a Hero, 1928, Editor's Choice, 1956, An Editor's Treasury, 1968, The Magazine Maze: A Prejudiced Perspective, 1980. Editor: The Inland Merchant, mag., 1920-24; editor bus. paper div. Western Newspaper Union, 1924-26; editor Am. Druggist, mag., 1926-34, Pictorial Rvw, 1934-37; mng. editor Good Housekeeping. 1937-38, editor, 1938-58, McCall's 1959-62; pres. McCall Corp., 1961-65; cons. Norton Simon, Inc., 1966—. Recipient Editor of Year award Mag. Editors Council, 1960, Home: 1474 3rd Ave New York NY 10028

MAYES, KATHLEEN, b. Beckenham, Kent, Eng., Feb. 16, 1931, came to U.S., 1959, d. Henry Francis and Gladys Clara (Goldsmith) Doran; m. Dorin Barry Mayes, Nov. 4, 1961. Author: The Sodium Watcher's Guide, 1984, The Salt-Watcher's Guide, 1986, Osteoporosis: Brittle Bones and the Calcium Crisis, 1986, Osteoporosis, 1987, The Fat Connection, 1987. Ed., Eng. scriptwrtr. BBC, London, 1948-59. Home: 6061 Berkeley Rd Goleta CA 93117

MAYFAIR, BERTHA, see Raborg, Frederick Ashton, Jr.

MAYFIELD, RITA, see Nipp, Francis Stuart

MAYHALL, JANE FRANCIS, b. Louisville, KY, May 10, 1922; d. Howard Wesley, and Loula Eliza (Bennett) Mayhall; m. Leslie George Katz, June 4, 1940. Author: Cousin to Human, 1960, Ready for the Ha-Ha, 1966, Givers and Takers 1, 1968, Givers and Takers 2, 1973; contrbr. to The Best American Short Stories, 1947-49, New Directions, 1949, Treasury of American Fiction, 1981, Treasury of American Poetry, 1978 and var. other anthologies. Student Black Mountain College, 1937-40; New School for Social Research, 1945-48. Teacher, New School for Soc. Res, NYC, 1947-48; tchr., Morehead College, Ky., 1965-67; tchr., Hofstra U., NY, 1977-78. Home: 15 W 67th St New York NY 10023

MAYMAN, MARTIN, b. NYC, Apr. 2, 1924; s. Abraham and Anna (Mann) M.; m. Rosemary Walker, Oct. 12, 1960 (div.); children—Sara, Stephen, Daniel. Author: Three Approaches to the Experimental Study of Subliminal Processes, 1973, (with K.A. Menninger and P. Pruyser) The Vital Balance, 1963, A Manual for Psychiatric Case Study, 2d ed., 1963; editor: Infant Research: The Dawn of Awareness, 1981. BS, CCNY, 1943; MS, N.Y.U., 1947; PhD, U. Kans., 1953. Editor: Psychoanalytic Inquiry, 1980—; adv. editor: Jnl Consulting Psychology, 1965-70, Psychotherapy, 1975—. Home: 3969 Pemberton Ln Ann Arbor MI 48105

MAYNARD, ROBERT CLYVE, b. Bklyn., June 17, 1937; s. Samuel Christopher and Robertine Isola (Greaves) M.; m. Nancy Hicks, Jan. 1, 1975; children: Dori J., David H., Alex Caldwell. Reporter Afro-Am. News, Balt., 1956; reporter York (Pa.) Gazette and Daily, 1961-67, reporter Washington Post, 1967-72, assoc. editor/ombudsman, 1972-74, editorial writer, 1974-77; editor, pub. Oakland (Calif.) Tribune, 1979—, owner, 1983—; former chmn. Inst. Journalism Edn.; Syndicatd columnist Universal Press Syndicate; dir. AP; trustee Found. Am. Communications. Mem. Am. Newspaper Pubs. Assn. (govt. affairs com.), Am. Press Inst. (Western region adv. bd.), Newspaper Advt. Bur. (bd. dirs.). Office: The Tribune Tower Oakland CA 94612

MAZLISH, BRUCE, b. NYC, Sept. 15, 1923; s. Louis and Lena (Reuben) M.; children—Anthony, Jared, Cordelia, Peter. Author: (with J. Bronowski) The Western Intellectual Tradition, 1960, The Riddle of History, 1966, In Search of Nixon, 1972, James and John Stuart Mill: Father and Son in the 19th Century, 1975, The Revolutionary Ascetic, 1976, Kissinger, The European Mind in American Policy, 1976, (with Edwin Diamond) Jimmy Carter, An Interpretive Biography, 1980, The Meaning of Karl Marx, 1984; editor: Psychoanalysis and History, 1963, rev. edit., 1971, The Railroad and the Space Program: An Exploration in Historical Analogy, 1965; assoc. editor: Journal Interdisciplinary History, The Psychohistory Rvw. BA, Columbia U., 1944, MA, 1947, PhD, 1955. Served with inf. and OSS AUS, 1943-45. Fellow Am. Acad. Arts and Scis. Home: 11 Lowell St Cambridge MA 02138

MAZUR, GAIL BECKWITH, b. Cambridge, MA, Nov. 10, 1937, d. Manuel and S. Mildred (Rosenberg) B.; m. Michael Mazur, Dec. 28, 1958; children—Daniel, Kathe. Author: Nightfire, 1978, The Pose of Happiness, 1986; contrbr. poetry to Poetry, Hudson Rvw, New Republic, Ploughshares, others; contrbr. articles to Boston Rvw, Boston Globe. BA, Smith Coll., 1959; MA, Lesley Coll., Cambridge, 1983. Dir. Blacksmith House Poetry Program, Cambridge, 1973—; poet-in-residence Emerson Coll., Boston, 1979-80; ed. Ploughshares, Cambridge, 1980—; instr. U. Mass., Boston, 1985; vis. lectr. Wellesley Coll., 1986. Recipient Creative Wrtg. award NEA, 1978. Mem. PSA (Gertrude Claytor award poetry 1980), PEN (bd. dirs. New Eng. chpt. 1982—). Address: 5 Walnut Ave Cambridge MA 02140

MAZZARO, JEROME LOUIS, b. Detroit, Nov. 25, 1934; s. Emmacolato and Maria Carmela (Pedalino) M. Author, 1960—, latest being The Figure of Dante, 1981, The Caves of Love: Poems, 1985, Rubbings: Poems, 1985; ed., Fresco, 1960-61, Modern Poetry Studies, 1970-79, The Poetry Review, 1985—. AB, Wayne St. U., Detroit, 1954, PhD, 1963; MA, U. Iowa, 1956. Instr., U. Detroit, 1958-61; asst. prof. St. Coll. at Cortland (NY), 1962-64; asst. prof. St. U. of NY at Buffalo, 1964—. Guggenheim Fellow, 1964-65, Hadley Fellow, Bennington (VT) Coll. Mem. PSA, Dante Soc. of Am. Home: 147 Capen Blvd Buffalo NY 14226

MC AFEE, VIRGINIA THURSTON, b. Sandersville, GA, Feb. 18, 1950; d. William Gordon and Nancy Catherine (Everett) Thurston; m. James Lotis McAfee, Jr., Feb. 8, 1975; children: Jamie, Jonathan. Weekly columnist Wrightsville (Ga.) Headlight. Wrkg. on non-fiction. BA, MEd, Ga. Coll. Tchr. Brentwood Schl., Sandersville, Ga., 1973—. Recipient award for Column Ga. Press Assn., 1984, 86. Home: Rt 1 Box 240B Wrightsville GA 31096

MC ALEAVEY, DAVID WILLARD, b. Wichita, KS, Mar. 27, 1946, s. Frank Leo and Jane Louisa (Ayers) McA.; m. Christina Dickson, Jan. 1970 (div. 1971); m. 2d, Katherine Ann Perry, Jan. 2, 1977; children—Maia Margaret, Andrew Athan. Author: Sterling 403, 1971, The Forty Days, 1975, Shrine, Shelter, Cave, 1980, Holding Obsidian, 1985, Washington and Washington Writing, 1986; ed.: Evidence of Community: Writing from the Jenny McKean Moore Community Workshops at George Washington University, 1984. MFA, Cornell U., 1972, PhD, 1975. Mem. faculty George Washington U., Washington, 1974—, assoc. prof. English, 1983—, assoc. dean Columbian Coll. Arts & Scis., 1986—; mem. lit. panel D.C. Commn. on Arts and Humanities, 1983—; bd. dirs. Poetry Comm. of Greater Washington D.C. Area, 1985—. Recipient Kreymborg prize, PSA, 1984. Mem. MLA, AWP, PEN, Wrtrs. Center Bethesda, PSA. Home: 3305 N George Mason Dr Arlington VA 22207

MC ALISTER, THOMAS ALLEN, (Tomasco Mykelystar), b. San Mateo, Calif., Oct. 3, 1948, s. Charles James and June Viola (Conrad) McA.; m. Darlene Jo Pertner, June 28, 1969; children—Dawn, Jennifer, Ryan. Author: The Semblance, 1978, Persquagle Poems, 1983. Student, West Valley Coll., Campbell, Calif. Pres. Tomasco Enterprises, Santa Clara, Calif., 1985—. Home: 2850 Mauricia Ave Santa Clara CA 95051

MC ANALLY, DON, b. Sewell, NJ, Oct. 27, 1913; s. James C. and Ina (MacLeod) McA.; m. Edith P. McKinney, Dec. 11, 1934; 1 dau., Shirley Ann English. Contrbr. articles to newspapers. Ed.: Daily Times, Woodbury, NJ, 1932-43, Pacific Oil Marketer, 1960-66, Calif. Sr. Citizen, 1977-84, Automotive Booster of Calif., 1974—, Oil and Automotive Marketing News, 1966—. Pub. Calif. Business woman, 1978. Grad. public schs., Woodbury. Ed. Owens-Ill. Glass Co., Glassboro, NJ, 1943-45, ed., publicity wrtr., 1945-47; asst. advt. mgr. Libbey-Owens-Ford Glass Co., Toledo, OH, 1947-53; product sales mgr., sales promotion mgr. LOF Glass Fibers, Toledo, 1953-59; owner Hovercraft of Southern Calif., 1975-76. Home: 4409 Indiana Ave La Canada CA 91011

MCANALLY, MARY E(LLEN), b. Vandalia, IL, Jan. 21, 1939; d. Virgil Pafford and Mary Frances (Handy) M.; m. Etheridge Knight, June 11, 1973 (div); children: Mary Tandiwe, Etheridge Bambata. Author; We Will Make a River (poems), 1979; ed. Warning: Hitchhikers May Be Escaping Convicts anthology of poetry from prisoners of Oklahoma), 1980, The Absence of the Father and The Dance of the Zygotes (poems), 1981; Poems from the Animal Heart, 1981, ed, Family Violence: Poems on the Pathology, 1982, ed, We Sing Our Struggle: A Tribute to Us All, 1982, ed, Meridel Le Sueur, Word Is Movement: Journal Notes from Atlanta to Tulsa to Wounded Knee, 1983; Coming of Age in Oklahoma (poems), 1987. Contrbr of poems, articles, and rvws to lit mags, including New Letters, Women: A Journal of Liberation, Woman-spirit, Dark Hose, Chrysalis, Milkweed Chronicle, Painted Bride Qtly, Primavera, Feminist Rvw, Gar, Gryphon, Velvet Wings, Oakwood, West End, Off Our Backs, Nimrod, and South and West. Poery ed, Nimrod and Sister Advocate; contrbg ed, Sez. BA (cum laude), Univ of Tulsa, 1962; BD, Princeton Theological Sem, 1965; MA, Columbia Univ, 1968, additional grad study. Ordained Presbyterian clergywoman and ecumenical theologian. Instrctr, Spelman Coll, Atlanta, Ga., 1962; asst chaplain, Trenton (N.J.) State Hospital for the Criminally Insane, 1963; asst to the chaplain, Rutgers Univ, New Brunswick, N.J., 1963-64; Christian educ dir Firs Presby. Ch. in Bartlesville, Okla., 1964; asst pastor Trinity Presby. Ch., NYC, 1964-65; admin asst in office of student world relaions, United Presbyterian Church in the U.S.A., N.Y.C., 1965-69; instr in coll discovery program, Staten Island Community College of he City Univ of N.Y., 1969; assoc ed, American Report (natl peace newspaper), NYC, 1969-71; instr, Upward Bound program, Lincoln Univ, Jefferson City, Mo, 1972-73; instr, extension program at federal prison, Univ of Mo., 1972-73; senior citizens supervisor, Indianapolis Settlements, Inc., 1973-74; supervisor, Volunteers in Service to America (VISTA), Legal Services Orgn, Indianapolis, 1974-75; dir of educ, Associated Migrant Opportunity Services, Indianapolis, 1975; dir, Young Women's Christian Assn (YWCA), Bloomington, Minn., 1975-77; dir, Women's Center, Tulsa, Okla., 1977-79; asst dir, Natl Indian Child Abuse and Neglect Resource Center, Tuksa, 1979-80; state coordinator, HeadStart Program, Claremore, Okla, 1980-81; dir, Shelter for Battered Women, Tulsa. 1981; state coordinator, Okla Religious Coalition fo Abortion Rights, 1981—; dean of students, Okla Jr. Coll, 1986—. Poet-in-reidence for both the Okla Arts and Humanities Cncl in a prison ars pogram and the Tulsa Art and Humanities Cncl, 1978-79. Mem: Natl Writers Union (charter mem, exec bd mem, Okla. state organizer, 1981-84), Individual Artists of Oklahoma, Open Door Arts Cooperative, Tulsa Women's Political Caucus, Democratic Women's Action Group, Poets for Peace, Tulsa Peace Fellowship. Beaudoin Gem Stone award for poery, 1977; Carl Sandburg award for poetry, 1978; NEA creative witing literary fellowship, 1981-82. Home: 76 North Yorktown Tulsa OK 74110

MC ARTHUR, BARBARA JEAN (Jean Martin), b. Dubuque, IA, July 7; d. James Laurence and Ada Virginia (Boone) Martin; m. William H. McArthur, Aug. 24, 1957 (div. 1975); children—Michele Jean, William Michael. Contrbr. chpt. to microbiology book; articles to profl. jnls. Wrkg. on biography of U.S. Appeals Ct. Judge Damon J. Keith; epidemiology textbook. Ed.: (with L. Arking) Nursing Clinics of North America: Infection Control, 1980; mem. editorial bd.: Infection Control, 1979—. B.S.N., DePaul U., 1956, M.S., 1957; M.S., U. Wash., 1971, Ph.D., 1976. Asst. prof. Knoxville Coll., TN, 1957-69; assoc. prof. Wayne State U., Detroit, 1976-78, prof., 1978—. Office: Wayne State U 5557 Cass Ave Detroit MI 48202

MC AULAY, SARA W., b. Washington, Aug. 23, 1940, d. Edward Allen and Marjorie Randolph (Brower) Willis; m. Douglas H. McAulay; 1 son, Michael B. Author: Catch Rides (novel), 1975, In Search of the Petroglyph (novel for young readers), 1978, Chance (novel), 1982. Wrkg. on short story collection, novel. BA, Calif. State U.-Hayward, 1971; MA, Fairleigh Dickinson U., 1978. Adj. prof. Fairleigh Dickinson U., Madison, NJ, 1976-78, Rutgers U., Newark, 1977-83; asst. prof. dept English Calif. State U.-Hayward, 1984—. N.J. State Council on Arts fellow, 1982, NEA fellow, 1985. Mem. AG, NWU. Office: Dept Engl Cal St U Hayward CA 94542

MC AULEY, MILTON KENNETH, b. Dunsmuir, CA, Apr. 23, 1919, s. William Clear McAuley and Grace (Frentress) Holmes; m. Maxine Emma Laurenson, Mar. 16, 1942; children—Patricia Louise, Barbara Ann, William Kenneth. Author: Hiking Trails of the Santa Monica Mountains, 1980, 4th edit., 1987, Hiking in Topanga State Park, 1981, 2d edit., 1984, Hiking Trails of Point Mugu State Park, 1982, Hiking Trails of Malibu Creek State Park, 1983, Wildflowers of the Santa Monica Mountains, 1985. Wrkg. on hiking guide. BS, U. Ill., 1956; teaching credential, Calif. Lutheran Coll., 1971. Pilot U.S. Air Force, 1941-61; applications engr. Navigation and Control Div., Bendix Corp., Los Angeles, 1961-70; ed., Canyon Publishing Co., Canogo Park, 1980-. Served to maj. USAF, 1941-61. Home: 8561 Eatough Ave Canoga Park CA 91304

MC AULIFFE, FRANK MALACHI, b. NYC, Dec. 3, 1926; s. Cornelius Jeremiah and Margaret (Harte) McA.; m. Rita Mary Gibbons, Mar. 17, 1951; children—Meg (Mrs. Rich Reed), Liz (Mrs. Archie Gollen), Mark Conn, Mary (Mrs. Scott Buonocore), Kathleen, Barbara Bridget, Luke. Author: Hot Town, 1956; series with Augustus Mandrell as protagonist Of All the Blood Cheek, 1962; Rather a Vicious Gentleman, 1968, For Murder I Charge More, 1971, The Maltese Falcon Commission, 1974, Bagman, 1979, Bodyguard, 1980. Served with USAAF, 1945. Recipient Edgar award MWA, 1971. Address: 1828 Swift Blvd Ventura CA 93003

MC AVOY, WILLIAM CHARLES, b. Cleve., Jan. 28, 1921; s. Charles William and Olive Charlotte (Connors) McA.; m. Jerry Ferguson, Jan. 8, 1945 (div. 1976); children—Carolyn (Mrs. Paul A. Kolodziej), Kathleen, Michael, Thomas, William, Elizabeth, John, Anne, David; m. 2d, Constance Bednall, Nov. 18, 1981. Author: American College Handbook of English Fundamentals (with W.E. Buckler), 1965, Dramatic Tragedy, 1971; editor: Twelfth Night: The Variorum Shakespeare, 1966, A New Variorum Edition of Shakespeare: Twelfth Night: A Bibliography to Supplement the New Variorum Edition of 1901, 1984; contrbr. articles to profl. jnls. AB, John Carroll U., 1946; MA, U. Ill., 1948, PhD, 1952. Served with USAAF, 1942-45. Mem. MLA, AAUP. Home: 2336 Manor Lake Ct Chesterfield MO 63017

MC BAIN, ED, see Hunter, Evan

MC BEE, DENIS, (Duke D'Realo), b. Martinsburg, WV, June 2, 1952, s. Marlin William Jr. and Doris Jean (Hite) McB. Ed., Beatniks from Space mag., 1980-86, The Death Collection, 1982; contrbr. Cab Art, Marginal Politics, Delirium, Popular Reality, others. Student public schls., Martinsburg. Mem. staff U. Mich., Ann Arbor, 1973—; ed., pub. Neither/Nor Press, 1980—. Mem. CCLM Poetry Resource Center Mich. Office: Box 8043 Ann Arbor MI 48107

MC BRAND, QUINTEN, see Rusk, Nance J.

MC BRAYER, NELLIE K., b. GA, June 17, 1924; d. Ernest C. and Ola (Elrod) Clark; m. N. L. McBrayer, Apr. 22, 1942 (div. Nov. 21, 1979); children—Neiene, Buman, Johnny, Rita. Contrbr. poems to anthols.; author songs. Nurse, Convalscent Home, GA, 1967—. Recipient Golden Poet award World of Poetry, 1987. Home: Rt 1 Box 1685 Dawsonville GA 30534

MC BREARTY, ROBERT GARNER, b. San Antonio, July 1, 1954; s. William Francis and Virginia Edna (Garner) McB.; m. Mary Ellen Metke, June 16, 1984. Contrbr. short stories to Pushcart, Miss. Rvw, Kans. Qtly, New England Rvw. BFA, Inst. Allende, 1978; MFA in English, U. Iowa, 1981. Free-lance writer, 1980—; artist-in-residence N.Mex. Arts Div., Santa Fe, 1983-84. Address: 317 Holly Oak Ln Alameda CA 94501

MC BRIDE, ELLA ANDREPONT, b. Cedar Point, LA, Dec. 11, 1919, d. Joseph and Ella (Franques) Andrepont; m. Joseph Monroe McBride, Oct. 18, 1940 (dec. 1968). Contrbr., ed.: Roses From Heaven, vol. I, 1984, vol. II, 1983, 2d edit., 1984. Wrkg. on Des Roses du Ciel. BS, U. Southwestern La., 1942, spl. edn. cert., 1968. Tchr. elem. and high schls. in Tex. and La., 1948-78. Home: 2401 N 8th St Orange TX 77630

MC BRINE, AVA JEAN, b. Waco, TX, Nov. 13, 1947; d. Jackson Seymor, Jr. and Ava Fay (Stallard) Row; m. Eugene Dale McBrine, Nov. 18, 1967; children—Andrew Dale, Michael Paul, Jonathan Scott. Contrbr. poems to anthols. Student McLennan Commun. Coll., 1985-86. Recipient Golden Poet award World of Poetry, 1987. Home: B-39 Nassau Park Lewes DE 19958

MC CABE, JAMES VICTOR, b. Balt., July 3, 1963; s. Kenneth Eugene and Joyce Priscilla (Kerch) McC. Contrbr. poems to anthols., lit. mags. Art salesperson Fine Art Galleries, Ocean City, MD, 1981-86; art representative Arthur James Galleries, Delray Beach, FL, 1986-87; coordinating ed. CRC Press, Inc., Boca Raton, FL, 1986—. Home: 60 Marine Way 3 Delray Beach FL 33483

MC CABE, JOHN CHARLES, III, b. Detroit, Nov. 14, 1920; s. Charles John and Rosalie (Dropiewski) McC.; m. Vija Valda Zarina, Oct. 19, 1958; children—Linard Peter, Sean Cahal and Deirdre Rose (twins). Author: Mr. Laurel and Mr. Hardy, 1961, rev. ed., 1987, George M. Cohan: The Man Who Owned Broadway, 1973, The Comedy World of Stan Laurel, 1974, Laurel & Hardy, 1975, (with G.B. Harrison) Proclaiming the Word, 1976, (with A. Kilgore and R. Bann) Charlie Chaplin, 1978; conslt. to James Cagney for autobiography Cagney by Cagney, 1976. PhB, U. Detroit, 1947; MFA in Theatre, Fordham U., 1948; PhD in English Lit, Shakespeare Inst., U. Birmingham, Eng., 1954. Chmn. Dept. Dramatic Art, NYU, 1956-69; author-in-residence, Lake Superior State Coll., Sault Ste.

Marie, Mich., 1970-87. Served with USAAF, 1943-45. Mem. Shakespeare Assn. and The Players. Home: Box 363 Mackinac Island MI 49757

MC CABE, MARGARET E., b. Bklyn., July 4, 1939, d. William H. and Margaret E. (Simmons) McCabe; children—Suzanne E. Wakeland, David W. Medsker. Co-author: Simple Cooperation in the Classroom, 1985, How to Stop Fighting with Your Kids, 1985, How to Say What You Mean, 1986, Cooperative Meeting Management, 1986. BA, San Jose State U., 1971, MS, 1972; EdD, U. Laverne (Calif.), 1983. Psychologist, adminstr. various schl. dists., Calif., 1973-83; author, conslt. Intl. Training Assoc., Willits, Calif., 1983—; adj. prof. Dominican Coll., San Rafael, Calif., 1984-87; pres. Leadership Success Inst., 1987-. Office: Box 1599 Willits CA 95490

MC CABE, VICTORIA, b. Clare, IA, May 29, 1948; d. Raymond William and Ruby Colleen (Egli) McCabe; m. Jeru Hense, June 23, 1981; children—Shannon, Keegan. Author: John Keat's Porridge, 1975, Until Death, 1980. Contrbr. poems to lit. mags. BA, U. Mo., 1970; PhD, U. Denver, 1982. Hon. prof. English, U. Colo., Colorado Springs, 1977—; poetry ed., Writer's Forum. Mem. AAP, AWP. Home: 2301 Forest Denver CO 80207

MC CAFFERTY, BARBARA TAYLOR (Taylor McCafferty), b. Louisville, KY, Sept. 15, 1946; d. Charles Allen and Marjorie Ozie (Meador) Taylor; m. Richard Clark Taylor, Oct. 15, 1966 (div. 1978; children—Geoffrey Richard, Christopher Allen, Rachael Emily; m. John Alexander McCafferty, Nov. 15, 1982. Contrbr. to Alfred Hitchcock's Mystery Mag. B.A., U. Louisville, 1980. Editorial asst. Genl. Electric Corp., Louisville, 1966-69; art dir. Schneider, DeMuth Advt., Louisville, 1980—. Home: Rt 1 Box 167 Lebanon Junction KY 40150

McCAHEY, JEANNE, see Hart, Jeanne

MCCALL, MABEL BUNNY, b. Bronx, NY, Feb. 6, 1923; d. James and Mabel Mildern (Johnson) McCall; m. Theodore Richard Ross, Oct. 31, 1947 (dec. Nov. 7, 1973). Song lyricist & contrbr. to anthologies, magazines, newspapers (poetry). Award of Merit certificate for poem "The Rape of the Lady Called Harlem," and three others; Golden Poet awards, 1985, 86, 87. Home: 41-12 10th St 4f Long Island NY 11101

MC CALLA, GARY EDWARD, b. Chickasha, OK, Mar. 20, 1931; s. Joseph Bailey and Marilouise (Klaeger) McC.; m. Dominique Stassinos, Dec. 17, 1955; children—Karine, Claudia, Eric, Christopher. Advt. and pub. relations mgr. Ideco div. Dresser Industries, Dallas, 1957-61; pub. Passport mag., Dallas, 1961-62; contractor NASA, Houston, Huntsville, Ala., 1962-65; with So. Living mag., Birmingham, Ala., 1965—, editor, 1969—. BA in Journalism, U. Okla., 1954. Served to 1st lt. AUS, 1954-57. Office: 820 Shades Creek Pkwy Birmingham AL 35201

MC CANN, CECILE NELKEN, b. New Orleans; d. Abraham and Leona (Reiman) Nelken; children—Dorothy Collins, Cecile Isaacs, Annette Lassen, Denise Bachman, Albert Hews III. Founder, editor, pub. Artweek mag., Oakland, Calif., 1970—; conslt. NEA, 1974-78, fellow in art criticism, 1976; contrbr. to profl. publs. Student, Vassar Coll., Tulane U.; BA, San Jose State Coll., 1963, MA, 1964; postgrad., U. Calif., Berkeley, 1966-67. Office: 1628 Telegraph Ave Oakland CA 94612

McCANN, JANET, b. Newark, Nov. 5, 1942; m. Hugh McCann; children: Stephanie, Hugh, Paul, Peter. Editor poetry jnl Piddiddle; author: (chapbook) How They Got Here (winner Natl. Looking Glass chapbook competition), 1984; co-author: (textbook) Creative and Critical Thinking, 1985; contbr. over 350 poems to mags. MA, U. Pitts., 1964, PhD, 1974. Faculty, Tex. A&M, College Station, 1969—, assoc. prof., English, 1983—. Home: 1000 Timm Dr College Station TX 77840

MC CANN, MARIAH, see McCumber, Marie McHargue

MC CANN, MICHAEL F., b. Toronto, Ont., Can., Jan. 19, 1943, came to U.S., 1964, s. Jack F. McCann and Bertha Alice (Singleton) Maher; m. Lois Kaggen, Sept. 26, 1984. Author: Health Hazards Manual for Artists, 1975, 3d rev. edit., 1985, Artist Beware: The Hazards and Precautions in Working with Art and Craft Materials, 1979; ed. Health Hazards in the Arts and Crafts, 1980. BSc with honors in Chemistry, U. Calgary, 1964; PhD in Chemistry, Columbia U., 1972. Sr. tech. wrtr., advertising product safety coordinator GAF Corp., NYC, 1972-75; dir. art hazards resource center Fdn. for Community of Artists, NYC, 1975-77; founder and exec. dir. Center Occupational Hazards, NYC, 1977—. Editor Art Hazards News. Office: Center Occup Hazards 5 Beekman St New York NY 10038

MC CARRISTON, LINDA, b. Chelsea, MA, July 30, 1943, d. William Thomas and Leona Marie (Parent) McC.; m. Michael La Combe, Aug. 21, 1965 (div. July 1977); children—Michael La Combe, David La Combe; m. Tom Absher, Jan. 19, 1979; children—Robin, Shannon, Matthew. Author: Talking Soft Dutch, 1984 (AWP selection in award series for poetry 1983); contrbr. poems and prose to Ga. Rvw, Ohio Rvw, Poetry, Ploughshares, Poetry N.W., Poetry Now, New Eng. Rvw, Tar River, others. BA, Emmanuel Coll., Boston, 1965; MFA, Goddard Coll., Plainfield, Vt., 1978. Mem. faculty summer writing program Goddard Coll., 1978, 79, mem. faculty undergrad. program, 1982; mem. faculty adult degree program Vt. Coll., Montpelier, 1979—. Recipient Grolier prize Grolier Bookshop, Cambridge, Mass., 1982; Vt. Council for Arts fellow, 1982; NEA fellow, 1984. Mem. AWP, New Eng. Am. Studies Assn. Home: Genl Deliv Chelsea VT 05038

MC CARTHY, EUGENE JOSEPH, b. Watkins, MN, Mar. 29, 1916; s. Michael John and Anna (Baden) McC.; m. Abigail Quigley, June 1945; children: Ellen, Mary, Michael, Margaret. Author: Frontiers in American Democray, 1960, Ditionary of American Politics, 1962, A Liberal Answer to the Conservative Challenge, 1964, The Limits of Power, 1967, The Year of the People, 1969, Other Things and The Aardvarketry, 1970, The Hard Years, 1975, Mr. Raccoon and His Friends, 1977, America Revisited, 1978, Ground Fog and Night, 1979, The Ultimate Tyranny, 1980, Contradictions and Contraries, 1983, Up 'Til Now, 1987; co-author: A Political Bestiary, 1978. A.B., St. John's U., Collegeville, Minn., 1935; A.M., U. of Minn., 1939. Address: Box 22 Woodville VA 22749

MC CARTHY, GERALD A., b. Nov. 28, 1947; s. William J. and Marie (Calamandrei) McC. Book of poems: War Story, 1977. Poems, stories, reportage in TriQtly., New Letters, Natl. Cath. Reporter, Ploughshares, Mid-Am. Rvw, Wis. Rvw, Northeast, others. Instr. St. Thomas Aquinas Coll., Sparkill, N.Y., 1985—. Mem. Vets. for Peace, Maine, 1986. Mem. P&W, AWP. CAPS fellow in poetry NYS Com. on Arts, 1981. Home: Box 248 Mountainville NY 10953

MC CARTHY, KEVIN MICHAEL, b. Dumont, NJ, Oct. 15, 1940; s. Dennis Leo and Dorothy Marie (King) McC.; m. Eileen Tabor Mullady, Apr. 22, 1967 (div. 1977); children—Catherine, Brendan; m. Cynthia Ann Wetzel, Aug. 13, 1983; children—Erin, Matthew. Author: Grammar and Usage, 1980, Saudi Arabia: A Desert Kingdom, 1986, The AVT Learning System in Writing, 1986, The History of Gilchrist County, 1986. Wrkg. on book on 19th century Fla. newspapers, Fla. lighthouses. B.A., LaSalle Coll., 1963; M.A., U. N.C., 1966, Ph.D., 1970. Peace Corps vol. Ceyhan High Sch., Turkey, 1963-65; assoc. prof. U. Fla., Gainesville, 1969—; Fulbright prof. Lebanese Natl. U., Beirut, 1971-72, King Saud U., Riyadh, Saudi Arabia, 1982-84. Mem. Marjorie Kinnan Rawlings Soc. (v.p.). Home: 3915 SW 18th St Gainesville FL 32608

MC CARTHY, MARY, b. Seattle, June 21, 1912; d. Roy Winfield and Therese (Preston) McC.; son—Reuel K. Wilson; m. James Raymond West, April 15, 1961. Author: The Company She Keeps, 1942, The Oasis, 1949, Cast a Cold Eye, 1950, The Groves of Academe, 1952, A Charmed Life, 1955, Sights and Spectacles, 1956, Venice Observed, 1956, Memories of a Catholic Girlhood, 1957, The Stones of Florence, 1959, On the Contrary, 1961, The Group, 1963, Mary McCarthy's Theatre Chronicles, 1963, Vietnam, 1967, Hanoi, 1968, The Writing on the Wall, 1970, Birds of America, 1971, Medina, 1972, The Seventeenth Degree, 1974, The Mask of State, 1974, Cannibals and Missionaries, 1979, Ideas and the Novel, 1980, Occasional Prose, 1985, How I Grew, 1987; contrbr. articles to natl. magazines. AB, Vassar Coll., 1933. Editor Covici Friede, 1936-37; ed. Partisan Rvw, 1937-38, drama critic, 1937-48; instr. lit. Bard Coll., 1945-56; instr. Sarah Lawrence Coll., 1948; Northcliffe lectr. Univ. Coll., London, 1980; Charles P. Stevenson Chair of Literature, Bard Coll., 1986—; Guggenheim fellow, 1949, 59; Natl. Inst. grantee, 1957; Horizon prize, 1949; Edward McDowell Medal, 1984, for outstanding contribution to literature; National Medal for Literature, 1984. Mem. Natl. Inst. Arts and Letters, Phi Beta Kappa. Home: PO Box 5 Castine ME 04421

MC CARTHY, ROSEMARY P., b. Newark, Oct. 21, 1928, s. Daniel J. and Nora Elizabeth (Connors) McCarthy Levien. Author: The Family Tree: The Connors-Walsh Family of Kiltimagh, County Mayo, Eire and the United States of America with Branches in Great Britain and Throughout the World, 1979; wrtr., ed. Intl. Family Tree Newsletter, 1979—; co-ed.: Long Island Hist. Soc. Genealogy Workshop Newsletter, Bklyn., 1979-80. Wrkg. on family history. BS in Nursing, St. John's U., 1963; MEd, Columbia U., 1973. Public health nurse Dept. of Health, NYC, 1981—, acting dist. suprvsg. nurse, CSD 23, Bklyn, 1986—; family historian, genealogist, archivist. Mem. Am. Pub. Health Assn., Bklyn. Hist. Soc., Soc. Old Brooklynites. Home: 899 Union St Brooklyn NY 11215

MC CARTNEY, DOROTHY WILSON, b. Stroudsburg, PA, June 12, 1914, d. George Zabriskie and Winifred Russell (Hanna) Wilson; m. John Richard McCartney, Jan. 23, 1943; children—Elaina Maureen, Michael Scott. Author:

Lemmus Lemmus and Other Poems, 1973; contrbr. short stories, poems to publs. in U.S., Ireland and Eng. BA, Pa. State U., 1934; MA, Cornell U., 1943. Tchr. pub. schls. various locations in Pa., 1936-42; music librarian Cornell U., Ithaca, N.Y., 1942-43; asst. librarian West Chester (Pa.) State U., 1962-65; freelance wrtr., 1950—; Film Perspectives pianist for silent movies, Wilmington, Del., 1954-65; Film Perspectives secy. & treas., 1955-65; asst. to. John R. McCartney, dir., 1955-65. Recipient Oscar Arnold Young Meml. book award N.C. Poetry Council, 1974, numerous prizes for poems from various state poetry socs. and Nat. Fedn. State Poetry Socs. Mem. Pa. State Poetry Soc., N.C. State Poetry Soc. (poetry contest judge), AAUW (pres. wrtrs. group 1952-53). Home: Box 29 Westtown PA 19395

MCCARTY, JESSE LOUIS HENRY, (Butch R., or T., Mudbone, Vivian Esmeralda Mudbone, Joe Keats), b. Pensacola, FL, Jan. 18, 1941; s. Owen and Gloria Mary (Castagnasso) McC.; m. Marilyn Janey Van Eaton, Jan. 20, 1964 (div. Oct. 1968); children: Gary McCarty Braithwaite, May Donna Tournabuoni, Mysara Catherine, Zoey Van Eaton. Author: Skyroses, 1980; Valentine's People, 1981; The Anthology of the Hegelbrost Family of Idaho, 1983; The History of Lincoln County, New Mexico, from 1875-1885, 1985; Up Front: The U.S.A. Bumpersticker Catalog, 1986, also numerous books privately printed; contrbr. poems to Am. Lit. Anthology. Wrkg. on novels, semifiction. Student George Washington U., 1962-66, UCLA, 1977-79. Book and movie reviewer Tube mag., Madison, Wis., 1970-73; pub. relations wrtr., sports info. dir. Gallaudet Coll., Washington, 1974-75; ed. Sierra Star, Oakhurst, Calif., 1976-77; asst. ed. monthly mag. UCLA, Westwood, 1977-79; freelance wrtr. and ed., 1979—. Mem. NWU, P&W. Address: 32 W Anapamu Apt. 400 Santa Barbara CA 93101

MC CAULEY, CAROLE SPEARIN, b. Great Barrington, MA, Apr. 18, 1939, d. Kenneth Waldo and Elizabeth Daignault (La Prise) Spearin; m. Arthur Leo McCauley, Nov. 14, 1964; 1 son, Brendan. Author: Six Portraits (fiction), 1973; Computers and Creativity, 1974; Happenthing in Travel On (novel), 1975; Pregnancy After 35, 1976; AIDS: Prevention and Healing with Nutrition, 1985; Surviving Breast Cancer, 1978, 1986; The Honesty Tree (novel), 1986; When Your Child Is Afraid... (co-author), 1988; contrbr. stories, articles, poetry, rvws to: Omni, Creative Computing, Feminist Art Jnl, numerous other publs. Wrkg. on fantasy novel series.Student, U. Besancon, France, U. Montpellier, France; AB, Antioch U., 1962. Assoc. ed. Panache mag., Princeton, N.J., 1969-74; staff wrtr. Orthopaedic Index, Middle Village, N.Y., 1980-82; free-lance wrtr., ed., IBM Tech. Pubns., White Plains, NY, and Warwick, England, 1981—. Recipient 5 awards for short-story writing. Mem. NWU (exec. com. Westchester local br.), Feminist Wrtrs. Guild. Home: 23 Buena Vista Dr Greenwich CT 06831

MC CAULL, JULIAN LINCOLN, b. Mpls., Feb. 22, 1936; s. John Dinsmore and Janet Shores (McGill) McC., m. Charlene Joan Hayden, July 15, 1961; children: John, Alison. Author: Train No. 8, 1987, The Hinge, 1984; co-author: Water Pollution, 1974; sr. ed.: Natl. Stat. Assessment of Rural Water Conditions in the US, 1982; contrbr. numerous articles to profl. jnls. BA, Princeton U. Sci. writer/ed. Modern Medicine, Mpls., 1962-68; co-founder Inst. Afro-Am. Studies, Mpls., 1968; adminstr./ed. Center for the Biology of Natural Systems at Wash. Univ., St. Louis, 1968-70; co-ed./pub. Environment Mag., St Louis, 1970-78; Assoc. ed. Bell Labs, 1978, sr. ed. Cornell Univ., 1979-82; writer/pub./owner Alcyone Publs, Ithaca, NY, 1982—. Mem. NASW. Addres: RR1 Box 137B Locke NY 13092

MC CLANE, KENNETH ANDERSON JR., b. NYC, Feb. 19, 1951, s. Kenneth Anderson and Genevieve Dora (Greene) McC.; m. Rochelle Evette Woods, Oct. 22, 1982. Author: Out Beyond the Bay, 1975, Moons and Low Times, 1978, To Hear the River, 1981, At Winter's End, 1982, A Tree Beyond Telling: Poems Selected and New, 1984. AB, Cornell U., 1973, MA, 1974, MFA, 1976. Instr. English, Colby Coll., Waterville, Me., 1974-75; asst. supr. seek program CCNY, 1978-79; assoc. prof. English Cornell U., Ithaca, N.Y., 1982—; Luce vis. assoc. prof. Williams Coll., Williamstown, Mass., 1984-85. Recipient Corson Morrison Poetry prize, 1973, George Harmon Coxe award in creative wrtg., 1973. Home: 114 Glenside Rd Ithaca NY 14850

MC CLARY, JANE MC ILVAINE, b. Middleburg, VA, d. William Cooper and Elizabeth (Walker) Stevenson; m. Robinson McIlvaine, June 3, 1939 (dec. 1956); 1 son, Stevenson; m. 2d, Nelson C. McClary, Dec. 15, 1956; 1 son, Christopher. Author: Front Page for Jennifer, 1950, It Happens Every Thursday, 1951, The Sea Sprite, 1952, Cintras Challenge, 1955, Stardust for Jennifer, 1956, My Antarctic Honeymoon, 1956, Coppers Chance, 1952, Cammies Choice, 1961, Cammies Challenge, 1962, Cammies Cousin, 1963, The Will to Win, 1966, To Win the Hunt, 1966, A Portion for Foxes, 1972, Maggie Royal, 1981. Columnist Washington Times-Herald, 1937-40, Middleburg (Va.) Chronicle, 1937-40; wrtr. Time, Inc., NYC, 1940-43; corr. Phila. Inquirer, 1945-56, INS- London Express, NYC, 1953; ed., pub. Downingtown (Pa.) Weekly Archive, 1946-56; freelance wrtr., novelist. Mem. Overseas Press Club, AG, NWU, Va. Center for Creative Arts. Home: Box 326 Middleburg VA 22117

MC CLATCHY, JOSEPH DONALD, b. Bryn Mawr, PA, Aug. 12, 1945; s. J. Donald and Mary Jane (Hayden) McClatchy. Author: Scenes from Another Life, 1981, Stars Principal, 1986; editor: Anne Sexton: The Artist and Her Critics, 1978, Recitative: Prose by James Merrill, 1986, Poets on Painters, 1987; poetry and articles in The New Yorker, NY Times Book Rvw, The New Republic, other jnls. AB summa cum laude, Georgetown U., 1967; PhD, Yale U., 1974. Instr., LaSalle College, Phila., Pa., 1968-71; asst. prof., Yale U., New Haven, CT, 1974-81; writer-in-res., CUNY, NYC, 1982; lectr. Princeton U., Princeton, NJ, 1981—. Awards: Gordon Barber Prize, PSA, 1984; Witter Bynner Prize, Am. Acad. & Inst. of Arts and Letters, 1985. Home: 54 West 16th St New York NY 10011

MC CLEERY, WILLIAM THOMAS, b. Hastings, NE, Sept. 15, 1911; s. Carl Kilburn and Vera Gertrude (Lowman) McC.; m. Martha Davenport, Oct. 3, 1936 (div. 1946); 1 son, Michael Carl; m. 2d, Ann Roan Robinson, Mar. 18, 1950; 1 son, Samuel Adams. Author: Wolf Story, 1947; Broadway plays Hope for the Best, 1945, Parlor Story, 1947, Conversations on the Character of Princeton, 1986; co-author: The Way to Go, 1974. AB, U. Nebr., 1931. Feature writer Omaha World Herald; Washington staff A.P., 1932-34; exec. editor A.P. Feature Service, 1935-38; editorial staff Life mag., 1938-39; Sunday editor PM, 1939-45; assoc. editor Ladies' Home Jnl, 1958-63; editor Univ. Princeton (N.J.) Qtly, 1964-77; lectr. in playwriting Princeton U., 1967-77. Home: 317 Edgerstoune Rd Princeton NJ 08540

MC CLERNON, CRYSTAL DAWN, b. Tucson, Apr. 11, 1960; d. Walter Jesse and Mary Belle (Scott) Whittaker; m. Bernard McClernon, Feb. 24, 1979. Contrbr. articles to mags. B.S. in Ed., Southwest Mo. State U., 1983. Ed., wrtr. Southwest Mo. State U., Springfield, MO, 1981-82; tchr. Bristow Public Schls., OK, 1983-85, Albuquerque Public Schls., 1985—; TV scriptwriter, Highfire Prodns., 1987—. Mem. NCTE. Home: 7200 Montgomery NE B-2 Ste 115 Albuquerque NM 87109

MC CLOSKEY, MARK, b. NYC, Feb. 1, 1938, s. John and Adele (Bernard) McC.; m. Bernadette Jeanne Maron, Feb. 3, 1962 (div. 1973); children—Daria, Adrian. Author: Goodbye, But Listen, 1968, All That Mattered, 1976, The Secret Documents of America, 1977; translator The Latin Poetry of George Herbert: A Bilingual Edition, 1965. Wrkg. on series of mystery novels. BA, Iona Coll., 1961; MA, Ohio U., 1963. Instr. Ohio U., 1963-64, asst. ed. Ohio U. Press, 1964-66; asst. prof. SUNY, Cortland, 1966-70, U. So. Calif., 1970-73, Calif. State U., Chico, 1973-77; instr. Occidental Coll., Los Angeles, 1977—, Glendale Coll., Calif., 1980—; wrtr.-in-residence Hollins Coll., Va., 1970. Recipient Theodore Roethke prize Poetry N.W., 1973; faculty fellow in creative writing SUNY Research Found., 1967, 68. Mem. AWP, NWU, PSA. Home: 1525 Dixon St Glendale CA 91205

McCLUNG, ROBERT M(ARHALL), b. Sept. 10, 1916; s. Frank A. and Mary A. (Goehring) M.; m. Gale Stubbs, July 23, 1949; children: William Mashall, Thomas Cooper. Author: (many of his books self-illustrated): Wings in the Woods, 1948, Sphinx: The Story of a Caterpillar, 1949, rev ed, 1981, Ruby Throat: The Story of a Hummingbird, 1950, Stripe: The Story of a Chipmunk, 1951, Spike: the Story of a Whitetail Deer, 1952, Tiger: The Story of a Swallowtail Butterfly, 1953, Bufo: The Story of a Toad, 1954, Vulcan, the Story of a Bald Eagle, 1955, Major: The Story of a Black Bear, 1956, Green Darner: The Story of a Dragonfly, 1956, Leaper: The Story of an Atlantic Salmon, 1957, Luna: The Story of a Moth, 1957, All About Animals and Their Young, 1958, Buzztail: The Story of a Rattlesnake, 1958, Little Burma, 1958, Whooping Crane 1959, Otus, the Story of a Screech Owl, 1959, Shag, Last of the Plains Buffalo, 1960, Whitefoot: The Story of a Woodmouse, 1961, Mammals and How They Live, 1963, Possum, 1963, Screamer Last of the Eastern Panthers, 1964, Spotted Salamander, 1964, Honker, the story of a Wild Goose, 1965. Caterpillars and How they Live, 1965, The Swift Deer, 1966, Ladybug, 1966, Moths and Butterflies and How They Live, 1966, The Mighty Bear, 1967, Horseshoe Crab, 1967, Black Jack, Last of the Big Alligators, 1967 Redbird: The Story of a Cardinal, 1968, Lost Wild America, the story of own Extinct and Vanishing Wildlife, 1969, Blaze: The Story of Striped Skunk, 1969, Aquatic Insects and How They Live, 1970, Thor, Last of the Sperm Whales, 1971 Bees, Wasps, and Hornets and How They Live, 1971, Scoop: Last of the Brown Pelicans, 1972, Treasues in the Sea, 1972, Samson Last of the California Grizzlies, 1973, Mice, Moose, and Men: How Populations Rise and Fall, 1973, How Animals Hide, 1973, Gypsy Moth: Its History in America, 1974, Creepy Crawly Things: Reptiles and Amphibians, 1974, Sea Star, 1975, Lost Wild Worlds: The Story of Extinct and Vanishing

Wildlife of the Eastern Hemisphere, 1976, Animals That Build Their Homes, 1976, Peeper, First Voice of Spring, 1977, Hunted Mammals of the Sea, 1978, America's Endangered Birds: Programs and People Working to Save hem, 1979, Snakes: Their Place in the Sun, 1979, The Amazing Egg, 1980, Vanishing Wildlife of Latin America, 1981. Rajpur, Last of the Bengal Tigers, 1982, Mysteries of Migration, 1983. Gorilla, 1984, The True Adventures of Grizzly Adams, 1985, Whitetail 1987. Lili, a Giant Panda of Sichuan, 1988, Ed and contrbr: Wild Animals of North America, Song and Garden Birds of North America, Water, Prey, and Game Birds of North America, Vacationland U.S.A. Contrbr to Grolier's New Book of Knowledge and to mags. AB, Princeton Univ, 1939; MS, Cornell Univ, 1948. Copywriter, McCann, Erickson, Inc. (adv. agency), N.Y.C., 1940-41, 1946-47; asst in animal depts, N.Y. Zoological Park, 1948-52, curator of mammals and bird, 1952-55; ed, Nal Geographic Soc, Washington, D.C., 1958-62; freelance writer and ed of children's books, 1955-58, 1962—. Military service: U.S. Navy Reserve, active duty as deck officer and naval aviator, 1941-46; became lieutenant commander. Religion: Protestant. Home: 91 Sunset Ave. Amherst MA 01002

MC CLURE, MICHAEL THOMAS, b. Marysville, KS, Oct. 20, 1932; s. Thomas and Marian Dixie (Johnston) McC.; m. Joanna Keera Kinnison, Oct. 10, 1954; 1 dau., Katherine Jane. Author TV documentaries, jnlsm. (Rolling Stone, LA Times, Vanity Fair), poetry books Hymns to St. Geryon, 1959, Dark Brown, 1961, The New Book, 1961, Ghost Tantras, 1964, Little Odes, 1967, Star, 1970, Rare Angel, 1974, September Blackberries, 1974, Jaguar Skies, 1975, Antechamber, 1978, Selected Poems, 1986; also author: Meat Science Essays, 1963, Freewheelin Frank Secretary of the Angels—As Told to Michael McClure, 1969, The Mad Cub, 1970, The Adept, 1971, Hail Thee Who Play, 1974, The Grabbing of the Fairy, 1978, Josephine the Mouse Singer, 1980 (Obie Award), Fragments of Perseus, 1983 (poems); playwright: The Beard (NYC prodn. received two Obies 1967), The Mammals, Gorf, 1976, General Gorgeous, 1976; Scratching the Beat Surface, 1982 (essays), Specks, 1985 (essays), VKTMS, 1985 (play). BA, San Francisco State Coll., 1955. Playwright-in residence, A.C.T., 1975 (Guggenheim fellow for poetry 1974), A.C.T. (recipient award for Poetry NEA 1974, 75), A.C.T. (Magic Theatre award 1974), A.C.T. (Playwright award Rockefeller Found., 1975). Office: New Direction 80 8th Ave New York NY 10011

MC COMISKEY, BRUCE THOMAS, b. Newton, MA, Nov. 13, 1963; s. Thomas Edward and Eleanor Mary (Carp) McC. Contrbr. poems to lit. mags., anthols.; articles to profl. jnls. B.A. in English Edn., Ill. State U., 1986; postgrad., 1987. Composition instr. Ill. State U., Normal, 1987—, instr. English as a second lang., 1987—. Recipient cert. of Merit, poetry, Yes Press, 1985. Mem. NCTE. Home: 2 Hawthorn Dr Hawthorn Woods IL 60047

MC CONKEY, JAMES R., b. Lakewood, OH, Sept. 2, 1921; s. Clayton Delano and Grace (Baird) McC.; m. Gladys Jean Voorhees, May 6, 1944; children—Lawrence Clark, John Crispin, James Clayton. Author: The Novels of E.M. Forster, 1957, Night Stand, 1965, Crossroads, 1968, The Tree House Confessions, 1979, Court of Memory, 1983, To a Distant Island, 1984, Kayo, 1987; editor: Chekhov and Our Age, 1985. BA, Cleve. Coll., 1943; MA, Western Res. U., 1946; PhD, U. Iowa, 1953. Dir. Morehead Writers Workshop, 1951-56, Antioch Seminar in Writing and Pub., Yellow Springs, Ohio, 1957-60. Served with U.S. Army, 1943-45. Guggenheim fellow, 1970; Eugene Saxon Meml. Trust Fund fellow, 1962; recipient NEA essay award, 1968, Am. Acad. and Inst. Arts and Letters award in lit., 1979. Home: Route 1 Box 360 Trumansburg NY 14886

MC CORD, CATHERINE GUMM, b. Flemington, WV, Dec. 15, 1926; d. Robert Bent and Wilma (Gibson) Gumm; m. Charles Monroe McCord, Aug. 31, 1946; children; Charles Robert and Ellen Elizabeth. Author: Of Butterflies and Buttercups (haiku), 1985; ed. Alligator Quills (anthol. 3d-grade student poems), 1987; poems in Napa Rvw, Haiku Jnl, Hibiscus, Farm Wife News, Sandcutters, newspapers. Student Univ. of Ariz., 1944-47; B.S. (Bus. Admin.), Univ. of San Francisco, 1978. Technical wrtr., Hughes Aircraft, Tucson, 1955-60; wrtr.-ed., Aerojet-Genl. Corp., Sacramento, Calif., 1964-82; communications conslt., Shingle Springs, Calif., 1979—; poet-conslt., Calif. Poets in the Schls., San Francisco, 1986—. Recipient, Ad Schuster Award (Grand Prize), Berkeley, 1983; 2d place Book Award, Calif. Press Women, 1986; World of Poetry Laureate ($15,000 Grand Prize), 1987. Mem. Calif. Poets in the Schls., Calif Press Women, Natl. Press Women. Home: 3641 Kimworth Ln Shingle Springs CA 95682

MC CORD, CHRISTIAN, see Pickerell, Rodney R.

MC CORD, HOWARD LAWRENCE, b. El Paso, TX, Nov. 3, 1932, s. Frank Edward and Sylvia Joy (Coe) McC.; m. Dora Garcia Ochoa, Apr. 19, 1953 (div. 1975); children—Colman Garcia, Robert Ochoa; m. 2d, Jennifer Sue Revis, July 25, 1975; children—Susannah Leigh, Julia Eden, Wyatt Edward Asher, Eva Ariella Siobhan. Author: The Arcs of Lowitz, 1982, The Great Toad Hunt and Other Expeditions, 1982, Walking Edges: A Book of Obsessional Texts, 1983, Jennifer, 1984, 19 other books since 1963. BA, U. Tex.-El Paso, 1957; MA, U. Utah, 1958. Mem. faculty Wash. State U., 1960-71; prof. creative wrtg. Bowling Green (Ohio) State U., 1971—, dir. creative wrtg. program, 1971-80. Woodrow Wilson fellow, 1957; recipient Fulbright award to India, 1965; D.H. Lawrence fellow U. N.Mex., 1971, Ohio Arts Council fellow, 1982, 86, NEA fellow, 1976, 83. Mem. WWA. Home: 15431 Sand Ridge Bowling Green OH 43402

MC CORDUCK, PAMELA, b. Liverpool, Eng., Oct. 27, 1940, came to U.S., 1946, d. William John and Hilda May (Bond) McCorduck; m. Joseph F. Traub, Dec. 6, 1969. Author: Familiar Relations (novel), 1971, Working to the End (novel), 1972, Machines Who Think (non-fiction), 1979, The Fifth Generation (non-fiction), 1983, The Universal Machine (non-fiction), 1985. AB, U. Calif.-Berkeley, 1961; MFA, Columbia U., 1970. Lectr. Columbia U., NYC, 1980—. Mem. PEN Am. Ctr. Exec. Bd., AG, NASW. Home: 450 Riverside Dr New York NY 10027

MC CORMACK, OLIVIA, see Horrigan, Patricia Ann

MC CORMICK, KENNETH DALE, b. Madison, NJ, Feb. 25, 1906; s. John Dale and Ida Pearl (Wenger) McC.; children: Dale, Kevin; m. Anne Hutchens, 1968; 1 son, John Bradley, With Doubleday and Co., Inc., 1930—, successively clk., mgr., bookshop, promotion mgr. pub. house, reader in editorial dept., chief assoc. editor, 1938, editor-in-chief, 1942-71, v.p., 1948-71, sr. cons. editor, 1971—; editorial cons. Franklin Library, 1975; contbr to: Publishers' Weekly. AB, Willamette U., 1928. Home: 670 West End Ave New York NY 10025

MC CORMICK, PATRICK M. J., (Mijael Chohn), b. Tracy, MN, June 21, 1952; s. John Thomas and Diane Adah (Louaire-Johnston) McC.; m. Jennie Kay Flickinger, Oct. 8, 1977; children—John Thomas, Angelique Ellen, Heather Dianne, Gloria Malory. Ed., The Victorian (nwsltr.), 1979-81; contrbr. articles & poems to The Regista, 1973-77; Am. Poetry Anthology, 1985. BA in Hist., Borromeo Coll. of Ohio, 1977. Asst. mgr., M.A.R.S., Akron, OH, 1977; dist. dir. Catholic Youth Org., Barberton, OH, 1978; youth minister/liturgist, Our Lady of Victory Catholic Ch., Tallmadge, OH, 1978-81; dir. relig. edn. St. Rose's Catholic Church, Proctor, MN, 1985—. Mem. NWC. Home: 1011 5th St S E Bemidji MN 56601

MC COWN, JOHN CLINTON, b. Fayetteville, TN, Mar. 7, 1952, s. James Edward and Mary Jane (Wallace) McC.; m. Cynthia Pasquinelli, Sept. 2, 1982; children: Caitlin Ann, Mary Alison. Author: (poems) Sidetracks, 1977, Wind Over Water, 1984; ed.: Ind. Rvw, 1982-83; founder, ed.: Beloit Fiction Jnl, 1984—; contrbr. poems and short stories to N.W., So. Poetry, Conn. Poetry, St. Andrews rvws, Coll. English, Bluefish, Kans. Qtly, Poetry Now, Mississippi Mud, Dan River Anthology, Anthology Mag. Verse, Yearbook Am. Poetry, Wind. BA, Wake Forest U., 1974, MA, 1978; MFA, Ind. U., 1985. Artist-in-res. Johnston Tech. Inst., N.C., 1976-78; capitol reporter Ala. Info. Network, Montgomery, 1978; instr. James Sprunt Coll., Kenansville, N.C., 1979; assoc. instr. U. Ala., Tuscaloosa, 1980-81, Ind. U., Bloomington, 1981-84; asst. prof. Beloit Coll., Wis., 1984—. Recipient Germaine Bree Book award Jackpine Press, 1977; award for documentary excellence AP, 1978; prize AAP, 1982. Mem. AWP. Home: 636 Harrison Ave Beloit WI 53511

MC COY, EASTON WHITNEY, b. New Brunswick, NJ, Jan. 30, 1918; d. William Orr and Ruth (Lessig) Orr; m. Glenn W. McCoy Jan. 1, 1940 (div. 1969); 1 dau.: Kathy Long. Co-pub. Bolivar Breeze newspaper, Bolivar, NY, 1946-53. Contrbtr. bk rvws to local newspapers. BS, Northwestern Univ., 1939. Home: 500 S Main Apt 816 Elkhart IN 46515

MC COY, J. J., see McCoy, Joseph Jerome, Jr.

MC COY, JIM, see Schmidt, George Neil

MC COY, JOSEPH JEROME, JR., (J.J. McCoy), b. Phila., Jan. 4, 1917; s. Joseph Jerome and Clair Josephine (Tinaro) McC.; m. Basia Barbara Kocyan, Apr. 13, 1948; children—Tara Irene, Liza Marie. Author: Pet Safety, In Defense of Animals (outstanding Science Book for Children award, Natl. Sci. Tchrs. Assn. and the children's Book Council, 1978), The Cancer Lady, A Sea of Troubles (Outstanding Sci. Bk. for Children, 1975, Jr. Lit. Guild Selection), Wild Enemies (Jr. Lit. Guild Selection, 1974), Our Captive Animals (Outstanding Sci. Bk. for Children, 1972) To Feed a Nation, Saving Our Wildlife, Shadows Over the Land, House Sparrows, The Nature Sleuths, Swans, The Hunt for the Whooping Cranes, World of the Veterinarian, Animal Servants of Man, Lords of the Sky, Complete Book of Dog Training and Care, Complete Book of Cat Health and Care.

AA in Agrl., Pa. State U.-University Park, 1942. Pres. Frenchtown Bd. Health, N.J., 1975; chmn. Shade Tree Commn., Frenchtown, 1977-80, sec., 1986-87, chmn., 1987. Served to sgt. U.S. Army, 1942-46. Mem. Hawk Mountain Sanctuary Assn., Natl. Geographic Soc. Home: 17 Fourth St Frenchtown NJ 08825

MC COY, KAREN KAWAMOTO, b. Twin Falls, ID, Oct. 2, 1953; d. George Joji and Florene Fumi (Otsuki) Kawamoto; m. Edward Lee McCoy, June 18, 1978; 1 son, Kevin. Contrbr. non-fiction articles, young adult story to children's mags. B.S. in Microbiology, Oreg. State U., 1978. Sales clrk. Oreg. State U. Bookstore, Corvallis, 1979-84; free-lance wrtr., 1984—. Mem. SCBW (Honorable Mention for Young adult fiction, 1987), Akron Manuscript Club (Honorable Mention for children's literature, 1986). Home: 2632 Monterey Wooster OH 44691

MCCOY, MAUREEN ELLEN, b. Des Moines. Author: Walking After Midnight (novel), 1985, Summertime (novel), 1987; contrbr. stories to: New Letters, Gt. River Rvw, Intro, other mags. BA, U. Denver, 1972; MFA, U. Iowa, 1983. Wrtg. fellow Fine Arts Work Center, Provincetown, Mass., 1983-85; wrtr.-in-residence Kalamazoo (Mich.) Coll., 1984; Schweitzer Fellow, State Univ. of NY, 1987-89. MacDowell Colony resident, Peterborough, N.H., 1983; recipient James A. Michener award Copernicus Soc., U. Iowa, 1985. Home: 8 Peyster St Albany NY 12208

MC COY, MILES EDWARD, b. Yakima, WA, Jan. 27, 1949; s. Miles Edward and Linda Lou (Smith) McC.; m. Carla Marie Laurent, Aug. 11, 1979; 1 son, Blake Edward. Ed.: OAN Digger, 1983—, OAN Directory & Buyer's Guide, 1983—, Farwest Show Program, 1984—; contrbr. articles to num. mags. inclg.: Amer. Nurseryman, 1979—, Capital Press, 1979-83, Ornamentals Northwest, 1979—, Garden Supply Retailer, 1985, Golf Course Mgt., 1984. BS with honors in Jnlsm., BS with honors in Horticulture, Oregon State U., 1977. Biological tech., USDA/ARS Hort. Lab., Corvallis, OR, 1977-80; informational rep., OSU, Corvallis, 1980-83; dir. of communic., OR Assn. of Nurserymen, Portland, OR, 1983—. Mem. Nursery Assn. Execs. Office: 2780 SE Harrison 204 Milwaukie OR 97222

MC COY, ROBIN RENEE, b. Portsmouth, VA, Jan. 1, 1957; d. Paul Dean and Bernadette Mary (Kascak) Hunley; m. Steven Davis McCoy, June 14, 1980; children—Robert James, Laura Renee. Contrbr. to Our World's Best Loved Poems, 1985. Wrkg. on poetry collection, children's story, short stories. Pharmacy tech. Gen. Med. Ctrs., Pomona, Calif., 1978-80; data analyst SAI Comsystems, Pomona, 1980-83; tax practitioner, Fontana, Calif., 1984—; supr. Transamerica, Upland, Calif., 1984—. Recipient Golden Poet award World of Poetry, Sacramento, 1985, 86. Address: 10400 Arrow Rt P-11 Rancho Cucamongo CA 91730

MC CRACKEN, DANIEL DELBERT, b. Hughsville, MT, July 23, 1930; s. Albert Kay and Blanche (Spear) McC.; m. Evelyn Edwards, 1952; children: Charles, Judith, Cynthia, Virginia, Rachel, Aliza, Thomas; m. Helen Blumenthal, 1980; 1 stepson, Michael Cohen. Author: Digital Computer Programming, 1957, (with H. Weiss and T.H. Lee) Programming Business Computers, 1959, A Guide to FORTRAN programming, 1961, A Guide to IBM 1401 Programming, 1962, A Guide to ALGOL Programming, 1962, A Guide to COBOL Programming, 1963, (with U. Garbassi) 2d ed., 1970, (with F.J. Gruenberger) Introduction to Electronic Computers, 1963, (with W.S. Dorn) Numerical Methods and FORTRAN Programming, 1964, A Guide to FORTRAN IV Programming, 1965, 2d ed., 1972, FORTRAN with Engineering Applications, 1967, Public Policy and the Expert, 1971, Numerical Methods with FORTRAN IV Case Studies, 1972, A Simplified Guide to FORTRAN Programming, 1974, A Simplified Guide to FORTRAN Programming, 1974, A Simplified Guide to Structured COBOL Programming, 1976, A Guide to PL/M Programming for Microcomputer Applications, 1978, A Guide to NOMAD for Applications Development, 1981, Engineers and Scientist with FORTRAN 79, 1984; editor: (with M. Mead, R.L. Shinn and J.E. Carothers) To Love or To Perish: The Technological Crisis and the Churches, 1972. BA in Math., Central Wash. U., 1950, 1951; student, NYU, 1958-59; M.Div., Union Theol. Sem., NYC, 1970. Address: 160 Cabrini Blvd New York NY 10033

MC CRAE, SHARON ELIZABETH, b. Morristown, NJ, Apr. 22, 1955; d. William Patrick and Alma Teresa (Tryder) McC. Editor: Chem. Equipment mag., 1982-84, Pharma News, 1986—. Contrbr. articles to newspapers, trade and bus. pubs. BS in Journalism, Ariz. State U., 1979. Reporter, Recorder Pub. Co., Bernardsville, N.J., 1980-82; acct. exec. Gilbert, Whitney & Johns, Whippany, N.J., 1984-86. Mem. Intl. Assn. Bus. Communicators, Natl. Assn. Female Execs. Home: 55 Whitehead Rd Morristown NJ 07960

MC CRAY, KATHERINE LEE, b. Rochester, NY, Aug. 1, 1961, d. Eugene Fred and Joan (Hannon) Wolfarth. Contrbr. articles to Health Assn. Newsletter. BA in Communication Arts, U. Dayton, 1983. Freelance wrtr., The Health Assn., Rochester, N.Y., 1983—; photog. lab. tehnician Visual Horizons, Rochester, 1984-87; camera operator, Visual Impressions, Rochester, 1987—. Home: 153 Ashland St 2 Rochester NY 14620

MC CRIE, ROBERT DELBERT, b. Sarnia, Ont., Can., Oct. 8, 1938; s. Robert Newton and Evelyn May (Johnston) McC.; m. Fulvia Madia, Dec. 22, 1965; children—Carla Alexandra, Mara Elizabeth. BA, Ohio Wesleyan Univ., 1960; MS, Univ. Toledo, 1962; postgrad, Univ. Chgo., 1962-63. Rsrchr. Connective Tissues Research Lab., Copenhagen, 1963; copywrtr. advt. agcys., 1965-70; pres., ed. Security Letter, Inc., 1970—; ed., pub. HBJ Publs., 1973-76; pres. Mags. for Medicine, Inc., 1972—. Editor: Behavioral Medicine, 1978-81, Security Letter Source Book, 1983—; contrbr. books and articles on security. Home: 49 E 96th St New York NY 10128

MC CRIMMON, JAMES MCNAB, b. Renton, Scotland, June 16, 1908; came to U.S., 1929, naturalized, 1939; s. John and Margaret (Patterson) McCrimmon; m. Barbara Smith, June 10, 1939; children: Kevin M., John M. Author: (with MacMinn and Hainds) Bibliography of the Writing of John Stuart Mill, 1945, Writing with a Purpose, 1950, Open Door to Education, (with Louttit and Babberton), 1951, From Source to Statement, 1968. BA, Northwestern U., 1932, MA, 1933, PhD, 1937. Home: 1330 W Indian Head Dr Tallahassee FL 32301

MC CULLAGH, JAMES CHARLES, b. London, Oct. 22, 1941, came to U.S., 1954, s. James Christopher and Violet (Smith) McC.; m. Lee Ann McConnell, June 1, 1968; children—Declan, Deirdre. Author: That Kingdom Coming Business (poetry), 1984, Bicycle Fitness Book, 1984. MA, Lehigh U., 1970, PhD, 1974. Pub. Bicycling, Emaus, Pa., 1979-83; v.p., ed. Rodale Press, Emaus, 1983-86, group v.p., editorial dir., 1985—. Home: 139 Martin St Allentown PA 18103

MC CULLOUGH, FRANCES MONSON, b. Quantico, VA, Oct. 23, 1938, d. George Edward and Frances (Fouche) Monson; m. David Willis McCullough, Nov. 22, 1965; children—Benjamin, Katherine. Ed. The Jnls. of Sylvia Plath, 1982, Holiday Home Cooking, 1986 (BOMC); editor of poetry anthologies Earth, Air, Fire & Water, Love Is Like the Lion's Tooth. Wrkg. on letters of Djuna Barnes. BA, Stanford U., 1960; postgrad. Brandeis U., 1961. Sr. ed. Harper & Row, NYC, 1964-80, The Dial Press, NYC, 1980-85; chmn. lit. panel NEA, 1980; cons. ed., Bantam Books, 1986—; cons. ed., Soho Press, 1986-. Recipient Roger Klein award for creative editing, 1971. Mem. PEN, AWP (bd. dirs. 1981-85), Women's Media Group. Home: 117 Villard Ave Hastings-on-Hudson NY 10706

MC CULLOUGH, KEN, b. Staten Island, NY, July 18, 1943; s. Robert Ervin and Barbara Marie (Midgley) McC.; 1 child, Galway. Author: The Easy Wreckage, 1971, Migrations, 1973, Creosote, 1976, Elegy for Old Anna, 1985, Travelling Light, 1986. BA, U. Delaware, 1966; MFA, U. Iowa, 1968. Asst. prof. Mont. State Univ., Bozeman, 1970-75; writer-in-residence SC Ednl. TV, Columbia, 1975-79; program spclst. Ia. Humanities Bd., Iowa City, 1982-83; academic adv. Univ. Iowa, Iowa City, 1983—, adj. asst. prof., 1982—. Lector, St. Mary's Ch., Iowa City, 1982—, Parish Council, 1986—. Recipient AAP award, NYC, 1966, Sri Chimnoy award, Jamaica, NY, 1980; fellow Helene Wurlitzer Fdn., Taos, NM, 1973, NEA, Washington, 1974. Mem. AWP, Natl. Assn. Academic Advs. Address: 831 N Dodge St Iowa City IA 52240

MC CULLY, EMILY ARNOLD, (Emily Arnold), b. Galesburg, IL, July 1, 1939; d. Wade Edward and Kathryn (Maher) Arnold; m. George McCully, June 3, 1961 (div.); children—Nathaniel, Tahaddeus. Author: (novels) A Craving, 1982, 2d ed., 1986, Life Drawing, 1986; (children's books) Picnic, 1984, First Snow, 1985, For I Shall Consider My Cat Jeoffry, 1985, The Show Must Go On, 1986, School, 1987, New Baby, 1988, Christmas Gift, 1988, You Lucky Duck, 1988, The Grandma Mixup, 1987. B.A., Brown U., 1961; M.A., Columbia U., 1964. Mem. PEN, AG, Hudson Valley WG. Reipient Graphic Excellence award New York Public Library and Bklyn. Museum, 1975; O. Henry Collection, 1977; award for fiction NEA, 1980, CAPS, 1981; Christopher Soc. award, 1985. Home: Box 212 Rural District Chatham NY 12037

MC CUMBER, MARIE MC HARGUE, (Mariah McCann), b. Columbus, GA; d. Walter Albert and Mabel Marie (McCann) McHargue; m. Jak H. McCumber, Nov. 26, 1956 (div. 1965); children—Guy Mitchell, John Mark. Author: Comprehensive Survey of Black History in the Chattahoochee Valley Area, 1979; contrbr. articles, poetry to newspapers. Owner, ed., pub. Trend Mag., Alma, Ga., 1970-75; freelance wrtr., 1975-80; sr. wrtr., ed. Brentwood Christian Press, Columbus, Ga., 1980—. Home: Box 8394 Columbus GA 31908

MC CUNN, RUTHANNE LUM, b. San Francisco, Feb. 21, 1946; m. Donald McCunn, June

15, 1965. Author: An Illustrated History of the Chinese in America, 1979, Thousand Pieces of Gold, 1981, Pie-Biter, 1983, Sole Survivor, 1985, Chinese American Portraits: Personal Histories 1828-1988, 1988. Wrkg. on novel. Co-editor: Chinese America: History and Perspectives annual, 1987—. B.A., U. Tex., 1968. Elem. schl. tchr. Santa Barbara Unified Schls., CA, 1970-73, English tchr. jr. high sch., 1974-78. Mem. Calif. State Library Scis. Bd., 1979, Calif. State Com. for Evaluation and Selection of Texts for State Adoption, 1979. Recipient Am. Book award Before Columbus Fdn., Berkeley, CA, 1984. Home: 1007 Castro St San Francisco CA 94114

MC CURDY, PATRICK PIERRE, b. Angers, France, Sept. 14, 1928, came to U.S., 1929, s. Joseph Alexander and Constance Yolande (de Boisferon) McC.; m. Eiko Yamada, May 31, 1953; children—Alan J., Wendy C., Alec J., Jeffrey R. BS in Chem. Engring., Carnegie Inst. Tech., 1949. Asst. ed. Chem. and Engring. News, Washington, 1960-61, asst. ed., NYC, 1961-62, bur. head, Frankfurt, W.Germany, 1962-65, bur. head Tokyo, 1965-67, mng. ed., Washington, 1967-69, ed., 1969-73; ed.-in- chief Chem. Week, NYC, 1973-80, 1986—; dir. tech. communications Dow Chem. Co., Midland, Mich., 1980-84. Served to 1st lt. U.S. Army, 1950-54. Recipient Jesse H. Neal Editorial Achievement award Am. bus. Press, NYC, 1978. Mem. profl. orgns. Home: 220A Riverside Ave Riverside CT 06878

MC CURRY, JAMES PATRICK, b. Hawthorne, CA, Oct. 3, 1943. Ed.: Delirium (poetry & fict. mag.), 1974-79; author: The Machine 1-12 plus Letter to Boulder, the Dragon; contrbr. of over 100 poems & writings to jnls & mags. inclg. Qtly West, Denver Qtly, Invisible City, Colorado State Review, Poetry Comics, Boundary 2, Writers Forum, Writers Jnl, Intermedia. Wrkg. on The Machine (13—), lifelong project. BA, Knox Coll., 1965; MA, CO State U., 1974; PhD, U. Denver, 1985. Instr., Carl Sandburg Coll., Galesburg, IL, 1980—. Woodrow Wilson Fellow, Yale, 1965-66. Home: Box 341 Wataga IL 61488

MC CUTCHAN, KENNETH PEVA, b. Vanderburgh County, IN, Apr. 21, 1913; s. Thomas W. and Lenora (Peva) McC. Author: Adventures of Isaac Knight, 1959, From Then Til Now, 1969, Pictorial Study of Old Vanderburgh County Court House, 1972, Saundersville, the English Settlement, 1978, At The Bend in the River, 1982. Contrbr. to Was It Yesterday, 1980, Where There's a Willard, 1986. Ed: Sunbeam Manufacturing Co. Parts Catalog, 1937-42. B.A., Evansville Coll., 1935; student Sorbonne, Paris, 1945. Veterans' counselor Ind. State Employment Service, 1946-47; radio announcer Sta. WIKY, Evansville, IN, 1947-73, retired. Mem. library com. Ind. Hist. Soc., Indpls., 1975-80; bd. dirs. Conrad Baker Fdn., Evansville, 1970-85, Wesselman Nature Ctr., Evansville, 1984, Evansville Museum, 1985—. Served to staff sgt. U.S. Army, 1942-45. Recipient Alumni cert. for excellence U. Evansville, 1979; named to Disting. Alumnus Hall of Fame, Central High Schl., Evansville, 1970. Home: 9100 N Green River Rd Evansville IN 47711

MC DANIEL, BONNY ELIZABETH, (Bonny E. Myers), b. Nevada City, CA, Oct. 5, 1936, d. Albert George and Eunice Alward (Bannon) Schofield; m. John Vance Myers, Dec. 15, 1956 (div. 1969); 1 son, Ronald Glenn; m. 2d, James Wesley McDaniel, Feb. 1, 1970; stepchildren—Lynn, Karen, Marti, James Jr., Mark. Contrbr. articles on animal psychology, genealogy to topical publs. Student Porterville (Calif.) Coll., 1984-86. Photojournalist, columnist, feature wrtr. Terra Bella (Calif.) News, 1984—; corr. Calif. Horsetrader, San Marcos, 1985—; ed. newsletters various orgns. Mem. Porterville Art Assn. (pres. 1980), Tule Tree Tracers (pres. 1984—). Office: Box 119 Terra Bella CA 93270

MC DANIEL, CHARLES-GENE, b. Luxora, AR, Jan. 11, 1931; s. Charles Waite and Edith Estelle (Kelly) McD. Contrbr. articles to The Progressive, The Nation, Quill, Consumer's Digest, Christian Century, Today's Health, Reader's Digest, other periodicals; mem. edl. bd. Toward Freedom, Chicago Sun-Times and Tribune, The Advocate, others. BS, Northwestern Univ., 1954, MS in jnlsm., 1955. Reporter Gazette and Daily, York, Pa., 1955-58; sci. wrtr. Chgo. bur. AP, 1958-79; assoc. prof. jnlsm., Roosevelt Univ., Chgo., 1979-84, prof., 1984-, chmn. dept., 1979—. Mem. AAUP, Fellowship of Reconciliation, ACLU, Natl. Gay and Lesbian Task Force, War Resisters Lg., Handgun Control Inc. Home: 5108 S Cornel Ave Chicago IL 60615

MC DANIEL, ROBBIE LEE, b. Henning, TN, Aug. 30, 1940; s. Cyrus Lawson and Melba Irene (Olds) Bray; divorced; children—Jay, Gigi, Doug, Ethyl, Johanna; m. Charles O. McDaniel, Sept. 2, 1983. Asst. ed., columnist: Harbor Herald Newspapers, 1971-73; ed. Square Dance Cookbook, 1976. Registered medical asst.; licensed Ill. insurance broker. Home: 1510 5th St Madison IL 62060

MC DARGH-ELVINS, EILEEN, b. Denver, Sept. 5, 1948, d. H.J. and Mary (Reinberg) McDargh; m. Bill Elvins; children—Todd, Holly, Heather. Author: How to Work for a Living and Still Be Free to Live, 1985; contrbr. to Off-Duty Mag., Los Angeles Times, Bus. to Bus., Orange County Register, Dawn Mag., Air Calif., Orange County Mag., Exec. BA in Speech and Communications, U. Fla., 1969; postgrad., U. Calif., Irvine. Tchr. pub. schls., Nassau, Fla., 1970-73; pub. relations dir. Amelia Island Plantation, Fla., 1973-78; corp. communications staff Comprehensive Care Corp., Newport Beach, Calif., 1978-79; sr. account exec. Gloria Zigner & Assocs., Newport Beach, 1980-81; prin. McDargh Communications, Laguna Niguel, Calif., since 1981. Mem. Calif. Press Women (dir.; 1st prize non-fiction writing, 1983-84), Nat. Speakers Assn., Women in Communications, Am. Soc. Tng. and Devel. Home: 23731 Montego Bay Laguna Niguel CA 92677

MC DARRAH, FRED WILLIAM, b. Bklyn., Nov. 5, 1926; s. Howard Arthur and Elizabeth (Swann) McD.; m. Gloria Schoffel, Nov. 5, 1960; children—Timothy Swann, Patrick James. Author: The Beat Scene, 1960, The Artist's World in Pictures, 1961, Greenwich Village, 1963, Museums in New York, 4th ed., 1983, Photography Marketplace 2d ed., 1977, Stock Photo and Assignment Source Book, 2d ed., 1984, Kerouac & Friends: A Beat Generation Album, 1984; coauthor: (with John Gruen) The New Bohemia, 1966, (with James J. Young) Guide for Ecumenical Discussion, 1970; editor: Executive Desk Diary, Saturday Rvw, 1962-64. Mem. staff Village Voice, NYC, 1959—, picture editor, 1971—. Served with AUS, 1944-47. Mem. AG. Home: 505 La Guardia Pl New York NY 10012

MC DERMOTT, MICHAEL JAMES, b. NYC, May 11, 1952; s. Eugene Michael and Therese Jane (Gignac) McD.; m. Kathleen Rose Nestor, Sept. 28, 1979; children—Jacqueline Rose, Sean Michael, Kathleen Marie. Ed./contrbr.: Meridian, 1977-79, Bronx Press Review, 1979, Jnl. of Legal Medicine, 1980, Food & Drug Packaging, 1980-81, Frozen Foods, 1981, Industrial Edn., 1981, Autoweek, 1981-82, Autosound & Communics., 1981-86, Fast Service, 1982, Chain Drug Review, 1982-86, Audio Times, 1983, Hotel-Motel Mgt., 1984, Mass Mkt. Retailers, 1984-86, Franchise Mag., 1985—. BA, Lenman Coll. Contrb. ed. CES Pub., NYC, 1980—; sr. ed. Harcourt, Brace, Jovanovich, NYC, 1981-82; mng. ed. Racher Press, NYC, 1982-84, exec. ed., 84-86, editorial dir., 85-86; ed. pub. dir., Franchise mag., NYC, 1986—. Home: RD8 Horsepound Rd Carmel NY 10512

MC DONALD, JULIE J., b. Iowa, June 22, 1929, d. Alfred Julius Jensen and Myrtle Petra (Faurschou) Petersen; m. Elliott Raymond McDonald, Jr., May 6, 1952; children—Beth McDonald Pearson, Elliott R. III. Novelist: Amalie's Story, 1970, Petra, 1978, The Sailing Out, 1982, The Ballad of Bishop Hill, 1986; author: Ruth Buxton Sayre (biography), 1980, Delectably Danish, 1982. BA, U. Iowa, 1951; postgrad., Iowa Wrtrs. Workshop, 1961. Women's ed. Register-Republic, Rockford, Ill., 1951-52; feature wrtr. Quad- City Times, Davenport, Iowa, 1962-83; arts wrtr. Argus, Rock Island, Ill., 1983—; lectr. Black Hawk Coll., Moline, Ill., 1965-66, St. Ambrose Coll., Davenport, 1974—. Recipient Media in Arts award Iowa Arts Council, 1975, Fiction award Friends of Am. Wrtrs., 1979, fiction winner, Natl. Fedn. of Press Women, 1983, 87. Mem. AG, Iowa Press Women. Home: 2802 E Locust St Davenport IA 52803

MC DONALD, WALTER ROBERT, b. Lubbock, TX, July 18, 1934, s. Charles Arthur and Vera Belle (Graves) McD.; m. Carol Ham, Aug. 28, 1959; children—Cynthia, David, Charles. Author: (poems) Caliban in Blue, 1976, Anything, Anything, 1980, Burning the Fence, 1981, Witching on Hardscrabble, 1985, The Flying Dutchman, 1987, After the Noise of Saigon, 1987; (chapbooks) One Thing Leads to Another, 1978, Working against Time, 1981; ed. (with F. Kiley) A Catch-22 Casebook, 1973, (with J.P. White) Texas Stories & Poems, 1978; contrbr. poems to Poetry, Am. Poetry Rvw, Atlantic Monthly, TriQtly. BA, Tex. Technol. Coll., 1956, MA, 1957; PhD, U. Iowa, 1966. Instr., asst. prof., assoc. prof. U.S. Air Force Acad., Colo., 1960-62, 65-71; assoc. prof. English, Tex. Tech U., Lubbock, 1971-75, prof., 1975-87, Paul W. Horn Professor, 1987; also dir. creative writing. Served to maj. USAF, 1957-71. Recipient poetry award Pa. Rvw, 1985; syndicated fiction awards PEN/NEA, 1985; NEA creative writing grantee, 1984. Mem. PEN, Conf. Coll. Tchrs. of English of Tex., Tex. Inst. Letters (best short story award 1976, poetry award 1976, 85), AWP, PSA, MLA. Home: 3804 52d St Lubbock TX 79413

MC DONELL, MARCELLA ANN, b. Los Angeles, Nov. 4, 1945; d. Francis D. and Mary E. (Hogan) McD.; children—Eric, Christine. Author autobiography: The House that Roared, 1963. Contrbr. poems to anthols. Wrkg. on anthol. of poems with water color illustrations of life in Am. B.A. in English, Marymount Coll., 1970. Owner Marcella's Handicrafts, Los Angeles, 1972—. Mem. AAP, APA. Recipient Best Wrtr. award Santa Monica Evening Outlook, 1964. Home: 320 Mesa Rd Santa Monica CA 90402

MC DONELL, ROBERT TERRY, b. Norfolk, VA, Aug. 1, 1944; s. Robert Meynard and Irma Sophronia (Nelson) McD.; m. Joan Raffeld Hitzig, June 15, 1981. Author: California Bloodstock, 1980. Student, U. Calif., Berkeley, 1962-63, San Jose State U., 1963-64; BA in Art, U. Calif., Irvine, 1967. With AP, NYC, 1970-72; reporter Los Angeles Weekly, 1972-73; asso. editor San Francisco mag., 1974-76, City mag., San Francisco, 1976-77; sr. editor San Francisco mag., 1977, Outside mag., San Francisco, 1978-79; founding editor Rocky Mountain mag., Denver, 1979-80; mng. editor Rolling Stone mag., NYC, 1980-83; asst. mng. editor Newsweek mag., NYC, 1983—. Home: 7 Gracie Sq New York NY 10028

McDOUGALL, JO GAROT, b. Little Rock, Dec. 15, 1935; d. Leon J. and Ruth M. (Merritt) Garot; m. Charles W. McDougall, July 10, 1955; children: Charla McDougall Stone, Duke. Contrbr. to Patterns of Poetry: A Book of Forms, Lit. Mag., So. Poetry, Tex., N.Mex. Humanities rvws, Nimrod, Poetry Miscellany, Intro, Maine Times, Ark. Times. BS in Home Econ., U. Ark., 1957, MFA in Creative Writing, 1986. Poetry fellow U. So. Maine, Gorham, summer 1981; lectr. English, U. Ark., Fayetteville, 1985-86, asst. prof., 1986—; lectr. English, Northeast La. U., Monroe, 1986—. Mem. South Central MLA, AWP. Office: Eng Dept Northeast La U Monroe LA 71209

MC DOWELL, MICHAEL GERALD, b. Detroit, Nov. 16, 1953, s. Kenneth Elroy and Virginia Jennifer McD. Contrbr. articles, interviews to Bucketful of Brains, The BOB, Goldmine, Nineteen. Student, Eastern Mich. U., 1971-73; BA, U. Mich., 1975. Ed., pub. Blitz Mag., Los Angeles, 1976—. Home: Box 48124 Los Angeles CA 90048

MCDOWELL, ROBERT A., b. Alhambra, CA, Apr. 8, 1953; m. Lysa A. Howard, July 6, 1985. Author: (chapbook) At the House of the Tin Man, 1983, (poems) Quiet Money, 1986; contbr. poems, essays, rvws. to Hudson Rvw., Chowder Rvw., Poetry, London Mag., Poetry Now, others; co-editor, pub. The Reaper nos. 1-13 (with Mark Jarman). BA, U. Calif.-Santa Cruz, 1974; MFA, Columbia U., 1976. Painter, McKune Graphics, Los Angeles, 1976-77; asst. prof. Ind. State U., Evansville, 1978-84; pub., editor Story Line Press, Santa Cruz, 1985—; cons. U. Calif., Santa Cruz, 1984—. Mem. CCLM. Home: 403 Continental St Santa Cruz CA 95060

MC EATHRON, MARGARET, b. Oconto, WI, Nov. 17, 1899, d. Robert and Paulina (Grashorn) Wittke; m. Charles Nixon McEathron, Aug. 11, 1923; children—Donyll, Adair, Marni Nixon, Ariel. Author: Your Child Can Learn to Read, 1939, 2d rev. ed., 1956, I Learn to Read Book 1, 1956, Book 2, 1956, ABCs of Reading phonics primer series with workbooks, numerous reading and phonics materials; co-author: Philip's Cousin Jesus—The Untold Story (novel, with F. Holmes), 1981, I Am Two Men (novel, with F. Holmes), 1983; 50 Years of Reading Helpers, 1986. MA, Golden State U. Literacy tutor The Reading House, Los Angeles, 1938—, now dir.; tchr. trainer Family Edn. Service, Orange County, Calrif., 1962-69; pub. adult literacy courses, Orange County, 1980. Recipient awards for literacy work; Mark Twain award, 1950; recipient Remarkable Sr. award Sr. Pub. Group, Los Angeles, 1984. Office: 1330 Oakmont Rd Seal Beach CA 90740

MC ELROY, COLLEEN JOHNSON, b. St. Louis, Oct. 30, 1935; d. Jesse Dalton and Ruth Celeste Johnson; m. David McElroy, 1968 (div. 1978); children—Kevin Duane, Vanessa Colleen. Author: The Mules Done Long Since Gone, 1973, Music from Home: Selected Poems, 1976, Winters Without Snow, 1979, Lie and Say You Love Me, 1981, A Country Under Its Original Name, 1984, Queen of the Ebony Isles, 1984, Bone Flames, 1987, Jesus and Fat Tuesday (short stories), 1987; play Follow the Drinking Gourd, 1987. BS, Kansas State U., Manhattan, 1958; MS, 1963; Ph.D., U. Wash., 1973. Recipient Creative Writing award NEA, 1978, Am. Book award Before Columbus Fdn., 1984; named Woman of Achievement, Matrix Table, Seattle, 1985. Home: 2616 4th Ave N 406 Seattle WA 98109

MC FARLAND, ANNE S., (Anne Southworth), b. Cleve., Mar. 12, 1940; d. Edward and Barbara Anne (Eberth) Southworth; m. Charles W. McFarland, June 9, 1964; 1 son, Michael E. Author: (with S.C. Griffin) Foster Parent Education Handbook, 1982. Ed.: Over the Back Fence, 1981-84. Wrkg. on books, Next Friend; the Jnl. of a Foster Parent, Life in the Breakdown Lane. A.B., Oberlin Coll., 1962; M.Library Sci., Case Western Reserve U., 1964; J.D., Cleve. State U., 1974. Attorney, Cleveland Heights, OH, 1974-86; assoc. law librarian U. Akron, 1986—. Trustee New Day Press, Cleve., 1982—. Home: 12699 Cedar Rd Cleveland Heights OH 44106

MC FARLAND, JOHN BERNARD, b. Cambridge, MA, Jan. 16, 1943, s. William Anthony and Louise Marie (Bagdasarian) McF. Author: The Exploding Frog and Other Fables from Aesop (Best-Illustrated Book, Parents Choice Mag.), 1981; contrbr. short fiction to Image, Wiggansnatch, Fiction '84, Ararat, Cricket, other mags; book rvws.: Seattle Weekly, 1977-81, Pacific Northwest, 1982-83, Lights, 1983-84. BS, MIT, 1964; postgrad. Harvard U., 1964-66; MA, ABD, Johns Hopkins U., 1974. Economist Fed. Res. System, Washington, 1970-71; research assoc. AMA, Chgo., 1972-74; study dir., cons. Am. Hosp. Assn., Chgo., 1975-76; economist, energy analyst U.S. Dept. Energy, Seattle, 1976-81. Mem. NWU, Soc. Childrens Book Wrtrs., Am. Econ. Assn. Home: 1015 W Howe St Seattle WA 98119

MC FEE, MICHAEL ALAN, b. Asheville, NC, June 4, 1954, s. William Howard and Lucy Katherine (Farmer) McF.; m. Belinda Anne Pickett, June 16, 1978; 1 son, Philip Pickett. Author: Plain Air, 1983; ed. The Spectator Reader, 1985. BA summa cum laude, U. N.C., 1976, MA, 1978. Book ed. Spectator Mag., Raleigh, N.C., 1980—; book reviewer sta. WUNC-FM, Chapel Hill, N.C., 1982—; vis. poet, U. N.C., Chapel Hill, 1984, U. N.C., Greensboro, 1985-86, Cornell U., Ithaca, N.Y., 1986-87, Lawrence U., Appleton, Wis., 1988. Recipient Discovery award The Nation mag., 1980, Pushcart prize, 1981-82; poetry fellow N.C. Arts Council, 1985-86, Ingram Merrill Fdn., NYC, 1986, NEA fellow, 1987. Mem. P&W, Nat. Book Critics Circle. Home: 2514 Pickett Rd Durham NC 27705

MC FEELY, LARAMIE J., b. Grand Rapids, MI, Jan. 8, 1933; s. Cecil Sylvester and Hazel Alice (Disbrow) McF.; m. Carol Francis Grooters, Mar. 28, 1958; children: Debra, Dennis, Linda, Gharles, Brian. Contrbr.: Cloth Doll, Country Craftmakers, Greener Pastures Gazette, Poetry Pulps, other publs. BS, Grand Rapids Jr. Coll., 1957. Arts and crafts exhibitor; accordionist various night clubs. Home: 7607 Woodbridge Box 12 Brohman MI 49312

MC FEELY, WILLIAM SHIELD, b. NYC, Sept. 25, 1930; s. William C. and Marguerite (Shield) McF.; m. Mary Drake, Sept. 13, 1952; children—William Drake, Eliza, Jennifer. Author: Yankee Stepfather: Gen. O.O. Howard and the Freedmen, 1968, the Black Man in the Land of Equality, 1969, Grant: A Biography, 1981; co-author: Responses of the Presidents to Charges of Misconduct, 1974. BA, Amherst Coll., 1952, LHD, 1982; MA, Yale U., 1962, PhD, 1966. Recipient Pulitzer Prize in biography, 1982, Francis Parkman prize, 1982; Morse fellow, 1968-69; fellow ACLS, 1974-75, Huntington Library, 1976, 83; Guggenheim fellow, 1982-83. Mem. AG. Home: 23 Ashfield Ln South Hadley MA 01075

MC FERREN, MARTHA DEAN, b. Henderson, TX, April 25, 1947; d. Manley Edward and Emma Louise (Turner) McFerren; m. Dennis Scott Wall, May 21, 1977. Author: Delusions of a Popular Mind, 1983, Get Me Out of Here, 1984, A Contour for Ritual, 1987. BS, North Texas State U., 1969, MLS, 1971. Librn., San Jacinto College, Houston, 1971-76; librn., Jefferson Parish Libraries, Metairie, La., 1976-81; librn., New Orleans Public Schools, La., 1984-85. Mem. P&W, PSA. Home: 4013 Royal St New Orleans LA 70117

MC GAUGHEY, KATHRYN ELIZABETH, b. Merna, NE, Feb. 3, 1918; d. George Allen and Rosa Nell (Pirnie) McEwen; m. William Allen McGaughey, May 16, 1935; children—Thelma, Sharon, Eloyce, George, Clifford, Richard, Ann. Author: Treasures, 1966, The Little Red hair, 1966, Gift of Laughter, 1972, Grandma's Love Notes, 1980, Poems for the Young at Heart, 1985. Contrbr. articles to popular mags., newspapers including Empire Mag., Good Housekeeping, Denver Post. Grad. public schls., Merna. Mem. Poetry Soc. Colo., We Write Colo. Home: 2995 Hawk St Denver CO 80221

MC GEE, COKEY, see Walters, Clara O.

MC GEE, DENNIS ALBERT, b. Columbus, OH, Sept. 8, 1953; s. Manley Lafayette and Elizabeth Marie (Cummins) McGee; m. Lizbeth Allyn Maxson, Sept. 30, 1984. Author: The Rescue, 1980, Love Without Hypocrisy, 1982; screenplay Born to Race (in prodn. 1986). Assoc. of Theology, The Way College of Biblical Research, 1976. Dept. super. The Way College (Rome City, IN), 1979-81; self-emplyd. contrct. 1981-84; ad. manag. Lindbert Nutrition (LA), 1984-85; scriptwrtr. Romax Productions (Studio City, CA), 1985—. Home: 10815 Camarillo St N Hollywood CA 91602

MCGEE, HUDSON, see Walters, Clara O.

MC GEE, PATRICK EDGAR, b. Chgo., Jan. 13, 1944; s. Ralph and Minnie (Crutcher) McG. Author: poetry in Many Voices—Many Lands anthology, APA anthol. Student Olive Harvey, Chgo. Machine Clerk, USPS, Chgo., 1977—. Home: 9433 S Indiana Chicago IL 60619

MC GIFFERT, MICHAEL, b. Chgo., Oct. 5, 1928; s. Arthur Cushman and Elisabeth (Eliot) McG.; m. Genevieve White, Aug. 13, 1960; m. Elizabeth Eastman, June 19, 1949 (div. 1959). Author: The Higher Learning in Colorado, 1964; ed.: The Character of Americans, 1964, rev. ed., 1969, Puritanism and the American Experience,

1969, (with Robert A. Skotheim) American Social Thought, 1972, God's Plot: The Paradoxes of Puritan Piety, 1972. BA, Harvard Coll., 1949; BD, Yale U., 1952, PhD, 1958; postgrad., Union Theol. Sem., 1949-50. Editor, William & Mary Qtly, 1972-. Home: 104 Ware Rd Williamsburg VA 23185

MC GINNISS, JOE, b. NYC, Dec. 9, 1942; s. Joseph Aloysius and Mary Leonard McG.; m. Christine Cook, Sept. 25, 1965 (div.); children—Christine, Suzanne, Joe; m. 2d, Nancy Doherty, Nov. 20, 1976; 2 sons: Matthew, James. Author: The Selling of the President, 1968, The Dream Team, 1972, Heroes, 1976, Going to Extremes, 1980, Fatal Vision, 1983. BS, Holy Cross Coll., 1964. Reporter Port Chester (N.Y.) Daily Item, 1964, Worcester (Mass.) Telegram, 1965, Phila. Bull., 1966, Phila. Inquirer, 1967-68. Office: c/o Janklow 598 Madison Ave New York NY 10022

MC GLYNN, BRIAN JAMES, b. Bronx, NY, Sept. 4, 1952; s. David Joseph and Marilyn Ann (Compton) McG. Contrbr. wrtr. and poet to numerous publs. including The Daily Californian, The Humanist; ed., The Manhattan Quarterly, 1972-73; co-ed., Rapscallion's Dream, 1980-83. Home: 4342 Kepler Ave Bronx NY 10470

MC GONIGLE, THOMAS, Author: In Patchogue, 1985, The Corpse Dream of N. Petkov, 1987, afterword to Season at Coole (by Michael Stephens), 1984; contrbr. to: Five Plus Five, 1984, Sermons in Paint, 1984; ed.: Adrift mag. Wrkg. on Empty American Letters. Ed., Univ. Coll., Dublin, Ireland, Hollins Coll., Va. Home: 239 E 5th St 4D New York NY 10003

MC GOON, CLIFFORD, b. Bismarck, ND, Dec. 18, 1939; s. Clifford D. and Norma S. (Gilbertson) McG.; m. Janice Magenta, May 30, 1965 (div. July 5, 1973); m. 2d, Nancy Schonfeld, May 31, 1986; 1 dau., Amie. Editor: Tire News, 1967, Hercules Mixer, 1968-76, Communication World mag., 1978—(Best Trade Mag., Western Pubs. Assn. 1983). BS in Communications, U. Ill., Champaign, 1963. Ed. corp. pubs. Armstrong Rubber Co., New Haven, 1967-68, Hercules Inc., Wilmington, Del., 1968-76; dir. Lake County Big Bros., Lakeport, Calif., 1976-78; v.p. communication Intl. Assn. of Bus. Communicators, San Francisco, 1978—. Mem. Pub. Relations Soc. Am., Am. Soc. Assn. Execs. Office: Intl Assn Bus Comm 870 Market San Francisco CA 94102

MC GOUEY, ROBERT, b. NYC, Nov. 6, 1928, s. Frank E. and Margaret Marie (Sullivan) McG.; m. Patricia Danford; children—Thomas, Kathleen, Michael. Contrbr. poetry: New Voices in American Poetry, 1980, Our Twentieth Century's Greatest Poems, 1982, American Poetry Anthology, 1985. Wrkg. on poetry. Served with USN, 1946-48; ETO. Freight conductor LI RR, Jamaica, N.Y., 1953-84, ret. Home: RD1 Box 115-C Hawley PA 18428

MC GOWAN, HAROLD, b. Weehawken, NJ, June 23, 1909, s. Sylvester and Grace (Kalbfleish) McG.; m. Anne C. McTierman, Jan. 15, 1938; children—Linda Anne, Harold Charles, Janice Marie. Contrbr. numerous short stories to various publs. DSc, Fla. State Community Coll. Pres. Harold McGowan Constrn. Co., NYC, 1945—, Islip (N.Y.) Stores, Inc., 1950—, Harold McGowan Real Estate Corp., N.Y., 1960—; chmn., pres. Atomic Research, Inc., N.Y., 1960—. Mem. Mensa. Office: Box 250 Central Islip NY 11722

MC GRAIL, HARRINGTON, see Weigel, Tom

MC GRATH, LEE PARR, b. Robstown, TX; d. James Carl and Margaret Marden (Russ) Parr; m. Richard J. McGrath, Nov. 5, 1955; children: John Parr, Margaret Lee, Maureen Alison. Author: Crative Careers For Women, 1968, Do-It-All-Yourself Needlepoint, 1971, What Is a Father?, 1969, What Is a Mother?, 1969, What Is a Grandmother?, 1970, What Is a Grandfather?, 1970, What Is a Brother?, 1971, What Is a Sister:, 1971, What Is a Friend?, 1971, What Is a Pet?, 1971, Celebrity Needlepoint, 1972, Housekeeping With Antiques, 1971. B.A., So. Methodist U., 1955. Book reviewer Dallas Morning News, 1953, New Orleans Times-Picayune, 1956; guet editor Mademoiselle mag., 1952. Reipient Prix de Paris Vogue, 1954. Mem. ASJA. Home: 1 Gracie Terrace New York NY 10028

MC GRATH, THOMAS, b. near Sheldon, ND, Nov. 20, 1916; s. James Lang and Catherine (Shea) M.; m. Eugenia Johnson, Feb. 13, 1960; children—1 son Thomas (Tomasito) Samuel Koan. Author: poems First manifesto, 1940, To Walk a Crooked Mile, 1947, Figures from a Double World, 1955; children's books About Clouds, 1959, The Beautiful Things, 1960; novel The Gates of Ivory, The Gates of Horn, 1957; poems Letter to an Imaginary Friend, Parts I and II, 1969, Parts III and IV, 1985, New and Selected Poems, 1964, The Movie at the End of World: Selected Poems, 1973, Letter to Tomasito, 1977. Passages Toward the Dark, 1982, Echoes Inside the Labyrinth, 1983. Contrbr. poetry, short stories, and criticism to lit. mags. Founder and editor with Eugenia McGrath, Crazy Horse; former asst. editor California Quarterly and other lit. mags. Author of about 20 documentary film strips. BA, U. N. Dak., 1939; MA, La. State U., 1940, Rhodes scholar, New College Oxford U., 1947-48. Instr. in English, Colby Coll., 1940-41; asst. prof. English Los Angeles State College of Applied Arts and Sciences (now California State College, Los Angeles), 1950-54; asst. prof. of English, C.W. Post. Coll., Long Island, N.Y., 1960-61; assoc. prof English, N. Dakota State U., Fargo, 1962-67; assoc. prof. English, Moorhead (Minn.) State Univ., 1969—. Served with USAAF, 1942-45. Amy Lowell travelling poet scholar, 1965-66, Guggenheim fellow, 1967-68, Bush Fdn. fellow, 1975-76, grantee Minn. State Arts Council, 1973, 79. Mem. Phi Beta Kappa. Home: 2211 S 9th St Minneapolis MN 55404

MC GRAW, ERIN, b. Inglewood, CA, Dec. 20, 1957, d. Clarence Thomas and Eva Marie (Begovich) McG.; m. Todd Vern Titterud, Dec. 5, 1981. Ed. Ind. Rvw, 1984-85; contrbr. to Crosscurrents, Four Quarters, N.Am. Rvw, Ga. Rvw, Beloit Fiction Jnl, Crazyhorse. AB in English, U.Calif., Davis, 1979; MFA in Fiction, Ind. U., 1986. Instr. English, DePauw U., Greencastle, Ind., 1985-86, asst. prof., 1986—. Recipient lit. prize Natl. Soc. for Arts and Letters, 1985. Mem. AWP. Home: Box 2444 Bloomington IN 47402

MC GRAW, KAREN KAY, b. Des Moines, Feb. 17, 1938, d. George Frederick and Lena Aarlene (Wilhelm) Hutchings; 1 dau., Karen. Author: The Land I Love the Best (novel), 1986, The Thirteenth Year, 1986. Wrkg. on novel. BA, U. No. Iowa, 1981. Tchr. Hawkeye Inst. Tech., Waterloo, Iowa, 1984-86; Crow Greek Reservation High Schl., Stephan, SD, 1986-. Mem. NCTE. Home: 1120 Cherrywood Dr Cedar Falls IA 50619

MC GUANE, THOMAS FRANCIS, III, b. Wyandotte, MI, Dec. 11, 1939; s. Thomas Francis and Alice Rita (Torphy) McG.; m. Portia Crockett, Sept. 8, 1962; 1 son, Thomas Francis; m. 2d, Loraine Buffett, 1977; dau. Anne Buffett and step-dau. Katherine Heather. Author: The Sporting Club, 1969, The Bushwhacked Piano, 1971, Ninety-Two in the Shade, 1973, Panama, 1978, An Outside Chance: Essays on Sport, 1980, Nobody's Angel, Something to Be Desired, 1983, To Skin a Cat, 1986; screenplays include The Bushwhacked Piano, 1970, Rancho Deluxe, 1973, Ninety-Two in the Shade, 1974, Missouri Breaks, 1974, Tom Horn, 1980; contrbr.: Sports Illustrated, 1969-73. Student, Mich. State U., 1958-62, Yale Schl. Drama, 1962-65; Wallace Stegner fellow, Stanford U., 1966. Recipient Richard and Hinda Rosenthal Fdn. award fiction Nat. Inst. Arts and Letters, 1972. Office: c/o Hawkins 71 W 23rd St New York NY 10010

MCGUIGAN, KATHLEEN BAILEY, (Kate Bailey), b. Washington, Mar. 5, 1966; d. William Thomas and Nancy Elizabeth (Mattingly) McG. Columnist: Knight Crier, 1983-84. Contrbr. articles, poems to anthols., lit. mags. Student Washington Coll., 1984—. Dir. public relations, inventory control Thickfilm Intl. Microelectronics, Indian Head, MD, 1986—. Mem. Am. Film Inst. Home: 28 Potomac Ave Indian Head MD 20640

MC GUIRE, WILLIAM, b. St. Augustine, FL., Nov. 8, 1917; s. William Joseph an Edna Laurie (Musgrave) McG.; m. Anne Georgia Collins, Nov. 13, 1947; children: John, Edward; m. Paula Van Doren, May 28, 1965; 1 dau., Mary. Author: Bollingen: An Adventure in Collecting the Past, 1982; co-author: Jelliffe: American Psychoanalyst and Physician, 1983; exec. ed. Collected Works of C.G. Jung, 1953-83; editor: The Freud/Jung Letters, 1974, C.G. Jung Speaking, 1977, Jung, Seminar on Dream Analysis, 1984; contbr.: catalogue of Mellon collection Yale U. Alchemy and the Occult. 1968, 78. A.B., U. Fla., 1938, M.A., 1939; postgrad., Johns Hopkins U., 1939-41. Reporter Balt. Sun, 1941, The New Yorker, NYC, 1943-46; info. offier U.N. Seretariat, 1946-49, Splcl. editor: Bollingen Series, Bollingen Fdn., 1949-56; mng. editor, 1956-67; assoc. editor; Bollingen Series, Princeton U. Press, 1967-83, Served with USNR, 1941-43. Address: 219 Washington Rd Princeton NJ 08540

MC HUGH, HEATHER, b. San Diego, Aug. 20, 1948, d. John Laurence and Eileen Francesca (Smallwood) McHugh. Author: Dangers, 1977, A World of Difference, 1981, A Cup of Sky, A Foot of Fire, 1986; translator: D'Apres Tout (poems by Jean Foullain), 1981. BA, Radcliffe Coll., 1969; MA, Denver U., 1972. Assoc. prof. SUNY-Binghamton, 1976-83; mem. faculty MFA program for wrtrs. Warren Wilson Coll., Swannanoa, N.C., 1976—; wrtr.-in-residence U. Wash., Seattle, 1984—. Home: 2 Michenor St Eastport ME 04631

MCILHANEY, SAM CARL, b. Albuquerque, May 19, 1939; s. George Truett McI. and Mary Elizabeth (Walker) Rich; m. Anna Marie Patricia Wiese, June 12, 1982; 1 dau., Amber Dinelle. Contrbr. articles, short stories on Am. southwest to mags., jnls. including Impact Mag., N.Mex. Mag., Conceptions Southwest, Dallas Times Herald, Country People. BA, U. N.Mex., 1967. Instr. in history Bernalilo High Schl., N.Mex., 1977—. Mem. Hist. Soc. N.Mex., NWC. Home: 649 Vancouver Rd SE Rio Rancho NM 87124

MC ILWAIN, WILLIAM FRANKLIN, b. Lancaster, SC Dec. 15, 1925, 1925; s. William Franklin and Docia (Higgins) McI.; m. Anne Dalton, Nov. 28, 1952 (div. 1973); children: Dalton, Nancy, William Franklin III; m. K. L. Brelsford, June 5, 1978. Author: The Glass Rooster, 1960, (with Walter Friedenberg) Legends of Baptist Hollow, 1949; collaborator: (with Newsday staff) Naked Came The Stranger, 1969, A Farewell to Alcohol, 1973; contbr. to: Reader's Digest, Harper's, Esquire, Atlantic Monthly. B.A., Wake Forest Coll., 1949; postgrad., Harvard, 1957-58. Various positions with Wilmington (N.C.) Star, 1943, Charlotte (N.C.) Observer, 1945, Jacksonville (Fla.) Jnl., 1945, Winston-Salem (N.C.) Jnl.-Sentinel, 1949-52, Richmond (Va.) Times-Dispatch, 1952-54; chief copy editor Newsday, Garden City, N.Y., 1954-57, day news editor, 1957-60, city editor, 1060-64, mng. editor, 1964-66, editor, 1967-70; writer-in-res. Wake Forest U., 1970-71; dep. mng. editor Toronto Star, 1971-73; mng. editor The Reord, Hackensack, N.J., 1973-77; editor Boston Herald Am., 1977-79; dep. editor Washington Star, 1979-81, exec. mng. editor, 1981; editor Ark. Gazette, 1981-82; editor New York Newsday, 1982—; exec. editor Sarasota (Fla.) Herald-Tribune, 1984—. Served with USMCR, 1944. Mem. ASNE, Soc. Nieman Fellows. Office: Box 1719 Sarasota FL 33578

MC INGVALE, JAMES WESLEY (JIM), b. Batesville, MS, Oct. 13, 1954; s. Wesley Albert and Letrice Virginia (Aston) McI.; m. Nancy Chrystabel Bush, Aug. 14, 1976, 1 dau., Elizabeth Brooke. Ed.: Naval Inst. Proceedings, Armed Forces Jnl., Marine Corps Gazette, Marine Engring. Log, Sea Power, Maritime Rptr., Design News, 1980—. BA, U. MS, 1976. Photographer, Ingalls Shipbuilding div., Litton, Pascagoula, MS, 1977-81, pubn. ed., 82-83, sr. pubn. ed., 83—. Mem. IABC. Home: 1034 Del Norte Cr Pascagoula MS 39567

MC INTYRE, CATHRYN, b. Pontiac, MI, Feb. 27, 1959. Ed., On The Edge, 1983—. BA in Engl., MI State U., 1984. Home: 129 Pleasant Ave 3 Arlington MA 01274

MC INTYRE, MAUREEN ANNE, b. Rekjavik, Iceland, Oct. 27, 1949, came to U.S., 1950, d. Charles Joseph and Muriel Rita (Brousseau) McIntyre. Author: (with Dennis Holloway) The Owner-Builder Experience, 1986. Contrbr. articles to mags. Columnist Longmont Times-Call, 1983-85. Editor, pub.: Home Resource Mag., 1984—. BA in English, Syracuse U., 1971. Owner, Old Curiosity Shop, Boulder, 1972-76; co-owner, builder Woody Constn., Boulder, 1976-81; dir. Colo. Owner Builder Ctr., Boulder, 1981-86. Recipient 1st prize for editorial excellence Soc. Mkgt. Profl. Services, 1985. Home: 116 Nugget Dr JSR Boulder CO 80302

MC INTYRE, VONDA NEEL, b. Aug. 28, 1948; d. H. Neel and Vonda Barth (Keith) McI. Author: The Exile Waiting, 1976, Dreamsnake, 1978 (Hugo award), Fireflood and Other Stories, 1979, The Entropy Effect, 1981, Superluminal, 1983, Barbary, 1986; editor: (with Susan Janice Anderson) Aurora: Beyond Equality, 1976. BS, U. Wash., Seattle, 1970. Recipient Nebula award, 1973, 78. Mem. SFWA, AG, Costeau Soc., ACLU, Space Studies Inst. Home: Box 31041 Seattle WA 98103

MC KAIN, DAVID W., b. Punsutawney, PA, Dec. 28, 1937; s. Charles Van Kirk and Ida Mary (Crawford) McKain; m. Sharon Daniels, June 28, 1967 (div. 1972); m. 2d, Margaret F. Gibson, Dec. 27, 1975; children—Joshua VanKirk and Megan Crawford. Author: Christianity: Some Non-Christian Appraisals, 1965, The Whole Earth: Essays in Anger, Appreciation and Hope, 1970, In Touch, 1975, The Common Life, 1982, Our Roots Go Deep, 1985. BA, U. of CT., 1959, PhD, 1969. Editor, McGraw Hill, NYC, 1963-65; prof., U. of CT., Groton, CT, 1969—; wrtr.-in-res., Phillips Acad., Andover, MA, 1984—. Awards: NEA Fellowship, 1982, AWP Award for Creative Nonfiction, 1988. Mem. PSA, AAP. Home: Watson Road Preston CT 06360

MC KEE, GERALD, b. Twin Falls, ID, Aug. 1, 1930; s. Floyd and Martha Elizabeth (Callihan) McK.; m. Mary Lois McMullin, Aug. 24, 1968 (div. 1972). Program ed. Audio-Digest Internal Medicine and Surgery (medical tape recordings), 1956-60; mng. ed. Audio-Digest Fdn., Glendale, CA, 1960-82; ed./pub. Directory of Spoken-Word Audio-Cassettes and Audio-Cassette Nwsltr., 1972—; ed. nwsltrs: Nutrition & the M.D., 1976—, Sports Medicine Digest, 1982—; Emergency Medical Care Digest, 1980-84, Van Nuys, CA. BA in Jnlsm., U. ID, 1952. Ed./pub. Cassette Info. Svcs., Glendale, CA, 1972—. Past pres. and fellow, AMWA. Home: 2915 Graceland Way Glendale CA 91206

MC KEE, JOHN DE WITT, b. Emporia, KS, Dec. 22, 1919; s. Lewis DeWitt and Mary Emma (Machen) McK.; m. Jeannette Marie Hervin, Apr. 23, 1956. Author: Two Legs to Stand On: My Battle with Cerebral Palsy, 1955, William Allen White: Maverick on Main Street 1975, Time of Trouble, Time of Triumph: A Centennial History of the First Presbytrian Church in Socorro, NM (1880-1980), 1984; (with Spencer Wilson) Socorro Photographer: Joseph Edward Smith. 1858-1936, 1974. Editor: (with S. Wilson and Jeannette H. McKee) Spanish Times and Boom Times: Toward an Architectural History of Socorro, New Mexico (Charles L. Nieman), 1972. BA, Kans. Wesleyan, Salina, 1943; MA, U. N.Mex., 1952, PhD, 1959. English instr. U. N.Mex., Albuquerque, 1958-59; asst. prof. N.Mex. Inst. Mining & Tech., Socorro, 1959-66, assoc. prof., 1966-70, prof., 1970-85, prof. emeritus, 1985—. Mem. N.M. Developmentally Disabled Planning Council, Sante Fe, 1974-81, chmn., N.Mex. Devel. Disability Planning Council, 1975-76. Recipient Who's Crippled? award Natl. Assn. Crippled Children & Adults, 1954, citation Kappa Tau Alpha, 1976. Mem. Rocky Mt. MLA, Am. Studies Assn., Western Am. Lit. Assn. SDX, Profl. Jnlsts. Soc., NM Folklore Soc., Socorro County Hist. Soc. Home: 1302 Vista Dr NW Socorro NM 87801

MC KEE, LOUIS, b. Phila., July 31, 1951, s. Louis Charles and Mary Jane (Barrett) McK.; m. Christine Caruso, Aug. 19, 1978 (div. 1982). Author: Schuylkill County, 1982, The True Speed of Things, 1984, Safe Water, 1986, No Matter, 1987; rvws. ed.: Carousel Qtly, 1974-77; ed.: Implosion (anthology), 1983, Mickle St. Rvw, 1983-84, Painted Bride Qtly, 1985—, Axe Factory Rvw, 1986—; contrbr. poetry: Am. Poetry Rvw, Poetry Now, Negative Capability, others; contrbr. rvws., criticism: Small Press Rvw, Gargoyle, Smudge, others. Wrkg. on poetry collection, book on Richard Hugo's poetry. BA, LaSalle Coll., 1973. Tchr. Judge Schl., Phila., 1973—. Mem. AAP, PSA, PEN, P&W. Home: 8460 Frankford Ave Philadelphia PA 19136

MC KENDRICK, JOSEPH EDWARD, JR., b. Portsmouth, VA, June 6, 1956; s. Joseph Edw. McK., Sr. and Gertrude Mina (Eckstein) McK. Ed.: Executive Excellence: Your Success Plan for Managing Tomorrow, 1984, Mgt. World mag., 1985—, Managing newsltr., 1987-, Mgrs. Career Letter, 1986—, The Generalist Nwsltr., 1981-86. BA, Temple U., 1979. Asst. ed. Administrative Mgt. Soc., Willow Grove, PA, 1979-83, ed., 83—, mgr., 86—. Home: 515 Plymouth Rd X-7 Plymouth Meeting PA 19462

MC KENNA, JAMES A., III, b. Washington, Oct. 15, 1945, s. James A. and Rebecca (Rial) McK., Jr.; m. Jane Orbeton; children—Timothy, Susan. Contrbr. poems to Lit. Rvw, Negative Capability, Portland Rvw of Arts, Pegasus, Jam Today, Wind Chimes, Kennebec, Black Fly Rvw, others. BA, U. Notre Dame, 1967; MS, Boston U., 1970; JD, Georgetown U., 1974. Asst. atty. gen. State of Maine Augusta, 1979—. Served to capt. U.S. Army, 1970-73. Home: 5 Summer St Augusta ME 04330

MC KENZIE, MALROY BERNARD, (Mal McKenzie), b. Steubenville, OH, Jan. 30, 1951; s. Willie James and Addie Mae (Byron) McK. Contrbr. poems to anthols., lit. mags. Wrkg. on book of poems, songwriting, posters, greeting cards. A.A., Cuyahoga Commun. Coll., 1972; B.A., Davis & Elkins Coll., 1974. Insurance salesman Fidelity Union Life, Washington, 1976-81; commn. salesman Woodward & Lothrop, Washington, 1977—; interview specialist U.S. Census Bureau, Washington, 1977—; Mem. Wrtrs. Center. Recipient Golden Poet award World of Poetry, 1987, Merit award Creative Enterprises, 1987, Honorable Mention, Write On, 1987. Home: 1369 Potomac Ave SE Washington DC 20003

MC KEOWN, TOM, b. Evanston, IL, Sept. 29, 1937; s. Thomas Shanks and Ruth Ann (Fordyce) McK. Author: The Luminous Revolver, 1974, Driving to New Mexico, 1974, The House of Water, 1974, Certain Minutes, 1978, Circle of the Eye, 1982, Invitation of the Mirrors, 1985; contrbr. numerous poems to nat. and internat. lit. jnls. and popular mags. AB in English, U. Mich., 1961, AM, 1962. Alpena Comm. Coll., 1962-64; U. of Wis., Oshkosh, 1964-68, 1983-87; poet-in-residence Stephens Coll., 1968-74, U. Wis., Stevens Point, 1976-81; Savannah Coll. Art & Design, 1982-83; reader NEA in Mo., Kans., Mich.; active poet-in-the-schls. program. Recipient Avery Hopwood award for poetry U. Mich., 1968; Wis. Arts Fellowship for Poetry, 1980; Yaddo Residence grantee; Wurlitzer Residence grantee; Ossabaw Island Project grantee; Va. Center Creative Arts grantee. Address: Box 82 North Beach Pentwater MI 49449

MC KEOWN, WILLIAM TAYLOR, b. Ft. Collins, CO, July 4, 1921; s. Stuart Ellison and Eunice Harris (Akin) McK.; m. Lorraine Laredo; children—Elizabeth Ellison, Katherine, Suzanne. Author: Weekly N.E.A. syndicated newspaper column America Afloat, 1959—; contrbr. fiction, non-fiction natl. mags., 1947—; author: Boating Handbook, 1956, Boating in America, 1960. AB, Bowdoin Coll., 1942, student, Columbia U. Grad. Schl., 1948. Editor Fawcett Library Series, 1953-56; founding editor True's Boating Yearbook, 1955-56, Popular Boating mag., 1956, editor-in-chief, 1956-62; travel editor Davis Publs.; outdoor/boating/travel editor Popular Mechanics, 1971-82; sr. editor Outdoor Life, 1983—. Test and fighter pilot USAAF, World War II; ETO. Office: Outdoor Life 380 Madison Ave New York NY 10017

MC KERNAN, JOHN JOSEPH, b. Omaha, May 11, 1942, s. John Joseph and Monica Louise

(Nagengast) McK.; m. Llewellyn McKinnie, Aug. 3, 1967; 1 dau., Kathleen Claire. Author: Walking Along the Missouri River, 1977; contrbg. author: Three Omaha Poets, 1978; ed.: Little Rvw, 1969—. Wrkg. on biog. of Weldon Kees. BA, U. Omaha, 1965; MA, U. of Ark., 1967; MFA, Columbia U., 1971; PhD, Boston U., 1980. Prof. English, Marshall U., Huntington, W.Va., 1967—. Mem. CCCC, NCTE. Office: Dept Eng Marshall Univ Huntington WV 25701

MC KERNAN, LLEWELLYN TERESA, b. Hampton, AR, July 12, 1941; d. Walter William and Christine Carrie (Dunne) McKinnie; m. John Joseph McKernan, Aug. 3, 1967; 1 dau., Katie Claire. Author poetry: Short and Simple Annals: Poems about Appalachia, 1979, 2d ed., 1982, More Songs of Gladness, 1987, Bird Alphabet, 1988. Contrbr. poems to anthols. B.A. with honors in English, Hendrix Coll., 1963; M.A. in English, U. Ark., 1966; M.A. in Creative Writing, Brown U., 1975. English instr. Ga. State U., Statesboro, GA, 1966-67; adj. prof. English, Marshall U., Huntington, WV, 1978—. Fellow, WV Arts and Humanities Commn., 1981; grantee WV Humanities Fdn., 1983, P&W, 1984. Address: 1012 Chesapeake Ct Huntington WV 25701

MC KINLAY, ELEANOR GRANTHAM, b. College Station, TX, Feb. 23, 1921; d. Guy EVerett and Margaret Agnes (Paul) Grantham; m. Joseph Eldon Hall, Apr. 14, 1945 (div. 1960); children: Diane M. Hall Dency, Thomas Grantham Hall; m. 2d, Donald McKinlay, June 23, 1962; children: Dale McKinlay Inloes, Scott Mckinlay. Contrbr.: Life, Penny Press Classic, Dog Fany, Games, The Villager, Solares Hill, Sundial, Fla. Keys Mag., Mainstream, Intl. Jnl of Victimology, Ladies Circle, Chesapeake Bay Mag., others. Wrkg. on travel articles. BA, Cornell U. Tchr. various schs. in Md., 1952-74. Served to lt. (j.g.) USN, 1943-45. Home: 996 99th St Ocean Marathon FL 33050

MC KINNEY, DONALD LEE, b. Evanston, IL, July 12, 1923; s. Guy Doane and Cora Redfield (Brenton) McK.; m. Mary Frances Joyce, Dec. 14, 1958; children—Jennifer Joyce, Douglas Guy. Salesman textbooks John Wiley & Sons, NYC, 1949-52; freelance writer mostly comic books with some short articles and fiction, 1952-54; asst. mng. editor True mag., NYC, 1955-62; articles editor Saturday Evening Post, 1962-69; spcl. features editor NY Daily News, 1969-70; mng. editor McCalls mag., NYC, 1969-86; prof. jnlsm., Univ. of SC, 1986-. Served with USNR, 1943-46. Home: 4810 Portobello Rd Columbia SC 29206

MC KINNEY, IRENE, b. Belington, WV, Apr. 20, 1939, d. Ralph and Celia (Phares) Durrett; m. Joseph D. McKinney, 1956 (div. 1974); children—Julia Marie, Paul Steven. Author: The Girl with the Stone in Her Lap, 1976, The Wasps at the Blue Hexagons, 1984; contrbr. rvws, poetry: Qtly West, Cimarron Rvw, Salmagundi, Quarry West, Plainsong, numerous other lit mags; co-founder, ed. Trellis, 1973-75; asst. ed. Qtly West, 1978. MA, W.Va. U., 1970; PhD, U. Utah, 1980. Mem. faculty W.Va. Wesleyan Coll., Buckhannon, 1970-71, Potomac State Coll., Keyser, W.Va., 1971-75, U. Calif.-Santa Cruz, 1977, U. Utah, Salt Lake City, 1980-81; asst. prof. English Hamilton Coll., Clinton, N.Y., 1981—; poet-in-res. W.Va. Arts and Humanities Council, 1975-76, S.C. Arts Commn., 1976. Recipient Utah Arts prize Utah Arts Council, 1981, Breadloaf scholarship, 1985; McDowell Colony fellow, 1982, Blue Mountain Center fellow, 1982, NEA fellow, 1986. Mem. PSA, MLA, AWP. Home: Rt 1 Box 118 Belington WV 26250

MC KUEN, PAMELA DITTMER, b. Glencoe, MN, Aug. 4, 1951; d. Lowell Leo and Yvonne Ester (Kopischke) Dittmer; m. Herman Henry Mickunas, Aug. 4, 1973 (div. July 2, 1976); m. Myle Joseph Ward, June 2, 1984. Contrbr. to Consumer Guide Best Buys 1986, Consumer Guide Best Buy 1987, Consumer Guide 1000's of Free Things, 1987. B.A., Elmhurst Coll., 1974. Tchr. fashion Ray Vogue Schl., Chgo., 1974-77; public relations dir. Pheasant Run Resort, St. Charles, IL, 1980-82; free-lance wrtr., 1978—. Mem. Fashion Group. Home: 551 Hillside Ave Glen Ellyn IL 60137

MC KUEN, ROD, b. Oakland, CA, Apr. 29, 1933. Author: poetry And Autumn Came, 1954, Stanyan Street and Other Sorrows, 1966, Listen to the Warm, 1967, Twelve Years of Christmas, 1968, In Someone's Shadow, 1969, With Love, 1970, Caught in the Quiet, 1970, Moment to Moment, 1971, Fields, of Wonder, 1971, The Carols of Christmas, 1971, Pastorale, 1972, And to Each Season, 1972, Beyond the Boardwalk, 1975, Come to Me in Silence, 1973, America—An Affirmation, 1974, Seasons in the Sun, 1974, Alone, 1975, The McKuen Omnibus, 1975, Celebrations of the Heart, 1975, The Sea Around Me: The Hills Above, 1976, Finding My Father, 1976, Hand in Hand, 1977, Coming Close to the Earth, 1977, Love's Been Good to Me, 1979, We Touch the Sky, 1979, An Outstretched Hand, 1980, Looking for a Friend, 1980, The Power Bright and Shining: Images of My Country, 1980, Too Many Midnights, 1981, Rod McKuen's Book of Days, 1981, The Beautiful Strangers, 1981, Watch for the Wind, 1982, 1984 Book of Days, 1983, The Sound of Solitude, 1983, Suspension Bridge, 1984, Another Beautiful Day, 1984, 1986 Book of Days, 1985, Valentines, 1986, Intervals, 1986. Pres. Stanyan Books, Cheval Books, Biplane Books, Rod McKuen Enterprises; v.p. Tamarack Books; Composer-lyricist; numerous motion picture, TV scores. Horatio Alger award, 1975; Humanitarian award 1st Amendment Soc., 1977; Brandeis Lit. Trust award, 1981; Sylvester Pat Weaver award for pub. broadcasting, 1981. Mem. Modern Poetry Assn., ASCAP, WG, Am. Guild Authors and Composers (Dir.). Home: Box G Beverly Hills CA 90213

MC LANATHAN, RICHARD, (Barton Kennedy), b. Methuen, MA, Mar. 12, 1916; s. Frank Watson and Helen (Kennedy) McL.; m. Jane Fuller, Jan. 2, 1942. Author: Images of the Universe: Leonardo da Vinci, The Artist as Scientist, 1966, The Pageant of Medieval Art, 1966, The American Tradition in the Arts, 1968, A Guide to Civilisation: The Kenneth Clark Films on the Cultural Life of Western Man, The Brandywine Heritage, 1971, Art in America, 1973, The Art of Marguerite Stix, 1977, National Gallery of Art, East Building: A Profile, 1978, Romantic America; catalogue of the inaugural exhbn. of Tampa Museum, 1979, World Art in American Museums, A Personal Guide, 1983, Gilbert Stuart, 1986; co-author: M. and M. Karolik Collection of American Paintings, 1815-1855, 1949; editor: Catalogue of Classical Coins, 1955; cons. editor: Art and Man, Nat. Gallery Art, 1969-76; adv. editor: The Great Controversial Issues: The Arts, 1978; decorative arts editor: Webster's Unabridged Dictionary, 1955; contrbr.: Am. Foundation Philanthropy, 1967. Grad., Choate Schl., 1934; AB, Harvard, 1938, PhD, 1951. Home: Stone School House Phippsburg ME 04562

MC LAUGHLIN, J. RICHARD, b. Jersey City, Apr. 13, 1939; s. John Russell and Ada Frances (Richard) McL.; m. Emily Lynn Springston, June 17, 1961; children—John Randall, Timothy Scott, Steven Lynn. Author: MacIdeas, 1985, tech. papers on computer-aided trng., 1979-80; contrbr. arts. to sev. computer users guides, 1976-81; wrkg. on war novel, non-fict. bk. abt. storytelling. BA, Ohio Wesleyan U., 1961; postgrad. U. Nebraska, 1964-65; Famous Writers' Schl., 1972. Security/intellig. officer, USAF, var. locats., 1961-70; computer prog. designer, Bell Tel. Labs., NJ, 1970-82; software consultant Scriptware, Inc., Hillsborough, NJ, 1981—; part-time writer, 1970—. Served to Capt., USAF, 1961-70. Campfire storyteller for scouts, church groups, YMCA groups. Home: 111 Flanders Dr Somerville NJ 08876

MC LAUGHLIN, JUNE, see Strong, Bethany

MC LAUGHLIN, MICHAEL, b. San Francisco, Mar. 8, 1954, s. Charles Elmer and Nancy Lee (Bennet) McL. Author: Ped Xing (poetry), 1977, Western People Show Their Faces (novel), 1987; contrbr. poetry to LA Wkly, Kinsey Report, Westwinds, others; contrbr. prose to Frank, Paragraph, The So. Calif. Anthol, Gargoyle, other publs.; contrbr. criticism, interviews: Small Press Book Rvw, various newspapers. BA in Creative Writing, U. Calif.-Santa Cruz, 1976; MProf. Writing, U. So. Calif., 1986. Educator, 1976-83; ed.-in-chief So. Calif. Anthology, Los Angeles, 1983-85; instr. Calif. Poets-in-Schls. program, Los Angeles, 1985—. Home: 626 Boccaccio St Venice CA 90291

MC LAUGHLIN, WILLIAM DE WITT, (William McLaughlin), b. Youngstown, OH, Aug. 26, 1918. Author poetry collections: Ourselves at One Remove, 1972, At Rest in the Midwest, 1982. BA, Western Res. U., 1948; MS, U. Wis., Madison, 1950. Tchr. pub. schls., Cleve., to 1983. Served as sgt. U.S. Army Air Corps, 1941-45; North Africa, Mediterranean. Grantee Ohio Arts Council, 1983. Home: 20865 Chagrin Blvd Cleveland OH 44122

MC LEOD, JAMES RICHARD, b. Spokane, Wash., Jan. 8, 1942; s. Richard (James) Leland and Bernice Lola (Smith) McL.; div. Jan. 1978; children: Brock, Rory; m. Judith Osterberg Sylte, June 10, 1982; children: Anne Sylte, John Sylte. Author: Theodore Roethke: A Manuscript Checklist, 1971; Theodore Roethke: A Bibliography, 1973; A Bibliographic Guide to Midwestern Literature, 1982; Contemporary American Poets: Contemporary American Authors Bibliographical Series, 1986; contrbr. to N.W. Rvw, Slackwater Rvw. BA in English, U. Wash., 1966; MA in English, Eastern Wash. U., 1969. Tchr. pub. schls., Spokane, 1966-69, Mukilteo, Wash., 1969-70; asst. prof. U. Idaho, Moscow, 1971-74, 80; instr. English, North Idaho Coll., Coeur d'Alene, 1980—, dir. Scottish Studies, 1980—. Named honored author Wash. States Arts Commn., 1972, Idaho State Library, 1976. Mem. NCTE. Home: 701 S 12th St Coeur d'Alene ID 83814

MC LINDEN, STEPHEN KERRY, b. Peoria, IL, July 27, 1955; s. William P. and Monna A. McL.; m. Leslie Cherie Jetton, May 18, 1984; children—Dustin, Alex, Cameron. Ed.: Harbinger, 1973-75, Prairie Sun, 1976, Western Courier, 1977-80, Accent, 1980-84, Weekly Log, 1980-86, Tradewinds, 1980-86, Helm, 1981-84. AA, IL Central Coll., 1975; BA in Jnlsm., West. IL U., 1980. Mng. ed. Western Courier, Macomb,

IL, 1979-80; publicity co-ord., Tradewinds ed., Pier 1 Imports, Inc., Ft. Worth, TX, 1980-85, communics. mgr. 1985—. Mem. IABC. Home: 2403 Norwich Ct Arlington TX 76015

McMAHON, PAT, see Hoch, Edward D.

MC MAHON, THOMAS ARTHUR, b. Dayton, OH, Apr. 21, 1943; s. Howard O. and Lucile (Nelson) McM.; m. Carol Joan Ehlers, June 20, 1965; children—James R., Elizabeth K. Author: (novel) Principals of American Nuclear Chemistry, 1970, 2d ed., 1971, McKay's Bees, 1979, Loving Little Egypt, 1987; (non-fiction) On Size and Life, 1983, Muscles, Reflexes, and Locomotion, 1984. B.S., Cornell U., 1965; Ph.D., Mass. Inst. Technology, 1970. Asst. prof. Harvard U., Cambridge, MA, 1970-74, assoc. prof., 1974-77, prof., 1977—. Home: 65 Crest Rd Wellesby MA 02181

MC MANUS, JAMES, b. NYC, Mar. 22, 1951; s. Kevin J. and Mary A. (Madden) McM.; m. Susan Romanelli, May 9, 1974; children—Bridget, James. Author: Antonio Salazar Is Dead, 1979, Out of the Blue, 1984, Curtains, 1985, Chin Music, 1985 (paper, 1986), Ghost Waves, 1988.; Contrbg. ed., Formations. Asst. prof. Schl. of the Art Inst., Chgo., 1981—. Fellow, NEA, 1979, 85, Ill. Arts Council, 1985; recipient fiction award Ill. Arts Council, 1982, 83, 84, 86, 87. Mem. PEN. Address: 933-1/2 Linden Ave Winnetka IL 60093

MC MARTIN, PAULA J., b. Escanaba, MI, Aug. 21, 1955; d. Michael James and Pauline Leona (Waeghe) McM. Ed., The Woman Bowler mag., 1981-86, WIBC Tournament Program, 1985—; WIBC pub. rel. mgr., 1986—. BA in Jnlsm., U. WI-Eau Claire, 1977. Rptr., Daily Chronicle, DeKalb, IL, 1977-78; assoc. ed. Sporting Goods Bus., NYC, 1978—; sports rptr. Beloit (WI) Daily News, 1978-79, Green Bay (WI) Press, 1979—. Mem. WICI, NWBW, BWAA, WBW, PRSA. Home: 10316 W Lincoln Ave West Allis WI 53227

MC MASTER, R. E., JR., b. Yoakum, TX, Sept. 16, 1947. Author: Cycles of War, 1977; Trader's Notebook, 1978, 79, 80; Wealth for All—Religion, Politics, and War, 1982; Wealth for All—Economics, 1982; No Time for Slaves, 1986. Editor: (Newsletter) The Reaper, 1977—. Student pub. schls., Tex. Mem. Think Tank on Econ. and Mil. Matters, U.S. Library of Congress, 1978. Mem. Natl. Futures Assn. Office: Box 39026 Phoenix AZ 85069

MC MATH, PHILLIP H., b. Memphis, Dec. 25, 1945, s. Sidney S. and Sarah Anne (Phillips) McM.; m. Helen Carol Belew, Mar. 9, 1968. Novelist: Native Ground, 1985. Wrkg. on novel. BA, U. Ark., 1968, JD, 1973. Ptnr. McMath Law Firm, Little Rock, 1973—. Bd. dirs. Ark. Lit. Soc., Ark. Opera Theater; sec. Porter Fund-A Lit. Prize, Little Rock, 1985—. Served to capt. USMC, 1967-70; Vietnam. Home: 5417 Hawthorne Rd Little Rock AR 72207

MC MILLAN, ELMA JOYCE, b. San Angelo, TX, Apr. 8, 1934; d. Mart M. and Florence Amanda (Wilson) Melton; m. John Richard McMillan, Apr. 3, 1959; children—John R., Darryl. Author: (novel) Far from the Sun, 1985.Wrkg. on novel set in Middle Ages. Student Angelo State Univ., 1952-53, U. Puerto Rico, 1971-73. Home: 211 Judith Dr Greenhurst Summerville SC 29483

MC MILLAN, KAREN ALICE, b. Wilmington, OH, Jan. 3, 1961; d. Thomas Carroll and Katharine (Battelle) McM. Ed., AgMax Ag-News, 1983-86; mng. ed. Animal Health & Nutrition, 1986—. BS, Ohio State U., 1983. Communics. spclst. AgMax, Inc., Frankfort, IN, 1983-86; Mem. Natl. Agri-Mktg. Assn. Home: 5069 Linden Rd Apt 4309 Rockford IL 61109

MC MILLAN, LEONA PEARL, b. Mammoth, WV, June 18, 1913; d. Frederick Newton and Sarah Frances (Agee) Barger; m. Clemmons Riddick McMillan, Nov. 26, 1947; 1 son, Robert Lee. Author: Hard Winters and Soft Coal, 1984. Student, Capital City Commercial College, Charleston, W. Va., 1940-41. Secy., W. Va. Health Dept., Charleston, 1941-59; secy./supv., Health and Rehabilitation Services, Miami, Fla., 1959-77. Home: 625-30 Avenue W Bradenton FL 33505

MC MILLAN, PATRICIA ANN, b. Bklyn., Nov. 26, 1946; d. Aleck and Virginia Patricia (Quirke) Dubatowka; m. Robert A. McMillan, June 27, 1970; 1 son, Matthew. Author: Wordplay for Holidays, 1978. Contrbr. articles, short stories, poems, prayers to profl. mags., popular mags. including Highlights for Children, Humpty Dumpty's Mag., Today's Catholic Tchr. Ed. parish religious edn. newsletters, 1985—. B.A. in Elem. Edn., Georgian Ct. Coll., 1968 Tchr. Sacred Heart Sch., Suffern, NY, 1968-70, Tappen Zee Elem. Schl., Piermont, NY, 1970-72, Blauvelt Elem. Schl., NY, 1972-73, St. Mary Schl., Fort Walton Beach, FL, 1974-75; elem. Tchr. St. Mary Magdalen Schl., Altamonte Springs, FL, 1977—. Mem. Fla. Freelance Wrtrs. Assn., Natl. Catholic Edn. Assn. Home: 208 Sheridan Ave Longwood FL 32750

MCMILLAN, PETER AIDAN, b. Dublin, Ireland, Feb. 6, 1959; came to U.S., 1980; s. Matthew and Ann Moira (MacDermott) McM. Ed. Illuminations, bi-annl. poetry jnl., 1982—; contrbr. to Dictionary Lit. Biography, Writing Lab Newsletter, James Dickey Newsletter. Wrkg. on vol. on contemporary Irish poetry. BA, Univ. Coll., Dublin, MA, 1980; PhD, U. S.C., 1985. Lectr. Asian div. U. Md., Tokyo, 1985—. Home: PSC Box 100 APO San Francisco CA 96328

MC MILLAN, SALLY HILL, b. Charlotte, NC, Oct. 12, 1949, d. Clarence Hutchins and Dorothy (Pope) Hill; m. Ralph Reiss McMillan, June 22, 1974; children—Sara Porter, Dorothy Bennett. Ed., pub. Bed and Breakfast regional guides, other books. BA, High Point (N.C.) Coll., 1971; MA, U. N.C., Charlotte, 1973. Asst. sales dir. U. N.C. Press, Chapel Hill, 1974-77; ed., pub. East Woods Press, Charlotte, 1977-86; acquisitions ed., Globe Pequot Press, and pub. consl., 1987-. tchr. Radcliffe Publs. Inst., Boston, summer 1983, Denver Publs. Inst., summer 1985, 86. Mem. Women in Communications (bd. dirs. 1979-82), Pubs. Assn. of South (pres. 1985-87). Office: 429 East Kingston Ave Charlotte NC 29203

MC MILLEN, WILLIAM EARL, b. Wisconsin Rapids, WI, Feb. 28, 1947; s. Rober Earl and Marion Christina (MacKenzie) McM.; m. Barbara Ann Fialkowski, Jan. 17, 1970; children—Christopher, Mark. Contrbr. criticisms, bibliographies, fiction, poems to lit. mags., anthols. BA, U. Wis.-Stevens Point, 1969; MS, Ohio U.-Athens, Ph.D., 1976. Lectr., Bowling Green State U., Ohio, 1977-78, conf. dir., 1978-82; asst. to pres. Med. Coll. of Ohio, Toledo, 1982—. Bd. dirs. Wood County (Ohio) Mental Health Bd., 1984—. Recipient 1st place for (play) The Peacock Colony, Bowling Green State U., 1980; Ohio Arts Council grantee, 1978. Home: 824 Oak Knoll Dr Perrysburg OH 43551

MC MOY, JOHN H., b. Washington, Oct. 4, 1953; s. John H. and Evie M. (Moseley) McMoy; m. Kendall B., June 19, 1976; Poetry in Encore, Wrtrs. Digest, Midwest Poetry Rvw, Nom de Plume, Poets of the Vineyard, other lit mags and anthologies. BA, Auburn U., 1976; MA, U. of Tenn., 1978. Sr. contract administrator, Saudi Arabian Ministry of Defense and Aviation, Jeddah, Saudi Arabia, 1978-85; real estate investor/writer, Marietta, GA, 1985—. Home: 2684 Forest Way Marietta GA 30066

MC MULLEN, BETTY A. , b. Woodward OK, Jan. 10, 1936; d. Isaac Milton and Evelyn May (Murphy) Beasley; m. William Davis Brown, Sept. 2, 1952 (div.); children: Kathie Cassidy, Konnie Smith, Karl Brown, Kurt Brown; m. 2d, Leon Franklin McMullen, Nov. 18, 1972. Author: I Came Back: Learning to Live Again, 1987 (illus.); poetry to litmags, anthologies. Student Northwestern Okla. State Univ., Alva, Okla. Bookkeeper, Int. Office Mgr. Ranger Electronics, Alva, 1970-75. Recipient various poetry awards. Mem. Poetry Soc. Okla., Okla. Wrtrs. Fedn., AAP, other poetry societies. Home: 1017 Walsh Ln Yukon OK 73099

MC MULLEN, EDWIN WALLACE, JR., b. Quincy, FL, Dec. 8, 1915; s. Edwin Wallace and Sara Della (Moore) McM.; m. Marian Elizabeth Hoper, June 9, 1946; children—William Wallace, Charles Edwin. Author: English Topographic Terms in Florida, 1563-1874, 1953; editor: Names, 1962-65, also articles; editor, contrbr.: Pubs, Place-Names, and Patronymics, 1980. BA, U. Fla., 1936; MA, Columbia U., 1939, PhD, 1950. Instr. English, Hazelton Undergrad Ctr., PA State Coll., 1946-48, State Univ. of Iowa, 1950-52; U.S. Civil Svc., Arlington, VA, Natl. Security Agcy, 1952-57; Sr. Reporter; asst. editor Merriam Webster Dictionary Co., 1957; asst. prof. English, Lehigh Univ., 1957-61; asst. prof. English, Fairleigh Dickinson Univ. (Madison Campusl, 1961, assoc. prof., 1962-71, prof. of English, 1972-82; founder, dir. Names Inst., 1962—; Chmn. publs. subcom. Morris County Tercentenary Com., N.J., 1962-63. Served with Signal Corps IntelligenceU.S. Army, 1942-46. Mem. Am. Names Soc. (pres. 1976), Modern Lang. Assn., Internat. Congress on Onomastic Scis., Internat. Linguistic Assn., Am. Dialect Soc. Home: 15 Rosewood Dr Madison NJ 07940

MC MULLEN, LEON F., b. Alva, OK, June 8, 1930; s. Charles E. and Nina A. (Marks) McM.; m. Judith J. Urban (div.), 1 son: Rodney Leon; m. 2d, Betty A. Brown, Nov. 18, 1972. Author: poetry in Anthologies; first poem pubd. won Golden Poet Award, World of Poetry; various honorable & spcl. mentions. Student Northwestern Oklahoma State Univ., Alva. General Expeditor, USPS, MPO, Oklahoma City. Mem. Poetry Soc. Okla., AAP. Home: 1017 Walsh Ln Yukon OK 73099

MC NAIR, ROGERS MAC GOWAN, see Branson, Branley Allen

MCNAMARA, ROBERT JAMES, b. NYC, Mar. 28, 1950; s. James Joseph and Doris Agnes (Maier) McN.; m. Bridget Culligan, Aug. 16, 1975 (div. 1987); 1 child, Caitlin Culligan. Contbr. poems to Chowder Rvw, Colorado Rvw, Epoch, Chariton Rvw, Kansas Qtly, Poetry Miscellany, others; contbr. articles to Contemporary Lit., Pacific Coast Philology; poetry editor L'Epervier Press, 1977—. BA, Amherst Coll., 1971; PhD, U. Wash., 1985. Instr. U. Colo., Boulder, 1976; poet-in-res. Rocky Mountain Writers Guild, Boulder, 1977-79; instr. Colo. State U., Ft. Collins, 1976-79, U. Wash., Seattle, 1985-87; lectr. U. Wash., Seattle, 1987-. Amherst Coll. Meml. fellow, 1973-74; McMurphy fellow U. Wash., 1983-84, NEA fellow, 1987. Mem. MLA, Philol. Assn. Pacific Coast. Home: 5733 25th NE Seattle WA 98195

MC NAMARA, ROBERT STRANGE, b. San Francisco, June 9, 1916; s. Robert James and Clara Nell (Strange) McN.; m. Margaret Craig, Aug. 13, 1940 (de.); children: Margaret Elizabeth, Kathleen, Robert Craig. Author: The Essence of Security, 1968; One Hundred Countries—Two Billion People: The McNamara Years at the World Bank; Blundering into Disaster, 1986. A.B., U. Calif., 1937; M.B.A., Harvard, 1939. Mem. Phi Beta Kappa. Served as lt. col. USAAF, 1943-46. Legion of Merit, Medal of Freedom, D.S.M.; recipient Prsdl. Medal of Freedom with distinction; Albert Einstein Peace Prize; Franklin D. Roosevelt Freedom from Want Medal; Am. Assembly Svc. to Democracy Award; Christian A. Harter Memorial Award; Sidney Hillman Fdn. Prize Award, 1986; Olive Branch Award for Outstanding Book on Subject of World Peace. Office: 1455 Pennsylvania Ave NW Washington DC 20004

MC NAMEE, DARDIS, bNYC, Sept. 23, 1948, d. Daniel Vincent McNamee and Barbara (Cooley) McNamee Dudley; m. Frederick Arthur Childs, May 21, 1983; children—Austin Hayward McNamee, Margaret Taylor McNamee. Contrbr. articles, feature articles to newspapers, mags. BA, Bryn Mawr Coll., 1970; Phila. Musical Academy, 1971-73. Prof. musician, 1973-79; entertainment wrtr. Albany (N.Y.) Times Union, 1981-83; asst. entertainment ed. Berkshire Eagle, Pittsfield, Mass., 1983; script wrtr. N.Y. State Mus., Albany, 1984-85; editor/associate publisher Capital Region Mag., Albany, 1985. Mem. Women's Press Club. Home: 295 Quail St Albany NY 12208

MC NEE, ZEIDA, see Fink, Barbara Arlene

MC NEILL, WILLIAM HARDY, b. Vancouver, B.C., Can., Oct. 31, 1917; s. John Thomas and Netta (Hardy) McN.; m. Elizabeth Darbishire, Sept. 7, 1946; children—Ruth Netta, Deborah Joan, John Robert, Andrew Duncan. Author Greek Dilemma, War and Aftermath, 1947, Report on the Greeks, 1948, History Handbook of Western Civilization, rev. and enlarged, 1969, America, Britain and Russia, Their Cooperation and Conflict, 1941-46, 1953, Past and Future, 1954, Greece: American Aid in Action, 1947-56, 1957, Rise of the West, a History of the Human community, 1963, 8th edit., 1975 (Nat. Book award, Gordon J. Laing prize), Europe's Steppe Frontier, 1500-1800, 1964, A World History, 3d edit., 1979, The Contemporary World, 2d edit., 1975, The Ecumene: Story of Humanity, 1973, Venice, the Hinge of Europe, 1081-1797, 1974, The Shape of European History, 1974, Plagues and Peoples, 1976, Metamorphosis of Greece since World War II, 1978, The Human Condition, An Ecological and Historical View, 1980, Pursuit of Power, 1982, The Great Frontier, 1983, Mythistory and Other Essays, 1986, Polyethnicity and National Unity in World History, 1986. Editor: Lord Acton, Essays in the Liberal Interpretation of History, 1967, (with others) Readings in World History, Vols. I-X, 1968-73, Human Migration, 1978, Jnl. Modern History, 1971-79, Jnl. Modern Greek Studies, 1983-86; bd. editors: Encyc. Britannica, 1981—; contrbr. numerous articles and reviews to profl. jnls., chpts. to books. BA, U. Chgo., 1938, MA, 1939; PhD, Cornell U., 1947. Faculty U. Chgo., 1947—, prof. history, 1957—, chmn. dept., 1961-67, Robert A. Millikan Disting. Service prof., 1969-87; emeritus, 1987-; pres. Demos Fdn., 1968-80, chmn. bd., 1980—. Served with AUS, 1941-46; lt. col. Res. ret. Fulbright Research scholar Royal Inst. Intl. Affairs, Eng., 1950-51; Ford Faculty fellow 1954-55; Guggenheim fellow, 1971-72, 86. Fellow Am. Philos. Soc., Am. Acad. Arts and Scis., Brit. Acad. Arts and Scis. (corr.), Royal Hist. Soc. (corr.); mem. Am. Hist. Assn. (council, del. ACLS; pres., 1985). Address: Box 45 Colebrook CT 06021

MC NERNEY, JOAN, b. Bklyn., July 13, 1945. Author poetry: Crossing the River Rubicon, 1975, Crazy Flowers (poetic coloring book), 1984, Noah's Daughters, 1984, The Moon Is New, 1987; contrbr. to High Coo, Poetry People, Modern Haiku, Snakeroots, Touchstone, other lit. publs. BA, N.Y. State Bd. Regents. Presenter poetry readings. Home: 1935 83d St F8 Brooklyn NY 11214

MC NIFF, THOMAS ALFRED JR., b. Boston, Feb. 20, 1940; s. Thomas A. and Loretta Marie (Glennon) McN.; m. Shirley Elizabeth Piston, Mar. 12, 1973. Contrbr. articles to newspapers. B.S., Boston U., 1965; M.A. in Edn., Boston State Coll., 1976. Reporter, Boston Herald, 1964-67; newsman AP, Boston, Portland, ME, 1967-70; free-lance jnlst., 1971—. Mem. SPJ. Home: 118 Grandview Ave Winthrop MA 02152

MC NULTY, JOHN BARD, b. Mokanshan, China, July 13, 1916; s. Henry Augustus and Edith (Piper) McN.; m. Marjorie Mead Grant, May 23, 1942; children—Henry Bryant, Sarah Bard. Author: Older Than the Nation—A History of the Hartford Courant, 1964, Modes of Literature, 1977, The Correspondence of Thomas Cole and Daniel Wadsworth, 1983; contrbr. articles to profl. jnls. BS, Trinity Coll., Hartford, 1938; MA, Columbia U., 1939; PhD, Yale U., 1944. Faculty Trinity Coll., 1939-84, prof. English, 1960-84, chmn. dept., 1966-72, James J. Goodwin prof., 1967-84. MLA, AAUP. Home: 8 Little Acres Rd Glastonbury CT 06033

MC PARTLIN, JOHN, b. International Falls, MN, July 10, 1918; s. Francis Joseph and Alice Madge (Green) McP.; children—Mary Magaret McPartlin Hudson, Fudson, Francis J., John. Author, pub. humorous verse books: A Bay Hello, 1964, Don't Laugh I'm Serious, 1976, Mating of Janie McBride, 1977; contrbr. verse: Paradise of the Pacific, Honolulu Star Bulltn., anthologies. Wrkg. on novel. Student St. Thomas Coll. City ed. Morning Star, Bemidji, Minn., 1936-37; served as MSgt. USAF, 1940-61; corr. UP, Mpls., 1946-47; ed. numerous weekly newspapers, Wayne and Macomb counties, Mich., 1961-77; freelance wrtr., 1977—. Recipient awards in short story contests. Home: Box 81 New Baltimore MI 48047

MC PETERS, SHARON JANESE, b. San Bernardino, CA, Oct. 17, 1951, d. Cecil Leide and Mary Iula (Tanner) McPeters; m. David Lee Benders; 1 dau., Angela Maureen. Contrbr. fiction: Buff, Black Mountain II Rvw, Buffalo Spree Mag.; contrbr. non-fiction: Women in Edn.; mem. edit. bd., contrbr. fiction, poetry: Escarpments. Editor: Cotton Mill Boy, 1985-86. Wrkg. on novel, short stories, poetry, editing. BA in English and Journalism, U. So. Calif., 1981 MA, in English, SUNY-Buffalo, 1983. Freelance wrtr., Buffalo, 1984—. Mem. P&W. Home: 11 Fairbanks Ave B-2 Kenmore NY 14223

MC PHAIL, GORDON JOHN, b. Cleve., May 19, 1925; s. Neil J. and Ethel (Bigelow) McP. m. Frances Berela, Jan. 10, 1986. Contrbr. editorials to newspapers, mags. including Albuquerque Jnl., N.Mex. Mag., Albuquerque Living Mag. BA, Miami U., Oxford, Ohio, 1949, M.A. Salesman, U.S. Steel, Pitts., 1951-53, Allegheny Intl. Steel, Los Angeles, 1953-60, Kennecot Copper, 1960-62, Chase Brass; free-lance wrtr., Albuquerque, 1986—; prin. Urban Beautification, Albuquerque, 1985—. Named Most Promising Writer, Classics Club, 1949. Mem. Writers Co-op, Artists Assn. Home and Office: 135 Garcia NE Suite A Albuquerque NM 87123

MC PHERSON, BRUCE RICE, b. Atlanta, Oct. 12, 1951; s. Thomas Coatsworth and Jane Ridgeley (Rice) McP. Ed.: Treacle Story Series, 1976-79, More than Meat Joy, 1979, Likely Stories, 1981. AB, Brown U., 1973; postgrad. U. Pa., 1974-75. Art dir. and prod. mng. Pub. Ctr. for Cultural Resources, NYC, 1979-82; ed.-pub. Treacle Press, Providence, Phila. and New Paltz, N.Y., 1973-82, changed to McPherson & Co., New Paltz, 1983—; ed. Woodbine Press, East Haven, R.I., 1976-78. Recipient Ed's award N.Y. State Council on the Arts, 1986. Office: Box 638 New Paltz NY 12561

MC PHERSON, JAMES ALLEN, (James Alan McPherson), b. Savannah, GA, Sept. 16, 1943; s. James Allen and Mable (Smalls) McP.; 1 dau., Rachel Alice. Author: Hue and Cry, 1969, Railroad, 1976, Elbow Room, 1977. Contrbr. articles to newspapers, popular mags. including Atlantic Monthly, Esquire, Washington Post; stories to anthols. Editor: 100 Years After Huck: Fiction by Men in America, 1984, Ploughshares, 1985, others. BA, Morris Brown Coll., 1965; LLB, Harvard U., 1968; MFA, U. Ia., 1971. Assoc. prof. Morgan State U., Balt., 1975-76, U. Va., Charlottesville, 1976-81; prof. English, U. Ia., Iowa City, 1981—. Mem. lit. panel NEA, Washington, 1977-80; judge CCLM writing awards Gen. Electric, NYC, 1983-84. Recipient award in Excellence, AAAL, 1970, Pulitzer prize, 1978; Guggenheim fellow, 1973, MacArthur fellow, 1981. Mem. PEN, ACLU, NAACP, WL. Home: 711 Randell St Iowa City IA 52240

MC PHERSON, MICHAEL MAC KENZIE, b. Hilo, Hawaii, Feb. 23, 1947, s. George Henry and Aileen June Winifred (MacKenzie) McP. Author: Singing with the Owls, 1982; contrbr. poetry, short fiction to Hawaii Rvw, Bamboo Ridge, Poetry Hawaii: A Contemporary Anthology, others, BA in English, U. Hawaii, 1974, MA in English, 1976. Ed., pub. HAPA, 1981-83. Grantee Hawaii State Fdn. for Culture and Arts, 1983. Mem. Hawaii Lit. Arts Council. Home: Box 4392 Kamuela HI 96743

MC PHERSON, SANDRA JEAN, b. San Jose, CA, Aug. 2, 1943, adopted d. Walter James and Frances (Gibson) McP. Author poetry collections: Elegies for the Hot Season, 1970, Radiation, 1973, The Year of Our Birth, 1978, Sensing, 1980, Patron Happiness, 1983, Pheasant Flower, 1985, Responsibility for Blue, 1985, Floralia, 1985. BA in English, San Jose State U., 1965. Vis. lectr. U. Iowa, Iowa City, 1974-76, 78-80; assoc. prof. dept. English, U. Calif., Davis, 1985—. Grantee NEA, 1974, 80, 85, Guggenheim, 1976, Ingram Merrill Fdn., 1972, 84, Oreg. Arts Commn., 1984-85. Office: Dept Engl Univ

Calif Davis CA 95616

MC QUADE, WALTER, b. Port Washington, NY, May 1, 1922; s. Walter P. and Theresa (Dwyer) McQ.; m. Ann Aikman, Nov. 25, 1950; children—Molly Elizabeth, Benjamin Barr, Kate Maud. Author: Schoolhouse, 1958, Cities Fit To Live In, 1971, Stress, 1975, The Longevity Factor, 1979, Architecture in the Real World, 1987. B.Arch., Cornell U., 1947. Writer Archtl. Forum mag., 1947-64; architecture and design critic The Nation, 1959-65, Life Mag., 1970-74; bd. editors Fortune mag., 1964—. Served with AUS, 1942-46. Ford Fdn. Fellow, 1960; co-recipient Grand prize Milan Trennale, 1960; recipient Howard Blakeslee award Am. Heart Assn., 1972; Penney award U. Mo., 1972. Fellow AIA (Architecture Critics' medal 1974). Home: 3 Grosvenor Pl Great Neck NY 11021

MC QUEEN, MARJORIE, b. Mexico City, Mar. 31, 1927, came to U.S., 1929, d. George Melvin and Marie Wynkoop; m. Halton Stephen McQueen, Mar. 8, 1952 (dec. 1982); children—Kathleen Marie, Stephen Halton, Patricia Ann, Michael Allen (dec. 1955). AA, San Antonio Coll., 1952, Coll. of the Desert, Palm Desert, Calif., 1980; BA, Poli. Sci., U. Calif.-Riverside, Calif., 1983. Ed., wrtr. U.S. Air Force, San Antonio, 1948-52; USDA, Indio and Riverside, Calif., 1976-83; USAF, Public Affairs, 1984-86; USAF Aerospace Audiovisual Service, Central Visual Information Library, San Bernardino, Calif., 1986—. Free-lance wrtr., photographer, 1952—. Vice president/publicity dir. Rancho Mirage (Calif.) C. of C., 1978-81. Contrbr. articles to numerous newspapers, magazines, company newsletters, education digests and U.S. Air Force publications and newsletters. Recipient numerous photography awards; winner Wrtrs. Digest contest, 1973. Mem. Natl. League Am. Pen Women, Inc., Photographic Society of America, AAUW, World Affairs Council, Older Women's League. Home: 4041 Pedley Rd 4 Riverside CA 92509

MC QUILKIN, ROBERT RENNIE, b. Paterson, NJ, May 13, 1936; s. William Winters and Eleanor Godwin (Atterbury) McQuilkin; m. Sarah Couch, July 16, 1960; children—Eleanor Godwin, Sarah Couch, Robert Rennie, Jr. Author: An Astonishment and an Hissing, 1982, North Northeast, 1985, We All Fall Down, 1987; poetry in The Atlantic Monthly, Poetry, Yale Rvw, others; contrbr. to Anthology of Magazine Verse and Yearbook of Am. Poetry, Apple: An Anthology of Upstate Poets, other anthols. BA, Princeton, 1958, MA, Columbia U., 1961. Instr., Phillips Academy, Andover, Mass., 1962-70; instr., Loomis Chaffee School, Windsor, CT, 1974-76; instr., Miss Porter's School, Farmington, CT, 1976—. Awards: NEA fellowship, 1984. Mem. PSA. Home: 21 Goodrich Rd Simsbury CT 06070

MC UMBER, KEITH DARREN, b. Pine County, MN, Apr. 9, 1942; s. Vern Richard and Ethel (Harris) Ludington. Contrbr. poems to lit. mags., anthols. Wrkg. on autobiography, poetry. Student U. Minn., 1972—76. Recipient Merit award for saving human life Am. Red Cross, 1978. Home: 4445 E Lake St 13 Minneapolis MN 55406

MC VAY, BARRY LEE, b. Washington, Sept. 18, 1951, s. Joseph John and Stella Frances (Walejko) McV.; m. Vivina Helen Freel, Mar. 14, 1981; 1 son, William Randall. Author: Getting Started in Federal Contracting, 1984, 2d ed., 1987; ed., Buying Surplus Property from the U.S. Government, 1987. BA, U. Va., 1973. Tech. wrtr. Tech. Services Corp., Alexandria, Va., 1973-74; contract specialist U.S. Army tank command, Detroit, 1974-76, mobility command, Ft. Belvoir, Va., 1976-81; contracting officer U.S. Def. Intelligence Agcy., Washington, 1981-82; procurement analyst U.S. Army material command, Alexandria, Va., 1982—; v.p., owner Panoptic Enterprises, Woodbridge, Va., 1982—. Home: 3911 Findley Rd Woodbridge VA 22193

MC WEY, MICHAEL, b. Worcester, MA, Dec. 1, 1953, s. Francis Edward and Louise Catherine (Daley) McW.; m. Katherine Alice Vail, July 26, 1974. Contrbr. short stories to Sou'wester, Apalachee Qtly, Seventeen Mag., Redbook. BA Boston Coll., 1978. Mem. Boston Authors Club. Home: 34 Sparks St Cambridge MA 02138

MEACHAM, ARTHUR PAUL, b. New Orleans, Aug. 25, 1946; m. Rebecca Massey, Dec. 22, 1967; children—Adrian, Heather, Shelton, Amy, Wesley. Columnist: The Comml. News, 1981-82. Contrbr. articles to religious mags. Wrkg. on books on Jewish feasts, Tabernacle in the Wilderness. BS in Elem. Ed., V. of So. Miss., 1968; M.A. in Biblical Studies, Pensacola Christian Coll., 1980; Ph.D. in Religious Edn., Bethany Theol. Seminary, 1987. Pastor, United Methodist Ch., Harperville, Miss., 1971-72, Southern Methodist Ch., Shreveport, LA, 1984—. Home: 5960 Thornhill Ave Shreveport LA 71106

MEACHAM, ELLIS KIRBY, b. Chattanooga, Sept. 5, 1913, s. C.W. Kirby and Jean (Ellis) M.; m. Jean Austin, Feb. 12, 1940; children—G.B. Kirby, Jere E. Author: The East Indiaman, 1968, On the Company's Service, 1971, For King and Company, 1976. AB, U. Chattanooga, 1935; JD, Vanderbilt U., 1937. Atty. various ptnrships, Chattanooga, 1937-72; city atty. City of Chattanooga, 1948-72, judge municipal ct., 1972-79. Recipient Maj. Award for Fiction, Friends of Am. Wrtrs., 1969. Mem. AG. Home: 414 S Crest Rd Chattanooga TN 37404

MECHEM, JAMES HARLAN, b. Wichita, KS, Oct. 31, 1923; s. Kirke Field and Katharine Celia (Lewis) M.; m. Phyllis Raymond Chase, Sept. 6, 1950; children—Chris, Greg, Terry, Geoff, Kirke. Reporter, copyreader: Wichita Eagle & Beacon, 1957-66; tech. wrtr.: Beech Aircraft, Wichita, 1966-78. Ed., pub.: (short stories) A Diary of Women, 1969, Out of Sight, 1971-76, (with Ann Menebroker) Slices, 1972; Redstart mag., 1987—. Served with U.S. Army, 1943-46. Home: 229 N Fountain Wichita KS 67208

MEAD, HARRIET COUNCILL, b. Franklin, VA, Jan. 11; d. Hutson and Ollie (Whitley) Councill; m. Berne Matthews Mead, Jr., Dec. 2, 1940; 2 sons: William W., Charles C. Author: The Irrepressible Saint, 1983. BA, Coll. William & Mary, 1935. County librarian Carroll County, Va., 1935-36; city librarian schl. bd., Suffolk, Va., 1936-41; media spclst. Orange County schls., Orlando, Fla., 1961-80. Mem. Orlando-Winter Park Jr. League, Fla., 1985-86, League of Women Voters, Natl. Soc. Colonial Dames; Cornell Art Gallery Assocs., Winter Pk., Fla., 1985-86. Mem. Orange County Schl. Librarians (pres. 1968-69), Fla. Council of Libraries. Address: 500 East Marks St Orlando FL 32803

MEADE, WALTER WATHEN, b. Cin., Sept. 20, 1930; s. Walter Wathen and Hilda Jane (Erbland) M.; m. Ellen Roddick, Nov. 4, 1977; 1 son, Luke. Author: short stories Saturday Evening Post, Redbook, Tex. Qtly, Seventeen, Cosmopolitan, others. BA, DePauw U. Mng. editor Reader's Digest, NYC, 1968-74, Cosmopolitan, 1974-75; editorial dir. Avon Books, The Hearst Corp., NYC, 1976-79, pub., 1979-81, pres., 1981—. Mem. Hunter Brook Assn., Yorktown, N.Y. Served with AUS, 1952-54; Korea. Home: Old Logging Rd Yorktown Heights NY 10598

MEATS, STEPHEN, b. LeRoy, KS, Mar. 16, 1944, s. Cecil Eugene and Ruby Irene (Dyer) M.; m. Mary Beth Williams, May 30, 1964 (div. 1983); children—John Isaac, Laura Elizabeth, Owen Williams; m. 2d, Ann Downes, Aug. 20, 1983; 1 stepson, Edward Kane Leins. Co-ed. Revolutionary War novels of W.G. Simms (8 vols.), 1976; ed. Writings of B.F. Perry (3 vols.), 1980; contrbr. scholarly pieces: Joscelyn, 1975, Florida and the Revolutionary South, 1976, Gyascutas, 1978, Casebook on Light in August, 1982, other publs.; contrbr. poetry: Little Balkans Rvw, Kansas Qtly, Blue Unicorn, other lit mags; asst. ed. UT Rvw, 1972-79, poetry ed. Midwest Qtly, 1984—. Student Kans. State U., 1962-65; BA, U. So. Car., 1966, MA, 1968, PhD, 1972. Asst. prof. English U.S. Air Force Academy, Colo., 1968-72; assoc. prof. English U. Tampa, Fla., 1972-79, chmn. humanities div., 1974-79; prof. English Pittsburg (Kans.) State U., 1979—, chmn. dept. English, 1979-85. Home: 104 S Olive St Pittsburg KS 66762

MEDCALF, ROBERT RANDOLPH, JR., b. Baltimore, MD, Jul. 23, 1949; s. Robert Randolph and Marie Jean (Bald) Medcalf; m. Cecelia Marie Johnson, June 3, 1967 (div. 1986); children—Rebecca Anastatia, David Augustine, John Randolph. Poetry collection: Strange Things Happen, 1981; editor: Apogee no. 1, 1981, Microcosm no. 1, 1984; poetry contrbr. to Amazing, Space & Time, StarLine, Green's Mag., other mags. AA, Community Coll. of Baltimore, 1971, US Army, (Ft. Meade, MD), 1971-79; wrtr., 1979—. Mem. Small Press Wrtrs. and Artists, Science Fiction Poetry Assoc. Office: Box 644 Biglerville PA 17307

MEDEIROS, PRISCA D. BICOY, b. Puuhoku, Molokai HI; Mar. 29, 1928 d. Petronilo and Paula Daniel Bicoy; m. Joseph Patro Medeiros, 1946; children—Nathalie Medeiros Wilson, Edwin Vincent, Paula Medeiros Anderson, Jacqueline Medeiros Moran, Theresa Medeiros Washington, Jolyn Medeiros Kalama. Contrbr., author, pub., 8 poetry bks; to various publs; 12 meditation bks; wrkg. on children's literature. Ed. Colls.: De Anza, CSM, Bryman. Artist; 1986 Song Wrtr.; Lyricist Chapel Recording Co. and Talent Assocs. of Mass.; 1985 Lyrical award; 1985 Best Song of the Month Award. Author pub. (Copyright) 9 song-poem Lyrics. Mem. Song Wrtrs. Club Am.; Natl. Acad. Song Wrtrs. Home: 85 Amherst Ave Menlo Park CA 94025

MEDIN, DONNA MAE, b. Mpls., Aug. 29, 1932; d. Donald Erb Clason an Alice Elizabeth (Anderson) Clason-Schaller; m. Wallace George Medin, Nov. 5, 1954; children—Daniel Wallace (dec.), Debra Joy, Diane Lynn. Contrbr. articles to newspapers, religious pubs. including Mpls. Star and Tribune, Good News, others. Grad. public schls., Mpls. Recipient Honorable Mention award Wrtr.'s Digest, 1979. Mem. Minn. Christian WG. Home: 753 Polk St Anoka MN 55303

MEDINA, KATHRYN BACH, b. Plainfield, NJ, d. Francis Earl and Elizabeth (Evans) Bach; m. Standish Forde Medina, Jr., Apr. 20, 1968. Editor for Peter Benchley, Maggie Scarf, Tennessee Williams, Agnes de Mille, C.D.B. Bryan,

Hedrick Smith, William Safire. BA, Smith Coll., 1965. With Doubleday & Co., NYC, 1965-85; v.p./sr. ed. Random House, 1985—. Office: RH 201 E 50 St New York NY 10167

MEDWID, STEPHEN, b. Tarrytown, NY, May 26, 1958; s. Andrew and Mary (Gaviluk) M. Contrbr. articles to mags., newspapers including USA Today, World Boxing, others. Contrbg. ed. Stan Fiscler's All-Time Hockey Trivia Book, 1980, The Zany Book of Hockey, 1980; assoc. ed.: The Ring Record Book, 1982, 83. Student Curry Coll., 1976-77; B.A. in Communications/Jnlsm., C. W. Post Coll., 1980. Staff wrtr. Action Sports Hockey Mag., NYC., 1979-80; publicist Top Rank Inc., NYC, 1980-81; baseball newsman, UPI Sports, 1982; contrbg. ed. The Ring Mag., N.Y.C., 1982-83; assoc. ed. G. C. London Pub. Co., Rockville Centre, NY, 1983-84; free-lance wrtr., 1984., Home: 327 Naniloa Dr Wailuku HI 96793

MEEK, JAY, b. Grand Rapids, MI, Aug. 23, 1937; s. Edwin and Shirley (Peterson) M.; m. Martha George, Aug. 29, 1966; 1 child, Anna. Author: (poems) The Week the Dirigible Came, 1976; Drawing on the Walls, 1980; Earthly Purposes, 1984. Ba, U. Mich., 1959; MA, Syracuse U., 1965. Guest mem. writing faculty Sarah Lawrence Coll., Bronxville, N.Y., 1980-82; assoc. prof. MIT, Cambridge, 1982-83; wrtr.-in-res. Memphis State U., fall 1984; assoc. prof. English, U. N.D., Grand Forks, 1985—. NEA grantee, 1973; Guggenheim fellow, 1986. Office: Box 8237 Eng Dept U ND Grand Forks ND 58202

MEEKER, DARCY SUE, b. Farragut, ID, May 29, 1946; d. Ermine Linsley and Margaret Alice (Painter) Meeker; M. Tom Bright, May 12, 1984. Columnist: Fla. Bus. Jnl., 1986—. Contrbr. articles on health, sci., communications to newspapers, mags. including St. Petersburg Times, Citrus & Vegetable, Health Mag., others. Ed.-in-chief: Research '87: Biocontrol, 1986. Wrkg. on fables, self-help book for women, bus. plans, slide-show graphics. B.A., U. Fla., 1969, M.A., 1981. Chief print news U. Fla., Gainesville, 1974-85, asst. prof. communications, 1985—. Mem. NASW (assoc.), Fla. Freelance Wrtrs. Assn., Agrl. Communicators Edn., Am. Agrl. Eds. Assn., Southern Assn. Agrl. Scientists, Gainesville World Future Soc. (founder), Gainesville Area Women's Network (sec., v.p., chmn.), Gainesville Area Innovation Network. Home: 1222 NW 34 Terrace Gainesville FL 32605

MEGLIN, NICK, b. Brooklyn, N.Y., July 30, 1935; divorced; children: Diane Elizabeth, Christopher Allard. Author: On-the-Spot Drawing, 1972, Fountain Pen Drawing, 1973, Superfan, 1973, Supefan...Again., 1974, The Art of Humorous Illustration, 1975, Honor the Godfather, 1976, Mad Stew, 1977, (with Al Jaffee) Rotten Rhymes and Other Crimes, 1978, (with George Woodbridge), A Mad Look at the Fifties, 1985, with Woodbridge) "Mad" Looks at the Sixties, 1987. Also au of The Pen. Au of animated films, TV Scripts, recorded songs, aicle Sunday Times, Sunday News Magazine, others. AA, Brooklyn/Queens Coll (now Brooklyn Coll of the City Univ of N.Y.), 1956; BFA, School of Visual Arts, NYC. Editor, Mad (magazine), N.Y.C., 1956—. Freelance writer, 1954—; freelance illustrator, 1956—. Ins tr, School of Visual Arts, NYC., 1972—, Military service: U.S. Army, illustrator, 1958-60. Office: Mad 485 Madison Ave New York NY 10002

MEHTA, VED (PARKASH), b. Lahore, India, Mar. 21, 1934; came to U.S., 1949; s. Amolak Ram and Shanti Devi (Mehra) M.; m. Linn Fenimore Cooper Cary, Dec. 17, 1983; children: Alexandra Sage Fenimore Cooper. and Natasha Cary Fenimore Cooper. Author: Face to Face, 1957 (Secondary Edn. Annl. Book award 1958), reissued 1967, 78, excerpts 1981, Walking the Indian Streets, 1960, rev. 1971, Fly and the Fly-Bottle, 1963, 2d ed. 1983, The New Theologian, 1966, (novel) Delinquent Chacha, 1967, Portrait of India, 1970, John Is Easy to Please, 1971, Mahatma Gandhi and His Apostles, 1977, The New India, 1978, Photographs of Chachaji, 1980, A Family Affair: India Under Three Prime Ministers, 1982, Three Stories of the Raj (fiction), 1986; autobiographical series: Daddyji, 1972, Mamaji, 1979, Vedi, 1982, The Ledge Between the Streams, 1984, Sound-Shadows of the New World, 1986; also numerous translations, articles and stories in newspapers and mags. BA, Pomona Coll., 1956; BA, MA Oxford U., 1959; MA, Harvard U., 1961. Staff writer The New Yorker NYC, 1961—; prof. lit. Bard Coll., Annandale-on-Hudson, N.Y., 1985-86; prof. of art and culture Sarah Lawrence College, writer and commentator TV documentary film Chachaji: My Poor Relation, PBS, 1978, BBC, 1980. Hazen fellow 1956-59; Harvard Prize fellow, 1959-60; Guggenheim fellow, 1971-72, 77-78; Ford Fdn. grantee, 1971-76; Pub. Policy grantee, 1979-82; MacArthur Prize fellow, 1982-87.Mem. Century Assn. (trustee 1973-75), Council Fgn. Relations. Office: The New Yorker 25 W 43d St New York NY 10036

MEIER, AUGUST, b. NYC, Apr. 30, 1923; s. Frank A. and Clara (Cohen) M.; author: Negro Thought in America, 1880-1915, 1963, (with Elliott Rudwick) From Plantation to Ghetto, 1966, 3d ed., 1976, Black Detroit and the Rise of the UAW, 1979, CORE: A Study In The Civil Rights Movement, 1942-68, 1973, Along the Color Line: Explorations in the Black Experience, 1976; editor: (with Francis Broderick) Negro Protest Thought in the Twentieth Century, 1966; (with Broderick and Elliott Rudwick) rev. ed. renamed Black Protest Thought in The Twentieth Century, 1971, (with Rudwick) The Making of Black America, 1969; Black Nationalism in America, 1970; co-editor: Black Leaders of the Twentieth Century, 1982; genl. editor: Negro in Am. Life Series, 1966-74, Blacks in the New World Series, 1972—; editorial adv. bd.: Booker T. Washington Papers, 1967—,Civil War History, 1970, Jnl Am. History, 1974-77, Marcus Garvey Papers, 1978-81. AB, Oberlin Coll., 1945; AM, Columbia U., 1949, PhD, 1957. Asst. prof. history Tougaloo (Miss.) Coll., 1945-49; research asst. to pres. Fisk U., 1953, asst. prof. history, 1953-56; asst., assoc. prof. history Morgan State Coll., Balt., 1957-64; prof. history Roosevelt U., Chgo., 1964-67, Kent (Ohio) State U., 1967-69, univ. prof., 1969—. Advanced grad. fellow ACLS, 1952; Guggenheim fellow, 1971-72; NEH fellow, 1975-77; Center for Advanced Study in Behavioral Scis. fellow, 1976-77. Mem. Am. Hist. Assn., So. Hist. Assn., Assn. Study Negro Life and History, Orgn. Am. Historians (del. to ACLS 1979-83). Home: 122 N Prospect St Kent OH 44240

MEIER, KAY, b. Chgo., Sept. 30, 1933, d. George and Kathryn (McQuade) Schuette; m. Fred William Meier, Sept. 11, 1954. Contrbr. poetry to Cape Rock, Gryphon, Soundings, Nettles and Nutmet, other lit mags. BS, No. Ill. U., 1958; MA, Northeastern Ill. U., Chgo., 1971. Tchr. English 1958—. Recipient Poet & Patrons prize, Chgo., 1984; winner Salute to Arts poetry contest Triton Coll., River Grove, Ill., 1985. Mem. Ill. Wrtrs. Home: 8403 W Normal Ave Niles IL 60648

MEINKE, PETER, b. Bklyn., Dec. 29, 1932; s. Harry Frederick Meinke and Kathleen (McDonald) Lewis; m. Jeanne Clark, Dec. 14, 1957; children—Peri, Peter, Gretchen, Timothy. Author: Underneath the Lantern, 1986, The Piano Tuner, 1986, Trying to Surprise God, 1981, Rat Poems, 1978, The Night Train and the Golden Bird, 1977, Lines from Neuchatel, 1974, Howard Nemerov, 1968, Very Seldom Animals, 1969, The Legend of Larry the Lizard, 1968, Night Watch on the Chesapeake, 1987. AB, Hamilton College, 1955, MA, U. of MI, 1961, PhD, U. of MN, 1965. Teacher, Mt. Lakes High School, Mt. Lakes, NJ, 1958-60; asst. prof., Hamline U., St. Paul, MN, 1961-66; director, writing workshop, Eckerd College, St. Petersburg, FL, 1966—. Awards: NEA Fellowships, 1974-75; Fulbright lectrshp. U. of Warsaw, Poland, 1978-79; PSA Awards, 1976, 1984; James Thurber wrtr.-in-res., Columbus, OH, 1987. Mem. PSA, PEN. Home: 147 Wildwood Lane SE St Petersburg FL 33705

MEINSTEIN, CRYSTAL ANN, b. Chgo., June 29, 1955; d. James Lee and Mary Jane (Johnson) Carlson; m. Ronald S. Meinstein, Apr. 1, 1978; children-Elizabeth Marie, Michelle Robin. A.A., Thornton Commun. Coll., 1975; B.A. magna cum laude, Bradley U., 1977. Contrbr. poems, short stories, play and book rvws. to mags., newspapers. Short story ed. Bradley Rvw., Peoria, IL, 1976; research reader Bacon's Clipping Bur., Chgo., 1979-80; needlecrafts instr. Moraine Valley Commun. Coll., Palos Heights, IL, 1984-86; free-lance wrtr., 1987—. Mem. Alsip Wrtrs. Club (founder, leader 1982-83), Muse Wrtrs. Club (program dir. 1984-85). Home: 9044 Chelmsford Swartz Creek MI 48473

MEISSNER, WILLIAM JOSEPH, b. July 11, 1948. Author poetry collections: Learning to Breathe Underwater, 1979, The Sleepwalker's Son, 1986. Dir. creative writing program St. Cloud (Minn.) State U., since 1972. Recipient NEA fellowship, 1982, Loft-McKnight award, 1982, PEN-NEA Syndicated Fiction awards, 1983, 85. Home: 618 6th Ave N Saint Cloud MN 56301

MEISTER, SHIRLEY VOGLER, b. Belleville, IL, July 11, 1936; d. Lester Vernon and Irene Rose (Huber) Vogler; m. Paul Philip Meister, Aug. 30, 1958; children: Donna Marie, Diane Mary, Lisa Marie. Contrbr. poetry to numerous publs.; newspaper columnist: The Criterion, Indpls., The Messenger, Belleville, Ill. BA in English summa cum laude, Ind. U. Purdue U. at Indpls., 1985. Past wrtr. ed. Belleville News-Democrat; past editorial asst. Actual Specifying Engrs. mag., The Diary of Alpha Kappa Psi; freelance wrtr. Recipient Margaret Church Meml. award for poetry, Purdue U., 1984, Merrill and Marjorie Swedlund Meml. award for journalism, Purdue U., 1985, H.L. Creek Meml. award for lit. criticism, 1985, other awards. Mem. AAP, Wrtrs.' Center Indpls., Christian Wrtrs. League Am., Nat. League Am. Pen Women. Home: 5948 Hillside West Dr Indianapolis IN 46220

MELHEM, D(IANA) H(ELEN), b. Bklyn.; d. Nicholas and Georgette (Deyratani) M.; div. 1972; children: Dana Marie Vogel, Gregory Melhem Vogel. Author: (poetry) Notes on 94th Street, 1972, 79, Rest in Love, 1975, 78, Children of the House Afire/More Notes on 94th Street 1976; Reaching Exercises: The IWWG

Workshop Book, 1981; Gwendolyn Brooks: Poetry and the Heroic Voice, 1987; ed..: Mosaic: Poems from an IWWG Workshop, 1983; contrbr. poetry to N.Y. Times, Nation, Confrontation, Bitterroot, Croton Rvw., Gnosis, Sun Dog, Steppingstones, Gargoyle, also others, essays and criticism to N.Y. Times Mag., Greenfield Rvw., VORT, Western Jnl. Black Studies, others; rep. in anthologies. BA cum laude, NYU, 1949; MA, CCNY, 1971; PhD, CUNY, 1976. Adj. lectr. CCNY, 1971, adj. asst. prof., 1981-82; adj. asst. prof. lit. Coll. S.I., CUNY, 1978; adj. assoc. prof. lit. and composition L.I. U., 1981-83; mem. faculty New School for Social Research, 1979, 1982-85; adj. prof. Union for Experimenting Colls. and Univs., 1985—; dir. regional writing workshops IWWG, 1977-80; disting. vis. artist Southampton Coll., 1978. Recipient NY Heart Assn. Media award, 1979; Calliope Poetry award, 1974; Marie T. Unger award Shelley Soc. N.Y., 1984; NEH fellow, 1980-81. Mem. PSA, PEN, AAP, P&W, MLA, DG, Phi Beta Kappa. Home: 250 W 94th St New York NY 10025

MELICK, ARDEN DAVIS, b. Irvington, NJ, Dec. 31, 1940; d. Arthur Laird and Bernice (Spies) D.; m. David Marvin Melick, Sept. 2, 1960 (div. 1982); children—Randolph, David, Douglas. Sr. ed. Mobil Travel Guide, 1966, 67, 68, 69; author: The Presidents: Tidbits & Trivia, 1979, Wives of the Presidents, 1972, 74, 76, 78, 80, 82, Dolley Madison, First Lady, 1970. AA, Centenary Coll., 1960; BA, Seton Hall U., 1973; MA, Syracuse U., 1979. Second v.p. & dir. p.r. Fidelity Union Bancorp., Newark, 1973-79; mgr. corp. communics. Suburban Propane Gas Corp., Morristown, NJ, 1979-83; dir. communics. & spec. asst. to Commissioner, NJ Dept Commerce, Trenton, 1983-85; dir. corp. communics. Natl. Distillers & Chem. Corp., NYC, 1985—. Trustee, Centenary Coll., Newark Boys Chorus Schl. Home: 11 Kendal Ave Maplewood NJ 07040

MELINO, EUGENE ANTHONY, b. Bronx, NY, Aug. 6, 1958; s. Eugene John and Mary (Santiago) Melino. Contrbr. to Seventeen. BS, New York U., 1980; MA, 1982. Contract wrtr. IBM Industry Pubns. (White Plains, NY), 1983—, Institute for Commns. Advancement (NYC), 1984—; contrbg. wrtr. HQ Mag. IBM Corp., 1985. Home: 1103 Ellsworth Ave Bronx NY 10465

MELLENDER, JOHN CLIFFORD, (Jack), b. Chgo., Nov. 10, 1943, s. William Crane and Lillian Ruth (Hardy) M. Contrbr. to Am. Poetry Anthology, Vol. I, 1982. BA in Creative Writing, San Francisco State U., 1975; MA, U. Calif., Berkeley, 1984. Address: 1200 Lakeshore Ste 4G Oakland CA 94606

MELLICHAMP, JOSEPHINE WEAVER, b. Helton NC, Sept. 30, 1923; d. James Thomas Hampton and Bonnie Clyde (Bauguess) Weaver; m. J.M. Stafford Smith, Dec. 15, 1944 (div. 1959); m. 2d, Stiles A. Mellichamp, Dec. 16, 1961; stepchildren—Stiles A. Jr., Joseph Capers III. Author: Senators from Georgia, 1976, Georgia Heritage, 1988; contrbr. articles: Atlanta Jnl., Constitution Mag., Grit, Modern Woodmen, others. AB, Emory and Henry Coll., 1943. Wrtr., historian Strode Pubs., Huntsville, Ala., 1975—; natl. adviser, dep. gov. Am. Biog. Inst. Research Assn. Mem. Nat. League Am. Pen Women, Southeastern Wrtrs.' Assn., Atlanta Wrtrs.' Club, Atlanta Hist. Soc., Village Wrtrs.' Group, other profl. orgns. Home: 1124 Reeder Circle NE Atlanta GA 30306

MELLOW, JAMES ROBERT, b. Gloucester, MA, Feb. 28, 1926; s. James Robert and Cecilia Margaret (Sawyer) M. Author: Charmed Circle; Gertrude Stein & Co., 1974, Nathaniel Hawthorne in His Times, 1980 (Am. Book award for biography 1983); Invented Lives: F. Scott and Zelda Fitzgerald, 1984; editor: The Best in Arts, 1962, New York: The Art World, 1963. BS, Northwestern U., 1950. Mem. staff Arts mag., 1955-65, exec. editor, 1961, editor, 1961-65, Indsl. Design, 1965-68; art critic The New Leader, 1964-72, Art Intl., 1965-69, NY Times, 1970-74. Served with USAAF, 1944-46. Address: Box 297 Clinton CT 06413

MELMAN, SEYMOUR, Author: Dynamic Factors in Industrial Productivity, 1956, Decision Making and Productivity, 1958, Peace Race, 1961, Our Depleted Society, 1965, Pentagon Capitalism, 1970, The Permanent War Economy, 1974, Profits Without Production, 1983; editor: Inspection for Disarmament, 1958, No Place To Hide, 1962, Disarmament; its Politics and Economics, 1962, In the Name of America, 1968, Conversion of Industry from a Military to Civilian Economy; A Series, 1970, The War Economy of the U.S., 1971. Home: 304 Mudd Columbia U New York NY 10027

MELTZER, DAVID, b. Rochester, NY, Feb. 17, 1937; s. Louis and Roseamunde (Lovelace) M.; m. Christina Meyer, Apr. 1, 1958; children—Jennifer, Margaret, Amanda, Adam Benjamin ben David. Author: numerous books of poetry, including Tens, Selected Poems, 1973, Six, 1976, Two-Way Mirror: Notebook on Poetry, 1977, The Art, The Veil, 1981, The Name: Selected Poetry, 1973-83; editor: The San Francisco Poets, 1971, Birth, 1973, The Secret Garden; Anthology of the Classic Kabbalah, 1977, Birth: Anthology of Ancient Texts, Songs, Prayers, and Stories, 1981, Death: An Anthology of Ancient Texts, Songs, Prayers, and Stories, 1983; editor, pub.: bi-annual Jnl, Tree, also Tree Books; song-writer: Serpent Power, 1968, Poet Song, 1970; soundtrack for Chance, 1978. Student, Los Angeles City Coll., 1955-56, U. Calif. at Los Angeles, 1956-57. CCLM grantee, 1973-74, 81; NEA writing grantee, 1974, for pub., 1975; Calif. Arts Council grantee, 1979. Office: Box 9005 Berkeley CA 94709

MELTZER, MILTON, b. Worcester, MA, May 8, 1915; s. Benjamin and Mary (Richter) M.; m. Hilda Balinky, June 22, 1941; children—Jane, Amy. Author: Mark Twain Himself, 1960, (with Walter Harding) A Thoreau Profile, 1962, Langston Hughes: a Biography, 1968, Bread and Roses, 1967, Brother, Can You Spare a Dime, 1968, Slavery: A World History, 2 vols., 1972, Hunted Like A Wolf: The Seminole War, 1972, The Right to Remain Silent, 1972, (with Langston Hughes and C. Eric Lincoln) Pictorial History of Black Americans, 1983, The Eye of Conscience, 1974, World of Our Fathers: The Jews of Eastern Europe, 1974, Remember the Days: A Short of History of the Jewish American, 1974, Never to Forget: the Jews of the Holocaust, 1976, Taking Root: Jewish Immigrants in America, 1976, Dorothea Lange: A Photographer's Life, 1978, The Human Rights Book, 1979; co-editor: Lydia Maria Child: Selected Letters, 1817-1880, 1982, The Chinese Americans, 1980, The Jewish Americans, 1982, Hispanic Americans, 1982, The Terrorists, 1983. Student, Columbia, 1932-36. Adj. prof. history U. Mass., Amherst, 1970-80. Served with USAAF, 1942-46. Mem. Am. Hist. Assn., Orgn. Am. Historians, AG, PEN. Address: 236 West End Ave New York NY 10023

MELUCH, REBECCA M., b. Garfield Heights, OH, Oct. 24, 1956; d. Andrew David and Emma Blanche (Klemstein) Meluch. Author: Sovereign, 1979, Wind Dancers, 1981, Wind Child, 1982, Jerusalem Fire, 1985. BA, U. N.C.-Greensboro, 1978; MA, U. Pa., 1981. Free-lance wrtr., model, actress, 1978—. Mem. SFWA. Home: 29520 Schwartz Rd Westlake OH 44145

MELZER, DOROTHY GARRETT, b. Dadeville, AL; d. Henry Oliver and Pattie (Newell) Garrett; m. John Henry Melzer, July 4, 1936 (dec. June 21, 1967); children—John T. S., Linn Garrett. Author: (Poetry) Sullivan's Island, 1980, One Woman, 1980, Donegal Journey, 1982; (play) Lift Up Thine Eyes, 1936. Contrbr. articles to profl. jnls., poems to lit. mags. Ed.: The Book of College Verse, 1938. Wrkg. on collected poems, collection of essays, travel articles. Ph.B., U. Chgo., 1926, A.M., 1932. Instr. creative wrtg., U. Mo., 1945-46; dir. forensics, assoc. prof. English, Georgetown Coll., KY, 1947-58; asst. prof. English, Auburn U., AL, 1958-75, retired. Recipient award Tenn. Poetry Soc., 1946, Sonnet prize Ala. Wrtrs. Conclave, (1929. Home: 848 Cahaba Dr Auburn AL 36830

MELZER, JOHN T.S., b, Ashland, OH, Sept. 9, 1938; s. John Henry and Dorothy (Garrett) M. Author: Fourteen Days to Field Spanish, 1985; contrbr. articles to publs. Wrkg. on dictionary of oilfield Spanish, transl. and editing jnl. of Peruvian viceroy, handbook for transl. 18th century Spanish. BA, Auburn U., 1961; MA, U. Va., 1964; PhD, Tulane U., 1978. Translator, drilling fluid engr. Oilfield Service Co., 1978-81; oilfield cons Gulf of Mexico, 1979—. Recipient fellowships in history, Latin-Am. history, geography. Office: 848 Cahaba Dr Auburn AL 36830

MENASHE, SAMUEL, b. NYC, Sept. 16, 1925; s. Berish and Brana (Barak) M. Author: The Many Named Beloved, 1961; No Jerusalem But This, 1971; Fringe of Fire, 1973; To Open, 1974, Collected Poems, 1986. BA, Queens Coll., 1974; Doctorat d'Universite, The Sorbonne, 1950. Instr. Bard Coll., Annandale-on-Hudson, N.Y., 1952-53, Post Coll., Greenvale, N.Y., 1961-62; self-employed French tutor, NYC, 1962—. Recipient award Longview Fdn., 1954. Mem. PEN. Home: 75 Thompson St Apt 151 New York NY 10012

MENDEL, ROBERTA JOAN, b. Cleve., Apr. 30, 1935, d. Jack and Gertrude Nadine (Katz) Bailus; m. Leonard Mendel, Mar. 24, 1957; children—Valerie Anne, Stuart Craig, Todd Rhys. Contrbr. to Earth's Daus., Vanderbilt Rvw, Earthwide Calendar, Broomstick, Women's Network, Unicorn, New Voices, Jewish Poems, Writing for Me, Dan River Anthology, Am. Poetry Anthology, Quiet Thoughts Anthology, also numerous other jnls. in U.S. and fgn. countries. BA magna cum laude, John Carroll U., 1971, MA, 1973. Assoc. tchr. John Carroll U., 1971-73; lectr., instr. Cuyahoga County Community Coll., 1975; hist. abstractor ABC-CLIO Press, Santa Barbara, Calif., 1976-86; ed./pub. The Pin Prick Press, Shaker Heights, Ohio, 1978—; sales agt. Hunter Realty, Lyndhurst, Ohio, 1983—. Mem. COSMEP, P&W, AG, AL, Feminist Wrtrs.' Guild. Home: 2664 S Green Rd Shaker Heights OH 44122

MENDELSOHN, HAROLD, b. Jersey City, Oct. 30, 1923; s. Louis and Bessie (Yulinsky) M.; m. Irene Sylvia Gordon, Apr. 10, 1949; 1 dau., Susan Lynn. Author: Mass Entertainment, 1966, (with David H. Bayley) Minorities and the Police: Confrontation in America, 1969, (with Irving Crespi) Polls, Television and the New Politics, 1970, (with others) Television and Growing Up; The Impact of Televised Violence, 1972, (with Garrett O'Keefe) The People Choose a President, 1976; editor: Mass Communications series, 1967-69; contrbr. article to profl. jnls. BS, CCNY, 1945; MA, Columbia U., 1946; PhD, New Schl. Social Research, 1956. Sr. survey analyst U.S. Dept. State, Washington, 1951-52; research assoc. Bur. Social Sci. Research, Am. U., Washington, 1951-56; assoc. mgr. mktg. communications McCann-Erickson Advt., NYC, 1956-58; assoc. dir. Psychol. Corp., NYC, 1958-62; prof. dept. mass communications U. Denver, 1962—, chmn., 1970-78, dean faculty of Social Sciences, 1984. Office: Ctr Pub Comm 2018 S Gaylord Denver CO 80208

MENDELSOHN, JACK, b. Cambridge, MA, July 22, 1918; m. Ruth P. Mendelsohn, Dec. 26, 1949 (div. 1969); children—Channing T., Deborah T., Kurt A.; m. Joan Silverstone Hall, Aug. 3, 1969; 1 stepdau., Lisabeth Hall. Author: Why I Am a Unitarian, 1960, God, Allah and Ju Ju, 1962, The Forest Calls Back, 1965, The Martyrs, 1966, Channing, The Reluctant Radical, 1971, Alone Together, 1979, The Freeze Movement as an Ethical Achievement, 1983, Being Liberal in an Illiberal Age, 1985. BA. Boston U., 1939; S.T.B., Harvard, 1945; ordained to ministry Unitarian Universalist Ch., 1945; minister in, Rockford, Ill., 1947-54, Indpls., 1954-59, DD (hon.), Meadville Theol Schl., U. Chgo., 1962; Arlinton St. Ch., Boston, 1959-69; sr. minister First Unitarian Ch. Chgo., 1969-79; minister First Parish in Bedford, Mass., 1979—; Officer of Instruction, Harvard Univ., 1979—; mem. adj. faculty Meadville Theol. Schl., U. Chgo., 1969-79. Mem. NAACP, ACLU. Address: 5 Ledgewood Dr Bedford MA 01730

MENDINI, DOUGLAS A., b. Morganville, NJ, June 13, 1953, s. Tullio F. Mendini and Helen V. (Jones) Mendini-Renninger. Contrbr. short stories: Modernsense, The Occasional Rvw., The Pale Fire Rvw., others; playwright: Katharine the Great, 1983, Arizona Cowboys, 1984, A Good Sport, 1985; contrbr. poetry to over 40 lit. mags. BA, Seton Hall U. Project coordinator Monmouth County Arts Council, Red Bank, N.J., 1976-77; freelance wrtr., 1980—. Mem. P&W. Home: 403 W 54th St 1D New York NY 10019

MENKUS, BELDEN (ALFRED JULIAN), b. Sacramento, CA, May 6, 1931; s. Julian Alfred and Ida M.; m. JoAnn Bozarth, Dec. 14, 1952; children—Neal, Belden Jr., Juli Ann. Founder & ed.: Records Mgt. Jnl., 1963-68, Computer Security, 1974-77, Data Processing Auditing Rpt., 1983-86; exec. ed. Jnl. of Systs. Mgt., 1979—; contrbr. to anthologies and pubns., inclg., Modern Office Technology, Administrative Mgt., The Culpeper Rpt. on Mktg., Computers & Security, Honeywell Support, Christianity Today, others. Self-employed, 1969—; certified as Systs. Professional, Info. Systs. Auditor, Office Automation Profl. Records Mgr. Served to Alc, USAF, 1953-57. Address: Box 85 Middleville NJ 07855

MENZIE, DONALD E., b. DuBois, PA, Apr. 4, 1922; s. James Freeman and Helga Josephine (Johnson) M.; m. Jane Cameron Redsecker, Nov. 6, 1946; children—Donald, William, John, Thomas. Author: Reservoir Mechanics, 1954, Waterflooding for Engineers, 1968, Applied Reservoir Engineering for Geologists, 1971, New Recovery Techniques, 1975. Contrbr. numerous articles to profl. jnls. Wrkg. on Enhanced Oil Recovery. B.S. in Petroleum and Natural Ga Engineering, Penn. State U., 1942, M.S., 1948, Ph.D., 1962. Asst. prof. U. Okla., Norman, 1951-55, assoc. prof., 1955-64, prof., 1964—; owner Petroleum Engineering Educators, Norman, 1971—. Home: 1503 Melrose Dr Norman OK 73069

MERCER, CHARLES, b. Stouffville, Ont., Can., July 12, 1917; s. Alfred and Alma (Hoover) M.; m. Alma Sutton, Feb. 21, 1940. Author: The Narrow Ledge, 1951, There Comes A Time, 1955, Rachel Cade, 1956, The Drummond Tradition, 1957, Enough Good Men, 1960 Pilgrim Strangers, 1961, The Reckoning, 1962, Gift of Life, 1963, The Trespassers, 1964, Beyond Bojador, 1965, Promise Morning, 1966, The Minister, 1969, Revolt in April, 1971, Castle on the River, 1975, Witch Tide, 1976 Murray Hill, 1980, Pacific, 1981; nonfiction Alexander The Great, 1963, Legion of Strangers, 1964, Miracle at Midway, 1977, Monsters in the Earth: The Story of Earthquakes, 1978, Statue of Liberty, 1979; also numerous short stories, articles. A.B., Brown U., 1939. Reporter Washington Post, 1939-42; reporter, feature writer, columinist A.P., N.Y.C., 1946-59; sr. editor G.P. Putnam's Sons, N.Y.C., 1966-79, v.p., 1075-79. Served to 1st lt. AUS, World War II, Korean War. Mem. Phi Beta Kappa. Address: 16 Peru St Edison NJ 08820

MERCER, LINDA LOU, (Taryn Scott), b. Martinsburg, WV, Nov. 29, 1945; d. Charles Albert and Dorothy Jane (Baldwin) M. Contrbr. articles to mags, co-author scripts, Skylarks and Best in Show. B.A., Case Western Reserve U., 1967, M.A. dramatic art, 1969. Technical wrtr. Naval Surface Weapons Center, Silver Spring, MD, 1969-80, combat systems analyst, 1980—. Producer, Montgomery County Cable Public Access TV, Rockville, MD, 1987—. Mem. Women in Film Video. Home: 10153 Sutherland Rd Silver spring MD 20901

MERCER, ETHEL VIOLA, b. Ashland, KS, Sept. 13, 1947; d. Elmo Freeman Lake and Helen Irene (Wimer) Lowman; m. Gilbert Frank Maggard, Aug. 22, 1965 (dec. June 1970); children: Frank, Deidra; divorced; children: Jesse Mercer, Jonelle Mercer. Author: A Child of the King, 1986. Diploma, Salt City Bus. Coll., Hutchinson, Kans., 1973. Recipient Golden Poet award World of Poetry, 1985. Home: Box 314 Ashland KS 67831

MEREDITH, MARILYN, b. Glendale, CA, Aug. 24, 1933, d. Murl Maurice and Genevieve Mona (Hoffman) Mitchell; m. Arnold D. Meredith, Oct. 24, 1951; children—Dana Van Scoy, Mark, Lisa Aguilar, Lori Cole, Matthew. Author: The Crabtrees, Tule River Patriarchs, 1984, A Little Help from a Friend, 1984, The Demon Fire, 1985, Trail to Glory, 1986. Wrkg. on horror novel. AA in Early Childhood Edn., Ventura Coll., 1974. Tchr. devel. disabled, 1969-79, disadvantaged children, 1979-80, pre-schl., 1980-81; adminstr. facility for devel. disabled adult women, 1981—. Mem. MWA, NWC, Small Press Writers and Artists. Home: 34755 Hwy 190 Porterville CA 93257

MEREDITH, MORRIS, see Meredith, William

MEREDITH, SCOTT, b. NYC, Nov. 24, 1923; s. Henry and Esta (Meredith); m. Helen Kovet, Apr. 22, 1944; children—Stephen Charles, Randy Beth Meredith Sheer. Author: Writing to Sell, rev. eds., 1960, 74, 87. Writing for the American Market, 1960, The Face of Comedy, 1961, George S. Kaufman and His Friends, 1974, The Science of Gaming, 1974, Louis B. Mayer and His Enemies, 1987; also stories, novelettes, serials and articles; editor: The Best of Wodehouse, 1949, The Best of Modern Humor, 1951, Bar One Roundup, 1951, The Week-End Book of Humor, 1952, Bar Two Roundup, 1952, The Murder of Mr. Malone, An Anthology of Craig Rice Stories, 1953, Bar Three Roundup, 1954, Bar Four Roundup, 1955, 2d series, 1956, Bar Five Roundup, 1956, (with Ken Murray) The Ken Murray Book of Humor, 1957, Bar Six Roundup, 1957, (with Henry Morgan) The Henry Morgan Book of Humor, 1958, (with Sidney Meredith) The Best from Manhunt, 1958, The Bloodhound Anthology, 1960, The Fireside Treasury of Modern Humor, 1963, Best Western Stories, 1964, Best Western Stories For Young People, 1965, (with P.G. Wodehouse) The Best of Humor, 1965, A Carnival of Modern Humor, 1966; contrbr.: articles on humor to Ency. Brit, 1954-59; articles on fiction writing to Oxford Ency, 1960-61. Educated privately; doctorate, Mercy Coll., Westchester Cty., NY, 1983. Writer numerous mag. stories; established Scott Meredith Lit. Agy., Inc., NYC, 1940, pres., 1942—. Served with USAAF, World War II. Home: Kings Point NY 11024

MEREDITH, TED JORDAN, b. Helena, MT, July 18, 1950; s. Edward Lee and Nelva (Jordan) M. Author: Northwest Wine, 1980, 2d ed., 1983, A Dictionary of American Wine (with Ralph Hutchinson and Richard Figel), 1985, The Wines and Wineries of America's Northwest, 1986. BA, U. Montana, 1971, MA 1973. Freelance writer/pub. Office: Box 911 Kirkland WA 98083

MEREDITH, WILLIAM, (Morris Meredith), b. NYC, Jan. 9, 1919; s. William Morris and Nelley (Keyser) M. Author: poems Love Letter from an Impossible Land, 1944, Ships and Other Figures, 1948, The Open Sea and Other Poems, 1958, Shelley, 1962, The Wreck of the Thresher and Other Poems, 1964; translation Alcools, 1964, Earth Walk; New and Selected Poems, 1970, Hazard, The Painter, 1975, The Cheer, 1980. AB, Princeton U., 1940, Woodrow Wilson Fellow, 1946-47. Copy boy, reporter N.Y. Times, 1940-41; instr. English, creative writing Princeton U., 1946, 47-48, 49-50; asst. prof. English U. Hawaii, 1950-51; mem. faculty Conn. Coll., 1955—, prof. English, 1965—; dir. Conn. Coll. Humanities-Upward Bound Program, 1964-68; poetry cons. Library of Congress, 1978-80; served with USAAF, 1941-42; to lt. USNR, 1942-46; PTO; to lt. comdr. USNR; Korea. Decorated Air Medal with oak leaf cluster; recipient Loines prize natl. Inst. Arts and Letters, 1966; Van Wyck Brooks award, 1971; mem. Natl. Inst. Arts and Letters. Office: Connecticut Coll PO Box 1498 New London CT 06320

MERIWETHER, JAMES BABCOCK, b. Columbia, SC, May 8, 1928; s. Robert Lee and Margaret (Babcock) M.; m. Nancy Anderson Callcott, July 29, 1955; children—Rebecca, Robert, George, Nicholas, Margaret. Author: The Literary Career of William Faulkner, 1961, others; editor: Essays, Speeches and Public Letters of William Faulkner, 1966, others; contrbr. articles to profl. jnls. BA, U. S.C., 1949; MA, Princeton U., 1952, PhD, 1958. Asst. prof. English U. Tex., Austin 1958-59; asst. prof. U. N.C., Chapel Hill, 1959-62, assoc. prof., 1962-64; prof. U. S.C., Columbia, 1964-70, McClintock prof. So. letters, 1970—, dir. So. Studies program, 1974-80. Served with U.S. Army, 1953-56. ACLS fellow, 1960-61; Guggenheim fellow, 1963-64. Mem. MLA Am., Bibliographical Soc. Am., Am. Studies Assn., French, German, Brit. assns. Am. Studies, Phi Beta Kappa. Home: 1400 Devonshire Dr Columbia SC 29204

MERIWETHER, NELL W., b. Taylorsville, MS, June 17, 1931; d. William Henry and Ora Rachel (Gregg) Wood.; m. Carl L. Meriwether Jr., Aug. 22, 1952; children—C. Lester III, Lindy Sue, Anita Marie, Lauren Lea. Author: Lauren and Papilion, 1983, Camping with Timmy, 1984, How to Write a Research Paper: A Guide for High School Students, 1984. Wrkg. on children's books, juvenile devotional book, writing edn. guide. BA, Miss. Coll., 1952; MEd, La. State U., 1972. Tchr. English East Baton Rouge Public Sch. System, La., 1968—. Mem. La. Wrtrs.' Guild. Home: 6444 Peggy St Baton Rouge LA 70808

MERKLING, FRANK, b. Washington, Jan. 20, 1924; s. Frank and Marie (Judd) M.; m. Erica Perl, Nov. 8, 1952; children—Melissa, Maria, Christian. Author: English libretto of Carmen for Met. Opera Co., 1951; co-author: The Golden Horseshoe, 1965; contrbr.: New Grove Dictionary of Music in the United States, 1st ed., 1986; contrbr. articles to profl. jnls. BA cum laude, Harvard U., 1949. Freelance writer, 1949-54; assoc. editor Opera News, 1954-57, ed. 1957-74; music and arts critic Danbury (Conn.) News-Times, 1978—. Served with USAAF, 1943-46. Home: Rt 3 116 Buckingham Rd New Milford CT 06776

MERNIT, SUSAN, b. NYC, Jan. 23, 1953; d. Arthur Harold and Marilyn (Riback) Mernit; m. Spencer Guy Jarrett, June 12, 1977; 1 son-Zachary Jarrett. Author: Angelic Alphabet, 1976, Tree Climbing, 1981; ed.: Hand Book Mag. 1979-84; contrbr. to Sat. Rvw, Working Woman, New York Times Book Rvw, McCall's, lit pubns., anthologies. BA, Bard Coll., 1974; MA, Ohio State U., 1978. Wrtr.-in-res. grant NEA, 1982-83. Office: 164 Sterling Pl Brooklyn NY 11217

MERRELL, JAMES LEE, b. Indpls., Oct. 24, 1930; s. Mark W. and Pauline F. (Tucker) M.; m. Barbara Jeanne Burch, Dec. 23, 1951; children—Deborah Lea Merrell Griffin, Cynthia Lynn Merrell, Stuart Allen. Author: They Live Their Faith, 1965, The Power of One, 1976, Discover the Word in Print, 1979, Finding Faith in the Headlines, 1985. AB, Ind. U., 1952; MDiv, Christian Theol. Sem., 1956; LittD, Culver-Stockton Coll., 1972. Ordained to ministry Christian Ch., 1956; assoc. editor World Call, Indpls., 1966-71; editor: The Disciple, St. Louis, 1974—; v.p. Christian Bd. Publ., 1976—. Home: 5347 Warmwinds Ct Saint Louis MO 63129

MERRIAM, EVE, b. Phila., July 19, 1916; children—Guy Michel, Dee Michel. Author: Real Book About Franklin D. Roosevelt, 1952, The Voice of Liberty, 1959, Figleaf, 1960, Basics, 1962, After Nora Slammed the Door, 1964; (poems) Family Circle, 1946, Tomorrow Morning, 1951, Montgomery, Alabama, Money, Mississippi and Other Places, 1956, The Double Bed from the Feminine Side, 1958, The Trouble with Love, 1961; A Gaggle of Geese, 1960, Mommies at Work, 1961; (poems) There is No Rhyme, 1964, Catch A Little Rhyme, 1965, Independent Voices, 1968, The Inner City Mother Goose, 1969, The Nixon Poems, 1970, Finding A Poem, 1970; Growing Up Female In America, 1971; (poems) A Husband's Notes About Her, 1976, Rainbow Writing, 1976, The Birthday Cow, 1978; Unhurry Harry, 1978, Ab to Zog, 1978; author, lyricist musicals: Inner City, 1971; The Club, 1976, At Her Age, 1979, Dialogue for Lovers, 1980; And I Ain't Finished Yet, 1982, Plagues for Our Time, 1983, Fresh Paint, 1986; co-editor: Male and Female Under 18, 1973; contrbr. to numerous mags., anthologies. Tchr. CCNY, NYU, 1966-69; lectr. on sexism in edn., 1974—. Recipient Yale Younger Poets Award, 1946; Collier's Star Fiction award, 1949; Obie award, 1977. Mem. Dramatist Guild Council. Address: 101 W 12th St New York NY 10011

MERRIAM, ROBERT LORING, b. Greenfield, MA, June 4, 1924; s. Louis Thayer and Alice (Abercrombie) Merriam; m. Mary McDonald, Dec. 21, 1957; children—Robert, Melinda, Susan, Abigail. Author: The Ancient Art of Skating, 1957, Abigail Challenges the Telephone Co., 1973, Pleasant Beth, 1975, The Darling Twins, 1976, John Carson, 1977, Moses Washington, 1978, J. Hamilton Rose, 1980, The Ants, 1981, Six Vignettes, 1981, Maple Sugar, 1984, Lucy Terry Prince, 1984, Eunice Williams, 1985. BA, Dartmouth, 1948. Asst. to pres. Greenfield Comm. Coll. (MA), 1975—; Headmaster Stoneleigh Burnham Schl. (Greenfield), 1970-75; dean of students, Deerfield Acad., 1948-70. Lt. (jg), USNR, 1943-46, Pacific. Home: Newhall Rd Conway MA 01341

MERRILL, AUGUSTUS LEE, b. Andalusia, AL, Feb. 11, 1946, s. Augustus Reid and Ruby Lee (Bray) M.; m. Mary Charles, Jan. 5, 1965 (div. 1975); m. 2d, Melinda Rose Guerra, Apr. 15, 1978; 2 daus., Meredith and Julia, 1 son, Bryce. Contrbr. poetry to Mikrokosmos, Steelhead, Madrona, Plainsong, numerous other lit publs.; co-ed.: The Lake Superior Rvw, 1976-78. BA, Washington and Lee U., 1968; MA, Ind. U., 1970. Prof. English Northland Coll., Ashland, Wis., 1970—; mem. peer rvw. panel Wis. Arts Bd., Madison, 1982-84. Wis. Arts Bd. fellow, 1980. Home: 217 3d St E Washburn WI 54891

MERRILL, JAMES, b. NYC, Mar. 3, 1926; s. Charles Edward and Hellen (Ingram) M. Author: First Poems, 1951; play The Immortal Husband, 1956, The Seraglio, 1957; poetry The Country of a Thousand Years of Peace, 1959; play The Bait, 1960; poetry Water Street, 1962, The (Diblos) Notebook, 1965, Nights and Days, 1967 (Natl. Book award), The Fire Screen, 1969, Braving the Elements, 1972, The Yellow Pages, 1974, Divine Comedies, 1976 (Pulitzer prize), Mirabell: Books of Number, 1978 (Natl. Book award for poetry 1979), Scripts for the Pageant, 1980 (Recipient Bollingen prize in poetry 1973), From the First Nine (Poems 1946-76), 1982, The Changing Light at Sandover, 1982. BA, Amherst Coll., 1947. Served with AUS, 1944-45. Mem. NIAL. Home: 107 Water St Stonington CT 06378

MERRILL, JOAN CAROLYN, b. Melrose, MA, Nov. 27, 1941; d. James Brian and Carolyn Louise (Fletcher) Miskelly; m. Richard Ward Merrill, June 12, 1965; children—Jennifer, Eric. Contrbr. poems to anthol. Editor, contrbr. articles: Shattuck-St. Mary's Schl. Mag., 1985-86. Editor brochures, contrbr. rvws.: North Am. Book Clubs, 1984. Student, U. N.H., 1961; MEd, Antioch U., Cambridge, Mass., 1978. Tchr. English, Berwick Acad., South Berwick, Maine, 1980-81, St. Thomas Aquinas High Schl., Dover, N.H., 1981-83; West Nottingham Acad., Colora, MD, 1986—; copywrtr., ed. North Am. Book Clubs, Dover, 1984; copywrtr., continuity ed. KYMN radio, Northfield, Minn., 1986; free-lance ed., 1984-86. Mem. City Edn. Com., North Olmstead, Ohio, 1975; ballot clrk. Town Office, South Berwick, 1976-78; trustee South Berwick Pub. Library, 1976-78. Address: West Nottingham Acad Colora MD 21917

MERRILL, MIMI, b. Los Angeles, Mar. 17, 1926; d. Reuben and Rebecca (Ludwig) Licker; m. Hymie Mehlman, Sept., 1944; 1 son, Bruce; m. 2d, Scott Williams, July, 1950; children—Scott, Diane; m. 3d, Ralph E. Merrill, Dec. 30, 1955; children—Wendi, David. Fiction and poetry in Wind Songs, College Poetry Rvw, other lit mags. BA, Cal. State U., Bakersfield, 1983. Wrtng. instr., Cal. State U., Bakersfield, 1983—. Home: Box 877 Ridgecrest CA 93555

MERRILL, SUSAN LEE, b. Providence, RI, Dec. 11, 1942, d. Gordon Merrill and Rachel (Von) Hodges; m. Frank J. Prezelski, Jan. 11, 1970 (div. 1983); children—Benjamin, Kate. Contrbr. poetry to N.Y. Qtly, Purchase Poetry Rvw, Kansas Qtly, other lit mags; contrbr. articles to Ms mag., Sexual Behavior, Intellectual Digest, others. BA in History with honors, SUNY-Purchase. Copywrtr. J. Walter Thompson, NYC, 1963-66; feature wrtr., reptr., The AP, NYC, 1973-75; mng. ed. Croton Rev., Croton-on-Hudson, N.Y., 1981-85; poetry tchr. Bd. Coop. Edn. Services, Yonkers, 1983-84; Yorktown, N.Y., 1985-86; creative wrtg. tchr., Croton-Harmon Schl. Dist., 1985—; reporter, feature wrtr., NY Times, 1987-; columnist, feature wrtr, Patent Trader Newspaper, Mt. Kisco, N.Y., 1985—; freelance textbk. ed. & wrtr., 1985—; bd. dirs. Croton Council on Arts, 1980-85. Mem. P&W. Home: 340 Grand St Croton-on-Hudson NY 10520

MERRILL, TOM, b. NYC Contrbr. poems to lit. mags. Attended Harvard U., Oxford U., England. Recipient Honorable Mention, Negative Capability, 1986. Judged Annual Lyric College Contest, 1985. Home: 17 Kazimer Dr Billerica MA 01821

MERTON, ROBERT K., b. Phila., July 5, 1910; m. Suzanne Carhart, 1934 (separated); children—Stephanie (Mrs. Thomas A. Tombrello), Robert C., Vanessa H. (Mrs. John K. Carroll). Author: Science Technology and Society in 17th Century England, 2d ed., 1970, Mass Persuasion, 2d ed., 1971, Social Theory and Social Structure, rev. ed., 1968, On the Shoulders of Giants, 1965, On Theoretical Sociology, 1967, The Sociology of Science, 1973, Sociological Ambivalence, 1976, Sociology of Science: An Episodic Memoir, 1979, Social Research and the Practicing Professions, 1982; co-author: The Focussed Interview, rev. ed., 1956, Freedom to Read, 1957; co-editor, co-author: Continuities in Social Research, 1950, Social Policy and Social Research in Housing, 1951, Reader in Bureaucracy, 1952, The Student-Physician, 1957, Sociology Today, 1959, Contemporary Social Problems, 4th ed., 1976, The Sociology of Science in Europe, 1977, Toward a Metric of Science, 1978, Qualitative and Quantitative Social Research: Papers in Honor of Paul F. Lazarsfeld, 1979, Sociological Traditions from Generation to Generation, 1980, Continuities in Structural Inquiry, 1981. AB, Temple U., 1931, MA, Harvard U., 1932, PhD, 1936. Tutor, instr. sociology Harvard U., 1934-39; prof., chmn. dept. Tulane U., 1939-41; asst. prof. to prof. sociology Columbia U., 1941-63, Univ. prof. emeritus, 1979—; adj. prof. Rockefeller U., 1979—; Paley lectr. Cornell Med. Schl., 1975; Fulbright lectr. U. Kyoto, 1967—. Common Wealth Award for Disting. Service to Sociology, 1979; MacArthur Prize fellow, 1983. Mem. Am. Philo. Soc., Natl. Acad. Edn., Natl. Acad. Scis., Natl. Inst. Medicine, History Sci. Soc. Office: Fayerweather Hall Columbia U New York NY

10027

MERZ, ROLLANDE, b. Waterville, ME, July 15, 1941, d. Roland Frederick and Marie Rose (Paradis) Bechard; children—Lisa Calnan, Robert Calnan. Author: Pictires: Life and Still Life (poetry), 1984; contrbr. poetry to Aegis, Bitterroot, Calliope, other lit mags; contrbr. articles to local newspapers, mags. BA, U. N.H., 1978; MFA, Vt. Coll., 1983. Typesetter, proofreader N.H. Times, Concord, 1972-73; copy ed. Newbury (Md.) Press, 1973-74; wrtr., ed. U. N.H., Durham, 1975—; ed. Natl. Prime Users Group, Framingham, Mass., 1984—. Recipient Lamont Hall Poetry award, 1984. Mem. Soc. children's Book Wrtrs., AWP. Home: Rural Route Strafford NH 03884

MESSER, ANDREA ELYSE, b. Freeport, NY, Apr. 4, 1952; d. Julius and Gloria Rhoda (Epstein) Messer. Contrbr. rvws., booklets, articles on mech. engring. to trade mags., newspapers, popular mags., profl. jnls. BA in Sci. and Culture, Purdue U., 1973; MS in Journalism: Sci. Communication, Boston U., 1976; Sci. wrtr., reporter Attelboro Sun Chronicle, Mass., 1975-76; tech. ed. Bell Labs., Whippany, N.J., 1976-79; sci. ed. Freund Pub. Co., Tel Aviv, Israel, 1979-80; tech. news wrtr., ed., Am. Soc. Mech. Engrs., N.Y.C., 1981—. Mem. Natl. Assn. Sci. Wrtrs. (assoc.), World Future Soc., N.Y. Acad. Sci., Planetary Soc. Home: 3051 Edwin Ave 2B Fort Lee NJ 07024

MESSER, RICHARD E., b. Fruita, CO, Aug. 26, 1938, s. Richard G. and Olga (Sauwerwein) M.; m. Gloria Welsch (dec. 1974); m. Dympna Callaghan, Dec. 21, 1985. Author: (poems) Love Apple, 1970; ed. The Monthly, 1965-68; contrbr. rvws, critical articles, poetry, and stories to Psychol. Perspectives, Mid-Am. Rvw, S.D. Rvw, Pig Iron, Transition, Christian Sci. Montitor, The Nation, Anima, Foothills, other periodicals, lit mags and jnls. BA, Colo. State Coll., 1961; MA, U. Colo., 1964; PhD, U. Denver, 1971. Asst. prof. English, Ark. State U., Jonesboro, 1971-75; assoc. prof. English, Bowling Green State U., Ohio, 1975—. Mem. AWP. Office: Dept Eng BG State U Bowling Green OH 43403

MESSERLI, DOUGLAS, b. Waterloo, IA, May 30, 1947; s. John H. and Lorna Mary (Casper) M. Author: Djuna Barnes: A Bibliography, 1976, Index to Periodical Fiction in English, 1965-69, 1977, River to Rivet: A Poetic Trilogy, 1984, Foreword and Commentary of Interviews by Djuna Barnes, 1985; ed.: Smoke and Other Early Stories (Djuna Barnes), Contemp. Am. Fiction, 1983. Wrkg. on 21 Poets of "Language," Maxims from Mother's Milk. MA, U.Md., 1974, PhD, 1979. Instr. Univ. Md., Coll. Pk., 1978-79; asst. protocol Columbia Univ., NYC, 1979—; pub. Sun & Moon Press, Los Angeles, 1976—; ed. Sun & Moon: Jnl. Lit. & Art, Washington, DC, 1976-79; prof. Temple U., Phila., 1979-84; dir. Contemporary Arts Edn. Project, Los Angeles, 1984—. Recipient Ed.'s grant CCLM, 1979. Mem. MLA, Assn. Am. Booksellers. Home: 6363 Wilshire Blvd 115 Los Angeles CA 90048

MESSING, ROBIN, b. Bklyn., July 3, 1953, d. Morris and Millie (Rottblatt) M.; m. Eric Alabaster, May 7, 1983. Contrbr. to: Sugar, Alcohol & Meat Dial-a-Poem Poets, Dodeca, Israel Today, Balt. Jewish Times, other publs. BA, Bklyn. Coll., 1974. Editorial asst. Doubleday & Co., Inc., NYC, 1978-83; tchr. N.Y. State Poets-in-Schls., NYC, 1978-85, Tchrs. & Wrtrs. Collaborative, NYC, 1978-85; freelance wrtr., ed. Curriculum Concepts, McGraw Hill Book Co., NYC, 1983—. Mem. P&W (Workshop award, 1984, 85). Home: 348A 14th St Brooklyn NY 11215

METCALF, PAUL C., b. East Milton, MA, Nov. 7, 1917, s. Henry K. and Eleanor M. (Thomas) M.; m. Nancy H. Blackford, May 31, 1942; children—Anne Metcalf Westmoreland, Adrienne Metcalf Weinmen. Author: Will West, 1956, Genoa, 1965, Patagoni, 1971, Apalache, 1976, The Middle Passage, 1976, Zip Odes, 1979, U.S. Dept. of the Interior, 1980, Both, 1982, The Island, 1982, Louis the Torch, 1983, Golden Delicious, 1985, (with Douglas Woolf) Broken Field Runner, 1972; contrbr. to anthologies including Am. Equation, Berkshire Anthology, Sparks of Fire, Am Americas Anthology; ed. Mulch 7, 1975. Vis. prof. U. Calif., San Diego, winters 1982, 85; wrtr.-in-residence Centrum Fdn., Port Townsend, Wash., winter, 1983, SUNY, Albany, spring 1984; panelist, judge NEA, 1980-82. Home: RFD 1 Box 26 Chester MA 01011

METIVIER, DONALD ANTHONY, (Don), b. Glens Falls, NY, Aug. 2, 1936, s. Anthony Henry and Grace Ann (Usher) M.; m. Laraine Helen Martin, Sept. 9, 1961; children—Donna Ann, Richard Kerry, Dianne L.T., Anthony Francis and Stephen Michael (twins), Robert M., Laurie Ann. Ed.: On Nordic Skiing, 1983. BS in Communications, Boston U., 1960. Sports dir. WWSC Radio, Glens Falls, N.Y., 1961-79; reporter Post-Star, Glens Falls, 1961-75, ed., 1975-81; ed., Ski Racing Mag., Waitsfied, Vt., 1981—. Recipient awards AP, 1976. N.Y. Sportswrtrs. Assn., 1979. Mem. Eastern Ski Wrtrs. Assn. (dir.), U.S. Ski Wrtrs. Assn. (past pres.), N.Y. Turf Wrtrs. Assn., Sigma Delta Chi. Home: 7 Kensington Rd Glens Falls NY 12801

METLITZKI, DOROTHEE, b. Koenigsberg, Germany, July 27, 1914; came to Israel, 1939; d. Israel Yosifovich and Rosa Rachel (Malbin) M.; m. Paul Kraus, June, 1944 (dec.); m. Boris Grdseloff, Feb. 4, 1945 (dec.); 1 dau., Ruth. Author: Melville's Orienda, 1961, The Matter of Araby in Medieval England, 1977. B.A. with honors, U. London, 1936, M.A., 1938; Ph.D., Yale U., 1957. Instr. Hebrew U., Jerusalem, 1939-44; Brit. Council lectr., Cairo, 1945-47; founder, sec. dept. affairs of Arab women Israel Fedn. Labor (Histadrut), 1949-53; lectr. U. Calif.-Berkeley, 1957-64, assoc. prof., 1964-66; sr. lectr. Yale U., 1966-76, prof. English, 1976-85; prof. emeritus of Eng., 1985—. Mem. Medieval Acad. Am., MLA. Office: 305 Crown St Yale U New Haven CTJ 06520

METRAS, GARY, (Leo), b. Holyoke, MA, Apr. 1, 1947, s. Albert Herve and Doris (Suprenant) M.; m. Natalie Lukiwsky, Oct. 19, 1968; childrn—Jason Gary, Nadia Mary. Author: Roses in Lyric Light: Love Poems (pamphlet), 1974, A Room Full of Walls (pamphlet), 1978, The Necessities (chapbook), 1979, The Yearnings (pamphlet), 1980, The Night Watches, 1981, Destiny's Calendar, 1985, Center of the Spiral (chapbook), 1985. BA in English, U. Mass., 1972; MA in Creative Writing, Goddard Coll., 1981. Ed., pub. Adastra Press, Easthampton, Mass., 1980—. Poetry fellow Mass. Artists Fdn., 1984. Home: 101 Strong St Easthampton MA 01027

METRESS, SEAMUS P., b. Southampton, NY, Sept. 25, 1933; s. James F. and Hilda (Gugel) M.; m. Eileen Ryan, Oct. 31, 1974. Author: (under name James F. Metress): ed, Man in Ecological Perspective, 1971, ed (with C. L. Brace) Man in Evolutionary Perspective, 1973, (with Thor A. Conway) A Guide to the Literature on the Dental Anthropology of Post Pleistocene Man (monograph), 1974; (under name Seamus P. Metress): (with Cary S. Kart and Eileen Metress) Aging and Health, 1978, (with Kart) Nutrition and Aging: A Bibliographic Survey, 1979, Listen, Irish People (poems), 1979, (with Sharon J. Rogers) A Guide to the Use of Library Sources in Anthropology, Sociology, and Applied Health Sciences, 1979, The Irish-American Experience, 1981, The Hunger Strike and the Final Struggle, 1983, (with Kart) Nutrition, Society, and Old Age, 1984, A Regional Guide to Informational Sources on the Irish in the United States and Canada, 1986, (with Kart and E. Metress) Aging, Health, and Society, 1988. Co-ed, Toledo Area Aboriginal Research Club Bulletin, 1972-75. BS, Univ of Notre Dame, 1955; MA, Columbia Univ, 1957; Ph. D., Indiana Univ., 1971. High School tchr of biology and coach in the public schools of Spring Valley, N.Y., 1955-57, and Saginaw and Fennville, Mich., 1957-64; instr in biology, Aquinas Coll, Saginaw, Mich., 1964-65; asst prof, Clarion (Pa.) State Coll, 1966-68, assoc prof of anthropology, 1968; assoc prof, Univ of Toledo (Ohio), 1969-76, prof of anthropology, 1976—. Member Irish Northern Aid Com. Mem: Celtic League Intl, American Anthropological Assn, Soc for Medical Anthropology, Catholic Historical Soc, Immigration History Soc, Clan na Gael, Irish Labor History Soc, Natl Assn for Interdisciplinary Ethnic Studies, Irish-American Cultural Inst. Outstanding Teacher award, Univ of Toledo, 1972. Home: 4625 Paisley Rd Toledo OH 43615

METZ, JERRED, b. Lakewood, NJ, May 5, 1943, s. Eli Joseph and Francis (Mininsohn) M.; m. Sarah Barker; children—Zachary, Ravenna Barker. Author: Speak Like Rain (poetry), 1975, The Terperate Voluptuary (poetry), 1975, Three Legs Up, Cold as Stone: Six Legs Down, Blood and Bone (poetry), 1978, Angels in the House (poetry), 1979, Drinking the Dipper Dry: Nine Plain- Spoken Lives (prose), 1980, Halley's Comet, 1910: Fire in the Sky (prose), 1985; contrbr. to Voices within the Ark, 1980, Voices from the Interior: Poets of Missouri, 1983, Gates to the New City, 1983, other anthologies; contrbr. poetry: Pig Iron, Grub Street, Phantasm, Little Mag., other lit mags; translator Hebrew poetry For a Few Hours Only, 1976. MA, U. R.I., 1967; PhD, U. Minn., 1972. Asst. prof. dept. English Webster Coll., St. Louis, 1973-77; exec. asst. to dir. Dept. Human Services, St. Louis, 1977-86; assoc. prog. dir., Cardinal Ritter Inst., 1986—. Home: 2318 Albion Pl Saint Louis MO 63104

METZ, ROBERT ROY, b. Richmond Hill, NY, Mar. 23, 1929; s. Robert Roy, Sr. and Mary (Kissel) M.; m. Susan Lee Blair, 1984; children: Robert Sumner, Christopher Roy. B.A., Wesleyan U., Middletown Conn., 1950. Copyboy N.Y. Times, 1951, asst. fgn. news desk, 1952; rewriteman cable desk I.N.S., 1953, overnight cable editor, 1954-56, asst. feature editor, 1956-58; asst. news editor Newspaper Eenterprise Assn., 1958, news editor, 1959-63, mng. editor, 1963-66, exec. editor, 1966-68, v.p., 1967-71, editorial dir., 1968-71, pres., editor, dir., 1972—; dir. Berkeley-Small Inc., 1974-77; chmn. Berkeley-Small Inc., 1976-77; v.p., dir. United Feature Syndicate, 1976-77, pres., editor, 1978; pres., editor, dir. United Media, 1978-; dir. Kartes Video Communics., 1986-87. Mem. Sigma Delta Chi, Sigma Nu. Home: 170 E 77th St New York NY 10021

METZGER, DEENA POSY, b. Bklyn., Sept. 17, 1936; d. Arnold and Bella (Shapiro) Posy; m. Reed Metzger; children: Marc, Greg. Author: Skin: Shadows/Silence, 1976; The Book of Hags, 1977; Dark Milk, 1978; The Axis Mundi Poems, 1981; Dreams Against the State (play), 1981, 86; The Woman who Slept with Men To Take the War Out of Them, 1981, 83, Tree, 1981, 83; contrbr. to Chrysalis, Semiotica, New Letters, Am. Jnl Psychiatry, The Sun, In These Times, Los Angeles Weekly, Anima, Dreamworks, A Casebook on Anais Nin, Rising Tides, Pleasures, also others. MA, UCLA, 1960; PhD, Intl. Coll., Los Angeles, 1975. Self-employed writing therapist, 1975—. Recipient 1st Acad. Freedom award Calif. Fedn. Tchrs., 1975; 1st annl. Vesta award in writing Woman's Bldg., Los Angeles, 1982; NEA creative writing fellow, 1978. Mem. PEN, DG. Home: 20666 Callon Dr Topanga Canyon CA 90290

METZGER, DIANE HAMILL, b. Phila., July 23, 1949; d. David A., Sr. and Eunice (Shelton) Hamill; m. Frank Allen Metzger, Aug. 29, 1969; 1 son, Jason Frank. Author: (poems) Coralline Ornaments, 1980. Contrbr. poems, fiction to lit. mags. AA, Northampton Coll., 1980; BA, Bloomsburg Univ., 1987. Tchg. asst. State Correctional Institution, Muncy, Pa., 1978-82; free-lance wrtr., 1982—. Treas. Pennsylvania Lifers Association, Muncy, 1986. Recipient 2d prize for poetry Phila Wrtrs. Conf., 1969; hon. mention for poetry PEN, 1978, 3d prize for fiction, 1981, 2st prize for poetry, 1985; hon. mention for poetry Wrtr.'s Digest, 1978, 85. Mem. ASCAP, Mensa. Home: 313 Barker St Ridley Park PA 19078

METZROTH, JANE PORVANCHER, b. NYC, Dec. 18, 1951; d. Jack and Gladys (Guppy) Porvancher; m. Veit-Thomas E. Metzroth, Dec. 18, 1971; children—Erik, Alexander. Author: Picking The Perfect Nanny, 1985. BA, Skidmore Coll., Saratoga Springs, NY, 1973. Consultant, William M. Mercer, NYC, 1973-76, manager benefits planning J.C. Penney, NYC, 1976-80; v.p. dir. human resources Salomon Brothers, Inc., NYC, 1980—. Office: Salomon Brothers 1 NY Plaza New York NY 10004

MEUDT, EDNA KRITZ, b. Wyoming Valley, WI, Sept. 14, 1906; d. John Wiliam and Kristine Marie (Neilsen) Kritz; m. Peter John Meudt, Oct. 10, 1924 (dec. 1972); children—Richard E. (dec. 1981), Howard E. (dec. 1937), Kathy E. Ott (dec. 1985), Christine Schakel, Christopher Meudt (grandson-word). Author: (poetry books) Round River Canticle, 1960, In No Strange Land (1st prize NLAPW, 1966), 1965, No One Sings Face Down, 1970, The Ineluctable Sea, 1975, Plain Chant for a Tree, 1980; (plays) A Case of Semantics, 1970, Promised Land: (1st prize Council for Wis. Wrtrs., 1978), Life and Times of Henry Dodge, 1977. Contrbr. poems & short stories to anthols. and mags, articles to mags., newspapers. Ed.: Anthol. Wis. Poetry, 1963, An Uplands Reader, 1979, 81, 86, The Country Poet (since 1985). Wrkg. on novel, collection of poetry. Grad. private schls., Madison, WI. Recipient Gold cup for lit. achievement Theta Sigma Phi, 1967; award for Distinction, U. Wis. Coll. Life Scis., 1977; Christopher Latham Sholes award for extraordinary service Council of Wis. Wrtrs., 1984; Notable Wis. Author, 1985, from Wis Lib. Assn.; Royal Order of Pegasus from Natl. Fedn. State Poetry Socs., 1987. Edna Meudt Narrative Poetry Contest, Wis. Fellowship of Poets, est. 1986. Mem. Wis. Fellowship Poets (co-founder, pres. 1954, 64), Natl. Fedn. State Poetry Socs. (pres., chancellor), Wis. Acad. Scis., Arts & Letters (v.p. 1974-75), Wis. Arts Bd. (chmn. creative writing panel 1976-78). Home: Rt 3 Dodgeville WI 53533

MEYER, CLARENCE, b. Milw., Feb. 5, 1903; s. Joseph Ernest and Celia (Hoedel) M.; children: Diane, Nancy, Dana, David. Author: The Herbalist, rev. 1960, American Folk Medicine, 1973, Herbal Recipes, 1978, Vegetarian Medicines, 1980, Herbal Aphrodisiacs, 1986; editor: Herbalist Almanac, 1939-78. Student Chgo. Art Inst. Treas. Ind. Botanic Gardens, Hammond, 1936-78; editor, artist, gardener, botanist. Address: Box 427 Glenwood IL 60425

MEYER, GEORGE IRA, b. Somerville, N.J., Mar. 30, 1958; s. Robert George and Mary Ann (Krall) M. BS, Juniata Coll., Huntingdon, Pa., 1980. Natl. coordinator, newsletter ed. Libertarians for Gay and Lestian Concerns, San Francisco, 1983—. Home:20 Ford St San Francisco CA 94114

MEYER, LINDA D., b. Santa Barbara, CA, Apr. 2, 1948, d. John Floyd and Dorothy Lucidie (Baker) Potter; m. D. Lee Meyer, Sept. 6, 1969; children—Joshua Scott, Matthew Sean. Author: The Cesarean (R)evolution, 1979, Responsible Childbirth, 1984, Safety Zone, 1984, I Take Good Care of Me!, 1986; ed.: Special Delivery, 1980, Help for Depressed Mothers, 1980, Private Zone, 1982, Help Yourself to SAFETY, 1985, Strangers Don't Look Like the Big Bad Wolf, 1985, Dial Zero for Help, 1985, It's Not Your Fault, 1985, Welcome Home Stranger, 1986. BA, San Jose U., 1971. Mem. Pacific Northwest Wrtrs. Conf. Office: Box 524 Lynnwood WA 98046

MEYER, M. YVONNE, SSM, b. St. Louis, MO, Aug. 8; d. Joseph and Rose Teresa (Patterman) M. Ed.: SSM Links, 1974—, Highlights, 1956-60, Rambling Rose, 1968-76, Hist. of St. Mary's Schl. of Nursing, 1977, Ad On, 1977-78; author: Time & Cost Study of Medical Record Library Procedures, 1950, An Administrative Manual for Medical Records, 1958, articles in natl. health jnls. BS cum laude, St. Louis U., 1949, MEd, 1952. Medical records adm. St. Louis U. Hosp., 1952-56, St. Mary's Hosp., Kansas City, MO, 1956-60, St. Mary's Health Ctr., St. Louis, 1960-63, St. Francis Hosp., Blue Island, IL, 1963-68; asst. prof. St. Louis U., 1955-63; asst. admin. Mount St. Rose Hosp., St. Louis, 1968-74; dir. pubn. Sisters of St. Mary, St. Louis, 1974—. Office: Sisters 1100 Bellevue Ave St Louis MO 63117

MEYER, MAGGI H., see Meyer, Margaret H.

MEYER, MARGARET H., (Maggi H. Meyer), b. Fargo, ND, Feb. 1, 1916, d. Manning Newell and Veda (Williams) Hatcher; m. William Claire Meyer, May 27, 1938 (div. 1948). Author: Mix with Love, 1977, Bod and Soul, 1978, More, 1979, And More, 1980, It Came with Me, 1981, Sign of No Time, 1982, How Is It, 1983, Changing, 1984; pub. seven anthologies for Bay Area Poets Coalition, plus eight yrs. monthly poetry letter; contrbr. poetry to Ally, Nail Down My Corner, Poets at Work, numerous other anthols. Interior designer 1946-62; secy., interviewer Citizens Fedl. Savgs. & Loan, Oakland, Calif., 1962-66; secy., tech. asst. ICC, San Francisco, 1967-82; lectr. poetry workshops; judge poetry contests. Mem. Bay Area Poets Coalition (newsletter ed.), Ina Coolbrith, Renegades and Alameda Poets (pres.). Home: 1527 Virginia St Berkeley CA 94703

MEYER, PUCCI, b. NYC, Sept. 1, 1944; d. Charles Albert and Lollo (Offer) M. B.A., U. Wis., 1966. Asst. editor Look mag., NYC, 1970-71, editorial asst., Paris, 1967-79; reporter Newsday, Garden City, L.I., N.Y., 1971-73; style editor N.Y. Daily News Sunday Mag., NYC, 1974-76, assoc. editor, 1977-82, editor, 1983—. Contbr. articles to various natl. mags. Recipient Pulitzer prize as mem. Newsday investigative team which wrote articles "The Heroin Trail," 1973. Mem. Women in Communications. Office: Daily News 220 E 42nd St New York NY 10017

MEYER, SUSAN E., b. NYC, Apr. 22, 1940; d. Ernest L. and Dorothy (Narefsky) M. B.A., U. Wis., 1962. Asst. editor Collier Books, NYC, 1962; mng. editor Watson-Guptill Publs., NYC, 1963-70; editor-in-chief Am. Artist mag., NYC, 1979-79; editorial dir. Am. Artist, Art and Antiques, Interiors, Residential Interiors, 1979-81; co-pub. Roundtable Press, Inc., 1981—; Dir. Ednl. Solutions, Inc., 1969-70; draft counselor Village Peace Center, 1967-70; tutor Empire State Coll., 1975-76; adj.-prof. Union Grad. Schl., 1976-78. author: Three Generations of the Wyeth Family, 1975, James Montgomery Flagg, 1974, 40 Watercolorists and How They Work, 1976, America's Great Illustrators, 1978, You Can Renovate Your Own Home, 1978, Rockwell's People, 1981, Pasteups and Mechanicals, 1982, Treasury of the Great Children's Book Illustrators, 1983, How to Draw in Pen and Ink, 1985, (with Kent) Watercolorists at Work, 1972; Editor: (with Guptill) Watercolor Painting Step-by-Step, 1966, (with Kent) 100 Watercolor Techniques, 1968, (with Kinstler) Painting Portraits, 1971, (with Craig) Designing with Type, 1971, (with Guptill) Rendering in Pen and Ink, 1976, Rendering in Pencil, 1977, 20 Landscape Painters and How They Work, 1977, 20 Oil Painters and How They Work, 1978, 20 Figure Painters and How They Work, 1979; Photographer: (with Buchman) Stage Makeup, 1971, Film and Television Makeup, 1973. Trustee Artists Fellowship, 1978-84, Little Red School House Inc., 1980-82, Art Table Inc., 1981-83. Treas. Am. Book Producers Assn. Office: 80 E 11th St New York NY 10003

MEYER, THEODORE E. (TED), b. Bethlehem, PA, Jan. 27, 1931; s. Charles Anthony and Frances (Grebner) M.; m. Irene Mary Mullen, June 30, 1953 (div. 1976); children—Timothy Fred, Patricia Kathleen. Author: Body Count, 1982, The Citizens Club, 1983; contrbr. genl. and travel articles and commentaries to local, natl. and intl. mags. BS in Gen. Educ., Armed Forces Inst., U.WI, 1968. Milit. intell. ed. security agency, Frankfurt, Germ., 1948-50; intell. ed. USA milit. intell., Kileen, TX, 1957-59; asst. mgr. Camelback, Tannersville, PA, 1970-80; novelist, free-lance writer & pub., Mey-House Books, Stroudsburg, PA, 1981—. Home: Box 794 Stroudsburg PA 18360

MEYERER, MARGARET CHRISTINE, b. Birmingham, AL, Mar. 13, 1924; d. Morton Cleveland and Maude (Powers) Renfroe; m. Albert Meyerer, Jr., Feb. 14, 1942 (dec. 1969); children: Albert C., Kristan K. Eloise May Meyerer Sahlstrom; m. 2d, Thomas J. Standfill, Dec. 23, 1973 (div. 1980). Author: Heartbreak, 1985; contrbr. poetry: Morning Advocate mag., several anthologies. Wrkg. on editing collection of letters from husband in World War II. BS, La. State U., 1965, MS, 1968. Tchr. public schs., Baton Rouge, 1965-68, Livingston, La., 1969-76. Mem. So. Wrtrs. Guild, La. State Poetry Soc., Baton Rouge Poetry Soc., New Era Poetry Club. Home: 625 Audubon Ave Baton Rouge LA 70806

MEYEROWITZ, STEVEN A., b. NYC, July 5, 1955. Contrbr. bus. articles to newspapers, mags., jnls. including The N.Y. Times, ABA Jnl., Newsday, Legal Times of N.Y., Prime Times. Wrkg. on book about failed corp. takeover. BA, Hofstra U., Hempstead, N.Y., 1975; JD, Harvard U., 1979. Office: 179 Radcliffe Dr East Norwich NY 11732

MEYERS, CAROLE TERWILLIGER, b. San Francisco, June 30, 1945, d. Earl Walter and Esther Mary (Furst) Terwilliger; m. Gene Howard Meyers, May 2, 1971; children—David Charles, Suzanne Michelle. Author: How to Organize a Babysitting Cooperative and Get Some Free Time Away from the Kids, 1976, Weekend Adventures for City-Weary People: Overnight Trips in Northern California, 1977, 80, 84, Getting in the Spirit: Annual Bay Area Cristmas Events, 1979, Eating Out with the Kids in San Francisco and the Bay Area, 1976, 80, 85; contrbr. to Berkeley Monthly, Image Mag., San Francisco Focus Mag., others. BA, San Francisco State Coll., 1968; teaching credential Fresno State Coll., 1969. Columnist San Jose (Calif.) Mercury News, 1978-79, Parents' Press, Berkeley, Calif., 1980—, Calif. mag., San Francisco, 1981—, Calif. Travel Report, Los Angeles, 1982-83, Goodlife mag., San Francisco, 1983. Mem. Northern Calif. BK. Publicist's Assn., Writer's Connection. Office: Box 6061 Albany CA 94706

MICHAELS, CAROL ANN, b. Phillipsburg, NJ, Dec. 27, 1948; d. James Theodore and Florence Helen (Smith) Bastedo; m. Harold Michaels, May 5, 1968 (div. Mar. 1972); 1 dau., Cher Ann Michaels. Contrbr. to World of Poetry, Writer's Digest, Sunshine Mag. Student pub. schls. Monmouth Jnct., NJ. Data control clrk, Brookstone Co., Petersborouggh, NH, 1976-78; teller, Security First Fed. Savings & Loan, Daytona, FL, 1978-79; data entry clrk. Harry Strauss & Sons, New Brunswick, NJ, 1980-82; waitress Jefferson House Rest., East Windsor, NJ, 1982—; office asst. II—data entry, Princeton (NJ) U., 1985—. Num. poetry awards. Home: 3-H Abbington Dr East Windsor NJ 08520

MICHAELS, ELIZABETH, see Lodwick, Teresa Jane

MICHAELS, IRENE, see Jurezyk, Irene Donohue

MICHAELS, JAMES WALKER, b. Buffalo, June 17, 1921; s. Dewey and Phyllis (Boasberg) M.; m. Frances Matthews, June 6, 1947; children: Robert Matthews, James Walker, Anne Phyllis. B.S. cum laude, Harvard U., 1942. Ambulance driver Am. Field Service, India and Burma, 1943-44; with USIS, New Delhi, also Bangkok, 1944-46; fgn. corr. UP, bur. mgr., New Delhi, 1946-50; with Forbes mag., NYC, 1954—, mng. editor, 1956-61, editor, 1961—. Contbr. articles to mags. Office: Forbes 60 Fifth Ave New York NY 10011

MICHAELS, JOANNE, b. NYC, Dec. 30, 1950; d. Lawrence William and Renee (Pome) Michaels; m. George Henry Fillingham, Dec. 24, 1975 (div. Nov. 27, 1979); m. 2d, Stuart Alan Ober, Sept. 20, 1981; 1 son—Erik Kenneth Michaels-Ober. Author: Living Contradictions: The Women of the Baby Boom Come of Age, The Best of the Hudson Valley and Catskills, 1988; contrbr. to: Redbook, Bride's, Village Voice, Hudson Valley, Fodor's USA (editor, 1976). BA, U. CT, 1972. Asst. ed. The Viking Press, NYC, 1972-74; ed. David McKay, NYC, 1974-77, St. Martin's Press, NYC, 1977-78; v.p. Beekman Pub., Woodstock, NY, 1978-82; ed.-in-chief Hudson Valley Mag., Woodstock, 1982-86; pub. JMB Publications, 1986—. Mem. AG, Wom. in Communications. Home: Box 888 Woodstock NY 12498

MICHAELS, LEONARD, b. NYC, Jan. 2, 1933; s. Leon and Anna (Czeskies) M.; m. (1) Priscilla Older, June 30, 1966; (3) Brenda Lynn Hillman, Aug. 10, 1977; children: (first marriage) Ethan, Jesse; (third marriage) Louisa. Author: Going Places (short stories), 1969, I Would Have Saved Them If I Could (short stories), 1975. Contrbr, Theodore Solotaroff, ed, American Rvw 26, 1977, contrbr, William Abrahams, ed, Prize Stories, 1980: The O'Henry Awards, 1980, ed (with Christopher Ricks) The State of the Language, 1980, The Men's Club (novel), 1981, City Boy (play adapted from stories in Going Places and I Would Have Saved Them If I Could), prod, N.Y.C. at the Jewish Repertory Theater, 1985, The Men's Club (screenplay based on novel of the same title), 1986. Short stories in The American Literary Anthology, sponsored by the NEA. Contrbr of short stories to many lit jnls and popular mags, including Esquire, Paris Rvw, Quarterly. Contrbg ed, Threepenny Rvw, 1980—; corresponding ed, Paris Rvw, 1980—. BA, New York Univ, 1953; MA, Univ of Mich, 1956, Ph.D., 1966. Instr, Paterson State Coll (now William Patterson State Coll of N.J.), 1961-62; asst prof of English, Univ of Calif, Davis, 1966-69; prof of English, Univ of Calif, Berkeley, 1970—, ed University Publishing review, 1977—. Vis prof at many univs, including Bard Coll., U. of Iowa, Johns Hopkins Univ, Univ of Alabama. Guest lectr in institutions in the U.S. and abroad. Quill Award, Mass Rvw, 1964 for Sticks and Stones (short story), and 1966, for The Deal (short story); National Bk Award nomination, 1969, for Going Places; Guggenheim fellow, 1969; NEH fellow, 1970; American Acad Award in Literature, Natl Inst of Arts and Letters, 1971, for published work of distinction; N.Y. Times Book Rvw Editor's Choice award, 1975, for I Would Have Saved Them If I Could; American Book Award nomination and Natl Book Critics Circle Award nomination, both in 1982, for The Men's Club; Natl Fndn of the Arts and Humanities prize, for short story in Transatlantic. Home: 409 Boynton Ave Kensington CA 94707

MICHAUD, MICHAEL ALAN GEORGE, b. Hollywood, CA, Aug. 22, 1938; s. George Emile and Nathalie Adele (Neagles) M.; m. Carmen Yvonne Mitchell, Sept. 1960 (div. 1963); m. M. Grace Russo, June 5, 1965; children: Jon C., Cassandra M., Jason M., Joshua M. Editor: Flotsam and Jetsam lit. ann., 1956; founding editor: Open Forum, 1974-76 (Honor award 1976); mem. editorial bd.: Fgn. Service Jour., 1977-79; author: Reaching for the High Frontier, 1986; contrbr. numerous articles, papers, book rvws., short stories to publications. BA, UCLA, 1960, MA, 1963; postgrad., Georgetown U., 1978-79. Commd. fgn. service officer Dept. State, 1963; numerous assignments in the Dept. of State and overseas; presently Dir. Office of Advanced Technology, Dept. of State. Recipient Superior Honor award Dept. State, 1966, Meritorious Honor award Dept. State, 1976; Una Chapman Fellow, 1983-84. Mem. Aviation/Space Wrtrs. Assn., Intl. Inst. Strategic Studies, AAAS, AIAA, Am. Astronautical Soc., Intl. Acad. Astronautics. Office: OES/SAT Dept. State Washington DC 20520

MICHEL, TRUDI, b. NYC, May 17, 1921, d. Isadore and Ruth (Goodman) Michel; widow; children—Rhoda, Peter, Vicki. Author: Inside Tin Pan Alley (novel), 1948, Until the Baby Cries (screenplay), 1983, How Far is it to the White Sun? (screenplay), 1985. Student Columbia U., NYC. Broadway producer Theatre Life Co., NYC, 1950-62; motion picture wrtr. Theater Life Co.-Movelevision Co., NYC, 1951—. Mem. AL. Home: 130 E 63d St New York NY 10021

MICHELS, MICHAEL E., b. Santa Monica, CA, Aug. 20, 1951; s. Lowell S. and Margaret E.(Anderson) M. Editor, contrbr.: Off Duty Mag., 1978—, Off Duty Hi-Fi Annual, 1978—, Off Duty Photoguide, 1980—, Auto Stereo, 1983, ALA Jnl, 1984, Consumers Digest, 1985. BS in Communication Arts, Calif. Polytechnic Inst., 1975. Tech. wrtr., engr. Soderberg Mfg. Co., Walnut, Calif., 1973-78; tech. ed. Off Duty Pubs., Costa Mesa, Calif., 1978—; guest lectr. UCLA Extension. Mem. Soc. Audio Engrs. (assoc.). Home: 9127 Westminster Ave Garden Grove CA 92644

MICHELSON, PETER F., b. Chgo., Dec. 25, 1935; s. Paul Orne and Inez Theil (Larson) M.; m. Donna F. Corwin, Dec. 29, 1958 (div. 1970); children: Kristen, Hilary; m. Marilyn D. Krysl, Feb. 14, 1976; 1 stepchild, Riva. Author: (poems) The Eater, 1972, Pacific Plainsong, 1978, 2d ed., 1986, When the Revolution Really, 1984; (criticism) The Aesthetics of Pornography, 1971; ed. Chgo. Rvw., 1961-64, Purple Sage, 1969-70; contrbg. ed. TriQtly, 1975-78; adv. ed. Another Chgo. mag.; contrbr. essays and poems to TriQtly, The Nation, New Republic, Chgo., New Orleans, N.Am., Oyez, Antioch rvws., Choice, Prairie Schooner, Another Chgo. mag., others, also in anthologies including New Poetry Anthology I, Young Am. Wrtrs., Wrtrs. under Thirty. BA, Whitman Coll., 1957; MA, U. Wyo., 1958; postgrad. U. Chgo., 1960-63. Asst. prof. U. Notre Dame, 1964-68, Northwestern U., 1971-74; freelance wrtr., Chgo., 1969-71; assoc. prof. English, U. Colo., Boulder, 1974—; assoc. ed., co-pub. Rolling Stock, 1981—. Recipient poetry award Ill. Arts Council, 1972; NEA poetry grantee, 1975. Home: 1070 Grant Pl Boulder CO 80302

MICHELSON, RICHARD, b. Bklyn., July 3, 1953, s. Maurice and Caroline (Jacknowitz) M.; m. Jennifer Baldwin; children—Marisa Lynne, Samuel Armstrong. Author: The Head of the Family, 1978, Tap Dancing for the Relatives, 1985. BA, SUNY-Albany, 1976; MFA, Goddard Coll., 1981. Owner, Intl. Galleries, Northampton, Mass., 1976—. Home: Box 657 Amherst MA 01004

MICHELUCCI, KATHERINE CORALEE BURCH, b. Elmira, NY, Feb. 12, 1943; d. Hobart Alexander and Margaret Leona (Marshall) B.; m. Ernesto Michelluci, Apr. 21, 1968; children—Pietro Ernest, Sara Ann. Author cookbooks: Nature at Its Best in Italian Food, 1978, Bread & Pizza, 1979; contrbr. to Family Circle, Woman's World, Woman's Day, Am. Edn., Vegetarian Times, Health Express, Scubapro, Diver, Rochester, New Homes. MA in Ital. Lang. & Lit., Middlebury Coll., 1967; PhD in For. Langs. & Lit., Florence (Italy) U., 1970. TV producer, Ch. 9, Syracuse, Ch. 21, Rochester, NY, 1975-77; prof. Eng. & langs. U. Rochester (NY), RIT, Syracuse (NY), 1970-80; prof., TV lctr. Illinois Coll., Jacksonville, IL, 1981-83; freelance writer/lectr., Jacksonville, IL, Blairstown, NJ, 1980-86. Mem. NWU, RWA, NJRWA. Address: Box 1212 Fairport NY 14550

MICHENER, JAMES ALBERT, b. NYC, Feb. 3, 1907; s. Edwin and Mabel (Haddock) M.; m. Patti Koon, July 27, 1935 (div.); m. Vange Nord,

Sept. 2, 1948 (div.); m. Mari Yoriko Sabusawa, Oct. 23, 1955. Author: Unit in the Social Studies, 1940, Tales of the South Pacific, 1947 (Pulitzer prize), The Fires of Spring, 1949, Return to Paradise, 1951, The Voice of Asia, 1951, The Bridges of Toko Ri, 1953, Sayonara, 1954, Floating World, 1955, The Bridge at Andau, 1957, Rascals in Paradise, (with A. Grove Day), 1957, Selected Writings, 1957, The Hokusai Sketchbook, 1958, Japanese Prints, 1959, Hawaii, 1959, Report of the County Chairman, 1961, Caravans, 1963, The Source, 1965, Iberia, 1968, Presidential Lottery, 1969, The Quality of Life, 1970, Kent State, 1971, The Drifters, 1971, A Michener Miscellany, 1973, Centennial, 1974, Sports in America, 1976, Chesapeake, 1978, The Covenant, 1980, Space, 1982, Poland, 1983; editor: Future of Social Studies for N.E.A., 1940. AB summa cum laude, Swarthmore Coll., 1929; AM, U. No. Colo., 1937; research study, U. Pa., U. Va., Ohio State U., Harvard U., U. St. Andrews, Scotland, U. Sena, Italy, Brit. Mus. London, 1930-33. Tchr. Hill Schl., 1929-31, George Schl., Pa., 1933-36; prof. Colo. State Coll. Edn., 1936-41; vis. prof. Harvard U., 1939-40; assoc. editor Macmillan Co., 1941-49; mem. adv. com. on arts State Dept., 1957; mem. adv. council NASA, 1980-83; mem. U.S. Adv. Commn. on Info., 1971. Sec. Pa. Constl. Conv., 1967-68. Served with USNR, 1944-45, PTO. Recipient U.S. Medal of Freedom. Home: Box 10 St. Michael's MD 21663

MICK, COLIN KENNEDY, b. Lansing, MI, Jan. 17, 1941; s. Allan Herbert and Lucille Kennedy M.; m. Ulla Kasperski, June 24, 1966. Author: Working Smart, 1984 (with Kerry Mason), The Financial Planners Guide to Using Personal Computers (with Jerry Ball), 1984, Mastering Your Money (with Kerry Mason), 1986. BA, U. AK, 1963; MA, Stanford U., 1969, PhD, 1972. Wrtr., U. AK, 1963, 1966-67; cons. Stanford U., 1969-72, research assoc. 1972-75; pres. Applied Communication Research, Palo Alto, CA, 1975-82; exec. producer Understanding Personal Computers, Palo Alto, CA, 1982—; dir. Decision Information Service, Palo Alto, CA., 1977—. Home: 2130 Hanover St Palo Alto CA 94306

MICKENS, RONALD ELBERT, b. Petersburg, VA, Feb. 7, 1943; m. Maria Kelker, Aug. 13, 1976; children—James Williamson, Leah Marie. Author: Nonlinear Oscillations, 1981, Difference Equations, 1987. Ed.: Mathematical Analysis of Physical Systems, 1985. Wrkg. on books on black scientists and discrete dynamic systems. B.A., Fisk U., 1964; Ph.D., Vanderbilt U., 1968. Prof., Fisk U., Nashville, 1970-81, Atlanta U., 1982—; visiting prof. Mass. Inst. Tech., Cambridge, MA, 1973-74; visiting scholar Vanderbilt U., Nashville, 1980-81; research scholar Joint Inst. for Lab Astrophysics, Boulder, 1981-82. Woodrow Wilson fellow, 1964-65; fellow Danforth Fdn., 1965-68, NSF, 1968-70, Ford Fdn., 1980-81. Home: 2853 Chaucer Dr SW Atlanta GA 30311

MICKLOS, JOHN JOSEPH, JR., b. Newark, DE, Mar. 15, 1956; s. John Joseph and Shirley (Sipple) M.; m. Deborah Jean Amsden, June 1, 1985. Co-author: Read-Reason-Write (elem. sch. workbook series), 1981; contrbr. chap. Reading (college text), 1981; contrbg. ed. Delaware Today mag., 1984-86; columnist Newark Post, 1987—; contrbr. articles: Real Estate Today, Jnl. of Reading, Reading Horizons, others. BS in Journalism, Ohio U., 1978. Staff wrtr. Internat. Reading Assn., Newark, Del., 1978-84, ed., 1984—. Mem. NWC, Ednl. Press Assn., Soc. Scholarly Pub., St. David's Christian Wrtrs. Assn. Address: Box 8139 Newark DE 19714

MIDDENDORF, JOHN HARLAN, b. NYC., Mar. 31, 1922; s. George Arlington and Margaret (Hofmann) M.; m. Beverly Bruner, July 14, 1943; children: Cathie Jean (Mrs. Robert B. Hamilton Jr.), Peggy Ruth (Mrs. Lawrene J. Brindisi). Contbr. articles, revs. to profl. jnls.; Editor: English Writers of the Eighteenth Century, 1971; asst. editor: Johnsonian News Letter, 1950-58; co-editor, 1958-78; editor, 1978—; assoc. editor: Yale ed. Works Samuel Johnson, 1962-66; genl. editor, 1966—. AB, Dartmouth Coll., 1943; AM, Columbia U., 1947, PhD, 1953. Lectr. English CCNY, 1946, Hunter Coll., 1946-49; faculty Columbia, 1947—, prof. English, 1965—, dir. grad. studies, 1971-74, vice-chmn., 1976-80. Served to lt. (j.g.) USNR, 1943-46. Faculty fellow Fund Advancement Edn., 1951-52; grantee Council Research Humanities, 1958-59, Am. Philo. Soc., 1962, ACLS, 1962, NEH, 1976-85. Mem. Univ. Seminar on 18th Cent. European Culture (chmn. 1973-75), Oxford Biblio. Soc., MLA, Conf. Brit. Studies, Econ. History Soc., Am. Soc. 18th Cent. Studies, AAUP. Home: 404 Riverside Dr New York NY 10025

MIDDLEBROOK, DAVID, see Rosenus, Alan Harvey

MIDDLEBROOK, DIANE WOOD, b. Pocatello, ID, Apr. 16, 1939, d. Thomas Isaac and Helen (Downey) Wood; m. Jonathan Middlebrook, June 14, 1963 (div. 1972); 1 dau., Leah Wood; m. Carl Djerassi, June 21, 1985. Author: Walt Whitman and Wallace Stevens, 1974, Worlds into Words: Understanding Modern Poems, 1979, Gin Considered as a Demon (poems), 1983; co-ed.: Coming to Light: American Women Poets in the Twentieth Century (with Marilyn Yalom), 1985. BA, U. Wash., 1961; PhD, Yale U., 1968. Mem. faculty Stanford (Calif.) U., 1966—, prof. English, 1984—; trustee resident artists program Djerassi Fdn., Woodside, Calif., 1979—. NEH fellow, 1982-83, Bunting fellow Radcliffe Coll., 1982-83, Stanford Humanities fellow, 1983-84. Mem. MLA, Wallace Stevens Soc. Home: 1101 Green St San Francisco CA 94109

MIDDLEKAUFF, ROBERT LAWRENCE, b. Yakima, WA., July 5, 1929; s. harold an Katherine Ruth (Horne) M.; m. Beverly Jo Martin, July 11, 1952; children: Samuel John, Holly Ruth. Author: Ancients and Axioms, 1963, The Mathers, 1971, The Glorious Cause: The American Revolution, 1763-1789, 1982. BA, U. Wash., 1952; PhD, Yale U., 1961. Instr. history Yale U., 1959-62; asst. prof. history U. Calif.-Berkeley, 1962-66, assoc. prof., 1966-70, prof., 1970-80, Margaret Byrne prof. history, 1980-83; dir. Huntington Library, Art Gallery an Bot. Gardens, San Marino, Calif., 1983—. Served to 1st lt. USMC, 1952-54 Korea. Recipient Bancroft prize, 1972, Commonwealth Club Gold medal, 1983; fellow ACLS, 1965, NEH, 1973. Mem. Am. Hist. Assn., Orgn. Am. Historians, Soc. Am. Historians, Colonial Soc. Mass. (corr.). Home: 1151 Oxford Rd San Marino CA 91108

MIDDLETON, DREW, b. NYC, Oct. 14, 1913; s. Elmer Thomas and Jean (Drew) M.; m. Estelle Mansel-Edwards, Mar. 31, 1943; 1 dau., Judith Mary. author: Our Share of Night, 1946, The Struggle for Germany, 1949, The Defense of Westrn Europe, 1952, These Are the British, 1957, The Sky Suspended, 1960, The Supreme Choice, 1963, The Atlantic Community, 1965, Retreat From Victory, 1973, Where Has Last July Gone?, 1974, Can American Win the Next War?, 1975, Submarine, 1976, The Duel of the Giants: China and Russia in Asia, 1978, Crossroads of Modern Warfare, 1983. B.S. in Journalism, Syracuse U., 1935, LL.D. (hon.), 1963. Reporter Poughkeepsie Evening Star, 1936-37; war corr. attached to Brit. Exped. Force in France and Belgium, 1939-40; attached as corr. U.S. Army and Navy in Iceland, 1941-42; Allied Forces, London, 1942; mem. staff. N.Y. Times, London, 1942; at Frankfurt, Berlin and at Intl. Mil. Tribunal trials, Nuremberg, Germany, 1945-46; chief corr. N.Y. Times to USSR, 1946-47, Germany, 1947-53, London, 1953-63, Paris, 1963-65, UN, 1965-68, European affairs corr., 1968-70, mil. corr., 1970—. Recipient Headliners Club award fgn. corr., 1943; U.S. Navy Cert. of Merit, 1945; U.S. Medal of Freedom, 1948; OBE (mil. div.), 1947. Office: NY Times 229 W 43d St New York NY 10036

MIDDLETON, JAMES FRANKLIN, b. Indpls., Jan. 17, 1946; s. Norman Wilbert and Mildred (Reynolds) M.; m. Margaret Suzan Kirby, Jan. 21, 1967; children: Shantell, Shannon, Paul, Adam, Joshua. Contrbr. numerous religious article to various periodicals. BRE, Grand Rapids Baptist Coll., 1977. Pastor Faith Baptist Ch., Plainwell, Mich., 1977-84, Eastmont Baptists Ch., Grand Rapids, Mich, 1984—. Served with US Army, 1965-66. Home: 231 Grand River DR Ada MI 49301

MIDDLETON, NORMAN G., b. Sarasota, FL, Jan. 21, 1935; s. Norman G. and Elizabeth (Quina) M.; m. Shirley Marie Nickels, Sept. 5, 1962 (dec. 1966); m. Judith Stephens Middleton, Aug. 1, 1968. Author: The Caverns of My Mind, 1985; contrbr. poetry: Coleridge in Memoriam, 1984, Odessa Poetry Rev., numerous other publs. BA, U. Miami, 1960; MSW, Fla. State U., 1962. Clin. social worker Meml. Hosp., Sarasota, Fla., 1964-66; pvt. practice psychotherapy, Sarasota, 1966—. Mem. profl. orgns. Home: 16626 Winburn Dr Sarasota FL 34240

MIELE, ANGELO, b. Formia, Italy, Aug. 21, 1922; came to U.S., 1952; s. Salvatore and Elena (Marino) M. Author: Flight Mechanics, 1962; editor: Theory of Optimum Aerodynamic Shapes, 1965; author also numerous research papers in aerospace engring., math. programming, optimal control theory and computing methods.; Editor: Mathematical Concepts and Methods in Science and Engineering, 1974—; editor-in-chief: Jnl Optimization Theory and Applications, 1966—; assoc. editor: Jnl Astronautical Scis, 1964—, Applied Mathematics and Computation, 1975—, Optimal Control Applications and Methods, 1979—. D.Civil Engring., U. Rome, Italy, 1944, D.Aero. Engring., 1946. Asst. prof. Poly. Inst. Bklyn., 1952-55; prof. Purdue U., 1955-59; dir. astrodynamics Boeing Sci. Research Labs., 1959-64; prof. astronautics, math. scis. Rice U., Houston, 1964—; Cons. Douglas Aircraft Co., 1956-58, Allison div. Gen. Motors Corp., 1956-58. Pres. Italy in Am. Assn., 1966-68. Decorated knight comdr. Order Merit Italy; recipient Levy Medal Franklin Inst. of Phila., 1974. Fellow AIAA, AAS, Intl. Acad. Astronautics, Acad. Scis. Turin (corr.). Home: 5330 Beverly Hills Ln 3 Houston TX 77056

MIELKE, WAYNE JOSEPH, b. Detroit, May 8, 1954; s. Donald Joseph and Beverly Jean (Magnotte) M.; m. Lynette Marie Heikka, 1986. B.A. in Intl. Relations, Mich. State U., 1982. Account exec. Booth Broadcasting, Detroit, 1983-84; mng. ed. Northeast Detroiter Newspapers, Detroit, 1984-85; dir. communications New Detroit, Inc., Detroit, 1985—. Mem. PRSA,

Detroit Press Club. Home: 24738 Kelly Rd East Detroit MI 48021

MIHALY, EUGENE BRAMER, b. The Hague, Netherlands, Nov. 11, 1934; s. Eddy and Cecile (Bramer) Kahn; stepson, Eugene Mikaly; m. Linda Davis, Oct. 7, 1978; children: Lisa Klee, Jessica; 1 stepson, Russell C. DuBrow. Author: Foreign Aid and Politics in Nepal: A Case Study, 1965; contbr.: Political Development in Micronesia, 1974, Management of the Multinationals, 1974; also articles to various publs. A.B. magna cum laude, Harvard U., 1956; Ph.D., London Sch. Econs. and Polit. Sci., 1964. Aviation/space editor Hartford (Conn.) Courant, 1960-61; dir. Peace Corps, Tanzania, 1967-68; dir. Peace Corps Office Proogram: Dev., Eval., Research, 1969-70; assoc. dir. Inst. Intl. Studies, U. Calif., Berkeley, 1970-72; pres. Mihaly Intl. Corp., 1972—. Trustee, mem. exec. com. World Affairs Council No. Calif., World Without War Council; pres. Pacific-Indonesia C. of C.; vice-chmn. Nigeria-U.S. Bus. Council. Served to lt. (j.g.) USNR, 1956-59. Home: 18 Manzanita Pl Mill Valley CA 94941

MIHALYI, LOUIS LEONARD, b. Glenfield, NY, June 10, 1921, s. Charles Zoltan and Mildred Lovina (Betz) M.; m. Bernice Helen Jones, Aug. 29, 1944; children—Karen, Charles D., Dale, Susan, Sherry, Mark. Contrbr. articles to newspapers, mags.; columnist Watertown (N.Y.) Daily Times, 1980—. BA, Cornell U., 1943; postgrad. various schs., N.Y. High schl. sci. tchr., Glenfield, N.Y., 1957-60, Turin, N.Y., 1960-80. Named Bulln. Ed. of Yr., Senecaland Dist., SPEBSQSA, 1982, 84. Home: RD 1 Box 163 Glenfield NY 13343

MIKESELL, SUZANNE D., b. Melrose, MA, Aug. 13, 1948, d. Robert John and Mary Elizabeth (Mursch) Desmond; m. Richard K. Kenney, July 26, 1968 (div. 1970); 1 son, Michael Peter; m. 2d, Stephen Dean Mikesell, Aug. 17, 1974; 1 dau., Melissa Aimee. Editor: Cooking on a Woodburning Stove, 1980, Please Keep on $moking, 1980, Natural Breast Enlargement, 1981, Pitching In, 1981, Charles The Clown's Guide to Children's Parties, 1982, Unicorns Are Real, 1983, Whose Child Cries, 1984, He Hit Me Back First, 1983, Reading, Writing & Rage, 1985, Learning to Live, Learning to Love, 1985, Project Self-Esteem, 1985, Feelings Alphabet, 1985, Free Flight, 1986, Openmind/Wholemind, 1986, Winning Them Over, 1986, Unconditional Love and Forgiveness, 1986. AA, Wheaton Coll., Norton, Mass., 1968; BA, U. Calif.-Davis, 1977. Editorial asst. Natl. Council on Crime and Delinquency, Davis, Calif., 1974-77, Intl. Dialogue Press, Davis, 1977-80; ed. Jalmar Press, Sacramento, 1980-81, sr. ed., Rolling Hills Estates, Calif., 1981—; sole proptr. Calif. Editorial, Davis, 1981—. Home: Box 1292 Davis CA 95617

MILES, CANDICE ST. JACQUES, b. Great Lakes, IL, Sept. 4, 1951; d. Omer Alcide and Marilyn Elizabeth (Scholl) St. Jacques; m. Bruce Fraley Miles, Apr. 1, 1973. Author: The Jewel of the Desert, 1985. Assoc. ed.: Mesa Mag., AZ, 1976-78; mng. ed.: Ariz. Living Mag., Phoenix, 1978-81. B.A., Ariz. State U., 1973. Free-lance wrtr., 1981—; tchg. asst. Ariz. State Univ., Dept. Eng., 1987—. Recipient New Playwright award Invisible Theatre, Tucson, 1986. Mem. WICI (Far Wet v.p. 1985-87, pres. Phoenix chpt. 1984-85), Wrtr.'s Refinery, Ariz. Authors Assn. Home: 6329 N 13th St Phoenix AZ 85014

MILES, JOHN RUSSIANO, (Jack Miles), b. Chgo., July 30, 1942; s. John Alvin and Mary Jean (Murphy) M.; m. Jacqueline Russiano, Aug. 23, 1980; 1 child, Kathleen Russiano Miles. Author: Retroversion and Text Criticism, 1985. LittB, Gregorian Univ., Rome, 1966; PhD, Harvard U., 1971. Prof., Loyola U., Chgo., 1970-74, U. Mont., Missoula, 1974-75; ed. Doubleday Pub. Co., NYC, 1976-78; exec. ed. U. Calif. Press, Los Angeles, 1978-85; book ed. Los Angeles Times, 1985—. Office: Book Rvw LA Times Mirror Sq Los Angeles CA 90053

MILLASICH, HAZEL ASHTON, b. Allison, IA, Feb. 20, 1902, d. Charles Elliot and Violetta Irene (Boswell) Ashton; m. Nicholas Jonathan Millasich, Dec. 26, 1926 (dec.); children—James N., Blanche D., Richard D., Roger D. Novelist and poet: Bitter Sweet, 1965, Of Lust and Love, 1977, Lights and Shadows, 1980, Crumpled Paper Stories, 1981, View from the Mountain, 1983. Home: 5749 Craner Ave North Hollywood CA 91601

MILLAY, M. J., see Miller, Martin Jessee

MILLER, ANITA, b. Chgo., Aug. 31, 1926, d. Louis and Clara Louise (Ruttenberg) Wolfberg; . Jordan Miller, Dec. 19, 1948; children—Mark Crispin, Bruce Joshua, Eric Lincoln. PhD, English, Northwestern Univ., 1972. Author: Arnold Bennett: An Annotated Bibliography, 1977, (with others) Behind the Front Page, 1983, and Fair Women, 1981; editor: The Liberty Cap, 1977, One Summer in Israel, 1978, I Sami, 1978, Murder at the Red October, 1981, Caroline Norton's Defense, 1982, Cold Stove League, 1983, Lapis, 1984, Science Fiction Dialogues, 1983, The Makeover, 1984, Young Man in Paris, 1984, Aunt Ella Stories, 1984, Mrs. O'Leary's Comet, 1985, Carlyle Simpson, 1986, One For the Money, 1985, Paperback Talk, 1985; author intro. to numerous books. Wrkg. on: Harriet Hosmer, ¡Feminismo! Mem. Read Ill. Comm., Springfield and Chgo., 1985. Mem. MLA. Office: Acad Chgo 425 N Michigan Chicago IL 60611

MILLER, ARTHUR, b. NYC, Oct. 17, 1915; s. Isadore and Augusta (Barnett) M.; m. Mary Grace Slattery, Aug. 5, 1940 (div.); children: Jane Ellen, Robert; m. Marilyn Monroe, June 1956 (div.); m. Ingeborg Morath, Feb. 1962; 1 dau. Playwright: Man Who Had All the Luck, 1944, Situation Normal, 1944, All My Sons, 1948 (NY Drama Critics award); later motion picture Death of a Salesman (NY Drama Critics Circle award, Pulitzer prize 1949); The Crucible, 1953 (Tony award); later motion picture View from the Bridge, 1966; Collected Plays, 1958, After the Fall, 1963, Incident at Vichy, 1964, A Memory of Two Mondays, 1955, The Price, 1956, Up from Paradise, The Archbishop's Ceiling, The American Clock, 1981; screenplay Playing for Time, 1981; author: novel Focus, 1945; novel (later screenplay) The Misfits, 1960; The Price, 1968, The Creation of the World and Other Businesses, 1972, In Russia, 1969; also story collection I Don't Need You Anymore, 1967; (with Inge Morath) Chinese Encounters, 1979, (memoir) Salesman in Beijing, 1984. A.B., U. Mich., 1938. Assoc. prof. drama U. Mich., 1973-74. Recipient Hopwood award for Playwriting U. Mich., 1936, 37; Theatre Guild Natl. Award, 1938; Antoinette Perry award, 1953; Gold Medal for drama Natl. Inst. Arts and Letters, 1959; Creative Arts award Brandeis U., 1970; Anglo-Am. award, 1966. Address: ICM, 40 W 57th St New York NY 10019

MILLER, BARBARA ANN, (Bobbi Miller), b. Ft. Bragg, NC Feb. 3, 1955; d. James Houston and Ada Neil (Graham) Rutan; m. Timothy Paul Miller, May 28, 1983; children-Naomi D., Rebecca S. Contrbr. articles to mags., newsletters including Profl. Communicator, Aztec Peak, Network: Mag. for Colo. Women, others. Contrbg. ed. Natl. Soc. Suspense and Fiction Wrtrs., 1986—, Profl. Communicator, 1987; cons. ed. NWC, 1985—; asst. ed. Scribe Student News, Denver, 1981-82; ed. Memo Placement News, Denver, 1981-82; ed. Memo Placement News, Denver, 1982-83; assoc. ed. CO Springer, Colorado Springs, 1983. A.A. in Jnlsm., Pikes Peak Commun. Coll., 1979; B.A. in Mass Media Communication, U. Colo., Colorado Springs, 1983-84; free-lance wrtr., ed., 1983—. Recipient 1st place for genl. overall excellence Rocky Mt. Collegiate Press Assn., 1980, 10th place for short story Sci. Fiction Wrtrs. of Earth, 1987. Mem. WIC, NWC, IWWG. Home: 2369 Washo Circle Colorado Springs CO 80915

MILLER, BONNIE MARY, b. Aurora, IL, July 21, 1956; d. Paul Eduard and Mary Frances (McKenna) Miller. Contrbr. short stories, poems, articles to Nit & Nit, Rhino, Towers, Unicorn, Chgo. Letters, Mainstream, Northern Star, Beacon, Dialogue; ed. Nelson-Hall Pubs. BA English Lit., Mundelein Coll., 1982. Freelance writer and ed., Chgo., 1979—:edl. dir., Dialogue Mag., Berwyn, Ill., 1985—. Recipient poetry award Mundelein Coll., Chgo., 1982, Josephine Lusk Fiction award, 1982, writing scholarship, 1982. Office: c/o Dialogue 3100 Oak Park Ave Berwyn IL 60402

MILLER, BRUCE WINSTERD III, b. Lawrence, KS, Nov. 25, 1951, s. Bruce Winsterd Miller, Jr. and Patricia Ann (Young); m. Mary Catherine Donnelly, Apr. 18, 1981; children—Evan Bruce, Thomas Nathaniel. Author: The Caner's Handbook, 1983, Septic Tanks a Guide to Their Care and Feeding, 1985, Handmade Silk Flowers, 1986. BA, U. Calif., Berkeley, 1974. Book Buyer Moe's Books, Berkeley, 1974-81; owner Phoenix Books, San Luis Obispo, Calif., 1981—; book reviewer San Luis Obispo Telegram Tribune, 1984—. Home: 1319 14th St Los Osos CA 93402

MILLER, CATHERINE DIANE, b. Pitts., Dec. 9, 1952; d. Harry Edgar and Denise (Liebert) M. Contrbr. short stories to Sinister Wisdom, Confrontation, Apalachee Qtly. BA in English-Writing, U. Pitts., 1979, MFA in Creative Writing, 1986. Editorial asst. Am. Philo. Qtly, Pitts., 1979-80, U. Pitts. Press, 1980-81; tech. ed. Westinghouse Co., Pitts., 1981-85, communications specialist, 1985—. Fellow Yaddo Wrtrs. Colony, 1985, Pa. Council on Arts, 1986. Home: 319 E Swissvale 2 Pittsburgh PA 15218

MILLER, CONNIE, see Ark, Connie Eileen

MILLER, DONALD LARRY, (Brandon Scotte), b. St. Paul, Apr. 10, 1964; s. Gary Garfield Miller and Marlene Ann (Robertson) Ableiter; m. Sherrie Dawn, Sept. 15, 1984. Author: (poetry) Rememberance of Love Past, 1986. Ed: The Nightmare Express (newsltr.), 1986—; Terror Time Again (anthol.), 1987. Home: 262 Sherburne 2 St. Paul MN 55103.

MILLER, HARRIETT PUFFER, b. Kansas City, MO, Jan. 17, 1919; d. Paul Hubbard and Elvira Suzanne (Nelson) Puffer; divorced; children—Gary Hugh, Christina Joyce. Author: (children's serialized book) Western Trailer Life, 1946 (cassette/record) A Child's World of Stories, Poems & Mother Goose, 1984. contrbr. articles to mags. including Western Home Furnisher, Western Fabrics, Curtains & Draperies,

Western Upholstery Mag., Aim Plus; curricula material to public schls. Mng. ed. Western Trailer Life, 1946-47; ed. Service Publ, 1947-50. B.Edn., U. Miami, 1963; Diploma, Inst. of Children's Lit., 1985. Tchr. Dade County Public Schls., Miami, 1963-81. Home: 2180 Alamanda Dr North Miami FL 33181

MILLER, HOPE RIDINGS, b. Bonham, TX.; d. Alfred Lafayette and Grace (Dupree) Ridings; m. Clarence Lee Miller. Author: The Life and Times of Diplomatic Washington, 1969, Great Houses of Washington, 1969, Scandals in the Highest Office: Facts and Fiction in the Private Lives of Our Presidents, 1973; cassette tape Circling Lafayette Square, 1976. BA, U. Tex.; MA, Columbia; DLitt, Austin Coll. Society editor Washington Post, 1938-44; Washington corr. Town and Country mag., 1944-46, The Argonaut mag., 1945-49; assoc. editor Diplomat mag. 1952-55, editor-in-chief, 1956-66; TV prodn. staff Metromedia, Inc., 1966-70; Washington editor Antique Monthly, 1975—; mem. editorial adv. bd. Horizon mag., 1978—. Mem. Washington Press Club (past pres.), Columbia Hist. Soc., Am. News Women's Club, AG, Natl. Trust Hist. Preservation, Corcoran Gallery Art Assocs. Home: 1868 Columbia Rd NW Washington DC 20009

MILLER, IRA, b. Phila., Mar. 21, 1955, s. Sidney and Shirley (Steinman) M. Novelist: Seesaw, 1983 (translated to German, 1984; Spanish, 1985). BA cum laude in English, Clark U., 1977. Instr. English, tennis coach Fairleigh Dickinson U., Teaneck, N.J., 1985—; head counselor Antigua (W.I.) Adventure summer camp, summers 1977—. Home: 509 North St Teaneck NJ 07666

MILLER, JAMES EDWIN, JR., b. Bartlesville, OK, Sept. 9, 1920; s. James Edwin and Leona (Halsey) M.; m. Barbara Anderson, July 3, 1944; children: James E. III, Charlotte Ann. Author: a Critical Guide to Leaves of Grass, 1957, (with Bernice Slote and Karl Shapiro) Start with the Sun, 1960, Walt Whitman, 1962, Reader's Guide to Herman Melville, 1962, F. Scott Fitzgerald: His Art and His Technique, 1964, J.D. Salinger, 1965, Quests Surd and Absurd: Essays in American Literature, 1967, Word Self, Reality: The Rhetoric of Imagination, 1972, T.S. Eliot's Personal Waste Land, 1977, The American Quest for a Supreme Fiction: Whitman's Legacy in the Personal Epic, 1979; Editor: Complete Poetry and Selected Prose of Walt Whitman, 1959, Myth and Method: Modern Theories of Fiction, 1960, Dimensions of Poetry, 1962, Dimensions of the Short Story, 1964, Whitman's Song of Myself: Origin, Growth, Meaning, 1964, Dimensions of Literature, 1967, The Arts and the Public, 1967, Theory of Fiction: Henry James, 1972. B.A., U. Okla., 1942; M.A., U. Chgo., 1947, Ph.D., 1949. Asst. prof. English U. Nebr., Lincoln, 1953-56, prof., chmn. dept. 1956-62, prof. English U. Chgo., 1962—, chmn. dept. 1978-84, Helen A. Regenstein prof. lit., 1983—; Fulbright lectr., Italy, 1958-59, Kyoto, Japan, 1968, Australia, 1976, visiting prof., sorbonne, Paris, 1984-85, fall 1986. Served to capt. AUS, 1942-46; Served to capt. U.S. Army, 1950-52. Recipient Walt Whitman award Poetry Soc. Am., 1958, Poetry Chap Book award, 1961; Guggenheim fellow, 1969-70; NEH sr. fellow, 1974-75. Mem. MLA, NCTE (editor Coll. English 1960-66, pres. 1970), Am. Studies Assn., AAUP (council 1964-67), Midwest MLA (pres. 1961-62). Home: 5536 S Blackstone Ave Chicago IL 60637

MILLER, JANE RUTH, b. NYC, Apr. 27, 1949; d. H. Walter and Florence (Freed) Miller. Author: The Greater Leisures, 1983, Black Holes, Black Stockings, 1985. MA, CA St., Humboldt, CA, 1975; MFA, U. Iowa, 1977. Asst. prof. Goddard College, Plainfield, VT, 1977-80; visiting poet Writers Community, NYC,1983-84; vis. poet, U. IA, 1984-86. Fellowship, NEA, 1985, Residency Grant, Wurlitzer Fdn., Taos, NM, 1985, 88. Office: U IA 436 EPB Iowa City IA 52240

MILLER, JAY EARL, b. Barberton, OH, s. Jesse Earl and Ada Edith (Overholt) M.; m. Elizabeth Wilhelmina Streine, June 6, 1936 (div. 1960); children—Jay Streine, Ned Gregg, Lyn Ellen Miller Clark; m. 2d, Mary Louise Wathen, July 7, 1983. Author: Engineering with Rubber, 1949, A Study of the Scientific Manpower Problem of the United States, 1957, The Public Will Decide: PR the Way It Is, 1986; freelance cartoonist, 1985—. Wrkg. on novel. Student Kent (Ohio) State U. Mem. editorial staff Detroit Free Press, 1935-36; advt. mgr. B.F. Goodrich Co., Akron, Ohio, 1936-48, Western dir. public relations, Los Angeles, 1948-66, corp. dir. public relations, Akron, 1966-73. Home: Box 75-65A 9 Newberry Trl Garden City SC 29576.

MILLER, JEROME K., b. Great Bend, KS, Apr. 18, 1931; s. Walter J. and Kathleen M. (Kliesen) M. Author: Applying the New Copyright Law, 1979, The Copyright Directory, 1985; contrbr. articles on copyright to profl. jnls; book reviewer for Resources for Tech. Learning, 1972-74. BA, Emporia State U., 1965; AMLS, U. Mich., 1966; MA, U. Kans., 1973; EdD, U. Colo., 1976. Pres. Copyright Info. Services, 1983—. Mem. ALA. Address: Box 1460 Friday Harbor WA 98250

MILLER, JIM WAYNE, b. Leicester, NC, Oct. 21, 1936; s. James Woodrow and Edith (Smith) M.; m. Mary Ellen Yates, Aug. 17, 1958; children: James Yates, Fred Smith, Ruth Ratcliff. Author: (poems) Copperhead Cane, 1964, Dialogue with a Dead Man, 1974, 78, The Mountains Have Come Closer, 1980, Vein of Words, 1984, Nostalgia for 70, 1986; (ballads) The More Things Change the More They Stay the Same, 1971; translator poetry of Emil Lerperger, The Figure of Fulfillment, 1975, The Salzach Sibyl, 1986; I Have a Place: The Poetry of Jim Wayne Miller, color video (Centre Films). AB in English, Berea Coll., 1958; PhD in German and Am. Lit., Vanderbilt U., 1965. NDEA fellow Vanderbilt U., Nashville, 1960-63; prof. Western Ky. U., Bowling Green, 1963—. Recipient Topaz award Sigma Tau Delta, 1969; award for research and creativity Western Ky. U., 1976; Thomas Wolfe award Western N.C. Hist. Assn., 1980. Home: 1512 Eastland Bowling Green KY 42101

MILLER, JOSEPH HILLIS, b. Newport News, VA, Mar. 5, 1928; s. Joseph Hillis and Nell (Critzer) M.; m. Dorothy Marian James, Apr. 2, 1949; children: Robin Leigh, Matthew Hopkins, Sarah Elizabeth. Author: Charles Dickens: The World of His Novels, 1958, The Disappearance of God, Five Nineteenth-Century Writers, 1963, Poets of Reality, Six Twentieth-Century Writers, 1965, The Form of Victorian Fiction, 1968, Thomas Hardy: Distance and Desire, 1970, Fiction and Repetition, 1982, The Linguistic Moment, 1985, The Ethics of Reading, 1986. Editor: Modern Lang. Notes, 1953-61, ELH, 1953—; mem. adv. bd.: Diacritics, 1975—, Ga. Rvw, 1975—, Critical Inquiry, 1974—, Poetics Today, 1970—, Oxford Lit. Rvw, 1978—, Studies in English Lit, 1979—, Genre, 1980—. BA, Oberlin Coll., 1948; MA, Harvard U., 1949, PhD, 1952; MA, Yale U., 1972. Instr. English Williams Coll., Williamstown, Mass., 1952-53; mem. faculty Johns Hopkins U., Balt., 1953-72, prof. English, 1963-68, prof. English and humanistic studies, 1968-72, chmn. dept. English, 1964-68; prof. English Yale U., New Haven, 1972-75; prof. English and comparative lit., 1979-86; dir. lit. maj., 1980-83; Distinguished Prof. of English and Comparative Lit., U. of Calif., Irvine, 1986—; dir. NEH Summer Seminars, 1974, 77, 80. Guggenheim fellow, 1959-60, 65-66; NEH sr. fellow, 1975, 86; Carnegie fellow U. Edinburgh, 1981. Mem. MLA, Coll. English Assn, New Eng. Coll. English Assn. (pres. 1975-76). Home: 4 Locke Ct Irvine CA 92715

MILLER, KATHRYN SCHULTZ, b. Cin., June 25, 1954; d. Harold Eugene and Joan Ann (Puterbaugh) Schultz; m. Barry Ingram Miller, July 21, 1977. Author: The Very Bestest Present, 1980, I Think I Can, 1980, Poe! Poe! Poe!, 1982, I'm a Celebrity, 1982, Choosing Sides for Basketball, 1982, Blue Horses, 1982, You Don't See Me, 1985, Haunted House, 1985, The Shining Moment, 1987, A Thousand Cranes, 1988. B.S., U. Cin., 1977. Artistic dir. ArtReach Touring Theatre, Cin., 1976—. Bd. dirs. Ohio Theatre Alliance, Columbus, OH, 1979-86, Cin. Commn. on the Arts, Cin., 1983-85; panel mem. Ohio Arts Council, Columbus, 1980, 81. Fellow Ohio Arts Council, 1985; recipient Zeta Phi Eta award Children's Theatre Assn. Am., 1983, Post-Corbett award Cin. Post, 1985, Outstanding Work in Theatre award Ohio Theatre Alliance, 1987. Mem. Dramatists Guild, Am. Asn. Theatre for Youth. Office ArtReach 3074 Madison Rd Cincinnati OH 45209

MILLER, KATHY COLLARD, b. Huntington Park, CA, June 28, 1949, d. Richard Chester and Vivian Grace (Dauer) Collard; m. David Lawrence Miller, June 20, 1970; children—Darcy, Mark. Author: Out of Control, 1984; When Love Becomes Anger, 1985; articles in numerous mags. including Mothering, Charisma, Power for Living, Horizon, and Family Life Today. Address: Box 1058 Placentia CA 92670

MILLER, LESLIE ADRIENNE, b. Medina, OH, Oct. 22, 1956, d. Ray Glen and Martha (Ferguson) Miller; m. William Neven Simonds, Aug. 12, 1978 (div. 1980). Contrbr. poetry to Open Places, Prairie Schooner, Primavera, Nit & Wit, other lit mags; contrbr. rvws. to Open Places, Lit. Mag. Rvw. MA in English, U. Mo., 1980; MFA in Poetry, U. Iowa, 1982. Dir. creative writing program Stephens Coll., Columbia, Mo., 1983—; mng. ed. Open Places, Columbia, 1985—. Recipient Pres.'s award Ohio Jnl, 1985. Mem. P&W. Office: Dept Eng Stephens Coll Columbia MO 65215

MILLER, LEW, see Miller, Louis A.

MILLER, LINDA DIANNE, b. Galion, OH, June 8, 1947; d. Carl William and Doris Jean (Bechtol) Miller; m. Louis Lee Kimberlin, Sr., Mar. 5, 1966 (div. Mar. 5, 1970); children—Kimberly Ann, Louis Lee; m. Ronald Belvins (div.); m. Fredrick Walters (div.). Contrbr. essay, articles to mags., newspapers. Wrkg. on poetry, true life story of self-help, articles on religion. Degree in Cosmetology, Marion State Beauty Acad., 1973; A.A., Mansfield Bus. Coll., 1982. Reporter, Country Music Assn., Marion, OH, 1972-76; telephone representative Sears Tele-Marketing, Mansfield, OH, 1987—. Home: 475

Portland Way N Apt 4 Galion OH 44833

MILLER, LOUIS ADAM, (Lew Miller), b. Louisville, Apr. 4, 1917; s. Edward M. and Charlotte (Hoeferle) M.; m. Jean E. Culberson, July 12, 1952; children—Mark L., Douglas E., Gregory O., Rebecca Ann. Author: Your Divine Connection, 1978, repubd. as Miracles Can Happen to You, 1985; (tape cassette) Miracles, 1983. Contrbr. short stories, articles on religion, philosophy-psychology, adventure, advt.-mktg. to mags. BA in Mktg., U. Louisville, 1952. Wrtr., ed. Dunne Press, 1935-36; sales corr. Peerless Mfg. Corp., Louisville, 1936-42; dir. advt. Ky. Rural Elec., 1947-54; prin. Lew Miller Advt., Louisville, 1949-54; dir. promotions Lou Theatrical Assn., 1953-56; creative supr. mktg. Gen. Electric, Louisville, 1956-85; mktg. consl., lectr., 1985—. Bd. dirs. St. Joseph Inf., Louisville, 1972-77; dir. pub.-promotion Crusade for Freedom, 1950-52. Served as 1st lt. U.S. Army, 1942-47. Recipient Battlefield commn. U.S. Army, 1945; 4 coll. scholarships, 1936-49; named Hero of Month, Disabled Am. Vets., 1951. Mem. Louisville Advt. Club, 4th Cavalry Assn. (pres. 1949-50). Home: 1614 Dundee Way Louisville KY 40205

MILLER, LYNN RUTH, b. Toledo, Oct. 11, 1933, s. I.R. and Ida Ruth (Schwartz) M. Creator, wrtr., starred in The Little Playhouse, PBS ednl. TV program, CBS affiliate, Toledo, 1960-62; contrbr. articles to Christian Sci. Monitor, Good Housekeeping, Modern Maturity, numerous other periodicals. BA in Edn., U. Mich., 1955; MEd, U. Toledo, 1960; MA in Communications, Stanford U., 1964. Free-lance feature and fiction wrtr., 1970—. Recipient hon. mention short story competition Ursus Press, 1985. Home: 441 Brighton St Pacifica CA 94044

MILLER, M. HUGHES, b. Phila., July 3, 1913; s. Samuel Maximillian and Sarah (Hughes) M.; m. Doris Gloria Ross, Jan. 1, 1936 (div.); children: Bruce Hyatt, Stephen Hughes; m. Mala Powers, May 17, 1970. A.B., Muhlenberg Coll., 1931; M.A., U. Pa., 1932. Editorial writer Phila. Pub. Ledger, 1929-32; editor Lehigh Valley Review, 1933; mgr. Natl. Advt. Service, 1933-36; mgr. coll. pub. Prentice-Hall, 1936-37; staff pub. relations Earl Newsom & Co., 1937-39; gen. mgr. book pub. Am. Edn. Press, publs. dir. Current Sci. and Aviation,v.p., gen. mgr. Charles E. Merrill, also Wesleyan U. Press, 1939-56; v.p. new pub. Am. Book-Stratford Press, Inc., 1956-58; pres. Bobbs Merrill Co., Inc., 1959-63, Book Publishers Enterprises, Inc., NYC, 1963—; editorial dir. Child's First Encyc.; editor Dictionary of Basic Words, Am. edit. Blyton Secret Seven Series; mem. edn. bd. Education mag.; governing editorial bd. Mil. Pub. Inst.; pres. Hughes Miller Pubs. Projects, Inc., Four Seasons Estates, Inc., Lake Tahoe, Calif.; chmn bd. Inter-Assoc. Book Pub. Cons., 1966—; exec. com., dir. Devon Group, Inc. (formerly Gen. Edn. Services corp.); dir., chmn. acquisition com. Am. Book-Stratford Press, Inc.; founder Weekly Children's Book Club, 1953. Mem. Am. Film Inst. (charter), Am. Childhood Assn. Natl. Council Social Studies, Profl. Bookmen Am. (past pres., founder mem.), Assn. Childhood Edn. Intl. (dir.), Am. Inst. Graphic Arts (chmn. textbook clinic), Am. Textbook Pub. Inst. (chmn. plans and program 1954-56, dir.), Am. Assn. Schl. Adminstrs., Assn Supervision and Curriculum Devel. NEA, PEN London and Los Angeles (exec. com.), Am. Natl. Theatre Acad. (dir. 1973—), Ohio Soc. of N.Y., Intl. Reading Assn. Home: 10543 Valley Spring Ln North Hollywood CA 91602

MILLER, MARGUERITE ELIZABETH, (Teresa Moore), b. Grayslake, IL, July 2, 1917; d. Elmer Elwood and Elizabeth Margaret (Krusemarck) Burge; m. William David Miller, Jan. 19, 1940 (dec. Jan. 31, 1972); children—William G., David A., Steven E., Elizabeth R., Brian C. Author: Swords & Camellias, 1985; contrbr. short stories to mags. including True Romance, true Story, True Confessions. wrkg. on sequel to Swords & Camellias, book series on the occult. Student DePauw U., 1936-38. Coyp ed. Herald-Argus, LaPorte, IN, 1973-76; piano, organ tchr. Good Sounds Sch., LaPorte, 1976-79, Roxy Music Sch., LaPorte, 1979-87. Home: 3002 N County Rd 50 W La Porte IN 46350

MILLER, MARILEE LOIS, b. Morton, WA, Sept. 17, 1937, d. Carl A. and Esther M. (Anderson) Miller. Author: Landis, Pillar of the Church, Hypocrite and Murderer, 1983, Case of the Creative Miscreants, 1983, There's a Place of Understanding, 1986, For the Young at Heart, 1985, Dew on Ev'ry Blade of Grass, 1986. Grad. Art Instrn. Schls., Mpls., 1968. Wrtr., producer, ed., television series Soundings, Coos Bay, Oreg., 1977-80; columnist Coquille Valley Sentinel, 1981-83; owner, ed., pub. Kindred Joy Publs., Coquile, Oreg., since 1983; freelance wrtr. Grantee Oreg. Comm. for Humanities, 1979-80. Home: 554 W 4th St Coquille OR 97423

MILLER, MARK DAWSON, b. Eldorado, OK, Jan. 2, 1919, s. Archibald Roy and Ruby Earle (Thorp) M.; m. Dene Grant, Jan. 25, 1942; children—Kim Brett, Eric Bruce. Author: Wine, a Gentleman's Game, Wrkg. on romance illustration collection. Student U. Okla., Chouinards Art Inst. Prin. Mark Miller-Illustrator, NYC, Eng., France and Germany, 1949-71, Benmarl Wine Co., Marlboro, N.Y., 1971—, Gallery in a Vineyard, 1984—. Mem. Illustrators Soc. N.Y. Address: Benmarl Vineyards Marlboro NY 12542

MILLER, MARTIN JESSEE, (M. J. Millay), b. North Lake, IL, May 20, 1950; s. John Michel and Constance (Ottley) M.; m. Linda Pfluger, 1968 (div.); m. Janette Hazel Oldenburg, Sept. 18, 1971; children—Heather Lynn Faith, Jerorgia Kay. Author: Shaffer: Man of Mystery?, 1984; (plays) La La Land, 1986, The Liberated Woman and the Emancipated Mouse, 1986. A.A., Elgin Commun. Coll., 1978; B.A. in Communications, Judson Coll., 1985. Emergency crises counselor Baptist Family Services, Elgin, IL, 1982-84; mental health technician Elgin Mental Health Clinic, 1984—. Dir. Mixed Co. Theatre Co., Elgin, 1979-87. Served with U.S. Army, 1968-70. Named Best Dir., Mixed Co. Theatre Co., Elgin, 1979-87. Served with U.S. Army, 1968-70. Named Best Dir., Mixed Co. Threatre Co., 1983. Home: 331 Tulsa Carpentersville IL 60110

MILLER, MAUREEN, (Polking), b. Breda, Iowa, May 9, 1922; d. Anthony and Elsabe Anne (Brey) Polking; m. Martin H. Miller, Oct. 28, 1943 (dec. Sept. 1968); children: Martin A., Susan A., Daniel K. Author: For Growth and Getting Along Together, 1975; contrbr. to Readings in Educational Psychology: Contemporary Perspectives, 1976; Help Your Child for Life, 1978; To Share with Your Children—Activities To Help Them Feel Worthwhile, 1978; Family Communication: Keeping Connected in Changing Times, 1980; also filmstrip scripts, program materials, essays, articles for bus. newspapers, essays, poetry to newspapers, mags. and jnls. PhB, Creighton U., 1942; MS, Iowa State U., 1971. Freelance wrtr., 1958—; tchr. dept. community and adult edn. Des Moines Pub. Schls., 1972-77; seminar leader, speaker, 1977-82; instr. English, Drake U., 1981—. Home: 1018 Cummins Pkwy Des Moines IA 50311

MILLER, NATHAN, b. Balt., May 26, 1927; s. David and Jennie (Miller) M.; m. Jeanette Martick, Feb. 22, 1963. Author: Sea of Glory: The Contenental Navy Fights for Independence 1775-1783, 1974, The Founding Finaglers: Corruption in American History, 1976, The U.S. Navy: An Illustrated History, 1977, The Roosevelt chronicles, 1979, The Naval Air War: 1939-1945, 1980, FDR: An Intimate Biography, 1983, 1983; coauthor: The Belarus Secret, 1982; contbr. to: Inside the System, 1970, The Chesapeake Bay in the Era of the American Revolution, 1976, Franklin D. Roosevelt: His Life and Times, 1984. B.A., U. Md., 1950; M.A., 1951. With Balt. Sun, 1954-69; corr. Washington bur., 1966-69; assoc. editor Editorial Research Reports, Washington, 1970-71, Kiplinger Washington Letters, 1971; guest editor Washington Journalism Rev., 1977-78; mem. edl. bd., Nautical and Aviation Pub. Co., Baltimore, Md.; Cons. to Nat. Park Service on naval history Am. Revolution, 1974-76. Served with USNR, 1945-46. Recipient award for pub. service reporting Am. Polit. Sci. Assn., 1961. Mem. AG, Washington Ind. Writers Assn., Am. Film Inst. Home: 1933 19th St NW Washington DC 20009

MILLER, PAMELA B., b. Balt., June 19, 1952; d. Merton Howard and Eleanor (Cohen) M.; m. Richard Julian Chwedyk, June 4, 1977. Author: (poetry chapbook) Fast Little Shoes, 1986; contrbr. poems to Lucky Star, Chgo. Poetry Letter News, Overtures, Skywriting, Oyez Rvw, The Windflower Home Almanac of Poetry, Snakeroots, Out There, other lit mags. Student Roosevelt U., 1972-74; BA with honors, Columbia Coll., Chgo., 1981. Customer service corr. Ency. Brit., Chgo., 1977-78; wrtr./asst. mkgt. mgr., W. Braun Co., Chgo., 1981-84; brand naming project mgr. Brand Group, Inc., Chgo., 1984-86; copywriter, The Balcor Co., Skokie, 1987—. Vol. worker Chgo. Journalism Rvw, 1975. Recipient lit. award for poetry Ill. Arts Council, 1980. Mem. AAP (assoc.), P&W. Home: 7538 N Bell Apt 3A Chicago IL 60645

MILLER, PHILLIP EDWARD, b. Waterloo, IA, May 29, 1935; s. Joe Monroe and Elva Katherine (Groom) M.; m. Cathy Ann Love, Sept. 15, 1962; children—Eric Anthony, Bryan Edward, Stefan Patrick, Gregory Joseph. Editor and researcher: Proceedings of Ia. Acad. Sci., 1963, 64, Schl. Sci. and Math., 1964, 69, Am. Biology Tchr., 1968, Minn. Sci. mag., 1974-77, Proceedings of Intl. Tech. Communication Conf., 1979. BA in Sci. Edn., U. Northern Ia., 1961; MA in Sci. Edn., U. Ia., 1964. Tchr. physics and chemistry Millersburg Community High Schl., Ia., 1961; researcher, supervising tchr. U. Ia., Iowa City, 1962-64; biology instr., area coordinator literacy ctr. Western Ky. U., Bowling Green, 1964-66; sci. wrtr. U. Wis., Madison, 1966-68; assoc. news ed., journalism instr. Mich. State U., East Lansing, 1968-74; asst. prof. agrl., forestry and home econs. U. Minn., St. Paul, 1974-77; supr., sr. ed. atomic energy div. Du-Pont, Aiken, S.C., 1977—. Served to sgt. U.S. Army, 1955-58. Recipient gold medal and numerous awards for marksmanship, 1953-58; 1st place in sci. writing Argonne Univs. Assn., 1973; cert. for profl. achievement in sci. tchg. State of Ia. Bd.Pub. Instr., 1974; Blue ribbon for superior writing and editing Am. Assn. Agrl. Coll. Eds., 1975, Blue ribbon for best four-color periodical, 1976; Top 10 Dist. Bulltn. in world award Toastmasters Internat., 1985. Mem. Soc. Tech. Communication, Phi Delta Kappa, Sigma Xi.

Home: 343 S Chesterfield St Aiken SC 29801

MILLER, RAYMOND RUSSELL JR., b. Elizabeth, NJ, Apr. 19, 1944; s. Raymond Russell and Marie Susan (Iantosca) M.; m. Susan Mildred Lynch, Mar. 2, 1984. Author: (nonfiction) (with James McCloy) The Jersey Devil, 1976; (plays) Sweetness and Light, 1975, The Bar-Side, 1982, Coupling, 1983. Contrbr. articles to profl. jnls. B.A., Washington U., 1966; M.A., U. Del., 1969, Ph.D., 1974. Prof. English, Wilmington Coll., New Castle, DE, 1973—. Recipient Robin Taylor award Long Island U., 1975. Mem. MLA, NCTE. Home: 1830 N Lincoln St Wilmington DE 19806

MILLER, ROBERT JAMES, b. Detroit, Sept. 18, 1923; s Robert Paul and Desdemona (Jelinek) M.; m. Beatrice Diamond, Nov. 6, 1943; children: Karla M., Erik T., Terin T. Author: Monasteries and Culture Change in Inner Mongolia, 1959; contbr. numerous articles to profl. publs.; editor: Religious Ferment in Asia, 1974, Robotics: Future Factories, Future Workers. A.B. in Oriental Civilization, U. Mich., 1948; Ph.D. in Anthropology, U. Wash., 1956. Asia research fellow U. Wash., 1948-50, instr. in anthropology, 1950; research anthropologist Inner Mongolia Project, 1955-56; asst. prof. anthropology U. Wis., Madison, 1959-61, prof., 1965—, chmn. dept. anthropology, 1965–69, 76-78, prof. South Asian studies, 1959—. Served with USCG, 1942-44. Smithsonian fellow, 1970-72; Fellow Am. Anthrop. Assn., AAAS; mem. Assn. Asian Studies, AAUP, Council Anthropology and Edn. (dir. 1980—, chmn. com. on edn. futures 1981-84), Indian Anthropol. Assn. (founding), World Future Soc., Bioelectromagnetics Soc. Office: U Wis 5329 Social Sci Bldg Observatory Dr Madison WI 53706

MILLER, ROBERT JAMES, b. Dunn, NC, Jan. 14, 1933; s. Robert James and Edith (Crockett) M.; m. Patricia L. Shaw, Sept. 29, 1984; children: Patricia Ann, Susan Ballantine, Nancy Crockett. Author: The Assimilation of Nitrogen Compounds by Tree Seedlings, 1957, Some Ecological Aspects of Dry Matter Production, 1962, Liberal Arts and the Individual, 1972, Liberal Arts: an Educational Philosophy, 1973, Laboratory Notebook: General Biology, 1976, Educational Malpractice, 1984. B.S., N.C. State U., 1956; M.F., Yale U., 1962, M.S., 1965, Ph.D., 1967; J.D., N.C. Central U., 1984. Home: 3404 Lake Boone Trail Raleigh NC 27607

MILLER, ROBERTA DAVIS, b. Oklahoma City, Aug. 18, 1931; d. Robert Rutter and Lenora (Baldwin) Davis; married; children: Wendy, Jane, Elisabeth Whelan. Student, Okla. U., 1948-50, Central State U., 1950-51. Editor Golden Books, Western Pub. Co., 1963-71; pub. Sesame St. Mag., Electric Co. Mag., Children's TV Workshop, 1971-76; editor-in-chief Pizzazz Mag., Cadence Pub. Co., 1976-78; v.p., dir. lit. properties United Media Enterprises, 1978-85, intl. pub., 1986—. Cartoonist Soc., News-woman's Club N.Y. Office: 200 Park Ave. New York NY 10166

MILLER, RONALD R., b. Phila., June 27, 1933; s. Rudolph Wilhelm and Jessie Herbster (Cloward) M.; m. Winona K. Graf, Dec. 18, 1954; children—Marjorie, Curtis, Christoper, Matthew. Contrbr. articles, poetry, fiction, to mags. including Bus. Mgt., Constructor, Eastern Boating, Beachcomber. Pres., Barbetta/Miller Advt., Fairfield, N.J., 1961-73, Ronald R. Miller & Co., Caldwell, N.J., 1975-84; v.p. Hagen Communications Inc., Upper Montclair, N.J., 1973-74; freelance wrtr., Beach Haven Terrace, N.J., 1984—. Served with U.S. Air Force, 1953-57. Mem. Long Beach Island Writers Club, Long Beach Island Hist. Assn. (exec. com. 1983—), Boating Writers Intl. Home: 117 E Maryland Ave Beach Haven Terrace NJ 08008

MILLER, SHARON CHARLOTTE, b. Chgo., Aug. 30, 1949; d. Anthony Valerian and Mildred Josephine (Urban) Sujka; m. Thomas Earl Miller, Oct. 2, 1976. Author plays: Procrastination, 1980, Kiwi Birds, 1982. Contrbr. features, interviews, travel article to newspapers, mags. including Woman's World, Chgo. Tribune, Chgo. Life Mag. A.A. with honors, Robert Morris Coll., 1969; B.A. with honors in Radio/TV, Columbia Coll., 1979. On-air hostess Channel 66, Joliet, IL, 1981-82; on-air interviewer, producer Sta. WJRC, Joliet, 1983, 1984, 1984; airline hostess Am. Airlines, Chgo., 1970—; pub. Double M, Joliet, 1983—; free-lance wrtr., 1972—. Home: 21645 Nadia Dr Joliet IL 60436

MILLER, SHIRLEY CASEY, b. Los Angeles, May 11, 1932; d. Clarence Edmund and Erminie (Juaire) Gaffers; m. Paul H. Casey, Sept. 27, 1952 (div. 1974); children: Timothy Patrick, Michael Paul, Maureen Denise Casey Berk; m. 2d, Thomas W. Miller, May 11, 1976 (div. Mar., 1985). Author and ed.; Mexico West Cookbook; ed: Mexico West newsletter, 1976-81, The Baja Book, Angler's Guide to Baja Calif., World of Calif. Gray Whale. Student Pasadena (Calif.) City Coll. Secy.-treas. Baja Trail Publs., Huntington Beach, Calif., 1975-81, ed. Mexico West, 1976-86, exec. dir. Mexico West Travel Club, Costa Mesa, 1981—. Mem. Outdoor Writers Assn. American, Mexican Tourism Orgn. (secy.). Address: 2424 Newport Blvd Ste 91 Costa Mesa CA 92627.

MILLER, STEPHEN M., b. Appleton, WI, Aug. 18, 1939; s. Marvin James Miller and Ruth (Hamblin) Woolsey; children: Daniel, David. Author: The Last Camp in Am., 1982, Backwaters (poetry), 1985, Early Am. Waterfowling, 1986. BA, U. Iowa, 1964. Asst. exec. dir. Ducks Unlimited, NYC, 1965-66; mng. ed. Davis Publs., NYC, 1966-69; jnls. mgr. Univ. of Wis. Press, Madison, 1969—. Wis. Arts Bd. Literary Fellowship, 1987. Address: 17 N Franklin Ave Madison WI 53705

MILLER, THOMAS BENTLEY, b. Kalamazoo, MI, Apr. 18, 1950; s. Lester W. and Elsie Marie (Bentley) M. Author: North Channel Cruising Kit, 1987. Contrbr. articles to boating mags. wrkg. on Georgian Bay and Lake Michigan Cruising Kits. Founder, 4th Coast Communications, 1986—. Served U.S. Army, 1969–72. Home: 4228 Twin Terrace Kalamazoo MI 49002

MILLER, THOMAS EUGENE, b. Bryan, TX, Jan. 4, 1929, s. Eugene Adam and Ella Lucille (Schroeder) M. Contrbr.: Tex. Jurisprudence, Am. Law Reports Annotated, Fedl. Procedural Forms, numerous other legal publs. Author: book published under pseudonym. Wrkg. on novel, legal publs. BA, Tex. A&M U., 1950; MA, U. Tex.-Austin, 1956, JD, 1966. Ed. Bancroft-Whitney Co., San Francisco, 1966—. Mem. NWC, Press Club San Francisco, numerous profl. orgns. Home: 2293 Turk Blvd Apt 5 San Francisco CA 94118

MILLER, WALTER JAMES, b. McKee City, NJ, Jan. 16, 1918; s. Walter Theodore and Celestia Anna (Simmons) M. Author, co-author or ed. 60 books and 999 TV-radio scripts inclg. The Annotated Catch-22, From Auden to Vonnegut: Writers I Have Known, Kurt Vonnegut's Slaughterhouse-Five—A Critical Commentary, 1973, The Annotated Jules Verne (BOMC), 1976, Making An Angel (poetry), 1977, English for Office Careers, 1982, Upton Sinclair's The Jungle, 1983, How to Write Book Reports, 1984. BA, Bklyn. Coll., 1941; MA, Columbia, 1952. Asst. prof. Poly. Inst., Bklyn., 1946-55; asst. prof. Colo. State Univ., Ft. Collins, 1955-56; prof. English, NYU, NYC, 1958-84, emeritus, 1984—. Served U.S. Army Inf., 1943-46. Spcl. award Engrs. Council, 1964; Charles Angoff Poetry award, The Literary Rvw, 1983. Mem. PEN Am. Ctr., AG, P&W. Home: 100 Bleecker St 17E New York NY 10012

MILLER-JACOBSON, JAN BARBARA, b. Detroit, May 29, 1952; d. Leonard Manuel and Tobie K. Sikov; m. Ronald Miller, Aug. 17, 1974 (div. 1982); m. 2d, Daniel Melvyn Jacobson, June 30, 1984. Author: Amphoto Guide to Framing & Display, 1980; ed.: The Professional Guide to Green Plants, 1975. Ed.: The Photographer's Answer Book, 1978, Retouching from Start to Finish, 1979, Big Valley Mag., 1980-81, Innovations Mag., 1987—, Florist Mag., 1974-76, FTD News, 1974-76, The Rangefinder, 1976-79; contrbr. articles: Ariz. Home guide, Designers West, Phoenix Living, Peterson's Photographic, Los Angeles Times, other publs. BA, Mich. State U. Communications ed. CIGNA Healthplans, Glendale, Ariz., 1981-84; dir. communications US Adminstrs., Los Angeles, Ariz., 1984-85; exec. dir. Care Net, Phoenix, 1985-87; pres. JB Communications, Phoenix, 1987—. Mem. Women in Communications, Natl. Assn. Television Arts & Scis., Am. Soc. Bus. Press Eds. (past pres.), Valley Press Club Calif. (past v.p.). Office: JB Commun 8007 N 7th Ave Phoenix AZ 85021

MILLETT, KATHERINE MURRAY, (Kate Millet)b. St. Paul, Sept. 14, 1934; m. Fumio Yoshimura, 1965. Author: Sexual Politics, 1970, The Prostitution Papers, 1973, Flying, 1974, Sita, 1977, The Basement, 1979, Going to Iran, 1982. BA magn cum laude, U. Minn., 1956; postgrad. with 1st class honors, St. Hilda's Coll. Oxford, Eng., 1956-58; PhD, Columbia, 1970. Instr. English U. N.C. at Greensboro, 1958; tchr. Barnard Coll., 1964-68; tchr. English Bryn Mawr (Pa.) Coll.; distinguished vis. prof. Sacramento (Calif.) State Coll., 1973—. Sculptor, Tokyo, Japan, 1963; co-producer, co-dir.: film Three Lives, 1970; sculptor with one woman shows, Minami Gallery, Tokyo, Judson Gallery, Greenwich Village, 1967, Noho Gallery, NYC, 1976, 78, 80, Women's Bldg., Los Angeles, 1977. Mem. CORE, from 1965; chmn. edn. com. NOW, 1966; active supporter women's liberation groups. Address: Putnam 200 Madison Ave New York NY 10016

MILLHAUSER, STEVEN, bNYC, Aug. 3, 1943, s. Milton and Charlotte (Polonsky) M.; m. Cathy Anne Allis, June 16, 1984; 1 child, Jonathan David. Author: Edwin Mullhouse: The Life and Death of an American Writer, 1972, Portrait of a Romantic, 1977, In the Penny Arcade, 1986, From the Realm of Morpheus, 1986; contrbr. stories to New Yorker, Grand Street, Antaeus, Hudson Rvw. BA, Columbia U., 1965; postgrad. Brown U., 1969-72. Grad. asst. Brown U., Providence, 1976-77; vis. assoc. prof. English, Williams Coll., Williamstown, Mass., 1986-87. Recipient Prix Medicis Etranger, France, 1975; NEA fellow, 1986, Award in Lit., Am. Acad. and Inst. of Arts and Letters, 1987. Home: 32 South St. Williamstown MA 01267

MILLIS, CHRISTOPHER, b. Hartford, CT, May 27, 1954, s. Joseph Anthony and Margaret Mary (FitzGerald) M.; m. Nina Davis, July 30, 1977. Playwright: The Shining House, 1979, Poems for the End of the World, 1982, The Magnetic Properties of Moonlight, 1984. Contrbr. poetry to CutBank, Stone Country, Orbis, Hanging Loose, other lit mags; contrbr. criticism to Lit. Mag. Rvw, Small Press Book Rvw, Black American, Artspeak, others. Co-author: Approaching Grammar, 1986. BA, Wesleyan U., 1976; MA, NYU, 1982. Instr. English NYU, 1980-84; prof. English Fordham U., Bronx, N.Y., 1984-85, U. Mass.-Boston, 1985-86; Fulbright Fellow, 1986-87; prof. wrtg., Hobart and William Smith Colleges, 1987-. Yaddo fellow, 1981, 85; Va. Center for Arts fellow, 1983; grantee N.Y. Arts Council, 1984, winner Poetry Competition Phoenix Fdn., Barcelona, Spain, 1985. Mem. P&W, DG, PSA. Home: 11 Bearse Ave Dorchester MA 02124

MILLMAN, LAWRENCE B., b. Kansas City, MO, Jan. 13, 1946; s. Daniel S. and Zelma E. (Lawrence) M. Author: Our Like Will Not Be There Again, 1977, Hero Jesse, 1982, Smell of Earth and Clay, 1985, Parliament of Ravens, 1986. BA, Washington U., 1968; MA, Rutgers U., 1969, PhD, 1973. Asst. prof. Univ. Minn., Minneapolis, 1977-78; prof. Univ. Iceland, Reykjavik, 1982; adv. MFA program, Goddard Coll., Montpelier, Vt., 1981-83; lectr. Harvard extension, Cambridge, Mass., 1985. Fellow Bush Fdn., 1979, Fulbright Fdn., 1982, Guggenheim Fdn., 1983. Wrkg. on translations of Eskimo folktales. Address: Box 1582 Cambridge MA 02238

MILLS, BARBARA KLEBAN, b. Manchester, England (arrived in U.S., 1951); d. Arthur Cosnahon and Elizabeth (Moss) Mills; m. Eugene Kleban, Feb. 10, 1951 (div. 1979). Diploma, Greenwood College. Business reporter Time (NYC), 1956-70; features ed. Playboy (Chicago), 1970-77; correspondent People (Chicago), 1977—. Home: 1200 N Lake Shore Dr Chicago IL 60610

MILLS, DAN SAM PAXTON, (Dan Rain), b. Chgo., Feb. 1, 1924; s. Harry Paul and Jessie Louise (Dean) M. Author poetry: Toward Daylight, 1968, novel: Desert of Children, 1976; contrbr. poetry and prose to New Pioneer, Prairie Grass, Empty Window Rvw, Ia. City Creative Reading Series Mag. BA, U. Mich.-Ann Arbor, 1948; MA in Creative Writing, U. Tex., 1968. Proofreader J. Walter Thompson, NYC, 1948-49; text ed. Univ. Tex. Press, Austin, 1960-61; ed. Ia. City Creative Reading Series Mag., Ia., 1974-78; pub. Pearce Douglas Press, Iowa City, 1975-82. Served to pfc, US Army, 1943-45, USA. Address:560 Everett Ave Palo Alto CA 94301

MILLS, GUSSIE, b. Mt. Edgecumbe, AK, Sept. 25, 1975; s. George Norris and Joyce (Brown) M. Author: Cannery Kid, 1985. Home: 182 Front St Hoonah AK 99829

MILLS, JAMES SPENCER, b. Milw., May 20, 1932; s. Ralph Erskine and Elisabeth Amsden (Stevens) M. Author: The Panic in Needle Park, 1966, The Prosecutor, 1969, Report to the Commissioner, 1972, One Just Man, 1974, On the Edge, 1975, The Seventh Power, 1976, The Truth About Peter Harley, 1979, The Underground Empire, 1986. Student, Erskine Coll., 1950-51; BA, Princeton U., 1956. Reporter Worcester (Mass.) Telegram and Evening Gazette, summer 1955, Corpus Christi (Tex.) Caller Times, 1958, UPI, 1959; reporter, writer, editor Life mag., 1960-66. Served with UNSR, 1956-58. Address: Nesbit ICM 40 W 57th St New York NY 10019

MILLS, MARGARET ANN, b. Oregon City, OR, Nov. 9, 1949; d. John franklin and Edith Marie (Bilger) Schenck; m. Rodney Jesse Mills, Oct. 5, 1968; children—John, Jeffrey, Megan. Contrbr. articles to religious mags., lit. mags. B.A. in English, Northwest Nazarene Coll., 1971. Free-lance wrtr., 1972—. Home: 909 S 19th St Nampa ID 83651

MILLS, PAUL LANCE, b. Washington, June 15, 1951, s. Goodwin Goldstein and Rebelle Eve (Chrablow) M. Contrbr. to Renaissance mag., Stroker mag., G.E.M. mag., The Coop Songbook, others; performance poet under the name "Poez" in NYC, San Francisco, London, Paris. Student Boston U., 1969-71. Grantee P&W, 1982. Mem. AFTRA. Home: 107 Clinton St Apt 15 New York NY 10002

MILLS, RALPH JOSEPH, JR, b. Chgo., Dec. 16, 1931; s. Ralph Joseph and Eileen (McGuire) M.; m. Helen Daggett Harvey, Nov. 25, 1959; children: Natalie, Julian, Brett. Author: Theodoroe Roethke, 1963, Contemporary American Poetry, 1965, Richard Eberhart, 1966, Edith Sitwell, 1966, Kathleen Raine, 1967, Creation's Very Self, 1969, Door to the Sun-Poems, 1974, Cry of the Human, 1975, A Man to His Shadow: Poems, 1975, Night Road/Poems, 1978, Living with Distance: Poems, 1979, With No Answer: Poems, 1980, March Light (poems), 1983; For a Day (poems), 1985, Each Branch: Poems 1976-85, 1986, editor: On the Poet and His Craft—Selected Prose of Theodore Roethke, 1965, Selected Letters of Theodore Roethke, 1968, The Notebooks of David Ignatow, 1973, Open Between Us: Essays, Reviews and Interviews of David Ignatow, 1980. BA, Lake Forest Coll., 1954; MA, Northwestern U., 1956, PhD, 1963. Tchr. English, Am. lit. U., Chgo., 1959-65; prof. English U. Ill. at Chgo. 1965—. Recipient prize for poetry Soc. Midland Authors, 1980, awards for poetry Ill. Arts Council, 1979, 83, 84; English Speaking Union fellow, 1956-57, Carl Sandburg Prize, 1984. Home: 1451 N Astor St Chicago IL 60610

MILLWOOD, PAMELA EVELYN, b. Gainesville, ga., June 4, 1958; d. Cecil Benson Sr. and Evelyn Mae (Bruce) Millwood. Poetry in anthologies; mem. editorial com. Agriculture in Georgia Classrooms: A Resource Guide Kindergarten Through Fourth Grade, 1986. BS, Berry Coll., 1981, MED, 1985. Tchr. elem. schls. Chattooga County Bd. Edn., Summerville, Ga., 1981—. Mem. Chatooga Edn. Assn. (newsletter ed.), other edn. orgns. Home: 105 N Congress St Summerville GA 30747

MILNE, ROBERT SCOTT, b. Dighton, MA, Sept. 3, 1917, s. Walter Irving and Dorothy Andrews (Probst) M.; m. Gabrielle Kuranda, June 30, 1957. Author: Opportunities in Travel Careers, 1976, 3d ed., 1985; contrbr. travel articles to Atlantic, Aloha, USIA, 8 encycs., numerous periodicals and newspapers. BA, Clark U., Worcester, Mass., 1940. Ed. U. Hawaii Press, Honolulu, 1953-54, Scott Meredith Lit. Agcy., NYC,1954-55; asst. ed. Collier's Encyc., NYC,1956-63, assoc. ed. Encyc. Americana, NYC,1963-72; ed., pub. Travelwriter Marketletter, NYC,1975—. Recipient Silver Tankard for excellence Soc. Am. Travel Wrtrs., 1980. Mem. Council Wrtrs. Orgns., Travel Journalists Guild, ASJA, Naval Intelligence Professionals, N.Y. Travel Wrtrs. Assn., Media Alliance, NWU. Home: Old Knollwood Rd Elmsford NY 10523

MILNE, TEDDY (MARGARET), b. Delaware, OH, Oct. 17, 1930; d. Philip Frederick and Emily (Powell) Mayer; m. Alexander Wilson Milne, Apr. 24, 1965 (Dec. dec. 3, 1982); children—Timmon, Peter, James., Author: A Walk Around Portsoy, 1979, A Walk Around Cullen, 1980, Be Your Own Boss, 1982, Choose Love, 1986, Anthony, 1986, Peace Porridge One, 1987, Compassionate Democracy, 1987; (songs) War Is a Dinosaur, 1987. Contrbr. songs, articles to anthols., newspapers, mags. including True Story, Boston Globe, others. B.A., Boston U., 1951; student U. Paris, 1953-54. Ed. public relations Northampton Schl. for Girls, MA 1960-62; wrtr., copyeditor Daily Hampshire Gazette, Northampton, 1960-67; free-lance wrtr., 1979-80; ed. Laser, Northampton, 1982—, Peace Devel. Fund, Amherst, MA, 1984-86; ed., pub. Pittenbruach Press, Northampton, 1986—. Mem. steering com. Banffshire Arts Guild, Cullen, Scotland, 1975-80. Mem. COSMEP. Home: 15 Walnut St Northampton MA 01060

MILOFSKY, DAVID, b. NYC, June 11, 1946; s. Bernard and Ruth Bryan (Dorsey) M.; m. Jaqueline C. Thaler, May 15, 1972; 1 dau., Jennifer Claire. Author: (novel) Playing from Memory, 1981; script editor: Earplay (drama project of Natl. Pub. Radio), 1974-77; documentary Isaac Bashevis Singer, A Literary Portrait, 1978; contrbr. articles and rvws. to N.Y. Times Mag., Chgo. Tribune, Prairie Schooner, Redbook, others. Assoc. editor The Denver Qtly, 1983-84, editor, 1984—. BA, U. Wis., 1969, MA, 1971; MFA, U. Mass., 1977. Mem. MLA, AWP (dir.'s council). Bernard DeVoto fellow Bread Loaf Writers Conf., 1981.; Colo. Endowment for Hunanities grantee, 1986; NEA grantee, 1986; recipient Harvey Swados prize U. Mass., 1976. Home: 1770 Krameria Way Dever CO 80224

MILON, ELLA MAE, b. Conroe, TX, May 22, 1926; d. Haywood Gibson McFarland and Mavis Eulen (Driscoll) McCaghren; m. David Fred Engel, Sept. 7, 1946 (div. Feb. 12, 1960); children—Sherry Diane Wallis, Barbara Kay Mings, Stephen David; m. Carl Eugene Milon, May 21, 1960. Contrbr. articles to mags. including Dog World Mag., Shetland Sheepdog Mag., others; poems to mags., anthols. Student U. Tex., Austin, 1943-45. Recipient Silver Poet award World of Poetry, 1986, Golden Poet award, 1987. Mem. Greater Lafayette Kennel Club. Home: RR 1 Box 90 Frankfort IN 46041

MILOSZ, CZESLAW, b. Lithuania, June 30, 1911; came to U.S., 1960, naturalized, 1970; s. Aleksander and Weronika (Kunat) M. Author: books The Captive Mind, 1953, Native Realm, 1968, Post-War Polish Poetry, 1965, The History of Polish Literature, 1969, Selected Poems, 1972, Bells in Winter, 1978, The Issa Valley, 1981, Separate Notebooks, 1983, The Land of Ulro, 1984, The Unattainable Earth, 1985. MJuris, U. Wilno, Lithuania, 1934; LittD (hon.), U. Mich., 1977. Programmer Polish Natl. Radio, 1935-39; diplomatic service Polish Fgn. Affairs Ministry, Warsaw, 1945-50; vis. lectr. U. Calif., Berkeley, 1960-61, prof. Slavic langs. and lits., 1961-78, prof. emeritus, 1978—. Recipient Prix Litteraire Europeen Les Guildes du Livre, Geneva, 1953, Neustadt Intl. prize for lit. U. Okla., 1978, citation U. Calif., Berkeley, 1978, Nobel prize for lit., 1980; Natl. Culture Fund fellow,1934-35; Guggenheim fellow, 1976. Mem. Polish Inst. Letters and Scis. in Am., PEN Club in Exile. Office: Dept Slavic Langs U Calif Berkeley CA

94720

MILTNER, EMILY R., b. NYC, Feb. 18, 1908; d. John and Emily Elizabeth (Roy) Cunningham; m. Andrew Martin Miltner, July 25, 1931 (dec. Feb. 16, 1982); 1 son: Donald. Author: poetry; working on collection of poems. Student Miller Business College (NYC), Writers Schl. (corr., CT). Mem. APA. Home: 470 Paradise Isle Blvd Hallandale FL 33009

MILTNER, ROBERT FRANCIS, b. Cleve., Feb 25, 1949; s. Eugene C. and Jeanne A. (Higgins) M.; m. Linda Ann Smith, Dec. 22, 1974; children—Alison Elizabeth, Ross Patrick. Author: (textbooks) British Literature I, 1984; World History I, 1985; World History II, 1986; World Culture and Geography, 1987; Catcher in the Rye Resource Unit, 1987. Contrbr. articles, poems to lit. mags., profl. jnls., anthols. Assoc. ed., contrbr.: TAP Social Studies Newsletter, 1986—. Wrkg. on chapbook, poetry manuscript, ednl. texts. B.A. in English, Xavier U., 1971; M. Ed., John Carroll U., 1987. English tchr. Holy Family High Sch., Denver, 1975-77, Padua High Sch., OH, 1977-87; coord. devel. edn. Kent State U.-Stark Campus, Canton, OH, 1987—. Summer writing fellow Center for Learning, Rocky River, OH, 1983-87; recipient Athenaeum Poetry prize Xavier U., 1971, Sweeney award in English, 1971. Home: 204 Beck Rd Avon Lake OH 44012

MILTON, BARBARA, b. St. Louis, Jan. 1, 1947, d. John Sutcliff and Winifred (Scully) M. Author: A Small Cartoon (stories), 1983; contrbr. fiction to Paris Rvw, Quarto, Sundog, other publs. BA, Manhattanville Coll., 1968; MEd, Harvard U., 1969. Tchr. math., cons. Manhattan Country Schl., NYC, 1973-85-, Cathedral Schl., NYC, 1985—. Recipient Pushcart prize, 1983; McDowell fellow, 1985. Home: 292 Riverside Dr New York NY 10025

MILTON, EDITH, b. Karlsruhe, Germany, May 31, 1931, came to U.S., 1946, d. Bruno and Helene (Heidingsfeld) Cohn; m. Jack Ryan Bownfield, Sept. 22, 1951 (div. 1956); m. 2d, Peter Winslow Milton, June 3, 1961; children—Jeremy Lawrence, Naomi Helen. Novelist: Corridors, 1967; contrbr. stories to Yale Rvw, Kenyon Rvw, Helicon Nine, Best Short Stories of 1982, others; contrbr. rvws., articles to Parnassus, N.Y. Times Book Rvw, New Republic, others. BA, CCNY, 1958; PhD, Yale U., 1964. Instr. CCNY, 1959, Md. Inst., Balt., 1961-67, Keene (N.H.) State Coll., 1972, 73, Community Edn., Peterborough, N.H., 1979, 80, 84—. MacDowell Colony fellow, Peterborough, 1981. Mem. P&W. Home: Box 237 Francestown NH 03043

MILTON, HILARY (HERBERT, b. Jasper, AL, April 2, 1920; s. Hilary Herbert and Erline (Moore) M.; m. Patty Sanders, Sept. 26, 1952; children: Michelle Sanders, David Rodgers. Author: Steps to Better Writing (instruction book), 1962, The Gitaway Box 9 novel), 1968, The House of God and Minnie Mae (novel), 1969, The Tipple Bell (novel), 1970, November's Wheel, 1976, Emergency! 10-33 on Channel 11! (novel), 1977, Nowhere to Run, 1978, Mayday! Mayday! (novel; filmed for television by the ABC network), 1979, The Longest Highway (novel), 1979, Blind Flight, 1980, Brats and Mr. Jack, 1980, Shutterbugs and Car Thieves, 1980, 1981, Tornado!. 1983, Two from the Dead (novel), 1983. Plot-It-Yourself-Horror Series: Craven House Horrors, 1982, Nightmare Store, 1982, Space Age Terrors, 1983, Horror Hotel, 1983, Escape from High Doom, 1984, Fun House Terrors, 1984, Museum of the Living Dead, 1985, Dungeon Demons, 1985. Au of writing instuction manuals. Contrbr of articles on U.S. space activities to encyclopedias. Contrbr of articles to educational and government publications. Attended Ala. Polytechnic Inst. (now Auburn Univ.), 1938, and Birmingham-Southern/Coll, 1939-40; AB, Univ of Ala., 1948, MA, 1949. Instr in business wrting, Univ of Ala., Tuscaloosa, 1948-51; civilian educational specialist in Montgomery, Ala., U.S. Dept of the Air Force, 1951-52, information specialist in St. Louis, Mo., 1952-55, editorial dir, Washington, D.C., 1955-56, speech writer in Washington, D.C., 1956-62; report writer, Natl Aeronautics and Space Administration, Washington, D.C., 1962-70 full-time researcher and witer, 1970-71; writer-in-residence, Samford Univ, Birmingham, Ala., 1970-84; writer, 1984—. Spcl lectr at George Washington Univ, 1960. Member: Alabama Acad of Distinguished Authors. November's Wheels named most notable book for 1976 by the Ntl Council of Social Studies Children's Book Council; Mark Twain Awad, Charlie May Simon Award, Georgia Book Award, and Iowa Children's Choice Award nominations for Blind Flight; Juvenile Lit. Award, Ala. Libray Assn, 1983, for The Brats and M. Jack; Golden Archer Award, 1983, for Tornado! Military service: U.S. Amy Air Forces, 1942-45. Home: 3540 Oakdale Dr Birmingham AL 35223

MILTON, JOHN RONALD, (Christopher Garrard), b. Anoka, MN, May 24, 1924, s. John Peterson and Euphamia Alvera (Swanson) M.; m. Leonharda Allison Hinderlie, Aug. 3, 1946; 1 dau., Nanci Lynn. Author: The Loving Hawk (poetry), 1961, Western Plains (poetry), 1964, The Tree of Bones, 1965, This Lonely House, 1968, Conversations with Frank Waters, 1971, Oscar Howe: The Story of an American Indian (biography), 1972, The Tree of Bones and Other Poems, 1973, Conversations with Frederick Manfred, 1974, Crazy Horse: The Story of an American Indian (biography), 1974, The Blue Belly of the World, 1974, Notes to a Bald Buffalo (novel), 1976, South Dakota: A Bicentennial History, 1977, The Novel of the American West (criticism), 1980; ed.: Three West, 1970, American Indian II, 1971, The Literature of South Dakota, 1976; contrbr.: Critical Essays on the Western American Novel, 1980, Siouxland Heritage, 1982, Great Plains Poetry Anthology, 1982, Encyclopedia of Frontier and Western Fiction, 1983, Green Isle in the Sea, 1986, numerous others; author intro. to books on Western heritage. Founder, editor, South Dakota Rvw, 1963—. Chmn. Dakota Press, U. S.D., 1968-81. BA, U. Minn., 1948, MA, 1951; PhD, U. Denver, 1961. Instr. Augsburg Coll., Mpls., 1949-57; assoc. prof., then prof. Jamestown (N.D.) Coll., 1957-63; prof. English U. S.D., Vermillion, 1963—. Served with U.S. Army, 1943-46; PTO. Hill Fdn. grantee, 1966, 69, 70, 71; Helene Wurlitzer Fdn. fellow, Taos, N.Mex., 1965; NEA fellow, 1976; recipient Gov.'s Award, S.D. Arts Council, 1978, Western America award for achievement, 1984, S.D. Arts Cncl. Fiction Fellowship, 1987. Mem. Western Lit. Assn. (pres. 1971), Delta Phi Lambda. Home: 630 Thomas St Vermillion SD 57069

MILTON, WILHELM, see Linser, Paul William

MINAHAN, JOHN ENGLISH, b. Albany, NY, Apr. 30, 1933; s. John English and Constance Madeline (Langdon) M.; m. Verity Ann Hill, Apr. 27, 1966. Author: novels A Sudden Silence, 1963, The Passing Strange, 1965, Jeremy, 1973, Sorcerer, 1977, Nine/Thirty/Fifty-Five, 1977, Almost Summer, 1978, Nunzio, 1978, The Complete American Graffiti, 1979, Eyewitness, 1981, The Great Hotel Robbery, 1982, The Great Diamond Robbery, 1983, Mask, 1984, The Face Behind the Mask, 1985, The Great Pyramid Robbery, 1987, The Great Harvard Robbery, 1987; biography The Dream Collector, 1972; translation from French The Fabulous Onassis, 1972; screenplays A Sudden Silence, 1965; The Passing Strange, 1979; TV play First Flight, 1968; contbg. editor book and theater revs.: Miami Herald, 1983—; also articles in N.Y. Times, Saturday Rev., Time-Life Spcl. Reports. Student, Cornell U., 1955-57, Harvard U., 1957-58, Columbia U., 1958-60. Staff writer Time mag., 1960-61; chief TV writer J. Walter Thompson Co., NYC, 1961-65; freelance writer, NYC, 1965-73, Los Angeles, 1976-79; editor, pub. American Way mag., NYC, 1973-76; contrbg. editor Los Angeles mag., 1978-79; cons. Universal-MCA Inc., 1976-79. Recipient Doubleday award, 1960. Mem. Natl. Soc. Lit. and Arts. Address: c/o J. L. Mairs/Norton 500 Fifth Ave New York NY 10110

MINCZESKI, JOHN, . Author (poetry): The Spiders, 1979, The Reconstruction of Light, 1981. Wrkg. on chapbook of poems on Judy Garland; recently completed vol. poetry: Kinds of Flight. Writer-in-the-schl. COMPAS, St. Paul, 1975—. Fellow and grantee, Minn. State Arts Bd., 1976, 79; Bush Fdn. fellow, St Paul, 1982; NEA fellow, 1984, Loft/McKnight award for prose, 1986. Address: 1300 Dayton St St Paul MN 55104

MINER, ROBERT GORDON, b. Blue Island, IL, Jan. 29, 1923; s. Glen Ernest and Catherine (Leytze) M.; m. Betty Anne Clegg, May 23, 1944; children: Patricia L. (Mrs. Vaughn E. Clark), Stephen C., David N. Author: Handbook of Gardening, 1966, Complete Gardening Guide, 1969; Student, Knox Coll., 1941-42; MBA, U. Chgo., 1950; grad., U.S. Army Command and Gen. Staff Coll., 1968. Payroll auditor Employers Group Ins. Cos., 1946-49; advt. salesman Cole & Mason (pubs. reps.), 1949-54, partner, 1955-56; asst. pub. Flower Grower mag., Williams Press, 1956-61, pub., 1961-67; owner Media Design Assoc., Westport, Conn., 1967-71; pres. Early Am. Soc., Inc. (pub. Early Am. Life), Harrisburg, Pa., 1971-81; owner, pub. Old Main Books, 1981—. Served from 2d lt. to capt. AUS, 1942-46; col. Res. ret. Decorated Bronze Star. Home: 74 W Main St Mechanicsburg PA 17055

MINER, VALERIE, b. NYC, Aug. 28, 1947; d. John Daniel and Mary Gill (McKenzie) M. Author: (novels) Blood Sisters, 1982; Movement, 1982; Murder in the English Department, 1983; Winter's Edge, 1985, All Good Women, 1987; co-author: Tales I Tell My Mother, 1978; Her Own Woman, 1985; More Tales, 1986; contrbr. stories, essays and rvws. to N.Y. Times, Saturday Rvw, Christian Sci. Monitor, Ms, Mademoiselle, Conditions, other jnls. BA, U. Calif., Berkeley, 1969, MA, 1970. Wrtr., 1970—; lectr. univs. and colls., 1970—, U. Calif., Berkeley, 1977—. Council on Ednl. Devel. grantee, 1977, 79, 82, 83; NEH grantee, 1981. Mem. PEN (freedom to write com. 1983—), NBCC, NWU, MLA. Office: 301 Campbell Hall U Calif Berkeley CA 94720

MINES, JEANETTE MARIE, b. Chamberlain, SD, Sept. 9, 1948; d. Leo Francis and Anna Elizabeth (Leiferman) M.; m. John J. Ryan, Aug.14, 1971 (div. June 12, 1985); 1 dau., Marie. Author: Reckless, 1983, Another Chance, 1985, Misjudged, 1986, Risking It, 1988. B.A. Coll.

St. Theresa, 1970; M.Ed., U. Ill., 1978. Tchr. Proviso West High Schl., Hillside, IL, 1977-83; lectr. U. Ill., Chgo., 1984-87, Loyola U., Chgo., 1987—. Mem. Ind. Wrtrs. Chgo., CRRT, NOW. Home 800 S Wesley Oak Park IL 60304

MINNFEE, EDNA MAE, b. Warren, TX, Apr. 3, 1936, d. Shaw Whittie and Lydia Mae (Baltimore) Moore; m. Lester Walker, Sept. 15, 1951 (div. 1970); children—Linda Marie, Lester Jr.; m. 2d, Maurice Loyce Minnfee, Feb. 16, 1973. Author: That Great Year 2001, 1982. Lyricist Three Star Gold, Richmond, Calif., 1977—; wrtr., composer Am. Song Festival, 1981—, High Voltage Band, 1984—. Home: 168 9th St Richmond CA 94801

MINOT, STEPHEN, b. Boston, May 27, 1927, s. William and Elizabeth (Chapman) M.; m. Mollie Lowrance (div.); 1 child, Stephen Reid; m. Virginia Stover, 1955; children—Nicholas William, Chrystos. Author: Chill of Dusk, 1964, Crossings, Stories by Stephen Minot, 1975, Ghost Images, 1979, Surviving the Flood, 1981, Three Genres, The Writing of Poetry, Fiction, and Drama, 1965, 4th ed., 1987, Reading Fiction, 1984; contrbr. short stories to The Atlantic, Harpers, Kenyon, Va. Quarterly, Sewanee, Paris, So., N.Am., Mo., Am. Poetry rvws, Redbook, Playboy, Carleton Miscellany, Ploughshares, Qtly Rvw Lit., Antaeus, also included in O. Henry Prize Stories, The Best Am. Short Stories. AB, Harvard U., 1951; MA, Johns Hopkins U., 1955. Instr., asst. prof. Bowdoin Coll., 1955-58; asst. prof. U. Conn., Hartford, 1958-59; asst. prof., assoc. prof., prof. Trinity Coll., Hartford, 1959-81; wrtr.-in-residence Johns Hopkins U., 1974-75. Served with USAAF, 1944-45. Recipient Atlantic First award Atlantic Monthly, 1962; Eugene F. Saxton Meml. Fdn. fellow, 1963; NEA fellow for writing, 1976-77, 81-82. Home: 69 Hickory Hill Rd Simsbury CT 06070

MINSHULL, RUTH ELLEN, b. Battle Creek, MI, Oct. 9, 1926; d. Vernon Bradley and Lora Minerva (Percy) Convis; m. Robert Minshull, June 5, 1948 (div. 1965); children—Paul R., Lee S. Works include: Miracles for Breakfast, 1968, How to Choose Your People, 1972, Ups and Downs, 1974, How to Cure the Selfish, Destructive Child, 1978, Logic Puzzles, 1980, The Secrets of Making Layouts for QuickPrinting, 1982, Free Money! How to Win Sweepstakes—According to the Judges, 1985. Student, Albion Coll., 1946-47. Office: Box 117 Northport MI 49670

MINTON, JOHN DEAN, b. Cadiz, KY, July 29, 1921 John Ernest and Daisy Dean (Wilson) M.; m. Betty Jo Redick, June 8, 1947; children: John Dean, James Ernest. Author: The New Deal in Tennessee, 1932-1938, 1979; contbr. articles to profl. jnls. AB in Edn, U. Ky., 1943, MA in History, 1947; Ph.D., Vanderbilt U., 1959. Instr. history U. Miami, Fla., 1951; tchr. Broward County Pub. Schl. System, U. Miami evening div., 1951-53; prin. Trigg County (Ky.) High Schl., 1953-58; prof. history Western Ky. U., Bowling Green, 1958—, dean Grad. Coll., 1964-71, v.p. for adminstrv. affairs, 1970-79, interim pres., 1979, v.p. for student affairs, 1981—. Served with USNR, 1943-46. Mem. NEA, Ky. Edn. Assn., So. Hist. Assn., Ky. Hist. Soc., Bowling Green C. of C. (bd. dirs.), Phi Alpha Theta, Phi Eta Sigma, Kappa Delta Pi. Home: 645 Ridgecrest Dr Bowling Green KY 42101

MINTY, JUDITH, b. Detroit, Aug. 5, 1937; d. Karl Jalmer and Margaret (Hunt) Makinen; m. Edgar Sheldon Minty; children: Lora Ann, John Reed, Ann Sheldon. Author: Lake Songs and Other Fears, 1974, Yellow Dog Jnl, 1979, Letters to My Daughters, 1980, In the Presence of Mothers, 1981, Counting the Losses, 1986; contrbr. articles, stories and poetry to Atlantic Monthly, Seneca Rvw, Ladies' Home Jnl, Barat Rvw, Poetry, Hawaii Rvw, others. BS, Ithaca Coll.; MA, W. Mich. U., 1973. Vis. poet Central Mich. Univ., Mt. Pleasant, 1978-79, Interlochen Center, 1980-81, Univ. Calif., Santa Cruz, 1981-82; vis. assoc. prof. Syracuse Univ., NY, 1979-80; assoc. prof. Humboldt State Univ., Arcata, Calif., 1982—. Mem. PSA, P&W, AWP, NCTE, PEN. Address: Dept Eng Humboldt St U Arcata CA 95221

MIRABELLA, GRACE, b. Maplewood, NJ, June 10, 1930; d. Anthony and Florence (Bellofatto) M.; m. William G. Cahan, Nov. 24, 1974. B.A. Skidmore Coll., 1950. Mem. exec. trng. program Macy's, NYC, 1950-51; mem. fashion dept. Saks Fifth Ave., NYC, 1951-52; with Vogue mag., NYC, 1952-54, 56—, assoc. editor, 1965-71, editor-in-chief, 1971—; mem. pub. relations staff Simonetta & Fabiani, Rome, Italy, 1954-56; hon. bd. dirs. Catalyst; lectr. New Schl. Social Research. Adv. bf. Columbia Schl. Journalism. Recipient Outstanding Grad. Achievement award Skidmore Coll., 1972. Mem. Women's Forum N.Y. Office: Vogue 350 Madison Ave New York NY 10017

MIRSKY, MARK JAY, b. Boston, Aug. 11, 1939; s. Wilfred Saul and RuthSylvia (Lessler) M.; m. Kinger Channah Grytting, Sept. 1, 1980; children: Israel, Ruth Sylvia. Author: Thou Worm Jacob, 1967, Proceedings of the Rabble, 1971, Blue Hill Avenue, 1972, The Secret Table, 1975; essayist: My Search for the Messiah, 1977. BA, Harvard Coll., 1961; MA, Stanford U., 1965. Lectr. CCNY, 1965-66, lectr. to asst., 1967-70, 70-74, assoc. prof., 1975-80, prof. English, 1980—, dir. MA in English, 1978-84. Editor: Fiction Mag., NYC, 1972-84. Founding mem. Tchrs. and Writers, NYC, 1967, The Fiction Collective, 1974; bd. cons. CCLM, 1974-75. Served with USAFR, 1962-68. Woodrow Wilson Found. fellow, 1961-62; NEH sr. fellow, 1981-82; Creative Artists Pub. Service Program fellow, 1982-83; recipient editor's award NEA-CCLM, 1980. Mem. PEN. Office: CCNY Convent Ave & 38th St New York NY 10031

MIRTSOPOULOS, CHRISTOS, (Christos Konstantinos Ziros), b. Danbury, CT, May 5, 1947, s. Pantelis and Irene Cula (Zirou) M. Wrkg. on nonfiction detective stories, children's book, sci. fiction-fantasy stories. BFA, Pratt Inst., 1969, MFA, 1975; assoc. ed. Reese Pub., Inc., NYC, Official Detective Stories mag., Master Detective mag., True Detective mag., 1971-82; mng. ed. Reese Communications, Inc., NYC, on same magazines, 1982—. Home: 27-47 27th St Astoria NY 11102

MISFELDT, TERRY C., b. Chippewa Falls, WI, May 22, 1950; s. Clyde C. and Louise M. (Herman) M.; m. Kristine A. Kieffer, Nov. 23, 1979; children—Genevieve Louise, Gabrielle Leigh, Geoffrey Raymond. Writer/ed.: Link nwsltr., 1983—, The Concept nwsltr., 1983—, Future mag., 1979—, The Total Executive, 1984-85, The Badger, 1979; ed.: Springboard mag., 1985, Stress Endurance Manual, 1984; contrbr. to The Thorp Courier, 1976-79. BS, U. WI-La Crosse, 1972. Audiovisual trnee., I.T.T.Thorp Corp., Thorp, WI, 1973-75; photographer, Misfeldt Photography, Thorp, 1975-76; photojnlst. The Thorp Courier, 1976-79; mng. ed., Future, U.S. Jaycees, Tulsa, 1979-81, ed., 81-83, dir. pubns., 83—. Mem. IABC, Jaycees Intl. Trainer's Circle. Developer Time Block Mgt. Office: Jaycees 4 West 21st St Tulsa OK 74114

MISHLER, CLIFFORD LESLIE, b. Vandalia, MI, Aug. 11, 1939; s. Nelson Howard and Lily Mae (Young) M.; m. Sylvia M. Leer, Feb. 27, 1976; children: Sheila, Sharon, Susan. Student, Northwestern U., 1957-58. Author, pub., annl. edits. Annl. Studies U.S. and Can. Commemorative Medals and Tokens, 1958-63; assoc. editor Numismatic News, Krause Publs., Iola, Wis., 1963-64, editor, 1964-66, numismatic editor all publs., 1966-75, pub. all numismatic publs., 1975-78, exec. v.p., pub. all products, 1975—; mem. coins and medals adv. panel Am. Bicentennial Commn., 1976; mem. annl. assay Commn. U.S. Mint, 1973. Co-author: Standard Catalog of World Coins; contbr.: articles New Book Knowledge, annl., 1969-81. Life fellow Am. Numismatic Soc.; life mem. Am. Numismatic Assn. (Medal of Merit, 1983; Farran Zebbe distinguished svc. award, 1984), Token and Medal Soc. (editor jnl 1964-69, pres. 1976-78, Disting. Service award 1966, 80), mem. Soc. Intl. Numismatics (award of excellence, 1981). Home: 385 E State St Iola WI 54945

MISSEY, JAMES LAWRENCE, b. San Bernardino, CA, July 9, 1935; s. Lawrence William and Ida Lena (Rhodes) M.; m. Mary Jane Saunders, June 5, 1965 (div. Aug. 1975); 1 dau., Elizabeth Saunders; m. 2d, Catherine Ann Dugan, Dec. 27, 1980. Author: The Eve of Revolution: An Antiwar Memoir, 1985. Contrbr, fiction to lit. mag. BA, Pomona Coll., 1957; MA, U. Pa., 1959. PhD, 1963. Instr. English, Beloit Coll., Wis., 1962-64; asst. prof. English, Denison U., Granville, Ohio, 1964-66; asst. prof. to assoc. prof. English, U. Wis., Stevens Point, 1966—. Home: 818 Bukolt Ave St Stevens Point WI 54481

MISTRIC, MARY ANN, b. Opelousas, LA, Aug. 24, 1932; d. Russel and Mary (Nicko) Batalio; m. Carl L. Mistric, June 28, 1952; children—Julie Mistric Carter, Russel, Kathleen Mistric Gunby, Cory Paul, Jo Ann Mistric Caso. Contbr.: La. Lit. Legacy, L'Arpenteur Louisiane, New Beginnings, Better Days & Happy Endings. Poetry in anthologies. Wkg. on short story, novel. Student public schs., Opelousas. Mem. La. Wrtrs.' Guild (asst. dir. 1983—), So. Wrtrs.' Guild (co-ed. Write Right 1984—). Home: 4833 Southwind Dr Baton Rouge LA 70816

MITCHELL, BARBARA JOANNE, b. Clinton, IL, May 24, 1940; d. Merle and Dorothy Carlene (McBride) Edmiston: m. David Walter Mitchell, May 17, 1978. Columnist: The Northwest Herald, Crystal Lake, IL, 1985-87. Contrbr. articles to mags., newspapers including Chgo. Tribune, Ill. Mag., Capper's, others. B.A. with honors in History, Douglass Coll., 1982. Med. Transcriptionist Middlesex Genl. Univ. Hosp., New Bruswick, NJ, 1983-84, Spotswood, NJ, 1984-85; free-lance wrtr., 1985—. Mem. AAUW. Home: 441 Piedmont St Waterbury CT 06706

MITCHELL, BETTY JO, (BJ Mitchell), b. Coin, IA, May 2, 1931; m. John Lewis Mitchell, July 7, 1951 (div. 1963). Author: ALMS: A Budget Based Library Management System, 1983; co-author: Cost Analysis of Library Functions: A Total System Approach, 1978, How to See the U.S. on $12 a Day (Per Person, Double Occupancy), 1982; contrbr. to Library Effectiveness: A State of the Art, 1980; ed.: Yesterday's Lifestyles, Today's Survival: The Life of A Real

Ozark Mountain Hillbilly, 1983. BA, Southwest Mo. State U., 1952; MLS, U. So. Calif., Los Angeles, 1967. Assoc. dir. libraries Calif. State U., Northridge, 1971-81; owner, pub. Viewpoint Press, Tehachapi, Calif., 1981—; mgr. info. systems rent control bd. City of Santa Monica, Calif., 1984—. Mem. ALA. Home: 135 31st St Hermosa Beach CA 90254

MITCHELL, ENID, b. Shawnee, OH, Sept. 21, 1919; d. Charles Thomas and Hazel (Robertson) Mitchell. Ed., Contrbr.: Gift From My Mother (by Hazel Robertson Mitchell), 1965; contrbr. poetry: Scimitar and Song, Poetry Press, Am. Poetry Showcase 1985, Best New Poets of 1986, numerous others. Wrkg. on psychic jnl., poetry, plays. Student Ohio State U., 1946. Home: 1665 Summit St Columbus OH 43201

MITCHELL, LOFTEN, b. Columbus, NC, Apr. 15, 1919; s. Ulysses Sanford and Willia (Spaulding) M.; m. Helen Marsh, Sept. 30, 1948; 2 sons. Playwright: Blood in the Night, performed 1946, A Land Beyond the River, performed 1957, Star of the Morning (story of Black entertainer, Bert Williams), Cartoons for a Lunch Hour, 1978, (with Irving Burgie) Ballad for Bimshire; musical, produced on Broadway, 1963-64; Produced: plays Harlem Showcase; Author: Black Drama: The Story of the American Negro in the Theater, 1967, The Stubborn Old Lady, 1972, Voices of Black Theatre, 1975, Bubbling Brown Sugar, 1975; contbr. radio scripts, screenplays, articles on theatre to mags., newspapers. Studied playwriting at CCNY, 1937-38; grad., Talladega (Ala.) Coll., 1943; postgrad. in playwriting, Columbia U., 1947-51. Formerly social investigator Dept. Welfare, NYC; tchr. State U. N.Y., Binghamton. Served with USNR. Recipient Guggenheim award for creative writing, 1958-59; Rockefeller Fdn. grantee, 1961; Harlem Cultural Com. award, 1969. Mem. DG, Am. Soc. African Culture, NAACP. Office: 3217 Burrie Rd Vestal NY 13850

MITCHELL, MARIA, b. Chgo., d. William Carl and Marie (Prunty) Mitchell; m. James E. Hayes, July 1969; children—James Justin, William. Contrbr. short stories to N.Am. Rvw, Ball State U. Forum, Newstories, other lit mags. Wrkg. on novel. BA, U. Ill., 1967. Promotions and public relations wrtr. CBS Chgo., public relations wrtr. J. Walter Thompson, Chgo. Honorable mtn. WD fiction contest, 1986, The Conn. Wrtr., 1987. Mem. PEN Midwest, P&W. Home: 431 Sheridan Rd Kenilworth IL 60043

MITCHELL, PAUL DAVID, b. Feb. 11, 1959; s. Charles Ray and Beverly Jean (Barham) M. Ed.: The Tearsheet, 1982-83, World Dredging & Marine Construction Mag., 1984—. BA in Communics., Cal. State-Fullerton, 1982. Editorial asst. Orange County Register, Santa Ana, CA, 1982-83; assoc. ed., World Dredging Mag., Irvine, CA, 1983-84, ed., 1984—. Home: 1433 Superior Newport Beach CA 92663

MITCHELL, ROBERT WAYNE, (John Quatrain, Buick MacRane), b. Los Angeles, May 31, 1950; s. Ralph Miles and Evelyn Lucille (Porter) M.; m. Ann Elizabeth St. John, Aug. 14, 1976; children—Navid Sean, Ian Mathew, Bahiyyih Luz, Nathan Ezra. Contrbr. poems to anthols. Contrbg. ed. Weather Report, Ecce Homo. Student Moorpark Coll., Calif. Mem. Ruidoso WG, Alamo Writers Bloc (founder). Home: 1006 Indian Wells Rd Alamogordo NM 88310

MITCHELL, ROGER, b. Boston, Feb. 8, 1935, s. Roger and Virginia (Garrett) M.; m. Sally Hayden, Feb. 15, 1959 (div. 1976); children—Molly, Bridget; m. 2d, Judith Roman, July 22, 1980. Author: Letters from Siberia and Other Poems, 1971, Moving, 1976, Homage to Beatrix Potter, 1978, To Recommend Renewal, 1984, A Clear Space on a Cold Day, 1986, Adirondack, 1987. AB, Harvard U., 1957; PhD, Manchester (Eng.) U., 1963. Ed., pub. Minn. Rvw, Bloomington, Ind., 1973-81; prof. English Ind. U., Bloomington, 1975—; dir. Ind. U. Wrtrs.' Conf., 1975-85. Recipient Borestone Mountain award, 1973; PEN Intl. award, 1977; Lilly Fellowship, 1985; NEA Creative Writing Fellowship, 1986. Mem. AWP. Home: 1010 E 1st St Bloomington IN 47401

MITCHELL, W.J.T., b. Anaheim, CA, Mar. 24, 1942; s. Thomas Miles and Leona Marie (Gaertner) M.; m. Janice Misurell, Aug. 11, 1968; children: Carmen, Gabriel. B.A., Mich State U., 1963; M.A., Johns Hopkins U., Ph.D., 1968. Asst. prof. Ohio State U., Columbus, 1968-73, assoc. prof., 1973-77; prof. English art and design U. Chgo., 1977—; prof. Schl. Criticism and Theory Northwestern U., Evanston, Ill., 1983; vis. prof., Univ. of Canterbury, Christ/church, NZ, 1987; editor Critical Inquiry U. Chgo. Press. 1978—. Author: Blake's Composite Art, 1978, Iconology, 1986; editor: Language of Images, 1980 (outstanding issue of a learned jnl Conf. Editors Learned Jnls 1981), On Narrative, 1982, Politics of Interpretation, 1983, Against Theory, 1985. NEH fellow, 1976, 86; Guggenheim fellow, 1982; Am. Philo. Soc. grantee, 1967, 72, mem. MLA, Am. Soc. 18th Century Studies, Conf. Editors Learned Jnls, Johnson Soc., PEN, Acad. of Lit. Studies. Office: Dept Eng U Chgo 1050 E 59th St Chicago IL 60637

MITCHELL, WILLIAM RICHARD, b. McLoud, OK, Dec. 3, 1930; s. Thomas Weley and Nancy Elizabeth (Gregg) M.; m. Dorthy Faye Miller, June 19, 1949; children—Michael Anthony, Danie Richard, Janet Elaine Mitchell Thibodeau. Author: English in Faith—Learning Studies, 1973. Contrbr. poems to lit. mags., anthols.; fiction in anthol. B.A., Okla. City U., 1952; M.A., Boston U., 1957; Ph.D. U. Okla., 1969. Instr. to prof. Okla. Baptist U., Shawnee, 1953—, dean arts & scis., 1973-82. Served with U.S. Army, 1953-55. Mem. Conf. on Christianity & Lit., NCTE. Home: 4011 N Chapman Shawnee OK 74801

MITCHNER, GARY L., b. Middletown, OH, June 23, 1946, s. Richard Milton and Christine Louise (Newcomb) M.; m. Marilyn Ann La Bath, June 14, 1969; children—Natasha, Theodore, Therese. Ed. Western Ohio Jnl, 1980—; contrbr. poems to Shenandoah, Great Lakes Rvw, Cin. Poetry Rvw, others. BA, Wilmington Coll., 1967; MA, U. Mich., 1971. Instr. U. Cin., 1980—; prof. Sinclair Community Coll., Dayton, Ohio, 1971—. Recipient Elliston poetry award U. Cin., 1983. Mem. NCTE. Home: 108 Patterson Rd Dayton OH 45419

MITFORD, JESSICA, b. Batsford Mansion, Eng., Sept. 11, 1917; d. Lord and Lady Redesdale; m. Esmond Romilly, June 1937; 1 dau., Constancia; m. Robert Treuhaft, June 21, 1943; 1 son, Benjamin. Authur: autobiography Daughters and Rebels, 1960; The American Way of Death, 1963, The Trial of Dr. Spock, 1969, Kind and Usual Punishment—The Prison Business, 1973, A Fine Old Conflict, 1977, Poison Penmanship: The Gentle Art of Muckraking, 1979, Faces of Philip: A Memoir of Philip Toynbee, 1984. Address: 6411 Regent St Oakland CA 94618

MITGANG, HERBERT, b. NYC, Jan. 20, 1920; s. Benjamin and Florence (Altman) M.; m. Shirley Kravchick, May 13, 1945; children: Esther, Lee, Laura. Writer, producer: film documentaries including Henry Moore: Man of Form, D-Day Plus 20 Years, Sandburg's Prairie Years, Anthony Eden on Vietnam; Author: Lincoln as They Saw Him, 1956; novel The Return, 1959; The Man Who Rode the Tiger: The Life and Times of Judge Samuel Seabury, 1963 (Gavel award ABA), Working for the Reader, 1970; novel Get These Men Out of the Hot Sun, 1972; The Fiery Trial: A Life of Lincoln, 1974; novel The Montauk Fault, 1981; novel Kings in the Counting House, 1983; Editor: Washington, D.C. in Lincoln's Time, 1958, Civilians Under Arms: Stars and Stripes, Civil War to Korea, 1959, The Letters of Carl Sandburg, 1968, America at Random, 1969, Spectator of America, 1971, Abraham Lincoln: A Press Portrait, 1971; play Mister Lincoln, 1980; contbr. to New Yorker, Art News, The Nation, The Progressive. L.L.B., St. John's Law Schl., 1942. Bar: N.Y. bar 1942. Screen writer Universal-Intl. Pictures, 1945; copy editor, reviewer N.Y. Times, NYC, 1945-54; supervising editor Sunday Times drama sect., 1955-62; editorial writer, mem. editorial bd. N.Y. Times, 1963-64, 67-76, publishing, cultural corr., 1976—; asst. to pres., exec. editor CBS News, 1964-67. Mem. exec. bd. Newspaper Guild of N.Y., CIO, 1948-49. Army corr., mng. editor Stars and Stripes, Oran-Casablanca and Sicily edit., 1943-45, six battle stars, Knight, Order of Merit (Italy). Fellow Soc. Am. Historians; mem. AL (council 1962—, pres. fund 1976—), AG (pres. 1971-75), Internat. PEN. Office: NY Times 229 W 43rd St New York NY 10036

MITTELMARK, ABRAHAM, b. NYC, Sept. 26, 1926; s. Joseph and Minnie (Weintraub) M.; m. Janice Francis Smith, Dec. 15, 1949 (div. 1984); children—Margo Ann, June Lisa; m. 2d, Anna Armida Vanacore, April 6, 1985; 1 dau., Alyson. Tech. editor: CIBA Pharmaceutical, Summit, N.J., 1960-64; newsletter editor: N.J. Acad. of Sci., 1960-69. BA, N.Y. U., 1950; postgrad. Bklyn. Coll., 1950-53. Med. wrtr. Warner-Chilcott, Morris Plains, N.J., 1964-67; copywriter Benton & Bowles, NYC, 1972-74; freelance wrtr. in advt., North Plainfield, N.J., 1967-72, Califon, N.J., 1974—. Served U.S. Army, 1945-46, Phillipines campaign, sgt., medical corps. Mem. Am. Med. Wrtrs. Assn., 1956-72. Home: RD 2 Box 29 Califon NJ 07830

MIULLO, NATHANIEL JEROME, b. Utica, NY, Sept. 14, 1957; s. Nathaniel Joeseph and Mary Teresa (Curri) M.; m. Carol Lynne Higgins, Dec. 4, 1986. Contrbr. articles to profl. jnls. Wrkg. on short stories, environmental technical articles, poetry, interviews with govt. officials. B. Engineering, SUNY Maritime, 1979. Marine engineer Cleveland Cliffs' Iron Ore Co., Cleve., 1979-80; environmental engineer U.S. Environmental Protection Agy., Denver, 1981—. Author of first hazardous waste treatment permit in U.S.A. Recipient Bronze medal U.S. Environmental Protection Agy., 1983. Mem. Air Pollution Control Assn., Soc. Naval Architects Marine Engineers, Natl. Geographic Soc., Natl. Arbor Day Fdn. Home: 506 E Oak St Lafayette CO 80026

MIZE, JOE HENRY, b. Colorado City, TX, June 14, 1934; s. Kelly Marcus and Birtie (Adams) M.; m. Betty Bentley, Mar. 16, 1966; 1 dau., Kelly Jean. Author: (with J.G. Cox) Essentials of Simulation (translated into Japanese

1970), 1968, Prosim V: Instructor's Manual, 1971, Student's Manual, 1971, (with C.R. White and George H. Brooks) Operations Planning and Control, 1971, (with J.L. Kuester) Optimization Techniques with Fortran, 1973, (with W.C. Turner and K.E. Case) Introduction to Industrial and Systems Engineering, 1978 (named Book of Yr., Am. Inst. Indsl. Engrs. 1979); editor: (with J. Fabrycky) Prentice Hall International Series in Industrial and Systems Engineering, 1972—. BS in Indsl. Engring, Tex. Tech. Coll., 1958; MS (Research Found. grantee) in Indsl. Engring, Purdue U., 1963, PhD, 1964. Indsl. engr. White Sands Missile Range, N.Mex., 1958-61; assoc. prof. engring. Auburn (Ala.) U., 1964-69, dir. 1965-66; prof. engring. Ariz. State U., Tempe, 1969-72; prof., head Sch. Indsl. Engring. and Mgmt. Okla. State U., Stillwater, 1972-80, dir. Univ. Ctr. for Energy Research, 1980—; various mfg. firms, 1964—. Mem. Am. Inst. Indsl. Engrs. (exec. v.p. 1978-80, pres. 1981-82), Natl. Soc. Profl. Engrs., Inst. Mgmt. Scis., Council Indsl. Engring. Acad. Dept. Heads (chmn. 1976-76). Office: Ctr for Energy OK State U Stillwater OK 74078

MIZE, SHIRLEY J., b. Jacksonville, AL; d. Zebbie A. and Emily (Burgess) Johnston; one daughter, two sons. Author: Time Changes Everything, 1979. Contrbr. poems to anthols. Wrkg. on La. hist. fiction book, book about Tenn. horse farm, children's short stories. Grad. public schls., Jacksonville. Recipient Best Short Story award Bama Wrtrs. lub, 1967. Mem. Broadcast Musi Inc. Home: Decatur AL 35601

MOCK, JESSE ALEXANDER, JR, b. Forsyth County, NC, Sept. 17, 1920; s. Julius Alexander and Edna Elizabeth (Walker) M.; m. Dorothy Jeane Moreland, Oct. 11, 1947; children: Jeffrey Arden, Deverie Jeane, Danci Noella, Jon Adlai. A.B. in Journalism, U. N.C., 1947. Washington corr. various newspapers and radio stas., 1947-51, McGraw-Hill Pub. Co., 1951—; successively asst. to editor, prodn. editor, sr. editor Elec. World mag., 1953-70; assoc. editor to editor-in-chief Elec. Week newsletter, 1970-83; editor books on engring. ethics, civil def., natl. security. Peace activist, draft counselor. Recipient Jessie H. Neal award for editorial excellence in bus. journalism, 1961. Mem. Natl. Press Club. Home: 46 Skyland Dr Pisgah Forest NC 28768

MODIC, STANLEY JOHN, b. Fairport Harbor, OH, Dec. 29, 1936; s. Frank and Mary (Zakrajsek) M.; m. Albina DiMichele, May 27, 1961; children: Mark Francis, Laurel Marie. B.S. in Commerce, Ohio U., 1958. Reporter The Telegraph, Painesville, Ohio, 1960-63, city editor, 1964-65; asst. editor Steel Mag., Cleve., 1965-67, news editor, 1968-70, Industry Week (formerly Steel Mag.), Cleve., 1970-72, exec. editor, 1972, editor, 1972—. Municipal clk. Fairport Harbor, 1960-61; Mem. ASME, Am. Soc. Bus. Press Editors, Am. Fedn. Musicians, Sigma Delta Chi (pres. Cleve. chpt. 1975-76), Press Club of Cleveland. Home: 5842 Woodhill St Painesville OH 44077

MODICA, TERRY ANN, b. Bethlehem, PA, Feb. 27, 1955; d. Donald Raymond and Pamela Elaine (Gilmore) Repsher; m. Ralph Edward Modica, Nov. 28, 1975; children—David Ralph, Tammy Christina. Author: Press Your Way to Better Health with Body Buttons, 1984, How to Get Free Advertising, 1986. Contrbr. articles to mags. Editor: Diocesan newsletter, Trenton Diocese, N.J., 1981-82, Cath. Ch. newsletter, Freehold, N.J., 1985-86. Student Albright Coll., 1973-74, New Paltz U., 1974-75. Free-lance wrtr., proml. cons., Freehold and Jackson, 1982—. Team leader Worldwide Marriage Encounter, Trenton Diocese, 1984-85. Mem. St. Davids Christian Wrtr.'s Assn., IWWG, Natl. Evang. Wrtrs.' Soc. Home: RD 4 340 Pfister Rd Jackson NJ 08527

MOEBIUS, WILLIAM, b. Milwaukee, WI, Sept. 22, 1941; s. Carl W. and Janet (Smith) Moebius; m. Miriam Rutherford, June 27, 1964 (div. 1983); children—Corinna, Matthew, Margaret; m. 2d, Pamela Esler, July 28, 1985. Author: Elegies and Odes, 1969. Poems in New Poetry Anthology, 1969, Niagara Frontier Rvw, Panache, other lit mags; translation: Oedipus at Colonus in An Anthology of Greek Tragedy, 1972, poetry of Philodemus, Hedylus, and Killactor, in The Greek Anthology, 1974. BA, Lawrence U., 1963; PhD,SUNY at Buffalo, 1970. Assoc. prof., U. of Mass., Amherst, 1971-85. Mem. Children's Lit. Assoc., PSA, NCTE, Am. Comp. Lit. Assoc., Am. Guild of Organists. Home: 544 Bay Rd South Amherst MA 01002

MOFFITT, JOHN, b. Harrisburg, PA, June 27, 1908, s. John Jordan and Edith Victoria (Kelker) M. Author: (poems) This Narrow World, 1958, The Living Seed, 1962, Adam's Choice, 1967, Escape of the Leopard, 1974, Signal Message, 1982, Journey to Gorakhpur: An Encounter with Christ beyond Christianity, 1972, The Road to Now, 1982; ed., contrbr. A New Charter for Monasticism, 1970; contrbr. poems to America, Antioch, Kenyon, Saturday, Sewanee, Va. Qtly rvws, Atlantic Monthly, Chelsea, Modern Age, Prairie Schooner, others; contrbr. articles on mysticism and interreligious ecumenism to Ethics, Theol. Studies, America, Christian Century, Catholic World, Am. Ecclesiastical Rvw, Cistercian Studies, Vita Monastica, others. AB, Princeton U., 1928; grad. in composition Curtis Inst. Music, 1932. Novice, monk Ramakrishna Order of India, N.Y., 1933-35, 39-63; copy ed., poetry ed. America mag., NYC, 1963-70, poetry ed., 1970—. Address: c/o Am Mag 106 W 56 St New York NY 10019

MOHLENBROCK, ROBERT HERMAN, JR, b. Murphysboro, IL, Sept. 26, 1931; s. Robert Herman and Elsie (Treece) M.; m. Beverly Ann Kling, Oct. 19, 1957; children: Mark William, Wendy Ann, Trent Alan. Author: A Flora of Southern Illinois, 1957, Plant Communities of Southern Illinois, 1963, Ferns of Illinois, 1967, Flowering Plants of Illinois: Flowering Rush to Rushes, 1970, Flowering Plants of Illinois: Lilies to Orchids, 1970, Grasses of Illinois, 1972, 73, Forest Trees of Illinois, 1973, Guide to the Vascular Flora of Illinois, 1975, Spring Wildflowers of Carlyle-Rend-Shelbyville Lakes, 1975, Sedges of Illinios, 1976, Hollies to Loasas in Illinois, 1978, Distribution of Illinois Vascular Plants, 1968, Prairie Plants of Illinois, 1979, Hunter's Guide to Illinois Flowering Plants, 1980, Flowering Plants of Illinois: Willows to Mustards, 1980, You Can Grow Tropical Fruit Trees, 1980, Flowering Plants of Illinois: Magnolias to Pitcher Plants, 1981, Wildflowers of Roadside Fields and Open Habitats in Illinois, 1981, Giant City State Park, An Illustrated Handbook, 1981, Flowering Plants of Illinois: Basswoods to Spurges, 1982, Where Have All the Wildflowers Gone?, 1983, Field Guide to the U.S. National Forests,1984, Guide to the Vascular Flora of Illinois, rev. & enlarged ed., 1986, Flowering Plants of Illinois: Smartweeds to Birches, 1986, Macmillan's Field Guide to North American Wildflowers, 1987, . . . to North American Trees, 1987. BA, So. Ill. U., 1953; MS, 1954; PhD, Washington U., St. Louis, 1957. With dept. botany So. Ill. U., Carbondale, 1957—, chmn. dept., 1966-79, prof., 1966-85, disting. prof., 1985—. Trustee Ill. Nature Conservancy, Mo. Native Plant Soc.; mem. Ill. Nature Preserves Com. Mem. Am. Fern Soc., Assn. So. Biologists, So. Appalachian Bot. Club, chmn. No. Am. Plant Specialist Group, Species Survival Commn. Home: 1 Birdsong Dr Carbondale IL 62901

MOIR, ALFRED KUMMER, b. Mpls., Apr. 14, 1924; s. William Wilmerding and Blanche (Kummer) M. Author: (with others) Art in Italy, 1600-1700, 1965, The Italian Followers of Caravaggio, 2 vols, 1967, Caravaggio's Copyists, 1976, Caravaggio, 1982; editor: (with others) Seventeenth Century Italian Drawings in the Collection of Janos Scholz, 1974, European Drawings in the Santa Barbara Museum of Art, 1976, Regional Styles of Drawing in Italy 1600-1700, 1977, Old Master Drawings from the Feitelson Collection, 1983, Old Master Drawings from the Collection of John and Alice Steiner, 1985. AB, Harvard U., 1948, AM, 1949, PhD, 1953. Instr. to assoc. prof. Newcomb Coll., Tulane U., 1952-62; mem. faculty U. Calif. at Santa Barbara, 1962—, prof. art, 1964—, chmn. dept., 1963-69, dir. Edn. Abroad Program, Italy, 1978-80; art historian in residence Am. Acad. Rome, 1969-70, 80; Pres. So. Calif. Art Historians, 1964-66, 67-69; chmn. Tri-Counties Com. to Rescue Italian Art, 1967-68. Trustee Santa Barbara Free Sch., 1968-69; gov. Brooks Inst. Art Gallery, 1968-69; adj. curator, UCSB Art Museum, 1984—. Served with AUS, 1943-46. Mem. AAUP, Coll. Art Assn., Medeival Acad. Am., Soc. Archtl. Historians, Soc. Fellows of Am. Acad. in Rome, Ateneo Veneto (Venice). Address: Dept. Art Hist U Calif Santa Barbara CA 93106

MOISE, EDWIN EVARISTE, b. New Orleans, Dec. 22, 1918; s. Edwin Evariste and Annie Josephine (Boatner) M.; m. Mary Lorena Leake, May 28, 1942 (div. 1980); children: Edwin Evariste, Claire Mary. author: Elementary Geometry from an Advanced Standpoint, 1963, (with Floyd L. Downs, Jr.) Geometry, 1964, Number Systems of Elementary Mathematics, 1965, Calculus: Part I, 1966, Calculus: Part II, 1967, Geometric Topology in Dimensions 2 and 3, 1977, Introductory Problem Courses in Analysis and Topology, 1982. B.A. Tulane U., 1940; Ph.D. in Pure Math., U. Tex., 1947; M.A. (hon.), Harvard, 1960. From Asst. prof. to prof. math., U. of Mich., 1951-60; James Bryant Conant prof. edn. and math. Harvard U., 1960-71; Disting. prof. Queens Coll., CUNY, 1971-80, 81-87; Emeritus, 1987. Hudson prof. Auburn U., 1981-81; Temp. mem. Inst. Advanced Study, Princeton, 1949-51, 56-57. Served with USNR, 1942-46. Fellow AAAS; mem. Am. Math. Soc. (mng. editor bulltn. 1958-63, v.p. 1973-74), Math. Assn. Am. (v.p. 1965, pres. 1967-68), MLA. Home: 118-17 Union Turnpike Apt 16-B Forest Hills NY 11375

MOJTABAI, ANN GRACE, b. Bklyn., June 8, 1937, d. Robert and Naomi Cecelia (Friedman) Alpher; m. Fathollah Mojtabai, Apr. 1960 (div. 1966); children—Chitra, Ramin. Author: Mondome, 1974, The 400 Eels of Sigmund Freud, 1976, A Stopping Place, 1979, Autumn, 1982, Blessed Assurance, 1986. BA, Antioch Coll., 1958; MA, Columbia U., 1968, MLS, 1970. Lectr. philosophy CUNY, 1966-68; librarian CCNY, 1970-76; fellow Radcliffe Inst. Ind. Study, Cambridge, Mass., 1976-78; vis. asst. prof. English NYU, 1978; Briggs-Copeland lectr. in English Harvard U., Cambridge, 1978-83; wrtr.-in-residence U. Tulsa, 1983—. Guggenheim fellow, 1981-82; recipient Richard Hinda Rosenthal award AAIAL, 1983, Lillian Smith Award, So. Regional Council, 1986. Mem. Phi Beta Kappa, PEN, Mark Twain Soc. Home: 2102 S Hughes St Amarillo TX 79109

MOLD, HERMAN, see Baizer, Eric

MOLERO, WILSON JOSEPH, b. Verret Village, LA, Mar. 5, 1909; s. Charles Matthew and Camille (Nunez) M.; m. Annie Cecilia Webber; children—Wilson, Mary Anne. Poet, lyricist; poetry in anhologies. Student St. Bernard Parish Schs. Served with U.S. Army, 1942-45; ETO. Home: 74 W Claiborne Sq Chalmette LA 70043

MOLINE, JUDITH ANN, b. Chgo., Jan. 10, 1941, d. Robert William and Ella Louise (Morton) Moline: 1 child, Karl Ibrahim. Author: English For the Complementary Cycle in Lebanon, 4 vols., 1979-81, Paragraph Writing Made Easy, 1981, The Islamic Architecture of Lebanon (pamphlet), 1982; contrbr. to Kunst des Orients IX, XXI, a.a.r.p. XIII, Berytus XXVII, also others. Wrkg. on novel set in Middle East, short stories, poetry collection. BA, U. Calif., Santa Barbara, 1965; MA, NYU, 1967, Am. U. Beirut, 1975. Reading cons. Intl. Coll., Beirut, 1968-70, tchr., 1980-84; dir. learning lab. Beirut U. Coll., 1970-72; instr. Haigazian Coll., Beirut, 1973-75; lectr. Am. U. Beirut, 1975-80; mem. adj. faculty Syracuse U., N.Y., 1984-86. Home: 13001 Country Ridge Dr Germantown MD 20874

MOLITOR, GRAHAM THOMAS TATE, b. Seattle, Apr. 6, 1934; s. Robert Franklin and Louise Margaret (Graham) M.; m. Carlotta Jean Crate, July 30, 1960; children: Graham Thomas Tate, Anne Therese, Christopher Robert. Contrbg. editor: Food Tomorrow Newsletter, 1976-77, Focus on Tomorrow, 1970-77; bd. editors, Hudson Inst. Study of World Food Problems, 1975-77; assoc. ed.: Bus. Tomorrow Newsletter, 1977-79; bd. advs.: New Mktg. Technologies Monitor, 1983-85; co-ed.: A Look at Business in 1990—White Hs. Conf. on the Indsl. World Ahead, 1972. BS, U. Wash., 1955; LLB, Am. U., 1963. Bar: D.C. 1963. Legis. counsel U.S. Hs. of Reps., Washington, 1961-63; D.C. counsel, asst. dir. govt. relations Nabisco, Inc., Washington, 1964-70; dir. govtl. relations Gen. Mills Inc., Washington, 1970-77; pres. Pub. Policy Forecasting, Inc., 1977—. adj. prof. Grad. Schl. Bus., Am. U., Washington, 1969-75, 79—; mem. White House Adv. Com. on Social Indicators, 1975-76; del. White House Conf. on Youth, 1970; bd. dirs. First Global Conf. on the Future, Inc., Can., 1980—. Served to 1st lt. U.S. Army, 1958-61. Recipient Disting. Service award Grocery Mfrs. Am., 1973-74, Am. Mgmt. Assn., 1973. Mem Washington Bus.-Govt. Relations Council, World Future Soc. (v.p. & dir.) 1981—. Office: 9208 Wooden Bridge Rd Potomac MD 20854

MOLLENHOFF, CLARK RAYMOND, b. Burnside, IA., Apr. 16, 1921; s. Raymond Eldon and Margaret Pearl (Clark) M.; m. Georgia Giles Osmundson, Oct. 13, 1939 (div. Jan. 1978); children: Gjore Jean, Jacquelin Sue Mollenhoff Montgomery, Clark Raymond; m. Jane Cook Schurz, July 12, 1981. Author: Washington Cover-Up, 1962, Tentacles of Power, 1965, Despoilers of Democracy, 1965, The Pentagon, 1967, George Romney: Mormon in Politics, 1968, Strike Force, 1972, Game Plan for Disaster, 1976, The Man Who Pardoned Nixon, 1976, The President Who Failed, 1980, Investigative Reporting: From Courthouse to White House, 1981. Student, Webster City Jr. Coll., 1938-41; LL.B., Drake U., 1944, Harvard U., 1949-50; LL.D., Drake U., 1961, Iowa Wesleyan Coll., 1966, Simpson Coll., 1974. Bar: Iowa 1944, D.C. 1970, U.S. Supreme Ct. 1970, Fed. Ct. 1944. Washington bur. Cowles Publs., 1950-69; spl. counsel to Pres. U.S., 1969-70; bur. chief Des Moines Register, Washington, 1970-77; prof. journalism an law Washington and Lee U., Lexington, Va., 1976—; exchg. fellow, Univ. Coll., Oxford, 1980, 85. Served to lt. (j.g.) USNR, 1944-46. Recipient Heywood Broun award, 1956; Pulitzer prize for nat. reporting, 1958; William Allen White Meml. award U. Kansas, 1964; Soc. Profl. Journalists-Sigma Delta Chi fellow, 1980. Office: 207 Reid Hall Wash & Lee Lexington VA 24450

MOLNAR, THOMAS, b. Budapest, Hungary, June 26, 1921; s. Alexander and Aurelie (Blon) M. Author: Bernanos, His Political Thought and Prophecy, 1960, The Future of Education, 1961, The Decline of the Intelletual, 1962, The Two Faces of American Foreign Policy, 1962, Africa, A Political Travelogue, 1965, Utopia, the Perennial Heresy, 1967, Sartre, Ideologue of Our Time, 1968, Ecumenism or New Reformation?, 1968, The Counter-Revolution, 1969, La Gauche vue d'Animal politique, 1974, The European Dilemma, 1974, God and the Knowledge of Reality, 1974, Le Socialisme sans visage, 1976, Authority and Its Enemies, 1976, Christian Humanism, A Critique of the Secular City and its Ideology, 1978, Le modèle dé figuré, l 'Amérique de Tocqueville à Carter, 1978, Theists and Atheists, A Typology of Non-Belief, 1980, Politics and The State: A Catholic View, 1982, Le Dieu Immanent, 1982, Tiers-Monde, Idéologie, Réalité, 1982, L'Eclipse du Sacre, 1986, The Pagan Temptation, 1987. M.A. in French Lit., Université de Bruxelles, 1948, M.A. in Philosophy, 1948; Ph.D., Columbia U., 1952; PhD Honoris Causa, U. Mendoza (Argentina), 1986. Prof. French and world lit. Bklyn. Coll., 1957—; adj. prof. European intellectual history L.I.U., 1967—; guest prof. poli. philosophy Potchefstroom U., South Africa, 1969; guest prof. philosophy Hillsdale Coll., Mich., 1973-74; vis. prof. Yale U., 1983. Home: 142 West End Ave New York NY 10023

MOLONEY, TERRENCE PATRICK, (Terry), b. Los Angeles, Apr. 7, 1960, s. Gerald John Moloney and Dolores (Dietrich) Bradley. Contrbr. to So. Calif. Mag., 1982; feature wrtr., ed. Daily Trojan, U. So. Calif., 1978-82. BA in Journalism, U. So. Calif., Los Angeles, 1982. Contrbg. ed. Entrepreneur Mag., Los Angeles, 1982-84; rock video wrtr. Flash in the Pan Prodns., Los Angeles, 1984-85; copywrtr., screenwrtr. Mem. Screen Actors Guild, AFTRA, TV Acad. Arts and Scis., Pub. Relations Soc. Am. Home: 1209 Via Descanso Palos Verdes Estates CA 90274

MOMADAY, NAVARRE SCOTT, b. Lawton, OK, Feb. 27, 1934; s. Alfred Morris and Natachee (Scott) M.; m. Gaye Mangold, Sept. 5, 1959; children: Cael, Jill, Brit; m. Regina Heitzer, July 21, 1978; 1 dau., Lore. Author: The Complete Poems of Frederick Goddard Tuckerman, 1965, House Made of Dawn, 1968, The Way to Rainy Mountain, 1969, Angle of Geese and Other Poems, 1973, The Gourd Dancer, 1976, The Names, 1976, Man Made of Words, 1987. AB, U. N.Mex., 1958; AM, Stanford U., 1960, PhD, 1963. Asst. prof., assoc. prof. English, U. Calif., Santa Barabara, 1962-69, prof. English and comparative lit., Berkeley, 1969-72, Stanford U., 1972-80, U. Ariz., Tucson, 1980—; Cons. NEH, NEA, 1970—. Trustee Museum of Am. Indian, Heye Found, NYC, 1978—. Guggenheim fellow, 1966; Recipient Pulitzer prize for fiction, 1969; Disting. Service award Western Lit. Assn., 1983. Mem. MLA, Am. Studies Assn., PEN. Office: Dept English U Ariz Tucson AZ 85721

MOMSEN, WILIAM LAURENCE, b. Rio de Janeiro, Brazil, Dec. 2, 1932; s. Richard Paul and Dorothea Anne (Harnecker) M.; m. Diane A. Travis, 1956 (div. 1967); children: Will, Sandra. Engr., JPL, Pasadena, Calif., 1962-69; owner, operator Change Wheel and Tire, North Hollywood, Calif., 1970-75; tech. writer Associated Writers, Monrovia, Calif., 1977-79; editor, pub. Nautical Brass Mag., Montrose, Calif., 1980—. Served with U.S. Army, 1957-60. Fellow Eta Kappa Nu. Office: Box 744 Montrose CA 91020

MONACO, JAMES, b. NYC, Nov. 15, 1942, s. George C. and Susanne M.C. (Hirschland) M.; m. Susan R. Schenker, Oct. 24, 1976; children—Andrew, Charles, Margaret. Author: The New Wave: Godard, Truffaut, Chabrol, Rohmer, Rivette, 1976, How to Read a Film: The Art, Technology, Language, History and Theory of Film and Media, 1977, 2d ed., 1981 (pub. in German 1980, Japanese 1983, Dutch 1984, Italian 1985, also Chinese), Celebrity: The Media as Image Makers, 1978, Media Culture: Television, Radio, Records, Books, Newspapers, Movies, 1978, Alain Resnais: The Role of Imagination, 1979, American Film Now: The People, The Power, The Money, The Movies, 1979 (pub. in German and Japanese 1985), Who's Who in American Film Now, 1981, 2d ed., 1987, The Connoisseurs Guide to the Movies, 1985; contrbr. to numerous books and publs. on film; free-lance film critic, commentator. AB with honors, Muhlenberg Coll., 1963; MA, Columbia U., 1964, also postgrad. Mem. faculty CUNY, 1964, 68-70, chmn. dept. English, 1969; mem. faculty New Schl. Social Research, 1967—; adj. prof. NYU, 1977; lectr. U.S. and Europe. Mem. WG, AG, Am. Book Pub. Assn., Assn. Am. Pubs. Office: Baseline 838 Broadway New York NY 10003

MONAGHAN, MARY PATRICIA, b. Bklyn., Feb. 15, 1946; d. Edward Joseph and Mary Margaret (Gordon) Monaghan; m. Roland Wulbert, July 1984; children—Rachel, Joanna. Author: The Book of Goddesses and Heroines, 1981; editor: Hunger and Dreams: The Alaskan Women's Anthology, 1983, Unlacing: Ten Irish-American Women Poets, 1987. BA, U. of Minn., 1967, MA, 1971; MFA, U. of Alaska, 1981. Publicity Dir., Walker Art Center, Mpls., MN, 1972-73; editor, Minn. Public Radio, St. Paul, 1973-74; aide, Alaska State Legislature, Juneau, 1975; instr., Tanana Valley Comm. College, Fairbanks, AK, 1977—; founder and pres., Firewood Press, Fairbanks, AK, 1975—. Home: 486 Oopik Fairbanks AK 99709

MONCRIEF, RUTH, see Oglesby, Ted Nathan, Jr.

MONCRIEFFE, HYACHINTH WILLIAMS, b. Jamaica, W.I., Sept. 8, 1945, d. George Cornell and Maud Louise (Marshall) Williams, came to U.S., 1967; m. Moncrieffe; children—Denise Caroline, Eton Warren, Maxine Antonnette. Contrbr. poetry: Black and In Brooklyn, Nat. Poetry Anthology, Poetry Press, Suwanee Poetry, other lit mags; author: The Unlimited Mind (poetry), 1983. BS in Community Health and Health Adminstrn., St. Joseph's Coll., 1981; AA in Nursing, U. Albany, 1982; MA in Profl. Human Services, N.Y. Inst. Tech., 1984. Nursing supvr., tchr. Recipient numerous awards for poetry. Mem. Am. Film Inst., P&W, Songwrtrs. Club Am., ASCAP, AAP. Office: Box 615

Brooklyn NY 11216

MONK, SEAN CHARLES, (Pat), b. Rochester, Kent, England, Feb. 5, 1916 (arrvd. USA March 1947); s. Ernest F.J. and Mary Annie (Jones) M.; m. Emma Pearl Butler; children—Paddy, Colleen, Deirdre, Kelly, Heather. Author: The Essence of Clock Repair, 1983; contrbr. articles to Horological Times, Independent Jeweler, other trade jnls., The Peace Officer, Police Chief. Wrkg. on book of Irish short stories, poems. Student Rochester Jr. Tech. (England), graduate Electrical and Wireless Schl. (RAF, England). Served WWII Sgt., RAF. Mem. International Rotary; Economic Club, Detroit; British Horological Institute (fellow.); Mich. Watchmaker's Guild, Inc.; American Watchmaker's Institute. Home: 1223 Cedarholm Ln Bloomfield Hills MI 48013

MONNETT, JOHN HAMILTON, b. Kansas City, MO, May 21, 1944; s. Howard Norman and Hazel Marie (Hamilton) M.; m. Linda Louise Chambers, Dec. 28, 1973. Author: A Rocky Mountain Christmas, 1987; (with Michael McCarthy) Colorado Pofiles: Men and Women Who Shaped the Centennial State, 1987. B.S., Kansas State U., 1967; M.A., San Jose State U., 1973; Ph.D., U. Northern Colo., 1980. Di. continuing edn. Commun. Coll. of Denver, 1981-86; prof. history Cochise Coll., Douglas, AZ, 1971-78, Metro State Coll., Dener, 1984—. Home: 4638 Starboard Dr Boulder CO 80301

MONROE, MARY, b. Choctaw County, AL, Dec. 12, 1951, d. Otis Nicholson and Ocie (Kirksey) Bonner; m. Joseph Monroe, Jan. 19, 1969 (div. 1971); children—Michelle, Jacqueline Susann. Novelist: The Upper Room, 1985. Student public schls., Alliance, Ohio. Secy. Bechtel Corp., San Francisco, 1974-83; clrk.-typist Pacific Gas and Electric Co., San Francisco, 1983—. Mem. Oakland Black Wrtrs. Guild, Intl. Women's Wrtrs. Guild. Home: 41 Sutter St San Francisco CA 94104

MONTALVO, JOSE LUIS, b. Piedra Negras, Mexico, Sept. 9, 1946; children—Jose Luis, John Lawrence, Canela. Author: (bilingual poetry) Pensamientos Capurados, 1977, A Mi Que!, 1983. Contrbr. poems to anthols., lit. ms. Wrkg. on collection of poems, Black Hat Poems; bilingual play, The Village Virgin; collection of short stories in Spanish, La Niebla en Tejas. A.A., San Antonio Coll., 1973; B.A., St. Mary's U., 1975. Night mgr. Tex. Youth Commun., San Antonio, 1984—. Home: Box 12691 San Anonio TX 78212

MONTANA, J. D., see Hughes, Walter J., Sr.

MONTE, BRYAN ROBERT, b. Cleve., Nov. 3, 1957; s. Robert Pete and Mary Martha (Debus) M. Contrbr. poems, articles, short stories to anthols., books, mags., newspapers. Editor: No Apologies, 1983—; poetry selection com.: The Brown Jnl of the Arts, 1984. BA in English, U. Calif.-Berkeley, 1983; MA in Creative Writing, Brown U., 1986. Calif. poet in the schls., San Francisco, 1983-84; tech. wrtr. Brown U. Library, Providence, 1984-86; asst. bibliographer John Carter Brown Library, German-Americana project, Providence, 1986—; wrtg. spclst. Milford Pub. Schls., 1986-87. Recipient Youth and Creative Arts award The Saints Herald, Independence, Mo., 1976-78, Joan Yang Meml. Poetry prize U. Calif., Berkeley, 1982. Mem. MLA. Home: 2058 Mars Ave Lakewood OH 44107

MONTELIUS, SUSAN ANN, b. Reserve, LA, July 2, 1956; d. Gilbert Hunter and Frances Mae (Miano) M.; 1 foster child, Gisela Espinoza Hernandez. Author: Words, Inspiration and Lovers, 1986. contrbr. poems to anthols. Grad. public schls., Marerro, LA. Enlisted U.S. Navy, 1978—. Contrbr. Holiday Letters for Needy Children, 1985-87. Recipient award of Merit, World of Poetry, 1986, Talent, 1987; Golden Poet award World of Poetry, 1985, 86. Home: 516 Willowbrook Dr Gretna LA 70056

MONTEREY, HONEY, see Noah, Hope E.

MONTGOMERY, CATHERINE ANN, (Kate Sullivan), b. Cleveland, OH, Jan. 13, 1928; d. John Edward and Ann Gertrude (O'Neil) Sullivan; m. Jerry D. Montgomery, Apr. 8, 1947; 1 son—Patrick V. Editor: Cerebrations of C. Kism, 1983; author, publisher: The Eunuch Maker, 1984, B.B.N. 1983—; Western Reserve Mag, 1976, Portage Mail Mag., 1977, Women of the Plains-Leisure Books, 1977. Student Akron U. Nurse (LPN) St. Thomas Hospital (Akron, OH), 1961-70; freelance wrtr., 1970-86; editor B.B.N. (Akron, OH), 1976—. Pres. Akron Manuscript Club. Home: 1319 Pitkin Ave Akron OH 44310

MONTGOMERY, CATHIE MARION, (Cathie M. Douglas), b. Los Angeles, July 6, 1950; d. Gordon and Elaine (Harrington) Douglas; m. David Allen Montgomery, May 13, 1982; 1 son, Michael Andrew. Contrbr. sports and non-fiction articles to mags. including Family Pet, Soccer Am., Am. Dane. Reporter: Daily Reporter, Derby, Kans., 1979. BA in Speech and Drama, English, Drury Coll., Springfield, Mo., 1972; postgrad. Wichita State U., 1973-74. Proofreader, Letters Inc.-KPN Typographics, Wichita, Kans., 1978-82; newsletter contrbr. Animal Welfare Alliance, Wichita, 1980-83; free-lance wrtr., Wichita, 1984—. Vice pres. Kans. Humane Soc. Womens Aux., Wichita, 1977-78; Wichita Wings Orange Army Booster Club, 1981-86; Mem. AG of Am. Home: 101 W Dorrell Wichita KS 67233

MONTGOMERY, DAVID BRUCE, b. Fargo, ND, Apr. 30, 1938· David William and Iva Bernice (Trask) M.; m. Toby Marie Franks, June 11, 1960; children: David Richard, Scott Bradford, Pamela Marie. Author: (with Glen L. Urban) Management Science in Marketing, 1969, (with Massy and Morrison) Stochastic Models of Buying Behavior, 1970, (with Day et al.) Planning: Cases in Computer and Model Assisted Marketing, 1973, (with others) Consumer Behavior: Theoretical Sources, 1973, (with G.J. Eskin) Data Analysis, 1975; assoc. editor: Strategic Mgmt. Jnl. BS E.E., Stanford U., 1960, MBA, 1962, M.S. in Stats, 1964, PhD Mgmt. Sci., 1966. Asst. prof. mgmt. M.I.T., 1966-69, assoc. prof., 1969-70, Stanford U., 1970-73, prof. mktg. and mgmt. sci., 1973-78, Robert A. Magowan prof. mktg., 1978—; prin. MAC Inc. Home: 960 Wing Pl Stanford CA 94305

MONTGOMERY, GEORGE, b. Jersey City, Feb. 12, 1938, s. George and Elizabeth (Stokes) M.; m. Anna Golz, Dec. 1960 (div. 1983); children—Rachel, Rebekah, Patrick. Author: Mary Jane Papers, 1967, Moonblood, 1967, Mae West Batallion of Women Lost to My Control, 1983, Kingston, A City, 1984; e.: Blue Belt Anthology, Yowl Newsletter; contrbr. poetry, stories to mags and jnls, including Moody Street Irregulars. Columnist Kingston (N.Y.) Daily Freeman, 1977—. Address: Box 40 Rosendale NY 12472

MONTGOMERY, JOHN, see Gomery, Douglas

MONTGOMERY, JOHN DICKEY, b. Evanston, IL, Feb. 15, 1920; s. Charles William and Lora Kathryn (Dickey) M.; m. Jane Ireland, Dec. 19, 1954; children: Faith, Patience, John. Author: The Purge in Occupied Japan, 1953, Forced to Be Free, 1957, The Politics of Foreign Aid, 1962, Foreign Aid in International Politics, 1967, Technology and Civic Life, 1974, Aftermath: Tarnished Outcomes of American Foreign Policy, 1986; Co-author: The State Versus Socrates, 1954, Cases in Vietnamese Administration, 1959, Traditions, Values and Socio-Economic Development, 1961, Approaches to Development: Politics, Administration and Change, 1966, Education and Training in Developing Countries, 1961, Political and Administrative Development, 1969, Policy Sciences and Population, 1975, Values and Development: Appraising Asian Experience, 1976, Decentralization and Development, 1983, Americans as Proconsuls, 1984; author, co-editor: Patterns of Policy: Comparative and Longitudinal Studies of Population Events, 1979, International Dimensions of Land Reform, 1984; editor: Public Policy, 1964-69. AB, Kalamazoo Coll., 1941, AM, 1942, LLD, 1962; AM, Harvard, 1948, PhD, 1951. Chmn. dept. govt., Harvard Univ., 1980-84; Ford Fdn. Prof of Intl. Studies, 1984-. Home: 36 Hyde Ave Newton MA 02158

MONTGOMERY, JOHN McVEY, b. Spokane, WA, May 2, 1919; s. John McVey and Bel Gretchen (Murray) M.; m. Frances Nancy Cooney, May 2, 1948 (div. June 2, 1952); 1 dau., Laura. Contbr. to mags. including, Tempus Fugit, Kerouac, others; also anthologies Beat Indeed! Kerouac Graffiti. BS, U. Calif.-Berkeley, 1940; MLS, George Peabody U., 1958. Librarian, various libraries in Calif., 1950-72; postal clrk. U.S. Post Office, San Francisco, 1973-87; pub. Kerouaciana, Fels & Firn Press. Served with AUS, 1942-43. Recipient Alfred Longeuil Poetry prize UCLA, 1969, Grand Prize, APA, 1986. Mem. Am. Alpine Club, Marin Poetry Ctr. Home: 33 Scenic Ave San Anselmo CA 94960

MONTGOMERY, KATE, see Kaluse, Kathryn Ann

MONTGOMERY, MARION, b. Upson County, GA, Apr. 16, 1925, s. Marion H. and Lottie Mae (Jenkins) M.; m. Dorothy Carlisle, Jan. 20, 1951; children—Priscilla, Lola Dean, Marion III, Heli, Lewellyn. Author: Dry Lightning (poems), 1960, The Wandering of Desire (novel), 1962, Darrell (novel), 1964, Ye Olde Bluebird (novella), 1967, The Gull and Other Georgia Scenes (poems), 1969, Ezra Pound: A Critical Essay, 1970, T.S. Eliot: An Essay on the American Magus, 1970, The Reflective Journay Toward Order: Essays on Dante, Wordsworth, Eliot, and Others, 1973, Fugitive (novel), 1974, Eliot's Reflective Journey to the Garden, 1979, The Prophetic Poet and the Spirit of the Age: Vol. I, Why Flannery O'Connor Stayed Home, 1981, Why Poe Drank Liquor, 1983, Why Hawthorne Was Melancholy, 1984, Concerning Virtue and Modern Shadows of Turning, 1987, Possum and Other Receipts for the Recovery of "Southern Being," 1987. AB, U. Ga., 1950, MA, 1951; postgrad. U. Iowa, 1954-56. Asst. dir. U. Ga. Press, Athens, 1950-52; mem. faculty dept. English U. Ga., Athens, 1964—; mng. ed. Western Rvw., Iowa, 1957-58. Home: Box 115 Crawford GA 30630

MONTGOMERY, RUTH SHICK, b. Sumner, IL; d. Ira Whitmer and Bertha (Judy) Shick; m. Robert H. Montgomery, Dec. 26, 1935. Author: Once There Was a Nun, 1962, Mrs. LBJ, 1964, A Gift of Prophecy, 1965, A Search for the Truth,

1966, Flowers at the White House, 1967, Here and Hereafter, 1968, Hail to the Chiefs, 1970, A World Beyond, 1971, Born to Heal, 1973, Companions Along the Way, 1974, The World Before, 1976, Strangers Among Us, 1979, Threshold to Tomorrow, 1983, Aliens Among Us, 1985, Herald of the New Age, 1986. Student, Baylor U. and Purdue U., LLD, 1956, Baylor U.; LLD, Ashland Coll., 1958. Reporter Waco News-Tribune; women's editor Louisville Herald-Post; feature writer St. Louis Post-Dispatch, Indpls. Star; news reporter Chgo Tribune; Washington corr. NY Daily News, 1944-55; fgn. corr., intermittently 1946-68; spl. Washington corr. Intl. News Service, 1956-58; syndicated columnist Capital Letter King Features, Hearst Headline Service, 1958-68. Recipient Front Page award Indpls. Press Club, 1957; George Holmes Journalism award, 1957; Most Valuable Alumna award Baylor U., 1967. Mem. Washington Press Club (pres. 1950-51, gov. 1951-54), Natl. Press Club, White House Corrs. Assn., State Dept. Corrs. Assn., only woman selected to cover Pres. Roosevelt's funeral, 1945. Home: 3115 Gulf Shore Blvd PH2 Naples FL 33940

MOODY, R. BRUCE, b. Flushing, NY, Sept. 22, 1933; s. Albert and Kathleen May Cook (Coles) M.; 1 dau., Amanda Sidonie Moody. Author: The Decline and Fall of Daphne Finn, 1966; contrbr. stories to The New Yorker, 1965, Works, Michigan Quarterly, Botteghe Oscure; contrbr. poetry to The Little Mag.; staff writer The National Lampoon; theater critic The Sante Fe Rptr., 1980-81. BA, Columbia Coll., 1958; MA, Hunter Coll., 1970; PhD, CUNY, 1974. Served in U.S. Army, 1953-55. Office: Box 9555 Berkeley CA 94709

MOODY, ROBERTA LYNN, b. McKeesport, PA, Aug. 26, 1958; d. Paul Robert and Frances Wilma (Flading) Huttenhower; m. Roger Leslie Moody, Nov. 20, 1982; 1 son, Scott. Contrbr. articles to mags., newspapers. B.A. in Jnlsm., U. Mo., 1980. Newspaper reporter Houma Daily Courier, LA, 1981-83; advt. sales representative Sta. KCIL-FM, Houma, 1983-84; free-lance wrtr., 1985—. Recipient News Media award La. Assn. Educators, 1982. Mem. Am. Sewing Guild (publicity chmn. 1986). Home: 3340 Foxridge Dr Colorado Springs CO 80916

MOODY, RODGER, b. Williamsport, IN, Feb. 18, 1950; s. Edward Gene and Joyce Elaine M.; m. Denise Maria Wallace, Dec. 17, 1982; children: Dashiell Gage, Julian George. Editor Silverfish Rvw; poetry in Poet and Critic, Poetry Now, Dreamworks, Mississippi Mud, Nimrod, Willow Springs, other lit mags. BA in English Lit., U. Oreg., 1976, MFA in Creative Writing, 1978. Writing fellow Fine Arts Work Ctr., Provincetown, Mass., 1983-84, 87-88, postgrad. teaching fellow Oreg. State Prison (for U. Oreg.), Salem, 1985-86. Mem. CCLM, AWP, Lan Lit. Guild (bd. dirs.). Home: 207 E 30th St Eugene OR 97405

MOOG, FLORENCE EMMA, b. Bklyn., Jan. 24, 1915; d. George Alfred and Freda (Ott) M. Author: Structure and Development of Vertebrates, 1949; co-author: Life Science, 1955. A.B., N.Y.U., 1936; Ph.D., Columbia U., 1944; Merck postdoctoral fellow, Cambridge (Eng.) U., 1954-55; Instr. biology U. Del., 1940; research asso. Washington U., St. Louis, 1942-45, mem. faculty, 1945—, prof. biology, 1958—, chmn., 1975-77; mem. study sect. human embryology and devel. NIH, 1966-70; Charles Rebstock Prof., 1976-84, prof. emeritus, 1984—. Mem. Soc. Devel. Biology, Am. Soc. Zoologist, Soc. Gen. Physiology, AAAS (com. council affairs 1981-83), Union Concerned Scientists, Sigma Xi. Office: Dept. Biol Wash Univ St Louis MO 63130

MOOK, JAMES, b. El Dorado, AR, June 1, 1939. Author: Up from Despair, 1978; columnist UALR Forum, 1979. Contrbr. articles on public affairs, poems, short stories to newspapers, mags. including Veterans' Voices, Kaliedoscope. Wrkg. on short story, collection of poems, novel. A.A., Southern Ark. U., 1979. Golf instr. Veterans Administration Med. Ctr., North Little Rock, AR, 1981-87. Served with USAF, 1957-61. Recipient Golden Poet award World of Poetry, 1985, 86, 87; award Phoenix Wrtr.'s Club, 1986. Home: 3301 W Roosevelt Rd 30 Little Rock AR 72204

MOON, WARREN G., b. Westfield, Mass., Mar. 2, 1945; s. G.F.W. and N.E. (Noblecourt-Richaud) M. Book rvw. editor: Am. Jnl Archaeology, 1983-86; editor, author: Ancient Greek Art and Iconography, 1983, Green Vase Painting in Midwestern Collections, 1980; mem. editorial bd.: Wis. Acad. Rvw and Heartland Jnl; founder and co-genl. ed. Wis. Studies in Classics, monograph series, 1982—; contrbr. World Book Encyc. 1983. MA, Tufts U., 1967, U. Chgo., 1969, PhD, 1974. Instr. art history U. Wis., Madison, 1970-73, asst. prof., 1973-75, assoc. prof. art history and classics, 1975-80; prof. art history and classics U. Wis., Madison, 1980—; research curator Elvehjem Mus. Art U. Wis., Madison, 1975—; guest curator Art Inst. of Chgo., 1975-80. Chmn. bd. dirs. Center Gallery, Madison, 1982-83; bd. dirs. Creative Arts Over Sixty, Wis., 1981—. Inst. for Research in Humanities vis. fellow, 1975. Mem. Archaeol. Inst. Am., Coll. Art Assn., Midwest Soc. Art Historians, Wis. Acad. Scis., Arts and Letters. Office: Elvehjem Mus U. Wis Madison WI 53706

MOONE, JOSEPH LEANDERS, (J. L. Moon, J. Leanders Moon, Leanders Moore, Tee Windjammer), b. Greensboro, NC, May 3, 1953; s. Joe and Dorothy (Moore) M. Contrbr. poems to anthols. Diploma in Cooking, Denmark Tech. Schl., 1974. Recipient Merits of Song Writing award TALENT, 1977. Mem. S.C. Soc. Poets. Home: 327 W Gary St Clinton SC 29325

MOONEY, JAMES HUGH, b. Pitts., Aug. 18, 1929; s. James H. and Kathryn A. (Hall) M.; m. Eileen Jane Casey, July 30, 1960; children: Mark Hall, Sean Francis, Annina Marie, James Matthew, Lorelei Jane, Paul Adam, Kathryn Celeste. BA in Journalism, Duquesne U., Pitts., 1957. With advt. dept., then editorial dept. Pitts. Post-Gazette, 1953-61; writer-editor Natl. Observer, 1961-77, Natl. Geographic, 1977-79; editor Fdn. News mag., Washington, 1979-81; press secy. Congressman Mickey Edwards of Okla., Washington, 1982; asst. natl. editor Washington Times, 1982-83; editor Status Report, 1983—. Mem. European Assn. of Sci. Editors. Served with AUS, 1951-53. Home: 13820 N Gate Dr Silver Spring MD 20906

MOONEY, MICHAEL MORSE, b. Milw., Sept. 17, 1939; s. Richard Francis and Kathryn (Morse) M.; m. Kathryn Jane Wilson, Sept. 3, 1964; 1 dau., Sheila Ruth. Author: (novella) Names, 1979; (short stories) Squid Soup, 1980. BA, Dartmouth Coll., 1961; PhD, Edinburgh U., Scotland, 1968. Asst. prof. Moorhead St. Coll., Minn., 1967-79; lectr. U. Wis., Milw., 1970-77; ptnr. DeToro Mgmt., Milw., 1977-85; secy. Robert Marshall Co., Milw., 1985-86. Recipient Best Book-Length Fiction award Wis. Council of Wrtrs., 1980; creative writing grantee NEA, 1982. Home: 2824 N Murray Ave Milwaukee WI 53211

MOORE, BRIAN, b. Belfast, N. Ire., U.K., Aug. 25, 1921; came to U.S. 1960; s. James Bernard and Eileen (McFadden) M; m. Jean Denney, Oct. 1967; 1 son, Michael. Author: The Lonely Passion of Judith Hearne, 1955, The Feast of Lupercal, 1957, The Luck of Ginger Coffey, 1960, An Answer from Limbo, 1962, The Emperor of Ice Cream, 1965, I Am Mary Dunne, 1968, Fergus, 1970, The Revolution Script, 1971, Catholics, 1972, The Great Victorian Collection, 1975, The Doctor's Wife, 1976, The Mangan Inheritance, 1979, The Temptation of Eileen Hughes, 1981, Cold Heaven, 1983, Black Robe, 1985. The Color of Blood, 1987. Grad. St. Malachy's Coll., 1939. Recipient Quebec Lit. prize, 1958, U.S. Nat. Arts and Letters award, 1961, Fiction award Gov.-Gen. Can., 1961, 75; W.H. Smith award, 1975. Guggenheim fellow, 1959, Can. Council sr. fellow, 1962, 76; Scottish Arts Council Intl. fellow 1983. Home: 33958 Pacific Coast Hwy Malibu CA 90265

MOORE, DAISY SEALE, b. Meridian, MS, Apr. 10, 1933; d. Cecil Ray Seale and Mildred (Sharp) Mallini; widow; children—Ray Bryan, Gary Alan, Michael David, Paul Edwin. Contrbr. poems to anthols. B.A. Cum laude, William Carey Coll., 1962; M.Ed., Livingston U., 1969. Tchr. public schls., Linden, AL, 1968-70, Fairhope, AL, 1970-77, Mobile, AL, 1978—. Recipient Golden Poet award World of Poetry, 1987. Mem. Pensters, NEA, Ala. Edn. Assn., Delta Kappa Gamma. Home: 608 Hancock Rd Fairhope AL 36532

MOORE, DIANNE-JO, (Jodi Vernon) b. Cadillac, MI., Feb. 7, 1946; d. Vernon Leroy and Alice Mae (Hansen) Moore. Contrbr.: Ladies' Home Jnl., McCalls, Redbook, San Francisco Chronicle, Grand Rapids Press, numerous other nat. mags. and newspapers; ed. Midriff Messenger, mid-Mih. chap. Natl. Assn. to Aid Fat Americans. BA, Aquinas Coll., 1981. Caseworker Mih. Dept. Social Services, Grand Rapids, 1964-78; freelance wrtr., 1981—. Mem. NWC. Home: 545 Eastern Ave NE Grand Rapids MI 49503

MOORE, DONALD JOHN, b. Morristown, NJ, Aug. 25, 1959; s. Donald Joseph and Beatrice Irene (Heeb) M.; M. Brenna Lauren Stein, June 20, 1987. Mng. editor (newspaper) Guidon, 1979-80, editor-in-chief, 1980-81. Contrbr. to World Poetry, A New Day anthols., Odessa Poetry Rvw. BA in English and History, Norwich U., Northfield, Vt., 1977-81; MA in English, Seton Hall U., 1985. Cons. SMC Tech. Support, Bridgewater, N.J., 1982-84; fin. clk. AT&T Communications, Morristown, 1984-87. Recipient Creative Writing award Natl. Soc. Arts and Letters, 1977, Golden Poet Award, 1986, 87. Home: 1 Woodstone Rd Basking Ridge NJ 07920

MOORE, DOROTHY N(ELSON), b. Bruce, SD, Oct. 30, 1915; d. Nels T. and Millie (Amundson) Nelson; m. Raymond S. Moore, June 12, 1938; children: Dennis Raymond, Dorothy Kathleen (Mrs. Bruce D. Kordenbrock), Mai Tokizaki-Lim (foster daughter). Author: (with Raymond S. Moore) Better Late Than Early, 1975, Program Helps for Kindergarten, 1977, (with R.S. Moore and others) School Can Wait, 1979, (with R.S. Moore) Exploring Early Childhood (correspondence course), 1979, contrbr (with R. S. Moore), Kar E. Schaefer, Uwe Stave, and Wolfgang Blankenburg, eds, Individualization Process and Biographical Aspects of Disease, 1979, (with R.S. Moore) Home-Grown Kids (sequel to School Can Wait), 1981, (with R.S. Moore, Penny Estes Wheeler, and others) Homespun Schools: Teahing Children at Home—What Parents Are Doing and How They Are Doing It, 1982, (with Kahleen Kordenbrock, Julene Oswald, R.S. Moore, and Dennis R. Moore) Hometyle Teaching: A Handbook for Parents and Teachers, 1984, (with R.S. Moore) Home Made Health, 1986, (with D. S. Moore, D.R. and Kordenbrock), Home Built Discipline, 1987. Juveniles: (all with R.S. Moore) Guess Who Took the Battered-Up Bike: A Story of Kindness, 1985, Oh No! Miss Dent's Coming to Dinner, 1985, Quit? Not Me! A Story of Dependability, 1985. Au of church school curriculum material. Au of Understanding Children, a column in Worker. Contrbr to educational jnls. Attended Long Beach State Coll (now Calif. State Univ, Long Beach), Univ of Calif. at Los Angeles, and Univ of Southern Calif.; BA, Pacific Union Coll, 1937; MA (with highest honors), Emmanuel Missionary Coll (now Andrews Univ) 1959, grad study, 1976. Tchr of shorthand, Pacific Union Coll, Angwin, Calif., 1935-37; elementary school tchr in South Whitier, Calif., 1937-41 and Artesia, Calif., 1943-44; preschool tchr in Angwin, 1947-51; teacher of English as a fgn lang at schools and preschools in Sodeguaramachi, Chiba-Ken, Japan, 1951-56; reading supervisor at school in Takoma Pak, Md., 1957-60, 1964-67; organizer and dir of Cerebral Palsy Center, Loma Linda (Calif.) Univ, 1960-62; tchr of shorthand and typing in Keene, Tex., 1962-64; cons in early childhood educ, Hinsdale, Ill., 1967-70; church preschool dir & part-time lectr in remedial reading and childhood educ, Andrews Univ, Berrion Springs, Mich., 1970-83. Lectr a Indiana Univ. Seminar leader; cons in the U.S., Japan, and the Philippines. Address: 36211 SE Sunset View Washougal WA 98671

MOORE, ERCELLE, b. Basco, IL, Sept. 6, 1903; d. Wiley and Amanda Carolyn (Tiemann) O'Brien; m. LaRue Emmett Davis (dec. 1955); m. 2d, Arthur E. Moore (dec. 1985). Author short-story collections: Christmas at Crossroads, 1976, Crossroads, Oklahoma, 1979, Jesus Gave Them to Me, 1981, Scarecrows, 1983; poetry collections: I March to My Own Drum, 1953, More Over Walt Whitman, 1977, The Long and the Short of Them, Out of My Mind; contrbr. poetry, short stories to numerous newspapers and small mags. Wrkg. on fiction. Attended jr. coll., Kansas City, Mo. Past med. tehnologist, fashion model. Recipient Wrtr.'s Digest awards. Books included in Western history collection, U. Okla. Home: 5300 W 96th St Indianapolis IN 46268

MOORE, FRANCES F., b. Portland, OR, Dec. 20, 1943, d. Harold M. and Alma L. (Warren) Townsend; m. Marion F. Moore, Sept. 21, 1961; children—Victoria Lyn, Deborah Kaye, Diann Renee, William Daniel. Contrbr. to Am. Poetry Anthology, Our World's Best Loved Poems, Our World's Most Beloved Poems, New Voices in Am. Poetry, Hearts on Fire, A Treasury of Poems on Love, Words of Praise anthols. AA, Solano Community Coll., Suisun, Cal. Exec. secy. U.S. Army and U.S. Army, various locations, 1961-73; exec. secy. U.S. Air Force Civil Service, 1961-87; Travis AFB, Cal., 1983-; editor Fedl. Women's Program, 1983-84. Recipient 3 award of merit certs. World of Poetry, 1984, Golden Poet Award, 1985, Silver Poet Award, 1986. Home: 2125 Capitola Way Fairfield CA 94533

MOORE, GEOFFREY HOYT, b. Pequannock, NJ, Feb. 28, 1914; s. Edward H. and Marian (Leman) M.; m. Ella C. Goldschmid, July 12, 1938 (dec. June 2, 1975); children: Stephen, Peter, Kathleen, Pamela; m. Melita H. Riley, Sept. 28, 1975. Author: (with W.A. Wallis) A Significance Test for Time Series, 1941, Production of Industrial Materials in World Wars I and II, 1944, Statistical Indicators of Cyclical Revivals and Recessions, 1950, The Diffusion of Business Cycles, 1955, Measuring Recessions, 1958, Business Cycle Indicators, 1961, Tested Knowledge of Business Cycles, 1962, (with J. Shiskin) Indicators of Business Expansions and Contractions, 1966, (with P. Klein) The Quality of Consumer Installment Credit, 1967, The Anatomy of Inflation, 1969, The Cyclical Behavior of Prices, 1971, How Full is Full Employment?, 1973, Slowdowns, Recessions and Inflation, 1975, An Inflation Chronology, 1977, Business Cycles, Inflation and Forecasting, 1983, (with P. Klein) Monitoring Growth Cycles in Market-Oriented Countries, 1985, (with M. Moore) International Economic Indicators, 1985. BS, Rutgers U., 1933, MS, 1937; PhD, Harvard, 1947. Dir. Center for Intl. Bus. Cycle Research, 1979—; commr. labor statistics Dept. Labor, 1969-73; adj. scholar Am. Enterprise Inst., 1975—; assoc. prof. econ. NYU, 1947-48; vis. lectr. Columbia U., 1953-54, sr. research scholar, 1983—. Mem. N.Y. State Council Econ. Advisers, 1973-74. Fellow Am. Statis. Assn. (pres. 1968), Natl. Assn. Bus. Economists; mem. Am. Econs. Assn., Conf. Bus. Economists, Natl. Economists Club. Home: 1711 Valley Rd New Canaan CT 06840

MOORE, HARRISON LYMAN, b. Boston, Oct. 25, 1946; s. Charles Lothrop and Alice Lyman M. Contrbr. to Epson Soft World. B.A., Harvard Coll., 1969; M.B.A., M.S. in Jnlsm., Columbia U., 1973. Assoc. ed. Inc. Mag., Boston, 1979-81; contrbg. ed. Harvard Bus. Rvw., Cambridge, MA, 1987—. Recipient 2d place for non-fiction Wrtr.'s Digest, 1987. Home: 24 Payson Rd Belmont MA 02178

MOORE, HARRY E., JR, b. Frankfort, KY, Feb. 15, 1918; s. Harry E. and Julia (Shryock) M.; m. Eleanor Heyburn Stewart, Sept. 11, 1944; children—Leslie Heyburn Baskin, Harry E. Author: Pursuit of Values, 1970, Values for Freedom, 1972, How to Plan and Carry Out Your Own Groupwork Agency Study, 1974, Money: Raising and Managing Funds for Human Svcs., 1984; wking. on (with Jane Mallory Park) Mgt. Dynamics: Chars. of Successful Human Svcs. Orgns. AB, Georgetown (KY), 1941; BD, Crozer, 1943. Youth prog. dir., YMCA, Watertown, NY, 1946-49, Amsterdam, NY, 49-52; assoc. exec., YMCA, Plainfield, NJ, 1952-57, exec. dir., 1957-75; pres. Groupwork Today, Inc., So. Plainfield, NJ, 1975—. Office: Box 258 South Plainfield NJ 07080

MOORE, HARVIELEE ANN OFFUTT, b. Deming, NM, June 8, 1948, d. Ira Joe and Louella Carolyn (Chandler) Offutt; m. Samuel Tolbert Moore, July 23, 1977. Ed.: Galleon, 1966-67, The Sunburst (founder), 1968—, The Roadrunner, 1976-78; contrbr. to Natl. Tchrs.' Poetry Anthology, Warwhoop, other publs. Wrkg. on book of poems, tchr. curriculum materials. BA cum laude McMurry Coll., 1967; MA, Western N.Mex. U., 1975. Writing tchr. Deming (N.Mex.) High Schl., 1967-69, 70—, chmn. dept. English, 1980—, dir. Southwest Wrtrs. Guild, Deming, 1970-71. Recipient scholarship U. Colo. Wrtrs.' Conf., 1966, Grand Prize for writing program N.Mex. Research and Study Council, 1984, First Place Prize for Sunburst Program, 1985. Mem. NCTE, Phi Delta Kappa, other ednl. orgns. Home: Box 763 Deming NM 88031

MOORE, HONOR, b. NYC,Oct. 28, 1945; d. Paul and Jenny (McKean) Moore. Contrbr. poetry to 13th Moon, Feminist Studies, The Nation, New West, Chrysalis, Village Voice, others; articles to MS., Harpers, Boston Globe, others; author: Mourning Pictures (verse play), 1974; ed. The New Women's Theatre: 10 Plays by Contemporary Women, 1977. BA, Radcliffe Coll., 1967. Dir. poetry series Manhattan Theatre Club (NYC), 1971-74; vis. scholar Jas. Madison U., 1980; adjunct prof. in dramatic wrtg. NYU, 1980-81. Playwrtg. grant, NY State Council on Arts, 1975; Creative Wrtg. Fellowship (poetry), NEA, 1981. Mem. PEN, Feminist Wrtrs. Guild, bd. dirs. P&W, 1975—. Home: Box 305 Kent CT 06757

MOORE, JANICE TOWNLEY, b. Atlanta, Apr. 29, 1939, d. Alvin Mountville and Edith Fern (Davis) Townley; m. Carl Stanley Moore, Nov. 26, 1965; 1 son, Mark. Contrbr. poetry to Appalachian Heritage, Negative Capability, Chattahoochee Rvw, Confrontation, numerous other lit. mags.; poetry ed.: Ga. Jnl. BA, LaGrange (Ga.) Coll., 1961; MA, Auburn (Ala.) U., 1963. Instr. English Young Harris (Ga.) Coll., 1963—. Winner All Nations Poetry Contest, Triton Coll., River Grove, Ill., 1980. Mem. South Atlantic MLA, Ga. State Poetry Soc. Office: Dept Eng Young Harris Coll Young Harris GA 30582

MOORE, JOHN NORTON, b. June 12, 1937; s. William Thomas and Lorena (Norton) M.; m. Barbara Schneider, Dec. 12, 1981. Author: Law and the Indo-China War, 1972 (Phi Beta Kappa award), Law and the Grenada Mission, 1974, The Secret War in Central America, 1986; editor: Law and Civil War in the Modern World, 1976, (with Lillich) Readings in International Law, 1979, The Arab-Israeli Conflict, 3 vols, 1976; bd. editors: Am. Jnl Intl. Law, Consortium on Intelligence; contbr. articles on oceans policy, natl. security, congressional-exec. relations in fgn. policy to profl. jours. A.B. in Econ., Drew U., 1959; LL.B. with honors, Duke U., 1962; LL.M., U. Ill., 1965; Yale U. Law Schl., 1965-66. Bar: Fla. 1962, Ill. 1963, Va. 1969, D.C. 1972, U.S. Sup. Ct. 1972, U.S. Customs Ct. 1978, U.S. Ct. Customs and Patent Appeals 1980. Assoc. Prof. law U. Va. Law Schl., 1966-69, prof., 1969-76, dir. grad. program, 1969—; adj.-prof. Georgetown Law Center, 1978—; Walter L. Brown prof. law, dir. Center for Oceans Law and Policy, U. Va., 1976—, dir., 1982, Center Law and Natl. Security; cons. in field. Mem. State Dept. Adv. Bd. on Law of Sea, 1977—; chmn. oceans policy com. Republican Natl. Com. Fellow U. Calif., (Berkeley) Intl. Legal Studies Program, 1963. Chmn. bd. dirs., U.S. Inst. of Peace, 1985—. Mem. ABA (vice Chmn. sect. Intl. Law and chmn. com. on law and nat. security), Am. Law Inst., Council Fgn. Relations, Phi Beta Kappa. Drafted U.S. sponsored treaty to prevent spread of terrorism, 1972. Home: 824 Flordon Dr Charlottesville VA 22901

MOORE, JOHN REES, b. Washington, Oct. 15, 1918, s. John Brooks and Florence Du Bois (Rees) M.; m. Betty Lucille Drawbaugh, July 16, 1954; children—Steven Abel, Sarah Brooks. Author: Masks of Love and Death (on the plays of W.B. Yeats), 1971; ed.: The Idea of An American Novel (with Louis D. Rubin, Jr.), 1961, The Sounder Few (with R.H.W. Dillard and George Garrett), 1971; ed. The Hollins Critic, 1963—.

MA, Harvard U., 1942; PhD,Columbia U., 1957. Mem. faculty U. Ga., Athens, 1946-47, Carnegie Inst. Tech., Pitts., 1947-48, Lehigh U., Bethlehem, Pa., 1948-50, Columbia U., NYC,1955-57; prof. Hollins Coll., Roanoke, Va., 1957-85, prof. emeritus, 1985—; del. to Kahlil Gibran Intl. Festival, Beirut, 1970. Grantee Mellon Fdn., 1960, 66, Ford Fdn., 1970-71, Can. Embassy, 1976. Home: 7038 Goff Rd Hollins VA 24019

MOORE, LEANDERS, see Moone, Joseph Leanders

MOORE, LENARD DUANE, b. Jacksonville, NC, Feb. 13, 1958; s. Rogers Edward and Mary Louise (Pearson) M.; m. Marcille Lynn Gardner, Oct. 15, 1985; 1 child, Maiisha. Author: Poems of Love and Understanding, 1982, The Open Eye, 1985; contrbr. poems to Steppingstones, Intl. Poetry Rvw, Black Am. Lit. Forum, New Directions, Modern Haiku, Crosscurrents, others; contrbr. articles to Writers West, Writers Jnl, Dragonfly, Poets Crossroads; contrbr. rvws. and criticism to The Black Scholar, HAI. Poet-in-residence Mira Mesa Br. Library, San Diego, 1983; acting advisor Pacific Qtly Moana, 1982-83; tchr. Calif. Poets in Schls. Program, 1983; regional dir. Intl. Black Writer's Conf., 1982-83. Student, U. Md., N.C. State U. Served with U.S. Army, 1978-81. N.C. Haiku Soc. press grantee, 1985. Mem. PSA, AAP, Haiku Soc. Am. (Haiku Mus. Tokyo award 1983). Home: 5625 Continental Way Raleigh NC 27610

MOORE, LORRIE (MARIE L.), b. Glens Falls, NY, Jan. 13, 1957, d. Henry Thomas Jr. and Jeanne Lorena (Day) Moore. Author: Self-Help, 1985, Anagrams, 1986; contrbr. rvws. and articles to Ms., Mademoiselle, NY Times Book Rvw, Epoch; contrbr. short stories to Cosmopolitan, fiction intl., Story Qtly, Fiction Network, other publs. BA, St. Lawrence U., 1978; MFA, Cornell U., 1982. Lectr. Cornell U., Ithaca, N.Y., 1982-84; asst. prof. dept. English U. Wis.-Madison, 1984—. Recipient Award Series in Short Fiction, AWP, 1983; Granville Hicks Meml. fellow Yaddo Fdn., Saratoga Springs, N.Y., 1983. Mem. AWP, AG. Office: Dept Eng U WI 600 N Park St Madison WI 53706

MOORE, MARILYN M., b. Honolulu, Sept. 1, 1932; d. Peter Martin and Viola Hulda (Thesman) Janzen; m. Joseph Cleve Moore, Apr. 4, 1953; children—Shirley, Joseph, Linden. Author: Baking Your Own: Recipes and Tips for Better Breads, 1982. AA, Stephens Coll., 1951; BA, U.MO, 1953. Bread baking tchr., 1962—; free-lance writer, 1982—. Home: Box 424 Hoopeston IL 60942

MOORE, MAURINE, (Len O'Dell), b. Lamar, CO, Feb. 27, 1932; d. Gomer and Helen O'D.; divorced; children—Vivian, Jill Wood. Author: Income Graphology, 1978, Sex in Handwriting, 1983, Who Could I Tell?, 1985, After Abuse, 1987. B.A., Univ. of Colo., 1954; M.S., U. Wy., 1973. Tchr. public schls. Cheyenne, WY, 1970-73; graphologist Write Cons., Cheyenne, 1973-84; wrtr. Creative Communications, Cheyenne, 1984—. Mem. NWC, WWA, Wy. Wrtrs. Home: 5462 Walker Rd Cheyenne WY 82009

MOORE, MARK HARRISON, b. Oak Park, IL, Mar. 19, 1947; s. Charles Eugene and Jean (McFeely) M.; m. Martha Mansfield Church, June 15, 1968; children: Phoebe Sylvina, Tobias McFeely, Gaylen Williams. Author: Buy and Bust: The Effective Regulation of an Illicit Market in Heroin, 1977, (with others) Dangerous Offenders, 1985; editor:(with Joel Fleishman and Lance Leibman) Public Duties, 1980, (with Dean Gerstein) Alcohol and Public Policy, 1981. Student, Phillips Acad., 1962-65; BA Yale U., 1969; MPublic Policy, Harvard U., 1971, PhD, 1973. Teaching fellow, instr. public policy J.F. Kennedy Schl. Govt., Harvard U., Boston, 1971-73, asst. prof., 1973-74, 75-76, assoc. prof., 1976-79, Guggenheim prof. criminal justice policy and mgmt., 1979—; chief planning officer Drug Enforcement Administrn., U.S. Dept. Justice, Washington, 1974-75; cons. U.S. Dept. Justice, 1975-76, 81. Mem. Assn. Schls. Public Policy and Mgmt. Home: 134 Watson Rd Belmont MA 02178

MOORE, MONA, b. Milford, CT, Jan. 3, 1952; d. Joseph Philip and Maureen (Baird) M. Contrbr. to Brooks Community Nwsprs., Suburban News, Yale New Haven Magazine. BA, U. VT, 1974. Ed., Jax Fax Magazine, Darien CT, 1978-86. Home: Box 21667 Ft. Lauderdale FL 33335

MOORE, NAN K., see Moore, Nancy Lorene

MOORE, NANCY LORENE, (Nan K. Moore), b. Geneseo, KS, Sept. 10, 1938; d. Ivan Kenneth and Silvey Maureen (Spencer) Keaton; m. William Charles Moore, Sr., June 18, 1960; children—William Charles, Amy Carol. Contrbr. poems to lit mags, anthols.; children's stories, melodies and lyrics, non-fiction to mags. BS, Bethany Coll., Lindsborg, Kans., 1960; Tchr. Cert., Kans. State U., Manhattan, 1961, 63, postgrad., 1986—. Elem. tchr. Junction City pub. schls., Kans., 1962-85; tchr. English and jnlsm. Junction City Jr. High Schl., 1985—. Mem. Junction City Edn. Assn., Kans. Natl. Edn. Assn., NEA, Internat. Reading Assn., Midwest Chaparral Poets, Kans. Authors Club (2d place for essay 1981, 2d place hon. mention for poetry 1982). Home: 1035 Lakeview St Box 202 Milford KS 66514

MOORE, PHYLLIS LEE, b. Tampa, FL, Sept. 5, 1953; d. Howard Hudson and Marguerite Janice (Beggs) Moore. Contrbr. short stories to Apalachee Qtly, Miss. Rvw, Mich. Qtly Rvw, Sundog; poetry in Apalachee Qtly, Sundog. BA in Humanities, Fla. State U., 1979, MA in English, 1981. Tchg. asst. Fla. State Univ., Tallahassee, 1980-82, Univ. Ill., Chgo., 1982—, asst. to dir. creative wrtg. program, 1986—. Address: 5245 N Glenwood Ave Chicago IL 60640

MOORE, RAYMOND S., b. Glenda, CA, Sept. 24, 1915; s. Charles David and Dorothy (Holcomb) M.; m. Dorothy Nelson, June 12, 1938; children: Dennis Raymond, Dorothy Kahleen (Mrs. Bruce D. Kordenbrock), Marie Tokizaki-Lim (foster daughter). Author: (for books coauthored with his wife and others, see entry Moore, Dorothy Nelson) Science Discovers God, 1953, rev ed, 1978, Michibiki, 1956, A Guide to Higher Education Consortiums: 1965-66, 1967, Consortiums in American Higher Education, 1967, Adventist Education at the Crossroads, 1976, Balanced Education, 1976, The Abaddon Conspiracy, 1985. Contrbr: Marvin J. Taylor, ed, Religious Education, 1961, Lawrence C. Howard, ed, Inter-institutional Cooperation in Higher Education, 1967, Sidney S. Letter, ed, New Prospects for the Small Liberal Arts Coll, 1968, (with Dennis R. Moore and Robert D. Moon) Bernard Johnston, ed, Educ. Yrbk, 1973-74, 1973, (with D.R. Moore and Moon) J. Wesley Little and Arthur J. Brigham, eds, Emerging trategies in Early Childhood Educ, 1974, (with D.R. Moore) Dwight Allen, ed, Controversies in Educ., 1974 Carter Smith, ed, The Day Care Case, 1974, (with D.R. Moore) E. Paul Torrance and William F. White, eds, Issues and Advances in Educational Psychology, 2d ed, 1975, (with D.R. Moore and Moon) Robert C. Granger, Robert C. Young, and Joseph H. Stevens, Jr., Analysis and Critique of Early Childhood Educational Programs, 1976, (with D.R. Moore) Readings in Early Childhood Education, 1977-78, 1977, (with D.R. Moore) Readings in Early Childhood Education, 1978-79, 1978, (with D.R. Moore and Moon) Issues in Urban Education, 1978, John R. Hranitz and Anne Marie Nodkes, eds, Working with the Young Child, 1978, (with D.R. Moore) Wayne L. Wolf, ed, Education Today, 1979, Parents and Children, 1986. Also contrbr. to Walter Hahn, ed, Introduciton to Education, 1973; and to more than 40 coll textbooks. Contrbr to numerous journals, including Phi Delta Kappan. Jnl of Schl Health, Education Record, School and Society, Natl Edn Assn Jnl, and Jnl of Teacher Edn; to profl jnls in Japan, the Philippines, Germany, and Australia, and to religious jnls. AB, Pacific Union Coll, 1938; M. Ed., Univ of Southern Calif., 1946, D. Ed., 1947. Tchr at public schls in Calif., 1938-40, principal, 1940-41, superintendent, 1945-46; dir of grad studies and shmn, dept of edn and psychology, Pacific Union Coll, Angwin, Calif., 1947-51; pres, Nihon Sanōiku Gakuin Cool, Chiba-Ken, Japan, 1951-56; pres and grad dean, Philippine Union Coll, Manila, 1956-57; chmn dept of edn and psychology, Emmanuel Missionary Coll (now Andrews Univ), Berrien Springs, Mich, 1957-60; v pres, Loma Linda (Calif) Univ, 1960-62; pres and prof, Southwestern Union Coll, Keene, Tex., 1962-64; gradprogram officer, U.S. Office of Edn, Washington, D.C., 1964-67; founder, Hewitt Fndn, Washougal, Wash. (formerly Hewitt Research Center, Berrien Springs and California), 1964—, pres and chief exec officer, 1969-86. Dir of Seventh-day Adventist church school system in Japan, 1951-56; coordinator of work-study com, White House Conference on Children and Youth, 1960; exec v.p., Cedar Springs Fndn, Loma Linda, Calif., 1964-69; dir, Smithsonian Conference on Intercultural Edn, 1967; exec dir, Center for Advanced Intl Studies, Chicago, 1967-69; co-dir, FIrst World Conference on Intercultural Edn, Univ of Chicago, 1968, 1967-68; adj prof of higher edn, Andrews Univ, 1970-83; lectr, Western Michigan Univ, Kalamazoo, 1972-78, and at Indiana University, South Bend, 1978—, other schls. Facult mem, Univ of Nevada Natl Coll of Juvenile and Court Judges, 1982—. Lectr on higher edn to various confs and groups, including Natl Safety Congress, 1959, 1961, College Presidents Conf, 1967, Assn for Higher Edn, 1967, Univ of Wis. Conf on Developing Institutions, 1967, and Carnegie Conf on Cluster Colls, 1968. Expert witness in more than 40 trials in the U.S. and Canada. Cons on higher edn to numerous institutions, including The White House, U.S. Dept of Edn, Japan Ministry of Edn and Ministry of Agriculture, Conn. Commn on Higher Edn, and Ga. State Dept of Edn. Member: American Men of Science, Phi Delta Kappa. Commendation from Japanese imperial family, 1952, for work in distributive edn. and work-study programs; Philippine congressional commendation and presidential citation, 1957; citation from White House Conf on Children and Youth, 1960, for planning and coordination of work-study coms; commendation from Intl Acad for Preventive Medicine, 1975-76, for research in early childhood edn; Phi Delta Kappa commendation, 1976, for distinguished service and leadership in edn. Military service: U.S. Army, 1941-46; became major. Home: 36211 South East Sunset View Wahougal WA 98671

MOORE, RICHARD, b. Stamford, CT, Sept. 25, 1927, s. James Howard and Gertrude (Ehrhardt) M.; children—Stephanie, Tania, Claudia. Author: A Question of Survival (poetry collection), 1971, Word from the Hills: A Sonnet Sequence in Four Movements, 1972, Empires (narrative poetry), 1981, The Education of a Mouse (narrative poetry), 1983; contrbr. essays to Am. Music Tchr., Math. Mag., Ga. Rvw, other publs.; contrbr. poetry, prose to Sat. Rvw, Harper's Mag., The Listener (Eng.), Mademoiselle, numerous other publs. BA, Yale U., 1950; MA, Trinity Coll., 1955. Mem. faculty New Eng. Conservatory, Boston, 1965—. Mem. PEN, PSA, New Eng. Poetry Club. Home: 81 Clark St Belmont MA 02178

MOORE, ROBERTA LYNN, (Roberta Mortensen), b. South Bend, IN, Feb. 10, 1952; d.Robert Blake and Lydia Margeret (Hicks) Mortensen; m. Marv Ray Moore, Feb. 18, 1978; children—William Blake, Caressa Leann. Contrb. poem, articles to anthol., newspapers. Wrkg. on Christmas play, two adult novels, child's book about the sun. Home: 3775 Olive Rd Plymouth In 46563

MOORE, ROBERT LAURENCE, b. Houston, Apr. 3, 1940; s. Walter Parker and Zoe Alma (McBride) M.; m. Annette Hillin, Aug. 12, 1963 (dec. 1969); m. 2d, Elizabeth Ann Miller, Aug. 28, 1971 (div. 1987); m. 3d, Lauris McKee, July 26, 1987; children: Todd Andrew (dec.), Patrick McBride, Alissa Marie, Greta Lee. Author: European Socialists and the American Promised Land, 1970, In Search of White Crows, Spiritualism, Parapsychology and American Culture, 1977, Religious Outsiders and the Making of Americans, 1986; editor: The Rise of an American Left, 1973. BA, Rice U., 1962; MA, Yale U., 1964, PhD, 1968. Asst. Prof. history Yale U., New Haven, 1968-72, Cornell U., Ithaca, N.Y., 1972-74, assoc. prof., 1974-78, chmn. dept., 1980-83, prof. Am. history, 1978—. Recipient John Addison Porter prize Yale U., 1968; Fulbright fellow, Netherlands, 1966-67; NEH fellow, 1975-76; Rockefeller Fdn. fellow, 1979-80; Morse fellow Yale U., 1969-70. Mem. Am. Hist. Assn., Orgn. Am. Historians, Am. Studies Assn. Office: McGraw Hall Cornell U Ithaca NY 14853

MOORE, ROBERT LOWELL, JR, (Robin Moore) b. Boston, Oct. 31, 1925; s. Robert Lowell and Eleanor (Turner) M.,; Joan Friedman, Sept. 20, 1952 (div. 1956); 1 dau., Margo Joan; m. Olga Troshkin. Author: Pitchman, 1956, The Devil to Pay, 1961, The Green Berets, 1965, The Country Team, 1967, Fiedler, 1968, The French Connection, 1969, The Khaki Mafia, 1971, The Fifth Estate, 1974, (with Xaviera Hollander) The Terminal Connection, 1976, Dubai, 1976, Mafia Wife, 1977, The Banksters, 1977, Rhodesia, 1977, Only the Hyenas Laugh, 1978, The Big Paddle, 1978, Search and Destroy, 1978, (with Julian Askin) The Gold Connection, 1980. Grad., Middlesex Scl., Concord, Mass., 1943, Belmont Hill Schl., 1944; AB, Harvard U., 1949. European corr. Boston Globe, 1947; ind. TV producer, N.Y.C., 1949-52; dir. pub. relations Sheraton Corp. Am., Boston, 1952-54, dir. advt. and pub. relations, 1954-56. Served as staff sgt. USAAF, World War II. Mem. Am. Hotel Assn., Assn. Natl. Advertisers. Developed pvt. TV closed circuit network for hotels. Address: Manor Bks 45 E 30th St New York NY 10016

MOORE, ROSALIE, (Rosalie Brown), b. Oakland, CA, Oct. 8, 1910; d. Marvin Alonzo and Anna Teresa (Wooldridge) M.; m. William Louis Brown, June 30, 1942 (dec. 1964); children: Deborah Brown Turrietta, Celia Brown, Camas Brown Timmel. Author: (poems) The Grasshopper's Man and Other Poems, 1949, Year of the Children, 1977 (Pulitzer prize nominee), Of Singles and Doubles: A Collection of Poems, 1979; co-author (with husband under name Rosalie Brown) 7 children's books, 1954-64. BA with highest honors in English, U. Calif., Berkeley, 1932, MA, 1934. Instr. Coll. of Marin, Calif., 1965-76; instr. extended edn. dept. Mills Coll., Oakland, Calif., 1979-80. Recipient Charlels Sergel award for poetic drama U. Chgo., 1938; award in lit. Albert Bender Fnd., 1943; winner Yale Poetry Series, 1949; Guggenheim fellow, 1950, 51. Mem. PEN, Marin Poetry Ctr., Activist Poetry Group (founding mem.), Phi Beta Kappa. Home: 1130 7th St Apt B-26 Novato CA 94945

MOORE, SHEROR CATON, b. Alabaster, AL, June 19, 1943; d. Peter Jackson and Mary (Smith) Caton; m. Obie Rudolph Moore, June 25, 1960; children—Obie David, Jimmy Darrell. Author: (poems) Only the Ice Cream Shows, 1985. Contrbr. poems to anthols. Wrkg. on book of children's poetry. Recipient cert. of Merit, Am. Poetry Assn., 1986. Home: Rt 6 Box 95 Montevallo AL 35115

MOORE, TERESA, see Miller, Marquerite Elizabeth

MOORE, VIRGINIA BLANCK, b. Ceylon, MN, Apr. 6, 1915; d. George F. and Hazel Dora (Gideon) Blanck; m. Robert R. Moore, Oct. 22, 1944 (dec.), 1 son, Nathan R. Author: Seeing Eye Wife, 1960; Editor: Lyrical Iowa, 1974—. Contrbr. poems, articles to mags, newspapers including Ideals Mag., Cath. Digest, Toronto Star Weekly, Capper's, Wall St Jnl. BA, U. Ia., 1938. Coordinator info. services Ia. Children's and Family Services, Des Moines, 1964-81. Recipient 1st, 3d prizes Natl. Fed. State Poetry Socs., 1985. Mem. Ia. Poetry Assn., Phi Beta Kappa, Kappa Tau Alpha. Home: 1724 E 22nd St Des Moines IA 50317

MOORMAN, ROSEMARY LUCILLE, b. Marion, IN, Nov. 1, 1957; d. Bueford Paul and Mary Elizabeth (Thomas) Shaffer; m. Ralph Eugene Moorman, Dec. 12, 1980; children—Elizabeth Ramona, Ralph Eugene Jr. Contrbr. poetry to publs. by: Quill Books, Am. Poetry Assn., N.Y. Poetry Fdn., others. Wrkg. on poetry, songs, children's stories. BS in Nursing, Marion Coll. Nurse, Marion Genl. Hosp., Ind., 1981-87, Community Dialysis, Marion, Ind., 1987. Home: 6644 West 400 South Swayzee IN 46986

MOOSE, RUTH MORRIS, b. Albemarle, NC, Aug. 24, 1938; d. Ardie Lloyd and Vera (Smith) Morris; m. Talmadge Moose, June 17, 1956; children—Lyle Morris, Barry Neal. Author: To Survive, 1979, Finding Things in the Dark, 1980, The Wreath Ribbon Quilt and Other Stories, 1986; short stories numerous magazines inclg. Atlantic, Redbook, Ladies Home Journal; contrbr. poetry to Prairie Schooner, Nation, others. BA with honors, Pfeiffer Coll., Misenheimer, NC, 1985. Feature wrtr. Charlotte (NC) News, 1979-81; contrbr. ed. The New Renaissance, Arlington, MA, 1983; ed. Arts Journal, Asheville, NC, 1984—. Home: Rt 2 Box 469 Albemarle NC 28001

MORAFF, BARBARA, b. Paterson, NJ, Apr. 19, 1939, d. Richard and Frances (Mittleman) Morraff; children—Alesia, Marco. Author: The Life, 1978, Eat Me, Drink Me, 1978, Learning to Move, 1982, Telephone Company Repairman Poems, 1983, Ariadne's Thread, 1982, Potterwoman, 1983, Contra La Violencia, 1985, Deadly Nightshade, 1986. Wrkg. on novel, poetry book, non- fiction essays. Coordinator Vt. Artisans, Strafford, 1974-75. Home: RR 1 Strafford VT 05072

MORALES, see Burton, Mary Alice

MORAN, JOHN CHARLES, (J. S. Gael, Sean O'Morain), b. Nashville, Oct. 4, 1942; s. John Charles and Rachel Louise (Heflin) M.; m. Olga Cristina Robleda, Aug. 17, 1967; children—John Charles, Louis Patrick, Olga Cecilia Veronica. Author: An F. Marion Crawford Companion, 1981, Seeking Refuge in Torre San Nicola, an Introduction to F. Marion Crawford, 1980, In Memoriam: Gabriel Garcia Moreno 1875-1975, 1975. Editor: Francesca da Rimini (F. Marion Crawford), 1980, A Mystery of the Campagna (Baroness Anne Crawford von Rabe), 1983, The Romantist, 1977—. BA in English, George Peabody Coll., 1967, MLS, 1968. Dir., F. Marion Crawford Meml. Soc., Nashville, 1957—; bus. cons., La Ceiba, Honduras, 1981—. Home: Aptdo Postal 276 La Ceiba Honduras. Office: 3610 Meadowbrook Ave Nashville TN 37205

MORANT, MACK BERNARD, b. Holly Hill, SC, Oct. 15, 1946; s. Mack and Jannie (Gilmore) M. Author: Lines for the Mind, 1978, The Insane Nigger, 1979, Teacher/Student Work Manual: A Model for Evaluating Trad'l U.S. Hist. Textbooks, 1980; ed., pub. var. other works. BS in Bus. Adm., Voorhees Coll., 1968; MEd, U. Mass., 1972, CAGS, 1973; EdD, 1976. Tchr., Norway Neese Schl. Dist., Orangeburg, SC, 1968-71; deputy dir. Commun. Action, Marion, SC, 1977-81; dir. Minority Development, SC State Coll., Orangeburg, 1982-84; placement dir. VA. State U., Petersburg, VA, 1985—. Mem. ABBA. Home: 2235-C Ft Sedgwick Apts Petersburg VA 23805

MORDECAI, CAROLYN L., b. Philipsburg, PA, Jan. 14, 1936, d. Lewis Stein and Rosalie Marion (Tamler) Stein; children—Diane Mordecai, Leonard Mordecai. Author: Gourd Craft: Growing, Designing & Decorating Ornamental and Hardshelled Gourds, 1978, Finding Love in the '80s, 1984, 2d ed. re-titled The Complete Singles Guide to Dating & Mating, 1986. BS, Pa. State U., 1957. Feature wrtr. Pitts. Suburban Community Newspapers, 1973-74; freelance wrtr., NYC,1973-78; ed. Bus. News, Pvt. Industry Council, Pleasant Gap, Pa., 1983; mem. pub. and mktg. staff Nittany Press, State College, Pa., 1984—. Home: 1006 Golfview Ave State College PA 16801

MORENO, CATHERINE HARTMUS, b. Portland, OR, Feb. 9, 1935, d. Lawrence Eugene and Catherine Evelyn (Spall) Hartmus; m. Ralph Moreno, June 9, 1956 (dec.); children—Iana Kiri, Shonquis Crystal. Ed., pub. Hartmus Press, Mill Walley, Calif., 1972—. BA, U. Calif.-Berkeley, 1957, MLS, 1959. Librarian Calif. State U., San Francisco, 1959-62, U. Calif.-Berkeley, 1962—. Mem. COSMEP. Home: 23 Lomita Dr Mill Valley CA 94941

MORENO, EUSEBIO CARLOS, b. Dominican Republic, Aug. 14, 1960; came to U.S., 1977; s. Ramon and Carmen (Cruz) M. Author: (with poet Michele D'Uva) A Journey to Universal Poetry, 1984; contrbr. poetry to anthologies and newspapers. AA, CCNY, 1984, BA, 1986. Trans. English/Spanish, Universal Pubs., NYC, 1983—. Mem. Universalist Schl. of Lit. (co-founder). Home: 155 Ridge St 3G New York NY 10002

MOREY, KATHLEEN JOHNSON, b. Mpls., Dec. 13, 1946; d. Truman Henry and Maryon (Brady) Johnson; m. John P. Morey, Sept. 13, 1969 (div. April 1986); 1 son, John Truman. Author: Otto Shares a Hug and a Kiss, 1983, Otto Shares a Giggle, 1984, Otto Shares a Tear, 1984, Otto Shares a Fright, 1984. BA in English, Mt. St. Mary's Coll., Los Angeles. Interior designer Designs on You, Newport Beach, Calif., 1975-82; writer, illustrator, pub. kid-love unltd., Newport Beach, 1982—. Recipient poetry award Mother Cabrini Soc., 1969, Atlantic Monthly, 1969. Mem. Soc. Children's Book Writers, So. Calif. Council Lit. for Children and Young Adults. Home: 2036 Galaxy Dr Newport Beach CA 92660

MORGAN, DAVID PAGE, b. Monticello, GA, Mar. 17, 1927; s. Kingsley John and Juliet Freda (Gardner) M.; m. Margaret Joyce Blumer, Oct. 20, 1961. Student, Corpus Christi (Tex.) Jr. Coll., 1947-48. 1961. Student, Corpus Christi (Tex.) Jr. Coll., 1947-48. Reporter Taft (Tex.) Tribune, 1947-48; with Kalmbach Publishing Co., Milw., 1948—; editor Trains mag., 1953—, corp. secy. 1960-78, editorial v.p., pub. Better Camping mag., 1963-70; pub., editor Airliners Internat. mag., 1973-74. Author: True Adventures of Railroaders, 1954, Steam's Finest Hour, 1959, Canadian Steam! The Mohawk That Refused to Abdicate and Other Tales, 1975. Served with USAAF, 1945-46; served with USAF, 1950-51. Mem. Ry. and Locomotive Hist. Soc., Natl. Ry. Hist. Soc., Rocky Mountain R.R. Club, R.R. Pub. Relations Assn. Home: 12990 W Bluemound Rd Elm Grove WI 53122

MORGAN, ERNEST, b. St. Cloud, MN, July 6, 1905; s. Arthur Ernest and Urania (Jones) M.; m. Elizabeth Morey, 1931 (dec. 1971); children: Arthur, Jenifer, Benetta, Lee; m. Christine Fredericksen Wise, Dec. 1983. Author: (manual) Dealing Creatively with Death, 1962, 10th ed. 1985. Founder, pres., chmn. bd. Antioch Pub. Co. Yellow Springs, Ohio, 1926—; pub. Yellow Springs News, 1941-49; adminstr. Arab relief UNRWA in Palestine, Gaza, 1949-50; co-founder Arthur Morgan Schl., Celo Health Edn. Corp., Celo Community, Burnsville, N.C., 19622. Chmn. Socialist Party of Ohio, 1940's; co-founder Continental Assn. Funeral and Meml. Socs., 1963—. Mem. Natl. Hospice Orgn., Assn. for Death Edn. and Counseling, Intl. Typographical Union (local pres.), Am. Humanist Assn. Home: 1901 Hannah Branch Rd Burnsville NC 28714

MORGAN, (GEORGE) FREDERICK, b. NYC, April 25, 1922; s. John Williams and Marion Haviland (Burt) M.; m. Constance Canfield, Dec. 20, 1942 (div. Aug. 1957); children—Gaylen, Seth D., Veronica, George F.; m. Rose Fillmore, Aug. 14, 1957 (div. Aug. 1969); m. Paula Deitz, Nov. 30, 1969. Author: A Book of Change, 1972, Poems of the Two Worlds, 1977, The Tarot of Cornelius Agrippa, 1978, Death Mother and Other Poems, 1979, The River, 1980, Refractions, 1981, Northbook, 1982, Eleven Poems, 1983, The Fountain and Other Fables, 1985. AB, magna cum laude, Princeton Univ., 1943. Founder The Hudson Rvw, 1947, ed., pres., 1947—. Chmn. adv. council dept. Romance langs. and lits. Princeton Univ., 1973—. Named Chevalier de l'Ordre des Arts et des Lettres by French govt., 1984. Served with U.S. Army, 1943-45. Office: Hudson Rvw 684 Park Ave New York NY 10021

MORGAN, JAMES, b. Jackson, MS, Jan. 24, 1944; s. Leger James and Laura Patti (Kincannon) M.; m. Linda Reisdorf; children—James David, Matthew Kincannon. Editor: Hallmark Cards, Inc., Kansas City, Mo., 1968-72, Kansas City Mag., 1972-73, TWA Ambassador Mag., St. Paul, 1973-78; articles editor: Playboy Mag., Chgo., 1978-86; editorial dir. Southern Mag., Little Rock, 1986—. BA, U. Miss.-Oxford, 1966, MA, 1968. Mem. ASME, Sigma Delta Chi. Office: 201 E Markham Little Rock AR 72201

MORGAN, JANET F., see Daly, Janet Morgan

MORGAN, JANET MARIE FAIN, b. Akron, OH, Oct. 4, 1956; d. Ronald Arden and Rita Liberty (Lepera) Fain; m. Robert Edward Morgan, Sept. 1, 1984; children—Matthew, Katie, Thomas. Author: Nora Mill Granary Cookbook I, 1983, Nora Mill Granary Cookbook II, 1984, Nora Mill Granary Cookbook III, 1987. Contrbr. poem to anthol. B.A. in Psychology, Piedmont Coll., 1984. Mgr. Nora Mill Granary, Helen, GA, 1982-86; owner Morgans Schl. of Etiquette, Augusta, GA, 1987—. Home: 313 Gardners Mill Court Martinez GA 30907

MORGAN, LANIER VERNON, b. Lena, MS; s. Sam N. and Lona (Lewis) M.; divorced; children—Vernon, Vanessa; m. Evelyn Simmons, June 15, 1976; children Tynanva, Sandra, Daryl, Harold, Andy. Author: The Understanding and Modification of Delinquent Behavior, 1985. B.S. in Social Sci., Jackson State U., 1959, M.S. in Guidance Counseling, 1978. Dir. Youthwork Program, Wiona, MS, 1963-78; tchr. social studies public schls., Lexington, MS, 1963-78; youth counselor, Regional Detention Center, Flint, MS, 1978—. Home: 750 Tilden St Flint MI 48505

MORGAN, LEIGH, see Glaefke, Deborah S.

MORGAN, MARABEL, b. Crestline, OH, June 25, 1937; d. Howard and Delsa (Smith) Hawk; m. Charles O. Morgan, Jr., June 15, 1964; children: Laura Lynn, Michelle Rene. Author: The Total Woman, 1973, Total Joy, 1976, The Total Woman Cookbook, 1980, The Electric Woman, 1985. Ed., Ohio State U. Pres. Total Woman, Inc., Miami, Fla., 1970—; pub. speaker. Office: Total Woman 1300 NW 167th St Miami FL 33169

MORGAN, NEIL, b. Smithfield, NC, Feb. 27, 1924; s. Samuel Lewis and Isabelle (Robeson) M.; m. Caryl Lawrence, 1945 (div. 1954); m. Katharine Starkey, 1955 (div. 1962); m. Judith Blakely, 1964; 1 dau., Jill. Author: My San Diego, 1951, It Began With a Roar, 1953, Know Your Doctor, 1954, Crosstown, 1955, My San Diego 1960, 1959, Westward Tilt, 1963, Neil Morgan's San Diego, 1964, The Pacific States, 1967, The California Syndrome, 1969, (with Robert Witty) Marines of the Margarita, 1970, The Unconventional City, 1972, (with Tom Blair) Yesterday's San Diego, 1976, This Great Land, 1983. AB, Wake Forest Coll., 1943. Columnist San Diego Daily Jnl., 1946-50; columnist San Diego Evening Tribune, 1950—, assoc. editor, 1977-81, editor, 1981—; syndicated columnist Morgan Jnl, Copley News Service, 1958—; lectr.; cons. on Calif. affairs Bank of Am., Sunset mag. Served to lt. USNR, 1943-46. Recipient Ernie Pyle Meml. award, 1957, Bill Corum Meml. award, 1961, Disting. Service citation Wake Forest U., 1966; Grand award for travel writing Pacific Area Travel Assn., 1972, 78; named Outstanding Young Man of Year San Diego, 1959. Mem. AG, ASNE, Explorers Club. Home: 7930 Prospect Pl La Jolla CA 92037

MORGAN, ROBERT B., b. NYC, Sept. 17, 1931, s. Charles W. and Paula A. (von Mottus) M.; m. Bente P. Poulsen, Apr. 1962 (div. 1980); children—Lars A., Sven S., Kirsten U. BME, NYU, 1955; postgrad. U. Conn., 1983-84. Sr. research adminstr. Electrical Power Research Inst., Palo Alto, Calif., 1962-74; mgr. research Am. Soc. Civil Engrs., NYC, 1974-79; ed. Electrical Systems Design Mag., Cos Cob, Conn., 1979—. Home: 190 Sharp Hill Rd Wilton CT 06897

MORGAN, ROBERT RAY, b. Hendersonville, NC, Oct. 3, 1944, s. Clyde Ray and Fannie Geneva (Levi) M.; m. Nancy Keith Bullock, Aug. 6, 1965; children—Benjamin, Laurel, Nancy Kathryn. Author: Zirconia Poems, 1969, Red Owl: Poems, 1972, Land Diving, 1976, Trunk & Thicket, 1978, Groundwork, 1979, Bronze Age, 1981, At The Edge of the Orchard Country, 1986. BA in English, U. NC, Chapel Hill, 1965; MFA in Writing, U. NC, Greensboro, 1968. Mem. faculty Cornell U., Ithaca, N.Y., 1971—, prof. English, 1983—. NEA fellow, 1968, 74, 82, 87; NY Fdn. for The Arts Fellow, 1986; recipient Eunice Tietjens prize for poetry, 1979, Southern Poetry Rvw prize, 1975. Home: 105 N Wood Rd Freeville NY 13068

MORGAN, SILVER, see Burke, Ruth

MORGAN, SPEER, b. Fort Smith, AR, Jan. 25, 1946; s. Charles Donald and Betty (Speer) M.; m. Virginia Townsend, Aug. 20, 1968; 1 dau., Caitlin Derbyshire. Author: Frog Gig and Other Stories, 1975, Belle Starr: A Novel, 1979, Brother Enemy, 1981, The Assemblers, 1986; ed. The Mo. Rvw, 1974—. BA, U. Ark., 1968; PhD, Stanford U., 1972. Prof. English and creative writing Univ. Mo., Columbia, 1972—. Mem. AWP. Address: 717 Hilltop Dr Columbia MO 65205

MORGAN, W. ROBERT, b. Arkansas City, KS, Jan. 6, 1924, s. Louis S. Morgan and Betty (Starner) Linn; m. Willa June; children—Marilyn, Robert Hall. Author: The Perfect Horse, Justin Morgan—Founder of Breed, Chairman Mao's Big Red Book, Morgan Horse of the West. BA, Stanford U., 1948, LLB, 1949. Practice law, San Jose, Calif., 1949—. Pres. Triton Mus., Santa Clara, Calif., 1974—. Mem. Morgan Horse Assn. Home: 9500 New Ave Gilroy CA 95020

MORGANS, JAMES PATRICK, b. Red Oak, IA, Dec. 25, 1946; s. Ord Herald and Bernice Josephine (Johnson) M.; m. Judith Ann Rosenquist, Apr. 29, 1967; children—Patrick James, Meredith Joy. Contrbr. non-fiction articles to trade mags. including Farm Supplier, Am. Nurseryman Mag., Southern Florist, Rural Mo. Wrkg. on non-fiction articles, novel. B.A., Tarkio Coll., Mo., 1969; postgrad. Ia. U., Northwest Mo. State U. Traffic mgr. Mt. Arbor Nursery, Shenandoah, Ia., 1972-75; terminal mgr. Crouse Cartage Co., Shenandoah, 1975-78; buyer, mgr. Brandeis Stores, Omaha, Nebr., 1978-80; mgr. regional sales Precision Labs., Northbrook, Ill., 1980-83; free-lance wrtr., Shenandoah, 1983—. Mem. Soc. Am. Baseball Research. Home: 1105 Maple St Shenandoah IA 51601

MORGENSTERN, DAN MICHAEL, b. Munich, Germany, Oct. 24, 1929; came to U.S., 1947, naturalized, 1947; s. Soma and Ingeborg Henrietta (von Klenau) M.; m. Elsa Schocket, Mar. 31, 1974; children: Adam Oran, Joshua Louis. Student, Brandeis U., 1953-56. Editor Brandeis U. Justice, 1955-56; editoral asst. N.Y. Post, 1957-58; N.Y. corr. Jazz Jnl, London, 1958-61; assoc. editor, then editor-in-chief Metronome, 1961; editor Jazz, 1962-64; assoc. editor Down Beat, 1964-67; editor, 1967-73; lectr. jazz history Peabody Instn., Balt., 1978—; vis. prof., sr. research fellow for Am. Music, Bklyn. Coll., 1979; dir. Inst. Jazz Studies, Rutgers U., 1976—♦. dirs. Jazz Inst. Chgo., N.Y. Jazz Mus. Producer: ann. 10-concert series Jazz in the Garden, Museum Modern Art, N.Y.C., 1961-66; co-producer: concert series Jazz on Broadway, 1963, Just Jazz; 10 program TV series, Public Broadcasting Service, 1971; (Recipient Grammy award for best album notes 1973, 74, 76, 81); author: The Jazz Story: An Outline History, 1973, Jazz People, 1976; translator, editor: (Joachim E. Berendt) The New Jazz Book, 1962, rev. edit., 1957; co-editor Annl. Rvw Jazz Studies, 1982—. Served with U.S. Army, 1951-53. Deems Taylor award ASCAP, 1977. Mem. Natl. Acad. Rec. Arts and Scis. (gov. 1971—, trustee 1976-79, 81-84, 86, v.p. 1979-83, 1st v.p. 1983—), NEA (chmn. jazz adv. panel 1971-73, cons. music programs 1973-80), Music Critics Assn., PEN, AG. Home: 365 West End Ave New York NY 10024

MORGENSTERN, FRIEDA HOMNICK, (Wanda Blank), John A. Carberry), b. Bklyn., Oct. 4, 1917, d. David and Sadie (Englander) Homnick; m. Melvin DeWitt Morgenstern, Mar. 11, 1956; 1 son, Lewis Bayard. Contrbr. to NY Times, Los Angeles Times, Life and Health, Our Family (Canada), Highlights for Children, numerous other periodicals; San Diego corr. Natl. Jewish Post and Opinion; freelance wrtr., playwright, lit. agent. BA, UCLA, 1952. Exec. secy. Am. Broadcasting Co., NYC, after college; asst. to Barbara Walters, 1976-78; wrtr. Adv. Bd. on Women City of San Diego for Women's Opportunities Week, 1982. Mem. AG, DG, Calif. Press Women (past treas., winner interview category Annual Wrtrs. Competition 1983, 85). Home: 3634 7th Ave San Diego CA 92103

MORIARTY, MORGAN JOHANNA, b. Milw., May 14, 1955; d. Richard Glenn Winans and Maureen Ann (O'Connor) Crowley; m. Romuald Leo McBride III, May 22, 1987. Contrbr. to St. Louis Woman, Acme Press, St. Louis Mirror. Wrkg. on novel, short stories. English major, LaSalle Coll., 1973; jnlsm. major, U. Mo., 1982. Records clrk. Police Dept., Evansville, IN, 1984-86, dispatcher, 1986—. Home: 705 SE 4th St Evansville IN 47713

MORICE, DAVID JENNINGS, (Joyce Holland, Dr. Alphabet), b. St. Louis, Sept. 10, 1946, s. Gilbert Jennings and Lillian Gertrude (Murray) M. Author children's books: A Visit from St. Alphabet, 1982, Dot Town, 1984, The Happy Birthday Handbook, 1984; playwright: A Light Draw, 1977, Stargazers, 1978; poetry collections: Poems, 1971, Tilt, 1971, Paper Comet, 1974, Snapshots from Europe, 1974, Poetry City, USA, 1977, Jnd-Song of the Golden Gradrti, 1977, Quicksand Through the Hourglass, 1979, Poetry Comics, 1981, A Tourist's Guide to Computers, 1985; ed. mags.: Gum, 1970-73, Matchbook (as Joyce Holland), 1973, Speakeasy, 1976-80, Poetry Comics, 1979-82. BA in English, St. Louis U., 1969; MFA in poetry, U. Iowa, 1972. Tchr. Iowa Arts Council, Des Moines, 1975-80; computer typesetter U. Iowa, Iowa City, 1980-83, computer operator, 1984-85; intl. admissions asst. Washington U., St. Louis, 1985-86. Address: Box 585 Iowa City IA 52240

MORITZ, CHARLES FREDRIC, b. Cleve., Jan. 23, 1917; s. Frederic and Alberta (Hartwig) M. BA, Ohio State U., 1942; student, Harvard, 1946-47, Columbia, 1947-48; BS in L.S., Middlebury (Vt.) Coll., 1948, MA, 1950. Asst. librarian rare book room and reference dept. Yale Library, 1948-50; mem. staff N.Y. Pub. Library, 1950-52; asst. prof. Grad. Schl. Library Service Rutgers U., 1955-58; editor Current Biography, 1958—. Author: book reviews for Booklist, 1952-55. Served with AUS, 1942-45. Mem. ALA, Bibliog. Soc. Am. Home: 518 W 232d St New York NY 10063

MORRESSY, JOHN, b. Bklyn., Dec. 8, 1930; s. John Emmett and Jeanette Agnes (Geraghty) M.; m. Barbara Turner, Aug. 11, 1956. Author: The Blackboard Cavalier, 1966, The Addison Tradition, 1968, Starbrat, 1972, Nail Down the Stars, 1973, A Long Communion, 1974, The Humans of Ziax II, 1974, Under a Calculating Star, 1975, The Windows of Forever, 1975, A Law For the Stars, 1976, The Extraterritorial, 1977, Frostworld and Dreamfire, 1977, Drought on Ziax II, 1978, Ironbrand, 1980, Graymantle, 1981, Kingsbane, 1982, The Mansions of Space, 1983, Other Stories, 1983, The Time of the Annihilator, 1985, A Voice for Princess, 1986, The Questing of Kedrigern, 1987. BA, St. John's U., 1953; MA, NYU, 1961. Instr. English St. John's Univ., Bklyn., 1962-66; asst. prof. English Monmouth Coll., W. Long Branch, NJ, 1966-67, prof. Franklin Pierce Coll., Rindge, NH, 1968—; visiting writer, Worcester Consortium, Mass., 1977, Univ. Maine, Orono, 1977-78, Lynchburg Coll., Va., 1987; wrtr.-in-res., Franklin Pierce Coll., 1978—. Recipient Balrog award Sword and Shield, 1984. Served to Cpl. US Army, 1953-55, Germany. Mem. SFWA, AG. Address: Apple Hill Rd East Sullivan NH 03445

MORRIS, CECELIA MALTBY, b. Rigewood, NJ, July 8, 1916; d. Edward Julius and Grace (Maltby) Daniels; m. John Dalryple Hare, July 28, 1951 (de. Feb. 25, 1955); 1 dau., Sandra Florence. Contrbr. poems to anthols. Grad. private schl., The Hague, Holland. Instr. dance Mary Binney Montgomery Dancers, Phila., 1939-42; cosmetics demonstrator Lit Brothers, Phila., 1956-59. Recipient Honorable Mention awards World of Poetry, 1985, Golden Poet award, 1985, 86, 87. Home: 401 S Evergreen Ave 431 Woodbury NJ 08096

MORRIS, EDMUND, b. Nairobi, Kenya, May 27, 1940; came to U.S., 1968, naturalized, 1979; s. Eric Edmund and May Catherine (Dowling) M.; m. Sylvia Jukes, May 18, 1966. Author: The Rise of Theodore Roosevelt (Pulitzer prize for biography, Am. book award 1980). Student, Rhodes U., Grahamstown, S. Africa, 1959-1960. Address: 240 Central Park South New York NY 10019

MORRIS, ELIZABETH J., b. Rogers City, MI, Mar. 30, 1934, d. Paul Vivian and Janet (Alp) Thornley; m. Thomas Patrick Morris, Aug. 23, 1957; children—Thomas Jr., Catherine, Marianne. Contrbr. short stories to numerous lit. mags.; 2 full-length plays stage read, 1 one-act produced on radio, 1 in local theater, 1987. Newspaper wrtr., columnist Jnl. Newspapers, Bethesda, Md., 1972-82; lib. asst., 1981-84; word processor and active volunteer for 10 years, Wrtr.'s Center, Bethesda; project asst. PEN Syndicated Fiction Program, Bethesda, 1984-87. Mem. P&W. Home: 8708 Ewing Dr Bethesda MD 20817

MORRIS, MARNA JAY, b. Amityville, NY, Sept. 14, 1949; d. Theodore Sylvan and Bernice Rose (Plotnick) Berusch; m. Joel Rosenstock, Aug. 29, 1971 (div. Sept. 12, 1978); children—Scott Adam, Todd Stuart; m. 2d, James L. Morris, III, Aug. 9, 1985. Contrbr. articles to mags., newsletters including Country Rhythms, Mainstream Am., Philip Morris Derby Tabloid. Wrkg. on articles. B.A., SUNY-Cortland, 1970; post-grad. U. Louisville, N.Y., 1982—. Elem. tchr. Middle Country Community Schl. Dist., Centereach, N.Y., 1970-71; spcl. ed. tchr. St. John's Schl., Brussels, Belgium, 1971-76, Jefferson County Pub. Schl., Louisville, 1978-82; pres. Star Drive, Inc., Louisville, 1982—, M/J Morris, Inc., Louisville, 1985—. Mem. Natl. Assn. Female Execs., Fraternal Order Police, Country Music Assn., NEA, Ky. Retired Tchr. Assn. Home: 504 Palisades Ct Louisville KY 40223

MORRIS, MARY, b. Chgo., May 14, 1947, d. Sol H. and Rosalie (Zimbroff) Morris. Author: Vanishing Animals & Other Stories, 1979, Crossroads (novel), 1983, The Bus of Dreams (short stories), 1985, The Waiting Room (novel), 1989, Nothing to Declare (travel memoir), 1987. BA, Tufts Coll., 1969; MPhil, Columbia U., 1977. Ed. Beacon Press, Boston, 1969-72; mem. faculty Rutgers U., N.J., 1979; prof. Princeton (N.J.) U., 1980-86; prof., U. of Calif., Irvine, 1987-. NEA fellow, 1978, Guggenheim fellow, 1980; recipient Rome Prize in Lit., AAIAL, 1980. Mem. PEN. Home: 137 W 75th St New York NY 10023

MORRIS, MARY ELIZABETH, b. Ironton, OH, Mar. 2, 1913; d. J. Boyd and Elizabeth (Jones) Davis; m. Donald McLeon Pond, Dec. 10, 1934; m. William Morris, Feb. 8, 1947; children: Ann Elizabeth (Mrs. Paul S. Downie), Susan Jane, John Boyd, William Frazer, Mary Elizabeth, Evan Nathanael. Student, Ohio State U., 1930-34. Editor No. Star, Columbus, Ohio, summers 1930-31; editor Ohio Republican Woman, 1930-32; reporter Columbus Citizen, 1931-34; free lance writer, editor, 1934-41; founder labor sect. A.R.C., Washington, 1941, chief, 1941-45. Co-author: syndicated daily newspaper column Words, Wit and Wisdom, Norris Assocs., 1953—; exec. editor: Xerox Intermediate Dictionary, also Xerox Beginning Dictionary, 1973, Ginn Intermediate Dictionary, 1974, Weekly Reader Beginning Dictionary, 1974, Ginn Beginning Dictionary, 1974; Author: (with William Morris) The Word Game Book, 1959, 2d edit., 1975, Dictionary of Word and Phrase Origins, Vol. I, 1962, Vol. II, 1967, Vol. III, 1971, Harper Dictionary Contemporary Usage, 1975, 2d edit., 1984, The Morris Dictionary of Word and Phrase Origins, 1977, Words, Wit and Wisdom, 1978. Mem. Theta Sigma Phi. Home: 355 Sound Beach Ave Old Greenwich CT 06870

MORRIS, RICHARD W., b. Milw., June 16, 1939, s. Alvin Harry and Dorothy Lydia (Wissmueller) M. Author: He Dreamed, 1967, Prey, 1968, Don Giovanni Meets the Lone Ranger, 1970, Reno, Nevada, 1971, Plays, 1973, The Board of Directors, or Grape-Nuts, 1975, Poetry Is a Kind of Writing, 1975, Light, 1979, The End of the World, 1980, The Fate of the Universe, 1982, Evolution and Human Nature, 1983, Dismantling the Universe, 1983, Time's Arrows, 1985, The Nature of Reality, 1986, The Word and Beyond (with others), 1982; ed.: Camels Coming mag., 1965-68, Camels Coming Press, 1967-73; assoc. ed. San Francisco Book Rvw, 1971-72. Wrkg. on non-fiction. BS, U. Nev.-Reno, 1962, PhD, 1968; MS, U. N.Mex., 1964. Exec. dir. COSMEP, San Francisco, 1968—, ed. COSMEP Newsletter, 1969—. Office: Box 703 San Francisco CA 94101

MORRIS, ROBERT MCQUARY, b. Levelland, TX, Feb. 6, 1933; s. Arthur Garfield and Vera (Gardner) M.; m. Mary Pauline (Erschoen) Oct. 15, 1966; 1 son—Peter. Author: Hit and

Run (novel), 1986; fiction, articles to L.A. Times, lit and commercial mags. Fiction ed. West Coast Writer's Conspiracy. Coord. Sierra University Writer's Institute, 1985. BA, jnlsm., Univ. of Houston. AUS 1953-55 (Japan). Reporter, Wave Pubns., 1961-63; probation ofcr., LA county, 1963-85. Freelance, 1985—. Home: 8001 Kittyhawk Ave Los Angeles CA 90045

MORRIS, WILLIAM, b. Boston, Apr. 13, 1913; s. Charles Hyndman and Elizabeth Margaret (Hanna) M.; m. Jane Frazer, Aug. 7, 1939; m. Mary Elizabeth Davis, Feb. 8, 1947; children: Ann Elizabeth Morris Downie, Susan Jane, John Boyd, William Frazer, Mary Elizabeth, Evan Nathanael. AB, Harvard U., 1934. Instr. English and Latin, Newman Schl., 1935-37; mem. staff coll. dept. G.&C. Merriam Co., 1937-43; mng. editor Grosset & Dunlap, 1945-47, exec. editor, 1947-53, editor-in-chief, 1953-60; exec. editor Encyc. Intl., 1960-62; editor-in-chief Grolier Universal Encyc., 1962-64, Am. Heritage Dictionary, 1964-72, Xerox Intermediate Dictionary and Weekly Reader Beginning Dictionary, 1971—. Author: William Mororis on Words for The Bell-McClure Syndicate, 1953-68, (with Mary Morris) Words, Wit and Wisdom for Los Angeles Times Syndicate, 1968-75, United Feature Syndicate, 1975—; cons. editor: Funk & Wagnalls New Standard Dictionary, intl. ed. 1954-58, Funk & Wagnalls New Coll. Standard Dictionary, 1958-60; author: It's Easy to Increase Your Vocabulary, 1957, (with Mary Morris) The Word Game Book, 1959, Dictionary of Word and Phrase Origins, vol. I, 1962, vol. II, 1967, vol. III, 1972, Your Heritage of Words, 1970, Harper Dictionary of Contemporary Usage, 1975, 2d edit., 1984, Morris Dictionary of Word and Phrase Origins, 1977, 2d edit., 1987; editor: Words: The New Dictionary, 1947, Berlitz Self-Teacher Language Books, 1949-53; creator: William Morris Vocabulary Enrichment Program, 1964; editor: Young People's Thesaurus Dictionary, 1971; contbr. to: Newsbreak. Ind. candidate for Vice Pres. U.S., 1976. Served to lt. (j.g.) U.S. Maritime Service, 1943-45. Mem. NCTE, Coll. English Assn., ALA. Home: 355 Sound Beach Ave Old Greenwich CT 06870

MORRIS, WRIGHT, b. Central City, NE, Jan. 6, 1910; s. William H. and Grace (Osborn) M.; m. Mary E. Finfrock, 1934 (div. 1961); m. Josephine Kantor, 1961. Author: My Uncle Dudley, 1942, The Man Who Was There, 1945, The Inhabitants, 1946, The Home Place, 1948, The World in the Attic, 1949, Man and Boy, 1951, The Works of Love, 1952, The Deep Sleep, 1953, The Huge Season, 1954, The Field of Vision (Natl. Book award 1956), Love Among the Cannibals, 1957, The Territory Ahead, 1958, Ceremony in Lone Tree, 1960, The Mississippi River Reader, 1961, What a Way to Go, 1962, Cause for Wonder, 1963, One Day, 1965, In Orbit, 1967, A Bill of Rites, A Bill of Wrongs, a Bill of Goods, 1968, God's Country and My People, 1968, Wright Morris: A Reader, 1970, Fire Sermon, 1971, War Games, 1971, Love Affair, A Venetian Journal, 1972, Here is Einbaum, 1973, A Life, 1973, About Fiction, 1975, Real Losses, Imaginary Gains, 1976, The Fork River Space Project, 1977, Earthly Delights, Unearthly Adornments: The American Writer as Images Maker, 1978, Plains Song, 1980 (Am. Book award) Will's Boy, 1981, Photographs and Words, 1982, Solo: An American Dreamer in Europe, 1933-34, 1983, collected stories, 1984-86, 1986. Student, Pomona Coll., 1930-33. Recipient Robert Kirsch award for body of work, 1981; Guggenheim fellow, 1942, 46, 54. Mem. NIAL, AAAS. Office: Harper & Row 10 E 53d St New York NE 10022

MORRISEY, THOMAS, b. Dwight, IL, Mar. 8, 1952; s. Thomas James and Mary Ann (Masley) M.; m. Patricia Eileen Long, Dec. 29, 1972. Author: 20 American Peaks and Crags, 1978. Wrkg. on novel. BA with honors in English, U. Toledo, 1977, MA, 1979; MFA in Creative Writing, Bowling Green State U., 1982. Freelance wrtr., 1974-83; spl. project ed. Ceco Pub. Co., Warren, Mich., 1983-85, ed., v.p., 1986—, features ed. Friends mag., 1983-85, exec. ed., 1987—; sr. sci. wrtr. Gen. Motors Co., Warren, 1985-86. Mem. SATW. Home: 11480 S Crestline Dr Romeo MI 48065

MORRISON, ALEXANDER DAMIEN, see Stumpo, Carmine DeRogatis

MORRISON, APRIL DAWN, b. Bar Harbor, ME, Mar. 1, 1971; d. Mertic Arthur and Etta (Buswell) Morrison. Poetry in anthologies. Wrkg. on poetry. Student private schl., Newcastle, Me. Home: HC 62 Box 246 New Harbor ME 04554

MORRISON, DENISE ANNETTE, b. Malone, NY, d. Louis and Dorothea Louise (Howell) Papineau; children—Paul A., Gwen A., Amy J., Adam C., Kim M., Scot A., Angel Lynn. Contrbr. to Am. Poetry Anthology, 1986, Hollywood Gold Record Album, 1986. Student Jefferson Community Coll., Watertown, N.Y., 1984; degree in travel theory and computer operations, Metro Inst. of Travel, Syracuse, N.Y., 1986. Asst. med. reference librarian House of Good Samaritan Hosp., Watertown, N.Y., 1985—. Home: Box 25 Lyons Falls NY 13368

MORRISON, FRANK, (Mickey Spillane), b. Bklyn., Mar. 9, 1918; s. John Joseph and Catherine Anne Spillane; m. Mary Ann Pearce, 1945; children—Kathy, Ward, Mike, Carolyn; 2nd m. Sherri Malinou, Nov. 1964 (div); 3rd m. Jane Johnson of Marion, S.C. Author: mystery-suspense novels I, The Jury, 1947, Vengeance is Mine! (filmed in 1957), My Gun Is Quick, 1950 (filmed in 1957), The Big Kill, 1951, One Lonely Night, 1951, The Long Wait, 1951 (filmed in 1954), Kiss Me, Deadly, 1952 (filmed in 1955), Tough Guys, 1960, The Deep, 1961, Day of the Guns, 1964, The Snake, 1964, Bloody Sunrise, 1965, The Death Dealers, 1965, The Twisted Thing, 1966, The By-Pass Control, 1967, The Delta Factor, 1967 (filmed), Survival: Zero, 1970, Me, Hood, Hiller Mine, The Flier, Return of the Hood, Tomorrow I Die, 1984; children's book The Day the Sea Rolled Back, 1979; many others; also author: The Girl Hunters, 1962; author screenplay, 1963; starred in role of Mike Hammer: TV series premiered, "Mickey Spillane's Mike Hammer," 1958; as of 1987, 14 years with Miller Lite Beer TV commercials. Attended Fort Hays Kans. State Coll. Scripter, asst. editor, Funnies, Inc., in 1940s. Served to capt. USAF, World War II. Office: Mysterious Press 129 W 56th St NYC NY 10019

MORRISON, GRACE, see Chalip, Alice Grace

MORRISON, J. KEN, b. Salem, OR, Oct. 19, 1950; s. James M. and Frances J. M.; m. Jenni Raies, Sept. 4, 1976; children—Brent James, Shelby Melaka. Ed. & contrbr. Chain Saw Age Mag., 1979—; contrbr. to Oregon Business, Wood N Energy, Scies a Moteur. BA in Environmental Sci., Willamette U., 1973. Skiffman F/V Marjie Ann, Kodiak, AK, 1969-73, 76, 78; skipper M/V Del Rio, Anacortes, WA, 1974; sci. instr. Clatskanie (OR) Jr. H.S., 1977-78; ed./prod. mgr. Chain Saw Age, Portland, OR, 1979—. Office: Chain Saw 3435 N E Brdway Portland OR 97232

MORRISON, LAURA MARY, b. Summit, NJ, July 17, 1927; d. Fredrick Robert and Kathryn Bernedette (Ryan) M. Author: The Calculus of Variations and the Maximum Principle: Methods of Optimization for Dynamic Systems, 1964, Integration in Thought and Behavior: a Neuropsychological Theory, 1984. MS in Math., NYU, 1962; MA in Psychology, New Sch. Social Research, 1970. Ops. research analyst Esso R&E, Florham Park, N.J., 1962-65, Union Carbide Corp., NYC, 1965-67, Eastern Airlines, NYC, 1967-70; dir. research and devel. Harbor Pub. Co., NYC, 1979—. Mem. Mensa, Art Students League NYC. Office: Harbor Pub 80 N Moore St New York NY 10013

MORRISON, LILLIAN, b. Oct. 27, 1917, Jersey City, NJ; d. William and Rebecca (Nehamkin) M. Author: poetry, The Ghosts of Jersey City, 1967, Miranda's Music (with J. Boudin), 1968, The Sidewalk Racer, 1977, Who Would Marry a Mineral?, 1978, Overheard in a Bubble Chamber, 1981, The Break Dance Kids, 1985; anthologist, Yours Till Niagara Falls, 1950, Black Within and Red Without, 1953, A Diller, A Dollar, 1955, Touch Blue, 1958, Remember Me When This You See, 1961, Sprints and Distances, 1965, Best Wishes, Amen, 1974; articles in library jnls. BS, mathematics, Douglass College, Rutgers, 1938; BS, library science, Columbia Univ., 1942. Librarian, NY Pub. Lib., 1942-68; genl. ed., Crowell Poets Series (21 vols.), 1963-74; genl. ed., Crowell Poems of the World Series, 1966-74; lectr., Columbia Univ., Rutgers Univ., 1960-61; ed. Books for the Teen Age, 1968-82; coord. Young Adult Svcs., NY Pub. Lib., 1968-82. Wrkg. on vol. of poems, new poetry anthol. Mem. Authors Guild, PSA, Phi Beta Kappa. Home: 116 Pinehurst Ave New York NY 10033

MORRISON, MADISON, b. June 28, 1940. Author: Girls, 1976, Poems, 1977, Sleep, 1981, O, 1982, Light, 1983, Revolution (with Dan Boord), 1985, Selected Poems, 1985, Realization, I, 1986. BA, Yale U, 1961; AM, Harvard U, 1962, PhD, 1969. Tchg fellow Harvard Univ., 1963-65; lectr. Univ. Md., Overseas div.,1965-67; asst. prof. Univ. Okla., 1969-74, assoc. prof. 1974-86, prof. 1986—. Recipient Ingram Merrill Fdn. award, 1979; NEA Creative Writing fellow, 1980; NEH seminar award, 1980. Address: 420 W Eufaula St Norman OK 73069

MORRISON, MARVIN L., b. Montgomery, AL, Sept. 15, 1940; s. Delwin Russell and Stella Mable (Whidden) M.; m. Janet Faith Lewis, Jan. 29, 1965 (div. May 31, 1984); children—Spencer Lee, Chadwick David. Author: Word City; A New Language Tool, 1981, Wordfinder: The Phonic Key to the Dictionary, 1987 (rev. of Word City). A.B., Toccoa Falls Coll., 1962; Th.M., Dallas Theol. Seminary, 1966. Address: Box 305 Stone Mountain GA 30086

MORRISON, SUSAN GAYNELLE, b. Olathe, KS, Oct. 21, 1958, d. Earl DeWayne and Beverly Ann (Lloyd) M. Contrbr. poems to anthols. Wrkg. on Vietnam Vets. book, greeting cards. Student Natl. Coll. Bus., Kansas City, Mo., 1980. Qual. control inspector, Broadway Collection, Lenexa, Kans., 1983—. Home: 207 Colleen Gardner KS 66030

MORRISON, SUSAN ORINDA, (Indigo), b. Pontiac, MI, Jan. 2, 1948; d. John Elwood and Millicent Elaine (Truit) Orvis; m. Mahlon Lewis, June 25, 1978. Contrbr. poems to anthols., newspapers. Cert. in Cosmetology, Murrays Beauty Acad., 1969. Librarian public schl., Waterford, MI, 1965-66; waitress Meeting Place, Lewiston, MI, 1983-84. Recipient Golden Poet award World of Poetry, 1987, Honorable Mention, 1987. Home: Rt 1 Box 34 S Bourne Lewiston MI 49756

MORRISON, TONI, (Chloe Anthony Morrison) b. Lorain, OH, Feb. 18, 1931; d. George and Ella Ramah (Willis) Wofford; children: Harold Ford, Slade Kevin. Author: The Bluest Eye, 1970, Sula, 1974, Song of Solomon, 1977, Tar Baby, 1983, Beloved, 1987. B.A., Howard U., 1953; M.A., Cornell U., 1955. Tchr. English and humanities Tex. So. U., 1955-57, Howard U., 1957-64; editor Random House, N.Y.C., 1965—. Mem. AG (council). Office: 201 E 50th St New York NY 10022

MORROW, GEORGE TELFORD II, b. Oakland, CA, Aug. 25, 1943, s. George Telford and Elizabeth (Hirschboeck) M.; m. Joan Helen Schieferstein, Apr. 1971. Contrbr. articles, book rvws. to local newspapers. BA with honors, Rutgers U., 1965; MA, Brown U., 1967; JD cum laude William Mitchell Coll. Law, 1977. Dir., pub. Minn. State Register, St. Paul, 1975-77; sole practice law, Mpls., 1977-84; v.p., secy. and genl. counsel United Health Care Corp., Minnetonka, Minn., 1984—. Mem. legal orgns. Office: United Health 9900 Bren Rd E Minnetonka MN 55343

MORROW, SHEILA ANN, b. Detroit, July 4, 1936; d. Howard Henry and Mildred Marjorie (Jones) Baker; m. Wildred Russell Rooen (div. May 31, 1966); children—Kent R., Marjorie V., Bruce E., Scott L.; m. Glenn Gordon Hutton (div. Feb. 1976); 1 dau., Glenda G.; m. Lyle Harold Morrow, Dec. 27, 1980. Author handbook: How to Be a Good Carrier for Fun and Profit, 1985. Columnist: Brightmoor Jnl., 1981-82. Lyricist: No Matter Where You Are, 1987. B.A., Wayne State U., 1979, M.A., 1981. Newsletter ed. DeRoy Tenants Council, Detroit, 1977-79, Mature & Returning Students, Detroit, 1978-81; mgr. Kari Louise Originals, Detroit, 1980—. Home: 15803 Hazelton Detroit MI 48223

MORROW, WILLIAM L, (C. Cummins Catherwood), b. Sanford, NC, Nov. 14, 1943; s. Lee Edwin and Rosalie M. (Parrish) M. Contrbr. poems to anthols. Wrkg. on 2 novels. Student Wake Forest U., 1963—64, Trenton State Coll., 1968—69. Detective, N.J. State Police, 1966—71; area mgr. AT&T, 1971—. Home: Box 9023 Englewood CO 80111

MORSE, CARMEL LEI, b. Spokane, WA, June 15, 1953; d. John Ola and Billie Jean (Garrett) Lindgren; m. David Scott Morse, June 21, 1980; 1 dau. by previous marriage, Theresa Jean Keaton. Author: Audio Visual Primer, 1983. BFA, Wright State U., 1979. Audio-visual librarian Wright Library, Dayton, Ohio, 1983-84; gen. mgr. Brookline Visual Arts Svcs., Inc., Dayton, 1980—. Recipient hon. mention Ohio Poetry Days, 1979; Wright State U. scholar, 1977. Club: Miami Valley Student Filmmakers (coordinator 1977-79). Home: 130 Watervliet Ave Dayton OH 45420

MORSE, MARGARET PATRICIA, (Peggy Mansfield Morse), b. Boston, Feb. 25, 1912; d. John Edward and Margaret Agnes (Gaffney) Mansfield; m. Carroll Burton Morse, Aug. 17, 1931 (dec. Nov. 6, 1973); children—Patricia, Carole A., M. Rita, Edward, R. Michael, George F., John M. Contrbr. numerous poems to anthols., newspapers; short stories to newspaper. Wrkg. on short stories, poems. Student Inst. Children's Writing Lit., 1977-79, Cape Cod Commun. Coll., 1981-82, 82-83. Billing and payroll clrk. George Frost Co., Shirley, MA, 1947-60; accounting & administrative asst., Fort Devens, MA, 1960-80, retired. Home: 1183 County Rd Cataumet MA 02534

MORSE, PEGGY MANSFIELD, see Morse, Margaret Patricia

MORTEMORE, LENORE MARY, b. Batavia, NY, Apr. 25, 1927; d. Hans Peter and Mary Theresa (Balintfy) Cartensen; m. Donald William Mortemore (div. 1971); children—Jeffrey Craig, Denise Lenore, Derrick Lance, Janell Dianne. Author: Individualized Instruction in the Washington Local Schools, 1970. Contrbr. short story, poems to local newspaper, anthol. Wrkg. on short stories, poems, biography. Med. technologist Riverside Hosp., Toledo, OH, 1957-59; tchr. biology Bedford Public Schls, Temperance, MI, 1959-60; tchr. sci. Toledo Public Schls., 1962-65, Washington Local Schls., Toledo, 1965—. Recipient Outstanding Educator award Tchr.'s Assn. Washington Local Schls., 1983; Silver Poet award World of Poetry, 1986, Golden Poet award, 1987. Home: 3923 Brockton Dr Toledo OH 43623

MORTENSEN, ROBERTA, see Moore, Roberta Lynn

MORTIMER, WILLIAM JOHN, b. Bklyn., July 21, 1934, s. John Joseph and Mary Agnes (Hennessy) M.; m. Patricia Marie Wagner, Feb. 4, 1956; children—Bill, Theresa, Mary Lou, Tony, John, Gloria, Gina. Contrbr. articles: Point-of-Purchase Advt. Inst., Intl. Trade News. BA, St. John's U.; MS, Columbia U. Ed. Ahrens Pub. Co., N.Y.C., 1955-60; ed., pub. Automotive Retailer, Inc., Southport, Conn., 1960-68; sales-mktg. mgr. Consolidated Foods, Medina, Ohio, 1968-71; pub. Mortimer Communications, Fairfield, Conn., 1971—. Mem. profl. orgns. Home: 461 Skytop Dr Fairfield CT 06432

MORTON, ANNE MARIE JUDITH, b. Lackawanna, NY, July 11, 1965; W. Roger and Joan F. (Ash) M.; Editor-contributor: Emerson Review, 1987. Wrkg. on short stories & (novel) Holidays & Other Disasters. B.F.A. Emerson College, 1987; postgrad. Harvard University 1987—. Arhitectural photographer, Weathershield Mfg. 1983-86; prod. asst. Duck Productions, Boston, 1985-1986; Producer, WBZ—radio, Boston, 1987—. Home: 326 Dartmouth St Boston MA 02116

MORTON, FREDERIC, b. Vienna, Austria, Oct. 5, 1924; s. Frank and Rose (Ungvary) M.; m. Marcia Colman, Mar. 28, 1957; 1 dau., Rebecca. Author: novels The Hound, 1947, The Darkness Below, 1949, Asphalt and Desire, 1952, The Witching Ship, 1960, The Schatten Affair, 1965, Snow Gods, 1969, An Unknown Woman, 1976, This Forever Street, 1984; biography The Rothschilds, 1962, A Nervous Splendor—Vienna 1888/9, 1979; Crosstown Sabbath, 1987 (nonfiction); books transl. into 14 langs.; contrbr. to: publs. including Martha Foley's Best Am. Short Stories; other anthologies, N.Y. Times, Harper's mag., Atlantic mag., Nation, Playboy, Esquire, N.Y. Mag., Hudson Rvw., others; columnist: Village Voice. B.S., Coll. City N.Y., 1947; M.A., New Sch. Social Research, 1949. Recipient Author of Year award Natl. Anti-Defamation League, B'nai B'rith; Hon. Professorship award Republic of Austria, 1980; Golden Badge of Honor, City of Vienna, 1986; Dodd, Mead Intercollegiate Lit. fellow, 1947; Yaddo residence fellow, 1948, 50; Breadloaf Writer's Conf. fellow, 1947; Columbia U. fellow, 1953. Mem. AG (exec. council), P.E.N. Home: 110 Riverside Dr New York NY 10024

MOSCOVIT, ANDREI, see Yefimov, Igor

MOSELEY, WILLIAM, b. Todd County, KY, Nov. 3, 1935, s. John Preston and Mary Agnes (Swope) M. Playwright: Scenes from a Non-Marriage (with Edward Albee and others), 1981; contrbr. short stories to Best Am. Short Stories 1968, Pilgrims: An Anthology of Readings, 1971, One-Act Plays for Acting Students, 1987, mags including Epoch, Florida Rvw, Prairie Schooner; author radio-drama for prodn. in NYC, Ky. AB in English, U. Ky., 1958; MA in English, U. So. Calif.-Los Angeles, 1965. Instr. creative wrtg. Brevard Community Coll., Cocoa, Fla., 1971-73, mem. adj. faculty, 1974—; adj. faculty in wrtg. U. Central Fla., Orlando, 1985—; vis. wrtr. summer workshop Eastern Ky. U., Richmond, 1973, 83; freelance wrtr., 1970—; lit. dir. Space Coast Playwrights Workshop. Recipient Balch Fiction award Va. Qtly Rvw, 1967, Boyle Playwriting prize U. Va., 1984; grantee Fla. Arts Council, 1983. Home: 19 Alexander St Rockledge FL 32955

MOSER, DONALD BRUCE, b. Cleve., Oct. 19, 1932; s. Donald Dyman and Kathryn (McHugh) M.; m. Penny Lee Ward, Dec. 10, 1975. B.A., Ohio U., 1957; postgrad., Stanford U., 1957-58, U. Sydney, 1959-60. With Life mag., 1961-72. West Coast bur. chief, 1964-65, Far East bur. chief, 1966-69, asst. mng. editor, 1970-72; freelance writer, 1972-77; exec. editor Smithsonian mag., Washington, 1977-80, editor, 1981—. Author: The Peninsula, 1962, The Snake River Country, 1974, A Heart to the Hawks, 1975, Central American Jungles, 1976, China-Burma-India, 1978; contbr. articles to numerous mags., jnls. Served with U.S. Army, 1953-55. Stegner fellow, 1957-58; Fulbright scholar, 1959-60. Mem. Phi Beta Kappa. Office: Smithsn Mag 900 Jefferson Dr Washington DC 20560

MOSER, HAROLD DEAN, b. Kannapolis, NC, Oct. 31, 1938; s. Walter Glenn and Angie Elizabeth (Allen) M.; m. Carolyn Irene French, Mar. 28, 1964; children: Andrew Paul, Anna Elizabeth. AA, Wingate Coll., 1959; BA cum laude, Wake Forest U., 1961; MA Univ. fellow, Wake Forest U., 1963; PhD Ford fellow, U. Wis., 1977. Tchr. Robert B. Glenn High Schl., Winston-Salem, N.C., 1961-62; instr. history Chowan Coll., Murfreesboro, N.C., 1963-64; Teaching asst dept. history U. Wis., Madison, 1967-79; Nat. Hist. Publ. Commn. fellow The papers of Daniel Webster (Dartmouth Coll.), Hanover, N.H., 1971-72, asst. editor, 1972-73, assoc. editor, 1973-76, co-editor, 1976-77, editor corr. series, 1978-79; editor dir. The Papers of Andrew Jackson, 1979—; research prof. in history, U. of Tenn. Mem. Am. Hist. Assn., So. Hist. Assn., Orgn. Am. Historians, Soc. Historians of Early Am. Republic, Assn. for Documentary Editing, Tenn. Hist. Soc. Home: 9605 Tallahassee Ln Knoxville TN 37923

MOSER, NORMAN CALVIN, b. Durham, NC, Oct. 15, 1931; s. William Monroe and Myrtle Sarah (Jordan) M.; m. Hadassah Haskale, July 1966 (div. 1971); m. Yolanda Ponce Chirinos de Jesus, Nov. 17, 1977 (div. 1982); 1 son, David Preston. Student, U. Md., Ulm, Germany, 1955-56, U. Pacific, 1958; BA, San Francisco State U., 1961; MA in Lang. Arts, San Francisco State

U., 1966; postgrad., U. Wash., 1962, U. B.C., Can., 1963. Co-pub. weekly tabloid Bay Window (name later changed to Bay Area Arts Rvw), San Francisco, 1957-59; editor lit. mag. Transfer, San Francisco State U., 1959-61; editor, pub. Illuminations, Berkeley, Calif., 1965—; freelance writer. Singer-actor, Am. Guild Variety Artists, 1950-53; actor in plays and films; author: Jumpsongs, 1973, A Shaman's Songbook/ Poems & Tales, 1975, I Live in the South of My Heart, 1980, Open Season, 1980, The Shorter Plays & Scenarios of Norm Moser, 1981, El Grito del Norte & Other Stories, 1984; contrbr. to anthologies Because You Talk, 1976, Travois, 1976, Living Underground, 1973, Contemporary Literary Scene, 1974, Red Clay Reader, 1968, Green Isle in the Sea, 1986, others; contrbg. editor: Grande Ronde Rvw, 1969-71, Reader, 1968, Other Side, 1982, others; staff editor, writer: The Gar, 1972-74; contrbr. numerous articles, stories, poems and rvws. to lit. mags, anthologies and newspapers. Home: 2110 9th St B Berkeley CA 94710

MOSES, CLAIRE GOLDBERG, b. Hartford, CT, June 22, 1941, d. Abraham R. and Pauline (Hurwich) Moses; m. Arnold Moses, Sept. 11, 1966; children—Lisa, Leslie. Author: French Feminism in the Nineteenth Century, 1984; ed., mgr. Feminist Studies, 1977—. AB, Smith Coll., 1963; MPhL, George Washington U., 1971, PhD,1978. Assoc. European ed. Bus. Intl., NYC,1965-67; asst. professorial lectr. George Washington U., Washington, 1972-76; staff assoc. Am. Hist. Assn., Washington, 1976; assoc. prof. women's studies U. Md., College Park, 1977—. Recipient Joan Kelly prize Am. Hist. Assn., 1985; named Md. Woman of Letters, Women Legislators of Md., 1986. Mem. Am. Hist. Assn., Natl. Women's Studies Assn., Soc. French Hist. Studies. Office: Women's Studies Program U Md College Park MD 20742

MOSES, ELBERT RAYMOND JR., b. New Concord, OH, Mar. 31, 1908; s. Elbert Raymond and Helen Martha (Miller) M.; m. Mary Miller Sterrett, Sept. 21, 1933 (dec. 1984); 1 son, James Elbert; m. 2d, Caroline Mae Entenman, June 19, 1985. Author: Effective Speaking, 1956, 2d edit., 1957, Phonetics: History and Interpretation, 1964, Three Attributes of God, 1983; contrbr.: Am. Speech and Hearing Mag., Jnl. Am. Speech, Speech Monographs, Vet.'s Voices; poetry in anthologies. Wrkg. on non-fiction book. AB, U. Pitts., 1932; MSc, U. Mich., 1934, PhD, 1936. Mem. faculty dept. speech U. N.C., Greensboro, 1936-38, Ohio State U., Columbus, 1938-46, State U. Charleston, Ill., 1946-56, Mich. State U., East Lansing, 1956-59; prof. speech Clarion U. Pa., 1959-71, emeritus, 1971—. Recipient numerous awards from civic, mil. and govt. orgns. Fellow Am. Biog. Inst. (life), World Lit. Acad. (life); mem. World Inst. Achievement (winner essay competition 1985). Home: 2001 Rocky Dells Dr Prescott AZ 86303

MOSES, WILLIAM ROBERT, b. Alexandria, MN, Dec. 24, 1911; s. W.J. Barr and Annette M. (Peacock) M.; m. Elizabeth B. Petway, Apr. 3, 1935; 1 son, Edwin P. Author poems: Identities, 1965, Passage, 1976, Not Native, 1979, Double View, 1984. PhD, Vanderbilt U., 1939. English instr. Hendrix Coll., Conway, AR, 1935-36, WA St. U., 1936-39, U. IL, 1939-42; asst., assoc., full prof. KS St. U., 1950-82; retired 1982—. Served USNR, 1942-46. Home: 314 Denison Ave Manhattan KS 66502

MOSEY, CARON LEE, b. Flint, MI, Feb. 25, 1956; d. Robert Hayes and Betty Ruth (Spence) Covert; m. Neil Dean Mosey, Jr., Nov. 15, 1975; children—Sean Kempton, Loren Ansley. Author: America's Pictorial Quilts, 1985, Contemporary Quilts from Traditional Designs, 1987. Contrbr. articles to mags. on quilts and quilting. Owner, Quilted Art, Flushing, MI, 1983—. Recipient Citizen's Bank award, Flint, 1985. Mem. NWC, Am. Quilters Soc., Am. Intl. Quilt Assn. Home: 191 Park Ave Flushing MI 48433

MOSIER, JOHN, (Peter Quint), b. Bentonville, AR, July 9, 1944; s. Wilbur and Helen (Friedel) M.; m. Sarah Elizabeth Spain, Dec. 7, 1985; children by previous marriage: Therese, Katherine, Elise. Author: Institutional Research, A Review of the Literature, 1974, Women and Men Together, 1978, Handbook of Latin American Popular Culture, 1985, World Cinema Since 1945, 1986; editor Americas Mag., 1979—, New Orleans Rvw, 1978—; contbr. numerous profl. jnls, mags. BA, Tulane U., 1964, MA, 1966, PhD, 1968. Exec. secy. acad. affairs Loyola U., New Orleans, 1969-74; assoc. dir. Film Buffs Inst., New Orleans, 1975—; prof. English, 1986-. Home: 3524 Audubon Trace Jefferson LA 70121

MOSKOW, SHIRLEY BLOTNICK, b. Cambridge, MA, May 27, 1935; d. Samuel and Mollie (Pearl) Blotnik; m. Richard Sumner Moskow, Dec. 18, 1955; children—Jeffrey Howard, Neal Lewis. B.S., Boston U., 1957. Contrbr. chpt. on estate planning to book; Human Hand & Other Ailments: Letters to the New England Journal of Medicine, 1987. Wrkg. on non-fiction history of 19th Century Americans, novel. Book rvwr. Norfolk Pilot, VA, 1957-60; reporter The News-Tribune, Waltham, MA, 1970—76, lifestyle ed., 1976-82; free-lance wrtr., 1960—. Mem. SPJ (pres. 1982-83), NLAPW. Home: 31 Slocum Rd Lexington MA 02173

MOSLEY, SANDRA SHERRILL, b. Memphis, Aug. 12, 1946; d. Lewis Marion and Geraldine (Tanner) Sherrill; m. John H. Mosley, Jan. 21, 1967; children-John H., Tracy, Janet, Timothy. Columnist, Millington Star, TN, 1963-64. Contrbr. articles, poems, short stories to mags., newspapers including Lady's Circle, Rural Ga., Good Housekeeping, others. Wrkg. on articles, short stories, poems, novel. Student U. Tenn., 1964-67. Billing clrk. Ford dealership, Millington, 1968-69; tutor pvt. high sch., Ludowici, GA, 1979-85; free-lance wrtr., 1986—. Home: 152 Roth Rd Jesup GA 31545

MOSS, GRAVE YARD, b. Birmingham, AL, Nov. 25, 1946; s. Joseph Edward, Sr. and Annie Pearl (Black) M.; m. Cythia Graves, Nov. 22, 1966 (div.); 1 son, Carlton Graves; m. Gloria Jean Stallworth, Feb. 8, 1986; Children—Morgan Virginia, JoAnn Carmesha. Author: Grave Yard Moss Is Still Alive, 1987. Contrbr. poems to numerous anthols. Wrkg. on 2 books of poetry; collection of personalities from youth. Student Detroit Bus. Coll., 1975-76. Wayne State Coll., 1976-77. Inspector Ford Motor Co., Flat Rock, MI, 1972-73; salesman various orgns., Detroit and Atlanta, 1974-75; postal clrk. U.S. Postal Service, Detroit, 1976—. Home: 8566 Prest St Detroit MI 48228

MOSS, MARK DOUGLAS, b. NYC, s. Lyman Roger and Renee (Gruber) Moss. Editor: Sing Out! Magazine, 1982—. Student Pennsylvania State U., three years. Office: Box 1071 Easton PA 18044

MOSS, ROSE, (R. Johannes), b. Johannesburg, S. Africa, Jan. 2, 1937, d. David Hirsch and Yetta (Eidesas) Rappoport; 1 son, Duncan John. Novelist: The Terrorist, 1979, republished as The Schoolmaster, 1981, The Family Reunion, 1974; contrbr. stories to Cimarron Rvw, Twigs, Hudson River Anthology, Echad, numerous other lit mags; contrbr. articles to English in Africa, World Lit. Today, Pacific Qtly, Present Tense, others. MA, U. Natal, 1959; MBA, Boston U., 1983. Mem. faculty U. S. Africa, Pretoria, 1961-63, U. Mass., Boston, 1968-69, Wellesley (Mass.) Coll., 1972-82; free-lance ed., wrtr., Cambridge, Mass., 1984; assoc. Synectics, Cambridge, 1984-87; pres. Rose Moss Assocs., 1987-. McDowell Colony fellow, 1976, 79; guest wrtr. Yaddo Colony, 1977; Mellon Fdn. fellow, 1980; winner short fiction project, PEN, 1985. Mem. PEN. Home: 580 Walnut St Newton MA 02160

MOSSE, GEORGE L., b. Berlin, Sept. 20, 1918; U.S., 1939, naturalized, 1945; s. Hans Lachmann-Mosse and Felicia M. Author: The Struggle for Sovereignty in England, 1950, The Holy Pretence, 1957, The Reformation, 1953, 2d ed., 1963, The Crisis of German Ideology, 1964, The Culture of Western Europe, 1961, 2d ed., 1974, Nazi Culture, 1966, Germans and Jews, 1970, The Nationalisation of the Masses, Political Symbols and Mass Movements in Germany, 1975, (with H. Koenigsberger) Europe in the Sixteenth Century, 1968, Nazism, 1978, Towards the Final Solution: A History of European Racism, 1978, Masses and Men, Nationalist and Fascist Perceptions of Reality, 1980, German Jews Beyond Judaism, 1985, Nationalism and Sexuality, 1985; editor: Police Forces in History, 1975, International Facism, 1979; co-editor: Europe in Review, 1957, Jnl Contemporary History, 1966—, (with Bella Vago) Jews and Non-Jews in Eastern Europe, 1975; contrbr.:New Cambridge Modern History. Student, Cambridge (Eng.) U., 1937-39; BS, Haverford Coll., 1941; PhD, Harvard U., 1946; DLitt, Carthage Coll., 1973, DLitt, Hebrew Union Coll., 1987. From instr. to assoc. prof. State U. Iowa, 1944-55; from assoc. prof. to prof., U. Wis., 1955—, Bascom prof. history, 1964—; Koebner prof. history, Hebrew U., 1979—, fellow Inst. Contemporary Jewry, Hebrew U., 1974—; sr. fellow Australian Natl. U., 1972, 79. Bd. dirs. Wiener Library, London, 1974—, Leo Baeck Inst., NYC,1978—; bd. overseers Tauber Inst., Brandeis U., 1980—. Recipient Premio Storia Aqui, 1975, Premio Prezzolini, 1975—. Mem. AAUP (chmn. Iowa Conf. 1954-55), Am. Soc. Reformation Research (pres. 1962), Am. Soc. Church. History (council 1969-73), Am. Hist. Assn., Am. Acad. Arts and Science, Phi Beta Kappa. Home: 36 Glenway St Madison WI 53705

MOTIER, DONALD, b. Harrisburg, PA, May 17, 1943; s. Donald Boyd and Mary Ruth (Thompson) Miller. Author: (poems) Faces of Being, 1971; On the Hound and Other Prose-Poems, 1978; Just Friends: A Novel and Two Short Stories, 1984; contrbr. poetry to Write On, Quadernia di Poesia, Human Liberation Rvw., Hermes, Apprise, Moody Street Irregulars, also others. AA, York Jr. Coll., Pa., 1963; BA in Philosophy, Millersville State U., Pa., 1970. Library asst. Harrisburg Pub. Library, 1970-76; freelance wrtr., 1977—; library tech. State Library Pa., Harrisburg, 1978—. Home: Box 198 Federal Sq Station Harrisburg PA 17108

MOTT, MICHAEL CHARLES ALSTON, b. London, Dec. 8, 1930 (arrvd. USA 1966), s. Eric Alston and Margaret Bart (Berger) M.; m. Margaret Ann Watt, May 6, 1961; children—Sophie Jane and Amanda Margaret (twins). Author: (novels) The Notebooks of Susan Berry, 1964,

Helmet and Wasps, 1966; (children's novels) Master Entrick, 1965, The Blind Cross, 1969; (poetry) Absence of Unicorns, Presence of Lions, Counting the Grasses, Corday, 1987; author (biography) The Seven Mountains of Thomas Merton, 1984; contrbr. of over 200 poems to anthologies and lit mags, lead rvws. to major met. newspapers. Matriculations, Oriel Coll., Oxford, Eng., 1951; BA with honors, London U., 1971. Instr. Kenyon Coll., Gambier, Ohio, 1966-70; wrtr.-in-res. Emory U., Atlanta, 1970-77, Coll. William and Mary, Va., 1978-79, 85-86; prof. English, Bowling Green State U., Ohio, 1980—; asst. ed. Adam Intl. Rvw, 1956-66; poetry ed. Kenyon Rvw, 1967-70. Served to 2d lt. inf., Brit. Army, 1949-50. Recipient Gov. of Ga.'s award in fine arts, 1974; award The Christophers, 1984; Ohioana award, 1985; Nancy Dasher award, Ohio Coll. Eng. Assn., 1985; Olscamp research award Bowling Green State U., 1985; Guggenheim fellow, 1979-80. Mem. AG, AWP; fellow, Royal Geographical Soc.. Home: 128 N Maple St Bowling Green OH 43402

MOULTON, VIRGINIA NODINE, b. Aurora, IL, June 10, 1925; d. Ralph Harold and Margaret (Woerpel) Nodine; m. Richard Wentworth Moulton, Sept. 20, 1946; children—Richard Wentworth, David Nodine. Contrbr. articles to mags., newspapers including Gold Coast Mag., Pickett Mag., Orlando Sentinel, others. A.A., Endicott Coll., 1945. Staff wrtr. public relations dept. St. Michael Coll., Winooski, VT, 1969-73; corr. Orlando Sentinel, FL, 1973–76; reporter Vero Beach Press Jnl., FL, 1976–78; dir. public relations The Moorings, Vero Beach, 1978-87; pres. Moulton Media Management, Vero Beach, 1987—; Accredited Public Relations Professional. Mem. Fla. Public Relations Assn. (state dir. 1984-85, mem. accreditation bd., 1986-88, chpt. pres. 1983-85; Pres.'s award 1984), Am. Heart Assn. 9state dir. 1986–87, 87-88), Natl. Assn. Real Estate Eds., Fla. Freelance Wrtrs.' Assn. Home: 900 Bowline Dr Vero Beach FL 32963

MOUNTJOY, ROBERTA JEAN, see Sohl, Jerry

MOY, JAMES S., b. Chgo., Sept. 12, 1948; s. Robert Fook Shew and Ann Ngan Kwan (Chin) M.; m. Penelope Marguerite Leavitt, Mar. 4, 1978; 1 dau., Jennifer Anne Leavitt-Moy. Ed., Theatre Jnl., 1982-85, assoc. ed., 1986—; contrbr. to Themes in Drama, Theatre Survey, Theatre Research Intl., Theatre Quarterly, Theatre Hist. Studies, High Performance, Histoire du Theatre au Canada, Nineteenth Century Theatre Research, Theatre Jnl. AB in Art, U. IL, 1971, AM in Theatre, 1973, PhD in Theatre, 1977. Instr., U. TX, 1977-79; asst. prof. U. OR, 1979-81, U. WI, 81-84; assoc. prof. U. WI,1984—. Mem. MLA, Am. Soc. for Theatre Research, Am. Theatre Assn. Home: 3121 Oxford Rd Madison WI 53705

MOYNAHAN, JULIAN LANE, b. Cambridge, MA, May 21, 1925; s. Joseph Leo and Mary (Shea) M.; m. Elizabeth Rose Reilly, Aug. 6, 1945; children—Catherine, Brigid, Mary Ellen. Author: Sisters and Brothers, 1960, The Deed of Life, A Critical Study of D.H. Lawrence, 1963, Pairing Off, 1969, Vladimir Nabokov, 1971, Garden State, 1973, Where the Land and Water Meet, 1979; editor: The Viking Portable Thomas Hardy, 1977; contrbr. rvws. and criticism to NY Times Book Rvw, others. Mem. Pulitzer Prize in Fiction jury, 1983, chmn., 1988. AB, Harvard U., 1947, A.M., 1951, PhD,1957. Cataloguer, rare books asst. Boston Pub. Library, 1948-49, 51; teaching fellow Harvard U., 1951-53; instr. English Amherst Coll., 1953-55; instr., asst. prof. English Princeton, 1955-63; Fulbright lectr. Am. and English lit. Univ. Coll., Dublin, 1963-64; assoc. prof English Rutgers U., 1964-66, prof., 1966—, disting. prof., 1976—; Gauss lectr. Princeton U., 1975. Bicentennial preceptorship Princeton, 1960-63, grants-in-aid Am. Council Learned Socs., Am. Philo. Soc. Served with AUS, 1943-44. Creative writing award Natl. Fdn. Arts, 1966; Ingram-Merrill award, 1967; NEH fellow, 1975; Guggenheim fellow, 1983-84. Mem. MLA, AAUP, PEN. Home: 3439 Lawrenceville Rd Princeton NJ 08540

MOZESON, ISAAC ELCHANAN, b. Vancouver, B.C., Can., Nov. 20, 1951 (arrvd. USA 1953), s. Leon M. and Bernice (Tuniss) M.; m. Lois Stavsky, July 4, 1978; children—Sau Wai Ching, Daniel Reyes. Author: The Word—The English from Hebrew Dictionary: Revealing the Hebrew Sources of English, 1986, The Watcher and Other Poems, 1986; book rvw. ed. Judaica Book News mag., 1981-84; weekly book columnist, "Speaking of Books," The Jewish Press newspaper, 1982-85; ed., contrbr. Ten Jewish American Poets, 1982. BA, Yeshiva Coll., 1973; MA, CCNY, 1975; postgrad. NYU, 1975-79. Instr. English, Yeshiva U., NYC, 1975-79, Bramson ORT Tech. Inst., NYC, 1980—. Recipient award for religious poetry N.Y. Poetry Forum, 1980, 81. Mem. P&W. Home: 24 Fifth Ave New York NY 10011

MOZZER, ALANNA JEAN, b. Cumberland, MD, Mar. 17, 1952; d. Alexander John and Anna May (Kucynski) M. Columnist: Published!, 1986-87, Wrtrs. Alliance Newsletter, 1985–86, Chips off the Wrtrs. Block, 1985-86. Contrbr. book rvws., articles, news releases to mags., newsletters, books; planetarium scripts. Field ed.: Teaching Exceptional Children, 1985—; John Proctor and Some of His Descendants (Leland Proctor), 1985, Island Women, 1984, Am. Assn. Univ. Women Bulltn., 1978-79; editorial asst.: (script) The Invisible Universe, 1985. B.A., U. Hartford, 1974; M.A., George Washington U., 1977. Planetarium lectr., instr. So. Museum, Springfield, MA, 1982—; spcl. ed. tchr. Easthamp-High Schl., MA, 1982—. Recipient Commendation for column Rhyme Time, Story Time, Mystery Time, 1986, Honorable Mention, Byline, 1986. Mem. NEA. Home: 144 White St Springfield MA 01108

MOZINSKI, CATHLEE RAE, b. Fergus Falls, MN, Feb. 20, 1940; d. Charles LeRoy and Audrey Bertell (Wooodard) Jaren; m. Stephen Francis Mozinski, Sept. 5, 1964; children—Stephen Roy, Lora Ann. Contrbr. articles: Ind. Profl., Gainsville (Fla.) Sun, numerous other publs. Wrkg. on fiction. Freelance wrtr., 1982—; wrtr. Fla. Bus. Jnl., Gainsville, 1982-83; pub., ed. Women to Women News, Gainesville, 1983-86; editorial asst. Pinellas Park (Fla.) News, 1984-85. Mem. Nat. Fedn. Press Women, Fla. Freelance Wrtrs. Assn. Home: 1475 NW 21st Ave Gainesville FL 32605

MUCK, TERRY CHARLES, b. Batavia, NY, June 24, 1947, s. Webster Charles and Oaklie Mae (Floyd) M.; m. Judith Lee Keim, Sept. 19, 1972; children—David, Paul, Joseph. Author: Liberating the Leader's Prayer Life, 1985, When to Take a Risk, 1986. MDiv, Bethel Sem., 1972; PhD, Northwestern U., 1977. Ed. U.S. Handball Assn., Skokie, Ill., 1977-80; ed., sr. v.p. Christianity Today, Inc., Carol Stream, Ill., 1980—. Fulbright-Hayes grantee, Sri Lanka, 1976-77. Home: 602 S Gables Blvd Wheaton IL 60187

MUDBONE, BUTCH R., (T.) see McCarty, Jesse Louis Henry

MUDBONE, VIVIAN ESMERALDA, see McCarthy, Jessie Louis Henry

MUELLER, LORAINE DOROTHY, b. Sanborn, MN, Nov. 9, 1920, d. Charles Henry and Bertha Augusta (Pankonin) Schwanke; m. Rev. Stanley Karl Mueller, Sept. 6, 1939; children—Eileen Mueller Dunlap, Jeanette Mueller Marvel. Author: A Mountain and A Miracle, 1971; contrbr. poetry, inspirational stories to: Venture, Pasque Petals, Anthology on World Brotherhood and Peace, Prairie Poets, numerous other publs.; poetry columnist local newspaper. Ed. North Park Coll., Huron (S.D.) Coll. Cert. lay speaker United Meth. Ch., 1956—; participant Evangel. Mission, Porto Allegre and Cruz Alta, Brazil, 1962. Recipient Golden Poet award World of Poetry, 1984, 86. Mem. S.D. State Poetry Soc., League Minn. Poets, Southern Minn. Poetry Society, Natl. Fedn. State Poetry Socs.. Home: 761 Center St Trace MN 56175

MUESING-ELLWOOD, EDITH ELIZABETH, b. NYC, Sept. 18, 1947, d. Carl Earl and Elsbeth (Bushbeck) Muesing; m. William Adonis Gene Ellwood, Sept. 15, 1980; children—Jeanie Elizabeth, Colin Gene, Caroline Ada. Author: The Alternative to Technological Culture, 1983, United States Democracy: Myth vs. Reality, 1985; contrb. poetry: Dragonfly: A Quar. of Haiku, Windchimes, Orphic Lute, Ram: The Letterbox, Poets Pride, other lit. publs. Wrkg. on non-fiction, haiku. BA, Fordham U., 1969; MA, NYU, 1971. Freelance wrtr. Acad. Research Group, Rutherford, N.J., 1975-82; pub. Colin-Press, Bklyn., 1985-87. Fellow World Lit. Acad; prof. mem. NWC; mem. NWU, Intl. Women's Writing Guild, Women in Scholarly Pub. Home: 128 Dean St Brooklyn NY 11201

MUJICA, BARBARA LOUISE, b. Altoona, PA, Dec. 25, 1943; d. Louis and Carol Frieda (Kline) Kaminar; m. Mauro Mujica Dec. 26, 1966; children: Lillian, Mariana, Mauro. Author: A-LM Spanish, Level I, 1969 (rev. ed., 1974), Level II, 1970 (rev. ed., 1974), Level III, 1971, Level IV, 1973; Nuevas lecturas, 1974, Lecturas para pensar y discutir, 1972, Readings in Spanish Literature, 1975, Calderon's Characters: An Existential Point of View, 1980, Pasaporte, 1980, (rev. ed., 1984), Aqui y ahora, 1979, Entrevista, 1982, Iberian Pastoral Characters, 1986. M.A., Middlebury in France (Paris), 1965; Ph.D. New York Univ., 1974. Editor, pub., Verbena: Bilingual Rvw of the Arts, Wash. D.C., 1979-85; sr. assoc. ed., The Washington Rvw, 1983—; dir. El Retablo Spanish Language Theatre, 1985—. NEH Summer Inst. faculty, 1980; reading grant P&W, 1984; Spanish Govt. Grant, Ministry of Culture, Spain, 1987. Mem. MLA, AAUP, Wrtrs. Ctr., Am Assn. of Teachers of Spanish and Portuguese. Home: 7811 Lonesome Pine Ln Bethesda MD 20817

MULARI, MARY ELIZABETH, b. Biwabik, MN, Oct. 6, 1947; d. Arvid John and Helmi Viola (Peramaki) Koski; m. Barry A. Mulari, Aug. 12, 1972. Author: Designer Sweatshirts, 1983, Applique Design Collection, 1984, More Designer Sweatshirts, 1986. BS, U. Minn.-Duluth, 1970. Tchr. jr. high schl. Benson, Minn., 1970-71, Minn. schls., 1971-73; owner Aurora Surplus Store, Aurora, Minn., 1973—; freelance author and tchr., Aurora, 1982—. Mem. Community Edn. Arts Comm., Aurora, 1980—, trustee Library Bd., 1984—. Mem. AAUW. Address: 18 South Fifth St West Aurora MN 55705

MULFORD, PHILIPPA GREENE, b. NYC, May 29, 1948; d. Philip Murray and Constance (Clarke) Greene; m. R. Edward Mulford, Sept. 29, 1978. Author: The World is My Eggshell, 1986, If It's Not Funny, Why Am I Laughing?, 1982. BA, Skidmore College, Saratoga Springs, NY, 1971. Feature wrtr./reptr., Clinton Courier, Clinton, NY, 1971-73; exec. dir., Central NY Community Arts Council, Inc., Utica, NY, 1971-78. Home: Box 14 Norton Ave Clinton NY 13323

MULLER, GEORGENE K., b. Jamaica, NY., May 27, 1950; d. Robert Henry Sr. and Lois Alene (Kase) Muller; m. Raymond Eric Classen (div. 1974); children: Rachel Marie, Amanda Lee. Contrbr. numerous articles to various mags. Wkg. on high tech. articles. BA, Western Conn. State U., 1979. Sr. wrtr. Branson Sonic Power Co., Danbury, Conn., 1982-84; public relations coordinator Data Switch Corp., Shelton, Conn., 1984-85; pres. Muller Communications Group, Danbury, Conn., 1985—. Mem. Women in Communications, Soc. Profl. Journalists. Office: 54 Sand Pit Rd Danbury CT 06810

MULLINS, HELENE, b. New Rochelle, NY, July 12, 1899, d. Timothy J. and Marie (McCall) Gallagher; m. Ivan Mullins, 1920; m. 2d, Linne Johnson, 1958 (dec.). Author: Convent Girl, 1931, Balm in Gilead, 1931, Streams from the Source, 1938, The Mirrored Walk, 1970, others. Wrkg. on poems, autobiographical novel. Home: 16 W 16 St 2 PN New York NY 10011

MULLINS, RONALD GIFT, b. Adel, IA, June 6, 1938; s. Kenneth Wiley and Gladys Lorene (Gift) M.; m. Hattie Jo Pursglove, Aug. 17, 1963; children—Gretchen Pursglove, Margaret Criswell, Lesley Lorene. Author: A Hist. of The Continental Insurance Co., 1978, A Little About A Few Cutters, 1980. BA, U. IA, 1962. Mgr. community relns. Abex Corp., Mahwah, NJ, 1964-70; ed. pubns. Otis, NYC, 1970-76; dir. employee communics. Continental Corp., NYC, 1976—. Gold Quill award, IABC, 1979. Dir., treas. Council Communic. Mgt. Address: 580 Main E-164 New York NY 10044

MUNGIN, HORACE L., b. Younges Island, SC, Aug. 5, 1941; s. Horace Steel and Margaret (Morrison) M.; m. Gussie Sanders, July 11, 1964; children: Vaughn, Kevin, Malcolm. Author: (poetry) Dope Hustler's Jazz, 1969, Now See Here, Homes, 1970; How Many Niggers Make Half a Dozen, 1972; syndicated columnist Sleepy Willie, 1979-82; contrbr. poetry to Poet's Corner, articles to N.Y. Times, Amsterdam News. BA in English, Fordham U., 1975. Ed. Free Spirit Press, NYC, 1968-71; ed.-in-chief Black Forum Mag., Bronx, N.Y., 1975-78, poetry ed., 1978-80; pub., ed. Presstime, Bronx, 1982-84; newsletter ed. Nubian Soc., Bronx, 1982—. Served with U.S. Army, 1960-63. Recipient lit. achievement award Lincoln Square Community Ctr., 1983. Mem. P&W, So. Black Wrtrs. Assn. Home: 800 Concourse Village Bronx NY 10451

MUNOZ, CARLOS, JR., b. El Paso, TX, Aug. 25, 1939; s. Carlos Garcia and Clementina (Contreras) Munoz; m. Graciela Rios, Dec. 18, 1977; children—Carlos, Marina, Genaro, Daniel, Marcelo. Author. Quest for Identity and Power, 1988, Politics and the Chicano, 1974. BA, Cal. State U., 1968, PhD,Claremont Graduate, CA, 1973. Instr., Cal. State U., Los Angeles, 1968-69; lectr. Pitzer College, Claremont, CA, 1969-70; asst. prof., UC Irvine, 1970-76; assoc. prof., UC Berkeley, 1976—. Served with US Army, 1959-62. Mem. Am. Poli. Sci. Assoc., (co-founder) Natl. Assoc. for Chicano Studies, Chicano Council of Higher Ed. Home: 3078 Birmingham Dr Richmond CA 94806

MUNSAT, STANLEY MORRIS, b. Rutland, VT, Apr. 12, 1939; s. Leo and Ethel (Geron) M.; children—Steven, Tobin. Author: The Concept of Memory, 1967; Editor: The Analytic Synthetic Distinction, 1971; genl. editor: (with A.I. Melden) Wadsworth Basic Problems in Philosophy Series; Mem. editorial bd.: Philo. Research Archives; contrbr. articles to profl. jnls. AB, Cornell U., 1960; MA, U. Mich., 1962, PhD,1965. Asst. prof. U. Calgary, Alta., Can., 1963-66; asst. prof. philosophy U. Calif., Irvine, 1966-68, assoc. prof., 1968-71, prof., 1971-72; prof. philosophy U. NC, Chapel Hill, 1972—. Mem. Am. Philo. Assn. Home: 817 Shady Lawn Rd Chapel Hill NC 27514

MUNSTERBERG, HUGO, b. Berlin, Germany, Sept. 13, 1916; came to U.S., 1935, naturalized, 1941; s. Oskar and Helen (Rice) M.; m. Marjorie Bowen, June 26, 1943; 1 dau., Maujorie. Author: A Short History of Chinese Art, 1949, Twentieth Century Painting, 1951, Landscape Painting of China and Japan, 1955, The Arts of Japan, 1957, The Folk Art of Japan, 1958, The Art of the Chinese Sculptor, 1960, The Ceramic Art of Japan, 1963, Zen and Oriental Art, 1965, Mingei, 1965, Buddhist Bronzes of China, 1967, Art of the Far East, 1968, The Art of India and Southeast Asia, 1970, Oriental Sculpture, 1971, Dragon in Chinese Art, 1972, The Arts of China, 1972, A History of Women Artists, 1975, The Art of Modern Japan, 1977, Die Kunst Asiens, 1980, Dictionary of Chinese and Japanese Art, 1981, Japanese Prints, 1982, The Crown of Life, 1983, Symbolism in Ancient Chinese Art, 1986. AB, Harvard, 1938, PhD, 1941. Asst. prof. fine arts Mich. State U., 1946-49, assoc. prof., 1949-52; prof. art history Intl. Christian U., Tokyo, 1952-56, State U. N.Y. Coll. at New Paltz, 1958-78, chmn. dept. 1968-75; art critic Arts mag., 1957-60; adj. prof. Parsons Schl. Design, 1979—; vis. prof. Bard Coll., 1978-88. Served with AUS, 1942-46. Mem. Japan Soc. Home: 48 Elting Ave New Paltz NY 12561

MURATORI, FRED, b. Derby, CT, Apr. 30, 1951. Contrbr. poems to Poetry N.W., The Spectator, Tendril, Qtly West, CutBank, Miss., New Eng., So. Poetry, Lit., Chariton, So. Humanities rvws, Poets On, Hollins Critic, Confrontation, others; rvws. and essays to N.W., Chariton, Chowder rvws, Library Jnl. BA, Fairfield U., 1973; MA, Syracuse U., 1977, MLS, 1981. Adj. instr. Syracuse U., N.Y., 1978-79, 85; document analyst ERIC, Syracuse, 1979-81; reference librarian Cornell U., Ithaca, N.Y., 1981—. Home: 511 N Tioga St Ithaca NY 14850

MURPHY, DIANA SUE GROGAN (DIM), b. Memphis, TN, Dec. 29, 1947; d. William Thomas and Mary Zuleika (Underwood) G.; children—John William Grogan Murphy, Karen Alayne Murphy, Donna Phyllis Grogan Murphy. Contrbr. to Ms., Glamour, Memphis Press Scimitar, Tri State Defender, Ocean Spring Record, Biloxi Sun Herald, Miss. Press Register; pub. & ed., The Meta Star. BA, Memphis State, 1971, postgrad. also. With VISTA, Atlanta, GA, & So. Carolina, 1972; tch. asst., special ed., Memphis city schls., 1973-74; with Stunning Stouts, Biloxi, MS, 1976-83; subst. tchr. Ocean Springs (MS) Schls., 1984-85. Home: 116 Arbor Vista OceanSprings MS 39564

MURPHY, JOY WALDRON, b. Boston, Nov. 4, 1942; d. Albert and Agnes Waldron; m. Larry E. Murphy, 1982; children—April Roots, Logan Roots, Ellen Roots. Contrbr. articles to mags., newspapers including Smithsonian Mag., Phoenix Mag., Artists of the Rockies, Albuquerque Jnl, Detroit News, Boston Globe. BA in English, Coll. Sant2 Fe, 1977; postgrad. U. N.Mex., 1978-79. Wrtr., ed. Harvard U., Cambridge, Mass., 1962-66; tchr. lang. Berlitz Sch. of Langs., Seattle, Wash., 1971-73; pub. info. officer Secy. of State & Health & Environment, N.Mex., 1978-80; singer, guitarist hotels, Wash., N.Mex., 1972-84; free-lance wrtr., 1979—. Address: Box 5815 Santa Fe NM 87502

MURPHY, KAY ANN, b. Paris, IL, Sept. 28, 1942, d. Bernard Leo and Berna Georgia (Richey) Herrington; m. Ted Drake Murphy (div. 1971); children—David Allen, Scott Augustus, Melissa Ann. Author: The Autopsy (poetry collection), 1985; contrbr. poetry to Poetry, Anthology of Mag. Verse and Yearbook of Am. Poetry, Seneca Rvw, Spoon River Qtly, other publs.; contrbr. to Black Warrior Rvw. BA, Eastern Ill. U., 1976; MFA, Goddard Coll., 1980. Poet Ill. Arts Council, Chgo., 1978-83; instr. Danville (Ill.) Area Community Coll., 1978-84, U. New Orleans, 1984—. Mem. AWP, NCTE. Home: 6731 Gen Diaz New Orleans LA 70124

MURPHY, MICHAEL, b. Glen Rock, WY, Nov. 16, 1930. Author: (novels) A Wisp of Straw, 1956, The Floater, 1959, The Big Squeeze, 1962, The Will Rides the Wind, 1965, One of the Twelve, 1970, Hemingsteen, 1977 (Outstanding Novel of Yr. award Chgo. Fdn. for Lit. 1978), A.K.A. Ormond Sacker, 1980; Vincent Starrett: In Memoriam, 1976; ed. Starrett Versus Machen, 1981, (textbook) Of America, 1969; co-author, ed. Late, Later & Possibly Last, 1972. AB, U. Chgo., 1954, MA, 1955; PhD, U. Okla., 1957. Recipient disting. fiction award Malkin Meml. Fnd., 1978. Mem. Baker Street Irregulars. Home: 4304 McCausland St Louis MO 63109

MURPHY, PATRICE ANN, (Pat Murphy), b. Spokane, WA, Jan. 9, 1955; d. James F. and Katherine (Kordyban) M. Author: (novels) The Falling Woman, 1986; The Shadow Hunter, 1986; contrbr. short stories to Elsewhere, Amazing Sci. Fiction Stories, Isaac Azimov's Sci. Fiction Mag., also others. BA, U. Calif., Santa Cruz, 1976. Ed./wrtr. Sea World, San Diego, 1978-81, Exploratorium, San Francisco, 1982—. Mem. SFWA. Home: 1325 Lincoln Way Apt 6 San Francisco CA 94122

MURPHY, PATRICK DENNIS, b. Joliet, IL, Oct. 19, 1951, s. William P. Murphy and Evelyn (Reed) Spinozzi; m. Elaine Lim, June 15, 1977 (div. 1979); m. Bonnie Izumi Iwasaki, June 5, 1982. Co-ed.: Essentials: The Theory of Fiction, 1987. The Poetic Fantastic: Essays on the Fantastic in Poetry, 1987; contrbr. critical essays: Am. Poetry, Extrapolation, Virtual Image, other publs.; contrbr. poetry, revs. to Earthwise, Poet News, Parnassus Lit. Jnl, Pinchpenny, Quickenings, numerous other lit mags and anthologies. BA with honors, UCLA, 1973; MA with honors, Calif. State U.-Northridge, 1983; PhD, U. Calif.-Davis, 1986. Asst. prof. English, Indiana Univ. of Pa., 1987-. Mem. MLA, Western Lit. Assn., Intl. Assn. of Fantastic in Arts. Home: 242 Philadelphia St Indiana PA 15705

MURPHY, SHEILA E., b. Mishawaka, IN, Apr. 5, 1951, d. Thomas Timothy and Bernadean (Flynn) M. Author: Virtuoso Bird, 1981, Late Summer, 1984, Appropriate Behavior, 1987, The

Truth Right Now, 1987, Practical Motivation Handbook, 1986, Memory Transposed into the Key of C, 1986, With House Silence, 1986. BA, Nazareth Coll., Kalamazoo, 1973; MA, U. Mich., 1974; PhD, Ariz. State U., 1980. Asst. prof. Bay de Noe Coll., Escanaba, Mich., 1974-76; grad. assoc. Ariz. State U., Tempe, 1977-78; instr. English, Mesa Coll., Ariz., 1978-80; mgmt. devel. specialist Ramada Mgmt. Inst., Phoenix, 1980-85, dir., 1985—. Home: 3701 E Monterosa St Phoenix AZ 85018

MURPHY, THOMAS JAY, b. Suffolk, VA, Jan. 13, 1959; s. Willie Thomas and Rebecca (Seward) Murphy. Editor-in-chief: Red Bass Magazine, 1981—; contrbg. ed.: Art Papers, 1985—; contrbr. to High Performance, The Guardian, In These Times, Tallahassee Democrat, Pacific News Service, other nwspprs. and mags. BS in Jnlsm. Florida A&M U. Art critic Tallahassee Democrat (FL), 1985—. Home: 839A W St Augustine Tallahassee FL 32304

MURPHY, WALTER FRANCIS, b. Charleston, SC., Nov. 21, 1929; s. Walter Francis and Ruth (Gaffney) M.; m. Mary Therese Dolan, June 28, 1952; children: Kelly Ann, Holly Ann. Author: Congress and the Court, 1962, Elements of Judicial Strategy, 1964, Wiretapping on Trial, 1965, (with C.H. Pritchett) Courts, Judges and Politics, 4th edit., 1986, (with M. Danielson) American Democracy, 10th edit., 1983, Modern American Democracy, 1969, (with J. Tanenhaus) The Study of Public Law, 1972, (with J. Tanenhaus, D. Kastner) Public Evaluations of Constitutional Courts, 1974, (with J. Tanenhaus) Comparative Constitutional Law, 1977, The Vicar of Christ, 1979, (with D. Lockard) Basic Cases in Constitutional Law, 2d ed., 1987, The Roman Enigma, 1981, (with J. Fleming and W. Harris) American Constitutional Interpretation, 1986, Upon This Rock, 1987; book rvw. editor: World Politics, 1972-78; contbr. numerous articles to profl. jnls. A.B. magna cum laude, U. Notre Dame, 1950; A.M., George Washington U., 1954; Ph.D., U. Chgo., 1957. Served to capt. USMC, 1950-55; col. Res., ret. Decorated D.S.C., Purple Heart; recipient Chgo. Found. for Lit. award, 1980; Guggenheim fellow, 1973-74; NEH fellow, 1978-79. Fellow AAAS. Home: 240 Western Way Princeton NJ 08540

MURPHY, WINIFRED LEE, b. San Francisco, Aug. 6, 1931; d. John Joseph and Ida Loretta (Drady) Schamle; m. Owen James Murphy, July 7, 1962; children—Dana, Megan. Humor and feature articles in var. publs. and mags. including Life, San Francisco Examiner, Lady's Circle, Women's Day.. BA, San Francisco State U., 1954. TV prod./dir., KQED TV, San Francisco, 1954-72; columnist, Terra Linda News, CA, 1962-81; columnist, feature writer, Marin Scope, CA, 1981—. Home: 43 Fowler Court San Rafael CA 94903

MURR, DANNY LEE, (Dan Murry), b. Elyria, OH, May 30, 1930; s. Kenneth James and Wanda Bernice (Pixley) M.; m. Elizabeth Walker Bangs, Feb. 21, 1951 (div. 1967); children—Nancy, Kathleen, Tracee, David; m. 2d, Dorothy Ann Grada, Nov. 25, 1972. Contrbr. articles: Ill. PGA Ann., Chgo. Golfer, Sporting News Coll. Football mag., Fisherman's Handbook, numerous other publs. Wrkg. on short stories, novel. Student Ariz. State U., 1976. Sportswrtr., wire ed. The Reflector-Herald, Norwalk, Ohio, 1960-61; reporter, sportswrtr. The Jnl., Lorain, Ohio, 1961-63; sportswrtr. The Fla. Times-Union, Jacksonville, 1963-69; dir. public edn. Am. Cancer Soc., Jacksonville, 1970-71; sports ed. St. Augustine (Fla.) Record, 1971-73; sportswrtr. Gainesville (Fla.) Sun, 1973-75, Jnl.-Gazette, Ft. Wayne, Ind., 1976-78; sports ed. Morning Courier, Urbana, Ill., 1979, Beacon News, Aurora, Ill., 1979—. Named Boxing Wrtr. of Yr., World Boxing Assn., 1982-83; recipient award No. Ill. Newspaper Assn., 1980, 82; recipient cert. of merit UPI, 1979, Natl. Softball Media Assn., 1985. Mem. Natl. Sportscasters & Sportswrtrs. Assn. Home: 2050 W Illinois St Apt 2-J Aurora IL 60506

MURRAY, CHARLES (ALAN), b. Newton, IA, Jan. 8, 1943; s. Alan B. and Frances B. (Patrick) M.; m. (1) 1966, Suchart Dej-Uion, div. 1981; children—Narissa, Sara; (2) Catherine B. Cox, July 29, 1983; d., Anna. Author: (with Louis A. Cox), Beyond Probation, 1979, Safety Nets and the Truly Needy, 1982, contrib. to Crime and Public Policy, ed. James Q. Wilson, 1983, Losing Ground: American Social policy 1950-1980, 1984; articles in the Atlantic, Harper's, The American Spectator, and others. BA cum laude in history, Harvard, 1965, Ph. D. in pol. sci., Massachusetts Institute of Technology, 1974. Volunteer in Peace Corps, 1965-70 in rural Thailand; Washington head-quarters, American Institute for Research, research scientist, 1974-79, chief scientist 1979-81; consultant, 1981—; senior research fellow, Manhattan Institute for Policy Research, 1981-83. Address: MIPR 131 Spring St New York NY 10012

MURRAY, GERALD EDWARD, (G.E.), b. Buffalo, Dec. 17, 1945; s. Gerald Edward and Mary (Heffron) M.; m. Joanne Burns, Oct. 9, 1971; children: Caitlin Anne, Michael Brendan, Megan Elizabeth. Author poetry: A Mile Called Timothy, 1972, Holding Fast, 1974, Gasoline Dreams, 1978, Repairs (Devins award winner), 1979; A-Z: A New Letters Reader, 1982; contbr. Heartland II, 1975, Morrow Anthology of Young Am. Poets, 1985. BA, Canisius Coll., 1968; MA, North Coll., 1970. Instr. English Northeastern U., Boston, 1968-71; asst. public relations mgr. Allstate Ins., Northbrook, Ill., 1971-73; public relations dir. Amco Inds., Carol Stream, Ill., 1973-75; poetry columnist Chicago Sun-Times, 1975-84; sr. vp Burson-Marsteller, Chgo., 1975-87; exec. vp. Golin-Harris Communications, Chicago, 1987-.Cons (poetry), World Book Encyc's Year Book, contrbg. ed.; cons., Safer Fdn., Chgo., 1985, Greater Chgo Food Depository, 1983-84. Recipient Ill. Arts Council awards for poetry, 1977, 78, 79, 81, 86. Mem. Chgo. Press Club, PRSA, Natl. Investor Relations Inst. Address: 933 N Columbian Oak Park IL 60302

MURRAY, HUGH T. JR., b. New Orleans, Nov. 15, 1938, s. Hugh T. and Millie (Higgins) M. Author: The Negro in Depression and War, Prelude to Revolution, 1930-45, 1969, Civil Rights History-Writing and Anti-Communism: A Critique, 1975, The Scorpion and the Phoenix: Poetry of Defeat, Despair, Death and Defiance, 1983, Gay Life, 1986; contrbr. to NY Times Book Rvw, Phylon, Village Voice, numerous other publs. BA, Tulane U., 1960, MA, 1963. Asst. prof. So. U., New Orleans, 1967-69; research asst. Herbert Aptheker, NYC,1972-75, Richard Plant, NYC,1984; guest lectr. Martin Luther U., Halle, German Dem. Rep., 1971-72, Karl Marx U., Leipzig, German Dem. Rep., 1977-78. Mem. Am. Hist. Assn. Home: 90-11 35th Ave Jackson Heights NY 11372

MURRAY, JOHN JOSEPH, b. Bath, ME, July 2, 1915; s. John Joseph and Ida (King) M.; m. Helen Elizabeth Tomson, Jan. 30, 1942; children—John Joseph III, Michael Tomson. Author: A Student Guidebook to English History, 1947, An Honest Diplomat at the Hague, 1956, Amsterdam in the Age of Rembrandt, 1967, George I, the Baltic and the Whig Split, 1969, Antwerp in the Age of Plantin and Breughel, 1970, It Took All of Us, 1982, Flanders and England, 1985; editor: Essays in Modern European History, 1952, The Heritage of the Middle West, 1958; contrbr. articles, book rvws. to Am., fgn. hist. jnls.; author, narrator TV scripts for comml. TV. AB, U. Maine, 1937; MA, Ind. U., 1938; PhD,UCLA, 1942. Editor Douglas Aircraft, 1938-45; instr. history Ohio State U., 1945; instr. Northwestern U., 1945-46; asst. prof. Ind. U., 1946-49, assoc. prof., 1949-54; prof. Coe Coll., 1954—, chmn. history dept., 1955—, Henrietta Arnold prof., 1977-80, Arnold prof. emeritus, 1980—; historian Iowa Light and Power Co., 1980—. Fulbright research scholar U. Leiden, Netherlands, 1951-52; fellow Folger Shakespeare Library, Washington, 1954, summer 1959; sr. research fellow, 1973-74; Guggenheim fellow, 1968-69; fellow Royal Hist. Soc. (Eng.), Historisch Genootschop (Netherlands), Karolinska Forbundet (Sweden); mem. Cedar Rapids Art Assn., Am. Hist. Assn. Home: 2318 26th St Dr SE Cedar Rapids IA 52403

MURRAY, LEE WINSLOW, b. Balt., Apr. 29, 1949; s. Wilson and Catherine (Rose) M.; m. Toni Lynn Murray, Dec. 7, 1974; children—Kristi, Lee. BA in Poli. Sci., U. Cin., 1971. Ed./pub. Beverage Jnl., Balt., 1974—; assoc. pub. Times Pub., Towson, MD, 1979—; pres. Murray Communics., 1977—. Mem. Balt. Pubs. Assn. Office: Bev Jnl 2 West 25th St Baltimore MD 21218

MURRAY, RUTH MILDRED, b. Branford, FL, May 2, 1921; d. James Wesley Wood and Sepher Virginia (Hall) Wood Stinson; m. Mathew Josia Burns, Jr., Apr. 19, 1939 (dec. 1945); 1 son, Mathew Wesley (dec. 1987); m. 2d, Clifford Harold Murray, May 22, 1946 (dec. 1969); children: Linda Ruth Murray Hartley, Rudolph Earl. Poetry in anthologies. Home: 2800 Sophia St Bldg J Apt 5 Jacksonville FL 32205

MURRAY, STEVEN T., b. Berkeley, CA, Oct. 7, 1943, s. Steven T. and Verna F. (Hottel) M.; m. Tiina K. Nunnally, Oct. 5, 1985. Contrbr. translations from German, Danish, and Norwegian: The Best from the Rest of the World: European Science Fiction, 1976, Berkeley Fiction Rvw., 1982, Scandinavian Rvw, 1982; translator: The Sardine Deception (by Leif Davidsen), 1986, Witness to the Future (by Klaus Rifbjerg), 1987. Student Stanford U., 1961-64; BA in Creative Writing, Calif. State U.,-Hayward, 1972; postgrad. U. Calif.-Berkeley, 1981-82. Freelance tech. translator, lit. translator, Calif. and Wash., 1974—; owner, typographer Fjord Press Typography, Berkeley, Calif. and Seattle, 1976—; ed., pub. Fjord Press, Seattle, 1981—. Recipient Van de Bovenkamp-Armand G. Erpf Translation award Columbia U., 1985. Mem. ALTA, PEN. Address: Box 16501 Seattle WA 98116

MURRAY, VIRGINIA R., b. Lynchburg, VA, Nov. 8, 1914; d. Otho Dabney and Ruth Drucilla (Leslie) Riley; m. Herbert Henry Murray, Feb. 27, 1943; children—Ruth Murray Byram, Robert Riley. Contrbr. poetry: Poem, The Lyric, Negative Capability, over 20 other lit. mags.; poetry in anthologies. Wrkg. on poetry. AB, Randolph-Macon Women's Coll., 1936; postgrad., U. Va., 1938-40, George Washington U., 1946-47. Tchr. various schls. in Va., 1936-43, Huntsville, Ala., 1963-72. Recipient poetry awards. Mem. Ala. State Poetry Soc. (poet laureate contest winner, 1983), Natl. League Am. Penwomen, Huntsville Lit. Assn., ednl. orgns. Home: 8905 Strong Dr SE Huntsville AL 35802

MURRAY, WILLIAM STANTON, b. Bismarck, ND, Dec. 26, 1916; s. John Kenneth and Paula Emma (Wagner) M.; m. Nancy Anne deWaard, June 17, 1950; children—Katharine Mary, John Stanton, Patricia Ann. Author: Song of the Dusty Stars, 1970, rev. ed., 1985. LLB, U. of North Dakota, 1937, JD, 1939. Self-employed attorney, Bismarck, ND, 1939—. Home: 112 Riverside Park Rd Bismarck ND 58501

MURRIE, MICHAEL HOWARD, b. Alton, IL, Apr. 20, 1951; s. Clifford Paul and Natalie M.; m. Jacquelyn Dale Dunsworth, Aug. 19, 1972; children—Daniel, Benjamin, Susanna. Contrbr. article for trade mag.; author scripts for TV and video. Wrkg. on articles and research on TV news administration. B.A., Harding U., 1973; M. A., U. Mo., 1977. Bur. chief, reporter Sta. KFSM-TV, Ft. Smith, AK, 1973-74; news producer Sta. KATV-TV, Little Rock, 1974-75, Sta. KOCO-TV, Oklahoma City, OK, 1977; news producer, anchor Sta. KOMU-TV, Columbia, MO, 1976; news producer, ed., Sta. KSDK-TV, St. Louis, 1977-86; asst. prof. Ohio Weleyan U., Delaware, 1986—. Recipient Emmy for outstanding achievement in news broadcasting Natl. Acad. TV Arts Scis., 1985. Mem. Radio-TV News Dirs. Assn., Assn. Edn. Jnlsm. aand Mass Communication. Home: 630 Presidential Way Delaware OH 43015

MURRY, DAN, see Murr, Danny Lee

MUSAFIA, JUDITH N, b. Los Angeles, Mar. 14, 1941, d. Kenneth Elwood and Burnadetta Sophie (Suydam) Gross; m. Julien Musafia, June 7, 1962 (div. 1976); children—Dimitri, Dominik. Contrbr. to Christian Science Monitor, San Luis Obispo Telegram Tribune; columnist Five Cities Telegram Press Recorder, 1977; book critic Los Angeles Times, 1977-78; music critic Long Beach Ind. Press-Telegram, 1975-76. BA in English, Calif. State U., Long Beach, 1973. Freelance wrtr., musician, 1977—; columnist San Luis Obispo (Calif.) Telegram Tribune, 1984—, also music critic, feature wrtr.; pub. relations Local Library Users, United Calif. Central Coast, 1977. Music Critics Assn. of U.S. and Can. Intl. fellow, 1976; winner Short Story prize Santa Barbara Wrtrs. Conf., 1980. Mem. Public Corp. for Arts, Long Beach, Calif., AAUW. Home: 1518 Manhattan Ave Grover City CA 93433

MUSE, HELEN ELIZABETH, b. Detroit, Jan. 18, 1917; d. Clyde Franklin Sr. and Ethel Marilla (Worth) Muse. Author: Green Pavilions, 1961 (2d edit. 1976); contrbr. Deaf Am. Mag., Rome News-Tribune; excerpted in a History of Public Education in Georgia 1734-1976, 1979. Wrkg. on novels. BA, Gallaudet Coll., 1943, teaching cert., 1956; postgrad. Shorter Coll., 1961. Tchr. Ga. Schl. for the Deaf, Cave Spring, 1956-57, 59-80. Home: 7219 Cave Spring Rd SW Cave Spring GA 30124

MUSINSKY, GERALD, b. Pitts., 1954, s. Stephen John and Irene (Racko) M. Author: (poetry) Steel Living, 1984; asst. ed. Energy and Environment, 1978; ed. Mill Hunk Herald, Night Times, Creative Pittsburgh, Ideas & Images. BA, U. Pitts., 1978, MA, 1981. Instr. writing CCAC, Boyce Campus, Monroeville, Pa., 1983-85; wrtr.-in-res. Ky. Arts Council, 1984-85; lit. cons. Famous Rider Cultural Ctr., Pitts., 1984—. Mem. AWP, P&W. Pitts. Poetry Exchange. Home: B-12 Concord Plz 5540 Covode St Pittsburgh PA 15217

MUSKA, NICK, (Nicholas F.) (Miklos Szabo, Nick Norton), b. Lorain, Ohio, Aug. 23, 1942; s. Nicholas Michael and Anna Caroline (Weigl) M.; m. Susan Avril Hartman, May 21, 1965; 1 child, Samuel Michael. Author: Elm: Warehouse Poems, 1979, Living My Nightlife Out Under The Sun, 1987; ed.: From Inside Out; A Collection of Inmate Writings, 1980; Alternatives: A Guide to a Collection of Small Press Books, (with Joel Lipman), 1984; Three Key West Sunsets, 1985; contrbr. poems to Antioch Mag., Wabash Rvw., The Last Village Idiot, transls. pub. by Chgo. Rvw. AB in Lit., Antioch Coll., 1965; MA in English, U. Calif., Santa Barbara, 1967. Instr. Am. lit. Wabash Coll., Crawfordsville, Ind., 1972-74; instr./coordinator inmate arts Lucas County Jail/Toledo House of Corrections, 1978—; artist-in-edn., Ohio Arts Council, 1978—; poet-in-residence Holland Elem. Sch., Ohio, 1985-87; coordinator Toledo Poets Ctrs., 1975—. Winner poetry competition U. Toledo, 1975; recipient community impact award Arts Commn. Greater Toledo, 1983; Gov.'s award for arts in Ohio, 1985; Regents fellow U. Calif., 1967-68. Mem. Wrtrs. Resource Ctr. Toledo. Home: 534 Nesslewood Toledo OH 43610

MUSKE, CAROL ANNE, b. St. Paul, MN, Dec. 17, 1945; d. William Howard Muske and Elizabeth K. Kuchera; m. David C. Dukes, Jan. 31, 1983, 1 dau., Annie Cameron. Author: Camouflage, 1975, Skylight, 1981, Wyndmere, 1985; contrbr. rvws. to NY Times, LA Times; poetry in numerous lit mags. and anthologies. BA, Creighton U., 1967; MA, State U. of Calif., San Fran., 1970. Visiting Poet, U. of Iowa, 1983; prof., U. of Southern Cal., LA, 1984—. Awards: Guggenheim Fellowship, 1981, NEA Fellowship, 1984. Mem. PEN, P&W, PSA, AG. Home: 225 S Lorraine Blvd Los Angeles CA 90004

MUSSO, LAURIE DUSTON, b. Springfield, MA, Jan. 6, 1919, d. Arthur Given and Laura Estelle (Clark) Duston; m. Vincent J. Musso, Sept. 5, 1946; children—Dean Duston, Dwight Vincent. Co-author, ed., illustrator, pub.: Some Tales of Mother Earth and Her Children, 1983; contrbr. to Western Poetry Mag. Qtly, Dreams in Print. Wrkg. on juvenile hist. series. Student U. Wash., 1936, 37, U. Calif.-Berkeley, 1943, 44. Owner, ed. Megan's World, Fullerton, Calif., 1982—. Served with USN, 1944-45. Mem. Soc. Children's Book Wrtrs., Natl. League of Am. Pen Women, Pub. Assn. So. Calif., COSMEP. Recipient awards Calif. Fiction Wrtrs. Club. Home: 1820 Skyline Dr Fullerton CA 92631

MWADILIFU, MWALIMA IMARA, see Alexander, E. Curtis

MYCUE, EDWARD DELEHANT, b. Niagara Falls, NY, Mar. 21, 1937; s. John Powers and Ruth Agnes Taylor (Delehant) M. Author: Damage Within the Community, 1973, Root Route and Range: The Song Returns, 1979, The Singing Man My Father Gave Me, 1980, Edward (poems), 1987. BA, North Tex. State U., 1959. Mem. PEN, NWU, PSA. MacDowell fellow, 1974. Home: Box 640543 San Francisco CA 94164

MYER, CHARLES B(ERNARD), (Carl Dugan), b. Rio Piedras, P.R., Apr. 4, 1954, s. Carl Lee and Florence O. (Cooper) M.; m. Rebecca Marie Goodwin, Mar. 23, 1985. Playwright: Portrait of Judas, 1973, Living Water, 1974, The Baptist, 1978, Closed on Mondays, 1977, Sunday Breakfast, 1981, Broken Doll (musical), 1973, Lazz (musical, with Paul Allen), 1982, A Thousand Cranes for Peace (musical, with Paul Allen), 1984; author: Best of Backstages, 1981-85 (compendium of original columns), 1985, Arts in Santa Clara County, 1985; ed. Mascot, 1979-85, Westplan, 1983-84. AS, Contra Costa Coll., 1973; BS in Planning, Calif. Poly. U., 1976. Planning aide City of El Cerrito, Calif., 1974; data analyst Met. Transp. Commn., Berkeley, Calif., 1976-77; advance planner City of Santa Maria, Calif., 1977-78; sr. planner City of Gilroy, Calif., 1978—; columnist Gavilan Newspapers, Gilroy, 1981—. Winner 1st place playwrtg. competition, MASC, 1973. Mem. Calif. Confedn. Arts, Musicians and Actors, Serving the Community (MASC). Home: Box 2296 Gilroy CA 95021

MYERS, BOB, b. Prairie Grove, AR, Sept. 16, 1949; s. Charles P. and Vera J. M. Author: Good Old Hillmont High, 1979. MA in Communication, U. Kans., 1971, postgrad. Producer Mystery Forum Prodn., Independence, MO, 1984—. Address: 16503 Third St N Independence MO 64056

MYERS, BONNY E., see McDaniel, Bonny Elizabeth

MYERS, GAIL ELIZABETH, b. Oakland, CA, June 3, 1949, d. Theadore Glen and Elizabeth Jean (Burrill) M.; m. Raymundo Tellez Enriquez, Aug. 29, 1982; 2 sons, Alejandro and Andres. Contrbr. articles to Grassroots Newspaper, Calif. Tchr., Radical Tchr., Perspective Newspaper (also ed.), Exposition Newspaper (also ed.), numerous other publs. BA in Psychology, Mills Coll., 1970; MA in Early Childhood Edn., San Francisco State U. Tchr. various schls. in Calif., 1972-77; reporter, ed. Grassroots newspaper, Berkeley, Calif., 1978-80; public info. officer Alamedo Co. Spcl. Edn., Hayward, Calif., 1980-81; script-wrtr., producer Enriquez & Myers Slide Shows, San Francisco, 1981—; ed. Calif. Fedn. Tchrs., Oakland, 1984—; tchr. public relations class Media Alliance, San Francisco, 1981-85. Mem. Media Alliance, United Tchrs. Communications Assn. (recipient awards for Perspective newspaper 1985, 87. Home: 816-32d Ave San Francisco CA 94121

MYERS, GEORGE, JR., b. Harrisburg, PA, July 10, 1953; s. George F. and Virginia (Doepke) M; m. Shelly Hower, Oct. 7, 1984. Author: An Amnesiac on the Verge of Heaven, 1976, Nairobi, 1978, The News, 1985, An Introduction to Modern Times, 1982, Natural History, 1975, Alphabets Sublime, 1986, Bodies of Water, 1987, Epiphanies: The Prose Poem Now, 1987. BA in English, Baldwin-Wallace Coll, 1975; student, U Nairobi-E.Africa, 1973. Reporter Patriot-News, Harrisburg, Pa., 1977-83, wire ed./columnist, 1983-84; book ed. Columbus Dispatch, Ohio, 1984—. Recipient Ohio Arts Council fellowship in criticism, 1985. Address: Dispatch 34 S Third St Columbus OH 43216

MYERS, J. JAY, b. Detroit, July 31, 1919, s. Fred Maxfield and Glenna Pearl (Wallace) M.; m. Phyllis Byers, Aug. 1, 1941 (dec. 1958); children—Sandra Fay, Andrew Jay; m. 2d, Charlotte Elaine Will, Dec. 27, 1958; 1 dau., Susan Ruth. Author: The Revolutionists, 1971, Red Chiefs and White Challengers, 1972, Enchanting New Mexico, 1985; contrbr. to: World Over, Viva Mag., N.Mex. Mag., Detroit News, numerous other periodicals. Wrkg. on historical novel. BA, Wayne U., 1941, MEd, 1944. Tchr. public schls., Birmingham, Mich., 1942-78; freelance wrtr., photographer, Sante Fe, 1978—. Mem. Rocky Mountain Outdoor Wrtrs. and

Photographers. Home: Rt 7 Box 109JM Sante Fe NM 87505

MYERS, JACK ELLIOTT, b. Lynn, MA, Nov. 29, 1941; s. Alvin George and Ruth Libby (Cohen) M.; m. Nancy Leppert, June 15, 1967 (div. May 8, 1979); children—Benjamin, Seth; m. 2d, Willa Naomi Robins, Aug. 15, 1981; 1 child, Jacob. Author: Black Sun Abraxas, 1970, (wth photographer David Akiba) Will It Burn?, 1974, The Family War, 1977, I'm Amazed That You're Still Singing, 1981, Coming To the Surface, 1984, As Long As You're Happy, 1986. Ed.: A Trout in the Milk: Portrait of Richard Hugo, 1980. Co-ed.: New American Poets of the 80's (with Roger Weingarten), 1984, The Longman Dictionary and Handbook of Poetry (with Michael Simms), 1985. BA, U. Mass., 1970; MFA, U. Iowa, 1972. Assoc. prof. English, So. Meth. U., Dallas, 1975—; faculty Vt. Coll. MFA Program, Montpelier, 1980—. Mem. PEN, AWP, Tex. Assn. Creative Writing Tchrs., Tex. Inst. Letters. Recipient poetry award Tex. Inst. Letters, 1978; NEA fellow, 1982, 86; Yaddo Corp. fellow, 1978; Natl. Poetry Series winner, 1985. Home: 9940 Northcliff Dr Dallas TX 75218

MYERS, ROGER W., b. Horton, KS, Jan. 7, 1946; s. Walter E. and Jewell K. (Dawson) m.; m. Linda B. Whichello, Sept. 11, 1971. Contrbr. articles to mags. including Wrtr.'s Digest, Adweek, Screen, others. B.S. in Jnlsm., U. Kans., 1968; M.S. in Jnlsm., Northwestern U., 1969. Creative supvr. Needham, Harper & Steers, Chgo., 1975-76, Benton & Bowles, Chgo., 1976-78; exec. v.p. Burch Myers Cuttie Inc., Chgo., 1980-85; pres. Myers Roach & Prtnrs., Chgo., 1978-80, Mycomm Enterprises, Inc., Lake Forest, IL, 1985—. Recipient 1st place for fiction Wrtr.'s Digest, 1974, CLIO award, 1974, 76, 83, ANDY award N.Y. Ad Club, 1975, 76, 78, 82, 83, ADDY award Chgo. Ad Club, 1982, 83, 84, 85, 86. Mem. NWC, Ind. Wrtrs. Chgo. Home: 105 E Stone Ave Lake Forest IL 60045

MYERS, SUE ANN, b. Battle Creek, MI, Sept. 30, 1957; d. Harold Stanley and Beverly Ann (Gorham) Warkoczeski; m. Deryl Lee Myers, Sept. 12, 1975; children—Derick Lee, Kimberly Ann, Stacey Ann. Contrbr. poems to anthols. Wrkg. on new poetry, short story. Grad. public schls., Union City, MI. Home: 3428 E V Ave Vicksburg MI 49097

MYLES, SYMON, see Follett, Kenneth Martin

MYKELYSTAR, TOMASCO, see McAlister, Thomas Allen

MYNATT, CECIL FERRELL, (Skip Ferrel), b. Knoxville, May 10, 1920; s. Cecil F. and Ethel May (Ma) M.; m. Louise Courier, Dec. 5, 1975 (div. Feb. 20, 1086); children—Matthew, Cecilia, Martha, Melissa, Richard. Author: Depression, How to Cope, 1986. Contrbr. article to profl. jnl., poem to anthol. Wrkg. on What Psychiatry Can and Cannot Do for You; fiction, Rhoda; My Dream: A Primer of Mental Illness. B.S., U. Tenn., 1956, M.D., 1962. Practice of medicine specializing in psychiatry, Las Vegas, 1978-86; Joe Taullifer center, Lawton, OK, 1986—. Home: 34 SW 50th Lawton OK 73505

MYNATT, ELAINE SIMPSON, b. Mobile, AL, Nov. 25, 1947, d. Romeo Ezra Simpson and Faye (Austin) Estes; m. Jimmy Fredrick Baugh, Sept. 11, 1966 (div. 1978); children—Richard, Suzanne; m. 2d, Fred Richard Mynatt, Apr. 17, 1978; 1 dau., Beth. Author: Remarriage Reality, 1984; ed.: Koinonia Cooking, 1982, Louisiana Men Are Dinamight, 1983. Wrkg. on marriage self-help book. BA, Carson-Newman Coll., Jefferson City, Tenn., 1968. Tchr. pub. schls. various locations in La. and Tenn., 1968-78; pub., wrtr. Elm Publs., Knoxville, Tenn., 1982—. Mem. WG, AL. Office: Box 23192 Knoxville TN 37933

NADER, RALPH, b. Winsted, CT, Feb 27, 1934; s. Nadra and Rose (Bouziane) N. Author: Unsafe at Any Speed, 1965, rev., 1972, Working on the System: A Manual for Citizen's Access to Federal Agencies, 1972; co-author: What To Do with Your Bad Car, 1971, Action for a Change, 1972, You and Your Pension, 1973, Taming the Giant Corporation, 1976, Menace of Atomic Energy, 1977, The Lemon Book 1980; editor: Whistle Blowing: The Report on Professional Responsibility, 1972, The Consumer and Corporate Accountability, 1973; co-editor: Corporate Power in America, 1973, Verdicts on Lawyers, 1976, Who's Poisoning America, 1981; co-author: The Big Boys: Power & Position in American Business, 1986; contrbg. editor: Ladies Home Jnl, 1973-82. A.B. magna cum laude, Princeton U., 1955; LL.B with distinction, Harvard U., 1958. Served with AUS, 1959. Recipient Nieman Fellows award, 1965-66. Address: Box 19367 Washington DC 20036

NADLER, DOROTHY (DOT) LURIA, b. New Haven, June 15, d. Mandel and Bascia (Hamburg) Luria; widowed; children—Morton, Gerry Nadler Gould. Contrbr. poetry: Hearts on Fire (Love Poems), Our 20th Century's Greatest Poems, Our Best Beloved Poems, numerous others; "Data by Dot" column for 8 years. Wrkg. on book. Student NYU and Allied Art Inst. Freelance wrtr.; arts techr. Home: Box 117 Jeffersonville NY 12748

NAGEL, RICHARD, b. Geneva, IL, July 18, 1957; s. Ralph Arthur and Mary Ann (Schewalter) N. Contrbr. acticles to popular mags. City ed. Press Pubs., Elmhurst, IL, 1979-80; mng. ed. the Geneva Republican, 1985-87. B.S. in Jnlsm., U. Ill., 1979. Comedian, The Improv, NYC, 1981-85. Recipient Best Sports Wrtg. award Northern Ill. Newspaper Assn., 1986, Best Bus. Story award, 1986. Mem. Profl. Comedian's Assn. Home: 202 N Fifth St Geneva IL 60134

NAGLEE, DAVID INGERSOLL, b. Somers Point, NJ, Sept. 15, 1930; s. Jacob Hann, III and Dorcus Smith (Ingersoll) N.; m. Elfriede Elsa Kurz, Sept. 6, 1952; children—David Stephen, Joanna Jane, Deborah Ruth, Miriam Louise, Joy Ann. Author: History of the Methodist Church at Port Norris, N.J., 1962, Hauls of Holy Ivy, 1974, In Praise of More Folly, 1982, From Font to Faith: John wesley on infant Baptism & The Narture of Children, 1987; (poems) On Authors of Anonymous Letters, 1970, Bay of Fundy Fishing, 1971, Ode to Kudzu, 1979, Hope—Upon the Death of a Child, 1983, The New Idolatry: Computers, 1985. Author numerous hymns. B.A., Houghton Coll., 1953; Th.M., Crozer Theol. Seminary, 1959; M.A., Temple U., 1963, Ph.D., 1966. Minister, Methodist Church, Ellicottville, NY, 1953-56, Cumberland County, NJ, 1956-66; prof. LaGrange Coll., GA, 1966—, Flora Glenn Candler prof., 1971—; adj. prof. San Francisco Theol. Seminary, 1975, Southern Union Coll., Wadley, AL, 1978—, Candler Schl. Theol., Atlanta, 1979—. Served with U.S. Navy Res., 1947-54. Recipient Grayson M. Bradley award LaGrange Coll., 1973. Mem. Ga. Philosophical Soc., Soc. Christian philosophers, Am. church History Soc. Home: 804 Piney Woods Dr LaGrange GA 30240

NAHRA, NANCY ANN, b. Bangor, ME, May 11, 1947; d. John Joseph and Mary Hilda (Fowler) Nahra; m. F.E. Romer, Sept. 9, 1972 (div. 1979); m. Willard Sterne Randall, Oct. 19, 1985; children: Lucy Randell (b. April 11, 1987). Co-author: Visual Communication Through Signage, 1975; contrbr. to Urban Signage Forum, American Poetry Anthology, 1985; articles and poems in profl. jnls. BA, Colby College, 1968; MA, Stanford U., 1971; PhD cand. Princeton U., 1981. Editorial asst., Random House, NYC, 1971-72; editor/res. dir., Institute of Signage Research, Palo Alto, CA., 1972-77; lectr., OH State U., Columbus, 1977-79; instr., Princeton U., NJ, 1979-81, 1982-83; instr., Ecole Normale Superieure, Paris, France, 1981-82; lectr., U. of VT, Burlington, 1983—; dir. VT Overseas Studies Program, Nice, France, 1987-88. Winner John Masefield Award, PSA, 1987. Mem. AAP, PSA. Home: 20 West Canal St Winooski VT 05404

NAIL, DAWSON B., b. Greenfield,OK, Aug. 4, 1928, s. Eli Thomas and Vera Lucretia (Dawson) N.; m. Joye Ann Hough, July 30, 1955 (dec. 1969); children—Charles, Thomas, Penny, Gaye; m. Patsy Joan Gillespie, Aug. 4, 1972; stepchildren—Cynthia, Douglas. Ed.: The Business Behind the Box (by Les Brown), 1978, The Professor and the Commission (by Barry Cole and Malcolm Oettinger), 1979, The Evening Stars (by Barbara Matasou), 1983. BA, Southwestern Okla. U., 1950; MA, Okla. State U., 1955. Reporter Broadcasting mag., Washington, 1955-64; v.p., exec. ed. Television Digest, Inc., Washington, 1964—. Mem. Natl. Press Club, Soc. Profl. Journalists, Broadcast Pioneers. Office: TV Digest 1836 Jefferson Pl Washington DC 20036

NAILLON, VALERINE, (Valerine R. Shaw), b. Baker, OR, Mar. 13, 1960; d. Kenneth Wayne and Rose Zannah (Lloyd) Shaw; m. Ronald Dean Naillon, Mar. 2, 1985; 1 son, Jason Anthony. Contrbr. short stories to children's mags. Grad. public schs., Baker. Home: 34 Edison Dr Groton CT 06340

NAKADATE, NEIL EDWARD, b. East Chicago, IN, Sept. 1, 1943, s. Katsumi James and Mary (Marumoto) N.; m. M.M. Ivie, Dec. 29, 1972 (div. 1980); children—Nathaniel R., Nicholas K., Laurel K. Author: Robert Penn Warren: A Reference Guide, 1977, Robert Penn Warren: Critical Perspectives, 1981, (with others) England in Literature, 1979, Language: Structure and Use, 1981, Writing in the Liberal Arts Tradition: A Rhetoric with Readings, 1985. AB, Stanford U., 1965; PhD,Ind. U., 1972. Asst. prof. English, U. Tex., Austin, 1970-77; asst. prof. English, Iowa State U., Ames, 1977-80, assoc. prof., 1980-85, prof., 1985—. Mem. NCTE, Conf. Coll. Composition and Communication, Soc. for Study Multi-Ethnic Lit. U.S., Am. Lit. Section MLA. Home: 903 Burnett Ave Ames IA 50010

NAKATSUKA, LAWRENCE KAORU, b. Hanalei, HI, Jan. 27, 1920; s. Ichiro and Yone (Hashizume) N.; m. Minnie Yamauchi, Aug. 5, 1948; children—Paul Takashi, Roy Hiroshi, Laura Naomi. Hawaii corr. Christian sci. Monitor, 1950-53, Pacific Citizen, 1947-57. Reporter, asst. city ed. Honolulu Star Bulltn., 1939-52. Nieman Fellow, Harvard Univ., 1951-52. Press sec. Governor of Hawaii, Honolulu, 1953-60; legislative asst. U.S. Senator, Washington, 1963-76; v.p., dir. government affairs Chamber of Commerce of Hawaii, Honolulu, 1976-83, retired, 1983—. Home: 1335 Palolo Ave Honolulu HI 96816

NANFRIA, LINDA JEAN, b. Everett, MA, Nov. 27, 1949, d. Salvatore and Doris May (Mitton) Nanfria. Author: How to Publish an Organization Newsletter, 1976, Beat the Supermarket, 1979, A History of San Mateo Bar Association, 1984, A History of the Sausalito Yacht Club, 1985. BA, Calif. State U., Chico, 1974. PR manager/editor, Kaiser/Permanente, Oakland, CA, 1976; mng. edit., PAS Publishing, Daly City, CA, 1982; self-employed with Misc. Ink & Co., Menlo Park, CA, 1977—. Mem. Writer's Connection, Cupertino, 1987. Home: 228A O'Connor St Menlo Park CA 94025

NARELL, IRENA PENZIK, b. Sanok, Poland, Sept. 17, 1923; arrd. U.S.A., 1939; d. Abraham and Antonina (Katz) Penzik; m. Murray Narell, July 29, 1945; children: Jeff, Andrew. Author: Ashes to the Taste, 1961, Invisible Passage, 1969, Joshua, Fighter for Bar Kochba, 1978, Our City, the Jews of San Francisco, 1981; transl.: Holy Week; contrbr. to anthologies: Woman Who Lost Her Names, 1980, The Am. Jewish Woman, 1981, Family, 1987. BA, Columbia U., 1941-45. Secy. to Permanent Rep. Polish del. UN, NYC, 1946-52; co-owner Art Originals Gallery, NYC, 1958-60; mngr. The Steel Bandits, NYC, 1964-69; project dir. bicentennial exhibit J.L. Magnes Mus., Berkeley, Calif., 1975; freelance writer and lectr. Chapt. pres. Am. Jewish Congress, Queens, NY, 1966. Recipient Agnon Prize, NYU, NYC, 1956, Natl. Jewish Book award, NYC, 1979. Mem. NWU, Inst. Hist. Study. Address: 5949 Estates Dr Oakland CA 94611

NARGI, JANICE MARY, b. Milford, MA, Apr. 28, 1951; d. Edward L. and Blanche L. (McCarthy) N. Contrbr. articles to bus. mags. Newsletter ed. Women of Boston Directions, 1986—; ed.: People to People Quarterly, 1986, The Lighthouse Letter, 1986—. B.A., U. Mass., 1973; M.A., Assumption Coll., 1979. Entertainment ed., wrtr. Milford Daily News, 1976-78; schl. adjustment counselor Mendon-Upton Schls., upton, MA, 1979-86; owner, wrtr. JMN Pubs., Framingham, MA, 1981—. Pres. Milford Theartre Guild, 1975-77. Home: 260 Union Ave 29 Framingham MA 01701

NASAR, JACK LEON, b. Great Neck, NY, Mar. 31, 1947; s. Leon and Frieda (Dweck) N.; m. Judy Deloris Johnson, May 20, 1981; 1 dau., Joanna. Author: Environmental Aesthetics: Theory, Research and Application, 1988. Contrbr. articles to profl . jnls, & newspapers. B.S., Washington U., 1969; M.S., N.Y. U., 1973; Ph.D., Penn. State U., 1979. Asst. prof. U. Tenn., Knoxville, 1977-80; assoc. prof. Ohio State U., Columbus, 1980—. Home: 3003 Sudbury Rd Columbus OH 43221

NASH, ALANNA K., b. Louisville, KY, Aug. 16, 1950, d. Allan and Emily (Derrick) Nash. Author: Dolly, 1978, rev. ed., 1988, Behind Closed Doors: Talking with the Legends of Country Music, 1987, Jessica Savitch, 1988; contrbr. to N.Y. Times, Esquire, Stereo Rvw, other periodicals; contrbr. to Improving College Reading, 1978, Artists of American Folk Music, 1986, Reading Skills Handbook, 1987, The Great Book of Country Music, 1988. BA, Stephens Coll., 1972; MS, Columbia U., 1974. Popular music crit, Louisville Courier-Jnl., 1977; wrtr., producer radio syndication WHAS-Louisville Prodns., 1980; pres. Alandale Prodns., Louisville, 1981—. Mem. Sigma Delta Chi. Home: 703 Alta Vista Rd Louisville KY 40206

NASH, GRACE CHAPMAN, b. Garrettsville, OH, Nov. 19, 1909; d. Gale Joseph and Florence Estelle (Blackmarr) Chapman; m. Ralph Nash, Oct. 24, 1936; children—Ralph Stanley, Gale Blackmarr, Roy Leslie. Seventeen texts for Nash Music with Children Series; numerous articles on education for professional mags.; biographical books: That We Might Live, 1984, Christmas Poems of Grace C. Nash (1940-1985), 1985. AB, Ohio Wesleyan U., 1930; MA in music Chicago Musical Coll., 1936. Author/clinician in child development: Music, Language & Movement (US, Canada, Europe), 1968—, dir. grad. studies Orff, Kodaly, Laban (Northern Arizona U.), 1977—. Mem. Arizona Authors Assoc. Home: Box 1753 Scottsdale AZ 85252

NASH, JAY ROBERT III, b. Indpls., Nov. 26, 1934; s. Jay Robert and Jerrie Lynne (Cosur) N.; m. Janice Patricia Schwartz, Sept. 15, 1962 (div.); children—Lee Travis, Andrea Lynne; m. Judith Ann Anetsberger; son, Jay Robert Nash IV, Nov. 10, 1984. Author: Bloodletters and Badmen, 1973, On All Fronts, 1974, Hustlers and Con Men, 1976, Look for the Woman, 1981, Zanies: A Narrative Encyclopedia of the World's Greatest Eccentrics, 1982, Crime Movie Quiz Book, 1983, The Dillinger Dossier, 1983, others; ed./pub., Motion Picture Guide (vol. 1, 1985, vols. 2-6, 1986). Editor Milw. Lit. Times, 1961; editor Antioch (Ill.) News, 1962; mng. editor Am. Trade Mags., Chgo., 1962-66; editorial dir. PRM Corp., Chgo., 1967; editor-in-chief Chgo. Land mag., 1967-70; freelance writer, Chgo., 1970—; editor, pub. Lit. Times, 1961-70. Mem. AG, Midland Authors. Address: 2934 Indian Hill Wilmette IL 60091.

NASLUND, ALAN JOSEPH, b. Chinook, MT, Apr. 12, 1941; s. Harvey Clifford and Thelma Ruth (Williams) N.; m. Charlotte Ferree, 1962; 1 child, Andra Johanna; m. Sena Kathryn Jeter, Oct. 7, 1973; 1 child, Flora Kathryn. Poetry editor The Louisville Rvw, 1980-81; writer book rvws. The Courier-Jnl., 1981-84; fiction and poetry in numerous newspapers, mags, and rvws. MA in English, U. Mont., 1973; PhD in English, U. Louisville, 1982. Instr. English, Bellarmine Coll., Louisville, 1981-82; asst. prof. English, Hanover Coll., Ind., 1982-85, Pikeville Coll., Ky., 1985-86; assoc. faculty, Indiana U., Purdue U. at Indianapolis, 1986-87. Editor River City Rvw, Louisville, 1985—, co-editor, 1984-85. Mem. MLA. Home: 2028 Emerson Ave Louisville KY 40205

NASSIFF, TONIUS, see Stephens, Thomas M.

NATANSON, MAURICE ALEXANDER, b. NYC, Nov. 26, 1924; s. Charles and Kate (Scheer) N.; m. Lois Janet Lichenstein, Jan. 21, 1949; children:Charles, Nicholas, Kathy. Author: A Critique of Jean-Paul Sartre's Ontology, 1951, The Social Dynamics of George H. Mead, 1956, Literature, Philosophy, and the Social Sciences, 1962, The Journeying Self, 1970, Edmund Husserl, 1973, Phenomenology, Role, and Reason, 1974; editor: The Problem of Social Reality (Alfred Schutz), 1962, Philosophy of the Social Sciences, 1963, Essays in Phenomenology, 1966, Psychiatry and Philosophy, 1969, Phenomenology and Social Reality, 1970, Phenomenology and the Social Sciences, 1973), (With Henry W. Johnstone, Jr.) Philosophy, Rhetoric, and Argumentation, 1965; cons. editor: Philosophy Phenomenological Research, 1960-84, Indiana-Northwestern U. Press Studies Phenomenology Existential Philosophy, 1963—, Jnl. Value Inquiry, 1967—, Philosophy and Rhetoric, 1968—, Medicine and Philosophy, 1975; book rvw. editor: Man and World, 1968-78, Selected Studies Phenomenology Existential Philosophy, 1973—; mem. editorial adv. bd.: phenomenology and Human Scis., 1981—. Recipient Natl. Book award Philosophy and Religion, 1974. Mem. am. Philo. Assn. (Alfred Schutz lectr. 1969), Soc. Phenomenology Existential Philosophy mem. exec. com. 1964-68), Intl. Phenomenological Soc. Home: 428 Humphrey St New Haven Ct 06511

NATHAN, LEONARD EDWARD, b. Los Angeles, Nov. 8, 1924; s. Israel and Florence (Rosenberg) N.; m. Carol Gretchen Nash, June 27, 1949; children—Andrew Peter, Julia Irene, Miriam Abigail. Author: Western Reaches, 1958, The Glad and Sorry Seasons, 1963, The Matchmaker's Lament, 1967, The Day the Perfect Speakers Left, 1969, The Tragic Drama of William Butler Yeats, 1963, Flight Plan, 1971, Without Wishing, 1973, The Likeness, 1975, Coup, 1975, Returning Your Call, 1975, The Transport of Love: The Meghaduta by Kalidasa, 1976, Teachings of Grandfather Fox, 1977, Lost Distance, 1978, Dear Blood, 1980, Holding Patterns, 1982, Carrying On: New and Selected Poems, 1985; also record Confessions of a Matchmaker, 1973; translator: Songs of Something Else, 1982, Grace and Mercy in Her Wild Hair, 1982, (with Czelaw Milosz) Happy as a Dog's Tail (poems by Anna Swir). Student, Ga. Tech., 1943-44, UCLA, 1946-47; BA summa cum laude, U. Calif.-Berkeley, 1950, MA, 1952, PhD,1960. Instr. Modesto (Calif.) Jr. Coll., 1954-59; prof. dept. rhetoric U. Calif.-Berkeley, 1960—, chmn. dept., 1968-72. Served with AUS, 1943-45. Recipient Phelan award, 1955; Longview prize, 1961; award in lit. Natl. Inst. Arts and Letters, 1971; Poetry medal Commonwealth Club, 1976, 81; U. Calif. Creative Arts fellow, 1961-62, 73-74; U. Calif. Humanities research fellow, 1983-84; Am. Inst. Indian Studies fellow, 1966-67; Guggenheim fellow, 1976-77. Home: 40 Beverly Rd Kensington CA 94707

NATHAN, NORMAN, b. NYC, Nov. 19, 1915, s. Michael and Fannie (Levine) N.; m. Frieda Agin, July 21, 1940; children—Linda Nathan Kuzmack, Michele, Lois Anne. Author: Though Night Remain (poetry), 1959, Judging Poetry (textbook), 1961, The Right Word (vocabulary text workbook), 1962, Writing Sentences (text workbook), 1964 Short Stories (anthology textbook), 1969, Prince William B., 1975; contrbr. short stories to Oui, Can. Forum, Malahat Rvw, Victorian, others; contrbr. poems to Mindscapes, Sat. Evening Post, Prairie Schooner, Wascana Rvw, other lit mags, anthols and textbooks; contrbr. articles to Shakespeare Qtly., English Jnl, Jnl Higher Edn., others. AB, NYU, 1936, MA, 1938, PhD,1947. Prof. English Syracuse U., Utica, N.Y., 1949-68, Fla. Atlantic U., Boca Raton, 1968—. Mem. MLA. Home: 1189 SW Tamarind Way Boca Raton FL 33486

NATHAN, ROBERT STUART, b. Johnstown, PA, Aug. 13, 1948, s. Alex David and Bernice (Fadenhecht) N. Novelist: Amusement Park, 1977, Rising Higher, 1981, The White Tiger, 1987; contrbr. articles to Harper's, Cosmopolitan, N.Y. Times, other periodicals. BA cum laude, Amherst Coll., 1970. White House corr. Natl. Public Radio, Washington, 1976-77; novelist, journalist. Mem. AG. Address: Markson Agcy 44 Greenwich Ave New York NY 10011

NAUMAN, FRANCES IRMA, (Frances Wolf), b. Phoenix, AZ, Apr. 20, 1914; d. Arthur August Wilhelm and Zelia Irma (Pratt) Wolf; m. St. Elmo Nauman, Apr. 29, 1934 (div. 1963); children—St. Elmo, Diana Frances Nauman Jones. Author: Freeway Verse, 1976, I Love Los Angeles,

1984, California Majic, 1984. AA, U. So. Colo., 1945. Tchr., secy., 1945-66; exec. secy. Automobile Club of S. CA, Los Angeles, 1967-75, Crocker Bank, Los Angeles, 75-79; legal secy. Choate & Choate, Los Angeles, 1979-86. Mem. CA Federation Chaparral Poets, Poets Laureate Internatl., S.W. Art Assn. Address: 1918 N Whitney Ave Hollywood CA 90068

NAVASKY, VICTOR SAUL, b. NYC, July 5, 1932; s. Macy and Esther Blanche (Goldberg) N.; m. Anne Landey Strongin, Mar. 27, 1966; children—Bruno, Miri, Jenny. Author: Kennedy Justice, 1971 (Natl. Book Award nominee), Naming Names, 1980 (Am. Book Award 1981), (with Christopher Cerf) The Experts Speak, 1985. AB, Swarthmore Coll., 1954; LL.B., Yale U., 1959. Spcl. asst. to Gov. G. Mennen Williams, Mich., 1959-60; editor, pub. Monocle Mag., 1961-65; editor N.Y. Times mag., 1970-72, ed.-in-chief, The Nation mag., NYC, 1978—; vis. scholar Russell Sage Fdn., 1975-76; Ferris Prof. journalism Princeton U., 1976-77. Served with U.S. Army, 1954-56. Guggenheim fellow, 1974-75. Mem. AG, PEN, Phi Beta Kappa. Office: The Nation 72 Fifth Ave New York NY 10011

NAVON, ROBERT, b. NYC, May 18, 1954; s. Jack and Estelle N.; m. Hariclia Michailidou, Mar. 3, 1983 (div. 1985); m. Victoria (Ellie) Arroyo, Jan. 24, 1986. Author: Patterns of the Universe, 1977, Autumn Songs: Poems on Love, Beauty, Nature and Life, 1983; editor: The Platonic Theology Vols. I and II, 1985, The Pythagorean Writings: Hellenistic Texts from the 1st Century B.C.-3d Century A.D., 1986 (also wrote intro.), The Neoplatonic Writings of Numenius, 1987. BA, Lehman Coll., 1975; MS, SUNY-Geneseo, 1978; MA studies, philo., New Schl., 1982-86; PhD cand., Univ. of Kansas, 1986—; public lectr. in comparative religions, 1976-77. Librarian N.Y. Inst. Tech., 1978-79; office worker and real estate salesman NYC, 1979-83; tchr. English, NYC high schls., Bklyn., 1983-86; founder and ed., Selene Books Publications, 1983—. Active, Am. Platform Assn., 1976-78. N.Y. State Regents scholar, 1971. Mem. Am. Philo. Assn., Soc. for Ancient Greek Philosophy, Phi Beta Kappa. Address: Box 548 Lawrence KS 66044

NAWROCKI, TOM L., b. Chgo., May 11, 1947, s. Joseph T. and Pearl (Olszowy) N.; m. Denise Ann Gaffney, Dec. 22, 1983. Founding co-ed. Hair Trigger Mag., 1977; contrbr. articles to: So. Illinoisan, Egyptian, Virgin Mule, Wrtg. from Start to Finish, other publs. BA, Columbia Coll., Chgo., 1977; MA, Loyola U., Chgo., 1985. Instr. creative wrtg. Columbia Coll., Chgo., 1977-85, dir. freshman wrtg. program, 1986—; wrtg. cons. Chgo. Schl. System, 1980. Home: 1120 W Loyola St Chicago IL 60626

NAYER, LOUISE BEDFORD, b. NYC, Nov. 22, 1949; d. Herman Rafael and Dorothy Dennison (Daubert) N.; m. James Joseph Patten, Dec. 17, 1984; children: Sarah Anne, Laura Julia; 1 stepchild, Bonnie Lynne. Author: Keeping Watch, 1981; contrbr. poems to Unicorn, Contact II, Snapshots, Remington Rvw, Louisville Rvw. BA in Comparative Lit., U. Wis., 1971; MA in Humanities, SUNY, Buffalo, 1976. Instr. English, U. Calif. Extension Ctr., San Francisco, 1977-79, Coll. of San Mateo, Calif., 1982—, City Coll. San Francisco, 1985—; artist-in-residence Calif. Arts Council, 1979-82. Mem. P&W. Home: 626Spruce St San Francisco CA 94118

NAYLOR, LOIS ANNE MC CREA, b. Pitts., Sept. 14, 1948; d. Earle D. and Helen Jane (Martin) McCrea; m. Gary W. Naylor; children—Michelle, Kristi, Jeff. Contrbr. articles, booklets to profl. jnls., popular mags., books including Seventeen Mag., Communication: Journalism Edn. Today. Columnist, reporter, feature wrtr. Ankeny Press Citizen, 1976-79. BLS, U. Ia., 1983. Free-lance wrtr., Ankeny, Ia., 1979-82; dir. writing ITA, Inc., West Des Moines, Ia., 1982—. Chairperson publicity Intl. Yr. of the Child, 1979, Ankeny's Annual Celebration, 1980-81. Recipient 3d prize for master columnist Ia. Press Assn., 1978, Addy award Advt. Profls. Ia., 1984. Mem. Intl. Assn. Bus. Communicators (awards of Excellence 1984, 85, 86), awards of Merit 1984, 85). Home: 117 NW Coral Ln Ankeny IA 50021

NAYLOR, PHYLLIS REYNOLDS, b. Anderson, IN, Jan. 4, 1933, d. Eugene Spencer and Lura Mae (Schield) Reynolds; m. Thomas Anthony Tedesco, Sept. 9, 1951 (div. 1960); m. 2d, Rex Vaughn Naylor, May 26, 1960; children—Jeffrey, Michael. Author: Crazy Love: An Autobiographical Account of Marriage and Madness, 1977, In Small Doses, 1979, Revelations, 1979, Unexpected Pleasures, 1986, also 52 books for children and young adults; contrbr. short stories to numerous publs. Wrkg. on adult novel. BA, Am. U. Recipient Golden Kite award Soc. Children's Bookwrtrs., 1978, Notable Book award ALA, 1982, 85, 86, Edgar Allan Poe award MWA, 1985, Child Study award Bank Street Coll., 1983, the Young Adult Book Award in South Carolina (S.C. Assn. Schl. Libns.), 1985-86. Mem. Children's Book Guild Washington, AG, PEN. Home: 9910 Holmhurst Rd Bethesda MD 20817

NAYLOR, ROBERT L., b. Niagara Falls, NY, May 16, 1934; s. Robert Kingman and Louise Veronica (Meehan) N.; m. Kathleen Jane Storm, Dec. 29, 1956 (div. Aug. 1978); m. 2d, Donna Rose Acquaviva, Aug. 1, 1981; children—Kathleen, Bridget, Robert, James; stepchildren—Joseph, Theresa, Anthony, David, John, Lawrence, Mary. Contrbr. to Christian Sci. Monitor, New York Times, Changing Times, Washington Post, others; ghost collaborator Miles To Go, 1983. Student Penn. State U. Asst. Sunday mag. ed. Detroit Free Press, 1972-74; Sunday mag. ed. The Buffalo Courier-Express, 1974-78; asst. features ed. Sunday mag. The Detroit News, 1978-79; sr. PR acct. exec. Williard, Thomas & Durocher, Detroit, 1979-82; deputy features ed. The Washington Times, 1982-83; editorial dir. The Horse Digest, Leesburg, VA, 1983—. Served to PFC, U.S. Army, 1956-58. Home: Rt 1 Box 505 Kearneysville WV 25430

NAYLOR, RUTH EILEEN, b. Bluffton, OH, Sept. 3, 1934; d. Clifford Carver and Wanuneta Rosetta (Doudna) Bundy; m. Stanley Fred Naylor, Sept. 25, 1954; children—Kimberly Anne Naylor McCullough, Geoffrey Alan. Contrbr. poems to anthols., religious mags., newpapers and newsletters. Wrkg. on songwriting for opera. B.A., Bluffton Coll., 1971; M.A., Bowling Green State U., 1976. Secondary tchr. Bluffton Exempted Schls., 1972-84; assoc. pastor First Mennonite Ch., Bluffton, 1984—. Home: 123 Villanova Dr Bluffton OH 45817

NEAL, AVON, b. Morgantown, IN, July 16, 1922; s. Orval Francis and Goldie Agnes (Prather) N.; m. Ann Elizabeth Parker, Oct. 31, 1964. Author: Rubbings from Early American Stone Sculpture, 1963, Ephemeral Folk Figures, 1969, Molas: Folk Art of the Cuna Indians, 1977, Pigs and Eagles, 1978, Scarecrows, 1978, Early American Stone Sculpture Found in the Burying Grounds of New England, 1981, Los Ambulantes, 1982; contrbr. articles to profl. jnls. Student, Long Beach (Calif.) Coll.; MFA, Escuela de Bellas Artes, Mex., 1949. Artist-in-residence Altos de Chavon, Dominican Republic, 1983, 84; mem. advisory bd. Mus. Am. Folk Art, 1968-71, Dublin Seminar for New Eng. Folklife, 1976-78; propr. Thistle Hill Press; lectr., radio and TV appearances. Served with USN, World War II. Ford Fdn. grantee, 1962-64; Artists Fdn. Mass. fellow, 1979. Home: Thistle Hill North Brookfield MA 01535

NEAL, JAMES EDWARD JR., b. Toledo, Apr. 23, 1933; s. James Edward and Lois Catherine (Campbell) N.; children—Lynette Ann, David Evan. Author: Effective Phrases for Performance Appraisals: A Guide to Successful Evaluations, 1978 (4th ed., 1986), Your Slice of the Melon: A Guide to Greater Job Success, 1985. BBA, U. Toledo, 1955, MA, U. Ill-Champaign, 1957. Mgr. sales services Champion Spark Plug Co., Toledo, 1957—; founder Neal Publs., Perrysburg, Ohio, 1978—. Mem. Am. Mktg. Assn., Meeting Planners Intl., COSMEP. Address: 109 Holly Ln Perrysburg OH 43551

NEBEL, HENRY MARTIN, JR., b. NYC, Sept. 29, 1921; s. Henry Martin and Margaret (Naumann) N.; m. Sylvia Sue Fuller, July 13, 1967; children—Althea, Keith, Grant, Blake. Author: N.N. Karamzin, a Russian Sentimentalist, 1966, Selected Prose of N.M. Karamzin, 1967, Selected Aesthetic Works of Sumarokov and Karamzin, 1981, others; author articles and translations of Russian topics; editor, contrbg. editor various jnls. BA, Columbia U., 1943, MA, 1950, PhD, 1960. Researcher analyst Natl. Security Agcy., Arlington, Va., 1949-50, U.S. Mcht. Marine Acad., Kings Point, N.Y., 1955-56, Duke U., Durham, N.C., 1956-57; mem. faculty Northwestern U., Evanston, Ill., 1957—, prof. Russian lit., 1960—. Served with USAF, 1943-45. Mem. Am. Assn. Tchrs. Slavic and East European Langs., Soc. for Eighteenth-Century Lit., AAUP. Office: K-C Hall 148B NWU Evanston IL 60201

NEBEL, LAURIE JEAN, b. Charles City, IA, Mar. 13, 1957; d. Leonard and Mary Jean (Bennor) Kristiansen; m. Robert W. Nebel, Feb. 18, 1982. Author: Charles City—Quality of Life, 1986, Synapse, 1983-85, Growing to Market, 1984. B.A. in Communication Arts, Wartburg Coll., Waverly, Ia., 1979. News dir. KWBG radio sta., Boone, Ia., 1979-82, KBAB radio sta., Indianola, Ia., 1982-83; reporter, ed. Indianola Record Herald, 1982; wrtr., ed. Salsbury Labs, Inc., Charles City, Ia., 1983-86, advt. mgr., 1986—. Trustee Nashua Community Schl. Found., 1986—. Named Outstanding Sr. Journalism Student, Wartburg Coll., 1979. Mem. Natl. Assn. Agrl. Marketers, Soc. Collegiate Journalists. Home: 100 Dawn Dr Nashua IA 50658

NEE, KAY BONNER, b. Plummer, MN, Oct. 26; d. David Thomas and Helena (Franken) Bonner; m. William Joseph Nee; children—Christopher, Nicole, Lisa, Rachel. Contrbr.: Powhatan, the Story of an American Indian, Your Child's World, Preparing Children for the 21st Century, 1973, Living Married, 1975, Catholic Mi-s, Messenger of the Sacred Heart, other publs. Wrkg. on novels, play. BA with honors, Coll. St. Catherine; postgrad., U. Minn. Freelance writer, public relations and advt. agcys., Mpls. and St. Paul, 1957-68; freelance wrtr., dir. radio, TV, film, 1968-72; exec. dir. Minn. Assn. Social Service Agcys., St. Paul, 1972-81; v.p.

Pederson, Herzog & Nee Advt., Mpls., 1981—. Mem. North Suburban Center for Arts (pres.), AFTRA, Minn. Press Club, Northwest Advt. Council. Home: 219 Logan Pkwy Fridley MN 55432

NEEDHAM, RICHARD LEE, b. Cleve., Jan. 16, 1939; s. Lester Hayes and Helen (Bender) N.; m. Irene Juechter, Aug. 7, 1965; children—Margaret, Richard, Trevor. BA, Denison U., 1961; MA, U. Mo., 1967. Copy editor Sat. Rvw, NYC, 1967-68; editor-in- chief Preview Intl., NYC, 1968-69; financial and N.Y. editor Instns. mag.; also editor Service World Internat., NYC,1969-70; copy dir. American Home mag., NYC,1970-71; exec. editor Ski mag., NYC,1971-74, editor, 1974—, Ency. of Skiing, 1978. Broadcaster: Ski Spot, CBS Radio, 1978-83, "On the Slopes," 1984-85; Lowell Thomas award winner, 1985. Author: 50 Years of Skiing in North America, 1987. Served to lt. USNR, 1961-65. Mem. U.S. Ski Writers Assn., Eastern Ski Writers Assn., Overseas Press Club. Home: 115 Old Post Rd Croton-on-Hudson NY 10520

NEELD, JUDITH, b. Norwood, MA, Aug. 24, 1928; d. Carleton Warburton and Edith Mary (Wilson) Phillips; m. Richard Hoagland Neeld, Sept. 11, 1948; children—Gordon Phillips, Nancy Alison Neeld Vander Veen. Author: Scripts For A Life in Three Parts, 1978; poetry, articles, rvws. in Poetry Rvw, Mid-American Rvw, Kansas Qtly, Crosscurrents, others. Student, Denison U., Granville, OH, 1946-48. Managing ed., Patterns Magazine, Denville, NJ, 1973; ed., Stone Country Press, MA, 1976-84; ed., Stone Country Magazine, 1974—. Awards: Emily Dickinson, PSA 1985. Mem. PSA. Home: Box 132 Menemsha MA 02552

NEESE, RUBY S., b. Whitsett, NC, Oct. 20, 1930; d. Greer George and Pauline (Greeson) Shaw; m. Henry F. Neese, July 24, 1948; children—Henry F., Daniel A., Benton C., Jeffrey S. Author: Truths in Rhyme, 1985; contrbr. to Grit, Woman's Household, Burlington Times, other newspprs. Student pub. schls., Liberty, NC. Fire Dept. volunteer, Liberty NC. First pl. Laureate, United Amateur Press, 1982-83, first pl. Laureate, UAPAA, 1983. Home: Rt 3 Box 83 Liberty NC 27298

NEI-NEI, see Williams, Irene Mae

NEIDIGH, KIM LEE, b. Ft. Wayne, Ind., May 1, 1952; s. Paul Gilpen and Greta Louise (Shaffer) N. Contrbr. poetry and fiction to Bloodrake, Beyond,Grue, Persona, other lit mags, articles to INFO. Jnl., Fate, Crux, other periodicals. AAS, San Antonio Coll., 1972; BS, S.W. Tex. State U., San Marcos, 1976. Mem. P&W, Soc. for Investigation of the Unexplained. Home: 231 Radiance Ave SanAntonio TX 78218

NEIER, ARYEH, b. Berlin, Germany, Apr. 22, 1937; came to U.S., 1947, naturalized, 1955; s. Wolf and Gitla (Bendinska) N.; m. Yvette Celton, June 22, 1958; 1 son, David. Author: Dossier, 1975, Crime and Punishment: A Radical Solution, 1976, Defending My Enemy, 1979, Only Judgment, 1982; co-editor series of handbooks on rights of Americans, 1972-78; mem. editorial bd.: The Nation, 1978-86. B.S., Cornell U., 1958; LL.D. (hon.), Hofstra U., 1975, Hamilton Coll., 1979, Exec. dir. League Indsl. Democracy, N.Y.C., 1958-60; assoc. editor Current mag., NYC., 1960-63; exec. dir. N.Y. Civil Liberties Union, 1965-70; field devel. officer ACLU, 1963-64, exec. dir NYC., 1970-78; dir. 20th Century Fund Project on Litigation and Social Policy, 1978-81; lectr. Sch continuing Edn., NYU, 1968-69, Police Acad., 1969-70. Commr. juvenile justice standards project Am. Bar Assn.—Inst. for Judicial Administrn; vice chmn. Helsinki Watch Com., 1981—, Ams. Watch Com., 1981—, Asia Watch Com., 1985—. Recipient Gavel award am. Bar Assn., 1974. Fellow N.Y. Inst. for Humanities. Office: 36 W 44th St New York NY 10036

NEIGER, MICHAEL ALAN, b. Petoskey, MI, Oct. 2, 1953; s. Arthur Bart and Virginia N. Author: Latent Fingerprint Handbook, 1983, The Impact of Law Enforcement Professionalism on the Ability and Willingness of Police Departments to Utilize Forensic Science Services, 1985, Freelance Writing Opportunities, 1987, Marking Device Sales Opportunities, 1987, Michigan Cold-Water Fishing Directory, 1987. A.S., Northern Mich. U., 1974, B.S., 1975; M.S., Wayne State U., 1980, Ph.D., 1985. Laboratory specialist Crime Laboratory, Madison Heights, MI, 1979—; freelance wrtr., 1982—; ed., pub. Consumer Pubs., Inc., Sterling Heights, MI, 1986—. Home: 5057 Corey Ct Sterling Heights MI 48310

NEIL, FRED APPLESTEIN, b. Balt., Nov. 26, 1933; s. Frank and Mollie (Schapiro) Applestein; m. Sheila Tilles, Aug. 30, 1959 (div. May 1980); children—Jan Alan Neil, Brian Mark Applestein, Gail Renee Applestein; m. Dawn Francis Fisher, July 6, 1986. Contrbr. articles to mags., newspapers, newsletters. Ed., contrbr. Lafayette Square newsletter, 174-82, Fedl. Hill Newsletter, 1974-82, Greater Penn. Ave. Newsletter, 1974-82, MPCA News Letter, 1982—, Md. Rehabilitation Assn. News Letter, 1985—, Front & Center newsletter, 1980—. Wrkg. on Reaching the Media from Rehabilitation Prospective, The Media and Successful Vocational Rehabilitation Programs. B.A., U. Md., 1959. News and sports ed. Sta WITH, Balt. 1959-60; dir. news and sports Sta. WCBM, Metromedia, Balt., 1960-69; press officer Mayor william Donald Schaefer, Balt., 1970-71; genl. mgr. Balt. Banners World Team Tennis League, 1971-72; pres. Fred Neil Assoc., P.R., Balt., 1972—; staff specialist public info. Md. Rehabilitation Center, Balt., 1980—. Served with U.S. Army, 1956-58. Recipient award for spot reporting Chesapeake AP, 1967, award for in-depth sports reporting, 1967, 69. Mem. Md. Rehabilitation Assn. (pres. 1985, 87), Md. press Club, Balt. Sports Reporters Assn. (pres. 1964), Balt. Press Reporters Assn. (pres. 1965). Home: 4608 Learned Sage Ellicott City MD 21043

NELL, T. W., see Brady, Dan Phillip

NELMS, SHERYL LYNNE, b. Marysville, Kans., Dec. 3, 1944; d. Edwin Andrew and Margaret Eva (Smith) N.; m. Aug. 9, 1963 (div. July 1984); children: Julie Lynne Baker, Benjaman Edward Baker, David Alan Baker; m. 2d, Danny C. Pennington, June 3, 1986. Author: (poetry) Their Combs Turn Red in the Spring, 1984; contrbg. ed. Streets, 1980—, Byline, 1980—; contrbr. over 2000 poems to lit. and comml. mags. BS, S.D. State U., 1979; postgrad. U. Tex., Arlington, 1980-81. Typist, customer service rep., claims examiner N&N Ins. Co., Hurst, Tex., 1983-85; ins. adjustor Va. Life Ins. Co., Ft. Worth, 1985-86; ins. & securities sales, Tucson, 1986. Mem. WWA, Okla. Wrtrs. Fedn. (v.p.), Dallas-Ft. Worth Wrtrs. Workshop. Mem. Natl. League of Am. Pen Women, Soc. Southwestern Authors, Tucson Author's Resource Ctr., RWA. Address: Box 31595 Tuscon AZ 85751

NELSEN, HART MICHAEL, b. Piperstone, MN, Aug. 3, 1938; s. Noah I. and Nova (Ziegler) N.; m. Anne Kusener, June 13, 1964; 1 dau., Jennifer. Author: (with Anne K. Nelsen) Black Church in the Sixties, 1975; co-author: The Religion of Children, 1977, Religion and American Youth, 1976; editor: (with others) The Black Church in America, 1971; adv. editor: Sociol. Qtly, 1976-82; assoc. editor: Sociol. Analysis, 1977-80, Rvw Religious Research, 1977-80; editor, 1980-84; mem. editorial bd.: Social Forces, 1983-86. BA, U. No. Iowa, 1959, MA, 1963; MDiv, Princeton Theol. Sem., 1963; PhD,Vanderbilt U., 1972. Asst. prof. sociology Western Ky. U., Bowling Green, 1965-70, assoc. prof., 1970-73, Catholic U. Am., 1973-74, prof., 1974-81, chmn. dept. sociology, 1974-77, 81; prof. sociology La. State U., Baton Rouge, 1981-84, chmn. dept. sociology, head dept. rural sociology, 1981-84; dean Coll. of Lib. Arts, prof. of soc., PA State U., 1984—. Mem. Assn. Sociology Religion, Religious Research Assn. (pres. 1986-87), Soc. Sci. Study Religion, Am. Sociol. Assn., So. Sociol. Soc., Brit. Sociol. Assn. Office: 110 Sparks PA State Univ University Park PA 16802

NELSON, BOBBY JACK, b. Hatchel, TX, Sept. 9, 1938. Novels: The Last Station, 1972, Brothers, 1975, The Pull, 1986, The Devil to Pay, 1980 (with other); author: Coast-to-Coast, 1965; wrkg. on The Boy's Place (novel) to be published 1987. Address: 94 Pleasant Valley Wimberley TX 78676

NELSON, CHARLES LAMAR, b. Oxford, MS, June 9, 1917; s. Charles Robert and Willie Aline (Welch) N.; m. Lena Mae Reaves, Oct. 1, 1940; 1 son, Timothy Lamar. Author: (poems) The Marble Urn, 1941, William Faulkner: The Anchorite of Rowan Oak, 1973, A Chain that Breaks a Man, 1975; (prose) (with David Goforth) Our Neighbor, William Faulkner, 1977. Contrbr. poems to anthols, articles to books, newspapers. BA, U. Miss., 1946, MA, 1947. Tchr., prin., guidance counselor various pub. schls., Miss., Ark., Tenn., Ga., Mo. 1940-72; welfare agt. Adams County Welfare Dept., Natchez, Miss., 1958-59; Caledonia High Schl., Miss., 1972-82; retired. Served with USN, 1942-45. Recipient Top Area Mgr. award World Book Encyclopedia & Childcraft, 1959; cert. of Appreciation, USN, 1973, Pres. Gerald Ford, 1976. Fellow Intl. Acad. Poets; Natchez Poetry Soc. (co-founder and 1st pres. 1959-60), Miss. Poetry Soc. (treas. 1964-65), Columbus Poetry Soc. (co-founder and 1st pres. 1980-81), Assn. Christian Poets (co-founder and chmn. pub. 1984-85), William Faulkner Soc. Intl. Poets (founder and 1st pres. 1985-86). Home: 712 S 19th St Oxford MS 38655

NELSON, CURTIS SCOTT, b. Crowley, LA, May 28, 1929; s. Curtis Scott and Sylvia Faye (Sarver) N.; m. Elizabeth Elaine Friesen, June 30, 1961; children—Sarah Elizabeth, Peter Scott. Author poetry chapbook: After Summer; contrbr. poetry to Villager, Parnassus, Rhyme Time, New Earth Rvw, other publs.; contrbr. short stories to Hob-Nob, Hoosier Challenger, Story Time. BA, McNeese State U., 1953; MA, La. State U., 1964. Instr. English North Tex. State U., Denton, 1964-66; assoc. prof. English McNeese State U., Lake Charles, La., 1967—. Mem. NCTE, MLA (South Central sect.), Phi Kappa Phi. Home: Route 3 Box 456 Lake Charles LA 70605

NELSON, GINGER K., b. Hackensack, NJ, Jan. 21, 1939; d. Sholto Douglas and Louise Julia (Martens) Kirk; m. Fritz E. Nelson, III, Feb. 14, 1964; children—Linda, Fen, Danny,

Misty. Contrbr. short stories to mags. B.A., Coll. Misericordia, 1960. Library asst. Simi Valley Library, CA, 1976-78; substitute tchr. public schs., Prince Georges County, MD, 1979-81; aerobics dance tchr. Performance Productions, Camp Springs, MD, 1981-83. Recipient 2d place for short story Armed Forces Wrtrs.' League, 1973. Mem. Ala. Wrtrs.' Conclave (2d place for article 1986). Home: 12014 Comanche Trail Huntsville AL 35803

NELSON, JO ANN, b. Del Norte, CO, Feb. 5, 1946; s. John Clifford and Eva Frances Nelson. Contrbr. poetry to The Archer, Daily Meditations, Deros, Poetry Seattle, San Fernando Poetry Jnl, Voices for Peace, On the Edge, short story to Alma. BA, U. Colo., 1968. Tchr. pub. schls. Towson, Md., 1968-70, Colorado Springs, Colo., 1970-73; office mgr. Wolf Creek Ski Devel. Corp., South Fork, Colo., 1973-75; owner, mgr., chef La Mariposa Restaurant, South Fork, 1975-80; real estate salesman Balzotti & Co., Seattle, 1980—; co-owner Catehpenny Books, 1987—. Home: 3518 NE 147 St Seattle WA 98155

NELSON, JOHN ALLAN, b. Mayfield, KY, June 24, 1952; s. Edward and Martha (Baker) N.; m. Mary Jane Auxier, Sept. 14, 1974; 1 dau., Julie. Editor, contrbr.: The Citizen Voice & Times, 1984—. Contrbr. articles, chap. to book, mags. BA in Journalism, Eastern Ky. U. Safety dir. Southeast Coal Co., Irvine, Ky., 1974-85. Chmn. Bluegrass Pvt. Industry Council, Levington, Ky., 1984-86; bd. dirs. Health Help, Inc., McKee, Ky., 1985-86; chmn. Estill County Ednl. Task Force, Irvine, 1985-86. Recipient Best Local Column award Ky. Weekly Newspaper Assn., 1985. Mem. Soc. Profl. Journalists. Home: 12014 Comanche Trail Huntsville AL 35803

NELSON, KENT, b. Cin. Author: The Tennis Player and Other Stories, 1978, Cold Wind River (novel), 1981; contrbr. short stories to lit mags. Recipient Emily Clark Balch Prize Va. Qtly, 1975; NEA fellow, 1978, Best Am. Short Stories, 1987; Ingram Merrill Fellowship, 1986-87. Home: 1604 W Cheyenne Rd Colorado Springs CO 80906

NELSON, LIZA, b. Wilkes-Barre, PA, Mar. 14, 1950, d. Charles Mendel and June (Kuffler) Nelson; m. Richard Judson Brown, Nov. 25, 1977; children—Jacob, Hilary-Rose. Playwright: Not Just Kidstuff, 1980. Wrkg. on play. BA, U. Mich., 1972; MFA, Vt. Coll., 1984. Ed., drama critic Atlanta Gazette, 1973-79; dramaturg Alliance Theater, Atlanta, 1979-82; instr. Ga. State U., Atlanta, 1984—; expert panelist Fulton County Arts Council, Atlanta, 1986. Recipient Poetry Award, Callanwolde Arts Center, Atlanta, 1984. Mem. AWP. Home: 811 N Highland Ave Atlanta GA 30306

NELSON, MICHELLE HOGHLAND, b. Denver, Jan. 3, 1953; d. A. R. and Char (Wetsel) Hoghland; m. Barry Thomas Nelson, Nov. 29, 1975; children—Brandt, Ashley. Author: (filmstrips) A Visit with Health E. Elf, 1986, Safety with Health E. Elf, 1986, How to Succeed in School, 1987. Contrbr. short stories, articles, biographies to popular mags. including The Runner Mag., Ednl. Oasis, Baby Talk. B.S., U. Northern Colo., 1975; Tchg. Cert., U. Denver, 1977. English tchr. Jefferson County public schs., Littleton, CO, 1977-85; free-lance wrtr., 1985—. Publicity chairperson Littleton Depot Art Gallery, 1987; active Channel Six Public TV, Denver, 1987. Mem. SCBW. Home: 8001 S Harrison Circle Littleton CO 80122

NELSON, MILDRED, b. Washington County, AR, Mar. 28, 1915, d. Herbert Sylvester and Nettie Victoria (Ingalls) Pearson; m. Arthur Lee Nelson, July 7, 1935; children—Jerry Arthur, Victoria Lee. Novelist: Taste of Power, 1964, The Dark Stone, 1972, The Island, 1973; contrbr. poetry to Negro Digest, Oneoto Rvw, Chgo. Jewish Forum, McCall's, other publs., Light Year '86 anthology. BA, U. Ark., 1936. Recipient PEN Syndicated Fiction award 1984, 1st prize Shakespearean sonnet, World Order of Poets, 1985. Mem. AG, AL, P&W. Home: 954 Candlelight Pl La Jolla CA 92037

NELSON, MILO GABRIEL, b. Clinton, IA, Jan. 13, 1938; s. Grant August and Alice (Gabriel) N.; m. Sara Anderson, Aug. 27, 1966; 1 dau., Jennifer S.; m. 2d, Nancy Melin, Feb. 15, 1980. Author: Idaho Local History, 1976; coeditor: The Bookmark, 1970-78; contrbg. editor: Serials Rvw, 1978—, Reference Services Rvw, 1980—, Library Hi Tech, 1983—. BA in History, Drake U., 1960; MA in English, U. Wis., Madison, 1968, MLS, 1970. Humanities librarian U. Idaho Library, Moscow, 1970-78; editor Wilson Library Bull., H.W. Wilson Co., Bronx, N.Y., 1978—. Served with U.S. Army, 1961-63. Mem. ALA, Spcl. Libraries Assn., N.Y. Library Assn., New Eng. Library Assn., Idaho Library Assn. (editor Idaho Librarian 1975-78). Home: 42 Grandview Dr Mount Kisco NY 10549

NELSON, RAY FARADAY, b. Schenectady, NY, Oct. 3, 1931; s. Walter Hughes and Marie (Reed) Nelson; m. Kirsten Enge, Oct. 4, 1957; 1 son, Walter Nelson. Author: Ganymede Takeover, 1964, Blake's Progress, 1975, Then Beggars Could Ride, 1976, The Ecolog, 1977, Revolt of the Unemployables, 1978, Dimension of Horror, 1979, The Prometheus Man, 1982, Timequest, 1985; short fiction in Weird Tales, Amazing Stories, Nova, and other science fiction mags. BA, U. of Chgo., 1960. Freelance cartoonist, 1950-55; commercial artist, Artcraft Poster Co., Oakland, CA, 1955-57; folksinger, Paris, 1957-60; prog., U. of CA, Berkeley, 1961-64, freelance wrtr., 1964-77; co-owner, Big Cat Bookstore, Albany, CA, 1977—. Awards: Best SF of the Year, Doubleday/Ace, 1963, Jack London Award, Calif. Writer's Club, 1983. Home: 333 Ramona Ave El Cerrito CA 94530

NELSON, ROBIN COLEMAN, b. Phila., Sept. 16, 1935; s. John Coleman and Alice Elizabeth (Bloecher) N.; m. Patricia Ann Frank, Jan. 10, 1958; children—Alison, Christopher, Meredith. Author: Louisiana Man, 1971. Student, Pa. State U., 1953-55; BA in English, Columbia U., 1958. With F.W. Dodge Corp., 1958-59, Red Bank (N.J.) Register, 1960-65, Printer's Ink mag., 1966-72, Signature mag., 1973-77; exec. editor Popular Mechanics mag, NYC, 1977-82; editor/editorial dir. Best Publs. Inc., NYC, 1982—. Served with USAF, 1955-57. Home: 5 Center St Cresskill NJ 07626

NELSON, RODNEY, b. Fargo, N.D., Nov. 13, 1941; s. Rudolph Anton and Eva (Gunderson) N. Author: (poems) Oregon Scroll, 1976, Vigil, 1979, Red River Album, 1982, Popcorn Man, 1982, Thor's Home, 1984; (novel) The Boots Brevik Saga, 1978, The Green God, 1982, Home River, 1984, Villy Sadness, 1987. Editor: Dakota Arts Quarterly, 1979-84. Home: Box 3247 Fargo ND 58108

NELSON, VERA JOYCE, b. Dayton, WA, July 22, 1903; d. Isaac Newton and Nina Ethel (Butler) Newkirk; m. Caleb Alfred Nelson (dec.); 1 dau., Betty Ruth Schuld. Author: Webs From An Old Loom, 1952, Moccasin Prints West, 1955, Elder I.N. Newkirk Sr., 1969, The Scent of the Water, 1975, Swish of the Ski, 1978, David Douglas on the Columbia, 1978. BS, Portland State College, 1957. Secr., Phil Grossmayer Ins., Portland, 1924-26; secy., Pacific Trading Co., Portland, 1924; secy., Fred Lockley, Portland, 1945-47. Mem. PSA. Home: 1969 SW Park Ave Portland OR 97201

NELSON, VIRGINIA (GINI) L., b. Donnellson, IL, Mar. 29, 1918; d. Samuel Martin Nelson and Blanche Ella (Hawkins) Nelson Mathewson. Ed.: Scalpel & Tongs, Am. Jnl. Med. Philately, 1971-73; columnist Judaica Post, 1980-82; contrbr. numerous philatelist publs. Wrkg. on hist. novel. Student public schls., Decatur, Ill. Wrtr. N.Y. Diabetes Assn., N.Y.C., 1962-64, Montgomery County Heart Assn., Hillsboro, Ill, 1986—; newsletter ed. Ill. Audubon Soc., Hillsboro, 1986—. Mem. NWC. Home: 1961 E Union Box 384 Litchfield IL 62056

NELSON-HUMPHRIES, TESSA, b. Wakefield, England, Apr. 17, came to U.S., 1955; naturalized, 1975; m. Kenneth Nelson Brown, June 1, 1957 (dec. July 5, 1962); m. Cecil H. Unthank, 1963 (dec. 1979). Contrbr. articles, poems in anthols., lit. mags., popular mags. BA, London Univ., 1950; M.A., U. N.C., 1965; Ph.D. in English, U. Liverpool, United Kingdom, 1974. Dir. English, Windsor Coll., Buenos Aires, Argentina, 1958-59; lectr. in English, U. N.M., 1960-62; prof. English, Cumberland Coll., Williamsburg, KY, 1964—. Mem. SCBW, Soc. Women Wrtrs. & Jnlsts. (Julia Cairns Silver trophy for poetry 1978), NCTE. Home: York Cottage Rt 4 Box 944 Williamsburg KY 40769

NEMEROV, HOWARD, b. NYC, Mar. 1, 1920; s. David and Gertrude (Russek) N.; m. Margaret Russell, Jan. 26, 1944; children—David, Alexander Michael, Jeremy Seth. Author: (verse) Image and the Law, 1947; (novel) The Melodramatists, 1949; (verse) Guide to the Ruins, 1950; (novel) Federigo, or the Power of Love, 1954; (verse) The Salt Garden, 1955; (novel) The Homecoming Game, 1957; (verse) Mirrors and Windows, 1958; (short stories) A Commodity of Dreams, 1959; (verse) New and Selected Poems, 1960; (verse, including 2 plays) The Next Room of the Dream, 1962; Poetry and Fiction: Essays, 1963, Journal of the Fictive Life, 1965, The Blue Swallows, 1967, Stories, Fables and Other Diversions, 1961; (essays) Reflections on Poetry and Poetics, 1962; (verse) Gnomes and Occasions, 1973; The Western Approaches, Poems, 1973-75, 1975, Collected Poems, 1977; (essays) Figures of Thought, 1978; (verse) Sentences, 1980, Inside the Onion, 1984; New and Selected Essays, 1984; contrbr. critical writings to various periodicals. AB, Harvard U., 1941. Instr. English, Hamilton Coll., Clinton, NY, 1946-48; became mem. faculty lit. and langs. Bennington Coll., 1948; former prof. English, Brandeis U.; writer-in-residence Hollins (Va.) Coll., 1962; Fannie Hurst prof. creative lit. Washington U., St. Louis, 1969, now Edward Mallinckrodt disting. univ. prof. English; conslt. poetry in English, Lib. of Congress; assoc. ed. Furioso 1946-51. Served as pilot RAF, 8th A.F., USAAF, 1942-45. Bowdoin prize essayist Harvard Coll., 1940; Kenyon Rvw fellow fiction, 1955; recipient Blumenthal prize Poetry mag., 1958; 2d prize short story competition Va. Qtly Rvw, 1958; award for novel Natl. Inst. Arts and Letters, 1961; Arts award Brandeis U., 1963; St. Botolph's Club (Boston) Arts award, 1967; Theodore Roethke Meml. prize for poetry, 1968; Frank O'Hara Meml. prize Poetry mag., 1971; Natl.

Book award in poetry, 1978; Pulitzer prize in poetry, 1978; Wilma and Roswell Messing, Jr. award St. Louis U., 1979; Bollingen prize for poetry, 1981; Guggenheim fellow, 1968; Wallace Stevens poetry fellow Yale U., 1983. Fellow Am. Acad. Arts and Scis., Acad. Am. Poets; mem. Natl. Inst. Arts and Letters, Am. Acad. Arts and Letters. Home: 6970 Cornell Ave St. Louis MO 63130

NEMETZ, CHRISTINE ARAX, (Christine Arax), b. Orange, NJ, May 26, 1961; d. Victor Franklin and Valentine Anne (Bozian) N. Mng. ed.: Psychiatric Quarterly, 1983, Jnl of Primary Prevention, 1983, Qualitative Sociology, 1982-83, Clinical Social Work Jnl, 1983, The Psychoanalytic Rvw, 1983, Dreamworks, 1983, Legal Aspects of Medical Practice, 1985-87, Practical Gastroenterolgy, 1985-87; copy ed. numerous jnls, 1983-87. BA in Eng. Lit., Southwestern at Memphis, 1982. Rptr., Regional Weekly News, East Hanover, NJ, 1981-85; sr. mng. ed. Human Scis. Press, NYC,1982-83; tech. writer Union Bank, Los Angeles, 1984; assoc. ed. Pharmaceutical Communications, Long Island City, NY, 1985-87. Mem. AMWA. Home: 423 East 83rd St New York NY 10028

NEMIROW, JILL KARIN, b. Pitts., July 18, 1961; d. Alfred B. and Gladys J. (Urban) Nemirow. Contrbr. articles to popular mags. including Total Fitness Mag., Teenage, Am. Health, Reader's Digest. Columnist (news) The Record, 1986—, Dateline Jnl, 1986—. Editor, contrbr. The Bergen News, 1984-85. BA in Theater Arts, Rutgers U., New Brunswick, N.J., 1983. Reporter, The Paterson News, N.J., 1986, Dateline Jnl., Clifton, N.J., 1986—; free-lance wrtr., 1986—; asst. lifestyle ed., staff wrtr., Herald News, 1987. Recipient 1st place Am. Health Mag., 1986, Recovery Rm., N.J., 1986. Mem. Noah's Ark Animal Welfare, Intl. Women's Wrtg. Guild, Self-Employed Wrtr.'s Artist's Network. Home: 17 Second St Clifton NJ 07011

NEPO, MARK EVAN, b. Bklyn., Feb. 23, 1951, s. Morris and Renee (Rothman) N.; m. Anne Patricia Myers, Apr. 29, 1979. Author: (poems) A Memory as Sweet as You Make It, 1973, Arena from Within the I, 1977, God, the Maker of the Bed, and the Painter, 1988; contrbr. poetry to Antaeus, Kenyon Rvw, Southern Rvw, Sewanee Rvw, other lit mags. BA, SUNY, Cortland, 1973; DA, SUNY, Albany, 1980. Tchr. English, Ichabod Crane High Schl., Valatie, N.Y., 1974-77; lectr. English dept. Skidmore Coll., Saratoga Springs, N.Y., 1980-83, SUNY, Albany, 1980—. Mem. P&W, AWP. Home: 116 Horizon View Dr East Greenbush NY 12061

NERSESIAN, ROBERT S., b. Englewood, NJ, July 31, 1950; s. Serop S. and Elsie L. (Nazarian) N.; m. Allyn R. Sitjar Feb. 28, 1981; 1 dau., Sara. Ed., Focus mag., 1981-82; playwright: A Kids' Cabaret, 1985, Presents of Mind, 1985, The Greatest Girls' Softball Team at Sussex County, 1986, Self-Defense, 1986, The Wanderers, 1986, Who Are These Clowns? 1986, The Monster Murder Mystery, 1986, Where Is Stafford T. Wellington, 1987, The Boss, 1987, Taking the Bait, 1988; contrbr. to N.Y. Times, Newsday, Learning, others. BA, U. VA, 1972; MFA, Yale U., 1975. Actor, Yale Repertory Theatre, New Haven, 1972-75; playwright, NYC, 1975—; freelance pub. relns. writer, NYC, 1975—; pub. relns. mgr. AT&T, NYC, 1981—; adjunct prof. Fairleigh Dickinson U., Madison, NJ, 1985. Gold medal, NY Intl. Film & TV Fest., 1984. Mem. PRSA, IABC. Home: 58 Glenside Trail Sparta NJ 07871

NESBIT, ROBERT CARRINGTON, b. Ellensburg, WA, July 16, 1917; s. Sidney Shaw and Verna Mildred (Carrington) N.; m. Marie Richert, Nov. 24, 1942. Author: He Built Seattle: A Biography of Judge Thomas Burke, 1961, Wisconsin, A History, 1973 (award of merit Am. Assn. State and Local History 1975), The History of Wisconsin, Vol. III, Urbanization & Industrialization, 1873-93, 1985. B.A., Central Wash. Coll., 1939; M.A., U. Wash., 1947, Ph.D., 1957. Tchr. Cashmere (Wash.) Pub. Schs., 1939-41; state archivist, Wash., 1951-57; administrv. asst. Wash. Dept. Gen. Adminstrn., 1958-59, supr. purchasing, asst. dir., 1959-62; assoc. prof., chmn. dept. history Extension Div. U. Wis., Madison, 1962-68, prof., assoc. chmn. dept. history,1967-80.Served with USAAF, 1941-46. Wis. History Found. grantee, 1971-72; NEH grantee, 1980-82. Home: 2406 S Fir St Olympia WA 98501

NESOM, RUTH EVELYN, b. Tickfaw, LA, Nov. 10, 1916; d. George Wilburn and Cornelia (Arbuthnot) N. Contrbr. poems to anthols., articles, book rvw., poems to mags., newspapers. Wrkg. on hist. article, other articles. B.S., Southeastern La. U., 1938; M.A., La. State U., 1948. Tchr., librarian public schls., LA. U., 1938; M.A., La. State U., 1948. Tchr., librarian public schls., LA, 1938-72; librarian universities (NSU, LSU, Tulane), and for govt. in Europe and Japan. free-lance wrtr., poet. Recipient 1st place for poem La. State Poetry Soc., 1980, 84, 85. Mem. AAP. Address: 119 Florence Dr Hammond LA 70401

NESS, EVALINE, (Mrs. Arnold A. Bayard), b. Union City, OH, Apr. 24, 1911; d. Albert and Myrtle Woods (Carter) Michelow; m. Arnold A. Bayard, Nov. 1959. Author, illustrator: Josefina February, 1963, Gift for Sula Sula, 1963, Pavo and the Princess, 1964, Exactly Alike, 1964, A Double Discovery, 1965, Sam Bangs and Moonshine, 1966, The Girl and the Goatherd, 1969, Do You Have the Time, Lydia, 1971, Yeck Eck, 1973, Marcella's Guardian Angel; author, designer: Fierce: The Lion, 1980, American Colonial Paper House, Paper Palace, Four Rooms from the Metropolitan Museum, Victorian Paper House, Shaker Paper House; recipient 1st prize painting Corcoran Schl. Art 1945, Caldecott medal children's books 1967. Student, Muncie (Ind.) State Tchrs. Coll., 1931, Chgo. Art Inst., 1933, Corcoran Art Schl., 1945, Art Students League, NYC,1947, Accademia de Belle Arti, Rome, Italy, 1950. Tchr. children's art classes Corcoran Schl. Art, Washington, 1945-46, Parsons Schl. Design, NYC,1959-60; fashion illustrator Saks Fifth Ave., NYC,1946-49; mag. and advt. illustrator, 1946-49, illustrator numerous books, 1959—. Address: 303 Cocoanut Row Palm Beach FL 33480

NESTLE, JOAN, b. NYC, May 12, 1940, d. Jonas and Regina N. Contrbr.: Womanews, Sinister Wisdom, Bad Attitude, Body Politic, Gay Community News, other publs.; ed.: Lesbian Herstory Archives Newsletter. MA, NYU, 1965. Tchr. writing Queens Coll., CUNY, 1966—; cofounder Lesbian Herstory Archives/Lesbian Herstory Ednl. Fdn., Inc., NYC, 1973—; speaker, lectr. ednl. and cultural orgns. Mem. P&W. Home: 215 W 92d St New York NY 10025

NETT, ANN T., see Capek, Antoinette A.

NEUGARTEN, BERNICE LEVIN, b. Norfolk, NB, Feb. 11, 1916; d. David L. and Sadie (Segall) Levin; m. Fritz Neugarten, July 1, 1940; children—Dail Ann, Jerrold. Author: (with R.J. Havighurst) American Indian and White Children: A Social-Psychological Investigation, 1955, Society and Education, 1957, Personality in Middle and Late Life, 1964, (with R.J. Havighurst et al.) Adjustment to Retirement, 1969, (with R.P. Coleman) Social Status in the City, 1971; editor: Middle Age and Aging, 1968, Age or Need? Public Policies for Older People, 1982; assoc. editor: Jnl Gerontology, 1958-61; Human Devel., 1962-68. BA, U. Chgo., 1936, PhD,1943; DSc (hon.), U. So. Calif., 1980. Research assoc. Com. on Human Devel., U. Chgo., 1948-50, asst. prof., 1951-60, assoc. prof., 1960-64, prof., 1964-80, chmn., 1969-73; prof. edn. and sociology Northwestern U., 1980—; chmn. council com. on univ. women, 1969-70; mem. tech. com. research and demonstration White House Conf. on Aging, 1971; tech. adv. com. on aging research HEW, 1972-73; natl. adv. council Natl. Inst. on Aging, 1975-76, 78-81, Fedl. Council on Aging, 1978-81; dep. chmn. White House Conf. on Aging, 1981. Recipient Am. Psychol. Found. Teaching award, 1975, Disting. Contrbn. award Am. Psychol. Assn., 1980; Disting. Psychologist award Ill. Psychol. Assn., 1979; named to Chgo. Sr. Citizens Hall of Fame, 1983. Fellow AAAS, Am. Psychol. Assn., Am. Sociol. Assn., Gerontol. Soc. Am. (pres. 1968-69, Kleemeier award for research in aging 1971, Brookdale award for disting. contrbn. 1982); Sandoz Intl. Prize for Research in Gerontology, 1987; mem. Am. Acad. Arts and Scis., Intl. Assn. Gerontology, Inst. Medicine of Nat. Acad. Scis. (sr.). Home: 5801 Dorchester Ave Chicago IL 60637

NEUGEBOREN, JAY, b. Bklyn., May 30, 1938; s. David and Anne (Nassofer) N.; m. Betsey Bendorf, June 7, 1964 (div. 1983); children: Miriam, Aaron, Eli; m. Judy Karasik, Oct. 13, 1985. Author: Big Man, 1966, Listen Ruben Fontanez, 1968, Corky's Brother, 1969, Parentheses: An Autobiographical Journey, 1970, Sam's Legacy, 1973, An Orphan's Tale, 1976, The Stolen Jew, 1981, Before My Life Began, 1985; editor: The Story of Story Magazine, 1980. BA, Columbia U., 1959; MA, Ind. U., 1963. Preceptor, Columbia U., NYC, 1964-66; vis. writer Stanford U., Calif., 1966-67; prof. SUNY-Old Westbury, 1969-70; prof., resident writer U. Mass., Amherst, 1971—. Fellow Guggenheim Fdn., NEA, Mass. Council on Arts; recipient Transatlantic Rvw Novella award, 1967, PEN Syndicated Fiction prize (4), 1983-86, Edward Lewis Wallant award for best novel of 1985, Kenneth Smilen/Present Tense award for best novel of 1981 Am. Jewish Com. Office: U Mass Dept Eng Amherst MA 01003

NEUHARTH, ALLEN HAROLD, b. Eureka, SD, Mar. 22, 1924; s. Daniel J. and Christina (Neuharth) N.; m. Loretta Fay Helgeland, June 16, 1946 (div. 1972); children: Daniel J. II. Jan; m. Lori Wilson, Dec. 31, 1973 (div. 1982). Reporter Rapid City (S.D.) Jour., 1948; sports writer Mitchell (S.D.) Daily Republic, 1949; staff writer A.P., Sioux Falls, 1952-54; with Miami (Fla.) Herald, 1954-60; asst. mng. editor, pub, SoDak Sports, Sioux Falls, 1952-54; with Miami (Fla.) Herald, 1954-60; asst. mng. editor, 1958-60; asst. exec. editor Detroit Free Press, 1960-63; genl. mgr. Times-Union and Democrat and Chronicle, Rochester, N.Y., 1963-66; exec. v.p. Gannett Co., Inc., 1966-70, pres., 1970-84, chief exec. officer, 1973—, chmn., 1978—; founder and chmn. USA TODAY, 1982—; dir. Gannett News Service, Inc. and other subs. B.A. cum laude, U. S.D., 1950; student, Am. Press Inst., Columbia, 1956, 62, 63. Served with inf. AUS, 1943-46, ETO, PTO. Decorated Bronze Star; recipient Horatio Alger award, 1975. Mem. Am. Newspaper Pubs. Assn. (dir. 1968-82, chmn., pres. 1978-80). Office: 1100 Wilson Blvd Arlington VA 22209

NEUMAN, DONALD BERNARD, b. Milw., Sept. 17, 1934; s. Harry Morris and Ida (Nashinsky) N.; m. Barbara Heavenrich, Feb. 3, 1957; children: Phillip, Michael, Joel, Laura. Author: Sciencing for Tots, 2d edit, 1972, Creative Activities for Young Children, 1975, 2d edit, 1979, Science Activities for Young Children, 1978, When the Trolleys Were Stopped Cold, 1983, The Early Days of Stretcars in Milwaukee, 1983. BS, U. Wis., 1956; MA in Teaching, Mich. State U., 1966; PhD in Sci. Edn, Mich. State U., 1968. Tchr. pub. schls., Milw., 1960- 65; asst. instr. edn. Mich. State U., East Lansing, 1966-68; prof. curriculum and instrn., sci. edn. U. Wis.-Milw., 1968—, chmn. dept. curriculum and instrn., 1974-78, coordinator and headmaster Coll. for Kids, 1981—; cons. Head Start Program; project dir. Educating Young Bus Drivers. Mem. schl. bd. Milw. Hillel Acad., 1971—. Served to 1st lt. M.S.C. AUS, 1957-59. Acad. Year Inst. fellow NSF, 1965-66. Mem. AAAS (council), Phi Delta Kappa, Kappa Delta Pi. Home: 941 E Sylvan Ave Milwaukee WI 53217

NEUMAN, STEPHANIE SELLORS, b. Pueblo, CO, Dec. 14, 1945; d. John Sellors, Jr., and Margaret (Sorsen) Sellors; m. Robert Louis Bolton, Sept. 28, 1982; children—Robert J. Bolton, Lu-Ann Bolton, Cathleen Bolton. Author: Feelings: Everybody Has Them, 1984; ed. and pub.: Sleep with the Angels, 1985. BA, Miami U., 1963; MA, PhD, Case Western Reserve U. Research dir. Mental Dev. Ctr., Cleve., 1976-78; psychologist Cleve. Metro. Gen. Hosp., 19781; asst. prof. Psych., Case Western Reserve U., Cleve., 1979-82; psychologist, Brecksville, OH, 1978—; pub. SNB Pub., Inc., 1984—. Mem. COSMEP. Home: 10603 Glen Forest Trail Brecksville OH 44141

NEUMANN, ROBERT GERHARD, b. Vienna, Austria, Jan. 2, 1916; s. Hugo and Stephanie (Taussky) N.; m. Marlen Eldredge, July 27, 1941; children—Ronald E., Gregory W. Author: The Government of the German Federal Republic, 1966, European and Comparative Government, 4th ed., 1968, Toward a More Effective Executive-Legislative Relationship in the Conduct of America's Foreign Policy, 1977; contrbr.: The Austrian Solution, 1982. Editorial writer: Los Angeles Times, 1952-59. Diplome superieur, U. Rennes, France, 1936; diploma Consular Acad., Geneva Schl. Intl. Studies, 1937; student, U. Vienna, 1938; MA, Amherst Coll., 1940; PhD, U. Minn., 1946. Instr. State Tchrs. Coll., Oshkosh, Wis., 1941-42; lectr. U. Wis., 1946-46; asst. prof. UCLA, 1947-52, assoc. prof., 1952-58, prof., 1958-70, dir. Inst. Intl. and Fgn. Studies, 1959-65, chmn. Atlantic and West European Program, 1965-66; U.S. ambassador to Afghanistan, Kabul, 1966-73, to Morocco, Rabat, 1973-76, to Saudi Arabia, Jidda, 1981; vice chmn. Center for Strategic and Intl. Studies. Georgetown U., 1980-81, cons., 1980-81, sr. advisor, 1980-81, dir. Middle East Programs, 1980-81; cons. policy planning council Dept. of State, Ford Fdn., Rand Corp., also sec. def. Chmn. intl. relations sect.; vice chmn., trustee Moroccan-Am. Fdn., 1982—; vice chmn. Am.-Saudi Bus. Roundtable, 1982-83, chmn., 1984—. Served from pvt. to 1st lt. AUS, 1942-46. Fulbright fellow, France, 1954-55; decorated Legion of Honor, France, 1957; officer cross Order of Merit, Fedl. Republic of Germany, 1963. Home: 4986 Sentinel Dr Bethesda MD 20816

NEUMEYER, KATHLEEN, b. Indpls., June 11, 1944; d. Wilford C. and Barbara (Crise) Marshall; children—Andrew R., Kari. BSJ, Northwestern U., 1966. Reporter, UPI, Los Angeles, 1966-73; contrbr. ed. Los Angeles Mag., 1976—. Mem: Sigma Delta Chi, ASJA. Home: 9796 Burnley Pl Beverly Hills CA 90210

NEVILLE, EMILY CHENEY, b. Manchester, CT, Dec. 28, 1919; d. Howell and Anne (Bunce) Cheney; m. Glenn Neville; children—Emily Tam, Glenn H.H., Dessie, Marcy, Alec. Author: books including Seventeen Street Gang, 1966, Traveler from a Small Kingdom, 1968, Fogarty, 1969, Garden of Broken Glass, 1975; recipient Newbery award for It's Like This Cat, 1964, Jane Addams award for Berries Goodman 1966. Address: Keene Valley NY 12943

NEVIUS, BLAKE REYNOLDS, b. Winona, MN, Feb. 12, 1916; s. Blake Reynolds and Helena (MacLean) N. Author: Edith Wharton, 1953, Robert Herrick, 1962, Ethan Frome: The Story with Sources and Commentary, 1968, The American Novel: Sinclair Lewis to the Present, 1970, Ivy Compton-Burnett, 1970, Cooper's Landscapes: An Essay on the Picturesque Vision, 1975; editor: Nineteenth-Century Fiction, 1965-71, 80-83. BA, Antioch Coll., 1938; MA, U. Chgo., 1941, PhD, 1947. Teaching asst. English dept. U. Ill., 1941-42; mem. faculty UCLA, 1947—, prof. English, 1961-83, prof. emeritus, 1983—. Served with AUS, 1942-45; ETO. Decorated Bronze Star; recipient award Humanities Inst., U. Calif., 1967, 71, award for disting. career as editor Conf. Editors of Learned Jnls, 1982; Fulbright lectr., Germany, 1953-54; Guggenheim fellow, 1962-63; Rockefeller Ctr. at Bellagio fellow, 1982. Mem. MLA, Intl. Assn. Univ. Profs. English. Home: 4009 Woodcliff Rd Sherman Oaks CA 91403

NEWBAUER, JOHN ARTHUR, b. Newport, RI, Apr. 24, 1928; s. John Arthur and Theo Caroline (Trewhella) N.; m. Marilyn Mahler, Oct. 14, 1956; children—April, Dana, Miranda. BA, U. Calif.-Berkeley, 1951. Sr. editor and writer sci. and engring., rocket devel. dept. U.S. Naval Ordnance Test Sta., China Lake, Calif., 1951-56; editor-in-chief Astronautics and Aeronautics jnl, NYC,1963-83; ed.-in-chief Aerospace America, 1984-87; aquisitions ed. Aerospace America, 1987—; adminstr., tech. pubs., Am. Inst. Aeronautics and Astronautics, 1982—. Assoc. fellow AIAA, Brit. Interplanetary Soc. Home: 356 Bay Ridge Ave Brooklyn NY 11220

NEWBOUND, BETTY J., b. Detroit, July 13, 1928; d. Harry Arnold and Emily Sibilla (Beckert) Seuhr; m. William Howard Newbound, Sept. 28, 1951; children: Laurie Ann, Emalee Kay. Author: Southern Potteries Blue Ridge Dinnerware, Book 1, 1980, Book 2, 1984, Guide to Values of American-Made China & Pottery, 1983, Glass Collectors Almanac, 1988; contrbr. articles to collector publs. Home: 4567 Chadsworth St Union Lake MI 48085

NEWBY, IDUS ATWELL, b. Hawkinsville, GA, Oct. 3, 1931; s. Idus A. and Nomie Bell (Floyd) N. Author: Jim Crow's Defense, 1965, Challenge to the Court, 1967, The Development of Segregationist Thought, 1968, Black Carolinians, 1973, The South: A History, 1978; editor: The Civil War and Reconstruction, 1971. BS, Ga. So. Coll., 1951; MA, U.S.C., 1957; PhD, U. Calif. at Los Angeles, 1962. Asst. prof. history Western Wash. State Coll., 1962-63, Calif. State Coll., Fullerton, 1963-66; assoc. prof. history U. Hawaii, 1966 —, prof. history, 1970—. Served with USAF, 1951-55. Mem. Am., So. hist. assns., Orgn. Am. Historians, Assn., Study Negro History and Life. Home: 2533 Ala Wai Blvd Honolulu HI 96815

NEWCOMB, WILBURN WENDELL, b. St. Louis, July 1, 1935; s. Wilburn and Mary Minerva (Cutchin) N.; m. Sharon Ruth Moeller, Feb. 5, 1956 (div. 1968); children—Karen Ruth, Emily Rose, Suzanne; m. 2d, Lorraine Clara Gorrell, May 24, 1969; 1 dau., Rachel Claire. Author: Lute Music of Shakespeare's Time, 1965, Studien zur Lautenpraxis, 1968, Woodstove Handbook, 1974. MA, Indiana U., 1960; PhD, U. Goettingen, Germany, 1967. Assoc. prof. SUNY-Binghamton, 1968-70, U. Victoria, B.C., 70-73; correspondent Daily News Record, Charlotte, NC, 1977-80; assoc. ed. Textile World, Atlanta, 1980; ed. America's Textiles, Atlanta, 1981—. Fulbright fellow, 1960-62. Home: Box 4B Rt 1 Edgemoor SC 29712

NEWGAARD, PATRICIA ANN, b. Des Moines, Jan. 16, 1944, d. John Richard and Kathyren Ann (Husted) Dutcher; m. Thomas Fredrick Newgaard, Aug. 6, 1962; children—Patrick Thomas, Sarah, Beth Ann, Israel Benjamin Eric. Contrbr. poetry to For Poetry, The Art of Poetry, Potpourri, numerous other lit. mags. and anthologies. Cert. Inst. Children's Lit., 1981. Pub. Bright Ideas, Des Moines, 1974—; v.p. mktg. Co. Devel. Corp., Des Moines, 1982—. Recipient Golden Poet award World of Poetry, 1985. Home: 915 45th St Des Moines IA 50303

NEWLIN, MARGARET RUDD, b. NYC, Feb. 27, 1925, d. James H. and Marie (McLaughlin) Rudd; m. Nicholas Newlin, Apr. 2, 1956 (dec. July 1976); children—James, David, Robert, Thomas. Author: (prose under name Rudd) Divided Image: A Study of Blake & Yeats, 1953, Organiz'd Innocence: The Story of Blake's Prophetic Books, 1956; (poetry under name Newlin) The Fragile Immigrants, 1971, Day of Sirens, 1973, The Snow Falls Upward: Collected Poems, 1976, The Book of Mourning, 1982, Collected Poems, 1963-1985, 1986. Various teaching and coll. adminstrv. positions. Natl. Book award nominee in poetry, 1977; AAUW and Am. Philo. Soc. fellow, 1948-51; NEA fellow, 1976. Mem. PSA, AL, AG. Home: Shipley Farm Secane PA 19018

NEWMAN, CHARLES, b. St. Louis, May 27, 1938; s. Charles H. and June (Toney) N. Author: novels New Axis, 1968, The Promisekeeper, 1971, There Must Be More to Love Than Death, 1976; non-fiction A Child's History of America, 1973; contrbr. short stories to various mags. and anthologies including Best American Short Stories of 1971, 77; editor: New Writing from East Europe, 1968, New American Writers Under Thirty, 1970, The Art of Sylvia Plath, 1970, Nabokov: Criticism and Reminiscences, Translations and Tributes, 1970, Literature in Revolution, 1972, Prose for Borges, 1974; founder, editor: TriQtly Rvw, 1964-75; adv. editor, 1975—; contrbr. articles to profl. jnls, mag., newspapers. BA summa cum laude, Yale, 1960; postgrad. Balliol Coll. Oxford (Eng.) U., 1960-62. Instr. English Northwestern U., Evanston, IL, 1964-65, asst. prof., 1965-68, assoc. prof., 1968-73, prof., 1974-75; prof., chmn. The Writing Seminars Johns Hopkins, 1975-77; Dir. CCLM, NEA, Washington, 1968-74; dir. PEN, 1976 —. Recipient Midland Authors Soc. Distinguished Service award, 1973; Distinguished Service award Friends of Lit., 1973; Zabel prize innovative writing Natl. Inst. Arts and Letters, 1975; Woodrow Wilson fellow, 1960-61; Fulbright grantee, 1961-62; Rockefeller grantee for creative writing, 1967-68; NEA Creative Writing fellow, 1973; Ingram Merrill grantee creative writing, 1974; Guggenheim fellow, 1974-75. Address: Box 65 Volney VA 24379

NEWMAN, LESLEA, b. Bklyn., Nov. 5, 1955. Author: Just Looking for my Shoes (poetry), 1981, Good Enough to Eat (novel), 1986, Love Me Like You Mean It (poetry), 1987. Poetry and fiction in Common Lives, Conditions, Heresies, Sojourner, The Sun, Suicide Notes, others. 1986. BS in Edn., U. Vt., 1977; Cert. in Poetics, Naropa Inst., Boulder, Colo., 1981. Assoc. wrtr. Valley Advocate, Hadley, Mass., 1983-86; tchr. U. Mass. Continuing Edn., Amherst, 1983-85, Holyoke (Mass.) Community Coll., 1983-85, Hampshire Coll., Amherst, 1986. Mem. P&W, Feminist Wrtrs. Guild. Home: 50 Hawley St Northampton MA 01060

NEWMAN, P(AUL) B(AKER), b. Chgo., May 12, 1919, s. Paul Jones and Virginia Evelyn (Murray) N.; m. Anne Reese Royall, Feb. 27, 1945 (dec.); children—Betsy, William. Author poetry books: The Cheetah and the Fountain, 1968, Dust of the Sun, 1969, The Ladder of Love, 1970, Paula, 1975, The House on the Saco (N.C. Poetry Soc. Best Book of Poetry award), 1978, The Light of the Red Horse, 1981, The G. Washington Poems, 1986. BS in Physics, U. Chgo., 1940, PhD in English, 1958; MFA in Creative Wrtg., U. Iowa, 1951. Lectr. U. P.R., Mayaguez, 1956-58; asst. prof. Kans. State U., Manhattan, 1959-63; assoc. prof. Queens Coll., Charlotte, N.C., 1963-67, prof., 1967—. Served to capt. USAF, 1941-45; ETO. William Billings Fiske fellow U. Chgo., 1955; recipient Roanoke-Chowan award N.C. Lit. and Hist. Assn., 1968, 71. Mem. MLA, English-Speaking Union, AAUP. Home: 2215 Hassell Pl Charlotte NC 28209

NEWMAN, RACHEL, b. Malden, MA, May 1, 1938; d. Maurice and Edythe Brenda (Tichell) N.; m. Herbert Bleiweiss, Apr. 6, 1973. BA, Pa. State U., 1960; cert., N.Y. Schl. Interior Design, 1963. Accessories editor Women's Wear Daily, NYC,1964-65; designer, publicist Grandoe Glove Corp., NYC,1965-67; assoc. editor McCall's Sportswear and Dress Merchandiser mag., NYC,1967; mng. editor McCall's You-Do-It Home Decorating, 1968-70, Ladies Home Jnl Needle and Craft mag., NYC,1970-72; editor-in-chief Am. Home Crafts mag., NYC,1972-77; fashion dir. Good Housekeeping mag., NYC,1977-78, home bldg. and decorating dir., 1978-82; editor Country Living mag., 1978—; ed. Country Cooking mag., 1985—. Mem. N.Y. Fashion Group, Natl. Home Fashions League, Am. Soc. Interior Designers, ASME. Address: Country Living Mag 224 W 57th St New York NY 10019

NEWMAN, RICHARD ALAN, b. Watertown, NY, Mar. 30, 1930; s. Gordon Leon and Belle (Burton) N.; m. Peggy J. Hoyt, Oct. 23, 1964 (div. 1978); stepchildren—David W. Bauer, Paul W. Bauer, Nancy E. Bauer. Author: Black Index, Bless All Thy Creatures, Lord, Lemuel Haynes; author (Afro-American Education), (Black Access: A Bibliography). BA Maryville Coll., 1952; M.Div., Union Theol. Sem., 1955; postgrad., Syracuse U., 1959-61, Harvard U., 1966. Ordained to ministry Presbyn. Ch., 1955, demitted, 1977; minister Westminster Presbyn. Ch., Syracuse, N.Y., 1955-59; instr. religion Vassar Coll., Poughkeepsie, N.Y., 1962-63; prof., chmn. dept. social scis. Boston U., 1964-73; sr. editor G.K. Hall Co., Boston, 1973-79; exec. editor Garland Pub. Co., NYC, 1978-81; cons. N.Y. Pub. Library, 1981—. Mem. Am. Acad. Religion, Soc. for African Ch. History, Animal Protection Inst. Am. Home: 143 E 37th St New York NY 10016

NEWMAN, RUBY M., b. Mazarn, AR, May 31, 1909; d. Edmon Morgan and Sarah Elizabeth (Knox) Adams; m. Miles L. Newman, Mar. 16, 1933 (dec. 1977); children—Lois, Audine, Carl, Virgil, Bernice, Marshall, Geneva, Virginia. Author, pub.: Thorns and Roses (novel), 1981, Tour for Seven (novel), 1977, Rebel Preacher (novel), 1979, Family Collection (verse and prose), 1976. Student Henderson State Tchr.'s Coll., 1930-31. Tchr. rural Garland County, Ark., 1930s; wrtr., 1974—. Office: MN Pub Co Box 27 Bonnerdale AR 71933

NEWMARK, LEONARD DANIEL, b. Attica, IN, Apr. 8, 1929; s. Max Jacob and Sophie (Glusker) N.; m. Ruth Broessler, Sept. 16, 1941; children—Katya, Mark. Author: Linguistic History of English, 1963, Spoken Albanian, 1981, Standard Albanian, 1982. AB, U. Chgo., 1947; MA, Ind. U., 1951, PhD,1955. Instr. English U. Ill., Urbana, summer 1951; assoc. prof. English Ohio State U., 1954-62; assoc. prof. linguistics Ind. U.-Bloomington, 1962-63; prof. linguistics U. Calif.-San Diego, La Jolla, 1963—, chmn. dept., 1963-71, 79-85, head program in Am. lang. and culture, 1979-84. Fellow ACLS; mem. Linguistics Soc. Am. Home: 2643 St Tropez Pl La Jolla CA 92037

NEWSON, EULA MAE, (Elise Marcia Wynne), b. Fruitland Park, FL; Dec. 27, 1931; d. I.C. and Henrietta (Harris) Newson. Contrbr. articles on antiques and collectibles to numerous publs.; author: Did Justice Get Justice?, 1964. AA, John Jay Coll. of Criminal Justice; BA, CUNY, 1978, BA, 1979; jnlsm. certificate, London (England) School of Journalism, 1983. Pres., House of Great Creations, NYC,1964—. Silver medal, Inventor's Soc., 1964; Gold Medal, 1967. Mem. NWC. Home: 175 W 137th St New York NY 10030

NEWTON, DEBRA IRWIN, (Debbi Newton, Debbi Irwin), b. Framingham, MA, Jan. 9, 1959; d. Chester Maxwell, Jr. and Peggy Joyce (Lephew) Irwin; m. Ralph Clinton Newton, Jr., July 25, 1981; 1 dau., Kiley Ann. Contrbr. articles to Natl. Guard mags., civilian newspapers. Asst. ed.: Constitution Guard Newspaper, 1983-84, ed. Women's Page, 1984-85. Student Eastern Conn. State Coll., 1977-78. Enlisted Army Natl. Guard, 1979, advanced through ranks to sgt.; wrtr., photographer 130 th PAD, Conn. Army Natl. Guard, Hartford, 1979—, wrtr., ed., photographer, 1983-86, asst. broadcast supvr. public affairs detachment, 1983—. Home: 33 Park St Thomaston CT 06787

NEWTON, JAMES JOHN, b. Elmira, NY, Oct. 12, 1949; s. Walter James and Helen Lucille (Schaefer) N.; m. Susan Willa Muse, Feb. 2, 1980; children—Danielle, Stephanie, David. Author: A Practical Guide to Emergency Response Planning, 1987, Environmental Auditing, 1987, A Generator's RCRA Program, 1987. Contrbr., field ed.: Pollution Engineering Mag., 1985—. B.S., SUNY, Buffalo, 1971, M.S., 1974, 76. Environmental engineer U.S. Environmental Protection Agy., Atlanta, 1976-85, AZS Corp., Atlanta, 1985-87, The Chester Engineers, Atlanta, 1987—. Served to sgt. U.S. Army, 1971-77. Mem. NWC, Am. Soc. Civil Engineers, Natl. Soc. Profl. Engineers, Am. Soc. Safety Engineers. Home: 766 Copley Ct Stone Mountain GA 30088

NEY, JAMES WALTER EDWARD COLBY, b. Nakaru, Kenya, July 28, 1932; s. Reginald Osborne and Elizabeth Grace Colby (Aikins) N.; m. Joan Marie Allen, June 12, 1954; children—Cheryl Lyn, James Allen Colby, Peter Cameron. Author: Readings on American Society, 1969, Exploring in English, 1972, Discovery in English, 1972, American English for Japanese Students, 1973, Linguistics, Language Teaching and Composition in the Grades, 1975, Semantic Structures for the Syntax of the Modal Auxiliaries and Complements in English, 1981, others. AB, Wheaton Coll., 1955, AM, 1958; EdD., U. Mich., 1963. Cons. Dade County (Fla.) Schls., 1961-62; mem. Faculty U. Ryukyus, Okinawa, 1962-64, Mich. State U., 1964-69; mem. faculty Ariz. State U., Tempe, 1969—, prof. English, 1974—; pres. Ariz. Bilingual Council, 1973-74. Mem. Am. Linguistic Assn., MLA, NCTE, Can. Linguistic Assn., Am. Assn. Nurse Anesthetists (council on practice). Office: Ariz State Univ Tempe AZ 85281

NIATUM, DUANE, b. Seattle, Feb. 13, 1938, s. Dorothy Lorraine (Patsey) Babinger; 1 son, Marc. Author: After the Death of an Elder Klallam, 1970, A Cycle for the Woman in the Field, 1973, Taos Pueblo and Other Poems, 1973, Ascending Red Cedar Moon, 1974, Carriers of the Dream Wheel, 1975, Digging Out the Roots, 1977, Turning to the Rhythms of Her Song, 1977, To Bridge the Dream, 1978, Songs for the Harvester of Dreams, 1981, Pieces, 1981, Raven and the Fear of Growing White, 1983; contrbr. to numerous anthologies, newspapers, mags. BA, U. Wash.; MA, Johns Hopkins U. Tchr., freelance ed. Mem. PEN. Address: Mayo's 4516 NE 50th St Seattle WA 98105

NICHOLAS, MICHAEL, see Palumbo, Michael Nicholas

NICHOLAS, NANCY, b. NYC, Oct. 15, 1939; d. Jesse David and Elizabeth (Hess) Wolff; m. Charles Simmons, Sept. 17, 1977. Student, Radcliffe Coll. Tutotial dir. Harlem Edn. Program, NYC; then writer Scholastic Press, NYC, Scope mag.; editor Alfred A. Knopf, Inc., 1967—; appeared in film "Lianna," 1983. Office: 201 E 50th St New York NY 10022

NICHOLS, ELIZABETH L., b. Fort Scott, Kans., Nov. 12, 1922; d. Bernard and Lucy E. (Bachmann) McGuire; m. David E. Nichols, 1947; 1 son, Peter David. Author: Orff Instrument Source Books, vols. 1,2; Tune Into Limericks with Orff Instruments; Symphonic Senryu, Fractured Flute; articles in Music Educator's Jnl., Musicator, Orff Echo. MS, Kans. State U., 1961; Edn. Spclst., Ball State U., 1968-70. Prof. music Ball State Univ., Muncie, Ind., 1967-85; vis. prof. Univ. BC, Vancouver, Can., 1975-77. Mem. Sigma Alpha Iota. Address: 3006 Lydia Ave Topeka KS 66614

NICHOLS, JAMES RICHARD, b. Troy, NY, June 29, 1938; s. Elmer James and Mary Esther (Crandell) N.; m. Adelaide Claire Corbin, July 4, 1962 (div. Nov. 1976); children—James Harrison, Jonathan Carver; m. 2d, Carla Susan Hutchinson, Apr. 5, 1981 (div 1986). Author: Children of the Sea, 1977, Art & Irony, 1981, On Miracle Ground, 1982, Afterwords, 1986. BA, Union Coll., 1961; MA, U. N.C.-Chapel Hill, 1966, Ph.D., 1967. Prof., Muskingum Coll., New Concord, Ohio, 1969-86; head, Eng. & Philo. Dept., Georgia So. Coll., 1987—. Mem. Cambridge Wrtr.'s Workshop, Lawrence Durrell Soc.,AAUP, MLA. Home: 405 Zetterower Rd Statesboro GA 30458

NICHOLS, SARAH HOW-REE, b. Modoc, KS, Apr. 19, 1933; d. Roy Ramond and Minnie Lorena (Haury) Yount; m. Melvin Eugene Nichols, Sr., 1950; children—Jeanne Minest Lundgren, Melvin Eugene, Chad Josef. Contrbr. poems to anthols. BA, Garden City Comm. Coll., 1972. Sec., Trail City Art, Coolidge, Kans., 1980-81; pres. Kans. Poets 5, Garden City, 1983-84. Recipient award Edward A. Follot Poetry Competition, 1984, 85, 86; Best Poets award World of Poetry, 1985, Golden Poet award, 1985, 86; named New Poet Four, URSES Press, 1984. Mem. Natl. Fedn. State Poetry Socs., Kans. Wrtrs. Assn. Home: 407 Magnolia Garden KS 67846

NICHOLS, SHARON D., b. Laramie, WY, Oct. 4, 1936; d. Kenneth B. and Catherine I. (Linford) Dickensheets; m. Ted M. Nichols, June 14, 1957; children—Jon S., Lynne M., Lorri K. BA, U. WY, 1977. Tchr., Mtn. View Pub. Schl. (WY), 1957-58, Sunrise Pub. Schl. (WY), 1958-59; ed. Wyoming Trucker, Casper, WY, 1965—; ad. asst. Wyoming Trucking Assn., Casper, 1965-85, mng. dir.-CEO, 1985—. Mem. NFPW, Wyoming Press Women. Office: Wyo Trucking 555 N Poplar Casper WY 82602

NICHOLS, STEPHEN GEORGE, JR., b. Cambridge, MA, Oct. 24, 1936; s. Stephen George and Marjorie (Whitney) N.; m. Mary Winn Jordan, June 22, 1957 (div. 1972); children—Stephen Frost, Sarah Winn; m. 2d, Edith Karetzky, 1972; stepchildren: Laura Natalie Karetzky, Sarah Alexandra Karetzky. Author: Formulaic Diction and Thematic Composition in the Chanson de Roland, 1961, The Songs of Bernard de Ventadorn, 1962, Romanesque Signs: Early Medieval Narrative and Iconography, 1983, Images of Power, 1985, Mimesis: from Mirror to Method, Augustine to Descartes, 1982. Editorial bd.: French Rvw, 1968—, Medievalia et Humanistica, 1974—, Medievalia, 1974—, Oliphant, 1974—, PMLA, 1980. AB cum laude, Dartmouth Coll., 1958, Universite d'Aix-Marseilles, France, 1958-59; PhD,Yale U., 1963. Asst. prof. French UCLA, 1963-65; assoc. prof. comparative lit. U. Wis.-Madison, 1965-68, chmn. dept., 1967-68; prof. Romance langs. and comparative lit. Dartmouth Coll., 1968—, chmn. dept. comparative lit., 1969-74, 78, 79-82, chmn. dept. Romance langs., 1975-77, assoc. dir. fgn. study program, 1970-78, chmn. dept. French and Italian, 1982-85, faculty Dartmouth Inst., 1980-85; prof. Romance langs., U. of PA, 1985—. NEH fellow, 1978-79. Mem. Acad. Lit. Studies, Dante Soc., Intl. Comparative Lit. Assn., New Eng. Medieval Assn., MLA, Medieval Acad. Am., Societe Rencesvals, Assn. Internat. des Etudes Francaises. Home: 220 St Mark's Sq Philadelphia PA 19104

NICHOLSON, F.C. (FRANCES COSTLEY), b. Lynn, MA, Aug. 7, 1964; d. George T. and Frances (Costley) N. Sci/tech wrtr., contrbr. environmental articles to Boston mag. B.S. in Jnlsm., Northeastern U., 1987. Mem. NWU. Home: 43 Fuller St Lynn MA 01905

NICHOLSON, SUSAN JANE BROWN, b. Clinton, IA, July 29, 1942; d. William rthur and Martha Jane (Hoffman) Brown; m. James Hamilton Nicholson, May 2, 1963; children—Lora Lee, James Arthur. Author: Teddy Bears on Paper, 1985, Mickey Mouse Merchandise, 1986; contrbg. author (yearly) Warman's Americana and Collectible Guide; columnist Post Card Collector, Barr's Post Card News. Contrbg. ed. Spinning Wheel, 1976-82, Collector's Showcase, Antique Toy World, Doll Reader, Teddy Bear and Friends; Am. ed. The Post Card Collector's Gazette, 1976-80. B.S., Iowa State U., 1975, post-grad., 1975—. Office: Box 595 Lisle IL 60532

NICKERSON, SHEILA B., b. NYC, Apr. 14, 1942, d. Charles Cantine and Mavis (McGuire) Bunker; m. Martinus Hoffman Nickerson, Sept. 5, 1964; children—Helen, Thomas, Samuel. Author: Letter from Alaska and Other Poems, 1972, To the Waters and the Wild: Poems of Alaska, 1975, In Rooms of Falling Rain (novel), 1976, Songs of the Pine-Wife (poetry), 1980, Waiting for the News of Death (poetry chapbook), 1982, Writers in the Public Library (non-fiction), 1984, On Why the Quilt Maker Became a Dragon (poetry), 1985, Feast of the Animals (poetry), 1987; playwright: The Enchanted Halibut, 1981; contrbr. poetry to Gilt Edge, permafrost, Crab Creek Rvw, Tar River Poetry Rvw, other lit mags; contrbr. to Pushcart Prize anthology, 1985-86; co-ed.: Lemon Creek Gold. A Jnl of Prison Lit., 1979-84, Juneau 2000 Proceedings, 1982; mem. editorial bd.: On People and Things Alaskan, 1982. BA, Bryn Mawr Coll., 1964; PhD, Union Grad. Schl., 1985. Wrtr.-in-residence Alaska State Council on Arts, 1974, Alaska State Library, 1979; ed. Alaska Fish & Game, Juneau, 1985—. Alaska Poet Laureate, 1977-81; Alaska State Council on Arts fellow, 1986. Mem. Colo. Author's League, Denver Women's Press League, Natl. League Am. Pen Women. Home: 540 W 10th St Juneau AK 99801

NICKLAUS, (CHARLES) FREDERICK, b. Columbus, OH, Jan. 19, 1936, s. Charles Frederick and Effie (Fiedler) N. Author books of poetry: The Man Who Bit the Sun, 1964, Cut of Noon, 1971; contrbr. poetry to Poetry, Prairie Schooner, Pivot. other lit mags., N.Y. Times Book of Verse, 1971. BFA, Ohio State U., 1957. Ed. Columbia U. Press, 1966-72. McDowell Colony fellow, Peterborough, N.H., 1980. Home: 241 E 73d St New York NY 10021

NICKOLAS, GEORGE TOM, b. Davenport, IA, July 3, 1933, s. Thomas George and Gladys Maxine (Ritter) N.; m. Vera Irene Cummings, Dec. 7, 1963; children—Michael Thomas, Michele Lynn. Author: Veterans Directory, 1966, Handbook for an American, 1968; author tech. papers, articles. BA in Econs., Augustana Coll., 1959; MS, Fla. Inst. Technology, 1975. Owner, operator Nickolas' Tax Service, Davenport, Iowa, 1957—; contracting officer U.S. Army Armament Command, Rock Island, Ill., 1974-77, dv. chief., 1977—. Served with USN, 1951-55; retired on disability. Mem. contract mgmt. orgns. Home: 4426 El Rancho Dr Davenport IA 52806

NICKSON, RICHARD, b. Artesia, NM, Jan. 9, 1917, s. Guy William and Lora (Mummert) N.; m. Mary-Louise Huse, Aug. 31, 1947; children—Guy, Joel, Gregory. Author: Staves: A Book of Songs, 1977, Philip Freneau: Poet of the American Revolution, 1981; lyricist (for music by Benjamin Lees): Songs of the Night, 1958, Cyprian Songs, 1961, Three Songs for Contralto, 1968; contrbr. poetry to Calif. Qtly, Crazy Horse, other lit mags; contrbr. articles to Theatre Annl., Occident, Modern Drama, others; editor: The Independent Shavian, 1978—; film scripts include: Adventure in Art, Carolina, House of Life, Couriers from the Sky, The Atlanta Campaign. BA, U. N.C., 1946, MA, 1947; PhD,U. So. Calif.-Los Angeles, 1957. Asst. prof. Eastern N. Mex. U., Portales, 1958-60; assoc. prof. William Paterson Coll., Wayne, N.J., 1960-66, prof., 1966-85. Mem. Bernard Shaw Soc. (pres. 1975—). Home: 205 W 19th St New York NY 10011

NIE, NORMAN H., b. St. Louis, Apr. 1, 1943; s. Ben Phillip and Lucille Rose (Blacker) N.; m. Carol Phyllis Tietelbaum, May 31, 1964; children—Lara, Anne. Author: Participation in America: Political Democracy and Social Equality, 1972, The Changing American Voter, 1976, Participation and Political Equality, 1978, also articles. BA, Washington U., St. Louis, 1964; MA, Stanford U., 1964, PhD, 1971. Asst. prof. U. Chgo., 1968-72, assoc. prof., 1972-77, prof. poli. sci., 1977—; sr. study dir. Natl. Opinion Research Center, 1969—; pres. SPSS, Inc., Chgo., 1975—. Recipient Woodrow Wilson Fdn. Book award, 1976; Gladys M. Kammerer award, 1972; NSF grantee, 1973-76; 20th Century Fund grantee, 1974-75. Mem. Am. Poli. Sci. Assn., Am. Assn. Public Opinion Researchers, AAUP, Assn. Data Processing Service Orgns., Inc. Office: SPSS 444 N Michigan Ave 3300 Chicago IL 60611

NIEMI, NICOLE, b. Toledo, July 18, 1957, d. Roman Walter Marchewka and Gisele Brandt; m. W. Loren Niemi, July 13, 1984. Team author: Options in Rhetoric, 1980; author: Women of Courage, 1985, (plays) Premadonna Boatride, 1985, Tangled Vines, 1985, Beauty and the Beast, 1986, The Bandbox, 1986, Daddy Dada, 1986, The Banquet, 1987%ntrbr. poetry to Vermillion Lit. Project, Midwest Qtly, Poetry, Passages North, Spoon River Anthology, Calif. Qtly, Fallout, Poetry Motel, others; asst. ed. Where mag. BA in Creative Writing, Metro State U. Participant Breadloaf Wrtrs. Conf., 1984. Recipient Lake Superior Wrtr.'s award St. Louis County Arts and Heritage Assn., 1983, Mpls. and St. Paul Mayors Pub. Art award, 1986. Mem. NWU, P&W, Women's Art Registry Minn., Playwrights Ctr., The Loft. Address: 51 Melbourne Ave SE Minneapolis MN 55414

NIGG, JOSEPH EUGENE, (Joe Nigg), b. Davenport, IA, Oct. 27, 1938, s. Joseph John and Hollis Ellen (Garnant) N.; m. Gayle Marie Madsen, Aug. 1960 (div. 1979); children—Joseph Conrad, Michael Scott. Author: The Book of Gryphons, 1982, The Strength of Lions and the Flight of Eagles, 1982, A Guide to the Imaginary Birds of the World, 1984, Winegold (short stories), 1985; contrbr. stories to Epoch, Etcetera, Foothills, numerous other lit mags; asst. ed. Essays in Lit., 1974-75; co-ed. Pendragon: A Jnl. of the Creative Arts, 1981-85; fiction ed. Wayland Press, 1986 —. MFA, State U. Iowa, 1963; PhD, U. Denver, 1975. Mem. faculty Western State Coll., Gunnison, Colo., 1965-70, U. Denver, 1970-75; freelance wrtr., Denver, 1975-79; assoc. ed. Liniger's Real Estate, Denver, 1979-81; ed.-in-chief Re-Max Intl., Denver, 1981—. Mem. Colo. AL (Top Hand award for nonfiction book 1983, 85), Rocky Mountain WG (named Mary Chase Author of Yr. 1984). Home: 1114 Clayton St Denver CO 80206

NIGHTINGALE, BARBRA, b. Chgo., Aug. 6, 1949; d. Arthur A. and Geraldine (Smith) Evans; m. Oscar Allen, Aug. 3, 1968 (div. Dec. 29, 1970); m. 2d, Preston S. Nightingale, Nov. 23, 1977; 1 dau., Kimberly Beth Allen. Author: Lovers Never Die, 1981, Prelude to a Woman, 1986; contbr. poetry and interviews lit jnls; wrkg on Songs I Cannot Sing. BS, Fla. Intl. U., MA, Fla. Atlantic U. With Oschner Med. Center, New Orleans, 1973-75, Univ. Miami Med. Center, Fla.,

1975-76, Southeastern Med. Center, N. Miami Beach, Fla., 1976-79; faculty Broward Community Coll., Hollywood, Fla., 1983—, Univ. Miami, 1986—. Recipient first prize, Fla. Intl. Univ, Miami, 1982, Fla. State Poets Assn., 1983. Mem. S. Fla. Poetry Inst. (pres., 1982-86), Natl. League Am. PEN Women, Natl. Fedn. State Poetry Socs., AAP. Address: 2231 N 52d Ave Hollywood FL 33021

NIGRO, FELIX ANTHONY, b. Bklyn., Aug. 8, 1914; s. Vincent and Katherine (Tempone) N.; m. Edna Helen Nelson, July 28, 1938; children—Lloyd G., Kirsten F. Author: Public Administration: Readings and Documents, 1951, Public Personnel Administration, 1951, Modern Public Administration, 1984, 6th ed., (with Lloyd G. Nigro) New Public Personnel Administration, 1986, 3d ed. (with Lloyd G. Nigro), Management-Employee Relations in the Public Service, 1969, Readings in Public Administration, 1983 (with Lloyd G. Nigro). AB, U. Wis., 1935, MA, 1936, PhD in Poli. Sci, 1948. Various positions U.S. Govt. and UNRRA, 1937-46; mem. staff Griffenhagen & Assocs., 1946-47; asst. prof. govt. U. Tex., 1948-49; asst. prof. pub. adminstrn., U. of P.R., 1948-49, assoc. prof., 1954-56; asst. prof. pub.admin., Fla. State U., 1951-52; field cons. Inst. Inter-Am. Affairs, 1952-54; sr. assoc. J.L. Jacobs & Co. (mgmt cons.'s), Chgo., 1954; lectr. UN Advanced Schl. Pub. Adminstrn. (C.A.), 1956-57; prof. govt. So. Ill. U., 1957-61; prof. poli. sci. San Diego State Coll., 1961-65; Charles P. Messick prof. pub. adminstrn. U. Del., 1965-69; prof. poli. sci. U. Ga., 1969-82; prof. emeritus, 1982; prof. grad. program adminstrn. Rider Coll., 1982-85. Mem. Natl. Acad. Pub. Adminstrn., Am. Arbitration Assn., Am. Soc. Pub. Adminstrn., Intl. Personnel Mgmt. Assn., Indsl. Relations Research Assn. Home: 199 West View Dr Athens GA 30606

NILSEN, RICHARD HALDOR, b. Gloversville, IL, Jan. 20, 1948; s. Nils Christian and Catharine Wilber (Vibbard) N.; m. Lynda Joy Canary, Aug. 23, 1969; children: Christa, Cara, Kenneth. Ghostwriter: Intended for Pleasure, 1977; contrbr. article to Guideposts, poems to Epoch, Poetry Now, Buffalo Spree, Christianity Today, Anththesis, For the Time Being, Ariel II, Lantern, others. BA, Houghton Coll., 1970; MFA, MA, U. Ark., 1976. Instr. Ark. Inst. Theology, Fayetteville, 1976-82; owner, mgr. bookstore, Fayetteville, 1977-82; freelance wrtr., writing instr. Writers Block, Gloversville, N.Y., 1984—. Recipient intl. poetry prize Triton Coll., 1983; N.Y. State Council on Arts grantee, 1986. Home: RD 1 Box 235 Johnstown NY 12095

NIMNICHT, NONA VONNE, b. Loveland, CO, Mar. 17, 1930, d. Jacob C. and Ruth (Kroh) Ulrich; children—Glenda Nimnicht Northup, Mark, Kara. Author: In the Museum Naked, 1978; contrbr. poetry to Aldebaran Rvw, Blue Unicorn, Calyx, Zyga Mag., other lit mags. MA in English, Colo. State U., Ft. Collins, 1966, U. Calif., Berkeley, 1969. Reporter Rawlins (Wyo.) Daily Times, 1952-53; corr. Saratoga (Wyo.) Sun, 1953-54; soc. ed. Northern Wyo. Daily News (Worland), 1954-56; instr. English Colo. State U., Ft. Collins, 1966-67, Merritt Coll., Oakland, Calif., 1973-78. Wurlitzer Fdn. for Arts resident, Taos, N.Mex., 1980; recipient James D. Phelan award Montavalo Center for Arts, Saratoga, Calif., 1981; creative writing fellow NEA, 1984, 85. Mem. The Poetry Center. Home: 303 Adams St 210 Oakland CA 94610

NIMS, JOHN FREDERICK, b. Muskegon, MI, Nov. 20, 1913; s. Frank McReynolds and Anne (McDonald) N.; m. Bonnie Larkin, Sept. 11, 1947; children—John (dec.), Frank, George (dec.), Sarah Hoyt, Emily Anne. Author: The Iron Pastoral, 1947, A Fountain in Kentucky, 1950, The Poems of St. John of the Cross, 1959, rev., 1979, Knowledge of the Evening, 1960, Of Flesh and Bone, 1967, Sappho to Valery: Poems in Translation, 1971, 80, Western Wind, 1974, 83, The Kiss: A Jambalaya, 1982, Selected Poems, 1982; contrbr.: Five Young American Poets, 1944, The Complete Greek Tragedies, 1959; also anthologies, mags.; editor: Ovid's Metamorphoses, 1965, Harper Anthology of Poetry, 1981; assoc. editor: The Poem Itself, 1960; editorial adviser, Princeton U. Press, 1975-84. AB, U. Notre Dame, 1937, MA, 1939; PhD,U. Chgo., 1945. Mem. faculty U. Notre Dame, 1939-45, 46-52, 54-58, U. Toronto, 1945-56, Bocconi U., Milan, Italy, 1952-53, U. Florence, Italy, 1953-54, U. Madrid, 1958-60, Harvard U., 1964, 68-69, summer 1974, U. Ill.-Urbana, 1961-65, U. Ill., at Chgo., 1965-73, 1977-85, Bread Loaf Writers Conf., 1958-71, Bread Loaf Schl. English, 1965-69, U. Fla., fall 1972, 73-77; Margaret Scott Bundy prof. lit. Williams Coll., fall 1975; prof. lit. Coll. of Charleston, spring 1981; mem. editorial bd. Poetry mag., 1945-48, vis. editor, 1960-61, editor, 1978-84; Phi Beta Kappa poet Harvard U., 1978. Recipient Harriet Monroe Meml. award Poetry mag., 1942, Guarantors prize, 1943, Levinson prize, 1944, Disting. fellowship AAP, 1982; Fulbright grantee, 1952, 53; Smith Mundt grantee, 1958, 59; Natl. Found. Arts and Humanities grantee, 1967-68; award for creative writing Am. Acad. Arts and Letters, 1968; Creative Arts citation in Poetry Brandeis U., 1974; fellow Inst. Humanities U. Ill., 1983-84, Guggenheim fellow, 1986. Address: 3920 Lake Shore Dr Chicago IL 60613

NINKOVICH, THOMAS, b. Fresno, CA, Dec. 26, 1943; s. Dan and Louise (Metkovich) N. Author: Reunion Handbook, 1983, Go to Your Reunion!, 2d ed. of Reunion Handbook, 1987. Dir. Natl. Reunion Assn., Nevada City, Calif., 1981—. Served with USN, 1965-67. Office: Box 295 Nevada City CA 95959

NIPP, FRANCIS STUART, (Rita Mayfield), b. Rushville, IN, Dec. 23, 1914; s. Carl Van and Ethel Maud (Fry) N.; m. Mary Ellen Wood, Jan. 4, 1941; m. 2d, Rita Ann Mayfield, April 1, 1960. Contrbr. articles, reviews to var. publs. AB, Indiana U., 1937; MA, U. of Chgo., 1938. Edit., Encyclopedia Brittanica, Chgo., 1956-60, sr. edit., 1967-83; sr. edit., World Book Year Book, 1961-62; asst. ed., Scott, Foresman, Chgo., 1964-67, consl. ed. Who's Who in U.S. Writers, Editors & Poets, 1985—. Home: 1130 S Michigan Ave Chicago IL 60605

NIPS, NICK L., see Bennett, John M.

NISBET, ROBERT A, b. Los Angeles, Sept. 30, 1913; s. Henry S. and Cynthia (Jenifer) N.; m. Emily P. Heron (div.); children—Martha Rehrman, Constance Field; m. 2d, Caroline Burks Kirkpatrick; 1 dau., Ann. Author: The Quest for Community, 1953, Human Relations in Administration, 1956, Emile Durkheim, 1965, The Sociological Tradition, 1966, Tradition and Revolt, 1968, Social Change and History, 1969, The Social Bond, 1970, The Degradation of the Academic Dogma, 1971, The Social Philosophers, 1973, rev. ed., 1983, The Sociology of Emile Durkheim, 1974, Twilight of Authority, 1975, Sociology as an Art Form, 1976, History of the Idea of Progress, 1980, Prejudices: A Philosophical Dictionary, 1982, Conservation, 1986, Making of Modern Society, 1986; co-editor: Contemporary Social Problems, 1961, 66, 71, 76, History of Sociological Analysis, 1978; bd. editors: Am. Jnl Sociology, 1970-74; mem. publ. com.: The Public Interest, 1976-85; mem. editorial bd.: The American Scholar, 1975-80. AB, U. Calif., 1936, MA, 1937, PhD,1939; LHD, Hofstra U., 1974. Instr. social instns. U. Calif. at Berkeley, 1939-43, asst. dean, 1942-43, 46, asst. prof. social instns., 1943-48, assoc. prof. sociology, 1948-52; prof. sociology U. Calif., Riverside, 1953-72, vice chancellor, 1960-63, dean, 1953-63; Albert Schweitzer prof. humanities, Columbia Univ., 1974-78, emeritus, 1978—; resident scholar Am. Enterprise Inst., Washington, 1978-80, adj. scholar, 1980—; prof. history and sociology U. Ariz., 1972-74; Rieker lectr. U. Ariz., 1956; lectr. all univs., Calif., 1961, Guggenheim fellow, 1963-64; Cooper lectr. Swarthmore Coll., 1966; John Dewey lectr. John Dewey Soc., 1970; William A. Neilson research prof. Smith Coll., 1971-72; Blazer lectr. U. Ky., 1971; Phi Beta Kappa Natl. vis. scholar, 1971-72; Johns Hopkins Centennial scholar, 1975-76; W.G. Sumner lectr. Yale U., 1976; Leon lectr. U. Pa., 1982; Benjamin Rush lectr. Am. Psychiat. Assn., 1983. Mem. Natl. Council Humanities, 1975-78; bd. dirs. ACLS, 1974-79. Served with AUS, 1943-45; PTO. Rockefeller Fdn. grantee, 1975-78; recipient Ingersoll Award in Humanities, 1985. Fellow Am. Acad. Arts and Scis., Mem. Am. Philo. Soc., Soc. Am. Historians; mem. Société Europèene de Culture, Columbia Soc. Fellows, Institut Internationale de Sociologie, Phi Beta Kappa. Address: 2828 Wisconsin Ave NW Washington DC 20007

NISCHAN, GERDA M., b. Frankenthal, Germany, March 24, 1940; d. Otto and Barbara (Hock) Baumann; m. Prof. Bodo Nischan, Aug. 31, 1968; 1 son, Michael. Contrbr. to U.S. and European jnls and anthologies. Student, European schools. Secretary, German Consulate, Phila., 1967-69; editor, Arts Council Publications, Greenville, SC, 1985—. Mem. NC Poetry Society. Home: 115 Wilkshire Dr Greenville NC 27834

NISSENSON, HUGH, b. NYC, Mar. 10, 1933, s. Charles and Harriette (Dolch) N.; m. Marilyn Claster, Nov. 10, 1962; children—Katherine, Kore. Author: A Pile of Stones, 1965, Notes from the Frontier, 1968, In the Reign of Peace, 1972, My Own Ground, 1976, The Tree of Life, 1985. BA, Swarthmore (Pa.) Coll., 1955. Mem. PEN, AG, Home: 411 West End Ave New York NY 10024

NITSO, EVELYN AGNES, b. Biwabik, MN, Nov. 30, 1934; d. Wayne and Laila (Mohonen) Holmes; m. Prentice Eugene Nitso, Feb. 2, 1959. Author: The World We Live In, 1984; Gospel Stories for Children, 1984; A Little of This and a Little of That, 1984; 2 albums, 170 songs. Contrbr. poems to anthols. Served with USAF, 1954-62. Mem. Mpls. Poetry Soc. Home: 2000 Park Ave S Apt 201 Minneapolis MN 55404

NITZSCHE, JANE CHANCE, see Chance, Jane

NIVEN, LAURENCE VAN COTT, b. Los Angeles, Apr. 30, 1938; s. Waldemar Van Cott and Lucy Estelle (Doheny) N.; m. Marilyn Joyce Wisowaty, Sept. 6, 1969. Author: Gift from Earth, 1970, All the Myriad Ways, 1971, (with David Gerrold) The Flying Sorcerers, 1971, Neutron Star, 1968, World of Ptavvs, 1966, Ringworld, 1969, (with Jerry Pournelle) The Mote in God's Eye, 1974, Protector, 1973, The Flight of the Horse, 1973, Tales of Known Space, 1975, World Out of Time, 1976, The Magic Goes Away, 1978, Inferno, 1975, Lucifer's Hammer, 1977, Oath of Fealty, 1981, The Ringworld Engineers, 1980, The Patchwork Girl, 1979, (with Steven Barnes) Dream Park, 1981; free-lance writer, contrbr. stories to mags., also TV scripts. Student, Calif. Inst. Tech., 1956-58; BA in Math, Washburn U., 1962. Recipient Nebula award, Hugo award (5), Best Intl. Sci Fiction award, Lens award. Mem. SFWA, Los Angeles Sci. Fantasy Soc. Address: 136 El Camino Dr Beverly Hills CA 90620

NIXON, DAVID MICHAEL, b. Batavia, NY, Jan. 21, 1945, s. Duncan A. and Esther M. (Gillard) N.; m. Barbara Fisher, June 11, 1978. Author poetry chapbook: You See Me in the Trees, 1979; ed.: Some Things Make Us Strong (poetry chapbook), 1975; contrbr. poetry to anthologies: On Turtle's Back, 1978, Apple, 1979, Voices for Peace Anthology, 1983, Gypsy Special, 1986; contrbr. poetry: kayak, Small Pond, Gargoyle, Seditious Delicious, other periodicals. BA in English, Hobart Coll., 1967. Tchr. The Poetry Workshop of Rochester, N.Y., 1969-84, organizer, 1973-84; tchr. poetry schls. and libraries. Home: 21 Oak Hill View Rochester NY 14611

NIXON, SALLIE WHITE, b. Henderson, NC, Oct. 7, 1914; d. Wallace and Annie Lee (Harris) White; m. Caldwell Westmoreland Nixon, Jul. 8, 1942; 1 son—Caldwell Westmoreland. Contrbr. to various lit jnls; poetry collections: Surely—Goodness & Mercy, 1965, Second Grace, 1977. BA, U. of Nebraska, 1972. Retired tchr. Bd. mem. NC Arts Council, Raleigh, 1977-80. John Masefield Award, PSA, 1971, Gustav Davidson Award, 1973; University Prize, AAP, 1973; Vreeland Award, U. of Nebraska, 1973. Mem. PSA, NC Poetry Soc., Lincoln Arts Council. Home: 321 N Aspen St Lincolnton NC 28092

NIZALOWSKI, EDWARD MICHAEL, b. Jersey City, NJ, Nov. 4, 1947; s. Edward Mike and Helen (Nichipor) N. Author: (pamphlet) Hitory of the Tioga County Courthouse, 1982. Contrbr. articles to hist. mags. Author, ed. newsletter of Newark Valley Hist. Soc., 1983—. Wrkg. on family history. B.A. in English, SUNY-Potsdam, 1970; b.S. in Edn., SUNY-Cortland, 1978. Jazz musician, 1981-83; librarian high schl., Newark Valley, NY, 1985—. Recipient award of Merit for writings in Afro-Am. history Regional Conf. of Hist. Agys., 1985. Home: Rt 2 Box 251 Berkshire NY 13736

NIZALOWSKI, JOHN ANTHONY, b. Endicott, NY, Feb. 4, 1956; s. Edward Michael and Helen (Nichapor) N.; m. Patricia Anne Wnek, July 13, 1981. Contrbr. poetry to New River Free Press, Owego Rvw, New Horizons, Harvest from the Hills; articles in The Mountain Laurel, Macrobiotics Today; fiction in Blueline, Engineer's Forum; book rvws. in Jayland, Monochrome, Hard Row to Hoe, The Roanoke Times, World News. BA in English and History, SUNY, 1974-78; MA in English, U. Delaware, 1978-80. Instr. in English Univ. Delaware, Newark, 1980-81, Va. Tech., Blacksburg, 1981-86. Mem. Appalachian Writers Assn. Address: Box 252 Brown Rd RD2 Berkshire NY 13736

NOAH, HOPE E., b. NYC, Sept. 17, 1943, d. Mortimer Edward and Anne Yvonne (Forscher) Shaff; m. Lester V. Noah, Oct. 30, 1969 (div. 1985); children—Meredith Ayn, Allison Jane. Author: The Conversant Chef, 1988. Wrkg. on cookbook. BS in Speech, Emerson Coll., 1965. Columnist, cons. Single Times, N.Y.C., 1984—; columnist Bergen News, Palisades Park, N.J., 1982—; dir. creative advt., columnist Today newspapers, Wayne, N.J., 1982-84; ed.-in-chief N.J. Singles Mag., Totowa, 1985, Dynasty Media Pub. Co., Englewood Cliffs, N.J., 1985-86; small bus. cons., advt. and public relations, 1982—; columnist, "A Single Look," 1984—; "Cross Over the Bridge," 1987—; & for Spotlight Mag., 1986—. Home: 26 Leone Ct Glen Rock NJ 07452

NOBLE, DAVID WATSON, b. Princeton, NJ, Mar. 17, 1925; s. Charles John and Agnes Catherine (Konow) N.; m. Lois Marie Keller, Aug. 2, 1944; children—David Watson, Jeffrey, Douglas, Patricia. Author: The Paradox of Progressive Thought, 1958, Historians Against History, 1965, The Eternal Adam and the New World Garden, 1968, The Progressive Mind, 1970, 2d ed., 1981, (with Peter N. Carroll) The Restless Centuries: A History of the American People, 1973, 2d ed., 1979, The Free and the Unfree, 1977, (with David A. Horowitz and Peter N. Carroll) Twentieth Century Limited: A History of Recent America, 1980; The End of American History, 1985. BA, Princeton, 1948; MA, U. Wis., 1949, PhD,1952. Instr. U. Minn., Mpls., 1952-55, asst. prof., 1955-58, assoc. prof., 1958-65, prof., 1965—; lectr. Am. studies seminar Kyoto (Japan) U., summer 1980; vis. prof., Univ. of Salzburg (Austria), 1985. ACLS fellow, 1951. Mem. Phi Beta Kappa. Home: 2089 Commonwealth Ave St Paul MN 55108

NOBLE, NICHOLAS R., see Cole, E(ugene) R(oger)

NOCERINO, KATHRYN M., b. NYC, Feb. 6, 1947; d. Theodore C. and Jean (Renc) Nocerino. Author: Death of the Plankton Bar & Grill, 1987, Candles in the Daytime, 1985, Wax Lips, 1980; poetry in The Dream Book: An Anthology of Italian-American Women's Writing, 1985; poetry and rvws in Contact/II, Win Magazine, Home Planet News, others. MSW, Hunter College, NYC,1972. Assoc. editor, Manhattan Poetry Rvw, 1982-83; div. dir., NYC HRA Office of Financial Mgmt., 1984—. Mem. PSA, P&W. Home: 139 West 19th St New York NY 10011

NOLAN, AGNES PETERS, b. Salem, VA, June 24, 1908; d. James Sidney and Sara Lee (Robertson) Peters; m. Robert Wilson Nolan, Mar. 2, 1936; 1 son, Gordon Churchill. Contrbr. articles, short stories to numerous mags., newspapers including Jack and Jill, Delaware Today, others. Ed.: Historic Landmarks of Delaware (B. H. Macdonald), 1976. The HMR Story, 1966. B.A., U. Richmond, 1929; M.A., U. Del., 1957. Assoc. prof. Young Harris Coll., GA, 1935-36; tchr. Langley Air Force Base Schl., Hampton, VA, 1945-48; wrtr., producter Sta. WTAR, Sta. WGH, Norfolk and Newport News, VA, 1947-51, sta. WHYY-TV, Wilmington, DE, 1963-65. Mem. Jamestown Soc., Richmond, VA, 1950-87, Wilmington Operar Soc., 1965-87; active, Diamond State Branch, Natl. League of Am. Pen Women, 1962—. Recipient 1st place for children's radio Billboard Mag., 1948; script awards Phila. Wrtrs., 1953, 57, 67, 85, NLAPW, 1974. Home: Box 69 Cokesbury Village Hockessin DE 19707

NOLAND, CHARLES EUGENE, b. Miami, Mar. 11, 1930; s. Byrl E. Noland and Tenney C. (Garrett) Noland Harris; divorced; children—Richard, John, Kathryn, Kenneth. Contrbr. articles to numerous mags., newspapers. Bus. ed. Tampa Times, 1974-75; mng. ed. Tampa Sports, 1977-78; Frostproof News, 1979—. Wrkg. on humorous fiction, humorous columns. B.A. cum Laude, U. Miami, 1951, postgrad., 1954-55. Reporter, Miami Herald, 1950-51; staff corr., regional exec. UP, Miami, Atlanta, Tampa, 1951-67. Recipient award for humor column Fla. Press Assn., 1983, award for newspicture, 1983, Best Advt. Theme award, 1986; Press award Justice for Children, Inc., Lakeland, FL, 1986; Press award Justice for Children, Inc., Lakeland, FL, 1986; numerous others. Home: Box 831 Frostproof FL 33843

NOLAN, PAUL THOMAS, b. Rochester, NY, Apr. 4, 1919; s. John J. and Anna (Sweeney) N.; m. Peggy Hime, June 1, 1947; children—John Michael, Peter Andrew, Elizabeth Anne. Author: Round-The-World Plays, 1961, One-Act Plays of Lee Arthur, 1962, Chaucer for Children, 1963, Writing the One-Act Play, 1964, Death for the Lonely, 1964 (Natl. Workshop Players award), Three Plays by John W. Crawford, 1965, Marc Connelly, 1969, Drama Workshop Plays, 1969, Describing People, 1970, The Loneliest Game, 1971, Hedda Gabler, South, 1972, Last Week I Was Ninety- Five, 1973, Squeak to Me of Love, 1973, Between Hisses, 1973; (with James Burke) The Highwayman, 1975, The Eavesdrop Theatre, 1976, John Wallace Crawford, 1981, Folk Story Plays, 1982. Student, Aquinas Inst. Rochester, 1933-37; BA, Central Ark. U., 1947; MA, Tulane U., 1949, PhD,1953. Instr. English, dir. News Bur. Central Ark. U., 1947; asst. prof. English, dir. pub. relations Centenary Coll. of La., 1948-54; Ford Fdn. vis. prof. Ark. State U., 1954-55; prof. English, Dupre prof. humanities U. Southwestern La., Lafayette, 1955—. Served with USAAF, 1942-45. Mem. MLA, Playwrights' Theatre La., Am. Studies Assn. Home: 219 Renee Ave Lafayette LA 70503

NOLEN, WILLIAM ANTHONY, b. Holyoke, MA, Mar. 20, 1928; s. James Robert and Katherine Margaret (Dillon) N.; m. Joan Helene Scheibel, Nov. 289, 1953; children—James, Joan, William, Anna, Julius, Mary. Author: The Making of a Surgeon, 1970, A Surgeon's World, 1972, Healing: A Doctor in Search of a Miracle, 1974, Surgeon Under the Knife, 1976, The Baby in the Bottle, 1978, A Surgeon's Book of Hope, 1980; columnist, McCall's mag. AB, Holy Cross Coll., 1949; MD, Tufts U., 1953. Diplomate: Am. Bd. Surgery. Intern Cornell surg. div. Bellevue Hosp., NYC, 1953-54, resident in surgery, 1954-55, 57-60; surgeon Litchfield (Minn.) Clinic, 1960—; mem. staff Meeker County Hosp., Litchfield, Minn., chief dept. surgery, 1960-79, 84—; attending surgeon Hennepin County Hosp., U. Minn., Mpls., 1962-69. Served as capt. M.C. USAR, 1955-57. Fellow ACS. Home: 421 Marshall Ave N Litchfield MN 55355

NOLIN, LILLIAN RENEE, b. Lindenhurst, NY, Feb. 8, 1923, d. Edward John and Lillian (Branston) McGraw; m. James B. Nolin, Jan. 30, 1946; children—James, Joel. Author: Beyond the Veil, 1984; contrbr. poetry to Poetry Broadcast, America Speaks. Wrkg. on book, poetry anthology. Student, public schls., Lindenhurst, N.Y. Newswrtr. Lindenhurst Star, 1941-44, 46-55, Newsday, Bay Shore, N.Y., 1944-45, Babylon (N.Y.) Town Leader, 1955-60, Babylon Beacon, 1960-73, South Bay's Newspaper, Lindenhurst, 1973—. Home: 481 N Alleghany Ave Lindenhurst NY 11757

NOLLET, LOIS SOPHIA, (Diana Delmore), b. Mpls., Nov. 30, 1921; d. James Harold and Nora Agnes (Flanagan) McMahon; m. Anthony R.

Nollet, Jan. 18, 1943; children—Alice, Monica, James, Michael, David, Claire. Author: Leonie, 1982, 3d ed., 1985; Anthea, 1983, 3d ed., 1985; Dorinda, 1985, Cassandra, 1986, Melissande, 1987. Wrkg. on Araminta. B.S., Coll. of St. Catherine, 1944. Mem. RWA. Home:2412 Kingman Dr Wilmington DE 19810

NOLTE, CHARLES WINFIELD, b. Lewiston, MT, June 23, 1945; s. Glen O. and Hilda M. (Lohof) N.; m. Janet Rene Richards, Aug. 24, 1976; children—Michele, Melinda. Author:, ed. Innkeeping World, 1976—. Stud. pvt. schl., Zellwood, FL. Sales mgr. Rimrock Lodge, Billings, MT, 1965-70; owner/mgr. Alpine Lodge, Bozeman, MT, 1970-72; v.p. Amer. Inns, Billings, 1972-76; pub. Innkeeping World, Seattle, WA, 1976—. Address: Box 84108 Seattle WA 98124

NOLTE, JUDITH ANN, b. Hampton, IA, Sept. 17, 1938; d. Clifford P. and Sigrid M. (Johnson) N.; m. Randers H. Heimer, May 7, 1971. BS, U. Minn., 1960; MA in English, NYU, 1965. Tchr. English Middletown (N.Y.) High Schl., 1960-62, High Schl. of Commerce, NYC, 1962-64; merchandising editor Conde Nast Publs., NYC, 1964-69; editor-in-chief Am. Baby mag., NYC, 1969—, Weight Watchers mag., 1980-83; hostess Am. Baby Cable TV Show. Office: 575 Lexington Ave New York NY 10022

NOONAN, CAMERON, see Dillmann, Nancy Cameron

NORBECK, EDWARD, b. Prince Albert, Sask., Can., Mar. 18, 1915; came to U.S., 1923, naturalized, 1941; s. Gabriel and Hannah (Norman) N.; m. Jeanne Lewellen, Sept. 22, 1940 (dec. Oct. 14, 1944); m. 2d, Margaret Roberta Field, Feb. 18, 1950 (div. Nov. 8, 1976); children—Hannah Field, Edward Crosby, Seth Peter; m. 3d, Katherine Shannon, Oct. 6, 1977; children—George T. Shannon, David C. Shannon, Albert P. Shannon. Author: A Japanese Fishing Community, 1954, Pineapple Town—Hawaii, 1959, Religion in Primitive Society, 1961, Changing Japan, 1965, 2d ed., 1976, Religion and Society in Modern Japan, 1970, Religion in Human Life, 1974, From Country to City: Takashima Urbanized, 1978. Editor: Prehistoric Man in the New World, 1964, The Study of Personality: An Interdisciplinary Appraisal, 1968, The Study of Japan in the Behavioral Sciences, 1970, The Anthropological Study of Human Play, 1974, Ideas of Culture, Sources and Uses, 1976, Forms of Play of Native North Americans, 1979; Goodyear series regional anthropology, 1970-78. Student, Wash. State Coll., 1936-37; BA in Oriental Langs. and Lit., U. Mich., 1948; MA in Oriental Civilizations, U. Mich., 1949; PhD in Anthropology, U. Mich., 1952. Instr., then asst. prof. anthropology U. Utah, 1952-54; asst. prof. U. Calif. at Berkeley, 1954-60; mem. faculty Rice U., 1960—, chmn. dept. anthropology and sociology, 1960-71, 78-79, prof. anthropology, 1962—, dean humanities, 1965-67, dir., 1966-69, dir. grad. program in behavioral sci., 1969—; vice pres. Tourmaline Press, 1970-81; vis. disting. humanist U. Colo., 1982. Served to 2d lt. AUS, 1943-47. Fellow Am. Anthrop. Assn., Explorers Club, AAAS; mem. Am. Ethnol. Soc., Soc. for Sci. Study Religion, Japanese Soc. Ethnology, Assn. for Asian Studies, Asia Soc., Assn. for Anthrop. Study of Play, Phi Beta Kappa. Office: Dept Anthropology Rice Univ Houston TX 77001

NORDAN, LEWIS ALONZO, b. Jackson, MS, Aug. 23, 1939; stepson Gilbert Russell Bayles and Sara Ruth (Hightower) Bayles; m. Mary Mitman, Apr. 28, 1962 (div. Jan. 1983); children—Russell Ammon (dec.), John Robert (dec.), Lewis Eric; m. 2d, Alicia Blessing, July 3, 1986. Author short stories: Welcome to the Arrow-Catcher Fair, 1983, The All-Girl Football Team, 1986. BA, Millsaps Coll., 1963; MA, Miss. State U., 1966; PhD, Auburn U., 1973. Vix. writer Univ. Ark., Fayetteville, 1981-83; asst. prof. Univ. Pitts., 1983—. Served to JO3, USN, 1958-60, USS Saratoga. Address: 521 Gettysburg St Pittsburgh PA 15206

NORDHAUS, JEAN, b. Baltimore, MD, Nov. 14, 1939; d. Herbert Lee and Minna Esther (Cantor) Friedberg; m. Robert Riggs Nordhaus, June 27, 1964; children—Ronald Edward, Hannah. Author: A Language of Hands, 1982, A Bracelet of Lies, 1987. BA, Barnard College, 1960; PhD, Yale, 1969. Asst. prof., Federal City Coll., Washington, DC, 1971-74; dance ed., Washington Rvw, poetry coord., Folger Shakespeare Library, Washington, DC, 1980-83. Mem. PSA, P&W, The Comm. for Poetry. Home: 623 East Capitol St SE Washington DC 20003

NORGARD, ELIZABETH ANN, b. Fairbury, NB, Nov. 13, 1962; d. Carl Edwin and Margery Anice (Cossel) Norgard.; m. Butch Cossel; children: Mandy, Joshua, Christopher. Contrbr. poetry: Our Western World's Most Beautiful Poems, Remembrances of Love, Rhyme and Reason. Home: Box 415 Golden City MO 64748

NORINE, A., see Williams, Alberta Norine

NORMAN, JACKIE DELOIS, b. Kinta, OK, June 13, 1941; d. John A. and Ina E. (Wortham) N.; divorced; children—Kimberly A. Marshall, Timorhy G. Ewer. Contrbr. poems to anthols., lit mags. B.A., North Tex. State Univ., 1976. Substitute tchr. Nashville Metro Schls., TN, 1981-87. Mem. Fort Worth Poetry Soc. (Poetry award for Sandia, 1978), Poetry People, BPW. Home: 800 Warwick Bedford TX 76022

NORRIS, CAROLE VERONICA, b. Balt., Mar. 21, 1948; d. Robert John and Clarice Xavier (Barnes) N. B.A., Morgan State U., Balt., 1971. Intl. reporter Evening Sun, Balt., 1970-71; news coordinator Sta. WBAL-TV, Balt., 1971-72; intern. reporter Washington Star, 1972; gen. assignment reporter Phila. Inquirer, 1972-73; asso. producer Sta. WHYY-TV, Wilmington, Del., 1973-75; assignment editor Sta. WPVI-TV, Phila., 1975-76; hostess, radio news task show Sta. WEAA-FM, Balt., 1976-77; editor-in-chief Impact, Washington, 1979-81; dir. dept. public relations Nat. Office for Black Catholics, 1979-81; coordinator for devel. and info. sves. Archdiocese of Newark, 1981—; dir. Office of Black Ministry Roman Cath. Diocese of Bklyn., 1982—. Washington Journalism Center fellow, 1972. Mem. Cath. Press Assn. (chmn. com. for black concerns, mem. Hispanic-Black Caucus 1981), 1979-81, Assn. for Rights of Catholics in the Ch., Intl. Peace Research Assn., Assn. Black Journalists, 1973-76. Home: 149 Sterling St 18 Brooklyn NY 11225

NORRIS, DIANE LEE, b. Jackson, MI, Apr. 20, 1941; d. Leland Clyde and Arlene C. (Forsythe) Ellis; m. Robert Henry Norris, June 21, 1969; children—Joanna Marie, Sherri Lynn. Author: (children's books) Another Christmas Carol, 1985, A Very Special Valentine, 1985, Just Be Patient, 1987, Nightsounds, 1987; A Christmas Tapestry, 1986. Contrbr. series on bus rider safety to newspaper. Diploma, Inst. Children's Lit., 1982. Machine operator Shelby Bus. Forms, OH, 1963-70; schl. bus driver Buckeye Central Schl., New Washington, OH, 1979—. Producer, dir. children's TV program to promote reading Sta. WZZAE, Bucyrus, OH, 1984-85. Home: 6083 Dickson Rd New Washington OH 44854

NORRIS, EILEEN C., b. Chgo., Mar. 3, 1953; d. Williamk J. and Marie Carmody Norris; m. R. Bruce Dold, July 10, 1982; children—Megan, Kristen. Contrbr. articles: Crain's Chicago Business, Advertising Age Mag., Electronic Media Mag., Veterinary Practice Management Mag., numerous other publs. BA in Journalism, No. Ill. U., 1978. Reporter Chgo. Tribune, 1978-81; assoc. ed. Bus. Ins. Mag., Chgo., 1981-83; freelance wrtr., 1983—. Mem. NWU. Home: 5340 W Belle Plaine St Chicago IL 60641

NORRIS, KATHLEEN, b. Washington, July 27, 1947; d. John Heyward and Lois Ferne (Totten) Norris; m. David J. Dwyer. Author poems: Falling Off, 1971, The Middle of the World, 1981; contrbr. poet numerous anthologies and mags including WomanPoet: The West, 1985, A Geography of Poets, 1979, The Nation, Prairie Schooner. BA, Bennington College, VT, 1969. Program asst. AAP, NYC,1969-74; pres. and manager Leaves of Grass, Inc., Lemmon, SD, 1974—, asst. librarian Lemmon (SD) Library, 1976—; poet- in-residence ND Arts Council, Fargo, ND, 1979—. Big Table Poetry Series Award, Follett Publishers, 1971, CAPS Grant, Creative Artists Public Service Program, NYC,1972, Fine Arts Work Center Fellowship, Provincetown, MA, 1972. Mem. PSA. Home: Box 570 Lemmon SD 57638

NORRIS, ROGER HENRY, b. Bklyn., June 6, 1940; s. Paul George and Ruth Muriel (Hegeman) N.; m. Patricia Ann Groner, Nov. 29, 1968; children—Krista Leigh, Alec Scott, John Brian, Lara Nicole, Contrbr. poems to anthols., nonfiction to newspapers. B.S. in bus. admin., Penn. Military Coll., 1963. Insurance agent Clark Group, Middlesex, NJ, 1986—. Served with U.S. Navy, 1963-67. Home: 37 Kensington Rd Madison NJ 07940

NORRIS, WAYNE BRUCE, b. Passaic, NJ, Mar. 13, 1947; s. Harold Quittman and Helen Margaret (Currey) N.; m. Maryann Nora Cassidy, May 17, 1971; 1 son, Brian Eric. Author: The Big Book of Photocopier Humor (re-printed as You Don't Have to be Crazy to Work Here, But It Sure Helps). BA in Physics, U. Calif.-Santa Barbara, 1965-69. Physicist Rockwell Intl., Thousand Oaks, Calif., 1969-72; environ. cons. Norris Assocs., Santa Barbara, 1974-78, computer cons., 1981-85; computer analyst Jet Propulsion Lab, Pasadena, Calif., 1972-74, ITT Fed. Electric, Vandenberg AFB, 1973-74; deep sea diver-tender Oceaneering Intl., Santa Barbara, 1978; airline owner Norris Airways, 1978-81; physicist Genl. Research Corp., Santa Barbara, 1985—. Congressional candidate, Democratic party, 1984, 86; pres., MADD, Santa Barbara, 1985-86. Mem. IEEE, ACM, Assn. Old Crows. Address: 215 Palisades Dr Santa Barbara CA 93109

NORTH, CHARLES LAURENCE, b. NYC, June 9, 1941; s. Monroe Daniel and Viola (Utstein) N.; m. Paula dePillis, June 2, 1963; children: Jill, Michael. BA, Tufts U., 1962; MA, Columbia U., 1964. Author: Lineups, 1972, Elizabethan and Nova Scotian Music, 1974, Six Buildings, 1977, Leap Year: Poems 1968-78, 1978, Gemini (with Tony Towle), 1981; editor: (with James Schuyler) Broadway, A Poets and Painters Anthology, 1979; poetry in Poetry mag., The

Yale Lit., The Little Mag., Sun and Moon, United Artists, The World, others; criticism in Art in America, Language, Am. Bk. Rvw., others. Freelance editor Thomas Y. Crowell, NYC, 1965-66; adj. prof. English, poet-in-residence, Pace U., NYC, 1967—. Recipient Poets Fdn. award, 1972; NEA fellow, 1979. Home: 251 W 92d St New York NY 10025

NORTH, HELEN FLORENCE, b. Utica, NY; d. James H. and Catherine (Debbold) N. Author: Sophrosyne: Self-Knowledge and Self-Restraint in Greek Literature, 1966, From Myth to Icon: Reflections of Greek Ethical Doctrine in Literature and Art, 1979; translator: John Milton's Second Defense of the English People, 1966; editor: Interpretations of Plato: A Swarthmore Symposium, 1977; co-editor: Of Eloquence, 1970; editor: Jnl History of Ideas; mem. editorial bd.: Catalogus Translationum et Commentariorum, 1979—. AB, Cornell U., 1942, MA, 1943, PhD 1945. Instr. classical lang. Rosary Coll., River Forest, Ill., 1946-48; mem. faculty Swarthmore Coll., 1948—, prof. classics, 1961—, chmn. dept., 1959—. Centennial prof. classics, 1966-73, Kenan prof., 1973-78; vis. asst. prof. Cornell U., 1952—; vis. assoc. prof. Barnard Coll., 1954-55; vis. prof. LaSalle Coll., Phila., 1965, Am. Schl. Classical Studies, Athens, 1975; Blegen disting. vis. research prof. Vassar Coll., 1979. Bd. dirs. ACLS, 1977—; grantee ACLS, 1943-45, 1973, fellow, 1971-72; Fulbright fellow, Rome, 1953-54; fellow AAUW, 1963-64; NEH sr. fellow, 1967-68; NEH Coll. Tchrs. fellow, 1983-84; Martin classical lectr. Oberlin Coll., 1972; Guggenheim fellow, 1958-59; 1975-76. Mem. Am. Philol. Assn. (dir. 1968—, pres. 1976—, Charles J. Goodwin award of merit 1969), Classical Assn. Atlantic States, Catholic Commn. Intellectual and Cultural Affairs (chmn. 1968-69), Am. Acad. Arts and Scis., Soc. Religion Higher Edn., Phi Beta Kappa. Home: 604 Ogden Ave Swarthmore PA 19081

NORTHACKER, ALFRED AUSTIN, b. Scranton, PA, May 2, 1915; s. Carl Herbert and Beryl Stratton (Austin) N.; m. Marion Clara Leonard, Apr. 26, 1941; 1 son, Mark Austin. Contrbr. articles, book revs., bus. commentary to numerous trade and spl. interest publs. in U.S., England, Germany, S.Africa, Australia, India, Belgium, Can., Brazil and Netherlands. BBA in Fgn. Trade, MBA in Commerce, PhD in Internat. Mgmt. With M.W. Kellogg Co., Hackensack, N.J., 1936-81, ret. as mem. of exec. br.; cons., 1981—. Ed., pub. Ocala Shrine Club newsletter, Ocala Billiken Club newsletter. Home: 46 Chinica Dr Timucuan Island Summerfield FL 32691

NORTHART, LEO JOSEPH, b. Pitts., Aug. 23, 1929; s. Leo Joseph and Mozelt Larue (Ellington) N.; m. Thelma Irene Harvey, Dec. 20, 1948; children—Leo Joseph III, Pamela Leigh. Author: (with William H. Baumer) Buy, Sell, Merge: How to Do It, 1971. AB, U. N.C., 1952, MA, 1953. Advt. and sales promotion copywriter Gen. Electric Co., Schenectady, 1953-56; Dept. editor Chem. Week mag., NYC, 1956-60; intl. div. mgr. Am. Mgmt. Assn., NYC, 1960-63; dir. publs. Copley Intl. Corp., NYC, 1963-68; editorial dir. Johnston Intl. Pub. Corp., NYC, 1968-74; editor Pub. Relations Jnl of Pub. Relations Soc. Am., NYC, 1974-84; founder, prtnr. Creative Resource Group (editorial cons. and services firm), NYC, 1983—; Cons. Westinghouse Intl., UN; lectr. Advanced Wrtg. Course, Profl. Developmental Inst; Intl. Execs.; Inst., Intl. Study and Research Inst.; mem. adv. bd. Rutgers U. Inst. Intl. Bus.; mem. Select Businessmens Com. on Fgn. Trade, NYC. Served with USMC, 1946-48. Mem. World Trade Writers New York (pres. 1965), N.Y. Bus. Press Editors, ASME, Sigma Delta Chi. Home: 25 Meadow Pl Freehold NJ 07728

NORTHEN, HELEN, b. Butte, MT, d. John Alfred and Amelia Sigred (Anderson) N. Author: Social Work with Groups, 1968, Clinical Social Work, 1983; contrbr. chap. to Advancing Social Work Practice in the Health Care Field, 1983; co-ed. (with Robert Roberts) Theories of Social Work With Groups, 1976; contrbr. articles to profl. jnls. AB, U. Wash., 1939; MSW, U. Pitts., 1944; PhD, Bryn Mawr Coll., 1953. Mem. faculty U. So. Calif., Los Angeles, 1953—, prof. emeritus, 1984—. Home: 1707 Micheltorena St Los Angeles CA 90026

NORTHWAY, MARTIN, b. Kenosha, WI, Dec. 2, 1947, s. Leonard Ellis and Mary (Kleszewski) N.; m. Nancy Feller, Dec. 13, 1969 (dec. 1985); children—Heather, Andrew. Contrbr. numerous features and articles to natl. and regional mags., newspapers. Undergraduate, Am. History, U. Chgo., 1966-70. Ed. Chgo. Rap, 1971-74; prodn. mgr. The Alternative, Bloomington, Ind., 1975-76; mng. ed. Brown County Dem., Nashville, Inc., 1976-79; free-lance wrtr., 1979—; assoc. Ampersand Assocs., Inc., Chgo., 1979—; pres. Highlander Press, Chgo., 1982—; scriptwrtr. Frame One, Chgo., 1983-84. Recipient Newswriting award Hoosier State Press Assn., 1978. Home: 1600 Washington Evanston IL 60202

NORTON, NICK, see Muska, Nick

NOTTLE, DIANE, b. Northampton, PA, Jan. 25, 1955; d. Thomas Clifford and Eva May (Kostenbader) N. Contrbr. articles to Boston Globe, Polaroid Newsletter. Ed.: Do-Ahead Dining (Malabar Hornblower), 1986, A History of the Harvard Music Association (Arthur Hepner), 1987. B.A. in Jnlsm. and Political Sci., Penn. State U., 1975; M. Liberal Studies, Boston U., 1981. Copy ed. Roanoke Times, VA, 1975-76; asst. city ed. Rochester Democrat & Chronicle, NY, 1976-79; layout/makeup/slot ed. Boston Globe, 1979-86; adj. prof. Emerson Coll., Boston, 1986—; free-lance wrtr., ed., 1986—. Mem. NWU. Home: 27 Temple St 5 Boston MA 02114

NOURSE, ALAN E(DWARD), (Doctor X, Al Edwards), b. Des Moines, Ia., Aug. 11, 1928; s. Benjamin Chamberlain and Grace (Ogg) N.; m. Ann Jane Morton, 1952; children: Benjamin, Rebecca, Jonathan, Christopher. Author: (novels) Trouble on Titan (Junior Literary Guild selection), 1954, A Man Obsessed, 1954, rev. ed publ as The Mercy Man, 1968, Rocket to Limbo, 1957, Scavengers in Space, 1959, (with J.A. Meyer) The Invaders Are Coming, 1959, Star Surgeon, 1960, Raiders from the Rings, 1962, The Universe Between, 1965, The Bladerunner, 1974, The Practice, 1978, The Fourth Horseman, 1983. Nonfiction: So You Want to Be a Doctor, 1957, rev ed, 1963, (with brother, William B. Nourse) So You Want to Be a Lawyer, 1958, So You Want to Be a Scientist, 1960, Nine Planets, 1960, rev ed, 1970, (with E. Halliday) So You Want to Be a Nurse, 1961, (with J. Webbert) So You Want to Be an Engineer, 1962, (with Geoffrey Marks) The Management of a Medical Practice, 1962, So You Want to Be a Physicist, 1964, (with the editors of Life) The Body, 1964, So You Want to Be a Chemist, 1964; under pseud. Dr. X, Intern, 1965; So You Want to Be a Surgeon, 1966, (with C. Meinhardt, Jr.) So You Want to Be an Architect, 1969, Universe, Earth and Atom: The Story of Physics, 1969, Ladies Home Journal Family Medical Guide, 1973, The Outdoorsman's Medical Guide, 1974, Vitamins: A Concise Guide, 1977, Inside the Mayo Clinic, 1979, (with Janice Keller Phelps) The Hidden Addiction and How to Get Free, 1986, The Elk Hunt: A Search for Solutions to Coronary Artery Disease, 1986. Juveniles: Junior Intern, 1957, Venus and Mercury: A First Book, 1972, The Backyard Astronomer, 1973, The Giant Planets: A First Book, 1974, The Asteroids: A First Book, 1975, Viruses: A First Book, 1976, rev ed, 1982, Lumps, Bumps and Rashes: A Look at Kids' Diseases: A First Book, 1976, Clear Skin, Healthy Skin: A Concise Guide, 1976, Fractures, Dislocations and Sprains: A First Book, 1978, Hormones: An Impact Book, 1979, Menstruation: A First Book, 1980, Your Immune System: A Firs Book, 1982, Herpes: An Impsct Book, 1985, AIDS: An Impact Book, 1986. Short story collections: Tiger by the Tail and Other Science Fiction Storie, 1960 (publ in England as Beyond Infinity, 1964), The Counterfeit Man and Other Science Fiction Stories, 1963, Psi High and Others, 1967, Rx for Tomorrow: Tales of Science Fiction, Fantasy and Medicine, 1971. Au of column Family Doctor and contrbg ed, Good Housekeeping, 1976—. Contrbr of articles and short stories, sometimes under the pseudonym Al Edwards, to numerous periodicals, including Saturday Evening Post, Argosy, Playboy, Astounding Science Fiction, Better Homes and Gardens, and Boys Life; contrbr to medical jnls. BS, Rutgers Univ, 1951; MD, Univ of Pa., 1955. Intern, Virginia Mason Hospital, Seattle, Wash., 1955-56; freelance writer in North Bend, Wash., 1956-58; partner, North Bend Medical Clinic, 1958-64; freelance writer, 1964—. Member: AMA, Science Fiction Writers of America (pres, 1968-69), Washington State Medical Soc, King County Medical Soc, Alpha Kappa Alpha. Junior Book Award from Boys Clubs of America, 1963, for Raiders from the Rings; Washington State Governor's Award from Governor's Festival of the Arts, 1966, 1974. Military service: U.S. Navy Hospital Corps, 1946-48. Home: Rt 1 Box 173 Thorp WA 98946

NOVAK, JOSEPH, see Kosinski, Jerzy Nikodem

NOVAK, MICHAEL (JOHN), JR., b. Sept. 9, 1933; s. Michael John and Irene (Sakmar) N.; m. Karen Ruth Laub, June 29, 1963; children: Richard, Tanya, Jana. Author: novels The Tiber was Silver, 1961, Naked I Leave, 1970; nonfiction: Belief and Unbelief, 1965, The Experience of Nothingness, 1970, The Rise of the Unmeltable Ethnics, 1972, Choosing Our King, 1974, The Joy of Sports, 1976, The Guns of Lattimer, 1978, The American Vision, 1978; The Spirit of Democratic Capitalism, 1982, Confession of a Catholic, 1983, Moral Clarity in the Nuclear Age, 1983, Freedom with Justice, 1984, Human Rights and the New Realism, 1986, Character and Crime, 1986, Will It Liberate, 1986. A.B. summa cum laude, Stonehill Coll., North Easton, Mass., 1956; B.T. cum laude, Gregorian U., Rome, 1958; M.A., Harvard U., 1965; LL.D., Keuka (N.Y.) Coll., 1970, Stonehill Coll., Mass., 1977; L.H.D., Davis and Elkins (W.Va.) Coll., 1971, LeMoyne (N.Y.) Coll., 1976, Sacred Heart U., 1977, Muhlenberg Coll., 1979, D'Youville Coll., 1981, Boston U., 1981, New Eng. Coll., 1983, Rivier Coll., 1984, Marquette Univ., 1987. Teaching fellow Harvard U., 1961-63; asst. prof. Stanford U., 1965-68; assoc. prof. philosophy and religious studies State U. N.Y., Old Westbury, 1968-71; provost Disciplines Coll., SUNY, Old Westbury, 1969-71; Ledden-Watson disting. prof. religion Syracuse U., 1977-79; 1976, syndicated columnist, 1976-80, 84—; resident scholar in religion and public policy Am. Enterprise Inst., Washington, 1978—; George Frederick Jowett chair, Religion & Public Policy, 1983, dir. Social and Political Studies, 1987. U.S. rep. UN Human Rights Commn., 1981-83; assoc. editor Commonweal mag., 1966-69; contrbg. editor Christian Century, 1967-80, Christianity and Crisis, 1968-76, Jnl Ecumenical Studies, 1967—, This World, 1982—, Catholicism in Crisis, 1982—; religion editor Natl. Rev., 1979-86; judge Natl. Book awards, 1971, DuPont Broadcast Journalism awards, 1971-80; mem. Bd. Intl. Broadcasting, 1983—; Presdtl. Task Force, Project Economic Justice, 1985—; Cncl. of Scholars, Lib. of Congress, 1986—; speechwriter natl. poli. campaigns, 1970, 72. Address: Am Enterprise Inst 1150 17th St Washington DC 20036

NOVAK, MICHAEL PAUL, b. Chgo., July 6, 1935, s. Joseph Francis and Mae Barbara (Killian) N.; m. Julie Callanan, July 12, 1958; children—Brian, Christina. Author: The Leavenworth Poems, 1972, Sailing by the Whirlpool (poetry), 1978; contrbr. poems, essays, stories, translations to Kenyon Rvw, Hudson Rvw, Denver Qtly, numerous other lit publs.; book reviewer of Kansas City Star, 1972-78; creator audio-visual presentation: A Geography of Kansas Poetry. Wrkg. on poetry. BA, Catholic U., 1957; MFA, U. Iowa, 1962. Instr. English Ill. State U., Normal, 1961-63; assoc. prof. English St. Mary Coll., Leavenworth, Kans., 1963—. NEA summer seminar fellow CUNY, 1977, NYU, 1981, sr. fellow Mellon Fdn., U. Kans., 1982; recipient poetry award Kansas City Star, 1969, 70, Kans Qtly, 1973. Office: Saint Mary Coll Leavenworth KS 66048

NOVAK, ROBERT LEE, (Indiana Bob), b. Olney, IL, Sept. 4, 1933; s. Edward and Beulah (Nicholas) N. Author poetry: At the Splinter House, 1971, Sleeping with Sylvia Plath, 1983; short stories; book: Writing Haiku from Photographs, 1977. BA, Wabash Coll., 1955; PhD,U. Okla., 1972. Prof. Purdue Univ., Ft. Wayne, Ind., 1960-74, Ind. Univ., 1974—; ed. the Windless Orchard, 1970—. Mem. MLA, Kappa Sigma. Home: 6718 Baytree Dr Fort Wayne IN 46825

NOVELLO, DON, b. Ashtabula, OH, Jan. 1, 1943; s. Augustine and Eleanor (Finnerty) N. Author: The Lazlo Letters, 1977; film Gilda Live, 1980; contrbr. articles to Playboy, Rolling Stone, Washington Post. BA, U. Dayton, 1964. Comedy writer, NBC-TV, including Smothers Brothers Show, 1975, Van Dyke & Company, 1976, Saturday Night Live, 1978-80; television producer: SCTV, NBC-TV, 1982; rec. artist, Warner Bros. Records. Mem. WG Am., SAG, AFTRA. Office: Workman Pub 1 W 39th St New York NY 10018

NOWAK, EDWARD, JR., (Haddie), b. Boston, Sept. 6, 1920; s. Edward and Julia (Danielo) N.; m. Mary Louise Johnson, June 27, 1945; children—Kenneth, John, Peter, Kristina, Thomas. Contrbr. articles to mags., newspapers. Contrbg. ed.: Offshore New England Mag., 1977-83; regional ed.: The Fisherman Mag., 1982—. Student Boston U., 1940-43. Genl. sales mgr. Bigelow & Dowse Co., Needham, MA, 1960-62; dir. specialized sales Decatur Hopkins, Taunton, MA, 1962-77; cons. fishing, outdoor equipment sales, Needham, 1977—. Mem. Northeast OWA. Home: 20 Churchill Ln Needham MA 02192

NOYES, STANLEY (TINNING), b. San Francisco, Apr. 7, 1924, s. James Goodman and Winifred (Tinning) N.; m. Nancy Black, Mar. 12, 1949; children—Frank Garniss, Charles De St. Maurice, Julie Hoyt. Author: No Flowers for a Clown (novel), 1961, Shadowbox (novel), 1970, Faces and Spirits (poems), 1974, Beyond the Mountains Beyond the Mountains (poems), 1979, Western (fiction chapbook), 1980, The Commander of Dead Leaves (poems), 1984; co-ed.: The Indian Rio Grande: Recent Poems from 3 Cultures (with Gene Frumkin), 1977. AB, U. Calif.-Berkeley, 1950, MA, 1951. Asst. prof. Calif. Coll. Arts and Crafts, 1953-61; vis. lectr. Coll. Santa Fe, 1965-71; lit. arts coordinator N. Mex. Arts Div., 1972-86. MacDowell Colony fellow, Peterborough, N.H., 1967. Mem. Rio Grande Wrtrs. Assn. (mem. bd. dirs., 1976-78), PEN. Home: 634 E Garcia St Santa Fe NM 87501

NTUBE, DOMINIC KWANG, b. Nkwenfor, Kumba, Cameroon, Jan. 23, 1950, came to U.S., 1980; s. John Akoh Ehoh and Hannah Mbi Akoh. Co-author: From Debt to Development: Alternatives to the International Debt Crisis, 1985. Contrbr. articles on African econ., developmntl. issues to mags, jnls. BA (hons.) in Hist., Dip. Law, Cameroon Univ., Yaounde, 1974, 1980; MA, Johns Hopkins U., Washington, 1982; postgrad. PhD cand. Howard U., 1983—. Prof., Ministry of Edn., Mbalmayo, Cameroon, 1977-80; sr. ed. Transnatl. Research Co., Washington, 1981-83; research asst. Natl. Rural Electric Coop. Am., Washington, 1983-84; ed., co-founder Yaounde Times Mag., Washington, 1983—; policy analyst Bread for the World, Washington, 1984—; guest lectr. U.S. Fgn. Service Inst., Arlington, Va., 1982, 85. Mem. Mayor's Intl. Task Force on Africa, Washington, 1982. Mem. Smithsonian Inst., Fgn. Press Ctr. Home: 1474 Columbia Rd No 304 Washington DC 20009

NUGENT, WALTER TERRY KING, b. Watertown, NY., Jan. 11, 1935; s. Clarence A. and Florence (King) N.; m. 1955; children: Katherine, Rachel, David, Douglas, Terry, Mary; in. Suellen Hoy, 1986. Author: The Tolerant Populists, 1963; Creative History, 1967, 2d edit., 1973; The Money Question During Reconstruction, 1967; Money and American Society 1865-1880, 1968; Modern America, 1973; From Centennial to World War: American Society 1876-1917, 1977; Structures of American Social History, 1981. A.B., St. Benedict's Coll., 1954, D. Litt., 1968; M.A., Georgetown U., 1956; Ph.D., U. Chgo., 1961. Instr. history Washburn U., 1957-58; asst. prof. Kans. State U., 1961-63; asst. prof. history Ind. U., 1963-64, asso. prof., 1964-68, prof., 1968-84, assoe. dean Coll. Arts and Scis., 1967-71, asso. dean overseas study, 1972-76, chmn. history dept., 1974-77; Tacks Prof. Hist., Univ. of Notre Dame, 1984—; vis. prof. U. Hamburg, 1980, U. Warsaw, 1982; mem. Fulbright Selection Com., 1980-87, Newberry Library fellow, 1962; Guggenheim fellow, 1964-65; Paley lectr. and Fulbright vis. prof. Hebrew U. Jerusalem, 1978-79; Huntington Library fellow, 1979, 85. Mem. Am. Hist. Assn., Orgn. Am. Historians, Authors Guild Am., Ind. Assn. Historians. Home: 481 Decio Hall Notre Dame IN 46556

NULL, KATHLEEN "CASEY", b. Glendale, CA, May 20, 1949, d. William Robert and Dorothy B. (Van Schoonhoven) Hardy; m. Kip Emerson Null, May 27, 1979; children—Jason, Michael, Christopher, Kiera. Author-photog.: From Here to Maternity, 1987; contrbr. poetry, features and fiction to Sentinel, Ensign Mag., New Era, Family Journal, Red Book and The Artist. Wrote script for "Let Them Be Children,": PBS documentary. BA, Brigham Young U. Columnist, The Sentinel, Phoenix, AZ, 1983—; freelance writer, artist, and photographer, 1973—. mem. Assoc. Latter Day Media Artists, Assoc. Photographers International, CA. Women Writers. Home: 16562 Patricia Ln Huntington Beach CA 92647

NUNN, WILFRED (BILL), b. Granby, MO, Oct. 22, 1926; s. Roy Sterling and Effie Beatrice (Stoneman) N; m. Mary Flo Spence, June 10, 1950 (div. May, 1980); children: David, Jeanne; m. 2d, Rebecca Susannah O'Hanlon, Sept. 5, 1980; children: Susan, David. Author: Eye of the Eagle, 1982, Missouri by Bill Nunn, 1983, Bill Nunn's Column Book, 1984. BJ, U. Mo. Reporter/city ed. Daily News, Independence, Mo., 1950, Post-Tribune, Jefferson City, Mo., 1950-52. Address: Rt Bonnots Mill MO 65016

NURKSE, ALAN D., b. NYC, Dec. 13, 1949. Contrbr. poems to lit. mags., anthols. Translator: Words and Time (Alaide Koppa de Solorzano), 1985. Wrkg. on hist. narrative poems, love poems. BA, Harvard U., 1970. Fellow NEA, 1983. Mem. Amnesty Intl. Home: 208 Prospect Park W 4B Brooklyn NY 11215

NYE, NAOMI SHIHAB, b. St. Louis, March 12, 1952; d. Aziz and Miriam Naomi (Allwardt) Shihab; m. Michael Nye, 1978; 1 son-Madison Cloudfeather, 1986. Works include: Tattooed Feet, 1977, Eye-to-Eye, 1978, On the Edge of the Sky, 1982, Different Ways to Pray, 1980, Hugging the Jukebox, 1982, Yellow Glove, 1986. BA, Trinity U., 1974. Poet-in-the-Schools, TX Comm. on the Arts, 1974-86; poetry lectr., U. of TX at San Antonio, 1984; poetry lectr., U. of Calif. at Berkeley, 1982; modifier transl. for PROTA project, 1982—; freelance lectr., workshops. Mem. Texas Inst. of Letters, PEN. Home: 806 South Main San Antonio TX 78204

NYERGES, CHRISTOPHER JOHN, b. Pasadena, CA, Jan. 11, 1955; s. Frank and Marie N. Author: Urban Wilderness, 1980, Wild Greens & Salads, 1982, Guide to Wild Food, 1978 (2d rev. ed., 1982); booklets include The Book of Carob, 1980, Dowsing, 1980, A Bicyclist's Guide to Food, 1980, The Maya, 1984, The Mystery of the Sphinx, 1984, Exploring Human Traits via Animal Characteristics, 1985; co-author: Why Weapons? 1982, Rotten Apple Report, 1986, What Causes Gas, 1987, The Science of Persona Pretenders, 1987; columnist Copley News Service, 1980—, Pasadena Star News, 1976—, Perspective column for Foothill Newspapers, 1985—. Leader wilderness field trips Los Angeles County, 1974—; tchr. survival courses Los Angeles County, 1983—; tchr. "Writing for Survival," 1983—. Mem. Natl. Rifle Assn., MENSA. Address: Box 42152 Los Angeles CA 90042

NYMAN, MARY MALLON, b. Evanston, IL, July 26, 1935; d. Horace Taft and Emily Louise (Seiter) Mallon; m. Daniel Currier Nyman, June 20, 1959 (div. 1977); children—Robert, Emily, John, Helen, Daniel. Author: The Season's Edge and Other Poems, 1983; contrbr. poetry: Poetic Justic, other lit. publs. and newspapers. Wrkg. on teen adventure book. AB, Wheaton Coll., 1957; AM, Boston U., 1959. Instr. English, Boston U., 1962-70, Fisher Coll., 1972-74; tchr. Wareham (Mass.) High Sch., 1976—. Mem. NCTE, other ednl. orgns. Home: Box 642 Wareham MA 02571

OANDASAN, WILLIAM, b. Santa Rosa, CA, Jan. 17, 1947; s. William Cortes and Bernita (Potter) Oandasan; m. Georgiana "Joey" Paisano, Oct. 28, 1973; children—Anne, Bernite. Author: Round Valley Verses, 1986, Round Valley Songs, 1984, Moving Inland, 1983, A Branch of California Redwood, 1981; co-editor: Chicano Poetry Anthology Series, 1980-81; editor: A, a jnl of contemporary lit., 1976-82; Chicago Uptown Indian Poetry Anthol., 1981, American Indian Culture and Research Jnl, 1981-86. Program host KPFK (Los Angeles), 1986—. BA, U. of Calif., 1974; MA, U. of Ill., Circle Campus, 1981; MFA, Norwich U., 1984. Learning specialist Truman Coll. (Chicago), 1980-81; senior ed. UCLA (Los Angeles), 1981—. Am. Bk. Award, Before Columbus Fdn., 1985. Mem. MLA, AWP; Exec. Dir. A Writers Circle. Home: 2132 Penmar Ave 5 Venice CA 90291

OAKLEY, LEAH FITZGERALD, b. Hartselle, AL, Nov. 29, 1932; d. Frank Wood and Bertie (Almon) Fitzgerald; m. Joel Daniel Oakley, May 17, 1952; 1 dau., Teresa Anne. Contrbr.: Pathophysiology: Adaptations and Alterations in Function (by B. Bullock, Rosenthal), 1984, Mosby Assess Test (by Saxton and others), 1986, Jnl. Ala. Acad. Sci., Jnl. Psychosocial and Mental Health Services, Jnl. Gerontological Nursing, other profl. mags. Assoc. Nursing, John C. Calhoun Community Coll., 1971; MS in Nursing, U. Ala.-Birmingham, 1981. Nurse, educator, 1971—; psychiatric nursing instr. Wallace State Community Coll., Hanceville, Ala., 1985—. Recipient profl. and acad. awards. Mem. AAUW, numerous profl. orgns. Home: 405 Beard St SW Decatur AL 35601

OATES, JOYCE CAROL, b. Lockport, NY, June 16, 1938; d. Frederic James and Caroline (Bush) O.; m. Raymond Joseph Smith, Jan. 23, 1961. Author: By the North Gate (stories), 1963, The Sweet Enemy (play), 1965, With Shuddering Fall, 1965, Upon the Sweeping Flood (stories), 1966, A Garden of Earthly Delights, 1967, Women in Love (poems), 1968, Expensive People, 1968, Them, 1969 (Natl. Book Award 1970), Anonymous Sings, 1969, The Wheel of Love (stories), 1970, Love and Its Derangements (poems), 1970, Wonderland, 1971, The Edge of Impossibility (essays), 1971, Marriages and Infidelities (stories), 1972, Angel Fire (poems), 1973, Do With Me What You Will, 1973, Sunday Dinner (play produced at Am. Place Theatre), 1970, The Poetry of D.H. Lawrence, 1973, Dreaming America (poems), 1973, The Hungry Ghosts (stories), 1974, The Goddess and Other Women, 1974, New Heaven, New Earth (essays), 1974, Miracle Play (play), 1974, Where Have You Been (stories), 1974, The Poisoned Kiss and Other Portuguese Stories, 1975, The Seduction and Other Stories, 1975, The Assassins, 1975, Crossing the Border (stories), 1976, Childwold, 1976, The Triumph of the Spider Monkey, 1977, Night-Side (stories), 1977, Men Whose Lives Are Money (poems), 1978, Son of the Morning, 1978, Unholy Loves, 1979, Cybele, 1979, All the Good People I've Left Behind (stories), 1979, Bellefleur, 1980, A Sentimental Education, 1981, Contraries: Essays, 1981, Angel of Light, 1981, A Bloodsmoor Romance, 1982, Mysteries of Winterthurn, 1984, Daisy (play prod. at Cubioulo Theatre, NYC), 1980; editor: Scenes from American Life, 1973, Ont. Rvw, The Best American Short Stories, 1979. BA, Syracuse U., 1960; MA, U. Wis., 1961. Prof. English U. Detroit, 1961-67, U. Windsor, Ont., Can., from 1967; writer-in-res., Princeton U., 1978—. Recipient O. Henry Prize Story award, 1967-68; Guggenheim fellow, 1967-68. Mem. AAIAL. Office: 185 Nassau St Princeton NJ 08540

OATMAN, ERIC FURBER, b. NYC, Nov. 6, 1939, s. Frederic and Margery (Ward) O.; m. Jane Langenbacher, Nov. 28, 1969; 1 dau., Alison. Ed.: Medical Care in America, 1978, Crime and Society, 1979, Prospects for Energy in America, 1980, Barron's Booknotes (The Jungle, 1984, Tom Sawyer, 1985, As I Lay Dying, 1985). AB, Hamilton Coll., 1961; MFA, U. Iowa, 1972. Assoc. ed. Sr. Scholastic mag., NYC, 1973-75, Jr. Scholastic mag., NYC, 1975-76; ed.-in-chief Scholastic Search mag., NYC, 1976-83, Scholastic Update mag., NYC, 1983-86; edl. dir., Custom Mag. Div., 1986—. Recipient awards Ednl. Press Assn. Am., 1974, 78, 82, 83, 84, 86,87. Home: 318B Greenwich St New York NY 10013

O'BARR, JEAN FOX, b. Chgo., Nov. 6, 1942, d. Robert Warren and Jean (Stewart) Fox; m. William McAlston, Sept. 4, 1965; children—Claire Anne, Emily Catherine. Author: Shindano: Swahili Essays and Other Stories (with Johannes Mlela), 1971, Third World Women: Factors in Their Changing Status, 1976, Perspectives on Power: Women in Africa, Asia and Latin America, 1982; contrbg. ed.: Language and Politics (with W.M. O'Barr), 1976, Cell Leaderrs in Tanzania (with Joel Samoff), 1986; ed.: Passbook Number F. 47927: Women and the mau Mau in Kenya, 1985; contrbr. articles, chaps. to poli. sci. publs., articles, monographs to continuing edn. publs., book and film rvws. to sociol. publs. AB, Ind. U., 1964; MA, PhD, Northwestern U., 1970. Adj. assoc. prof. poli. sci. Duke U., Durham, N.C., 1969—, dir. continuing edn., 1969-82, dir. women's studies, 1982—; ed. Signs: Jnl of Women in Culture and Soc., Durham, 1985—. Office: Signs 207 E Duke Bldg Durham NC 27708

OBER, STUART A., bNYC, Oct. 2, 1946, s. Paul Ober and Gertrude (Stollerman) Greenberg; m. Joanne Michaels, Sept. 20, 1981; 1 son, Erik. Author: Everybody's Guide to Tax Shelters, 1980, rev. ed., 1982, various tax shelter trng. manuals; ed.-in- chief The Ober Income Letter, 1983—; pub. The Tax Shelter Blue Book, 1984—. BA with honors, Wesleyan U., 1968; lic., Sorbonne U., Paris, 1972; post-grad. CUNY, 1972-74. Tax shelter specialist various cos., NYC, 1972-79; pres. Securities Investigations, Inc., Woodstock, N.Y., 1979—. Chmn. bd. dirs. Woodstock Playhouse, 1985-87. Home: Box 888 Mill Hill Rd Woodstock NY 12498

O'BRIAN, FRANK, see Garfield, Brian Wynne

O'BRIEN, BEATRICE MARIE, b. Elizabeth, NJ, June 18, 1920, d. William Charles and Ida Mae (Stevens) Kahl; m. George Mathew O'Brien, Jan. 20, 1945; children—Bonnie, Dennis, Bill, Maureen, Lisa, Lynn. Author: I Looked Out One Morning (juvenile), 1979, No Small Twig (poetry), 1984; contrbr. poetry to Mozart Park, Dragonfly, The Villager, numerous other publs. Nurse, U.S. Navy, 1943-45. Dir. Poets Theatre, Hornese, N.Y., 1980—. Winner Pa. Poetry Soc. Animal Kingdom contest, 1979; recipient several Best of Issue awards. Home: RD 2 Box 155 Cohocton NY 14826

O'BRIEN, DARCY, b. Los Angeles, July 16, 1939; s. George and Marguerite (Churchill) O'B.; m. Ruth Ellen Berke, Aug. 26, 1961 (div. 1968); 1 dau., Molly; m. Suzanne Beesley, Feb. 27, 1987. Author: The Conscience of James Joyce, 1968; W.R. Rodgers, 1971; Patrick Kavanagh, 1975; A Way of Life, Like Any Other (Ernest Hemingway Fdn. award 1978); Moment By Moment, 1978; The Silver Spooner, 1981, Two of a Kind, 1985. AB, Princeton U., 1961; postgrad., Cambridge (Eng.) U., 1963-64; MA, U. Calif., Berkeley, 1963, PhD,1965. Prof. English, Pomona Coll., 1965-77; prof. modern letters U. Tulsa, 1978—. U. Ill. Center for Advanced Study fellow, 1969-70; Mellon Fdn. fellow, 1973-74; Guggenheim fellow, 1978-79. Mem. James Joyce Soc., PEN. Office: Dept Eng U Tulsa Tulsa OK 74104

O'BRIEN, JOHN THOMAS, b. Chgo., Nov. 10, 1945, s. William Francis and Ruth Fransis (Burke) O'B.; m. Jeanne Marie Russell, Dec. 21, 1968; children—Kathleen, Emmett, William, Kevin. Author: Interviews with Black Writers, 1973, No Signs from Heaven: Theological Tradition and the Modern Literary Imagination, 1975; contrbr. articles, interviews to Listening, Studies in Black Lit., Canto, Syntaxis, other publs.; contrbr. book rvws. to Chgo. Sun-Times, Washington Post, others. MA, U. Ill.-Chgo., 1971; PhD, No. Ill. U., 1975. Prof. English, DePaul U., Chicago, 1987; ed., pub. Rvw Contemporary Fiction, 1980—, Dalkey Archive Press, Elmwood Park, 1984—; panelist on lit., Ill. Arts Council, 1982-85. Mem. MLA, CCLM, Conf. Eds. Learned Jnls. Office: 1817 79th Ave Elmwood Park IL 60635

O'BRIEN, KATHARINE, b. Amesbury, MA, d. Martin W. and Catherine (Higgins) O'Brien. Author: Sequences, 1966, Excavation and Other Verse, 1967; poetry in Saturday Review, Christian Science Monitor, New York Times, many others; music: "When I Set Out for Lyonnesse," 1947. AB, Bates College, 1922; AM, Cornell U., 1924, PhD,Brown U., 1939. Instr. to prof. and chairman, math. dept., College of New Rochelle, New Rochelle, NY, 1925-36; instr. and head, math. dept., Deering High School, Portland, ME, 1940-71; lectr., U. of Maine, Portland, 1962-73; lectr., Brown Univ., summers 1962-1965, 67 (NSF Inst.) Mem. PSA, NY Acad. of Sciences, Math. Assoc. of Am., Phi Beta Kappa. Home: 130 Hartley St Portland ME 04103

O'BRIEN, PENNY, b. Adana, Turkey, Jan. 24, 1928 (arrd. U.S.A. 1929); d. Paul William and Persis (Carney) Penningroth; m. James Michael O'Brien, June 6, 1950; children—Michael, Paul, Kathi, Richard. Pub., ed., wrtr., RESources, 1970-81; ed., New York State Reporter. BA, Univ. of Iowa, 1949; MSE (early childhood), SUNY, Binghamton, 1977. Newsltr. wrtg., Binghamton, NY, 1984—. Mem. Women's Natl. Book Assn., 1985—; Southern Tier Children's Lit. Guild, 1982—. Home: 43 Hooper Rd Endwell NY 13760

O'BRIEN, SUSAN BARBARA, b. NYC, Jan. 2, 1954; d. Daniel William and Madeline (Kriedler) Winfield; m. Donald P. O'Brien, Mar. 28, 1983; 1 son, Brendan. Contrbr. short story to Jr. Trails Mag., article to Fla. Nursing News. Wrkg. on short stories, articles. Nursing Diploma, Long Island Coll. Hosp., 1973; Cert., Inst. Children's Lit., 1986. Registered nurse Long Island Coll. Hosp., Brklyn., 1973-82, Sun City Hosp., Sun City Center, FL, 1982—. Home: 737 Kingston Ct Apollo Beach FL 33570

OBSTFELD, RAYMOND, (Jason Frost, Don Pendleton, Pike Bishop, Carl Stevens). Author: (as Raymond Obstfeld) The Golden Fleece, 1979, Dead-End Option, 1980, Dead Heat (Edgar Allen Poe award), 1981, Dead Bolt, 1982, The Remington Factor, 1985, Redtooth, 1986, Brainchild, 1986, The Masked Dog, 1986, The Whipping Boy, 1987; (as Jason Frost) Warlord series (also screenplay), 1983-85, Invasion USA, 1985; (as Don Pendleton) Bloodsport, 1982, Flesh Wounds, 1983, Savannah Swingsaw, 1985, The Fire Eaters, 1986; (as Pike Bishop) Judgement at Poisoned Well, 1983, Diamondback, 1983; (as Carl Stevens) Dagger: The Centaur Conspiracy, 1983, Dagger No. 2: Ride of the Razorback, 1984; author poetry: The Cat with Half a Face, 1978; contrbr. poetry to Encore, Hourglass, Hartford Courant, other lit. publs.; contrbr. stories to Dogsoldier, Crook's Mag., Not-So-Pvt. Eye, others; contrbr. articles to numerous mags., newspapers; book reviewer Armchair Detective. BA, U. Redlands, 1972; postgrad. U. Calif.-Santa Barbara, 1972-73; MA, U. Calif.-Davis, 1976. Asst. prof. dept. English Orange Coast Coll., Costa Mesa, Calif., 1976—. Mem. MWA, Am. Film Inst. Home: 190 Greenmoor St Irvine CA 92714

OCHESTER, ED, b. Bklyn., Sept. 15, 1939; s. Edwin Otto and Viola (Bachtle) O.; m. Clarinda Horner, June 19, 1965; children—Edwin Hall, Elizabeth Britten. Author poems: Dancing on the Edges of Knives, 1973; The End of the Ice Age, 1977, Miracle Mile, 1984, Weehawken Ferry, 1985, Changing the Name to Ochester, 1986. BA, Cornell U., 1961; MA, Harvard U., 1962. Assoc. English prof. U. Pitts., 1977—; ed. U. Pitts. Press Poetry Series, 1978—. Devins Award, U. Mo. Press, 1973, Fellowship, Pa. Council on the Arts, 1981, 83, 85, Fellowship, NEA, 1984. Mem. PSA, PEN, AWP. Home: RD 1 Box 174 Shelocta PA 15774

O'CONNELL, JEFFREY, b. Worcester, MA, Sept. 28, 1928; s. Thomas Joseph and Mary (Carroll) O'C.; m. Virginia Kearns, Nov. 26, 1960; children—Mara, Devin. Author: (with R.E. Keeton) Basic Protection for the Traffic Victim, 1965; After Cars Crash: The Need for Legal and Insurance Reform, 1967; (with Arthur Myers) Safety Last: An Indictment of the Auto Industry, 1966; (with R.E. Keeton, John McCord) Crisis in Car Insurance, 1968; (with Wallace Wilson) Car Insurance and Consumer Desires, 1969; The Injury Industry, 1971; (with Rita James Simon) Payment for Pain and Suffering, 1972; Ending Insult to Injury: No-Fault Insurance for Products and Services, 1975; (with Roger Henderson) Tort Law, No-Fault and Beyond, 1975; The Lawsuit Lottery: Only the Lawyers Win, 1979. Grad. cum laude, Phillips Exeter Acad., 1947; AB cum laude, Dartmouth Coll., 1951; JD, Harvard U., 1954. Bar: Mass. 1954, Conn., 1954, Va., 1983, hon. admittance to Ark., Minn. bars. Instr. speech Tufts U., 1953-54; with firm Sherburne, Powers & Needham, 1954-57, Hale & Dorr, Boston, 1958-59; asst. prof. then assoc. prof. law U. Iowa Coll. Law, 1959-62; assoc. dir. automobile claims study Harvard Law Schl., 1963-64; assoc. prof. law U. Ill. Coll. Law, 1964-65, prof., 1965-79; prof. law U. Va. Law Schl., 1980-83, John Allan Love prof., 1983—; mem. Center for Advanced Study, 1980-83; vis. fellow Center for Socio-Legal Studies, Wolfson Coll., Oxford (Eng.) U., 1973, 79; Bd. dirs. Consumers Union, 1970-76. Served as 1st lt. USAF, 1954-57. Guggenheim fellow, 1972-73, 79-80. Mem. ABA, Phi Beta Kappa. Home: 4 Oak Circle Charlottesville VA 22901

O'CONNELL, RICHARD, b. NYC, Oct. 25, 1928; s. Richard James and Mary Ellen (Fallon) O'C; m. Milda Maria Klapatanskas, Sept. 27, 1955 (div.); children—Richard James, Ilona Maria; m. Beryl Evelyn Reeves, Nov. 14, 1978. Author: From an Interior Silence, 1961, Cries of Flesh and Stone, 1962, New Poems and Translations, 1963, Brazilian Happenings, 1966, Terrane, 1967, Thirty Epigrams, 1971, Irish Monastic Poems (transl.), 1975, The Word in Time (selected transl. of Antonio Machado), 1975, Sappho (selected transl.), 1975, Lorca (selected transl.), 1976, Middle English Poems (transl.), 1976, More Irish Poems (transl.), 1976, Epigrams from Martial (transl.), 1976, One Hundred Epigrams from the Greek Anthology (transl.), 1977, Hudson's Fourth Voyage, 1978. Editor: Apollo's Day, 17th Century Songs, 1969; Atlantis Edits., 1962—, Poetry Newsletter, 1971—. BS, Temple U., 1956; MA, Johns Hopkins, 1957. Instr. English Temple U., Phila., 1957-61; asst. prof., 1961-69, asso. prof., 1969—; guest lectr. poetry dept. writing seminars Johns Hopkins U., 1961-74; participant Poetry in Schools Prog., Pa. Council Arts, 1971-73; Fulbright lectr. Am. lit U. of Brazil, Rio de Janeiro, 1960, U. Navarre, Pamplona, Spain, 1962-63. Served with USN, 1948-52. Recipient Contemporary Poetry Prize, 1972. Mem. PEN, MLA, AWP, Walt Whitman Poetry Center (dir.), Lit. Fellowship Phila. Home: 220 Rices Mill Rd Wyncote PA 19095

O'CONNOR, DENNIS PATRICK, b. Washington, IN, Mar. 17, 1955, s. James Daniel and Anna Louise (Colvin) O'C.; m. Paula Marie Fey, Nov. 12, 1983. Contrbr. articles to Living Single mag., Columbia Mag., Wrtr.'s Digest, other publs. Wrkg. on children's non-fiction. AB in Journalism, Ind. U., 1977. Sports ed. Recorder Newspapers, Edgewood, Ky., 1982-83; assoc. ed. The Messenger, Covington, Ky., 1983-84; mng. ed. Cin. Suburban Press, 1984—; instr. wrtg., Discovery Ctr., Cincinnati, 1986—. Recipient awards Ky. Press Assn., Catholic Press Assn. Mem. NWC, Cin. Eds. Assn., Sigma Delta Chi. Home: 1335 Amsterdam Rd Park Hills KY 41011

O'CONNOR, PHILIP F., b. San Francisco; m. Delores O'Connor (div.); children—Dondi, John, Christopher, Erin, Justin. Author: Old Morals, Small Continents, Darker Times (short stories), 1971, A Season for Unnatural Causes (short stories), 1975, Stealing Home (novel), 1979, Ohio Woman (novella), 1985, Defending Civilization (novel), 1988. BA, U. San Francisco, 1954; MA, San Francisco State U., 1961; MFA, U. Iowa, 1963. Prof. Bowling Green (Ohio) State U., 1967—. Served to 1st lt. U.S. Army, 1954-56. Mem. AWP, PEN. Home: 520 Lorraine Ave Bowling Green OH 43402

O'DELL, LEN, see Moore, Maurine

O'DELL, MARY ERNESTINE, b. Beckley, WV, Sept. 8, 1935; s. Ernest Forbis and Doris Mary (Truman) Houck; m. Daniel Moss Beam, Feb. 22, 1958 (div. May 1985); children: Robert Duke, Dorothy Karen; m. 2d, James R. O'Dell, Aug. 30, 1986. Author: (poetry) Homefolks, 1984; Blue Air and Wheels, 1985; contrbr. to Maternal Legacy, Cambric Poetry Project III, Fellowship of the Poet, 1986. AB, Transylvania U., Lexington, Ky., 1957; MA, Western Ky. U., 1978. Tchr. elem. schls. Jefferson County Bd. Edn., Louisville, 1958-60, Larue County Bd. Edn., Hodgenville, Ky., 1968—. Recipient 1st place award Mid-South Poetry Consortium, 1986. Mem. Ky. Poetry Soc. (secy.; 1st place award 1984, 85). Home: Rt 3 Box 3 Hodgenville KY 42748

O'DELL, SCOTT, b. Los Angeles, 1898; s. Bennett Mason and May Elizabeth (Gabriel) O'D. Author: Woman of Spain, 1934, Hill of the Hawk, 1947, (with William Doyle) Man Alone, 1953, Country of the Sun, 1957, The Sea Is Red, 1958, Island of the Blue Dolphins (Newbery medal 1961, Rupert Hughes award 1960, Hans Christian Andersen award of merit 1962, William Allen White award 1963, German Juvenile Intl. award 1963, Nene award 1964, OMAR's award 1985), 1960, The King's Fifth (Newbery honor book 1967, German Juvenile Intl. award 1969), 1966, The Black Pearl (Newbery honor book 1968), 1967, (with Rhoda Kellogg) The Psychology of Children's Art, 1967, The Dark Canoe, 1968, Journey to Jericho, 1969, Sing Down the Moon (Newbery honor book 1971), 1970, The Treasure of Topo-el-Bampo, 1972, The Cruise of the Arctic Star, 1973, Child of Fire, 1974, The Hawk That Dare Not Hunt By Day, 1975, Zia, 1976, The 290, 1976, Carlota, 1977, Kathleen, Please Come Home, 1978, The Captive, 1979, Sarah Bishop, 1980, The Feathered Serpent, 1981, The Spanish Smile, 1982, The Amethyst Ring, 1983, The Castle in the Sea, 1983, Alexandra (Parent's Choice award 1984, Florida State Historical award 1985), 1984, The Road to Damietta, 1985, Streams to the River, River to the Sea, (Parents Choice award, 1986); Scott O'Dell Historical Novel Award, 1987, The Serpent Never Sleeps, 1987. Student, Occidental Coll., 1919, U. Wis., 1920, Stanford, 1920-21, U. Rome, Italy, 1925. Recipient Hans Christian Andersen Intl. medal 1972, U. So. Miss. medallion 1976, Regina medal 1978, FOCAL award 1981. Mem. AG. Address:Houghton Mifflin 2 Park St Boston MA 02108

ODEN, GLORIA CATHERINE, b. Yonkers, NY, d. Redmon Stanley and Ethel Eva (Kincaid) Oden; m. John Price Bell, July 20, 1978. Author: Resurrections, 1978, The Tie That Binds, 1980. BA, Howard U., 1944, JD, 1948. Asst. prof. U. Md. Baltimore County, Catonsville, 1971-75, assoc. prof., 1975-83, prof., 1983—. Office: Univ Md Catonsville MD 21228

ODOM, KAREN D., see Davenport, Karen Odom

O'DONNELL, LAURENCE GERARD, b. Bklyn., June 30, 1935; s. Thomas Edward and Dorothy (Clark) O'D.; m. Joan M. Coniglio, Jan. 9, 1960; children: Christopher, Carolyn, Jeffery, Anthony. A.B., Holy Cross Coll., 1957. With Wall St. Jnl., 1958—, reporter, NYC, 1958-66, chief Detroit Bur., 1966–74, asst. mng. editor, NYC., 1974-77, mng. editor, 1977-83, assoc. editor, 1983—. Mem. AP Mng. Editors Assn., Am. Soc. Newspaper Editors. Office: 200 Liberty St New York NY 10281

O'DONNELL, RICHARD MICHAEL, b. Elyria, OH, Nov. 17, 1951; s. Alfred Peter Joseph Jr. and Mary Josephine (Keyes) O'D.; m. Kathleen Ann Farahay; children—Richard Jr., Patricia, Sean, Kathleen. Author: Rice Wine, 1983, Where's Santa Claus?, 1985, Santa's Workshop, 1985; contrbr. chapbook, Disk Network; ed. and contrbr. Telescope, Diskazine, Intro 14. BA, Oberlin Coll.; MFA, Bowling Green State U. Pres. Bookward Pub., Grafton, Ohio, 1981—. Recipient individual artist fellowship, Ohio Arts Council, Columbus, 1984-86. Mem. AWP. Address: 2219 Grafton Rd Grafton OH 44044

O'DONNELL-LEACH, KAREN, b. Pawtucket, RI, June 5, 1951; d. William R. and Regina G. (Dowling) O'Donnell; m. David Leach, Sept. 10, 1979. Editor: ISDN Information Sourcebook, 1986, Telecommunications Information Sourcebook, 1987, Fiber Optic Reprint Series, 1987. BA, U. Mass., 1975; MLS, U. Mich., 1978. Archivist, Archives Am. Art, Boston, 1981; Data Analyst, Info. Access, Belmont,

Calif., 1982-86; Info. Specialist, IGI Consulting, Boston, 1986—. Home: 8 Everett St Boston MA 02130

O'DONOHOE, NICHOLAS BENJAMIN, b. Charles City, IA, Oct. 31, 1952; s. James E. and Beth (Larson) O'D.; m. Lynn Anne Evans, Aug. 5, 1978. Author: April Snow, 1984, Wind Chill, 1985, Open Season, 1986. BA, Carleton Coll., 1975; PhD, Syracuse U., 1983. Instr., Va. Tech. U., Blacksburg, 1981-83, asst. prof., 1983—. Mem. MWA, Newman Community. Home: 905 Preston Ave Blacksburg VA 24060

OEHSER, PAUL HENRY, b. Cherry Creek, NY, Mar. 27, 1904; s. Henry Christian and Agnes Theodosia (Abbey) O.; m. Grace M. Edgbert, Oct. 4, 1927; children—Gordon Vincent, Richard Edgbert. Author: Sons of Science, the Story of the Smithsonian Institution and Its Leaders, 1949; Fifty Poems, 1954; The Smithsonian Institution, 1970; (poems and essays) The Witch of Scrapfaggot Green, 1981; The Smithsonian Institution, 1983; contrbr. articles, rvws., verse to mags., jnls, encys., news publs.; gen. editor: United States Ency. of History, 1967-68. Student, U. Iowa, 1924; AB, Greenville (Ill.) Coll., 1925; postgrad., Am. U., 1926-30. Asst. editor Bur. Biol. Survey, Dept. Agr., 1925-31; editor U.S. Nat. Mus., Smithsonian Instn., 1931-50; chief editorial and publs. div., pub. relations officer Smithsonian Instn., 1950-66, research assoc., 1966—; editor sci. publs. Natl. Geog. Soc., 1966-78; mng. editor Jnl Washington Acad. Scis., 1939-59; editor Proc. 8th Am. Sci. Congress, Dept. State, 1941-43. Fellow Washington Acad. Scis.; mem. Philo. Soc. Washington, Am. Ornithol. Union, Biol. Soc. Washington, Wilderness Soc., Thoreau Soc. Am. (pres. 1961), Washington Biologists' Field Club (pres. 1964-67), Cosmos Club of Washington, Literary Soc. of Washington. Home: 9012 Old Dominion Dr McLean VA 22102

OELSCHLAEGER, RENEE LOUISE, b. St. Louis, Dec. 25, 1948; d. Norman Arthur and Marion Ruthe (West) Stricker; m. Dennis Lee Oelschlaeger, Dec. 20, 1969; children—Amanda Lea, Abigail Marie, Adam Wesley, Andrew Edward. Contrbr. poems, articles, short stories to mags., newspapers, anthols. Cert., Emmaus Bible Schl., 1968; student John Brown U., 1968-70. Comml. teller LaSalle Natl. Bank, Chgo., 1967-68; census enumerator U.S. Census Bur., Siloam Springs, AR, 1970; sec. to v.p. personnel Trinity Universal Insurance Co., Dallas, 1970-74; free-lance wrtr., 1974—. Recipient numerous awards for poetry Ark. Wrtrs. Conf., Ozark Wrtrs., AG, 1982-87. Mem. Springdale P&W (past sec., awards for poetry and prose 1984, 85, 86, Poets' Roundtable Ark. (awards for poetry 1982, 84, 85, 86), Natl. Fedn. State Poetry Socs. (awards for poetry 1983, 85, 86). Home: 835 N West End St Springdale AR 72764

OFFIT, SIDNEY, b. Balt., Oct. 13, 1928; s. Barney and Lillian (Cohen) O.; m. Avodah Crindell Komito, Aug. 8, 1952; children—Kenneth, Michael Robert. Author: He Had it Made, 1959, The Other Side of the Street, 1962, Soupbone, 1963, Topsy Turvey, 1965, The Adventure of Homer Fink, 1966, The Boy Who Made a Million, 1968; short stories Not All the Girls Have Million Dollar Smiles, 1971; Only a Girl Like You, 1972, What Kind of Guy Do You Think I Am?, 1977; series sports books for boys, 1961-65, also essays, rvws., short stories; book editor: Politics Today, 1978-80. BA, Johns Hopkins U., 1950. Editorial staff Mercury Publs., NYC,1952-53, Macfadden Publs., 1953-54; contrbg. editor Baseball mag., Washington, 1955-58; adj. prof. creative writing N.Y. U., 1977—; assoc. editor Intellectual Digest, 1970-72, sr. editor, 1972-74; lectr. creative writing New Schl. Social Research, 1965—; curator George Polk Awards for Journalism, 1977—; mem. natl. bd. Natl. Book Com., 1973-75; commentator Channel 5 TV, NYC,1975-85. Mem. AG, AL, Am. Center of PEN. Home: 23 E 69th St New York NY 10021

OFFSEY, SOL, b. NYC, Mar. 3, 1922; s. Abraham and Sadie (Feldman) O.; m. Shirley Zelda Halperin, July 25, 1952 (dec. Oct. 1979); children—Lloyd, Elana. Author: (short stories) Edifice, 1985; (TV script) Heed the Falling Sparrow, 1958. Contrbr. poems, fiction to anthols. Student Columbia U. Import specialist U.S. Customs Service, NYC, 1961-76, retired. Home: 1721 Dahill Rd Brooklyn NY 11223

OFHAND, JACK, see Coe, Joe Ann

O'GARA, ELAINE JANET, b. Topeka, Dec. 8, 1944; d. Maurice and Anne Emily (Lehenbauer) O'Gara; m. Robert Burnap Shapiro, Oct. 8, 1977. Contrbr. to Acorns, Travel Writers Markets, Potrero View, Noe Valley Voice. BA, Valparaiso U., 1962-66; MA, U. Wis., 1966-68; MS, NE. U., Boston, 1977-78. Freelance writer, San Francisco, 1976—; pub. Winterbourne Press, Berkeley, Calif., 1984—. Coordinator, Intl. Vol. Service, San Francisco, 1970-71; vol., Recreation Center for the Handicapped, SF, 1979-80; singer, San Francisco Bach Choir, 1979—; bd. dirs. San Francisco Leagaue of Urban Gardeners, 1982-84. Mem. Calif. Writers Club, Pub. Mktg. Assn., Writers Connection, Media Alliance, Marin Self Publishers Assn. Address: Box 7548 Berkeley CA 94707

OGBURN, CHARLTON, b. Atlanta, Mar. 15, 1911; s. Charlton and Dorothy (Stevens) O.; m. Mary C. Aldis, June 6, 1945 (div. 1951); 1 son, William O. Porter; m. Vera Weidman, Feb. 24, 1951; children—Nyssa, Holly. Author: The White Falcon, 1955, The Bridge, 1957, Big Caesar, 1958, The Marauders, 1959, U.S. Army, 1960, The Gold of the River Sea, 1965, The Winter Beach, 1966, The Forging of Our Continent, 1968, The Continent in Our Hands, 1971, Winespring Mountain, 1973, The Southern Appalachians: A Wilderness Quest, 1975, The Adventure of Birds, 1976, Railroads: The Great American Adventure, 1977, The Mysterious William Shakespeare: The Myth and the Reality, 1985. SB, Harvard, 1932; grad., Natl. War Coll., 1952. Writer Alfred P. Sloan Fdn., 1937-39; book reviewer BOM Club, 1940-41; Officer U.S. Dept. of State, 1946-57. Served to capt. AUS, 1941-46; India-Burma. Home: 403 Hancock St Beaufort SC 29902

OGDEN, GEORGINE LUCILE, (Georgine Prokopov), b. Middletown, NY, Nov. 3, 1925; d. George Timlow and Lucile Greenleaf (Gumaer) Ogden; m. Theodore Sergius, Oct. 4, 1968. Author: Orange Poems, 1987. Contrbr. poetry to Voices of the Majestic Sage, 1984, Treasures of the Precious Moments, 1985, Bird Verse Portfolios, 1985, BIPA (Faith), 1984, 85, American Poetry Anthology, 1983, 85. BA, U. of Wisconsin, 1947; MIA Columbia U., 1949; PhD, U. of London, 1958. Assoc. prof. poli. sci. and history Upper Iowa Coll. (Fayette), 1967-73; admin. aide Orange Co. Executive's Off. (Goshen, NY), 1975-77; dir. of research Westchester Co. Dept. of Health (White Plains, NY), 1981-83; data analyst Hudson Valley HSA (Tuxedo, NY), 1977-81, 1984—. Home: Box 578 Beverly Hills FL 32665

OGILVIE, FAN S., b. Charleston, WV, May 29, 1944, d. Frederick Marshall and Elizabeth Morehead (Brightwell) Staunton; m. Donald Gordon Ogilvie, June 18, 1966; children—Jennifer Braemar, Adam Christopher. Author: The Other Side of the Hill; contrbr. poems to D.C. Gazette, Three Sisters. BA, Smith Coll., 1966; MA, George Washington U., 1971. Tchr./poetry dir. St. Thomas's Day Schl., New Haven, 1977-80; poet-in-residence Nightingale-Bamford Schl., NYC,1982-85; dir. workshop Martha's Vineyard Wrtrs. Workshop, 1982-83; tchr. English, poet, short story wrtr., since 1972; produced, acted-in The Prodigious Hickey, Am. Playhouse Robert F. Kennedy Meml., Washington, 1985. Recipient commendation Chester H. Jones Fdn., 1985. Mem. AAP, PSA, 92d Street Y Poetry Ctr. Home: 3129 N St Washington DC 20007

OGILVIE, LLOYD JOHN, b. Kenosha, WI, Sept. 2, 1930; s. Varde Spencer and Katherine (Jacobson) O.; m. Mary Jane Jenkins, Mar. 25, 1951. Author: A Life Full of Surprises, 1969, Let God Love You, 1974, If I Should Wake before I Die, 1973, Lord of the Ups and Downs, 1974, You've Got Charisma, 1975, Cup of Wonder, 1976, Life Without Limits, 1976, Drumbeat of Love, 1977, When God First Thought of You, 1978, The Autobiography of God, 1979, The Bush Is Still Burning, 1980, The Radiance of the Inner Splendor, 1980, Congratulations, God Believes in You, 1981, Life as It Was Meant to Be, 1981, The Beauty of Love, The Beauty of Friendship, 1981, The Beauty of Caring, The Beauty of Sharing, 1981, God's Best for My Life, 1981, God's Will in your Life, 1982, Ask Him Anything, 1982, Commentary on Book of Acts, 1983, Praying with Power, 1983, Falling into Greatness, 1983, Freedom in the Spirit, 1984, Making Stress Work For You, 1984, The Lord of the Impossible, 1984, Why Not Accept Christ's Healing and Wholeness, 1984, If God Cares, Why Do I Still Have Problems? 1985, The Other Jesus, 1986. Genl. editor: Communicator's Commentary of the Bible, 1982—. BA, Lake Forest Coll., 1952, Garrett Theol. Sem., 1956; postgrad., New Coll., U. Edinburgh, Scotland, 1955-56; DD, Whitworth Coll., 1973; LHD, U. Redlands, 1974; D.Humanities, Moravian Coll., 1975. Office: 1760 N Gower St Hollywood CA 90028

OGLESBY, THEODORE NATHANIEL JR., (Ruth Moncrief), b. Pine Grove, GA, June 14, 1932; s. T. N. and Ruth (Moncrief) O.; m. Betty Mitchell, June 12, 1953; children—Reggie, Lydia. Ed. edit page: The Times, Gainesville, GA., 1953. Program dir. Sta. WBGR, Jesup, GA, 1953-54; news dir. Sta. WDUN, Gainesville, 1956-59; pub. The Tribune, Gainesville, 1959-70. Mem. Ga. Press Assn. (dir. 1964-70; numerous awards for best personal column, editorial writing, most fearless editorial, religious editorial, feature writing, best news photograph, best editorial page, 1961—, Natl. Conf. Editorial Wrtrs., Reserve Officers Assn. Home: Box 663 Gainsville GA 30503

O'GORMAN, NED, b. 1931; married; 1 son, Richard. Author: The Night of the Hammer, 1961, Adam Before His Mirror, 1963, The Buzzard and the Peacock, 1965, The Harvesters' Vase, 1968, The Storefront: A Community of Children on Madison Avenue and 129th Street, 1970; children's book The Blue Butterfly, 1971; poetry The Flag the Hawk Flies, 1972, The Wilderness and the Laurel Tree: A Guide for Parents and Teachers on the Observation of

Children, 1972, The Children Are Dying, 1978; Terrible Steel, Perfected Crystal: Anthology of Spiritual Readings, 1981; sr. editor: Jubilee mag., 1962-65; editor: Prophetic Voices: Ideas and Words on Revolution, 1969, Seabury Press. AB, St. Michael's Coll., LHD, 1983; A.M., Columbia U., Guggenheim fellow, 1956, 62; Rockefeller Fdn. Centre for Study fellow, Eng., 1972, Bellagio, Italy, 1977. Address: 60 W 66th St New York NY 10023

O'GRADY, HENRY, see Brady, Henry Grady

O'GRADY, THOMAS JOSEPH, b. Balt., Aug. 226, 1943, s. Thomas Joseph and Sallie Mapp (Dennis) Grady; m. Frances Anne Griesser, June 21, 1966 (div. 1971); m. 2d, Bronwyn Regina Southworth, July 17, 1971; children—Ethan Southworth, Ryan Dennis. Author: Unicorn Evils, 1977, Establishing a Vineyard, 1980, The Farmville Elegies, 1981; translator poems by Jaroslav Siefert: The Casting of Bells, 1982, Mozart in Prague, 1985, Eight Days, 1985. BA, U. Balt., 1966; MA, Johns Hopkins U., 1967. Poet-in-residence Hampden-Sydney (Va.) Coll., 1974—, founder, ed. The Hampden-Sydney Poetry Rvw, 1974—; owner, vintner Rose Bower Winery, 1974—. Recipient Ed.'s award NEA, 1976, Leache Prize for Poetry, Chrysler Mus., Norfolk, Va., 1977, Impact Book award Commentators Press, 1980. Home: Box 126 Hampden-Sydney VA 23943

O'HALLORAN, JUDY MACKENZIE, b. Mobile, AL, Jan. 4, 1946; d. John Paul and Marion (Dunn) Mackenize Bender; m. Roger Edward O'Halloran, Aug. 10, 1968; children—Sean C., Ryan M., Casey P. Contrbr. articles to mags. Wrkg. on Down Syndrome and Positive Parenting B.S., Fla. State U., 1968. Tchr. public schls., Tallahassee, FL, 1969–72, Ft. Myers, FL, 1975-78; free-lance wrtr., 1986—. Mem. Fla. Freelance Wrtrs. Assn., Cape Coral Wrtrs. Club. Address: 4874 Lema Ct North Fort Myers FL 33913

O'HANLON, ALVIN MERLE, b. East Liverpool, OH, Oct. 19, 1932; s. George Anthony and Adelaide (Schonn) O. Author: Reflections Sharing Thoughts: One-on-One, 1986. B.A. in Bus. Administration and Econ., Chapman Coll., 1972. Enlisted U.S. Air Force, 1951, advanced through grades to major, 1972; internal auditor Am. Express, N.Y.C., 1973-80; real estate broker, Ft. Lauderdale, FL, 1980-86; free-lance wrtr. Phoenix Press, Port Charlotte, FL, 1986—. Mem. Natl. Assn. Ind. Pubs., Fla. Freelance Wrtrs. Assn., Fla. Pubs. Group. Home: 2787 E Oakland Pk Blvd Suite 211 Fort Lauderdale FL 33306

O'HARA, WILLIAM F., JR., b. Buffalo, NY, Apr. 21, 1953; s. William F. and Jane O'Hara. Pres./pub./ed. International Sport Fishing Publications, Inc. Publications: O'Hara's 1984 International Sport Fishing Tournament Directory, O'Hara's 1985-86 International Sport Fishing Tournament Directory, Sport Fishing Along the Mexican Coasts, Mexican Sport Fishing News, International Fishing Charters, Lodges and Camps. Editor: Nautica mag. (intl. ed.). Student San Jose, CA pub. schls. Office: 11000 Metro Parkway Ft Myers FL 33912

O'HERIN, TIMOTHY PATRICK, b. St. Louis, Feb. 18, 1955; s. Edward Francis and Zoe Constance (Leuer) O'H. Contrbr. articles to newspapers, mags. Assoc. ed.: Okla. Pub., 1987. B.A. in Jnlsm., U. Mo., 1978. Reporter, Daily Standard, Sikeston, MO, 1978-80, Daily Oklahoman, Oklahoma City, 1981-85; mng. ed. Friday Newspaper, Oklahoma City, 1985; field representative U.S. Senator Don Nickles, Oklahoma City, 1986; mng. mem. services Oklahoma Press Assn., Oklahoma City, 1987. Home: 3125 NW 50 Oklahoma City OK 73112

OHMANN, RICHARD MALIN, b. Cleve., July 11, 1931; s. Oliver Arthur and Grace (Malin) O.; m. Carol Alice Burke, June 25, 1955; children—Sarah Malin, William Burke. Author: Shaw: The Style and the Man, 1962, (with others) The Logic and Rhetoric of Exposition, 3d ed., 1969, English in America: A Radical Critique of the Profession, 1976, Politics of Letters, 1987; editor: Coll. English, 1966-78. BA, Oberlin Coll., 1952; MA, Harvard, 1954, PhD, 1960. Guggenheim fellow, 1964-65; Rockefeller fellow, 1982-83. Mem. MLA. Address: Dept of Eng Wesleyan U Middletown CT 06457

OISTEANU, VALERY, (Eyestone), b. Karaganda, USSR, Sept. 3, 1943, came to U.S., 1973, s. Mihail and Bella (Iosovici) O.; m. Sandra Rosescu, Mar. 23, 1967 (div. 1972); m. 2d, Ruth Friedman, Dec. 3, 1973. Author: Prosthesis, 1970, Underground Shadows, 1977, Underwater Temples, 1979, Do Not Defuse, 1982, Vis-A-Vis Ball, 1985. MS in Chemistry, Polytech. U., Bucharest, Romania, 1966. Producer, host Romanian Radio-TV, Bucharest, 1967-72; announcer Voice of Israel, Tel Aviv, 1972-73; freelance radio journalist, NYC,1973-84; tchr. public schls., NYC,1985—. Served as capt. Romanian Army, 1966-67. Mem. P&W. Home: 170 2d Ave 2A New York NY 10003

OKENSON, LOIS WILEY, b. NYC, Jan. 5, 1919; d. Lewis June and Isabel Augusta (Treen) Wiley; m. George Paul Okeson, May 13, 1944; children—David, Steven, Jeffrey, Neil. Contrbr. articles to Family Motor Coaching, Christian Home, Second Spring. B.A., Montclair State Tchrs. Coll., 1939. With Beauty Counselor and Vanda Cosmetics, Andover, NJ, 1959-79; freelance wrtr., 1979—. Home: Rt. 2 Box 142 Starr SC 29684

OKINS, ELLIOTT EUGENE, b. Auburn, WA, Aug. 27, 1915, s. Elliott Marvin and Lila Muriel (Palmer) O.; m. Antonia Patricia Ojeda, Dec. 23, 1938 (dec. Feb. 6, 1987); children—Lila Rosalie Okins Earnest, Michael Elliott. Author: To Spy or Not To Spy, 1986, How to Care for a Mentally Impaired Person, 1986. Ed., U. N.Mex., Blackstone U. Enlisted U.S. Navy, 1935, advanced through grades to Lt. Cdr., 1955, ret. 1960; served with office of county clrk., San Diego, 1960-75, chief depy. county clrk., 1974-75. Mem. mil. orgns. Home: 871 Bergamont Dr Henderson NV 89015

O'KIRWAN, SEAMUS, b. Albany, NY, May 30, 1950; s. James and Mary (Monahan) Kirwan; divorced; children—Seamus, Mary Shannon. Author corporate annual reports; contrbr. articles to bus. mags. Author: Managing Information Media in the Automated Office, 1983, Shawmut Bank's ABCs of Financing College Education, 1983. B.S., Manhattan Coll. Mgr. news oeprations, Doremus & Co., 1970-74; corp.relations mgr. Merrill Lynch & Co., 1974-76; Dir. editorial services N.Y. State Bankers Assn., 1976-78; administr. financial communications B F Goodrich Co., Akron, OH, 1978—-81; pres. O'Kirwan & Assocs., South Boston, MA, 1981—. Recipient Silver anvil PRSA, 1976, Nichols award Natl. Assn. Investment Clubs, 1979, 80, Mead Library of Ideas award Mead Paper, 1980, Hatch award Boston Ad Club, 1983. Home: 15 Thomas Park South Boston MA 02127

OKRENT, DANIEL, b. Detroit, Apr. 2, 1948, s. Harry and Gizella (Adler) O.; m. Cynthia Boyer, June 23, 1969 (div. 1977); m. 2d, Rebecca Kathryn Lazear, Aug. 28, 1977; children—John Lazear, Lydia Adler. Author: Nine Innings, 1985; contrbr. to Rotisserie League Baseball, 1984; ed.: The Ultimate Baseball Book, 1979; contrbr.: Sports Illustrated, N.Y. Times, Esquire, other publs. BA, U. Mich., 1969. Ed. Alfred A. Knopf, Inc., NYC, 1969-73; editorial dir. Grossman Pubs., NYC, 1973-76; ed.-in-chief Harcourt Brace Jovanovich, NYC, 1976-77; pres. Hilltown Press, Inc., Worthington, Mass., 1977—, Tex. Monthly Press, Inc., Austin, 1979-83; ed., pres. New Eng. Monthly, Inc., Haydenville, Mass., 1983—. Mem. ASME, AG, Soc. Am. Baseball Research. Office: Box 446 Haydenville MA 01039

OLAFSON, HARLAN NESTOR, b. Mpls., May 18, 1928, s. Nestor Olaf and Gladys Evangeline (Lund) O.; m. Joyce Violet Johnson, June 23, 1945; children—Gay, Gary, Lindy Lou. Wrtr., ed. Anvil mag., December mag.; wrtr. So. Oreg. Horse Racing Assn. Newsletter. MA, Maria Sanford JHS, Mpls. Office mgr. Pioneer Aluminum Co., Los Angeles, 1955-58, Heat Engring. and Supply Co., San Gabriel, Calif., 1959-63; v.p., gen. mgr. Indsl. Heater Sales Co., East Los Angeles, 1963-65; natl. sales mgr. Rama Corp., San Jacinto, Calif., 1966-69. Mem. Marxist Hist. Soc., AARP, So. Oreg. Horse Racing Assn. (pres.). Home: 1684 Stringer Gap Rd Grants Pass OR 97527

OLDER, JULIA D., b. Chgo., May 25, 1941; d. David Drake and Martha Louise (Dalrymple) Older. Works include: Oonts and Others (poems), 1982, A Little Wild (poems), 1987; Menus A Trois (with Steve Sherman), BOMC selection, 1987, Endometriosis, 1984, Cooking Without Fuel, 1982, Soup and Bread, 1978, Appalachian Odyssey, 1977. BA, U. of Mich., 1963; MFA, Instituto Allende, Mexico, 1969. Children's book editor, Putnam Pub. Co., NYC,1969-70; editor and reviewer, New Hampshire Times, 1975-77; freelance wrtr. and musician, 1973—. Wrkg. on Hermaphroditus in America (booklength dramatic narrative poem). Mem. PSA, New England Poetry Club. Home: Box 174 Hancock New Hampshire 03449

OLDHAM, JOE, b. Bklyn., Aug. 1, 1943. Editor Car Model OLR Pub., North Arlington, N.J., 1966-68; assoc. editor Automobile Intl. Johnston Intl. Publs., NYC, 1968-70; spcl. projects editor Magnum-Royal Publs., NYC,1970-72; book devel. editor Hearst Corp., NYC,1972-77, editor Motor Mag., 1977-81, exec. editor Popular Mechanics, 1981-85, ed.-in-chief, 1985—. BS, NYU, 1965. Mem. Intl. Motor Press Assn. (pres. 1973-74, 81-82), ASME, Am. Auto Racing Writers and Broadcasting Assn. Office: Hearst 224 W 57th St New York NY 10019

OLDKNOW, ANTONY, b. Peterborough, Eng., Aug. 15, 1939; arrd. US, 1966; s. William Fleming and Gertrude Ada (Webster) O. Author: (poetry) The Lost Allegory, 1966, Positive Poems for Twentieth Century Anglo-Saxons, 1967, Tomcats and Tigertails, 1968, Verses for the Beast, 1971, Sonnets by Oldknow, 1972, Anthem for Rusty Saw and Blue Sky, 1975, Consolation for Beggars, 1978, More Sonnets by Oldknow, 1980, Miniature Clouds, 1982, Ten Small Songs, 1985; fiction: The Rod of the Lord, 1969; transl. Old English: The Seafarer, 1981; ed: Poets of the Red River, 1976; contrbr. poetry, transl. from French and Old English, fiction to Poetry, The Nation, Antioch Rvw, Lit Rvw, Poetry Now, Cutbank, Chelsea, So. Poetry Rvw, Madrona, Samisdat, others. BA, U. Leeds, England, 1961, MEdn, 1963; MS, U. Edinburgh, Scotland, 1964; PhD, U. ND, 1983. Asst. prof. linguistics Univ. Laval, Quebec, Can., 1964-66; asst. prof. English ND State Univ., Fargo, 1966-72; instr. Univ. ND, Grand Forks, 1972-76; academic coordinator Univ. Wis., Stevens Pt, 1976-84 (interrupted); traveling writer Plains Distrib., Fargo, 1980-81; asst. prof. English Mankato State Univ., Minn., 1982-83; instr. English Univ. Kans., Lawrence, 1984-87; asst. prof. Eng. Eastern NM U., Portales, 1987—. Lit. grants panelist, Wis. State Arts Bd., Madison, 1978-82, artists-in-res. program, 1980-84; poets-in-the-schl. program, ND State Arts Bd., Bismarck, 1971-72. Recipient lit. grant ND Arts Bd., 1972, Wis. Arts Bd., 1978, 81; U. ND Poetry Prize, Grand Forks, 1973. Mem. P&W, AWP, MLA. Address: 927 W 16th Ln Portales NM 88130

OLDS, SHARON, b. San Francisco, Nov. 19, 1942. Author: Satan Says, 1980, The Dead and the Living, 1984, The Gold Cell, 1987. BA, Stanford U., 1964; PhD,Columbia U., 1972. Adj. prof., New York U., 1983-86; poetry wrkshp. leader, Sarah Lawrence College, Bronxville, NY, 1984; vis. prof., SUNY, Purchase, NY, 1986; prof., Brandeis U., Waltham, Mass., 1986—. Awards: NEA Fellowship, 1981; Guggenheim Fellowship, 1982; Lamont Award AAP, 1985; Natl. Book Critics Circle Award (Poetry), 1985. Mem. PEN, PSA, AG. Address: Knopf 201 E 50th St New York NY 10022

OLESHANSKY, DAVID SAM, b. Detroit, Feb. 20, 1957; s. Nathan and Ruth (Shumaker) O.; m. Deborah Joan Feinstein, Sept. 14, 1986. Author: I Hear Pancakes Folding, 1986. Contrbr. poems to lit. mags. B. Genl. Studies with distinction, U. Mich., 1978; MFA in Creative Writing, Am. U., 1986. Recipient Hopwood award for poetry U. Mich., 1975, 78. Mem. NCTE. Home: 3414 Rodman St NW Washington DC 20008

OLIPHANT, DAVE, b. Fort Worth, July 18, 1939; s. Mosby Davis and Dorothy Marie (Keetch) O.; m. Maria Isabel Jofre, Jan. 28, 1967; children: Dario Alejandro, Elisa. Author poems: Brands, 1972, Taking Stock, 1973, Lines & Mounds, 1976, The Killdeer Crying, 1977 (ed.), Footprints, 1978, Austin, 1985; ed. The New Breed, 1973, Washing the Cow's Skull, 1981; essays: On a High Horse, 1983; transl.: If Poetry Is to Be Written Right, 1977; text: Civilization & Barbarism, 1979. Ed. Prickly Pear Press. MA, U. Tex.-Austin, 1964-65; PhD, N. Ill. U.-DeKalb, 1969-74; asst. prof. English dept. Univ. Tex., Austin, 1976-78; sr. ed. Harry Ransom Humanities Research Center, Austin, 1979—. Mem. Tex. Inst. Letters. Address: 1402 Mimosa Pass Cedar Park TX 78613

OLIVER, LINDA, see Bell, Victor L.

OLIVER, MARY, b. Maple Heights, OH, Sept. 10, 1935; d. Edward William and Helen Marie (Vlasak) O.; Author: No Voyage and Other Poems, 1963, enlarged ed., 1965, The River Styx, Ohio, 1972, The Night Traveler, 1978, Twelve Moons, 1979, American Primitive, 1983, Dream Work, 1986. Student, Ohio State U., 1955-56, Vassar Coll., 1956-57. Chmn. writing dept. Fine Arts Work Center, Provincetown, 1972, 73, mem. writing com., 1984. Yale Rvw Recipient Shelley Meml. award, 1970; Cleve. Arts prize for lit., 1979; Achievement award AAIAL, 1983; Pulitzer prize for poetry, 1984; others. NEA fellow, 1972-73; Guggenheim fellow, 1980-81. Mem. PSA, PEN. Home: Box 338 Provincetown MA 02657

OLIVER-PICKETT, CHERYL KAY, b. Oklahoma City, OK, Aug. 27, 1949; d. William Riley and Sara Elizabeth (Lewis) Foster; m. Jerry Clinton Oliver, Jan. 3, 1969 (div. Nov. 1973); 1 dau., Charlotte Maja; m. Richard Philip Pickett, Jan. 14, 1977. Contrbr. articles to profl. jnls. B.A., Central State U., 1978; postgrad. Metropolitan State Coll., 1980-83. With Veterans Administration Hosp., Oklahoma City, 1977-78; bookkeeper Colo. Med. Center, Denver, 1979; researcher U. Colo. Health Scis. Center, Denver, 1979—. Home: 1859 Niagara St Denver CO 80220

OLMSTED, ROBERT WALSH, (Richard S. Danbury III), b. Washington, Mar. 15, 1936; s. Victo Hugo and Frances Nicholas (Walsh) O.; m. Elaine Bennett, May 7, 1958; children: Lori O. Bowman, Suzanne O. Helms, Julie Elizabeth, James Robert Mason. Author: Northern Lights, 1969, First Christmas Ever, 1973, Shadows on Casseopia, 1976, Wild Strawberries at 3,000 feet, 1986; editor numerous books; author poems and short stories. BA, Mansfield State U., 1969; MA, U. Maine, 1971; PhD, U. Mass., 1981. Pres. Conservatory of Am. Letters, editor Northwoods Press, Thomaston, Maine, 1972-86; exec., mng. editor Conservatory Am. Letters, Thomaston, 1986—. Served with USAF, 1955-58. Office: Box 88 Thomaston ME 04861

OLNEY, JAMES, b. Marathon, IA, July 12, 1933; s. Norris G. and Doris B. (Hawk) O.; 1 child, Nathan. Author: Metaphors of Self: The Meaning of Autobiography, 1972; Tell Me Africa: An Approach to African Literature, 1973; The Rhizome and the Flower: The Perennial Philosophy—Yeats and Jung, 1980; ed.: Autobiography: Essays Theoretical and Critical, 1980. BA, State U. Iowa, 1955; MA, Columbia U., 1958, PhD, 1963. Fulbright lectr. Cuttington Coll., Liberia, 1967-69; vis. prof. Northwestern U., 1974, Amherst Coll., 1978-79; prof. English, N.C. Central U., Durham, 1970-83; Voorhies prof. English, La. State U., Baton Rouge, 1983—, ed. Southeern Review. NEH sr. fellow, 1975-76; fellow Guggenheim Fdn., 1980-81, Natl. Humanities Ctr., 1980-81. Mem. MLA. Home: 1744 Pollard Pkwy Baton Rouge LA 70808

OLSEN, DONALD D., b. Mpls., Aug. 7, 1931; s. Harold D. and Marion (Kelly) Olsen; m. Miriam V. Anderson, Mar. 13, 1960; children—Kristen, Eric, Frederick, Sten, Jonathan. Poetry contrbr. to Minnesota Rvw, Tennessee Poetry Jnl, Great Lakes Rvw, Crazy Horse, Spoon River Qtly, other lit mags; editor/publisher: established Ox Head Press, 1966. BA, U. of Minnesota, 1959, MA, 1964. Librarian U. of Minnesota (Morris, MN), 1964-65; acquisitions librarian U. of Wisconsin (Menomonie, WI), 1965-69, Southwest State U. (Marshall, MN), 1969—. Sgt., US Army, 1951-53, US. Home: Rt 3 Box 136 Browerville MN 56438

OLSEN, HUMPHREY ADONIRAM, b. Caterham, Surrey, Eng., Sept. 3, 1909; came to US, 1916; s. Alfred Berthier and Mary Henrietta Huntington (Poole) O.; m. Grace Elizabeth Elliott, Feb. 1, 1948; 1 dau., Alice Rosemary. Ed. and pub.: Snowy Egret (lit. natural history mag.), 1922, Artful Codger, 1984-86; contrbr. biology book rvws., Choice, 1964-70. BA, U. Mich., 1931, A.M.L.S., 1946; MA in Edn., U. Ky., 1941. Librarian and English tchr. Pikeville Coll., Pikeville, KY., 1949-56, Shorter Coll., Rome, Ga., 1957-62. Vincennes Univ., Vincennes, Ind., 1962-67, Cumberland Coll., Williamsburg, Ky., 1968-75. Mem. Choice (editorial council 1967-69), Wilson Ornithol. Soc., Ky. Ornithol. Soc. Home: 107 S 8th St Williamsburg KY 40769

OLSEN, RICHARD ELLISON, b. NYC, Feb. 2, 1941; s. Harold Burgher and Gladys Estelle (Ellison) O. Author: Karl Marx, 1978. BS, Union Coll., 1958-62; MA, Brown U., 1969, PhD, 1971. Prof. Adelphi Univ., Garden City, NY, 1971—. Served as Health Service officer, USPHS, 1963-65, Las Vegas. Mem. Am. Philo. Assn. Address: 1 Univ Pl 15N New York NY 10003

OLSEN, TILLIE, b. NE, Jan. 14, 1912; d. Samuel and Ida (Beber) Lerner; m. Jack Olsen; children—Karla, Julie, Kathie, Laurie. Author: Tell Me A Riddle, 1962, Yonnonidio: From the Thirties, 1974, Rebecca Harding Davis: Life in the Iron Mills, 1973, Silences, 1978; short fiction published in 61 anthologies. Grad. high schl. Writer-in-res. or vis. faculty English Amherst Coll., 1969-70, Stanford U., 1972, M.I.T., 1973-74, U. Mass., Boston, 1974; cons. on lit.; reader and lectr. Recipient NEA award, 1967; Am. Acad. Natl. Inst. award for distinguished contrbn. to Am. letters, 1975; Ford Fdn. grantee, 1959, Stanford writing fellow, 1956; Radcliffe Inst. fellow, 1962-64; Guggenheim fellow, 1975-76. Mem. AG, PEN. Home: 1435 Laguna St San Francisco CA 94115

OLSEN, W. SCOTT, b. Kansas City, MO, Nov. 6, 1958, s. Fred and Joyce Jean (Ansel) O.; m. Maureen Ann Kliegel, June 8, 1985. Contrbr. stories to Ozark Rvw, Midlands, Uncle, Pulpsmith, Unknowns, Kans. Qtly. BA, U. Mo., 1979, MA, 1981; MFA, U. Mass., 1985. Vis. asst. prof. Lander Coll., Greenwood, S.C., 1985—, ed. New Voices, 1986; presenter papers to profl. confs. Mem. MLA, NCTE, P&W. Home: 225 Rock Knoll Dr Greenwood SC 29646

OLSON, CLARENCE ELMER, JR., b. Edgerton, WI, July 1, 1927; s. C. Elmer and Helen (Turnbull) O.; m. Arielle North, Sept. 4, 1954; children—Randall Jack, Christina North, Jens Sterling Elmer. News editor Edgerton Reporter, 1953; photographer, writer Madison (Wis.) Capitol Times, 1953-59; writer St. Louis Post-Dispatch Pictures mag., 1959-65, asst. editor, 1965-68; asst. mng. editor Careers Today mag., Delmar, Calif., 1968-69; book editor St. Louis Post-Dispatch, 1969—. BS, U. Wis., 1950. Served with USNR, 1945-46. Mem. Natl. Book Critics Circle. Home: 236 N Elm Ave Webster Groves MO 63119

OLSON, CLAYTON LEO, b. NYC, May 1, 1947, s. Clayton Telesphore and Helen Veronica (Sullo) O. Co-pub. Food Combining Simplified, 1983, Food Combining Recipe Book, 1985. Student Miami Dade Coll., 1974-75, St. Michael's Coll., Winooski, Vt., 1965-69. Pres. William James Work Co., Santa Cruz, Calif., 1977-79; dir. William James Assn., Santa Cruz, 1979—; pres., newsletter ed. The Fruition Project, Santa Cruz, 1979—. Office: Box 7800 Santa Cruz CA 95061

OLSON, JANE VIRGINIA, b. Chgo., Dec. 14, 1916; d. Oscar Wilford and Mary (Bowles) O.; m. William M. Gooden, Feb. 16, 1955 (div. 1957). Copy editor Atlantic Monthly mag., Boston, 1942-46; copy editor Vogue mag., NYC, 1946-49; tech. editor Ill. Geol. Survey, Urbana, 1949-55; sci. and social sci. editor Yale U. Press, New

Haven, 1958-69; editor Am. Scientist mag., New Haven, 1969-80, sr. cons. editor, 1981—. BA, U. N.Mex., 1939. Home: 60 Ardmore St Hamden CT 06517

OLSON, KAY MELCHISEDECH, b. Nov. 16, 1948; d. John William and Carol Louise (Born) Melchisedech; m. John Olson, Sept. 5, 1970 (div.); children—Jennifer Marie, Nathan John. Author, Day Trips (travel guide). BA, U. MN, 1971. News ed. Post Nwsprs., New Hope, MN, 1971-73; ed. National Car Rental, Mpls., 1974-76; free-lance writer, 1976-82; ed. Garden Supply Retailer, Mpls., 1982—. Mem. Garden Writers Assn. Am., Am. Assn. Nurserymen. Office: Garden Supply 12400 Whitewater Dr Minnetonka MN 55343

OLSON, KIRBY, b. Mason City, IA, Sept. 16, 1956, s. Arne Leroy and Joanne Barbara (Wilson) O.; m. Joellyn Jean Rock, Aug. 2, 1983. Contrbr. to Oink!, Grimoire, Pinchpenny, Fat Tuesday, other lit mags.; translator works of Philippe Soupault; ed. small press mag. Future Tense. BA, Evergreen State Coll., 1979. Secy. U. Wash., Seattle, 1981—. Mem. CODA, P&W. Office: Box 959 Seattle WA 98111

OLSON, LAWRENCE, b. Memphis, May 7, 1918; s. Lawrence A. and Wanda (Liddell) O.; m. Jeane E. Noordhoff, Dec. 19, 1941; children: Alexandra Lyman, Sarah Liddell. Author: The Cranes on Dying River and Other Poems, 1947, Dimensions of Japan, 1963, Japan in Postwar Asia, 1970. BA, U. Miss., 1938; MA, Harvard U., 1939, PhD, 1955. Served to lt. (j.g.) USN, 1942-46. Ford fellow, 1952-54; Rockefeller fellow, 1963; Fulbright research fellow Japan, 1973-74; Woodrow Wilson Intl. Center for Scholars fellow, 1979-80. Home: Box O Middle Haddam CT 06456

OLSON, LYNN, b. Chgo., March 23; s. Ellen (Nelson) Olson. Author: Classroom Tested Techniques for Elementary Teachers, 1973, Sculpting with Cement; Direct Modeling in a Permanent Medium, 1981, 82, 83, 85, 87; writer/illustr. numerous mag. articles. Sculptor, wrkg. with original techniques for direct cement sculpture. Home: 4607 Claussen Ln Valparaiso IN 46383

OLSON, MARK WILLIAM, b. Chgo., July 3, 1946; s. David Cornelius and Dorothy Ilene (Pomeroy) O.; m. Joan Lea Toms, Aug. 17, 1969. BA, Wheaton Coll., 1968; M.Div., Bethel Theol. Sem., 1971; MS in Journalism, Northwestern U., 1972. Editorial asst. Venture Mag., Wheaton, Ill., 1965-66, Harvest Publs., Chgo., 1966-68; freelance writer, 1972; sr. high editor David C. Cook Pub. Co., Elgin, Ill., 1973-74; mng. editor The Other Side Mag., Phila., 1974-77, editor, 1977—. Mem. Associated Church Press, Evang. Press Assn. Home: 1405 Sunken Rd Box 3948 Fredericksburg VA 22402

OLSON, RICHARD GEORGE, b. St. Paul, Nov. 4, 1940; s. George Henry and Lenore Marie (Dickhudt) O.; m. Kathleen Tina Argento, June 23, 1962; 1 dau., Karlin Marie. Author: Science as Metaphor, 1970, Scottish Philosophy and British Physics, 1975, Science Deified and Science Defied, 1982. BS, Harvey Mudd Coll., 1962; MA, Harvard U., 1963, PhD,1967. NEH Younger Humanist fellow. Home: 5869 Sunset Ranch Rd Riverside CA 92506

OLSON, TOBY, b. Berwyn, IL, Aug. 17, 1937; s. Merle Theodore Olson and Elizabeth (Skowbo) Potokar; m. Anne Yeomans, 1963 (div.); m. Miriam Meltzer, Nov. 27, 1967. Author: (novels) The Life of Jesus, 1976, Seaview, 1982, The Woman Who Escaped from Shame, 1986, Utah, 1987; (poetry) We Are the Fire, 1984; ed. Writing Talks, 1983. BA, Occidental Coll., 1965; MA, L.I. U., 1968. Assoc. dir. Aspen Wrtrs.' Workshop, Colo., 1964-68; asst. prof. L.I. U., Bklyn, 1968-74; mem. faculty New Schl. for Social Research, 1966-73; prof. English, Temple U., Phila., 1975—. Served with USN, 1957-63. Recipient award in poetry CAPS, 1974; PEN/Faulkner award PEN South, 1983; fellow in fiction Pa. Council on Arts, 1983, NEA, 1985, Guggenheim Fdn., 1985, Rockefeller Fdn. Fellow, 1987. Mem. PEN Am. Ctr., P&W. Home: 329 S Juniper St Philadelphia PA 19107

OLSZTYNSKI, JAMES C., b. Chgo., Feb. 23, 1947; s. John W. and Frances (Krawczyk) O.; m. Jennifer Cox, June 17, 1972; children—Kathryn Louise, Ellen Frances. Contrbr. to Chgo. Tribune, Reader, New Petroleum Retailer, Nutshell, Chgo. Illini. BA, U. IL, 1974; MA, U. IL, 1979. Assoc. ed. Supply House Times, Skokie, IL, 1977-83; ed. Plumbing & Mechanical, Skokie, 1983—. Served to Sp4, U.S. Army, 1966-68. Home: 1229 Washington Ave Wilmette IL 60091

OLVERA, JOE, b. El Paso, TX, July 21, 1944, s. Dario Ceniceros and Francisca (Jimenez) O.; div.; children—Nila, Malintzin. Author: Voces de la gente, 1972, Chicanismo: A Culture Trip, 1981; Drugs: Frankly Speaking, 1982, High Times: The Effects of Drugs in Humans, 1982, Strange Dream in Calexico Motel Room, 1986, Book of Thailand. Grad. U. Tex.-El Paso; postgrad., Columbia U. Editorial asst. Tonatinh/Punta Sol, Berkeley, Calif., 1975-78; trng. devel. specialist Southwest Trng. Inst., El Paso, 1978-82; reporter, columnist Herald-Post, El Paso, 1982-85; exec. dir. Fourth Estate Cons., El Paso, 1985—; cand. for mayor, El Paso, 1985. Recipient Drama award Colo. Council for Spanish Surnamed, 1972, investigative reporting award UPI, 1984; grantee NEH, 1981. Mem. Natl. Assn. Hispanic Journalists (founding mem.), P&W. Home: 9206 Yucatan St El Paso TX 79907

OMAN, ELIZABETH ANN, b. Hibbing, MN, Mar. 1, 1940; d. Wanner Godfrey and Florence (Engstrom) Oman; m. L. James Fletcher, July 10, 1975; stepchildren—Roderich, Patricia, Douglas. Contrbr. articles to computer, genealogy, travel mags., newspapers. Wrkg. on travel and computer articles. B.A., Carleton Coll., 1962; M.A., U. Minn., 1964. Instr. U. Minn., Duluth, 1967-69; asst. prof. U. Wis., Stevens Point, 1970-74, Nebr. Wesleyan U., Lincoln, 1974-75; free-lance wrtr., 1984—. Active Lindsborg Arts Council, KS, 1984—, AAUW, 1985—. Recipient 3d place for essay Minn. Police OFficers, 1956. Home: 800 N Second Lindsborg KS 67456

O'MARA, DEBORAH LYNN, b. Chgo., Oct. 17, 1957; d. Frank Bishop and Eva Rose (Spitz) Rothman; m. James Patrick O'Mara; 1 son, James Joseph. Columnist: Security Gazette, England, 1984-87. contrbr. to Collectibles Illustrated. Ed.: ICG Railroad, Chgo., 1979-83; mng. ed.: Cahners Pub., des Plaines, IL, 1983—. B.S. in Jnlsm., Northern Ill. U., 1979. Recipient Neal award Assn. Bus. Press Eds., 1983-87, Best News/Photography award Assn. Railroad Eds., 1982, 83, Cahners Achievement award Cahners Pub. Co., 1986. Mem. SPJ, Chgo. Assn. Bus. Press Eds. Home: 6132 Overhill Chicago IL 60631

O'MARA MC MAHON, PEGGY NORREEN, b. Kenosha, WI, May 14, 1947; d. Oliver Edward and Ruth Helen (Slater) O'Mara; m. John William McMahon, May 27, 1973; children: Lally, Finnie, Bram, Nora. Ed.: Mothering Mag., 1980—, Immunization Booklet, Circumcision Booklet, Midwifery and the Law; ed. and contrbr.: Mother Poet, Poetry and Photography anthology, 1983; contrbr. intro.: Ended Beginnings, 1984. BS, U. Wis., Milw., 1970. Spcl. edn. tchr. Zia Schl., Alamogordo, N.Mex., 1972-73; MBA coordinator U. Utah, Holloman AFB, N.Mex., 1973; freelance writer, 1974—; ed. Mothering Mag., Albuquerque, 1978-79. Bd. dirs. Midwifery Trng. Inst., Albuquerque, 1984—; consumer mem., N.Mex. Midwifery Adv. Bd., Sante Fe, 1985—. Recipient 1st place award Natl. Fedn. Press Women, 1984. Mem. Natl. Assn. Homebased Businesswomen, N.Mex. Press Women (1st place ed. award, 1984, 1st place page layout award, 1984). Address: Rt 7 Box 124K Sante Fe NM 87505

O'MAREY, RAUGETTZ, see Aquila, Napolean E. M.

OMBU, CLAUDIO, see Keating, John Roderick

O'MEL, LORI, see Harrell, Lori O'Mel

O'MORAIN, SEAN, see Moran, John Charles

OMURA, JAMES MATSUMOTO, b. Winslow, WA, Nov. 27, 1912; s. Tsurumatsu and Harue (Higashi) Matsumoto; widowed; children—Yoshito (dec.), Utaka (James M.), Hanako, Taeko, Chikara (dec.); m. 2d. Haruko (Motoishi); children: Gregg, Kiyoshi, Wayne Stanley. Contrbr. articles, critiques, rvws., commentaries, short stories, poems, essays to mags., newspapers. Ed.: New Japanese Am. News, 1933-34, New World Daily News, 1934-35, New World Sun, 1935-36; ed., pub.: Current Life Mag., 1940-42; ed., public relations Rocky Shimpo Tri-Weekly, 1944, 47. Wrkg. on memoirs. Grad. public schls., Seattle. Pres. Omura Landscape Service, Denver, 1946-79. Widely known as lone Japanese-American voice against World War II eviction of Japanese-Americans from West Coast, and their subsequent war-long detention in camps. Home: 1455 S Irving St Denver CO 80219

ONEAL, JOSEPH ALLEN, see Hughes, Walter J., Sr.

O'NEAL, REAGAN, see Rigney, James Oliver, Jr.

O'NEAL, WINSTON JAMES, JR., b. Fort Wayne, IN, Nov. 25, 1948; s. Winston James and Mary Margaret (Burns) O'N.; m. Amelia van Singel, July 11, 1970. Contrbr. to books and periodicals: Blues Who's Who, Down Beat, Rolling Stone, Chicago Defender, Chicago Reader, Chicago Tribune, Blues Unlimited, Boston Real Paper, Melody Maker, 1969—. BSJ, Northwestern U., 1970, MSJ, 1974. Co-pub. Living Blues Mag., Chgo., 1970-83, co-ed., 1970—. Pubns.ed. Ctr. Study Southern Culture, 1986—. Mem. Blues Fdn., Natl. Acad. Recording Arts & Scis. Home: Box 1771 University MS 38667

O'NEIL, WAYNE, b. Kenosha, WI, Dec. 22, 1931; s. L.J. and Kathryn (Obermeyer) O'N.; married; children—Scott Leslie, Patrick Sean, Elizabeth Erla. Author: (in Chinese) English Transformational Grammar, 1981, Linguistics and Applied Linguistics, 1983; contrbr. articles to profl. jnls. AB, U. Wis., 1955, AM, 1956, PhD, 1960. Served with U.S. Army, 1952-54. Fulbright fellow in Iceland, 1961; ACLS study fellow M.I.T., 1964-65. Mem. Linguistic Soc. Am., MLA. Office: MIT Dept Linguistics Cambridge MA 02139

O'NEILL, PETER J., b. Cullins, County Sligo, Ireland, came to U.S., 1930, s. Michael and Ellen (Grady) O'N.; m. Bridie Queenan, Nov. 25, 1936; children—Peter J. II, Margaret, Patricia, Teresa. Author: Geneological History of the O'Neills of Ulster, Ireland, 1984. Ed. in Ireland. Columnist Irish World, NYC, 1974-84. Home: Box 56 Freehold NY 12431

O'NEILL, WILLIAM LAWRENCE, b. Big Rapids, MI, Apr. 18, 1935; s. John Patrick and Helen Elizabeth (Marsh) O'N.; m. Elizabeth Carol Knollmueller, Aug. 20, 1960; children—Cassandra Leigh, Catherine Lorraine. Author: Divorce in the Progressive Era, 1967, Everyone Was Brave: The Rise and Fall of Feminism in America, 1969, Coming Apart: An Informal History of America in the 1960s, 1971, The Last Romantic: A Life of Max Eastman, 1978, A Better World: The Great Schism: Stalinism and the American Intellectuals, 1982, American High: The Years of Confidence, 1945-60, 1986. AB, U. Mich., 1957; MA, U. Calif., Berkeley, 1958, PhD,1963. NEH fellow, 1979-80. Home: 232 Harrison Ave Highland Park NJ 08904

OPPENHEIM, LUCY LINDA, b. Greenwich, CT, Dec. 4, 1959; d. Philip Morris and Isadora (Becker) O. Contrbr. articles, rvws. to newspapers, mags. Ed.: Mental Health Assn. of Anne Arundel County Newsletter, 1986; coal industry reports. A.A. in Genl. Studies, Tompkins-Cortland Commun. Coll., 1978; B.A. in Liberal Arts, St. John's Coll., 1982. Assoc. ed. The Publick Enterprise, Annapolis, MD, 1984-85; production asst., Pasha Pubs., Roslyn, VA, 1985-86; free-lance wrtr., ed., 1986—. Mem. Washington Ind. Wrtrs. Address: 17C Heritage Ct Annapolis MD 21401

OPPENHEIMER, JOEL LESTER, b. Yonkers, NY, Feb. 18, 1930; s. Leopold and Kate Blanche (Rosenwasser) O.; m. Rena Mary Margaret Julia Ann Furlong, June 5, 1952 (div. June 1959); children—Nicholas Patrick, Daniel Eben; m. 2d, Helen Joan Bukberg, June 5, 1966 (div. Nov. 1977); children—Nathaniel Ezra, Lemuel Shandy Davin, Theresa Maria; m 3d, Theresa Marie Maier. Nov. 10, 1984. Author: poems The Dutiful Son, 1956, The Love Bit, 1961, In Time, 1969, On Occasion, 1973, The Woman Poems, 1975, Names, Dates, and Places, 1979, Just Friends/Friends and Lovers, 1980, At Fifty, 1982, New Spaces, 1985; play The Great American Desert, 1961; non-fiction The Wrong Season, 1973, Marilyn Lives!, 1981; lectures, Poetry The Ecology of the Soul, 1983; stories Pan's Eyes, 1974. Student, Cornell U., 1947-48, U. Chgo., 1948-49, Black Mountain Coll., 1950-53. Freelance writer, 1966—; columnist Village Voice, 1970-84, NH Times, 1985-87; dir. Poetry Project, St. Mark's Chapbook. in the Bowery, 1966-68, Tchrs. and Writers Collaborative, 1969; poet-in-residence City Coll., CUNY, 1969-82; assoc. prof. New England Coll., 1982—; vis. poet St. Andrews Presbyn. Coll., 1977—. CAPS Program grantee N.Y. State Council on Arts, 1971; NEA fellow, 1979, 80. Mem. AG, PSA, PEN. Home: Box 281 Henniker NH 03242

OPRE, THOMAS EDWARD, b. Evansville, IN, Nov. 6, 1943; s. William Jennings and Ruth (Strouss) O.; m. Norlin Kay Hartley, June 20, 1965; children—Thomas Andrew, William Hartley. Author numerous articles in outdoor and travel fields. Sports and outdoor writer Decatur (Ill.) Herald & Rvw, 1965-66; outdoor editor Detroit Free Press, 1966—; midwest field editor Field and Stream mag., 1971-81; editorial dir. Gt. Lakes Sportsman mag., 1972-75; editor-at-large and sports vehicles editor Outdoor Life mag., 1981—. AB in Journalism, Ind. U., 1965. Natl. Writer's award Safari Club Intl., 1977, Deep Woods Writing award OWAA, 1977. Intl. Wildlife Fdn. Award, 1983, Environmental Quality Award, EPA, 1979. Mem. Outdoor Writers Assn. Am., Assn. Gt. Lakes Outdoor Writers, Mich. Outdoor Writers Assn. Home: 6193 Kinyon Dr Brighton MI 48116

ORBEN, ROBERT, b. NYC, Mar. 4, 1927; s. Walter August and Marie (Neweceral) O.; m. Jean Louise Connelly, July 25, 1945. Author: The Encyclopedia of One-Liner Comedy, 1971, 2500 Jokes to Start 'Em Laughing, 1979, 2100 Laughs for All Occasions, 1983, 2400 Jokes to Brighten Your Speeches, 1984, numerous other books of humor for performers and public speakers. Humor and speech writer for entertainment personalities, bus. execs., politicians, 1946—; speechwriter Pres. Gerald R. Ford, 1974-75; spcl. asst. to pres., dir. White House speechwriting dept., Washington, 1976-77; editor Orben's Current Comedy, Wilmington, Del., 1971—; lectr. in field, cons. in field. TV writer: Jack Paar Show, 1962-63, Red Skelton Hour, 1964-70; Mem. WG. Address: 1200 N Nash St Arlington VA 22209

OREAR, JAY, b. Chgo., Nov. 6, 1925; s. Leslie and Edna (Tragnitz) O.; m. Jeanne Bliven, Mar. 10, 1951; children—Scott, Robin, Wendy; m. Virginia Watts, Sept. 6, 1974. Author: Nuclear Physics, 1951, Fundamental Physics, 1961, Programmed Manual, 1963, Statistics for Physicists, 1958, Physics, 1979. Ph.B., U. Chgo., 1944, PhD, 1953. Served with USNR, 1944-46. Fellow Am. Phys. Soc. (editor Forum Newsletter 1972—). Home: 20 Sun Path Ithaca NY 14850

O'REILLY, JACKSON, see Rigney, James Oliver, Jr.

O'REILLY, SUE ANN, b. Zanesville, OH, Apr. 1, 1950; d. Clyde E. and Margaret A. (Pfiefer) Perine; m. Thomas M. O'Reilly, July 21, 1973; children—Sean, Kelly. Columnist: Around Our House, 1985-86. Contrbr. numerous feature stories to newspapers. B.S. in Interperonal Communication, Ohio U., 1972; postgrad. Miami U., 1978-85. Social worker Goodwill Ind., Zanesville, 1973-74; bookkeeper, Central Trust Co., Zanesville, 1975-76; stringer Fairfield Echo, OH, 1985-86, Oxford Press, OH, 1987—. Home: 3127 Harris Rd Hamilton OH 45013

OREKA, DONNA, see Jakubowski, Donna Marie

OREL, HAROLD, b. Boston, Mar. 31, 1926; s. Saul and Sarah (Wicker) O.; m. Charlyn Hawkins, May 25, 1951; children—Sara Elinor, Timothy Ralston. Author: Thomas Hardy's Epic-Drama: A Study of "The Dynasts," 1963, The Development of William Butler Yeats, 1885-1900, 1968, English Romantic Poets and the Enlightenment: Nine Essays on a Literary Relationship, in Studies in Voltaire and the Eighteenth Century, vol. CIII, 1973, The Final Years of Thomas Hardy, 1912-1928, 1976, Victorian Literary Critics, 1984, The Literary Achievement of Rebecca West, 1986, The Victorian Short Story, 1986, The Unknown Thomas Hardy: Lesser-Known Aspects of Hardy's Life and Career, 1987; contrbg. author: Thomas Hardy and the Modern World, 1974, The Genius of Thomas Hardy, 1976, Budmouth Essays on Thomas Hardy, 1976; co-editor: The Thomas Hardy Rev, 1975—; editor: The World of Victorian Humor, 1961, Six Essays in Nineteenth Century English Literature and Thought, 1962, Thomas Hardy's Personal Writings: Prefaces, Literary Opinions, Reminiscences, 1966, British Poetry 1880-1920: Edwardian Voices, 1969, The Nineteenth-Century Writer and his Audience, 1969, Irish History and Culture, 1976, The Dynasts (Thomas Hardy), 1978, The Scottish World, 1981, Rudyard Kipling: Interviews and Recollections, 2 vols., 1983, Victorian Short Stories, 1987. BA cum laude, U. N.H., 1948; MA, U. Mich., 1949, PhD,1952; postgrad., Harvard U., 1949. Teaching fellow U. Mich., 1948-52. Served with USN, 1944-46. Grantee ACLS, 1966; NEH grantee, 1975; grantee Am. Philo. Soc., 1964, 80. Home: 713 Schwarz Rd Lawrence KS 66044

ORESICK, PETER MICHAEL, b. Ford City, PA, Sept. 8, 1955; s. Peter and Mary (Gernat) O.; m. Stephanie Flom, Nov. 26, 1977; children—William, Jacob, David. Author: The Story of Glass, 1977, Other Lives, 1985, An American Peace, 1985. BA, U. Pitts., 1977, MFA, 1981. Tchr. Pitts. pub. schs., 1978-80; adj. faculty U. Pitts., 1982—; mgr. mkgt. and promotion U. Pitts. Press, 1985—. Recipient prize AAP, 1980; fellow Pa. Arts Council, 1984. Mem. AWP. Office: Press 127 N Bellefield Ave Pittsburgh PA 15260

ORFALEA, GREGORY MICHAEL, b. Los Angeles, Aug. 9, 1949, s. Aref Joseph and Rose Mary (Awad) O.; m. Eileen Margaret Rogers, Aug. 4, 1984; 2 sons, Matthew Rogers and Andrew Aref. Author books: Pictures at an Exhibition, 1977, Before the Flames: A Quest for the History of Arab Americans, 1988, The Capital of Solitude, 1988; monographs: Arms Build-Up in the Middle East, 1981, U.S.-Arab Relations: The Literary Dimensions, 1984; contrbr. essays, poems, fiction to numerous lit mags and anthols; editor: Three Sisters Mag., 1971-72, Annual Report, Greater Anchorage Area Borough Dept. of Parks and Recreation, 1974, With a Bandage I Manage, 1978, Wrapping the Grapeleaves, 1982, (with Sharif Elmusa) Grape Leaves, 1988. AB in English, Georgetown U., 1971; MFA, U. Alaska, 1974. Jnlst. Northern Va. Sun, Arlington, 1971-72; instr. English, Santa Barbara City Coll., Calif., 1974-76; Artist in Residence, Miramonte Elem. Schl., Los Angeles, 1977-78; tchr. Emerson Prep. Schl., Washington, 1984-85; wrtr.-ed. Dept. of Commerce, Washington, 1985-86; wrtr. -ed. SBA, Washington, DC, 1986—. Grants: Calif. Arts Council, 1977, Middle East Peace Research Inst., 1983, Fdn. for Transnational Projects, 1985; first prize, World Lebanese Cultural Union, Beirut, 1975; Edmund A. Bunn Award for Journalistic Excellence, Georgetown U., 1971. Mem. PSA. Home: 1778 Hobart St NW Washington DC 20009

ORFIELD, OLIVIA FULLER, b. Charleston, SC, Apr. 5, 1922; d. Rex George Fuller and Olivia Moorer (Connor) Fuller Hogue; m. Horace Maxwell ("Barney") Orfield, Aug. 5, 1950; children—John Erik and Daniel Gregory. Author: Death Trap, 1979, Uses of Love, Bird of Paradise on the Far Side of Echo (plays); Vortex, 1981, The Nose of Low. BA with Honours in Engl., Rice U., 1943. Secy. to exec. dir. AP, New York, 1943-44; asst. to asst. to pub. Newsweek, New York 1944-45; "Girl Friday" to theatre prod. Alfred de Liagre, Jr., New York, 1945-

47; MS. rdr. Bobbs- Merrill's Yg. People's Books, New York, 1969-70; ed. prism press, Houston, TX, 1980—. Mem. Authors Unltd. of Houst., DG, IWWG. Home: 11706 Longleaf Ln Houston TX 77024

ORGEL, STEPHEN (KITAY), b. NYC, Apr. 11, 1933; s. Samuel Zachary and Esther (Kitay) O. Author: the Jonsonian Masque, 1965, (with Roy Strong) Inigo Jones, 1973, The Illusion of Power, 1975; editor: Ben Jonson's Masques, 1969, Marlowe's Poems and Translations, 1971, The Renaissance Imagination, 1981; editor-in-chief: English Literary History, 1980-85. AB, Columbia, 1954; PhD,(Woodrow Wilson fellow), Harvard, 1959. ACLS fellow, 1968, 73; NEH sr. fellow, 1982-83. Mem. MLA, Renaissance Soc. Am., Shakespeare Assn. Am. Office: Dept Eng Stanford U Stanford CA 94305

ORLEN, STEVE, b. Holyoke, MA, Jan. 12, 1942; s. Milton H. and B. Florence (Belkin) Orlen; m. Gail Barbara Marcus, Aug. 11, 1969; 1 child, Cozi Andreas Marcus Orlen. Author: Sleeping On Doors, 1976, Separate Creatures, 1977, Permission to Speak, 1978, A Place At The Table, 1981; poetry in New English and U.S. Poems, 1977, The Ardis Anthology of New American Poetry, 1977, other anthols. BA, U. of Mass., 1964; MFA, U. of Ia., 1965-67. Prof., U. of Arizona, Tucson, 1967—. Awards: NEA Fellowship, 1974, 1980, 1985. Mem. PSA. Home: 436 South Fifth Tucson AZ 85701

O'RILEY, PATRICK ADELBERT, b. Hudson, SD, Arp. 20, 1941; s. Robert Charles and Dorothy Veronne (Miller) O.; m. Janice Kay Howe, July 29, 1981; 1 dau., Kimberly. Contrbr. poems, short stories to lit. mags. including Hueuos Southwest, Conceptions Southwest, Blue Spruce Jnl. B.U.S., U. NM, 1986. Served to E-3 U.S. Army, 1957-63. Home: 625 Grove St SE "C" Albuquerque NM 87108

ORLOCK, CAROL E., b. San Diego, Feb. 17, 1947, d. James C. and Anna Elizabeth (Saylor) Gibson; m. John Orlock (div.). Novelist: The Goddess Letters, 1987; contrbr. stories to Calyx, Clinton St. Qtly, Iron Country Anthology, other publs. BA, Pa. State U., 1968; MA, San Francisco State Coll., 1968. Instr. Olympic Coll., Bremerton, Wash., 1974-78; lectr. U. Wash. Extension, Seattle, 1976—, coordinator wrtg. program, 1982—. Wash. State Arts Commn. Fiction Wrtg. fellow, 1984-85; recipient Publ. Project award King County Arts Commn., 1985-86. Mem. Feminist Wrtrs. Guild. Home: 920 2d Ave W Seattle WA 98119

ORNSTEIN, ROBERT, b. NYC, Nov. 3, 1925; s. Max and Frances (Saphire) O.; m. Doris L. Robbins, Aug. 19, 1951; children—Suzanne Ruth, Lisa, Adam Samuel. Author: The Moral Vision of Jacobean Tragedy, 1960, A Kingdom for a Stage, 1972; also articles; films A Poet's World, 1973, Sidewalks and Similes, 1973, Dead Ends and New Dreams, 1973, In the Last Days, 1973; author, producer, dir.: ednl. films Harpsichord Building in America, 1976, The Staging of Shakespeare, 1976, The Poetry of Robert Frost, 1976; editor: Shakespeare's Problem Comedies, 1961, (with Hazelton Spencer) Elizabethan and Jacobean Comedy, 1964, Elizabethan and Jacobean Tragedy, 1964. BA, NYU, 1948; MA, U. Wis., 1949, PhD, 1954. Served E.E. AUS, 1944-46; ETO. Fulbright scholar, London, 1951-52; Guggenheim fellow, 1961-62; NEH fellow, 1976. Mem. MLA, Shakespeare Assn. Am. (pres. 1977-78), Renaissance Soc. Home: 3122 Woodbury Rd Shaker Heights OH 44120

O'ROURKE, LAWRENCE MICHAEL, b. Phila., Mar. 12, 1938, s. Lawrence M. and Margaret M. (Higgins) O'R.; m. Patricia Coe, Aug. 26, 1967; children—Christopher, Katharine, Jennifer, Timothy. Ed.: The American Teacher, 1982; author: Between God & Caesar (with others), 1985, Geno—A Biography, 1986. AB, Villanova U., 1959; JD, Georgetown U., 1970. Bur. chief Phila. Bulltn., Washington, 1970-80; dep. asst. sec. U.S. Dept. Edn., Washington, 1980; pvt. law practice, 1981—.White House corr. St. Louis Post-Dispatch, Washington, 1981—. Mem. Overseas Wrtrs., Gridiron Club, White House Corrs. Assn. Home: 3904 Rosemary St Chevy Chase MD 20815

O'ROURKE, SEAMUS, see Green, Theo

O'ROURKE, SHEILA ANNE, b. Wallace, ID, Oct. 16, 1941; d. George Jerimiah and Goldie Edith (Wamsley) O'Rourke; m. Michael Stearns, Feb. 23, 1963; children—Timaree, Peter, Caitlin; m. 2d, Fred Carpenter, June 2, 1979. Contrbr. poems var. mags. in US and Mex.; author, poetry Your Silence Speaks, 1985. Student, Long Beach College, CA., 1962. Mem. NWC. Home: 18381 Vista del Lago Yorba Linda CA 92686

O'ROURKE, WILLIAM ANDREW, b. Chgo., Dec. 4, 1945; s. William Andrew and Elizabeth (Kompare) O'R.; m. Marion Teresa Ghilarducci, July 9, 1986. Author: The Harrisburg 7 and the New Catholic Left, 1972, The Meekness of Isaac, 1974, Idle Hands, 1981, Criminal Tendencies, 1987. Editor: On the Job, 1977. BA, U. Mo. at Kansas City, 1968; MFA, Columbia U., 1970. Instr. journalism Kean Coll., Union, N.J., 1973; creative wrtg. tchr., Rutgers U., 1975-78, Mount Holyoke Coll., 1978-81; U. Notre Dame, 1981—. Fine Arts Work Center fellow, Provincetown, Mass., 1970-72; James Thurber wrtr.-in-res., Thurber House, Columbus, Ohio, 1984; recipient CAPS award N.Y. State Council on the Arts, 1975; NEA creative writing fellow, 1981-82. Mem. AG. Office: Dept Eng U Notre Dame Notre Dame IN 46556

ORR, EDWARD CARL, b. San Diego, Jan. 28, 1943; s. Edward Carl and Mildred Eugene (Gordon) Orr; m. Carol Jean Heller, Dec. 12, 1965; children—Nichole, Tiffany, Arianne. Contrbr. poems to numerous pubs., including Yankee, Christian Science Monitor, NY Times, South Humanities Rvw; author: Masking and Unmasking: Poems about Art, 1981; Enigmas: After de Chirico, 1986. BA, Bradley, U., 1965, MA, IL State U., 1972. Tchr. Peoria Pub. Schls., 1965-85. Home: 1013 West Bradley Ave Peoria IL 61606

ORR, ELAINE L., b. Washington, Aug. 14, 1951; d. Miles D. and H. Rita (Rooney) Orr. Author: The Right Word: Guidelines for Avoiding Sex-biased Language (with M.R. Dishman), 1985; contrbr.: Giants in Management, 1985, Public Adminstrn. Times, Peace Inst. Reporter; co-ed. newsletter for internat. and comparative adminstrn. sect. of Am. Soc. for Public Adminstrn., 1984—. Wrkg. on play, novel, articles on lang. equity, nuclear disarmament, mgmt. techniques. BA, U. Dayton, 1972; MA, Am. U., 1974. With U.S. Gen. Acctg. Office, Washington, 1974-86, dir., internat. liaison, 1980-86, ed. Internat. Jnl. Govt. Acctg., 1983-86; freelance wrtr., 1986—; assoc. ed. The Bureaucrat: Jnl. for Public Mgrs., Washington, 1987—. Mem. Washington Ind. Wrtrs., Nat. Press Club, Am. Soc. for Public Adminstrn., Wrtrs.' Center. Home: 9 Pine Ave Takoma Park MD 20912

ORR, LINDA, b. Atlanta, Apr. 20, 1943, d. Henry Hammett and Marianna (DeNoyelles) Orr. Author: Jules Michelet: Nature, History, and Language, 1976, A Certain X (poems), 1980; contrbr. to Antaeus, Paris Rvw, Antioch Rvw, Secret Destinations: Writers on Travel, 1985. BA, Duke U., 1965; PhD,Yale U., 1971. Asst. prof. Swarthmore (Pa.) Coll., 1974-75; asst., then assoc. prof. Yale U., New Haven, 1975-80; assoc. prof. dept. romance langs. Duke U., Durham, N.C., 1980—; vis. assoc. prof. U. Calif.-Berkeley, 1980. Mem. P&W, N.C. Wrtrs. Network, MLA. Office: Dept Rom Langs Duke Durham NC 27706

ORRMONT, ARTHUR, b. Albany, NY, July 3, 1922, s. William and Leona (Kaufman) Goldberg; m. Lora Orenstein, Oct. 4, 1956 (div. 1965). Author: Love Cults and Faith-Healers, 1961, (with Marion Aten) Last Train Over Rostov Bridge, 1962, Indestructible Commodore Perry, 1962, Amazing Alexander Hamilton, 1964, Master Detective: Allan Pinkerton (Jr. Lit. Guild selection), 1965, Chinese Gordon: Hero of Khartoum, 1966, Fighter Against Slavery: Jehudi Ashmun, 1966, Mr. Lincoln's Master Spy: Lafayette Baker, 1966, Diplomat in Warpaint: Chief Alexander Gillivray of the Creeks, 1967, Richard Burton, 1969, James Buchanan Eads: The Man Who Mastered the Mississippi, 1970, (with Joseph Lauro) Action Priest, 1970, Requiem for War: The Life of Wilfred Owen, 1972; ed. (with Leonie Rosenstiel) Lit. Agents of N.Am., 1984. BA, U. Mich., 1945; postgrad. Cornell U., 1945. Assoc. ed., head edit. dept. Farrar, Straus & Co., NYC, 1945-51; sr. ed. Popular Library, NYC, 1951-55; exec. ed. Fawcett Books, N.Y.C., 1955-57; pres., edit. dir. Author Aid Assocs., NYC, 1968—; ed. Natl. Hall of Fame Biography Series, 1970-72; lectr. in creative wrtg. CCNY, 1961, Columbia U., 1967. Mem. Jamesians. Office: Author Aid 340 E 52d St New York NY 10022

ORTEGA, ISABEL, see Leonard, Phyllis G.

ORTH, KEVIN ROBERT, b. Cleve., Nov. 10, 1961; s. Robert Franklin and Margery (Erdman) O. Contrbr. poems, book rvws., articles to lit. mags., anthols., newspapers; translator of Borges and Neruda to lit. mag. Contrbg. ed.: View After Dark Mag., Columbus, OH, 1983-86; mng. ed.: The Booster, Columbus, 1984; manuscript ed.; Ohio State U. Press, Columbus, 1986—. B.A., Ohio State U., 1983. Pres., Orth Communications, Columbus, 1982—. Trustee Jefferson Acad. Music, Columbus, 1986—. Grantee Ohio Arts Council, 1984. Mem. PSA. Home: 4217 N High St Columbus OH 43214

ORTIZ, EUGENE DENIS, b. Chgo., Apr. 15, 1956; s. Herbert Mendosa and Pearl Mary (Santos) O.; m. Ladona Sue Davis, July 22, 1978. B.A. in Humanities, T. A. Edison State Coll. 1985. Ed., pub. The Wrtr.'s Nook News, Chardon, OH, 1985—. Mem. NWC, COSMEP, Pubs. Assn. N.Am. Address: 10957 Chardon Rd Chardon OH 44024

ORTIZ, ROXANNE DUNBAR, b. San Antonio, Sept. 10, 1938; d. Moyer Haywood and Edna Louise (Curry) Dunbar; m. Daniel Callarman, July 5, 1958 (div. June 1964); 1 child, Michelle. Author: The Great Sioux Nation: Oral History of the Sioux-US Treaty, 1977; Roots of Resistance: History of Land Tenure, New Mexico, 1680-1980, 1980; Indians of the Americas:

Human Rights and Self-Determination, 1984; ed. Economic Development in American Indian Reservations, 1979; American Indian Energy Resources, 1980; contrbr. articles to Jnl Ethnic Studies, Human Rights US Style, Irredeemable America, others. BA in History, San Francisco State U., 1963; PhD in History, UCLA, 1974. Instr. UCLA, 1965-68, Suffolk U., Boston 1968-69; prof. ethnic studies Calif. State U., Hayward, 1974—. Grantee NSF, 1978-79, Ford Fdn., 1979-80; NEH research fellow, 1980-81. Home: 275 Grand View Ave Apt 103 San Francisco CA 94114

OSBORN, CAROLYN CULBERT, b. Nashville, July 11, 1934, d. William and Katherine (Truett) Culbert; m. Joe Allen Osborn, June 11, 1955; children—William, Claire, Celia. Author: A Horse of Another Color, 1977, The Fields of Memory, 1984; contrbr. short stories to Corral, Antioch Rvw, Ascent, Cimarron Rvw, numerous other lit mags and anthologies. BA in Journalism, U. Tex.-Austin, 1955, MA, 1959. Instr. English U. Tex.-Austin, 1968-78; prtnr. Culbert-Osborn Cattle, Evant, Tex., 1973—; free-lance wrtr., 1957—. Recipient awards Tex. Books in Rvw, 1977, Tex. Inst. Letters, 1978, PEN Syndicated Fiction award, 1985. Home: 3002 Gilbert St Austin TX 78703

OSBORNE, JOHN WALTER, b. Bklyn., Aug. 19, 1927; s. Douglas Walter and Gertrude Ann (Purcell) O.; m. Frances Patricia Hannon, Aug. 2, 1958; 1 son, David. Author: William Cobbett: His Thought and His Times, 1966, The Silent Revolution: The Industrial Revolution in England as a Source of Cultural Change, 1970, John Cartwright, 1972; co-editor, A Grammar of the English Language by William Cobbett, 1983; contrbr. articles to profl. jnls; Editor: Jnl of Rutgers U. Libraries, 1975-80. BA, Rutgers U., 1957, MA (Louis Bevier fellow), 1959, PhD,1961. Am. Philo. Soc. grantee, 1966, 75. Home: 24 Helen Ave West Orange NJ 07052

OSBORNE, MAGGIE ELLEN, (Margaret St. George), b. Hollywood, CA, June 10, 1941; d. William Edward and Zelma Lucille (King) Prather; m. Charles Carter, 1965 (div. 1972); 1 son, Zane Earl; m. 2d, George Muncy Osborne II, Apr. 29, 1972. Novelist: Alexa, 1980, Salem's Daughter, 1981, Portrait in Passion, 1981, Yankee Princess, 1982, Rage to Love, 1983, Flight of Fancy, 1984, Winter Magic, 1986, Castles and Fairy Tales, 1986, The Heart Club, 1987, Chase the Heart, 1987, Where There's Smoke..., 1988, Heart's Desire, 1988. Mem. Romance Wrtrs. Am. (past pres.; named Romance Wrtr. of Yr. 1984). Home: Box E Dillon CO 80435

OSGOOD, CHARLES EGERTON, b. Somerville, MA, Nov. 20, 1916; s. Merrill White and Ruth Madeline (Egerton) O.; m. Cynthia Luella Thornton, June 27, 1939; children—Philip Thornton, Gail Ruth. Author: Method and Theory in Experimental Psychology, 1953, The Measurement of Meaning, 1957, An Alternative to War or Surrender, 1962. BA, Dartmouth, 1939, DSc, 1962; PhD, Yale, 1945. Research assoc. Yale, 1945-46; asst. prof. psychology U. Conn., 1946-49; assoc. prof. psychology U. Ill., 1949-52, prof. communication, psychology, 1952—, dir., 1957-66, 1965—. Guggenheim fellow. Mem. Am. Acad. Arts and Scis., natl. Acad. Scis., Linguistic Soc. Am. Home: 304 E Mumford Dr Urbana IL 61801

O'SHAUGHNESSY, KATHLEEN KOLBE, b. Nyack, NY, June 19, 1951; d. John Joseph and Mary Preston (Searing) O.; m. Donald Edison Stearns, June 29, 1974 (div.); 1 dau., Kelly Alicia. Contrbr. poem to Greensboro Rvw., Aura; article to Critical Essays on Toni Morrison. BA in English, Tufts Univ., 1973; M.A. in English, U. N.H., 1974; M.F.A. in Creative Writing, U. N.C.-Greensboro, 1986. Instr., U. Ala., Birmingham, 1986—. Mem. South Atlantic MLA, AWP. Home: 538-D S 47th St Birmingham AL 35222

OSTERMAN, SUSAN, b. Phila., Aug. 21, 1949; m. Douglas Owen Roberts, Mar. 2, 1983. Author: Silence and Slow Time (poetry), 1975, Strip Mining (poetry), 1986; contrbr.: Cat Fancy, Gnosis Anthology, Transom Mag., Howling Dog Mag., other publs. BA, Columbia U., 1967-71, MAT, 1975; MA, CCNY, 1977. Ed. A.L. Fierst, Lit. Agt., NYC, 1971-73, Columbia U. Press, NYC, 1973-75; instr. N.Y. Inst. Tech., NYC, 1975-76, Coll. New Rochelle, NYC, 1977—. Mem. P&W (recipient cash awards), Mensa. Home: 610 W 115th St Apt 94 New York NY 10025

OSTERWEIL, WENDY, b. Chgo., May 26, 1953; d. Jerry Osterweil and Lucy Edwards; m. Eli Goldblatt, June 2, 1985. Editor: Alternative Press Publishers of Children's Books: A Directory, 2d ed. 1985. BS, Temple U., 1979; MFA, U. Wis., 1986. Art tchr. Pa. Sch. for Deaf, Phila., 1979-80, Germantown Acad., Ft. Washington, Pa., 1980-83; tchr. After Schl. Day Care, Madison, Wis., 1985—; coordinator Alternative Press Collection, Coop. Children's Book Ctr., Madison, 1984-86. Home: 905C Eagle Hts Madison WI 53705

OSTRANDER, (WILLIS) FREDERICK, b. Berkeley, CA, Apr. 23, 1926, s. Willis Frederick and Grace (Jackson) O.; m. Nancy Majors, Jan. 2, 1950; children—Margaret, Adam, Daphne, John. Author: The Hunchback and the Swan, 1978; contrbr. to Blue Unicorn, Galley Sail Rvw, Mark in Time-Portraits and Poetry in San Francisco, numerous other publs. Wrkg. on poetry. BA, U.Calif.-Berkeley. Appraiser, then exec. v.p. Twin Pines Fed. Savs. & Loan, Berkeley, 1962-84; self-employed real estate appraiser, Berkeley, 1984—; dir. Lawrence Hart Inst. Activist-Modernist Lit. Home: 2741 Woolsey St Berkeley CA 94705

OSTRIKER, ALICIA, b. NYC, Nov. 11, 1937, d. David and Beatrice (Linnick) Suskin; m. Jeremiah P. Ostriker, Dec. 1, 1958; children—Rebecca, Eve, Gabriel. Author: Vision and Verse in William Blake, 1965, Songs, 1969, Once More Out of Darkness and Other Poems, 1974, A Dream of Springtime: Poems 1970-77, 1978, The Mother-Child Papers, 1980, A Woman Under the Surface, 1982, Writing Like a Woman, 1983, Stealing the Language: The Emergency of Women's Poetry in America, 1986, The Imaginary Lover, 1986; ed.: The Complete Poems of William Blake, 1977. BA, Brandeis U., 1959; PhD, U. Wis., Madison, 1964. Mem. faculty dept. English Rutgers U., New Brunswick, N.J., 1965—, prof., 1972—. Poetry fellow NEA, 1976-77, Guggenheim Fdn., 1984-85, Rockefeller Fdn. fellow, 1982. Mem. MLA, PEN. Home: 33 Philip Dr Princeton NJ 08540

OSWALD, ERNEST JOHN, b. NYC, Jan. 20, 1943, s. Ernest and Theresa (Wagner) O. Author poetry collection: Apricot Two Step, 1977; contrbr. poetry to Windscherm (Netherlands), N.Y. Qtly, Small Pond Rvw, Eureka Rvw, other publs. AS, Bronx Community Coll., 1967; BA, Fordham U., 1973. Clk. Fawcett Publs., NYC,1969-73; poetry ed. Heirs Mag., San Francisco, 1973-82; legal asst. Fireman's Fund, San Francisco, 1984-85; case asst., Hassard, Bonnington, Rogers & Huber, San Francisco, 1986—. Mem. P&W. Home: 128 Laguna St San Francisco CA 94102

OTT, GIL, b. Abington, PA, Feb. 27, 1950; s. Edwin Mahlon and Hazel Marie (Allen) O. Author: Maize, 1979, the children, 1981, Ladder (Spectacular Diseases in the UK), 1984, For the Salamander, 1985, within range, 1986, Traffic, 1985, The Yellow Floor, 1987; single artist issue of Origin mag., 1982; contrbr. to Paper Air, Ironwood, Tamarisk, The Difficulties, Oars, Text, Heat, Origin. Ed./pub. Singing Horse Press, Phila., 1976—; dir. devel. Painted Bride Art Center, Phila., 1981—. Mem. CCLM (ed. fellowship, NYC, 1985); recipient Pa. Cncl. on the Arts Fellowship in Poetry, 1986. Address: Box 40034 Philadelphia PA 19106

OTTO, WAYNE RAYMOND, b. Fremont, WI, Oct. 22, 1931; s. Henry F. and Edna A. (Wohlt) O.; m. Shirley J. Bergen, Oct. 13, 1953 (div.); 1 dau., Eleni. Co-author: Teaching Adults to Read, 1967, Administering the School Reading Program, 1970, Wisconsin Design for Reading Skill Development, 1972, Corrective and Remedial Teaching, 1966, rev., 1973, 80, Focused Reading Instruction, 1974, Merrill Linguistic Reading Program, 1975, Objective Based Reading, 1976, Speedway: The Action Way to Speed Read, 1975, The School Reading Program, 1978, Steck-Vaugn Adult Reading, 1978, How to Teach Reading, 1979, Atari Speed Reading, 1983, Meeting the Challenge, 1985; co-editor: Remedial Teaching, 1969, Reading Problems: A Multidisciplinary Approach, 1977, Reading Expository Text, 1982; exec. editor: Jnl. Ednl. Research, 1969—; assoc. editor: Reading Psychology Qtly, 1979—. BS, U. Wis., River Falls, 1953, MS, 1959, PhD,1961, U. Wis. Served with USMCR, 1953-55. Mem. Intl. Reading Assn. (chmn. studies and research com. 1975-77, advisory editor 1979—), Natl. Reading Conf. (dir., advisory editor jnl 1975-78), Am. Rdg. Forum (dir. 1984-85). Home: 3383 Sugar Maple Ln Verona WI 53593

OVEREND, ROBERT BENJAMIN, JR., b. Evanston, IL, May 12, 1943; s. Robert Benjamin O., Sr., and Leah Mary (O'Leary) O.; m. Rita Marie Heiberger, June 29, 1968; 1 dau., Katharine Marie. BA, De Paul U., 1965; MA, Loyola, 1968. Tchr., St. Norbert's Schl., Northbrook, IL, 1967; asst. ed. Kiwanis Mag., Chgo., 1967-70; assoc. ed., Traffic Safety, Chgo., 1970-80, ed., 1980—. Home: 7333 N Ridge Blvd Chicago IL 60645

OVERMAN, MARJORIE MOORE, b. Goldsboro, NC, Jan. 27, 1919; d. Ezra Alexander Moore and Mallie Preston (Edwards) Moore; m. Thell Becton Overman, May 16, 1942; children—Etta Overman Mitchell, Ann Overman Yates. Book of original verse: The Edge of Forever, 1984; reg. contrbr. to the Wallace Enterprise. AB, Guilford Coll., 1940. Homemaker, 1942-60; social case worker Dept. Public Welfare (Kenansville, NC), 1960-64; adult probation/parole officer Dept. Corrections (Raleigh, NC), 1964-79. Home: 323 E Cavenaugh St Wallace NC 28466

OVERTON, JANE TAYLOR, b. Jonesboro, AR, Aug. 12, 1935; d. Lewis Earl and Alma (Nichols) Taylor; m. James Winston Overton, Nov. 3, 1953; children—Daniel Earl, Rebecca Lou, James Winston II. Author: The Potter's Clay (poetry), 1984; contrbr. poetry, stories: Hilton Head Islander, Island Packet, Miss. Poetry Soc. Jnl., others; poetry in anthologies. Wrkg. on poetry, children's book, novels. Student public schls., Greenville, Miss. Home: 71 Fairfield Ave Holyoke MA 01040

OVERTON, RONALD ERNEST, b. Bay Shore, NY, July 23, 1943, s. Ernest and Hazel (Hallock) O.; m. Linda Lahikainen, Sept. 5, 1970; children—Ned, Peter, Eve. Author poetry collections: Dead Reckoning, 1979, Love on the Alexander Hamilton, 1985; contrbr. poetry to Kayak, Salmagundi, Shenandoah, Bluefish, many other mags. and jnls; From the Belly of the Shark anthology, 1973; contrbr. prose: Am. Poetry Rvw, Andover Rvw, St. Mag., others. BA, SUNY-Stony Brook, 1966, MA, 1967. Instr. Barrington (R.I.) Coll., 1967-69; poet-in-residence N.Y. State Poets in Schls. Program, 1974-84, Phillips Acad., Andover, Mass., summer 1979; adj. mentor Empire State Coll., N.Y., 1982-84; adj. lectr. SUNY- Stony Brook, 1983—. NEA creative wrtg. fellow, 1976-77. Home: 16 Beaver Ln East Setauket NY 11733

OVESEN, ELLIS, see Smith, Shirley Mae

OWEN, EILEEN EDMUNDS, b. Concord, NH, Feb. 27, 1949; d. Edward Scott and Olive Lydia (Ames) Edmunds; m. John David Owen, June 19, 1971. Author: Facing the Weather Side, 1985; ed. Signpost Mag., 1984, Back Door Travel Newsletter, 1985, 86, Globetrotting, 1985; contrbr. to Arts & Artists, Cin. Poetry, Seattle rvws, Clay and Pine, Dark Horse, Sojourner, Tar River Poetry, Poetry N.W., other lit mags. Assoc. ed. Signpost Mag., Lynnwood, Wash., 1983-85; artist-in-res. Ucross Fnd., Wyo., 1984; ed., office mgr. Europe Thru the Back Door, Edmonds, Wash., 1985—. Home: 2709 128th St SE Everett WA 98208

OWEN, MARY JANE, b. Evanston, IL, June 8, 1936; d. Hugh Samuel McKeown and Lois Edna (Markee) Dugan; divorced; 1 child, India. Author: The Volunteer Path to Employment, 1984 (Outstanding Govt. Pub., Natl. Assn. Govt. Communicators 1985), New Resources: Volunteers Who Happen to be Disabled, 1984. Contrbr. articles to newspapers, mags. concerning disability. Contrbg. ed. The Disability Rag, 1984—, Mainstream Mag., 1985—. Ed. DCEH Perspectives, 1980—. BFA in Fine Arts and Painting, U. N.Mex., 1956; MSW, U. Calif.-Berkeley, 1967. Asst. prof. San Francisco State U., 1968-71; paralegal, tchr. Ctr. for Ind. Living, Berkeley, 1973-76; adminstr. Univ. Yr. in Action program Peralta Community Coll., Berkeley, 1976-78; spcl. asst. to assoc. dir. ACTION, Washington, 1978-80; wrtr., ed. Pres.'s Com. on Employment of the Handicapped, Washington, 1980—. Bd. dirs. Ctr. Ind. Living, 1948—; chmn. bd. Disability Focus, Inc., Washington, 1986—. Mem. Am. Assn. Disability Communicators (bd. dirs. 1984—), Washington Ind. Wrtrs., Natl. Assn. Social Workers, Natl. Rehab. Assn. Home: 2032 Belmont Rd NW 226 Washington DC 20009

OWEN, SUE ANN, b. Clarinda, IA, Sept. 5, 1942; d. Theodore Reynold and Elizabeth Jeanne (Roderick) Matthews; m. Thomas Charles Owen, Aug. 29, 1964. Author: Nursery Rhymes for the Dead, 1980; contrbr. poetry to The Nation, Poetry, Anthology of Mag. Verse, The Best of Intro. BA, U. Wis., 1964; MFA, Goddard College, Plainfield, Vt., 1978. Poet in the Schools, Arts & Humanities Council, Baton Rouge, 1980-81, visiting artist 1982—. Mem. PSA, AWP, P&W, Arts & Humanities Council. Home: 2015 General Cleburne Baton Rouge LA 70810

OWENS, CHRISTOPHER G., b. Brunswick, GA, July 14, 1961; s. Henry E. Owens Jr. and Elizabeth S. (Grumbles) Owens Newton. Contrbr.: La Prensa, Focus, The Orlando Runner. Wrkg. on career help book. BA in Communications, U. Central Fla., 1985. Asst. mgr. Rawlings Sporting Goods, Orlando, 1982—. Home: 5437B Lake Margaret Dr Orlando FL 32812

OWENS, ROCHELLE, b. Bklyn., Apr. 2, 1936; d. Max and Molly (Adler) Bass; m. George Economou, June 17, 1962. Author: plays The String Game, 1965, Istanboul, 1965, Futz, 1967, Homo, 1966, Beclch, 1966, Futz and What Came After, 1968, He Wants Shih, 1969, Farmers Almanac, 1969, The Queen of Greece, 1969, Kontraption, 1970, The Karl Marx Play, 1971, O.K. Certaldo, 1975, Emma Instigated Me, 1976, The Widow and the Colonel, 1977, Mountain Rites, 1977, Sweet Potatoes, 1978, Who Do You Want, Peire Vidal, 1982; Oklahoma Too (video), 1987; poetry Not Be Essence That Cannot Be, 1961, Salt and Core, 1969, I am The Babe of Joseph Stalin's Daughter, Poems from Joe's Garage, The Joe 82 Creation Poems, The Karl Marx Play & Others, The Joe Chronicles, Part 2, Four Young Lady Poets, 1962, Shemuel, 1979, French Light, 1984, Constructs, 1985, W.C.Fields in French Light, 1986, How Much Paint Does the Painting Need, 1987; editor: Spontaneous Combustion; film Futz, 1969. Fellow, Yale Schl. Drama, 1968. Founding mem. N.Y. Theatre Strategy. Prod., host of radio series The Writers Mind, 1985. Ford Fdn. grantee, 1965; Guggenheim fellow, 1971; CAPS grantee, 1973; NEA grantee, 1974; Rockefeller Fdn. grantee, 1974; honors N.Y. Drama Critics Circle; Obie award, 1967. Mem. DG, ASCAP. Address: 1401 Magnolia St Norman OK 73069

OZARK, CHILLY, see Childress, William Dale

OZICK, CYNTHIA, b. NYC, Apr. 17, 1928; d. William and Celia (Regelson) O.; m. Bernard Hallote, Sept. 7, 1952; 1 dau., Rachel Sarah. Author: Trust, 1966, The Pagan Rabbi and Other Stories, 1971, Bloodshed and Three Novellas, 1976, Levitation: Five Fictions, 1982, Art and Ardor: Essays, 1983, The Cannibal Galaxy, 1983, The Messiah of Stockholm, 1987. BA cum laude with honors in English, NYU, 1949; MA, Ohio State U., 1950. Recipient Rea Award for the Short Story, 1986; Mildred and Harold Strauss Living award Am. Acad. Arts and Letters, 1983; Guggenheim fellow, 1982. Address: Knopf 201 E 50th St New York NY 10022

OZMENT, STEVEN, b. McComb, MS, Feb. 21, 1939; s. Lowell V. and Shirley M. (Edgar) O.; m. Andrea Todd Foster, Apr. 30, 1977; 2 daus., Amanda and Emma; children by previous marriage: Joel, Matthew, Katherine. Author: Homo Spiritualis, 1969, The Reformation in Medieval Perspective, 1971, Mysticism and Dissent, 1973, The Reformation in the Cities, 1975, (with others) The Western Heritage, 1979, 2d ed., 1982, The Age of Reform, 1980; winner Schaff prize (Am. Book Award nominee 1980), Reformation Europe: A Guide to Research, 1982, When Fathers Ruled: Family Life in Reformation Europe, 1983, Magdalena and Balthasar: An Intimate Portrait of Life in 16th-Century Europe, 1986; (with others) The Heritage of World Civilizations, 1986; editorial bd.: Archive for Reformation History, 1976—, Sixteenth Century Jnl, 1976—, Jnl Am. Acad. Religion, 1972-77, Jnl Hist. Ideas, 1976—. BA, Hendrix Coll., 1960; BD, Drew Theol. Schl., 1964; PhD,Harvard U., 1967; MA (hon.), Yale U., 1975. Morse fellow, 1970-71; Guggenheim fellow, 1978. Home: 69 High Rd Newbury MA 01950

PACHECO, JAVIER BARRALES, (Harvey Patch), b. Palo Alto, CA, Apr. 22, 1949; s. Marcelino Buitron and Mary (Barrales) P. Contrbr. poems to lit. mags. including Electrum, Grito Del Sol, One More Canto. BA in Music History, San Francisco State U., 1974; MA in Ethnomusicology, UCLA, 1986. Tchg. asst. music dept. UCLA, 1984-85, bibliographer Chicano studies research ctr., 1985-86; translator Lion's Gate Films, Santa Monica, Calif., 1984-85; freelance musician, arranger, San Francisco, 1980-82; cons. Raices de Mex., Ballet Folklorico, East Palo Alto, Calif., 1985-86. Bd. dirs. Concilio de Arte Popular, Calif., 1977-79. Mem. Hispanic Musicians Assn. (bd. dirs. 1985-86), Soc. Ethnomusicology, Natl. Assn. Chicano Studies, Am. Fedn. Musicians. Home: 5162 Berryman Ave Culver City CA 90230

PACK, LOLA KATHRYN LEE, (Lola Lee Pack, L. Kathryn Pack), b. Johnston Co., NC, Apr. 14, 1924; d. Louis Roger and Allie Catherine (West) Lee; m. Roy L. Pack, Mar. 6, 1943; children—Wesley Watson, Loucinda Catherine, Joseph Patrick. Contrbr. to Uwharrie Rvw, Bay Leaves, Young Publications, Spafaswap, Fayetteville Observer, other jnls. Student Worth's Bus. Coll. Eligibility Spec. Social Services (NC), 1967-72; fulltime homemkr. Recognized by NC Poetry Soc. 1971, 81, 82, 83, by Poetry Cncl. of NC, 1969, 79, 80, 83. Mem. NC Poetry Soc. Home: Rt 1 Box 472 Linden NC 28356

PACK, ROBERT M., b. NYC, May 19, 1929; s. Carl and Henrietta (Langbert) P.; m. Patricia Powell, June 7, 1961; children—Erik, Pamela, Kevin. Author poetry: The Irony of Joy, 1955, A Stranger's Privilege, 1959, Guarded by Women, 1963, Home from the Cemetery, 1969, Nothing But Light, 1972, Keeping Watch, 1976, Waking to My Name: New and Selected Poems, 1980, Faces in a Single Tree: A Cycle of Monologues, 1984, Affirming Limits: Essays on Morality, Choice and Poetic Form, 1985, Clayfeld Rejoices, Clayfeld Laments: A Sequence of Poems, 1987. BA, Dartmouth Coll., 1951; MA, Columbia U., 1953. Dir. Bread Loaf Writers' Conf., 1973—. Fulbright fellow, 1956-57; recipient awards Natl. Council of Arts, Natl. Arts and Humanities. Home: RD 2 Cornwall VT 05753

PACKARD, VANCE OAKLEY, b. Granville Summit, PA, May 22, 1914; s. Philip Joseph and Mabel (Case) P.; m. Mamie Virginia Mathews, Nov. 25, 1938; children—Vance Philip, Randall Mathews, Cynthia Ann. Author: Animal IQ, 1950, The Hidden Persuaders, 1957, The Status Seekers, 1959, The Waste Makers, 1960, The Pyramid Climbers, 1962, The Naked Society, 1964, The Sexual Wilderness, 1968, A Nation of Strangers, 1972, The People Shapers, 1977 (Notable Book of 1977, ALA), Our Endangered Children, 1983. BA, Pa. State U., 1936; MS, Columbia U., 1937. Reporter Centre Daily Times, State College, Pa., 1936; columnist Boston Record, 1937-38; writer, editor Assoc. Press Feature Service, 1938-42; editor, staff writer Am. mag., 1942-56; staff writer Collier's mag., 1956; lectr. reporting, mag. writing Columbia, 1941-44, NYU, 1945-57. Mem. Soc. Mag. Writers (pres. 1961), AG. Home: 87 Mill Rd New Canaan CT 06840

PACKIE, SUSAN, b. Maplewood, NJ, Oct. 5, 1946; d. John Welch and Dorothy Verna (Rappaport) P. Author, illustrator: Yanticaw, 1985, Castles in the Air, 1986, Spathiphylla and Limes,

1986. BA, Columbia U., 1976; MA, New Schl., NYC, 1978. Tchr. art St. Joseph's Hosp., Paterson, N.J., 1973-77; editorial asst. NOK Pub., N.Y.C., 1979; tutor Bloomfield Coll., Newark Hosp., Passaic Coll., N.J., 1979-81; instr. Malcolm-King Coll., N.Y.C., 1981-83; staff wrtr. Inside Joke, NYC, 1984—. Recipient 1st prize for poetry N.J. mag., 1982; Hon. Mention for poetry N.Am. Mentor Mag., 83, 84, cert. Merit, 1985; Hon. Mention for poetry Hoosier Challenger, 1984, Calli's Tales, 1985. Home: 10-D Belleview Ct Belleville NJ 07109

PADEN, ROBERTA LEE, b. Colby, KS, Feb. 15, 1938; d. Homer Ernest and Harriet Eloise (McCafferty) P.; m. Gregory Grosbard (div.) Aug. 10, 1963; children—Guy Lee and Gayle Rachel Grosbard. Author: Otros Amigos series (trans.) tchrs. guides; Who Am I? (workbook); edited supplemental bilingual reading series, Santillana Pub. Co. BA, Wichita State Univ., 1968. Eng. lang. ed./trans., Santillana Pub. Co., 1977-79; project ed., Curriculum Concepts Inc., 1979-80; project control analyst, Drexel Burnham Lambert, 1981—. Home: 330 W 86 New York NY 10024

PADGETT, RON, b. Tulsa, June 17, 1942. Author poetry: Bean Spasms, 1967, Great Balls of Fire, 1969, Toujours l'amour, 1976, Tulsa Kid, 1979, Triangles in the Afternoon, 1979; translator: The Poet Assassinated (by Guillaume Apollinaire), 1984. BA, Columbia U., 1964. Dir. Poetry Project, NYC,1978-80; dir. publs. Tchrs. & Wrtrs. Collaborative, NYC,1981—. Fulbright fellow Inst. Intl. Edn., Paris, 1965; recipient Poets Fdn. award, 1964, 69; translation grantee NEA, 1983, NY State Council on Arts, 1984; Guggenheim, 1986. Mem. Blaise Cendrars Intl. Soc. Home: 342 E 13th St New York NY 10003

PAGE, RUTH W., b. Phila., Mar. 8, 1921; d. Morris and Hilda Wilhelmina (Hjerpe) Wolf; m. Proctor H. Page, Mar. 8, 1945; children—Candace, Patti Ruth, Robert Hull. Ed., Suburban List, 1957-77, National Gardening, 1969—; contrbr. book & theatre rvws. to Burlington Free Press. BA, Swarthmore Coll. Asst. to exec. sec'y. Book Pub. Bureau, NYC; ed. Suburban List, Essex Jct., VT, 1957-77, National Gardening, Burlington, VT, 69—. Office: Gardening Assn 180 Flynn Ave Burlington VT 05401

PAGE, SUSAN, see Stone, Susan Gail

PAGE, WILLIAM HOWARD, b. Cleveland, TN, Dec. 5, 1929; s. Ruble Dixon and Florence Bell (Whitehead) P.; m. Nancy Ellen Kennedy, June 4, 1955; 1 son, Vincent Howard. Author poetry: Clutch Plates, 1976, The Gatekeeper, 1982, Bodies Not Our Own, 1986; contrbr. poetry to over 100 mags. inclg. The Southern Rvw, Chariton Rvw, The Midwest Qtly, Cimarron Rvw, Southwest Rvw, Ploughshares. MA, Geo Peabody Coll., 1957; MFA, Bowling Green State U., 1978. Instr. W. Tex. State Univ., Canyon, 1957-59; instr. to asst. prof. Troy State Univ., Ala., 1959-62; assoc. prof. Memphis State Univ., Tenn., 1962—, founding ed. Memphis State Rvw, 1980—. Recipient Walter R. Smith Disting. Book award, Memphis State Univ., 1985. Home: 5551 Derron Ave Memphis TN 38115

PAGELS, ELAINE HIESEY, b. Palo Alto, CA, Feb. 13, 1943; d. William McKinley and Louise Sophia (Boogaert) H.; m. Heinz R. Pagels, June 7, 1969. Author: The Johannine Gospel in Gnostic Exegesis, 1973, The Gnostic Paul, 1975, The Gnostic Gospels, 1979. BA, Stanford U., 1954, MA, 1965; PhD, Harvard U., 1970. NEH grantee, 1973; Mellon fellow Aspen Inst. Humanistic Studies, 1974; Hazen fellow, 1975; Rockefeller fellow, 1977-78; Guggenheim fellow, 1978-79; MacArthur Prize fellow, 1981-83. Office: 1819 Hall Princeton NJ 08540

PAGLIO, LYDIA ELIZABETH, b. Providence; d. Victor and Lydia Anne (DiPrete) P. Editorial asst. Sport mag., NYC,1971-72; assoc. editor True Experience, also True Love mags., NYC,1972-73; editor True Experience mag., 1973-81; edl. cons. 1981-83; editor Dell Pub., NYC,1983-84, sr. editor, director Candlelight Romances, 1984-87; sr. ed., Zebra Books, 1987; dir. publicity Dancer's World, Springfield, Mass., 1978-80. Mem. Editorial Free-lance Assn. (dir.), 1981-83. BA, N.Y. U. Address: 41 W 82d St New York NY 10024

PAINTER, CHARLOTTE, Author: Who Made the Lamb, 1965, Confession from the Malaga Madhouse, 1971, Revelations: Diaries of Women, 1975, Seeing Things, 1975, Gifts of Age, 1985. MA, Stanford U., 1963. Lectr. Stanford (Calif.) U., 1963-69, U. Calif.-Berkeley, -Santa Cruz, -Davis, 1971-75; assoc. prof. San Francisco State U., 1975—; disting. vis. wrtr. Eastern Wash. U., Spokane, 1983. Radcliffe Inst. fellow, 1966-68; grantee NEA, 1972. Home: Box 3446 Oakland CA 94609

PAIR, JOYCE MORROW, b. Newnan, GA, July 1, 1931; d. Glenn Moore Morrow and Catherine Elizabeth (McGee) Buchanan; 1 child, Vicki Lyn Pair Eubanks. Contrbr. poetry to Ga. State Rvw, Chattahoochee Rvw; ed.: James Dickey Newsletter, 1984—. Wrkg. on book of philosophy and fiction of F. Scott Fitzgerald. MA, Ga. State U., 1975, PhD, 1983. Chrysler Corp., Atlanta, 1957-68; assoc. prof. English, DeKalb Coll., Dunwoody, Ga., 1978—. George Sparks fellow, 1974. Mem. MLA, South Atlantic MLA, Coll. English Assn. Home: 1131 Kingstown Ct Decatur GA 30033

PAK, HYUNG WOONG, b. Ham-Hoong, Korea, Nov. 6, 1932; arrd. U.S., 1955, naturalized, 1968; s. Kyung-Koo and Myung-Sook (Lee) P.; m. Alexandra Theresa Badarak, 1960; m. Diana Lee Stenen Woodruff, 1975; children—Jonathan Tong-Hee, Michelle Hyun-Mi Lee. Author: The Pacific Rim. Editor, Chgo. Rvw, 1958-63, cons., 1963-65; assoc. editor Ency. Britannica Press, Chgo., 1963-64, sr. editor social scis. and humanities, 1964-66; dir. instructional materials div. and sales mgr. schl. and coll. div. Bantam Books, NYC, 1966-69; v.p., editorial dir. Instructional Media Am., NYC, 1969-70; gen. mgr. schl. dept. Appleton-Century-Crofts/New Century, 1970-72; v.p., editorial dir. D. Van Nostrand Co., NYC, 1972-74, pres., 1974-76, Chatham Sq. Press, NYC, 1976-83; pub. Urizen Books, Inc., NYC, 1978-81; exec. v.p. Bus. Software mag., Palo Alto, Calif., 1984; cons. Modern Age: Qtly Rvw, 1962-63. AB, U. Chgo., 1958. Served with Republic Korea Army, 1950-54. Home: 1015 Sharpless Rd Philadelphia PA 19126

PALAY, SANFORD LOUIS, b. Cleve., Sept. 23, 1918; s. Harry and Lena (Sugarman) P.; m. Victoria Chan Curtis, 1970; children: Victoria Li-Mei, Rebecca li-Ming. Author: The Fine Structure of the Nervous System, 1970, 2d edit., 1976, Cerebellar Cortex, Cytology and Organization, 1973; Editor: Frontiers of Cytology, 1958, The Cerebellum, New Vistas, 1981. AB, Oberlin Coll., 1940; MD (Hoover prize scholar 1943), Western Res. U., 1943. Editorial bd.: Exptl. Neurology, 1959-76, Jnl. Cell Biology, 1962-67, Brain Research, 1965-71, Jnl. Comparative Neurology, 1966—, Jnl. Ultrastructure Research, 1966—, Jnl. of Neurocytology, 1972—, Exptl. Brain Research, 1965—76, Neurosci, 1975—, Zeitschrift fur Anatomie and Entwicklungsgeschichte, 1968; co-mng. editor, 1978—; editor-in-chief: Jnl. Comparative Neurology, 1981—; mem. adv. bd. editors: Jnl. Neuropathology and Exptl. Neurology, 1963—, Intl. Jnl. Neurosci, 1969-74, Tissue and Cell, 1969—; contbr. articles to profl. jnls. Served to capt. M.C. AUS, 1946-47. Recipient 50 Best Books of 1974 award Intl. Book Fair, Frankfurt, Germany, Best Book in Profl. Readership award Am. Med. Writers Assn., 1975; Guggenheim fellow, 1971-72. Fellow Am. Acad. Arts and Scis. Home: 78 Temple Rd Concord MA 01742

PALEY, GRACE, b. NYC, Dec. 11, 1922; d. Isaac and Mary (Ridnyik) Goodside; m. Jess Paley, June 20, 1942; children—Nora, Dan.; m. 2d, Robert Nichols, 1972. Author: The Little Disturbances of Man, 1959, Enormous Changes at the Last Minute, 1975; stories in Atlantic, Esquire, Ikon, Accent, others. Ed., Hunter Coll., NYU. Recipient Literary award for short story writing Natl. Inst. Arts and Letters, 1970; elected to Am. Acad. and Inst. Arts and Letters, 1980; Guggenheim fellow. Home: 126 W 11 St New York NY 10011

PALLISTER, JAN, see Pallister, Janis L.

PALLISTER, JANIS LOUISE, b. Rochester, MN, Jan. 12, 1926; d. George L. and Edith Marion (Reed) Pallister; m. Clinton Colby, (div. 1962). Author, 1971—, latest being At the Eighth Station, 1983, Sursum Corda, 1982. PhD, U. MN, 1964. Instr., Black Hills Coll., Spearfish, SD, 1948-50, Colby Coll., Waterville, ME, 1959-61; instr. Bowling Green (OH) St. U., 1961-78, prof. 1978-85, prof. emeritus 1985—. Columbia U. Translation Award, 1978, NEH Fellowship, 1980, Natl. Translators Assoc. best translation prize, 1982, Can. Govt. Research Grant, 1984. Mem. AAUP, MLA, AATF. Home: 211 State St Bowling Green OH 43402

PALLOTTA, GAIL CASSADY, b. Charlotte, NC, Jan. 7, 1942; d. Henry Gibbs and Evelyn (Mathis) Cassady; m. Frederick Vance Pallota, Apr. 8, 1972; 1dau., Laurie Elizabeth. Contrbr. articles to numerous mags. including Atlanta, Inside Cobb, The State, Ga. Jnl., Mother Earth News, Lady's Circle. Contrbr. poems to anthols. Ed.: Linefill, Atlanta, 1967-68. A.B. in English, Western Carolina U., 1964; Pub. Cert., Emory U., 1967. Asst. ed. W.R.C. Smith, Atlanta, 1964-65; editorial asst. Life Insurance Co. of Ga., Atlanta, 1965-67; copywrtr. Philip Denton Advt., Atlanta, 1968-70; free-lance wrtr., 1972—. Instr. writing workshops Marietta, GA, 1985—. Home: 251 Hunting Creek Dr Marietta GA 30068

PALMATIER, ROBERT ALLEN, b. Kalamazoo, July 22, 1926; s. Karl Ernest and Cecile (Chase) P.; m. Marion Dolores Babilla, Dec. 21, 1946; children: David Eugene, Denise Marie. Author: A Descriptive Syntax of the Ormulum, 1969, A Glossary for English Transformational Grammar, 1972. BA magna cum laude, Western Mich. U., 1950, MA, 1955; PhD, U. Mich., 1965. Served with AUS, 1944-46; ETO. Mem. Linguistic Soc. Am., MLA. Home: 1326 Hardwick Ave Kalamazoo MI 49002

PALMER, CHARLENE NOEL, b. Los Angeles, Feb. 23, 1930; d. Robert and Ruth (Galfond) Goldenberg; m. David Walter Palmer, June 16, 1951; children—Stephen David, Charna Ruth,

Nicholas Alan, Renee Elizabeth. Author: Long Stems Colored, 1953; poems in numerous anthols, inclg. Peace or Perish, Anthology, Voices for Peace, Anti-War Poems Anthology, vol. 2, and lit mags. including Chicago Omnibus, Christian Century, The Living Church, Odyssey, others. Student UCLA, 3-1/2 yrs. Parish secy. St. Paul's Church (Flint, MI), 1985—. Home: 1634 Cromwell Ave Flint MI 48503

PALMER, DAVID WALTER, b. Detroit, Nov. 24, 1928, s. Walter Samuel and Elizabeth Ruth (Besancon) P.; m. Charlene Goldenberg, June 16, 1951; children—Stephen David, Charna Ruth, Nicholas Alan, Renee Elizabeth. Author: Quickly, Over the Wall (poems and paintings), 1966; ed. Beloit Poetry Jnl, 1964-67; regular reviewer for Library Jnl, 1962-66; contrbr. to numerous lit mags. BA, UCLA, 1951, MLS, 1961. Library dir. Rockford (Ill.) Coll., 1964-68, Baldwin-Wallace Coll., Berea, Ohio, 1968-74, U. Mich., Flint, 1974—. Mem. PSA, ALA, Riemenschneider Bach Inst. Home: 1634 Cromwell Ave Flint MI 48503

PALMER, ROBERT FRANKLIN, JR., b. Little Rock, June 19, 1945; s. Robert Franklin and Marguerite (Bowers) P. Author: Baby, That Was Rock and Roll: The Legendary Leiber and Stoller, 1978, A Tale of Two Cities: Memphis Rock and New Orleans Roll, 1979, Deep Blues, 1981, The Rolling Stones, 1983. BA in English, U. Ark., Little Rock, 1967. Assoc. editor: Changes mag., 1969-70; freelance writer on music, 1970—; music critic: contemporary and exptl. music, jazz and pop N.Y. Times, 1976—; contrb. editor, jazz columnist: Penthouse. Address: NY Times 229 W 43d St NewYork NY 10036

PALUMBO, MICHAEL NICHOLAS, (Michael Nicholas), b. Fremont, Calif., Feb. 13, 1960, s. Michael Veto and Leona Lucille (Harvey) P. Author: Together As One (novel), 1986; contrbr. to San Francisco Examiner, M. Mag., People Mag., Life Mag. BA in Sociology, U. Calif., Berkeley, MS in Social Psychology. Home: 27346 Parkside Dr Hayward CA 95452

PANICH, PAULA MARIE, b. Akron, OH, Nov. 6, 1947; d. Milan and Juanita M. (Gaichin) P.; m. William Linsman, Aug. 15, 1981; 1 dau., Ilana Panich-Linsman. Author: (with Nora Burba) The Desert Southwest, 1987. Contrbr. articles to mags. including Ariz. Republic, Southwest Profile, others. Regional ed.: Am.'s Greatest Walks, 1986; contrbg. ed.: Phoenix Home & Garden, 1984—. B.A., Ariz. State U., 1969; postgrad. U. Calif.-Berkeley (SF campus), 1970-74. Account exec. Bozell & Jacobs, Phoenix, 1979-80; owner P. Panich Public Relations, Phoenix, 1981-84; public relations officer Heard Museum, Phoenix, 1986-87; free-lance wrtr., 1973—. Founder Urban Focus, Phoenix, 1980. Recipient Honorable Mention for non-fiction Wrtr.'s Digest, 1986. Mem. Camelback Lit. Soc. (founder). Home: 4426 N 46th Pl Phoenix AZ 85018

PANICHAS, GEORGE ANDREW, b. Springfield, MA, May 21, 1930; s. Andrew and Fotini (Dracouli) P. Author: Adventure in Consciousness: The Meaning of D.H. Lawrence's Religious Quest, 1964, Epicurus, 1967, The Reverent Discipline: Essays in Literary Criticism and Culture, 1974, The Burden of Vision: Dostoevsky's Spiritual Art, 1977, The Courage of Judgment: Essays in Criticism, Culture and Society, 1982; editor: Mansions of the Spirit: Essays in Literature and Religion, 1967, Promise of Greatness: The War of 1914-1918, 1968, The Politics of Twentieth-Century Novelists, 1971, The Simone Weil Reader, 1977, Irving Babbitt: Representative Writings, 1981, Irving Babbitt In Our Time (with Claes G. Ryn), 1986, Modern Age: the First Twenty-Five Years. A Selection, 1987; editorial advisor: Modern Age: A Qtly Rev., 1971-77; assoc. editor, 1978-83; editor, 1984—; adv. bd.: Continuity: A Jnl of History, 1984—; Earhart Fdn. grantee, 1982; mem. of the Richard M. Weaver Fellowship Awards com., 1983—, Ingersoll Prizes Jury Panel, 1986; co-dir. Conf. on Irving Babbitt, 1983, Academic Bd. of Natl. Humanities Inst., 1985—; contrbr. articles and rvws to profl. jnls. BA, Am. Intl. Coll., 1951, LittD (hon.), 1984; AM, Trinity Coll., Conn., 1952; PhD,Nottingham (Eng.) U., 1962. Fellow Royal Soc. Arts (U.K.). Home: 4313 Knox Rd 402 College Park MD 20740

PANITT, MERRILL, b. Hartford, CT, Sept. 11, 1917; s. Irving and Anna (Shear) P.; m. Marjorie Hoover, Apr. 2, 1942; 1 son, Jeffrey. Reporter United Press, 1937-39; pub. relations ofcl. Mo. Pub. Expenditure Survey, 1939-41; with Triangle Publs., Inc., Phila., 1946—; TV columnist Philadelphia Inquirer, 1949-53, adminstrv. asst. to pres., 1948-53; mng. editor TV Guide, 1953-59, editor, 1959-73, editorial dir., 1973—; also editorial dir. TV Digest, TV Factbook (trade publs.), 1959-61; editor TV Guide Roundup in 1960. Co-author: Soldier's Album, 1946. BJ, U. Mo. Served to maj. AUS, 1941-46. Home: 389 Eaton Way West Chester PA 19380

PANKOWSKI, ELSIE MARIE, b. Ross, ND, Jan. 31, 1933, d. Frank Henry and Geraldine Delores (Richards) Cvancara; m. John Thomas Pankowski, Apr. 12, 1952; children—Geri, Daryl. Contrbr. poetry to Montana Arts, Snapdragon, Northwest Mag., Christian Sci. Monitor, numerous other pubsl. Mem. Mont. Inst. of Arts (state wrtr.'s chmn., bd. dirs. 1982-83, acting secy. Great Falls Wrtrs. Group), Great Falls Arts Assn. Home: 1404 11th Ave S Great Falls MT 59405

PANOFSKY, HANS ARNOLD, b. Kassel, Germany, Sept. 18, 1917; came to U.S., 1934, naturalized, 1944; s. Erwin and Dora (Mosse) P.; m. Margaret Ann Riker, July 24, 1943; children Ruth Alice Morgan-Jones, Anne Davison. Author: Introduction to Dynamic Meteorology, 1955, (with Glenn Brier) Some Applications of Statistics Meteorology, 1958, (with John L. Lumley) Structure of Atmospheric Turbulence, 1964, AB, Princeton, 1938; PhD, U. Calif. at Berkeley, 1941; postgrad. Sch. USN, 1980, Colo. State U., 1982; Erskine fellow U. Canterbury, N.Z., 1983. Guggenheim fellow, 1960. Home: 6222 Agee St Apt 5 San Diego CA 92122

PANOZZO, MICHAEL EDWARD, b. Chgo., Apr. 18, 1958; s. Lawrence Cornelius and Antoinette (Rigoni) P.; m. Ellen Elizabeth Kunka, July 24, 1982. BA in Jnlsm., Marquette U., 1980. Ed., Billiards Digest, Chgo., 1980—. Office: Billiards 875 N Michigan Ave Chicago IL 60611

PANSHIN, ALEXEL, b. Lansing, MI, Aug. 14, 1940; s. Alexis John and Lucie (Padget) P.; m. Cory Seidman, June 4, 1969; children—Adam, Tobiah. Author: Heinlein in Dimension, 1968, Rite of Passage, 1968, Star Well, 1968 The Thurb Revolution, 1968, Masque World, 1969, Farewell to Yesterday's Tomorrow, 1975, (with Cory Panshin) SF in Dimension, 1976, rev. ed., 1980, (with Cory Panshin) Earth Magic, 1978; Transmutations: A Book of Personal Alchemy, 1982, (with Cory Panshin) The World Beyond the Hill, 1988. Student, U. Mich., 1958-60; BA, Mich. State U., 1965; MA, U. Chgo., 1966. Founder Elephant Books, 1982. Recipient Hugo award 25th World Sci. Fiction Conv., 1967; Nebula award for Rite of Passage, 1968. Home: RDI Box 168 Riegelsville PA 18077

PANTZER, ALFRED KIVU, b. Focsani, Romania, Feb. 2, 1925, came to U.S., 1971, s. Kivu M. and Betty K. (Muhlstein) P.; m. Eugenia Pantir, Feb. 2, 1966. Contrbr. articles to NY Allegro Musicians mag., music edn. mags. in Romania. Wrkg. on instrumental singing book. MA, Columbia U., 1978, EdD candidate, 1979. Ed. Romanian Music Editing House, 1952-58; founder 1976, since pres. Center for Music Literacy, NYC. Home: 45-25 42d St Apt 4C Long Island City NY 11104

PAOLANO, MARY, b. Barberton, OH, Oct. 11, 1918; d. Frank and Josephine (Kosir) Platner; m. Aldo R. Paolano, June 10, 1939; children—Mary Jo, Jeffrey, Susan McKiernan, John, Eugene, Jane Mitchell. Contrbr. articles to mags., newspapers. Grad. public schls., Barberton. Organist, St. Andrew's Episopal Ch., Barberton, 1962—. Mem. Akron Manuscript Club. Home: 6752 Cleve-Mass Rd Clinton OH 44216

PAOLUCCI, ANNE (ATTURA), b. Rome; d. Joseph and Lucy (Guidoni) Attura; m. Henry Paolucci. Author: (with H. Paolucci) Hegel on Tragedy, 1962; From Tension to Tonic: The Plays of Edward Albee, 1972; Pirandello's Theater: The Recovery of the Modern Stage for Dramatic Art, 1974, Poems Written for Sbek's Mummies, Marie Menken, and Other Important Persons, Places, and Things, 1977, Eight Short Stories, 1977, short stories Sepia Tones, 1985; plays include Cipango!, 1985, Minions of the Race, published as book, 1978; poem Riding the Mast Where It Swings, 1980; editor, author: introduction Dante's Influence on American Writers, 1977; founder, genl. editor: Rvw. Natl. Lits., 1970—, CNL/Qtly World Report, 1974—. BA, Barnard Coll.; MA, Columbia U., Ph.D., 1963. Mem. faculty English dept. Brearley Schl., N.Y.C., 1957-59; asst. prof. English and comp. lit. CCNY, 1959-69; univ. research prof. St. John's U., Jamaica, N.Y., 1969—, prof. English, 1975—, acting head dept. English, 1973-74, chmn. dept. English, 1982—; director, Doctor of Arts Degree Program in English, 1982—; Fulbright lectr. in Am. drama U. Naples, Italy, 1965-67; spcl. lectr. U. Urbino, summers, 1966-67, U. Bari, 1967, Univs. Bologna, Catania, Messina, Palermo, Milan, Pisa, 1965-67; disting. adj. vis. prof. Queens Coll., CUNY; bd. dirs. World Centre for Shakespeare Studies, 1972—; founder, exec. dir. Council on Natl. Lits., 1974—; mem. exec. com. Conf. Editors Learned Journals-MLA, 1975—; del. to Fgn. Lang. Jnls, 1977—; mem. adv. bd. Commn. on Tech. and Cultural Transformation, UNESCO, 1978—; mem. acad. council Shakespeare Globe Theatre Centre, 1981—. Award Women's Press Club, N.Y., 1974, Order of Merit, Rep. of Italy, 1987, Liberty Medal, 1986; Natl. Council on the Humanities, 1986—. Mem. Intl. Shakespeare Assn., Shakespeare Assn. Am., Renaissance Soc. Am., Renaissance Inst. Japan, Intl. Comparative Lit. Assn., Am. Comparative Lit. Assn., MLA, Am. PEN, Hegel Soc. Am., Dante Soc. Am., Pirandello Soc., Natl. Soc. Lit. and Arts. Office: Saint John's U Jamaica NY 11439

PAPALEO, JOSEPH, b. NYC, Jan. 13, 1927; s. Giusseppe and Rosa (Sammartina) P.; m. Tonie Piazza, Sept. 30, 1982. Author: (novella) Arete,

1960; (novels) All the Comforts, 1969, Out of Place, 1971; contrbr. poetry to Paris Rvw, short stories to New Yorker, Commentary, Harper's, Accent, Epoch, Transatlantic, Remington rvw, Montrealer, Attenzione, Penthouse. BA, Sarah Lawrence Coll., 1947; MA, Columbia U., 1951; diploma U. Florence, 1952. Tchr. Fieldston Sch., N.Y.C., 1953-59; prof. Sarah Lawrence Coll., Bronxville, N.Y., 1960—. Served with USAAF, 1942-46; PTO. Recipient prize for poetry Ramapo Coll., 1978; Guggenheim fellow, 1974. Home: 139 Lee Ave Yonkers NY 10705

PAPE, SHARON BARBARA, b. NYC,Jan. 15, 1947, d. Mitchell and Adele Karen (Freidin) Fine; m. Dennis Michael Pape, Aug. 27, 1967; children—Jason Ian, Lauren Michele. Author: Ghost Fire (novel), 1983, The Godchildren (novel), 1986; contrbr. short story to Redbook. BA, Queens Coll., 1968. Tchr. public schls., Jericho, N.Y., 1969-72. Home: 5 Meroke Ct Huntington Station NY 11746

PAPP, VINCENT, see Vishnisky, Morris Irving

PARADIS, PHILIP M., b. New Britain, CT, Feb. 11, 1951, s. Norman and Claire P.; m. Marjorie Hull, May 27, 1978. Poetry collection: Tornado Alley, 1986; contrbr. nonfiction to Midwest Qtly, Tex. Rvw, Cimarron Rvw; contrbr. poetry to Coll. English, Tar River Poetry, Kans. Qtly, Pembroke Mag., other jnls; poetry ed. Midland Rvw, 1985; contrbg. ed. Poet & Critic, 1985—. MA in English, U. Utah, Salt Lake City, 1981; PhD in English, Okla. State U., Stillwater, 1984. Lectr. Okla. State U., Stillwater, 1980-85; adj. asst. prof. English Iowa State U., Ames, 1985—. Winner 1st prize poetry, Conn. Poetry Circuit, 1976, Acad. Am. Poets, 1982; grantee Conn. Arts Council, 1977. Mem. MLA, NCTE, AWP. Office: Dept Engl 203 Ross Hall Iowa State U Ames IA 50011

PARADISO, K. L., (Kate Eden) b. Rochester, NY, Aug. 12, 1946; d. James Arthur and Jane Lange (Herbert) Lenhard; m. Joseph Michael Paradiso, Apr. 14, 1972. Author: Sacred Heart Parish: 1936-1986, 1986, The History of Sacred Heart—1887-1987, 1986; (with Betty Peterson) The Shepherd newsletter, 1986—. Contrbr. poem to anthol. A. Genl. Studies, Cochise Coll., 1986. Payroll auditor Parmelee Electric Co., Willcox, AZ, 1979-80; secy., administrative asst. Cochise Coll., Willcox, 1983—. Home: Rt 1 Box 758 Willcox AZ 85643

PARENTE, AUDREY, b. Torrington, CT, Jan. 3, 1948; d. Alfred Joseph and Gloria Angela (Capitani) Riccucci; m. Anthony Parente, June 29, 1968; children: Peter Anthony, David Anthony. Contrbr. to Real Estate Today, Grit, Byline, Cat Fanciers, The Inkling, The Horror Show, Central Fla. Mag., Golden Years, others; ed. and pub. SPWAO newsletter, 1985. AS in legal sci., Post Coll. Self-employed, Ormond Beach, Fla., 1982—. Bd. dirs., Friends of Ormond Beach Pub. Library, 1985. Mem. Natl. League Am. Pen Women, Ormond Writers League, Small Press Writers and Artists Orgn. Address: 411 Main Trail Ormond Beach FL 32074

PARHAM, ROBERT RANDALL, b. Takoma Park, MD, Apr. 21, 1943; s. O. Lee and Lavon Louise (Marshall) P.; m. Dorothy Ann Van Hook, July 31, 1965; children: Misty Dawn, Thomas Orion. Author: Sending the Children for Song, 1975; contrbr. to Rolling Stone, S.W. Rvw. BA, Belmont Coll., Nashville, 1965; MA, Fla. State U., 1970, PhD, 1980. Instr. English, Francis Marion Coll., Florence, S.C., 1970-76, asst. prof., 1978-81, assoc. prof., 1981—, chmn. dept., 1985—. Recipient W. Gilmore Simms prize S.C. Poetry Soc., 1973. Mem. NCTE, MLA. Home: 233 Creek Dr Quinby SC 29501

PARIS, MATTHEW LIONEL, b. Bklyn., Apr. 9, 1938, s. Morris and Selma (Lippman) P.; m. Marian Palm, June 3, 1985; 1 son, Noah. Novelist: Mystery, 1973, The Holy City, 1979; contrbr. to December, Pulpsmith, Lotus, Newsart, numerous other lit publs.; ed.: Bklyn. Lit. Rvw, 1980-86, Prospect Park Vintage Poets Series, 1980-86. Supr. NYC Dept. Parks, Bklyn., 1980—; adj. prof. L.I. U., Bklyn., 1980-83; dir. poetry readings, musical concerts with poetry theatre groups. Dir. Poets for City Schls., Bklyn., 1974—. Home: 850 E 31st St C6 Brooklyn NY 11210

PARISH, BARBARA SHIRK, b. Lincoln, KS, Nov. 28, 1942, d. Henry Lee and Effie Iola (Rohe) Shirk; m. Harlie Albert Parish, Jr., Aug. 30, 1964; 1 dau., Shannon Jeannine. Contrbr. poetry, fiction to Small Pond, Wind, Prairie Schooner, Plainswoman, Ky Poetry Rvw, others. BA in English, Ft. Hays State U., 1964; MA in English, U. Mo., 1966, MLS, 1968. Cataloger U. Louisville, 1968-69, reference librarian, 1971-72; freelance wrtr., 1972—. Recipient Poetry Reading award Tenn. Arts Commn., 1981, and poetry award through Plainswoman, North Dakota Arts Council, 1987. Mem. Ky. State Poetry Soc., Beta Phi Mu. Home: 4293 Beechcliff Ln Memphis TN 38128

PARISI, JOSEPH (ANTHONY), b. Duluth, MN, Nov. 18, 1944; s. Joseph Carl Parisi and Phyllis Susan (Quaranta) Schlecht. Co-editor: The Poetry Anthology, 1912-77, 1978; articles and rvws. in Yale Rvw, Ga. Rvw, Shenandoah, TriQuarterly, Poetry, Modern Philology, Chgo. Tribune, Chgo. Sun-Times, Sewanee Rvw, Contemporary Poets, others. BA with honors, Coll. St. Thomas, St. Paul, 1966; MA, U. Chgo., 1967, PhD with honors, 1973. Assoc. editor Poetry Mag., Chgo., 1976-83, acting editor, 1983-85; adj. prof. English, U. Ill., Chgo., 1978—; editor Poetry Mag., Chgo., 1985—. Mem. Modern Poetry Assn. (devel. dir.), Newberry Library Assocs. Alvin Bentley Fdn. scholar, 1963; U. Chgo. fellow, 1966-69. Home: 3440 N Lake Shore Dr Chicago IL 60657

PARK, CHUNG I., b. Chang-won, Kyungnam, Korea, Aug. 25, 1938; arrived U.S. Aug., 1969; s. Zung S. and Bong-y (Chu) P.; m. Jung Yol (Yoo), Aug. 30, 1969; children—Charlotte, Sue, Andrew. Compiler and ed.: Best Sellers & Best Choices, 1980-83. Best Books by Consensus, 1984—. Reporter/Writer for The COINT Reports, 1980—. MSLS, U. So. Calif., 1971; postgrad., U. Ill.-Urbana, 1975. Reference librarian Malcolm X Coll., Chgo., 1972—.Mem. ALA, Am. Soc. Info. Sci., World Future Soc. Home: 9302 Parkside Morton Grove IL 60053

PARKER, ALLISON, see Clyne, Patricia Edwards

PARKER, ARRI SENDZIMIR, b. NYC, Oct. 22, 1948; d. Michael George and Jane (Harkness) Sendzimir; m. William Ted Parker, Jr., June 21, 1979; children—Win, Jessica. Editor: La Feuille d'Avis des Halles (Paris), 1971-74, The Women's Newspaper, 1982—. BA, U. of Pennsylvania, 1971; MBA Columbia Business, 1977. Field translator Bechtel/France (El Eulma, Algeria), 1974-84; assist. regional mgr. Parsons Brinckerhoff Intl. (NYC), 1977-79. Second place, publications, New Jersey Press Women, 1985, first place, publications, N.J. Press Women, 1987. Mem. New Jersey Press Women, SPJ. Office: Box 1303 Princeton NJ 08542

PARKER, BARRY RICHARD, b. Penticton, B.C., Can., Apr. 13, 1935; s. Gladstone F. Parker and Olive Vizer; m. Gloria Elizabeth Haberstock, Dec. 9, 1960; 1 child, David. Author: Concepts of Cosmos, 1984; Einstein's Dream, 1986, Search for a Super Theory, 1987; Creation, 1988; contrbr. numerous articles to Astronomy, Sky and Telescope, others. BA, U. B.C., 1959, MSc, 1961; PhD, Utah State U., 1967. Asst. prof. Weber State Coll., Ogden, Utah, 1963-66; prof. physics dept. Idaho State U., Pocatello, 1967—. Recipient 3d place sci. writing award McDonald Obs., 1981, 1st place, 1984. Home: 750 Fairway Dr Pocatello ID 83201

PARKER, EDNA MAE, b. nr. Leith, ND., Mar. 17, 1910; d. Jacob Wade and Erma Anna (Meyers) Good; m. Laurence Yale Parker, Aug. 19, 1938 (dec. 1950). Author: Every Memory Precious, vol. 1, 1983, My Unforgettable ABCS, vol. 2, 1985, My Backyard Jungle, vol. 3, 1987, Twenty Years in the Post Office, vol. 4, 1987; poetry in anthologies. Wrkg. on non-fiction, poetry. Student public schs., Freeport, Ill. Postmaster U.S. Postal Service, Cedarville, Ill., 1960-80. Member Cedarville Area Hist. Soc., Newspaper Inst. Am., other orgns. Home: 125 W Cherry St Cedarville IL 61013

PARKER, FRANKLIN, b. NYC, June 2, 1921; m. Betty June Parker, June 12, 1950. Author: African Development and Education in Southern Rhodesia, 1960, Africa South of the Sahara, 1966, George Peabody: A Biography, 1971, The Battle of the Books: Kanawha County, 1975, What Can We Learn from the Schools of China?, 1977, British Schools and Ours, 1979; co-author: John Dewey: Master Educator, 2d ed., 1961, Government Policy and International Education, 1965, Church and State in Education, 1966, Strategies for Curriculum Change: Cases from 13 Nations, 1968, Dimensions of Physical Education, 1969, International Education: Understandings and Misunderstandings, 1969, Understanding the American Public High School, 1969, Education in Southern Africa, 1970, Curriculum for Man in an International World, 1971, Administrative Dimensions of Health and Physical Education Programs, Including Athletics, 1971, Education and the Many Faces of the Disadvantaged, 1972, The Saber-Tooth Curriculum, meml. ed., 1972, Accelerated Development in Southern Africa, 1974, Myth and Reality: A Reader in Education, 1975, Six Questions: Controversy and Conflict in Education, 1975, Crucial Issues in Education, 6th ed., 1977; series editor American Dissertations on Foreign Education, A Bibliography with Abstracts: vol. 1, Canada, 1971, Vol. 2, India, 1972, vol. 3, Japan, 1972, vol. 4, Africa, 1973, vol. 5, Scandanavia, 1974, vol. 6, China, 1975, vol. 7, Korea, 1976, vol. 8, Mexico, 1976, vol. 9, South America, 1977, vol. 10, Central America, 1978, vol. 11, Pakistan and Bangladesh, 1979, vol. 12, Iran and Iraq, 1980, vol. 13, Israel, 1980, vol. 14, Middle East, 1981, vol. 15, Thailand, 1983, vol. 16, Asia, 1985, vol. 17, Pacific, 1986, vol. 18, Philippines, 1986, vol. 19, Australia and New Zealand, 1987, vol. 20, British Isles, 1988; series editor: (with Betty June Parker) Education in Puerto Rico and of Puerto Ricans in the U.S.A., 1978, Women's Education—A World View: Annotated Bibliography of Doctoral Dissertations, vol. 1, 1979, U.S. Higher Education: A Guide to Information Sources, 1980, Women's Education—A World

View: Annotated Bibliography of Books and Reports, vol. 2, 1981, Education in the People's Republic of China, Past and Present: Annotated Bibliography, 1986; cons. editor: Jnl Thought, 1965-80, Western Carolina U. Jnl Edn., 1969-76, W.Va. U. Mag., 1969-78, Ednl. Studies; Eng., 1975-77, Rvw of Edn., 1977—, CORE (Collected Original Resources in Edn.), 1977—, Intl. Jnl African Hist. Studies, 1977—, Edn. Digest, 1976-80, U.S.A. Today, 1981—; contrbr. to: Ammericana Annl., 1961—, Collier's Yearbook, 1965-72, Compton's Yearbook, 1965-66, Dictionary of Am. Biography, 1951-55, Dictionary of Scientific Biography, Encyc. of Edn., 1971, McGraw-Hill Encyc. of World Biography, 1973, Acad. Am. Encyc., 1979, Random House Dictionary (unabridged), 1984, Reader's Digest Almanac and Yearbook 1968-73; others. BA, Berea (Ky.) Coll., 1949; MS, U. Ill., 1950; Ed.D., George Peabody Coll. Tchrs. of Vanderbilt U., 1956; research fellow, Univ. Coll. Rhodesia, 1957-58, Rhodes-Livingstone Inst. Social Research, Africa, 1961-62. Served with USAAF, 1942-46. Sr. Fulbright research scholar, 1961-62. Mem. U.S.A. Comparative and Intl. Edn. Soc., Appalachian Writers Assn.; others. Address: Box 5774 CEE No Ariz U Flagstaff AZ 86011

PARKER, IOLA B., b. Portland, OR, Feb. 9, 1905; d. Walter Newton and Zina (Boen) Ford; m. J. St. John Parker, Jan, 8, 1937; hildren—George Walter, Rozina. Contrbr. articles, stories to newspapers, popular mags., profl. jnls. including Guideposts, Smithsonian, Early Am. Life, numerous others. Wrkg. on mag. articles. B.S. Fla. Southern Coll., 1928; postgrad. U. Fla., U. Pitts. Tchr. si. and math public high shls., Lakeland, Arcadia and Bradenton, FL, 1928-54; asst. prof. chemistry Poinr Park Coll., Pitts., PA, 1954-72. Home: Rt 5 Box 152 Oakland MD 15220

PARKER, JEAN, see Sharat Chandra, G. S.

PARKER, JOYCE CAVE, (Turnik), b. Washington, July 12, 1948; d. Normal Emanuel and Madge Felecia (Gordon) Cave; divorced; 1 child, Arnese Shirell Parker. Contrbr. poems to anthols. Wrkg. on collection of poems. BA equivalent, Dept. Agrl. Grad. Schl., Washington, 1979; postgrad. Prince George Community Coll., 1979. Secy. Fed. Govt., Washington, 1974-75, adminstrv. clrk., 1975-77, program asst., 1977-79, program analyst, 1979-80, equal opportunity asst., 1980; secy., pub. affairs asst. D.C. Govt., Washington, 1981—. Active PTA, Washington, 1973-85. Recipient Superior Performance award Dist. Govt., 1984, Outstanding Performance award, 1985; named Employee of Yr. finalist Theodore Hagans, Jr., Washington, 1985. Mem. Employees Devel. Assn. Home: 4620 Brooks St NE Apt 2 Washington DC 20019

PARKER, MAYNARD MICHAEL, b. Los Angeles, July 28, 1940; s. Clarence Newton and Virginia Esther (Boyce) P.; m. Judith Daren Seaborg, Dec. 11, 1965 (div.); 1 dau., Francesca Lynn; m. 2d, Susan Fraker, Sept. 15, 1985; 1 son: Nicholas Maynard. BA, Stanford U., 1962; MA, Columbia U., 1963. Reporter Life mag., 1963-64, corr. Hong Kong Bur., 1966-67; corr. Hong Kong Bur. Newsweek, 1967-69, Saigon bur. chief, Vietnam, 1969-70, chief Hong Kong Bur., 1969-73, sr. natl. affairs editor, 1975-77, asst. mng. editor, 1977-80, exec. editor, 1980-82, editor, 1982—, mng. editor Newsweek Intl., NYC,1973-75. Contrbr. articles to Fgn. Affairs, Fgn. Policy, Reporter, Atlantic. Served to 1st lt. inf. U.S. Army, 1964-66. Mem. Council on Fgn. Relations, ASME. Home: 9E 96th St New York NY 10128

PARKER, NANCY WINSLOW, b. Maplewood, NJ, Oct. 18, 1930; d. Winslow Aurelius and Beatrice (Gaunt) Parker. Author, illustrator: The Man with The Take-Apart Head, 1974, The Party at the Old Farm, 1975, Mrs. Wilson Wanders Off, 1976, Love from Uncle Clyde, 1977, The Crocodile Under Louis Finneberg's Bed, 1978, The President's Cabinet, 1978, The Ordeal of Byron B. Blackbear, 1979, Puddums, The Cathcarts' Orange Cat, 1980, Poofy Loves Company, 1980 (ALA Notable Book, 1980), The Spotted Dog, 1980, The President's Car, 1981, Cooper, The McNallys' Big Black Dog, 1981, Love from Aunt Betty, 1983, The Christmas Camel, 1983, The United Nations from A to Z, 1985, Bugs, With Joan Richards Wright, 1987, Paul Revere's Ride, 1985, Aren't You Coming, Too?, 1987, General Store, 1988; illustrator: Oh, A Hunting We Will Go!, 1974, Warm as Wool, Cool as Cotton, the Story of Natural Fibers, 1975, The Goat in the Rug, 1976, Willy Bear, 1976 (Christopher 1976), Sweetly Sings the Donkey, 1976, The Substitute, 1977, Hot Cross Buns and Other Old Street Cries, 1978, No Bath Tonight, 1978, My Mom Travels a Lot, 1981 (Christopher 1981). BA, Mills Coll., 1952; student Schl. Visual Art, NYC, Art Students League. Pub. relations exec. N.Y. Soccer Club, NYC,1961-63; with RCA, NYC,1964-67; art dir. Appleton-Century-Crofts, NYC,1968-70; staff designer Holt Rinehart & Winston, NYC,1970-73; freelance writer, illustrator, 1974—. Jane Tinkham Broughton fellow, 1975. Mem. Soc. Illustrators, Graphic Artists Guild. Home: 51 E 74th St New York NY 10021

PARKER, PAT, b. Houston, Jan. 20, 1944, d. Ernest Nathaniel and Marie Louise (Anderson) Cooks; children—Cadssidy Brown, Anastasia Dunham-Parker. Author poetry books: Child of Myself, 1971, Pit Stop, 1974, Womanslaughter, 1978, Movement in Black, 1978, Jonestown and Other Madness, 1985; contrbr. to Plexus, Amazon Poetry, I Never Told Anyone, Home Girls, other anthologies, mags. and newspapers. Dir. Oakland (Calif.) Feminist Women's Health Center, 1978—; founder Black Women's Revolutionary Council, Oakland, 1980. Office: Aya Ent 1547 Palos Verdes Mall Walnut Creek CA 94569

PARKHURST, LOLITA, b. Chgo., Jan. 22, 1926; d. Peter and Julia (Wegmann) Kitcheos; div.; children: Sheri, James, David, Kathleen, John, Debra. Poetry published in Am. Poetry Assn. anthologies. BA, Valparaiso U., 1950; MA, Western Mich. U., 1967. Tchr. English Bloomingdale (Mich.) Public Schls., 1963—. Home: 1037 N 46th St Pullman MI 49450

PARKHURST, LOUIS GIFFORD, JR., (John Charles Edwards), b. Broken Arrow, OK, Aug. 13, 1946, s. Louis Gifford and Martha Gertrude (Kendall) P.; m. Patricia Ann Kirkham, June 8, 1968; children—Jonathan Edward, Kathryn Elizabeth. Author: Francis Schaeffer: The Man and His Message, 1985; compiler, ed. works of Charles G. Finney: Principles of Prayer, 1980, Principles of Victory, 1981, Principles of Liberty, 1983, Answers to Prayer, 1983, Principles of Holiness, 1984, Principles of Union with Christ, 1985, Principles of Love, 1986, Principles of Sanctification, 1986, Principles of Devotion, 1987, Principles of Discipleship, 1988, Principles of Revival, 1987; ed.: Pilgrim's Prayer Book (John Bunyan), 1986; compiler, ed.: The Believer's Secret of the Abiding Presence (by Andrew Murray and Brother Lawrence), 1986, The Believer's Secret of Spiritual Power (by Andrew Murray and Charles G. Finney), 1987, The Art of Life (Edith Schaeffer and Floyd Hosmer, illus.), 1987. BA, U. Okla., 1969, MA, 1974; MDiv, Princeton Theol. Sem., 1973. Ordained minister, 1st Christian Ch., 1973, pastor 1st Christian Ch., Rochester, Minn., 1977—; instr. philosophy Minn. Bible Coll., Rochester, Minn., 1981—; founder, pres. Christian Life Study Center, Rochester, 1981—. Office: Box 7024 Rochester MN 55903

PARKINSON, THOMAS FRANCIS, b. San Francisco, Feb. 24, 1920; s. T.F. and Catherine (Green) P.; m. Ariel Reynolds, Dec. 23, 1948; children—Katherine, Chrysa. Author: Men, Women, Vines, 1959, Thanatos, 1965, rev. ed., 1975, Protect the Earth, 1970, Homage to Jack Spicer, 1970, W.B. Yeats, Self-Critic and the Later Poetry, 2 vols., 1971; What the Blind Man Saw, 1974 (verse drama); The Canters of Thomas Parkinson, 1977 (verse); Hart Crane and Yvor Winters: Their Literary Correspondence, 1978; Poets, Poems, Movements, 1987; ed.: A Casebook on the Beat, 1960, Masterworks of Prose, 1961, Robert Lowell, 1969. AB summa cum laude, U. Calif.-Berkeley, 1945, MA, 1946, PhD,1948. Asst. prof. English, U. Calif.-Berkeley, 1948-53, assoc. prof., 1953-60, prof. English, 1960—, spcl. asst. to chancellor, 1979-81; vis. asst. prof. Wesleyan U., CT, 1951-52; Fulbright prof. U. Bordeaux, France, 1953-54, U. Frankfurt, Germany, 1954, Nice and Grenoble, France, 1965-66; vis. prof. U. Wash., Seattle, 1968; vis. lectr. Oxford (England) U., 1969; vis. prof. U. York (England), 1970; mem. lit. panel NEA, 1971-74; Sr. Research Fellow, NEH, 1984-85; vis. Sr. Research Fellow, St. John's College (Oxford), 1984-85; Guggenheim fellow, 1957-58; Inst. Creative Art fellow, 1963-64, sr. research Fellowship, NEA, 1984-85. Am. Philo. Soc. Travel grantee, 1957, 68; Humanities research prof., 1969-70, 80-81, ACLS grant, 1985. Mem. AAUP, MLA. Home: 1001 Cragmont Berkeley CA 94708

PARKS, MARY LU, b. Akron, OH, Mar. 27, 1928; m. Robert Gillen Parks, Apr. 19, 1950; children—Laura Parks Carr, Martha Parks Colwell, Mary Parks Stier. Contrbr. numerous articles to floral trade publs. BSci, U. Tenn. Product mgr. Ball Seed Co., West Chicago, Ill., 1974-80; pub., owner Florascope, Glen Ellyn, Ill., 1980—. Winner Publications Award, BPI, 1984. Office: 9 Office Park Circle 210 Birmingham AL 35223

PARLATORE, ANSELM, b. Bklyn., Dec. 7, 1943. Author: Hybrid Inoculum, 1976, The Circa Poems, 1975, Provisions, 1972; contrbr. poems to numerous mags and anthols. Editor, Granite, 1972-75; Bluefish, Southampton, NY, 1982—. Address: Box 1601 Southampton NY 11968

PARMAN, FRANK, see Parman, James Frank

PARMAN, JAMES FRANK, (Frank), b. Cordell, OK, Feb. 28, 1938; s. James Franklin and Lauretta Lee (Wright) P. Author: Daybook of Western Heroes: Poems From An Outlaw Calendar, 1977, This Land, Your Land, My Land, 1979, (co-author) Architecture in Oklahoma: Landmark & Vernacular, 1978; contrbr. to Southwest: A Contemporary Anthol., 1977; ed.: territory of Oklahoma: lit. & the arts, 1979-85; co-ed. var. pubs. Student, U. OK, 1956-62, Columbia U., 1963-64. Co-ed., Point Riders Press, Cottonwood Arts Fndn., Norman, OK, 1974—; ed./pub. renegade, Norman, 1984—; co-ed./ed. Point Riders Press/renegade, Norman, 1974—. Librettist fellowship, NEA, 1975-76; playwright in residence, SUNY, Buffalo, 1970-72. Mem.

NWU, PEN. Home: 829 South Pickard Norman OK 73069

PARNELL, MICHAEL, see Elman, Richard

PARQUE, RICHARD ANTHONY, b. Los Angeles, Aug. 10, 1935; s. Joe and Helen Margaret (Muto) P.; m. Vo Thi Lan, May 1, 1975; children—Kenneth, James, Phat. Author: Sweet Vietnam, 1984, Hellbound, 1985, Firefight, 1986, Flight of the Phantom, 1987, A Distant Thunder, 1988. Contrbr. articles to mags.; poems to anthols., lit. mags.; opinions and commentaries to newspapers including Los Angeles Daily News, Los Angeles Herald Examiner, others. B.A., Calif. State U., Los Angleles, 1958, M.A., 1966; postgrad. U. Redlands, 1966-67. Pres., Parque Cons. Assocs., Los Angeles, 1971-77; corp. dir. edn. and training Ralph M. Parsons Co., Pasadena, CA, 1977-78; free-lance technical and creative wrtr., 1978—; adj. faculty San Diego State U., CA, 1966-68, Calif. State U., Los Angeles, 1980, U. Calif. Los Angeles, 1982. Mem. AG, AL, NWC, AAP. Home: Box 327 Verdugo City CA 91046

PARROTT, WANDA SUE, b. Kansas City, MO, Feb. 12, 1935, d. William Raymond and Lois Marie (Cain) Childress; m. Edward Anthony Parrott, 1962 (div. 1971); 1 son—Edward Anthony. Author: Understanding Automatic Writing, 1973, Understanding the Aura, 1975, Aldena—The Diary of an Unborn Soul, 1986; contrbr. articles to Rosicrucian Digest, others. Staff wrtr., ed. Los Angeles Herald Examiner, 1968-74; mem. Intl. Communications Council Rosicrucian Order, San Jose, Calif., 1984-85. Named Outstanding Feature Wrtr., Hearst Corp., NYC,1968, 70, 71, 72. Mem. Book Publicists So. Calif., Los Angeles Gold Quill Lit. Circle (founder 1985), Los Angeles Authors' Club, Women in Pub. Affairs. Address: Box 1790 Studio City CA 91604

PARTCH, KENNETH PAUL, b. Mt. Vernon, NY, June 22, 1925; s. Edward Augustus and Grace Jane (Crabb) P.; m. Dorothy Sophia Iversen, July 16, 1953; children—Marjorie, Stephen, Jessica. Contrbr.: Crowell-Collier Ency. AB, Bklyn. Coll., 1949. Mng. ed. Moore Pub. Co., 1955, Chain Store Age Mag., 1955-59, Sales Mgt. Mag., 1961; ed. Food Topics Mag., 1961-68; dir. mktg. Grocery Mfrs. Am., 1969-70; ed. Chain Store Age-Supermarket Group, NYC,1970-77; cons. to supermarket industry, 1977-80; ed. and publs. dir. Supermarket Bus. Mag., 1980—; vp/edl. Fieldmart Media, Inc., 1984—. Home: 20 Devils Garden Rd South Norwalk CT 06854

PARTEE, BARBARA HALL, b. Englewood, NJ, June 23, 1940; d. David B. and Helen M. Hall; m. Morriss Henry Partee, 1966 (div. 1971); children—Morriss M., David M., Joel T.; m. 2d, Emmon Werner Bach, Nov. 2, 1973. Author: Fundamentals of Mathematics for Linguists, 1979; (with Stockwell and Schachter) The Major Syntactic Structures of English, 1972; Subject and Object in Modern English, 1979; ed.: Montague Grammar, 1976; mem. editorial bd.: Language, 1967-73, Linguistic Inquiry, 1972-79, Theoretical Linguistics, 1974—, Linguistics and Philosophy, 1977—. BA with high honors in Math., Swarthmore Coll., 1961; PhD in Linguistics, MIT, 1965. Asst. prof. UCLA, 1965-69, assoc. prof., 1969-83; assoc. prof. linguistics and philosophy U. MA, Amherst, 1972-73, prof., 1973—; fellow Ctr. for Advanced Study in Behavior Scis., 1976-77. Recipient Chancellor's medal U. MA, 1977; NEH fellow, 1982-83. Mem. Linguistic Soc. Am. (pres., 1986), Am. Philo. Assn., Assn. Computational Linguistics. Home: 50 Hobart Ln Amherst MA 01002

PARTRIDGE, DIXIE LEE, b. Afton, WY, July 6, 1943; d. LeVon Elmo and Clara Leath (Moser) Henderson; m. Jerry A. Partridge, Aug. 20, 1963; children—Kimberly, Darcy, Lezlee, Karen, Tyler, Justin. Author: Deer in the Haystacks, 1984; (anthol.) From Seedbed to Harvest, 1985, Toward Solomon's Mountain, 1986. Contrbr. poems to Qtly West, Centennial Rvw, Ks. Qtly, Christian Sci. Monitor, to Mont. Rvw, Writers Forum, Id. Wildlife, Ellensburg Anthol., Ind. Rvw. BA, Brigham Young U., 1965. Recipient 1st Place, Wash. World Poetry Day, Poetry Scribes of Spokane, 1984, 85, 1st Place in lit. and belief contest Brigham Young U., 1985. Mem. Mid-Columbia Writers, Wash. Poets Assn. (William Stafford awards, honorable mentions 1979, 80, 82, 1st Place in tradition contest 1986), 1986 Poetry Broadside Award, Washington State, Ellensburg Arts Council. Home: 1817 Marshall Ct Richland WA 99352

PASCARELLA, PERRY JAMES, b. Bradford, PA, Apr. 11, 1934; s. James and Lucille Margaret (Monti) P.; m. Carol Ruth Taylor, May 4, 1957; children—Cynthia, Elizabeth. Author: Technology—Fire in a Dark World, 1979, Humanagement in the Future Corporation, 1981, The New Achievers, 1984; contrbg. author: Optimistic Outlooks, 1982, Creating a Global Agenda, 1984; contrbr. articles to profl. pubs. AB, Kenyon Coll., 1956; postgrad. Coll. of William and Mary, 1957, George Washington U., 1958. Credit rptr. Dun & Bradstreet, Cleve., 1956-60; asst. ed. Steel Mag., Cleve., 1961-63, assoc. ed., 1963-67, bus. ed., 1968-69; mng. ed. Industry Week Mag., Cleve., 1970-71, exec. ed., 1971-86, ed.-in-chief, 1986—, lectr. in field. Carnegie scholar, 1952-56; recipient Disting. Svc. award Kenyon Coll., 1975, 81. Mem. World Future Soc., Natl. Assn. of Bus. Economists. Home: 30413 Windsor Dr Bay Village OH 44140

PASCOE, PATRICIA HILL, b. Sparta, WI, June 1, 1935; d. Fred Kirk and Edith (Kilpatrick) Hill; m. D. Monte Pascoe, Aug. 3, 1957; children: Sarah, Ted, Will. Contrbr.: Denver Mag., Denver Bus., Denver Post, Colo. Statesman, numerous other publs. BA, U. Colo., 1957; MA, U. Denver, 1968, PhD, 1982. Reporter Capitol News Service, Denver, 1985; freelance wrtr., 1984—. Mem. Soc. Profl. Journalists, Denver Women's Press Club, Rocky Mountain MLA. Home: 744 Lafayette St Denver CO 80218

PASCOE, VALENTINE, see Simpson, Joanne

PASTAN, LINDA, b. NYC,May 27, 1932; d. Jacob and Bess Olenik; m. Ira Pastan, June 14, 1953; children—Stephen, Peter, Rachel. Author: A Perfect Circle of Sun, 1971, Aspects of Eve, 1975, The Five Stages of Grief, 1978, Waiting for My Life, 1981, PM/AM: New and Selected Poems, 1982, A Fraction of Darkness, 1985. BA, Radcliffe, 1954; MA, Brandeis, 1957. Awards: NEA Fellowship; Di Castagnola Award (PSA), Bess Hokins Prize, Poetry Mag., Maurice English Award. Home: 11710 Beall Mt Rd Potomac MD 20854

PASTERNAK, CEEL, b. Dearborn, MI, July 17, 1932; d. James A. and Dorothy A. (Waggener) Waldsmith; m. R. Michael, July 11, 1959 (div. 1969); children—Nicholas M., Lissa J. Ed., The Internal Auditor Jnl., 1982—, The Practice of Modern Internal Auditing, 2d ed., rev., 1981. BS in Jnlsm., MI State U., 1954. Women's ed./p.r. Mt. State Tel./Mfg., Denver/Miami, 1956-69; ed./p.r. Lantana (FL) Boat, Palm Beach (FL) Life, 1970-76; prod. mgr. Spray mag., Winter Park, FL, 1977-79; ed. Inst. of Int. Audit., Altamonte Springs, FL, 1979-83, mgr./ed., 1983—. Mem. FL Mag. Assn. Office: Internal Auditor 249 Maitland Altamonte Springs FL 32792

PATCH, HARVEY, see Pacheco, Javier Barrales

PATERSON, LIN RICHTER, b. Paterson, NJ, Apr. 15, 1936; d. Meyer and Evelyn (Letz) Notkin; m. Howard S. Richter, Dec. 27, 1955; children—Michael, Ronni; m. 2d, Walter David Paterson, Aug. 26, 1982. Author: (with Fred Belliveau) Understanding Human Sexual Inadequacy, 1970. BA, Bryn Mawr Coll., 1957. Copy ed. W.B. Saunders Co., Phila., 1957-58; freelance med. ed., Boston, 1958-65; med. ed. Lahey Clinic Fdn., Boston, 1965-68; ed. med. div. Little, Brown & Co., Boston, 1968-79, ed.-in-chief, 1979-83; v.p., gen. mgr. book div., Appleton-Century-Crofts, East Norwalk, CT, 1983-84, pres., 1984—. Mem. Am. Med. Pubs. Assn. Office: Appleton & Lange 25 Van Zant St East Norwalk CT 06855

PATITZ, DOLORES ROSE, (D. Bauer-Patitz), b. Glidden, Wis., April 12; d. George M. and Anne Sabina (Bay) Bauer; m. James T. Patitz, 1952; children—Zondra Rose, Teresa Ann. Contrbr. poems to lit. mags., anthol. AA in Bus., Bus. Coll., Duluth, Minn., 1952; undergrad. U. Wash., 1953-54, U. Minn., 1950-51; U. Wis.-Milw., 1957. Bus. mgr., acct. Glidden Pub. Scl., 1972—, fed. programs coordinator, 1975—; forensic judge Wis. Forensic Assn., Madison, 1977—. Dir. drama Peeksville Leaguers 4-H Club, Glidden, 1967—; actor, dir. lighting Community Theater Group, Port Townsend, Wash., 1949-51; dir., actor Chippewa Players Drama Group, Glidden, 1978—; adv. fin. Glidden Pub. Schl. Bldg. Program, Glidden, 1985-86. Recipient Dramatic Arts award Chippewa Players, 1980. Home: RR 1 Box 189 Glidden WI 54527

PATLER, LOUIS, b. Hackensack, NJ, Oct. 29, 1943, s. Samuel and Connie (Vilardi) Patler; m. Catherine Louise Smith, July 5, 1978; children—Kale, Elina, Caitlin, Johana, Kellin. Author: Eloisa, 1979, An American Ensemble, 1980; ed.: Convivio, 1984, American Trend Report, 1979, 80, 81, 83; contrbr. poetry to Hawk-Wind, ACTS, Black Box, Root Drinker, Padma, others. BA, UCLA, 1965; MA, San Francisco State U., 1968; PhD, Wayne State U., 1972. Poet-in-res. World Campus Afloat, Orange, Calif., 1970-74; mem. grad. poetics faculty New Coll. Calif., San Francisco, 1972-87; grad. poetics faculty, Antioch U.S.F., 1987—; wrtr. Shannon Assocs., Montreal, Can., 1979—; ed. Am. Trend Report, Sausalito, Calif., 1979—. Grantee CCLM, 1975, 76; recipient editing award NEA, 1976. Home: 36 Shell Rd Mill Valley CA 94941

PATRICK, KIT, see Carpenter, Patricia

PATRICK, SAM J., b. Owensboro, KY, Aug. 8, 1937; s. John Terrance and Pearl (Cole) P.; m. Joyce L. Schvler, children—Christy, Daniel, Angela, Tharasa, Jill, Melissa. Author: How to Reduce Vandalism in our High Shools, 1983, Leesport High, 1984, Rodney, 1987, The Umpire, 1987; columnist: The Clermont Sun, 1987—. Contrbr. articles, short stories to numerous newspapers, mags. Wrkg. on 3 novels, screenplay. B.S., Georgetown Coll., 1959; M.A., Spalding Coll., 1975; Ed.S., U. Cin., 1978. Dir. marketing Ohio Blueprint Co., Cin., OH, 1979—. Home:

9495 West Ave Cincinnati OH 45242

PATTERSON, BECKY, see Crader, Rebecca Jane

PATTERSON, CHARLES WILSON, b. New Britain, CT, Aug. 5, 1935; s. Robert Fenton and Ann Janet (Wilson) Patterson. Author: Anti-Semitism: The Road to the Holocaust and Beyond, 1982, Thomas Jefferson, 1987, Social Perspectives of Protestant Journals during the Depression of 1893-97, 1970. Contrbr. to World History: Patterns of Civilization, 1983; contrbr. to various jnls. Ed., City and State in the Developing World, 1968. BA, Amherst College, 1958; MA, Columbia Univ., 1960; BD, Episcopal Theological Schl., 1963; PhD, Columbia U., 1970. Teacher var. schls. 1964-71; faculty member New School for Social Research, NY, 1971-81; tchr., Calhoun School, NY, 1981-84; assoc. editor, Scribners, 1985. Mem. AG, NWU, PEN, Editorial Freelancers Assoc. Home: 545 West End Ave New York NY 10024

PATTERSON, RAYMOND RICHARD, b. NYC, Dec. 14, 1929, s. John Tollie and Mildred Lena (Clemens) P.; m. Boydie Alice Cooke, Nov. 16, 1957; 1 child—Ama. Author: 26 Ways of Looking at a Black Man and Other Poems, 1969, Elemental Blues, 1983. AB, Lincoln U., Pa., 1951; MA, NYU, 1956. Instr. English, Benedict Coll., Columbia, S.C., 1958-59; tchr. pub. schls., NYC,1959-68; assoc. prof. English CCNY, 1968—. Served with U.S. Army, 1951-53. Recipient Poetry award PSA, 1950; grantee NEA, 1969; CAPS fellow, 1977. Mem. PSA, Walt Whitman Birthplace Assn., PEN Am. Ctr., 1983. Home: 2 Lee Ct Merrick NY 11566

PATTERSON, SCOT G., b. Minneapolis, March 30, 1953; s. Gerald R. and Joan E. (Hodecker) Patterson. Editor-in-Chief: A Social Learning Approach, Vol. I: Families with Aggressive Children, 1975, Vol. II: Observation in Home Settings, 1978, Vol. III: Coercive Family Process, 1982, other books in field of psychology. BS, U. of Oregon, 1977. Editor-in-Chief Castalia Publishing Company (Eugene, OR), 1975—. Home: 2485 McMillan St Eugene OR 97405

PATTERSON, TIMOTHY DALE, (Timothy James), b. Patuxent River, Md., Jan. 19, 1949; s. James Earl and Beverly Lavon (Reid) P.; m. Pamela Kay Zemke, Nov. 25, 1972. Author: Other Men's Women, 1985. Reporter Southeast Daily News, 1975-78. Editor: Fluor mag., 1982-84, Omnia mag., 1984-85. Contrbr. annual reports, corp. pubs., fin. communications. B.A. in Journalism, Calif. State U.-Long Beach, 1975; MA in Communications, Brigham Young U., 1982. Editorial dir. Fluor Corp., Irvine, Calif., 1978-84; mag. ed. Allied Corp., Morristown, N.J., 1984-85; free-lance wrtr., Bedminster, N.J., 1985—. Served to cpl. U.S. Army, 1969-71. Recipient award of Distinction, Los Angeles County Press Club, 1977. Mem. Pub. Relations Soc. Am., Soc. Profl. Journalists, Somerville (N.J.) C. of C. Home and Office: 51 Stone Run Rd Bedminster NJ 07921

PATTERSON, VERONICA SHANTZ, b. Rochester, NY, Feb. 19, 1945; d. Edgar Moore and Margaret (McLean) Shantz; m. Evan Rice Patterson, June 11, 1968; children: Carrie, Sara. Author: (poetry) How To Make a Terrarium, 1987; contrbr. poems to So. Poetry, Ind., Croton, La., Colo., Cumberland Poetry, Poetry-North, Colo.-North, N.Mex. Humanities rvws, Kalliope, Sou'wester, Spoon River Qtly., Buckle, Descant, Cape Rock, Concerning Poetry, others. BA, Cornell U., 1966; MA, U. Mich., 1967; EdD, U. No. Colo., 1983. Colo. Council on Arts and Humanities fellow, 1984-85. Mem. Phi Beta Kappa. Home: 2425 Agate Dr Loveland CO 80538

PATTON, MICHAEL QUINN (HALCOLM), b. Pewee Valley, KY, Sept. 5, 1945; s. James Quinn and Eleanor (Powell) P.; m. Jeanne Louise Campbell, June 2, 1977; children—Brandon, Julius, Charmagne. Author: Alternative Evaluation Paradigms, 1975, Utilization-Focused Evaln., 1978, 2d ed., 1986, Qualitative Evaln. Methods, 1980, Creative Evaln., 1981, 2d ed., 1987, Practical Evaln., 1982, Culture & Evaln., 1985. How to Use Qualitative Methods, 1987. Ed., Journal of Extension, 1988. PhD, U. WI,1973. Dir., MN Ctr. for Soc. Research, Mpls., 1975-80, Caribbean Proj., U. MN, St. Paul, 1980-84; prog. dir., Intl. Office, St. Paul, 1984—, pres., American Evaluation Assn., 1988. Myrdal award, Evaln. Research Soc., 1984. Mem. Am. Evaln. Assn., Am. Sociol. Assn. Home: 2199 St Clair Ave Saint Paul MN 55105

PATTY, ANN ELIZABETH, b. Frankfurt, IN, Mar. 22, 1951; d. William Joseph and Frances (O'Connor) Patty; m. Robert S. Withers; 1 dau.—Sophia Alba. BA, U. Calif.-Berkeley, 1974. Assoc. ed. Dell Pubs. Co., NYC, 1975-77; sr. ed. Pocket Books, NYC, 1977—; ed.-in-chief Poseidon Press, NYC, 1982—. Office: Pocket Books 1230 Ave of Americas New York NY 10020

PAUGH, THOMAS FRANCIS, b. Newark, Mar. 15, 1929; s. George Ruel and Gladys (Organ) P.; m. Martha Anne Freeze, Apr. 19, 1954; children—Jennifer Paugh Kopp, Lawrence David. BA, Colgate U., 1952. Photog./rptr. Ridgewood News (NJ), 1954-55; rptr. Bergen Record, Hackensack, NJ, 1955-56; regional ed. Outdoor Life, Miami, FL, 1977-78; assoc. ed. Sports Afield, NYC,1957-62, mng. ed., 62-67, field ed., Miami, 67-76, ed., NYC,1978—. Served to 1st. Lt., USAF, 1952-54. Mem. ASME, OWAA, Soc. of Illustrators. Office: Sports Afield 250 W 55 St New York NY 10019

PAUL, AILEEN, see Phillips, Aileen

PAUL, DAVID TYLER, b. NYC, Nov. 18, 1934; s. Samuel H. and Margaret (Tyler) P.; children—Sarah, Adam David. Author: Harbor Tug, 1967, Tugboat Adventure, 1967. Student, Colgate U., 1953-54, Haverford Coll., 1954-56; BFA, R.I. Schl. Design, 1959; cert. in firemanics, SUNY, 1976, video prodn., Pace U., 1980. Account supr. Meriden Gravure Co., CT, 1959-60; art dir., prodn. mgr. juvenile books Macmillan Co. 1960-62; art dir. Popular Boating Mag., 1962-64; design dir. Parents Mag. Press, 1964-66; dir. design Random House, Inc., 1966-69; v.p., mng. ed. Abelard-Schuman Ltd. & Criterion Books, 1969-70, pres., 1970-71; propr. Graphics Cons.; pub. Drake Pubs., Inc., 1973-74; dir. Photo- Media, Ltd.; co-fndr., ed. The Fire Islander Mag., 1975-77; mng. ed. Northeastern Indsl. World mag., 1976-77; exec. ed. for video and audiovisual, mng. ed. Cambridge Book Co., 1977-81; ind. I.T.V. producer, 1981—. Recipient awards Soc. Illustrators, Lithographers and Printers Natl. Assn., Graphic Arts Council Chgo. Mem. Am. Inst. Graphic Arts. Home: 540 E Gravers Ln Wyndmoor PA 19118

PAUL, DORIS JESSIE, b. Upland, IN., Aug. 16, 1903; d. Burton Allison and Bessie Belle (Smith) Atkinson; m. Wilson Benton Paul, June 24, 1930; 1 dau., Margery Ellen Paul Grier. Author: The Navajo Code Talkers, 1973, A Picture of Persia (with M. Ali Issari), 1977, What is Cinema Verite? (with Issari), 1979; contrbr. over 400 articles to 39 different periodicals; composer children's song books, church choir anthems. BA, Taylor U., 1926, B Music Edn., 1930; M Music, U. Mich., 1935. Music instr., choral dir. numerous schs. and univs., 1929-32, 42—47; freelance wrtr. Home: 1420 Somerset Close East Lansing MI 48823

PAUL, JAY SNYDER, b. Albany, NY, Apr. 15, 1945; s. Jay Evans and Margaret Janette (Snyder) P.; m. Joanne Carol Hasfurter, Aug. 20, 1966; 1 dau., Catherine Elizabeth. Contrbr. stories, essays, and poems to Pikestaff Rvw, New England Rvw, Cimarron Rvw, Poetry Northwest, Chicago Rvw., Abraxas, others. BA in English, Hartwick Coll., 1962-66; MA, Mich. State U., 1968, PhD in English, 1971. Asst. prof. English, No. Ill. Univ., DeKalb, 1971-73, 74-78; administrv. intern Ill. State Univ., Normal, 1973-74; prof. English Christopher Newport Coll., Newport News, Va., 1978—. Exec. comm. Va. Humanities Conf., 1981-85, pres., 1984-85; bd. dirs., Colony Recreation & Civic Assn., Newport News, 1983—, vice-pres. 1985—. Mem. AWP, NCTE. Address: 7 Sylvia Ln Newport News VA 23602

PAUL, SANDRA K., b. June 6, 1938; d. Benjamin and Eleanor Miriam (Epstein) Koodin. Ed., Electronic Publishing Business, 1983-86, assoc. pub., 1986—. BA, Hunter College, 1962, MA, 1965. Consultant, J.K. Lasser & Co., NYC,1960-64; research asst. Hunter Coll., NYC,1964-65; staff Random House, NYC,1967-78; pres. SKP Assocs., NYC,1978—. Mem. NYBPE, Amer. Soc. for Info. Sci. Office: SKP 160 Fifth Ave New York NY 10011

PAUL, WILLIAM BRUCE, (Bil), b. Whitehall, WI, Sept. 4, 1943; s. Harry Burns and Roberta (Wilcox) Paul; m. Lorraine Welch, Dec. 6, 1980; children—Katherine Jewell, Ian Alan. Author: The Tri-X Chronicles, 1971, Crossing the USA the Short Way: Bicycling a Mississippi River Route, 1978, Bicycling California's Spine: Touring the Length of the Sierra Nevada, 1980; ed. Mailmen's Dog Stories, 1979. BA, San Francisco State U., 1971; MA, Lone Mountain Coll., 1976. Owner Alchemist/Light Publishing (San Mateo, CA), 1971—; communications specialist with UPS, 1986—; sales rep. USPS (San Francisco), 1983—. SP5, US Army, 1963-66, Europe, Vietnam. Home: Box 5183 San Jose CA 95150

PAULIE, b. New Iberia, LA, Dec. 2, 1947; d. Jared Young Sr. and Wilda (Andrews) Gilmore; m. Tami Marie Allen, Sept. 12, 1987. Author, illustrator, pub.: The Wrong Foot (with Melissa Gelhaus), 1984, The Nowhere Man Affair (Huggy award, Zebra, FanQ award, Alexander Award Spy-Con.) Media West 1986; ed., pub., artist: Blond Blintz Bulletin-Dirtball Dispatch, 1978, Partners, 1979, Gryffon's Star, 1979, Jelly Baby Chronicles vol. 1, 1980, vol. 2, 1981, vol. 3, 1983, vol. 4, 1985, Roscius Maximus I, 1982, Roscius Maximus 2, 1984, 11 & 2 no.1, 1986, no.2, 1987, no.3, 1987. Wrkg. on novellas. Cert. Chgo. Acad. Fine Arts, 1970; student Western Mich. U., 1980-82. Ed., pub. Otter Limits Press, Boyne City, Mich., 1979—. Address: Box 99 Boyne City MI 49712

PAULK, WILLIAM (ESTON), b. Rebecca, GA, Mar. 7, 1929; s. William Eston and Beulah (Taylor) P. Author: Green Jade Bowl, 1955, Earth Chant, 1956, The Beholden Hills, 1984 (Oscar Arnold Young Meml. award, Poetry Council of

NC, 1985); contrbr. to Ga. Rvw, Green River Rvw, Appalachian Heritage, Chattahooche Rvw, Cumberlands, Davidson Misc., Laurel Rvw, and other jnls; play, The Gallery, 1964. BA in English, U. Ga., 1950, MA in English, 1954. Instr. Univ. Ga., Athens, 1954-57; tchr. The Darlington Schl., Rome, Ga., 1957-59; assoc. prof. Western Carolina Univ., Cullowhee, NC, 1959—.0 Address: Box 311 Cullowhee NC 28723

PAULSEN, NORMAN DEITRICH, b. Lompoc, CA, Feb. 3, 1929; s. Charles and Eileen (Chapman) P.; m. Patricia Ann DeCataldo, Aug. 3, 1981. Author: Christ Consciousness, 1985. Founder, prin. The Builders, Salt Lake City, 1980—, Wells, NV, 1980—, Santa Barbara, CA, 1968-80, Regency Affiliates, Wells, 1984—. Home: Big Springs Ranch Oasis Wells NV 89835

PAULSON, ALAN CHARLES, b. Milw., Dec. 1, 1947; s. Robert Clyde and Dorothy Ann (Lohneis) P. Contrbr. articles on naural history, biology, art, panoramic photography, northern engineering, coral reefs, the Arctic, aviation, weapons to mags. Ed.: Hydroelectric Power in Twentieth Century Alaska, 1983, Environmental Atlas of Alaska, 1984, Building in the Norh, 1985; ed., contrb.: A Solar Design Manual for Alaska, 1981. B.S. in Zoology, U. Wis., 1970; M.S. in Zoology, U. Alaska, 1973. Free-lance wrtr., 1977-78; ed. U. Alaka, Fairbanks, 1978-86, Inst. of Northern Engineering, Fairbanks, 1986—. Recipient Fejes Book Writing award U. Alaska, 1984, named Alaskan Wrtr. of Yr., 1977. Mem. Intl. Soc. Panoramic Photographers, Natl. Press Photographers Assn. Home: 1349 Chena Ridge Rd Fairbanks AK 99709

PAVLICH, WALTER DAVID, b. Portland, OR, Aug. 8, 1955, s. George Mathew and Eleanor LaVerne (Johnson) P. Author: Loadstones, 1984, Ongoing Portraits, 1985, Of Things Odd & Therefore Beautiful, 1987. BA, U. Oreg., 1978; MFA, U. Mont., 1980. Cons. Mont. Arts Council, Missoula, 1981-83, Contemporary Crafts Assn., Portland, Oreg., 1982-86, Eastern Oreg. Arts Council, LaGrande, 1984-86. Calif. Artists-in-the-Schls., San Francisco. Oreg. Arts Commn. fellow, 1984-85; recipient Ruth Lake Memorial Award (PSA), 1985; scholarship Bread Loaf Wrtrs.' Conf., Vt., 1984. Home: 4629 SE Reedway Portland OR 97206

PAWLAK, MARK JOSEPH, b. Buffalo, May 29, 1948; s. Joseph Andrew and Eleanor (Prorok) P.; m. Mary F. Bonina, Aug. 21, 1982; 1 child, Andrai Pawlak Whitted. Author: (poems) The Buffalo Sequence, 1978, All the News, 1984; contrbr. to anthologies Blood of Their Blood: Anthology of Polish-American Poets, 1980, Blood to Remember, American Poets on the Holocaust, 1986. Wrkg. on booklength poem about civil war in El Salvador. BS in Physics, MIT, 1970. Elem. tchr. Santa Barbara Free Sch., Calif., 1970-71, Group Schl., Cambridge, Mass., 1971-74, 77-80; poet-in-residence Worcester Pub. Schls. System, Mass., 1974-76; instr. math. skills U. Mass.-Boston/Harbor Campus, 1980—. Home: 173A Rindge Ave Cambridge MA 02140

PAYNE, MARY, see Santomauro, Mary Elizabeth

PAYNE, MICHAEL DAVID, b. Dallas, Jan. 17, 1941; s. Fred G. Payne and Jocie Marie (Kirkham) Lundberg; m. Laura Asherman, Dec. 26, 1973; children—Jeffrey, Albert, Edward. Author: Contemporary Essays on Style, 1969, Irony in Shakespeare's Roman Plays, 1974, Shakespeare: Contemporary Critical Approaches, 1979, Text, Interpretation, Theory, 1985, Perspective, 1986, Self, Sign, and Symbol, 1987, Criticism, History, Intertextuality, 1987. Student, U. Calif.-Berkeley, 1958-59, 61; BA, So. Oreg. Coll., 1962; PhD, U. Oreg., 1969. Tchr. English, Medford (Oreg.) Sr. High Schl., 1962-63; instr. English, U. Oreg., Eugene, 1963-69; asst. prof., prof. English, Bucknell U., Lewisburg, PA, 1969—, chmn. dept. history, 1980-82, chmn. dept. English, 1982—., Presdl. prof., 1982—, John P. Crozer Prof. of English; ed. Bucknell Rev., 1984—; dir. Bucknell U. Press, 1972-76. Recipient Lindback award for disting. tchg., 1976; Folger Shakespeare Lib. fellow, 1973; NEH fellow, 1974; Bucknell Alumni fellow, 1978-79. Mem. Shakespeare Assn. Am., Natl. Council Tchrs. of English, AAUP, MLA, Coll. English Assn. Home: 1704 Jefferson Ave Lewisburg PA 17837

PAYNE, PEGGY, b. Wilmington, NC, Jan. 8, 1949, d. Harry Eugene and Margaret (Tucker) Payne; m. Robert Marcus Dick II, Dec. 8, 1983. Contrbr. to N.Y. Times, Cosmopolitan, McCall's, Sci. Digest, other mags. and newspapers, first novel accepted for publ., 1988. BA, Duke U., 1970. Freelance wrtr., 1972—. NEH fellow, 1979; recipient Crucible Fiction award, 1978. Mem. AG, ASJA, Soc. Am. Travel Wrtrs. Office: 611 W North St Raleigh NC 27603

PAYTON, RANDI, see Payton, Randolph Randi

PAYTON, RANDOLPH RANDI, (Randi Payton), b. Camden, NJ, July 5, 1954; s. Robert Bobby and Adele (Ingram) P.; m. Regina Davis, July 28, 1981; children—Kimatni, Orisha, Imasonghe. Author: How to Start an Independent School, 1986. Contrbr. articles to newspapers including Washington Post. BA in Journalism, U. D.C., 1983. With pub. relations dept. Community Warehouse, Washington, 1978-82, Nat. Ctr. for Neighborhood Enterprise, 1986—; news wrtr., pub. affairs WPFW radio, Washington, 1981-83; reporter Washington-Afro-Am. Newspaper, 1984-86; free-lance wrtr. Washington Post newspaper, 1983-84, self-employed, 1986—. Coordinator pub. relations Friends of Coll. Here Come, Washington, 1986; WHMM ch. 32, Howard U., 1986—. Served with USMC, 1973-77. Mem. Alliance Third World Journalists, Washington Ind. Wrtrs. Home: 1205 Columbia Rd NW Washington DC 20009

PEABODY, RICHARD MYERS, (Jr), b. Washington, Mar. 14, 1951; s. Richard Myers and Rachael (Hudson) Peabody. Editor: Gargoyle Mag., 1976—, DC Magazines: A Literary Retrospective, 1982, Mavericks: Nine Independent Publishers, 1983; contrbr. to A Writer's Guide to Washington, 1983, Washing. Post Book World, Columbus Dispatch, other nwspprs.; author: Diet of Earthworms, 1985, I'm in Love with the Morton Salt Girl, 1979, I'm in Love with the Morton Salt Girl/Echt & Ersatz, 1985. BA in English U. of Maryland, 1973; MA in Literature American U., 1975. Workshop instr. St. John's Coll. (Annapolis, MD), 1985—. Panelist Lit. Advisory Panel, DC Comm. on Arts & Human., 1985-87, co-founder Wash. Writing Archive project at George Wash. U., 1985. Office: Box 30906 Bethesda MD 20814

PEACOCK, MOLLY, b. Buffalo, NY, June 30, 1947; d. Edward Frank and Pauline Ruth (Wright) Peacock; Author: And Live Apart, 1980, Raw Heaven, 1984. BA magna cum laude, Harpur College, 1969; MA with honors, Johns Hopkins U., 1977. Admin. and lectr., The State U. of NY at Binghamton, 1970-76; lectr., Johns Hopkins U., Baltimore, 1977-78; poet-in-res., Delaware Arts Council, Wilmington, 1978-81; educator, Friends Seminary, NYC, 1981—. Home: 321 East 71st St 5F New York NY 10021

PEARCE, FLOYD EARL, (Zachary Pearce), b. Lewis, IA; s. Earl Wilis and Florence Lucille (Chubick) P. Bookbinder Cardoza Binding, San Francisco, 1960-70; printer, bookbinder, owner The Pterodactyl Press, San Francisco, 1970-82, Cumberland, Iowa, 1983—. Bd. dirs. Iowa State Univ. Agrl. Ext., Atlantic, 1984—, Cass County Arts Council, Atlantic, 1985—, v.p., 1986—, pres., 1987; fin. comm. City of Cumberland, 1985—, councilman, 1986-90. Recipient 2 Honor Book awards Chicago Book Clinic, 1985. Home: Box 205 Cumberland IA 50843

PEARCE, ROY HARVEY, b. Chgo., Dec. 2, 1919; s. Walter Leslie and Esther (Bruesch) P.; m. Marie Jeanette Vandenberg, Feb. 8, 1947; children—Joanna Vandenberg, Robert Elliott. Author: The Savages of America, 1953, rev. 1965, The Continuity of American Poetry, 1961, Historicism Once More, 1969; ed.: Colonial American Writing, 1950, rev. ed., 1968, Tales and Sketches of Nathaniel Hawthorne, 1982, (with Cady, Hoffman) The Growth of American Literature, 1956, (with Charvat, Simpson) Centenary Edition of the Works of Nathaniel Hawthorne, 1972—, (with Miller) The Act of the Mind, 1965, Experience in the Novel, 1968, Pacific Coast Philology, 1978, (with Almond and Chodorow) Progress and Its Discontents, 1982; editorial bd.: ELH, 1946-75, Am. Lit., 1978-80, PMLA, 1976-79. BA, U. Calif.-Los Angeles, 1940, MA, 1942; PhD, Johns Hopkins U., 1945. Instr. English, Ohio State U., 1945-46, assoc. prof., prof. English, 1949-63; asst. prof. English U. Calif.-Berkeley, 1946-49; prof. Am. Lit., U. Calif.-San Diego, 1963—, assoc. dean grad. studies and research, 1968-71, dean grad. studies, 1972-75; vis. prof., lectr. Johns Hopkins, Salzburg Seminar Am. Studies, Claremont Grad. Schl., U. Bordeaux, Tchrs. Coll. Columbia. Recipient Poetry Chap Book award PSA, 1962; Am. Council Learned Socs. research fellow, 1948, 58, 59; fellow Com. Midwestern Studies, 1950; faculty study fellow, 1950-51; Fund For Advancement Edn. fellow, 1953-54; Guggenheim fellow, 1975-76. Fellow Am. Anthrop. Assn., AAAS; mem. MLA, Am. Hist. Assn., AAUP, Am. Studies Assn., NCTE, Internat. Assn. U. Profs. English, Modern Humanities Research Assn. Home: 7858 Esterel Dr La Joll CA 92037

PEARL, ERIC, see Elman, Richard

PEARLMAN, WILLIAM D., (Bill Pearlman), b. Los Angeles, Aug. 19, 1943, s. Jack C. and Mary Jane (Vandervort) P.; m. Lynn Williams, June 9, 1973; 1 child, Wave. Author: Surfing Off the Ark (poems 1965-69), 1970, Inzorbital (novel), 1974, An Elegy for Prefontaine, 1977; contrbr. to Io, Truck, Stooge, Denver Post; ed. Fervent Falley, 1972-75. BA, UCLA, 1966; MA, U. N.Mex., 1976. Lectr. U. N.Mex., Albuquerque, 1968-69, 76-77, counselor Mental Health Center, 1983-84; counselor Open Door Clinic, Seattle, 1978-79, Counseling Center, Bernalillo, N.Mex., 1979-81. Home: Box 613 Placitas NM 87043

PEARLSON, FREDDA S., b. Bklyn., June 19, 1949; d. Martin Victor and Sally (Sellinger) P. Contrbr. poetry to Stone Country, Feminist Renaissance, Wis. Rvw., Calif. Qtly, Chrysallis, other lit. mags. BA in English and Econ., Bklyn. Coll., 1970. Owner FSP Communications, NYC,

1978—; mng. ed. The Feminist Renaissance, NYC, 1983—. Home: 350 Bleeker St New York NY 10014

PEARN, VICTOR, b. Jacksonville, IL, Mar. 6, 1950, s. Forest Seaman and Dephim (Weaver) P.; divorced; children—Spirit, Dede. Contrbr. poetry to Coloradan, The Scrivener, Alchemist Rvw, Archer, numerous other lit mags. BA, Sangamon State U., Springfield, Ill., 1976; MA in English Lit., U. Colo., Boulder, 1983. Teaching Poetry Workshop at U. Colo., Boulder. Served with USMC, 1969-72. Home: 745 30th St. 3 Boulder CO 80303

PEARSON, JEAN ELIZABETH, b. Bethlehem, PA, Sept. 1, 1945, d. Harold E. and Ruth E. Pearson. Co-author of Kvinnliga Forfattare (Women Authors), lit. history pub. in Swedish, 1983; ed. of Mickle Street Rvw No. 7, "Whitman and the Earth," 1985; contrbg. ed. of MSR, 1983—. Poetry in Am. Poetry Rvw, Earth's Daughters, Christian Science Monitor, Sparks of Fire: Blake in a New Age, Milkweed Chronicle. BA, Moravian Coll., 1967; MA, Cornell U., 1971, PhD,1980. Instr., Moravian Coll., 1974-79; jnlst. in Sweden, 1979-80; asst. prof., Moravian Coll., 1981-85; freelance wrtr. and ed., 1985—. Mem. MLA, Women in German, PSA, ALTA. Office: Box 417 Bethlehem PA 18016

PEATTIE, NOEL RODERICK, (Garbanzo Bean), b. Menton, France, Nov. 28, 1932; came to U.S., 1933; s. Donald Culross and Louise Heegaard (Redfield) P. Author: (with Donald C. Peattie) A cup of sky, 1950; author: The living Z, 1974; editor, pub. Sipapu, 1970—; pub. Konocti Books, four poetry titles and several broadsides, 1973—; proprietor Cannonade Press, 1978—. BA, Pomona Coll., 1954; MA, Yale U., 1955; MLS, U. Calif.-Berkeley, 1961. Librarian Calif. State U., Los Angeles, 1961-66, U. Calif., Davis, 1966—. Mem. COSMEP (bd. dirs. 1974-76), CCLM, Western Ind. Pubs. (pres. 1978-79), Alternative Press Syndicate, ALA, Calif. Poetry Bibliographeers, chmn, 1987—. Home: Rt 1 Box 216 Winters CA 95694

PEAVY, LINDA, b. Hattiesburg, MS, Nov. 5, 1943; d. Wyatt Gaines and Claribel (Hickman) Sellers; m. Howard S. Peavy, Dec. 21, 1962; children: Erica, Don. Author: (with Jeri Day) Complete Book of Rockcrafting, 1978; Have a Healthy Baby, 1979; (with illus. Ronald Himler) Allison's Grandfather, 1981; (with Andrea Pagenkopf) Grow Healthy Kids, 1980; (with Ursula Smith) Food Nutrition and You, 1982, Women Who Changed Things, 1983, Dreams into Deeds, 1985; (chapbook) A Feathered Shadow, 1984; editor: Canyon Cookery, 1980; poetry and short stories pub. in Tex. Rvw, South Dakota Rvw, Cottonwood, Sunrust, Poets On, Pudding, New Oxford Rvw, others. BA in English, Miss. Coll., 1964; MA in Engish, U. N.C., 1971. Tchr. Central High Sch., Jackson, Miss., 1964-66, Glen Oaks High Schl., Baton Rouge, La., 1966-69; Instr. English Okla. Bapt. U., Shawnee, 1970-74; poet/writer in schls. Mont. Arts Council, 1982-84, 86; freelance writer, 1974—. Recipient Paladin award Mont. Hist. Soc., 1985. Mem. AG, Soc. Children's Book Writers, AAUW, Natl. Women's Studies Assn., Mont. Inst. of Arts. Home: 521 S 6th Bozeman MT 59715

PECK, MARIE JOHNSTON, (Marie E. Johnston), b. New Haven, CT., Aug. 15, 1932; s. James Howard and Marie (Voigt) Johnston; m. Austin Monroe Peck, July 19, 1952 (div. 1959). Author: Mythologizing Uruguayan Reality in the Works of Jose Pedro Diaz. Editor: Brown v. Board of Education of Topeka: The Case of the Century, 1986. Wrkg. on articles, translations involving Latin Am. BA with distinction, U. N.Mex., 1968, PhD, 1974. Wrtr., coordinator bilingual edn. U. N.Mex., Albuquerque, 1976-78; curriculum wrtr. Albuquerque pub. schs., 1980-81; instr. humaniities Johnson Co. Community Coll., Overland Park, Kans. 1985-86; freelance wrtr., ed., Southwestern Images, Inc., N.Mex. and Kans., 1978—; cons., Brown U. Topeka Project, Merriam, Kans., 1984—. Bd. dirs. Operation SER, Jobs for Progress, Inc., Colorado Springs, Colo., 1972-74, Mid-Coast Community Radio, Kansas City, Mo., 1986—. Fulbright sr. scholar, Uruguay, Argentina, 1981-82, fellow, Organization of Amer. States (Uraguay, 1970), fellow, Natl. Defense Foreign Language, U.S. Govt. Title VI Program, 1967-71. Mem. AATSP, Fulbright Alumni Assn., Latin Am. Studies Assn., MLA. Home: 8226 Johnson Dr Shawnee Mission KS 66202

PECK, RICHARD WAYNE, b. Decatur, IL, Apr. 5, 1934; s. Wayne Morris and Virginia (Gray) P. Author books for adolescents inclg.: Are You in the House Alone?, 1977 (Edgar Allen Poe award 1977), Father Figure, 1978, Secrets of the Shopping Mall, 1979; Sounds and Silences, 1970 (poetry anthology); contrbr. articles on architecture and local hist. to N.Y. Times. Student, Exeter (Eng.) U., 1954-55; BA, DePauw U., 1956; MA, So. Ill. U., 1959. Mem. faculty Schl. Edn., Hunter Coll., 1965-71; asst. dir. Council Basic Edn., Washington, 1969-70; lectr. in field. English-Speaking Union fellow Jesus Coll., Oxford (Eng.) U., 1973. Mem. AG, AL. Home: 155 E 72d St New York NY 10021

PECKENPAUGH, ANGELA J., b. Richmond, VA, Mar. 21, 1942, d. Clarence Hazelton and Mary Gibson (Chamberlayne) Johnson; m. C. W. Peckenpaugh (div.). Author: Letters from Lee's Army, 1979, Discovering the Mandala, 1981, A Book of Charms, 1983, Refreshing the Fey, 1986; contrbr. to anthologies: Moving to Antarctica, Poetry Out of Wisconsin, The Liar's Craft, The Five Petalled Blossom, Dear Winter, Gathering Place of the Waters, Eleven Wisconsin Poets; contrbr. poems to Va. Qtly Rvw, Cream City Rvw, Lamp in the Spine, Panache, Calliope, other lit mags; pub., ed. Sackbut Rev., 1978-81. BA, Denison U., 1965; MA, Ohio U., 1966; MFA in Writing, U. Mass., 1978. Dir. devel. Milw. Inst. Art and Design, 1975-77; dir. Writing Program for Adults U. Wis., Milw., 1978-82; asst. prof. English U. Wis., Whitewater, 1982—. Grantee, CCLM, 1980, NEA, 1981, Wis. Arts Bd., 1981. Mem. Feminist Wrtrs. Guild, Council Wis. Wrtrs., Wis. Regional Wrtrs., AWP, Wis. Alliance Authors & Pubs, Poetry Bd., Wisconsin Acad. Rvw. Home: 2513 E Webster Pl Milwaukee WI 53211

PECOS, BILL, see Sherman, William David

PEDERSON, CYNTHIA SUE, b. Oklahoma City, Sept. 11, 1956, d. Stephen and Elizabeth Jean (Badders) Daniels; m. Ronald Melvin Pederson, June 20, 1979. Author: Earthcolors, 1982, Spoken Across a Distance, 1982; contrbr. poems to Midwest Qtly, Little Balkans Rvw, A Confluence of Poems, Sunflower Petals, Cottonwood Rvw, Naked Man; ed. Inscape, 1980, 84; Ligature Press; contrbr. rvws., short fiction, articles, essays, broadsides to various publs. BA in English, Washburn U., 1978; MA in English, U. Kans., 1983. Tchr. pub. schl., Topeka, 1978-80, Shawnee Country Day Schl., Topeka, 1984-85; adj. instr. Washburn U., Topeka, 1986—; adj. instr. Friends U. Mem. Kans. Wrtrs. Assn., Kans. Poetry Soc., Headwaters Wrtrs. Orgn. Home: 1521 College Ave Topeka KS 66605

PEDOE, DANIEL, b. London, England, Oct. 29, 1910; came to U.S., 1962, naturalized, 1972. Co-author: Methods of Algebraic Geometry, 3 vols., 1947-53; author: Circles, 1957, Gentle Art of Mathematics, 1958, Projective Geometry, 1963, A Course in Geometry, 1970, Geometry and the Liberal Arts, 1976. BA, Magdalene Coll., Cambridge, Eng., 1933, PhD,1937; postgrad. Princeton U., 1935-36. Instr. Southampton U., Birmingham U., Eng., 1936-47; Leverhulme research fellow Cambridge (Eng.) U., 1947-48; reader U. London, 1948-52; prof. U. Khartoum, 1952-59, U. Singapore, 1959-62, Purdue U., 1962-64; prof. math. U. Minn., Mpls., 1964-81. Recipient Lester R. Ford award for expository writing Math. Assn. Am., 1968. Mem. Math. Assn. Am. Home: 1956 E River Terr Minneapolis MN 55414

PEEBLES, MARVIN L., b. Phila., Mar. 10, 1944, s. Hurley G. and Sammie Keith (Ervin) P. Author: Model Code for Student Rights, Responsibilities and Conduct, 1969, Own Worst Enemies: Local Charity Unmasked, 1984; ed.: Consequences, 1977-86, Community Service Bus., 1978—, Annl. Directory of Mgmt. Resources for Community Based Orgns., 1979—, Directory of Consultants and Mgmt. Trng. Programs Intended for Local Nonprofit Orgns., 1981—; contrbr. to Student Lawyer Jnl, Police Times, Law and Order, others. BA, Pa. State U., 1966; JD, Villanova U., 1969. Criminal justice specialist Alameda Regional Criminal Justice Planning Bd., Oakland, Calif., 1974-77; staff aide Legal Dept. San Francisco Unified Schl. Dist., 1977-78; cons., pub., ed., wrtr., prin. MLP Enterprises, San Francisco and Phila., 1977—. Office: MLP Box 18918 Philadelphia PA 19119

PEELE, ROGER, b. Chapel Hill, NC, Dec. 24, 1930; s. Joseph Emmett and Catherine (Graves) P.; m. Diana Egan, June 15, 1963; children—Amy, Holly, Rodney. Contrbr. articles to profl. jnls. Wrkg. on clinical, administrative and forensic issues in Am. psychiatry.A.B., U. N.C., 1955; M.D., U. Tenn., 1960. Acting superintendent Saint Elizabeth's Hosp., Washington, 1975-77, asst. superintendent, 1974-75, 77-79, chair psychiatry dept., 1979—, dir. Overholser div. of training, 1979—; chief clinical officer D.C. Commn. on Mental Health Services Administration, Washington, 1987—. Home: 12919 Asbury Dr Fort Washington MD 20744

PEHRSON, BARBARA J., (Barbara J. Pehrson-Thomas), b. Salt Lake City, Feb . 14, 1928; d. Lester Myron and Cathryn Arlene (Thomas) Pehrson. Co-author: Bits and Pieces on Being a Woman, 1984; author: Generic Selling, 1987; contrbr. Home Builders Mag. Wrkg. on nonfiction, salesmanship handbook. BA, U. Guanajuato, Mex. Owner, pres. Builders Task Force, Denver, 1983-87, Pehrson-Thomas Consulting Firm, Denver, 1987—. Office: 999 18th St Suite 1000 Denver CO 80220

PEKRUL, KIMBERLY ANN, (Theolyn Pekrul Sharmel), b. Battle Creek, MI, Mar. 23, 1960; d. Melvin C. and Sharon J. (Buchanan) Upson; m. Mark D. Pekrul, July 14, 1979; children—Heather Lynn, Christopher Daryl. Columnist: Reed City News, 1985-87. Contrbr. articles to mags., newspapers; author video scripts. Ed., contrbr.: Trinity Tokens newsletter, 1983-87. Student Ferris State Coll., 1978-79; Diploma, Inst. Children's Lit., 1987. Pres., chief exec. officer Cedar Ridge Advt. and Communications Agy.,

Reed City, MI, 1987—; free-lance wrtr., 1981—. Bd. dir. Reed City Public Library, 1986—. Grantee SCBW, 1985. Mem. SCBW. Home: Rt 3 Box 437-A Reed City MI 49677

PELLEGRINI, RUBY LOUISE, (Ruby Sealy), b. Miami, Fla., Jan. 20, 1962; d. Henry Warren and Priscilla (Stradchuk) Sealy; m. Joseph Patrick Pellegrini, Nov. 30, 1985. Poetry in anthologies. AA in Journalism, Central Fla. Community Coll., 1986. Reporter, feature wrtr., columnist, Big Sun News, Ocala, Fla., 1986. Mem. Christian Wrtrs. Fellowship. Home: Box 266 Belleview FL 32620

PELLEGRINO, CHARLES R., b. NYC, May 5, 1953, s. John and Jane (McAvinue) P.; m. Tige, Aug. 20, 1977; widowed April 1986. Author: Chariots for Apollo: The Making of the Lunar Module (with Joshua Stoff), 1986, Time Gate: Hurtling Backward Through History, 1985, Darwin's Universe: Origins and Crises in the History of Life (wtih Jesse A. Stoff), 1986, Flying to Valhalla: The Science Behind the Fiction (with Jim Powell), 1988, Her Name, "Titanic," 1988. Interstellar Communication and Travel (with Isaac Asimov and others), 1988, Atlantis: The End of a Dream, 1988. BA, L.I. U., 1975, MS, 1977; PhD, Victoria U., N.Z., 1982. Mem. AAAS, Planetary Soc., Brit. Interplanetary Soc. Home: 118 Pine St Rockville Centre NY 11570

PELLETT, KENT LOUIS, b. Salem, MO, Feb. 12, 1904; s. Frank Chapman and Ada Eugenie (Neff) P.; m. Marie Summerbell, June 23, 1929; children—Franklin Carlyle, David Louis, Susan Joy Pellett Penn. Author: (series) Lives of Famous Beekeepers, 1929, Private Lives of the Pioneers, 1938-40, Outlaws Iowa Can't Forget, 1939; Pioneers in Iowa Horticulture, 1941, Livestock Feeding, 1952. Co-owner, co-ed.: Lehigh Valley Angus and Fort Dodge Ind., 1929-35; Co-Op-Co News, 1943-67; mng. editor: Soybean Digest, 1942-73, Soybean Blue Book annl., 1947-73. BS, Ia. State Coll., 1928. Secy. Hudson Comml. Club, Hudson, Ia., 1943; pres. Ia. State Commons Club, Ames, 1927-28. Recipient meritorious svc. award Am. Soybean Assn., 1968, Godfather award, 1973. Home: Hudson IA 50643

PELLINGTON, J. RICHARD, b. Orange, NJ., Feb. 22, 1922, s. John Russell and Susan Florence (McDonough) P. Student Seton Hall U., 1946-51, Reporter Ocean County Daily Observer, Toms River, N.J., 1967-80, ed. People section, 1981-86; actor, dir. various N.J. theater orgns., 1940—. Served with USN, 1942-45. Home: 3810 5th St. E 221 Bradenton FL 33508

PELTON, TIMOTHY JOHN, b. Bloomsburg, PA., Sept. 22, 1956, s. John Henry and Ann Marie (Kessler) P.; M. Eleanor R. Bird, May 23, 1987. Contrbr. articles to: Sci. Digest, Popular Sci., Omni, other publs. BA, Pa. State U., 1978. Freelance wrtr., University Park, Pa., 1978; reporter, photographer Press-Enterprise, Bloomsburg, Pa., 1979-80; freelance wrtr., photographer, Bloomsburg, 1980-83, editorial designer, 1983-84; ed. Underwater USA, Bloomsburg, 1984—. Mem. Soc. Profl. Journalists, AAAS. Office: Underwater USA 3185 Lackawanna Ave Bloomsburg PA 17815

PELZER, DAVID ALAN, b. Cin., Nov. 19, 1950; s. Raymond Joseph and Wanda (Campbell) P.; m. Kathleen Marie Henson, Aug. 2, 1980; children—Jeremy, Justin. BS, Cons. Nat. Res., U. CA-Berkley, 1974; MS, Ag. Jnlsm., U. WI, 1982. Ednl. aids ed. National 4-H Council, Chgo., 1978-80; mng. ed. Farm Futures Mag., Milw., 1982-85; ed. Agri. Finance Mag., Skokie, IL, 1985—. Office: Century Comm 5520 Touhy Skokie IL 60077

PENDLETON, DON, see Obstfeld, Raymond Loeb

PENDLETON, JAMES DUDLEY, b. Ft. Bragg, NC, Dec. 12, 1930, s. James Dudley II and Lottie (Alexander) P.; children—Lelia, Eve, Caroline. Playwright: The Defender, 1961, The Oakes of Mamre, 1963, Nightsong, 1964, The Brief and Violent Reign of Absalom, 1968, The Trial of Judas, 1968, The Obscene Verse of Magdalene Randallman, 1972, A Last Supper, 1972, Ralegh, 1982; author television plays, radio dramas, magazine articles. B, Davidson (N.C.) Coll., 1952; MA, U. N.C.-Chapel Hill, 1956-58. Instr. N.Y. City Community Coll., Bklyn., 1954-56; prof. Va. Commonwealth U., Richmond, 1958—. Served as capt. U.S. Army, 1952-54. Recipient award N.C. Schl. of Arts, Winston-Salem, 1972, Rochester (Minn.) Civic Theater award, 1978, O'Neill Drama for TV award Eugene O'Neill Theater Center, NYC, 1979, 80. Mem. DG. Home: Box 5382 Richmond VA 23220

PENICK, JOHN EDGAR, b. Langley, VA, Jan. 2, 1944; s. Edgar C. and Bessie (Beene) P.; m. Nell Inman, July 23, 1966; children—Lucas, Megan. Contrbr. articles, chpt. to books including Tchr. Edn., Phi Delta Kappan, Curriculum Rvw, Edn. Digest, Focus on Excellence. BS, U. Miami, 1966, MA, 1969; PhD, Fla. State U., 1973. Tchr. Jackson High Schl., Miami, 1967-70; tchr., dir. Loyola U. Chgo., 1973-75; prof. U. Ia., Iowa City, 1975—. Recipient writing award Assn. Edn. Tchrs. Sci., 1978; Fulbright fellow (2), 1985, fellow USIA, 1986. Fellow Ia. Acad. Sci.; Outstanding Sci. Educator, 1987, Assn. for the Education of Tchrs. in Sci. mem. Natl. Sci. Tchrs. Assn. (2 Ohaus awards for innovation in tchg. 1982, 86), Natl. Assn. Sci. Tchrs. Office: 789 Van Allen Hall Iowa City IA 52242

PENN, JEAN COX, b. Chgo., Jan. 26, 1944, d. Carl Otto and Esther (Aberman) Watson; m. Richard Cox, Oct. 29, 1966 (div. 1967); m. 2d, Richard Arlen Penn, June 24, 1971. Contrbr. to Playboy, Cosmopolitan, Los Angeles Mag., Los Angeles Times, numerous others. BA in Jnlsm., U. So. Calif., Los Angeles, 1965. Reporter Orange Coast Daily Pilot, 1966-69; pub. info. dir. Calif. Mus. Sci. and Industry, Los Angeles, 1970-72; corr. Women's Wear Daily, 1972-77; sr. ed. Los Angeles Mag., 1983—. Home: Apt 5 824 18th St Santa Monica CA 90403

PENN, PENNETTA, see Dudley, Peggy Loucelle

PENNER, HELEN, b. McMahon, Saskatchewan, Canada, Feb. 26, 1937; d. Jacob and Annie (Hiebert) Knelsen; m. Henry Dyk, May 9, 1953 (de. July 24, 1953); 1 son, Victor; m. Mel Penner, Sept. 2, 1955; children—Steven, Jerald, Kevin, Lori. Author: Early Memories, Bks. I & II, 1986; Which Way? (transl. of grandfather's jnl. from Russia to Canada, 1842), 1987. Contrbr. poems to anthols. Wrkg. on 16th poetry bk. Grad. public schls., Edmonton, Alberta, Canada. Sec. High Level Echo, Alberta, 1973; lunchroom supvr. Vista Heights Sch., Calgary, Alberta, 1982—. Home: 1711 Valleyview Rd NE Calgary Alberta T2E 6G1 Canada

PENNER, JONATHAN DAVID, b. Bridgeport, CT, May 29, 1940; s. Sidney Lincoln and Leonore (Koskoff) P.; m. Lucille Toby Recht, Apr. 21, 1968; children: Benjamin, Daniel. Author: Going Blind, 1977; The Intelligent Traveler's Guide to Chiribosco, 1983; Private Parties, 1983. BA, U. Bridgeport, 1964, MFA, U. Iowa, 1966, MA, 1972, PhD, 1975. Postdoctoral fellow Edinburgh U., Scotland, 1977-78; asst. prof. English, U. Ariz., Tucson, 1978-83, assoc. prof., 1984—; vis. asst. prof. Vanderbilt U., 1984. Recipient Drue Heinz lit. prize U. Pitts. Press, 1983; fellow NEA, 1976, 83, Guggenheim Fnd., 1977, Fulbright Fdn., 1984. Mem. NBCC, PEN Am. Ctr. Home: 2232 E Seneca St Tucson AZ 85719

PENZER, MARK, b. Bklyn., Nov. 22, 1932; s. Ed and Fay (Weinberg) P.; m. Eileen Malen, Aug. 12, 1962; children—Matthew, Nicole; m. Nydia Rey, Nov. 25, 1985. Author: The Motorboatman's Bible, 1965, The Powerboatman's Bible, 1977. BBA, CCNY; JD, Fordham U. Freelance writer, 1950-53; editorial asst. Hearst mags., NYC,1955, asst. ed., 1956, assoc. ed., 1957-66; ed.-in-chief Rudder Mag., 1967-69, editorial dir., 1970-74; ed.-in-chief True, 1970-73, ed.-at-large, 1973-75; pub., ed.-in-chief Jnl Energy Medicine, 1978-81; Medicare Hearing Officer, 1981-82; tchr. creative writing Dade County Off Campus Edn., Prof. Bus. Communication, Fla. Intl. Univ; exec. certified instr., DMA. Office: 15507 Braemar Ct Miami Lakes FL 33014

PEPER, GEORGE FREDERICK, b. Nyack, NY, Jan. 25, 1950; s. Gerhard Wilhelm and Doris Elene (Bargfrede) P.; m. Elizabeth Marshall White, May 20, 1978; 1 son—Timothy William. Author: Scrambling Golf, 1977, golf's Supershots, 1982, Masters Tournament annls., 1983, 84. BA in English and Comparative Lit., Princeton U., 1972; postgrad. Yale U., 1973. Assoc. ed. Winchester Press, NYC, 1973-75; communications dir. Met. Golf Assn., NYC, 1976; assoc. ed., exec. ed. Golf Mag., NYC, 1976-78, ed., 1979—. Mem. Golf Writers Assn. Am., Met. Golf Writers Assn., ASME, Golf Collectors Soc. Office: Golf Mag 380 Madison Ave New York NY 10017

PEPPERS-JOHNSON, MARY LYNNE, b. St. Louis, July 29, 1960, d. Gerald Franklin and Beverly Joyce (Kunhart) Peppers; m. Stephen Lee Johnson, Sept. 7, 1985. Contrbg. ed.: The Am. Bench, 1985-86, The Am. Bar, 1986. BA, U. of the Pacific. Public relations asst. Calif. Soc. Profl. Engrs., Sacramento, 1982-84; assoc. ed. R.B. Forster & Assocs., Sacramento, 1984-86; mng. ed. Calif. Pharmacists Assn., Sacramento, 1986—. Office: Calif Pharm Assn 1112 I St Suite 300 Sacramento CA 95814

PEREIRA, TERESINHA ALVES, b. Belo-Horizonte, Brazil, Nov. 1, 1934; came to U.S., 1960; d. Pindaro de Paula and Maria Albertina (Alves) Pereira; m. Heitor Martins, Oct. 31, 1958 (div. 1977); children—Luzia, Emilia; m. Pedro Melendez, Mar. 2, 1978; children—Pedro Alberto, Luis Carlos. Author: Torre de Mitos, 1972, Tienda de Rondas, 1973, El Amor de los Narcisos, 1974, Aliens, 1975; (poems) A Rosa no Tempo das Cerejeiras em Flor, 1974; (fiction) Mundo Cao, 1974, Peligro: Los Angeles se Caen, 1974; (essays) La Trayectoria de Julio Cortazar en la Ficion Moderna, 1974; O Realismo Magico de Clarice Lispector, 1974, La Literatura Antillana, 1986. Ed.: Intl. Poetry Yearbook and Mag., 1980—, New Wave mag., Poetry Mag. 1975—, Lit, Lit. Mag. 1973—, Directory of International Wrtrs. and Artists, 1980—. Wrkg. on influence of soviet poetry in Brazilian contemporary revolutionary poetry. Tchr. Cert., Instituto de Educacao, Brazil, 1952; B.A., U.

Minas Gerais, Brazil, 1960; Ph.D., U. N.M., 1972. Asst. prof. U. Colo., Boulder, 1975-80, assoc. prof., 1980—. Recipient Natl. 1st prize Servico Nacional Teatro, Brazil, 1972; Gold medal Acad. of Pontzen, Italy, 1979, Ateneu Angrense, Brazil, 1980; named Poet of Yr., Canadian Soc. of Poets, 1977. Mem. Intl. Wrtrs. Assn. (pres.), World Poetry Soc. Office: U Colo Campus Box 278 Boulder CO 80309

PERKINS, JAMES ASHBROOK, b. Covington, KY, Feb. 7, 1941, s. Harry Dimmit and Juanita (Ashbrook) P.; m. Jane Allen, June 17, 1963; children—James Allen, Jeffrey Ashbrook. Author: The Amish: 2 Perceptions, 1976, Billy-the-Kid, Chicken Gizzards and Other Tales, 1977, The Woodcarver, 1978, The Amish: 2 Perceptions 2, 1981. BA, Centre Coll., Danville, Ky., 1963; MA, Miami U., Oxford, Ohio, 1965; PhD,U. Tenn., Knoxville, 1972. Instr. Memphis State U., 1965-67, U. Tenn., Knoxville, 1972-73; asst. prof. Westminster Coll., New Wilmington, Pa., 1973-79, assoc. prof., 1979—. NEH fellow, 1978, 81, 85; recipient Sr. Poetry award Miss. Arts Festival, Jackson, 1971. Mem. P&W, NWU AWP. Office: Westminster Coll Box 32 New Wilmington PA 16172

PERKINS, MERLE LESTER, b. West Lebanon, NH, Apr. 16, 1919; s. Charles Elisha and Ethel (Armstrong) P.; m. Barbara Marion Cunningham, June 16, 1951; children—Elizabeth Cunningham, Janet Blair. Author: The Moral and Political Philosophy of the Abbe de Saint-Pierre, 1959, Voltaire's Concept of International Order, 1965, Jean-Jacques Rousseau on History, Liberty, and National Survival, 1968, Jean-Jacques Rousseau on the Individual and Society, 1974, Diderot on the Time-Space Continuum, 1982, Montesquieu on International Rivalry and War, 1986. AB, Dartmouth, 1941; AM, Brown U., 1942, PhD in French, 1950. Instr. in French, Brown U., 1948-50, U. Chgo., 1950-53; mem. faculty U. Calif.-Davis, 1953-67, prof. French, 1963-67, chmn. dept. fgn. langs., 1962-65, chmn. dept. Italian and French, 1965-67; prof. French, U. WI, 1967—, Pickard Bascom prof. French, 1983—, chmn. grad. studies in French, 1967-74, 77—; Parker fellow Dartmouth, 1941-42; Edwards fellow Brown U., 1948-49; MLA grantee, 1956-57; Penrose Fund Grantee Am. Philo. Soc., 1956-57, 72-73, 74-75; Fulbright research grantee, France, 1960-61, 67-68. Mem. Am. Assn. Tchrs. French, Philol. Assn. Pacific Coast, MLA, Intl. Assn. for 18th-Century Studies, Modern Humanities Research Assn. Address: Dept Fr 1220 Linden Dr Madison WI 53706

PERKINS, MICHAEL, b. Lansing, MI, Nov. 3, 1942, s. William and Virginia (Davis) P.; m. Renie Fay Schoemaker (dec. 1968); children—Leslie Michael, Djuna Elizabeth, Zachary Alexander. Author: Evil Companions, 1968, Down Here, 1970, The Secret Record, 1976, The Persistence of Desire, 1977, Praise in the Ears of Clouds, 1983; ed.: Ulster Arts mag., 1978-79, Troia (by Bonnie Bremser), 1969, Covering Ground (by Donald Phelps), 1969, The Black Mountain Book (by Fielding Dawson), 1969, Angel (by Ray Bremser), 1965, Down Here mag., 1965-68; contrbr.: Young Beats: Literary Bohemians in Post War America, Younger Critics of North America, Macmillan Dictionary of 20th Century Science- Fiction. BA, Ohio U., 1963; postgrad., CCNY, 1966. Ed. Tompkins Sq. Press, NYC., 1965-68, Croton Press, Ltd., NYC., 1967-72, Milky Way Prodns., NYC, 1970—; wrtr.-in-residence Crandall Library, Glens Falls, N.Y., 1985; co-dir. Performances in Words and Music, Kleinert Arts Center, Woodstock, N.Y., 1983—; panelist N.Y. Fdn. for Arts, 1985. Mem. AG, NBCC. Home: RR 1 Box 56 Glenford NY 12433

PERLMAN, JOHN NIELS, b. Alexandria, VA, May 13, 1946; s. Ellis Sherman and Birthe Elaine (Jessen) P.; m. Janis Lynn Hadobas, May 26, 1966; 1 child, Nicole Jeanne Kachina. Author: Kachina, 1971; Three Years Rings, 1972; Nicole, 1976; Notes Toward a Family, 1976; Swath, 1978; Self Portrait, 1979; Homing, 1983; A Wake of, 1984; co-ed. Room: A Poetry Mag., 1986—. BA, Ohio State U., 1969; MS in Edn., Iona Coll., 1982. Cons. in poetry NEA, 1971; vis. poet to Wyo. community colls. Wyo. Arts Council, 1971-72; vis. poet Poets in Schls., NYC, 1972-73; tchr. creative writing/English, Mamaroneck Pub. Schls., N.Y., 1973—. Recipient prize AAP, 1969. Home: 1632 Mamaroneck Ave Mamaroneck NY 10543

PERLMAN, MARK, b. Madison, WI, Dec. 23, 1923; s. Selig and Eva (Shaber) P.; m. Naomi Gertrude Waxman, June 7, 1953; 1 dau.—Abigail Ruth. Author: Judges in Industry: A Study of Labor Arbitration in Australia, 1954, Labor Union Theories in America, 1958, 2d ed., 1976, The Machinists: A New Study in American Trade Unionism, 1962, (with T.D. Baker) Health Manpower in a Developing Economy, 1967; ed.: The Economics of Health and Medical Care, 1974, The Organization and Retrieval of Economic Knowledge, 1977, (with G.K. MacLeod) Health Care Capital: Competition and Control, 1978, Festschrifts (Sir John Barry, Edgar M. Hoover), 1972. Co-editor Cambridge Surveys of Contemporary Economics series; mng. ed. Jnl Economic Lit, 1968-81; cons. ed., later editorial cons. USIA publ., Portfolio on Intl. Econ. Perspectives, 1972—; ed. Joseph Schumpeter Intellectual Soc., 1986—. BA, MA, U. WI, 1947; PhD,Columbia U., 1950. Asst. prof. U. Hawaii, 1951-52, Cornell U., 1952-55; asst. prof., then assoc. prof. Johns Hopkins U., 1955-63; prof. econ., hist. and pub. health U. Pitts., 1963—, chmn. dept., 1965-70, univ. prof., 1969—; disting. vis. scholar Beijing Chinese Natl. Acad. Soc. Scis., 1983; Rockefeller Fdn. resident scholar, Italy, 1983. Soc. Sci. Research Council fellow, 1949-50; Ford Fdn. fellow, 1962-63. Mem. Inst. for Advanced Study, 1981-82, Am. Econ. Assn., Royal Econ. Soc., Intl. Union Sci. Study Population, Econ. Hist. Assn., Hist. Econ. Soc. (pres., 1985). Home: 5622 Bartlett St Pittsburgh PA 15217

PERLMAN, SUSAN GAIL, b. NYC, Dec. 29, 1950; d. Philip and Pearl P.; Hunter Coll., 1967-71. Copywriter, Blaine Thompson Advt., NYC, 1968-71; copywriter J. C. Penney Co., NYC, 1971-72; exec. info. officer Jews for Jesus, San Francisco, 1972—; editor Issues mag. 1978—; articles in Moody Monthly, Christian Life, Christianity Today, Eternity, Good News Broadcaster, Presbyterian Life; article in J. D. Douglas, ed., The Work of an Evangelist, 1984. Speaker and cons.; asst. coordinator Lausanne Consultation on Jewish Evangelism; bd. dirs., Jews for Jesus; mem. Lausanne Com. for World Evangelization; mem. Intl. Council Bibl. Inerrancy, Congress on Bible Com.; del. Conservative Baptist Assn. Am. Office: Jews for Jesus 60 Haight St San Francisco CA 94102

PERLMUTTER, PHILIP, b. NYC, July 10, 1925; s. Hyman and Bella P.; married; children—Jeff, Cathy. Author: Jewish Sports Champions, 1963, Builders of Israel, 1964, More Jewish Sports Champions, 1973. Contrbr. articles, short stories to mags. B.A., N.Y.U., 1950; M.A., Columbia U., 1954 Exec. dir. Am. Jewish Commun., Boston, 1960-75, Jewish Commun. Relations Council of Greater Boston, 1975—. Home: 281 Waban Ave Newton MA 02168

PERNOLL, MARTIN LESTER, b. Lakeview, OR, Dec. 10, 1939; s. Martin V.P.; m. Elizabeth Lush, June 25, 1961 (div. Feb. 1987); children—Kristin Ann, Martin William. Author: Current Obstetric & Gynecological Diagnosis & Treatment, 1987. B.S., U. Oreg., 1962; M.D., U. Tex., Galveston, 1963. Asst. prof. U. Oreg. Med. Center, Portland, 1970-72, assoc. prof., 1972-78; chmn., prof. Tulane U. Schl. Medicine, New Orleans, 1978—. Served to major U.S. Air Force, 1968-70. Home: 6325 Paris Ave New Orleans LA 70122

PERRI, CAROL SUE, b. Memphis, Oct. 3, 1946, d. Charles Nicholass and Jean Marie (Conger) Smith; m. Samuel Anthony Perri, Aug. 22, 1965; children—Catherine, Samuel Jr., Susan. BA, Calif. State U., Sacramento, 1986. Wrtr., asst. ed. The Intercom, Sacramento Army Depot newspaper, 1982, Crossroads mag., Sacramento, 1983; wrtr. People on Parade, 1982, Sacramento Sports, 1983; ed. The Calif. Hwy. Patrolman, 1983—; guest ed. Am. River Coll. Wrtrs.' Seminar, 1984, 85, Calif. State U.-Sacramento Wrtrs.' Seminar, 1985. Mem. Sacramento Press Club, Sigma Delta Chi. Home: 4971 Moddison Ave Sacramento CA 95819

PERRY, BETH, b. Oklahoma City, OK, Apr. 4, 1928; d. Warren Edward Bentley and Ollie Antoinette (Kerr) Bentley; m. Kenneth Alvin Perry, June 3, 1945; children—Pamela Lynn, Scott Kenneth, Angela Beth. Contrbr. articles to mags., newspapers including Oklahoma City Times, Fla. Times Union, Jacksonville Jnl., North Light Mag. B.A., U. North Fla., 1978, B.F.A. magna cum laude, 1983. Mem. Art League of Jacksonville, Jacksonville Water-color Soc., DuPont Creative Writing Group. Home: 7926 Praver Dr West Jacksonville FL 32217

PERRY, CHARLES E., b. Rogersville, AL, Oct. 10, 1932; s. George Shellie and Kate Pauline (Waddell) P.; m. Carolyn Sue Bailey, Aug. 18, 1962; children—Charles Eric, Delana Carol. AB in History, Jacksonville State U., 1964. Radio announcer WAVU, Albertville, AL, 1957-62; assoc. ed. The Reporter, Albertville, 1957-62; rptr.-state ed. Huntsville Times (AL), 1966-70; ed. Poultry Meat Mag., Cullman, AL, 1971-74; comm. dir. S.E. Poultry & Egg Assn., Atlanta, 1974-76; ed. Poultry Digest, Cullman, 1980—. Served to Cpl., US Army, 1953-55. Home: 215 Miller St Albertville AL 35950

PERRY, MARION J.H., b. Takoma, MD, June 2, 1943; d. Armin Werner and Adah Hubbard (Porter) Helz; m. Franklin A.H. Perry, July 17, 1971; children—Judith Aurelia, Scott Hubbard. Author: Icarus, 1980, The Mirror's Image, 1981, Establishing Intimacy, 1982; editor: Reflections: Then and Now (Mildred Crombie), 1981. MA, U. of Ia., 1966, MFA, 1969; MA, SUNY, Buffalo, 1979, PhD,1986. Instr., West Liberty State College, W. Lib., W.Va., 1966-68; instr., Albright Coll., Reading, Pa., 1968-70; instr., SUNY, Buffalo, NY, 1970-74; instr., Erie Comm. College, Orchard Pk., NY, 1975—. Mem. PSA, P&W. Home: 123 Park Pl East Aurora NY 14025

PERRY, NINA DIAMOND, b. Phila., Apr. 1, 1956; d. William W. and Adele (Plotnick) Diamond; m. David C. Perry, Feb. 16, 1986. Contrbr. numerous articles to popular mags. including South Fla. Home & Garden, Starweek TV., others; humorous scripts to "Pandemonium" on Sta. WLRN-FM, Miami, 1984—. contrbg. ed.: Miami/South Fla. Mag., 1982—; ed./designer: Bus. Rvw., 1985-86. Student Fla. State U., 1974-80. Dir. Creative services Sta. WECA-TV, Tallahassee, 1981-82; free-lance wrtr., 1982—. Mem. Fla. Freelance Wrtrs. Assn., Am. Film Inst. Home: 11535-B SW 109 Rd Miami FL 33176

PERRY, ROBIN L., b. NYC, Dec. 27, 1917, s. Clinton McKesson and Natalie Livingston (Forbes) P. Author: The Woods Rider, 1973, The Road Rider, 1974, Color Photography, 1975, The Trials Motorcyclist, 1975, Welcome for a Hero (novel), 1976, Photography for Professionals, 1976, Creative Professional Photography, 1979, Shadows of the Mind, 1986, The Toy Soldiers, 1986; contrbr. writing, illustrations to N.Y. Times, Popular Photography, Time, Wrtr.'s Digest, other periodicals. Freelance photography illustrator, wrtr. Served to maj. U.S. Army. Photographic exhbns. include tours in Belgium, Denmark, Germany, France, England and U.S.; photographs and writings in Archive of Contemporary Am. History, U. Wyo. Fellow Royal Photographic Soc., Internationale Societe Photographe. Address: 541 Nightingale Dr Indialanitic FL 32903

PERRY, SUSAN, b. NYC, Jul. 16, 1946; d. Daniel Carr and Frances (Farkash) Selden; m. John Lakkis (div. Jul. 1981); children—Simon John, Kevin Michael; 2nd m. Stephen Gregory Perry, Sept. 3, 1983. Contrbr. to Seventeen, Gifted Children Monthly, Los Angeles Times, Los Angeles Mag., LA Parent, Valley Mag., Woman's World, USA Today, other mags. BA, UCLA, 1968; MA, Pacific Oaks Coll., 1978. Ed.: LA Parent Mag. (Burbank, CA), 1980-82, Hollywood Post (LA), 1983; PR rep. Cultural Affairs Dept., City of LA, 1983; freelance wrtr. 1980—. Mem. Indep. Wrtrs. Southern CA. Home: 2715 Lakewood Ave Los Angeles CA 90039

PERRY, THOMAS KENNEDY, b. Anderson, SC, Feb. 11, 1952; s. Thomas Edsel and Betty Jean (Whitten) P.; m. Donna Marie Adams, May 16, 1981. Contrbr. articles, poems to anthols., lit. mags., newspapers. Wrkg. on comprehensive history of textile baseball history in S.C., novel. B.A. in English, Wake Forest U., 1974, M.A. in English, 1977. Personnel generalist Kendall Co., Pelzer and Newberry, SC, Boson, 1981-86; asst. personnel mgr. Am. Fiber & Finishing Inc., Newberry, 1986—. Home: 2103 Evans Circle Newberry SC 29108

PERSICO, JOSEPH EDWARD, b. Gloversville, NY, July 19, 1930; s. Thomas Louis and Blanche (Perrone) P.; m. Sylvia La Vista, May 23, 1959; children—Vanya, Andrea. Author: My Enemy My Brother: Men and Days of Gettysburg, 1977; The Spiderweb, 1979; Piercing The Reich: The Penetration of Nazi Germany by American Secret Agents during World War II, 1979, The Imperial Rockefeller: A Biography of Nelson A. Rockefeller, 1982. BA, SUNY-Albany, 1952; postgrad. Columbia U., 1955. Writer staff Gov. NY State, Albany, 1955-59; commd. fgn. svc. officer USIA, Buenos Aires, Argentina, Rio de Janeiro, Brazil, 1959-62; exec. asst. to commr. NY State Health Dept., Albany, 1963-66; chief speechwriter Gov. NY State, Albany, 1966-74, v.p. U.S., Washington, 1975-77. Mem. AG. Address: Box 108 Albany NY 12260

PERSKY, MORDECAI (MORT), b. Savannah, GA, Oct. 28, 1931; s. Nathan and Esther (Surasky) P.; m. Janet P. Holley, Oct., 1953 (div. 1962); 1 dau.—Lisa; m. 2d, Yolanda Kelley, Apr. 9, 1964 (div. 1974); m. 3d, Judith P. Rossner, Jan. 7, 1979 (div. 1984). AB, USC, 1953. Sports writer Augusta (Ga.) Herald, 1953-54, Atlanta Constn., 1954-56; ed., columnist Augusta Herald, 1956-58; copy ed. Miami (Fla.) Herald, 1958-62; Sunday layout ed. N.Y. Herald Tribune, 1962-64; Sunday ed. Detroit Free Press, 1964-67, asst. mng. ed., 1967-70; asst. to exec. ed. Phila. Inquirer, 1970-71; ed.-in-chief, v.p. Family Weekly Mag., NYC, 1971-76; mng. ed. Phila. Daily News, 1976-77; editorial dir. new publs. Playboy Enterprises, Inc., Chgo. and NYC, 1977-81; ed. Oui Mag., Los Angeles, 1980-81; founder One Woman Mag., NYC, 1983. Recipient medal Art Dirs. Club Detroit, 1965, 66; certificate of merit Art Dirs. Club N.Y., 1966-67; participant (as editor) Pulitzer prize for Detroit Free Press coverage of 1967 riots. Mem. ASME, Assn. Sunday and Feature Eds. Home: 74 Fifth Ave New York NY 10011

PERSKY, ROBERT SAMUEL, b. Jersey City, Jan. 5, 1930, s. Benjamin and Ethel (Soman) P.; m. Marilyn S. Bernstein (div.); children—Steven D., Joshua S., Laura R.; m. Lila L. Mukamal, June 28, 1987; Author: The Artist's Guide to Getting and Having a Successful Exhibition, 1985; The ARTnews Guide to Tax Benefits for Collectors, Dealers, Investors, 1986; ed.: Photographic Art Market, vol. III, 1985; columnist Art Bus. News, 1983—. Ed. Photographic Arts Center, NYC,1980, Photograph Collector's Newsletter, NYC,1980—; mem. adv. bd. Catskill Center for Photography, Woodstock, NY, 1983—. Mem. Assn. Intl. Photography Art Dealers, Am. Soc. Mag. Photographers, Am. Photographic Hist. Soc. Home: 302 W 86th St New York NY 10024

PERTSCHUK, MICHAEL, b. London, Jan. 12, 1933 (U.S. citizen born abroad); s. David and Sarah (Baumander) P.; m. (1) Carleen Joyce Dooley, Sept. 1954 (div. Dec. 1976), children: Mark, Amy; (2) Anna Phillips Sofaer, Aprl 1977. Author: Revolt Against Regulation: The Rise and Pause of the Consumer Movement, 1984, Giant Killers, 1986. BA, Yale Univ., 1954, LLB, Schl. of Law, 1959. Law clerk, Chief Judge Gus J. Solomon, U.S. Dist. Ct., Ore., 1959-60; assoc., Hart, Rockwood, Davies, Biggs and Strayer, Portland, 1960-62; legis. asst U.S. Sen. Maurine B. Neuberger, Orgegon, 1962-64; staff counsel, U.S. Sen. Commerce Com., 1964-68, chief counsel, 1968-77; chairman, Federal Trade Commission, 1977-81, commissioner, 1981-84; Fellow, Wilson Ctr., Smithsonian, 1984-85; Codir. Advocacy Institute, 1984—. Member: Natl. Acad. of Public Admin., bd. member, Common Cause. Address: Advocacy 1730 M St NW Washington DC 20036

PESSEN, EDWARD, b. NYC, Dec. 31, 1920; s. Abraham and Anna (Flashberg) P.; m. Adele Barlin, Nov. 25, 1940; children—Beth, Abigail, Dinah, Jonathan, Andrew. Author: Most Uncommon Jacksonians, 1967, Jacksonian America, 1969; rev. ed., 1978, Riches, Class and Power Before the Civil War, 1973, The Log Cabin Myth: The Social Backgrounds of the Presidents, 1984; author & ed.: New Perspectives on Jacksonian Parties and Politics, 1969, Three Centuries of Social Mobility in America, 1974, Jacksonian Panorama, 1976, The Many-Faceted Jacksonian Era, 1977, co-author of more than 60 additional books; editorial bd. N.Y. History, Labor History, Jnl Early Republic. BA, Columbia U., 1947, MA, 1948, PhD,1954. History lectr. CUNY, 1948-54; assoc. prof. history Fisk U., Nashville, 1954-56; prof. history S.I. Community Coll., 1956-70; prof. history Baruch Coll. and Grad. Ctr., 1970-72, Disting. prof. history, 1972—. SUNY Research Fdn. grantee, 1968; Guggenheim fellow, 1977; Rockefeller Fdn. fellow, 1978; CUNY Research Fdn. fellow, 1979, Fulbright lectr. in Am. history at Moscow State U., U.S.S.R., 1985. Mem. Am. Hist. Assn., Am. Antiquarian Soc., Orgn. Am. Historians, pres. Soc. Historians of Early Am. Republic, 1985-86. Home: 853 E 18th St Brooklyn NY 11230

PESSOLANO, LINDA, b. Springfield, MA, July 2, 1946, d. Angelo Charles and Claire Virginia (Snowman) P. Contrbr. poems to Foolscap, Sojourner, Stone County, So. Poetry Rvw, essay to Foolscap. AB, Smith Coll., 1968; MAT, Simmons Coll., 1969; MFA in Poetry, Warren Wilson Coll., Swannanoa, N.C., 1984. Tchr. English, Brookline High Schl., Mass., 1969-81, 1982-86; full-time wrtr., 1986—. Recipient commendation for poetry Pub. Schls. Brookline, 1985. Fellow AWP. Home: 51 High St Newton Upper Falls MA 02164

PETER, LAURENCE JOHNSTON, b. Vancouver, B.C., Can., Sept. 16, 1919; s. Victor C. and Vicenta (Steves) P.; m. Irene J. Howe, Feb. 25, 1967; children—John, Edward, Alice, Margaret. Author: Prescriptive Teaching, 1965, (with Raymond Hull) The Peter Principle: Why Things Always Go Wrong, 1969, The Peter Prescription: How to Make Things Go Right, 1972, The Peter Plan: A Proposal for Survival, 1975, Competencies for Teaching, 4 vols., 1975, Peter's Quotations: Ideas for Our Time, Peter's People and Their Marvelous Ideas, 1979, (with Bill Dana) The Laughter Prescription, 1982, Why Things Go Wrong or The Peter Principle Revisited, 1984; Processes of Teaching, 1985; The Peter Pyramid or Will We Ever Get the Point. BA, Western Wash. State Coll., 1967, M.Ed., 1958; Ed.D., Wash. State U., 1963; LHD (hon.), Heidelberg Coll., Tiffin, Ohio, 1982. Tchr., B.C., 1941-47; instr. B.C. Prison, Burnaby, 1947-48; guidance cslr., Vancouver, 1948-64; instr. U. B.C., 1964; asst. prof. U. So. Calif., Los Angeles, 1964-66, assoc. prof., 1966-69, prof., 1969-70; dir., Evelyn Frieden Center for Prescriptive Teaching, 1967-70; adj. prof. U. Calif., Turlock; panel mem. rev. bd. HEW, 1969-70; ret., 1970, ind. research and writing projects, 1970—. Recipient Phi Delta Kappa research award U. So. Calif., 1970, Canadian Univs. Assn. Alumni award, Disting. Alumnus Awards Western Wash. State Coll., Wash. State U., Will Rogers Top Hand award, 1979, Noble Prize, Assn. for Promotion of Humor, Intl. Affairs, Paris, 1984. Mem. AAUP, PEN, AFTRA, AG. Home: 2332 Via Anacapa Palos Verdes Estates CA 90274

PETERFREUND, STUART SAMUEL, b. Bklyn., June 30, 1945, s. Harold and Gloria Doris (Doller) P.; m. Carol Jean Litzler, Sept. 12, 1981. Author: The Hanged Knife and Other Poems, 1970, Harder Than Rain (poetry), 1977, Interstatements (poetry), 1986; ed.: Romanticism Past and Present, 1979—, Soc. for Lit. and Sci. newsletter, 1985—, Center for Lit. Studies annl. proceedings, 1985—. MFA, U. Calif., Irvine, 1968; PhD, U. Wash., 1974. Asst. prof. U. Ark., Little Rock, 1975-78; asst. prof. Northeastern U., Boston, 1978-82, assoc. prof. dept. English, 1982—. Poetry fellow So. Fedn. State Arts Assns., 1977. Mem. Soc. for Lit. and Sci., MLA, P&W. Office: Dept Eng Northeastern U 360 Huntington Ave Boston MA 02115

PETERS, CLARICE, see Kwock, Laureen C.

PETERS, JOAN KAREN, b. NYC, May 10, 1945, d. Daniel and Bette (Gurenseig) Peters; m. Peter Passell, Apr. 25, 1985. Author: Manny & Rose (novel), 1975; contrbr. articles to Encyc. of Women Wrtrs., 1979; ed. Anatomy of Melancholy (by Robert Burton), 1979. BA, U. Chgo., MA, PhD in Comparative Lit. Inst. English Middlebury (Vt.) Coll., 1970-72; asst. prof. English CUNY, 1972-74, Rutgers U., New Brunswick, N.J., 1974-76. Home: 380 W 12th St New York NY 10014

PETERS, LOUISE, see Sekoll, June Louise

PETERS, ROBERT, b. Eagle River, WI, Oct. 20, 1924, s. Charles Harry Samuel and Dorothy Jane (Keck) P.; m. Jean Powell, Oct. 1950 (div. 1969); children—Robert II, Meredith, Richard, Jefferson. Author: Songs for a Son (poems), 1967, The Sow's Head and Other Poems, 1968, The Gift to be Simple, 1975, Gaugin's Chair: Selected Poems, 1977, The Picnic in the Snow, 1982, What Dillinger Meant to Me, 1983, Hawker, 1984, Kane, 1985, Shaker Light, 1987, Ludwig, 1986; author: The Crowns of Apollo: Swinburne's Principles of Literature and Art, 1965, The Peters Black and Blue Guide to Literary Journals, vol. I, 1983, vol. II, 1985, vol. III, 1987. The Great American Poetry Bake-Off, vol. I, 1980, vol. II, 1982, vol. III, 1987; ed.: The Poets Now Series, 1982—; co-ed.: The Letters of John Addington Symonds, 1967-69; author acting scripts: Mad Ludwig, 1983, The Blood Countess, 1985. BA, U. Wis., 1948, MA, 1949, PhD,1952. Assoc. prof. Wayne State U., 1958-63; prof. English, U. Calif.-Riverside, 1963-68, U. Calif.-Irvine, 1968—. Served to maj. USAF, 1943-46; ETO. Guggenheim fellow, 1966-67, NEA fellow, 1974; letters, working drafts included in spcl. collections Spencer Library, U. Kans., Lawrence. Mem. PEN, PSA (Di Castagnola prize 1983). Home: 9431 Krepp Dr Huntington Beach CA 92646

PETERS, VICKIE JANN, b. Los Angeles, May 1, 1951, d. Edward and Elsie Neuvert; m. Milan James Peters; 1 son, Milan Anthony. Wrtr., ed.: AADE Reference Manual for Evaluation of Diabetes Education Programs, 1982; contrbr. articles to nursing publs. BS, Mt. St. Mary's coll., 1973; MS, Calif. State U.-Los Angeles, 1977, MA, 1978. Mem. nursing and edn. staff Valley Presbyn. Hosp., Van Nuys, Calif., 1973-86; mem. editorial bd. The Diabetes Educator, 1980-84. Home: 4228 Laurelgrove Ave Studio City CA 91604

PETERS, WILLIAM, b. San Francisco, July 30, 1921; s. William Ernest and Dorothy (Wright) P.; m. Mercy Ann Miller, Oct. 12, 1942 (div. 1968); children—Suzanne Peters Hilton, Geoffrey Wright, Jennifer, Gretchen Peters Daniel. Author: Passport to Friendship—The Story of the Experiment in International Living, 1957, The Southern Temper, 1959, (with Mrs. Medgar Evers) For Us, The Living, 1967, A Class Divided, 1971, A More Perfect Union, 1987; producer, writer, dir. TV documentaries: The Eye of the Storm, 1971, Suddenly An Eagle, 1976, Death of a Family, 1979, A Bond of Iron, 1982, A Class Divided, 1985; exec. prod. Boswell's London Journal, 1985, others. BS, Northwestern U., 1947. Account exec. pub. relations J. Walter Thompson Co., Chgo., 1947-51; mem. fiction staff Ladies' Home Jnl, 1951-52; article ed. Woman's Home Companion, 1952-53; freelance writer, 1953-62; producer: CBS Reports for CBS News, 1962-66; free-lance writer, film dir. and TV producer/exec. producer, NYC, 1966-82; dir. Yale U. Films, 1982—; cons. race relations, 1959—, hist. TV documentaries, 1976—. Recipient Benjamin Franklin mag. award, 1954, Peabody TV award, 1963, 70, 76; Golden Gavel award Am. Bar Assn., 1963; Schl. Bell Award NEA, ,64, Sydney Hillman Fdn. Prize Award, 1986; Emmy Award, 1986. Mem. Dirs. Guild Am., WGA. Home: 3108 Long Hill Rd Guliford CT 06437

PETERSON, CHARLOTTE A., b. Casper, WY, July 14, 1945, d. Louis Philip and Charlotte Marie (Reeves) House; 1 dau, Lisa. Author: Anatomy of Beauty, 1976; contrbr. articles to Cosmopolitan, Hoof & Horn Nat. Rodeo Cowboys Assn. Jnl., Data News, other publs. Ed., U. So. Colo., U. Wyo. Staff wrtr. Communications Pub. Co., Denver, 1972-74; dir. mktg. Hilton Corp., Casper, Wyo. 1974-76; woner, mgr. Studio 9, Casper, 1976- 79; staff mgr. AT&T Info. Systems, Morristown, N.J., 1979—; owner, mgr. advt. agcy. Peterson Prodns., 1976-78; freelance wrtr., 1974—. Mem. Ariz. Authors Assn. Home: 5 Meadowlark St Hackettstown NJ 07840

PETERSON, CHESTER, JR., b. Salina, KS, Mar. 24, 1937; s. Chester Nels and Erma Ann (Reed) P.; divorced; children: Joy, Nels, Erik, Ragnar; m. Miyoko Ikegami, May 21, 1982. Contrbr. articles to Air Progress, Aero, Folio, AOPA Pilot, Guns, Travel Wkly, Successful Farming, Farm Jnl., Kans. Bus. News, Hawaii, The Wrtr., Police Marksman, others, chpt. to The Writer's Handbook. BS, Kans., State U., 1959, BS, 1960. Assoc. ed. Successful Farming, Des Moines, 1960-64; creative contact exec. Gardner Advt., St. Louis, 1964; freelance wrtr., 1963-73; pub.-ed. Simmental Shield, Lindsborg, Kans., 1973—. Recipient cert. of merit N.Y.C. Art Dirs. Club, 1975. Mem. Agrl. Eds. Am., Livestock Publs. Council, Am. Soc. Mag. Photographers, Sigma Delta Chi, NWC. Home: Box 71 Lindsborg KS 67456

PETERSON, DONALD ROBERT, b. Sandstone, MN, Apr. 1, 1929; s. Martin Theodore and Margaret (Dezell) P.; m. Lois Ruth Taylor, Dec. 31, 1951 (div. 1975); children—Wyatt A., Winston B., Whitney C. (dec.), Westley D., Webster E.; m. 2d, Edie Tannenbaum, Aug. 31, 1975; 1 son, Ryan Kerry. Founding ed. Car Collector Mag., 1977—; contrbd. chapter to Complete Handbook of Automobile Hobbies; articles to Business Atlanta Mag., The Classic Car Mag. BS, Gustavus Adolphus, 1952. Auditor, General Mills, Mpls., 1952-53; underwriter Prudential Ins., Mpls., 1953- 64, North Central Life, St. Paul, 64-65; asst. cashier Northeast State Bank, Mpls., 1966-67; pres. First State Bank, Murdock, MN, 1967-73; ed. Car Collector Mag., Atlanta, 1977—. Served to S1, USN, 1946-47. Citation for Dist. Svc., Classic Car Club Amer., 1965. Mem. Soc. Automotive Hist. Mayor, City of Murdock, MN, 1973-74. Home: 1400 Lake Ridge Court Roswell GA 30076

PETERSON, ERIC CLINTON, b. Derby, CT, Dec. 13, 1944; s. Richard Jersey and Marie Natalie (Vulcu) P.; m. Georgia Diane Chrampanis, Dec. 8, 1972 (div. Feb. 25, 1981); 1 dau., Samantha; m. 2d, Phyllis Ann Latino, Oct. 17, 1982. Monthly govt. affairs columnist Shopping Ctr. World; bi-monthly columnist Stores Mag. BA, Ohio Wesleyan U., 1967. Asst. ed. Chain Store Age, NYC,1970-72; assoc. ed. Shopping Ctr. World, NYC,1972-75, ed., 1975-77; pub. affairs ed. ICSC, NYC,1977-81; ed.-in-chief Business Facilities, Red Bank, NJ, 1981-87. Served to Spec. 5, US Army, 1968-69, Vietnam. Mem. ABP, Am. Econ. Devel. Council. Office: Bus Fac 121 Monmouth St Red Bank NJ 07701

PETERSON, KAREN LYNN, b. Buffalo, Dec. 3, 1952; d. Bertil Leonard and Jean Anne (Ripton) Peterson. Contrbr. Radical Teacher, 1981; Room of Our Own (poetry jnl), 1976—, Common Ground, Western N.Y. Women's News Journal, 1983—; ed. Works & Days, interdisciplinary journal, 1979-80. BA, Wells Coll., 1974; MLS, SUNYAB, 1976. J.D. SUNYAB, 1987. Area co-ord. Browsing Lib./Music Rm., SUNYAB, Buffalo, 1978-79, tchg. fellow, English Dept., 1978-81, lectr./instr. SUC/B & SUNYAB, 1982, law lib. clk. Sears Law Lib., SUNYAB, 1983—; editing and research asst. to Dr. Sarah Slavin, for APSA research, SUC/B, Buffalo, 1982—, law library clerk, 1983-87. Home: S-5068 Lake Shore Rd Hamburg NY 14075

PETERSON, ROBERT, b. Denver, June 2, 1924; s. Ernest F. and Alice (Morris) P.; 1 child, Laurel D. Glenn. Author: Home for the Night, 1962; The Binnacle, 1967; Wondering Where You Are, 1969; Lone Rider, 1976; Under Sealed Orders, 1976; Leaving Taos, 1981 (Natl. Poetry Series award 1981); The Only Piano Player in La Paz, 1985, Waiting for Garbo: 44 Ghazals, 1987. BA, U. Calif., Berkeley, 1974; MA, San Francisco State Coll., 1956. Ed. Contact mag., 1959-61; instr. poetry workshop San Francisco State Coll., 1963-64; post-in-res. Reed Coll., Portland, Oreg., 1969-71; ed./contest judge Brigadoon Corp., Santa Cruz, Calif., 1983—. Served with AUS, 1943-45; ETO; PTO. NEA poetry grantee, 1967; Amy Lowell traveling fellow, 1972-73. Mem. AG, PEN, PSA. Home: PO Box 1213 Capitola CA 95010

PETERSON, SHARON MARIE, b. Catskill, NY, Dec. 29, 1947; d. Clyde Sidney McCoon and Amelia (Parslow) Dewes; m. Gerald Warner Burson, Aug. 1964 (div. 1973); m. Bruce Kent Peterson, Feb. 3, 1973 (div. 1986); children—Mark Peterson, Robb Peterson. Author, ed., pub. Images series of profl. guidelines for bus. executives, 1987-88; poetry in anthologies. Wrkg. on novel, nonfiction. BA, Ariz. State U., 1968. Mgmt. cons., 1975-80; founder, rpes. Exec. Assistance Programs, Scottsdale, Ariz., 1980—. Home: Scottsdale AZ

PETESCH, NATALIE L(EVIN) M(AINES), b. Detroit, MI; d. Samuel and Anna (Goldman) Levin; m. (1) John Maines, Dec. 21, 1945 (div. Jan., 1959); (2) Donald Anthony Petesch, Aug. 30, 1959; children: (1st mar.) Rachel Maines; (2d mar.) Nicholas Donald. Author: After the First Death, There Is No Other (short story collection), 1974, The Odyssey of Katinou Kalokovich (novel), 1974, Two Novels: The Long Hot Summers of Yasba K. (and) The Leprosarium, 1978, publ. as Seasons Such as These, 1979, Soul Clap Its Hands and Sing (short story collection), 1980, Duncan's Colony (novel), 1982, Wild with All Regret (short story collection), 1985, Flowering Mimosa (novel), 1986. Work in anthologies, including, Elizabeth Canar and Cecile Vye, eds, Different Drummers, 1973, Gay Rubin, ed, Michigan Hot Apples: An Anthology of Michigan Writers, 1973, Margaret Kaminski, ed, Moving to Antarctica, 1975, Theodore Solotaroff and Shannon Ravenel, eds, Best American Short Stories of 1978, 1978, Fiction Omnibus, 1979, and The Best of the California Quarterly, 1975-1985, 1986. Contrbr of short stories to lit jnls. Attended Wayne State Univ, Detroit, Mich. BS, Boston Univ, 1955; MA, Brandeis Univ, 1956; Ph.D., Uni of Texas at Austin, 1962. Spcl instr, Univ of Texas at Austin, 1959-60, instr in British and Am lit, 1963-65; asst prof of British and Am lit, San Francisco State Coll (now Univ), San Francisco, 1961-62;

asst. prof of British and Am lit, 1961-62, Southwest Texas State College (now Univ), San Marcos, full-time writer, 1965—. Distinguished Vis Prof in Creative Writing, Univ of Idaho, Jan., 1982. Iowa School of Letters award for short fiction, 1974, for After the First Death, There Is No Other; Kansas Quarterly Fiction Award, 1976; First Prize, Louisville Review fiction competition, 1978; New Letters Summer Prize Book award, 1979, for Seasons Such as These; Pa. Council on the Arts literary fellow, 1980; Dobie-Paisano fellow in lit nomination, 1981; Swallow's Tale Prize for short fiction, 1985, for Wild with All Regret. Address: 6320 Crombie St Pittsburgh PA 15217

PETITJEAN, JEAN, see Kleinhans, Theodore John

PETRAKIS, HARRY MARK, b. St. Louis, June 5, 1923; s. Mark E. and Stella (Christoulakis) P.; m. Diane Perparos, Sept. 30, 1945; children—Mark, John, Dean. Author: Lion at My Heart, 1959, The Odyssey of Kostas Volakis, 1963, Pericles on 31st Street, 1965 (nominated Natl. Book award), The Founder's Touch, 1965, A Dream of Kings, 1966 (nominated Natl. Book award), The Waves of Night, 1969, Stelmark: A Family Recollection, 1970, In the Land of Morning, 1973, The Hour of the Bell, 1976, A Petrakis Reader, 28 Stories, 1978, Nick the Greek, 1979, Days of Vengeance, 1983, Reflections on a Writer's Life and Work, 1983; contrbr. short stories to Atlantic Monthly, Sat. Eve. Post, Harper's Bazaar, Country Beautiful (story included in Prize Stories, also O. Henry Award 1966). Student, U. IL, 1940-41, LHD, 1971; LHD, Governor's State U., 1980, Hellenic Coll., 1984. Freelance writer, tchr., lectr.; tchr. workshop classes in novel, short story; McGuffey vis. lectr. Ohio U., Athens, 1971; writer-in-res. Chgo. Pub. Lib., 1976-77, Chgo. Bd. Edn., 1978-79. Recipient awards Friends of Am. Writers, Friends of Lit., Soc. Midland Authors, Carl Sandburg award. Mem. AG, PEN, WGA-West. Address: 80 East Rd Dune Acres Chesterton IN 46304

PETRIE, FERDINAND RALPH, b. Hackensack, NJ, Sept. 17, 1925; s. Archibald John and Bessie (Rutherford) P.; m. Phyllis C. Haddow, Oct. 19, 1951; children—Beth, David. Author: Drawing Landscapes in Pencil, 1979; illustrator: The Drawing Book, 1980, The Color Book, 1981, The Alkyd Book, 1982, Watercolorist's Guide to Painting Trees, 1983, WGP Skies, 1984, WGP Water, 1985; designer U.S. commemorative stamp design, 2 Zaire commemorative stamps, 1980. Advt. cert., Parson's Schl. Design, NYC,1949; student Art Students League, 1947-49, Famous Artists Course in Illustration, 1958-59. Illustrator J. Gans Assocs., NYC,1950-69; freelance illustrator, artist, 1969—; owner, Petrie Gallery, Rockport, MA, 1971—. Mem. Am. Watercolor Soc., Artists Fellowship, Rockport Art Assn., Am. Artists Profl. League, Grand Central Gallery, NJ Watercolor Soc. Address: 51 Vreeland Ave Ruitherford NJ 07070

PETROSKI, CATHERINE, b. St. Louis, Sept. 7, 1939, d. Robert J. and Mary (Stirling) Groom; m. Henry Petroski, July 15, 1966; children—Karen, Stephen. Author: Gravity and Other Stories, 1981, Beautiful My Mane in the Wind, 1983, The Summer That Lasted Forever, 1984; contrbr. to Tex. Stories and Poems, Having Been There, Stories for Free Children, MS, N.Am. Rvw, Prairie Schooner, Va. Qtly, Miss. Rvw, others. BA, MacMurray Coll., 1961, D.Lit. (hon.), 1984; MA, U. Ill., 1962. Staff wrtr./ed. NCTE, Champaign, Ill., 1967-68; freelance wrtr., 1968—; wrtr.-in-residence Ill. Arts Council, Chgo., 1976-78; lectr. U. N.C., Chapel Hill, 1982, Duke U., Durham, N.C., 1983. Bridgman scholar Bread Loaf Wrtrs. Conf., 1974, Allan Collins fellow, 1982; NEA writing fellow, 1977-78, 83; Yaddo fellow/resident, 1980, 84. Mem. AG. Home: 2501 Perkins Rd Durham NC 27706

PETROSKI, HENRY, b. NYC, Feb. 6, 1942, s. Henry Frank and Victoria Rose (Grygrowych) P.; m. Catherine Ann Groom, July 15, 1966; children—Karen Beth, Stephen James. Author: To Engineer Is Human: The Role of Failure in Successful Design, 1985, Beyond Engineering: Essays and Other Attempts To Figure without Equations, 1986; contrbr. poems to Poetry, Shenandoah, Descant, Prairie Schooner, other mags and anthols, essays to N.Y. Times, Washington Post, Tech. Rvw, Va. Qtly, others. BME, Manhattan Coll., 1963; PhD, U. Ill., 1968. Instr. U. Ill., Urbana, 1965-68; asst. prof. U. Tex., Austin, 1968-74; engr. Argonne Natl. Lab., Ill., 1975-80; assoc. prof. dept. civil and environ. engring. Duke U., Durham, N.C., 1980-87; prof., 1987—, dir. grad. studies, 1981-86. Recipient lit. award Ill. Arts Council, 1976. Home: 2501 Perkins Rd Durham NC 27706

PETROVIC, DRAGUTIN, see Domac, Dragutin Charles

PETRY, ANN, b. Old Saybrook, CT, Oct. 12, 1908; d. Peter Clark and Bertha Ernestine (James) Lane; m. George David Petry, Feb. 22, 1938; 1 dau., Elizabeth Ann. Author: (novels) The Street, 1946, Country Place, 1947, The Narrows, 1953; (short stories) Miss Muriel and Other Stories, 1971; (books for young people): The Drugstore Cat, 1949, Harriet Tubman Conductor on the Underground Railroad, 1955, Titula of Salem Village, 1964, Legends of the Saints, 1970. PhG, Conn. Coll. of Pharmacy; Litt.D (hon.), Suffolk U., 1983. Mem. AG, AL, PEN. Home: 113 Old Boston Post Rd Old Saybrook CT 06475

PETT, SAUL, b. Passaic, NJ, Mar. 18, 1918; s. Nathan and Ida (Litsky) P.; m. Leanore Green, Feb. 23, 1951 (dec. July 1978); children—Amy Pett Unger, Kathy Pett Harpster, Sukey. Ed., co-author: The Torch is Passed, 1963, Lightning Out of Israel, 1967. BA in Journalism, U. MO, 1940. Reporter-writer Intl. News Svc., Detroit, Chgo., NYC, 1940-46, AP, NYC, 1946-64; spcl. corr., NYC, 1964—. Recipient jnlsm. medal U. MO, Columbia, 1956, genl. rptg. award Sigma Delta Chi, 1963, Fgn. Corr. award Overseas Press Club, NYC, 1964, top performance award AP Mng. Eds., NYC, 1965, best nwspr. writing award Am. Soc. Nwspr. Eds., 1981, Pulitzer prize for feature writing, 1982. Office: AP 50 Rockefeller Pl New York NY 10020

PETT, STEPHEN, b. Salt Lake City, June 3, 1949; s. James Arthur and Ethelyn (Cannon) P.; m. Clare Cardinal, Dec. 28, 1975; children—Morgan, Walker. Author: (poems) Pulpit of Bones, 1974, (novel) Sirens, 1987. Contrbr. poems to anthol., lit. mags.; short stories to lit. mags. BA, Colo. Coll., 1971; MA, Hollins Coll., 1974; PhD, U. Utah-Salt Lake City, 1980. Poet-in-the-schls. Utah Arts Council, Salt Lake City, 1975-80; copy wrtr. KALL-radio sta., Salt Lake City, 1980; asst. prof. Marshall U., Huntington, W.Va., 1981-83, Ia. State U., Ames, 1983—. Co-chmn. Symposium on the Am. Indian, Ames, 1986, 87. Recipient Honors List award for story The Face of the Waters, Best Short Stories of 1981, 1982, 1st place for novel Quint's Eden, W.Va. Wrtrs.' Assn., 1982, 1st place for short story, Iowa Arts Council Literary Awards Competition, 1986, 1st place Fiction Network Short Fiction, 1986. Home: 818 7th St Ames IA 50010

PETTIT, MICHAEL EDWIN, b. Lubbock, TX, Aug. 9, 1950; s. A. Edwin and Eugenia (Cowden) P.; m. Dara Wier; children—Emily and Guy. Author: American Light, 1984, Cardinal Points, 1988; ed. Black Warrior Rvw, 1981-82; Contrbr. poems to Kenyon Rvw., Morrow Anthology of Younger American Poets, Mo. Rvw, Mass Rvw, others. BA, Princeton U., 1972; MFA, U. Ala., 1983. Instr. U. Ala., Tuscaloosa, 1984-85; lectr. Mt. Holyoke Coll., Mass., 1986-87, asst. prof. Mount Holyoke Coll., 1986—. NEA creative wrtr.'s fellow 1985. Home: 504 Montague Rd Amherst MA 01002

PETTY, ANNE C., b. Panama City, FL; d. William Albert and Clara Louise (Tucker) Cotton; m. William Howard Petty, June 6, 1964; 1 dau., April Anne. Author: (programmed textbook) (with James F. Wilkey) Principles of Learning, 1974; One Ring to Bind Them: Tolkien's Mythology, 1984. Contrbr. chpt. to Emerson: Collected Essays, 1971; articles to profl. jnls., popular mags. including Electronic Edn., Fla. Living, Tallahassee Mag., others. Contrbr., ed. instructional modules, promotional brochures and posters, textbook curriculum materials, scripts, videotape, slidetape, computer-assisted instruction; founder, contrbg. ed. Tenn. St. Rag., 1980; editor-in-chief (newsletter) Lifeline, 1984-86; contrbg. ed. Apalachee Today, 1987—. BA, Fla. State Univ., 1967, MA, 1970, PhD in English, 1972. Projects ed. Ctr. for Ednl. Tehnology, Tallahassee, 1973-75; pubs. cons. Fla. Div. of State Planning, Tallahassee, 1975-76; freelance wrtr., ed., Tallahassee, 1976-79; wrtr., ed. Ctr. for Vocational Edn., Tallahassee, 1984-86; editorial coord. Ctr. for Instructional Devel., Tallahassee, 1986—. Asst. artistic dir. Tallahassee Ballet Co., 1983-84; promotional wrtr. Tallahassee Symphony Orchestra, 1985. Recipient Challenge prize Fla. Endowment for the Humanities, 1984; prize for poetry, juvenile article, genl. non-fiction Fla. State Wrtrs. competition, 1986, Honorable Mention for essay, 1987. Mem. Fla. Freelance Wrtrs. Assn., NWC, Tallahassee Wrtrs. Assn. (founding mem.), Assn. Ednl. Technology and Communications, Fla. Folklore Soc., Fla. Lit. Coalition, Fla. Adult Edn. Assn., Fla. State Dance Assn. Home: Rt 3 Box 5355 Crawfordville FL 32327

PETTY, MILANA MC LEAD, b. Milw., Oct. 24, 1954; d. Karl H. and Dorothy Evelyn (Nelson) MCL.; m. Jeffrey Ray Petty, Dec. 30, 1978. Exec. ed. Florida Gulf Coast Home Buyer's Guide, 1979—. AA, St. Petersburg Jr. Coll., 1974; BA in Mass. Comm./Mag. Edit., U. So. Fla., 1976. Ed., Restaurant Nwsltr., St. Petersburg, FL, 1975-77; assoc. ed. Fla. Bldr. Mag., Tampa, FL, 1975-78, St. Petersburg (FL) Times/Retail Times Nwsltr., 1978; exec. ed. Baker Pubns./ Living Mag., Tampa, 1979—. Ed. of Year, Baker Pubns., 1981, 84. Pres. Fla. Mag. Assn., 1987. Home: 2427 14th St North St Petersburg FL 33704

PETZAL, DAVID ELIAS, b. NYC, Oct. 21, 1941; s. Henry and Aline Born (Bixer) P.; m. Arlene Ann Taylor, May 29, 1974. Author: The .22 Rifle, 1972; ed.: The Experts Book of the Shooting Sports, 1972, The Experts Book of Upland Game and Waterfowl Hunting, 1975, The Experts Book of Big-Game Hunting in North America, 1976. BA, Colgate U., 1963. Ed., Maco Publs., NYC,1964-69; mng. ed. Davis Publs.,

NYC,1969-70; features ed. Hearst Publs., NYC,1970-72; mng. ed. CBS Publs., NYC,1972-79, ed., 1979-83, exec. ed., 1983—. Home: Box 219 Bedford NY 10506

PETZINGER, WILLIAM CHARLES, b. Morristown, NJ, Mar. 29, 1960; s. William Charles and Margaret Mary (Yannotta) P. Contrbr. to nwsprs. & mags., 1982—, inclg. NJ Herald, NJ Monthly, NJ Goodlife, Star-Ledger, Morristown Daily Record, Daily Advance, Courier-News. BA, Montclair State, 1982. Writer Media Masters, Parsippany, NJ, 1982-83; pub. relns. March of Dimes, Fairfield, NJ, 1983-86; acct. exec., Poppe Tyson Advertising & Public Relations, Union NJ, 1986—; var. freelance positions. Home: 142 Springdale Ave Yardville NJ 08620

PEYRE, HENRI MAURICE, b. Paris, Feb. 21, 1901; s. Brice and Marie (Tuvien) P.; came to U.S., 1925; 1 son—Brice. Author: The Failures of Criticism, 1967, Historical and Critical Essays, 1968, Dostoevsky and French Literary Imagination, 1975, What Is Romanticism, 1977; contrbr. articles to profl. jnls. Ecole Normale Superieure, Paris, 1920. Mem. faculty French univs., Bryn Mawr Coll., Yale U.; distinguished prof. French Grad. Center, CUNY, 1969—. Mem. Am. Philo. Soc., AAAS. Address: 290 North Ave Westport CT 06880

PEYTON, HELEN E., b. Silent Run, KY, Sept. 10, 1921; d. William Benjamin and Pernicia H. (Franklin) Hart; m. John M. Peyton, Dec. 16, 1939; children: Betty J. and Patricia H. (Johnson). Author: Some Early Pioneers of Western Kentucky, Their Ancestors and Descendants, 1984, 2d ed., 1988. Writer, Trails Away, Greenville, MI, 1986. Student 3 yrs., Marine Valley Community Coll., Palos Hills, Ill. Home: 7719 W 91st St Hickory Hills IL 60457

PFEIFFER, J(OHN) DOUGLAS, b. Quebec City, Can., Oct. 29, 1927; s. Gordon Edward and Dorothy Douglas (Young) P.; came to U.S., 1950, naturalized, 1955; m. Virginia Mae Sturgess, Nov. 8, 1958. Author: Skiing with Pfeiffer, 1958, 62, Ten Secrets of Skiing (for Bob Beattie), 1965, Skiing Simplified, 1972, Skiing—The Killy Way, 1972, Skiing Skills, 1980; writer, narrator films: To Test a Ski, 1974, Freestyle, Prostyle, 1975; contrbr. articles to mags.; TV sports commentator. BA, Long Beach State Coll., 1961. Dir. ski schl. Snow Summit, Big Bear Lake, CA, 1953-63; tchr. Big Bear Lake, 1955-56, Newport Beach (CA) pub. schls., 1960-63; natl. ed. Skiing Mag., NYC,1963-64; dir. ski schl., Loveland Basin, CO, 1964-65; ed.-in-chief Skiing, Skiing Area News, Skiing Area Guide, Skiing Intl. Yearbook, Skiing Trade News, NYC,1965-74, ed.-at-large, 1975-86; contrbg. ed. Skiing Mag., Ski Mag. Inducted into Natl. Ski Hall of Fame, 1987 Home: Box 1806 Big Bear Lake CA 92315

PFEIFFER, JOHN WILLIAM, b. Wallace, ID, July 10, 1937; s. John William and Mary Loretta (Schmidt) P.; m. Judith Ann Cook, Dec. 14, 1973; children—Heidi Erika, Charles Wilson. Author: Applied Strategic Planning (with Goodstein and Nolan), 1986; Instrumentation in Human Relations Training, 1973, 2d ed., 1976; Reference Guide to Handbooks and Annuals, 1975, 3d ed., 1981; ed.: Strategic Planning: Selected Readings, 1986; A Handbook of Structured Experiences for Human Relations Training, 10 vols., 1969-85; The Annual Handbook for Group Facilitators, 10 vols., 1972-81; The 1982, 83, 84, 85, 86 Annuals for Facilitators, Trainers and Cons.; editor: Group and Organizations Studies: Intl. Jnl for Group Facilitators, 1976-79. BA, U. MD, 1962; PhD (fellow), U. IA, 1968; JD, Western State U., 1982. Instr. U. MD, 1965-67; dir. adult edn. Kirkwood (IA) Community Coll., 1967-69; dir. ednl. resources Ind. Higher Edn. Telecommunications Systems, Indpls., 1969-72; pres. Univ. Assocs., San Diego, 1972-80, 83—; adj. tchr. Ind. U., 1969-72, Purdue U., 1971-72. Home: 2610 Inyaha Ln La Jolla CA 92037

PFEIL, JOHN FREDERICK, (Fred), b. Port Allegany, PA, Sept. 21, 1949; s. Robert Karl and Harriett Marie (Herriman) P.; m. Anne Elizabeth Krosby, June 9, 1981. Author: Shine On and Other Stories, 1987; Goodman 2020, 1986; ed. Minn. Rvw., 1982- 85; co-ed. The Year Left: An American Socialist Yearbook, vols. I & II, 1985 and 1987; contrbr. to Fiction Intl., Mo., Sewanee, Minn. (2d place for short story 1981), GA., Pawn, Chouteau rvws., Boundary 2, Mississippi Mud, Coll. English, Story Qtly., Boston U. Jnl (1st place for short story 1978), Spectrum, Ploughshares, Place, others. BA summa cum laude, Amherst Coll., 1971; AM, Stanford U., 1973. Instr English, Stephens Coll., Columbia, Mo., 1976-79; asst. prof. English, Oreg. State U., Corvallis, 1979-85, Trinity Coll., Hartford, Conn., 1985—. NEA fellow, 1981; Oreg. Arts Comm. fellow, 1982. Mem. P&W, AWP, Marxist Lit. Group. Home: 31 Monroe St Hartford CT 06114

PFINGSTON, ROGER CARL, b. Evansville, IN, April 6, 1940; s. Walter Carl and Esther Ora (Sandage) Pfingston; m. Nancy Lee Weber, Dec. 16, 1962; children—Brett, Jenna. Works include: The Circus of Unreasonable Acts, 1982, Goose Bones, 1985, Something Iridescent, 1987; poems and short fiction in New Letters, Ascent, Chicago Tribune, The Nation, and other mags. and anthologies. AB, Indiana U., 1962, MS, 1967. Tchr., Virginia Beach, Va. pub. schls., 1964-65; tchr., Univ. High School, Bloomington, IN, 1967-72; tchr., Bloomington High School North, IN, 1972—. With US Navy, 1962-64. Awards: NEA Fellowship, 1978. Mem. PSA. Home: 4020 Stoutes Creek Rd Bloomington IN 47401

PHANTOM, D. S., see Skrabanek, Donald W.

PHELAN, FRANCIS J., b. Pitts., May 29, 1925; s. James P. Phelan and Annie O'Donnell; m. Anne Francis Cavanaugh, June 14, 1975. Author: How to Found Your Own Religion, 1963, Four Ways of Computing Midnight, 1985. MA, Notre Dame, 1959; PhD, University Coll., Dublin, Ireland, 1966. Chair, Engl. Dept., U. Portland, 1962-63; dir. Irish Studies, Stonehill Coll., N. Easton, MA, 1972-80. Pushcart Prize, 1982. Address: Eng Dept Stonehill Coll N Easton MA 02357

PHELAN, THOMAS ANTHONY, b. NYC, Jan. 20, 1928, s. Thomas Francis and Kathleen (Langdon) P.; m. Anna Mary Ward, Aug. 31, 1957; children—Thomas, Theresa, Barbara, William. Contrbr. poetry: Byline mag., Arulo mag., Calli's Tales, gen. interest newspapers; contrbr. Am. Poetry Anthology, 1982-83, Hearts of Fire Anthology, 1984, Am. Poetry Showcase, 1985, numerous others. Wrkg. on haiku, poetry, screenplay. Investigator William J. Burns Agy., NYC, 1952-55; detective NYC Police Dept., 1955-66; pres., dir. Universal Detectives, Inc., NY and NJ, 1966—. Recipient NY Poetry Soc. award, 1985, Golden Poet award World of Poetry, 1985, 86. Mem. Bergen Poets, AAP, Fla. State Poets Assn., Natl. Fedn. State Poetry Socs. Home: 51 Phelps Ave Bergenfield NJ 07621

PHILIP, A.G. DAVIS, b. NYC, Jan. 9, 1929; s. Van Ness and Lillian (Davis) P.; m. Kristina Drobavicius, Apr. 25, 1964; 1 dau.—Kristina Elizabeth Elanor. Exhibitor 2d Annl. Photography Regional, Albany, NY, 1980; author (with M. Cullen and R.E. White) UBV Color—Magnitude Diagrams of Galactic Globular Clusters, 1976; ed.: The Evolution of Population II Stars, 1972, Multicolor Photometry and the Theoretical HR Diagram (with D.S. Hayes), 1975; Galactic Structure in the Direction of the Galactic Polar Caps (with McCarthy), 1977; In Memory of Henry Norris Russell (with Hayes), 1977; The HR Diagram (with D.S. Hayes), 1978; Problems in Calibration of Multicolor Systems, 1979; Spectral Classification of the Future (with M.F. McCarthy), 1979; X-Ray Symposium, 1981; Astrophysical Parameters for Globular Clusters (with Hayes), 1981; The Nearby Stars and the Stellar Luminosity Function (with A.R. Upgren), 1983; Calibration of Fundamental Stellar Quantities (with Hayes and L. Pasinetti), 1984; Horizontal-Branch and UV Bright Stars, 1985; Spectroscopic and Photometric Classification of Population II Stars, 1986. BS, Union Coll., 1951; MS, N.M. State U., 1959; PhD, Case Inst. Tech., 1964. Tchr. physics, math. and chemistry Brooks Schl., 1954-59; instr. Case Inst. Tech., 1962-64; asst. prof. astronomy U. N. Mex., 1964-66, SUNY-Albany, 1966-67, assoc. prof., 1967-76, prof. astronomy Union Coll., Schenectady, 1976—, astronomer Dudley Obs., 1967-81, ed. Dudley Obs. Reports, 1978-81; astronomer Van Vleck Obs., Wesleyan U., 1982—, editor contrbns. of VV obs., 1983; dir., secy.-treas. N.Y. Astron. Corp.; pres., treas. L. Davis Press, Inc., 1982—; pres., treas. Inst. for Space Observations, 1986. Fellow Royal Astron. Soc., AAAS. 1st U.S. observer Soviet 6M telescope, 1980, Trustee for Astrophysical Research, 1986—. Home: 1125 Oxford Pl Schenectady NY 12308

PHILIPSON, MORRIS, b. New Haven, June 23, 1926; s. Samuel and Edith (Alderman) P.; m. Susan Antonia Sacher, Apr. 26, 1961; children—Nicholas, Jenny, Alex. Author: Outline of Jungian Aesthetics, 1963, Bourgeois Anonymous, 1964, The Count Who Wished He Were a Peasant: A Life of Leo Tolstoy, 1967, Paradoxes, 1969, Everything Changes, 1972, The Wallpaper Fox, 1976, A Man in Charge, 1979, Secret Understandings, 1983; ed.: Aldous Huxley on Arts and Artists, 1960, Aesthetics Today, 1961, Automation: Implications for the Future, 1962, (with Clapp, Rosenthal) Foundations of Western Thought, 1962. Diploma, U. Paris, 1947; BA, U. Chgo., 1949, MA, 1952; PhD in Philosophy, Columbia U., 1959. Instr. English lit. Hofstra Coll., 1954-55; instr. philosophy Juilliard Schl. Music, 1955-56, 57-58; lectr. Hunter Coll., 1957-60; ed. Vintage Books, Alfred A. Knopf, Inc., NYC, 1959-61, Modern Lib., also trade books Random House, Pantheon Books, 1961-65; sr. ed. Basic Books, NYC, 1965-66; exec. ed. U. Chgo. Press, 1966-67, dir., 1967—. Office: 5801 S Ellis Ave Chicago IL 60637

PHILLABAUM, LESLIE ERVIN, b. Cortland, NY, June 1, 1936; s. Vern Arthur and Beatrice Elizabeth (Butterfield) P.; m. Roberta Kimbrough Swarr, Mar. 17, 1962; children—Diane Melissa, Scott Christopher. BS, PA State U., 1958, MA, 1963. Editor PA State U. Press, 1961-63; ed.-in-chief U. NC Press, 1963-70; assoc. dir., ed. LA State U. Press, Baton Rouge, 1970-75, dir. 1975—. Mem. Assn. Am. Univ. Presses. Home: 670 Burgin Ave Baton Rouge LA 70808

PHILLIPS, AILEEN PAUL, b. Waycross, GA, June 2, 1917; d. John Preston Phillips and Edna (Samuelson) DeGrofft; children—Celia Paul, Kathleen, Frederick Bartholomew. Author: Kids Cooking, 1970, Kids Indoor Gardening, 1972, Kids Camping, 1973, Candies Cookies Cakes, 1974, Kids Cooking Complete Meals, 1975, Kids Cooking Without a Stove, 1975, 2d edit., 1985, Kids Fifty-State Cookbook, 1976; Kids Outdoor Gardening, 1978, Kids' Diet Cookbook, 1980 (Natl. Sci. Tchrs. award 1980). Contrbr. articles to newspapers, mags., jnls. BA, Highlands U., Las Vegas, N.Mex., 1980. Owner, mgr. Aileen Paul Assoc., Pub. Relations & Info. Cons., NYC, 1954-77; info. specialist U.S. Consumer Product Safety Commn., Dallas, 1977-79; dir. community relations Wheelwright Mus. Am. Indian, Sante Fe, 1982-85; free-lance wrtr., 1954—. Mem. N.Mex Press Women, Rocky Mt. Outdoor Wrtrs. (bd. dirs.), Soc. Childrens' Book Wrtrs. Home and Office: 2562 Avenida de Isidro Sante Fe NM 87505

PHILLIPS, EDWIN ALLEN, b. Lowell, FL, Mar. 18, 1915; s. William Henry and Jane (Goodman) P.; m. Margaret Ellen Knight, Jan. 16, 1942; children—Ellen Knight, Nancy Jane. Author: Methods of Vegetation Study, 1959, Field Ecology, 1964, Basic Ideas in Biology, 1971; co-author: Basic Demonstrations in Biology, 1971, The Environment and Organisms: An Ecosystem Approach, 1971-74; revision plant sections 4th ed., Biological Science, An Inquiry into Life, 1977, The Local Environment, 1979; editorial bd.: Vegetation, 1955-74. AB, Colgate U., 1937; MA, U. MI, 1940, PhD, 1948. Instr. botany Colgate U., Hamilton, NY, 1946-48; prof. botany Pomona Coll., Claremont, CA, 1948—, chmn. dept. botany, 1973-77; vis. prof. plant ecology U. MI Biol. Sta., summers 1955-56, 58, 70-71; cons., mem. steering om. U. Hawaii Fundamental Approach to Sci. Teaching Study, 1969—; cons. Govt. India, AID, summers 1964-65; mem. research adv. bd. San Dimas Exptl. Forest, 1957—; participant AID Sci. Edn. Survey, State Dept., Indonesia, 1972; researcher Kenya Natl. parks, 1972. Recipient Wig Distinguished Prof. award Pomona Coll., 1966; NSF fellow Harvard U., summer 1959, Oxford U., 1961-62. Fellow AAAS; mem. Am. Inst. Biol. Scis., Bot. Soc. Am., Am. & Brit. bryological socs., Ecol. Soc. Am., Soc. Am. Naturalists. Home: 1201 N College Ave Claremont CA 91711

PHILLIPS, KEVIN PRICE, b. NYC, Nov. 30, 1940; s. William Edward and Dorothy Virginia (Price) P.; m. Martha Eleanor Henderson, Sept. 28, 1968; children—Andrew, Alexander. Author: The Emerging Republican Majority, 1969, Electoral Reform and Voter Participation, 1975, Mediacracy, 1975, Post-Conservative America, 1982, Staying on Top: The Business Case for a National Industrial Strategy, 1984; ed. and pub.: The American Political Report, 1971—, Business and Public Affairs Fortnightly, 1979—. Student U. Edinburgh, Scotland, 1959-60; AB, Colgate U., 1961; LLB, Harvard U., 1964. Admin. asst. to Congressman Paul Fino, 1964-68; spcl. asst. to campaign mgr. Nixon for Pres. Com., 1968; spcl. asst. atty. genl. U.S., 1969-70; syndicated nwspr. columnist King Features, 1970-83; pres. Am. Polit. Research Corp., 1971—; commentator CBS (Spectrum), 1978—. Mem. NY, DC bars. Home: 5115 Moorland Ln Bethesda MD 20014

PHILLIPS, LOUIS JAMES, b. Lowell, MA, June 15, 1942, s. Louis James and Dorothy (Perkins) P.; m. Patricia Louise Ranard, Sept. 26, 1971; children—Ian, Matthew. Author: The Man Who Stole the Atlantic Ocean, 1971, Theodore Jonathan Wainwright is Going to Bomb the Pentagon, 1973, The Animated Thumbtack, Railroad, Dollhouse & All Round Surprise Book, 1975, The Brothers Wrong & Wrong Again, 1977, Funky Facts, 1979, Freaky Facts, 1981, Sneakers (with Karen Markoe), 1981, The Handy Book of Football: Facts, Stars & Feats (with Arnie Markoe), 1981, Women in Sports: Facts, Stars & Feats (with Karen Markoe), 1981, The Handy Book of Baseball: Facts, Stars & Feats, 1981, The Upside Down Riddle Book, 1981, The Illustrated Book of Baseball Rules (with Arnie Markoe, 1982), Oops!, 1982, 505 Movie Questions Your Friends Can't Answer, 1983, How Do You Get A Horse Out of the Bathtub, 1984, The Crazy Bones Dictionary, 1981, The Film Buff's Calendar, 1980; author poetry: Celebrations & Bewilderments, 1979, All the Natural Cruelty of Things, 1980, All That Glows Sees, 1981, Bulkington, 1983; playwright: Arbuckle's Rape, 1976, Warbeck, 1980, The Last of the Marx Brothers Writers, 1981, The Envoi Messages, 1985. BA, Stetson U., 1964; MA, U. N.C., 1965; MA, CUNY, 1967. Adj. prof. humanities Schl. Visual Arts, NYC, 1977—. NEA playwriting fellow, 1981; recipient PEN Syndicated Fiction award, 1983, 85; co-winner Swallow Tale's Press Poetry Competition, 1984. Mem. DG. Home: 447 E 14th St New York NY 10009

PHILLIPS, MARGARET IMOGENE, b. Anderson, AL, Jan. 25, 1926; d. Leonard H. and Ruby E. (Thomas) Burgess; m. Jasper Nelson Phillips, Sept. 7, 1943; children—Richard Nelson, Vicky Sue. Author: (biography) Doctor of the Cotton Patch, 1968, Governors of Tennessee, 1978; (meditations) Songs of the Good Earth, 1979. Contrbr. short stories to Bridge; columnist: Florence Herald, 1956-59, Florence Times, 1966-67, Giles Free Press, Democrat Union, thens Limestone Covrier, 1962-67. Ed: Poetry by Almon McConnel, 1967. B.S. in English and Sociology, U. North Ala., 1971, M.A. in Edn., 1976. Farm feature wrtr. Southern Farm Pub., Nashville, 1966-68; tchr. public shls., Lavderdale County, Florence, AL, 1971-86; free-lance wrtr., 1986—. Home: Box 443 Lexington AL 35648

PHILLIPS, MEREDITH BOWEN, b. Oshkosh, WI, July 5, 1943; d. William Hugh and Patricia (Meredith) Bowen; m. Larry C. Pearson, Aug. 23, 1964 (div. Mar., 1972); children—Chris Pearson, Jeremy Pearson; m. 2d, Peter F.C. Phillips, Aug. 5, 1972; 1 son, Evan Phillips. Author: The Child's Peninsula, 1979, Death Spiral, Murder at the Winter Olympics, 1984. BA, Stanford U., 1965. Editor, Perseverance Press, Menlo Park, CA, 1979—. Mem. MWA, CWA, Peninsula Pub., Writers Connect. Office: Perseverance Press Box 384 Menlo Park CA 94026

PHILLIPS, MICHAEL JOSEPH, b. Mar. 2, 1937, Indpls., s. Joseph J. and Bernice Rebecca (Farmer) P. Author poetry: Kinetics & Concretes, 1971, The Concrete Book, 1971, 8 Page Poems, 1971, Love, Love, Love, 1973, Concrete Sonnets, 1973, Concrete Haiku, 1975, Visual Sequences, 1975, Abstract Poems, 1978, Underworld Love Poems, 1979, Selected Love Poems, 1980, Indy Dolls, 1982, Superbeuts, 1983; contrbr. numerous anthologies, mags., newspapers and jnls. BA cum laude, Wabash Coll., 1959; postgrad. NYU, 1960-62, Oxford (Eng.) U., 1969, 71, Harvard U., 1970; MA, Ind. U., 1964, PhD, 1971; postdoctoral student Free Univ. Indpls., 1972-75, Butler U., 1973-75, Ind. U.-Purdue U. Indpls., 1975, Cambridge (Eng.) U., 1978, Oxford U., 1978. Mem. faculty Free Univ. Indpls., 1973, 77-79; vis. fellow Harvard U., 1976-77. Mem. Intl. Comparative Lit. Assn., MLA, Am. Comparative Lit. Assn., Soc. Study Midwestern Lit., Mensa, Phi Beta Kappa. Home: 101 S Glenwood Ave W Bloomington IN 47401

PHILLIPS, ROBERT SCHAEFFER, b. Milford, DE, Feb. 2, 1938, s. Thomas Allen and Katheryn Augusta (Schaeffer) P.; m. Judith Bloomingdale, June 27, 1963; 1 son, Graham Van Buren. Author: Inner Weather, 1966, The Land of Lost Content, 1970, Aspects of Alice, 1971, Moonstruck, 1973, The Confessional Poets, 1973, Denton Welch, 1974, William Goyen, 1978, The Pregnant Man, 1978, Last and Lost Poems of Delmore Schwartz, 1979, Running on Empty, 1981, Stories of Noel Coward, 1984, Letters of Delmore Schwartz, 1985, Stories of Denton Welch, 1986, Personal Accounts, 1986, The Ego Is Always at the Wheel, 1986. BA, Syracuse U., 1960, MA, 1962. Advt. exec., NYC,1963—, v.p., creative supr. J. Walter Thompson, 1976-85; creative supr. BBDO, 1985—, Award in Literature, AAAL, 1987; Yaddo fellow, Saratoga Springs, N.Y., 1981; N.Y. State CAPS fellow, 1977. Mem. PEN, NBCC, PSA. Home: Box AF Katonah NY 10536

PHILLIPS, SUSAN ELIZABETH, b. Cin., Dec. 11, 1947; d. John Aller and Louesa Coate Titus; m. William C. Phillips, Jr., June 26, 1971; children—Ty, Zachary. Author: (with Claire Kiehl) The Copeland Bride, 1983, Risen Glory, 1984, Glitter Baby, 1987. BFA, Ohio U. Tchr., Columbus (OH) pub. schls., 1966-71, curric. coord., 71-73. Critic's Choice, Best New Histl. Romance Writer, Romantic Times, 1985; Silver Medallion, Histl. Rom., RWA, 1985, Fiction Writer's Monthly Award, 1986. AG. Mem. RWA. Address: 1134 Hobson Mill Dr Naperville IL 60540

PHILLIPS, WILLIAM, b. NYC; s. Edward and Marie (Berman) P.; m. Edna M. Greenblatt. Author: A Partisan View, 1983, A Sense of the Present, 1967; ed.: Short Stories of Dostoyevsky, Great American Short Novels; co-ed.: The Partisan Review Anthology. BS, CCNY; MA, NYU; postgrad. Columbia U. Ed., Partisan Review, 1934—; former cons. ed. Dial Press, Criterion Books, Random House, Chilmark Press; instr. Columbia U., 1945; lectr. New Schl. Social Research; vis. lectr. U. Minn., 1953, Sarah Lawrence Coll., 1951-54, 56-57; assoc. prof. NYU, 1960, 61-63; prof. English, Rutgers U., 1963-78; prof. Boston U., 1978—. Mem. Gov. NJ Com. on Arts, 1964-66; arts adv. gp. Bus. Com. for Arts; Pres. Carter's Task Force for Arts and Humanities; Guggenheim fellow, 1977; Rockefeller Fdn. grantee, 1977-78; NEH fellow, 1978—. Mem. ALMA, CCLM, AL, PEN. Home: 101 W 12th St New York NY 10011

PHILLIS, YANNIS ANASTASIOS, b. Nafplion, Greece, Mar. 3, 1950 (arrvd. USA 1976), s. Anastasios and Philipia Phillis; m. Nili Boren; children—Anastasia, Philip. Author: (poetry) Starting in Nafplion, 1975, Arctic Zone, 1976, Zarathustra and the Five Vespers, 1985, (nonfiction) The Last Gasp of Planet Earth, 1984. PhD, UCLA, 1980. Research asst. UCLA, 1977-78, teaching asst., 1978-80; asst. prof. Boston U., 1980—. Served to 2d lt. Greek Army, 1973-75. Home: 35 Country Rd Chestnut Hill MA 02167

PIATNOCHKA, RUTH ANN, b. Newark, Apr. 24, 1955; d. Timothy and Mary (Demsyn) Piatnochka. Contrbr. articles, stories to mags., newspapers, Editor: Evan. Bapt. Herald, 1979—.

BA, Rutgers U., Newark, 1977; MA, Columbia U., 1983. Tutor English, Prudential Ins. Co., Newark, 1975-76, Rutgers U., Newark, 1976-77; adminstrv. asst. pub. relations Slavic Missionary Service, South River, N.J., 1977-79. Mem. Russian- Ukrainian Evang. Bapt. Union USA (exec. com.), Evang. Press Assn. (recipient Mel Larson Journalism scholarship 1981). Home: 2794 Audrey Terr Union NJ 07083

PICANO, FELICE, b. NYC, Feb. 22, 1944; d. Felice John Picano and Anne (DelSanto) Galluccio. Author: (novels) Smart As the Devil, 1975, Eyes, 1976, The Mesmerist, 1977, The Lure, 1979, Late in the Season, 1981, House of Cards, 1984; (memoirs) Ambidextrous: The Secret Lives of Children, 1985; (plays); Immortal! (adaptation of An Asian Minor), 1986; (novella) An Asian Minor, 1982; editor: A True Likeness: Lesbian and Gay Writing Today, 1980; also poetry and short stories. BA, Queens Coll., City U. N.Y., 1964. Pub. SeaHorse Press Ltd., NYC, 1977—. Mem. AG, PEN, WG. Home: 307 W 11th St New York NY 10014

PICCIONE, ANTHONY, b. Sheffield, AL, July 3, 1939, s. Nicholas Piccione and Martha (Crawford) March; m. Ginny Marie Lance; children—Lisa, Rachel, Sarah, Todd. Author: Anchor Dragging (poetry), 1977, 1980 (2nd printing), Seeing It Was So, 1986; chapbooks: Then It Was My Birthday, 1982, In a Gorge with a Friend, 1979, Nearing Land, 1975, While Leaning Over to Say Something, 1977; pamphlets. MA, U. Tex., El Paso, 1965; PhD, Ohio U., 1969. Asst. prof. No. Ill. U., Dekalb, 1968-70; assoc. prof. SUNY-Brockport, 1970—, vis. prof. Second Fgn. Lang. Inst., Beijing, China, 1982-83. Writing fellow SUNY, 1975, 76, 78, 79. Mem. AAP, NWU. Home: 110 Clark St. Brockport NY 14420

PICKARD, JOHN BENEDICT, b. b. Newton, MA, Oct. 4, 1928; s. Greenleaf Whittier and Helen (Liston) P.; m. Margaret Suzanne Dederich, Nov. 24, 1956; children—Stephen, Ellen, Nathaniel, Thaddeus, John Samuel. Author: John Greenleaf Whittier: An Introduction and Interpretation, 1961, Legends of New England by J.G. Whittier, 1965, Emily Dickinson, 1967, Memorabilia of John Greenleaf Whittier, 1968, The Letters of John Greenleaf Whittier, 3 vols., 1975, Whittier and Whittierland, 1976; contrbr.: American Writers, 1979, Samuel Kipnis Film Collection, 1982, Bibliography of J.G. Whittier, 1987. BA, Holy Cross Coll., 1950; postgrad., Boston Coll., 1950-51; PhD, U.WI, 1954. Instr. U. Calif. (Far East Extension), 1956; asst. prof. English Rice U., Houston, 1956-63; assoc. prof. U. FL, Gainesville, 1963-68, prof. 1968—. Am. Philo. Soc. grantee, 1962, 67, 69. Mem. MLA, South Central MLA. Office: Dept Eng U FLa Gainesville FL 32611

PICKENS, KEL NORRIS, b. Tulsa, OK, May 15, 1949; s. Norris Ira and Georgia Marie (Hollis) P.; m. Jan Vaughan, Feb. 10, 1970 (div. 1973); 1 son, Jeffrey Scott; m. Betty Carolyn Meyer, Mar. 20, 1980. Author: The Music of Our Language, 1983; (plays) Radio Station K-I-D-S, 1983, The Colors of Life, 1987. ontrbr. article to mag.; children's radio scripts Sta. KSP1 1981—. Ed.: Payne County Peace Network Newsletter, 1986. B.S. in Jnlsm., Okla. State U., 1971, M.A. in History, 1976. Sales cons. Sta. KSPI, Stillwater, OK, 1981-85; sales mgr. Sta. KVRO, Stillwater, 1985-86, Jnl. Monthly Newspaper, Stillwater, 1986—. Media spokesperson Sunbelt Alliance, Tulsa, 1976-80. Recipient Best 30-Second Radio comml. for Okla., Okla. Assn. Broadasters, 1982, Outstanding Achievement in Broadcasting award for children's programming, 1984, 85, 86; Outstanding Contrbrs. to Okla. Musicians award Jam Mag., 1983. Home: 115 Melrose Stillwater OK 74074

PICKERELL, RODNEY R., (Christian McCord), b. Boise, ID, June 14, 1938, s. Jack Marvin and Harriet Fern (Zimmer) P.; m. Margery Janice Louther, July 24, 1959; children—Ric, Dan, Laurie, Clairissa. Novelist: Across the Shining Mountains, 1986. BA, U. Idaho, 1979. With Sears, Roebuck Co., 1958—, fixture coordinator, San Bruno, Calif., 1985—Home: 41447 Carmen St. Fremont CA 94539

PICKLE, HAL B(RITTAIN), b. Ennis, TX, Jan. 16, 1929; s. Oren M. and Bessie Mae (Beard) P.; m. Anna Lucille Toupal, June 27, 1953; children: Debra Lyn, Karen Kay, Eric Brian, Lance Oram. Author: Personality and Success: An Evaluation of Personal Characteristics of Succesful Small Business Managers, 1964, (with Royce L. Abraham-son) Introduction to Business: Text and Cases, 1972, 4th ed, 1980, (with Abrahamson) Introduction to Business: Readings, 1972, 2d ed, 1974, (with Abrahamson) Introduction to Business: Study Guide, 1972, 2d ed, 1974, 3d ed publ as Introduction to Business: Study Guide and Readings, 1977, 6th ed, 1986, (with Abrahamson) Introduction to Business: Instrucor's Manual, 1972, 6th ed, 1986, (with Rucks) The Impact of Water Pollution Abatement on Competition and Pricing in the Alabama Textile Industry, 1973, (with Rowe) The Impact of Water Pollution Abatement on Competition and Pricing in the Alabama Steel Industry, 1973, (with Rucks and Sisson) The Economic Benefits of Abating Water Pollution in the Steel, Textile, and Paper Industries in Alabama, 1973, (with Abrahamson) Small Business Management, with study guide and instructor's manual, 1976, 4th ed, 1986, (with Abrahamson) Administracion de Empresas, 1982, (with Abrahamson) Introduction to Business, 5th ed, 1983, 6th ed, 1986, (with Abrahamson) Introduction to Business: Test Bank, 5th ed, 1983. BBA, North Texas State Coll (now Univ), 1959, MBA, 1960; Ph.D., Univ of Arkansas, 1964. Assoc prof of management, Southwest Texas State Univ, San Marcos, 1962-69; prof of management, Auburn (Ala.) Univ, 1969-73; pres, Hal B. Pickle (research and consulting firm), Austin, Tex., 1973-75; assoc prof, St. Edward's Univ, Austin, 1975-78, prof, 1978—. Pres, Auburn Business Consultants, Inc., 1972—. Member: Acad of Management, Natl Cncl of Small Business Management Development. Outstanding Educator of America Award, 1971 and 1972; research grants from Natl Sci Fndn, 1971, Small Business Administration, 1971, and Office of Water Resources, 1971-73. Military service: U.S. Army, Engineers, 1950-52. Home: 4905 Saddle Drive Austin TX 78727

PIEL, GERARD, b. Woodmere L.I., NY, Mar. 1, 1915; s. William F.J. and Loretto (Scott) P.; m. Mary Tapp Bird, Feb. 4, 1938; children—Jonathan Bird, Samuel Bird (dec.); m. 2d, Eleanor Virden Jackson, June 24, 1955; 1 dau.—Eleanor Jackson. Author: Science in the Cause of Man, 1961, The Acceleration of History, 1972; transl.: Le Scienze, 1968, Saiensu, 1971, Ciencia, 1976, Pour La Science, 1977, Spektrum der Wissenschaft, 1978, Ke Xue, 1979, V Mire Nauki, 1983. AB magna cum laude, Harvard U., 1937, Sci. ed. Life Mag., 1938-44; asst. to pres. Henry J. Kaiser Co., 1945-46; organizer (with Dennis Flanagan, Donald H. Miller, Jr.), pres. Sci. Am., Inc., 1946—; pub. mag. Sci. Am., 1947—. Recipient George Polk award, 1961, Kalinga prize, 1962, Bradford Washburn award, 1966, Arches of Sci. award, 1969, Rosenberger medal U. Chgo., 1973; named Pub. of Year Mag. Pubs. Assn., 1980. Fellow Am. Acad. Arts and Scis., AAAS; mem. Council Fgn. Relations, Am. Philo. Soc., Natl. Acad. Scis. Inst. Medicine. Office: Sci Am 415 Madison Ave. New York NY 10017

PIERCY, MARGE, b. Detroit, Mar. 31, 1936; d. Robert Douglas and Bert Bernice (Bunnin) Piercy; M. Ira Wood, 1982. Author: Breaking Camp, 1968, Hard Loving, 1969, Going Down Fast, 1969, Dance The Eagle to Sleep, 1970, (with Bob Hershon, Emmett Jarrett and Dick Lourie) 4-Telling, 1971, Small Changes, 1973, To Be of Use, 1973, Living in the Open, 1976, Woman on the Edge of Time, 1976, The High Cost of Living, 1978, The Twelve-Spoked Wheel Flashing, 1978, Vida, 1980, The Moon Is Always Female, 1980, Braided Lives, 1982, Fly Away Home, 1984, (with David Ira Wood) The Last White Class (play), 1979, Parti-Colored Blocks for a Quilt (essays), 1982, Circles on the Water (poetry), 1982, Stone, Paper, Knife (poetry), 1983, My Mother's Body (poetry), 1983, Gone to Soldiers, 1987; adv. ed.: APHRA, 1975-78, Poetry on the Buses, 1979-81. AB, U. Mich., 1957; MA, Northwestern U., 1958. Instr. Ind. U. (Gary ext.), 1960-62; poet-in-res. U. Kans., 1971; distinguished vis. lctr. Thomas Jefferson Coll., Grand Valley State Colls., 1975; vis. faculty Women's Writers Conf., Cazenovia (N.Y.) Coll., 1976, 78, 80; wrtr.-in-res., Ohio State U., 1985, Ellison Poet at U of Cincinnati, U. of Cincinnati, 1986; cons. NY State Council on Arts, 1971, Mass. Fdn. for Humanities and Council on Arts, 1974; advisory panel in lit., Mass. Council on Arts and Humanities, 1986—. Bd. Mass. Fdn. Humanities and Public Policy, 1978-85; Writer's board, Mass. Council on the Arts and Humanities, 1985-86. James B. Angell scholar; Lucinda Goodrich Downs scholar; recipient Orion Scott award in Humanities, poetry and fiction awards, Avery Hopwood Contest, 1956, 57, Borestone Mountain Poetry Award, 1968, 74, Lit. award Gov. Mass. Commn. on Status on Women, 1974, NEA Award, 1978. Mem. AG, AL, NWU, PEN, PSA, Mass. Council on the Arts and Humanities, 1986—. Address: Box 943 Wellfleet MA 02667

PIERMAN, CAROL J., b. Lima, OH, Oct. 16, 1947; d. James Henry and Ellin J. (Frey) Pierman. Author: Passage, 1977, The Naturalized Citizen, 1981; contbr. to Three Rivers Poetry Jnl, Lit Mag Rvw, Cimarron Rvw, Painted Bride Quar, Contact/II, Salthouse, Centennial Rvw, Open Places, Carolina Qtly, Ascent, others. Hearing Harry Say; short stories and essays. BA, Bowling Green State U, MFA, PhD. Program CCLM, NYC, 1973-76; asst. prof. Southern Ill. Univ., Carbondale, 1980- 86; assoc. ed. River Styx. Recipient Ill. Arts Council fellowship, 1985. Mem. P&W. Address: Box 324 Ottawa OH 45875

PIIRTO-NAVARRE, JANE MARIE, (Jane Piirto, Jeanne Marina), b. Ishpeming, MI, Dec. 19, 1941, d. George Isaac and Helmi Helena (Eskilinen) Piirto; m. Paul Edward Navarre, Aug. 29, 1963 (div. 1980); children—Steven David, Denise Ruth. Novelist: The Three-Week Trance Diet, 1985; contrbr. stories, poems to S.D. Rvw, Sing, Heavenly Muse!, Bitterroot, Der Schlopen Dopen, Poetry Now, other lit mags; contrbr. to anthologies: A Change in Weather, Midwest Woman Poets, They Came to School Dressed as Flowers, 73 Ohio Poets, others. BA magna cum laude, No. Mich. U., 1963; PhD, Bowling

Green State U., 1977. Ednl. cons. Hardin County Schls., Kenton, Ohio, 1977-79, Monroe County Ind. Schl. Dist., Mich., 1979-83; prin. Hunter Coll. Campus Schls., 1983—. Lit. chair Ohio Arts Council, Columbus, 1983—. Ohio Arts Council fellow, 1982. Office: Campus Schls 71 E 94th St New York NY 10128

PIKE, LAWRENCE, b. Detroit, Dec. 2, 1932, s. Maurice and Mae (Adelson) P.; m. Janet Muir, Aug. 19, 1962 (div. 1972); children—Joshua, Nathaniel. Author: Now That Good Jack Armstrong's Gone, 1980, Hideout Matinees, 1981; contrbr. poetry, articles to Kayak, N.Y. Qtly, Works, Counter/Measures, Green River Rvw, Studies in Contemporary Satire, Song, Windsor Rvw, Passages North, contemporary Miochigan Poetry, others. BA, U. Mich., 1954, MA, Wayne State U., 1972. Tchr. Macomb Community Coll., Warren, Mich., 1964—; tchr. creative writing in schls., Mich. Council for Arts, 1978—. Grantee Mich. Council for Arts, 1983. Home: 117 E Bloomfield St Royal Oak MI 48073

PILAC, PAMELA ANN, b. Aug. 28, 1954; d. Francis James Lach and Florence Jacqueline (Friese) Lach Zavacky; m. Thomas M. Piljac, Aug. 23, 1975. Author: The Bride's Thank you Writing Guide, 1983, The Bride to Bride Book, 1983, Newlywed: A Survival Guide to the First Years of Marriage, 1985, You Can Go Home Again: The Career Woman's Guide to Leaving the Work Force, 1985, The Groom to Groom Book, 1983. Student Purdue U. Office mgr. Gen. Electric Credit Corp., Portage, Ind., 1973-81, Bryce- Waterton Publs., Portage, 1982—. Office: BW Publs 6411 Mulberry Ave Portage IN 46368

PILCER, SONIA HANNA, b. Augsburg, Germany, Feb. 3, 1949; came to U.S., 1950; d. Benjamin and Lusia (Gradon) P. Author: (novels) Teen Angel, 1978, Little Darlings, 1980, Maiden Rite, 1982, I-Land,: Manhattan in Monologue, 1987; contbr. poetry to lit. mags. BA, Queens, 1970. Prof., CCNY, 1978-83, Hofstra U., 1980, Hebrew U. in Jerusalem, 1983, Writer's Voice, 63rd St. YMCA, NYC, 1985—, Worker's Ctr. for Edn., 1986. Yaddo fellow, 1979; McDowell fellow, 1980, N.Y. Fdn. for the Arts fiction fellow, 1987. Mem. PEN, WG. Home: 172 W 79th St New York NY 10024

PILCHER, EDITH, b. NYC,Aug. 14, 1928, d. Isaac Bendow and Estelle (Stich) Bendow; m. Valter Ennis Pilcher, June 24, 1950; children—Steven, Dorothy. Author: Castorland: French Refugees in the Western Adirondacks, 1793-1814, 1985; contrbr. articles to N.Y. State Conservationist, Adirondac, Adirondack Life, Union Coll. Mag.; contrbr. chpt. to Village Technology Handbook, 1968; author tourist publs. on Ethiopian regions. BA, Syracuse U., 1950; postgrad. Union Coll., Schenectady, N.Y., 1956-60. Wrtr., ed. N.C. State Coll., Raleigh, 1951-52; wrtr. Ethiopian Tourist Agcy., Addis Ababa, 1968-69; freelance wrtr., 1970—; commd. wrtr. Adirondack Mountain Res., St. Huberts, N.Y., 1985—. Mem. Adirondack Research Ctr. Home: 1714 Wendell Ave Schenectady NY 12308

PILGRIM-GURACAR, GENEVIEVE, (Bulbul), b. Chgo., Feb. 3, 1936, d. Robert Cushman and Virginia (Braun) Leland; m. Celik Mehmet Guracar; children—Ismayil Mustafa, Osman Yunus. Author, cartoonist: The Not So Helpless Female, I'm Not for Women's Lib...But, Dissecting Doctor Medicorpse, Everybody's Studying Us, Sugar Daddy's A Sticky Myth, Pulling Our Own Strings, Our Bodies Ourselves, 1984, Plant Closures, Aging, Ageism and Society, Surviving America, The Ribbon; contrbr. cartoons: Off Our Backs, NOW News, LNS, U.A.W. Local Union Press Assn., Union Communications Service, Impact Visuals, Pax Et Libertas, Grassroots, other feminist, labor & peace publs. BS in Design, U. Mich., 1959. Publisher Arachne Pub. Co., Mountain view, Calif., 1971—; founder Needle & Thread Arts Soc., video producer, 1983—; speaker ednl. and humanist orgns. Mem. Graphic Arts Guild. Home: 1113 Sladky St Mountain View CA 94040

PILIBOSIAN, HELENE ROSE, b. Boston, June 26, 1933; d. Khachadoor and Yeghsa (Haboian) Pilibosian; m. Hagop Sarkissian, Sept. 17, 1960; children—Sharon, Robert. Author: The Meaning of the ADL, 1977, Carvings from an Heirloom, 1983; contrbr. Armenian Mirror Spectator, Ararat Qtly, Kans Qtly, N. American Mentor Mag., Charlatan, Author & Journalist, anthologies incl. Armenian N. American Poets, Armenian American Poets, 1965, Natl. Fedn. State Poetry Socs., 1984, and others. AA, Harvard, 1960. Ed. Armenian Mirror Spectator, Watertown, Mass., 1964-66, co- ed., 1976-81; freelance writer, 1981, proofreader, Harvard Univ., Cambridge, Mass., 1981—. Recipient 1st prize in poetry, Armenian Allied Arts Assn., 1971, Pteranodon award, Natl. Fedn. State Poetry Socs., 1984, Wind Lit. Jnl. award Ky. Poetry Soc., 1982. Mem. Natl. Assn. Armenian Studies and Research, Cambridge. Home: 171 Maplewood St Watertown MA 02172

PILLIPS, WILLIAM JOHN, see Grabowski, William John

PILPEL, HARRIET FLEISCHL, b. NYC, d. Julius and Ethel (Loewy) Fleischl; m. Robert Cecil Pilpel; children—Judith Ethel (Mrs. Alan Appelbaum), Robert Harry. Author: (with Theodora Zavin) Your Marriage and the Law, 1952, 64, Rights and Writers, 1960, (with Morton D. Goldberg) A Copyright Guide, 1960, (with Minna Post Peyser) Know Your Rights, 1965; writer, lctr., TV discussant on marriage and family law, lit. and entertainment law, constl. law, civil liberties, birth control, abortion, status of women, problems of sr. citizens and legal profession; mem. editorial adv. bd. Jnl Marriage and Family Counseling; bd. eds. Performing Arts Rvw; contrbr. Pub.'s Weekly Mag. BA, Vassar Coll.; MA in International Relations and Pub. Law, LLB (Kent scholar), Columbia U.; DHL (hon.), Queens Coll., Charlotte, NC, 1981. Research asst. Columbia Law Schl., 1934-35; sr. partner Greenbaum, Wolff, & Ernst; now counsel Weil, Gotshal & Manges. Past mem. com. on polit. and civil rights Pres. Kennedy's Commn. on Status Women; mem. spcl. task force on status women Pres. Johnson's Citizens' Adv. Com.; project dir. HEW Study on Family Planning, Contraception, Vol. Sterilization and Abortion; chmn. panel law and planned parenthood Intl. Planned Parenthood Fedn.; genl. counsel Planned Parenthood-World Population; counsel Assn. for Voluntary Sterilization; cochairperson com. on law, social action and urban affairs Am. Jewish Congress; bd. dirs. Population Resource Center; mem. adv. com. New Women's Career Program; mem. Women's Forum, past trustee NY Ethical Culture Soc., Women's Law Fund; mem. com. on freedom and equality of access to info. ALA; mem. natl. adv. bd. Center for the Book, Lib. of Cong. Recipient SIECUS award, 1973, Margaret Sanger award, 1974, Louise Waterman Wise Laureate award, 1978, Earl Warren Civil Liberties award, 1978, annl. medal for excellence Columbia U. Law Schl. Alumni Assn., 1980, Allard K. Lowenstein award, 1981. Fellow Am. Bar Fdn.; mem. Am. Assn. Marriage Counselors, Am. Acad. Matrimonial Lawyers, Copyright Soc. USA, Assn. Bar City NY, Am., Fed. Bar Assns., NY County Lawyers Assn., ACLU, Lawyers Alliance for Nuclear Arms Control, Am. Law Inst., PEN, ASJA. Home: 70 E 96th St New York NY 10028

PILPEL, ROBERT H., b. NYC, Feb. 16, 1943, s. Robert C. and Harriet F. (Fleischl) P.; m. Madelaine F. French, June 6, 1982. Author: Young Men with Unlimited Capital (with others), 1974, Churchill in America, 1976, To the Honor of the Fleet (fiction), 1979, Between Eternities (fiction), 1985. BA (with Great Distinction), Phi Beta Kappa, Stanford U., 1963; JD, Yale U., 1966. Freelance wrtr., Rome and NYC,1971—. Major, USAF reserve. Fulbright fellow, Rome, 1970-71. Mem. AG. Home: 322 W 57th St New York NY 10019

PINCHOT, ANN, b. NYC; 1 dau., Susan. Novelist: Hear This Woman!, 1958, Hagar, 1960, 52 West, 1962, Vanessa, 1978, Certain Rich Girls, 1979, Doctors and Wives, 1980, The Luck of the Linscotts, 1982, A Moment in the Sun, 1984, The Man Chasers, 1970, The Heart Doctors' Heart Book, 1974. Home: 88 Maltbie Ave Stamford CT 06902

PINE, JOHN CHRISTOPHER, b. NYC, Oct. 12, 1922, s. Sherwood Wilson and Margaret Hugh (Wallace) P.; m. Doris Johanna Roederer, Nov. 20, 1948; children—Dick, Victoria. Author: 199 Ways to Review a Book: A Librarian's Readings in the Novel of the Sixties, 1971, Block Island, 1982, Cliff Walk, 1985, Chinese Camp and Other California Poems, 1986. BA, U. Mont., 1951; MLS, U. Wash., 1956. Asst. lit. div. Rochester (N.Y.) Public Library, 1957-62; reader's adviser, head adult services Smithtown (N.Y.) Public Library, 1963-78. Mem. Walt Whitman Assn., Calif. Library Assn. Home: 1230 Uplands Dr El Dorado Hills CA 95630

PINKHAM, MARY ELLEN, b. Mpls., June 4, 1946; d. Albert Franklin and Pearl Eleanor (Mattson) Higginbotham; m. Sherman Francis, Jr., Mar. 14, 1970; 1 son—Andrew. Author: Mary Ellen's Best of Helpful Hints, 1976, Mary Ellen's Best of Kitchen Hints, 1980, Mary Ellen's Best of Helpful Hints II, 1981. Student pub. schools. Syndicated nwspr. columnist "Mary Ellen's Self-Help Diet" and "Mary Ellen's Hints," 1979—; TV personality, 1979—; pres., chmn. bd. Mary Ellen Enterprises, Inc., 1976—. Mem. AFTRA. Office: 6414 Cambridge St Saint Louis Park MN 55426

PINSKER, SANFORD SIGMUND, b. Washington, Sept. 28, 1941; s. Morris David and Sonia (Molliver) P.; m. Ann Shifra Getson, Jan. 28, 1968; children: Matthew, Beth. Author: The Schlemiel as Metaphor, 1971; The Languages of Joseph Conrad, 1974; The Comedy that "Hoits," 1976; Conversations with Contemporary American Writers, 1985; (poetry) Still Life, 1974, Memory Breaks Off, 1984, Whales at Play, 1986, The Uncompromising Fictions of Cynthia Ozick, 1987, William Stafford, Richard Hugo, and David Wagoner: Three Poets of the Pacific Northwest, 1987. Teaching asst. U. Wash., 1963-67; asst. prof. English, Franklin and Marshall Coll., Lancaster, Pa., 1967-74, assoc. prof., 1974-85; prof. 1986—; vis. prof. U. Calif., Riverside, 1973, 75; Fulbright sr. lectr., Belgium, 1984-85. NEH scholar, 1971. Home: 700 N Pine St Lancaster PA 17603

PINSKY, ROBERT NEAL, b. Long Branch, NJ, Oct. 20, 1940; s. Milford Simon and Sylvia (Eisenberg) P.; m. EllenJane Bailey, Dec. 30, 1961; children—Nicole, Caroline, Elizabeth. Author: Landor's Poetry, 1968, Sadness and Happiness, 1975, The Situation of Poetry, 1977, An Explanation of America, 1980, History of My Heart, 1984. BA, Rutgers U., 1962; PhD,Stanford U., 1966. Mem. English faculty U. Chgo., 1967-68, Wellesley Coll., 1968-80; prof. English U. Calif., Berkeley, 1980—; poetry ed. New Republic Mag., 1978—; vis. lectr. Harvard U.; Hurst prof. Washington U., St. Louis. Recipient Artists award AAAL, 1979, Saxifrage prize, 1980; Guggenheim fellow, 1980, William Carlos Williams Award PSA, 1984. Mem. PEN. Office: Engl Dept U Calif Berkeley CA 94720

PIPES, RICHARD EDGAR, b. Cieszyn, Poland, July 11, 1923; s. Mark and Sophia (Haskelberg) P.; came to U.S., 1940, naturalized, 1943; m. Irene Eugenia Roth, Sept. 1, 1946; children—Daniel, Steven. Author: Formation of the Soviet Union, rev. ed., 1964, Karamzin's Memoir on Ancient and Modern Russia, 1959, Social Democracy and the St. Petersburg Labor Movement, 1963, Europe Since 1815, 1970, Struve: Liberal on the Left, 1870-1905, 1970, Russia Under the Old Regime, 1974, Struve: Liberal on the Right, 1905-1944, 1980, U.S.-Soviet Relations in the Era of Detente, 1981, Survival Is Not Enough, 1984; ed.: Russian Intelligentsia, 1961, (with John Fine) Of the Russe Commonwealth (Giles Fletcher), 1966, Revolutionary Russia, 1968, Collected Works in Fifteen Volumes (P. B. Struve), 1970, Soviet Strategy in Europe, 1976. Student, Muskingum (Ohio) Coll., 1940-43; AB, Cornell U., 1945; PhD, Harvard U., 1950. Mem. faculty Harvard, 1950—, prof. history, 1963-75, Frank B. Baird Jr. prof. history, 1975—; assoc. dir. Russian Research Ctr. 1962-64, dir., 1968-73; sr. cons. Stanford Research Inst., 1973-78; dir. Eastern European and Soviet affairs Natl. Security Council, 1981-82. Mem. exec. com. Com. on Present Danger, 1977—; chmn. Govt. Team B to Rev. Intelligence Estimates, 1976; mem. Reagan transition team State Dept., 1980. Guggenheim fellow, 1956, 65; felllow ACLS, 1965, Ctr. for Advanced Study in Behavioral Scis., Stanford, CA, 1969-70. Fellow AAAS; mem. Council Fgn. Relations. Home: 17 Berkeley St Cambridge MA 02138

PIQUETTE, MARICE ANN, b. Lowell, MA, Dec. 8, 1954; d. Donald Ray and Florence Lillian (Jelly) Janow; m. Jean C. Piquette, Aug. 22, 1972; children—Renee Michelle, Laura Denise. Contrbr. articles to mags., newspapers. Author: Sidney—The Miracle of a Seed, Student Rutgers U., 1973-76; B.A., U. Central Fla., 1981. With public relations Tasty Maid, Piscataway, NJ, 1975-76; office mgr. Nationwide Insurance Co., Orlando, FL, 1980-87. Recipient Golden Apple award Orange County ADDitions Program, Orlando, 1985. Home: 7814 Barberry Dr Orlando FL 32811

PIRSIG, ROBERT MAYNARD, b. Mpls., Sept. 6, 1928; s. Maynard Ernest and Harriet Marie (Sjobeck) P.; m. Nancy Ann James, May 10, 1954 (div. Aug. 1978); children—Christopher (dec. Nov. 17, 1979), Theodore; m. 2d, Wendy L. Kimball, Dec. 28, 1978; 1 dau.—Nell. Author: Zen and the Art of Motorcycle Maintenance, 1974. BA, U. Minn., 1950, MA, 1958. Recipient Award AAAL, 1979; Guggenheim fellow, 1974—. Mem. Soc. Tech. Communicators. Office: Morrow 105 Madison Ave New York NY 10016

PISAR, SAMUEL, b. Bialystock, Poland, Mar. 18, 1929; s. David and Helaina (Suchowolski) P.; m. Judith Frehm, Sept. 2, 1971; 1 dau.—Leah; children by previous marriage—Helaina, Alexandra. Author: Coexistence and Commerce, 1970, Les dames de la Paix, 1971, Of Blood and Hope, 1980, La Ressource Humaine, 1983. LLB, U. Melbourne, Australia, 1953; LLM, Harvard U., 1955, JSD, 1959; DES, U. Paris, 1966; LLD, 1969. Legal counsel UNESCO, 1956-59; practitioner intl. law Paris, New York, Washington and London, 1959—; lectr. U. Paris, 1974; mem. President J.F. Kennedy Task Force Fgn. Econ. Policy19,60; adv. State Dept., 1961; cons. joint econ. com. U.S. Cong., 1962. Mem. ABA, NY, Calif., DC Bar Assns., Am. Judicature Soc., Gray's Inn (London). Made U.S. Citizen by special act of Cong., 1961. Office: 575 Madison Ave New York NY 10022

PITT, CHRISTINE A., b. Ashtabula, OH, Jan. 8, 1952; d. Edward J. and Helen B. (Jakubowski) Pitt. Poetry in numerous anthologies. Quality assurance technician Premix, Inc., North Kingsville, Ohio. Home: 5818 Washington Blvd Ashtabula OH 44004

PITT, SUZANNE FRANCES, b. Toledo, Mar. 21, 1946, d. Oliver Frederic and Dorothy Josephine (Uhl) Senn; m. Timothy Lee Moffatt, Dec. 23, 1967 (div. 1972); m. 2d, William Sterling Pitt, Jan. 24, 1975; children—Anne Elizabeth, Joseph Robert, Alice Rose. Contrbr. poetry to The Fairly Free Thinker, Turn, Turn, Turn, Foreground, other lit mags. AA, Foothill Coll., Los Altos, Calif., 1968, AS, 1976; BA, Evergreen State Coll., Olympia, Wash., 1973. Freelance wrtr., 1965—; comml. fisherman, Eureka, Calif., 1973-75, 85—; tchr. health scis. Coll. of Redwoods, Eureka, 1976-77; physician asst., Eureka, 1977-83. CPR, first air instr. ARC, 1964—; registered interpreter Registry Interpreters for Deaf, Silver Spring, Md. Home: 3127 Pigeon Point Rd Eureka CA 95501

PITTORE, CARLO, see Stanley, Charles J.

PITTS, EUGENE, III, b. Louisiana, MO, Aug. 3, 1940; s. Eugene and Leora Mae (Shetley) P.; m. Sharon Lee Green, May 5, 1973; children—Eugene IV, Stefan Gregory. Grad. Northwestern U., 1962. Editor, Audio Magazine, NYC. Office: CBS Mags 1515 Broadway New York NY 10036

PIZER, DONALD, b. NYC, Apr. 5, 1929; s. Morris and Helen (Rosenfeld) P.; m. Carol Hart, Apr. 7, 1966; children—Karin, Ann, Margaret. Author: Hamlin Garland's Early Work and Career, 1960, Realism and Naturalism in Nineteenth-Century American Literature, 1966, The Novels of Frank Norris, 1966, The Novels of Theodore Dreiser, 1976, Twentieth-Century American Literary Naturalism: An Interpretation, 1982. BA, UCLA, 1951, MA, 1952, PhD,1955. Mem. faculty Tulane U., 1957—, prof. English, 1964-72, Pierce Butler prof. English, 1972—, Mellon prof. humanities, 1978-79. Guggenheim fellow, 1962; ACLS fellow, 1971-72; NEH fellow, 1978-79. Mem. MLA. Home: 6320 Story St New Orleans LA 70118

PLANTINGA, ALVIN, b. Ann Arbor, MI, Nov. 15, 1932; s. Cornelius A. and Lettie Gertrude (Bossenbrook) P.; m. Kathleen Ann DeBoer, June 16, 1955; children—Carl, Jane, Harry, Ann. Author: God and Other Minds, 1967, The Nature of Necessity, 1974, God, Freedom and Evil, 1974, Does God Have A Nature?, 1980. AB, Calvin Coll., 1954; MA, U. MI, 1955; PhD, Yale U., 1958. Instr. Yale U., New Haven, 1957-58; assoc. prof. Wayne State U., Detroit, 1958-63; prof. Calvin Coll., Grand Rapids, MI, 1963-82; prof. U. of Notre Dame, South Bend, IN. 1982—; dir. NEH, Grand Rapids, 1974-78. Fellow Ctr. Advanced Study inn Behavioral Scis., 1968-69; Guggenheim fellow, 1971-72; fellow NEH, 1975-76; vis. fellow Balliol Coll., Oxford, Eng., 1975-76, Gifford lect. U. of Aberdeen, Scotland, 1987. Mem. Am. Philo. Assn., Soc. Christian Philosophers. Home: 50505 Hollyhock Rd South Bend IN 46637

PLATH, JAMES WALTER, b. Chgo., Oct. 29, 1950; s. Norman Arthur and Audrey Marie (Kuester) P.; m. Carol Lynn Jacobson, Nov. 15, 1973 (div. Aug. 18, 1980); children—Amy, Sheri, Brian, Cory. Contrbr. poetry to anthology, Gathering Place of the Waters, 1983, and publs. inclg. Another Chgo. Mag., Nit & Wit, Abraxas, Spoon River Qtly, Blue Unicorn. BA, English, Calif. State U.-Chico, 1980; MA, English, U. Wis.-Milw., 1982. Substitute tchr. County schls., Butte, Calif., 1975-80; tchg. asst. English dept., Univ. Wis., Milw., 1980-86; founding ed. and pub. Clockwatch Rvw. Recipient of Tinsley Helton Dissertation Fellowship, 1987. Mem. AAP, Council for Wis. Writers, CCLM. Address: 737 Penbrook Way Hartland WI 53029

PLATT, EUGENE, b. Charleston, SC, Feb. 20, 1939, s. Paul Calhoun and Estell Annie (Bell) P. Author poetry collections: coffee and solace, 1970, an original sin, 1974, South Carolina State Line, 1980; author poetry chapbooks: Six of One/ Half Dozen of the Other, Allegheny Reveries; contrbr. poetry: Bitterroot, Crazy Horse, Icarus, Tar River Poets, numerous other lit mags; ed.: A Patrick Kavanagh Anthology, 1973, Don't Ask Me Why I Write These Things, 1974, The Turnings of Autumn, 1976, An Outer Banks Anthology; poetry ed. Sandlapper, 1974-78; assoc. ed. Tinderbox. BA, U. S.C.; diploma in Anglo-Irish Lit., Trinity Coll., Dublin, 1970; MA in English, Clarion State Coll.; postgrad. Fla. State U. Mem. staff Bur. Indian Affairs, 1976-78, New Orleans Outer Continental Shelf Office, Bur. Land Mgmt., 1978-79, U.S. Commn. on Civil Rights, 1980-83; now with U.S. Dept. Labor, ed. Preservation Progress newsletter; poet-in-schls., Ala., Fla., Pa., S.C. and Va. Recipient Hart Crane and Alice Crane Williams Meml. Fund award, Va. Ctr. Creative Arts fellow.Address: 2044 Medway Rd Charleston SC 29412

PLAUT, MARTIN EDWARD, (Paul Marttin, Harrison Hopkins), b. Leipzig, Germany, Feb. 19, 1937; s. Otto L. and Hannah (Lowenstein) P.; came to U.S. 1939, naturalized 1946; m. Sharon Evert, Sept. 10, 1965; children—Benjamin Bogart, Anne, Susan. Author: Heartsblood (as Paul Marttin), 1970, Cocoa Blades, 1972, Grand Rounds (as Harrison Hopkins), 1974, Doctor's Guide to You and Your Colon, 1982. AB, Brown U., 1958; MD, Tufts U., 1962. Intern Buffalo (NY) Genl. Hosp., 1962-63; resident Buffalo Genl Hosp. and fellow infectious diseases New Eng. Med. Ctr., Boston, 1964-67; asst. prof. medicine SUNY, Buffalo, 1967-72, assoc. prof. medicine, 1972-79, prof. medicine, 1980—; assoc. chief medicine Sisters of Charity Hosp., Buffalo, 1981—; private practice medicine, specializing in infect. dis. Address: 2157 Main St Buffalo NY 14214

PLAZYK, JUDY LYNN, b. Elgin, IL, Dec. 25, 1960; d. Daniel John and Rose G. (Pieczynski) P. Author: (with Rosalie Hewitt and Vicky Miller)

Composing with Wordstar, 1986, 2d ed., 1987. Wrkg. on computer-assisted composition text using PFS: Profl. Write. B.A., Hope Coll., 1983; M.A., Northern Ill. U., 1986. English instr. Northern Ill. U., DeKalb, 1984-86; asst. mng. ed. Year Book Med. Pubs., Chgo., 1987—. Recipient Merit award STC, 1986. Recipient of natl. award for innovative curriculum from Am. Assn. of State Colleges and Universities, 1987. Home: 150 Pauline Dr Elgin IL 60123

PLEIBEL, FRED, see Glass, Herbert

PLIMPTON, GEORGE AMES, b. NYC, Mar. 18, 1927; s. Francis T. P. and Pauline (Ames) P.; m. Freddy Medora Espy, 1968; children—Medora Ames, Taylor Ames. Author: Rabbit's Umbrella, 1956, Out of My League, 1961, Paper Lion, 1966, The Bogey Man, 1968, Mad Ducks and Bears, 1973, One for the Record, 1974, Shadow-Box, 1976, A Sports Bestiary, 1982, Fireworks, 1984, Open Net, 1985, Curious Case of Sidd Finch, 1987; ed. Writers at Work vols., 1957, 63, 67, 76, 81, 84, 86; ed.-in- chief, Paris Rvw, 1953—. AB, Harvard U., 1948, MA Cambridge U., 1950. Dir. Am. Lit. Anthol. program, 1967-71; assoc. ed. Harper's mag., 1972-81. Address: 541 E 72d St New York NY 10021

PLOEGER, KATHERINE MARIE, b. San Francisco, June 12, 1955, d. Richard Collins and Bonnie (Daugherty) Ploeger. Author: Tips for Women Travelers, 1980, The Weather Handbook-USA, 1983, The Book of Cruise Comparisons (3 vols.), 1986; contrbr. travel articles, photographs to var. U.S. newspapers, Castlee Publs., Traveletter Series, other publs.; designer promotional materials. AA, Canada Community Coll., 1975; BA, San Diego State U., 1978. Office: Box 50964 Palo Alto CA 94303

PLOTNIK, ARTHUR, b. White Plains, NY, Oct. 1, 1937; s. Michael and Annabelle (Taub) P.; m. Meta Von Borstel, Sept. 6, 1960 (div. 1979); children—Julia Nicole, Katya Michelle; m. 2d, Mary Phelan, Dec. 2, 1983. Author: The Elements of Editing: A Modern Guide for Editors and Journalists, 1982, The Man Behind the Quill: Jacob Shallus, Calligrapher of the U.S. Constitution, 1987; 22 pseudonymous novels, articles, TV scripts. BA, State U.NY, Binghamton, 1960; MA, U. IA, 1961; MS in L.S., Columbia U., 1966. Genl. rptr., reviewer Albany (NY) Times Union, 1963-64; freelance writer, 1964-66; ed. Librarians Office, Lib. of Cong., 1966-69; assoc. ed. Wilson Lib. Bull., Bronx, NY, 1969-74; ed.-in-chief Am. Libs., Chgo., 1975—; exec. prod., Library Video Mag, ALA, Chgo., 1986-; journalism faculty, Columbia Coll. Chgo., 1987-. Bd. dirs. Am. Book Awards, 1979-82; bd. advs. Univ. Press of Am., 1982—. Fellow Iowa Writers Wkshop. Creative Writing, 1961; recipient award Ednl. Press Assn. Am., 1973 (3) 77, 82, 83. Mem. ALA, EPAA. Home: 2120 Pensacola Chicago IL 60618

PLUCKER, CHARLOTTE ANN, (Charlotte Hall-Meier), b. Rochelle, IL, Oct. 8, 1955; d. Allen Dean Braddy and Shirley June (Taylor) McKinley; m. Jeffrey Lee Plucker, Mar. 7, 1986. Editor: Precious Metals Trading Handbook, 1983, Investment Strategies for Financial Security: 1984 and Beyond, 1984. Contrbr. articles to bus. mags. Student Kishwaukee Jr. Coll., 1974-80; B.A., Northern Ill. U., 1987. Trading asst Consorcio Panamericano de Inversionistas, S.A., San Jose, Costa Rica, 1980-81; co-owner, adminstr. Meier & Assoc., Chgo., DeKalb, IL, 1981-84; asst. newsroom supvr. DeKalb News Service, 1987. Copyproofer CPA Exam. Rvw., Dekalb, 1987. Home: 610 Emmert Dr Box 342 Sycamore IL 60178

PLUME, NONA DEXTROSE, see Fuller, Mike Andrew

POBO, KENNETH GEORGE, b. Elmhurst, IL, Aug. 24, 1954, s. Louis George and Myrtle Mae (Swanson) P. Author poetry collections: Musings from the Porchlit Sea, 1979, Billions of Lit Cigarettes, 1981, Evergreen, 1985, A Pause Inside Dusk, 1986. PhD, U. Wis., Milw., 1983. Instr. U. Tenn., Knoxville, 1983—. Mem. MLA. Home: 2751 Jersey St Knoxville TN 37919

POCHODA, ELIZABETH TURNER, b. Chgo., Dec. 13, 1941; s. Frederick William and Frances (Franklin) Turner; m. Philip Pochoda, May 12, 1968; 1 dau.—Ivy. Author: Arthurian Propaganda, 1970. BA, Conn. Coll., 1963; MA, U. PA, 1964, PhD, 1968. Lit. ed. Nation Mag., NYC, 1976-82; ed. Vanity Fair Mag., NYC, 1982—. Office: Vanity Fair 350 Madison Ave New York NY 10017

POCHODA, PHILIP M., b. NYC, Mar. 20, 1940; s. Samuel Bernard and Pearl Miriam (North) P.; m. Elizabeth Turner, May 12, 1968; 1 dau.—Ivy. BA, Amherst Coll., 1961; BS, MIT, 1961; PhD, Princeton U., 1969. Asst. prof. sociology and history U. PA, Phila., 1966-76; sr. ed. Pantheon Books, NYC, 1977-80; dir. Anchor Press, Dial Press and Dolphin Books Doubleday, NYC, 1981—. Home: 247 Clinton St Brooklyn NY 11201

PODHORETZ, NORMAN, b. Bklyn., Jan. 16, 1930; s. Julius and Helen (Woliner) P.; m. Midge Decter, Oct. 21, 1956; children—Rachael, Naomi, Ruth, John. Author: Doings and Undoings, The Fifties and After in American Writing, 1964, Making It, 1968, Breaking Ranks, 1979, The Present Danger, 1980, Why We Were in Vietnam, 1982, The Bloody Crossroads, 1986; ed.: The Commentary Reader, 1966. AB, Columbia, 1950; BHL, Jewish Theol. Sem., 1950, LLD (hon.), 1980; BA (Kellett fellow), Cambridge (Eng.) U., 1952, MA, 1957; LHD (hon.), Hamilton Coll., 1969. Assoc. ed. Commentary, 1956-58, ed.-in-chief, 1960—; Looking Glass Lib., 1959-60. Fulbright fellow, 1950-51. Mem. Council on Foreign Relations, Comm. on the Present Danger, Comm. for the Free World. Office: 165 E 56th St New York NY 10022

POE, KATRINE LAURA, b. Oskaloosa, IA, Sept. 29, 1958; d. Jimmy Edward and Donna Faye (Fisher) P. Contrbr. numerous poems to lit. mags., anthols. Wrkg. on novel with Catherine Porri; editing poery collections, non-fiction articles. B.A., Clarke Coll., 1980; postgrad. U. Madrid, 1979, U. Hawaii, 1981-82. Home: 6151 N Winthrop Ave 1108 Chicago IL 60660

POELLOT, RAYMOND ALBERT, b. Longmont, CO, June 24, 1955; s. Charles Herman Poellot; m. Patti Johneece, Aug. 28, 1977 (dec. Apr. 17, 1979). Contrbr. poems to lit. mags., anthols. Wrkg. on romance novels, short horror stories. A.A. in Bus. Administration, Commun. Coll. Balt., 1982; B.S. in Bus. Administration, Morgan State U., 1985. Mng. ed. The Progressive News, Jessup, MD, 1980-85; communications specialist Patuxent Inst., Jessup, 1985—. Served with U.S. Marine Corps, 1975-79. Recipient Merit cert. World of Poetry, 1984, 85, Golden Poet award, 1985, 86. Home: Box 700 Jessup MD 20794

POGREBIN, LETTY COTTIN, b. NYC, June 9, 1939; d. Jacob and Cyral (Halpern) Cottin; m. Bertrand B. Pogrebin, Dec. 8, 1963; children—Abigail and Robin (twins), David. Author: How to Make It in a Man's World, 1970, Getting Yours: How to Make the System Work for the Working Woman, 1975, Growing Up Free: Raising Your Child in the 80's, 1980, Stories for Free Children, 1982, Family Politics, 1983, Among Friends, 1986; contrbr. to N.Y. Times, other mags., nwsprs. AB cum laude with spcl. dist. in Engl. and Am. Lit., Brandeis U., 1959. V.p. Bernard Geis Assoc., NYC,1960-70; columnist The Working Woman column Ladies Home Jnl, 1971-81, Hers column, NY Times, 1983, In Person column, Newsday, 1986; ed. Ms. Mag., NYC,1971—; Poynter fellow Yale U., 1982; fellow MacDowell Colony, 1979; governing council AG, 1986; lectr. women's & family issues, friendship, changing roles of men & women, employment, non-sexist child rearing & edn., Judaism & feminism. Bd. dirs. Action for Child.'s TV, Ms. Fdn., Pub. Ed. Assn., Women's Action Alliance. Mem. AL. Address: Ms Mag 119 W 40th St New York NY 10018

POGUE, FORREST CARLISLE, b. Eddyville, KY, Sept. 17, 1912; s. Forrest Carlisle and Frances (Carter) P.; m. Christine Brown, Sept. 4, 1954. Author: The Supreme Command, 1954, George C. Marshall: Education of a General, Vol. 1, 1963, Ordeal and Hope, 1939-42, Vol. 2, 1966, Organizer of Victory, 1943-45, Vol. 3, 1973, Statesman, 1945-59, Vol. 4, 1987; co-author: The Meaning of Yalta, 1956; contrbr.: Command Decisions, 1960, Total War and Cold War, 1962, D Day: The Normandy Invasion in Retrospect, 1970, America's Continuing Revolution, 1975, The War Lords, 1976, Bicentennial History of the United States, 1976; contrbg. ed.: Guide to American Foreign Relations Since 1700, 1983. AB, Murray (KY) State Coll., 1931; MA, U. KY, 1932; Am. exch. fellow, Inst. des Hautes Etudes Internationales, U. Paris, France, 1937-38; PhD,Clark U., 1939, LHD, 1975; Litt.D., Washington and Lee U., 1970, U. KY, 1983; LLD, Murray State U., 1970. Instr. Western KY State Coll., 1933; instr., assoc. prof. Murray State Coll., 1933-42; mem. hist. sect. U.S. Forces, ETO, 1944-46; with Office Chief Mil. Hist., Dept. Army, 1946-52; sometime professorial lectr. George Washington U.; ops. research analyst Ops. Research Office, Johns Hopkins, U.S. Army Hdqrs., Europe, Heidelberg, Germany, 1952-54; prof. history Murray State Coll., 1954-56; dir. George C. Marshall Research Center, Arlington, VA, 1956-64, George C. Marshall Research Lib., 1964-74, exec. dir. George C. Marshall Research Fdn., 1965-74, biographer, 1974—; life trustee, mem. adv. com. Marshall Papers; dir. Dwight D. Eisenhower Inst. Hist. Research, Natl. Mus. Am. Hist., Smithsonian Instn., 1974-84; adv. com. on Eisenhower papers; adj. fellow Woodrow Wilson Intl. Ctr. Scholars, 1974-77; Dist. vis. prof. VA Mil. Inst., 1972; past chmn. Am. Com. on Hist. 2d World War; former mem. adv. grps. Air Force, Army, and Navy Hist. offices; chmn. adv. com. Senate Hist. Office; adv. com. Former Mems. Congress; natl. advisor KY Oral Hist. Commn. Trustee Harry S. Truman Inst. of Truman Lib.; trustee U.S. Capitol Hist. Soc., mem. adv. com. Natl. Hist. Soc. Hon. fellow U.S. Mil. Hist. Research Collection. Mem. Oral Hist. Assn. (past pres.), U.S. Commn. on Mil. Hist., Orgn. Am. Historians, Soc. Am. Historians, NEA. Address: 1111 Army-Navy Dr Arlington VA 22202

POHL, FREDERIK, b. NYC, Nov. 26, 1919; s. Fred and Anna Jane (Mason) p; M. Carol

Metcalf Ulf, Sept. 15, 1952 (div. Aug. 1982); children: Frederik IV, Ann, Karen, Kathy; m. 2d, Elizabeth Anne Hull, July 27, 1984. Author: more than 100 books inclg. The Space Merchants and other novels (many with C. M. Kornbluth), Man Plus, Gateway, Jem, The Years of the City, Black Star Rising, Chernobyl, 1987, The Coming of the Quantum Cats. Ed. Popular Publs, 1939-43, asst. circulation mgr. Popular Sci., 1947-50, Galaxy 1960-69, exec. ed. Ace Books, 1971-72, Bantam Books, 1973-79; copywriter Thwing & Altman, 1946. Served with USAF, 1943-45. Recipient 6 Hugo awards, 2 Nebula awards, Am. Book award, 2 John W Campbell Intl awards, Edward E. Smith award, Popular Culture Assn. award, Prix Apollo (France), others. Mem./fellow AAAS, British Interplanetary Soc.; mem. SFWA (past pres.), World Sci. Fiction (past pres.), AG (mid-west chair), NY Acad. Sci., others. Address: 855 S Harvard Dr Palatine IL 60067

POINDEXTER, JOSEPH BOYD, b. NYC, July 4, 1935; s. Everton Gentry and Elinor (Fuller) P.; m. Holly McNeely, Oct. 20, 1976; children—Matthew McNeely, Owen McNeely AB, Harvard U., 1957. Asst. mng. ed. Bus. Wk, 1963-67; sr. ed. Dun's Rev., 1967-70, asst. mng. ed., 1970-73; ed. MBA Mag., 1973-76, exec. ed., 1974-76, Juris Doctor, 1974-76, Med. Dimensions, 1974-76, New Eng., 1974-76; sr. ed. East/West Network, NYC,1976-77, exec. ed., 1977-83; sr. ed. Money Mag., 1985; sr. ed. Life Mag., 1986. Home: 213 Warren St Brooklyn NY 11201

POIRIER, RICHARD, b. Gloucester, MA, Sept. 9, 1925; s. Philip and Annie (Kiley) P. Author: The Comic Sense of Henry James, 1960, In Defense of Reading, 1962, A World Elsewhere, 1966, The Performing Self, 1971, Norman Mailer, 1973, Robert Frost: The Work of Knowing, 1977, The Renewal of Literature, 1987; ed.: Raritan Qtly, 1981—. AB, Amherst Coll., 1949; MA, Yale U., 1951; PhD,Harvard U., 1959; student U. Paris, France, 1944-45; postgrad Cambridge (Eng.) U., 1952-53; HHD, Amherst Coll., 1978. Mem. faculty Williams Coll., 1950-52, Harvard U., 1953-63; Disting. prof. English, Rutgers U., 1963—; v.p. Lit. Classics of U.S., Inc.; dir. Harpers Mag.; bd. dirs. PEN, 1984-86; ed. Partisan Review, 1963-73, O. Henry Prize Stories, 1961-65. Bd. dirs. Natl. Book Critics Circle. Mem. Am. Acad. Arts & Scis. Home: 104 W 70th St New York NY 10023

POIS, ROBERT AUGUST, b. Washington, Apr. 24, 1940; s. Joseph and Rose (Tomarkin) P.; m. Anne Marie Messerschmitt, July 2, 1972; children—Haia Rebecca, Erica Leah, Emily Tamara. Author: Friedrich Meinecke and German Politics in the 20th Century, 1972, The Bourgeois Democrats of Weimar Germany, 1976, Emil Nolde, 1982, National Socialism and the Religion of Nature, 1986 AB, Grinnell (Iowa) Coll., 1961; MA, U. WI, 1962, PhD, 1965. Mem. faculty U. Colo. Boulder, 1965—, prof. history, 1975—. Woodrow Wilson fellow, 1961. Home: 1521 9th St Boulder CO 80302

POLAK, JULIE STARK, b. Crestline, OH, Sept. 11, 1945; d. John Eugene and Leslie Jean (Sigars) Stark; m. Leonard J. Polak, Mar. 18, 1973; children—Christopher, Zeus, Sarina, Libby, Sterling, Lance. Conrbr. numerous articles to mags., newspapers, including Chgo. Tribune, others. B.S., Ohio State U., 1972, M.A., 1974. Tchr. public schls., Galion, OH, 1972—. Home 607 S Sandusky Ave Bucyrus OH 44833

POLEC, STANLEY WALTER, b. Philadelphia, PA, June 9, 1930; s. Albert and Agnes (Witko) P. Author: poetry in Wide Open Mag., Poets at work, other litmags and anthols. Wrkg. on short biographies of noted Polish-Americans. Graduate Technical H.S., Phil., 1949, Natl. Radio Inst., 1956. Employee Heintz Mfg. Col., Sears, Roebuck, Philco Corp., William Laird & Assoc., Phil.; freelance wrtr., 1985—. Mem. P&W, Natl. Wrtrs. Club. Home: 3943 Priscilla St Philadelphia PA 19140

POLETTE, NANCY (JANE), b. Richmond Heights, MO, May 18, 1930; d. Willard A. and Alice (Colvin) McCaleb; m. Paul L. Polette, Dec. 23, 1950; children: Pamela (deceased), Paula, Keith, Marsha. Author: Basic Library Skills, 1971, Library Skills for Primary Grades, 1973, Developing Methods of Inquiry: A Source Book for Elementary Media Personnel, 1973, In Service: School Library/Media Workshops and Conferences, 1973, The Vodka in the Punch and Other Notes from a Library Supervisor, 1975, (with Marjorie Hamlin) Reading Guidance in a Media Age, 1975, ed, Helen Saunders, The Modern School Library, 2d ed, 1975, E Is for Everybody: A Manual for Bringing Fine Picture Books into the Hands and Hearts of Children, 1977, 2d ed, 1982, (with Hamlin) Celebrating with Books, 1978, Katie Penn, 1978, (with Hamlin) Exploring Books with Gifted Children, 1980, Picture Books for Gifted Programs, 1981, Three R's for the Gifted: Reading, Writing, and Research, 1982, Tangles (picture book), 1983, The Thinker's Mother Goose (picture book), 1983, Books and Real Life: A Guide for Gifted Students and Teachers, 1984, The Research Book for Gifted Programs, 1985, The Reader's Alamanac, 1986, The Research Almanac, 1986, The Book Bag, 1986. Computer software: Who Stole Cinderella's Slipper, 1983, Mother Goose for Young Thinkers, 1983, The Revenge of Rumpelstiltskin, 1983, The Pied Piper Pipes Again, 1983. Also au of tapes and transparencies series for library use and of film script, Anne's Journeys, 1983. Ed, Miller-Brody Newbery Literary Activities Pack Program, 1974-75. Mem of bk rvw staff, School Library Jnl, 1972-73. Contrbr to jnls. AA, William Woods Coll, 1950; B.S. Ed., Washington Univ, St. Louis, Mo., 1962; MS Ed., Southern Illinois Univ, 1968; grad study, Univ of Mo, 1972-73. Elementary school tchr in Jefferson Co., Mo., 1950-51, and in Ritenour, Mo., 1954; elementary school tchr, Pattonville School District, Maryland Heights, Mo., 1955-65, co-ordinator of elementary school materials, 1965-80; instr, Southern Illinois Univ at Edwrdsville, 1968-78; instructor (1970) to assoc. prof of educ (1979—), Lindenwood Coll, St. Charles, Mo. Ed-in-chief, Book Lures, Inc. Lectr and wokshop leader, 1968—. Educational cons., ECA, Denver, Colo., 1977-80. Mem bd dirrs of Leukemia Guild of Mo., 1959-70, and of Ill., 1959-70. Member: ALA, American Assn of School Librarians, NCTE, Assn for Supervision and Curriculm Development, Mo. Library Assn, Mo. Assn of School Librarians (vice-pres, 1973-74), Mo. State Teachers Assn, Suburban Library Assn, Chicago Children's Reading Round Table. Home: 203 San Jose Court O'Fallon MO 63366

POLICOFF, SUSAN LEWIS, b. Richmond, VA, Jun. 24, 1944; d.Leonard David and Naomi (Lewis) Policoff; m. Edward Silver, 1967 (div. 1973); 1 dau.—Lea Rose Policoff. Contrbr. to Suppression, New Morning, Second Coming, Bay Guardian, Rolling Stone, other newspprs., mags. BA in English, History, State U. of NY at Albany, 1967. Co-ed. Suppression Antiwar & Literary Mag. (Albany, NY), 1968-69; caretaker House boarding farm (Ypsilanti, MI), 1974-75. Home: 2807 Milvia St Berkeley CA 94703

POLITE, CARLENE HATCHER, b. Detroit, Aug. 28, 1932, d. John and Lillian (Cook) Hatcher; children—Glynda, Lila. Author: The Flagellants, 1966, 67, 68, 69 (nominee for Pulitzer and Faulkner prizes 1967), Sister X & The Victims of Foul Play, 1975. Assoc. prof. SUNY, Buffalo, 1971—; panelist, juror NEA, 1982, N.Y. State Council on Arts, 1981, N.Y. Fdn. on Arts, 1985. Home: 390 Linwood Ave Apt 4 Buffalo NY 14206

POLITE, FRANK C., b. Youngstown, OH, Sept. 18, 1936, s. Jacob Joseph and Nancy Marie (Zarella) P.; 1 child, Charlene Ann Miller Khepri; m. 2d, Dorothea Lynn Bailik, Sept. 18, 1983. Author: Letters of Transit, 1979, The Pool of Midnight, 1983; contrbr. poetry: New Yorker, N.Am. Rvw, RiverStyx, Harper's, The Nation, Poetry, Yellow Silk, others. Lectr. U. Md., Europe, 1983—. Recipient Individual Artist award Ohio Arts Council, 1980. Home: 44 N Schenley Ave Youngstown OH 44509

POLKING, KIRK, b. Covington, KY, Dec. 21, 1925; Henry and Mary (Hull) P. Author: Oceans of the World: Our Essential Resource, 1983, The Private Pilot's Dictionary and Handbook, 1986, Let's Go to an Atomic Energy Town, 1968, Let's Go See Congress at Work, 1966, Let's Go with Henry Hudson, 1964, Let's Go with Lewis & Clark, 1963; ed. Writer's Digest Forum, 1976—, num. books inclg.: Law and the Writer, 1985, Writer's Encyc., 1985, Freelance Jobs for Writers, 1984, Artist's Market, 1975, Beginning Writer's Answer Book, 1984, Writer's Mkt., 1971, How to Make Money in Your Spare Time by Writing, 1971. Student, Xavier U., U. Cin. Asst. ed. Writer's Digest, Modern Photog., asst. circ. mgr., Cin., 1948-52; circ. mgr. Farm Quarterly, Cin., 1952-57; freelance writer, Cin., 1957-62; ed. Writer's Digest, F & W Pubns., Cin., 1963-72, Spec. Projs., 1973-75; dir. Writer's Digest Schl., and ed., WDS Forum, Cin., 1976—. National Headliner, WIC, 1970. Mem. AG, WIC, Natl. Lg. Am. PEN Women, NFPW. Home: 529 Constitution Sq Cincinnati OH 45255

POLLAK, FELIX, b. Vienna, Nov. 11, 1909, came to U.S., 1939, s. Geza and Helene (Schneider) P.; m. Sara Allen, June 23, 1950. Author: Castle and the Flaw, 1963, Say When, 1969, Voyages to the Inland Sea II (with James Hearst and John Woods), 1972, Ginkgo, 1973, Subject to Change, 1978, Prose & Cons, 1983, Tunnel Visions, 1984, Benefits of Doubt, 1987; contrbr. Perspectives on Pornography, 1970, The Little Mag. in Am., 1978; contrbr. prose, poetry to over 100 lit. mags. and quars. Wrkg. on selected poems, translations. DrJur, U. Vienna, 1953; MA in Library Sci., U. Mich., 1948. Curator rare books and spcl. collections U. Wis.-Madison, 1959-74, prof. emeritus, 1974—. Recipient Borestone Mountain Poetry award, 1965; winner poetry awards Council Wis. Wrtrs., 1973, 78, 82, 84. Home: 3907 Winnemac Ave Madison WI 53711

POLLAK, RICHARD, b. Chgo., Apr. 5, 1934; s. Robert and Janet (Spitzer) P.; m. Merle Ann Winer, Mar. 26, 1961 (div. 1979); 1 dau.—Amanda; m. 2d, Diane Walsh, Mar. 6, 1982. Author: Up Against Apartheid, 1981, The Episode, 1986; ed.: Stop The Presses, I Want To Get Off!, 1975. Student Knox Coll., 1952-54; BA in English, Amherst Coll., 1957. Rprtr., Worcester (Mass.) Teleg. & Gazette, 1957; polit. rprtr.

Evening Sun, Balt., 1959-64; assoc. ed. Newsweek, NYC,1964-67; asst. ed. Honolulu Star Bull., 1967-68; freelance writer, NYC,1968-71; co-fdr., ed. More Mag., NYC,1971-76; tchr. Yale U., 1977, NYU, 1977, 82-86; lit. ed. The Nation, 1980-81. Cons. Ford Fdn., 1970-72, Poynter fellow Yale U., 1977. Mem. PEN. Home: 404 Riverside Dr New York NY 10025

POLLAN-COHEN, SHIRLEY, b. NYC; d. Benjamin and Anna Rose (Flatow) Pollan; children: Robert B., Linda T. Contrbr. to Connections, Grub Street, Bronx Roots I and II, Garland, Heiroglyphics Press, also anthologies. Adminstrv. asst. Bronx Community Coll., N.Y., 1967—; columnist Bronx Chronicle, 1976; performing poet. Mem. P&W, Bronx Poets and Wrtrs. Alliance (sec. 1980-81, publicity dir. 1981-83, dir. 1983—). Address: Jerome Ave. Station Box 627 Bronx NY 10468

POLLET, ELIZABETH, b. NYC, June 27, 1922; d. Joseph Pollet and Emily Hannah (Smith) Scarlett; m. Delmore Schwartz, 1949 (div. 1957). Author: A Family Romance, 1950; contrbr. to Solo, New World Writing No. 4; ed. Portrait of Delmore: The Journals and Notes, 1939-1959, 1986. BA, U. Chgo., 1948; MA, NYU, 1965, PhD, 1978. Adj. lectr. Hunter Coll., 1978- 80; adj. asst. prof. NYU, 1982—. Home: 463 West St Apt D-817 New York NY 10014

POLLET, SYLVESTER, b. Kingston, NY, June 28, 1939, s. Joseph and Betty Heap (Strassburger) P.; m. Margaret A. Keleshian, Oct. 13, 1973. Author poetry collection: Entering the Walking-Stick Business, 1982; contrbr. poems to New Eng. Rvw, Beloit Poetry Jnl, Puckerbrush Rvw, numerous other lit mags and jnls; contrbr. poetry to anthologies: New Maine Writing, Maine Moments in N.Y., New Eng. Poetry, Maine Poets Festival Anthology, Light Year '87. BA in English, Dartmouth Coll., 1961; MA in English, U. Me., Orono, 1985. Book rvw. ed. Sagetrieb, Natl. Poetry Fdn., Orono, 1984—; lect. creative writing Univ. Me., Orono, 1985—. Mem. NWU, New Eng. Arts Fdn., Maine Touring Artists Program. Home: RFD 2 Box 3630 East Holden ME 04429

POLLIO, RALPH THOMAS, b. Bronx, NY, Nov. 1, 1948, s. Thomas and Dolores (Miccioli) P.; m. Rita Lucia Napolitano, Sept. 29, 1974; 1 son, Christopher. BCE, Manhattan Coll. Founder, ed., pub. Eastern Basketball Publs., West Hempstead, N.Y., 1975—. Served to Sgt., USANG, 1969-74. Mem. U.S. Basketball Wrtrs. Assn. (1st place award for best mag. feature 1984). Mag. Pubs. Assn., ASME, ASCE. Office: EBP 7 May Ct West Hempstead NY 11552

POLLITT, KATHA, b. NYC, Oct. 14, 1949, d. Basil Riddiford and Leanora (Levine) P. Author: Antarctic Traveller, 1982; contrbr. poetry to New Yorker, The Atlantic, Grand Street, Poetry, Antaeus, Shenandoah, New Republic, Pequod, other mags., The Morrow Anthology of Younger American Poets, other anthols. Student, Harvard U.-Radcliffe Coll., 1967-72, Columbia U. Schl. Arts, 1973-75. Freelance critic numerous jnls. including N.Y. Times Book Rvw, The Nation, The Atlantic, MS, Mother Jones, Yale Rvw, Harpers, 1975—; lit. ed. The Nation, 1982-84; lectr. Princeton U., 1984. NEA grantee, 1984; Fulbright writer's program in Yugoslavia grantee, 1985. Mem. NBCC (bd. dirs. 1984-86, award in poetry 1983). Home: 317 W 93rd St New York NY 10025

POLOME, EDGAR CHARLES, b. Brussels, Belgium, July 31, 1920; s. Marcel Felicien and Berthe (Henry) P.; came to U.S. 1961, naturalized, 1966; m. Julia Josephine Schwindt, June 22, 1944 (dec. May 1975); children—Monique (Mrs. John Ellsworth), Andre; m. 2d, Barbara Baker Harris, July 11, 1980. Author: Swahili Language Handbook, 1967, Language in Tanzania, 1980, Language, Society and Paleoculture: Essays, 1982; ed. Old Norse Literature and Mythology, 1969, The Indo-Europeans in the 4th and 3rd Millennia, 1982; co-ed.: Jnl. Indo-European Studies, 1973—, The Mankind Qtly, 1980—. BA, Universite Libre de Bruxelles, 1941, PhD, 1949; MA, Cath. U. Louvain, 1943. Instr. Germanic lang. Athenee Ville de Bruxelles, 1942-56; prof. Dutch Belgian Natl. Broadcasting Corp., Brussels, 1954-56; prof. linguistics U. Belgian Congo, 1956-61; prof. Germanic, Oriental, African langs. and lits. U. Tex., Austin, 1962—, chmn. dept., 1969-76, Christie and Stanley Adams Jr. Centennial Prof. of Liberal Arts, 1984—; Fulbright prof. U. Kiel, 1968; Ford Fdn. team dir. Tanzania survey, 1969-70. Mem. Linguistics Soc. Am., Am. Oriental Soc., MLA, African Studies Assn., Am. Anthrop. Assn., Indogermanische Gesellschaft, Societas Linguistica Europa, Societe de Linguistique de Paris, Am. Inst. Indian Studies. Home: 3403 Loyola Ln Austin TX 78723

POLSBY, NELSON WOOLF, b. Norwich, CT, Oct. 25, 1934; s. Daniel II and Edythe (Woolf) P.; m. Linda Dale Offenbach, Aug. 3, 1958; children—Lisa, Emily, Daniel R. Author: Congress and the Presidency, 3d edit., 1976, Congress: An Introduction, 1968, Political Promises, 1974, Community Power and Political Theory, 2d ed., 1980, (with Geoffrey Smith) British Government and its Discontents, 1981, Consequences of Party Reform, 1983, (with Aaron Wildavsky) Presidential Elections, 6th ed., 1984, Political Innovation in America, 1984; ed.: (with R.A. Dentler and P. Smith) Politics and Social Life, 1963, Congressional Behavior, 1971, Reapportionment in the 1970's, 1971, The Modern Presidency, 1973, (with F.I. Greenstein) Handbook of Political Science, 8 vols., 1975, (with R.L. Peabody) New Perspectives on the House of Representatives, 3d ed., 1977, What If?, 1982; book rvw. ed. Transaction, 1968-71; mng. ed. Am. Poli. Sci. Rvw, 1971-77. AB, Johns Hopkins, 1956; MA, Yale U., 1958, PhD, 1961. Instr. U. WI, 1960-61; from asst. prof. to prof. Wesleyan U., Middletown, CT, 1961-68; prof. poli. sci. U. CA-Berkeley, 1967—. Fellow Social Sci. Research Council, 1959, Brookings Instn., 1959-60, Ctr. Advanced Study Behavioral Scis., 1965-66; Ford Fdn., 1970-71, Guggenheim Fdn., 1977-78, Roosevelt Ctr., 1982-83. Fellow AAAS; mem. Am. Poli. Sci. Assn., Am. Sociol. Assn., Council on Foreign Relations. Mem. com. on pub. engring. policy Natl. Acad. Engring., 1973-76, commn. on vice presidential selection Democratic Natl. Com., 1973-74, Yale U. Council, 1978—. Home: 1500 Leroy Ave Berkeley CA 94708

POMERANTZ, CHARLOTTE, b. Bklyn., July 24, 1930; d. Abraham L. and Phyllis (Cohen) P.; m. Carl Marzani, Nov. 12, 1966; children—Gabrielle Rose, Daniel Avram. Author children's books: The Bear Who Couldn't Sleep, 1965, The Moon Pony, 1967, Ask the Windy Sea, 1968, Why You Look Like You Whereas I Look Like Me, 1968, The Day They Parachuted Cats on Borneo, 1971 (chosen for Intl. Year of the Child 1977-78), The Princess and the Admiral, 1974 (Jane Addams Children's Book Award), The Piggy in the Puddle, 1974, The Ballad of the Long Tailed Rat, 1975, Detective Poufy's First Case, 1976, The Mango Tooth, 1977, The Downtown Fairy Godmother, 1978, The Tamarindo Puppy and Other Poems, 1980 (an ALA Notable Book), Noah's and Namah's Ark, 1981, If I Had a Paka (poems in 11 langs.), 1982, Buffy and Albert, 1982, Posy, 1983, Where's the Bear, 1983; co-author, lyricist musical Eureka, 1980. BA, Sarah Lawrence Coll., 1953. Spcl. editorial asst. Einstein on Peace, 1960; ed. A Quarter Century of Un-Americana, 1963. Address: 260 W 21st St New York NY 10011

POMEROY, CLAIRE, see Ice, Ruth

POMEROY, IRA LEWIS, b. Athens, LA, Dec. 17, 1924, s. Ira and Catherine (Albright) Pomeroy; m. Carol Croeni, Aug. 28, 1969; children—Cheryl, Nancy, Brenda, Sue, Louann. Author: Ira L. Pomeroy Collected Poems, 1983. BA, UCLA, 1950; DO, Des Moines Osteopathic College, 1954; MD, Calif. Coll. Med. (UCI Med.), 1962. Mem. OMA, OCAAFP. Home: 1132 Fraley Garden Grove CA 90630

PONICSAN, DARRYL, b. Shenandoah, PA, May 26, 1939; s. Frank and Ann (Kuleck) P; m. Cecilia; children: Lorena, Dylan. Author: The Last Detail, 1970, Golden Grove, 1971, Andoshen, Pa, 1972, Cinderella Liberty, 1972, The Accomplice, 1974, Tom Mix Died for Your Sins, 1975, The Ringmaster, 1977, An Unmarried Man, 1980; contrbr. to Am Heritage, 1977; wrkg on film projects. BA, Muhlenberg Coll, 1959; MA, Cornell U, 1965. Served to lt, USN, 1961-65, 6th fleet. Recipient screenwriter of the year award, NAACP, 1973. Address: Box 1596 Ojai CA 90265

PONIEWAZ, JEFF, b. Milw., Sept. 28, 1946. Author: Raygun and The Hostages, 1984, Dolphin Leaping in the Milky Way, 1985; contrbr. poetry to Los Angeles Times, Greenpeace Chronicles, Earth First!, Blake Times, Appeal to Reason, Wisconsin Poets Calendar, Ocooch Mountain News, Brewing: 20 Milwaukee Poets, Gathering Place of the Waters: 30 Milwaukee Poets, New Blood, Touchstone, New Age Mag., Crazy Shepherd, others. BA, U. Wis., 1970, MFA, 1973, postgrad. 1983. Active poets-in-schls. program, Wis., 1972-82; tchr. creative writing, U. Wis., Milw., 1983—. Contest winner AAP, 1973. Home: 4540 S 1st St Milwaukee WI 53207

PONTE, JOSEPH GONSALVES JR., b. New Bedford, MS, Aug. 9, 1925; s. Joseph G. and Adelaide (Santos) P.; m. Jean Moore, June 16, 1956; children—Wendy J., Joseph M., Malcolm M. Contrbr. numerous chpts., tech. and trade articles on food tech. to books, profl. jnls., trade mags. B.A., Northwester U., 1956; M.S., U. Minn., 1958. Technologist, Am. Inst. of Baking, Chgo., 1954-56; mgr. research services ITT Continental Baking, Rye, NY, 1958-75; prof. Kans. State U., Manhattan, 1975—. Active Manhattan Arts Council, 1984-86, Friends of Art, Manhattan, 1984-86. Mem. Am. Assn. Cereal Chemists, Inst. Food Tech., Sigma Xi. Home: 3110 Cindella Dr Manhattan KS 66502

PONTICELLO, MATTHEW, b. Bklyn., Apr. 18, 1948; s. Philip and Marion (Sorentino) P.; m. Jeanelle Driggers (div. 1976); 1 dau., Kimberly. Author: (poems) The Poet Blossomed, 1984, A Rosebird in the American Dream, 1985; (screenplay) Peola; (short film) Behind the Lines; (film) Bloodbath. Student Union Coll., 1974-76. Ed. co. newspaper Thomas & Betts, Raritan, N.J., 1972—. Home: 128 E 3d Ave Roselle NJ

07203

POOKA, I. M., see Bonnett, Kendra R.

POOLE, CAROLYN ANN, b. Chgo., Jan. 4, 1931; d. Russell Poole and Martha Elizabeth (Hirsch) Hampton. Contrbr. poems to lit. mags., anthols. B.A., Valparaiso U., 1953; M.S. in Edn., Southern Ill. U., 1970. Recreational therapist Ill. Sold & Sail Home, Quincy, 1966-68; free-lance poet, 1957—. Recipient Outstanding Dramatic Achievement award Valparaiso U. Players, 1953. Home: 3806 First St Park City IL 60085

POOLE, JAY MARTIN, b. Clinton, OK, Aug. 6, 1934; s. Cleo Lloyd and Arlie (Martin) P. BA, U. Tulsa, 1957, postgrad., 1958-60; MLS, U. OK, 1970. Reference librarian, spcl. programs librarian U. Wash., 1970-73; head reference dept. SUNY, Buffalo, 1973-74; head librarian undergrad. library U. Texas, Austin, 1974-79; editor Choice mag., 1979-81; asst. dir. collection devel. Texas A & M U., College Station, 1982. Recipient Outstanding svc. to librarianship citation U. OK, 1979. Mem. ALA, Pacific N.W. Lib. Assn., Wash. Lib. Assn., Texas Lib. Assn., Southwestern Lib. Assn., Natl. Book Critics Circle, Soc. Scholarly Pubs. Office: Evans Library Texas A & M College Station TX 77843

POOLE, KATHLEEN ZADA, b. Cheverlly, MD, Oct. 18, 1953; d. Arhie Franklin and Zada Margaret (Hung) P. Contrbr. articles to mags. including Nursing, Laboratory Management Mag. B.S. in Nursing, U. Fla., 1975. Presentations ed. Martin Marietta, Orlando, FL, 1983; mkgt. dir. West Lake Hosp., Longwood, FL, 1983-85; free-lance copywrtr., wrtr., 1979-83, 85—. Recipient Healthcare Advt. award Healthcare Mkgt. Report, Atlanta, 1987. Home 759 Phoenix Ln Oviedo FL 32765

POPKIN, ROY SANDOR, b. NYC, Mar 4, 1921; s. Louis and Zelda (Feinberg) P.; children by previous marriage—Gail Ohnsman, Raymond Louis; m. Mary O'Rourke, June 26, 1971. Author: The Environmental Science Services Administration, 1967, Desalination, Water for the World's Future, 1969, The Technology of Necessity, 1970. Contrbr. chpts. on natural disasters to books; articles to mags. including Readers Digest, Catholic Digest, numerous others. Student U. N.C., 1938-39, N.Y. U., 1939-41. Reporter Overseas News Agcy., N.Y.C., 1939-41; publicist Philip Schuyler Assoc., N.Y.C., 1940-42; publicist Am. Red Cross, Brklyn., 1942-43, asst. exec. dir., 1943-44, asst. natl. dir., blood program, 1943-44, asst. dir. disaster services, 1960-81, asst. natl. dir., blood program, 1943-44, asst. dir. disastr services, 1960-81, deputy natl. dir. service, 1981-84, retired. Mem. AG. Home: 2111 Hanover St Silver Spring MD 20910

PORTER, ANDREW BRIAN, b. Cape Town, South Africa, Aug. 26, 1928; s. Andrew Ferdinand and Vera Sybil (Bloxham) P.; came to U.S., 1972. Author: A Musical Season, 1974, Wagner's Ring, 1976, Music of Three Seasons, 1978, Music of Three More Seasons, 1981, Wagner's Tristan and Isolde, 1981, The Tempest, 1985 Musical Events 1980-1983, 1987; ed.: Musical Times, 1960-67; co-ed.: Verdi's MacBeth: A Sourcebook, 1983; editorial bd.: New Grove Dictionary of Music and Musicians, 18th ed. BA, MA, Univ. Coll., Oxford, Eng., 1952. Music critic Fin. Times, London, 1950-74; Bloch Prof. U. Calif., Berkeley, 1981. Mem. Royal Musical Assn. Am. Music Ctr., Am. Musicol. Soc., ASCAP, Am. Inst. Verdi Studies, Donizetti Soc. Office: NYer 25 W 43d St New York NY 10036

PORTER, BERN, b. Porter Settlement, ME, Feb. 14, 1911; s. Lewis Harden and Etta Flora (Rogers) P. Author 73 books. Wrkg. on Sweet End, Book of Porter, Bern (3 titles in progress). BS, Colby Coll., 1932; ScM, Brown U., 1933. Chmn. bd. Bern Porter Internat., Belfast, Maine, 1926—. NEA fellow, 1981. Fellow Intl. Acad. Poets London (founding), Soc. Writers and Pubs., Centro Studi E Scambi Internzzionali, Rome; mem. Maine Writers and Pubs., PEN, Carnegie Authors. Home: 22 Salmond Way Belfast ME 04915

PORTER, DARWIN FRED, b. Greensboro, NC, Sept. 13, 1937; s. Numie Rowan and Hazel Lee (Phillips) P. Author: Frommer Travel Guides to: England, 1964, Spain, 1966, Scandinavia, 1967, Los Angeles, 1969, London, 1970, Lisbon/Madrid, 1972, Paris, 1972, Morocco, 1974, Rome, 1974; Frommer/Pasmantier Travel Guides to: Portugal, 1968, England, 1969, Italy, 1969, Germany, 1970, France, 1970, the Caribbean, Bermuda, the Bahamas, 1980, Switzerland, 1984, Austria and Hungary, 1984, Prentice Hall Press Travel Guides to Scotland and Wales, 1986, Bermuda and The Bahamas, 1986; novels: Butterflies in Heat, 1976, Marika, 1977, Venus, 1982. BA, U.Miami, 1959. Bur. chief Miami Herald, 1959-60; v.p. Haggart Assocs., NYC,1961-64; editor, author Arthur Frommer Inc., NYC,1964-67, Frommer/Pasmantier Pub. Corp., 1967-84, Prentice Hall Press, 1985-88. Recipient Silver Award Intl. Film and TV Festival N.Y., 1977. Mem. Soc. Am. Travel Writers, Smithsonian Assocs. Home: 75 St Marks Pl Staten Island NY 10301

PORTER, DONALD, b. New Orleans, Apr. 16, 1939, s. D.R. and Olga Porter; m. Diane Taxson; children—Katherine, Victoria. Author: Inner Running, 191977, Sight Unseen, 1978, Apache War Cry, 1981, Kowa Fires, 1983. BA, U. Sewanee, 1960; BA, MA, Kings Coll., Cambridge, Eng., 1962. Vice-pres. Relco., Inc., NYC,1967-75; pres. Wrtg. Workshop, NYC,1977—; pres. Ariel Fund, 1982—; chmn. Relco, Inc., NYC,1985—. Mem. MWA. Home: 120 W 70th St New York NY 10023

PORTER, HARLAN DAVID, b. Tuscola, IL; s. Franklin Lee, Sr. and Sarah Nancy (Dallas) P. Columnist, Tuscola Rvw., 1983—. Contrbr. articles, poems to Straight mag., Ill. History mag., Am. Poetry Anthol., others. Reporter, Tusola Rvw., 1983-86, mng. ed., 1986—. Student Southern Ill. U., 1983-84, Parkland Coll., 1984—. Freelance wrtr., photographer, 1981—. Dir. Tuscola Chamber of Commerce, 1986—, Museum Assn. of Douglas ounty, Tusola, 1985; curator Ervin House, Tuscola, 1984—. Mem. Intl. Thespian Soc. Home: 607 E. Newkirk Tuscola IL 61953

PORTER, JANET KAY, b. Charleston, WV, June 29, 1945; d. Arthur Russell and Nellie Arlene Smith; m. Charles Franklin Hayes, May 8, 1967 (div. Sept. 14, 1978); children—Michael Kevin, Jim Kenneth; m. Michael Pell Porter, Feb. 13, 1983. Contrbr. articles to Sun Press Newspapers, Honolulu Mag. Ed.: Ka'upena newsletter, 1984-87, The Leaflet newsletter, 1985-87; faculty advisor: Harvest mag., 1985-87. B.S. in Edn., W.V. U., 1967; M.A. in English, U. Hawaii, 1974. High sch. tchr. Hawaii Baptist Acad., Honolulu, 1974-76; lectr. U. Hawaii, Honolulu, 1976-78; instr. lang. arts Leeward Commun. Coll., Pearl City, HI, 1978—. Mem. Hawaii Councils Tchrs. English, Arts Council Hawaii, Hawaii Lit. Arts Council. Home: 972 Kealaolu Ave Honolulu HI 96816

PORTER, JOE ASHBY, (Joseph A.), b. Madisonville, KY, July 21, 1942; s. Lawrence and Margaret (Wise) P. Author: Eelgrass, 1977, The Kentucky Stories, 1983; (as Joseph A. Porter) The Drama of Speech Arts, 1979. BA, Harvard U.; PhD, U. Calif.-Berkeley. Instr. Shoreline Community Coll., Seattle, 1977-78; asst. prof. Univ. Va., Charlottesville, 1970-73, Univ. Balt., 1976-77, Towson State Coll., 1976-77, Murray State Univ., KY, 1978-80, Duke Univ., Durham, NC, 1980—. Recipient NEA fellowship, 1979-80, 85-86; syndicated fiction award, PEN, 1983, 84. Mem. AWP, MLA, Southeastern Renaissance Conf. Address: 2411 W Club Blvd Durham NC 27705

PORTER, J(ENE) M(ILES), b. Wichita, KS, Aug. 21, 1937; s. Gilbert and Vernice (Nash) P.; m. Susan Margaret Speer; children: Edmund, Cliff, Tom, Julia, Jeannette. Author: ed, United States Foreign Policy and South Vietnam, 1966, ed, Contemporary Developments in the Theory and Practice of Communism, 1967, ed and au of intro, Martin Luther: Selected Political Writings, 1974, ed, Sophia and Praxis: The Boundaries of Politics, 1984, ed (with Richard Vernon) Unity, Plurality and Politics, 1986, ed, Classics in Political Philosophy,. Contrbr of articles and rvws to political sci and history jnls., and Queen's Qtly. BA, Park Coll, 1959; MA, Univ of Wyoming, 1960; Ph.D., Duke Univ, 1967. Asst prof of American government and political philosophy, Drury Coll, Springfield, Mo. 1963-67; asst prof of poli sci, Univ of Saskatchewan, Saskatoon, 1967-70, assoc prof, 1970-76, prof of pol sci, 1976—, assoc head of dept, 1978-79. Vis scholar, Tulane Univ, 1974-75, Pomona Coll., 1980-81. Program dir, Intl Seminar for Philosophy and Political Theory, 1981. Member: Canadian Poli Sci Assn (mem bd dirs, 1980—), American Poli Sci Assn, Conf for the Study of Political Thought, Phi Gamma Mu, Phi Kappa Phi. Grant from Natl Humanities Faculty, 1974, Canada, 1980, Kemper Educ and Charitable Fund, 1981, and Earhart Fndn, 1981. Office: Dept of Political Studies U Saskatchewan Saskatoon Saskatchewan Canada S7N OWO

PORTER, MARGARET EVANS, b. Macon, GA, Mar. 4, 1959; d. Fred William and Mariann (Chappell) Evans; m. Christopher John Porter, Oct. 6, 1984. Author: (film scripts) Golden Moments in the Golden Isles, 1981, An Introduction to Denver's C. Henry Kempe Center, 1985, Denver's Housing Options: CHOICE, 1985; (MA thesis) Cable News Network: A Descriptive Analysis of Turner's News Channel, 1983; (instr.'s manual) Mass Media Research: An Introduction, 2d., 1987;; (novel) Heiress of Ardara, 1988. B.A., Agnes Scott Coll., 1980; M.A., U. Ga., 1983. Asst. dir. Consumer Pulse of Denver, 1983-84. Recipient cert. of Merit, U. Ga., 1976; named Outstanding Young Women of Am., 1983. Mem. RWA, Rocky Mountain Fiction Wrtrs., Am. Film Inst., Jane Austen Soc. North Am., AG. Home: 5742 S Pierson St Littleton CO 80127

PORTER, SYLVIA, b. Patchogue, L.I., NY, June 18, 1913; d. Louis and Rose (Maisel) Feldman; m. Reed R. Porter, 1931; 1 dau.—Cris Sara; 1 stepson—Sumner Campbell Collins; m. 2d, James F. Fox, 1979. Author: Sylvia Porter's Income Tax Guide, pub. annually 1960—, Sylvia Porter's Money Book—How to Earn It, Spend It, Save It, Invest It, Borrow It, and Use It to

Better Your Life, 1975, paperback edit., 1976, Sylvia Porter's New Money Book for the 80's, 1979, Sylvia Porter's Your Own Money, 1983; co-author (with J.K. Lasser) Managing Your Money; ed.-in-chief Sylvia Porter's Personal Finance Mag.; syndicated columnist Universal Press. BA magna cum laude, Hunter Coll., 1932; postgrad. Schl. Bus. Admin. NYU. Founder weekly newsletter "Reporting on Goverments"; assoc. N.Y. Post, 1935-77, N.Y. Daily News, 1978—. Office: 1271 Ave of Americas New York NY 10020

PORTUGAL, PAMELA RAINBEAR, see Walatka, Pamela Portugal

POSAMENTIER, EVELYN, b. NYC, Aug. 7, 1951, d. Ernest and Alice (Pisk) Posamentier. Author: Elise (chapbook), 1979; contrbr. to Am. Poetry Rvw, Chrysalis, Volition, Poetry Motel; contrbr. poetry to Networks: An Anthology of San Francisco Bay Area Women Poets, 1979. BA in Creative Wrtg., San Francisco State U., 1974, MA in Creative Wrtg., 1977. Recipient Sylvia and Irving Wallace Poetry prize AAP, 1977. Home: 210 Hoffman Ave San Francisco CA 94114

POSNANSKY, MERRICK, b. Bolton, Lancashire, Eng., Mar. 8, 1931; s. Simon and Dora (Cohen) P.; came to U.S., 1977; m. Eunice Sarah Lubega, Feb. 10, 1962; children—Sheba, Tessa, Helen. Ed.: Nile Quest, 1962, Prelude to East African History, 1966; joint ed. The Archaeological and Linguistic Reconstruction of African History, 1982; guest ed. Jnl New World Archaeology, 1982, 1986. BA, U. Nottingham, Eng., 1952, PhD, 1956; Dip. Arch., Peterhouse, Cambridge U., Eng., 1953. Warden of prehist. sites Royal Natl. Parks, Nairobi, Kenya, 1956-58; curator Uganda Museum, Kampala, 1958-62; asst. dir. Brit. Inst. in Eastern Africa, Kampala, 1962-64; dir. African studies Makerere U. Coll., Kampala, 1964-67; prof. archaeology U. Ghana, Legon, 1967-76; prof. history and anthropology UCLA, 1976—, chmn. archaeology program, 1979-81; dir. Inst. of Archaeology, 1984, chmn. adv. com. African Studies Ctr., 1983—; chmn. Hist. Monuments Commn. Uganda, 1964-67. Fellow Soc. Antiquaries of London; mem. Uganda Soc., Soc. Hist. Archaeology, African Studies Assn., UCLA Friends of Archaeology. Home: 19010 Los Alimos St Northridge CA 91326

POST, JONATHAN VOS, b. NYC, Sept. 3, 1951; s. Samuel Herbert and Patricia Francis (Vos) P.; m. Dr. Christine Mary Carmichael, Feb. 14, 1986. Wrtr. sci., fantasy, sci. fiction, poems, art and music criticism, dramas, radio and TV scripts. Wrkg. on comic novel, sci. fiction novel, book on computer futures, relationship between sci. and poetry, screenplay. BS in Math., Calif. Inst. Tech., 1973, BS in Poetry, 1973; MS in Computer, U. Mass., 1975, postgrad., 1975-77. Software engr. Jet Propulsion Lab., Pasadena, Calif., 1983-84, Voyager mission planning engr., 1984-85; cons., pub., chief exec. officer Computer Futures Inc., Pasadena, 1985—; chief exec. officer Emerald City Pub.; exec. asst. to the Pres., Konigsberg Instruments Inc., Pasadena, CA, 1981-; sec. Beverly Hills Mgmt. Assocs. Recipient 1st prize Amy Woodward Fisher Meml. poetry contest Nat. League Am. Penwomen-Poetry Scribes Spokane, 1980; 1st place for poetry Tacoma Wrtrs. Club, 1983. Mem. SFWA, MWA, P&W, Sci. Fiction Poetry Assn. Office: EC Pub 385 S Catalina No 231 Pasadena CA 91106

POST, RICK ALAN, b. Denver, Sept. 15, 1962; s. John Dunbar and Marilyn (Vance) P. Author: Campus Guide to Drinking, 1984, MASP: Multipath Analysis Software Package (govt. publ.), 1985. BS in Bus., U. Colo., 1984. Freelance wrtr., Denver, 1986—. Pres. Accident Press, Dillon, Colo., 1984—. Office: Box 1665 Dillon CO 80435

POSTER, CAROL, b. NYC, Aug. 5, 1956, d. William Shakespeare and Constance (Hammett) Poster. Author: Blackbird (poems), 1979, Deceiving the Worms (poems), 1984; contrbr. to Antigonish Rvw, Bitterroot, Blue Grass, Kans. Qtly, Laughing Unicorn, numerous other lit mags in U.S., U.K., N.Z., India and Switzerland; contrbr. fiction to Atticus Rvw, Ploughshares, Reflect, other periodicals; ed.: Princeton Arts Jnl, 1974-75, Poems Pennyeach, 1975, Amaryllis Rvw, 1985—; arts ed. Hollins Columns, 1976; assoc. ed. Product, 1980; dance ed. The Event, 1985—. BA cum laude, Hollins (Va.) Coll., 1977. Freelance wrtr., theater dir., 1974—; owner, mgr. Amaryllis Software, Salt Lake City, 1984—; newsletter ed. Zero Pop. Growth (Salt Lake City), 1985—; programmer N.Am. Weather Cons., Salt Lake City, 1986—. Mem. P&W, AWP, Broadway Drama Guild. Address: 535 Parkview Dr Park City UT 84060

POSTON, DAVID L., b. Greensboro, NC, Aug. 15, 1953, s. Joseph B. and Mary M. (Inman) Poston; m. Linda Fay Farmer, Feb. 22, 1985; 1 son, David L. II. Author materials on work safety and unions for various companies. Home: 201 Cannon Ave Greer SC 29651

POTEETE, ROBERT ARTHUR, b. Perry, AR, Aug. 29, 1926; s. Arthur and Ruby (Farish) P.; m. Frances Reynolds, Feb. 15, 1951 (dec. Mar. 1969); children—Anthony R., Julia Anne, Richard A.R. (dec. Sept., 1973). Contrbr. articles to popular mags. BA, U. Central Ark., 1948; postgrad. Medill Schl. Jnlsm., Northwestern U., 1948-49. Rptr. Ark. Gazette, 1949; rptr., day city ed., asst. news ed., asst. Sunday ed. N.Y. Herald Tribune, 1950-66, mng. ed., Paris, 1963-65; sr. ed. Saturday Evening Post, NYC,1966-69; mng. ed., ed. Psychology Today, Del Mar, CA, 1969-73; mng. ed. New Publs., Playboy Enterprises, Inc., Chgo., 1973-74; sr. ed. Money Mag., 1974-76; ed.-in-chief Am. Illustrated mag. USIA, Washington, 1976—. Mem. ASME, Inner Circle. Home: 2500 Q St NW 644 Washington DC 20007

POTOK, CHAIM, b. NYC, Feb. 17, 1929, s. Benjamin Max and Mollie (Friedman) P.; m. Adena Sara Mosevitzky, June 8, 1958; children—Rena, Naama, Akiva. Author: The Chosen, 1967, The Promise, 1969, My Name is Asher Lev, 1972, In the Beginning, 1975, Wanderings, 1978, The Book of Lights, 1981, Davita's Harp, 1985, Theo Tobiasse: Artist in Exile, 1986. BA summa cum laude, Yeshiva U., 1950; PhD, U. Pa., 1965. Mng. ed. Conservative Judaism, NYC,1964-65; ed. Jewish Publ. Soc., Phila., 1965-74, spcl. projects ed., 1974—. Nominated for Natl. Book award, 1968; recipient Edward Lewis Wallant prize, 1968, Athanaeum award, 1971. Mem. PEN, DG, WG. Home: 20 Berwick Rd Merion PA 19131

POTOKER, EDWARD MARTIN, b. Newark, June 13, 1931; s. Benjamin and Bessie (Linn) P.; m. Berit Maria Arneberg, Sept. 3, 1958; 1 son—Eric Benjamin. Author: The Corn Grain, 1956, Ronald Firbank, 1969, John Brain, 1978; contrbr. Ency. World Lit. in the 20th Century, Groliers Ency. Intl., The Dartmouth Alumni mag., Ramparts; book reviewer: N.Y. Times Book Rvw, 1962—, Saturday Rvw, 1965—; ed.: The Ronald Firbank-Carl Van Vechten Correspondence, A Tragedy in Green and When Widows Love: Two Stories by Donald Firbank, 1978; founding mem. Jnl Critical Analysis, 1969, AB, Dartmouth Coll., 1953; MA, Columbia U., 1955, PhD,1964; postgrad U. Munich, Germany, 1955-56. Mem. editorial staff New Yorker Mag., 1957-58; instr. English U. Rochester, 1958-59; lectr. English Hunter Coll., 1960; mem. faculty CCNY, 1960—, asst. prof. English, 1966—, Bernard M. Baruch Coll., NYC,1968-72; assoc. prof. Bernard M. Baruch Coll., NYC,1972-79, prof. 1979—, chmn. dept. English, 1971, 76—. Mem. AAUP, MLA. Home: 186 Riverside Dr New York NY 10024

POTTER, CLARKSON NOTT, b. Mendham, NJ, May 17, 1928; s. John Howard Nott and Margaretta (Wood) P.; m. Ruth Delafield, June 14, 1949 (div. Aug. 1965); children—Howard Alonzo, Christian, Margaretta, Edward Eliphalet; m. 2d, Pamela Howard, Nov. 26, 1973 (div. Apr. 1976); 1 son—Jack Rohe Howard-Potter; m. 3d, Helga Maass, Oct. 31, 1981. Author: Writers, Editors and Moneymen, 1988. BA, Union Coll., 1950. With Doubleday & Co., NYC,1950-57; sr. ed., advt. mgr., mng. ed. Dial Press, NYC,1958-59; founder, ed.-in-chief Clarkson N. Potter Inc., NYC,1959-76; dir., ed.-in-chief Barre Pub. Co. Inc., MA, 1974-76; pres. The Brandywine Press, NYC,1976-80; lit. agt., publishing cons., Jamestown, RI, 1980—; bd. dirs., v.p. Pub. Center for Cultural Resources Inc., NYC,1973—. Home and Office: 5 Westwood Rd Jamestown RI 02835

POTTER, MARK, see Hollabaugh Mark

POTTERFIELD, PETER LOUNSBURY, b. Jacksonville, FL, Oct. 3, 1949; s. Jack Maxwell and Peggy Lou (Lounsbury) P. Contrbr. to: Atlanta Constitution, 1972- 73, Outside Mag., 1985. BA, U. FL, 1971. Arts ed. Sante Fe Reporter, 1975-77; ed. Northwest Skier, Seattle, 1977-79, Pacific Northwest Mag., 79—. Mem. Am. Soc. Mag. Eds., SPJ. Office: Pacific NW Mag 222 Dexter Ave Seattle WA 98119

POTTS, CHARLES, b. Idaho Falls, ID, Aug. 28, 1943; s. Verl Stanley and Sarah Mildred (Gray) P.; m. Judith Ellen Silverman, Mar. 28, 1977; 1 child, Emily Karen. Author: Little Lord Shiva, 1969; The Trancemigracion of Menzu, 1974; The Golden Calf, 1975; The Opium Must Go Thru, 1976; (autobiography) Valga Krusa, 1977; (poems) Rocky Mountain Man, 1978; contrbr. poetry to Wild Dog, Aldebran Rvw, Kaleidoscope, The Smith, other lit mags. BA, Idaho State U., 1965. Founder, pub. Litmus Inc., 1966-81; instr. Walla Walla Community Coll., Wash., 1981—; real estate broker Century 21, Dale Snider Realtors, 1984—. Home: 350 S Palouse Walla Walla WA 99362

POULIN, A., JR., b. Lisbon, ME, Mar. 14, 1938. Author: In Advent: Poems, 1972, Catawba: Omens, Prayers and Songs: Poems, 1977, The Widow's Taboo: Poems after the Catawba, 1977, The Nameless Garden: Poems, 1978, The Slaughter of Pigs: A Sequence of Poems, 1981, A Momentary Order: Poems, 1987; editor: Contemporary American Poetry, 1971, 4th ed. 1985, A Ballet for the Ear: Interviews, Essays, and Reviews (John Logan), 1983; co-editor (with David A. DeTurk) The American Folk Scene: Dimensions of the Folksong Revival, 1967; (translator) Duino Elegies and the Sonnets to Orpheus (German poems by Rainer Marie Rilke), 1977, Saltimbanques (French prose poems by Rainer Maria Rilke), 1979, The Roses and the

Windows (French poems by Rainer Maria Rilke), 1979, Poems (French poems by Anne Herbert), 1980, The Astonishment of Origins (French poems by Rainer Maria Rilke), 1982, Orchards (French poems by Rainer Maria Rilke), 1982, The Migration of Powers (French poems by Rainer Maria Rilke), 1984, The Complete French Poems of Rainer Maria Rilke, 1986; poems, translations, essays, revs. and interviews pub. in Atlantic Monthly, Paris Rvw, Kenyon Rvw, New Directions, Esquire, Poetry Northwest, The Nation, others; also numerous anthologies; contrbg. editor The American Poetry Rvw, 1972—; founding editor and pub. BOA Editions, Ltd., 1976—. Chmn. Div. Humanities, St. Francis Coll., U. New Eng., 1969-71; asst. to pres. for curriculum planning and devel., 1970-71; dir. Brockport Writers Forum, Dept. English, SUNY-Brockport, 1972-75, prof. English. Mem. lit. panel N.Y. State Council on Arts, 1977-80; founding exec. dir. N.Y. State Lit. Ctr., Inc., Brockport/Fairport, 1978- 80; cons. various lit. and arts orgns. assoc. Danforth Fdn., 1970—; fellow and grantee Research Fdn. of SUNY, 1972, 73, 74, 77, 79; NEA fellow, 1974, 82; poetry fellow NY Fdn. Arts, 1986; Embassy of Can., 1982; recipient Transl. award Columbia U., 1977; residencies Yaddo, 1977, 80. Home: 92 Park Ave Brockport NY 14420

POUNCY, MATTIE HUNTER, b. Princeton, NJ, July 20, 1924, d. Thomas and Margaret (Jordan) Hunter; m. Hillard Warren Pouncy, Oct. 12, 1947; 1 son, Hillard III. Author: Reach a Little Deeper, 1986, In Search of Self, 1987. BS, Tuskegee U., 1948; MA, Trenton State Coll., 1977. Tchr. public schls. throughout N.J., 1955—; presenter workshops. Home: 157 Mansgrove Rd Princeton NJ 08540

POWDERS, DONNA JO, b. Morris, OK, July 20, 1942; d. Everett Walter and Doretha Lavern (Beaver) Stubbs; m. Alvin Leroy Powders, Nov. 6, 1959; children—Dennis Alvin, Alan Leroy. Novel: A Man of Few Words, 1984. Contrbr. articles, short stories to mags., newspapers including Tulsa County News, Intl. Christian News, others. Wkg. on young adult novel, suspense novel. Secy, Scovil & Sides Hardware, Tulsa, OK, 1967—.Mem. Okla. Wrtrs. Fedn., Tulsa Nightwriters (treas. 1986, 87). Home: 6832 S 32d W Ave Tulsa OK 74132

POWELL, BEVERLY JO, (Taylor Powell), b. Tucson, Dec. 13, 1940; d. Joseph Alma and Avonelle Davis (Mills) Taylor; m. Wayne Fisher Powell, Nov. 28, 1958; children—Susan Lynne Powell Deason, Catherine Joanne. Author: Remote Sensing of the Environment, 1973, The Manager's EEO Guidebook, 1988; columnist Jet Jnl., 1964-69; contrbr.: Women Winning (two chaps.), 1976, Maricopa Lawyer, 1987. Wrkg. on mysteries, non-fiction. Ed. Maricopa Community Coll., 1964-67, Ariz. State U., 1969. Investigator EEOC, various locations, 1972-78, chief personnel and ops. services, Phoenix, 1978-79, compliance supr., Phoenix, San Diego and Los Angeles, 1979-86; ptnr. firm Brown, Powell & Duff, 1986—. Mem. MWA, Romance Wrtrs. Am. Home: 5545 N Quail Run Rd Paradise Valley AZ 85253

POWELL, CYNTHIA ANNE, b. Balt., Apr. 21, 1958; d. Malcolm Haney and Annette (Dixon) Powell. Contrbr. articles: The Private Funding Advisor, College Marketing Alert, other publs. BA, Seton Hill Coll., 1980. Mem. public relations staff Mt. St. Mary's Coll., Emmitsburg, Md., 1981-85; asst. to pres. 70001 Ltd., Washington, 1985-86; dir. mktg.-communications Albion (Mich.) Coll., 1986—. Mem. EWA, Women in Communications. Office: Albion Coll 501 E Michigan Ave Albion MI 49224

POWELL, TAYLOR, see Powell, Beverly Jo

POWELL, ENID LEVINGER, b. NYC, Nov. 24, 1931, d. Herbert R. and Selma E. (Sherman) Levinger; m. Bert Powell, Nov. 5, 1950; children—Pip, Jon. Co-author (with Pamela Printer): The Big Steal, 1980, The Divorce Handbook, 1982; contrbr. to The Purple Turtle, Kittens & Children. MA in English, Creative Wrtg., U. Ill., Chgo., 1978. Freelance wrtr., 1950—; CBS program The Young and The Restless, 1984—. Mem. WG. Home: 1340 N Astor St 907 Chicago IL 60610

POWELL, EVAN ARNOLD, b. Asheville, NC, Sept. 5, 1937; s. Arnold Elmore and Mary Elizabeth (Reighard) P.; children—Angela, Trip, Scott. Author: The Complete Guide to Home Appliance Repair, 1974, rev. edit., 1984; The Popular Science Book of Home Heating (and Cooling), 1984; tech. cons., contrbg. ed.: The Homeowner, 1983—; contrbr. to: Homeowner's How To Treasury, 1976, Popular Sci. Homeowner's Encyc., 1975, 78, Arete Encyc., 1980, Carolina Outdoors; contrbg. ed.: Motorcamping Handbook; columnist: Housepower, Checkpoint. Student, N.C. State U., 1954-55; BA, Furman U., 1958. Tech. svc. dir. product engring. and tng. Sears Roebuck & Co., 1959-73; feature writer Popular Sci. mag., NYC, 1969-73, S.E. ed., Greenville, S.C., 1973—; instr. Greenville Tech. Coll., 1967-70. Producer, commentator: T.V. features Checkpoint, WYFF-TV, Multimedia. Recipient ALMA awards Assn. Home Appliance Mfrs., 1972, 73, 75, 77-78, 79-80, award Major Appliance Consumer's Action Panel, 1975, NEH, 1978. Mem. ASJA. Office: Chestout Mt Rt 1 Box 322A Traveler's Rest SC 29690

POWELL, JOSEPH EDWARD, b. Ellensburg, Wash., Jan. 22, 1952, s. Arthur George and Dorothy Jean (Davis) P. Author: Counting the Change, 1986; contrbr. poetry to Ariel, Alaska Qtly Rvw, Arachne, Crab Creek Rvw, Poetry, Seattle Rvw, Taurus, other publs.; cono rvws. to Humanist, San Francisco Rvw. of Books. BA in English Lit., U. Wash., 1975; MA in English Lit., Central Wash. U., 1978, BA in Edn., 1982; MFA, U. Ariz., 1981. Instr. Central Wash. U., Ellensburg, 1982-83, 84—. Winner 1st place, Sun Dog, Fla. State U., 1982, Book award, Qtly Rvw of Lit., 1986. Mem. AWP. Home: Rt 1 Box 504 Ellensburg WA 98926

POWELL, RICHARD PITTS, b. Phila., Nov. 28, 1908; s. Richard Percival and Lida Catherine (Pitts) P.; m. Marian Carleton Roberts, Sept. 6, 1932 (dec. Nov. 1979); children—Stephen Barnes, Dorothy Louise; m. 2d, Margaret M. Cooper, 1980. Author mysteries: Don't Catch Me, 1943, All Over but The Shooting, 1944, Lay That Pistol Down, 1945, Shoot If You Must, 1946, And Hope to Die, 1947, Shark River, 1950, Shell Game, 1950, A Shot in the Dark, 1952, Say It with Bullets, 1953, False Colors, 1955; author novels: The Philadelphian, 1957, Pioneer, Go Home, 1959, The Soldier, 1960, I Take This Land, 1963, Daily and Sunday, 1965, Don Quixote, U.S.A., 1966, Tickets to the Devil, 1968, Whom the Gods Would Destroy, 1970, Florida: A Picture Tour, 1972; (as Jeremy Kirk) The Build-Up Boys, 1951; contrbr. short stories, articles, serials to mags. AB, Princeton, 1930. Rptr. Phila. Evening Ledger, 1930-40; with N.W. Ayer & Son, Phila., 1940-58, mem. pub. relations dept., 1940-42, charge info. svcs., 1949-58, v.p. 1951-58. Home: 1201 Carlene Ave Fort Myers FL 33901

POWER, MARJORIE, b. NYC, Oct. 31, 1947; d. Lawrence Magnus and Regina (Rothbaum) Strauss; m. Max Singleton Power, Dec. 9, 1979; 1 son, Erik. Author: Living With It: Poems by Marjorie Power, 1983; poetry in lit mags including The Poetry Rvw, The Seattle Rvw, Plainsong, and Stone Country. BA, San Francisco State U., 1969. Mem. PSA, Wash. Poets' Assoc., Northwest Renaissance. Home: 5608 Boston Harbor Rd Olympia Washington 98506

POWERS, ANNE, b. Cloquet, MN, May 7, 1913; d. John Patrick and Maud (Lynch) P.; m. Harold A. Schwartz, Aug. 22, 1938; children—Weldon, Lynn. Author: The Gallant Years, 1946, Ride East, Ride West, 1947, No Wall So High, 1949, The Ironmaster, 1951, The Only Sin, 1953, The Thousand Fires, 1957, Ride With Danger, 1958, No King But Caesar, 1960, Rachel, 1973, The Four Queens, 1977, The Royal Consorts, 1978, The Young Empress, 1979, Possession, 1979, Eleanor, The Passionate Queen, 1981. Student, U. MN, 1932-33. Lectr., instr. writing Marquette U., Milw., instr. creative writing. Headliner of Yr. award Wisconsin Women in Communication, 1983. Mem. Allied Authors, Fictioneers. Home: 3800 N Newhall St Milwaukee WI 53211

POWERS, JAMES FARL, b. Jacksonville, IL, July 8, 1917; s. James Ansbury and Zella (Routzong) P.; m. Elizabeth Alice Wahl, Apr. 22, 1946; children—Katherine, Mary, James, Hugh, Jane. Author: Prince of Darkness and Other Stories, 1947, The Presence of Grace, 1956, Morte D'Urban, 1962 (Natl. Book Award 1963), Look How the Fish Live, 1975. Student, Northwestern U., 1938-40. Tchr. writing courses St. John's U., Collegeville, MN, 1947, 1975—, Marquette U., 1949-51, U. MI, 1956-57; writer-in-res. Smith Coll., 1965-66. Guggenheim fellow, 1948; grantee Natl. Inst. Arts and Letters, 1948; Rockefeller fellow, 1954, 57, 67. Mem. Natl. Inst. Arts and Letters. Office: Knopf 201 E 59th St New York NY 10022

POWERS, JOHN R., b. Chgo., Nov. 30, 1945; s. John Francis and JuneRose (Tampier) P. Author: The Last Catholic in America, 1973, Do Black Patent Leather Shoes Really Reflect Up?, 1975, The Unoriginal Sinner and The Ice Cream God, 1977; musical version of Do Black Patent Leather Shoes Really Reflect Up?, 1979. BS in Sociology, Loyola U., Chgo., 1967; MA in Radio, TV and Film, Northwestern U., 1969, PhD, 1975. Elem. and jr. high schl. tchr., Chgo., 1967-68; asst. prof. speech Northeastern Ill. U., Chgo., 1972-79. Office: Contemporary Bks 180 N Michigan Ave Chicago IL 60601

POWERS, THOMAS MOORE, b. NYC, Dec. 12, 1940; s. Joshua Bryant and Susan (Moore) P.; m. Candace Molloy, Aug. 21, 1965; children—Amanda, Susan, Cassandra. Author: Diana: The Making of A Terrorist, 1971, The War at Home, 1973, The Man Who Kept the Secrets: Richard Helms and the CIA, 1979, Thinking About the Next War, 1982. BA, Yale U., 1964. Reporter Rome (Italy) Daily American, 1965-67, UPI, NYC, 1967-70; free-lance writer, 1970—. Recipient Pulitzer prize for natl. rptg., 1971. Mem. PEN. Office: Hitzig 34 Gramercy Pk New York NY 10003

POYER, DAVID, b. DuBois, PA, Nov. 26, 1949; s. Leonard Poyer; m. Kelly Lea Fisher, July 3,

1986. Novels: White Continent, 1980, The Shiloh Project, 1981, Star Seed, 1982, The Return of Philo T. McGiffin (Top Young Adult Novel, Book List 1983), 1983, Stepfather Bank, 1987, The Dead of Winter, 1988, The Med, 1988; (nonfiction) Insiders Guide to Outer Banks of N.C., 1978—. Contrbr. sci. fiction, articles to mags. including Analog, Isaac Asimov's, others. B.S., U.S. Naval Acad., 1971; M.A., George Washington U., 1986. Commissioned Ensign U.S. Navy, 1971, advanced through grades to Lt. Commander, USNR. Mem. AG. Home: 3659 Riverside Ave Jacksonville FL 32205

POYNTER, DANIEL FRANK, (Dan Poynter), b. NYC, Sept. 17, 1938; s. William Frank and Josephine E. (Thompson) P. Author numerous books including The Parachute Manual, 1972, 1977, 1984, Parachuting, The Skydivers' Handbook, 1978, Parachute Rigging Course, 1977, Parachuting Instructor/Examiner Course, 1969, Parachuting Manual with Log, 1976, Hang Gliding, 1973, Manned Kiting, 1974, Frisbee Players' Handbook, 1978, Toobee Players' Handbook, 1981, Self-Publishing Manual, How to Write, Print and Sell Your Own Book, 1979, Publishing Short-Run Books, 1980, Book Fairs, 1981, Business Letters for Publishers, 1981, Computer Selection Guide, 1983, Word Processors and Information Processing, 1982, Publishing Forms, 1985, Parachuting Manual for Square/ Tandem Equipment, 1985; author over 400 tech. and popular articles pub. in various mags., chpts. in encycs. and other books; author monthly column in Parachutist mag., 1963—; editor Spotter news mag., 1965-74; past editor Para-News-briefs publ.; author numerous tech. reports for USPA. BA in Social Sci., Calif. State U.-Chico, 1960; postgrad. San Francisco Law Sch., 1962-63. Recipient Meritorious Achievement award Central Atlantic Sport Parachute Assn., 1968, numerous other certs. of appreciation. Mem. U.S. Parachute Assn. (25-Yr. Cert. of Membership 1986, Achievement award 1981, Gold Parachutists Wings 1972), Parachute Industry Assn. (pres. 1985, 86). Home: RR 1 Box P Goleta CA 93117

PRANCE, JUNE E., (Catherine Hill), b. Hudersfield, Yorkshire, England (arrvd. USA 1948); d. George H. and Beatrice (Hill) Shaw. Author: Commercial Art Techniques, 1976, British Recipes for American Cooks, 1972; contrbr. to various poetry anthologies, various US, British & Commonwealth publications. BA in Arts & Sciences, Jnlsm. Florida State, 1961; MA in Education, U. of South Florida, 1976. Promo. dir. Tampa Tribune Co. (FL), 1963-68; graphics instr., dept. head U. of South FL, 1968—; ed./publ. British Digest Illustrated (Riverview, FL), 1979—. Publicity dir. The Les Evans Fund for Handicapped Children, Essex, England. Mem. London Press Club. Home: 10104 Tucker Jones Rd Riverview FL 33569

PRAIRIE SAGE, THE, see Barnes, Jerry Neal

PRANGE, MARNIE, b. Portsmouth, VA, May 5, 1953, d. Arthur Jergen and Sarah Elizabeth (Bowen) Prange. Ed.: Black Warrior Rvw, 1979-81; mng. ed.: Mo. Rvw, 1982; contrbr. poetry to Poetry Now, Poetry Northwest, River Styx, Window, numerous other publs. MA, Hollins Coll., Roanoke, Va., 1977; MFA, U. Ala., 1983. Instr. U. Mo., Columbia, 1981-82, U. Louisville, 1983-84, Fla. Intl. Un., Miami, 1985—; asst. prof. No. Ariz. U., Flagstaff, 1984-85. Mem. AAP, AWP, P&W. Home: 4561 Post Ave Miami Beach FL 33140

PRASHKER, BETTY A., b. NYC, d. Ellis and Lillian B. Arnoff; m. Herbert Prashker, Dec. 12, 1950 (div. 1972); children—Susan Herman, Lucy, Marti. BA, Vassar Coll. Asst. ed. Doubleday & Co., Inc., NYC,1946-51, sr. ed., editorial dir., v.p., 1965-82; copywriter Denhard & Stewart, NYC,1961-63; sr. ed. Coward- McCann, Inc., NYC,1963-65; ed.-in-chief, v.p., assoc. pub., Crown Pubs., Inc., NYC,1982-83. Chmn. genl. pub. div. Assn. Am. Pubs., NYC. Mem. governing bd. dirs. Fund for Artists Colonies, NYC,1983—, Women's Media Group. Office: Crown 225 Park Ave New York NY 10003

PRATER, RUBY MARIAN, (Ruby Cone) b. Elkhart, IN, Jan. 5, 1915; d. Harold Van Namee Replogle and Blon Marie (Newell) Hibshman; m. Richard Cone, June 30, 1945 (dec. Mar. 17, 1985); children—Gary, Dennis, Terry and Richard Cone and Sharel Kidder and Jayna Eash; m. Glen Prater, Apr. 26, 1986. Columnist: Truth Pub., Elkhart, IN, 1960-75, Tribune, South Bend, IN, 1965-75, Comml., Leesburg, FL, 1976-87; author: (booklet) P.M.-It Works, 1972. Contrbr. articles to mags., newspapers including Mobile Home Living, Kalamazoo Gazette, others. Ed., contrbr. Tavares Citizen, Eustis, FL, 1975-76. Wrkg. on live story of a man. Student U. Ind., 1950-52. Recipient Spcl. award A Noticia, Sao Paulo, Brazil, 1973, Bronze plaque, Truth Pub. Co., 1975. Home: 151 Tara Dr Tavares FL 32778

PRATT, JOHN CLARK, b. St. Albans, VT, Aug. 19, 1932, s. John Lowell and Katharine (Jennison) P.; m. Dolores Barghausen, Jan. 27, 1955 (div. Feb. 1968); children—Karen Bartleson, Sandra, Pamela, John Randall; m. Doreen Kleerup, June 28, 1968; stepchildren—Lynn Goodman, Christine Smith. Author: The Meaning of Modern Poetry, 1962, John Steinbeck, 1970, The Laotian Fragments, 1974, 85, Vietnam Voices, 1984, Writing from Scratch: The Essay, 1987; co-author (with Tim Lomperis) Reading the Wind: The Literature of the Vietnam War, 1986; ed. One Flew Over the Cuckoo's Nest (Ken Kesey), 1973, (with Victor Neufeldt) George Eliot's Middlemarch Notebooks, 1979. BA, U. Calif., Berkeley, 1954; MA, Columbia U., 1960; PhD, Princeton U., 1965. Instr. English, U.S. Air Force Acad., Colorado Springs, Colo., 1960-62, asst. prof., 1965-69, assoc. prof., 1970-73, prof., 1973; prof. English, Colo. State U., Ft. Collins, 1975—; Fulbright lectr., Portugal, 1974-75, USSR, 1980. Served to lt. col., USAF, 1954-74, Vietnam. George Harper McClean fellow Princeton U., 1962-65. Mem. Rocky Mountain Am. Studies Assn., Colo. Seminars (bd. dirs.). Home: 3409 Canadian Pkwy Fort Collins CO 80524

PRATT, MARJORIE JEAN, b. Dorchester, MA, Sept. 5, 1936; d. Alvin Eugene and Dorothy (Bradford) Snell; m. Roger Lee Jackson (div.); 1 son, Bradford; m. Milo Harry Young, Jr. (div.); 1 dau., Valerie; m. Charles Pratt (div.); 1 dau., Kimberly. Contrbr. articles on boating, humor, how-to, antique boat restoration to mags. including Southern Star, Offshore, others. A.A. in Human Services Merrimack Coll., 1977, B.A. in Sociology, 1979; M.A. Antioch U., 1980. Psychotherapist, counselor Tri City Mental Health Ctr., Malden, MA, 1976-84; assessment counselor Northeast Career Sch., Malfen, 1984-86; family counselor Forest Hills Meml. Park, Palm City, FL, 1986—. Home: 9801 S AIA Unit 1204 Jensen Beach FL 33457

PRATT, PAUL W., b. New Castle, PA, Oct. 9, 1946; s. Paul N. and Ann D. (Morella) P. Ed.: Veterinary Practice Mgt., 1979, Lab. Profiles of Small Anim. Diseases, 1980, Equine Med. and Surgery, 1982, Feline Med., 1983, Lab. Procedures for Anim. Health Technicians, 1985, Medical Nursing for Anim. Health Techs., 1985, Modern Veterinary Pract., 1978—, Veterinary Computing, 1982—, DVM Mgt., 1985—. BS, PA State U., 1968; VMD, U. PA, 1973. Assoc. veterinarian, Dr. R.J. Straley, Belefonte, PA, 1973, Society Hill Vet. Hosp., Phila., 1974-75, Kirkwood Anim. Hosp., Newark, DE, 1976-77; vet. med. officer Food & Drug Admin., Rockville, MD, 1977-78; ed. Amer. Veterinary Pubns., Santa Barbara, CA, 1978-86, pub., 1986—. Mem. Amer. Vet. Med. Assn. Working on: Milking Your Cows for All They're Worth. Office: AVP 5782 Thornwood Dr Goleta CA 93117

PRATT, WILLIAM CROUCH, JR., b. Shawnee, OK, Oct. 5, 1927; s. William Crouch and Irene (Johnston) P.; m. Anne Cullen Rich, Oct. 2, 1954; children—Catherine Cullen, William Stuart, Randall Johnston. Author: The Imagist Poem, 1963, The Fugitive Poets, 1965, The College Writer, 1969, College Days at Old Miami, 1984, The Influence of French Symbolism on Modern American Poetry, 1985; contrbr. essays, translations, poems, rvws. to lit jnls, books. BA, U. OK, 1949; MA, Vanderbilt U., 1951, PhD,1957. Rotary Intl. fellow U. Glasgow, Scotland, 1951-52; instr. English Vanderbilt U., 1955-57, Miami U., Oxford, OH, 1957-59, asst. prof., 1959-64, assoc. prof., dir. Freshman English, 1964-68, prof., 1968—; adviser Ohio Poetry Circuit, 1964—; Fulbright-Hays lectr. Am. lit., prof. Am. lit. Univ. Coll., Dublin, Eire, 1975-76; resident scholar Miami U. European Ctr., Luxembourg, 1976; lectr. Yeats Intl. Summer Schl., Sligo, Eire, 1979, 81-83. Mem. MLA, NCTE, CCCC, Intl. Contemp. Lit. and Theatre Soc., Soc. Study So. Lit. Home: 212 Oakhill Dr Oxford OH 45056

PRENTISS, TINA M., (Thalia Prescott, Terri Putnam) b. Boston, Nov. 19, 1911; d. Ernest and Isabelle Chubb (Boice) McLean; m. Goodwin Ryder Prentiss, Mar. 13, 1937 (dec. 1986); children—Earle Lawrence, Paul Murray. Included in Story of American Artists' Group, 1945, Artists/USA, 1979-80, 81-82, Woman Artists in America, 1975; columnist, feature wrtr.: Craft Horizons, Boston Today, 1976-79, Intl. Travel News, Christian Sci. Monitor, Boston Globe, Boston Herald & Traveller, Famous Artists Mag., numerous others. Wrkg. on self-enrichment book. BSE, Mass. Coll. Art, Boston, 1933; also studied at Harvard U., DeCordova Mus., Columbia U., U. Kans., Queens U., NYU, Canada, and abroad. Tchr. art Boston Schl. Dist.,1960-68; freelance wrtr., painter, sculptor, 1926—. Recipient numerous art awards. Mem. local, regional and natl. arts orgns. Home: 136 Eames St Wilmington MA 01887

PRESCOTT, STEVE, b. Harrisburg, PA, Nov. 14, 1964; s. Roy Eugene and Gail Lee (Gilman) P. Staff writer Nassau Weekly, 1986; contrbr. to Creative Computing, Nibble, The WU Rvw. BA in Computer Sci., Princeton U., 1987. Writer/ programmer Stoner Assocs. Inc., Carlisle, PA, 1983-84; programmer/p.r. rep. Nixdorf Computer AG, Paderborn, W. Germ., 1985; video prodn. assist. & AAAS fellow Health & Sci. Communic., Mpls., MN, 1986. Home: 2 Creekside Ln Camp Hill PA 17011

PRESCOTT, THALIA, see Prentiss, Tina M.

PRESS, SIMONE NAOMI JUDA, b. Cambridge, MA, Apr. 12, 1943, d. Walter and Renee (Molino) Juda; m. Steven Eric Press, June 14,

1969; children—Corinna Nicole, Valerie Gabriella. Author: (poetry) Thaw, 1974, Lifting Water, 1979, (play) Willing (produced in Detroit, 1983, off-off Broadway, NYC,1985). BA, Bennington Coll., 1965; MA, Columbia U., 1967. Assoc. prof. English, Siena Heights Coll., Adrian, Mich., 1973—; playwright- in-residence Attic Theatre, Detroit, 1983-86; artistic dir. Young People's Theater, Ann Arbor, Mich., 1985—. Grantee Mich. Council for Arts, 1973—, Kellogg Fdn., 1983-86. Mem. DG (assoc.). Home: 2215 Chaveer Ct Ann Arbor MI 48103

PRESTBO, JOHN ANDREW, b. Northwood, ND, Sept. 26, 1941; s. Oscar Bernt and Jeanne (Schol) P.; m. Darlene Parrish, Aug. 14, 1965; children—Bradford Jonathan, Laura Christine. Co-Author (with Frederick C. Klein) News and the Market, 1974; ed.: This Abundant Land, 1975, Dow Jones Commodities Handbook, 1976-79; author: Sleuthing, 1976. BS, Northwestern U., 1963, MS, 1964. Rptr., writer Wall Street Jnl, Chgo., 1967-74, staff ed., page 1, NYC,1974-75, commodities ed., 1975-77, bur. chief, Cleve., 1977-81, market ed., NYC,1984—; v.p. editorial Dow Jones Radio 2, Inc., Princeton, NJ, 1981-83. Recipient Econ. Reporting award Inc. Natural Gas Assn., U. MO, 1967, achievement/bur. writing award G.M. Loeb, 1968. Home: 14 Charleston Dr Skillman NJ 08558

PRESTON, JOHN, b. Framingham, MA, Dec. 11, 1945, s. John and Nancy (Blood) P. Author fiction: Franny, the Queen of Provincetown, 1983, Mr. Benson, 1983, Sweet Dreams, 1984, Golden Years, 1984, Deadly Lies, 1985, Stolen Moments, 1986, Secret Dangers, 1986, Lethal Silence, 1986, I Once Had a Master and Other Tales of Erotic Love, 1984, Entertainment for a Master, 1986, Love of a Master, 1987, The Heir, 1987. author non-fiction: Classified Affairs: A Gay Man's Guide to the Personals (with Frederick Brandt), 1984, Safe Sex: The Ultimate Erotic Guide (with Glenn Swann), 1986 ed.: Hot Living: Erotic Tales about Safer Sex, 1985; contrbr. to The Alternative Press Annual, The Christopher Street Reader. Wrkg. on gay erotic series. BA, Lake Forest Coll., 1968; cert. in sexual health U. Minn. Med. Schl., 1973. Recipient Jane Chambers Playwriters award, Meridien Theatre, 1984; named Wrtr. of Yr., Weekly News, Miami, Fla., 1985. Mem. NWU, Me. Wrtrs. and Pubs. Alliance. Home: Box 5314 Portland ME 04101

PRESTON, MARCIA, b. El Reno, OK, Oct. 10, 1944; d. Paul H. and Atha Belle (Fry) Snyder; m. Paul Preston, Aug. 26, 1963; children—Jeffrey Allen, Andrew Dean. Contrbr. articles to mags., newspapers, lit. mags. including Woman's World, Flower & Garden, 'Teen, Amtrak Express, others. B.A., M.A. Central State U. Editorial asst. Outdoor Okla. Mag., Oklahoma City, 1965-66; ed., pub. Byline Mag., Edmond, OK, 1986—; ed. Persimmon Hill Mag., Oklahoma City, 1986—; free-lancer, 1967. Mem. Okla. City Wrtrs. (past pres.), Okla. Wrtrs. Fdn. (bd. dir.), WIC. Home: Box 130596 Edmond OK 73013

PRESTON, SONDRA KAY, b. Clarinda, IA, Mar. 19, 1947; d. Richard Jackson Bloomfield and Bette Ruth (Baxter) Elsey; m. Dennis Jenson, Nov. 7, 1964 (div. Jan. 1971); children—Christopher Bryan, Angela Dawn; m. Russell Paul Kline, Aug. 11, 1984. Book rvw. columnist: Midwest Art, 1985—, Art Gallery Intl., 1985—, Tulsa World newspaper, 1980—. Contrbr. numerous articles, book rvws. to mags., newspapers. B.S., U. Nebr., 1973. Assoc. ed. Pennwell Pub. Co., Tulsa, 1980-84; free-lance wrtr., ed., 1984—. Recipient 1st prize for short story Tulsa County Friends of Public Library, 1978, Honorable Mention for short story, 1985. Home: 18107 E 3d St Tulsa OK 74108

PRICE, MAURICIA, b. Shanghai, Kiangsu, People's Republic China, Jan. 7, 1925, came to U.S., 1927; d. Maurice Thomas and Bertha Olivia (Attaway) Price. Author: Beyond the Gates, 1979, On the Wing, 1982, Among the Whisperings, 1986. Contrbr. poems to lit. mags., anthols., yearbooks. BS, U. Calif.-Berkeley, 1945; MA, San Francisco State Coll., 1958. Tchr. nursery schl. Richmond Schls., Calif., 1948- 50; tchr. kindergaretn and primary grades Richmond Unified Schl. Dist., 1950-83, retired. Recipient Merit award N.Am. Mentor, 1973, 74, 86, Golden Poet award World of Poetry, 1985, 86; named Poet of Yr., J. Mark Press, 1973. Mem. Alvarado-Richmond Assn. Childhood Edn. (corr. sec. 1978—), Calif. Retired Tchrs. Assn. (newsletter ed. 1985—), Delta Kappa Gamma (legislative chair 1984—). Home: 800 Arlington Ave El Cerrito CA 94530

PRICE, REYNOLDS, b. Macon, NC, Feb. 1, 1933; s. William Solomon and Elizabeth (Rodwell) P. Author: A Long and Happy Life, 1962 (William Faulkner Fdn. award notable 1st novel, 1962), The Names and Faces of Heroes, 1963, A Generous Man, 1966, Love and Work, 1968, Permanent Errors, 1970, Things Themselves, 1973, The Surface of Earth, 1975, Early Dark, 1977, A Palpable God, 1978, The Source of Light, 1981, Vital Provisions, 1982. AB summa cum laude, Duke U., 1955; B.Litt. (Rhodes Scholar), Merton Coll., Oxford (Eng.) U., 1958; Litt.D., St. Andrews Presbyn. Coll., 1978, Wake Forest U., 1979. Mem. faculty English Duke U., 1958—; asst. prof., 1961-68, assoc. prof. 1968-72, prof., 1972-77, James B. Duke prof., 1977—, acting chmn., 1983; writer-in-res. U.N.C., Chapel Hill, 1965, U. KS, 1967, 69, 80, U.N.C., Greensboro, 1971; Glasgow prof. Washington & Lee U., 1971; faculty Salzburg Seminar, 1977. Recipient Sir Walter Raleigh award, 1962, 76, 81; award Natl. Assn. Ind. Schls., 1964; Guggenheim fellow, 1964-65; fellow NEA, 1967-68, lit. adv. panel, 1973-76, chmn. 1976; Natl. Inst. Arts and Letters award, 1971; Bellamann Fdn. award, 1972; Lillian Smith Award, 1976; N.C. award, 1977. Home: 4813 Duke Station Durham NC 27706

PRICE, RICHARD, b. NYC, Oct. 12, 1949; s. Milton and Harriet (Rosenbaum) P.; m. Judith P. Hudson, Sept. 26, 1985; children: Anne Morgan Price Hudson. Author: The Wanderers, 1974, Bloodbrothers, 1976, Ladies Man, 1978, The Breaks, 1982. Screenplay for feature film The Color of Money, in 1986. BS, Cornell U., 1971; MFA, Columbia U., 1976. Mem. PEN, WGA. CAPS grantee NY State, 1982; NEA grantee, 1982. Office: 684 Broadway New York NY 10012

PRICE, S. DAVID, b. Oklahoma City, Mar. 22, 1943, s. Stanley Erwin and Helen Merle (Foster) P.; 1 dau., Alicia Kim. Author: Summer Snow: Twenty-One Poems, 1977; contrbr. poetry to The Tex. Rvw, The Wrtr., Encore, Driftwood East, other publs.; contrbr. articles to The Explicator, Counsel, The Frontiersman, other publs. Ed. Biblical Integrity. BA, Central State U., Edmond, Okla., 1971, MA, 1972; PhD, Okla. State U., 1980. Reporter The Daily Oklahoman, Oklahoma City, 1959-66, 70; reporter, religion ed. The Oklahoma Jnl, Midwest City, 1970; instr. English Okla. State U., Stillwater, 1974-80, Rose State Coll., Midwest City, Okla., 1980-81. Recipient numerous journalistic and wrtg. awards. Mem. P&W. Home: 405 W Britton 106-S Oklahoma City OK 73114

PRICE, V. B., b. Los Angeles, Aug. 30, 1940, s. Vincent L. Jr. and Edith Barrett (Williams) P.; m. Sandra Rae Greenwald, 1961 (div. 1963); children—Barrett Jody, Keir Christopher; m. 2d, Nancy Lee Rini, Jan. 4, 1969. Author: The Cyclops' Garden (poetry), 1969, Semblances (poetry), 1976, Documentaries (poetry), 1985, Monsters (nonfiction, with Vincent Price), 1982; contrbr. poetry to N.Mex. Qtly, Southwest Rvw, NY Qtly, numerous other lit mags; contrbr. articles to mags. and newspapers. BA, U. N.Mex., 1962. City ed. N.Mex. Ind., Albuquerque, 1971-78; ed. Century Mag., Albuquerque, 1978-83, ed. N.Mex. Mag., Santa Fe, 1984-85; architecture critic Albuquerque Jnl., 1983-85; columnist Albuquerque Tribune, 1985—; architecture ed. ARTSPACE, Albuquerque, 1985—. Bd. trustees Albuquerque Mus., 1971-78; mem. N. Mex. Humanities Council, 1979-85; chmn. lit. panel N.Mex. Arts Div., Santa Fe, 1981-83. Ford Fdn. fellow, 1960-62, grantee NEA, 1978. Mem. PSA. Home: 2026 Candelaria Rd NW Albuquerque NM 87107

PRICE, WILLIAM, b. Wenatchee, WA, Sept. 27, 1938; s. T.M. and Margaret (Batterton) P.; m. Aida Minet Keshishian, June 25, 1966; children: Susan, Jennie. Author: The Potlatch Run, 1986; contrbr. to Evergreen, Rio Grande revs., Sat. Eve. Post, Yakima, Cold-drill. AA, Wenatchee Valley Coll., 1958. Mgr. communications McKinsey & Co., NYC, 1979—. Fellow Creative Arts Pub. Service, 1978, NEA, 1973. Mem. AG. Home: 292 Clermont Ave Brooklyn NY 11205

PRIESTLEY, OPAL LEE, (Lee Priestley), b. Iola, KS, Aug. 30, 1904; d. Edmond and Bess (Dorsa) Shore; m. Orville E. Priestley, June 14, 1926 (dec. Feb. 13, 1967); children—Joseph Shore, Orville Eugene. Author: Rocket to the Stars, 1959, Murder Takes the Baths, 1960, A Teacher for Tibbey, 1960, Rocket Mouse, 1961, A Second Look for Avis, 1961, Believe in Spring, 1964, The Too-Two Twins, 1965, Meow, 1968, Now for Nola, 1970, The Sound of Always, 1975, American's Space Shuttle, 1978, The Giant Who Wanted Company, 1979. Contrbr. articles to newspapers, anthols., textbooks, mags., profl. jnls. Student U. Okla., 1925-28; BA, N.Mex. State U.-Las Cruces, 1950. Tchr. pub. high schls., Drumright, Okla. and Crowley, La., 1926-45, U. Okla., Norman, 1947-65, N.Mex. State U., Las Cruces, 1976-86. Bd. dirs. Good Samaritan Retirement Home, Las Cruces, 1970-86; chmn. Branigan Meml. Library, Las Cruces, 1968-84; pres. bd. dirs. Rio Grande Hist. Collections, Las Cruces, 1970-74, Dona Ana Drug & Crime Commn., Las Cruces, 1975-78. Recipient Zia award N.Mex. Press Assn., 1960, 73; named Woman of Achievement, N.Mex. State U., Las Cruces, 1967, Hall of Honor named in recognition County Hist. Soc., 1977. Mem. N. Mex. Press Women (bd. dirs. 1950-60), Altrusa, Phi Kappa Phi, Delta Kappa Gamma. Home: 426 N Miranda Las Cruces NM 88005

PRIGOGINE, ILYA, b. Moscow, Jan. 25, 1917; s. Roman and Julie (Wichmann) P.; m. Marina Prokopowicz, Feb. 25, 1961; children: Yves, Pascal. Author: (with R. Defay) Traite de Thermondynamique, conformement aux methodes de, Gibbs et de De Donder, 1944, 50, Etude Thermodynamique des Phenomenes Irreversibles, 1947, Introduction to Thermodynamics of Irreversible Processes, 1962, (with A. Bellemans, V. Mathot) The Molecular Theory of Solutions, 1957, Statistical Mechanics of Irreversible Processes, 1962, (with others) Non Equilibrium Thermodynamics, Variational Techniques and Stability, 1966, (with R. Herman) Kinetic Theory of Vehicular Traffic, 1971, (with R. Glansdorff) Thermodynamic Theory of Structure, Stability and Fluctuations, 1971, (with G. Nicolis) Self-Organization in Nonequilibrium Systems, 1977, From Being to Becoming-Time and Complexity in Physical Sciences, 1979, Order Out of Chaos, 1983, La Nouvelle Alliance, Les Metamorphoses de la Science, 1979. Ph.D., Free U. Brussels, 1942. Address: U Texas Austin TX 78712

PRIORE, FRANK VINCENT, b. College Point, NY, Oct. 20, 1946, s. Frank Joseph and Fortunata (Varisco) P.; m. Catherine Wilhelmina Schutt, July 20, 1968; children—Lorraine Margaret, Virginia Frances. Author: Pick a Boy—Any Boy, 1978, George Who?, 1979, Son of "A Christmas Carol", 1979, Off with His Head!, 1980, Alias (MS) Santa Claus, 1980, Vampires are a Pain in the Neck, 1983, Go, Go, Go, UFO!, 1984, The Parables of Jesus, 1985, Holiday Plays, 1985, Lessons of Jesus, 1986. Grad. N.Y. Acad. Theatrical Arts, 1968. Standards engr. EDO Corp., College Point, N.Y., 1969—; dir. Colonial Players, Bayside, N.Y., 1968-73. Home: 5-12 125th St College Point NY 11356

PRITCHARD, MELISSA BROWN, b. San Mateo, CA, Dec. 12, 1948; d. Clarence John and Helen Lorraine (Reilly) Brown; m. Daniel Hachez, June 1973 (div. 1976); m. Mark Timothy Pritchard, May 1977; children: Noelle Katarina, Caitlin Skye. Contrbr. short stories to Ontario Rvw, Prairie Schooner, Ascent, Kenyon Rvw other lit mags, O. Henry Prize Stories, 1984. Wrkg. on editing Story Qtly No. 25, research for 2d novel. BA, U. Calif., Santa Barbara, 1970; postgrad. Western Wash. State Coll., 1976-77; ed. Story Quar., 1984-87. Recipient awards for stories Ill. Arts Council, 1980, 81, 83; NEA fellow, 1982-83; James D. Phelan award San Francisco Fdn., 1982; Flannery O'Connor Award for Short Fiction, 1986; IAC fellowship, 1986-87, honorary citation, PEN/Nelson Algren Award, 1987. PEN/NEA Syndicated Fiction winner, 1985. Home: 2510 Isabella Evanston IL 60201

PRITCHARD, PARM FREDERICK, (Pritch), b. Peoria, IL, Dec. 10, 1914; s. Ralph Waldo and Flora E. (Kountz) P.; m. Patricia Jane Chose, Dec. 24, 1937; children—Parm H., James C., Wendy Jane Geer, Leslie Elizabeth Desloovere. Ed., pub.: Utility Purchasing and Stores, 1962-87, Electric Utility Fleet Mgmt., 1981-87. B.S. in Mechanical Engrng., Stevens Inst. of Tech., 1936. Production mgr. to mktg. mgr. McGraw-Hill Pub. Recipient award for excellence Cahners Pub. Co., 1966. Office: Pritchard Pub P O Box 960 Durham NH 03824

PRIVETTE, WILLIAM HERBERT, b. Salisbury, NC, Dec. 30, 1949; s. William C. and Lena W. (Milholen) P.; m. Karen Cecilia Perten, May 20, 1972; children—Heath, Rebekah, Ian. Syndicated outdoor columnist: Fins, Feathers, and Friends, 1986, 87; columnist: Southwestern Woodsmen, 1987. Contrbr. articles to outdoor mags. Conservation ed.: Fur-Fish-Game, 1987. contrbg. ed.: Fly Fishing Heritage, 1987. Wrkg. on book, The Compleat Outdoors with Murphy. A.B., Duke U., 1972; M.Div., U. South, 1975. Asst. rector St. Johns Parish, Fayetteville, NC, 1975-78; rector Christ Ch., Fayetteville, NC, 1978-81; rector St. Thomas Paris, Ahoskie, NC, 1981-85; dir. edn. and communication St. Paul's Ch., Dayton, OH, 1985—. Mem. NWC, OWAA. Home: 401 Wiltshire Blvd Dayton OH 45419

PROFFER, ELLENDEA CATHERINE, b. Phila., Nov. 24, 1944; d. Joseph and Helen (Jardine) McEnness; m. Carl Ray Proffer, Oct. 1967. Author: The Early Plays of Mikhail Bulgakov, 1971, The Silver Age of Russian Culture, 1975, Double Wedding, 1982, Bulgakov, 1983; ed.: Ardis Anthology of Recent Russian Lit., 1975, Ardis Anthology of New Amer. Poetry, 1977, Tsvetaeva: A Photo Biography, 1980, Russian Liter. TriQtly, 1971—, Regency Miss, 1978; co-ed.: Ardis Anthology of Russian Futurism, 1980, Contemp. Russian Prose, 1982. BA, U. MD, 1966; MA, Ind. U., 1968, PhD, 1971. Asst. prof. Slavic, Wayne State U., Detroit, 1970-71; assoc. prof. humanities U. MI, Dearborn, 1972-73; co-founder, pres., owner Ardis Pubs., Ann Arbor, 1971—. NDEA fellow 1968-69. Mem. Am. Assn. Advancement of Slavic Studies, PEN. Home: 2901 Heatherway St Ann Arbor MI 48104

PROKOP, MICHAEL STEPHEN, b. Warren, OH, Oct. 31, 1953, s. Michael and Elizabeth Jane (Markovich) P. Author: Divorce Happens to the Nicest Kids, 1986, Kid's Divorce Workbook, 1986; contrbr. to Coll. Student Jnl, Psychologist's Corner. BA cum laude in Psychology, Kent (Ohio) State U., 1976; MEd in Sch. Psychology, Bowling Green (Ohio) State U., 1978. Dir. activity therapy Fallsview Mental Health Center, Cuyahoga Falls, Ohio, 1975-76; intern schl. psychologist Richland County Schls., Mansfield, Ohio, 1977-78; schl. psychologist Warren (Ohio) City Schls., 1978; cons. psychologist Devel. Clinic, Warren, 1979—; dir. stress reduction clinic Warren YMCA, 1981—. Mem. Northwestern PEN, Wrtrs. Club. Office: Box 1443 Warren OH 44482

PRONZINI, BILL JOHN, (William Pronzini), b. Petaluma, CA, Apr. 13, 1943; s. Joseph and Helene (Guder) P.; m. Brunhilde Schier, July 28, 1972. Author 47 novels (including under pseudonymns), 3 books of nonfiction, 1971—; first novel The Stalker, 1971; ed. 55 anthologies; contrbr. numerous short stories to publs. Coll. student 2 yrs. MWA Scroll award, Best First Novel, 1972. Mem. WGA-West, MWA. Office: Box 1349 Sonoma CA 95476

PROPST, NELL BROWN, b. Birmingham, AL, Sept. 23, 1925; d. Buren J. and Leila Alice (Williams) Brown; m. Thomas Keith Propst, Oct. 7, 1949; children—Thomas Kim, Joel Keith, Koger Lewis, Holly Elizabeth. Author: (play) Premiere for Two, 1945, Where the Buffalo Roamed, 1959, The Seekers (1st prize Colo. Federated Women's Clubs, 1954), 1954, The Cage Experiment (award Colo. AL, 1975), 1973; Forgotten People, A History of the South Platte Trail, 1979, Those Strenuous Dames of the Colorado Prairie, 1982, The Boys from Joes, a Colorado Basketball Legend, 1987. Contrbr. articles to mags. B.A., Samford U., 1945; M.A., U. Denver, 1949. Tchr., dir. Northeastern Jr. Coll., Sterling, CO, 1947-78, 70-72; free-lance dir., speaker, 1947—. Mem. WWA, NWC, AL, DG. Home: Bar Three Ranch Box 218 Merino CO 80741

PROSEN, ROSE MARY, b. Cleve., d. Josef and Rose (Barle) Prosen. Author: Poems (chapbook), 1971, O The Ravages, 1975, Apples (chapbook), 1980, Thank You Michelangelo: Love Poems to a Married Man, 1980; contrbr. poetry to Anthology of Slovenian American Literature, Italian Americana, Slovenski Koledar, Epos, numerous other lit. publs. BS in Ed., Kent (Ohio) State U., 1956; MA in Brit. Lit., John Carroll U., Cleve., 1962.Instr. English Kent State U., 1963-65; prof. English Cuyahoga Community Coll., Cleve., 1965-84; lectr., wrtr., 1984—. Winner Hart Crane Meml. Poetry prize, U. Calif., Davis, 1975. Mem. Multi-Ethnic Lit. Soc. U.S., Poets' League Greater Cleve. Address: Box 506 2300 Overlook Rd Cleveland Heights OH 44106

PROSSER, HAROLD LEE, (Justin W. Pinoak, Tishamingo Firestone) b. Springfield, MO, Dec. 31, 1944; step-son Frank, son Marjorie M. (Firestone) Hart; m. Grace Eileen Wright, Nov. 4, 1971; 2 daus., Rachael Maranda and Rebecca Dawn. Author: Dandelion Seeds, 1974, The Capricorn and Other Fantasy Stories, 1974, The Lamb, The Tiger and the Sphinx, 1975, The Cymric and Other Occult Poems, 1976, The Day of the Grunion and Other Stories, 1977, Goodbye, Lon Chaney, Jr., Goodbye, 1978, Summer Wine, 1978, Am. Fantasy Lit., 1980, Am. Short Fiction, 1981, Mo. Short Fiction, 1985, Robert Bloch, 1987, Charles Beaumont, 1987, Phoenix, 1986, Twentieth Century Sci. Fiction Writers (2d ed.), 1986, Poul Anderson, 1988, Frank Herbert, 1987, Desert Woman Visions: 100 Poems, 1987; contrbr. to more than 900 publs. in var. fields since 1963; wrkg. on autobiographical sketches, children's lit, film studies, fiction, a screenplay. BS in Sociol. So. Mo. State U., 1974, MSED in Social Sci., 1982. Sociol. instr. So. Mo. State U., Springfield, MO, 1982-85. Mem. Capricorn Seven Research Soc. (founder), Sci. Fiction Research Assn., Fantasy & Horror Writers of Am. Address: Box 3922 Springfield MO 65808

PRUCHA, CHRISTINE A., (Christine A. Verstraete), b. Chgo., Dec. 7, 1955; d. Seraphien S. and Marcia M. Shatholt Verstraete; m. David Prucha, Nov. 14, 1982. Contrbr. articles to Chgo. Tribune, 1980-82, Highland Park News & Lake Forester, 1983—; bus. features to newsletters. Asst. ed., contrbr.: Good Shepherd Visitor, 1985—. A.A. in Jnlsm., Wright Jr. Coll., 1976; B.A. in Jnlsm., Columbia Coll., 1979. Free-lance wrtr. Robin F. Pendergrast Marketing Firm, Northfield, IL, 1986—; part-time staff wrtr. Pioneer Press, Highland Park, IL, 1983—. Recipient Outstanding Merit award Amy Fdn., 1986. Home: 3321 N Oleander Ave Chicago IL 60634

PRUST, SUSAN LUZADER, (S. D. Luzader), b. Clarksburg, WV, Jan. 6, 1954; d. William Thomas and Norma Leigh (Pritt) Luzader; m. Randall Scot Prust, Dec. 29, 1973; children—Justin Scot, Steven Michael. Contrbr. articles to mags. including AMA News, Ariz. highways, Ariz. Living, Phoenix Home and Garden , Ariz. Mag. Ed.: Canyon Courier, Evergreen, CO, 1976, IEA News, 1981-82, Treasury of Kathe Kruse Dolls, 1984. B.S. in Jnlsm., Ariz. State U., 1974. Vol., Casa de los Ninos, Tucson, 1986—. Home: 5100 W Camino Del Desierto Tucson AZ 85745

PRYDE, MARION JACKSON, b. Washington, Dec. 6, 1911; d. Samuel Claybourne and Ann Eliza (Barnett) Jackson; m. Paul Lanier Pryde, Mar. 24, 1940; children—Paul Lanier, Marilyn A. Pryde Sims. Author: Distinguished Negroes Abroad, 1946. Contrbr. articles to newsletters, jnls., bulltns. Wrkg. on revising Distinguished Negroes Abroad. A.B., Howard U., 1954, M.A., 1968. Elem. tchr. public schls., Washington, 1931-69; tchr. special edn. public schls., Washington, 1970-74. Home: 7464 Seventh St NW Washington DC 20012

PRYOR, HUBERT, b. Buenos Aires, Argentina, Mar. 18, 1916; s. John W. and Hilda A.

(Cowes) P.; came to U.S., 1940; m. Ellen M. Ach, 1940; children—Alan, Gerald, David; m. 2d, Roberta J. Baughman, 1959; m. 3d, Luanne Williamson Van Norden, 1967 (div. 1982). Grad., St. George's Coll., Argentina, 1932; student U. London, Eng., 1934-36. Corr. in S. Am. for UP, 1937-39; pub. relations rep. Pan Am. Airways in Buenos Aires, 1939-40; rptr. N.Y. Herald Tribune, 1940-41; writer, dir. short-wave newsroom CBS, 1941-46; asst. mng. ed. Knickerbocker Weekly, 1946-47; sr. ed. Look Mag., 1947-62; creative supr. Wilson, Haight & Welch, 1962-63; ed. Science Digest, 1963-67; mng. ed. Med. World News, 1967; ed. NRTA Jour. Modern Maturity, 1967-82; editorial dir. Dynamic Years, 1977-82; publs. coordinator Modern Maturity, Dynamic Years, 1982-84; adj. cons., wrtr., 1985—. Eds. Address: 3520 S Ocean Blvd Palm Beach FL 33480

PRYOR, MARK WAYNE, b. Clarksville, TN, May 6, 1958; s. Wheeler Wayne and Mary Judith (Hunt) P.; m. Susan Digby Ramsay, June 1, 1980; children: Wheeler Hunt, Sadie Augusta. Ed. Food People Mag., 1983-86, The Culpepper Letter, 1986—. BA, U. of the South, 1980. Freelance writer, Atlanta, 1981; assoc. ed. Food People Mag., Atlanta, 1982, ed. & v.p., 1983-86; ed. The Culpepper Letter, Atlanta, 1986—. Office: Culpepper 400 Perimeter Ctr Atlanta GA 30346

PUGLISI, ANGELA AURORA, b. Messina, Italy, Jan. 28, 1949; came to U.S., 1954, naturalized, 1980; d. Vittorio and Carmela (Alizzi) P. Author: Toward Excellence in Education through the Liberal Arts, 1984. Contrbr. poems to lit. mags., anthols. B.A. with honors Dunbarton Coll., 1972; M.F.A., Calif. U., 1974, M.A. in Art History, 1976, M.A. in Modern Lang., 1977, Ph.D. in Comparative Lit., 1983. Wrtr., cons. U.S. Dept. Edn., Washington, 1983-85; instr. continuing edn., Catholic U., Washington, 1974-85, lectr. modern lang. and lit., 1985-86; lectr. Georgetown U., Washington, 1986—. Founding mem. Italian Cultural Ctr.-Casa Italiana, Washington; bd. dirs. Senese Ednl. Enterprises, Inc. Recipient cert. of Appreciation for outstanding service to edn. and edn. reform efforts U.S. Dept. Edn., 1985. Mem. Corcoran Coll. of Art Assn., Natl. Assn. Women Execs. Home: 3003 Merritt Ct Berkshire MD 20747

PURCELL, HENRY, (Hank), b. Fall River, MA,Sept. 6, 1929; s. Henry Roy and Loretta Angela (Daley) P.; m. Suzie J. Winters Nov. 2, 1957 (dec.); children: Mike, Debbie, Terry (dec.) Author: Poems from the Front (chapbook), 1950 Monkey on My Back (chapbook), 1952, Poetry-from Hell aka Attica (chapbook), 1986, Computer-aided Book Reading Now, 1987, How to Decide your Values, 1987; articles and poetry in numerous periodicals. AA, Cayuga Coll., NY; LLB, Blackstone Law Coll.,Chgo., 1968. Legal activities, Natl. Lawyers Guild, 1974-86. Publisher, Lollipop Power Press,1985—. Served to cpl., U.S. Army, Korea, 1945-51. Mem. Natl. Lawyers Guild, ACLU, War Resisters League, COSMEP. Home: Box 1784 Madison Sq Sta New York NY 10159

PURCELL, PAUL E., b. Valdosta, GA, Dec. 3, 1959; s. Eugene T. and Audrey Louise (Garrett) P. Author: The Complete Guide to Home-made Income, 1985. Student Valdosta State Coll. Pres. P & P Publs., Atlanta, 1984—. Home: 2550 Akers Mill Rd Apt L 10 Atlanta GA 30339

PURCELL, ROYAL, b. Vincennes, IN, Apr. 7, 1921; s. George William and Ella (Rosenbaum) Purcell. Author: The Concept of Being Human, 1985, Ethics, Morality, and Mores, 1986; contrbr. to Aviation Age, Florida Illustrated, Los Angeles Daily News, Washington Star, others. BA, Indiana U., 1941; MA, Fletcher School of Law and Diplomacy, 1943; MLS, Indiana U., 1972. Writer/editor, 1946—. T/Sgt., US Army, 1943-46, PTO. Office: 806 W Second St Bloomington IN 47401

PURDON, ERIC SINCLAIRE, b. Manila, Philippines, Oct. 25, 1913; s. Eric St. Clair and Mary (Morgan) P.; m. Mary Benjamin; children—Henry Prime, Eric St. Clair, Pamela Purdon Link. Author: The Valley of the Larks, 1939, Battle Report, 1947, Black Company, 1972. B.S., Trinity Coll., 1935; M.S., Boston U., 1955. Ed., Farrah & Rinehart, N.Y.C., 1937-41. U.S. Navy, 1941-63. Public relations Dept. of Commerce, Washington, 1963-64; with commun. relations Job Corps, Washington, 1964-73. Mem. NPC. Home: 449 Harwood Rd MD 20776

PURDY, JAMES, b. 1923. Author: Don't Call Me by My Right Name, 1956, Dream Palace, 1956, Color of Darkness, 1957, Malcolm, 1959, The Nephew, 1960, Children Is All (play), 1962, Eventide, 1963, Cabot Wright Begins, 1964, Eustace Chisholm and The Works, 1967, An Oyster Is A Wealthy Beast, 1967, Mr. Evening, 1968, Jeremy's Version, 1970, On The Rebound, 1970, The Running Sun (poetry), 1971, I Am Elijah Thrush, 1971, Sunshine Is an Only Child, 1973, Sleepers in Moon Crowned Valleys, 1974, The House of the Solitary Maggot, 1974, In a Shallow Grave, 1976, A Day After the Fair, 1977, Narrow Rooms, 1978, I Will Arrest the Bird That Has No Light (poetry), 1978, Lessons and Complaints, 1978, Sleep Tight, 1978, Proud Flesh (4 short plays), 1980, Mourners Below, 1981, The Berry- Picker and Scrap of Paper, Two Plays, 1981, On Glory's Course, 1984, In the Hollow of His Hand, 1986, The Brooklyn Branding Parlors (poetry), 1986 The Candles of your Eyes (Collected Stories, 1968-1987), 1987. Address: 236 Henry St Brooklyn NY 11201

PURDY, SUSAN, b. NYC, Feb. 28, 1942; d. Angelo Paul and Josephine (Pocoroba) Galietta; m. Richard L. Purdy, Oct. 13, 1962 (div.); children—Richard Lawrence, Brennan Paul. Contrbr. articles to Good Housekeeping, Aero, Woman's World, The Builder, The Writer, other pop. mags; contrib. ed. House in the Hamptons Intl.; contrbr. Writer's Hdbk, 1986. Student, Lindenhurst NY pub. schls. Freelance writer, NY, 1981—. Mem. ASJA. Home: 30 Liberty Ave Lindenhurst NY 11757

PURENS, ILMARS ULDIS, b. Augsburg, Germany, Mar. 23, 1947, came to U.S., 1950, s. Janis Edgar and Natalia (Silins) P. Author: Accordion Music (poetry), 1979, Emblems (poetry), 1985. MA in English, NYU, 1971, MFA in Film and TV, 1976. Ind. film maker. Woodrow Wilson fellow NYU, 1968-69; NDEA scholar NYU Inst. Film. and TV, 1974-76. Home: 1244 Bel Aire Dr Daytona Beach FL 32018

PURSIFULL, CARMEN MARIA, b. NYC., Sept. 1, 1930; d. Pedro C. and Ana Maria (Gonzalez) Padilla; m. John M. Pursifull, Aug. 12, 1962; children—Adrienne M. Ramos Lindsey, Rajiam. Author poetry collection: Carmen by Moonlight, 1982; contrbr. poetry: The Americas Rvw, Matrix, Harmony, Miss. Valley Rvw, Lit. Mag., Village Works, Parnassus, Korone, Raza Cosmica, numerous other lit. publs. and newspapers. Wrkg. on autobiography in narrative verse. Student public schls., Bronx, NY. Mem. Red Herring Poetry Workshop, Rockford Wrtrs. Guild, Conservatory Am. Letters. Home: 809 W Maple St Champaign IL 61820

PURVES, ALAN CARROLL, b. Phila., Dec. 14, 1931; s. Edmund Randolph and Mary Carroll (Spencer) P.; m. Anita Woodruff Parker, June 18, 1960 (dec. 1975); children—William Carroll, Theodore Rehn; m. 2d, Anne Hathaway Nesbitt, July 14, 1976. Author: The Essays of Theodore Spencer, 1968, The Elements of Writing about a Literary Work, 1968, Testing in Literature, 1971, How Porcupines Make Love, 1972, Literature and the Reader, 1972, Responding, 1973, Literature Education in Ten Counties, 1973, Educational Policy and International Assessment, 1975, Common Sense and Testing in English, 1975, Evaluation in English, 1976, Achievement in Reading and Literature: New Zealand in International Perspective, 1979, Evaluation of Learning in Literature, 1980, Achievement in Reading and Literature: The U.S. in International Perspective, 1981, The Implementation of Language and International Schools, 1981, Becoming Readers in a Complex Society, 1982, An International Perspective on the Evaluation of Written Composition, 1982, Experiencing Children's Literature 1984, How to Write Well in College, 1984, Contrastive Rhetoric, 1987, General Education, 1988; ed.: Research in the Teaching of English, 1971-77. AB, Harvard U., 1953; MA, Columbia, 1956, PhD,1960. Lectr. Hofstra Coll., 1956-58; instr. Columbia, 1958-61; asst. prof. English Barnard Coll., NYC,1961-65; examiner in humanities Ednl. Testing Svc., 1965-68; pres. Wonalancet (N.H.) Corp., 1967-70, 75-77; assoc. prof. English, U. IL, Urbana, 1968-70, prof., 1970-73, prof. English edn., 1973, dir., 1976-86; pro f. Edn. and Hum., SUNY-Alb, 1986-; dir. center for Writing and Literacy, 1987-§aff assoc. Central Midwest Regional Ednl. Lab., St. Ann, MO, 1968-70. Mem. NCTE, Newcomen Soc. (hon.), IL Assn. Tchrs. Eng., Natl. Conf. Research Eng., IL Conf. Eng. Edn., Am. Ednl. Research Assn., Intl. Assn. for Eval. of Ednl. Achievements chmn, 1986-89. Home: Box 344 Melrose NY 12121

PURVIANCE, DONALD GENE, b. Attica, IN, Aug. 30, 1936, s. Charles Gerald and Mary Louise (Clawson) P.; m. Sue Carolyn Fox, Jan. 15, 1961; children—Gary Phillip, Amy Lynn, Charles Ronald. Ed. Canard Anthology, 1984; contrbr. fiction to Quarterly West, Va. Qtly Rvw, Canard Anthology, The Liar's Craft. MFA, U. Iowa, 1977. Home: 1867 Navajo Pl Escondido CA 92025

PUTMAN, KAREN FLORENCE, b. Freeport, IL, July 7, 1941; d. Glenn Koch and Lois P. (Oswalt) Schoenhardt; m. Robert A. Putman, Oct. 19, 1979; children—Sue Warneke, Jeffrey, Kaye Curtis. Soc. columnist: Minnetonka Pilot, Mound, MN, 1963-71; columnist: Laker News, Spring Park, MN, 1971, Maverick News, Excelsior, MN, 1972, Enterprise News, 1974-75, Freeport Advertiser, IL, 1976, Daily Gazette, Sterling, IL, 1982-83. Contrbr. features to Laker News, 1971-72, Freeport Advertiser, 1977-78, Daily Gazette, 1980-83. Student U. Minn., 1969, 73. Asst. ed. Maverick Pub., Excelsior, 1973-75; advt. exec. Freeport Advertiser, 1976-78; staff wrtr., photographer, advt. Daily Gazette, 1980-83; free-lance wrtr. Freeport Jnl., 1986-87, Rockford Register Star, IL, 1987—. Recipient 2d Best State Promotion for farm sect. Natl. Advt. Pubs. Assn., 1977. Home: Box 286 Freeport IL 61032

PUTNAM, ROBERT E., b. Mt. Sterling, IL, Sept. 13, 1933; s. John Harold and Florence

Pauline (Curran) P.; m. Linda J. Wiant, Aug. 30, 1960; children—Justine, Robbie, Dylan. Co-editor: Young Poets of Illinois, 1959; Author: Fundamentals of Carpentry, 1967, Concrete Block Construction, 3d ed., 1973, Bricklaying Skill and Practice, 3d ed., 1974, Architectural and Building Trades Dictionary, 3d ed., 1974, Fundamentals of Carpentry: Tools, Materials and Practices, 5th ed., 1977, Basic Blueprint Reading: Residential, 1980, Builder's Comprehensive Dictionary, 1984, Construction Blueprint Reading, 1985, Building Trades Blueprint Reading, 1986, Motorcycle Operation and Service (co-author), 1986, Welding Print Reading, 1986. BA, U. IL, 1959; MA, Roosevelt U., 1969. Assoc. engr. Western Electric Co., Chgo., 1960-62; with Am. Tech. Pubs., Inc., Chgo., 1964-82, ed.-in-chief, 1973-82, v.p. editorial, 1980-82. Home: 256 Lester Ave Park Forest IL 60466

PUTNAM, TERRI, see Prentiss, Tina M.

PUZO, MARIO, b. NYC, Oct. 15, 1920; married; children—Anthony, Joey, Dorothy, Virginia, Eugene. Author: Dark Arena, 1955, The Fortunate Pilgrim, 1965, The Runaway Summer of Davie Shaw, 1966, The Godfather, 1969, The Godfather Papers and Other Confessions, 1972, Inside Las Vegas, 1977, Fools Die, 1979; screenwriter: The Godfather, 1972, The Godfather, Part II, 1974, Earthquake, 1974, Superman, 1979, Superman II, 1980. Ed. Columbia U., New Schl. for Social Research; lit. reviewer various mags., former ed. Male Mag. Recipient Acad. Awards for best screenplay with Francis Ford Coppola, The Godfather, 1972, The Godfather, Part II, 1974. Address: Putnam's 200 Madison Ave New York NY 10016

PYLE, KENNETH BIRGER, b. Bellefonte, PA, Apr. 20, 1936; s. Hugh Gillespie and Beatrice Ingeborg (Petterson) P.; m. Anne Hamilton Henszey, Dec. 22, 1960; children—William Henszey, Anne Hamilton. Author: The New Generation in Meiji Japan, 1969, The Making of Modern Japan, 1978; ed. Jnl Japanese Studies, 1974—. AB magna cum laude, Harvard U., 1958; PhD,Johns Hopkins U., 1965. Asst. prof. Wash. U., 1965-69, assoc. prof., 1969-75, prof. history and Asian studies, 1975—, dir. Henry M. Jackson Schl. Intl. Studies, 1978—; vis. lectr. in history Stanford U., 1964-65; vis. assoc. prof. history Yale U., 1969-70. Ford Fdn. fellow, 1961-64; Fulbright-Hays fellow, 1970-71; Social Sci. Research Council-ACLS fellow, 1970-73, 77, 83-84. Mem. Assn. Asian Studies, Am. Hist. Assn. Home: 8416 Midland Rd Bellevue WA 98004

PYNCHON, THOMAS, b. Glen Cove, NY, May 8, 1937; s. Thomas R.P. Author: V (Faulkner Prize, best 1st novel of 1963, 1964), The Crying of Lot 49, 1966 (Rosenthal Fdn. award Natl. Inst. Arts and Letters, 1967), Gravity's Rainbow, 1973 (Natl. Book Award), Mortality and Mercy in Vienna, 1976; Slow Learner, 1984 (short story collection); contrbr. short stories to publs. inclg. Sat. Eve. Post. BA, Cornell U., 1958. Former editorial writer Boeing Co., Seattle. Address: Little Brown 34 Beacon St Boston MA 02106

PYNSON, JOHN, see de Vinck, Jose M.

PYROS, JOHN, b. Weathersfield, CT, Jan. 9, 1931, s. Andrew John and Anastasia (Kalograkos) P. Author: Mike Gold, Dean of Proletarian Literature, 1979, William Wantling, 1981; ed., pub. Dramatika Mag., 1968—; contrbg. ed.: Contact II, other publs. BA, Bklyn. Coll., 1953. Served with U.S. Army, 1953-55. So. Fellowship Fdn. fellow, 1967. Home: 429 Hope St Tarpon Springs FL 34689

QUAGLIANO, ANTHONY JOHN, b. Bklyn., Oct. 17, 1941. Author: Language Drawn and Quartered (poems), 1975, Fierce Meadows (poems), 1981; ed.: Charles Bukowski issue Small Press Rvw, 1973, Reuel Denney issue Poetry Pilot, 1986; contrbr. poetry to over 70 mags, including the New York Qtly, Rolling Stone, New Letters, Kayak, Hawaii Rvw, anthols, jnls, articles to Encyc. of Psychology, 1984, Creativity and Science, 1986. BA, U. Chgo., 1963. Recipient Pushcart prize, 1976, Clark award in poetry, U. Hawaii, 1979, Poetry on the Bus award City of Honolulu, 1985, 86, 87. Mem. Hawaii Lit. Arts Council. Home: 509 University Ave 902 Honolulu HI 96826

QUATRAIN, JOHN, see Mitchell, Robert Wayne

QUEENAN, JOSEPH MARTIN, JR., (Gavin Borg, Rackham Tweedy, Roberto Blancos, Max Wadier), b. Phila., Nov. 3, 1950; s. Joseph Martin and Agnes Catherine (McNulty) Q.; m. Francesca Jane Spinner, Jan. 7, 1977; 1 dau., Bridget Noelle. Author 40 short pieces fiction pubd. in Sport, North 1981, Players, Mag. of Fantasy & Sci. Fict., Pulpsmith, Verbatim. BA, St. Joseph's Univ., 1972. Ed.-in- chief: Uncle Sam, NYC,1982-83, Amer. Bus., NYC,1982-86, Better Living, NYC,1983-86, Moneysworth, NYC,1984-86; freelance writer. Office: Am Bus Mag 1775 Broadway New York NY 10019

QUENELLE, JOHN DUFF, b. Jasper, AL, Mar. 9, 1946; s. John Albert and Jane Elizabeth (Sartain) Q.; children by previous marriage—David Brantley, Laura Duff; m. Patricia Clotfelter, Oct. 3, 1982; 1 son, John Peter Clotfelter-Quenelle. Editor-in-chief: Cumberland Law Rvw., 1973-74. B.A., Vanderbilt U., 1968; J.D., Cumberland Schl. Law, 1974. Bar: Ala., 1974. Assoc. attorney firm Johnston, Barton, et al., Birmingham, AL, 1974-79, prtnr., 1979-81; producer, v.p. Raven Cliff Productions, Birmingham, 1981-83; free-lance wrtr., 1983—. Served to 1st lt. U.S. Army, 1968-70. Home: 1325 Fourteenth Ave S Birmingham AL 35205

QUERRY, RONALD BURNS, b. Washington, Mar. 22, 1943; s. Woodrow Burns and Beverly (Downer) Corbett; m. Isabel Lindsay, Jan. 10, 1964 (div. 1965); 1 dau., Isabel Kathleen; m. 2d, Elaine Breece Stribling, May 14, 1984. Author: I See By My Get-Up (That I Am a Cowboy), 1986. Contrbr. articles to newspapers, mags. Editor: Growing Old at Willie Nelson's Picnic, 1983. BA, Central State U., (Okla.), 1969; MA, N.Mex. Highlands U., 1970; PhD, U. N.Mex., 1975. Prof. English, U. Okla., Norman, 1979-83; free-lance wrtr., 1983—. Mem. NWU, N.Mex. Cattlemen's Assn. Home: Box 268 El Prado NM 87529

QUILA, PHOLLEY M., see Auila, Napolean E. M.

QUIMBY, WILLIAM ROBERT (BILL), b. Tucson, Sept. 30, 1936; s. Isaac William Q. and Helen Gertrude (Dixon) Miller; m. Jean Potts, Mar. 30, 1956; 1 dau., Stephanie Jean. Ed./designer SCI Record Book of Trophy Animals, eds. IV, V, & VI; contrbr. to num. outdoor & shooting mags., 1967—. BS, U. AZ, 1959. Outdoor ed. Tucson (AZ) Citizen, 1967—; pubns. dir. Safari Mag., Tucson, 1983—. Mem. OWAA, AZ OWA. Named Conservn. Communicator of Year, AZ Wildlife Fedn., 1970; num. awards, AZ Press Club, 1967-86. Office: Safari 5151 E Brdwy Tucson AZ 85711

QUINN, BERNETTA VIOLA, OSF b. Lake Geneva, WI, Sept. 19, 1915; d. Bernard Franklin and Ellen Quinn. Author: The Metamorphic Tradition in Modern Poetry, 1955, Design in Gold, 1957, Give Me Souls, 1958, To God Alone the Glory, 1960, Ezra Pound, An Introduction to the Poetry, 1973, Randall Jarrell, 1981, Dancing in Stillness, 1983; wrkg. on Randall Jarrell in Retrospect: A Reading of the Poems. AB, Coll. of St. Teresa, 1942; MA, Catholic U. Am., 1944; PhD, U. Wis.-Madison, 1952. Tchr. St. Priscilla Schl., Chgo., 1937-40, Cathedral High Schl., Winona, Minn., 1942-43, St. Augustine High Schl., Austin, Minn., 1944-46, 52-53, Coll. of Ste. Teresa, Winona, 1946-69, Allen Univ., Columbia, SC, 1969-73, Norfolk State Univ., Va., 1973-81. Mejii Gakuin Univ. and Univ. of the Sacred Heart, Tokyo, Japan, 1976-77. Mem. Alston Wilkes Soc. for Prison Rehab., Columbia, SC, 1969—; Inst. in Prison Rehab., Norfolk, Va., 1978-81. Recipient NEH fellow, 1967, NEA fellow 1968, MacDowell Colony fellow 1972, 84, 85; Rockefeller Fdn. fellow, Villa Serbelloni, Italy, 1975; fellow, Va. Center for the Creative Arts, 1979, 83, 84, 85; hon. LLD, Siena Coll., Loudonville, NY, 1974. Mem. William Carlos Williams Soc., PEN, PSA, AAP, AWP. Address: Assisi Heights Rochester MN 55903

QUINN, JOHN COLLINS, b. Providence, Oct. 24, 1925; s. John A. and Kathryn H. (Collins) Q.; m. Lois R. Richardson, June 20, 1953; children—John Collins, Lo-anne, Richard B., Christopher A. AB, Providence Coll., 1945; MS, Columbia U. Schl. Jnlsm., 1946. Successively copy boy, rptr., asst. city ed., Washington corresp., asst. mng. ed., day mng. ed. Providence Jour.-Bull., 1943-66; with Gannett Co. Inc., Rochester, NY, 1966—; exec. ed. Rochester Democrat & Chronicle, Times-Union, 1966-71, genl. mgr. Gannett News Svc., 1967-80, v.p. parent co., 1971-75, sr. v.p. news and info., 1975-80, sr. v.p., chief news exec. parent co., 1980-83, exec. v.p. Gannett Co., ed. USA TODAY, 1983—. Named to R.I. Hall of Fame, 1975. Mem. AP Mng. Eds., ASNE. Home: 365 South Atlantic Ave Cocoa Beach FL 32931

QUINN, SALLY, b. Savannah, GA, July 1, 1941; d. William Wilson and Bette (Williams) Q.; m. Benjamin Crowninshield Bradlee, Oct. 20. 1978; 1 child, Josiah Quinn Crowninshield Bradlee. Author: We're Going to Make You a Star, 1975, (novel) Regrets Only, 1986. Grad., Smith Coll. Reporter, Washington Post, 1969-73, 74—; co-anchorperson CBS Morning News, NYC, 1973-74. Address: 3014 N St NW Washington DC 20007

QUIRK, LAWRENCE JOSEPH, b. Lynn, MA, Sept. 9, 1923; s. Andrew Lawrence and Margaret (Connery) Q. Author: The Films of Joan Crawford, 1968, Robert Francis Kennedy, 1968, The Films of Ingrid Bergman, 1970, The Films of Paul Newman, 1971, The Films of Fredric March, 1971, foreword to anthol. Photoplay Magazine, 1971, The Films of William Holden, 1973, The Great Romantic Films, 1974, The Films of Robert Taylor, 1975, The Films of Ronald Colman, 1977, The Films of Warren Beatty, 1979, The Films of Myrna Loy, 1980, The Films of Gloria Swanson, 1984, Claudette Colbert: An Illustrated Biography, 1985, Bette Davis: Her Films & Career, 1985, Lauren Bacall: Her Films and Career, 1986, Jane Wyman: The Actress and the Woman, 1986, The Complete Films of William Powell, 1986, Margaret Sullavan: Child of

Fate, 1987, Norma Shearer, A Biography, 1988; (novel) Some Lovely Image (Walt Whitman award, 1976), 1976. Film critic to Motion Picture Herald, Motion Picture Daily, Current Screen, Screen Slants; articles to mags., newspapers including N.Y. Times, Variety, others. Owner, ed.: Quirk's Rvws., 1972—. Wrkg. on Merle Oberon: A Biography, Greer Garson: A Celebration. B.A., with honors, Suffolk U., 1949; postgrad. Boston U., 1949-50. Dir., James R. in Retrospect: A Reading of the Poems. AB, Coll. of St. Teresa, 1942; MA, Catholic U. Am., 1944; PhD, U. Wis.-Madison, 1952. Tchr. St. Priscilla Schl., Chgo., 1937-40, Cathedral High Schl., Winona, Minn., 1942-43, St. Augustine High Schl., Austin, Minn., 1944-46, 52-53, Coll. of Ste. Teresa, Winona, 1946-69, Allen Univ., Columbia, SC, 1969-73, Norfolk State Univ., Va., 1973-81. Mejii Gakuin Univ. and Univ. of the Sacred Heart, Tokyo, Japan, 1976-77. Mem. Alston Wilkes Soc. for Prison Rehab., Columbia, SC, 1969—; Inst. in Prison Rehab., Norfolk, Va., 1978-81. Recipient NEH fellow, 1967, NEA fellow 1968, MacDowell Colony fellow 1972, 84, 85; Rockefeller Fdn. fellow, Villa Serbelloni, Italy, 1975; fellow, Va. Center for the Creative Arts, 1979, 83, 84, 85; hon. LLD, Siena Coll., Loudonville, NY, 1974. Mem. William Carlos Williams Soc., PEN, PSA, AAP, AWP. Address: Assisi Heights Rochester MN 55903

QUINN, JOHN COLLINS, b. Providence, Oct. 24, 1925; s. John A. and Kathryn H. (Collins) Q.; m. Lois R. Richardson, June 20, 1953; children—John Collins, Lo-anne, Richard B., Christopher A. AB, Providence Coll., 1945; MS, Columbia U. Schl. Jnlsm., 1946. Successively copy boy, rptr., asst. city ed., Washington corresp., asst. mng. ed., day mng. ed. Providence Jour.-Bull., 1943-66; with Gannett Co. Inc., Rochester, NY, 1966—; exec. ed. Rochester Democrat & Chronicle, Times-Union, 1966-71, genl. mgr. Gannett News Svc., 1967-80, v.p. parent co., 1971-75, sr. v.p. news and info., 1975-80, sr. v.p., chief news exec. parent co., 1980-83, exec. v.p. Gannett Co., ed. USA TODAY, 1983—. Named to R.I. Hall of Fame, 1975. Mem. AP Mng. Eds., ASNE. Home: 365 South Atlantic Ave Cocoa Beach FL 32931

QUINN, SALLY, b. Savannah, GA, July 1, 1941; d. William Wilson and Bette (Williams) Q.; m. Benjamin Crowninshield Bradlee, Oct. 20. 1978; 1 child, Josiah Quinn Crowninshield Bradlee. Author: We're Going to Make You a Star, 1975, (novel) Regrets Only, 1986. Grad., Smith Coll. Reporter, Washington Post, 1969-73, 74—; coanchorperson CBS Morning News, NYC, 1973-74. Address: 3014 N St NW Washington DC 20007

QUIRK, LAWRENCE JOSEPH, b. Lynn, MA, Sept. 9, 1923; s. Andrew Lawrence and Margaret (Connery) Q. Author: The Films of Joan Crawford, 1968, Robert Francis Kennedy, 1968, The Films of Ingrid Bergman, 1970, The Films of Paul Newman, 1971, The Films of Fredric March, 1971, foreword to anthol. Photoplay Magazine, 1971, The Films of William Holden, 1973, The Great Romantic Films, 1974, The Films of Robert Taylor, 1975, The Films of Ronald Colman, 1977, The Films of Warren Beatty, 1979, The Films of Myrna Loy, 1980, The Films of Gloria Swanson, 1984, Claudette Colbert: An Illustrated Biography, 1985, Bette Davis: Her Films & Career, 1985, Lauren Bacall: Her Films and Career, 1986, Jane Wyman: The Actress and the Woman, 1986, The Complete Films of William Powell, 1986, Margaret Sullavan: Child of Fate, 1987, Norma Shearer, A Biography, 1988; (novel) Some Lovely Image (Walt Whitman award, 1976), 1976. Film critic to Motion Picture Herald, Motion Picture Daily, Current Screen, Screen Slants; articles to mags., newspapers including N.Y. Times, Variety, others. Owner, ed.: Quirk's Rvws., 1972—. Wrkg. on Merle Oberon: A Biography, Greer Garson: A Celebration. B.A., with honors, Suffolk U., 1949; postgrad. Boston U., 1949-50. Dir., James R. Quirk Meml. Film Symposium and Research Ctr., and donor of James R. Quirk Award to distinguished film figures, 1971—. Served to sgt. U.S. Army, 1950-53. Home: 74 Charles St New York NY 10014

RAATZ, PATRICIA ANNE TIRRELL, b. Woburn, MA, Aug. 15, 1946; d. Gerard Thomas and Wanda Hope (Cheek) Tirrell; m. Aaron Frederick Raatz; children—Patrick Andrew, Erin Francise, Sean Tirrell. Author: You Can Lose Weight and Keep It Off, 1978; advice columnist Northern News, 1967-69; nutrition columnist Rockdale Citizen, 1976-78; contrbr. articles: Purpose mag., Transitions Abroad, Natural Food and Farming, Mature Years, numerous other publs. Wrkg. on novel, non-fiction, articles for trade, religious and regional publs. BS, No. Mich. U., 1974; postgrad., Loyola U., New Orleans. Dietary cons., Conyers, Ga., 1976-80; freelance wrtr., 1983—. Mem. Nat. League Am. Pen Women. Home: Box 1281 Conyers GA 30207

RABE, BERNIECE LOUISE, b. Parma, MO, Jan. 11, 1928; d. Grover Cleveland and Martha (Green) Bagby; m. Walter Henry Rabe, July 30, 1946; children—Alan, Brian, Clay, Dara. Author: (young adult fiction) Rass (Best of Decade award Schl. Library Jnl. 1974), 1973, Naomi, 1975, The Girl Who Had No Name, 1977, (SCBW Golden Kite Award, 1978), The Orphans (SMA award 1979), 1978, Who's Afraid?, 1980, Margaret's Moves, 1987, A Smooth Move, 1987, Joey Caruba, 1988, Margo's Rehearsal for the Big Time, 1988; (picture books) The Balancing Girl (Notable Book of Yr. award Am.Library Assn., 1983), 1982, Can They See Me, 1976, Two Peas in a Pod, 1974. Contrbr. short stories to children's mags. including Cricket; articles to World Book, Encyc. Britannica, others; short stories to adult quarterlies. B.A. in Edn., Natl. Coll. Edn., 1963; M.A., Columbia Coll., 1988. Writing instr. Columbia Coll., Chgo., 1987-88; art instr. Barrington Countryside, IL, 1965-66, Chgo. Jr. Schl., 1967-68. Mem. Soc. Midland Authors (bd. dirs.), Off Campus Wrtrs. (bd. dirs.), Fox Valley Wrtrs. (bd. dirs.). Home: 860 Willow Ln Sleepy Hollow IL 60118

RABINER, SUSAN, b. Bklyn., May 5, 1948; d. Nathan M. and Gloria (Bodinger) Rabbiner; m. Alfred G. Fortunato, Mar. 27, 1974; children—Anna, Matthew. BA cum laude, Goucher Coll., 1969. Asst. ed. Random House, NYC, 1969-72; ed. Oxford U. Press, NYC,1973-79, sr. ed., 1980-87; sr. ed., St. Martin's Press, NYC, 1987—; vis. lectr. Yale U., New Haven, 1983, 1984. Home: 1009 Brent Dr Wantagh NY 11793

RABORG, FREDERICK ASHTON, JR., (Canyon Kern, Bertha Mayfair, Wolfe Bronson, Dick Baldwin), b. Richmond, VA, Apr. 10, 1934, s. Frederick Ashton and Marguerette (Smith) R.; m. Eileen Mary Bradshaw, Oct. 19, 1957; children—Frederick Ashton III, Donald Wayne, Marguerette Jeannette Raborg Cluck, Wayne Patrick, Jayne Alyson Raborg Davis, Kevin Douglas. Author: Gin Street Rhythms, 1972, Why Should the Devil Have All the Good Tunes?, 1972, many others; Contrbr. short stories to Sports Afield, Chic, Short Story Intl., Prairie Schooner, Old Hickory Rvw, Richmond Qtly, Cavalier, Dude, Gent, Rogue, Dapper, Grit, The Horn Book, Nugget, Sepia, Sir!, Swank, Topper, Velvet, Stag, Class, Catholic Home, The Church Herald, Marriage and Family Living, Purpose, others; contrbr. poetry to Ladies' Home Jnl, East West Jnl, Tendril, The Cape Rock, Epos, Grit, Poetry Australia, Japanophile, Modern Haiku, Little Balkans Rvw, Mendocino Rev., Our Navy, The Oregonian, Wind, Revista/Rvw Interamericana, River City Rev., Chesapeake Bay mag., Sisters Today, Stone Country, Studia Mystica, Westways, others; contrbr. to Dramatics, Los Angeles Herald Examiner, Portland Chronicle, many others. BA in English Lit., Calif. State U., Bakersfield, 1973, postgrad., 1974-75. Ed. Pantry mag., Bakersfield, 1963-65, The Oildale News, Bakersfield, 1969-70; columnist Bakersfield News Bull., 1969-72; book and drama critic Bakersfield Californian, 1972-78; ed., pub. AMELIA mag., Bakersfield, 1983—. Actor, crew mem. Bakersfield Community Theatre, 1969-74; playwright Bakersfield Theatre Guild, 1973-74; bd. dirs. Playwrights, Actors Conservation Theatre, Bakersfield, 1975-78; instr. Bakersfield Coll., 1970-74. Recipient Intl. Intercollegiate award Class mag., 1970, Guideposts award, Guideposts mag., 1973, Intl. Thespians Assn. award Dramatics mag., 1976, U.S.-Netherlands 200 award, The Netherlands, 1982. Mem. AG, DG. Home: 329 E St Bakersfield CA 93304

RABY, ELAINE MILLER, b. Ethel, LA, Sept. 2, 1938; d. George and Gertrude (Haynes) Miller; m. C. T. Raby, Apr. 15, 1967; children—Dwight, Iris Yvette, Wayne Anthony, Eric Clyde, Trudi E'Layne. Contrbr. poems to anthols. Wrkg. on poetry, book of life experiences. B.A., Southern U., 1960. Tchr. parish schls., Ethel, LA, 1960-67, Baton Rouge, LA, 1967-82, retired. Mem. La. Assn. Educators, NEA. Home: 2737 Brandywine Dr Baton Rouge LA 70808

RACCAH, DOMINIQUE MARCELLE, b. Paris, Aug. 24, 1956, came to U.S., 1965; naturalized, 1973; d. Paul Mordechai and Colette (Gomarah) R.; m. Raymond W,. Bennett, III, Aug. 20, 1980; children—Marie, Lyron, Doran. Ed.: Financial Sourcebooks; Sources: Financial Research, Marketing Surveys and Services, 1987. B.A., U. Ill., Chgo., 1978; M..S., U. Ill., 1981. Research analyst Leo Burnett Advt., Chgo., 1980-81, research supvr., 1981-84, assoc. research dir., 1984-87; pub. Financial Sourcebooks, Naperville, IL, 1987—. Mem. Bank Mktg. Assn., Am. Mktg. Assm., Chgo. Book Clinic, Chgo. Women Pub. Office: Financial Sourcebooks 26 N Webster St Naperville IL 60540

RACHLIN, HARVEY, b. Phila., June 23, 1951, s. Philip and Mazie (Drucker) R. Author: The Songwriter's Handbook, 1977, The Encyclopedia of the Music Business (Best Reference Book of Yr., Library Jnl, 1982), 1981, Love Grams, 1983, The Money Encyclopedia (Best Reference Book of Yr., Library Jnl, 1985), 1984, The Kennedys, A Chronological History: 1821-Present, 1986. BA in Biology, Hofstra U., 1973. Instr. Five Towns Coll., Seaford, N.Y., 1978-84. Mem. ASCAP (Deems Taylor award, 1982). Home: 252 Robby Ln Manhasset Hills NY 11040

RACHLIN, NAHID, b. Abadan, Iran, June 6, 1944; arrd. U.S. 1961; d. Manoochehr and Parvin; m. Howard Rachlin, 1965. Author: (novels) Foreigner, 1978, Married to a Stranger, 1983; contrbr. stories to Redbook, Fiction, Minn. Rvw, Four Quarters, Shenandoah, Confrontation, Prism Intl., Ararat; contrbr. rvws. to NY Times Book Rvw, Newsday. BA, Lindenwood Coll.,

1961-65. Adj. asst. prof. Creative Writing NY Univ. Continuing Edn., NYC, 1978—; wrtr.-in-res. Marymount Manhattan Coll., fall 1986. Recipient Doubleday award Columbia U., NYC, 1974; Bennett Cerf award, Columbia U., 1975; Wallace Stegner Fellow, Stanford U., Palo Alto, Calif., 1975-76; NEA grantee, Washington, 1979. Mem. PEN (Syndicated Fiction Project, 1983). Address: 501 E 87 St New York NY 10028

RACKLEY, AUDIE NEAL, b. Oney, OK, Oct. 11, 1934; s. Emmet Irvin and Jesse Lela (Morrison) R.; m. Willie Mae Holsted, Aug. 26, 1956; children—Leicia Leann, Renee, Audette Marshelle. BS in Animal Sci., Okla. State U., 1957. Mgr. Hissom A. and M. Farm, Okla. State U., Sand Springs, 1957, Grad. of Distinction, Okla. State U., 1987; swine herdsman Okla. State U., 1959-61; field rep., advt. salesman Cattleman Mag., Ft. Worth, 1961-67; pub. relations and field rep. Am. Angus Assn., St. Joseph, MO, 1967-70; dir. advt. Quarter Horse Jnl, Amarillo, TX, 1970-72, ed., mgr. 1972—; pres. Am. Horse Publs., 1976—; 1st v.p., Livestock Publications Council. Mem. Am. Horse Publs., Soc. Natl. Assn. Publs. Home: Rt 4 Box 58 Amarillo TX 79119

RACKOW, SYLVIA, b. NYC, May 21, 1931; d. Isaac and Regina (Friedman) Frieder; m. Paul Rackow, Sept. 12, 1962; children—Julianna, Samantha, Isadora. Contrbr. to numerous mags. including Seventeen, Travel & Leisure, Black Enterprise, columnist Greenwich Village News, NY State Pharmacist, 1960-62, Medical News, 1963-65, contrib. ed. Our Town, 1986—. BA, Hunter Coll., NYC,1955; MA, Columbia U., 1958. Pub. relations dir. NY St. Pharm. Soc., NYC,1960-62; media relations coordinator NY St. Medical Soc., NYC,1963-65; public relations cons. Rackow Assoc., NYC,1966—; instr. IA St. U., 1965-66; lectr. The City College, NYC,1966-69; adj. lectr. John Jay Coll., NYC,1975-78; Manhattan Community Coll., NYC,1983—; Empire State Coll. (SUNY), 1986—. Freelance wrtr., jnlst., ed. 1978—. Drama assistantship, U.CT, 1958. Mem. AG, AL. Home: One Washington Sq Village New York NY 10012

RADAVICH, DAVID ALLEN, b. Boston, Oct. 30, 1949. Author poetry: Slain Species, 1980; chapbooks of poems Britain and US, 1975-77; contrbr. poems and short pieces Chapman, Counterpoint, Krax, Muse, Omens, Orbis, Outrigger, Success, Trends, Weyfarers (all UK), Eureka (Sweden); Funnel, Rhein-Neckar Zeitung, Die Zeit (all W. Ger.); Poetry-Windsor-Poesie (Can.); Flame, Kans. Qtly, Lit Mag Rvw, Louisville Rvw, Lyrical Iowa, Now Mag, Poets On; contrbr. rvws. to Kans. City Star/Times, others; four plays. BA, U. Kans.-Lawrence, 1971, PhD, 1979. Fulbright lectr. Univ. Stuttgart, W. Ger., 1979-81; instr. Iowa State Univ., Ames, 1982-84; prof. Eastern Ill. Univ., Charleston, 1984—. Recipient 3d prize poetry, Kans. Qtly, 1974; 1st prize poetry, Tell-Tale Mag, Bolton, England, 1978; 1st prize Intl. Verse Competition, Coventry, England, 1982; 3rd prize poetry, Success Mag, Peterborough, England, 1983. Mem. Fulbright Alumni Assn, Intl. Poetry Soc., DG, Ill. Wrtrs. Home: 422 Harrison St Charleston IL 61920

RADCLIFFE, ELEANOR SCHROEDER, (Ellie Radcliffe), b. Detroit, Apr. 23, 1914; d. Walter William and Clara (Riske) Schroeder; m. Carlyle Eugene Radcliffe, Apr. 29, 1939 (dec. Sept. 1978); children—Carolyn, Barbara, Robert. Contrbr. poems to anthols., newspaper, local pubs. Secy. Minnatonka, Copper Harbor, MI, 1968-75; secy., seurity officer Presbyterian Towers, St. Petersburg, FL, 1985—. Recipient Merit award World of Poetry, 1986, 87, Silver Poet award, 1986, Golden Poet award, 1987. Home: 430 Bay St NE Apt 901 Saint Petersburg FL 33701

RADCLIFFE, JANETTE, see Roberts, Janet

RADFORD, RICHARD FRANCIS, JR., (Lynne Critchley, Amy Lyndon, Dick Radford), b. Boston, Feb. 15, 1939, s. Richard Francis and Lorraine (Lally) R.; m. Lynne S. Critchley, Aug. 20, 1966; children—Amy Lynne, Richard III. Author: Opal Moon (novel), 1980, One White Rose (novel), 1980, Tournamelnt of Love (novel), 1980, Having Been There, 1979, Dream of Spring (novel), 1982, Golfer's Book of Trivia, 1985, Trooper, 1986, Drug Agent, U.S.A., 1987. BA with honors, Boston State Coll., 1979. Cons. substance abuse Alcohol Consumption Awareness, Inc., Boston, 1975—. Home: 8 Juniper St. 29 Brookline MA 02146

RAE, MICHELLE LAUREN, b. Pitts., Nov. 11, 1968; d. J.L. and Helen Rae (Hampton) Spray. Poetry in anthologies. Wrkg. on poetry. Student Bauder Coll., Ft. Lauderdale, Fla. Mem. Am. Poetry Assn., World of Racing. Home: 1103 Londonwood St Brandon FL 33511

RAEFF, MARC, b. Moscow, USSR, July 28, 1923; s. Isaak and Victoria (Bychowsky) R.; came to U.S., 1941, naturalized 1943; m. Lillian Gottesman, Sept. 24, 1951; children—Anne, Catherine. Author: Siberia and the Reforms of 1822, 1956, M.M. Speransky—Statesman of Imperial Russia, 1957, Origins of the Russian Intelligentsia, 1966, Imperial Russia—The Coming of Age of Modern Russia 1682-1825, 1971, Understanding Imperial Russia, 1983, The Well Ordered Police State, 1983; contrbr. Am. and European jnls. Baccalaureat, Lycee, 1942; MA, Harvard U., 1947, PhD,1950. From instr. to assoc. prof. history Clark U., 1949-61; mem. faculty Columbia U., 1961—, prof. Russian history, 1965—, Bakhmeteff prof. Russian studies, 1973—; vis. prof. U. Wash., 1952-53, Free U. Berlin, 1966, Sorbonne, Paris, 1960-61, Acad. Scis. USSR, 1965, 68, 72, Max Planck Inst. Fur Geschichte, Gottingen, Germany, 1972, 74, All Souls Coll., Oxford, Eng., 1976, U. Tubingen (Germany), 1981, Harvard U., 1982, U. Heidelberg, 1983. Guggenheim fellow, 1957-58, 1987-88; fellow Social Sci. Research Council, 1958-61; Fulbright lectr. U. Paris, 1960-61; sr. research fellow NEH, 1967-68, 83-84. Home: 479 Knickerbocker Rd Tenafly NJ 07670

RAFAEL, DON, see Yalkovsky, Rafael

RAFALSKY, STEPHEN MARK, (Steve Levin, Mark Stevens), b. NYC, Mar. 21, 1942; s. Richard Levin and Stephanie Gertrude (Von Muller-Deham) R.; m. Jacqueline Harding, Mar. 29, 1986; children by previous marriages: Suzanne Elizabeth, Lisa Nadine. Author: True Image, 1977; A Poet Arises in Israel, 1978; Haiku Sandwich: for Anne Waldman, 1978; Elegiac Feelings Un-Amerikan, 1978; Tripping Again, 1979; Folly 9& Wisdom: Love Poems, 1979; Ed., pub.: Writings from Young Poets, 1981; A Fire in the Lake, 1983; ed.: The Lightning Herald: Un Journal de Poetes Terribles, 1978—. Teaching asst. spcl. edn. classes Children's Annex, Kingston, N.Y., 1979-84, Rhinebeck Country Sch., N.Y., 1985-86. Served with USMC, 1959-61. Address: Box 371 Woodstock NY 12498

RAFFA, JOSEPH, b. Hartford, CT, Aug. 26, 1947; s. Joseph and Regina (Slattery) R.; m. Merrily Friedlander, June 28, 1975; 1 dau., Laura. Author: Death Depends on Our Dark Silence, 1986, No Archeologist Ever Dug Up an Erection, 1987; contrbr. poetry, short stories, articles: Crosscurrents, N.Y. Qtly., numerous others in US, Can. and Eng. Wrkg. on novel, book on poetry of Michael S. Harper. M. Ed., Columbia U., 1977, PhD, 1984. Adj. prof. George Washington U., Washington, 1984—; dir. First Thursday Poetry and Prose Series, Takoma Park, Md., 1985—. Mem. AAP, MLA. Home: 3213 Edgewood St Kensington MD 20895

RAFFEL, BURTON NATHAN, b. NYC, Apr. 27, 1928; s. Harry L. and Rose (Karr) R.; m. Elizabeth Clare Wilson, Apr. 16, 1974; children: Wendy Gabrielle, Kezia Beth, Shifra Simma, Brian. Author: (criticism/history) The Development of Modern Indonesian Poetry, 1967. The Forked Tongue: A Study of the Translation Process, 1971, Why Re-create?, 1973, Introduction to Poetry, 1971, Robert Lowell, 1981, T.S. Eliot, 1982, How to Read a Poem, 1984, American Victorians: Explorations in Emotional History, 1984, Ezra Pound: The Prime Minister of Poetry, 1985, Poets, Politicians, and Con Men, 1986; (bibliography) Guide to Paperback Translations in the Humanities: A Teacher's Handbook, 1976; (anthologies/collections) Poems, 1971, Signet Classic Book of American Stories, 1985, Signet Classic Book of Contemporary American Stories, 1986, Forty-One Stories of O. Henry, 1984, Possum and Ole Ez in the Public Eye, 1985; (translations) Poems from the Old English, 1960, rev. edit. 1964, Beowulf, 1963, (with Nurdin Salam) Chairil Anwar: Selected Poems, 1963, An Anthology of Modern Indonesian Poetry, 1964, rev. edit. 1970, Sir Gawain and the Green Knight, 1970, The Complete Poetry and Prose of Chairil Anwar, 1970, Russian Poetry under the Tsars, 1971, Selected Works of Nikolai S. Gumilev (with Alla Burago), 1972, (with Alla Burago) Complete Poetry of Osip E. Mandelstam, 1973, Horace: Selected Odes, Epodes, Satires, and Epistles, 1973, (with James Hynd, David Armstrong, and W.R. Johnson) Horace: Ars Poetica, 1974, (with Harry Aveling) Ballads and Blues: Selected Poems of W.S. Rendra, 1974, A Thousand Years of Vietnamese Poetry (with N.N. Bich, W.S. Merwin), 1975, The Bull Hide (La Pell de Brau), 1978, Selected Poems of Alexander Pushkin (with Alla Burago), 1979, The Essential Horace, 1983, (with Zuxin Ding) Gems of Chinese Poetry, 1986, Chretian de Troyes, Yvain 1987; (poetry) Mia Poems, 1968, Four Humours, 1979, Changing the Angle of the Sun-Dial, 1984, Grice, 1985. BA cum laude, Bklyn. Coll., 1948: MA, Ohio State U., 1949; J.D., Yale U., 1958. Wrkg. on Introduction to Literature, The Art of Translation, Readings and Documents in the History of Prosody; poetry and fiction. Instr. English, SUNY-Stony Brook, 1964-65, asst. prof. English, 1965-66; assoc. prof. SUNY-Buffalo, 1966-68; vis. prof. Haifa U., Israel, 1968-69; prof. English and classics U. Tex., Austin, 1969-71; sr. tutor (dean), Ontario Coll. of Art, Toronto, 1971-72; vis. prof. Humanities York U., Toronto, 1975-75; vis. prof. Emory U., 1974; sr. editor (freelance) McDonnell Douglas Co., Denver, 1985—; prof. English U. Denver, 1975—; Atty. Milbank, Tweed, Hadley & McCloy, NYC, 1958-60. Bar: N.Y. 1959. Grantee Am. Philo. Soc., 1962, 63, Research Fdn. State N.Y., 1964, 65; recipient Frances Steloff prize for fiction, 1978. Mem. Natl. Humanities Faculty. Home: 765 Harrison St Box 6326 Denver CO 80206

RAFFERTY, CAROLYN BANKS, (Carolyn Banks), b. Pitts., Feb. 9, 1941, d. Philip Jacob and Victoria Ann (Zbel) Dogonka; m. Robert R. Rafferty, Aug. 26, 1984; son by previous marriage, Donald Banks. Author: Mr. Right, 1979, The Darkroom, 1980, The Adventures of Runcible Spoon, 1980, The Girls on the Row, 1983, Patchwork, 1986. MA, U. Md., 1968. Mem. PEN, AG, NBCC, MWA. Home: 16111 FM 969 Austin TX 78724

RAFFERTY, KEVIN PATRICK, b. Hollywood, CA., Oct. 7, 1955; s. Loren Eugene and Rose Marie (Fusano) R.; m. Patricia Ann Supancic, Sept. 27, 1980; 1 son, Kevin Patrick Jr. AA in Philosophy, St. John's Sem.; BA in Art, Calif. State U.-Fullerton. Scope wrtr. Walt Disney Imagineering, Glendale, Calif., 1979-84, sr. scope wrtr., 1985-87, show design wrtr., 1987—; communications ed. So. Calif. Edison Co., Rosemead, 1984-85. Home: 2704 N Vista Heights Rd Orange CA 92667

RAFFERTY, LARRY E., b. Whittier, CA, Feb. 5, 1942; s. Charles E. and Mabel G. (Allen) Rafferty; m. Meryl Natchez, May, 1969; children—Micah, Niam, Lisa, Tulley. Ed./publ. Hit & Run Press; titles include: Late Show (Michael Shepler), 1974, 12 Winter Haiku (Adrienne Ross), 1977, The Indio Trash Compactor Murders (Shepler), 1979, Night Train (Larry Rafferty), 1981, Sentimental Journey (Jim Chapson), 1985. BA in English, Cal. State, LA, 1967. Genl. partner L.E. Rafferty & Assoc. (Lafayette, CA), 1982—. Small Press Grant, NEA, 1977. Mem. Pacific Ctr. for The Book Arts. Home: 1725 Springbrook Rd Lafayette CA 94549

RAGAN, JAMES, b. Duquesne, PA, Dec. 19, 1944; s. John and Teresa (Jakuba) R.; m. Debora Ann Skovranko, May 29, 1982; 1 child, Tera Vale. Author: (poetry) In the Talking Hours, 1979; Womb-Weary, 1986; transl. in Japan (poetry) Tokyo Special, 1980; contrbr. poetry to Ohio, N.W., Ind., So. Poetry, Greenfield, Windsor, Bellingham, Minetta, West Coast Poetry rvws, Poetry N.W., Shenandoah, Denver, N.Y. quars., Crosscurrents, So. Calif. Anthology, Lotus, Confrontation, other lit mags; produced plays include Saints, The Gandy Dancers, Commedia. BA, St. Vincent Coll., Latrobe, Pa., 1966; MA, Ohio U., 1967, PhD, 1971. Asst. prof. Ohio U., Athens, 1971-72, U. Tex., El Paso, 1979-81; dir., prof. writing program U. So. Calif., Los Angeles, 1982—; Fulbright sr. lectr. poetry, Yugoslavia, 1984. Recipient Emerson Poetry Prize, Ohio U., 1971, Billee Murray Denne poetry award Lincoln Coll., Ill., 1981. Mem. WG Am., PSA, AWP. Office U So Calif DCC 201 Los Angeles CA 90089

RAGAN, ROY ALLEN, b. Indianapolis, Sept. 9, 1929; s. Paul Elden and Nora Elvira (Merritt) R.; m. Frankie M. Jones, Dec. 11, 1974; children: Paul, Kevin, Sheryl, Mark, Gregory. BA, Indiana Univ., Bloomington, 1956. Agent, Lincoln Natl. Life, Indianapolis, 1957-60; asst. ed., Rough Notes Co., Inc., 1960-65; tchr. Indpls. public schls., 1965-67; mng. ed. Rough Notes Co., Inc., Indianapolis, 1967-70, ed., 1970-81; ed. Life & Health Publications, Rough Notes Co., Inc., 1981—. Editor or compilor/editor of 41 books dealing with insurance and editor of 281 monthly issues of Insurance Sales Magazine. Author: Direct Mail Letters, 1980. Served with AUS, 1948-52. Mem. Natl. Assn. of Life Underwriters, Natl. Assn. of Health Underwriters, Natl. Wrtrs. Club. Home: 7618 W St. Clair St Indianapolis IN 46214

RAGAN, SAMUEL TALMADGE, (Sam) b. Berea, NC, Dec. 31, 1915; s. William Samuel and Emma Clare (Long) R.; m. Marjorie Usher, Aug. 19, 1939; children—Nancy, Ann Talmadge. Author: (poems) The Tree in the Far Pasture, 1964, To the Water's Edge, 1971, Journey into Morning, 1982, Back to Beginnings, 1984; The New Day, 1964, The Democratic Party—Its Aims and Purposes, 1961, Dixie Looked Away, 1965. BA, Atlantic Christian Coll., 1936. Exec. ed., News and Observer (Raleigh, NC), 1941-69; ed.-pub., The Pilot (Southern Pines), 1969—. Poet Laureate of NC (since 1982); pres. NC Press Assn., 1974; pres., AP Managing Eds. Assn., 1963-64; chmn. Freedom of Information, Am. Soc. of newspaper Eds., 1968. Mem. Sigma Delta Chi, NC Writers Conf. Home: 255 Hill Rd Southern Pines NC 28387

RAH, A. KALID, see Bowart, Walter Howard

RAHL, CECILIA MAY N, b. Yonkers, NY, Oct. 10, 1931, d. John Steven and Helen (Minar) Novotny; m. Ernest Rahl, June 6, 1952; children—Andrea, Lydia Rahl Kaplan and Marian Rahl Snik. Author books of poetry: The Hollow and The Hill, 1977, Friends, 1979, Comparisons, 1979; contrbr. poetry to Poet, Eminent Poet Series, Sayeeda Publs., Madras, India, Zinger Anthology, 1985; contrbr. articles to United Slovanic Am. League Newsletter, Herald Statesman, Home News and Times. Student Mercy Coll., Dobbs Ferry, N.Y., 1984-87, Student Iona Coll., 1987-. Office asst. City Ct. Yonkers, 1967—. Corr. sec. United Slovanic Am. League, Yonkers, 1975-76, secy., 1977-78; mem. Slovak World Congress. Mem. World Poetry Soc. (award, Madras, India, 1982), Bronxville Wrtr.'s Group, Calif. Fedn. Chapparrel Poets (Robert Frost chpt.). Home: 130 Theo Fremd Ave M3 Rye NY 10580

RAIN, DAN, see Mills, Dan Sam P.

RAINBOW, THOMAS, b. Syracuse, NY, Mar. 3, 1948; s. William Robert and Lois E. (Werner) Rainbow. Author: Last Call for Alcohol, 1976, Saloon, 1976, The Last Barstool, 1977, The Longest Drive, 1981, Blue Highway, 1982, Sunset Grill, 1983. BA, Syracuse U., 1972. Owner Desperado's (Gerogetown, DC), 1976-80; Greenskeeper Wildwood Golf Course (Cicero, NY), 1980-84; foreman, Clay Hwy. Dept. (NY), 1985. Sgt., USAF, 1968-72, Far East. Home: 113 Chestnut Rd North Syracuse NY 13212

RAINES, KATHLEEN JANE, b. Muskogee, OK, Nov. 6, 1946; d. John Dyas and Kathleen (DeGroot) Parker; m. Richard Ross Raines, Aug. 25, 1971; children—Christopher Brian, Rebecca Alyson, William Benjamin. Author: Behavior and Species Specificity of Two Kansas Gastropods, 1974, Guidelines for Increasing Wildlife on Farms and Ranches with Ideas for Supplemental Income Sources for Rural Families, 1984, Friends in Deed: A Course in Helping Build Supportive Friendships, 1986; articles in Coll. Life, Emporia Gazette, others. BMusEd, Coll. Emporia, 1969; M.S., Kans. State Tchrs. Coll., 1974, postgrad., 1982—. Substitute tchr. pub. schs., var. Kans. schls., 1983—. Music therapy aide Lyon County Retarded Childrens Ctr., Emporia, 1965-70; tchr. free univ. project Coll. Emporia, 1970. Recipient Outstanding Service award Lankenau Hosp., Phila., 1963-65; Cert. of Achievement, U. Innsbruck-Mayerhofen Campus, Austria, 1969, Natl. Outdoor Leadership Schl., 1970. Mem. Mu Phi Epsilon (Outstanding Sr. award 1969-70; life mem.), Okla. Hist. Soc. (life), Am. Malacological Union, Kans. Assn. Children with Learning Disabilities. Home: 403 Vine St Wamego KS 66547

RALSTOR, ADAM, see Wiliamson, Richard

RAMANUJAN, MOLLY, (Shouri Daniels), b. Kerala, India, came to U.S., 1961, d. Kurien Chacko and Leah (Mikhail) Daniels; m. A.K. Ramanujan, June 7, 1962; children—Krittika Maya, Krishna Shauri. Novelist: The Yellow Fish, 1966, The Salt Doll, 1978, A City of Children, 1986; author short fiction, lit. criticism. Wrkg. on book-length essay, fiction writing manual. MA, Bombay U. and Ind. U.; PhD Com. on Social Thought, U. Chgo., 1986. Founder, dir. Clothesline Schl. Fiction, Chgo., 1979—; lectr. Center Continuing Edn., U. Chgo., 1984—; dir. Chgo. Writing Inst., 1985—. Ed., pub. Clothesline Rvw, vol. 1, nos. 1-3, containing 128 stories by 52 Illinois wrtrs., 1986. Recipient Fulbright Smith-Mundt award, 1961-62, Best Fiction award Ill. Arts Council, 1978, Best Lit. Criticism award Ill. Arts Council, 1982, PEN Syndicated Fiction award, 1985. Mem. Soc. Midland Authors. Home: 5629 Dorchester St Chicago IL 60637

RAMBACH, PEGGY DIANE, b. Manhasset, NY, Mar. 14, 1958, d. Harvey Wolfe Rambach and Patricia Jane (Scharlin) Taylor; m. Andre Jules Dubus, Dec. 16, 1979; 1 child, Cadence Yvonne Rambach Dubus. Author: (chapbook) When the Animals Leave, 1986; contrbr. short stories to Intro 13, Crazyhorse, Fiction Network. BA, Tufts U., 1980; MA, U. N.H., 1982; MFA, Vt. Coll., 1984. Instr. composition Bradford Coll., Mass., 1982-84; instr. writing ctr. U. Ala., Tuscaloosa, 1985; owner One on One Writing, Haverhill, Mass., 1985—; condr. pvt. writing workshops. named outstanding wrtr. Pushcart Prize Anthology, 1984. Mem. AWP. Home: 753 E Broadway Haverhill MA 01830

RAMEY, DIANE ELFRIEDE, b. San Francisco, Apr. 1, 1949; d. Lester Carl (stepfather) and Ingeborg E. (Michael) Christensen. Contrbr. numerous poems to lit. mags., anthols. Student Valparaiso U., 1966-71. Legal secy. Burns & Figa, Denver, 1982-84, free-lance, 1984-86, Sherman & Howard, Denver, 1986-87; free-lance wrtr., 1987—. Recipient Golden Poet Award World of Poetry, 1987, Honorable Mention, 1987. Home 3540 S Pearl 507 Englewood CO 80110

RAMIREZ, JOAN E., b. Mpls., Sept. 14, 1943, d. William Edward and Marcella Marie (Schmitz) Winship; m. David Joseph Ramirez. Contrbr. articles to Twin City Rose Newsletter, Chez Nous, Minn. Affirmative Action Digest. Wrkg. on hist. research at Univ. of Calif., Berkeley, Dept. of Minority and Women's Studies, "The Mexican-American in Minnesota." Ed.-in-chief La Voz News Mag., Mpls., 1970—. Office: Box 19206 Diamond Lake Sta Minneapolis MN 55419

RAMSAY, ETHEL DAVIS, b. Salisbury, NC, June 15, 1905; d. Angier Bryant and Ada Catherine (Taylor) Davis; m. William James Ramsay, June 3, 1934 (dec. Feb. 5, 1972); children—Mary Catherine Boudrie, William James, Richard Corum, Robert Davis, Frances Ethel (dec.). Contrbr. poems to anthols. A.B., Duke U., 1926, M.A., 1928; postgrad. U.N.C., 1929-33. Tchr. Tuscalum Coll., Greenville, TN, 1962-63, Columbia Basin Coll., Pasco, WA, 1963-70, retired. Recipient Poetry award NLAPW, 1980; award for children's unpublished fiction Friends of the Public Library, Tulsa, OK, 1985. Home: 11611 E 84th Ct N Owasso OK 74055

RAMSDALE, DAVID ALAN, (Taishin), b. Winfield, KS, Sept. 18, 1950. Author of Sexual Energy Ecstasy. Contrbr. to Meditation, Romantic Times, The Men's Jnl, Mothering, others. Wrkg. on books on sex, meditation, Buddhism. BA, U. Calif.-San Diego, 1974. Pub., Peak Skill Pub. Co., Playa Del Rey, Calif., 1984—; public speaker. Mem. COSMEP. Office: Box 1449 Goleta CA 93116

RAMSEY, CHARLES FREDERIC, JR., b. Pitts., Jan. 29, 1915; s. Charles Frederic and Ethel (Runnette) R.; m. Amelia Johnston, Apr. 16, 1948 (dec. Jan. 1979); children—Loch, Martha, Alida. Author: Jazzmen, 1939, A Guide to Longplay Jazz Records, 1954, Been Here and Gone, 1960, Where The Music Started, 1970; recordings incl.: Prose du Transsiberien et de la Petite Jeanne de France, 1967, Fasola, 53 Shape-Note Folk Hymns, 1970, 16 Poems by Sterling A. Brown Read by Sterling A. Brown; film documentaries incl.: Music of the South, 1957, The Evangelists, 1957, The American Revolution of '63, Anatomy of Pop, 1966, Mississippi: A Self Portrait, 1966, The Songmakers, 1967, Image of America, 1967; contrbr. photographs: La Musique, 1967, Histoire du Jazz, 1967, Le Sud au Temps de Scarlette, Focus Intl. Ency., The Story of the Blues, 1969, others. BA cum laude, Princeton U., 1936. Editorial, book design, Harcourt, Brace & Co., NYC,1936-39; writer information svc. Dept. Agr., 1941-42; freelance writer Voice Am., Dept. State, 1942—; music ed. Charm Mag., NYC,1946-52, Sat. Rvw, 1950—; recordist, anthologist Folkways Records; seminars in history Am. informal music Solebury Schl., New Hope, PA, 1962—; Inst. Jazz Studies; ednl. programming cons. Rutgers U.; biog. writer Time-Life Records; cons. Time-Life Books; councillor Soc. Ethnomusicology, 1961-63; bd. advisors William Ransom Hogan Jazz Archive, Tulane U., 1981—; TV writer, producer, CBS, NBC, ABC, Tulane U. Recipient Prix France-Amerique, Princeton, 1936, Best Textbook Design award Am. Inst. Graphic Arts, 1939, Jnlsm. Fund Silver Pen award, 1960, Peabody award to co-producers NBC-TV, 1964; Natl. Brotherhood award to co-producers, writers NBC news documentary, 1967; Guggenheim fellow, 1953, 55; NEH fellow, 1974-75; Ford Fdn. fellow, 1975-76. Address: The Federal Twist RD 2 Stockton NJ 08559

RAMSEY, FRANK B., b. Muncie, IN, July 10, 1902; s. Earl E. and Blanche Banta (Sleeper) R.; m. Mildred Read, Apr. 9, 1933 (dec. Apr. 1, 1985). Ed. Indiana Medicine, Jnl. Indiana State Med. Assn., 1949—. AB, IN U., 1924, MD, 1927. Served to Col., AUS, 1940-45, PTO. Mem. AMA, AMWA, Amer. Coll. of Surgeons. Home: 1401 W 52d St Indianapolis IN 46208

RAMSEY, JAROLD W., b. Bend, OR, Sept. 1, 1937, s. A.S. and Wilma (Mendenhall) R.; m. Dorothy Quinn, Aug. 16, 1959; children—Kate, Sophia, John. Author poetry collections: The Space Between Us., 1970, Love in an Earthquake, 1973, Dermographia, 1982; Coyote Goes Upriver (play), 1985; ed.: Coyote Was Going There: Indian Literature of the Oregon Country, 1977, Reading the Fire: Essays in the Traditional Indian Literature of the Far West, 1983. BA with honors, U. Oreg., 1959; PhD,U. Wash., 1964. Asst. prof. English, U. Rochester, N.Y., 1965-70, assoc. prof., 1980-81, prof. English, 1982—; vis. prof. English, U. Victoria, B.C., Can., 1975-76. Recipient Borestone Mountain Best Poem award, 1972, 75, 76, Lillian Fairchild prize, Fairchild Fdn., Rochester, 1973, Don Walker award Western Lit. Assn., 1979, Helen Bullis Poetry Prize, Poetry NW, Seattle, 1985; grantee NEA, 1974, 76, Ingram Merrill Fdn., 1975. Mem. MLA, Am. Folklore Assn., Assn. for Study of Am. Indian Lit. Home: 519 Wellington Ave Rochester NY 14619

RAMSEY, MICHAEL KIRBY, b. Center, TX, Oct. 22, 1948; s. John Donece and Avis Molene (Shofner) R.; m. Catherine Mittis Gay, June 19, 1978; 1 son, John Michael. Author: (textbook) Foundations of Clinical Laboratory Science, 1986. Contrbr. articles to profl. jnls. B.S., Northwestern State U., 1972; M.S., North Tex. State U., 1981, Ph.D., 1984. Med. tehnologist All Saints Hosp., Ft. Worth, 1978-83; asst. prof. med. technology Northeastern La. U., Monroe, 1983—. Served with U.S. Air Force, 1976-80. Home: 1802 Nancy Dr Ruston LA 71270

RANA, KIRANJIT S., II, b. Kashmir, India, Sept. 5, 1946; came to U.S., 1981; s. Jagjit S. and Bhagwant S. (Dugal) Aurora. Editor: L.S.D. Psychotherapy (Stanislav Grof), 1978, Once a Month (Katharina Dalton) 1978, Drinking Problems Family Problems (Marie-Louise Meyer), 1979, Awakening of Consciousness (Carl Hulsmann), 1980, Exclusively Female (Linda Ojeda), 1982, All Mighty: A Study of the God Complex (Horst Richter), 1983, Dynamics of Couples Therapy (Jurg Willi), 1983; transl.and editor: Intrance: Fundamental Psychological Patterns of the Inner and Outer World (C.J. Schuurman), 1984, Getting High In Natural Ways, 1986, Tales of the Comet, 1986. B. Tech., Indian Inst. Tech., Kharagpur, India, 1969; grad. diploma in labor welfare and social work, Calcutta U., 1972. Personnel officer Metal Box Co. of India, Calcutta, 1970-73; editor Sufi Pub. Co., Dockenfield, Surrey, 1975-76; chief editor Servire Group, Katwijk, The Netherlands, 1976-81; v.p. Hunter House Inc., Claremont, Calif., 1981-84, pub. and pres., 1984—. Mem. of the Board, Publishers Marketing Assn, 1986. Office: Box 1302 Claremont CA 91711

RAND, ANTHONE, see Rose, Patricia Anthone

RANDALL, JAMES HAMILTON ZWINGE, see Randi, James

RANDI, JAMES, (Randall James Hamilton Zwinge), b. Toronto, Ont., Can., Aug. 7, 1928; s. G. Randall and M. Alice Zwinge. Author: The Magic of Uri Geller, 1975, (with Bert Sugar) Houdini, His Life and Art, 1976, Flim-Flam, 1981, Test Your ESP Potential, 1983, The Faith Healers, 1987. Student, Oakwood Collegiate Inst., Toronto, 1940-45. Mem. editorial bd.: Skeptical Inquirer, 1976—. Home: 12000 NW 8th St Plantation FL 33325

RANDOLPH, JOHN DENSON, b. Balt., Oct. 28, 1938; s. John W. and Jean (Belden) R.; m. Mary Galbo, Nov. 30, 1963; children—Mary Victoria, Kathy, John Jr. Author: Fishing Basics, 1981, Backpacking Basics, 1982, numerous freelance articles for Outdoor Life, Sports Afield, Field and Stream, Vermont Life. BA, Williams Coll., 1962. Writer, Brattleboro Reformer (VT), 1968; county ed. Bennington Banner (VT), 1969; ed./pub. Vermont Sportsman, Bennington, 1969-78; mng. ed. Fly Fisherman, Dorset, VT, 1978-82, ed., 1982—; mng. ed. Backpacker, Dorset, 1982; ed.-in-chief Country Jnl Magazine, 1986—. Served to Capt., USMCR, 1963-66. Home: 3204 N Scenic Rd Harrisburg PA 17109

RANER, BERTHA FRANCES, (Bea Raner), b. Mpls., Mar. 3, 1915, d. Walter Cornelious and Rosa May (Ruggles) Kelsey; m. Lloyd Harold Cook, Oct. 1932 (div. 1935); children—Esther Corrine, Dolores Gay; m. 2d, Albert William Oliver, 1937 (div. 1945); children—Alberta Rose, Wilma Jean; m. 3d, Howard Duncan Raner, 1947 (div. 1959). Author book of poetry, short subjects, From the Heart, 1980; contrbr. poetry to World Treasury of Great Poems, 1980, short story to Pittsburg (Calif.) Post Dispatch, 1981. AA, Diablo Valley Jr. Coll., 1971. Address: 105 Reef Dr Pittsburg CA 94565

RANIA, ALBERT NUNZIO, b. Camden, NJ, Oct. 13, 1966; s. Nunzio Albert and Gloria Elizabeth (Grant) R. Contrbr. poetry to anthols.: Am. Poetry Anthol. v. IV, 1985, Voices in Poetics: A Modern Treas., 1985, Riders of the Rainbow, 1986, The Natl. Poetry Anthol., 1986, Words of Praise, A Treas. of Relig. and Inspirational Poetry, 1986. Award for outstanding poetic achievement, YES Press, 1985. Home: 1427 Boxwood Dr Hilltop NJ 08012

RANIERI, LORRAINE MARY, (April Showers), b. Phila., Dec. 5, 1943; d. Charles R. and Jennie (Forte) Cavallaro; m. Frank J. Ranieri, Oct. 3, 1964, children—Frank, III, Joanne. Contrbr. poems to anthols.; song lyrics to Columbine Record Corp., 1985. Wrkg. on collection of poems, short stories. B.A. in Journalism, Gloucester County Coll., Sewell, N.J. Free-lance wrtr., Pitman and Mantua, N.J., 1974—. Recipient Outstanding Poetic Achievement award Yes Press, 1985, 4 spcl. mention awards World of Poetry, 1984-85; named Golden Poet World of Poetry, 1985, 87. Mem. Southern N.J. Poetry Soc. (publicity com. 1984-85). Home: 146 McCarthy Ave Mantua NJ 08051

RANKIN, SUSAN JEWEL, b. Springfield, MO, June 20, 1949; d. Owen Robert and Naomi Ruth (Hartpence) Williams; m. Gerald Lee Steese, Jan. 10, 1970 (div. 1976); 1 son, Steven; m. 2d, Bob Lee Rankin, Nov. 22, 1977. Contrbr. numerous articles: Glendale News Press, Ariz. Republic, Holbrook Tribune, N.Y. Gilbert & Sullivan Soc., Much Ado About Mensa, other publs., wrtr., ed. house organs for Council for Exceptional Children, Gilbert & Sullivan Soc. Wrkg. on novels. Student No. Ariz. U., 1966-68, 71, 84, Northland Pioneer Coll., 1976-85. Asst. adminstr. spl. edn. Winslow (Ariz.) Public Schs., 1979-86; mgr. KJ Enterprises, Inc., Winslow, 1986-87; med. records technician Neurology Center No. Ariz., Flagstaff, 1987—. Home: 141 Navajo Dr Winslow AZ 86047

RANK, MAUREEN JOY, b. Oskaloosa, IA, June 8, 1947, d. Maurice Stanley and Ada Florence (Groenenboom) Johnston; m. Michael F. Rank, May 27, 1972; children—Holly, Scott. Author: God Can Make It Happen (with Russ Johnston), 1975, Dynamic Praying for Exciting Results (with Russ Johnston), 1979, Turn Your Dreams Into Reality (with Russ Johnston), 1982, Free to Grieve, 1985; freelance book ed. Wrkg. on books on female sexuality. BS, Iowa State U., 1969. Office: 1310 E Main St Knoxville IA 50138

RANSOM, DANA, see Gideon, Nancy A.

RANSOM, BILL, b. Puyallup, WA, June 6, 1945; s. William Bertsell and LaVerne May (Marcoe) R.; 1 dau., Hali Kalae. Author: poems Finding True North, 1974, Waving Arms at the Blind, 1975, Last Rites, 1978, Last Call, 1983, The Single Man Looks at Winter, 1983; novels (with

Frank Herbert) The Jesus Incident, 1979, The Lazarus Effect, The Ascension Factor; contrbns. to numerous lit mags, including Tendril, Prairie Schooner, NY Qtly, Ironweed, Hawaii Rvw. BA, Edn., Univ. Wash., 1970. Carpenter, 1980-81; free-lance jnlst. (Central Am.), 1982-83; emergency medical tech., 1983—. Mem. Intl. Machinists, Aerospace Workers, PSA, P&W. Home: Box 531 Port Townsend WA 98368

RAPHAEL, DAN AMBROSE, (Mara Fish), b. Fargo, ND, June 7, 1952; s. Raymond John and Ceceilia Agnes (Banaszek) Dlugonski; m. Melba Joyce Jones; 1 child, Orion Lorenz. Author: (books of poetry) Polymerge, 1979, Dawn Patrol, 1979, Zone du Jour, 1981, To Taste, 1983, Attention Spotcheck, 1983, The Matter What Is, 1984, Bop Grit Storm Cafe, 1985, Rain Away, 1987; editor, pub. NRG mag., 1976—. BA, Cornell U., 1973; MFA, Bowling Green State U., 1975. Substitute tchr. Pitts. Pub. Schs., 1975-76; janitor Shakespeare Festival, Ashland, Oreg., 1976-77; meat carver Beecher Meats, Portland, Oreg., 1977-78; mail carrier U.S. Postal Service, Portland, 1978-81; motor vehicles rep. Oregon DMV, Portland, 1983—. Project coordinator Portland Poetry Festival, 1985—. Home: 6735 SE 78th Portland OR 97206

RAPHAEL, MORRIS CHARLES, b. Natchez, MS, July 31, 1917; s. Charles Mansour and Rose (Karooz) R.; m. Seartha Lorenzo, 1940 (dec. 1954); 1 son, Morris Jr.; m. 2d, Helen Louise Hofstetter, May 24, 1958; children: Rose Anne, John. Author, pub.: The Battle in the Bayou Country, 1976, Weeks Hall-the Master of the Shadows, 1981, The Weeks Hall Tapes, 1983, How Do You Know When You're in Acadiana, 1984, Mystic Bayou, 1985, Murder on the Teche Queen, 1987. Wrkg. on screenplay. City ed. Franklin (La.) Banner Tribune, 1954-56; author, pub. Morris Raphael Books, New Iberia, La., 1975—. Recipient Edward J. Moore award Deep South Wrtrs. Orgn., 1970, Jefferson Davis Award, United Daughters of Confederacy, 1974. Mem. La. Wrtrs.' Guild, Attakapas Hist. Assn., La. Hist. Assn. Home: 1404 Bayou Side Dr New Iberia LA 70560

RAPHAEL, PHYLLIS, b. NYC, May 22, 1937, d. Samuel and Rose (Beck) Raphael; m. Robert Chartoff, Dec. 1956 (div. 1970); children—Jennifer, William, Julie. Author: They Got What They Wanted, 1972, Beating the Love Affair Rap and Other Tales, 1983; contrbr. to Cosmopolitan, Harper's, McCalls, Village Voice, Penthouse, Vogue, others. BA, Barnard Coll., 1959. Tchr. wrtg., Columbia U., 1978—. Mem. PEN, P&W, winner PEN Syndicated Fiction Award, 1987. Home: 390 West End Ave New York NY 10024

RAPOPORT, DANIEL, b. NYC,Jan. 19, 1933; s. David and Ida (Bernstein) R.; m. Maxine Barczak; children—Victoria, Andrew, Adam. Author: Inside the House: An Irreverent Guided Tour through the House of Representatives from the Days of Adam Clayton Powell to those of Peter Rodino; mag. and nwspr. articles. BA, U. Ill., 1954. With UPI, Washington, 1958-72; free-lance writer, 1972—; fdr., pres., Farragut Pub. Co., Washington, DC, 1984—. Nieman fellow, 1970-71. Mem. Washington Ind. Writers (pres. 1982-83). Home: 3804 Jenifer St NW Washington DC 20015

RAPP, LEA BAYERS, b. Bklyn., July 19, 1946; d. Irving and Adele (Emanuel) Bayers; m. Stanley J. Rapp, Sept. 3, 1966; children—Ilana, Justin. Author: Put Your Kid in Show Biz, 1986, business and personal improvement books as work-for-hire; lectr. and workshop leader; syndicated columnist Things for Free, 1977-80; (play) Smiling Faces. Contrbr. to mags., newspapers including USA Today, N.Y. Times, Christian Science Monitor, Playbill, Sunday N.Y. Daily News, N.Y. Post, Tech. Photography Mag., Amelia Literary Mag. Student, Bklyn. Coll., Rutgers U.-New Brunswick, N.J. Mem. ASCAP, N.J. Press Women, Natl. Fedn. Press Women, AG, AL of America award winning feature journalist-NJPW. Office: 82 Marsh Ave Sayreville NJ 08872

RASKIN, ELLEN, b. Milw., Mar. 13, 1928; d. Sol and Margaret (Goldfisch) Raskin; m. Dennis Flanagan, Oct. 17, 1966; 1 dau.—Susan Kuhlman Metcalfe. Writer & illustrator children's books, inclg. Nothing Ever Happens on My Block, 1966, The World's Greatest Freak Show, 1971, Twenty-two, Twenty-three, 1976, The Westing Game, 1978 (John Newbery medal, 1979). Student, U. WI, Madison, 1945-48. Instr. in illustration Pratt Inst., 1963, Syracuse U., 1976; guest lectr. U. Berkeley, 1969, 72, 77. Freelance illustrator, NYC, 1955-68. Recipient Distinctive Merit award Art Dirs. Clubs, 1958, Silver medal, 1959; citation of merit Soc. Illustrators, 1966, 70, 71; Best Picture Book award World-Jnl-Tribune, 1966; Honor Book award Boston Globe-Horn Book, 1973; citation Bklyn. Mus. Art, 1973, 74; Edgar Allan Poe Spcl. award MWA, 1975; Newbery Honor Book award ALA, 1975; Best Fiction award Boston Globe-Horn Book, 1978; Notable Wisconsin Author, 1981; book named to Am. Inst. Graphic Arts 50 Books of Yr., 1966, 68; N.Y. Times 10 Best Books, 1966, 68. Mem. AG, Graphic Artists Guild. Home: 12 Gay St New York NY 10014

RASLEY, ALICIA TODD, (Michelle Venet, Elizabeth Todd), B. Hammond, IN, Dec. 29, 1955; d. Robert Marion and Jeanne Marie (Pustek) Todd; m. Jeffrey Scott Rasley, July 7, 1974; 1 son, James Joseph. Author: The Reluctant Lady, 1982, The Earl's Intrigue, 1984. Ed.: Using Apple Works, 1986, Rapids of Change, 1987. B.A. in English, Butler U., 1980, M.S. in Radio and TV, 1984. Editorial asst. Ind. Hist. Soc., Indpls., 1980-81; press aide Ind. Attorney Genl., Indpls., 1982-83; writing instr. Ind. U., Indpls., 1985—; free-lance wrtr., ed., 1982—. Mem. RWA. Home: 6422 Ralston Indianapolis IN 46220

RASMUS, JOHN A., b. St. Louis, Mar. 20, 1954; s. Robert Nelson and Annette Elizabeth (Avery) R. Asst. ed. Chgo. mag., 1975-76, assoc. ed., 1976-78, editorial dir., 1978-79; mng. ed. Outside mag., Chgo., 1979-84, ed., 1984—. Adjunct instr., Medill Grad. School of Journalism, Northwestern U. 1985-86. Recipient Natl. Mag. Award for gen. excellence ASME, 1984. Home: 1547 N Dearborn St Chicago IL 60610

RASS, REBECCA RIVKA, b. Tel-Aviv, Israel, Dec. 9, 1936, came to U.S., Mar. 1971, d. Meir and Rachel (Berger) Wilcher; 1 dau., Enid. Author: From A to Z, 1969, Word War I and Word War II (poetic fables), 1973, From Moscow to Jerusalem (nonfiction), 1976, The Fairy Tales of My Mind (fiction), 1978, The Mountain (fiction), 1982; contrbr. short story to Solo, 1978. BA, Empire State Coll., N.Y., 1977; MFA, Bklyn. Coll., 1979. Cultural corr. Yedioth Ahronoth, Tel Aviv, 1965—; lectr. CCNY, 1971-78; asst. prof. Pace U., NYC,1979—, Queens Coll., N.Y., 1979—, Manhattan Community Coll., NYC,1985—. Mem. P&W. Home: 54 West 16th 14C New York NY 10011

RATCH, JERRY, b. Chgo., Aug. 9, 1944, s. Otto Joseph and Bess (Mika) R.; m. Mary Ann Hayden, Oct. 23, 1972; stepchildren—Erin, John, Matthew, Thomas. Author books of poetry: Puppet X, 1973, 76, Clown Birth, 1975, The Suburban Poem, 1975, Osiris, 1977, Chaucer Marginalia, 1979, Rose, 1979, Chairman, 1982, Hot Weather: Selected, 1982, Helen, 1985, Lenin's Paintings, 1986. BA in English, U. Ill., 1967; MFA in Wrtg., U. Calif.-Irvine, 1970. Broker Mason-McDuffie, Berkeley, Calif., 1981-85, Coldwell-Banker, Berkeley, 1985—. Mem. West Coast Print Center (dir.). Home: 1536 Walnut St Berkeley CA 94709

RATEAVER, BARGYLA, b. Ft. Dauphin, Madagascar, Aug. 3, 1916, came to U.S., 1935, d. Eugene Alaric and Margaret (Schaffnit) Rateaver; 1 child, Gylver. Author: Organic Method Primer, 1973; ed., pub., reprints on organic agriculture and related matters; contrbr. numerous articles to Let's Live, Earth Times, Health Qtly, Organic Jnl, others. BA, U. Calif.-Berkeley, 1943, MLS, 1959; MS, U. Mich., 1950, PhD,1951. Tchr., lectr., plant researcher, 1930—. Grantee Longwood Gardens, Pa., 1955; recipient numerous awards in field. Mem. Intl. Fedn. Organic Agr. Movements, Acres, USA. Home: 9049 Covina St San Diego CA 92126

RATIGAN, WILLIAM, b. Detroit, Nov. 7; s. Bernard Joseph and Bertie (Laing) R.; m. Eleanor Dee Eldridge, Sept. 12, 1935 (dec.); children—Patricia Lee (Mrs. Arthur A. Ranger), Anesta Colleen (Mrs. Arthur J. Pelton), Bobbie Laing (dec.), Shannon Leitrim. Author poetry: NBC War Poems, 1945, Great Lakes Chanteys, 1948-56; author books: Soo Canal, 1954, 68, Young Mr. Big, 1955, Hiawatha and America's Mightiest Mile, 1955; ed.: The Adventure of Captain McCargo, 1956, Straits of Mackinac, 1957, The Blue Snow, 1958, Tiny Tim Pine, 1958, Adventures of Paul Bunyan and Babe, 1958, The Long Crossing, 1959, Highways Over Broad Waters, 1959, Great Lakes Shipwrecks & Survivals, Carl D. Bradley Book, 1960, Daniel J. Morrell book, 1969, Conflicts Within Counseling and Guidance, 1964; co-author: Theories of Counseling, 1965, 72, School Counseling: View from Within, American Schl. Cslrs. Assoc.'s First Yearbook, 1967, Great Lakes History: Steamer Edmund Fitzgerald Ed.: Great Lakes Shipwrecks & Survivals, 1977; contrbr. to Curtis Pub. Co., other mags., 1946—; Great Lakes Reader, 1966, 78, Encyc. Americana, 1968—. Student U. Detroit, 1931, 33; AB, U. Tenn., Chattanooga, 1935; MA, Mich. State U., 1961, PhD, 1963. Continuity dir., producer NBC, Denver, 1937-40, pioneered news dept. 1939, supr., 1940-42; mng. news ed. Western div., supr. commentators and war corrs., PTO, 1942-45, news ed., scriptwriter, 1945; staff mem. NDEA Counseling and Guidance Inst. of Mich. State U., 1962; sr. extension lectr. Mich. State U., 1962—; vis. lectr. Fla. State U., 1965, U. Wis., 1966, 68, U. Miami, 1967; fdr. The Dockside Press, 1953; mem.-at-large Adv. Council Naval Affairs, 1957—; cons. Smithsonian Instn., tech. devel. Great Lakes craft, 1959—. Named Chief Ottawa tribe, Opwananiian Kanotong, Interpreter of Dreams, 1957; recipient Distinguished Alumni award U. Tenn., 1963, Dean Jr. Coll., 1966. Office: Dockside Press 1 Shipyard Row Charlevoix MI 49720

RATKOVIC, MARGARET JEANNE, (Gigi Ratkovic), b. Newark, Feb. 10, 1960; d. Cameron and Margaret Emily (Kroll) R. Contrbr. poems to anthols. B.A. in English, Seton Hall U., 1982. Proofreader Burrelle's Press Clipping

Service, Livingston, NJ, 1983-85; lrk. Controller Prudential Insurance Co., Florham Park, NJ, 1985-86. Recipient cert. of Merit for poem Nashville Newsletter, 1979. Mem. Am. Film Inst., Natl. Assn. of Unknown Players Home: 12 Manor Rd Livingston NJ 07039

RATNER, ROCHELLE, b. Atlantic City, NJ, Dec. 2, 1948; d. Herman and Esther (Tischler) Ratner. Author: A Birthday of Waters, 1971, Variations on a Theme in Blue, 1971, False Trees, 1973, Paul Colinet: Selected Prose Poems, 1976, The Mysteries, 1976, Pirate's Song, 1976, The Tighrope Walker, 1977, Quarry, 1978, Combing the Waves, 1980, Sea Sir in a Grave Ground Hog Turns Toward, 1980, Hide & Seek, 1980, Practicing to Be a Woman, 1982, Trying to Understand What It Means to Be a Feminist, 1984, Bobby's Girl, 1986. Poetry columnist Soho Weekly News, NYC, 1976-82; exec. ed. Am. Book Rvw, NYC, 1977—; ed. Hand Book, NYC, 1978-82; small press columnist Library Jnl., NYC, 1985; editor NUKUG newsletter, NYC, 1985—. Mem. PEN. Address: 314 E 78 St New York NY 10021

RATTEE, MICHAEL DENNIS, b. Holyoke, MA, Feb. 27, 1953, s. Arnold Lawrence and Helen Gertrude (Rogers) R.; m. Daphne Herwig, Aug. 25, 1971 (div. 1973); 1 child, Kiev; m. 2d, Hannelore Helga Quander, Sept. 4, 1977. Author: Mentioning Dreams (poetry), 1985, Calling Yourself Home (poetry), 1986; ed.: Prickly Pear poetry jnl.; contrbr. poetry to Blue Unicorn, Cut Bank, Negative Capability, other lit. mags. Student U. Vt., 1975-76. Co-dir. Mosaic Reading Series, Tucson, Ariz., 1979—. Home: 2833 E Kaibab Vista Tucson AZ 85713

RATZLAFF, KEITH ALAN, b. Henderson, NV, July 29, 1953; s. D.P. and Marie R. (Friesen) R.; m. Treva Reimer, Sept. 6, 1975. Author chapbooks: Out Here, 1984, 4x4, 1983. BA, Bethel Coll., 1976, MFA, Ind. U., 1983. Assoc. instr. Ind. Univ., Bloomington, 1980-83; asst. prof. Quincy Coll., Ill., 1984; instr. Central Coll., Pella, Iowa, 1984—. Mem. MLA, AWP. Address: 907 Washington Pella IA 50219

RAUCH, IRMENGARD, b. Dayton, OH, Apr. 17, 1933; d. Konrad and Elsa (Knott) Rauch; m. Gerald F. Carr, June 12, 1965; children—Christopher, Gregory. Author: The Old High German Diphthongization: A Description of a Phonemic Change, 1967; ed.: (with others) Approaches in Linguistic Methodology, 1967, Spanish ed., 1974, Der Heliand, 1974, Linguistic Method: Essays in Honor of Herbert Penzl, 1979, The Signifying Animal: The Grammar of Language and Experience, 1980, Language Change, 1983; contrbr. to profl. jnls. Student Natl. U. Mex., summer 1954; BS with honors, U. Dayton, 1955; MA, Ohio State U., 1957; postgrad. (Fulbright fellow), U. Munich, W. Germany, 1957-58; PhD, U. MI, 1962. Instr. German and linguistics U. WI, Madison, 1962-63, asst. prof., 1963-66; assoc. prof. German, U. Pitts., 1966-68; assoc. prof. German and linguistics U. IL, Urbana, 1968-72, prof., 1972-79, U. Calif.-Berkeley, 1979—. Research grantee U. WI, summer 1966, U. IL, 1975-79, Eastern IL U., 1976, NEH, 1978, U. CA-Berkeley, 1979—; travel grantee NSF, Linguistics Soc. Am., 1972; Guggenheim fellow, 1982-83. Mem. Linguistics Soc. Am., MLA, Am. Assn. Tchrs. German, Societas Linguistica Europaea, Intl. Linguistic Assn., AAAS, AAUP, Phonetics Assn., Semiotic Soc. Am. (pres. 1982-83). Home: 2282 Clear View Circle Benicia CA 94510

RAUTERKUS, MARK, b. Pitts., May 16, 1959; s. Leo Michael and Audrey (McElligott) R. Ed.-in-chief: Great States Swimming News mag., 1982—, Swimming News Mag., 1986 Wrkg. on data transfer on computers for swimming. B.S. in Jnlsm., Ohio U., 1982; postgrad. Baylor U., 1983. head swim coach Peoria Area Water Wizards, IL, 1983-86, New Trier Swim Club, Winnetka, IL, 1986-87. Tchr. water safety Am. Red Cross 1976—. Recipient Spirit award Ill. Swimming Championships, 1985, 86; named Coach of Yr., Lincolnland Swim Conf., IL, 1984. Mem. Am. Swim Coaches Assn. (bd. sec. local chpt.), U.S. Swimming. Office: Box 99 Winnetka IL 60093

RAUTH, RUTH BINKLEY, b. Chgo., Dec. 1, 1929; d. John Herman and Mildred G. (Forsyth) Krueger; m. Robert L. Binkley, Dec. 22, 1951 (div); children—Steven J., Dale R., Keith M.; m. 2d, James W. Rauth, Apr. 28, 1984. Author: Promises in the Wind (poetry), 1981; contrbr. poetry: Bardic Echoes, Spindrift, Dream Shop, numerous other publs.; contrbr. feature articles: Christian Home, Good Living, Mature Years, others. Wrkg. on poetry book, mystery novel. B.A., U. Mo., 1951. Advt. sales rep. Milford (Ohio) Advertiser, 1975-76, advt. mgr., 1976-78; advt. mgr. Terrace Park (Ohio) Village Views, 1978-87; workshop coordinator Bethesda Scarlet Oaks, Cin., 1983-87. Mem. Ohio Poetry Assn. (v.p., winner competitions), Greater Cin. Wrtrs.' League (pres.), Verse Wrtrs.' Guild Ohio, Eastern Hills Book Club. Home: 414 Western Ave Terrace Park OH 45174

RAUZIN, ERICA MEYER, b. Atlanta, June 29, 1949, d. Sylvan Hugh and Anne (Heineman) Meyer; m. Alan Howard Rauzin, Apr. 22, 1979; 1 child, Dara Heineman. BA, U. N.C., 1971; MA, Columbia U. Schl. Jnlsm., 1972. Reporter St. Petersburg (Fla.) Times, 1972-74, Coral Gables (Fla.) Times Guide, 1975-76; ptnr. Hunt-Meyer Public Relations, Miami, Fla., 1978-81; v.p. editorial Meyer Publs., Miami, 1981—; ed. Miami-South Fla. mag., 1981—, ed. South Fla. Home & Garden Mag., 1984—. Recipient Herbert Bayard Swope News Writing award, 1976; Gavel Award Cert. of Merit, 1977. Mem. Women in Communications. Home: 1030 14th St Miami Beach FL 33139

RAVENEL, SHANNON, b. Charleston, SC, Aug. 13, 1938; d. Elias Prioleau and Harriett Shannon (Steedman) R.; m. Dale Purves, MD, May 25, 1968; children—Sara Blake, Harriett. V.P. & Sr. Ed. Algonquin Books, Chapel Hill, NC, 1982—. Annual ed. Best Amer. Short Stories, vols. 63-71, 1978—, in conjunction with Guest Eds.: Theodore Solotaroff, Joyce Carol Oates, Stanley Elkin, Hortense Calisher, John Gardner, Anne Tyler, John Updike, Gail Godwin, Raymond Carver, Ann Beattie. BA in Eng. Lit., Hollins Coll., 1960., Advt. writer Holt, Rinehart & Winston, NYC,1960-61; editorial secy. Houghton Mifflin Co., Boston, 1961-64, editorial reader, 1964-66, ed. trade books, 1966-71. Bd. mem. Univ. City Pub. Lib. (MO), 1985—, Wash. Univ. Lib., Bookmark Soc., St. Louis, 1985—. Mem. PEN. Office: Box 2225 Chapel Hill NC 27515

RAWE, FRANCIS ANTHONY, b. Lexington, KY, Mar. 28, 1941; s. William Thurber and Roseann (Clancy) R.; m. Lula May Zopp, Sept. 26, 1961; children—Ellen, Anthony. Author: St. Michaels (non-fiction), 1985, Irish Short Stories, 1986; contrbr.: Persimmon Hill, Denver Catholic Register. Wrkg. on modern western novel. AA, El Paso Coll. Cattleman, Rawe Cattle Co., Calhan, Colo., 1979—. Home: 27195 W Ramah Rd Calhan CO 80808

RAWLINS, SUSAN ELIZABETH, b. Chico, CA, Nov. 16, 1941; d. Jack Leo and Elizabeth (Oser) Rawlins; m. Stanley Ira Kramer, Aug. 14, 1983. Contrbr. poems, articles to lit. mags., anthols. Editor: The Lover Within (J. B. Henderson), A Western Portal of Culture (Mark A. Wardrip). BA, U. Calif.-Berkeley; MA, San Francisco State U. Tchr. Richmond Pub. Schls., Calif., 1964-84. Home: 1517 Ada St Berkeley CA 94703

RAWSON, ELEANOR S., m. Kennett Longley Rawson; children—Linda, Kennett Longley. V.p., exec. ed. David McKay Co.; exec. v.p. Rawson, Wade Publishers, Inc.; exec. v.p. Rawson Assocs. div. Scribner Book Cos.; v.p. Scribner Book Cos.; tchg. staff Columbia U., 1956-57; lectr. NYU, New Schl., NYC. Former editorial staff, writer Am. Mag.; free-lance writer for radio, mags., nwsprs.; fiction ed. Collier's Mag. Mem. Women's Natl. Book Assn., PEN, Overseas Press Club Am., Women's Forum, Women in Media. Home: 23 Brewster Ln Setauket NY 11733

RAY, BOBBI, see Madri, Alberta Marie

RAY, DAVID EUGENE, b. Sapulpa, OK, May 20, 1932; s. Dowell Adolphus and Catherine (Jennings) R.; m. Suzanne Judy Morrish, Feb. 21, 1970; children: Winifred, Wesley, Samuel, Sapphina. Author: X-Rays, 1965, Dragging the Main, 1968, A Hill in Oklahoma, 1972, Gathering Firewood, 1974; poems inspired by the Ghazals of Ghalib: Enough of Flying, 1977; The Mulberries of Mingo, 1978, The Tramp's Cup, 1978 (William Carlos Williams award Poetry Soc. Am.), The Touched Life: New Poems and Selected, 1982, Not Far From the River, 1983, On Wednesday I Cleaned Out My Wallet, 1985, Elysium in the Halls of Hell, 1986, New Zealand, 1987; editor: Chgo. Rvw, 1956-57, The Chgo. Rvw Anthology, 1959, Epoch, 1960-64; From the Hungarian Revolution, 1966, New Letters, 1971—, (with Robert Farnsworth) Richard Wright: Impressions and Perspectives, 1973, (with Jack Salzman) A Jack Conroy Reader, 1979, (with Judy Ray) New Asian Writing, 1979, From A to Z: 200 Contemporary American Poets, 1981, (with Amritjit Singh) India: An Anthology of Contemporary Writing, 1982, (with Judy Ray) New Letters Readers I and II, 1984. BA, U. Chgo., 1952, MA, 1957. Instr. Cornell U., Ithaca, N.Y., 1960-64; instr. Reed Coll., Portland, Oreg., 1964-66; lectr. U. Iowa, Iowa City, 1969-70; assoc. prof. Bowling Green (Ohio) State U., 1970-71; prof. English U. Mo.-Kansas City, 1971—; vis. prof. English Syracuse (N.Y.) U., 1978-79, U. Rajasthan, India 1981-82, U. of Otago, Dunedin, New Zealand, 1987. Recipient Young Writers award New Republic, 1958; William Carlos Williams award, 1979; Woursell Found., U. Vienna (Austria) fellow 1966-71; NEA fellow in creative writing, 1983; winner Sotheby's Arvon Internat. Poetry Contest, 1983; recipient N.T. Veatch award for disting. research and creative activity U. Mo.-Kansas City, 1982, PEN Syndicated Fiction Project award, 1983, 84, 85, 86; Thorpe Menn award, 1983. Mem. PEN, AAUP, PSA; elected mem. CCLM Grants Com., 1975, 79. Home: 5517 Crestwood Dr Kansas City MO 64110

RAY, SHIRLEY G., b. Oklahoma City, Sept. 24, 1934; d. Roy A. and Ethyl (Northcutt) Gaumer; m. James C. Ray, Oct. 24, 1951; children—Cynthia Ray-Shipp, Kenneth S. Ray, Karen Ray-

Mason. Ed./contrbr. Wine Country Mag., 1981—. BA, UC-Berkeley, 1972. Organic farmer, Shirley Farms, Clayton, CA, 1974-82; photog. ed., Wine Country Mag., Benicia, CA, 1981-83, mng. ed., 1983, ed., 1983—. Home: Box 451 Clayton CA 94517

RAY, SUZANNE JUDY, b. Petworth, Sussex, Eng., Aug. 20, 1939 (arrived USA 1969), d. Wilfrid Tom Huxtable and Doris Ella (Bird) Morrish; m. David Eugene Ray, Feb. 21, 1970; 1 child, Sapphina. Author: (poems) Pebble Rings, 1980; co-ed. (with David Ray) New Asian Writing, 1979; contrbr. poems, stories to anthols and mags. Secy. to registrar Kakerere U., Kampala, Uganda, 1961-64; secy. Transition mag., Kampala, 1965-67; assoc. ed. New Letters mag., Kansas City, Mo., 1971-85; radio producer New Letters on the Air, U. Mo.-Kansas City, 1977-78, 82—. Recipient award World Order Narrative Poets. Mem. PSA. Home: 5517 Crestwood Dr Kansas City MO 64110

RAYMOND, ILENE HELEN, b. Phila., Oct. 13, 1954; d. Aaron and Emma (Nathans) Raymond; m. Jefferey Scott Rush, Aug. 14, 1983; 1 son, Alexander Matthew. Contrbr. stories Phoebe, Mademoiselle, Playgirl, O.Henry Prize Stories, 1985 (O.Henry prize, Doubleday, 1985), Editor's Choice: Best Am. Stories. AB, Brandeis U., 1976; MFA, U. Iowa Writers Workshop, 1983. Pub. relations dept. Blue Cross & Blue Shield, Washington, DC, 1976-78; editor BNA, Washington, 1978-81; instr. Penn. State Univ., Univ. Park, Pa., 1983—. Mem. AWP. Address: 167 Hillview Ave State College PA 16801

RAYMOND, JAMES C., b. New Orleans, July 2, 1940; s. Lucien H. and Ethel (Bordeaux) R.; m. Ginny T. Raymond, Nov. 23, 1968; children: Jeanne-Marie, Leslie. Author: Writing (Is an Unnatural Act), 1980; Clear Understandings: A Guide to Legal Writing (with Ronald L. Goldfarb), 1983; ed. Literacy as a Human Problem, 1982; James B. McMillan: Essays in Linguistics . . . (with I. Willis Russell), 1977; contrbr. Classical Rhetoric and Modern Discourse, 1985. AB, Spring Hill Coll., 1965; PhD, U. Tex., 1973. Prof. English Univ. Ala., Tuscaloosa, 1973—; editor College English, 1985—. Mem. NCTE, MLA, CCCC. Address: 1220 Queen City Ave Tuscaloosa AL 35401

RAYMOND, MARK WESLEY, b. Modesto, CA, Oct. 12, 1950, s. Fern Eldridge Raymond and Ruth Corrine (Newey) Sesser. Contrbr. to Mendocino Grapevine, Soldier Mag., others. News ed. Clarion, Rohnert Park, Calif., 1969-71; ed. Reveille, Cloverdale, Calif., 1971-72; city ed. Ukiah (Calif.) Daily Jnl, 1977-78, mng. ed., 1978-79; asst. ed. Pointer View, U.S. Mil. Acad., West Point, N.Y., 1984-87. Served with U.S. Army, 1983-87. Home: 925 Brommer St Santa Cruz CA 95062

RAYMOND, MONICA E., b. NYC, Feb. 9, 1949, d. Boris Mark and Dorothy Ann (Silk) Raymond. Contrbr. poetry, prose to Village Voice, Heresies, Sinister Wisdom, Tendril, other publs. BA, U. Chgo., 1968; MA, Columbia U., 1972. Tchr. writing Lehman Coll., NYC,1973-76, Bentley Coll., Waltham, Mass., 1982-84, Harvard U., Cambridge, Mass., 1985—. Recipient Writing award BOM Club, 1968, Mass. Arts lottery grant, 1986, poetry res., Boston MBTA Artstops program, 1986, resident Cummington Community of Arts, 1984. Mem. P&W, PSA. Home: 53 Kelly Rd Cambridge MA 02139

RAYMOND, (MYRTLE) ROBY, b. Alfred, ND, May 4, 1920; d. John J. Klundt and Myrtle Robison; m. Robert A. Knight, Apr. 14, 1945 (div.); children—William Atherton, Richard Robison, James Everett; m. Harry C. Raymond, June 23, 1962. Contrbr. articles to newspapers, alumni and popular mags. including Conn. Mag., World Tennis; author med. pamphlets, brochures, financial reports. B.S. in Jnlsm., Northwestern U., 1945; M.S. in Communication, Fairfield U., 1975. Dir. pubs. Yale-New Haven Hosp./Med. Center, CT, 1962-75; adj. prof., public relations cons. U. New Haven, West Haven, CT, 1975-77; dir. communication/public affairs Armstrong Rubber Co., New Haven, 1977-87; owner Raymond Enterprises, exec. speech wrtg. bureau. Mem. PRSA (v.p. South Central Conn. chpt.), IABC (Merit award for spl. pub./speech 1982. Address: Box 8867 New Haven CT 06532

RAZ, HILDA, b. Rochester, NY, May 4, 1938; d. Franklyn Emmanuel and Dolly (Horwich) Raz; m. Frederick Martin Link, June 9, 1957 (div. 1969); children—John Franklin and Sarah; m. 2d, Dale Marion Nordyke, Oct. 4, 1980. Contrbr. poems and criticism to North Am. Rvw, The Pa. Rvw, Denver Qtly, Whole Notes, All My Grandmothers Could Sing, Pebble, Nebr. Poets, Prairie Schooner; contrbr. chap. on "feminist poets" in Twentieth-Century American Poetry, 1987. BA, Boston U., 1956-60. Asst. dir. Planned Parenthood of Mass., 1960-62; edl. asst. Prairie Schooner, 1969-72, contrbrg. editor, 1972-75, poetry editor, 1976—, acting editor, 1980-81, 1985, ed., 1987-. Bd. dirs., Planned Parenthood League of Lincoln, Neb., 1978-83. Recipient Bread Loaf scholarship in poetry, 1985, for editors, 1974. V.p., AWP Bd. of Dir. 1987-88. Mem. AWP (dir., 1986 —), AAP. Address: 960 Cotner Blvd Lincoln NE 68510

RAZ, JO ANNE, see Hrascinski, JoAnne Victoria

READER, DENNIS JOEL, b. Santa Cruz, CA, Sept. 4, 1939, s. Dale Ray and Margaret Grace (Jacob) R.; m. Karen A. Theriot, June 13, 1964; children—Nicole, Erica, Joel. Author: Coming Back Alive, 1981; co-ed.: The vision of This Land, 1976; contrbr. short fiction and poetry to various lit mags. MA, Calif. State U., San Francisco, 1967; PhDU. Calif., San Diego, 1971. Mem. faculty Western Ill. U., Macomb, 1967-79, assoc. prof., 1976-79. Home: 2045 Green Valley Rd Watsonville CA 95076

REAKER, BETH ANN, b. Plymouth, IN, July 29, 1956; d. Dale Franklin and Phyllis Darlene (Schaal) R. Ed.: The Enquirer, Bremen, IN, 1982-83; city ed.: The Pilot-News, Plymouth, 1983-85; asst. ed.: Culver Alumnus Mag., 1985—. B.S., Ball State U., 1978. Reporter, Herald-Tribune, Batesville, IN, 1979; asst. dir. pubs. Culver Ednl. Fdn., IN, 1985—. Recipient 2d place for best news series in a daily, Hoosier State Press Assn., 1985. Home: 807 W Washington St Plymouth IN 46563

REARDON, EDWARD HYLAND, b. Medford, MA, July 20, 1942; s. Robert Francis and Margaret Mary (Hyland) R.; m. Carol Jean Guiliano, Aug. 6, 1966 (div. 1971); children—Jeanne, Connie, Barbara. Author (plays) The Blue Hotel, 1969, The Wake, 1969, Creation Script, 1970, The Morning the Oak Tree Bled, 1970, Lure of the Devil's Triangle, 1975, Dollar Scholar, 1981, that Indian Summer, 1985. Contrbr. numerous short stories to Hi-Time Pubs. A.B. in English Lit., Spring Hill Coll., 1964; M.F.A. in Theatre, Fla. State U., 1969. Staff fiction wrtr. Hi-Time Pubs., Milw., 1971-74; resource tchr. Broward Adult Edn., Fort Llauderdale, FL, 1972-77; owner, operator, actor The Competition Repertory, Fort Lauderdale, 1975-76; wrtr., program developer Instructional TV, Fort Lauderdale, 1977—. Active Fort Lauderdale Art Museum, 1987—. Recipient Best Play award Miami Playwrights Festival, 1985. Mem. Fla. Motion Picture TV Assn., DG, Fla. Freelance Wrtrs. Assn. Home: 1220 NW 9th Ave Fort Lauderdale FL 33311

REARDON, JANET MAUK, see Farrant, Elizabeth

REAVIS, CHARLES G., b. Endicott, NY, March 23, 1948, s. Charles Gillespie and Georgia Lunga Reavis; m. Jana Allen; children—Charles. Author: Home Sausage Making, 1981, rev. ed., 1987. BA, State University of NY, Binghamton, 1970. Home: 2711 Watson Blvd. Endwell NY 13760

RECK, W(ALDO) EMERSON, b. Gettysburg, OH, Dec. 28, 1903; s. Samuel Harvey and Effie Drustella (Arnett) R.; m. Hazel Winifred January, Sept. 7, 1926 (dec. Aug. 2, 1983); children—Phyllis Jean Reck Welch, Elizabeth Ann Reck Lada. Author: Public Relations, a Program for Colleges and Universities, 1946, The Changing World of College Relations, 1975, Father Can't Forget, 1982, A. Lincoln: His Last 24 Hours, 1987. Contrbr. numerous articles on Revolutionary and Civil Wars, Abraham Lincoln and hist. subjects to mags., books. Ed.: Publicity Problems, 1939, College Publicity Manual, 1948, Morning Guide, 1940. Wrkg. on articles. A.B., Wittenberg U., 1926; M.A., U. Iowa, 1946; LL.D., Midland Coll., 1949. Dir. public relations Colgate U., Hamilton, NY, 1940-48; v.p. Wittenberg U., Springfield, OH, 1948-70; free-lance hist. wrtr., 1970—. Reipient Frank Ashmore award ouncil for Advancement & Support of Edn., 1977, Wittenberg Medal of Honor, 1982. Mem. SPJ, Am. Coll. Pub. Relations Assn. (pres. 1940-41; Disting. Service award 1942, Outstanding Ahievement award 1944, 47). Home: 3148 Argonne Ln N Springfield OH 45503

RECTOR, LIAM, b. Washington, Nov. 21, 1949; m. Mary Rector; 1 dau., Virginia. Author: The Sorrow of Architecture (poems), 1984; contrbr. poetry to Paris Rvw, Shenandoah, Kayak, Partisan Rvw,other lit mags and anthologies; contrbr. criticism to Lit. Mag. Rvw, Hudson Rvw. BA, U. Md., 1974; MA, Johns Hopkins U., 1978. Dir. poetry programs Folger Shakespeare Library, Washington, 1978-80, 83; programs assoc. AAP, NYC, 1980-81; co-dir. Martha's Vineyard Poetry Workshop, Vineyard Haven, Mass., summers 1982, 83; program specialist NEA Lit. Program, Washington, 1983-85; Guggenheim fellow 1986; poetry ed. Calvert Rvw, U. Md., 1974; ed.-at-large Black Box lit. qtly on tape cassettes, 1979-80; grants panelist D.C. Commn. for Arts and Humanities, 1979. NEA fellow, 1980. Home: 3120 Abell Ave Baltimore MD 21218

REDDING, JAY SAUNDERS, b. Wilmington, DE; s. Lewis Alfred and Mary Ann (Holmes) R.; m. Esther Elizabeth James, Aug. 19, 1929; children—Conway Holmes, Lewis Alfred. Author: To Make a Poet Black, 1939, No Day of Triumph, 1942 (Mayflower award), Stranger and Alone, 1950, They Came in Chains, 1950, On Being Negro in America, 1951, (with Ivan E. Taylor) Reading for Writing (coll. textbook), 1951, An American in India, 1954, The Lonesome Road, 1958, The Negro, 1967; ed.: (with

A.P. Davis) Cavalcade, 1971; contrbr. arts., essays, rvws to nat. mags.; editorial bd. American Scholar, 1954-62, 70-73. Student, Howard Schl., Wilmington, 1912-23, Lincoln U., PA, 1923-24; PhD Brown U., 1928; AM, U. Scholar, 1932-33, D.Litt., 1963, Columbia U., 1933-34. Tchr. Morehouse Coll., Atlanta, 1929-31, Louisville Municipal Coll., 1934-36, So. U., 1936-38; prof. English Hampton Inst., 1943-66, Johnson prof. creative lit. until 1966; dir. div. research and publ. NEH, Washington, 1966-70, cons., 1970—; Ernest I. White prof. Am. studies and humane letters Cornell U., 1970-75, emeritus, 1975—; vis. prof. English Brown U., 1949-50; fellow in humanities Duke U., 1964-65; bd. fellows Brown U. Corp., 1969-81; hon. cons. Am. culture Lib. of Cong., 1973-76; exchange lectr. Dept. State, India, 1952; Am. Soc. African Culture exchange lectr., Africa, 1962; bd. dirs. Am. Council Learned Socs., 1975—, Ctr. for Advanced Studies, U. VA, 1976—. Rockefeller Fdn. fellow, 1940-41; Guggenheim fellow, 1944-45, 59-60; recipient Mayflower award N.C. Hist. Soc., 1944; cited by NY Amsterdam News for distinction, 1944, by NY Pub. Lib. for outstanding contrib. to interracial understanding, 1945, 46, by Natl. Urban League for outstanding achievement, 1949. Mem. fiction award com. Nat. Book Award, 1955, Nat. Book Com. (life mem.), Assn. for Study of Negro Life and Hist., Am. Folklore Soc., MLA. Home: 310 Winthrop Dr Ithaca NY 14850

REDDOUT, DONNA JANE, b. Tulsa, OK, Nov. 3, 1947; d. Elmer James and Loena Mae (Betremieux) Balcom; m. Terry Allen Reddout, Nov. 5, 1971 (dec. Oct. 2, 1976); 1 dau., Zara Teresa. Contrbr. articles to profl. jnls., popular mags. Ed.: Lawton Home & Lifestyle, 1980. Wrkg. on articles, book on writing. B.A., Okla. State U., 1970; M.A., U. Ark., 1973. Instr., Cameron U., Lawton, OK, 1976-79; training analyst, Telos Fed. Systems, Lawton, 1980—. Mem. Natl. Soc. Performance and Instruction, Am. Soc. Training Devel. Home: 820 NW 35 St Lawton OK 73505

REDENIUS, MARY PALMER, b. Champaign, IL, Apr. 5, 1942; d. Clark Francis and Alice Mary (McGinnis) Palmer; m. Richard Dean Redenius, Apr. 29, 1962; children: Jon Michael, Thomas Clark, Andrew Edward, Brendan Peter. Ed. Potomac Potpourri, 1970-79, Souper Salads cook-book, 1978; contrbr.: Phoebe, William and Mary Rev., Fairfax Jnl. BA, George Mason U., 1985; MA candidate, U. Colo., 1986. Mem. public relations staff Grad. Sch. Public Affairs, U. Colo., Boulder, 1986—. Home: 1731 Hawthorne Ave Boulder CO 60302

REDFORD, ROBERTA CARLY, b. Laramie, WY, Mar. 11, 1951. Contrbr. articles to mags., newspapers including Los Angeles Herald-Examiner, Grit, Great Lakes Travel & Living. Wrkg. on novel about profl. basketball. B.S. in Criminal Justice, U. Wyo. Home: 4136 S 490 East 18 Murray VT 84107

REECE, WAYNE GAIL, b. Muncie, IN, Mar. 23, 1935; s. Charles Sutton and Helena Cleota (Harbaugh) R.; m. Jo Ellen Bentley, May 19, 1973; children—Marcie Jennings, Angela Davidson, Kirsten Dodson, Kendra Gray. Author: The Christ Who Reigns Over Us, 1982, Living Through Divorce, 1987, Daily Bible Study, Mar.-May, 1988, 1988; lessons God of Creation, 1985; study guide In Search of Hope, 1979; playlet No Longer Outsiders, 1972. Contrbr. articles, study guides, bulltn. inserts to mags. Ed.: Christian Action, 1970-71, Cross-Talk, 1971-73, Adult Bible Studies, 1974-79, Self-Instruction Study Bible Series, 1977-79. Wrkg. on manuscript on relationship between sports and life/faith. B.A., DePauw U., 1957; M.Div., Southern Methodist U., 1960. Ed. United Methodist Pub. House, Nashville, 1970-79; pastor 1st United Methodist Ch., Kalamazoo, MI, 1979-85, Big Rapids, MI, 1985—. Home: 202 S Warren Big Rapids MI 49307

REED, ALISON TOUSTER, b. Nashville, Jan. 29, 1952; d. Oscar and Eva K. Touster; m. Robert Murphy, May 12, 1979; children: Julia, Jeremy. Author: The First Movement, 1974, Bid Me Welcome, 1976; contrbr. to Poem, DeKalb Lit. Arts Jnl, So. Poetry Rvw, Carolina Qtly, Colo. State Rvw, Outerbridge, others, BA, Vanderbilt U., 1971-76, MA (Merrill Moore award), 1976-77. Tchg. fellow Vanderbilt Univ., Nashville, 1976-80; tchr. Tenn. State Univ., Nashville, 1980. Recipient Ind. Univ. Fdn. prize in poetry, 1976. Mem. Phi Beta Kappa, PSA, AAP (poetry prize, 1971). Address: 5303 Lancelot Rd Brentwood TN 37027

REED, DALPHA MAE, (Georgia Folkman), b. Pekin, IL, Dec. 30, 1921; d. James McDonald and Myona B. (Folkman) Williams; m. Max W. Conn, Mar. 30, 1943 (dec. Aug. 27, 1944); m. Vern C. Reed, Sept. 14, 1947; children—Lynn Beresoff, Janise Kee, Jill Keturi. Contrbr. articles to mags. including War Cry Mag., Jr. Discoveries, Home Life, Sr. Am. News, True Romance Mag.; puzzles to Boys and Girls, Sr. Hi Challenge. Part-time student Ill. Commun. Coll., Free-lance court reporter, 1956—. Mem. NWC. Home: 100 Montrose Ave East Peoria IL 61611

REED, DAVID STUART, b. St. Petersburg, FL, Feb. 9, 1950, s. Stuart William and Nancy Fenton (Meddaugh) R. Contrbr. articles to: Esquire, Travel & Leisure, Ultra Sport, Financial Planner, Men's Fitness, Americana, Connoisseur, airline mags and other publs.; columnist (syndicated wkly), The Business Traveler, San Francisco Chronicle Features syndicate; contrbr. to Fodor's Guide to Los Angeles, 1984-85. Student, Vanderbilt U., 1967-69; BA summa cum laude, U. N.H., 1976. Features ed. Travel Agt. Mag., NYC1978-83; freelance wrtr., Los Angeles, 1983—. Mem. SATW, Hollywood Heritage, Adoptees Liberty Movement Assn., Home: 2126 Lyric Ave Los Angeles CA 90027

REED, ISHMAEL SCOTT, b. Chattanooga, Feb. 22, 1938; s. Bennie Stephen and Thelma (Coleman) R.; m. Carla Blank; children—Timothy Brett, Tennessee Maria. Author: The Freelance Pallbearers, 1967, Yellow Back Radio Broke Down, 1969, Mumbo Jumbo, 1972, The Last Days of Louisiana Red, 1974, Flight to Canada, 1976, The Terrible Twos, 1982; author poetry: Catechism of the Neo-American HooDoo Church, 1970, Conjure, 1972, Chattanooga, 1973, Secretary to the Spirits, 1978; essayist: God Made Alaska for the Indians, 1981, Shrovetide in Old New Orleans, 1978; ed.: 19 Necromancers From Now, 1970; collaborator (with Carla Blank and Suzushi Hanayagi) in multi-media Bicentennial mystery The Lost State of Franklin (winner Poetry in Pub. Places contest 1975). Dir. Reed & Cannon Co.; assoc. fellow Calhoun House, Yale U., 1983—; co-pub. Quilt Mag.; sr. lectr. U. Calif.-Berkeley; mem. usage panel Am. Heritage Dictionary; exec. producer video soap opera (Personal Problems), assoc. ed. Chmn. Berkeley Arts Commn.; adv. chmn., CCLM. Recipient award Natl. Inst. Arts and Letters, 1975, ACLU award, 1978, Michaux award, 1978; NEA writing fellow, 1974; Guggenheim fellow, 1975. Mem. AG, PEN. Address: 1610 Madrone Ln Davis CA 95616

REED, JOHN THEODORE, b. Camden, NJ, Jul. 5, 1946; s. Theodore and Marian Theresa (Simonsick) R.; m. Margaret C. Tunnell, May 31, 1975; children—Daniel, Steven, Michael. Author: Apartment Investing Check Lists, 1978, Aggressive Tax Avoidance for Real Estate Investors, annually 1981-87, Sensible Finance Techniques for Real Estate Investors, 1984, other books on real estate investment; ed., pub., Real Estate Investors' Monthly (newsletter). BS Military Science, West Point, 1968; MBA, Harvard, 1977. Mgmnt. trainee Crocker Bank (San Francisco), 1977-78; senior ed. Real Estate Investing Letter (Norwalk, CT), 1976-86; owner/ed. Reed Publishing (Danville, CA), 1981—. Mem. AG, Natl. Assn. Real Estate Editors. Home: 342 Bryan Dr Danville CA 94526

REED, JOSEPH WAYNE, JR, b. St. Petersburg, FL, May 31, 1932; s. Joseph Wayne and Gertrude (Cain) R.; m. Lillian Craig (Kit), Dec. 10, 1955; children—Joseph McKean, John Craig, Katherine Hyde. Author: English Biography in the Early Nineteenth Century, 1801-38, 1966, Faulkner's Narrative, 1973, Three American Originals: John Ford, William Faulkner, and Charles Ives, 1984; ed.: Barbara Bodichon's American Diary, 1972, (with W.S. Lewis) Horace Walpole's Family Correspondence, 1973, (with F.A. Pottle) Boswell, Laird of Auchinleck, 1977. BA, Yale U., 1954, MA, 1958, PhD1961. Research asst. Yale Lib., 1956-57; instr. English, Wesleyan U., Middletown, CT, 1960-61, asst. prof., 1961-67, assoc. prof., 1967-71, prof., 1971—, chmn. dept., 1971-73, 1975-76, 1985-86; prof. of Eng. and Am. Studies, 1986; vis. lctr. Yale U., 1974; lectr. U.S. Dept. State and USIS, Can., India, Nepal, 1974. Chmn. bd. trustees Yale Library Assocs. Home: 45 Lawn Ave Middletown CT 06457

REED, KIT, b. San Diego, d. John Rich and Lillian (Hyde) Craig; m. Joseph Reed, Dec. 10, 1955; children—McKean, John Craig, Katherine Hyde. Novelist: Mother Isn't Dead She's Only Sleeping, 1961, At War As Children, 1964, The Better Part, 1967, Armed Camps, 1970, Cry of the Daughter, 1971, Tiger Rag, 1973, Captain Grownup, 1976, The Ballad of T. Rantula, 1979, Magic Time, 1981, Fort Privilege, 1985; author short story collections: Mr. Da V. and Other Stories, 1967, The Killer Mice, 1976, Other Stories And: The Attack of the Giant Baby, 1982, The Revenge of the Senior Citizens, Plus, 1986, Catholic Girls, 1987; author: Story First, the Writer as Insider (textbook), 1982, Fat (anthology), 1974, The Bathyscaphe (radio play), 1979; contrbr. short stories to periodicals, anthologies in U.S., U.K., Japan and France. BA, Coll. Notre Dame of Md., 1954. Past reporter St. Petersburg (Fla.) Times, New Haven Register; freelance wrtr., 1959—; adjunct . prof. English, Wesleyan U., 1974—. Guggenheim fellow, 1964-65, Rockefeller fellow, Aspen Inst., 1976; grantee Abraham Woursell Fdn., 1965-70. Mem. PEN, WG. Home: 45 Lawn Ave Middletown CT 06457

REED, LILLIAN CRAIG, (Kit), b. San Diego, June 7, 1932; d. John Rich and Lillian (Hyde) Craig; m. Joseph Wayne Reed, Jr., Dec. 10, 1955; children—Joseph, John, Katherine. Author: Mother Isn't Dead, She's Only Sleeping, 1961, At War as Children, 1964, The Better Part, 1967, Mr. Da V. and Other Stories, 1967, Armed Camps, 1969, Cry of the Daughter, 1971, Tiger

Rag, 1973, Captain Grownup, 1976, The Killer Mice, 1976, The Ballad of T. Rantula, 1979, Magic Time, 1980, Other Stories and The Attack of the Giant Baby, 1981, Story First, The Writer as Insider, 1982, The Bathyscaphe, 1979 (radio play). BA in English, Coll. Notre Dame, Balt., 1954. Rprtr., St. Petersburg (Fla.) Times, 1954-55, New Haven Register, 1956-59; free-lance writer, 1959—; vis. prof. of English, Wesleyan U. (CT), 1974—; USIS lectr., India, 1974. Named New England Newspaperwoman of Year, New Eng. Women's Press Assn., 1958, 59; Guggenheim fellow, 1964-65. Mem. PEN, AG, WG (East). Address: 45 Lawn Ave Middletown CT 06457

REED, LOIS MARY, b. Rockham, SD, Dec. 14, 1919; d. Leonard Lorenzo and Coral (Bentley) Wintersteen; m. Harold Thomas Reed, May 3, 1941; children—Richard T., Russell D., Curtis L., Carla J., Harold J. Contrbr. poems, short stories, articles to numerous mags., newspapers, anthols. including Ariz. Mag., Empire Mag., The Phoenix Gazette, Farm Jnl., others. Natl. secy. Com. to Combat Huntington's Disease, NYC. 1973-79, pres. Ariz chpt., Phoenix, 1973-79. Home: 506 W Oregon Phoenix AZ 85013

REED, PAUL, b. San Diego, CA, May 28, 1956; s. Sigurd William Hustoft and Melva (Moffat) Reed. Author: Facing It, 1984, Serenity, 1987; contrbr. to San Francisco Chronicle, Bay Area Reporter. BA in History and Anthropology, Cal. State U., 1978; MA in Anthropology, U. of Cal., 1981. Editor Ten Speed Press/Celestial Arts (Berkeley, CA), 1981—. Home: Box 14793 San Francisco CA 94114

REED, REX, b. Ft. Worth, Oct. 2, 1938; s. Jimmy M. and Jewell (Smith) R. Author: Do You Sleep in the Nude?, 1968, Conversations in the Raw, 1969, Big Screen, Little Screen, 1971, People Are Crazy Here, 1974, Valentines and Vitriol, 1977, Travolta to Keaton, 1979; (novel) Personal Effects, 1986. BA, LA State U., 1960. Film critic Holiday Mag., Women's Wear Daily, 1968-71; music critic Stereo Rvw., 1968-75; film critic NY Daily News, 1971-75; syndicated columnist Chgo. Tribune-NY Daily News Syndicate, 1971—. Address: Tri-News 220 E 42d St New York NY 10017

REED, SALLY ANN, b. Dayton, OH, June 7, 1947; d. William A. Reed and Camille (Teresa) Hannan; m. R. Craig Sautter, Aug. 22, 1970. Contrbr. articles to profl. jnls, NY Times, other periodicals. Editor: Instructor Mag., 1975-80, The Selective Guide to Colleges, 1985; (newsletter) College Bound, 1986—. BA, Ind. U.-Bloomington, 1969, Tchg. Cert., 1970; postgraduate NYU, 1975. Feature wrtr. Fort Wayne Jnl Gazette, 1972-73; free-lance journalist, 1980—. Mem. Edn. Press Assn. Am. (treas., bd. dirs.; 8 awards for feature articles 1976-80), Edn. Wrtrs., Ind. Wrtrs. Chgo. Home: 7658 N Rogers Ave Chicago IL 60626

REEDER, HUBERT, b. Plainfield, NJ, Mar. 17, 1948; s. Henry M. and Algalee (Shephard) Reeder. Contrbr. to poetry anthologies. Award of Merit from World of Poetry, 1984, 85; Golden Poet Award, 1987. AS, accts., Essex County Coll. (Newark), 1976; BS, accts., Rutgers Univ., 1985. Address: Coopers & Lybrand, 80 Park Plaza Newark NJ 07102

REEDY, GEORGE EDWARD, b. East Chgo., IN, Aug. 5, 1917; s. George Edward and Mary (Mulvaney) R.; m. Lillian Greenwald, Mar. 22, 1948 (dec); children—Michael Andrew, William James. Author: Who Will Do Our Fighting for Us?, 1969, The Twilight of the Presidency, 1970, The Presidency in Flux, 1973, Lyndon B. Johnson, A Memoir, 1982, The U.S. Senate: Paralysis or Search for Consensus, 1986, The Twilight of the Presidency: Johnson to Reagan, 1987; contrbr.: numerous mags. and nwsprs. BA in Sociology, U. Chgo., 1938; DJC, Nashota Sem., 1981. Reporter, Phila. Inquirer, summer 1937; congl. corr. U.P.I., 1938-41, 46-51; staff cons. armed svcs. preparedness subcom. U.S. Senate, 1951-52, staff dir. minority policy com., 1953-54, staff dir. majority policy com., 1955-60; spl. asst. to Vice Pres. Lyndon B. Johnson, 1961-63; press sec. to Pres. Johnson, 1964-65; pres. Struthers Research and Devel. Corp., Washington, 1966-68; dir. & v.p. planning Struthers Wells Corp., NYC, 1966-68; spl. cons. to Pres. Johnson, 1968-69; writer, lectr., cons., 1969-72; Founding Fellow, The Woodrow Wilson Intl. Ctr. for scholars, 1970; dean, Nieman prof., Coll. Jnlsm Marquette U., Milw., 1972-77. Mem. Pres. Nat. Adv. Commn. Selective Service, 1966-67, Marine Sci., Engring. Resources, 1967-68. Home: 2535 N Stowell Ave Milwaukee WI 53211

REEDY, JERRY EDWARD, b. Aberdeen, SD, Feb. 4, 1936; s. Robert Emmett and Helen Mary (Issenhuth) R.; m. Susan Mary Rogers, June 22, 1968; children-Megan Marie, Erin Elizabeth, Matthew Robert-Emmett, Thomas Walter. AB, U.Notre Dame, 1958; MA, U. SD, 1961. Area ed. Red Wing (Minn.) Daily Republican Eagle, 1959-60; instr. in Engl., U. SD, 1960-61; with Better Homes & Gardens Mag., Des Moines, 1961-69; instr. in English, Drake U., Des Moines, 1966-68; ed.-in-chief, contrbg. author Odyssey Mag., Chgo., 1969-78; instr. in English, Barat Coll., Lake Forest, IL, 1976-77; freelance ed., writer & photog. for natl. mags. and metro. daily nwsprs., 1978—; travel ed. Better Homes and Gardens Brides Book, 1983-84. Mem. Soc. Am. Travel Writers, Midwest Writers. Home and Office: 3542 Pine Grove Chicago IL 60657

REEDY, PENELOPE MICHAL, b. Everett, WA, June 5, 1947 d. Ralph Warner Croner and Patricia Ann (Elzea) Leek; m. Jim Reedy, Oct. 2, 1971; children: Patricia, Katherine, James, Edward. Editor Redneck Rvw of Lit., 1975—; author article in mags., N.Y. Times Book Rvw. Grad. Lake Stevens High Schl., Wash. Ranch wife, Fairfield, Idaho, 1971—. Mem. Assn. for Humanities in Idaho, 1982-86, Western Lit Assn. Home: Rt 1 Box 1085 Fairfield ID 83327

REES, ELOISE RODKEY, b. Edmond, OK, Jan. 28, 1918; d. Earl Antone and Emma P. (Weaver) Rodkey; m. Kenneth Walter Rees, Oct. 1, 1940; children—Kenneth Rodkey, Carol Eloise, Robert W. Novelist: Gloomsday Sun, 1979, Ms. President, 1999, 1979, Once in Six Thousand Years, 1979; contrbr. articles: Home Life, Countryside mag., The Edmond Sun. Wrkg. on non-fiction, novels. BA in Drama, U. Okla., 1939, MA in Drama, 1940. Freelance wrtr., 1970—; bd. dirs. Heartland Exploration, Oklahoma City, 1979—, Rees Crosstimber Farms, Oklahoma City, 1980—; pres. Grandkids' Energy, Oklahoma City, 1987. Mem. Oklahoma City Wrtrs.' Assn., Oklahoma Romance Authors. Home: Rt 1 Box 218R Edmond OK 73034

REESE, DEBORAH DECKER, b. Milw., Aug. 12, 1950; d. Ernst and Sophia (Karolewicz) Decker; m. Clyde William Reese, Oct. 22, 1983; 1 son, Robert Ernst. Contrbr. articles, essays, photos on automobiles and automobile-related topics to mags. Wrkg. on biography of Johnny Rutherford. Student U. Wis., Milw., 1979-83. Free-lance wrtr., 1982—. Mem. NWC, Beta Phi Gamma. Home: 4858 S Hoyt St Littleton CO 80123

REESE, HARRY EUGENE, b. Fort Worth, TX, Oct. 9, 1946, s. Harry Alpha and Betty Lee (Ogletree) R.; m. Sandra Liddell Paulson, Sept. 24, 1977. Author poetry books: Unknown Friends, 1976, arplines, 1980, An Argument for Reorganizing the Calendar, 1984; contrbr. to anthology: New Work(s): 10 Contemporary Poets, 1981; contrbr. poetry to Kans. Qtly, Intro 6, Hyperion, Loon, other lit mags. BA, U. Calif. Santa Barbara, 1968, MA, 1971; MA, Brown U., 1975. Asst. Copper Beech Press, Providence, 1973-75; poet- in-schls. R.I. State Council on Arts, 1973-75; pub., ed., printer, artist Turkey Press, Cranston, R.I., Berkeley, Calif., Isla Vista, Calif., 1974—; lectr. art U. Calif., Santa Barbara, 1978—; co-founder Visible Light Gallery, Santa Barbara, 1979-80. Grantee NEA, 1976, 77, 79, 81, Calif. Arts Council, 1979-80; artist-in-residence Calif. Arts Council, 1979-80. Home: 6746 Sueno Rd Isla Vista CA 93117

REEVE, AGNESA LUFKIN, b. Waco, TX, Jan. 1, 1927; d. Philo King and Agnes (McGill) Burney; m. Marshall Perry Reeve, July 13, 1985. Author: From Hacienda to Bungalow: Houses of Northern New Mexico, 1860-1912, 1988.BA, Southern Meth. U., 1947, MA, 1967; PhD, U. N. Mex., 1983. Instr. El Centro Coll., Dallas, 1967-79, Southern Meth. U., Dallas, 1969-74, Santa Fe Community Coll., 1983-85. Free lance writer, 1975—. Bd. dir. Hist. Sante Fe Found., 1979—, chmn, 1983-85. Mem. Hist. Soc. N.Mex. Home: 30 Old Arroyo Chamisa Rd Sante Fe NM 87505

REEVE, F.D., b. Phila., 1928; m. Ellen Swift. Author: The Red Machines, 1968, Just over the Border, 1969, The Brother, 1971, White Colors, 1973 (fiction), In the Silent Stones, 1968, The Blue Cat, 1972 (verse), Nightway, 1987; ed./transl. Five Short Novels by Turgenev, 1961, Anthology of Russian Plays, 1961, 63, 75, Soviet Russian Short Stories, 1963, Contemporary Russian Drama, 1968, An Arrow in the Wall, 1987. Founding editor Poetry Rvw, 1982-84. PhD Columbia U., 1958. Prof. Wesleyan U. (Conn.), 1962—; visiting lecturer Yale U. (Conn.), 1972—. Exchange Prof. ACLS/USSR Academy of Sciences, 1961; AAIAL award in lit., 1970; award from PEN (fiction), 1985, 86. Mem. PEN, Poets House (dir.). Home: RR Box 206 Mt Holly VT 05758

REEVES, TIMOTHY SCOTT, b. Salem, OH, Oct. 4, 1953; s. Arthur Theodore and Barbara (Schmidt) R.; m. Susan Marie Hare, May 29, 1976; children—Amanda, Benjamin, Christopher. Ed., Farm & Dairy Newspaper, 1978—. BS, Ohio State U., 1976. Pub. relns. dir. Ag. Tech. Inst., Wooster, OH, 1976-77, E. Indiana PCA, Hartford City, IN, 1977-78; ed. Farm & Dairy News, Salem, OH, 1978—. Mem. Nwspr. Farm Eds. of Amer. Office: 185 E State St Box 38 Salem OH 44460

REGLIER, ANNA LEE KATHERINE, b. Pontiac, MI, Mar. 10, 1926; d. Joseph Wiley and Gertrude Anna (Bruns) Howell; m. Stanley Eugene Regier, Apr. 14, 1947; children: Lee Joseph Richard, Stephen Eugene. Reporter Alcona Herald, Harrisville, Mich., 1969-78, Alcona Rev., Lincoln, Mich., 1969-78, Bay City (Mich.) Time, 1972-79. Wrkg. on romance novels. Home: 3202 S North Lake Trail Glennie MI 48737

REGINALD, ROBERT, b. Fukuoka, Kyushu, Japan, Feb. 11, 1948, came to U.S., 1949; s. Roy Walter and Betty Jane (Kapel) Burgess; m. Mary Alice Wickizer, Oct. 15, 1976; stepchildren—Richard Albert Rogers, Mary Louise Reynnells. Author: 38 published books, esp.: Cumulative Paperback Index, 1973, Contemporary Science Fiction Authors, 1975, Things to Come, 1977, Science Fiction & Fantasy Literature, 1979 (Suppl., 1988), Tempest in a Teapot, 1983, Lords Temporal & Lords Spiritual, 1985, Futurevisions, 1985; ed. 6 reprint series, 2 jourmnals, 1 newsletter, 15 monographic series.AB with honors, Gonzaga U., Spokane, Wash., 1969; MS in Library Sci., U. Southern Calif., 1970. Prof., librarian Calif. State U., San Bernardino, 1970—; ed. Newcastle Pub. Co., North Hollywood, Calif., 1971—; pub., ed. The Borgo Press, San Bernardino, 1975—. Mem. SFWA, Sci. Fiction Research Assn., Pubs. Mkgt. Assn., NEA., Ca. Faculty Assn. Home: Box 2845 San Bernardino CA 92406

REGISTER, VICTORIA SMITH, b. Miami, Nov. 27, 1944, 1944; d. Harry Lee and Frankie (Hutchins) Smith; m. George Robert Register, III, Sept. 14, 1966 (div. Feb. 28, 1982); children—George Robert, Harry Rhett. Author: Study Skills Guide, 1984. Contrbr. articles to Episcopal Quarterly, Glamour, Fla. Alligator, Family Therapist, Networker. Ed.: What Can I Do to Help the Environment, 1972. B.A. in English, U. Fla., 1965, M.A. in English, 1982. Tchr. English, Columnbia County schs., Lake City, FL, 1966-68; adj. instr. U. Fla., Gainesville, 1972-73; asst. dir. admissions Episcopal High Sch., Jacksonville, FL, 1973—. Mem. Intl. Reading Assn. Home: 1044 Cherry St Jacksonville FL 32205

REGNIER, STEPHEN JOSEPH, b. Kankakee, IL, Apr. 26, 1950; s. Russell Joseph and Rose Marie (LeBeau) R.; n. Deborah Ann Balek, Dec. 29, 1973; children—Kimberley Marie, Lindsay Sharon. Author: Writing for Publication in Rehabilitation, 1980, Portraying Persons with Disabilities in Print, 1981. Contrbr. to Galaudet Encyc. of Deaf People and Deafness, 1987. Ed.: Rehabilitation: 25 Years of Concepts, Principles, Perspectives, 1985, Handbook on Stuttering (Oliver Bloodstein), 1987. B.A., Northern Ill. U., 1972. Info. specialist Natl. Easter Seal Soc., Chgo., 1976, assoc. ed., wrtr., 1976-78, ed. Rehabilitation Lit., 1978-86, freelance wrtr., 1982—, editorial specialist, 1987—. Mem. AMWA, ASME. Home: 2308 Central Rd Rolling Meadows IL 60008

REGOR, SIWEL, see Lewis, Roger

REHBOCK, NANCY E., b. NYC, Mar. 21, 1959, d. Gerhard Bruno and Mary Catherine (Watson) Rehbock. Editor: All Across America People are Dying to be Happy and Gay, 1986. BS, Iona Coll., New Rochelle, N.Y., 1982; MA, NYU, 1987. Ed. Blood Moon Press, Ridgewood, N.Y., 1984—. Home: 60-25 67th Ave Ridgewood NY 11385

REHNS, MARSHA LEE, (Faith Lieber), b. Balt., Dec. 23, 1946; d. Fred and Ruth (Lieber) R.; m. Walter Richard Arnheim, Sept. 5, 1971; children—Ethan Robert, Phillip Milton. Ed.: Surgical Advances, 1969-71, Mims Mag., 1975-76, Human Nature Mag., 1977-79, Odyssey Mag., 1979-80, Childbirth Educator Mag., 1981—, Childbirth '84, '85, '86; contrbr. to: Sci. Digest, Weight Watchers, Prime Time, Sci.'80, 1979-81. BS, U. Pitts., 1967; M.Phil., Yale, 1969. Ed., Sci. & Med. Pub., NYC1971-75, Haymarket Pub., London, 1975-76, Human Nature Mag., NYC1977-79, Public Broadcasting Assoc., Boston, 1979-80, American Baby, Inc., NYC 1981—. Mem. NASW, ASME. Office: Am Baby 575 Lexington Ave New York NY 10022

REICH, HERB, b. NYC; s. Herman S. and Hattie (Davis) R.; m. Gerri Toog, Aug. 8, 1960; children—Amanda Suri, Elizabeth Jo. Ed.: Odyssey Sci. Lib. Encyc. of Engineering Signs and Symbols, 1965, Dict. of Physics and Mathematics Abbrevs., Signs and Symbols, 1965, Dict. of Eletronics Abbrevs., Signs and Symbols, 1965; contrbr.: Random House Dict. of the Eng. Lang., 1967, The Greatest Revue Sketches, 1982; TV writer, 1950-55: Broadway Open House, Milton Berle Texaco Star Theatre, All-Star Revue, Tonight Show. BA, Bklyn Coll., 1950; MA, Bklyn Coll, and Kings County Hosp., 1951; postgrad. Columbia U., 1951-54. Staff writer NBC-TV, NYC and Los Angeles, 1955-57; research coord. Inst. for Motivational Research, Croton-on-Hudson, NY, 1958-59; research dir. Scientist and Engr. Technol. Inst., NYC, 1960-64; mng. ed. SETI Pubs. Inc., NYC, 1961-64; sr. ed. Odyssey Press, NYC, 1964-65; ed. dir. Profl. and Tech. Progs. Inc., NYC, 1966-72; dir. Behavioral Sci. Book Svc., NYC, 1966-72; dir. behavioral scis. prog. Basic Books Inc., NYC, 1973-79; ed. intersci. div. John Wiley & Sons Inc., NYC, 1979—. Office: Wiley 605 Third Ave New York NY 10158

REID, BENJAMIN LAWRENCE, b. Louisville, May 3, 1918; s. Isaac Errett and Margaret (Lawrence) R.; m. Jane Coleman Davidson, July 15, 1942; children—Jane Lawrence Reid McAnulty, Colin Way. Author: Art by Subtraction: A Dissenting Opinion of Gertrude Stein, 1958, William Butler Yeats: The Lyric of Tragedy, 1961, The Man from New York: John Quinn and His Friends, 1968 (Pulitzer Prize, 1969), The Long Boy and Others: Eighteenth Century Studies, 1969, Tragic Occasions: Essays on Several Forms, 1971, The Lives of Roger Casement, 1976. AB, U. Louisville, 1943, DHL, 1970; AM, Columbia U., 1950; PhD, U. Va., 1957. Faculty Iowa State Coll., Ames, 1946-48, Smith Coll., Northampton, Mass., 1948-51, Sweet Briar (Va.) Coll., 1951-57; prof. English, Mt. Holyoke Coll., 1957—, Andrew Mellon prof. humanities, 1972—. Mem. AAUP, MLA. Home: 1 Greenwood Ln South Hadley MA 01075

REID, JANET KAY, b. Tulsa, Mar. 1, 1952; d. Roy Lee and Sybil B. (Holloway) R. BS in Advt. & Pub. Relns., OK State U., 1974; Communics. co-ord. Frito-Lay, Inc., Dallas, 1975-76; ed. The SPAN, Austin Industries, Dallas, 1976-77, First Family, InterFirst Bank, Dallas, 1977-79; dir. communics. Assn. of Oilwell Servicing Contractors, and mng. ed. Well Servicing Mag., Dallas, 1979-85, ed./pub., 1985—. Mem. IABC. Office: 6060 N Central Expy Dallas TX 75206

REID, JOYCE EDNA, b. Pensacola, FL, Sept. 14, 1941; d. Grady W. and Edna (Clark) Babb; m. Ronald L. Reid, Sept. 4, 1960; children—Melissa, Amber. Contrbr. articles to mags., newspapers including Mother Earth News, Flagstaff Woman, Ariz. Sun Times, Home Life, Vibrant Living, others. Ed., pub.; Ariz. Singles, 1987—. Student Judson Coll., 1959-60, U. Calif., 1962. Mem. Yreka City Council, CA, 1972-73, Happy Camp sch. bd., CA, 1973-74; pres. Magic Curtain Productions, Flagstaff, AZ, 1985-86. Mem. Network Singles Pubs., NWC. Home: 1911 E Ranier Loop Flagstaff AZ 86004

REID, RANDALL, b. Paso Robles, CA, Oct. 4, 1931, s. Clyde Carson Reid and Esther Lyman (Howe) Smith; m. Earline Mason, July 31, 1954 (div. 1981); children—Katharine Giovanna, Eric Reid; m. 2d, Judith Ames Whitenack, Feb. 14, 1982. Author: The Fiction of Nathanael West: No Redeemer, No Promised Land, 1967, Lost and Found, 1975; contrbr. short stories: Prize Stories 1973: The O. Henry Awards, TriQtly, Carolina Qtly, other lit mags., anthology Last Night's Stranger, 1982. BA, San Francisco State U., 1959; MA, Stanford U., 1961, PhD1966. Asst. prof. U. Chgo., 1966-69, assoc. prof., 1969-71; dir., dean Deep Springs (Calif.) Coll., 1969-75; prof. English U. Nev., Reno, 1975—; Fulbright prof. U. Alexandria, Egypt, 1981-82. Woodrow Wilson fellow, 1959-60, NDEA fellow, 1965-66, NEH fellow, 1972-73. Home: 1530 Hillside Dr Reno NV 89503

REIFLER, SAMUEL, b. Poughkeepsie, NY, Mar. 27, 1939; s. Nathan Reifler and Martha (Gold) Myers; m. Niloufer Marker, Sept. 4, 1985; 1 dau. by previous marriage, Nelly Reifler. Author: I Ching—A New Interpretation for Modern Times, 1973; Ed.: Regulation News, 1976-83, Barrytown Explorer, 1979-82, Telecommunications Alert, 1984—; contrbr.: Esquire mag., Harper's Bazaar, Stories for the Sixties, New Directions 47, others. Ed. Regulation News, Rhinebeck, NY, 1976-83, Barrytown (NY) Explorer, 1979-82, Telecommunications Alert, NYC1984—. Home: Hollow Road Clinton Corners NY 12514

REILLY, NANCY O., b. Springfield, MA, June 16, 1951, d. Edward Houston and Elizabeth Miriam (Witzenfeldt) Reilly. Author: Hoodwink (play), Everything Eats Something Crys (play), Presto Sold! (poems); performance poet-playwright: The Second Coming to No Final End, 1981, In The Range of Dangerous Intentions, 1982; presenter readings produced and funded by The Performing Garage—p&w, 1983—. BA, N.D. State U.; postgrad. U. Ariz. Asst. R. Schechner Theater, NYC, 1978-80; founding mem. Re Cher Chez Theater, NYC, 1980-82; assoc. Wooster Group Theater, NYC, 1983—; producer reading series for wrtrs. and filmmakers. Grantee P&W, 1985—; Edward Albee Wrtrs.' Colony fellow, Montauk, N.Y., summer 1985. Mem. P&W. Home: 106 Greenwich St Apt 10 New York NY 10006

REINHARDT, MADGE, b. Grand Forks, ND, Nov. 29, 1925, d. James Melvin and Cora Lee (Cook) Reinhardt; m. Rolland Russel Ritter, Sept. 9, 1951; children—Susan, Karen, Daniel. Novelist: You've Got to Ride the Subway, 1977, The Year of the Silence, 1978, The Voice of the Stranger, 1982, The Unclean Bird, 1986; contrbr. articles to Scripps-Howard syndicate, Mpls. Tribune, Christian Sci. Monitor. Wrkg. on mystery novel series. BA, U. Nebr., 1947. Advt. copywrtr. dept. stores, Mpls., 1951-53; freelance wrtr., St. Paul, 1954—. Mem. COSMEP, P&W, Women's Inst. Freedom of the Press. Home: 1803 Venus Ave St Paul MN 55112

REINMAN, JACOB J., b. Bklyn., Dec. 27, 1947; s. Leib and Yetta (Krasniansky) R.; m. Shami Rubin, June 15, 1970; children—Devora, Chaim, Berel, Shulem Mordechai. Author: Shufra Dishtara: A Study of the Theory and Philosophy of Talmudic Contractual Law, 1982; (Jewish classic) Menoras Hamaor: The Light of Contentment, 1982, Menoras Hamaor: The Three Festivals, 1982, Menoras Hamaor: Parents and Children, 1983, Menoras Hamaor: The Days of Teshuvah, 1983, Menoras Hamaor: The Minor Festivals, 1986, Menoras Hamaor: The Mitzvah of Tzedakah, 1983; (hist. fiction) The Promised

Child, 1984, The Dream, 1984, The Year of the Sword, 1985, Twilight, 1985, The Imposter, 1986, The Purple Ring, 1986, Envoy from Vienna, 1987. The Marrano Prince, 1988. Ed.: The Laws of Muletzah, 1981, The Soul Thirsts Still, 1984, The Captive Sultan, 1985, The Jew in Exile, 1986, Skullcaps 'n Switchblades, 1987, Williamsburg, 1987. B.A. in Judaic Studies, Guraryeh Inst., Ph.D. in Talmudic Law, Beth Medrash Govoha. Pub., ed. C.I.S. Communication Inc., Lakewood, NJ, 1984—. Home: 674 8th St Lakewood NJ 08701

REIS, ROBERT M., b. NYC, Oct. 27, 1960, s. Stefan and Meta (Mayer) R. BA in Journalism, NYU, 1982. Ed. Motel-Hotel Insider Newsletter, 1983—, Real Estate Insider Newsletter, 1983—, both with Atcom Publishing Co., NYC. Office: Atcom 2315 Broadway New York NY 10024

REISS, ALVIN, b. Ft. Still, Okla., Oct. 31, 1932, s. Clarence Gustave Alvin and Mabel Alma (Craig) R.; m. Audrey Anna Spencer, Sept. 1, 1951 (div. 1975); children—Belinda, Karen Reiss Wilson. Author: (plays) River Children, (produced 1984), The Smallest Giant, (various prodns.); contrbr. to Diamond Anthology, American Theatre Critics, McCall's, Mississippi Valley Rvw, others; contrbr. writer Matinee at the Bijou, PBS, 1984-85. Student So. Oreg. Coll., U. Oreg., 1950-51. Program dir. Sta. KBOY-FM, Medford, Oreg., 1966-69; news dir. Sta. KYJC, Medford, 1969-73; staff writer, film and drama critic Mail Tribune, Medford, 1969—. Recipient 1st award for TV drama Birmingham Festival Arts, 1963, 4th award, 1964; Western States Playwriting award Very Little Theater, Eugene, Oreg., 1965. Mem. Am. Theatre Critics Assn., PSA (John Masefield award 1965), AL, DG, Soc. Profl. Journalists. Home: Box 597 Jacksonville OR 97530

REISS, JAMES, b. NYCJuly 11, 1941; s. Joseph and Cecilia (Blocksberg) R.; m. Barbara Eve Klevs, June 21, 1964; children—Heather Eve, Crystal Jo. Author poems: The Breathers, 1974, Express, 1983; biography: Self-Interviews: James Dickey 1984; contrbr. poetry to numerous mags and anthols including The New Yorker, Esquire. BA, U. Chgo., 1963, MA, 1964. Visiting poet & assoc. prof. Queens College, CUNY, 1975-76; English instr. Miami (OH) U., 1965-69, asst. prof. 1969-73, assoc. prof. 1973-81, prof. 1981—. Discovery Award, 92nd St YMCA, NYC1974, NEA Fellowship, 1974, CAPS Award, NY St. Council on the Arts, 1975, 78, Big Apple Poetry Award, 1976, Individual Artist Grant, Ohio Arts Council, 1980, 81, N.Y. Fdn. for the Arts Poetry Fellowship, 1987. Mem. PEN, PSA, MLA. Home: 1290 Madison Ave New York NY 10128

REISS, TIMOTHY JAMES, b. Stanmore, Eng., May 14, 1942, s. James Martin and Margaret Joan (Ping) R.; came to U.S., 1964; m. Dorothy Jeano Weisinger, Aug. 13, 1966 (div.); children—Matthew James W., Suzanna Jean, Justin Timothy. Author: Toward Dramatic Illusion, 1971, Tragedy and Truth, 1980, Discourse of Modernism, 1982, Uncertainty of Analysis, 1988; ed.: (with others) Opening Up the Disciplines, 1982, Tragedy and the Tragic, 1983, Science, Language and the Perspective Mind, 1973. BA with honors, Manchester U., Eng., 1964; MA, U. Ill., 1965, PhD1968. Instr. French, U. Ill., Urbana, 1967-68; instr., asst. prof. Yale U., New Haven, 1968-73; assoc. prof., prof. comp. lit. U. Montreal, Can., 1973-84, prof. comp. lit., French, philos. Emory U., Atlanta, 1983-87; Prof. and Chmn., Comp. Lit.,NYU, 1987-. Fellow, Royal Soc. of Canada, 1983—, Am. Acad. of Lit, 1986-. Mem. MLA, Can. Assn. Comp. Lit., Intl. Comp. Lit. Assn., Can. Soc. REsearch in Semiotics. Office: Comp Lit NYU New York NY 10003

REITER, LORA K., b. Beloit, KS, Jan. 15, 1939; d. Loren J. and Lora D. Reiter. Contrbr. poems to regional jnls. BA in Psychology, Ottawa U., 1982; PhD in English, Kans. U., 1975. Grad. asst. St. Louis Univ., Mo., 1962-64; instr. Kalamazoo Coll., Mich., 1964-67; prof. English Ottawa Univ., Kans., 1969—. Recipient Rotary Internal fellowship, Danforth fellowship. Address: Box 59 Ottawa Univ Ottawa KS 66067

REITZ, MICHELLE MASTRUSERIO, b. Cin., Oct. 31, 1954; d. Michael Nicholas and Jean Elaine (Stahl) Mastruserio; m. Daniel John Reitz, Sr., May 27, 1971; children—Heather, Jennifer, Daniel, Katherine. Author: How to Succeed in a Home Business, 1986. Contrbg. ed.: Black Wizardry, 1980. Student Austin Peay State U., 1979-80, Coll. Mt. St. Joseph, 1984—. Marketing spclst. Warner Amex Cable, Cin., 1983-85; owner, mgr. Printed Pages, Cin., 1985—. Office: Box 11336 Cincinnati OH 45211

RENALDI, LUIGI, see Farley, M. Foster

RENDER, SYLVIA LYONS, b. Atlanta, June 8, 1913; d. Lewis Rudolph and Mamie Beatrice (Foster) Lyons; m. July 14, 1935 (div. 1943); 1 son—Frank Wyatt II. Author: Charles W. Chesnutt, 1980; ed.: The Short Fiction of Charles W. Chesnutt, 1974, rev. ed. 1981. BS, Tenn. State U., 1934; postgrad. U. Chgo., 1934-35; MA, Ohio State U., 1952; PhD, George Peabody Coll. for Tchrs., 1962. Instr., Fla. A&M U., Tallahassee, 1952-56, asst. prof. Eng., 1960-62, assoc. prof., 1960-62, prof., 1962-63, N.C. Central U., Durham, 1964-75; mem. adj. faculty George Peabody Coll. for Tchrs., Nashville, 1970, George Washington U., Washington, 1974-77; specialist in Afro-Am. Hist. and culture, manuscript div. Lib. of Cong., Washington, 1973-82; freelance lectr., cons. Afro-Am. Hist. and criticism, research & writer in lit., Alexandria, WA, 1983—. Address: 6429 Princeton Dr Alexandria VA 22307

RENO, SUSAN BENNEKEMPER, b. Jersey City, NJ, July 3, 1954; m. Edward Anthony Reno, July 1, 1982; children—Daniel Noland, Christine Amanda. AB, Vassar Coll., 1976. Asst. ed. Intl. Lit. Mgmt., NYC, 1977-78; freelance wrtr./ ed., 1978-84; assoc. ed. Accord, Inc., NYC, 1984-85; culture ed. The World & I, Washington, 1985—. Home: 5306 85th Ave 2B New Carrollton MD 20784

RENSBERRY, RICHARD J., b. Alpena, MI, June 13, 1952, s. Raymond Vernal and Lydia (Heath) R.; m. Kathryn Brashear, June 1, 1980. Contrbr. poetry to Touchstone Jnl, Poetry Press chapbooks and anthols, New World anthols, Wide Open Mag. of Poetry, others. AS, Alpena (Mich.) Community Coll., 1972; student Mich. State U., 1972-76. Dancer East Lansing Dance Theatre, Mich., 1974-76; minister Ch. of Scientology, Berkeley, Calif., 1980—; painter, Berkeley, 1980—. Home: 725 Talbot St Albany CA 94706

RENSHAW, CHALRES CLARK, JR., b. Chgo., Aug. 22, 1920; s. Charles Clark and Nanna Lou (Nysewander) R.; m. Elizabeth Campbell Fly, Apr. 11, 1953 (div. Jan. 1960); 1 dau.—Nina Renshaw Griscom. Contrbr. to World Book Ency. Year Book, 1963. Student Trinity Coll., Hartford, CT, 1939-41. Reporter, featr. wrtr., bk. critic Chgo. (IL) Herald-Am., 1943-46; assoc. ed. Finance Mag., Chgo., 1947; wrtr., articles ed. Amer. Wkly., NYC1948-61; sr. ed., asst. mng. ed., mng. ed. World Bk. Ency. Yr. Bk., Chgo., 1962-67; freelance wrtr., NYC1968-70; sr. ed. Natl. Wildlife Mag., Milw., 1970-72; ed. Prism, AMA, Chgo., 1972-75; ed.-in-chief socioecon. publs., AMA, Chgo., 1975-78, v.p., ed. dir. consumer bk. div., 1981-85. Home: 1360 N Lakeshore Dr Chicago IL 60610

RENWICK, GLORIA RAINEY, b. Portland, OR, Aug. 20, d. Edward Terry and Mary (Leekley) Rainey; m. Edward Shield Renwick, Oct. 20, 1962; children—Elese M., Edward R., Walter J. Author: Strictly Business, 1982, Winners, 1985. BS, UCLA, 1959; MPW, U. So. Calif.-Los Angeles, 1987. With J.C. Penney, Inc., Los Angeles, 1959-64; free-lance modeling instr., Pasadena, Calif., 1964-68; communications cons. MBA program U. So. Calif., Los Angeles, 1985—. Mem. Romance Wrtrs. Am. Home: 1500 Normandy Dr Pasadena CA 91103

REPLANSKY, NAOMI, b. NYCMay 23, 1918; d. Sol and Fannie (Ginsberg) Replansky. Author: Ring Song, 1952; poems in NY Qtly, Missouri Rvw, The Nation, Poetry, other mags; also in A Geography of Poets, Women Working, No More Masks, other anthols. BA, UCLA, 1956. Mem. PEN, PSA. Home: 146 W 76th St New York NY 10023

REPOSA, CAROL COFFEE, b. San Diego, Oct. 18, 1943, d. Horace Otha Coffee and Jane Allen (Shindler) Crow; m. Richard E. Reposa, Dec. 30, 1967 (div. Dec. 1985); children—Ruth Erica, Adam Thomas. Contrbr. poems to Descant, Passages North, Inlet, Pax, Tex. Observer, English in Tex., Romance Langs. Jnl, Trinity Rvw, Day Tonight/Night Today, Imagine, Anthology of Mag. Verse/Yearbook Am. Poetry, Am. Muse, From Hide and Horn, Sesquicentennial Anthology of Texas Poetry, Artists Alliance Revue. BA in English, U. Tex., Austin, 1965, MA in English, 1968. Instr. English, San Antonio Coll., 1970-71, 81—, Trinity U., San Antonio, 1980-81. Mem. PSA, NCTE, Conf. Coll. Tchrs. English. Home: 263 W Hermine St San Antonio TX 78212

RETTIE, JOHN GARNER, b. London, July 1, 1949; s. John Kerr and Dorothea Garner (Barker) Rettie; m. Lisa Winn, Feb. 25, 1984. Contrbr. articles to numerous mags. on auto topics in the US and Europe. Student, Leeds U., England, 1967-70. Editor, Import Motors and Parts, N. Hollywood, CA, 1982-86; W. Coast Ed., Ward's Communications, Detroit, MI, 1986—; freelance wrtr., 1973—.Mem. Guild of Motoring Writers, American Racing Press Assn., Intl. Motoring Press Assn. Home: 655 Catania Way Santa Barbara CA 93105

REUL, RICHARD PHILIP, b. Roselle, NJ, Oct. 1, 1921, s. George Philip and Gladys Evelyn (Insel) R.; m. Jean Gwendolyn Lyda, Apr. 1, 1945 (dec. 1974); children—Douglas Eric, Lawrence Kendall (dec.). Author: Conflict Orientation as a Management Technique (UCLA seminar), 1972; contrbr. tech. articles to aerospace mags. BSME, Purdue U., 1942. Various engring. positions to 1975; sr. cons. Abacus Programming, Downey, Calif., 1975-77; sr. systems engr. Martin Marietta Co., El Segundo, Calif., 1977-79, Rocketdyne, Canoga Park, Calif., 1979-87. Mem. NWC, numerous profl. engring. orgns. Home: Box 2557 Pahrumb NV 89041

REUTER, FRANK THEODORE, b. Kankakee, IL, Mar. 18, 1926; s. Frank and Evelyn Marie (Scott) Theodore; m. Kathleen Ann Pester, June 16, 1951; children—Mark, Stephen, Christopher, Ann, Katherine. Author: West Liberty State College: The First 125 Years, 1963, Catholic Influence on American Colonial Policies, 1898-1904, 1967, Trials and Triumphs: George Washington's Foreign Policy, 1983. BS, U. Ill., 1950, MA, 1959, PhD1960. Instr. West Liberty (WV) State Coll., 1960-62; asst. prof. Texas Christian U. (Fort Worth), 1962-66, assoc. prof. 1966-71, prof. history, 1971—, dean, 1970-75, chair dept. history, 1980-83. Served with USNR, 1944-46. Mem. Orgn. Am. Historians, Phi Beta Kappa, Am. Hist. Assn., Soc. Historians Early Republic, Soc. Historians Am. Fgn. Relations. Home: 3617 Winifred Dr Fort Worth TX 76133

REUTHER, DAVID LOUIS, b. Detroit, Nov. 2, 1946; s. Roy Louis and Fania (Sonkin) Reuther; m. Margaret Alexander Miller, July 21, 1973; children—Katherine Anna, Jacob Alexander. Author: Fun To Go, a Take-Along Activity Book (with Roy Doty), 1982, Save- the-Animals Activity Book, 1982, The Hidden Game of Baseball (with John Thorn and Pete Palmer), 1984; editor (with John Thorn): The Armchair Quarterback, 1982, The Armchair Aviator, 1983, The Armchair Mountaineer, 1984, The Armchair Book of Baseball, 1985, The Armchair Angler, 1986. BA, U. Mich.-Ann Arbor, 1968. Tchr. Lewis-Wadhams Schl. (Westport, NY), 1969-71; asst. dir. Children's Book Council (NYC), 1971-73; editor children's books Macmillan Publishing Co. (NYC), 1973-76; sr. ed. children's books, Four Winds Press/Scholastic (NYC), 1976-82; vp., editor-in-chief Morrow Jr. Books (NYC), 1982—; mem. Natl. Sci. Tchrs. Assn.-Children's Book Council (bd. dirs.,p 1985; treas., 1986-87) Joint Com., 1982—. Mem. AG, ALA. Home: 271 Central Park W New York NY 10024

REWALD, JOHN, b. Berlin, Germany, May 12, 1912 (arrvd. U.S., 1941, naturalized, 1947); s. Bruno and Paula (Feinstein) Rewald; m. Estelle Haimovici, 1939 (div.); 1 son, Paul; m. 2d, Alice Bellony, 1956 (div.). Author: Gauguin, 1938, Maillol, 1939, Georges Seurat, 1943, Camille Pissarro, Letters to His Son Lucien, 1943, Sculptures of E. Degas, 1944, History of Impressionism, 1946, Renoir Drawings, 1946, Pierre Bonnard, 1948, Paul Cezanne, 1948, Post-Impressionism—From Van Gogh to Gauguin, 1956, Gauguin Drawings, 1958; others. Student U. Hamburg, 1931, U. Frankfort-on-Main, 1931-32; DLettres U. Pariis, 1936. Curator pvt. collection John Hay Whitney; assoc. Museum Modern Art (NYC), 1943—; prof. dept. art U. Chgo., 1963-71; disting. prof. grad. center CUNY, 1971—. Home: 1075 Park Ave New York NY 10128

REXINE, JOHN EFSTRATIOS, b. Boston, June 6, 1929; s. Efstratios John and Athena (Glekas) Rexine; m. Elaine Lavrakas, June 16, 1957; children—John Efstratios, Jr., Athena Elisabeth, Michael Constantine. Author: Solon and His Political Theory, 1958, Religion in Plato and Cicero, 1959, rev. ed., 1968, The Educated Man (with Andreas Kazamias, Paul Nash, Henry Perkinson), 1965, A Pictorial History of Greece (with Thomas Spelios, Harry J. Psomiades), 1967, The Hellenic Spirit: Byzantine and Post Byzantine, 1981, An Explorer of the Realm of Art, Life, and Thought: A Survey of the Works of Philosopher and Theologian Constantine Cavarnos, 1985; contrbg editor: The Hellenic Chronicle, 1952—; book rvw. columnist, 1972—; mng. editor, 1959-60; assoc. editor: Greek Orthodox Theol. Rvw, 1960-67; editorial adv. bd., 1967—; asst. editor: Helios, 1976-79; assoc. editor: Diakonia, 1971—; Classical Outlook, 1977-79; book rvw. editor classics and modern Greek: The Modern Lang. Jnl, 1977-79, contrbg ed., Greek Accent, 1983—; edl. bd. mem. Jnl of Modern Hellenism, 1984—; edl. adv. bd. Holy Cross Orthodox Press, 1984—; edl. adv. bd. Classical and Modern Literature, 1985—. AB, Harvard, 1951, AM, 1953, PhD1964; Litt.D. (hon.) Hellenic Coll./Holy Cross Greek Orthodox Schl. of Theology, 1981; Lic. Theol. (hon.) Center for Traditionalist Orthodox Studies, 1986. Instr. humanities Brandeis U., 1955-57; instr. classics Colgate U., 1957-60, asst. prof. classics, 1960-64, assoc. prof., 1964-68, prof. 1968—, Charles A. Dana prof. classics, 1977—, chair dept. classics, 1964-72, 1985—; dir. div. univ. studies, 1969-72, dir. div. humanities, 1972-84, chair dept. classics, slavic and Oriental langs., 1972-73, acting chair, 1976, assoc. dean faculty, 1973-74, acting dean faculty, 1977-78; dir. Colgate-IBM Corp. Inst. Liberal Arts Program for Execs., 1969-71, 78, 79, 81-86, vis. prof. Greek and classical mythology Coll. Year in Athens, Greece, fall 1972-73; Fulbright-Hays sr. research scholar Am. Schl. Classical Studies, Athens, 1979-80; Mem. program bd. div. Christian edn. Natl. Council Chs. Christ, 1969-72; vp Inst. for Byzantine and Modern Greek Studies, 1974—; Certificate of Distinguished Svc., Inst. of Intl. Edn., 1984. Mem. Am. Philol. Assn., Medieval Acad. Am., Am. Classical League, Classical Assn. Atlantic States, Classical Assn. Empire State, Helicon Soc. (pres., 1956-57); The Hamilton Club (vice-chmn., 1985; pres., 1986). Home: RD 2 Spring St Box 78B Hamilton NY 13346

REYERSON, DENNIS ORVILLE, b. Madison, MN, June 3, 1939. Contrbr. articles to mags., newspapers including St. Cloud Daily Times, The Cath. Florester, The Nat. Future Farmer. Gags and one-liners to cartoonists and comedians, inclg. Joan Rivers. Diploma in mechanics, Lively Vo-Tec, 1981; BA, St. Cloud State U., 1983. Career counselor U.S. Navy, 1957-79; facilitator of quality circle program, State of Minn., 1984—. Home: 24625 22 Ave St Cloud MN 56301

REYES, CARLOS, b. Marshfield, MO, June 2, 1935, s. Herman Carroll King and Alice Day; m. Barbara Anne Hollingsworth, Sept. 1958 (div. 1971); children—Michael Hollingsworth King, Amy Sofia, Rachel Kathleen Reyes, Nina Heloise; m. 2d, Karen Ann Stoner, May 21, 1978. Author poetry books: The Windows, 1967, The Prisoner, 1973, The Orange Letters, 1976, The Shingle Weaver's Journal, 1980, At Doolin Quay, 1982, Nightmarks, 1986; founder, ed.: Potpourri intl. poetry mag., 1964-68, Estro, 1964, The Wine Press, 1964-68; ed.: Pleigo (Am.-Can. broadsheets), 1964-68; founder, ed., pres.: Trask House Books, Inc., 1968—; co-ed.: Hubbub (semi-annl. poetry mag.), 1982—. BA, U. Oreg., 1961; MA, ABD U. Ariz., 1965. Poet-in-residence Artists in Schls. program Contemporary Crafts, Portland, Oreg., 1981—, Oreg. Arts Fdn., Portland, 1982—, Wash. Arts Commn., Olympia, 1985—. Grantee Oreg. Arts Commn., 1982; Yaddo fellow, 1985. Home: 2754 SE 27th St Portland OR 97202

REYNOLDS, ANN, see Bly, Carol McLean

REYNOLDS, BENJAMIN JAMES, (Ben Barry), b. Bellingham, WA, Feb. 4, 1952; s. Thomas Burnett Barry and Jacqueline Ann (Harding) Reynolds. Author: (with Kendra Kopelke, William G. Durden) Writing Instruction for Verbally Talented Youth: The Johns Hopkins Model, 1984. Contrbr. articles to profl. jnls., lit. mags., newspapers. B.A., Duke U., 1974; M.A., Johns Hopkins U., 1978. Instr. Md. Wrtr.'s Council, Balt., 1980-83; instr. continuing edn. Johns Hopkins U., Balt., 1984—, sr. instr. Center for Talented Youth, 1978—. Panel mem. Md. State Arts Council, 1980-83, Mid-Atlantic States Arts Consortium, 1984. Recipient Fiction prize Black Warrior Rvw., 1978. Mem. NCTE. Home: 702 Benston Pl Baltimore MD 21210

REYNOLDS, BILLIE ILES, b. Oakland, CA, Mar. 26, 1929; d. Walter Finley and Frances O. (Blakesley) Iles; m. William Vern Reynolds, June 23, 1950 (dec. Dec. 9, 1981); children—Gil, Cindy, Wendy, Christy. Author: Planning Is the Key, 1984, Family Care Package, 1985; columnist on the arts: Emerald Empire News, 1957-58. Contrbr. articles to mags., trade jnls., newsletters. Ed., contrbr.: Natl. Sch. Bus. Report, 1971-82; ed.: Oregon Blue Book, 1970-71. Wrkg. on article, revision of Planning Is the Key. Student Ariz. State U., 1948-49, Chemeketa Commun. Coll., 1969. Asst. to exec. dir. Natl. Sch. Transportation Assn., Washington, 1967-76, exec. dir., 1976-82; exec. dir. Ariz. Landscape Contractors Assn., Scottsdale, AZ, 1984-86; representative Integrated Resources Equity Corp., Scottsdale, 1986—. Mem. Ariz. Soc. Assn. Execs. Home: Box 5766 Scottsdale AZ 85261

REYNOLDS, DAVID, see Kenyon, Bruce Guy

REYNOLDS, DENISE ANNETTE, b. San Diego, CA, June 26, 1960; d. Edward Charles and Vilma Elizabeth (Brooks) Reynolds; m. Paul S. Loya, Jr. June 26, 1979 (div. Sept., 1981). Contrbr. to Serenade Poetry Qtly, Midwest Poetry Rvw, Black Creek Rvw, Poetry Today, others. Student Utah pvt. schls. Federal Asst. St. Planning Office (S.L.C., UT), 1981-82; exec. secretary, 1982—; editor Daring Poetry Qtly, (Canton, OH), 1985—. Mem. P&W. Home: Box 203 Minerva OH 44657

REYNOLDS, JAMES A., b. Tulsa, OK, Feb. 5, 1929; s. Bruce and Anna (Williams) R.; m. Anne Prisco, May 3, 1953; children—Jan Reynolds Bodanyi, Bruce M. Reynolds. Mag. ed.: Medical Economics, 1963-80, Home, 1980-82, RN, 1983—. BA, OK A & M, 1949; MS, Syracuse U., 1954. Legislative corresp., United Press, Albany, NY, 1950-54; news ed. Congressional Qtly, Washington, 1954-55; Washington corresp. Wall Street Jnl, 1955-59; editorial staff National Geographic, Washington, 1959-63; mng. ed., Washington ed., exec. ed. Medical Economics, Oradell, NJ, 1963-80; ed. Home, Oradell, 1980-82, ed. RN, Oradell, 1983—. Served to cpl., US Army, 1951-53. Mem. NPC, NYBPE, SPJ, ASME. Home: 405 Oradell Ave Oradell NJ 07649

REYNOLDS, JOHN DANA, b. Bethesda, MD, Sept. 20, 1945, s. Dana Drummond and Lorna Woollacott (Murphy) R. Wrtr., ed. Employee Benefits Report, 1984—. BS in Econ, W.Va. U., 1967, MA, 1973; JD, Rutgers U., 1979. Dir. pension mktg. Prudential Ins. Co., Newark, 1973-81; asst. v.p. Noble, Lowndes & Becker, East Orange, N.J., 1982-85; ed. Employee Benefits Report, Warren, Gorham & Lamont, N.Y.C., 1984—; freelance employee benefits cons., South Orange, N.J., 1985—. Home: 378 Warwick Ave South Orange NJ 07079

REYNOLDS, LORRAINE PHYLLIS, (Reine Eliasen), b. Mpls., Dec. 29, 1919, d. Emil C. F. and Helen Lorraine (Grandmaitre) Eliasen; m. Roy S. Daniel, June 12, 1937 (div. 1944); 1 dau., Marlene Daniel Cruikshank; m. Aubrey M. Reynolds, Sept. 23, 1959. Author: Happy Holiday or How Not to Travel in a Luxurious Land Yacht, 1970; wrtr. fashion brochures, fashion show commentary. Student Marie Fontayne Sch. Fashion Modeling, 1941-42, writing course at Everybody's Village, Palm Springs, Calif., 1968-69, Pasadena Playhouse, 1945-46; model, showroom sales staff, mgr., stylist fashion industry, Los Angeles, 1942-55; fashion show producer Palm Springs Women's Club, Calif., 1963-71; freelance wrtr., 1969—. Office: Cruikshank 4028 Malva Terr Fremont CA 94536

REYNOLDS, (MARJORIE) MOIRA DAVISON, (Marna Moore), b. Bangor, Northern Ireland, June 22, 1915 (parents Am. citizens); d. Asa Francis and Marjorie Racy (Bolton) Davison; m. Orland Bruce Reynolds, Sept. 4, 1954; 1 son, Ronald Davison. Author: Clinical Chemistry for the Small Hospital Laboratory, 1969, Aim for a job in the Medical Laboratory, 1972, rev. ed., 1982, The Outstretched Hand/Modern Medical Discoveries, 1980, Margaret Sanger, 1981, Uncle Tom's Cabin and Mid-Nineteenth Century United States/Pen and Conscience, 1985, Nineteenth-Century American Women of Note/Thoroughfare for Freedom, 1988. B.A., Dalhousie U., 1937; M.A., Boston U., 1949, Ph.D., 1952. Head laboratory dept. Porter Hosp., Middlebury, VT, 1963-68; free-lance wrtr., 1969—. Trustee Peter White Public Library, Marquettee, MI, 1983—. Home: 225 E Michigan St Marquette MI 49855

REYNOLDS, PAMELA CHRISTINE SCHROM, b. Chgo., July 13, 1945; d. Frank Joseph Schrom and Gladys Louise (Gustafson) Volkert; m. David Robert Reynolds, Aug. 23, 1969. Contrbr. to Chgo. Daily News, Chgo. Reader. BA in Engl., U. IL-Chgo., 1967; MS in Jnlsm., Medill Schl./Northwestern U., 1974. Assoc. ed. Natl. Sporting Goods Assn., Chgo., 1974-78, The Guarantor mag., Chicago Title Ins. Co., Chgo., 1978-81; ed. PTA Today, National PTA, Chgo., 1981—. Excellence in ednl. jnlsm. award, EDPRESS, 1982, 83, 84, 85. Mem. SPJ, EDPRESS. Office: PTA 700 N Rush St Chicago IL 60611

REYNOLDS, SIDNEY RAE, b. Alliance, NE, June 27, 1956, d. Harold Edward and Dolores Jean (Bestol) James; m. Eddie Ellis Reynolds, May 24, 1975; 1 dau., Ashley Dawn. BS, Kans. State U., 1977. Asst. ed. Mich. Farmer, Harvest Publs., Lansing, 1978-79, assoc. ed., 1979-80; assoc. ed. Kansas Farmer, Harvest Publs., Topeka, 1980-82; ed. Coastal Plains Farmer Mag., SpecAg Publs., Raleigh, N.C., 1982-87, editorial dir., 1984—, exec. ed. Peanut Farmer, 1985—, exec. ed. Flue Cured Tobacco Farmer, 1987—, exec. ed. The Rice Jnl. Mem. Am. Agrl. Eds. Assn., Soc. Profl. Journalists. Home: 512 Brookfield Rd Raleigh NC 27609

RHEINHEIMER, KURT, b. Balt., Apr. 28, 1946, s. Walter Heinrich Rheinheimer and Mildred Eloise (Hurt) Elmendorf; m. Melanie Baker, Apr. 11, 1970; children—Eric Hurt, Carl Baker. Contrbr. short stories to Mich. Qtly Rvw, Redbook, Black Warrior Rvw, numerous other publs. BA, Towson State U., 1969; MA, Creighton U., 1972. Rehab. mgr. Eastern Nebr. Retardation Center, Omaha, 1971-75; dir. rehab. services Assn. Retarded Citizens, Roanoke, Va., 1976-83; ed. Roanoker Mag., Leisure Pub. Co., 1983—. Work cited in Best Am. Short Stories, 1975, 85, 86, Pushcart Prize, 1977, 82, 85; recipient Black Warrior Rvw Fiction award, 1982, Lawrence prize Mich. Qtly Rvw, 1984. Home: 1848 Blenheim Rd SW Roanoke VA 24015

RHO, LORRAINE THERESE, (Marguerite), b. Kealia, HI, d. Anthony Souza and Mary (Vierra) Craveira; m. Edward Rho. Founding ed., pub. Rocky View, 1968; ed.-in-chief Ampersand, 1971—, Maui Today, 1971—, At Wailea, 1971—, A&B Week, 1971—; contrbr. poetry numerous publs.; contrbr. articles, columns to trade and gen. interest publs. BJ, U. Mo.; continuing studies U. of Naples, Hawaii. Reporter Garden Island, Honolulu, Advertiser; wrtr., arts ed. Examiner, Independence, Mo.; wrtr. Newsday, Kingston, Jamaica; assoc. ed. Playthings, NYC; ed. Raymond Records, N.Y., reporter, feature wrtr. Rome Daily American; publs. mgr. Alexander & Baldwin, Inc., Honolulu, 1970— freelance wrtr., ed., communications cons. Wrkg. on novel, short stories, poetry, TV script, guidebook. Recipient Silver and Golden Poet awards World of Poetry, 1985, 86, numerous journalistic awards. Accredited mem. Intl. Assn. Bus. Communicators (Gold Quill award 1981). Office: Box 3440 Honolulu HI 96801

RHOADES, AMANDA, see Malott, Adele Renee

RHOADES, JACQUELINE JO, b. Chgo., Mar. 8,1941; d. James Paul and Geraldine (Maxwell) Rhoades; children—Michael Kreeger, Cynthia Kreeger. Author: (with M. McCabe) Simple Cooperation in the Classroom, 1985; (with McCabe) How to Stop fighting with Your Kids, 1985; (with McCabe) How to Say What You Mean, 1986; (with McCabe) Cooperative Meeting Management, 1986. BS in Sociology, Long Beach State U., 1969; MS in Edn., Mount St. Mary's Coll., Los Angeles, 1973. Spcl. edn. tchr., Los Angeles Unified Schl. Dist., 1970-76; resource specialist Willits Unified Schl. Dist., Calif., 1976-81; edn. specialist Spcl. Ed. Resource Network, Calif. Dept. Edn., 1981-85; adj. prof. Dominican Coll., San Rafael, Calif., 1982—; wrtr., cons. Intl. Trng. Assocs., Willits, 1985—. Recipient Merit award for outstanding service Dominican Coll., 1985. Mem. AAUW. Home: Box 1431 Willits CA 95490

RHODE, ROBERT THOMAS, b. Pine Village, IN, July 25, 1954; s. Joseph Curtis and Ida Marie (Coan) R. Author: Dealing with Censorship, 1979, Sunrust, 1985, Artemis, 1985, National Collegiate Honors Council Report, 1985. BS, Ind. U.-Bloomington, 1976, MA, 1978, PhD, 1981. Assoc. instr. Ind. U., Bloomington, 1976-81; asst. prof. English, dir. honors Northern Ky. U., Highland Heights, 1981—. Mem. Ky. Honors Roundtable (pres.), Mid-East Honors Assn. (v.p.), Natl. Collegiate Honors Council. Home: 1321 Alexandria Pike No B3 Fort Thomas KY 41075

RHODES, DAVID MARK, b. Lamar, CO, Nov. 23, 1951, s. Don Leon and Doris Nadine (Ditlow) R.; m. Jeannette Marie Griffin, Mar. 10, 1978. Author: Never Marry A Virgin, Stanly, 1972, Me in the Middle, 1972. Student Colo. State U., Ft. Collins, 1970-72. Actor Iron Springs Chateau, Manitou, Colo., 1971-72; wrtr. Apollo Pub. Co., Woodbridge, Conn., 1970-74; owner, gen. mgr. Gold Hill Cinema, Woodland Park, Colo., 1975-77; wrtr. Walt Disney Imagineering, Glendale, Calif., 1977—. Home: 1224-B S Cypress Ave Ontario CA 91761

RHODES, NORMAN LEONARD, b. Phila., Feb. 25, 1942; s. Harry and Anne R. Author: (play) Something to Eat, 1983, (catalog essay) Robert Wilson: A Theater of Dreams, 1986. Editor: (catalog) Abstraction: Abstraction, 1986. BA, Temple U., 1964; MFA, Carnegie Mellon U., 1986. Mem. DG. Home: 24 Fifth Ave New York NY 10011

RHODES, RICHARD LEE, b. Kansas City, KS, July 4, 1937; s. Arthur and Georgia Saphronia (Collier) Rhodes; m. Linda Iredell Hampton, Aug. 30, 1960 (div. 1974); children—Timothy James, Katherine Hampton; 2nd m. Mary Magdalene Evans, Nov. 26, 1976. Author: The Inland Ground, 1970, The Ungodly, 1973, The Ozarks, 1974, Holy Secrets, 1978, Looking for America, 1979, The Last Safari, 1980, Sons of Earth, 1981, The Making of the Atomic Bomb, 1987. Contrbr. articles to natl. mags. BA, Yale U., 1959. Contrbg. editor Harper's mag. (NYC), 1970-74, Playboy, 1974—. Served with USAF, 1959, 60-61. Guggenheim fellow, 1974-75; NEA fellow, 1978-79; Ford Fdn. fellow, 1981-83. Address: Janklow Assoc 598 Madison Ave New York NY 10022

RHUE, MORTON, see Strasser, Todd

RICCARDS, MICHAEL PATRICK, b. Hillside, NJ, Oct. 2, 1944; s. Patrick and Margaret M.(Finelli) R.; m. Barbara Dunlop, June 16, 1970; children—Patrick, Catherine, Abigail. Author: Reflections on American Political Thought, 1973, The Making of American Citizenry: An Introduction to Political Socialization, 1973, A Republic If You Can Keep It, 1987; verse plays: Lincoln, Devil and Daniel Webster, Robin Hood, Alexander, Ty Cobb and The Great American Past Time. BA, Rutgers U., 1966, MA, 1967, M Phil, 1969, PhD, 1970. Spcl. asst. to chancellor Dept. of Higher Edn., Trenton, N.J., 1969-70; asst. then assoc. prof. SUNY-Buffalo Coll., 1970-77; dean arts and scis. U. Mass., Boston, 1977-82; provost, Hunter Coll., 1982-83, prof., 1982-86; pres. St. John's Coll., Santa Fe, New Mexico, 1986—. Served with USNG, 1967-73. Fulbright fellow to Japan, 1973-74; Scholar Diplomat, U.S. State Dept., 1976; NEH fellow, 1976-77; Henry Huntington fellow, 1977. Office: Pres Office: St. John's Coll Santa Fe NM 87501

RICCI, NAOMI C., b. Schenectady, NY, Oct. 30, 1942; d. Dominick Ralph and Yolanda Loretta (Carboni) Ricci. Author: The American Muse—A Treasury of Lyric Poetry, P.S. My Heart Belongs to You, Ashes to Ashes, other bks. of poetry. Student pub. schls. Schenectady, NY. Insurance underwrtr. Jardine Insur. Brokers (Schenectady), 1962-65; exec. secy. General Electric Co. (Schenectady), 1965—. Home: 1631 Foster Ave Schenectady NY 12308

RICCINTO, PATRICK JOHN JR., b. Syracuse, N.Y., May 3, 1943; s. Patrick John and Carol (Zona) R.; m. Alice Faye Nunnery, Aug. 1, 1964; children—John, Mary, Elizabeth, Carol, Patrick III. Novelist: The Shepherds, 1986. Wrkg. on novels, short stories. BA in Sociology, Park Coll., 1976; MEd, Ga. State U., 1979. Served to Lt. Col., U.S. Army, 1962-87; job placement officer for disabled, Goodwill Industries, Columbus, Ga., 1987—. Home: 4026 King Arthur Pl Columbus GA 31907

RICE, CAROLYN J., b. Hammond, Ind., Dec. 31, 1952, d. Warren E. and Helen (Kruit) Rice. Contrbr. articles to Yachting, Eastern Airline Rvw, Campus USA, Mt. Sinai Med. Ctr. publs. BA, Hunter Coll., 1984. Communications specialist U.S. Navy, Newport News, Va., 1973-76; asst. v.p. Offshore Sailing Schl., NYC1977-81; dir. internal communications Mt. Sinai Med. Ctr., NYC1982—. Mem. NWC., IABC. Home: 32-50 70th St New York NY 11370

RICE, CLOVITA, b. Fayetteville, AR, July 17, 1929; d. Elmer and Mary Ola (Scotts) Powers; m. Clarence Rice, Dec. 12, 1949; children—Joe David, Robbi Ann, Vicki Lee. Author: Blow out the Sun, and Red Balloons for the Major; poems and articles in mags. and newspapers. BA, U. of Ark., 1964, MSE, 1965. Tchr., Little Rock publ. schls., 1965-76; ed., Voices Intl., Little Rock, 1969-85. Mem. PSA, Natl. Lg. of Am. Pen Women, Poets Roundtable of Ark. Home: 1115 Gillette Dr Little Rock AR 77207

RICE, DONALD LEE, b. East Greenwich, RI, Aug. 5, 1938, s. Walter Lewis and Edna Mary (Tunnicliff) R.; m. Dotti Lee Bundy, May 20, 1961; 1 son, Aaron. Author: How to Publish Your Own Magazine, 1978; ed.: The Agitator, 1972, Mammals: A Clipbook, 1979, Birds: A Clipbook, 1980, Fishes, Reptiles, and Amphibians: A Clipbook, 1981, The Friendly Stars, 1982, The New Testament: A Pictorial Archive from 19th Century Sources, 1986; playwright: The President's Coming, 1970, The Tryouts, 1973, The Situation on Earth, 1974, Software, 1980; contrbr. short stories, satires, poetry to Newsart, Unicorn, Scholia Satyrica, Vile, other periodicals. Student Urbana (Ohio) Jr. Coll., 1959-61. Tech. ed. Cooper-Bessemer, Mt. Vernon, Ohio, 1966-71; ed. Schism, Mt. Vernon, 1971-75; pres. D.L. Rice & Assocs., Mt. Vernon, 1975—. Recipient Playwright award Ohio Arts Council, 1974. Home: 1109 W Vine St Mount Vernon OH 43050

RICE, (ETHEL) ANN, b. South Bend, IN, July 3, 1933; d. Walter A. and Ethylan Maude (Worden) Rice. AB, Nazareth Coll., 1955. Editorial asst. Ave Maria mag. (Notre Dame, IN), 1955-63, asst. editor, 1963-64, Today mag. (Notre Dame), 1963-64, Scott, Foresman & Co. (Chgo.), 1964-67; editor U. Notre Dame Press, 1967—. Office: U Notre Dame Press Notre Dame IN 46556

RICE, PATRICIA ANNE, b. Walden, NY, July 23, 1949; d. Abner Hasbrouck Birch and Dorothy Anne Gillespie; m. Donald Wayne Rice, Feb. 14, 1969; children—Corinna Anne, Derek Wayne. Author: Love's First Surrender, 1984, Lady Sorceress, 1985, Moonlight Mistress, 1985, Love Betrayed, 1987. Student U. Ky.-Lexington, 1967-68; BS, Murray State U., 1979. CPA, Reed & Co., Mayfield, Ky., 1982—. Bd. dirs. Purchase Area Arts Council, Mayfield, 1985—. Mem. AAUW (state auditor 1983-84). Home: 237 N 6th St Mayfield KY 42066

RICE, STANLEY TRAVIS, JR., b. Dallas, Nov. 7, 1942; s. Stanley Travis and Margaret Nolia (Cruse) Rice; m. Anne O'Brien, Oct. 14, 1961. Author: Some Lamb, 1975, Whiteboy, 1977 (Edgar Allen Poe award Acad. Am. Poets 1977), Body of Work, 1983. BA, San Francisco State U., 1964, MA, 1965. Prof. English and creative writing San Francisco State U., 1964—; asst. dir. Poetry Center, 1964-72, chmn. dept. creative writing, 1980—. Grantee NEA, 1966; writing fellow, 1972; Recipient Joseph Henry Jackson Award, 19683. Office: 1600 Holloway St San Francisco CA 94132

RICE, WILLIAM C., b. Washington, May 4, 1955, s. Frank A. and Ann Craig (Sutton) R. Contrbr. to Chronicles of Culture (later, Chronicles), Calif. Rvw, Collegiate Microcomputer, Sierra, Michigan Rvw. other periodicals. BA, U. Va., 1975, MA, 1979. Lectr. U. Pa., Phila., 1982-84; instr. Temple U., Phila., 1984-85; dir. writing Tyler Schl. Art, Phila., 1985—. Resident fellow Va. Center for Creative Arts, Sweet Briar, 1982. Mem. AWP. Home: 805 Spring St Ann Arbor MI 48103

RICH, ADRIENNE, b. Balt., May 16, 1929; d. Arnold Rice and Helen Elizabeth (Jones); m. Alfred Conrad (dec. 1970); children—David, Paul, Jacob. Author: A Change of World, 1951, The Diamond Cutters and Other Poems, 1955, Snapshots of a Daughter-in-Law, 1963, Necessities of Life: Poems, 1962-65, 1966, Leaflets, Poems, 1965-68, Necessities of Life: Poems, 1965-68, 1969, The Will to Change, 1971, Diving into the Wreck, 1973, Poems Selected and New, 1950-74, 1975, Of Woman Born: Motherhood as Experience and Institution, 1976, 10th Anniversary Ed., 1986; The Dream of a Common Language: Poems, 1974-77, 1978, On Lies, Secrets and Silence: Selected Prose, 1966-1978, 1979, A Wild Patience Has Taken Me This Far; Poems, 1978-81, 1981, The Fact of a Doorframe: Poem, 1978-81, Your Native Land, Your Life: Poems, 1986, Blood, Bread and Poetry: Selected Prose, 1986; co-editor: Sinister Wisdom, 1980-83; contrbr. to numerous anthologies. AB, Radcliffe Coll., 1951. Tchr. workshop YM-WHA Poetry Center (NYC), 1966-67; vis. lectr. Swarthmore Coll., 1967-69; adj. prof. writing div. Columbia U., 1967-69; lectr. CCNY, 1968-70, instr., 1970-71, asst. prof. English, 1971-72, 74-75; Fannie Hurst vis. prof. creative lit. Brandeis U., 1972-73; prof. English Douglass Coll., Rutgers U., 1976—; Clark lectr. and Disting. vis. prof. Scripps Coll., 1983—; disting. vis. prof. San Jose State U. 1984-86; prof. of English and Feminist Studies, Stanford U., 1986—. Recipient Yale Series of Younger Poets award, 1951; Ridgely Torrence Meml. award PSA, 1955; Natl. Inst. Arts and Letters award poetry, 1961; Bess Hikin prize Poetry mag., 1963; Eunice Tietjens Meml. prize, 1968; Shelley Meml. award, 1971; Natl. Book award, 1974; Fund for Human Dignity award Natl. Gay Task Force, 1981., Ruth Lilly Poetry Award; Brandeis Creative Arts Commission Medal in Poetry, 1987. Address: Norton 500 5th Ave New York NY 10036

RICH, ALAN, b. Boston, June 17, 1924; s. Edward and Helen (Hirshberg) Rich. Author: Careers and Opportunities in Music, 1964, Music: Mirror of the Arts, 1969, Listeners Guides to Classical Music, Opera, Jazz, 3 vols., 1980, The Lincoln Center Story, 1984; also articles. AB, Harvard, 1945; MA, U. CA- Berkeley, 1952. Alfred Hertz Meml. Traveling fellow in music (Vienna, Austria), 1952-53; asst. music critic Boston Herald, 1944-45, NY Sun, 1947-48; contrbr. Am. Record Guide, 1947-61, Saturday Rvw, 1952-53, Mus. Am., 1955-61, Mus. Qtly, 1957-58; tchr. music U. CA (Berkeley), 1950-58; program and music dir. Pacifica Fdn., FM radio, 1953-61; asst. music critic NY Times, 1961-63; chief music critic, editor NY Herald Tribune, 1963-66; music critic, editor NY World Jnl. Tribune, 1966-67; contrbg. editor Time mag., 1967-68; music and drama critic, arts editor Calif. mag. (formerly New West), 1979-83, contrbg. editor, 1983—; genl. editor Newsweek mag., 1983—; tchr. New Schl. for Social Research, 1972-75, 77—, U. So. CA Schl. Jnlsm., 1980-82, Calif. Inst. Arts, 1982—; artist-in-res. Davis Center for the Performing Arts City U. (NY), 1975-76. Recipient Deems Taylor award ASCAP, 1970, 73, 74. Mem. Music Critics Circle NY (secy. 1961-63, chair 1963-64), NY Drama Critics Circle, Am. Theatre Critics Assn. Home: 2925 Greenfield Ave Los Angeles CA 90064

RICH, FRANK HART, b. Washington, June 2, 1949; s. Frank Hart Rich and Helene Bernice (Aaronson) Fisher; m. Gail Florence Winston, Apr. 25, 1976; 1 son—Nathaniel Howard. BA in Am. history and lit., Harvard U., 1971. Co-editor Richmond Mercury (VA), 1972-73; sr. editor, film critic New Times mag. (NYC), 1973-75; film critic NY Post, 1975-77; film and TV critic Time (NYC), 1977-80; chief drama critic NY Times, 1980—. Mem. NY Drama Critics Circle. Office: NY Times 229 W 43rd St New York NY 10036

RICH, JOHN, see Devereux, John

RICH, MARK DAVID, b. Chgo., Nov. 1, 1958; s. Charles Mark and Kikue (Kikuchi) Rich. Poetry contrbr. to Anti-War Poems II, 1985, Alternate Lives, 1986, Poly, 1986, other anthologies, Poem, Breathless Mag. Expressions, Riverside Qtly, Pandora, other lit mags; ed.: Treaders of Starlight, 1974 & 76; co-ed: The Magazine of Speculative Poetry, 1984—. BA, Beloit Coll., 1980. Theater/arts revwr. Beloit Daily News (WI), Janesville Gazette (WI); freelance wrtr./artst. Mem. Science Fiction Poetry Assn. Office: Box 564 Beloit WI 53511

RICHARD, ALICE, see Hirschel, L. Anne

RICHARD, MICHEL PAUL, b. NYC, Sept. 30, 1933; s. Paul Antoine and Virginia (Stromborg) R.; m. Peggy Jean Richard, 1987; children—Michele Lyn, Kevin George, Paul Erik, Dana Francis. BA, U. Chgo., 1951, MA, 1955; PhD, NYU, 1967. Author: Exploring Social Space, 1973, Without Passport, 1987; ed: Thoughts for All Seasons mag, 1976—; contrbr. intro to Social and Cultural Dynamics, Four Psychologies Applied to Edn. Social sci. analyst NIMH, Bethesda, Md., 1960-63; asst. prof. sociol., Converse Coll., Spartanburg, SC, 1957-58; lectr. Brklyn Coll., 1963-65; assoc. prof. Dickinson Coll., Carlisle, Pa, 1965-68, SUNY, Geneseo, 1968—. Pres., Mental Health Assn of Livingston County, NY, 1984. Address: 15 Second St Geneseo NY 14454

RICHARDS, CAROLYN BAXTER, b. Corpus Christi, TX, Dec. 29, 1926, d. Mainer Maurice and Alma Burnice (Agnew) McCrorey; m. Jay Edward Richards, Oct. 23, 1945; children—Mainer, Regina Richards Langley, Dorothy Richards Rosier. Wrkg. on romance novels. Student Del Mar Jr. Coll., 1944-45, Yuba Coll., 1961-62. Women's ed. Oroville (Calif.)-Mercury Register, 1963-70, asst. news ed., lifestyle ed., 1980-85; women's ed. Antelope Valley Press, Palmdale, Calif., 1970-80. Recipient Local Column award Calif. Newspaper Pub. Assn., 1982. Home: 3275 Orange Ave Oroville CA 95966

RICHARDS, CYNDI, see Richeson, Cena Golder

RICHARDS, ELIZABETH GLAZIER, b. NYC, Apr. 7, 1959; d. Benjamin Thomas and Cordelia (Creamer) Richards. Contrbr. stories, essays and poetry Dickinson Rvw, NER/BLQ, Radcliffe Qtly, Syracuse Poems and Stories, Oxford mag, Sequoia, Dialtone, The Harvard Advocate (contrbg. editor); wrkg. on collection of short stories: Tell Me How Things Are, and a collection of poetry. BA in Writing, Stanford U., 1980-82; MA in Writing, Syracuse U., 1982-84. Creative writing fellow Syracuse Univ., NY, 1982-83, tchg. asst., 1983-84, 85-86, instr. English, 1984-85; tech. writer Genigraphics, Liverpool, NY, 1985. Counsellor, Planned Parenthood, Syracuse, 1985-86. Mem. AWP, Signet Soc. Address: 70 E 96th St New York NY 10128

RICHARDS, JEFF, b. Washington, Oct. 11, 1944, s. Robert Kenneth Richards and Helen Elizabeth (Greene) Richards Schaub; m. Cornelia Mary Suzanne Callahan, June 18, 1976. Contrbr. poems, short stories, novel excerpts to Sand Rvw, Phoebe, G.W. Rvw, Houston Chronicle. Wrkg. on novel. BA, Denison U., 1968; MA, Hollins Coll., 1976. Continuity wrtr. WKYR radio, cumberland, Md., 1966-67; newsletter ed. R&B Assocs., Washington, 1968-70; tchr. high schls., Phila., 1971-74; prof. U. Ala., George mason U., Am. U., 1977—, George Washington U., Washington, 1985—; mem. editorial bd. Black Warrior Rvw, 1976-78. Mem. AWP, Washington Ind. Wrtrs., Glen Echo Wrtrs. Center. Home: 3631 39th St NW B314 Washington DC 20016

RICHARDS, JERROLD ALLEN, b. Helena, MT, June 1, 1949; d. Jerrold Reeves and Jean Belle (Calkins) R. Author: Nuclear War and You: Before, During, After, 1984. BA, U. Oreg., 1975. Owner, operator Aamco Transmissions, Corvallis, Oreg., 1977-81; acct. Champion Intl., Eugene, Oreg., 1975-77. Mem. ACLU, Common Cause. Office: Box 19446 Portland OR 97219

RICHARDS, MARY FALLON, b. Bliss, NY, 1920; d. Martin Leo and Lydia Belle (Merville) Fallon: m. John C. Richards, June 5, 1943; children—Barbara, James, David, Paul, Jean. Columnist Del. Today, 1978. Contrbr. articles to Ancestry Mag., Del. Today, Nat. Genealogical Soc. Quarterly, Wilmington Evening News. Co-ed.: Del. Genealogial Soc. Jnl., 1982—; ed.: Del-Gen-Data Bank, 1986. Wrkg. on Del. Genealogical material. B.S., Nazareth Coll., 1941. Profl. genealogist, 1975—. Bd. dirs. St. Michael's Day Nursery, Wilmington, DE, 1964-74, pres., 1969-74; bd. dirs. St. David's Day Nursery, Wilmington, 1975-79, pres., 1977-79. Mem. Del. Genealogical Soc. (bd. dirs.), Nat. Genealogical Soc., Nat. Genealogical Computer Group, Genealogical Soc. of Penn. Home: 3 Little Leaf Ct Wilmington DE 19810

RICHARDS, RAMONA POPE, b. Gadsden, AL, May 1, 1957; d. Jesse Ray and Jimmie Lou (Waldrop) Pope; m. Pat James Richards, Jr., May 30, 1982. Contrbr. articles to mags. including High Adventure, The Disciple, Space Grits, Autoduel Qtly. Editor: Ideals mag., 1985-87, Apex 1986—. BA, Middle Tenn. State U., 1979, MA, 1984. Library asst. Middle Tenn. State U., Murfreesboro, 1976-79, projectionist, 1976-80, tchg. asst., 1979-80; editorial sec. Abingdon Press, Nashville, 1981-85. Mem. Soc. Creative Anachronism, Middle Cumberland Archeol. Soc., Mythopoeic Soc. Home: 304 Fieldrest Dr Nashville TN 37211

RICHARDSON, BETTY JOYCE, b. Louisville, Feb. 14, 1935; d. Robert Frank and Dora (Freiberg) Ritchie; m. Robert L. Crain, 1952 (div. 1954); 1 son, Victor L.; m. Kermit T. Hoyenga, 1960 (div. 1968); m. John Atkins Richardson, 1969 (div. 1979). Author: Sexism in Higher Education, 1974, John Collier, 1983, Serving Together: A Century of Firefighting in Madison County, Ill., 1984. Contrbr. articles, rvws., rvw. essays to profl. jnls. Wrtr., soc. ed. Springfield News & Sun, OH, 1957-61; mem. editorial bds. Papers on Llang. and lit., Prairie Shooner, others. B.A., U. Louisville, 1957; M.A., U. Nebr., 1963, Ph.D., 1968. Asst. prof. to prof. Southern Ill. U., Edwardsville, 1968—. Mem. MLA, Midwest MLA, AG. Home: 20A Fox Meadow Ln Edwardsville IL 62025

RICHARDSON, JAMES, b. Bradenton, FL, Jan. 1, 1950, s. James Everette and Betty (Behrer) R.; m. Constance W. Hassett, July 15, 1978; 2 daus., Constance R. Hassett. and Catherine W. Richardson. Author: Reservations: Poems, 1977, Thomas Hardy: The Poetry of Necessity, 1977, Second Guesses: Poems, 1984, Vanishing Lives: Style & Self in Tennyson, D.G. Rossetti, Swinburne and Yeats, 1987. AB, Princeton U., 1971; MA, U. Va., 1973, PhD1975. Asst. prof. English, Harvard U., 1975-80; dir., creative wrtg. prog., Princeton U., 1980—. Fellowships: NEH, 1978, State Council on the Arts, 1985. Mem. PEN, MLA, AWP, PSA. Home: 5 Civic Center Dr 19 East Brunswick NJ 08816

RICHARDSON, JAMES ROBERT, (Jim), b. Willmar, MN, June 12, 1946; s. Robert David and Patricia Marion (Jones) R.; m. Cassie Lucille Speight, June 8, 1976; children—Rachel, Susanna Carol, James Robert. Author: Foundations for Living, 1983, Praying in the Holy Ghost, 1983. Founder, ed.: The Gospel Truth, 1973—; city ed.: Anchorage Times, 1969-76. B.A. in English, Macalester Coll., 1968. Home: 8035 Lloyd Dr Anchorage AK 99502

RICHARDSON, KEN EDGAR, b. Louisville, Aug. 25, 1952; s. Ray Laymon and Roberta Lee (Baxter) R.; m. Janice Louise Priest, Jan. 3, 1981. Author: (with Douglas & Steven Cobb) Hands on Paradox 1986. Contrbr. articles to profl. jnls. Asst. editor: The Paradox User's Jnl., 1985-86. B.A., U. of Louisville, 1977; MA in Psychology, Spalding U., 1980; MBA, Bellarmine Coll., 1984. Program coordinator Ind. Vocat.-Tech. Coll., Sellersburg, Ind., 1976-79; surgical tech., Jewish Hosp., Louisville, 1973-76, transplant coordinator, 1979-81, adminstr., 1981-84; administr. U. Louisville, 1984-85; wrtr. Cobb Group Inc., Louisville, 1985—. Mem. adv. com. Dept. Edn.-Health Occupations, Frankfort, KY., 1982, Dept. Health-High Blood Pressure Program, Louisville, 1982-83; pres. Natl. Kidney Fdn., Louisville, 1984-86; exec. dir. Ky. Donors Affiliates, Inc., 1986-; bd. dirs. Ohio Valley Renal Disease Network, Frankfort. Served with USN, 1969-73. Recipient Vol. Service award Natl. Kidney Fdn., 1982, 83, Outstanding Achievement award, 1984. Mem. Natl. Renal Administrs. Assn., Ky. Med. Group Mgmt. Assn., Louisville Bd. Realtors (assoc.), Cousteau Soc. Home: 6610 Morocco Dr Louisville KY 40214

RICHARDSON, LINDA F., b. Pocatello, ID, May 13, 1951; d. Kenneth W. and Gwen I. (Van Sickle) R. Author: (pamphlet) Chemicals—Their Benefits & Risks: A Future Imperfect, 1980. Contrbr. articles to mags. Wrkg. on Shoshone Indian hist. novel, English history novel. B.S. in Sociology, Id. State U., 1973. Home: 302 S 4th Apt A Sandpoint ID 83864

RICHARDSON, MIDGE TURK, b. Los Angeles, Mar. 26, 1930; d. Charles Aloysius and Marie Theresa (Lindekin) Turk; m. Hamilton Farrar Richardson, Feb. 8, 1974. Author: The Buried Life: A Nun's Journey, 1971, Gordon Parks; A Biography for Children, 1971; also articles. BA, Immaculate Heart Coll., 1951, MA, 1956; postgrad. U. CA, Santa Barbara, Duquesne U., U. Pitts. Mem. Immaculate Heart Community, Roman Catholic Ch., 1948-66; asst. to dean Schl. Arts (NYU), 1966-67; coll. editor Glamour mag. (NYC), 1967-74; editor-in-chief Co-Ed mag., editorial dir. Forecast and Co-Ed mags. (NYC), 1974-75; ed.-in-chief, Seventeen mag. (NYC) 1975—; lectr. Tishman seminars Hunter Coll. (NYC), 1975-77. Recipient award Outstanding Women in Pub., 1982. Mem. ASME. Office: 850 3rd Ave New York NY 10022

RICHESON, CENA GOLDER, (Velma Chamberlain, Cyndi Richards), b. Oregon City, OR, Apr. 11, 1941; d. Robert Burton and Mabel Zoa (Hainline) Golder; m. Jerry Richeson, June 3, 1961; children: Ivan, Kevin. Author: (as Velma Chamberlain) For Love's Sake, 1980; (as Cyndi Richards) Love Is Where You Find It, 1984, Go for Broke, 1988; Wild West Show (hist. articles), 1987. Contrbr. articles to consumer periodicals. AA, Diablo Valley Coll., Pleasant Hill, Calif., 1962; BA in English, Calif. State U., Hayward, 1972. Instr. Shasta Coll., Redding, Calif., 1974-76; tchr. Liberty Union High Schl., Brentwood, Calif., 1985—. Recipient prize for article Wrtr.'s Digest, 1976; 3d prize for article Williamette Wrtrs., 1976. Mem. P&W, WWA, Soc. Children's Book Wrtrs., Calif. Wrtrs. Club, Zane Grey's West Society. Address: Box 268 Knightsen CA 94548

RICHEY, BRUCE RADFORD, b. Crayne, KY, Nov. 9, 1951, s. Ish Hardin and Lillian (Wyatt) R.; div., 1 son, Jeremy Ross. Author: If I Were Lost, 1978, The New Yorker in Me, 1982, Titles of June, 1985, The Silence in My Cry, 1986. Wrkg. on poetry books. AA, Western U. Personnel dir. Rossal, Inc., Bloomington, Ind., 1982-85; prin. Richey & Assocs., Inc., Bowling Green, Ky., 1985—. Named Greenwich Poet, Greenwich Village Poets, 1980, Southern Poet, So. Poetry Soc., 1984. Mem. Am. Poetry Assn., ASCAP. Home: 720 Ridgeview Dr 1203 Frankfort KY 40601

RICHEY, RODNEY PAUL, b. Elwood, IN, Jan. 18, 1957; s. Paul Marlin and Lois Eileen (Cade) R. Contrbr. articles to Am. Classic Screen, Grub St., Muncie, IN, 1977. B.S. in English Lit., Ball State U., 1979, M.A. in English Composition, 1980. Instr. freshman English, Ball State U., 1979-83; feature wrtr., Muncie Star, 1983—; script wrtr. Media Ind., Indpls., 1986—. Recipient Achievement in Writing award NCTE, 1974, Best Feature Story award Hoosier State Press Assn., 1983, Honorable Mention for best feature Sigma Delta Chi and SPJ, 1987. Mem. SPJ. Home: 2901 W Ethel Ave Muncie IN 47304

RICHMAN, ALAN, b. Bronx, NY, Nov. 12, 1939; s. Louis and Sonia (Carity) Richman; m. Kelli Shor, June 21, 1964; children—Lincoln Seth Shor, Matthew Mackenzie Shor. Author: Czechoslovakia in Pictures, 1969, A Book on the Chair, 1968. BA, Hunter Coll., 1960. Reporter Leader-Observer (weekly newspaper) (NYC), 1960-61; asst. editor Modern Tire Dealer (publ.) (NYC)19,62-64; assoc. editor ASTA Travel News (NYC), 1964-65; pub. relations rep. M.J. Jacobs Inc. (NYC), 1965-66; mng. editor Modern Floor Coverings (NYC), 1966-68; editor Bank Systems & Equipment (NYC), 1968-79, Health Care Products News, 1976; assoc. pub. Bank Systems & Equipment, 1969-71, co-pub., 1971-73, pub., 1973-79; editorial dir. Natl. Jeweler (NYC), 1979-81; editor Health Foods Bus., editorial dir. Army/Navy Store and Outdoor Merchandiser, 1981—, The Pet Dealer, 1983—. Served with AUS, 1961-62. Recipient Jesse H. Neal certificate merit Am. Bus. Press, 1973. Mem. NY Bus. Press Editors Assn. Home: 5 Clayton Rd Morganville NJ 07751

RICHMAN, ELLIOT, (Hymen Abdul Zuma), b. Phila., Nov. 3, 1941, s. Harry and Fay (Forman) R.; m. Sara Miller, July 11, 1965; children—Stephanie, Heath. Contrbr. poetry to MAAT, Impetus, The Windless Orchard, Thunder Sandwich, The Poetry Rvw, Black Bear Rvw, Deros, Poetry Newsletter, Broken Streets, Esprit, Centennial Rvw, Bogg, Modern Haiku, Gypsy, Cicada, Abbey, Parnassus, Adirondac, Mickle Street Rvw, The Baltimore Sun, Deros, Fat Tuesday, The Poetry Newsletter, The Poetry Rvw, others; rvw in Esprit. BA, Pa. State U., 1963; MA, San Francisco State U., 1967. Advisory bd. Esprit mag. 1986—. Tchr. Clinton Community Coll., Plattsburgh, N.Y., 1976—, Maximum Security Prison, Dannemora, N.Y., 1977—. Address: 4 University Pl Plattsburgh NY 12901

RICHMAN, JORDAN PAUL, b. Bklyn., Sept. 2, 1931; s. Abraham and Dora (Goldstein) R.; m. Barbara Mencher, Dec. 25, 1954 (div. Oct. 1960); m. Vita Gittelman, June 28, 1963; 1 dau., Kitty. Columnist: The Sun Newspaper, 1980-82, Sunbelt Building Jnl., 1986. Contrbr. articles to Ariz. Bus. Gazette; Samuel discussions of aml. Johnson & Swift in Enlightenment Essays, U. of Dayton Rvw., The New Rambler. Ed.: Encyc. of Silk Screen Printing, 1986; MORE: Move on Rehab Experiene, 1987, The Aids Forum Newsletter, 1987. Wrkg. on the Mexican Wolf Recovery Program. Brooklyn College, 1955; M.A., N.Y. U., 1957; Ph.D., U. N.M., 1961. Instr. U. Colo., Boulder, 1961-62; assoc. prof. U. Bloomsburg, PA, 1963-71; part-time lectr. Ariz. State U., Tempe, 1983-84, Ottawa U., Phoenix, 1985; free-lance wrtr., 1985—. Mem. Soc. for Humanistic Judaism, Am. Philatelic Soc. Home: 1302 E Coronado Rd Phoenix AZ 85006

RICHMAN, STEVEN MARK, b. Bklyn., Jan. 12, 1955; s. David and Sheila Elaine (Raskin) R.; m. Barbara Jeanne Bishop, Nov. 20, 1983; 1 son, Justin Bradley. Contrbr. fiction to Plateau, poetry to Modern Haiku, New Jersey Living, Seton Hall Legislative Jnl, New Jersey Lawyer; part-time rptr. Hightstown Gazette, 1973-75; contrbr. to Highway Assist. Progs.: A Histl. Perspect., 1978, 1979 Annual Survey of Am. Law. BA, Drew U., 1977; JD, NYU, 1980. Private pract. law, 1980—. Mem. NJ Bar Assn., Am. Bar Assn. Home: 7 Hancock Ct East Windsor NJ 08520

RICHMOND, STEVEN ALLAN, b. Los Angeles, Jan 24, 1941; s. Abraham and Elsie R. Author: Poems, 1964, Long Dongs, 1966, Hitler Painted Roses, 1966, Earth Rose, 1971 (Wormwood award, 1974), Red Work, Black Widow, 1976, Wildseed, 1977, Lifshin & Richmond, 1977, Venice Jones, 1978, Prospects, 1983, Charlene Rubinski, 1983, Gagaku, 1985, Gagaku Avenue, 1987, Santa Monica Poems, 1987. BS, UCLA, 1962, LLB, 1965. Address: 137 Hollister Ave Santa Monica CA 90405

RICHNAK, BARBARA M., b. Schenectady, NY Sept. 18, 1936; d. Daniel S.V. and Helen A. (Kashuba) Budnick; m. Dr. Louis Richnak Aug. 31, 1957; children—Susan, Joel, Christopher. Author: A River Flows: The Life of Robert Lardin Fulton, 1984, Silver Hillside: The Life and Times of Virginia City, 1985; contrbr. articles to various publs. including San Francisco Chronicle and California Living. BA, Penn. State U., 1957. Asst. editor, The AOPA Pilot Magazine, 1958-62; reporter, Tahoe World, 1975-79. Address: Box 2237 Olympic Valley CA 95730

RICHTER, FRANK, b. Chgo., may 25, 1916, s. George J. and Elizabeth (Boehm) R.; m. Lorraine Anderson, Apr. 19, 1947 (div. 1983); children—Mary, Nora; m. 2d, Teresita Meana, Sept. 16, 1983. Ed., Northwestern U. Asst. ed. Rock Products mag., Chgo., 1938-41; assoc. ed. U.S. Corps of Engrs., Columbus, Ohio, 1941-45; cofounder, ed., pub. Modern Railroads, Chgo., 1945-70, co-founder Appliance Mfr. and Traffic Mgmt., pub. Progressive Railroading, Chgo., 1970—, both with Murphy-Richter Pub. Co. Writer on RR & transportation subjects, 1945—. Lectr. on spclzd. indstrl. and tech. jnlsm., Northwestern U. Schl. Jnlsm. Home: 1116 Greenleaf Ave Wilmette IL 60091

RICHTER, HARVENA, b. Reading, PA, Mar. 13, 1919; d. Conrad and Harvena (Achenbach) R. Author: The Human Shore, 1959, English edit., 1960, Virginia Woolf: The Inward Voyage, 1970. Editor: The Rawhide Knot & Other Stories (Conrad Richter), 1978, Writing to Survive: The Private Notebooks of Conrad Richter, 1988. Contrbr. short stories, essays, poems in mags., anthols. BA, U. N.Mex., 1938; MA, NYU, 1955, PhD, 1967. Advt. copywriter Saks Fifth Ave., NYC, 1942-43, May's 1943-46; copy chief, Elizabeth Arden, 1946-47; advt. dir. I. Miller, NYC, 1947-48; feature wrtr. various news services, 1949-53; inst. English, NYU, 1953-66; prof. English, U. N.Mex., Albuquerque, 1969—. Writing fellow, Yaddo, 1962, 63, AAUW, 1964-65; Colony fellow McDowell Assn., 1965-66; residency fellow Wurlitzer Fdn., 1968, 73, 74. Mem. AG, Rio Grande Wrtr.'s Assn. Home: 1932 Candelaria Rd NW Albuquerque NM 87107

RICKARDS, CATHERINE ISABELLA, b. nr. Laurel, DE, May 18, 1916; d. Samuel Stanford and Laura Emma (King) LeCates; m. George Harold Rickards, May 18, 1937 (dec. 1986); 1 son, George Bruce. Poetry in anthologies. Wrkg. on short stories. Student public schs., Salisbury, Md.; student creative writing, Wor-Wic Tech. Community Coll. Ins. agent Bankers Life & Casualty Co, Chgo., 1951-79, ret. Home: 315 Buena Vista Ave Salisbury MD 21801

RICKETTS, MARY JANE GNEGY, (Marijane G. Ricketts), b. Mt. Lake Park, MD, July 16, 1925; d. Clyde Columbus and Zelda Adaline (Stemple) Gnegy; m. Aubrey Eugene Ricketts, Apr. 9, 1950; children—Kenneth David, Jennifer Alison. Author: Is It the Onions Making Life Pungent?, 1986. Contrbr. numerous poems to lit. mags., anthols. B.A., W.V. Wesleyan Coll., 1947; Diploma in Comml. Arts, Strayer Bus. Coll., 1949. Secy., Montogomery County Public Schls., MD, 1962-85, part-time secy., 1985—. Recipient 1st prize Byline Mag., 1983, Annual Lit. award for poetry, 1986; award of Excellence, DeLong and Assocs., Annapolis, MD, 1985, 86, 87, 1st prize, 1987; award for excellence E. A. Fallot, 1985; 3d prize Poetry Press, 1985; award Ursus Press, 1985, 86. Mem. PSA, Natl. Fedn. State Poetry Socs. (3d prize 1986, 1st Honorable Mention 1986), Md. State Poetry Lit. Soc., Wrtrs. League Washington, Wrtr.'s Center Bethesda. Home: 10203 Clearbrook Pl Kensington MD 20895

RIDDLE, MAXWELL, see Bowart, Walter Howard

RIDEOUT, WALTER BATES, b. Lee, ME, Oct. 21, 1917; s. Walter John and Helen Ruth (Brickett) Rideout; m. Jeanette Lee Drisko, Aug. 2, 1947; children—Linda Carolyn, Richard Bates, David John. Author: The Radical Novel in the United States, 1900-1954, 1956; editor: Letters of Sherwood Anderson (with Howard Mumford Jones), 1953, A College Book of Modern Verse, 1958, and A College Book of Modern Fiction, 1961 (with James K. Robinson), The Experience of Prose, 1960, I. Donnelly, Caesar's Column, 1960, American Poetry (with G.W. Allen and J.K. Robinson), 1965, Sherwood Anderson: Collection of Critical Essays, 1974. AB, Colby Coll., 1938; MA, Harvard U., 1939, PhD1950. Teaching fellow English Harvard U., 1946-49, asst. prof., summer 1954, prof., summer 1969; from instr. to assoc. prof. English Northwestern U. (Evanston, IL), 1949-63; dir. program Bell System execs., 1957-58, 59-61; prof. English U. WI (Madison), 1963—, Harry Hayden Clark prof. English, 1972—, dept. chmn., 1965-68, sr. vis. prof. Inst. Research in Humanities, 1968-69; vis. prof. U. Hawaii, summer 1977; Disting. lectr. (Fulbright grantee) English Kyoto Am. Studies Summer Seminar (Kyoto, Japan), 1981. Fellow, Newberry Lib., 1951; Guggenheim, 1957; recipient MidAmerica Award, Soc. for Study of Midwestern Literature. Mem. AAUP, ACLU, MLA, Phi Beta Kappa. Home: 1306 Seminole Hwy Madison WI 53711

RIDGEWAY, JAMES FOWLER, b. Auburn, NY, Nov. 1, 1936; s. George L. and Florence (Fowler) Ridgeway; m. Patricia Carol Dodge, Nov. 1966; 1 son—David Andrew. Author: The Closed Corporation, 1969, Politics of Ecology, 1970, The Last Play, 1973, New Energy, 1975, Energy-Efficient Community Planning, 1979, Who Owns the Earth, 1980, Smoke (with Alexander Cockburn), 1978, Political Ecology (with Alexander Cockburn), 1979, Powering Civilization, 1983. AB, Princeton U., 1959. Assoc. editor New Republic (Washington), 1962-68, contrbg. editor, 1968-70; editor Hard Times, 1968-70, Elements, 1974-80; assoc. editor Ramparts, 1970-75; assoc. fellow Inst. for Policy Studies, 1973-77; mem. Pub. Resource Center, 1977—; staff writer Village Voice, 1973—. Served with Army N.G., 1959. Home: 3103 Macomb St NW Washington DC 20008

RIDL, JACK ROGERS, b. Sewickley, PA, April 10, 1944; s. Charles Gerald and Elizabeth Ann (Rogers) Ridl; m. Julie Ann Garlinghouse, June 25, 1983; 1 dau., Meredith. Author: The Same Ghost, 1984; editor: Social Psychology, 1983, Psychology, 1986; poetry in Yankee, The Georgia Rvw, Southern Poetry Rvw, other lit mags. BA, Westminster College, 1967, MEd, 1970. Asst. dean of admissions, Colgate, Hamilton, NY, 1967-68; asst. dir. admissions, U. of Pittsburgh, 1968-70; assoc. prof., Hope College, Holland, Mich., 1970—. Mem. AAP, PSA. Home: 2309 Auburn Ave Holland MI 49424

RIDOLPHI, LUCY ELIZABETH, b. Montgomery, AL, Mar. 11, 1957; d. Julian Maddox and Lucy Elizabeth (Howard) R. Contrbr. articles to mags., newspapers inluding Timber Proessing, Ala. Jnl., others. Ed.: Ala. Today, 1984-85, Huntingdon Bulltn., 1985—. B.A., Huntingdon Coll.,1979; postgrad., Auburn U., 1981-83. Public relations asst. Huntingdon Coll., Montgomery, AL, 1977-79, news bur. dir., 1985—; editorial asst. Hatton, Brown Pub., Montgomery, 1979-81, Ala. Tourism & Travel, Montgomery, 1983-84; production asst. Ala. Public TV, Montgomery, 1984-85. Mem. Public Relation Council Ala., Montgomery Assn. Bus. Communicators, NWC. Home: 2845 Zelda Rd Apt C-4 Montgomery AL 36106

RIED, GLENDA E., b. Toledo, June 20, 1933; d. Glenn Jeffries and Fola Follette (Ford) Thompson; m. Richard Theodore Ried, Mar. 23,

1963 (dec. Feb. 1979); 1 son, Richard Glenn Ried. Co- author Careers in Acctg., 1984; ed. & contrbr. The Woman CPA, 1983-86; contrbr. The CPA Jnl, 1986. BBAd., cum laude, U. Toledo, 1955, MBA, with highest honors, 1961. Instr., U. Toledo, 1959-61, asst. prof., 1962-73, assoc. prof., 1974-80, professor of acctg., 1981—. CPA, OH, 1960. Office: U Toledo 2801 W Bancroft Toledo OH 43606

RIEGLE, KAREN DEWALD, b. Akron, MI, Dec. 12, 1951; d. William and Barbara Lou (Prime) Dewald; m. Timothy James Riegle, Oct. 23, 1976; children—Jeffrey, Sarah. Contrbr. book rvws., articles on lit. topics to mags. B.A. in English, Mich. State U., 1973, M.A. in English, 1974, M.A. in Reading, 1977. Dir. learning resources center Alpena Commun. Coll., MI, 1976-80; instr. Suomi Coll., Hancock, MI, 1980-81; free-lance instr. Huron Intermediate Schl., Bad Axe, MI, 1985—, St. Clair County Commun. Coll., Port Huron, MI, 1986—, Saginaw Valley State Coll., MI, 1986—. Mem. Intl. Reading Assn., Phi Beta Kappa. Home: 418 E Woodworth St Bad Axe MI 48413

RIEMER, RUBY, b. Mt. Carmel, PA, Aug. 18, 1924, d. Benjamin and Ida (DeLuge) Riemer; m. Neal Riemer, Sept. 15, 1946; children—David, Jeremiah, Seth. Contrbr. poetry: Poet Lore, Ascent, Pivot, The Nation, Anthology of Magazine Verse, numerous other lit. mags.; contrbr. articles to Stone Country, Polity, Exquisite Corpse, American Book Rvw, Belles Lettres, Women and Polities, Philosophy of the Social Sciences, others. BA, Temple U., 1946; MA, Boston U., 1950. Lectr. U. Wis.-Milw., 1965-72, Drew U., Madison, N.J., 1976—. Grantee N.J. State Council on Arts, 1985-86. Home: Village Rd Box 210 Green Village NJ 07935

RIES, RICHARD RAYMOND, b. Mpls., Nov. 12, 1953; s. Ortwin Herald Raymond and Phyllis Arlene (Seaberg) R.; m. Julie Anne Graves, July 13, 1970; 1 stepchild, Jay Michael Langsford. Contrbr. articles, short stories on travel, personalities, how-to-do its, motorcycling to mags. Grad. public schls., Fridley, MN. Free-lance wrtr., 1984—. Home: Rt 3 Box 12 Madison IN 47250

RIFKIN, JEREMY CHICAGO, 1945; m. Donna Wulkon. Author: Common Sense II, 1972, ed., with John Rossen, How to Commit Revolution American Style, 1972, Own Your Own Job, 1977, with Randy Barber, The North Will Rise Again: Pensions, Politics and Power in the 1980s, 1978, with Ted Howard, Who Should Play God, 1977, and The Emerging Order: God in the Age of Scarcity, 1977, Entropy, 1980; with Nicanor Perlas, Algeny, 1983; Declaration of a Heretic, 1985. BA in econ., Wharton School Of Finance, U. of Penn., MA, in intl. affairs, Fletcher School of Law and diplomacy, Tufts U. Organized against the Vietnam War, including mock war trials, worked for Volunteers in Service for America (VISTA). Founded People's Bicentennial Commission, 1971; co-dir. People's Business Commission and founded successor, Foundation on Economic Trends, 1977. Lecturer on bioengineering at college campuses. Office: Fdn on Econ Trends 1130 17th St. NW Washington DC 20036

RIGBY, RICHARD NORRIS, b. Boston, July 1, 1935, s. Richard Norris and Hazel (Foster) R.; children—Christopher, Nan, Betsy. Co-ed. (with Ann Breen): Urban Waterfronts '83: Balancing Public-Private Interests, 1984, Caution: Working Waterfront: The Impact of Change on Marine Enterprises, 1985, Urban Waterfronts '84: Toward New Horizons, 1985, Fishing Piers: What Cities Can Do, 1986. AB, Williams Co.., 1957. Reporter Enterprise News, High Point, Charlotte, N.C., 1958-64; ed., staff mem. various marine orgns., Washington, 1969-74; wrtr., ed. Dept. Commerce, Washington, 1974-81; co-dir. Waterfront Center, Washington, 1982—. NEA grantee, 1984. Office: Waterfront 1536 44th St NW Washington DC 20007

RIGGS, DIONIS COFFIN, b. Edgartown MA Aug. 6, 1898, d. Thomas M. and Mary Wilder (Cleaveland) Coffin; m. Sidney Noyes Riggs, June 25, 1922; children—Alvida, Ann, Cynthia. Author: From Off Island (Best Seller 1940), 1940, People to Remember, Sea Born Island (poetry); contrbr. poetry to Christian Sci. Monitor, Cat Fancy, Poet Lore, Yankee, other publs.; contrbr. translations of Turkish poetry to Denver Qtly, Mundus Artium, Spirit, other lit. jnls. Ed. N.J. State Tchrs. Coll., Newark. Mem. PSA, Poetry Soc. Va., Poetry Soc. Ga., New Eng. Poetry Club. Home: Box 41 West Tisbury MA 02575

RIGGS, LYNN SPENCER, b. Indpls., Mar. 25, 1946; s. Ivan N. and Ella Alberta (Spencer) R.; m. Judy Ann Embry, Nov. 12, 1966; children—Joseph Ray, Ella Irene. Contrbr. articles to auto mags., newspapers including Car and Driver, Auto Racing Digest, Inpls. Star, others. Home: 1224 S Belmont Indianapolis IN 46221

RIGNEY, JAMES OLIVER, JR., (Robert Jordan, Reagan O'Neal, Jackson O'Reilly, Chang Lung), b. Charleston, SC, Oct. 17, 1948; s. James Oliver and Eva May (Grooms) R.; m. Harriet Stoney Popham McDougal, Mar. 28, 1981; 1 son, William Popham McDougal. Author: (as Reagan O'Neal) The Fallon Blood, 1980, The Fallon Pride, 1981, The Fallon Legacy, 1982; (as Jackson O'Reilly) Cheyenne Raiders, 1982; (as Robert Jordon) Conan the Invincible, 1982, Conan the Defender, 1982, Conan the Unconquered, 1983, Conan the Triumphant, 1983, Conan the Magnificant, 1984; Conan the Destroyer, 1984, Conan the Victorious, 1984. Contrbr. (as Chang Lung) dance rvws. for mags. BS in Physics, Citadel, 1974. Nuclear engr. U.S. Civil Service, 1974-78; freelance wrtr., 1978—. Mem. SFWA. Home: 129 Tradd St Charleston SC 29401

RIKER, LEIGH BARTLEY, (Lin Mallory), b. Akron, OH, May 24, 1941; d. Robert Andrew and Mona (Perry) Bartley; m. Donald Kay Riker, Oct. 30, 1965; children—Scott, Hal. Author: Heartsong, 1985, Acts of Passion, 1985. Wrkg. on novels, Morning Rain and Blessed Events; short stories. B.A. in English, Kent State U., 1963. Sec. U. Kans., Lawrence, 1966-68; administrative asst. Am. Assn. for the Advancement of Sci., NYC, 1968-70; free-lance wrtr., 1977—. Mem. Friends of the Library, Hamden, CT, 1986—. Mem. AG, NWC. Home: 166 Mather St Hamden CT 06517

RIKHOFF, JEAN., Author: (novels) Dear Ones All, 1961, Voyage In, Voyage Out, 1963, Rites of Passage, 1966, Buttes Landing, 1973, One of the Raymonds, 1974, The Sweetwater, 1976, Where Were You in '76?, 1978; (juveniles) Writing About the Frontier: Mark Twain, 1963, Robert E. Lee: Soldier of the South, 1968; (anthology) The Quixote Anthology, 1968; contrbr. articles, poems, short stories to mags. including The Writer, New Republic, Quixote, others. BA in English, Mt. Holyoke Coll., 1948; MA in English, Wesleyan U., 1949. Philosophy asst. Carleton Co.., Northfield, Minn., 1949-50; editorial asst. Gourmet Mag., 1952-54; instr. English, U. Md. Overseas Program, 1954-57; founder, editor Quixote Rvw, 1954-60; prof. English, Adirondack Community Coll., Glens Falls, N.Y., 1969—; founder, editor Glen Falls Rvw, Loft Press, Loft Players. Eugene Saxton fellow in creative writing Harper's Mag., 1958; NEH fellow, 1972; SUNY fellow, 1973, 79. Home: 42 Sherman Ave Glens Falls NY 12801

RILEY, JOCELYN CAROL, b. Mpls., Mar. 6, 1949, d. G.D. Riley and D.J. (Berg) Jacobson; m. Jeffrey Allen Steele, Sept. 4, 1971; children—Doran Riley, Brendan Riley. Novelist: Only My Mouth Is Smiling, 1982, Crazy Quilt, 1984. Contrbr. rvws. to Book Rvw Digest, Contemporary Lit. Criticism, Small Press Rvw. BA in English Lit., Carleton Coll., 1971. Mng. ed. Carleton Miscellany, Northfield, Minn., 1971; mktg. asst. Beacon Press, Boston, 1971-73; freelance wrtr., novelist, 1973—; producer, 1986—, Her Own Words. Recipient Best Books for Young Adults award for Only My Mouth Is Smiling, ALA, 1982, Arthur Tofte Meml. award Council Wis. Wrtrs., 1982, 86. Writer's Cup, 1985. Mem. Women in Communications (pres. 1984-85), AG, NBCC, PEN, Assn. Multi-Image (pres. 1985-87). Office: Box 5264 Hilldale Madison WI 53705

RILEY, MICHAEL DAVID, b. Lancaster, PA, June 10, 1945; s. Charles Bernard and Sarah Marie (Stetter) R.; m. Anne Mary Waller, June 18, 1966; children—Erin Elizabeth, Devin Michael. Author poetry: Scrimshaw: Citizens of Bone, 1987; contrbr. poetry to many jnls and mags inclg. So. Humanities Rvw, Ariz. Qtly, Yearbook of Am. Poetry, Kans. Qtly, Tex Qtly, Separate Doors, Third Eye, PermaFrost, Passaic Rvw; contrbr. essays on T.S. Eliot, Samuel Johnson, Maurice Merleau-Ponty; ed. Old Red Kimono, 1978-80. BA, U. Scranton, 1967; MA, Ohio U., 1969, PhD, 1973. Asst. prof. English Floyd Jr. Coll., Rome, Ga., 1973-78, Penn. State Univ., Wilkes-Barre, 1978-81, Reading campus, 1981—. Mem. MLA. Address: 1705 Lititz Pike Lancaster PA 17601

RILEY, MILLIE WILLETT, b. Jonesboro, AR, Aug. 23, 1935; d. William Otis and Mildred (Phelps) W.; m. Sydney M. Stolbach, May 31, 1959 (dec. Sept. 6, 1966); m. 2d, Paul Joseph Riley, July 19, 1969; children—Rachele, Erin. BS, Iowa State U., 1956. Advtg. copywriter The Hecht Co., Washington, 1956-60; ed., Teen Times, Future Homemakers Amer., Washington, 1966-69; writer/ed. Dateline, Amer. Home Econs. Assn., Washington, 1981-84, What's New in Home Econs., Phila., 1982-86; freelance writer/ed., Washington, 1969—, var. pamphlets & kits for educators; contrbr.: Today's Edn., J.C. Penney Forum, Quilter's Nwsltr./Mag., Fairfax Chronicles. Mem. Washington Independent Writers, Washington Ed Press. Home: 1734 P Street NW Washington DC 20036

RILEY, REBECCA, see Cissom, Mary Joan

RILLY, CHERLYL ANN, b. Detroit, June 17, 1952; d. John Charles and Dorothy Frances (Ozanich) R. Author: 4 air personality humor books including Triviallaneous & Book of Days. Contrbr. articles to mags., newspapers including Woman's Day, Bridal Guide, others. Student Oakland Commun. Coll., 1974, Birmingham Bloomfield Art Assn., 1975. Staff wrtr. Contemporary Comedy, Dallas, 1982—; creator, satirist The Heeda Hooper Show, Southfield, MI, 1983; cartoonist Tex. Gardener Mag., Waco, 1984—; spl. feature wrtr. C & G Pubs., Warren, MI, 1984-86; contrbg. ed. Heritage Mag., St. Clair

Shores, MI, 1986—; free-lance wrtr., 1977—. Mem. NWC. Address: 20028 Woodmont Harper Woods MI 48225

RIMM, VIRGINIA MARY, b. NYC, July 18, 1933; d. John Henry and Margaret Elizabeth (Whittle) Kelly; m. Charles B. Rimm, May 26, 1957; children: Catherine Elizabeth, Kenneth Charles, Michael John, Suzanne Patricia, Edward Robert, Nancy Anne, Jeanne Therese. Contrbr. articles and/or photos to Maine Life, Yankee, Upcountry, Christian Herald, Me. Organic Farmer & Gardener, Woman's Natl. Farm and Garden, Treasure Trove, others. BS, Columbia U., 1950-52, RN, 1952-55. Head librarian Stanford Free Library, Stanfordville, NY, 1964-69; local corres. Repl. Jnl, Belfast, Me., 1972-74; district corr. Bangor Daily News, Me., 1974-79; ed./pub. New England Sampler, Monore, Me., 1980—. Mem. Waldo County Coop Ext. Service Exec. Bd., 1975-77, Waldo County Genl. Hosp. Bd. of Incorporators, 1981—, press, Penobscot Bay Growers' Assn, 1982, all Belfast. Address: Box 306 Belfast ME 04915

RIMMER, CHRISTINE L., b. San Jose, CA, Jan. 28, 1950, d. Thomas Retzer and Auralee (Strand) Smith; m. Rodney Dean Rimmer, July 11, 1970. Contrbr. poetry to Neworld mag., Anthology of Mag. Verse, 1979; short story to Crosscurrents; short play to: West Coast Plays; author: The Road Home, 1987, Arena of the Heart, 1988. BFA, Calif. State U., Sacramento, 1973; tradeschl., H.B. Studios, NYC1975, 76. Winner 1st pl. for poetry, Neworld Creative Writing Competition, Los Angeles, 1978, Fiction award Crosscurrents mag., 1981, Bronze Star Halo award So. Calif. Motion Picture Council, 1984. Mem. WG, DG. Home: 1649 E 61st St Long Beach CA 90805

RINALDI, NICHOLAS MICHAEL, b. Bklyn., Apr. 2, 1934, s. Frank Anthony and Rose (Lopena) R.; m. Jacqueline Tellier, Aug. 29, 1959; children—Tina, Paul, Stephen, David. Author: The Resurrection of the Snails, 1977, We Have Lost Our Fathers, 1982, The Luftwaffe in Chaos, 1985 (poetry), Bridge Fall Down, 1985 (novel); contrbr. poems to Yale Rvw, New Am. Rvw, Carolina Qtly, other lit mags. MA, Fordham U., 1960, PhD1963. Instr., asst. prof. St. Johns U., 1960-66; lectr. CUNY, 1966; assoc. prof. Columbia, 1966; prof. U. Conn., 1972; prof. Fairfield U., Conn., 1966—. Awards: Lit. Rvw. Charles Angoff Poetry Awd., Neg. Capability Eve of St. Agnes Poetry Awd., N.Y. Poetry Forum Awd., All Nations Poetry Awd. Mem. MLA, PSA, Assoc. Wrtg. Programs. Home: 190 Brookview Ave Fairfield CT 16432

RINARD, SALLY STEDMAN, b. July 4, 1947; d. Richard I. and Frances (O'Brien) R. Author, Pretensions (novel), 1985; book reviewer, Greensboro (NC) News & Record; copy ed. Good Housekeeping Mag., 1970-72; rptr., feature writer, Women's Wear Daily, also W, 1972-82. BA, U. SC, 1968; postgrad. U. NC, 1969-70. Home: 30 E 72nd St New York NY 10021

RIND, SHERRY, b. Seattle, Mar. 29, 1952, d. Martin B. and Bernice (Mossafer) R.; m. John Welliver, July 15, 1984. Author: The Whooping Crane Dance, 1981, The Hawk in the Back Yard, 1985; contrbr. articles to The Watchbird, poetry to Poery N.W., So. Poetry Rev., Crescent Rev., Fine Madness, also others; ed. Zoo News. Wrkg. on novel and poetry collection. BA, U. Wash., 1973, MA, 1977. Instr. Seattle Arts Commn., 1977-78, Shoreline Community Coll., Seattle, 1977-82, Bellevue Community Coll., Wash., 1984-86. Recipient Louisa Kern award U. Wash., 1982; prize for poetry Anhinga Press, 1984, NEA Fellowship, 1986. Mem. P&W, Pacific N.W. Wrtrs. Conf. Home: 6509 210th Ave NE Redmond WA 98053

RING, MARGARET R., b. Bethesda, MD; d. John J. and Anne M. R. Ed., Liquid Chromotography Lit.: Abstracts & Index, 1984-85, Gas Chromotography Lit.: Abstracts & Index, 1984-85, Jnl. Analytical Toxicology, 1984-85, Byline—AAMA, 1985—, Professional Medical Asst., 1985—. BA, Northwestern U., 1979. Medical asst. Fairhaven Med. Ctr., Mundelein, IL, 1979-80; admin. asst. Amer. Osteopathic Assn., Chgo., 1980-81; writer/ed. Sargent-Welch Scientific Co., Skokie, IL, 1981-84; mng. ed. Preston Pubns., Niles, IL, 1984-85; dir. editorial svcs. Am. Assn. Medical Assts., Chgo., 1985—. Mem. AAAS, Soc. Natl. Assn. Pubns., secy./treas., AMWA. Office: Am Assn of Med Assts 20 N Wacker Chicago IL 60606

RINGLER, SHARON MATTILA, b. Laurium, MI, May 25, 1948; d. Fred Felix and Mary-Lou (Eckloff) Mattila; m. John Robert Ringler, Jr., Aug. 26, 1967 (div. Dec. 17, 1973); children—Jay Robert, Jo'el Renee. Ed.: Computing Hints for Instructor's Using the Sperry 1100/80, 1982, Instructor's Guide to Computerized Test Scoring, 1982, Sperry 1100 Reference Manual, 1983, Control Language Reference Card for Sperry Exec 1100, 1983, Sperry Univac 1100 Software Overview, 1983, Guide to Using Demand Terminals at MTU, 1983, Guide to the MTU Graphics Lab, 1984, Introduction to Computer Services, 1984, The Conversion Connections, 1985-86, Sperry 1100 Editor Reference Card, 1985, VM/CMS Handbook: A user Guide and Reference Manual, 1986, Micresoft Fortran Supplement, 1987, Reference Card to Facilities and Services, 1987, Text Processing on the IBM 4381: User's Guide to GML and Script, 1987, ACS Newsletters, 1982—. Wrkg. on ACS Policies and Procedures, Software Directory for the IBM 4381. B.S. in Social Scis., Mich. Technological U., 1979. Asst. mgr. Downtowner Motel, Houghton, MI, 1967-71; credit management trainee Sears, Roebuck, Hayward, CA, 1979-81; documentation coord. academic computing services Mich. Technological U., Houghton, 1982—. Recipient 1st place for ACS Newsletter, Assn. Computer Machines Spl. Interest Group on Univ. and Coll. Computing Services, 1984, 2d place for ACS Newsletter, 1986. Home: 703 W Memorial Dr Houghton MI 49931

RINKEL, MARGARET ELIZABETH, b. Macon, GA, Jan. 16, 1928; d. William Henry and Margaret Elizabeth (Tarver) Causey; m. Gene K. Rinkel, Aug. 4, 1950; children—Stephen Dwight, Karen Ruth Smith. Author: articles in Ideas for Teaching English in the Junior High and Middle Schools, 1980, Classroom Practices in the Teaching of English, 1986. Contrbr. articles, poems to profl. jnls., anthols; chpt. to High Interest, Easy Reading, 1987. Ed.: Newsletter of Ill. Assn. Tchrs. English, 1983—. B.A., Greenville Coll., 1950; M.Ed., U. Ill., 1967. English tchr. public schs., Mahomet, IL, 1963—. Assoc. mem. Coll. of Edn., U. Ill., 1981—, mem. area communication com., 1977—; mem. task force Champaign County Mental Health Bd., IL, 1974-75. Recipient Governor's Master Tchr. award Ill. State Bd. Edn., 1984, Disting. Cooperating Tchr. award Dept. Secondary Edn., U. Ill.-Urbana, 1985. Mem. NCTE, Ill. Assn. Tchrs. English, NEA, Ill. Edn. Assn., Mahomet-Seymour Edn. Assn. Home: 404 N Weathering Dr Mahomet IL 61853

RINZLER, CAROL GENE EISEN, b. Newark, Sept. 12, 1941; d. Irving Y. and Ruth (Katz) Eisen; m. Carl Rinzler, July 21, 1962 (div. 1976); children—Michael Franklin, Jane Ruth. Author: Frankly McCarthy, 1969, Nobody Said You Had to Eat Off the Floor, 1971, The Girl Who Got All the Breaks, 1980, Your Adolescent: An Owner's Manual, 1981, How to Set Up for a Mah-Jongg Game and other Lost Arts (with J. Gelman), 1987; contrbr. articles and rvws. to various periodicals. AB, Coucher Coll., 1962; JD, Yale U., 1980. Bar: NY State bar 1981-; Supreme Ct., 1984. Editor Charterhouse Books, Inc. (NYC), 1971-73, publ. 1973-74; articles editor Glamour Mag. (NYC), 1974-77; book critic Washington Post and syndicated, 1974—, columnist Mademoiselle, 1981-86. Cosmopolitan, 1983—; contrbg. editor Pub. Weekly, 1983-87; assoc. firm Cahill Gordon & Reindel (NYC), 1980-86; counsel firm Rembar & Curtis (NYC), 1986—. Judge (nonfiction) Natl. Bk. Awards, 1987. Mem. Friends of Scarlett O'Hara, Women's Media Group (pres. 1984-85), Natl. Book Critics Circle, PEN (exec. bd., 1986-), AG. Home: 1215 Fifth Ave New York NY 10029

RIORDAN, MICHAEL, b. Springfield, MA, Dec. 3, 1946; s. Edward John and Evelyn Anna (Hnizdo) R., m. Linda Michele Goodman, Apr. 8, 1979. Author: The Solar Home Book, 1976 (with Bruce Anderson) ed: Energy Primer, 1978. The Wind Power Book, 1981, A Golden Thread, 1980, The Ecology of Freedom, 1982, The Day After Midnight, 1982; contrbr. to Sci. Annual, 1984. SB in Physics, MIT, 1968, PhD in Physics, 1973. Research assoc. MIT, Cambridge, Mass., 1973-75; ed. and pub. Cheshire Books, Palo Alto, Calif., 1976-85; instr. Cabrillo Coll, Aptos, Calif, 1978-80; cons. physicist Am. Univ., Washington, 1985; scientist Univ. Rochester, NY, 1985—. Dir., No. Calif. Solar Energy Assn., Berkeley, 1979-80, vp, 1981; treas. Cuesta La Honda Guild, Calif. Mem. Am. Physical Soc., Sigma Xi. Address: Box 130 La Honda CA 94020

RISHEL, MARY ANN MALINCHAK, b. Port Vue, PA, July 12, 1940, d. Michael and Helen G. (Stash) Malinchak; m. Thomas Rishel, Nov. 5, 1966. Contrbr. to Red Cedar Rvw, Hudson Rvw, Cornell Rvw, Shankpainter. BA, U. Pitts., 1962, MA, 1969; MFA, Cornell U., 1979. Instr. Ithaca (N.Y.) Coll., 1975-82, asst. prof., 1982—. Recipient Best Am. Short Story award Houghton Mifflin, 1978; Provincetown Fine Arts Work Center fellow, 1984-85. Mem. P&W, World Humor and Irony Assn., Coll. Communication and Composition Assn. Home: 1331 Ellis Hollow Rd Ithaca NY 14850

RITCHEY, DAVID, b. Shelbyville, KY, May 26, 1940; children—Adam Parker, Joy Elizabeth. Author: A Guide to the Baltimore Stage in the Eighteenth Century, 1982. Contrbr. articles to profl. jnls., popular mags., newspapers including Chrisian Sci. Monitor, USA Today, others. B.A., Georgetown Coll., 1962; Ph.D., La. State U., 1971. Recipient awards for speechwriting, editorial writing, feature writing, radio writing IABC, 1984, 85, 86, 87; awards for radio writing, feature writing PRSA, 1986, 87. Home: 1421 N Univ Apt N-322 Little Rock AR 72207

RITCHIE, MICHAEL KARL, (Michael Karl), b. Cin., Nov. 23, 1946. Author: For Those in the Know (poems), 1976, Night Blindness (poems), 1976, Closing Down the Hearth (poems), 1983; non- fiction ed., contrbg. ed. Mid-Am. Rvw. MFA, U. Iowa, 1975, PhD, Bowling Green State U., 1986. Fgn. expert Xi'an Fgn. Langs. Inst., People's Republic of China, 1984-

85; instr. English Bowling Green (Ohio) State U., 1985—. Office: Dept Eng Bowling Green State U Bowling Green OH 43403

RITTBERG, ELLEN POBER, b. Bklyn., May 5, 1952; d. Nathan and Pearl Pober; m. Israel Rittberg Nov. 21, 1975; children—Jay, Mathew, Kim. Author plays: Sci Fi, 1985, Sabbath Elevator, 1985, Just a Quiet Evening At Home, 1984. BA, Boston U., MA, SUNY, Buffalo; staff writer and L.I. ed., Jewish Week. Freelance wrtr. Recipient Sigma Delta Chi awd., 1984; Folio awd. Best Public Affairs Show, 1984. Mem. DG, Press Club of Long Island. Home: 40 Island St Plainview NY 11803

RITTER, JEFFREY MICHAEL (JEFF), b. Harrisburg, PA, Nov. 27, 1960; s. Arnold Ritter and Rae (Brown) Kooseman. Editor, Broadside Mag., NYC, 1983—. BA, Hampshire Coll., 1982; MA, Bowling Green State U., 1984. Recipient Plebney Award Plebney Graphics Fdn., 1985. Office: Box 1464 1995 Broadway New York NY 10023

RITZ, JOSEPH P., b. Chgo., Nov. 6, 1929; m. Ann M. Girard, July 26, 1958; children—Joanne, Michael, Robert, Jonathan, Margaret. Author: The Despised Poor, 1966; playwright: Copy Desk, 1985; contrbr. articles, humor to Chgo. Tribune, Seattle Times, Toronto Globe, others. Wrkg. on play. Student Seattle U., 1951-52; BS in Journalism, Marquette U., 1955. Reporter Leader-Herald, Gloversville, N.Y., 1955-57, Jnl.-Courier, New Haven, 1957-59, Evening News, Newburg, N.Y., 1961-64; asst. news dir. Fordham U., NYC1959-61; reptr., copy ed. Buffalo Courier-Express, 1964-82; labor ed., columnist Buffalo News, 1983—. Served with U.S. Army, 1948-51. Recipient Disting. Pub. Affairs Reporting award Am. Poli. Sci. Assn., 1966; Page One awds. 1967, 69, 70, 73, 75, 81; Sigma Delta Chi awd. for Best Column, 1986. Mem. Newspaper Guild (pres. Buffalo chap. 1973-75). Home: 6301 Smith Rd Hamburg NY 14075

RIVERA, LOUIS REYES, b. Bklyn., May 19, 1945; s. Louis Alfonso and Amelia (Pardo) R.; m. Barbara Killens, Nov. 2, 1974; children: Abiba, Barra, Kutisa. Author: Who Pays the Cost, 1977; This One for You,1983; ed. (poetry) Poets in Motion,1976, Love—A Collection of Young Songs, 1977, Womanrise, 1978, (prose) Portraits of the Puerto Rican Experience, 1984; contrbr. to West End mag., Sunbury Jnl, Caliban, Bookmark, Areito, Universal Black Wrtr., Black Nation, West SideWords, The Paper, also anthologies. Wrkg. on hist. poems. BA, CCNY, 1974. Pub. Shamal Books, NYC, 1976—; adj. prof. poetry and drama Coll. of New Rochelle, 1982; poet-in-residence Bronx Community Coll., 1982; vis. lectr. Afrikan Poetry Theatre, Jamaica, N.Y., 1980—; instr. creative writing Pratt Inst., 1983—. Mem. Black Wrtrs. Union (founding mem., former chmn.), Am. Wrtrs. Congress, Met. Lit. Assn. (bd. dirs.), Calabash Poets Workshop (founding mem.). Office: Gen PO Box 16 New York NY 10116

RIVERA, MIQUELA CARLEEN, b. Sant 2 Fe, Aug. 1, 1954; d. R. Arthur and Marie (Lujan) R. Columnist: Tucson Citizen, 1986—. Contrbr. articles to Hispanic Engineer, U.S. Black Engineer, Vista Mag. B.A., N.M. State U., 1976; M.A., Mich. State U., 1979, Ph.D. in Clinical Psychology, 1981. Con., edn. dir. La Frontera Mental Health Ctr., Tucson, 1981-85; psychologist Contact, Inc., Tucson, 1985—; private practice psychologist, Tucson, 1985—. Bd. dir. Hispanic Profl. Action Com., Tucson, 1986-88. Mem. Exec. Women's Council, Am. Psychological Assn., Ariz. Bd. Psychologist Examiners. Home: 1801 N Camino de La Cienega Tucson AZ 85719

RIVERA, VICKI LAURA, b. Champaign, IL, Feb. 15, 1945; d. Abraham and Sylvia (Reiss) Tatz; m. Wilfredo Rivera, July 1, 1982; 1 son, Pablo Sungja. BA, Wilkes Coll., 1966. Staff wrtr. Bell Telephone Labs., Murray Hill, N.J., 1966-67, Bank of Am., San Francisco, 1970-73; women's ed. Clarksville Leaf-Chronicle, Tenn., 1968-69; ed. Way of the World mag., Washington, 1975-76, News World Communications, NYC, 1976-85, The World & I mag., Washington, 1986—. Home: 404 Charter Oak Ct Waldorf MD 20601

RIVERO, ANDRES, b. Havana, Cuba, June 18, 1936, came to U.S., 1959; s. Andres and Isabel (Collado) R., m. Pilar Funcia, May 19, 1959; children—Andres, Juan Carlos, Teresa. Author: (short stories) Somos Como Somos, others. BA, U. Vilanova, Havana, 1959. Ed., Spanish Today Mag., Miami, 1968—. Fellow, NEA, 1979. Home: 77515 W 132 Ct Miami FL 33183

RIVERS, JOAN, b. 1937; d. Meyer C. Molinsky; m. Edgar Rosenberg, July 15, 1965 (dec. 1987); 1 dau., Melissa. Author: The Life and Hard Times of Heidi Abromovitz, 1984 (autobiography) Enter Talking, 1986; originator, author: screen play TV movie The Girl Most Likely To, ABC, 1973; cable TV spcl. Joan River and Friends Salute Heidi Abromovitz, 1985; author: film Having a Baby Can Be a Scream, 1974; coauthor, dir.: film Rabbit Test, 1978. B.A., Barnard Coll., 1958. Nat. syndicated columnist, Chgo. Tribune, 1973-76; creator: CBS TV series Husband and Wives, 1976-77. Address: Sammeth Org 9200 Sunset Blvd Suite 1001 Los Angeles CA 90069

RIXON, ROBERT N., b. Roselle Park, NJ, Nov. 11, 1948, s. Joseph Samuel Rixon and Maizie (Amidon) Kusky. Author: Prima Facie (poetry), 1980, The Strand (poetry), 1984; ed.: The Refinery Radio Tapes, 1986; contrbr. to Option Mag., Action, Planet Detroit, Village Voice, New York Qtly, numerous other mags. Student Ramapo Coll., 1974-76. Tchr. Linden (N.J.) Music Studio, 1984—; freelance wrtr., 1980—; host poetry program WFMU-FM, 1981—. Home: 322 Mitchell Ave Linden NJ 07036

RIZZUTO, JAMES JOSEPH, b. Trenton, NJ, Mar. 2, 1939; s. Sabastian Stephen and Neljane Helen (Downing) R.; m. Shirley Anne Ozaki, Apr. 29, 1962; children—Rahna Reiko, Leticia Anne, James Anthony. Author: How to Prepare for College Board Achievement Tests, Math Level I, 1969, Modern Hawaiian Gamefishing, 1976, Polynesian Fishing Almanac, 1980; Fishing Hawaii Style, vol. 1, 1983, vol. II, 1987, vol. III, 1988; columnist: West Hawaii Today, 1970—; Hawaii corr.: Marlin, 1986—. Contrbr. articles to Field and Stream, Fishing World. Assoc. ed.: Hawaii Fishing News, 1980—; Hawaii ed.: Salt Water Sportsman, 1981—, Western Outdoors, 1982—. B.A. in Geology, Rutgers U., 1960; MALS in Mathematics, Wesleyan U., 1972. Head mathematics dept. Hawaii Preparatory Acad., Kamuela, 1969-75, 1987—, head lower and middle schl., 1975-86, dir. faculty devel., 1986-87. Governor, Pacific Gamefish Research Fdn., Kailua-Kona, HI, 1984—. Mem. Natl. Council Tchrs. Mahematics, Hawaiian Intl. Billfish Assn. (commissioner 1974—). Home: Box 635 Kamuela HI 96743

RIZZUTO, SHARIDA ANN, b. New Orleans, July 17, 1948; d. Samuel David and Vivian Catherine (O'Hern) R. Contrbr., ed.: The Collinsport Record, 1983—, The Vampire Jnl., 1984—, Baker St. Gazette, 1987—, The Haunted Jnl., 1987—, Horizons West, 1987—, Poison Pen Wrtrs.' News, 1987—, Movie Memories, 1987—, Sleuth Jnl., 1987—, Students of Sci., 1987—; ed.: Nocturnal News, 1985—, The Collinwood Jnl., 1986—, Deep South Jnl., 1987—, Horizons Beyond, 1987—. Wrkg. on annuals: The Lovecraft Rvw., The Poe Jnl., The Salem Jnl.; mystery and horror anthols. and novels. Student U. New Orleans, 1975-82. Bookstore mgr. Ye Oldee Curiosity Shoppe, New Orleans, 1972-73; pub., ed. Baker St. Pubs., New Orleans, 1983—, M.O.R.G.U.S., New Orleans, 1987. Friends of the Jefferson Parish Library, Matairie, LA, 1987—. Mem. NWC, MWA, Horror Wrtrs. Am., Ntl. Assn. Ind. Pubs. Home: 353 Vinet Ave Jefferson LA 70121

ROADARMEL, PAUL DOUGLAS, b. Ithaca, NY, May 28, 1942; s. Kenneth Roadarmel and Catherine Bobel. Author: The Kaligarh Fault, 1979, Beach House 7, 1986, BFA, Syracuse U., 1964, MA, 1970. Art tchr. Stockbridge Schl., Munnsville, NY, 1964-65; Peace Corps art dir./health dept., Hariana State, India, 1966-68; tchr., comm. artist, Bangkok, Thailand, 1968; tchr. Indian Hill Arts Wkshp., Stockbridge, MA, 1970-73, The Dalton Schl., NYC, 1975-77; seminar instr. NY State Council Arts, Syracuse, 1984; freelance artist & writer. Mem. MWA. Home: 118 East 91st St New York NY 10128

ROBB, THOMAS BRADLEY, b. Chgo., May 5, 1932; s. Paul Bradley and Rhyllis Rena (Barber) R.; m. Shirely Mae Kolouch, Aug. 21, 1953 (div. June 20, 1982); children—Marcia Lynn Bergen, J. Scott, Judith Lorraine, James Douglas, Rebecca Ruth; m. Elizabeth Lee Wilbanks, Nov. 2, 1982. Author: The Bonus Years: Foundations for Ministry with Older Persons, 1968, Senior Center Operation, 1978, Senior Center Administration, 1978. B.A., Ariz. State U., 1953; B.D., San Francisco Theol. Seminary, 1957, Th.M., 1964, Th.D., 1970. Administ., Westminster-Canterbury, Richmond, VA, 1974-76; program dir. Natl. Council on Aging, Washington, 1976-80; dir. Presbyterian Office on Aging, Atlanta, 1981—. Mem. Natl. Interfaith Coalition Aging (sec.), Gerontogical Soc. Am., Am. Soc. Aging, Natl. Council Aging. Home: 624 Avery St Decatur GA 30030

ROBBINS, CATHERINE CODISPOTI, b. NYC, Mar. 1, 1941; d. Guido and Victoria (Lijoi) Codispoti; m. Richard G. Robbins, Jr., Apr. 2, 1966; children—Carla, Nicholas. Contrbr. articles to newspapers, popular mags. including The N.Y. Times, Advantage Mag., N.M. Mag. Reporter Albuquerque Jnl., Impact Mag., 1980-82, Albuquerque News, 77-79; reporter, wrtr., ed., N.M. Ind., 1972-77; city ed. N.M. Sun, 1982-83. B.S. in English, Columbia U., 1965; M.A. in English, N.Y. U., 1969; Trustee Chamber Orchestra of Albuquerque, 1983-86. Recipient numerous awards Albuquerque Press Club. Mem. N.M. Press Women (numerous awards), NFPW (numerous awards). Home: 224 12th St NW Albuquerque NM 87102

ROBBINS, DOREN RICHARD, b. Los Angeles, Aug. 20, 1949, s. Ralph and Florence (Gurstein) R.; 1 dau., Samantha Juliet. Author: Detonated Veils, 1976, The Roots and the Towers, 1980, Seduction of the Groom, 1982, Time of the Devils (broadside), 1985, In-Terminal Rose (broadside), 1985, Sympathetic Manifesto, 1987; co-founder, ed., pub.: Third Rail: A Journal of Politics and the Arts, 1975-82; contrbr. poetry to over 40 periodicals and anthologies. Home: 12540 Rubens Ave Los Angeles CA 90046

ROBBINS, HAROLD, b. NYC, May 21, 1916; m. Lillian Machnivitz (div.); 2nd m. Grace Palermo; children—Caryn, Adreana. Author: Never Love a Stranger, 1948, The Dream Merchants, 1949, A Stone for Danny Fisher, 1952, Never Leave Me, 1953, 79 Park Avenue, 1955, Stiletto, 1960, The Carpetbaggers, 1961, Where Love Has Gone, 1962, The Adventurers, 1966, The Inheritors, 1969, The Betsy, 1971, The Pirate, 1974, Lonely Lady, 1976, Dreams Die First, 1977, Memories of Another Day, 1979, Goodbye, Janette, 1981, Spellbinder, 1982, Descent from Xanadu, 1984, The Storyteller, 1986. Student pub. schls. NYC. In food factoring bus. until 1940; shipping clk. Universal Pictures (NYC), 1940-46. Office: Berner & Gitlin 7 W 51st St New York NY 10019

ROBBINS, MARTIN, b. Denver, CO, July 10, 1931; s. Sam and Evelyn (Bricker) Robbins; m. Judith Ann Fisher, July 31, 1977; stepson—Stanton Emerson Fisher Wortham. Author: A Refrain of Roses, 1965, A Reply to the Headlines, 1970, A Week Like Summer, 1979, A Year with Two Winters, 1984; poetry in Webster, Greenfield, Sewanee, Poetry rvws and other lit mags. MA, State U. of Ia., 1959; PhD, Brandeis U., 1968. Asst. prof., Northeastern U., Boston, 1963-73; instr., Harvard College, Cambridge, Mass., 1973-76; instr., Radcliffe Seminars, Cambridge, 1976—. Mem. PSA, PEN, New England Poetry Club. Home: 19 Houston St West Roxbury MA 02132

ROBBINS, RICHARD LEROY, b. Los Angeles, Aug. 27, 1953; s. Richard Leroy and Irene Cecilia (Annand) Robbins; m. Candace Lee Black, Sept. 8, 1979; 2 sons, Keenan. and Lewis. Author: The Invisible Wedding, 1984, Toward New Weather, 1979; contrbr. to Where We Are: The Montana Poets Anthology, 1980, Rain in the Forest, Light in the Trees: Contemporary Poetry From the Northwest, 1983. AB, San Diego State U., 1975; MFA, U. of MT, 1979. Editor/publ., Cafeteria, Missoula, MT, 1975-81; ed./publ., Cutbank/Smokeroot Press, Miss., MT, 1977-79, wrtr.-in-res., MT Arts Council, Miss. MT, 1979-81; asst. and assoc. prof., Mankato ST. U., Mankato, MN, 1984—. Mem. AWP, MLA, Assn. of Teachers of Tech. Writing. Home: 236 Clark St Mankato MN 56001

ROBBINS, TOM, b. Blowing Rock, NC, 1936; m. Terrie (div.); 1 child—Fleetwood Starr. Author: biography Guy Anderson, 1965; fiction Another Roadside Attraction, 1971, Even Cowgirls Get the Blues, 1976, Still Life with Woodpecker, 1980. Student Washington and Lee U., Richmond Profl. Inst. (now VA Commonwealth U.). Former copy editor Richmond (VA) Times-Dispatch, Seattle Times, Seattle Post-Intelligencer. Served with USAF. Address: Houghton Mifflin 1 Beacon St Boston MA 02108

ROBERTS, BARBARA BAKER, b. Calera, AL, May 9, 1934; d. Horace Claude and Eva Theresa (Aldridge) Baker; m. Edmund W. Roberts, Apr. 17, 1954; children—Neena Gretchen, Edmund Keith. Contrbr. articles, poetry, short stories, book rvws. to lit. mags., newspapers, popular mags. including Montevallo Rvw., Birmingham Mag., Ala. Farmer. Co-ed.: Maps in the Samford University Library, 1977, Early History of Calera, AL, 1980. Wrkg. on article on Thomas Hardy and John Ruskin. BA, Alahama Coll. (now Univ. of Montevallo) 1954; M.A., Samford U., 1969; Ph.D., U. Ala., 1985. Research asst. Samford U. Library, Birmingham, AL, 1975-78; teaching asst. U. Ala., Tuscaloosa, 1979-82; asst. prof. English, Samford U., Birmingham, 1986—; free-lance wrtr., 1986—. Docent, Birmingham Museum of Art, 1971-74. Mem. Shelby County Hist. Soc. (pres. 1976-77), Ala. Hist. Assn., South Atlantic MLA, Magi City Wrtrs., NCTE, Ala. Council Tchrs. of English, AAUW, Samford U. Faculty Women's Club. Home: 2735 Smyer Rd Birmingham AL 35216

ROBERTS, BONNIE LESLIE, b. Florence, AL, Sept. 30, 1949; d. James William Brooks and Sarah Elizabeth (Hall) Gibbs; m. James Steven Roberts, Sept. 5, 1970; 1 dau., Jennifer Elizabeth. Contrbr. poems to numerous lit. mags., anthols. including Ky. Poetry Rvw., Amelia Mag., Poetry Australia, Proof Rock, Sands, Piedmont Lit. Rvw., others. B.S., Auburn U., 1971; postgrad., U. of South, 1981-85, U. Dijon, France, 1972, Vanderbilt U., 1974, U. Ala., 1977, 78. Tchr. English and French, Decatur High Sch., AL, 1971-74; social worker child welfare Dept. of Pensions & Securities, Huntsville, AL, 1974-76; poet arts-in-edn. Ala. State Council on the Arts, Montgomery, 1984—. Mem. Ala. State Poetry Soc., Huntsville Lit. Assn., Assn. Applied Poetry (patron). Home: 3628 GreenBrier Dr Huntsville AL 35810

ROBERTS, DELMAR L., b. Raleigh, NC, Apr. 9, 1933, s. James Delmar and Nellie Brocklebank (Tyson) R. Ed.: The Best of Legal Economics, 1979, 35 books for various authors. BA in Textiles, N.C. State U., 1956; MA in Journalism, U. S.C., 1974. Ed.-in- chief, editorial v.p. Sandlapper Mag., Columbia, S.C., 1968-73; assoc. ed. S.C. History Illustrated, Columbia, 1971; mng. ed. Legal Econ. mag., ABA, Chgo., 1974—. Mem. Soc. Profl. Journalists, Kappa Tau Alpha. Home: 1028 Old Birch Dr Blythewood SC 29016

ROBERTS, DIANE HILL, b. Goldsboro, NC, Dec. 11, 1947; d. Giles and Bonnie (Moore) Hill; m. Toby Roberts, Aug. 16, 1969, children—Daniel. Contrbr. American Poetry Anthology, 1984, Poetry Today, A Carolina Literary Companion, The Best of the Editor's Desk, American Muse; Wayah Rvw, Arts Journal, Chapbook Down the Dirt Road, 1986; co-editor, Neuse River Anthology. MA, North Carolina State U., 1981. Engl. instr., Lenoir Community College, Kinston, NC, 1980—. Home: Rt 2 Box 236 Goldsboro NC 27530

ROBERTS, JANET LOUISE, (Louisa Bronte, Rebecca Danton, Janette Radcliffe), b. New Britain, CT, Jan. 20, 1925; d. Walter Nelson and Marjorie Mae (Miller) Roberts. Author: numerous books, including Jewels of Terror, 1970, Weeping Lady, 1971, Love Song, 1971, The Curse of Kenton, 1972, Marriage of Inconvenience, 1972, My Lady Mischief, 1973, The Dancing Doll, 1973, The First Waltz, 1974, Jade Vendetta, 1976, Island of Desire, 1977, Golden Lotus, 1979, Silver Jasmine, 1980, Flamenco Rose, 1981, Scarlet Poppies, 1983; as Rebecca Danton: Sign of the Golden Goose, 1972, Fire Opals, 1977, Ship of Hate, 1977, Star Sapphire, 1979, Ruby Heart, 1980, French Jade, 1982; as Louisa Bronte: Lord Satan, 1972, Her Demon Lover, 1973, The Vallette Heritage, 1978, The Van Rhyne Heritage, 1979, The Gunther Heritage, 1981; as Janette Radcliffe: The Blue-Eyed Gypsy, 1974, Gentleman Pirate, 1975, The Heart Awakens, 1977, Scarlet Secrets, 1977, Hidden Fires, 1978, Stormy Surrender, 1978. BA, Otterbein Coll., 1946; MSLS Columbia U., 1966. Reference librarian Dayton and Montgomery County (Ohio) Public Library, 1966-78. Mem. ALA, Ohio Library Assn., AG. Office: Garon-Brooke 415 Central Pk W New York NY 10025

ROBERTS, JANET MARIE, (Janet Marie), b. Sparta, WI, Jan. 30, 1947, d. Leo Harold and Ruby LaVonne (Nienast) Wittler; m. T.C.W. Roberts, Jr., May 18, 1985. Author poetry books: Hearts Core, 1974, eye of the Needle, 1979, Reaping Song, 1981, Toyshop of the Mind, 1981; Focus on the Heart, Hypertension & the Heart, 1984; contrbr. poetry to Manhattan Poetry Rvw, N.J. Poetry Anthology, Strand; contrbr. articles to The Princeton Packet, Wis. State Jnl, others. BS, U. Wis.-Madison, 1971, MS, 1974, MA, 1974. Adj. prof. Rider Coll., Trenton State Coll., 1981-83; assoc. ed. Vintage, 1976; assoc. ed. to ed.-in-chief, Doubleday, 1975; food ed. Macmillan, 1984; med. ed. McGraw Hill, 1984; instr. Fordham U., Bronx, N.Y., 1984-85; tchr. Hotchkiss Schl., Lakeville, Conn., 1985-86; ed., cons., NYC, 1979; publicist Guggenheim Mus., NYC, 1984; Poets-in-Schls. program, NYC, 1979, N.J. State Council on Arts, 1983-85, fellowship, 1985, VCCA Residency, 1986; Seefurth Fdn. fellow U. Wis., 1971. Mem. MLA, AWP, P&W. Home: 16 Stony Brk Lane Princeton NJ 08540

ROBERTS, JIM JOSEPH, b. Ansonia, CT, Sept. 11, 1947; s. Thadeus Joseph and Louise (Callahan) Sosnowski; m. Gail Elizabeth Prentice, Sept. 21, 1968 (div. Apr. 74); m. 2d, Naomi Ruth Nyquist, Aug. 18, 1985; children—Jeanette, David, Katie. Author numerous TV and radio documentaries, hist. programs including Ed Murrow: Father of TV News, 1972, The Hurricane Hunt, 1972, Blizzards, 1973, Guilty though Found Innocent, 1974, Elena: The Not so Lovely Lady, 1985, The Hobo Trail, 1986, Time to Live: Time to Die, 1984. BA cum laude in Journalism, U. R.I.-Kingston, 1973. Wrtr., reporter WNTS-radio, Indpls, 1975-76, WQAD-TV, Moline, Ill., 1976-79; wrtr., ed. WPRI-TV, Providence, 1979-82, WLOX-TV, Biloxi, Miss., 1983-86; head wrtr. EduVision, Gulfport, Miss., 1985—. Recipient Best Documentary award AP, 1978, Ill. Broadcasters, 1978; Runner-up for best documentary Miss. AP, 1985, 3d place for documentary 1985, Best News Cast Award, Assoc. Press, 1985, 86, 87. Mem. Soc. Profl. Journalists, Am. Fedn. TV Radio Artists, Screen Actors Guild, Radio/TV News Dirs. Assn. Home: 4809 Courthouse Rd Gulfport MS 39501

ROBERTS, LEONARD ROBERT, (Len Roberts), b. Cohoes, NY, Mar. 13, 1947, s. Raymond Richard and Margery (Trudeau) R.; m. Denise Patricia Geiger, Nov. 11, 1972 (div. 1980); m. 2d, Nancy Jean Crane, Dec. 31, 1982; children—Tamara, Bradford, Joshua. Author poetry collections: Cohoes Theater, 1980, From the Dark, 1984, The Driving (chapbook), 1986, Sweet Ones, 1987; contrbr. poetry to Ga. Rvw, Ohio Rvw, Va. Qtly Rvw, Mo. Rvw, numerous other jnls and mags. BA, Siena Coll., Albany, N.Y., 1970; MA, U. Dayton (Ohio), 1971; PhD, Lehigh U., Bethlehem, Pa., 1975. Assoc. prof. Northampton County Area Community Coll., Bethlehem, 1974-83; vis. asst. prof. Lafayette Coll., Easton, Pa., 1983—. Recipient Pa. writing award Pa. Council on Arts, 1981, 86, writing award NEA, 1984. Mem. Pa. Artists in Edn., P&W. Home: 1791 Wassergass Rd Hellertown PA 18055

ROBERTSON, HOWARD WAYNE, (Lee Douglas), b. Eugene, OR, Sept. 19, 1947; 2 daus. Chapbook: to the fierce guard in the Assyrian Saloon, 1987; contrbr. poems to Assembling, Croton Rvw, Yet Another Small Magazine, Yellow Silk, Negative Capability, Pinchpenny, others. BA, U. Oreg., 1970, MA, 1978; MLS, U. So. Calif., 1975. Librarian U. Oreg., Eugene, 1975—. Office: Library Univ Oreg Eugene OR 97403

ROBERTSON, JERI JANE, b. Augsburg, Germany, June 10, 1960, came to U.S., 1965; d. Jerry Carlton and Deana Jane (Knight) R. Ed.: Color You Beautiful by P. B. Christian, 1987. A.A. in Jnlsm., Glendal Comm. Coll., 1980; B.S. in Jnlsm., Ariz. State U., Tempe, 1982. Reporter, Verde Ind., Cottonwood, AZ, 1983-85; tchr. Glendale Commun. Coll., AZ, 1985—; ed. Foothills Sentinel, Cave Creek, AZ, 1985—. Mem. Ariz. Press Club (2d place for investigative story on open meetings law 1983), Western Newspapers (editorial com.). Home Box 4521 Cave Creek AZ 85331

ROBERTSON, JOHN, see Bensink, John Robert

ROBERTSON, MARY E., b. Charleston, AR, Apr. 28, 1937; d. Thomas Winfield and Esther (Scherer) R.; m. Peter Lawrence Marchant, Oct. 28, 1961; children—Jennifer Esther, Piers Adam. Books pub.: Jordan's Stormy Banks and Other Stories, 1961, (for children) Jemimalee, 1977 and Tarantula and Red Chigger, 1980, After Freud, 1981, The Clearing, 1982, Speak, Angel, 1983. Stories in Mademoiselle, Seventeen, Stand, Mississippi Rvw, Carolina Rvw, Ascent, Kans. Qtly, Aspen Anthology, Redbook, Va. Qtly, Seattle Rvw, Outerbridge, MS. MA, U. Ark., 1959; MFA, U. Iowa, 1961. Lectr. SUNY-Brockport, 1979-81; writer-in-residence Western Wash. U., Bellingham, 1981, 83; fiction faculty MFA program for writers Warren Wilson Coll., Swannanoa, N.C., 1983—. Mem. P&W, NWU. Recipient 1st prize Mademoiselle Coll. Fiction Contest, 1958; Orgn. Am. Pen Women scholar, 1980; winner AWP award in the novel, 1980; NEA fellow in fiction, 1983. Home: 3238 Brick Schoolhouse Rd Hamlin NY 14464

ROBERTSON, PAT, see Robertson, Thomas Patrick, Jr..

ROBERTSON, PHIL, b. Ukiah, CA, July 5, 1925, s. Glenn F. and Ida H. (Phillips) Seward; m. June King Robertson, Nov. 24, 1956; children—Richard Dunn, Gene Manson, William Dunn, James Dunn. Contrbr. articles to Newsweek, Sunset, Los Angeles Mirror, San Francisco Examiner, other natl. mags. and newspapers. BA in Journalism, San Jose State U., 1948. Reporter Enterprise-Record, Chico, Calif., 1948-50, 56-62; statehouse reporter UP, Denver, 1950-54; mng. ed. Evening Free Lance, Hollister, Calif., 1962-68; adminstrv. service officer Monterey County Probation Dept., Salinas, Calif., 1968-82; stringer AP, 1958-68, San Francisco Chronicle, 1957-63. Recipient citation AP Mng. Eds. Assn., 1961. Home: 18120 Berta Canyon Salinas CA 93907

ROBERTSON, THOMAS PATRICK, JR., (Pat Robertson), b. Greenville, SC, Aug. 1, 1938; s. Thomas Patrick and Joyce Elizabeth (Bridges) R.; m. Dorothy Janice Hammond, Apr. 9, 1966; children—Sean Patrick, Michael Benjamin. Reporter The State Newspaper, Columbia, SC, 1960-62; ed., columnist The Newberry Observer, SC, 1962; city ed. The Evening Herald, Rock Hill, sC, 1962-64; Piedmont bur. chief The State Newspaper, Rock Hill, 1965-67, state news ed., Columbia, 1967-69, outdoors ed., 1984—; city ed. The Columbia Record, Columbia, 1969-73, outdoor wrtr., 1977-84. Contrbr. articles to outdoor mags. including Outdoor Life. Sporting Classics, S.C. Wildlife. Student Spartanburg Jr. Coll., 1956-57; B.A. in Jnlsm., U. S.C., 1961. Recipient Meritorious Service award S.C. Wildlife and Marine Resources Commn., 1982, Harry R. E. Hampton Woods and Waters award for excellence in natural resource reporting S.C. Wildlife Fdn., 1982; named Conservation Communicator of Yr., S.C. Wildlife Fdn., 1978, Jnlst. of Yr., 1983; Shriners Sportsman of Yr., Great Falls Shrine Club, 1985. Mem. OWAA (Easton Waterfowl Festival Wrtrs. award 1986), SC Outdoor Press Assn., Southeastern Outdoor Press Assn. Home: Rt 2 Box 153 Blythewood SC 29016

ROBINETT, BETTY WALLACE, b. Detroit, June 23, 1919; d. Henry Guy and Beulah (Reid) Wallace; m. Ralph F. Robinett, Apr. 10, 1952 (dec. div. 1960); 1 son—Richard Wallace. Author: Manual of American English Pronunciation (with C.H. Prator), 1972, 4th ed. 1985; Teaching English to Speakers of Other Languages, Substance and Technique, 1978; Second Language Learning: Contrastive Analysis, Error Analysis and Related Aspects (with J. Schachter), 1983. BA, Wayne State U., 1940; MA, U. Mich., 1941, PhD, 1951. Instr. admin. asst. English Lang. Inst., U. Mich. (Ann Arbor), 1945-50; cons. Dept. Edn. (San Juan, PR), 1950-51, 52-57; lect. English, U. Mich., 1951-52, 55-56; assoc. prof. English InterAm. U. (San German, PR), 1957-59; asst. prof., prof. linguistics, Ball State U., 1959-68; prof. English and linguistics U. Minn. (Mpls.), 1968—, dir. program in English as a second lang., 1968-80, acting asst. vp acad. affairs, 1979-80, assoc. vp acad. affairs, 1980—. Home: 1909 E River Terr Minneapolis MN 55414

ROBINETT, ROBENA DELITE, b. Oakland, MD, May 19, 1953; d. Blair and Jean (Leighton) Robinett. Contrbr.: The Banner newspaper, Easton, Md., Daily Times, Salisbury, Md., numerous coll. publs. Wrkg. on poetry, naturalist book. AA, Chesapeake Coll., 1973; BS, Salisbury State Coll., 1983. Tchr. Salisbury, Md., 1985; sci. cons. Orion Research Assocs., Centreville, Md., 1986-87. Home: 110 S Liberty St Centreville MD 21617

ROBINS, CORINNE, b. NYC, July 31, 1934, d. Sydney D. and Lillie (Kupsky) Robins; m. Salvatore Romano, June 19, 1964; 1 dau., Joyce. Author: The Pluralist Era: American Art 1968-81, 1984, Art in the 7th Power (poetry chapbook), 1985; contrbr. short story: Contemporary American Fiction, 1983; contrbr. poetry: Artist & Critic, Confrontation, Lips, New Letters, Blue Smoke; contrbr. articles: Artscribe, Soho Weekly News, Feminist Art Jnl, Womanart, others. Student New Schl. Social Research. Assoc. ed. ARTS Mag., NYC 1978—; assoc. ed., art book ed. Am. Book Rvw, NYC, 1984—; instr. art history Schl. Visual Arts, NYC, 1978; vis. assoc. prof. Pratt Inst., Bklyn., 1978—. Art critics fellow NEA, 1978. Mem. Internat. Critics Assn., P&W, PSA. Home: 83 Wooster St New York NY 10012

ROBINS, NATALIE, b. Bound Brook, NJ, June 20, 1938; m. Christopher C. H. Lehmann-Haupt, Oct. 3, 1965; children—Rachel, Noah. Author: Wild Lace (poems), 1960, My Father Spoke of His Riches (poems), 1966, The Peas Belong on the Eye Level (poems), 1972, Eclipse (poems), 1981, co-author, Savage Grace (non-fiction), 1985. BA, Mary Washington Coll., 1960. Address: ICM 40 W 57th St New York NY 10019

ROBINS, ROE, see Rogers, Robert Willis

ROBINS, SHAUNA, see Hall, D. Elaine

ROBINSON, CORA GUINN, b. Dallas, June 2, 1958; d. Richard Louis and Odessa Venora (Fry) G. Mng. ed. Houston Defender Newspaper, 1981-82; ed. Transmission, 1984—. B.S. in Jnlsm., Tex. Tech U., 1980. Communications represenative Contemporary Communications, Houston, 1979-80; communications specialist Port of Houston Authority, 1980-81; media relations coord. Meml. Hosp. System, Houston, 1982-84; ed. co. pubs. Houston Lighting & Power, 1984—. Named Notable Woman of Tex., Emerson Pub., 1984-85. Mem. IABC, WICI. Home: 2750 Holly Hall 1802 Houston TX 77054

ROBINSON, JAMES ARTHUR, b. Blackwell, OK, June 9, 1932; s. William L. and Ethel Bell (Hicks) Robinson. Author: National and International Decision Making (with R.C. Snyder), 1961, Congress and Foreign Policy Making, rev. ed., 1967, House Rules Committee, 1964. AB, George Washington U., 1954, DPS (hon.), 1977; MA, U. OK, 1955; PhDNorthwestern U., 1957; LLD (hon.), Kyungpook (Korea) Natl. U., 1979. Instr. poli. sci. Northwestern U. (Evanston, IL), 1958-59, asst. prof., 1959-62, assoc. prof., 1962-64; prof. poli. sci. Ohio State U. (Columbus), 1964-71; dir. Mershon Center, 1967-70, vp acad. affairs, provost, 1969-71; pres. prof. poli. sci. Macalester Coll. (St. Paul), 1971-74, pres. and prof. of polit. Sci., management, and educational leadership, The U. of W. Fla. (Pensacola), 1974—.Home: Pres Office U West Florida Pensacola FL 32514

ROBINSON, JAMES KEITH, b.Waterman, IL, July 24, 1916; s. John Beveridge and Margaret Ethel (McCoy) R.; m. Pamela Ruth Lyne, July 11, 1945; 2 sons, Christopher Lyne, Nicholas Keith. Edited: A College Book of Modern Verse (with Walter B. Rideout), 1958, A College Book of Modern Fiction (with Walter B. Rideout), 1961, Am. Poetry (with G.W. Allen and W.B. Rideout), 1965; Thomas Hardy: The Mayor of Casterbridge, 1977, A Rededication to Scholarship, 1980. BA, U. Tenn.-Knoxville, 1934-38; MA, Harvard U., 1940, PhD, 1949. Served to Ensign, USN, 1942-43, lt. jg. 1944-45, lt., 1945-56, lt. commndr., 1945-46, inactive lt. commndr., 1946-51. Recipient Dexter Traveling fellowship, Harvard Univ., England, 1947, faculty fellowship, 1952; Taft faculty research fellowship, Univ. Cincinnati, 1971, grad. schl. fellow, 1979, Disting. career award for tchg., 1985. Mem. MLA, AAUP, Address: 444 Riddle Rd Cincinnati OH 45220

ROBINSON, JOHN DELYN, b. Chgo., Jan. 23, 1946; s. Delyn Lavelle and Bonnie Lee R.; m. Dianne Luby, June 26, 1971 (div. 1980), m. 2d, Marsha Bernice Gilford, Aug. 15, 1982. Author: January's Dream (novel), 1985. Wrkg. on novel, Legends of the Lost.; contrbr. theatre and book rvws. to Rhode Island Rvw, political journalism: The Citizen Advocate, Intl. Herald Tribune. BBA, St. Ambrose Coll., 1964-68; MA in Writing U. NH, 1976-77. Instr. English Bryn Mawr Schl., Chgo., 1968-72, Timberlane high schl., Plaistow, NH, 1974-78, McIntosh Coll., Dover, NH, 1979-80, White Pines Coll., Chester, NH, 1981-84; asst. prof. English Bradford Coll., Mass., 1983-85; self- employed writer Portsmouth, NH, 1986—. Mem. AG, AL Am.,

AWP. Address: 39 Cass St Portsmouth NH 03801

ROBINSON, KATHERINE PRENTIS WOODROOFE, (Mrs. M. Richard Robinson, Jr.), b. Detroit, Oct. 20, 1939; d. Robert William and Lindsay Prentis Woodroofe; m. Richard Robinson, Jr., May 17, 1968. BA, Smith Coll., 1961. With Scholastic Mags., Inc. (NYC), 1961—; asst. editor Lit. Cavalcade Mag., 1963-64; assoc. editor, mng. editor Scholastic Scope mag., 1965-67, editor, 1967—; also editor Scope Play Series, Scope Activity Kits. Home: 156 W 88th St New York NY 10024

ROBINSON, KATHLEEN SHELLEY, b. San Jose, CA, Mar. 28, 1948, d. Francis Warren and Evelyn Irene (Flanagan) Robinson. Author teleplays for Magnum, P.I., 1982, 83. Wrkg. on screenplay. AA, Coll. San Mateo, 1968; BA in History, U. Calif.-Berkeley, 1970. Adminstrv. asst. Computer Curriculum Corp., Palo Alto, Calif., 1980-84; exec. secy. Grace Ventures Corp., Cupertino, Calif., 1984-85; secy. Stanford U., Calif., 1985—. Vol. VISTA, Washington, 1968. Mem. Wrtr.'s Connection, Media Alliance. Home: 275 E O'Keefe St 14 Palo Alto CA 94303

ROBINSON, KAYLAINE, b. San Francisco, July 30, 1933, d. Robert Nasmyth and Katherine Margaret (Miller) Miller; m. Theodore Albert Robinson, June 6, 1970; children—Kim Kaylaine Williams, Kevin Paul Nasmyth Hart, Lisa Lorayn Hart. Contrbr. to The Wheel, The Drifter, Panorama, Goldweb Publs., Scenic 88 Fun Times. AA, Sacramento Jr. Coll., 1952, BA, 1954. Wrtr., mng. ed., Scenic 88 Fun Times, Pioneer, Calif.; wrtr. Amador Dispatch, Jackson. Home: Box 340 Pioneer CA 95666

ROBINSON, LEONARD WALLACE, b. Malden, MA, Nov. 9, 1912; s. Henry Morton and Ellen Elizabeth (Flynn) R.; m. Patricia McKenna Goedicke, May 18, 1972; 1 child, Roderick Wallace. Author: (novels) The Man Who Loved Beauty, 1976; The Assassin, 1969 (also pub. as With Time Running Out); (poetry) In the Whale, 1983; ed.: The Road to Janowska (Leon Wells), 1963. Student, Columbia U., 1931-35; postgrad. New Schl. for Social Research, 1941-44; MA, U. Guanajuato, Mex., Reporter/wrtr. New Yorker mag., NYC, 1942-46; mng. ed. Esquire mag., 1952-54; fiction ed.-in-chief Colliers mag., NYC, 1956, exec. ed. Holt Reinhardt and Winston, NYC, 1957—. Fellow MacDowell Colony; mem. PEN. Home: 310 McLeod Ave Missoula MT 59801

ROBINSON, MARCELA, b. Panama, Feb. 15, came to U.S., 1970, d. James and Beatrice (Yard) Robinson. Scriptwrtr.: The Little School on the Island, 1983, Roommates, 1983. MA, Calif. State U., Northridge, 1976. Tchr. public schls., Sepulveda, Calif.; prin. Marcela Prodns., Van Nuys, Calif., 1983—. Office: Box 4951 Panorama City CA 91412

ROBINSON, RAYMOND KENNETH, b. NYC, Dec. 4, 1920; s. Louis Harry and Lillian (Hoffman) Robinson; m. Phyllis Cumins, Sept. 19, 1949; children—Nancy, Stephen, Tad. Author: Mario Lanza Story, 1960, Ted Williams, 1962, Stan Musial: Baseball's Durable Man, 1963, Speed Kings of the Basepaths, 1964, Greatest World Series Thrillers, 1965, Greatest Yankees of Them All, 1968, Baseball's Most Colorful Managers, 1969, Baseball, paperback series, 1958-75, Oh Baby, I Love It! (with Tim McCarver), 1987; anthologized in Best Sports Stories of the Year, 1958, 59, Fireside Book of Baseball, 2 editions. BA, Columbia, 1941; postgrad. Columbia Law Schl., 1941-42. Mng. editor Mag. Mgmt., 1950-56; editor Real mag., 1956-57; mng. editor Pageant mag., 1957-59; sr. editor Coronet mag., 1959-61; articles editor Good Housekeeping mag., 1961-69; mng. editor Seventeen mag., 1969-79, exec. editor, 1979—. Served with AUS, 1942-46. Mem. ASME. chmn, Alumni Advisory Bd., Columbia Mag. Home: 530 E 90th St New York NY 10128

ROBINSON, SUSAN HAND, (Susan Hand), b. Summit, NJ, Oct. 1, 1942, d. Darwin Clifford and Pattie Ruth (Neff) Hand; m. Stephen Manning Robinson, June 20, 1970 (div. 1983); 1 son, Morgan Manning. Contrbr. stories to N.Am. Mentor Mag., Epoch. BA magna cum laude, Radcliffe Coll., 1964; MA, Columbia U., 1966; MFA, Warren Wilson Coll., 1986. Tchr., Englewood, N.J., 1967-70; free-lance wrtr., ed., Ill. and Mass., 1970—. Woodrow Wilson fellow, 1965. Mem. AWP, Phi Beta Kappa. Home: 25 Pleasant St Newton Centre MA 02159

ROBINSON, WILLIAM WHEELER, b. Elizabeth, NJ, Oct. 4, 1918; s. Henry Pearson and Clare Stearns (Wheeler) Robinson; m. Jane Dimock, Feb. 27, 1942; children—William Wheeler, Martha Robinson Bliss, Alice. Author: The Science of Sailing, 1960, New Boat, 1961, A Berth to Bermuda, 1961, Where the Trade Winds Blow, 1963, Expert Sailing, 1965, Over the Horizon, 1966, The World of Yachting, 1966, Better Sailing for Boys and Girls, 1968, The America's Cup Races (with H.L. Stone), 1970, Legendary Yachts, 1971, rev. 1978, The Sailing Life, 1974, Right Boat for You, 1974, Great American Yacht Designers, 1974, America's Sailing Book, 1976, A Sailor's Tales, 1978, Cruising, the Boats and the Places, 1981, South to the Caribbean, 1981, Where to Cruise, 1984, Islands, 1985, Caribbean Cruising Handbook, 1986, 80 Years of Yachting. 1987; contrbr. numerous articles to profl. jnls. BA, Princeton U., 1939. Traffic rep. Traffic dept. Eastern Airlines (NYC), 1939-41; mgr. pub. relations Elco Yacht Div. (Bayonne, NJ), 1945-57; sportswriter Newark Evening News (NJ), 1947-55; sportswriter, syndicated columnist Newark Star-Ledger, 1955-57; assoc. editor Yachting Mag. (NYC), 1957-67, editor, exec. vp, 1967-78, editor-at-large, 1979-86; ed.-at-large, Cruising World Mag. (Newport, R.I.), 1987—; mem. exec. bd. Sea Ventures (Ft. Hancock, NJ), 1974-77; pres. Princeton Club of NY, 1984—; writer radio, TV shows on boating; freelance writer. Served with USNR, 1941-45. Mem. Cruising Club Am. (historian 1972-77). Home: 14 Oyster Bay Dr Rumson NJ 07760

ROBY, KINLEY EDMUND, b. Westbrook, ME, Aug. 2, 1929; m. Mary Wilson Linn, Feb. 3, 1951. Author: A Writer at War, 1972, The King, The Press and the People, 1975, Joyce Cary, 1984, T.S. Eliot: The Sweeney Motive, 1985. AB, U. Maine, 1951, M Ed., 1956; PhDPA State U., 1970. Prof. English Northeastern U. (Boston), 1970—, chair dept. 1981—. Mem. MLA. Office: Northeastern U 360 Huntington Ave Boston MA 02115

ROCHON, EDWIN WATERBURY, b. Butte, MT, Jan. 29, 1918; s. Clarence G. and Edna (Waterbury) Rochon; m. Thelma Parrish, Mar. 7, 1943. Author: short stories This Week mag, 1961-65. BA, Princeton, 1940; MA, Columbia, 1962. Copy reader NY Herald Tribune, 1948-52, NY Daily News, 1961-63; columnist NY World- Telegram and Sun, 1953-61; fin. editor House and Home mag. (NYC), 1963-78, mng. editor, 1977-79; staff editor Bus. Week mag., 1979-82. Served AUS, 1941-45, lt. col. Res. Ret. Home: 310 1st Ave New York NY 10009

ROCKSTEIN, MORRIS, b. Toronto, Ont., Can., Jan. 8, 1916 (came to U.S. 1923); s. David and Mina (Segal) Rockstein. Sr. Author: Biology of Human Aging, 1978; editor: Physiology of Insecta, 6 vols., 1973-74, Physiology and Pathology of Human Aging, 1975, Nutrition, Longevity and Aging, 1977; author: Miscellaneous Collections, Entomol. Soc. Am., 1982—. AB, Brooklyn Coll., 1938; MA, Columbia U., 1941; PhD, U. Minn., 1948; cert. Oak Ridge Inst. Nuclear Studies, 1950. Research asst. entomology U. Minn., 1941-42; asst. prof., assoc. prof. zoophysiology Wash. State U. (Pullman), 1948-53; asst. prof., assoc. prof. physiology NYU Schl. Medicine (NYC), 1953-61; prof. physiology U. Miami Schl. Medicine, 1961-81, chair, sci. adv. bd. Anorexia Nervosa Inst. (Melbourne, FL), 1983—. Served with USAAF, 1942-46. Home: 8045 SW 107 Ave Miami FL 33134

RODDIN, MICHAEL IAN, b. Fresh Meadows, NY Aug. 21, 1955; s. William J. and Helen I. (Always) R.; m. Laura K. Greaves, May 25, 1983; children—Shannon Lee, Kayla Michelle. Contrbr. to Warrior Press, Fort Riley Post, Army mag., others. Ed.: Kennedy Kaserne Newsletter, 1981-82, The Informer, 1984-86, Kaleidoscope, 1984-85. B.S. in English, U. Maine, 1979; M.S. in Systems Management, U. Southern Calif., 1986. Commissioned Capt. U.S. Army, 1973, advanced through grades to capt., 1979—, instr. Ft. Dix, NJ, 1973-75, personnel mgr., Fulda and Frankfurt, Wet Germany, 1979-83, publi8c relations dir., Ft. Riley, KS, 1983-86, advt. project officer, Ft. Sheridan, IL, 1986—. Recipient Keith L. Ware Award U.S. Army, 1984, 85, Silver Poet award World Poetry Press, 1986. Mem. Assn. U.S. Army, Nat. Assn. Govt. Communicators, NWC, Natl. Freelancers Assn. Home: 334 S Seymour Ave Mundelein IL 60060

RODGERS, MARY COLUMBRO, b. Aurora, OH, Apr. 17, 1925, d. Nicola D. and Nazarena J. (DeNicola) Columbro; m. Daniel Richard Rodgers, July 24, 1965; children—Daniel Robert III, Mary Patricia, Mary Kristine. Author numerous books, monographs including: Cross-Component English Teaching: New Design Units, 1970, Language Arts Lessons for a Career Curriculum: Grades 7-8, National Open University: Design for Synthesis Between Collegiate and Paracollegiate Educational Systems in the United States, 1973, A Short Course in English Composition, 1976, Open University English Teaching, 1945-85: Conceptual History and Rationale, 1985, History of the Am. Open Univ., 1965-85, 1986, Essays in English Pedagogy in the American Open University, 1987; author: Christmas Lullaby, A Play, 1942, Sister Saints: A Musical Production, 1943, A Shakespearean Sonnet Set to Music, 1957, Two Song Poems for Children. 1960, New Moon and Other Poems, 1941 to 1961, 1963, A Packet of Poems for Children, 1970, Chapbook of Children's Literature, 1977 BA, Notre Dame Coll., Cleve., 1957; MA, Western Res. U., 1962; PhD, Ohio State U., 1965; EdD, Calif. Natl. Open U., 1975, DLitt, 1978. Founder, chancellor Open Univ. Am., the research archetype, Hyattsville, Md., 1965; founder Md. Natl. Open U., Hyattsville, 1972, Natl. Open U., Washington, 1973, Calif. Natl. Open U., Sacramento, 1975, Nev. Natl. Open U., Carson City, 1978. Fulbright teaching-research fellow, U. Rome, 1964-65; recipient Poetry prize Open U. Am., Hyattsville, Md., 1968. Mem. PSA, NCTE, Fellowship of Catholic Scholars, profl. orgns. Home: 3916 Commander Dr Hyattsville MD 20782

RODIECK, PATRICIA ANNA, b. Niagara Falls, NY, July 18, 1938; d. Walter Sherman and Laura Anna (Wiseman) Johnson; div. 1977; children: Arlo Eugene, Jorma Leonard. Works include Crabshell Brief, 1979-83; ed. Self-Determination: An Examination of the Question and its Application to the African-American People (James Forman) 1981; The Invisible Empire: The Ku Klux Klan Impact on History (W.L. Katz), 1986. BA, Colby Coll., 1960; research asst. Sydney U., Australia, 1963; student Natl. Art Schl., Sydney, 1964-66.; potter, Sydney, 1965-78; pres. Open Hand Pub. Inc., Seattle, 1981-83, Washington, 1983—. Mem. Women's Natl. Book Assn., Washington Pubs. Assn. Home: 600 E Pine Suite 565 Seattle WA 98122

ROE, INA LEA, b. Wheat, TN, Nov. 25, 1930; d. William Ernest and Lucile Marie (Zimmerman) Gallaher; m. Donald Roe, Aug. 15, 1961. BA, BS U. Tenn, 1952; MS Temple U., 1961. Technologist for doctors (Knoxville, TN), 1952-58; technologist Meml. Hosp. (Chattanooga), 1958-59; mem. faculty dept. med. tech. Temple U. (Philadelphia), 1961-75, prof. 1973-75, clin. prof., 1975—; editor-in-chief Am. Jnl Med.Tech. (Houston), 1970—; cons. med. lab. sci. edn. programs, 1970—. Home: Rt 1 Box 236-A Spring City TN 37381

ROECKER, W(ILLIAM) A(LAN), b. Madison, Wis., Jan. 17, 1942, s. Alan Wallace and Maxeen Athol (Spees) R.; m. Margaret Dee Horn, Dec. 27, 1963 (div. 1972); m. Deborah Sue Huntsman, Dec. 31, 1984. Author: (poems) Willamette, 1970, You Know Me, 1972, Closer to the Country, 1976; ed. Stories That Count, 1971; contrbr. stories and poetry to Quixote, Trace, WHR, Inscape, also other lit mags. Wrkg. on poems and articles for sportfishing and hang gliding publs.; assoc. ed. South Coast Sportfishing mag., Los Angeles, 1987. BS, U. Oreg., 1966, MFA, 1967. Grad. asst. English dept. U. Oreg., 1966-67; instr., asst. prof. English dept. U. Ariz., Tucson, 1968-75; freelance wrtr.., 1976—; wrtr., editor Windsport mag., San Diego, 1981-82; field ed., Today's Fisherman mag., 1985—. Recipient Gray prize for hang gliding journalism, 1985. NEA grantee, 1973. Home: 379 N Vulcan St Encinitas CA 92024

ROES, NICHOLAS A., b. Jersey City, Dec. 26, 1952; s. Nicholas Rocco and Mimi (Maresca) R.; m. Nancy Bennett, Nov. 26, 1977. Author: Helping Children Watch TV, 1982, America's Lowest Cost Colleges, 1985. BS, U. Bridgeport, 1974, MA, 1983, 9th ed., 1987; Syndicated Column, Wall St. Casino. Ed., Teacher Update Newsletter, 1977—. Address: Box 205 Saddle River NJ 07458

ROETS, LOIS SCHELLE, b. Breda,IA, Mar. 4, 1937; d. Charles and Mary Ann (Goecke) Schelle; m. Philip Roets, June 7, 1969; children—Jacqueline, Ron. Author: Public Speaking, 1984, Writing Fiction, 1985, Leadership, 1986; lyricist, songwriter 10 ballads, Student Projects—Ideas & Plans, 1987, Philosophy and Philosophers, 1987. BS, Viterbo Coll., 1964; MS, U. Wis.-Madison, 1975; EdD, Inst. Adv. Studies, St. Louis, 1984. Tchr. pub. schls., Ia. and Wis., 1961—, freelance wrtr., 1977—. Mem. Am. Educators Research Assn., Natl. Assn. Gifted Children, Natl. Writers Club. Home: 407 W Cherry Box 51 New Sharon IA 50207

ROFFMAN, ROSALY DE MAIOS, b. NYC, June 1, 1937, d. Murray and Sylvia (Fleishman) DeMaios; m. Bernard Roffman, May 30, 1964; 1 son, Peter. Contrbr. poetry to Sojourner, Centennial, New Oregon Rvw, Poets On, numerous other lit mags; publs. ed. Threepenny Papers, Honolulu, 1960-63; presenter poetry readings. BA with honors in Lang. and Lit., CCNY, 1960; MA in English, U. Hawaii, 1967. Wrtr. TV Guide, 1960-61, Council St. Travel, NYC, 1962-63; tchr. U. Hawaii, Honolulu, 1961-63; instr. CCNY, 1963-65, Gakushuin U., Tokyo, 1962; assoc. prof. Indiana U. of Pa., 1965—, chair Asian Studies, 1985-86. Grantee NEH, 1980, Jungian Inst. Mem. PSA, AAUP. Home: 15 Forbes Terr Pittsburgh PA 15217

ROGERS, DONALD JOSEPH, b. Chgo., Dec. 13, 1945; s. Joseph Paul and LaVerne Joan (Trudan) R.; m. Nancy Benning Kelly, Aug. 12, 1978. Author: Banned! Book Censorship in the Schools, 1987, Press versus Government, 1986; ed. Law in American History, 1983; contrbr. to Four Psychologies Applied to Education, 1975, The Book of Macintosh Software, 1985, also periodicals Elem. Schl. Jnl, Annals Am. Acad. Poli. and Social Sci., Curriculum Adv. Service Rvw, Best Sellers, Nibble Mag., Weekend World, Chgo. Tribune. AB, U. Notre Dame, 1967; MA, Northeastern Ill. U., 1973. Tchr. pub. schls., Northlake and Northfield, Ill., 1968-76; wrtr./producer Soc. for Visual Edn., Chgo., 1976-78, Encyc. Brit. Ednl. Corp., Chgo., 1978-81; freelance wrtr., 1981—. Recipient award for best social studies filmstrip Natl. Ednl. Film Festival, 1984. Home: 515 N Bristol Ln Schaumburg IL 60194

ROGERS, FAITH ELAINE, b. Darby,PA, Feb. 13, 1945; d. Raymond Bailey and Elfriede Dorothea (Otto) R.; m. William E. Ingalls, Nov. 4, 1966 (div. Mar. 1974); 1 dau., Ursula Rogers-Ingalls. BS in Jnlsm., U. Co, 1967. Editorial asst. Wadsworth Pub. Co., Belmont, CA, 1967-68; staff ed. Geol. Soc. Amer., Boulder, CO, 1973-81, editorial co-ord., 1981-84, mng. ed., 1984—. Mem. AESE, SSP. Office: Box 9140 Boulder CO 80301

ROGERS, PATTIANN, b. Joplin, MO, Mar. 23, 1940; d. William Elmer and Irene Christine (Keiter) Tall; m. John Robert Rogers, Sept. 3, 1950; children: John Ashley, Arthur William. Author: The Expectations of Light, 1981, The Tattooed Lady in the Garden, 1986; contrbr. to Morrow Anthology of Younger American Poets, 1985, New American Poets of the 80's, 1985. BA,U. Mo., 1961; MA, U. Houston, 1981. Vis. asst. prof. So. Methodist Univ., Dallas, 1985, Univ. Houston, 1986. NEA grantee, 1982; Guggenheim fellow, 1984; recipient Voertman Poetry award, Tex. Inst. Letters, 1982; Tietiens Prize in Poetry, 1982; Pushcart prizes, 1984, 85. Mem PEN, P&W, Tex. Inst. Letters. Address: 11502 Brookmeadows Stafford TX 77477

ROGERS, PAULINE BONNIE, b. Springfield, MA, Apr. 6, 1949, d. Paul and Gertrude (Alley) Rogers. Author television movies: Glass Houses, Paying for Love, Other Victims. BA, Am. Intl. U., Springfield, Mass.; MA, Hunter Coll., NYC, 1971. Publicist Merv Griffin Prodns., Los Angeles, 1976-82; free-lance wrtr., 1976—. Mem. WGA. Home: 1380 Midvale Ave Apt 208 Los Angeles CA 90024

ROGERS, ROBERT WENTWORTH, b. Boston, Dec. 1, 1914; s. Lester Frances and Elizabeth (Gill) Rogers; m. Jeanne Francis Way, May 18, 1946 (dec. 1955); foster children—Susan Way, Sarah Wentworth; 2nd m. Elizabeth Belcher Yudkin, Nov. 23, 1956; 1 son—John Parker; foster children—Michael Yudkin, David Yudkin. Author: The Major Satires of Alexander Pope, 1955; editorial bd.: Jnl. English and Germanic Philology, 1954-66. AB U. Mich., 1936 MA Harvard, 1937, PhD, 1942. Instr. English, sr. tutor Dunster House, Harvard, 1946-48; asst. prof. English U. Ill. (Champaign-Urbana), 1948-51, asso. prof. 1951-55, prof., 1955—, exec. sec. dept. English, 1953-57, acting head, 1956-57, head dept. 1957-64, dean, 1964-79, dean emeritus, 1979—; mem. Commn. on Arts and Scis., Natl. Assn. State Univs. and Land Grant Colls., 1972-74. Served from ensign to lt. (s.g.) USNR, 1942-46. Mem. MLA, NCTE (adv. council 1960-62), Midwest MLA (pres. 1960), AAUP, Natl. Assn. Chmn. Depts. English (secy-treas. 1963-64), Phi Beta Kappa. Home: 1117 Mayfair Rd Champaign IL 61821

ROGERS, ROBERT WILLIS, (Roe Robins), b. Mason, TN, Aug. 31, 1912; s. Bennie Willis and Anna Muriel (Eubank) R.; m. Dorothy J. Armstrong, Sept. 7, 1935; children—Robert Armstrong, William Edward, Mary Carolyn. Author: National Reporting Handbook, 1956 (Superior Service award from US Dept. Agr.), and SCS-USDA Annual Reports, The Rogers of Belmont-Mason, Tennessee, 1982, Rogers & Fraser-Founders, 1983, Giles Rogers, Pioneer Immigrant to King and Queen County, Virginia, 1984; ed.: The Rogers of Reedy Branch, Dinwiddie County, Virginia (by Ginger Rogers), 1983. Wrkg. on hist. novel, genealogy, biography. B Engring., U. Tenn., 1932; postgrad., US Dept. Agr. Grad. Sch., 1945-48. With US Dept. Agr., 1935-68, cons. engr., Tenn., 1935-43, chief reports div., Washington, 1943-68; real estate broker, Chevy Chase, Md. Recipient of many awards from hist. and genealogy socs. Home: 4701 Willard Ave Chevy Chase MD 20815

ROGERS, ROSEMARY, b. Panadura, Ceylon, Dec. 7, 1932; d. Cyril and Barbara (Jansz) Allan; m. Summa Navaratnam (div.); children—Rosanne, Sharon; 2nd m. Leroy Rogers (div.); children—Michael, Adam; 3rd m. Christopher Kadison. Author: novels Sweet Savage Love, 1974, The Wildest Heart, 1974, Dark Fires, 1975, Wicked Loving Lies, 1976, The Crowd Pleasers, 1978, The Insiders, 1979, Lost Love, Last Love, 1980, Love Play, 1981, Surrender to Love, 1982, The Wanton, 1985. BA, U. Ceylon. Writer features and pub. affairs info. Associated Newspapers Ceylon (Colombo), 1959-62; secy. billeting office Travis AFB (CA), 1964-69; secy. Solano County Parks Dept. (Fairfield, CA), 1969-74; part-time reporter Fairfield Daily Republic. Mem. AG, AL Am. Office: NAL 1633 Broadway New York NY 10010

ROGERS, THOMAS N.R., b. Bronxville, NY; s. Joel Townsley and Winifred Woodruff (Whitehouse) R.; m. Maureen Eileen Delaney (div.); 1 son, Joel. Contrbr. articles to Washington Post, Daily Iowan, Carousel; stories Shankpainter, Three Sisters, Harpers, This World, So. Humanities Rvw, Nimrod., North American Rvw. BA, Geo. Washington U., 1966; MFA, U. Iowa, 1977. Columnist Daily Iowan, Iowa City, 1985—. Recipient fellowships Fine Arts Work Ctr., 1979, 80, NEA, 1981-82; first place award Iowa Arts Council lit., 1984; winner PEN syndicated fiction competition, 1984, 86. Address: 800 Kimball Rd Iowa City IA 52240

ROGERSON, LYNDA GAIL, b. Bangor, ME, Sept. 2, 1948; d. John Albin and Helen Julia (Domagala) Nelson; m. George Roger Lambert, Feb. 22, 1969 (div. Apr. 1972); 1 dau., Lara Lyn; m. Michael Mont Rogerson, Oct. 21, 1978; children—Kaelyn Mae, Sarah Grace. Author: Veterans Resources Handbook, 1976, Before You Write Your Resume, 1983, Health Promotion Programming in the Department of Corrections, 1985. B.A., U. Colo., 1971, M.A., 1978; postgrad. U. Northern Colo., 1981-87. Veterans certification officer Pikes Peak Commun. Coll., Colorado Springs, CO, 1974-81, career devel. specialist, 1981-83; career cons. Lynco Assocs., Colorado Springs, 1977—. Mem. Am. Soc. Training Devel. (v.p. Pikes Peak chapt.), Am. Assn. Counseling Devel., Natl. Assn. Female Execs. (exec. dir. network exchange for women), Bus. Profl. Women. Home: 2930 Marilyn Rd Colorado Springs CO 80909

ROGIN, GILBERT LESLIE, b. NYC, Nov. 14, 1929; s. Robert I. and Lillian Carol (Ruderman) Rogin. Author: The Fencing Master, 1965, What Happens Next?, 1971, Preparations for the Ascent, 1980. AB, Columbia, 1951. Mng. editor Sports Illus. (NYC), 1979-84; mng. ed. Discover, 1984—. Served with AUS, 1952-54. Recipient award for creative work in lit. Am. Acad. Inst. Arts and Letters, 1972. Home: 42 W 10th St New York NY 10011

ROGOW, ZACK, b. NYC, May 8, 1952, s. Leon and Mildred (Weisfeld) R.; m. Anne Sachs, July 6, 1986. Author: Glimmerings, 1979, Make It Last, 1983, A Preview of the Dream, 1985; co-translator: The Dice Cup (by Max Jacob), 1979. BA cum laude, Yale U., 1975; MA, CUNY, 1977. Contrbg. ed. Home Planet News, NYC1980—; co-ed. Slow Motion Mag., NYC1985—. Home: Sachs 733 31st Ave San Francisco CA 94121

ROHMANN, PAUL HENRY, b. Bklyn., Feb. 15, 1918; s. Henry August and Elizabeth (Zaiser) Rohmann; m. Christabel Grover, May 31, 1941; children—Christopher, Eric, Margaret Moore, Kimberly. Contrbr. to scholarly publs. BA, Antioch Coll., 1940. Editor Air Tech. Service Command. US Army Air Force, Wright Field, 1942-45; asst. mgr. Antioch Press (Yellow Springs, OH), 1945-57, dir. 1957-69; editor Antioch Rvw, 1957-67; assoc. dir. Kent State U. Press (Ohio), 1969-73, dir. 1974-85. Mem. Assn. Am. Univ. Presses (dir. 1980-82). Home: Rt 3 Box 731 Putney VT 05346

ROHRBACH, PETER THOMAS, (James P. Cody), b. NYC, Feb. 27, 1926; s. James P. and Kathryn F. (Foley); m. Sheila Sheehan, Sept. 21, 1970; 1 dau., Sarah. Author 15 books, latest being Journey to Carith, 1966, The Disullusioned, 1969, Conversation with Christ, 1981, Stagecoach East, 1982, American Issue, 1984. Wrkg. on book on Am. history. A.B. in Philosophy, Catholic U. Am., 1952, M.A. in Edn., 1953. Mem. AG, PEN, Washington Ind. Wrtrs. Home and Office: 9609 Barkston CT Potomac MD 20850

ROHRBERGER, MARY, b. New Orleans, Jan. 22, 1929, d. Adolf and Flora (Ketry) Rohrberger. Author: Hawthorne and the Modern Short Story: A Study in Genre, 1966, An Introduction to Literature, 1968, Reading and Writing About Literature, 1970, The Art of Katherine Mansfield, 1977, Story to Anti-Story, 1979; contrbr. numerous articles to regional, natl. and intl. jnls. BA in English, Newcomb Coll., New Orleans, 1950; MA, Tulane U., 1952, PhD, 1961. Mem. faculty Okla. State U., Stillwater, 19,61—, prof., 1971—, asst. to dean Coll. Arts and Scis., 1980-83, dir. curricular affairs Coll. Arts and Scis., 1983-m. Mem. MLA, NCTE, Phi Beta Kappa. Office: 201 Life Scis E Okla State U Stillwater OK 74078

ROHRER, LILA BORG, (Susie), b. Davenport, IA, Jan. 29, 1929; d. Clarence Eugene Borg and Mabel (Ginter) Brandt; m. Donald Dean, Aug. 1, 1948; children—Jeanne, Jane, Soonee Joan. Author: Ethic Iowa, 1985. Contrbr. short stories, articles, poems to anthols., mags. including Midwest Poetry Rvw., Best of Ed.'s Desk, Odessa Poetry Rvw. BA in Art Edn., U. Ia., 1965, MA in Art Edn., 1968. Tchr. HLV Community Schls., Victor, Ia., 1968—; corr. Cedar Rapids Gazette, Ia., 1985—, Bklyn. Free Press, Bklyn., Ia., 1985—. Mem. AAP, Delta Kappa Gamma. Home: Box M Victor IA 52347

ROHRS, WILHELM HERMANN, b. Lippstadt, Germany, Sept. 7, 1932, came to U.S., 1957; s. Wilhelm Franz and Luise Anna (Liebern) R.; m. Heidi Buchler, May 28, 1955; 1 dau., Angelika. Contrbr. poems to numerous anthols.; working on Farewell Cycle, 1986—, entirely in German (25 poems), Jessica Cycle, 1976-87. Cartographer degree, Coll. Engring., Frankfurt, Germany, 1953. Freelance cartographer, 1953—. Recipient Honorable Mention award World of Poetry Press, 1983, 85, 86, 87,Golden Poet award, 1985, 86, 87. Home: 82 Jacoby St Maplewood NJ 07040

ROLFE, BARI, b. Chgo., July 20, 1916; d. Max and Doris (Fellin) Wicks. Author: Behind the Mask, 1977, Commedia dell'Arte, A Scene Study Book, 1977, Movement for Period Plays, 1985; editor: Mime Bibliography, 1978, Farces, Italian Style, 1978, Mimes on Miming, 1980; articles in Theatrical Movement, A Bibliographical Anthology, 1986. Mime, dancer, choreographer, cons., dir., tchr., writer in schls., univs., cos., TV, theatres U.S. and abroad, over 50 yrs. Mem. Am. Theatre Assn. Home: 434 66th St Oakland CA 94609

ROLLE, ANDREW, b. Providence, Apr. 12, 1922; m. Frances Johanna Squires, Dec. 1945 (div.); children—John Warren, Alexander Frederick, Julia Elisabeth; 2nd m. Myra Moss, Nov. 1983. Author: Riviera Path, 1946, An American in California, 1956, reprinted, 1982, The Road to Virginia City, 1960, Lincoln: A Contemporary Portrait (with Allan Nevins, Irving Stone), 1961, California: A History, 1963, rev. ed., 1969, 78, Occidental College: The First Seventy-Five Years, 1963, The Lost Cause: Confederate Exiles in Mexico, 1965, The Golden State, 1967, rev. ed., 1978, California, A Student Guide, 1965, Los Angeles, A Student Guide, 1965; editor: A Century of Dishonor (Helen Hunt Jackson), 1964, The Immigrant Upraised, 1968, Life in California, 1972, Gli Emigrati Vittoriosi, 1973, Essays and Assays (with George Knoles, others), 1973, Studies in Italian American Social History (with Francesco Cordasco, others), 1975, Los Angeles: The Biography of a City (with John Caughey, others), 1976, Conflict in America (with Allan Weinstein, others), 1977, The Italian Americans: Troubled Roots, 1980, Los Angeles: From Pueblo to Tomorrow's City, 1981, Occidental College: A Centennial History, 1986. BA, Occidental Coll., 1943; MA, UCLA, 1949, PhD, 1953; grad. So. Calif. Psychoanalytic Inst., 1976. Am. vice consul (Genoa, Italy), 1945-48; vis. prof. U. Calif. (Los Angeles), 1975, 76; editorial assoc. Pacific Hist. Rvw, 1952-53; from asst. prof. to prof. Occidental Coll., 1953-62, prof., chmn. dept. history, 1962, 65-66, 73-74, Cleland prof. history, 1965—. Served to 1st lt. M.I. AUS, 1943-45, 51-52. Recipient award of merit Am. Assn. State and Local History; silver medal Italian Ministry Fgn. Affairs; Commonwealth award for non- fiction; Huntington Library-Rockefeller Fdn. fellow; resident scholar Rockefeller Fdn. Center, Bellagio, Italy. Home: 2105 Adair San Marino CA 91108

ROLLEFSON, ANNA MAE MAXINE, b. Ventura, IA, Nov. 22, 1924; d. Selmer Eli and Anna Caroline (Nelson) Moore; m. Harvey Rollefson, Aug. 1, 1949; children—Vicki Rollefson Dickenson, Cindy Rollefson Wooge. Author poetry: Reflections (book), 1985, poems in local nwspr. & church messenger; publisher of Reminiscing the Good Old Days (short stories and poems), and a Christmas Story for Children, The Smallest Reindeer. Student pub. schls., Ventura, IA. Homemaker & poet. Golden poet award, World of Poetry, 1985 Home: RR 4 Box 78 Forest City IA 50436

ROLLINGS, ALANE, b. Savannah, GA; d. Harry Evan and Irma Lee (Pittman) Rollings; m. Richard G. Stern, Aug., 1985. Author: Transparent Landscapes, 1984. BA, MA, U. Chgo. Lectr. Loyola Univ., Chgo., 1985—. Address: 5455 S Ridgewood Ct Chicago IL 60615

ROLLOFF LANGWORTHY, CAROL LEMAY, (Carol Rolloff), b. Pollock, SD, Mar. 18, 1942; d. Harold Theodore and Myrtle May (Ehnert) DeBoer; m. Anthony A. Rolloff, May 26, 1964 (div. Aug. 13,1977); 1 dau., S. Alexis; m. 2d, Russell L. Langworthy, Dec. 22, 1981; stepchildren—Mark W., Peter R. Contrbr. articles to Twin Cities mag., travel features to newspapers, articles to profl. jnls. BA, Macalester Coll., 1964; MA, U. Denver, 1980. Copy ed. Mpls. Tribune, 1966; reporter St. Paul Dispatch Pioneer, 1966-69; editorial asst. U. Denber, 1971-73; grants coordinator Macalester Coll., St. Paul, 1976-79; dir. pub. info. Coll. of St. Catherine, St. Paul, 1979-81; research assoc. Carleton Coll., Northfield, Minn., 1981—. Mem. Women Hist. of Midwest (pres.), Am. Studies Assn., Minn. Press Club. Home: 310 E Fifth St Northfield MN 55057

ROLOFF, MICHAEL, b. Berlin, Dec. 19, 1937 (came to US, 1950, naturalized, 1952); s. William and Alexandra (Von Alvensleben) Roloff. Author: (fiction) Darlings and Monsters, 1991. The Hunger Artists, 1990, Breakup under Analysis, 1992. (The Darlings and Monsters Quartet); (poetry) Headshots, 1984, It Won't Grow Back, 1985; screenwriter: Feelings, 1982, Darlings and Monsters, 1983, The Graduation Party, 1984; translator numerous books from German, including works by Peter Handke, Hermann Hesse, Nelly Sachs, F.X. Kroetx, Rolf Hochhuth, H.M. Enzensberger; playwright: Wolves of Wyoming, 1985, Palombe Bleu, 1986, Schizzohawk, 1986, The Last Time Can Be the Best Time, 1986, The Mama/Papa Boy/Girl After Dinner Theater, 1986; contrbr. to NY Times Book Rvw. BA, Haverford Coll., 1958; MA, Stanford U., 1960. Editor, Farrar, Straus & Giroux (NYC), 1966-70; lit. agt. Lantz-Donadio Agcy., 1970-72; sr. editor Continuum Books, Seabury Press (NYC), 1972-75; pub. mgr. Urizen Books, Inc. (NYC), 1975-81; mem. Yale Repertory Theatre, 1979-80. Participant cultural exchange program ICA, 1980. Mem. PEN (exec. com. 1977-81). Home: Box 6754 Malibu CA 90264

ROLLYSON, CARL, b. Miami, FL., Mar. 2, 1948; s. Carl Emerson and Emily (Sokolik) R.; m. Charlotte Hollander, May 17, 1969 (div. 1981); 1 dau., Amelia; m. 2d, Lisa Paddock, Nov. 5, 1981. Author: Uses of the Past in the Novels of William Faulkner, 1984, Marilyn Monroe: A Life of the Actress, 1986, Lillian Hellman: Her Legend and Her Legacy, 1988; contrbr. articles, book revs., film revs. to various publs. Wrkg. on biography of Martha Gellhorn. BA, Mich. State U., 1969; MA, U. Toronto, 1970, PhD, 1975. Mem. faculty Wayne State U., Detroit, 1976-87, asst. dean, 1985-87; assoc. dean Baruch Coll., CUNY, 1987—. Fulbright fellow, Poland, 1979-80. Mem. MLA, Orgn. Am. Historians. Home: 23 Lexington Ave Apt 918 New York NY 10010

ROLOFSON, KRISTINE NANCY, b. Charleston, SC, Dec. 9, 1951; d. Donald Lloyd and Ottis Mary (Scheverman) Winslow; m. GLen Edwin Rolofson, Sept. 26, 1970; children—Benjamin, William, Nancy. Author: (novel) The Crowded Heart, 1987. Owner, Holiday Shores Cafe, Hope, ID, 1984-85, Signature Wallcoverings, Hope, 1985—. Bd. dirs. Meml. Commun. Ctr. Assn., Hope, 1982-85. Mem. RWA. Home: Box 193 Hope ID 83836

ROMANO, FRANK J., b. Bklyn., June 20, 1941; s. John Lewis and Rose Marie (Perrino) R.; m. Joanne L., Aug. 30, 1962; children—Richard M., Robert J. Author: Handbook of Composition Input, 1972, How to Build a Profitable Nwspr., 1973, Automated Typesetting—The Basic Course, 1974, Don't Call A Cold Type, 1975, The Type Encyc., 1985, Machine Wrtr. & Typesetting, 1986. BA, Bklyn. Coll., 1967. Asst. ad. mgr., Mergenthaler, Bklyn., 1960-67; pres. FR Assoc., NYC, 1967-70; mgr. mktg. comm. Compugraphic, Wilmington, MA, 1970-72ɲb. Typeworld, Salem, NH, 1973—. Served to PO1, USNR, 1962-70. Mem. Natl. Composition Assn., Assn. Graphics Arts Consultants. Dwiggins Award, Bookbuilder, 1985. Office: Box 170 Salem NH 03079

ROMANO, NICK JOSEPH, b. East Chicago, IN, Dec. 6, 1951, s. Russell Paul and Iona Jean (Radcliff) R.; m. Judith Luckett, Aug. 6, 1983; 1 son, Christopher Russell. BA, U. of Indpls., 1973. Sportswrtr. Muncie (Ind.) Newspapers, Inc., 1973-74; mng. ed. Harcourt Brace Jovanovich, Cleve., 1974-77, Cahners Pub. Co., Chgo., 1977-78; ed., pub. Golf Digest/Tennis, Inc., Trumbull, Conn., 1978—, dir. trade publs., 1984—. Mem. Am. Bus. Pubs., Golf Wrtrs. Assn. Am., U.S. Tennis Wrtrs.' Assn. Office: Golf Digest 5520 Park Ave Trumbull CT 06611

ROMJUE, JOHN LAWSON, (Nickell Romjue), b. Washington, Oct. 4, 1936; s. Lawson and Joanne (Hutchinson), R.; m. Ingeborg Gertrud Schaefer, Mar. 25, 1961; children: Martin, Kristin. Author: From Active Defense to Airland Battle: The Development of Army Doctrine, 1973-82, 1984, also other hist. monographs; contrbr. short stories to Mo., Cimarron, Roanoke rvws., DeKalb Lit. Arts Jnl, Wrtrs. Forum 8, Beyond Baroque, Sou'wester, AURA Literary/Arts Rvw, 1987, Writers Forum 8 and 13, articles to Christianity and Crisis, Air U., Mil. rvws., Newport News Daily Press, Chronicles of Culture, rvws. to Russian Lit. Tri Qtly, Worldview, Mil. Affairs, Natl. Def., also other jnls. BA in History, U. Mo., 1962, MA in Modern European History, 1963. Command historian U.S. Army Combat Devels. Experimentation Command, Ft. Ord, Calif., 1969-74; staff historian U.S. Army Tng. and Doctrine Command, Ft. Monroe, Va., 1974-83, dept. staff historian field programs, 1983-85, chief hist. research, 1985—. Served with U.S. Army, 1957-61. Fulbright scholar Heidelberg U., 1963-64. Mem. Am. Hist. Assn., Tidewater Wrtrs. Anns. Home: 410 Willow Oaks Blvd Hampton VA 23669

ROMTVEDT, DAVID WILLIAM, b. Portland, OR, June 7, 1950, s. Arthur William and Borgny Brunhild (Romtvedt) Young. Author: Loaf of Bread and a Bus Ticket Home, 1982, Moon, 1984, Free and Compulsory for All, 1984; asst. ed.: Writing from the World, 1976; translator: Rincon Poetico, 1975, Letters from Mexico, 1987. BA, Reed Coll., 1972; MFA, Iowa Wrtrs.' Workshop, 1975. Asst. prof. Natl. U. Rwanda, Butare, 1976-77; poet-in-residence various art councils, pvt. orgns. and colls. throughout U.S., 1978-85; fellow U. Tex.-Austin, 1985-86, 1987. NEA fellow, 1979. Mem. P&W. Home: 457 N Main St Buffalo WY 82834

RONA, DONNA C., b. Jacksonville, FL, Oct. 6, 1954, d. Robert H. and Veneda L. Cook; m. Peter A. Rona, 1974; 1 dau., Jessica R. Author: Handbook of Environmental Permitting, 1986; contrbr. articles, tech. reports to numerous profl. publs. BS in Ocean Engring., Fla. Atlantic U., 1973; MS in Mech. Engring., U. Miami, 1976. Pres. Rona Coastal Consulting, Key Biscayne, Fla., 1979—; adj. prof. Nova U., Ft. Lauderdale, Fla., 1980—; ed. Jnl Coastal Research, Ft. Lauderdale, 1983—. Office: Box 490102 Key Biscayne FL 33149

RONE, WILLIAM EUGENE, JR., b. Atlanta, Nov. 7, 1926; s. William Eugene and Marguerite (Kellet) Rone; m. Margaret Louise Banks, July 17, 1953; 1 son—James Kellett. Author: Biography of Max Hirsch, 1956. AB Wofford Coll., 1949; LL.B. U. SC, 1951; grad. US Army Command and Gen. Staff Coll., 1974. With The State (newspaper) (Columbia, SC), 1950—, city editor, 1962-65, assoc., editor, 1966-69, editorial page editor, 1969—; SC corr. So. Edn. Reporting Service (Nashville), 1962-68; columnist Raleigh News & Observer (NC), 1968—, Atlanta Jnl.—Constn., 1973-84. Served with USNR, 1945-46. Recipient SC AP award for reporting in depth, 1962. Mem. Am. Soc. Newspaper Editors, Natl. Conf. Editorial Writers. Home: 726 Fairway Ln Columbia SC 29210

ROOD, FRANK WILLIAM, b. Bellingham, WA, July 25, 1905; s. William Frank and Cora Belle (Fink) R.; m. Ella Louise Buss, Apr. 9, 1937; a child, Lou Betty. Author: Americanizing America, 1984. Employment tax auditor Dept. of Employment, El Centro and Chico, CA, 1940-65. Mem. St. Petersburg Wrtrs. Club (fellow). Home: Hotel Huntington Suite 333 226-4th Ave S Saint Petersburg FL 33701

ROOK, PEARL NEWTON, b. Neward, Mar. 26, 1923; d. Paul DeVere and Pearl Lucille (Schribner) Newton; m. Robert Eugene Chittenden, Dec. 30, 1942 (dec. Dec. 30, 1944); m. 2d, Douglas Lee Rook, Mar. 5, 1948; children—Pamela, Douglas, Sandra. Author: (poems) Shifting Sands, 1971, Hidden Universe, 1974; (with Douglas L. Rook) Sound of Thought, 1977, Where Still The Source Endures, 1986. Poetry editor: Newark Courier, 1966-81, soc. editor, 1967-68; poetry editor: Rochester Democrat and Chronicle, N.Y., 1973-82. BA in English, Hobart & William Smith Coll., 1978. Recipient Cert. of Merit, N.Am. Mentor, 1983. Mem. Natl. League PEN Women (pres. N.Y. chpt., 1st prize, 1983), Rochester Poets (recording sec. 1970-72), Sodus Bay Waterways Assn. (pres. 1979-80). Home: 126 Williams St Newark NY 14513

ROONEY, ANDREW AITKEN, b. Albany, NY, Jan. 14, 1919; s. Walter S. and Ellinor (Reynolds) Rooney; m. Marguerite Howard, Apr. 21, 1942; children—Ellen, Martha, Emily, Brian. Author: Air Gunner (with O.C. Hutton), 1944, The Story of Stars and Stripes, 1946, Conquerors' Peace, 1947, The Fortunes of War, 1962, A Few Minutes with Andy Rooney, 1981, And More By Andy Rooney, 1982, Pieces of My Mind, 1984, Word For Word, 1986. TV programs include An Essay on War, Mr. Rooney Goes to Washington, Mr. Rooney Goes to Dinner; regular commentator-essayist: 60 Minutes, 1978—. Student Colgate U., 1942. Writer-producer CBS-TV News, 1959—; newspaper columnist Tribune Co. Syndicate, 1979—. Served with AUS, 1941-45. Recipient awards for best-written TV documentary Writers Guild Am., 1966, 68, 71, 75, 76, Emmy awards, 1968, 78, 81, 82. Address: CBS 521 W 52 St New York NY 10019

ROORBACH, DOUGLAS E., b. Cape May Court House, NJ, Feb. 1, 1959; s. J. Arthur and R. Rebecca (Chew) R.; m. Laurie J. Braaten, Nov. 20, 1982. Ed.: Referee, 1979, Frontier, 1983, Print & Graphics, 1984-85, Quick Printing, 1985-86, Publishing Trade, 1985-86, Cape May County Gazette-Leader, 1981—. BA in Communics., Houghton Coll., 1981; MA in Pubns. Design, U. Balt., 1983. Dir. of devel., Houghton Acad. (NY), 1982-84; ed. Print & Graphics, Washington, 1984-85; mng. ed., then ed. Quick Printing, Ft. Pierce, FL, 1985—; mng. ed. Publishing Trade, Ft. Pierce, 1985-86, ed., 1987-. Home: 462 SW Molloy St Port St Lucie FL 34984

ROOSE, CHRISTINA, b. Pomona, CA, Dec. 15, 1944; d. Kenneth Davis and Gretchen (Burns) Roose. Ed., pub. Nexus newsletter, 1983—; columnist Library Jnl., 1984—; contrbr. chap.: Online Searching, 1984, Children and Books, 1986; contrbr. articles: Library Jnl., Ill. Libraries, RQ, other profl. publs. BA, Kalamazoo Coll., 1966; MA, U. Minn., 1969. Prin., Roose Research, Evanston, Ill., 1980—; dir. reference N. Suburban Library System, Wheeling, Ill., 1975—. Mem. ALA. Home: 1206 Simpson St Evanston IL 60201

ROOSE-CHURCH, LISA ANN, b. Barstow, CA, Apr. 23, 1964; d. James D. and Beverly Jean (Roose) Robinson; m. Raymond Church, Aug. 16, 1986. Poetry in anthologies. Wrkg. on romance novel, short stories, poetry. Ed. Poetry magic, 1987—. BS, Central Mich. U. Corr. Morning Sun, Mt. Pleasant, Mich., 1986; now freelance wrtr. Mem. Women in Communications, Soc. Profl. Journalists. Home: Box 521 Potterville MI 48876

ROOT, WILLIAM PITT, b. Austin, MN, Dec. 28, 1941; s. William Pitt and Bonita Joy (Hilbert) Root; m. Judith Carol Bechtold, 1965 (div. 1970); 1 dau.—Jennifer Lorca. Author: The Storm and Other Poems, 1969, Striking the Dark Air for Music, 1973, Coot and Other Characters, 1977, Fireclock, 1981, Reasons for Going it on Foot, 1981, In the World's Common Grasses, 1981, Faultdancing, 1986, Salmondream: Selected Poems (Scotland), 1987; transl.: Selected Odes of Pablo Neruda, 1983; collaborated (with filmmaker Ray Rice) on poetry films Song of the Woman and The Butterflyman (Orpheus award 1st Intl. Poetry Film Festival, 1975), 7 for a Magician, 1976, Faces, 1981. BA, U. Wash., 1964; MFA, U. NC (Greensboro), 1967; postgrad. Stanford U., 1968-69. Asst. prof. Mich. State U., 1967-68; tchr. writing Mid-Peninsula Free U., 1969; wrtr.-in-residence Amherst Coll., U. Southwestern La., 1976, U. Mont., 1978, 80, 83-86; vis. wrtr.-in-res. U. Mont., 1978; with poet-in-schls. program state art councils, Oreg., Miss., Idaho, Ariz., Vt., Mont., Wyo., Wash., Tex., 1971—; Distinguished writer-in-res. Wichita State U., 1976. Rockefeller Fdn. grantee, 1969-70; Guggenheim grantee, 1970-71; NEA grantee, 1973-74: US/UK Bicentennial Exchange Artist, 1978-79. Address: c/o Bruce McGrew Box E Oracle AZ 85623

ROPER, JOHN EDGAR, b. Oklahoma City, OK, Nov. 9, 1962; s. Leon Edgar and Lois (Williamson) R.; m. Joyce Arlene Huffaker, Dec. 29, 1984. Contrbr. articles to mags., newspapers. Ed.: The Harvest, 1987. B.A. in English, Central State U., Dir. develop. English Lang. Center, Edmond, OK, 1985-86; tchr. English/Spanish/sci. Oak Creak Ranch Schl., Sedona, AZ, 1986-87; free-lance wrtr., 1987—. Recipient award for essay Okla. Freedom Forum, 1980. Home: Box 174 Cornville AZ 86325

ROQUEMORE, ANNE MICKLER, b. Chattanooga, TN, Dec. 3, 1950; d. Jacob Ernest Mickler and Dorothy Ann (McCarver) Mickler Sparks; m. Perry Crawford Roquemore, Jr., Sept. 3, 1969; 1 son, Chris. Contrbr. articles, poems to newspapers, mags. including Woman's Day, Christian Sci. Monitor, Home Mechanics, Early Am. Life, others. Ed., features ed. Cable TV Times, Montgomery, 1978-80; pub. mgr. Ala. League of Municipalities, Montgomery, 1986—. Wrkg. on short stories, editing. B.A., U. Ala., 1973. Recipient Honorable Mention, Wrtrs. Digest Mag., Cin., 1983, 85. Home: 5764 Bridle Path Ln Montgomery AL 36116

ROREM, NED, b. Richmond, IN, Oct. 23, 1923; s. Clarence Rufus and Gladys (Miller) Rorem. Author: The Paris Diary of Ned Rorem, 1966, Music from Inside Out, 1967, The New York Diary, 1967, Music and People, 1968, Critical Affairs, 1970, Pure Contraption, 1973, The Later Diaries, 1974, An Absolute Gift, 1978, Setting the Tone, 1983, Paul's Blues, 1984, The Nantucket Diaries, 1987, Perfect Pitch, 1988; contrbr. articles to various newspapers and mags. Student, Northwestern U., 1940-42, Curtis Inst. Philadelphia, 1943; BA, Julliard Schl. Music, 1946, MA, 1948; DFA (hon.), Northwestern U., 1977. Slee prof., composer-in-residence Buffalo U., 1956-61; prof. composition U. Utah, 1965-67. Mem. PEN, ASCAP, AAIAL, Soc. of Friends. Address: B & H 24 W 57th St New York NY 10019

ROSBERG, ROSE, b. NYC; d. Nathan and Dora R. Author poems: Trips—Without LSD, 1969; contrbr. poetry to Images, KS Qtly, others. BA, Hunter College; BLS, Pratt Institute. Tchr., NYC Board of Edn. Mem. PSA. Home: 880 W 181 St New York NY 10033

ROSE, DANIEL ASA, b. NYC, Nov. 20, 1949, s. Gilbert J. and Anne (Kaufman) R.; m. Laura Love, Nov. 30, 1974 (div. 1983); children—Alexander, Marshall. Novelist: Flipping For It, 1987; contrbr. short stories to New Yorker, Partisan Rvw, So. Rvw, others; included in anthologies: O. Henry Prize Stories 1980, New World Literature (Budapest), 1982, Reading Commitment (college textbook), others; contrbr. articles: Esquire, NY Times, Vanity Fair, Traveler, others. AB, Brown U., 1971. Ed. The Spectator, Somerset, Mass., 1972-75; freelance wrtr., 1975—; contrbg. ed. Success Mag., NYC1984—. Winner O. Henry Prize, 1980. Home: 138 Bay State Rd Rehoboth MA 02769

ROSE, ELEANOR, see Ruocchio, Patricia Jeanne

ROSE, GILBERT PAUL, b. NYC, Aug. 6, 1939; s. Wiliam R. and Sylvia (Lanzet) Briefstein; m. Nancy Gortz, June 11, 1961; children—Dorothy, Rebecca. Editor: Plato's Crito, 1980, Plato's Symposium, 1981, Plato's Republic, Book I, 1983. AB, U. CA (Berkeley), 1963, PhD, 1969; postgrad. U. WI, 1963-64. Instr. to assoc. prof. Swarthmore Coll. (PA), 1967-81, prof. dept. classics, 1981—, Old Dominion fellow, 1970-71; Mellon grantee, 1974-75. Mem. AAUP. Office: Swarthmore Coll Swarthmore PA 19081

ROSE, IRENE, see Wildgrube, Irene W.

ROSE, JOEL, b. Los Angeles, Mar. 1, 1948; s. Milton and Edna (Greenfield) R.; m. Catherine Texier; child: Celine Texier-Rose. Editor and established Seneca Rvw., 1968-70; editor/pub. Between C&D, 1984—; co-ed with Catherine Texier: Between C & D: Anthology of the Lower East Side Literary Mag., 1988 author: (novel) Kill the Poor, 1986; short stories in Bomb, New Observations, Confrontation, Jeopardy, Northwest Passage, Autrement (Paris), others; films Billy Omansky, Chastity Goes to College, It's Not Superstition; TV scripts, Miami Vice (with Miguel Pinero), others; also articles in mags. and other publs.; two non-fiction books. BA, Hobart Coll., 1970; MFA in Writing, Columbia U., 1973. Freelance writer, 1975—. N.Y. State Council on Arts grantee, 1986; NEA, 1986-87. Mem. CCLM., Poets and Writers. Home: 255 E 7th St New York NY 10009

ROSE, LOUISE BLECHER, b. Bklyn., June 3, 1943, d. Ezra and Rhoda (Ettenson) Blecher. Novelist: The Launching of Barbara Fabrikant, 1975; contrbr. stories, articles to Redbook mag., Cosmopolitan mag. BA, Sarah Lawrence Coll., 1965; MA, Columbia U., 1967. Asst. prof. St. Joseph's Coll., Bklyn., 1967-86, Sarah Lawrence Coll., Bronxville, N.Y., 1975-83, Columbia U., NYC, 1983-86, Yeshiva U., NYC, 1986—. Grantee N.Y. State Council on Arts, NEA. Home: 295 Central Park W New York NY 10024

ROSE, MARK ALLEN, b. NYC, Aug. 4, 1939; s. Sydney Aaron and Rose (Shapiro) Rose; m. Rachel Warner Liebes, 1979; 1 son—Edward; 1 stepson—Jonah Liebes. Author: Heroic Love, 1968; fiction, Golding's Tale, 1972; Shakespearean Design, 1972, Spenser's Art, 1975, Alien Encounters, 1981; editor: Twentieth Century Views of Science Fiction, 1976, Twentieth Century Interpretations of Antony and Cleopatra, 1977, Bridges to Science Fiction (with Slusser and Guffey), 1980. AB, Princeton U., 1961; B.Litt., Merton Coll., Oxford U. (England), 1963; PhD, Harvard U., 1967. From instr. to assoc. prof. English Yale U., 1967-74; prof. English U. IL (Urbana), 1974-77, U. CA (Santa Barbara), 1977—. Woodrow Wilson fellow, 1961, Henry fellow, 1961-62, Dexter fellow, 1966, Morse fellow, 1970-71, NEH fellow, 1979-80. Mem. MLA, Renaissance Soc. Am., Shakespeare Soc. Am. Home: 859 Jimeno Rd Santa Barbara CA 93103

ROSE, PATRICIA ANTHONE, (Anthone Rand), b. Joliet, IL, June 18, 1930; d. George Leland and Barbara Elizabeth (Meyer) Rand; divorced; children—Stephanie, David, Karen, Claudia. Author: The Solar Boat Book, 1979, The Solar Boat Book Revised, 1983. Mem. AG. Home: 4770 Snook Dr SE St Petersburg FL 33705

ROSE, PHYLLIS, b. NYC, Oct. 26, 1942; d. Eli and Minnie (Selesko) Davidoff; m. Mark Rose, June 10, 1965 (div. 1975); 1 son—Teddy. Author: Woman of Letters: A Life of Virginia Woolf, 1978, Parallel Lives: Five Victorian Marriages, 1983, Writing of Women, 1985; book reviewer: The Nation, NY Times Book Rvw, Washington Post Book World, The Atlantic. BA, Radcliffe Coll., 1964; MA, Yale U., 1965; PhD, Harvard U., 1970. Teaching fellow Harvard U. (Cambridge, MA), 1966-67; acting instr. Yale U. (New Haven), 1969; asst. prof. Wesleyan U. (Middletown, CT), 1969-76, assoc. prof., 1976-81, prof. English, 1981—; vis. prof. U. CA (Berkeley), 1981-82. NEH fellow, 1973-74; Rockefeller fellow, 1984-85; Guggenheim fellow, 1985. Mem. PEN, Natl. Bk. Critics' Circle. Home: 74 Wyllys Ave Middletown CT 06457

ROSE, REGINALD, b. NYC, Dec. 10, 1920; s. William and Alice (Obendorfer) Rose; children—Jonathan, Richard, Andrew, Steven; m. Ellen McLaughlin July 6, 1963; children—Thomas, Christopher. Author TV plays, including: Twelve Angry Men, 1954, The Sacco Vanzetti Story, 1959, The Defenders, 1961-65; film scripts include Crime in the Streets, 1956, Twelve Angry Men, 1957, Baxter!, 1973, Somebody Killed Her Husband, 1978, The Wild Geese, 1978, The Sea Wolves, 1980, Whose Life Is It Anyway?, 1981, Escape From Sobibor, 1987; plays include Black Monday, 1962, Twelve Angry Men, 1958, The Porcelain Year, 1965; books include Six TV Plays, 1956, The Thomas Book, 1972. Student CCNY, 1937-38. Pres. Defender Prodn., Inc., 1961—. Recipient Emmy awards 1954, 62, 63, WG of America Laurel Award for Lifetime Achievement, 1987, numerous others. Address: 20 Wedgewood Rd Westport CT 06880

ROSE, WENDY (BRONWEN) ELIZABETH, b. Oakland, CA, May 7, 1948; m. Arthur Murata, Mar. 11, 1976. Author: Hopi Roadrunner Dancing, 1973; Long Division, 1976; Academic Squaw, 1977; Poetry of the Indian, 1978; Builder Kachina, 1979; Aboriginal Tattooing in California, 1979; Lost Copper, 1980; What Happened when Hopi Hit New York, 1982; Halfbreed Chronicles, 1985; contrbr. to numerous anthologies. AB, U. Calif., Berkeley, 1976, MA, 1978. Wrtr.-speaker, 1967—; instr. native Am. studies/ethnic studies U. Calif., Berkeley, 1979-83, Calif. State U., Fresno, 1983-84, Fresno City Coll., 1984—. Mem. MLA (commn. on lang. and lit. of Am.), PEN, Assn. for Study Am. Indian Lits., Natl. Assn. Ethnic Studies. Home: 3182 E Palo Alto Fresno CA 93710

ROSEMONT, FRANKLIN, b. Chgo., Oct. 2, 1943; s. Henry P. and Sally Kaye (Janiak) R.; m. Penelope Bartik, May 13, 1965. Author: The Morning of a Machine Gun (poems), 1968, The Apple of the Automatic Zebra's Eye (poems), 1970, Andre Breton and the First Principles of Surrealism, 1978; ed.: What Is Surrealism?, 1978, Surrealism and Its Popular Accomplices, 1979, Marvelous Freedom, 1976, Isadora Speaks, 1981, You Have No Country! Workers' Struggle Against War, 1984, Mr Block: 24 IWW Cartoons, 1984, Haymarket Scrapbook, 1986, Manifesto on the Position and Direction of the Surrealist Movement, 1970; ed.-in-chief Arsenal: Surrealist Subversion, 1970—. Address: Kerr Publg 1740 W Greenleaf Chicago IL 60626

ROSEN, DAVID HENRY, b. Portchester, NY, Feb. 25, 1945, s. Max and Barbara (Middendorf) R.; m. Deborah Jean Voorhees, June 30, 1973; children—Sarah, Laura, Rachel. Author: Lesbianism: A Study of Female Homosexuality, 1974, Medicine as a Human Experience (with David Reiser), 1984, Henry's Tower, 1984. AB in Psychol. Biology, U. Calif.-Berkeley, 1966; MD, U. Mo., 1970. Mem. faculty U. Calif. Med. Center, San Francisco, 1974-82; assoc. prof. psychiatry and medicine, U. Rochester (N.Y.) Med. Center, 1982-86, Frank McMillan Prof. of Analytical Psychology and Psychiatry & Behavioral Science, Texas A & M U., 1986-. Recipient numerous med. and teaching awards. Mem. Am. Psychiatric Assn., AMA, Soc. Health and Human Values. Home: 1315 Angelina College Station TX 77840

ROSEN, GERALD ROBERT, b. NYC, Nov. 17, 1930; s. Sol and Essie (Shapiro) Rosen; m. Lois Lehrman, May 9, 1958; 1 son—Evan Mark. BS, IN U., 1951, MA, 1953. Intelligence analyst Dept. Def. (NYC), 1955-58; assoc. editor Challenge: The Mag. of Econ. Affairs (NYC), 1959-61, mng. editor, 1961-64, 65-66; sr. editor Dun's Rev. (NYC), 1964-65, natl. affairs editor, 1967-77, exec. editor, 1977—; fin. corr. Westinghouse Broadcasting Co. Served with CIC US Army, 1953-55. Mem. Soc. Am. Bus. and Econ. Writers, NY Fin. Writers Assn., White House Corrs. Assn., Natl. Press Club. Home: 1623 Clifton Ave Columbus OH 43203

ROSEN, MICHAEL J., b. Columbus, OH, Sept. 20, 1954. Author: A Drink At the Mirage, 1984; editor: Thurber and Columbustown; contrbr. poems, stories and reviews to The Atlantic, The New Yorker, The Nation, Grand Street, Paris Rvw, Shenandoah, Prairie Schooner, Epoch, Bloomsbury Rvw, others. BS in Zoology, Ohio State U., 1976; MFA, Columbia U., 1981. Artist in schls. Ohio Arts Council, 1978-84; freelance artist, illustrator and designer, 1981—; instr. Ohio State Univ., 1983-85; lit. dir. The Thurber House, Columbus, Ohio, 1983—. Fellow: NEA, 1984, Ingram Merrill Fdn., 1982, 83, Ohio Arts Council, 1981, 85; recipient Ohioana Library award, 1985. Mem. PEN, PSA (Gustav Davidson award, 1985). Home: 1312 E Broad St Columbus OH 43205

ROSEN, NORMA, b. NYC, d. Louis and Rose (Miller) Gangel; m. Robert S. Rosen, Aug. 23, 1960; children—Anne, Jonathan. Author: Joy to Levine! (novel), 1962 Green (short story collection), 1967, Touching Evil (novel), 1970, At the Center (novel), 1982, The Miracle of Dora Wakin (play), 1985; contrbr to N.Y. Times Hers weekly essay, Nov. 1982-Feb. 1983, essay on Jonah in The Hebrew Bible, 1987. Wrkg. on novel. BA, Mt. Holyoke Coll., 1946; MA, Columbia U., 1953. Tchr. creative wrtg. Coll. New Rochelle, N.Y., 1976-85, Yale U., 1983, NYU, 1985—. Grantee Eugene F. Saxton Fdn., 1960, N.Y. State CAPS, 1975; Radcliffe Inst. fellow, 1971-73. Home: 11 Mereland Rd New Rochelle NY 10804

ROSENAU, JAMES NATHAN, b. Philadelphia, Nov. 25, 1924; s. Walter Nathan and Fanny Fox (Baum) Rosenau; m. Norah McCarthy, Aug. 5, 1955 (dec. July 5, 1974); 1 dau.—Heidi Margaret.; m. 2d, Pauline Vaillaucourt June 14, 1987. Author: Public Opinion and Foreign Policy, 1961, National Leadership and Foreign Policy, 1963, The Drama of Politics, 1973, Citizenship Between Elections, 1974, The Scientific Study of Foreign Policy, 1980, American Leadership in World Affairs, 1984. AB, Bard Coll., 1948; AM, Johns Hopkins U., 1949; PhD, Princeton U., 1957. Instr. Rutgers U. (New Brunswick, NJ), 1949-54, asst. prof., 1954-60, assoc. prof., 1960-62, prof., 1962-70, Ohio State U. (Columbus), 1970-73; prof. poli. sci. U. So. CA (Los Angeles), 1973—; research asst. Inst. Advanced Study (Princeton, NJ), 1953-54; research assoc. Princeton U. (NJ), 1960-70; dir. Schl. Intl. Relations U. So. CA (Los Angeles), 1976-79; dir. Schl. Intl. Relations Inst. Transnatl. Studies (Los Angeles), 1973—. Served with US Army, 1942-46. Ford Fdn. fellow, 1958-59; Guggenheim Fellowship, 1987-88; researchgrantee NSF, 1970, 73, 78, 79, 83; recipient stipend NEH, 1976. Home: 1700 San Remo Dr Pacific Palisades CA 90272

ROSENBAUM, SYLVIA P., b. Bklyn.; d. Jack and Ida Olga (Kanover) Portugal; m. Murray N. Rosenbaum, Mar. 19, 1961; 1 son—Robert. Author: Ribbons, 1976, Carrousel, 1981; contrbr. poetry to Bitterroot, Sunstorm, Orbis, Voices Intl., Poetry Today, Wind Mag. others. Second Prize NWC, 1978; first prize Natl. Fed. of State Poetry, Florida, 1973, 80. Mem. FL State Poet. Soc., Poets' Study Club of Terre Haute. Home: 10 Heritage Ct Valley Stream NY 11581

ROSENBERG, BRUCE ALAN, b. NYC, July 27, 1934; s. Howard Alyne and Audrey (Olenick) Rosenberg. Author: The Art of The American Folk Preacher, 1970, Custer and the Epic of Defeat, 1976, The Code of the West, 1981, The Spy Story, 1987, Can These Bones Live, 1988; asst. editor: Chaucer Rvw, 1967-79, Jnl Am. Folklore, 1970-79. BA, Hofstra U., 1955; MA, PA State U., 1962; PhD, 32 Ohio State U., 1965. Mem. faculty U. CA (Santa Barbara), 1965-67, U. VA (Charlottesville), 1967-69, PA State U., State College, 1969-77; prof. English lit. and Am. civilization Brown U., 1977—; Fulbright lectr. (Warsaw, Poland), 1981. Served with US Army, 1955-57. Recipient James Russell Lowell prize, 1970, Chgo. Folklore prize, 1970, 76, ACLS fellow, 1967, NEH fellow, 1976-77, Guggenheim fellow, 1982-83. Mem. MLA, Am. Folklore Soc. Home: Box 1892 Providence RI 02912

ROSENBERG, CHARLES ERNEST, b. NYC, Nov. 11, 1936; s. Bernard and Marion (Roberts) Rosenberg; m. Carroll Ann Smith, June 22, 1961 (div. 1977); 1 dau.—Leah; 2nd m. Drew Gilpin Faust, June 7, 1980; 1 dau.—Jessica. Author: The Cholera Years: The United States in 1832, 1849, and 1866, 1962, The Trial of the Assassin Guiteau: Psychiatry and Law in the Gilded Age, 1968, No Other Gods: On Science and Social Thought in America, 1976, The Care of Strangers: The Rise of America's Hospital System, 1987. BA, U. Wis., 1956; MA, Columbia U., 1957, PhD, 1961. Fellow Johns Hopkins U. (Baltimore), 1960-61; asst. prof. U. Wis., 1961-63; assoc. prof. U. Penn. (Philadelphia), 1965-68, prof. history, 1968—, chmn. dept., 1974-75, 79-83; Bd. dirs. Mental Health Assn. Southeastern PA, 1973-75, Library Co., Philadelphia 1981-, exec. bd. Orgn. of Amer. Historians, 1986-88. Natl. Inst. Health Research grantee, 1964-70, Guggenheim fellow, 1965-66, NEH fellow, 1972-73, Rockefeller fellow, 1975-76, Inst. for Advanced Study, 1979-80, fellow Ctr. for Advanced Study in the Behavioral Sciences, 1983-84, member Inst. of Medicine, 1985-, Am Acad. of Arts and Sciences, 1986-. Home: 435 S 45th St Philadelphia PA 19104

ROSENBERG, EVA, b. Budapest, Hungary, March 5, 1953 (arrived in US May 8, 1962); d. Tibor and Aranka R. Author: It's Your Business: Tax Preparation for the Self-Employed, annually, 1983—; Tax Anxiety Xperience, a T.A.X. Planning Guide, annually, 1985—; Building a Tax Planning Practice, 1985, co-author, The Educator's Tax Planning Handbook, 1986-87; financial column in The Barnstormer, 1984-85. BA in Accounting, Calif. State U., 1977, MBA in Intl. Business, Calif. State U., Fullerton, 1982. Accountant Ernst & Whinney, CPA's (Newport Beach, CA), 1978, Lester Witte & Co., CPA's (Newport Beach, 1978-79, instr. V.S.C. Interactive Instructional Television Newwork; owner Indep. Rsch. Svcs. Van Nuys, (CA), 1980—. Acting Treas. Friends of Irvine Fine Arts Cntr., 1984-85. VP Programs Professional Women's Network, pres. and fdr. Southcoast Assn. for Female Executives. Office: 14553 Delano St. Suite 316 Van Nuys CA 91411

ROSENBERG, JAY FRANK, b. Chgo., Apr. 18, 1942; s. Sandor and Laura (Fried) Rosenberg; m. Regina M. Faltin, Aug. 7, 1980; stepson—Glen Faltin; children by previous marriage—Joshua Conrad (dec.), Leslie Johanna. Author: The Impoverished Students' Book of Cookery, Drinkery and Housekeepery, 1964, Linguistic Representation, 1974, The Practice of Philosophy, 1978, One World and Our Knowledge of It, 1980, Thinking Clearly About Death, 1983, The Thinking Self, 1986, Philosophieren, 1986; contrbr. essays, papers in philosophy to profl. jnls; editor: Readings in the Philosophy of Language (with Charles Travis), 1971. BA, Reed Coll., 1963; MA, U. Pitts., 1964, PhD, 1966. Faculty U. NC (Chapel Hill), 1966—, prof. Philosophy, 1974, asst. chmn. dept., 1975-76, 77-78, dept. chmn., 1984—, Taylor Grandy Prof. of Philosophy, 1987-. Mem. AAUP, Am. Philo. Assn., Southern Society for Philosophy and Psychology, North American Kant Soc. Home: 715 Williams Circle Chapel Hill NC 27514

ROSENBERG, JERRY MARTIN, b. NYC, Feb. 5, 1935; s. Frank and Esther (Gardner) Rosenberg; m. Ellen Young, Sept. 11, 1960; children—Laura, Elizabeth. Author: Automation Manpower and Education, 1966, The Computer Prophets, 1969, The Death of Privacy, 1969, Dictionary of Business and Management, 1978, Dictionary of Banking and Financial Services, 1982, Inside the Wall Street Journal, 1982, Dictionary of Computers, Data Processing and Telecommunications, 1983, The Investor's Dictionary, 1986. BS, Coll. City NY, 1956; MA, Ohio State U., 1957; certificate Sorbonne, 1958; PhD, NYU, 1963. As st. prof. Cornell U. Schl. Indsl. and Labor Relations, 1961-64; asst. prof. Columbia, 1964-68; pvt. practice cons. (NYC), 1968-71; assoc. prof. City U. NY, 1971-74; prof. mgmt. Lehman Coll., City U. NY, 1977-80; prof. bus. adminstrn. and mgmt. dept., grad. schl. of mgmt., chmn. Rutgers U. (Newark), 1980—. Recipient Fulbright and French Govt. awards, 1957. Home: 515 Tulfan Terr Riverdale NY 10463

ROSENBERG, JOHN DAVID, b. NYCApr. 17, 1929; s. David and Dorothy Lilian (Shatz) Rosenberg; m. Maurine Ann Hellner, June 11, 1972; 1 son—Matthew John. Author: The Darkening Glass: A Portrait of Ruskin's Genius, 1961, The Fall of Camelot: A Study of Tennyson's Idylls of the King, 1973, Carlyle and the Burden of History, 1985; editor: Ruskin, 1963, Mayhew, 1968, Swinburne, 1968, Tennyson, 1975; contrbr. essays and rvws. on English lit. to NY Times Book Rvw, Harper's mag., Hudson Rvw and profl. jnls. BA, Columbia Coll., 1950, Clare Coll., Cambridge U., 1953, MA, 1958, Columbia U., 1951, PhD, 1960. Lectr. in English, Columbia U. (NYC), 1953-54, asst. prof., 1962-65, assoc. prof., 1966-67, prof. English, 1967—, dir. of grad studies in English, 1986—; editor-in-chief Columbia Rvw, 1949-50; cons. Harvard, Yale, Princeton U. presses. Recipient Clarke F. Ansley award for Voice in the Wilderness: A Study of John Ruskin, 1960, Council for Research in Humanities grant-in-aid, 1965; ACLS fellow, 1965-66, 79; Guggenheim fellow, 1968-69; NEH fellow, 1982-83. Mem. MLA, Tennyson Soc., Ruskin Assn. Home: 435 Riverside Dr New York NY 10025

ROSENBERG, MAURICE, b. Oswego, NY, Sept. 3, 1919; s. Samuel and Diana (Lishansky)

Rosenberg; m. Ruth Myers, Dec. 7, 1941 (dec. Nov. 1945); 1 son—David Lee; 2nd m; Gloria Jacobson, Dec. 19, 1948; children—Joan Myra, Richard Sam. Author: Elements of Civil Procedure (with Harold Korn, Hans Smit and Jack Weinstein), 1962, 3rd edit., 1976, Conflict of Laws (with Willis Reese), 7th edit., 1977, The Pretrial Conference and Effective Justice, 1964, Justice on Appeal (with Paul Carrington and Daniel Meador), 1976, Appellate Justice in New York (with James D. Hopkins and Robert MacCrate), 1982; editor: Dollars, Delay and the Automobile Victim, 1968, Law and social Research (with Lloyd Ohlin), 1977. AB Syracuse U., 1940; LLB Columbia, 1947. Bar: NY bar, 1947. Law sec. to judge NY Ct. Appeals, 1947-49; asso. firm Cravath, Swaine & Moore (NYC), 1949-53, Austrian, Lance & Stewart, 1953-56; prof. Columbia U. Law Schl., 1956, Nash prof., Harold R. Medina prof. procedural jurisprudence, 1973— ; on leave, 1979-81; dir. Project Effective Justice, 1956-64, Walter E. Meyer Research Inst. Law, 1965-71; spcl. asst. to atty. genl. US, 1976, 81; cons. US Dept. Justice, 1977-79, asst. atty. genl. US, 1979-81; lectr. US, Asia and Europe: mem. faculty Nat. Coll. State Trial Judges; mem. Mayor NYC Com. on Judiciary, 1962-77; chmn. Adv. Council Appellate Justice, 1970-75, Council on Role of Cts., 1978-80; chmn. asv. council Natl. Center for State Cts., 1975-77. Served with AUS, 1941-45; ETO. Home: 10 Hunting Ridge Rd White Plains NY 10605

ROSENBERG, NANCY SHERMAN, b. New York, NY, June 21, 1931; d. Monroe and Gertrude (Horn) Sherman; m. Lawrence C. Rosenberg, July 15, 1951; children—Eric, Mark, Constance, Elizabeth. Author: The Boy Who Ate Flowers, 1960, Gwendolyn the Miracle Hen, 1961 (Herald Tribune Children's Spring Book Festival Award, 1961), Gwendolyn and the Weathercock, 1963, (with Dr. Lawrence Rosenberg), The Story of Modern Medicine, 1966, Miss Agatha's Lark, 1968, New Parts for People (with Dr. Reuven K. Snyderman), 1968, How to Enjoy Mathematics with Your Child, 1970, Vaccines and Viruses (with Dr. Louis Z. Cooper), 1971; also 4 study modules in math., 1980; contrbtr. articles on math, and edn. to profl. jnls. BA Bryn Mawr Coll., 1952. Home: 28 Fanshaw Ave Yonkers NY 10705

ROSENBERGER, FRANCIS COLEMAN, b. Mar. 22, 1915, s. George L. and Olive (Robertson) R.; m. Lucinda Tavenner, Apr. 30, 1941 (dec.1960); m. 2d, Paulette Dionne, Feb. 18, 1961 (div. 1962); m. 3d, Astra Brennan, Dec. 12, 1966. Author: The Virginia Poems, 1943, XII Poems, 1946, One Season Here: Poems, 1976, An Alphabet (poems), 1978, The Visit (poems), 1984; ed.: Virginia Reader: A Treasury of Writings from the First Voyages to the Present, 1948, 1972, American Sampler: A Selection of New Poetry, 1951, Jefferson Reader: A Treasury of Writings about Thomas Jefferson, 1953, Harley Martin Kilgore: Memorial Addresses Delivered in Congress, 1956, Records of the Columbia Historical Society of Washington, D.C. (8 vols.), 1961-80, Of Prisons and Justice: A Selection of the Writings of James V. Bennett, 1964, The Robinson-Rosenberger Journey to the Gold Fields of California, 1849-1850: The Diary of Zirkel D. Robinson, 1966, Washington and the Poet (anthology), 1977; contrbr. poetry to anthologies and periodicals; contrbr. book revs. to numerous publs. JD, George Washington U., 1942. Lawyer, wrtr., ed.; mem. legal and legis. staff U.S. Senate, 1942-78; guest scholar Brookings Instn.; adviser U.S. delegations to intl. Confs., Geneva, 1955, 56, 73. Recipient Natl. Poetry Center award N.Y. World's Fair, 1939. Home: 6809 Melrose Dr McLean VA 22101

ROSENBLATT, PAUL, b. Bklyn. Feb. 16, 1928; s. Abraham and Mildred (Brower) Rosenblatt; m. Joan Barbara Shufro, June. 17, 1956; children—Abram, David. Co-author: A Certain Bridge: Issac Bashevis Singer on Literature and Life, 1971, rev. edit., 1979, John Woolman, 1969; Editor: The Cliff Dwelers, 1973 (Henry Blake Fuller). BA Bklyn. Coll., 1949, MA, 1951; PhD Columbia U. 1960. Instr. Bklyn. Coll., 1955-58; mem. faculty U. Ariz. (Tuscon), 1958—, prof. English, 1970—, acting head dept. Romance langs., 1973-75, dean, 1975-82; Regent Hays-Fulbright prof. Am. lit. Fed. U. (Rio de Janeiro, Brazil), 1968-69, 72-73; Fulbright prof. U. Cuyo (Mendoza, Argentina), 1969; mem. bd. acad. visitors Am. Grad. Schl. Intl. Mgmt., 1975—; mem. various panels div. Nat. Endowment Humanities, 1976—; mem. Ariz. Council Humanities and Pub. Policy, 1975—; mem. commn. on arts and scis. Nat. Assn. State Univs. and Land Grant Colls., 1979-82. Served wih U.S. Army, 1953-55. Recipient award So. Books Competition, 1979, Silver Medallion City of Florence (Italy), 1983. Mem. MLA; hon. life mem. Am. Lit. Assn., Brazil. Office: 445 Modern Lang Bldg U Ariz Tucson AZ 85721

ROSENBLATT, RUTH, (Ruth Benjamin),b. Tacoma, Wash., Mar. 5, 1934, d. David and Rebecca (Shallit) Turteltaub; m. Arthur Rosenblat lt, Aug. 5, 1956; children—Paul, Judy. Novelist: Naked at Forty, 1984; contrbr. poetry to: Caravan, Hoosier Challenger, Bitterroot, other publs. BA, Sarah Lawrence Coll., 1956. Prodn. asst. Coronet mag., N.Y.C., 1956-57; editorial asst. Hillman Periodicals, N.Y.C., 1957-59; part-time asst. P&W, 1984-86. Mem. AG. Home: 1158 Fifth Ave New York NY 10029

ROSENBLUM, MARTIN JACK, (Cicero De Westbrook), b. Appleton, WI, Aug. 19, 1946; s. Sander and Esther Pearl (Ressman) R; m. Maureen Rice, Sept. 6, 1970; 2 daus., Sarah Terez, Molly Dvora. Author: Home, 1970, Bright Blue Coats, 1970, Settling Attention, 1970, The Werewolf Sequence, 1974, Scattered On: Omens & Curses, 1975, Protractive Verse, 1975, As I Magic, 1976, Divisions One, 1979, Born Out, 1983, Brite Shade, 1984, Burning Oak, 1985, Carl Rakosi, 1986, Still Life, 1986, A Volf An Eynzamer, 1986; Geographics, 1986, Music Lingo, 1986, Stone Fog, 1987, Conjunction, 1987, Black lit Frontier, 1987; contrbr. Albatross One, 1969, Brewing: 20 Milw. Poets, 1972; ed., An Objectivist Casebook, 1987. MA in Writing and Lit, UW-Milw, 1971, PhD in Mod. Poetry (Knapp fellow, 1975, 76), 1980. Lectr. English, Univ. Wis., Milw., 1970-80; dir. Writing Labs Marquette Univ., Milw, 1972; exec. dir. Lawyers for the Creative Arts, Chgo., 1980; admissions spclst. and academic adv. Dept Edl. Opportunity, Univ. Wis., Milw, 1980—. Mem. Colt Collectors Assn, Natl Rifle Assn. Recipient AAP award, NYC, 1970, Sterling Library award, Yale Univ, 1976. Address: 2521 East Stratford Ct Shorewood WI 53211

ROSENBURG, ROBERT KEMPER, b. Balt., June 10, 1920; s. Abel Abraham and Marion (Kemper) R. Pub. 12 vols. of poetry. Founder, editor Linden Press, Balt., 1960—. Spcl. student Johns Hopkins U., 1951-65. Mem. Natl. Soc. Crippled Children and Adults. Home: 3601 Greenway Baltimore MD 21218

ROSENFELD, ARNOLD SOLOMON, b. NYC, Apr. 18, 1933; s. William and Sarah (Cohen) Rosenfeld; m. Ruth Doris Lilly, Sept. 30, 1956; children—William Bennett, Jonathan Andrew, Lauren. Editor: A Thomason Sketchbook, 1969. Student U. Houston, 1951; Profl. Journalism fellow, Stanford, 1967. Mem. staff Houston Post, 1953-67; asso. editor Detroit mag. Detroit Free Press, 1967; editor Detroit mag., 1968; mng. editor Dayton Daily News, 1968-76, editor, 1976-80; exec. editor Dayton Daily News and Jour. Herald, 1980—. Served with AUS, 1951-53. Recipient Editorial Writing award A.P. Mng. Editors Assn. TX, 1966; Media award Nat. Assn. Mental Health, 1976. Mem. ASNE. Home: 3711 Hidden Hollow Dr Austin TX 78731

ROSENGARTEN, DAVID, b. NYC., Jan. 25, 1950, s. Leonard and Lorraine (Stein) R.; m. Constance Crimmins Childs, Oct. 15, 1983. Assoc. ed.: A Dictionary of American Wines, 1985; contrbr. articles to Wine Spectator, Theater Jnl, Bon Appetit, Video Rvw. BA cum laude, Colgate U., 1971; PhD, Cornell U., 1980. Lectr. Cornell U., Ithaca, N.Y., 1979-80; asst. prof. Skidmore Coll., Saratoga Springs, N.Y., 1980-83; columnist, corr. The Wine Spectator, San Francisco, 1985—. Shubert Fdn. playwriting fellow, N.Y.C., 1971; John McVoy fellow Cornell U., 1977-79. Mem. P&K Wine Media Guild, Am. Inst. Wine and Food. Office: Wine Spec 400 E 51st St New York NY 10022

ROSENMAN, JOHN BROWN, b.Cleve., Apr. 16, 1941; s. Isidor and Mona Brown R.; m. Jane Palmer, Sept. 7, 1967; children—Lori March, David Gerald. Author: The Best Laugh Last, 1981. Contrbr. short stories, poems to lit mags., anthols. Wrkg. on sci. fiction novel. B.A. in English and Polit. Sci., Hiram Coll., 1963; M.A. in English, Kent State U., 1966, Ph.D., 1970. Asst. prof. Lakehead U., Thunder Bay, Ont., Can., 1970-74, Elizabeth City State U., N.C., 1981-82, Norfolk State U., Va., 1982—; assoc. prof. Claflin Coll., Orangeburg, S.C., 1974-81. Recipient 1st Book award McPherson & Co., 1981. Mem. MLA, SAMLA,CEA, SPWAO, CLA, Horror Wrtrs. Am. Home: 6229 Auburn Dr Virginia Beach VA 23464

ROSENSTEIN, IRA, b. Bklyn., June 28, 1947; s. Joseph and Mildred (Garfinkel) R. Author: Left On the Field to Die (long poem pub. in 3 parts) 1: Timothy Richardson, 1982, 2. Yehudi Weismann, 1982, 3. Peter Koslov, 1984; Twenty-Two Sonnets, 1986. Mrkg. on poetry and plays. BF, Queens Coll., 1968; MFA, Brandeis U., 1972. Piano music buyer Schirmer Music Store, NYC, 1984—. Address: Box 3102 Long Island City NY 11103

ROSENSTIEL, LEONIE, b. NYC, Dec. 28; d. Raymond and Annette (Bitterman) R. Author: The Life and Works of Lili Boulanger, 1978, Nadia Boulanger: A Life in Music, 1982. Contrbr. articles, book rvws., translations, record liner notes to music anthols., mags. Translator: Musica Enchiriadis, 1976. Assoc. editor Current Musicology, 1969-71, spcl. projects editor, 1971-73; editor, contrbr., author: Schirmer History of Music, 1982; editor: (with Arthur Orrmont) Literary Agents of North America, 1983—; Freelancers of North America, 1982—. AB, Barnard Coll., 1968; MA, Columbia U., 1970, MPhil, 1973, PhD, 1974; diploma Mexican Natl. Inst. Fine Arts, 1975. Founder, dir. Manhasset Chamber Ensemble, N.Y., 1974-76; pres. Research Assocs. Intl., NYC, 1980—; cons. ed., 1976—. Trustee, Profl. Childrens Schl., NYC, 1972-74. Regents scholar N.Y. State, 1964-69; fellow Rockefeller Fdn., 1978-79; grantee ACLS, 1978. Mem. AG, AL. Office: Box 6503 Grand Central

PO New York NY 10163

ROSENSTOCK, FRANCYNE N., b. NYC, Jan. 29, 1951; d. Max and Gloria (Weisser) R. Contrbr. to Country Living, Hartford Courant, Hudson Valley Mag., Milw. Jnl, N.Y. Post, Phila. Enquirer, Times-Herald Record. Wrkg. on novel. BA, U. Miami, 1974; MPA, U. Hartford, 1980. Ed. Annl. Report to Residents, Town of West Hartford, Conn., 1979; self-employed polit. cons., Avon, Conn., 1980-82; writer-ed./pub. rel. cons., Ellenville, NY, 1982—; adj. prof. Ulster County Community Coll., Stone Ridge, N.Y., 1984-85. Founder ShoWriter Assocs., 1985, pub. rel. liason, RDAC, Goshen, N.Y., 1986-. Home: Box 52 Ellenville NY 12428

ROSENTHAL, ABBY JANE, b. NYC, June 4, 1946, d. Milton Paul and Thelma (Drogin) Rosenthal; m. Thomas E. Johnson, Jr., June 12, 1981; 1 dau., Hannah Elizabeth. Author: Faithful (poetry), 1986; contrbr. poetry, prose: Bloomsbury Rvw, Hollins Critic, Carolina Qtly, Alaska, Qtly Rvw, others. BA, Cornell U., 1968, MFA, 1978. Tchr. Ithaca (N.Y.) Coll., 1978-79, U. Wyo., Laramie, 1981-84, Yeshiva of the South, Memphis, 1984-85. Mem. P&W. Home: 650 S Greer St Memphis TN 38111

ROSENTHAL, ABRAHAM MICHAEL, b. Sault. St. Marie, Ont., Can., May 2, 1922 (came to U.S. 1926, naturalized 1951); s. Harry and Sarah (Dickstein) Rosenthal; m. Ann Marie Burke, Mar. 12, 1949; children—Jonathan Harry, Daniel Michael, Andrew Mark. Author: 38 Witnesses; co-author: One More Victim; co-editor: The Night the Lights Went Out, The Pope's Journey to the United States; contrbtr.: articles Foreign Affairs. BS in Social Sci. CCNY, 1944, LL.D, 1974; hon, degree SUNY, 1984. Staff NY Times, 1944—, UN corr., 1946-54, assigned India, 1954-48, Warsaw, Poland, 1958-59, Geneva, Switzerland, 1960-61, Tokyo, 1961-63, met. editor, 1963-66, asst. mng. editor, 1967-68, asso. mng. editor, 1968-69, mng. editor, 1969-77; Pres. Fgn. Corr. Assn. India, 1957. Pulitzer prize for intl. reporting, 1960, Number One award Overseas Press Club, 1960, George Polk Meml. award, 1960, 65, Page One award Newspaper Guild NY, 1960, Hon. award Assn. Indians in Am., 1974. Office: NY Times 229 W 43rd St New York NY 10036

ROSENTHAL, DAVID H., b. NYC, Nov. 21, 1945, s. Macha Louis and Victoria Mildred (Hemmelstein) R. Author: Eyes on the Street (poems), 1974; translator: Four Postwar Catalan Poets, 1978, Modern Catalan Poetry: An Anthology, 1979, The Time of the Doves (by Merce Rodoreda), 1980, Two Stories by Merce Rodoreda, 1983, Tirant lo Blanc (by Joanot Martorell and Joan Marti de Galba), 1984, My Christina and Other Stories (by Merce Rodoreda, 1984). MA, NYU, 1971; PhD, CUNY, 1977. Grantee NEH, 1978-80, Joint U.S.-Spanish Comm., Madrid, 1981; ACLS fellow, 1985-86. Mem. N.Am. Catalan Soc. Home: 785 West End Ave 8E New York NY 10025

ROSENTHAL, DOUGLAS EURICO, b. New York, NY, Feb. 12, 1940; s. Jacob and Edna Louise (Muir) Rosenthal; m. Erica Switzen Kremen, Nov. 12, 1967; children—Benjamin Muir, Rachel Elizabeth. Author: (with Baker and others) Antitrust Guide for International Operations, 1977, Lawyer and Client: Who's in Charge?, 1974, 2nd rev. edit., 1977; (with Knighton) National Laws and International Commerce: The Problem of Extraterritoriality; contrbtr. articles to profl. publs. BA Yale U., 1961, LLB, 1966, PhD in Poli. Sci., 1970; postrad (Henry fellow) Balliol Coll. Oxford U. (Eng.), 1962; MA Columbia U., 1963. Bar: NY, 1968, US Supreme Ct., 1976, DC, 1980. Project dir. Russell Sage Found. (NYC), 1968-70; asoc. firm Fried, Frank, Harris Shriver & Jacobson (NYC), 1970-74; asst. chief fgn. commerce sect., antitrust div. Dept. Justice (Washington), 1974-77, chief, 1977-80; partner firm Sutherland, Asbill & Brennan (Washington), 1980—; reporter Am. Law Inst.—Am. Bar Assn. Model Lawyer Peer Rev. System, 1980; speaker USIA (Australia, Engl., Can., W. Ger., Japan.) Home: 1666 K St NW Washington DC 20006

ROSENTHAL, JACOB, (Jack Rosenthal), b. Tel-Aviv, Palestine, June 30, 1935 (came to US 1938, naturalized 1943); s. Manfred and Rachel (Kaplan) Rosenthal; Prin. author: Kerner Commn. Report on Urban Riots, 1968; natl. urban corr.: Life mag., 1968-69; urban corr.: NY Times, Washington, 1969-73; asst. Sunday editor, mag. editor, 1973-77; dep. editorial page editor, 1977—. AB, Harvard U., 1956. Reporter, editor Portland Oregeonian, Reporter, 1950-61; asst. dir., dir. public info. US Dept. Justice (Washington), 1961-66; exec. asst. to undersecy. state, 1966-67; Kennedy fellow Harvard Inst. Politics, 1967-68. Recipient Best Editorial award Intl. Labor Press Assn., 1961, Loeb award, 1973, Pulitzer prize for ediorials, 1982. Office: NY Times 229 W 43rd St New York NY 10036

ROSENTHAL, M.L., b. Washington, Mar. 14, 1917; s. Jacob and Ethel (Brown) Rosenthal; m. Victoria Himmelstein, Jan. 7, 1939; children: David, Alan, Laura. Author: (with A.J.M. Smith) Exploring Poetry, 1955, 73, The Modern Poets: A Critical Introduction, 1960, A Primer of Ezra Pound, 1960, Blue Boy on Skates: Poems, 1964, The New Poets: American and British Poetry since World War II, 1967, Beyond Power: New Poems, 1969, The View from the Peacock's Tail: Poems, 1972, Randall Jarrell, 1972, Poetry and the Common Life, 1974, 83, She: A Sequence of Poems, 1977, Sailing into the Unknown: Yeats, Pound, and Eliot, 1978, Poems, 1964-80, 1981, The Modern Poetic Sequence: The Genius of Modern Poetry (with Sally M. Gall), 1983; The Poet's Art, 1987, As for Love: Poems & Translations, 1987; editor: Selected Poems and Two Plays of WB. Yeats, 1962, 73, Selected Poems and Three Plays of W.B. Yeats (rev.), 1987; The William Carlos Williams Reader, 1966, The New Modern Poetry: An Anthology of American and British Poetry since World War II, 1967, 69, 100 Postwar Poems, British and American, 1968; coeditor: Chief Modern Poets of Britain and America, 1970; genl. ed.: Poetry in English: An Anthology, 1987; translator: The Adventures of Pinocchio: Tale of a Puppet, 1983. BA U. Chgo., 1937, MA, 1938; PhD, NYU, 1949. Faculty Mich. State U., 1939-45; faculty NYU (NYC), 1945—, prof., 1961—; founder, dir. Poetics Inst., 1977-79; poetry editor The Nation, 1956-61, Humanist, 1970-78, Present Tense, 1973—; vis. specialist US Cultural Exchange Programs (Germany), 1961, (Pakistan), 1965, (Poland, Rumania, Bulgaria), 1966, (Italy and France), 1980; vis. prof. U. PA, 1974, U.Zurich, 1984; vis. poet, Israel, 1974, Yogoslavia, 1980, Disting. Scholar Exchange Program, China, 1983; dir. summer seminar NEH, 1981, 83; dir. NEH Inst. (poetic) 1985. Mem. adv. com. Natl. Book Com. 1964-67; mem. Bollingen award com., 1968-70; chmn. Delmore Schwartz Meml. Award, 1970—; mem. creative arts awards lit. jury Brandeis U., 1976—; ACLS Fellow, 1942, 50-51; Guggenheim fellow, 1960-61, 64-65; Explication Fdn. Award, 1984 Mem. AAUP, PEN, MLA, Phi Beta Kappa. Home: 17 Bayard Ln Suffern NY 10901

ROSENTHAL, ROBERT, b. Giessen, Germany, Mar. 2, 1933 (came to US 1940, naturalized, 1946); s. Julius and Hermine (Kahn) Rosenthal; m. Mary Lu Clayton, Apr. 20, 1951; children: Roberta, David C., Virginia. Author: Experimenter Effects in Behavioral Research, 1966, enlarged edit., 1976, Meta-analytic procedures for Social Research, 1984, Judgment Studies, 1987; (with Lenore Jacobson) Pygmalion in the Classroom, 1968, (with others) New Directions in Psychology 4, 1970, Sensitivity to Nonverbal Communication: The PONS Test, 1979, (with Ralph L. Rosnow) The Volunteer Subject, 1975, Essentials of Behavioral Research, 1984, Understanding Behavioral Science, 1984, Contras Analysis, 1985, (with Brian Mullen) BASIC Meta-analysis, 1985, editor: (with Ralph L.) Artifact in Behavioral Research, 1969, Rosnow) Skill in Nonverbal Communication, 1979, Quantitative Assessement of Research Domains, 1980, (with Thomas A. Sebeok) The Clever Hans Phenomenon: Communication with Horses Whales, Apes and People, 1981, (with Peter D. Blanck and Ross Buck) Nonverbal Communication in the Clinical Context, 1986. AB UCLA, 1953, PhD, 1956; Diplomate: clin. psychology Am. Bd. Examiners Profl. Psychology. Clin. psychology trainee Los Angeles Area VA, 1954-57; lectr. U. So. Calif., 1956-57; acting instr. UCLA, 1957; from asst. to assoc. prof. coordinator clin. tng. U. ND, 1957-62; vis. assoc. prof. Ohio State U., 1960-61; lect. Boston U., 1965-66; lectr. clin. psychology Harvard U., 1962-67, prof. social psychology, 1967—. Guggenheim fellow; sr. Fulbright scholar. Home: 12 Phinney Rd Lexington MA 02173

ROSENUS, ALAN HARVEY, (David Middlebrook), b. Chgo., July 9, 1940, s. Isadore and Beatrice (Frey) R.; m. Linda Wynne, Sept. 15, 1965. Author: The Old One (novel, as David Middlebrook), 1973, Devil Stories (short stories), 1979; ed., author introduction: Unwritten History: Life Amongst the Modocs (by Joaquin Miller), 1972, 82, Selected Writings of Joaquin Miller, 1976; contrbr. to Confluence, New America, Jettlag, Fifty Wetern Writers, other lit. publs. Wrkg. on novel, hist. introduction. BA, Brown U., 1962, MA, San Francisco State Coll., 1966, DA in Am. Lit., U. Oreg., 1972; postgrad. Stanford U., 1962, U. Iowa, 1967-69. Instr. English San Francisco State U., 1963-65, Coll. of Marin, Kentfield, Calif., 1965-66, Coe Coll., Cedar Rapids, Iowa, 1968-69; ed.-in-chief Urion Press, Eugene Oreg., 1972-79, San Jose, Calif., 1980—. Grantee NEA, 1979. Mem. Comm. Small Mag. Eds. and Pubs. Home: 20621 Lomita Ave Saratoga CA 95070

ROSENZWEIG, PHYLLIS D., b. NYC, Dec. 27, 1943, d. Bernard and Beatrice (Doctor) Rosenzweig. Author: Seventeen Poems, 1975; contrbr. to Roof, Telephone, Sun & Moon, Washington Rvw. BA, Hunter Coll., 1964; MA, Inst. Fine Art, NYU, 1970. Poetry ed. Washington Rvw, 1982-84, assoc. ed., 1984—; ed., pub. Primary Writing, Washington. Home: 1545 18th St NW 116 Washington DC 20036

ROSIER, JAMES LOUIS, b. Chgo., Mar. 14, 1932; s. Escol MacFarland and Maudellen (Hamblin) Rosier; m. Katherine Lee Allen, Sept. 10, 1955; children—Meredith Lee, Paul Carick, Jessica Holly. Author/co-author: The Vitellius Psalter, 1962, Poems in Old English, 1962, The Norton Reader, 1965—, Philological Essays, 1970, Old English Language and Literature, 1972, Aldhelm: The Poetic Works, 1984; asst. editor:

Middle English Dictionary, 1961-63. Student DePauw U., 1949-51; BA Stanford U., 1953, PhD, 1957; postgrad., Freie U. (Berlin, West Germany), 1954-55. Instr. Cornell U. (Ithica, NY), 1957-60, asst. prof., 1960-61, U. Mich. (Ann Arbor), 1961-63; asso. prof. English U. PA (Philadelphia), 1963-68, prof. English philology, 1968—, chmn. grad. sudies, 1977-79; vis. asso. prof. U. Chgo., 1965; honors examiner Manhatanville Coll. (NY), 1970-71, Swarthmore Coll. (PA), 1972-73, 81-82; cons. Binghamton Med. Studies, Can. Council, ACLS grantee, 1960, Am. Philo. Soc. grantee, 1964, 71; Guggenheim fellow, 1964-65; U. PA Research Fdn. grantee, 1983. Mem. MLA, Medieval Acad. Am., Soc. Study Medieval Lang. and Lit., Dictionary Soc. Am. (co-founder, exec. bd. 1977—, vp, pres.-elect. 1983—), Renaissance Soc. Am. Home: 508 Cedar LN Swarthmore PA 19081

ROSNER, ANN, see Seaman, Barbara

ROSS, ANDREA PATRICIA, b. Bronx, NY, Sept. 29, d. Stephen and Louise Alice (Lord) Ross. Author children's books: Chester the Little Black Earth Ant, 1980, Rock Little Flowers, 1984, Seymour, 1985, Poenisha, 1986, Oscar Crab and Rollo Car, 1986; Pogosticks (children's play), 1986;, Too Much Fun, 1988; contrbr. to Am. Poetry Assn. anthology. Wrkg. on children's stories, poems, songs, play. Student U. Knoxville, then U. Cin. Costumer, playwright: Playhouse in the Park, Cin., 1968-70, Am. Conservatory Theatre, San Francisco, 1970-71, The Acting Co., Juilliard Schl., NYC, 1971-73, Dance Theatre Harlem, NYC, 1973-81, CBS Broadcast Center, NYC, 1981—. Recipient of Golden Poet Award, Silver Poet Award, Am. Poetry Assn. for poem, Just a Word. Home: 467 Central Park W Apt 6E New York NY 10025

ROSS, DAVID, b. NYC, Sept. 26, 1929, s. Samuel Ross and Helen Haas. Author: Three Ages of Lake Light, 1962; poetry ed. Advance!, 1976, Golden Horses: Poetry for a New Civilization, 1976; contrbr. poems to New Yorker Book of Poems, Golden Horses, The Nation, Poetry, Kulchur, New Yorker, Mich. Qtly Rvw, Transatlantic Rvw, and Essays N.Y. Times Book Rvw, Kulchur, Mich. Qtly Rvw, Advance!. Student Champlain Coll., 1947-49, Syracuse U., 1949. Tchr. lit. New Schl. for Social Research, NYC, 1962-67; condr. poetry workshop Antioch U./West, Los Angeles, 1976-77. Address: Haas 170 E Hartsdale Ave Hartsdale NY 10530

ROSS, DORTHY MARCUSSEN, b. Pleasant Plains, IL, Jan. 31, 1933; d. Russell Jens and Frances Marie (Ferguson) Marcussen; m. Franklin North Ross, Feb. 14, 1954; children—Dana, Peter Douglas, Frances Ann. Author: Fundraising for Youth, 1984. Contrbr. poems to anthols. Student Western Ill. U., 1950-51. Exec. secy. Office of Governor, Springfield, Il, 1971-72; exec./legal secy. Ill. Dept. of Conservation, Springfield, 1972-87. Mem. NPW (state secy. 1982-84), Ill. State Poetry Soc. (state secy. 1980-82), RWA (secy. Heart & Scroll chpt.). Home: Compass Point Farm Rochester IL 62563

ROSS, GLEN ERNEST, b. Stilwell, OK., Aug. 7, 1929, s. George James and Jennie Elizabeth (Garrison) R.; m. Renee Chaussee, July 12, 1963; childen—Erica L., Anne Adrir. Author: (novel) The Last Campaign, 1962; ed. Just a Passin' Through; ontrbr. to El Universal, N.Mex. Qtly, Baraza, Army mag., American Men at Arms, Success in Writing. BA, U. Colo., 1955; MA, U. Ams., Mexico City, 1962. Ed. English sect. El Universal, Mexico City, 1958-59; tchr. Spanish and French, Jefferson High Schl., Hobbs, N. Mex., 1961-66; grad. instr. U. Colo., Boulder, 1966-67; asst. prof. English, Central State U., Edmond, Okla., 1967—. Served with U.S. Army, 1948-52. Home: 648 Reynolds Rd Edmond OK 73013

ROSS, JAMES FRANCIS, b. Providence, Oct. 8, 1931; s. James Joseph and Teresa Marie (Sullivan) Ross; m. Kathleen Marie Fallon, Dec. 1, 1956; children—Seamus, Ellen, Richard Fallon, Therese. Author: Philosophical Theology, 1969, 2nd edit., 1980, Introduction to Philosophy of Religion, 1970, Portraying Analogy, 1981; translator, editor: Suarez on Formal and Universal Unity, 1964; editor: Studies in Medieval Philosophy, 1971. AB Cath. U. Am., 1953, MA. 1954; PhD Brown U., 1958; JD U. PA, 1974. Bar: PA bar, 1975. Instr., then asst. prof. Philosophy U. Mich., 1959-61; asst. prof. U. PA, 1962-65, asso. prof., 1965-68, prof., 1968—, chmn. Philosophy dept. and grad. group in Philosophy, 1966-7-, 81-83; Rackham research fellow U. Mich., 1960-61; NIH spl. Research fellow, 1970; NEH fellow, mem. Inst. advanced Study, Princeton, 1975-76; vis. prof. Brown U., summer 1977; assoc. mem. Darwin Coll., Cambridge U. (England) 1982-83, 83—, Guggenheim fellow, 1982-83. Office: 315 Logan Hall U PA Philadelphia PA 19104

ROSS, LEE A., b. Norwood, MA, July 17, 1945; s. Dorothy B. (Blaisdell) R.; m. Melinda Christine Mason, Aug. 12, 1972; children—Allan, Katherine. Contrbr. articles to ednl. publs. BS, Tenn. Wesleyan Coll., 1972; MS, Auburn U., 1973; Ednl. Specialist, Ark. State U., 1984. Guidance counselor Strong Schl., Marianna, Ark., 1974-77; prin. Greene County Tech. Schl. Dist., Paragould, Ark., 1977—. Served with U.S. Army, 1965-68; Vietnam. Mem. profl. ednl. orgns. Home: Box 512 Paragould AR 72451

ROSS, LEONA CURTIS, b. Kingfield, ME, Oct. 10, 1953; d. Linwood Carlton Curtis and Anna May (LeMay) Smith; m. Robert Blynn Ross, July 17, 1971 (dec. Aug. 13, 1973); children—Jason James, Justin Linwood. Author: Resurrexit, 1986. Wrkg. on murder mystery. Student U. Maine, 1985—. Clrk., Maxwell's Market, West Farmington, ME, 1986; clrk. return dept. G. H. Bass Co., Wilton, ME, 1987. Home: Rt 2 Box 2227 Farmington ME 04938

ROSS, MARILYN ANN (ANN MARKHAM), b. San Diego, Nov. 3, 1939; d. Glenn James and Dorothy Verna (Scudder) M.; m. Clayton Theodore Heimberg (div.); m. Tom Ross, May 25, 1977; children: Scott, Steven, Kevin, Laurie. Author: Discover Your Roots, 1977, Creative Loafing, 1978, Encyclopedia of Self-Publishing, 1978, Be Tough or Be Gone, 1983, Complete Guide to Self-Publishing, 1985, How to Make Big Profits Publishing City & Regional Books, 1987; editor: The UNcook Book, 1980, A Bridge to Yesterday, 1982, Buffalo Management and Marketing, 1983, The Natl. Survey of Op-Ed Pages, 1986. Student San Diego State U., 1977-78. Dir. mktg. South Bay Trade Schls., San Diego, 1972-78; mgr. Mervyns Dept. Store, San Diego, 1977-78; pres. Communication Creativity, Saguache, Colo., 1978—; co-founder About Books, Inc., Saguache, 1978—. Bd. dirs. Ch. Religious Sci., San Diego, 1979. Mem. AG, ASJA, NWS, San Diego Women in Bus. (founding, bd. dirs. 1980), San Luis Valley Writers Guild (co-founder 1985), Saguache C. of C. (vol. head 1981—). Recipient Best Non-Fiction Book award Press Women, 1978, 79. Home: County Rd FF38 Saguache CO 81149

ROSS, RAYMOND SAMUEL, b.Milw., Apr. 14, 1925; s. Samuel and Agnes Tobina (Thorkildsen) R.; m. Ricky Reichmann, June 19, 1948; children—Mark G., Scott R. Author: Persuasion: Communication and Interpersonal Relations, 1974, Essentials of Speech Communication, 2d ed., 1984, Understanding Persuasion, 2d ed., 1985, Speech Communication: Fundamentals and Practice, 8th ed., 1988, Small Groups in Organizational Settings, 1988; (with others) The Air Force Staff Officer, 1960, Communicative Arts and Sciences of Speech, 1967; (with Mark Ross) Relating and Interacting: An Introduction to Interpersonal Communication, 1982. Ph.B., Marquette U., 1949, M.A., 1950; Ph.D., Purdue U., 1954. Prof. Wayne State U., Detroit, 1958-85, prof. emeritus, 1985—; disting. visiting prof. Pepperdine U., Malibu, CA, 1986. Mem. Speech Communication Assn., Am. Psychological Assn., Address: 12745 Avondale Ln Traverse City MI 49684

ROSS, ROBERT E. (Bob), b. Ainsworth, NE, Aug. 16, 1944, s. Edwin F. and Alice K. Ross. Author: Solitary Confinement (poetry), 1977; co-ed.: CutBank, 1982-83; ed.: Shitepoke, 1985; contrbr. poems, fiction to lit mags. MA, U. Ariz., 1972; MFA, U. Mont., 1983. Mem. faculty dept. English U. Alaska, Fairbanks, 1984-86. Served to 2d lt. USAF. Home: 2404 Raymond Missoula MT 59802

ROSS, ROSEANNA GAYE, b. Lancaster, OH, Nov. 22, 1949; d. Eugene Francis and Vonna LaVerne (Thacker) R.; m. Robert A. Crook, Dec. 29, 1971 (div. Mar. 1979); 1 dau., Collette Suzanne Crook; m. 2d, Timothy Scott Foster, Nov. 26, 1982; 2 sons: Marshall Ross Foster, Brennan Ross Foster. Pubns. incl.: Lancaster Eagle Gazette Nwspr., 1971-78, Jnl. Volunteers with Delinquents, 1972, Health Values: Achieving High Level Wellness, 1977, Health Communic. Nwsltr., 1979-80, Ednl. Gerontology, 1982, ERIC Clearing—House—Resources in Edn., 1985. BSEd, Ohio U., 1971, PhD, 1982; MA, Ohio State U., 1972. Engl. tchr. Stanberry Freshman H.S., Lancaster, OH, 1973-74; part-time instr. Hocking Tech. Coll., Nelsonville, OH, 1972-77, Ohio U., Lancaster, 72-80; asst. prof. & forensics dir. St. Cloud State (MN) U., 1980-84, assoc. prof. communics. & internship dir., 1984—. MN Dept. Edn. grant, 1985. Mem. Internatl. Communic. Assn., other prof. orgns. Home: 32202 Cty Rd 1 St Cloud MN 56303

ROSS, STANLEY ROBERT, b. NYC, Aug.m 8, 1921; s. Max George and Ethel (Aks) Ross; m. Lenore Jacobson, Oct. 7, 1945 (div. 1975); children—Steven David, Alicia Ellen, Janet Irene; m. 2d, Geraldine D. Gagliano, Dec. 18, 1977. Author: Francisco I. Madero, Apostle of Mexican Democracy, 1955, 2nd ed., 1977; co-author, co-editor: Historia Documental de Mexico, 2 vols., 1964; editor: Is the Mexican Revolution Dead?, 1965, rev. edit., 1975, Comp. Fuentes de la Historia Contemporanea de Mexico: Periodicos Y Revistas, 2 vols, 1966-67, 3 vols., 1978-80, Latin America in Transition, 1970, (Paul Kennedy) The Middle Beat, 1971, Views Across the Border: The United States and Mexico, 1978; co-editor: Criticas constructivas del sistema politico Mexicano, 1973, U.S. Policies Toward Mexico: Perceptions and Perspectives, 1979, The Illegal Alien from Mexico: Policy Choices for an Intractable Issue, 1980, Ecology and Development of the Border Region, 1983; adv. editor: The Americas, 1956-70; co-editor: United States Relations with Mexico: Context and Content, 1981, Buenos Aires: 400 Years, 1982; contrbg. editor: The Handbook of Latin

American Studies, 1960-70; mng. editor: Hispanic American Hist. Rvw, 1970-75. AB, Queens Coll., 1942; MA, Columbia U., 1943, PhD, 1951. Instr. History Queens Coll., 1946-48; from instr. to prof. history U. Nebr., 1948-62; prof. history, chmn. dept. State U. NY (Stony Brook), 1962-66; acting dean Coll. Arts and Scis., 1963-66, dean, 1966-68, prof. history, dir. Inst. Latin Am. Studies U. TX (Austin), 1968-71, provost arts and scis., 1971-72, provost, 1972-73, vp, provost, 1973-76, prof. history, coordinator research program, 1976—, Ashbel Smith prof. history, 1983, CB Smith Sr. Centennial chair in US-Mexico Relations, 1983—; coordinator Office of Mexican Studies, 1980—. US natl. mem. comm. on history Pan Am. Inst. Georgraphy and History, 1969-73; mem. joint com. Latin-Am. studies ACLS-Social Sci. Research Council, 1968-71. Served to 1st lt. USAAF, 1943-46. Home: 102 Canyon Rim Dr Austin TX 78746

ROSS, STEVEN SANDER, b. Boston, May 29, 1946; s. Eli Woodrow and Lillian Faye (Arrick) Ross; m. Nancy Lawrence Bush, June 23, 1970; children—Marion Joyce, Heather Rebecca, Leah Elizabeth. Editor: Air and Water News, McGraw-Hill Pub. Co., NYC, 1970-72, New Engr. mag., MBA Communications, NYC, 1972-79; asso, editor: Chem. Engring. mag., 1972; editorial dir., New Engr. mag., 1978-79; mng. editor: Boardroom Reports, 1979-80; editor-in-chief: Direct Mag., 1981—; author: Construction Disasters, 1983; co-author: Product Safety and Liability: A Desk Reference, 1979; Editor: Environment Regulation Handbook, 1973—, Land Use Planning Substances Sourcebook II, 1980; co-editor: McGraw-Hill's 1972 Report on Business and the Environment, 1972. BS in Physics, Rensselaer Poly. Inst., 1969; MS in Jnlsm., Columbia, 1970. Dir. spl. projects Environ, Info. Center (NYC), 1974—; assoc. McNamee Cons. Co., 1981—. Home: 120 Irving St Box L Leonia NJ 07605

ROSS, SUSAN, see Fass, Susan R.

ROSS, THEODORE JOHN, b. Boston, Oct. 3, 1924; s. Samuel and Rita (Newman) R.; m. Rhoda Pollack, Dec. 25, 1956; children: Richard, Jonathan, Laurence. Ed. anthology Film and the Liberal Arts, 1970, (with Huss) Focus on the Horror Film, 1972; contrbr. to New Republic, Dissent, New Politics, December, Psychoanalytic, Mass., Chgo., Fairleigh Dickinson U. Bus. rvws, Take One, Film Heritage, Film Qtly., Lit./Film Qtly., Coll. English, Qtly Rvw, Film Studies, Encoder, Thought in Prose, Mass Media and Mass Man, Focus on the Western, Renaissance of the Film, also others. Wrkg. on Philip Larkin's collected criticism, study on films of Joseph Losey. BA, Clark U., 1948; MA, Columbia U., 1949. Editorial asst. Wise Publs., NYC, 1949-51; instr. W.Va. U.,1952-55, Wayne State U., 1956-60; asst. prof. to prof. Fairleigh Dickinson U., Madison, N.J., 1960—. Served with AUS, 1943-46; ETO. N.J. Commn. on Humanities grantee, 1978. Mem. NCTE, N.E. MLA, Popular Culture Assn. South. Home: 2 Woodley Rd Morristown NJ 07960

ROSS-BREGGIN, VIRGINIA (GINGER) FAYE, B. Mineola, NY, Feb. 25, 1951; d. Philip Cole and Jean (Heissenbuttel) Ross; m. Peter Roger Breggin, July 4, 1984; children—Alysha Ulan, Benjamin Jay Breggin. Contrbr.: Huntington Herald Press, Freedom Jnl., The Truth About Drugs, Mideast Bus. Exchange, The Humanist. Wrkg. on book of photoessays. Formerly reporter, Huntington (Ind.) Herald Press; ed., exec. ed. Freedom Jnl., Los Angeles; public relations officer, asst. advt. dir. Michael Baybak & Co., Beverly Hills, Calif.; now freelance photojournalist, Bethesda, Md. Work displayed in exhibitions, competitions, Md., M.C., Colo., and Calif. Home: 4628 Chestnut St Bethesda MD 20814

ROSSET, LISA KRUG, b. NYC, Nov. 11, 1952; d. George William and Rita (Earle) Krug; m. Barney Rosset, Nov. 5, 1980; 1 dau.—Chantal. BA magna cum laude Smith Coll., 1974; MA Columbia U., 1976 Editor Latin Am. Series and general editor, Grove Press (NYC), 1976-86. Mng. ed. Aperture, 1987—. Mem. Phi Beta Kappa. Office: Aperture 20 E 23 St New York NY 10010

ROSSITER, CHARLES M., b. Balt., Dec. 11, 1942, s. Charles M. and Margaret E. (Wallace) R.; m. Mary Ellen Munley, June 8, 1978; 1 dau., Erika Lynn. Author: Communicating Personally, 1975, Human Potential Guide to Dynamic Personal Growth, 1984, Thirds, 1985. Wrkg. on poetry, fiction. BS, U. Md., 1965, MA, PhD, Ohio U., Athens, 1970. Assoc. prof. U. Wis.-Milw., 1969-79, Hood Coll., Frederick, Md., 1980-84; sr. researcher, Pacific Inst., Bethesda, MD, 1985—; sr. researcher, Research Fdn. of SUNY at Albany, 1987—; freelance wrtr., cons., Washington, 1979-85. Mem. Nat. Assn. Poetry Therapy, Wrtr.'s Center. Home: 158 Western Ave Albany NY 12203

ROSSMAN, PARKER, b. Enid, OK, May 20, 1919; s. George P. and Vera E. (Jacobs) R.; m. Jean F. Fleming, June 6, 1951; children—Kristen-Anne, George III, Mary-Michelle. Author non-fiction: Sexual Experience, 1978, Hospice, 1979, After Punishment What?, 1980, Computers: New Opportunities..., 1984, Family Survival: Coping With Stress, 1984, Helping People Care on the Job, 1985, Computers: Bridges to the Future, 1985, Dreams and Demons, 1988. BA, U. Okla., 1941; BD, U. Chgo., 1944, PhD, Yale U., 1953. Author-in-residence Central Philippines U., 1982-83. Mem. AL, AG, PEN. Home: Box 382 Niantic CT 06357

ROSSNER, JUDITH, b. NYC, Mar. 31, 1935; d. Joseph George and Dorothy (Shapiro) Perelman; children: Jean, Daniel. Author: To the Precipice, 1966; Nine Months in the Life of an Old Maid, 1969; Any Minute I Can Split, 1972; Looking for Mr. Goodbar, 1975; Attachments, 1977; Emmeline, 1980; August, 1983. Attended CCNY 1952-54. Address: Bach Agcy 747 3rd Ave New York NY 10017

ROSSON-DAVIS, BARBARA ANN, b. San Mateo, CA, Aug. 30, 1946, d. James Thurman and Elaine Helen (Dellos) Rosson; m. 2d, Steven L. Davis, Oct. 5, 1979; 1 son, Matthew Ross. Contrbr. to lit. jnls and anthologies including: Beatitudes, Voices of the Wineland, Green River Rvw, The Pilot, Intl. Poetry Rvw, Carolina Qtly, Michigan Rvw. BA cum laude, San Francisco State U., 1969; postgrad., U. Calif.-Berkeley, 1973, 74, 75. Poet-in-schls., Napa and St. Helena, Calif., 1976-77; mgr. Tayloring, San Francisco, 1977-78; asst.-dir. Vorpal Gallery, San Francisco, 1973-76; dir. Eidolon, San Francisco, 1978-79; founder, dir. Poetry Center Southeast, Guilford College, N.C., 1980-83; lit. chair O. Henry Festival, Greensboro, N.C., 1984. Winner 1st award Napa Coll. Wrtrs. Conf., 1975. Mem. N.C. Wrtrs., N.C. Poetry Soc. Home: 5205 Hilltop Rd Jamestown NC 27282

ROSTKY, GEORGE HAROLD, b.NYC, Feb. 28, 1926; s. Morris and Mary (Wyloge) Rostky; m. Rhoda Thelma Bornstein, June 29, 1950; children—Mark, Lisa. BEE CCNY, 1957. Asso. editor Electronic Design (NYC), 1957-61, editor-in-chief (Rochelle Park, NJ), 1971-78; editorial dir./assoc. pub. Electronic Engring. Times (Manhasset, NY), 1978-86; securities analyst McDonnell & Co. (NYC), 1961-62; editorial dir. Mactier Pub. Co. (NYC), 1962-71; founder Geo. Rostky Assocs. Mkt. Research, 1986. US Dept. Commerce industry tech. rep. to US Electronics Catalog Exhbn. (India), 1980. Served with AUS, 1942-45. Recipient Indsl. Mktg. award for editorial excellence, 1964, Neal awards, 1967, 74, 75, 77. Home: 39 Cumberland Ave Great Neck NY 11020

ROTH, DUANE A., (Dewey Roth), b. Bluffton, IN, Aug. 2, 1957, s. Clarence E. and Georgina D. (Smith) R.; m. Debbie Ann Brewer, June 9, 1979; children—Angel Brooke, Shonda Diane, Curtis Emanuel. Contrbr. to Straight Mag., Christian Standard. Wrkg. on narrative of gospel accounts. BS, Cin. Bible Coll., 1984. On-air personality sta. WXKE, Ft. Wayne, Ind., 1976-77, sta. WFWR-WCMX-Fm, Ft. Wayne, 1977-78; minister of youth and edn. Cedar Creek Ch. of Christ, Leo, Ind., 1984—. Home: 10 Surrey Ln Apt 114 Grabill IN 46741

ROTH, HENRY H., July 19, 1933; s. Bernard Brandeis and Sara (Abelson) R.; m. Sylvia Grossberg, June 12, 1955 (div. Aug. 1987); children—Stephen, Anna, Susan. Author: (fiction) The Cruz Stories, 1973, Jackdaw (NEA Award), 1975, In Empty Rooms, 1980; (plays) Postscripts, 1981, The Prisoner, 1983, Don't Be Late, 1983, The Country Gentlemen, 1984, The Sublet, 1985; (filmscripts) Five and Dime Dreams, 1982, The Cruz Brothers and Miss Malloy (film produced), 1980. Contrbr. numerous short stories to lit mags, numerous anthols. B.A., NYU., 1955. Tchr., wrtr.-in-residence Rockland Center for the Arts, West Nyack, NY, 1979-82; lectr. CUNY, 1981—; tchr. high schl. upward bound Columbia U., NYC, 1985. Judge, Dejur Creative Writing Award, 1987; judge Pennsylvania fiction fellowships; leader numerous writing workshops. Yaddo fellow, 1980; novel grantee NEA, 1975. Mem. PEN. Home: 1 Haven Ct Nyack NY 10960

ROTH, JOHN KING, b.Grand Haven, MI, Sept, 3, 1940; s. Josiah V. and Doris Irene (King) Roth; m. Evelyn Lillian Austin, June 25, 1964; children—Andrew Lee, Sarah Austin. Author: Freedom and the Moral Life, 1969, Problems of the Philosophy of Religion, 1971, American Dreams, 1976, A Consuming Fire, 1979, Approaches to Auschwitz (with Richard L. Rubenstein), 1987, The Questions of Philosophy (with Frederick Sontag), 1987. BA Pomona Coll., 1962; student Yale U. Div. Sch., 1962-63, MA, 1965, PhD, 1966. Asst. prof., 1971-76, Russell K. Pitzer prof. Philosophy, 1976—, vis. prof. Philosophy Franklin Coll. (Lugano, Switzerland), 1973; Fulbright lectr. Am. studies U. Innbruck (Austria), 1973-74; vis. prof. Philosophy Doshisha U. (Kyoto, Japan), 1981-82; vis. prof. Holocaust Studies U. Haifa (Israel), 1982. Spl. advisor US Holocaust Meml. Council, Washington, 1980—. Danforth grad. fellow, 1962-66; Graves fellow, 1970-71; NEH fellow, 1976-77. Home: 1648 Kenyon Pl Claremont CA 91711

ROTH, JUDITH PARIS, b. Bklyn., Dec. 29, 1949, d. Leonard Paris and Leah (Kaminsky) Small; m. Bryan L. Roth, M.D., PhD, Sept. 1, 1985; 1dau., Rachel Annaliese (Feb. 11, 1987).

Author: The Essential Guide to CD-ROM, 1986; contrbr. to Software Rvw., Popular Computing, High Technology, EITV, other profl. mags.; contrbr.: Conservation in the Library, 1983. BA, George Washington U., 1970, MLS, Syracuse U., 1971, MSW, Catholic Univ. of Am., 1985. Research assoc. Essex Corp., Alexandria, Va., 1976-78; info. mgr. IPPRC, McLean, Va., 1978-80; ed.-in-chief Optical Information Systems, Meckler Corp., Westport, Conn., 1981—. Mem. ALA. Home: 2157 Evans Ct Apt 304 Falls Church VA 22043

ROTH, JUNE DORIS SPIEWAK, b. Haverstraw, NY, Feb. 16, 1926; d. Harry I. and Ida (Glazer) Spiewak; m. Frederick Roth, Jul. 7, 1945; children—Nancy, Robert. Author: The Freeze and Please Homefreezer Cookbook, 1963, The Rich and Delicious Low-Calorie Figure Slimming Cookbook, 1964, Thousand Calorie Cookbook, 1967, How to Use Sugar to Lose Weight, 1969, Fast and Fancy Cookbook, 1969, How to Cook Like a Jewish Mother, 1969, The Take Good Care of My Son Cookbook for Brides, 1969, The Indoor/Outdoor Barbecue Book, 1970, The Pick of the Pantry Cookbook, 1970, Let's Have a Brunch Cookbook, 1971, Edith Bunker's All in the Family Cookbook, 1972, The On-Your-Own Cookbook, 1972, Healthier Jewish Cookery: The Unsaturated Fat Way, 1972, Elegant Desserts, 1973, Old-Fashioned Candymaking, 1974, Salt-Free Cooking with Herbs and Spices, 1975, The Troubled Tummy Cookbook, 1976, Cooking for Your Hyperactive Child, 1977, The Galley Cookbook, 1977, The Food/Depression Connection, 1978, Aerobic Nutrition, 1981, The Allergic Gourmet, 1983, Living Better with a Special Diet, 1983, The Pasta Lover's Diet Book, 1984, The Executive Success Diet, 1986. Student Pa. State U., 1942-44; grad. Tobé Coburn Sch., 1945; BA Thomas Edison Coll, 1981; MS U. Bridgeport, 1982. Nationally syndicated newspaper column "Special Diets," 1979—; recipe developer The Pritikin Program for Diet and Exercise, 1979. Mem. Authors League Am., Am. Soc. Journalists and Authors (pres. 1982-83), Newspaper Food Editors and Writers Assn., Newspaper Features Council, Natl. Fedn. Press Women, Natl. Press Club. Address: 1057 Oakland Ct Teaneck NJ 07666

ROTH, MARTHA, (Martha Vanceburg), b. Chgo., May 1, 1938; d. Joseph Russel and Sylvia (Weinstein) Silverman; m. Martin Roth, June 7, 1957; children—Molly Dulcinea, Jennifer Margaret, David Sebastian. Author: The Life (play), 1979, The Promise of a New Day, 1984, In Border Crossings, 1984, Waitress Journal, 1986. Certificat, U. Paris, 1957; AB, U. Chgo., 1958. Man. ed. Modern Medicine, New York, 1975-78; man. ed, Contemp. Sociology, Mpls., 1983-86; exec. ed. Hurricane Alice, Mpls., 1983—. Mem. NWU. Office: 270 Lind Hall 270 Church St Minneapolis MN 55455

ROTH, PHILIP, b. Newark, Mar. 19, 1933; s. Herman and Bess (Finkel) R.; m. Margaret Martinson, Feb. 22, 1959 (dec. 1968). Author: Goodbye, Columbus, 1959 (Natl. Bk. Award), Letting Go, 1962, When She Was Good, 1967, Portnoy's Complaint, 1969, Our Gang, 1971, The Breast, 1972, The Great American Novel, 1973, My Life as a Man, 1974, Reading Myself and Others, 1975, The Professor of Desire, 1977, The Ghost Writer, 1979, A Philip Roth Reader, 1980, Zuckerman Unbound, 1981, The Anatomy Lesson, 1983, The Counterlife, 1987. AB, Bucknell U., 1954; MA, U. Chgo., 1955. Tchr. English U. Chgo., 1956-58; mem. faculty Iowa Writer's Wkshp., 1960-62; wrtr.-in-res. Princeton U., 1962-64; vs. wrtr., SUNY at Stony Brook, 1966, 67, U. Pa., 1967-77. Served with AUS, 1955-56. Guggenheim fellow, 1959-60; Ford Fdn. grantee, 1965; Rockefeller fellow, 1966. Mem. Am. Inst. Arts and Letters. Address: Farrar Straus 19 Union Sq W New York NY 10003

ROTHBERG, ABRAHAM, b. NYC, Jan. 14, 1922; s. Louis and Lottie (Drimmer) Rothberg; m. Esther Conwell, Sept, 30, 1945; 1 son—Lewis Josiah. Author: Abraham, Eyewitness History of World War II, 1962, The Thousand Doors, 1965, The Heirs of Cain, 1966, The Song of David Freed, 1968, The Other Man's Shoes, 1969, The Boy and the Dolphin, 1969, The Sword of the Golem, 1971, Aleksandr Solzhenitsyn: The Major Novels, 1971, The Heirs of Stalin: Dissidence and the Soviet Regime, 1953-1970, 1972, The Stalking Horse, 1972, The Great Waltz, 1978, The Four Corners of the House, 1981; editor: US Stories, 1949, Flashes in the Night, 1958, Anatomy of a Moral, 1959, A Bar-Mitzvah Companion, 1959, Great Adventure Stories of Jack London, 1967; contrbtr. articles, essays, stories, poems to various publs., anthologies, collections. AB Bklyn. Coll, 1942; MA U. Iowa, 1947; PhD, Columbia U., 1952. Chmn. editorial bd. Stateside (mag.) (NYC), 1947-49; instr. English, creative writing Columbia U. (NYC), 1948; instr. English, humanities Hofstra Coll. (Hempstead, NY), 1947-51; prof. English St. John Fisher Coll. 1973-83, chmn. dept. English, 1981-82; editor-in-chief Free Europe Press (NYC), 1952-59; mng. editor George Braziller, Inc. (NYC), 1959, New Leader (mag.) 1960-61; cons. editor New Jewish Encyc., 1960-62; writer, editorial cons. European corr. Natl. Observer (Washington), Manchester Guardian (England), 1962-63; sr. editor Bantam Books, Inc. (NYC), 1966-67; cons. editor The New Union Prayer Book (NYC), 1975. Served with AUS, 1943-35. Ford Fdn. Fellow, NYC, 1951-52; Recipient John H. McGinnis Meml. award for essay, 1973-74, Lit. Award Friends of Rochester Library, 1980. Home: 340 Pelham Rd Rochester NY 14610

ROTHENBERG, JEROME DENNIS, b. New York, NY, Dec. 11, 1931; s. Morris and Estelle (Lichtenstein) Rothenberg; m. Diane Brodatz, Dec. 25, 1952; 1 son—Matthew. Author: numerous books of poetry and prose, including Between, 1967, Technicians of the Sacred, 1968, Poems for the Game of Silence, 1971, Shaking the Pumpkin, 1972, America a Prophecy, 1973, Revolution of the Word, 1974, Poland/1931, 1974, A Big Jewish Book, 1978, A Seneca Journal, 1978, Vienna Blood, 1980, Pre-Faces, 1981, Symposium of the Whole, 1983, That Dada Strain, 1983 New Selected Poems, 1986; editor, pub., Hawk's Well Press, NYC, 1958-65, Some/Thing mag., 1966-69, Alcheringa: Ethnopoetics, 1970-76, New Wilderness Letter, 1976-86. BA CCNY, 1952; MA U Mich., 1953. With Mannes Coll. Music (NYC), 1961-70; vis. prof. U. Calif. (San Diego), 1971, 78-84, U. Wis. (Milwaukee), 1974-75, San Diego State U., 1976-77, U. Calif. (Riverside), 1980; vis. Aerol Arnold prof. English U. So. Calif., 1983, vis. prof. U. Oklahoma (Norman), 1985; vis. N.Y. State Writer-in-Residence, State U. N.Y. (Albany), 1986; Professor, State U. N.Y. (Binghamton), 1986—; poet, freelance writer, 1956—. Served with AUS, 1953-55. Recipient award in poetry Longview Fdn., 1960, Before Columbus Fdn. Am. Book award, 1982; Wenner-Gren Fdn. grantee-in-aid for research in Am. Indian Poetry, 1968; Guggenheim fellow in creative writing, 1974; NEA poetry grantee, 1976. Mem. PEN Am. Center, New Wilderness Found. Home: 1026 San Abella Dr Encinitas CA 92024

ROTHMAN, HOWARD, b. Phila., Sept. 26, 1953; s. Edwin and Ida (Steinman) R.; m. Patricia Myers, Apr. 20, 1975; 1 dau., Anna Leigh. Co-author (with Robert Rubman, M.D.) Future Vision, 1987; contrbr. articles: Am. Way, Nation's Bus., Guest Informant, Denver Bus. Jnl., Phila. Inquirer, Tampa Tribune, numerous other publs. Wrkg. on articles, non-fiction. BA in Journalism, Pa. State U., 1974. Staff wrtr. Germantown Courier, Phila., 1976-77; ed. Southeast Sentinel, Denver, 1977-80; assoc. ed. Jackson Hole Guide, Jackson, Wyo., 1980-82; freelance wrtr., 1982—. Recipient awards Wyo. Press Assn., 1981, Fountainhead Media Awards, 1986. Mem. WWA, U.S. Ski Wrtrs.' Assn., Am. Medical Wrtrs. Assn. Home: 2351 S Josephine St Denver CO 80210

ROTHSTEIN, ERIC, b. Bklyn., Mar. 12, 1936; s. Emil and Charlotte (Spielberger) Rothstein; m. Marian Grunwald, June 20, 1965; div. Nov. 26, 1985. Author: Restoration Tragedy: Form and the Process of Change, 1967, George Farquhar, 1967, Systems of Order and Inquiry in Later Eighteenth-Century Fiction, 1975, Restoration and Eighteenth-Century Poetry, 1660-1780, 1981, The Design of Carolean Comedy, 1988. AB Harvard U., 1957; PhD Princeton U., 1962. Instr. U. Wis. (Madison), 1961-63, asst prof. English, 1963-66, assoc. prof., 1966-70, prof, 1970-82, Edgar W. Lacy prof. English, 1982—. Fellow ACLS, 1973; NEH fellow, summer, 1980; Humanities Research Institute, 1985. Home: 417 Ridge St Madison WI 53705

ROTHSTEIN, MARILYN E., b. Oxford, MA, Sept. 5, 1938, d. Louis Anthony and Leslie Anna (Fortin) Kemp; m. Sewall Wallace Craig, May 1960 (dec. 1962); m. Jack H. Rothstein, Sept. 19, 1964; children—Chris Laurence, Rachel Ann, Sarah Isa. Author: Self-Advocacy for Senior Citizens, 1978, The Court System in New York State, 1980, What Every Citizen Should Know: A Guide to Local Government, 1980; contrbr. articles to 1985 New Book of Knowledge, Amtrak Express, Woman's World, Sports Parade, Glass mag., other publs. MA in English, Siena Coll., 1966. Wrtr. Cornell U. Extension, Albany, N.Y., 1975-82; freelance wrtr., Delmar, N.YU., 1982—. Mem. N.Y. State Women's Press Club. Office: 18 Pinedale Ave Delmar NY 12054

ROTTMAN, GORDON LEROY, b. Seaside, OR, Feb 24, 1947; s. Carl Fredrick and Dorris R.; m. Barbara Paulette Brown, July 6, 1971 (div. June 18, 1983); m 2d, Enriqueta Guillermina Garza Medina, June 19, 1983; children: Joseph, Melanie, Mario, Angelina. Author: US Army Spcl. Forces, 1952-84, 1985, Warsaw Pact Ground Forces, 1987, US Army Rangers, 1942-86, 1987; contrbr. to Trading Post Mag, Red Thrust Star, Army Trainer Mag. Enlisted US Army, 1967, advanced through grades to sgt 1st class, 1975; weapons spclst. 7th Spcl. Forces Group, Ft. Bragg, NC, 1968-69, 5th Spcl. Forces Group, Vietnam, 1969-70, Res. Cont. Group, Houston, 1970-74; squad leader 143d Infantry, Houston, 1974-75, ops. sgt., 1975-80, trng. NCO, 1980—. Adv., Explorer Scouts, Houston, 1977-82. Recipient Fourth Estate award for excellence in mil. jnlsm., US Army Forces Command, 1983, 84. Mem. Am Soc. Mil. Insignia Collectors. Address: 406 Hohldale Houston TX 77091

ROTZINGER-PADDEN, KARIN MARIE, b. East Patchogue, NY, Sept. 1, 1962, d. Engelbert Joseph and Marie Frances (Murgia) Rotzinger; m. Robert Michael Padden, Dec. 29, 1985. Contrbr. to: Computer Systems News, Computer Retail News, Electronic Buyers News, Information Week. Wrkg. on children's books, articles. AA with honors, Suffolk Community Coll., 1982; BA magna cum laude, St. Joseph's Coll., 1984. Asst. ed. Computer Retail News, Manhasset, N.Y., 1985—, Computer Systems News, Manhasset, 1985—; freelance wrtr. Home: Ferndale Pl Montauk NY 11954

ROUECHÉ, BERTON, b. Kansas City, MO, Apr. 16, 1911; s. Clarence Berson and Nana (Mossman) Roueché; m. Katherine Eisenhower, Oct. 28, 1936; 1 son—Bradford. Author: Black Weather, 1945, Eleven Blue Men, 1954, The Incurable Wound, 1958, The Last Enemy, 1957, The Delectable Mountains, 1959, The Neutral Spirit, 1969, A Man Named Hoffman, 1965, A Field Guide to Disease, 1967, Annals of Epidemiology, 1967, What's Left: Reports on a Diminishing America, 1969, The Orange Man, 1971, Feral, 1974, Fago, 1977, The River World, 1978, The Medical Detectives, 1980, The Medical Detectives II, 1984, Special Places, 1982; editor: Curiosities of Medicine, 1963. BJ U. Mo., 1933. Reporter Kansas City Star, St. Louis Glove-Democrat, St. Louis Poist-Dispatch, 1934-44; staff writer New Yorker Mag. 1944—; exec. com. Health Research Com. NYC. Recipient Laker Journalism award med. reporting, 1950, 60; annual award Natl. Council Infant and Child Care, 1956, Am Med. Writers Assn., 1963; Journalism Award AMA, 1970; U. Mo. honor award for disting. Journalism, 1981; Am. Acad. and Inst. Arts and Letters award in Lit., 1982; Lewis Thomas Award of the Am. Coll. of Physicians, 1987. Home: Stony Hill Rd Amagansett NY 11930

ROUNDS, KATHLEEN LINDA, b. Niagara Falls, NY., Nov. 18, 1948, d. Harry William and Cleo Lillian (Ferguson) Faery; m. Robert Roger Rounds, Sept. 17, 1966; children—Vicki, Dean, Valerie, Adam. Contrbr. articles to Yankee mag., Buffalo Mag., Discover Niagara; ed.: Equine Update, 1983. Wrkg. on novels. AA, Niagara Community Coll. Feature wrtr. Union Sun & Jnl., Lockport, N.Y., 1982-84. Freelance wrtr. Home: 6422 Rounds Rd Newfane NY 14108

ROUTE, DEBORAH, A., b. Detroit, MI, Dec. 18, 1953; d. William Daniel and Lucille Audrienne (Cummins) Route. Poetry in Centennial Rvw, Labyris, Red Cedar Rvw., Calliope, People's Voice, other lit. mags. and anthologies. BA, Michigan State U., 1976, MA, 1979-82. Instr., Lansing Community College, MI, 1979-82; editor, Labyris Press, Lansing, MI, 1982—. instr., U. of Wis., Platteville, 1982—; Kentucky Artist in Residence, KAC Lexington, KY, 1984-86. Mem. AWP, PSA, WFOP. Home: 260 N Elm Platteville WI 53818

ROVNER, ARKADY, b. Odessa, USSR, Jan. 28, 1940, came to U.S., 1974, s. Boris and Sima R.; m. Victoria Andreyeva, Aug. 5, 1979; 1 son, Anton, Author: Guests from the Provinces (short stories), 1975, Kalalatsy (novel), 1980, Bubbles of the Earth (short stories), 1985; contrbr.: Apollo-77, Time and Us, City, Echo, other lit publs. MA in Philosophy, Moscow State U., 1965; PhD in Philosophy, Columbia U., 1987. Ed., translator Acad. Social Scis., Moscow, 1969-73; founding ed. Gnosis Press, N.Y.C., 1975—; adj. faculty New Sch. Social Research, NYU, George Washington U., 1975—. Grantee Roothbert Fund. Mem. PEN. Office: Box 42 Prince St Sta New York NY 10012

ROWAN, CARL THOMAS, b. Ravenscroft, TN, Aug. 11, 1925; s. Thomas David and Johnnie (Bradford) Rowan; m. Vivien Louise Murphy, Aug. 2, 1950; children—Barbara, Carl Thomas, Geoffrey. Author: South of Freedom, 1953, The Pitiful and the Proud, 1956, Go South to Sorrow, 1956, Wait Till Next Year, 1960, Just Between Us Blacks, 1974. Student, Tenn. State U., 1942-43, Washburn U., 1943-44; AB in Math, Oberlin Coll., 1947; MA in Journalism, U. Minn., 1948. Copywrtr. Mpls. Tribune, 1948-50, staff wrtr., 1950-61; dep. asst. secy. State for pub. affairs Dept. of State, 1961-63; US ambassador to Finland (Helsinki), 1963-64; dir. USIA (Washington), 1964-65; syndicated columnist Chicago Daily News, Pubs. Hall Syndicate, 1965—. Recipient Sidney Hillman Award for best newspaper reporting, 1952; award for best genl. reporting on segregation cases pending before U.S. Supreme Ct. Sigma Delta Chi, 1954; fgn. corr. medallion for articles on India, 1955; fgn. corr. medallion for articles on S.E. Asia, coverage of Bandung Conf., 1956; Communications award in Human Relations Anti-Defamation League B'nai B'rith, 1964; George Foster Peabody award for TV spcl. Race War in Rhodesia, 1978. Office: 3251-C Sutton Pl NW Washington DC 20016

ROWE, BEVERLY HOPE, b. Carrollton, MO, Jan. 6, 1933; d. William Calhoun and Neva Roberta (Tatman) Hope; m. Charles Hines Rowe, May 24, 1975. Contrbtr. to Wee Wisdom Mag., Christian Science Monitor, Macy-West Newspprs., Assoc. Press. AB Denison U., 1954. Feature ed./report. The Reporter-Dispatch (White Plains, NY), 1962-64; PR wrtr. Hearst Mag. Corp. (NYC), 1970s; Communications wrtr. Tilden Midtown Democreatic Club (NYC), 1985—. Hon. Ment. Medical Art., Nation'l MS Society, 1969. Mem. Overseas Press Club. Home 61 Lexington Ave New York NY 10010

ROWE, MELANIE, see Browning, Pamela

ROWE, MYRA, b. Mt. Holly, AR, Mar. 4, 1927; d. Tillman and Hazel (Blasingame) Owen; m. W.C. Rowe, Dec. 29, 1945; children: Cindy, Sandy, Suzanne, Bill. Author hist. romances: Wild Embrace, 1985, Louisiana Lady, 1986, Cajun Rose, 1987, River Temptress, 1987, Treasure's Golden Dream, 1988; contrbr. articles: Romance Wrtrs.' Report, Fiction Wrtrs.' Mag., Romantic Times. BA in English, So. Ark. U.; MA in English, Northeast La. U. Tchr. English, Jones County JC, Ellisville, Miss., 1968-72, River Oaks High Schl., Monroe, La., 1972-73, 75-76. Mem. Nat. League Am. Pen Women, Romance Wrtrs. Am. Home: 428 Eastlake Rt 4 Monroe LA 71203

ROWE, WILLIAM MORFORD, JR., b. Dover, NJ, Feb. 11, 1937; s. William Morford and Helen Marie (Garanyi) R.; m. Janette B. Bauer, Jan. 22, 1976. Author: Robotics Directory, 1984, 3d ed., 1986, Fiber Optics Technical Directory, 1984, 3d ed., 1986, Programmable Controller Directory, 1986, Robot Comparison Charts, 1985, 2d ed., 1986, Fiber Optics Comparison Chart, 1986. Student Muhlenburg Coll., 1955-57, Fairleigh Dickinson U., 1958-60. Exec. v.p. Kniep Assocs. Inc., Randolph, N.J., 1971-75; free-lance wrtr., Rockaway, N.J., 1975-81; owner, pub. Tech. Data Pub. Corp., Mt. Arlington, N.J., 1981—. Mem. Am. Assn. Artificial Intelligence, Soc. Mfg. Engrs., Digital Eqpt. Computer Users Soc. Home: 91 N Bertrand Rd Mount Arlington NJ 07856

ROYKO, MIKE, b. Chgo., IL, Sept. 19, 1932; s. Michael and Helen (Zak) Royko; m. Carol Joyce Duckman, Nov. 7, 1954 (dec. Sept., 1979); children—M. David, Robert F. Author: Up Against It, 1967, I May Be Wrong but I Doubt It, 1968, Boss—Richard J. Daley of Chicago, 1971, Slats Grobnik and Some Other Friends, 1973, Sez Who? Sez Me, 1982, Like I Was Sayin', 1984. Student, Wright Jr. Coll., 1951-52. Reporter Chicago North Side Newspapers, 1956; reporter, asst. city editor Chicago City News Bur., 1956-59; reporter columnist Chicago Sun-Times, 1978-84; columnist Chicago Tribune, 1984—. Served with USAF, 1952-56. Recipient Heywood Broun award, 1968, Pulitzer prize for commentary, 1972, named to Chicago Press Club Journalism Hall of Fame, 1980. Mem. Chicago Newspaper Reporters Assn. Office: Tribune 435 N Michigan Ave Chicago IL 60611

ROZAKIS, ROBERT H., b. NYC, April 4, 1951; s. Louis Nicholas and Sylvia (Kitter) Rozakis; m. Laurie Neu, April 5, 1974; children—Charles, Samantha. BBA, Hofstra U., 1973. Asst. editor, DC Comics, NYC, 1973-76, asst. prod. manager, 1976-81, prod. manager, 1981-87; prod. dir. 1987—; writer, 1974—. Work included in Superman Exhibition at Smithsonsian Institution, 1987. Awards: Hofstra U. Man of the Year 1972. Home: 62 Sunset Ave Farmingdale NY 11735

ROZENSTAIN, S(HEFRAH) ANN, b. Calgary, Alta., Can., July 30, 1928, d. Yale and Jennie (Margolis) Rozenstain. Contrbr. articles to Vibrant Life, Christian Single, Grit, Adventist Rev., other publs.; ed. ch. and orgn. newslettes. BS, Pacific Union Coll., 1951. Library clk. San Bernardino (Calif.) County Library, 1959-77; secy. U.S. Air Force, San Bernardino, 1985—; freelance wrtr. for Redlands Daily Facts, San Bernardino Sun-Telegram. Recipient photography awards U.S. Air Force, 1985. Mem. Photog. Soc. Am., Natl. League Am. Pen Women. Home: Box 218 Loma Linda CA 92354

RUARK, GIBBONS, b. Raleigh, NC, Dec. 10, 1941, s. Henry Gibbons and Sarah Elizabeth (Jenkins) R. Author: A Program for Survival, 1971, Reeds, 1978, Keeping Company, 1983, Small Rain, 1984; co-ed. The Greensboro Reader, 1968. AB, U. N.C., 1963; MA, U. Mass., 1965. mem. faculty U. Del., Newark, 1968—, prof. English, 1983—. Recipient Natl. Arts Council award, 1970, NEA fellowship, 1979, 86, Saxifrage Prize, 1984. Home: 708 Bent Ln Newark DE 19711

RUBEN, ANN MOLIVER, b. Pitts., Jan. 9, 1925; d. Max and Fannie (Landy) Moliver; m. Gershon Ruben, June 26, 1943; children—Stephen, Richard, David. Author: Our Teachers Are Crying: A Positive Approach to Solving Classroom Problems, 1975, How to Make Your Spouse Your Best Friend, 1975, The CAMM Program, 1980, How I Grew Up to be a Happy Child, 1983. B.S. in Elem. Edn., U. Pitts., 1961, M.Ed. in Counseling Edn., 1965, Ph.D. in Higher Edn., 1969. Educational cons. U. Pitts., 1967-72; assoc. prof. Barry U., Miami Shores, 1972-76; psychologist, Miami, 1975—. Recipient Outstanding Service award Veterans Adminstration, Pitts., 1958. Fellow Am. Orthopsychiatric Assn.; mem. Am. Assn. Counseling Devel., Am., Fla. assna. marriage family therapist. Home: 6948 Crown Gate Dr Miami Lakes FL 33014

RUBENSTEIN, ELAINE J., b. NYC, Oct. 6, 1949, d. Ira Aaron and Mirah (Slater) Rubenstein. Contrbr. poetry to So. Poetry Rvw, Cin. Poetry Rvw, Wrtrs. Forum, Poetry, other lit mags. BA, U. Calif.-Berkeley, 1973; MFA, U. Calif.-Irvine, 1980. Instr. English Irvine Valley

Coll., 1980—; ed. The Elephant-Ear, Irvine, 1982-84, 86—. Home: 1295 Fairywood Ln Laguna Beach CA 92651

RUBENSTEIN, SHARON LYNN, b. Los Angeles, Aug. 30, 1945; d. Harry and Sylvia (Resnick) Rubenstein; m. John J. Svehla, Nov. 12, 1976. Contrbr. poems to lit. mags., anthols. Wrkg. on poems on youth, neighborhoods, love. Student Pierce Coll., 1963-65. Named Feature Poet, The Poet, 1984, Broken Sts., 1985, 87. Home: 4391 Sunset Blvd 371 Hollywood CA 90029

RUBIN, DAVID M., b., Cleve., May 19, 1945, s. Arthur Louis and Gertrude (Berkowitz) R.; m. Christina Press, Aug. 22, 1971. Author: A Region's Press, 1971, Mass Media and the Environment, 1973, Report of the Public's Right to Information Task Force, 1979, Media: An Introductory Analysis of American Mass Communications, 1982, War, Peace and the News Media, 1983. BA, Columbia U., 1967; MA, Stanford U., 1968, PhD, 1972. Asst. prof. journalism NYU, N.Y.C., 1971-75, assoc. prof., 1976-85, prof., 1985—; co-dir., Ctr. for War, Peace, and the News Media, NYU, 1985—. Head Task Force on Pub.'s Right to Know-Pres.'s Three-Mile Island Commn., Washington, 1979 (cert. of appreciation); mem. discipline com. in communications Council Intl. Exchange of Scholars, Washington, 1982—; chmn. communications media com. ACLU, NYC., 1984—; bd. dirs. Com. to Protect Journalists, NYC., 1985—. Mem. Assn. Edn. in Journalism and Mass Communications (elected to profl. freedom and responsibility com. 1980-85, recipient Krieghbaum Under 40 award 1981). Home: 110 Bleecker St Apt 19B New York NY 10012

RUBIN, DIANA KWIATKOWSKI, b. NYC, Dec. 30, 1958, d. Leo R. and Gladys Ellen (Dempsey) Kwiatkowski; m. Paul Louis Rubin, Jan. 4, 1986. Author: Panorama, 1979, The Poet Pope, 1980, View from This Side of Heaven, 1982. Mem. Wrtrs. Community, AAP, P&W. Home: 12 Gales Rd Edison NJ 08837

RUBIN, LARRY JEROME, b. Bayonne, NJ, Feb. 14, 1930; s. Abraham Joseph and Lillian (Strongin) R. Author: (poems) The World's Old Way, 1963, Lanced in Light, 1967, All My Mirrors Lie, 1975. Contrbr. poems to lit. mags., anthols.; articles on English and Am. lit. to profl. jnls. BA, Emory U., 1951, MA, 1952, PhD, 1956. Instr. English to assoc. prof. Ga. Tech., Atlanta, 1956-73, prof. English, 1973—. Recipient Lit. Achievement award Ga. Wrtrs. Assn., 1963, Sidney Lanier award Oglethorpe U., 1964, John Holmes Meml. award Poetry Soc. N.H., 1965, Ga. Poet of Yr. award Dixie Council of Authors and Journalists, 1967, 75, award Kansas City Star, 1969, Ga. Authors Series award Ga. Southern Coll., 1975; Poetry Contest winner Triton Coll., 1980, PSA, 1961, 73; Smith-Mundt fellow, 1961-62, Fulbright fellow, 1966-67, 69-70, 71-72. Mem. PSA, MLA. Home: Box 15014 Druid Hills Br Atlanta GA 30333

RUDIN, ARNOLD JAMES, b. Pitts., Oct. 7, 1934, s. Philip G. and Beatrice (Rosenbloom); m. Marcia Ruth Kaplan, July 27, 1969; children—Eve Sandra, Jennifer Anne. Co-ed.: Evangelicals & Jews in Conversation, 1977, Evangelicals & Jews in an Age of Pluralism, 1984, Twenty Years of Catholic-Jewish Relations, 1986, A Time to Speak-The Evangelical Jewish Encounters, 1987. co-author: Prison or Paradise? The New Religious Cults, 1980, Why Me? Why Anyone?, 1986; author: Israel for Chrisians: Understanding Modern Israel, 1983. BA, George Washington U., 1955; MA, Hebrew Union Coll., 1960. Ordained rabbi, 1960; USAF CHAPLAIN, 1960-62 asst. rabbi Congregation B'nai Jehudah, Kansas City, Mo., 1962-64; rabbi Sinai Temple, Champaign, Ill., 1964-68; asst. dir. interreligious affairs Am. Jewish Com., N.Y.C., 1968-83, dir. nat. inter-religious affairs, 1983—. DD (hon.), Hebrew Union Coll., 1985. Home: 129 E 82d St Apt 9B New York NY 10022

RUDIN, MARCIA RUTH, b. Pueblo, CO, Sept. 28, 1940; d. Max Kaplan and Elisabeth (Neu) Abrams; m. James Rudin July 27, 1969; children—Eve Sandra, Jennifer Anne. Co. Author: Prison or Paradise? The New Religious Cults (with James Rudin), 1980, Why Me? Why Anyone? (with James Rudin and Hirshe Jaffe) 1986; articles and revws. in NY Times, NY Daily News, The New Leader, Catholic Digest, Dialogue and other periodicals and prof. jnls. BA, philo. and relig., Boston Univ., 1962; MA, relig., jointly Columbia Univ. and Union Theological Seminary, 1965. Tchr. history of relig., Brooklyn Friends School, 1965; philo., history of relig., philo. of ed., William Paterson Coll., 1965-69. Mem. Phi Beta Kappa, ed. bds. The Cult Observer, Cultic Studies Jnl. Home: 129 E 82 Apt. 9-B New York NY 10028

RUDMAN, MARK, b. NYC, Dec. 11, 1948, s. Charles Rudman and Marjorie Louise (Levy) Strome; m. Madelaine Bates; 1 son, Samuel. Author: In the Neighboring Cell, 1982, The Mystery in the Garden (chapbook), 1985, Robert Lowell, 1983, The Ruin Revived, 1986, By Contraries and other poems, 1986; ed.: Secret Destinations: Writers on Travel, 1985; translator: My Sister-Life and the Sublime Malady (Boris Pasternak), 1985, Square of Angels (Bohdan Antonych). BA, New Schl. Social Research, 1971; MFA, Columbia U., 1974. Ed. Pequod, N.Y.C., 1975—; wrtr.-in-residence York Coll.-Queens, 1984—; prof. NYU, 1985—. CCLM and NYSCA ed.'s fellow, 1981, Ingram Merrill fellow, 1983. Mem PEN (translation fellow 1976),NBCC, PSA. Office: Dept Eng NYU 19 University Pl New York NY 10003

RUDY, DOROTHY L., (D.L. Rudy), b. Hamilton, OH, June 27, 1924, d. William H. and Marjorie D. (Rammel) Richardson; m. Willis Rudy, Jan. 31, 1944; children—Dee Dee, Willis Philip (dec.), Willa. Author: Quality of Small, 1971, Psyche Afoot, 1978, Grace Notes to the Measure of the Heart, 1979; contrbr. poetry to Poetry Encyc. of Women Poets, Scimitar and Song, Bitterroot, other lit. publs.; ed. N.Y. Poetry Forum anthology for Bicentennial. Wrkg. on book on Am. women poets. BA, Queens Coll., 1945, MA, Columbia U., 1948; postgrad. Radcliffe-Harvard U., 1948-49. Tchr. various schls. N.Y., Mass. and N.J., 1948-60, 62-64; prof. English Worcester (Mass.) Jr. Coll., 1960-62, Montclair State Coll., Upper Montclair, N.J., 1964—. Grantee Am. Poets Fellowship, 1978; winner 1st prize for lyric poem Scimitar and Song, 1973. Mem. PEN Women, P&W, N.Y. Poetry Forum, Bergen Poets. Home: 161 W Clinton Ave Tenafly NY 07670

RUFF, HOWARD JOSEPH, b. Berkeley, CA, Dec. 27, 1930; s. Wilson Rex and Rena Mayberry (Braley) Ruff; m. Kay Franc Felt, Apr. 18, 1955; children—Lawrence, Eric, David, Pamela, Sharon, Patty, Anthony, David, Tim, Lisa, Debbie, Terri Lynn. Author: How to Prosper during the Coming Bad Years, 1979, Howard Ruff from A to Z, 1980, Survive and Win in the Inflationary Eighties, 1981, Making Money, 1983. Student Brigham Young U., 1950-54. Stockbroker, 1955-60; owner speed-reading franchises (CA), 1960-68; distbr. food supplements, 1971-75; chmn. bd. Target Pubs.; editor The Ruff Times, 1975—. Served with USAF, 1955-59. Office: Box 31 Springville UT 84663

RUFFIN, MARK ANTHONY, b. Chgo., Sept. 24, 1956; s. Simmie Hents Ruffin and Willa Elizabeth (O'Domes) Hammond; m. Rogina Faye Phillips, Dec. 9, 1981; children—Kenyatta Hents-Phillips, Sidney Bechet-Mandela. Contrbr. articles to Chi. Sun-Times, mags., including Ill. Entertainer, Jazz Line, Chgo. Mag., others. Ed.-in-chief: Uhuru-Sasa, 1976-77; jazz ed.: Chgo. Scene Mag., 1985-86, Chgo. Mag., 1985—. Wrkg. on articles, biography of Chick Corea. Student Southern Ill. U., 1974-77. Operations engineer Sta. WBEZ, Chgo., 1980; jazz dir. Sta. WDCB-FM, Glen Ellyn, IL, 1980-85; music dir. Sta. WBEE/Heritage Commn., Chgo., 1985—. Recipient cert. of Appreciation, Loyola U., Chgo., 1986. Mem. AFRTA. Home: 1124 Nichols Ln Maywood IL 60153

RUFFIN, PAUL DEAN, b. Millport, AL, May 14, 1941; s. David Clarence and Zealon (Robinson) R.; m. Sharon Krebs, June 16, 1973; 1 dau., Genevieve Baptiste. Works include: Mississippi Poets, 1976, The Texas Anthology, 1979, Lighting the Furnace Pilot, 1980, Our Women, 1982, The Storm Cellar, 1985. PhD, U. Southern Miss., 1974. Assoc. prof. Eng., Sam Houston State U., 1975—. Mem. AWP, TACWT. Home: 2014 Ave N1/2 Huntsville TX 77340

RUFFOLO, LISA M., b. Milw., Sept. 23, 1956; d. Edward E. and Helen G. (Monticelli) Ruffolo. Contrbr. Northern New England Rvw, Abbey, Miss. Mud, New Oreg. Rvw, Beloit Fiction Jnl, others; author: Holidays (short fiction). BA, UW-Madison, 1979; MA, Johns Hopkins U., 1980. Tchr. fiction wrtg., U. Wisc., 1986—. Mem. Soc. Tech. Writers, Women in High Tech, AWP. Recipient Mich. Council for the Arts grant, 1983; Wis. Arts Bd. fellowship, 1984. Address: 720 E. Gorham Madison WI 53703

RUFFUS, STEPHEN, b. NYC, Apr. 6, 1949; s. Socrates and Kalliope (Stephanopoulos) R.; m. Kathy Diane DeNayer, Sept. 30, 1982; children: Hether, Jessica. Ed.: Because My Cupboards Were Empty and Filled with Darkness, 1977; Swimming in a Garden Free, 1986; poetry ed. Qtly West, 1976-78; contrbr. to Westigan Rvw Poetry, Western Humanities Rvw, others. Postgrad. U. Utah. Artist-in-residence Utah Arts Council, Salt Lake City, 1977—, Salt Lake Arts Council, Salt Lake City, 1979-81; instr. U. Utah, Salt Lake City, 1985—. Recipient Coll. award AAP, 1977; 1st place for poetry Utah Arts Council, 1980, 81, 2d place for poetry vol., 1983. Home: 118 Clinton Ave Salt Lake City UT 84103

RUGGIA, JAMES CHARLES, b. Hackensack, NJ, Apr. 15, 1954; s. Nicolo Mario and Frances Linette (Caubet) R.; m. Sharon Lee Guynup, 1 child. Author: Crossing the Border, Selected Poems of James Ruggia, 1986; ed. (with Mark Rogers) Ferro Botanica mag., 1983; ed. St. Mark's Poetry Project Newsletter, 1985-86, also anthologies; contrbr. articles and poems to Pan Am Clipper, MD Mag., Ehtap mag., New Blood, The World, Ferro Botanica, Big Scream, also others. Wrkg. on travel and history articles, Am. psalms. BA in Lit., Ramapo Coll. Poet, tchr. Wrtrs. in Schls., Hoboken, N.J., 1982-83. Recipient William Carlos Williams award Williams Ctr., Paterson, N.J., 1979; N.J. Council on Arts fellow, 1983. Home: 813 Willow Ave

Hoboken NJ 07030

RUGGIERI, HELEN, b. South Plainfield, NJ, Aug. 30, 1938; d. James Gordon and Lily (Middleton) Mitchell; m. Ford F. Ruggieri, Mar. 9, 1963; children: Maria, Ford M., Andrea. Author: (poetry) The Poetess, 1980, Concrete Madonna, 1982, Rock City Hill Exercises, 1983; (how-to book) Petals & Spice; nonfiction, Mother Earth News, lit mags. Ed. Uroboros Books, 1978—, Allegany Poetry, 1976-77, Uroboros, 1978-83. BA, Pa. State U., 1960; MA, St. Bonaventure U., 1972. Adj. instr. Jamestown Community Coll., Olean, NY, 1981—, U. Pitts., Bradford, 1985—. Mem. AWP, Wrtrs. Collective, Niagara Erie Writers. Home: 111 N 10th St Olean NY 14760

RUGOFF, MILTON, b. NYC, Mar. 6, 1913; s. David and Jennie (Joseph) Rugoff; m. Helen Birkenbaum, Jan. 31, 1937; 1 dau.—Kathy. Author: Donne's Imagery, 1940, Penguin Book of World Folk Tales, 1949, The Great Travelers, 1960, Prudery and Passion: Sexuality in Victorian America, 1970; editor: Britannica Encyc. American Art, 1973, The Wild Places, 1974, The Beechers: An American Family in the Nineteenth Century, 1981. BA Columbia U., 1933, MA, 1934, PhD, 1940. Editor Alfred A. Knopf, Inc., 1943-47, The Mag., 1947-48, Readers Subscription Book Club, 1953; editor, vp, Chanticleer Press (NYC), 1948—. Served with AUS, 1943-46. Office: 424 Madison Ave New York NY 10017

RUHL, STEVEN, b. Lock Haven, PA, July 14, 1954; s. Harold E and Janet L. (English) R. Author poetry: No Bread Without the Dance, 1979, Beauty and the Beast, 1982, Dead Lift, 1983; ed. mags.: Jukebox Terrorists with Typewriters, 1984—, Tightrope, 1982; contrbr. poetry to Oyez Rvw, Barney, Beatniks from Space, Fell Swoop, Luna Tack, B City, Prairie Schooner, Loon, Yankee, Small Pond, Coll. English, Anaesthesia Rvw, others. Student Pa. State U., 1975-76. Profl. musician; chief contrbrg. writer Amherst Bulletin, Amherst, Mass., 1981—. Performer, treas., Mustard Seed Troupe (artists against nuclear war), Amherst, 1981-84; organizer Media Task Force WE Mass Weapons Freeze campaign, 1981-82. Poetry fellow Mass. Artists Fdn., Mass. Council Arts & Humanities, 1978; Amherst Arts Council grantee, 1985. Address: Box 1220 Belchertown MA 01007

RUHLAND, ELIZABETH A., b. Buffalo, NY, Mar. 7, d. Leopold Anthony and Irene Sophie (Klimeczko) Wolasz, NY Anthology, 1987. Contrbr. to Am. Poetry Anthology, 1986. Student Canisius Coll., 1984—. Systems adminstr. TRW systems div., Buffalo, 1970-76, Goldome Bank, Buffalo, 1976—.Recipient of Golden Poet Award, World Poetry Assn., 1987. Home: 738 Niagara St 5 Buffalo NY 14213

RUNCIMAN, LEX, b. Portland, OR, Feb. 13, 1951; s. Alexander and Helen Geneva (Martindale) R.; m. Deborah Jane Berry, Sept. 11, 1971; children—Elizabeth, Jane. Author: (book of Poems) Luck, 1981. Co-ed.: Where We Are: The Montana Poets Anthology, 1978, Northwest Variety: Personal Essays by Regional Authors, 1986. MFA in English/Writing, U. Mont., 1977; PhD in English, U. Utah, 1981. Ed. CutBank, Missoula, MT, 1976-77; teaching fellow in English, U. UT, Salt Lake City, 1978-81; ed. Qtly West, Salt Lake City, 1981; instr. English, Oreg. State U., Corvallis, 1981-85, writing lab. coordinator, 1985—; ed. Arrowood Books, Corvallis, 1985-m. Mem. PSA, AWP, NCTE. Recipient Clarice Short teaching award U. Utah English Dept., 1981. Home: 2695 NW Royal Oaks Corvallis OR 97330

RUNKLE, MARY ARVELLA, b. Queen City, MO, July 24, 1934; d. Millard Alfred and Clio Naomi (Tade) Turner; m. Don Lavern Runkle; children—Patricia, Donna, Carol, Neal, Craig. Author: Strange Animals & Photos, 1978. Contrbr. articles to agrl. mags. including Farm & Ranch Living, Farm Woman. Editor: Animal World, 1980-82. Corr., newspaper wrtr., photographer Ottumwa Courier, Ia., 1964-74; news feature wrtr., photographer Bloomfield Newspapers, Ia., 1974-80, mng. ed., 1982-84; free-lance wrtr., photographer, Bloomfield, 1984—. Mem., pub. relations Davis County Tourism Corp., Bloomfield, 1986. Recipient Reading award for writing Davis County Reading Council, 1984. Mem. Ia. Press Women (numerous 1st place awards for writing 1975-80), Ottumwa Camera Club, Ottumwa Area Wrtrs. Home: RR 9 Bloomfield IA 52537

RUOCCHIO, PATRICIA JEANNE, (Eleanor Rose), b. New Haven, June 18, 1958; d. William Robert and Margaret Anna (Strom) Ruocchio. Contrbr. articles: The Am. Jnl. Psychiatry (transl. to German), N.Y. Times, Splash mag., Hosp. and Community Psychiatry, Boston Herald; contrbr. to Abnormal Psychology: Current Perspectives (by Bootzin and Acocella), 5th edit., 1987. Wrkg. on book on World War I protest poetry, articles, essays. AB, Harvard U., 1982. Freelance wrtr., Boston, 1982—. Home: 115 Mill St Belmont MA 02178

RUPPERT, JAMES K., b. Buffalo, Jan. 15, 1949, s. Kenneth and Marjorie (Nichols) R.; m. Terry Boren, Mar. 17, 1984; 1 child, Koren. Author: Natural Formations, 1982, Red Bluffs, 1987; contrbr. to Studies in American Indian Literature, 1983, Southwest: A Contemporary Anthology, 1980., Red Bluffs, 1988. MA in English, Purdue U., 1972; PhD in English, U. N.Mex., 1981. Chmn. communications Navajo Community Coll., Tsaile, Ariz., 1977-80, U. N.Mex.-Gallup, 1980-85; chmn. genl. studies U. N.Mex.-Valencia, Belen, 1985-87; New Mexico Tech, 1987—; Fulbright lectr. U. Munich 1982-83; contrbg. ed. Contact II. Mem. Assn. Study of Am. Indian Lit., MLA, Multi-ethnic Lit. Soc. of U.S. Home: 1628 Cornell St SE Albuquerque NM 87106

RUSH, JEFFREY S., b. Phila., July 17, 1950, s. M. Frank and Renee (Carol) Rush; m. Ilene Helen Raymond, Aug. 14, 1983; 1 son, Alexander Matthew. Contrbr. articles, rvws to Telescope, Wide Angle, Magill's Cinema Annl. BA in Visual Studies, Harvard U., 1972; MFA in Screen Writing and Directing, Am. Film Inst., Los Angeles, 1977; MFA in Fiction, U. Iowa, 1982. Wrtr. Neil Israel Co., Los Angeles, 1979; instr. Calif. State U.-Dominguez Hills, 1980, U. Iowa, Iowa City, 1981-83; asst. prof. Pa. State U., University Park, 1983—. Teaching-Writing fellow U. Iowa, 1981-82, James Michener fellow, 1983; grantee Pa. Council on Arts, 1985. Mem. Soc. Cinema Studies, Univ. Film and Video Assn. Office: 103 Arts Bldg Pa State Univ University Park PA 16802

RUSHING, JANE GILMORE, b. Pyron, TX, Nov. 15, 1925; d. Clyde Preston and Mabel Irene (Adams) Gilmore; m. James Arthur Rushing, Nov. 29, 1956; 1 son—James Arthur. Novels include Walnut Grove, 1964, Against the Moon, 1968, Tamzen, 1972, Winds of Blame, 1983 Mary Dove, 1974, The Raincrow, 1977, Covenant of Grace 1982, (with Kline A. Nall) books include Evolution of a University, Texas Tech's First Fifty Years, 1975. BA Tex. Tech U., 1944, MA, 1945, PhD, 1957. Reporter Abilene Reporter-News (TX), 1946-47; tchr. TX high schs., 1947-54; inst. U. Tenn., 1957-59; instr. to asst. prof. Tex. Tech U., intermittently, 1959-68. LeBaron R. Barker, Jr., Fiction award, 1975, Emily Clark Balch Award, 1961, Texas Literary Award for Fiction, 1984. Mem. TX Inst. Letters, AG, AL. Home: 3809 99th St Lubbock TX 79413

RUSHTON, THEODORE ALLAN, b. Orillia, Ontario, Canada, Jan. 9, 1938; came to U.S., 1967; s. Harold and Mildred Irene (Jewell) R.; m. Mary Edith McKenzie, June 2, 1966. Contrbr. articles to newspapers including Orillia Packet and Times, Barrie Examiner, Gallup Ind., Mesa Tribune, Ariz. Bus. Gazette. Ed.: Mesa Ind., Mesa, AZ, 1985-86, EVg Mag., Tempe, AZ, 1986—, Gallup Ind., NM, 1967-71, Tucson Citizen, 1971-74, APEA News, Phoenix, 1976-78. B.S. in Engineering, U. Waterloo, 1963. Press sec. Governor of Ariz., Phoenix, 1974-78; political wrtr. Mesa Tribune, Phoenix, 1978-83; free-lance wrtr., 1983-85. Recipient Investigative Reports award Ariz. Press Assn., 1980, 82; Best editorials award N.M. Press Assn., 1971, Best Columns award, 1971, Best Photography award, 1969, 71. Home: 410 W McNeil Dr Phoenix AZ 85041

RUSINIAK, YVONNE LUBOV, b. Detroit, Nov. 16, 1945; d. Stephen Luke and Luba (Dudra) R. Author: Exotic Tea, 1970, Jasmine Days, 1974, Playground Poems, 1981. Contrbr. poems to newspapers, anthols. Ed.: History's Mill, 1981; (with Naomi Long Madgett) Many Voices, One Dream, 1973, Yes, I've Been There, 1973. Wrkg. on poetry collection. Actress, 1964-68; spcl. activities instr. in creative dramatics and poetry for children and teens Detroit Recreation Dept., 1969-76; secy. Holy Ghost Russian Orthodox Ch., Detroit, 1979—. Mem. Poetry Research Center Mich. Home: 19928 Westphalia Detroit MI 48205

RUSK, NANCE J., (Mariah Jerme, Quinten McBrand, Clifford Hanger), b. Denver, Apr. 18, 1957; d. Robert Nevels and Billie Louise (Rosenthal) Rusk. Author (as Mariah Jerme): Copy One, 1979, Putney Collection, 1979, Balanced Ride, 1980, The Outside, 1980, The Year of the Moon, 1980, Indian on a Painted Pony, 1980, The Future's Past, 1982, Valley of Souls, 1982, Bad Dreams, 1982, Going Shopping, 1982, What Words, 1982, From There to Here, 1983, Shot Dead on a Saturday Night, 1984, Countless Words, 1985, My New Job, 1987, Shades of Summer, 1987, Does it Exist?, 1987; (as Clifford Hanger): Joe Stack, 1984; (as Quinten McBrand): Painting on the Wall, 1986, The Burned Paintings, 1986. Wrkg. on poetry, lyrics, novel, filmscript. Assoc. Applied Sci, Pima Coll., 1987. Legal asst., Tucson, Ariz., 1987—. Mem. NWC. Home: Urman Esq 240 N Stone Ave Tucson AZ 85701

RUSS, JOANNA, b. NYC Feb. 22, 1937; d. Evarett and Bertha (Zinner) Russ. Author: Picnic on Paradise, 1968, And Chaos Died, 1970, The Female Man. 1975, We Who Are About To, 1977, Kittatinny: A Tale of Magic, 1978, The Two of Them, 1978, On Strike Against God, 1980; How To Suppress Women's Writing, 1983, Extra(Ordinary) People, 1984, and Magic Mommas, Trembling Sisters, Puritans & Perverts, 1985; also numerous Short Stories. BA in English, Cornell U., 1957; MFA in Playwriting and Dramatic Lit., Yale, 1960. Lectr, in English Cornell U., 1967-70, asst. prof., 1970-72; asst. prof. English Harpur Coll., State U. NY (Binghamton), 1972-75, U. Colorado, 1975-77; assoc. prof. U. Wash., 1977—. Mem. MLA, Sci. Fiction Writers Am. (Nebula award for best short story, 1972 and Hugo Award for s.f. novella, 1983.) Address: Dept Engl GN-30 U Washington Seattle WA 98195

RUSS, LAWRENCE, b. Detroit, Aug 18, 1950; m. Marion Long, May 31, 1977. Author: The Burning Ground, 1981; anthologies: Intro No. 6, The Third Coast, Anthology of Mag. Verse and Yearbook of Am. Poetry; The Nation, The Iowa Rvw, Va. Qtly Rvw, NY Qtly, Ironwood, Yankee, Parabola, New Age Jnl, others; contrbr. essays and rvws. to Contemp. Poets of the English Lang., Parabola, New Age Jnl, Granite, others. BA, U Mich-Ann Arbor, 1972, JD, 1977; MFA, U Mass-Amherst, 1974. Asst. Atty. genl., State of Conn., Hartford, 1986—; prin. atty. Trager and Trager, PC, Fairfield, Conn, 1981-86. Mem. lit. comm., Gov's. Council for the Arts, 1971-72; vol. atty., Lawyers for the Creative Arts, Chgo., 1978-80, Conn. Vol. Lawyers for the Arts, 1982—; chmn. edn. sub-comm., 1987-88, vice-chmn., 1986-87, Conn. Bar Assn. Arts Law comm., 1985-86. Mem PSA, Conn. Bar Assn. Address: 245-49 Unquowa Rd Fairfield CT 06430

RUSS, LISA, see Spaar, Lisa Russ

RUSSEL, CAROL ANN MARIE, b. Fargo, ND, Sept 18, 1951; d. Norman Eugene and Joyce Elaine (Myhre) Russell/South; m. Michael Walter Schlemper, July 19, 1986. Author: The Red Envelope, 1984; ed. GiltEdge, New Series; contrbr. Columbia, Poetry Northwest, Ohio Rvw, Cutbank, Cafe Solo, Mont Gothic, Prairie Schooner, Ploughshares, Nimrod, Tendril, Willow Springs, Sonora Rvw, Qtly West, NJ Poetry Jnl, Poet & Critic, others. BA,St Cloud State U, 1969-73; MA, U Mont, 1974-75, MFA1976-78;/cand. PhD U. Nebr., 1985—. Tchg. asst. Univ. Mont., Missoula, 1974-75, U. Nebr., Lincoln, 1985—; program mgr. CCESP Univ. Mont., 1975-81; asst. prof. Tarkio Coll., MO., 1981-85. Chair, GiltEdge, New Series, Missoula, 1978-81, poetry ed., Cutbank mag., 1975. Mem. Delta Kappa Gamma, PSA, AWP, Mo. Philol. Assn. Address: 467-L Whalley Ave New Haven CT 06511

RUSSELL, FRANCIS, b. Boston, MA, Jan. 12, 1910; s. Leo Spotten and Ethel May (Kent) Russell; m. Sharon Soong, mar. 5, 1966 (div. 1981); 1 dau.—Sara; m. Rosalind Lawson, 1984. Author: Three Studies in 20th Century Obscurity, 1954, Tragedy in Dedham, 1962, The Great Interlude, 1964, The World of Durer, 1967, The Shadow of Blooming Grove, 1968, The Making of the Nation, 1968, The Confident Years, 1969, Forty Years On, 1970, The Horizon Concise History of Germany, 1973, A City in Terror, 1975, The President Makers from Mark Hanna to Joseph P. Kennedy, 1976, Adams: An American Dynasty, 1976, The Secret War, 1981, Sacco-Vanzetti: The Case Resolved, 1986, The knave of Boston, 1987. Student U. Breslau, Germany, 1931-32; AB, Bowdoin Coll., 1933; AM, Harvard U., 1937. Wrtr. for various Irish, English and Am. publs., 1946—. Served to capt. Can. Army, 1941-46. Soc. of Am. Historians Fellow, Guggenheim fellow, 1964-65. Recipient Friendship award Fed. Republic of Germany. Dir. Goethe Soc. Address: The Lindens Sandwich MA 02563

RUSSELL, HELEN ROSS, b. Myerstown, PA, Feb. 21, 1915; d. George Smith and Helen Louise (Boyd) R.; m. Robert Stanley Russell, Sept. 24, 1960. Ed., Nature Study Jnl., 1978—; author books: City Critters, 1969, 75, The True Book of Buds, 1970, Clarion the Killdeer, 1970, Winter Search Party, 1971, The True Book of Springtime Tree Seeds, 1972, 10 Minute Field Trips, 1972, Earth, the Great Recycler, 1973, Foraging for Dinner, 1975, Wave Hill Trail Guide, 1978; author field trip guides: Winter, 1972, Soil, 1972, Small Worlds, 1972, Water, 1973. BS, Lebanon Valley Coll., 1943; MA, Cornell U., 1947, PhD, 1949; DHL, Lebanon Valley Coll., 1973. Tchr. pub. high schls., Lebanon & Berks Co., PA, 1934-43; prof. biology State Coll., Fitchburg, MA, 1949-56, chr. sci. dept., 1952-56, acad. dean, 1956-66; freelance author, consultant, New Jersey, 1967—; ed. Nature Study Jnl, Am. Nat. Study Soc., 1978—. Eva L. Gordon award for Children's Sci. Lit., 1976; NY State Outdoor Ed. Lit. Award, 1982; Candance Stevenson Awards prose writing, 1980, 82, 84, 85. Mem. AAAS, Am. Nature Study Soc. Address: 44 College Dr Jersey City NJ 07305

RUSSELL, SANDRA LITTLE, b. Pitts., Nov. 6, 1946; d. William Leo and Evelyn (Sentner) Russell; children: Russell, Wendy. Author/contrbr.: Entangled, 1976, Pegasus, 1976, To Banbury Cross and Back, 1976, Crossroads Anthology, 1979, Aspen Anthology No. 10, 1980, Swift Kick, 1982, Sunrust, 1984, Croton Rev, 1985, Amelia, Ball State U. Forum, The Informer (opera libretto; prod Tex Opera Theater, Rutgers U., 1985, Duke U., 1986). BA in English, Georgian Ct. Coll.; postgrad, U. Pitts. Brooklyn Coll., 1987. Mem CODA. Address: 508 Simonton St Key West FL 33040

RUSSELL, SHARMAN APT, b. Edwards AFB, CA, July 23, 1954, d. Milburn Grant and Fay Lorrie Apt; m. Peter Russell, Jan. 24, 1986; 1 dau., Maria. Author: Built to Last: The Architectural History of Silver City (with others), 1986, Frederick Douglass, 1987; contrbr. fiction to Quarry West, Ascent, Touchstone, other lit publs. BS, U. Calif.-Berkeley, 1976; MFA, U. Mont., 1980. Reporter El Paso Times, Silver City, N.Mex., 1981; writing instr. Western N.Mex. U., Silver City, 1981—. Mem. Soc. Children's Book Wrtrs., P&W, AWP. Home: Rt 15 Box 2560 Mimbres NM 88049

RUSSELL, THOMAS LYON, b. Wrexham, Great Britain, Feb. 9, 1946; came to U.S., 1947; naturalized, 1947; s. Thomas Lyon and Monica Eve (Yeo) R.; m. Irma L. Stephens, Mar. 21, 1947; children—Nathaniel, Anna. Contrbr. poems, short stories to lit. mags., anthols. BA, 1968, MA, 1974, Ph.D., Kans. U., 1981. Tchr., ed. Kans. U., Lawrence, 1974-81; asst. prof. N.Y.U., NYC, 1983-84; dir. creative writing Memphis State U., 1984-87. Fellow Carnegie Fnd., 1984, NEA, 1986; recipient award Pushcart Anthol., 1985, Seaton Hall award Kans. Quarterly, 1986. Mem. Kans. Wrtr.'s Conf., Tenn. Wrtr.'s Assn., AAUP. Office: English Dept Memphis State U Memphis TN 38152

RUSSELL, TIMOTHY, b. Steubenville, OH, May 25, 1951; s. Charles William and Ruth (Roush) R; m. Josephine Dolan, July 17, 1971; children: Shane, Ivan, Violet, Laurel. Contrbr. Poetry Northwest, West Branch, Pa. Rvw. BA, W. Liberty State Coll., 1977; MA, U. Pitts., 1979. Laborer Weirton Steel, Weirton, W Va, 1973—. Served to sgt, US Army, 1970-72. Recipient 2d place award, AAP, Univ. Pitts., 1979, 1st prize (novel) W. Va. Writer's Inc., 1987, 1st prize (play) W. Va. Writer's Inc., 1987. Mem. W. Va. Writers, W.Va. Poetry Soc., PSA, P&W. Address: 3336 Elm St Weirton WV 26062

RUSSO, RICHARD, b. Johnstown, NY, July 15, 1949, s. James W. Russo and Jean (LeVarn) Findlay; m. Barbara Marie Russo; children—Emily, Kate. Novelist: Mohawk, 1986; contrbg. ed.: Puerto del Sol; contrbr. short fiction to Mss, Prairie Schooner, Mid-Am. Rvw, Sonora Rvw, others. PhD, U. Ariz., 1980, MFA, 1981. Tchr. fiction, So. Ill. U., Carbondale. Pa. Council of Arts fellow, 1983. Mem. AWP. Home: Rt 9 Box 23A Carbondale IL 62901

RUSTA, "B", see Benson, Clara Mays

RUSTY, , see Hayes, James Russell

RUTHERFORD, BRETT, b. Connellsville, PA, Oct. 16, 1947; s. Donald T. and Lena Jean (Ullery) R. Author: Songs of the I and Thou, 1968, City Limits, 1971, The Pumpkined Heart, 1973, Whippoorwill Road: The Supernatural Poems, 1985, Anniversarium: The Autumn Poems, 1984, Prometheus on Fifth Avenue, 1987, Piper (with others), 1987; ed.: May Eve: A Festival of Supernatural Poems, 1975, Last Flowers: The Romance Poems of E.A. Poe and S.H. Whitman, 1987. Wrkg. on two novels, three poetry collections. Pres. The Poet's Press, NYC, 1969-85, NYC and Providence, R.I., 1985—; dir. publs. Nat. Assn. Printers and Lithographers, Teaneck, N.J., 1974-81. Mem. AAP, Am. Printing History Assn. Home: 255 Transit St Providence RI 02906

RUTSALA, VERN, b. McCall, ID, Feb. 5, 1934; m. Joan Colby, Apr. 6, 1957; children—Matthew, David, Kirsten. Author poetry collections: The Window, 1964, Small Songs, 1969, The Harmful State, 1971, Laments, 1975, The Journey Begins, 1976, Paragraphs, 1978, The New Life, 1978, Walking Home from the Icehouse, 1981, The Mystery of Lost Shoes, 1985, Backtracking, 1985, Ruined Cities, 1987; ed.: British Poetry 1972, 1972. Wrkg. on poetry collections, short fiction. BA, Reed Coll., 1956; MFA, U. Iowa, 1960. Mem. faculty Lewis and Clark Coll., Portland, Oreg., 1961—, prof. English, 1977—; vis. prof. U. Minn., Mpls., 1968-69, Bowling Green (Ohio) State U., 1970. NEA fellow, 1974, 79, Guggenheim fellow, London, 1982-83. Mem. PEN, PSA. Home: 2404 NE 24th Ave Portland OR 97212

RUTKOVSKY, PAUL MICHAEL, b. Oct. 15, 1947; s. Paul and Genevieve (Wojtkun) R.; m. Frances Irene Cutrell, Aug. 22, 1970. Author: Commodity Character, 1982, Catalogue, 1983, Center Quarterly, Vol. 5 No. 6, 1984, I Am Siam, 1984, Artist's Books, Critical Anthology and Sourcebook, 1985,Macartist (computer drawings), 1985; editor Doo Daa Florida, Vol. 1 No. 1-5, 1982—, Get, Vol. 1 No. 1-3, 1985—. BFA, Memphis Coll. Art, 1970; MFA, U. Ill., 1972. Instr. painting U. Ill., Champaign, 1972-73; instr. art dept. U. New Haven, 1976-82; dir., editor Papier Mache Video Inst., New Haven, 1978-82; instr. art dept. So. Conn. State U., New Haven, 1977-81; asst. prof. Paier Coll.. of Art, Hamden, Conn., 1980-82, Fla. State U., Tallahassee, 1982—; Active, Polit. Art Documentation/Distbn., NYC, 1983—. Editing grantee Haymarket Found., 1978; fellow NEA, 1979, Conn. Commn. on Arts, 1980, Fla. Cultural Affairs, 1983; visual artist New Haven Arts Council, 1982, fellow Ctr. for Advanced Visual Studies, MIT, 1986-87. Home: 227 Westridge Dr Tallahassee FL 32304

RUTSKY, LESTER, b. NYC, May 23, 1924, s. Samuel and Bess (Millman) R.; m. Elaine Rutsky, Aug. 30, 1959. Contrbr. to Coin World, N.Y. Daily News, Economist Newspapers, other newspapers. Winner numerous poetry contests; recipient Paul Elliot Meml. award Poetry Soc. Mich., 1982. Mem. Poetry Soc. Mich., Ind. State Fedn. Poetry Clubs, AAP. Home: 2930 W 5th St Brooklyn NY 11224

RUYN, LIZA, see Chowdhury, Debi Elizabeth

RUZIC, NEIL PIERCE, b. Chgo., May 12, 1930; s. Joseph Francis and Ida (Pierce) Ruzic; m. Carol W. Kalsbeek, Apr. 14, 1950; 1 son—David Neil. Author: There's Adventure in Meteorology, 1958, There's Adventure in Civil Engineering, 1958, Stimulus, 1960, The Case for Going to the Moon, 1965, Where the Winds Sleep, 1970, Spinoff 1976, 1976, Blueprint for an Island for Science, part 1, 1976, part 2, 1977, Open-Ocean Polyculture, 1979, Emerging Technologies, 1985. Student, Loyola U., 1946-47; BS in Journalism, Psychology and Science, Northwestern U., 1950. Corr., Costa Rica, Latin Am., 1949; writer with various newspapers including Michigan City News-Dispatch (IN), 1950-52; dir. publs. IIT Research Inst. (Chicago), 1954-58; fndr. Industrial Research Neil Ruzic & Co. (Chicago), 1973—; cons. to NASA, 1973-78; fndr.Island for Sci., 1976-86. A founder, bd. dirs. Natl. Space Inst.; founder & pres., Little Stirrup Cay Ltd., Bahamas. Served with AUS, 1952-54. Office: Box 527 Beverly Shores IN 46301

RYAN, MARGARET, b. Trenton, NJ, June 23, 1950, d. Thomas Michael and Anna Cornelia (Jansen) Ryan; m. Steven Paul Lerner, Aug. 29, 1974; 1 dau., Emily. Author: Filling Out A Life (poems), 1982; contrbr. poetry to Intro 6, Epoch, Pivot, Amelia, other publs. BA, U. Pa., 1972; MA, Syracuse U., 1974. Recipient Pushcart prize, 1979-80. Mem. P&W. Home: Box 12 Old Chatham NY 12136

RYAN, MARY ELIZABETH, b. Manchester, NA, Aug. 19, 1953, d. Leo Thomas and Lorraine Doris (Joseph) R. Author: Dance a Step Closer, 1984; contrbr. to Young Miss mag., McCall's, Pub. Weekly, St. Anthony Messenge, Co-Ed, Woman's Own, Dolly, Face-to-Face. Wrkg. on sequel to Dance a Step Closer. BFA, NYU, 1977; MA U. Wash., 1987. Mem. staff New Yorker, N.Y.C., 1978-80; editorial cons. Andrews & Robb, Seattle, 1983-84; student coordinator Seattle U., 1984; ed. Wordcrafters N.W., Seattle, 1984-85; mem. legal staff Bogle & Gates, Seattle, 1985-86; lectr. to sch. and library assns. Recipient outstanding children's book award U. Iowa, 1985; Stegner fellow Stanford U., 1982-83; Hoynes fellow U. Va., 1982; Carnegie Fund grantee, 1984, 85. Mem. AG, Pacific N.W. Wrtrs., AFTRA. Home: 312 Harvard Ave E Apt 102 Seattle WA 98102

RYAN, MICHAEL JOSEPH, b. Boston, May 20, 1953; s. Walter Joseph and Lorraine Marie (McCarty) R.; m. Deborah Ann Boles, Oct. 27, 1979; children—Jennifer, Kevin. Wrkg. on: The Roxbury Rogue: James Michael Curley, novels. Contrbr. articles to newspapers, mags. including Boston Herald, Boston Globe, others. Ed.: Bay State Briefs, 1982—; Annual Report of Mass. Trial Court, 1982-86. BA in History, Boston State Coll., 1976; MS in Jnlsm., Boston U., 1979. Corr., Boston Globe, 1979; reporter Daily Transcript, Dedham, MA, 1979-82; public info. officer Mass. Trial Ct., Boston, 1982—. Home: 35 Aldis Ln Wrentham MA 02093

RYAN, NANCY MARIE, b. Johnson City, NY; d. Edward P. and Margie (Devine) Ryan. Chapbook: Shades of Green and Darkness, 1981; contrbr. poetry to Midwest Poetry Rvw., Vega, Bardic Echoes, New England Sampler, other poetry mags, anthologies. BA and MA Albany State Teachers Coll. Teacher Weedsport Central High (NY), Universidad de la Fontera (Temuco, Chile), Guilderland Central High (NY). First prize Midwest Poetry Rvw contest. Beverwyck Dr Guilderland NY 12084

RYAN, PAT, see Wilson, Patricia Ann

RYLANDER, EDITH MAY, b. Orland, CA, Apr. 3, 1935; d. Thomas Charles and Ellen Louisa (Burnett) Alcock; m. John Donald Rylander, July 24, 1948; children—Daniel, Shireen, Eric. Coauthor What's In A Poem, 1972; columnist, Morrison County Record, Long Prairie Leader, St. Cloud Daily Times; contrbr. articles to The New Farm, 1979, 80, poetry to Milkweed Chronicle, Loonfeather, Arts in Soc., Antioch Rvw., Sing Heavenly Muse!, others. BA, San Jose State, 1957. Instr. St. Cloud State (MN) U., 1966-67; columnist Morrison County Record, Little Falls, MN, 1981—, Long Prairie (MN) Leader, 1981—, St. Cloud (MN) Daily Times, 1983—; freelance writer. Bush arts fellow, 1980. Address: Rt 1 Grey Eagle MN 56336

RYPEL, THADDEUS CHESTER, (Ted Rypel), b. Cleve., Nov. 13, 1949; s. Chester S. and Genevieve J. (Labus) R.; m. Christine Antoinette Torok, Sept. 30, 1972; children—Jennifer, Michael, Elizabeth, John. Author: Deathwind of Vedun, 1982, Samurai Steel, 1982, Samurai Combat, 1983, Fortress of Lost Worlds, 1985, Knights of Wonder, 1986. A.A., Cuyohoga Commun. Coll., 1976. Ed. Union Gospel Press., Cleve., 1971-74; night mgr. Fisher-Fazio, Cleve., 1974-85; salesman Cox Cable, Parma, OH, 1985-86; asst. mgr. Mr. Z Video, Parma, 1986—. Home: 1817 Alvin Ave Cleveland OH 44109

SABATINE, JEAN ANN, b. Uniontown, PA, July 19, 1941; d. Frank and Jane (Klus) S.; m. David Samuelson (div. 1975); m. David Hodge, Aug. 20, 1977. Author: Techniques and Styles of Jazz Dancing, 1969, The Actor's Image: Movement Training for Stage and Screen, 1983. Contrbr. articles to profl. jnls., newsletters, Anthol. of Am. Jazz Dance. B.A. in Drama, Syracuse U., 1963; M.S. in Dance and Drama, U. Utah, 1967. Asst. prof. drama State U. N.Y., Buffalo, 1971-72; assoc. prof. drama, head movement program Penn. State U., University Park, 1972-80; prof. drama, head movement/dance program U. Conn., Storrs, 1980—. Mem. Am. Dance Guild, New England Theater Conf., Assn. Theater in Higher Edn. Home: 406 Chaffeeville Rd Storrs CT 06268

SABIN, ARTHUR J., b. Chg., Sept. 21, 1930; m. Sandra G. Greenstein, Dec. 21, 1952; Children—Neal, Karen. Author: Pilot Training—You Can Learn to Fly, 1979, All About Suing & Being Sued, 1981. Contrbr. numerous articles to profl. jnls., others. Wrkg. on novel, articles, column. A.B., Roosevelt U., 1952; A.M., Northwestern U., 1953; L.D., John Marshall Law Sch., 1959. Prof. history Northeastern Ill. U., Chgo., 1962-75; prof. law John Marshall Law Sch., Chgo., 1972—. Mem. bd. edn. Niles Township High Schs., Skokie, IL, 1966-68. Served to corporal U.S. Army, 1953-55. Named Outstanding Alumni, John Marshall Law Sch., 1978. Mem. Ill. State Bar Assn., WG, NWC. Home: 710 Strawberry Hill Glencoe IL 60022

SABLE, BARBARA KINSEY, b. Astoria, NY, Oct. 6, 1927; d. Albert and Verna (Rowe) Kinsey; m. Arthur Sable, Nov. 1973. Author workbook: Fundamentals of Music for Non-Music Majors; The Vocal Sound, 1982; contrbr. poetry: Poetry Parade, Goliards, White Rock Rev., others; contrbr. article: Music Rvwl., Jnl. Musicological Research, Musical Heritage Rvw., other publs. BA, Wooster (Ohio) Coll., 1949; MA, Columbia U., 1950; DMus, Ind. U., 1966. Prof. Northeast Mo. State U., Kirksville, 1962-64, U. Calif.-Santa Barbara, 1964-69, U. Colo.-Boulder, 1969—; assoc. ed. Nat. Assn. Tchrs. of Singing Bulltn. Mem. profl. orgns. Home: 3430 Ash Ave Boulder CO 80303

SACHS, BLANCHE, b. Cairo, Egypt, Jan. 31, 1933, came to U.S., 1955, naturalized, 1960; d. Salomon Joseph and Flore (Aghion) Cohen; m. Lester Marvin Sachs, Jan. 27, 1957; children—Jared Ethan (dec.), Deborah Eve. Contrbr. articles, poems to mags., newspapers. B.A. in Sociology/Psychology, Southern Ill. U., 1956; postgrad. Balt. Hebrew Coll., 1965-68. Substitute tchr. public schls., Balt., 1964-74; tour guide Md. His. Soc., Balt., 1984—; French tour guide Balt.-Rent-A-Tour, Balt., 1987. Mem. Balt. Wrtr.'s Alliance (2d prize for poetry 1986, Honorable Mention for short story 1986), Intl. Women's WG. Home: 8823 Stonehaven Rd Randallstown MD 21133

SACHS, EDWARD K., (Yitzhawk Butterfield), b. Balt., Feb. 13, 1924; s. Abraham and Anna (Kamfner) S.; m. Elizabeth Newton, June 14, 1951; children—Ramsey Michelle, Hunter William. Author: (novel) Combo, 1944; (novella) All the People, All the Places, All the Things, 1966-69. Contrbr. fiction, non-fiction, humor, rvws., interviews to mags. Editor: Joe Must Go (Julian Messner), 1954-55. Publisher: Yitzhawk Butterfield Epistle & Journal. Wrkg. on novel. Student U. Ill.-Champaign, 1941-42. Dir. pub. relations Joe Must Go., 1953-56; exec. v.p. The Dorset Group, 1968—. Mem. Am. Newspaper Guild. Home: 820 W Belmont Chicago IL 60657

SACKETT, DONNA C., b. Bklyn., Nov. 26, 1949; d. Benjamin Ritchie and Florence M. (Bender) Gurdison; m. R. A. Sackett, July 28, 1973 (div. 1987). Editor: IMLR Newsletter, Sophia Newsletter, 1975-77, Dialogue mag., 1985-87. B.A. with high honors, Douglass Coll., 1977; M.S., Rutgers U., 1981. Training cons. PRUPAC, Holmdel, NJ, 1977-82, personnel cons., 1982-85; ed. The Prudential, Newark, 1985—. Home: 7 East Wilson Circle Red Bank NJ 07701

SACKETT, ERNEST L., b. Spokane, WA, Aug. 31, 1928; s. Elmer Alvin and Eudora M. (Gifford) S.; m. Florence C. Seefeldt, Sept. 1955 (div. June 1971); m. 2d, Esther L. Paulsen, Aug. 1, 1971. Author: The Endless Scheme of Life 1949, An Artist's West, 1967, Random Poems, 1971, Selected Poems, 1952, Birthday Matches, 1979, 12 Ways to Sell Your Old, Used and Rare Books, 1976, Rhyme with Ease, 1982, Color-Vision for the Blind, 1983, Rhyme 'n Match Crossword Puzzles, 1983, A Baker's Dozen: Keepsake, 1983, Home from the Sea: The Story of the Ship Ashore, 1985. Editor: Newsletter of Rogue River Chpt. Council of Blind Grants Pass, 1984-85. Wrkg. on biography of Robert Wright. BS in Elem. Edn., Southern Oreg. State C., 1959. Tchr. pub. schls., Tendoy and Kellogg, Idaho, Chewelah, Wash., Trail, Oreg.; tchr., librarian pub. schl. Grants Pass, Oreg., 1958—86; dir., Sackett Publications, 1976—. NEA, Soc. Children's Book Wrtrs. Home: 100 Waverly Dr Grants Pass OR 97526

SACKS, OLIVER (WOLF), b. London, July 9, 1933, s. Dr. Samuel and Dr. Muriel Elsie (Landau) S.; Author: Migraine: The Evolution of a Common Disorder, 1970; Awakenings, 1973; A Leg to Stand On, 1984; The Man Who Mistook His Wife for a Hat and Other Clinical Tales, 1985. BA, Queen's College, Oxford U., 1954, MA, B Ch, 1958, internship Middlesex Hosp., London, 1959, further study U. of Calif., Los Angeles, 1960-65. Albert Einstein College of Med., NYC, prof. neurology, 1965—. Mem. Am. Acad. of Neurology. Home: 119 Horton St Bronx NY 10464

SADLER, MARK, see Lynds, Dennis

SADLER, NORMA JEAN, b. Youngstown, OH, June 13, 1944; d. Anthony James and Ann (Hlasta) Narky; m. Jeffrey Allen Sadler, Aug. 20, 1966. Author: Mirabelle's Country Club for Cats & Other Poems, 1986. Contrbr. articles to profl. jnls., poems to mags. BA in English, UCLA, 1966; MA, Calif. State U.-Long Beach, 1967; PhD in Curriculum and Instruction, U. Wis.-Madison, 1973. Elem. tchr., Sun Prairie, Wis., 1967-68, Middleton, Wis., 1968-69; tchr. jr. high schl., Middleton, 1969-70; prof. Boise State U., Id., 1984—. Recipient 1st Place, Bronze medallion for poem Triton Coll., River Grove, Ill., 1981. Mem. Children's Lit. Assn. Home: 795 River Heights Dr Meridian ID 83642

SADOFF, IRA, b. NYC, Mar. 7, 1945, s. Robert and Yvette S.; m. Dianne Fallon, July 29, 1968. Author: Settling Down (poems), 1975, Palm Reading in Winter (poems), 1978, Maine: Nine Poems, 1981, A Northern Calendar (poems), 1982, Uncoupling (novel), 1982, Emotional Traffic (poems), 1988. BS, Cornell U., 1966; MFA, U. Oreg., 1968. Wrtr.-in-residence Antioch Coll., Yellow Springs, Ohio, 1972-77; assoc. prof. Colby Coll., Waterville, Me., 1977—; vis. asst. prof. Hampshire Coll., Amherst, Mass., 1976; vis. assoc. prof. U. Va., Charlottesville, 1981-82. Bread Loaf Wrtrs. Conf. fellow, 1976; prof. Bread Loaf Schl. of English, 1984, 86; NEA Creative Arts fellow, 1980-81. Mem. PEN, PSA. Home: RD1 Box 730 N Vassalboro ME 04962

SAFFORD, DAN SCOTT, (Roy Ingersoll), b. San Diego, Nov. 30, 1950. Contrbr. stories to Crucible, Wrtrs. Forum, Kansas Qtly, Sawmill, other publs.; contrbr. poetry to Manhattan Mercury, Touchstone; contrbr. articles to Lit. Mag. Rvw., The Writing Instr.; ed.: Touchstone, 1982-83; assoc. ed.: Lit. Mag. Rvw, 1980-82. BA in English, Utah State U., 1975; MA in English, Kans. State U., 1980. Instr. Kans. State U., Manhattan, 1976-82; author/ed. Boeing Aerospace, Seattle, 1986—. Mem. AWP, NCTE. Home: 4213 S 303 St Auburn WA 98002

SAFIRE, WILLIAM, b. NYC, Dec. 17, 1929; s. Oliver C. and Ida (Panish) Safire; m. Helene Belmar Julius, Dec. 16, 1962; children—Mark Lindsey, Annabel Victoria. Author: The Relations Explosion, 1963, Plunging into Politics, 1964, Safir's Political Dictionary, 1968, rev. edit., 1972, 78, Before the Fall, 1975, Full Disclosure, 1977, Safire's Washington, 1980, On Language, 1980, What's the Good Word?, 1982, (with Leonard Safir) Good Advice, 1982, I Stand Corrected, 1984, Take My Word For It, 1986, Freedom (novel), 1987. Student Syracuse U., 1947-49. Reporter NY Herald Tribune Syndicate, 1949-51; corr. WNBC-WNBT, Europe and Middle East, 1951; radio-TV producer WNBC (NYC), 1954-55; vp Tex McCrary, Inc., 1955-60; pres. Safire Pub. Relations, Inc., 1960-68; spcl. asst. to Pres. Nixon (Washington), 1969-73; columnist NY Times (Washington), 1973—. Served with AUS, 1952-54. Recipient Pulitzer Prize for Disting. Commentary, 1978. Address: NY Times 1000 Connecticut Ave NW Washington DC 20036

SAFRAN, CLAIRE, b. NYC; d. Simon and Flora (R) Safran; m. John Milton Williams, June 8, 1958; 1 son—Scott Edward. Contbr. to maj. nat. mags., 1972—. BA in English cum laude, Bklyn. Coll., 1951. News editor Photo Dealer mag., 1951-53; asso. editor TV Radio Mirror, 1954-58; mng. editor Photoplay mag., 1958-61; editor TV Radio Mirror, 1961-65, IN mag., 1965-67; asso. editor Family Weekly mag., 1967-68; editor Coronet mag., 1968-71; contbg. editor Redbook, 1974-77; exec. editor, 1977-78, contbg. editor, 1979-81; roving editor Reader's Digest, 1983—. Recipient Media award Am. Psychol. Found., 1977; finalist Penney-Missouri Mag. Awards, 1977; Merit award in Journalism Religious Public Relations Council, 1978; honorable mention journalism awards Am. Acad. Pediatrics, 1979; 1st pl. nat. editorials Odyssey Inst. Media Awards, 1979, 80, 86; Matrix award Women in Communication, 1982, 83, 84; American Society of Journalists and Authors Award, 1984; American Academy of Family Physicians Journalism Award, 1984; William Harvey Award, 1984. Mem. Am. Soc. Journalists and Authors. Home: 53 Evergreen Westport CT 06880

SAFRAN, VERNA, see Tomasson, Verna

SAFRANSKY, SY, b. NYC March 31, 1945; s. Harry and Rose (Druy) Safansky; m. Norma Frances Tappe, Jul. 31, 1983; children Mara, Sara. Ed. The Sun Magazine (Chapel Hill, NC), 1974—. Office: The Sun 412 W Rosemary St Chapel Hill NC 27514

SAGAN, CARL EDWARD, b. NYC, Nov. 9, 1934; s. Samuel and Rachel (Gruber) Sagan; m. Ann Druyan; children by previous marriages—Dorion Solomon, Jeremy Ethan, Nicholas; 1 dau.—Alexandra. Author: Atmospheres of Mars and Venus, 1961, Planets, 1966, Intelligent Life in the Universe, 1966, Planetary Exploration, 1970, Mars and the Mind of Man, 1973, The Cosmic Connection, 1973, Other Worlds, 1975, The Dragons of Eden, 1977, Murmurs of Earth: The Voyager Interstellar Record, 1978, Broca's Brain, 1979, Cosmos, 1980, Contract, 1985, (novel) Comet, 1985; editor: Icarus: Intl. Jnl Solar System Studies, 1968-79, Planetary Atmospheres, 1971, Space Research, 1971, UFO'S: A Scientific Debate, 1972, Communication with Extraterrestrial Intelligence, 1973; editorial bd.: Origins of Life, 1974—, Icarus, 1962—, Climatic Change, 1976—, Science 80, 1979-82. AB with genl. and spcl. honors, U. Chgo., 1954, BS, 1955, MS, 1956, PhD, 1960. Miller research fellow U. CA-Berkeley, 1960-62; vis. asst. prof. genetics Stanford med. Schl., 1962-63; astrophysicist Smithsonian Astrophys. Obs. (Cambridge, MA), 1962-68, asst. prof. Harvard U., 1962-67; mem. faculty Cornell U., 1968—, prof. astronomy and space scis., ,70—, David Duncan prof., 1976 ,dir. Lab. Planetary Studies, 1968—, assoc. dir. Center for Radiophysics and Space Research, 72-81; pres. Carl Sagan Prodns. (Cosmos TV series), 1977—; nonresident fellow Robotics Inst., Carnegie-Mellon U., 1982—. Mem. various adv. groups NASA and Natl. Acad. Scis., 1959—; mem. council Smithsonian Instn., 1975—; vice-chair working group moon and planets, space orgn. Intl. Council Sci. Unions, 1968-74; lectr. Apollo flight crews NASA, 1969-72; chair U.S. del. Joint Conf. U.S. Natl. and Soviet Acads., Sci. on Communication with Extraterrestrial Intelligence, 1971; responsible for Pioneer 10 and Voyager 1 and 3 interstellar messages; judge Natl. Book Awards, 1975; mem. fellowship panel Guggenheim Fdn., 1976—. Pulitzer prize for lit., 1978, Hugo award, 1981. Mem. AG. Address: Space Sci Cornell Univ Ithaca NY 14853

SAGAN, KATHYRNE V., b. NYC, Feb. 7, 1952, d. Harry J. and Zita M. (Kane) S. BA, Fordham U., 1973; MA in English, U. Ill., Urbana, 1977. Ed. Dell Pub. Co., 1977-83; fiction ed. Redbook mag., NYC, 1983—. Home: 121 W 79th St New York NY 10024

SAGAN, MIRIAM ANNA, b. NYC, Apr. 27, 1954; d. Eli Jacob and Frimi (Giller) Sagan; m. Robert Winson Sycamore, Oct. 10, 1982. Works include: Dharmakaya, 1986, Eyebrows of Geese, 1986, Leaving the Temple, 1985, Aegean Doorway, 1984, Talking You Down, 1983, Visions Edge, 1978, Dangerous Body, 1976. BA, Harvard, 1975; MA, Boston U., 1977. Edit., Aspect Magazine, Somerville, MA, 1976-79; ed., Zephyr Press, Somerville, 1979-87; freelance wrtr., 1979—; artist-in-res. with New Mexico, 1986-88. Mem. PSA, P & W. Home: 626 Kathryn St Sant Fe NM 87501

SAGER, DONNA LAYNE (Donna Layne), b. Carlsbad, NM, July 17, 1956; d. Donald Iris and Charlotte Ellen (Oseland) Roberts; m. Stephen James Anderson, Aug. 23, 1976 (div. Mar. 1982); children—Christopher James, Andrew Don; m. 2d. Norman Harvery Sager, July 30, 1982; step-children—Melodee, David, Eric. Contrbr. poems in various anthologies. Wrkg. on: manuscripts. Student pub. schls., El Paso, X, U. TX, El Paso, 1975-77; AA, Empire St. Coll., NY, 1987. Freelance wrtr. 1982—. Hon. Mention, Golden Poet of the Year, World of Poetry Press, Sacramento, 1985. Home: 35 Adam Silver Creek NY 14136

SAHGAL, PAVAN, b. Srinagar, Kashmir, India, May 17, 1949, came to U.S., 1974, s. Krishan K. and Krishna (Dhawan) S. Contrbr. articles to Venture mag., Sci. Digest, Collector Investor, other publs.; contrbr. poetry: PEN mag., Anthology of Indo-Anglican Poetry, 1973. MS in Journalism, Columbia U., 1975. Freelance wrtr., NYC, 1980-81; corp. fin. ed. Pensions and Investment Age, NYC, 1981-84; ed.-in-chief Wall St. Computer Rvw, 1984—. Home: 49 Park Ave New York NY 10016

SAID, EDWARD W., b. Jerusalem, Palestine, Nov. 1, 1935; s. Wadie A. and Hilda (Musa) Said; m. Mariam Cortas, Dec. 15, 1970; children—Wadie, Najla. Author: Joseph Conrad and the Fiction of Autobiography, 1966, Beginnings: Intention and Method, 1975, Orientalism, 1978, The Question of Palestine, 1979; editor: Literature and Society, 1979, Covering Islam, 1981, The World, the Text, and the Critic, 1983, After the Last Sky, 1986. AB, Princeton U., 1957; AM, Harvard U., 1960, PhD, 1964. Tutor history and lit. Harvard U., 1961-63; inst. Columbia U., 1963-65, asst. prof. English, 1965-67, assoc. prof., 1968-70, prof., 1970-77, Parr prof. English and comparative lit., 1977—; vis. prof. Harvard U., 1974; fellow Center for Advanced Study in Behavioral Scis. (Palo Alto, CA), 1975-76; Christian Gauss lectr. in criticism Princeton U., spring 1977; vis. prof. humanities Johns Hopkins, spring 1979; Carpenter prof. U. Chgo., 1983. Social Sci. Research fellow, 1975; Guggenheim fellow, 1972-73; Recipient Lionel Trilling award Columbia U., 1976, Recipient, René Wellek Award, American Am. Comp. Lit. Assn., 1985. Mem. MLA, Assn. Arab Am. U. Grads. (past vp) NY Council Fgn. Relations, PEN. Office: Hamilton Hall Columbia Univ New York NY 10027

SAINER, ARTHUR, b. NYC, Sept. 12, 1924; s. Louis and Sadie (Roth) Sainer; m. Maryjane Treloar, Apr. 18, 1981; children—Douglas M., Stephanie M., Jane M., Ross M. Editor: Village Voice, 1962; author: plays The Burning Out of 82, 1985, Sunday Childhood Journeys to Nobody at Home, 1980, Images of the Coming Dead, 1980, After the Baal-Shem Tov, 1979, Carol in Winter Sunlight, 1977, The Children's Army Is Late, 1974; The Radical Theatre Notebook, 1975; reporter: NEA, Washington, 1979-82. BA, Washington Sq. Coll., NYC, 1946; MA, Columbia U., 1948. Tchr. Bennington Coll. (VT), 1967-69, Adelphi U. (Garden City, NY), 1974-75, S.I. Community Coll., 1974-75; faculty Wesleyan U. (Middletown, CT), 1977-80, Hunter Coll. (NYC)1980-81; assoc. prof. theatre Middlebury Coll. (CT), 1981-83, play dir. Boat Sun Cavern, 1983; drama critic Village Voice (NYC)1961-80; play dir. Lord Tom Goldsmith at Theatre for New City (NYC), 1979, Witnesses at Open Space, 1977. Panelist VT Council on the Arts, Montpelier, 1982, 83, NY. State Council on the Arts, 1976-78. Ford Fdn. grantee, 1979, 80; recipient grant Office for Advanced Drama Research, U. Minn., 1967, award for Grab Your Hat, John Golden Fdn., 1946, Berman Awd. for Sunday Childhood Journeys..., 1984. Address: 565 W End Ave New York NY 10024

ST. CLAIR, PHILIP, b. Warren, OH, Apr. 30, 1944; s. Harvey Lee and Ruth (Sutton) St. C. Author: In the Thirty-Nine Steps, 1980; At the Tent of Heaven, 1984; Little-Dog-of-Iron, 1985; ed.: Frederic Remington: The American West, 1979. BA, Kent State U., 1970, MA, 1972, MLS, 1974; MFA, Bowling Green State U., 1985. Ed. Volair Ltd. Pub. Co., Kent, Ohio, 1976-79; assoc. Western Res. Pub. Services, Kent, 1979-81; instr. Kent State U., 1981-83, Bowling Green State U., Ohio, 1985-86, Southern Ill. Univ. at Carbondale, 1986-. Home: 813 S University No J Carbondale IL 62901

ST. CLOUD, ALDEN, see Salchert, Brian Arthur

ST. CYR, NAPOLEON JOSEPH, b. Franklin, NH, May 8, 1924; s. Wilfred Joseph and Odile Ann (LaMontagne) St.C. Author: (poetry) Pebble Ring, 1966, The Stones Unturned, 1967; contrbr. to numerous mags.; ed. and pub., The Small Pond Mag. of Lit., 1969—; ed. poetry, Cider Mill Press. BS, U.N.H., 1953; Masters, Fairfield U., 1960, cert. of advanced study, 1967. Elementary tchr., Trumbull, CT, 1955-65, Fairfield, CT, 1965-79. Numerous poetry judgings, incl. Natl. Book Awards. Mem. CCLM, COSMEP, AARP. Home: 50 Shirley Dr Stratford CT 06497

ST. GEORGE, MARGARET, see Osborne, Maggie Ellen

SAINT-JACQUES, ALFRED JOSEPH, b. Lausanne, Switzerland, Sept. 17, 1956, came to U.S., 1959, s. Alfred Joseph and Kiki (Cambus) Saint-J. Contrbr.: Respiratory Medicine Today, Dermatology News, Rheumatology News, several gen. interest publs. Wrkg. on travel and consumer health articles. BA in Journalism and Communications, Fordham U., 1979. Reporter Yonkers (N.Y.) Home News & Times, 1979; reporter, photographer Eastside Express-Westsider, NYC, 1979; asst. ed. Acad. Communications, NYC, 1979-83, spcl. projects ed., 1983-85; freelance wrtr., 1985—; mng. ed. Immunology & Allergy Practice, NYC, 1985—. Office: Immun & All Prac 116 W 32d St New York NY 10001

ST. MAWR, ERIN, see Kennedy, J. H.

SALANTRIE, FRANK, b. Newburgh, NY, Jan. 25, 1926; s. Edward F. and Mary (Caltabiano) S.; m. June Pines, Nov. 25, 1970; children (previous marriages) Judith Broz, Eugene Katz, Mary Frances, Frank. Ed. and pub. The Original Art Report, Chgo., 1967—; real estate assoc. Century 21-Stanmeyer, Chgo., 1985—. Served to s/sgt. USAF, WWII, PTO. Mem. Natl. Artists Equity Assn. Home: 3854 N Ridgeway Ave Chicago IL 60618

SALAS, FLOYD FRANCIS, b. Walsenburg, CO, Jan. 24, 1931; s. Edward and Anita (Sanchez) S.; m. Velva Daryl Harris, Sept. 1948 (div. 1970); 1 child, Gregory Francis. Author: (novels) Tattoo the Wicked Cross, 1967; What Now My Love, 1970; Lay My Body on the Line, 1978; ed., contrbr. Word Hustlers, 1976, To Build a Fire, 1976, Stories and Poems from Close to Home, 1986. BA, San Francisco State U., 1963, MA in Creative Writing, 1965. State coordinator poetry in schls. San Francisco State U., 1973-76; prof. English, U. Calif., Berkeley, 1977-78, Foothill Coll., Los Altos Hills, Calif., 1979—, Sonoma State U., Rohnert Park, Calif., 1984—. Recipient Joseph Henry Jackson award San Francisco Fdn., 1964; Rockefeller Fdn. scholar, Mexico City, 1958-59; Eugene F. Saxton fellow Harper & Row, 1965; NEA fellow, 1978; James P. Lynch Meml. fellow U. Calif., Berkeley, 1977, Bay Area writing project fellow, 1984. Home: 1206 Delaware St Berkeley CA 94702

SALAZAR, BARBARA M., b. Hernandez, NM, Oct. 1, 1949; d. Arsenio Manuel and Mary Martha (Madrid) Montano; m. John Gilbert Salazar, Apr. 23, 1966; children—Melissa Tammy, Mark John, Jason Louis. Author: (poems) Life, Don't Hold It In, 1984. Contrbr. poems to anthols. Student Northern N.Mex. Community Coll., 1981—. Tchr.'s aide Espanola Elem. Schl., N.Mex., 1974-76, Espanola Jr. High Schl., 1976-80; group secy., administrv. service specialist Los Alamos Natl. Lab., N.Mex., 1981—. Recipient Merit Certificate award World of Poetry, 1983, 84, 85, 86, Golden Poet award, 1985, 86. Home: Box 894 Espanola NM 87532

SALCHERT, BRIAN ARTHUR (Alden St. Cloud), b. Fond du Lac, WI, Jan. 16, 1941, s. John Joseph and Seviah Elizabeth (Morse) S.; m. Janice Marie Binnebose, June 12, 1965. Author: Rooted Sky, 1972, January 1976, 1977, 12 Sonnets from 1976, 1981, First Pick, 1982, and the extremely rare Teasings, 1986; contrbr. to anthologies: Minn. Poets Anthology, 1973, Wis. Rvw fifth season, 1980, Wisconsin Poets' Calendar: 1982, Wisconsin Poets' Calendar: 1983; contrbr. poetry to Wis. Rvw, RFD, Studia Mystica, Seems, Sou' wester, Bitterroot, other lit mags; co-ed.: Karamu, 1967-70, Road Apple Rvw, 1971, 72. BA in English, Wis. State U., Oshkosh, 1965; MFA in English, U. Iowa, 1967. Instr. English, Eastern Ill. U., Charleston, 1967-70, U. Wis., Oshkosh, 1970-72; night auditor Holiday Inn-West, Gainesville, Fla., 1982—. Home: 3530 SW 24th Ave Lot 41 Gainesville FL 32607

SALE, MARILYN MILLS, b. Bklyn., Jan. 5, 1928; d. Philip J. Mills and Mildred (Leetracker) Smith; m. William M. Sale, June 13, 1953 (div. 1967); children—Elizabeth W., David K. BA, Smith Coll., 1949; M.Ed, Washington U., 1968. Asst. editor Rinehart & Co. (NYC), 1950-53, Cornell U. Press (Ithaca, NY), 1953-57, asst. mng. editor, 1971-76, action dir., 1982-83, mng. editor, 1983—; humanities editor PA U. Press (Phila.), 1969-71. Mem. Women in Scholarly Pub. Office: Press 124 Roberts Pl Ithaca NY 14850

SALEH, DENNIS, b. Chgo., Dec. 8, 1942, s. William and Kathryn (McKoy) S.; m. Michele Johnson, Sept. 13, 1969; children—Brandon, Bree. Author: Just What the Country Needs, Another Poetry Anthology, 1971, Palmway (poetry), 1976, Rock Art: The Golden Age of Record Album Covers, 1978, 100 Chameleons (poetry), 1978, Science Fiction Gold: Film Classics of the 50s, 1979, First Z Poems, 1980, This Is Not Surrealism, 1987. BA in Psychology, Calif. State U.-Fresno, 1964; MFA in Creative Wrtg., U. Calif.-Irvine, 1968. Lectr. U. Calif., Riverside and Santa Cruz, 1968-71, Calif. State U., San Diego and Fresno, 1972-74, U. Calif. Extension, Fresno and Santa Cruz, 1974-75; ed., pub. Comma Books, Inc., Seaside, Calif., 1976—. Home: 1996 Grandview St Seaside CA 93955

SALERNO, NICHOLAS ANDREW, b. Chgo., June 21, 1936; s. Nicholas A. and Lucia (Pollara) S. Author: Strategies in Prose, 1968; Composition & Literary Form, 1972; contrbr. articles to Victorian Poetry, 20th Century Literature, Etudes Anglaises, Arion, Coll. English, Am. Imago, Shakespeare Qtly, others. BA, Ariz. State U., 1957, MA, 1959; PhD., Stanford U., 1962. Prof. English and film history Ariz. State U., Tempe, 1961—, chmn. dept. English, 1982—; film critic Sta. KAET, PBS, 1970-82, Sta. KXTV, ABC, 1979-82, Scottsdale Progress, 1981— Phoenix Mag., 1983—; host Cinema Classics: The Goldwyn Touch, PBS, 1980-82. Served to capt. U.S. Army. Grantee Natl. Fnd. Arts and Humanities, 1967, NEA, 1975, 76. Mem. MLA, Am. Film Inst., Univ. Film and TV Assn. Home: 7718 E Cypress St Scottsdale AZ 85257

SALFORD, HERBERT WETHERBEE, b. Poughkeepsie, NY, Aug. 7, 1911; s. William Arthur and Belle (Wetherbee) Saltford; m. Beatrice Anton, Sept. 30, 1933; children—Arthur G., Richard A., Marcia J., Linda B. Contrbr. to Yankee, House and Garden, Travel, Old Farmer's Almanac, The New York Times, The Christian Science Monitor, other newspprs. and mags. BS in Agriculture, Cornell U., 1933. Production mgr. Schatz Mfg. Co. (Poughkeepsie), 1942-46; Supt. of Parks (Poughkeepsie), 1965-71. Mem. Garden Wrtrs. Assn. of Amer. Home: 27 Bancroft Rd Poughkeepsie NY 12601

SALINGER, JEROME DAVID, b. NYC, Jan. 1, 1919; s. Sol and Miriam (Jillich) Salinger; m. Claire Douglas, 1953 (div. 1967); children—Mathew, Peggy. Author: Catcher in the Rye, 1951, Nine Stories, 1953, Franny and Zooey, 1961, Raise High the Roof Beam, Carpenters, 1962, Seymour—An Introduction, 1963; contrbr. stories to New Yorker mag.; story Uncle Wiggly in Connecticut produced as motion picture My Foolish Heart. Student Valley Forge Mil. Acad.; student, Columbia U. Served to sgt. AUS, 1942-46. Office: Ober 40 E 49th St New York NY 10017

SALINGER, PIERRE EMIL GEORGE, b. San Francisco, June 14, 1925; s. Herbert and Jehanne (Bietry) S.; m. Renee Laboure, Jan. 1, 1947; children: Marc (dec.), Suzanne, Stephen; m. Nancy Brook Joy, June 28, 1957; m. Nicole Helene Gilmann, June 18, 1965; 1 son, Gregory. Author: With Kennedy, 1966, On Instructions of My Government; editor: A Tribute to John

F. Kennedy, 1964, A Tribute to Robert F. Kennedy, 1968, Je Suis un Americain, 1975, La France et lke Nouveau Monde, 1976, America Held Hostage—The Secret Negotiations, 1981, The Dossier, 1984. B.S., U. San Francisco, 1947. Reporter, night city editor San Francisco Chronicle, 1946-55; West Coast editor, contbg. editor Collier's mag., 1955-56; press sec. to U.S. Senaor Kennedy, 1959-60, to; Pres. Kennedy, 1961-63, to, Pres. Johnson, 1963-64; contbg. corr. ABC for Europe, 1977—, Paris bur. chief, 1979—; chief fgn. corr. ABC News, 1983—. Served with USNR, World War II. Decorated Legion of Honor France; Navy and Marine Corps medal. Mem. Nat. Press (Washington). Address: ABC Pub Relns Office 1330 Ave of Americas New York NY 10019

SALISBURY, RALPH JAMES, b. Fayette County, IA, Jan. 24, 1926; s. Charles and Olive Ione (McAllister) Salisberry; m. Eleanor Joyce Hurlbert, Apr. 9, 1948 (div. 1969); children: Jeffrey Charles, Brian Floyd; m. Ingrid Darlene Wendt, Apr. 23, 1969; 1 child, Erin Marie. Author: (poems) Ghost Grapefruit and Other Poems, 1972; Pointing at the Rainbow: Poems from a Cherokee Heritage, 1980; Spirit Beast Chant, 1982; Going to the Water: Poems of a Cherokee Heritage, 1983; A White Rainbow: Poems of a Cherokee Heritage, 1985; ed.: A Nation Within, 1983; contrbr. to Modern Poetry Western Am., Out of This World, Earth Power Coming, Songs from This Earth, others. Ed.-in-chief, Northwest Rvw, 1963-68, poetry ed., 1960; ed. Western Rvw, 1950. BA, U. Iowa, 1948, MFA, 1951. Prof. English, U. Oreg., Eugene, 1960—; vis. prof. Fresno State Coll., 1969-70; sr. Fulbright lectr. J.W. Goethe U., Frankfurt, W. Ger., 1983. Served with USAAF, 1944-46. Recipient award Chapelbrook Fdn., 1966. Home: 2377 Charnelton Eugene OR 97405

SALKIND, NEIL JOSEPH, b. Newark, Apr. 27, 1947. Author: Child Development, 1976, 5th ed., 1986, Thories of Development, 1980, 2d ed., 1983. Contrbr. articles to profl. jnls. BA, U. Md., 1969, PhD, 1973. Research assoc., Natl. Inst. Edn., Washington, 1972-74; prof., U. Kans., Lawrence, 1974—. Mem. APA, Soc. Research Child Devel. Home: 734 Indiana Lawrence KS 66044

SALM, PETER, b. Hameln, Germany, Aug. 23, 1919 (came to U.S., 1938); s. Uri and Helen (Hahlo) Salm B.; m. June Macy, Aug. 10, 1958; 1 son—Anthony. Author: Three Modes of Criticism, 1968, German transl., 1970, The Poem as Plant, 1971; translator: (Goethe) Faust I, 1962, rev. ed., 1985, Pinpoint of Eternity, 1986. BA, UCLA, 1961; PhD, Yale U., 1958. Asst. prof. German Wesleyan U. (Middletown, CT), 1958-63; assoc. prof. German Case Western Res. U. (Cleve.), 1963-65, chair modern langs., until 1976, prof. comparative lit. and German, 1976—. Served to tech. sgt. CIC, US Army, 1942-46. Mem. MLA. Office: Case Wstrn U Dept Comp Lit Cleveland OH 44106

SALMON, JOHN HEARSEY MC MILLAN, b. Thames, New Zealand, Dec. 2, 1925 (came to U.S., 1969); s. John Hearsey and Elizabeth (McMillan) Salmon. Author: The French Religious Wars in English Political Thought, 1959, A History of Goldmining in New Zealand, 1963, Cardinal de Retz, 1969, Society in Crisis—France in The 16th Century, 1975, Renaissance and Revolt: Essays in the Intellectual and Social History of Early Modern France, 1987; editor: The French Wars of Religion, 1967; co-editor: Francogallia (Francois Hotman), 1972. MA, U. New Zealand, 1951; M Litt., Cambridge (Eng.) U., 1957; Litt.D., Victoria U., 1970. Prof. history U. New S. Wales (Sydney, Australis), 1960-65; prof. history dean humanities U. Waikato (New Zealand), 1965-69; Marjorie Walter Goodhart prof. history Bryn Mawr Coll., 1969—. Fellow Royal hist. Cos. Home: 1853 County Line Rd Villanova PA 19085

SALTERBERG, SUSAN KAY, b. Fairfield, IA, Mar. 24, 1960; d. Earl John and Isabelle Mary (Auwaerter) S. Asst. pubns. adminstr., U. No. Iowa, 1986—; contrbr. articles to Colorado Cowboy, The Clydesdale News, EPIC/Salute; photography to The Horse Digest, EPIC/Salute. BA, Central Coll., Pella, IA, 1982. Pub. relns. jnlst. Freiberg-Frederick & Assoc., Cedar Falls, IA, 1982-83; mng. ed. Freiberg Publs., Cedar Falls, 1983-86. Mem. WIC, Amer. Horse Publs. Office: 169 Gilhrist Cedar Falls IA 50614

SALVATORE, MICHAEL JOSEPH, b. Hartford, CT, Dec. 2, 1934; s. Dominic J. Salvatore and Jennie E. (Johnson) Salvatore-Dewey; m. Catherine P. O'Donnell, Aug. 31, 1957; children—Pat, Frank, Joseph. Contrbr. articles to newspapers, mags. including Conn. Mag., English Jnl., others. B.A., Hillyer Coll. 1956; M.A., U. Conn., 1960. Reporter, Jnl. Inquirer, Manchester, CT, 1964-78, Hartford Pubs., Enfield, CT, 1978-82; tchr, English chairman East Windsor High Sch., CT, 1960—. Active East Windsor Hist. Soc., 1969—, South Windsor Hist. Soc., CT, 1986—, Conn. Hist. Soc., 1987—. Mem. East Windsor Edn. Assn. (past pres.), NCTE, Conn. Council Tchrs. English, Conn. Edn. Assn. Home: 56 Greenfield Dr South Windsor CT 06074

SAMPERI, FRANK V., b. Bklyn., May 19, 1933, s. Gaetana S.; m. Dolores Jean Volz, Jan. 10, 1964; children—Claudia, David. Author books of poetry: Song Book, 1960, Of Light, 1965, Branches, 1965, Morning and Evening (portfolio), 1967, Crystals, 1967, The Triune, 1969, The Prefiguration, 1971, Quadifariam, 1973, The Fourth, 1973, Lume Gloriae, Infinitesimals, 1974, Alfa ed O, 1976, Sanza Mezzo, 1977, The Kingdom, 1978, A Remotis, 1979, Letargo, 1980, The Bow Window, 1986. Served with U.S. Army, 1953-55; Korea. Home: 10622 Camden Ave Sun City AZ 85351

SAMPSON, CAROL ANN, b. Wabash, IN, Dec. 5, 1942, d. John Roland Bennett and Virginia Ann (Garthwait) Bennett Mulhulland; m. John Russell Arrison, III, (div.); children—Tracy, John. BS cum laude, Woodbury U., 1975. Pres., prin. designed Carol Sampson Interior Designs, Inc., Riverside, Calif., 1974—; house and home ed. Inland Empire Mag., Riverside, 1978—. Office: Sampson Int 6876 Indiana Ave Riverside CA 92506

SAMUELS, ALFRED PUTNAM, JR., b. Charlottesville, VA, July 11, 1926; s. Alfred P. and Elsie Mae (Bias) S.; divorced; children—Richard Allen, Dorothy Frances. Ed.: The Virginian, 1970, The Post, 19—. Grad. public schls., Chgo. Pres. Aco Games, The Allen Co., Charlottesville, 1951-76, The Allen Co. of Okla., Norman, 1972-76, Pubs. Syndication Intl., Washington, 1984—. Served with U.S. Navy, 1943-46. Home: 2211 Forister CT Norman OK 73069

SAMUELSON, GEORGIA JAMIE, b. Bklyn., Feb. 22, 1950; d. George James Dedeoglou and Zbada Mahfouz; m. Richard Michael Lingua, Mar. 9, 1968 (div. Dec. 31, 1979); 1 son, Richard Aleander; m. Kirby Gale Samuelson, Dec. 27, 1980. Columnist "On the Job Front". Contrbr. articles to mags., newspapers, profl. jnls. Assoc. ed. Calif. Job Jnl., 1982—. Editor, CCCPA Reports. Mem. adv. bd. Bay Area Library and Info. System; past pres. Friends of the Alameda Free Library, 1985; Mem. NWC, Media Alliance, Employment Mgnt. Assn., Calif. Commun. Coll. Placement Assn. (vp). Address: 1446 Sixth St Alameda CA 94501

SANBERG, PAUL RONALD, b. Coral Gables, FL, Jan. 4, 1955; s. Bernard and Molly (Spector) S. Author: Over the Counter Drugs: Harmless or Hazardous, 1986, Prescription Narcotics: The Addictive Painkillers, 1986. Contrbr. numerous articles to profl. jnls., books. Ed.: Bird Behaviour, 1983—. B.Sc. with honors, York U., 1976; M.Sc., U. British Columbia, Toronto, Canada, 1979; Ph.D., Australian Natl. U., Canberra, 1981; Graduate Diploma in Sci. Edn., Western Australian Inst. Technology, Perth, 1985. Asst. prof. Ohio U., Athens, 1983-86; assoc. prof. U. Cin., 1986—. Office Dept of Psych U Cin Cincinnati OH 45267

SANCHEZ, FRANCISCO P., b. Las Maria's, P.R., Aug. 10, 1960, came to U.S., 1968, s. Francisco Vargas Sanchez and Nereida (Figueroa) Aquino. Contrbr. poetry to Am. Poetry Assn., Poetry Press, N.Y. Poetry Soc., others. Student Marist Coll., Poughkeepsie, N.Y., 1980-81. Tutor Hunter Coll., NYC, 1981-82; security investigator Mag Investigations, NYC, 1982-84; machinist X-L Plastics, Clifton, N.J. Home: 235 4th St Apt 7 Passaic NJ 07055

SANCHEZ, NANCY EILEEN, b. Miami, Aug. 20, 1956; d. Edward Alden and Virginia Leone (Brown) Blanton; m. Mark Bishop Sanchez, Dec. 30, 1979 (div. Dec. 20, 1985). Feature wrtr. Rome News Tribune, GA, 1982-83. Ed. mags.: Coastlines, GA, 1985, DNR Outdoor Report, 1986-87; assoc. ed.: Darien News, GA, 1983-85.. B.S. in Jnlsm., U. Fla., 1979. Public relations asst., ed. Meml. Hospital, Jacksonville, FL, 1981-82; communicator, ed. Dept. Natural Resources, Brunswick, GA, 1985—. Recipient 1st place for features Ga. Press Assn., 1982, 83, 2d place for features, 1983. Home: 1805 1/2 Bruce Dr Saint Simons Island GA 31522

SANCHEZ, RICARDO, b. El Paso, TX, Mar 29, 1941; s. Pedro Lucero and Lena C. (Gallegos) S.; m. Maria Teresa Silva, Nov. 22, 1964; children: Rikard-Sergei, Libertad-Yvonne, Jacinto Temilotzin. Author: Los Cuatro, 1971, Canto y Grito Mi Liberacion, 1971, Mano a Mano, 1972, Liberation of a Chicano Mind, 1973, Hechizo-spells, 1975, Milhaus Blues y Gritos Nortenos, 1979, 80, Brown Bear Honey Madnesses, 1982, Amsterdam Cantos, 1983, Selected Poems, 1986, Perdido: A barrio story, 1985. PhD, Union Grad. Schl., 1973-75. Assoc. prof. Univ. Utah, Salt Lake City, 1977-80, depy. dir. project SER, 1980-81; psychiatric trainer Brown Schls., Austin, Tex., 1982; assoc. dir. Noel Therapeutic, Austin, 1981-82; owner, mgr. Paperbacks y mas, San Antonio, Tex, 1983—; arts columnist Express-News, San Antonio, 1985-86. Trustee, San Antonio Library System, 1985-87; dir, Poetry Tejas Intl., San Antonio, 1983—, founder/mgr., Poets of Tejas Reading Series, San Antonio, 1982—; lit. panel, NEA, Washington, 1979-82, Tex. Commn. Arts, Austin, 1982-85. Recipient Key to the City award, City Council, Pueblo, Colo, 1975; Outstanding prof. award, Chicano Student Assn., Univ. Utah, 1979; Ford Fdn. fellow, 1973, 74. Address: 730 W Elsmere San Antonio TX 78212

SAND, GEORGE X., (Brett Barton), b. Manahawkin, NJ; m. Phyllis Philibert, 1940 (dec. 1971); children—Gail Drillot, Karen Alt; m. Lou Burke, 1973; children—Brenda Townsend, Charles Huff, Jr. Author: Skin and Scuba Diving, 1964, Salt-Water Fly Fishing, 1970, The Everglades Today, 1971, Iron-Tail, 1971, Complete Beginner's Guide to Fishing, 1974, Never Quit, 1981. Named 1st Outstanding Conservationist, State of Fla., 1950. Mem. Fla. Motion Picture TV Assn. Home: 1412 Winkler Ave Fort Myers FL 33901

SANDBURG, HELGA, b. Maywood, IL, Nov. 24, 1918; d. Carl and Lilian (Steichen) S.; m. George Crile, Jr., Nov. 9, 1963; children by previous marriage—John Carl Steichen, Paula Steichen Polega. Author: novels The Wheel of Earth, 1958, Measure My Love, 1959, The Owl's Roost, 1962, The Wizard's Child, 1967; nonfiction Sweet Music, A Book of Family Reminiscence and Song, 1963; (with George Crile, Jr.) Above and Below, 1969; poetry The Unicorns, 1965; To A New Husband, 1970; young adult novels Blueberry, 1963; Gingerbread, 1964; juveniles Joel and the Wild Goose, 1963; Bo and the Old Donkey, 1965, Anna and the Baby Buzzard, 1970; collection of short stories Children and Lovers: 15 Stories by Helga Sandburg, 1976; biography A Great and Glorious Romance: The Story of Carl Sandburg and Lilian Steichen, 1978; also numerous short stories; rep. in collections.; Contbr.: short stories, poems, articles to popular mags. Student, Mich. State Coll., 1939-40, U. Chgo., 1940. Dairy goat breeder, also personal sec. to father, 1944-51; sec. manuscripts div., also for keeper of collections Library of Congress, 1952-56; adminstrv. asst. for papers of Woodrow Wilson, 1958-59; writer, lectr., 1957—. Recipient Va. Qtly Rvw. prize for best short story, 1959, Borestone Mountain poetry award, 1962, Poetry award Chgo. Tribune, 1970; 2d prize 7th Annl. Kans. Poetry Contest; grantee Finnish Am. Soc. and Svenska Inst., 1961. Mem. AG, PSA, Am.-Scandinavian Fdn. Address: 2060 Kent Rd Cleveland OH 44106

SANDER, LAWRENCE D., Ed.: Day Timer Newspaper, 1977-79, Onion City Bureaucrat, 1983-86; contrbr. to Jepson Jabber, The Planetary Newsletter, Vacaville (Calif.) Reporter, The Bark. Student San Francisco State U., 1985—. Assoc. dir. Sanoby Pub. Group, Arcata, Calif. and Vacaville, Calif., 1983—. Office: Sanoby 700 Brookside Dr Vacaville CA 95688

SANDERLIN, GEORGE, b. Balt., Feb. 5, 1915, s. George B. and Charlotte (Brady) S.; m. Owenita Harrah; children—Frea, Sheila, David, John. Author: College Reading: A Collection of Prose, Plays and Poetry, 1953, St. Jerome and the Bible, 1961, Effective Writing and Reading (with James I. Brown), 1962, First Around the World: A Journal of Magellan's Voyage, 1964, St. Gregory the Great, 1964, Eastward to India: Vasco da Gama's Voyage, 1965, Effective Writing, 1966, Across the Ocean Sea: A Journal of Columbus's Voyage, 1966, 1776: Journals of American Independence, 1968, The Sea-Dragon: Journals of Francis Drake's Voyage Around the World, 1969, Benjamin Franklin: As Others Saw Him, 1971, Bartolome de Las Casas: A Selection of His Writings, 1971, the Settlement of California, 1972, A Hoop to the Barrel: The Making of the American Constitution, 1974, Washington Irving: As Others Saw Him, 1975, Mark Twain: As Others Saw Him, 1978; contrbr. articles to Modern Lang. Notes, Speculum, Chaucer Rvw., Parents' Mag., numerous other publs. Wrkg. on history of the bible, BA, Am. U., 1935; PhD, Johns Hopkins U., 1938. Prof. English U. Me., Orono, 1938-55, San Diego State U., 1955—. Home: 997 Vista Grande Rd El Cajon CA 92019

SANDERLIN, OWENITA HARRAH, (Kathryn Kenny), b. Los Angeles, June 2, 1916, d. Owen Melville Harrah and Marigold (Whitford) Fry; m. George William Sanderlin, May 30, 1936; children—Frea Elizabeth, Sheila Mary, David George, John Owen. Novels: Jeanie O'Brien, 1965, Tennis Rebel, 1978, Match Point, 1979; biography, Johnny, 1968, 69, 78; non-fiction: Creative Teaching, 1971, Teaching Gifted Children, 1973 (with Ruth Lundy) Gifted Children: How to Identify and Teach Them, 1979; juvenile fiction: (as Kathryn Kenny) Trixie Belden: Mystery of the Queen's Necklace, 1979; contrbr. articles, short stories, poems to Saturday Evening Post, Jack and Jill, Catholic Digest, Ladies' Home Jnl, Parents, others, also books and anthologies. BA summa cum laude, Am. U., Washington, 1937; teaching credential, San Diego State U., 1969. Freelance wrtr., speaker at confs., 1940—; tchr. English, creative writing, speech, drama, Orono, Me. and San Diego; cons. gifted programs San Diego City Schls., 1972-74, 1980—. Mem. Scripps Clinic and Research Fdn., La Jolla, Calif., 1984—. Mem. Book Publicists San Diego. Address: 997 Vista Grande Rd El Cajon CA 92019

SANDERS, DEBRA FAYE, b. Amarillo, TX, July 1, 1952; d. Douglas Eugene and Gloria Elizabeth (Jamison) S. Author songs recorded on Where No Man, The Final Frontier, Free Fall and Other Delights. Contrbr. poems to newspapers, anthols. Cert., Atlanta Sch. Interior Design, 1972, Inst. Children's Lit., 1987; student Georgia Tech U., 1969-71. Secy. Plantation Pineapple Co., Honolulu, 1978—. Recipient Golden Poet award World of Poetry, 1985, 86, 87, Honorable Mention for poetry, 1985, 86, 87. Mem. Hawaii Mensa (past pres.), Planetary Soc. Home: 1415 Victoria St 206 Honolulu HI 96822

SANDERS, LAWRENCE, b. Bklyn., 1920. Author: The Anderson Tapes, 1970 (Edgar award MWA), The Pleasures of Helen, 1971, Love Songs, 1972, The First Deadly Sin, 1973, The Tomorrow File, 1975, The Tangent Objective, 1976, The Marlow Chronicles, 1977, The Second Deadly Sin, 1977, The Tangent Factor, 1978, The Sixth Commandment, 1979, The Tenth Commandment, 1980, The Case of Lucy Bending, 1982. BA, Wabash Coll., 1940. Staff mem. Macy's Dept. Store (NYC), 1940-43; editor and writer of stories for various mags., editor Mechanix Illus., Sci. and Mechanics, free-lance writer for men's mags., 1946-68; novelist, 1969—. Served as sgt. USMC, 1943-46. Office: Putnam 200 madison Ave New York NY 10016

SANDERS, LEONARD MARION, JR., b. Denver, Jan. 15, 1929; s. Leonard Marion and Jacqueline (Thomas) Sanders; m. Florene Lovette Cooter, Aug. 21, 1956. Author: Four-Year Hitch, 1961, The Wooden Horseshow, 1964, The Seed (pseudonym Dan Thomas), 1969, How Fort Worth Became the Texasmost City, 1973, The Marshal of Stud Horse Flats, 1975, The Hamlet Warning, 1976, The Hamlet Ultimatum, 1979, Sonoma, 1981, Act of War, 1982, Fort Worth, 1984. Student U. Okla., 1946-49, 51, 54, 57. Mem. staff Enid News-Eagle (OK), 1949; Daily Oklahoman, 1950-51; mng. editor Okla. Publisher, 1954; mem. staff Wichita Falls Record- News (TX), 1954-56, Norman Transcript (OK), 1957, Ft. Worth Star-Telegram, 1958-79, fine arts editor, book page editor, 1964-79. Served with USNR, 1952-53. Mem. AG, WWA, SFWA, MWA, TX Inst. Letters. Home: 4200 Clayton Rd W Fort Worth TX 76116

SANDERS, RONALD, b. Union City, NJ, July 7, 1932; s. George Harry and Rose (Rachlin) Sanders; m. Beverly Helen Gingold, Mar. 19, 1967. Author: Israel: The View from Masada, 1966, The Downtown Jews, 1969, Reflections on a Tea Pot, 1972, Lost Tribes and Promised Lands, 1978, The Days Grow Short: The Life and Music of Kurt Weill, 1980, The High Walls of Jerusalem, 1984, Shores of Refuge, 1988; co-editor: Socialist Thought: A Documentary History, 1964. BA summa cum laude, Kenyon Coll., 1954; MA, Columbia, 1957. Lectr. history Queens Coll. (Flushing, NY), 1958-65; assoc. editor Midstream mag. (NYC)1965-73, editor, 1973-75. Home: 49 W 12th St New York NY 10011

SANDERS, SCOTT RUSSELL, b. Memphis, TN, Oct 26, 1945; s. Greeley Ray and Eva Mary (Solomon) S; m. Ruth Ann McClure, Aug. 24, 1967; children: Eva Rachel, Jesse Solomon. Author: D.H. Lawrence, 1974, Wilderness Plots, 1983, Fetching the Dead, 1984, Wonders Hidden, 1984, Terrarium, 1985, Hear the Wind Blow, 1985, Stone Country, 1986, Bad Man Ballad, 1986, The Paradise of Bombs, 1987; ed. The Audubon Reader, 1986; contrbr. fiction and essays to lit mags. BA, Brown U., 1967; PhD, Cambridge U., England, 1971. Prof. English Ind. Univ., Bloomington, 1971—; lit. ed. Cambridge Rvw, England, 1969-71; fiction ed. Minn Rvw, 1976-80; contrbr. ed. North Am. Rvw, 1982—; columnist on fiction Chgo Sun-Times, 1977-84. Address: 1113 E Wylie St Bloomington IN 47401

SANDIFER, LINDA PROPHET, b. Rigby, ID, Dec. 18, 1951; d. David D. and Virginia M. (Chiles) Prophet; m. Van R. Sandifer, Jr., July 31, 1976; children: Amanda, Bonny, Emily. Author: Tyler's Woman, 1985; Pride's Passion, 1986, Heart of the Hunter, 1987. Mem. Romance Wrtrs. Am., Idaho Wrtrs. League (1st place for adult fiction 1983, 85, Wrtr. of Yr. award 1985). Home: Rt 1 Box 141 Idaho Falls ID 83401

SANDLER, IRVING HARRY, b. NYC, July 22, 1925; s. Harry and Anna Sandler; m. Lucy Freeman, Sept. 4, 1958; 1 dau.—Catherine Harriet. Author: The Triumph of American Painting: A History of Abstract Expressionism, 1970, The New York School: Painters and Sculptors of the Fifties, 1978, Alex Katz, 1979, Al Held, 1984. BA, Temple U., 1948; MA, U. PA, 1950; PhD, NYU, 1976. Instr. in art history NYU, 1960-71; prof. art history SUNY, Purchase, 1971; art critic NY Post (NYC)1960-65. Served with USMC, 1943-46. Guggenheim fellow, 1965; NEA fellow, 1977. mem. Coll. Art Assn., Intl. Assn. Art Critics. Home: 100 Bleecker St New York NY 10012

SANDLER, LUCY FREEMAN, b. NYC, June 7, 1930; .d Otto and Frances (Glass) Freeman; m. Irving Sandler, Sept. 4, 1958; 1 dau.—Catherine Harriet. Editor: Essays in Memory of Karl Lehmann, 1964, Art, the Ape of Nature: Studies in Honor of H.W. Janson, 1981; author: The Peterborough Psalter in Brussels, 1974, The Psalter of Robert De Lisle in the British Library, 1983, Gothic Manuscripts, 1285-1345, 1986; asst. editor: The Art Bull., 1964-67; editor: Monograph Series, 1970-75; mem. editorial bd.: Jnl Jewish Art, 1978. BA, Queens Coll., 1951, MA, Columbia U., 1957; PhD, NYU, 1964. Asst. prof. NYU (NYC), 1964-70, assoc. prof., 1970-75, prof. fine arts, 1975-85, Helen Gould Sheppard

Prof. of Art Hist., 1985—, chair dept., 1975—; editorial cons. Viator, UCLA, 1983—. NEH fellow, 1967-68. Mem. Coll. Art Assn. (pres., 1981-84), AAUP. Home: 100 Bleecker St New York NY 10012

SANDLER, ROBERTA, b. NY, May 3, 1943; m. Martin Sandler, Mar. 31, 1964. Contrbr. articles to mags., newspapers including N.Y. Times, Chgo. Tribune, Miami Herald, Milw. Jnl., Family Circle, Harper's, Ladies'Home Jnl., others. Free lance wrtr., 1977—; tchr. writing for mags., newspapers, Boca Ration, FL, 1984—. Recipient Bronze medal for disting. health jnlsm. Am. Chiropractic Assn., 1987. Mem. Intl. Women's WG, Fla. Freelance Wrtr.'s Assn. (lectr. 1986 —). Office: 3835 NW 27th Ave Boca Raton FL 33434

SANDS, EDITH SYLVIA ABELOFF, (Mrs. Abraham M. Sands), b. Bklyn.; d. Louis and Jennie (Goldstein) Abeloff; m. Abraham M. Sands, June 5, 1932; children—Stephanie Lou, John Eliot. Author: How to Select Executive Personnel, 1963; contrbr. articles to profl. jnls; editor jnl industry studies for investment decisions. BA, Adelphi Coll., 1932; MBA, Baruch Schl. Bus. Adminstrn., CCNY, 1956; PhD, NYU, 1961. Asst. prof. LIU (Bklyn.), 1961-65, assoc. prof., 1965-69, prof., 1969-81, prof. fin. emeritus, 1981—, chair dept. finance, 1962-72; prof. fin., chmn. Touro Coll. (NYC)1981—. Mem. AAUP. Home: 874 Carroll St Brooklyn NY 11215

SANDS, MELODY GAIL, b. Lake Charles, LA, July 26, 1955; d. Harry Myron and Sandra Zoe (Love) S. Contrbr. articles to mags., newspapers. B.S. in Jnlsm., Ohio U., 1977. Ed., Athens News, Inc., OH, 1977-87, part-owner, v.p., 1978—; free-lance wrtr. Chgo. Sun Times, 1987—. Recipient Hugh M. Hefner First Amendment award for print jnlsm. Playboy Fdn., 1982. Home: Rt 1 Box 62D New Plymouth OH 45654

SANDY, STEPHEN MERRILL, b. Mpls., Aug. 2, 1934; s. Alan Francis and Evelyn Brown (Martin) S.; m. Virginia Scoville, Oct. 11, 1969; children—Clare, Nathaniel. Author: Stresses in the Peaceable Kingdom, 1967, Roofs, 1971, The Raveling of the Novel, 1980, The Hawthorne Effect, 1980, Flight of Steps, 1982, Riding to Greylock, 1983, To a Mantis, 1987, Man in the Open Air, 1988. BA, Yale U., 1955; AM, Harvard U., 1959, PhD, 1963. Vis. prof. U. Tokyo, 1967-68, Brown U., Providence, R.I., 1968-69; vis. lectr. U. R.I., Kingston, 1969; faculty Bennington Coll., Vt., 1969—, prof.: faculty Harvard Univ., 1963-67, faculty Harvard Summer Schl., 1986—. Grantee Vt. Council on Arts, Ingram Merrill Fdn., 1985. Home: Box 524 North Bennington VT 05257

SANFELICI, ARTHUR HUGO, b. Haledon, NJ, May 23, 1934; s. Hugo and Anna (Schilder) S.; m. Betty Louise Van Riper, Aug. 10, 1957; children—Brian Arthur, Amy Elizabeth, Gary Hugh, Bruce Richard. Editor, compiler: Yesterday's Wings. Student, Lehigh U., 1952-55. Assoc. editor Flying Mag. (NYC)1961-64; mng. editor Am. Aviation Mag. (Washington), 1964-68; dist. sales mgr. Gates Learjet Co. (NYC)1969-71; exec. editor Airport World Mag. (Westport, CT), 1971-74; mng. editor Pilot mag., 1975-79, editor AOPA Newsletter, AOPAirport Report, Genl. Aviation Natl. Report, 1979—. Served with USAF, 1955-60. Mem. Aviation and Space Writers Assn., Aircraft Owners and Pilots Assn. (asst. vp). Home: 5 Oak Shade Rd Sterling VA 22170

SANFIELD, STEVE, b. Cambridge, MA, Aug. 3, 1937, s. Harold and Rose (Silverman) S.; m. Jacqueline Desire Bellon, Jan. 4, 1969 (div. 1976); 1 son, Aaron Mikhal; m. 2d, Sarah Ruth Sparks, Sept. 6, 1985. Author: Water Before and Water After, 1974, Backlog, 1975, A Fall From Grace, 1976, Wandering, 1978, The Confounding, 1980, 40 Days and 40 Nights, 1983, A New Way, 1983, A Natural Man—The True Story of John Henry, 1986, Chasing the Cranes, 1986; translator: Only the Ashes, 1981; assoc. ed.: Kuksu, 1975-78; contrbg. ed.: Zero, 1978-81. BA, U. Mass., 1958. Newswrtr. CBS News, Los Angeles, 1959-61; storytelling cons. Ednl. Media Assn., Port Townsend, Wash., 1980-86, Centrum Fdn., Port Townsend, 1980—; artistic dir. Sierra Storytelling Festival, Nevada City, Calif., 1985-86; bd. dirs. Am. Storytelling Resource Center, Santa Cruz, Calif., 1980-84, bd. dirs. North Columbia Schoolhouse Cultural Ctr., 1980—. Grantee Calif. Arts Council Artist-in-Schls. program, 1977-80, Sierra County Arts Council, 1982-85; winner 1st prize annl. haiku contest Haiku Zasshi Zo, Seattle, 1985. Mem. Natl. Assn. Preservation and Perpetuation of Storytelling, NWU, Society of Children's Book Wrtrs. Home: 22000 Lost River Rd Nevada City CA 95959

SANFORD, DAVID BOYER, b. Denver, Mar. 4, 1943; s. Filmore Bowyer and Alice Irene (Peterson) Sanford. Author: Who Put the Contrbr. in Consumer?, 1972, Me and Ralph, 1976; editor, co- author: Hot War on the Consumer, 1970. BA with honors, U. Denver, 1964; MS in Journalism with honors, Columbiaa U., 1965. With New Republic mag. (Washington), 1965-76, mng. editor, 1970-76, Politics Today (formerly Skeptic) (Santa Barbara, CA), 1976-78, contrbg. editor, 1978-79; editorial writer Los Angeles Herald Examiner, 1978-79; mng. editor Harper's mag. (NYC), 1979-80; editor Wall St. Jnl mag., 1980-81; sr. spcl. writer Wall Street Jnl, 1981—; syndicated columnist, 1970-71; commentator Canadian Broadcasting Corp., 1967-76. Centennial scholar, 1960-64; NY Newspaper Guild fellow, 1964-65. Mem. AG. Home: 118 Prospect Park W Brooklyn NY 11215

SANFORD, GERALDINE A., b. Sioux Falls, SD, Aug. 1, 1928, d. Francis Meredith and Opal Mae (Weimer) Jones; m. Dayton Marshall Sanford (div. 1972); children—Scott Elliot, Melissa Drue, Corey Todd, Craig Marshall, Reed Meredith. Contrbr. articles, poems to lit mags. BA, Augustana Coll., Sioux Falls, 1971; MA in English, U. S.D., Vermillion, 1977. Editorial asst. SD Rvw, 1983—. Mem. P&W. Home: 306 W 36th St Sioux Falls SD 57105

SANFORD, TERRY, b. Laurinburg, NC, Aug. 20, 1917; s. Cecil and Elizabeth (Martin) Sanford; m. Margaret Rose Knight, July 4, 1942; children—Elizabeth Knight, Terry. Author: But What About the People?, 1966, Storm Over the States, 1967, A Danger of Democracy, 1981. AB, U. NC, 1939, JD, 1946. Bar: NC 1946. Asst. dir. Inst. Govt., U. NC, 1940-41, 46-48; spcl. agt. FBI, 1941-42; practiced in Fayetteville, 1948-60; prtnr. Sanford, Adams, McCullough & Beard (Raleigh, NC), 1965—; gov. State of NC, 1961-65; pres. Duke U. (Durham, NC), 1969-85; public gov. Am. Stock Exchange, 1977-83; Dir. Study of Am. States, Duke U., 1965-68; chair ITT Intl. Fellowship Com., Am. Council Young Polit. Leaders. Served to 1st lt. AUS, 1942-46. Home: 2500 Auburn St Durham NC 27706

SANTARLASCI, STEPHEN M., b. Phila., Mar. 28, 1952; s. Joseph H., Sr. and Rosemary T. (Donovan) S.; m. Pamela R. Fairhurst, May 29, 1976; 1 dau., Michelle L. Ed.: The Mutual Mag., 1979—. B.A. in English Lit., U. Va., 1974. Asst. to pres., ed. Mutual Beneficial Assn. of Rail Transportation Employees, Inc., Phila., 1975-86. Home: 11 Sycamore Ct Paoli PA 19301

SANTINI, ROSEMARIE, b. NYC. Author: The Secret Fire, The Sex Doctors, A Swell Style of Murder, 1986, The Secret Fire: A Study of How Women Live Their Sexual Fantasies, Forty- One Grove Street; fiction and nonfiction in Women's World, LHJ, Penthouse, Playboy, Family Circle, other periodicals, anthols.; television: All My Children, bks. I, II, III. Ed. True Story Magazine; tchr. wrtg., Baruch Coll., NYU. Mem. Author's Guild, P&W, PSA, SAJA, DG, Natl. Academy of Television Arts and Sciences. Office: Lord Agcy 660 Madison Ave New York NY 10022

SANTOMAURO, MARY ELIZABETH, (Mary Payne), b. Monticello, UT, Mar. 24, 1935, d. Dexter Airl and Stella Gladys (Hicks) Hurley; m. Vincent Richard Santomauro, Feb. 27, 1954; children—Michael, Patrick, Paul, Theresa, Rose. Author: Rest of Afternoon Was Watermelon, 1979; contrbr. poetry to Union City Outlook, Adventures in Poetry, Quickenings, Creative with Words, numerous other lit. publs.; contrbr. articles to Money Engr., Ye Olde Greensheet Jnl, Conservative Digest, numerous other publs. Admin. secy. to dir. mktg. Audiotronics, Los Angeles, 1979-81; prodn. clk. Greensheet shopper, Van Nuys, Calif., 1981—. Recipient Golden Poet award World of Poetry, 1985. Home: Box 489 Woodland Hills CA 91365

SANTOS, SHEROD, b. Greenville, SC, Sept. 9, 1949, s. Sherod and Sarah Simpson (Gossett) S.; m. Lynne Marie McMahon; 1 child, Benjamin Hart. Author: (poems) Accidental Weather, 1982; contrbr. poetry to New Yorker, The Nation, Poetry, Paris Rvw, other mags. MFA, U. Calif., Irvine, 1978, PhD, U. Utah, 1982. Asst. prof. Calif. State U., San Bernardino, 1982-83; assoc. prof. English, U. Mo., Columbia, 1983—. Recipient Oscar Blumenthal prize Poetry mag., 1983, Delmore Schwartz Meml. award NYU, 1983, Robert Frost Poet award, 1984; grantee Ingram-Merrill Fdn., 1983, Guggenheim Fdn., 1984, NEA, 1987. Home: 500 W Broadway Columbia MO 65203

SAPIRO, LELAND, (Yogi Borel, Moses Maimonides, Jr.), b. Chgo., Apr. 14, 1924; s. Aaron and Janet (Arndt) S. Contrbr. Rhodomagnetic Digest, Lovecraft Symposium, Writer's Digest, COSMEP Newsltr.; ed. Riverside Qtly, 1964—. BA, U. Calif.-Berkeley, 1950; MA, UCLA, 1953. Instr. Calif. State Univ., Fullerton, 1961-62; lectr. U. So. Calif., Los Angeles, 1962-64; tchg. asst. U. Saskatchewan, Saskatoon, Can., 1962-64; lectr. U. Regina, Can., 1967-73; instr. U. Wis., Sheboygan, 1980-81; asst. prof. Coker Coll., Hartsville, S.C., 1981-83; tchg. asst. U. Tex., Richardson, 1983—. Served as staff sgt. USMC, 1942-46. Mem. MLA, Math. Assn. Am., COSMEP. Home: 2809 Custer 264 Richardson TX 75080

SAPP, EVA JO, b. San Antonio, Feb. 4, 1944, d. Herschel and Ada (Rasdon) Barnhill; m. David Paul Sapp, July 6, 1968; children—Lesley, Michael. Contrbr. fiction to N.Am. Rvw, Thornleigh Rvw, Epoch, The Sun, Kans. Qtly, Long Pond, Washington Rvw, Intro 15. BA, U. Mo., 1976, MA, 1982. Editorial asst. Mo. Rvw, Columbia, 1978-80, genl. fiction advisor, 1980-81, assoc. ed., 1981—; grad. tchr. U. Mo., Columbia, 1980-85, vis. lectr., 1985—. Recipient 2d place Mahan award U. Mo., 1981, 1st place award, 1983-84, McKinney prize, 1984. Mem. AWP, P&W. Home: 1000 Maplewood Columbia MO 65203

SARDEN, CLAUDIA, b. Waterbury, CT, Jan. 11. 1958; d. Claude, Sr. and Clementine (Young) Moss; m. Avery Monroe Sarden, June 30, 1982; 1 son, Avery Monroe, Author: Dolly: Memoirs of a High School Graduate, 1987. Contrr. poems to anthols., short stories to mag. B.S. in English Edn., Tuskegee U., 1980; M.A. in English Edn., Ga. State U., 1985. Secondary English tchr. Phoenix City Middle Schls., AL, 1980-82, DeKalb County Schls., Decatur, GA, 1981—. Home: 5348 Cayuga Ct Lithonia GA 30038

SARGEANT, NANCY REARDON, b. Providence, Oct. 30, 1933; d. Vincent and Margaret M. (Mackenzie) Reardon. Contrbr. to anthologies. B.Ed., RI Coll., 1955; MA, Boston U., 1958. Tchr. (Warwick, RI), 1955-57, 58-60, (Denver), 1957-58, (Burlington, MA), 1960-63; editor Houghton Mifflin Co. (Boston), 1963-67, supervising editor, 1967-74, exec. editor schl. reading dept., 1974-85, edl. dir., 1985—, reading cons. Mem. Intl. Reading Assn., New England Reading Assn., Bookbuilders. Office: One Beacon St Boston MA 02107

SARGENT, ROBERT STRONG, b. New Orleans, May 23, 1912; s. Harry B. and Hilah Estill (White) Sargent; m. Mary Jane Barnett, July 21, 1985. Author: Aspects of a Southern Story, 1983, A Woman From Memphis, 1981, Now Is Always the Miraculous Time, 1977. BS, Miss. State U., Starkville, Miss., 1933. Eng., Dept. of Defense, Wash., D.C., 1947-72. Served with US Navy, 1943-46. Mem. PSA. Home: 1435 4th St SW B-111 Washington DC 20024

SARRIS, ANDREW GEORGE, b. Bklyn., Oct. 31, 1928; s. George Andrew and Themis (Katavolos) Sarris; m. Molly Clark Haskell, May 31, 1969. Author: The Films of Josef Von Sternberg, 1966, Interviews with Film Directors, 1967, The Film, The American Cinema, both 1968, Confessions of a Cultist, 1970, The Primal Screen, 1973, The John Ford Movie Mystery, 1976, Politics and Cinema, 1978. AB, Columbia, 1951. Film critic Village Voice (NYC), 1960—; editor-in-chief Cahiers du Cinema in English; instr. Schl. Visual Arts, 1965-67, asst. prof. NYU, 1967-69; assoc. prof. films Columbia Schl. Arts (NYC)1969-81, prof., 1981. Served with Signal Corps AUS, 1952-54. Guggenheim fellow, 1969. Mem. Am. Film Inst. (dir.), Soc., Cinema Studies, Natl. Soc. Film Critics, NY Film Critics. Home: 19 E 88th St New York NY 10028

SARSON, EVELYN PATRICIA, see Kaye, Evelyn Patricia

SATCHELL, CAROL ALEXIS, b. Richmond, VA, Oct. 3, 1945; d. James Edward and Myrtle Ann (Lewis) Satchell; m. Russell Henry Gaines, Jr., Dec. 22, 1961 (div. 1980); children: Russell III, Myrtle, Kim, Aldophus, Helen. BS in English Lit., Va. Union. In sales, Richmond, 1981-83; cashier Pantry-Pride, Richmond, 1983-85; TV broadcaster J. Sears, 1984-85; radio broadcaster WDYL-FM, Chester, Va., 1984-86; ed. and pub., pres., Satchell's Pub. Co., Richmond, 1984-87. Mem. NOW, Natl. Orgn. Colored Women, NAACP. Address: 3124 Fifth Ave Richmond VA 23222

SATTER, MARLENE YVONNE, (Lee Barwood), b. Jersey City, NJ, Apr. 11, 1952; d. Henry Joseph and Jeanne Theresa (Calley) Barwood; m. Jack Wallace Satter, July 28, 1973. Author: (radio script) The Bells of Aedan Marsh, 1987. Contrbr. articles to mags., anthols. including Ellery Queen's Mystery Mag., Space and Time, Weirdbook, others. B.A. in French, Pace U., 1973. Technical ed., wrtr., 1973—. Mem. WORDS: The Ark. Lit. SOc., MWA, SPWAO, IWWG, Heart of Ozarks Theater Co. Office: Box 715 Salem AR 72576

SATTERFIELD, BEN, b. Bangor, ME, June 10, 1945; s. Hoyt O'Neal and Trudie Elizabeth (Bennett) S. Pub. poems, short stories, articles, one-act plays, other works in numerous publs. both popular and lit., such as Caper, Hustler, Gentleman's Companion, Knave, Men, Pub, S.C. Rvw, Nit & Wit, The Round Table, Earthwise, Southwest Rvw, Clock Radio, Uncle, Tex. Rvw, Alfred Hitchcock's Mystery Mag., Manhunt, Mike Shayne Mystery Mag., others. PhD, U. Tex., 1976. Served to capt. USAF, 1965-70; Vietnam. Mng. ed. Oasis Press, Austin, Tex., 1976-80, Impala Press, Austin, 1980—; most recent publ. edited: Twisted Planet Tails (fiction anthology), 1985. Home: 2710 La Mesa Dr Austin TX 78704

SATTLER, HELEN RONEY, b. Newton, IA, Mar. 2, 1921; d. Louie Earl and Hazel Iona (Cure) Roney; m. Robert Edward Sattler, Sept. 30, 1950; children—Richard Allan, Kathryn Ann Sattler Gatz. Author: Kitchen Carton Crafts, 1970, Holiday Gifts, Favors and Decorations, 1971, The Beginning to Read Puzzle Book, 1971, Sockcraft, 1972, The Eggless Cookbook, 1972, Recipies for Art and Craft Materials, 1973, Jar and Bottle Craft, 1974, Train Whistle, 1977, Nature's Weather Forecasters, 1978, Dollars from Dandelions, 1979, Brain Busters, 1980, Dinosaurs of North America, 1981, No Place for a Goat, 1981, Smallest Witch, 1981, Noses Are Special, 1982, Morgan the Whale, 1982, The Illustrated Dinosaur Dictionary, 1983, Fish Facts and Bird Brains, 1984, Baby Dinosaurs, 1984, Sharks, the Super Fish, 1986, Pterosaurs, the Flying Reptiles, 1987, Whales, Nomads of the Sea, 1987. Wrkg. on The World's Eagles and Tyrannosaurus and His Kin. B.S. in Edn., Southwest Mo. State Coll., 1946. Children's librarian public library, Kansas City, MO, 1948-49; tchr. Southwest Missouri, 1941-48, Lago Colony Schl., Aruba, 1949-50. Recipient Honor award Boston Globe/Hornbook, 1981, Outstanding Contribution to Children's Lit. award Central Mo. State U., 1984. Mem. Bartlesville Wordweavers, Okla. Wrtr.'s Fedn. (Cherub award 1979, 82), SCBW (Golden Kite award 1981, 84), AG. Home: 1245 Grandview Bartlesville OK 74006

SAUL, JOHN WOODRUFF, III, b. Pasadena, CA, Feb. 25, 1942; s. John Woodruff and Adeline Elizabeth (Lee) Saul. Author: Suffer The Children, 1977; Punish the Sinners, 1978, Cry for the Strangers, 1979, Comes the Blind Fury, 1980, When the Wind Blows, 1981, The God Project, 1982, Nathaniel, 1984; also other novels under pseudonyms. Student, Antioch Coll., 1959-60, Cerritos Coll., 1960-61, Mont. State U., Missoula, 1961-62, San Francisco State Coll., 1963-65. Bd. dirs. Deattel Theatre Arts, 1978-80. Mem. AG. Office: Rotrosen 318 E 51st St New York NY 10022

SAUNDERS, CATHERINE RUGGIE, b. Chgo, Oct. 17, 1951, d. Alexander Neal and Bernadine P. (Schaefer) Ruggie. Editor: Irises, 1978, Valentine, 1980, Meadowlark, 1981, Cross-Stitch, 1982; Night Shift, 1982 (contrbr.) Southwest Pass, 1983, Cold Snap, 1985 (contrbr.); illustrator: Roadsalt, 1976, Harry Grow Round the Mulberry Bush, 1975, Through a Prism Into White, 1973, Crackerjack Harry and His Box of Magic, 1974, Tulips, 1986, Lullaby, 1987; contrbr. to: Demon Letting, 1976 (illus.), New Am. Graphics., Datelines: 1978 Writer's Issue. Wrkg. on poetry chapbooks. MA, U. Wis.-Madison, 1975, MFA, 1976. Lectr. U. Wis., Madison, 1977-78; instr. Evanston Art Center, Ill., 1978-80, Columbia Coll., Chgo., 1979-80; asst. prof. Cameron U., Lawton, Okla., 1980-83, St. Assoc. Prof., Xavier Coll., Chgo., 1983—; vis. designer Sch. of Art Inst., Chgo., 1985—. Winner 1st place poetry contest Poets & Patrons Ann., 1979; grantee Cameron U., 1982. Artists Fellowship, Ill. Arts Council, 1986. Mem. Am. Printing History Assn., Soc. Typographic Arts, World Print Council. Home: 215 Gale River Forest IL 60305

SAUNDERS, DERO AMES, b. Starkville, MS, Sept. 27, 1913; s. Madison and Erin (Hearon) Saunders; m. Beatrice Nair, May 23, 1936; children—David, Richard. Contrbg. author: Why Do People Buy?, 1953, The Changing American Market, 1954; editor: The Portable Gibbon, 1952, The Autobiography of Edward Gibbon, 1961; co-editor: The History of Rome, 1958; chair editorial bd: Dartmouth Alumni mag., 1983—. AB, Dartmouth Coll., 1935; AM, Columbia U., 1938. Lectr., lecture mgr., contrbr. to various mags., 1936-42; with Fgn. Econ. Admin. (Washington and Cairo, Egypt), 1943-45, chief, 1945; assoc. editor Fortune mag., 1945-57; vp Med. and Pharm. Info. Bur., 1957-59; lectr. Hunter Coll., 1960-61, 67—; assoc. editor Forbes mag., 1960-62, sr. editor, 1962-66, exec. editor, 1966-81; contrbg. editor, 1982—. Home: 446 W 22nd St New York NY 10011

SAUNDERS, DORIS EVANS, b. Chgo., Aug. 8, 1921; d. Alvesta Stewart and Thelma (Rice) Evans; m. Vincent E. Saunders, Jr., Oct. 28, 1950 (div. Aug. 1963); children—Ann Camille Vivian, Vincent E. III. Host: radio program The Think Tank, 1971-72; writer, producer: TV show Our People, 1968-70; co-author: Black Society, 1976; assoc. editor: Negro Digent mag., 1962-66; editor: The Day They Marched, 1963. The Kennerdy Years and the Negro, 1964, DuBois: A Pictorial Biography, 1979, Wouldn't Take Nothin' for My Journey (L. Berry), 1981; compiler, editor: The Negro Handbook, 1966, The Ebony Handbook, 1974; pub. Kith and Kin. BA, Roosevelt U., 1951; MS, MA, Boston U., 1977. Sr. library asst. Chgo. Pub. Library, 1942-66, dir. book div., 1961-66, 73-77; prof. coordinator print journalism Jackson State U. (MS), 1977—; Dishng. minority lectr. U. Miss., Oxford, 1986; pres. Ancestor Hunting, Inc, Chgo, 1982—; dir. community relations Chgo. State Coll., 1968-70; columnist Chgo. Daily Defender, 1966-70, Chgo. Courier, 1970-73; staff. asso. Office of Chancellor, U. IL at Chgo. Circle, 1970-73. Secy. bd. Black Acad. Arts and Letters; past bd. dirs. South Side Com. Art Center, Chgo. Mem. Soc. Profl. Journalists, Natl. Assn. Media Women, Inc. Address: Box 2413 Chicago IL 60690

SAUNDERS, RUBIE AGNES, b. NYC, Jan. 31, 1929; d. Walter St. Clair and Rubie Gwendolyn (Ford) Saunders. Author: books, inclg. Calling All Girls Party Book, 1966, Marilyn Morgan, R.N., 1969, Marilyn Morgan's Triumph, 1970, Concise Guide to Baby Sitting, 1972, Concise Guide to Smart Shopping and Consumerism, 1973, Quick and Easy Housekeeping, 1977; The Beauty Book, 1983. BA, Hunter Coll., City U. NY, 1950. Editorial secy. Parents Mag. Enterprises, Inc. (NYC)1950-51, editorial asst.,

1951-53, asst. editor, 1953-54, mng. editor, 1955-60; editor Young Miss mag., 1960-80, editorial dir., 1967-80; instr. Inst. Children's Lit., 1980—. Bd. dirs. Feminist Press; secy. New Rochelle Council on Arts; elected to New Rochelle Bd. of Education, 1986-91. Home: 26 Glenwood Ave New Rochelle NY 10801

SAUNDERS, SALLY LOVE, b. Bryn Mawr, PA, Jan. 15, 1940; d. Lawrence and Dorothy (Love) Saunders. Poet: poems publ. in various periodicals; author: Pauses, 1978, Fresh Bread, 1982; contrbr. poems to newspapers. Student, Sophia U., Tokyo, Japan, 1963, U. PA, Columbia; BS, George Williams Coll., 1965. Tchr. Shipley Schl., Bryn Mawr, 1962-65, Agnes Irwin Schl. (Wynnewood, PA), 1964-65, Montgomery County Day Schl. (Wynnewood), 1962, Miquon Schl. (PA), Waldron Acad. (Merion, PA), 1965-66, Haverford Schl. (PA), 1965-66, Friends Se. Schl. (NYC)1966-68, Ballard Schl., 1966-67, Lower Merion Schl. (Ardmore, PA), nights 1967-71, Univ. Settlement House (Phila.), 1961-63, Navajo Indian Reservation (Fort Defiance, AZ), 1963, Young Men's Jewish Youth Center (Chgo.), 1964-65, Margaret Fuller Settlement House (Cambridge, MA), 1958-61; poetry therapist PA Hosp. Inst., 1969-74, also drug rehab. house (Phila.). Mem. AAP, Natl. Fedn. State Poetry Therapy Assn. (VP), Avalon OR., AG, Natl. Writers Club, Pen and Brush Club, JN, PA Poetry socs., Cath. Poetry Soc., FL State Poetry Soc, Pen and Pencil Club. Address: No. 36 C 1420 Locust St Philadelphia PA 19102

SAUTTER, R. CRAIG, b. Indpls., IN, Jan. 27, 1947, s. Robert Underwood and Virginia Belle (Mittendorf) S.; m. Sally Ann Reed Aug. 22, 1970. Poetry in Madison Rvw, Velvet Wings, Assembling, Central Park, Midway Rvw, other lit mags, NY Times, Chicago Tribune, Chicago Mag., Instructor, Electronic Learning, Illinois Issues, Jnl Soc. Midwestern Lit. BA, Indiana U., 1969; MA Philos., U. of Wis., 1972. Field Coord. Natl. Urban Lg., 1972-75; poet-in-residence, Livingston, Steuben, Wyo. counties, NY, 1976-78; Sr. Wrtr., Bradford Exchg., 1979-83; free-lance wrtr., Chgo., 1977—; philo., poli., lit., creative wrtg. tchr., DePaul U., 1980—. Contrbr. to Power of the Ballot, Select Guide to Colleges, ReadAbility (text) series, 1980; position paper wrtr., H. Washington, Mayor Chgo., 1983. Poetry ed., December mag., 1979—. Poet, IAC, 1985—. Mem. IWOC, Club d'Ronde. Home: 7658 N Rogers Ave Chicago IL 60626

SAVAGE, ROTH, see Kehrer, Daniel M.

SAVAGE, THOMAS U., (Tom Savage), b. NYC, July 14, 1948; s. Thomas U. and Anna (Joyce) S., Jr. Author: Personalities, Jim Brodey Books, 1978; (poems) Slow Waltz on a Glass Harmonica/Filling Spaces, 1980; contrbr. to City Mag., World, Telephone, The Little Mag., Abraxas, Portable Lower East Side, East Village Eye, Appearances, Blue Smoke, Ink, Little Caesar, River Styx, Roof, others; rep. in anthologies The Full Deck Anthology, Knock Knock. BA, Bklyn. Coll., 1969; MS, Columbia U., 1980. Ed. Roof Mag., 1976-77; ed. Gandhabba, 1983—; workshop leader Poetry Project, NYC, 1984-85. PEN grantee, 1978; CCLM fellow, 1984. Mem. P&W. Home: 622 E 11th St New York NY 10009

SAVETH, EDWARD NORMAN, b. NYC, Feb. 16, 1915; s. Isidor and Eva (Vasa) Saveth; m. Harriet Ostler, June 22, 1975; 1 son by previous marriage—Henry. Author: American Historians and European Immigrants, 1947; author, editor: Understanding the American Past, 1954, Henry Adams, 1963, American History and the Social Sciences, 1964; revisions editor: Encyc. Americana, 1962; contrbr. numerous articles to mags. BSS, CCNY, 1935; MA, Columbia U., 1937, PhD, 1946. Prof. history Grad. Faculty New Schl. for Social Research (NYC), 1960-63; Fulbright prof. Kyoto U. (Kyoto, Japan), 1964-65; prof. Dartmouth Coll, 1965-66; Disting. prof. SUNY-Fredonia, 1967—; lectr. USIA (Nepal), 1965, (Morocco), 1977; Fulbright prof. Hebrew U. (Jerusalem), 1981. Mem. Am. Hist. Assn., Orgn. Am. Historians. Home: 24 Westley Dr Fredonia NY 14063

SAVICKY, RANDOLPH PHILIP, b. Flushing, NY, Apr. 21, 1953, s. Joseph W. and Monica E. (Savage) S.; m. Barbara Panos, Dec. 22, 1979. Pres., RPS Communications; contrbr. articles to Newsday, Village Voice, Jazz Mag., Sound and Communications, Muses, New York Post, Music and Sound Output, other publs. BA in Journalism, SUNY-New Paltz, 1975. Editorial asst. Newsday, Garden City, N.Y., 1975-78; ed. Good Times, Greenvale, N.Y., 1978-80, Pharmacy Times, Port Washington, N.Y., 1980, Surgical Rounds, Port Washington, 1980-83; ed.-in-chief, Pro Sound News, NYC, 1983—; consultant Audio. Engineering Soc. Daily, Kitchen and Bath Bus. Daily. Mem. Sigma Delta Chi, N.Y. Press Club, L.I. Press Club. Office: Box 1122 Murray Hill Sta New York NY 10016

SAVOIE, TERRENCE MAURICE, b. Milw., Sept. 29, 1946, s. Maurice P. and Marie R. (Godin) S.; m. Donna Rae Meyer, Oct. 1, 1945; children—Pamela, Megan, Benjamin. Contrbr. poetry to Ploughshares, Black Warrior Rvw, Porch, 1981 Anthology of Mag. Verse and Yearbook of Am. Poetry, other publs. BA, Divine Word Coll., Epworth, Iowa, 1968; MA, U. Iowa, 1975. Tchr. public schls., Davenport, Iowa, 1975—. Home: 2219 Scott St Davenport IA 52803

SAVOY, DOUGLAS EUGENE, b. Bellingham, WA, May 11, 1927; s. Lewis Dell and Maymie (Janett) Savoy; m. Elvira Clarke, Dec. 5, 1957 (div.); 1 son—Jamil Sean (dec.); 2nd m. Sylvia Ontaneda, July 7, 1971; children—Douglas Eugene, Christopher Sean, Sylvia Jamila. Author: Antisuyo, The Search for Lost Cities of the High Amazon, 1970, Vilcambamba, Last City of the Incas, 1970, The Cosolargy Papers, vol. 1, 1970, vols. 2-3, 1972, The Child Christ, 1973, Arabic ed., 1976, Japanese ed., 1981, The Decoded New Testament, 1974, Arabic ed., 1981, The Millennium Edition of the Decoded New Testament, 1973, On The Trail of the Feathered Serpent, 1974, Code Book and Community Manual for Overseers, 1975, Prophecies of Jamil: First Prophecy to the Americas, 1976, Second Prophecy to the Americas, 1976, The Secret Sayings of Jamil: The Image and the Word, vol. 1, 1976, vol. 2, 1977, Project X—The Search for the Secrets of Immortality, 1977, Prophecy to the Races of Man, 1977, Solar Cultures of the Americas, 1977, Dream Analysis, 1977, Vision Analysis, 1977, Christoanalysis, 1978, The Essaei Document: Secrets of an Eternal Race, 1978, Millennium ed., 1983 The Lost Gospel of Jesus: Hidden Teachings of Christ, 1978, Millennium ed., 1984, Secret Saying of Jamil, vol. 4, 1978, Prophecy to the Christian Churches, 1978, The Sayings, vol. 3, 1978, vol. 4, 1979, Solar Cultures of Oceania, 1979, Prophecy of the End Times, 1980, Solar Cultures of Israel, The Holy Kabbalah and Secret Symbolism, vols. 1 and 2, 1980, Solar Cultures of China, 1980, Christotherapy, 1980, Christophysics, 1980, Christodynamics, 1980, Code Book of Prophecy, 1980, The Sayings, vol. 5, 1980, vol. 6, 1981, Solar Cultures of India, 1981, Prophecy on the Golden Age of Light and the Nation of Nations, vol. 5, 1981, Solar Cultures of Israel, 1981, The Counsels, 1982, Prophecy of the Universal Theocracy, vol. 6, 1982, Prophecy of the New Covenant, 1982, The Book of God's Revelation, 1983, Miracle of the Second Advent, 1984; numerous others; contrbr. articles on Peruvian cultures to mags., also articles on philosophy and religion. Student, U. Portland. Engaged in newspaper publishing, West Coast, 1949-56, began explorations in jungles east of Andes in Peru to prove his theory that high civilizations of Peru may have had their origin in jungles, 1967; pres., founder Andean Explorers Fdn. and Ocean Sailing Club, Reno; ordained minister; D.C.L.; Trustee in Trust and Episcopal Head Bishop of Intl. Community of Christ; chancellor, founder Sacred Coll. of Jamilian Theology; founder, pres. Jamilian U. of Ordained; pastor Chapel of Holy Child (Reno, NV). Served with AS USNR, 1944-46. Mem. Geog. Soc. Lima, AG, Explorers Club (N.Y.C.). Home: 2025 La Fond Reno NV 89509

SAVREN, SHELLEY, b. Cleve., June 7, 1949, s. Albert E. and Helen (Wieder) S.; 1 child, Talia. Author: (poems) Gathering My Belongings, 1983, Photo Album, 1987; contrbr. poetry to Poet's Pride, Day Tonight/Night Today, Deepest Valley Rvw, San Diego Mag., Maize, Cafe Solo, numerous others. Poet tchr. Calif. Poets in Schls., San Diego, 1976-86, San Diego Unified Schl. Dist., 1986-88; poet-in-res. Chula Vista City Schls., Calif., 1978-86; artist-in-res. Calif. Arts Council, San Diego, 1979-82 and 1986-88; grant recipient COMBO/Ntl. Ednowment for the Arts, 1986-87. mng. ed. The Longest Revolution, 1979-82. Mem. AWP, Calif. Poets in Schls., Fdn. for the Community of Artists. Home: 4604 Niagara Ave San Diego CA 92107

SAWYER, BARBARA JEAN, b. Ft. Bragg, CA, May 31, 1920, d. Robert Dixon and Esmeralda (Wolvin) Magner; m. Harvey Haywood Greene, Dec. 18, 1933 (dec. 1941); 1 dau., Ellen Ann; m. 2d, Bruce Garrett Sawyer, Sept. 1, 1952. Staff wrtr. The View, 1977; wrtr., ed. newsletters, 1981—. Wrkg. on novel, short stories. Student Fresno City Coll., 1961-62. Staff wrtr. Citizens' Communications Com., Mountain View, Calif., 1977. Home: 33303 Mission Space 13 Union City CA 94587

SAWYER, CORINNE HOLT, b. Chisholm, MN, Mar. 4, 1924; d. Grover Justine and Grace Margaret (Ueland) Holt; m. Robert Turnham Rickert, Sept. 2, 1947 (div. Sept. 1965); m. Hugh Alton Sawyer, Jr., Aug. 22, 1966 (dec. Aug. 1968). Author: The Case of John Darrell, Minister & Exorcist, 1962; adaptor Huckleberry Finn for children's theatre, 1946; contrbr. articles to The Best of Pogo, Studies in Popular Culture, Jnl Popular Film & TV, Jnl Geography, Jnl Popular Culture; ed. The 4077 Newsletter, 1983-85. BA, U. Minn., 1945, MA, 1947; PhD, Birmingham U., Engl., 1954. Instr. speech and English, U. Md. Overseas, Engl., 1954-58; coordinator closed circuit TV, East Carolina U., Greenville, N.C., 1958-66; prof. English, Clemson U., S.C., 1966—, dir. acad. spl. programs, 1982—. Mem. Popular Culture Assn. (Russell B. Nye award 1986). Home: 123 Houston St Clemson SC 29631

SAWYERS, JUNE, b. Glasgow, Scotland, Oct. 8, 1957; came to U.S., 1966; d. Thomas Charles Sawyers and Elizabeth Muir Lawson Porter. Columnist: Chgo. Tribune Sunday Mag., 1986—. Author hist. brochure for Lincoln Park C of C, 1983; contrbr. articles to Chgo. Tribune, Stagebill, Backstage. Ed., pub.: Celtic Fringe, 1986—. Wrkg. on books. B.A. in English/History, Northeastern Ill. U., 1980. Advt. coord. Putman Pub. Co., Chgo., 1981-83; copy ed., researcher Feature Group News Service, Chgo., 1985-86; ed. Jacobsen Pub. Co., Chgo., 1984—. Mem. Chgo. Women Pub. Home: 6145 W Giddings Chicago IL 60630

SAXON, DIRK, see Ewing, Jack

SAXTON, LA VERNE YOUNG, b. De Queen, AR, Feb. 26, 1921; d. Elmer Joseph and Elizabeth Morris (Jones) Young; m. Winfield Carey Saxton, Mar. 1, 1946; children—Becky, Beth, Carrie, Billy, James, Josie. Contrbr. non-fiction, inspirational articles, articles, poems to mags., newspapers including Woman's Day, Wrtr.'s Digest, Guideposts. Columnist: Madison County Herald, 1982. Billing clrk. Herb Battery, Kansas City, MO, 1947-48; free-lance wrtr., 1968—. Served as WAVE in U.S.N. Radio Intelligence, 1943-45. Recipient trophy for poem Madison-Ridgeland Acad., MS, 1974; several awards Greenwood Arts Festival, MS. Home: 303 Hwy 51 N Madison MS 39110

SAXTON, MARK, b. Mineola, NY, Nov. 28, 1914; s. Eugene Francis and Martha (Plaisted) Saxton; m. Josephine Porter Stocking, June 27, 1940 (dec. 1967); children—Russell Steele, Martha Porter. Author: Danger Road, 1939, The Broken Circle, 1941, The Year of August, 1943, Prepared for Rage, 1947, Paper Chase, 1964, The Islar, 1969, The Two Kingdoms, 1979, Havoc in Islandia, 1982; rvws. for NY Herald-Tribune Books, 1957-62. AB, Harvard U., 1936. Newspaper, mag. and radio work, 1936-38; asst. editor Farrar & Rinehart (NYC), 1938-43; assoc. editor Rinehart & Co., 1946; exec. editor William Sloane Assoc., 1946-50; editor McGraw-Hill Book Co., 1950-52; promotion mgr., editorial adviser Harvard U. Press (Cambridge, MA), 1952-68; editor-in-chief, dir. Gambit, Inc. (Ipswich, MA), 1968-80; mem. staff Breadloaf (VT) Writers Conf., summers 1947-51, 60. Served to Lt. (j.g.) USNR, 1943-46. Home: 41 E 28 St New York NY 10016

SAYKO, GENE J., b. Trenton, NJ, Feb. 14, 1939; s. Eugene and Margaret (Deak) Szajko; m. Kathleen Angela Zuczek, Apr. 25, 1964; children—Elizabeth, Kathleen, Jennifer. BS, Rider Coll., 1961. Copywriter, Flacks-Abramshon, Trenton, NJ, 1959-60; newswriter Radio WTTM, Trenton, 1960-61; rptr./city ed. Burlington County Times, Willingboro, NJ, 1961-64; rptr./asst. mng. ed. Trenton Times (NJ), 1964-81; ed. Metropolitan Purchasor, 1981-85; ed. Mercer Bus. Mag., Trenton, 1981—. Served to Sp4, U.S. Army, 1957-58. Mem. Bucks County Press Assn., Burlington County Press Assn. Office: Box 8307 Trenton NJ 08650

SAYRE, ROBERT FREEMAN, b. Columbus, OH, Nov. 6, 1933; s. Harrison M. and Mary (White) Sayre. Author: The Examined Self: Benjamin Franklin, Henry Adams and Henry James, 1964 and 1988, Adventures, Rhymes and Designs of Vachel Lindsay, 1968, Thoreau and the American Indians, 1977; ed.: Thoreau's "A Week . . . , Walden, Maine Woods, Cape Cod," 1985. PhD, Yale U., 1962. Instr. English U. IL, Urbana, 1961-63; Fulbright lectr. Lund U. (Sweden), 1963-65, Montpellier, France, 1984; mem. faculty U. Iowa, 1965—, prof. English, 1972—; dir. inter-profl. seminars NEH, 1978, 79. Guggenheim fellow, 1973-74. Mem. Am. Studies Assn., Midwestern MLA. Address: Eng Dept Univ Iowa Iowa City IA 52242

SCALES, ALTHEA E., b. Bklyn., Apr. 6, 1951, d. Rufus and Ida (Boone) Scales. Contrbr. short stories to Touch Mag., Radar, Teens Today, other mags.; contrbr. poetry to Northwoods Jnl, Young Publs., Poetry Press. BS in Bus. Edn., Bernard Baruch Coll., 1976; MA in Bus. Edn., NYU, 1980. Bus. education instr., 1976-87. Presently secretary, Citicorp/Citibank. Mem. NWC. Home: 187-50 Hilburn Ave Saint Albans NY 11412

SCARBROUGH, GEORGE ADDISON, b. Benton, TN, Oct. 20, 1915, s. William Oscar and Louise Anabel (McDowell) S. Author: (poetry) Tellico Blue, 1949, The Course Is Upward, 1951, Summer So-Called, 1956 (named one of best books of yr. N.Y. Times), New and Selected Poems, 1978, (novel) A Summer Ago, 1986; contrbr. to 17 anthologies, over 50 periodicals, including Coll. English, Natl. Forum, Atlantic, Harper's, Sat. Rvw Lit., New Republic, Qtly Rvw Lit., Sewanee, Chgo., Vanderbilt Poetry, Miss., S.W. rvws, Poetry. BA, Lincoln Meml. U., Harrogate, Tenn., 1947; MA, U. Tenn., 1954. Tchr. secondary schls. and jr. colls., 18 yrs.; staff poetry reviewer Chattanooga Times, 40 yrs. Recipient Borestone Mountain award, 1961, Mary Rugeley Ferguson poetry award Sewanee Rvw, Sheena Albanese Meml. prize in poetry Spirit Mag., Outstanding Tennessean award in lit., 1978. Home: 100 Darwin Ln Oak Ridge TN 37830

SCARINO, MARIANNE CANNAVA, b. Bklyn., Nov. 10, 1951, d. Giuseppe and Rachel Ann (Bonsignore) Cannava; m. Luigi Roberto Scarino, July 21, 1973. Contrbr. to Riverrun, PC Mag., Graduating Engr., Computer Careers. BA summa cum laude, Bklyn. Coll., 1983. Recipient Whiteside poetry award Bklyn. Coll., 1982, Lois Goodman short story award, 1983, Grebanier sonnet award, 1983. Home: 553 Brighton 10 Ct Brooklyn NY 11235

SCHAAF, FREDERICK CARL, b. Cumberland, NJ, Dec. 8. 1954; s. Frederick Carl and Olive Jean (Ireland) S.; m. Mame Lena Hockenbury, Oct. 20, 1984. Author: Wonders of the Sky, 1983, (with Guy Ottewell) Mankind's Comet, 1985; ed. Dark Skies for Comet Halley Jnl., 1984-86; contrbr. to Astronomy Mag., Old Farmer's Almanac, Mother Earth News Almanac, Atlantic City Press, Sky and Telescope, Sci., Smithsonian's Scientific Event Alert Network Bulln., others. AB in Engl. lit., Muhlenberg Coll., 1978; MA in Engl. lit., SUNY-Binghamton, 1980. Home: 706 E St Millville NJ 08332

SCHAAF, RICHARD EDMUND, (Mike Mathews)b. Akron, OH, June 2, 1949; s. Edmund Richard and Marjorie Helen (McCormick) S.; m. Betty Jean Schlatter, Oct. 14, 1972; children—Michael Steven, Matthew Donald. Assoc. ed. The Dairyman mag., 1969; mng. ed. Training: The Mag. of Human Resources Devel., 1980-81; business historian: St. Paul: A Modern Renaissance, 1986, City of Lakes: An Illustd. Hist. of Mpls., 1982; co-author Wheelchair Bowling: A Complete Guide to Bowling for the Handicapped, 1980; natl. ed. AAA World; sr. ed. Dazzle; contrbg. ed. Wing Elite; contrbr. arts to mags. incl.: Redbook, TWA Ambassador, Corporate Rpt., New West, Calif. Bus., Playgirl, The Exec., others, 1975—. BA in Jnlsm., San Jose State U., 1975. Freelance writer, Newport Beach, CA, 1975-80; mng. ed. Training mag., Mpls., 1980-81; bus. ed. Twin Cities Public TV, St. Paul, 1982-83; sr. writer Hill & Knowlton, Mpls., 1983-84, sr. ed., The Webb Co., St. Paul, 84-85; instr., mag. writing, U. MN, 1985; acct. supvr. Dunstan & Assocs., Mpls., 1985-86; freelance writer/author/consultant, 1986—. Mem. SPJ, MN Press Club. Home: 14080 Garland Ave S Apple Valley MN 55124

SCHAAP, JAMES CALVIN, b. Oostburg, WI, Feb. 17, 1948, s. Calvin and Jean Harriet (Dirkse) S.; m. Barbara Kaye Van Gelder, June 27, 1972; children—Andrea Jane, David Michael. Author: Sign of a Promise and Other Stories, 1979, CRC Family Portrait, 1983, Intermission, Breaking Away with God, 1985, Thirty-Five and Counting, 1986, Home Free, 1986. BA, Dordt Coll., 1970; MA, Ariz. State U., 1974; PhD, U. Wis.-Milw., 1985. Prof. Dordt Coll., Sioux Center, Iowa, 1976-80, 82—. Recipient working scholarship Bread Loaf Wrtrs. Conf., Middlebury, Vt., 1980. Mem. MLA. Home: 347 3d Ave NE Sioux Center IA 51250

SCHAAP, RICHARD JAY, b. NYC, Sept. 27, 1934; s. Maurice William and Leah (Lerner) Schaap; m. Barbara M. Barron, June 20, 1956 (div. 1967); children—Renee Beth, Michelle Anne; 2nd m. Madeleine Gottlieb, Aug. 29, 1967; children—Jeremy Albert, Joanna Rose; 3rd m. Patricia Ann McLeod, May 17, 1981; children—Karen Joan, David Maurice. Author (26 books), RFK, 1967, Turned On, 1967, (with Jerry Kramer) Instant Replay, 1968, Distant Replay, 1985, (with Jimmy Breslin) 44, 1980, Steinbrenner!, 1982. BS, Cornell U., 1955; MS, Columbia U., 1956. Sr. editor Newsweek (NYC), 1956-63; city editor NY Herald Tribune, 1964-66; correspondent NBC (NYC), 1971-80; ABC (NYC), 1980—. Served to Lt. U.S. Army, 1957-58. Office: ABC 47 W 66th St New York NY 10023

SCHAAR, FRANCES ELIZABETH, b. Fond du Lac, Wis., Mar. 25, 1911, d. Leon Gustav and Anne Fredricka (Hoppe) Schaar. Contrbr. numerous articles to Jnl Am. Med. Assn., Jnl Lab. and Clin. Medicine, Jnl Pediatrics, other profl. publs. MS, U. Wis.-Madison, 1938; MD, U. Ill., 1946. Practice medicine specializing in pediatrics, Mpls., 1953-70; dir. employee health service Univ. Hosps., U. Minn., Mpls., 1970-73; student health service physician No. Ill. U., 1973-78; instr. continuing edn. for nurses Normandale Community Coll., North Hennepin Community Coll., Mpls., 1978—. Home: 8115 Kentucky Ave Minneapolis MN 55438

SCHACHT, RICHARD LAWRENCE, b. Racine, WI, Dec. 19, 1941; s. Robert Hugo and Alice (Munger) S.; m. Marsha Ruth Clinard, Aug. 17, 1963; children—Eric Lawrence, Marshall Robert. Author: Alienation, 1970, Hegel and After, 1975, Nietzsche, 1983, Classical Modern Philosophers, 1984. BA, Harvard U., 1963; MA, Princeton U., 1965, PhD, 1967; postgrad., Tubingen U., 1966-67. Asst. prof. U. IL, Urbana-Champaign, 1967-71, assoc. prof., 1971-80, prof., 1980—; vis. prof. U. Oreg., 1969, U. Pitts., 1973, U. Mich., 1979; vis. scholar Tubingen U., 1975. Mem. AAUP, Am. Philo. Assn., N. Am. Nietzsche Soc., Intl. Sociol. Assn. Office: U IL 810 S Wright St Urbana IL 61801

SCHACHTER, HINDY LAUER, b. NYC, May 8, 1945, d. George and Doris (Trenk) Lauer; m. Irving Schachter, Dec. 4, 1967; 1 child, Amanda Cathleen. Author: Public Agency Communication, 1983; contrbr. poems and stories to Midstream, Jewish Frontier, Response; articles to New Leader, Pub. Adminstrn. Rvw, Pub. Personnel Mgmt. PhD, Columbia U., 1978. Asst. prof. N.J. Inst. Tech., Newark, 1979-84, assoc. prof., 1984—. Home: 420 E 64th St New York

NY 10021

SCHAEFER, VERNON JOSEPH, b. Dundee, MN, Dec. 30, 1919; s. Joseph Nicholas and Magdalen Rosalia (Knott) S. Author: We Ate Gooseberries, 1974; columnist Courier, 1959-76; syndicated columnist rural newspapers, 1974-87. Student St. Mary's Coll., Winona, Minn., 1937-39; St. Paul Seminary, 1939-45. Ordained priest Roman Cath. Ch., 1945. Priest Cath. Ch., Winona, Minn., 1945-86. Mem. Natl. Wrtrs. Club. Home: Box 1057 Eyota MN 55934

SCHAEFFER, SUSAN FROMBERG, b. Bklyn., Mar. 25, 1941; d. Irving and Edith (Levine) Fromberg; m. Neil J. Schaeffer, Oct. 11, 1970; children—Benjamin Adam, May Anna. Author: (poems) The Witch and the Weather Report, 1972, Granite Lady, 1974, Rhymes and Runes of the Toad, 1975, Alphabet for the Lost Years, 1976, The Bible of the Beasts of the Little Field, 1980; (novels) Falling, 1973, Anya, 1974, Time in Its Flight, 1978, Love, 1981, The Madness of a Seduced Woman, 1983, Mainland, 1985, The Injured Party, 1986; (short fiction) The Queen of Egypt, 1980; (children's novel) The Dragons of North Chittendon, 1986. BA, U. Chgo., 1961, MA, 1963, PhD, 1966. Asst. prof. Brklyn. Coll., 1967-71, assoc. prof., 1971-73, prof., 1973-84, Broeklundian prof. English, 1984—. Recipient Edward Lewis Wallant award Prairie Schooner, 1984, Friends of Lit. award, 1984, Lawrence award, 1984; Poetry award Centennial Rvw., 1985; O. Henry award, 1978; Guggenheim fellow, 1984-85. Mem. PSA, AG, PEN. Home: 783 E 21st St Brooklyn NY 11210

SCHAFER, EDWARD HETZEL, b. Seattle, Aug. 23, 1913; s. Edward Hetzel and Lillian (Moorehead) Schafer; m. Phyllis Brooks, Sept. 7, 1971; children from previous marriage—Tamlyn, Julian, Kevin. Author: The Empire of Min, 1954, Tu Wan's Stone Catalogue of Cloudy Forest, 1961, The Golden Peaches of Samarkand, 1963, Ancient China, 1967, The Vermilion Bird, 1967, Shore of Pearls, 1970, The Divine Woman, 1973, Pacing the Void, 1977, Mirages on the Sea of Time, 1985; editor: Jnl Am. Oriental Soc., 1958-64; contrbr. articles to profl. jnls. AB in anthropology, U. Calif., Berkeley, 1938, PhD in oriental langs., 1947; MA, U. Hawaii, 1940; postgrad., Harvard U., 1940-41. Lectr. in Oriental langs. U. Calif., Berkeley, 1947, asst. prof. Oriental langs., 1947-53, assoc. prof., 1953-58, prof., 1958-69; Agassiz prof. Oriental langs. and lit., 1969—. Served with USNR, 1941-46. Guggenheim fellow, 1953-54, 68-69. Mem. Am. Oriental Soc. (past pres.), Medieval Soc. Am. Home: 60 Avis Rd Berkeley CA 94707

SCHAIN, RICHARD, b. New York, NY, Oct. 16, 1930; s. Maurice and Beatrice (Gaier) Schain; m. Melanie Dreisbach, Aug. 15, 1980; 1 son—Eliot Schain. Author: Affirmations of Reality, 1982, Philosophical Artwork, 1983, A Contemporary Logos, 1984, Sententiae, 1984, Sentences in Small Spaces, 1985. AB, MD New York U. Assoc. prof. U. of Nebraska (Omaha), 1962-66; prof. UCLA (Los Angeles), 1967-83. Capt. US Air Force, 1955-57, US. Home: Box 517 Glen Ellen CA 95442

SCHALLER, GEORGE BEALS, b. Berlin, May 26, 1933; s. George Ludwig S. and Bettina (Byrd) Iwersen; m. Kay Suzanne Morgan, Aug. 26, 1957; children: Eric, Mark. Author: The Mountain Gorilla, 1963 (Wildlife Soc. 1965), The Year of the Gorilla, 1964, The Deer and the Tiger, 1967, The Serengeti Lion, 1972 (Natl. Book award 1973), Golden Shadows, Flying Hooves, 1973, Mountain Monarchs, 1977, Stones of Silence, 1980, The Giant Pandas of Wolong, 1985. B.S. in Zoology, U. Alaska, 1955; B.A. in Anthropology, 1955; Ph.D. in Zoology, U. Wis., 1962. Fellow Ctr. Advanced Study in Behavioral Scis., Stanford U., 1962; fellow Guggenheim Fdn., 1971. Office: New York Zool Soc Bronx Park Bronx NY 10460

SCHANSTRA, CARLA ROSS, (Ross Child, Chris Thomson), b. Berwyn, IL, Sept. 4, 1954; d. Caroles Schanstra and Heather Millar (Thomson) Alonso. Contrr.: Chgo. Tribune, Wrtr.'s Showcase, The Book Mart, numerous other publs. Wrkg. on plays, poetry. BA, Western Ill. U., 1976; postgrad., U. Ill., Chgo., 1980-81. Assoc. ed. Hitchcock Pub. Co., Wheaton, Ill., 1976-80; assoc. product mgr. Advanced Systems Inc., Elk Grove Village, Ill., 1980-81; tech. wrtr. Profl. Computer Resource, Oak Brook, Ill., 1982; sr. tech. wrtr. AT&T Bell Labs., Naperville, Ill., 1982—. Mem. Wrtrs. Workshop (co-founder), Soc. Tech. Communication (Award of Excellence 1985), Dramatists Guild. Home: 2 S 709 Winchester Circle Warenville IL 60555

SCHAPIRO, NANCY, b. St. Louis, Apr. 24, 1929, d. Julius and Dena (Oxenhandler) Cohen; m. Edward D. Schapiro, Nov. 28, 1950; children—Barbara Schapiro Scott, Ellen Schapiro Axelbaum, Jane Schapiro Brown. BA, Washington U., 1950, MA, 1965. Asst. ed. Perspective, St. Louis, 1960-74; ed., pub. Webster Rvw, St. Louis, 1974—; adj. prof. Webster U., St. Louis, 1974-82. Office: Webster 470 E Lockwood St Webster Groves MO 63119

SCHAPPES, MORRIS U(RMAN), b. Kamenets-Podolsk, Podolia, Ukraine, May 3, 1907, came to U.S., 1914, s. Haim (Shapshilevich) and Alta Ida (Urman) Shapiro; m. Sonya Laffer, Apr. 6, 1930. Author: Letters from The Tombs, 1943, Selections Prose and Poetry Emma Lazarus, 1944, 5th ed., 1982, The Letters of Emma Lazarus, 1949, A Documentary History of the Jews in the U.S., 1654-1965, 1950, 3d ed., 1971, The Jews in the U.S.A., 1654-1954, A Pictorial History, 1958, 2d ed., 1965, Emma Lazarus' "An Epistle to the Hebrews," 1986; contrbr. articles, poetry to: Sat. Rvw, N.Y. History, Jewish Life, Morning Freiheit, numerous other publs. Wrkg. on revision of The Jews in the U.S.A., A Pictorial History. BA, CCNY, 1928; MA, Columbia U., 1930. Mem. editorial bd. Jewish Life monthly, NYC, 1946-56; ed.-in-chief Jewish Currents monthly, NYC, 1957—; tutor, Eng. dept., CCNY, 1928-41, adj. prof. history Queens Coll., CUNY, 1972-76. Recipient Tercentenary award Emma Lazarus Fedn. Jewish Women's Clubs, 1954, Zhitlovsky award Zhitlovsky Fdn. Jewish Secular Edn., 1969, Holocaust Meml. award N.Y. Soc. Clin. Psychologists, 1979. Mem. Am. Jewish Hist. Soc., Jewish Hist. Soc. N.Y. (bd. dirs. 1984—), Am. Hist. Assn. Home: 700 Columbus Ave 8E New York NY 10003

SCHARDEIN, SANDRA WILD (KATHERINE SELBY), b. Bethesda, MD, Sept. 21, 1946; d. Gelbert Selby Wild, Sr. and Dorothy Marcella (Klapatch) W.; m. David Lee Schardein, Aug. 10, 1968; children—Thomas, Amy, Paul. BA cum laude, Ursuline Coll., 1968; postgrad., U. Louisville, 1971-73. Student asst. English Dept. Ursuline Coll., Louisville, KY, 1964-68; claims adj. Liberty Mutual Ins., Louisville, 1968-73; admin. asst. Neighborhood Dev. Corp., Louisville, 1974-79; ed. Kentuckiana Purchasor, Louisville, 1983—. Office: Box 35428 Louisville KY 40232

SCHECTER, JOEL R., b. Washington, June 21, 1947. Author: Durov's Pig: Clowns, Politics and Theatre, 1985, plays; contrbr. essays to Drama Review, Nation, New York Times, In These Times, Partisan Rvw, Brecht Yearbook, American Theatre; ed.: THEATER Mag., 1977—. BA, Antioch Coll., 1969; MFA, Yale U., 1972, DFA, 1973. Lectr., New School for Soc. Research, NYC, 1974; asst. prof. SUNY, Stonybrook, NY, 1974-77; literary adv. Amer. Place Theater, NYC, 1974-77; asst. & assoc. prof. Yale School of Drama, New Haven, 1977—. Mem. Brecht Soc. Office: Drama Schl 222 York St New Haven CT 06520

SCHEDLER, GILBERT WALTER, b. Vancouver, BC, Can., Mar. 11, 1935; s. Oscar August and Margaret (Barth) S; m. Pat Blumenthal, 1964 (div. 1973); children: Christopher, Rachel; m. 2d, Nancy Dunkak, 1975 (div. 1983) 1 dau., Sara. Author: College Study Guide in Am Lit (2 vols.), 1966; poems: Waking Before Dawn, 1978, Making Plans, 1980, That Invisble Wall, 1985. BD, Concordia Seminary, 1957-60; MA, Wash. Univ., 1960-63; PhD, U. Chgo., 1964-70. Vicar St. Matthew Luth. Ch., NYC, 1958-59; instr. Wash. Univ. St Louis, Mo, 1962-63; asst. prof. Wittenberg Univ., Springfield, Ohio, 1963-64; assoc. prof. Callison Coll., Stockton, Calif., 1967-76; prof. Coll. of the Pacific, Stockton, 1977—. Recipient NDEA fellowship, Washington U, 1960-63; IIE scholarship, U. Edinburgh, Scotland, 1963; Rockefeller Doctoral fellowship, 1966-7. Address: 1718 Oxford Way Stockton CA 95204

SCHEEL, MARK W., b. Emporia, KS, Jan. 25, 1943; s. Dale Alvord and Ethyle Lillian (Hundertmark) S. Contrbr. poetry to Encore, Heritage of Kans., Samisdat, Little Balkans Rvw, Pudding Mag., Rhyme Time, Cincinnati Poetry Rvw., Art/Life, The Gauden State. Contrbr. short stories to Artifact, Telescope, Sunrust, The Researcher Chronoscope, Facet. Contrbr. articles to Cycle Guide, Emporia State Research Studies, Nit & Wit, Writer's Newsletter, Alura Qtly, Listen, Pteranodon, Emporia Gazette, Star. BA, U. Kans., 1967; postgrad. Emporia Kans. State Coll., 1976-77. Asst. field dir. ARC, U.S., Vietnam, Thailand, W.Ger., Eng., 1968-72, field rep., Ft. Worth, 1973; teaching asst. Emporia Kans. State Coll., 1976; freelance writer, farm worker, Emporia, 1978—, creative wrtg. inst., Upward Bound, Emporia State U., 1986. Vol. Friends of Library, Emporia, 1978—; vol. researcher Poets & Writers, Inc., NYC (for Kans. region), 1980, 82, 84, 87; contest judge Emporians for Nuclear Disarmament (essay contest), Lyon County, Kans., 1983. Mem. Kans. Writers Assn., Natl. Writers Club, NWU. 1st place story contest Emporia Gazette, 1983, featured poet, Piedmont Literary Rvw. 10-Yr. Anthol., 1986; 8th place NWC book manuscript contest, 1986. Home: RR 2 Emporia KS 66801

SCHEELE, ROY MARTIN, b. Houston, Jan. 10, 1942, s. Elmer Martin and Hazel Ilene (McChesney) S.; m. Frances McGill Hazen, June 26, 1965; children—Evan, Christof. Author: Grams & Epigrams (broadside, poems), 1973, Accompanied (poetry chapbook), 1974, Noticing (poetry chapbook), 1979, The Sea-Ocean (poetry collection), 1981, Pointing Out the Sky (poetry), 1985 (nominee, 1986 William carlos Williams Award); contrbr. poetry to Prairie Schooner, Poetry, Sewanee Rvw, other publs., anthologies; contrbr. essays, rvws. to Pebble, S.C. Rvw, Southwest Rvw, others. BA, U. Nebr., 1965, MA, 1971. Instr. in English, U. Tenn., Martin, 1966-68, Theodor Heuss Gymnasium,

Waltrop, W.Ger., 1974-75; instr. classics Creighton U., Omaha, 1977-79; vis. lectr. classics U. Nebr., Lincoln, 1980-81; instr. English as 2d lang. Midwest Inst., Doane Coll., Crete, Nebr., 1982—. Winner 1st prize John G. Neihardt Fdn., Bancroft, Nebr., 1983. Home: 2020 S 25th St Lincoln NE 68502

SCHEIDHAUER, LYNN IRENE, b. Pitts., Feb. 11, 1955; d. W. Phillip and Dolores Marie (Bahler) S. Contrbr. article to mags. Ed.: Forward, 1977-79, Profile (award of Merit, NPRA, 1980), 1981-85, On the Land, 1981-85, Bankers at their Best, 1985, Suburbanite, 1985-86. B.A. magna cum laude in Writing, U. Pitts., 1977. Ed., dir. public info. Hood Coll., Frederick, MD, 1979-81; ed., mgr. internal communications Nature Conservancey, Alington, VA, 1981-85; ed. Suburban Bank, Bethesda, MD, 1985-86; regional mktg. officer, Sovran Bank, 1986—. Recipient Quill and Scroll Award Am. Newspaper Pubs., 1972. named Most Valuable Staffer, 1973. Mem. SPJ, IABC, Wrtrs. Center. Home: 11652 S Laurel Dr 3A Laurel MD 20708

SCHEIN, JEROME, b. Mpls., May 27, 1923, s. Adolph and Jeanette (Green) S.; m. Enid Gordon, Apr. 18, 1982. Author: The Deaf Community, 1968, The Deaf Population of the United States, 1974, Speaking the Language of Sign, 1984. Wrkg. on book on deafness. PhD, U. Minn., Mpls., 1958. Mem. faculty U. Wis., Madison, 1958-59, Fla. State U., Tallahassee, 1959-60, Gallaudet Coll., Washington, 1960-68; dean U. Cin., 1968-70; prof. NYU, NYC, 1970—; chair of deaf studies, Gallaudet Univ., 1986-87. Recipient Intl. medal World Fedn. of Deaf, Rome, 1975. Mem. N.Y. Soc. for Deaf (pres. 1976-86). Home: 1703 Andros Isle J-2 Coconut Creek FL 33066

SCHELL, JONATHAN EDWARD, b. NYC, Aug. 21, 1943; s. Orville H. and Marjorie Bertha Schell. Author: The Village of Ben Suc, 1967, The Military Half, 1968, The Time of Illusion, 1975, The Fate of the Earth, 1982, The Abolition, 1984. Staff writer New Yorker Mag., 1967—. Office: NY Mag 25 W 43rd St New York NY 10036

SCHELL, ROLFE FINCH, b. Keeseville, NY, Nov. 28, 1916; s. Lindsley Bernard and Helen (Finch) S.; m. Elizabeth Blandy, Oct. 28, 1938 (div. 1970); children—Elizabeth, Barbara, Lynn; m. 2d, Lois Wilcox, Dec. 5, 1971. Author: Album Maya, 1973, Aloysius Alligator, 1966, DeSoto Didn't Land at Tampa, 1965, Eat, Fast and Stay Slim, 1967, Florida's Fascinating Everglades, 1963, 1,000 Years on Mound Key, 1962, Schell's Guide to Eastern Mexico, 1973-74, Schell's Guide to Eastern Mexico 1975, Tigger, 1966, Yank in Yucatan, 1963. Wrkg. on, translation of Popol Vuhtia Pala, 1560 Mayan book. EE, Cornell U.; Rensselaer Poly. Inst. Freelance wrtr., 1956-66, 71-75; owner, ed. Mad Shopper newspaper, Fort Myers Beach, Fla., 1968-71. Home: 175 Bahia Via Fort Myers Beach FL 33931

SCHEPP, BRAD JEFFREY, b. Phila., Sept. 14, 1955; s. Marvin J. and Arlene Lois (Pincus) S.; m. Debra Ann Sorkowitz, Aug. 21, 1977; 1 dau., Stephanie Ruth. Author: (with Stephen Hastie) The Complete Passive Solar Home Book, 1985 (cited by LJ as among best sci-tech bks. 1985). Contrbr. articles, chpts. on energy, agoraphobia, job hunting to books, trade, profl., genl. interest pubs. Contrbg. editor: Home Remedies—Cures for America's Dwellings, 1981. BA in Communications, Rutgers Coll., New Brunswick, N.J., 1977. Wrtr., ed. The Franklin Inst., Phila., 1979-83; features wrtr. Inst. for Sci. Info., Phila., 1983-84; assoc. ed. Datapro Research Corp., Delran, N.J., 1984—. Telephone vol. Contact, Atlantic County, Atlantic City, N.J., 1977; mem. Solar Lobby, Washington, 1979—. Recipient Authors cert. N.J. Inst. Tech., 1986; recipient Award for Journalistic Excellence, Datapro Research Corp., 1987. Mem. AG, AL Am., Mid-Atlantic Solar Energy Assn. (bd. dirs.). Home: 601 Windsor Pl Moorestown NJ 08057

SCHERMAN, SUSAN LOUISE, b. Hoboken, N.J., Apr. 20, 1953; d. Everett Harold and Louise Annetta (Becker) S.; m. John Alfred Pendenza, Oct. 6, 1979. Author: Community Health Nursing Care Plans: A Guide for Home Health Care Professionals, 1984. BA in Health Sci., Jersey City State Coll., 1978; R.N., St. Mary Sch. Nursing, Hoboken, 1974. Supvr. pub. health nursing Hoboken Pub. Health Nursing Service, 1980-83; nurse cons. N.Y. County Health Services Rvw. Orgn., NYC, 1983-86; nurse cons. Bower & Gardner, NYC Mem. Soc. Scribes, Natl. Intravenous Therapy Assn. Home: 7 Cooper Pl Weehawken NJ 07087

SCHEVILL, JAMES ERWIN, b. Berkeley, CA, June 10, 1920; s. Rudolph and Margaret (Erwin) S.; m. Margot Helmuth, Aug. 2, 1966; children (by previous marriage): Deborah, Susanna. Author: poems Tensions, 1947, The American Fantasies, 1951; (biography) Sherwood Anderson: His Life and Work, 1951; musical play High Sinners, Low Angels, 1953; (poems) The Right to Greet, 1956; (biography) The Roaring Market and the Silent tomb, 1956; (verse play; commd. Nat. Council Chs. and Central Congl. Ch., Providence 1954) The Bloody Tenet, 1957; Selected Poems, 1959, The Cid, 1961, Private Dooms and Public Destinations; (play for voices; commd. Natl. Council Chs.) Voices of Mass. and Capital A, 1962; The Stalingrad Elegies, 1964, The Black President and Other Plays, 1965, The Buddhist Car, 1968, Violence and Glory; Poems, 1962-68, 1969, Lovecraft's Follies; (play) Breakout: In Search of New Theatrical Environments, 1973; (poems) The Buddhist Car and Other Characters, 1973, Pursuing Elegy: A Poem about Haiti, 1974; (play) Cathedral of Ice, 1975; (novel) The Arena of Ants, 1977; The Mayan Poems, 1978; (poems) Fire of Eyes: A Guatemalan Sequence, 1979; The American Fantasies: Collected Poems, 1945-81, 1983, Collected Short Plays, 1986, The Invisible Volcano (long poem), 1985, Oppenheimer's Chair (play), 1985, Collected Short Plays, 1986, Ambiguous Dancers of Fame: Collected Poems 1945-1986, Vol. II, 1987. B.S., Harvard U., 1942, M.A., Brown Univ., Hon. Dr. of Humane Ltrs., Rhode Island Coll., 1986. Mem. faculty San Francisco State Coll., 1959—, dir. Poetry Center, 1961-67, prof. English, 1968; prof. Brown U., 1968—. Served with AUS. 1942-46. Recipient Performance prize Natl. Theatre Competition, 1945; fellow Fund Advancement Edn., 1953-54; 2d prize Phelan Biography Competition, 1954; 2d prize Phelan Drama Competition, 1958; Fromm Fdn. commn., 1959; Ford Fdn. grantee, 1960-61; Rockefeller fellow, 1964; Roadstead Fdn. award, 1966; Gov.'s Award in Arts, R.I., 1975; Guggenheim fellow, 1981-82; McKnight Fellowship in Playwriting, 1984; 1985 Poetry Prize, The Centennial Rvw., Mich. State Univ. Home: 17 Keene St Providence RI 02906

SCHICK, JAMES BALDWIN MC DONALD, b. Lafayette, IN, Oct. 3, 1940; s. George Baldwin Powell and Grace Elizabeth (McDonald) S.; m. Marjorie Krask, Aug. 17, 1963; 1 son, Robert McDonald. Contrbr. articles to The History Tchr., Orgn. Am. Historians Newsletter, The Midwest Qtly, History Microcomputer Rvw, The Practice of History and Social Sci., Social Science Microcomputer Rvw; ed.-in-chief: Midwest Qtly, 1981—, History Microcomputer Rvw, 1985—, The Practice of History and Social Sci., 1977—. MS, U. Wis., 1963; PhD, Ind. U.-Bloomington, 1971. Instr. U. Kans., Lawrence, 1966-67; asst. prof. history Pitts. State Univ., Kans., 1967-72, assoc. prof., 1972-79, prof., 1979—. Precinct committeeman Dem. Party Kans., Pitts., 1976—. Recipient of grant from Commn. on Bicentennial for U.S. Constitution. Mem. Am. Hist. Assn., Orgn. Am. Historians. Home: 607 West Euclid Pittsburg KS 66762

SCHICKEL, RICHARD, b. Milw., Feb. 10, 1933; s. Edward J. and Helen (Hendricks) Schickel; children—Erika Tracy, Jessica Avery. Author: The World of Carnegie Hall, 1960, The Stars, 1962, movies: The History of an Art and an Institution, 1964, The Gentle Knight, 1964, The Disney Version, 1968, The World of Goya, 1968, Second Sight: Notes on Some Movies, 1972, His Picture in the Papers, 1974, Harold Lloyd: The Shape of Laughter, 1974, The Men Who Made the Movies, 1975, The World of Tennis, 1975, The Fairbanks Album, 1975, Another I, Another You, 1978, Singled Out, 1981, Gary Grant, 1984, W. W. Griffith, 1984, Intimate Strangers: The Culture of Celebrity, 1985; co-author: Lena, 1965. The Platinum Years, 1974; co-editor: film 67-68, 1968; producer, dir., writer: TV series The Men Who Made the Movies, 1973; producer-writer: TV spl. Life Goes to the Movies, 1976, SPFX, 1980; producer, writer, dir.: Funny Business, 1978, Into the Morning: Willa Cather's America, 1978, The Horror Show, 1979, James Cagney: That Yankee Doodle Dandy, 1981. BS U. Wis., 1955. Sr. editor Look mag., 1957-60, Show mag., 1960-63; self-employed, 1963—; film critic Life mag., 1965-72, Time mag., 1965; lectr. in history art Yale, 1972, 76. Guggenheim fellow, NY Film Critics. Address: 311 E. 83d St New York NY 10028

SCHICKER, GLENN EARL, b. Houghton Lake Heights, MI, Apr. 27, 1950; s. Earl Joseph and Doreen Estelle (Yaster) S.; m. Christine Diane Ball, May 14, 1972; children: Mathew, Joshua. Contrbr. articles: Christian Living, Home Life, Good News Broadcaster, John Milton Mag., Moody Monthly, Youth Alive!, Gurney's Gadening News, Grit, numerous other publs. BA, Central Mich. U., 1972. Reporter Houghton Lake (Mich.) Resorter, 1972, reporter, ed., 1974—. Served with U.S. Army, 1972-74. Home: 5070 North Cut Rd Roscommon MI 48653

SCHIEFFELIN, LAURIE GRAHAM, b. Evanston, IL, Nov. 22, 1941; d. Thomas Harlin and Mary Elisabeth (Stoner) Graham; m. George McKay Schieffelin, Dec. 12, 1980. Student, Mt. Holyoke Coll., 1959-61; BA, U. CO., 1963. Editor, Charles Scribner's Sons (NYC), 1969—. Bd. dirs. Musicians Emergency Fund. Mem. PEN. Office: 115 Fifth Ave New York NY 10003

SCHILLER, HERBERT I., b. NYC, Nov. 5, 1919; s. Benjamin Franklin and Gertrude (Perner) Schiller; m. Anita Rosenbaum, Nov. 5, 1946; children—Daniel T., P. Zachary. Author: Mass Communications and American Empire, 1969, Superstate: Readings in the Military-Industrial Complex, 1970, The Mind Managers, 1973, Communication and Cultural Domination, 1976, Who Knows: Information in the Age of the Fortune 500, 1981, Information and the Crisis Economy, 1984; editor: Qtly Rvw Econ. and Bus., 1963-70, National Sovereignty and Intl. Communication, 1979. BSS, CCNY, 1949; MA, Columbia, 1941; PhD, NYU, 1960. Teaching fellow CCNY, 1940-41; lectr. econ., 1949-59; economist U.S. Govt., 1941-42, 46-48; mem. faculty Pratt Inst. (Bklyn.), 1950-63, prof. econ., chair dept. social studies, ,62-63; research assoc. prof. Bur. Econ. and Bus. Research U. IL at urbana, 1963-65, research prof., 1965-70; prof. communications U. CA at San Diego, 1970—; lectr. Bklyn. Acad. Music, 1961-66; vis. fellow Inst. Policy Studies (WA), 1968; vis. prof. U. Amsterdam (Netherlands), 1973-74; Thord-Gray vis. lectr. U. Stockholm, 1978; vis. prof. communications Hunter Coll., City U. NY, 1978-79. Served with AUS, 1942-45; MTO. Mem. AAAS, Intl. Assn. mass Communication Research (VP), Intl. Inst. Communications (trustee 1978-84), AAUP. Home: 7109 Monte Vista La Jolla CA 92037

SCHIMMEL, CAROLINE FEAREY, b. NYC, June 2, 1944; d. John Lawrence and Mary Lavell (White) Fearey; m. Stuart Barr Schimmel, Apr. 14, 1977. Co-editor: Thomas W. Streeter Collection, vols. 5-7, 1968-70, John Fass: Printer, 1978, Aucassin and Nicolette: A Bibliography, 1976, A Bibliography of Materials Containing Information on Decorated Paper, 1982. AB, U. Pa., 1967; MLS, Columbia U., 1976. Cataloguer, appraiser rare books Sotheby Parke Bernet (NYC), 1968-70; asst. editor Limited Editions Club, 1970-73; exec. secy. Bibliog. Soc. Am. (NYC), 1969-81; researcher Am. Book Prices Current (NYC), 1978-80. Mem. Guild Book Workers (pres.). Home: 2 Beekman Pl New York NY 10022

SCHIRM, KAREN MARIE, b. La Crosse, WI, Nov. 19, 1946; d. Perry Drake and Marjory Eloise (Quarterman) Anderson; m. William Lee Schirm, Sept. 24, 1966; children—Kristi Lee, John Brian. Ed.: River City Rvw, 1976—, Midwestern 4-Wheeler, 1979—; contrbg. wrtr.: United's Voice, 1979—; contrbr.: National Poetry Anthology, 1962, Petersen's 4 Wheel & Off Road Mag., Tri-Power, Dirt News. Student pub. schls., La Crosse, WI. Home: 3118 Howry St La Crosse WI 54603

SCHLACHTER, GAIL ANN, b. Detroit, Apr. 7, 1943; d. Lewis E. and Helen (Blitz) Goldstein; children—Sandra Elyse, Eric Brian. Author: Lib. Sci. Disserts.: An Annotd. Bibliog., 1925-72, 1974, Directory of Internships, 1975, Minorities & Women: A Guide to the Ref. Lit. in the Soc. Sciences (Choice Outstanding Acad. Bk., 1977), 1976, Directory of Finl. Aids for Women, 1978—, for Minorities, 1984— (biennial pubs.), and numerous other lib. and finl. aid pubs. BA, U.C. Berkeley, 1964; MA in Hist./Educ., U.WI, 1966; MA in Lib. Sci., U.WI, 1967; PhD in Lib. Sci., U.MN, 1971; MPA, U.S.C., 1979. Head Commons Lib., U.WI, Madison, 1967-68; asst. prof. U. So.CA, Los Angeles, 1971-74; lib. dept. head CA State U. Library, Long Beach, 1974-76; asst. lib. dir. U. CA, Davis, 1976-81; v.p. & gen. mgr. ABC-CLIO, Santa Barbara, CA, 1981-85; pres. Reference Svc. Press, Los Angeles, 1985—. Mem. ALA, Calif. Lib. Assn. Office: 3540 Wilshire Blvd 310 Los Angeles CA 90010

SCHLAFLY, PHYLLIS STEWART, b. St. Louis, Aug. 15, 1924; d. John Bruce and Odile (Dodge) Stewart; m. Fred Schlafly, Oct. 20, 1949; children—John F., Bruce S., Roger S., Phyllis Liza Forshaw, Andrew L., Anne V. Author, pub: Phyllis Schlafly Report, 1967—; author: A Choice Not an Echo, 1964, The Gravediggers, 1964, Strike From Space, 1965, Safe Not Sorry, 1967, The Betrayers, 1968, Mindszenty The Man, 1972, Kissinger on the Couch, 1975, Ambush at Vladivostok, 1976, The Power of the Positive Woman, 1977, Equal Pay for UNequal Work, 1984, Child Abuse in the Classroom, 1984, Pornography's Victims, 1987. BA, Washington U. (St. Louis), 1944, JD, 1978; MA, Harvard U., 1945; LLD, Niagara U., 1976. Bar: Ill. bar 1979, D.C. bar 1984, Mo. bar 1985, Supreme Court bar, 1987. Syndicated columnist Copley News Service, 1976—; pres. Eagle Forum, 1975—. Mem. IL Commn. on Status of Women, 1975-85; natl. chair Stop ERA, 1972—; mem. Ronald Reagan's Def. Policy Adv. Group, 1980, Commn. on the Bicentennial of the U.S. Constitution, 1985-91. Address: 68 Fairmount Alton IL 62002

SCHLEEF, HELEN IDA, b. Sioux City, IA, Apr. 4, 1914. d. Ture and Nell May (Lawrey) Carlson; m. Carl Schleef, Apr. 21, 1934 (dec. 1982); 1 dau., Patricia. Author: A Window to Art, 1967; contrbr. poetry to N.Am. Mentor Mag., Iowa Poetry Day Brochures, Lyrical Iowa, numerous other publs.; contrbr. art and poetry articles Cherokee (Iowa) Daily Times. Matron, cook Cherokee County (Iowa) Jail, 1947-67. Recipient Poetry Achievement award, 1970, numerous other awards. Mem. Cherokee Wrtrs. Home: 608 W Cedar St Cherokee IA 51012

SCHLESINGER, ARTHUR (MEIER), JR., b. Columbus, OH, Oct. 15, 1917; s. Arthur M. and Elizabeth (Bancroft) Schlesinger; m. Marian Cannon, 1940 (div. 1970); children—Stephen Cannon, Katharine Kinderman, Christina, Andrew Bancroft; 2nd m. Alexandra Emmet, July 9, 1971; 1 son—Robert Emmet Kennedy. Author: Orestes A. Brownson, 1939, The Age of Jackson, 1945, The Vital Center, 1949, The General and the President (with R.H. Rovere), 1951, The Crisis of the Old Order, 1957, The Coming of the New Deal, 1958, The Politics of Upheaval, 1960, Kennedy or Nixon, 1960, The Politics of Hope, 1963, A Thousand Days, 1965, The Bitter Heritage, 1967, The Crisis of Confidence, 1969, The Imperial Presidency, 1973, Robert Kennedy and His Times, 1978, The Cycles of American History, 1986; film reviewer: Show mag., 1962-64, Vogue, 1967-72, Saturday Rvw, 1977-80, Am. Heritage, 1981-82. AB, Harvard U., 1938, mem. Soc. of Fellows, 1939-42; postgrad. Cambridge U. (England), 1938-39. With OWI, 1942-43, OSS, 1943-45; assoc. prof. history harvard U., 1946-54, prof., 1954-61; vis. fellow (Inst. Advanced Study), Princeton (NJ), 1966; Schweitzer prof. humanities City U. NY, 1966—; spcl. asst. to Pres. of U.S., 1961-64; Mem. jury Cannes Film Festival, 1964; Mem. Adlai E. Stevenson campaign staff, 1952, 56; trustee Twentieth Century Fund, Robert F. Kennedy Meml.; bd. dirs. John F. Kennedy Library, Harry S. Truman Library Inst. Served with AUS, 1945. Recipient Pulitzer prize for History, 1946, Pulitzer prize for Biography, 1966, Natl. Book award, 1966, 79, Natl. Inst. Arts and Letters Gold Medal for History, 1967, Fregene prize for lit. (Italy), 1983. Office: 33 W 42nd St New York NY 10036

SCHLEY, JAMES POWRIE, b. Milw., Nov. 13, 1956, s. Edward George and Imogene (Powrie) S. Ed.: Writing in a Nuclear Age, 1985. BA, Dartmouth Coll., 1979; MFA, Warren Wilson Coll., Swannanoa, N.C., 1986. Co-ed, New Eng. Rvw, Hanover, N.H., 1980—; mem. small press tech. assistance adv. bd. NEA, New Eng., 1983-84. Bread Loaf Wrtrs.' Conf. scholar, 1983; grantee N.H. Commn. on Arts, 1984. Office: Box 170 Hanover NH 03755

SCHLIPF, FREDERICK A., b. Fargo, ND, Sept. 14, 1941; s. Stewart and Ruth (Sulerud) S.; m. Diane Hillard, Aug. 7, 1965; 1 son—Karl Frederick Hillard Schlipf. Author: The New York Public Library: A Background Paper, 1965, Trends in Branch Lib. Use Related to Commun. Characteristics, 1966, Copying and Duplicating Practices in Am. Educ., 1966; ed. The Hist. of Champaign County, 1984 (reprint of 1905 ed.), Combined 1893, 1913 and 1929 Atlases of Champaign County, Ill., 1984, Collective Bargaining in Illinois, 1975, Upon a Quiet Landscape: The Photographs of Frank Sadorus (with Raymond Bial), 1983, and others; contrbr. reviews & articles to mags. and jnls. BA, Carleton Coll., 1963; MA, U. Chgo., 1966, PhD, 1973. Instr., U. Chgo., 1966-70; asst. prof. U. IL, 1970-74, adjunct prof., 1974—; exec. dir. The Urbana Free Library (IL), 1974—. Mem. ALA, IL. Lib. Assn. Home: 804 West Vermont Urbana IL 61801

SCHMADEKA, DELORES, (Delores Stacy), b. Pierce, ID, Mar. 15, 1933; d. Charles W. and Margaret Ione (Bigelow) Stacy; m. William H. Schmadeka, May 28, 1977; children—Randolph Marshall, Rodney Marshall (dec.). Author: Whatever Happened to the Kids from Pierce?, 1985, Love, Chrissie, 1986. BS in Edn., U. Id.-Moscow, 1963; MA in Gen. Studies, Oregon State U., 1967. Tchr. Ind. pub. schls., Lewiston, Id., 1963-66, 69— Cut Bank Jr. High Schl., Mont., 1967-69. Me. NEA, Am. Bus. Women's Assn., Id. Wrtr.'s League, Pacific Northwest Wrtr.'s Conf. Home: 504 Karin Ave Lewiston ID 83501

SCHMIDT, ANDREA GERTRUD, b. Varel, W.Germany, Aug. 18, 1960; came to U.S., 1968; d. Heinz Horst and Helga Gertrud (Dubig) Schmidt; m. William Benjamin Carver, Jr., June 15, 1979 (div. 1981); children—William Carver III (dec.), Anthony Schmidt, Eric Schmidt, Jeremy Schmidt (dec.). Contrbr. puzzles: Dell Puzzle Mags., Official Puzzle Mags., Penny Press Puzzle Mags. Home Box 312 Elkhart IN 46515

SCHMIDT, DIANE JOY, b. Lake Forest, IL, Oct. 10, 1953, d. Dr. John L. and Miriam E. (Friedman) Schmidt. Author: The Chicago Exhibition, 1985; contrbr. photographic portfolio to Abstract Relations (by T. E. Connor), 1980; contrbr. photographs and photo essays to genl. interest publs., including Chicago, Chicago Tribune, Time, The Reader, and publ. in Germany, France, Japan. BA, Prescott Coll., 1974; BFA, R.I. Schl. Design, 1976. Photographer, wrtr., Chgo., 1977—. Recipient NEA Midwest Regional Visual Arts Fellowship, 1987. Home: 2259 Sheridan Rd Highland Park IL 60035

SCHMIDT, GEORGE NEIL, (Neil Flanigan, Laura Del Vecchio, Jim McCoy), b. Rlizabeth, NJ, Sept. 28, 1946; s. Neil George and Mary (Lanigan) S.; m. Linda Haase, Aug. 22, 1970 (div. Oct. 1985). Contrbr. numerous articles on public edn. in Chgo. to edl. mags. Wrkg. on book: Omnipotence Ids a Four-Letter Word: The Strange Case of James Moffat; articles. B.A., U. Chgo., 1969. Assoc. ed. Substance Monthly Jnl., Chgol, 1975—; English Tchr. Amundsen High Schl., Chgo., 1984—. Recipient Merit cert. Intl. Reading Assn., 1983, Disting. Achievement award EO Press Assn., 1983. Mem. NWU. Home: 5018 N Hermitage Chicago Il 60640.

SCHMIDT, TOM V., b. San Francisco, Apr. 5, 1939, s. Winston Rowland and Irma (Liljequist) S.; m. Karen Jean Toepfer Aug. 20, 1976; 1 child, Alyssa Emily. Contrbr. to New Am. and Can. Poetry, Poetry Reading, Antioch Rvw, Field,

Hanging Loose, Pinchpenny, Poet News, others. BA, San Francisco State U., 1962, MA, 1965. Instr. English, American River Coll., Sacramento, 1965-76; artistic dir., clarinetist Backwoods Jazz, Nevada City, Calif., 1981—; clarinetist The Baret Bros., Davis, Calif., 1984—; poet-in-res. pub. schls., Rio Linda, Calif. Recipient award James D. Phelan Fdn., 1970. Mem. Sacramento Poetry Ctr. (Buffalo Club poetry award 1984). Home: 8036 Clalifornia Ave Fair Oaks CA 95628

SCHMITT, BETTY J., b. Dodge City, KS, Jan. 12, 1936; d. Eddie Vernon and Velda Esther (Fullerton) Lembright; m. Eugene F. Cave, July 5, 1953 (div. Nov. 1970); children—Vance, Brett; m. John E. Schmitt, Dec. 26, 1973. Contrbr. poems. to anthols. Wrkg. on short story, novels. Diploma, Wrtr.'s Inst., 1985. Contract specialist Dept. Housing and Urban Devel., Denver, 1980-86, contracting officer, 1986—. Recipient Golden poet award World of Poetry, 1985, 86, 87, Honorable Mention, 1983-86, Spcl. Mention cert., 1984. Home: 1348 S Drexel Way Lakewood CO 80226

SCHMITZ, DENNIS, b. Dubuque, IA, Aug. 11, 1937; s. Anthony and Roselyn (Schwartz) Schmitz; m. Loretta D'Agostino; children—Anne, Sara, Martha, Paul, Matthew. Author: We Weep for Our Strangeness, 1969, Double Exposures, 1971, Goodwill, Inc., 1976, String, 1980, Singing, 1985. BA, Loras College, 1959; MA, U. of Chgo., 1961. Instr., Ill. Inst. of Tech., Chgo., 1961-62; instr., U. of Wis., Milw., 1962-66; prof., Cal. State U., Sacramento, 1966—. Awards: Guggenheim fellowship, 1978. NEA fellowship, 1976, 1985. Mem. AWP, PEN, PSA. Home: 1348 57th St Sacramento CA 95819

SCHMUHL, MARIAN HOBBS, b. Washington, June 18, 1945; d. Robert Boyd and Barbara A. (Davis) Hobbs; m. Edward H. Schmuhl, Jan. 22, 1972; children—Edward Jr., Suzanne K. Ed.: Iris Soc. Mass. Newsletter, 1981-84, Region One Am. Iris Soc. Bulltn., 1983-86, The Medianite publ. of Median Iris Soc., 1984—; contrbr. articles to spl. interest publs. Wrkg. on bulltn. editing. BA, Tufts U., 1967. Librarian Arthur D. Little, Inc., Cambridge, Mass., 1967-75. Home: 7 Revolutionary Ridge Rd Bedford MA 01730

SCHNEEBAUM, TOBIAS, b. NYC, Mar. 25, 1922, s. Jacob and Rivka (Ehrenfreund) S. Author: Keep the River on Your Right, 1969, Wild Man, 1979, Asmat: Life with the Ancestors (with Gunter Konrad and Ursula Konrad), 1981, Asmat Images, 1985. BA, CCNY; MA, Goddard Coll. Lectr. in primative art New Schl., 1984—. Fulbright fellow, Peru, 1955, 56; CAPS fellow, 1974; Rockefeller Rdn. fellow, 1984; grantee JDR 3d Fund, Asmat, Indonesia, 1975, 80. Me. PEN. Home: 463 West St Apt 627A New York NY 10014

SCHNEEMAN, PETER HENRY, b. St. Paul, Sept. 18, 1937, s. Lambert Joseph and Edith Rosetta (Fritz) S.; m. Liane Truetsch, Sept. 12, 1964; children—Kristin, Andrea. Author: Through the Finger Goggles: Stories, 1982; contrbr. stories to New Am. Rvw, Am. Rvw, Salmagundi, numerous anthols. BA, U. Minn., Mpls., 1960, MA, 1967, PhD, 1972. Asst. prof. Pa. State U., 1971-81, assoc. prof. dept. English, 1982—. Yaddo fellow, 1973, 81; sr. Fulbright lectr. in Am. Lit., Bucharest, Romania, Council for Intl. Exchange Scholars, 1978; fiction writing fellow Pa. Council on Arts, 1981, 85; Commonwealth speaker, Pa. Humanities Council, 1985. Mem. AWP. Office: Burrowes Bldg Pa State University Park PA 16802

SCHNEEMANN, CAROLEE, b. Fox Chase, PA, Oct. 12, 1939. Author: Parts of a Body House Book, 1972, Cezanne, She Was a Great Painter, 1974, ABC—We Print Anything—in the Cards, 1977, More Than Meat Joy: Complete Performance Works & Selected Writings, 1979. Contrbr. articles to books. Student pub. schols. Founding mem. Judson Dance Theater, NYC, 1962; dir., founder Kinetic Theater, NYC, 1964; adv. Performing arts Jnl, NYC, 1982-84, High Performance Mag., 1985—. Fellow, CAPS, 1978-79, NEA, 81, 85; grantee N.Y. State Council on the Arts, 1968. Mem. Women Artist Filmmakers. Home 114 W 29th St New York NY 10001

SCHNEIDER, BEN ROSS, JR., b. Ben Ross and Jean Kimball (Taylor) S.; m. Mackay McCord; children—Devon, Ben III, Nicholas, Mackay. Author: Wordsworth Portraits: a Biographical Catalogue, 1950, Wordsworth's Cambridge Education, 1957, Themes and Research Papers (with H.K. Tjossem), 1961, The Ethos of Restoration Comedy, 1971, Travels in Computerland, 1974, Index to the London State, 1660-1800, 1978, My Personal Computer and Other Family Crises, 1984; contrbr. articles on lit. and computing to various publs. BA, Williams Coll., 1942; postgrad. Cambridge (Eng.) U., 1949-50; PhD, Columbia U., 1955. Mem. faculty Lawrence U., Appleton, Wis., 1955—, prof. emeritus. Served as sgt., U.S. Army, 1942-45. Grantee NEH, 1971-75, U.S. Steel Fdn., 1971-73, Mellon Fdn., 1973-78, Am. Philo. Soc., 1975-78, ACLS, 1975-78. Fellow Royal Soc. Arts; mem. MLA, Soc. Theatre Research (U.K.), Am. Soc. Eighteenth Century Studies, Shakespeare Assn. Am. Home: 826 E Alton St Appleton WI 54911

SCHNEIDER, C. REX, b. Butler, PA, Feb. 22, 1937, s. Cyril Leo and Alice Elizabeth (Jewell) S. Author, illustrator: The Wide- Mouthed Frog, 1980, Ain't We Got Fun?, 1982, And That's Not All, 1985; illustrator children's lit. for Schoolzone, Troll Press, Stemmer House, others. BS in Art Edn., Ball State U., 1959. Art ed. Performance Weekly Newspaper, 1972-74; graphics dir. Gerstung Intersport, Balt., 1974-80; freelance wrtr., illustrator, Balt., 1976—. Recipient Silver Medal, Atlanta Intl. Film Festival, 1969. Mem. Graphic Artists Guild. Home: 70038 Treasure Island Union MI 49130

SCHNEIDER, DUANE BERNARD, b. South Bend, IN, Nov. 15, 1937; s. William H. and Lillian L. (Pitchford) Schneider; m. JoAnne Bennett, Feb. 1, 1959 (div. Nov., 1986); children—Jeffrey, Eric, Lisa, Emily. Author: An Interview with Anais Nin, 1973, A Thomas Wolfe Collection, 1977, (with others) Anais Nin: An Introduction, 1979; contrbr. numerous articles to scholarly jnls. BA, Miami U. (Oxford, OH), 1958; MA, Kent State U., 1969; PhD, U. CO, 1965. Instr. engring., English U. CO, 1960-65; asst. prof. English Ohio U. (Athens), 1965-70, assoc. prof., 1970-75, prof., 1975—; dir. Ohio U. Press, 1986—; chair dept. English, 1983-86, chair Faculty Senate, 1981-83; editor, pub. Croissant & Co., 1968—. Mem. Thomas Wolfe Soc. (trustee, pres., 1979-81), MLA. Home: 3363 Windfall Ridge Athens OH 45701

SCHNEIDER, VIRGINIA DEE, b. Chgo., Aug. 3, 1914; d. Joseph S. and Marie D. (Rumins) Dee; m. Raymond E. Schneider, May 9, 1936 (dec. 1979); childen—Cathy Sue, Kenneth. Contrbr.: Lady's Circle, Grit, True Romance, New World, Parent's, Modern Maurity, Bread, Catholic Digest, Children's Playmate, numerous other publs.; poetry in anthologies. Wrkg. on novel, inspirational fiction. Student public and parochial schls., Chgo. Freelance wrr., 1964—; lit. chmn. St. Gerald's Ch., Oak Lawn, Ill., 1968-70; public relations chmn. Garden Sch. for Handicapped, Oak Lawn, 1966-76, Brother James Ct., Springfield, Ill., 1976-86. Mem. NWC. Home: 135 Cottonwood Cove Estates Springfield IL 62702

SCHNEIDER, YVETTE E., b. NYC, Nov. 19; d. Martin Gerald and Elaine (Schulman) Schneider. Author: Title of Truth (poetry chapbook), 1984, Power of Hunger (poetry chapbook), 1985, The Healing (essays, poetry), 1986, Under the Skin of the City (poetry chapbook), 1987. Wrkg. on novel. Ed., pub. Poetessa Press, East Rockaway, N.Y., 1984—. Mem. AG, IWWG, AAP, Feminist Writing Guild. Office: Box 420 East Rockaway NY 11518

SCHNEPF, MAX OWEN, b. Rock Rapids, IA, Oct. 26, 1941; s. Arthur Paul and Ida Louise (Oehmke) S.; m. Linda Lee Massa, Nov. 29, 1963; children—Max Otis, Michael Jon, Molly Anne. Ed.: Farmland, Food and the Future, 1979. Editor: Jnl of Soil and Water Conservation, 1965—; contrbr. Soil Conserv.: Assessing the National Resources Inventory, vol. 2, 1986. BS in Jnlsm./Fish & Wildlife, Iowa State U., 1964. Ed. of publs. Iowa Conservation Commn., Des Moines, 1964-65, Soil Conserv. Soc. of Amer., Ankeny, IA, 1965—. Mem. Soc. for Technical Communic., Council of Biology Eds., The Wildlife Soc., Amer. Soc. of Agronomy. Office: Soil Cons 7515 N E Ankeny Rd Ankeny IA 50021

SCHNITZER, CHRISTINE A., b. Dayton, OH, June 26, 1955; d. Edward Allen and Dolores (Ritchie) Hildbold. Assoc., Columbus Tech. ints. Pub.:...having writ...1984-87; Pub. Vimach Assocs., Columbus, Ohio, 1984-86; graphic artist Am. Ceramic Soc., 1985-87, mng. ed. Ceramic Abstracts, Am. Ceramic Soc., 1987—. Address: 3161 Columbus St Grove City OH 43123

SCHNURR, CONSTANCE BURKE, b. Lynn, MA, Feb. 5, 1932; d. John Edmund, Jr., and Beatrice Therese (Feero) Burke; m. William Bernhardt Schnurr, Nov. 28, 1959. Author, illustrator: (juvenile) The Crazy Lady, 1969. BA, Wellesley Coll., 1953; postgrad. Columbia U., 1960-62. Curatorial asst. Essex Inst., Salem, Mass., 1957-59; adminstrv. asst. Rockefeller U., 1970-75; personnel specialist FMC Corp., Phila., 1976—. Home: 124 Boxwood Ln Cinnaminson NJ 08077

SCHNURR, WILLIAM BERNHARDT, b. Utica, NY, Feb. 8.; s. Herman Albert and Eileen Rosemary (Casey) S.; m. Constance Burke, Nov. 28, 1959. Author: Johnnie Death, 1974. Contrbr. articles to popular mags. BA, Syracuse U., Utica, 1950. Wrtr., supvr. Young & Rubicam, Inc., NYC, 1951-60; free-lance wrtr., NYC, 1960-75, Cinnaminson, N.J., 1975—. Recipient Best Comml. of Yr., Advt. Age Mag., Best Campaign of Yr., Madison Ave. Mag., 5 awards N.Y. Art Dirs. Club, 3 awards Mus. Modern Art, 7 Clio awards. Mem. WG, Screen Actors Guild, Equity, Am. Fedn. TV Radio Artists. Home: 124 Boxwood Ln Cinnaminson NJ 08077

SCHOECK, RICHARD JOSEPH, b. NYC, Oct. 10, 1920; s. Gustav J. and Frances M. (Kuntz), Schoeck; m. Reta R. Haberer, 1945 (div. 1977); children—Eric R., Christine C., Jennifer A.; m. 2d, Megan S. Lloyd, Feb. 19, 1977.

Author: The Achievement of Thomas More, 1976, Intertextuality and Renaissance Texts, 1984, more than 100 scholarly articles and papers; editor: Delehaye's Legends of the Saints, 1961, Editing 16th Century Texts, 1966; (Roger Ascham), The Scholemaster, 1966, Shakespeare Qtly, 1972-74; gentl. editor: The Confutation of Tyndale, 3 vols., 1973; co-editor: Voices of Literature, 2 vols., 1964, 66, Chaucer Criticism, 2 vols., 1960, 61, Style, Rhetoric and Rhythm: Essays by M.W. Croll, 1966; former genl. editor: Patterns of Literary Criticism; spcl. editor: Canada vol. Rvw Natl. Literatures, 1977, Sir Thomas Browne and the Republic of Letters, 1982; mem. editorial bds. profl. jnls. MA, Princeton U., 1949, PhD, 1949. Instr. English Cornell U., 1949-55; asst. prof., then assoc. prof. U. Notre Dame, 1955-61; prof. English U. Toronto, 1961-71; head dept. English St. Michael's Coll., 1965-70; prof. vernacular lit. Pontifical Inst. Medieval Studies (Toronto), 1964-71; dir. research activities Folger Shakespeare Library also dir. Folger Inst., Renaissance and 18th Century Studies, 1970-74; adj. prof. English Cath. U. Am., 1972; prof. English, medieval and renaissance studies Cath. U. Am., 1972; prof. English, medieval and renaissance studies U. MD, 1974-75; prof. English and humanities U. CO (Boulder), 1975—, chair dept. integrated studies, 1976-79; Vincent J. Flynn prof. letters Coll. St. Thomas, 1960; vis. prof. Princeton U., 1964; cons. NEH; bd. dirs. Natural Law Inst., U. Notre Dame; Fellow Assn. Advancement Edn., 1952-53, Yale U., 1959-60, Can. Council, 1967-68, Guggenheim Fellow, 1968-69, Fulbright Research Fellowship (France, Holland), res. scholar Herzog August Bibliothek, 1986, emeritus Univ. of Colorado, 1987. Served with U.S. Army, 1940-46. Mem. Intl. Assn. Neo-Latin Studies (pres. 1976-79), MLA, PEN, Intl. Assn. U. Profs. English. Home: 4628 Tanglewood Trail Boulder CO 80301

SCHOELL, WILLIAM, b. NYC, Nov. 30, 1951; s. William Theodore and Caroline (Bauman) S. Author novels: Spawn of Hell, 1984, Shivers, 1985, Late at Night, 1986, Bride of Satan, 1986, Saurian, The Dragon, 1988; non-fiction: Stay Out of the Shower: 25 Years of Shocker Films Beginning with Psycho, 1985. Ed. Macabre Newsletter, assoc. ed. Quirk's Rvw. BA, Castleton (VT) St. College, 1973. Home: Box 117 Village Sta New York NY 10014

SCHOENBAUM, SAMUEL, b. NYC, Mar. 6, 1927; s. Abraham and Sarah (Altschuler) Schoenbaum; m. Marilyn Turk, June 10, 1946. Author: Internal Evidence and Elizabethan Dramatic Authorship, 1966, Shakespeare's Lives, 1970, William Shakespeare: A Documentary Life, 1975 (Distinguished Service award Soc. Midland Authors, 1976), William Shakespeare: A Compact Documentary Life, 1977, William Shakespeare: The Globe and the World, 1979, William Shakespeare: Records and Images, 1981; editor: (with K. Muir) A New Companion to Shakespeare and Others, 1985, Studies, 1970, Shakespeare Renaissance Drama, 1964-73. BA, Bklyn. Coll., 1947; MA, Columbia U., 1949, PhD, 1953, DLitt (hon.), Susquehanna U., 1986. Mem. faculty Northwestern U., 1953-75, Franklyn Bliss Snyder prof. English Lit., 1971-75; Disting. prof. English U. City NY, 1975-76; Disting. prof. Renaissance lit. U. MD, 1976—, dir. Center for Renaissance and Baroque Studies, 1981—; vis. prof. King's Coll. (London), 1961, U. Chgo., 1964, 65, Columbia, 1966, U. Wash., 1968; Mem. adv. com. Intl. Shakespeare Conf., 1972—; exec. bd. Shakespeare Qtly; mem. adv. council Am. Trust for Brit. Library; trustee emeritus Folger Shakespeare Library, Shakespeare Assn. Am., 1976-79. NEH Sr. fellowship, 1973-74. Mem. MLA. Home: 613 Constitution Ave NE Washington DC 20002

SCHOENBERGER, NANCY, b. Oakland, CA, Dec. 3, 1950, d. Sigmund Bernard and Betty Ellen (Beydler) Schoenberger. Author: The Taxidermist's Daughter (First Book award Mont. Arts Council), 1979, Girl on a White Porch (Devins award U. Mo. Press), 1987; contrbr. poetry to Antaeus, Cutbank (Richard Hugo Meml. award for poetry 1985), Ploughshares, other lit mags; contrbr. stories, rvws. to Three Penny Rvw, Cutbank, Gulfstream. BA, La. State U., 1972, MA, 1974; MFA, Columbia U., 1981. Instr. U. Mont., Missoula, 1975-78; vis. artist Poetry in Schls., Mont. Arts Council, 1978-79; assoc. producer N.Y. Center for Visual History, NYC, 1981-82; workshop instr. AAP, NYC, 1983—, dir. programs, 1982—. NEA poetry fellow, 1984; Rockefeller Fdn. resident at Study and Conf. Center, Bellagio, Italy, 1985; recipient Editor's Choice award for poetry Columbia: A Mag. of Poetry and Prose, 1985, other awards. Mem. PSA (Mary Carolyn Davies Meml. award 1984). Home: 406 E 83d St Apt 4B New York NY 10028

SCHOENFELD, MYRON R., b. NYCNov. 10, 1928, s. George M. and Rhoda (Kahn) S.; m. Gloria Toby Edis, June 14, 1959; children—Bradley Jon, Glenn Murray, Dawn Rhoda, Melody Lynn. Contrbr. articles to sci. jnls, essays and short stories to numerous publs.; ed.-in-chief Jnl Cardiovascular Ultrasonography; mem. editorial bd. Indian Jnl Med. Ultrasound. BA, Univ. Coll., NYC, 1948; MA, Columbia U., 1949; MD, Chgo. Med. Schl., 1953. Practice medicine, Yonkers, N.Y., 1960-76, Scarsdale, N.Y., 1977—; pres. Life-Line Spcl. Med. Services, Scarsdale, 1978—. Office: 2 Overhill Rd Scarsdale NY 10583

SCHOOLFIELD, HENRY PALMER JR. (HANK), b. Reidsville, NC, July 5, 1928; s. Henry Palmer S., Sr., and Nannie Margaret (Wheeler) S.; m. Thelma Elizabeth Henderson, Sept. 4, 1949; 1 dau., Judith Lynn Schoolfield Harris. Contrbr. articles on motor racing to num. pubns. BA in Jnlsm., U. NC, 1951. Wire ed. & city staff Winston-Salem (NC) Sentinel, 1951-53; exec. sports ed. Winston-Salem Jnl. & Sentinel, 1953-61; producer & dir. Universal Racing Network, Winston-Salem, 1964-82; ed. & pub. Southern MotoRacing, Winston-Salem, 1964—; pres. & CEO Universal Services, Inc., Winston-Salem, 1961—. Served to midshipman, USMC and USNR, 1946-49. Myers Bros. Meml. award, Most Outstanding Contrbn. to Motor Racing, Natl. Motorsport Press Assn., 1962. Mem. NMPA. Office: Box 500 Winston-Salem NC 27102

SCHOR, LYNDA, b. Bklyn., Apr. 18, 1938, d. Louis and Julia (Schleifer) Nyfield; children—Alexandra, Timothy, Zachary. Author: Appetites, 1975, True Love & Real Romance, 1979; contrbr. fiction and articles to Fiction Mag., Village Voice, Redbook, Mademoiselle, MS, Minn., Bellingham rvws, Feminist Studies, Psyche Critique, Playboy, Gentlemen's Qtly, to anthologies Fine Lines, Redbook's Finest Fiction, On the Job, Words To Go, Last Night's Stranger, Bitches & Sad Ladies, also others. BFA, Cooper Union. Wrtr. CETA Artists Program, NYC1978-80, CUNY, 1983; vis. wrtr-in-residence Fla. Intl. U., Miami, 1983-84; tchr. Lang Coll., New Schl. for Social Research, NYC, 1985—. Fellow MacDowell Colony, 1978, 79, 82, 83, Blue Mountain Ctr., 1985. Mem. PEN, P&W, AAAT, NWU. Home: 463 West St New York NY 10014

SCHOTT, PENELOPE SCAMBLY, b. Washington, Apr. 20, 1942, d. Elihu and Marian (Goldstein) Schott; m. Eric Sweetman; children—Daniel Kramer, Rebecca Kramer. Author: My Grandparents Were Married for Sixty-five Years, 1977 (poems), A Little Ignorance, 1986 (novel). BA in History, U. Mich., Ann Arbor, 1963; PhD in English, CUNY, 1971. Asst. prof. Rutgers U.; coord. accel. programs Somerset County Coll., N. Branch, N.J.; assoc. research scientist Educational Testing Service, Princeton, N.J., 1983-87. Hopwood Awards, U. Mich.; PSA Award. Home: Box 215 Rocky Hill NJ 18553

SCHRAG, PETER, b. Karlsruhe, Germany, July 24, 1931 (came to U.S., 1941, naturalized, 1953); s. Otto and Judith (Haas) Schrag; m. Melissa Jane Mowrer, June 9, 1953 (div. 1969); children—Mitzi, Erin Andre; 2nd m. Diane Divoky, May 24, 1969 (div. 1981); children—David Divoky, Benaiah Divoky. Author: Voices in the Classroom. 1965, Village School Downtown, 1967, Out of Place in America, 1971, The Decline of the Wasp, 1972, The End of the American Future, 1973, Test of Loyalty, 1974, (with Diane Divoky) The Myth of the Hyperactive Child, 1975, Mind Control, 1978; contbr. articles. AB Amhers Coll., 1953. Reporter El Paso (TX) Herald Post, 1953-55; asst. sec., asst. dir. publs. Amhers Coll., 1955-56, instr. Am. Studies, 1960-64; assoc. edn. editor Sat. Rvw., 1966-68, exec. editor, 1968-69; editor Change mag., 1969-70; editor at large Saturday Rvw, 1969-72; contbg. editor Saurday Review/Education, 1972-73; editorial adv. bd. The Columbia Forum 1972-75; editorial bd. Social Policy, 1971—, contbg. editor, 1975—, More, 1974-78, Inquiry, 1977-80; editorial page editor Sacramento Bee and McClatchy Newspapers, 1978—; vis. lectr. U. Mass. Sch. Edn., 1970-72; fellow in profl. journalism Stanford U. (Palo Alto, CA), 1973-74; lectr. U. CA at Berkeley, 1974-78. Mem. Center for Investigative Reporting. Office: Sac Bee 21st & Q Sts Sacramento CA 95813

SCHRAMM, DARRELL G.H., b. Hazen, ND, Jan. 25, 1943, s. Helmuth Herbert and Alma Magdalena (Reinhardt) S. Author: Silences, Bones and Angled Rain (poetry), 1974; contrbr. poetry to Mouth of the Dragon, No Apologies, Xanadu, other lit mags; contrbr. stories to Samisdat, North Country, Greyledge Rvw, other lit mags; contrbr rvws. to San Francisco Rvw of Books, Advocate, Small Press Rvw, Boston Gay Rvw. BA, Chico (Calif.) State U., 1965, then postgrad. Tchr. Stuart Hall Schl., San Francisco, 1978—. Mem. NCTE, AAP. Home: 236 Lexington St San Francisco CA 94110

SCHRAMM, RACHEL FLEISCHAMNN, (Rickie Fleischmann), b. Nurenberg, Germany, Oct. 19, 1929; arrd. U.S.A. Nov. 1938; d. Samuel and Ida (Wechsler) Fleischmann; m.Max Schramm, June 25, 1950; children: Diana Holtzman, Janet Gelman. Author articles and stories in Sun-Sentinel, Palm Beach Post, Boca Raton News, Ledger Dispatch, Virginian Pilot, The Record newspapers, Golden Years, The Southern Outlook, Florida Living, Boca Raton Magazine, Modern Salon, Florida Parent, other magazines, numerous newsletters, playbills. Student Wm. & Mary College, Fairleigh Dickinson Univ. Schl. representative and reporter for local newspapers; admin. asst., public relations; admin. asst., trade jnl.; freelance wrtr. Mem. Fla. Freelance Wrtrs. Assn., Natl. League of Am Pen Women, The Book Group, The Writers Group. Home: 10663 Boca Ln Boca Raton Fl 33428

SCHREIBER, MARK, b. Cin, July 8, 1960; s. Gary and Suzanne (Landsbaum) S; 1 son, Mark. Author: Princess in Exile, 1984. Address: 7835 New Bedford Ave Cincinnati OH 45237

SCHREIBER, RON, b. Chgo., Jan. 25, 1934; s. Paul Richard and Adeline Vlasta (Wencl) S. Author: Living Space, 1971; Moving to a New Place, 1974; False Clues, 1977; Against That Time, 1978; Tomorrow Will Really Be Sunday, 1984; ed.: things mag., 1964-66, Hanging Loose mag. and press, 1966—, 31 New American Poets, 1968. BA, Wesleyan U., Middletown, Conn., 1955; MA, Columbia U., 1959, PhD, 1967. Asst. ed. Columbia U. Press, 1958-61; mem faculty Columbia U., 1959-67, Rutgers U., Newark, 1960-61, U. Mass., Boston, 1967—. Served with U.S. Army, 1955-57. Home: 9 Reed St Cambridge MA 02140

SCHREIBER, SUZANNE E., b. Robinson, IL, Feb. 24, 1936; d. Jack and Ida C. (Fader) Landsbaum; m. Gary M. Schreiber, June 6, 1958; children—Mark A., Ben S., Ellen B. Author: Yoga for the Fun of It! Hatha Yoga for Preschool Children, 1980. BS in Elem. Edn., Ind. U., 1958. Tchr. Frick Elem. Schl., Pitts., 1958-60; Kids' Yoga Spclst. Jewish Community Ctrs., Cin., 1974—; ed., pub., author Sugar Marbel Press, Cin., 1980—; creator and performer tv series "Focus on Fitness" WPTO-TV, Oxford-Dayton, Ohio, 1985—. Recipient Kovod award Jewish Community Ctr., Cin., 1984. Mem. Pi Lambda Theta, Cin. Yoga Tchrs. Assn., Dayton Yoga Tchrs. Assn., Natl. Assn. Television Arts & Scis. Home: 1547 Shenandoah Ave Cincinnati OH 45237

SCHRICHTE, DELLZELL, (Dellzell Chenoweth), b. NYC, Sept. 5, 1962; d. Christian William and Goldie (Badogiannis) Chenoweth; m. David Rex Schricte, Dec. 20, 1985. Contrbr. articles: Impact! mag., Downtown Planet, Lake Forest Papers, TheHerald, Arlington Heights, Ill., others. Wrkg. on novel. BA in English with honors, Lake Forest Coll., 1984; postgrad., U. Hawaii-Manoa, 1986—. Staff wrtr. The Beat mag., Honolulu, 1986—; Westside story, 1987—; editorial asst. This Week mags., Honolulu, 1986—87; ed.-in-chief, Auto Hawaii, "The Car Magazine," both in Honolulu, 1987. Mem. U. Hawaii Pd. of Publications, Natl. Wrtrs. Club. Home: 411 Hobron Ln 911 Honolulu HI 96815

SCHRIENER, JUDY A., b. Denver, Oct. 11, 1949. Marketing columist: Ariz. Republic, 1985—. Contrbr. articles to mags., newspapers including ADWEEK Mag., Advt. Age, Advt. Age, others. Wrkg. on book on how to get publicity. B.S. in Psychology, Colo. State U., 1972. Dir. advt. Moore & Co. Realtors, Denver, 1978-79, Ariz. State Lottery, Phoenix, 1981-82; printing salesman, Phoenix, 1979-81; free-lance wrtr., 1981—. Mem. Phoenix Advt. Club, Phoenix Press Club, Ariz. Press Club (2d place for feature writing 1987, 3d place for feature writing 1987), Investigate Reporters & Eds. Address: Box 7233 Phoenix AZ 85011

SCHRIER, ARNOLD, b. NYC, May 30, 1925; s. Samuel and Yetta (Levine) Schrier; m. Sondra Weinshelbaum, June 12, 1949; children—Susan Lynn, Jay Alan, Linda Lee, Paula Kay. Author: Ireland and the American Emigration, 1958, The Development of Civilization, 1961-62, Modern European Civilization, 1963, Living World History, 1964, Twentieth Century World, 1974, History and Life: The World and Its People, 1977, A Russian Looks at America, 1979. Student Bethany Coll., 1943-44, Ohio Wesleyan U., 1944-45; BS, Northwestern U., 1949, MA, 1959, PhD, 1956. Asst. prof. history U. Cin., 1956-61; assoc. prof., 1961-66, prof., 1966—, dir. grad. studies history, 1969-78, Walter C. Langsam prof. modern European history, 1972—; vis. asst. prof. history Northwestern U. (Evanston, IL), 1960; vis. assoc. prof. history IN U. (Bloomington), 1965-66; vis. lectr. Russian history Duke U., 1966; disting. vis. prof. US Air Force Acad., 1983-84; dir. NDEA Inst. World History for Secondary Schl. Tchrs., U. Cin., 1965. Served with USNR, 1943-46, 52-54. Home: 9155 Peachblossom Ct Cincinnati OH 45231

SCHROEDER, CHERYL ANN, b. Mpls., Sept. 20, 1960; d. Dennis Hubert Schroeder and Jane Ilean Zacher. Editor: Mpls. Br. Cystic Fibrosis Found. newsletter, Mpls. Jaycees Newsletter. Contrbr. articles to mags., newspapers. B.A. in Journalism, U. Minn., 1984. Ed. extension classes U. Minn., Mpls., 1984-85; extension asst. promotions Anoka County Extension Service, Minn., 1985-86; free-lance wrtr., 1986-87; marketing dir. recreation services; Naval Sta., Long Beach, CA. Mem. Romance Wrtrs. Am. home: 24425 Seelye Brook Dr Saint Francis MN 55070

SCHROEDER, GARY STEVEN, b. Chgo., Feb. 15, 1951, s. George William and Atta Evelyn (Dipert) S.; m. Lynne Marie Dittrich, May 10, 1986. Author: The Slender Name (poetry), 1980, Mistaken Lights (poetry), 1985; ed.: Pendragon—A Jnl of the Arts, 1983-84, Wayland Press, 1985, Peak Flow, 1986, 87. BS, Met. State Coll., Denver, 1978; profl. cert. in respiratory therapy, St. Anthony Hosp., Denver, 1983. Cardiopulmonary critical care specialist Porter Meml. Hosp., Denver, 1983-87, respiratory therapist Am. Respiratory Care Services, 1987—. Recipient Lit. award Colo. Assn. Respiratory Therapy Edn., 1983, 85. Mem. NWU. Home: 675 S Sherman St Denver CO 80209

SCHROEDER, KATHLEEN AUDREY, b. Jersey City, NJ, Oct. 10, 1959; d. William D. and Audrey Ann (Tjarks) S. News correspondent Sta. WOBM-FM, Toms River, NJ (Job Performance commendation 1980-81), 1980-81; columnist Lakewood Town News, NJ, 1981; reporter Ocean County Reporter, Toms River, 1981; wrtr., reporter, photographer Wall Herald, Wall Township, NJ, 1983-84; staff wrtr. The Leader, Point Pleasant Beach, NJ, 1985. Contrbr. articles to lit. mags., newspapers. Wrkg. on articles, murder mystery, collection of humorous anecdotes. Named Most Valuable Staffer, Jersey Jnl., Jersey City, 1973. Home: 22 Commodore Dr Bricktown NJ 08723

SCHROEDER, MIKE F., b. Rochester, MN, Dec. 23, 1957; s. Derald and Elsie S. BA in Mass Communics., St. Cloud State U., 1981. Ed., Viking Rptr., Bloomington, MN, 1981; sports writer St. Cloud Daily Times (MN), 1982; sports info. dir. St. Cloud State U. (MN), 1982-84; mng. ed. Amer. Hockey Mag., Colorado Springs, CO, 1984—. Office: Hockey Assn 2997 Broadmr Vly Colorado Springs CO 80906

SCHROEDER, ROBERT ENGLE, b. Washington, Mar. 1, 1929; s. Robert Brett and Rilla Murray (Engle) S.; m. Jean Alison Stevenson, July 5, 1955. Author: Invesigations on the Gray Snapper, 1971, Something Rich & Strange, 1985. Contrbr. article to World Book Encyc. BA, Univ. of Md., 1954; Ph.D., U. Miami, 1964. Ind. researcher Chattem Drug & Chemical Co., Islamorada, FL, 1966-68; mng. dir. Mariculture Ltd., Grand Cayman, British West Indies, 1968-72; contractor Nat. Cancer Inst., Washington, 1972-81. Mem.AAAS. Home: 21661 Pearl St Box 633 Alva FL 33920

SCHUCK, MARJORIE MASSEY, b. Winchester, VA, Oct. 9, 1921, d. Carl Frederick Massey and Margaret Harriet (Parmele) Eastman; m. Ernest George Metcalfe, Dec. 2, 1943 (div. 1949); m. 2d Franz Schuck, Nov. 11, 1953 (dec. 1958). Contrbr. poetry to NY Times. Ed., pub.: Poetry Venture mag., 1968-79, Poetry Venture Qtly Essays, 1968-71, Poetry Venture Anthology, 1972; ed.: From Heyday to Mayday (by George H. Longstaff), 1983, The Prophet Jakob Lorder Predicts Coming Catastrophies and the True Christianity (by Kurt Eggenstein), 1985; founding pres., pub., ed. Valkyrie Pub. House, 1980—, ed., pub. The Valkyrie Newsletter, 1986—. Student U. Minn., 1941-43, Schl. Social Research, 1948, NYU, 1952, 54-55. Co-dir., assoc. ed. The Villanor Inter. Cultural Forum, Tampa, FL. Home: 8245 26th Ave N Saint Petersburg FL 33710

SCHUDY, PATRICIA HELLINGEN, b. Boonville, MD, Nov. 27, 1939; d. Charles J. and Matilda M. (Scheidt) Hellinger; m. Robin Colby Schudy, Jan. 16, 1964; children—Eric M., Kristin L., Anne C., Scott A., Brian J. Contrbr. to With All Sails Set, 1979, Kansas First Families at Home, 1982. Co-editor, In Sunshine and in Shadow, 1986. Contrbr. articles to mags., newspapers including Kansas!, Midwest Living, KC Star, Town Squire, Video Systems; columnist Kansas City Star Sunday Mag., 1983-86. AB in English, Mt. St. Scholastica, Atchison, Kans., 1960. Asst. dir. schl.-classroom program People-to-People, Inc., Kansas City, Mo., 1963-64; free-lance wrtr. Kansas City Star and Kansas City Star Sunday Mag., 1976-86; dir. pub. relations Rockhurst High Sch., Kansas City, 1980-85; v.p. Findlay/Schudy & Assoc., Overland Park, Kans., 1983—; field ed. Better Homes and Gargens mag. Meredith Corp., Des Moines, 1985—. Bd. dirs. Peace Links, 1984—. Recipient 3d place for feature article Reader's Digest Wrtrs. Conf., 1985. Mem. Central Exchange, Friends of Art, Nelson Gallery. Home: 9200 Manor Rd Leawood Rd KS 66206

SCHUFF, KAREN ELIZABETH, b. Highland Park, MI, June 1, 1937; d. Ernest Jack Bishop and Helen Wanda (Novak) Spector; m. Henry Clifton Schuff, Sept. 7, 1955; children—Deborah Elaine, David Lawrence. Author: Barefoot Philosopher, 1968, Come, Take My Hand, 1968, Of Rhythm and Cake, 1970, Of June I Sing, 1979, Green as April, 1987. Contrbr. poems o anthols., lit. mags. Recipient 1st prize for essay Creative Writing Center, Houghton Lake, MI, 1987. Mem. Poetry Soc. Mich., Ky., Penn. state poetry socs. Home: 15310 Windemere Ave Southgate MI 48195

SCHULBERG, BUDD, b. NYC, Mar. 27, 1914; s. Benjamin P. and Adeline (Jaffe) Schulberg; m. Virginia Ray, July 23, 1936; 1 dau.—Victoria; 2nd m. Victoria Anderson, Feb. 17, 1943; children—Stephen, David; 3rd m. Geraldine Brooks, July 12, 1964; 4th m. Betsy Anne Langman, June 9, 1979; children—Benn Stuart, Jessica. Screen writer, Hollywood, 1936-39; contrbr. short stories, articles to leading natl. mags. and anthologies; author: What Makes Sammy Run?, 1941 (co-author libretto for the Broadway musical, 1964), The Harder They Fall, 1947, The Disenchanted, 1950 (selected one of 3 outstanding works of fiction for 1950 by ALA and natl. book critics); vol. short stories Some Faces In The Crowd, 1953; screenplay On the Waterfront (NY Critics award, Fgn. Corrs. award, Screen

Writers Guild award, Acad. Award for best story and screenplay), 1954; novel Waterfront, 1955 (Christopher award); screen adaptation The Harder They Fall, 1955; screenplay A Face In The Crowd, 1957 (German Film Critics award); Wind Across the Everglades, The Disenchanted (Broadway play) 1958-59, From the Ashes: Voices of Watts, 1967 (Emmy award 1966), Sanctuary V, 1969, The Four Seasons of Success, 1972, Loser and Still Champion: Muhammed Ali, 1973, (with Geraldine Brooks) Swan Watch, 1975, Everything that Moves, 1980, Moving Pictures: Memories of a Hollywood Prince, 1981, Writers in America, 1983. Contrbr. to Sports Illustrated, Life, NY Times Book Rvw, Playboy. AB, Dartmouth Coll., 1936; LLD, 1960. Dir. Douglass House Watts Writers Workshop; founder, chmn., Frederick Douglass Creative Arts Center (NYC)1971. Served as Lt. (j.g.) USNR, 1943-46. Journalism award Dartmouth Coll., spcl. award for Watts Writers Workshop, New Eng. Theater Conf., 1969, Amistad award, award for work with black writers Howard U. Mem. DG, ASCAP, AG, Writers Guild East, PEN. Address: Dorese 41 W 82nd St New York NY 10024

SCHULDT, MICHAEL BRUCE, B. El Paso, TX, July 31, 1951; s. Arthur William and Vera Veronica (Coffee) S., m. Lori Lyn Meek, Aug. 10, 1985. Ed.: The World Book Encyc., 1978-88, contrbr. to Ind. English, 1986. B.A., Northern Ill. Ul, 1976. Asst. ed. World Book Inc., Chgo., 1977-81, sr. ed., 1981, staff ed., 1981-83, subject ed. physcial scis., 1983-87; editorial mgr. Mobil Travel Guide, Deerfield, Il, 1987; freelance ed,. wrtr,. 1987—. Address: 711 River Rd. Unit 611 Des Plaines Il 60016

SCHULER, ROBERT JORDAN, b. San Mateo, CA, June 25, 1939; s. Edward and Georgia Ruth (Goebel) S.; m. Carol Florence Forbis, Sept. 7, 1963; children: Sally, Edward Anthony, Michael. Author: Seasonings, 1978, Axle of the Oak, 1978, Where is Dancer's Hill?, 1979, Morning Raga, 1980, The Red Cedar Scroll, 1981, Floating Out of Stone, 1982, Music for Monet, 1984, Lasser: Things Lost, 1987. contrbr. poetry to Dakotah Terr., Tar River Poetry, Spoon River Qtly, other lit mags. AB in poli. sci. (with honors) Stanford U., 1961; MA in comparative lit., U. Calif.-Berkeley, 1965; Yale, Special Danforth Fellow, 1969-70; PhD program, U. Minn., 1986. Instr. in English Menlo Coll., Menlo Park, Calif., 1965-67, Shimer Coll., Mt. Carroll, Ill., 1967-78; assoc. prof. Univ. Wis.-Stout, Menomonie, 1978—. Address: 511 Sunset Dr Menomonie WI 54751

SCHULER, RUTH WILDES, b. Salem, MA, Feb. 11, 1933, d. Wilbur Leighton and Mary Eddie (Bryant) Wildes; m. Charles Albert Schuler, Sept. 8, 1954; children—Steven Charles, Jeanne Leigh. Author: Dreaming in the Dawn, 1980, An American in the Age of Aquarius, 1980, Beneath the Mushroom Cloud, 1984, Daughter from the Other Side of the Drawbridge, 1977, Born of Buffalo Bone, 1978, Portraits of a Poet Passing Through, 1978, February's Child, 1979, Prophet's Return From Exile (poetry), 1984, Beware of the Wolves (poetry), 1982, Princess in an Ivory Tower, 1985, Of Porcupines and Death (short stories), 1985; ed.: Dragon Fire, Dancing Dogs & Dangling Dreams, 1978, The Calico Sphinx, 1977, Trends no.8—Native American Poetry, 1983. Editor: Prophetic Voices, intl. lit mag. BA, San Francisco State U., 1957, MA, 1971. Recipient awards Berkeley Poets, Ina Coolbirth Circle, Contra Costa County Fair, N.Y. Poetry Forum. Home: 94 Santa Maria Dr Novato CA 94947

SCHULLER, MARY ANN, b. Marion, OH, Apr. 26, 1952; d. John and Anna May (Wolf) S. Author: Geometric Mazes, 1980, Hobby Word Search Puzzles, 1980, Wordles, 1981, Pun Fun, 1985, The Riddle-a-Day Riddle Book, 1986, Summer Diary, 1987, Wros-tonne and Other Sostories of Science Fantasy, 1987. Contrbr. short stories, articles to mags. including TV Guide, Child Life, Jack and Jill. B.A., Wittenberg U., 1974; M.A., U. Dayton, 1985. Tchr. Northwestern Local Schls., Springfield, OH, 1974—. Co-dir. Northwestern Spring Musical Play, Springfield, 1976—. Home: 613 Villa Rd Springfield OH 45503

SCHULMAN, MARY, b. Petrograd, Russia, July 20, 1910, d. Isidore and Anna Kuperstein; came to U.S., 1923; m. Milton Schulman, Aug. 20, 1938; 1 dau., Joan Schulman Braman. Author: Moses Hess: Prophet of Zionism, 1963; contrbr. numerous poems to mags. and other publs.; translator Yiddish poetry into English. BA, Hunter Coll., 1933; MS in Edn., CCNY, 1963, MA in Russian, 1965; PhD, Columbia U., 1984. Tchr. public schls., NYC, 1960-75; freelance translator, 1984—. Recipient Kappa Delta Pi award, CCNY edn. honor, 1965, Leopold Schepp Fdn. Scholarship, Hunter Coll., 1929-33. Home: 3322 Bainbridge Ave Bronx NY 10467

SCHULMAN, SARAH M., b. NYC, July 28, 1958. Author: The Sophie Horowitz Story (novel), 1984, Girls, Visions and Everything (novel), 1986, 6 plays; contrbr. short story: Things that Divide Us, 1985. Fulbright fellow, 1984-85. Home: 406 E 9th St New York NY 10009

SCHULTE, RAINER, b. Germany, July 8, 1937; s. Hans and Hedwig (Keller) Schulte. Author: Poetry The Suicide at the Piano, 1969, The Other Side of the Word, 1978, The Book of Isolation, 1981; editor-in-chief: Mundus Artium; editor: Giant Talk: An Anthology of Third World Writing, 1975, Needle Off Center: A Multi-Media Show, 1973, Translation Rvw; co-editor: Continental Short Stories: The Modern Tradition, 1968; translator: Selected Poetry (Yvan Goll), 1981. MA, U. Mainz, Germany, 1962; PhD in Comparative Lit., U. Mich., 1965. Prof. comparative lit. Ohio U., 1965-75; prof. comparative lit. and humanities U. Tex. at Dallas, 1975—. Home: 605 W Lamar St McKinney TX 75069

SCHULTZ, MICHAEL EDWARD, b. Salisbury, MD, Nov. 28, 1953; s. Edward Charles and Ella Mae (Galloway) S.; m. Linda Lou Liggett, Aug. 4, 1979 (div. Jan. 15, 1987); children—Jery Dale, Melinda Elaine; m. Colleen Marie Dudley, Aug. 25, 1987. Contrbr. poems to anthols. B.S. in Occupational Edn., Southern Ill. U., 1986. Enlisted, U.S. Navy, 1971, now serving as division chief PCU Topeka, Groton, CT, 1986—. Mem. Nashville Songwriters (assoc.), Am. Poetry Assn. Home: 150 B Military Hwy Gales Ferry CT 06335

SCHULTZ, NANCY LUSIGNAN, b. Pittsfield, MA, July 6, 1956; d. Henri Theophil and Carolyn (Budrow) Lusignan. Contrbr. to Soundings East, North Shore: Sunday, Qtly Rvw Wines, Cambridge Chronicle, The Sextant; ed. articles for Nation's Bus., Jnl Acctg. Res. BA, Coll. of the Holy Cross, 1975-78; PhD, Boston Coll., 1979-84. Asst. prof. English Salem State Coll., Mass., 1983—, faculty adv., Florence Luscomb Women's Ctr., 1983—. Mem. MLA, Nathaniel Hawthorne Soc. Address: 269 Summer St Somerville MA 02144

SCHULTZ, PHILIP (ARNOLD), b. Rochester, NY, Jan. 6, 1945; s. Samuel Benjamin and Lillian B. (Bernstein) S. Author: (poems) Like Wings (Am. Acad. and Inst. Arts and Letters award), 1979, Deep Within the Ravine (Lamont Poetry Selection, AAP), 1984, My Guardian Angel Stein, 1986; numerous poems, short stories to lit mags. Wrkg. on novel to be titled Swagger. BA, San Francisco State Univ., 1967; MFA, Univ. of Iowa, 1971. Wrtr.-in-res., Kalamazoo Coll., 1971-72; lectr. in creative wrtg., Univ. of Mass. at Boston, 1973-75; tchr. creative wrtg., NYU, 1978—, dir. creative wrtg. program, NYU, 1983—, founder and dir. Writers Studio, a private schl. for wrtrs., 1984—. State Council for the Arts fellow, NY, 1976, 80; NEA fellowship, 1981; Fulbright grantee, 1983; NY Fdn. for the Arts Award in Poetry, 1985. Mem. PSA, PEN, AG. Home: 78 Charles St 212 New York NY 10014

SCHULZE, FRANZ, JR., b. Uniontown, PA, Jan. 30, 1972; s. Franz and Anna E. (Krimmel) Schulze; m. Marianne Gaw, June 24, 191961; children—F.C. Matthew, Lukas. Author: Art, Architecture and Civilization, ,69, Fantastic Images: Chicago Art Since 1945, 1972, 100 Years of Chicago Architecture, Stealing Is My Game, 1975, Mies van der Rohe: A Critical Biography, 1986. Student Northwestern U., 1943; PhB, U. Chgo., 1945; BFA Schl. Art Inst. Chgo., 1949, MFA, 1960; postgrad. Acad. Fine Arts, Munich, Germany, 1956-57. Instr. art Purdue U., 1950-52; chair dept. art Lake Forest Coll. (IL), 1952-58, artist-in-res., 1958-61, prof. art, 1961—, Hollender prof. art, 1974—; art critic Chgo. Daily News, 1962-78, Chgo. Sun Times, 1978—; contrbg. editor Art News, 1958-64, 73—, Inland Architect, 1975—; Chgo. corr. in art Christian Sci. Monitor, 1958-62, Art in Am., 1965-73; Art Intl., 1966-67; art and architecture critic The Chicagoan, 1973-74; mem. vis. com. dept. art U. Chgo., 1974—. Trustee Ragdale Fdn., Lake Forest, 1981—. Ford Fdn. fellow, 1964-65; Graham Fdn. for Advanced Studies in the Fine arts fellow, 1971, 81; NEH fellow, 1982; Skidmore Owings's Merrill Fdn. fellow, 1983. Home: 872 Northmoor Rd Lake Forest IL 60045

SCHULZE, KENNETH W., b. Lakewood, OH, Apr. 18, 1951; s. Arthur Paul and Edna Esther (Solada) S. Contrbr. to var. media inclg. Overtures, Writer's Bloc, Nexus, Sci. Fi. Chronicle, The Mind's Eye, Performance in Blood (Honorable Mention National Writer's Club Book Contest, 1984), The Poet, Supernova, Chicago Sheet, Infinitum, Stag, Embassy Casette, Panache, Horizons Beyond. BA, U. Mich., 1973. Editorial asst. Commerce Clearing House, Chgo., 1974-76, Amer. Bar Assn. Press, Chgo., 1977-79; ed. Year Book Medical Pub., Inc., Chgo., 1979-82. Finalist, Katherine Anne Porter Prize for Fiction Contest, 1984; first runner-up, Competition 38, Fantasy & Science Fiction Mag., 1985; second place, Intl. Writers of the Future Contest, 1985. Mem. SFWA. Address: 22455 Lake Road Rocky River OH 44116

SCHUMACHER, GENNY, see Smith, Genny Hall

SCHUMACHER, JULIE ALISON, b. Wilmington, Del., Dec. 2, 1958, d. Frederick George and Winifred Jean (Temple) Schumacher; m. Lawrence Rubin Jacobs. Contrbr. short stories to The Quarterly, Four Quarters, Calif Qtly, New Letters; contrbr. book rvws. to The Nation; included in Best Am. Short Stories 1983. BA,

Oberlin (Ohio) Coll., 1981; MFA, Cornell U., 1986. Assoc. ed. P.W. Communications, NYC1983-85; fiction ed. Epoch Mag., Ithaca, N.Y., summer 1985; temp. lectr. Cornell U., Ithaca, 1985—. Home: 313 S Aurora St Ithaca NY 14850

SCHUTTE, WILLIAM METCALF, b. New Haven, CT, May 9, 1919; s. Louis Henry and Anna (Metcalf) Schutte; m. Susan Roberts McDowell, May 15, 1943 (dec. Sept. 1965); children—Scott, Kirk, Kim; m. Anne Cole Jacobson, Dec. 21, 1967. Author: Joyce and Shakespeare: A Study in the Meaning of Ulysses, 1957, Communication in Business and Industry (with E.R. Steinberg), 1960, rev. ed., 1983, Personal Integrity (with Steinberg), 1961, Twentieth Century Interpretations of Joyce's A Portrait of the Artist as a Young Man, 1968; author: Index to Recurrent Elements in Joyce's Ulysses, 1982; contrbr. articles to profl. jnls. Grad. Hotchkiss Schl., 1937; BA, Yale U., 1941, MA, 1947, PhD, 1954. Mem. faculty Carnegie Inst. Tech., 1947-60, assoc. prof. English, 1955, asst. to pres., 1956-58; mem. faculty Lawrence U., 1960-84, Lucia R. Briggs prcf. English, 1965-84, prof. emeritus, 1984—; dir. London Center, 1975-76; faculty fellow Newberry Library Seminar Assoc. Colls., Midwest (Chgo), 1969-71; cons. in communications. Bd. govs. Attic Theatre (Appleton), 1961-67, pres., 1964-67. Recipient Carnegie Corp. Teaching award Carnegie Inst. Tech., 1954. Mem. MLA, Renaissance Soc. Am., Wis. Hist. Soc., Shakespeare Assn. Am. Home: 4 Brokaw Pl Appleton WI 54911

SCHUYLER, JAMES MARCUS, b. Chgo., Nov. 9, 1923; s. Marcus James and Margaret (Connor) Schuyler. Author: poetry Salute, 1960, May 24th or So, 1966, Freely Espousing: Poems, 1969, The Crystal Lithium, 1972, A Sun Cab, 1972, Hymn to Life: Poems, 1974, The Home Book: Prose and Poems, 1951-70, 1977, The Morning of the Poem, 1980, Collabs (with Helena Hughes), 1980, A Few Days: Poems, 1985; fiction Alfred and Guinevere, 1958, A Nest of Ninnies (with John Ashbery), 1969, What's for Dinner?, 1978, Diary Early in '71, 1982; libretto A Picnic Cantata (with Paul Bowles), 1955. Student, Bethany Coll., 1941-43, U. Florence, 1947-48. Me. Staff Mus. Modern Art (NYC), 1955-61; critic Art News mag. Frank O'Hara prize Poetry mag., 1969; Natl. Inst. Arts and Letters award, 1976; Pulitzer prize for poetry, 1981; NEA grantee, 1971, 72; AAP fellow; Guggenheim fellow, 1981. Office: Groffsky 2 Fifth Ave New York NY 10003

SCHWANZ, H. LEE, b. Lorimor, IA, Apr. 23, 1923; s. Arthur I. and Rae E. (Coffery) S.; m. Kathleen Jesse Boland, Sept. 1, 1947; children—Michael L., Leslie A. Schwanz Satran, Stephen E., Susan E. Schwanz Pigorsch. Ed./contrbr. arts to Country Gentleman, Farm Profit, PCA Farming, National Wildlife, Big Farmer, FarmFutures, Buying for the Farm, Archery World, SnoTrack; books: The Family Poultry Flock, 1981, Rabbits for Food and Profit, 1982. BS, IA State U., 1947. Farm rptr. Cedar Rapids (IA) Gazette, 1947-50; assoc. ed. Country Gentleman, Phila., 1950-55; ed. Agricultural Publ., Milw., 1956-59; pub. Market Communics., Milw., 1960-80, Elmbrook Pub., Brookfield, WI, 1980—. Served to Capt., U.S. Army, 1943-46, ETO. Mem. Sigma Delta Chi. Home: 2645 Maple Hill Lane Brookfield WI 53005

SCHWARTZ, JEFFREY, b. Cleve., Feb. 29, 1952, s. Daniel E. and Doris (Ottenberg) S.; m. Betsy A. Bowen, Aug. 19, 1984. Author: Contending with the Dark, 1978; contrbr. poetry: The Little Mag., Hanging Loose, Nantucket Rvw, Night House Anthology, numerous other lit. publs.; co-ed. Aspect Mag., 1975-76. BA, Boston U., 1974, MA, U. Mass., 1978, DA, Carnegie-Mellon U., 1985. Instr. English Southwestern Mass. U., North Dartmouth, 1978-80, Bristol Community Coll., Fall River, Mass., 1979-81, Sewickley Acad., Pitts., 1985—; cons. Bread Loaf Schl. English, Middlebury, Vt., 1984—. Winner AAP Prize, 1977; NEH fellow, 1981; Recipient Adamson award for poetry, 1982, 83, 84, for nonfiction, 1984. Mem. AWP. Home: 365 S Atlantic Ave Pittsburgh PA 15224

SCHWARTZ, JOSEPH, b. Milw., Apr. 9, 1925; s. Alfred George and Mary (Wutchek) Schwartz; m. Joan Jackson, Aug. 28, 1954; 1 son—Adam. Author: A Reader for Writers, 3rd ed., 1971, Perspectives on Language, 1963, Province of Rhetoric, 1965, Poetry: Meaning and Form, 1969, Hart Crane: A Critical Bibliography, 1970, Hart Crane: A Descriptive Bibliography, 1972, Exposition, 2nd ed., 1971, Hart Crane: A Reference Guide, 1983; editor: Renascence mag. BA, Marquette U., 1946, MA, 1947; PhD, U. WI, 1952. Teaching asst. Marquette U. (Milw.), 1946-47, instr. 1947-48, 50-54, asst. prof., 1954-59, assoc. prof., 1959-64, prof., 1964—, chair dept. English, 1963-75; teaching fellow U. WI, 1948-50. Mem. Phi Beta Kappa, Alpha Sigma Nu. Home: 8516 W Mequon Rd 112 N Mequon WI 53092

SCHWARTZ, KESSEL, b. Kansas City, MO, Mar. 19, 1920; s. Henry and Dora (Tananbaum) Schwartz; m. Barbara Lewin, Apr. 3, 1947; children—Joseph David, Deborah, Edward, Michael. Author: The Ecuadorian Novel, 1953, An Introduction to Modern Spanish Literature, 1967, The Meaning of Existence in Contemporary Hispanic Literature, 1969, Vicente Aleixandre, 1970, Juan Goytisolo, 1970, A New History of Spanish American Fiction, 1972 (named Outstanding Acad. Book of Year, Am. Assn. Coll. and Research Librarians), Studies on Twentieth Century Spanish and Spanish American Literature, 1983; co-author: A New History of Spanish Literature, 1961, A New Anthology of Spanish Literature, 1968; assoc. editor: Hispania, 1965-84; editorial adv. bd: Anales de Literatura Espanola Contemporanea Folio. BA, U. MO, 1940, MA, 1941; PhD, Columbia U., 1953. Asst. instr. U. MO, 1940-42; dir. cultural centers in Nicaragua, Ecuador, cultural observer in Costa Rica State Dept., 1946-48; instr. Hofstra, Hamilton, Colby colls., 1948-53; asst. prof. U. VT, 1953-57; assoc. prof., then prof. modern lang., chair dept. U. Ark., 1957-62; prof. modern langs. U. Miami (FL), 1962—, chair dept., 1962-64, 74-83, dir. grad. studies, 1964-65, 83—; vis. prof. U. NC (Chapel Hill), 1966-67. Served with AUS, 1942-46. Mem. AATSP, Asociacion Internacional de Hispanistas. Home: 6400 Maynada Coral Gables FL 33146

SCHWARTZ, LLOYD, b. Bklyn., Nov. 29, 1941; s. Samuel and Ida (Singer) S. Author: These People, 1981; ed. Elizabeth Bishop and Her Art, 1983; contrbr. Eating the Menu, 1974, Poesia della Metamorfosi, 1984, Ecstatic Occasions, Expedient Forms, 1986. Ed. Ploughshares, 1979; classical music ed. Boston Phoenix, 1978—. Contrbr. poems, articles, Atlantic, Am Rvw, NY Times, New Republic, Opera Qtly, other periodicals, lit mags. BA, Queens College; PhD, Harvard. Assoc. prof. Eng., Boston State College, 1971-82; prof. Eng., Univ. Mass., 1982—. Deems Taylor Award, ASCAP, 1980. Mem. PEN/New England, PSA, New England Poetry Club. Home: 27 Pennsylvania Ave Somerville MA 02145

SCHWARTZ, LYNNE SHARON, b. Mar. 19, 1939; d. Jacob M. and Sarah (Slatus) Sharon; m. Harry Schwartz, Dec. 22, 1957; children—Rachel Eve, Miranda Ruth. Author: Rough Strife, 1980, Balancing Acts, 1981, Disturbances in the Field, 1983, Acquainted with the Night, (stories), 1984, We Are Talking About Homes (nonfiction), 1985, The Melting Pot and Other Subversive Stories, 1987. Free-lance editor; translator; adj. lectr. English, Hunter Coll., 1971-77; vis. lectr. U. Iowa Writers' Workshop, 1982-83; Boston U., 1984-85; Columbia U., 1984; Rice U., 1987. BA, Barnard Coll., 1959, MA; Woodrow Wilson Natl. fellow, Bryn Mawr Coll., 1961; postgrad. NYU, 1967-72. Assoc. editor The Writer mag., Boston, 1961-63; editorial dir. Calliope Records, spoken records (Boston), 1962-64; pub. relations writer Operation Open City, NY Urban League (NYC), 1965-67. Fiction selected for Pushcart Prize III; Best American Short Stories, 1978, 79; O. Henry Prize Stories, 1979; Guggenheim fellowship for fiction, 1984, NEA, 1985. Address: Harper & Row 10 E 53rd New York NY 10022

SCHWARTZ, ROBERTA CHRISTINE, b. Detroit. Contrbr. numerous articles: Discovery mag., Detroit Free Press, Detroit News, Heritage mag., Glass Art mag., Chgo. Tribune, other nat. and regional publs. Wrkg. on travel articles. BA, Marygrove Coll., 1960; MA, PhD, Wayne State U., 1968. Radio ed., UPI, Washington, DC, 1961-63. Assoc. prof. Oakland U., Rochester, Mich., 1980—; pres. Roberta Schwartz Assocs., Inc., Rochester, 1980—. Interviewer for WDTR (Detroit), other public radio stations. Mem. Hemingway Soc., Nat. Conf. Editorial Wrtrs. Home: 397 Tourangean Dr Rochester MI 48063

SCHWARTZ, STEVEN R., b. Chester, PA, May 3, 1950, s. Benjamin and Jeannette S.; m. Emily M. Hammond, May 25, 1985. Author: To Leningrad in Winter: Stories by Steven Schwartz, 1985; contrbr. stories to Prize Stories 1983: The O.Henry Awards, Epoch, Antioch Rvw, San Francisco Chronicle, other publs. BA in Psychology, U. Colo., 1973; MFA, U. Ariz., 1981. Instr. U. New Orleans, 1982-84; asst. prof. English Colo. State U. Fort Collins, 1984—. Recipient PEN Syndicated Fiction award, 1985, Breakthrough award U. Mo. Press, 1985. Mem. AWP. Home: 627 Whedbee St Fort Collins CO 80524

SCHWARTZ, TERRY WALTER, b. Cin., Oct. 23, 1950, s. Walter Schwartz and Myrna Joann (Whitworth) Sandipher; m. Linda Diann Bretches (div. 1979); 1 son—Joshua David. Contrbr. poetry to Our Western World's Greatest Poems, 1984. AA, Cuyamaca Community Coll., El Cajon, Calif., 1983; postgrad. San Diego State U., 1983—. Recipient Award of Merit, World of Poetry, 1983, 1984; Golden Poet Award, World of Poetry, 1985, 86. Home: 3903 Conrad Dr Apt 84 Spring Valley CA 92077

SCHWARTZ, TONY (ANTHONY), b. Manhattan, NY., Aug. 19, 1923, s. Samuel and Esther (Levy); m. Reenah Lurie, Sept. 27, 1957; children—Michaela and Anton. Author: The Responsive Chord, 1973, Media: The Second God, 1982. Pratt Institute (NYC.), cert. in advertising design, 1944. Civil Service graphic artist for the U.S. Navy, 1944-45; art director, Graphic Institute, 1945-50; art director, Wexton Co. (adv.), 1950-52. Sound studies: collected and catalogued 20,000 folk songs and stories from 52 countries; weekly radio program WNYC, 1946-72, Prix Italia, World Radio Festival, 1956. In-depth audio profile of Postal Zone 19, N.Y.C. Folkway Records sound documentaries, incl. New York 19, Nueva York (Puerto Rican sounds), 1,2,2 and a Zing, Zing, Zing (children's street games and songs), You're Stepping on My Shadow. Sounds for television commercials (Cannes Film Festival prize for Coca Cola commercial); Venice Film Fetival for documentary film sound in My Own Backyard to Play In. Presented recordings in musical education programs at Columbia Univ., Hunter College, New york University, Town Hall, Museum of Modern Art. Columns on sound for Art Direction and Popular Photography. Advertising column for MIN (Media Industry Newsletter, 1972 to present), Saturday night concerts, the Baq Room, Manhattan, 6 years. Political television commercials from 1964, public service commercials, Instructor, Media & Public Health, Harvard University, School of Public Health. Address: 455 W 56th St New York NY 10019

SCHWARTZ, WILLIAM JEFFREY, b. Columbus, OH, Dec. 25, 1957; s. William Earl Schwartz and Nancy Lee (Miller) Gardner; m. Cynthia Elaine Perez, June 20, 1981; 1 son, Christopher Alan. Contrbr. articles to newspapers. Wrkg. on book on profl. baseball players. A.A., John Wesley Coll., 1979; B.A., Mount Vernon Nazarene Coll., 1981. COord. info. services Mount Vernon Nazareen Coll., OH, 1981—; info. dir. Mid-Ohio Conf., Mount Vernon, 1983—, Natl. Assn. of Intercollegiate Athletics (NAIA), Mount Vernon, 1984—. Recipient 2d place for baseball press guide Coll. Sports Info. Dirs. Am. and Natl. Collegiate Baseball Wrtrs. Assn., 1984, 87, 1st place, 1986, 3d place for best sports story/best news story Mount Vernon News, 1983. Mem. Natl. Collegiate Baseball Wrtrs. Assn., Coll. Sports Info. Dirs. Am., Football Wrtrs. Assn. Am. U.S. Basketball Wrtrs. Assn., NAIA Sports Info. Dirs. Assn. Home: 18 Buena Vista Ave Mount Vernon OH 43050

SCHWARTZMAN, LOIS PHOEBE, b. Durham, NC, Feb. 23, 1937; d. William and Ida (Etkin) Zuckerman; m. Edwin Schwartzman, Jan. 27, 1962; children—Miriam, Susan, Judith, Anne, Ruth. Contrbr. to Working Mother Mag., Teen Beat Mag. B.A. in English, Rutgers U., 1972. Jnlst., News Transcript, Freehold, NJ, 1985—; free-lance wrtr., 1980—. Home: 147 Jackson Mills Rd Freehold NJ 07728

SCHULZE, ENIKA HERMINE, b. Hardenberg, Netherlands, Sept. 26, 1938, came to U.S., 1955, d. Hendrick Jan and Maria Martha (Rienksma) Grooters; m. David W. Pearson, May 2, 1959 (div. 1975); m. Richard H. Schulze, Aug. 29, 1987. BA, U. Okla., 1970; MBA, So. Meth. U., 1976. Pres., mng. ed. Legal Ass. Today, Inc., Dallas, 1983—, pres. Pearson Pubs. Co. Mem. profl. orgns. Office: Legal Asst 6060 N Central Expwy Dallas TX 75206

SCHWARZ, JOYCE A., b. Cleveland, OH, d. Frank Anton and Ann Marie (Stefani) Habart. Articles in pop. mags. including McCalls, American Girl; author Cooking With Frozen Vegetables, 1978, Entertaining with Brandy, 1979. BS, Ohio U., 1968; MA, U. of Southern Cal., Los Angeles, 1984. Asst. ed., Ladies Home Journal, NYC, 1968-69; assoc. ed. American Girl magazine, NYC, 1969-71; dir. of publs., U. of San Francisco, 1971-77; acct. supvsr., Foote Cone & Belding, San Francisco, 1977-79; vp, Fawcett McDermott Cavanagh, Hon. HW, 1979-82; pres., Joyce A. Schwartz & Assoc., Los Angeles, 1982-m. Mem. Women in Film, Public Relations Society of America, Acad. of Tel. Arts and Sci. Home: 1616 N. Poinsettia 420 Los Angeles CA 90046

SCHWED, PETER, b. NYC, Jan. 18, 1911; s. Frederick and Bertie (Stiefel) Schwed; m. Antonia Sanxay Holding, Mar. 6, 1947; children—Katharine Holding (Mrs. Eric F. Wood), Peter Gregory, Laura Sanxay, Roger Eaton. Author: Sinister Tennis, 1975, God Bless Pawnbrokers, 1975, The Serve and the Overhead Smash, 1976, Hanging in There, 1977, The Education of a Woman Golfer (with Nancy Lopez), 1979, Test Your Tennis IQ, 1981, Turning the Pages, 1984 Overtime, 1987, How to Talk Tennis, 1988; compiler: The Cook Charts, 1949; editor: Great Stories From the World of Sports (with H.W. Wind), 1958, The Fireside Book of Tennis (with Allison Danzig), 1972; contrbr. articles to periodicals. Grad. Lawrenceville (NJ) Schl., 1928; student Princeton, 1929-32. Asst. vp Provident Loan Soc. (NY), 1932-42; with Simon & Schuster, Inc. (NYC), 1946-84, vp exec. editor, 1957-62, exec. vp., 1962-66, pub. trade books, 1966-72, chair editorial bd., 1972-82, editorial chair emeritus, 1982-84, dir., 1966-72. Served to capt. F.A. AUS, World War II. Mem. AG, PEN. Home: 151 W 86th St New York NY 10024

SCHWEITZER, DARRELL CHARLES, b. Woodbury, NJ, Aug. 27, 1952; s. Francis Edward Schweitzer and Mary Alice (Schilling) Lalli. Author: (criticism) Conan's World & Robert E. Howard, 1979, The Dream Quest of HP Lovecraft, 1978; (short stories) We Are All Legends, 1981, Tom O'Bedlam's Night Out & Other Strange Excursions, 1985; (novel) The Shattered Goddess, 1982; (with G. Scithers and John M. Ford) On Writing Science Fiction: The Editors Strike Back, 1981; ed. Exploring Fantasy Worlds, 1985; Discovering Modern Horror Fiction, 1985, also others; contrbr. fiction, essays, rvws. and columns to Twilight Zone, Night Cry, Amazing Stories, Sci. Fiction Rvw, Phila. Inquirer, also others. BA in Geography, Villanova U., 1974, MA in English, 1976. Asst. ed. Isaac Asimov's Sci. Fiction Mag., Phila., 1977-82, Amazing Stories, Phila., 1982-86. Home: 113 Deepdale Rd Strafford PA 19087

SCHWERIN, DORIS, b. Peabody, MA, June 24, 1922, d. Harry and Mary (Polivnick) Halpern; m. Jules V. Schwerin, Mar. 2, 1946; 1 son, Charles Norman. Author: Diary of a Pigeon Watcher, 1976, Leanna, 1978, The Tomorrow Book (children's book), 1984, Rainbow Walkers, 1985, The Tree that Cried (children's book), 1985. Ed. Juilliard Schl., Boston U. Mem. PEN, AL, AG, Dramatists Guild, ASCAP. Home: 317 W 83d St New York NY 10024

SCHWERNER, ARMAND, b. Antwerp, Belgium, May 11, 1927 (arrd. US, 1936); s. Elie and Sara S. Author: The Lightfall, 1963, The Domesday Dictionary (with Donald Kaplan), 1963, (if personal), 1968, The Tablets I-VIII, 1968, Seaweed, 1969, The Tablets I-XV, 1971, The Bacchae Sonnets, 1974, The Tablets I-XVIII (tape ed.), 1974, Redspell, 1975, Tablets XVI, XVII, XVIII, 1975, This Practice, Tablet XIX and other poems, 1976, Bacchae Sonnets, 1977, the work , the joy and the triumph of the will, 1978, Philoctetes, translated from the Greek (cassette), 1978, Sounds of the River Naranjana and the Tablets I-XXIV, 1983; contrbns. to numerous anthols. BA, MA, Columbia Univ., 1950, 1964. Prof., Coll. of Staten Island, 1964—. NEA creative writer's fellowships, 1973, 79, 87, CAPS creative wrtg. fellowship, 1973, 75. Mem. PEN, PSA. Home: 30 Catlin Ave Staten Island NY 10304

SCHWIRIAN, ANN, b. Mt. Vernon, Wash., July 4, 1934, d. Willard Wesley and Katherine Clara (Fleek) Gustafson; m. James Andrew Schwirian, Sept. 12, 1953; children—George, Janna, Kay, Susan. Contrbr. to Pacifica Nexus, If Poetry, Talisman, Odessa Poetry Rvw, Riders of the Rainbow, numerous other publs. AA, Skyline Community Coll., San Bruno, Calif., 1977; BA, San Francisco State U., 1980, MA, 1983. Recipient Spcl. Commendation award San Francisco Browning Soc., 1983. Mem. Pacifica Women Wrtrs. Support Group. Home: 20 Point Reyes Way Pacifica CA 94044

SCOBIE, ITHA, b. Bklyn., Aug. 5, 1950, d. Philip and Mildred Verowitz; 1 dau., Risa. Author: There for the Taking, 1979; contrbr. to Out There, Coldspring Jnl, VoiceFree (Dublin, Ireland), The Fred (London), other small press publs. Student Schl. Visual Arts, NYC. Tchr., cons. Creative Edn. Center, Woodstock, N.Y., 1977-79, N.Y. Poets-in-Schls. project, NYC, 1979—. Mem. P&W. Home: 20 Desbrosses St New York NY 10013

SCOPPETTONE, SANDRA VALERIE, b. Morristown, NJ, June 1, 1936; d. Casimiro Radames and Helen Katherine (Greis) Scoppettone. Picture books: Suzuki Beane, 1961, Bang Bang You're Dead, 1968; novels: Trying Hard to Hear You, 1974, The Late Great Me, 1976, Some Unknown Person, 1977, Happy Endings Are All Alike, 1978, Such Nice People, 1980, Long Time Between Kisses, 1982, Innocent Bystanders, 1983, Playing Murder, 1985. Recipient Eugene O'Neill award, 1972. Home: 131 Prince St New York NY 10012

SCOTT, AMANDA, see Scott-Drennan, Lynne Ellen

SCOTT, ELIZABETH ANN, (Liz), b. Pitts., KS, July 6, 1951; d. John Clark and Virginia Lee (Huffman) S. Author: Public Relations Handbook, 1978, 79, Foreign Trade and the Hand Glass Industry, 1979; ed., contrbr. numerous articles to Glass News and its predecessor National Glass Budget, 1978—. BA, Geneva Coll., 1972. Mgr., Liz Scott Enterprises, Pitts., PA, 1976—; mng. ed. Glass News, Pitts., 1978—. Office: 803 South Negley Ave Pittsburgh PA 15232

SCOTT, JONNIE MELIA DEAN, b. Kansas City, KS, June 15, 1957; d. James Dean and Ida Lorena (Cornett) Helm; m. Michael Lee Scott, Jan. 4, 1975; children—James Michael, John Tillman Helm.Contrbr. poems to anthols. Wrkg. on book of religious poems. Grad. public schs. Kansas City. Named one of Best New Poets of 1986, Am. Poetry Assn., 1986. Home: 5221 Crest Dr Kansas City KS 66106

SCOTT, MICHAEL K., see McKay, Scott Michael

SCOTT, PATRICIA JEANNE, b. Wheeling, WV, Aug. 22, 1942; d. Robert and Teresa (Cerutti) S.; m. Norman Scott; 1 daughter, Shay Bartlett. Contrbr. articles on the law to profl. mags., popular mag; author law-related edn. programs. B.A. in Political Sci., Western Coll., 1964; postgrad Loyola Coll., Balt., 1985—. Tchr. public schls., Annapolis, MD, 1966-87, Elkton, MD,

1987—. Home: 13 Revere Pl The Hunt Club Newark DE 19702

SCOTT, TARYN, see Mercer, Linda Lou

SCOTT, WALTER RAY, b. Sulphur Well, KY, Aug. 19, 1913; s. John William and Eudora Elma (Finn) S.; m. Verna Bruister, Dec. 12, 1938; children—Neila Sharron Scott Darnaby, Daryl Elana Scott Gilpin. Author: A Pictorial Study of Mammoth Cave, 1949, Big Bend National Park—Land of Dramatic Contrasts, 1950. Student Lindsey-Wilson Coll., Columbia, Ky., 1931, Murray State U., 1934-35, Western Ky. State U., 1935. Photographer U.S. Engrs., Mobile, Ala., 1941-42; dir. pub. relations and photography Natl. Park Concessions, Inc., Mammoth Cave, Ky., 1946-67; dir. Ky. Dept. tourism, Frankfort, Ky., 1967-81; free-lance wrtr., photographer, Frankfort, 1981—. chmn. dist. Ky. Schl. Bds. Assn., Bowling Green, Ky., 1963-64. Served as CPO (photog.) U.S. Navy, 1942, 46. Recipient 1st place for calendar competition Westfield Ins. Co., 1986. Mem. Soc. Am. Travel Wrtrs. (1st place for travel photograph 1984, 85, 86), Midwest Travel Wrtrs. Assn., Ky. Outdoor Press Assn. Home: 1220 Chinook TL Frankfort KY 40601

SCOTT-DRENNAN, LYNNE ELLEN, (Amanda Scott)b. Salinas, CA, Aug. 7, 1944; d. Lionel Burr and Ellen (Lowell) Scott; m. Terry Richard Drennan; 1 son—James Richard. Author: The Fugitive Heiress, 1981, The Kidnapped Bride, 1983, The Indomitable Miss Harris, 1983, Ravenwood's Lady, 1983, Affair of Honor, 1984, Summer Sandcastle, 1984, Lady Hawk's Folly, 1985, Lady Escapade, 1985, Lord Abberley's Nemesis, 1986, Lady Meriel's Duty, 1987, Mistress of the Hunt, 1987, Sweet Thunder, 1987, Lady Brittany's Choice, 1987. BA, Mills Coll., 1966; MA, San Jose State U., 1968. Teacher Salinas City Schls. (CA), 1968-71. Mem. Child Abuse Services Cncl., 1980-84, Child Molest Protocol Comm., 1983-84. Best Regency Author, Romantic Times Mag., 1983-84, Best Sensual Regency, 1983-84 Romance Writer's of Amer.'s Golden Medallion for Best Regency of 1986. Mem. Romance Wrtrs. of Am. Home: 137 Rambling Dr Folsom CA 95630

SCOTT-MCBRIDE, NANCY FORSYTH, b. Carbondale, IL, June 21, 1940; d. Walter and Marie (Shepherd) Forsyth; m. Robert Scott, Feb. 7, 1959 (div. Oct. 1972); children—Jennifer, Ryan, Robby; m. 2d, Scott McBride, Sept. 27, 1984. Contrbr. poetry to numerous mags. and anthologies including Village Voice, NY Quarterly, Ten Years & Then Some. BS, Northwestern U., 1959. Editorial board NY Quarterly Poetry Jnl, 1970-75. Greenburg Poetry Prize, NY St. Council for the Arts, 1982, 83, Best Anti-nuclear Poem, Social Responsibility, 1985. Mem. PSA, P&W. Home: 1 Hillside Terr Irvington NY 10533

SCOTTE, BRANDON, see Miller, Donald Larry

SCRIMGEOUR, JAMES RICHARD, b. Holden, MA, July 29, 1938; s. John Harold and Alice Beatrice (Le Poer) S.; m. Christine Xanthakos, Oct. 13, 1963; children: John David, Mary Xanthi, James Dimitri. Author: Sean O'Casey, 1978; Dikel, Your Hands and Other Poems, 1979; ed.: What Is That Country Standing Inside You, 1976; co-ed. Pikestaff Forum, Vols. I-VII, 1977—, Pikestaff Rev., Vols. I-III; Sticklewort and Feverfew (Robert Sutherland), 1980; The Horse We Lie Down In (Frannie Lindsay), 1981; contrbr. articles to Modern Drama, Scandinavian Studies, Sean O'Casey Rvw, Mass. Studies in English. BA in English, Clark U., 1963; MA in English, U. Mass., 1968, PhD in English, 1972. Grad. asst. U. Mass., Amherst, 1967-71; asst. prof. Ill. State U., Normal, 1971-78; asst. prof., assoc. prof. prof. English, Western Conn. State U., Danbury, 1979—. Served with U.S. Army, 1957-59. Home: 36 Caldwell Dr New Milford CT 06776

SCULLY, JAMES JOSEPH, b. New Haven, CT, Feb. 23, 1937; s. James and Hazel Ruth (Donovan) S.; m. Arlene Marie Steeves, Sept. 10, 1960; children—John, Aaron, Deirdre. Author: The Marches, 1967, Avenue of the Americas, 1971, Santiago Poems, 1975, Scrap Book, 1977, May Day, 1980, Apollo Helmet, 1983; (with Grandin Conover) Communications, 1970. Translator: (with C. J. Herington) Prometheus Bound (Aeschylus), 1975; (with Maria Proser) Quechua People Poetry, 1977; (with Maria Proser and Arlene Scully) De Repente/All of a Sudden (Teresa de Jesus), 1979; (with Arlene Scully) Poetry and Militancy in Latin America (Roque Dalton), 1981. Ed.: Modern poetics, 1965, Modern Poets on Modern Poetry, 1966. Student Southern Conn. State U., 1955-57; B.A., U. Conn., 1959. Instr., Rutgers U., New Brunswick, NJ, 1963-64; asst. prof. to prof. U. Conn., Storrs, 1964—. Guggenheim fellow; fellow NEA, Ingram Merrill Fdn.; recipient Lamont Poetry award AAP, 1967, Contrbr.'s prize The Far Point, 1969, Jenny Taine Meml. award Mass. Rvw., 1971, Translation award Islands and Continents, 1980, award for bookcover design Bookbuilders of Boston, 1983. Mem. PEN. Home: 250 Lewiston Ave Willimantic CT 06226

SCULLY, JAMES JOSEPH, b. New Haven, Feb. 23, 1937, s. James and Hazel Ruth (Donovan) S.; m. Arlene Marie Steeves, Sept. 10, 1960; children—John, Deirdre. Author: The Marches, 1967, Avenue of the Americas, 1971, Santiago Poems, 1975, Scrap Book, 1977, May Day, 1980, Apollo Helmet, 1983; ed.: Modern Poetics, 1964, Modern Poets on Modern Poetry, 1965; translator (with C.J. Herington) Prometheus Bound, by Aeschylus, 1975, (with Maria A. Proser) Quechua Peoples Poetry, 1977, (with Proser and wife) De Repente/All of a Sudden, 1979. Wrkg. on critical/theoretical essays. BA, U. Conn., 1959, PhD, 1964. Instr. Rutgers U., New Brunswick, N.J., 1963-64; asst. prof., assoc. prof., prof. U. Conn., Storrs, 1964—. Recipient Lamont award AAP, 1967; Guggenheim fellow, 1973; NEA fellow, 1977. Mem. PEN, PSA. Home: 250 Lewiston Ave Williamantic CT 06226

SEAGER, WILLIAM RALPH, b. Geneva, NY, Nov. 3, 1911, s. William Thomas and Ellen Bessie (Nichols) S.; m. Ruth Marie Lovejoy, Dec. 11, 1932; children—Ralph William, Douglas Byron, Keith Allen. Author books of verse: Songs from a Willow Whistle, 1956, Beyond the Green Gate (Pub.'s Award 1958), 1958, Christmas Chimes in Rhyme, 1962, The Sound of an Echo, 1963, Cup, Flagon, and Fountain, 1965, A Choice of Dreams, 1970, Wheatfields & Vineyards, 1975, Little Yates and the United States, 1976, the Manger Mouse and Other Christmas Poems, 1977, Hiding in Plain Sight, 1982, The Love Tree, 1985; co-author corr. course on writing poetry for Christian Authors' Guild. LittD, Keuka Coll., 1970. Carrier, clrk. U.S. Post Office Dept., Penn Yan, N.Y., 1938-68; asst. prof. Keuka Coll., Keuka Park, N.Y., 1960-82; now prof. emeritus; poet, lectr., dir. poetry workshops, 1954—. Mem. P&W. Served with U.S. Navy, 1944-45. Home: 311 Keuka St Penn Yan NY 14527

SEAGULL, SAMANTHA SINGER, (Sandra Lee Mayer, Luana Lee Kimm, Tanya Fu-Chiang Liu, Tamminy Barkley, Leah Alexandre), b. Mpls., July 16, 1942; d. Irvin Carlos and Evelyn Sophia (Lindgren) Mayer; m. Vernon Arlan King, Mar. 1, 1968 (div. Mar. 28, 1970); children—Lu Jeanna Kay, Melonie Ann, Chrystian Wayn. Contrbr. numerous poems to anthols. Wrkg. on poems, children's books (prose and poetry), song lyrics, Chinese proverbs, Japanese haiku. Student U. Minn., 1964-66, Drama Schl., Los Angeles 1959-60, currently student at Anoka-Ramsey Comm. Coll. Recipient 6th prize Clover Poetry Assn., 1975, 19 awards World of Poetry, 1983-86, 9 Hon. Mention awards Ursus Press, 1984-86, 4 Poetry awards Trouvere Co., 1985. Address: Box 1106 Minneapolis MN 55440

SEALE, JAN EPTON, b. Pilot Point, TX, Aug. 28, 1939; d. Thomas H. and Margaret B. (Pittman) Epton; m. Carl Seale, Apr. 4, 1958; children—Ansen, Erren, Avrel. Author: Bonds, 1978, 2d ed., 1981, Sharing the House, 1982. BA, U. Louisville, 1960; MA, North Tex. State U., 1970. Instr. English, North Tex. State U., Denton, 1970-71, Pan Am. U., Edinburg, Tex., 1973-83; cons., wrtr., 1983—. Fellow, NEA, 1982. Home: 400 Sycamore McAllen TX 78501

SEALE, JOSEPH LLOYD, b. Colon, Republic of Panama, Sept. 24, 1919, came to U.S., 1951, naturalized, 1957; s. Eugene Flavius and Emily (Neptune) S.; m. Virginia Augusta Lewis De Seale, Dec. 9, 1939; children—Elvia Carol Brown, Joseph L., Maicela. Contrbr. poems. to anthols., lit. mags.; article to mag. B.B.A., CCUY, 1961. Home: 855 SW Early Terrace Port Charlotte FL 33981

SEALY, RUBY, see Pellegrini, Ruby Louise

SEAMAN, BARBARA, (Ann Rosner), b. Bklyn., Sept. 11, 1935; d. Henry Jerome and Sophie Blance (Kimels) Rosner; m. Gideon Seaman, Jan. 13, 1957 (div.); children—Noah Samuel, Elana Felicia, Shira Jean; m. 2d, Milton Forman, Apr. 18, 1982. Author: The Doctors' Case Against the Pill, 1969, rev. ed., 1980, Free and Female, 1972, Women and the Crisis in Sex Hormones (with G. Seaman), 1977, Women's Health Care: A Guide to Alternatives, 1983; contrbg. author: foreword to Lunaception, 1975, new foreword, 1982; The Bisexuals, 1974, Career and Motherhood, 1979; author: (play) I Am a Woman, 1972; contrbr. to various anthologies including Rooms with No View, 1974; narrator: (film) Taking Our Bodies Back, 1974; contrbr. editorials and rvws. to newspapers, popular mags.; books and articles translated into Spanish, German, Dutch, Turkish, Japanese, Hebrew, French, Italian. BA, Oberlin Coll., 1956, cert. in advanced sci. writing Columbia U. Schl. Journalism, 1968. Columnist, contrbg. editor Ladies' Home Jnl (NYC), 1965-69; editor child care and edn. Family Circle (NYC), 1970-73; contrbg. editor Omni mag., 1978; cons. FYI, ABC-TV, 1979-80; tchr. Coll. New Rochelle, 1975, Sagaris Inst., 1975; co-founder Natl. Women's Health Network, 1975—; vp Women's Med. Center (NYC), 1971-73; mem. ERA Emergency Task Force, 1979—; mem. adv. council Feminist Press (Old Westbury, NY), 1975—; mem. adv. bd. Feminist Center for Human Growth and Devel., 1979—, Women's History Library (Berkeley, CA), 1973—; mem. steering com. Women's Forum, 1974; mem. adv. bd. NOW (NY), 1973, Women's Guide to Books, 1974, Jewish Women for Affirmative Action (Evanston, IL), 1973—, Jnl Women and Health, 1975—, Jewish Feminist Orgn. NYC, 1975—.

Recipient citation for books as first to raise issue of sexism in health care as world-wide issue Library of Congress, 1973, citation as author responsible for patient package inserts on prescriptions HEW, 1970, Matrix award, 1978; inviting com. Am. Writers Congress. Mem. Columbia U. Seminar on Women in Soc., ASJA, Natl. Assn. Sci. Writers, PEN, NEW, AL, Women's Ink. Address: 734 Noyes Evanston IL 60201

SEAMAN, SYLVIA SYBIL, (Francis Sylvin), b. NYC, Nov. 8, d. Nathaniel and Felicia (Bleet) Bernstein; m. William Seaman, Dec. 27, 1925; children—Gideon, Jonathan. Author: Rusty Carrousel (as Francis Sylvin, with Frances Wexler), 1943, Miracle Father (as Francis Sylvin), 1952, Test Tube Father, 1967, How to be a Jewish Grandmother, 1979, Always a Woman, 1965. BA, Cornell U., 1922; MA, Columbia U., 1926. Tchr., librarian public schls., NYC, 1922-25. Mem. AL. Home: 244 W 74th St New York NY 10023

SEATH, OLGA WINNIFRED HANNA, b. Columbus City, IA, Feb. 9, 1899; d. Lindlay Branson and Sara Leona (Shaum) Hanna; m. Dr. Kenneth Lynde, 1917; children: Barbara, Eleanore; m. Russell Seath, 1925; children—Dorothy, Marianne, Robert. Author poetry books: Poems by Olga, 1985, The Rest of the Story, 1985, Olga's Love Addiction, 1985. Wrkg. on book on Jesus' teaching. Address: Hughes 4301 Orange Grove North Fort Myers FL 33903

SEATOR, LYNETTE HUBBARD, b. Chgo., Mar. 23, 1929, d. Alvin Glen and Thelma May (Mulnix) Hubbard; m. Gordon Douglas Seator, June 8, 1949; children—Pamela, Penelope, Patricia, Glen. Contrbr. poetry to Spoon River Qtly, Praxis, Open Places, Kalliope, Pulpsmith, other lit mags. MA, U. Ill., 1966, PhD, 1972. Instr. Western Ill. U., Macomb, 1966-67; prof. Ill. Coll., Jacksonville, 1967—, Harry J. Dunbaugh disting. prof., 1976; artist-in-residence Ill. Arts council, 1984-86. Danforth assoc., 1976; NEH fellow Columbia U., 1979. Mem. P&W, AAUP, MLA (women's caucus). Home: 1609 Mound Ave Jacksonville IL 62650

SEAVER, JAMES EVERETT, b. Los Angeles, Oct. 4, 1918; s. Everett Herbert and Gertrude Lillian (Sharp) Seaver; m. Virginia Stevens, Dec. 20, 1940; children—Richard Everett, William Merrill, Robert Edward. Author: The Persecution of the Jews in the Roman Empire, 313-438 AD, 1942, also articles. AB, Stanford U., 1940; PhD, Cornell U., 1946. Asst. instr. history Cornell U., 1940-42, 44-46; instr. Mich. State U., 1946-47; mem. faculty U. Kans. (Lawrence), 1947—, prof. history, 1960—, pres. faculty, 1972-74, 82-83. Fulbright-Hays grantee, Italy, 1953-54, Israel, 1963-64; Carnegie grantee, Costa Rica, 1966-67. Home: 600 Louisiana St Lawrence KS 66044

SEBEOK, THOMAS ALBERT, b. Budapest, Hungary, Nov. 9, 1920 (came to U.S., 1937, naturalized, 1944); s. Dezso and Veronica (Perlman) Sebeok; m. Eleanor Lawton, Sept. 1947; 1 dau.—Veronica C.; 2nd m. Jean Umiker, Oct. 1972; children—Jessica A., Erica L. Editor-in-chief: Semiotica, 1968—, Current Trends in Linguistics, 1963—, Approaches to Semiotics, 1968-74; editor: Studies in Semiotics, 1974—; genl. editor: Advances in Semiotics, 1974; contrbr. numerous articles to profl. jnls. BA, U. Chgo., 1941; MA, Princeton, 1943, PhD, 1945. Mem. Faculty IN. U. (Bloomington), 1943—, Distinguished prof. linguistics, 1967—, prof. anthropology, prof. Uralic and Altaic studies, fellow Folklore Inst., mem. Russian and East European Inst., chair Research Center for Lang. and Semiotic Studies, chair grad. program in Semantic Studies; mem.-at-large Natl. Acad. Scis.-NRC; Linguistic Soc. Am. prof., 1975; cons. Ford Fdn., Guggenheim Fdn., Wenner-Gren Fdn. for Anthrop. Research, U.S. Office Edn., NSF, fellowship div. Natl. Acad. Scis., Can. Council; panel mem. for linguistics NEA, 1966-67; exchange prof. Natl. Acad. Scis.-USSR Acad. Scis., 1973. Mem. Intl. Assn. Semiotic Studies, Linguistic Soc. Am., Am. Assn. Machine Translation and Computational Linguistics. Home: 1104 Covenanter Dr Bloomington IN 47401

SEGAL, CHARLES PAUL, b. Boston, Mar. 19, 1936; s. Robert and Gladys (Barsky) Segal; children—Joshua Hawley, Thaddeus Gabriel. Author: Landscape in Ovid's Metamorphoses, 1969, The Theme of the Mutilation of Corpse in the Illiad, 1971, Tragedy and Civilization: An Interpretation of Sophocles, 1982, Poetry and Myth in Ancient Pastoral: Essays on Theocritus and Virgil, 1981; Dionysiac Poetics and Euripides' Bacchae, 1982, Interpreting Greek Tragedy, 1986, Pindar's Mythmaking: The Fourth Pythian Ode, 1986, Language and Desire in Seneca's Phaedra, 1986; editor: The Heroic Paradox, 1982, A Rhetoric of Imitation: Literary Memory in Virgil and Other Latin Poets, 1986, Roads to Paradise: Reading the Lives of the Early Saints, 1987. Editorial bd.: Am. Jnl Semiotics, 1981; Scholars Press, 1982; Helios, 1985—, MD, 1985—, Quad. Catalans de Cultura Clàssica, 1986—. AB, Harvard U., 1957, PhD, 1961; postgrad. (Fulbright scholar) Am. Schl. Classical Studies, Athens, Greece, 1957-58. Teaching fellow, classics tutor Harvard U., 1959-61, instr., 1963-64; asst. prof. classics U. PA (Phila.), 1964-65, assoc. prof., 1965-67, assoc. prof. Brown U., 1968-70, prof., 1970—, prof. classics and comparative lit., 1978—, chair classics, 1978-81; Benedict prof. classics, prof. comparative lit., 1980-86; prof. classics and comp. lit., Princeton U., 1987—; jr. fellow Center for Hellenic Studies, 1967-68, sr. fellow, 1986; vis. prof., prof.-in-charge Intercollegiate Center for Classical Studies (Rome), 1970-72; vis. prof. Brandeis U., 1974; vis. dir. studies Ecole Hautes Etudes (Paris), 1975-76; Fulbright exchange lectr. U. Melbourne (Australia), 1978; vis. prof. Greek Columbia U., 1979; participant 1st and 2nd Soviet/Am. Semiotics Colloquia, Am. Council Learned Socs./USSR Acad. Scis., 1980-83; cons. in field; mem. exec. council Center Semiotics, Brown U., 1979—; chair and mem. curriculum rev. com. Brown U., 1982-84. ACLS fellow, 1975; Guggenheim fellow, 1981-82; NEH fellow, 1977, 1985-86; Recipient Prix de Rome Am. Acad. in Rome, 1961-63. Resident in Classics, Am. Acad. in Rome, 1986. Mem. Am. Philol. Assn., Am. Comparative Lit. Assn., Classical Assn. New Eng., Virgilian Soc., Intl. Ovid Soc., Societa Italiana per lo Studio dell Antichita Classica. Home: 77 Randall Road Princeton NJ 08540

SEGAL, ERICH, b. Bklyn., June 16, 1937; s. Samuel Michael and Cynthia (Shapiro) Segal; m. Karen Llona Marianne James, June 10, 1975; 1 dau. Author, narrator: TV spcl. The Ancient Games, 1972, rebroadcast 1976, TV spcl. Olympathon '80; novels: Love Story, 1970, Fairy Tale, 1973, Oliver's Story, 1977, Man, Woman and Child, 1980, The Class, 1985; book and lyrics: Sing Muse, 1961-62; play: Odyssey, 1974; author screenplays: The Beatles' Yellow Submarine, The Games, Love Story (Golden Globe Award), R.P.M., Oliver's Story, A Change of Seasons, Man, Woman and Child. Author: Roman Laughter: The Comedy of Plautus, 1968, rev. ed., 1985; editor: Euripides: A Collection of Critical Essays, 1968, Oxford Readings in Greek Tragedy, 1983, Plato's Dialogues, 1984; co-editor: Caesar Augustus: Seven Essays, 1984; editor, translator: Plautus: Three Comedies, 1969, Scholarship on Plautus, 1965-1976, 1981. AB, Harvard U., 1958, AM, 1959, PhD, 1965. Teaching fellow humanities, Harvard U., 1959-63; vis. lectr. Yale U., 1964-65, asst. prof. 1965-68, assoc. prof. classics and comparative lit., 1968-73; vis. prof. Classical philology U. Munich (Germany), 1973; vis. prof. classics Princeton U., 1974-75, Tel Aviv U., spring 1976; vis. prof. comparative lit. Dartmouth Coll., fall 1976-80; vis. fellow Wolfson Coll., Oxford U., 1978, 79, 80; adj. prof. classics Yale U., 1981—; hon. research fellow University Coll. (London), 1983—; mem. exec. com. Natl. Adv. Council, Peace Corps, 1970; jury mem. Cannes Film Festival, 1971, Natl. Book Award (Arts and Letters), 1971. Guggenheim fellow, 1968; Presidential Commendation for service to Peace Corps, 1971. Mem. Acad. Lit. Studies. Office: Rm 1106 119 W 57th St New York NY 10019

SEGAL, JONATHAN BRUCE, b. NYC, May 12, 1946; s. Clement and Florence Lillian (Miller) Segal; m. Haidi Kuhn, June 30, 1974. Contrbr. articles to popular journals. BA, Washington Coll., 1966. Writer, editor NY Times (NYC)1966-73; editor Quadrangle/NY Times Book Co. (NYC)1974-76; sr. editor Simon & Schuster (NYC), 1976-81; vp, exec. editor, editor-in-chief, edl. dir. Times Books (NYC)1981—; ed.-at-large, Random House, 1985—. Home: 115 E 9th Apt 12E New York NY 10003

SEGAL, LORE, b. Vienna, Austria, Mar. 8, 1928 (came to U.S., 1951, naturalized, 1956); d. Ignatz and Franzi (Stern) Groszmann; m. David I. Segal, Nov. 3, 1960 (dec.); children—Beatrice Ann, Jacob Paul. Author: Other People's Houses, 1964; (novel) Lucinella, 1976, (novel) Her First American, 1986; (children's books) All the Way Home, 1973, Tell Me a Trudy, 1977; The Story of Mrs. Brubeck and How She Looked for Trouble and Where She Found Him, 1981, The Story of Mrs. Lovewright and Purrless Her Cat, 1985; translator: (with W.D. Snodgrass) Gallows Songs, 1968, The Juniper Tree and Other Tales from Grimm, 1973; contrbr. short stories, articles, to NY Times Book Rvw, Partisan Rvw, New Republic, The New Yorker, others. BA in English Bedford Coll., U. London, Engl., 1948. Prof. writing div. Schl. Arts, Columbia U., also Princeton U., Sarah Lawrence Coll., Bennington Coll.; prof. writing U. IL (Chgo.). Guggenheim fellow, 1965-66; Council Arts and Humanities grantee, 1968-69; Artists Public Service grantee, 1970-71; CAPS grantee, 1975; NEA grantee, spring 1982; NEH grantee, 1983, AAIAL Award, 1986, NEA grantee, 1987. Address: 280 Riverside Dr New York NY 10025

SEGERSTROM, JANE ARCHER, b. Los Angeles, CA, Feb. 1, 1930; d. Francis Gaden and Lyda Mary (Comer) Archer; m. Clifford Charles Segerstrom, Feb. 1, 1951; children—John Archer, Carol Anne. Author: Look Like Yourself and Love It, 1980. BS, George Pepperdine U., 1951. Instructor adult program Long Beach City Coll. (CA), 1956-64; pres. Triad Interests, Inc. (Houston, TX), 1974, publisher, 1980; pres. Tri-D Consultants, 1983—. Mem. Wmn. in Communications, Assn. of Fashion and Image Consultants, Assn. of Image Consultants, Home Economists in Bus., Fashion Group, Am. Soc. for Training and Development. Home: 10811

Riverview Dr Houston TX 77042

SEID, RUTH, (Jo Sinclair), b. Bklyn., July 1, 1913; d. Nathan and Ida Seid. Author: Wasteland, 1946 (re-issued 1987), Sing at My Wake, 1951, The Long Moment, play, 1951, The Changelings, 1955 (re-issued 1985), Anna Teller, 1960; short stories anthologies Theme and Variation in the Short Story, 1938, Of the People, 1942, America in Literature, 1944, This Way to Unity, 1945, Social Insight Through Short Stories, 1946, Cross Section, 1946, This Land, These People, 1950; contrbr. short story to anthologies A Treasury of American Jewish Stories, 1948, The American Judaism Reader, 1967, Tales of Our People, 1969; mags., including Readers Digest (Recipient Harper's Prize novel award, 1946, 2nd prize natl. TV competition Fund for Republic, 1956, Annl. Fiction award Jewish Book Council Am. 1956, annl. award Ohioana Library 1956, 61, Brotherhood Week certificate of recognition NCCJ, 1956, Lit. award Cleve. Arts prize, 1961, Wolpaw Play Writing grant Jewish Community Centers, Cleve, 1969.) Grad. John Hay High Schl., Cleve. Various clerical jobs, publicity work, 1943-46; asst. dir. publicity dept. Greater Cleve. chpt. A.R.C., 1945-46. Mem. AG, PEN. All archives: Mugar Meml Library of Boston Univ. Home: 1021 Wellington Rd Jenkintown PA 19046

SEIDEL, FREDERICK LEWIS, b. Feb. 19, 1936; s. Jerome Jay and Thelma (Cartun) Seidel; children—Felicity, Samuel. Author: (poetry) Final Solutions, 1963, Sunrise, 1980 (recipient Lamont poetry prize, 1979, American Poetry Rvw. prize, 1979, Natl. Book Critics Circle award for poetry 1980). AB Harvard U., 1957. Paris editor Paris Rvw., 1960-61, adv. editor, 1961—; lectr. English Rutgers U. (New Brunswick, NJ). Address: 251 W 92d St New York NY 10025

SEIDENBAUM, ART DAVID, b. Bronx, NY, May 4, 1930; s. William G. and Lida (Aretsky) Seidenbaum; children—Kyle Scott, Kerry Kai. Author: Los Angeles 200: A Bicentennial Celebration (Harry Abrams), 1980. BS, Northwestern U., 1951; postgrad. Harvard U., 1951-52. Reporter Life mag. (NYC), 1955-59, corr., Los Angeles, 1959-61; W. Coast bur. chief, contbg. editor Saturday Evening Post (Los Angeles), 1961-62; columnist Los Angeles Times, 1962-78, editor book review sect., 1978-85, ed. Opinion sect., 1985—. Office: LA Times Mirror Sq Los Angeles CA 90053

SEIDENSTICKER, EDWARD GEORGE, b. Castle Rock, CO, Feb. 11, 1921; s. Edward George and Mary Elizabeth (Dillon) Seidensticker. Author: Kafu The Scribbler, 1965, Japan, 1961, Low City, High City, 1983; Translator: The Tale of Genju (by Murasaki Shikibu), 1976. BA, U. CO, 1942; MA, Columbia U., 1947; postgrad. Harvard. U., 1947-48. With U.S. Fgn. Service, Dept. State, Japan, 1947-50; mem. faculty Stanford U., 1962-66, prof. 1964-66; prof. dept. Far Eastern lans. and lit. U. Mich., Ann Arbor, 1966-77; prof. Japanese Columbia U., 1977—. Served with USMCR, 1942-46. Recipient Natl. Book Award, 1970; citation Japanese Ministry Edn., 1971; Kikuchikan prize, 1977; Goto Miyoko prize, 1982. Mem. Am. Oriental Soc., Assn. for Asian Studies. Home: 445 Riverside Dr New York NY 10027

SEIDMAN, HUGH, b. Bklyn., Aug. 1, 1940, s. Monas and Susan (Grossman) S. Author: (poetry) Collecting Evidence, 1970, Blood Lord, 1974, Throne/Falcon/Eye, 1982; ed. anthologies Westbeth Poets, 1971, Equal Time, 1972. BS, Bklyn. Poly., 1961; MS, U. Minn., 1964; MFA, Columbia U., 1969. Vis. wrtr. Yale U., 1971, 73; wrtr.-in-residence City Coll. CUNY, 1972-75, Wilkes Coll., Wilkes-Barre, Pa., 1975, Wichita State U., Kans., 1978, Coll. William and Mary, 1982; mem. faculty New Schl. for Social Research, NYC, 1976—; vis. asst. prof. Washington Coll., Chestertown, Md., 1979; vis. lectr. U. Wis., 1981, Columbia U., 1985. NEA writing fellow, 1972, 85. Mem. PEN, PSA, AG, AL. Home: 463 West St H960 New York NY 10014

SEIFERLE, REBECCA ANN, b. Denver, Dec. 14, 1951, d. Arthur Mase and Mary Kathryn (Thornton) Seiferle; m. Phillip Joseph Valencia, Aug. 11, 1978; children—Ann Clair, Maria Rose. Contrbr. poetry: Descant, Embers, Yes, Poetic Justic, Negative Capability, numerous other lit. mags. BA, SUNY-Albany, 1982. Freelance wrtr., 1976—; poet-in-schl., N.Mex. Arts Div., 1976. Winner poetry contests; recipient Bernie Babcock award Voice Intl., 1983. Mem. P&W, Feminist Wrtrs.' Guild. Home: Box 1131 Bloomfield NM 87413

SEITZ, NICHOLAS JOSEPH, b. Topeka, KS, Jan. 30, 1939; s. Frank Joseph and Lydia Natalie (Clerico) Seitz; m. Velma Jean Pfannenstiel, Sept. 12, 1959; children—Bradley Joseph, Gregory Joseph. Author: (with Dave Hill) Teed Off, 1977, Superstars of Golf, 1978, (with Tom Watson) Getting Up and Down, 1983; contrbr. articles to profl. jnls.; anthologized in Best Sports Stories. BA, U. OK, 1966. Sports editor Manhattan Mercury (KS), 1960-62, Norman Transcript (OK), 1962-64, OK Jnl. (Oklahoma City), 1964-67; mem. staff Golf Digest mag. (Norwalk, CT), 1967—, editor, 1973—; editorial dir. Golf Digest and Tennis, 1982—; syndicated golf instrn. and commentary CBS Radio Network; commentary ESPN TV Network. Named OK sports Writer of Year Natl. Sportswriters and Sportscasters Assn., 1965; winner contests Natl. Basketball Writers Assn., Golf Writers Assn. Home: 36 Hunt St Rowayton CT 06853

SEKLER, EDUARD FRANZ, b. Vienna, Austria, Sept. 30, 1920 (came to U.S., 1955); s. Eduard Jacob and Elisabeth (Demmel) Sekler; m. Mary Patricia May, July 20, 1962. Author: Pointhouses in European Housing, 1952, Wren and His Place in European Architecture, 1956, Proportion, a Measure of Order, 1965, Historic Urban Spaces I-IV, 1962-71, Proposal for the Urbanistic Conservation of Patan Durbar Square, 1980, Joseph Hoffmann, The Architectural Work, 1982, 1985, (with others) Kathmandu Valley, The Preservation of Physical Environment and Cultural Heritage, 2 vols., 1975, Le Corbusier at Work: The Genesis of the Carpenter Center for the Visual Arts, 1977, Dipl. Ing., Tech, U., Vienna, 1945; student Schl. Planning and Regional Research, London, Eng., 1947; PhD, Warburg Inst., London U., 1948; AM (hon.), Harvard, 1960. Partner archtl. firm Prehsler and Sekler, Vienna, 1945—; teaching asst., lectr. faculty architecture Tech. U., Vienna, 1945-54; vis. prof. architecture Harvard, 1954-56, assoc. prof., 1956-60, prof., 1960—, Osgood Hooker prof. visual art, 1970—; coordinator studies Carpenter Center Visual Arts, 1962-65, dir., 1966-76, chair dept. visual and environmental studies, 1968-70; expert mem. intl. com. hist. monuments UNESCO, 1951-54. Guggenheim fellow, 1961-62, 62-63. Fellow Am. Acad. Arts and Scis., fellow, US/ICOMS, 1986; mem. Intl. Council Monuments and Sites, Soc. Archtl. Historians. Home: 21 Gibson St Cambridge MA 02138

SEKOLL, JUNE LOUISE, (Louise Peters), b. Amsterdam, NY, Oct. 9, 1931, d. Dewey Samuel and Elsie (Hall) Petterson; m. Ferd Ralph Sekoll, Apr. 27, 1957; children—Ferd II, Frank, Sandra, Sarah, Anna, Marietta, Peter. Author: Dreams Never Die (novel), 1980. BS, Cornell U., 1954. Reporter Daily Reporter, Wellsville, N.Y., 1955-57, Hornell (N.Y.) Tribune, 1977-81; ed. Country Folks, Palatine Bridge, N.Y., 1981—; owner, pub., ed. Ridge Runner, Andover, N.Y., 1985—. Mem. Newspaper Farm Eds. Am. (historian 1986—), Northeast Farm Communicators (pres. 1984-86), Romance Wrtrs. Am., Creative Wrtrs. of Southern Tier-Niagara Erie Wrtrs. Home: Rock Creek Rd Greenwood NY 14839

SELAK, BARBARA S., see Tarila, B. Sophia

SELBY, KATHERINE, see Schardein, Sandra Wild

SELF, EDWIN FORBES, b. Dundee, Scotland, June 15, 1920; s. Robert Henry and Agnes (Dick) Self; m. Dorothy McCloskey, Nov. 1, 1942; children—Joan, Robert; 2nd m. Gloria Eileen Winke Wade, Aug. 18, 1951; children—Winke, Carey. AB in Polit. Sci. Dartmouth, 1942. Advertising manager La Jolla (CA), 1947-48; bus. manager Frontie Mg. (Los Angeles), 1949-55; editor, publ. San Diego Mag., 1948—; publisher cons. for San Francisco mag.; pub. cons. Washingtonian Mag. Spcl. award 1st Annl. City and Regional Mag. Conf., 1977. Mem. San Diego C. of C., City and Regional Mag. Assn. US Home: Box 85409 San Diego CA 92138

SELIG, KARL-LUDWIG, b. Wiesbaden, Germany, Aug. 14, 1926 (naturalized, 1948); s. Lucian and Erna (Reiss) Selig. Author: The Library of Vincencio Juan de Lastanosa, Patron of Gracian, Geneva, 1960, also numerous articles, revs.; editor: (Thomas Blundeville) of Councils and Counselors, 1963, (with A.G. Hatcher) Studia Philologica et Litteraria in Honorem L. Spitzer, 1958, (with J.E. Keller) Essays in Honor of N. B. Adams, 1966, U. NC Studies in Comparative Lit., 1959-61, Bull. Comediantes, 1959-64; asso. editor: Modern Lang. Notes, 1955-58; mng. editor: Romance Notes, 1959-61; co-editor: Yearbook of Comparative Lit., Vol. IX, 1960; editorial bd.: Coleccion Tamesis, London, 1962-79, Romanic Rev., 1969—, Teaching Lang. Through Lit., 1978—; assoc. editor: Hispania, 1969-74, Ky. Romance Qtly., 1973—; gen. editor: Revista Hispánica Moderna, 1971—; mem. natl. advd. bd: MLA. Intl. Bibliography, 1978—; editorial bd.: Yale Italian Studies, 1976-80. BA, Ohio State U., 1946, MA, 1947; student. U. Rome, Italy, 1949-50; PhD, U. Tex., 1955. Asst. prof. Romance Langs. and lit. Johns Hopkins, 1954-58; assoc. prof. U. NC, 1958-61, u. MN, 1961-63; vis. prof. U. TX, 1963-64, prof. Romance langs. and lit., 1964-65; Hinchliff prof. Spanish lit. Cornell U., 1965-69, dir. grad. studies in Romance lit., 1966-69; prof. Spanish lit. Columbia, 1969—. Mem. MLA Am. (secy., then chair Romance sect. 1965-66, chair comparative lit., 1973), Am. Assn. Tchrs. Spanish and Portugese, Am. Assn. Tchrs. Italian, Mediaval Acad. Am., Modern Hunamities Research Assn., Internatl. Assn. Hispanists, Am. Comparative Lit. Assn., Coll. Art Assn., Acad. Lit. Studies. Home: 30 E 37th St New York NY 10016

SELIGMAN, DANIEL, b. NYC, Sept. 25, 1924; s. Irving and Clare (O'Brien) Seligman; m. Mary Gale Sherburn, May 23, 1953; children—Nora, William Paul. Student, Rutgers U., 1941-42; AB, NYU, 1946. Editorial asst. New Leader, 1946;

asst. editor Am. Mercury, 1946-50; assoc. editor Fortune, 1950-59, editorial bd., 1959-66, asst. mng. editor, 1966-69, exec. editor, 1970-77, assoc. mng. editor, 1977—; sr. staff editor all Time, Inc. (publs.), 1969-70. Home 190 E 72nd St New York NY 10020

SELL, JILL, b. Cleve., June 22, 1950; d. Charles F. and Betty (Greenly) Veleba; children—Kenneth E., Daniel Adam. Author poetry: Teddy Bears and Tears, 1982, Tree Bark, 1988. Contrbr. articles to mags., newspapers. B.S. in English/Ednl. Media, Kent State U., 1972, postgrad., 1975. East coast ed. Bedder News, Lewiston, ID, 1977-81; ed., columnist News Leader/Bulltn., Northfield, OH, 1977-81; spcl. assignment reporter Plain Dealer, Cleve., 1984—, Akron Beacon Jnl., OH, 1986—, Cleve. Mag., 1987. Lit. workshop coord. Cuyahoga Valley Natl. Recreation Area, Brecksville, OH, 1987; founder, coord. Cleve. Metroparks Poetry in the Park, Brecksville, 1984—. Recipient 1st place for poetry Ohio Poetry Day, 1986, 2d place for poetry, 1987. Mem. NFPW, Ohio Press Women (Editorial Writing award 1987). Home: 7666 N Gannett Rd Sagamore Hills OH 44067

SELLARS, NIGEL ANTHONY, b. Bermingham, England, Oct. 2, 1954; s. Robert William and Florence (Thompson) S.; m. Vicki S. Brown, Dec. 17, 1981. Contrbr. poems to anthols., mags. Wrkg. on novel, The Floating World. B.A. in Psychology, U. Okla., 1977, B.A. in Jnlsm., 1980, M.A. in Jnlsm., 1984. Sports reporter Moore Monitor, OK, 1981-82, city hall reporter, 1982-83, mng. ed., 1983-84; suburban affairs reporter Daily Oklahoman, Oklahoma City, OK, 1984-86, edn. wrtr., 1986—. Recipient Marshall Gregory award Okla. Edn. Assn., 1986, Carl Rogan award AP, 1987. Home: 912 Hardin Dr Norman OK 73072

SELLERS, BETTIE MIXON, b. Tampa, FL, Mar. 30, 1926; d. William Skeen and Rebecca (Pursley) Mixon; div.; children: Carol, David, Molly. Author poetry: Westward from Bald Mountain, 1976, Appalachian Carols, 1976, Spring Onions and Cornbread, 1978, Morning of the Red-Tailed Hawk, 1981, Liza's Monday, 1986; wrkg on poetry collections, These Battlements Are Ours. BA, La Grange Coll., 1956-58; MA, U Ga, 1965-66. Chair div. Humanities Young Harris Coll., Ga, 1975-85, Goolsby Prof. English, 1986. Recipient Caroline Wyatt Meml. award, Atlanta Writers Club, 1981, 83, 85; Daniel Whitehead Meml. award, Ga. State Poetry Soc., 1984; Poet of the Year award, Dixie Council of Authors/Jnlists., 1982, 84. Mem. Delta Kappa Gamma (publicity chair, 1978—), Ga. State Poetry Soc. (pres., 1981-83), Ga. Council Arts (lit. bd.), Ga. Endowment for the Humanities (lit. bd., 1985—), Southeastern Conf. Tchrs. English (poetry coordinator), South Atlantic MLA, Appalachian Writers Assn. Address: Box 274 Young Harris GA 30582

SELLERY, J'NAN MORSE, b. Oakland, CA, Jan. 3, 1928; d. Raymond Stephen and Minna Esther (Bourus) Morse; m. Austin R. Sallery, Aug. 30, 1947; children—Stephen Brooke, Edward Austin, Margaret Joan, John Merritt. Author: (with William O. Harris) Descriptive Bibliography of Elizabeth Bowen, 1981. Contrbr. poems to lit. mags. Editor: (with John B. Vickery) Goethe's Faust Part I Essays in Criticism, 1969, The Scapegoat: Some Literary Permutations, 1972; assoc. editor, contrbr., Psychol. Perspectives, 1969—. BA, U. Calif.-Riverside, 1965, MA, 1967, PhD, 1970. Asst. prof. English, Harvey Mudd Coll., Claremont, Calif., 1970-74, assoc. prof. English, 1974-80; assoc. prof. English, Claremont Grad. Schl., 1975-80; prof. English, Harvey Mudd Coll. and Claremont Grad. Schl., 1980—. Mem. MLA (regional rep. women's studies 1986—), AAUW (chair women higher edn. 1980-86), Intl. Fed. Univ. Women, Philol. Assn. Pacific Coast. Home: 1923 Lassen Ave Claremont CA 91711

SELLIN, ERIC, b. Phila., Nov. 7, 1933; s. Thorsten and Amy (Anderson) Sellin; m. Birgitta Sjoberg, Jan. 25, 1958; children—Frederick, Christopher. Author: The Dramatic Concepts of Antonin Artaud, 1968, The Inner Game of Soccer, 1976, Soccer Basics, 1977; books of poetry Night Voyage, 1964, Trees at First Light, 1973, Tanker Poems, 1973, Borne Kilometrquie, 1973, Marginalia, 1979, Crepuscule prononge a El Biar, 1982, Nightfall over Lumbumbashi, 1982, Night Foundering, 1985; editor: Africana Jnl, 1983-87; contrbr. articles to profl. jnls and anthologies. BA, U. PA, 1955, MA, 1958, PhD, 1965. Asst. instr. French U. PA (Phila.), 1955-56, 1957-58, 1959-60; lctr. Am. lit. U. Bordeaux (France), 1956-57; instr. French Clark U. (Worcester, MA), 1958-59; lctr. creative writing U. PA, 1960-62; instr. French Temple U. (Phila.), 1962-65, asst. prof., 1965-67, assoc. prof. 1967-70, prof., 1970—, chair dept. French and Italian, 1970-73, founder, dir. Center for Study of Francophone Lit. of North Africa, 1981—; editor CELFAN Rvw, 1981—; USIS lectr. Africa and Near East, 1981, 82, 83, 85. Mem. Am. Assn. Tchrs. of French, MLA, AAUP, African Lit. Assn. Home: 312 Kent Rd Bala- Cynwyd PA 19004

SELSAM, MILICENT ELLIS, b. Bklyn.; d. Israel and Ida (Abrams) Ellis; m. Howard Selsam, Sept. 1, 1936; 1 son—Robert. Author, editor: numerous books including The American Travels of Alexander von Humboldt, 1962 (Gold Medal award Boys Club Am.), Let's Get Turtles, 1965, (with J. Bronowski) Biography of an Atom, 1965 (Thomas A. Edison award), Penny's Animals and How He Put Them in Order, 1966 (Boys Club Am. jr. book award), How to Be a Nature Detective, 1966, How Animals Tell Time, 1967, Questions and Answers About Ants, 1967, The Tiger, 1969, Hidden Animals, 1969, Egg to Chick, 1970, How Puppies Grow, 1972, Is This a Baby Dinosaur?, 1972, A First Look at Leaves, 1972, A First Look at Fish, 1972, A First Look at Mammals, 1973, Harlequin Moth, 1975, Popcorn, 1976, The Amazing Dandelion, 1977, Land of the Giant Tortoise, 1977, Sea Monsters of Long Ago, 1977, Tyrannosaurus Rex, 1978, A First Look at Sharks, 1979, Night Animals, 1980, Backyard Insects, 1981; (adult) The Don't Throw it Grow it Book of Houseplants, 1977; juvenile sci. editor, Walker and Co. Pubs. AB, Bklyn. Coll., 1932; MA, Columbia U., 1934, M,Ph., 1979. Recipient Eva L. Gordon award Am. Nature Study Soc., 1964; Four-Leaf Clover award Lucky Book Club, 1973; Washington Children's Book Guild award, 1978. Mem. Am. Nature Study Soc., AG. Home: 100 W 94th St New York NY 10025

SELTZER, JOANNE, b. Detroit, Nov. 21, 1929; d. Samuel Zellman and Ethel (Levin) Zellman Benz Goldstein; m. Stanley Seltzer, Feb. 10, 1951; children—Laura, Ellen, Andrew, Cindy. Author: Adirondack Lake Poems, 1985; contrbr. lit mags, other periodicals, including Village Voice, Willow Springs, anthols. BA, Univ. of Michigan, 1951; MA, Coll. of St. Rose, 1978. Freelance writer, 1973—. Mem. Feminist Writers' Guild, PSA, AWP. Home: 2481 McGovern Dr Schenectady NY 12309

SELZLER, BERNARD JOHN, b. Strausberg, ND, May 23, 1939; s. John and Mary Lillian (Schmidt) S.; m. Carma Jean Brandner; children—Nicolee Johnson, Darin. Editor: (with Hudson & McGuire) Business Writing: Concepts and Applications, 1983. BS Minot State Coll., 1965; MS, East Tex. State U., 1971, EdD, 1974. Tchr. Grand Forks pub. schls., N.D., 1966-69; assoc. prof. communication U. Minn., Crookston, 1969—. Mem. Minn. Humanities Commn., St. Paul, 1982—. Served with USN, 1957-61. Me. NCTE, Minn. Council Tchrs. English. Home: 129 Campbell Rd Crookston MN 56716

SEMMEL, BERNARD, b. NYC, July 23, 1928; s. Samuel and Tillie (Beer) Semmel; m. Maxine Loraine Guse, Mr. 19, 1955; 1 son—Stuart Mill. Author: Imperialism and Social Reform, 1960, Jamaican Blood and Victorian Conscience, 1963, The Rise of Free Trade Imperialism, 1970, The Methodist Revolution, 1973, John Stuart Mill and the Pursuit of Virtue, 1984, Liberalism and Naval Strategy, 1986; editor: Occasional Papers of T.R. Malthus, 1963; editor, translator: Halevy's The Birth of Methodism in England, 1971; editor: Jnl Brit. Studies, 1969-74, Marxism and the Science of War, 1981. BA, CCNY, 1947; MA, Columbia U., 1951, PhD, 1955; postgrad., London Schl. Econ., 1959-60. With Natl. Citizens Commn. for Pub. Schls. and Council for Fin. Aid to Edn. (NYC), 1951-55; asst. prof. history Park Coll. (Parkville, MO), 1956-60; mem. faculty SUNY (Stony Brook), 1960—, prof. history, 1964—, chair dept., 1966-69; vis. prof. Columbia U., 1966-67, assoc., seminar in social and poli. thought, 1968—; cons. Council Intl. Exchange of Scholars, NEH, also chair panel for Ralph Waldo Emerson prize, 1979. Home: 6 Woodbine Ave Box 1162 Stony Brook NY 11790

SENDAK, MAURICE BERNARD, b. Bklyn., June 10, 1928; s. Philip and Sadie (Schindler) Sendak. Author, illustrator: Kenny's Window, 1956, Very Far Away, 1957, The Sign on Rosie's Door, 1960, The Nutshell Library, 1963, Where the Wild Things Are, 1963 (Caldecott medal 1964); illustrator: A Hole Is to Dig, 1952, A Very Special House, 1954, I'll Be You and You Be Me, 1954, Charlotte and the White Horse, 1955, What do You Say, Dear?, 1959, The Moonjumpers, 1960, Little Bear's Visit, 1962, Schoolmaster Whackwell's Wonderful Sons, 1962, Mr. Rabbit and the Lovely Present, 1963, The Griffin and the Minor Canon, 1963, Nikolenka's Childhood, 1963, The Bat-Poet, 1964, Lullabies and Night Songs, 1965, Hector Protector and As I Went Over the Water, 1965, Zlateh the Goat, 1966, Higglety Pigglety Pop, Or There Must Be More to Life, 1967, In the Night Kitchen, 1970, The Animal Family, 1965, In The Night Kitchen Coloring Book, 1971, Pictures By Maurice Sendak, 1971, The Juniper Tree and Other Tales from Grimm, 1973, Outside Over There, 1981; writer, dir., lyricist: TV animated spcl. Really Rosie, 1975; opera set and costume designer for The Magic Flute, 1981. Student, Art Students League, NYC, 1949-51. Address: Harper & Row 10 E 53rd St New York NY 10022

SENDLER, DAVID A., b. White Plains, NY, Dec. 12, 1938; s. Morris Sendler and Rose (Gaskin) S.; m. Emily Irene Shimm, Oct. 17, 1965; children—Matthew, Karen. BA, Dartmouth, 1960; MS, Columbia Schl. Jnlsm., 1961. Assoc. ed. Sport Mag., NYC, 1964-65; exec. ed. Pageant Mag., NYC, 1965-71; ed. Today's Health, Chgo., 1971-74; sr. ed. Parade, NYC, 1974-75; arts. ed. Ladies Home Jnl, NYC, 1975-76; mng.

wd. TV Guide, Radnor, PA, 1976-79, exec. ed., 1979-80; ed. Panorama Mag., Rosemont, PA, 1980-81; co-ed. TV Guide, Radnor, PA, 1981—. Served to spclst. 5th class, U.S. Army, 1961-63. Mem. Assn. Mag. Eds., SPJ. Office: TV Gd 100 Matsonford Rd Radnor PA 19088

SENGPIEHL, JUNE SHIRLEY, b. Buffalo, Jan. 3; d. Sherman Henry and Anna Mae (Gosley) Cline; m. Paul M. Sengpiehl, June 29, 1963; children—Jeffrey, Chrystal. Contrbr.: Teens Today, Gospel Carrier, Contact, Vista, Family Life Today, Seek, Rosicrucian Digest, numerous other publs. Wrkg. on romantic mystery novel, articles, short fiction, children's books. Student Syracuse U., 1954-55, Mich. State U., 1956-58. Mem. NWC. Home: 727 N Ridgeland Ave Oak Park IL 60302

SENNETT, JOHN PATRICK, b. Chgo., Dec. 31, 1952, s. Morton William and Nancy Anne (Sennett) S. Contrbr. to Miss. Valley Rvw, Crow Call, Derby City, Bloodroot, Washout Rvw, numerous other mags. Wrkg. on poetry, songwriting. BA, U. Wis.-Madison, 1975; BS, Devry Inst. Tech., Chgo., 1985. Ed.-in-chief Magic Changes, Warrenville, Ill., 1978—, The Amplifier, Chgo., 1982-85; sr. tech. assoc. AT&T Bell Labs., Naperville, 1985—. Grantee Helene Wurlitzer Colony for Arts, Taos, N.Mex., 1975, 76, Edna St. Vincent Millay Colony, Austerlitz, N.Y., 1977; winner 1st pl. Devry 1st Annl. Writing Contest, Chgo., 1985, Poetry Soc. Ga. contest. Mem. IEEE, Instrument Soc. Am., Poets for Peace. Home: 25424 Emerald Green Dr F Warrenville IL 60555

SENTI, R. RICHARD, (William N . James), b. Pratt, KS, Dec. 29, 1946, s. Milton M. and Virginia P. (Richard) S.; m. Mary E. Mack, Aug. 31, 1984. Contrbr.: Monterey (Calif.) Life Mag., Well-Being Mag., Alive Mag., Sierra Mag., local newspapers, BS in Journalism, Kans. U., 1968. Advt. supr. Armstrong World Co., Lancaster, Pa., 1968-72; media specialist, photographer Ariz. State U., Tempe, 1973-74; freelance photographer, wrtr., graphic designer, Santa Cruz, Calif., 1975-81; ed. Darkroom Photography Mag., San Francisco, 1981—. Co-recipient Maggie awards Western Publs. Assn., 1982—. Mem. Natl. Press Photographers Assn., Western Publs. Assn., Light Gathering. Home: 2308 Howe St Berkeley CA 94705

SENZ, LAURIE S., b. NYC, July 13, 1957; d. Fred Louis and Marilyn Dorothy (Gravitz) Senz; m. David M. Emmer, Oct. 9, 1983. Contrbr. articles to mags., newspaper including Saturday Evening Post, Chgo. Tribune, Boston Herald, NYT Syndicate, Newsday, others. B.A., SUNY, 1979. Managing ed. The Best Gold Coast Fashion & Lifestyle, Ft. Lauderdale, FL; travel ed. The Jewish Times, Boca Raton, FL. Mem. NLAPW, FFWA, South Fla. Wrts. Assn. (lectr.) Home: 9220 SW 14 St Apt 3209 Boca Raton FL 33428

SERPENTO, B. JAMES, b. Lincoln, NB, June 16, 1960; s. Silvio Bernard and Madonna Patricia (Boatwright) S. Playwright: Baby Talk pubd. in Plays, 1985. BA in Speech, Iowa State U., Ames, 1985; dir./instr. DSM Comm. Coll., Des Moines, 1985; asst. Indiana U., Bloomington, 1985-86. Playwriting award, Am. Theatre Actors, 1985; Shiner Merit award, Natl. Soc. Arts & Letters, 1985; Bloomington Playwrights Project Playwriting Contest winner, 1987. Assoc. mem DG. Address: 703 W Gourley Pike 31 Bloomington IN 47401

SERVAIS, DONNA J., b. Marinette, WI, Oct. 20, 1946; m. John G. Servais, July 5, 1972; children—Jessica, Casey. Author: Life to Life: A Women's Portrait Album, 1986; contrbr. to Primipara: Jnl of Wis. Women, Catalyst, Houston County Gazette, Poems/Fields and other open places. MA in English, U. Wis.-Madison, 1978; ME- PD Profl. Devel., U. Wis.-LaCrosse, 1983. Tchr. La Crosse Schl. Dist., 1984-85; instr. bus. communications U. Wis.-LaCrosse, 1985-86; instr. English, Winona State U., MN, 1986—. Mem. Midwest Wrtr.'s Guild, AAUW (newsletter ed. Appleton, Wis. br., 1976). Home: Rt 1 Box 167 La Crescent MN 55947

SETH, VIKRAM, b. Calcutta, India, June 20, 1952; s. Premnath and Leila (Sewth) S. Author: Mappings: A Chapbook of Poems, 1980, From Heaven Lake: Travels Through Sinkiang and Tibet, 1983, The Humble Administrator's Garden: Poems, 1985, The Golden Gate: A Novel in Verse, 1986. Diploma, Nanjing U., People Republic of China, 1982; MA with Honors, Oxford U., 1975; M.A., Stanford U., 1977. Sr. ed. Stanford U. Press, Calif., 1985-86. Recipient Thomas Cook Travel Book Award, 1983; Commonwealth Poetry Prize for Asia, 1985; fellow Ingram Merrill Fdn., 1985, Guggenheim fellow, 1986. Home: 7 Teenmurti Ln New Delhi India 110 011

SETTLE, MARY LEE, b. Charleston, WV, July 29, 1918; d. Joseph Edward and Rachel (Tompkins) Settle; m. William Littleton Tazewell, Sept. 2, 1978; 1 son—Christopher Weathersbee. Author: The Love Eaters, 1954, The Kiss of Kin, 1955, O Beulah Land, 1956, Know Nothing, 1960, Fight Night on a Sweet Saturday, 1964, All The Brave Promises, 1966, The Clam Shell, 1971, Prisons, 1973, Blood Tie, 1977, The Scapegoat, 1980, The Killing Ground, 1982. Student, Sweet Briar Coll., 1936-38. Assoc. prof. Bard Coll. (Annandale-on-Hudson, NY), 1965-76; vis. lectr. U. Va., 1978-82, U. Iowa, 1976. Served with Women's Aux., RAF, 1942-43. Recipient Merrill Fdn. award, 1974, Natl. Book award, 1978. Home: 524 Pembroke Ave Norfolk VA 23507

SETTLES, CHERYL LYNNE, b. Denver, July 10, 1947; d. Leonard Joseph and Erma Merle (Horan) Yanick; m. James Leonard Settles, June 4, 1966 (div. May 13, 1987); children—Tanya Lynne, Daniel James, Contrbr. articles to mags., newspapers including Denver Post, Tchr. Mag., others. B.A. magna cum laude in Elem. Edn., Metro State Coll., 1979. Secy., Custom Craftsmen, Inc., Littleton, CO, 1986-87; central overdues clrk. Jefferson County Library, Lakewood, CO, 1987—. Mem. Intl. Reading Assn. Home: 9310 W Ontario Dr Littleton CO 80123

SETTLES, WILLIAM FREDERICK, b. Aurora, IL, Sept. 24, 1937; s. Arnold Joseph and Cleo Dorothy (Frazier) S.; m. June A. Cooper, Dec. 22, 1967; children: Amanda Jo, Caryn Beth. Author: Communist Life Revisited, 1982; syndicated weekly newspaper column "Life Under Communism," 1965-67; articles in numerous publs. including The Herald, The Clearing House, Northern Alumnus, Stride. BS No. Ill. U., 1959; MS, 1961. Asst. prof. edn. Western Ill. U., Macomb, 1970-72 (ret). Mem. NEA (life), Ill. Edn. Assn. Recipient Tchr. medal Freedom Fdn., 1966, Newspaper award, 1968. Home: Box 1121 Aurora IL 60507

SEUNG, THOMAS KAEHAO, b. Jungju, Korea, Sept. 20, 1930; s. Maengzeung and Hwaksil (Baek) Seung; m. Kwihwan Hahn, May 29, 1965; children—Hyunjune Sebastian, Kwonjune Justin, Haesue Florence. Author: The Fragile Leaves of the Sibyl, 1962, Kant's Transcendental Logic, Cultural Thematics, 1976, 1969, Structuralism and Hermeneutics, 1982, Semiotics and Thematics, 1982. BA, Yale U., 1958, MA, 1961, PhD, 1965. Instr. Yale U., 1963-65; asst. prof. Fordham U., 1965-66; mem. faculty dept. philosophy U. Tex. (Austin), 1966-86, prof., 1972-86; H.B. Alexander Prof. Hum., Scripps Coll., 1986-87; Jesse H. Jones Regents Prof. in Liberal Arts, Univ. of Texas at Austin, 1987—. Office: Phil Dept Univ of Texas Austin TX 78712

SEVANDAL, MARCIANA ASIS SAGUN, (Marian Andal), b. Catarman, Philippines, Mar. 9, 1912, came to U.S., 1974, d. Ambrosio Ambil Asis and Dominga (Reyes) Sagun; m. Simeon Enriquez Sevandal (dec.); children—Patria Sevandal de Los Reyes, Libertad Sevandal Dial, Virgilio Asis Sevandal, Rizalina Sevandal Bayon, Simeon Asis Sevandal, Violeta Sevandal Hilao, Adelpha Sevandal Mabulay. Author playlets: World Brotherhood, 1950, Royalty in My Native Land, 1969, The Nativity of the Child Jesus, 1981; contrbr. poetry World of Poetry. Ed., Philippines. Tchr., head tchr., schl. prin. then dist. supr. Bur. Public Schls., Philippines, 1930-73; chief ed. Newsletter, WODRAD, 1984—. Recipient Golden Poet awards World of Poetry, 1985, 1986, 1987. Mem. World of Poetry. Home: 50 Rizal St Apt 206 San Francisco CA 94107

SEWALL, RICHARD BENSON, b. Albany, NY, Feb. 11, 1908; s. Charles Grenville and Kate (Strong) S.; m. Mathilde Parmelee, Mar. 13, 1940 (dec.); children: Stephen, Richard, David. Author: (with others) The Age of Johnson, 1949, Tragic Themes in Western Literature, 1955; The Vision of Tragedy, 1959, The Lyman Letters, New Light on Emily Dickinson and Her Family, 1965, The Life of Emily Dickinson, 2 vols., 1974; editor: (with R. W. Short) Short Stories for Study, 1941, (with L. Michel) Tragedy: Modern Essays in Criticism, 1963, Emily Dickinson: Twentieth Century Views, 1963. BA, Williams Coll., 1929; PhD, Yale U., 1933. Instr. English, Clark U., Worcester, Mass., 1933-34; faculty Yale U., New Haven, 1934—, instr., asst. prof., assoc. prof., 1934-59, prof., 1959-76. Recipient Natl. Book award for biography, 1974, PSA award for biography, 1974; Litt.D., Williams Coll., 1975; LHD, Albertus Magnus Coll., 1975. Fellow AAAS. Home: 63 Downs Rd Bethany CT 06525

SEWARD, DOYLE ADAM JR., b. Texarkana, AR, Sept. 24, 1956; s. Doyle Preston Seward and Rena (Cooper) Adams. Contrbr. articles to lit. mags., newspapers including Kans. Speech Jnl., lower case, Cow Creek Rvw., others. Ed.: Wyoming World News, 1982-87, The Limen, 1985-86; co-ed.: Call to Action, 1987-88. Cartoonist, Chgo. Maoon, 1987-88. A.B., Louisiana Coll., 1982; A.M., Pittsburg State U., 1984, AMRS, Divinity Schl., U. Chgo., 1988. Instr. mass media Open U., U. Chgo., 1985; reference asst. Meadville Seminary, Chgo., 1984—; night minister First Unitarian Ch., Chgo., 1984—. Recipient 1st prize lower case, 1986. Home: 5701 S Woodlawn Chicago IL 60637

SEWARD, WILLIAM WARD, JR., (Leigh Rives) b. Surry, VA, Feb. 2, 1913; s. William Ward and Elizabeth (Gwaltney) Seward; m. Virginia Leigh Widgeon, Dec. 27, 1941; children—Virginia R., Leigh W. Author: The Quarrels of Alexander Pope, 1935; editor: The Longer Thou Livest the More Fool Thou Art (W. Wagner), 1939, Literature and War, 1943, Skirts of the Dead Night, 1950, Foreword to Descent of the White Bird (Barbara Whitney), 1955, Contrasts in Modern Writers, 1963, My Friend Ernest Hemingway, 1969; editorial bd.: Lyric Virginia Today, 1956. AB, U. Richmond, 1934, MA, 1935; grad. fellow, Duke U., 1938-38, 40-41. English tchr. pub. schls., 1935-38; instr. U. Richmond, 1939-40, summer 1944; head English dept. Greenbrier Mil. Schl., 1941-42; prof., head English dept. Tift Coll., 1942-45; faculty Old Dominion U. (Norfolk, VA), 1945, 47—, prof., 1957-77, prof. emeritus, 1977—, head dept. English, 1947-61; lectr. U. Va. extension div., 1952-54. Recipient Charles T. Norman medal for best grad. in English U. Richmond, 1934. Mem. Poetry Soc. Va. (pres, 1952-55), Poetry Soc. Am., Va. Writers Club, Intl. Mark Twain Soc. (hon.). Home: 701 Cavalier Dr Virginia Beach VA 23451

SEWELL, ELIZABETH, b. Coonoor, India, Mar. 9, 1919, became U.S. citizen, 1973, d. Robert Seymour and Dorothy (Dean) Sewell. Author: The Structure of Poetry, 1951, The Dividing of Time (novel), 1951, Paul Valery: The Mind in the Mirror, 1952, The Field of Nonsense, 1952, The Singular Hope (novel), 1955, The Orphic Voice, 1960, Now Bless Thyself (novel), 1962, Poems 1947-1961, 1962, The Human Metaphor, 1964, Signs and Cities (poems), 1968, To Be a True Poem (essays), 1979, An Idea (memoir), 1983, Acquist (poems), 1984; contrbr. poetry, articles: Parnassus, Studia Mystica, The Lion and the Unicorn, Antigonish Rvw, numerous other lit. publs. BA, Cambridge (Eng.) U., 1942, MA, 1945, PhD, 1949. Educator, 1951—; prof. English, Hunter Coll., CUNY, 1971-74; Joe Rosenthal prof. humanities, U. N.C., Greensboro, 1974-77; prof. humanities Mercer U., Macon, Ga., 1984-86. Recipient Natl. Award, AAIAL, 1981, Zoe Kincaid Brockman Poetry award N.C. Poetry Soc., 1985. Mem. PEN, NWU. Home: 854 W Bessemer Ave Greensboro NC 27408

SEWELL, JOAN MARSHALL, b. Nashville, Nov. 5, 1936; d. Willie Eston and Omer Lee (Denney) Marshall; m. S.S. Sewell, Dec. 8, 1956; children—Gina, Donna, Lisa, Sheila. Contrbr: Scholastic mag., Early Years, Today's Edn., Guideposts, Farm Family, Mosaic, numerous other publs.; wrtr., designer tri-fold pamphlets for bus. and service orgns. Wrkg. on articles, short stories, children's book. AB, Ga. State U., 1961, EdS, 1980; MEd, U. Ga., 1971. Tchr. Gwinnett County Schls., Lawrenceville, Ga., 1966—. Mem. ednl. orgns. Home: 4864 Five Forks Trickum Rd Lilburn GA 30247

SHAARA, MICHAEL JOSEPH, JR., b. Jersey City, June 23, 1929; s. Michael Joseph and Florence Alleene (Maxwell) Shaara; m. Helen Elizabeth Krumwiede, Sept. 16, 1950 (div. June 1980); children—Jeffrey, Lila. Author: The Broken Place, 1968, The Killer Angels, 1974, The Herald, 1981, Soldier Boy, 1982. BS, Rutgers U., 1951; postgrad., Columbia U., 1952, U. Vt., 1953-54. Assoc. prof. English Fla. State U. (Tallahassee), 1961-73; writer, producer, performer courses ednl. TV, 1961-65. Served with AUS, 1946-47. Recipient Pulitzer Prize for fiction, 1975; award for excellence in med. journalism AMA, 1966. Mem. AAUP. Home: 3019 Thomasville Rd Tallahassee FL 32312

SHACKLEFORD, RUBY P., b. Wilson, NC, Dec. 17, 1913; d. Joshua W. and Sallie (Poole) Paschall; m. Richard W. Shackleford. Author poetry: Dreamer's Wine, Poems, Visual Diary and Poems, Poems 4, Ascend the Hill, Bamboo Harp. BA, UNCG, 1933, MA UNC-Ch, 1950. Tchr. elem. schl. Wilson County, NC, 1933-35, secondary schl., var. counties, 1935-61; asst. prof. English Atlantic Christian Coll. Wilson, 1961-78. Recipient Haiku prize, Piedmont Lit. Rev., free verse prize, Pa. Poetry Annual. Mem. NC Poetry Soc (pres., 1978-80, winner sonnet contest), Delta Kappa Gamma Omicron (pres., 1957-59), NC Assn. Educators (dist. secy. 1964-65). Address: Rt 5 Box 407 Wilson NC 27893

SHADDOCK, DAVID ROBERT, b. Los Angeles, June 5, 1948, s. Hyman Louis and Toby Lorraine (Spivak) S.; m. Toby Furash, Apr. 29, 1984. Author: Dreams Are Another Set of Muscles, 1986; contrbr. articles to Whales, A Celebration, Peace or Perish, New Age Jnl, Poetry Flash; contrbr. poems to numerous mags., inclg. Mother Jones, Hanging Loose, Panjandrum Rvw. BA in English, U. Calif. at Berkeley, 1969; MA in Psychology, Antioch U., San Francisco, 1982. Child-care tchr. U. Calif. at Berkeley, 1972-84; family therapist Youth Advocates, San Anselmo, Calif., 1984-85; psychotherapist in pvt. prac., Oakland, Calif., 1983—. First prize, Intl. Peace Poetry Competition, 1984. Home: 1209 Kains Ave Berkeley CA 94706

SHADOVITZ, DAVID JAY, b. Princeton, NJ, Mar. 21, 1954; s. Ralph and Edith S.; m. Kesako Fowler; children—Michael, Laurie, Patricia. Ed.: Coal Industry News, Petrochemical Equipment News, Computer Dealer, 1977—. BA, Trenton State Coll.; MA, Stephen F. Austin. Assoc. ed., Gordon Pubns., Morristown, NJ, 1977-79, ed. 80-82, editorial dir./assoc. pub., Randolph, NJ, 82—. Office Box 1952 Dover NJ 07801.

SHADWELL, DELVENIA GAIL, b. Funkhouser, IL, May 20, 1938; d. Louis Walker and Nelle Evelyn (Stewart) S. Author: The Speech Teacher, 1960, A Project Text in Speech Fundamentals, 1970, 2d ed., 1974, The Generic Speaker, 1985. Contrbr. article to Woman Engineer. B.S. in Edn., Eastern Ill. U., 1960, M.S. in Edn., 1961; Ph.D., U. Ill., 1967. Asst. prof. Chgo. City Coll., 1965-67; instr., dir. forensics Elgin Commun. Coll., IL, 1967-76, 1984—, instructional dean, 1976-84. Mem. NWC. Home: 165 N Lyle Elgin IL 60123

SHAIL, LINDA GRACE, b. Norwich, CT, Nov. 7, 1947; d. James Leonard and Alice Lillian (Webb) Meagher; m. Joseph Walter Meagher Shail, Aug. 4, 1973; children—Joseph, Meghan, Maureen, Joshua. Contrbr. to various mags., inclg. Health Explorer, Medical Detective, Turtle, Humpty Dumpty. BA, Western CT St. College, Danbury, 1970. Lab. technician Danbury (CT) Hosp., 1968-71, Strong Memorial Hosp., Rochester, NY, 1973-74; tchr. Waterbury (CT) Catholic High Schl., 1971-73; substitute tchr. Penn Yan (NY) Central Schls., 1981—. Home: 4848 Main St Box 121 Hall NY 14463

SHAINIS, MURRAY J., b. Bronx, NY., June 6, 1926, s. Henry and Lena (Edelman) S.; m. Hilda Gertler, June 28, 1953; children—Daniel, Julie, Janet. Author: Small Plant Production Planning and Control, 1957, Engineer as Manager, 1972, 6th rev. ed., 1986, Office Furniture Industry, 1974, Project Management, 1975, Engineering Management: People and Projects, 1976, 3d rev. ed., 1985, Operations Manager's Desk Book, 1982, Managing Contracted Professional Services, 1986. Wrkg. on engring. book. BEE, CCNY, 1949; MME, Bklyn. Poly. Inst., 1957, MS in Mgmt., 1970. Registered profl. engr., N.Y. State, 1954; pres. Murray J. Shainis, Inc., Beechhurst, N.Y., 1969—. Office: 157-11 9th Ave Beechhurst NY 11357

SHANER, RICHARD CLARK, b. Brookline, Mass., Feb. 21, 1948, s. Richard Bernhardt and Hazel Laura (Clark) S.; m. Mary Carol Edwards, June 24, 1972. Author: A Nantucket Bestiary, 1981; ed. Peregrine Anthology, 1978; contrbr. articles, poems to various Am. and Can. mags. and jnls. BA, U. Mass., 1971, MA, 1973. Poem Gilman Pond Mountain sandblasted into platform bricks at Davis Sq. Sta., Mass. Transit Authority, Cambridge Arts Council, 1982. Mem. P&W. Home: 10 Spring St Hingham MA 02043

SHANGE, NTOZAKE, b. Trenton, NJ, Oct. 18, 1948; d. Paul T. and Eloise Williams. Author: (plays) For Colored Girls Who Have Considered Suicide/When the Rainbow Is Enuf, 1976; Negress, 1977, A Photograph: Lovers in Motion, 1977, Where the Mississippi Meets the Amazon, 1977, From Okra to Greens, 1978, Magic Spell 7, 1979, Boogie Woogie Landscapes, 1980, Mother Courage, 1980, Mouths, 1981; (operetta) Carrie, 1981; author: Books for Colored Girls, 1975, Sassafrass, 1976; contrbr. poetry, essays and short stories to numerous mags. and anthologies, including Third World Women, Chgo. Rvw, Am. Rag, Sojourner, Womansports; performing mem.: Sounds in Motion Dance Co., performed in various jazz/poetry collaborations. BA in Am. Studies cum laude, Barnard Coll., 1970; MA in Am. Studies (NDEA fellow), U. So. Calif., 1973. Mem. faculty Sonoma State U., 1973-75, Mills Coll., 1975, CCNY, 1975, Douglass Coll., 1978. Recipient award Outer Critics Circle, 1977; OBIE award, 1977, 80; Audelco award, 1977; Frank Silvera Writer's Workshop award, 1978; poetry award Los Angeles Times book prizes, 1981; Guggenheim fellow, 1981. Mem. Actors Equity, Natl. Acad. TV Arts and Scis., AAP, DG, PEN Am. Center, P&W, NY Feminist Art Guild. Office: St Martin's 175 Fifth Ave New York NY 10010

SHANKS, HERSHEL, b. Sharon, PA, Mar. 8, 1930; s. Martin and Mildred (Freedman) Shanks; m. Judith Alexander Weil, Feb. 20, 1966; children—Elizabeth Jean, Julia Emily. Author: The Art and Craft of Judging, 1968, The City of David, 1973, Judaism in Stone, 1979; also articles; co-editor: Recent Archaeology in the Land of Israel, 1984. BA, Haverford Coll., 1952; MA, Columbia, 1953; LL.B., Harvard, 1956. Bar: DC 1956. Trial atty. Dept. Justice, 1956-59; pvt. practice (Washington), 1959—; partner firm Glassie Pewett, Bebee & Shanks, 1964—; editor Bibl. Archaeology Rvw (Washington), 1975—, Bible Rvw (Washington), 1984, Moment (Washington), 1987; Pres. Bibl. Archaeology Soc., 1974, Jewish Educational Ventures, Inc, 1987. Home: 5208 38th St NW Washington DC 20015

SHANNON, CHRISTINA, see Bone, Brenda Kay

SHANNON, DON MICHAEL, (Dale Shoal), b. Chgo., Aug. 16, 1948; s. Donald Gray and Olga Rita (Kraus) S. Author: Techniques and Strategies for Playing Propaganda 1987, Playing Winning Linguishtik, 1987, Yesterday's Child, 1986, Atom and Eve, 1987, Upchuck Papers, 1987. Wrkg. on assorted sci. fiction and ednl. essays. B.A., U. New Orleans, 1979, M.Edn., 1984. Asst. recreation supvr. Jefferson Parish Recreation Dept., Metairie, LA, 1976-80; tchr. Jefferson Parish Public Schls., Metaiie, 1980—. Home: 4421 Herrmann St C Metairie LA 70006

SHAPIRO, ERIN PIZZEY, b. Feb. 19, 1939, d. Cyril Carney and Dardaniel Balfor; m. Jeffrey Scott Shapiro, Dec. 17, 1980; children—Cleo, Amos, Francis, Richard, Luch Grandel, Keita, Amber. Author: Scream Quietly or the Neighbors will Hear, 1974, Infernal Child, 1977, Slut's

Cookbook, 1981, Prone to Violence, 1982, Erin Pizzey Collects, 1983, The Water Shed, 1983, In the Shadow of the Castle, 1984, Pleasure Palace, 1985, First Lady, 1986. Founder Women's Aid shelter movement. Recipient Nancy Astor award for journalism, 1985. Home: 10 Conchas Loop Santa Fe NM 87505

SHAPIRO, NAOMI K., b. Madison, Wis., July 18, 1941, d. Sam and Sara (Sweet) Shapiro; m. Earl Epstein, Jan. 12, 1964 (div. 1978); children—Andrea E., Eden B.; m. 2d, Ray Spitz, Feb. 6, 1982. BA, U. Wis.-Madison, 1963, MA, 1966. Publs. specialist Am. Soc. Trng. and Devel., Madison, 1979-80; communications dir. Natl. Assn. Advt. Pubs., Madison, 1980-82; pub. Brilliant Ideas for Pubs., Madison, 1982—; pres. Creative Brilliance Assocs., Madison, 1982—. Mem. Sales and Mktg. Execs., Intl., Women in Communications. Office: Box 4237 Madison WI 53711

SHAPLEN, ROBERT MODELL, b. Phila., Mar. 22, 1917; s. Joseph and Sonia (Modell) Shaplen; m. Martha Lucas, Apr. 10, 1953 (div. 1962); 1 son—Peter Lucas; 2nd m. June Herman, Mar. 31, 1962; children—Kate, Jason; 3rd m. Hsia Hsun Hsia, June 8, 1984. Author: A Corner of the World, 1949, Free Love and Heavenly Sinners, 1954, A Forest of Tigers, 1956, Kreuger: Genius and Swindler, 1960, Toward the Wellbeing of Mankind: 50 Years of the Rockefeller Foundation, 1962, The Lost Revolution, 1965, Time out of Hand: Revolution and Reaction in the Southeast Asia, rev., 1970, The Road from War, rev., 1971; (introduction), The Face of Asia, 1972, A Turning Wheel, 1979, Bitter Victory, 1986; also numerous articles, TV documentaries. BA, U. Wis., 1937; MS in Journalism, Columbia U., 1938; postgrad. (Nieman fellow), Harvard U., 1947-48. Reporter NY Herald Tribune, 1937-43; S.W. Pacific War corr. Newsweek mag., 1943-45, Far East bur. chief (Shanghai), 1945-47; writer Fortune mag., 1948-50; mem. fgn. staff Collier's mag., also fgn. corr. 15 newspapers, 1950-52; staff writer New Yorker mag., 1952—, Far East corr. (Hong Kong), 1962-78; disting. vis. Marsh prof. communications U. Mich., 1980. Office: New Yorker 25 W 43rd St New York NY 10036

SHARAT CHANDRA, G.S., (Jean Parker), b. India, May 3, 1938; arrd. USA Sept., 1963; s. G. Shankara and Lalithamma (Venkatamma) Chetty; m. Jane, Sept. 1, 1966; children—Bharat, Shalini, Anjana. Author poetry: Bharata Natyam Dancer, 1968, April in Nanjangud, 1971, Once or Twice, 1974, The Ghost of Meaning, 1978, Heirloom, 1982; collection short stories, 1982, Aliens, 1986, Logic to Their Fate, 1986; editor Kamadhenu, 1970-75; fiction and poetry in 5 countries. BA and BL, U. Mysore, India, 1953-58; LLM, U. Toronto, 1964-66; MFA, U. Iowa, 1966-68. Asst. prof. Iowa Wesleyan, Mt. Pleasant, 1969-72, Wash. State Univ., Pullman, 1972-78; prof. Univ. Malaysia, Kuala Lumpur, 1978-79; asst. prof. Univ. Mo. Kans. City, 1983—; wrtr.-in-res., Purdue U., 1985, U. of Hawaii, 1987. Recipient poetry award Fla. State Arts Council, Tallahassee, 1980; NEA vis. artist, 1981. Mem. AWP, MLA. Address: 9916 Juniper Overland Pk KS 66207

SHARE, DONALD SETH, b. Cleve., Jan. 24, 1957, s. Leonard and Carol (Robey) S. Author: The Histories, 1980, Poems for Wives and Sphinxes, 1982, Giant Steps, 1987; ed.: Litmus Paper, 1984—. AB, Brown U., 1978; MS, Simmons Coll., 1979; MA, Boston U., 1988. Assoc. librarian Bryant Coll., Smithfield, R.I., 1980-82; tech. services librarian Rice U., Houston, 1982-85; data analyst METRO, Houston, 1985-86. Second place, Robert Fitzgerald translation prize, 1987. Reader: Partisan Rvw, 1986—, P&W, ALA. Home: 340 Shady Woods Cove Memphis TN 38119

SHARMEL, THEOLYN PEKRUL, see Pekrul, Kimberly A.

SHARP, ARTHUR GLYNN, b. Waterbury, CT, Feb. 2, 1941; s. Edward Parr and Margaret Lorraine (Colbert) S.; m. Elizabeth Alice O'Meara, Dec. 26, 1966; children—Thomas Edward, Kristine Elizabeth. Contrbr. numerous articles to newspapers, mags. including Hartford Courant, Am. West, Civil War Times Illustrated, Women's Circle. B.A., U. Hartford, 1969; M.A., Trinity Coll., 1972. Computer operaor Travelers Cos., Hartford, CT, 1964-69, data processing specialist, 1969-74, sr. tech. wrtr., 1974-86, personnel communications adminstr., 1986-87. Home: 35 Ashwell Ave Rocky Hill CT 06067

SHARP, DONNA LEE, (Albertson), b. Lakewood, NJ, Aug. 21, 1951; d. Donald Gene and Dorothy Ann (Wortelman) Sharp; m. Panayoti Athanasio, Aug. 8, 1969 (div. Nov. 1975); 1 son, Theodore Lee Athanasio; m. 2d, David Vogel Albertson, Dec. 17, 1975; children—Alice Naomi Albertson, Holly Kristine Albertson. Author num. poems. Student Ocean County Coll., 1986. Poet/songwriter. Mem. Ocean County Writers' Assn., Blue Grass and Old Time Music Assoc. of NJ, O.C. Poets Collective, O.C. Artists Guild. Home: 388 Coolidge Ave Bayville NJ 08721

SHARP, SHARON ANNETTE ANDREWS, b. Birmingham, AL., Dec. 26, 1952; d. Joseph Wheeler, Jr., and Ann Langley (Steele) Andrews; m. Bobby Huel Sharp Dec. 26, 1972; 1 child, Lindley Colin. Contrbr. articles, book rvws. to profl. jnls., books. Co-editor: (with Margaret Murray) 1984: The Human Imperative—Technology and the Humanities in Perspective, 1986; copy editor: Health Today, 1986, Consumer Behavior, 1987, Freedom to Be, 1986, The Creative Edge, 1986, Generating Prose, 1987, Keeping in Touch, 1987, Intro. to Sociology, 1987, Babies and Their Mothers, 1987, Own Your Own Franchise, 1987, Ethical Dexision-Making Style, 1987, Processes in Technical Writing, 1987, Adj. and Growth in a Changing World, 3d. ed., 1987. BA summa cum laude in English, Duke U., 1974; MS in Family Relations, U. Ky-Lexington, 1977; PhD in Family Studies, Va. Tech., 1980. Coordinator health edn. Va. Tech. Student Health Services, Blacksburg, 1979-80; ass. prof. family & human devel. and sociology Miss. U. for Women, Columbus, 1980-84; editorial asst. encyc. of So. Culture, Ctr. for the Study of Southern Culture, U. Miss., Oxford, Miss., 1985-86; free-lance wrtr. ed., Oxford, 1984-87, Boone, 1987—. Mem. Phi Beta Kappa, Am. Sociol. Assn., Natl. Council on Family Relations, Edl. Freelancers Assn., Women's Natl. Bk. Assn., Southeastern Council on Family Relations (newsletter ed. and sec., 1985-87, pres., 1987-89)1987—), Miss. Council on Family Relations (1st v.p. 1983-84, pres. 1984-85, Southern Sociol. Soc. Home: Box 3345 Boone NC 28607

SHARPE, MYRON EMANUEL, b. Chester, PA, Sept. 10, 1928; s. Abraham Maxwell and Emma (Friedman) Sharpe; m. Carole S. Brafman, Mar. 27, 1983; children—Susanna, Matthew, Elizabeth. Author: John Kenneth Galbraith and the Lower Economics, 1973; editor: The Liberman Discussion: A New Phase in Soviet Economic Thought, 1966, Reform of Soviet Economic Management, 1966; co- editor: The Challenge of Economics, 1977; editor, pub.: Challenge: The Mag. of Economic Affairs, 1973—; co-founder, publ.: Social Policy, 1970-72. BA, Swarthmore Coll., 1950; MA, U. Mich., 1951; postgrad., 1951-54; pres. Modern Factors Corp. (Phila.), 1957; founder, chair bd., pres., M.E. Sharpe, Inc. (Pub.), White Plains, NY, 1958—; econ. cons., 1956—; co- founder, pres. M. E. Sharpe, Ltd. (Arts and Antiques) (New Canaan, CT), 1981-83; Founder, exec. dir. com. to Save the Life of Henry Spetter, 1974; co-founder, coordinator Initiative Com. for Natl. Econ. Planning, 1974-76. Home: 121 Ferris Hill Rd New Canaan CT 06840

SHATTUCK, ROGER WHITNEY, b. NYC, Aug. 20, 1923; s. Howard Francis and Elizabeth (Colt) Shattuck; m. Nora Ewing White, Aug. 20, 1949; children—Tari Elizabeth, Marc Ewing, Patricia Colt, Eileen Shepard. Author: The Banquet Years, 1958, poems Half Tame, 1964, Proust's Binoculars, 1963, Marcel Proust, 1974 (Natl. Book award 1975), The Forbidden Experiment, 1980, The Innocent Eye, 1984; editor or co-editor: Selected Writings of Guillaume Apollinaire, 1950, Mount Analogue (Rene Daumal), 1959, The Craft and Context of Translation, 1961, Selected works of Alfred Jarry, 1965, Occasions by Paul Valery, 1970; mem. editorial bd.: PMLA, 1977-78. Grad., St. Paul's Schl., Concord, NH, 1941; BA, Yale, 1947. Information officer UNESCO (Paris, France), 1947-48; asst. editor Harcourt, Brace & Co., 1949-50; mem. Soc. Fellows, Harvard, 1950-53, instr. French, 1953-56; faculty U. Tex., Austin, 1956-71, prof. English, French, 1968-71, chair dept. French and Italian, 1968-71; Commonwealth prof. French, U. Va., Charlottesville, 1974—; Fulbright prof. of Am. lit. and civilization, U. of Dakar, Senegal, 1984-85; adv. bd. Natl. Translation Center, 1964-69, chair, 1966-69; provediteur gen. Coll. de Pataphysique (Paris), 1961—. Special award, Amer. Inst. and Acad. of Arts and Letters, 1987. Served to capt. USAF, 1942-45. Office: Dept Fr Cabell Hall U Va Charlottesville VA 22903

SHAUGHNESSY, PHYLLIS B., b. Batavia, NY, Aug. 10, 1934, d. Daliton Garfield and Elizabeth (Green) Votes; m. Thomas Patrick Shaughnessy, Aug. 20, 1955; children—Kathleen, Thomas, Patrick, Michael, Patricia, Daniel. Author: I Am Who I Am, 1984; contrbr. articles and stories to Mature Living, Family Festivals, Parish Monthly. Free-lance wrtr., 1950-81; religious edn. coordinator St. Columba Ch., Caledonia, N.Y., 1970-82. Home: 3273 South Dr Caledonia NY 14423

SHAW, ARNOLD, b. NYC, June 28, 1909; s. David and Sarah (Coller) Shaw; m. Ghita Milgrom; children—Mindy Sura, Elizabeth Hilda. Author: Lingo of Tin Pan Alley, 1950, The Money Song, 1953, Belafonte, 1960, Sinatra: 20th Century Romantic, 1968, The Rock Revolution: What's Happening in Today's Music, 1969, The World of Soul, 1970, The Street that Never Slept: NY's Fabled 52nd St., 1971, The Rockin' 50s, 1974, 52nd St.: The Street of Jazz, 1977, Honkers and Shouters: The Golden Years of Rhythm & Blues, 1978, Music Scene, New Book of Knowledge Annuals, 1970-86, Sinatra: The Entertainer, 1982, Dictionary of American Pop/Rock, 1982, The Jazz Age: Popular Music in the 1920s, 1987; editor: Mathematical Basis of the Arts by Joseph Schillinger, 1948; co-editor: Schillinger System of Musical Composition, 1946; composer: Sing a Song of Americans, 1941,

A Man Called Peter and Other Songs, 1956, Mobiles for Piano, 1966, Stabiles for Piano, 1968, Plabiles for Piano, 1971, One Finger Piano, Kiss Me Another, Night Lights, A Whirl of Waltzes for Piano, 1974, The Mod Moppet: 7 Nursery Rip-Offs for Piano, 1975, They Had a Dream: An American Musical Odyssey, 1975-76, The Bubble-Gum Waltzes, 1977, An American Sonata, 1978, Snapshots of Three Friends, 1980, The Lights of Christmas/Chanukah, 1980, Felicidad!, 1981, The Promise of Easter/Passover, 1981, Snapshot of Guido, 1985, The IASPM Preludes, 1986, The Desert Suite for Piano, 1987. MA, Columbia U., 1931. Exec. editor Musette Pubs. (NYC), 1941; dir. pub. relations, advt. Big Three Music Corp., 1944; edit Swank mag., 1945; dir. pub. relations, adv. Leeds Music Corp., 1946; vp, genl. profl. mgr. Duchess Music Co., 1949, Hill & Range Songs, 1953, Edward B. Marks Music Corp., 1955-66; lectr. Julliard Schl. Music, 1945, New Schl., 1957, Farleigh Dickinson U., 1964-65, U. Nev., Reno, U. Okla., 1971, U. Nev., Las Vegas, 1977—; mem. natl. adv. bd. Fisk U. Inst. for Research in Black Music. Pianist on radio, 1926; orch. leader, 1932; TV producer-narrator-writer- composer: series Curtain Time-Great Musicals; host: Window on the Arts, 1972-73. Mem. AG, Am. Musicological Soc., ASCAP (Deems Taylor award 1968, 79), Am. Guild Authors and Composers, co- chair Intl. Assn. for Study of Popular Music, 1984—; mem. exec. com., IASPM, 1985—; Black Popular Music in America, 1986; dir., Popular Music Research Ctr., 1985—. Address: 2288 Gabriel Dr Las Vegas NV 89119

SHAW, BYNUM GILLETTE, (Bob Gillette), b. Alamance County, NC, July 10,1923; s. William Carroll and Martha Alice (Saunders) S.; m. Louis N. Brantley, 1948 (dec. 1980); children: Bonnie Shaw Fowler, Susan Shaw Huffstetler; m. Emily C. Rushworth, 1982 (dec. 1985); m. Charlotte E. Reeder, 1986. Author: (novels) The Sound of Small Hammers, 1962, The Nazi Hunter, 1968, Days of Power, Nights of Fear, 1980; (history) Divided We Stand: The Baptists in American Life, 1974; (with Edgar E. Folk) W.W. Holden: A Political Biography, 1982; contrbr. to N.Y. Times, New Republic, Moneysworth, Esquire, others. BA, Wake Forest Coll., 1951.Copy ed., reporter, Wash. corr., chief German bur. Balt. Sun, 1951-61, editorial wrtr., 1962-65; prof. journalism Wake Forest U., Winston-Salem, 1965—. Recipient Sir Walter Raleigh award N.C. Hist. Book Club, 1969. Mem. NC Wrtrs. Conf. Home: 2700 Speas Rd Winston-Salem NC 27106

SHAW, DORENE LEE, (Dorene Lee Wolshaw), b. Lennex, CA, Aug. 16, 1925, d. Lee Samuel and Cora Irene (Roush) Langford; m. Frank Williams Heinz, Nov. 2, 1946 (div. 1966); 1 son, Ken Lee; m. 2d, Ryan Donald Williams, July 4, 1970. Contrbr. poetry to N.Y. Poetry Soc. Anthology, 1985; Am. Poetry Anthology, vol. IV, 1985; The Art of Poetry, 1985; Masterpieces of Modern Verse; Words of Praise, vol. II, 1986, Best New Poets of 1986, 1987, Lords of Light in Song, 1965-87; completed decipherment of holy ark of covenant, a poetic treatise entitled Sword, Wings, and Lovers, 1962-84. Address: Box 1762 Bishop CA 93514

SHAW, FRAN WEBER, b. Hartford, CT, June 16, 1947, d. Barnett and Elizabeth Weber; m. R. David Shaw, Nov. 22, 1970; 1 child, Blake. Author: 30 Ways to Help You Write, 1980; coauthor: Grammar and Composition, 1984, 86; ed. Myriads lit mag; contrbr. to Self, Biz, Laureate, other publs. Wrkg. on novel, business writing instruction book and video, "Write It Up!" AB magna cum laude, Barnard Coll., 1969; AM, Stanford U., 1971; PhD, Union Grad. Schl., Cin., 1973. Past faculty Famous Wrtrs. Schl., Westport, Conn.; asst. prof. English U. Conn., Stamford, 1977—; writing cons. Effective Writing Consultants, Weston, Conn.; lectr. Norwalk Community Coll., Loretto Heights Coll., U. Colo., U. Hartford; writing workshop leader local and natl. orgns. Winner Sounds of Young America Contest, 1965; Danforth Fdn. fellow, 1969, Woodrow Wilson Fdn. fellow, 1969. Mem. NCTE, Phi Beta Kappa. Home: Box 1212 Weston CT 06883

SHAW, GRACE GOODFRIEND, (Mrs. Herbert Franklin Shaw), b. NYC; d. Henry Bernheim and Jane Elizabeth (Stone) Goodfriend; m. Herbert Franklin Shaw; 1 son—Brandon Hibbs. Student Bennington Coll.; BA magna cum laude, Fordham U., 1976. Successively reporter Port Chester Daily Item (NY); editorial coordinator World Scope Encyc. (NYC), assoc. editor Clarence L. Barnhart, Inc. (Bronxville, NY); freelance writer for reference books; sr. editor, coll. dept. Bobbs-Merrill (NYC), mng. editor, exec. editor trade div., 1979-80, pub., 1980—; editing supr. World Pub. Co. (NYC), 1965-68, mng. editor, 1968-69, sr. editor, 1969; mng. editor Peter H. Wyden Co. (NYC), 1969-70; assoc. editor Dial Press (NYC), 1971-72, sr. editor, 1972, David McKay Co. (NYC), 1972-75, Grosset & Dunlap, 1975-77; chief Editor Today Press, 1977-79. Home: 85 Lee Rd Scarsdale NY 10583

SHAW, JANET, b. Springfield, IL, Sept. 30, 1937; d. Russel Henry and Sarah Nadina (Boardman) Fowler; m. Thomas Joseph Beeler, Aug. 22, 1959 (div. Sept. 1977); children—Laura, Kristin, Mark; m. 2d, Robert Clyde Shaw, Sept. 12, 1977. Author poems: How To Walk On Water, 1973, Dowry, 1978; short story collection: Some Of The Things I Did Not Do, 1984; children's novel, Kirsten Larson, 1986; novel: Taking Leave, 1987. AA, Stephens Coll., Columbia, MO, 1957; BA, Goucher College, Baltimore, 1959. Lecturer, U. WI, 1980, 82, 85, 86; wrtr.-in- res. Assoc. Colls. of the Twin Cities, St. Paul, 1983; visiting wrtr. Edgewood College, Madison, WI, 1984. Devins Award, U. MO Press, 1978, Individual Artist Fellowship, WI Arts Board, 1981, 82. Home: 10 Blue Spruce Trail Madison WI 53717

SHAW, LEROY ROBERT, b. Medicine Hat, Alta, Can., Jan. 15, 1923 (came to U.S., 1923, naturalized, 1947); s. Roy Albert and Ruby Ida (Johnson) Shaw; m. Ida Rosmarie Mannaberg, June 29, 1959; children—Dion Desmond, Melissa Amanda. Author: Witness of Deceit: Gerhart Hauptmann as Critic of Society, 1958, The Playwright and Historical Change: Dramatic Strategies in Brecht, Hauptmann, Kaiser, Wedekind, 1970, Focus on German for Beginners, 1965, (with others) Focus on German for Intermediates, 1965, In einer deutschen Stadt, 1960, Review and Progress in German, 1959; editor: (with introduction) The German Theatre Today, 1963. AB, U. Calif. at Berkeley, 1946, MA, 1948, PhD, 1954; postgrad., U. Zurich, 1949-50, U. Vienna, 1950. Instr. German, humanities Reed Coll., 1951-53; from instr. to assoc. prof. German U. Tex. at Austin, 1953-65; prof. German U. Wis. at Milw., 1965-68, U. Ill. at Chgo., 1968—. head dept. 1979-85; vis. Fulbright prof. German Trinity Coll. (Dublin, Ireland), 1966-67. Mem. Am. Assn. Tchrs. German, MLA, Midwest MLA, AAUP, Brecht Soc. Home: 1137 N Euclid Ave Oak Park IL 60302

SHAW, LI KUNG, b. Hubei, China, Oct. 29, 1915; came to U.S., 1975, s. Yue Shang and Yau Sou (Lee) S.; m. Ton San Le, Jan. 1, 1941; children: Carlos, Julia, Delia, Juan, Pedro, Cora. Author:A Mathematical Model of Life and Living, 3 Vols., 1959-74, Purposive Biology, 1982, The Shell-Corner Method, 1984. Wrkg. on design of palm-sized keyboard to operate Chinese language computer. BS, Chiao Tung U., Shanghai, 1937; M. Engring., Central U., Chungking, 1939. Aero.engr. Chinese Air Force, China, 1939-45; chief, air transport div. Ministry of Comm., China, 1945-49; owner pvt. bus., Hong Kong, 1949-52; indsl. engr. ACINDAR, Shell, Argentia, 1953-63; owner pvt. bus., Argentina and U.S., 1964-76; writer, 1977—. Dir. China Air Transport Soc., Nanking, 1948, Argentine Ops. Research Soc., Buenos Aires, 1959. Mem. Chinese Lang. Computer Soc. Home: 2530 33d Ave San Francisco CA 94116

SHAW, MARTHA L., b. Stoneham, MA, Jan. 21, 1961; d. Ronald E. and Barbara I. (Chick) Shaw. Contrbr.: Spirit Wings, Boston Globe, Silver Wings, Sword of the Spirit, Calli's Tales, Night Roses, Once Upon a Poet, Chasing Rainbows, numerous others. Mem. Chrisian edn. staff S. Luke's Ch., Chelsea, Mass., 1975-83, St. Paul's Ch., Malden, Mass., 1984—; with Broadway Nat. Bank, Chelsea, 1979—. Mem. Christian Wrtrs.' League Am. Home: 148 Clark Ave Chelsea MA 02150

SHAW, STANFORD JAY, b. St. Paul, May 5, 1930; s. Albert G. and Belle (Jaffey) Shaw; m. Ezel Kural, June 6, 1967; 1 dau.—Wendy Miriam Kural. Author: The Financial and Administrative Organization and Development of Ottoman Egypt, 1966, The Budget of Ottoman Egypt, 1969, Between Old and New: The Ottoman Empire under Sultan Selim III, 1971, History of the Ottoman Empire and Modern Turkey, vol. 1, Empire of the Gazis: The Rise and Decline of Ottoman Empire, 1280-1808, (with Ezel Kural Shaw) vol. 2, Reform, Revolution and Republic: The Rise of Modern Turkey, 1808-1975, 1976-77; editor-in-chief: Intl. Jnl Middle East Studies, 1968-83. BA, Stanford U., 1951; MA, Princeton U., 1955, PhD, 1958; MA (hon.), Harvard U., 1966. Research fellow Center Middle Eastern Studies, Harvard U., 1958-60, asst. prof. Turkish, 1960-65, assoc. prof. Turkish history, 1965-68; prof. Turkish, Nr. Eastern history UCLA, 1968—; mem. exec. bd. Am. Research Inst. Turkey, 1964-68, 75—. Mem. Middle East Studies Assn., Middle East Inst., Royal Asiatic Soc., Am. Hist. Assn., Intl. Soc. Oriental Studies, Turkish Hist. Soc. Office: History Dept U Calif Los Angeles CA 90024

SHAW, VALERINE R., see Naillon, Valerine R.

SHAW-GALVEZ, ENRIQUE, see Bell, Victor L.

SHEA, DONALD RICHARD, b. Mpls., July 15, 1926; s. John James and Marjorie (Jennings) Shea; m. Mary Patricia Donovan, June 4, 1948; children—Barbara, John, Marjorie, Kathleen. Author: The Calvo Clause: A Problem of Inter-American and International Law and Diplomacy, 1955; editor: Business and Legal Aspects of Latin American Trade and Investment, 1976; sr. editor: Reference Manual on Doing Business in Latin America, 1979; contrbr. to: Encyc. Americana. BA, U. Minn., 1947, MA, 1949, PhD, 1953. Prof. poli. sci. U. Wis. at Milw., 1949—, chair dept. poli. sci., 1957-61, dir. Inst. for World Affairs, 1960-63, spcl. asst. to chancellor, 1962-

64. adminstr. Peace Corps Trng. Center, 1962-69, dean Intl. Studies and Programs, 1963-70, dir., 1976—, cons. Ford Fdn., 1966-68. Bd. dirs. World Affairs Council Milw., Inst. World Affairs, Milw. Intl. Student's Center. Served with USNR, 1944-46. Home: 3346 N Summit Ave Milwaukee WI 53211

SHEA, GERALD JAMES, b.Galesburg, IL, Sept. 13, 1949; s. James Phillip and Joleene Ann (Moore) S.; children—Colin William, Brynn Nadine. Author: Carl Sandburg in Galesburg January 9-10, 1953, 1984, Adda & Juanita the discovery and restoration of the Carl Sandburg birthplace, 1985, Poems West from Ballina, 1987. Ed., wrtr., photographer Woodstock Newsletter, IL, 1981-82. B.A. in English, Western Ill. U., 1971, M.S. in Edn., 1975. Tchr. public schls., Crystal Lake, IL, 1975-87, McHenry County Coll., Crystal Lake, 1980-87. Mem. Profl. Photographers Am. Home: 30 S Oak St Crystal Lake IL 60014

SHEAFFER, M.P.A., b. Chambersburg, PA, d. Joseph Mifflin and Annie Parks (Moore) Sheaffer. Poetry in Philadelphia Poets, Sandcutters, All Seasons Poetry Newsletter, Poetry, Greenwood Rvw, other lit mags. BS, Shippensburg U.; MA, Tulane, MA, Rosary College, Graduate School of Fine Arts in Florence, Italy; MA, NYU; PhDTulane. Prof., Millersville, U. of Pennsylvania, Millersville, Pa.; editor, Volo International Newsletter, Millersville, Pa. Mem. PSA, CAA, CEA, Mod. Poetry Assoc., Women in the Arts. Address: Dept Eng Millersville U Millersville PA 17551

SHEAHEN, ALLAN, b. Cleve., June 28, 1932. Author: Guaranteed Income: The Right to Economic Security, 1984. ed. Natl. Masters Running News, monthly, 1979—; contrbr. to America, Commonweal, Runner, Runner's World, Running Mag. BA, Denison U., 1953. Office: Box 2204 Van Nuys CA 91404

SHECTMAN, ROBIN, b. Dayton, OH, Nov. 14, 1948, d. Jerome J. and Linda Frances (Bradley) Slutzky; m. Stephen Shectman; children—Nicholas, Sarah. Ed. Altadena (Calif.) Rvw, 1978—; contrbr. poetry to Yankee, Calif. Qtly, Blue Unicorn, numerous other publs. Office: Box 212 Altadena CA 91001

SHEEHAN, NEIL, b. Holyoke, MA, Oct. 27, 1936; s. Cornelius Joseph and Mary (O'Shea) Sheehan; m. Susan Margulies, Mar. 30, 1965; children—Maria Gregory, Catherine Fair. Author: The Arnheiter Affair, 1972, A Bright Shining Lie: John Paul Vann and America in Vietnam, 1988; contrbr. to The Pentagon Papers, 1971, also articles, book rvws. to popular mags. AB cum laude, Harvard U., 1958; Litt.D., Columbia Coll., Chgo., 1972. Vietnam Bur. chief UPI (Saigon), 1962-64; reporter NY Times (NYC, Djakarta, Saigon, Washington), 1964—. Served with AUS, 1959-62. Recipient Louis M. Lyons award for conscience and integrity in journalism, 1964, Silver medal Poor Richard Club, Phila., 1964, certificate of appreciation for best article on Asia Overseas Press Club Am., 1967, 1st Annl. Drew Pearson prize for excellence in investigative reporting, 1971, Columbia Journalism award, 1972, Sidney Hillman Fdn. award, 1972, Page One award Newspaper Guild NY, 1972, citation of excellence Overseas Press Club, 1972. Obtained Pentagon Papers, 1971. Home: 4505 Klingle St NW Washington DC 20016

SHEEHY, GAIL HENION, b. Mamaroneck, NY, Nov. 27, 1937; d. Harold Merritt and Lillian Rainey (Paquin) Henion; m. Albert F. Sheehy, Aug. 20, 1960 (div. 1967); 1 dau.—Maura; 1 foster dau.—Mohm. Author: (novel) Lovesounds, 1970; Panthermania: The Clash of Black Against Black in One American City, 1971, Speed Is of the Essence, 1971, Hustling: Prostitution in Our Wide-Open Society, 1973, Passages: Predictable Crises of Adult Life, 1976, Pathfinders, 1981, Spirit of Survival, 1986. BS, U. Vt., 1958, fellow, Journalism Schl., Columbia U., 1970. Traveling home economist J.C. Penney & Co., 1958-60; fashion editor Rochester Democrat & Chronicle, 1961-63; feature writer NY Herald Tribune (NYC)1963-66; contrbg. editor New York mag., 1968-77; contrbr. to NY Times Mag., Parade, Vanity Fair, New Republic, Washington Post. Recipient Front Page award Newswomen's Club NY, 1964, 73; Natl. Mag. award Columbia U., 1973; Penney-Mo. Journalism award U. Mo., 1975. Mem. PEN, AG, P&W. Office: Morrow 105 Madison Ave New York NY 10016

SHEFTEL, BEATRICE K., (Kerry Little, B. K. Tortoric), b. Bklyn., Jan. 24, 1945; d. Salvatore Sebastion and Frances (Trapani) Tortorici; m. Robert Sheftel, Oct. 12, 1963; 1 son, Robert Francis. Contrbr. poems, aticles to mags., lit. mags., anthols. Ed.: Romantic Book Guide, 1982-84, Manch Commun. Coll. Cougar, 1985-86, sr. ed.: Coventry, 1986—. ed.: Applause (selected poetry and prose), 1988. Former ed. Spirit of Muse, author of 2 chapbooks. Assoc. Sci., Manch Commun. Coll., 1986; B.Genl. Sci., U. Conn., 1987. Mem. WIC, Conn. Poetry Soc., Conn. Wrtrs. League, Wit Wisdom Wrtrs. Club. Home: 24 Farm Dr Manchester CT 06040

SHELBY, JOYCE YOUNG, b. Augusta, GA, Mar. 17, 1947, d. Nathaniel Thomas and Prudence (Bolden) Young; children—Gail Ann-Marie, Claybrone III. BA, Spelman Coll., Atlanta, 1968; MS in Journalism, Columbia U., 1969. Reporter Pitts. Post-Gazette, 1969, WQED-TV, Pitts., 1969-71, WHUR-FM, Washington, 1971-72; public info. officer Consumer Info. Center, Washington, 1972-74; ed. Georgetown Today, Georgetown U., Washington, 1974-75; adj. faculty Grad. Schl. Journalism, Columbia U., NYC, 1975-81, asst. prof., 1981—. Recipient Golden Quill award Pitts. Press Club, 1970. Home: 605 W 113th St 62 New York NY 10025

SHELDON, SIDNEY, b. Chgo., Feb. 11, 1917; s. Otto and Natalie (Marcus) Sheldon; m. Jorja Curtright, Mar. 28, 1951; 1 dau.—Mary. Author: The Naked Face, 1970, The Other Side of Midnight, 1975, A Stranger in the Mirror, 1976, Bloodline, 1977, Rage of Angels, 1980, Master of the Game, 1982, If Tomorrow Comes, 1985; creator, writer, producer: Nancy, The Patty Duke Show, Hart to Hart, I Dream of Jeannie; author: plays including Roman Candle, Jackpot, Dream With Music, Alice in Arms, Redhead; writer screenplays including Billy Rose's Jumbo, The Bachelor and the Bobby-Soxer, Easter Parade, Annie Get Your Gun; writer, dir.: Dream Wife; writer: Anything Goes, Never Too Young; writer, dir: Buster Keaton Story; recipient Acad. Award for screenplay The Bachelor and the Bobby-Soxer 1947, Tony award for Redhead 1959, WG Am. Screen awards for Easter Parade, 1948, Annie Get Your Gun 1950. Ed. Northwestern U. Started as reader, Universal and 20th Century Fox Studios. Served with USAF, World War II. Office: Morrow 105 Madison Ave New York NY 10016

SHELL, COURTNEY, see Bone, Brenda Kay

SHELLENBERGER, VERNA S, b. Meyersdale, PA, Apr. 1, 1915; d. John F. and Mary E. (Seiler) Siegner; m. Philbert Shellenberger, Jan. 12, 1957 (div. Feb. 20, 1975). Contrbr. poems to anthols. Student, Phila. Acad. Schl. Music. Office clrk. Acme Mkts., Phila., 1952—75. Pianist L & S Rest Home, Atco, N.J., 1975-86. Recipient Golden Poetry award World of Poetry, 1985. Home: 123 S Oak Ave Mount Ephraim NJ 08059

SHELNUTT, EVE B., b. Spartanburg, SC, Aug. 29, 1941; m. Mark Logan Shelton. Short story collections: The Love Child, 1979, The Formal Voice, 1982, The Musician, 1987. Chapbook-fiction: Descant, 1981. Poetry collection: Air and Salt, 1983. Stories pub. in anthologies: O. Henry Prize Stories, 1975, Stories of the Modern South, 1981, The Third Coast, 1982, Ohio Rvw Ten-Yr. Retrospective, 1983, From Mt. San Angelo, 1984, The Ploughshares Reader, 1985, An American Christmas, 1986; also stories in Mother Jones, Am. Rvw, Agni Rvw, Prairie Schooner, others. Book forthcoming The Musician. Also numerous fiction and poetry readings at colls. and univs. BA, U. Cin., 1972; MFA, U. N.C., 1973. Assoc. prof. Western Mich. U., Kalamazoo, 1974-80, U. Pitts., 1980—. Office: Dept Eng 501 Cathedral Pittsburgh PA 15260

SHELTON, MARK LOGAN, b. Chgo., May 19, 1958; s. Roscoe Wilbur and Rose Catherine (Schanes) S.; m. Eve Shelnutt, May 29, 1982. Contrbr. fiction to Pa. Rvw, Passages North, Backspace, The Trial Balloon; poetry in Ohio Jnl, Westigan Rvw, Intro, 3 Rivers Poetry; nonfiction in Pitts. Post-Gazette, Pitts. Press, Ohio Mag, Pittsburgh Mag. Contrbg. ed. Pittsburgh Mag., 1986—. BA, Western Mich. U., 1980; MFA, U. Pitts., 1982. Instr. Community Coll., Allegheny County, Pa., 1982-83; media coordinator Presbyterian Hosp. Pitts., 1985; instr. Univ. Pitts., 1983. Mem. Am. Medical Writers Assn., Nat. Assn. Advancement Sci. Address: Box 276 Laughlintown PA 15655

SHELTON, NICOLINA (NIKKI), b. New Rochelle, NY; d. Angelo and Filomena Sylvester. Travel ed. U.S. Hispanic Affairs Mag.; contrbg. ed.: Travel Agent Mag., Travel Holiday Mag., TravelAge East Mag., Airfare Interline Mag., Catholic N.Y. Nwspr., R & R Eur-Network Mag., Gannett-Westchester Nwsprs., Turismondo Travel Mag., Il Tempo Mag., contrbr. num. arts. to profl. & popular mags. & nwsprs. Pub. relns. spec. House of Seagram's, NYC, 1952-61; acct. exec. Fletcher Richards Adv., NYC, 1962-64; dep. p.r. dir. U.S. Pavilion, N.Y. World's Fair, 1964-65; p.r. dir. Loewy, Stempel Adv., NYC, 1969-70; news and info. spec. GAF Corp., NYC, 1971-73; press relns. off. Paul Andrews P.R., NYC, 1973-82; freelance writer, 1982—. 6 natl. first prizes for arts. & feats., num. other creative writing awards. Mem. N.Y. Publicity Club, N.Y. Tourism Press Assn., Caribbean Tourism Assn., N.Y.C. Police Press Corp. Home: 21 Rhodes St New Rochelle NY 10801

SHELTON, RICHARD, b. Boise, ID, June 24, 1933, s. Leonard Pryor and Hazel Josephine (Ashlock) S.; m. Lois Bruce, Dec. 24, 1956; 1 child, Brad Scott. Author: Journal of Return, 1969, The Tattooed Desert, 1971, The Heroes of Our Time, 1972, Calendar, 1972, Of All the Dirty Words, 1972, Among the Stones, 1973, Chosen Place, 1975, You Can't Have Everything, 1975, Desert Water, 1977, The Bus to Veracruz, 1978, A Kind of Glory, 1982, Selected Poems: 1969-81, 1982, Hohokam, 1986, The Other Side of the Story, 1986, (filmscripts) Sonoran: The Hidden Desert, 1979, Another Day,

1980, The Sound of Water, 1983. BA, Abiline Christian U., 1958; MA, U. Ariz., 1961. Instr. English, U. Ariz., 1960-69, asst. prof., 1970-74, assoc. prof., 1974-79, prof., 1979—. Served with U.S. Army, 1956-58. Recipient U.S. award Intl. Poetry Forum, 1970; NEA fellow, 1976. Mem. AWP (pres. bd. dirs.), PEN-PSA, Natl. Fedn. State Poetry Socs. Home: 1548 Plaza DeLirios Tucson AZ 85745

SHEPHERD, CATHERINE, b. Atmore, AL, June 16, 1915, d. Joseph Elijah and Mary Inda (Pugh) Cunningham; m. Emmett Hill Shepherd, Jan. 27, 1945; children—Mary Lu, Paul Hill, Joseph Emmett. Ed. Leclaire Newsletter, 1951; contrbr. to The Ray of Gamma Sigma Epsilon, Chem. Abstracts Service, The Upper Room, The Prayer Tower, Annals of N.Y. Acad. Scis., Fla. Rvw (1st prize for poetry 1984). Wrkg. on popular sci. book for adults, fantasy and sci. books for children. BS, U. Ala., 1938; postgrad. U. Chgo. Bacteriologist, researcher, 1938-46, 59-66; grad. research asst. U. South Fla., Tampa, 1966-67; dir. children's ministry 1st United Methodist Ch., Clearwater, Fla., 1970-76; freelance wrtr., 1976—. Mem. Soc. Children's Book wrtrs. Home: 2748 Avocado Dr Clearwater FL 33519

SHEPHERD, GARY KEVIN, b. Danville, IL, July 15, 1957; s. Gerald Shepherd and Evelyn Mae (Craig) Shepherd-McCraw; m. Joyce Marie Eannarino, May 13, 1980; children—Jason, Bridget, Timothy. Corr. Southern Illinoisan, 1986-87; contrbr. articles to newspapers, mags. including Ill. Fishing News, Humanist, Adventure Mag., others. Ed.: Jasper Jnl., 1981-83, Southern Ill. Wrtr., 1985, Southern Ill. Peace Coalition newsletter, 1985-1987, Jasper County Hist. Soc. newsletter, 1982-1983, Newton Arts Council newsletter, 1982-1983. B.A. in English, Jnlsm., Southern Ill. U., 1979. Library clrk. Southern Ill. U., Carbondale, 1980-81; reporter Newton Press-Monitor, IL, 1981-84; owner, mgr. Book Depot, Carbondale, 1984—; free-lance wrtr., 1984—. Recipient Young Wrtrs.' Essay award Am. Humanist Assn., 1987. Mem. Southern Ill. WG (pres. 1986). Home: 1505 W Tripoli Carbondale IL 62901

SHER, STEVEN J., b. Bklyn., Sept. 28, 1949, s. Albert and Miriam R. (Ginsberg) S.; m. Nancy A. Green, Mar. 11, 1978; children—Kyla M., Ari D. Author: Nickelodeon (poetry), 1978, Persnickety (poetry), 1979, Caught in the Revolving Door (poetry), 1980, Trolley Lives (poetry), 1985, Silverman's Tomb and Other Stories, 1987; co-ed.: Northwest Variety (essays), 1987. BA in Sociology, CCNY, 1970; MA in Journalism, U. Iowa, 1973; MFA in Poetry, Bklyn. Coll., 1978. Mem. faculty Bklyn. Coll., 1977-78, dir. creative wrtg. prog., Spalding U., Louisville, Ky., 1979-81; instr. English Oreg. State U., Corvallis, 1981-86; asst. prof. Eng., U. NC, Wilmington, 1986—; freelance ed., Appleton-Century-Crofts, Swan Publ., People & Places mag., Bitterroot. Office: Dept Eng Univ NC Wilmington NC 28403

SHERBURNE, DONALD WYNNE, b. Proctor, VT, Apr. 21, 1929; s. Hermon Kirk and Alma May (Bixby) Sherburne; m. Elizabeth Statesir Darling, July 30, 1955; children—Kevin Darling, Nancy Elizabeth, Lynne Darling. Author: A Whiteheadian Aesthetic, 1961, A Key to Whitehead's Process and Reality, 1966; editor: Soundings—An Interdisciplinary Jnl, 1980-85; co-editor: Corrected Edition of Whitehead's Process and Reality, 1978. AB, Middlebury Coll., 1951; BA, Balliol Coll., Oxford U., 1953; MA, Yale U., 1958, PhD, 1960. Instr. philosophy Yale, 1959-60; asst. prof. Vanderbilt U. (Nashville), 1960-64, assoc. prof., 1964-68, prof. philosophy, 1968—, chair dept., 1973-80. Served with U.S. Army, 1954-56. Home: 227 Leonard Ave Nashville TN 37205

SHERER, BILLEE JEAN, b. Kirksville, Mo., Aug. 11, 1948; d. Gail and Irene (Davis) S. Author: Potpourri: The Art of Fragrance Crafting; (manual) The Grant Wood AEA Guide to Newsletter Production; contrbr. to Linker, Iowa Journalist, Grit, Career World, On the Line, School Shop, Cedar Rapids Gazette, Washington Evening Jnl., Anamosa-Eureka-Jnl., others. BA in Psychology, N.E. Mo. State Coll., 1970; MA in Guidance, 1972; MA in Journalism, U. Iowa, 1984. Guidance counselor Adair County R-II, Brashear, Mo., 1974-76, Shellsburg Community Coll., Iowa, 1976-85; pub. inf. specialist Grant Wood Area Edn. Agy., Cedar Rapids, Iowa, 1985—. Murray journalism scholar U. Iowa, 1984. Home: 3949 Crestwood Dr NW Cedar Rapids IA 52405

SHERIDAN, CHARLES STEVE, b. Montgomery, AL, Apr. 23, 1958; s. Charles Harold and Edith Maryln (Dawson) S.; m. Kathy Dawn Bert, Apr. 7, 1986; children—Chrisopher, Stephen. Contrbr. articles to mags. Ed.: Auminae, 1984. Student Auburn U., 1986-87, Fla. State U., 1983=84. Editor: The Progress, Prattville, AL, 1984-85, ed., 1985-86; mng. ed. The Autauga Times, Prattville, 1986—. Recipient Best Commun. Series award Ala. Press Assn., 1985, 1st place for Best Series, 1986. Home: Rt 3 Box 367A Prattville AL 36067

SHERMAN, JAMES RICHARD, b. Luverne, MN, Aug. 20, 1935, s. Russell Alfred and Blanche Leona (Peterson) S.; m. Merlene Gail Thorson, June 6, 1957; children—Christopher James, Eric Emerson, Lincoln Everett. Author: How to Overcome a Bad Back, 1979, Stop Procrastinating—Do It!, 1980, Rejection, 1981, Get Set . . . Go!, 1982, Escape to the Gunflint (novel), 1983, Middle Age Is Not a Disease, 1985. Wrkg. on self-help books. BA, U. Colo.-Boulder, 1963, MPS, 1964; PhD, U. No. Colo., 1967. Asst. chancellor Minn. Jr. Coll. System, St. Paul, 1968-72; sr. cons. Ednl. Mgmt. System, Edina, Minn., 1971-79; owner, mgr. Pathway Books, Golden Valley, Minn., 1979—. Mem. Minn. Ind. Pub. Assn. (sec.), Minn. Book Pub. Roundtable, Upper Midwest Booksellers Assn. Address: 700 Parkview Terr Golden Valley MN 55427

SHERMAN, JOE, b. Lebanon, NH, Apr. 19, 1945, s. George David and Lula Maud (Hopkins) S.; m. Margaret Cohen, June 11, 1972; 1 son, Andrew James. Author: The House at Shelburne Farms, 1986, A Thousand Voices, 1987; contrbr. articles to Yankee Mag., New Eng. Rvw, Fine Homebldg., numerous other publs. BBA, U. Mich., 1968; MBA, U. Mass., 1970. Vice-pres. Am. Intl. Travel, Los Angeles, 1970-72; freelance wrtr. Mem. NWU. Home: Box 22 Montgomery VT 05470

SHERMAN, ROBERT T., b. Evanston, IL, Aug. 19, 1937; s. Robert T. and Jean Palmer (Dawes) S.; m. Patricia Lou Naumes, Oct. 19, 1974. Editor & pub.: Letters from the Gold Rush, 1980. BS, Marietta Coll., 1960. Comml. artist The Shoppers Mart, Chgo., 1964-65, Penny Saver, Midlothian, 1965-66, State-Wide Ins., Chgo., 1965-66; computer programmer MICA, Chgo., 1966-67, Alesdan Inc., Chgo., 1967-68; tech. adv. Harris Bank, Chgo., 1968—. Treas. Glenview Art League. Address: 3516 Lawson Rd Glenview IL 60025

SHERMAN, STEVE BARRY, b. Los Angeles, July 26, 1938, s. Gene Franklin and Genevieve Marie (McLaughlin) S. Author: ABCs of Library Promotion, 1971, Home Heating with Coal, 1980, The Haagen-Dazs Book of Ice Cream, 1982, Basic Yankee, 1984, The Maple Sugar Murders (fiction), 1987; co- author: (with Julia Older) Appalachian Odyssey, 1977, Soup and Bread, 1978, Menus à Trois, 1987. Contrbr. articles to Esquire, Alaska, Yankee, Country Jnl, Parents, The N.Y. Times, Christian Sci. Monitor, Boston Globe Sunday Mag., N.H. Profiles, Home Energy Digest, Technology Illustrated, New Shelter, Publishers Weekly, Bus. N.H., Historic Preservation, New Home, others. BA in Philosophy, Loyola U., Los Angeles, 1960, MA in Communications, 1965; MSLS, UCLA, 1967. Tchr., research librarian, Alaska, 1964-68; reporter Daily News, Anchorage, 1969; freelance wrtr., 1970—; feature wrtr. N.H. Times, Concord, 1975-78. Address: Box 174 Hancock NH 03449

SHERMAN, WILLIAM DAVID, (Pecos Bill), b. Phila., Dec. 24, 1940, s. Louis and Gertrude (Benn) S. Author: (poems) The Springbok, 1973, The Hard Sidewalk, 1974, 75, The Horses of Gwyddno Garanhir, 1976, Heart Attack & Spanish Songs in Mandaine Land, 1981, Duchamp's Door, 1982, Mermaids, 1986, She Wants To Go to Pago-Pago, 1986; guest ed. Sixpack No. 5; contrbr. to numerous mags. and jnls, included in anthology matieres d'Angleterre. AB, Temple U., 1962; MA, SUNY, Buffalo, 1964, PhD, 1968. Scriptreader Rank Films, London, 1975-77; founder, ed.-pub., designer Branch Redd Books, 1976—; tchr. phys. ed. Samuel Pepys Schl., London, 1979-80; full-time poet, wrtr., 1984—; lectr. Am. studies U. Hull, Eng., 1967-68; lectr. Am. lit. Univ. Coll. Wales, Aberystwyth, 1969-72. Home: Box 46466 Philadelphia PA 19160

SHERRY, JAMES TERENCE, b. Phila., Dec. 30, 1946, s. Fred Richard and Shirley (Socolof) S.; m. Lee Frances Sahlins, June 13, 1968. Author: Part Songs, 1979, In Case, 1981, Converses, 1983, Popular Fiction, 1985, The Word I Like White Paint Considered, 1986, In the American Tree, 1986. AB, Reed Coll., 1968. Ed. ROOF Mag., NYC, 1976-79; pres. Segue Fdn., NYC, 1977—; freelance wrtr., NYC, 1972—. Woodrow Wilson Fdn. fellow, 1968; recipient CAPS awd., 1983. Mem. Alliance Lit. Orgns., P&W, Igor Fdn. Home: 300 Bowery St New York NY 10012

SHERWIN, JAMES LELAND (LANNY), b. Cleve., Apr. 29, 1950; s. James nelson and Kathleen (Burke) S.; m. Phyllis Better, Aug. 14, 1977 (div. 1978). Owner, pub., ed.: Gulfshore Life, 1977-86, Naples-on-the-Gulf, 1980-86, Central Fla. Mag., 1982-84, PBA Horizons, 1984-85, Traditions, 1984-86, Ft. Myers Mag., 1985-86, Reflections, 1985-86, Images, 1985-86, Wrkg. on mystery novel. BA in English, Lehigh U., 1972. Wrtr., photographer Chagrin Valley Times, Chagrin Falls, Ohio, 1975-77; pres. Gulfshore Pub. Co., Inc., Naples, Fla., 1977-86, Sherwin Communications, Inc., Naples, 1987—. Winner article competition Fla. Freelance Wrtrs.' Assn., 1987. Mem. Fla. Mag. Assn. (pres.; recipient Gen. Excellence award 1982, 83, 85, 86, Best of Show Photograph award 1983), Office: Sherwin Comm 672 Hickory Rd Naples FL 33963

SHERWIN, JUDITH JOHNSON, see Johnson, Judith Evelyn

SHERWOOD, EVELYN RUTH, b. Boston, June 6, 1929; d. Arnold L. and Eleanor L. (Kershaw) Snell; m. John D. Flynn, Nov. 2, 1947 (div. 1970); children—Gail M., Thomas A., John D., Brian A., Peter K., Elizabeth A.; m. Donald F. Sherwood, July 10, 1977. Contrbr. poems to lit. mags. Mem. editorial staff Kalliope jnl., 1980-87. B.A., Fla. State U., 1979, M.L.S., 1980. Librarian, Grenfield Elem. Sch., Jacksonville, FL, (1980—. Home: 3054 Cobblewood Ln W Jacksonville Fl 3225

SHESTACK, MELVIN BERNARD, b. Bklyn., Aug. 18, 1931; s. David and Sylvia Pearl (Saffran) Shestack; m. Jessica Gifford, Feb. 13, 1965; 1 dau.—Victoria J. Producer, writer: documentary The Forgotten American, ,67; author: The Country Music Encyclopedia, 1974; co-author: filmscript The Soul, 1978, Secrets of Success, 1980, "How'm I Doing?": The Wit and Wisdom of Ed Koch, 1981. AB, U. So. Calif., 1953; postgrad., U. Rochester, NY U., New Schl. Social Research. Assoc. editor Sat. Eve. Post, 1965-67; staff producer CBS-TV News, 1967-69; assoc. producer sta. WOR-TV, 1970; exec. editor True mag. (NYC), 1971-75, editor-in-chief, 1975; editor In The Know mag. (NYC), 1975—; exec. dir. Ponca Inst. Am. Studies, 1976-80; exec. editor Antelope Classics, Empire Edits., 1977—; vp, dir. spcl. projects Montcalm Pub. Co., 1980—. Served with AUS, 1953-55. Recipient Brown-Nickerson award for best religious radio program, 1967. Home: 4 Great Jones St New York NY 10012

SHETTERLY, WILLIAM HOWARD, b. Columbia, SC, Aug. 22, 1955; s. Bob E. and Joan Mary (Fikkan) S.; m. Emma Lucinda Bull, Oct. 17, 1981. Author: Cats Have No Lord, 1985, Witch Blood, 1986; ed. (with Emma Bull) Liavek, 1985, The Players of Luck, 1986, Wizard's Row, 1987. Wrkg. on Dogland, a fantasy, The Tangled Lands, a prequel, the 4th Liavek anthology (with Emma Bull). BA in English Lit., Beloit Coll., 1976. Editorial asst. Berkley Books, NYC, 1976; prodn. aid John Wiley & Sons, NYC, 1977; actor NYC, 1978-79; mgr. Shetterly Enterprises, Rat Rapids, Ont., Can., 1980-84; pub. Steel Dragon Press, Mpls., 1984—. Mem. SFWA. Address: Box 7253 Powderhorn Sta Minneapolis MN 55407

SHEVIN, DAVID A., b. Rochester, NY, June 1, 1951; s. Nathan and Ella (Drexler) S. Author: Postcard: Bebe 1909, 1978, Camptown Spaces, 1978, The Stop Book, 1978, Something Like a Monkey, 1981, What Happens, 1983; contbr. to anthologies: Voices Within the Ark, 1980, Itinerary 2, 1975, Intro No. 7,, 1975, Intro No. 10, 1980; contbr. to jnls: Blue Unicorn, Cin. Poetry Rvw, Confrontation, Dacotah Terr., Loon, Louisville Rvw, Rolling Stone, WIN, others. BA, Lewis & Clark Coll., 1973; MFA, Bowling Green State U., 1976; Phd, U. Cin., 1986. Instr. English Univ. Cin., 1976-81, Miami Univ., 1986-87, asst. prof. English, Tiffin Univ., 1987—. staff AFTRA, Cin., 1981-85. New Jewish Agenda, Central Am. Task Force, 1985—. Address: 142½ N Washington St Tiffin OH 44883

SHIDELER, ROSS PATRICK, b. Denver, Apr. 12, 1936; s. Byron H.S. and Trudy (Shideler). Author: (monograph) Voices Under The Ground: Themes and Images in the Poetry of Gunnar Ekelof, 1973; Per Olov Enquist—A Critical Study, 1984; translator: (play) The Night of the Tribades (by Per Olov Enquist), 1977; assoc. ed. Swedish Bk Rvw, 1985—, ed. bd. U. Neb. Scandinavian Lit. in translation series, 1986—. BA, San Francisco State U., 1958; MA, U. Stockholm, 1963; PhD, U. Calif. at Berkeley, 1968. Instr. in comparative lit. U. Calif. at Berkeley, 1967-68; asst. prof. English Hunter Coll. (NYC), 1968-69; asst. prof. Scandinavian lang. and comparative lit. UCLA, 1969-73, assoc. profl, 1973-79, prof., 1979—. Mem. MLA, Soc. Advancement Scandinavian Studies, Am. Comparative Lit. Assn., DG. Office: Comp Lit 405 Hilgard Los Angeles CA 90024

SHIELDS, DAVID J., b. Los Angeles, July 22, 1956; s. Milton and Hannah (Bloom) S. Author novels: Heroes, 1984, Dead Languages, 1988; contrbr. short fiction and criticism to Iowa Rvw, Chgo Rvw, James Joyce Qtly, No Light, San Francisco Chronicle, Hellcoal, Issues; screenplay of Heroes in development with prod. co. BA, Brown U., 1974-78; MFA, Iowa Writers Workshop, 1978-80. Instr. Univ. Iowa, Iowa City, 1980; UCLA, 1985; asst. prof. St. Lawrence Univ., Canton, NY, 1985-86, 1987-88. Recipient NEA fiction grant, 1982, Ingram Merrill Fdn. award, 1983, PEN fiction competition, 1985, Ludwig Vogelstein Fdn. grant, 1986. Mem. PEN, Authors Guild, MLA, AWP, P&W, WG of Am. Address: 14 Jay St Canton NY 13617

SHIELDS, STEVEN LAYNE, b. Logan, UT, Apr. 22, 1956; s. Wayne Ross and Carol (Nulph) S.; 1 son, Christopher. Asst. editor, Nauvoo Neighbor, 1975, Plaza Magazine, 1978, John Whitmer History Journal, 1986; editor, Restoration, 1981—. BS in Bus. Admin., U. Phoenix, 1986. Exec. asst. to pres. Horizon Pub., Bountiful, Utah, 1979—; pres. Restoration Research, Bountiful, 1981—. Home: 453 W 1500 S Bountiful UT 84010

SHIH, JOAN CHUNG-WEN, b. Nanking, China, came to U.S., 1948, naturalized, 1960; d. Cho-kiang and Chia-pu (Fang) Shih. Author: Injustice to Tou O, 1972, The Golden Age of Chinese Drama: Yuan Tsa-chu, 1976, Return from Silence: China's Writers of the May Fourth Tradition, 1983. BA, St. John's U., Shanghai, 1945; MA, Duke U., 1949, PhD, 1955. Asst. prof. Chinese Stanford U., 1961-64, Pomona Coll., Claremont, Calif., 1965-66; prof., chmn. dept. East Asian langs. and lit., George Washington U., Washington, 1971—. Mem. Sino-Am. Cultural Soc. (bd. dirs. 1971-76), Chinese Lang. Tchrs. Assn. (chmn.). Home :2500 Va Ave NW Apt 602-S Washington DC 20037

SHINN, DUANE, (Dunk), b. Auburn, CA, Nov. 13, 1938; s. Archie Wilbur and Iola (Eisley) S.; m. Beverly Jane Luman, Aug. 27, 1960; children: Kurt, Kendra, Garin, Garth. Author: How to Read Music, Creative Arranging, Teach Yourself All About Chords, 34 others, plus 400 cassette covers, 27 videos. BA, So. Oreg. State Coll., MA. Freelance musical performance and writing; pub. Duane Shinn Publs., Oreg. Address: Box 700 Medford OR 97501

SHIPLER, DAVID KARR, b. Orange, NJ, Dec. 3, 1942; s. Guy Emery J. and Eleanor (Karr) Shipler; m. Deborah S. Isaacs, Sept. 17, 1966; children—Jonathan Robert, Laura Karr, Michael Edmund. Author: Russia: Broken Idols, Solemn Dreams, 1983 (Overseas Press Club award), Arab and Jew: Wounded Spirits in a Promised Land, 1986 (Pulitzer Prize); contrbr. articles to natl. mags. AB, Dartmouth Coll., 1964. News clk. NY Times, 1966-67, news summary writer, 1968, reporter metro. staff, 1968-73, fgn. corr. Saigon bur., 1973-75, fgn. corr. Moscow bur., 1975—, bur. chief Moscow bur., 1977-79, chief Jerusalem bur., 1979-84, guest scholar, Brookings Instn., 1984-85, corr. NY Times, Washington bur., 1985—, chief diplomatic corr., 1987—. Served with USNR, 1964-66. Recipient award for disting. reporting Soc. Silurians, 1971; award for disting. pub. affairs reporting Am. Poli. Scis. Assn., 1971; Page One award (with others) for most crusading newspaper, 1973; award NY chpt. Sigma Delta Chi, 1973; co-recipient George Polk award, 1982. Mem. NY Newspaper Guild, AG. Office: NY Times 1000 Conn Ave Washington DC 20036

SHIPLETT, JUNE ELIZABETH LUND, b. Mayfield Heights, OH, June 17, 1930; d. Arthur Ellsworth and Gladys Margaret (Eames) Lund; m. Charles Eugene Shiplett, Jan. 7, 1950; children—Maureen, Geraldine, Yvonne, Laura. Author: The Raging Winds of Heaven, 1978, Reap the Bitter Winds, 1979, Journey to Yesterday, 1979-83, The Wild Storms of Heaven, 1980, Defy the Savage Winds, 1980, Return to Yesterday, 1983, Thunder in the Wind, 1983, Wild Winds Calling, 1984, Beloved Traitor, 1985, Winds of Betrayal, 1987, Lady Wildcat, 1987. Wrkg. on Farewell the Winds of Heavan. Grad. public schls., Mayfield Heights. Switchboard operator Ohio Bell, Mayfield Heights, 1948-50, profl. Answering Service, Mayfield Heights and Mentor, OH, 1967-77. Bd. trustees Mentor Public Library, 1982—. Mem. AG, RWA. Home: 5509 Chestnut St Mentor-On-The-Lake OH 44060

SHIPLEY, ROBERT HOPKINS, b. Kalamazoo, Mich., Apr. 11, 1945, s. Robert Clement and Jean (Hopkins) S.; m. Janet Long, June 2, 1968 (div.); children—Kimra, Jennifer. Author: Flooding and Implosive Therapy: Direct Therapeutic Exposure in Clinical Practice, 1983, QuitSmart: A Guide to Freedom from Cigarettes, 1985, QuitSmart Self-Hypnosis (cassette tape), 1985; contrbg. author: The Heart Book, 1981, Behavioral Medicine in General Medical Practice, 1982. BS in Psychology, Mich. State U., 1967; MA, PhD in Clin. Psychology, U. Iowa, 1972. Mem. staff Mid-Mo. Mental Health Ctr., Columbia, 1972-77; asst. prof. psychiatry U. Mo., Columbia, 1972-77; staff psychologist VA Med. Center, Durham, N.C., 1977-80, chief psychology service, 1980—; assoc. prof. psychiatry Duke U. Med. Center, Durham, 1980—, dir. Quit Smoking Clinic, 1977—. Mem. profl. psychol. assns. Office: Psych Serv VA 508 Fulton St Durham NC 27705

SHIPLEY, THOMAS E. JR., b. Kingsport, Tenn., Mar. 22, 1924; s. Thomas E. and Blanche (Dykes) S.; m. Sarah Virginia Doane, Aug. 27, 1948; children: Thomas Doane, Ardin Leigh.Contrbr. articles: Tooling & Production, American Metal Market, Abrasive Engineering Society Magazine, numerous other trade publs. BSEE, Va. Poly. Inst. With Gen. Electric Co., various locations, 1950-65; pres. Machine Tool Sale Co., Birmingham, Mich., 1977—. Served with USN, 1944-46; ETO. Mem. Bus. and Profl. Advt. Assn., profl. orgns. Home: 1150 Suffield St Birmingham MI 48009

SHIPPEY, FREDERICK ALEXANDER, b. Troy, NY, Aug. 21, 1908; s. William Dean and Jennie (Rankin) S.; m. Melda B. Haynes, June 17, 1938; children—Melda Jean Shippey Pike, Stuart Haynes Shippey, Ed./contrbr., Review of Religious Research, 1959-64; author: Church Work in the City, 1952, City Church and Social Class, 1958, Six Research Studies, 1960, Protestantism in Suburban Life, 1964, Ethnic Population and The Methodist Church, 1970; contrbr. chapters to: Cities and Churches, 1962, Institutionalism and Church Unity, 1963, Sociology in Use, 1965, The Sociology of Religion, 1967, Ency. of World Methodism, 1970. AB, Syracuse, 1935; BD, Yale U., 1938; PhD, Northwestern U., 1947. Minister, Stanford Methodist Church, Schenectady, NY, 1938-44; dir. research & surveys, Meth. Bd. Missions, United States, 1944-51; prof. Drew U., Madison, NJ, 1950-75, prof. emeritus, 75—. Mem. Am. Sociol. Assn., Relig. Research Assn. Home: 52 Fairview Ave Madison NJ 07940

SHIPPEY, JUANITA WATERS, b. Memphis, Feb. 28, 1946; d. Joseph Oliver Mary Pauline (Beard) Waters; m. Stirling Clarke Shippey, Oct. 28, 1966; children—Mary Elizabeth, Miriam Annette, Raymund Pearce. Author: Kids' Action Songs, 1976, Kids' Action Art, 1980; columnist: The Georgia Storyteller, The Telegraph, Georgia Mountain Newspaper; contrbr. articles: Commerce News. Wrkg. on curriculum books, juvenile fiction, folklore, non-fiction. BSEd cum laud, U. Ga., 1976; MSEd, N. Ga. Coll., 1983. Tchr. public schs., Cleveland, Ga., 1978—; freelance wrtr. Mem. ednl. orgns. Home: Box 627 Cleveland GA 30528

SHIRER, WILLIAM LAWRENCE, b. Chgo., Feb. 23, 1904; s. Seward Smith and Bessie Josephine (Tanner) Shirer; m. Theresa Stiberitz, 1931 (div. 1970); children—Eileen Inga, Linda Elizabeth. Author: Berlin Diary, 1941, End of a Berlin Diary, 1947, The Traitor, 1950, Midcentury Journey, 1952, Stranger Come Home, 1954, The Challenge of Scandinavia, 1955, The Consul's Wife, 1956, The Rise and Fall of the Third Reich, 1960 (Natl. Book award 1961), The Rise and Fall of Adolf Hitler, 1961, The Sinking of the Bismarck, 1962, The Collapse of the Third Republic, 1969, 20th Century Journey, 1976, Gandhi—A Memoir, 1979, The Nightmare Years, 1984; contrbr. to Harper's, others. AB, Coe Coll., 1925, Litt.D. (hon.). Journalist, Paris ed. Chicago Tribune, 1925-26, fgn. corr., 1926-33, Universal News Service, 1935-37; became Continental rep. CBS, 1937; warr corr., 1939-45, commentator, 1945-47; commentator on Mutual network, 1947-49. Mem. AG (pres.), PEN, Council on Fgn. Relations, Fgn. Policy Assn. Address: Box 487 34 Sunset Ave Lenox MA 01240

SHIRLEY, GLENN DEAN, b. Payne County, OK, Dec. 9, 1916; s. Ellis Dean and Effie Teresa (Knorr) Shirley; m. Carrie Mabel Jacob, 1946; children—Glenda Lea, Kenneth Ellis. Author: books of western history and personalities, including Toughest of Them All, 1953, Six-Gun and Silver Star, 1955, Law West of Ft. Smith: A History of Frontier Justice in the Idian Territory, 1834-1896, 1957, 7th ed., 1982, Pawnee Bill: A Biography of Gordon W. Lillie, 1958, 4th ed., 1981, Buckshin and Spurs: A Gallery of Frontier Rogues and Heroes, 1958, Outlaw Queen, 1960, Heck Thomas, Frontier Marshal: The Story of a Real Gunfighter, 1962, Born to Kill, 1963, Henry Starr, Last of the Real Badmen, 1965, 2nd ed., 1976, Buckskin Joe: The Unique and Vivid Memoirs of Edward Jonathan Hoyt, Hunter-Trapper, Scout, Soldier, Showman, Frontiersman and Friend of the Indians, 1840-1918, 1966, Shotgun for Hire: The Story of "Deacon" Jim Miller, Killer of Pat Garrett, 1970, The Life of Texas Jack: Eight Years a Criminal— 41 Years Trusting in God, 1973, Red Yesterdays, 1977, West of Hell's Fringe: Crime, Criminals and the Federal Peace Officer in Oklahoma Territory 1889-1907, 1978, Temple Houston, Lawyer with a Gun, 1980, Belle Starr and Her Times: The Literature The Facts and The Legends, 1982; contrbr. numerous short stories, novelettes and factual articles to Western pulps, fact-detective and men's mags. and genl. markets, to anthologies; former contrbg. editor: Westerner, Old Trails, Oklahoma Monthly. Diploma, NY Inst. Photography, 1941, Intl. Criminologist Schl., 1948, Delehanty Inst., 1949, Okla. Inst. Tech., 1950; LL.B., LaSalle U., Chgo., 1940. Capt., asst. chief Stillwater Police Dept. (OK), 1936-57; criminal dep. Payne County Sheriff's Office, 1957-59; asst. chief security Okla. State U. (Stillwater), 1959-69; publs. specialist, asst. dir. Okla. State U. Press, 1969-79, ret., 1980; free-lance writer (Stillwater), 1980—, lectr. in field. Recipient Okla. Literary Endeavor award, 1960; introduced into Okla. Journalism Hall of Fame, 1981. Mem. Okla. Writers Fedn. (past pres., life mem.), WWA, Western History Assn., Natl. Assn. Outlaw and Lawman History, Oklahoma Heritage Assn., Inst. Great Plains, Assocs. Western History Collections (trustee), Oklahoma State Hist. Soc., Kans. State Hist. Soc., Mont. State Hist. Soc. Address: Box 824 Stillwater OK 74076

SHNAYERSON, ROBERT BEAHAN, b. NYC, Dec. 8, 1925; s. charles and madalene (Griffin) Beahan; m. Lydia Conde Todd, Dec. 23, 1950 (dec. Sept. 1973); children—Michael, Kate; 2nd m. Laurie Platt Winfrey, June 9, 1980; 1 dau.—Maggie. Author: The Illustrated History of the Supreme Court of the United States, 1986. AB, Dartmouth, 1950. Reporter NY Daily News, 1946; reporter Life mag. (NYC), 1950-54; corr. Time-Life News Service, 1954-56; contrbg. editor Time mag., 1957-59, edn. editor, 1959-64, law editor, 1964-67, sr. editor, 1967-71; editor-in-chief Harper's Mag. 1971-76; editor, pub. Quest Mag., 1976-81, Technology mag., 1981-82; editorial dir. Science Digest, 1986. Served with USNR, 1943-46. Home: 118 Riverside Dr New York NY 10024

SHOAL, DALE, see Shannon, Don Michael

SHOCKLEY, ANN ALLEN, b. Louisville, June 21, 1927, d. Henry and Bessie (Lucas) Allen; children—W. Leslie, Jr., Tamara Ann. Author: Loving Her, 1974, The Black and White of It, 1980, Say Jesus and Come to Me, 1982; co-ed.: (with Sue P. Chandler) Living Black American Authors, 1973, (with E.J. Josey) A Handbook of Black Librarianship. BA, Fisk U., 1948; MLS, Case Western Res. U., 1959. Asst. librarian Del. State Coll., Dover, 1959-60; asst., then assoc. librarian U. Md. Eastern Shore, Princess Anne, 1960-69; assoc. librarian, archivist, assoc. prof. library sci. Fisk U., Nashville, 1969—. Recipient Natl. Short Story award AAUW, 1962, Black Caucus award for newsletter editing ALA, 1975, Hatshepsut award for lit. Comm. for Visibility of Other Black Women, NYC, 1981, Martin Luther King Black Author award Interdenominational Ministers Fellowship, Nashville, 1982. Mem. AG, ALA, Soc. Am. Archivists, Assn. Black Women Historians. Home: 5975 Post Rd Nashville TN 37205

SHOMAKER, GORDON ALEXANDER JR., b. Denver, Mar. 21, 1926; s. Gordon Alexander and Louise L. (Feuerstein) S. Author: (poems) The Arrow of the Years, 1976; (plays) Joshua, 1962, Fountain of Youth, 1983, World Citizen, 1983 Literary Detectives, 1985. Contrbr. short story to Gryphon. B.A., U. S.C., 1947; M.A., U. Colo., 1953. Instr., Quinnipiac Coll., New Haven, 1955-58, Wis. State U., River Falls, 1967. Served with U.S. Navy, 1944-54. Mem. Theater of Original Plays, Saint Paul United Methodist Ch. Home: 613 W Grant Ave Pueblo CO 81004

SHOEMAKER, LYNN HENRY, b. Racine, WI, Mar. 31, 1939, s. William and Gretchen (Gall) S.; m. Christine Annette Moore, June 1966 (div.); 1 dau., Erica. Author poetry collections: Coming Home, 1973, Curses and Blessings, 1978, Hands, 1982. BA, Harvard U., 1961; MA, U. S.D., 1961, DA, SUNY-Albany, 1982. Asst. prof. Yankton (S.D.) Coll., 1962-63; instr. Calif. State U., Los Angeles, 1966-67, East Los Angeles Jr. Coll., 1970-71, Ithaca (N.Y.) Coll., 1977-78, U. Kans., Lawrence, 1982—. Mem. AWP, MLA. Address: 172 N. Esterly Ave Whitewater WI 53190

SHOLL, ELIZABETH (BETSY) NEARY, b. Lakewood, OH, June 12, 1945, d. John Schenck and Beatrice (Scott) Neary; m. John Douglas Sholl, June 17, 1967; children—Matthew, Hannah. Author: Changing Faces, 1974, Appalachian Winter, 1978, Room Overhead, 1986; contrbr. poetry to Field, Agni Rvw, West Branch, other lit mags. BA, Bucknell U., 1967; MA, U. Rochester, 1969. Instr. MIT, Cambridge, 1972-76; freelance lectr., Va., 1976-83; instr. U. So. Me., Portland, 1983—; artist-in-residence Me. Arts Commn. 1984—. Grantee Appalachian Woman Grants for Wrtrs., 1980-81. Mem. New Eng. Wrtrs. for Survival, AAP, Alice James Poetry Cooperative, Me. Wrtrs. & Pubs. Alliance. Home: 24 Brentwood St Portland ME 04103

SHOMER, ENID, b. Washington, D.C., Feb. 2, 1944; d. Philip and Minnie (Magazine) Steine; m. Arthur Shomer, Sept. 15, 1966; children—Nirah, Oren. Author: The Startle Effect, 1983, Florida Postcards, 1987, Stalking the Florida Panther, 1987. Poetry in California Qtly, Poetry, New Letters, other lit mags. Fiction and nonfiction in The Florida Rvw, Black Warrior Rvw, Woman's World, other mags. Contrbr. to Blood to Remember: American Poets on the Holocaust, 1986, Touching Fire: Erotic Writing by Women, 1986. BA, Wellesley College, 1965; MA, U. of Miami, 1974. Lectr., U. of Miami, Coral Gables, Fla., 1974-80. Winner Eve of St. Agnes prize, 1985, Washington prize, 1985, Writer's Digest Writing Competition in poetry, 1986, poetry prize of the Cincinnati Poetry Rvw, 1986, Jubilee Press Chapbook Competition, 1986. Mem. PSA, Home: 4781 NW 8th Ave Gainesville FL 32605

SHOR, CYNTHIA LYNCH, b. Des Moines, Mar. 27, 1947, d. Patrick Henry and Gladys Elizabeth (Huggard) Lynch; m. Stephen Alan Shor, June 14, 1969; children—Jeremy Andrew, Elizabeth Ann. Contrbr. poetry: Calli's Tales, Black Maria, Alura Quar., Confrontation, other publs. Wrkg. on poetry chapbook, short fiction. BA, NYU, 1969; MA in Lit., Am. U., 1971. Poet, tchr. Poets-in-the Schls., N.Y., 1985—; Arts' Partners, NY, 1986—. Bread Loaf Wrtrs. Conf., Middlebury, Vt., 1984. Mem. AAP, PSA, IWWG. Home: 4 Grassfield Rd Kings Point NY 11024

SHOR, MURRAY, b. Bronx, NY, Jan. 12, 1932; s. Sol and Sarah Edith (Stein) S.; m. Joan Ann Stolmaker, Dec. 25, 1952; children—Joyce Rise, Tama Jill, Morton Seth. BA, Bklyn. Coll., 1957. Reptr., Courier-Freeman, Potsdam, NY, 1957-58; reptr., The Citizen, Denville, NJ, 1958-60; ed. Rockland Independent, Suffern, NY, 1960-62; Rockland County ed., The Record, Hackensack, NJ, 1962-68; exec. ed. Chain Store Age, NYC, 1968-71; ed. Shopping Center World, NYC, 1971-73; ed./pub. MJJTM Pub., Suffern, 1973—; founded Shopping Ctr. Digest, 1973, Directory of Major Malls, 1980, Factory Outlet World, 1982. Served to CPL, U.S. Army, 1952-54. Office: Box 2 Suffern NY 10901

SHORE, HERBERT, b. Phila., June 6, 1924; s. Meyer and Francies (Smiler) Shore; m. Yen Lu Wong, Dec. 23, 1977; children—Norman Jon, Pia Ilyen Wong, Maya Iming Wong. Author: Come Back Africa, 1970, Ashes Dark Antigone, 1972, Toward the World of Tomorrow, 1978, Cultural Policy, 1981, Cicada Images, Moulting, 1983, Seek to Be Human, 1985, Beginnings Are Born in Memory, 1986, Shi-Me, 1987. BA, U. Pa., 1942; postgrad., Columbia U., 1946-48, Dramatic Workshop New Schl., 1946-48, Stanford U., 1948-53; MA, Stanford U., 1958; PhD, Intl. Coll., 1983. Author, dramatist, theatre dir. and dramaturg, 1956—; dir. Council Tech. and Cultural Transformation, 1974—; prof., dir. div. drama U. So. Calif., 1979—; founding dir. TNR: The New Repertory, 1972; cons. UNESCO, 1974—; provost Intl. Coll., 1983—; dir. plays for theatre and TV, author plays, also cantata. Served with USMC, 1943-46. Recipient Writers' Digest prize for fiction, 1963. Mem. Am. Film Inst., AAP, Soc. Writers and Poets, MLA, Am. Theatre Assn., African Studies Assn. Office: Div Drama U So Cal Los Angeles CA 90089

SHORTRIDGE, CHARLES EMIL, b. San Francisco, Mar. 11, 1941, s. Cleophus Donald and Clara Winifred (Raymond) S.; m. Portia Maire Scott, Mar. 17, 1962; children—Aree Destinae, Charnell La Vette, Cherylyn Nae Vonne. Author: Kitchen Thoughts, 1969, Poetrysoul, 1976, Poems for Poets, 1980, Lyrical Letters, 1985. Student, San Francisco City Coll., 1964. Chef So. Pacific Ry., Oakland, Calif., 1971-78; funding coordinator Fin. Intermediary, San Francisco, 1979-81; pres. Chasno's Prodns., San Francisco, 1981—. Recipient 1st place award Transp. Writers, 1975, peers 1st place award Calif. Poets, 1984. Mem. Am. guild Authors and Composers, Broadcast Music Industry, Golden Gate Poets (v.p. 1981-83), Rhythm Writers (pres. 1984—). Home: 68 Lausanne Ave Daly City CA 94014

SHOT, DANNY, b. NYC, Sept. 8, 1957; s. Siegfried and Doris (Mendheim) Schott; m. Caroline Doncourt, Nov. 23, 1985. Contrbr. poems and short stories to lit mags including New Blood, Kings of the World, NY Qtly, Big Scream, Ferro Botanica. Editor: Long Shot I-V, 1981—. BA, Rutgers Coll., 1980. Tchr. English, Samuel Gompers Voc. and Tech. H.S., Bronx, NY, 1986—. Chairman, Big Buster Fdn., mem. United Fedn. of Tchrs. Home: 211 York St Jersey City NJ 07302

SHOVALD, ARLENE ELIZABETH, b. Stambaugh, MI, Apr. 14, 1940; d. William Lawrence and Dorothy Mary (Scott) Mellstrom; m. Robert Paul Shovald, June 20, 1959; children—Robert, Terri, Rick, Anne. Reporter: Mountain Mail, 1980—. Author: (novel) Kill the Competition, 1987; contrbr. articles to mags., newspapers including Modern Maturity, Womans World, Denver Post, Romance Digest, others. Ed.: The Reporter, Iron River, MI, 1975-79. Grad. public schs., Iron River. Free-lance wtr., 1960—. Mem. NWC, Iron County Pess Assn. (founder), Upper Peninsula Wrtrs. Club (founder; Upper Peninsula Wrtr. of Yr. 1976). Home: 1124 D St Salida CO 81201

SHOWERS, APRIL, see Ranieri, Lorraine M.

SHREVE, SUSAN RICHARDS, b. Toledo, May 2, 1939, d. Robert Kenneth Richards and Helen Elizabeth (Greene) Richards Schaub; m. Porter G. Shreve, May 26, 1962; children—Porter, Elizabeth, Caleb, Katharine. Author: A Fortunate Madness, 1974, A Woman Like That, 1974, Children of Power, 1979, Miracle Play, 1981, Dreaming of Heroes, 1984, Queen of Hearts, 1987; author children's books: The Nightmares of Geranium Street, 1977, Family Secrets, 1978, Loveletters, 1978, The Bad Dreams of a Good Girl, 1982, The Flunking of Joshua Bates, 1984, The Revolution of Mary Leary, 1983, How I Saved the World on Purpose, 1985, Lucy Forever and Miss Rose Tree, 1986. BA, U. Pa., 1961; MA, U. Va., 1969. Prof. English George Mason U., Fairfax, Va., now Jerry McKean Moore chair of wrtg.; vis. prof. fiction Columbia U., NYC, 1982—. Guggenheim fellow, 1978-79; grantee NEA, 1982. Mem. PEN (pres. PEN/Faulkner 1985), Washington Ind. Wrtrs., Children's Book Guild, AG. Home: 3518 35th St NW Washington DC 20016

SHRODES, CAROLINE, b. Madison, MN; d. George Hamilton and Clara (Blasing) Shrodes. Co-editor: Patterns for Living, 1940, 43, 47, 49, 55, Psychology through Literature, 1943, Reading for Rhetoric, 1959, 67, 75, 79, Reading for Understanding, 1969, The Conscious Reader, 1974, 78, 85, 88. PhB, U. Chgo., 1928, MA, 1934; PhD, U. CA, Berkeley, CA, 1949. Prof., chmn. English dept. San Francisco St. U., 1946-73; core faculty Union Graduate Schl., Cincinnati, 1973—. Mem. Am. Psychological Assn., MLA. Home: 89 Cloud View Rd Sausalito CA 96965

SHRUM, CHRISTINE RUTH, (Christine King Schrum), b. Phoenix, Oct. 29, 1949; d. James Leland Andrew and Elsie Lorraine (Baptista) King; m. Harvey Earl Shrum, Oct. 10, 1970; children: David Earl, Lorraine Ellen. Poetry pub. in Pine Cone Press, Big Spring Herald, Natl. Soc. Pub. Poets, and World of Poetry Press anthologies, Our Twentieth Century's Greatest Poems, Today's Greatest Poems and Our World's Best Loved Poems. Wrkg. on autobiography, vol. of poems. Student Lassen Coll., 1974-81. Credit clk. Montgomery Ward, Big Spring, Tex., 1967-70; cashier J.C. Penney Co., Napa, Calif., 1970; crisis line vo., Lassen Family Services, Susanville, Calif., 1981-84; freelance poet, 1976—. Recipient 2 Awards of Merit, 1986, World of Poetry Press, 1983, 84, Golden Poet award, 1985, Silver Poet Award, 1986, honorable mention, Ctr. for Literary Competition, winter 1986, 3 honorable mention certs., World of Poetry, 1986, 1987. Home: 471-050 Cottonwood Rd Susanville CA 96130

SHUGRUE, JAMES LEONARD, b. Chgo., Mar. 22, 1948; s. Leonard Eugene and Anne Coletta (Hogan) S.; m. Lisa M. Steinman, July 23, 1984. Contrbr. poems to lit. mags. Editor: Hubbub, 1983—. Ed. St. Gregory's H.S. Bookbuyer, Portland State Bookstore, Oreg., 1979-81, Powell's Books, Portland, 1981—. Pres. Portland Poetry Festival, 1983, bd. dirs., 1985—; judge AAP prize Lewis and Clark Coll., Portland, 1984. Home: 5344 SE 38th Portland OR 97202

SHULDINER, HERBERT, b. Bklyn., Jan. 10, 1929; s. Philip and Jennie (Lazar) Shuldiner; m. Julie Abrauanel, June 23, 1951; children—Janet, Beverly, Albert. Editor: (with E.V. Heyn) The Popular Science Book of Gadgets, 1981. BA, NY U., 1956. Various positions NY Mirror (NYC), 1946-63; reporter Popular Sci. (NYC), 1963, writer, asst. city editor, assoc. editor, sr. editor, 1976, group editor consumer info., 1976-80, exec. editor, 1980-85; editor, 1985—; freelance writer, 1963-79; columnist Outdoor Life mag. (NYC), 1976-78. Served with U.S. Army, 1950-52. Mem. Natl. Assn. Sci. Writers. Office: Pop Sci 380 Madison Ave New York NY 10017

SHULEVITZ, URI, b. Warsaw, Poland, Feb. 27, 1935 (came to U.S., 1959, naturalized, 1965); s. Abraham and Szandla (Hermanstat) Shulevitz. Author, illustrator: The Moon in My Room, 1963, One Monday Morning, 1967, Rain Rain Rivers, 1969, Oh What a Noise, 1971, Dawn, 1974, The Treasure, 1979 (Caldecott Honor Book 1980), Writing with Pictures: How to Write and Illustrate Children's books, 1985, The Strange and Exciting Adventures of Jeremiah Hush, 1986; illustrator: The Fool of the World and the Flying Ship, 1968 (Caldecott medal 1969), The Twelve Dancing Princesses, 1966, Soldier and Tsar in the Forest, 1972, The Fools of Chelm, 1973, The Touchstone, 1976, Hanukah Money, 1978, The Lost Kingdom of Karnica, 1979, The Golem, 1982. Student, Tel-Aviv Inst., 1953-55; Tchrs. Cert., Tchrs. Coll. Israel, 1956; student, Bklyn., Museum Art Schl., 1959-61. Instr. illustrating and writing of children's books The New School, 1970—; dir. illustrating and writing of children's books Hartwick Coll., 1974—. Served with Israeli Army, 1956-59. Mem. AG. Address: FS&G 19 Union Sq W New York NY 10003

SHULMAN, IRVING, b. Bklyn., May 21, 1913; s. Max and Sarah (Ress) Shulman; m. Julia Grager, July 9, 1938; children—Joan, Leslie. Author: (novel) The Amboy Dukes, 1947, Cry Tough, 1949; (film) The Big Brokers, 1951, City Across the River; (novel) The Square Trap, 1953; film version Rebel Without a Cause; (novel) Good Deeds Must be Punished, 1956, Calibre, 1957, The Velvet Knife, 1959; (short stories) The Short End of the Stick, 1959; (biography) The Roots of Fury, 1961, Harlow, 1964, Valentino, 1967; (social study) Jackie: The Exploitation of a First Lady, 1970; (novel) The Devil's Knee, 1973, Saturn's Child, 1976. AB magna cum laude, Ohio U., 1937; AM, Columbia U., 1938; PhD, UCLA, 1972. Personnel technician, statistician, administrv. officer, info. specialist various govt. agcys., 1941-47; faculty dept. English George Washington U., 1943-47; teaching asst. UCLA, 1962-64; asst. prof. English dept. Calif. State Coll. (Los Angeles), 1964-65; author, collaborator various screen plays. Mem. MLA, AAUP, WG Am., Acad. Motion Picture Arts and Scis., Am. film Inst. Address: W E Stein 9454 Wilshire Blvd Beverly Hills CA 90212

SHULMAN, MAX, b. St. Paul, Mar. 14, 1919; s. Abraham and Bessie (Karchmer) Shulman; m. Carol Rees, Dec. 21, 1941 (dec. 1963); children—Daniel, Max, Peter, Martha; m. Mary G. Bryant, 1964. Free-lance writer, 1942—; Author: Barefoot Boy with Cheek, 1943 (musical comedy version produced 1947), The Feather Merchants, 1944, The Zebra Derby, 1946, Sleep Till Noon, 1949, Rally Round the Flag, Boys, 1957; (with Julius J. Epstein) The Tender Trap; play, 1954, I Was a Teen Age Dwarf, 1959, Anyone Got a Match?, 1964; musical comedy How Now Dow Jones, 1967, Potatoes Are Cheaper, 1971; also short stories in Mademoiselle, others; author: TV series Dobie Gillis. AB, U. Minn., 1942. Served with USAF, 1942-44. Mem. AG, DG. Address: Benjamin ICM 8899 Beverly Blvd Los Angeles CA 90048

SHULVASS, MOSES AVIGDOR (TOBIAS MEYERSON), b. Plonsk, Poland, July 29, 1909; came to U.S., 1948; s. Meyer and Rebecca (Michelson) S.; m. Celia Anne Cemach, Apr. 4, 1935; children: Phyllis, Ruth. Author: The Jews in Wuerzburg during the Middle Ages (German), 1934, Bibliographical Guide to Jewish Studies (Yiddish), 1935, Rome and Jerusalem (Hebrew),

1944, Chapters from the Life of Samuel David Luzzatto (Hebrew), 1951, The Jews in the World of the Renaissance (Hebrew), 1955, In the Grip of Centuries (Hebrew), 1960, Between the Rhine and the Bosporus, 1964, From East to West, 1971, The Jews in the World of the Renaissance (English), 1973, Jewish Culture in Eastern Europe: The Classical Period, 1975, The History of the Jewish People, Vol. I: The Antiquity, 1982, Vol. II: The Early Middle Ages, 1983, Vol. III: The Late Middle Ages, 1985; editor: Jewish Historical Texts Series, 1948-52, Perspectives in Jewish Learning, Vol. 2, 1966; editor Italy Qtly., 1945; contbr. to scholarly and lit. jnls. Ordained rabbi Tahkemoni Rabbinical Sem., Warsaw, 1930; PhD magna cum laude, U. Berlin, 1934; DHL honoris causa, Spertus Coll. of Judaica, 1974. Freelance author, lectr., Israel, 1935-47; prof. Jewish history Balt. Hebrew Coll., 1948-51; prof. Jewish history Spertus Coll. of Judaica, Chgo., 1951—, chmn. dept. grad. studies, 1952-71, now Disting. Service prof. Jewish history. Active in Jewish cultural and religious orgns. Recipient La-Med prize La-Med Fdn., 1956, Solomon Goldman Creativity award Anshe Emet Synagogue, Chgo., 1981; grantee Rosaline Cohn Scholars Fund, Chgo., 1980-85; research grantee Meml. Fdn. Jewish Culture, NYC, 1968-69. Fellow Am. Acad. Jewish Research; mem. Ctr. Jewish-Christian Studies of Chgo. Theol. Sem. (assoc.), Jewish Book Council Am.(mem.-at-large natl. com.), Hist. Soc. Israel (bd. dirs. 1945-48), Hebrew PEN of Am., Yiddish PEN of Am. Home: 2733 W Greenleaf Chicago IL 60645

SHUMSKY, ZENA, see Collier, Zena

SHURA, MARY FRANCIS, see Craig, Mary Francis Shura

SHURTLEFF, WILLIAM ROY, b. Oakland, CA, Apr. 28, 1941, s. Lawton Lothrop and Barbara Anne (Reinhardt) S.; m. Akiko Aoyagi, Mar. 10, 1977. Author: The Book of Tofu, 1975, 83, The Book of Miso, 1976, 83, The Book of Kudzu, 1977, Miso Production, 1977, 81, The Book of Tempeh, 1979, 85, Tofu & Soymilk Production, 1979, 83, Tempeh Production, 1980, 86, Soyfoods Industry and Market: Directory and Databook, 1983, 84, 85, Soymilk Industry and Market: Worldwide and Country-by- Country Analysis, 1984, 1987, History of Tempeh, 1984, 85, Tofutti and Other Soy Ice Creams: Non-dairy Frozen Dessert Industry and market, 1985, Thesaurus for SOYA, Computerized Bibliographic Database, 1985, 86, Bibliography of Soybeans and Soyfoods: 1100 B.C. to the 1980s, and History of Soybeans and Soyfoods: Past, Present and Future, 1988. BA with honors, Stanford U., 1963, BSc, 1967, MA in Edn., 1967. Dir. Soyfoods Center, Lafayette Calif., 1976—. Home: Box 234 Lafayette CA 94549

SHY, JOHN WILLARD, b. Dayton, OH, Mar. 23, 1931; s. Willard Alden and Margaret (Brush) Shy. Author: Guerrillas in the 1960s, 1962, Toward Lexington, 1965, A People Numerous and Armed, 1976. BS, U.S. Mil. Acad., 1952, MA, U. Vt., 1957; PhD, Princeton U., 1961. Instr. history Princeton U., 1959-62, asst. prof., 1962-66, assoc. prof., 1966-68; prof. history U. Mich., 1968—; Fulbright prof. U. London, 1975-76; Harmsworth prof. Oxford U., 1983-84. Office: History Dept U Mich Ann Arbor MI 48109

SHYRE, PAUL, b. NYC, Mar. 8, 1926; s. Louis Phillip and Mary (Lee) Shyre. Playwright: The Child Buyer, 1964, A Whitman Portrait, 1967, Ah Men!, 1968; adapted, performer: Pictures in the Hallway, 1956, I Knock At The Door, 1957, U.S.A., 1959; adapted, dir.: Drums Under the Windows, 1960, Will Rogers USA, 1972, Paris Was Yesterday, 1980; author: Carl Sandburg: Echoes and Silences, PBS Am. Playhouse series, 1982, Eugene O'Neill: A Glory of Ghosts, 1986 (San Francisco Intl. Film Festival Spcl. Jury Award, 1986), PBS, Hizzoner!, PBS, 1982-83 (Emmy award, 1986). Student, U. Fla., Gainesville, 1945, Am. Acad. Dramatic Arts, NYC, 1946-47. Prof. dept. theatre arts Cornell U., 1980. Recipient NY Drama Desk, 1957, Obie, 1957, Creative Arts Brandeis U., 1958. Mem. WG, Dramatists Guild, Soc. Dirs. and Choreographers, AFTRA, Screen Actors Guild. Home: 162 W 56th St New York NY 10019

SIATOS, THOMAS JOHN, b. Los Angeles, Sept. 13, 1923; s. John and Kaleope (Kontos) Siatos; m. Farrel Dale Solberg, Aug. 17, 1957; 1 dau.—Dena Ann. BS in Bus. Adminstrn., U. Calif. at Los Angeles, 1949. Engaged in banking and life ins. bus., 1950-53, free-lance writer firearms and hunting, 1953—; mng. editor Western Outdoor Pub. Co. (Los Angeles), 1954-58; editor Guns and Ammo mag. pub. Petersen Pub. Co. (Los Angeles), 1958-64; editorial dir. Petersen Publishing Co., 1964-65; pub. Guns & Ammo mag., 1965-73, exec. pub., 1973—, Hunting Mag., also Outdoor Specialty Books, 1973—, corporate vp, 1975—. Served with USMCR, 1942-45; PTO. Office: 8490 Sunset Blvd Los Angeles CA 90069

SIEBERT, SHIRLEY E., b. Chgo., Nov. 1, 1920; d. John Gregory and Christine (Kozeny) Ebner; m. C. Stuart Siebert, Apr. 13, 1946; 1 dau., Patricia Siebert Cinquini. Syndicated columnist So This is Housekeeping (newspaper), Farm News Roundup (radio); contrbr. articles: Gambling Times, Today in Michiana, People in Action, Business Today, Rotarian, Ford Times. Wrkg. on mag. articles. BS in Speech, Northwestern U. Reporter, night city ed. Transradio Press, Chgo., 1942-44; account exec. J. Walter Thompson Co., Chgo., 1944-46; columnist Derus Media Service, Chgo., 1946-52; with Siebert & Demmy Mktg., Chgo., 1963-74, Siebert Mktg. Services, St. Joseph, Mich., 1981—; freelance wrtr., 1982—. Mem. NWU. Home: 1248 Point O'Woods Dr Benton Harbor MI 49022

SIEGEL, CAROLYN LEE, b. Dayton, OH, July 2, 1951; d. Frederick Francis and Margaret Amelia (Sauer) Davidson; m. Gary Alan Siegel, Feb. 29, 1972; 1 son, Joshua Aslan. Author: White Hall—The Clay Estate, 1985, Jemima, 1986. Wrkg. on biography of Cassius Macellus Clay. B.A., U. Ariz.-Tucson, 1973; M.A., Eastern Ky. U., 1978. Tchr., Lochiel Elem. Schl., Ariz., 1973-74, Williamstown Elem. Sch., Ky., 1979-80; free-lance wrtr., Richmond, Ky., 1984—. Mem. Ky. Hist. Soc. Home: 1721 Red House Rd Richmond KY 40475

SIEGEL, MARTIN, (Marc Heller), b. Newark, Oct. 3, 1925; s. Samuel and Gussie (Heller) S.; m. Shirley Siskind, Dec. 8, 1950 (div. Apr. 1968); children: Judy, David; m. Cherie Sherman, May 1, 1970; step-children: Pamela, Sandra, Philip. Co-author: (novel) Wake Me When Its Over, 1955; author: (poetry) Reflections on a War, 1961; (essay) Warfare—The Ultimate Madness, 1962; ed., contrbr. to articles on environ. issues. Wrkg. on novel and photo-journalism book. BSc, Rutgers U., PhD. Exec. v.p. systems John Wiley & Sons, Bethesda, Md., 1970-75; dir. pub. relations Equitable Environ. Health, Rockville, Md., 1975-77; dir. bus. devel. Biospherics Inc., Rockville, 1977-79; pres. Siegel-Houston & Assocs., Washington, 1979—. Served with AUS, 1943-45; ETO. Home: 5108 Lupine Ct Rockville MD 20853

SIEGEL, ROBERT HAROLD, b. Oak Park, IL, Aug. 18, 1939, s. Frederick William and Charlotte Lucille (Chance) S.; m. Roberta Ann Hill, Aug. 19, 1961; children—Anne Lenaye, Lucy Blythe, Christine Elizabeth. Author: The Beasts & The Elders (poetry), 1973, In A Pig's Eye (poetry), 1980, Alpha Centauri (fiction), 1980, Whalesong (fiction, Matson award Friends of Lit., 1982), 1981, The Kingdom of Wundle, 1982, The Wyrm of Grog, 1986. BA, Wheaton Coll. (Ill.), 1961; MA, Johns Hopkins U., 1962, PhD, Harvard U., 1968. Asst. prof. English Dartmouth Coll., Hanover, N.H., 1967-75; prof. English, U. Wis.-Milw., 1976—; vis. lectr. creative wrtg. Princeton (N.J.) U., 1975-76; McMannes vis. prof. Wheaton Coll., 1976. Recipient Soc. Midland Authors Award for Poetry, 1974, 81, Prairie Schooner poetry prize, 1977; U. Wis. research fellow, 1978, 84, Ingram Merrill Fdn. fellow, 1979, NEA fellow, 1980. Mem. AWP, AG, Council Wis. Wrtrs. Address: Box 413 Milwaukee WI 53201

SIEGEL, WILLIAM MORDECAI, b. Hartford, CT, July 13, 1950, s. Jacob Israel and Annette (Alberts) S.; m. Cheryl Savageau; 1 son, Christopher Charles. Poetry in: Below the Salt, 1974; contrbg. ed.: Worcester Rvw, 1984, 85. BA in History, Clark U., 1972. Sr. wrtr. Data Gen Corp., Westboro, Mass., 1975-84, Apollo Computer Inc., Chelmsford, Mass., 1984—; vis. lectr. U. Lowell (Mass.), 1984—; vis. artist Shrewsbury (Mass.) high schl., 1983. Dir. Worcester County Poetry Assn. (pres. 1985-86), Jazz Worcester (publicity chmn. 1984-85), Worcester Com. Against Registration for Draft, Worcester County Coalition for Disarmament. Home: 19 Walnut Hill Dr Worcester MA 01602

SIEKERT, ROBERT GEORGE, b. Milw., July 23, 1924; s. Hugo Paul and Elisa (Kraus) S.; m. Mary Jane Evans, Feb. 17, 1951; children—Robert Jr., John E., Friedrich A.P. Ed.: Cerebral Vascular Diseases, Third Conference, 1961, Fourth Conf., 1965, Fifth Conf., 1966, Sixth Conf., 1968, Cerebrovascular Survey Report, 1970, 76, 80. BS, Northwestern U., 1945, MS, 1946, MD, 1948. Instr. to prof. Mayo Medical Sch., Rochester, MN, 1955-73, prof. neurology, 1973—; ed. Mayo Clinic Proceedings, Rochester, 1982—. Served to Lt. j.g., USN, 1950-52. Mem. profl. orgns. Alpha Omega Alpha, Northwestern U., 1948. Office: Mayo Clinic Rochester MN 55905

SIENKIEWICZ, JULIAN, see Martin, Julian

SIEVER, RAYMOND, b. Chgo., Sept. 14, 1923; s. Leo and Lillie (Katz) Siever; m. Doris Fisher, Mar. 31.1945; children—Larry Joseph, Michael David. Author: (with others) Geology of Sandstones, 1965, Sand and Sandstone, 1972, 86, Earth, 4th ed., 1986, Planet Earth, 1974, Energy and Environment, 1978. BS, U. Chgo., 1943, MS, 1947, PhD, 1950; MA (hon.), Harvard U., 1960. With Ill. Geol. Survey, 1943-44, 47-56, geologist, 1953-56; research assoc., NSF sr. postdoctoral fellow Harvard U., 1956-57, mem. faculty, 1957—, prof. geology, 1965—, chair dept. geol. scis., 1968-71, 76-81; assoc. geology Woods Hole Oceanographic Instn. (MA), 1957-65; cons. to industry and govt. 1957—. Served with USAF, 1944-46. Recipient Best Paper award Soc. Econ. Paleontologists and Mineralogists, 1957. Home: 38 Avon t Cambridge MA 02138

SIGEL, EFREM, b. NYC, Apr. 29, 1943; s. Benjamin M. and Dorothy (Birnbaum) S.; m. Frederica Evan; children—Jonathan, Matthew. Author: Kermanshah Transfer, 1973, Crisis!, 1979, Videotext: The Coming Revolution in Home/Office Information Retrieval, 1979, Video Discs, 1980, Future of Videotext, 1982. BA, Harvard, 1964, MBA, 1968. Tchr., Peace Corps, Ivory Coast, 1964-66, NYC schools, 1965-69; ed.-in-chief Knowledge Industry Pub., White Plains, NY, 1970-83; pres. Communcs. Trends, Inc., Larchmont, NY, 1983—. Home: 15 Rose Hill Ave New Rochelle NY 10804

SIGNER, BILLIE TOUCHSTONE, (B. Touchstone Hardaway, Billie L. Touchstone, Billie Touchstone Hardaway), b. Hattiesburg, MS, May 26, 1930, d. Burt Warren and William Mary (Hegwood) Touchstone; m. Hal T. Hardaway, Mar. 19, 1950 (div. 1981); children—Terry, Bonnie, Kay, Anthony, Timothy, Mary; m. 2d, John Merritt Singer, Jan. 15, 1982. Author: Beaver City, 1985, One Small Drum, 1985 (juvenile historical fiction); Redneck Country Cookin', 1980; These Hills My Home, A Buffalo River Story, 1985; contrbr. stories and articles to numerous periodicals. Ed., pub. J&B Books, Albany, N.Y., 1984—. Mem. Soc. Children's Book Wrtrs., numerous hist. socs. Home: Rt 2 Box 53-A Homer LA 71040

SIKES, DAVID GLENN, b. Sweetwater, TX, Dec. 27, 1942; s. Amos Talmage and Deliah Mae (Bozeman) S.; m. Carla Faye Cody, Aug. 4, 1983; children—Tony, Kathryn, Allison, Christopher, Mary. Author: Twenty First Century Sales, 1980, Advanced Interviews and Interrogations, 1981, Typology of a Terrorist, 1987. Wrkg. on Cops Don't Cry, Robed Clowns and Court Jestores, Spider Line. B.A., Shaw U., 1975; Ph.D., Columbia Pacific U., 1987. Undersheriff Clear Creek County Sheriff's Dept., Georgetown, CO, 1982-85; pvt. investigator, Litleton, CO, 1985-86; deputy sheriff Araphahoe County Sheriff's Dep., Litleton, 1986—. Served with U.S. Army, 1964-78. Decorated Meitorious Service metal, 1977. Home: 6143 S Fairfield St Littleton CO 80120

SIKES, SHIRLEY RUTH, b. Manhattan, KJS, Oct. 3, 1928; d. Herbert Hiram and Susan Grace (Dickman) King; m. William Edward Sikes, Dec. 24, 1949; 1 child, Stephanie Grace. Contrbr. to Bull. of Menninger Clinic, Women's Day, Reporter, Lit., Transatlantic, Arkansas River, Sonora rvws, Kans., Denver Qtlys., Four Quarters, Calyx, others. BS, Kans. State U., Manhattan, 1950, postgrad., 1955-56. Dick jockey Sta. KMAN, Manhattan, 1958-59; exec. v.p. Leonardville State Bank, Kans., 1985—. Named One of 100 Outstanding Wrtrs. in U.S., Pushcart Press, 1981. Mem. AG, IWWG, P&W. Home: 403 W Elk St PO Box 149 Leonardville KS 66449

SILAG, BILL, b. White Plains, NY, July 31, 1946; s. William J. and Jeanne (Gallagher) S.; m. Pamela Kay Watts; children—Phoebe Graves, Lucy Gallagher, Megan Renee, Eric Eugene. Contrbr. articles, rvws. to profl. jnls. including Am. Qtly, Ia. Ofcl. Register, Wis. Mag. History, Jnl Hist. Geography. BA, Cornell U., 1969; Ph.D., U. Ia., 1979. Instr. U. Pitts., 1976-77; sr. ed. State Hit. Soc. Ia., Iowa City, 1979-82; mng. ed. Ia. State Univ. Press, Ames, Ia., 1985—. Trustee, State Hist. Soc. Ia. Recipient Jacob Swisher award State Hist. Soc. Ia., 1973. Office: Ia S U Press 2122 S State Ave Ames IA 50010

SILBER, JOAN KAREN, b. Millburn, NJ, June 14, 1945, d. Samuel Sanford and Dorothy (Arlein) Silber. Author: Household Words (novel), 1980, In the City (novel)1987; contrbr. book rvws. to MS., Newsday, Village Voice. BA, Sarah Lawrence Coll., 1967; MA, NYU, 1979. Mem. faculty NYU, 1981-84, Sarah Lawrence Coll., Bronxville, N.Y., 1985—, Sarah Lawrence Writing Inst. for Adults, 1984-85, Warren Wilson Coll., Swannanoa, N.C., 1986—. Recipient NEA, 1986, NYFA, 1986, Guggenheim fellow, 1984-85; recipient Ernest Hemingway award PEN-Ernest Hemingway Fdn., 1981. Mem. PEN, P&W, AG. Home: 43 Bond St New York NY 10012

SILBERMAN, CHARLES ELIOT, b. Des Moines, Jan. 31, 1925; s. Seppy I. and Cel (Levy) Silberman; m. Arlene Propper, Sept. 12, 1948; children—David, Richard, Jeffrey, Steven. Author: Crisis in Black and White, 1964, The Myths of Automation, 1966, Crisis in the Classroom, 1970, The Open Classroom Reader, 1973, Criminal Violence, Criminal Justice, 1978, A Certain People, 1985; contrbg. ed.: Reconstructionist mag. AB, Columbia U., 1946, postgrad. in econ., 1946-49; instr. econ. Columbia U., 1948-53; assoc. editor Fortune mag., 1953-60, mem. bd. editors, 1961-71; dir. Study Law and Justice, 1972-79, dir. The Study of Jewish Life, 1979-85; mem. joint commn. on juvenile justice standards ABA; dir. Carnegie Corp. Study Edn. Eucators, 1966-69. Served to lt. (jg) USNR, 1943-46. Home: 535 E 86th St New York NY 10028

SILBERT, LAYLE, b. Chgo.; d. Morris and Rose (Davidson) Silbert; m. Abraham Aidenoff (dec.). Author: Imaginary People and Other Strangers (short stories), 1985, Making a Baby in Union Park Chicago (poems), 1983; short stories and poems in var. lit mags. BA, U. of Chgo.; MA, U. of Chgo. Freelance photographer and writer. Mem. PEN, PSA, Amer. Soc. of Mag. Photographers, Prof. Women Photographers. Home: 505 LaGuardia Place 16C New York NY 10012

SILBEY, PAULA J., b. Washington, Dec. 11, 1946; d. Samuel M. and Dorothy L. (Lebman) Silbey. Contrbr. to House Beautiful, Art & Antiques, Stagebill, Dance Mag., Weight Watchers Mag., other mags. BFA, Ithaca Coll., 1968; cert. in Journalism Price Schl. of Advertising & Journalism, 1970. Pub. rel. asst. Phila. Orch., 1968-71; PR dir., St. Louis Symphony, 1972-74; PR dir., Milw. Performing Arts Ctr., 1974-77; sr. acct. exec. Zigman-Joseph-Skeen (Milwaukee, WI), 1977-79, NW Ayer (NYC)1980-82; freelance wrtr., 1982—. VP, Women in Comm., SE WI chapter, 1975. Mem. Ed. Freelnce. Assoc., ASJA. Home: 19 Barrow St 4A New York NY 10014

SILESKY, BARRY, b. Mpls., July 1, 1949; s. Sidney L. Silesky and Layah (Schneider) Sperling; m. Loren Delorenzo, Aug. 24, 1973 (div. 1980); m. 2d, Sharon Solwitz, June 13, 1982. Author: Twin Cities Family Fun Guide, 1980; In the Ruins, 1983; ed. Another Chgo. Mag. 1980—, Banyan Press Anthology, 1980; contrbr. poetry to Grand St., Greenfield Rvw, Southwest Rvw, Ascent, Oyez Rev, Oink!, Black Warrior Rvw, Yankee, Poetry Northwest, Anthology of Mag. Verse and Yearbook of Am. Poetry; contrbr. prose to North Am. Rvw, Poetry Now; book rvws. to Chgo. Mag., 1980-86, Chgo. Tribune, 1984-86; Am. Bk. Rvw, 1987. BA, Northwestern U., 1967-71; MA, U. Ill.-Chgo., 1974-76. Recipient winner's award Innovative fiction contest, Center Press, Ranchos of Taos, NM, 1983; Ill. Arts Council fellowships, 1985, 86, 87. Mem. NWU, P&W. Address: 3709 N Kemore Chgo IL 60613

SILLIMAN, RON, b. Pasco, WA, Aug. 5, 1946; s. Glenn Sherman and Patricia Ruth (Tansley) S; m. Rochelle Myra Nameroff, Oct. 31, 1965 (div. 1972); m. Krishna Evans, April 6, 1986. Works include: Crow, 1971, Mohawk, 1973, Nox, 1974, Sitting Up, Standing, Taking Steps, 1978, Ketjak, 1978, Tjanting, 1981, Bart, 1983, ABC, 1984, Paradise, 1985, The Age of Huts, 1986. Student, San Francisco State U., 1966-69; student, U. of Calif., Berkeley, 1970-71. Lectr. SF State U., 1981; lectr., U. of Cal. at San Diego, 1982; wrtr.-in-res., New College of Cal., SF, 1982; poet-in-res., Cal. Inst. of Integral Studies, SF, CA., 1982—. Awards: NEA Fellowship, 1979, Poetry Ctr. Bk. Awd., 1985. Mem. PSA, MLA, Media Alliance. Home: 13 Porter St San Francisco CA 94110

SILVA, BEVERLY, b. Los Angeles; d. Cecilio and Marian (Langstaff) Cruz; m. Edwin Silva, Mar. 8, 1956 (div. 1969); children: Geof, Carla, Madelyn, Joy; m. Juvencio Garcia, Nov. 19, 1982. Author: The Second Street Poems, 1983; The Cat and Other Stories, 1986; contrbr. poetry to Women Talking, Women Listening, Mango Off Our Backs, The Poet, other lit mags. BA in English, San Jose State U., 1971, MA in English, 1976. ESL instr. Met. Adult Edn., San Jose, Calif., 1977—; poet-cons. Poetry in Schs., San Jose, 1979; instr. English Gavilan Coll., Gilroy, CA. Named Favorite Poet, Poetry Orgn. Women of No. Calif., 1978. Mem. IWWG, Bay Area Poets Coalition, Fem. Wrtrs. Guild. Home: 2155 Lanai Ave Apt 53 Jan Jose CA 95122

SILVA, JOAN YVONNE, b. Bloomfield, NE, Mar. 8, d. Leslie Edwin and Rosamond Merle (Stephens) Downie; m. Robert Joseph Silva (div. 1973); m. 2d, Ralph M. Kniseley. Contrbr. poetry: Pteranodon, Gryphon, Slipstream, other lit. mags. Wrkg. on novel. Ed., U. Oreg., U. Tenn. Freelance wrtr. Co-ed./pub., The Signal, Network Intl. Mem. Idaho Wrtrs. League (winner 1st pl. Open Title Article 1984), NWC, AAP. Office: PO Box 9 Emmett ID 83617

SILVER, DAVID FRANCIS, b. San Francisco, Jan. 26, 1957, s. Frank George and Marjorie Frances (Anderson) S.; m. Ramona Marie Dennis, Oct. 15, 1983. Author: Callous Dreams, 1980, Photography and the Expressive Dimensions of Man, 1983, Hardly a Day Goes By, 1985; wrtr./ed. And Now, a Few Words,..., 1981; contrbr. to Amazing, Americana, Am. Collector, Am. Jnl Anthropology, Analog, Atlantic, Cornucopia: An Anthology of Contemporary Poetry, others. BA in Anthropology, San Francisco State U., 1981. Tchr. scis. Calif. Acad. Scis., San Francisco, 1978-81, research assoc., 1981—; tchr. photography Dept. Recreation and Parks, San Francisco, 1982—; tchr. sci. and math. Drew Coll. Prep. Schl., San Francisco, 1983-84; tchr. biology St. Paul's High Schl., San Francisco, 1984—; ed./pub. B.A.P.A. Photo-History Jnl, Profiles in Wonder, INPHO Photo-History Jnl, Poetically Speaking. Mem. Intl. Photog. Hist. Orgn. (pres.), Bay Area Photographica Assn. Office: Box 16074 San Francisco CA 94116

SILVER, GARY LEE, b. Findlay, OH, Feb. 5, 1948; s. Charles Edward and Eileen Mae (La Rue) S.; m. Hallie Ann Yundt, Jan. 3, 1976. Genl. ed. Ralph W. Secord Press, 1983—, ed. Big Two-Hearted, 1985—; rvwr. edl. media for Curriculum Rev, 1981-85; contrbr. stories and poems to Carolina Qtly Penny Dreadful, Small Pond Mag, Itinerary: Fiction, and others; bk. rvw. ed. Library Software Rvw, 1986—. BS in

Edn., Bowling Green State U., 1970, MFA, 1972; MLS, Ind. U., 1975. Asst. head librarian, Kendallville public library, Ind., 1972-74; AV/TV coordinator Riverview high schl.; Sarasota Fla., 1976-80; dir. Bartow County Library System, Cartersville, Ga., 1980-83; Mid-Peninsula Library Coop., Iron Mountain, Mich., 1983—. Recipient distinctive fiction listing, Martha Foley's Best Stories of 1974. Mem. ALA, Mich. Library Assn (edl. bd. 1984-85), COSMEP. Address: Rt. 2 Box 45 Stephenson MI 49887

SILVER, MARC S., b. Balt., Dec. 26, 1951; s. Donald Leon and Shirley Elinor (Freeman) S.; m. Marsha Lee Dale, June 8, 1980; 1 dau., Maya Dale Silver. Ed. The B'nai B'rith Intl. Jewish Monthly, 1981—; contrbr. to NY Times, Balt. Sunpapers, Present Tense, Washington Post. BA, U. MD, 1973. Assoc. ed. Balt. Jewish Times, 1974-79; freelance writer, 1980-81; ed. The Jewish Monthly, Washington, 1981—. Mem. Amer. Jewish Press Assn. Office: Jewish Mthly 1640 RI Ave N W Washington DC 20036

SILVER-LILLYWHITE, EILEEN, b. Balt., Jan. 6, 1953; d. Stanley Marvin and Harriet Zelda (Cohen) Silver; m. Harvey Lillywhite, Dec. 12, 1976; 1 son, Jacob Thomas. Author: All That Autumn, 1983; contrbr. poetry to Ohio Rvw, Mo. Rvw, Seattle Rvw, Crazy Horse, Kans. Qtly, others. MFA, Columbia U., 1980; PhD, U. Utah, 1985. Asst. prof. Towson State Unive., Md., 1984—. Address: 629 Glynita Cr Reisterstown MD 21136

SILVERBERG, ROBERT, b. NYC, s. Michael and Helen (Baim) S.; m. Barbara Brown, 1956 (div. 1986); m. 2d Karen Haber, 1987. Author: novels Thorns, 1967, The Masks of Time, 1968, Hawksbill Station, 1968, Nightwings, 1969, To Live Again, 1969, Tower of Glass, 1970, The World Inside, 1971, Son of Man, 1971, A Time of Changes, 1971, Dying Inside, 1972, The Book of Skulls, 1972, Born With the Dead, 1974, Shadrach in the Furnace, 1976, Lord Valentine's Castle, 1980, Majipoor Chronicles, 1982, Lord of Darkness, 1983, Valentine Pontifex, 1983, Gilgamesh the King, 1984, Tom O'Bedlam, 1985, Star of Gypsies, 1986; non-fiction Lost Cities and Vanished Civilizations, 1962, The Great Wall of China, 1965, The Old Ones: Indians of the American Southwest, 1965, Scientists and Scoundrels: A Book of Hoaxes, 1965, The Auk, the Dodo and the Oryx, 1966, The Morning of Mankind: Prehistoric Man in Europe, 1967, Mound Builders of Ancient America: The Archaeology of a Myth, 1968, If I Forget Thee, O Jerusalem: American Jews and the State of Israel, 1970, The Pueblo Revolt, 1970, The Realm of Prester John, 1971. BA, Columbia U., 1956. Recipient Hugo award World Sci. Fiction Conv., 1956, 69, Nebula award Sci. Fiction Writers Am., 1970, 72, 75, 86. Mem. SFWA (pres. 1967-68). Address: Box 13160 Station E Oakland CA 94661

SILVERMAN, AL, b. Lynn, MA, Apr. 12, 1926; s. Henry and Minnie (Damsky) Silverman; m. Rosa Magaro, Sept. 9, 1951; children—Thomas, Brian, Matthew. Author: Warren Spahn, 1961, Best from Sport, 1961, (with Phil Rizzuto) The Miracle New York Yankees, 1962, Mickey Mantle, Master Yankee, 1963, World Series Heroes, 1964, (with Paul Horung) Football and the Single Man, 1965, The Specialist in Pro Football, 1966, Sports Titans of the 20th Century, 1968, (with Frank Robinson) My Life Is Baseball, 1968, More Sport Titians of the 20th Century, 1969, Joe DiMaggio, The Golden Year, 1969, I Am Third (with Gale Sayers), 1970, Foster and Laurie, 1974. BS, Boston U., 1949. Assoc. editor Sport mag., 1951-52; sports editor True mag., 1952-54; asst. editor Argosy mag., 1954-55; free-lance mag. writer, contrbr. Sat. Eve. Post, Coronet, Pageant, This Week, Am. Weekly, Am. Heritage, Sat. Rvw, others, 1955-60; editor-in-chief Saga mag., Impact mag., Sport Library, Sport mag., 1960-72; exec. vp, editorial dir. BOMC, 1972—, pres., chief operating officer, 1981. Mem. AG. Home: 311 Rosedale Ave White Plains NY 10605

SILVERMAN, ALBERT JAMES, b. Balt., Sept. 4, 1906; s. David and Sara (Whiteman) S.; widowed; children—Sally, David, Tom. Author: Baltimore, City of Promise, 1953, Unseen Harvests, 1986. Contrbr. articles to mags. Wrkg. on mag. article. B.S., Johns Hopkins U., 1933, M.A., 1952. Instr., Johns Hopkins U., Balt., 1958-73; head history dept. Balt. Polytechnic Inst., 1958-74. Home: 2826 Damascus Ct Baltimore MD 21209

SILVERMAN, HERSCHEL, b. Port Chester, NY, Apr. 17, 1926, s. Isadore and Ella Esther (Jacobson) S.; m. Laura Rothschild, June 23, 1945; children—Elaine Esther, Jack. Author poetry collections: Krishna Poems, 1970, Nite Train, 1975, April, 1975, Vietnam Newsreels after 'The Times', 1975, Timepiece, 1981, Reflections for Gene Noce, 1981, Nine de Koonings for Marian Courtney, 1982, Getting It Together, 1981, Bouquet for Maggie, 1982, Fool, 1983, Humm, 1983, Jazz and the Changes, 1984; ed., pub.: All My Roads (by Jonathan London), 1983, Pasacaglia (by Theodore Enslin), 1982, Longitude Poems (by Pamela Margoshes), 1983. Student Seton Hall U., 1955-57. Owner, mgr. Hersch's Beehive Candy Store, Bayonne, N.J., 1952-86; ed., pub. Beehive Mag. of Contemporary N.J. Poetry, Bayonne, 1984—. Served with USN, WWII, Korea. N.J. Council on Arts poetry fellow, 1980-81. Mem. Poetry Soc. N.J. Home: 47 E 33d St Bayonne NJ 07002

SILVERMAN, KENNETH EUGENE, b. NYC, Feb. 5, 1936; s. Gustave and Bessie (Goldberg) Silverman; m. Sharon Medjuck, Sept. 8, 1957; children—Willa Zahava, Ethan Leigh. Author: Timothy Dwight, 1969, A Cultural History of the American Revolution, 1976, The Life and Times of Cotton Mather, 1984; editor: anthology Colonial American Poetry, 1968; compiler: Selected Letters of Cotton Mather, 1976; mem. editorial bd.: Early Am. Lit., 1969-72, 77-80; editorial bd., The William and Mary Qtly., 1984-87; editorial bd., Amer. Lit., 1987—. Advisory coun., Inst. of Early Amer. History and Culture, 1984-87. BA, Columbia U., 1956, MA, 1958, PhD, 1964. Instr. English U. Wyo. (Laramie, 1958-59; preceptor in English Columbia U. (NYC), 1962-64; prof. English, grad. adviser in Am. civilization, NY U. (NYC), 1964—. Bancroft Prize in Am. history, 1985, Pulitzer Prize for biography, 1985. Mem. MLA (chair Early Am. lit. group 1975), PEN Am. Office: NYU Dept Eng 19 Univ Pl New York NY 10003

SILVERS, ROBERT B., b. Mineola, NY, Dec. 31, 1929; s. James J. and Rose (Roden) Silvers. Editor: Writing in America, 1960; translator: La Gangrene, 1961. AB, U. Chgo., 1947; grad., Ecole des Sci. Politiques, Paris, 1956. Press secy. to Gov. Bowles of Conn., 1950; mem. editorial bd. Paris Rvw, 1954—; assoc. editor Harper's mag., 1959-63; co-editor NY Rvw Books, 1963—. Served with AUS, 1952-53. Office: 250 W 57th St New York NY 10107

SILVERS, VICKI, b. NY, Jan. 22, 1941; d. Louis Meyers and Diane (Aronson) Cohen; divorced; children—Lisa Melanie, Jullette Joy. Author: (picture book) Sing a Song of Sound, 1973. Contrbr. poems to mags., newspapers, anthols. Wrkg. on picture books for children and poetry. Grad. public schs., Bklyn. Home: 60 Nobel St Brentwood LI NY 11717

SILVERSTEIN, SHELBY, (Shel Silverstein), b. Chgo., 1932. Author: Lafcodio, The Lion Who Shot Back, Uncle Shelby's ABZ Book, Giraffe and a Half, The Giving Tree, Now Here's My Plan, 1976, Uncle Shelby's Zoo; Don't Bump the Glump, Where the Sidewalk Ends, 1974, The Missing Piece, 1976, The Missing Piece Meets the Big O, 1981; (drawings) Different Dances, 1979, Who Wants a Cheap Rhinoceros, 1983; composer: Comin' After Junny, Boa Constrictor, A Boy Named Sue, One's On the Way. Former corr. Stars and Stripes (Pacific area); now cartoonist, writer Playboy Mag. Address: Harper & Row 10 E 53rd St New York NY 10022

SILVERTON, MICHAEL JOHN, b. White Plains, NY, Mar. 17, 1935; m. Felicia Thorn, Dec. 3, 1979; children from previous marriage—Seth, Alexandra. Contrbr. poetry: Wormwood Review, Poetry Now, Prairie Schooner, The Nation, Some/Thing, others; poems in 3 anthologies ed. by Wm. Cole; coordinated poetry readings for The New School for Social Research (NYC); produced poetry broadcasts for WNYC and Pacifica Radio; at present writes the column "Random Noise" for the bi-monthly record-review mag Fanfare. Home: 459 12th St Brooklyn NY 11215

SILVEUS, MARI L., b. Warsaw, IN, Oct. 29, 1957; d. Richard F. and Lula F. (Setser) S. Co-Ed. Nuggets, 1984—; contrbr. to Courier-Jnl Mag., Emergency Librarian, Wallpaper Jnl, Indpls. Mag., Sycamore, Indpls. Monthly, Dog World, Canine Chronicle, Nuggets, Dog Fancy, Pure-Bred Dogs/Amer. Kennel Gazette. BA in Journalism and Polit. Sci., Ind. U., 1980. Communications rep. Dow Chem. Co., Freeport, Tex., Midland, Mich., 1979-81; freelance wrtr., 1982—. Mem. Dog Wrtrs. Assn. Am. Home: 10061 W Stogsdill Rd Bloomington IN 47401

SIMCOE, ANNELL LACY, b. Wellington, TX, May 22, 1941; d. Robert Milton and Edith (Cummings) L.; m. Melvin John Simcoe, Oct. 10, 1973; children—Michael Robert, Stephen Wayne. Ed.: Delta Pi Epsilon Jnl, 1985—, Jnl Voc. & Tech. Edn., 1985—, Jnl Edn. for Bus., 1984—, Natl. Bus. Edn. Assn. Yrbk., 1969; author: The Professions and Ethics: Views and Realities, 1986, Keyboarding for The Automated Office 1, 2, & 3, 1986, Keyboarding, 1986. BS, Texas Woman's U., 1962, MA, 1963; PhD, Ohio State U., 1968. Tchr., Dalhart (TX) Pub. Schs., 1963-64; instr. U. TX-Arlington, 1964-66; research assoc., Ohio State U., Columbus, 1966-68; asst. prof. GA State U., Atlanta, 1968-70; prof. Rutgers U., New Brunswick, NJ, 1970—. Mem. Am. Edn. Research Assn. Home: 52 Long View Dr Green Brook NJ 08812

SIMIC, CHARLES, b. Beograd, Yugoslavia, May 9, 1938 (came to U.S., 1954, naturalized, 1971); s. George and Helen (Matijevich) Simic; m. Helen Dubin, Oct. 1964; children—Anna, Philip. Author: poems What the Grass Says, 1967, Somewhere Among Us a Stone Is Taking Notes, 1969, Dismantling the Silence, 1971, White, 1972, Return to a Place Lit by a Glass of Milk, 1974, Biography and a Lament, 1976, Charon's Cosmology, 1977, Classic Ballroom Dances, 1980, Austerities, 1982, Selected Poems 1963-83, 1985, Unending Blues, 1986; translator, editor: (with C.W. Truesdale) Fire Gardens, 1970, (with Mark Strand) Another Republic, 1976; translator: The Little Box, 1970, Four Modern Yugoslav Poets, 1970; contrbr. poems to mags. and anthologies. BA, NY U., 1967. Editorial asst. Aperture, Qtly of Photography (NYC), 1966-69; prof. English Calif. State U. (Hayward), 1970-73, U. NH (Durham), 1973—. Served with U.S. Army, 1961-63. Recipient PEN Intl. award for translation, 1970, Edgar Allan Poe award, 1975, Natl. Inst. Arts and Letters and AAIAL award, 1976. Home: Box 192 Strafford NH 03884

SIMKIN, PENELOPE PAYSON, b. Portland, ME, May 31, 1938; d. Thomas and Caroline Wood (Little) Payson; m. Peter Simkin, Aug. 9, 1958; children—Andrew, Caroline, Elizabeth, Mary. Author: Talking about Childbirth, 1975, NAPSAC Consumer Guide to Alternative Birth Services, 1978. Contrbr. articles to mags. Editor, author NAPSAC Directory of Alternative Birth Services and Consumer Guide, 1978, 3d ed., 1982; editor: ICEA Rvw., 1976-78, (with Anderson) Birth—Through Children's Eyes, 1981; (with Whalley and Keppler) Pregnancy, Childbirth and the Newborn, 1984; (with Kitzinger) Episiotomy and the Second Stage of Labor, 1984-86; assoc. editor: Birth: Issues in Perinatal Care and Edn., 1986. BA in English, Swarthmore Coll., 1959; Cert. in Physical Therapy, U. Pa., 1961. Childbirth educator Childbirth Edn. Assn. of Seattle, 1968—; pres., ed. Pennypress, Inc., Seattle, 1978—; cons. & faculty Seattle Midwifery Schl., 1984— Mem. Intl. Childbirth Edn. Assn. (v.p. 1976-78, bd. dirs. 1972-78; bd. cons. 1986—), NOW, Midwives' Assn. Wash. (1st annual award for contrbns. to midwifery, 1984, secy., 1983—), Regional Assn. Childbirth Educators Puget Sound (adv. bd. 1979-85). Office: Pennypress 1100 23d Ave E Seattle WA 98112

SIMMERMAN, JIM, b. Denver, Mar. 5, 1952, s. Wade Darrow and Jane Eleanor (Flowers) S. Author poetry collections: Home, 1983, Once Out of Nature, 1988; poetry ed.: Iowa Jnl Lit. Studies, 1980, Shankpainter, 1984-85; editorial cons. New Oxford Book of English Verse, 1984; contrbg. ed. Pushcart Prize XI: Best of the Small Presses, 1986; contrbr. poems to over 70 jnls and anthols. BA in Edn., U. Mo., Columbia, 1973, MA in English, 1976, MFA in Creative Writing, U. Iowa, 1980. Instr. English, U. Mo., Columbia, 1976; teaching asst. U. Iowa, Iowa City, 1979-80; instr. English, No. Ariz. U., Flagstaff, 1977-78, 81-83, asst. prof., 1983—; poetry cons. Tuba City (Ariz.) Public Schls., 1983; mem. lit. panel Ariz. Commn. on Arts; judge Ariz. Poetry Soc., 1985. Creative writing fellow Ariz. Commn. on Arts, 1983, Fine Arts Work Center, Provincetown, Mass., 1984-85, NEA, 1984-85; grantee No. Ariz. U., 1983, 84, 85, 86. Mem. P&W, AWP. Office: Box 6032 No Ariz U Flagstaff AZ 86011

SIMMONS, DR. GEORGE, see Kramer, Philip Earl

SIMMONS, SHIRLEY J(OYCE LESLIE), b. NYC, July 24, d. Mike and Kate (Leslie) Simmons. Contrbr. poetry to univ. and small press publs.; honor entire issue Freedom's Child, 1983; contrbr. songs, lyrics, spcl. material to Art & Oxygen, 1985. BBA, Pace U., 1965; student Am. Theater Wing Wrtrs. Workshop, 1950. Mem. N.Y. Film Club, P&W. Home: Box 7496 GOP NY 10116

SIMMONS, VIRGINIA ANNE, see Wolf, Virginia Simmons

SIMMS, AMI, b. Detroit, Nov. 12, 1954; d. Leonard W. and Beebe (Gottesman) Moss; m. Steven W. Simms, June 19, 1977; 1 dau., Jennifer Rachel. Author: How to Improve Your Quilting Stitch, 1986, 2d ed., 1987, Invisible Applique, 1986, Little Ditties, 1986. Contrbr. numerous articles to quilting mags., anthols. B.A., Kalamazoo Coll., 1976; postgrad. Western Mich. U., U. Mich., 1977-84. Tchr. Davison Commun. Schls., MI, 1978-81, Mott Adult High Schl., Flint, MI, 1982-83; contrbg. ed. Quilt Mag., 1986—; quilting lectr./workshop leader, 1982—. Home: 2228 Mallery St Flint MI 48504

SIMON, HAROLD, b. Bronx, NY, May 9, 1953; s. Lester Simon. Contrbr. arts. to: Essex Gazette, 1982, Petersen's PhotoGraph mag., 1986; author essays N.J. State Museum, 1985, 86. BS, Hunter Coll. CUNY, 1976. Dir., The Simon Gallery, Montclair, NJ, 1981—; pub./ed. Strategies: The Self-Promotion Newsletter for Photographers, Montclair, 1984—. Mem. Soc. for Photographic Edn., COSMEP. Office: Box 838 Montclair NJ 07042

SIMON, JACQUELINE ANN, b. Baton Route, LA, Apr. 17, 1943, d. Jean Arthur Simon and Eula Louise (Tate) Jones; m. James Doyle Colthart, Mar. 14, 1981; 1 stepson, Christopher. Contrbr. to Christmas in Texas, 1979, A Texas Christmas, 1983, Her Work, 1984, Of Hide and Horn, 1985; Redbook, Domestic Crude, Dialog, other publs. Wrkg. on novel. BS, La. State U., 1964, MA, 1968. Mktg. dir. Johnson-Loggins, Inc., Houston, 1971-75; instr. Houston Community Coll., 1976-81; freelance wrtr., 1981—; instr. Rice U. Continuing Ed. Program, 1986—. Recipient Wrtr. Recogition award Tex. Commn. on Arts, 1981, Houston Discovery price PEN Southwest, 1982. Home: 3603 Blue Bonnet Blvd Houston TX 77025

SIMON, JO ANN (Joanna Campbell), b. Norwalk, CT, Nov. 2, 1946; d. Charles Lester and Joephine F. (Berglund) Haessig; m. Kenneth Campbell, Sr., Dec. 27, 1969 (div. 1975); children—Kimberly, Kenneth. Author: Love Once in Passing, 1981, The Thoroughbred, 1981, Hold Fast to Love, 1982, Secret Identity, 1982, Love Once Again, 1983, Love Notes, 1983, The Caitlin Triology, 1984, 2d ed., 1985, Beloved Captain, 1988, A Horse of Her Own, 1988. Student Nowalk Commun. Coll., 1965-66. Asst. to v.p. Hanson & Orth Inc., Darien, CT, 1972-81. Recipient Bronze Porgie, West Coast Rvw. of Books, 1983; Time Travel award Romantic Times, 1984, Reviewer's Choice for fantasy, 1984. Mem. AG, RWA (bd. dirs. 1982-84). Home: 39 Mountain St Box 426 Camden ME 04843

SIMON, JOHN OLIVER, b. NYC, Apr. 21, 1942, s. Bernard Aaron Simon and Frances Cassandra (Kehrlein) Adler; 1 dau., Kia; 1 stepdau., Lorelei Bosserman. Author 13 books and chapbooks of poetry including: Roads to Dawn, 1968, Rattlesnake Grass, 1978, Neither of Us Can Break the Other's Hold: Poems for my Father, 1981, Confronting the Empire (bilingual with translations into Spanish by Monica Mansour and Alberto Blanco), 1985; contrbr. poetry to Alcatraz, Hanging Loose, Nimrod, Contact II, Chelsea, numerous other lit. publs. BA with highest honors, Swarthmore (Pa.) Coll., 1964; MA in English, U. Calif.-Berkeley, 1966; postgrad. Center for Open Learning, 1974-75. Staff poet Calif. Poets-in-Schls., 1971—. exec. dir., 1978-81, project dir. Calif. Heritage Poetry Curriculum, Oakland Unified Schl. Dist., 1982—; project dir. introducing poets-in-schls. teaching techniques to Mex. poets, funded by Witter Bynner Fdn. Mem. PEN, ALTA, PSA. Home: 2209 California St Berkeley CA 94703

SIMON, MAURYA, b. NYC, Dec. 7, 1950; d. Robert Leopold Simon and Baila Goldenthal; m. Robert Edward Falk, June 17, 1973; 2 daus., Naomi, Leah. Author: The Enchanted Room, 1986. BA, Pitzer Coll., 1978-80; MFA, U. Calif.-Irvine, 1982-84. Vis. lectr. Pitzer Coll., Claremont, Calif., 1983-84, 86-87, Univ. Calif., Riverside, 1984—. Recipient Univ. award, AAP, NYC, 1983; first prize Natl. Fedn. State Poetry Socs., Mecanicsburg, Ohio, 1984. Mem. PSA, AAP, MLA. Address: Box 0203 Mt. Baldy CA 91759

SIMON, PAUL, b. Eugene, OR, Nov. 29, 1928; s. Martin Paul and Ruth (Troemel) Simon; m. Jeanne Hurley, Apr. 21, 1960; children—Sheila, Martin. Author: Lovejoy: Martyr to Freedom, 1964, Lincoln's Preparation for Greatness, 1966, A Hungry World, 1966, (with Jeanne Hurley Simon) Protestant-Catholic Marriages Can Succeed, 1967, You Want to Change the World? So Change It, 1971; co-author: The Politics of World Hunger, 1973, The Tongue- Tied American: Confronting the Foreign Language Crisis, 1980; The Once and Future Democrats: Strategies for Change, 1982; The Glass House: Politics and Morality in the nation's Capital, 1984; Beginnings: Senator Paul Simon Speaks to Young Americans, 1986. Author of wkly. newspaper column, 1948—; contrbr. articles to periodicals, including Harper's. Student, U. Oreg., 1945-46, Dana Coll., Blair, NE, 1946-48, LL.D., 1965. Pub. Troy Tribune (IL), 1948-66; mem. Ill. House of Reps., 1955-63, Ill. Senate, 1963-69; lt. gov. Ill., 1969-73; fellow John F. Kennedy Inst. Politics Harvard, 1973; prof. public affairs Sangamon State U. (Springfield, IL), 1973; mem. 94th-98th Congresses from 24th District Ill., mem. U.S. Senate, 99th Congress. Served with CIC AUS, 1951-53. Recipient Am. Poli. Sci. Assn. award, 1957; named Best Illionis Legislator 7 times. Office: 462 Dirksen Bldg Washington DC 20510

SIMON, ROBERT L., b. Bklyn., May 12, 1941; s. J.L. and Frances S. Simon; m. Joy, Sept. 27, 1967; children—Bruce, Marc. Author: The Individual and the Political Order, 1978, 2d ed., 1986; Sports and Social Values, ,85; assoc. editor: Ethics: An Intl. Jnl of Social, Legal and Poli. Philosophy, 1979—. BA, Lafayette Coll., 1963; PhD, U. Pa., 1969. Instr. Lafayette Coll. (Easton, PA), 1967-68; prof. Hamilton Coll. (Clinton, NY), 1968—, William R. Kenan Jr. prof. philosophy (Clinton, 1981-85. Mem. Am. Philo. Assn., AAUP. Office: Hamilton Coll Clinton NY 13323

SIMON, ROGER MITCHELL, b. Chgo., Mar. 29, 1948; s. Sheldon and Pauline (Odess) Simon; m. Marcia Kramer, May 15, 1977. Editor: The Advisor, U. Ill., 1970; contrbr.: free-lance articles to Playboy mag., TV Guide, others. BS, U. Ill., 1970. Reporter City News Bur. Chgo., 1970; columnist Waukegan News-Sun (IL), 1970-72, Chgo. Sun-Times, 1972-84, Baltimore Sun, 1984—; work syndicated by Los Angeles Times Syndicate; columnist Chgo. mag.; Recipient Page One award Chgo. Newspaper Guild, 1972, 74, 75, 77, 78, 79, 82, 1st place award for public service UPI, 1974, 80, 82, 83, Silver Gavel award Am. Bar Assn., 1975, 76, 79, Natl. Merit award Assn. Trial Lawyers Am., 1975, 76, Disting. Reporter award Inland Daily Press Assn., 1975,

1st place award for column, AP, 1976, 77, 78, 80, Peter Lisagor award Headline Club, 1980, 83. Office: LA Times Syndicate Times Mirror Sq Los Angeles CA 90053

SIMON, WERNER, b. Bremen, Germany, June 5, 1915 (came to U.S., 1937, naturalized, 1941), s. Louis and Elise (Halle) Simon; m. Elizabeth Strawn, Apr. 24, 1939. Author: (with Dr. R.D. Wirt) Differential Treatment and Prognosis in Schizophrenia, 1959; contrbr. articles on schizophrenia, suicide, drug addiction, music therapy to publs. Student, U. Frankfurt, Germany, 1932-36; M.D., U. Berne, Switzerland, 1937. Intern Lutheran Hosp. (Omaha), 1937-38, resident psychiatry, 1938-39; resident physician Cherokee State Hosp. (Cherokee, IA), 1939-41; psychiatrists Vets. Hosps. (Palo Alto, CA, American Lake, WA), 1941-44, VA Hosp. (St. Cloud, MN), 1946-48, chief psychiatry (Mpls.), 1948-71, prof. psychiatry U. Minn. Med. Schl. (Mpls.), 1956-71, clin. prof. psychiatry and medicine, 1971—; cons. Hastings State Hosp. (MN), 1960-73, Hennepin County Gen. Hosp., 1971—, VA Hosp. (Mpls.), 1971-82. Served as Capt. M.C., AUS, 1944-46. Home: 8915 River Ridge Rd Minneapolis MN 55420

SIMONSMEIER, LARRY MARVIN, b. Swea City, IA, Sept. 16, 1944; s. Marvin J. and Irene (Rohlf) Simonsmeier; m. Constance E. Miller, Dec. 18, 1966; children—David, Stephen. Assoc. editor: Pharmacy Law Digest, 1981—. BS, Drake U., 1967; JD, U. Denver, 1973. Staff pharmacist Osco Drug (Chgo.), 1967-68; pharmacy mgr. Macy's Drug (Loveland, CO), 1968-70; asst. prof. pharmacy law Wash. State U. (Pullman), 1974-79, dean, assoc. prof., 1979—. Office: Coll Phar Wash State U Pullman WA 99164

SIMONY, MAGGY, (Anne Stenholm), d. Seth and Anna (Stenholm) Magnuson; m. William J. Simony (dec. 1973); children—Stephen, Christine, Maria. Author: (as Anne Stenholm) Travel Agency: A How-to-do-it Manual for Starting One of Your Own, 1979, (as Maggy Simony) The Traveler's Reading Guide—Ready-made Reading Lists for the Armchair Traveler, 1987. Home: Box 1385 Meredith NH 03253

SIMPSON, EDWIN L., b. Jackson, OH, Feb. 29, 1948; s. Edwin F. and Doris B. (Radcliffe) S.; m. Sonja Lee Tackett, May 10, 1974; children—Jeremiah E., David T. Author: How to Get Rich With Your Microcomputer, 1982, The Complete Home Business Guide, 1985. BS, Ohio U., 1971. Ed. and pub. Home Business News, Jackson, OH, 1985—. Home: 12221 Beaver Pike Jackson OH 45640

SIMPSON, ETHEL CHACHERE, b. Opelousas, LA, July 22, 1937; d. John Elliott and Annie Margaret (Trahan) Chachere; m. Roy Vergil Simpson, Jr.; children—Michel Miles, Christopher Lawrence. Author: Simpkinsville and Vicinity: Arkansas Stories of Ruth McEnery Stuart, 1983; Tulip Evermore: William Paisley and Emma Butler, Their Lives in Letters, 1985; Arkansas in Short Fiction, 1986. Wrkg. on pictoral hisory of U. Ark., cultural history of Fayetteville, Ark. 1920-80. B.A., U. South-westen La., 1958; M.A., U. Ark., 1960, Ph.D., 1977. Instr. English, U. Md., College Park, 1960-64; asst. prof. English, U. Southeastern La., hammand, 1964-69; instr. foreign lang. U. Ark., Fayetteville, 1969-74, bibliographer, 1983—. Home: 409 Oliver Ave Fayetteville AR 72701

SIMPSON, GEDDES WILSON, b. Scranton, PA, Aug. 15, 1908; s. Frank Morton and Mary Elizabeth (Wilson) S.; m. Blanche May Thomas, Oct. 21, 1933; children—Mary, Frank, Blanche, Geddes Jr. Contrbr. chapter to AVI pub. Potatoes: Prodn., storing, processing, arts, in Jnl Econ. Entomol., Annals Ent. Soc. Am., Am. Potato Jnl, Jnl Ag. Research, Bulletins Me. Agric. Exp. Sta. AB, Bucknell, 1929; MA, Cornell, 1931, PhD, 1935. Asst. entomologist, Maine AES, Orono, 1931-42, assoc. entom., 43-54, entom., 55-74; prof. of entom. L.S. Agric., Orono, 1954-74; prof. emeritus, 1974—; ed.-in-chief Am. Potato Jnl., Orono, 1974—; asst. to dir., Maine AES, 1976—. Hon. life mem. Potato Assn. Am., Entomol. Soc. Am. Fellow AAAS, Phi Beta Kappa. Home: 15 Cedar St Orono ME 04473

SIMPSON, LOUIS ASTON MARANTZ, b. Jamaica, W.I., Mar. 27, 1923; s. Aston and Rosalind (Marantz) Simpson; m. Jeanne Claire Rogers, 1949 (div.1954); 1 son—Louis Matthew; m. 2d, Dorothy Mildred Roochvarg, 1955 (div. 1979); children—Anne Borovoi, Anthony Rolf; m. 3d, Miriam Bachner, 1985. Author: Poems The Arrivistes, 1949, Good News of Death, 1955, A Dream of Governors, 1959, At the End of the Open Road, 1963, Selected Poems, 1965, Adventures of the Letter I, 1971, Searching for the Ox, 1976, Caviar at the Funeral, 1980, The Best Hour of the Night, 1983, People Live Here: Selected Poems 1949-1983, 1983; books Riverside Drive, 1962, James Hogg, A Critical Study, 1962, North of Jamaica, 1972, Three on the Tower: The Lives and Works of Ezra Pound, T.S. Eliot and William Carlos Williams, 1975, A Revolution in Taste: Studies of Dylan Thomas, Allen Ginsberg, Sylvia Plath and Robert Lowell, 1978, A Company of Poets, 1981, The Character of the Poet, 1986; editor: An Introduction to Poetry, 1967, The New Poets of England and America, 1957. Higher schs. certificate, Munro Coll., Jamaica, 1939; BS, Columbia U., 1948, AM, 1950, PhD, 1959; D.H.L., Eastern Mich. U., 1977. Editor Bobbs-Merrill Pub. Co., NYC, 1950-55; instr. Columbia U., 1955-59; prof. English U. Calif. at Berkeley, 1959-67, State U. NY at Stony Brook, 1967—. Served with AUS, 1943-45. Pulitzer prize for poetry 1964, Columbia University Medal for Excellence, 1965, Jewish Book Council award for poetry, 1981, Elmer Holmes Bobst award, 1987. Address: Box 91 Port Jefferson NY 11777

SIMPSON, NANCY CAROLYN, b. Miami, FL, Dec. 16, 1938, d. Clyde Taylor and Mamie Jewell (Cofer) Simpson; m. Ernest William Brantley, Feb. 1, 1957 (div. 1978); children—Jeffrey Taylor, Timothy Reid, Jeremy Quoc Phong. Author: Across Water, 1983, Night Student, 1985; contrbr. poetry: Nimrod, Southern Poetry Rvw, New Va. Rvw, Ga. Rvw, Confrontation, Anthology of Mag. Verse and Yearbook of Am. Poetry, others. BS in Edn., Western Carolina U., 1979; MFA in Writing, Warren Wilson Coll., 1983. Tchr. exceptional students Hayesville (N.C.) High Schl., 1975—; bd. trustees N.C. Wrtrs. Network, Durham, 1985, 86, creative writing instr., 1986. Mem. P&W, AWP. Home: Rt 2 Cherry Mountain Rd Hayesville NC 28904

SIMPSON, WINIFRED ROUSE, b. Detroit, Nov. 22, 1937; d. Frank Edwin and Winifred Mayme (Ramsey) Rouse; m. Phillip Dean Simpson, Dec. 22, 1960; children—John, Matthew, Frederick. Author: I Can Help, Mommy, 1986, Hello, World, You're Mine?, 1987. Contrbr. short stories to children's mags., anthol. Wrkg. on juvenile novel, mystery. BS, Colo. Coll., Colorado Springs, 1959. Tech. illustrator Kaman Aircraft, Colorado Springs, 1960, Hewlett-Packard, Palo Alto, Calif., 1960-63, Colorado Springs, 1965-69. Pres. Columbia Elem. Schl., PTA, Colorado Springs, 1970-72; Mem. Soc. of Children's Book Wrtrs., Kappa Kappa Gamma. Home: 25 Birch Pl New Providence NJ 07974

SIMS, JAMES HYLBERT, b. Orlando, FL, Oct. 29, 1924; s. James W. and Anna L. (Hylbert) Sims; m. Ruth Elizabeth Gray, Jan. 3, 1944; children—James W., Timothy C., Suzannah C., C. Andrew, John M. Author: Biblical Allusions in Shakespeare's Comedies, 1960, The Bible in Milton's Epics, 1962, Dramatic Uses of Biblical Allusion in Marlowe and Shakespeare, 1966, Milton and Scriptural Tradition: The Bible into Poetry, 1984. Assoc. editor: Seventeenth-Century News, 1968—. BA, in English and History, U. Fla., 1949, MA, 1950, PhD in English Lit., 1959. Instr. English Tenn. Temple Coll., 1950-51; pres., instr. English Tri-State Bapt. Coll., (Evansville, IN), 1951-54; instr. English U. Fla. (Gainesville), 1955-57, 58-59; prof. English Tift Coll. (Forsyth, GA), 1959-61, Austin Peay State U. (Clarksville, TN), 1961-66, U. Okla. (Norman), 1966-76; prof. English and dean Coll. Liberal Arts U. So. Miss. (Hattiesburg), 1976-82, vp acad. affairs, 1982—. Served with USN, 1943-46. Mem. MLA, Milton Soc. Am. (pres. 1976), Atlantic MLA, South Central MLA, South Central Renaissance Conf. (pres. 1983), Southeastern Renaissance Conf., Conf. Christianity and Lit. Home: 3103 Delwood Dr Hattiesburg MS 39401

SIMSON, JOANNE (Valentine Pascoe), b. Chgo., Nov. 19, 1936; d. Kenneth Brown and Helen Marjorie (Pascoe) Valentine; m. A. F. Simson, June 1960 (div.); 1 dau., Maria; m. 2d, M. L. Smith Nov. 1971 (div.); children—Elisabeth, Briana. Contrbr. fiction to lit. mag. Editorial bd. Anatomical Record. BA in Biology, Kalamazoo Coll., 1959; PhD in Anatomy, SUNY-Syracuse, 1969. Asst. prof. pathology Med. U. S.C., Charleston, 1970-75, assoc. prof. anatomy, 1976-82, prof. anatomy, 1983—. Ed. newsletter Amnesty Intl., Charleston, 1982-85; tchr. religious edn. Circular Ch., Charleston. Home: 1760 Pittsford Cr Charleston SC 29412

SINCLAIR, MARJORIE PUTNAM, b. Sioux Falls, SD, Nov. 27, 1913, d. Frank Israel and Sue Gertrude (Reed) Putnam; m. Gregg M. Sinclair, May 20, 1939 (dec. 1976); m. 2d, Leon Edel, May 30, 1980. Author: Kona, 1947, The Wild Wind, 1950, Nahienaena, Sacred Daughter of Hawaii, 1976, The Path of the Ocean, 1982, The Place Your Body Is (as Marjorie Edel), 1984; translator: The Poems of T'ao Chi'en, 1953, A Grass Path: The Poems of Kotomichi Okuma, 1955. Wrkg. on poetry book, novel. MA, Mills Coll., 1937. Prof. English, U. Hawaii, Honolulu, to 1980, prof. emeritus, 1980—. Recipient Hawaii Award for Lit., State Fdn. on Culture and the Arts, 1981. Home: 3817 Lurline Dr Honolulu HI 96816

SINGER, FRIEDA, b. NYC, June 4, d. Charles and Esther (Mariansky) S.; m. Morris Shapiro, June 25, 1978; stepchildren—Sheryl Levine, Eileen Robbins. Ed. Daughters in High School, 1974-75; book reviewer 100 Tested Books for the Reluctant Reader, 1967, 72; contrbr. poetry to Perceptions, Infinity Mag., Poetry in Performance, Blood to Remember: Am. Poets on the Holocaust, South Fla. Poetry Rvw. Wrkg. on book of poetry based on interviews with holocaust survivors. Student Columbia U., 1957-58; MA in Creative Writing, CCNY, 1985. Tchr. English and drama High Schl. Fashion, NYC, 1955-

59; tchr. English and creative writing Norman Thomas High Schl., NYC, 1959-79. Named Poet of Yr., N.Y. Poetry Forum, 1981, CAAA genl. excellence in poetry awards, 1986, FFWA award in traditional verse, 1986, 1987, World Order of Narrative Poets Browning award for dramatic monologue and Ted Hughes award for poem on man/men, 1986 Golden Poet Award, World of Poetry, 1987. Mem. PSA, AG, AL, South Fla. Poetry Inst., Shelley Soc. (10th Anniversary award 1984, Irma Rhods award 1985). Home: 161-08 Jewel Ave Flushing NY 11365

SINGER, ISAAC BASHEVIS, b. Radzymin, Poland, July 14, 1904 (came to U.S., 1935, naturalized, 1943); s. Pinchos Menachem and Bathsheba (Zylberman) Singer; m. Alma Haimann, Feb. 14, 1940; 1 son—Israel. Author: Satan in Goray, 1935, The Family Moskat, 1950, Gimpel the Fool, 1957, The Magician of Lubin, 1960, The Spinoza of Market Street, 1961, The Slave, 1962, Short Friday, 1964, In My Father's Court, 1966, The Manor, 1967, The Seance, 1968, The Estate, 1969, A Friend of Kafka, 1970, Enemies, A Love Story, 1972, A Crown of Feathers, 1973, Passions, 1976, Lost in America, 1981, The Collected Stories of Isaac Bashevis Singer, 1982, The Golem, 1982, Love and Exile, 1984; also books for children including A Day of Pleasure, 1970 (Natl. Book award). Student, Rabbinical Sem., Warsaw, Poland, 1920-27; Litt.D. (hon.), L.I. U., 1979. With Hebrew and Yiddish publs. in Poland, 1926-35, Jewish Daily Forward (NYC), 1935—. Recipient Epstein Fiction award, 1963; Playboy award for best fiction/short story, 1967; Poses Creative Arts award, 1970; Natl. Book awards, 1970, 74; Nobel Prize for lit., 1978. Mem. Am. Acad. Arts and Scis. Address: 209 W 86th St New York NY 10024

SINGER, KURT DEUTSCH, b. Vienna, Austria, Aug. 10, 1911 (came to U.S., 1940, naturalized, 1951); s. Ignaz Deutsch and Irene (Singer) Singer); m. Hilda Tradelius, Dec. 23, 1932; children—Marian Alice Birgit, Kenneth Walt; 2nd m. Jane Sherrod, Jan., 1955. Author: The Coming War, 1934, Germany's Secret Service in Central America, 1943, Spies and Saboteurs in Argentina, 1943, Duel for the Northland, 1943, White Book of the Church of Norway, 1944, Spies and Traitors of World War II, 1945, Who are the Communists in America?, 1948, 3000 Years of Espionage, 1951, World's Greatest Women Spies, 1952, Kippie the Cow, juvenile, 1952, Gentlemen Spies, 1953, The Man in the Trojan Horse, 1954, World's Best Spy Stories, 1954, Charles Laughton Story; adapted TV, motion pictures, 1954, Spy Stories and Asia, 1955, More Spy Stories, 1955, My Greatest Crime Story, 1956, My Most Famous Case, 1957, The Danny Kaye Saga; My Strangest Case, 1958, Spy Omnibus, 1959, Spies for Democracy, 1960, Crime Omnibus Spies Who Changed History, 1961, Hemingway—Life and Death of a Giant, 1961, True Adventures in Crime, Dr. Albert Schweitzer, Medical Missionary, 1962, Lyndon Baines Johnson—Man of Reason, 1964, Ho-i-man, 1965, Kurt Singer's Ghost Omnibus, 1965, Kurt Singer's Horror Omnibus: The World's Greatest Stories of the Occult, The Unearthly, 1965, Mata Hari—Goddess of Sin, 1965, Lyndon Johnson—From Kennedy to Vietnam, 1966, Weird Tales Anthology, 1966, I Can't Sleep at Night, 1966, Weird Tales of Supernatural, 1967, Tales of Terror, 1967, Famous Short Stories, 1967, Folktales of the South Pacific, 1967, Tales of the Uncanny, 1968, Gothic Reader, 1968, Bloch and Bradbury, 1969, Folktales of Mexico, 1969, Tales of the Unknown, 1970, Tales of the Macabre, 1971, Ghouls and Ghosts, 1972, Satanic Omnibus, 1973, Gothic Horror Omnibus, 1974, Dictionary of Household Hints and Help, 1974, They Are Possessed, 1976, True Adventures into the Unknown, 1980, I Spied—And Survived, 1980,m Target Books of Horror, vols. 1-4, 1984-86; editor: UN Calendar, 1959-68. Student, U. Zurich, Switzerland, 1930, Labor Coll., Stockholm, 1936; PhD, Div. Coll. Metaphysics, Indpls., 1951. Escaped to Sweden, 1934; founder Ossietzky Com. (successful in release Ossietzky from concentration camp); corr. Swedish mag. Folket i Bild, 1935-40; founder Niemoller Com.; pub. biography Goring in Eng. (confiscated in Sweden), 1940; co-founder pro-Allied newspaper Trots Allt, 1939; corr. Swedish newspapers in U.S., 1940; editor News Background, 1942; lectr. U. Minn., U. Kans., U. Wis., 1945-49; radio commentator WKAT, 1950; corr. N. Am. Newspaper Alliance (NYC), 1953—; chair bd. Singer Communication Inc.; dir. Oceanic Press Service (Buena Park, CA); author, editor underground weekly Mitteilungsblatter (Berlin), 1933. Mem. UN Speakers Research Com., UN Children's Emergency Fund. Address: 3164 Tyler Ave Anaheim CA 92801

SINGER, MARCUS GEORGE, b. NYC, Jan. 4, 1926; s. David Emanuel and Esther (Kobre) Singer; m. Blanche Ladenson, Aug. 10, 1947; children—Karen Beth, Debra Ann. Author: Generalization in Ethics, 2nd ed., 1971; editor: Morals and Values, 1977, American Philosophy, 1986; contrbr.: Essays in Moral Philosophy, 1958, Encyc. of Philosophy, 1967, Skepticism and Moral Principles, 1973, Acad. Am. Encyc., 1982, World Book Encyc., 1984, 86, Gewirth's Ethical Rationalism, 1984, Morality and Universality, 1985, New Directions in Ethics, 1986; co-editor: Introductory Readings in Philosophy, 2nd ed., 1974, Reason and the Common Good, 1963, Belief, Knowledge and Truth, 1970. AB, U. Ill., 1948; PhD (Susan Linn Sage fellow), Cornell U., 1952. Asst. in philosophy Cornell U. (Ithaca, NY), 1948-49, instr. philosophy, 1951-52, U. Wis. at Madison, 1952-55, asst. prof., 1955-59, assoc. prof., 1959-63, prof. philosophy, 1963—, chair dept. philosophy, 1963-68; chair philosophy dept. U. Wis. Center System, 1964-66; dir. pub. lectr. series Royal Inst. Philosophy (London), 1984-85; vis. fellow Birkbeck Coll., U. London, 1962-63; research assoc. U. Calif. at Berkeley, 1969; vis. Cowling prof. philosophy Carleton Coll. (Northfield, MN), 1972; vis. prof. humanities U. Fla. (Gainesville), 1975; vis. fellow U. Warwick, 1977, 84-85; vis. Francis M. Bernardin disting. prof. humanities U. MO. (Kansas City), 1979; hon. research fellow Birkbeck Coll., U. London, 1984-85. Served with USAF, 1944-45. Mem. Am. Philo. Assn. (pres. 1985-86), Royal Inst. Philosophy, AAUP, Aristotelian Soc., Mind Assn., Wis. Acad. Scis., Arts and Letters. Home: 5021 Regent St Madison WI 53705

SINGER, NORMAN, b. Chgo., Aug. 10, 1932, s. Robert and Rene (Duquesne) S. Novelist: Curtain of Flesh, 1968, The Pornographer, 1968, The Babysitter, 1968, The Hungry Husband, 1969, The Lay of the Land, 1969, The Man Who Raped San Francisco, 1969, The Girl Explosion, 1971, Coming on Strong, 1972, The Girl Who Licked the World, 1975, The Cannibals Next Door, 1975, The Shakedown Kid, 1976, Diamond Stud, 1976; ghostwrtr., ed. over 85 books. Student Columbia U., U. Calif. Extension-San Francisco. Freelance wrtr. Mem. AL, Am. Address: 1847 Hayes St San Francisco CA 94117

SINGER, SARAH BETH, b. NYC, July 4, 1915; d. Samuel and Rose (Dunetz) White; m. Leon Eugene Singer, Nov. 23, 1938 (widowed 1980); children—Jack, Rachel. Author: Magic Casements, 1957, After the Beginning, 1975, Of Love and Shoes, 1987. contrbr. poetry to NY Times, McCalls, CSM, Bitterroot, N.Mex. Qtly, other lit mags and to anthologies, including American Women Poets, 1976, Yearbook of American Poetry, 1981, The Best of 1980, 1981 C.W. Post Chapbook, Judaism, The Jewish Frontier, The Lyric, etc.; cons. editor: Poet Lore, 1975-81. BA, NYU, 1934; postgrad., New Schl. Social Research, 1961-63. Tchr. creative writing Hillside Hosp. (Queens, NY), 1966-74; Samuel Field YMCA (Queens), 1980-82. Recipient Stephen Vincent Benet award Poet Lore, 1968, 71; prizes from The Ntl. League of Amer. Penwomen, The Lyric, and Eve's Legacy. Mem. Natl. League Am. Penwomen, PSA (vp 1974-78, exec. dir. L.I. 1979-84, James Joyce award 1972, Consuelo Ford award 1973, Gustav Davidson award, 1974, 1st prize award 1975, Celia Wagner award 1976), P&W. Address: 2360 43rd Ave East Unit 415 Seattle WA 98112

SINGH, SWAYAM PRABHA, b. Bangalore, Mysore, India, Aug. 26, 1945; s. Kripal Ananda and Sharada (Bai) Singh; m. Kesava B. Singh, June 15, 1967; children—Jyothi Kiran, Naveen Raj. Author: Learn to Cook Without Preservatives, Eat East Indian Way, 1980, Swayam's Authentic Cookbook of India, 1987, Journey From India (autobiography) vol. 1, 1988, vol. 2, 1989; ed. newsletters. Wrkg. on holistic health cookbook. Ed. St. Philominas Coll., Mysore City, India. Founder 1979, since pres. Singh Seven Seas Publs., Lansing, Mich; pres. Unique foods of India, Lansing, 1984—, Unique Inns of America, Lansing, 1987—; Unique Universal Gourmet Club, 1984—; freelance wrtr. Home: 2311 Meadowcroft Dr Lansing MI 48912

SINGLETON, JOAN VIETOR, b. Los Angeles, Nov. 8, 1951; d. Carl William and Elizabeth Anne (Caulfield) Vietor; m. W. Alexander Sheafe, Apr. 23, 1977 (div. 1981); m. Ralph Stuart Singleton, Dec. 21, 1984. Co-author: (screenplays) MIA—Missing in Action, 1982, The Baja Blaze, 1984; pub. 6 books on motion picture prodn./reference. BA, Hollins Coll., 1972. Owner, operator Joan Vietor Enterprises (pub. relations firm), Los Angeles, 1975-80; with acquisitions dept. Warner Bros., Burbank, Calif., 1980-81; freelance writer, Los Angeles, 1981—; pres. Lone Eagle Pub. Co., Beverly Hills, Calif., 1982—. Mem. Pubs. Mktg. Assn. (bd. dirs.). Office: 9903 Santa Monica Blvd. Beverly Hills CA 90212

SIROF, HARRIET TOBY, b. Oct. 18, 1930, d. Herman and Lillian (Miller) Hockman; m. Sidney M. Sirof, June 18, 1949; children—Laurie, David, Amy. Author juvenile novels: A New-Fashioned Love Story, 1977, Save the Dam!, 1981, That Certain Smile, 1982, The Real World, 1985, Anything You Can Do, 1986; author: The IF Machine, 1978, The Junior Encyclopedia of Israel, 1980; contrbr. short stories to N.Am. Rvw, Descant, Inlet, other anthologies and mags. BA, New Schl. Social Research, 1962. Writing instr. South Shore Adult Center, Bklyn., 1977-83, Long Island U., Bklyn., 1978-79, Bklyn. Coll., 1980-81, 84—, St. Johns U., Jamaica, N.Y., 1978—. Mem. AG, IWWG. Address: 792 E 21st St Brooklyn NY 11210

SITKA, WARREN, see Levi, Steven C.

SIVACK, DENIS, b. Little Falls, NY, Jan. 1, 1942; s. Albert Frederick and Helen Jane (DeForrest) S.; m. Veronica M. Balken, 1976 (div. 1982). Contrbr. poetry to Apogee, Catholic

World, Cloud Marauder, Commonweal, Epos, Espirit, Expatriate, L.I., Nassau rvws, For Now, Gnosis, Group 74, Hierophant, N.Y. Qtly, N.Y. Times, Sanskaras, The Smith, articles to N.Y. Running News On the Run, also Essays on the Work of Frederick Sommer. BA, Siena Coll., 1963; MA, Fortham U., 1965, postgrad. Instr. English, Mercy Coll., Dobbs Ferry, N.Y., 1964-67, asst. prof., 1967-69; lectr. English, Kingsborough Community Coll., Bklyn., 1969-71, asst. prof., dir. of freshman English, 1971—; book artist; photographer. Mellon fellow CUNY, 1986. Mem. NWU, P&W, N.Y. Poets Coop. (charter), Ctr. for Book Arts (secy). Home: 1165 E 54th St Apt 4F Brooklyn NY 11234

SIVERD, BONNIE, b. Greensburg, PA, Dec. 11, 1949; d. Charles and Helen (Kantorczyk) Shulock; m. Robert Joseph Siverd, Jan. 8, 1972; 1 son, Robert Joseph. Author: Count Your Change: A Woman's Guide to Sudden Financial Change, 1983, The Working Woman Financial Advisor, 1987. Contrbtr. articles, chpts. to books, jnls., mags. including Continental mag., N.Y. Habitat mag., numerous other. B.S. in Foreign Service, Georgetown U., 1971. Wrtr., Congessional Quarterly, Washington, 1971-73; reporter, researcher Time mag., N.Y.C., 1973-78; staff ed. Bus. Week, N.Y.C., 1978-81; personal finance analyst Cable News Network, N.Y.C., 1986-87; contrbg. ed. Working Woman, N.Y.C., 1981—. Home: 90 Partidge Rd Stamford CT 06903

SKAFTE, MARJORIE DORIS, b. Osseo, WI, Aug. 1, 1921, d. Nels E. and Regina B. (Severson) Westegard; m. Lloyd A. Skafte, Feb. 14, 1942 (div. 1979); children—Merilee Skafte Main, Patricia Skafte Pearman, Linwood, Robert. Student St. Olaf Coll., U. Minn. Ed. Ojibway Press, Duluth, 1964-71; ed. Harcourt Brace Jovanovich, Duluth, 1964—, pub., 1971—. Home: 4311 Tioga St Duluth MN 55804

SKALA, MARY JANE, b. Cleve., Dec. 13, 1948; d. Charles Roger and Dorothy Jane (Hauselman) Day; m. Philip Henry Snyder, June 27, 1970 (div. Sept. 1979); 1 dau., Sara Lynn; m. Robert Skala, Apr. 16, 1983 (div.); 1 son, Matthew Robert. Contrbr. articles to mags. Student Muskingum Coll., 1966-68; B.A. with honors, Michigan State U., 1970. Reporter Sun Newspapers, Cleve., 1972-81; asst. ed. Chessie System Railroad, Cleve., 1981-84, ed., 1984-85; public info. specialist Cuyahoga Commun. Coll., Cleve., 1987; ed. new Cleveland Woman mag., 1987—. Recipient Best Sports Story award Suburban Newspapers Am., 1975, Best Sports Feature award Ntl. Newspaper Assn., 1975, Best Overall Pub. award Assn. Railroad Eds., 1982, 84. Mem. SPJ, IABC (past bd. dirs.), Ohio Press Women. Home: 7662 Birchmont Chagrin Falls OH 44022

SKELTON, IRA STEVEN, b. Greenville, SC, Mar. 18, 1949; s. Ira Gordon and Jennie Louise (Campbell) S., Jr. Ed. P.E.T.: Potty Effectiveness Training (L.T. Raskind), 1977; editorial asst. Fitzgerald/Hemingway Annl., 1971, 72. contrbr. to U. S.C. lit. mag. The Crucible, Voices: Jnl Am. Acad. Psychotherapists. Wrkg. on uncollected papers and collected works of Alfred Adler. BA, Stetson U./U. S.C., 1972; postgrad. U. S.C., 1973-74, 76-77, 78, 80. Composition specialist State Printing Co., Columbia S.C., 1982-84; research assoc. U. S.C., Columbia, 1985; dir. Crown Agy., Columbia, 1985—; exec. dir. Great Works Fdn., 1985—; res. asst. prof., Schl. of Med., Dept. Pediatrics, U. of S.C., 1986—. Grantee Columbia Adlerian Soc., 1985, Fairfield Arts Council, 1986. Home: 220 W Durst Ave Greenwood SC 29646

SKEMER, ARNOLD MARIUS, b. NYC, Dec. 22, 1946; s. Alex and Lillian (Farber) S.; m. Leslie Helen Weiner, June 3, 1979; children: Roland, Melanie. Author: The Famine, 1985. BA, Queens Coll., 1968. Ed. Phrygian Press. Mem. COSMEP, Network Ind. Pubs. of Greater N.Y. Home: 58 09 205th St Bayside NY 11364

SKINNER, KNUTE (RUMSEY), b. St. Louis, MO, April 25, 1929; s. George Rumsey and Lidi (Skjoldvig) S.; m. Jeanne Pratt, 1953 (div. 1954), child—Frank; m. 2d Linda Ann Kuhn, March 30, 1961 (div. 1978), children—Dunstan, Morgan; m. 3d Edna Faye Kiel, March 25, 1978. Author: Stranger with a Watch, 1965, A Close Sky over Killaspuglonane, 1968, In Dinosaur Country, 1969, The Sorcerers: A Loatian Tale, 1972, Hearing of the Hard Times, 1981, The Flame Room, 1983, Selected Poems, 1985; ed. Bellingham Rvw, 1977—; contrbr. poetry, short stories to textbooks, periodicals. Student, Culver-Stockton Coll., 1947-49; BA, Univ. Northern Colo., 1951; MA, Middlebury Coll., 1954; PhD, Univ. of Iowa, 1958. Inst. Eng., 1955-56, 57-58, 60-61, U. of Iowa; asst. prof. Eng., Okla. Coll. for Women, 1961-62; lectr. creative wrtg., Western Washington Univ., 1962-71, assoc. prof. Eng., 1971-73, prof., 1973—; pres. Signpost Press, Inc., 1983—. NEA fellowship, 1975. Mem. PSA, Am. Comm. Irish Studies, Wash. Poets Assn. Home: 412 N State St Bellingham WA 98225

SKIPPER, DONALD BRUCE, b. Bayonne, NJ, Sept. 28, 1945; s. J. G. S.; m. Nadia Maria Franovich, May 25, 1979; children—Richard, Jonathan. Contrbr. articles o Armor Mag., Aviation Digest, others. BA, Wilmington Coll., 1967; M.S., U. Southern Calif., 1976. Commissioned 2d Lt. U.S. Army, 1968, advanced through ranks to lt. col., 1986, prof. St. Leo Coll., Atlanta, 1980—; mgr. ODT program, Ft. McPherson, GA, 1980-84; prof. Coll. of St. Francis, 1985—; mgr. training program, 1984-86; branch chief, Ft. Gillem, GA, 1986—. Recipient 1st place Writing award Aviation Diget, 1974, 4th Estate award U.S.A. Forces Command, 1981, Minute Man award Natl. Guard Bur., 1982; named Instr. of Yr., St. Leo Coll., 1986. Mem. Army Aviation Assn. Home: 827 Four Winds Ln Jonesboro GA 30236

SKLAR, GEORGE, b. Meriden, CT, June 1, 1908; s. Ezak and Bertha (Marshak) Sklar; m. Miriam Blecher, Aug. 22, 1935; children—Judith, Daniel, Zachary. Author: (with Albert Maltz) plays Merry Go Round, produced, Avon Theatre, NY, 1932, Peace on Earth, (with Albert Maltz), Theatre Union, 1933, Stevedore (with Paul Peters), Theatre Union, 1934, Parade (with Paul Peters), Theatre Guild, NYC, 1935, Life and Death of An American, produced by Fedl. Theatre Project, 1939; novel The Two Worlds of Johnny Truro, 1947; (with Vera Caspary) play Laura; produced at Cort Theatre, NYC, 1947; novel The Promising Young Men, 1951, The Housewarming, 1953, The Identity of Dr. Frazier, 1961; play And People All Around, 1966 (1966-67 selection Am. Playwrights Theatre), Brown Pelican, 1972. BA, Yale, 1929; postgrad. dept. drama, 1929-31. Mem. DG, AG. Address: 530 Fuller Ave Los Angeles CA 90036

SKLAR, MORTY E., (Mickey Sky), b. Sunnyside, NY, Nov. 28, 1935; s. Jack and Selma (Ehrlich) S.; m. Shelley Sterling, Aug. 1981 (div. Nov. 1983). Author: The Night We Stood Up For Our Rights, 1978; contrbr. poetry to: A to Z: 200 Contemporary Am. Poets, 1981, Abraxas, 1977, 1985, Open Places, 1985, others. BA in Engl., U. Iowa, 1975. Ed./pub. The Spirit That Moves Us Press, Iowa City, 1975—. Mem. CCLM. Orig. Engl. lang. publisher of poetry of Jaroslav Seifert, 1984 Nobel Prize winner. CCLM editor's grant, 1985. Office: Box 1585 Iowa City IA 52244

SKLAR, ROBERT ANTHONY, b. New Brunswick, NJ, Dec. 3, 1936; s. Leon George and Lilyn (Fuchs) Sklar; m. Kathryn Sue Kish, Nov. 27, 1958 (div. 1979); children—Leonard, Susan; m. 2d, Adrienne E. Harris, June 11, 1982. Author: F. Scott Fitzgerald, The Last Laocoon, 1967, Movie-Made America: A Cultural History of American Movies, 1975, Prime-Time America: Life on and Behind the Television Screen, 1980; editor: The Plastic Age, 1917-1930, 1970—; edl. bd. & bk. rvw. ed., CINEASTE mag.; contrbr. essays, articles, rvws. to publs. AB summa cum laude, Princeton U., 1958; student, U. Bonn, West Germany, 1959-60; PhD, Harvard, 1965. Rewriter AP (Newark), 1958-59; staff reporter Los Angeles Times, 1959; asst. prof. program Am. culture U. Mich. at Ann Arbor, 1965-69, assoc. prof. history, 1969-75, prof. history, 1975-76, mem. natl. humanities faculty, 1972-73; vis. prof. U. Auckland (New Zealand), 1970, U. Tokyo, 1971, Bard Coll., 1975-76; cultural historian, writer on movies, TV, Am. culture and soc.; prof. cinema NYU 1977—, chair dept. cinema studies, 1977-81. Guggenheim fellow, 1970-71, Rockefeller Fdn. Humanities fellow, 1976-77. Mem. Am. Studies Assn. (vp 1971), Soc. Cinema Studies (pres. 1979-81). Address: 284 Lafayette St New York NY 10012

SKOCHLAS, JOHN, b. Holyoke, MA, Nov. 12, 1949. Author: A Lilac Rebellion, 1985. Wrkg. on: Bohemian Banquet (novel). BA, Holy Cross Coll., 1971. Novelist. Address: Box 433 Northampton MA 01061

SKOYLES, JOHN, b. NYC, Dec. 11, 1949, s. Gerard Francis Xavier and Olga (Bertolotti) S.; m. Maria Flook, June 9, 1984; 1 dau., Kate. Author book of poetry: A Little Faith, 1981. AB, Fairfield (Conn.) U., 1971; MA, MFA, U. Iowa, 1974. Asst. prof. So. Meth. U., Dallas, 1976-79; chmn. writing comm. Fine Arts Work Center, Provincetown, Mass., 1979-81; mem. writing faculty Sarah Lawrence Coll., Bronxville, N.Y., 1981-84; dir. MFA program for wrtrs. Warren Wilson Coll., Swannanoa, N.C., 1984—. Fine Arts Work Center writing fellow, 1974-75, 75-76; grantee NEA, 1976; N.Y. State Arts Council poetry fellow, 1983. Home: 403 W Connally St Black Mountain NC 28711

SKRABANEK, DONALD W., (D.S. Phantom), b. Baytown, TX, Nov. 18, 1951, s. Vernon E. and Alice Hazel (von Roeder) S.; m. Anne Rose Souby, Apr. 21, 1981; children—Alana Elizabeth, Ava Marlies. Author: Texas Rising (novel), 1978, Kitty Torture, 1979, 81, Publishing Tactics, 1980, Fear of the Retro-Image (one-act play), 1981; ed., compiler: Texas Publishers & Publications Directory (grantee NEA-Tex. Commn. on Arts, named best reference work Border Regional Library Assn.), 1980, 82, Freelance Opportunities in Texas Publishing, 1982, Phantom Phrases (anthology of cosmic fiction), 1982, The Best of KTQ Magazine, 1982; ed.: KTQ Mag., 1980-81; contrbr.: Lone Star Mag. of Humor, Pawn Rvw, N.Mex. Humanities Rvw, other publs. BA in English, U. Houston, 1974, MA, 1976. Freelance wrtr., 1974—, ed., 1980—; owner, pub., ed. S&S Press, Austin,

Tex., 1978—. Mem. Tex. Circuit, Tex. Assn. Creative Writing Tchrs. Office: Box 5931 Austin TX 78763

SKY, MICKEY, see Sklar, Morty E.

SLAPPEY, MARY MC GOWAN, b. Kitrell, NC, Nov. 22, 1914; d. Walter Gordon and Mary Jouvette (McGowan) S. Author: Exploring Opportunities for Women in Military Service, 1986. Contrbr. poems to anthols., prose, non-fiction to mags., trade jnls. Author: novels— Glory of Wooden Walls, Forever Love, Sallie Robbin, Plum Blossom. A.B., George Washington U., 1947; J.D., Intl. Schl. Law, 1977. Free-lance wrtr., 1970—. Recipient Laurel Wreath, Poet Laureates Intl., 1978. Mem. Federal Poets (pres. 1976-78). Home: 4500 Chesapeake St NW Washington DC 20016

SLATKIN, MARCIA, b. NYC, Jan. 27, 1943; s. Benjamin and Doris (Prager) Smilowitz; m. Dan Slatkin, June 9, 1963 (div. May 1976); children: Heidi, Rebecca. Author: (poems) Poems: 1973-81, Mothers and Daughters, 1984; contrbr. fiction to San Francisco Chronicle, Newsday, poetry to Xanadu, Street Mag., N.Mex. Poetry Rvw, also others. BA, Queens Coll., 1963; MA in English, NYU, 1964, postgrad., 1972. Tchr. cello Brentwood High Schl., L.I., N.Y., 1972-74; tchr. English, Comsewogue High Schl., Port Jefferson Station, L.I., 1974—. Recipient Walt Whitman award for poetry, 1976; syndicated fiction project award PEN, 1985, 86. Mem. P&W. Home: Box 2036 Setauket NY 11733

SLATOFF, WALTER JACOB, b. NYC, Mar. 1, 1922; s. Ellis and Jeannette (Armstrong) S.; m. Jane Metzger, Sept. 10, 1946; children: Joan, Donald. Author: Quest for Failure: A Study of William Faulkner, 1960; With Respect to Readers: Dimensions of Literary Response, 1970; The Look of Distance: Reflections on Suffering and Sympathy in Modern Literature—Auden to Agree, Whitman to Woolf, 1985; co-ed. Epoch mag., 1956-84. BA, Columbia U., 1943; MA, U. Mich., 1950, PhD, 1955. Freelance wrtrs., 1946-49; instr. English, Cornell U., Ithaca, N.Y., 1955-58, asst. prof., 1958-64, assoc. prof., 1964-70, prof., 1970—. Served with AUS, 1943-46; ETO. Home: 23 Renwick Hgts Rd Ithaca NY 14850

SLAVITT, DAVID RYTMAN, (Henry Sutton, David Benjamin), b. White Plains, NY, Mar. 23, 1935, s. Samuel Saul and Adele Beatrice (Rytman) S.; m. Lynn Nita Meyer, Aug. 27, 1956 (div. 1977); children—Evan Meyer, Sarah Slavitt Bryce, Joshua Rytman; m. 2d, Janet Lee Abrahm, Apr. 16, 1978. Author poetry: Suits for the Dead, 1961, The Carnivore, 1965, Day Sailing, 1968, The Eclogues of Virgil, 1971, Child's Play, 1972, The Eclogues and the Georgics of Virgil, 1972, Vital Signs: New and Selected Poems, 1975, Rounding the Horn, 1978, Dozens, 1981, Big Nose, 1983, The Elegies to Delia of Albius Tibullus, 1985, The Tristia of Ovid, 1986, The Walls of Thebes, 1986; author fiction: Rochelle, or Virtue Rewarded, 1967, Feel Free, 1968, Anagrams, 1970, ABCD, 1972, The Outer Mongolian, 1973, King of Hearts, 1976, Jo Stern, 1978, Cold Comfort, 1980, Ringer, 1982, Alice at 80, 1984, The Agent (with Bill Adler), 1986, The Hussar, 1987; novelist as Henry Sutton: The Exhibitionist, 1967, The Voyeur, 1968, Vector, 1970, The Liberated, 1973, The Sacrifice, 1978, The Proposal, 1980; as Lynn Meyer: Paperback Thriller, 1975; as Henry Lazarus: That Golden Woman, 1976; as David Benjamin: The Idol, 1979, Observing Physicians (nonfiction), 1987; ed. Land of Superior Mirages: New and Selected Poems of Adrien Stoutenberg, 1986. BA, Yale U., 1956; MA, Columbia U., 1957. Assoc. ed. Newsweek mag., NYC, 1958-65; asst. prof. U. Md., College Park, 1977; assoc. prof. Temple U., Phila., 1978-80; lectr. Columbia U., NYC, 1985-86, lectr. Rutgers U., 1987—. Recipient award Pa. Council on Arts, 1985. Home: 523 S 41st St Philadelphia PA 19104

SLEDD, JAMES HINTON, b. Atlanta, Dec. 5, 1914; s. Andrew and Annie Florence (Candler) Sledd; m. Joan Webb, July 16, 1939; children—Andrew, Robert, James, John, Ann. Author, editor of books on linguistics, contrbr. articles to profl. jnls. BA, Emory U., 1936, Oxford U., 1939; PhD, U. Tex., 1947; postdoctoral studies, U. Mich., 1948, U. Chgo., 1951. Instr. English U. Chgo., 1945-46, asst. prof., 1948-55, assoc. prof., 1955-56; asst. prof. Duke, 1946-48; assoc. prof. U. Calif. at Berkeley, 1956-59; vis. prof. U. Ceylon, 1959-60; prof. Northwestern U. (Evanston, IL), 1960-64, U. Tex. (Austin), 1964-85; vis. prof. U. Mich., summer 1956, U. London, 1963, U. Wash., summer 1963, Mont. State U., summer, 1967, others; now ret. Mem. MLA, Linguistic Soc. Address: Box 5311 Austin TX 78763

SLIM, MEMPHIS, see Sullivan, Larr Michael

SLOAN, JAMES PARK, b. Greenwood, SC, Sept. 22, 1944; s. James Park and Alice Catherine (Gaines) Sloan; m. Jeanette Carol Pasin, July 25, 1968 (div. June 1987); children—Eugene Blakely, Anna Jeanette. Author: War Games (Best First Novel award Gt. Lakes Colls. Assn. 1971), 1971 (Peggy McPhaul award Midwestern Writers Assn. 1971), The Case History of Comrade V, 1972 (Friends of Lit. award 1972), The Last Cold-War Cowboy, 1987; contrbg. editor: Am. Pen Qtly, 1974—. BA, harvard U., 1968. Mem. faculty U. Ill., Chgo. Circle, 1972—, assoc. prof. English, 1976—, chair program for writers, 1976-79. Served with USAR, 1964-67, Vietnam. Address: Dept Eng Univ Ill Chicago IL 60680

SLOTKIN, RICHARD SIDNEY, b. Bklyn., Nov,. 8, 1942; s. Herman and Roselyn B. (Seplowitz) Slotkin; m. Iris F. Shupack, June 23, 1963; 1 son—Joel Elliot. Author: Regeneration Through Violence: The Mythology of the American Frontier, 1600-1860, 1973 (Albert Beveridge award Am. Hist. Assn.), (with J.K. Folsom) So Dreadful a Judgement: Puritan Responses to King Philip's War, 1675-1677, 1978, The Crater: A Novel of the Civil War, 1980, The Fatal Environment: The Myth of the Frontier in the Age of Industrialization, 1800-1890, 1985 (Little Big Horn Associates Literary Award). BA, Bklyn. Coll., 1963; PhD, Brown U., 1967; MA (hon.), Wesleyan U., 1976. Mem. faculty Wesleyan U. (Middletown, CT), 1966—, prof. English, 1976—, Olin prof., 1982—, chair dept. Am. studies, 1976. Recipient Don. D. Walker prize AQ; Award for Distinguised Achievement, Brown Univ. Grad. Schl. Mem. Society of Amer. Historians, Am. Film Inst., MLA, ASA, AHA, AAUP. Address: Eng Dept Wesleyan U Middletown CT 06457

SLOWINSKI, EMIL JOHN, b. Newark, Oct. 12, 1922; s. Emil John and Helen (Zaworski) Slowinski; m. Emily Dayton, June 16, 1951; children—David A., Walter D., Nathan T., Amy H., Marya R. Author: (with W.L. Masterton) Chemical Principles, 1966, 6th ed., 1985, Chemical Principles in the Laboratory, 1969, 4th ed., 1985, Mathematical Preparation for General Chemistry, 1970, Elementary Mathematical Preparation for General Chemistry, 1974, 2nd ed., 1982, Chemical Principles in the Laboratory with Qualitative Analysis, 1974, Qualitative Analysis and the Properties of Ions in Aqueous Solution, 1971, Chemistry, 1980. BS, U. Mass., 1946; PhD, MIT, 1949. Instr. Swarthmore Coll., 1949-52; instr., asst. prof., assoc. ,rof. U. Conn., 1952-64; prof. chemistry Macalester Coll., St. Paul, 1964—, chair dept., 1964-70; NSF sci. faculty fellow Oxford U., 1960-61; Natl. Acad. Scis. Exchange prof. U. Warsaw, 1968-69. Served with AUS, 1943-46; ETO. Mem. Am. Chem. Soc., AAUP. Office: Dept Chem Macalester Coll St Paul MN 55105

SLUDIKOFF, STANLEY ROBERT, b. Bronx, NY, July 17, 1935; s. Harry and Lillie (Elberger) Sludikoff; m. Ann Paula Blumberg, June 30, 1972; children—Lisa Beth, Jaime Dawn, Bonnie Joy. Author: (under pen name Stanley Roberts): Winning Blackjack, 1971, How to Win at Weekend Blackjack, 1973, Robert's Rules of Gambling, 1977, Gambling Times Guide to Blackjack, 1983, The Beginner's Guide to Winning Blackjack, 1983, According to Gambling Times: The Rules of Casino Games, 1983, The Casino Gourmet, 6 vols., 1984, Casinos of the Caribbean, 1984; Gambling Times Guide to Casino Games (4-part video), 1986. B.Arch., Pratt Inst., 1957; grad. student, U. So. Calif., 1960-62. Lic. architect, real estate broker. Project planner Robert E. Alexander, F.A.I.A. & Assos. (Los Angeles), 1965-66, Daniel, Mann, Johnson & Mendenhall (City and Regional Planning Cons.), 1967-70; pres., publisher Gambling Times Inc., also Two Worlds Mgmt., Inc. (Los Angeles), 1971—; pres. Las Vegas TV Weekly, also Postal West, (Las Vegas), 1975—; founder Stanley Roberts Schl. Winning Blackjack, 1976; instr. city and regional planning program U. So. Calif., 1960-63. Served to lt. col. U.S. Army Res.; Meritorious Svc. medal, 1985. Recipient commendation from mayor Los Angeles for work on model cities funding, 1968. Home: 17437 Tarzana St Encino CA 91316

SMALLENBURG, HARRY RUSSELL, b. Burbank, CA, July 17, 1942, s. Harry Walter and Carol Jane (Thornton) S.; m. Renee June DeYoe, Mar. 27, 1962 (div. 1972); 1 dau., Elizabeth Anne; m. 2d, Deborah Katherine Outland, Sept. 15, 1974 (div. 1987); 1 dau., Jessamyn Ellen. Contrbr. to: New Art Examiner, Art Rvw, At Art Center, Ency. Brittanica Annual, 1987, Exposure, 1987, other publs. PhD, U. Calif.-Berkeley, 1971; MFA in Photography, Cranbrook Art Acad., Bloomfield Hills, Mich., 1978. Asst. prof. English Wayne State U., Detroit, 1970-76; prof., dept. chmn. Center for Creative Studies, Detroit, 1976—; publs. dir. Art Center Coll. Design, Pasadena, Calif., 1984-85. Mem. MLA. Home: 730 E Tujunga St Apt D Burbank CA 91501

SMARIO, THOMAS MICHAEL, b. Oakland, CA, Mar. 5, 1950, s. Babe and Ida (Ralston) S.; m. Marilyn Louise Bechtle, Dec. 6, 1980; children—Doug, Tim, Michelle. Author: The Soles of My Shoes, 1975, Lines, 1978, Luckynuts & Real People, 1979, The Cat's Pajamas, 1982, Spring Fever, 1985, Handbook of Orthopaedic Casting, 1987. AA, Laney Coll., 1970. Poet-in-residence Oregon Arts Commn., Salem, 1976-78; orthopedic technician Good Samaritan Hosp., Portland, Oreg., 1977-78, Kaiser Edn., Portland, 1978—. Mem. Oreg. State Poetry Assn., Portland Poetry Festival, P&W. Home: 11900 SE Foster Pl Portland OR 97266

SMART, WILLIAM EDWARD JR., b. Jefferson City, MO, Feb. 28, 1933, s. William Edward and May Ferne (Whiteside) S.; m. Marymartha Kistenmacher, July 26, 1955 (div. 1975); children—Paul, David, Fern; m. 2d Juliana Frosch, Dec. 26, 1976 (div. 1987); children—Sarah, Jessie. Ed.: Eight Modern Essayists, 1965, 73, 80, 85, Women & Men/Men & Women, 1975, From Mt. St. Angelo, 1984; contrbr. short stories, poems, essays to Kenyon Rvw, New Republic, WIND, other publs. Wrkg. on novel. AB, Kenyon Coll., 1955; MA, U. Conn., 1960. Mem. faculty dept. English Skidmore Coll., Saratoga Springs, N.Y., 1960-64, Sweet Briar (Va.) Coll., 1966—; dir. Va. Center for Creative Arts, Swwet Briar, 1975—. Grantee Fulbright Fdn., Eng., 1964-66; fellow Va. Center for Creative Arts, 1974, 75, Tyrone Guthrie Centre, Ireland, 1983, 85; vis. artist Am. Acad. in Rome, 1985. Home: Mount San Angelo Sweet Briar VA 24595

SMELSER, NEIL JOSEPH, b. Kakoka, MO, July 22, 1930; s. Joseph Nelson and Susie Marie (Hess) Smelser; m. Helen Thelma Margolis, June 10, 1954 (div. 1965); children—Eric Jonathan, Tina Rachel; 2nd m. Sharin Fateley, Dec. 20, 1967; children—Joseph Neil, Sarah Joanne. Author: (with T. Parsons) Economy and Society, 1956, Social Change in the Industrial Revolution, 1959, Theory of Collective Behavior, 1962, The Sociology of Economic Life, 1963, 2nd ed., 1975, Essays in Sociological Explanation, 1968, Comparative Methods in the Social Sciences, 1976, (with Robin Content) The Changing Academic market, 1980, Sociology, 1981, end edit., 1984; editor: (with W.T. Smelser) Personality and Social Systems, 1963, 2nd ed., 1971, (with S.M. Lipset) Social Structure and Mobility in Economic Development, 1966, Sociology, 1967, 2nd ed., 1973, (with James Davis) Sociology, a Survey Report, 1969, Karl Marx on Society and Social Change, 1973, (with Gabriel Almond) Public Higher Education in California, 1974, (with Erik Erikson) Themes of Work and Love in Adulthood, 1980, (with Jeffrey Alexander, Bernhard Giesen, Richard Münch) The Micro-Macro Link, 1987. BA, Harvard U., 1952, PhD, 1958; BA, Magdalen Coll., Oxford (Eng.) U., 1954, MA, 1959; grad. San Francisco Psychoanalytic Inst., 1971. Mem. faculty U. Calif. at Berkeley, 1958—, prof. sociology, 1962—, asst. chancellor ednl. devel., 1966-68; assoc. dir. Inst. Intl. Relations, 1969-73, 80—, Univ. prof. sociology, 1972, dir. edn. abroad program for U.K. and Ireland, 1977-79; bd. dirs. Fdn. Fund for Research in Psychiatry, 1967-70; bd. dirs. Social Sci. Research Council, 1968-71, chair, 1971-73; trustee Center for Advanced Study in Behavioral and Social Scis., 1980-86, chair, 1984-86, mem. subcom. humanism Am. Bd. Internal Medicine, 1981-85; editor Am. Sociol. Rvw, 1962-65; advisory editor Am. Jnl Sociology, 1960-62; mem. com. econ. growth Social Sci. Research Council, 1961-65; chair sociology panel Behavioral and Social Scis. survey Natl. Acad. Scis. and Social Sci. Research Council, 1967-69; mem. com. on basic research in behavioral and social scis., 1980-81, chair, 1982-83, co-chair, 1984-86. Home: 109 Hillcrest Rd Berkeley CA 94705

SMERALDI, FLORENCE G. STARK, b. NYC, 1938, d. Arthur and Mary (Kraus) Stark; m. Mario L. Smeraldi, Sept. 11, 1960; children—Lisa J., Eric M., Ed.: Wave Hill Newsletter, 1981-83, Jewish Meml. Hosp. Newsletter, 1983-84; contrbr. Cannon Ball Express, Community Network Yellow Pages, Bronx NOW. BS, CUNY, 1979. Asst. to exec. dir. Lincoln Sq., NYC, 1984-85; exec. secy./fundraiser The Blue Card, NYC, 1985—, consultent and spkr. to not-for-profit organizations. Home: 3400 Fort Independence St New York NY 10463

SMETZER, MICHAEL BERNIE, b. Terre Haute, IN, Mar. 25, 1948; s. Bernie Franklin and Viola Irene (Dyer) S. Contrbr. poetry fiction, rvws. to City Moon, Cottonwood, Kans. Qtly, Open House, Hanging Loose, New Letters, Poetry Now, others. BA, Purdue U., 1971; MA, Valparaiso U., 1972; MFA, Bowling Green State U., 1985. Lectr. Univ. Kans., Lawrence, 1979-83, 85—, ed. Naked Man, Lawrence, 1981—, ed. Grad News Paper, 1978-79, ed.-in-chief Cottonwood Rvw, 1974-78; tchg. fellow Bowling Green State Univ., Oh., 1983-85, asst. ed. Mid-Am. Rvw, 1984-85. Mem. AWP, MLA, Kansas Wrtrs. Assn. Address: 947 Mississippi St Apt A Lawrence KS 66044

SMILEY, TERAH LEROY, b. Oak Hill, KS, Aug. 21, 1914; s. Terah Edward and Frances Angelina (Huls) Smiley; m. Marie Lemley, July 1935; 1 dau.—Terrie Lucille Scheele; 2nd m. Winifred Whiting Lindsay, June 10, 1947; children—John, Maureen, Kathlyn; 1 stepdau.—Margaret Ann Taylor. Editor: (with James H. Zumberge) Polar Deserts and Modern Man, 1974, The Geological Story of the World's Deserts, 1982, (with T.L. Pewe) Landscapes of Arizona: The Geological Story, 1984. Student, U. Kans., 1934-36; MA, U. Ariz., 1949. With U.S. Natl. Park Service, 1939-41, U.S. Immigration Service, 1941-42; research Lab. of Tree-Ring, U. Ariz. (Tucson), 1946-60, dir., 1958-60, dir. geochronology labs., 1957-67, head dept., 1967–70, chmn. Intl. Conf. on Forest Tree Growth (Tucson), 1960; vice chair. U.S. Com. on Intl. Assn. for Quaternary Research, Natl. Acad. Sci., 1961-66; mem. 1st Intl. Hydrological Decade, Natl. Acad. Sci., 1964-66;, genl. chmn. Intl. Conf., 1969, Am. Assn. for the Advancement of Science; served with USNR, 1942-45. Home: 2732 N Gill Ave Tucson AZ 85719

SMILEY, VIRGINIA KESTER, (Tess Ewing), b. Rochester, NY, Feb. 21, 1923, d. Harold P. and Isabell (Fleming) Kester; m. Robert Porter Smiley, Sept. 8, 1945; children—Suzanne P., Kimberly D. Author: (juvenile fiction) Little Boy Navajo, 1954, The Buzzing Bees, 1956, Swirling Sands, 1958, A Horse for Matthew Allen, 1972, Fuji Stick (in A Sun That Warms), 1970, Sugarbush Spring, 1985, Love in the Wings, 1987; (romances) Cove of Fear, 1974, Guest at Gladehaven, 1972, Mansion of Mystery, 1973, Nurse Karen's Summer of Fear, 1979, Tender Betrayal, 1984, A Haven for Jenny, 1969, Under Purple Skies, 1972, Love Rides the Rapids, 1980, Starburst, 1982, High Country Nurse, 1970, Nurse of the Grand Canyon, 1973, Nurse for Morgan Acres, 1973, Nurse for the Civic Center, 1974, Libby Williams—Nurse Practitioner, 1975, Lisa Hunt—Pediatric Nurse, 1976, Nurse Delia's Choice, 1977, Nurse Kate's Mercy Flight, 1968, Sugarbush Nurse, 1981; contrbr. articles, short stories to numerous youth and family publs. Mem. Romance Wrtrs. Am., MWA, Soc. Children's Book Wrtrs. Address: 669 Webster Rd Webster NY 14580

SMITH, A. ROBERT, b. York, PA, Feb. 13, 1925; s. Arthur R. and Inez (Dunnick) Smith; m. Elizabeth McDowell Morgan, May 28, 1967; children—Mrs. Dana C. Cutler, Philip S. Morgan IV, Edward A.M. Morgan, Elizabeth A. Morgan. Author: The Tiger in the Senate, 1962 (with Eric Sevareid and Fred J. Maroon) Washington: Magnificent Capital, 1965, (with James V. Giles) An American Rape, 1975. BS, Juniata Coll., 1950; postgrad., George Washington U., 1950. Washington corr. Eugene Register-Guard (OR), 1951-78; Portland Oregonian, 1953-72; assoc. editor Virginian-Pilot, Norfolk, Va., 1978-83; editor Assn. Research and Enlightenment mag. (Virginia Beach, VA), 1984—. Served with USNR, 1943-46; PTO. Address: Box 595 Virginia Beach VA 23451

SMITH, ALAN HARVEY, b. Wilkes-Barre, PA, May 4, 1920; s. Harold Daniel and Florence (Sugden) Smith; m. Rugh Zimmerman, Nov. 3, 1944; 1 dau.—Jill Clerihew. BA, Bucknell U., 1941; MA, Columbia U., 1951; postgrad., Harvard U., 1948-49. Tchr. Lewisburg High Schl. (PA), 1941-42; instr. English Rensselaer Poly. Inst. (Troy, NY), 1946-48; asst. editor Americana Annual, Grolier, Inc. (NYC), 1950-53, sr. asst. editor, 1953-58, assoc. editor, 1958-59, Encyc. Americana (Danbury, CT), 1959-65, exec. editor, 1965-81, editor-in-chief, 1981—. Served with USNR, 1942-45. Office: Grolier Sherman Trnpk Danbury CT 06816

SMITH, ANNE MOLLEGEN, b. Meridian, MS; d. Albert Theodore and Ione (Rush) Mollegen; m. David Fay Smith; 1 dau., Amanda Wetherbee Smith. Ed., Redbook's Famous Fiction (anthology), 1977. BA, Smith Coll. Fiction ed., Redbook, 1967-77, mng. ed., 1978-81, ed.-in-chief, 1981-83; exec. ed. Glamour, 1983; ed.-in-chief Working Woman Mag., 1984—; co-chair of bd. Nuclear Times mag., 1986-m. Mem. Women's Media Group, Editors Organizing Comm. Natl. Mag. award, fict., ASME/Columbia U. Schl. Jnlsm., 1974. Office: WW 342 Madison Ave New York NY 10173

SMITH, ANNIE, see Smith, Louise Hamilton

SMITH, BARBARA HERRNSTEIN, b. NYC, Aug. 6, 1932; d. Benjamin and Ann (Weinstein) Brodo; m. Richard J. Herrnstein, May 28, 1951 (div. Aug. 1961); 1 dau.—Julia; 2nd m. Thomas H. Smith, Feb. 21, 1964 (div. Nov. 1974); 1 dau.—Deirdre Maud. Author: Poetic Closure: A Study of How Poems End, 1968, On the Margins of Discourse: the Relation of Literature to Language, 1978; editor: Discussions of Shakespeare's Sonnets, 1969; mem. editorial bd.: Critical Inquiry, PMLA, 1978-80; assoc. editor: Poetics Today. Student, CCNY, 1950-52; BA summa cum laude, Brandeis U., 1954, MA, 1955, PhD, 1965. Instr. English Sanz Schl. Langs. (Washington), 1956-57; teaching and research asst. Brandeis U., 1959-61, instr. dept. English and Am. lit., 1961-62; faculty div. lit. and langs. Bennington Coll. (VT), 1962-74; vis. lectr. Annenberg Schl. Communications, U. PA, 1973-74, prof. English and communications, 1974—, dir. Center for Study Art and Symbolic Behavior, 1979, univ. prof., 1980—; Judge William Riley Parker prize com. MLA, 1970-71; mem. bd. judges Explicator Award, 1975—; mem. supervising com. English Inst., 1977—; pres. Acad. Lit. Studies, 1983-84. Recipient Christian Gauss award, 1968, Explicator award, 1968. Mem. MLA, AAAS, Acad. Lit. Studies, Soc. for Critical Exchange. Address: 4632 Larchwood Ave Philadelphia PA 19143

SMITH, BERNITA LOUISE, b. Beloit, KS, Mar. 25, 1952, d. Raymond Lewis and Louise Frances (Yost) Smith. Contrbr. short stories: Children's Digest, R-A-D-A-R, Youth! Editor's Desk, Alive! For Young Teens; contrbr. poetry: Byline mag., Clubhouse, Ideals. Editor's Desk, Our Little Friend; contribr. non-fiction arts.; Byline mag., Editor's Desk, KANSAS! mag. Wrkg. on juvenile fiction, poetry, song lyrics. Student public schs., Downs, Kans. Photographer, wrtr. Brush Art Corp., Downs, 1970-77, head copywrtr., 1978-83; freelance wrtr., 1983—. Winner competitions Byline mag., 1986 6th dist. of

Kansas Author's Club, 1986; Editor's Desk mag., 1987. Home: Rt 1 Box 46 Downs KS 67437

SMITH, BERTIE REECE, b. Monroe, NC, Nov. 16, 1913; d. Allen Clinton and Lula Cora (Jones) Reece; m. Reginald Lowell Smith, Dec. 24, 1932 (dec. May 1980); children—Reginald Lowell, Wayne Reece. Contrbr. poetry to Lace and Pig Iron, 1931, A Time for Poetry, 1966, Quaderni di Poesia, 1977, Colonnades, 1981, Masters of Modern Poetry, 1981, Soundings in Poetry, 1981, Rainbows, 1985. Ed. Ideal Business College, Queens College. Sr. Service Reviewer, Equifax, Inc., Charlotte, NC, 1933-83; personnel dir. Southern Engineering, Charlotte, 1957-58. Hon. mention, Carl Sandburg Award, NC Poetry Soc., 1976. Mem: NC Poetry Soc., Natl. Federation of Poetry Socs., AAP. Home: 1012 Keystone Ct Charlotte NC 28210

SMITH, BRIDGET ANN, b. Washington, Sept. 30, 1949; d. Bernard Diamond and Catherine Frances (Mullins) S.; m. James Beale Asper, Aug. 30, 1975; children—Sarah Asper-Smith, Brenna Asper-Smith. Author: Color in Rain Country, 1981, On People and Things Alaskan, 1983, Death of an Alakan Princess, 1988. B.A. in Edn., U. Alaska, 1972; M.A. in Psychology, Catholic U. Am., 1973. Clinician, Mental Health Clinic, Juneau, AK, 1976-79; counsellor Parent Aide Program, Juneau, 1981-85; guardian ad litem Superior Ct., Juneau, 1982-85; lectr. in psychology U. Alaska, Juneau, 1974—. Home: 137 Sixth St Juneau AK 99801

SMITH, C. RAY, b. Birmingham, AL, Mar. 3, 1929; s. Calvin Ray and Sara Amanda (Kelly) Smith; m. Leslie Armstrong, Dec. 17, 1971 (div.); 1 son—Sinclair Scott. Author: books, including The American Endless Weekend, 1972, Supermanerism: New Attitudes in Post Modern Architecture, 1977, AIGA Graphic Design USA: 1, 1980; co-author (with Allen Tate) Interior Design in the Twentieth Century, 1986, Interior Design in Twentieth Century America: A History, 1987; editor: The Theatre Crafts Book of Costume, 1973, The Theatre Crafts Book of makeup, Masks and Wigs, 1974; contrbr. articles to newspaper, profl. jnls, periodicals, encys. BA in English, Kenyon Coll., 1951; MA, Yale U., 1958; student, Royal Acad. Dramatic Art, London, 1956-57. Asst. editor Interior Design mag., 1959-60; from assoc. editor to sr. and features editor Progressive Architecture mag., 1961-70; editor Theatre Crafts Mag., 1969-74; editor-in-chief Interiors and Residential Interiors mags., 1974-76; design ed. Unique Homes mag., 1986—; free-lance author, editor lectr.; cons. pub. relations, design; tchr. Parsons Schl. Design (NYC), 1978-84, Fashion Inst. of Technology (NYC), 1985—. Served with AUS, 1952-54; ETO. Home: Box 32 Krumsville PA 19534

SMITH, CAROL STURM, b. Trenton, NJ, Oct. 28, 1938, d. Joseph and Sarah (Kleinman) Sturm; m. Stanley Palmer Smith, Mar. 14, 1964 (div. 1980); 1 dau., Sharian Dove; m. 2d, Wesley Edmund Beaumont, Nov. 21, 1981. Co-author: The Complete Kitchen Guide, 1968, 77, The Cookbook Library (18 vols.), 1968-69, 84; author: For Love of Ivy, 1968, What's Up, Doc?, 1972, The End, 1975, Fat People, 1975, Renewal, 1982, The Right Time, 1982, Partners, 1982, Only a Dream, 1984; collaborator: The Child and the Serpent (by Sy Cook), 1980. BA, NYU, 1961. Asst. ed. Coward- McCann, NYC, 1961-63; assoc. ed. G.P. Putnam & Sons, NYC, 1963-64, New Am. Library, NYC, 1965-66. Grantee N.Y. State Council on Arts, 1972; MacDowell Colony fellow. Mem. AG, PEN. Home: Box 63A Scotch Rd Pennington NJ 08534

SMITH, CHARLES, (Charles Wasegaboah), b. Zanesville, OH, July 13, 1947; s. George Elmer MacMillen and Mary Lydia Smith; m. Brenda Joyce Fries, Apr. 4, 1976. Author, lecturer; resource guide & training progam for small retail operator, 1981, Security Poser series, 1982. Contrbr. articles to mags. A.A.S. in Safety-Security Technology, Ohio U., 1984, B.Criminal Justice, 1985. Mgr. Seaway Distributing Inc., Newark, OH, 1971-80; owner Smith Exec. Services, McArthur, OH, 1980—; prof. ind. studies Ohio U., Athens, 1986—. Home Rt 1 Box 47B McArthur OH 45651

SMITH, CHERYL S., b. Congers, NY, Feb. 14, 1949, d. George Woodrow and Margaret Pearl (Springstead) Smith. Playwright: The Writing Life, 1984; contrbr. episode story idea, dialogue to M*A*S*H, 1972; contrbr. articles to San Jose Mercury News, Oceanic Soc. publ. Student, Cedar Crest Coll., Allentown, Pa., 1971. Communications mgr. Litton Industries, Orangeburg, N.Y., 1971-72; ed. Prentice Hall, Englewood Cliffs, N.J., 1972-77; public relations specialist Natl. Info. Systems, Cupertino, Calif., 1982-86. Recipient writing awards Maltese Falcon Soc., San Francisco, 1983, Wrtr.'s Digest, 1985, Florida Freelance Wrtrs. Assn., 1985, Finalist Twentieth Century Fox Comedy Competition, 1987. Home: 241 Friar Way Campbell CA 95008

SMITH, CHESTER LEO, b. Kansas City, MO, Jan. 23, 1922; s. Chester Leo and Alameda Mariposa (West) Smith; m. Ann Smith; 1 dau.—Blithe. Author: Midway 4 June, 1942, 1962; editor: (Wu Han): The Dismissal of Hai Jui, 1968; contrbr. stories to Collier's, Am. Legion mag.; producer: plays My Empress Eva Darling, The Last Execution, Images of Che, Cross-Examination at Auschwitz. BA, U. Chgo., 1942; JD, Harvard U., 1948. Bar: IL, 1949, CA, 1951. Asst. to vp Cuneo Press (Chgo.), 1948-49; individual practice (Los Angeles), 1951—. Served to 1st lt. A.C. USMCR, 1942-45. Decorated Air medal (3). Address: Box 49590 Los Angeles CA 90049

SMITH, CHRISTINA ANN, b. Los Angeles, CA, Jul. 26, 1947; d. Robert Baron and Susan (Jonasky) Baron; m. John Hylas Smith, Sept. 3, 1966; children—Bryon Thomas, Wesley Hayes. Author: Kingsmate, 1978, Chivo, 1979, The Ring, The Parish, 1980. BA, U. of Calif., Santa Barbara. Asst. mgr. legal rights Lorimar Productions (Culver City, CA), 1982—. Home: 9046 Reading Los Angeles CA 90045

SMITH, CLARA MAY FREEMAN, b. Flushing, MI, Aug. 28, 1912; d. Arthur Milton and Anna Bell (Rush) Freeman; m. Russell Frederick Smith, Dec. 21, 1952 (dec.); step-children: Adelaide Smith Harris, Margaret Ann smith Condon, James Edwad. Author history of Lincoln Consolidated Training schl. affiliated with Eastern Mich. Univ. on file at Libray of Congess and Eastern Mich. U. Library. MA, Northwestern U., 1942; PhD, U. Mich., 1962. Retired tchr. Home: 1003 Pearl St Ypsilanti MI 48197

SMITH, DAVID CHARLES, b. Mt. Clemens, MI; s. Arthur Patrick and Harriett (Dickson) S.; m. Isabelle Johnston, Apr. 6, 1957; children—Shannon, Erin, Geoffrey, Timothy. Co-author The Search for Johnny Nicholas, 1982; contrbr. to New York Times, Parade, Ford Times, Washington Post, Michigan Living, others; rptr. Detroit Times, 1959, Toledo Blade, 1961, Wall Street Jnl., 1961-65; finl. ed. Detroit Free Press, 1965-70; ed. Ward's Auto World, 1971—. BA, U. MI, 1958. Staff rptr. Detroit Times, 1959, bus. ed., 1960; staff rptr. Toledo Blade, 1961, Wall St. Jnl., Cleve./Los Angeles, 1961-65; finl. ed. Detroit Free Press, 1965-70; ed./v.p. Ward's Auto World, Detroit, 1971—. Served to Cpl., USMC, 1952-54. Mem. SABEW, Detroit Press Club, Internat. Motor Press Assn., Detroit Auto Writers Group. Num. awards inclg. Pulitzer Prize awarded entire staff Detroit Free Press, 1967. Home: 7355 Chula Vista LN Birmingham MI 48010

SMITH, DAVID JEDDIE, b. Portsmouth, VA, Dec. 19, 1942; s. Ralph Gerald Smith and Catherine Mary (Cornwell) Easter; m. Deloras Mae Weaver, March 31, 1966; children, David J., Lael Cornwell, Mary Catherine. Works include: The Roundhouse Voices: Selected and New Poems, 1985, Local Assays, 1985, In the House of the Judge, 1983, Gray Soldiers, 1984, Southern Delights, 1984, Onliness, 1981, Homage to Edgar Allan Poe, 1981, Dream Flights, 1981, Goshawk, Antelope, 1981, Cumberland Station, 1981. BA, U. of Va., 1965; MA, Southern IL U., 1969; PhD, OH U., 1976. Asst. prof., Cottey College, Nevada, MO, 1974-75; assoc. prof., U. of Utah, Salt Lake City, 1976-80; assoc. prof., U. of Fla., Gainesville, 1981-82; prof., Va. Commonwealth U., Richmond, 1982—. With USAF, 1969-72. Awards: NEA grant, 1976, 1981; Guggenheim fellowship, 1981, Lyndhurst fellowship, 1987. Mem. AWP, MLA. Home: 2821 E Brigstock Rd Midlothian VA 23113

SMITH, DAVID LIONEL, (D.L. Crockett-Smith), b. Tuskegee, AL, Feb. 3, 1954; s. David Alexander Smith and Thelma Leontyne (Crockett) Adams; m. Vivian A. Cooke-Buckhoy, June 15, 1980; 1 child, Nikita L. Author: Cowboy Amok (poems), 1987. Contrbr. to The Best of the Best, Black Scholar, Open Places, Minn. Rvw, First World, Cumbaya, New Collage. BA, New Coll., Sarasota, Fla., 1974; PhD, U. Chgo., 1980. NEH summer intern, Washington, 1976; asst. prof. English, Williams Coll., Williamstown, Mass., 1980-87, assoc. prof. 1987—. Mem. MLA, Popular Culture Assn. Home: Old State Rd Berkshire MA 01224

SMITH, DEBBI LYNN, (Deborah M. Smith), b. Snoqualamie, WA, June 17, 1959; d. Jacob Martin and Bonnie Beth (Vince) Myers; m. Robert Lawrence Smith, June 2, 1979. Contrbr. poems to anthols. Student Towson State U., 1987—. Administrative asst. Hydrogen Research Center, College Station, TX, 1981-85, cons., 1985—, lobbyist, 1987—. Mem. Am. Bus. Women's Assn. (fellow). Home: 374 Jaimie Ct Glen Burnie MD 21061

SMITH, DONNETTA KAY, (Donnie Smith), b. Quincy, IL, June 5, 1944; d. Donald Richard and Helena Fern (Epperson) Bowen; m. John Dale Smith, Nov. 27, 1968; 1 dau., Melissa Juliet; children by previous marriage—Donald James Whitaker, Rodger Bryan Whitaker. Contrbr. feature and tech. articles to mags., newsletters, newspapers including Capper's Weekly, Keokuk Daily Gate City, CornsTalk, Interior Motives, Lamplighter, The Christian Standard, The Lookout, others. Home: 150 Walte Ln Keokuk IA 52632

SMITH, FRANCINE DENISE, b. Willard, OH, Nov. 1, 1949; d. Maynard Deyo and Dorothy Lucille (Franklin) Doan; m. Larry Woodrow Smith, June 26, 1970; children—Lynn Marie (dec.), Stephanie Amber, Cortney Elaine. Contrbr. poem to anthol. Wrkg. on short story,

"The Love for Our Dying Child," poems. Press take away operator R. R. Donnelly & Son, Willard, 1967-70; line person R. R. Donnelly Printing & Son, Willard, 1970-72, sewer operator, 1972—. Recipient Silver Poet award World of Poetry, 1986. Home: 37 Brooks Ct Plymouth OH 44865

SMITH, FRANK KINGSTON, b. Philadelphia, Jan. 11, 1919; s. Frank and Marion (Owen) S.; m. Marianne von Hiller, June 25, 1941; children: Frank Kingston Smith, Jr., Douglas von Hiller Smith, Hugh Gregory Smith. Author: Weekend Pilot, 1957, Flights of Fancy, 1959, I'd Rather Be Flying!, 1961, Computer Guide, 1961, How to Take Great Photos from Airplanes, 1979, Private Pilot's Survival Manual, 1979, Legacy of Wings, 1981, Weekend Wings, 1982, Aviation and Pennsylvania, 1981, Flying the Bahamas, 1983, Aviation and World Progress, 1982. Columnist, Flying, 1958-68, Air Progress, 1968-73; contrbtg. ed. Plane & Pilot, 1973-77, AOPA Pilot, 1977-83; featured columnist, Sport Aviation, 1984—; contrbr. Wings/Air Power, Professional Pilot; wrtr. technical svcs. manuals for Airport Services Management (1964-73), technical monographs for DOT/FAA Civil Air Patrol. AB, Trinity Coll., LLB, Temple Univ. Associate to partner, Philadelphia law firms 1945-63; pres. Natl. Aviation Trades Assn., Washington, DC, 1963-73; partner, Beckman & Smith, Washington, DC, 1973-78. Lt. Cdr., USNR, 1942-46, SoWesPac. Wrkg. on three books, nonfiction. Home: Six W Aberdeen Rd Ocean City NJ 08226

SMITH, GENNY HALL, (Genny Schumacher), b. San Francisco, July 6, 1921; d. Hayes and Mollie (Cykler) Hall; m. Gerhard Schumacher, 1948; m. Ward Conwell Smith, Jan. 7, 1968. Co-author, ed.: The Mammoth Lakes Sierra: A Handbook for Roadside & Trail, 1959, rev. 1964, 1969, 1976; Deepest Valley: A Guide to Owens Valley, Its Roadsides and Mountain Trails, 1962, 78; author, ed. Historic Mammoth Postcards, 1971; Historic Owens Valley Postcards, 1975; ed. Earthquakes & Young Volcanoes along the Eastern Sierra Nevada, 1982, Old Mammoth, 1982, Doctor Nellie: The Autobiography of Dr. Helen MacKnight Doyle, 1983, The Lost Cement Mine, 1984. BA, Reed Coll., 1943. Ed. Sierra Club Outings Com., San Francisco, 1965-68, Jr. Bach Festival Assn., Berkeley, Calif., 1966-68; pub. Genny Smith Books, Mammoth Lakes, Calif., 1976—. Mem. Bookbuilders West, Phi Beta Kappa. Home: 1304 Pitman Ave Palo Alto CA 94301

SMITH, GORDON ROSS, b. Monmouth County, NJ, May 23, 1917; s. Mortimer Dickerson and Elizabeth Clara (Ross) Smith; m. Jane Pakenham, Aug. 29, 1948; children—Gordon Ross, Corinna Pakenham. Author: A Classified Shakespeare Bibliography, 1936-58, 1963, Essays on Shakespeare, 1965; cons. editor: Jnl History of Ideas; editorial bd.: Film Forum Rvw, Columbia U., 1948-49. BS, Columbia U., 1948, MA, 1949; PhD, PA State U., 1956. Instr. English, Waynesburg Coll. (PA), 1949-50; instr. English, PA State U., 1950-56, asst. prof., 1956-59, assoc. prof., 1959-63, prof., 1963-66; Folger Shakespeare Library fellow, 1958; Fulbright lectr. Royal U. Malta, 1962-63; prof. English, Temple U. (Phila.), 1966-84, prof. emeritus, 1984—. Served with AUS, 1943-46. Mem. Shakespeare Assn. Am., PA Hist. Soc., Intl. Shakespeare Assn. Home: 35 Red Oak Rd Oreland PA 19075

SMITH, HAROLD LEE, b. Atlanta, Jan. 15, 1930; s. Howard Lee and Lillie Mae (Helton) S.; m. Elizabeth Sharp, Nov. 18, 1951. Author: A Beacon for Christ, 1984. Contrbr. articles and pamphlets. Ed.: Rambler Mag., 1960-65, Southeastern Florist Mag., 1962-63, Fabricator Mag., 1962-65, Southern Pest Control Jnl., 1962-69. Student, Ga. State U., 1954-60. Owner, Smith Enterprises, Smyrna, 1974—. Mem. Smynna City Council, 1960-63, mayor, 1970-73. Served with U.S. Navy, 1948-52. Recipient Key Man award Ga. Jaycees, 1962, 63, 64; named Citizen of Yr., Kiwanis Club of Smyrna, 1970, Jr. Woman's Club, Symrna, 1970-71. mem. Optimist Intl., Smyrna Hist. Geneological Soc. (pres. 1985—). Home: 825 Austin Dr Smyrna GA 30080

SMITH, JACK CLIFFORD, b. Long Beach, CA, Aug. 27, 1916; s. Charles Franklin and Anna Mary (Hughes) Smith; m. Denise Bresson, June 17, 1939; children—Curtis Bresson, Douglas Franklin. Author: Three Coins in the Birdbath, 1965, Smith on Wry, 1970, God and Mr. Gomez, 1974, The Big Orange, 1976, Spend All Your Kisses, Mr. Smith, 1978, Jack Smith's LA, 1980, How to Win a Pullet Surprise, 1982, Cats, Dogs and Other Strangers at My Door, 1984. Student, Bakersfield Coll., 1937-38. Reporter Bakersfield Californian, 1937-38, Honolulu Advertiser, 1941-42, UPI, Sacramento, 1943, Los Angeles Daily News, 1946-49, Los Angeles Herald-Express, 1950-52, Los Angeles Times, 1953-58, columnist, 1958—. Served with USMC, 1944-45. Home: 4251 Camino Real Los Angeles CA 90065

SMITH, JANE DAVIS, (Jane Maxwell), b. LaPorte, Ind., May 18, 1949; d. Edward Moffett and Katherine Frances (Foutz) Davis; m. Donald Lee Smith, Apr. 15, 1967; children—Heidi Joanne, Alison Renee, Steven Michael, Scott Edward Moffett Davis Smith. Contrbr.: The Camper Times. Wrkg. on health article. Student U. Elkhart, various writing seminars. Mem. Staff U. Notre Dame, Ind., 1967-71. Mem. NWC, SCBW. Home: 139 Timber Ln South Bend IN 46615

SMITH, JEANETTE GOATES, b. Salt Lake City, June 27, 1961; d. Delbert Tolton and Claudia (Tidwell) Goates; m. Bret Gerald Smith, Apr. 23, 1982; children—Brandon, Spencer. Author: Children Who Govern Themselves, 1988. Contrbr. articles to Hartford Woman, New Haven County Woman, Vibrant Life, Lady's Circle, Bus. Properties. B.A. in Communications, Brigham Young U., 1982. Home: 41 Fox Run Rd Waterbury CT 06708

SMITH, JEFF DAVID, b. Waukesha, WI, Oct. 31, 1969; s. Joel David and Alyce Lynn (Rupp) S. Contrbr. articles to newspapers, mags. Asst. sports ed., columnist: The Community-Advertiser, Columbus, IN, 1987—. Student Ind. U., 1987—. Graphic designer The Advertiser, Columbus, 1986-87; sports wrtr. The Community, Columbus, 1986-87. Recipient Excellence in Jnlsm. award Ball State U., 1985, Journalistic Excellence award Ind. U., 1986, 2d place, Honorable Mention, Jesse Suart Lit. Festival, 1987. Mem. Ind. Press Assn. (Harvey award for column 1986). Home: 4520 Mission Ct W Columbus IN 47203

SMITH, JESSIE CARNEY, b. Greensboro, NC, Spet. 24, 1930; d. James Ampler and Vesona Bigelow Carney; m. Frederick Douglas Smith, Dec. 22, 1950 (div.); 1 son—Frederick Douglas. Author: Black Academic Libraries and Research Collections; compiler: Minority American Women: A Biographical Directory; editor: Ethnic Genealogy: A Research Guide; compiler: Images of Blacks in American Culture, 1986; editorial bd.: Choice, 1969-74; contrbr. articles to profl. jnls. BS, NC A and T State U., 1950; student, Cornell U., fall 1950; MA, Mich. State U., 1956; AM, George Peabody Coll. Tchrs., 1957; PhD, U. IL, 1964. Head cataloger, instr. library sci. Tenn. State U., 1957-60; teaching asst. U. IL, 1961-63; coordinator library service, asst. prof. Tenn. A. and I. State U., 1963-65; univ. librarian, prof. Fisk U., 1965—, dir. library trng. insts., 1970-79, dir. Themes in the Black Am. Experience: A Learning Library Program, 1980-84, fed. relations officer, 1976-78; lectr. Peabody Library Schl., George Peabody Coll. for Tchrs., 1969—, Ala. A. & M. U., 1971, U. Tenn., 1973; cons. So. Assn. Colls. and Schls., 1968—, U.S. Office for Civil Rights, 1979—; Sec. COSATI Subcom. on Negro Research Libraries, 1970-73; mem. Biomed. Library Review Com., 1972-76; cons. gen. programs div., library programs HEW, 1978—; lectr. cons. black lit. and black collections. Dir. library study Tenn. Higher Edn. Commn., 1974. Bd. dirs. Bethlehem Center, Nashville, 1965-68. Office: Fisk U Lib 17th Ave N Nashville TN 37203

SMITH, JO ANNE, b. Mpls., Mar. 18, 1930; d. Robert Bradburn and Virginia Mae Smith. Author: JM409 Casebook and Study Guide, 1976, Mass Communications Law Casebook, 1979, 2nd ed., 1981. BA, U. Minn., 1951, MA, 1957. Wire and sports editor Rhinelander Daily News (WI), 1951-52; staff corr., night mgr. UP (Mpls.), 1952-56; interim instr. U. NC (Chapel Hill), 1957-58; instr. U. Fla. (Gainesville), 1959-65, asst. prof. journalism, communications, 1965-68, assoc. prof., 1968-76, prof., 1976—, Disting. lectr., 1977; dir. Fla. Freedom of Info. Clearing House. Mem. Women in Communications, Soc. Profl. Journalists, Assn. Edn. in Journalism. Home: 208 NW 21 Terr Gainesville FL 32603

SMITH, JOHN EDWIN, b. Bklyn., May 27, 1921; s. Joseph Robert and Florence Grace (Dunn) Smith; m. Marilyn Blanche Schulhof, Aug. 25, 1951; children—Robin Dunn, Diana Edwards. Author: Royce's Social Infinite, 1950, Value Convictions and Higher Education, 1958, Reason and God, 1961, The Spirit of American Philosophy, 1963, The Philosophy of Religion, 1965, Religion and Empiricism, 1967, Experience and God, 1968, Themes in American Philosophy, 1970, Contemporary American Philosophy, 1970, The Analogy of Experience, 1973, Purpose and Thought: The Meaning of Pragmatism, 1978; translator: (R. Kroner): Kant's Weltanschauung, 1956; gen. editor, Yale ed.: Works of Jonathan Edwards; editorial bd.: Monist, 1962—, Jnl Religious Studies, Philosophy East and West, Jnl Chinese Philosophy, The Personalist Forum, Logos, Jnl of Speculative Philosophy, Faith and Philosophy. AB, Columbia U., 1942, PhD, 1948; BD, Union Theol. Sem., NYC, 1945; MA (hon.), Yale U., 1959; LL.D., U. Notre Dame, 1964. Instr. religion and philosophy Vassar Coll., 1945-46; from instr. to asst. prof. philosophy and religion Barnard Coll., 1946-52; mem. faculty Yale U., 1952—, prof. philosophy, 1959—, chair dept., 1961-m, Clark prof. philosophy, 1972—; vis. prof. Union Theol. Sem., 1959, U. Mich., 1958; guest prof. U. Heidelberg, Germany, 1961; Suarez lectr. Fordham U., 1963; pub. lectr. King's College, Univ. London, 1965; Aquinas lectr. Marquette U., 1967; Warfield lectr. Princeton Theol. Sem., 1970; Fulbright lectr. Kyoto U., Japan, 1971; Sprunt lectr. Union Theol. Sem. VA, 1973; Mead-Swing lectr. Oberlin Coll., 1975; H. Richard Niebuhr lectr. Elmhurst Coll., IL, 1977; Merrick lectr. Ohio Wesleyan U., 1977; Roy Wood Sellars lectr. Bucknell U., 1978; O'Hara lectr. U. Notre Dame,

1984; mem. adv. com. Natl. Humanities Inst., New Haven, 1974, dir., 1977—. Home: 300 Ridgewood Ave Hamden CT 06517

SMITH, KATHLEEN KEER MCGOWAN, b. Newark, Mar. 8, 1918; d. Theo F. and Florence Ethel (MacRae) Keer; m. H. Allenby, July 28, 1949 (div. 1977); 1 dau., Kathy Breeden Allenby Ryan (dec. 1968); m. 2d, John F. McGowan, Apr. 24, 1981 (dec.); m. 3d, Bev Smith, Sept. 4, 1987. Contrbr. articles to civic orgn. publs.; poetry in anthologies. Wrkg. on poetry. BA, Smith Coll.; postgrad., Columbia U. Artist, painter. Recipient award for paintings. Home: 583 North Lake Way Palm Beach FL 33480

SMITH, KELLIE MICHELLE, (Kellie Cunningham), b. Berkeley, CA, July 28, 1965, d. Qutbuddin Loren Rue and Bhakti (Banning) Smith. Contrbr. to Am. Poetry Anthol, 1984, Dairy Goat Jnl. Student Calif. State U., Chico, 1983—. Home: 1133 W Sacramento Ave Apt 15 Chico CA 95926

SMITH, LARRY R., b. Steubenville, OH, Feb. 11, 1943; s. Delbert R. and Jean Rae (Putnam) S.; m. Ann Zaben, July 3, 1965; children—Laura, Brian, Suzanne. Author poetry books: Growth, 1978, Echo Without Sound, 1981, Scissors, Paper, Rock, 1982, Across These States, 1984; lit. biography: Kenneth Patchen, 1978, Lawrence Felinghetti, 1983; contrbr. articles Dict. Lit. Biography, poetry to many publs. BA, Muskingum Coll., 1965; MA, Kent State U., 1970, PhD, 1974. High schl. tchr. Euclid, Ohio, 1965-68; prof. English Bowling Green State Univ.-Firelands Coll., Huron, Ohio, 1970—; mng. ed. The Plough: N. Coast Rvw, 1983—; ed. and pub. Bottom Dog Press, Firelands Coll., Huron, 1984—. Founding mem. Firelands United Campuses to Prevent Nuclear War, Voices for Peace. Recipient Ohio Arts Council publ. grants, 1982, 83, 85. Mem. P&W. Home: 813 Seneca St Huron OH 44839

SMITH, LEON L., SR., b. Kansas City, KS, Jan. 3, 1931; s. Fred Louis and Elizabeth Viola (Flinn) Romi; children—Leon, Jerry, Judy, Beverly; m. 2d, Georgia Jean Mogelberg, Oct. 22, 1975. Author: A Guide To Laurel and Hardy Movie Locations, 1982, Following The Comedy Trail, 1984. AA, East Los Angeles Junior Coll., 1959. Home: 6519 Paseo El Greco Anaheim Hills CA 92807

SMITH, LIZ, b. Ft. Worth, Feb. 2; d. Sloan and Sarah Elizabeth (McCall) S. Author: The Mother Book, 1978. B.J., U. Tex., 1948. Editor Dell Publns., N.Y.C., 1950-53; assoc. producer CBS Radio, 1953-55, NBC-TV, 1955-59; assoc. on Cholly Knickerbocker newspaper column, N.Y.C., 1959-64; film critic Cosmopolitan mag., 1966—; freelance mag. writer, also staff writer Sports Illus. columnist Chgo. Tribune-N.Y. Daily News Syndicate, 1976—; TV commentator WNBC-TV, N.Y.C., 1978—; Address: NY Daily News 220 E 42d St New York NY 10017

SMITH, LOUISE HAMILTON, (Annie Smith), b. Columbus, Miss., Sept. 12, 1926; d. Onnie Felto and Mary Cordelia (Stewart) Hamilton; m. Felton Lomax Smith, June 11, 1948; children: Roger Felton, Katrina Louise, Sheila Renae. Contrbr. to Christian Sci. Monitor, Grit, Woman's Day, Natl. Features Syndicate, True Romance, True Story. Wrkg. on children's picture book, short stories and novel. Student Miss. U. for Women, 1955. Operator South Central Bell Telephone Co., Columbus, 1946-78. Home: 1524 Bell Ave Columbus MS 39701

SMITH, MARK RICHARD, b. Charlevoix, MI, Nov. 19, 1935; s. Marcus Grey Smith and Nellie Elizabeth (Van Eeuwen) Miller; m. Anthea Mae Eatough, May 23, 1963; children: Heidi, Matje, Maida, Gudrun. Author: (novels) Toyland, 1965; The Middleman, 1967; The Death of the Detective, 1974; The Moon Lamp, 1976; The Delphinium Girl, 1980; Doctor Blues, 1983; Smoek Street, 1984. AB, Northwestern U., 1960. Prof. English, U. N.H., 1976—, dir. grad. writing, 1981-85; wrtr.-in-residence Hollins Coll., Va., 1981; Thornton wrtr.-in-residence Lynchburg Coll., Va., 1984; vis. prof. English, U. Tex., Austin, 1986; Fulbright sr. lectr., Yugoslavia, 1985. Writing grantee Rockefeller Fdn., 1965, Ingram Merrill Fdn., 1976, 77, NEA, 1976; Guggenheim Fdn. fellow, 1968. Home: Box 261 Juniper Ln York Harbor ME 03911

SMITH, MICHAEL TOWNSEND, b. Kansas City, MO, Oct. 5, 1935; s. Lewis Motter and Dorothy (Pew) Smith; m. Michele Marie Hawley, 1974; children—Julian Bach, Alfred St. John. Author: (fiction) Getting Across, 1962, Near the End, 1965, Automatic Vaudeville, 1970, High Points of Youth, 1980; (poetry) American Baby, 1975; plays I Like It, 1961, The Next Thing, 1963, A Dog's Love, 1965, Captain Jack's Revenge, 1970, Country Music, 1971, Double Solitaire, 1973, Prussian Suite, 1973, A Wedding Party, 1974, Cowgirl Ecstasy, 1976, Heavy Pockets, 1981, One Hundred Thousand Songs, 1982, Turnip Family Secrets, 1983; (translation) Life Is Dream, 1978; (critical jnl) Theatre Trip, 1969; editor: (anthologies) Eight Plays from Off-Off-Broadway, 1966, The Best of Off-Off-Broadway, 1969; More Plays from Off-Off-Broadway, 1966. Student, Yale U., 1953-55. Theatre critic Village Voice (NYC), 1959-68, 1970-74, assoc. editor, 1962-65; curator, judge Obie awards for theatre, 1962-68, 1970-74; tchr. New Schl. Social Research, 1964-65, Hunter Coll., 1972; playwright mem. Open Theatre (NYC), 1962-66; dir. Theatre Genesis (NYC), 1971-74; arts editor Taos News (NM) m 1977-78; music critic New London Day (CT), 1982—; instrument maker, adminstr. Zuckemann Hapsichords Inc., 1975-76, 79—. Recipient creative art citation in theatre Brandeis U., 1965; Obie award, 1971; Rockefeller Fdn. award, 1976. Address: 86 Main St Westerly RI 02891

SMITH, MONTE, see Smith, V. LaMonte

SMITH, MURIEL JOAN, b. Elizabeth, NJ, Nov. 23, 1936; d. Vincent dePaul and Gladys Magdalen (Van Den Bergh) Slavin; m. James Edward Smith, Jr., May 7, 1955; children—Kathy Plamara, Michelle McNamee, James E., Tracie Marie. Reporter, Daily Record, Long Branch, NJ, 1957-63, Highlands Star, Atlantic Highlands, NJ, 1960-66; reporter The Courier, Middletown, NJ, 1966-72, assoc. ed., 1972-86, ed., 1986—. Mem. N.J. Press Assn. (award for Enterprise Reporting, 1968), Natl. Newspaper Assn. Home: 135 Highland Ave Highlands NJ 07732

SMITH, PATRICK DAVIS, b. Mendenhall, MS, Oct. 8, 1927; s. John D. and Nora Jane (Eubanks) S.; m. Iris Doty, Aug. 1, 1948; children—Jane Smith Schneider, Patrick D. Author: (novels) The River Is Home, 1953, The Beginning, 1967, Forever Island, 1973, Angel City, 1978, Allapattah, 1979, A Land Remembered, 1984. Contrbr. short stories, essays, articles to mags. wrkg. on book on Majorie Kinnan Rowlings. B.A., U. Miss., 1947, M.A., 1959. Dir. public relations Hinds Jr. Coll., Raymond, MS, 1959-62, U. Miss., Oxford, 1962-66, Brevard Commun. Coll., Cocoa, FL, 1966—. Bd. dirs. Council for Fla. Libraries, Ft. Lauderdale, 1987, Brevard Mus., Cocoa, 1987; active Brevard Arts Council, Cocoa, 1987. Recipient Outstanding Author award Gannett Fla. Today, 1987. Mem. Fla. Space Coast Wrtrs. Conf. (Outstanding Fla. Author 1987), AG, Space Coast Public Relation Assn. Home: 1370 Island Dr Merritt Island FL 32952

SMITH, PATRICK D., b. Mendenhall, MS, Oct. 8, 1927, s. John D. and Nora Jane (Eukanks) S.; m. Iris Doty, July 1, 1948; children—Jane L. Smith Schneider, Patrick D. Jr. Novelist: The River Is Home, 1953, The Beginning, 1967, Forever Island, 1973, Angel City, 1977, Allapattah, 1980, A Land Remembered, 1984. BA, U. Miss., 1947, MA in English, 1959. Dir. public relations Hinds Jr. Coll., Raymond, Miss., 1959-62, U. Miss., Oxford, 1962-66, Brevard Community Coll., Cocoa, Fla., 1966—. Mem. Space Coast Public Relations Assn., AG, Council for Support and Advancement of Edn. Home: 1370 Island Dr Merritt Island FL 32952

SMITH, R(OBERT) E., JR., b. Holyoke, MA, Mar. 10, 1943, s. Robert Edward and Margie Norma (Edes) S.; m. Pauletta Verett, July 28, 1968. Contrbr. to Cimarron Rvw, Best Am. Short Stories 1982, Pawn Rvw, Tex. Rvw, numerous other lit. publs. BA, Harding Coll., Searcy, Ark., 1964; MFA, U. Oreg., 1966; PhD, U. Mo., 1969. Prof. dept. communications Purdue U., West Lafayette, Inc., 1969—. Mem. Soc. for Study Midwestern Lit., Western Lit. Assn. Home: 520 Terry Ln West Lafayette IN 47906

SMITH, RICHARD JAY, b. NYC, June 13, 1930; s. Jacob and Rose (Adelman) Smith; m. Jane Grosfeld, Dec. 17, 1955; children—Lisa Jill, Tracey Elizabeth, James Andrew. Contrbg. editor: Reoperative Surgery, 1964, Understanding Surgery, 1967, Encyc. Child Care, 1967, Flynn's Hand Surgery, 1974, Operative Surgery, The Hand, 1977, Advances in Surgery II, 1977, Vascular Surgery, 1977, MGH Textbook of Emergency Medicine, 1978, Management of Peripheral Nerve Problems, 1980, The Practice of Hand Surgery, 1981, Operative Hand Surgery, 1982. BA, Brown U., 1951; MD, NY Med. Coll., 1955. Diplomate: Am. Bd. Orthopaedic Surgery. Surg. intern 3d surg. div. Bellevue Hosp. (NYC), 1955-56; resident orthopaedic surgery Hosp. Joint Diseases (NYC)1957-60, attending orthopaedic surgeon (hand surgery), 1966-72, chief hand surgery, 1968-72; asst. clin. prof. orthopaedic surgery Albert Einstein Coll. Medicine, 1964-72; assoc. clin. prof. orthopaedic surgery Mt. Sinai Schl. Medicine, City U. NY, 1967-72; clin. prof. orthopaedic surgery Harvard Med. Schl., 1972—; chief hand surgery dept. orthopaedic surgery Mass. Gen. Hosp. (Boston), 1972—. Served as lt. comdr. USPHS, 1960-62. Home: 9 Blake Rd Weston MA 02193

SMITH, RICHARD KEANE, (Rick Smith), b. NYC, Mar. 2, 1942; s. William Arthur Smith and Mary Frances (Nixon) Latessa; m. Lynda Hart, May 30, 1980. Author: Exhibition Game, 1973; (rec.) Hand to Mouth, 1981; ed. Stonecloud mag., 1975, 76, 77; Conversation with a Dying Friend, 1976. Wrkg. on book on rehab. of head-injured adult. BA in Lit., Bard Coll., 1965; MS in Rehab. Counseling, Calif. State U., Los Angeles, 1974. Clin. coordinator Rancho Transitional Living Residence, Downey, Calif., 1984—. Mem. ASCAP, Natl. Acad. Rec. Arts and Scis., Natl. Rehab. Assn. Home: 1735 Wayne St Pomona CA 91767

SMITH, ROBERT CLARKE, b. Sioux Center, IA, Mar. 12, 1940; s. Alfred William and Elizabeth (Clarke) Smith; m. Marjorie Fairchild Heyne, Dec. 25, 1965 (div.); 1 son—Geoffrey; 2nd m. Suzan Leigh Morrow, Dec. 30, 1969 (div.); 3rd m. Lorene E. Cary, Aug. 27, 1983; 1 dau.—Laura. Author: (with Min S. Yee and Donald K. Wright) The Driver's Handbook, 1974. Student, Drake U., 1958-60; BA, U. Iowa, 1962; AM, U. Chgo., 1963; postgrad., 1965-66. Instr. English Valparaiso U. (IN), 1963-65, Northwestern U. (Evanston, IL), 1966-69, Tex. A&M U., (College Station), 1969-70; sr. editor Today's Health (Chgo.), 1971-73; assoc. travel editor Saturday Rvw (San Francisco), 1973; mng. editor The Great Escape (Mill Valley, CA), 1973-74, Columbia Journalism Rvw (NYC), 1974-78, TV Guide (Radnor, PA), 1979—; assoc. in jnlsm. Grad. Schl., Columbia U., 1976-78; lectr. jnlsm. Temple U., 1985—. Office: TV Guide Radnor PA 19088

SMITH, ROBERT ELLIS, b. Providence, Sept. 6, 1940, s. Ronald Bancroft and Clarice (Evans) S.; m. Kathryn Ritter; children—Mark, David. Author: Privacy: How to Protect What's Left of It, 1980, Workrights, 1983, Big Brother Book of Lists, 1984, Block Island Trivia, 1985, Celebrities and Privacy, 1985, Compilation of State and Federal Privacy Laws, 1975, 76, 80, 81, 84. BS, Harvard U., 1962; JD, Georgetown U., 1975. Reporter Detroit Free Press, 1962-63, 66, Newsday, Garden City, N.Y., 1967-71; ed. The Southern Courier, Montgomery, Ala., 1965-66; asst. dir. Office for Civil Rights, HEW, Washington, 1971-73; pub. Privacy Jnl., Washington, 1974—; practice law, Washington, since 1976. Del. to Democratic Natl. Conv., 1976; commr. D.C. Human Rights Commn., 1982-85. Recipient Love joy award Village Voice, 1985. Mem. AG, NWU, Washington Ind. Wrtrs. (bd. dirs. 1982-83). Office: Box 15300 Washington DC 20003

SMITH, ROBERT LETTON, b. Winston-Salem, NC, April 10, 1928; s. Robert Edward and Mary Juliet (Letton) Smith; m. Nancy Jordan, Dec. 21, 1958; 1 dau., Julia Letton. Author: Refractions, 1979; poems in Shenandoah, Western Hum. Rvw, Georgia Rvw, other lit mags. BA, OH Wesleyan U. English tchr., NYC public schools, 1964—. PFC, US Army, 1953-55. Mem. PSA. Home: 271 E 78th St New York NY 10021

SMITH, RODNEY T., b. Washington, April 13, 1948; s. Roland McCall and Mary Helen (Thaxton) Smith; m. Nadya Belins, Feb. 20, 1985. Works include: Waking Under Snow, 1975, Good Water, 1979, Rural Route, 1981, Beasts Did Leap, 1982, From the High Dive, 1983, Roosevelt Unbound, 1985, Birchlights, 1985. MA, Appalachian State U., 1975; BA, U. of NC, 1970. Wrtr.-in-res., Auburn U., Auburn, AL, 1975—. Awards: Texas Review Poetry Awd., 1985; John Masefield Awd., PSA, 1981. Mem. MLA, PSA, AAP. Home: 1709 2nd Ave Opelika AL 36801

SMITH, SHARON KAY, b. Huntington, WV, Oct. 9, 1954, d. Earl R. and Elizabeth Amanda (Tackett) Smith; m. Jack Edward Smith, Oct. 12, 1973; children—Jacklynn Amanda, Shannon Beth. Ed., wrtr.: On Center, 1984-86, Centerpieces, 1986—; ed.: The Achiever, 1985-86; wrtr. The Daily Independent, 1984—. Wrkg. on novel, contemporary poetry. AA, Ashland (Ky.) Community Coll., 1986. Public relations rep. Paramount Arts Center, Ashland, Ky., 1984-85; mktg. dir. Jesse Stuart Fdn., Ashland, 1986—; freelance wrtr., 1984—. Mem. Intl. Assn. Bus. Communicators, Natl. Assn. Female Execs. Home: 3524 Sharon Ct Catlettsburg KY 41129

SMITH, SHERYL L., b. Chgo., Dec. 23, 1947; d. James F. and Dorothy Geraldine (Arnesson) S. Poetry ed. Riverside Quar., 1975—; contrbr. critical articles on sci. fiction to Riverside Quar., Gorbett, Ibid, also others. BA in English, U. Ill., Chgo., 1968. Ed., secy. Research & Decisions, San Francisco, 1983-84; software tester Analytica Corp., Fremont, Calif., 1984-85; software technician Forefront-Ashton Tate, Sunnyvale, Calif., 1985-86; software tester, Borland Intl., Scotts Valley, Calif., 1986—. Home: 515 Saratoga Ave 2 Santa Clara CA 95050

SMITH, SHIRLEY MAE, (Ellis Ovesen), b. New Effington, SD, July 18, 1923, d. Einar Walstrup and Augustina Maria (Ovesen) Johansen; m. Thor Lowe Smith, Aug. 27, 1949; children—Theodore Lowe, Glen Everett. Author poetry books: Gloried Grass, 1970, Haloed Paths, 1973, To Those Who Love (with Helen Carter King), 1974, The Last Hour, 1975, Lives Touch, 1976, A Time for Singing (award Natl. League Am. Penwomen), 1977, A Book of Praises, 1977, Beloved, 1980, Another Man's Moccasins, 1982, The Green Madonna, 1984, The Keeper of the Word, 1985, The Flowers of God, 1985, The Wing Brush, 1986, "Streets of Fire," 1986, Bird Poems, Vol. 1 and 2, 1987. MA cum laude, U. Wis.-Madison, 1948; tchr. credentials and tchr. of English, San Jose State U., 1963. Tchr. Freshman Eng., U. of Wis., 1946-48; poetry tutor Los Altos, Calif., 1960s—; founder Citizens United for Rural Environment, Los Altos, 1972. Grantee Am. Poetry Fellowship Soc.; recipient numerous poetry awards, named Town Poet, Los Altos Hills, Calif., 1972. Hon. Doctorate of Lit., World Acad. of Arts and Culture, 1986 Mem. Calif. State Poetry Soc. (pres. 1975-76), pfl. mem., PSA,NWC, Calif. Wrtrs. Club, Pacific Art League, Peninsula Poets (founder, now pres.), Natl. League Am. Penwomen, Natl. Fedn. State Poetry Socs., Calif. Fedn. Chaparral Poets, World Congress Poets, United Poets Laureate Intl. Home: Box 482 Los Altos CA 94023

SMITH, SUE FRANCES, b. Lockhart, TX, July 4, 1940; d. Monroe John Baylor and Myrtle (Krause) Mueck; m. Michael Vogtel Smith, Apr. 20, 1963 (div. July 1977); 1 dau.—Jordan Meredith. B. Journalism, U. Tex., 1962. Feature writer, photographer Corpus Christi Caller Times, 1962-64; feature writer, editor Chgo. Tribune, 1964-76; features editor Dallas Times Herald, 1976-82; asst. mng. editor (for features), Denver Post, 1983-84, assoc. ed., 1984—. Home: 1216 E 10th Ave Denver CO 80218

SMITH, SUSAN ROSS, b. Portland, OR, May 17, 1945, d. Thomas Henry Ross and Winifred (Davies) Sanders; m. Stephen John Smith, June 10, 1967; children—Teresa Lynn, Brian Thomas. Author: Happy Birthday, A Guide to Special Parties for Children, 1983. BS, Portland State U., 1966. Tchr. Oreg. schls., 1967-79; author, pub., distbr. White Pine Press, West Linn, Oreg., 1983—. Home: 505 SW Long Farm Rd West Linn OR 97068

SMITH, TERENCE FITZGERALD, b. Brynmawr, PA, Nov. 18, 1938; s. Walter W. and Catherine M. (Cody) Smith; m. Phyllis Ann Charnley, June 20, 19,64; children—li Reed, Christopher Wellesly. BA, U. Notre Dame, 1960. Reporter Stanford Adv. (CT), 1960-62, NY Herald Tribune (NYC), 1963-65; with NY Times (NYC), 1965—, fgn. corr., Israel, Thailand, Vietnam bur. chief, 1969-70, diplomatic corr., Washington, 1970-72, chief corr., Israel, 1972-76, dep. fgn. editor, 1976-77, chief White House corr., 1978-81, sr. corr. Washington bur., 1981, editor Washington Talk page, 1981-85; Washington corr. CBS Morning News, 1985—; lectr., free-lasnce writer, radio, TV appearances. Mem. Overseas Writers Assn. Home: 1309 29th St NW Washington DC 10007

SMITH, V. LA MONTE, (Monte Smith), b. Ogden, Utah, Apr. 30, 1938, s. Ralph L. Smith and Nellie (Blackwell) Avery; m. Sue Key, Dec. 13; 1 son, Ralph L. Author: A Different Drummer: A Case Study of Systemic Intrusions and Dysfunction, 1977, The Techniques of North American Indian Beadwork, 1983, Quill and Beadwork of the North American Indian: A Sourcebook, 1984, 28 Patterns of the 18th-19th Century Frontier, 1985; ed.: The Techniques of Porcupine Quill Decoration Among the Indians of North America, 1982, Techniques of Beading Earrings, 1984, Crow Indian Beadwork, 1984, More Techniques of Beading Earrings, 1985. MA, Cornell U., 1975, PhD summa cum laude, 1978. Pres. Eagle Feather Trading Post, Inc., Ogden, Utah, 1976—. Woodrow Wilson fellow, 1972, Ford fellow, 1977. Mem. WWA, Rocky Mountain Book Pub. Assn., Phi Beta Kappa. Home: 706 W Riverdale Rd Ogden UT 84405

SMITH, WARD, see Goldsmith, Howard

SMITH, WILBUR STEVENSON, b. Columbia, SC, Sept. 6, 1911; s. George W. and Margaret Rebecca (Stevenson) S.; m. Sarah E. Bolick, Dec. 22, 1934; children: Sarah, Margaret, Stephanie. Author: (with N. Hebden) State City Relationships in Highway Affairs, 1950, (with T. Matson, F. Hurd) Traffic Engineering, 1955, tech. bulltns., reports, traffic surveys. B.S., Univ. S.C., 1932, M.S. magna cum laude, 1933, LL.D., 1963; postgrad., Harvard U., 1936-37; L.H.D., Lander Coll., 1975. Office: 1330 Lady StSuite 609 Columbia SC 29201

SMITH, WILMA JANICE, b. Pryor, OK, Aug. 15, 1926; William Henry and Mary Jo (Buffington) Bell; m. Merle Thomas Smith, Apr. 30, 1948. Country music features, Sepia, 1970's; Elvis Presley articles var. pubns., 1977-80; poetry in several major publs., 1986, 87; writer bio sketches of stars and liner notes, record album jkts. Student OK A & M, 1946, OK Schl. Accountancy, 1947. Secy. Acad. Country Music, Hollywood, CA, 1976-78; pub. relns. staff, Mickey Gilley, So. Calif., 1975-82; colum., feat. writer Country Music Rev., Tulsa, 1977-80; major feature art. on open-heart surgery in Let's Live mag., 1982; contrbg. ed. Nashville Star Rptr., 1976-78; publicist U. IL Press, Urbana, 1975-76; contrbr. photog. Lerner Books, Mpls., 1976-80; stringer Country Music mag., NYC, 1986—; promotional wrtg. for singers, film actors, 1987—. Mem. Acad. Country Music, Calif. Country Music Assn; Smithsonian Assoc., 1985-87 and 88. Home: 503 N Platina Dr Diamond Bar CA 91765

SMITH, WM. HOVEY, (Alphred E. Farnagle), b. Sandersville, GA, Dec. 10, 1941; s. William Hovey Smith and Frances (Ward) Summerlin. Author: Geology of the Tennille Lime Sinks, Washington County, Georgia, 1983, Kaolin Deposits of Central Georgia, 1983, Guide to Homes and Plantations of the Thomasville (Georgia) Region, 1984, Geology of Bortow County, Georgia, 1985, Farnagle's Fables for Children and Adults, 1984, The Not So Goody Gum Drop Shop: A Play, 1984. Ed.: Plain Words About AIDS, 1985, 3d ed., 1988. Wrkg. on rev. ed. of Plain Words about AIDS and Spanish ed. B.S., U. Ga., 1963; M.S., U. Alaska, College, 1970. Geologis, Lindgren Exploration Co., Wayzata,

MN, 1970-74, Heinrich Geoex, Tucson, 1975-77, Resource Assocs. of Alaska, Fairbanks, 1977-83; pres. Whitehall Press Budget Pubs., Sandersville, GA, 1983—. Mem. Natl. AIDS Network, Intl. Soc. AIDS Edn., Am. Inst. Mining Engineers. Home: RT 1 Box 603 Sandersville GA 31082

SMITH, WILLIAM JAY, b. Winnifield, LA, Apr. 22, 1918; s. Jay and Georgia (Campster) Smith; m. Barbara Howes, Oct. 1, 1947 (div. June 1965); children—David Emerson, Gregory Jay; m. 2d, Sonja Haussmann, Sept. 3, 1966. Author: Poems, 1947, Celebration at Dark, 1950, Laughing Time: Nonsense Poems, 1955, Poems, 1947-57, Boy Blue's book of Beasts, 1957, Puptents and Pebbles: A Nonsense ABC, 1959, The Spectra Hoax, 1961, (with Louise Bogan) The Golden Journey: Poems for Young People, 1965, The Tin Can and Other Poems, 1966, Poems from France, 1967, Mr. Smith and Other Nonsense, 1968, New and Selected Poems, 1970, The Streaks of the Tulip: Selected Criticism, 1972, Poems from Italy, 1973, Venice in the Fog, 1975, The Telephone, 1977, Laughing Time, 1980, The Traveler's Tree, New and Selected Poems, 1980, Army Brat: A Memoir, 1980, A Green Place: Modern Poems, 1982, (with Emanuel Brasil) Brazilian Poetry 1950-1980, Jules Laforgue, Moral Tales, 1985, collected Translations: Italian, French, Spanish, Portugese, 1985, (with Dana Gioia) Poems from Italy, 1985, (with Leif Sjoberg) Harry Martinson, Nature Poems, 1985. BA, Washington U., St. Louis, 1939, MA, 1941; postgrad., Columbia U., 1946-47, Oxford U., 1947-48, U. Florence, Italy, 1948-50; Litt.D., New Eng. Coll., 1973. Asst. in French Washington U., 1939-41; instr. English and French Columbia U., 1946-47; lectr. English Williams Coll., 1951, poet-in-res., lectr. English, 1959-64, 66-67; Ford Fdn. fellow Arena Stage (Washington), 1964-65; writer-in-res. Hollins Coll., 1965-66, prof. English, 1967, 70-80, prof. emeritus, 1980; cons. poetry Library of Congress (Washington), 1968-70, hon. cons. in Am. letters, 1970-76; vis. prof., acting chair writing div. Schl. Arts, Columbia U., 1973, 74-75; mem. jury Natl. Book award, 1962, 70, 75. Served to lt. USNR, 1941-45. Elected mem. Am. Acad. and Inst. of Arts & Letters, 1975, VP for lit., 1986; poet-in-res., Cathedral of St. John the Divine, 1986—. Jury Neustadt Intl. prize for lit., 1978; prize Poetry mag., 1945, 64; Henry Bellamann Major award, 1970; Russell Loines award Natl. Inst. Arts and Letters, 1972; Gold Medal of Labor, Hungarian Peoples Republic, 1978; Golden Rose New Eng. Poetry Soc., 1979. Mem. AAIAL, Am. Assn. Rhodes Scholars, AAP, AG (council), PEN. Home: 1675 York Ave Apt 20 K New York NY 10128

SMITH, Z. Z., see Westheimer, David

SMOKE, JUDITH MCCOLL, b. San Diego, Aug. 9, 1942, d. Hal Herbert and Ella Ruth (Dunn) McColl; m. Robert Morrow Slater, July 11, 1966 (div. 1978); 1 son, Robert Morrow Jr.; m. 2d, Clinton Hamilton Smoke, June 1, 1983. Wrtr., ed. operating manuals, reports, other profl. materials, 1983—; contrbr. poetry, book rvws. Low County News and Rev., Charleston, S.C., 1974-76. AB, U. S.C., 1966; MBA, William Carey Coll., 1986. Instr. tech. writing Cape Feat Tech. Inst., Wilmington, N.C., 1976-79; account exec. New Hanover Broadcasting Corp., Wilmington, 1979-81; promotion mgr. Atlantic Telecasting Corp., wrtr., producer scripts WECT-TV, Wilmington, 1981-82; tech. wrtr. Computer Scis. Corp., Natl. Space Technology Labs., Miss., 1983—; publicity dir., publ. ed. Arts Council of Lower Cape Fear, Wilmington, 1979-83. Mem. Intl. Assn. Bus. Wrtrs. Home: 8 Willow Circle Gulfport MS 39503

SNIDER, CLIFTON MARK, b. Duluth, MN, Mar. 3, 1947; s. Allan George and Rhoda Marion (Tout) S. Author (poetry): Jesse Comes Back, 1976, Bad Smoke Good Body, 1980, Jesse and His Son, 1982, Edwin: A Character in Poems, 1984. BA, Calif. State U., 1969, MA, 1971; PhD, U. NM, 1974. Adj. instr. Long Beach City Coll., Calif., 1975—, Cerritos Coll., Norwalk, Calif., 1982—, Calif. State Univ., Long Beach, 1974—. Address: 1246 Appleton St Long Beach CA 90802

SNIDER, RUTH, see Hoeppner, Iona Ruth

SNODGRASS, ANN A., b. Sigourney, IA, May 5, 1958, d. Rodney G. and Barbara L. (Sampson) Snodgrass. Contrbr. poetry to Antioch, Paris, Sonora rvws, Crosscurrents, other lit mags; contrbr. translations to Pan's Rvw, New Letters, Quarry West. BA in English, U. Iowa, 1980; MA in English, Johns Hopkins U., 1981. Asst. Toothpaste Press, Iowa City, Iowa, 1978-79, Grilled Flowers Press, Iowa City, 1979-80; editorial asst. Johns Hopkins U. Press., Balt., 1980-81; poetry reader Ploughshares, Boston, 1981-82; poetry ed. Qtly West, Salt Lake City, 1983-85, ed., 1985—. Recipient Renato Poggioli award PEN Am. Center, NYC, 1985. Mem. AWP. Address: Eng Dept U Utah Salt Lake City UT 84112

SNODGRASS, TOD JOHN, b. San Diego, June 7, 1945; s. John Philip Snodgrass and Edith (Capps) Rudrauff; m. Birgit H. Moll, June 13, 1982; children: Sean Tod, Danial, Jerime, Danica Britney. Author: Office Purchasing Guide, 1985, 86; ed. The Secretary's Friend, 1986. Student San Diego State U. Pres. Snodgrass Stationery & Prts., Inc., Gardena, Calif., 1972-85; pub. Lowen Pub., Rancho Palos Verdes, Calif., 1985—. Mem. Pubs. Mktg. Assn., COSMEP. Address 2464 Rue Le Charlene 140 Rancho Palos Verdes CA 90274

SNODGRASS, W. D., (S.S. Gardons, Will McConnell), b. Wilkinsburg, PA, Jan. 5, 1926; s. Bruce DeWitt and Jesse Helen (Murchie) S.; m. Kathleen Ann Brown, June 20, 1985; children: Cynthia (by 1st marriage); Russell, Kathy (stepdaughter) (by 2nd marriage). Author: (poetry) Heart's Needle, 1959, After Experience, 1967, (under pseudonym S.S. Gardons) Remains, 1970, The Fuehrer Bunker, 1977, If Birds Build with Your Hair, 1979, These Trees Stand, 1981, The Boy Made of Meat, 1982, Magda Goebbels, 1983, The Four Seasons, 1984, D.D. Byrde Calling Jennie Wrenne, 1984, Remains (rev. under name W.D. Snodgrass), 1985, Selected Poems, 1987, The Death of Cock Robin, 1987; (trans.) Gallows Songs (Christian Morgenstern), 1967, Six Troubadour Songs, 1977, Traditional Hungarian Songs, 1978, Six Minnesinger Songs, 1983. Student Geneva Coll., 1943-44, 46; BA, State U. of Iowa, 1949, MA, 1951, MFA, 1953, postgrad., 1953-55. With dept. English, Cornell U., 1955-57, U. Rochester, 1957-58, Wayne State U., 1959-67, English and speech depts. Syracuse U., 1968-77; Disting. Vis. prof. Old Dominion U., 1978-79; Disting. Vis. prof. U. Del., Newark, 1979, Disting. prof. creative writing and contemporary poetry, 1980—. Wrkg. on The Fuehrer Bunker. Served with USN, World War II. Fellow, Hudson Rev., 1958-59, Guggenheim Found., 1972-73, AAP, 1973, Ingram-Merrill, 1979; grantee Nat. Inst. Arts and Letters, 1960, Ford Found., 1963-64, Nat. Council on Arts, 1966-67, Ctr. Advanced Study, 1983-84; recipient Ingram-Merrill award, 1958, Longview Lit. award, 1959, Spl. Citation, PSA, 1960, Pulitzer Prize in Poetry, 1960, Guiness Poetry award (Gt. Britain), 1961, Miles Modern Poetry award, 1966, Bi-Centennial medal William and Mary Coll., 1976, Centennial medal Govt. of Romania, 1977. Fellow Natl. Inst. Arts and Letters, PSA, AAP, PEN, OG (assoc.). Home: 308 Delaware Circle Newark DE 19711

SNOOK, HERBERT EDGAR, b. Beacon, NY, Jan. 24, 1945; s. Willett A. and Elizabeth (Edgar) S., m. Linda S. Dolan, Feb. 27, 1981; children—Lynn Anne, Stacey Lynn, Matthew Aaron, Aaron Dolan. Contrbr. articles to mags. including Extra 2200 S., Model Railroad Cratsman, Model Railroader, Trains. Staff ed.: CTC Bd. Railroad Mag., Oroville, CA, 1987—; mng. ed.: Charlotte Monthly Mag., Port Chalotte, FL, 1987—. Wrkg. on column on autograph collecting. Attended Dutchess CC, 1963-64. Municipal Police Training in Police Sci., Iona Coll., 1967. Police officer City of Beacon, NY, 1966-78. Freelance wrtr. Address: Box 80902 Port Charlotte FL 33949

SNOW, BONNIE, b. Cleve., May 14, 1952; d. William and Elaine Ruth (Spero) Sosnowsky; m. Steven R. Glave. Author: They Call Me Duchess, But My Name Is . . . , 1975, She Lays Eggs for Gentleman (one-woman show), 1977, I Always Talk to Cabdrivers, 1986; contbr. to LI Rvw, Milkwood; wrkg. on new poetry; music for her rock 'n' roll band, Vinyl Virgin. BA, Northwestern U., 1970-71; MA, Occidental Coll., 1974-75. Secy. Met. Mus. Art, Research to Prevent Blindness, Bon Bon Prodns., Acad. Scis., all NYC. Recipient 1st place award, San Francisco State Univ., 1974. Mem. AFTRA, Songwriters Guild, P&W, NY Poetry Soc. Address: 188A E 93 St New York NY 10128

SNOW, ROBERT LAWRENCE, b. Indpls., May 17, 1949; s. Paul Allen and Martha Jane (Fisher) S.; m. Melanie Gay, Apr. 26, 1980; children—Alan Fitzpatrick, Melissa Ann. Contrbr. articles, short stories to mags. including Reader's Digest, Natl. Centurion, Police Mag., others. A.S. in Criminal Justice, Ind. U., 1973, B.S. magna cum laude in Psychology, 1975. Field training coord. Indpls. Police Dept., 1978-80, dir. planning, 1980-86, chief exec. officer, 1986—. Bd. dirs. Emergency Med. Services Council, Indpls., 1980—; public safety representative Med. Technical Advisory Council, Indpls., 1980—. Recipient One of Ten Best Stories of Yr. award Police Mag., 1981, 82; named Outstanding Young Man of Yr., Natl. Jaycees, 1982. Home: 5114 E Heathwood Dr Indianapolis IN 46237

SNYDAL, JAMES MATTHEW, b. Williston, ND, May 6, 1949, s. Arthur Joseph and Doris Olive (Gores) S,; m. Kathryn Jean Church, July 25, 1970. Contrbr. to Permafrost, Floating Poetry Gallery, Poem the Nukes, Pebble, numerous other lit mags. Wrkg. on jnl of English authors. BA. U. Wash., 1982—; v.p. Had We But, Inc., Seattle, 1984—; ed. Fine Madness, Seattle, 1986—. Mem. P&W. Home: 11034 Old Creosote Hill Rd Bainbridge Island WA 98110

SNYDER, GARY SHERMAN, b. San Francisco, May 8, 1930; s. Harold Alton and Lois (Wilkie) Snyder; m. Masa Uehara, Aug. 6, 1967; children—Kai, Gen. Author: poems Riprap, 1959, Myths and Texts, 1960, Six Sections from Mountains and Rivers without End, 1965, A Range of Poems, 1966, The Back Country, 1968; prose Earth House Hold, 1969; poems Regarding Wave, 1970, Turtle Island, 1974; prose The

Old Ways, 1977, He who Hunted Birds in His Father's Village, 1979, The Real Work, 1980; poetry Axe Handles, 1983; prose Passage through India, 1984, poetry Left Out in the Rain, 1986. BA, Reed Coll., 1951; postgrad., Ind. U., 1951-52, U. Calif. at Berkeley, 1953-56. Gen. Lookout Mount Baker Forest, 1952-53; research in Japan, 1956-57, 59-64; lectr. U. Calif. at Berkeley, 1964-65; prof. U. Calif., Davis, 1986—. Poetry award Natl. Inst. Arts and Letters; Pulitzer prize for poetry, 1975. Address: 18442 MacNab Cypress Rd Nevada City CA 95959

SNYDER, NANCY ELLEN, b. Portland, ME, Aug. 25, 1935; d. Harry Gilbert and Mildred (Cushing) Hanson; m. Bruce Judson Snyder, Oct. 30, 1954; children: Dara Christine Snyder Cummins, Meena Ellen. BA, U. Wash., 1982. Wrtr. Titusville (Fla.) Star Advocate (Gannett Corp.), 1962-64, ed., 1965-69; wrtr.-ed Fournier Pub. Co., Seattle, 1970-73; freelance wrtr., 1973-82; staff wrtr. Delta Airlines, Atlanta, 1984—. Wrkg. on mystery novel. Home: 303 So River Farm Dr Alpharetta GA 30201

SNYDER, SUSAN BROOKE, b. Yonkers, NY, July 12, 1934; d. John Warren and Virginia Grace (Hartung) Snyder. Author: The Comic Matrix of Shakespeare's Tragedies, 1979; editor: Divine Weeks and Works of DuBartas, 1979; editorial bd.: Shakespeare Qtly, 1972—. BA, Hunter coll., CUNY, 1955; MA, Columbia U., 1958, PhD, 1963. Lectr. Queens Coll., CUNY, (NYC), 1961-63; instr. Swarthmore Coll. (PA), 1963-66, asst. prof. English lit., 1966-70, assoc. prof., 1970-75, prof., 1975—, Eugene M. Lang research prof., 1982-86. Folger Library sr. fellow, 1972-73; NEH fellow, 1967-68; Guggenheim Fdn. fellow, 1980-81. Mem. MLA. Office: Dept Eng Swarthmore Coll Swarthmore PA 19081

SNYDER, ZILPHA KEATLEY, b. Lemoore, CA, May 11, 1927; d. William Solon and Dessa E. (Jepson) Keatley; m. Larry Alan Snyder, June 18, 1950; children—Susan Melissa, Douglas Clark, Benton Lee (foster son). Author: Season of Ponies, 1964 (ALA notable book 1975), The Velvet Room, 1965 (Jr. Lit. Guild, Arrow Book Club), Black and Blue Magic, 1966 (Arrow Book Club, tape and film strip), The Egypt Game, 1967 (Newbery honor book, 1st prize Spring Book Festival, NY 1967, Lewis Carroll shelf award, George Stone recognition of merit); ALA notable book, recipient., filmstrip and tape Eyes in the Fishbowl, 1968, Today is Saturday, 1969, The Changeling, 1970 (Christopher medal, Jr. Lit. Guild, Arrow Book Club), The Headless Cupid, 1971 (Newbery honor book, Hans Christian Andersen Intl. honor list, Christopher medal, Jr. Lit. Guild, William Allen White award, recipient., filmstrip and tape), The Witches of Worm, 1972 (Newbery honor book, ALA notable book, recipient.), The Princess and the Giants, 19733, The Truth About Stone Hollow, 1974, Green-sky Trilogy: Below the Root, 1975 (Jr. Lit. Guild) And All Between, 1976, Until the Celebration, 1977 (Jr. Lit. Guild); novel for adults Heirs of Darkness, 1978, The Famous Stanley Kidnapping Case, 1979 (sequel to The Headless Cupid), A Fabulous Creature, 1981, Come On, Patsy, 1982; The Birds of Summer, 1983 (Los Angeles PEN award 1983), Blair's Nightmare (Jr. Lit. Guild), 1984, The Changing Maze, 1985, And Condors Danced, 1987. BA, Whittier Coll., 1948. Tchr., 1948-62; master tchr. U. Calif., Berkeley, 1959-61; Public speaker. Mem. AG. Home: 52 Miller Ave Mill Valley CA 94941

SOBCZYNSKA, DANUTA, (Diana Karazim), b. Grajewo, Bialystok, Poland, Jan. 9, 1944 (came to US, Aug. 8, 1962); d. Francis and Genovefe (Barycki) Karazim; m. Walt Sobczynski; children—Andrew, Annette. Publisher: The Songwriters' Expo., 1984—. BA, Hunter College, 1968, MSW, 1978; postgrad. NYU. Director Human Multiservice Assoc. (Brooklyn, NY), 1980—; program dir. POMOC Inc. (Brooklyn), 1985—. Golden Poet Award, World of Poetry, 1985. Mem. NASW. Office: Song Expo 215 29th St Brooklyn NY 11226

SOBEL, LESTER ALBERT, bNYC, Oct. 3, 1919; s. David and Ray Dorothy (Mendelson) Sobel; m. Eileen Lucille Helfer, May 3, 1953; children—Martha Lorraine, Sharon Ruth, Jonathan William. Author: National Issues, 1956, Space: From Sputnik to Gemini, 1965, South Vietnam: U.S.-Communist Confrontation in South-East Asia, Vol. 1, 1966, Vol. 2, 1969, Vol. 3, 1977, Vol. 4, 1980, Civil Rights, 1967, Russia's Rulers: The Khrushchev Period, 1971, Chile and Allende, 1974, Political Terrorism, Vol. 1, 1975, Vol. 2, 1978, Presidential Succession, 1975, Kissinger and Detente, 1975, Argentina and Peron, 1975, Cancer and the Environment, 1979, Peace-Making in the Middle East, 1980, Media Controversies, 1981. BBA, CCNY, 1942. Mem. editorial staff Facts on File, 1946—, editor-in hief, 1960-73; vp Facts on File, Inc., 1964-80, sr. contrbg. editor, 1980—; editor-in-chief News Year, 1960-63, News Dictionary, 1964-73, Interim History, 1964-75, editor Reality, 1976—. Served with AUS, 1942-45; ETO. Decorated Bronze Star. Home: 226 Porterfield Pl Freeport NY 11520

SOBIN, A. G., see Sobin, Anthony

SOBIN, ANTHONY, b. Washington, July 18, 1944; s. Walter and Theda Anne (Guymer) S.; 1 child, Melissa. Author: The Sunday Naturalist, 1982; contrbr. to numerous jnls and lit mags including Poetry, Am. Poetry Rvw, Poetry N.W., Paris Rvw, Partisan Rvw, New Letters. BA in English, tulane U., 1966; MFA in Poetry, U. Iowa, 1969; PhD in English, U. Utah, 1975. Assoc. prof. English and creative writing grad. writing program Wichita State U., Kans., 1970—; vis. prof. U. Tex., Austin, 1983. Recipient 1st prize for poetry Kans. Qtly, 1974-85, poetry award Utah Council for Arts, 1974, 81; NEA creative writing fellow, 1975. Office: Eng Dept Wichita State U Wichita KS 67208

SOBLESKIE, PATRICIA ANGELA, b. Akron, OH, Dec. 9, 1947; d. Francis Edward and Juliette Delores (Delisa) McCormick; m. Edward Allan Sobleskie, Dec. 16, 1967; children—Kimberly, Edward. Contrb. poems, articles to mags., anthols., newspapers including Daily Guideposts, Grit, Woman's World, Wrtr.'s Digest, others. Wrkg. on articles. A.A. magna cum laude, Albany Jr. Coll., 1984. Bookkeeper 1st Nat. Bank., Albany, GA, 1968-74; writing instr. Life Office Management, Atlanta, 1981—. Recipient Outstanding Achievement in Jnlsm. award Albany Jr. Coll., 1984. Home: 305 Johnson Rd Albany GA 31705

SOBOL, DONALD J., b. NYC, Oct. 4, 1924; s. Ira J. and Ida (Gelula) Sobol; m. Rose Louisa Tiplintz, Aug. 14, 1955; children—Diane, Glenn (dec. 1983), Eric, John. Author: more than 50 books; syndicated newspaper feature Two Minute Mystery Series; numerous short stories for adults and children. BA, Oberlin Coll., 1948. Mem. editorial staff New York Sun (NYC), 1948, L.I. Daily Press, 1949-51; with R.H. Macy's Co., 1953-54; free-lance writer, 1954—. Served with AUS, 1943-46. Recipient awards. Mem. AL Am., MWA, Soc. Children's Book Writers. Office: McIntosh & Otis 475 5th Ave New York NY 10017

SOCOLOW, ELIZABETH A., b. NYC, June 15, 1940, d. Ralph Maurice and Frances Irene (Goldberg) Sussman; div.; children—David Jacob, Seth Lewis. Author: Laughing at Gravity: Conversations with Isaac Newton, 1988. Contrbr. to Ploughshares, Berkeley Poets Coop. Mag., MS. Mag, Nantucket Rvw, New York Qtly., New England Rvw/Breadloaf Qtly, Nimrod Mag.; poetry ed. PSLS, rotating mng. ed. U.S. 1 Worksheets. BA, Vassar Coll., 1962; MA, PhD. Harvard U., 1963, 67; tchr. high schl. English Lakewood Prep. Poet-in-schls., N.J. State Council on Arts, 1984-86, coordinator reading series, Arts Council of Princeton, 1985—, Barnard Women Poets Prize, 1987. Mem. MLA, P&W. Home: 64 Pine St Princeton NJ 08542

SODARO, ROBERT J., b. Norwalk, CT, Sept. 23, 1955; s. Henry J. and Marie (Calise) S. Author: Trivia Mania: Commercials & Ads, 1984. Contrbr. articles to mags. including Amazing Heroes, Guide to Computer Living, numerous others. Ed.: Amazing Heroes, 1982, Comics Jnl., 1982-83, Videogaming and Computer Gaming Illustrated, 1983-84, Ahoy!, 1983-85, The Guide to Computer Living, 1985-87, Add-Ons Buyer's Guide & Handbook, 1985, Comics Interview, 1987; Created and wrtg. action/adventure spy comic, Agent Unknown, for Renegade Press. BS in Media Studies, Sacred Heart U., 1978. Free-lance wrtr., 1985—. Home: Box 1081 Fairfield CT 06432

SOFFER, ALFRED, b. South Bend, IN, May 5, 1922; s. Simom Mordicai and Bessie Molly (Rokach) S.; m. Isabel Marie Weintraub, July 22, 1956; children—Jonathan, Joshua, Gil. Ed.-in-chief Chest, 1969—; co-ed. Heart & Lung, 1974-83; chief ed. Archives of Internal Medicine, 1976-86; editorial bd., Jnl. of AMA, 1976—, Respiration, 1976—; author 45 articles on cardiac disease, 2 books on cardiology, 150 editorials in peer-review medical jnls. BA, U. WI, 1943, MD, 1945. Served to Capt., USMC, 1946-48. Fellow Am. Coll. Cardiology, Am. Coll. Physicians. Consultant to White House and HEW on medical jnls., 1972-74; consultant on research in Israel and Far East to Secy. of HEW, 1972-74. Office: Am Coll. of Chest Phys 911 Busse Hwy Park Ridge IL 60068

SOHL, JERRY, (Nathan Butler, Sein Mei Sullivan, Roberta Jean Mountjoy), b. Los Angeles, Dec. 2, 1913, s. Fred and Florence (Wray) S.; m. Jean Gordon, Oct. 28, 1943; children—Allan, Martha Jane, Jennifer. Author: The Haploids, 1952, The Transcendent Man, 1953, Costigan's Needle, 1953, The Altered Ego, 1954, Point Ultimate, 1955, Prelude to Peril, 1956, The Mars Monopoly, 1956, The Time Dissolver, 1956, One Against Herculum, 1959, The Odious Ones, 1959, Night Slaves (Fawcett Gold Medal), 1963, The Lemon Eaters, 1967, The Spun Sugar Hole, 1971, The Anomaly, 1971, The Underhanded Chess, 1973, The Resurrection of Frank Borchard, 1973, Dr. Josh (Fawcett Gold Medal), 1974, Mamelle (Fawcett Gold Medal), 1974, Supermanchu, 1974, Underhanded Bridge, 1975, Blow Dry, 1976, I, Aleppo, 1976, Mamelle, The Goddess, 1977, Night Wind, 1981, Kaheesh, 1983, Death Sleep, 1983, Black Thunder, 1983; contrbr. stories: Playboy, Galaxy, Space, The New Mind, other publs.; screenwrtr.: Twelve Hours to Kill, 1960, Die, Monster, Die, 1965, Night Slaves, 1970;

staff wrtr. TV series: Star Trek, Alfred Hitchcock Presents, The New Breed; contrbr. episodes: Twilight Zone, Naked City, Outer Limits, numerous others. Wrkg. on novels. Mem. SFWA, WG, AG. Home: 3020 Ash Ct Thousand Oaks CA 91360

SOKOLNIKOFF, NICHOLAS, see Homesley, Horace Edward

SOLDO, JOHN J., b. Bklyn., May 16, 1945, s. Victor and Mildred (Ferrari) S.; m. Martha Schwink, Aug. 24, 1968 (div. Apr. 1971). Author: Delano in America, 1974, The Tempering of T.S. Eliot, 1983, Odes & Cycles, 1983, In an Arid Clime, 1985; also over 400 pub. poems, jnl articles, lit. essays. BA magna cum laude, Fordham U., 1966; MA, Harvard U., 1968, PhD, 1972. Mem. faculty Wells Coll., 1971-72, CUNY, 1972-73; Columbia U., 1973-77, Eastern N.Mex. U., Portales, 1978-84, L.I. U., Southampton, N.Y., 1986—. Recipient award for poetry Intl. Acad. des Beaux Arts, 1976, also numerous regional awards. Mem. P&W, N.Y. Poetry Forum, Bklyn. Poetry Circle, N.Mex. Poetry Soc. (chancellor). Home: 238 Ave U Brooklyn NY 11223

SOLER, DONA K., b. Grand Rapids, MI, March 7, 1921; d. Melbourne A. and Katherine Anne Welch; 1 dau.—Suzette Maria. Author books: What God Hath Put Together, 1983, Our Heritage From the Angels, 1984, Expose the Dirty Devil, 1984, Anthology of Verse, 1985, For Love of Henry, 1985, Greyball, 1986, House of Evil Secrets, 1986. Student, public and parochial schls., Grand Rapids, MI. Editor and pub. of Orange Coast Catholic Newsletter, 1970-73; editor Lake Riverside Communicators Newsletter, 1974-79; editor and pub. of Psychic Exchange News and Research Monthly, 1979—. Home: 2604 Willo Ln Costa Mesa CA 92627

SOLLOV, JACQUES, b. Cornwall, Ont., Can., Aug. 3, 1935, s. Joseph and Elise (Collins) S. Author, ed.: The Temple of Love, 1979, Reborn Again in the Kingdom, 1982, Gold of the Stars, 1983; contrbr: Our World's Most Beloved Poems Anthology, 1984. Wrkg. on poetry collection. BEE, UCLA, 1965. Project analog. engr. NASA and Aerospace Research Pilot Schl., Calif., 1965-70 (assist Astronaut trng., Gemini & Apollo projects); pilot trainer Lockheed Aircraft Corp., Palmdale, Calif., 1971—. Recipient Silver medal Universal Acad. Switzerland, 1983, Golden Poet award World of Poetry, 1985, Silver Poet Award, 1986. Mem. AG, P&S, Am. Film Inst. Office: Box 1332 Dept S-0111 Lowell MA 01853

SOLONCHE, JOEL R., b. NYC, July 16, 1946; s. Abraham and Sally (Karp) S.; m. Joan I. Siegel, Dec. 31, 1972. Contbr. to anthologies: 1985 Anthology of Am. Verse, Blood to Remember: contbr. to Am. Scholar, Crosscurrents, Cumberland Poetry Rvw, Dark Horse, Salmagundi, Lyric, Negative Capability, Pinchpenny, Poem, Poetry Northwest, Poets On, Pulpsmith (Madeline Sadin award), Small Pond, others. BS, NYU; MA, SUNY-New Paltz. Address: Box 99 Blooming Grove NY 10914

SOLOTAROFF, TED, b. Elizabeth, NJ, Oct. 9, 1928; s. Ben and Rose (Weiss) S.; m. Virginia Ruth Martin, Dec. 27, 1982; children: Paul, Ivan, Jason, Isaac. Author: Red Hot Vacuum, 1970, A Few Voices in My Head, 1987. Editor: Age of Enormity, 1962; Writers and Issues, 1969; Many Windows, 1982. Contbr. articles to profl. jnls. B.A., U. Mich., Ann Arbor, 1952; M.A., U. Chgo., 1956. Assoc. editor Commentary Mag., 1960-66; editor Book Week, N.Y. Herald Tribune, 1966, Am. Review, New Am. Library, 1966-70, New Am. Review, Simon & Schuster, 1970-72, Am. Review, Bantam Books Inc., 1972-79; sr. editor Harper & Row Inc., 1979—; Lectr. lit. and creative writing U. Chgo., Yale U., CCNY, U. Calif.-Berkeley, Columbia U., U. Mich. Served with USN, 1946-48. Recipient Irita Van Doren award Am. Pub. Assn., 1972; Creative Arts award Brandeis U., 1973; Lucille Medwick award Am. PEN, 1980. Home: 54 Morningside Dr New York NY 10025

SOLTER, ALETHA LUCIA, b. Princeton, NJ, Dec. 21, 1945; d. Josef Maria and Anna-Tonette (Hegland) Jauch; m. Kenneth Marc Solter, July 10, 1971; children: Nicholas, Sarah. Author: The Aware Baby: A New Approach to Parenting, 1984. M. in Biology, U. Geneva, Switzerland, 1969; PhD in Psychology, U. Calif.-Santa Barbara, 1975. Instr. history of sci. Pub. High Schl., Geneva, Switzerland, 1967-68; lab. asst. Inst. Environ. Stress, U. Calif., Santa Barbara, 1969-70, lectr. introductory psychology, 1975-76, postdoctoral research asst. dept. edn., 1980-81; instr. parenting Continuing Edn. Div., Santa Barbara City Coll., 1985—; pub. Shining Star Press, Goleta, Calif., 1984—. NSF predoctoral trainee, 1972-74; predoctoral fellow Natl. Inst. Mental Health, 1974-75. Home: 104 Saint Ives Pl Goleta CA 93117

SOLWITZ, SHARON DEE, b. Pitts., Dec. 10, 1945, d. Myron Joseph and Ruth Rose (Berez) Solwitz; m. Barry Thomas Silesky, June 13, 1982. Contrbr. to Mademoiselle, New Am. Wrtg., Another Chicago Mag., Telescope, Kans. Qtly., Other Voices, Nimrod. BA cum laude in English, Cornell U., 1968; MA, U. Ill.-Chgo., 1978, MFA, 1981. Freelance wrtr., filmmaker, Chgo., 1969-79; artist-in-edn., Ill. Arts Council, 1983—; fiction ed. Another Chgo. Mag., 1984—; vis. lectr. Sch. of Art Inst. Chgo., 1984—. Recipient lit. award Ill. Arts Council, 1983; Kansas Arts Council fiction prize, 1986; Katherine Anne Porter fiction prize (Nimrod), 1986, Illinois Arts Coun. grant, literary award, 1987. Home: 3709 N. Kenmore Ave Chicago IL 60613.

SOLZHENITSYN, ALEXANDER, b. Kislorodsk, Russia, Dec. 11, 1918; m. Natalya Reshetovskaya. Author: novel One Day in the Life of Ivan Denisovich, 1962, We Never Make Mistakes, 1963, The First Circle, 1968, The Cancer Ward, 1968, Stories and Prose Poems, 1971, August 1914, 1972, The Gulag Archipelago, 1918-1956, Part I, 1974, Part II, 1975, Part III, 1976, The Oak and the Calf, 1975, Letter to the Soviet Leaders, 1975, From Under the Rubble, 1976, Detentte: Prospects for Democracy and Dictatorship, 1976, Warning to the West, 1976, Lenin in Zurich, 1976, The Novel Lecture, 1973; narrative poem Prussian Nights, 1977; (Harvard U. commencement address), A World Split Apart, 1978, The Mortal Danger: Misconceptions About Soviet Russia and the Threat to America, 1980, Victory Celebrations, 1983; plays Love-Girl and the Innocent, 1970, Candle in the Wind, 1974, Three Plays, 1985. Corr. student in philology, Moscow Inst. History, Philosophy and Lit., 1939-40; degree in math. and physics, U. Rostov, 1941; Litt.D., Harvard U., 1978. Arty. officer Russian Army, World War II. Recipient Nobel prize for lit., 1970, Templeton prize, 1983. Mem. Am. Acad. Arts and Scis. Imprisoned under Premier Joseph Stalin on unnamed polit. charges, 1945-53; exiled to Siberia, 1953; wrote and taught; freed from exile, 1956; after release taught at secondary schl. in Ryazan; exiled from USSR, 1974. Address: FS&G 19 Union Sq W New York NY 10003

SOMERFIELD, NEIL, b. Hereford, England, May 31, 1953, came to U.S., 1983; s. Dennis William and Muriel (Stone) S.; m. Eileen Mary Smith, June 15, 1985; 1 son, Harvey James. Wrkg. on (film story) The Shanachie, (film story and screenplay) Ben-Gurion, (documentary), Communism's Forgotten Victims. Chmn., creative dir. Somerfield & Williams Ltd., London, 1981-83; pres. The Somerfield Film Group, Inc., Wellesley, MA, 1983—. Recipient award Designers and Art Dirs. Club, London, 1982, Silver award Campaign Mag., 1982, Gold award, Best in Show award Art Dirs. Club, Boston, 1985, Intl. Film & TV Festival awards, 1985, 86. Mem. Dir. Guild Am. Home: 47 Curve St Wellesley MA 02181

SOMERS, MARGARET LEE, (Margaret Simmons), b. Tacoma, Apr. 6, 1941; d. Floyd Leland and Daisy Jane (Campbell) S. Contrbr. articles, reports, short stories, poems to trade jnls., profl. pubs., lit. mags., anthols. Author, ed.: (with D. H. Ford) Plan for Higher Education in Pennsylvania, 1967. Ed.: An Intellectual Autobiography (Joseph Novak), 1977; numerous technical and public relations pieces. B.A., Penn. State U., 1967; M.A., Kans. U., 1969; Ph.D., Cornell U., 1974. Visiting asst. prof. U. Ky., Lexington, 1977-81; asst. prof. U. Minn., St. Paul, 1981-85; staff tutor in English, U. Cin., 1986—. Named Tchr. of Yr., U. Ky. Dept. Mechanical Engineering, 1981. Mem. NCTE, TABC. Office: Box 21028 Cincinnati OH 45212

SONENBERG, MAYA, b. NYC, Feb. 24, 1960, d. Jack Sonenberg and Phoebe (Rubin) Helman. Contrbr. short fiction to Grand Street, Gargoyle, Chelsea. BA, Wesleyan U., Middletown, Conn., 1982; AM in fiction, Brown U., 1984. Writing tutor Brown U., Providence, 1982-84, intern advisor, teaching fellow in fiction, 1984; teaching asst. in English, Choate Rosemary Hall, Wallingford, Conn., 1983, lectr. Sonoma State Univ., Rohnert Park, CA, 1986. Winchester fellow, 1982; Brown U. fellow, 1982-83. Mem. AWP. Home: 2435 1/2 McKinley Ave Berkeley CA 94703

SONENSCHEIN, DAVID WALTER, b. Terre haute, IN, Feb. 22, 1941, s. Benjamin and Mary Catherine (Olds) S. Author: Some Homosexual Men, 1983; ed.: Soc. for Sci. Study of Sex, 1969-71, Jnl. Popular Culture, 1969-71, Med. Aspects of Human Sexuality, 1970-73, Childhood Sensuality Circle, 1982-84, The Rag, 1969-73, ARG, 1982-83; contrbg. author: Readings in General Sociology, 1969, Sociology and the Student, 1970, The Social Dimension of Human Sexuality, 1972, Things in the Driver's Seat, 1972, Side Saddle on the Golden Calf, 1972, Homosexuality: A Changing Picture, 1973,Sex Research: Studies from the Kinsey Institute, 1976, The Popular Culture Reader, 1978, Forbidden Fruits: Taboos and Tabooism in Culture, 1984; contrbr. articles to acad. and popular publs.; contrbr. to The Rag, GALA Rvw, Gay Community News, others. BA in Anthropology-Philosophy, U. Ariz., 1965; MA, Ind. U., 1968; postgrad., U. Tex.-Austin, 1968-71. Home: Box 15744 San Antonio TX 78212

SONNENBERG, BEN, b. NYC, Dec. 30, 1936, s. Benjamin and Hilda (Caplan) S.; m. Wendy Adler (div. 1974); m. 2d, Susan de Verges (div. 1977); m. 3d, Dorothy Gallagher, Mar. 10, 1981; children—Susanna, Emma, Saidee. Author: Jane Street, 1967, Mole Wedding, 1969; ed.: Grand Street, 1981—, A Grand Street Reader, 1986;

contrbr. articles: The Nation, Yale Rvw, London Mag. Mem. PEN. Home: 50 Riverside Dr New York NY 10024

SONNENBLICK, EDMUND H., b. New Haven, Dec. 7, 1932, s. Ira J. and Rosalind (Helfaud) S.; m. Linda Bland, 1954; children—Emily, Charlotte, Annie (dec.). Ed., contrbr.: Mechanisms of Contraction of the Normal and Failing Heart, 1968, other texts; contrbr. over 400 articles to profl. jnls.; ed.-in- chief: Progress in Cardiovascular Diseases, 1972—; ed.: Yearbook of Cardiovascular Medicine and Surgery, 1973—, The Heart (by J. Willis Hurst), 1981; sr. ed.: Cardiovascular Medicine, 1976-79, Cardiovascular Rvws. and Reports, 1979—; mem. editorial bd. numerous profl. publs. BA, Wesleyan U., 1954; MD, Harvard U., 1958. Olson prof. medicine Albert Einstein Coll. Medicine, Bronx, N.Y., 1984—, dir. Cardiovascular Center, 1985—. Served as sr. asst. surgeon USPHS, 1960-62. Mem. Phi Beta Kappa. Home: 138 Goodwives River Rd Darien CT 06820

SOOS, RICHARD A. JR., b. Passaic, NJ, Apr. 24, 1955, s. Richard A. and Shirley M. (Schneider) S.; m. Ann C. Fajilan, May 15, 1976 (div. 1979); m. 2d, Beverly J. Somerville Dauphinais, Mar. 15, 1980; children—Erin Marie, Sarah Elizabeth, Richard Alphonse. Author poetry books: Why Poetry, 1972, Reality is a Drunken Feeling, 1979, Patient Rains, 1982, A Foreign Landscape, 1984; ed. Seven Stars Poetry mag., 1972-80. Owner, mgr. Carpentr's Constrn., San Jose, Calif., 1980—; pres. Realities Library. Home: 2745 Moneterey Hwy Apt 76 San Jose CAJ 95111

SORENSEN, CAMEY, b. Boston, May 31, 1933; d. John and Rose (De Francesco) Alabiso; m. Charles Frederick, Sept. 2, 1961; 1 son, Richard Frederick. Author: It Could Happen to You, 1981. Contrbr. articles to newspapers, mags.; author songs. Secy., Àlford Manufacturing Co., Woburn, MA, 1984—. Office: Box 113 Woburn MA 01801

SORENSON, CHRISTINE, see Stevens, Christine Hyde

SORENSON, SHARON O., b. Evansville, IN, Aug. 15, 1943; d. Orville Charles and Viola Caroline (Savage) Blaser; m. Charles E. Sorenson, July 24, 1965. Author: Everyday Grammar and Usage Simplified and Self-Taught, 1982, 4th ed., 1987, Student's Guide to Writing Better Compositions, 1986, Webster's New World Student Writer's Handbook, 1988; author teaching aids; contrbr. numerous articles to trade and profl. publs. BA, Evansville Coll., 1964; MA, U. Evansville, 1967. Tchr. English Evansville (Ind.)-Vanderburgh Sch. Corp., 1964-79, dir. writing lab., 1980-86; adj. faculty U. Evansville, 1974-79, 87—; language arts cons., 1985—; freelance wrtr., 1979—; guest lectr. Midwest Wrtr.'s Conf., Muncie, Ind., 1981-84; judge Ohio Valley Wrtr.'s Assn., 1984; guest speaker ann. convention NCTE, Los Angeles, 1987. Recipient Hilda Maehling Fdn. fellowship, 1983. Mem. NCTE, Natl. Writing Centers Assn. Home: 10776 Altheide Rd Mount Vernon IN 47620

SORRELLS, ROBERT TALIAFERRO, b. NYC, Sept. 15, 1932, s. John Harvey and Ruth Given (Arnett) S.; m. Marjorie Dillman Baker, Mar. 10, 1962; children—Walter Arl, Ruth Lindsey. Contrbr.: Am. Rvw., S.C. Rev., Snowy Egret, December mag., other lit mags and anthologies. BA, Vanderbilt U., 1956, MA, 1957; MFA, U. Iowa, 1965. Asst. prof. Clemson (S.C.) U., 1965-70, ed., wrtr., 1983-85; freelance wrtr. (film script, radio programs for S. C. Edn'l. Radio Network, etc.). Clemson, 1972—. Grantee NEA, 1978, S.C. Comm. for Humanities, 1981; recipient PEN-NEA Syndicated Fiction award, 1983. Mem. AWP, So. Humanities Conf., South Atlantic MLA. Home: 1607 Bexhill Dr Knoxville TN 37922

SORRENTINO, GILBERT, b. Brklyn., Apr. 27, 1929; s. August E. and Anne Marie (Davis) Sorrentino; m. Victoria Ortiz; children—Jesse, Delia, Christopher. Author: The Darkness Surrounds Us, 1960, Black and White, 1964, The Sky Changes, 1966, The Perfect Fiction, 1968, Steelwork, 1970, Imaginative Qualities of Actual Things, 1971, Corrosive Sublimate, 1971, Splendide-Hotel, 1973, Flawless Play Restored, 1974, A Dozen Oranges, 1976, white Sail, 1977, Sulpiciae Elegidia/Elegiacs of Sulpicia, 1977, The Orangery, 1978, Mulligan Stew, 1979, Aberration of Starlight, 1980, Selected Poems, 1958-80, 1981, Crystal Vision, 1981, Blue Pastoral, 1983, Something Said: Essays, 1984, Odd Number, 1485. Student, Bklyn. Coll., 1949-51, 54-56. Editor Grove Press (NY), 1965-70; tchr. Columbia U., 1966, Aspen Writers Workshop, 1967, Sarah Lawrence Coll., 1972, The New Schl. for Social Research, from 1976; NEH chair in lit. U. Scranton, 1979; prof. English Stanford U. (CA), 1982—. Served with US Army, 1951-53. Recipient Samuel Fels award in fiction CCLM, 1974; John Dos Passos prize, 1981; CAPS program grantee, 1974-75; NEA grantee, 1975-76, 1978-79. Mem. PEN Am. Center. Address: Morris Agcy 1350 Ave of Ams New York NY 10019

SORSOLEIL, LORI MARIE, b. Mpls., Mar. 8, 1962; d. Clark Roger Van Horn and Joyce Ann (Hake) Hayes. Author: You Must be Cristal, 1978, Make Way for Weird, 1985, contrbr. to anthols. Wrkg. on sci. fiction novel. B.A., Bemidji State U., Minn. 1986. Mem. Soc. Collegiate Journalists, Mensa. Home: 302 Kay Ave Bemidji MN 56601

SOSTCHEN, CINDY, b. Bklyn., Sept. 5, 1957, d. William and Jean (Keller) Sostchen. Contrbr. poetry to Earthwise Calendar, Voices Intl, John Frost's Anthol. (1986). AAS with honors, Kingsborough Community Coll., 1978. Legal secy. firm Bower & Gardner, NYC, 1979—. Mem. Fla. Poets Assn. Home: 50 Shore Blvd Brooklyn NY 11235

SOUCY, BARBARA MARIE, b. Lackawanna, NY, Apr. 2, 1949, d. Rob Roy Charles and Alvina Ruth (Anstett) Olver; children—Thomas Charles Olver, Patrick James Manning, Matthew Cadell Bender. Author: Wonders (poetry), 1986. Wrkg. on autobiography. Tchr. New Penn Beauty Schl., Olean, N.Y., 1983—; emergency med. technician Hinsdale (N.Y.) Fire Dept., 1979—. Home: 3865 Canal St Hinsdale NY 14743

SOUDER, MARK STEPHEN, b. Independence, MO, Sept. 28, 1956; s. Arnold and Lois Eileen (Hawbaker) S. Editor/publisher: Florist & Grower, 1983-86, Sign of the Times—A Chronicle of Decadence in the Atomic Age, twice yearly, 1981—. Graduate Evergreen State Coll., 1980. Composition foreman Typeface Typesetting (Portland, OR), 1984; publisher Studio 403 (Portland), art director Kustom Printing/Journal and Bulletin Agcy. (Seattle, WA). Office: Box 70672 Seattle WA 98107

SOURIAN, PETER, b. Boston, Apr. 7, 1933; s. Zareh Missak and Zabelle (Bayentz) S.; m. Eve Jeanne Pocquet, Sept. 25, 1971; children—Mark, Delphine. Novels: Miri, 1957, The Best and Worst of Times, 1961, The Gate, 1965. Articles, fiction and rvws. in various publs. BA, Harvard U., 1955. Served to Sp. 5, U.S. Army, 1957-59. Prof. English, Bard Coll., Annandale-on-Hudson, 1965—; TV critic The Nation, 1975-80. Mem. PEN. Home: 30 E 70th St New York NY 10021

SOUTHWORTH, Anne, see McFarland, Anne S.

SOUTHWORTH, MILES F., b. Monroe, MI, May 16, 1935, s. Dwight and Erdine (Moyer) S.; m. Donna Kay Burley, Mar. 11, 1938; children—Sandra, Carrie. Author: Color Separation Techniques, 2d edit., 1979, Pocket Guide to Color Reproductions, 1979. BS, U. Mich., 1960; EdM, U. Rochester, 1967. Prof. Rochester (N.Y.) Inst. Tech., 1961-85, dir. Schl. of Printing, 1985—. Mem. graphic arts orgns. Home: 3100 Bronson Hill Rd Livonia NY 14487

SOWELL, CAROL ANN, b. Memphis, Oct. 8, 1946; d. Searcy Leo and Reba (Walls) Sowell. Ed.: Letting Go with Love: The Grieving Pocess (by Nancy O'Connor), 1984, The Dancing Healers (by Carl Hammerschlag), 1987; contrbr. articles: Modern Maturity, Prime Times, Grit, The Woman Engr., numerous others. BA in English, Tulane U., 1968; MA in Journalism, U. Mich., 1970. Asst. ed. School Shop, Ann Arbor, Mich., 1970-72; reporter Parsons (Kans.) Sun, 1972-74; gen. mgr. Green Valley (Ariz.) New, 1975-79; reporter, asst. ed. Ariz. Daily Star, Tucson, 1979-82; freelance wrtr., ed., Tucson, 1982—. Mem. Nat. Fedn. Press Women (finance chmn. Ariz. chap.), Authors Resource Center. Home: Box 43924 Tucson AZ 85733

SPAAR, LISA RUSS, (Lisa Russ), b. Elizabeth, NJ, Mar. 17, 1956, d. Warren Kenneth and Kay Lynne (Smith) Russ; m. A. Peter Spaar, June 6, 1981. Author chapbooks: Blind Boy on Skates, 1985; Cellar, 1983, contrbr. poetry to Va Qtly Rvw, Tendril, Crazyhorse, Intro 13, Stone Country, The Greenfield Rvw, numerous other lit mags; contrbr. to anthologies: Selections: Univ. & Coll. Poetry Prizes, 1973-78, 1980, Anthology of Mag. Verse and Yearbook of Am. Poetry, 1984, Pocket Poems, 1985. BA in English, U. Va., 1978, MFA, 1982. Instr. English, James Madison U., Harrisonburg, Va., 1982-85, North Tex. State U., Denton, 1985—. Hoyns poetry fellow U. Va., 1980-81; recipient lit. award Va. Commonwealth U.-AAUW, 1984. Mem. AWP, P&W, AAP (prize 1977). Office: Dept Eng N Tex State U Denton TX 76203

SPAHL, GARY MICHAEL, b. Middletown, CT, Oct. 19, 1960; s. Raymond John and Betty Ann (Boucher) S. Author: Coming Out: An Anthology, 1988. Wrkg.on cookbook, Moths in the Pantry; collection of essays, experimental piece. Student U. Mass., 1978-80; B.S. in Mass Communication, Emerson Coll., 1984. Tchr. elem. schls., Boston, 1985—; fundraiser Sta. WGBH-TV, Boston, 1985-86; free-lance copywrtr. Media-Mania, Boston, 1985—, The Philipson Agcy., Boston, 1985—. Recipient award for best produced public service announcement Alpha Epsilon Rho, 1984, 1st place for essay Wrtr.'s Refinery, Phoenix, 1987, Dore Schary Humanitarian Filmmaking award Anti-Defamation League of B'nai B'rith, 1985; grantee Mass. Arts Council, 1985. Mem. NWU. Home: 22 Eldridge Rd Boston MA 02130

SPANIER, MURIEL, b. NYC, Apr. 21, 1928; d. Frederick David Spanier and Sophia Roth; m. Nathan Marcuvitz, June 30, 1948; children—Andrew, Karen. Author: (novel) Staying Afloat, 1985. Contrbr. short stories to popular mags. including Saturday Evening Post, Ingenue, others. B.A., Hunter Coll., 1984. Copywriter Grey Advt., NYC, 1960-64; wrtr., ed. Sussman & Sugar, NYC, 1965-70; adj. lectr. English, Queens Coll., 1975-78. Mem. PEN, P&W. Home: 7 Ridge Dr E Great Neck NY 11021

SPARKS, (THEO) MERRILL, b. Mount Etna, IA, Oct. 5, 1922; s. David G. and Ollie M. (Hickman) S. Contrbr. poetry and poetry transl. to Poems, 1961; (in Russian) Picture Gallery, 1965; Anima Eroica, 1968; Iconography, 1969; Arts of Russia, 1970; Primer of Experimental Poetry, 1971; Sergei Bongart, 1982, N.Y. Rvw of Books, Choice, Coastlines, Unicorn Folios, Poetry N.Y., Lyrical Iowa, Western Rvw, other lit mag; translator/ed. (with Vladimir Markov) Modern Russian Poetry, 1966 (PEN Intl. Transl. Award 1968); composer: over 1000 songs; chamber cantata, Anima Eroica (with Vernon Duke) 1966 (Cross of Merit, Rome, 1966); musical, Icaria, prod. 1986. Wrkg (with Ricardo Sauro) on translating poems of Alfonsina Storni. Student U. Besancon, France, 1946; BA, U.So. Calif., 1948; postgrad. U. Iowa 1948-51; Columbia U., 1951-52. Voice/piano entertainer, 1953—. Served with AUS, 1943-46, ETO, MTO. Mem. Modern Poetry Assn., Authors Guild, Songwrtrs. Protective Assn., Am. Fedn. Musicians, Rotary Intl. Home: Box 12 Mount Etna IA 50855

SPATZ, RONALD M., b. NYC, Apr. 10, 1949, s. John R. and Estelle (Jacobs) S. Ed. Icarus, 1979-80; exec. ed., fiction ed., founding ed. Alaska Qtly Rvw, 1981—; contrbr. fiction to Panache, Telescope, In the Dream Light, other lit mags and anthologies. BA, U. Iowa, 1971, MFA, 1973. Mem. faculty U. Mo., Columbia, 1973-74, Western Mich. U., Kalamazoo, 1974-78, Mo. Western State State Coll., St. Joseph, 1979-80; assoc. prof., dir. creative writing program U. Alaska, Anchorage, 1980—. Grantee Mich. Council for Arts, 1976, 78; NEA creative writing fellow, 1982; Alaska State Council on Arts fiction writing fellow, 1985. Mem. AWP. Home: 2396 E 47th St Anchorage AK 99507

SPAW, JUNE, b. Bloomington, IN, Aug. 10, 1925; d. Velber and Rhetta (Adams) Jasper; m. Millard Spaw, Sept. 1, 1951; children—Rhonda Clemens, Doretta Herrlinger. Author: (poetry) From the Thicket, 1970. B.A., Berea Coll., 1948; postgrad. U. Cin., 1963-67. Tchr. math and English Eubank High Sch., KY, 1960-63, St. Bernard-Elmwood Place Schs., St. Bernard, OH, 1963-85, retired. Recipient Golden Poet award World of Poetry, 1986. Mem. Appalachian Poetry Assn. Home: 2581 Ansel Rd Science Hill KY 42553

SPEARS, MONROE KIRK, b. Darlington, SC, Apr. 28, 1916; s. James Monroe and Lillian (Fair) Spears; m. Betty Greene, Sept. 3, 1941; 1 dau.—Julia Herndon. Author: The Poetry of W.H. Auden: The Disenchanted Island, 1963, Hart Crane, 1965, Dionysus and the City: Modernism in Twentieth Century Poetry, 1970, Space against Time in Modern American Poetry, 1972, The Levitator and Other Poems, 1975, American Ambitions: Selected Essays on Literary and Cultural Themes, 1987; editor: (with H.B. Wright) The Literary Works of Matthew Prior, 2 vols. 1959, W.H. Auden: A Collection of Critical Essays, 1964, The Narrative Poetry of Shakespeare, 1968; ed., Sewanee Rvw, 1952-61; adv. editor, 1961-73. AB, AM, U. SC, 1937; PhD, Princeton U., 1940; D. Letters (hon.), U. of South, 1983 Instr. English U. Wis., 1940-42; asst. prof., then assoc. prof. English Vanderbilt U., 1946-52; prof. English U. South, 1952-64; Libbie Shearn Moody prof. English Rice U., 1964-86, emeritus 1986—; vis. prof. Swarthmore Coll., 1961-62; mem. adv. council dept. English Princeton U., 1960-66, Christian Gauss lectr., 1975; dir. NEA Seminars for Coll. Tchrs. Rice U., 1975, 78. Served to capt. AUS and USAF, 1942-46; ETO. Home: Carruthers Rd Sewanee TN 37375

SPECTOR, ROBERT DONALD, b. NYC, Sept. 21, 1922; s. Morris and Helen (Speigel) Spector; m. Eleanor Helen Luskin, Aug. 19, 1945; children—Stephen Brett, Eric Charles. Author: English Literary Periodicals, 1966, Tobias George Smollett, 1968, Par Lagerkvist, 1973, Arthur Murphy, 1979, Tobias Smollett: A Reference Guide, 1980, The English Gothic, 1983; editor: Essays on the Eighteenth Century Novel, 1965, Great British Short Novels, 1970, 9 other vols. English and Am. lit., rvws. and articles. BA, LIU, 1948; MA, NYU, 1949; PhD, Columbia U., 1962. Instr. LIU (Bklyn.), 1948-59, asst. prof., 1959-62, assoc. prof., 1962-65, prof. English, 1965—, chair dept. 1970-75, dir. humanities and communication arts, 1975—, chair senate, 1966-67, 69-70; editor, cons. Johnson Reprint Corp., 1967—. Served with USCGR, 1942-46. Mem. MLA, PEN. Home: 1761 E 26th St Brooklyn NY 11229

SPEER, ALLEN PAUL III, b. Boonville, NC, Sept. 4, 1951; s. Allen Paul and Frieda (Hinshaw) S. Editor: Hemlocks and Balsams, 1980 (vol. 6, 1985). BS in Social Sci., Appalachian State U., 1973, MA in Poli. Sci., 1975; Ed. D., U. N.C.-Greensboro, 1986. Tchr. Boonville Schl., Boonville, N.C., 1976-77, Lees McRae Coll., Banner Elk, N.C., 1977. Recipient Outstanding Educator's award Lees McRae Coll., 1980. Mem. Phi Theta Kappa (Mosal Scholar, 1985), Appalachian Writers Assn., N.C. Writers Assn. Home: Box 537 Banner Elk NC 28604

SPEER, BETTY JEAN, (Rebecca St. Columb), b. Berrien Co. MI, May 14, 1931; d. Graydon Leroy and Clara Alice (Birr) Wilson; m. Richard McCord Speer, Sept. 1, 1957; children—Richard J., Shawn-Ann, Erin E., Julie S., Serena C. Author: Jenny Saw, April Next Door, Madam President. Wrkg. on Legend of the Clouds. Home: 4066 E Ridgewood Las Vegas NV 89120

SPEER, GARRY WAYNE, b. Gulfport, MS, Dec. 11, 1957; s. Lee Albert, Jr. Speer and Carrie Lee (Cruthirds) Beech; m. Sandra Marie Lubin, Aug. 10, 1981; 1 dau., Cynthia Danielle. Contrbr. poems, short stories to anthols., newspaper. Wrkg. on poetry, short stories, novels, photojnlsm. A.A., Phillips Coll., 1987. Entertainment ed. The Lion's Roar, Hammond, LA, 1982-84; lab. technician for SE La., New Orleans, 1987—. Recipient Golden Poet award World of Poetry, 1986, 87. Home: 2608 Hyman Pl New Orleans LA 70131

SPEER, LAUREL, b. Los Angeles, Mar. 3, 1940; d. George Frank and Helen (Fischer) Elmendorf; m. Donald Pierce Speer, Jan. 27, 1962 (div. May 29, 1987); children—Kirsten, Marshall Patton, Stephen Anthony. Author: (poems) A Bit of Wit, 1979, Lovers & Others, 1980, Don't Dress Your Cat in an Apron, 1981, Hokum/Visions of a Gringa, 1982, The Hobbesian Apple, 1982, T. Roosevelt Tracks the Last Buffalo, 1982; (fiction) The Hundred Percent Black Steinway Grand, 1979; (plays) The Self-Mutilation of an Aged Apple Woman, 1980; (poems) (with Stuart McCarty) I'm Hiding from the Cat, 1983, One Lunch, 1984, Weird Sister 1, 1984, Vincent et al., 1985, The Scandal of Her Bath, 1986, Second Thoughts Over Bourget, 1987. Wrkg. on Very Frightened Men, Cold Egg. Student Stanford U., 1958-60; B.A., U. Calif., Los Angeles, 1962; postgrad. U. Southern Calif., 1962-63. Home: 2041 E Waverly Tucson AZ 85719

SPEICHER, RITA L., b. NYC, May 14, 1954. Author: Night Lives/Other Lives, 1978. Contrbr. poems, stories to mags. B.A., Bklyn. Coll., 1966; M.A., NYU, 1967. Prodn. asst., coordinator Graphic Curriculum, NYC, 1964, 65, 67, 68; coordinator TV, Jewish Theol. Seminary, NYC, 1969-70; founder Women's Wrtr.'s Ctr., Cazenovia, N.Y., 1975-82, Freehand, Inc., Provincetown, Mass., 1982—. Recipient Poetry award Community Artists Pub. Service, NYC, 1981; named Trailblazer of the Arts, NOW,1980. Mem. Feminist WG, Women's Studies Assn. Home: 40 Commercial Provincetown MA 02657

SPELMAN, PHILIP OHEL, b. South Haven, MI, July 21, 1923; s. Ohel Bostwick and Gertrude (Englesby) S.; m. Margaret Rankin, Dec. 13, 1938; children—Sara Marie, Philip Scott, Wendy Ruth, Tanya Marie, Mark Frederick, Margaret Opel. Editor/publisher: You and the Law, 1978, Impotence: How to Overcome It, 1987, Love & Revolution; 101 Years of the Automobile, 1988. Contrbr. numerous articles to mags., newspapers including American Mag., Colliers, Sci. Digest, others. B.A., Mich. State U., 1948; Ph.D., Wayne State U., 1984. Assoc. ed. Motor News Mag., Detroit, 1948-55; public relations dir. McCann-Erickson, Detroit, 1955-57, Young & Rubicam Inc., Detroit, 1957-70; pres. Spelman Productions, Southfield, MI, 1970—; dir. communications State Bar of Mich., Lansing, 1974—. Recipient award Pic Mag., 1947, Mark Twain Midwest Travel Wrtrs. Award, 1954, 55. Mem. Adcraft Club Detroit, Detroit Press Club, PRSA. Home: 26941 Pebblestone Rd Southfield MI 48034

SPENCE, GERALD LEONARD, b. Laramie, WY, Jan. 8, 1929; s. Gerald W. and Esther Sophie (Pfleeger) Spence; m. Anna Wilson, June 20, 1947; children—Kip, Kerry, Kent, Katy; m. 2d, LaNelle Hampton Peterson, Nov. 18, 1969. Author (with others) Gunning for Justice, 1982, Of Murder and Madness, 1983, Trial by Fire, 1986. BSL, U. Wyo., 1949, LL.B, 1952. Bar: WY, 1952, US Ct. Claims 1952. Sole practice (Riverton, WY), 1952-54, county and pros. atty. (Fremont County, WY), 1954-62; prtnr. Spence, Moriarity & Schuster (Jackson, WY), 1978—; lectr. legal orgns. and law schls. Office: Box 548 Jackson WY 83001

SPENCER, DICK III, b. Dallas, Jan. 28, 1921; s. Richard and Jessie (Burden) Spencer; m. Jo Anne Nicholson, July 24, 1943 (div. May, 1983); children—Barbara Jo Spencer Corpolongo, Richard Craig (dec.), Debra Jean; m. 2d, Vivian King, June 4, 1983. Author: Editorial Cartooning, 1949, Pulitzer Prize Cartoons, 1951, Beginning Western Horsemanship, 1959, Intermediate Western Horsemanship, 1960, Horse Breaking, 1967. BA, U. Iowa, 1942. With promotion dept. Look mag., 1945-47; editor U. Colo. (Boulder), 1950-51; editor Western Horseman mag. (Colorado Springs), 1951-69, pub., 1969—. Served with AUS, 1942-45; ETO. Home: 14050 Roller Coaster Rd Colorado Springs CO 80908

SPENCER, JAMES RICHARDSON, b. Basin, Wyo., Mar. 7, 1986, s. Frank John and Emma Ruth (Hoover) S.; m. Margaretta Long, Oct. 5, 1966; children—Erin, Jaime. Author: Beyond Mormonism: An Elder's Story, 1984, Have You Witnessed to a Mormon Lately?, 1986; contrbr.: Christian Life, Christian Reader. Wrkg. on nonfiction. Ed., Ricks Coll., Ariz. State U. Staff wrtr. various newspapers, Idaho, 1972-80; pastor Shiloh Christian Center, Idaho Falls, 1980—. Mem. Natl. Wrtrs. Assn. Office: Box 3804 Idaho Falls ID 83403

SPENCER, JEAN W., b. Phila., d. E. Russell and Grace (Albright) Wigfield; m. John M. Spencer; children—Lu-Anne, Pamela. Author: Exploring Careers as a Computer Technician, 1985, Exploring Careers in the Electronic Office, 1986. Photographer/wrtr.: Images: Women in Transition, 1976. Graduate Ventura (Calif.) Coll. Pub. relations info. officer Oxnard (Calif.) Coll., 1975—. Mem. Presbyn. Wrtrs. Guild, Calif. Wrtrs. Club, Soc. Children's Book Wrtrs., Pub. Info. Communications Assn. Home: 1534 Loma Dr Camarillo CA 93010

SPENCER, MARK MORRIS, b. Richmond, VA, Feb. 12, 1956, s. Howard Regan and Evelyn (Morris) S.; m. Diana Lynn Harvey, July 20, 1980; 1 dau., Krista Lynn. Contrbr. short stories Fiction 84, Fla. Rvw, NM Humanities Rvw, The Mac Guffin, Chariton Rvw, Beloit Fiction Jnl, SD Rvw, Laurel Rvw, Gambit, Half Tones to Jubilee, Writers' Bar-B-Q; non-fiction in Critique, Am. Inst. Discussion Rvw, Hawaii Rvw. BA, U. Cin., 1979; MFA, Bowling Green State U., 1981. Instr. English SW Mo. State Univ., Springfield, 1983-87, asst. prof. English, Cameron Univ., Lawton, OK, 1987—. Address: 1920 NW Kinyon Lawton OK 73502

SPERRY, ROGER WOLCOTT, b. Hartford, CT, Aug. 20, 1913; s. Francis B. and Florence (Kraemer) S.; m. Norma G. Deupree, Dec. 28, 1949; children: Glenn Tad, Janeth Hope. Editorial bd.: Behavioral Biology. Contbr. articles to profl. jnls., chpts. to books. Mem. editorial advisory bds.: Exptl. Neurology, Exptl. Brain Research, Neuropsychologia, Intl. Jnl of Neuroscience, Zygon, Behavioral Biology, Perspectives in Biology and Medicine. B.A., Oberlin Coll., 1935, M.A., 1937, Ph.D., U. Chgo., 1941, Research fellow Harvard and Yerkes Labs., 1941-46; research brain orgn. and neural mechanism. Albert Lasker Basic Med. Research award, 1979; co-recipient William Thomas Wakeman Research award Natl. Paraplegia Found., 1972, Claude Bernard sci. journalism award, 1975, Disting. research award Intl. Visual Literacy Assn., 1979; Nobel prize in Physiology/medicine, 1981; Realia Award of Inst. for Advanced Philosophic Research, 1986. Fellow AAAS, Am. Acad. Arts and Scis., Am. Psychol. Assn; mem. Royal Acad. (fgn. mem.), Natl. Acad. Scis.. Office: 1201 E California St Pasadena CA 91125

SPEVAK, TERYL A., b. Los Angeles, Nov. 20, 1951; d. Ezra Charles and Marie Helen (Courturier) Spevak. Contrbr. articles: Michigan Natural Resources, Dog World, Pure-Bred Dogs/Am. Kennel Gazette, other publs. BA in Zoology, UCLA, 1974, PhD in Zoology, 1979. Freelance wrtr., ed., 1985—; assoc. ed. Setters, Inc. mag., Santa Barbara, Calif., 1987—. Home: 4807 Leland Rd Laingsburg MI 48848

SPIEGELMAN, WILLARD LESTER, b. St. Joseph, MO, Dec. 29, 1944; s. Jay and Edith Henriette (Bowman) S. Author: Wordsworth's Heroes, 1985; editor Southwest Rev., 1984—; contbr. James Merrill: Essays in Criticism, 1983; contbr. articles to Studies in Romanticism, Salmagundi, Parnassus, Keats-Shelley Jnl, Comparative Literature, others. AB, Williams Coll., 1966; AM, Harvard U., 1967, PhD, 1971. Prof. English, So. Meth. U., 1971—. Recipient Perrine prize Phi Beta Kappa, 1981; NEH/Rockefeller Fdn. grantee, 1984, 85-86. Mem. MLA, Wordsworth-Coleridge Soc. Home: 6019 Bryan Pkwy Dallas TX 75206

SPIELBERG, PETER, b. Vienna, Austria, July 2, 1929, came to U.S., 1939; m. Elaine Konstant; children—Christine, Ivan. Author: Bedrock (short stories), 1973, Twiddledum Twaddledum (novel), 1974, The Hermetic Whore (short stories), 1977, Crash- Landing (novel), 1985. BA, CCNY, 1952; MA, NYU, 1956, PhD, U. Buffalo, 1961. Prof. English, Bklyn. Coll., CUNY, 1961—, mem. fiction writing staff MFA program, 1974—. NEA writing fellow, 1980. Mem. PEN. Home: 321 W 24th St New York NY 10011

SPIELER, FRANCIS JOSEPH, b. Glasgow, Scotland, May 23, 1943 (came to U.S., 1955, naturalized, 1974); s. Ludwig and Rachel (Neuer) Spieler; m. Gene Ellen Bobker. BA in Comparative Lit., CCNY, 1967. Staff editor NY Times, 1963-73; sr. editor Penthouse Publs., 1973-75; music critic Harper's Monthly, 1976—; adj. prof. journalism NYU, 1975; sr. editor SoHo Weekly News, 1975-76; editorial cons., ind. literary agt. Home: 410 W 24th St New York NY 10011

SPIESS, ROBERT CLAYTON, b. Milw., Oct. 16, 1921; s. Oscar Joseph and Myrtle Ruth (Koken) S. Works include: The Heron's Legs, 1966, The Turtle's Ears, 1971, Five Caribbean Haibun, 1972, The Shape of Water, 1982, The Bold Silverfish and Tall River Junction, 1986. BS, U. Wisc., 1947, MS, 1948. Ed./pub., Modern Haiku, Madison, WI, 1978—. NEA awards: 1979, 80, 81. Office: Box 1752 Madison WI 53701

SPILKA, MARK, b. Cleve., Aug. 6, 1925; s. Harvey Joseph and Zella (Fenberg) Spilka; m. Ellen Potter, May 6, 1950 (div. Dec. 1965); children—Jane, Rachel, Aaron; m. 2d, Ruth Dane Farnum, Jan. 18, 1975; stepchildren—Betsy, Polly. Author: The Love Ethic of D.H. Lawrence, 1955, Dickens and Kafka: A Mutual Interpretation, 1963, Virginia Woolf's Quarrel with Grieving, 1980; editor: D.H. Lawrence: A Collection of Critical Essays, 1963, Towards a Poetics of Fiction: Essays from Novel: A Forum on Fiction, 1967-76, 1977; mng. editor: Novel: A Forum on Fiction, 1967-77; editor, 1978—. BA magna cum laude, Brown U., 1949; MA, IN U., 1953, PhD, 1956. Editorial asst. Am. Mercury, 1949-51; instr. U. Mich., 1954-58, asst. prof., 1958-63; assoc. prof. Brown U., Providence, 1963-67, prof., 1967—, chair English dept., 1968-73; pres. Conf. Editors of Learned Jnls, MLA, 1974-75; pres. Dickens Soc, MLA, 1986. Served with USAF, 1944-46. Mem. MLA, AAUP. Home: 294 Doyle Ave Providence RI 02906

SPILLANE, MICKEY, see Morrison, Frank

SPINA, ANGELA MARIE, b. Roseau, MN, Mar. 26, 1964, d. James William and Rita Louise (Foster) Brewster; m. Stacy Ernest Spina, June 29, 1985. Contrbr. to World Treasury of Great Poems, Family Treasury of Great Poem and Mysteries, Am. Poetry Anthology. Student U. Minn.-Crookston, 1982-84. Recipient Golden Poet awards World of Poetry, 1985, 1986. Home: 603 Riverview Dr Warroad MN 56763

SPINA, VINCENT, b. Bklyn., July 6, 1944, s. Salvatore and Mary (Curcio) S.; m. Rosa Lidia Sanchez, Aug. 21, 1971; 1 son, Juan Carlos. Contrbr. poetry to books, mags. including: Ediciones Pliegos, 1986, Italo-Peru, 1975, Antiediciones Villa Miseria, 1972, Calliopes Corner, The Hoboken Terminal, Smackwarm, The Atavist. Wrkg. on book of poetry. MA, NYU, 1976, PhD, 1982. Mem. faculty NYU, N.Y.C., 1978-82, Boricua Coll., Bklyn, 1983-84, Rutgers U., Newark, 1985—. Mem. MLA, P&W. Home: 32-05 35th Ave Astoria NY 11106

SPINGARN, LAWRENCE PERREIRA, b. Jersey City, NJ, July 11, 1917; s. Joseph Kalman and Anne (Birnbaum) S.; m. Priscilla Rudolph, Dec. 26, 1943 (div. April 15, 1947), Sylvia Georgina Wainhouse, June 19, 1949. Author: Rococo Summer & Other Poems, 1947, The Lost River: Poems, 1951, Letters from Exile: Poems, 1961, Madame Bidet & Other Fixtures: Poems, 1970, Poets West: Contemporary Poems from the Eleven Western States (ed.), 1975, The Blue Door & Other Stories, 1977, The Black Cap: A Story, 1978, The Dark Playground: Poems, 1979, The Belvedere: A Story, 1982, Moral Tales, 1983, Mapping the Wilderness: Poems, 1987; contrbr. to anthols., periodicals, lit mags. BSS, Bowdoin Coll, 1940; MA, Univ. of Michigan, 1948. Librarian, Lib. of Cong., 1941-43; freelance wrtr., ed., 1943-59; tchr. Pomona Coll., UCLA, 1948-49, 54-57; prof. of Eng., Valley Coll., 1959-85; publisher, Perivale Press, 1968—. Mem. Intl. Inst. of Arts & Letters, PSA, PEN. Office: Perivale 13830 Erwin St Van Nuys CA 91401

SPIRES, ELIZABETH, b. Lancaster, OH, May 28, 1952; d. Richard Clarence and Elizabeth Sue (Wagner) Spires; m. Madison Smartt Bell, June 15, 1985. Author children's book: The Falling Star, 1981; poetry: Globe, 1981, Swan's Island, 1985; contrbr. poetry to numerous mags and anthologies including The New Yorker, The New Republic, Poetry, The New Criterion, The Morrow Anthology of Younger Am. Poets. BA, Vassar Coll., Poughkeepsie, NY, 1974; MA, Johns Hopkins U., 1979. Visiting asst. prof. Washington Coll., Chestertown, MD, 1981, Johns Hopkins U., 1984-85; poet-in-res. Loyola Coll., Baltimore, 1981-82; asst. prof. Goucher Coll., Towson, MD, 1982-86. W.K. Rose Fellowship, Vassar Coll., 1976, NEA Fellowship, 1981, Individual Artist's Grant, MD St. Arts Council, 1982, Ingram Merrill Award, 1982, Amy Lowell Traveling Poetry Scholarship, 1986-87. Home: 420 Ferson Ave Iowa City IA 52240

SPITTER, THE, see Bennett, John M.

SPIVACK, KATHLEEN, b. Sept. 22, 1938, Bronxville, NY; d. Peter F. and Doris (Schmitz) Drucker; children—Nova, Marin Spivack. Author: Flying Inland, 1973, The Jane Poems, 1974, Swimmer in the Spreading Dawn, 1981, The Beds We Lie In, 1986, The Honeymoon, 1986. Contrbr. articles, essays, poems, short stories to Atlantic Monthly, Encounter, New Yorker, lit mags. BA, Oberlin College, 1959; MA, Boston Univ., 1964. Instr. Boston Univ., 1963-65; psychologist, Brandeis Univ., 1965-69; director, Advanced Wrtg. Wrkshop, Watertown, 1971—. NEA Fellowship, 1978; Radcliffe Inst. Bunting Fellowship, 1969-71; PSA Hemley Prize, 1978. Mem. PSA. Wrkg. on personal memoir of Robert Lowell, Anne Sexton. Home: 52 Spruce St Watertown MA 02172

SPIVAK, MELVIN EZRA, b. Bklyn., June 1, 1937; s. Harry and Pauline Rose (Rogosin) S. Contrbr. poems to lit. mags., anthols. Grad.

public schls., Brklyn. With maintenance Victory Meml. Hosp., Brkly., 1970-75, retired. Home: 2120 N Pacific Ave Apt 188 Santa Cruz CA 95060

SPRAGUE, BRENDA LEE, b. Wichita, KS., Feb. 17, 1953; d. Verner Anton and Gloria Lee (Johnson) Bertelsen; m. Robert William Sprague, June 20, 1981; children: Nelson Van Robert, Rianna Lee. Contrbr.: Phenomenological Research in Rhetoric, Language and Communication, Phenomenology in Rhetoric and Communication, Southern Illinoisan Newspaper. BS, So. Ill. U., 1976, MS, 1978; ABD/PhD, Ohio U., 1981. Freelance wrtr., Carbondale, Ill., 1983—; instr. John A. Logan Coll., Carterville, Ill., 1983—. Mem. Nat. League Am. Pen Women. Home: 1005 W Walnut St Carbondale IL 62901

SPRAGUE, WILLIAM LEIGH, b. Weatherford, OK., July 28, 1938; s. Frank W. and Eula L. (Miley) S. Ed.: Glance, 1977-82, Our Christian Church Heritage: Journeying In Faith, 1979, Shirt-Sleeve Ministries: Christian Laity in Action, 1981; contrbg. ed.: Vanguard, 1977-82; contrbr. chaps.: Partners in New Possibilities, 1981, Put Love First, 1982; contrbr. articles to numerous publs. BA, Phillips U., 1960, BD, 1964; STM, Boston U., 1966. Dir. services to homeowners Community Interfaith Housing, Indpls., 1982-85; program coordinator Harbor Light Center, Salvation Army, Indpls., 1985—; freelance wtr., 1966—. Mem. Associated Wrtrs. Ind. (newsletter ed.). Home: 1135 Aqua Vista Dr Apt B Indianapolis IN 46229

SPRINGER, NANCY CONNOR, b. Livingston, NJ, July 5, 1948, d. Harry E. and Helen (Wheeler) Connor; m. Joel H. Springer, Sept. 13, 1969; children—Jonathan, Nora. Novelist: The Book of Suns, 1977, The White Hart, 1979, The Silver Sun, 1980, The Sable Moon, 1981, The Black Beast, 1982, The Golden Swan, 1983, The Book of Vale, 1983, Wings of Flame, 1985, Chains of Gold, 1986, A Horse to Love (juvenile), 1987, Madbond, 1987, Mindbond, 1987 (Vols. I and II, Sea King Trilogy, Chance: and Other Gestures of the Hand of Fate (collection), 1987, Not on a White Horse (juvenile), 1987; contrbr. short stories: Fantasy Book, 1982, Goldmann Fantasy Foliant I, Magic in Ithkar, Moonsinger's Friends, Top Fantasy, Fantasy and Science Fiction, other publs.; contrbr. poetry: Fantasy Book, Echoes, Star*Line, other publs. BA, Gettysburg Coll., 1970. Mem. Central Pennsylvania Writers' Org., Soc. of Children's Book Writers, SFWA. Home: 360 W Main St Dallastown PA 17313

SPURGEON, DICKIE ALLEN, b. Vanduser, MO, Maar. 4, 1936; s. Royal Allen and Nellie Delorah (Myers) Spurgeon. Editor Sou'wester mag.; assoc. editor: Papers on Language and Literature; editor: Tudor Translations of the Colloquies of Erasmus, 1972, Three Tudor Dialogues, 1978. PhD, U. Ill., 1967. Asst. prof. U. Md., 1967-71; prof. So. Ill. U., Edwardsville, 1971—. Recipient Ill. Arts award Ill. Arts Council, 1981, 83; Best Tex. Short Story award Tex. Arts Com., 1983; Genl. Electric Writers award, 1984. Home: 602 Hillsboro Edwardsville IL 62025

SQUIRE, ROCHELLE BRENER, (Shelley Brener Squire, Rochelle Brener), b. Syracuse, NY, Feb. 27, 1945; d. Eugene Seymour and Evelyn (Grossman) Brener; m. Donald A. Squire, Jan. 10, 1965; children—Barry Evan, Karen Lee. Author chapbook: The Bottom Line, 1974; contrbr. poetry to PackRat, 1975; contrbr. wrtr. and photojournalist, The Communicator, 1980, The Answer, 1981. BA, Russell Sage College, Troy, NY, 1974. Stringer, photographer Hearst News, Albany, NY, 1973-75; drama critic and features wrtr. KITE Mag., various, NY, 1973-79; ed. Woman Locally Mag., Albany, 1975; contrbr. ed., artist Poetry Forum, Tustin, CA, 1975-76; freelance poet, photographer, 1974—. Hon. mention, Am. Song Festival Lyric Open, 1979, 81. Hon. mention, Am. PEN Women. Mem. NWC, P&W, Professional Photographers of America, PSA, Assoc. Photographers Intl., Intl. Freelance Photographers. Home: 69 Huntersfield Rd Delmar NY 12054

SQUIRE, SHELLEY BRENER, see Squire, Rochelle Brener

SQUIRES, (JAMES) RADCLIFFE), b. Salt Lake City, May 23, 1917; s. Edward Frederic and Janet Melvina (McNeil) Squires; m. Eileen Mulholland, Sept. 19, 1946 (dec. Sept. 1976). Author: Cornar, 1940, Where the Compass Spins, 1951, The Loyalties of Robinson Jeffers, 1956, The Major Themes of Robert Frost, 1963, Frederic Prokosch, 1964, Fingers of Hermes, 1965, The Light under Islands, 1967, Allen Tate, 1971, Waiting in the Bone, 1973, Gardens of the World, 1981, Journeys, 1983; editor: Allen Tate and His Work, 1972, BA, U. Utah, 1940; AM, U. Chgo., 1946; PhD, Harvard, 1952. Instr. Dartmouth, 1946-48; Fulbright prof., U. Salonica (Greece), 1956-60; mem. faculty U. Mich (Ann Arbor), 1952—, prof. English, 1963-81; editor Mich. Qtly Rvw, 1971-77. Served with USNR, 1941-45. Address: Dept Eng U. Michigan Ann Arbor MI 48109

SQUIRES, JAMES ROBERT, b. Oakland, CA, Oct. 14, 1922; s. Harry Edwin and Ruby (Fulton) Squire; m. Barbara Lyman, Jan. 20, 1946; children—Kathryn Elizabeth, Kevin Richard, David Whitford. Author: (with W. Loban, M. Ryan) Teaching Language and Literature, 1961, 69, (with R.K. Applebee) High School English Instruction Today, 1969, (with B.L. Squire) Greek Myths and Legends, 1967, Teaching English in the United Kingdom, 1969, A New Look at Progressive Education, 1972, Exemplary Practices in Composition, 1986; editor: Teaching of English 76th Yearbook Natl. Soc. Study Edn., 1977, Dynamics of Language Learning, 1986. BA, Pomona Coll., 1947; D.Litt., 1966; MA, U. Calif. at Berkeley, 1949, PhD, 1956. Tchr. secondary schl. (Oakland, CA), 1949-54; supr. lectr. English edn. U. Calif. at Berkeley, 1951-59; prof. English U. IL (Urbana), 1959-67; exec. sec. NCTE, 1960-67; editor-in-chief, sr. vp Ginn & Co. (Lexington, MA), 1968-74, sr. vp, pub., 1975-80, sr. vp dir. research and devel., 1980-82, sr. vp, sr. cons., 1983—; pres. Natl. Conf. Research in English, 1982-83; exec. cons., 1985—. Served with AUS, 1943-45. Recipient Creative Scholarship award Coll. Lang. Assn., 1961. Mem. MLA, NCTE, Intl. Reading Assn., CCCC. Home: 43 Round Hill Rd Lincoln MA 10773

SRODA, GEORGE, b. Stevens Point, WI, Apr. 3, 1911; s. Frank and Johanna (Okray) Sroda; m. Susan Rekoske, Jun. 19, 1934; children—Richard, Thomas. Author: No Angle Left Unturned—Facts About Nightcrawlers; Life Story of Herman the Worm. Home: Amherst Jct WI 54407

STABLEIN, MARILYN ESTELLE, b. Los Angeles, Aug. 22, 1946, d. Paul Justus and Thelma Rachel (Hogevoll) Zulch; m. William George Stablein, Jan. 22, 1971; children—William Paul Jr., Ann Sunita. Author: Ticketless Traveler, 1982, The Census Taker: Tales of a Traveler in India and Nepal, 1985; contrbr. stories to Miss. Rvw, Crazyhorse, Domestic Crude, Clinton St. Qtly, others; contrbr. poetry to Afterthought, Poetry Seattle, The Light, Dragonfly, others; contrbr. articles to Natl. Observer, Tibet Soc. Bull., Poetry Exchange, others. BA in Creative Writing, U. Wash., 1981; MA in Creative Writing, U. Houston, 1984. Founding pub. Wash'n Press, Seattle, 1980—; lit. events organizer Bumbershoot, Seattle, 1981, 82, pres. Grad. English Soc., Houston, 1983, 84; exec. dir. The Literary Center, Seattle, 1985—. Cullen Grad. fellow U. Houston, 1982-83, recipient Brazos Fiction award, 1984; recipient award King County Arts Commn., Seattle, 1985; NEA fellow in arts mgmt., 1985. Mem. Seattle Freelances, Phi Beta Kappa, Omicron Delta Kappa. Home: 5210 16th St NE Seattle WA 98105

STACY, DELORES, see Schmadeka, Delores

STACY, PAULINE FRENCH, b. Pratt, KS, Feb. 22, 1915; d. Leo Walter and Bessie Rosanna (Branson) French; m. Larcel Romain Stacy, July 21, 1934; children—Grace Romaine, Rosanna Pauline. Author: (poetry) You Shall Not Want, 1975, For As Long As We Both Shall Love, 1975; (how-to) Ventriloquists: Here's How!, 1976. Contrbr. short stories, articles, photography, poetry to mag., anthols. Wrkg. on romance novel. B.A., Ariz. State U., 1960; M.S., Fort Hays Kans. State U., 1971. Tchr. pvt. and public schs., Kans., 1960-71; program specialist Harvest Pub. Co., Clev., 1978-80; free-lance wrtr., artist. Mem. AAUW, Mensa. Home: HCR 2 Box 10 Meade KS 67864

STADTER, PHILIP AUSTIN, b. Cleve., Nov. 29, 1936; s. John M. and Mary Louise (Jones) Stadter; m. Lucia Angela Ciapponi, July 6, 1963; children—Paul, Maria, Mark. Author: Plutarch's Historical Methods, 1965, The Public Library of Renaissance Florence, 1972, Arrian of Nicomedia, 1980; editor: The Speeches of Thucydides, 1973. BA, Princeton U., 1958; MA, Harvard U., 1959, PhD, 1963. Instr. U. NC (Chapel Hill), 1962-64, asst. prof., 1964-67, assoc. prof., 1967-71, prof., 1971—, chair dept. classics, 1976-86. Office: U NC Dept Classics Chapel Hill NC 27514

STADTLER, BEATRICE HORWITZ, b. Cleve., June 26, 1921; d. David and Minnie (Gorelick) Horwitz; m. Oscar Stadtler, Jan. 31, 1945; children—Dona Stadtler Rosenblatt, Sander, Miriam Stadtler Rosenbaum. Author: Once Upon a Jewish Holiday, 1963, The Story of Dona Gracia, 1969, The Adventures of Gluckel of Hamlen, 1967, Rescue From the Sky (in Hebrew), 1972, Personalities of the Jewish Labor Movement, 1972, The Holocaust: A History of Courage and Resistance, 1975 (prize outstanding juvenile book Natl. Jewish Welfare Bd. 1975); film strip The Adventures of Mirkee Pirkee and Danny Dollar, 1963 (prize Natl. Council Jewish Audio Visual Materials 1963); libretto rock opera Solomon the King; also articles, stories; author: weekly column Cleve. Jewish News, 1964-70, Boston Jewish Advocate, 1970—. Secy. Cleve. Dept. Pub. Health and Welfare, 1940; secy., dept. mgr., Fedl. Pub. Housing Authority, Cleve., 1943; primary supr. Temple Beth Shalom Religious Schl. (Cleve.), 1953; registrar Cleve. Coll. Jewish Studies, 1958; asst. editor Israel Philatelist, 1975—; speaker on holocaust. Home: 24355 Tunbridge Ln Beachwood OH 44122

STAFF, LA VADA FALKNER, (Katie LaVee), b. Miami, AZ, Mar. 30, 1924, d. Carroll Franklin and Velma (Medlock) Falkner; m. Virgil C. Staff, June 17. 1949. Contrbr. poetry to Am. Poetry Anthology, 1985. Wrkg. on novels. RN, Paradise Valley Schl. Nursing, 1948. Nurse hosps. in Mass., Calif., 1949—. Mem. NWC, profl. orgns. Home: 1700 Sonoma Ave Berkeley CA 94707

STAFFORD, BYRON DONALD, b. Wembley, England, May 14, 1946, came o U.S., 1970; s. Walter James and Lillian Jesse (Postbeschild) Bransom; m. Anna Mae, Mar. 18, 1973; children—Michelle Lee, Leah Jeanette. Contrbr. articles to mags., newpapers. Student Fich Inst., London, 1965-66. Recipient award Mead Pub., 1986. Home: Box 1746 Snowflake AZ 85937

STAFFORD, JAN, b. Spruce Pine, NC, June 13, 1951; d. Grady Johnson and Iris Mary (Saunders) S. Author: Ms. Midas, 1975, On Wry (poetry), 1979, Bizarro In Love, 1986; contrbr. fict. & poetry to Cellar Door, The Wild Iris, New South Writing, Chrysalis, Berkeley Barb, others. BA, U.NC, 1973. Radio announcer, WHOA-AM, Hato Rey, Puerto Rico, 1974-75; asst. ed. San Jose Post-Record (CA), 1976-78, Committee on Research, U.CA-Berkeley, 81-83; ed. Western Office Dealer Mag., San Francisco, 1983-85, Am. Office Dealer, San Francisco, 85—. Office: 22 Battery St Ste 510 San Francisco CA 94111

STAFFORD, MARILYN, see Terschluse, Marilyn Ann

STAFFORD, WILLIAM EDGAR, b. Hutchinson, KS, Jan. 17, 1914; s. Earl Ingersoll and Ruby Nina (Mayher) Stafford; m. Dorothy Hope Frantz, Apr. 8, 1944; children—Bret William, Kim Robert, Kathryn Lee, Barbara Claire. Author: Down in my Heart, 1947; poems West of Your City, 1960, Traveling Through the Dark, 1962 (Natl. Book award 1963), The Rescued Year, 1966, Allegiances, 1970, Someday, Maybe, 1973, Stories That Could Be True, New and Collected Poems, 1977, Writing the Australian Crawl, 1978, Things That Happen Where There Aren't Any People, 1980, Sometimes Like a Legend, 1981, A Glass Face in the Rain, 1982; regular contrbr. to periodicals. BA, U. Kans., 1937, MA, 1946; PhD, State U. Iowa, 1954; Litt.D., Ripon Coll., 1965; L.H.D., Linfield Coll, 1970. Faculty Lewis and Clark Coll. (Portland, OR), 1948-80, prof. English, 1960-80; faculty San Jose State Coll. (CA), 1956-57, Manchester Coll. (IN), 1955-56; cons. poetry Library of Congress (Washington), 1970. Ednl. secy. civilian publ. service sect. Ch. of Brethen, 1943-44. Mem. AAUP, MLA, NCTE, Modern Poetry Assn. Home: 1050 Sunningdale Lake Oswego OR 97034

STAFFORD, WILLIAM TALMADGE, b. Marianna, FL, Oct. 31, 1924; s. William H. and Lovie L. (Lamb) Stafford; m. Frances Marie McKeown, June 12, 1949 (div. 1981); children—Melinda, Jocelyn, Kathleen; 2nd m. Ruth Ann Miller, Sept. 17, 1981. Author: A Name, Title and Place Index to the Critical Writings of Henry James, 1975, Books Speaking to Books, 1981; also articles, rvws; editor: Melville's Billy Budd and the Critics, 2nd ed., 1968, James's Daisy Miller, 1963, Twentieth Century American Writing, 1965, Perspectives on James's The Portrait of a Lady, 1967, Studies in The American, 1971, Henry James Novels, 1871-1880, 1983, Henry James Novels 1881-1886, 1985. BA with honors, U. Fla., 1948; MA, Columbia U., 1950; PhD, U. KY, 1956. Research asst. Columbia U. Press, 1950; part-time instr. U. KY, 1950-53; mem. faculty Purdue U., 1953—, prof. English, 1966—; vis. prof. U. KY, 1966, Columbia U., 1967, Tulsa Grad. Inst. Modern Letters, 1973; Fulbright prof., Finland, 19,63-64, Yugoslavia, 1970-71; editor Modern Fiction Studies, 1956—; cons. Ednl. Testing Service, 1958-70, Coll. Entrance Exam. Bd., 1964-70. Served with AUS, 1943-46. Mem. Phi Beta Kappa, Intl. Assn. Univ. Profs. English, MLA. Former mem: Midwest MLA, NCTE, Popular Culture Assn. Home: 717 Salisbury St West Lafayette IN 47906

STAHL, JAYNE LYN, b. NYC, 1949, d. David Darwin Stahl and Ethel Terry (Strauss) Siegel. Author: (plays) Max's Donuts, James, (critical work) Poe and the Pathology of Reason; chapbook: Courtroom Chrysanthemum, 1967; contrbr. poetry to Podium Mag., N.Y. Qtly, Pulpsmith, Yearbook of Modern Poetry, numerous other lit mags. BA summa cum laude, SUNY-Buffalo, 1972; MA, San Francisco State U., 1986. Mem. AAP, P&W. Home: 1415 Franklin St San Francisco CA 94109

STAHLER, CHARLES, Author: Vegetarianism for the Working Person, 1986, Healthy Holidays, 1984, I Love Animals and Broccoli, 1985, No-Cholesterol Passover Recipies, 1986. Contrbr. articles to vegetarian, nutrition mags., newsletters. Wrkg. on The Ethical Entrepreneur. Office: Box 1463 Baltimore MD 21203

STALLWORTHY, JON HOWIE, b. London, Jan. 18, 1935 (came to U.S., 1977); s. John Arthur and Margaret (Howie) Stallworth. m. Jull Meredith Waldock, June 25, 1960; children—Jonathan Meredith, Philippa Margaret, Nicholas Kyd. Author: biography Wilfred Owen, 1974; lit. criticism Between the Lines, 1963, Vision and Revision, 1969; poetry Root and Branch, 1969, Hand in Hand, 1974, The Apple Barrel, 1974, A Familiar Tree, 1978, The Aztec Sonata, 1986; translator: Alexnder Blok Selected Poems, 1974, Boris Pasternak Selected Poems, 1983; editor: Wilfred Owen: Complete Poems and Fragments, 1983, The Oxford Book of War Poetry, 1984. BA, Oxford U., 1958, B.Litt., 1964. Editor Oxford U. Press (London), 1959-70, dep. acad. pub., 1974-77; vis. fellow All Souls Coll., Oxford U., 1970-71; editor Clarendon Press, Oxford, 1970, dep. acad. pub., 1974-77; vis. fellow All Souls Coll., Oxford U., 1970-71; editor Clarendon Press, Oxford, 1971-74; Anderson prof. English Cornel U. (Ithaca, NY), 1977—; dir. Poetry Book Soc. (U.K.), 1962-78; mem. Arts Council Lit. Panel (U.K.), 1965-68. Served to lt. Brit. Army, 1953-55. Recipient Duff Cooper award, 1974, W.H. Smith & Son Lit. award, 1975, E.M. Forster award Am. Assn. Arts and Lit., 1976. Home: 1456 Hanshaw Rd Ithaca NY 14850

STALZER, DAVID, b. Kansas City, MO, Sept. 1, 1914; s. Theodore Jean and Jessie Eunice (Wadley) S.; m. Romano Hortense, May 1938; children—Lance, Robin. Contrbr. poems to numerous lit. mags., including Kauri, Epos, Quixote, Impetus, Dog River Rvw, anthols., newspapers Ed.: The Eagle, 1939. Wrkg. on novel, Cannibals & Cabbages. Mem. P&W, Stone Ridge Poetry Workshop, Hudson Valley Wrtrs. Sculptor and seller of rare books. Home: 31 Rhinecliff Rd Rhinebeck NY 12572

STAMBLER, IRWIN, b. NYC, Nov. 20, 1924; s. Sidney and Bess S.; m. Constance, Nov. 5, 1950; children—Amy, Alice, Lyndon, Barrett. Author: Encyclopedia of Popular Music, 1965; Great Moments in Auto Racing, 1965, Automobiles of the Future, 1966; (with Grelun Landon) Encyclopedia of Country, Folk & Western Music, 1969, Golden Guitars: Story of Country Music, 1971, New Encyclopedia of Folk, Country & Western Music, 1982 (Reference Book of Yr., Library Jnl.) Guitar Years: Pop Music from C&W to Hard Rock, 1970; Great Moments in Stock Car Racing, 1971; Unusual Autos of Today & Tomorrow, 1972; Speed Kings: World's Fastest Humans, 1973; Women in Sports, 1974; Supercars and the Men who Race Them, 1975; Bill Walton, Super Center, 1975; Encyclopedia of Pop, Rock & Soul, 1975, rev. 1976, new ed. 1988; Catfish Hunter, The $3 Million Arm, 1976; Here Come the Funny Cars, 1976; Minibikes and Small Cycles, 1977; Racing the Sprint Cars, 1979; Dream Machines: Vans and Pickups, 1980; Off-Roading, 1984. Student Tex. A&M; B.S. in Engring., NYU, Bronx, 1947, M.S., 1949. Design engr., project engr. Chase Aircraft, NYC, 1951-53; design/structure engr. Republic Aviation, Farmingdale, N.Y., 1953-55; engring. ed. Space/ Aeronautics, N.Y.C., 1955-66, Western ed. Research and Development, 1967—; assoc. ed. Gas Turbine World, Beverly Hills, Calif., 1975—; pub., editorial dir. Alternative Energy, Beverly Hills, 1980—, Tech. Forecasts, Beverly Hills, 1969—. Baseball coach Little League, Beverly Hills, 1976-79. Served to sgt. U.S. Army, 1944-46. Home: 423 Beverwil Dr Beverly Hills CA 90211

STAMBLER, PETER LANE, b. Washington, Nov. 17, 1944, s. Bernard and Elizabeth (Dickey) S.; m. Jeanne Sims, Dec. 23, 1971 (div. 1982); children—Brian, Alexa, Meredith; m. 2d, Nancy Jean Techlin, Oct. 27, 1984; stepchildren—Laura, Kristen. Author: Wilderness Fires (poetry), 1981, Clara's Husband (play), 1983, Witnesses (poetry), 1984, Unsettled Accounts (poetry), 1987, Copper Country (play), 1986; contrbr. poetry to Shenandoah, Beloit Poetry Rvw, Abraxas, Cimarron Rvw, numerous other lit mags. BA, Yale U., 1966; MFA, Carnegie-Mellon U., 1968; PhD, Syracuse U., 1974. Instr. N.C. Schl. Arts, Winston-Salem, 1968-71; asst. prof., then assoc. prof. U. Wis., Green Bay, 1975-87, full prof. 1987; prin. lctr. Hong Kong Baptist Coll, 1987—. Recipient Best Book award (Wilderness Fires), Council Wis. Wrtrs., 1982, Best Play award (Clara's Husband), 1984, (Copper Country) 1987; Recipient New Play award Ill. State U., 1983 (Clara's Husband), Wis. Public Radio Drama award (The Badger), 1983. English Dept Hong Kong Baptist Coll 224 Waterloo Rd Kowloon Hong Kong

STAMPER, LORI, b. Ft. Rucker, AL, Sept. 8, 1959. Contrbr. articles to The Crimson White, The Army Flier, Headliner Mag., When Mother Calls. Sports ed.: Corolla, 1980-81, Myriad Mag., 1980; ed.: Providerfax, 1987; ed., contrbr.: C & B Advisory, 1987, Update, 1987, Health Care Response, 1987. B.A. in Jnlsm., U. Ala., Tuscaloosa, 1982. Wrtr., Martin Advt., Birmingham, AL, 1982-84; wrtr., producer Central Bank of the South, Birmingham, 1984-85; communications specialist Blue Cross & Blue Shield of Ala., Birmingham, 1986-87, Direct Banking Ctr., South Trust Bk., Birmingham, 1987—. Mem. Ad Club (Addy award for advt. excellence 1984, 85). Home: Box 59824 Birmingham AL 35259

STANDING, SUE, b. Salt Lake City, UT, Apr. 14, 1952; d. Erwin Albert and Beverly (Farnes) Standing. Author: Amphibious Weather, 1981, Deception Pass, 1984; poetry to American Poetry Rvw, Nation, Ploughshares, Poetry Northwest, other lit mags. AB, Oberlin Coll., 1974; MA, Boston U., 1977. Lectr. Wellesley Coll.

(MA), 1979; wrtr.-in-res. Wheaton Coll (Norton, MA), 1979—; consultnt. JFK School of Govt., Harvard U. (Cambridge, MA), 1981—; mentor Lesley Coll. (Cambridge), 1984—. NEA Grant, 1984. Mem. PSA, AWP. Home: 44 Gordon St Allston MA 02134

STANDISH, CRAIG PETER, b. NYC, June 5, 1953; s. Peter and Violet (Oldham) S.; m. Susan Kay, May 25, 1974; 1 child, Ian Craig. Author: A Sheep Baas at the Moon, Poor Richard; contrbr. to numerous mags. and newspapers including Steinbeck Qtly, South & West, World's Best Poets of 1974, Piedmont, Dog River, Mendocino rvws, Parnassus, Calliope's Corner, New Voices, Poet's Corner, Art Mag.; contrbr. to books including Oak Ridge Year Book, Lyrical Treasures, The Poet, American Poetry Anthology, American Muse, Dan River Anthology, Hearts on Fire. Student broadcast journalism Williamsport Community Coll., 1973-75. Home: 1009 N Solandra Dr Orlando FL 32807

STANFORD, DONALD ELWIN, b. Amherst, MA, Feb. 7, 1913; s. Ernest Elwood and Alice (Carroll) Stanford; m. Edna Goodwin, July, 1937 (div. 1946); 1 son—Don David; 2nd m. Maryanna Peterson, Aug. 14, 1953. Author: New England Earth, 1941, The Traveler, 1955, In the Classic Mode: The Achievement of Robert Bridges, 1978, Revolution and Convention in Modern Poetry, 1983; editor: The Poems of Edward Taylor, 1960, Dictionary of Literary Biography, vol. 18, 1981, Dictionary of Literary Biography, vol. 20, 1983, Selected Letters of Robert Bridges, 2 vols., 1982, Humanities Series, 1963-66, The So. Rvw, 1963-83; mem. adv. bd.: Hopkins Qtly, 1981—. BA, Stanford U., 1933, PhD, 1953; MA, Harvard U., 1934. Instr. LA State U. (Baton Rouge), 1949-50, asst. prof. English, 1953-54, assoc. prof., 1954-62, prof., 1962-79, Alumni prof. English, 1979-83, Alumni prof. emeritus, 1983—; vis. prof. Duke U. (Durham, NC), 1961-62, Tex. A&M U. (College Station), 1984. Mem. PEN, MLA, South Atlantic MLA. Home: 776 Delgado Dr Baton Rouge LA 70808

STANG, RICHARD, b. NYC, July 3, 1925; s. Benjamin and Shirley (Duckor) Stang; m. Sondra Judith Selvansky, June 17, 1946; children—David, Elizabeth, Samuel. Author: The Theory of Novel in England, 1850-1870, 1959; editor: Discussions of George Eliot, 1960. BA, Columbia U., 1958, MA, 1949, PhD, 1958. Asst. prof. Carleton Coll. (Northfield, MN), 1958-61; prof. English lit. Washington U. (St. Louis), 1961—. Served with AUS, 1943-46; ETO. Home: 6310 Pershing Ave St Louis MO 63130

STANGER, ILA, b. NYC, Oct. 13, 1940; d. Jack Simon and Shirley Ruth (Nadelson) Stanger. BA, Bklyn. Coll., 1961. Feature and travel editor Harper's Bazaar (NYC), 1969-75; exec. editor Travel and Leisure mag. (NYC), 1975-85; ed.-in-chief, Food and Wine mag. (NYC), 1985—; freelance writer on arts, features and travel. Mem. NY Travel Writers, Am. Soc. Mag. Editors. Home: 115 W 71st St New York NY 10023

STANLEY, CHARLES J., (Carlo Pittore), b. NYC, May 14, 1943; s. Stanford A. and Estelle S. Author: The Adventures of Carlo Pittore, 1979; The Man With An Egg, 1982; ed. Yurtyet, 1979; Maine Moments in NY, 1979; Colleagues, 1979. BA in English, Tufts Coll., 1966; postgrad adv. painting, Bklyn Mus. Art Schl., 1977-78. Address: Acad. of Carlo Pittore Bowdoinham ME 04008

STANLEY, JOHN W., b. Santa Maria, CA, Feb. 20, 1940; s. Myron Gilbert and Frances (Hartman) S.; m. Erica Jones, June 15, 1962; children: Russ Maurus, Trista Karolina. Author: The Great Comics Game, 1966, the Monster Movie Game Book, 1974, World War III, 1976, The Dark Side (with Kenn Davis), 1976, Viva Knievel!, 1977, Bogart '48 (with Kenn Davis), 1980, The Creature Features Movie Guide, 1981, 2d ed., 1984. BA, San Francisco State U. writer/ed. San Francisco Chronicle, 1962—; host/producer/writer KTVU-TV, Oakland, Calif., 1979-84. Recipient Edgar nomination, MWA. Address: 1082 Grand Teton Dr Pacifica CA 94044

STANSBERRY, DOMENIC JOSEPH, b. Washington, Mar. 15, 1952, s. Chadwick Leroy and Theresa (Mussolino) S.; m. Gillian Concley, Mar. 22, 1986. Author: The Spoiler; contrbr. to Ploughshares, Mississippi Mud, Hartford Courant, Daily Hampshire Gazette. MA, Colo. State U., 1980; MFA, U. Mass., 1984. Instr. U. New Orleans, 1984-87; vis. lectr. Tulane U., New Orleans, 1985-86. Recipient Mel Cohen award for nonfiction, Ploughshares, 1985. Home: W 1230 Sprague No 14 Spokane WA 99201

STANTON, MAURA, b. Evanston, IL, Sept. 9, 1946; d. Joseph Patrick and Wanda Grace (Haggard) Stanton; m. Richard Cecil, April 10, 1972. Author poetry: Cries of Swimmers, 1984, Snow on Snow, 1975; novels: Molly Companion, 1977. BA, U. of Minn., 1969; MFA, U. of Iowa, 1971. Instr. SUNY at Cortland, NY, 1972-73; asst. prof., U. of Richmond, Va., 1973-77; asst. prof., Humboldt State U., Calif., 1977-78; asst. prof., U. of Arizona, 1978-82; disting. wrtr.-in-res., Mary Washington College, 1981-82; assoc. prof., Indiana U., 1982—. Awards: NEA fellowship, 1974, 1982; Lawrence Fdn. Prize, Mich. Quarterly Rvw, 1982. Address: Dept Eng Indiana U Bloomington IN 47405

STANTON, PRISCILLA ANNE, b. NYC, Mar. 21, 1953, d. Herbert G. and Claire E. (Freedman) Stanton, stepdau. Greta (Wertheimer) Stanton. Ed.: Box 241, Poetry and Arts mag., 1975; contrbr.: Casebook in Organizational Communications (by Eugene Marlow), 1982. BA in English, Rutgers U., 1975; MA in Public Communications, Fortham U., 1983. Admin., wrtr. ASME, NYC, 1983-84, staff ed. ASME Student News, 1984—; radio scriptwrtr., producer sta.-WBAI, 1982-83; reporter Our Town newspaper, 1985—; tutor Literacy Vols. Am., NYC, 1984. Home: 210 E 21st St New York NY 10010

STAP, DONALD L., b. Kalamazoo, Aug. 14, 1949, s. Elmer and Ruth Evangeline (Lukins) S.; m. Kristine Anda Austrins, Apr. 17, 1971; 1 child, Benjamin Valdis. Author: A Vanishing Species; contrbr. poetry to Poetry, Poetry N.W., N.Am. Rvw, Mass. Rvw, Am. Scholar, Prairie Schooner, others; articles to Sierra, Intl. Wildlife, Backpacker, Modern Maturity, Am. Way, Chicago, Travel & Leisure; book reviewer Chgo. Tribune, Chgo., Milw. Jnl. BA, Western Mich. U., 1972; PhD, U. Utah, 1978. Asst. prof. English, Western Mich. U., Kalamazoo, 1978-82, U. Central Fla., Orlando, 1985—; freelance wrtr., 1982-85. Mich. Council for Arts creative artist grantee, 1982-83; NEA fellow, 1986. Home: 3741 Sutter's Mill Circle Casselberry FL 32707

STAPLETON, KATHARINE LAURENCE, b. Holyoke, MA, Nov. 20, 1911; d. Richard Prout and Frances (Purtill) Stapleton. Author: Justice and World Society, 1944, The Design of Democracy, 1949, H.D. Thoreau: A Writers Journal, 1960, Yushin's Log and Other Poems, 1969, The Elected Circle: Studies in the Art of Prose, 1973, Marianne Moore: The Poet's Advance, 1978. AB, Smith Coll., 1932; postgrad., U. London, Eng., 1932-33. Registrar Mass. Pub. Employment Service, 1933-34; faculty Bryn Mawr Coll., 1934—; prof. English and Poli. theory, 1948-64, chair dept. English, 1954-65, Mary E. Garrett prof. English, 1964-80, prof. emeritus, 1980—. Mem. bd. sponsors Natl. Com. for an Effective Congress. Recipient Lindback Fdn. award, 1980. Mem. AAUP, MLA, Renaissance Soc., Thoreau Soc. Home: 229 N Roberts Rd Bryn Mawr PA 19010

STARKE, LINDA, B.A. in Sociology, Beloit Coll., 1970. Editor: State of the World (Worldwatch Inst.), 1984, Our Common Future (World Comm. Envir. & Devel.), 1987, numerous reports from Office of Technology Assessment of U.S. Congress and Natl. Acad. of Scis. Ed., outreach liaison Worldwatch Inst., Washington, 1976-82; free-lance ed., 1982—. mem. Wash. Ind. Wrtrs. (formerly bd. dirs.), Assn. Editorial Bus. (bd. dirs.). Home: 1789 Lanier Pl NW Washington DC 20009

STARLING, THOMAS, see Hayton, Richard Neil

STARMER, RONNIE, b. Cortland, NY, Feb. 12, 1952, s. Cecil and Vee (Ferro) S.; m. Connie Lee Karpinski; 1 son, Jacob Travis. Contrbr. to: A Search for Soul, Magic of the Muse, Transition, La Traviata, other publs. BA, Syracuse U., 1976; MA, SUNY-Cortland, 1982. Tchr. public schls., Whitney Point, N.Y., 1976-80, Livingston Manor, N.Y., 1981—. Home: RD 2 Box 399 Livingston Manor NY 12758

STARR, CHESTER, b. Centralia, MO, Oct. 5, 1914; s. Chester Gibbs and Nettie (Glore) Starr; m. Gretchen Daub, July 15, 1940; children—Jennifer (Mrs. Michael Johnson), Deborah (Mrs. Gene Sessions), Richard G., Thomas J.J. Author: Roman Imperial Navy, 1941, From Salerno to the Alps, 1948, Emergence of Rome, 1950, Civilization and the Caesars, 1954, Origins of Greek Civilization, 1961, History of Ancient World, 1965, Rise and Fall of Ancient World, 1965, Awakening of the Greek Historical Spirit, 1968, Athenian Coinage, 480-499 B.C., 1970, Ancient Greeks, 1971, Ancient Romans, 1971, Early Man, 1973, Political Intelligence in Classical Greece, 1974, Economic and Social Growth of Early Greece, 1977, Essays on Ancient History, 1979, Beginnings of Imperial Rome, 1980, The Roman Empire: A Study in Survival, 1982, Flawed Mirror, 1983, Individual and Community, 1984, Past and Future in Ancient History, 1986. AB with distinction, U. MO, 1934, LLD, 1981, MA, 19,35; PhD, Cornell U., 1938, LLD, U. Ill., 1987. Faculty U. Ill. at Urbana, 1940-70, prof., history, 1953-70, chair div. humanities, 1953-55, chair dept. history, 1960-61; prof. U. Mich. (Ann Arbor), 1970—, Bentley prof., 1973-83, Hudson prof., 1981; cons. World Book, 1963-67, Encyc. Americana, 1966—. Served from 1st lt. to lt. col. AUS, 1942-46; MTO. Decorated Bronze Star; Croce di Guerra (Italy). Home: 2301 Blueberry Ln Ann Arbor MI 48103

STARR, JAN, see Stewart, June

STARR, WILLIAM J., b. Concordia, KS., May 23, 1923; s. Robert Ellis and Kathryn (Kelly) S.; m. Constance Laura Koebelin, June 21, 1947; children: Kathleen, Teresa, Gregory, Timothy, Judith, William Jr., Michael, David. Author: Scored for Listening, 1959, Perceiving Music,

1962, Music Scores Omnibus, 1964, Basic Piano Skills, 1971, Suzuki Violinist, 1976, To Learn with Love, 1983. Music, Eastman Sch. BMusic, 1944, MMusic, 1947. Prof. music U. Tenn., Knoxville, 1949-82, chmn. dept. music, 1977-82; adj. prof. music U. Colo., Boulder, 1982—. Served as lt. (j.g.) USN, 1944-46; PTO. Home: 402 Pine Tree Ln Boulder CO 80302

STARR-WHITE, DEBI, see Livingston-White, Deborah J. Halemah

STARZAK, MICHAEL EDWARD, b. Woonsocket, RI, Apr. 21, 1942, s. Michael and Ida Dolores (Bielagus) S.; m. Anndrea Lee Zahorak, July 22, 1967; children—Jocelyn Ann, Alissa Michelle. Author: The Physical Chemistry of Membranes, 1984, numerous research publs. ScB, Brown U., 1963; PhD, Northwestern U., 1968. Mem. faculty U. Calif.-Santa Cruz, 1968-70; asst., then assoc. prof. chemistry SUNY-Binghamton, 1970—. Mem. profl. sci. orgns. Office: Dept Chemistry SUNY Binghamton NY 13901

STATON, JOHANNA BILBO, b. Ithaca, NY, Aug. 23, 1939, d. Jean Straughan and Ellen Ruth (Elliott) Bilbo; m. Richard Denis Staton, Jan. 20, 1968; children—Christopher Elliott, Valerie Wing. Contrbr. book revs., articles, fiction: Jack and Jill, Odyssey, Stories, Instructor, Sarasota (Fla.) Herald-Tribune and Journal. Wrkg. on children's novels. BA, Rollins Coll., 1961; MS in Journalism, Northwestern U., 1964. Asst. then assoc. ed. Jack and Jill, Curtis Pub. Co., Phila., 1965-69; tech. copy ed. Auerbach Pub., Pennsauken, N.J., 1976-80; med. copy ed. Franklin Inst. Press, Phila., 1981-83; proofreader, ed. Radio Only and Inside Radio, Cherry Hill, N.J., 1983-84; ed. Instructor's Read-Aloud Anthology, Instructor Books, NYC, 1984; ed. Ultrapure Water, Tall Oaks Pub. Co., Voorhees, N.J., 1984—. Home: 224 E Homestead Ave Collingswood NJ 08108

STAUFFER, DOROTHY HUBBELL, b. Chicago, June 10, 1905; d. Richard Sinclair and Bessie Louise (Seymour) Hubbell; m. Walter Stauffer, Feb. 8, 1931 (dec. Aug. 25, 1944); children: Dorothy Louise Stauffer Dreher, John Richard Stauffer. Author: Lights and Shadows: A Partially Fictitious Autobiography, 1915-31. Tchr. H.S. English, Tiskilwa, Ill., 1928-31; owner, operator, grocery, Tiskilwa, 1944-55; English tchr. or librarian, various highschools, Ill., 1953-66; librarian, Northern Ill. Univ., 1966-74; housemother, Chi Omega Sorority, Bradley Univ., 1975-80, Wrkg. on narrative genealogy-history of Hubbells from 1639. AB, English, highest honors, Univ. of Illinois, 1928; MSEd., Northern Illinois Univ., 1966, MA Lib Sci, 1969. Mem. DZ, Phi Beta Kappa, DAR. Home: 215 W 6th St Apt 1010 Peoria IL 61605

STEADMAN, JOHN MARCELLUS, III, b. Spartanburg, SC, Nov. 25, 1918; s. John Marcellus and Medora Rice (Rembert) Steadman. Author numerous books, 1967—, latest publs. Disembodied Laughter: Troilus and the Apotheosis Tradition, 1972, The Lamb and the Elephant: Ideal Imitation and the Context of Renaissance Allegory, 1974, Epic and Tragic Structure in Paradise Lost, 1976, Nature into Myth: Medieval and Renaissance Moral Symbols, 1979, The Hill and the Labyrinth: Discourse and Certitude in Milton and his Near-Contemporaries, 1984, Milton's Biblical and Classical Imagery, 1984, The Wall of Paradise: Essays on Milton's Poetics, 1985, Milton and the Paradoxes of Renaissance Heroism, 1987. Co-editor: A Milton Ency., vols. I-IX, 1978-83; editor: Huntington Library Qtly, 1962-81. AB, Emory U., 1940, MA, 1941, DHL (hon.), 1976; MA (T.W. Hunt scholar), Princeton U., 1948; PhD (Proctor fellow), Princeton U., 1949. Instr. English GA Inst. Tech., 1941-42; asst. prof. U. NC, 1949-51; ind. study and research in English lit., 1953-61; research assoc., then sr. research assoc. Henry E. Huntington Library (San Marino, CA) 1962—; mem. faculty U. CA (Riverside), 1966—, prof. English, 1967—, faculty research lectr. 1977; vis. disting. prof. City U. NY, fall 1974. Served to capt. USAAF, 1942-46; served to capt. USAF, 1951-52. Mem. Milton Soc. Am. (pres., 1973, honored scholar 1976). Office: Dept Eng U Calif Riverside CA 92521

STEADMAN, MARK S., b. Statesboro, GA, July 2, 1930; s. Mark S. and Marie Marcella (Hopkins) S.; m. Joan Marie Anderson, Mar. 29, 1952; children—Clayton DeWitt, Todd Anderson, Wade Hopkins. Author: McAfee County, 1971, reissued, 1985, (Fr. trans., Quoi neuf en Georgie, 1974; Ger. transl., Schwarze Chronik, 1975), A Lion's Share, 1976. BA in English, Emory U., 1951; MA, Fla. State U., 1956, PhD, 1963. Prof. English, Clemson U., S.C., 1957—; vis. assoc. prof. Am. lit Am. U., Cairo, Egypt, 1968-69; Fulbright lectr. Leningrad State U., U.S.S.R., 1983. Fellow, NEA, 1979-80. Mem. South Atlantic MLA. Home: Rt 3 Box 215-B Central SC 29630

STEARNS, JON ROD, (Nicholas Drake), b. Tampa, FL, May 19, 1958; s. Howard Ford and Rosemary (Lee) S. Author: (poems) Distortions Of, 1985, The Body Eclectic, 1986. Contrbr. poems, short stories to lit mags, anthols. Editor Galeria '86, Hills Comm. Coll. BA in History, U. Tampa, 1980; MA in History, U. South Fla., 1986. Recipient Estelle J. Zbar Poetry award U. South Fla. English Dept., 1986. Mem. Phi Alpha Theta. Home: 1602 W. Richardson Pl Tampa FL 33606

STEBBINS, ESTHER SIGNE, b. Whitinsville, MA, July 9, 1947; d. Cecil Reginald and Helen Elizabeth (Metcalf Wheeler. Contrbr. poems to anthols. Grad. public schs., East Douglas, MA. Garage attendant Hertz Rent-A-Car, Atlanta, 1981—. Recipient Merit cert. World of Poetry, 1985, Golden Poet award, 1985, Silver Poet award, 1986. Home: 628 Coleman St Apt 1 Hapeville GA 30354

STECK, CAROL R., b. Cin., Nov. 20, 1954; d. Richard M. and June I. (Van Buskirk) Reid; m. Robert M. Steck, Aug. 19, 1978; 1 dau., Victoria Carol. Supvr., employee communications, Feedback Mag., The Moogolog, Moog Connection, The Moog Employee Handbook. BA in English, Marietta Coll., 1976; MA in Pub. Relations, Syracuse U., 1977. Asst. dir. pub. relations Millard Fillmore Hosp., Buffalo, 1978-80; acct. exec. Weil, Levy and King, Buffalo, 1980; supr. employee communications Moog Inc., Elma, N.Y., 1980—. Mem. Pub. Relations Soc. Am., Intl. Assn. Bus. Communicators. Home: 257 Olean St East Aurora NY 14052

STEEL, DANIELLE FERNANDE, b. NYC, Aug. 14, 1947; d. John and Norma (Stone) Schuelein-Steel. Author: Going Home, 1973, Passion's Promise, 1977, Now and Forever, 1978, The Promise, 1978, Season of Passion, 1979, Summers End, 1979, To Love Again, 1980, The Ring, 1981, Loving, 1980, Love, 1981, Remembrance, 1981, Palomino, 1981, Once in a Lifetime, 1982, Crossings, 1982, A Perfect Stranger, 1982, Thurston House, 1983, Changes, 1983, Full Circle, 1984, Family Album, 1983, Secrets, 1983, Kaleidoscope, 1987; (non-fiction) Having a Baby, 1984; contbr. poetry to mags., including Cosmopolitan, McCall's, Ladies Home Jnl., Good Housekeeping. Student, Parsons Schl. Design, 1963, NYU, 1963-67. Copywriter Grey Advtg., San Franciso, 1973-74. Office Dell Pubs One Dag Hammarskjold Plaza New York NY 10017

STEELE, FRANK PETTUS, b. Tuscaloosa, AL, Jan. 13, 1935; s. Frank Pettus and Zeila (Stovall) Steele; m. Peggy Myrick, Apr. 27, 1958; children—Carolyn, Nancy. Author: Walking to the Waterfall, 1969, Poems, 1972; editor: Poetry Southeast: 1950-70, 1969, Plainsong, 1979—. Co-editor: Tennessee Poetry Jnl, 1967-68. BA, U. of AL, 1960; Ed D U. of TN, 1968. English tchr. Baylor School (Chattanooga, TN), 1960-64, Webb School (Knoxville, TN), 1964-67, U. of TN (Martin), 1967-68, Western Kentucky U. (Bowling Green), 1968—. NEA grant for Plainsong, 1983-84, 1984-85. Mem. South Atlantic MLA. Home: 152 Meadowlark Tr Rt 8 Bowling Green KN 42101

STEELE, ROBERT BAINUM JR., b. Little Rock, June 30, 1937; s. Robert Bainum and Mamie Eleanor (Walters) S.; m. Bettina Nemec, Mar. 29, 1956; children—Lia A. Hanna, Andrea Thrasher, Mark V., Melanie. Author: (poems) A Gallery of Moonmen, 1968. Contrbr. poems, articles to mags., anthols., newspapers. B.S. in English, U. Central Ark., 1963, M.S. in English, 1983. Musician, U.S. Navy Band Washington, 1956-59; tchr. various high schs., colls., AR, 1963-83; free-lance wrtr., 1959—. Served with USN, 1955-59. Recipient Coll. Writing award Atlantic Monthly, 1961. Home: 1939 Broken Arrow Dr North Little Rock AR 72118

STEELE, TIMOTHY REID, b. Burlington, VT, Jan. 22, 1948, s. Edward William Steele, Jr., and Ruth (Reid) Gjessing; m. Catherine Fuller, Sept. 27, 1969 (div. 1973); m. 2d, Victoria Lee Erpelding, Jan. 14, 1979. Author: Uncertainties and Rest, 1979, The Prudent Heart, 1983, Nine Poems, 1984, On Harmony, 1984, Short Subjects, 1985, Sapphics Against Anger and Other Poems, 1986; contrbr. poems, rvws and essays to Poetry, Threepenny Rvw, Paris Rvw, numerous other publs. BA, Stanford U., 1970; PhD, Brandeis U., 1977. Lectr. Calif. State U., Hayward, 1973-74, Stanford (Calif.) U., 1975-77, UCLA, 1977-83. Lectr. Univ. of Calif. Santa Barbara, 1986; assoc. prof. Calif. State Univ. Los Angeles, 1987—. Recipient Wallace Stegner Fellowship in creative writing Stanford U., 1972-73, John Simon Guggenheim Meml. Fdn. fellowship, 1984-85. Acad. of Amer. Poets' Peter I.B. Laven Younger Poets Award, 1986, Commonwealth Club of Calif. Medal for Poetry, 1986, Los Angeles Ctr. of PEN Literary Award for Poetry, 1987. Mem. AAP, MLA. Home: 2811A Arizona Ave Santa Monica CA 90404

STEGALL, PAULINE M, b. Wheatcroft, KY, Apr. 3, 1923; d. Rutherford Birchard and Edna Roberts Morgan; m. Darrell Eugene Stringer, Apr. 27, 1946 (dec. 1969); children—Cynthia Dawn Stringer Hart, Darilyn Jill, Paul Eugene; m. 2d, Wallace Theodore Stegall, Apr. 5, 1980. Contrbr. to The Church Musician, Illinois Baptist, Christian Singles, The Livingston Ledger, School Musician, Bluegrass Music News, Western Recorder. Bachelor of Music Edn., Murray State U., 1944, Master's of Music Edn., 1971. Supvr. of music, Willow Springs (MO) Pub. Sch., 1944-46; choral dir. Livingston County Schs., KY, 1962-87; owner-operator Morgan's Dept.

Store, Salem, KY, 1969-86; private music tchr., MO & KY, 1939—; state corresp. Western Recorder, Middletown, KY, 1985—. Wilbur C. Fields Writing Incentive award, 1986 2nd and 3rd awards, 1987. Home: Box 78 Salem KY 42078

STEGEMAN, WILLIAM H., (Bill) b. Aztec, NM, Sept. 7, 1914; s. Gerret Fredrick Stegeman and Lena Olive (Rathjen) Covert; m. Jeanne Olivette Stallings, 1940 (dec. 1963); 2nd m. Judith Joyce Henniger, Jul. 20, 1966; 1 son—William G., stepchildren—Jeffrey Ross Stacy, Valerie Jo Stacy. Author: Living in the Kindergarten, 1950, Living in the Primary Grades, 1955, Curriculum in America, 1960; wrkg. on Pop Ivers Takes a Holiday, Secrets of Mulungutti. AB, UCLA, 1937; PhD in Ed. U. of CA, 1947. Prof. State U. (Chico, CA), 1947-53; Deputy Supt. City Schools (San Diego), 1953-76; freelance consult. and wrtr., 1976—. Mem. Governor's Youth Commission (Sacramento), 1950-60, Urban Renewal Comm. (San Diego), 1955-63. Field Dir., Am. Red Cross, 1942-45, Europe. Library Award, Caldecott Library, 1951. Home: 4835 Bram Ave Bonita CA 92002

STEGNER, STUART PAGE, b. Salt Lake, UT, Jan. 31, 1937, s. Wallace Earle and Mary (Page) S. Author: Escape into Aesthetics, 1968, The Edge, 1969, Hawks and Harriers, 1972, Sportscar Menopause, 1977, American Places, 1981, Islands of the West, 1985. BA, Stanford U., 1959, PhD, 1964. Asst. prof. Ohio State U., Columbus, 1965-68; prof. U. Calif.-Santa Cruz, 1968—. Assoc. dir. Peace Corps, Ecuador, 1970-72. NEA fellow, 1979, NEH fellow, 1980, Guggenheim fellow, 1981. Home: 2574 Pine Flat Santa Cruz CA 95060

STEGNER, WALLACE EARLE, b. Lake Mills, IA, Feb. 18, 1909; s. George Henry and Hilda Emilia (Paulson) Stegner; m. Mary Stuart Page, Sept. 1, 1934; 1 son—Stuart Page. Author: numerous books, 1937—, including The Women on the Wall, 1950, The Preacher and the Slave, 1950, Beyond the Hundredth Meridian, 1954, The City of the Living, 1956, A Shooting Star, 1961, Wolf Willow, 1963 (Blackhawk award), The Gathering of Zion, 1964, All the Little Live Things, 1967 (Commonwealth Club gold medal 1968), The Sound of Mountain Water, 1969, Angle of Repose, 1971 (Pulitzer prize 1972), The Uneasy Chair: A Biography of Bernard DeVoto, 1974, The Spectator Bird, 1976 (Natl. Book award 1977), Recapitulation, 1979; editor numerous texts; contrbr. articles to mags.; editor-in-chief: Am. West, 1966-69. AB, U. Utah, 1930, D.Litt., 1968; MA, U. IA, 1932, PhD, 1935; postgrad., U. Calif., 1932-33, LHD, 1969; D.Litt., Utah State U., 1972; LLD, U. Sask., 1973; DHL, Santa Clara U., 1979, DLitt, U. Wis., 1986. Instr. English Augustana Coll. (Rock Island, IL), 1933-34, U. Utah, 1934-37, U. Wis., 1937-39; instr. English Harvard, 1939-45; prof. English Stanford, 1945—, Reynolds prof. humanities, 1969-71. Recipient Little Brown & Co. prize for novelette Remembering Laughter 1937; O. Henry 1st prize for short story 1950; Robert Kirsch award, 1980. Mem. AAAS, AAIAL. Home: 13456 South Fork Ln Los Altos Hills CA 94022

STEIER, RODNEY DEAN, b. Hartford, CT, July 19, 1949; s. Richard S. and Eleanor (Glater) S.; m. Elena Vira, May 15, 1977; children: Lydia, Teddy, Drew, Julia. Author: Kevin, 28 Days to Satori; ed. Ohio Seduction (Pat Bizzaaro, Settan (Scott Norris), Pruning the Annuals (Cynthia Macdonald), Issuing of Scars (Terry Stokes), The Flesh-Eating Horse (Dave Kelley); ed., pub. Bartholomew's Cobble, 1976. BA, Springfield, Coll., 1971; MA, Miami U., Oxford, Ohio, 1972. NEA grantee, 1978. Home: 19 Howland Rd West Hartford CT 06107

STEIN, DAVE, see Richman, Elliott

STEIN, DONA LUONGO, b. Boston, May 16, 1935, d. Frank Joseph and Regina (Bigler) Luongo; m. Robert Allen Stein, July 8, 1961 (div. Sept. 1985); 1 child, Benjamin Allen. Author: Children of the Mafiosi, 1977; contrbr. to Cameos, Small Press Women Poets, Poems, A Celebration, Introduction of Literature, Anthology of Magazine Verse and Yearbook of American Poetry, Sojourner, Worcester Rvw, Ploughshares, Denver Qtly, Puerto del Sol, Poetry Rvw, others. AB, Clark U., 1960, MA, 1969; MFA, Warren Wilson Coll., 1984. Asst. prof. Inst. English, Lasell Jr. Coll., Auburndale, Mass., 1969-75; part-time instr. Fitchburg State Coll., Mass., 1976-80; lectr. Tufts U., Medford, Mass., 1981-83; instr. continuing edn. Brandeis U., Waltham, Mass., 1983; adj. asst. prof. Bentley Coll., Waltham, 1984—. Mass Arts Council poetry fellow, 1976; Margaret Bridgman scholar in poetry Bread Loaf, 1977; poetry residence fellow Wurlitzer Fdn., 1980-81; poetry fellow Yaddo, 1985; poetry fellow and scholar Montalvo Ctr. for Arts, 1985, Stegner fellow, Stanford U., 1986-87. Mem. PSA, P&W, AWP, Poets for Peace. Home: 361 Wolcott St Auburndale MA 02166

STEIN, EDWARD DALTON, see Tucker, Charles Christopher

STEIN, GEORGE HENRY, b. Vienna, Austria, May 18, 1934 (came to U.S., 1939, naturalized, 1948); m. Dorothy Ann Lahm, Nov. 22, 1963; 1 son—Kenneth. Author: The Waffen SS: Hitler's Elite Guard at War, 1939-45, 1966 (transl. into German, 1967, French, 1967, Spanish, 1973, Portuguese, 1970); contrbr. articles on modern European history to scholarly publs.; editor: Hitler, 1968; contrbr. book rvws. to hist. jnls. BA with honors (NY State Regents scholar), Bklyn. Coll., 1959; MA in History (Regents fellow), Columbia U., 1960; PhD in History (Pres.'s fellow), Columbia U., 1964. Lectr. history City Coll., CUNY, 1962-63; instr. dept. history Columbia U. (NYC), 1963-65, asst. prof., 1970—, disting. teaching prof., 1973—, vice-chair grad. affairs, 1974-76, vp acad. affairs, 1976-85, vp acad. affairs and Provost, 1985—; manuscript evaluator and cons. to numerous publishers, 1964—. Served with USAF, 1953-57. Office: VP Acad Aff SUNY Binghamton NY 13901

STEIN, HERMAN DAVID, b. NYC, Aug. 13, 1917; s. Charles and Emma (Rosenblum) Stein; m. Charmion Kerr, Sept. 15, 1946; children—Karen Lou Gelender, Susan Stein Bennett, Naomi Elizabeth. Author: The Curriculum Study of the Columbia University School of Social Work, 1960; co-author: The Characteristics of American Jews, 1965; editor: (with Richard A. Cloward) Social Perspectives on Behavior, 1958, Planning for the Needs of Children in Developing Countries, 1965, Social Theory and Social Invention, 1968, The Crisis in Welfare in Cleveland, 1969, Organization and the Human Services, 1981; mem. editorial bd.: Administr. in Social work, 1976—. BSS, CCNY, 1939, MS, Columbia U., 1941, D. Social Welfare, 1958; LHD, Hebrew Union Coll.-Jewish Inst. Religion, 1969. Family Case worker, dir. pub. relations Jewish Family Service (NYC), 1941-45; mem. faculty Columbia Schl. Social Work (NYC), 1945-47, 50-64, prof. 1958-64, dir. research center, 1959-62; dean Schl. Applied Social Scis. Case Western Res. U. (Cleveland) 1964-68, provost for social and behavioral scis., 1967-71, provost univ., 1969-72 and 1986-88; div. Global Currents Lctr. Series, 1982—. Univ. prof., 1972—; fellow Center for Advances Study in Behavior Scis., 1974-75, 78-79; lectr. Schl. Social Work, Smith Coll. 1950-63, Harvard Schl. Public Health, 1971—. Office: Pardee Hall Case Westrn Cleveland OH 44106

STEIN, JOSEPH, (Barry Kluff), b. Columbus, OH, Dec. 25, 1912; s. Aloysius John and Rose Elizabeth (Trogus) S.; m. Loma Jean Talboy, Mar. 4, 1944; children: Nancy, Thomas, James, Carol, Mary, Lucy, Eric. Author: Lift Is Where You Find It, 1985; The Newsroom Dragonfly, 1974 (co-author); contrbr. articles to The Oregonian, NW Mag; corres., The Washington Post, 1976-77. Aviation ed. Oreg. Jnl, Portland, 1946-54; with public affairs dept NASA, Washington, 1954-71; freelance writer, Oreg., 1971—; pub. The Zig Zag Papers, 1984—. Counselor/therapist, Menal Health Clinic, Oregon City, 1971—. Served to lt. comdr., USNR, 1943-66. Mem. Helicopter Assn. Intl., Am. Helicopter Soc., Aviation Writers Assn., Airborne Law Enforcement Assn. Address: 70796 Barlow Tl Box 247 Zig Zag OR 97049

STEIN, JULIA A., b. Pitts., July 1, 1946. Author: (poetry) Under the Ladder to Heaven, 1984; assoc. and contrbg. ed. Electrum, 1983, ed., 1984; assoc. ed. West End Press, 1985. BA in Sociology, U. Calif., Berkeley, 1968; MA in Psychology, Calif. State U., Los Angeles, 1970. Ludwig Vogelstein Fdn. poetry grantee, 1985. Mem. AAP (finalist Whitman competition 1983), NWU. Home: 819 N Sierra Bonita Ave Los Angeles CA 90046

STEIN, MURRAY WALTER, b. Yorkton, Sask., Can., Sept. 2, 1943, s. Walter and Jennette (Reiman) S.; m. Jan Ohmstede, Jan. 1976; 1 son—Charles Christopher. Author: In Mid-Life, 1984, Jung's Treatment of Christianity, 1985; editor: Chiron: A Review of Jungian Analysis, 1984—; contrbr. chpts: Fathers and Mothers, 1976, Facing the Gods, 1978, Jungian Analysis, 1983. BA, Yale U., 1965, M.Div., 1969; PhDDiploma, C.G. Jung Inst./Zurich; U. Chgo., 1984. Jungian analyst, Wilmette, Ill., 1976—; gen. prtnr. Chiron Publs., Wilmette, 1983—; tchg. analyst, C.G. Jung Inst., Chgo. Home: 75 Tudor Pl Kenilworth IL 60043

STEIN, ROBERTA KATCHEN, b. Allentown, Pa., June 7, 1941; d. Harry William and Selma (Kessler) Katchen; m. Michael Roger Stein, Aug. 27, 1967; children: Eytan Moshe, Talya Margalit. Contrbr. numerous articles to Chgo. Tribune. BA, Queens Coll. Asst. ed. Tri-Qtly, Evanston, Ill., 1970-71; freelance ed., 1978-82; freelance wrtr., ed., 1982—; ed. archtl. records Chgo. Art Inst., 1982. Mem. Ind. Wrtrs. Chgo. Home: 8826 Ewing Ave Evanston IL 60203

STEINBACH, MEREDITH LYNN, b. Ames, IA, Mar. 18, 1949; d. Christopher Gene and Joy Janice (Johnson) Steinbach; m. Charles Ossian Hartman, May 9, 1979; 1 son, Zachary. Author: Zara, 1982. Contrbr. stories to lit. mags., anthols. B.Gen. Studies, U. Ia., 1973, M.F.A., 1976. Wrtr.-in-residence Antioch Coll., Yellow Springs, Ohio, 1976-77; vis. lectr. in fiction Northwestern U., Evanston, Ill., 1977-79; vis. asst. prof. U. Wash., Seattle, 1979-82; Bunting fellow of Radcliffe Coll., Harvard U., Cambridge, Mass., 1982-83; asst. prof. Brown U., Providence, R.I., 1983—. Fellow, NEA, 1978. Agent: Borchardt 136 E 57th St New York NY

10022

STEINBERG, BERNHARD EVANBAR, (B.H. Evanbar), b. Kingsbridge, NY, June 18, 1900, s. Murray Charles and Sara (Sprinborg) S.; m. Roberta Riman, Feb. 13, 1932; children—Bernard, Michael Evanbar. Author, medical book: Infections of the Peritoneum, 1944; cartoon book: It Was My Idea, 1952; Development of Character and Intelligence, 1987; assoc. ed. Leukemia Abstracts, 1954-64; contrbr. over 200 articles to med. and hosp. jnls. Wrkg. on plays, fiction. BA, Fordham U., 1918; MD, Boston U., 1922. Chief pathologist, dir. Inst. Med. Research, Toledo, 1926—; lectr. forensic medicine, cons. in forensic pathology; assoc. clinical prof., Loma Linda Univ. Schl. of Medicine, 1965—. Served with USPHS, 1954-64. Recipient numerous awards, fellowships in medicine. Mem. DG, WG. Home: 20342 Seaboard Rd Malibu CA 90265

STEINBERG, DAVID, b. NYC, July 14, 1944; s. Bert and Sophie (Axelrod) S.; m. Susan Black, Sept. 2, 1967 (div. May 15, 1980); 1 child, Dylan Joshua. Author: Doing Your Own School, 1972, If I Knew the Way, 1975, Welcome, Brothers, 1976, Fatherjournal: Five Years of Awakening to Fatherhood, 1977, Beneath This Calm Exterior, 1982; editor: Working Loose, 1971, Yellow Brick Road, 1974; contrbr. Manifesto, 1970, The Future of the Family, 1972, Seasons of Rebellion, 1972, Men in Difficult Times, 1981, Men without Masks, 1980. Currently editing Erotic by Nature, a collection of conscious, imaginative, erotic writing and photography. BA, Oberlin Coll., 1965. Writer, editor, Santa Cruz, Calif., 1971—. Mem. Calif. Antisexist Men's Polit. Caucus, Berkeley, 1984—, Nat. Orgn. Changing Men, 1984—; organizer Calif. Men's Gathering, Santa Cruz, 1982. Office: Box 2992 Santa Cruz CA 95063

STEINBRINK, JEROLD C., b. Erie, PA, Aug. 13, 1953, s. Fred Harvey and Virginia Mary (Pifer) S.; m. Mary Anne Mennite, Apr. 18, 1981. BA in Journalism, Temple U., 1976. Asst. ed. publs. Food Fair, Inc., Phila., 1966-77; sr. ed. Indsl. Distributor News, Chilton Co., Radnor, Pa., 1977-78, ed., 1978-80, ed.-in- chief, 1980-84, ed.-in-chief Indsl. Maintenance and Plant Operation, 1984—. Mem. BPA. Home: 114 Merion Ave Narberth PA 19072

STEINER, BARBARA ANNETTE, b. Dardenelle, AR, Nov. 3, 1934; d. Hershel Thomas and Rachel Julia (Stilley) Daniel; m. Kenneth Earle Steiner, Aug. 4, 1957 (div. Jan. 1980); children—Rachel Anne, Rebecca Sue. Author: (children's and teens books) Biography of a Polar Bear (Outstanding Sci. Book of Yr., Natl. Sci. Tchr's Assn. and Children's Book Council, 1972, Juvenile Nonfiction book Colo. AL, 1973), 1972, Your Hobby: Stamp Collecting, 1972, Biography of a Wolf, 1973, Biography of a Desert Bighorn, 1974, Biography of a Kangaroo Rat (Juvenile Nonfiction Book award AL, 1977), 1976, Biography of a Killer Whale, 1977, Biography of a Bengal Tiger, 1978, But Not Stanleigh, 1980, Stanleigh's Wrong-Side-Out-Day, 1982, Secret Love, 1982, The Searching Heart, 1982, Hat Full of Love (Best Juvenile Fiction Book, Colo. AL, 1984), 1983, Secret of the Dark, 1984, See You in July, 1984, Is There a Cure for Sophomore Year (Best Teen Fiction Book, Colo. AL, 1986), 1986, Life of the Party, 1986, The Night Before, 1986, Sweet Revenge, 1986, If You Love Me, 1986, Oliver Dibbs to the Rescue (Best Juvenile Fiction Book, Colo. AL, 1986), 1986, Oliver Dibbs and the Dinosaur Cause (Best Juvenile Book, Colo. AL, 1987), 1986, Sunny Side Up, 1987, I'm Nobody, Who are You?, 1987, Tennis Novel, 1987, Valerie, 1988, Kristin, 1988; (with Kathleen Phillips) Creative Writing: A Handbook for Teaching Young People (Best Adult Nonfiction Book, Colo. AL, 1986), 1985, The House of Whispering Aspen, 1985, Echoes of Landre House, 1986, Creative Writing: A Workbook of More Ideas for Young People, 1988. B.S. in Engineering, Henderson State U., 1955; M.S. in Education, U. Kans., 1958. Reading specialist Boulder Public Schs., Nederland, CO, 1966-68; continuing edn. tchr. in writing U. Colo., Boulder, 1979—; free-lance wrtr., 1987—. Recipient Best Juvenile Article award Colo. AL, 1972, Juvenile Poetry award, 1981; Disting. Instr. award U. Colo, 1985. Mem. SCBW (bd. dirs.). Home: 3584 Kirkwood Pl Boulder CO 80302

STEINGASS, DAVID HERBERT, b. Elyria, OH, July 12, 1940, s. Herbert Edward and Katherine (Lutsch) S.; m. Susan Eliott Ross; m. 2d, Stephanie Lee Edwards, Dec. 1, 1955; 1 son, Brook Robert. Author poetry collections: Body Compass, 1968, American Handbook, 1973. MA, U. Me., Orono, 1964; MFA, U. Calif., Irvine, 1968. Wrtr.-in-residence La. State U., Baton Rouge, 1964-66, U. Wis., Madison and Stevens Point, 1968-74; poet-in-the-schls., various locations in Wis., 1975—. McDowell fellow, 1970; NEA creative writing fellow, 1971. Home: 1510 Drake St madison WI 53711

STEINHOFF, WILLIAM RICHARD, b. Chgo., Feb. 13, 1914; s. William Richard and Nellie (Mulligan) Steinhoff; m. Rosannah Jenne Cannon, Jan. 6, 1940. Editor: (with others) Modern Short Stories, 1951, The Image of the Work, 1952; (with A. Carr) Points of Departure, 1960, George Orwell and the Origins of 1984, 1975 (pub. in England as The Road to 1984), Utopia Reconsidered—Comments on 1984, pub. in No Place Else—Explorations in Utopian and Dystopian Fiction. AB, U. CA at Berkeley, 1938, MA, 1940, PhD, 1948. Mem. Faculty U. Mich. (Ann Arbor), 1948—, prof. English lit., 1963—; vis. prof. U. Aix-Marseilles (France), 1964-65; Sr. Fulbright Lectr., Gadjah Mada U., Yogyakarta, Indonesia, 1984-86, prof. emeritus, U. Mich., 1983-84, sr. Fulbright lctr., Comenius Univ., Bratislara, Czechoslovakia, 1987-88. mem. exec. com. CCCC, 1959-60. Chair Mich. Commn. Tchr. Certification, 1961-62. Served to 2nd lt. AUS, 1943-46. Home: 519 Onodaga St Ann Arbor MI 48104

STEINMAN, LISA MALINOWSKI, b. Willimantic, Conn., Apr. 8, 1950, d. Zenon S. and Shirley B. (Nathanson) Malinowski; m. James A. Steinman, Apr. 18, 1968 (div. 1980); m. James L. Shugrue, July 23, 1984. Author: Lost Poems, 1976, Made in America, 1987; contrbr. articles, poetry and rvws. to Contemporary Lit., Ironwood, Threpenny Rvw, Williams Rvw, numerous other lit mags. BA, Cornell U., 1971, MFA, 1973, PhD1976. Asst. prof. Reed Coll., Portland, Oreg., 1976-82, assoc. prof.19,82—. Bd. dirs. Portland Poetry Festival. Breadloaf Wrtrs. Conf. scholar, 1981; Oregon Arts Commn. poetry fellow, 1983, NEA fellow, 1984; Rockefeller Scholar-in-res., Poetry Ctr., 1987-88; Pablo Neruda Poetry Prize, 1987. Mem. MLA. Office: Reed Coll 3203 SE Woodstock St Portland OR 97202

STEMME, FRED GEORGE, b. Chgo., Oct. 17, 1939; s. Harry Albert and Mabel (Rainey) S.; m. Jeanne Gibson, June 10, 1977. Contrbr. poems to anthols, lit jnls. BA, Calif. State U.-Fullerton, 1971. Area mgr. Quality Care, Des Moines, 1978-81; br. mgr. Western Temporary Services, Mission, Kans., 1981-82; mgr. Terminix Intl., Merrian, Kans., 1982-83; agt. Farmers Ins. Group, Overland Park, Kans., 1983—. Home: 9126 W 73d St 105 Shawnee Mission KS 66204

STENHOLM, ANNE, see Simony, Maggy

STENT, GUNTHER SIEGMUND, b. Berlin, Germany, Mar. 28, 1924 (came to U.S., 1940, naturalized, 1945); s. George and Elizabeth (Karfunkelstein) Stent; m. Inga Lofsdottir, Oct. 27, 1951; 1 son—Stefan Loftur. Author: Papers on Bacterial Viruses, 2nd ed., 1966, Molecular Biology of Bacterial Viruses, 1963, Phage and the Origin of Molecular Biology, 1966, The Coming of the Golden Age, 1969, Function and Formation of Neural Systems, 1977, Morality as a Biological Phenomenon, 1978, Paradoxes of Progress, 1978, Molecular Genetics, 2nd ed., 1978; mem. editorial bd.: Jnl. Molecular Biology, 1965-68, Genetics, 1963-68, Zeitschrift fur Verebungslehre, 1962-68, Annl. Rvws. Genetics, 1965-69, Annl. Rvws. Microbiology, 1966-70. BS, U. IL, 1945, PhD, 1948; (hon.) D. Sc. York U., Toronto, Ont., Can., 1984. Research Asst. U. IL, 1945-48; research fellow Calif. Inst. Tech., 1948-50, U. Copenhagen (Denmark) 1950-51, Pasteur Inst. (Paris, France) 1951-52; asst. research biochemist U. CA (Berkeley), 1952-56, faculty, 1956—, prof. molecular biology, 1959—, prof. arts and scis., 1967-68, chair molecular biology, 1980—, dir. virus lab., 1980—. Home: 145 Purdue Ave Berkeley CA 94708

STENZEL, LARRY G., b. July 20, 1949. Author: Tales to Tell, 1978, Afraid of the Dark, 1981, Lillie Seline's Confession, 1982, A Vacation from Worry, 1984. BA, U. Minn., 1971. Office: Powell Pub 2201 I St Sacramento CA 95816

STEPHENS, CHRISTOPHER P., Ed., pub.-in-chief Ultramarine Pub. Co., Inc., Hastings-On-Hudson, N.Y., 1973—. Office: Box 303 Hastings-On-Hudson NY 10706

STEPHENS, EDWARD CARL, b. Los Angeles, July 27, 1924; s. Carl Edward and Helen Mildred (Kerner) Stephens. Author: novels A Twist of Lemon, 1958, One More Summer, 1960, Blow Negative!, 1962, Roman Joy, 1965, A Turn in the Dark Wood, 1968, The Submariner, 1974. AB, Occidental Coll., 1947; MS, Northwestern U., 1955. Advt. exec. Dancer-Fitzgerald-Sample Inc. (NYC), 1955-64; prof. Medill Schl. Journalism, Northwestern U. Evanston, IL, 1964-76; prof., chair dept. adv. S.I. Newhouse Schl. Pub. Communications Syracuse U. (NY), 1976-80, dean, 1980—; cons. Foote, Cone & Belding Communications. Served as destroyer officer USN, 1943-46; PTO; served as submarine officer USN, 1950-53; Atlantic; served as capt. USNR, 1968. Decorated Purple Heart. Mem. Am. Acad. Advt. (pres., 1976-77), Assn. Edn. Journalism and Mass Communication, AL, Natl. Acad. TV Arts and Scis. Home: 125 Tejah Ave Syracuse NY 13210

STEPHENS, GLENN ARTHUR, b. Ft. Collins, CO, Sept. 11, 1926; s. Miles Earnest and Gertrude Luella (Salyer) S.; m. Lorraine Helen Zell, Jan. 19, 1957; children—Brian Paul, Linda Kay. Author: Kriegies, Caterpellars and Lucky Bastards, 1987. Contrbr. articles to mags. Machinist, Woodward Governor Co., Ft. Collins, 1961-85, retired. Mem. NWC. Home: 2455 Cheviot Dr Fort Collins CO 80526

STEPHENS, MARTHA T., b. Waycross, GA, Mar. 19, 1937; m. Jerome Stephens, 1965; children—Daniel, Paige, Shelley. Novelist: Cast a Wistful Eye, 1977 (condensed in Redbook mag.); ed.: The Pig and Other Stories; author: The Question of Flannery O'Connor, 1973. PhD, Ind. U. Prof. English, U. Cin., 1967—. Yaddo and Ragdale artist colony resident; grantee Ohio Arts Council. Office: Dept. Eng Univ Cin Cincinnati OH 45221

STEPHENS, REED, see Donaldson, Stephen Reeder

STEPHENS, THOMAS M. (Tonuis Nassiff), b. Youngstown, OH, June 15, 1931; s. Thomas and Mary (Hanna) S.; m. Evelyn V. Kleshock, July 1, 1955. Author: Implementing Behavioral Approaches in Schools, 1975, Directive Teaching, 1976, Teaching Skills to Children with Learning and Behavioral Disorders, 1977, Social Skills in the Classroom, 1978, Teaching Children Basic Skills, 1982, Criterion Referenced Curriculum, 1982, Teaching Mainstreamed Students, 1982. Contrbr. numerous articles, book chpts., columns to profl. jnls., mags.; author monographs. B.S., Youngstown Coll., 1955; M.Ed., Kent State U., 1957; Ed.D., U. Pitts., 1966. Administr. Title IESEA, Ohio Dept. of Edn., Columbus, 1960-66; assoc. prof. U. Pitts., 1966-70; prof., assoc. dean Ohio State U., Columbus, 1970—. Recipient Talisman award Ohio Assn. for Children with Learning Disabilities, 1979; named Outstanding Tchr. Educator, Charles E. Merrill, 1985. Home: 1753 Blue Ash Pl Columbus OH 43229

STEPHENSON, KATHRYN LYLE, b. Kansas City, MO, July 30, 1912; d. Clay Wheeler and Sue (Vertrees) Stephenson; m. Jack M. Mosely (div.); children—Kathryn Sue, Jack M. Editor: Jnl of Plastic and Reconstructive Surgery, 1965-67, Year Book of Plastic Surgery, 1967-77; contrbr. chapters to Symposium on Medical Writing, Everywoman's Health, 1980-82, 1985; author: Plastic and Reconstructive Surgery (with E.C. Padgett), 1948. BA, U. of Arizona, 1934; MD, U. of Kansas, 1941. Staff Los Angeles Children's Hosp., 1950-54; private pract. (Santa Barbara), 1919-78. Home: 780 Rockbridge Rd Santa Barbara CA 93108

STEPHENSON, SHELBY, b. Benson, NC, Jun. 14, 1938; s. W. Paul and Maytle Samantha (Johnson) Stephenson; m. Linda Letchworth Wilson, Jul. 30, 1966; children—Jacob Winsor, Kate. Chapbooks: Middle Creek Poems, 1979, Carolina Shout!, 1985; contrbr. to Ohio Review, Hudson Review, Poetry Northwest; editor, Pembroke Magazine, 1979—. BA, U. of NC, 1960; MA, U. of Pittsburgh, 1967; PhD, U. of Wisconsin, 1973. Chair, English Campbell U. (Buies Creek, NC), 1974-78; prof. Engl. Pembroke State U. (NC), 1978—. Pres. NC Literary & Historical Assoc. (Raleigh), 1982-83. The Playwright's Fund of NC Award, 1985. Mem. AWP, PSA, AAP. Home: 355 E Conn Ave Southern Pines NC 28387

STERLING, GARY CAMPBELL, b. Hollywood, CA, Oct. 10, 1941; m. Shirley Carol, Sept. 9, 1962; 1 son, Derek James. Contrbr. poems to anthols. Editor: Poetry UCR, 1964. BA, U. Calif.-Riverside, 1965; MA, Calif. State U.-Los Angeles, 1975. Tchr. English, John Marshall High Schl., Pasadena, Calif. 1985—. Ed. Friends of Altadena Library Newsletter, Calif. Recipient Martin Luther King, Jr. award U. Calif., Irvine, 1986; named Tchr. of Yr., Pasadena Edn. Assn., 1979. Mem. Poets for Peace (charter), Pasadena Fedn. Tchrs. (past v.p.), Phi Delta Kappa, Delta Phi Upsilon (hon.) Home: 2396 Highland Ave Altadena CA 91001

STERN, AARON, b. Germany, May 20, 1918; s. David and Helen (Schurek) Stern; m. Bella Tcherniawska, Jan. 1940; children—Edith, David. Author: Ethnic Minorities in Poland, 1937, Nazi Atrocities in Europe; The Making of a Genius, Principles of the Total Education Submersion Method, The Joy of Learning, The Naked Truth—Observations of an Iconoclast; numerous sci. papers. Student gymnazium, Warsaw U., Plock, Poland, 1937-38; BA, Bklyn. Coll., 1956; MA Equiv., Columbia U., 1957, Jewish Theol. Sem. Am. Originator Total Edn. Submersion Method; conducted schl. based on method in Displaced Persons Camp (Germany), 1948-81; lect. on method at univs., 1949—. Conducted landmark study of Head Start Program for HEW, 1974; active participant desegregation of pub. facilities, voters registration; active presdl. campaigns senators Eugene McCarthy, George McGovern. Nominated for Pulitzer prize, 1977-80. Mem. AG, AL Am. Home: 2485 NE 214th St North Miami Beach FL 33180

STERN, ARTHUR CHARLES, b. Salem, MA, Oct. 20, 1957, s. Henderson Arthur and Marjorie Farnsworth (Green) S. Author: Over 40 and Fabulous, 1984. BFA, U. So. Calif. Mng. ed. Laufer Publs., Hollywood, Calif., 1980-81; features ed. Gambling Times Inc., Hollywood, 1982; mng. ed. DS Publs., Cresskill, N.J., 1983; ed. The Rangefinder Pub. Co., Santa Monica, Calif., 1984—. Office: Rangefinder 1312 Lincoln Blvd Santa Monica CA 90406

STERN, MADELEINE BETTINA, b. NYC, July 1, 1912; s. Moses Roland and Lillie (Mack) Stern. Author: The Life of Margaret Fuller, 1942, Louisa May Alcott, 1950, Purple Passage: The Life of Mrs. Frank Leslie, 1953, Imprints on History: Book Publishers and American Frontiers, 1956, We the Women: Career Firsts of Nineteenth Century America, 1962, So Much in a Lifetime: The Story of Dr. Isabel Barrows, 1965, Queen of Publishers' Row: Mrs. Frank Leslie, 1966, The Pantarch: A Biography of Stephen Pearl Andrew, 1968, Heads and Headlines: The Phrenological Fowlers, 1971, Books and Book People in 19th Century America, 1978, Antiquarian Bookselling in the United States: A History from the Origins to the 1940s, 1985; (with Leona Rostenberg) Old and Rare: Thirty Years in the Book Business, 1974, Between Boards: New Thoughts on Old Books, 1978; editor: Women on the Move, 4 vols., 1972, Victoria Woodhull Reader, 1974, Louisa's Wonder Book—An Unknown Alcott Juvenile, 1975, Behind a Mask: The Unknown Thrillers of Louisa May Alcott, 1975, Plots and Counterplots: More Unknown Thrillers of Louisa May Alcott, 1976, Publishers for Mass Entertainment in 19th-Century America, 1980, A Phrenological Dictionary of 19th-Century Americans, 1982, Critical Essays on Louisa May Alcott, 1984, A Modern Mephistopheles and Taming a Tartar by Louisa May Alcott, 1987; co-editor (with Joel Myerson and Daniel Shealy), The Selected Letters of Louisa May Alcott, 1987, A Double Life: Five Unknown Thrillers by Louisa May Alcott, 1988. BA, Barnard Coll., 1932; MA, Columbia U., 1934. Tchr. English NYC High Schls., 1934-43; prtnr. Leona Rostenberg Rare Books (NYC), 1945—, Leona Rostenberg and Madeleine B. Stern Rare Books, 1980—; co-founder Antiquarian Booksellers Ctr. (NY), 1962. Mem. Phi Beta Kappa, MLA, AL, APHA, Ms Soc. Home: 40 E 88th St New York NY 10128

STERN, PHILIP MAURICE, b. NYC, May 24, 1926; s. Edgar Bloom and Edith (Rosenwald) Stern; m. Helen Phillips Burroughs Sedgwick, Aug. 30, 1957; children—Henry D., Michael P., Helen P., David M., Eve; m. Nellie L. Gifford, June 14, 1975; 2nd m. Helen Markel, Feb. 9, 1980. Author: The Great Treasury Raid, 1964, (with George de Vincent) The Shame of a Nation, 1966, (with Helen B. Stern) Oh, Say Can You See: A Bifocal Tour of Washington, 1966, The Oppenheimer Case: Security on Trial, 1969, The Rape of the Taxpayer, 1973, Lawyers on Trial, 1980. AB magna cum laude, Harvard, 1947; postgrad., Georgetown U. Law Center, 1975-76; LHD (hon.), colgate U., 1974. Reporter, editorial writer New Orleans Item, 1948; legislative asst. U.S. Rep. Henry M. Jackson, 1949-50, U.S. Senator Paul Douglas, 1951-52; personal asst. Wilson W. Wyatt, campaign mgr. to Adlai E. Stevenson, 1952; dir. research Democratic Natl. Com., also sr. editor Dem. Digest, 1953-56; editor No. VA Sun (Arlington), 1957-60, editor, pub., 1960; dep. asst. secy. of state for pub. affairs, 1961-62, writer, author, 1962—; spcl. assignment reporter, natl. staff Washington Post, 1974-75; founder Fund for Investigative Journalism, 1968, Stern Community Law Firm, Stern Concern, 1970, Ctr. for Pub. Financing of Campaigns, 1975-76, Citizens for Common Sense in Natl. Defense, 1982, Ams. for Fair Elections, 1983, Project for Investigative Journalism on Money in Politics, 1983; founder, co-chair Citizens Against PACs, 1984. Home: 3409 Newark St NW Washington DC 20016

STERN, RICHARD GUSTAVE, b NYC, Feb. 25, 1928; s. Henry George and marion (Veit) Stern; m. Gay Clark, Mar. 14, 1950 (div. Feb. 1972); children—Christopher Holmes, Kate Macomber, Andrew Henry, Nicholas Clark; m. 2d, Alane Rollings. Author: Golk, 1960, Europe or Up and Down with Baggish and Schreiber, 1961, In Any Case, 1962, Teeth, Dying and Other Matters, 1964, Stitch, 1965, 1968: A Short Novel, An Urban Idyll, Five Stories and Two Trade Notes, 1970, The Books in Fred Hampton's Apartment, 1973, Other Men's Daughters, 1973, Natural Shocks, 1978, Packages, 1980, The Invention of the Real, 1982; A Father's Words, 1986 (non- fiction) The Position of the Body, 1986; Collected Stories, 1988; editor: Honey and Wax, 1966. BA, U. NC, 1947; MA, Harvard, 1950; PhD, State U. IA, 1954. Faculty U. Chgo., 1955—, prof. English, 1965—; vis. lectr. U. Venice (Italy), 1962-63, U. Heidelberg (Germany), 1949-50, U. CA at Santa Barbara, summer, 1964, 68, State U. NY at Buffalo, summer, 1966, Harvard, 1969, U. Nice, 1970. Recipient Friends of Lit. award, 1963, fiction award Natl. Inst. Arts and Letters, 1968, Carl Sandburg award for fiction, 1979, IL Arts Council awards, 1979, 81, medal of merit for the novel, AAIAL, 1985. Address: Dept English U Chgo Chicago IL 60637

STERN, RICHARD MARTIN, b. Fresno, CA, Mar. 17, 1915; s. Charles Frank and True (Aiken) Stern; m. Dorothy Helen Atherton, Dec. 20, 1937; 1 adopted dau.—Mary Elisabeth Emery (Mrs. Robert Vinton). Writer: short stories and serials for natl. mags. including Redbook, 1945; author: The Bright Road to Fear, 1958, Suspense, 1959, The Search for Tabatha Carr, 1960, These Unlucky Deeds, 1961, High Hazard, 1962, Cry Havoc, 1963, Right Hand, Opposite, 1964, I Hide, We Seek, 1964, The Kessler Legacy, 1967, Merry Go Round, 1969, Brood of Eagles, 1969, Manuscript for Murder, 1970, Murder in the Walls, 1971, You Don't Need an Enemy, 1972, Stanfield Harvest, 1972, Death in the Snow, 1973, The Tower, 1973, The Power, 1974, The

Will, 1976, Snowbound Six, 1977, Flood, 1979, The Big Bridge, 1982, Wildfire, 1986; editorial bd.: The Writer. Student, Harvard U., 1933-36. Genl. advt., radio and newspaper pub. and promotion Hearst Corp., 1936-37; dehydrator foreman Boothe Fruit Co. (Modesto, CA), 1938-39; mfg. engr. Lockheed Aircraft Corp. (Burbank), 1940-45. Mem. MWA (Edgar award 1959, exec. vp 1962-64, pres. 1971), Brit. Crime Writers Assn., AG. Office: Brandt & Brandt 1501 Broadway New York NY 10036

STERNLIEB, BARRY F., b. NYC, Dec. 29, 1947; s. Harold and Jeannette (Silverman) S.; m. Maureen Elizabeth Moroney, Oct. 26, 1969; 2 daus., Kirsten, Kyla. Author: Fission, 1986; contrbr. poetry to West Coast Poetry Rvw, Chowder Rvw, Beloit Poetry Jnl, Xanadu, Scree, Sou'wester, Rapport, Poetry Miscellany, Wind Lit Jnl, Poetry NOW, Poetry Northwest, Hiram Poetry Rvw, other lit mags and anthols. BA, Fairleigh Dickinson U., 1964-68. Tchr. NYC, 1968-73, Pittsfield, Mass. 1973—. Address: State Rd Richmond MA 01254

STETLER, RUSSELL DEARNLEY, JR., b. Phila., Jan. 15, 1945, s. Russell Dearnley and Martha E. (Schultz) S. Author: The Battle of Bogside, 1970; co-ed.: The Assassinations, 1975. BA, Haverford (Pa.) Coll., 1966; postgrad. New Schl. Social Research, 1966-67. Lectr. Hendon Coll., London, 1968-69; ed. Ramparts Press, Palo Alto, Calif., 1971-72; reporter, ed. Internews, Berkeley, Calif., 1973-78; tchr. Caribbean Schl., Ponce, P.R., 1978-80; pvt. investigator, San Francisco, 1980—. Office: 2176 Union St San Francisco CA 94123

STEVENS, ANDREW L., b. Woodstock, OH, Jan. 7, 1936; s. Raymond H. and Ruth M. (Penn) Stevens; m. Theresa A. Bell, Sept. 29, 1956; children—Terry, Brian, Michelle, Micah. B.S., Ohio State U., 1958, M.S., 1963. Vocational agrl. tchr. Richwood High Schl., OH, 1958-63; ed. The Ohio Farmer/HBJ Pubs., Columbus, OH, 1963—. Mem. Am. Agrl. Eds. Assn., ASBPE. Home: 20920 Pherson Pike Williamsport OH 43164

STEVENS, ANDREW L., b. Woodstock, OH, Jan. 7, 1936, s. Raymond H. and Ruth M. (Penn) S.; m. Theresa A. Bell, Sept. 29, 1956; children—Terry, Brian, Michelle, Micah. BS, Ohio State U., 1958, MS, 1963. Assoc. ed. HBJ Publs., The Ohio Farmer, Columbus, Ohio, 1963-75, ed., 1975—. Mem. Am. Agrl. Eds. Assn. Office: HBJ Publs 1350 W 5th Ave Columbus OH 43212

STEVENS, A(RTHUR) WILBER, JR., b. Bklyn., Aug. 16, 1921; s. Arthur Wilber and Isabella Ellen (MacGibbon) Stevens; m. Marjorie Athene Rogers, Feb. 15, 1955 (dec. Feb. 1979); children—Arthur Wilber III, Christopher Rivers; m. Loucinda Wilder Davis, Feb. 12, 1983. Author-editor: Poems Southwest, 1967, Stories Southwest, 1973; author: Pocatello, The World Is Going to End up in Burma; co-editor: Anthology of Contemporary Anglo-Indian Poetry, 1981; contbr. poems and articles to profl. journs.; editor, pub. lit mag: Interim, 1944-45, 1985—. AB, Brown U., 1942; MA, U. WA, 1956, PhD, 1957. Teaching fellow, assoc., then instr. U. WA (Seattle), 1944-54; vis. lectr., then asst. prof. Idaho State U. (Pocatello), 1954-60; assoc. prof., chair dept. English, 1961-64; Fulbright prof. Am. and English lit. U. Mandalay (Burma) and U. Chulalongkorn (Thailand), 1956-57; Fulbright prof. Am. lit. U. Brazil (Rio de Janeiro), 1959; prof., chair Center Lang. and Lit. Studies, Prescott Coll. (AZ), 1966-69, provost, 1968-71, dir. Prescott Coll. Pres., 1968-73, prof. English and comparative lit., 1972-73; prof. English and Humanities U. Nev. (Las Vegas), 1973—, dean, 1973-75; dramatic and music critic Billboard, 1947-54, Intermountain, 1954-64, Seattle Home News 1947-53, Prescott Courier and The Paper, 1966-73, Las Vegas Rev.-Jour., 1973-77, Las Vegas Sun, 1977-84; KLAV Radio Sta., The Las Vegas: theatre critic, Las Vegas Rvw Jnl, 1984—. Bd. dirs. Orme Schl., Prescott, 1969-73. Mem. Music Critics Assn., Am. Theatre Critics Assn., MLA, Rocky Mountain MLA, AAUP. Home: 3770 Forestcrest Dr Las Vegas NV 89121

STEVENS, BARBARA CONSTANCE, b. Birkenhead, Eng., July 7, 1924, came to U.S., 1948; d. Cecil Vaughan and Susan Dixon (Capener) Crapper; m. Murry Stevens, Aug. 15, 1948; children—Maureen Holman, Susan Chambers, Nancy Evertz, Scott, Trish. Contrbr. poems to lit. mags. Editor: (poetry newsletter) Serendipity, 1979-85, Pasque Petals, 1983—. Student pub. schls., Eng. Pres. Community Playhouse, Sioux Falls, S.D., 1972-75, Sioux Empire Arts Council, Sioux Falls, 1976. Mem. S.D. State Poetry Soc. (pres. 1975-80), Natl. Fedn. State Poetry Soc. (pres. 1985-87, membership chmn, 1987—). Home: 909 E 34th St Sioux Falls SD 57105

STEVENS, C(LYSLE) J(ULIUS), (John Stevens Wade), b. Smithfield, ME, Dec. 8, 1927, s. Earl Wade and Leanora May (Witham) S.; m. Stella Rachel Taschlicky, June 13, 1954. Poetry collections: First Poems, 1954, Climbs, 1962, (with John Judson) Two from Where It Snows, 1964, Poems from the Lowlands (Dutch and Flemish translations), 1966, Gallery, 1969, The Cats in the Colosseum, 1972, Well Water and Daisies, 1974, Each to His Own Ground, 1976, Waterland (Dutch translations), 1977, Some of My Best Friends Are Trees, 1977, Homecoming, 1978, Up North, 1980, Gaston Burssens (Flemish translations); contrbr. to Western Humanities Rvw, Queens Qtly, The Nation, Prairie Schooner, Colo. Qtly, N.Mex. Qtly, N.Y. Times, Dubliner, West Coast Rvw, Prisms, Film Qtly, El Corno Emplumado, Midwest Qtly, Coll. English, Confrontation, Jeopardy, Carleton Miscellany, Antigonish Rvw, others, also to numerous anthologies. BA, Conn. State Coll., 1952. Served with U.S. Army, 1944-46. Address: Box 5 Weld ME 04285

STEVENS, CARL, see Obstfeld, Raymond

STEVENS, CHRISTINE HYDE (Christine Brown, Christine Sorensen), b. Elmhurst, IL, Apr. 11, 1926; d. Christopher C. and Helene (Hyde) Brown; m. Robert E. Sorensen, July 18, 1954 (dec. Dec. 18, 1974); m. Lee D. Stevens Sr., Apr. 10, 1981. Contrbr. articles to mags., newspapers, cookbook; author greeting cards. Asst. ed., wrtr.: Ill. Edn., Springfield, IL, 1949-51; assoc. ed.: The Kalamazoo Mag., MI, 1964-66; newsletter ed.: Kalamazoo County Chamber of Commerce Bulltn., 1967-68; ed., wrtr. Children's Charter of the Courts of Mich. Bulltn., 1967-71. B.Music, DePauw U., 1948. Home: Woodland Lakes 48 5401 Hwy 17-92 W Haines City FL 33844

STEVENS, ELISABETH, b. Rome, NY, Aug. 11, 1929; d. George May and Elisabeth (Stryker) S.; m. Robert C. Schleussner, Mar. 12, 1966 (div. Mar. 13, 1977); 1 dau., Laura. Author: Elisabeth Stevens Guide to Baltimore's Inner Habor, 1981; (short stories) Fire & Water: Six Stories, 1982; (poems) Children of Dust: Portraits & Preludes, 1985. Art critic, reporter Washington Post, 1965-66; art critic Wall St. Jnl., 1969-72, Trenton Times, 1974-77, Balt. Sun, 1978-87. Fellow NEA, 1973-74, MacDowell Colony, Peterborough, NH, 1981, Va. Ctr. for Creative Arts, 1982, 83, 84, 85, 86, Ragdale Fdn., 1984; grantee Md. State Arts Council, 1986. Mem. Coll. Art Assn., Am. Studies Assn., MLA, Popular Culture Assn., Balt. Bibliophiles, Balt. Wrtrs.' Alliance. Home: 6604 Walnutwood Circle Baltimore MD 21212

STEVENS, HOLLY, b. Hartford, CT, Aug. 10, 1924; d. Wallace and Elsie Viola (Kachel) Stevens; m. John Martin Hanchak, Aug. 5, 1944 (div. Sept. 1951); 1 son—Peter Reed Hanchak; m. 2d, Duncan Stephenson, Aug. 24, 1957 (div. Dec. 1965). Author: Souvenirs and Prophecies: The Young Wallace Stevens, 1977; editor: Letters of Wallace Stevens, 1966, The Palm at the End of the Mind: Selected Poems and a Play by Wallace Stevens, 1971. Student, Vassar Coll., 1941-42, U. CT, 1951-53. Fire underwriter Aetna Life Affiliated Cos. (Hartford), 1942-46; purchasing asst. Trinity Coll. (Hartford), 1955-64; secy. Yale, 1966-68; advt. mgr. Yale Rvw, 1968-69, bus. mgr., 1969-77; cons. CT Public Radio, 1979; founder, dir. New Eng. Poetry Circuit, 1963-68, mem. selection com., 1972—; founding mem. Poetry Center Trinity Coll. Home: Joshua Cove Guilford CT 06437

STEVENS, MARK, see Rafalsky, Stephen Mark

STEVENS, R. L., see Hoch, Edward D.

STEVENS, ROBERT JAY, b. Detroit, July 25, 1945, s. Jay Benjamin and Louise Ann (Beyreuther) S.; m. Dahlia Jean Conger, Aug. 15, 1970; children—Sandra Lee, Julie Ann. Ed., Huron Coll., Wayne State U. Staff wrtr. Automotive News, Detroit, 1968-71; asst. ed., ed. Cummins Pub. Co., Oak Park, Mich., 1971-78; ed. Chevrolet Jnl, Sandy Corp., Warren, Mich., 1978-79; ed. Cars & Parts mag., Amos Press, Inc., Sidney, Ohio, 1979—. Served with U.S. Army, 1966-68; Vietnam. Decorated Bronze Star, Air Combat medal. Mem. Soc. Automotive Historians, Detroit Auto Wrtrs. Office: Box 482 Sidney OH 45365

STEVENS, SUZANNE, see Wagner-Stevens, Tina Marie

STEVENSON, JOHN EDWARD, b. Balt., Jan. 14, 1952; s. James Reilly and Pearl (Johnson) S.; m. Janelle Diane Bloemker, Apr. 12, 1975. Contrbr. articles: Balt. Evening Sun, Hartford Courant; author radio play: The Black Ace and The Mystery Squadron, 1984. BA, BS, St. Johns Coll., 1983. Producer radio sta. WCBM, Balt., 1984, sta. WFBR, Balt., 1984-86; columnist Pollution Engring., Chgo., 1985-86; ed., photographer Spotlight on Edn., Higganum, Conn., 1986-87, Conn. edition Hosp. News, 1987; wrtr. Nat. Journalism Center, Washington, 1986; freelance wrtr., photographer, Middletown, Conn., 1987—. Mem. profl. photog. orgns. Home: 215 Pine St Middletown CT 06457

STEVENSON, WILLIAM HENRI, b. London, June 1, 1924; s. William and Alida (Deleporte) Stevenson; m. Glenys Rowe, July 28, 1945; children—Andrew, Jacqueline, Kevin, Sally. Author: Travels In and Around Red China, 1957, Rebels in Indonesia, 1964, Chronicles of the Israeli Air Force, 1971, A Man Called Intrepid, 1976, Ninety Minutes at Entebbe, 1976, The Ghosts of Africa, 1981; producer: TV documentaries; movie screenplays include The Bushbabies, 1970. Student, Royal Navy Coll., 1942. Fgn. corr. Toronto Star (Ont., Can.), 1948-

58; Toronto Globe and Mail, 1958-63; Ind. TV News (London, Eng.), 1964-66, CBC, 1966-77; ind. writer, broadcaster, 1977—. Served as aviator Royal Navy, 1942-45. Mem. AG. Office: Gitlin Agcy 7 W 51st St New York NYK 10019

STEVER, MARGO TAFT, b. Cin., Mar. 4, 1950, d. David Gibson Jr. and Katharine Longworth (Whittaker) Taft; m. Donald Winfred Stever, Jr., July 31, 1976; children—David, James. Contrbr. poetry to New Eng. Rvw, Poet Lore, Poetry Now, Croton Rvw, Chelsea, West Branch, numerous other lit mags, No More Masks, Voices for Peace Anthology; contrbr. photographs to The Movement Towards a New America, 1970, Celebrating in Action, 1971, The Harvard Advocate, 1970, Connection, 1979. AB, Radcliffe Coll., 1972; EdM, Harvard U., 1975; postgrad. Sarah Lawrence Coll., 1985—. Tchr. learning disabled children The Krebs Schl., Lexington, Mass., 1975-76; asst. dir. N.H. Civil Liberties Union, Concord, 1976-77; co-dir. Sleepy Hollow Poetry Series, Warner Library, Tarrytown, N.Y., 1983—. Finalist numerous poetry competitions, 1981—. Mem. P&W, NWU. Home: 157 Millard Ave North Tarrytown NY 10591

STEWARD, D. E., b. 1936. Author: Four Stories, 1978, Contact Inhibition, 1985, A Letter to a Writer Down the Line, 1987. Home: Box 1239 Princeton NJ 08542

STEWARD, HAL DAVID, b. East St. Louis, IL, Dec. 2, 1918; s. Owen Bob Steward and Margaret Alice Martin. Author: Thunderbolt, 1948, The Successful Writer's Guide, 1970, Money Making Secrets of the Millionaires, 1972; (novels) The Spy and the Pirate Queen, 1965, Assasins' Hideaway, 1966. Contrbr. numerous articles to natl. mags. Reporter: Los Angeles Examiner, 1961-62, San Diego Union, 1962-64; exec. ed.: The Daily Chronicle, Centralia, WA, 1974-77; roving corr. The Newsletter on Newsletters, Rhinebeck, NY, 1985—. B.S., Boston U., 1961; Ph.D., Columbia Pacific U., 1979. Freelance wrtr., 1965-74, 80-85. Served to lt. col. U.S. Army, 1937-61. Mem. AG, SPJ, Aviation/Space Wrtrs. Assn. Home: 4725 W Quincy Ave 1004 Denver CO 80236

STEWARD, NANNCY JEAN (Steele Derringer), b. Fort Collins, CO, Apr. 11, 1953; d. Kenneth L. and H. Jean (Donegan) S. Columnist: Silver Quill, 1971. Contrbr. articles, poems to newspapers, anthols., lit. mags. B.A., Colo. State U., 1981. Staff wrtr. public relations Sta. KCSU-FM, Fort Collins, 1980; intern Colubine Cablevision, Fort Collins, 1981; copywriter Orion Images, Denver, 1982-85; free-lance wrtr., 1986—. Recipient Golden Poet award World of Poetry, 1987. Mem. SPJ. Home: Box 149 Fort Collins CO 80522

STEWART, ANN HARLEMAN, see Harleman, Ann

STEWART, CHERE LYNN, b. Ashland, KY, Aug. 27, 1955; d. James Henry and Fannie Mae (Ison) Steward; m. James Edgar Newman; children—James E., Shannon Michael, Angela Kathryn. Contrbr. articles to profl. jnls. Research ed.: The Escalade, 1982-83. A.A. in Communications, U. Ky., 1980; B.A. in Research Psychology, Marshall U., 1983; postgrad. Morehead U., 1986—. Domestic violence counselor Pathways, Inc., Ashland, 1984-85; ind. advt. cons. Steele Plastics, Ashland, 1985; consumer behavioral and creative advt. cons., communications cons., 1985—. Mem. NWC. Home: 2013 W Ike Patton Dr Ashland KY 41101

STEWART, DONALD C., b. Kansas City, MO, June 24, 1930; s. Charles Allen and Harriet X (McTaggart) S.; m. Patricia Louise Pettepier, June 3, 1955; 2 daus., Ellen Marie, Mary Catherine. Author: The Authentic Voice, 1972, The Versatile Writer, 1986; contrbr. to Historical Rhetoric, The Present State of Scholarship in English, Essays on Classical Rhetoric and Modern Discourse, Traditions of Inquiry. BA, U. Kans., 1948-52, MA, 1952-55; PhD, U. Wis., 1955-62. Instr. Univ. Ill., Urbana, 1962-63, asst. prof., 1963-68; asst. prof., Kans. State Univ., Manhattan, 1968-75, assoc. prof., 1975-81, prof., 1981—. Recipient research grant, ACLS, 1981. Mem. CCCC (pres., 1983), NCTE (exec. com., 1983), Kans. Assn. Tchrs. English (pres., 1984). Address: Dept Eng Kans State U Manhattan KS 66506

STEWART, EUGENE JOEL, b. Albuquerque, Feb. 22, 1960; s. Clarence and Doris Eloris (Hughes) S.; m. Patricia Ann Ransom, Apr. 26, 1986; 1 dau., Ishiria Nyree Ransom. Contrbr. poems to anthols. Student Arapahoe Commun. Coll., 1978-81. Purchasing asst. Denver Federal Ct., Lakewood, CO, 1977-81; printer/mgr. Scotties Sprint Print, Englewood, CO, 1981—; power distributor U.S. Army Reserves, Aurora, CO, 1986—. Recipient Honorable Mention, Intl. Press, 1981; 9 Merit awards World of Poetry, 1983-87, Golden Poet award, 1985, 86. Home: 3680 Pontiac St Denver CO 80207

STEWART, GARY, see Stewart, June

STEWART, HOLLIS KIMBALL, b. Little Rock, Oct. 29, 1953; s. Bill Dave and Ruth Evelyn (Hollis) S. Contrbr. poems, articles to lit. and popular mags. including Ark. Times, Ark. Econ. Report, Mikrokosmos. B.A. in English and Jnlsm., Harding Coll., 1975; M.F.A., Wichita State U., 1981. Lectr., U. Ark., Little Rock, 1981—; ed. Arkansas Jnl., Little Rock, 1981—. Home: 315 N Cedar Little Rock AR 72205

STEWART, JOFFRE LAMAR, b. Chgo., Apr. 17, 1925; s. Lamar and Cecilia Oneida (Bailey) S. Author: Poems and Poetry, 1982; contrbr. to Experiment, Oyez, The Bridge, The Word, Peace Action, Reader, Resistance News, Bluff, Nuclear Resister, Radix, others. BA, Roosevelt U., 1952. Served with AUS, 1944-45; ETO. Home: 2636 Calumet Apt 702 Chicago IL 60616

STEWART, JUNE GARY (Jan Starr, Rocky Jones, Gary Stewart), b. Melrose Park, IL, Mar. 15, 1931; d. Harry John and Stephanie (Stanislawa) Gary; m. James M. Stewart; children—Sue Anna, Linda, James, John. Author, ed.: Collector's Cookbook, 1984; (play) Lincoln, 1976. Contrbr. articles to books, mags., newspapers including Reader's Digest; columnist Lerner Life Newspapers, Skokie, IL, 1977-85; stringer Paddock Pubs., Arlington Heights, IL, 1966-70, reporter Bugle Pubs., Niles, IL, 1970-71, Suburban Tribune, Hillside, IL, 1971, Topics, Palatine, IL, 1975. Ed.: Nomda Mag., 1966, Reminder Pubs., Wheeling, IL, 1971-73. Wrkg. on cookbooks, homeowner's guide, sci. fiction, job market, advt. B.A., Northeastern U., 1973; postgrad. Norheastern U. Area representative Pickwick Pubs., Park Ridge, IL, 1976; merchandiser Walgreens Advt., Deerfield, IL, 1976-77; editorial dir. GS Pubs., Mt. Prospect, IL, 1983-84; v.p. marketing and advt. Gary Stewart Heating and Air Conditioning, Mt. Prospect, 1981-88 Editorial cons. Wheeling Hist. Book, 1984-85. Served with USAF, 1952-54. Recipient Poetry award Wilroy Farms, 1979. Mem. NWU, WG West, NWC. Home: 368 Park Ave Wheeling IL 60090

STEWART, KATHRYN, see McDonald, Kathryn Stewart

STEWART, MARY FLORENCE ELINOR, b. Sunderland, Country Durham, Sept. 17, 1916; d. Frederick A. and mary Edith (Matt,ews) Rainbow; m. Frederick H. Stewart, 1945. Author: Madam Will You Talk?, 1954, Wildfire at Midnight, 1956, Thunder on the Right, 1957, Nine Coaches Waiting, 1958, My Brother Michael, 1959, The Ivy Tree, 1961, The Moonspinners, 1962, This Rough Magic, 1964, Airs Above the Ground, 1965, The Gabriel Hounds, 1967, The Wind off the Small Isles, 1968, The Crystal Cave, 1970, The Little Broomstick, 1971, The Hollow Hills, 1973, Ludo and the Star Horse, 1974, Touch Not the Cat, 1976, The Last Enchantment, 1979, A Walk in Wolf Wood, 1980, The Wicked Day, 1983; also peoms, articles. BA, Durham U., 1939, MA, 1941. Lectr. in English Durham U., 1941-45, part-time lectr. English, 1948-58. Mem. PEN. Address: Morrow 105 Madison Ave New York NY 10016

STEWART, SHARON DIANE, b. Cleve., June 16, 1951; d. Elton Stewart and Mary Ruth (Speights) Boyland. Contrbr. technical articles, features to mags., newspapers; author technical maintenance manuals. Contrbr., ed.: Toastmasters newsletter, 1983-84; ed., pub. chmn. San Diego Chpt. of Natl. Acad. TV Arts and Scis. newsletter, 1983. B.S., San Diego State U., 1974; M.B.A., U. San Diego, 1977. Accounts pay supvr. Security Pac Finance, San Diego, CA, 1979-84; sr. accounting specialist Sun Savings & Loan, San Diego, 1984-85; pubs. specialist Turbomach, San Diego, 1985—; ensign, USNR. Bd. dirs. technical writing advisory com. San Diego Commun. Coll., 1984—. Recipient Honorable Mention for poem Mesa Coll., San Diego, 1983. Home: 3441 Ruffin Rd 1B San Diego CA 92123

STICKLE, CHARLES EDWARD, b. Clinton, IN, Jan. 1, 1941; s. Adolph E. and Myrtle E. (Steffey) S.; m. Marie J. Boatwright; children—Randy D., Troy A., Michelle L. Contrbr. poems to lit. mags., anthols. Wrkg. on poetry, articles on stress and frustration. B.A., U. Nebr., 1972; M.S., Troy State U., 1977. Enlisted as Airman Basic, U.S. Navy, 1959, advanced through grades to capt., 1982. Home: 317 Cornell Rd Montgomery AL 36109

STICKNEY, WALT CHRISTOPHER, b. New Orleans, Aug. 30, 1944. Author: To Night: Little David on Mouth-Harp, 1970; Cover My Souls, 1977; one n five minute pose-pomes, 1974; The Bethesda Preludes, 1983; How to Live With An Actor, 1986; ed. Piano, a flowing jnl, 1978—; 44 Covers for the Locked-Up n Locked-Out, 1975. BA, U. Pa., 1968. Grantee D.C. Commn. on Arts and Humanities, 1977, NEA, 1980, 81. Home: 1823 Madison St Ridgewood NY 11385

STIEFEL, JANICE J., b. Chgo., Jan. 4, 1936; d. Russell and Evelyn Agnes (Arnold) Johnson; m. John Louis Stiefel, Sept. 7, 1957; children: Kay Ellen, Mark John. Author: How To Plan A Bible Treasure Hunt, 1980; Secy., Cleaver-Brooks Co., Milw., 1953-57, Wis. Power & Light, Madison, 1957-59, Downing Box Co., Milw., 1959-60, Beautiful Savior Ch., Mequon, 1965-79; owner/pres. The Second Hand, Plymouth, Wis., 1970—. Address: R 3 Mullet LN Plymouth WI 53073

STIFF, ROBERT MARTIN, b. Detroit, Aug. 25, 1931; s. Martin Louis and Gladys Irene (Mathews) S.; m. Cindy Patricia Blumenfeld, Aug. 30, 1980; children—David, Amy, Kirsten. Reporter, photographer Painesville Telegraph, OH, 1953-55, bur. chief, city ed., 1955-57, 57-61; deskman, asst. city ed. St. Petersburg Times, 1961-62, sports ed., city ed., day ed., state ed., asst. mng. ed., 1962-67; ed. Evening Ind., St. Petersburg, 1967-84; exec. ed. Tallahassee Democrat, 1985—. B.A. in Radio, Jnlsm. Ohio State U., 1953. Mem. Am. Soc. Newspaper Eds. (bd. dirs.), Am. Soc. Newspaper Eds. Fdn. (bd. dirs.), Fla. Soc. Newspaper Eds. (past pres.), AP Assn. Fla. (past pres.), Home: 876 Maderia Circle Tallahassee FL 32312

STILES, MARTHA BENNET, b. Manila, Philippines; d. Forrest Hampton and Jane McClintock (Bennett) Wells; m. Martin Stiles; 1 son, John Martin. Author: One Among the Indians, 1962, The Strange House at Newport, 1963, Darkness Over the Land, 1966, Dougal Looks for Birds, 1972, James the Vine Puller, 1975, Tana and the Useless Monkey, 1979, The Star in the Forest, 1979. Landscapes, 1984, Sarah the Dragon Lady, 1986. Contrbr. fiction to mags., newspapers including Ingenue, Thoroughbred Record, N.Y. Times, others. Student William & Mary Coll., 1950-52; B.S., U. Mich., 1954. Recipient Hopwood award U. Mich., 1956, 58, Citation for contrbn. to children's lit. Central Mo. State U., 1978, short fiction award Frankfort Arts Found., 1984, 86. Mem. AG, U. Ky. Library Assocs., Detroit Women Wrtrs., Detroit Women Wrtrs., Friends of Bourbon County Library. Home: 861 Hume-Bedford Rd Paris KY 40361

STILLMAN, WILLIAM EVERETT (S. W. Everett), b. Midland, MI, Dec. 9, 1952; s. Dewitt S. and Carolyn (Stein) S.; m. Carol Schlemmer, June 15, 1974; children—Lauren Aletta, Mark Everett. Author: Christian Science Under the Nazi Regime, 1975, Poems Volume I, 1983, Of Brooks and Streams and Things, 1986. Wrkg. on novel, Tendrils of Power, Diary of an MBA. B.A., Principia Coll., 1975; M.B.A., Washington U., 1979. Genl. mgr. ROWI USA, St. Louis, 1979-82; N.Y. mgr. Christian Sci. Monitor, N.Y.C., 1983-84; natl. account mgr. Siemens Transmission, Phoenix, 1985—. Recipient Eagle of Achievement, bronze West German Government, 1975. Mem. Am. Marketing Assn. Home: 9510 N 47th Pl Phoenix AZ 85028

STILLWELL, MARY KATHRYN, b. Omaha, Sept. 1, 1944; m. Frank H.W. Edler, May 26, 1985. Author: (poems) Moving to Malibu, 1987; contrbr. poetry to Paris Rvw, N.Y. Qtly, Kans. Qtly, Mass. Rvw, Prairie Schooner, The Little Mag., Confrontation, others. AB, St. Mary Coll. Levenworth, Kans., 1966. Dir. of marketing and communications, Long Island Univ. Mem. P&W. Home: 245 Garfield Ave Mineola NY 11501

STINNETTE, CARLENE ROSALEE, b. Alamagordo, NM, Oct. 1, 1955; d. Carl Alden and Rosalee (Hankins) Moore; m. Bing Quinton Stinnette, May 25, 1974. Contrbr. poems to anthols., newspapers. Grad. public schls., Goodland, KS. Recipient Honorable Mention, World of Poetry, (3) 1983, 84, Golden Poet award, 1985, Silver Poet award, 1986. Mem. NWC. Home: 1302 Walnut Goodland KS 67735

STIRLING, DALE ALEXANDER, b. Riverside, CA, Oct. 5, 1956; s. Alexander James and Marilyn Ann (Garrett) S.; m. Stephanie Kay Fox, Jan. 17, 1981. Author: The Alaska Records Survey, 1986; editor, writer monographs Heritage North Publs. in History, Heritage North Reference Publs.; author over 50 hist. and reference works specializing in Alaska and Pacific Northwest history and culture. BA in History, U. Alaska, Anchorage, 1980; MA in History, Alaska Pacific U., 1984; cert. Modern Archives Inst., 1985; cert. in Records and Information Mgmt., Univ. of Washington, 1987. Historian, Alaska Dept. Natural Resources, Anchorage, 1980-86; editor Poetry North Rvw, Anchorage, 1980-85; historian/archivist/records mgr. Heritage North, Seattle, 1980—. Contrbr. poetry lo lit mags. Mem. Lit Artists Guild of Alaska (bd. dir., 1981-82), Friends of Anchorage Libraries (bd. dir., 1984-85), Northwest Oral History Assn. (Alaska del. 1984-86), Am. Assn. State and Local History (membership com. 1985-86), Soc. Am. Archivists, Assn. of Records Mgrs. and Administrs, Assn. of Image and Information Mgmt., Northwest Archivists,Natl. Assn. Bibliog. of History, Phi Alpha Theta; Alaska Pacific Univ. Master of Liberal Arts Advisory Bd., 1984-86. Home: 1417 NE 113th Seattle WA 98125

STIRNEMANN, S. A., b. Obion, TN. Editor: P'An Ku, 1981, 82, Coast Lines: A Literary Review, 1983-84, The South Fla. Poetry Rvw, 1984—. BA, Fla. Atlantic U., 1983, MA, 1985. Instr. English, Fla. Atlantic U., Boca Raton, 1985—. Recipient Poetry award Wrtr.'s Digest, 1981, Natl. League of Am. PEN Women, 1982, U. West Fla., 1982, Fla. Atlantic U., 1982, 83. Mem. South Fla. Poetry Inst. (pres. 1985-86), Fla. Freelance Wrtrs. Assn., AAP, AWP, Phi Kappa Phi. Home: 7190 NW 21st St Sunrise FL 33313

STISE, PAU, see Hise, Bob

STOCK, NORMAN, b. Bklyn., July 14, 1940; s. Harry and Hadassah (Belenky) S. Contrbr. poetry to Bitterroot, Overflow, Whereas, Meal, The Smith, N.Y. Qtly, New Eng. Rvw and Bread Loaf Qtly, Home Planet News, Hanging Loose, Brooklyn Rvw. BA, Bklyn. Coll., 1962; MLS, Rutgers U., 1967; MA in Engish, Hunter Coll., 1971. Reference librarian Monmouth Coll., 1966-67, Queens Borough Pub. Library, 1967-73, Bklyn. Coll., 1973-76; reference librarian Montclair State Coll., Upper Montclair N.J., 1976-77, collection devel. librarian, 1978-82, head collection devel./acquisitions, 1982—. Recipient New Voice award for poetry Wrtrs.'s Voice-West Side YMCA, 1984; Bread Loaf scholar, 1985, winner New York to the Heartland contest in poetry, 1986.. Mem. PSA. Home: 875 W 181st St Apt 5M New York NY 10033

STOCKING, MARION KINGSTON, b. Didier, PA, June 4, 1922; d. William Frank and Louise Anne (Schucholz) Kingston; m. David Mackenzie Stocking, Dec. 21, 1954 (dec. Nov. 21, 1984); 1 stepson, Frederick B. Author: Academic Writing, 1978. Ed.: the Beloit Poetry Jnl., 1955—, The Jnls. of Claire Clairmont, 1968; contrbg. ed. Shelley and His Circle, vol. 5, 1974. Wrkg. on editing letters of Claire and Charles Clairmont and Fanny Imlay. A.B., Mt. Holyoke Coll., 1943; Ph.D., Duke U., 1952. Asst. prof. to prof. emerita Beloit Coll., WI, 1954-84; faculty assoc. Coll. of Atlantic, Bar Harbor, ME, 1984—; owner, pub. Latona Press, Ellsworth, ME, 1978—. chair, lit. panel Maine Arts Comm., Augusta, 1985—. Mem. MLA, Keats-Shelley Assn. Home: Rt 2 Box 154 Ellsworth ME 04605

STOKES, PENELOPE JUNE, b. Charleston, MS, Mar. 11, 1950; d. James Richard and Betty (Baker) Stokes. Author: The Quest for Maturity: A Study of William Wordsworth's The Prelude, 1974, Ruth and Daniel: God's People in an Alien Society, 1986. Editor books for Zondervan, Bethany House, other trade pubs. BS, Miss. U. for Women, 1972, MA, 1973; PhD, U. Miss., 1978. Instr. English, U. Miss., Oxford, 1973-78; prof. English, Mid-South Bible Coll., Memphis, 1978-80; assoc. prof. St. Paul Bible Coll., 1980-85; free-lance wrtr., ed., Frost, Minn., 1985—. Recipient Louise Crump Writing award Miss. U. for Women, 1971; fellow U. Miss., 1973-74. Mem. Minn. Christian WG, Phi Kappa Phi, Sigma Tau Delta, Pi Tau Chi, Pi Gamma Mu. Home: Box 488 Frost MN 56033

STOKES, TERRY, b. Flushing, NY, Dec. 26, 1943; s. William John Stokes and Elaine Terry (Wesley) DeLarm. m. Amy Elder, Aug. 8, 1981; children—Max, Nadja. Works include: Balancing Out, 1968, The Lady Poems, 1969, The Night Ed Sullivan Slapped One of the Kessler Twins, 1970, The Satanic American Flag, 1970, Natural Disasters, 1971, Punching In, Punching Out, 1973, Crimes of Passion, 1973, Boning the Dreamer, 1975, High School Confidential, 1976, Issuing of Scars, 1979, Missing the Boat, 1985, Sportin' News, 1985. BA, U. of Hartford, 1965; MFA, U. of IA, 1967. Instr., Western Mich. U., Kalamazoo, 1967-71; poet-in-res., U. of Hartford, CT, 1971-75, NY State Poet-in-the-schools, 1973-76; assoc. prof., U. of Cincinnati, Ohio, 1977—. Mem. PEN, PSA. Home: 2328 Flora St Cincinnati OH 45219

STOKES, WILLIAM FOREST, b. Barron, WI, Sept. 11, 1931; s. Forrest Peter and Agnes Elizabeth (Hegel) Stokes; m. Betty Lou Buckley, July 14, 1956; children—Patricia, Larry, Scott, Rick, Michael. Author: Ship the Kids on Ahead, 1969, Slap Shot, 1975, You Can Catch Fish, 1976, Hi Ho Silver, Anyway, 1979. BS, U. WI, 1958. Reporter, Stevens Point Daily Journal (WI), 1958-59; reporter-columnist WI State Jour. (Madison), 1959-69; writer columnist Milw. Jour., 1969-82; columnist Chgo. Tribune, 1982—. Served with U.S. Army, 1951-54. Recipient Ernie Pyle Annl. Writing award Scripps-Howard Fdn., 1972. Home: 5604 Hempstead Rd Madison WI 53711

STOKESBURY, LEON, b. Oklahoma City, Dec. 5, 1945, s. Leon Burdet and Jennie Lee (Smith) S.; m. Susan Elisabeth Thurman, Oct. 12, 1980; 1 child, Erin Elisabeth. Author: Often in Different Landscapes, 1976, The Royal Nonesuch, 1984, The Drifting Away, 1986. MA, MFA, U. Ark., 1972; PhD, Fla. State U., 1984. Instr. Lamar U., Beaumont, Tex., 1972-75; vis. wrtr.-in-residence North Tex. State U., Denton, 1978-79, Hollins Coll., Roanoke, Va., 1980-81, U. Southwestern La., Lafayette, 1984; asst. prof. dept. langs. McNeese State U., Lake Charles, La., 1985—. Co-winner poetry competition AWP, 1975. Office: Dept Langs McNeese St U Lake Charles LA 70609

STOLOFF, CAROLYN, b. NYC, Jan. 14, 1927; d. Charles I. and Irma (Levy) S. Author: Stepping Out, 1971, Dying to Survive, 1973, In the Red Meadow, 1973, Lighter-Than-Night Verse, 1977, Swiftly Now, 1982, A Spool of Blue: New and Selected Poems, 1983; poems pub. in numerous mags. and anthologies including The New Yorker, The Nation, Partisan Rvw, Antioch Rvw, Prairie Schooner, Chelsea, others. BS in Painting, Columbia U., 1949. Asst. prof. art Manhattanville Coll., Purchase, N.Y., 1957-79, chmn. dept. art and art history, 1960-65, lectr. in English, 1969-74; vis. wrtr. Stephens Coll., Mo., 1975, Hamilton Coll., Clinton, N.Y., 1985. Bd. dirs. Audubon Artists, NYC, 1983-85; mem.

Amnesty Intl., NYC, 1983-85. Residence grantee MacDowell Colony, N.H., 1961, 62, 70, 76, Helene Wurlitzer Fdn., N.Mex., 1972, 73, 74, Ossabaw Island Project, Ga., 1976, R.I. Creative Arts Ctr., 1981, Michael Karolyi Meml. Fdn., Vence, France, 1983, Va. Ctr. for Creative Arts, 1985; recipient Theodore Roethke award Poetry Northwest, 1967, 1st prize for poetry The Miscellany, 1972, Natl. Council on Arts award, 1968. Mem. PSA, AG, N.Y. Artists Equity Assn. Home: 24 W 8th St New York NY 10011

STONE, ALISON JO, b. Framingham, MA, May 24, 1964; d. Harvey Stanley and Deanne Francis (Cohn) S. Contrbr. poems to lit. mags. B.A., Brandeis U., 1984; postgrad. N.Y. U., 1987—. Photographer's asst. LJE Photography, Brighton, MA, 1983-87; free-lance artist, 1983—. Recipient Henry and Ida Wilchinski Poetry prize Brandeis U., 1984, Louis D. Brandeis Scholar of the Creative Arts award, Brandeis U., 1984. Home: 33 Third Ave New York NY 10003

STONE, GAYLE HALLENBECK, b. Omaha, June 23, 1945, d. Paul Duane and Marian Lucille (Tice) Hallenbeck; m. Thomas F. Stone, Aug. 14, 1966 (div. 1984); children—Paul Franklin, Julia Louise; m. 2d, Dennis Lynds, Feb. 14, 1986. Author: (under pseudonym Nick Carter) Day of the Mahdi, 1984, The Mayan Connection, 1984, Pursuit of the Eagle, 1985, White Death, 1985, The Execution Exchange, 1985, Intimacy (by C. Edward Crowther, PhD, with Gayle Stone), 1986; contrbr. short stories to S.D. Rvw, Fla. Rvw. Wrkg. on 2 novels. BA, U. Iowa, Iowa City, 1967. Reporter Ariz. Republic, Phoenix, 1967; editor Gen. Electric—TEMPO, Santa Barbara, 1968-71; assoc. editor Santa Barbara Mag., Calif., 1983—; ed. Santa Barbara Mag., 1986; ed. Prime Real Estate Mag., 1987—; fiction writing instr. U. Calif., Santa Barbara, Ventura City Coll., 1981—. Recipient Outstanding Short Story award County of Santa Barbara, 1980. Address: 234 S Voluntario St F Santa Barbara CA 93103

STONE, JENNIFER, b. Tucson, Dec. 5, 1933; children—Paul, Peter. Author: Over by the Caves, 1977, Mind Over Media: Essays on Film and Television, 1987; contrbr. to: Berkeley Poetry Rvw, Mama Bears News, Plexus, Irish Qtly, numerous other lit. publs. BA, Mills Coll., Oakland, Calif., 1955; MA, San Francisco State U., 1975. Poetry ed. Shameless Hussy Press, Berkeley, Calif., 1977-78; TV critic Plexus mag., Oakland, 1979-83; columnist Grassroots, Berkeley, 1980-83; film critic The Berkeley Monthly, 1980-83; film, drama and lit. critic sta. KPFA, Public Radio, Berkeley, 1981—. Recipient wrtr.'s residency, Briarcombe, Bolinas Bay, Calif., Mar. 1982, Steepletop, Austerlitz, N.Y., Nov. 1985. Mem. Feminist Wrtrs. Guild. Home: 2931 Florence St Berkeley CA 94705

STONE, JOAN ELIZABETH, b. Port Angeles, WA, d. William David and Florence Iva (Burdick) Duncan; m. Donald Harwood Stone, July 9, 1949 (div. 1980); children—Bruce, Duncan, Duane, Todd, Anne. Author: The Swimmer and Other Poems, 1975, Seven Poems, 1978, A Letter to Myself to Water, 1981, Our Lady of the Harbor, 1986. BA magna cum laude, U. Wash., Seattle, 1970, MA, 1974, PhC, 1976. Asst. prof. English, U. Mont., Missoula, 1974, U. Wash., Seattle, 1975, Colo. Coll., Colorado Springs, 1977—. Recipient Pacific Northwest Wrtrs. award, 1968, AAP award, U. Wash., 1969, 70, 72; included in Borestone Mountain Best Poems of 1973, 1974. Home: 312 E Yampa St Colorado Springs CO 80903

STONE, JOHN, b. Jackson, MS, Feb. 7, 1936, s. John Henry and Pauline (Marler) S.; m. Lu Crymes, Aug. 16, 1958; children—John Henry, James Edwin. Author: (poems) The Smell of Matches, 1972, In All This Rain, 1980, Renaming the Streets, 1985; ed. Principles and Practice of Emergency Medicine, 1978, 2d ed., 1986; contrbr. to lit. and poetry anthologies, textbooks of internal medicine, cardiology. BA, Millsaps Coll., 1958; MD, Washington U., St. Louis, 1962. Instr. medicine Emory U. Schl. Medicine, Atlanta, 1968-69, asst. prof., 1969-72, assoc. prof., 1972-77, prof., 1977—, assoc. dean, dir. admissions, 1982—. Served to lt. comdr. USPHS, 1964-66. Recipient lit. achievement award for poetry Ga. Wrtrs.' Assn., 1973; named wrtr. of yr. in poetry Dixie Council Authors and Journalists, 1981; Literature Awd., Miss. Inst. Arts & Letters, 1985. Home: 3983 Northlake Creek Ct Tucker GA 30084

STONE, JULIE LYNN, b. Manistee, MI, Nov. 9, 1959; d. Richard Andrew and Karen Ann (Rademaker) Stone. Contrbr. poetry to Poems of the Heartland, Quiet Thoughts, Poetic Treasures, Images of the Mystic Truth, Dreams of the Heroic Muse, Dreams, Eternal Echoes, Earthshine, Am Poetry Anthology, Poet's Corner. AA, Muskegon Community Coll. Writer Lakeshore Times, N. Muskegon, Mich., 1980. Asst. Rep. Party, Muskegon, 1984. Mem. P&W, Muskegon Mus. Arts, MCC Fdn. Address: 3755 Henry St 106 Muskegon MI 49441

STONE, KENNETH MICHAEL, b. NYC, Oct. 18, 1942; s. Henry and Marion Edna S. Author numerous wks. inclg. Impious Fires, 1976, Breaking the Desire, 1982, Leaving Cloistered Safety, 1984, Boundaries, 1985; ed. Thirteen (poetry mag.), 1982—; contrbr. to numerous pubs. inclg. Poetic Justice, Salome, Ambrosia, Black Bear, Writers Lifeline, Mozart Park, Silver Wings. BA, Allegheny Coll., 1964; MS, USC, 1970. Officer, USAF, var. locats., 1964-74; deputy commissioner and staff dev. co-ord. Otsego County Dept. Soc. Svcs., Cooperstown, NY, 1974—. Poet of Yr., CSP World News, 1983; poet of the issue, The Sounds of Poetry, 1985. Mem. NA/PT, FSPA. Home: Box 392 Portlandville NY 13834

STONE, MARIE KIRCHNER, b. MN. Author: American Literature in the American Studies Approach, 1964, An Experiment Reports on Itself, 1974, Between Home and Community, 1976, Gifted Child, 1978, Ralph Tyler's Principle of Curriculum, Instruction, & Evaluation, 1985. Wrkg. on curriculum devel. M.A., U. Minn., 1985; Ph.D., Loyola U., Chgo., 1970-87. Educator, Franci W. Parker Schls., Am. Soc. Curriculum Developers, Academic Comm. of Natl. Acsn. of Ind. Schls., 1973-79, soc. for Study of Curriculum History, 1985-87. Home: 2130 Lincoln Park W Chicago IL 60614

STONE, MICHAEL ROBERT, b. E. St. Louis, IL, May 10, 1951; s. Robert Beckwith and Claire Dean (Kiggins) S.; m. Kristine Lynn Moss, Feb. 4, 1978; children—Leslie Michele, Stephanie Marie. Ed.: Fairview Heights Tribune, 1975-77, Mascoutah Herald, 1976-77, Clinton County News, 1976-77, Farm Impact, 1975-77; pub.: IAPES News, 1981—, Proceedings IAPES convent., 1981—, Perspective: essays & rvws. of issues in Employment Secur. and emp. & trng. progs., 1985—. BJ, U. MO, 1973, BA, 1974. Ed., Tribune, Fairview Heights, IL, 1975-77; mng. ed. Yelvington Pub., Mascoutah, IL, 1976-77; zoning officer City of Fairview, Fairview Heights, IL, 1977-81; exec. dir. Intl. Assn. Personnel in Employment Security, Frankfort, KY, 1981—. Home: 555 Poa Frankfort KY 40601

STONE, ROBERT ANTHONY, b. NYC, Aug. 21, 1937; s. C. Homer and Gladys Catherine (Grant) Stone; m. Janice G. Burr, Dec. 11, 1959; children—Deidre M., Ian A. Author: A Hall of Mirrors, 1967, Dog Soldiers, 1974 (Natl. Book award), A Flag for Sunrise, 1981, Children of Light, 1986, Outerbridge Reach, 1989; contrbg. author: Best American Short Stories, 1970, 71. Student, NYU, 1958-59; Stegner fellow, Stanford, 1962. Editorial asst. NY Daily News (NYC), 1958-60; novelist, 1960—; wirter-in-res. Princeton U., 1971-72; faculty Amherst Coll., 1972-75, 77-78, Stanford U., 1979, U. Hawaii-Manoa, 1979-80, Harvard U., 1981, U. Calif.-Irvine, 1982, NYU, 1983, U. Calif., San Diego, 1985, Princeton U., 1985. Served with USN, 1955-58. Recipient William Faulkner prize, 1967, Natl. Bk. award, 1975, John Dos Passos prize for lit., 1982, award in lit. AAIAL, 1982; recipient Mildred and Harold Strauss Livings ($50,000 annually for 5 years), 1987. Mem. PEN (exec. bd.). Office: Donadio 231 W 22nd St New York NY 10011

STONE, SUSAN GAIL, (Susan Page), b. Columbia, KY, June 22, 1957; d. Glenn Mitchell and Janet Sue (Wheeler) Stone; m. Huston Page, Nov. 28, 1981 (div. Nov. 22, 1985). Wrkg. on investigative stories. B.A., U. Ky., 1984. Feature wrtr. State Jnl., Frankfort, KY, 1984-86, news reporter, 1986—. Recipient 3d place for investigative reporting Ky. Press Assn., 1985. Mem. SPJ. Home: 221 W Broadway 2 Frankfort KY 40601

STOOP, NORMA MC LAIN, b. Panama Canal Zone, July 20, 1910, d. Harry Edward and Gladys (Brandon) McLain. Widowed, 1966. Contrbr. poetry to Atlantic Monthly, N.Y. Times, Quest, McCalls, many other publs.; contrbr. rvw., photography to Sat. Rev., Stuttgarter Nachrichten, Christian Sci. Monitor, La Depeche du Midi, others; contrbr. interviews, articles: After Dark, Manhattan Arts, others. Wrkg. on poetry, fiction and non-fiction. Student Penn Hall Jr. Coll., 1929, Carnegie Inst. Tech., 1929-30. Sr. ed. Dance Mag., NYC, 1969—, After Dark mag., NYC, 1969-82; entertainment ed. radio program Sr. Edition, sta.-WNYC,NYC, 1980-83; film critic, assoc. ed. Manhattan Arts, NYC, 1983—. Recipient Borestone Mountain Poetry award, 1973. Mem. Overseas Press Club, Natl. Assn. TV Arts and Scis., PSA, Dance Critics Assn., Natl. Soc. Profl. Journalists, Deadline Club. Home: 165 W 66th St Apt 21F New York NY 10023

STORR, JOHN FREDERICK, b. Ottawa, Ont., Can., Aug. 17, 1915, s. John and Alice Sarah (Twigge) S.; m. Barbara Rhoda Gordon, Aug. 15, 1942; 1 son, Gordon. Contrbr. articles to Aspects of Sponge Biology, other prof. publs.; author monographs. Master Queen's Coll., Nassau, Bahamas, 1942-45; tchr. Friends Schl., Bklyn., 1945-46; asst. prof. Adelphi Coll., Garden City, N.Y., 1946-52; research asst. prof. Miami (Fla.) U., 1955-58; assoc. prof. SUNY-Buffalo, 1958—. Mem. Alpha Epsilon Rho, numerous profl. orgns. Home: 41 Fairways Blvd Buffalo NY 14221

STOTZFUS, BEN FRANK, b. Sofia, Bulgaria, Sept. 15, 1927, s. B. Frank and Esther Alfrida (Johnson) S.; m. Judith Mattern Palmer, Nov. 8, 1975; children—Jan, Celia, Andrew. Novelist: The Eye of the Needle, 1967, Black Lazarus,

1972; author: Alain Robbe-Grillet and the New French Novel, 1964, Georges Chenneviere et L'Unanimisme, 1965, Gide's Eagles (MLA Scholar's Library), 1969, Gide and Hemingway: Rebels Against God, 1978, Robbe-Grillet: The Body of the Text, 1985; contrbr. short fiction, poetry to Kayak, Mosaic, Chelsea, other lit. publs.; contrbr. articles, essays to scholarly publs. BA, Amherst Coll., 1949; LittD, 1974; PhD, U. Wis.-Madison, 1959. Prof. French, comparative lit., creative writing, U. Calif.-Riverside, 1960—. Grantee Fulbright-Hays Fdn., 1955-56, 63-64, Camargo Fdn., 1983, 85. Mem. MLA, AWP, So. Comparative Lit. Assn., Assn. des Amis d'Andre Gide. Office: Dept Lit Langs U Calif Riverside CA 92521

STOUT, KATE, b. Pitts., Nov. 12, 1949, d. Frederick Lacey and Marjorie Bryce (Cope) Stout. Ed.: Building with Nantucket in Mind, 1978; contrbr. articles to McCall's, Saturday Rvw, NY Times, Bride's Mag., Working Woman, other publs. BA, Centre Coll., 1971; MA, Sussex U., Eng., 1975; MS, Columbia U., 1982. News dir. Channel 3-TV, Nantucket, Mass., 1979-80; researcher The Virginia Woolf Letters, vol. VI, Eng., 1979; ed. Nantucket Times, 1985; ed., pub. Nantucket Map & Legend, 1986—; founder, dir. Nantucket Wrtrs.' Workshop, 1976-85. Recipient Best Mag. Reporting award Met. Louisville Sigma Delta Chi, 1981, Louis & Pauline Cowan award Columbia U., 1982. Mem. NWC, ASJA. Office: 448 E 87th St 4B New York NY 10128

STOUT, THOMAS JAMES, b. Rochester, NY, Feb. 1, 1964; s. John H. and Alice L. (Ryan) S. Creator, Allegheny Rvw for undergraduate writer, 1983-86, also Allegheny Lit. Rvw. for Allegheny students, 1984-86. BS in Chemistry/English, Allegheny Coll., 1986. Editorial bd. Allegheny Rvw., Meadville, Pa., 1982-83, editor, 1983-85, sr. editor, 1985—. Pub. readings liaison Allegheny Coll., Meadville, 1985—. Lubrizol Corp. scholar, 1985-86. Mem. Phi Beta Kappa, Am. Chem. Soc. (student affiliate), Phi Lambda Upsilon. Home: 614 Heritage Dr Rochester NY 14615

STOYENOFF, NORMA JEANNE DAVIS, b. Wyandotte, MI, Mar. 26, 1932; d. Leo Frank and Genevieve Elyse (Budrysky) Davis; m. Fred Stoyenoff, Feb. 7, 1953; 1 dau., Jennifer Lynn. Contrbr. numerous articles and fiction to mags. including Woman's Day, Better Homes & Gardens, True Story, others. Wrkg. on novels, Summer of Fear, Love's Sweet Song. Grad. private schls., Wyandotte. Bookkeeper, Taepke Electric Co., New Boston, MI, 1950-51; secy. to asst. superintendent public schls., Romulus, MI, 1951-55. Home: 45290 Sunrise Ln Belleville MI 48111

STRACHAN, PATRICIA HARTING, b. St. Louis, July 27, 1948; d. William Harting and Elizabeth (Halliday) Bayer; m. William Bruce Strachan, Oct. 28, 1972. Editor: Coming Into the Country, 1977, The Right Stuff, 1979, Housekeeping, 1980, Edisto, 1984. BA, Duke U., 1970; postgrad., Radcliffe Coll., 1970. Editorial asst. to Robert Giroux, Farrar Straus & Giroux, Inc. (NYC), 1971-74, editor, 1975-80, exec. editor, 1980—. Mem. PEN (Roger Klein award for editing 1983). Office: FS&G Inc 19 Union Sq W New York NY 10003

STRAHAN, BRADLEY R., b. Boston, Sept. 3, 1937, s. Frank and Anna (Lessoff) S.; m. Anila Nand-Kishore, May 20, 1962 (div. 1978); children—Russel Rajindra, Barak David, Shanna Rebeka; m. 2d, Shirley G. Sullivan, Oct. 17, 1981; 1 son, Bryn David. Author: Love Songs for an Age of Anxiety, 1980, Poems, 1981; ed. Black Buzzard Illustrated Poetry Chapbook series, 1980—; ed.-in-chief Visions, The Intl. Mag. of Illustrated Poetry, 1979—; contrbr. poetry to Crosscurrents, Pulpsmith, Stone Country, Negative Capability, Hollins Critic, Poetry Australia, Christian Sci. Monitor, other publs., anthols. BA, Bklyn. Coll., 1960, MA, 1963. Ed., pub. Black Buzzard Press, Arlington, Va., 1979—; poetry coordinator Art Barn Assn., Washington, 1980—; poetry cons. Slavin Gallery, Washington, 1984—; lectr. various ednl. and cultural orgns. U.S. and Europe, USIA touring poet, 1980, 83, 85. Prize winner Shri Chinmoy Orgn., NYC1984, Passaic Poetry Center, N.J., 1985. Mem. Washington Area Wrtrs. Center. Home: 4705 S 8th Rd Arlington VA 22204

STRAND, MARK, b. Summerside, P.E.I., Can., Apr. 11, 1934 (came to US, 1938); s. Robert Joseph and Sonia (Apter) Strand; m. Antonia Ratensky, Sept. 14, 1961 (div. June 1973); 1 dau.—Jessica; 2nd m. Julia Runsey Garretson, Mar. 15, 1976; son—Thomas Summerfield. Author: Sleeping With One Eye Open, 1964, Reasons for Moving, 1968, Darker, 1970, New Poetry of Mexico, 1970, The Contemporary American Poets, 1969, 18 Poems for the Quechua, 1971, The Story of Our Lives, 1973, The Owl's Insomnia, 1973, The Sargentville Notebook, 1973, Another Republic, 1976, The Monument, 1978, The Late Hour, 1978, Selected Poems, 1980 (Recipit award Am. Acad. and Inst. Arts and Letters 1975, Edgar Allen Poe prize 1974), The Planet of Lost Things, 1983, ART of the Real: Nine American Figurative Painters, 1983, The Night Book, 1985, Mr. and Mrs. Baby, 1985, Rembrandt Takes a Walk, 1986, William Baily, 1987. BA, Antioch, 1957; BFA, Yale, 1959; MA, U. Iowa, 1962. Instr. English, U. Iowa, 1962-65; asst. prof. Mt. Holyoke Coll., 1967; vis. prof. U. Wash., 1968; vis. lectr. Yale, 1969-70, U. VA, 1976, CA State U. (Fresno), 1977, U. CA (Irvine), 1979; Bain-Swiggett lectr. Princeton, 1973; Hurst prof. poetry Brandeis U., 1974-75; vis. prof. U. VA, 1978, Wesleyan U., 1979, Harvard U., 1980; prof. U. Utah, 1981; adj. assoc. prof. Columbia U., 1969-72; assoc. prof. Bklyn. Coll., 1971-72; distinguished prof. U. Utah, 1987—. Fellowship of Acad. of Amer. Poets, 1979, John D. and Catherine T. Mac Arthur fellowship, 1987. Mem. AAIAL. Home: 716 4th Ave Salt Lake City UT 84103

STRANGE, CATHY LEE, (Paula Legendre), b. Boulder, Feb. 25, 1955; d. Robert Cannon and Margaret Elin (Turnquist) Strange; 1 son, James Bryan. Contrbr. article to Meditations for the Divorced, Daily Camera. B.S./with Honors in Mechanical Engineering, U. Colo., 1977. Engineering asst. Lawrence Livermore Lab., CA, 1976; mechanical engineer, 1977-80, technical wrtr., IBM Corp., Boulder, 1980—. Home: 4212B Monroe Dr Boulder CO 80303

STRASSER, TODD, (Morton Rhue), b. NYC, May 5, 1950, s. Chester and Sheila (Reisner) S.; m. Pamela Older; 1 child, Lia. Author: Angel Dust Blues, 1979, Friends Till the End, 1981, The Wave (as Morton Rhue), 1981, Rock N' Roll Nights, 1982, Workin' for Peanuts (made into movie), 1983, Turn It Up!, 1984, The Complete Computer Popularity Program, 1984, A Very Touchy Subject (made into movie), 1985. BA, Beloit (Wis.) Coll., 1974. Winner Best Book for Young Adults award Am. Library Assn. (Friends Till the End), 1983, (Rock N' Roll Night), 1984. Mem. Freedom to Read Fdn., Intl. Reading Assn., P&W. Home: 310 W 79th St New York NY 10024

STRATTON, THOMAS WILLIAM, (Tom), b. West Chester, PA, Mar. 23, 1946, s. William Braningham Stratton and Dorothy Alice (Carpenter) Spitzner; m. Margaret Elizabeth Letson, July 7, 1970; 1 dau., Carra Sage. Author: Buffalo Chips, Son of Buffalo Chips; contrbr. articles, satire to Cavalier, Crawdaddy, Natl. Lampoon, other publs.; cartoons published in N.Y. Times, Sat. Rvw, other natl. publs. BA in Art History, SUNY-Buffalo, BA in Sociology. Advt. artist Loblaw, Inc., Buffalo, 1970-71; free-lance cartoonist, wrtr., comedian. Fellow Natl. Cartoonist Guild. Home: S 4211 Lake Shore Rd Hamburg NY 14075

STRAUB, PETER FRANCIS, b. Milw., Mar. 2, 1943; s. Gordon Anthony and Elvena (Nilsestuen) Straub; m. Susan Bitker, Aug. 27, 1966; children—Benjamin Bitker, Emma Sydney Valli. Author: Marriages, 1973, Julia, 1975, If You Could See Me Now, 1977, Ghost Story, 1979 Shadow Land, 1982, Floating Dragon, 1983, The Talisman, 1984, Blue Rose, 1985, Koko, 1988. BA, U. WI, 1965; MA, Columbia U., 1966. English tchr. Univ. Schl. (Milw.), 1966-68. Mem. AG, AL. Home: Box 395 Greens Farms CT 06436

STRAUCH, RALPH E., b. Springfield, MA, May 14, 1937, s. Ralph E. and Cora Helen (McMath) S.; m. Merna Lynn Berkowitz, Sept. 14, 1958; children—Shar, David. Author: The Reality Illusion: How We Create the World We Experience, 1983; contrbr. articles, reports to numerous publs. BA, UCLA, 1959; MA, U. Calif.-Berkeley, 1964, PhD, 1965. Sr. mathematician Rand Corp., Santa Monica, Calif., 1965-76; cons. numerous corps., 1977-82; Feldenkrais tchr., pvt. prac., Pacific Palisades, Calif., 1982—. NSF fellow, 1963. Home: 1383 Avenida de Cortez Pacific Palisades CA 90272

STRAUS, AUSTIN GUY, b. Bklyn., June 12, 1939; s. Frederick and Roslyn (Bassin) S.; m. Anne Moody, Mar. 9, 1967 (div. 1977); 1 son, Sascha; m. 2d, Patrocinia Gonzalez, 1977 (div. 1978); m. 3d, Wanda Coleman, May 1, 1981; stepchildren: Tony, Tunisia, Ian. Contrbr. poems and art to anthologies, lit mags; contrbr. articles to Amnesty Intl.; ed. many books; rvws. and cartoon in Shattersheet. BA, in philosophy, Bklyn. Coll., 1958-61; MA, NYU, 1969. Freelance ed. and ghostwriter, NY, 1965—; tutor, York Coll., Jamaica, NY, 1975-76; ed. and reprinter AMS Press, Lenox Hill Press and others, NYC, 1975—; poetry workshop tchr. City Coll., Los Angeles, 1985—; poetry tchr., UCLA, 1986—. Antiwar Activist, Minority of One Mag. and var. orgns., New York, mid-1960s; vol. group leader, Amnesty Intl., San Diego, 1978, SW regional coordinator, Amnesty Intl., L.A. 1978-79;; office mgr., Campaign for Citizen's Police Rvw. Bd., Los Angeles, 1980; So. Calif. rep., Citizen's Party, Los Angeles, 1980. Mem. P&W. Address: Box 29154 Los Angeles CA 90029

STRAUSBAUGH, JOHN R., b. Balt., Oct. 31, 1951; s. J. Joseph and Thelma F. W. Author: (play) Animal Relations, 1981, Red Zone, 1985; Prose/Poems, 1982; (prose) Flying Fish, 1986. Contrbr. articles, rvws., short stories, poems to mags., lit mags., newspapers. Wrkg. on novel, video documentaries of Irish music, sequel to Red Zone. BA cum laude, U. Md.-Balt., 1974. Assoc. dir. Theatre Project, Balt., 1978-82; sr. wrtr. City Paper, Balt., 1978—; project dir. Cultural Policy Inst., Balt., 1986—; free-lance wrtr., 1982—. Recipient Way with Words Grand prize for poetry WAYE-radio, Balt., 1973. Mem. P&W. Home: 221 Ridgemede Rd Baltimore MD 21210

STRAUSS, DAVID LEVI, b. Junction City, KS, Mar. 10, 1953, s. Clifford Clemens and Amy Viola (Lee) S. Author: Manoeuvres: Poems 1977-79, 1980, Code of Signals: Recent Writings in Poetics, 1983; contrbr. to Acts, Hambone, Temblor, Credences, other lit mags; contrbr. to Afterimage, Artweek, Camerawork Qtly, other art mags.; ed., pub. ACTS; A Jnl of New Writing, 1982—. BA, Goddard Coll., 1976; postgrad. New Coll., San Francisco, 1981-86. Freelance wrtr., critic for various publs. Recipient Briarcombe award Briarcombe Fdn., Bolinas, Calif., 1983; NEA pub. grantee, 1985. Mem. CCLM. Home: 514 Guerrero St San Francisco CA 94110

STRAUSS, SALLY, b. St. Louis, May 1, 1925; d. Arthur and Frances (Somit) Rubinsky; m. Harry Strauss, Feb. 17, 1960; children: Gary, Linda, Michael, Lawrence. Author: Inner Rhythm: An Exciting New Approach to Stress-Free Living, 1984. Student San Francisco City Coll. Exec. secy. US Army Ordnance, San Francisco, 1942-45; reg. dir. No. Calif. City of Hope, San Francisco, 1957-67; exec. secy. and campaign coordinator Shaare Zedek Hosp. of Israel, San Francisco region, 1975-80. Mem. Med. Lib. Bd., Marshall Hale Meml. Hosp., 1976; winner, Writer's Digest Creative Writing Contest. Address: Chase Pub 1654 33rd Ave San Francisco CA 94122

STREET, JULIA MONTGOMERY, b. Concord, NC, Jan. 19, 1898; d. Samuel Lewis and Elizabeth B. (Norris) Montgomery; m. C.A. Street, Sept. 13, 1924 (dec. Feb. 2, 1968); children—Carol, Claudius. Author: Fiddler's Fancy, 1954, Moccasin Tracks, 1956, Dulcie's Whale, 1963, Drovovs' Gold, 1958, Candle Love Feast, 1961, North Carolina Parade, 1966, Judacalla's Handprint, 1969, others. AB U. of NC. Teacher NC pub. schls. (Rocky Mount), 1918-20, (Winston-Salem), 1923-24; free-lance wrtr. 1959—. Winner AAUW award for juvenile literature of year, 1956, 1963, 1967, Alumni Service Award, U. of N.C., for preserving N.C. history for school children, 1967. Mem. NC Wrtrs. Conf., secy., 1964. Home: 545 Oaklawn Ave Winston-Salem NC 27104

STREVINSKY, CHRISTINE MARIA, b. Poznan, Poland, Jan. 11, 1932; d. Antoni Szambelan and Broniskawa (Kierzek) Szambelan Wiatrowski Doremba; m. Veto Hnery Strevinsky, Oct. 23, 1954 (div. 1981); children: Phillip Anthony, Barbara Ann, Mitchell Alan. Author: The Dark Hour of Noon, 1982. Wrkg. on biography. BA, U. New Orleans, 1981, MA in English, 1984. Instr. Delgado Jr. Coll., New Orleans, 1984—. Mem. La. Wrtrs.' Guild, New Orleans Wrtrs.' Network. Home: 3700 Division St Apt 104 Metairie LA 70002

STRICKLAND, BRAD, see Strickland, William Bradley

STRICKLAND, JUDY EVELYN, b. Hampton, AR, July 2, 1947; d. Elton Austin and Janie Sue (Hayes) Evans; m. Larry Joe Strickland, May 24, 1969; 1 daughter, Tracy Jo. Contrbr. articles to lit. jnl., Calhoun County Accent. Ed., author: Haiku Collection, 1968; ed.: New Beginnings, 1977-78. Wrkg. on scripts, essays, short stories, romance novel. B.A., Southern Ark. U., 1969. English tchr. Hampton High Sch., AR, 1977-84, Strong High Sch., AR, 1986—. Mem. NCTE. Home: Rt 8 Box 486 El Dorado AR 71730

STRICKLAND, WILLIAM BRADLEY, (Brad Strickland), b. New Holland, GA, Oct. 27, 1947, s. Silas Henry and Eavleen (Watkins) S.; m. Barbara Ann Justus, June 8, 1969; children—Jonathan, Amy. Author: (novel) To Stand Beneath the Sun, 1986; contrbr. stories to mag. of Fantasy and Sci. Fiction, Isaac Asimov's Sci. Fiction Mag. MA, U. Ga., 1971, PhD, 1976. Chmn. humanities Truett-McConnell Coll., Cleveland, Ga., 1976-85; head secondary English dept. Lakeview Acad., Gainesville, Ga., 1985-87; asst. prof. English, Gainsville, Ga., 1987—. Mem. SFWA, South Atlantic MLA, Computer Wrtrs. Am. Home: Rt 2 Box 355 Oakwood GA 30566

STROMBERGER, THEODORE LEO, b. Canon City, CO, June 22, 1905, s. Gustav Adolph and Kate (Brennan) S.; m. Dorothy H. Stromberger, Aug. 26, 1939; children—Eric, Karla. Contrbr.: Western Advt., Harvard Bus. Rev., Profl. Engr., Christian Sci. Monitor, other mags., trade jnls., newspapers. Wrkg. on articles, fiction, poetry. MA, U. So. Calif. Advt. exec. 1939-80, now prin. Tx Stromberger Co., Pasadena, Calif. Home: 1040 S Orange Grove Blvd Apt 4 Pasadena CA 91105

STROM-PAIKIN, JOYCE ELIZABETH, (Joyce E. Danielson), b. Syracuse, NY, Oct. 25, 1946; d. Paul H. Strom and Elizabeth (Bartlett) Black; m. Frank J. Iaconis, May 31, 1963 (div. Mar. 25, 1974); children—Paul, Michael; m. Lester Paikin, June 26, 1982. Author: Medical Treason, 1977, Through the Light, 1982. A.A.S. in Nursing, Cayuga Commun. Coll., 1976; B.S. in Psychology, Nova U., 1978, M.S. in Psychology, 1980. Charge nurse St. Joseph's Hosp., Syracuse, 1974-77; owner, psychotherapist Psycho-Awareness, Inc., Tamarac, FL, 1980—. Recipient award for articles and features Wrtr.'s Digest, 1981. Home: 6112 NW 1st St Margate FL 33063

STRONG, BETHANY J., (June McLaughlin), b. Oklahoma City, June 13, 1906; d. Nicholas H. McLaughlin and Anna A. (Spuhler) Leonard; m. John D. Strong Sept. 2, 1928; 2 daus.: Patricia A., Virginia Maria. Author: The King's Ganeralissima, First Love, Favorite Son, Murder in the Mirror; wrkg. on non-fiction book: How The West Was Really Won. BS, Johns Hopkins U. Freelance writer/novelist/poet; ed. and pub. Parable Press, Amherst, Mass., 1977—. AAUW (pres. Conn. Valley br.), Am. Pen Women. Address: 136 Gray St Amherst MA 01002

STRONG, JANET KONHAUS, b. Carlisle, Pa., d. Frank Bishop and Ruth (Blessley) Konhaus; m. Edward Belleneny Strong, June 21, 1960; children—Susan Marie, Edward Bradley. Ed., pub. Bed & Breakfast Almanac of the World Renowned Napa Valley, 1981, 2d ed., 1983, Bed & Breakfast Almanac of California and Hawaii, 1985, Bed & Breakfast Ultramanager, 1985. BS in Edn., State U. Kutztown, Pa.; MA in Psychol. Services, Columbia U. Tchr. Mechanicsburg, Pa., 1954-58, Westfield, N.J., 1958-60, St. Helena, Calif., 1966-85; pub., ed. B&B Prodns., St. Helena, 1981—. Mem. Napa Valley Innkeepers Assn. (founder, pres. 1981), Bed & Breakfast Innkeepers Assn. Office: Box 295 Suite 400 Saint Helena CA 94574

STROUD, DREW MCCORD, b. Phoenix, AZ, Sept. 3, 1944. Author: The Majority Minority, 1974, Lines Drawn Towards, 1980, The Hospitality of Circumstance, 1987; editor and translator: Poamorio, 1985, Night of the Milky Way Railroad, 1984. BA, Harvard, 1966; MA, U. of AZ, 1985. Director of Intl. Promo., Kodansha Intl., Tokyo, Japan, 1977-80; editor-in-chief, SARU Press, Tucson, Tokyo, Buenos Aires, 1980—. Mem. PSA, AAP, Amer. Assn. of Tchrs. of Spanish and Portugese. Address: Box 1067 Sedona AZ 86336

STROZESKI, CHARLES, b. Somerville, N.J., Jan. 28, 1962; s. Leo Charles and Sophie (Borinski) S. Contrbr. poems to anthols. Wrkg. on collection of poetry. AAS, Somerset County Coll., Somerville, 1982. Home: 928 Huff Ave Manville NJ 08835

STRUCKHOFF, ROGER STEPHEN, b. Clinton, IA, Dec. 11, 1954; s. Paul Frederick and Norma Joann (Ashby) S.; m. Carol Kristine Long, Aug. 31, 1985. Prodn. editor: World Mining (English, Russian, Chinese edits.), World Coal, World Mining Latino, Portable Computer; assoc. editor: Latin Am. Mining Letter, Latino Mineras Noticias, Unix Rvw; sr. editor: Data Gen. Micro World, Epson World, Profl. Computing, Portable Computer Rvw; editor: PC Companion. BA, Knox Coll., Galesburg, Ill., 1977; postgrad. U. Calif-Berkeley, 1978-81. Ed., Miller Freeman Pubs., San Francisco, 1978-85, Camden Communications, Me., 1985—. Recipient Neil award, BPA, 1980. Mem. Boston Computer Soc., Boston Computer Mus., Smithsonian Inst. Home: 10A High St Camden ME 04843

STRUDWICK, DOROTHY J., b. Mpls., Jan. 31, 1918; d. James Watt and Marion C. (Bussey) S.; divorced; children—Dorothy Halla-Poe, Linda Jean Flanders. Contrbr. articles, poems, short stories in mags. including Ivory Tower, Golden Mag., Child Life, Ideals, others. BS in Edn., U. Minn. 1957; postgrad. Colo. Coll., Colorado Springs, Denver U., U. of Colorado, Boulder. English tchr. Bryant Jr. High Schl., Mpls., 1955-63, Portola Jr. High, Tarzana, Calif., 1963-64; research asst. Paul S. Amidon Assocs., Mpls., 1964-65; instr. creative writing Palmer Wrtrs. Schl., Mpls., 1965-71, retired; free-lance wrtr., 1971—. Mem Mpls. Wrtrs. Workshop. Home: 4101 Parklawn Ave No 213 Edina MN 55435

STUART, ANNE ELIZABETH, b. Lansing, MI, Nov. 5, 1956; d. Robert David and Marianne Stuart: m. Kenneth E. Parker. Contrbr. articles on women's issues, health/fitness, travel, medicine, nursing, careers, profiles to mags., newspapers, trade jnls., corporate pubs. including Boston Mag., Newsday, others. B.A. in English, Jnlsm., Mich. State U., 1979; M.S. in Jnlsm., Columbia U., 1986. Mng. ed. Mich. Nurse Mag., Lansing, 1979-80; reporter, ed. Star-Gazette/Telegam, Elmira, NY, 1980-83; reporter Knickerbocker News, Albany, NY, 1983-85, Newsday, Long Island, NY, 1985; free-lance wrtr., 1985—. Tchr. Brookline Adult and Commun. Edn. Program, MA, 1987—. Recipient 3d place N.Y. State AP, 1984; 1st place Sigma Delta Chi, (3) 1986. Mem. NWU. Home: 15 Thompson Dr 6 Randolph MA 02368

STUART, CAROLYN, see McDonald, Kathryn Stewart

STUART, DABNEY, b. Richmond, VA, Nov. 4, 1937; s. Walker Dabney, Jr. and Martha (Von Schilling) S.; m. Sandra Westcott, Jan. 20, 1983; children—Nathan, Martha, Darren. Author: The Diving Bell, 1966, A Particular Place, 1969, The Other Hand, 1974, Friends of Yours, Friends of Mine, 1974, Round and Round, 1977, Nabokov: The Dimensions of Parody, 1978, Rockbridge

Poems, 1981, Common Ground, 1982, Don't Look Back, 1987. Editor: (poetry and rvw.) Shanandoah, 1966-76, acting editor, 1970; (poetry) New Virginia Rvw, 1982; editorial bd. Poets in the South, 1976-81. AB, Davidson Coll., 1960; AM, Harvard U., 1962. McGuffey Prof. of Creative Wrtg., Ohio U., Spring 1975; poet-in-res. Trinity Coll., Spring 1978; poet-in-residence U. Va., Charlottesville, 1981, 82-83; prof. English, Washington & Lee U., Lexington, Va., 1965—. Recipient Dylan Thomas award PSA, 1965; fellow NEA, 1974, 82; Governor's Award for the Arts (VA), 1979, Guggenheim Fellowship, 1987-88. Mem. AG. Home: 30 Edmondson Ave Lexington VA 24450

STUART, DIANA, see Toombs, Jane Ellen

STUART, KIEL, b. NYC, 1951. Contrbr. to N.Y. Times, Christian Sci. Monitor, Commodore mag., Artist's mag., Art & Artists, Fantasy Book, Ampersand, Beyond. AA, Suffolk Community Coll., Selden, N.Y., 1972; BA, SUNY, Stony Brook, N.Y., 1975. Dir. Wrtrs. Alliance, 1979—, ed. newsletter, 1979—; ed. SFWA Forum, 1985—. AAUW grantee for lit. achievement, 1984. Mem. AG, SFWA. Home: 12 Skylark Ln Stony Brook NY 11790

STUART, SANDY, see Kaufman, Stuart J.

STUART, VIRGINIA ELAINE, b. Ayer, MA, Dec. 31, 1953; d. James Allen and Lorraine Alma (Pote) S.; m. John Ledyard Hill, Jr., June 7, 1980. Author: (with D. Freeman) Resources for Gifted Children, 1980; (with D.H. Graves) Write from the Start, 1985; contrbr. short stories, poems, essays to Aegis, Penumbra, Bradford Rvw, Write to Learn. BS summa cum laude in Botany and Plant Sci., U. N.H., 1975, MA in English, 1980. Editorial asst. Trillium Press, NYC, summer 1979; reader Redbook mag., N.Y.C., summer 1980; research asst. Writing Process Lab., U. N.H., Durham, 1981; ptnr., instr. Rule Assocs., Northwood, N.H., 1981-83; instr. English, U.N.H., Durham, 1980—; freelance wrtr., 1983—. Mem. NCTE, Phi Beta Kappa. Home: College Rd PO Box 176 Stratham NH 03885

STUDEBAKER, III, JOSEPH ELIZAH, b. U.S. Naval Hospital, Yokosuka, Japan, Feb. 5, 1956; s. Joseph Elizah and Sakako Morikawa S.; Mona McNally June 25, 1983; 1 dau.—Lisa Michelle. Author: A Collection of Thoughts, 1980; contrbr. to Ground, The Hoff; ed. Aerye, 1973-74; Ground, 1980-81. BS, Univ. of SC, Aiken, 1984; grad. work, Wolford Coll., Fort Hays State Univ. Tchr., Bishopville H.S. (SC), 1984—. Mem. NCTE, NEA. Home: 411 N Main St Bishopville SC 29010

STUDEBAKER, MICHAEL JOHN, b. Los Angeles, Feb. 2, 1949; s. Mulford B. and E. Barbara (Krantz) S. Author: Budget Skiers Guidebook—Western U.S., 1983, 85, Budget Vacationers Guidebook—Western U.S., 1984, 86. BBA, Calif. State U.-Fullerton, 1971; postgrad. Calif. State U.-Los Angeles, 1971-72, passed CPA exam, 1974. Jr. acct. Booth & Booth, Pasadena, Calif., 1972-73; sr. acct. Jay Wright, CPA, Sacramento, Calif., 1973-74; acctg. supr. Liken, Inc., Huntington Beach, Calif., 1974-76, Fed. Mogul Corp., Downey, Calif., 1976-77; pvt. practice pub. acctg., Whittier, Calif., 1977-83; pvt. practice travel counseling, Whittier, 1967-86; wrtr-pub. Glastonbury Press, Whittier, 1983—. Mem. Book Publicists So. Calif. Home: 12816 E Rose Dr Whittier CA 90601

STUDEBAKER, WILLIAM VERN, b. Salmon, ID, May 21, 1947, s. Robert R. and Betty L. (Silbaugh) S.; m. Judy Kay Infanger, Aug. 23, 1969; children—Tona, Robert, Tyler, Eric. Author poetry collections: Everything Goes Without Saying, 1978, Trailing the Raven, 1983, The Cleaving, 1985; contrbr.: Ohio Rvw, Tar River Poetry, Rain in the Forest, Light in the Trees: Contemporary Poetry from the Northwest, numerous other lit mags and anthologies. BA in History, Idaho State U., 1969, MA in English, 1972. Asst. prof. Coll. So. Idaho, Twin Falls, 1977—; vice- chmn. Idaho Commn. on Arts, Boise, 1982-85. Mem. Intermountain Artists and Wrtrs.' Fedn. (pres. 1977). Home: Rt 4 Box 7464 Twin Falls ID 83301

STUDER, CONSTANCE ELAINE, (Connie), b. Lodi, OH, Dec. 4, 1942; d. Lucien Kellogg Adams and Evelyn Lois (Motter) Browne; m. Kenneth Eugene Studer, Aug. 17, 1963 (div. April, 1974); 1 son, Christopher Eugene. Contrbr. poems to anthologies and mags. BA, Illinois College, Jacksonville, 1971; MA, U. of CO, Boulder, 1980. Protocol ed., Boulder Community Hospital, 1983—; owner/wrtr./ed., Wing Communications, Boulder, 1983—. Mem. NWC, AMWA. Home: 4518 Aberdeen Place Boulder CO 80301

STUDER-JOHNSON, MARIAN KAYE, b. Mpls., Apr. 13, 1954; d. Stanley Eugene and Mary Therese (Willette) Studer; m. Boyd Lee Johnson, Apr. 24, 1982; 1 dau., Rachel Carmen. Contrbr. articles, editor: Mankato Free Press newspaper, 1981-84, Arabian Horse Times mag., 1984—. B.S. summa cum laude, Mankato State U., 1981. Assoc. ed. Arabian Horse Times, Waseca, Minn., 1984-85, mng. ed., 1985-86, ed., 1986—; self-employed horse trainer, breeder. Recipient Franklin Rogers award Mankato State U., 1980, faculty award, 1981. Mem. Quarter House Assn. (sec.-treas. region 2 1986), Phi Kappa Phi. Home: Blue Willow Farm Rt 3 Box 102 Janesville MN 56048

STUHLMAN, DANIEL D., b. St. Louis, Oct. 7, 1950; s. Fred F. and Beverly (Cohen) S. Author: Whole Wheat Bread Recipes, 1979, My Own Hanukah Story, 1980, "Teacher, My Stomach Hurts!", 1980, My Own Pesah Story, 1981; editor: Library of Congress Subject Headings for Judaica, 1982, 83, 2d. ed. 1986; also author computer programs: Print-File, Secret-File, Employment Agency System. BHL, Jewish Theol. Sem., NYC, 1973; BA, Columbia U., 1973, MSLS, 1974. Librarian, Hebrew Union Coll., Cin., 1974-76, Beth Hillel, Wilmette, Ill., 1976—; pres. BYLS Computer Cons., Chgo., 1984—, BYLS Press, 1978—. Mem. ALA, Turbo Users Group, Assn. Jewish Libraries. Home: 6247 N Francisco Chicago IL 60659

STUMP, GAIL ALDEN, b. Carlinville, IL, July 19, 1951; d. Charles Robert and Claribelle (Otwell) Miller; m. John Andrew Stump, Aug. 15, 1970; children: Edward Andrew, William Matthew. Author: poetry to anthologies, inclg. Hearts on Fire, 1986, Pauses in Time, 1986, Best New Poets of 1986. Student Ill. State Univ., 1969-70, Univ. of Ill., Champaign, 1987—. Bank teller, Sterling, Ill., 1970-73; secy., dir. personnel, Unit No. 5, Sterling, Ill., 1973-75; secy., bookkeeper, Smeltzer Insurance, Rock Falls, Ill., 1987—. Home: 24269 Hillcrest Dr Sterling IL 61081

STUMPO, CARMINE DE ROGATIS, (Alexander Damien Morrison), b. Belmar, NJ, Feb. 18, 1963; s. Carmine and Anna (DeRogatis) S. Contrbr. short stories to lit. mags. including Viewpoint, Just Spring. Wrkg. on short stories, novel. A.S. in English, Broward Commun. Coll., 1986. Asst. med. examiner Coll. of Boca Raton, FL, 1983-85; English tutor Broward Commun. Coll., Pompano, FL, 1985-86; free-lance wrtr., 1986—. Mem. Natl. St. Rod Assn., Antique Automobile Club Am., Jr. Acad. Sci. Recipient cert. of Appreciation, Dau. Am. Revolution, 1977, Merit award St. Elizabeth Schl., Pompano, 1977, medal, plaque Serra Club, 1978, Merit award Sun-Sentinel Newspaper, Ft. Lauderdale, FL, 1981, Paul Harris Fellowship Award, 1987. Home: 621 Kensington Pl Wilton Manors FL 33305

STUPPLE, DONNA-MARIE KATHLEEN, b. Chgo., Jan. 14, 1945; d. Thomas P. and Marie R. (Kozlowski) Boland; m. H. Bruce Stupple, Aug. 10, 1968. Columnist: Newsletter for the Assembly for Computers in English, Jan.-Mar. 1987. Contrbr. articles to English Jnl., Ill. English Bulltn. B.S. in Enlgish, Loyola U., 1966, M.A. in English, 1968. Tchr. public schls., Park Ridge, IL, 1968. Mem. NCTE, Ill. Assn. Tchrs. English, Jane Austen Soc. N.Am., Assn. Computers in English. Home: 1035 Park Ave Deerfield IL 60015

STURDIVANT, FREDERICK DAVID, b. Whitewright, TX, Oct. 17, 1937; s. Wyatt A. and Juanita P. (Phillips) Sturdivant; m. Patricia A. Robinson, Dec. 22, 1959 (div. 1981); children—Kaira, Lisha, Brian; 2nd m. Teresa A. Mobley, Feb. 3, 1982. Author: (with others) Competition and Human Behavior, 1968, The Ghetto Marketplace, 1969, Managerial Analysis in Marketing, 1970, Growth Through Service: The Story of American Hospital Supply Corporation, 1970, Perspectives in Marketing Management, 1971, (with O. Smalley) The Credit Merchants: A History of Speigel, Inc., 1973, (with A. Andreasen) Minorities and Marketing: Research Challenges, 1977, Business and Society: A Managerial Approach, 2nd ed., 1981, (with L. Robinson) The Corporate Social Challenge, 3d ed., 1985 BS, San Jose State Coll., 1959; MBA, U. Ore. 1960; PhD, Northwestern U., 1963. Asst. prof. U. So. CA., 1964-67; assoc. prof. U. TX at Austin, 1967-70, Harvard, 1970-72; M. Riklis prof. bus. and its environment Ohio State U. (Columbus), 1972—; Prin. Mgmt. Analysis Center, Inc. (Cambridge, MA), dir. Progressive Corp. (Cleveland), 1973-81, State Savs. (Columbus); Mem. Task Force on Mktg. and Low-Income Consumers, Natl. Mktg. Adv. Com., Dept. Commerce, 1967-70; cons. Office Calif. Atty. Gen., 1966, Sen Charles Percy, 1968; mem. adv. council on urban affairs to lt. gov., TX, 1969-70; dir. research Robert N. Shamansky of Ohio Congl. Campaign, 1980. Home: 3180 Lake Shore Dr Chicago IL 60606

STYLES, TERESA JO, b. Atlanta, Oct. 19, 1950; d. Julian English and Jennie Marine (Sims) S. Contrbr. article to The Chart mag. Wkrg. on mystery novel. B.A. in English, Spelman Coll., 1972; M.A. in Film, Northwestern U., 1973. Production asst. Sta. WETV, Atlanta, 1974-75; assoc. producer CBS News, NYC., 1975-85; instr. Savannah State Coll., GA, 1985—. Mem. Hist. Savannah Fdn., 1987—. Recipient cert. for Blacks in Am., Columbia DuPont, 1979, for The Defense of the U.S. Ground Zero, 1981; cert. for What Shall We Do about Mother, Emmy, 1980; cert. for Teddy, Columbia DuPont and Emmy, 1979. Mem. WG East. Home: 216 E Jones Savannah GA 31401

STYRON, WILLIAM, b. Newport News, VA, June 11, 1925; s. William Clark and Pauline Margaret (Abraham) Styron; m. Rose Burgunder, May 4, 1953; children—Susanna Margaret, Paola Clark, Thomas, Claire Alexandra. Author: (novels) Lie Down in Darkness, 1951, The Long March, 1953, Set This House on Fire, 1960, The Confessions of Nat Turner, 1967 (Pulitzer prize 1968, Howells medal Am. Acad. Arts and Letters 1970), Sophie's Choice, 1979 (Am. Book award 1980), In the Clap Shack, This Quiet Dust, 1982; editor: Best Stories from the Paris Rvw, 1959; adv. editor: Paris Rvw, 1953—; editorial bd.: The Am. Scholar, 1970-76. Student, Christchurch Schl., Davidson Coll.; AB, Duke U., 1947, Litt.D, 1968. Fellow Am. Acad. Arts and Letters at Am. Acad. in Rome, 1953; fellow Silliman Coll., Yale, 1964—; hon. jury pres. Cannes Film Festival, 1983, Conn. Arts award, 1984. Decorated Commandeur de l'Ordre des Arts et des Lettres, Commandeur, Legion d'Honneur (France). Mem. Am. Acad. Arts and Scis., Natl. Inst. Arts and Letters. Home: RFD Roxbury CT 06783

SUGAR, BERT RANDOLPH, b. Washington, June 7, 1937; s. Harold Randolph and Anne Edith (Rosenweig) Sugar; m. Suzanne Davis, Nov. 22, 1960; children—Jennifer Anne, John-Brooks Randolph. Author: Where Were You When the Lights Went Out?, 1965, Sting Like a Bee (with Jose Torres and Norman Mailer), 1971, Inside Boxing (with Floyd Patterson), 1974, The Sports Collectors Bible, 1975, 77, 79, The Assassination Chain (with Sybil Leek), 1976, The Horseplayer's Guide to Winning Systems, 1976, Who Was harry Steinfeldt: and Other Baseball Trivia Questions, 1976, The Life and Times of Harry Houdini (with The Amazing Randi), 1976, Classic Baseball Cards, 1977, The Thrill of Victory, 1977, The SEC, Hit the Sign and Win a Free Suit of Clothes from Harry Finklestein, 1978, The Book of Sports Quotes, 1978, Collectibles: The Nostalgia Collectors Bible, 1980, The Ring Record Book, 1980, 81, 82, 83, The Great Fights, 1981, Baseball Trivia, 1981, 100 Years of Boxing, 1983, The Good, The Bad and the Ugly, 1985, Baseball's 50 Greatest Games, 1986, others; contrbr. articles to newspapers and magazines inclg. NY Times, USA Today, Village Voice, Inside Sports. BS, U. MD, 1957; MBA, U. MI, 1959, LL.B, 1960, JD, 1960; PhD candidate, Am. U., 1961. Bar: D.C. 1961. Practiced in Washington, 1961; pub., editor Baseball Monthly, 1961-62; account exec. McCann-Erickson (NYC), 1964-65; account supr., vp Papert, Koenig, Lois, 1965-66; dir. mktg., vp D'Arcy, MacManus, Maisius (NYC), 1967-70; pres., pub., editor Champion Sports Pub. Co., 1970-73; editor-in-chief Argosy, Imported Car Performance mags. (NYC), 1973-76; sr. vp Baron, Costello & Fine Advt. (NYC), 1976-77; editor, pub. The Ring mag., Boxing Illustrated, Campaigns mag., 1979-83. Media award Media Scope, 1969, certificate of merit Intl. Adv. Assn., 1977, Red Smith award as outstanding writer Intl. Boxing Writers Assn.; founder Joe Lapchick award, 1972; cofounder Black Athletes Hall of Fame, 1972. Mem. Boxing Writers Assn., ASME, Am. Poli. Items Collectors Assn., Football Writers Assn., Basketball Writers Assn. Home: 6 Southview Rd Chappaqua NY 10514

SUITER, SHEARY SUE, b. Eugene, OR, Nov. 8, 1951; d. F. William and Mina A. (Sheary) Clough; m. Larry J. Suiter, Dec. 31, 1977; stepchildren—Derrick L., Stacie R. Author: (young adult novels) The Right Kind of Guy, 1985, Boy Crazy, 1986. Contrbr. to Real Food Places, 1981. Contrbg. ed.: Alaska Outdoors Mag., 1983-86. Wrkg. on adult novel. A.Sci., Lane Commun. Coll., 1975; student in English, U. Oreg., 1971-73, Oreg. State U., 1969-70. Owner, operator Sportfishing Lodge, Soldotna, AK, 1980—; dental hygienist, Anchorage, 1986—. Mem. NWC, AG. Home: Box 91989 Anchorage AK 99509

SULKIN, SIDNEY, b. Boston, Feb. 2, 1918; s. Frank Sam and Celia (Glazer) S.; m. Naomi Ann Levenson, Oct. 4, 1950; 1 child, Jonathan Leigh. Author: (novel) The Family Man, 1962; Complete Planning for College, 1962, rev., edit., 1968; (play) Gate of the Lions, 1980 (produced by Invisible Theatre, Tucson 1982); The Secret Seed, Stories and Poems, 1984; (play) The Other Side of Babylon, 1984 (produced by Source Theatre, Washington 1984); (play) No More to Prophesy, 1986 (produced by Independent Eye Theater, Lancaster, Pa., 1987); co-ed. For Your Freedom and Ours, 1943; co-translator: Matthew the Young King (Korczak), 1945; contrbr. stories, poems and articles to Harpers, Saturday, Kenyon, Sewanee, N.Am., Va. Quar., Lit., S.W., Mich. Quar., S.D., Cimarron rvws, Qtly Rvw Lit. (contemporary poet award 1980), New Republic, N.Y. Times, O. Henry Prize Stories, Best American Short Stories, others. Chief Washington bur. Voice of Am., 1949-53; editorial dir. Natl. Issues Com., Washington, 1953-55; asst. ed. Changing Times mag., Washington, 1955-62, sr. ed., 1962-71, mng. ed., 1971-75, ed., 1975-81. Mem. PEN (Washington liaison 1985—), AG, Dramatists Guild, PSA, Nat. Press Club, Writers Watch (pres. 1986—). Home: 5012 Elsmere Pl Bethesda MD 20814

SULLIVAN, GLADYS ANN, b. Moline, KS, July 22, 1931, d. Paul Joseph Sr. and Grace Mina (Fleming) Welch; m. Donald Eugene Sullivan, Dec. 2, 1950, children—John Lee, Jerald Dean, Donna Ruth Sullivan Cornish. Contrbr. to Catholic Digest, Songwrtrs. Expo., Am. Poetry Assn., NY Poetry Soc. Wrkg. on poetry, lyrics. Mem. Nat. Songwrtrs. Am. Office: Box 894 El Dorado KS 67042

SULLIVAN, JAMES EDWARD, b. Cohasset, MA, July 11, 1928; s. James J., Jr. and Louise (Hyland) S.; m. Frances Elizabeth Lynch, Aug. 11, 1963 (dec. Oct. 1976); children: Julia Marietta, John Franklin Joseph. Contrbr. poems to Commonweal, Worcester Rvw., Gob, America, Barre Gazette. AB, Boston Coll., 1948, MA, 1950. Librarian Woods Meml. Library, Barre, Mass., 1967—. Recipient award Worcester County Poetry Assn., 1972. Mem. P&W. Home: Sunrise Ave Box 451 Barre MA 01005

SULLIVAN, JANET WRIGHT, b. New Orleans, July 18, 1926, d. Bidwell Albert and Olive (Higdon) Wright; m. George Sullivan, Dec. 23, 1951 (dec. 1978); 1 son, Philip Wright. Contrbr. to Newport Rvw, Northeast Jnl, West Hills Rvw, Negative Capability, The New Paper, Michigan Qrly. Rvw. Wrkg. on novel, poetry collection, short story collection. AB, Barnard Coll., 1948; MA, Brown U., 1954; MFA, Warren Wilson Coll., 1982. Assoc. prof English, Community Coll. R.I., Warwick, 1968—. Yaddo fellow, Saratoga Springs, N.Y., 1983, 84; MacDowell Colony fellow, Peterborough, N.H., 1984, 1987. Home: 156 Congdon St Providence RI 02906

SULLIVAN, JANICE CALHOUN, b. Greenwood, SC, Aug. 3, 1953; d. Furman and Carrie Lee (Speach) Calhoun; m. Ronald Sullivan, May 3, 1975 (div. Oct. 1978); 1 dau., Felicia Rochelle. Contrbr. poems to anthols., children's article to mag. Grad. public schls. Ninety Six, SC. Recipient Honorable Mention, Nashville Newsletter, 1982; 5 Honorable Mentions, World of Poetry, 1986-87, Golden Poet award, 1986-87. Home: 107 Althea St Greenwood SC 29646

SULLIVAN, JOHN PATRICK, b. Liverpool, Eng., July 13, 1930 (came to U.S., 1961); s. Daniel and Alice (Long) Sullivan; m. Mary Frances Rock, July 20, 1954 (div. 1963); m. 2d, Judith Patrice Eldridge, Apr. 7, 1967 (div. Apr. 1972); m. 3d, Judith Lee Godfrey, Apr. 21, 1973. Author: Ezra Pound and Sextus Propertius: A Study in Creative Translation, 1964; Petronius: The Satyricon and the Fragments (trans.), 1965; The Satyricon of Petronius: A Literary Study, 1968, Propertius: A Critical Introduction, 1977; The Jaundiced Eye, poems, 1976; Petronius, The Satyricon and Seneca, The Apocolocyntosis (trans.), 1978; also various classical, philosophical and lit. articles; editor: Critical Essays on Roman Literature: Elegy and Lyric, 1962; Critical Essays on Roman Literature: Satire, 1963; Ezra Pound, 1970; Women in the Ancient World: The Arethusa Papers, 1984; Arethusa mag., 1972-75, Arion Mag., 1961-70; Epigrams of Martial Englished by Divers Hands 16c-20c, 1987. BA, St. John's College, Cambridge U. (Eng.), 1955, MA, 1957; MA, Oxford U. (Eng.), 1957. Jr. research fellow Queen's Coll., Oxford U., 1954; fellow, tutor classics Lincoln Coll., 1955-62, dean, 1960-61; vis. prof. U. TX, 1961-62, assoc. prof. classics, 1962-63, prof. classics, 1963-69, chair dept., 1963-65; sr. fellow. NEAH, 1967-68; prof. arts and letters SUNY (Buffalo), 1969-78, provost arts and letters, 1972-75; prof. classics U. CA at Santa Barbara, 1978—; vis. fellow Clare Hall, Cambridge U. (Eng.), 1975-76, Gray lectr., 1978; vis. prof. U. Hawaii, 1977; Martin lectr. Oberlin Coll., 1976; vis. fellow Wolfson Coll., Oxford U. (Eng.), 1981; Guggenheim Fellow, 1984. Served with Brit. Army, 1948-49. Address: 1020 Palermo Dr Santa Barbara CA 93105

SULLIVAN, LARRY MICHAEL, (memphis slim), b. Memphis, July 30, 1948, s. Morris Kelly and Dorothy (McKee) S.; m. Mary Jo Hulme, Mar. 22, 1968 (div. 1971); 1 son, Mark Alexander; m. 2d, Kathryn Sue Curry, July 1, 1984. Contrbr. poetry: Snatsu Tu, other publs. Wrkg. on short stories. BS, U. Tenn., 1970, MS, 1976. Polit. corr. Knoxville Libra, Havana, Cuba, 1971; news ed. Great Speckled Bird, Atlanta, 1976; disability adjudicator State of Ga., Atlanta, 1976-81; disability analyst, State of Calif., Los Angeles, 1981-83, trainer, 1983-86, unit mgr., 1986—; staff wrtr. Free Venice (Calif.) Beachhead, 1981—; presenter poetry readings. Office: Box 1132 Venice CA 90294

SULLIVAN, P(ATRICIA) LANCE, b. Austin, TX, Feb. 15, 1950; d. Frederick Lee and Betty Ellen (Leonard) Stead; m. John Edward Sullivan, Jan. 1, 1978. Ed.: Atlanta Profl. Women's Directory, 1982-83, Atlanta Occupational Medicine Newsletter, 1985, The Preferred Press, 1984-86, Pen-Graphs, 1986-87; contrbr. articles: Atlanta Mag., Accent on Living; columnist: Go Mag., Images in Fashion, Best in Store, The Village Wrtr. BA in English Lit., Calif. State U.-Northridge, 1978. Graphic artist Hughes Research Labs., Malibu, Calif., 1971-79; freelance wrtr., artist, designer, ed., 1979—. Mem. Nat. League Am. Pen Women in Communications, Sigma Delta Chi. Home: 3746 Wieuca Rd NE Atlanta GA 30342

SULLIVAN, SEAN MEI, see Sohl, Jerry

SULLIVAN, WALTER SEAGAR, b. NYC, Jan. 12, 1918; s. Walter Seager and Jeanet E. (Loomis) Sullivan; m. Mary E. Barrett, Aug. 17, 1950;

children—Elizabeth Anne, Catherine Ellinwood, Theodore Loomis. Author: Quest for a Continent, 1957, White Land of Adventure, 1957, Assault on the Unknown, 1961, We Are Not Alone, 1964 (Intl. Non-Fiction Book prize 1965), Continents in Motion, 1974, Black Holes, the Edge of Space, the End of Time, 1979, Landprints, 1984; editor: America's Race for the Moon, 1962. BA, Yale U., 1940, HLD, 1969; HLD, Neward Coll. Engring., 1973; DSc, Hofstra U., 1974, Ohio State U., 1977. Mem. staff NY Times, 1940—; fgn. corr. Far East, 1948-50, UN corr., 1951-52, fgn. corr., Germany, 1952-56, chief sci. writer, 1960-62, sci. news editor, 1962-63, sci. editor, 1964. Served to lt. comdr. USNR, 1940-46; PTO. Recipient George Polk Meml. award in journalism, 1959; Westinghouse-AAAS award, 1963, 68, 72; Am. Inst. Physics-U.S. Steel Fdn. award, 1969; Sci. in Soc. journalism award Natl. Assn. Sci. Writers, 1976; Disting. Pub. Svc. award, Natl. Sci. Fdn., 1978; Public Welfare Medal, Natl. Acad. Scis., 1980. Office: NY Times Times Sq New York NY 10036

SULLIVAN, WILLIAM JOSEPH, b. Balt., May 2, 1931; s. William Joseph and Mary Ann (Vulgaris) S. Contrbr. poems to Celebration, Md. English Jnl, A Sampling of Poems, Johns Hopkins Mag; articles to Md. Highlights, Am. Jnl Obstetrics and Gyn.; MA, Johns Hopkins U., 1973. Lab. tech. dept. medicine Johns Hopkins Univ., Balt., 1954-70, cons. dept. ob-gyn, 1963-70; go-game instr. Mayor's office, Balt., 1975-81; math. instr. Towson State Univ., Md., 1974-80; English instr. Essex Community Coll., Balt., 1974-75; founder Prospect Press, Balt., 1974—; poet-in-the-schls. Md. State Arts Council, Balt., 1975—. Co-founder and trustee, Vols. Opposing Leakin Park Expressway, Balt., 1971—; pres., The Windsor Hill Assn., 1967-68. Mem. Am. Go Assn., No. Am. Mycological Assn. Address: 2707 Lawina Rd Baltimore MD 21216

SULTAN, STANLEY, b. NYC, July 17, 1928; s. Jack and Bess (Leinwand) S.; m. Florence Lehman, June 16, 1948 (div. Nov. 18, 1963); children—James Lehman, Sonia Elizabeth Sultan-Kemple; m. 2d, Betty Ann Hillman, May 10, 1966. author: The Argument of Ulysses, 1965, 2d ed., 1987, Yeats at His Last, 1975, Ulysses, The Waste Land and Modernism, 1977, Rabbi: A Tale of the Waning Year, 1978, Eliot, Joyce and Company, 1987. Contrbr. short stories, chpts. to anthols., books. BA, Cornell U., 1949; PhD, Yale U., 1955. Asst. ed. Natl. Lexicographic Bd., NYC, 1951-55; instr. English, Smith Coll., Northampton, Mass., 1955-59; asst. prof. to prof. English, Clark U., Worcester, Mass., 1959—. Mem. NWU, AAUP, Malone Soc., Intl. Assn. Study of Anglo-Irish Lit., DSA, NAACP, ACLU. Home: 25 Hardwick St Boston MA 02135

SUMMERLIN, SAM, b. Chapel Hill, NC, Jan. 1, 1928; s. Irl Whitaker and Adolpha (Askew) Summerlin; m. Cynthia Clare Cyr, Apr. 10, 1952; children—Sandi Claire, Thomas Anthony. Author: (with William L. Ryan) The China Cloud, 1968, (with Bruce Henderson) 1:33 In Memoriam John F. Kennedy, 1968, Latin America: The Land of Revolution, 1972 (with Bruce Henderson) The Super Sleuths, 1976; producer: TV documentaries China: An Open Door, 1972, Oscar: The Story Behind the Statue, 1972, Olympics: The Eternal Torch, 1972, The World in 1974: History As We Lived It, 1975, The Torch of Champions (Winter and Summer Olympics), 1976, 80, Portraits of Power: Those Who Shaped the 20th Century, 1978, Filmmakers Salute Oscar, 1978, 79, 80, Olympic Champions series, 1980. BA, U. NC, 1948. State reporter AP, Raleigh, NC, 1949-51, fgn. corr., Tokyo, 1941-54, Korea, 1951-54, acting Chief bur., Manila, 1953, chief corr., Carribean, 1954-55, C. Am., 1954-55, Havana, 1954-55, chief of bur. Buenos Aires, 1955-63, New Orleans, 1963-65, Latin Am. editor, 1965-70, depy world news editor, NYC, 1970-75; asst. editor, asst. genl. mgr. NY Times News Service, 1975-79, genl. mgr., 1979—; vp NY Syndicatiob Sales Corp., 1978-79, exec. vp, 1979, pres., 1979—. Served to lt. (jg) USNR, 1949-63. Recipient Bronze Hugo Chgo. Intl. Film Festival, Maria Moors Cabot award Columbia U., 1975. Mem. Natl. Assn. TV Program Execs., ASJA. Home: 4 Bird Ln Rye NY 10580

SUMMERS, ANTHONY J., b. Corona, CA, Oct. 13, 1953; s. Homer J. and Margaret Rose (Wagner) S.; m. Christina Margaret Hamburger, July 5, 1980; children: Christian J., Eric Michael. Author: Emergence: Metamorphosis; contrbr. to mags and jnls: Titmouse Rvw, Vagabond, The Smith, Taurus, Samisdat, The Smudge, Plat Detroit, others; ed./pub. Image Mag, 1972—; pub. Cornerstone Press, 1974—. BA in English lit., U. Mo., 1976. Adminstr. Natl. Supermarkets, Inc., St. Louis, 1970—. Address: 1825 Bender Lane Arnold MO 63010

SUMMERS, HOLLIS, b. Eminence, KY, June 21, 1916; s. Hollis S. and Hazel (Holmes) Summers; m. Laura Clarke, June 30, 1943; children—Hollis III, David Clarke. Author: (novels) City Limit, 1948, Brighten the Corner, 1952, The Weather of February, 1957, The Day After Sunday, 1968, The Garden, 1972, (with James Rourke) Teach You A Lesson, 1955; (poetry) Walks Near Athens, 1959, Someone Else, 1962, Seven Occasions, 1965, The Peddler and Other Domestic Matters, 1967 (Ohioana Poetry award 1968), Sit Opposite Each Other, 1970, Start from Home, 1972, Occupant Please Forward, 1976, Dinosaurs, 1977, After the Twelve Days, 1987; (short stories) How They Chose the Dead, 1973, Standing Room, 1984; editor: Kentucky Story, 1954, (with Edgar Whan) Literature: An Introduction, 1960, Discussions of the Short Story, 1963. AB, Georgetown Coll., 1937, Litt. D, 1965; MA, Middlebury Coll., 1943; PhD, State U. Iowa, 1949. Tchr. Georgetown Coll., 1944-49, U. KY, 1940-59, Ohio U., 1959—; Staff Writers Conf., Bread Loaf, VT, Antioch, Ohio, Morehead, KY, Grinnell, Iowa, others; lectr. arts program Assn. Am. Colls., 1958-63; Danforth lectr., 1963-66, 71; Fulbright lectr. U. Canterbury, Christchurch, NZ, 1978; mem. Ohio Council for Humanities. Recipient Poetry award Sat. Rvw, 1959, Ohio Arts Council award, 1976, NEA grantee. Nancy Dasher Award for best book by Eng. prof. in Ohio higher edn., 1986; Helen Krout Meml. award for outstanding poet in Ohio, 1987. Home: 181 N Congress St Athens OH 45701

SUMMERS, ROBERT SAMUEL, b. Halfway, OR, Sept. 19, 1933; s. Orson William and Estella Belle (Robertson) Summers; m. Dorothy Millicent Kopp, June 14, 1955; children—Brent, William, Thomas, Elizabeth, Robert. Author: (with Howard) Law, Its Nature, Functions and Limits, 1972, (with Hubbard and Campbell) Justice and Order Through Law, 1973, (with Bozzone and Campbell) The American Legal System, 1973, (with Speidel and White) Teaching Materials on Commercial Transactions, 1974, Collective Bargaining and the Public Benefit Conferral—A Jurisprudential Critique, 1976, (with White) The Uniform Commercial Code, 1980, (with Speidel and White) Teaching Materials on Commercial and Consumer Law, 1981, Het Pramatisch Instrumentalisme, 1981, Instrumentalism and American Legal Theory, 1982, Lon L. Fuller—Life and Work, 1984; editor: Essays in Legal Philosophy, vol. 1, 1968, vol. 2, 1971. BS in Poli. Sci., U. OR, 1955; postgrad. (Fulbright scholar), U. Southampton, Eng., 1955-56; LLB, Harvard U., 1959; postgrad. research, Oxford (Eng.) U., 1964-65, 74-75. Bar: OR, 1959, NY, 1974. Assoc. King, Miller, Anderson, Nash and Yerke (Portland, OR), 1959-60; asst. prof. law U. OR, 1960-63, assoc. prof., 1964-68; vis. assoc. prof. law Stanford U., 1963-64; prof. U. OR, 1968-69, Cornell U., 1969-76, McRoberts prof. law, 1976—; summer vis. prof. IN U., 1969, U. MI, 1974, U. Warwich (Eng.), 1975, U. Miami (FL), 1976-78, Australia Natl. U., U. sydney (Australia), 1977; research fellow Merton Coll., Oxford U., 1981-82; cons. Cornell Law Project in public schls. (NY), 1969-74, Law in Am. Soc. project Chgo. Bd. Edn., 1968-69; instr. natl. Acad. Jud. Edn., 1976—. Office: Cornell Law Schl Ithaca NY 14853

SUMMERSELL, CHARLES GRAYSON, b. Mobile, AL, Feb. 25, 1908; s. Charles Fishweek and Sallie Rebecca (Grayson) Summersell; m. Frances Sharpley, Nov. 10, 1934. Author: Historical Foundations of Mobile, 1949, Mobile: History of a Seaport Town, 1949, Alabama History for Schools, 1957, rev. ed., 1961, 70, 75, 82, 85, Alabama Past and Future, (with Howard W. Odum and G.H. Yeuell), 1941, rev. ed. (with G.H. Yeuell and W.R. Higgs), 1950, (with Frances C. Roberts) Exploring Alabama, 1957, rev. ed., 1961, The Cruise of CSS Sumter, 1965, (with Frances S. Summersell) Alabama History Filmstrips, 1961, (with Rembert Patrick and Frances S. Summersell) Florida History Filmstrips, (with W.T. Chambers and Frances S. Summersell) Texas History Filmstrips, 1965, The Cruise of CSS Sumter, 1965, (with Jerome Hausman and Frances Summersell) Ohio History Filmstrips, 1966, (with Andrew Rolle and Frances S. Summersell) California History Filmstrips, 1967, (with Robert Sutton and Frances S. Summersell) Illinois History Filmstrips, 1971; CSS Alabama Builder, Captain and Plans, 1985; editor: The Journal of George Townley Fullam, Boarding Officer of the Confederate Sea Raider Alabama, 1973; editor, author introduction: Colonial Mobile, 1975; editorial adv. bd.: American Neptune, 1946-83; editorial bd.: The AL Rvw., 1964-71; contbr. articles and rvws, to encys. and profl. jnls. AB, U. AL, 1929, AM, 1930; PhD, Vanderbilt U., 1940. Instr. history, 1947—; head dept. history, 1954-71; radio commentator (Tuscaloosa and Selma, AL), 1941-43. Served from lt. (j.g.) to lt. comdr. USNR, 1942-46; PTO comdr., 1954; officer charge Naval Intelligence Sch., 1951-53. Address: 1411 Caplewood Dr Tuscaloosa AL 35401

SUMMERVILLE, JAMES, b. Nashville, Oct. 27, 1947. Author: Educating Black Doctors: A History of Meharry Medical College,1983. Contrbr. story to Homewords: A Book of Tennessee Writers. BA, Univ. of Tenn., 1969; MA English, U. Ia., 1972; MA in History, Vanderbilt U., 1983. Asst. to vice-chancellor Vanderbilt U., Nashville, 1977-81; asst. ed. History News, Am. Assn. for State & Local History, Nashville, 1984—; cons., 1981-84. Dir. Hillsboro-West End Neighborhood Assn., Nashville, 1981—. Mem. Tenn. Hist. Soc. (Moore Meml. award 1975). Home: 2911 Woodlawn Dr Nashville TN 37215

SUMNER, STEPHEN I., b. Bronx, NY, July 19, 1941, s. Charles and Mollie (Kaufman) S.; m. Ellen Sumner, Apr. 22, 1967; children—Charles, Randi. Contrbr. to Logo & Ednl. Computing Jnl, Sanny Jnl. BA, Brandeis U., 1963; EdD, Columbia U., 1974. Sr. ed. Krell Software Co., St. James, N.Y., 1982—; ed. Logo and Ednl. Computing Jnl., Stony Brook, 1983—. Home: 205 Carol Ave Pelham NY 10803

SUNDBERG, NORMA JEAN, b. Thompson, OH, Feb. 21, 1933; d. Burton Roger and Helen (Stearns) Rohrbaugh; m. Albert Russell Sundberg, Apr. 15, 1952; children—Michelle, Paul, Sally, Wesley, Glen, Russell, Roger, Amy, Mark, Janet. Columnist: Jefferson Gazette, OH, 1984, Free Enterprise, Chardon, OH, 1980—. Contrbr. nonfiction poems to mags., newspapers, anthols. including Hoard's Dairyman, Christian Science Monitor, Farm Wife News, others. Ed.: Tower Bell newsletter, Jefferson, OH, 1974-84. Wrkg. on booklet of poems. A.A. in Genl. Studies, Kent State U., Ashtabula, OH, 1980. Freelance wrtr., 1952—; part-time instr. Kent State U., Ashtabula, OH, 1980—. Recipient Kaleidoscope award Kent State U. English Dept., 1978. Mem. Wrtrs. Western Reserve. Home: 1740 Mechanicsville Rd Rock Creek OH 44084

SUNG, YUAN-MING, (Syming) b. Sun City, Honan, China, Dec. 14, 1930, came to U.S., 1968, s. Tsi-Chean Sung and Shiao-Yong Young; m. Kay Sung, May 26, 1975. Author: The Civilization of a Desolate Island, 1955, Son of Star, 1956 (in Chinese); author: New BASIC in Systematic and Advanced Business Programming (in English), 1982. BA, Tamkong Coll., Taiwan. Ed. New Life Daily News, Taipei, Taiwan, 1958-68, China Times, N.Y.C., 1968-72; pres. Sym's Pub. Corp., NYC, 1982—. Home: 20 Confucius Plaza Apt 38K New York NY 10002

SUPLEE, CAROL JANET CUNNINGHAM, b. Cleve., Dec. 27, 1934, d. Lyman Emory and Evelyn Zelle (Smith) Cunningham; m. James R. Suplee, June 27, 1953; children—Karen April, James R., Jr., Debra Gail. Ed.: New Jersey's Aviation History (by H.V. Reilly). Wrkg. on history, biography, poetry. Columnist Levittown Life, Willingboro, N.J., 1964-66; wrtr., ed. Willingboro News Press, 1967-68; reporter, ed. Burlington County Herald, Mount Holly, N.J., 1968-72; reporter, feature wrtr. Burlington County Times, Willingboro, 1972-77, editorial page ed., 1977—. Recipient awards journalistic orgns. Mem. Nat. Conf. Editorial Wrtrs., Soc. Profl. Journalists, Women in Communications (chair freedom of info. com., Phila. chap. 1980-81). Home: 908 Cedar St Riverton NJ 08077

SURNAMER, SHULAMITH, see Caplan, Judith Shulamith Langer

SUSIE, see Rohrer, Lila Borg

SUSSKIND, HARRIET, b. Bklyn; d. Haskell and Gertrude (Citrin) Susskind; m. Dr. Robert E. Rosenblum, Oct. 11, 1953; children—Melinda, Mark, Andrea. Author: Of Grownups and Groupies, A Slow Way to Voices, This Heat, In a Different House; poetry and fiction in Connecticut Qtly, Hawaii Rvw, Georgia Rvw, Parnassus, MSS, other lit mags. AB, Hunter College; MA, Ohio State U. Instr., U. of Rochester, NY, 1957-63; prof., Monroe Community College, Rochester, NY, 1964—; reviewer, Gannett News Services, Rochester, NY, 1976-83; poet-in-res., SUC, Brockport, 1982-83. Awards: NEH Fellowship, 1980; Hackney Lit. Award, U. of Alabama, 1984. Mem. MLA. Home: 670 Mendon Rd Pittsford NY 14534

SUSSLER, BETSY RUTH, b. Hartford, CT, Feb. 5, 1952; d. Frank Sussler and Rita Louise (Lentz) Freedman. Pub., editor Bomb mag., a quar. on new art, literature, theatre and film. Student Newcomb Coll., 1968-70; BFA, San Francisco Art Inst., 1973. Vice-pres. Ctr. for New Art, NYC, 1981-85; pres. New Art Publs., NYC, 1986—. Office: New Art 177 Franklin St New York NY 10013

SUSSMAN, M. HAL, see Hallsten McGarry, Susan Joan

SUSSMAN, OCIE JONES, b. Opelika, AL, June 5, 1935; d. Isaac and Katie (Chislom)n Jones; m. Stephen Sussman, Aug. 16, 1963. Editor: Dimensions Jnl, 1976. BS, Bank St. Coll. Edn., NYC, 1970; PhD, Forham U., 1976. Tchr. Bklyn. publ schls., 1964-69; asst. dean labor coll. Cornell U., NYC, 1969-70; asst. prof. Bklyn. Coll., 1970-76; instr. lang. arts Ethical Culture Schl., NYC, 1976-85; prof. Burlington County Coll., Pemberton, N.J., 1985—. Recipient award Natl. Sci. Found., 1968, Ford Fdn., 1975, 76. Home: Shady Oaks Bldg 1 W Hampton St Pemberton NJ 08068

SUSSMAN, SUSAN, b. Chgo.; d. Emanuel and Edie (Levitt) Rissman; m. Barry Sussman, Sept. 21, 1963; children—Sy, Aaron, Rachael. Author: Hippo Thunder, 1982, There's No Such Thing as a Chanukkah Bush, 1984, Casey the Nomad, 1985, Don't Say Goodbye, 1985, Sweet Talk, 1985, Night After Night, 1986, Just Friends, 1986, Lies (People Believe) about Animals, 1987, One for You—One for Me, 1988, Hanukkah: Eight Lights Around the World, 1988, The Dieter, 1988; (children's musical) Let's Go for the Record (grant Hewlett/Packard Corp., 1986), 1986; columnist: Raquetball Everyone, 1981-82. Contrbr. articles, humor pieces, features to newspapers, mags. Contributing ed., My Own Magazine, Genl. Learning Corp, B.A., U. Ill., champaign, 1963. Mem. SCBW, Off-Campus Wrtrs. Workshop, Ill. Arts Alliance, CRRT, SMA. Office: Arts Center 927 Noyes Evanston IL 60201

SUTHERLAND, RAYMOND CARTER, b. Horse Cave, KY, Nov. 5, 1917; s. Raymond Carter and Nellie Ruth (Veluzat) Sutherland. Author: Medieval English Conceptions of Hell as Derived from Biblical, Patristic, and native Germanic Sources, 1953, The Religious Background of Swift's Tale of a Tub, 1958, The Mechanics of Versification, 1963. AB, U. KY, 1939, MA, 1959, PhD, 1953; Licentiate, Genl. Theol. Sem., NYC, 1942; postgrad., St. John's Theol. Sem., Camarillo, CA, 1948, Genl. Theol. Sem., NYC, 1979. Ordained priest Episcopal Ch., 1942; curate St. Luke's Ch. (Anchorage, Louisville), 1942-44; prof. English U. TN (Knoxville), 1953-57; mem. faculty GA State U. (Atlanta), 1957—, prof. English, 1965—, dir. English grad. studies, 1978—; lectr. Oriental ceramics. Served as chaplain AUS, 1944-47. Mem. MLA. Office: Dept Eng GA State U Atlanta GA 30303

SUTHERLAND, ROBERT D, b. Blytheville, AR, Nov. 4, 1937, s. Donald Charles and Opal Gladys (Gillispie) S.; m. Marilyn Fern Neufeldt, July 25, 1959; children—David Scott, Allan Philip. Author: Language and Lewis Carroll, 1970, Sticklewort and Feverfew (novel), 1980; ed.: On the Battlefield: Cairo, Illinois, 1970, The Horse We Lie Down In, Eight Poems (by Frannie Lindsay), 1980, Funeral, A Play (by Richard Dokey), 1982; contrbr. poems: This Awkward Mud, 1984, Light Year '87, 1986; ed.: Pikestaff Forum, 1977—, Pikestaff Rvw, 1979-82; contrbr. essays, articles, book rvws: College English, Children's Literature in Education, The Post-Amerikan, other lit. publs. Wrkg. on novel, short stories, poems. BA in English, Wichita State U., 1959; MA, PhD in English, U. Iowa, 1964. Prof. English, Ill. State U., Normal, 1964—. Recipient Juvenile Book Merit award for writing, illustrating Sticklewort and Feverfew, Friends of Am. Wrtrs., 1981. Mem. NCTE, Ill. Wrtrs., Linguistic Soc. Am. Office: Box 127 Normal IL 61761

SUTHERLAND, WILLIAM OWEN SHEPPARD, b. Wilmington, NC, Jan. 19, 1921; s. William Owen Sheppard and Mary Owen (Green) Sutherland; m. Madeline Ethel Cooley, Sept. 12, 1947; children—Madeline, William, John, Thomas. Author: Art of the Satirist, 1965; co-editor: The Reader, 1960, Six Contemporary Novels, 1961; An Index to 18th Century Periodicals, 1900, 1956. AB in English with honors, U. NC, 1942, MS, 1947, PhD, 1950. Instr. English U. NC (Chapel Hill), 1950-51; instr. Northwestern U. (Chicago), 1951-54; asst. prof. U. TX (Austin), 1954-58, assoc. prof., 1958-65, prof., 1965—, chair dept., 1983—, faculty humanist rep. Deans of Humanities of Southwest Conf., 1980; cons. Ednl. Testing Service and Coll. Bd., Princeton, NJ, 1965-72, NEH, Washington, 1978—. Mem. MLA, South Central MLA, AAUP, NCTE. Home: 3610 Highland View Austin TX 78731

SUTTON, DOROTHY MOSELEY, b. Todd County, KY, Oct. 11, 1938; d. John Preston and Mary (Swope) Moseley; m. William Sutton, Sept. 2, 1961; children—Mary Elizabeth, Dorothy Cassandra. Contrbr. poems, short stories to lit. mags, articles to profl. pubs. BA, Georgetown Coll., Ky., 1960; MA, U. Miss.-Oxford, 1963; PhD, U. Ky.-Lexington, 1981. Instr. Eastern Ky. U., Richmond, 1973-79, asst. prof., 1980-83, assoc. prof., 1984—, dir. vis. wrtrs. program, wrtg. conf. staff. Named Outstanding Young Woman of Am., Washington, 1974, chosen by James Dickey to study with him at Atlantic Ctr. for the Arts, 1981, attended Bread Loaf on Bingham Wrtg. Grant, 1987. Mem. Ky. Poetry Soc. (3 Poetry awards 1980-86; bd. dirs.), Ky. Philo. Assn., MLA. Home: 115 Southland Dr Richmond KY 40475

SUTTON, HENRY, see Slavitt, David Rytman

SVEHLA, JOHN JOHN, b. North Platte, NB; s. Anton and Gladis (Granger) S.; m. Sharon Lynn Rubenstein, Nov. 12, 1976. Author poems: Sun, 1975. Contrbr. numerous poems to anthols., lit. mags. Wrkg. on new idiom in nature poetry. Recipient 2d prize Calif. Fedn. of Chaparral Poets, 1977; 2d Honorable Mention, Penn. Poetry Soc., 1977, 3rd Honorable Mention, 1981; Finalist award Negative Capability, 1986; Honorable Mention, Am. Poetry Assn., 1986. Mem. Fla. State Poetry Assn. Home: 4391 Sunset Blvd 371 Hollywood CA 90029

SWAIM, ALICE MACKENZIE, b. June 5, 1911, Craigdam, Aberdeenshire, Scotland; d. Donald Campbell and Alice Annand (Murray) Mackenzie; m. William Thomas Swaim Dec. 27, 1932; children—Elizabeth Anne, Kathleen Mckenzie. Author: Let the Deep Song Rise, 1952, Up to the Stars, 1954, Sunshine in a Thimble, 1958, Crickets Are Crying Autumn, 1960, The Gentle Dragon, 1962, Pennsylvania Profile, 1966, Here, on the Threshold, 1966, Scented Honeysuckle Days, 1966, Beneath a Dancing Star, 1968, Beyond My Catnip Garden, 1970, Unicorn and Thistle, 1981, And Miles to Go, 1981, Children in Summer, 1983; also brochures, articles, bk reviews. Critic, Natl. Writers Club, 1953-55; col.,

Cornucopia, 1953-55; col., Carlisle, Pa., Evening Sentinel, 1956-70; 1st vp Am. Poetry Lg., 1964-70; consultant, Assoc. for Poetry Therapy, 1970-74, natl. contest judge, 1963-85; mktg. ed., Poetry Soc. of NH, 1974-85. Included in Borestone Mt. 100 best poems of Eng.-spkg. world, 1960; Am. Heritage Award, 1974. Mem. PSA, Am. Poetry Lg, Texas; Poetry Soc. of New Hampshire. Home: 322 N 2nd St Apt 1606 Harrisburg PA 17101

SWAN, FRANCES ADELE (FRANCES MUELLER SWAN), b. Ferguson, MO, Apr. 9, 1919; d. Robert John and Selma Helen (Sachse) Mueller; m. Donald Stewart Swan, May 2, 1959. Author: Through the Valley, 1978, Once Upon a Rhyme (book of poetry), 1984; freelance writer poems, short stories, articles, plays, scripts for children's mags. Student Sanford-Brown Bus. Coll., St. Louis County. Office worker with several cos., St. Louis, 1940-63. Home: 11533 Old St Charles Rd Bridgeton MO 63044

SWAN, GLADYS, b. NYC, Oct. 15, 1934; d. Robert J. and Sarah (Taub) Rubenstein; m. Richard Borders Swan, Sept. 9, 1955; children—Andrea, Leah. Author: On the Edge of the Desert, 1979, Carnival for the Gods, 1986, Of Memory and Desire, 1988. Contrbr. short stories to lit. mags., anthols. BA, Western N.Mex. U., 1954; MA, Claremont Grad. Sch., 1955. Prof. Franklin Coll., Ind., 1969-86; Disting. vis. wrtr. U. Tex., El Paso, 1984-85, Ohio Univ., 1986-87; faculty Vermont Coll., Montpelier, 1981—; assoc. prof. U. of Mo. Columbia, 1987—. Fellow, Lilly Endowment, 1975-76, Fulbright, Yugoslavia, 1988. Mem. AWP. Home: 2601 Lynnwood Dr Columbia MO 65203

SWANBERG, INGRID, b. Ross, CA, Sept. 4, 1947. Author: Flashlights (poetry chapbook), 1980, Letter to Persephone & Other Poems, 1984, The Little Door of Winter (poetry), 1986; contrbr. to Grand Ronde Rvw, Lips, Smokesignals, Northeast, other publs.; ed., pub. Ghost Pony Press, 1980—; ed.-in-chief Abraxas mag., 1981—. MA in English, Calif. State U., Sacramento, 1972; postgrad., U. Wis.-Madison, 1973-75. Recipient Award-Wis., Rhiannon Press, 1984. Mem. COSMEP, CCLM. Home: 2518 Gregory St Madison WI 53711

SWANDER, MARY LYNCH, b. Carroll, IA, Nov. 5, 1950; d. John Chester and Rita Marie (Lynch) Swander. Works: Needlepoint, 1977, Succession, 1979, Lost Lake, 1986, Driving the Body Back, 1986; contrbr. poetry to The Nation, Pequod, others. BA, U. Iowa, 1973, MFA, 1976. Wrtr.-in-res. Interlochen (MI) Arts Acad., 1982; asst. prof. Lake Forest (IL) Coll., 1976-79, asst. prof. Iowa State U., 1986—. Ingram-Merrill Award, 1980, Carl Sandburg Literary Award, Chgo. Public Library, 1982, Natl. Endowment for the Arts Award, 19897. Mem. PSA, AWP. Home: 931 Carroll Ave. Ames IA 50010

SWANGER, DAVID, b. Newark, Aug. 1, 1940; s. Saul and Pearl (Ginevsky) S.; m. Lynn Lundstrom, Apr. 5, 1969; children—Ana Lauren, Elissa Molly, Max Daniel. Author: The Poem as Process, 1974, Lemming Song, 1976, The Shape of Waters, 1978, Inside the Horse, 1981. Contrbr. poems to lit. mags. BA, Swarthmore, 1963; MA in Tchg., Harvard U., 1964, EdD, 1970. Prof. edn. and creative writing U. Calif., Santa Cruz, 1971—. Woodrow Wilson fellow, 1970; grantee Calif. Arts Council, 1978, NEA, 1979. Mem. Am. Assn. Aesthetics. Home: 1959 Pine Flat Rd Santa Cruz CA 95060

SWANN, BRIAN, b. Northumberland, Eng., Aug. 13, 1940, came to U.S., 1963; m. Roberta Swann. Author: (poetry) The Whale's Scars, 1975, Roots, 1976, Living Time, 1978, The Four Seasons, 1980, The Middle of the Journey, 1982, (fiction) The Runner, 1980, Elizabeth, 1981, Unreal Estate, 1981, Another Story, 1984, The Plot of the Mice, 1986, (juvenile) The Fox and the Buffalo, 1983, Water Became Bone, 1983; translator: The Collected Poems of Lucio Piccolo (with Ruth Feldman), 1972, Selected Poetry of Andrea Zanzotto (with Feldman), 1976, Shema: Collected Poems of Primo Levi (with Feldman), 1975, The Day Is Always New: Selected Poems of Rocco Scotellaro (with Feldman), 1980, The Dry Air of the Fire: Selected Poems of Bartolo Cattafi (with Feldman), 1981, Selected Poems of Tudor Arghezi (with Michael Impey), 1976, Primele Poeme/First Poems of Tristan Tzara (with Impey), 1975, Euripides' Phoenissae (with Peter Burian), 1981, The Moon of the Bourbons: Selected Poems of Vittorio Bodini (with Feldman), 1980, On the Nomad Sea: Selected Poems of Milih Cevdet Anday (with Talat Halman), 1980, Song of the Sky: Versions of Native American Poetry, 1985; ed.: Currents and Trends: Italian Poetry Today (with Feldman), 1979, Smoothing the Ground: Essays on Native American Oral Literature, 1983, I Tell You Now: Autobiographical Essays by Native American Writers (with Arnold Krupat), 1987, Recovering the Word: Essays on Native American Literature (with Krupat), 1987; contrbr. poetry, fiction to Paris Rvw, Antaeus, Salmagundi, New Yorker, other anthologies and jnls. BA, Cambridge (Eng.) U., 1962, MA, 1965; PhD, Princeton U., 1970. Mem. faculty Cooper Union, NYC1972—, prof. humanities and social sci., 1978—; assoc. ed. Chelsea; poetry ed. Amicus. Recipient John Florio Prize, 1977; grantee Creative Artists in Public Service, 1981, NEA fellow, 1979. Office: Cooper Union Cooper Street New York NY 10003

SWANN, LOIS, b. NYC, Nov. 17, 1944; d. Peter and Edith Marie (De Rose) Riso; div. 1979; children: Peter Burgess, Polly Lorraine. Author: The Mists of Manittoo, 1976; Torn Covenants, 1981; papers archived at Mugar Meml. Library, Boston U. Ed. The True Wayfaring Christian: Studies in Milton's Puritanism, 1987. BA, Marquette U., 1966. Ed. Peat, Marwick, Mitchell & Co., N.Y.C., 1980-81; publs. cons. Mfrs. Hanover Trust Co., N.Y.C., 1981—. Mem. AG, P&W. Home: 1 Midland Gardens Bronxville NY 10708

SWANN, ROBERTA, b. NYC, June 17, 1947, d. Louis and Eve Cheroff; m. Brian Swann, Feb. 15, 1980; children—Derek, Nicole. Author: Private parts, 1978, Women the Cildren the Men, 1979, Voices of the Third Age, 1986; contrbr. poetry, fiction to Chelsea, Poetry Now, Ploughshares, Anthology of Mag. Verse and Yearbook of Poetry, 1979, 80, 81, numerous other lit. mags. and anthols. Tchr. creative writing Cooper Union, New Schl., NYC; program dir. Great Hall, Cooper Union, Am. Jazz Orchestra. Home: 19 Stuyvesant Oval New York NY 10009

SWANSON, ELEANORA, (Veritas), b. NYC, Apr. 29, 1916; d. Reuben and Ida (Primoff) Dorfman; m. Dia el-chatti, Oct. 18, 1945 (div. 1965); children: Dawn, Aida, Omar; m. 2d, Rollan Swanson, Sept. 13, 1965. Author: Three Soldiers of Japan, 1980; edited: History of Japan (by Hugh Bonton), 1943. Student, Columbia U., 1942, Geo. Washington U., 1942, AB in Econ., 1960; Georgetown U. Foreign Svc. Schl., 1943, 1962. Writer, OWI, Washington, 1942-44; OPA, 1944-45; for Arabic newspapers, Damascus, Syria, 1949-56; editor, Public Health Reports, Washington, 1956-60; assoc. ed., Children, Washington, 1960-64; freelance wrtr., 1974—; asst. ed., Airfair, Los Angeles, 1977; faculty member, Village Ctr. of the Arts, Palm Springs, Calif., 1985—. Fellow, ACLS; mem. Village Center for the Arts, Palm Springs. Home: Box 784 Freeport NY 11520

SWANSON, GLADYS IRENE, b. Mpls., Feb. 22, 1922, 1922; d. Charle Edward and Mary Julia (Altman) Young; m. Carroll Alvin Swanson, Mar. 15, 1941 (div. May 15, 1954); children—Kalvin Carroll, Caryl Robert, Cinda Marie Swanson Mack. Contrbr. poems to anthols. Ed.: Line from Nine, 1976-84. Wrkg. on poetry, children's stories. Diploma, Mpls. Bus. Coll., 1956. Sec., Public Works, Mpls., 1956—. Home: 4431 Wentworth Ave S Minneapolis MN 55409

SWANSON, LAURENCE ALBERT, b. Monmouth, IL, June 29, 1941; s. Ronald Louis and Jeanne B.(McIntyre) S.; m. Patricia Pickens, Mar. 11, 1964. Editor, contrbr.: Turning Wheels mag., 1972—. B.Music, Boston U., 1963; MS in Edn., Western Ill. U., 1967; JD magna cum laude, Northern Ill. U., 1985. Dir. band pub. schl. dists., Colchester and Sciota, Ill., 1967-70; yardmaster and operator Burlington Northern RR, Aurora, Ill., 1970-82; sole practice law, Aurora, 1986—. Mem. ABA, Ill., Kane County bar assns. Home: Box 1040 Oswego IL 60543

SWANSON, ROY ARTHUR, b. St. Paul, Apr. 7, 1925; s. Roy Benjamin and Gertrude (Larson) Swanson; m. Vivian May Vitous, Mar. 30, 1946; children—Lynn Marie (Mrs. Gerald A. Snider), Robin Lillian, Robert Roy, Dyack Tyler, Dana Miriam. Author: Odi et Amo: The Complete Poetry of Catullus, 1959, Heart of Reason: Introductory Essays in Modern World Humanities, 1963, Pindar's Odes, 1974, Greek and Latin Word Elements, 1981; editor: Minn. Rvw, 1963-67, Classical Jnl, 1968-73; contrbr. articles to profl. jnls. Bd. dirs. Lutheran Studies, Inc. BA, U. Minn., 1948, BS, 1949, MA, 1951; PhD, U. Ill., 1954. Prin. Maplewood Elementary Schl. (St. Paul), 1949-51; instr. U. Ill., 1952-53, Inc. U., 1954-57; asst. prof. U. Minn. (Mpls.), 1957-61, assoc. prof., 1961-64, acting chair classics, 1963-64, prof. classics, chair comparative lit., 1964-65; prof. English Macalester Coll. (St. Paul), 1965-67; coordinator humanities program, 1966-67; prof. comparative lit. and classics U. Wis. at Milw., 1967-86, chair classics, 1967-70, chair comparative lit., 1970-73, 76-83, coordinator Scandinavian studies program, 1982—. Served with AUS, 1944-46. Recipient Disting. Teaching award U. Minn., 1962, U. Wis. at Milw., 1974. Mem. Am. Philol. Assn., Am. Comparative Lit. Assn., MLA, Soc. for Advancement Scandinavian Study. Home: 11618 N Bobolink Ln Mequon WI 53092

SWANSON, STEPHEN OLNEY, b. Mpls., Aug. 31, 1932; s. Carl R. and Dorothy B. (Olney) S.; m. Judith G. Seleen, June 10, 1957; children—Scott, Shelley, Noel, Kim, Brian. Author: What Does God Want Me to Do with My Life?, 1979, The Double Cross, 1980, For Every Body, 1981, Bible Readings for Men, 1984, Biblical Pictures of Bread, 1984, Brad Benson and the Secret Weapon, 1984, The Triumph, 1984, Faith Prints, 1985, When You Graduate, 1985, Biblical Pictures of Water, 1986, It Takes Two, 1987; The Life of Christ, 1987. Contrbr. poems to lit. mags. BA, St. Olaf Coll., 1950; Graduate in Theol., Luther Theol. Sem., 1958, BD, 1960; MA, U. Oregon, 1964,DArts, 1970. Asst. prof. English,

Tex. Luth. Coll., Seguin, 1966-70, Camrose Luth. Coll., Alta, Can., 1970-73; assoc. prof. English,St. Olaf Coll., Northfield, Minn., 1974—. Mem. P&W, Hymn Soc. Am., Minn. Christian WG. Home: 910 Saint Olaf Ave Northfield MN 55057

SWARD, ROBERT S., b. Chgo., June 23, 1933, s. Dr. Irving Michael and Gertrude (Huebsch) S.; m. Judith Essenson, Mar. 21, 1969 (div. 1972); children—Cheryl, Barbara, Michael, Hannah, Nicholas. Author: Advertisements (poetry), 1958, Uncle Dog & Other Poems, 1962, Kissing the Dancer (poetry), 1964, Thousand- Year-Old Fiancee (poetry), 1965, The Jurassic Shales (novel), 1975, The Iowa Poems, 1975, Six Poems, 1980, Poems: New & Selected (1957-1983): Half-A-Life's History, 1983, The Toronto Islands, 1983, The Three Roberts (with Robert Priest and Robert Zend) "On Love," 1984, Poet Santa Cruz, 1985; ed. Vancouver Island Poems, 1973, Cheers for Muktananda, 1976, CV-II (with Penny Kemp), 1981; contrbr. Penguin Animal Book of Poetry, 1967, Silver Screen (Neue Amerikanische Lyrik), 1970, The New Yorker Book of Poems, 1970, Contemporary American Poets, 1970, Poets of Canada, 1978, others. BA with honors, U. Ill., 1956; MA, U. Iowa, 1958. Poet-in-residence U. Iowa, 1966-67, Aspen Wrtrs.; Workshop; asst. prof. English U. Victoria, B.C., Can., 1969-73, U. of Calif. Extension, Santa Cruz, 1986—; ed. Hancock House Pubs., 1976-79. Guggenheim fellow, 1964-65, D.H. Lawrence fellow U. N.Mex., 1966-67, MacDowell Colony and Yaddo fellow, 1984; grantee Can. Council, 1981-84. Mem. NWU, League Can. Poets. Home: Box 7062 Santa Cruz CA 95061

SWARTHOUT, GLENDON FRED, b. Pinckney, MI, Apr. 8, 1918; s. Fred Harrington and Lila (Chubb) Swarthout; m. Kathryn Blair Vaughn, Dec. 28, 1940; 1 son—Miles. Author: Willow Run, 1943, They Came to Cordura, 1958, Where the Boys Are, 1960, Welcome to Thebes, 1962, (with Kathryn Swarthout) The Ghost and the Magic Saber, 1963, The Cadillac Cowboys, 1964, (with Kathryn Swarthout) Whichaway, 1966, The Eagle and the Iron Cross, 1966, Loveland, 1968, (with Kathryn Swarthout) The Button Boat, 1969, Bless the Beasts and Children, 1970, (with Kathryn Swarthout) TV Thompson, 1972, The Tin Lizzie Troop, 1972, Luck and Pluck, 1973, The Shootist, 1975, The Melodeon, 1977, Skeletons, 1979, (with Kathryn Swarthout) Cadbury's Coffin, 1982, The Old Colts, 1985; contrbr. short stories to mags. including New World Writing, Esquire. AB, U. Mich., 1939, AM, 1946; PhD, Mich. State U., 1955. Served with U. S. Army, 1943-45; ETO. Recipient Playwriting award Theater Guild, 1947, Hopwood award in fiction 1946, O. Henry Prize Short Stories 1960, Gold medal Natl. Soc. Arts and Letters, 1972, Spur award for best western novel Western Writers Am. 1975. Home: 5045 Tamanar Way Scottsdale AZ 85253

SWARTLEY, DAVID WARREN, b. Sellersville, PA, July 12, 1950; s. G. Merrill and Miriam Kulp (Landis) S.; m. Jane Ann Luke, Sept. 7, 1984; children—Kevin Stark, Scott Stark, Christopher Swartley. Author: My Friend, My Brother, 1980, My Little Georgie, 1983. B.A., Goshen Coll., 1977; M.S., Ind. U., 1981. Tchr. Middlebury Commun. Schs., IN, 1977-85; freelance wrtr., 1985—. Home: 601 Maplecrest Dr Goshen IN 46526

SWARTZ, BURTON EUGENE, (Burton Crane), b. Mpls., May 16, 1934; s. Harry Douglas and Ruth (Werner) S. Contrbr. articles to mags; lyricist with BMI Musical Theatre Wkshp, 1968-70, songs performed in NYC clubs and cabarets; gave poetry-jazz concerts in halls, clubs, on radio. BA, Calif. State U.-Los Angeles, 1960; MA, Columbia U., 1972. Tchr. English, NYC, Bd. Edn., 1972-84; instr. acting, NYC, 1985—. Recipient Best Essay award KLAC-TV and Grand Taste Co., 1952, WLIB-radio, 1976; Best Film award Tchrs. Coll., NYC, 1972. Mem. P&W. Home: 235 W 107 St New York NY 10025

SWENSON, GRACE STAGEBERG, b. Minn.; d. Nels and Nettie (Johnson) Stageberg; m. Olaf H. Swanson (dec. Sept. 30, 1978); children—Jon Stuart, Richard Lee. Author: Minnesota in Books for Young Readers, 1975, From the Ashes, The Story of the Hinckley Fire of 1894, 1979. BA, U. Minn.-Duluth; MA, U. Minn.-Mpls., 1973. Instr. music, art and English, pub. schls., Minn., Wis.; librarian pub. schl., Wayzata, Minn., 1963-84. Recipient Educator of Yr. award Jr. C. of C., Plymouth, Minn., 1976; named Career Tchr. of Yr., Wayzata Pub. Schls., 1981. Mem. Minn. Ednl. Media Orgn., local, state, natl. edn. assns., Delta Kappa Gamma (pres., named Woman of Achievement 1986). Home: 430 Magnolia Ln N Plymouth MN 55441

SWENSON, KAREN, b. NYC, July 29, 1936; d. Howard William and Dorothy (Trautman) Swenson. Author: An Attic of Ideals, 1974, East-West, 1980; contrbr. poetry to numerous anthologies including The New Yorker Book of Poems, 1969. BA, Barnard Coll., NYC1954-59; MA, NY U., 1971. Poet-in-residence Clark U., Worcester, Mass., 1976-77, U. ID & Denver U., 1979-80; asst. prof. Skidmore Coll., 1977-78, Scripps Coll., Claremont, CA, 1980-82; lectr. CCNY & Fordham U., 1982-85. Trans Atlantic (Review) Fellowship, NY, 1974. Mem. PSA, PEN, MLA, AWP, NWU. Home: 430 State St Bklyn NY 11217

SWENSON, MAY, b. Logan, UT, May 28, 1919; d. Dan Arthur and Margaret (Hellberg) Swenson. Author: Another Animal, 1954, A Cage of Spines, 1958, To Mix with Time, 1963, Poems to Solve, 1966, Half Sun Half Sleep, 1967, Iconographs, 1970, More Poems to Solve, 1971, (translated from Swedish) Windows & Stones (Tomas Transtromer), 1972, The Guess and Spell Coloring Book, 1976, New and Selected Things Taking Place, 1978, In Other Words, 1987. BS, Utah State U., hon. Dr. of Letters, 1987. Editor New Directions Press, 1959-66; mem. staff Breadloaf Writers Conf., 1976. Poet-in-res. Purdue U. (Lafayette, IN), 1966-67, U. NC (Greensboro), 1968-69, 75, Lethbridge U. (Alberta, Can., 1970), U. Calif. (Riverside), 1973. Recipient Natl. Inst. Arts and Letters award, 1960, Guggenheim Fdn. award, 1960, Brandeis U. award, 1967, Disting. Service Gold medal Utah State U., 1967; Shelley Meml. award Poetry Soc. Am., 1968, NEA grant, 1974, Bollingen prize in poetry Yale U., 1981, MacArthur Fellowship, 1987. Fellow Acad. Am. Poets (chancellor 1980). Mem. PSA, PEN Am. Ctr., AAIAL. Home: 73 Boulevard Sea Cliff NY 11579

SWIFT, MARY HOWARD DAVIDSON, (Mary Swift), b. Mineola, NY, Oct. 13, 1926; d. Howard Calhoun and Mary Perrine (Patterson) Davidson; children—Byron, Isabel, Bill, Lila (dec.). BA, Vassar Coll., 1950, MA, Catholic U., 1972; MA, Geo. Washington U., 1978. Writer Wash. Rvw, Washington, D.C., 1978—, mng. ed., 1983—. Bd. dirs. Wash. Project for the Arts, 1978-85, chmn., 1978-81; bd. dirs. Dist. Curators, Wash., 1985—. Home: 3233 Reservoir Rd NW Washington DC 20007

SWIGART, ROB, b. Chgo., Jan. 7, 1941, s. Eugene and Ruth Elyssa (Robison) S.; m. Jane Bugas, Mar. 26, 1969; children—Saramanda Nell, Tess Miranda. Novelist: Little America, 1977, A.K.A./A Cosmic Fable, 1978, The Time Trip, 1979, The Book of Revelations, 1981, Vector, 1986, Portal, 1988; Portal (entertainment software), 1986. Contrbr. to Women Poets of the World, 1983, book rvws. to San Francisco Chronicle, articles to Macworld, Family Learning, Calif. Living, other mags. BA, Princeton U., 1962; PhD, SUNY-Buffalo, 1972. Reporter Cin. Enquirer, 1963; text salesman Harper & Row, Denver, 1965-69; assoc. prof. English San Jose (Calif.) State U., 1972—. Mem. SFWA, AG, MWA. Home: 255 Cerrito Ave Redwood City CA 94061

SYKES, ROBERT H., b. Wheeling, WV, Dec. 1, 1927; s. Harry Franklin and Mary (McNichols) S.; m. Joanne Ellen Fast, Apr. 5, 1954; 2 daus.: Roberta-Jo, Sandra. Author: Proud Heritage at West Va., 1968, Invincible Invalid, 1983; contrbr. articles, studies in short fiction to Christian Evangelist, Communications Briefings, Library Jnl, Vidya, Greentree Rvw, Walt Whitman Rvw, Studies in Am. Lit.: ed. Harfod County Democrat, Vidya Jnl. AB, West Liberty Coll., 1955; PhD, U. Pitts. 1962. Feature writer Wheeling News Register, W. Va., 1947-51; prof. Bethany Coll., W. Va., 1955-68, West Liberty Coll., 1968-86. Served to s/sgt., US Army, 1948-52, Japan, Korea. Recipient Fulbright Exchange prof., 1964; Danforth Fdn. Disting. prof. award, 1963. Address: Point Breeze Dr Bethany WV 26032

SYLVESTER, JANET, b. Youngstown, OH, May 5, 1950. Author: (poems) That Mulberry Wine, 1985; contrbr. poems to Morrow Anthology of Younger Am. Poets, Arion's Dolphin, Io, Works, Agni, Bennington, Cimarron, Ont., Seneca rvws. BA, Goddard Coll., 1975, MFA, 1978. With acquisitions dept. AMS Press, Inc., NYC, 1977-79; editorial secy. Harvard Mag., Cambridge, Mass., 1984; Banister wrtr.-in-res. Sweet Briar Coll., VA, 1985-87. Recipient prize AAP-U. Utah, 1980; Grolier Poetry prize Grolier Book Shop, 1982. Home: Dept of English Univ of Utah Salt Lake City UT 84112

SYLVIN, FRANCIS, see Seamon, Sylvia Sybil

SYMING, , see Sung, Yuan-Ming

SZABO, MIKLOS, see Muska, Nick

SZERLIP, BARBARA L., b. Newark, Nov. 28, 1949; d. Stewart S. and Ziril (Weinstein) S. Author: Sympathetic Alphabet, 1975; The Ugliest Women in the World and Other Histories, 1978; ed.: California Treasurers: An Exploration in Museum Education for Children, 1978; contrbr. to anthologies, Four Young Women: Poems, Wonders; also articles in City Arts, San Francisco Mag., Credits, Vista, Natl. Geographic. Founder, ed. Tractor, small press lit mag, 1971-75. NEA fellow, 1976-77, 81-82; recipient Pushcart prize, 1977. Home: 532-B Lombard St San Francisco CA 94133

SZLADITS, LOLA LEONTIN, b. Budapest, Hungary, Mar. 11, 1923 (came to U.S., 1950, naturalized, 1956); d. Bodog and Margit (Stern) Abel; m. Charles Szladits, Oct.9, 1950. Author: Book Collecting: A Modern Guide, 1977, numerous exhbn. catalogs, 1969—. PhD, Peter Pazmany U., Budapest, 1946; postgrad., Columbia U., 1946-47, Sorbonne, U. Paris, Spring 1948; Dip. Lib., Univ. Coll., London U., 1950. Med. secy. Allied Control Commn., U.S. Forces in Hungary, 1945-46; Oriental librarian Courtauld Inst. Art (London), 1948-50; indexer Natl. Health Council, NYC, 1950-51; librarian, first asst. rare book room NY Acad. Medicine (NYC), 1951-55; first asst. Berg Collection, 1955-69; curator Berg Collection English and Am. Lit., 1969—; mem. council Princeton Library (NY), 1979—, Rosenbach Fdn. Library, 1980—, Dictionary Lit. Biography, 1981—. Mem. Bibliog. Soc. Am. (council 1976-82), English-Speaking Union, NY Hist. Soc., Keats-Shelley Assn. Am. (dir. 1974—). Office: NY Public Lib 476 Fifth Ave New York NY 10018

SZOGYI, ALEX, b. NYC, Jan. 27, 1929; s. Arpad and Vera Irene (Hoffman) Szogyi. Author: Anthologie d'Humour Français, 1970; translator: Grotowski (Temkine), 1972, also all of Chekhov's plays, and plays of Gorki, Giraudoux, Anouilh, Beaumarchais, Musset, Marquis de Sade, George Sand, Verga, Strinberg and Feydeau; translator and performer: Marriage of Figaro (Beaumarchais), 1982; editor: Candide (Voltaire), 1962, George Sand Studies, 1980, Vol. II, 1982; monthly columnist: Cook's Books, Bon Appetit mag., 1979-81. BA, Bklyn. Coll., 1950; MA, Yale U., 1954, PhD, 1958. Mem. faculty Yale U., 1952-55, Wesleyan U., 1955-61; mem. faculty Hunter Coll., NYC, 1961—, prof. Romance langs., 1971—, chair dept. 1970-77. Mem. MLA, Am. Assn. Tchrs. French, PEN (syndicated fiction award for short story 1983), Am. Comparative Lit. Assn., DG, Natl. Book Critics Circle. Home: 61 Jane St New York NY 10014

SZUCS, ANDREW ERIC, b. Cleve., Apr. 25, 1946; s. Andrew Elmer and Katherine (Krizsak) S.; m. Laura Jean Nyhan, June 4, 1971; children—Andrew Edward, Eric Stephen. Contrbr. articles to mags. Ed.: Air Force Logistics Command Annual Commander's Report, 1980-85, Wright State U. Coll. of Bus. and Administration Yearbook, 1987. B.A., U. Dayton, 1968; M.B.A., Wright State U., 1984. Public Affair Officer Wright-Patterson Air Force Base, OH, 1973-77, Pubs. Mgr. Air Force Logistics Command, 1977-85, Chief Pub. Div., 1985—. Served with U.S. Air Force, 1968-73. mem. NPC, Aviation/Space Wrtrs. Assn. (Midwest Region Jnlsm. award 1987). Home: 1135 Mint Springs Dr Fairborn OH 45324

SZULC, TAD, b. Warsaw, Poland, July 25, 1926 (came to U.S., 1947, naturalized, 1954); s. Seweryn and Janina (Baruch) Szulc; m. Marianne Carr, July 8, 1948; children—Nicole, Anthony. Author: Twilight of the Tyrants, 1959, The Cuban Invasion, 1962, The Winds of Revolution, 1963, Dominican Diary, 1965, Latin America, 1966, Bombs of Palomares, 1967, United States and the Caribbean, 1971, Czechoslovakia since World War II, 1971, Portrait of Spain, 1972, Compulsive Spy: The Strange Career of E. Howard Hunt, 1974, The Energy Crisis, 1974, Innocents at Home, 1974, The Illusion of Peace, 1978, Diplomatic Immunity, 1981, Fidel: A Critical Portrait, 1986. Student, U. Brazil, 1943-45. Reporter AP (Rio de Janeiro), 1945-46; corr. at UN for UPI, 1949-53; mem. staff NY times, after 1953, corr., Latin Am., 1955-61, with Washington bur., 1961-65, 69-72, assigned to Spain and Portugal, 1965-68, assigned to Eastern Europe, 1968-69; commentator fgn. policy, 1972—. Decorated Cross of Chevalier of Legion d'Honneur France. World Business Council Medal, Dr. Honorus Causa in Humane Ltrs., Amer. Coll. of Switzerland. Recipient Maria Moors Cabot gold medal Columbia U.; OPC award for best book on fgn. affairs, 1979, 87. Address: 4515 29th St NW Washington DC 20008

SZYDLOWSKI, MARY FRANCES, (Mary Vigliante, Mary Vigliante Szydlowski, Jarl Szydlow), b. Albany, NY; d. Frank Anthony and Nataly Agatha (Nicita) Vigliante; m. Frank Joseph Szydlowski; 1 dau.—Carrie Ann. Author: The Ark, 1978, The Colony, 1979, The Land, 1979, Source of Evil, 1980, Silent Song, 1980, Worship the Night, 1982 (reprinted 1985). BA, State U. of NY at Albany, 1971. Administrator NY State Dept. of Mental Hygiene (Albany), 1974-78. Treas. NOW (Albany), 1980-81. Mem. AG, AL, SFWA. Home: 92B Columbia Turnpike Rensselaer NY 12144

TABIN, JANET HALE, b. Joplin, MO, Apr. 21, 1946; d. Wilbur Elwood and Marie (Reeves) Hale; m. Lee E. Tabin, Apr. 21, 1979; children—Jennifer, William, John. Contrbr. articles to mags., books including New Standard Encyc., PTA Today, others. Wrkg. on book on fundamental econ. concepts at middle sch. reading level. B.A., Grinnell Coll., 1969; M.B.A., U. Chgo., 1979. Asst. ed. Standard Edn. Corp., Chgo., 1969-71; copywrtr. Spiegel, Inc., Chgo., 1971-73; copywrtr., ed. internal mag. Northern Trust Co., Chgo., 1974-76; mgr. marketing communications Motorola Tele-programs Inc., Schiller Park, IL, 1976-77; research supvr. Leo Burnett Co., Chgo., 1978-85; prin. Small Bus. Marketing Services, Glenview, IL, 1987—. Mem. Off-Campus Wrtrs. Workshop. Home: 2660 Roslyn Ln Highland Park IL 60035

TAFOYA, CATHY JO, b. Pensacola, FL, Aug. 24, 1953, d. Ernest Homer Joseph and Frances (Smith) Gosselin; m. Don Richard Maholland, Dec. 19, 1970 (div. 1978); children—Shawn Richard, Alphonsine Vera Elizabeth Tafoya. Contrbr. to Our Western World's Greatest Poems, 1983, Our World's Best Loved Poems, 1984; songwriter: "I Dream of You," 1983, "The Last Time," 1984. Student pub. schls., Alameda, Calif. Fellow World of Poetry (Golden Poet award 1985); mem. Natl. Wrtrs. Club, Wrtrs. Connection. Address: 1528 Stanton St Almeda CA 94501

TAGGART, JOHN P(AUL), b. Guthrie Center, IA, Oct. 5, 1942; s. Darrel F. and Pauline Taggart; m. Jennifer Anne James; children: Sarah Rose, Holly Kathleen. Author: (poetry) To Construct a Clock, 1971; The Pyramid Is a Pure Crystal, 1974; Prism and the Pine Twig, 1977; Dodeka, 1979; Peace on Earth, 1981; Dehiscence, 1983; Loop, 1987. BA in English and Philosophy, Earlham Coll., 1965; MA in English Lit., U. Chgo., 1966; PhD in Interdisciplinary Humanities, Syracuse U., 1974. Prof. Shippensburg U., Pa., 1969—. Recipient poetry prize Chgo. Rev., 1980, Ironwood, 1982; fellow Ford Fdn., 1965, NEA, 1976, 86, Pa. Council on Arts, 1983. Mem. Melville Soc. Home: 210 S Washington St Shippensburg PA 17257

TAGIURI, RENATO, b. Milan, Italy, Apr. 28, 1919; s. Giulia and Corrado Tagiuri; m. Consuelo Keller, May 5, 1946; children—Robert, Peter, John. Author: (with Petrullo) Person Perception, 1958, (with Litwin) Organizational Climate, 1968, (with Lawrence, Barnett and Dunphy) Behavioral Science Concepts in Case Analysis, 1968, (with Glover and Hower) The Administrator, 5th ed., 1973; contrbr. chpts. to books and encycs. BSc, McGill U., 1945, MSc, 1946; PhD, Harvard U., 1951. Mem. faculty Harvard U. 1951—, prof. social sci., 1962—; cons. to govt., pvt. orgns., 1951—. Home: 432 Concord Rd Weston MA 02193

TAGLIABUE, JOHN, b. Cantu (Como), Italy, July 1, 1923 (came to U.S. 1927); s. Battista and Adelaide (Boghi) T.; m. Grace Ten Eyck, Sept. 11, 1946; children—Francesca, Dina. Author: Poems (1941-58), 1959, A Japanese Journal, 1966, The Buddha Uproar, 1970, The Doorless Door, 1970, The Great Day (poems 1962-83), 1984; contrbr. lit mags, periodicals and anthols., poetry, travel jnl. sections, essays, short plays. Wrkg. on The Asia House Poems, A Shakespeare Notebook, The Mediterranean Poems. BA, MA, Columbia Univ., 1944, 45; grad. studies Univ. of Florence, Italy, 1950-52. Instr. Am. Univ. of Beirut, 1945-56; asst. prof., Alfred Univ., 1948-50; Fulbright lectr., Univ. of Pisa, 1950-52, Tokyo Univ., 1958-60, Fudan Univ. (China), 1984; prof., Bates Coll., 1953—. Mem. PSA, PEN. Home: 12 Abbott St Lewiston ME 04240

TAISHIN, see Ramsdale, David Alan

TAIT, ELIZABETH LEEDS, b. Moorestown, NJ, Aug. 1, 1906; d. George Hancock and Caroline Hornor (Leeds) Warwick; m. Colin F. Tait, June 23, 1928; children—Betsey Leeds Puth, William Woolman Tait. Author: Potpourri, 1984, Words, 1978. Student, Temple U., Philadelphia. Secy. treas., Burl. Co. Insurance Agents Assoc., 1955-60; chmn., Leaves of Grass, Mount Holly, NJ, 1977-80. Mem. Burlington County Poets. Home: 17920 Golf Blvd 907 Redington Shores FL 33708

TAIT, IRENE GRAYSON, b. New Orleans, Jan. 25, 1918; d. William Gordon and Louise Elizabeth (Duplantis) Grayson; m. Joseph Olier Tait, June 14, 1938; foster children—Jo Ann, Kathy. Columnist Key West Citizen, 1976-77; author: The Last Days, 1978, Demetria, 1987. Contrbr. articles, short stories to mags. including Better Homes and Gardens, True Detective Mag., Reader's Digest, others. Cert. in Jnlsm., Newspaper Inst. of N.Y., 1941, Navy Extension Schl., 1942. Corr., UPI, New Orleans, 1947-49; feature wrtr., The New Orleans Item, 1947-49; soc. ed., Sanford Herald, FL, 1950-52; asst. news ed., Sta. WLOF, Orlando, FL, 1952-54; family counsellor, Valdosta Counselling Service, GA, 1979—. Office: Box 3196 Valdosta GA 31604

TALAL, MARILYNN CAROLE GLICK, b. NYC; d. Philip Howard and Dorothy (Barchoff) Glick; m. Norman Talal, June 21, 1959; children—Andrew Henry, Melissa Ellen. Contrbr. poems to anthols., lit. mags. BA, Sarah Lawrence Coll., 1959; MA in Contemporary English Lit., Columbia U., 1963; Stella Erhart Fellow and PhD candidate, Univ. of Houston, 1987-88. Instructor, Univ. of Virginia, 1964-65; poet-in-residence, Bel Aire School, Tiburon, Calif., 1974-78; Poet in the schls. Calif. Poets in the Schls., San Francisco, 1978-82, county coordinator, 1979-82; tchg. assoc. U. Tex., San Antonio, 1982-85; writing cons., San Antonio, 1986—. Recipient 2d place Poetry award Poet's Round Table, Terre Haute, Ind., 1969, 1st place award for poetry Napa Valley Poetry Conf., 1981. Home: 106 Village Circle San Antonio TX 78232

TALAN, JAMIE LYNN, b. NYC, June 25, 1956; d. Jack Robert Talan and Suzanne Lois (Robinson) Habib; m. Norman Leonard Prusslin, Aug. 8, 1982. Contrbr. to numerous newspapers and mags, including New York Times, Self, McCall's. BA, SUNY, Stony Brook, NY, 1978. Ed., P&W Communications, NYC, 1979-81; medical wrtr., stringer NY Times, 1982-85; science reporter Newsday, Long Island, NY, 1985—. Mem. NASW. Home: 37 Montrose Dr Commack NY 11725

TALBOT, STROBE, b. Dayton, OH, Apr. 25, 1946; s. Nelson S. and Helen Josephine (Large) Talbott; m. Brooke Lloyd Shearer, Nov. 14, 1971; children—Devin Lloyd, Adrian Nelson. Translator, editor: Khrushchev Remembers, 1974, Khrushchev Remembers: The Last Testament, 1974; author: Endgame: The Inside Story of SALT II, 1979. BA, Yale U., 1968, MA (hon.), 1976; M.Litt. (Rhodes scholar), Oxford U. (Eng.), 1971. Eastern Europe corr. Time Mag., 1971-73, State Dept. corr. (Washington), 1973-75; White House corr., 1975-77, diplomatic corr. (Washington), 1977—; fellow Yale Corp., 1976-82; mem. panel on natl. security and future of arms control Carnegie Endowment for Intl. Peace. Recipient Edward Weintal prize for disting. diplomatic reporting, 1980, OPC award, 1983. Mem. Council Fgn. Relations, Am. Assn. Rhodes Scholars (bd. directors). Home: 2842 28th St NW Washington DC 20006

TALESE, GAY, b. Ocean City, NJ, Feb. 7, 1932; s. Joseph Francis and Catherine (DePaulo) Talese; m. Nan Ahearn, June 10, 1959; children—Pamela, Catherine. Author: New York—A Serendipiter's Journey, 1961, The Bridge, 1964, The Overreachers, 1965, The Kingdom and the Power, 1969, Fame and Obscurity, 1970, Honor Thy Father, 1971, Thy Neighbor's Wife, 1980; contrbr.: articles to Esquire, Harper's, others. Served to 1st lt. U.S. Army. Mem. PEN. Address: 109 E 61st St New York NY 10021

TALL, DEBORAH, b. Washington, Mar. 16, 1951, d. Max Michael and Selma (Donnerstein) Tall; m. David Weiss, Sept. 9, 1979; 1 dau., Zoe. Author: Eight Colors Wide, 1974, Ninth Life, 1982, The Island of the White Cow, 1986; contrbr. numerous poems to mags; ed. Seneca Rvw, 1982—. BA, U. Mich., 1972; MFA, Goddard Coll., 1979. Asst. prof. U. Balt., 1980-82, Hobart & William Smith Colls., Geneva, N.Y., 1982—. Recipient Hopwood award, U. Mich., 1972; Yaddo fellow, 1982, 84. Mem. AWP, AAP, NWU, PSA. Office: Hobart & William Smith Colls Geneva NY 14456

TALMADGE, JEFFREY D., b. Uvalde, Tex., Feb. 18, 1953. Contrbr. to Tex. Qtly, Greensboro Rvw, Gargoyle, other lit jnls. BA, Duke U., 1975; JD, U. Tex.-Austin, 1980. Press secy. Congressman Bob Krueger, Washington, 1975-77; lawyer firm Fulbright & Jaworski, Houston, 1980-85, firm Mullen, Berliner, MacInnes & Redding, Austin, Tex., 1985—. Grantee Mary Roberts Rinehard Fdn., 1975; recipient AAP award, 1975. Mem. Austin Wrtrs. League, Austin Lawyers and Accts. for Arts. Home: 5618 Bull Creek Austin TX 78756

TAMAYO, REVÊ, see Klyman, Anne Griffiths

TAMBUZI, JITU, see Byrd, Odell Richard, Jr.

TANA, PATTI, b. Santa Monica, CA, May 16, 1945; d. Jack and Ada (Selinger) Van Glubt; m. John Renner, June 24, 1975; 1 child, Jesse. Author: (poetry) How Odd This Ritual of Harmony, 1981, Ask the Dreamer Where Night Begins: Poems & Postscripts, 1986. Assoc. editor: (anthol.) Raining Leaves; editorial bd. Esprit Mag. BA, U. Mo., 1966; MA, 1968. Assoc. prof. Nassau Community Coll., Garden City, N.Y., 1971—. Recipient Irma Rhodes award Shelly Soc. N.Y., 1983, 1st prize for poetry Peninsula Pub. Library, Lawrence, N.Y., 1986; fellow NEH, 1977. Mem. PSA, P&W. Home: 462 W Beech St Long Beach NY 11561

TANNENBAUM, JUDITH NETTIE, b. Chgo., Feb. 13, 1947; d. Robert and Edith (Lazaroff) Tannenbaum; 1 dau., Sara Press. Author: The World Saying Yes, 1980, Living Here, 1983, Ten to Darkness, 1985. Contrbr. poems to anthol., lit. mags. BA in Poli. Sci., U. Calif.-Berkeley, 1968; MA in English, Sonoma State U., 1979. Now tchr. poetry San Quentin State Prison, Calif. Poets in the Schls., Calif. Heritage Poetry Program. Grantee Calif. Arts Council, 1986; Mendocino County Arts Council, 1983. Mem. Calif. Poets in Schls. Home: 1146 Washington 4 Albany CA 94706

TANNER, JOHN, see Matcha, Jack

TANOUYE, ELYSE TOSHIE, b. Honolulu, Sept. 6, 1955; d. Roy S. and Frances T. (Akita) T. Hawaii Business Mag., 1981—. BA, Reed Coll., 1979; postgrad., U. MO, 1985. Legislative aide, HI state senate, Honolulu, 1980-81; staff writer Hawaii Business, Honolulu, 1981-82, assoc. ed., 82-84, mng. ed., 84-85, ed., 85—. Award for Overall Excellence, HI Pubs. Assn., 1986. Mem. Investigative Rptrs. & Eds. Office: HI Bus Pub 825 Keeaumoku Waipau HI 96797

TANSILL, MEL, b. Balt., Mar. 30, 1954; s. Melvin Ellsworth and Jacqueline Joan (Byron) T. Contrbr. poems to anthol., articles to trade mags., newspapers. B.A. in Creative Writing, U. Balt., 1976, M.A. in Pubs., 1984. News/feature wrtr. Baltimore News Am., 1976-79; mgr. employee communications Equitable Bank, Balt., 1979-80, mgr. corporate communications Union Trust Co., Balt., 1980-81; pubs. chief Md. Port Administration, Balt., 1981-84, asst. public affair dir., 1984—. recipient Writing/Communications Excellence award United Way of Centrl Md., 1979, 80, cited for communications excellence Johns Hopkins U. Eisenhower Library, 1983. Mem. IABC (Writing Excellence award 1979, 80, 81, 82, 83, 84). Home: 123 W Ostend St Baltimore MD 21230

TAPELLINI, DONNA LYNN, b. Jersey City, Apr. 4, 1955; d. Donald and Marilyn (Kruse) T. Managing ed., Food & Beverage Marketing, 1987—; senior assoc. ed. Gralla Pubns., 1984-87. Degree in Jnlsm., Politics, NYU, 1984. Freelance writer poetry, short stories, non-fict. Mem. Natl. Pol. Sci. Assn., Kappa Tau Alpha. Home: 7200 Blvd East Apt 3F North Bergen NJ 07047

TAPLEY, LANCE E., b. Bar Harbor, ME, Oct. 5, 1944; s. Lyman and Barbara R. (Ferry) T.; m. Margaret Ann Libby; children: Isaac, Adam, Asa, Elias. Author: Ski Touring in New England, 1973, Ski Touring in New England and New York, 1975; contrbr. articles and stories to mags. AB, Dartmouth Coll., 1966; postgrad., U. Toulouse, France, 1967. Ed. and reporter San Francisco Chronicle, Providence Jnl, Portland Press Herald, 1967-71; ed. Coping Mag, Portland, Me., 1982-85; exec. dir. Me. Common Cause, Augusta, 1977-80; owner and pub. Lance Tapley Pubs., Augusta, 1983—; freelance writer, ME. and NYC, 1972—. Natl. bd. dirs., Common Cause, Washington, 1983—; dir. Me. Summer Inst., Augusta, 1984—. Natl. Center for Economic Alternative grantee, Washington, 1975. Mem. Me. Writers and Pubs Alliance. Address: 7 Elm St Augusta ME 04330

TAPPER, JOAN JUDITH, b. Chgo., June 12, 1947; d. Samuel Jack and Anna (Swoiskin) T.; m. Steven Richard Siegel, Oct. 15, 1971. BA, U. Chgo., 1968; MA, Harvard U., 1969. Manuscript ed. Chelsea House, NYC, 1969-71; assoc. ed. Scribners, NYC, 1971; free-lance ed., Washington, 1971-72; ed. National Acad. Scis., Washington, 1972-73; assoc. ed. Praeger Pub., Washington, 1973-74; editorial dir. New Republic Books, Washington, 1974-79; mng. ed. Special Pubns., Natl. Geographic, Washington, 1979-83; ed. Natl. Geographic Traveler, Washington, 1983—. Mem. ASME, SATW. Home: 224 Cape St John Rd Annapolis MD 21401

TAPPLY, WILLIAM GEORGE, b. Waltham, MA, July 16, 1940; s. Horace Gardner and Muriel Langley (Morgridge) T.; m. Alice Sandra Knight, Aug. 28, 1962 (div. Jan. 1967); m. Cynthia Ann Ehrgott, Mar. 7, 1970; children—Michael, Melissa, Sarah. Author: Death at Charity's Point, 1984, The Dutch Blue Error, 1985, Follow the Sharks, 1985, The Marine Corpse, 1986, Dead Meat, 1987, The Vulgar Boatman, 1988. Contrbr. articles to mags., newspapers including Sports Illustrated, Better Homes & Gardens, Boston Herald, others. B.A., Amherst Coll., 1962; M.A.T., Harvard U., 1963. Tchr. Lexington High Schl., MA, 1963—. Mem. AG. MWA, NEA. Home: 70 Hillside Ave Concord MA 01742

TAQUEY, CHARLES HENRI, b. Paris, France, Feb. 1912; s. Henri and Marguerite (Normand) Taquey; m. Ruth McVitty, Feb. 1, 1947; children—Antony, Chantal, Fleming. Author: German Financial Crisis, 1931, Richard Cobden, 1938, Trusts and Patents, 1946, Obstacles to Development in Indonesia, 1952, Fisheries in Cambodia, 1959, Against Full Employment, 1973, Democracy and Socialism, 1976, Transnational Corporations and the State, 1979, Beyond Free Trade, 1983. BS, Paris U., 1929; Laureat Ecole Libre des Sciences Politiques, 1933, Paris Law Schl., 1934. French Treasury rep. (Paris, London, Berlin, NYC), 1934-47; local currencies mgr. ECA, 1948-51; staff officer Exec. Office of Pres., 1952-57; fgn. service econ. officer Am. embassies (Phnom-Penh, Cambodia; Tunis, Tunisia; Kingston, Jamaica), also detailed to Dept. Commerce as dep. dir. fgn. activities mgmt., 1957-70; mgmt. cons., ecol. economist (intl. trade and resources recovery), 1970—; expert witness Intl. Trade Commn. and ways and means com. U.S. House of Reps., GAO, fgn. govts. Served as lt., French Army, 1940; lt., AUS, 1942-46; capt. 1952. Address: 1681 31st St NW Washington DC 20007

TARACHOW, MICHAEL, b. Milw., Dec. 27, 1954. Author: Waves, 1977, The Turning Point, 1982, Somewhere Music, Somehow Song, 1982, Dusk Music, 1987. BA, U. Wisc.-Milw., 1979. Ed./pub./printer Pentagram Press. Milw., 1974—. Recipient poetry award, Council for Wis. Writers, 1977. Mem. NY Typophiles, Am. Printing History Assn. Address: 212 North Second St Minneapolis MN 55401

TARASOVIC, MARCIA MARGARET, b. Bridgeport, CT, July 8, 1943; d. Thomas Joseph and Mary Louise (Foytho) T.; m. Joseph E. Dreiss, Mar. 4, 1967 (div. Sept. 1976); children: Kristin Bishop Dreiss-Tarasociv, Ingrid Ross Dreiss-Tarasovic. Contrbr. poetry to S.D. Rvw, Portland Rvw, Mill Hunk Herald, Wind, other lit mags and anthologies. BA, Chatham Coll., 1985. Profl. artist, Pitts., 1966-78; steelworker U.S. Steel Corp., Pitts., 1977-83, tchr., cons., 1976-83; communication cons. FAA Airway Facilities, Pitts., 1985-86; marketing coord., Buchanan Ingersoll Prof. Corp., 1986—. Mem. P&W. Home: Box 506 Sewickley PA 15143

TARBELL, JAMES, b. Spokane, WA, Dec. 11, 1949; s. Harry and Polly (Gallagher) T.; m. Judy Widmer, July 3, 1979; children: Shamli and Crescent. BA, Am. U. Ed. An Apple Press, Annapolis, Calif., 1983, The Ridge Times Press, 1984—. Bd. Dirs., Mendocino County Literacy, 1986. Address: Box 90 Mendocino CA 95460

TARILA, B. SOPHIA, (Barbara S. Selak), b. Chgo., Aug. 1, 1938; d. John Wallace and Sadie Maria (Kotila) Sampson; m. R. Daniel Selak, Dec. 29, 1961 (div. 1981); children—Mark, Eric, Terra. Author, pub.: an Esoteric Look at Hatha Yoga, 1980, Crystal Cosmos Network Directory II, New Age Marketing Resource Directory; ed.: The Downside of Up (by Marian Greenberg), Jose El Diablo (by Beatrice V. Baker), Quality Sound Engineering (by Sherman Keene), other. BA, Gettysburg Coll., 1960; MS, U. Wis.-Madison, 1965; PhD, U. Oriental Studies, Los Angeles, 1978. Ed. Verde Valley View, Cottonwood, Ariz., 1982; ed., designer Call of the Canyon mag., Sedona, Ariz., 1982-83; ed., designer First Editions, Sedona, 1984—; pub. associate Mystic Crystal Publs., Sedona, 1987—; ed.: The Crystal Sourcebook: From Science to Metaphysics. Mem. Cosmed, Pubs. Mktg. Assn. Home: Box 1158 Sedona AZ 86336

TARN, NATHANIEL, b. Paris, France, June 30, 1928; s. Marcel and Yvonne (Suchar) Tarn. Author: Old Savage/Young City, 1964, Penguin Modern Poets No. Seven: Richard Murphy, John Silkin, Nathaniel Tarn, 1965, Where Babylon Ends, 1968, The Beautiful Contradictions, 1969, October, 1969, A Nowhere for Vallejo, 1971, Lyrics for the Bride of God: Section: The Artemision, 1972, The Persephones, 1974, Lyrics for the Bride of God, 1975, The House of Leaves, 1976, Birdscapes, with Seaside, 1978. The Desert Mothers, 1985, At the Western Gates, 1985, Palenque, 1986, (with Janet Rodney) The Forest, 1978, Alashka, 1979, The Ground of Our Great Admiration of Nature, 1978; contrbg. author to numerous anthologies; translator: The Heights of Macchu Picchu (Pablo Neruda, 1966, Stelae (Victor Segalen), 1969, editor, co-translator: Contrbr. Cuba: An Anthology of Cuban Poetry of the Last Sixty Years, 1969, Selected Poems (Pablo Neruda), 1970. BA with honors, Cambridge U. (Eng.), 1948, MA, 1952; postgrad., Sorbonne, U. Paris, 1949-51; MA, U. Chgo., 1952, PhD, 1957; London Schl. Econs., 1953-58. Anthropologist, Guatemala, Burma, Alaska and others, 1952—; editor Cape Editions and founder-dir. Cape Goliard Press, J. Cape Ltd., 1967-69; vis. prof. State U. NY at Buffalo, and Princeton, 1969-70; prof. comparative lit. Rutgers U., 1970-84. Recipient Guiness prize for poetry, 1963. Home: Box 566 Tesuque NM 87574

TARNOPOLSKY, RAFAEL, b. Buenos Aires, Argentina, Sept. 12, 1922, came to U.S., 1961, s. Samuel and Tabel T.; m. Esther Singer, Apr. 18, 1948; children—Jerry, Joseph, Riva. Contrbr. sci. papers to Osteopathic Physician, Jnl Am. Osteopathic Assn., other profl. publs. BSc, Coll. Arnaldo, Brazil, 1939; MD, U. Minas, Brazil, 1947. Prof. Univ. Osteo. Medicine, Des Moines, 1976—. Served to 1st lt. M.C., Israeli Army, 1957-58. Mem. profl. orgns. Home: 3000 Grand Ave 714 Des Moines IA 50312

TARPLEY, FRED ANDERSON, b. Leonard, TX, Jan. 27; s. Fred Frost and Adele (McCorstin) T.; m. Jolene Connatser, Feb. 22, 1969; children—Ted, marie, Mark. Author: Place Names of Northeast Texas, 1969, From Blinky to Blue John: A Word Atlas of Northeast Texas, 1970, 1001 Texas Place Names, 1980, Jefferson: Riverport to the Southwest, 1984. BA, East Tex. State U., 1951, MA, 1954; PhD, La. State U., 1960. City ed. Galveston (Tex.) Daily News, 1951-52; tchr., Galveston Schl. System, 1951-52; prof. East Tex. State U., Commerce, 1957—. Fellow East Tex. Hist. Assn.; mem. Tex. Joint Council Tchrs. English (hon. life mem.), Am. Name Soc. (past pres.). Office: Dept Lit East Tex State U Commerce TX 75428

TARR, CURTIS W., b. Stockton, CA, Sept. 18, 1924; s. F.W. and Esther (Reed) Tarr; m. Elizabeth May Myers, 1955 (div. 1978); children—Pamela Elizabeth, Cynthia Leigh; 2nd m. Marilyn Van Stralen, 1979. Author: Private Soldier, 1976, By the Numbers, 1981. BA, Stanford U., 1948, PhD, 1962; MBA, Harvard U., 1950; LHD, Ripon Coll., 1965, Grinnell Coll., 1969, Lincoln Coll., 1980; LL.D., Lawrence U., 1974, Ill. Wesleyan U., 1980. Research asst., instr. Harvard U., 1950-52; vp Sierra Tractor & Equipment Co. (Chico, CA), 1952-58; staff mem. 2nd Hoover Commn., 1954-55; pres. Lawrence U. (Appleton, WI), 1963-69; asst. secy. for manpower and res. affairs Air Force, 1969-70; dir. SSS (Washington), 1970-72; under-secy. state for security assistance, 1972-73, acting depty. under-secy. state for mgmt., 1973; vp overseas devel. Deere & Co. (Moline, IL), 1973, vp parts distbn. and materials mgmt., 1973-81, vp mgmt. devel., 1981-83; dean Grad. Schl. Mgmt. Cornell U., 1984—; served with AUS, 1943-46; ETO. Home: 529 Cayuga Heights Rd Ithaca NY 14850

TARR, JOEL ARTHUR, b. Jersey City, May 8, 1934; s. Max Alfred and Florence (Levine) Tartalsky; m. Arlene Green, Sept. 2, 1956 (dec. June 1969); children—Michael Jay, Joanna Sue; 2nd m. Tova Brafman, Aug. 11, 1978; 2 dau.—Maya Leah, Ilana Aviel. Author: A Study in Boss Politics, 1971; editor: Patterns of City Growth, 1974, Retrospective Technology Assessment, 1977, Sister Cities, 1986. BS, Rutgers U., 1956, MA, 1957; PhD, Northwestern U., 1963. Asst. prof. Calif. State U. at Long Beach, 1961-66; vis. prof. U. Calif. at Santa Barbara, 1966-67; asst. prof. Carnegie- Mellon U. (Pitts.), 1967-70, assoc. prof., 1969-72, prof. history and pub. policy, 1973—, dir. program in tech. and soc., 1975—, co-dir., program in applied history and social sci., 1978—, acting dean, Schl. of Urban and Public Affairs, 1986. Bd. dirs. Action Housing, Pitts., 1983. Mem. Pub. Works Hist. Soc. (pres. 1982-83), Orgn. Am. Historians, Pub. History Assn. (natl. council), AAAS, Am. Soc. Environ. Home: 5418 Normlee Pl Pittsburgh PA 15217

TARRANT, MAE CROSS, b. Pleasanton, TX, Apr. 30, 1923, d. Dick Leo and Mary Lea (Burke) Cross; m. Billy Surles Tarrant, Mar. 13, 1965; children: Billy Lee; by previous marriage—Rita Beth Robinson Ramsey, Arin Forest Robinson III, Sharla Mae Robinson Lord; stepchildren: Jacquelyn Sue Tarrant Goolsby, Ronald Joe Tarrant. Contrbr. poetry: newspapers, magazines, bulletins, newsletters, and jnls. Wrkg. on poetry. BA, Sul Ross State U. Owner, operator Speed Queen Laundry, Chama, N.Mex. Home: Box 455 Chama NM 87520

TARRANT, MARY THERESA, b. Detroit, Dec. 6, 1966; d. Thomas Fenelon and Nydia (Cortez) Tarrant. Poetry in anthologies. Wrkg. on poetry. Student Henry Ford Community Coll. Home: 2521 Central Apt 2 Detroit MI 48209

TARVER, DAVID PAUL, b. Monroe, LA, Feb. 16, 1951, s. Lee and Lucille (Pope) T.; m. Debra Lynn Gallien, May 26, 1973; children—Dustin Paul, Josh Patrick. Author: Aquatic and Wetland Plants of Florida, 1978, 79; ed. Aquatic mag., 1982-85; contrbg. wrtr.: Standard Methods, 15th ed., 1978; contrbr. numerous articles to sci. jnls. BS in Wildlife Mgmt., Northwestern State U., 1973, MS in Botany, 1975. Biologist Fla. Dept. Natural Resources, Tallahassee, 1974-81; aquatic specialist Eli Lilly Co., Tallahassee, 1981—. Mem. Fla. Outdoor Wrtrs. Assn., Fla. Aquatic Plant Mgmt. Soc. (ed. 1982-85). Home: 1499 Morning Dove Rd Tallahassee FL 32312

TARZIK, JACK, b. Munich, Germany, Oct. 14, 1946, came to U.S., 1950, s. Bernard and Sophia (Lustig) T.; m. Miriam Schipper, May 27, 1975; children—Corey, Ita, Ari. Author:: Willing Captive, 1980; contrbr. short stories to periodicals. BA, Bklyn, Coll., 1970; MS, LI U., 1979. Home: 24 Paerdegat 4th St Brooklyn NY 11236

TATE, JAMES, b. Kansas City, MO, Dec. 8, 1943; s. Robert and Betty (Sears) Tate. Author: The Lost Pilot, 1967, The Notes of Woe, 1967, The Torches, 1968, rev. ed., 1971, Row With Your Hair, 1969, Shepherds of the Mist, 1969, The Oblivion Ha-Ha, 1970, Absences, 1972, Hottentot Ossuary, 1974, Viper Jazz, 1976, Riven Doggeries, 1979. BA, Kans. State Coll., 1965; MFA, U. Iowa, 1967. Vis. lectr. U. Calif. at Berkeley, 1967—; asst. prof. English Columbia U., until 1971; prof. English U. Mass. (Amherst), 1971—; poetry editor Dickinson Rvw. Recipient award for poetry Natl. Inst. Arts and Letters 1974. Home: 16 Jones Rd Pelham MA 01022

TATELBAUM, BRENDA LOEW, (Barbara Allyn), b. Boston, Apr. 1, 1951; d. Kenneth F. and Florence (Rosoff) Loew; m. Ira Rubin Tatelbaum, Aug. 23, 1970 (div. Apr. 25, 1983); children—Laura Rani Tatelbaum, Max Loew Tatelbaum. Author: Surprise Beach Ball, 1982, Eden Poems, 1982, Life Evolves from Living, 1983; contrbr. poetry to numerous mags. and nwsprs. BA, Boston U., 1971; MA, Brown U., 1973. Asst. lib. Brown U., Providence, 1973; speech tchr. Dartmouth Pub. Schls. (MA), 1974-78, Needham Pub. Schls. (MA), 1979; ed./writer Brush Hill Press, Milton, MA, 1979-84; pub./ed. Eidos Mag.: Erotic Entertainment for Women, Boston, 1984—. Mem. NEPC; Fellow, World Lit. Acad., Natl. Coalition Against Censorship, ACLU, NAFE. Home: 367 Brush Hill Rd Milton MA 02186

TATLOW, MARILYN ROSE, b. Columbia, MO, June 23, 1940, d. James Madison and Ivis Louise (Love) Silvey; m. Gary Arthur Tatlow, June 2, 1962; children—Jennifer Gay, Phillip Arthur, Rebecca Jane. Contrbr.: Chgo. Tribune, Missouri Life, Boston Herald Am., Conn. Wrtr., Modern Bride, The First Anthol. of Missouri Women Writers, 1986, other publs. Wrkg. on short fiction collection, hist. novel. AA, Columbia Coll., 1960; BA, Mo. U., 1962; MFA, Warren Wilson Coll., 1986. Weekly columnist The Paper, Moberly, Mo., 1977-78; staff reporter Columbia (Mo.) Insider, 1979-80; contrbg. ed. Family Jnl, Columbia, 1984; gardening columnist Moberly Monitor-Index, 1984-85; freelance wrtr. Mem. Mo. Wrtrs. Guild, Intl. Womens Writing Guild. Home: 10 Westwood Pl Moberly MO 65270

TAUBE, LESTER S., b. Trenton, NJ, June 5, 1920; s. John and Dora (Barker) T.; m. Eileen Winslade, Dec. 31, 1948 (div.); children—Mark,

Cheryl, John; m. 2d, Ursula Pohlmann, Feb. 1964 (div.); 1 dau., Erica. Author novels: The Grabbers (The Diamond Boomerang), Peter Krimsov, Myer For Hire, The Cossack Cowboy, The Lands of Thunder. Student Rutgers U., 1940; U.S. Command & General Staff, Ft. Leavenworth, KS, 1968. Pres. Taub Corp., Paris, France, 1962-68; freelance novelist, Ehrwald, Austria, 1969-75; econ. dev. off., State of NJ, Trenton, 1978—. Served to Colonel, U.S. Army, 1936-73, worldwide. Home: 26 Snowflower Ln Willingboro NJ 08046

TAUKE, BEVERLY HUBBLE, (Beverly Hubble), b. Danville, IL, Sept. 1, 1949; d. Ralph Tipton and Catherine (Shaw) Hubble; m. Thomas Joseph Tauke, Nov. 17, 1984. Contrbr. articles to mags. including Christianity Today, Moody Monthly, Christian Life. BRE, Bapt. Bible Coll., Clarks Summit, Pa, 1971; MA with high honor, Wheaton Coll., 1975. Head wrtr. pub. relations Moody Bible Inst., Chgo., 1971-74; wrtr., acct. asst. Domain Advt. Agcy., Wheaton, Ill., 1974-75; press secy, Reps. John Conlan & Delbert Latta, Washington, 1975-77, Bobby Richardson campaign, Rock Hill, S.C., 1976; faculty Daystar U. Coll., Nairobi, Kenya, 1977-80; dir. communications Senator Charles Grassley, Washington, 1980—; lectr. poli. communications univs. and profl. training programs, Ia. and Washington, 1981-86. Recipient Citizenship award Bapt. Bible Coll., 1971; named Outstanding Young Woman of Am., 1977-86; Mem. Women in Govt. Relations. Home: 400 O St SW 203 Washington DC 20024

TAUSCH, GERRY MARGARET, b. NYC, July 1, 1930; d. Arthur Joachim and Margaret (Mack) O'Sullivan; m. Ronald D. Tausch, Dec. 6, 1951; children—Clae M. Miller, Aleen M. O'Sullivan, Roland E., Tracy. Author: Glamour in the Kitchem: Recipes & Memoirs of a West Point Wife, 1982; columnist Our Town, 1982-84, Personal Perspectives in The Meeting Manager, 1985, Executive Style in Sarasota Herald Tribune, 1986—. Student Seton Hill Coll., 1947-49. Profl. speaker The Speaker's Connection, Sarasota, FL, 1975—, co-owner, co-dir., 1982—; free-lance celebrity image cons., 1971-82. Cofounder Asolo State Theate Celebrity Series, Sarasota, 1982. Named Top Female Exec., Bus. Jnl., Sarasota, 1986. Mem. Women Owner's Network (bus. mentor, Highest Visibility award 1986), Natl. Speakers Assn. (regional chpt. advisor 1986—; named Chpt. Mem. of Year 1986). Office: Spkr's Conn 3530 Pine Valley Dr Sarasota FL 34239

TAUSCH, SUSAN DIANE, (Quinn Lo), b. Miami Beach, FL, June 13, 1955; d. David Graver and Hildegard Else (Müller) Graver Farnam; m. Edward Frank Gulden Tausch, Dec. 5, 1976; 1 son, Anthony Mitchell. Author: Beyond Me (poetry), 1982, Patchwork Alleys (poetry), 1983, Passages (poetry), 1984, Forty Nights into the Sabaku (poetry), 1985, Distance to the Far Shore (poetry), 1986, Quinn Lo-Extremes (adult erotica), 1984; Silver Poet Award, 1986, Golden Poet Award, 1987; contrbr. to newspapers, anthologies and other publs. Wrkg. on poetry, adult erotica, song lyrics. Student public schs., Miami. Freelance artist, wrtr., photographer, Batavia, Ohio, 1976-85; dir. Avante Prodns., Batavia, 1985—. Mem. Am. Council for Arts, Contemporary Arts Center Cin., Fla. State Poets Assn. Address: Box 449 Batavia OH 45103

TAVEL, RONALD, b. George and Florence (Sterns) T. Novelist: Street of Stairs, 1968; contrbr. Partisan Rvw, Best of Off-Off Broadway, Elephantitis, numerous other publs.; drama ed. Bklyn. Lit. Rvw, 1983—, MA. U. Wyo. Artist-in-residence Yale Div. Schl., New Haven, 1975, 77; lectr., playwright-in-residence, Cornell U., Ithaca, N.Y., 1980-81; lectr. fgn. langs. Mahidol U., Bangkok, Thailand, 1981-82; commd. playwright Theater for the New City, NYC, 1983-87; distinguished visiting assoc. prof., Univ. of Colorado (Boulder), 1986-87. Winner Obie award (Boy on the Straight-Back Chair), 1969, (Bigfoot), 1973; grantee N.Y. Fdn. for the Arts Fellowship, 1986-87, Guggenheim Fdn., N.Y. State Council on Arts, NEA, Rockefeller Fdn., ZBS Fdn. Mem. N.Y. Theatre Strategy, Am. Theater Assn. Home: 438 W Broadway Apt 1 New York NY 10012

TAYLOR, ALEXANDER DOUGLAS, b. Rumford, ME, July 8, 1931; s. K. Austin and Anne Murray (McLeod) T. Author: (poetry) Stemmer i parken (transl. into Danish Peter Pulsen et al. bilingual ed.), 1984, Love Is a Terrible Light, 1983, Zadar, 1976; co-editor: (anthologies) Contemporary Danish Poetry, 1977, American Literature: Four Themes, 1966; numerous books trans. from Danish; over 200 publs. of poetry, fiction, essays, and trans. in mags. BA, Skidmore Coll., 1953; MA, U. Conn., 1964, PhD, 1970. Elem. tchr., Glen Falls, N.Y., 1954-55; sales rep. Eastern Corp., NYC, 1955-58; tchr. English, E.O. Smith, U. Conn., 1958-68, chmn. dept., 1964-68; Fulbright exchange tchr., Denmark, 1965-66; lectr. Magleaas Folk High Sch., Denmark, 1972; poet-in-residence Central Conn. State Univ., 1974,76; co-dir., editor Curbstone Press, 1975—; prof. English, Eastern Conn. State U., Willimantic, 1969— Fellow and grantee Conn. Commn. on Arts, 1973, Eastern Conn. State Univ. Fdn., 1974, NEH, 1975, 80, Yale Vis. Faculty Program, 1980, Augustinus Found., 1981, 82, NEA, 1983, Danish Ministry of Culture, 1974, 79, 83; recipient Conn. Arts award, 1981, Island and Continents Trans. award, 1979, 80. Mem. AAUP, Am. Lit. Translators Assn., Danish PEN. Home: 321 Jackson St Willimantic CT 06226

TAYLOR, BRUCE, b. Boston, Feb. 19; s. Edward H. and Barbara (Young) T.; m. Karen Leigh Jacobsen, July 4, 1983; 1 son, Noah Bruce. Author: Idle Trade: Early Poems, 1979, Everywhere the Beauty Gives Itself Away, 1976, The Darling Poems: A Romance, 1980; ed.: Eating the Menu, 1974, Upriver, 1979, 81, 84. BA, Bridgewater State, 1968; MA and MFA, U. Ark., 1972. Assoc. prof. Univ. Wis., Eau Claire, 1972—. Dir., Eau Claire Writers' Workshop, 1976—. Recipient Kenneth Patchen Poetry Award, Univ. Ark., 1972; Creative Writing Fellowship, Wis. Arts Bd., 1981; Fulbright Sr. Scholar, Seoul, S. Korea, 1981. Mem. PEN, AWP, Wis. Fellowship of Poets. Address: 1133 Barron St Eau Claire WI 54703

TAYLOR, CHARLES ANDREW (CHUCK), b. Cape Girardeau, MO, Feb. 25, 1950; m. Gloria Ross, May 20, 1971 (div. 1980); 1 son, Charles Andrew II. Author: Effective Ways to Recruit and Retain Minority Students, 1985, Cultural Retreat Handbook, 1985, Guide to Multicultural Resources, 1986, The Handbook of Minority Student Services, 1986. BS, SE Mo. State U., 1972; MS, U. Oreg., 1976. Fin. Aid counselor Univ. Wis., Madison, 1973-76, asst. to assoc. dean, 1983-84, dir. Oshkosh br., 1977-80; exec. dir. Civic Center Cape Girardeau, 1976-77, dir. Madison schls. Human Relation Dept, Madison, 1980-83; pub. Natl. Minority Campus Chronicle, Madison, 1982—. Deputy Adv., Wis. Gov.'s Office, Madison, 1980. EDPRESS, Intl. Black Writers Conf. Address: 4408 Village Ln Madison WI 53704

TAYLOR, CHARLES BRUCE, (Chuck), b. Mpls., Aug. 14, 1949, s. C. Bruce and Betty (Hall) T.; m. Margaret Adelle, Nov. 21, 1964 (div. 1977); m. 2d, Pat Ellis, Sept. 23, 1977. Poetry collections: Amerryka!, 1984, Ordinary Life, 1984, At the Heart of Things, 1986, Nothing's Impossible (prose poems), 1985; novel: Drifter's Story, 1986; essay collections: Only a Poet, 1984; fiction: Lights of the City: Stories from Austin, 1984. MA, U. Iowa, 1967; PhDNo. Ill. U., 1972. Mgr. Paperback Plus Books, Austin, Tex., 1981-82; prof., U. Tex., Austin, 1982-85, U. Tex., Tyler, 1985—. Lit. panelist Tex. Art Commn., Austin, 1985; artist-in-schls., Galveston Art Council, 1980-81. Winner poetry prize, Utah Arts Commn., 1979, Austin Book award, Tex. Circuit, 1984; grantee Tex. Arts Commn., 1985, 86. Home: Box 1385 Austin TX 78767

TAYLOR, CONCIERE MARLANA, (Carl Leader), b. NYC, Oct. 10, 1950, d. George Allen and Celestine-Winifred (Leader) Taylor. Contrbr. to Whetstone, Earth's Daughters, Rapunzel, Washout Rvw, other lit. publs. AA, Queensborough Community Coll., 1971; BFA, C.W. Post Coll.-L.I. U., 1974. Ed. Source lit. mag., Queens Council on Arts, Jamaica, N.Y., 1977-79, ed.-in-chief, 1979-81, lit. coordinator, dir. lit. arts div., 1979-81, now columnist, staff wrtr. for Profiles newspaper; freelance wrtr., ed. Winner prize New Worlds Anthology, 1980. Mem. PSA, P&W. Home: 67-08 Parsons Blvd Flushing NY 11365

TAYLOR, DOROTHY JEAN, (Morgan), b. West Liberty, KY, Jan. 20, 1950; d. Thomas Henry and Jane (Evans) Miller; m. Larry Wayne Taylor, Sept. 5, 1970. Contrbr. poems to anthols. Ed.: Case Managements Assn. of Southwest Ohio Newsletter, 1986-87. Assoc. Mental Helth Degree, Sinclair Commun. Coll., 1986; student Wright State U., 1986-87. Securities trading clrk. First Natl. Bank, Dayton, OH, 1977-85; case mgr. Commun. Living Center, Dayton, 1986—. Recipient Golden Poet award World of Poetry, 1985, 86. Home: 2831 Wyoming Dr Xenia OH 45385

TAYLOR, GEORGE FREDERICK, b. Portland, OR, Feb. 28, 1926; s. George Noble and Ida Louise (Dixon) Taylor; m. Georga Bray, Oct. 6, 1951; children—Amelia Ruth, Ross Noble. BS, U. Oreg., 1950. Reporter Astoria Budget (OR), 1950-52, Portland Oregonian, 1952-54; copy reader Wall St. Jnl, 1955-57, reporter, 1957-59, Detroit Bur. chief, 1959-64, Washington corr., 1964-68, asst. mng. editor (San Francisco), 1968-69, mng. editor (NYC), 1970-77, exec. editor, 1977—. Served to lt. USAF, 1955-57. Office: Cortlandt St New York NY 10007

TAYLOR, HENRY SPLAWN, b. Loudoun County, VA, June 21, 1942; s. Thomas Edward and Mary Marshall (Splawn) Taylor; m. Sarah Spencer Bean, June 12, 1965 (div. 1967); 2nd m. Frances Ferguson Carney, June 29, 1968; children—Thomas Edward, Richard Carney. Author: poems The Horse Show at Midnight, 1966, Breakings, 1971, An Afternoon of Pocket Billiards, 1975, Desperado, 1979, The Flying Change, 1985; textbook Poetry: Points of Departure, 1974; The Water of Light: A Miscellany in Honor of Brewster Ghiselin, 1976; co-translator: The Children of Herakles, 1981; contrbg. editor: Hollins Critic, 1971-78; editorial cons.: Magill's Literary Annl., 1972—; cons. editor: Poet Lore, 1977-85. BA, U. Va., 1965; MA, Hollins Coll., 1966. Instr. English Roanoke Coll. (VA), 1966-68; asst. prof. U. Utah, 1968-71; mem.

faculty Am. U., 1971—, prof. lit., 1976—, dir. MFA program in creative writing, 1982-84, dir. Am. Studies program, 1983-85; dir. U. Utah Writers' Conf., 1970-72; writer-in-res. Hollins Coll., spring 1978. Fellow NEA, 1978-86; Witter Bynner Poetry Prize, 1984, Pulitzer Prize in Poetry, 1986. Home: Box 85 Lincoln VA 22078

TAYLOR, JAMES ROBERT, III, (James Taylor), b. Balt., Nov. 25, 1950; s. James Robert and Marie Ann (McCubbin) T., Jr.; m. Rosemary Frances Pantaleo, June 22, 1980 (div. Jan. 1984). Author: Tigerwolves, 1982; Tricks of Vision, 1985; contrbr. poetry to Puerto Del Sol, Lips, Blind Alleys, other lit mags. BA, U. Md., Balt., 1973; MA, Johns Hopkins U., 1974. Pres. Dolphin-Moon Press, 1984—. Recipient poetry prize Sta. WAYE, Balt., 1972. Home: 29 N Kenwood Ave Baltimore MD 21224

TAYLOR, JOE W., b. Lexington, KY, Jan. 27, 1949, s. Mary Louise Cox; m. Tricia Lou Willey, Dec. 9, 1984. Contrbr. stories: Va. Qtly, S.C. Rvw, Sun Dog, TriQtly, other lit mags. PhD, Fla. State U. Editor, Swallow's Tale Press, 1983—. Part-time instr. Ga. State U., Atlanta, 1986—. Address: 736 Greenwillow Run Wesley Chapel FL 34249

TAYLOR, KEITH, b. Kelowna, B.C., Can., June 4, 1952; came to U.S., 1963; s. Donald M. and Joyce M. (Finlay) T.; m. Christine A. Golus, May 14, 1983. Author: Learning to Dance (collection of poems), 1985; editor The Borders Rvw (formerly Books from Borders), 1982—; articles, poems and rvws. pub. in Ann Arbor Mag., The Beloit Poetry Jnl, The Great Lakes Rvw, News Letters, Passages North, others. BA, Bethel Coll., 1975; MA, Central Mich. U., 1982. Creative writer in schls. Mich. Council for Arts, Detroit, 1980—. Home: 1715 Dexter Ann Arbor MI 48103

TAYLOR, MARTHA, see Dupes, Martha Gail

TAYLOR, MORRIS, b. Richmond, VA, Aug. 28, 1956; s. Morris and Lillie Mae (Lipscomb) T. Author: The Top of the Hill, 1987. Contrbr. articles to Brilliant Star, Spiritual Mothering Jnl., Am. Baha'i, Felbwship in Prayer, Ed.: (newspaper) Bermuda Baha'i, 1979-80. B.A., U. Va., 1978. Dept. supvr. Taft Productions, Doswell, VA, 1975-78; program coord. Bahai'i Natl. Center, Wilmette, IL, 1980-85; analysis supervisor Allstate Insurance Co., Northbrook, IL, 1986—. Home: 718 Mulford St Evanston IL 60202

TAYLOR, PAUL J., b. Waterbury, CT, Mar. 16, 1946; s. William O. and Mary E. (Plummer) T.; m. Margaret E. Siehr; children—Paul J., Jr., Benjamin J., Nathaniel W. Ed./pub. Better Health mag., 1979—. BA, Central CT State U., 1968. Pub. relns. spclst. CT Genl. Life Ins. Co., Bloomfield, 1969-73; v.p. Hosp. of St. Raphael, New Haven, 1973-86; pres. Inst. for Better Health, New Haven, 1984—; v.p. St. Raphael Corp., New Haven, 1986—. Mem. Am. Soc. Hosp. Mktg. & P.R., Acad. Hosp. P.R. Home: 249 Thornton St Hamden CT 06517

TAYLOR, (PAUL) KENT, b. New Castle, PA, Nov. 8, 1940, s. Paul D. Taylor and Goldie L. (McKee) Mihu; m. Joan Czaban; 1 son, Mark; m. 2d, Helen G. Hughes. Author: Selected Poems, 1963, Aleatory Letters, 1964, Fortuitons Motherfucer (with D.A. Levy), 1965, Late Stations, 1966, Torn Birds, 1969, Cleveland Dreams, 1971, Shit Outside When Eating Berries, 1971, Empty Ground, 1976, Driving Like the Sun, 1976; contrbr.: Wormwood Rvw, Glass Onion, Synapse, Cream City Rvw, numerous other lit mags. BA, Ohio Wesleyan U., 1962. Home: 1450 10th Ave San Francisco CA 94122

TAYLOR, PETER HILLSMAN, b. Trenton, TN, Jan. 8, 1917; s. Matthew Hillsman and Katherine Taylor; m. Eleanor Lilly Ross, June 4, 1943; children—Katherine Baird, Peter Ross. Author: A Long Fourth and Other Stories, 1948, A Woman of Means, 1950, The Widows of Thornton, 1954; play Tennessee Day in St. Louis, 1957, Happy Families Are All Alike, 1959, Miss Lenora When Last Seen, 1964, The Collected Stories of Peter Taylor, 1969, A Stand in the Mountains, 1968, Presences, 1973, In the Miro District and Other Stories, 1976, The Old Forest, 1985, A Stand in the Mountains, 1986, A Summons to Memphis, 1986. BA, Kenyon Coll., 1940. Mem. vis. com. dept. English Harvard U., 1966-83, lectr. in creative writing, 1973—; prof. English U. Va., 1967—. Recipient Natl. Acad. award fiction, 1950, Fulbright award, 1955. Home: 1841 Wayside Pl Charlottesville VA 22903

TAYLOR, RICHARD, b. Charlotte, MI, Nov. 5, 1919; s. Floyd Clyde and Marie Louise (Milbourn) Taylor; m. Thelma Maxine Elworthy, Jan. 14, 1944 (div. 1961); children—Christopher, Randall; 2nd m. Hylda Carpenter Higginson, Dec. 26, 1961; 1 stepdau.—Molly. Author: Metaphysics (Spanish, Dutch, Japanese, Portugese translations), 1963, rev., 1974, 83, Action and Purpose, 1965, Good and Evil, 1970, Freedom, Anarchy and the Law, 1973, With Heart and Mind, 1973, Having Love Affairs, 1982, Ethics, Faith and Reason, 1984; editor: Theism (J.S. Mill), 1957, Selected Essays (Schopenhauer), 1963 assoc. editor: Am. Philo. Qtly, 1972—; contrbr. articles to publs., U.S., Eng., Australia. AB, U. Ill., 1941; AM, Oberlin Coll., 1947; PhD, Brown U., 1951. Faculty Brown U., 1951-52, 53-63, prof. philosophy, 1958-63, chair dept. 1959-60, William Herbert Perry Faunce prof. philosophy, 1959-63; prof. philosophy grad. faculty Columbia, 1963-66; prof. philosophy U. Rochester, NY, 1966—, chair dept. 1966-69; Leavitt-Spencer adj. prof. philosophy Union Coll., 1981—. Served to lt. USNR, 1943-47. Mem. Am. Philo. Assn. Home: RD 3 Trumansburg NY 14886

TAYLOR, ROBERT LEWIS, b. So. IL, Sept. 24, 1912; s. Roscoe Aaron and Mabel (Bowyer) Taylor; m. Judith Martin, Feb. 3, 1945; children—Martin Lewis, Elizabeth Ann Taylor Peek. Author: Adrift in a Boneyard, 1947, Doctor, Lawyer, Merchant, Chief, 1948, W.C. Fields: His Follies and Fortunes, 1949, The Running Pianist, 1950, Professor Fodorski, 1950, Winston Churchill: An Informal Study of Greatness, 1952, The Bright Sands, 1954, Center Ring: The People of the Circus, 1956, The Travels of Jaimie McPheeters, 1958, A Journey to Matecumbe, 1961, Two Roads to Guadalupe, 1964, Vessel of Wrath: The Life and Times of Carry Nation, 1966, A Roaring in the Wind, 1978, Niagara, 1980; contrbr. to Reader's Digest, New Yorker, Saturday Evening Post, Life, Colliers, Esquire, Redbook. AB, U. Ill., 1930-33. Corr. Am. Boy mag., 1935; reporter St. Louis Post Dispatch, 1936-39. Profile writer New Yorker mag., 1939-63. Served as lt. comdr. USNR, 1942-46. Recipient Pulitzer prize for The Travels of Jaimie McPheeters, 1959, hon. mention award genl. reporting div. Sigma Delta Chi Disting. Service Awards, 1939. Mem. AG. Home: 5 Currituck Rd Newtown CT 06470

TAYLOR, ROBERT LOVE, JR., b. Oklahoma City, OK, Oct. 19, 1941, s. Robert Love Taylor and Willie Merle (Wiseman) Davis; m. Sue Ann Patterson, Sept. 9, 1962; children—Jennifer, Julia. Author: Loving Belle Starr, 1984, Fiddle and Bow, 1985; co-ed.: West Branch, 1977—. Stories in Georgia Rvw, Shenandoah, Western Humanities Rvw, Ohio Rvw, other lit mags. BA, U. Okla., 1966; MA, Ohio U., Athens, 1970, PhD, 1972. Tchr. public schls., Milw. and Willows, Calif., 1966-69; instr. Ohio U., Athens, 1969-72; prof. dept. English Bucknell U., Lewisburg, Pa., 1972—. NDEA fellow Ohio U., 1969-72, Pa. Council on Arts lit. fellow, 1983, 85. Mem. AG. Home: 265 Green St Mifflinburg PA 17844

TAYLOR, ROY G., b. Wayne County, NC, Dec. 7, 1918; s. Lewis G. Taylor and Kate (Turner) Taylor; 1 dau., Georgia Kay Page. Author: Sharecroppers: The Way We Really Were, 1984. Student, Wayne County NC public schools. Editor, Wilson Daily Times, Wilson, NC, 1981—. Home: 203 N Cone St Wilson NC 27893

TAYLOR, TELFORD, b. Schenectady, Feb. 24, 1908; s. John Bellamy and Marcia Estabrook (Jones) Taylor; m. Mary Eleanor Walker, July 2, 1937 (div.); children—Joan, Ellen, John Bellamy; m. 2d, Toby Barbara Golick, Aug. 9, 1974; children—Benjamin Waite, Samuel Bourne. Author: Sword and Swastika, 1952, Grand Inquest, 1954, The march of Conquest, 1958, The Breaking Wave, 1967, Two Studies in Constitutional Interpretation, 1969, Nuremberg and Vietnam, 1970, Courts of Terror, 1976, Munich: The Price of Peace, 1979. AB, Williams Coll., 1928, AM, 1932, LL.D., 1949; LLB, Harvard, 1932. Instr. history and poli. sci. Williams Coll., 1928-29; law clk. to U.S. circuit judge (NYC), 1932-33; asst. solicitor U.S. Dept. Interior (Washington), 1933-34; sr. atty. A.A.A., 1934-35; assoc. counsel U.S. Senate com. on interstate commerce, 1935-39; spcl. asst. to atty. genl. U.S., 1939-40; genl. counsel FCC, 1940-42; practiced with Taylor, Scoll, Ferencz & Simon; vis. lectr. Yale U. Law Schl., 1957-76, Columbia U. Law Schl., 1958-63, prof. law, 1963-74, Nash prof., 1974-76, emeritus, 1976—; prof. Cardozo Law Schl., 1976-77, 78—; vp prof. Harvard U. Law Schl., 1977-78; Fed. Spcl. master U.S. Dist. Ct. for So. Dist. NY, 1977-82; Adminstr. Small Def. Plants Administrn., 1951-52; counsel Joint Council for Edn. TV, 1951-61; chair NYC Adv. Bd. Pub. Welfare, 1960-63, mem., 1963-66. Commd. maj. M.I. service U.S. Army, 1942; lt. col. Gen Staff Corps, 1943; col. (assigned as mil. intelligence officer ETO, 1943-45); assoc. counsel, U.S. rep. for prosecution of war criminals, brig. gen., 1946. Recipient Natl. critics prize for non-fiction, 1979. Mem. AG. Home: 54 Morningside Dr New York NY 10025

TAYLOR, THEODORE LANGHANS, b. Statesville, N.C.,; s. Edward Riley and Elnora Alma (Langhans) T.; m. Gweneth Goodwin, Oct. 25, 1946 (div. Sept. 1977); children: Mark, Wendy, Michael; m. Flora McLellan, Apr. 18, 1982. Author: The Magnificent Mitscher, 1954; Fire on the Beaches, 1957; The Body Trade, 1967; People Who Make Movies, 1967; The Cay, 1969; Special Unit Senator, 1970; Air Raid: Pearl Harbor, 1970; The Children's War, 1971; The Maldonado Miracle, 1972; Rebellion Town, 1973; Teetoncey, 1974; Battle in the Arctic Seas, 1974; Teetoncey and Ben O'Neal, 1975; A Shepherd Watches, A Shepherd Sings, 1977; The Odyssey of Ben O'Neal, 1977; Battle Off Midway Island, 1978; Jule, 1979; The Trouble with Tuck, 1981; HMS Hood vs Bismarck, 1982; Sweet Friday Island, 1984; Rocket Island, 1985; The Cats of Shambala, 1985; Walking Up a Rainbow, 1986,

The Stalker, 1987. Press agt. Paramount Pictures, Hollywood, Calif., 1955-57; assoc. producer Perlberg-Seaton Prodns., Hollywood, 1957-61; free-lance producer, 1961-70. Served to lt. USN, 1944-54; PTO. Recipient Lewis Carroll Shelf award U. Wis., 1970; award for best nonfiction western WWA, 1977; Young Reader medal Calif. Reading Assn., 1984. Mem. SWG, AG. Home: 1856 Catalina St Laguna Beach CA 92651

TEAGAN, MARK TILDEN, b. Cambridge, MA, Mar. 16, 1945; s. John Edward and Gladys Marilyn (McGuinness) T. Contrbr articles to book; author case studies. Ed.: Patient Billing & Accounts Receivable, 1985, Admissions, Transfers, Discharges, 1985, Inpatient Registration, 1985, Accounts Payable, 1986, Medical Records Abstracting, 1986, Order Communications, 1986; Productivity Management in the Development of Computer Applications, 1985. B.A., Harvard Coll., 1967; M.B.A., Harvard Bus. Schl., 1976. Marketing support mgr. KeaMed Hospital Systems, Boston, 1981-85; mgr. pubs. Keane, Inc., Boston, 1982-86, marketing mgr., 1987—; free-lance wrtr., 1979-81. Mem. WG. Home: 54 Lewis Wharf Boston MA 02110

TEAGUE, BURTON WILLIAM, b. Portland, OR, Oct. 1, 1912, s. William Thomas and Bertie Mae (Bardo) T.; m. Sally Estes Reimer, July 30, 1938; children—Barbara Estes, Gregory Bardo. Author: Compensating Key Personnel Overseas, 1972, Financial Planning for Executives, 1973, Estate Planning for the Corporate Executive, 1974, Extra Pay for Service Abroad, 1975, The Economic Problem, 1975, Selecting and Orienting Staff for Service Overseas, 1976, Keeping the Incentive in Incentive Pay, 1977, The Board of Directors, 1977, Corporate Directorship Practices, 1978, Seven Steps to a Great Career, 1981, Compensating Foreign Service Personnel, 1982, Personal Money Management, 1984, Retirement Without Ulcers, 1985. ABA, Nichols Coll., 1933; JD, Ind. U., 1936. Spl. agt. FBI, Washington, 1942-46; freelance wrtr., cons., Short Hills, N.J., 1946-70, Basking Ridge, N.J., 1977—; sr. research assoc. The Conf. Bd., NYC, 1970-77. Mem. NWC. Home: 27 Dexter Dr N Basking Ridge NJ 07920

TEBBEL, JOHN, b. Boyne City, MI, Nov. 16, 1912; s. William and Edna (Johnston) Tebbel; m. Kathryn Carl, Apr. 29, 1939; 1 dau.—Judith. Author: An American Dynasty, 1947, The Marshall Fields, 1957, George Horace Lorimer and the Saturday Evening Post, 1948, Battle for North America, 1948, Your Body, 1951, The Conqueror, 1951, Touched with Fire, 1952, The Life and Good Times of William Randolph Hearst, 1952, George Washington's America, 1954, A Voice in the Street, 1954, The Magic of Balanced Living, 1956, The American Indian Wars, 1960, The Inheritors, 1962, The Epicure's Companion, 1962, David Sarnoff, 1963, Compact History of the American Newspaper, 1964, From Rags to Riches, 1964, Open Letter to Newspaper Readers, 1968, Compact History of American Magazines, 1969, A History of Book Publishing in the United States, 4 vols., 1972, 75, 78, 81, The Battle of Fallen Timbers, 1972, The Media in America, 1975, The Press and the Presidency, 1985, Between Covers, 1987. AB, Central Mich. Coll. Edn., 1935; MS, columbia U., 1937. City editor Isabella Co. Times-News (Mt. Pleasant, MI), 1935-36; writer Newsweek mag., 1937; reporter Detroit Free Press, 1937-39; feature writer, roto news editor Providence Jnl, 1939-41; mng. editor Am. Mercury, 1941-43; Sunday staff writer NY Times, 1943; assoc. editor E.P. Dutton & Co., 1943-47; asst. in journalism Schl. Journalism Columbia U., 1943-45; chair dept. journalism NYU, 1954-65, prof. journalism, 1949-76. Mem. Soc. Profl. Journalists. Home: 876-A Heritage Vlg Southbury CT 06488

TEGELER, DOROTHY, b. Effingham, IL, Oct. 12, 1950; d. Albert Bernard and Mildred Elizabeth (Haarmann) Tegeler; m. Steven Anthony Geisler, June 12, 1971 (div. Aug. 1984); children—Paul Anthony, Laura Ann. Author: Retiring in America, 1987, Hello Arizona 1987. Ed.: Insights, 1982-84, Credit Life and Disability Insurance, 1986, Author's Newsletter, 1986-87. Wrkg. on Moving to Ariz. B.S. in Edn., Ill. State U., 1971. Ed., McKnight Pub., Bloomington, IL, 1972-74, Ill. Farm Bur., Bloomington, 1982-84; pub., author Fiesta Books, Phoenix, 1986—; free-lance wrtr., 1974—. Pres. Ariz. Authors Assn. Mem. Phoenix Soc. Communicating Ats, COSMEP, Pubs. Marketing Assn. Home: Box 30555 Phoenix AZ 85046

TEGTMEIER, PATRICIA MAE READ, b. Portland, OR, May 27, 1937; d. Lawrence Arleigh Read, Jr. and Alice Margaret Aikins Read Moser; m. James Milton Tenney, June 9, 1962 (div. June 16, 1966); m. Albert A. Tegtmeier, Jr., Dec. 31, 1967; children—Ruth Selene, Matthew L. L. Contrbr. short stories, articles to mags., newspapers, newsletters including Alaska Woman Mag., New Horizons newspaper, others. A.A. with honors in Genl. Studies, Monterey Peninsula Coll., 1972; B.A. in English, U. Alaska, 1976. Pubs. technician State of Alaska, Anchorage, 1981-83; editorial asst. U.S. Dept. of Army, Ft. Richardson, AK, 1984—; free-lance wrtr., 1976—. Recipient Honorable Mention for short story Anchorage Lit. Project, 1977. Mem. Soc. Technical Communication. Home: 2101 Hillcrest Pl Anchorage AK 99503

TEISLER, DAVID A., b. Cleve., Dec. 26, 1953, s. E.G. and Margaret Rose (Szekely) T. Ed., contrbr.: QC Mag. of Queens County, NY C. of C. Corp. Relocation Program Series, Lookin' at Bklyn., NovaNews, The Natl Geographic Soc. Special Publ., numerous other publs. and video prodns. BFA, Bowling Green (Ohio State U., 1976; BEd, Cleve. State U., 1979. Mng. ed. Staten Island Mag., NYC, 1981-83; mng. ed., sr. wrtr. Motivational Communications, NYC, 1982-83; prodn. mgr. About Face, NYC, 1983-85; sr. wrtr., publs. ed. NCCI, NYC, 1985-87; dir of publ., The Soc. of Nuclear Medicine, NYC, 1987. Home: 262 Prospect Pl Brooklyn NY 11238

TEISON, HERBERT J., b. NYC, Nov. 22, 1927, s. Sam Bass and Ceilia Sidney Wokowisky; m. Kathleen Kolasky, June 24, 1968 (div. 1978). Contrbr. articles: Sat. Rvw, N.Y. Times, New Yorker, others. BS, CUNY, 1949. Publisher, Sat. Rvw Programs, 1960-75; founder, ed., pub. TravelSmart, 1976—, Travel Smart for Bus., 1980—. Mem. Soc. Am. Travel Wrtrs. Address: Dobbs Ferry NY 10522

TELLER, GAYL FLORENE, b. NYC, June 17, 1946, d. Reuben and Hilda (Eisgrau) Leibowitz; m. Michael Alan Teller, Aug. 14, 1965; 1 son, Paul. Contrbr. poetry to A Shout in the Street, Phoebus, Caesura, The Yellow Butterfly, Lyrical Fiesta, Jean's Jnl, Hartford Courant, Some Friends, Wyoming, the Hub of the Wheel, The Connecticut Writer. Author: At the Intersection of Everything You Have Ever Loved. MA in Curriculum and Teaching, Columbia U., 1969; MA in English, Queens Coll., CUNY, 1981. Tchr. English August Martin High Schl., Jamaica, N.Y., 1977-78; instr. Suffolk County Community Coll., Brentwood, N.Y., 1981-85, N.Y. Inst. Tech., Old Westbury, 1985—, Hofstra U., Hempstead, N.Y., 1985—. Winner Peninsula Library Poetry Competition, Lawrence, N.Y., 1984, 85, 1st Place Poem award Poetry of the Year, 1975, NFSPS (hon. mention), 1984, Artemis Poetry contest (hon. mention), 1987. Mem. Poetry Ctr., Modern Poetry Assn., Long Island Poetry Collective. Address: 1 Florence Ln Plainview NY 11803

TELSER, LESTER GREENSPAN, b. Chgo., Jan. 3, 1931; s. Asher and Edith (Greenspan) Telser; m. Sylvia R. Trossman, June 24, 1956; children—Joshua, Tamar. Author: Competition, Collusion and Game Theory, 1972, Functional Analysis in Mathematical Economics, 1972, Economic Theory and the Core, 1978, A Theory of Efficient Cooperation and Competition, 1987. AB, Roosevelt U., 1951; student, Harvard, 1951-52; AM, U. Chgo., 1953, PhD in Econ., 1956. Asst. prof. econ, Iowa State U., 1956; mem. faculty Grad. Schl. Bus. U. Chgo., 1958-65, faculty Dept Econ., 1965—; cons. to industry, 1964—. Served with AUS, 1956-58. Mem. Am. Econ. Assn., Am. Stat. Assn., Econometric Soc. Home: 1456 E 56th St Chicago IL 60637

TEMPLE, PENELOPE DENVER, see Thomas, Peter D.

TEMPLETON, FIONA ANNE, b. Bellshill, Scotland, Dec. 23, 1951; came to U.S., 1978; s. James and Norah (Monaghan) T. Author: Elements of Performance Art, 1976, London, 1984; contrbr. to Poetics Jnl, Boundary 2, JAA, Zone, Sun and Moon, Partisan Rvw, Musics, Wallpaper. Auditor, Aix en Provence U., France, 1972; MA with honors in French and Spanish, Edinburgh U., 1973; MA in Poetics, NYU, 1985. Translator, tchr., 1975—; co-dir., author, performer Theatre of Mistakes, London, 1975-79; dir. non-permanent performance co., NYC, 1980—. Recipient New Genres award NEA, 1983; Fund for Performance Art award Jerome Fdn., 1985; N.Y. Fdn. for Arts fellow, 1985; PEN Wrtrs. Fund, 1986. Mem. P&W. Home: 100 St. Mark's Pl Apt 7 New York NY 10009

TEMPLEMAN, KRISTINE HOFGREN, (Kira Thomassen), b. Rockville Centre, NY, Apr. 25, 1947; m. Thomas S. Templeman, June 25, 1983; children—Scott, Erica Hope. Contrbr. articles, chpts. to profl. jnl., scientific books. Newsletter ed. Assn. for Women in Sci., 1986-87; ed.: Quality Assurance in the Performance of Science, 1988. B.A., Fla. State U., 1970, M.S., 1973; Ph.D., U. Western Ontario, London, Canada, 1980. Research asoc. Dartmouth Med. Schl., Hanover, NH, 1985-86; staff scientist, wrtr. Health Effects Inst., Cambridge, MA, 1986-87; scientific ed., free-lance wrtr. Advantage Pubs., Cambridge, 1986—. Home: 12 Ten Hills Rd Somerville MA 02145

TENER, ROBERT L., b. Barberton, OH, May 1, 1924, s. Lawrence Edward and Ruby Margaret (Zeptner) T.; m. Barbara Ann Child (div. 1970); m. Carolyn Jane Albu, Jan. 3, 1971. Author: The Phoenix Riddle: A Study of Irony in Comedy, 1979; contrbr. articles to profl. publs. MA, Western Res. U., 1949, PhD, 1964. Asst. prof. Wilkes Coll., Wilkes-Barre, Pa., 1955-59; tchr. Milan High Schl., Ohio, 1959-60; prof. English, Kent State U., Ohio, 1960—. Mem. Modern Drama. Address: Eng Dept Kent State U Kent OH 44242

TENKILLER, LOUIS, see Homesley, Horace Edward

TENPAS, KATHLEEN MASON, b. Wickford, RI, Apr. 14, 1952, d. Harold R. and Verna Lee (White) Mason; m. Stanley Louis Tenpas, July 16, 1971; children—Julia Ann, Melissa Kay. Author: Country Woman, 1978, Hill Farm, 1985 (play produced 1987); contrbr. to: Aevum, Blueline, Farm Jnl, numerous other publs. AA, Jamestown Community Coll., 1984. Prtnr. in dairy farm, North Clymer, N.Y., 1972—; poet-in-schls., Sherman, N.Y., 1983; co-founder, prin. ed., Arachne: Hanging by a thread (now called Arachne, Inc.), to 1984. Recipient Spcl. Merit award Seed-In-Hand, 1982, award Natl. League Am. Pen Women, 1984. Home: RD 1 Box 314 North Clymer NY 14759

TERKEL, STUDS LOUIS, b. NYC, May 16, 1912; s. Samuel and Anna (Finkel) Terkel; m. Ida Goldberg, July 2, 1939; 1 son—Paul. Author: Giants of Jazz, 1956, Division Street America, 1966, Amazing Grace, 1959, Hard Times, 1970, Working, 1974, Talking to Myself, 1977, American Dreams: Lost and Found, 1980, PhB, U. Chgo., 1932, JD, 1934. Host of Studs Terkel Show,WFMT-FM, Chgo.; master of ceremonies, Newport Folk Festival, 1959, 60, Ravinia Music Festival, 1959, U. Chgo. Folk Festival, 1961, others; panel moderator, lectr., narrator films. Program, Wax Museum, winner 1st award as best cultural program in regional radio category Inst. Edn. by Radio-TV, Ohio State U., 1959, recipient Prix Italia, UNESCO award for best radio program East-West Values 1962, Communicator of Year award U. Chgo. Alumni Assn. 1969. Office: WFMT 303 E Wacker Dr Chicago IL 60601

TERRILL, ROSS GLADWIN, b. Melbourne, Australia (naturalized, 1979); s. Frank and Miriel (Lloyd) Terrill. Author: China Profile, 1969, China and Ourselves, 1971, 800,000,000: The Real China, 1972, R.H. Tawney and His Times, 1973, Flowers on an Iron Tree, 1975, The Future of China, 1978, The China Difference, 1979, Mao: A Biography, 1980, White-Boned Demon, 1984, The Australians, 1987; contrbr. numerous articles to Foreign Affairs. BA with 1st class honors, U. Melbourne; PhD, Harvard U., 1970. Tutor in poli. sci. U. Melbourne, 1962-63; staff secy. Australian Student Christian Movement, 1964-65; teaching fellow Harvard, 1968-70, lectr. govt., 1970-73, assoc. prof., 1974-78, research fellow East Asian studies, 1970—, dir. programs, 1974-78; contrbg. editor Atlantic Monthly, 1970-84; research fellow Asia Soc., 1977-79; freelance, 1978—. Recipient Natl. Mag. award, 1972, George Polk Meml. award outstanding mag. reporting, 1972, Sumner prize, 1970, Queen's Coll. exhbn. U. Melbourne, 1957. Mem. AG, Am. Poli. Sci. Assn. Home: 200 St Botolph St Boston MA 02115

TERRIS, SUSAN, b. St. Louis, June 5, 1937; d. Harold William and Myra Rae (Friedman) Dubinsky; m. David W. Terris, Aug. 31, 1958; children—Daniel, Michael, Amy. Author novels 1970—, latest include Stage Brat, 1980, No Scarlet Ribbons, 1981, Wings and Roots, 1982, Octopus Pie, 1983, Baby-Snatcher, 1984, The Latchkey Kids, 1986 Nell's Quilt, 1987. BA, Wellesley Coll., 1959; MA, San Francisco State U., 1966. Mem. AG, Soc. Childrens Book Wrtrs. Home: 11 Jordan Ave San Francisco CA 94118

TERRIS, VIRGINIA RINALDY, b. Bklyn., Aug. 26, 1917; d. Edward Sutherland and Edith (Staines) Rinaldy; m. Albert Terris, Feb. 14, 1942 (separated July 1969); children: Susan, Abby, David, Enoch. Author: (poetry) Tracking, 1976, Canal, 1981; co-ed.: The Many Worlds of Poetry, 1969; compiler: Woman in America, 1980; contrbr. articles, revs. and poems to Emily Dickinson Bulltn., Am. Women Writers, Am. Qtly., Contemporary Lit., New Yorker, Paris, Hampden-Sydney, Greenfield rvws, Nation, Poetry Now, Poetry East, Chelsea, Modern Poetry Studies, Ardis Anthology, also others. Freelance ed. Knopf, Harcourt Brace, also others, NYC, 1944-64; instr. to assoc. prof. Adelphi U., Garden City, N.Y., 1964-80, prof. English, 1980-83; self-employed wrtr., tchr., 1983—. Fellow Yaddo Colony, 1981, 83, Millay Colony for Arts, 1982, 84. Mem. PSA (ret. dir., 1983), MLA, PEN, Am. Studies Assn. Home: 393 S Grove St Freeport NY 11520

TERSCHLUSE, MARILYN ANN, (Marilyn Stafford), b. St. Louis, Nov. 18, 1956; d. Valerius Henry and Janet Marilyn (Dickerson) T. Author: The Inside Secrets to a Modeling Career!, 1982; The Missouri Creative Directory, 1982-83. BGS, U. Mo., 1979. Actress, model, 1974—; newscaster Sta. KMOX-CBS, St. Louis, 1979-80; entertainment reporter Sta. KPWR-FM, Los Angeles, 1986—; freelance wrtr., 1981—. Mem. AFTRA. Home: 727 Westbourne Dr Apt 112 West Hollywood CA 90069

TESTERMAN, JEAN LEIGHTON, b. Montrose, MD, Oct. 6, 1923; m. Andrew Testerman. Author: Cry Over Me, 1969, Eagle's Wings, 1973, Making It, 1985. Contrbr. articles to religious mags. B.A., Am. U., 1945; M.Edn., U. Md., 1962. Tchr. public schls., MD, 1975-85, State Penitentiary, Balt., 1985—. Coord. Vols. in Teaching and Learning, Howard County, MD, 1960's; cons. Md. Writing Project, 1981—. Home: 3634 Saint John's Ln Ellicott City MD 21043

TETLEY, ARTHUR RUSSELL, b. Kennett, MO, Oct. 22, 1930; s. Arthur Louis and Eva Ann (Owens) T.; m. Elizabeth Marie Schauwecker, Feb. 16, 1963; children: Mark, Douglas, Steve. Author: A Comprehensive Approach to the G5B-1 Gyro, 1963; Bird Taxidermy, 1982; contrbr. to Am. Hunter, Idaho Wildfowl, Waterfowler's World. Student pub. schls., Kennett. Specifications wrtr. Rockwell Intl., Seal Beach, Calif., 1964-69; specifications engr. Aerojet Nuclear Co., Idaho Falls, Idaho, 1969-76; sr. communications specialist EG&G Idaho, Inc., Idaho Falls, 1969—. Served with U.S. Army, 1951-54; Korea. Home: 775 Jeri Ave Idaho Falls ID 83402

TETLOW, EDWIN, b. Altrincham, Eng., May 19, 1905; s. William Chadwick and Mary (Entwhistle) Tetlow; m. Kathleen Whitworth Brown, Sept. 14, 1932; children—Susan Edwina (Mrs. Ray F. Bentley), Timothy Chadwick. Author: Eye on Cuba, 1966, The United Nations, 1971, The Enigma of Hastings, 1974; book reviewer: Christian Science Monitor; contrbr. Director mag. and Telegraph Sunday Mag., London. Student, Manchester U. (Eng.), 1924. Student journalist Daily Dispatch, Manchester, 1924-30. Mem. Staff Eve. News (London), 1930-33, Daily Mail (London), 1933-45; naval war corr., 1940-42; army war corr., 1942-45; Berlin corr. Daily Telegraph, 1945-50, NY corr., 1942-45; free-lance author, 1965—. Life mem. Fgn. Press Assn. (pres. 1964-65, mem. exec. bd. 1965—). Home: Peterskill House Alligerville High Falls NY 12440

TETREAULT, WILFRED F., b. Pawtucket, RI, July 31, 1927, s. Wilfred J. and Mabel (Fisher) T.; m. Catherine Calavlieri, June 1952; children—Thersa, Michael, Betsy. Author: Buying and Selling Business Opportunities, 1979, Starting Right in Your New Business, 1979, 10th ed., 1986, Business Appraisal, 1985, Financing Businesses, 1985, Listing Businesses, 1985, Starting Right in Obtaining Credit Cards, Auto, Home Business Loans, 1987. Ed. Brown U., R.I. Schl. Design. Corp. pres., mgr. Smith-Tetreault Corp., Bristol, R.I., 1958-60, Daisy Cup Corp., New Bedford, Mass., 1960-65; plant mgr. Bemiss-Jason, Inc., Palo Alto, Calif., 1968-70; real estate assoc. UBI, Inc., Santa Clara, Calif., 1976-78; pres. Mike's Union Co., Sunnyvale, Calif., 1974-76; chmn. bd. dirs. Am. Bus. Consultants, Inc., Sunnyvale, 1979—. Home: 1540 Nuthatch Ln Sunnyvale CA 94087

TEVLIN, MICHAEL F., b. NYC, Dec. 18, 1953; s. James Emmet and Eunice Marie (Roach) T. Writer, Lake Oswego Review, 1981-82, Valley Times, 1982-83; ed. AM News mag., 1983-86, Soaring mag., 1983-86. BA, SUNY-Oneonta, 1975; MA, U. OR/Sch. Jnlsm., 1981. Rptr., Lake Oswego (OR) Review, 1981-82, Valley Times, Beaverton, OR, 82-83; writer/ed. GranTree Corp.,Portland, OR, 1983-86; wrtr., Portland Genl. Elec., 1986—. Mem. IABC. Personality feat. award, SPJ, 1983. Address: 1042 Yates St Lake Oswego OR 97034

THAM, HILARY, see Goldberg, Hilary Tham

THAYNE, EMMA LOU WARNER, b. Salt Lake City, Oct. 22, 1924; s. Homer Candland and Grace (Richards) Warner; m. Melvin Erickson Thayne, Dec. 27, 1949; children: Rebecca, Rinda, Shelley, Diane, Megan. Author: (poetry) Spaces in the Sage, 1971, Until Another Day for Butterflies, 1973, On Slim, Unaccountable Bones, 1974, How Much for the Earth?, 1983; (poetry and prose) With Love, Mother, 1975, The Family Bond, 1977, A Woman's Place, 1977, Once in Israel, 1980; (novel) Never Past the Gate, 1975 (Book Club selection 1983); contrbr. essays to Joy, Turning Points, Blue Prints for Living, also monographs, non-fiction. Wrkg. on poetry and jnl acct. of 21 days in Soviet Union. BA, U. Utah, 1945, MA, 1970. Assoc. instr. English, U. Utah, Salt Lake City, 1946-76, instr. Inst. Religion, 1983-85; speaker at confs., seminars, workshops, 1975—; dir. Deseret News Pub. Co., Salt Lake City; vis. poet Poetry in Schls., 1972-76. Named Poet of Yr., Assn. for Mormon Letters, 1980, 85; grantee in field, 1982-85. Mem. AAP, Contemporary Authors, Phi Beta Kappa. Home: 1965 St. Mary's Dr Salt Lake City UT 84108

THEIBERT, PHILIP REED, b. Akron, OH, Sept. 22, 1952; s. Philip Richard and Ann (Connes) T.; m. Kathleen Coleman, Aug. 27, 1981; 1 dau., Claire. Author: (with Mark Pastin) Hard Problems of Management, 1985; Financial Planning Simplified, 1986. Contrbr. articles to mags. including New Management, Business Week Careers, Exec. Speaker, Tucson Mag. Reporter, Fulton Sun-Gazette, Mo., 1975-76; copywrtr. Owens Advt., Phoenix, 1976-80; ed. Ariz. Grocer Mag., Phoenix, 1980-81./B.A., Pomona Coll., 1975; M.A. in Creative Writing, Ariz. State U., 1986. Free-lance wrtr., 1981-84; corp. speechwrtr. Ariz. Public Service, Phoenix, 1985—. Eec. in residence Ariz. Sate U. Ctr. for Ethics, Tempe, 1984—; bd. dirs. Tempe Leadership Program, 1985. Mem. IABC, PRSA. Home: 42 W Vernon Phoenix AZ 85003

THERNSTROM, STEPHAN ALBERT, b. Port Huron, MI, Nov. 5, 1934; s. Albert George and

Bernadene (Robbins) Thernstrom; m. Abigail Mann, Jan. 3, 1959; children—Melanie Rachel, Samuel Altgeld. Author: Poverty and Progress, 1964, Poverty, Planning and Politics in the New Boston, 1969, The Other Bostonians, 1973, History of the American People, 1983; editor: Harvard Encyc. Am. Ethnic Groups; co-editor: Harvard Studies in Urban History. BS, Northwestern U., 1956; AM, Harvard, 1958, PhD, D1962. Instr. history Harvard, 1962-66, asst. prof., 1966-67, prof., 1973-81, Winthrop prod., 1981—; prof. Brandeis U., 1967-69, UCLA, 1969-73; Pitt. prof. Am history and instns. Cambridge U., 1978-79; dir. Charles Warren Ctr. for Research in Am. History, 1980-83. Recipient Bancroft prize, R.R. Hawkins award, Faculty prize Harvard U. Press, Waldo G. Leland prize. Home: Robinson Hall Harvard Cambridge MA 02138

THLIVERIS, ELIZABETH HOPE, b. Ft. Sam Houston, TX, Feb. 25, 1939; d. Robert Arthur and Bernice (Oden) Boyce; m. Thomas Allen Neyland (div. Feb. 2, 1960); children—Mark C., Carol A., Mary L., David A.; m. Tom Andrew Thliveris, June 23, 1960. Contrbr. poems to anthols. B.Music, U. Tex., 1959, M.Music, 1960. Tchr. Scottdale Schls., AZ, 1970-84, Paradise Valley Schls., Phoenix, 1986—. Recipient Golden Poet Award World of Poetry, 1985, 87, Silver Poet Award, 1986, 87. Mem. ASCAP, Songwriters Guild, Los Angeles Songwriters, Am. Choral Dirs. Assn. Home: 3302 E Cochise Rd Phoenix AZ 85028

THOM, JAMES ALEXANDER, b. Gosport, IN, May 28, 1933, s. Jay Webb and Julia Elizabeth (Swain) T. Novelist: Spectator Sport, 1978, Long Knife, 1979, Follow the River (N.Y. Times Bestseller list), 1981, From Sea to Shining Sea, 1984, Staying Out of Hell, 1985; contrbr. articles, rvws. to Sat. Evening Post, Natl. Geographic, Nuggets mag., Washington Post, others. AB, Butler U., 1961. Wrtr., columnist, ed. Indpls. Star, 1961-67; wrtr., ed. Rev. Pub. Co., Indpls., 1967-70, Sat. Evening Post Co., Indpls., 1970—; lectr. Ind. U., Bloomington, 1977-80. Mem. AG. Home: 10061 W Stogsdill Rd Bloomington IN 47401

THOMAS, ARTHUR LAWRENCE, b. Cleve., July 8, 1952; s. Anthony Leonard and Anne Louise (Rinkus) T. Author: Receational Wrestling, 1976, Bicycling Is for Me, 1978, Volleyball Is for Me, 1978, Fishing Is for Me, 1978, Backpacking Is for Me, 1979, Fencing Is for Me, 1979, Boxing Is for Me, 1979, Horseback Riding Is for Me, 1980, Wrestling Is for Me, 1980, Archery Is for Me, 1980, The Merry-Go-Round Book, 1981, Theater Publicity Handbook, 1982. Wrkg. on television and movie scripts. B.A., Baldwin-Wallace Coll., 1974; M.A., Kent State U., 1987. Theater critic Westlife, Westlake, OH, 1980—; drama dir. Brkly. City Schls., OH, 1980—, prof. Capitol U., Cleve., 1981—; tchr., cons. St. Ignatius High Schl., Cleve., 1982—. Grantee Marth Holden Jennings Fdn., 1977, 78, 79, 86, NEH, 1987. Mem. NCTE, ATCA, U.S. Inst. Theater Technology, Pioneer Drama Service (advisory bd.). Home: 12500 Edgewater Dr Lakewood OH 44107

THOMAS, BEVERLY PHYLLIS, b. Ashland, KY, June 11, 1938; d. Ernest Vincent Runyon and Samye Beaire (Maynard) Burns; m. Lawrence Winner Smith, Apr. 6, 1955 (div. Oct. 1957); 1 son, Jeffery Lawrence; m. Jack Lee Thomas (div. 1970); 1 dau., Samye Ann Thomas Davies. Contrbr. feature articles, bus. porfiles to mags. Newsletter ed.: Dateline Data Service, 1982—, Frick & Frack Revu, 1987—. Student Ohio U., 1976-77. Bookkeeper, Holiday Inn, Inc., Chillicothe, 1970-72; computer programmer Ross County Health Dept., Chillicothe, 1972-78; supvr. Dept. of Health, Columus, OH, 1978—. Mem. Ohio Commun. Theatre Assn. (delegate). Home: 1077 Rumsey Rd Columbus OH 43207

THOMAS, (CHARLES) DAVIS, b. Detroit, Dec. 20, 1928, s. Charles Richard and Nellie Clare (Davis) T.; m. Karin Ronnefeldt, Apr. 21, 1956; 1 son, Cord Alexander. Ed.: Moon, Man's Greatest Adventure, 1970, People of the First Man: Life Among the Plains Indians in their Final Days of Glory, 1976. BA in English, U. Mich., 1950. Reporter, staff corr. Life Mag., NYC and Los Angeles, 1954-60, mng. ed. Saturday Evening Post, Phila. and NYC, 1961-63; ed.-in-chief Ladies' Home Jnl, NYC, 1964-65; exec. ed. Holiday Mag., 1970, Travel & Leisure, 1971-75; ed. Down East Mag., Camden, Me., 1976—. Recipient annl. Book Award, Aviation Space Writers Assn., 1971. Home: 57 Megunticook St Camden ME 04843

THOMAS, DANIEL B., see Bluestein, Daniel Thomas

THOMAS, EVELYN F., b. Mineola, NY., June 5, 1922; d. David S. and Celia Thomas. Contrbr. poetry: Toward Solomon's Mountain: The Experience of Disability in Poetry, Kaleidoscope, anthologies. Wrkg. on poetry, travel-adventure book, novel, articles. BA in Art, Music, U. Mo., 1944; MLS, Fla. State U., 1958. Dir. libraries Instituto Cultural Peruano-Norteamericano, Lima, Peru, 1963-66; co-host TV program, Ministry of Edn., Lima, 1964; assoc. prof., liaison librarian Fla. Atlantic U., Boca Raton, 1967; behavioral scis. librarian Palm Beach County Community Mental Health Center, West Palm Beach, Fla., 1971-73; freelance wrtr., 1967—. Mem. South Fla. Poetry Inst. Address: 1200 45th St Van 109B West Palm Beach FL 33407

THOMAS, F(RANKLIN) RICHARD, b. Evansville, IN, Aug. 1, 1940, s. Franklin Albert and Lydia Elizabeth (Klausmeier) T.; m. Sharon Kay Myers, June 2, 1962; children—Severn Rhyl, Caerllion. Author: Fat Grass (poems), 1970, Alive with You This Day (poems), 1980, Frog Praises Night (poems), 1980, Heart Climbing Stairs (poems), 1985, Corolla, Stamen, and Style (poems), 1985, The Literary Admirers of Alfred Stieglitz, 1983; ed. The Landlocked Heart: Poems from Indiana, 1980, Centering Mag., 1971—, Years Press, 1971—. AB, Purdue U., MA, 1964; PhD, Ind. U., 1970. Asst. prof. Purdue U., Hammond, Ind., 1969-71; prof. Mich. State U., East Lansing, 1971—. Fulbright tchr., Denmark, 1974-75, lectr., 1985-86; MacDowell fellow, Peterborough, N.H., 1979. Mem. P&W, AWP, PEN, Mich. Poetry Council, Fulbright Alumni Assn., Soc. Study Midwestern Lit. Office: Bessey Hall MSU East Lansing MI 48824

THOMAS, GREGORY E., b. Washington, IN, Jan. 8, 1949; s. Clyde I. and Margaret J. (Newton) T.; m. Janet G. Williams, July 17, 1971; children—Laura E., Michael G. Contrbr. articles to automotive mags., other pubs. B.A., U. Evansville, 1971. Advt., bus. news mgr. Warrick Newspapers, Boonville, IN, 1971-74; reporter Washington Times-Herald, Washington, 1974-75; ed. Credithrift Financial, Evansville, IN, 1976—. Mem. IABC (founder, pres. Greater Evansville chpt., Silver Quill award of Excellence 1981, Silver Quill award of Merit 1984, Silver Quill Honorable Mention 1984). Home: 7925 Peach Blossom Ln Evansville IN 47115

THOMAS, HAZEL FOSTER, b. Sanford, NC, Oct. 13, 1923; d. Marshall Brown and Mary Currie (Foushee) Foster; m. William Chalmers Thomas, Nov. 29, 1943; children—Charlene, Patrice, William, Thomas. Author poems: Under Papa's Oak Tree, 1982; contrbr. to anthologies including Poetry Under The Stars, 1982, Soundings in Poetry. Student, Central Carolina Tech. Coll., Sanford, NC, 1978—. Two awards, NC Poetry Council, 1984; hon. mention, Top Records Songwriting contest, 1986. Mem. NC Poetry Soc., Friday Noon Poetry Club, Top Records Song Wrtrs. Assn. Home: Box 2246 Sanford NC 27330

THOMAS, JESSE JAMES, b. Greenfield, IN, Nov. 13, 1933; s. Jesse Brumfield and Evelyn Adella (Moss) T.; m. Mary Alice Jennings, Sept. 6, 1953; children: Carla, Claudia, Lisa, Jessica; (div. 1982); m. Bonnie Jean Grihalva, Oct. 29, 1983; children: Lance, Michelle, Michael, Dominique (stepchildren). Author: The Revolutionary Hero: A Phenomenological Study, 1972, The Youniverse: Gestalt Therapy and Non-Western Religions, 1978, Therapeutic Bedtime Stories, 1987; also chpts. of books in field. MTh, Garrett Theol. Sem., 1959; PhD, Northwestern U., 1967. Lectr. Northwestern U., Evanston, Ill., 1962-67; assoc. prof. Saginaw Valley State Coll., University Center, Mich., 1967-77; adj. faculty San Diego State U., 1979—, Calif. Schl. Profl. Psychology, San Diego, 1980—, pvt. practice Psychol. Services, La Jolla, 1977—. Mem. Am. Soc. Clin. Hypnosis, Calif. Assn. Marriage and Family Therapists, San Diego Soc. Sex Therapists and Educators, San Diego Soc. Clin. Hypnosis. Home: 11950 Navaja Ln El Cajon CA 92020

THOMAS, JOYCE CAROL, b. Ponca City, OK, May 25, 1938; d. Floyd Dave and Leona (Thompson) Haynes; children: Monica, Gregory, Michael, Roy. Author: (poetry) Bittersweet, 1973, Crystal Breezes, 1974, Blessing, 1975, Inside the Rainbow, 1982, Black Child, 1982; (novels) Marked by Fire, 1982 (Am. Book award 1983), Bright Shadow, 1983 (Coretta Scott King honor award ALA 1984), Water Girl, 1986, The Golden Pasture, 1986. BA, San Jose State U., 1966; MA, Stanford U., 1967. Vis. prof. English, Purdue U., Lafayette, Ind., spring 1984. Home: 2422 Cedar St Berkeley CA 94708

THOMAS, MARK ELLIS, b. Durham, NC, May 4, 1955; s. Ellis Porter and Nancy Margaret (Cantrell) T.; m. Kimberley Sands, May 17, 1984. Contrbr. poetry & scholarly articles to Coraddi, canadian Lit., Midwestern MLA Jrnl, Names, Little America,Coll. Poetry Rvw, Pegasus, William and Mary Rvw, Windhover, Explicator, Malcolm Lowry Rvw, Am. Notes and Queries, a-mongster, From the Viscera, So. Conscience. BA in English, NC State U., 1982, MA in English, Coll. of William and Mary, 1984; MFA, UNC-Greensboro, 1986, grad. students, Univ. of Ill., 1986—. Ironworker Daniels Construction, 1979-80. Mem. MLA, Midwestern MLA, AWP. Address: 714 South State St Champaign IL 61820

THOMAS, NORMAN CARL, b. Sioux Falls, SD, Feb. 16, 1932; s. Russell and Helen Victoria (Matson) Thomas; m. Marilyn Lou Murphy, Jan. 31, 1953; children—Robert, Margaret, Elizabeth, Anne. Author: Rule 9: Politics, Administration and Civil Rights, 1966, (with Karl A. Lamb) Congress: Politics and Practice, 1964, Education in National Politics, 1975, (with R.A. Watson) Presidential Politics, 1983; editor, contrbr.: The Presidency in Contemporary Context, 1975. BA, U. Mich., 1953; MA, Princeton,

1958; PhD, 1959. Instr. poli. sci. U. Mich. (Ann Arbor), 1959-62, asst. prof., 1962-65, assoc. prof., 1965-69; prof. Duke, 1969-71; prof. poli. sci. U. Cin., 1971-80, Charles Phelps Taft prof., 1980—, head dept., 1971-76, 81—; cons. Adminstrv. Conf. U.S., 1971-75. Served to lt. (j.g.) USNR, 1953-56. Recipient Disting. Service award U. Mich., Devel. Council, 1964. Mem. Am. Poli. Sci. Assn., Am. Soc. Pub. Adminstrn. Home: 510 Oliver Ct Cincinnati OH 45215

THOMAS, PETER D., (Penelope Denver Temple), b. Gloucester, Eng., May 11, 1928, came to U.S., 1965, s. Archibald Donald and Lucy Eleanor Anne (Packer) T. Author: Poems from Nigeria, 1967, Sun Bells (poems), 1974, Revealer of Secrets (folk tales), 1975, Songs of Gold: The Poetic Legacy of Nsukka, 1986; contrbr. to Don't Let Him Die (Christopher Okigbo Meml. Anthology), 1978; contrbr. poems, rvws. to African Arts, Lit. Rvw, Nigeria Mag., Green River Rvw, numerous other publs. BA, MA, Oxford, (Eng.) U., 1953. Lectr. U. Nigeria, Nsukka, 1960-65; vis. lectr. U. Utah, Salt Lake City, 1965-68; jr. fellow Mackinac Coll., Mackinac Island, Mich., 1968-69; prof. dept. English Lake Superior State Coll., Sault Ste. Marie, Mich., 1969—, ed. The Woods-Runner, 1970—, Danforth assoc., 1976—. Recipient Poetry award Utah State Inst. Fine Arts, 1967; Peter Thomas Collection started at Boston U. Libraries, 1969. Office: Lake Superior St Coll Sault Ste Marie MI 49783

THOMAS, ROBERT DICKINSON, b. Sacramento, CA, Oct. 2, 1945, s. Jack Irvin and Evelyn Lee (Barnett) T.; m. Jennifer Jean Abels, July 7, 1966 (div. 1974); children—Derek Michael (dec.), Kimberly Jean; m. 2d, Nicole Jean Pinard, Aug. 5, 1976; 1 stepson, William O. Stark. Contrbr. articles to Performing Arts Mag., Pasadena (Calif.) Star-News. BA in Journalism Calif. State U.-Los Angeles, 1977. Asst. dir. public relations Transamerica Fin. Corp., Los Angeles, 1977-79; mgr. publs. and media services Beneficial Standard Corp., Los Angeles, 1979-83; dir. communications, ed., pub. FORE mag., So. Calif. Golf Assn., North Hollywood, 1983—; classical music critic Pasadena Star-News, 1983—; public relations cons. Los Angeles Opera Theatre, 1982-83. Mem. Intl. Assn. Bus. Communicators (pres. Los Angeles chpt. 1984); recipient numerous awards. Home: 333 Stowe Terr Los Angeles CA 90042

THOMFORD, ARLINE GESINE, b. Zumbrota, Minn., June 19, 1932; d. William Carl and Gesine Emma (Stechmann) Yedke; m. James Anard Thomford, July 11, 1953; children—Peter, Paul, Joel. News wrtr., social editor: Zumbrota News, Minn., 1977-84. Contrbr. articles, photographs to bulltn., newspaper. AA, Rochester Community Coll., 1979. Tchr. Sunday schl. Christ Luth. Ladies Aid, Zumbrota, 1950, 71, 72, pres., secy., treas., 1970-86; leader Mineola Minuteman 4-H Club, Goodhue County, Minn., 1970-73. Home: Rt 2 Box 150 Zumbrota MN 55992

THOMPSON, CAROL LEWIS, b. NYC, Dec. 26, 1918; d. Jasper Robert and Freda (Rafalsky) Lewis; m. Elbert Paul Thompson, July 4, 1942; children—Timothy Lewis, Ellen, John, Abigail. AB, Wellesley Coll., 1940; MA, Mt. Holyoke Coll., 1942. Asst. editor Current History, 1943; assoc. editor, 1943-55; editor, 1955—, Encyc. of Developing Nations; assoc. editor Forum mag., 1945-49; contrbr. to Encyc. Brit., World Book Encyc. Mem. Am. Hist. Assn., Natl. Council Social Studies. Home: RR 1 Box 132 Furlong PA 18925

THOMPSON, DAVID JAMES, b. Gadsden, AL,Apr. 9, 1945; s. James Sawin and Ruth Eloise (Mafziger) T.; m. Sandra Sue Stromgren, Mar. 16, 1978; children—Jennifer, Erin. BS in Jnlsm., Portland State U., 1969. City desk writer, Oregon Jnl., Portland, 1967-70; free-lance photojnlst., Portland, 1970-79; tech. writer/engineer Tektronix, Portland, 1979-82; ed./pub. Micro Cornucopia, Bend, OR, 1981—. Office: Box 223 Bend OR 97709

THOMPSON, DEBORAH COLUSSY, b. Coral Gables, FL, Apr. 22, 1954; d. Dan Alfred and Helen (Graham) Colussy; m. Craig Sidney Thompson, Feb. 1, 1984. Assoc. ed. Travel & Leisure; ed. Adventure Road, Amoco Traveler, Signature, Carte Blanche nwsltr. BA, U. PA, 1973. Asst. ed. Travel & Leisure, NYC, 1978-83, assoc. ed., 83-85; ed. Citicorp Publishing, NYC, 1985-86; freelance writer, Pound Ridge, NY, 1986—. Home: Box 381 Cross Pond Rd Pound Ridge NY 10576

THOMPSON, EDWARD THORWALD, b. Milw., Feb. 13, 1928; s. Edward Kramer and Marguerite Minerva (Maxam) Thompson; m. Margaret Kessler, 1949; children—Edward T., Anne B., Evan K., David S.; 2nd m. Nancy Cale, May 28, 1966; 1 dau.—Julie; 3rd m. Susan L. Jacobson, Nov. 28, 1981. Grad. Lawrenceville Sch., 1945; S.B., Mass. Inst. Tech., 1949. Engr. Mobil Oil Co. (Beaumont, TX), 1949-52; asso. editor Chem. Engr. mag. (NYC), 1952-55; mng. editor Chem. Week mag. (NYC), 1955-56; aso. editor Fortune mag., 1956-60; with Reader's Digest (Pleasantville, NY), 1960—84, editor-in-chief, 1976-84; mag. cons., 1984. Recipient Golden Plate award Am. Acad. Achievement, 1977. Mem. ASME (exec. com.). Home: Beaver Dam Rd Box 189 Katonah NY 10536

THOMPSON, GARY ALLEN, b. Oxnard, CA, June 30, 1951, s. Mark Wesley and Harriett Jane (Wilson) T.; m. Cheri Lee Cain, Sept. 20, 1979; 1 dau., Tracy Lee. Author: Chumash (novel), 1986. Contrbr. stories, film rvws., articles to periodicals. BA in Poli. Sci., Calif. State U.-Long Beach, 1975. Mem. park staff Calif. Dept. Parks and Recreation, Point Migu, 1975-77; craftsman Pacific Bell, Torrance, Calif., 1977—. Mem. NWC. Home: 4622 W 149th St Lawndale CA 90260

THOMPSON, GERALD LUTHER, b. Rolfe, IA, Nov. 25, 1923; s. Luther and Sylva Carlotta (Larson) Thompson; m. Dorothea Vivian Mosley, Aug. 25, 1954; children—Allison M., Emily A., Abigail E. Author: (with J.G. Kemeny and J.L. Snell) Introduction to Finite Mathematics, 1957; co-author or author: Finite Mathematical Strucures, 1959, Finite Mathematics with Business Applications, 1962, Industrial Scheduling, 1963, Programming and Probability Models in Operations Research, 1973, Mathematical Theory of Expanding and Contracting Economies, 1976, Optimal Control Theory: Management Science Applications, 1981; assoc. editor: Inst. Mgmt. Scis. Jnl., 1966-69, BS in Elec. Engring., Iowa State U., 1944; MS in Math, MIT., 1948; PhD. U. Mich., 1953. Instr. math. Princeton, 1951-53; asst. prof. math. Dartmouth, 1953-58; prof. math. Ohio Wesleyan U., Delaware, 1958-59; assoc. prof. applied math. and indsl. adminstrn. Carnegie-Mellon U., Pitts., 1959-63, prof., 1963—, IBM prof. systems and operations research, 1980; cons. Prin. investigator Mgmt. Scis. Research Group, Carnegie-Mellon U. Rep. of Ins. Mgmt. Scis. to NRC. Served with USNR, 1943-46. Mem. Math. Assn. Am., AAAS, Econometric Soc., Inst. Mgmt. Scis., Operations Research Soc. Am. Home: 15 Wedgewood Ln Pittsburg PA 15215

THOMPSON, HUNTER STOCKTON, b. Louisville, July 18, 1939; s. Jack R. and Virginia (Ray) Thompson; m.; 1 son—Juan. Author: Hell's Angels, 1966, The Rum Diary, 1967, Fear and Loathing in Las Vegas, 1972, Fear and Loathing on the Campaign Trail '72, 1973, The Great Shark Hunt, 1977, (with Ralph Steadman) The Curse of Lono, 1982, The Silk Rd., 1984. Caribbean corr. Time Mag., 1959, NY Herald Tribune, 1959-60; South Am. corr. Natl. Observer, 1961-63; West Coast corr. The Nation, 1964-66; columnist Ramparts, 1967-68, Scanlan's, 1969-70; natl. affairs editor Rolling Stone, 1970-84; global affairs corr. High Times, 1977-82. Office: ICM 40 W 57th St New York NY 10019

THOMPSON, JACQUELINE, b. Morristown, NJ, Dec. 4, 1945. d. Bernard Lee Thompson and Dorothy (Bischoff) Hussa. Author: The Very Rich Book: America's Supermillionaires and Their Money—Where They Got It, How They Spend It, 1982, Future Rich: The Poeple, Companies and Industries Creating America's Next Fortunes, 1985; ed.: Image Impact: The Aspiring Woman's Personal Packaging Program, 1981, Image Impact for Men: The Business and Professional Man's Personal Packaging Program, 1985; ghostwriter: Color Wonderful: The Revolutionary Color, Wardrobe and Makeup Program, 1986, Upward Mobility: A Comprehensive Career Advancement Plan for Women Determined to Succeed in the Working World, 1982; ed., pub.: Directory of Personal Image Consultants, 1978, 79, 80-81, 82-83, 84-85, 86-87; researcher, contrbr.: What to Do with the Rest of Your Life: The Catalyst Career Guide for Women in the '80s, 1980; contrbr. articles to Forbes, Working Woman, Music Jnl, other publs. BA, Barnard Coll., 1969. Free-lance wrtr., public relations cons. Mem. ASJA. Address: 10 Bay St Landing Staten Island NY 10301

THOMPSON, LOU ANN, b. Dallas, Mar. 24, 1953; d. Houston Theodore and Eula Ernestine (Harmon) T. Contrbg. ed. N.Mex. Humanities Rev., 1985-86; contrbr. to Explicator, Lamar Jnl, Humanities, N.Mex. Humanities Rvw, Impact. BA summa cum laude, North Tex. State U., 1975; MA, La. State U., 1977; PhD, Tex. Christian U., 1984. Instr. La. State U., 1977-78, Lamar U., 1978-81, U. Tex., Arlington, 1982-83, Pan Am. U., Edinburg, Tex., 1984-85; teaching asst. Tex. Christian U., 1982-83; asst. prof. N.Mex. Inst. Mining and Tech., Socorro, 1985—. Mem. MLA, South Central MLA, Rocky Mt. MLA, CCCC, NCTE, Keats-Shelley Assn. Am. Home: 718 Liles Socorro NM 87801

THOMPON, LOUISE SAARI, b. Inglewood, CA, Aug. 28, 1943; d. Ferdinand Anton and Violet Elsie (Janu) Saari; m. Robert Allan Thompson, Nov. 27. 1970. Co-author: Egoshell, 1987. Contrbr. article to The Nautilus. B.A., Conn. Coll., 1980, M.A., 1982. Vice pres. research Spatialworld Corporation, Mystic, CT, 1984—. Mem. New England Estuarine Research Soc., Am. Assn. Advancement Sci. Home: 401 Factory Sq Mystic CT 06355

THOMPSON, PHYLLIS HOGE, (Phyllis Kirtley), b. Elizabeth, NJ, Nov. 15, 1926; d. Philip Barlow and Dorothy Morgan (Anderson) Hoge; m. John C. Rose, Oct. 6, 1951 (div. Nov. 20, 1962); children—Mead A., William S., John C. Rose Liao, Katherine B.; m. 2d, N. J. Thompson, June 3, 1964 (div. Mar. 12, 1969); m. 3d, Bacil F. Kirtley, May 14, 1983. Author: Artichoke and Other Poems, 1969, The Creation Frame, 1973, The Serpent of the White Rose, 1976, What the Land Gave, 1981, The Ghosts of Who We Were, 1986. Contrbr. poems to popular and lit. mags. Editor: Festival Hawaii, 1967, Haku Mele: Hawaii Poets in the Schools, 1968, 69 (project award NEH, 1968-69). BA, Conn. Coll., 1948; MA, Duke U., 1949; PhD, U. Wis.-Madison, 1957. Prof., U. Hawaii, Honolulu, 1964-83, retired. Dir., Poets in the Schls., Honolulu, 1966-72; mem. Hawaii Com. Humanities, Honolulu, 1979-81; bd. dirs. Hawaii Lit. Arts Council, Honolulu, 1973-80; mem. Hawaii Arts & Culture Council, Honolulu, 1972-74. Fellow, Yaddo; Danforth fellow. Mem. AAP, Rio Grande Wrtrs., Albuquerque Wrtrs. Home: 213 Dartmouth Dr SE Albuquerque NM 87106

THOMPSON, REBECCA, b. Dover, NH; d. Lawrence Clayton and Margaret Frances (Jordan) Thompson; m. Ted van Griethuysen, May 26, 1962. Contrr. poems, essays to lit. mags., anthols. Ed.: (poetry jnl.) Conn. River Rvw., 1987—; Poems from Mac's Harbor, 1987. Wrkg. on collection of poetry. B.A., U. N.H., 1958; M.A., Penn. State U., 1960. Tchr. ethics/poetry Aesthetic Realism Fdn., NYC, 1971-82; tchr. poetry Baldwin Ctr./Library Travelling Critiques, Stratford, CT, 1983—. Lit. adv. Arts Council, Stratford, 1987—. Mem. Conn. Poetry Soc. (pres. local chpt.), AAP. Home: 490 Sherwood Pl 1A Stratford CT 06497

THOMPSON, SANDRA JEAN, b. Chgo., Aug. 29, 1943; d. Russell Williard and Dorothy Alice (Eby) Thompson; m. George Allen Davis, Oct. 26, 1973 (div. Mar., 1981); 1 dau., Alexandra Thompson Davis; m. 2d, Lawrence Sierkese Kleinfeld, Apr. 12, 1981. Author: Close-Ups (short fiction), 1984; Wild Bananas (novel), 1986; contrbr. stories and articles to NY Times, Ms, Wash Rvw, Hanging Loose, Miami Herald. Wrkg. on a novel, Running Scared. BA, Ohio Wesleyan U.; MFA, CUNY-Bklyn. Staff writer St. Petersburg Times, Fla., July, 1983-84, asst. news features ed., 1984-86, news features ed., 1986—. Recipient Flannery O'Connor Award for Short Fiction, Univ. Ga. Press, Athens, 1983. Mem. AG, AWP, P&W. Address: 2973 68th Ave S St Petersburg FL 33712

THOMPSON, SUE ELLEN, b. Glen Ridge, NJ, July 19, 1948, d. Elliott Axel and Eleanor Jeanette (Bromley) Thompson; m. Stuart Lee Parnes, Nov. 15, 1979; 1 child, Thomasin Leah. Author: This Body of Silk, 1986; contrbr. poetry to Poet Lore, Denver Qtly, Seneca Rvw, New Letters, other lit mags. BA in English, Middlebury (Vt.) Coll., 1970; MA in English, Bread Loaf Schl. English, Middlebury, 1974. Bus. ed. Prentice-Hall, Waterford, Conn., 1971-78; freelance wrtr., Mystic, Conn., 1978—; assoc. ed. Tendril mag. Natl. Arts Club scholar Bread Loaf Wrtrs. Conf., Middlebury, 1982; selected for ConnTours touring artist program Conn. Commn. on Arts, 1984-86; recipient Samuel French Morse prize in poetry Northeastern Univ. Press, Boston, 1986. Home: Box 326 Mystic CT 06355

THOMPSON, THOMAS DWIGHT, (Dwight Thompson), b. Oklahoma, OK, Mar. 4, 1945; s. John Maples and Faye Elaine (Setters) Thompson; m. Nadine Marguerite Desloge, Oct. 22, 1966; children—Laurence Francoise, Matthew John, Gabrielle Mary. Author poetry: Through Chameleon Seas. BA, Southwestern State. Jobs include, dishwasher, rig roustabout, farmer, pea picker, prospector, song writer, real estate investor, lumberjack, fisherman, 1966-85. Home: 225 Piper Street Healdsburg CA 95448

THOMPSON, WILLIAM IRWIN, b. Chgo., July 1619 1938; s. Chester Andres and Lillian Margaret (Fahey) Thompson; m. Gail Joan Gordon, Feb. 3, 1960 (div. Jan. 1979); children—Evan Timothy, Hilary Joan, Andres Rhys; m. 2d, Beatrice Madeleine Rudin, Mar. 1, 1979. Author: Imagination of an Insurrection: Dublin, Easter, 1916, 1967, At the Edge of History, 1971, Passages about Earth, 1974, Evil and World Order, 1976, Darkness and Scattered Light, 1978, The Time Falling Bodies Take to Light, 1981, From Nation to Emanation, 1981, Blue Jade from the Morning Star, 1983. BA with honors in Philosophy, Pomona Coll., 1962; MA (Woodrow Wilson fellow), Cornell U., 1964; PhD (Woodrow Wilson dissertation fellow), Cornell U., 1966. Instr. humanities MIT, 1965-66, asst. prof., 1966-67, Old Dominion fellow, ,67, assoc. prof. humanities, 1968, York U. (Toronto, Ont., Can.), 1968-72, prof., 1973; vis. prof. religion Syracuse U. (NY), 1973; vis. prof. poli. sci. U. Hawaii, 1981; vis. prof. Celtic studies U. Toronto, 1984; founding dir. Lindisfarne Assocs., 1973—. Address: Box 130 Crestone CO 81131

THOMSON, CHRIS, see Schanstra, Carla Ross

THOMSON, SARAH ELIZABETH, b. Quincy, FL, Feb. 20, 1906; d. Paul Swainston and Elizabeth Gunn (Nicholson) T. Contrbr. essays, poetry, articles to anthols., mags., including Christian Science Monitor, Good Old Days Mag., Fla. Living Mag. B.A., Fla. State Coll. for Women, 1927; M.S., U. Mich., 1945. Prof. speech and communication Fla. State Coll. for Women and Fla. State U., Tallahassee, 1929-71; prof. emeritus Fla. State U., 1971—. Recipient First place for poetry The Poetry Reader, 1979, Honorable Mention award for short story Woman's Day, 1985. Mem. Am. Assn. Retired Tchrs., Natl. Speech-Communication Assn. Home: 530 Williams St Tallahassee FL 32303

THOMSON, VIRGINIA WINBOURN, b. Oakland, CA, Aug. 6, 1930; d. Harry Linn and Jennie Cook (Vineyard) T. Author: The Lion Desk, 1965; editor: Short Talks around the Lord's Table (Harry Linn Thomson), 1985. Wrkg. on two hist. novels. AA, San Mateo Coll., 1948; BA, San Jose State Coll., 1951; MA, U. Calif-Berkeley, 1952. Tchr. social sci., Capuchino High Schl., San Bruno, Calif., 1952-54, Watsonville High Schl., Calif., 1954-87; saleswoman, storyteller Home Interiors, San Mateo, Calif., 1963-64. Recipient Silver Pitcher award Home Interiors, 1964. Mem. Calif. Alumni Assn. (life), Natl. Geographic Assn. (life), AAUW, Phi Alpha Theta. Home: 215 Seville Way San Mateo CA 94402

THORMAN, RICHARD, b. NYC, Nov. 21, 1924, s. Lester K. and Helen T. (Tillis) T.; m. Margaret Spencer, Dec. 28, 1950 (div.); children—Adam, Thomas, Helen Barrett; m. Carolyn E. Lindsay, Aug. 7, 1984. Novelist: Bachman's Law, 1981; contrbr. stories to So. Rvw, Sewanee Rvw, Va. Qtly Rvw, Fiction; contrbr. poetry to Shenandoah, Spectrum. AB, Williams Coll., 1946; AM, Columbia U., 1948. Tchr. CCNY, 1948-50; wrtr. Natl. Acad. Scis., Washington, 1957-59, Voice of Am., Washington, 1984—; mem. arts adv. panel State of Md., 1985—. Recipient Goddard prize Tufts U., 1944, winner, Maryland Individual Artist Fellow in Fiction. Mem. Washington Wrtrs. Ctr. Home: 6721 Montell Ct Highland MD 20777

THORNDIKE, JOSEPH JACOBS JR., b. Peabody, MA, July 29, 1913; s. Joseph Jacobs and Susan Ellison (Farnham) Thorndike; m. Virginia Lemont, Sept. 7, 1940; children—John, Alan; 2nd m. Margery Darrell, Oct. 3, 1963; 1 son—Joseph Jacobs. Author: The Very Rich, 1976, The Magnificent Builders, 1978; editor: Seafaring America, 1974, Mysteries of the Past, 1977, Discovery of Lost Worlds, 1979, Mysteries of the Deep, 1980, Three Centuries of American Architects, 1981. AB, Harvard, 1934. Asst. editor Time Mag., 1934-36; assoc. editor Life Mag., 1936-46; mng. editor Life, 1946-49; pres. Thorndike, Jensen & Parton, Inc.; co-founder, sr. editor Am. Heritage Pub. Co., also vp. Home: 20 Cedar St Chatham MA 02633

THORNE, RICK JOSEPH, (Atma), b. Columbus, OH, Sept. 11, 1948; children—Shawn, Nahan, Michelle. Contrbr. to Kansas in Color, Peterson's Photographic Mag., Kans. Mag., Outdoor Ind. Mag., others. Pub.: Your Key to Success and Happiness, 1987. Wrkg. on pub. of Killed by Innocence, This Side of Hell, Ten Children's Books, The Book Called Feelings, 1000 Poems, 500 Song Lyrics, Sons of Thunder, Over the Horizon. Student in Mass Communications, Ind. U., 1971-73; Diploma, N.Y. Inst. Photography, 1977. Wrtr., photographer Ind. U. Newspaper, Indpls., 1970-72; prin. S.P. Pubs., Inc., Hollywood, FL, 1987—. Home: Box 223043 Hollywood FL 33020

THORNTON, DONALD RAY, (Don), b. Winnsboro, LA, Dec. 15, 1936, s. D.B. and Eutha (Cockerham) T.; m. Suzannah Smith; children—Kyla, Tribbey. Author: Outcry, 1960, Sounding, 1976, A Walk on Water, 1985; illustrator: Sucking on Rattlesnake Bones, 1976, Spare Poems, 1976, Cassandra, 1976, Eighteen Poems, 1976, Poetic Images, 1985, We Are Authors, Too, 1985, Mindscapes, 1985, Children Lore, 1985; contrbr. to Pawn Rvw, Black Creek Rvw, N.Y. Smith, Trovere's 5th Anniversary Wrtr.'s Book, numerous other publs.; ed.: Hypethral, 1984, Fantasy and Other Joys, 1981, Writeright, 1985, Whiffle. BA in Art Ed., La. Poly. U., 1960; MFA, La. State U., 1967. Artist-in-residence Coll. of Mainland, Texas City, Tex., 1973-76; set designer Am. Bicentennial Ballet, Houston, 1976; guest curator, designer Lafayette Natural History Mus., La., 1978. Recipient Book Publ. award La. Div. of Arts, 1981, Acadiana Arts Council, 1981, La. Reading Assn., 1985, St. Martin Parish Schl. Bd., 1986. Home: 1504 Howard St New Iberia LA 70560

THORNTON, MARY JANE, (Malia Lane), b. Honolulu, July 26, 1923, d. Harvey John and Mabel Wilma (Lane) Thornton. Author: Connections with the DC-8, 1960, Down Memory Lane, 1986. BA, U. Vt., 1946; MA, San Francisco State U., 1979. Reporter, columnist Fairchild Publs., NYC, 1948-49; ed. M.D. Publs., NYC, 1953-56; ed., wrtr. Liquidometer Corp., NYC, 1958-67; ed. ATS News, NYC, 1974—; mng. ed. Am. Thoracic Soc., NYC, 1967—; cons. Com. to Research TV Programming, NYC, 1970-71. Mem. AMWA, House Mag. Inst., Soc. Tech. Wrtrs. and Eds. Home: 16-28 Cedar Pl Oakdale NY 11769

THORPE, JAMES, b. Aiken, SC, Aug. 17, 1915; s. J. Ernest and Ruby (Holloway) Thorpe; m. Elizabeth McLean Daniells, July 19, 1941; children—James, John D., Sally Jans-Thorpe. Author: Bibliography of the Writings of George Lyman Kittredge, 1948, Milton Criticism, 1950, Rochester's Poems on Several Occasions, 1950, Poems of Sir George Etherege, 1963, Aims and

Methods of Scholarship, 1963, 70, Literary Scholarship, 1964, Relations of Literary Study, 1967, Bunyan's Grace Abounding and Pilgrim's Progress, 1969, Principles of Textual Criticism, 1972, 2nd ed., 1979, Use of Manuscripts in Literary Research, 1974, 2nd ed., 1979, Gifts of Genius, 1980, A Word to the Wise, 1982, John Milton: The Inner Life, 1983, The Sense of Style: Reading English Prose, 1987. AB, The Citadel, 1936, LL.D., 1971; MA, U. NC, 1937; PhD, Harvard U., 1941; Litt.D., Occidental Coll., 1968; LHD, Claremont Grad. Schl., 1968; HHD, U. Toledo, 1977. Instr. to prof. English Princeton, 1946-66; dir. Huntington Library, Art Gallery and Bot. Gardens (San Marino, CA), 1966-83; sr. research assoc. Huntington Library, 1966—. Served to col. USAF, 1941-46. Mem. MLA, Am. Antiquarian Soc., Am. Acad. Arts and Scis., Am. Philo. Soc. Home: 1199 Arden Rd Pasadena CA 91106

THORPE, STEPHEN J., b. Louisville, KY, Jan. 13, 1944, s. Virgil Leo and Elizabeth (Jackson) T.; m. Linda Karen Jensen, Apr. 1, 1967; 1 son, Richard LaVerne. Novelist: Walking Wounded, 1980; contrbr. short stories to Encounter, Calif. Qtly, Smackwarm; contrbr. articles to Western Horseman, Tex. Longhorn Scene, American Cowboy, other publs. BA in Philosophy, U. Wash., 1966; MA in English, U. Calif.-Davis, 1978. Mem. editorial bd. Calif. Qtly, Davis, 1972-75, bus. mgr., 1973-75; free-lance wrtr., 1970—. Mem. Sacramento Wrtrs.' Guild. Home: 536 C St Davis CA 95616

THORSON, ROBERT MARK, b. Edgerton, WI, Oct. 6, 1951; s. Theodore W. and Margaret (Anderson) T.; m. Kristine Elizabeth Hoy, Aug. 21, 1977; children—Karsten Adem, Tyler Curtis. Contrr. articles to Sci. Contrbr., ed.: (with others) Interior Alaska, A Journey Through Time, 1986; (with T. D. Hamilton, Katherine Reed) Glaciation in Alaska, The Geologic Record, 1986. B.S. in Earth Sci., Bemidji State U., 1973; M.S. in Geology, U. Alaska, Fairbanks, 1975; Ph.D. in Geology, U. Wash., 1979. Asst. prof. geology U. Alaska, Fairbanks, 1980-84, exec. dir. Alaska quaternary center, 1982-84; assoc. prof. geology U. Conn., Storrs, 1984—. Recipient Spcl. award for achievement U. Conn., 1986. Home: 9 Storrs Heights Rd Storrs CT 06268

THORSTAD, BRUCE, b. Mpls., Apr. 16, 1946; s. Harold Marlin and Agnes Helene (Bakken) T.; m. Ruth Clarice Pederson, Oct. 1, 1967; 1 dau., Holly Dana. Mag. ed.: Overseas Life, 1975-78, Holiday Inn Companion, 1977-78, Off Duty Europe, 1978-80, Off Duty America, 1980—. BA, U. WI, 1973. Ed., Overseas Life, Friedrichsdorf, W. Germany, 1975-78; ed. Holiday Inn Companion, Friedrichsdorf, 1977-78; European ed. Off Duty Europe, Frankfurt, Germany, 1978-80; U.S. ed., Off Duty Amer., Costa Mesa, CA, 1980—. Home: 17349 Los Amigos Circle Fountain Valley CA 92708

THRONE, MARILYN ELIZABETH, b. Cleve., Oct. 24, 1939, d. Charles George and Clara Elizabeth (Keiffer) Throne. Author preface: The Eye of the Beholder: Collected Poems by Malcolm Sedam, 1975; contrbr. numerous poems to Poem, Outerbridge, Cape Rock, Lyrical Voices, other publs. AB, Miami U., Oxford, Ohio, 1961, MA, 1962; PhD, Ohio State U., 1969. Mem. faculty Miami U., Oxford, 1964—, assoc. prof. dept. English, 1982—. Home: 631 Brill Dr Oxford OH 45056

THURMANN, HOLLIS (HOLLY LEIGH), b. Racine, WI, Aug. 7, 1946; d. Henry Thurmann Jr. and LaVonne Elma (Craig) Thurmann Hausen. Poetry in anthologies. Wrkg. on novel. Student Olivet Nazarene Coll., 1965, 66. Fin. coordinator H. W. Lochner, Inc., Chgo., 1980—. Home 73 Maple Ave Fox Lake IL 60020

TICHY, SUSAN ELIZABETH, b. Washington, Apr. 25, 1952; d. Joseph Charles, Jr. and Margaret Elizabeth (Bubb) Tichy; m. Lewis Michael O'Hanlon, Jan. 23, 1982. Author: The Hands in Exile, 1983; A Smell of Burning Starts the Day (poems), 1988.. Contrbr. poems, rvws. to lit. mags., anthols. BA, Goddard Coll., 1975; MA, U. Colo-Boulder, 1979 Visiting Assoc Prof., Ohio Univ., 1987, Colorado Council on Art sand Humanities Resident Artist, 1988. Recipient Poetry award Eugene Kayden Fdn., 1985, Pushcart Prize, 1986, Mem. P&W, NWU. Home: Box 357 Westcliffe CO 81252

TICKLE, PHYLLIS ALEXANDER, b. Johnson City, TN, Mar. 12, 1934. d. Philip Wade and Mary Katherine (Porter) Alexander; m. Samuel Milton Tickle, June 17, 1955; children—Nora, Mary, Laura, John, Philip Wade, Sam, Rebecca. Author: American Genesis (translated to Spanish), 1976, Of Snakes and their Skins, 1980, On Beyond Koch, 1981, The City Essays, 1982, On Beyond Ais, 1982, Tobias and the Angel (originally Puppeteers for Our Lady), 1982, What the Heart Already Knows (liturgical essays), 1985, Final Sanity (liturgical essays), 1987 Children of Her Name, 1987, Ordinary Time (liturgical essays), 1988; contrbr. to anthologies: Tigris and Euphrates, 1979, Windflower Almanac, 1980, Womanblood, 1981, Seabury in Memoriam, 1983, Samuel Johnson in Memoriam, 1984, Celebration in Poetry, 1986, others; guest ed.: Wrtrs. Circle, 1979, Chaff, 1979; contrbr. poetry: Images, Kudzu, Velvet Wings, Nexus, numerous other lit mags; columnist COSMEP Rural Rvw; reviewer, religious titles, Small Press Magazine, The Church News, other publs. BA, Eastern Tenn. State U., 1955; MA, Furman U., 1961. Mng. ed. St. Luke's Press, Memphis, 1975-82, sr. ed., 1982—; poetry coordinator Cumberland Valley Wrtrs. Conf., 1977-82; poet-in-res. Memphis Brooks Gallery, 1977—. Winner Polly Bond award, editorial bd. Diocese of West Tenn., 1985. Mem. Pub. Tennessee Humanities Council, Assn. of the South (chmn. 1984-85), Tenn. Lit. Arts Assn. (pres. 1984-85). Office: St Luke's 1407 Union Ave Memphis TN 38104

TIDD, CYNTHIA ANN, b. Elgin, IL, Dec. 4, 1956; d. Arthur Edward and Evelyn Ann (Dunovsky) T. Contrbr. short stories, poems o numerous mags., anthols. including Vega mag., The Villager mag., Jean's Jnl. Wrkg. on novel, short stories, poetry. Recipient 1st prize for short story Virginia Hardy's Oven, 1972. Home: 1606 S Princeton Ave Arlington Heights IL 60007

TIFFT, ELLEN, b. Elmira, NY, June 28, 1917, d. Halsey and Julia (Day) Sayles; m. Bela Tifft, July 17, 1938; children—Wilton, John, Nicol. Co-author: Carnival Woods (with Emily Katherine Harris); author chapbooks: A Door in a Wall, 1966, A Kissed Cold Kite, 1968, The Live-Long Day, 1972; contrbr. poetry, stories: New Yorker, Poetry, Yale Rvw, other publs. Wrkg. on novel, short fiction. Student Elmira (N.Y.) Coll., 1936-38. Recipient Annl. award Poetry Book Mag., 1953, White Mountain Press, 1981. Mem. PSA. Home: Del 342 RD 3 East Hill Elmira NY 14901

TIGER, MADELINE JOAN, b. NYC, Nov. 17, 1934, d. Howard Lang and Elinor (Hamburg) Tiger; m. Nov. 3, 1956 (div. 1975); children—Randall, Barbara Joan, Joseph, Timothy, Homer. Author: Electric Blanket, 1986, Toward Spring Bank, 1981, Keeping House in This Forest, 1977; co-author, Creative Writing: A Manual for Teachers, 1985; contrbr. poetry to Judaism, The Greenfield Rvw, Colo. State Rvw, Berkeley Poets Coop., Poets On, Worcester Rvw, Mother-Poet Anthology, others; contrbr. book rvws. to Home Planet News, Stone Country, New Directions for Women; contrbr. articles to Andover Rvw, Am. Poetry Rvw. BA, Wellesley Coll., 1956; MAT, Harvard U., 1957. Tchr. pub. schls., N.J., 1957-60; poet-in-residence N.J. State Council on Arts, 1973—. Creative writing fellow N.J. State Council on Arts, 1978, 80; recipient Fellowship of Citation, Columbia U. Schl. of Arts, 1985. Mem. PSA (Alfred North Kreymborg award 1975), PEN. Address: 15 Victoria Terr Upper Montclair NJ 07043

TIGGES, JOHN THOMAS, b. Dubuque, IA, May 16, 1932, s. John George and Madonna Josephine (Heiberger) T.; m. Kathryn Elizabeth Johnson, Mar. 22, 1954; children—Juliana, John, Timothy, Teresa, Jay. Author: The Legend of Jean Marie Cardinal (novel), 1976, Garden of the Incubus (novel), 1982, Unto the Altar (novel), 1985, They Came from Dubuque (biographies), 1983, Kiss Not the Child (novel), 1985, Milwaukee Road Narrow Gauge, The Chicago, Bellevue, Cascade & Western, Iowa's Slim Princess (history), 1985, Evil Dreams (novel), 1985, The Immortal (novel), 1986, Hands of Lucifer (novel), 1987, As Evil Does (novel), 1987, The Pack (novel), 1987; syndicated columnist, Tough Trivia Tidbits, 1983-87; columnist, contrbr. "Julien's Jnl," Dubuque Telegraph-Herald, "Memory Lane," 1979-80. Ed., Loras Coll., and U. Dubuque. Recipient World of Lit. award Carnegie-Stout Library, Dubuque, 1981. Mem. NWC, World Lit. Acad., Iowa Authors. Address: Box 902 Dubuque IA 52004

TIKTIN, CARL, b. Bklyn., June 27, 1930; s. Nathan Tiktin and Lena Slutsky; m. Colette Lafond, Sept. 30, 1955; children: Ross, Michelle, Hope, Laura. Author: The Hour Glass Man, 1978; Ron, 1979. Wrkg. on new novel. BA, Bklyn. Coll., 1955. Served with U.S. Army, 1951-53; Korea. Mem. PEN. Home: 87 Alta Ave Yonkers NY 10705

TILEY, SHARON KAY, b. Chambersburg, PA, June 21, 1952; d. John Lewis and Agnes Caroline (Kennedy) Tiley. BJ, U. Mo., 1974; MBA, Avila Coll., 1979. Advt. asst. Women in Bus. (Kansas City, Mo.), 1975-76; asst. public relations coordinator Am. Bus. Women's Assn. (Kansas City), 1975-76, public relations coordinator, 1976—, advt. mgr., 1976—; editor Women in Bus., 1979—; instr. Avila Coll. (Kansas City). Mem. Women's Polit. Caucus, 1978, editor MO ERA Coalition Newsletter, 1976, mem. MO host com. Natl. Republican Conv., 1976, secy. MO Fedn. Coll. Rep. Mem. Women in Communications, Intl. Assn. Bus. Communicators, Kansas City Bus. Communicators, LWV. Office: Box 8728 Kansas City MO 64114

TILLICH, HANNAH, b. Rothenburg Fulda, Germany, May 17, 1896; came to U.S., 1933; widowed Oct. 1965; children: Erdmuthe, Rene. Author: From Time to Time, From Place to Place, The Harbor Mouse; contrbr. to Confrontation, Winter Light. Home: 84 Woodslane Box 1334 East Hampton NY 11937

TILLINGHAST, RICHARD WILLIFORD, b. Memphis, TN, Nov. 25, 1940; s. Raymond Charles and Martha Borum (Williford) Tillinghast; m. Mary Graves, April 21, 1973; children—Joshua, Julia, Andrew, Charles. BA, Univ. of the South, 1962; MA, Harvard, 1963, PhD, 1970. Author: Our Flag Was Still There, 1984, The Knife and Other Poems, 1980, Sleep Watch, 1969. Asst. prof., U. of Cal., Berkeley, 1968-73; instr. College of Marin, 1976-79; asst. prof. U. of the South, Sewanee, TN, 1979-80; Briggs-Copeland lectr., Harvard, Cambridge, MA, 1980-83; assoc. prof., U. of Mich., Ann Arbor, 1983—. Mem. PSA, MLA, South Atlantic Language Assoc. Home: 1317 Granger Ave Ann Arbor MI 48104

TILLMAN, KAYLA LINN, b. Mayfield, KY, Sept. 16, 1962; d. Stanford Little and Barbara Ann (Burkhalter) Tillman. Contrbg. wrtr.: Progressive Farmer, Red and Black, Ugazine, other publs. BA in Journalism, U. Ga. Documentary wrtr. Ga. Public TV, Athens, 1984; copy wrtr. Total Video, Washington, 1985; city ed., Tifton (Ga.) Gazette, 1985-87; wrtr. Robbie Writes, Tifton, 1987—; ed./wrtr. Rowan & Assocs., Tifton, 1987—; ed. various newsletters. Recipient Documentary award Sigma Delta Chi, 1985. Mem. Kappa Tau Alpha. Home: 209 Love Ave Apt 202 Tifton GA 31794

TILTON, RAFAEL, (Madonna Elaine Tilton), b. Laurin, MT, Oct. 4, 1929; d. Charles Lester Tilton and Clara Mary (Nickol) Hansen. Author: Isidore Finds Time to Care, 1980, The Immortal Dragon of Sylene, 1982. Contrbr. chpts. to Concept Centered Curriculum, 1967, short story to Murder in Mind, 1985. Editor computer software manuals Minn. Ednl. Computing Corp., 1982, 83; asst. editor: Mpls. Spokesman, 1982—; contrbg. editor: Teacher Manual, Joy 6, A Religious Education Program for Intermediate Grades, 1979. BA in English, Edn., Coll. St. Teresa, Winona, Minn., 1959, MA in English, Fordham U., 1963. Joined Sisters of St. Francis, Roman Cath. Ch., 1949. Tchr. Cath. elem. schl., Austin and Rochester, Minn., 1951-59; tchr. English, Cath. high schl. in Minn. and Ohio, 1959-77; free-lance wrtr., wrtr.-in-residence Acad. Our Lady of Lourdes, Rochester, 1981, 85; copy ed. Sing Heavenly Muse!, 1982. Regional coordinator Minn. High School Press Assn., 1970-80; vol. Friendly Visitors, Winona, 1980-82; mem. Cable Commn., Winona, 1979-82. Recipient 2d place Cath. Press Assn. of U.S. and Can., 1982; 1st prize Stephen Maynard award Ky. State Poetry Soc., 1982; (2) 1st and 2nd prizes AAUW, 1983, 84, 85. Mem. Intl. Registry of Women Religious Artists, Loft-A Place for Lit. & Arts, Sing Heavenly Muse! (bd. dirs., (chair, 1987—), Delta Kappa Gamma (recording secy.), Third Age Programs (bd. dirs.). Address: Box 4900 Rochester MN 55903

TILTON, SISTER RAFAEL, see Tilton, Rafael

TIMMINS, LOIS FAHS, b. NYC, July 3, 1914; d. Charles Harvey and Sophia (Lyon) Fahs; children—Nancy Timmins Kirk, Kathy Fahs Timmins. Author: Swing Your Partner: Old Time Dances of New Brunswick and Nova Scotia, 1939, Understanding Through Communications, 1972, Life-Time Chart, 1978, Finding Words for Your Feelings, 1985 (booklet), 9 cassettes on Feelings and How to Cope with Them, 17 articles. MA, Columbia Tchrs. Coll., 1936, DEd, 1941. Asst. prof. Willimantic S.T.C. (CT), 1941-43, TX Woman's U., Denton, 1953-57; prof. staff Timberlawn Psych. Hosp., Dallas, 1957-80; prof. speaker/writer, Dallas, 1980—. Mem. COSMEP. Home: 6145 Anita St Dallas TX 75214

TINGHITELLA, STEPHEN, b. Bklyn., May 21, 1915; s. Michael and Carmela (Cestaro) Tinghitella; m. Inez Barbara Albertelli, May 20, 1945; children—Vilma, Stephen, John. Author: (with Jack W. Farrell) Physical Distribution Forum, 1973; sponsoring editor: Distribution & Transportation Handbook, 1970, Red Book on Transportation of Hazardous Materials, 1977. Student, Acad. Advanced Traffic, 1946-50. Traffic mgr. John Sexton & Co. (wholesale grocery distbn.) (Long Island City, NY), 1947-53; vp. Rupp Trucking Co. (NYC), 1953-56; dir. transp. Commerce and Industry Assn. NY (NYC), 1956-62; editor-in-chief Traffic Mgmt. mag. Cahners Pub. Co. (NYC), 1962—, pub., 1970—, vp, 1975—. Served to master sgt. AUS, 1942-46. Recipient Spcl. citation Pres's. Com. Employment of Handicapped, 1967, Editor's award Cahners Pub. Co., 1968, Editorial Achievement award Am. Bus. Press, 1974, 78. Office: 196 Boston Ave Massapequa NY 11758

TINNELL, (MARVIN) AL(LEN), b. Clarksburg, WV., Oct. 4, 1949; s. Marvin Ernest and Mary Martha (Hoffman) T.; m. Marcia Robin Johns, Jan. 26, 1974. Contrbr.: The Preston County Jnl., The Tampa Tribune, Dog Fancy mag., numerous others. Syndicated through CORD Inc. Wrkg. on legend, fiction, poetry. Home: 3317 Dorchester St Tampa FL 33611

TIPPETT, VIRGINIA MONROE, b. Cave City, KY, Nov. 19, 1901, d. John Glazebrook and Elizabeth Lucinda (Wilson) Monroe; m. James Campbell Tippett (dec. 1938); children—Jim, Mary Lucinda, Tom. Author: Jin and Jim's Love Story, 1984; contrbr. Second Spring. Wrkg. on novels, family histories. AB, Georgetown Coll., 1923. Sales mgr. F.E. Compton Pub. Co., Chgo., 1945-73, ret. Home: 1612 Chichester Ave Louisville KY 40205

TIPTON, CAROLYN LOUISE, b. Berkeley, CA, Aug. 19, 1950; d. James Lowell and Elizabeth Kolb (Coleman) Tipton; m. Frank Lada Kucera, Aug. 11, 1973. Contrbr. poems to anthols., lit. mags. Wrkg. on poetic translation of A la pintura. BA, U. Calif., Berkeley, 1973; MA, Stanford U., 1975; PhD. Calif.-Berkeley, 1987. Tchg. asst. U. Calif., Berkeley, 1978-79, assoc., 1979-80, 82, acting instr., 1982-84. Recipient Joan Lee Yang Meml. Poetry prize Undergrad. Council, U. Calif-Berkelely, 1973, Ina Coolbrith Meml. Poetry prize, 1973. Mem. ALTA, MLA, Phi Beta Kappa. Home: 4133 Balfour Oakland CA 94610

TISCHLER, MONTE MAURICE, b. NYC., June 9, 1931; s. Mortimore Harold and Lillian (Schnitzer) T. Freelance columnist: Sentinel-Echo, London, KY, 1984—. Student U. Chgo., 1948-50; B.S., Columbia U., 1963. Pres. Tischler Realty Co., NYC., 1976-79. Coordinator, Laural County Literacy Council, London, 1986. Home: Box 370 East Bernstadt KY 40729

TISSERAND, JACQUES, see Barnes, Jim Weaver

TIZOC, see Hruska, Elias Nicolas,

TOBIAS, ANDREW PREVIN, b. NYC, Apr. 20, 1947; s. Seth D. and Audrey J. (Landau) Tobias. Author: The Funny Money Game, 1972, Fire and Ice, 1976, The Only Investment Guide You'll Ever Need, 1978, Getting By on 100,000 a Year and Other Sad Tales, 1980, The Invisible Bankers, 1982, Managing Your Money, 1984, Money Angels, 1984. BA, Harvard U., 1968, MBA, 1972. Recipient Gerald Loeb award, 1984. Address: 683 NE 69th St Miami FL 33138

TOBIAS, RONALD BENJAMIN, b. Newark, Oct. 25, 1946; s. Irving Raymond and Elise (Jorish) Bean; m. Janet Stanley (div.); 1 child, Rory; m. Valerie Ann Jonsson, June 5, 1982. Author: Shoot To Kill, 1981; Our Man Is Inside, 1983; Terror en la Embajada, 1984; Kings & Desperate Men and Other Stories, 1985; contrbr. short fiction and non-fiction to Esquire, Statesman, Penthouse, Sports Afield, Kans. Qtly, Carolina Qtly, N.Y. Times, Antogonish Rvw., Descant, Mundus Artium, others. BA, Kans. State U., 1969; MFA, Bowling Green State U., 1970. Instr. Va. Commonwealth U., Richmond, 1974-78; assoc. prof. U. Tex., Dallas, 1978—. Mem. ALTA, AWP. Home: Rt 1 Box 365 Nevada TX 75073

TODD, ELIZABETH, see Rasley, Alicia Todd

TODD, RHESA, see Hutcherson, Harmon Harding

TODD, SAMUEL RICHARD, JR., b. Newburgh, NY, Aug. 29, 1940; s. Samuel Richard and Miriam Agnes (Walsh) Todd; m. Susan Burgess Bagg, Nov. 9, 1964; children—Emily, Margaret, Elinor. BA, Amherst Coll., 1962; postgrad., Stanford U., 1963-65. Advt. copywriter BBDO (NYC), 1962-63; free-lance writer (Los Altos Hills, CA), 1965-67; editor Houghton Mifflin (Boston), 1967-69; with Atlantic Monthly Co. (Boston), 1969—, assoc. editor, 1970-77, exec. editor, 1977-82, sr. editor, 1982-83; editor Richard Todd Books, 1983—; contrbg. ed. New England Monthly, 1984—. Office: Box 446 Haydenville MA 01039

TODD, WILLIAM BURTON, b. Chester, PA, Apr. 11, 1919; s. William Booth and Edith Hawkins (Burton) Todd; m. Ann Bowden, Nov. 23, 1969; children by previous marriage—Marilyn Chestnut Todd Guinn, Susan Linda Todd Kramer, Deborah Burton, Terence Kingsley. Author: New Adventures among Old Books, 1958, Prize Books: Awards Granted to Scholars, 1961, Bibliography of Edmund Burke, 1964, Directory of Printers: London 1800-1840, 1972, The White House Transcripts: An Enquiry, 1974, The Gutenberg Bible: New Evidence, 1982; editor: Goldsmith's Prospect of Society, 1954, Burke's Reflections on the Revolution in France, 1959, Thomas J. Wise Centenary Studies, 1959, (with E. Stenbock-Fermor) The Kilgour Collection of Russian Literature, 1959, Guy of Warwick, 1968, Suppressed Commentaries on the Wiseian Forgeries, 1969, Hume and the Enlightenment, 1974, (with R.H. Campbell and A.S. Skinner) Smith's Wealth of Nations, 1976, (with Paul Langford) Writings and Speeches of Burke, 1981, Hume's History of England, 1983—, Papers Bibliog. Soc. Am., 1967-81. BA, Lehigh U., 1940, MA, 1947, LHD (hon.), 1975; PhD, U. Chgo., 1949. Prof., head dept. English, Salem Coll.(NC), 1949-54; asst. librarian Houghton Library, Harvard U., 1955-58; assoc. prof. English, U. Tex. (Austin), 1958, prof., dir. bibliog. research, 1959-82, Kerr Centennial prof. English history and culture, 1982—; JRP Lyell reader in bibliography Oxford U. (Eng.), 1969-70; vis. fellow All Souls Coll., 1970; Andrew D. Osborn lectr. U. Western Ont., 1978; cons. Natl. Library Australia, 1973, NEH Research Tools Program, 1977-78; D. Nichol Smith lectr. Australian Natl. U. (Canberra), 1973; Cecil Oldman Meml. lectr. Leeds U. (Eng.), 1975; Intl. Library lectr., Leipzig, E. Ger., 1981; natl. adv. bd. Center for the Book, 1978—. Served to maj. inf. AUS, 1941-45; ETO. Recipient Oldman Meml. award and Marc Fitch bibliography prize, 1975. Mem. Pvt. Libraries Assn. (Eng.) Home: 2109B Expo Blvd Austin TX 78703

TOFFLER, ALVIN, b. NYC, Oct. 4, 1928; s. Sam and Rose (Albaum) Toffler; m. Adelaide Elizabeth Farrell, Apr. 29, 1950; 1 dau.—Karen. Author: The Culture Consumers, 1964, Future Shock, 1970, The Eco-Spasm Report, 1975, The Third Wave, 1980, Previews and Promises, 1983, The Adaptive Corporation. 1986. editor: Schoolhouse in the City, 1968, The Futurists, 1972, Learning for Tomorrow, 1974; contbg. editor: Art News; contrbr. editor: Art News. AB, NYU, 1949; LL.D (hon), U. Western Ont., Lit. D., U. Cin., Miami U., D.Sc., Rensselaer Poly. inst., Litt.D., Ripon Coll. Washington Corr. various newspapers, mags., 1957-59; assoc. editor Fortune, 1959-61; mem. faculty New Sch. for Social Research, 1965-67; vis. scholar Russell Sage Found., 1969-70; vis. prof. Cornell U. (Ithaca, NY), 1969; Cons. Rockefeller Bros. Fund., Inst. for Future, AT & T, Ednl. Facilities Labs., Inc., Address: Washington CT 06793

TOLAND, JOHN WILLARD, b. La Crosse, WI, June 29, 1912; s. Ralph and Helen Chandler (Snow) Toland; m. Toshiko Matsumara, Mar. 12, 1960; 1 dau.—Tamiko; children by previous marriage—Diana Toland Netzer, Marcia Toland. Author: Ships in the Sky, 1957, Battle: The Story of the Bulge, 1959, But Not in Shame, 1961, The Dillinger Days, 1963, The Flying Tigers, 1963, The Last 100 Days, 1966, The Battle of the Bulge, 1966, The Rising Sun, 1970 (Pulitzer prize for non-fiction), Adolf Hitler, 1976, Hitler, the Pictorial Documentary of His Life, 1978, No Man's Land, 1980, Infamy, 1982, Gods of War, 1985; also short stories. BA, Williams Coll., 1936; student, Yale Drama Schl., 1936-37; LHD, Williams Coll., 1968; U. Alaska, 1977, U. Conn., 1986. Mem. adv. council Natl. Archives. Mem. AG, Accademia del Mediterraneo, Western Front Assn. (hon. vp). Home: 1 Long Ridge Rd Danbury CT 06810

TOLBERT, CLEDITH CASSIDY, b. McBee, SC, Dec. 8, 1922; d. Elza and Alta Ellen (Winninger) Cassidy; m. Harry L. Tolbert (dec. 1982); children—Harry L., Larry E., John K., James L. Contrbr. poetry: Homespun mag., Farmers Guide, Ariz. Hwys., other periodicals; contrbr. articles, Indpls. Star, Indpls. News, Louisville Times, Louisville Courier-Jnl., other mags. and newspapers. Wrkg. on biography, book of poetry. Ed. Central Normal Coll., Danville, Ind. News ed. Springs Valley Herald, French Lick, Ind., 1958-82. DD(hon.), Ch. of Gospel Ministry, 1978. Home: Box 274 West Baden IN 47469

TOLCHIN, MARTIN, b., NYC, Sept. 20, 1928; s. Charles T. and Evelyn (Weisman) Tolchin; m. Susan Jane Goldsmith, Dec. 23, 1965; children—Charles, Karen. Author: (with Susan Jane Tolchin) To The Victor, 1971, Clout—Women Power and Politics, 1974, Dismantling America—The Rush to Deregulate, 1983. Student, U. Utah, 1947-49; LL.B., NY Law Schl., 1951. Reporter NY Times (NYC), 1954—. Served with US Army, 1951-53. Recipient Schaeffer Gold Typewriter award E.M. Schaeffer Co., 1967, Page One award, 1967, Sigma Delta Chi award, 1973, award for disting. reporting of Congress Everett M. Dirksen, 1983. Home: 5117 Wickett Terr Bethesda MD 20814

TOLEDANO, RALPH DE, b. Internat. Zone of Tangier, Aug. 17, 1916; m. Nora Romaine, July 6, 1938 (div.); children—James, Paul. Author: Seeds of Treason, 1950, Spies, Dupes and Diplomats, 1952, Day of Reckoning, 1955, Nixon, 1956, Lament for a Generation, 1960, The Greatest Plot in History, 1963, The Winning Side, 1963, The Goldwater Story, 1964, RFK: The Man Who Would be President, 1967, America, I-Love-You, 1968, One Man Alone: Richard M. Nixon, 1969, Cladue Kirk: Man and Myth, 1970, Little Cesar, 1971, J. Edgar Hoover: The Man in His Time, 1973, Hit and Run: The Ralph Nader Story, 1975, Let Our Cities Burn, 1975; poems: You & I, 1978, Devil Take Him, 1979; editor: Frontiers of Jazz, 1947; co-editor: The Conservative Papers, 1964; editor-in-chief: Political Success, 1968-69; mem. adv. bd.: Yale Lit. Mag., 1981—; contbr. to nat. mags. BA, Columbia Coll., 1938. Founder, co-editor Jazz Info., 1938-39; assoc. editor The New Leader, 1941-43; editor The Standard, 1946; mng. editor Plain Talk, 1946-47; pub. dir. Dress Joint Bd., Intl. Ladies Garment Workers Union, 1947-48; asst. editor Newsweek, 1948, natl. reports editor, 1950-60; Washington corr., 1956-60; syndicated columnist King Features, 1960-71, Natl. News Research Syndicate, 1971-74, Copley News Service, 1974—; chief Washington Bur., Taft Broadcasting Co., 1960-61; contbg. editor Natl. Rev., 1960—; pres. Natl. News-Research, 1960—, Anthem Books, 1970; editor-in-chief Washington World, 1961-62; mem. 20th Century Fund Task Force on Freedom Press, 1971-72. Served in OSS and as info. specialist in AUS, 1943-46. Recipient Freedoms Fdn. award, 1950, 61, 74, Americanism award VFW, 1953. Mem. Intl. Mark Twain Soc. (chevalier). Office: 825 New Hampshire Ave NW Washington DC 20037

TOLEDO-PEREYRA, LUIS HORACIO, b. Nogales, AZ, Oct. 19, 1943; s. Jose Horacio Toledo and Elia (Elvira) Pereyra; m. Marjean May Gilbert, Mar. 21, 1973; children—Alexander Horacio, Suzanne Elizabeth. Author: The Pancreas, Principles of Medical and Surgical Practice, 1985, Complications of Organ Transplantation, 1987. Ed: Basic Concepts of Organ Procurement, Perfusion, and Preservation, 1982. Wrkg. on C. Walton Lillehei: Life & Accomplishments; Organ Preservation. Collegio Regis, Hermosillo, Sonora, Mexico, 1960; M.D. summa cum laude, Natl. U. Mex., Mexico City, 1967; Ph.D., U. Minn., 1976. Chief surgical research, co-dir. transplantation Henry Ford Hosp., Detroit, 1977-79; chief transplantation, dir. research Mount Carmel Mercy Hosp., Detroit, 1979—. Recipient Med. Jnl. Manuscript award Henry Ford Hosp., 1979. Mem. AMWA. Office: Dept Transplant Mt Carmel Mercy Hosp 6071 W Outer Dr Detroit MI 48235

TOLLES, MARTHA, b. Oklahoma City, d. Willis and Natalie Mary (Dunbar) Gregory; m. Edwin Leroy Tolles, June 21, 1944; children—Stephen, Henry, Cynthia, Roy, James, Thomas. Children's books: Katie and Those Boys, 1974 (first published as Too Many Boys, 1965), Katie for President, 1976, Katie's Babysitting Job, 1985, Who's Reading Darci's Diary, 1984, Darci and the Dance Contest, 1985; contrbr. short stories to mags., anthologies. BA in English, Smith Coll., 1943. Genl. reporter Port Chester (N.Y.) Daily Item, 1943—; editorial bd. Pubs. Weekly, NYC1944—. Mem. Soc. Children's Book Wrtrs., Address: 860 Oxford Rd San Marino CA 91108

TOLLESON, EVANGELINE W., b. Shreveport, LA. Ed.: 1985, San Francisco Bus. Mag., 1985-87, ed. and art dir., 1987—. Student U. Ark., 1974-76; B.A. in Mass Media News, U. Tulsa, 1977. News reporter Shreveport Jnl., 1978-82; mgr. communications Shreveport Chamber of Commerce, 1982-85, ed. Shreveport Mag., 1985; mgr. pubns. San Francisco Chamber of Commerce, 1985—. Recipient Best of Show award Shreveport Advt. Fedn., 1983, (3) Gold awards, 1985. Mem. PRSA, San Francisco Advt. Club, Am. Chamber of Commerce Execs. (communications council, Grand awad for community viewbooks 1983, Grand award for membership materials, 1984). Office: SFB 465 California St 9th Floor San Francisco CA 94104

TOLLEY, TRESA GAIL, b. Decatur, IL, June 19, 1946; d. Jetson Edgar and Tressie (Gaston) Livingston; m. Bob Tolley, Aug. 17, 1965 (div. Apr. 19, 1970), 1 son, Bobby Gene. Contrbr. poems to anthols. Wrkg. on short stories, poetry, novel. B.A. in English, Southern Ill. U., 1974, M.S. in Secondary Edn./English, 1988. Office supvr. Southern Ill. U., Carbondale, 1976-79, staff clrk. acad. affairs, 1979—. Home: 305 E Freeman Carbondale IL 62901

TOM, CREIGHTON HARVEY, (Craig H. Tom), b. Oakland, Calif., Mar. 29, 1944; s. Harvey and Katheirne (Lew) T. Co-author: Distant Bugles, 1988, The Invisible War (novel), 1988; author tech. papers. Wrkg. on short stories, novels. MS in Stats., Colo. State U., 1972, PhD in Computer Sci., 1978. Astronaut candidate NASA, Johnson Space Center, Houston, 1980; cons., Golden, Colo., 1981; scientist, specialist ConTel Info. Systems, Littleton, Colo., 1981-84; sr. staff engr. Hughes Aircraft Co., Englewood, Colo., 1984—. Served to maj. U.S. Army, 1966-67; Southeast Asia. Decorated Bronze Star, Air medals. Mem. profl. orgns. Home: 7951 S Cedar St Littleton CO 80120

TOMASSON, VERNA, (Verna Safran), b. Bklyn., Mar. 25, 1932, d. Philip and Sally (Safran) Woskoff; m. Robert E. Tomasson, June 1961 (div. 1963); 1 son, Michael. Author: Womanstages (poetry), 1980; contrbr. poetry to Home Planet News, Eve's Legacy, Valhalla. BA in History, Antioch Coll., 1953; MFA in Drama, Columbia U., 1957. Tchr. N.Y.C. Bd. Edn., 1983—. Winner short story contest Wrtrs.' Digest, 1971, poetry contest Valhalla, 1981. Mem. P&W, N.Y. Play Shop (co-founder, dir.), Actors Equity Assn., DG. Home: 230 Park Pl Brooklyn NY 11238

TOMICH, NANCY ELLEN, b. Belleville, IL, May 17, 1945; d. John and Ethel Frieda (Bender) T.; m. Charles Puffenbarger, June 15, 1968 (div. June 1974); 1 dau., Megan; m. 2d, John. S. Zapp, May 22, 1976; 1 dau., Vanessa. Mng. ed., ed. U.S. Medicine, 1970—. BS, U. IL, 1967. Rptr., News-Jnl., Wilmington, DE, 1967-68; assoc. U. of IL Press, Champaign, 1968; edit. assoc. George Wash. U., Washington, 1967-70; mng. ed., U.S. Medicine, Washington, 1970-79, ed., 79—. Mem. NY Acad. Scis., NPC, SPJ. Office: U S Med 2033 M St NW Washington DC 20036

TOMKIEL, JUDITH IRENE, (Judy), b. St. Louis, MO, Nov. 4, 1949; d. Melvin Charles William and Mildred Neva (Kayhart) Linders; m. William George Tomkiel, Dec. 15, 1972; children—Sothy Ra William, Kimberli, Jennifer, Christopher. Catalogue: Custom Writer's Pins and Writer's Novelties, by The Idea Shoppe, 1985. Poetry to periodicals. Student Florissant, Mo., pub. schls. Owner The Idea Shoppe (Garden Grove, CA), 1983—. Golden Poet Award, 1987. Mem. Natl. Wrtrs. Club (Aurora, CO), Natl. Assn. Female Executives, Mail Order Business Board. Home: 13351 Hale Ave Garden Grove CA 92644

TOMKINS, CALVIN, b. Orange, NJ, Dec. 17, 1925; s. Frederick and Laura (Gravesl) Tomkins; m. Grace Lloyd Fanning, Sept. 11, 1948; children—Anne Graves, Susan Temple, Spencer;

m. 2d, Judy Johnston, Nov. 11, 1961 (div. Feb. 1981; m. 3d, Susan Cheever, Oct. 1, 1981; 1 dau.—Sarah Liley Cheever. Author: The Bride & The Bachelors, 1965, Merchants and Masterpieces, 1970, Living Well is the Best Revenge, 1971, Off the Wall, 1980. BA, Princeton U., 1948. Assoc. editor Newsweek mag. (NYC), 1955-57, genl. editor, 1957-59, staff wrtr, The New Yorker (NYC), 1960—. Served with USN. Mem. AL Am. Inc., PEN Am. Ctr. Address: New Yorker 25 W 43rd St New York NY 10036

TOMLINSON, GERALD (ARTHUR), b. Elmira, NY, Jan. 24, 1933; s. Arthur William and Margaret Delphine (Loomis) Tomlinson; m. Alexis M. Usakowski, Aug. 19, 1966; children—Eli, Matthew. Author: On a Field of Black, 1980, School Administrator's Complete Letter Book, 1984, Accountant's Complete Letter Book (co-author), 1987; Managing Smart (co-author), 1987; The Baseball Research Handbook, 1987; contrbr. to Ellery Queen's Mystery Mag., Alfred Hitchcock's Mystery Mag., other mags. BA, Marietta Coll., 1955; postgrad Columbia Law School, 1959-60. Senior ed. Holt, Rinehart (NYC), 1966-69; exec. ed. Silver Burdett Co. (Morristown, NJ), 1969-81; publisher Home Run Press (Lake Hopatcong, NJ), 1985—. SP3, US Army, 1956-58. Mem. MWA, NCTE, ASCD, SABR. Home: Box 432A Lake Hopatcong NJ 07849

TOMME, JOHN CARLIN, b. Chgo., June 29, 1930, s. John Carlin and Jessie (Clements) T.; m. Carol Joy Lundberg, Sept. 26, 1962 (div. Apr. 1967). Contrbr. to Reader (Chgo.), French Rvw. BA, U. Ill., 1952; D de l'U, U. Paris, 1969. Ed.-translator Agence France-Presse, Paris, 1959-60; instr. French, Northwestern U., 1962-63, Wright Coll., Chgo., 1963-66, No. Ill. U., DeKalb, 1967-71; research assoc. Coronet Films, Chgo., 1967; caseworker Ill. Dept. Pub. Aid, Chgo., 1973—. Served to lt (j.g.) USN, 1952-56. Ill. Arts Council grantee, 1980. Home: 658 W Cornelia Ave Chicago IL 60657

TOMPKINS, RALPH JOEL, b. Cross Creek, FL, Nov. 24, 1919; s. James Robert and Callie (Dunn) T.; m. Bonnie Louise Tigert, June 3, 1941; children—Burney, Ralph Waldo, Timothy B. (dec.), Daniel James. Author: Cracker Crumbs (poetry, folklore), 1974, Down the Green Road—A Gathering of Florida Legends, Folklore and Verse, 1988; contrbr. articles: The Youth's Instructor, Tampa Bay Mag., Brandon News, The Reporter, other local publs.; columnist Perry Newspapers, Fla., 1947-53. BSEd, Fla. So. U., 1947; MAEd, U. Fla., 1949. News reporter Am. Press, Lakeland, Fla., 1945-47; feature wrtr. Sanford (Fla.) Herald, 1952-53; tchr., schl. adminstr. various public sch. systems, Fla. from 1949; ed., pub. Timuquan Prodns., Tampa, Fla., 1987—. Mem. profl. orgns. Home: 2107 W Norfolk St Tampa FL 33604

TONG, BENJAMIN ROBERT, b. San Francisco. Author: The Way of the Taoist Warrior: Encounters with a Taoist Master in the West, 1987; contrbr. to numerous psychol. and ethnic studies periodicals. MA, San Francisco State U., 1970; PhD, Calif. Schl. Profl. Psychology, 1974; cert. Am. Conservatory Theater, San Francisco, 1975. Freelance wrtr., reviewer, 1971—; psychotherapist, cons., 1975—; lectr. ethnic studies San Francisco State U., 1975—; prof. Wright Inst. Grad. Schl. Psychology, Berkeley, Calif., 1979-86; research assoc. Inst. Study of Social Change, U. Calif.-Berkeley, 1980—. Mem. profl. orgns. Home: 1957 Stockton St San Francisco CA 94133

TONSING, CAROL E, b. Little Rock, d. Harold and Verda (Benn) Tonsing. Author: Men's Hair (with George Roberson), 1985, How to Buy the Fur that Makes You Look Like a Million (with Viola Sylvert), 1987; ghost-wrtr.: Lovescopes (Arlene Dahl), 1983, Always Beautiful (Kaylan Pickford), 1985, Sidney Omarr's Astrological Guides, 1987, 1988. BS, Simmons Coll., Boston, 1962. Home: 22 W 77th St New York NY 10024

TOOL, DENNIS CASLER, b. Biloxi, MS, Mar. 11, 1948, s. H. Warren and Dorothy Jeane (Casler) T.; m. T. Ruth Johnson, June 15, 1968 (div. 1970). Contrbr. poetry to Poetry Miscellany, So. Rvw, Poet Lore, Colo. State Rvw, other lit mags; contrbr. to Anthology of Mag. Verse and Yearbook of Am. Poetry. BA, U. Miss., Oxford, 1972, MFA, U. Ark., Fayetteville, 1980. Tech. translator, Paris, 1973-74; in-service instr. No. Miss. Center, Oxford, 1974-75; teaching asst. U. Ark., Fayetteville, 1975-80; lectr. English, U. Wyo., Laramie, 1981—. Recipient Dudley Fitts award in translation U. Ark., 1979. Mem. MLA, AWP, Am. Lit. Translators Assn. Home: 2941 Brookridge Ln Charlotte NC 28211

TOOMBS, JANE ELLEN, (Diana Stuart), b. Los Angeles, Dec. 27, 1926; d. James K. and Frances (Crooks) Jamison; m. Albert Jenke, June 24, 1949; children—James, Ellen, Ann, Bobbie Jane, Robert; m. 2d, John Edward Toombs, March 2, 1972. Wrks. include: The Scots, 1985, Shadowed Hearts, 1984, Restless Obsession, 1984, Arapaho Spirit, 1983, Tule Witch, 1973; Mem. Romance Writers of America. Home: 14 Roe St Cornwall-on-Hudson NY 12520

TOOMEY, JEANNE ELIZABETH (LIZ GRAY), b. NYC, Aug. 22; d. Edward Aloysius and Anna Margaret (O'Grady) T.; m. Peter E. Terranova, Sept. 28, 1951 (dec. 1968); children—Peter Edward, Sheila; m. 2d, James R. Gray, Dec. 5, 1972. Formerly columnist, News Tribune, Woodbridge, NJ; also nwspr. feat. writer. BA, Southampton Coll. of L.I.U., 1976. NY Women's Press Club award, 1961; Nevada State Press Assn. award, 1961-62. Mem. OPC, NY Press Club, Newswomen's Club of NY. Home: 914 Quincy St Albuquerque NM 87110

TOOS, A. J., see Grossman, Andrew Joseph

TOPKINS, KATHARINE, b. Seattle, July 22, 1927; d. Paul Joseph and Katharine (Crane) Theda; m. Richard Marvin Topkins, July 18, 1952; children—Richard, Joan, Deborah. Author: (novels) All the Tea in China, 1972, Kotch, 1965, (with Richard Topkins) Passing Go, 1968, Il Boom, 1974; also short stories. Student, Maryville Coll.; BS, Columbia U., 1949; MA, Claremont Grad. Schl., 1951. Home: 932 Via Casitas Greenbrae CA 94904

TOROSIAN, JEANNE WYLIE, b. Cin., Feb. 24, 1913; d. Clarence Raymond and Elizabeth Mahala (Shaw) Wylie; m. Edward Torosian, Feb. 7, 1942 (dec.). Author: Face to Face (novel), 1952, A Long Look Home (poems, watercolor paintings), 1983; contrbr. short stories: Atlantic Monthly, O. Henry Meml. Short Story Collection, McCall's mag., others; contrbr. poetry: Echoes from the Moon, Bear Tracks, Peak and Pairie, other lit. mags. BS, Northwestern U., 1933; MS, Wayne State U., 1936. instructor creative writing Wayne State U., Detroit, 1955-62, Mich. State U., Oakland, 1960-62, U. Utah, 1963-66; presenter workshops, classes in creative writing. Mem. Detroit Women Wrtrs. (life). Home: 1251 Country Club Dr Long's Peak Rt Estes Park CO 80517

TORTORIC, B. K., see Sheftel, Beatrice K.

TOSTESON, HEATHER, b. NYC, Nov. 7, 1950; d. Daniel Charles Tosteson and Penelope (Kinsley) Ellis; 1 son, Trevor Tosteson. Contrbr. fiction to Western Humanities Rvw, Cottonwood Rvw, Four Quartets; poetry in Fine Madness, Mid-Am Rvw, Small Pond, Cardinal, Intro 11, Anthology of Mag. Vèrse & Yearbook of Am. Poetry, Northwest Rvw, Beloit Poetry Jnl, Wind, Calliope, So. Poetry Rvw. BA, Sarah Lawrence Coll., 1971, MFA, UNC-Greensboro, 1977, PhD, Ohio U., 1982. Assoc. editor Greensboro Rvw, 1975-77; grad. tchg. fellow Ohio Univ., Athens, 1977-79; sci. writer/editor Univ. Calif., San Francisco, 1980-81. Mem. MLA, AWP, Phila. Writers Orgn. Address: 40 Pine Rd Chestnut Hill MA 02167

TOTH, SUSAN ERICKSON ALLEN, b. Ames, IA, June 24, 1940; d. Edward Douglas and Hazel Elvira (Erickson) Allen Lipa; m. Louis E. Toth, July 27, 1963 (div. 1974); 1 child, Jennifer Lee; m. James E. Stageberg, Feb. 9, 1985. Books: Blooming: A Small-Town Girlhood, 1981, Ivy Days: Making My Way Out East, 1984. Contrbr. stories and essays to Redbook, Harper's, N.Y. Times Book Rvw, McCalls, Cosmopolitan, Great River Rvw, N.Am. Rvw, others. BA, Smith Coll., 1961; MA, U. Calif.-Berkeley, 1963; PhDU. Minn., 1969. Instr. San Francisco State U., 1963-64; prof. Macalester Coll., St. Paul, 1969—. Mem. Natl. Book Critics Circle. Fellow Minn. State Arts Bd., 1980-81, Loft-McKinght, 1982, MacDowell Colony, 1984. Home: 4820 Penn Ave S Minneapolis MN 55409

TOUCHSTONE, BILLIE L., see Signer, Billie Touchstone

TOWNER, GEORGE RUTHERFORD, b. NYC, Sept. 15, 1933, s. Rutherford Hamilton and Marion (Washburn) T.; m. Danielle Lemoine, Apr. 30, 1985; children—Stephane, Diane, Philip. Author: The Architecture of Knowledge, 1980, Apple Pascal, 1985, Macintosh Workshop Assembler, 1986; ed.:H The Ecphorizer, 1982—. MA, U. Calif., Berkeley, 1957. Asst. dir. Kaiser Research Fdn., Richmond, Calif., 1958-60; pres. Berkeley Instruments, Oakland, Calif., 1962-67; chmn. bd. dirs. Towner Systems, San Leandro, Calif., 1968-78; cons., Sunnyvale, Calif., 1979—. Served with U.S. Army, 1957-58. Mem. Mensa (life). Home: 814 Gail Ave Sunnyvale CA 94086

TOWNLEY, JOHN MARK, b. Shawnee, OK, Aug. 18, 1932, s. Max Henry and Helen Betty (Hawk) T.; m. Erin Banahan, Feb. 7, 1980; children—Cynthia, Barbara, John Jr. Author: Conquered Provinces: Nevada Moves Southeast, 1864-1871, 1973, Turn this Water Into Gold: The Story of the Newlands Project, 1977, The Truckee Basin Fishery, 1844-1944, 1980, The Orr Ditch Case, 1913-1944, 1980, Alfalfa Country: Nevada Land, Water and Politics in the 19th Century, 1981, The Rush for Reese: Development of Central Nevada, 1982, Tough Little Town on the Truckee: 19th Century Reno, 1983; contrbr. articles: Ariz. and the West, Jnl of the West, Agrl. History, Indian Historian, other publs. BS in Geology, U. Tex.-Austin, 1954; MA, U. Nev., Reno, 1967, PhD, 1976. Dir. Nev. Hist. Soc., Reno, 1972-80, Gt. Basin Studies Center, Reno, 1980—. Home: 7115 Pembroke Dr Reno NV 89502

TOWNSEND, CHERYL ANN, (cat), b. Rochester, NY, May 21, 1957; d. Virgil Leslie Townsend and Nancy Alma (MacPherson) Kraus; m. Jerry Edward Grimm, June 24, 1982; stepchildren: Heidi, John, Josh, Danny. Author: Dancin' On Your Fingers, 1986; contrbr. to Up Aainst the Wall, Mother . . ., Vega*, Arulo!, Tiotis, Bogg, Random Weirdness, Planet Detroit, Thunder Sandwich, Black Bear, Fat Tuesday, Mockersatz, Lucky Star, Cat's Eye, Poetic Justice Parnassus, Slipstream, BalSun, others; chapbooks: An Ordinary Girl, 1985, Spcl. Orders to Go, 1985. Freelance model, Ohio, 1982—; ed./pub. Impetus, Implosion Press, Stow, Ohio, 1984—; police reserve, Stow, 1986—; paraprofl. Rape Crisis Center, Akron, Ohio, 1984—; store detective, Tallmadge, 1986. Address: 4975 Comanche Trail Stow OH 44224

TOWNSEND, GUY MANNERING, b. Memphis, Mar. 2, 1943; s. Hugh Jennings and Jonnie Inez (Ramer) T.; m. Cynthia Babette Schubert, Sept. 2, 1967 (div. Aug. 2, 1979), children—Stephanie Anne, Valerie Elizabeth; m. 2d, Jeanne Carol Horton, Apr. 19, 1980. Books: Rex Stout: An Annotated Primary and Secondary Bibliography, 1980, To Prove a Villain, 1985; contrbr. var. publs.; ed. and pub., The Mystery Fancier, 1976—; founder and pub., Brownstone Books, 1981—. BA, Ark. Polytech. Coll., 1965; MA, Memphis State U., 1968; PhD, Tulane U., 1974; JD Chase Coll. of Law, 1986. Asst. prof., Gulf Coast Jr. Coll., Panama City, Fla., 1968-69; instr. Yankton Coll., Yankton, S.D., 1971-74; asst. prof., Paine Coll., Augusta, GA, 1975-76; staff writer, Courier News, Blytheville, Ark., 1978-79, 80-81; assoc. ed. Practical Horseman Mag., West Chester, PA, 1981; Chief Probation Officer, 5th Judicial Dist., Madison, Indiana, 1983—. Mem. MWA, ABA. Home: 1717 Clinton St Madison IN 47250

TRACY, FRANK WILLIAM, JR., (William Tracy), b. Lawrenceville, IL, July 24, 1935; s. Frank William and Margaret Lulu (Rodgers) Tracy; m. Ruth Hargate, 1967 (div. 1973). Works include: Aramco and Its World, 1980, A Photographer on the Phoenician Coast, 1965; contrbr. to var. newspapers, mags., and anthologies in U.S. and abroad. BA, Duke U., 1957; MA, American U., Beirut, 1970. Tchr., Beirut and Saudi Arabia, 1957-66; asst. edit., Aramco World Magazine, Beirut, 1967-77; ed./wrtr., UNICEF, NYC, 1974-75; ed./wrtr., Arabian American Oil Co., Dhahran, Saudi Arabia, 1977-81. Served with U.S. Army, 1958-60. Mem. Screenwriters Assoc. of Santa Barbara. Clubs: MENSA, Kiwanis (Santa Barbara). Home: Box 2489 Santa Barbara CA 93120

TRACY, JAMES DONALD, b. St. Louis, Feb. 14, 1938; s. Leo W. and Marguerite M. (Meehan) Tracy; m. Nancy Ann McBride, Sept. 6, 1968; children—Patrick, Samuel, Mary Ann. Author: Erasmus: The Growth of a Mind, 1972, The Politics of Erasmus: A Pacifist Intellectual and His Political Milieu, 1979, True Ocean Found: Paludanus' Letters on Dutch Voyages to the Kara Sea, 1980, A Financial Revolution in the Habsburg Netherlands, 1985; ed.: Luther and the Modern State in Germany, 1986; editorial bd.: Sixteenth Century Jnl, 1979—; Erasmus of Rotterdam Yrbk., 1981—. BA, St. Louis U., 1959; MAS, Johns Hopkins U., 1960, Notre Dame U., 1961; PhD, Princeton U., 1967. Instr. U. Mich., 1964-66; instr. to prof. history U. Minn., 1966—.Home: 934 Portland Ave Saint Paul MN 55104

TRACY, STEPHEN V(ICTOR), b. Brockton, MA, Apr. 6, 1941; s. Edward and Patti (Atwood) Tracy; m. June W. Allison. Author: The Lettering of an Athenian Mason, 1975, First Fruits for the Pythais, 1982; co-author: book and audio-visual materials Greek Civilization, 1982; ed.: Studies Presented to Sterling Dow, 1985. BA, Brown U., 1963; MA, Harvard U., 1965, PhD, 1968. Asst. prof. Wellesley Coll. (MA), 1967-71; asst. prof. Greek and Latin Ohio State U. (Columbus), 1971-73, assoc. prof., 1973-77, prof., 1977—; mem. mng. com. Am. Schl. Classical Studies (Athens, Greece), 1974—, dir. summer session, 1975; chmn. comm. on pubns., 1985—. Office: OSU 414 University Hall Columbus OH 43210

TRAILS, MANY, see Cook, Rodney Edwin, Sr.

TRAILS, MAYETTE, see Kirk, Pearl Louise

TRAIN, JOHN, b. NYC, May 25, 1928; s. Arthur Cheney and Helen (Coster) Train; m. Maria Teresa Cini di Pianzano, 1961 (div. 1976); children—Helen, Nina, Lisa; 2nd m. Frances Cheston, July 23, 1977. Author: Dance of the Money Bees, 1973, Remarkable Names, 1977, Even More Remarkable Names, 1979, Remarkable Occurrences, 1978, Remarkable Words, 1980, The Money Masters, 1980, Remarkable Relatives, 1981, Preserving Capital, 1983, Famous Financial Fiascos, 1984, John Train's Most Remarkable Names, 1985, The Midas Touch, 1987. BA, Harvard U., 1950, MA, 1951; postgrad., Sorbonne, France, 1951-52. Founder, mng. editor Paris Rvw, 1952-54; pres. Train, Smith Counsel (and predecessor firms) (NYC), 1959—; columnist Forbes mag., 1977-82; columnist Harvard mag., 1982—; pres. Chateau Malescasse (Lamarque-Margaux, Bordeaux, France), 1970—. Chmn. Italian Emergency Relief Com., 1976-77,pres., Afghanistan Relief Committee, 1985—; trustee Harvard Lampoon, Cambridge, MA, 1974—. Served with U.S. Army, 1954-56. Office: 345 Park Ave New York NY 10022

TRAINER, ORVEL LEROY, b. Milliken, CO, Sept. 26, 1925; s. Charles Wesley and Elda May (Easton) Trainer; m. Joanne Irene Gasser, June 1, 1952; children—Ryan Thomas, Eric John. Author: novels Wakau, 1970, Ice Harvest, 1971, Ashes, 1972, Death Roads, 1979. BA, U. Colo., 1950, MA, 1955, PhD, 1960; diploma, U. Oslo, 1953. Lifetime teaching cert., Colo, Instr. in econs. U. Colo. (Boulder), 1959-60; asst. prof. econs. U. No. Colo. (Greeley, 1960-65, assoc. prof., 1965-70, prof. 1970—, dean Schl. Ednl. Change and Devel., 1974-75, dean Coll. Edn., 1981-82; founding dir. Educators Life Ins. Co. (Denver), 1963-68; dir. Read Constrn. Co. (Cheyenne, WO), 1968-69; dir., treas. Delta Dental Plan (Denver), 1981—; dir. Inst. New World Archaelogy (Chgo.), 1983—. Bd. dirs. Urban Renewal Authority, Greeley, 1971-72. Served with USN, 1943-46. Office: U No Colo Coll Arts & Sci Greeley CO 80639

TRAKAS, DENO, b. Charlotte, NC, Apr. 23, 1952; s. Pedro N. and Anna (Patterson) T.; m. Kathy Jackson, Aug. 10, 1974; children—Hayley, Dylan. Author: The Shuffle of Wings, 1987. Contrbr. poems to literary mags. including Denver Qtly, Kans. Qtly, Louisville Rvw. BA, Eckerd Coll., 1974; M.A., Tulsa U., 1976; Ph.D., U. S.C.-Columbia, 1981. Assoc. prof. Wofford Coll., Spartanburg, S.C., 1980—. Recipient Fiction Project award S.C. Arts Commn., 1985. Mem. South Atlantic MLA, NCTE. Home: 120 Winton Ct Spartanburg SC 29301

TRANBARGER, OSSIE ELMO, b. Apr. 6, 1914, d. Clarence Hosea and Matilda Anna (Bradely) Lasley; m. Jack Tranbarger (dec. 1981); 1 son, Matt. Contrbr.: Bitterroot, Cyclo-Flame, Driftwood East, Dragonfly, Haiku West, numerous other lit. mags. and anthologies. Wrkg. on haiku collection, poetry. Ed. Independence (Kans.) Community Coll. Ed. poetry column Independence News; guest ed. Midwest issue Poet, India; Am. ed. Phoenix Mag., Eng.; judge numerous haiku competitions. DHL, Intl. Fedn. Research Poetry, U. Asia; cited for Outstanding Contrbns. to Lit., Hayden Library, Ariz.; recipient numerous other awards. Mem. Natl. League Am. Penwomen (pres. Kans. chap. 1973-74), Fedn. Chaparral Poets, Kans. Authors Club, Ariz. State Poetry Soc., Poets Round Table Indiana. Home: 619 W Main St Independence KS 67301

TRAP, M., see Wicklund, Millie Mae

TRAUGOTT, ELIZABETH CLOSS, b. Bristol, Eng., Apr. 9, 1939; d. August and Hannah M. (Priebsch) Closs; m. John L. Traugott, Sept. 26, 1967; 1 dau.—Isabel. Author: A History of English Syntax, 1972, (with Mary Pratt) Linguistics For Students of Literature, 1980. Ed. (with A. terMeulen, J. Reilly, C. Ferguson) On Conditionals, 1986. BA in English, Oxford U., Eng., 1960, MA, 1964; PhD in English lang., U. Calif. at Berkeley, 1964. Asst. prof. English, U. Calif. at Berkeley, 1964-70; lectr. U. East Africa (Tanzania), 1965-66, U. York (Eng.), 1966-67; lectr., then assoc. prof. linguistics and English Stanford U. (CA), 1970-77, prof., 1977—, chair dept., 1980-85; Vice provost and Dean of Graduate Studies, 1985—. Mem. Linguistic Soc. Am. (exec. com.), Intl. Soc. Hist. Linguistics (pres. 1979-81), MLA, AAUW, AAUP. Office: Bldg 10 Stanford U Stanford CA 94305

TRAVIS, R(OSEMARIE) L., b. NYC, Aug. 7; d. Vincent Joseph and Yolanda (Corbani) Lavarello; m. Curtis Summer Travis, Aug. 27, 1955; children—Victoria, Barbara, John Howe. Contrbr.: Ind. Speech Jnl., Indpls. Convention Guide, Garden Mag., numerous regional newspapers; ed. church and civic orgn. publs. Wrkg. on mystery novels. BA in Journalism, Butler U., 1981. Reporter Hudson Dispatch, Union City, N.J., 1949-51, Colorado Springs Gazette-Telegraph, Colo., 1953; assoc. ed. Garden Mag., N.Y.C., 1951-53; public relations asst. Indpls. Convention Ctr., 1974-75; publicity dir. Indpls. Opera Co., 1977-78. Mem. NWC, Soc. Profl. Journalists. Home: 5707 N Pennsylvania St Indianapolis IN 46220

TREAT, LAWRENCE, b. NYC, Dec. 21, 1903; s. Henry and Daisy (Stein) Goldstone; m. Rose Ehrenfreund, 1943. Author: fiction Run Far, Run Fast, 1937, B as in Banshee, 1940, D as in Dead, 1941, H as in Hangman, 1942, O as in Omen, 1943, The Leatherman, 1944, V as in Victim, 1945, H as in Hunted, 1946, Q as in Quicksand, 1947, Over the Edge, 1948, F as in Flight, 1948, Trial and Terror, 1949, Big Shot, 1951, Weep for a Wanton, 1956, Lady, Drop Dead, 1960, Venus Unarmed, 1961, P as in Police, 1970; picture mysteries Crime and Puzzlement: 24 Solve-Them-Yourself Picture Mysteries, 1981, Crime and Puzzlement 2, 1982, You're the Detective, 1983, The Armchair Detective, 1983; editor: Murder in Mind, 1967, The Mystery Writer's Handbook, 1976, A Special Kind of Crime, 1982; originator: Police procedural and Detective picture puzzle; contrbr.: numerous short stories to mags, including Alfred Hitchcock's Mystery Mag., Ellery Queen's Mystery Mag., Red Book, others, also numerous anthologies. BA, Dartmouth Coll., 1924; LL.B., Columbia U., 1927. Recipient Edgar Allan Poe award Mystery Writers of Am., 1965, 78, prize Intl. Crime Writer's Contest, Stockholm, 1981, Mystery Wrtrs. of Am. Spcl. TV awd. for "Wake Me When I'm Dead," 1986. Mem. MWA (founder, past pres.), Boston Author's Club. Office: RFD Box 475A Edgartown MA 02539

TREBILCOCK, DOROTHY WARNER, b. Lansing, MI, July 8, 1926; d. Harold Herrick and Sarah Grace (Hardie) Warner; m. James M. Trebilcock, Aug. 25, 1950 (dec. Feb. 11, 1984); children—Amy Anne, Robert James. Author: Shield of Innocence, 1978. Contrbr. numerous articles, stories, poems to mags., newspapers, profl. jnls. including Sailing, Crossroads, WD, Modern Maturity, Jack and Jill, others. B.A., MIch. State U., 1948, M.A., 1973. Part-time tchr. colls. and univs., MI, 1968-80; research coord. Mich. State U., East Lansing, 1971-73; wrtr.-in-schl. Mich. Council for the Arts, 1980—. Recipient Centennial Song award Kappa Alpha Theta, 1970, Chrysalis award for essay Saginaw Valley State Coll., 1978. Mem. SCBW. Home: 109 N Gaylord Ave Ludington MI 49431

TRECKER, JANICE LAW, (Janice Law), b. Sharon, CT, June 10, 1941; d. James Ord and Janet (Galloway) Law; m. Jerrold B. Trecker, June 9, 1962; 1 son, James Harleigh. Author: Preachers, Rebels & Traders—Connecticut 1818-1865, 1975, Women on the Move, 1975, The Big Payoff, 1975, Gemini Trip, 1977, Under Orion, 1978, Shadow of the Palms, 1979, Death under Par, 1981, All the Kings Ladies, 1986. Contrbr. numeous articles, movie rvws., short stories to mags., newspapers. B.A., Syracuse U., 1962; M.A. in Lit., U. Conn., 1967. English tchr. Windsor Schs., CT, 1962-66; math tchr. Plant Jr. High, West Hartford, CT, 1967; history tchr., W. Hartford Sohls., 1984-85, theory of knowledge, 1987-88. free-lance wrtr., 1967—. Mem. AG. Home: 33 Westfield Rd West Hartford CT 06119

TREECE, PATRICIA, b. Yakima, WA, Nov. 22, 1938; d. Raymond Edward and Minnie (Sams) Treece; m. Ralph Sariego, Feb. 5, 1966; children—Christopher Adam, Katherine Melissa. Author: Soldier of God, 1982, A Man For Others, 1982, The Sanctified Body, 1982. BA magna cum laude, U. Ore., 1960; postgrad. UCLA, 1962-63, Middlebury (VT) Coll., 1962. Tchr., Inglewood High Schl. (CA), 1963-64, Arcadia High Schl. (CA), 1964-66; freelance wrtr., 1966—. Outstanding Senior Thesis, U. Ore., 1960, Phi Beta Kappa. Home: RR 1 Calabasas CA 91302

TREFETHEN, FLORENCE, b. Phila., Sept. 18, 1921, d. Otto Carl Johann and Emma Martha (Paessler) Newman; m. Lloyd MacGregor Trefethen, May 17, 1944; children—Gwyned, Lloyd Nicholas. Author of Writing a Poem, 1975; contrbr. poems, short fiction, articles, reviews to CSM, N.Y. Times, Harper's, other mags.; columnist, The Writer Mag., 1968-87; ed. (with Joseph F. McCloskey) Operations Research for Management, 1954. AB, Bryn Mawr Coll., 1943; MLitt, Cambridge U., England, 1950. Operations analyst Johns Hopkins U., Chevy Chase, Md., 1950-54; instr. English, Tufts U., Medford, Mass., 1959-66; lectr. English, Northeastern U., Boston, 1966-68; lectr. Radcliffe Inst., 1969-70, 72-73; exec. ed. Council on East Asian Studies, Harvard U., 1974—. Served to lt. j.g. with WAVES, 1943-45. Various prizes from PSA and New England Poetry Club; story chosen for O. Henry Best Short Stories of 1982. Mem. PSA, New England Poetry Club, Soc. of Scholarly Publishers. Home: 23 Barberry Rd Lexington MA 02173

TRELEAVEN, JOHN WATERLOO, b. Port Huron, MI, July 19, 1922, s.. Walter Peter and Margaret Emily (Green) T. Author: Basic Grammar and Composition for Technical Writing, 1963; ed., columnist Old Catholic Messenger, 1980-85. Wrkg. on self-help books. BA, Olivet Coll., 1944; LTh, Seabury-Western Theol. Seminary, 1947; STB, Temple U., 1952; DD (hon.), Western Theol. Coll., 1958; STD (hon.) Gen. Synod Old Catholic Ch., 1976. Instr. English RCA Institutes, NYC, 1962-70, Phillips Bus. Coll., East Orange, N.J., 1983-86, St. Clair County Coll., Port Huron, Mich., 1986—; bishop, rector All Souls' Ch., East Hanover, N.J., 1970-86. Home: 4653 Desmond Beach Port Huron MI 48060

TREMBLAY, WILLIAM ANDREW, (Bill), b. Southbridge, MA, June 9, 1940, s. Arthur Achilles and Irene Louise (Fontaine) T.; m. Cynthia Ann Crooks, Sept. 28, 1962; children—William Crooks, Benjamin Phillip, John Fontaine. Author: A Time for Breaking (chapbook), 1970, Crying in the Cheap Seats, 1971, The Anarchist Heart, 1977, Home Front, 1978, The Peaceable Kingdom (chapbook), 1978, Second Sun: New and Selected Poems, 1985, Duhamel: Ideas of Order in Little Canada, 1986; contrbr. to anthologies: Travelling America with Its Poets, 1976, Vietnam Perspectives, 1985, Carrying the Darkness, 1985; contrbr. poetry to Ironwood, Tar River Poetry, Chowder Rvw, Three Rivers Poetry Jnl, other lit. mags. AB, Clark U., 1962, MA, 1969; MFA, U. Mass., 1972. Instr., asst. prof. Leicester (Mass.) Jr. Coll., 1967-70; instr. Springfield (Mass.) Coll., 1972-73; mem. faculty Colo. State U., Fort Collins, 1973—, prof., 1983—. Fulbright-Hays lectr. LusoÅm. Comm., Lisbon, Portugal, 1979; NEH summer seminar with M.L. Rosenthal, NYU, poetics of modern poetry; NEA fellow for creative writing, 1985. Mem. AWP (dir.'s council 1985-86), Northeast MLA, High Plains Arts Center, CCLM, Western Lit. Assn. Home: 3412 Lancaster Dr Fort Collins CO 80525

TREMMEL, ROBERT ARNOLD, b. Sheldon, IA, Nov. 1, 1948; s. Arnold Nicholas and Roberta Agnes (Skilling) T.; m. Nancy Jane Shulke, Feb. 14, 1970; children: Jennifer Ann, Nicholas Robert Skilling. Ed. Kans. English, 1986—; contrbr. articles to Iowa English Bulltn., Freshman English News, Jnl of Teaching Writing, Kans. English, Ind. English, Toward Better Writing, Conn. English Jnl, Natl. Assn. Secondary Schl. Prins. Jnl, poetry to Iowa, Greensboro, Hiram Poetry, Great River, Cumberland Poetry, Cottonwood rvws, Ascent, Sou'wester, Poem, Cincinnati Poetry Rvw, North Dakota Qrtly, Zone 3, Whiskey Island Magazine, others. Wrkg. on poetry, research on rhetoric, composition, and students' poetry. BA, U. Iowa, 1971, MA, 1975, PhD, 1982. Tchr. English pub. schls., Lisbon, Iowa, 1971-73; grad. asst. rhetoric program U. Iowa, 1978-82; asst. prof. English, Washburn U., Topeka, 1982—. Mem. NCTE, Kans. Assn. Tchrs. English, CCCC. Office: Washburn U 1700 College St Topeka KS 66621

TRESCOTT, PAUL BARTON, b. Bloomsburg, PA, Nov. 22, 1925; s. Paul Henry and Stella (Potts) T.; m. Kathleen Colcord Carroll, Aug. 15, 1982; children by previous marriage—Jeffrey, Jill, Andrew. Author: Money, Banking and Economic Welfare (2 editions), 1960, 65, Financing American Enterprise, 1963, The Logic of the Price System, 1970, Thailand's Monetary Experience, 1971; contrbr. articles to: History of Political Economy, Jnl. of Money, Credit and Banking, Jnl. of Economic Issues, numerous other econs. publs. BA, Swarthmore Coll., 1949; MA, Princeton U., 1951, PhD, 1954. Vis. prof. econs. Thammasat U., Bangkok, Thailand, 1965-67; prof. Miami U., Oxford, Ohio, 1967-69, So. Meth. u., Dallas, 1969-76, U. Ill., Urbana, 1981, So. Ill. U., Carbondale, 1976—. Served as sgt. U.S. Army, 1944-46; ETO, Philippines. Mem. econs. orgns. Office: Dept Econ So Ill U Carbondale IL 62901

TREUTEL, LUCILE VERONICA, (Veronica Dale), b. Mobile, Ala., Oct. 10; d. Peter Joseph and Ann Louise (Rouse) Treutel. Contrbr. juvenile fiction, poetry to numerous publs.; poetry in anthologies. Wrkg. on novel, memoirs, song lyrics. BS in Edn., U. Ala., 1950. Former tchr. Mobile Pub. Schs. Mem. ednl. orgns. Home: 351 Conti St Mobile AL 36602

TRILLIN, CALVIN MARSHALL, b. Kansas City, MO, Dec. 5, 1935; s. Abe and Edyth Trillin; m. Alice Stewart, Aug. 13, 1965; children—Abigail, Sarah Stewart. Author: An Education in Georgia, 1964, Barnett Frummer is an Unbloomed Flower, 1969, U. S. Journal, 1971, American Fried, 1974, Runestruck, 1977, Alice, Let's Eat, 1978, Floater, 1980, Uncivil Liberties, 1982, Third Helpings, 1983, Killings, 1984, With All Disrespect, 1985, If You Can't Say Something Nice, 1987. BA, Yale U., 1957. Reporter, writer Time mag., 1960-63; staff writer New Yorker mag., 1963—; columnist Nation mag., 1978-85-; syndicated columnist, King Features Synd., 1986—. Office: New Yorker 25 W 43rd St New York NY 10036

TRINIDAD, DAVID ALLEN, b. Los Angeles, July 20, 1953; s. Rupert Manley and Joyce Madeline (Hockinson) T. Author: (poems) Pavane, 1981, Monday, Monday, 1985, Living Doll, 1986, November, 1986. Contrbr. poems to anthols., lit. mags. BA in English, Calif. State U.-Northridge, 1979. Poet-in-residence Dorland Mountain Colony, Temecula, Calif., 1979; ed. Sherwood Press, Los Angeles, 1981-85; tenant relations asst. City Housing Authority, Los Angeles, 1981—. Home: 1836½ N Edgemont St 4 Los Angeles CA 90027

TRISLER, HENRY FRANKLIN, JR., (Hank Trisler), b. Seattle, Sept. 14, 1937; s. Henry Franklin and Aileen Leatrice (Snyder) Trisler; m. Dorothy Alyce Kutsaleris, Aug. 1, 1959 (div. Aug. 1976); children—Kimberlee, Richard, Steven, Michael; m. 2d, Barbara Elaine Berman, April 2, 1979; children—Howard, Richard, Alayne. Author: No Bull Selling, 1982, No Bull Sales Management, 1985; publisher, The Trisler Times. Certificate General Motors Institute, Flint, Mich., 1957. Salesman various cos., 1957-70; Owner, Raintree Realtors, 1970-76; Owner, The Trisler Co., San Jose, Calif., 1976—. Address: 1416 Fruitdale Ave San Jose CA 95128

TROISE, FRED, b. NYC, May 28, 1937, s. Louis C. and Anne (Bivona) T.; m. Marie-Claire J. Tocco, Apr. 9, 1960; children—Douglas, Brigitte, Claudine. Contrbg. author: The Water Encyclopedia, 1970; co-author: Water Atlas of the United States, 1974; author reports, ed. seminar guides. BS, Bklyn Coll., 1960. Vice-pres. Water Info. Ctr., Syosset, N.Y., 1966—; ed. Ground Water Newsletter, 1984—. Mem. profl. geol. orgns. Home: 5 Beach Plum Dr Centerport NY 11721

TROTTA, ANNA MARIE, b. Bronx, NY, Aug. 17, 1937; d. Frank Joseph and Anna (Jacobson) Jessie; m. James Robert Trotta, Nov. 30, 1954; children: James Robert, Susan, Elizabeth, Michael, Cynthia. Author: (poetry) Loving, 1971; (humor) Hello Taxi Service, 1978; contrbr. poetry, humor, short stories to The Poet, Encore, Major Poets, Profl. Poet, Wrtr.'s Digest, Parents, Newsday, Inky Trails, Wrtr.'s Jnl, Ed.'s Desk, also numerous others. Student pub. schls., Bronx. Recipient Silver Poet award World of Poetry, 1986. Home: 5522 W Acoma Rd Glendale AZ 85306

TROUBETZKOY, DOROTHY ULRICH, b. Hartford, CT, d. George and Alice (Smith) Ulrich; m. Serge Sergeivitch Troubetzkoy; children—Daria T. Lewis, Sergei, Vilna T. Roorda. Author: Out of the Wilderness, 1957, Richmond, City of Churches, 1957, Bluebonnets and Blood, 1968, Sagamore Creek, 1969, Where is Christmas, 1968, The Petrarch Beat, 1979, Poems From Korea, 1982, Love in the Rain, 1986; Edited: Significant Addresses of the Jamestown Festival, 1957, Poetry Party, 1962; poetry and fiction in jnls. and lit mags; many natl awards. AB, U. of Chgo., postgrad, Columbia U. Columnist, ftr. wrtr. Richmond Times Dispatch, 1951-53; asst. ed., Virginia Wildlife, 1953-56; dir. Info. and Rsrch., City of Richmond, 1956-58; editor, Va. Cavalcade, 1959-63; editor, The Independent Virginian, 1972—. Mem. National Press Club, National Federation of Press Women (past pres.). Home: 2223 Grove Ave Richmond VA 23220

TROUT, KILGORE, see Farmer, Philip Jose

TROWBRIDGE, WILLIAM L., b. Chgo., May 9, 1941; s. Edwin A. and Mildred (Stockton) Trowbridge; m. Waneta Sue Downing, July 6, 1963; children—Jennifer, Sean, Randall. Author: The Book of Kong, 1986; poems in The Georgia Rvw, Poetry, Kenyon Rvw, Missouri Rvw, Prairie Schooner, Beloit Poetry Jnl, New Letters, other lit mags. AB, U. of Mo., Columbia, 1963, MA, 1965; PhD, Vanderbilt U., 1975. Prof., Northwest Mo. State U., Maryville, Mo., 1971—. Mem. PSA, AAUP, AWP. Home: 232 W First Maryville MO 64468

TROY, MARY DELPHINE, b. St. Louis, Aug. 23, 1948; d. Clarence Edward and Delphine Mary (Auchly) Troy; m. Pierre Wayne Davis, Sept. 22, 1984. Author: Duty, 1982, A Man Around the House, 1985; edited Hydropyrolysis of Biomass to Produce Liquid Hydrocarbon Fuels. BA, U. Mo., 1962-66; MFA, U. Ark., 1983-86. Tchr. Ursuline Academy, St. Louis, 1972-77, Univ. Ark., Fayetteville, 1983—; editor/writer Univ. Hawaii, Honolulu, 1978-83. Recipient John Gould Fletcher awd. for literary merit, 1986. Mem. Amnesty Intl. Address: 3516 Humphrey St Louis MO 63118

TRUDEAU, GARRY B., b. NYC., 1948; m. Jane Pauley; children: 1 son, 1 dau. (twins). Author: Any Grooming Hints for Your Fans, Rollie, But the Pension Fund was Just Sitting There, The Doonesbury Chronicles, Guilty, Guilty, Guilty, We Who Are About to Fry, Salute You: Selected Cartoons from In Search of Reagan's Brain, Vol. 2, Is This Your First Purge, Miss?, The Wreck of the Rusty Nail; contbr.: (with Nicholas von Hoffman) publs. including The People's Doonebury; many others (recipient Pulitzer prize, 1975). Grad., Yale U. and Yale U. Schl. Art and Achitecture. Creator: comic srip Doonebury; syndicated nationwide comic strip. Plays include: Doonesbury, 1983, Rapmaster Ronnie, A Patisan Review (with Elizabeth Swados), 1984. Address: Universal Press Syn 4400 Johnson Dr Fairway KS 66205

TRUDELL, SHARON, b. Ada, OK; d. Gilbert Michael and Virginia Arlene (House) Reekie; m. Norman Joseph Trudell, Feb. 12, 1980; children—Rebecca, Jessica. Contrbr. features to newspapers. Wrkg. on book for Enoch Kelly Haney. Student Seminole Jr. Coll., 1980-81, Livingston U., 1978-79. News ed. Wewoka Daily Times, OK, 1983; soc. ed. The Seminole Producer, OK, 1983-84; reporter/columnist Shawnee News-Star, OK, 1984-85; pub., ed. The Seminole Advocate, OK, 1986—. Recipient Spots News award AP, 1984. Home: Rt 1 Box 128 Seminole OK 74868

TRUE, JUNE AUDREY, (Audrey Day), b. Bklyn., Sept. 3, 1927; d. Harry Brown and Harriet May (Day) True; m. Nathan Albert, Sept. 30, 1949 (div. 1965); children—Paul, Ruth Albert Topper, William, Norman, Claude, Emily, Catherine; m. 2d, Norman Arlen Heap, Feb. 25, 1977. Author: Finding Out: Conducting and Evaluating Social Research, 1983. Contrbr. chaps., articles, research reports to profl. jnls. BA, Rutgers U., 1963, MA, 1966, PhD, 1972. Lectr. Douglass Coll., New Brunswick, 1967-70; asst. prof. Trenton State Coll., Ewing, N.J., 1970-81, assoc. prof., 1981—. Sec. CORE, Plainfield, N.J., 1964-67. Mem. N.J. Sociol. Soc. (pres.). Home: RD 1 Box 111 Stockton NJ 08559

TRUEDSON, GAIL VAN HORN, b. Mpls., June 20, 1951; s. Dean B. and Ruby Lucille (Scott) Van Horn; m. Everett Charles Truedson, July 3, 1982; 1 child, Amanda Lee Van Horn. Contbr. to numerous mags, jnls, and newspapers, 1968—. Family editor Marshall Ind., Minn., 1974-76; regional editor Dixon Evening Telegraph, Ill., 1977; editor legis. publs. Ill. State C. of C., Springfield, 1978; dir. pub. relations Ill. Savs. and Loan League, Springfield, 1979-82; asst. press sec. Lt. Gov. George Ryan, Springfield, 1983; editor Callan Pub., Inc., Mpls., 1984—. Named Outstanding Staffer, Mpls. Star and Tribune, 1969; recipient Best Investigative Journalism award Minn. Newspaper Assn., 1975. Mem. Pub. Relations Soc. Am., Women in Communications Inc., Sigma Delta Chi. Home: 3444 Portland Ave S No. 1 Minneapolis MN 55407

TRUEMAN, TERRY EARL, b. Birmingham, AL. Dec. 15, 1947, s. Sydney McDaniel and Jeanne E. (LaPine) T.; m. Linda L. Cooper, Feb. 1976 (div. 1970) m. 2d, Leslie G. Hanson, June 1970 (div. 1981); m. 3d, Ginger M. Ninde, Feb. 7, 1981; children: H. Sheehan McDaniel, Jesse Cruz Trueman. Contrbr. poems, short stories, articles, essays: Idiom (Australia), Wis. Rev., Parachute, Poetry Australia, numerous other lit. mags. Wrkg. on novel, short-story collection, poetry. BA, u. Wash., 1971; MS, Eastern Wash. U., 1975, MFA, 1985. Psychotherapist Spokane (Wash.) Mental Health, 1973-80; staff corr. Spokesman Rev. newspaper, Spokane, 1980—; ed. Northwest Artpaper, Seattle, 1985—. Home: Box 1107 Medical Lake WA 99022

TRUESDELL, CLIFFORD AMBROSE III, b. Los Angeles, Feb. 18, 1919; s. Clifford Ambrose and Yetta Helen (Walker) Truesdell; m. Beverly Poland, Nov. 18, 1939; 1 son—Clifford Ambrose IV; 2nd m. Charlotte Janice Brudno, Sept. 16, 1951. Author or co-author: 20 books including Mechanical Foundations, 1952, Classical Field Theories, 1960, Flexible and Elastic Bodies, 1960, Non-Linear Field Theories of Mechanics, 1965, Essays in the History of Mechanics, 1968, Rational Thermodynamics, 1969, Introduction to Rational Elasticity, 1973, Rational Continuum Mechanics, 1977, Concepts and Logic of Classical Thermodynamics, 1977, Maxwell's Kinetic Theory, 1980, Tragicomical History of Thermodynamics, 1980; An Idiot's Fugitive Essays on Science, 1983; Co-founder, co-editor: Jnl Rational Mechanics and Analysis, 1952-56; editor or co-editor: Leonhardi Euleri Opera Omnia Series II, vols. 10-13, 18-19, 1952-71; Handbuch der Physik, vols. 6a, 8-9, 1956-74; founder, editor: Archive for Rational Mechanics and Analysis, 1957-67; co-editor, 1967-86, editor, 1986—; founder, editor: Archive for History of Exact Sciences, 1960—, Springer Tracts in Natural Philosophy, 1962-66; co-editor, 1967-78; editor, 1979—; editorial bd.: Rendiconti del Circolo Matematico di Palermo, 1971—, Meccanica, 1974—, Nuovo Cimento, 1979—, Bollettino di Storia delle Scienze Matematiche, 1979—, Speculations in Science and Technology, 1980—. BS in Math, Calif. Inst. Tech., 1941, MS, 1942; cert. in mechanics, Brown U., 1942; PhD in Math, Princeton, 1943; Dott. ing. h.c., Politecnico di Milano, 1965; D.Sc., Tulane U., 1976; Fil.D. (hon.), Uppsala U., 1979, Dr. Phil., Basel U., 1979. Asst. in history, debating and math. Calif. Inst. Tech. (Pasadena), 1940-42; asst. in mechanics Brown U. (Providence), 1942; instr. math. Princeton U., 1942-43, U. Mich. (Ann Arbor), 1943-44; mem. staff radiation lab. Mass. Inst. Tech. (Cambridge), 1944-46; chief theoretical mechanics subdiv. U.S. Naval Ordnance Lab. (White Oak, MD), 1946-48; head theoretical mechanics sect. U.S. Naval Research Lab. (Washington), 1948-51; prof. math. Ind. U. (Bloomington), 1950-61; prof. rational mechanics Johns Hopkins (Balt.), 1961—. Home: 4007 Greenway Baltimore MD 21218

TRUJILLO, PAUL EDWARD, b. Belen, NM, Dec. 15, 1952, s. Juan Del Dios and Reina (Romero) T.; m. Rita Alice Martinez, Sept. 11, 1973; 1 dau., Erica Marie. Contrbr. to Bi-Lingual Rvw, Ceremony of Brotherhood, Santa Fe Poetry, Rio Grande Wrtrs. Assn. Qtly, others. BEE, N.Mex. State U., Las Cruces, 1976. Engr., 1973-81; lectr. U. N.Mex.-Valencia, Belen, 1981-84; tchr. Los Lunas (N.Mex.) High Schl., 1984-85, Belen High Schl., 1985—. Mem. Rio Grande Wrtrs. Assn. (bd. dirs. Albuquerque chpt. 1984—; winner 1st place for haiku 1980). Home: Box 396 Peralta NM 87042

TUCHMAN, BARBARA WERTHEIM, b. NYC, Jan. 30, 1912; d. Maurice and Alma (Morgenthau) Wertheim; m. Lester R. Tuchman, 1940; children—Lucy, Jessica, Alma. Author: The Lost British Policy, 1938, Bible and Sword, 1956, The Zimmerman Telegram, 1958, The Guns of August, 1962 (Pulitzer prize), The Proud Tower, 1966, Stilwell and the American Experience in China, 1971 (Pulitzer prize), Notes from China, 1972, A Distant Mirror, 19778, Practising History, 1981, The March of Folly, 1984. BA, Radcliffe Coll., 1933, D. Litt., Yale, 1940. Research asst. Inst. Pacific Relations, NYC, 1934, Tokyo, 1935; editorial asst. The Nation, NYC, 1936 Spain, 1937; staff writer War in Spain. London, 1937-38; Am. corr. New Statesman and Nation, London, 1939; with Far East news desk, OWI, NYC, 1944-45; Jefferson lectr., 1980; Mem. Smithsonian Council, 1971—. Trustee Radcliffe Coll., 1960-72, NY Public Library, 1980. Mem. AG, AL, Soc. Am. Historians (pres. 1971-73). Office Russell & Volk 551 Fifth Ave New York NY 10017

TUCKER, CHARLES CHRISTOPHER, (Edward Dalton Stein)b. Dallas, Aug. 26, 1950; s. Clyde W. and Bessie (Allen) T.; div. 1983; 1 son, Jason W. BA in English, North Texas State U., 1973, MA, 1975. Adjunct prof. English, Lamar U., Beaumont, TX, 1975-77; freelance writer, 1978-80; ed. Vision Mag., Dallas, 1980-81; assoc., exec. ed and columnist, D Mag., Dallas, 1982—. Katie award, Dallas Press Club, 1984, City and Regional Magazine Gold Medal for Best Commentary, 1985. Office: D Mag 3988 N Central Dallas TX 75204

TUCKER, HELEN W., b. Raleigh, NC, Nov. 1, 1926, d. William Blair and Helen Mae (Welch) Tucker; m. William Thad Beckwith, Jan. 9, 1971. Novels: The Sound of Summer Voices, 1969, The Guilt of August Fielding, 1971, No Need of Glory, 1972, The Virgin of Lontano, 1973, A Strange and Ill-Starred Marriage, 1978, A Reason for Rivalry, 1979, A Mistress to the Regent, 1980, An Infamous Attachment, 1980, The Halverton Scandal, 1980, A Wedding Day Deception, 1981, The Double Dealers, 1982, Season of Dishonor, 1982, Ardent Vows, 1983, Bound by Honor, 1984. BA, Wake Forest Coll., 1946; student, Columbia U., 1957-58. Newspaper reporter, N.C. and Idaho, 1946-51; radio copywrtr. sta. KDYL, Salt Lake City, 1952-53; copy supr. sta. WPTF, Raleigh, N.C., 1953-55; reporter Raleigh Times, 1955-57; editorial asst. Columbia Univ. Press, NYC, 1959-60; dir. publicity and publs., N.C. Mus. Art, Raleigh, 1967-70. Recipient Disting. Alumni award Wake Forest U., 1971. Address: 2930 Hostetler St Raleigh NC 27609

TUCKER, KAY HARTMAN, b. Lebanon, PA, May 27, 1957; d. Harvey Daniel and Marion Elizabeth (Gemmill) Hartman; m. Thomas Neil Tucker, May 2, 1987. Editor: Natl. Urban and Community Foretry Forum, 1983, NAACOG Newsletter, 1984—, Commonwealth Child Devel. Com. newslete, 1979. Contrbr. articles to numerous jnls., mag., newsletters. BA in journalism, Ind. U. of Pa., 1979. Intern, Commonwealth Child Devel. Com., Harisburg, Pa., 1979; adminsrv. asst. Washington Ctr. for Learning Alternatives, Washington, 1979-80; dir. big tree program Am. Forestry Assn., Washingon, 1980-83; editor NAACOG Orgn. Obstetric, Gynecologic, & Neonatal Nurses, Washington, 1983—; contrbr. writer Rock Creek Monitor, Washington, 1981-83. Vol. speaker Planned Parenthood of Met. Washington, 1983; vol. tutor Higher Acievement Program, Washington, 1986. Recipient Gold Circle award Am Soc. Assn. Execs., 1985. Mem. Greenpeace Intl., Am Forestry Assn., Natl. Water Conservation Coalition, Sigma Delta Chi. Home: 5310 Broad Branch Rd NW Washington DC 20015

TUCKER, MARTIN, b. Phila., Feb. 8, 1928, s. Herman and Sarah (Goldbert) T. Author: Africa in Modern Literature, 1967, Joseph Conrad, 1976, (poems) Homes of Locks and Mysteries, 1982 (English Speaking Union citation for achievement 1982); ed. Moulton's Library of Literary Criticism, 4 vols., 1968, Modern British Literature, 4 vols., 1967-75, Confrontation mag., 1970—; (CCLM editorial fellow, 1987); The Critical Temper, 4 vols., 1970-79, Modern Commonwealth Literature, 1978; contrbr. to New Republic, N.Y. Times Book Rvw, The Nation, Saturday Rvw, Commonweal, Epoch, Chgo. Rvw, New Letters, Village Voice, others. Wrkg. on Literary Exiles of the 20th Century. Prof. English, Bklyn. Ctr. Campus, L.I. U., 1958-84, C.W. Post Campus, Greenvale, N.Y., 1984—; feature wrtr. AP, Huntington, W.Va., 1954-55, N.Mex newspapers, Farmingville and Artesia, 1955-56. Recipient residence award Virginia Center for the Creative Arts, 1984, 1987, MacDowell Colony, 1977, 78, Trustees award for disting. achievement L.I. U., 1981; NEA edl. fellow, 1979. Mem. PEN (exec. bd. Am. Ctr. 1973—, wrtr. newsletter 1973-78), PSA (governing bd. 1985—), African Lit. Assn., AG, NBCC, MLA. Home: 90-A Dosoris Ln Glen Cove NY 11542

TUCKER, MELVIN JAY, b. Easthampton, MA, Mar. 3, 1931, s. Earle H. and Florence (Thompson) T.; m. N. Evelyn Tucker, June 27, 1953; children—Anne, Ellen, Michael. Author: The Life of Thomas Howard, Earl of Surrey and Second Duke of Norfolk, 1964; (with Sanders Laurie) Centering: Your Guide to Inner Growth, 1978 (pub. as Centering: The Power of Meditation in Eng. 1982); contrbr. chap. to History of Childhood, 1974 (also English, German, Spanish eds.); contrbg. ed. History of Childhood Qtly, 1973-76, Jnl Psychohistory, 1976-84. BA, U. of Mass., 1953, MA, 1954; PhD, Northwestern U., 1962. Instr. history Colby Coll., 1959-60; instr. humanities MIT, 1960-63; asst. prof., assoc. prof. history SUNY, Buffalo, 1963—, dir. grad. studies, 1979-85. Served to 1st lt. USAF, 1954-56. Recipient cert. of merit Buffalo and Erie County Hist. Soc., 1974; Ctr. for Medieval and Early Renaissance Studies fellow SUNY, Binghamton, 1970-77. Mem. Assn. for Bibliography of History (council 1983-84), Am. Hist. Assn., Conf. Brit. Studies. Home: 107 Willow Green Dr Tonawanda NY 14150

TUCKER, NANCY MEREDITH, b. Passaic, NJ, Mar. 29, 1946, d. Charles Lewis and Mildred June (Vitz) Tucker. BA, Mary Washington Coll. of U. Va., 1968. Editorial asst. F-D-C Reports, Inc., Washington, 1968-70, research asst. Council on Library Resources, Inc., Washington, 1971-72; ed. Military Market Mag., Springfield, Va., 1973—. Mem. Am. Soc. Bus. Press Eds. (dir.), Nat. Fedn. Press Women. Office: Mil Mkt Mag 6883 Comm Dr Springfield VA 22159

TUDOR, JIM PATRICK, b. Ft. Smith, AR, Nov. 20, 1946; s. W. A. and Gearldine (Batchelor) T.; m. Melanie Williford, Dec. 7, 1969; 1 son, Scott. Author: Telecommunication Study for Arkansas Legislature, 1975/Research Methods for the Treasure Hunter, 1978, Arkansas State Police Yearbook, 1979, History of the Arkansas State Police, 1982, Police Traffic Radar, 1984. Contrbr. articles to mags. Wrkg. on books on treasure sites of the South Central U.S., advanced photography for the intermediate coward. Student U. Ark., 1964-67. Trooper, Ark. State Police, Little Rock, 1968-70, sgt., 1970-71, lt., 1975-87; spl. asst. to dir. Crime Info. Ctr., Little Rock, 1971-75. Chief of staff Governor's Natural Resource Commn., Little Rock, 1983. Mem. Exchange Club (named Police Officer of Yr. 1971), Profl. Photographers Am., Am. Asn. Identification. Home: 6913 Yorkwood Dr Little Rock AR 72209

TUFTE, EDWARD ROLF, b. Kansas City, MO, Mar, 14, 1942; s. Edward E. and Virginia (James) Tufte. Author: Size and Democracy, 1973 (with R.A. Dahl), Data Analysis, 1974, Political Control of the Economy, 1978 (Kammerer award 1979), The Visual Display of Quantitative Information, 1983, Envisioning Information, 1988. BS, Stanford U., 1963, MS, 1964; PhD, Yale U., 1968. Asst. prof. pub. policy Princeton U., 1967-71, assoc. prof., 1971-74, prof., 1974-77, Yale U. (New Haven, CT), 1977—; pres. Graphics Press (Cheshire, CT), 1983—; cons. in field. Office: Yale U 124 Prospect St New Haven CT 06520

TUITT, RON S., b. Bronx, NY, Jan. 17, 1958; s. Julie Gay (Rivera) Hinds. Sr. writer, TV Guide, 1982—; contrbr.: Black Metro Mag., N.Y. Times, Washington Square News, Bridgewater Courier News. BS in Jnlsm., Soc., NYU, 1982. Stringer, The N.Y. Times, NYC, 1980-82; edit. asst. National Urban League, NYC, 1981; sr. writer TV Guide mag., NYC, 1982—. Home: 612 Chrome St North Brunswick NJ 08902

TULLY, ANDREW FREDERICK, JR., b. Southbridge, MA, Oct. 24, 1914; s. Andrew F. and Amelria (Mason) Tully; m. Mary Dani, Apr. 15, 1939 (div.); children—Martha Hardy, Mary Elizabeth, Sheila, Andrew Frederick, Mark; m. 2d, Barbara Witchell, Sept. 5, 1960 (div.); m. 3d, Mary Ellen Wood, Dec. 19, 1964; 1 son—John Spaulding. Author: Era of Elegance, 1947, Treasury Agent, 1958, A Race of Rebels, 1960, When They Burned the White House, 1961, CIA: The Inside Story, 1962, Capitol Hill, 1962, Berlin: Story of a Battle, 1963, Supreme Court, 1963, (with Milton Britten) Where Did Your Money Go?, 1964, The FBI's Most Famous Cases, 1965, The Time of the Hawk, 1967, White Tie and Dagger, 1967, The Super Spies, 1969, The Secret War Against Dope, 1973, The Brahmin Arrangement, 1974, Inside the FBI, 1979. Grad. high schl. Reporter Worcester Post (MA), 1936-38, Southbridge Evening News, 1933-36; editor, owner Southbridge Press, weekly, 1939-42; war corr. Boston Traveller, ETO, 1944-45; rewrite, feature NY World Telegram, 1945-47; free-lance, 1947-48; Washington bur. Scripps-Howard Newspapers, 1948-61; Washington columnist McNaught Syndicate; dir. United Dairy Equipment Co. (West Chester, PA). Recipient Ernie Pyle award for series on Soviet Russia, 1955, Headliners award, 1956. Mem. White House Corrs. Assn. Address: 2104 48th St NW Washington DC 20007

TUMPANE, JOHN D., b. Worcester, MA, Oct. 20, 1922. Playwright: The Gift of Tenyin, 1956; author: Scotch and Holy Water, 1981. BA, Yale U., 1944, MFA, 1949. Mgr. The Tumpane Co., 1958-76; freelance wrtr., Walnut Creek, Calif., 1976—; pub. St. Giles Press, Lafayette, Calif., 1981—. Office: Box 1416 Lafayette CA 94549

TURA, TESSI, see Heymont, George

TURCO, LEWIS PUTNAM, (Wesli Court) b. Buffalo, NY, May 2, 1934; s. Luigi and May Laura (Putnam) Turco; m. Jean Cate Houdlette, June 16, 1956; children—Melora Ann, Christopher Cameron. Works include: First Poems, 1960, Awaken, Bells Falling, 1968, The Book of Forms, 1968, The Inhabitant, 1970, Pocoangelini: A Fantography & Other Poems, 1971, Poetry: An Introduction Through Writing, 1973, Seasons of the Blood, 1980, American Still Lifes, 1981, The Compleat Melancholick, 1985, Visions and Revisions of American Poetry, 1986, The New Book of Forms, 1986, (by Wesli Court): Courses in Laments, 1977, Murgatroyd and Mabel, 1977. BA, U. of Conn., 1959; MA, U. of Iowa, 1962. Founding dir., Cleve. St. U. Poetry Ctr., 1961-64; prof. SUNY College, Oswego, 1965—; Vis. Prof., SUNY College, Potsdam, 1968-69; Bingham Poet-in-Res., U. of Louisville, 1982. With USN, 1952-56. Mem. PEN, PSA. Home: Box 362 Oswego NY 13126

TURKINGTON, GREGG MCPATRICK, (Half Gobo), b. Darwin, Australia, Nov. 25, 1967; came to U.S., 1975; s. Jarvis Albin Bock and Malvina (de la Parra) Halby, Editor Lexicon Devil, 1983; author: (play) Sandy's Gumption Summer, 1985; contbr. Yogi Cometbus Mag. and I.C.Y.M. Editor Breakfast Without Meat mag., 1983-84, co-editor, 1985-87. Co-founder Carolina Rainbow Found., San Francisco, 1983. Home: Office: 1827 Haight Rm 188 San Francisco CA 94117

TURNER, ALBERTA T., b. NYC, Oct. 22, 1919, d. Albert Chester and Marion Watson (Fellows) Tucker; m. William Arthur Turner, Apr. 9, 1943 (dec. 1984); children—Prudence M. Turner Richards, Arthur Brenton. Author poetry collections: Need, 1971, Learning to Count, 1974, Lid and Spoon, 1977, A Belfry of Knees, 1983; author textbook: To Make a Poem, 1982; editor: 50 Contemporary Poets, 1977, Poets Teaching, 1980, 45 Contemporary Poems, 1985. BA, Hunter Coll., 1940; MA, Wellesley Coll., 1941; PhD, Ohio State U., 1946. Lectr. Oberlin (Ohio) Coll., 1946-69; mem. faculty Cleve. State U., 1964—, dir. Poetry Center, 1964—, prof. English, 1978—; assoc. ed. Field mag., Oberlin, 1970—. Recipient Individual Artist's award Ohio Arts Council, 1980, Cleve. Artists award in Lit., Cleve. Women's City Club, 1985, Helen and Laura Krout Poetry award Ohioana Library Assn., 1986. Mem. PEN, Milton Soc. Am. Home: 482 Caskey Ct Oberlin OH 44074

TURNER, CAROLYN ANN, b. Murray, KY, Aug. 23, 1949; d. Huda Franklin and Bessie (Griffin) Turner. Contrbr. to Am. Poetry Anthology. BA, Murray State U., 1971, MA, 1985. English instr. Murray State Univ., Fort Campbell, Ky., 1973-74, Frayser Bapt. Schl., Memphis, 1977-79, Tabernacle Schl., Covington, Tenn., 1979-81, Hughes High Schl., Ark., 1981-83; grad. asst. English Murray State Univ., 1983-85, adj., 1985-86; grad. asst. English, Univ. of Missouri-Columbia, 1987—. Address: 809 Hurt Murray KY 42071

TURNER, DENISE DUNN, b. Cairo, IL, Aug. 2, 1947; d. Robert James and Helen Grace (Dunn) Watkins; m. Revis Eugene Turner, Dec. 22, 1967; children—Rebecca Jill, Stephen Robert. Author: Home Sweet Fishbowl, 1982, Scuff Marks on the Ceiling, 1986. Contrbr. numerous articles to mags., bible study series book. B.S., Southern Ill. U., 1970. Buyer, Stewart's, Louisville, 1970-73; reporter Middletown Jnl., OH, 1987—; freelance wrtr., 1975—. Wrtr. publicity Middfest Com., Middletown, 1986. Home: 217 Edith Dr Middletown OH 45042

TURNER, JEAN-RAE, b. Newark, Aug. 6, 1920; d. William Roberts and Jessie Edith (MacRae) T.; 1 dau., Margaret Ann Phillips Adams Richter Zeiger. Author: Along the Upper Road, A Hist. of Hillside, NJ, 1977, Elizabethtown and Union County, A Pictorial History, 1982. BS in Edn., Trenton State Coll., 1942; MA in Hist., Columbia U. Tchrs. Coll., 1944. Tchr., Hillside (NJ) pub. schls., 1942-45; rptr. The Elizabeth (NJ) Daily Jnl., 1945-79; columnist, The Citizen; librarian New Jersey Newsphotos, Newark, 1980—. Outstanding jnlst., NJ Daily Nwspr. Women, 1977. Mem. NJ Press Women, NJ Press Photographers, Natl. Press Photogs. Address: Box 241 Elizabeth NJ 07207

TURNIK, see Parker, Joyce Annetta

TUSIANI, JOSEPH, b. Foggia, Italy, Jan. 14, 1924 (came to U.S., 1947, naturalized, 1956); s. Michael and Maria (Pisone) Tusiani. Author: Dante in Licenza, 1952, Two Critical Essays on Emily Dickinson, 1952, Poesia Missionaria in Inghilterra Ed America, 1953, Sonettisti Americani, 1954, Melos Cordis; poems in Latin, 1955, Lo Speco Celeste, 1956, Odi Sacre; poems, 1958, The Complete Poems of Michelangelo, 1960, Rind and All, 1962, Lust and Liberty (The Poems of Machiavelli), 1963, The Fifth Season, 1963, Dante's Inferno (Introduced to Young People), 1964, Envoy from Heaven, 1965, Dante's Purgatorio (Introduced to Young People), 1969, Dante's Paradise (Introduced to Young People), 1970, Tasso's Jerusalem Delivered; verse transl., 1970, Boccaccio's Nymphs of Fiesole, 1971, Italian Poets of the Renaissance, 1971, From Marino to Marinetti, 1973, The Age of Dante, 1973, America the Free, 1976, Gente Mia and Other Poems, 1978. Dottore in Lettere summa cum laude, U. Naples, 1947, Litt.D., 1971. Lectr. in Italian lit. Hunter Coll., 1950-62; chair Italian dept. Coll. Mt. St. Vincent, 1948-71; vis. assoc. prof. NYU, 1956-64, city U. NY, 1971—; prof. Herbert H. Lehman Coll., 1971—; NDEA vis. prof. Italian Conn. State Coll., 1962. Recipient Greenwood Prize for poetry in Eng., 1956, Outstanding Tchr. award, 1969, Joseph Tusiani scholarship fund established in his honor at Lehman Coll., 1983. Mem. PSA, Cath. Poetry Soc. Am. (dir. 1958, Spirit gold medal 1968). Home: 2140 Tomlinson Ave Bronx NY 10461

TUTTLE, JUDITH AURRE, b. Rugby, Gt. Britain, Aug. 14, 1942, came to U.S., 1948, d. Fermin and Shirley (Powell) Aurre; m. Lyle Gilbert Tuttle, Dec. 16, 1982. Ed. Tattoo Historian, 1982—. BA, U. Fla., 1964. Tchr. Dade County public schls., Fla., 1964-65; TV instr., scriptwrtr. Govt. Am. Samoa, Pago Pago, 1966-76; sole practice real estate broker, San Francisco, 1979-81; prop. Tattoo Art Mus., San Francisco, 1982—. Office: Tattoo Art 30 7th St San Francisco CA 94103

TUTU, see Chowdhury, Debi Elizabeth,

TWEEDY, RACKHAM, see Queenan, Joseph Martin, Jr.

TWICHELL, CHASE, b. New Haven, CT, Aug. 20, 1950; d. Charles Pratt and Ann (Chase) Twichell. Author: Northern Spy, 1981, The Odds, 1986. BA, Trinity Coll., Hartford, CT, 1973, MFA, U. IA, 1976. Ed., Pennyroyal Press, W. Hatfield, MA, 1976-84; visiting asst. prof. Hampshire Coll., Amherst, MA, 1984-85; assoc. prof. U. AL, 1985—. Artists Fellowship, MA Artists Fdn., 1981, Fellowship, Bread Loaf Wrtrs. Conf., 1984, Fellowship, Wesleyan Wrtrs. Conf., 1985. Mem. PSA, AWP, AAP. Home: 2604 Lakewood Circle Tuscaloosa AL 35405

TWITTY, WILLIAM BRADLEY, b. Cherokee, AL, Jan. 5, 1920; s. Clarence Hudson and Lyda (Blackburn) T.; m. Gaila Norhington, May 22, 1941 (div. May 22, 1951); children—Tralelia, Camille, Gaila, Gina; m. Edith Bolling, May 22, 1951. Author: Y'all Come, 1962; (poems) The Flying Green Whale and Other Poems: 1964, 1965; (novel) Beyond the Leaves, 1966. Contrbr. articles to profl. jnls. Author, ed.: Spelling is Fun, 1955—, Colonial Handwriting: K-9, 1958—; ed.: Governments Under Which We Live & Civics, 1955—, Communicative Arts, 1955—, Alabama History, 1958—/Chemistry Lab Manual: 101, 102, 103, Genl. Chemistry, 1985—, Managing the Learning Process in Bus. Edn., 1986, It's a Long Way from Scooba, 1986, Elementary Math & Basic Algebra, 1987, Call Forth the Mighty Men, 1987, Duty & the Law, 1987. Wrkg. on Modern Poet series. B.A., U. Ala., 1943; LL.B., U. N.C., 1947. Vice pres. Colonial Press, Tuscloosa, AL, 1954-64, pres., Birmingham, AL, 1964-86, chmn., Bessemer, AL, 1986—. Served with U.S. Army, 1944-45. Home: 1237 Stevens Rd SE Bessemer AL 35023

TYE, HENRY JR., b. Detroit, Feb. 14, 1962; s. Henry Ollice and Frankie (Mays) T. Poetry in anthologies. Wrkg. on book of poetry, novel. BA in Psychology, U. Detroit, 1985. Youth counselor The Children's Center, Detroit, 1987—. Home: 3381 Charlevoix St Detroit MI 48207

TYLER, ANNE, (Mrs. Taght M. Modarressi), b. Mpls., Oct. 25, 1941; d. Lloyd Parry and Phyllis (Mahon) Tyler; m. Taghi M. Modarressi, May 3, 1963; children—Tezh, Mitra. Author: (novels) If Morning Ever Comes, 1964, The Tin Can Tree, 1965, A Slipping-Down Life, 1970, The Clock Winder, 1972, Celestial Navigation, 1974, Searching for Caleb, 1976, Earthly Possessions, 1977, Morgan's Passing, 1980, Dinner at the Homesick Restaurant, 1982, The Accidental Tourist, 1985; contrbr. short stories to natl. mags. BA, Duke U., 1961; postgrad., Columbia U., 1962. Home: 222 Tunbridge Rd Baltimore MD 21212

TYLER, ROBERT L., b. Virginia, MN, Feb. 11, 1922; s. Leon Meredith and Bessie Julia (Carver) T.; m. Molly Erlich, Dec. 17, 1947 (div. Sept. 1970); children—Deborah Pearl, Daniel Kurt; m. 2d, Gerry Ruth Sack, June 20, 1971; 1 son, Benjamin Leon. Author: Rebels of the Woods: the IWW in the Pacific Northwest, 1968, Walter Reuther, 1971; (poems) Deposition of Don Quixote, 1964, A Hearth of Mental Rock, 1985. Contrbr. articles to profl. jnls. essays, poems, to lit mags. Contrbg. editor: The Humanist, 1970—. BA, U. Minn. Mpls., 1948, MA, 1949; PhD, U. Oreg.-Eugene, 1953. Prof. history Ball State U., Muncie, Ind., 1956-66, Wagner Coll., Staten Island, N.Y., 1967-70, Southern Conn. State U., New Haven, 1970-84, retired; Fulbright prof. U. Guyana, Georgetown, 1966-67. Home: 41 Linden Dr Kingston RI 02881

TYRRELL, CALVIN E., (Stoney Lane), b. Endicott, NY; s. Curtis Sterling and Alice (Lindsey) T.; m. Linda Kay Crooks, Sept. 15, 1962; children—Robert Cottrell, Kimberly Ann Sexton. Author: Collected Thoughts Poems and Writings, 1986; (song) I'll See You in Tampa, 1985. Contrbr. poems to anthols. Wrkg. on book, music. Grad. public schs., North Kingstown, RI. Realtor, owner Fla. Assn. Realtors, Kissimmee, FL, 1973-84; district mgr. United Agys., Kissimmee, 1984-87, deputy property appraisor Osceola County, Kissimmee, 1987—. Mem. Osceloa Wrtrs. Club. Home: 917 Verona St Kissimmee FL 32741

TYTELL, JOHN, b. Antwerp, Belgium, May 17, 1939 (came to U.S., 1941); s. Charles and Lena (Gano) Tytell; m. Mellon Gregori, May 28, 1967. Author: Ezra Pound: The Solitary Volcano, 1987, Naked Angels, 1976, The American Experience, 1970; contrbr. articles to Am. Scholar, Partisan Rvw, others. BA, CCNY, 1961; MA, NYU, 1963, PhD., 1968. Grad reader NYU, 1963-67; lectr. Queens Coll. (NYC), 1963-68, assoc. prof., 1968-73, 1973-76, prof. English, 1977—; exec. editor Am. Book Rvw, 1979—; vis. prof. Rutgers U., 1980, U. Paris, 1983; cons. Natl. Humanities Faculty (GA), , ,78—. Home: 69 Perry St New York NY 10014

TZIMET, NAFTALI, see Cymet, Tyler Childs

UBELL, EARL, b. Bklyn., June 21, 1926; s. Charles and Hilda (Kramer) Ubell; m. Shirley Leitman, Feb. 12, 1949; children—Lori Ellen, Michael Charles. Producer: documentaries

Medicine in America, 1977, Escape from Madness, 1977; author: The World of Push and Pull, 1964, The World of the Living, 1965, The World of Candle and Color, 1969, How to Save Your LIfe, 1972, Mother/Father/You, 1980. BS, Coll. City Ny., 1948. With NY Herald Tribune, 1943-66, successively messenger, as. sec. to mng. editor, reporter, 1943-53, sci. editor, 1953-66, syndicated columnis, 1956-66; sci. commentator MBS, 1958-59; spcl. sci. editor WNEW (NY), 1962; health and sci. editor WCBS-TV (NYC), 1966-72, 78—; health editor Parade mag., 1983—; dir. TV news NBC News (NYC), 1972-76; producer spcl. broadcasts, 1976-78. Pres. Council Advancement Sci. Writing, Inc., 1960-66, bd. dirs., 1960—. Served as aviation radioman USNR, 1944-46. Recipient Mental Health Bell award NY State Soc. Mental Health, 1957, Albert Lasker med. journalism award, 1958; award for radio program Nat. Assn. Mental Health, 1962; Sci. Writers award AAAS, 1960; Empire State award, 1963; TV Reporting award NY Assoc. Press, 1969, 71; NY Emmy award, 1971; Smuelson award NY League for Hard of Hearing; Legal-Med. award Milton Halpern Library of Legal Medicine. Mem. Natl. Assn. Sci. Writers (pres. 1960-61), Nuclear Energy Writers Assn. (pres. 1965-66). Home: 114 West 27 New York NY 10001

UBELL, ROBERT NEIL, b. Bklyn., Sept. 14, 1938; s. Charles and Hilda (Kramer) U.; m. Rosalyn Deutsche, Sept. 24, 1976; children—Jennifer, Elizabeth. Author: (with Marvin Leiner) Children Are the Revolution, 1974; editor: Physics Today Buyers' Guide, 1984-86; exec. ed. Linguistics: The Cambridge Survey, 1987—; exec. ed. Pre-Med Handbook, 1986; Mem. Edl. Bd. ISI Press; pub. adv. comm., The Scientist, Bks. sub-comm., Am. Inst. of Physics; Pubns. Comm., Am. Inst. Biological Scis. BA, Bklyn. Coll., 1961; student, Acad. Fine Arts, Rome, Italy, 1959-60, City U. NY, 1961-62, Pratt Graphic Arts Workshop (NYC), 1972-73. Assoc. editor Nuclear Industry, Atomic Industrial Forum, 1962-64; editor Plenum Pub. Corp. (NYC), 1965-68, sr. editor, 1968-70, vp, editor-in-chief, 1970-76; editor The Sciences, NY Acad. Scis. (NYC), 1976-79; Am. pub. Nature (NYC), 1979-83; pub. Robert Ubell Assocs. (NYC), 1983—. Mem. NY Acad. Scis., Am. Inst. Biological Scis., Soc. for Scholarly Publishing, Natl. Assn. Sci. Writers, Council of Biology Editors, AAAS. Home: 54 W 11th St New York NY 10011

UCHILL, IDA LIBERT, b. Denver, Dec. 10, 1917; d. Paul and Fannie B. (Pepper) Libert; m. Sam Harry Uchill; children—Deborah Uchill Miller, Vicki. Author: Pioneers, Peddlers, and Tsadikim, 1957, 2d ed., 1979, Wetside Story Revisited, 1987, The Jewish Traveler, 1987. Contrbr. articles to mags., newspapers including Denver Post, Am. Tchr., others. B.A., U. Colo., 1939. Tchr. public schs., Denver, 1961-83. Mem. NLAPW, Colo. AL. Home: 795 S Jersey St Denver CO 80224

UDE, WAYNE RICHARD, b. Mpls., Mar. 23, 1946, s. Vernon Richard and Jeanne (Boutelle) U.; m. Marian Blue, July 15, 1983; children—James, Cheryl. Author: Buffalo and other Stories, 1975, 4th ed., 1978, Becoming Coyote (novel), 1981, 2d ed., 1985; contrbr. stories to Aspen Anthology, Lynx Mag., Salt Cedar, Scree, others; contrbr. essays, rvws. to Am. Book Rvw, Sunday Clothes, others; producer, host wrtr.-interview program sta. KMSU, 1985-86. BA, U. Mont., 1969; MFA, U. Mass., 1974. Ed. Colo. State Rvw, Ft. Collins, 1977-84; asst. prof., then assoc. prof. English Colo. State U., 1976-84; wrtr.-in-residence Mankato (Minn.) State U., 1984-86. Mem. Western Lit. Assn., AWP. Home: 513 Marshall St Mankato MN 56001

UDOVITCH, ABRAHAM LABE, b. Winnipeg, Man., Can., May 31, 1933 (came to U.S., naturalized, 1966); s. Benjamin Alexander and Minnie (Benson) Udovitch; children—Tamar, Miriam Esther. Author: Partnership and Profit in Medieval Islam, 1970; editor: Studia Islamica, 1975; editorial bd.: Jnl of Interdisciplinary History, 1970—, Intl. Jnl of Middle East Studies, 1975—; mem. exec. com.: Encyc. of Islam. BS, Columbia U., 1958, MA, 1959; PhD, Yale, 1965. Asst. prof. Middle East history Brandeis U., 1964-65, Cornell U., 1965-67; assoc. prof. Middle East history Princeton, 1968-71, prof., 1971—, chair dept. Nr. Eastern studies, 1973-77, 80—; bd. govs. Am. Research Inst. in Turkey, 1969—; dir. Middle East study panel Commn. on Critical Choices for Americans, 1974-76. Home: 11 College Rd Princeton NJ 08540

UHRMAN, ESTHER, b. New London, CT, July 7, 1921, d. David Aaron and Pauline (Schwartz) Uhrman. Author: Gypsy Logic (poetry), 1970, From Canarsie to Masada (novelette), 1975; contrbr. poetry, articles to trade mags., newspapers. Diploma in Design and Illustration, Traphagan Schl. Fashion, 1955; AA, NYC Tech. Coll., 1974; student, Cornell U., 1975-77; PhD, U. Danzig, Poland, 1977. Artist, wrtr. NYC, 1954—; asst. ed. Inside Detective-True Detective, NYC, 1977. Recipient. N.Y. State Podiker award, 1968, Golden Windmill Radio Drama award, Govt. of Holland, 1971. Fellow World Lit. Acad.; mem. Intl. Arts Guild. Home: 1655 Flatbush Ave Brooklyn NY 11210

UITTI, KARL DAVID, b. Calumet, MI, Dec. 10, 1933; s. Karl Abram and Joy (Weidelman) Uitti; m. Maria Esther Clark, Feb. 15, 1953 (div. Feb. 1973); children—Maria Elisabeth, Karl Gerard; 2nd m. Michelle Alice Freeman, Mar. 13, 1974; children—David Charles, Jacob Christian. Author: The Concept of Self in the Symbolist Novel, 1961, La Passion litteraire de Remy de Gourmont, 1962, Linguistics and Literary Theory, 1969, Story, Myth and Celebration in Old French Narrative Poetry (1050-1200), 1973; contrbr. numerous articles and rvws to scholarly jnls; editor: Edward C. Armstrong Monographs on Medieval Literature; mem. editorial bd.: Historiographica linguistica; mem. adv. council: Dictionary of the Middle Ages, Romance Philology. AB, U. Calif. at Berkeley, 1952, AM, 1952, PhD, 1959; student univs. Nancy and Bordeaux, 1952-54. Instr. Princeton U., 1959-61, asst. prof., 1961-65, assoc. prof., 1965-68, prof., 1968—, John N. Woodhull prof. modern langs., 1978—, chair dept. Romance langs., 1973-78. Guggenheim fellow, 1963-65, NEH Sr. fellow, 1976, ACLS grantee, 1986. Served with AUS, 1954-56. Mem. MLA, Linguistic Soc. Am., Medieval Acad. Am., Phi Beta Kappa, Societe linguistique romane. Home: 50 Grove Ave Princeton NJ 08540

ULANOV, BARRY, b. NYC, Apr. 10, 1918; s. Nathan A. and Jeanette (Askwith) Ulanov; m. Joan Bel Geddes, Dec. 16, 1939; children—Anne, Nicholas, Katherine; 2nd m. Ann Belford, Aug. 21, 1968; 1 son—Alexander. Author: The Recorded Music of W.A. Mozart, 1942, Duke Ellington, 1946, The Incredible Crosby, 1948, A History of Jazz in America, 1952, A Handbook of Jazz, 1957, Sources and Resources, 1960, Death: A Book of Preparation and Consolation, 1959, Makers of the Modern Theater, 1961, The Way of St. Alphonsus Liguori, 1961, Seeds of Hope in the Modern World, 1962, Contemporary Catholic Thought, 1963, The Two Worlds of American Art, 1965, The Making of a Modern Saint, 1966, (with James B. Hall) Modern Culture and the Arts, 1967, 72, Where Swing Came From, 1970, Swing Lives!, 1972, (with Ann Ulanov) Religion and the Unconscious, 1975, (with Ann Ulanov) Primary Speech: A Psychology of Prayer, 1982, (with Ann Ulanov) Cinderella and Her Sisters: The Envied and the Envying, 1983, The Prayers of St. Augustine, 1984, (with Ann Ulanov) The Witch and the Clown: Two Archetypes of Human Sexuality, 1986; co-translator: (with Joan Ulanov) The Last Essays of George Bernanos, 1955, (with Frank Tauritz) Joy out of Sorrow (by Mere Marie des Douleurs), 1958. AB, Columbia U., 1939, PhD, 1955; Litt.D., Villanova U., 1965. Editor Swing mag., 1939-41, Listen mag., 1940-42, Metronome mag., 1943-55, Metronome Yearbook, 1950-55; columnist Down Beat mag., 1955-58; instr. English Princeton U., 1950-51, Barnard Coll., 1951-56, asst. prof., 1956-59, assoc. prof., 1959-66, prof. 1966—, McIntosh Prof. of English, 1986—, chair dept., 1967-71, 79-82, chair program in the arts, 1975-79, 82—; adj. prof. religion Columbia U., 1966; assoc. editor The Bridge Yearbook of Inst. Judaeo-Christian studies, 1955-68. Mem. PEN, St. Thomas More Soc. (pres. 1955-56, 64-65), Conf. on Humanities, CCICA, The Conference of Anglican Theologians. Office: Barnard Coll New York NY 10027

ULISSE, PETER JAMES, b. New Britain, CT, Oct. 2, 1944, s. Peter John and Mary Margaret (Cesanek) U.; m. Gael Lynn Catabia, Dec. 30, 1967; children—Christian, Rebecca, Justin. Author poetry chapbooks: Triad, 1983, Wings & Roots, 1985; ed.: Conn. River Rvw, High Tide; contrbr.: Small Pond, Greyledge Rvw, Amanda Blue, other publs. AB, Providence Coll., 1966; MA, U. Va., 1967. Prof. Housatonic Community Coll., Bridgeport, Conn., 1970—; leader poetry workshops North Ave. Correctional Inst., Bridgeport, 1981; presenter poetry readings. Served to 1st lt. U.S. Army, 1968-70. Mellon fellow Yale U., 1981; winner poetry contest Different Drummer, 1978. Mem. Conn. Poetry Soc. (past v.p.), AAP. Home: 65 Rivercliff Dr Devon CT 06460

ULRICH, ANN CAROL, b. Madison, WI, July 17, 1952; d. Marvin Michael and Marion Ellen (Hughes) Schumacher; m. Jeffrey Lee Ulrich, Aug. 19, 1972; children—Ryan Ronald, Martin Andrew, Scott Jeffrey. Contrbr.: Career World mag., Alive for Young Teens, True Story, various community newspapers; ed., pub. The Star Beacon, 1987—. BA with honors, Mich. State U., 1975. Prodn. asst., circulation mgr. Snowmass (Colo.) Newspapers, 1980-84; typesetter Capital Citie Communications, Albany, Oreg., 1984-85; typesetter, ed., High Country Shopper, Paonia,Colo., 1985—; assoc. dir. UFO Contact Center Internat., Delta, Colo., 1986—; Pub. Earth Star Publications, Delta, CO, 1987—. Address: Box 174 Delta CO 81416

ULRICH, HOMER, b. Chgo., Mar. 27, 1906; s. Charles August and Alma Henrietta (Geewe) U.; m. Miriam Elizabeth North, Sept. 19, 1934; children—Karen E. Jones, David N. Ulrich, Gretchen M. Buzzell. Author: Chamber Music, 1948-66, The Education of a Concert-Goer, 1949, Symphonic Music, 1952, Famous Women Singers, 1952, Music: A Design for Listening, 1947, 62, 70, (with Bryce Jordan) Designed for Listening, 1957, 62, (with Paul A. Pisk) A History of Music and Musical Style, 1963, A Survey of

Choral Music and Musical Style, 1963, A Survey of Choral Music, 1973, Centennial History of the Music Teachers National Assn., 1976. MA, U. Chgo., 1939. Cellist & bassoonist, Chgo. Symphony Orch., 1929-35; head music dept. Monticello Coll., Godfrey, IL, 1935-38; prof. music U. TX, Austin, 1939-53; prof. & head dept. U. MD, College Park, 1953-72, prof. emeritus, 1972; ed. Amer. Music Teacher, Cin., 1972—. Honorary mem. Phi Beta Kappa, U. MD, 1971. Home: 3587 S. Leisure World Blvd Silver Spring MD 20906

UMPHENOUR, JILLIAN DARRELYN, b. Glendale, CA, June 5, 1957, d. Darrell Clyde and Mary Ellen (Burtis) Umphenour; m. Russell Grant Williams, Aug. 14, 1979 (div. 1982); 1 child, Aubrey (dec.). Contrbr. to Our World's Best Loved Poems, 1984, N.Y. Poetry Soc. Anthology, 1985. Wrkg. on poetry collection. AA, Orange Coast Coll., 1986. Drafter, illustrator D/Appolonia, Irvine, Calif., 1981; mech. drafter Am. Bentley Co., Irvine, 1981-85; electro-mech. drafter, Babcock, Inc., Anaheim, Calif., 1985—; free-lance wrtr., ad wrtr., Irvine, Calif., 1986—; music & movie critic (free-lance), Orange County Rvw, 1986—. Recipient Golden Poet award World of Poetry, 1985. Mem. NWC, Am. Film Inst. Home: 317 Iris Corona del Mar CA 92625

UN, see Amanuddin, Syed

UNGER, BURTON, b. NYC, June 25, 1939; s. Herman S. and Lillian (Israel) U.; m. Rhoda Kesler, Apr. 11, 1966; children—Laurel, Rachel. Assoc. ed. Local 1199 Drug and Hosp. News, 1965-67, High Fidelity Trade News, 1967-68; ed. Port Washington News, 1968-70, Small World mag., 1974082; pubns. ed. Volkswagen of Am., 1970-82; pubns. mgr. NJ Inst. Tech., 1982-83; pubns. supvr. Mercedes-Benz of N. Am., 1983—; contrbr. to Small Bus. Computer Mag., 1982-83. BA, Bklyn Coll., 1960; MS, Columbia Grad. Sch. Jnlsm., 1965. Most improved nwspr. award, NY Press Assn., 1968; graphic excell. awards, Printing Industries of NY, 1979, 80, 81. Mem. SPJ, IMPA. Home: 11 Elston Rd Upper Montclair NJ 07043

UNGER, DOUGLAS ARTHUR, b. Moscow, ID, June 27, 1952; s. Maurice Albert Unger and Ruth (Mann) Stoecker; m. Amy Burk, May 10, 1980; 1 stepdau., Erin. Author: Leavin the Land, 1984 (Best Novel, Soc. Midland Authors, 1985), El Yanqui, 1986. Wrkg. on novel. BA, U. Chgo., 1973; MFA, U. Ia., 1977. Instr. theater and dance Western Wash. U., 1980-82; asst. prof. creative writing program Syracuse U., N.Y., 1983—. Guggenheim fellow, 1985. Mem. PEN. Home: 124 S. Lorraine Ave Syracuse NY 13210

UNGERER, JEAN TOMI, b. Strasbourg, France, Nov. 28, 1931 (came to U.S., 1957); s. Theo and Alice (Essler) Ungerer; m. Miriam Lancaster; 1 dau.—Phoebe Alexis. Author: The Mellops Go Flying, 1957, Crietor, 1958, Adelaide, 1959, Emile, 1960, Inside marriage, 1960, Horrible, 1960, Rufus, 1961, Three Robbers, 1962, Snail Where Are You?, 1962, Herzinfarkt, 1962, The Mellops Go Underground, ,62, A Child-Phoebe Alexis, 1962, Underground Sketchbook, 1964, One Two Where Is My Shoe?, 1964, The Party, 1966, Orlando, 1966, Zeralda's Ogre, 1967, Moon Man, 1967, Ask Me a Question, 1968, The Hat, 1969, The Fornicon, 1969, Compromises, 1969, Beast of Monsieur Racine, 1971, I Am Papa Snap and These Are My Favorite No Such Stories, 1971, No Kiss for Mother, 1972, Spiegelmensch, 1972, T. Ungerer Fairy Tales, 1972, Amerika, 1974, Allumette, 1974, Totempole, 1976, A Great Song Book, 1978, Babylon, 1979, Politricks, 1979; artist, illus., cartoonist for natl. mags., illus. children's books, cartoon album. Student French and German Schools. Served with Mounted Police, 1953. Recipient honors for books NY Herald Tribune, gold medal Soc. of Illustrators, 1960, Intl. Children's Book Prize. Mem. Inst. Graphic Arts, PEN, AG. Office: Doubleday 245 Pk Ave New York NY 10017

UNTERBERGER, BETTY MILLER, b. Glasgow, Scotland, Dec. 27, 1923; d. Joseph C. and Leah Miller; m. Robert Ruppe, July 27, 1944; children—Glen, Gail, Gregg. Author: America's Siberian Expedition 1918-1920: A Study of National Policy, 1956, 69; editor: American Intervention in the Russian Civil War, 1969, Intervention Against Communism: Did the U.S. Try to Overthrow the Soviet Government, 1918-1920; contrbr. to Woodrow Wilson and the Revolutionary World, 1982; editorial adv. bd.: The Papers of Woodrow Wilson, Princeton U., 1982; bd. editors: Diplomatic History, 1981—, Red River Valley Hist. Rvw, 1975—. BA, Syracuse U., 1943; MA, Harvard U., 1946; PhD, Duke U., 1950. Asst. prof. E. Carolina U. (Greenville), 1948-50; assoc. prof., dir. liberal arts ctr. Whittier Coll. (CA), 1954-61; assoc. prof. Calif. State U. at Fullerton, 1961-65, prof., chair grad. studies, 1965-68; prof. Tex. A&M U. (College Station), 1968—; mem. U.S. Dept. Army Hist. Adv. Com., 1980-82, Natl. Hist. Publs. and Records Commn., 1980—. Trustee Am. Inst. Pakistan Studies, Villanova U., PA, 1981—. Recipient Disting. Teaching award Calif. State U. at Fullerton, 1966, All- Univ. Disting. Teaching award Tex. A&M U., 1975. Mem. Am. Hist. Assn., Orgn. Am. Historians, Soc. Historians of Am. Fgn. Relations, Rocky Mountain Assn. Slavic Studies. Office: Tex A&M Univ College Station TX 77843

UNTERECKER, JOHN EUGENE, b. Buffalo, Dec. 14, 1922; s. John G. and Bertha (Ellinger) Unterecker; m. Ann Apalian, Feb. 28, 1953 (div. 1973). Author: A Reader's Guide to W.B. Yeats, 1959, Lawrence Durrell, 1964, The Dreaming Zoo, 1965, Voyager: A Life of Hart Crane, 1969, Dance Sequence, 1975, Stone, 1977; editor: (with Frank Stewart) Poetry Hawaii: A Contemporary Anthology, 1979; contrbr. poetry to major mags. BA, Middlebury Coll., 1944; MA, Columbia U., 1948, PhD, 1958. Radio announcer WBN(Buffalo), 1944; Off-Broadway stock and TV actor, 1945-56; instr. Coll. City NY, 1946-58; mem. faculty Columbia, 1958-74, prof. English lit., 1966-74; faculty dept. English U. Hawaii (Honolulu), 1974—; vis. prof. U. Hawaii, 1969, U. Tex., 1974, Flinders U. (Australia), 1979; lectr. Yeats Intl. Summer Schl. (Ireland), 1972, 73-75, 77, 78, 79, 80; book reviewer NY Times, New Leader, Sat. Rvw. Pres. Hawaii Lit. Council 1975, mem. bd., 1975-78. Guggenheim fellow, 1964-65; Yaddo fellow, 1967, 68, 69, 70, 72, 74, 79; NEA fellow, 1980; Hawaii Award for Literature, 1985. Mem. AG, PEN, James Joyce Soc., Am. Com. Irish Studies, Am. Gloxinia Soc. Address: 1417 Alencastre St Honolulu HI 96816

UPDIKE, JOHN HOYER, b. Shillington, PA, Mar. 18, 1932; s. Wesley R. and Linda G. (Hoyer) Updike; m. Mary E. Pennington, June 26, 1953; children—Elizabeth, David, Michael, Miranda; m. 2d, Martha R. Bernhard, Sept. 30, 1977. Author: The Carpentered Hen, 1958, The Poorhouse Fair, 1959, The Same Door, 1959, Rabbit, Run, 1960, Pigeon Feathers, 1962, The Centaur, 1963 (Natl. Book Award), Telephone Poles, 1963, Olinger Stories; selection, 1964, Of the Farm, 1965, Assorted Prose, 1965, The Music School, 1966, Couples, 1968, Midpoint, 1969, Bech: A Book, 1970, Rabbit Redux, 1971, Museums and Women, 1972, Buchanan Dying, 1974, A Month of Sundays, 1975, Picked-Up Pieces, 1975, Marry Me, 1976, Tossing and Turning, 1977, The Coup, 1978, Too Far to Go, Problems, 1979, Rabbit Is Rich, 1981, Bech Is Back, 1982, Hugging the Shore, 1983, The Witches of Eastwick, 1984, Facing Nature, 1985, Roger's Version, 1986. Trust Me, 1987. AB, Harvard U., 1954; student Ruskin Schl. Drawing and Fine Art, 1954-55. With New Yorker mag., 1955-57. Recipient Rosenthal award natl. Inst. Arts and Letters, 1960, O'Henry Prize Short story winner, 1967-68, Macdowell medal, 1981, Pulitzer Prize, American Book Award, National Book Critics' Circle Award. Mem. Natl. Inst. Arts and Letters, Am. Acad. Arts and Scis. Office: Knopf 201 E 50th St New York NY 10022

UPHOFF, JOSEPH ANTHONY, JR., b. Colorado Springs, CO, Mar. 15, 1950; s. Joseph Anthony and Melva Corinne (Eitel) U. Works include: The House Is Green, 1983, Aikido, 1984, A Linguistic of Calculus Methods, 1984, (Castaneda) Dreaming and Stalking, 1985, The Murdering Magician, 1985, A Critique of John S. Wilson's Work (Dada), 1985, Logarithmic, Trigonometric, and Quadriatic Transforms, 1986, The Whispering Surgeon, 1986, Surrealist Philosophy, 1986, Psychic Ecology, 1987, Theoretical History, 1987, Existentialism in Art, 1987, The Ghost Dance, 1987, Modern Relativity, 1987. AA in Arts, El Paso C.C., 1975; BA, U. Colo., 1977. Artist. Mem. Poetry West. Office: 1025 Garner St Box 18 Colorado Springs CO 80905

UPTON, LEE, b. St. John's, MI, June 2, 1953; d. Charles William and Rose Mindwell (Thompson) Upton; m. Richard Buttny, July 22, 1980. Author: The Invention of Kindness, 1984; fiction, poetry in Yale Rvw, Poetry, Chgo. Rvw, Ascent, New Voices, other lit mags. MFA, U. of Mass., 1981; PhD Lit., SUNY-Binghamton, 1986. Instr., U. of Maryland, Asian Div., 1980-81; instr., Va. Commonwealth U., Richmond, 1982; tchr., SUNY-Binghamton, NY, 1983-1986; asst. prof., Lafayette College, 1986-1987; asst. prof., Grand Valley State College, 1987—. Pushcart Price, 1987. Mem. AWP, PSA. Home: 5674 Wacousta Rd Fowler MI 48835

UPTON, ROBERT CHAPMAN, JR., b. Houston, June 28, 1935; s. Robert Chapman and Rose (Leminski) U.; m. Clara Slocum, June 2, 1956; children—Robert, Gregory, Cynthia, Michael. Author: Consumers Guide to Mutual Fund, 1987; (play) Word from Our Sponsor, 1986; syndicated columnist: Financial Focus, 1978—. Contrbr. article to mags., trade jnls. B.A., St. Mary's U., 1956; M.A., Pepperdine U., 1965. Resident mgr. A.G. Edwards & Co., Alexandria, LA, 1968-78; limited ptnr. Edward D. Jones & Co., Alexandria, 1978—. Served to capt. U.S. Army, 1960-68. Home: One Kisatchie Ln Boyce LA 71409

UPTON, ROBERT J., b. Beardstown, Ill., Apr. 3, 1934; s. James Upton and Mary Catherine (Miller) Dreher; m. Patricia Anne Sloneker, June 6, 1961; children—Kathleen Upton-Finch, Jeffrey. Author: Who'd Want to Kill Old George?, 1977, A Golden Fleecing, 1978, Fade Out, 1985, 2d ed., 1986, Dead on the Stick, 1986. Fla. State Univ., Yale, 1961; L.L.B.; Stetson Law Schl., 1963. Served with U.S. Army, 1954-56. Home: 419 W 22d St New York NY 10011

URBANIAK, GEORGE CARL, b. Bklyn., Nov. 15, 1947, s. Joseph and Anna Helen (Yanak) U.; m. Joyce Lynn Bielcik, June 28, 1969; 1 son, Robert, Author: The Wayfarer, 1979, (screenplay 1984), Mirrorslave, 1979, Suddenly, By Chance... (screenplay), 1984; contrbr. to Psychic Pathways Newsletter, Moontides Mag. Student pub. schls., Elmhurst, N.Y. With NYC Dept. Water Resources, 1966-72; mgr. NYC Dept. Sanitation, 1972—. Home: 58-19 Cooper Ave Glendale NY 11385

URDANG, LAURENCE, b. NYC, Mar. 21, 1927; s. Harry Rudman and Annabel (Schafran) Urdang; m. Irena B. Ehrlich vel Sluszny, May 23, 1952 (div.); children—Nicole Severyn, Alexandra Stefanie. Compiler numerous books including: mng. editor: Random House Unabridged Dictionary, 1966; editor-in-chief: Random House College Dictionary, 1968, Random House Dictionary of Synonyms and Antonyms, 1960, NY Times Everyday Reader's Dictionary of Misunderstood, Misused, Mispronounced Words, 1972, Dictionary of Advertising Terms, 1977, Official Associated Press Almanac, 1973, 74, 75, CBS News Alamanc, 1976, Hammond Almanac, 1977, Picturesque Expressions, 1980, Illustrated Children's Dictionary, 1979, Basic Dictionary of Synonyms and Antonyms, 1979, The Synonym Finder, 1979, Collins English Dictionary, 1979, -Ologies & -Isms, 1978, 81, 86, Twentieth Century American Nicknames, 1979, A Treasury of Biblical Quotations, 1980, The Timetables of American History, 1981, Mosby's Medical and Nursing Dictionary, 1983, etc. (c. 130 dictionaries, encyclopedias, reference works, in all). BS, Columbia U., 1954, postgrad., 1954-58. Lectr. genl. linguistics NYU, 1956-61; assoc. editor dictionary dept. Funk & Wagnalls, Inc. (NYC), 1957; reference editor Random House, Inc. (NYC), 1957-61, dir. reference dept., 1962-69; pres. Laurence Urdang, Inc. (Old Lyme, CT. and Aylesbury, Eng.), 1969—; chair bd. Laurence Urdang Assocs., Ltd. (Aylesbury, Eng.), 1969-78; editor Verbatim (Old Lyme, Aylesbury), 1974—. Served with USNR, 1944-45. Mem. Linguistic Soc. Am., Am. Dialect Soc., EURALEX, Dict. Soc. of No. Am., Am. Soc. Indexers. Office: 4 Laurel Heights Old Lyme CT 06371

URIOSTE, PAT L., see Keuning, Patricia Dubrava

URIS, LEON, b. Balt., Aug. 3, 1924; s. Wolf William and Anna (Blumberg) Uris; m. Betty Katherine Beck, Jan. 5, 1945; children—Karen Lynn, Mark Jay, Michael Cady; 2nd m. Jill Peabody, Feb. 15, 1971. Author: Battle Cry, 1953, The Angry Hills, 1955, Exodus, 1957, Exodus Revisited, 1959, Mila 18, 1961, Armageddon, 1964, Topaz, 1967, QB VII, 1970, Trinity, 1976, Jerusalem, Song of Songs, 1981 (with Jill Uris) Ireland: A Terrible Beauty, 1975, The Haj, 1984; also screen writer. Ed. Balt. City coll. Served from pvt. to pfc., 2d Div., USMCR, 1942-46. Office: Doubleday 245 Park Ave New York NY 10017

UROFSKY, MELVIN IRVING, b. NYC, Feb. 7, 1939; s. Philip and Sylvia (Passow) Urofsky; m. Susan Linda Miller, Aug. 27, 1961; children—Philip Eric, Robert Ian. Author: Big Steel and Wilson Administration, 1969, Why Teachers Strike, 1970, A Mind of One Piece, 1971, American Zionism from Herzl to The Holocaust, 1976, We Are One!, 1978, Louis D. Brandeis and the Progressive Tradition, 1980, A Voice that Spoke for Justice: The Life and Times of Stephen S. Wise, 1981, A March of Liberty, 1987; co-editor: Brandeis Letters, 5 vols., 1971-78; ed. The Bill of Rights, the Supreme Court and the Law, 1986, ed. The Douglas Letters, 1987. AB, Columbia U., 1961, MA, 1962, PhD1968; J.D., U. Va., 1983. Instr. history Ohio State U., 1964-67; asst. prof. SUNY at Albany, 1967-74; prof. of history Va. Commonwealth U. (Richmond), 1974—. Recipient Kaplun award Jewish Book Council, 1976. Mem. Am. Jewish Hist. Soc. (chair acad. council, 1979-83), AHA, OAH. Home: 14301 Spring Gate Ct Midlothian VA 23113

USCHUK, PAMELA MARIE, b. Lansing, MI, June 10, 1948; d. George Wassill and Ella Marie (Smith) U.; Jerome Walter Gates, June 3, 1972 (div. Dec. 28, 1981). Author: (chapbooks) Light from Dead Stars, 1981, Sleeping under a Meteor Shower on the Straits of Juan De Fuca, 1983, Meditations Beside Kootenai Creek, 1984, Waiting for Rain, 1987; (pamphlet of poems) Loving the Outlaw, 1984; editor: (anthologies of children's poems) Fields with No Fences, 1983, Now, I Become, 1984; editor Cutbank 23, 24, & 25, 26, 1984—; guest poetry editor Intro 16, AWP, 1985. BA cum laude, Central Mich. U., 1970; MFA in Creative Writing, U. Mont., 1986. Lang. arts instr. Elk Rapids Middle Sch., Mich., 1975-79; poet-in-schs. Mont. Arts Council, Helena, Mont., 1983—; editor/arts anthology, 1984—; editor-in-chief Cutbank U. Mont., Missoula, 1984-86, poetry editor, 1984-85. Mem. Pine River Assn., Huxley, Mich., 1976-80, Natl. Wildlife Assn., Washington, 1976- 80, The Cousteau Soc., Washington, 1985-86; exec. dir. Mich. Trailwalkers Assn., Traverse City, 1975-80. Higher Edn. Mich. Edn. Dept., 1966-70; grad. fellow Central Mich. U., 1971; Centrum writing scholar, 1980; Bertha Morton scholar U. Mont., 1985-86. Mem. AWP, Creative Writing Club, (U. Mont.), Women Writers (Missoula). Home: 65 Plains Rd New Paltz NY 12561

UTADA, BETH BROWN, (Kaze Utada), b. Cleve., Mar. 7, 1953, d. James B. and Jeannette (Glover) Oliver; m. Otis Brown, Apr. 23, 1978 (div. 1981); children—Maria Helena Muriel, Otis; m. 2d, Yukio Utada, June 25, 1985; children—Connie, Andy. Author: Lightyears, 1982, Kaze, 1985, Boca Raton (cassette book), 1986; contrbr. articles, rvws., poems to Ampersand, Teaching Exceptional Children, Harambee Flame, Afro-Am. Affairs, other publs. Student pub. schls., Westtown, Pa., Bryn Mawr Coll. Mem. Poets and Prophets, Haiku Soc. Am., Delaware Valley Composers, PSA. Home: 4238 Chestnut St Apt 4 Philadelphia PA 19104

UTADA, KAZE, see Utada, Beth Brown

UTIGER, ROBERT DAVID, b. Bridgeport, CT, July 14, 1931; s. David Alfred Utiger and Aldine (Frey) Elliott; m. Sally Baldwin, Nov. 23, 1953; children—Jane, David, Nancy, Ed.- in-Chief Jnl. Clinical Endocrinology & Metabolism, 1983—; author 115 scientific papers, 49 editorials, book chapters, etc., 69 abstracts. AB, Williams Coll., 1953; MD, Washington U., 1957. Asst. prof. medicine, Washington U., 1965-69; assoc. prof. medicine, U. PA, 1969-73; prof. medicine, 73-79; prof. medicine U. NC, 1979—, named Caviness Prof., 1985. Phi Beta Kappa, 1953, Alpha Omega Alpha, 1957. Home: 101 Foxridge Rd Chapel Hill NC 27514

VACHE, WARREN WEBSTER, b. Bklyn., Nov. 27, 1914; s. George Webster and Marion (Boerckel) V.; m. Madeline Ida Sohl, Sept. 18, 1947; children—Warren W., Allan Robert. Author: This Horn for Hire (biog. Pee Wee Erwin), 1986; I Would Do Anything for You (biog. Claude Hopkins), Miss. Rag., Feb., Mar., April, 1986. Contrbr. jazz articles to music mags. including Jazz Jnl, Miss. Rag, Modern Drummer. Editor: Jersey Jazz 1974—; Fedn. Jazz 1985. Mem. Am. Fedn. Musicians (life), Am. Fedn. Jazz Socs. (v.p.), NJ Jazz Soc. (charter bd. mem.). Home: 836 W Inman Ave Rahway NJ 07065

VALENTI, DAN, b. Pittsfield, MA, Nov. 22, 1951, s. Michael Gino and Virginia Jean (Paoli) V. Author: Red Sox: A Reckoning, 1979, From Florida to Fenway, 1981, Cities Journey, 1981, Diary of a Sportscaster, 1982, The Third Berkshire Anthology, 1983, The Impossible Dream, 1987. Grapefruit League Rundown, 1988, December Sunlight, 1988. Contrbr. to USA Today, N.Y. Times, others; poetry extensively pubd. in Negative Capability, The Berkeley Poetry Review, Amelia, Piedmont Literary Review, TinWreath, others; extensively pubd. in trade and bus. press on "high technology." BA, Union Coll., 1974; MA, Syracuse U., 1975. Ed. Post-Standard, Syracuse, 1975-78; ed., columnist Times Leader, Wilkes-Barre, Pa., 1979-80; prin., Dan Valenti Communications, Pittsfield, Mass., 1980—. Pub., ed.-in-chief Literations small press (Cellerway Press imprint). Office: Box 1845 Pittsfield MA 01202

VALENTINO, TINA, b. Melrose Park, IL, Oct. 30, 1959, d. mary Ann (Montino) V. Contrbr. to The Lyric, Sunrust, Lambda Iota Tau Jnl, Ariel II, III, IV, Am. Poetry Anthology, Poetry Scope, Chgo. Sun-Times. Wrkg. on collection of columns focusing on events and people in Melrose Park; collection of poems (Winter Thunder). BA, Rosary Coll., River Forest, Ill. Ed., columnist West Suburban Press, Inc., Melrose Park, 1982—; ed. Star- Sentinel Newspapers, Melrose Park, 1982—. Recipient award for pub. info. excellence Proviso Assn. for Retarded Citizens, 1985, Am. Cancer Soc., 1984. Mem. PSA, Ill. Press Assn., No. Ill. Newspaper Assn. Home: 1708 N 22nd Avenue Melrose Park IL 60160

VALONE, THOMAS FRANCIS, b. Cheverly, MD, Mar. 3, 1951, s. Peter Louis Valone and Francis Irene (Locke) Derby. Author: The One-Piece Faraday Generator, 1985, 2d edit., 1986; contrbr. books: Konversion von Schwerkraft-Feld-Energie, 1981, The Emerging Energy Science, 1985, The Manual of Free Energy Devices and Systems, 1986; ed., contrbr. proceedings on profl. symposia; contrbr. articles: Sci. Digest, Pursuit, Magnets in Your Future, Vegetarian Voice, Energy Unlimited, numerous profl. publs. Wrkg. on environ. reader, other sci. books and articles. BS in Physics, BSEE, SUNY-Buffalo, 1974, MA in Physics, 1984; PE license, 1986. Research dir. Scott Aviation Co., Lancaster, N.Y., 1976-80; prof. Erie Community Coll., Buffalo, 1981—, Pres., Integrity Electronics & Research, Buffalo, NY, 1981–. Mem. physics orgns. Home: 558 Breckenridge St Buffalo NY 14222

VALUCHEK, ANDREW J., b. Nov. 20, 1911; s. Andrew and Celestine (Medlen) V.; m. Ethel Kana, Sept. 14, 1936 (dec. 1951; children: Lynn Valuchek De Beer, Jan Valuchek Clark. Author: All The Presidents' Women. Wrkg. on history book. Ed., NYU. Pub., ed. Czechoslovak Daily, N.Y.C., 1936-51; dir. nationalities div. Dem. Nat. Com., Washington, 1951-78; asst. to majority leader, U.S. House of Reps, Washington, 1978—. Mem. Natl. Press Club. Home: 9600 River Rd Potomac MD 20854

VALYS, SUSAN PATRICIA, b. Bridgeport, CT, Apr. 12, 1962, d. Anthony John and Suzanne

Mary (Huray) Valys. Contrbr. to: Roadrunner, Newsbasket, other publs. BA in Journalism, Trinity U.; postgrad. U. Tex.-San Antonio. Public relations asst. Southwest Research Inst., San Antonio, 1980-84; freelance wrtr. San Antonio Monthly Mag., 1983-84; account exec. Fawcett & Assocs., San Antonio, 1984-85; editor and comm. coord., H-E-B Food & Drugs, San Antonio, 1985—. Mem. Public Relations Soc. Am., Women in Communications (recipient scholarship 1983), Intl. Assn. Bus. Communicators, Sigma Delta Chi. Home: 2441 NE Loop 410 Apt 108 San Antonio TX 78217

VANCE, JOHN HOLBROOK, (Jack Vance), b. San Francisco, Aug. 28; s. Charles Albert and Edith (Hoefler) Vance; m. Norma Ingold, Aug. 24, 1946; 1 son—John. BA, U. Calif., Berkeley, 1942. Pub.: first story The World Thinker in Thrilling Wonder Stories, 1945; writer: six episodes Captain Video TV series, 1952; author: Dying Earth, 1950, Big Planet, 1957, The Man in the Cage, 1960, The Dragon masters, 1963, The Last Castle, 1967, Planet of Adventure 4 vols., 1968-70, Demon Prince series, 5 vols., 1964-81, Lyonesse, 1983, Lyonesse II: The Green Pearl, 1985, The Durdane Trilogy: The Anome, 1973, The Brave Free Men, 1973, The Asutra, 1974; numerous other novels. Served with U.S. Mcht. Marine, 1943-45. Recipient Edgar Allen Poe award MWA, 1960, Hugo award World Sci. Fiction Conv., 1964, 1967, Nebula award SFWA, 1967, Jupiter Award for Best Novelette of 1974, 1975, Lifetime Achievement Award, from World Fantasy Convention. Office: 6383 Valley View Rd Oakland CA 94611

VANCEBURG, MARTHA, see Roth, Martha

VANDER MOLEN, ROBERT L., b. Grand Rapids, MI, Apr. 23, 1947; s. Robert L. and Marjorie Ruth (Mollo) VM; m. Deborah Marie Stenman Dec. 16, 1980; 2 sons, Sean, Colin. Author poems: Blood Ink, 1967, The Lost Book, 1968, Variations, 1970, The Pavilion, 1974, Circumstances, 1978, Along the River, 1978. BA, Mich. State U.; MFA, U. Oreg. Instr. Grand Rapids Jr. Coll., Mich., 1975-79; house painter self-employed, Grand Rapids, 1981—. Address: 1569 Laughlin NW Grand Rapids MI 49504

VANDERBYLT, WHITEFORD, see Boyle, John E. Whiteford

VANDERSEE, CHARLES ANDREW, b. Gary, IN, Mar. 25, 1938; s. Harvey Frederick and Louise Amelia (Bauer) V. Contrbr. poems, articles to lit. mags., profl. jnls., anthols. Columnist, The Cresset, 1969-72, 82—. Editor: The Bread-Winners (John Hay), 1973; assoc. editor: The Letters of Henry Adams, 6 vols., 1982, 87. BA, Valparaiso U., 1960; MA, UCLA, 1961, PhD, 1964. Assoc. prof. English, U. Va., Charlottesville, 1970—, dean Echols scholars program, 1973—. Danforth fellow, 1960-64, Bruern fellow in Am. lit., U. Leeds, 1968-69, fellow ACLS, 1972-73; grantee NEH, 1977-86. Mem. MLA, Soc. Values in Higher Edn., Assn. Documentary Editing. Office: U Va Dept English Wilson Hall Charlottesville VA 22903

VANDERWEIDE, HARRY, b. Chelsea, MA, June 23, 1944; s. Harold Peter and Florence (Kulicke) V.; m. Lana Louise Bartolino, Mar., 1965; children—Bradley, Douglas, Elizabeth, Amanda. Ed., The Maine Sportman, 1972—; Maine ed., Outdoor Life Mag., 1976—; outdoor columnist, Maine Sunday Telegram, 1980; author/ed. 12 books on hunting, fishing, wildlife, inclg. The Maine Sportsman Book of Hunting; contrbr. articles photos. to Field & Stream, Salt Water Sportsman, others. Mem. New England OWA. Address: Box 365 Augusta ME 04330

VAN DE WATER, JOHN WARD, b. Wappingers Falls, NY, May 31, 1913; s. John Henry and Rosamond Augusta (Budd) Van de Water; m. Sara Jane Logan, Jun. 29, 1935; children—Peter Edgar, Jean Anne, John Gilbert, Gordon Budd. Author: Rural Living, 1977-85, Chichee's Trunk, 1980, Rock on the Hudson, 1984, Moonlight Sonorous, 1984. BS, St. Lawrence U., 1935; MA, State U. of NY, 1941. Director Bi-National Cntr—USIA (Tehran, Iran), 1960-62; Chair-Liberal Arts Jefferson Coll. (Watertown, NY), 1962-69. Home: Star Rt Canton NY 13617

VAN DOREN, CHARLES, b. NYC, Feb. 12, 1926; s. Mark and Dorothy (Graffe) Van Doren; m. Geraldine Bernstein, Apr. 17, 1957; children—Elizabeth, John C.L. Author: The Idea of Progress, 1967, The Joy of Reading, 1985, The Bank of Knowledge, 1988, Tuscan Places, 1989; editor: Annals of America, 20 vols., 1969, Webster's American Biographies, 1974, Great Treasury of Western Thought, 1977. BA, St. Johns Coll., 1947; MA, Columbia U., 1949, PhD (Cutting fellow), 1959. Instr. English Columbia, 1955-59; sr. assoc. Inst. for Philo. Research (Chgo.), 1960-67, assoc. dir., 1967—; vp editorial Encyc. Brit., Inc., 1973-82; chair Bradford Mountain Book Enterprises, Inc. (NYC), 1983—; pres. Praeger Pubs., 1974-75. Served with USAF, 1944-45. Mem. AG. Home: Box 69 Falls Village CT 06031

VAN DUSEN, HENRY HUGH, b. NYC, Apr. 27, 1934; s. Henry Pitney and Elizabeth (Bartholomew) Van Dusen; m. Geraldine Ann Rapf, Nov. 30, 1968; children—Caitlin Sarah, Norah Elizabeth. BA, Harvard U., 1956. Editorial asst. Harper & Row (NYC), 1956-60, asst. editor, 1960-62, assoc. editor, 1962-64, editor, mgr. paperback dept., 1965-85, sr. ed., 1985—, mem. pub. bd., 1986—. Home: Glendale Rd Ossining NY 10562

VAN DUYN, MONA JANE, b. Waterloo, IA, May 9, 1921; d. Earl George and Lora G. (Kramer) Van Duyn; m. Jarvis A. Thurston, Aug. 31, 1943. Author: Valentines to the Wide World, 1959, A Time of Bees, 1964, To See, To Take, 1970, Bedtime Stories, 1972, Merciful Disguises, 1973, Letters from a Father and Other Poems, 1982. BA, U. No. Iowa, 1942; MA, U. Iowa, 1943; D. Litt. (hon.), Washington U., St. Louis, 1971, Cornell Coll., Iowa, 1972. Instr. English U. Iowa, 1943-46, U. Louisville, 1946-50; lectr. English Univ. Coll., Washington U., 1950-67; poetry readings, 1970—; poetry editor, co-pub. Perspective, A Qtly of Lit., 1947-67; lectr. Salzburg (Austria) Seminar Am. Studies, 1973; adj. prof. poetry workshop Conf., Mass., 1974, 76, staff mem. Breadloaf Writers Conference, 1987, staff mem. writers conferences in Texas, Minnesota, Indiana, New York, Minnesota, Indiana, New York, 1987; prof., Washington Univ., 1987; recipient Bollingen prize, 1970; Natl. Book award, 1971; Eunice Tietjens award, 1956; Helen Bullis prize, 1964; Harriet Monroe award, 1968; Hart Crane Meml. award, 1968; Loines prize Natl. Inst. Arts and Letters, 1976. Recipient Sandburg prize Cornell Coll., 1982. Shelley Memorial Award, 1987. Mem. Natl. Inst. Arts and Letters, NEA grant, 1985, Chancellor AAP, 1985. Address: 7505 Teasdale Ave St Louis MO 63130

VAN DYKE, HENRY, b. Allegan, MI, Oct. 3, 1928, s. Henry L. and Bessie C. (Chandler) Van D. Novelist: Ladies of the Rachmaninoff Eyes, 1965, Blood of Strawberries, 1969, Dead Piano, 1971, Lunacy and Caprice, 1987. MA, U. Mich. Corr. Basic Books, Inc., NYC, 1958-67; wrtr.-in-res. Kent (Ohio) State U., 1969—. Recipient Hopwood award U. Mich., 1954, Guggenheim award, 1972, Lit. award AAIAL, 1974. Home: 40 Waterside Plaza New York NY 10010

VANGELISTI, PAUL LOUIS, b. San Francisco, Sept. 17, 1945, s. Nicholas Thomas and Josephine Marie (Zangani) V.; m. Margaret Catherine Dryden, Dec. 31, 1966 (div. 1980); children—Tristan, Simone. Author: Communion, 1970, Air, 1973, The Tender Continent, 1974, Iltenero continente, 1975, Pearl Harbor, 1975, The Extravagant Room, 1976, La stanza stravagante, 1977, 2 x 2, 1977, Remembering the Movies, 1977, Portfolio, 1978, Un grammo d'oro, 1981, Another You, 1981, Ora Blu, 1981, Abandoned Latitudes, 1983, Rime, 1983; translator: Our Positions (Corrado Costa), 1975, Another Earthquake (Franco Beltrametti), 1977, Various Devices (Adriano Spatola), 1978, Invasions (Antonio Porta), 1986, numerous others; ed.: Italian Poetry, 1960-80: from the Neo to the Post-Avantgarde, 1982; The New Polish Poetry, 1978, Specimen 73, 1973, Anthology of L.A. Poets, 1972; co-ed. Invisible City mag., 1971-82. BA, U. San Francisco, 1967, MA, U. So. Calif., 1972, PhD candidate. Ed., reviewer Hollywood Reporter, Los Angeles, 1972-73; cultural affairs dir. sta. KPFK, North Hollywood, 1974-82; tchr. Los Angeles Community Colls., 1981—, Otis Art Inst., Los Angeles, 1984—. W.R. Moses writing fellow, 1971, CCLM ed. fellow, 1981, NEA translators fellow, 1981; recipient Drama Award, Corp. Public Broadcasting, 1980. Mem. Am. Lit. Translators Assn. Home: 3132 Berkeley Cr Los Angeles CA 90026

VAN HOUTEN, LOIS M., b. Paterson, NJ, Oct. 30, 1918, d. William H. and Lillian (Rider) Daniels; m. Melvin E. Van Houten, May 15, 1942; children—Edward B., Jay W. Author: North Jersey Blues, 1972, Behind the Door, 1976, The Woman Who Warped with Doors, 1977, The Woman Wedged in the Window, 1979, All Those Bells, 1981; represented in Bergen Poets anthologies, 1974-85; contrbr. poems to Lips, Stone Country, Epos, Wormwood, other lit mags. Student William Patterson Coll., 1966-76. Vice pres. Bergen Poets, Bergen City, N.J., 1974-86. Grantee P&W of N.Y., Inc., 1978, City of Lyndhurst, N.J., Geraldine R. Dodge Fdn., 1980; N.J. State Council on Arts fellow, 1980-81, 84-85. Mem. P&W of NY, Inc. Home: 16 Harlow Crescent Fair Lawn NJ 07410

VAN ITALLIE, JEAN-CLAUDE, b. Brussels, May 25, 1936 (came to U.S., 1940); s. Hughes Ferdinand and Martha Mathilde Caroline (Levy) van Itallie. Author: plays War, 1963, Almost Like Being, 1965, I'm Really Here, 1965, America Hurrah, 1966 (Drama Desk, Outer Circle Critics 1967), The Serpent, 1968 (Obie 1969), A Fable, 1975, King of the United States, 1972, Mystery Play, 1973, Medea, 1979, Bag Lady, 1979, Tibetan Book of the Dead, 1983, Early Warnings, 1983, The Traveler, 1986, A Day in the Life (with Joe Chaikin), 1987; new English versions Chekhov's Seagull, 1973, Chekhov's Cherry Orchard, 1977, Chekhov's Three Sisters, 1982, Chekhov's Uncle Vanya, 1983, Genet's Balcony, 1985. AB, Harvard U., 1958; PhD (hon.), Kent State U., 1977. Tchr. theatre, playwrighting New Schl. for Social Research (NYC), 1966; playwright of ensemble Open Theatre, 1963-68; tchr. theatre, playwrighting Yale U. Schl. Drama (New Haven), 1969, 79, 84, Naropa Inst. (Boulder, CO), 1976-83, Princeton U. (NJ), 1976-88; NYU, 1981-88. Home: 744 Spruce St Boulder CO 80302

VAN MEER, MARY ANN, b. Mt. Clemens, MI, Nov. 22; d. Leo Harold and Rose Emma (Gulden) VanM.; stepmother: Ruth Helen Van Meer. Author: Traveling with Your Dog, U.S.A., 1976, How to Set Up a Home Typing Business, 1978, Freelance Photographer's Handbook, 1979, See America Free, 1981, Free Campgrounds, U.S.A., 1982, Free Attractions, U.S.A., 1982, VanMeer's Guide to Free Attractions, U.S.A., 1984, Van Meer's Guide to Free Attractions, U.S.A., 1984, Van Meer's Guide to Free Campgrounds, 1984. Publisher Natl. Health and Medical Trends, 1986—. Student Mich. State U., 1965-66, 67-68, Sorbonne U., Paris, 1968; B.A. in Edn., U. Fla., 1970. Pres. VanMeer Tutoring and Translating, N.Y.C., 1970-72, VanMeer Pubs., Inc., Clearwater, Fla., 1980—, VanMeer Media Advt., Inc., Clearwater, 1980—; free-lance wrtr., 1973-79; exec. dir., founder Natl. Centers for Health and Med. Info., Inc., Clearwater, 1982—; pres. Health and Medical Trends, Inc., 1987—. Mem. Am. Booksellers Assn., AG. Office: Box 1289 Clearwater FL 33517

VAN SCYOC, LINDA JANE, b. Shelbyville, IN, Jan. 10, 1951, Author: Ask, Advertising Survival Kit, 1975; poetry in anthologies. Wrkg. on poetry, non-fiction. BS, Ball State U., 1972, MA, 1974. Tchr. public schs. Greenfield, Ind., 1973-76, New Palestine, Ind., 1976-87; instr. Ball State. Ind. Vocat. Tech. Coll., Indpls., 1985—, U., Muncie, Ind., 1987— Home: RR 3 Box 166A New Palestine IN 46163

VAN SETERS, JOHN, b. Hamilton, Ont., Can., May 2, 1935; s. Hugo and Anna (Hubert) Van Seters; m. Elizabeth Marie Malmberg, June 11, 1960; children—Peter John, Deborah Elizabeth. Author: The Hyksos: A New Investigation, 1966, Abraham in History and Tradition, 1975, In Search of History, 1983, Der Jahwist als Historiker, 1987. BA, U. Toronto, 1958; MA, Yale U., 1959, PhD, 1965; Princeton Theol. Sem., 1962. Asst. prof. dept. Near Eastern studies Waterloo Luth. U., 1965-67; assoc. prof. Old Testament Andover Newton Theol. Schl., 1967-70; assoc. prof. dept. Near Eastern studies U. Toronto, 1970-76, prof., 1976-77; James A. Gray prof. Bibl. lit., dept. religious studies, U. NC, Chapel Hill, 1977—, chair, 1980—. Mem. Soc. Bibl. Lit., Am. Schls. Oriental Research, Soc. Study of Egyptian Antiquities, AAUP, Am. Oriental Soc. Home: 303 Hoot Owl Ln Chapel Hill NC 27514

VAN SICKLE, JOHN BABCOCK, b. Freeport, IL, Sept. 30, 1936; s. John rowley and mary Kathryn (Babcock) Van Sickle; m. Giulia Battaglia, Dec. 28, 1965. Author: The Design of Virgil's Bucolics, 1978; contrbr. articles, rvws. to profl. jnls; Atlantic states editor: Classical Jnl, 1978; corr. editor: Quaderni Urbinati di Dultura Classica, ,77; guest editor: Arethusa, 1976, 80. AB cum laude, Harvard U., 1958, PhD, 1966; AM, U. Ill., 1959. Instr., then asst. prof. classical studies U. Pa., 1965-71; vis. assoc. prof. classics Brown U., 1971-72; prof.-in-charge, vis. prof. Intercollegiate Center for Classical Studies (Stanford U.) Rome, 1972-74; assoc. prof. Bklyn. Coll. and Grad. Schl., CUNY, 1976-78, prof. classics and comparative lit., 1979—. Office: Brooklyn Coll Brooklyn NY 11210

VAN SPANCKEREN, KATHRYN, b. Kansas City, MO, Dec. 14, 1945; d. Warner John and Jacqueline (Jones) Van Spanckeren; m. Stephen Philp Breslow; 1 son, Paul Benjamin. Editor: John Gardner: The Critical Perspective, 1983; Thor's Hammer: Essays on John Gardner, 1985; Margaret Atwood, 1988; poetry and articles in American Poetry Rvw, Ploughshares, Dialectical Anthropology, other jnls and anthols. BA, U. of CA at Berkeley, 1967, MA, Harvard, 1969, PhD, 1976. Prof., Wheaton College, Norton, MA, 1974-79; prof., U. of Tampa, Fla., 1983—; editor, Aspect Magazine, 1975-78; editor, Margaret Atwood Newsletter, 1983—; co-edit., New Wilderness Letter, 1987—. Mem. PSA, MLA, SAMLA, D.H. Lawrence Soc. Home: 93 Martinique Ave Tampa FL 33606

VAN STEENBURGH, BARBARA JEAN, b. Parker, SD, Apr. 20, 1927; d. Bert K. and Alma Barbara (Weber) Fairchild; m. E. W. Van Steenburgh, Mar. 22, 1950; children—Tracy, Robert, Lesley. Contrbr. poems to lit. mags., anthols. Wrkg. on poetry chapbook, setting poems to music. B.A., Cornell Coll., 1949; M.S. in Edn., Northern Ill. U., 1978. Tchr. Dexter High Schl., MI, 1956-57, Malta High Schl., IL, 1972-77; freelance wrtr., 1977—. Chmn. publicity DeKalb Arts Commn., IL, 1983-85. Mem. DeKalb Wordwrights (founder), Ill. Wrtrs. Recipient Honorable Mention and 2d place, Poets & Patrons, 1982. Home: 817 Lucinda Ave DeKalb IL 60115

VAN TASSEL, KATRINA, b. May 29, 1921, d. C.B. and Alma (Bogue) Van T.; m. Tom T. Wuerth, Sept. 20, 1947; children—Christopher, Jonathan, Peter, Megan. Contrbr. poetry to Stone Country, Embers, Yankee, Poets On, Red Fox Rvw. BA, Bennington Coll., 1942; MA, Wesleyan U., 1979. Tchr., head drama dept. Guilford (Conn.) public schls., 1960-80; arts specialist Comprehensive Arts Program, New Haven public schls., 1983, 84, 85, 86, 87; lit. ed. Embers poetry jnl, 1981—. Recipient 1st Andrew Mt. Press chapbook awd. Mem. Conn. Poetry Soc., AAP, Guilford Poetry Group (chair 1976—). Home: 6 Broad St Guilford CT 06437

VAN VOGT, ALFRED ELTON, b. Man., Can., Apr. 26, 1912 (came to U.S., 1944, naturalized, 1952); s. Henry and Agnes (Buhr) Van Vogt; m. Edna Mayne Hull, May 9, 1939 (dec. 1975); m. 2d, Lydia I. Brayman, Oct. 6, 1979. Contbr. short stories to True Story Mag., 1932-36; author: radioplays, Can., 1935-38; short stories, novels including Null-A three, 1984, Computer Eye, 1985, Rogue Ship, 1985, The Silkie, 1985. Rep. trade papers, Western Ca., 1935-39. Recipient Anne Radcliffe Lit. award, 1968; guest of honor European Sci. Fiction Conv., Brussels, 1978 Mem. Calif. Assn. Dianetic Auditors (pres. 1958—), AG Am., SFWA. Address: Box 3065 Hollywood CA 90078

VAN WALLEGHEN, MICHAEL J(OSPEH), b. Detroit, Oct. 4, 1938; s. Joseph and Bernice Van Wallgehen. Author: The Wichita Poems, 1975, More Trouble With the Obvious, 1981. BA, Wayne State U., 1962; MA, U. Iowa, 1965. Instr. English Wichita State U., 1965-66, asst. prof., 1966-69; asst. prof. English U. Ill., Urbana, 1970-75, assoc. prof., 1975-81, prof. 1981—, fellow Center for Advanced Studies, 1983. Recipient 1st prize Borestone Mountain Poetry award 1966, Pushcart prize 1977, Ill. Arts Council award 1978, Lamont Poetry prize AAP, 1980, NEA fellow 1979, 87. Served with USN, 1956-58. Office: Dept Eng U Ill Urbana IL 61801

VAN WOERKOM, DOROTHY O'BRIEN, b. Buffalo, June 26, 1924; d. Peter Simon and Helen Elizabeth (Miller) O'Brien; m. John Van Woerkom, Feb. 22, 1961. Author: children's books including Stepka and the Magic Fire, 1974 (Best Religious Children's Book, Cath. Press Assn.), Journeys to Bethlehem, 1974, Meat Pies and Sausages, 1976, A Hundred Angels Singing, 1976, The Queen Who Couldn't Bake Gingerbread, 1974, Abu Ali, 1976, Tit for Tat, 1977, Harry and Shellburt, 1977, The Friends of Abu Ali, 1978, Donkey Ysabel, 1978, Alexandra the Rock-Eater, 1978, When All the World Was Waiting, 1979, Hidden Messages, 1979 (named an outstanding sci. trade book), Lands of Fire and Ice, 1980, Pearl in the Egg, 1980, Something to Crow About, 1982, Old Devil is Waiting, 1985, Tall Corn/Tall Tale, 1987; series editor: I Can Read a Bible Story, Concordia Pub. House, 1975. Student, Canisius Coll., 1948-50. Mem. AG, MWA. Home: 8826 McAvoy Dr Houston TX 77074

VAN WYNGARDEN, BRUCE, b. Louisville, Mar. 28, 1948; s. William Wells and Lucille Elizabeth (Hall) VanW.; m. Frances Epps Henderson, Nov. 25, 1978; children—Mary Moss, Andrew Wells. Contrbr. rvws. & essays to Washington Post, USA Today, Saturday Review, Historic Preservation, St. Louis Globe-Democrat; co-author Shock of Recognition, TBP 1986. Jnlsm. student, U. MO, 1966-71. Advt. rep. Columbia (MO) Daily Tribune, 1977-79; assoc. ed. Missouri Life Mag., Columbia, 1979-81; mng. ed. Saturday Review, Columbia, 1982-84, sr. ed., Washington, 1984-85; ed. Pittsburgh (PA) Mag., 1985—. Mem. NBCC. Home: 2334 Collins Rd Pittsburgh PA 15235

VARGAS, LAURA DENNISON, b. Toledo, Feb. 9, 1945, d. Stanley Richard Gould and Carol Frances (Krueger) Dennison; m. Daniel Solomon Vargas, July 31, 1984. Author: The Poetry of Laura Dennison, 1978, In Sun and Shade, 1985; contrbr. poetry to Oink 12!, Euterpe, Unicorn, Modern Images, other publs. BA, Wells Coll., 1966; MEd, Columbia U., 1975. Tchr. pub. schls. NYC, 1969-71, 86—; tchr. poetry workshop Dominican Acad., 1976, Roosevelt Hosp., NYC, 1975. Mem. P&W, IPA. Home: 2020 E 41st St 5B Brooklyn NY 11234

VARLEY, JOHN HERBERT, b. Austin, TX, 1947; s. John Edward and Joan Francis (Boehm) Varley; m. Anet Mconel, Oct. 10, 1970; children—Maurice McConnell, Roger McConnell, Stefan McConnell. Author: The Ophiuchi Hotline, 1977, The Persistance of Vision, 1978 (Best Novella of 1978, Hugo and Nebula awards); collected stories, 1978 (recipient Prix Apollo 1979); novel Titan, 1979, Wizard, 1980; collected stories The Barbie Murders, 1980; novel and screenplay Millennium, 1983; screenplay Galazy, 1978. Student, Mich. State U., 1965-67. Mem. WG Am. West. Address: 2030 W 28th St Eugene OR 97405

VARNUM-GALLANT, BILLIE MAE, (Billie Varnum), b. Elberton, GA, June 27, 1951; d. William Taft and Willie Mae (Harris) Varnum; m. Charles Lester Marsh, Nov. 10, 1973 (div. 1979); m. 2d, Mark Henry Gallant, S., Dec. 31, 1982. Contrbr. fiction, bus. articles to numerous publs. Wrkg. on writing textbook, articles. BA, U. Ga., 1973, MEd, 1976, EdS, 1978; PhD, Ga. State U., 1984. Mem. faculty Brenau Coll., Gainesville, Ga., 1979—, assoc. prof. humanities, 1985—. Mem. Am. Bus. Communication Assn., Assn. Profl. Writing Cons. Home: 3656 Browns Bridge Rd Apt Al Gainesville GA 30501

VARTNAW, WILLIAM R., b. Petaluma, CA, May 5, 1949, s. William Raphel and Valere Erna

(Marion) V. Author: In Concern: for Angels (poetry), 1984; contrbr. to Honeydew: an anthology, Yellow Brick Road, Tunnel Road, Berkeley Works, other lit mags. AB, U. Calif.-Davis, 1971. Pub., ed. Taurean Horn Press, San Francisco, 1974—. Home: 920 Leavenworth St 401 San Francisco CA 94109

VASTA, EDWARD, b. Forest Park, IL, Jan. 18, 1928, s. Joseph and Josephine (Malimaci) V.; m. Geraldine Stocco, Nov. 28, 1953; children—John Robert, Paula Lorraine, Joseph Edward, Catherine Ann, Barbara Josephine, Salvatore James. Author: The Spiritual Basis of Piers Plowman, 1965, Middle English Survey: Critical Essays, 1965, Interpretations of Piers Plowman, 1968, Chaucerian Problems and Perspectives, 1979. BA, U. Noitre Dame, 1952; MA, U. Mich., 1954; PhD, Stanford U., 1963. Prof. English, U. Notre Dame, Inc., 1969—. Served with USN, 1946-48. Fulbright scholar, Florence, Italy, 1952; Danforth Fdn. grantee, 1961; NEA creative writing fellow, 1980. Mem. MLA. Medieval Acad. Am., New Chaucer Soc. Home: 52140 Harvest Dr South Bend IN 46637

VAUGHAN, MARILOU TAYLOR, b. Detroit; d. robert Adams and Dorothea (Trauffer) Taylor; m. David Rodman Baughan, Jan. 2, 1960. BA, Eastern Mich. U., 1958; postgrad., Stanford U., 1959. Asst. editor Smithsonian mag. (Washington), 1974-76; assoc. editor New West mag. (Beverly Hills, CA), 1976-77; assoc. editor Archtl. Digest (Los Angeles), 1977-79; mng. editor Bon Appetit mag. (Los Angeles), 1978-82; editor Bon Appetit mag., vp Knapp Communications Corp. (Los Angeles), 1982—. Mem. ASME. Office: 5900 Wilshire Blvd Los Angeles CA 90036

VAUGHAN, SAMUEL SNELL, b. Phila., aug. 3, 1928; s. Joseph and Anna Catherine (Alexander) Vaughan; m. Jo LoBiondo, Oct. 22, 1949; children—Jeffrey Marc, Leslie Jane, Dana Alexander, David Samuel. Author: juveniles, Whoever Heard of Kangaroo Eggs?, 1957; New Shoes, 1961; The Two-Thirty Bird, 1965; history, The Little Church, 1969; satire, Little Red Hood, 1979; contrbr. to NY Times, Sunday Times of London, Daedalus, other mags., newspapers, books. BA, Pa. State U., 1951. Deskman, King Features Syndicate (NYC), 1951; asst. mgr., Doubleday Syndicate, 1952-54; advt. mgr., Doubleday & Co., Inc. (NYC), 1954-56, sales mgr., 1956-58, sr. editor, 1958-68, exec. editor and dep. editor-in-chief, 1968-70, pub., pres. pub. div., 1970-83, vp parent co., 1970-86, editor-in-chief, 1983-85; sr. vp and ed., adult trade, Random House (NYC), 1986—. Bowker lectr., 1976; faculty English dept. Columbia U., 1978—. Served with USMC, 1946-48. Home: 23 Inness Rd Tenafly NJ 07670

VAUGHN, BONNIE JEAN, b. Genoa, OH, Nov. 8, 1921; d. Carl William and Alice Sophia (Rolf) Emch; m. Richard Arthur Cook, Dec. 28, 1941 (dec. Nov. 26, 1958); children—Ronald Richard, Douglas Deane; m. Joseph Telford Vaughn, Sept. 9, 1961. Author (choir cantatas) Is It I?, 1982, Were You There?, 1983, The Long Journey, 1983, Love Came Down, 1984, At the Cross, 1985, Now Thank We All Our God, 1986, The Lord is Come, 1986. Student Bowling Green State U., 1939-41. Administrative secy. Brush Wellman Inc., Elmoe, OH, 1956—. Recipient 1st place for centennial hymn City of Pemberville, 1976, 1st place for sesquicentennial hymn Maumee Valley Presbytery, 1987. Home: 114 Cherry St Pemberville OH 43450

VAUGHN, JAMES MICHAEL, b. Evansville, IN, Dec. 21, 1939; s. Ray Chester and Mary Carol (Childress) V.; m. Patricia Rose Morrison, Nov. 10, 1973; 1 dau., Annelise Kristin. Contrbr. articles, editorials, featues to mags., newspaper. Ed. training manual/readings text: Road to Knighthood, 1962. Wrkg. on articles. B.S. in Bus. Administration Butler U., 1965; postgrad. (law) Ind. U., 1969-71; M.A. in Bus. Administration, Webster U., 1980; M.A. in Political Sci., Ball State U., 1987. Commissioned 2d lt. U.S. Army, 1966, advanced through ranks to major, 1978—. Mem. Orgn. Am. Historians, Indiana Hist. Soc., Assn. for State/Local Hist., Acad. of Poli. Sci. Home: 5221 Hedgerow Dr Indianapolis IN 46226

VAUGHN, PHOEBE JUANITA, b. Portsmouth, VA, Mar. 9, 1939; d. Samuel Franklin and Wynona Frances (Brabson) Fitzgerald; m. Lawrence Vaughn, Dec. 8, 1956 (div. Sept. 8, 1972); children—Darrell Anthony, Wendell Craig. Contrbr. poems to anthols. Wrkg. on 2 books of poetry, song lyrics, poetry. L.P.N., MMW, 1961; student Miami-Dade Coll., 1979-84. L.P.N. Catalano's Nurses, Hialeah, FL, 1974-85; freelance L.P.N., 1985—. Recipient Honorable Mention, World of Poetry, 1983, 87, Golden Poet award, 1987; cert. of Merit, Talent & Assoc. Co., Wollaston, MA, 1986. Mem. NWC, Songwriters Assn. Washington. Home: Box 7268 Silver Spring MD 20907

VAZAKAS, BYRON, b. NYC. Author poetry vols.: Transfigured Night, 1946, The Equal Tribunals, 1961, The Marble Manifesto, 1966, Nostalgias For A House of Cards, 1970; contrbr. nearly 250 poems to lit. publs. Amy Lowell travel fellow in poetry, Harvard U., 1962-64; recipient LittD (hon), Albright Coll., Reading, Pa., 1981, numerous art colony fellowships. Home: 1623 Mineral Spring Rd Reading PA 19602

VEAZEY, MARY VIRGINIA, b. Maplesville, AL, Apr. 5, 1943; d. Henry Vinson and Bonita Marie (Craig) Veazey. Contrbr. poetry: Twigs, Cimarron Rev., Poem, The Windless Orchard, other lit. mags.; poetry in anthologies. BA, U. Montevallo; MA, Auburn U. Home: Rt 1 Box 282 Maplesville AL 36750

VECOLI, RUDOLPH JOHN, b. Wallingford, CT, Mar. 2, 1927; s. Giovanni Battista and Settima Maria (Palmerini) Vecoli; m. Jill Cherington, June 27, 1959; children—Christopher, Lisa, Jeremy. Author: The People of New Jersey, 1965, Foreword to Marie Hall Ets, Rosa: The Story of an Italian Immigrant, 1970, Italian Americans, 1985; contrbg. author: Gli italiani fuori d'Italia, 1983, They Chose Minnesota: A Survey of the State's Ethnic Groups, 1981, Pane e Lavoro: The Italian American Working Class, 1980, Perspectives in Italian Immigration and Ethnicity, 1977, Immigrants and Religion in Urban America, 1977, The State of American History, 1970, The Reinterpretation of American History and Culture, 1973; editor, contbr. author: The Other Catholics, 1978; mem. editorial bd.: Jnl. Am. Ethnic History, Studi Emigrazione; contrbr. articles to profl. jnls. BA, U. Conn., 1950; MA, U. Pa., 1951; PhD, U. Wis., 1963. Fgn. affairs officer Dept. State, 1951-54; instr. history Ohio State U., 1957-59, Pa. State U., 1960-61; asst. prof. Rutgers U., 1961-65; assoc. prof. U. Ill., Champaign, 1965-67; prof. history, dir. Immigration History Research Center, U. Minn., Mpls., 1967—; vis. prof. U. Uppsala (Sweden), 1970. Bd. Am. Immigration and Citizenship Conf., mem. Minn. Humanities Comm. Served with USNR, 1945-46. Home: 610 E 58th St Minneapolis MN 55417

VELASCO, KATHY LYNN, b. Rockford, IL, Jan. 7, 1956; d. Marvin Mauritz and LaVonna Mae (Murphy) P. Asst., assoc., mng. ed., ed. The Fabricator, 1978—. BA in English & Broadcasting, Western IL U., 1978. Asst. ed., then assoc. ed., then mng. ed., The Fabricator, Rockford, IL, 1978-87. Ed. and V.P. of Operations, The Croyden Group, Ltd., 1987—. Office: 5411 East State St. Rockford IL 61108

VELTEN, KATHLEEN ANN, b. St. Petersburg, FL, Jan. 4, 1950; d. Conrad Theodore and Betty Foy (Dexheimer) V. Contrbr. short stories to mags. Ed.: Gordon Coll. Lit. Mag., 1969. B.A., Gordon Coll., 1971; postgrad. Bentley Coll., 1973-80. Operations analyst Federal Reserve Bank of Boston, 1979-84; marketing coord. Vanass Hangen Brustlin, Boston, 1985—. Home: 306 Summer St Arlington MA 02174

VENDLER, HELEN HENNESSY, b. Boston, Apr. 30, 1933; d. George and Helen (Conway) Hennessy; 1 son—David. Author: Yeats's Vision and the Later Plays, 1963, On Extended Wings: Wallace Stevens' Longer Poems, 1969, The Poetry of George Herbert, 1975, Part of nature, Part of Us, 1980, The Odes of John Keats, 1983, Wallace Stevens: Words Chosen Out of Desire, 1985; ed.: The Harvard Book of Contemporary American Poetry, 1985. AB, Emmanuel Coll., 1954; PhDHarvard U., 1960, U. Oslo (hon., 1980), D.Litt. (hon.), Smith Coll., Kenyon Coll., U. of Hartford, Union Coll., Columbia U. Instr. Cornell U. (Ithaca, NY), 1960-63; lectr. Swarthmore Coll. (PA), and Haverford Coll. (PA), 1963-64; asst. prof. Smith Coll. (Northampton, MA), 1964-66; assoc. prof. Boston U., 1966-68, prof., 1968-85; Fulbright lectr. U. Bordeaux (France), 1968-69; vis. prof. Harvard U., 1981-85, Kenan prof., 1985; poetry critic New Yorker, 1978—. Recipient Lowell prize, 1969, Explicator prize, 1969, award Natl. Inst. Arts and Letters, 1975, Natl. Book Critics Circle award, 1980, finalist, 1981. Mem. MLA (exec. council 1972-75, pres. 1980), English Inst. (trustee 1977-85), Am. Acad. Arts and Scis., Norwegian Acad. of Letters and Sci. Sr. Soc. of Fellows, Harvard. Home: 16 A Still St Brookline MA 02146

VENET, MICHELLE, see Rasley, Alicia Todd

VENEZKY, RICHARD LAWRENCE, b. Pitts., Apr. 16, 1938; s. Bernard Jacob and Isabelle (Zeisel) Venezky; m. Karen F. Gauz, Aug. 2, 1964; children—Dina Yael, Elie Michael. Author: The Structure of English Orthography, 1970, Testing in Reading, 1974; co-author: A Microfiche Concordance to Old English, 1981, Letter and Word Perception, 1980; The Ginn Reading Program, 1981; contrbr. chpts. to books, articles to profl. jnls; cons.: Oxford English Dictionary Supplement; adviser: for data processing Dictionary of Old English, 1971—; editorial/adv. com.: Computers and the Humanities, 1974, Visible Language, 1976, Doubleday Dictionary, 1975-77. BEE, Cornell U., 1961, MA, 1962; postgrad., U. Calif. at Berkeley, 1962-63; PhD, Stanford U., 1965. Systems programmer, tech. writer Control Data Corp. (Palo Alto, CA), 1962-65; asst. prof. English and computer scis., U. Wis. (Madison), 1965-69, assoc. prof. computer scis., 1969-74, prof., 1974-77, chair dept., 1975-77; Unidel prof. ednl. studies U. Del. (Newark), 1977—; vis. research assoc. Tel Aviv U., 1969-70, research fellow, 1973. Exec. comm. Jewish Fedn. of Del., 1985; fellow Am. Psychological Assn; Natl. Comm. on Research on English.

Home: 206 Hullihen Dr Newark DE 19711

VENINGA, JAMES FRANK, b. Milw., Aug. 26, 1944; s. Frank and Otila Ann (Mauch) V.; m. Catherine Martha Williams, Apr. 5, 1969; 1 dau., Jennifer. Ed.-in-chief Tex. Jrnl. Ideas, History and Culture, 1982—; ed.: The Biographer's Gift, 1983; co-ed.: Vietnam in Remission, 1985. BA, Baylor U., 1966; MA, Rice U., PhD, 1974. Ass. prof. U. St. Thomas, Houston, 1971-74; eec. dir. Tex. Com. for Humanities, Austin, 1975—; sr. lectr. U. Tex.-Austin, 1984, vis. prof., 1986. Office: Com for Humanities 1604 Nueces St Austin TX 78701

VENINGA, ROBERT LOUIS, b. Milw., Dec. 10, 1941; s. Frank and Otila (Mauch) V.; m. Karen Ann Smit, Dec. 29, 1969; 1 son, Brent Karl. Author: (with James P. Spradley) The Work/Stress Connection: How to Cope with Job Burnout, 1981, The Human Side of Health Admin., 1982, A Gift of Hope: How We Survive our Tragedies, 1985; contrbr. to profl. & scholarly jnls. BA, U. MN, 1963, MA, 1969, PhD, 1972; BD; North Am. Baptist Seminary, 1966. Assist. dean, Sch. of Pub. Health, U. MN, Mpls., 1972-76, assoc. dean, 1976-80, assoc. prof., 1976-85, prof., 1985—. Mem. Am. Pub. Health Assn. Office: 1260 Mayo Bldg. Box 197 U MN Minneapolis MN 55455

VENN, GEORGE ANDREW, b. Tacoma, Wash., Oct. 12, 1943, s. Ernest Fyfe and Beth Alice (Mayo) Fyfe Venn; m. Elizabeth Anne Cheney, July 26, 1966; children—Alicia Anne, Alex Andrew. Author: Sunday Afternoon: Grande Ronde, 1976, Off the Main Road, 1978, Marking the Magic Circle, 1987, contrbr. poetry to Fourteen Oregon Poets, 1976, Portland Poetry Festival Anthology, 1975, Rain in The Forest, Light in The Trees, 1983, other anthologies; contrbr. prose to Northwest Rvw, Western Am. Lit., Mont., Eastern Oreg. Lit. Supplement, others. BA, Coll. of Idaho, 1967; MFA, U. Mont., 1970. Touring wrtr. Western States Arts, Denver, 1976; prof. English Eastern Oreg. State U., La Grande, 1970-81, 1983-87, wrtr.-in-res., 1977—; fgn. expert English as 2d lang. Changsha (Hunan) Ry., 1981-82; book reviewer Northwest Pub.; mem. editorial bd. Northwest Folklore. Grantee Oreg. Arts Commn., 1971, 72, 73, 76, 77, 85, Sierra Club Fdn., San Francisco, 1973, Oreg. Com. for Humanities, 1981. recipient Pushcart prize for poetry, 1979. Mem. Western Lit. Assn., P&W, AWP. Home: Route 2 Box 2499 La Grande OR 97850

VENN, JONATHAN, b. Chgo., Dec. 24, 1950; s. Jack Arnold and Dorothy Almeda (McCambridge) V.; m. Carleen Harriet Stoskopf, Oct. 17, 1981; 1 dau., Marissa Ann. Contrb. article to profl. jnls. Mem. editorial rvw. bd. Jnl. Christian Healing, 1987—. B.S. with honors, Loyola U., Chgo., 1972; Ph.D., Northwestern U., 1977. Lectr., U. Md., Heidelberg, Federal Republic Gemany, 1982-83; clinical psychologist Balt. Gas & Electric, 1983—. Dir. Careerscope, Columbia, MD, 1984—. Home: 10840 Green Mountain Circle Columbia MD 21044

VENTURE, A. DAVID, see Hughes, Walter J., Sr.

VENUTI, LAWRENCE M., b. Phila., Feb. 9, 1953, s. Michael F. and Lucille L. (Rutigliano) V. Translator: Delirium (Barbara Alberti), 1980, A Scientific Autobiography (Aldo Rossi), 1981, Restless Nights: Selected Stories of Dino Buzzati, 1983 (Columbia U. Transl. Ctr. award 1983), Falling in Love (Francesco Alberoni), 1983, The Siren: A Selection from Dino Buzzati, 1984; contrbr. articles and reviews to Attenzione, Denver Qtly, Philadelphia Inquirer, Modern Fiction Studies, English Lit. Renaissance, Assays, Jnl Medieval and Renaissance Studies, Criticism, Boundary 2; contrbr. transl. of Italian poetry and prose to Antaeus, Chgo., Lit., New Orleans, Paris, Partisan, Mont. rvws, Fiction, Chelsea, Poetry Now, others. BA, Temple U., 1974; PhDColumbia U., 1980. Asst. prof. English, Coll. of New Rochelle, 1979, Iona Coll., 1980, Temple U., 1980-87; lectr. humanities Cooper Union, 1980, assoc. prof. English, Temple U., 1987. Recipient Premio di cultura award for transl. Govt. of Italy, 1984; NEA transl. fellow, 1982. Mem. ALTA, PEN (transl. com., Renato Poggioli award for transl. 1980). Home: 262 W 107th St 4B New York NY 10025

VER BECKE, W. EDWIN, b. Sidney, IA, July 21, 1913; s. Walter Earle and Dora Abbigail (Thorne) Verbeck; m. Eugenia Chaussey, 1954 (dec. 1969); 1 dau., Ghizella Anne Roumaia (dec.). Author: Poems of the Spirit, 1950, Poems, 1955, Line in Painting, 1955; contrbr. poems to anthols., lit. mags.; articles to schl. mags. Art ed.: Exploration Mag., 1935-37; ed.: Flight Mag., 1937, Circle Mag., 1940; founder, dir. Poetry Fdn., 1987. Student Tchrs. Coll., Duluth, MN, 1932, U. Minn., 1937. Dir., founder Sausalito Little Theatre, CA, 1954—; founder Drama Readers, Laguan Beach, CA, 1955-60. Bd. dirs. Arts Intl., Chgo., Worldwide Arts, Chgo. Recipient Spcl. award Orange County Art Assn., 1954. Mem. Am. Poetry Soc., Am. DG. Home: 840 8th Ave Suite 6M New York NY 10019

VERBY, JANE CRAWFORD, b. LaCrosse, WI, Oct. 3, 1923; d. Clarence Horatio and Belva Gertrude (Hatch) C.; m. John Edward Verby, June 15, 1946; children—John, Steven, Ruth, Karl. Author: How to Talk to Doctors, 1977, Patterns, 1986; contrbr. arts. to: Mpls./St. Paul Mag., 1983, Sunday Mpls. Tribune, 1979, Y Drych Mag., 1982, Western Mail Nwspr., 1978. BA, Carleton Coll., 1945. Proofreader, Mayo Clinic, Rochester, MN, 1945-46; Minnesota poll, Mpls. Tribune, 1946-47; word processor, Animal Fair, Edina, MN, 1984. Mem. NPW. Home: 9609 Washburn Ave S Bloomington MN 55431

VERCZ, CAROL ANN, b. Herkimer, NY, June 9, 1946; d. Steven and Frances Josephine (Grabinski) Osley; m. Peter Vercz. Author: The Soldier, America and Me, 1982, Beyond the Storm, 1985, In Pursuit of Honor, 1985, A Beautiful Love Story, 1985; Writers Do's and Don'ts, 1982, Helpful Hints for Writers, 1983, How Not to Get Published, 1983, How to Properly Prepare Poems for Publication, 1983; contrbr. articles and po8ms to regional and Canadian pubns., anthologies. Legal secy. degree, Syracuse Business Coll. Mem. natl. wrters. clubs. Home: RD No 1 Mohawk NY 13407

VERE, CORA ELIZA, b. West Newton, PA, June 15, 1919; d. Charles Edwin and Isabel Jewitt (Smith) Alter; m. Harry William Vere, June 28, 1939; children—Virginia Ann, Thomas Eric. Author: The Religious Implications of Hawthorne's Novels, 1963, One Hundred Years of the Episcopal Church, 1972, Beginnings, 1985. Wrkg. on novel, autobiographical essays. B.A., William Smith Coll., 1940; M.A., N.D. State U., 1963. Instr. English, Concordia Coll., Moorhead, MN, 1967-73, El Paso Commun. Coll., TX, 1973-81, (part-time) Pima Commun. Coll., Green Valley, AZ, 1981—. Mem. Green Valley Chamber Music Soc. (pres. 1985), AAUW, NLAPW. Home: 1352 Camino del Sol Green Valley AZ 85614

VERMILYA, CLAIRE (SZALA), b. Metz, MI, Dec. 12, 1919; d. Anthony and Bernice (Centala) Szala; m. Harlan E. Vemilya, July 29, 1940 (dec. July 12, 1968); children—Harlan J., Wayne A. Author: Bootlegger's Daughter, 1987. Wrkg. on poetry. Grad. public schls., Onaway, MI. Home: 210 Spruce St Onaway MI 49765

VERNON, DAVID HARVEY, b. Boston, Aug. 9, 1925; s. Bernard Nathan and Ida E. (Cohen) Vernon; m. Rhoda Louise Sterman, June 1, 1947; children—Amy Lynne, Charles Adam. Editor: (with Depew) General State Food and Drug Law, Annotated, 1955, Title XIV of the American Law of Mining, 1960, Conflict of Laws: Cases, Problems and Essays, 1973, supplement, 1979,. Contracts: Theory and Practice, 1980, Conflict of Law: Theory and Practice, 1982, Journal of Legal Education, 1987. AB, Harvard, 1949, LL.B., 1952; LL.M., NYU, 1953, JSD, 1960. Instr. NYU, 1953-54; asst. prof. law U. Houston, 1954-55; from asst. prof. to prof. law U. N.Mex. (Albuquerque), 1955-64; assoc. dean, prof. law U. Wash. (Seattle), 1964-66; prof. law U. Iowa, 1966—, dean, 1966-71; vis. prof. Schl. Law, Washington U. (St. Louis), 1974-75, U. Durham (Eng.), fall 1980, Victoria U. (Wellington, New Zealand), 1986. Bd. dirs. Wash. State Affiliate ACLU, 1964-66, Iowa Civil Liberties Union, 1966-72. Served with USNR, 1943-46. Pres., Assoc. of Am. Law Schls., 1983. Home: 327 Koser Ave Iowa City IA 52240

VERNON, HARRIET DOROTHY, b. Balt., June 10, 1914; d. John Archer and Harriet (Parkhurst) V. Contrbr. articles to newpapers, trade mags. Ed.: Good News, Govans United Methodist Church, 1974-80. B.A., Goucher Coll., 1935; M.Ed., Loyola Coll., 1958. Ed. Cross Currents, Central Md. Ecumenical Council, Balt., 1980-87; receptionist, proofreader Chronicle Newspaper, Balt., 1986—; Spcl. asst. Allegro Communications, 1986—. Home: 423 Notre Dame Ln Baltimore MD 21212

VERNON, JODI, see Moore, Dianne Jo

VERNON, RAYMOND, b. NYC, Sept. 1, 1913; s. Hyman and Lillian (Sonnenberg) Vernon; m. Josephine Stone, Aug. 9, 1935; children—Heidi, Susan Patricia. Author: Regulation of Stock Exchange Members, 1941, America's Trade Policy and GATT, 1954, Organizing for World Trade, 1956, Metropolis 1985, 1960, The Dilemma of Mexico's Development, 1963, Myth and Reality of Our Urban Problems, 1965, Manager in the International Economy, 1968, Sovereignty at Bay, 1971, Storm over the Multinationals, 1976, Two Hungry Giants, 1983, Exploring The Global Economy, 1985; editor: Public Policy and Private Enterprise in Mexico, 1964, How Latin America Views the U.S. Investor, 1966, The Technology Factor in International Trade, 1970, Big Business and the State, 1974, The Oil Crisis, 1976, State-owned Enterprises in the Western Economies, 1980; contrbr. articles to profl. jnls. AB cum laude, CCNY, 1933; PhD, Columbia U., 1941; MA (hon.), Harvard U., 1959. Statistician SEC, 1935-42, asst. dir. trading and exchange div., 1942-46; asst. chief intl. resources div. Dept. of State, 1946-48; became adviser on comml. policy, 1948, depy. dir. Office of Econ. Def. and Trade Policy, 1951, acting dir., 1954; staff mem. joint Presdl. Congl. Commn. on Fgn. Econ. Policy, 1953-54; planning and control dir. Hawley and Hoops, Inc., 1954-56; dir. NY Metropolitan Region Study, 1956-59; prof. Harvard U. Bus. Schl., 1959-80, dir. Harvard Devel. Adv.

Service, 1962-65, dir. Center for Intl. Affairs, 1973-78, prof. intl. relations, 1978-84; dir. Am. Gen. mutl. fund complex; lectr. Am. U., 1946-48, Princeton U., 1954-55, Swarthmore coll., 1955-56; adj. prof. Fletcher Schl. Law and Diplomacy, 1979-81; mem. Mission on Japanese Combines (Tokyo), 1946; mem. U.S. del. GATT, Geneva, 1950, Torquay, Eng., 1951, vice chair U.S. del., Geneva, 1952; spcl. cons. to undersecy. Dept. State, 1962, Dept. of Treasury, 1978-79; participant UN Conf. on Regional Devel. (Tokyo), 1958; visiting scholar, World Bank, 1987. Home: 1 Dunstable Rd Cambridge MA 02138

VERNON, SIDNEY, b. NYC., Nov. 12, 1906; widowed; children—Kenneth, Sheridan. Author: How to Understand People, 1982, Reach for Charisma, 1983. Contrbr. numerous articles to profl. jnls. Ed.: Robby's Revelry, 1985. B.S., CCNY, 1926; M.D., SUNY Downstate, 1930. Practice of medicine specializing in genl. surgery, Willimantic, CT, 1932—; pres. Rovern Press, Willimantic, 1982. Served to lt. col. U.S. Air Force, 1941-50. Home: 180 Birch St Willimantic CT 06226

VERRETTE, LOUISE MADELEINE, b. Fall River, MA, Mar. 30, 1949; d. Emile A. and Eveline J. (Marois) V. Contrbr. poems to anthols. B.A., Bridgewater State Coll., 1971, M.Ed., 1977. Data entry operator Bus. Research Corp., South Boston, MA, 1985-87; administrative asst. Dun & Bradstreet, Weston, MA, 1985—. Mem. Blackstone Valley WG (recording secy.). Home: 97 N Warren Ave Brockton MA 02401

VER STEEG, CLARENCE LESTER, b. Orange City, IA, Dec. 28, 1922; s. John A. and Annie (Vischer) Ver Steeg; m. Dorothy Ann De Vrie, Dec. 24, 1943; 1 son—John Charles. Author: Robert Morris, Revolutionary Financier, 1954, A True and Historical Narrative of the Province of Georgia, 1960, The American People: Their History, 1961, The Formative yers, 1607-1763, 1964, (Brit. edit.), 1965, The Story of Our Country, 1965, (with others) Investigating Man's World, 6 vols., 1970, (with Richard Hofstadter) Great Issues in American History, From Settlement to Revolution 1584-1776, 1969; editorial cons.: Papers of Robert Morris, vols. I-VI, 1973—, AB, Morningside Coll., 1943, MA, Columbia U., 1946, PhD, 1950. Lectr., then instr. history Columbia U. (NYC), 1946-50; mem. faculty Northwestern U. (Evanston, IL), 1950—, prof. history, 1959—, dean Grad Schl., 1975—; vis. lectr. Harvard U., 1959-60; mem. council Inst. Early Am. History and Culture (Williamsburg, VA), 1961-64, 68-72, chair exec. com., 1970-72; vis. mem. Inst. Advanced Study (Princeton, NJ), 1967-68; chair faculty com. to recommend Master Plan Higher Edn. in Ill., 1962-64; mem. bd. Grad. Record Exams, 1981—, Ctr. Research Libraries, 1980—. Served with USAF, 1942-45. Mem. Am. Hist. Assn. (nominating com. 1965-68, chair 1967-68, Albert J. Beveridge prize 1952), Orgn. Am. Historians (editorial bd. Jnl. Am. History 1968-72), So. Hist. Assn., AAUP. Home: 2619 Ridge Ave Evanston IL 60201

VERSTRAETE, CHRISTINE A., see Prucha, Christine A.

VERTREACE, MARTHA MODENA, b. Washington, Nov. 24, 1945; d. Walter Charles and Mattie Modena (Kendrick) V. Author: (poems) Second House from the Corner, 1986. Contrbr. numerous poems, book rvws., articles to lit. and popular mags., anthols. Editorial bd. Seams Mag., Chgo., 1986—. District of Columbia Teachers Coll., 1967; M.A. in English, Roosevelt U., 1972; Mph in Ed., Roosevelt Univ., 1973; M.A. in Religious Studies, Mundelein Coll., 1982. English tchr. Roosevelt High Schl., Gary, IN, 1967-72; instr. English, Kennedy-King Coll., Chgo., 1977-82, asst. prof. English, poet-in-residence, 1986—; asst. adj. prof. Rosary Coll., River Forest, IL, 1982-83. Mem. adv. bd. City Mag., Chgo. City Colls., 1985—; active Chgo. Call to Action, 1977—. Recipient 1st prize for poetry U. Chgo., 1985, Triton Coll., River Grove, IL, 1985, 86, 87, Natl. Fdn. of State Poetry Socs., Inc., LA, 1985; award for excellence in profl. writing Ill. Assn. Tchrs. of English, 1986; Lit. award Ill. Arts Council, 1987; others. Mem. Kappa Delta Pi, Pi Lambda Theta. Home: 5637 S Kenwood Ave Chicago IL 60637

VEUHOFF, HEINZ, b. Wiesbaden (Hessen) Germany, April 16, 1933 (arrd. U.S.A. 1959); s. Otto and Johanna (Raubach) V.; m. Helga Schiskowsky, May 12, 1956; children—Sigla Chirstine, Marc Alain. Author: Die Beiden Brueder, 1954; poems Methafischgebiss (with Heinz Fischer), 1959; series of one-copy and limited ed. books of papercuts, collages, monotypes, drawings, poems, 1960—; The Dorothy Day Book (one copy), 1965; contrbr. lit mags, periodicals, including Kansas Qtly, U&lc. Student, WKS (Wiesbaden), 1951-55. Creative dir., PFA, 1965—. Home: 43-05 72nd St Woodside NY 11377

VICKER, RAY, b. WI, Aug. 27, 1917; s. Joseph John and Mary (Young) Vicker; m. Margaret Ella Leach, Feb. 23, 1944. Author: How an Election Was Won, 1962, Those Swiss Money Men, 1973, Kingdom of Oil, 1974, Realms of Gold, 1975, This Hungry World, 1976, Dow-Jones-Irwin Guide to Retirement Planning, 1985; also numerous articles. Student, Wis. State U., Stevens Point, 1934, Los Angeles City Coll., 1940-41, U.S. Mcht. Marine Officers' Schl., 1944, Northwestern U., 1947-49. With Chgo. Jnl. Commerce, 1946-50, automobile editor, 1947-50; mem. staff Wall St. Jnl, 1950-83, European editor, London, Eng., 1960-75, sr. intl. corr., 1975-80, sr. natl. corr., 1980-83. Served with U.S. Merchant Marine, 1942-46. Recipient Outstanding Reporting Abroad award Chgo. Newspaper Guild, 1959, Best Bus. Reporting Abroad award E.W. Fairchild, 1963, 67, hon. mention, 1965, Bob Considine award, 1979, ICMA Journalism award, 1983. Home: 1209 Avenida Sevilla 2B Walnut Creek CA 94595

VICKERS, EDWARD DAVIN, b. Whigham, GA, Jan. 10, 1945; s. Eldridge Mathew Vickers and Eula Vickers (Bryant) Miller. Author: Echo in the Woods, 1979, 2d ed., 1984; ed.: The Reach of Song, Book 1, 1981, Book 2, 1982; contrbr.: Negative Capability, Chattahoochee Rvw., Tennessee Voices, Parnassus, Creative Loafing, other lit. mags. and rvws. BS in Math., Valdosta State Coll., 1966. Named Author of the Yr. in Poetry, Dixie Council Authors and Journalists, 1980, 82; recipient Daniel W. Hicky Natl. award Ga. State Poetry Soc., 1985. Mem. PSA, Village Wrtrs. Group, Natl. Fedn. State Poetry Socs. (v.p. 1981-85), Atlanta Wrtrs. Club (pres. 1978-79), Ga. State Poetry Soc. (founding pres. 1979-81). Home: Box 7695 Atlanta GA 30357

VICKERY, JIM DALE, b. Thief River Falls, MN, Mar. 27, 1951; s. James McClelland and Ella Mae (Huot) V.; m. Mary Beth Fandel, 1975 (div. Jan. 1981); m. 2d Christine Ann Trost, June 18, 1983. Author: Wilderness Visionaries, 1986; contrbr. arts. to: Canoe, Sierra, Audubon, Camping Jnl., Spiritual Life, Writer's Digest, Sacramento Bee, Sunday Clothes, St. Paul Pioneer Press, N.Y. Times, Canadian Geographic, others. BA in Theology, St. John's U., 1973; park ranger trng., Vermilion Comm. Coll., 1985-86. Contrbg. ed. Backpacking Jnl., 1976-79, Canoe Mag., 82—; feature writer Ely (MN) Echo, 1979-82; freelance writer, Ely, 1982—. Mem. nature orgns. Practicing woodsman & wilderness guide. Address: Box 762 Ely MN 55731

VIDAL, GORE, b. West Point, NY, Oct. 3, 1925; s. Eugene L. and Nina (Gore) Vidal. Author: novels Williwaw, 1946, In a Yellow Wood, 1947, The City and the Pillar, 1948, The Season of Comfort, 1949, A Search for the King, 1950, Dark Green, Bright Red, 1950, The Judgement of Paris, 1952, Messiah, 1954, Julian, 1964, Washington, D.C., 1967, Myra Breckinridge, 1968, Two Sisters, 1970, Burr, 1973, Myron, 1974, 1986, 1976, Kalki, 1978, Creation, 1981, Duluth, 1983, Lincoln, 1984; stories A thirsty Evil, 1956; plays Visit to a Small Planet; for TV and Broadway, 1957, The Best Man, 1960, Romulus, 1966, Weekend, 1968, An Evening with Richard Nixon, 1972; essays Rocking the Boat, 1962, Reflections upon a Sinking Ship, 1969; collected essays Homage to Daniel Shays, 1973, Matters of Fact and of Fiction, 1977, The Second American Revolution, 1982. Grad., Phillips Exter Acad., 1943. Mem. Pres.'s Adv. Com. on Arts, 1961-63; Democratic- Liberal candidate for U.S. Congress, 1960, candidate for Dem. nomination from Calif. for 1982; co-chiar The People's Party, 1970-74. Served with AUS, 1943-46. Address: Random Hs 201 E 50th St New York NY 10022

VIERECK, PETER, b. NYC, Aug. 5, 1916; s. George S. and Margaret (Hein) V.; m. Anya de Markov, June 1945 (div. May 1970); children—John-Alexis, Valerie Edwina (Mrs. John Gibbs); m. Betty Martin Falkenberg, Aug. 30, 1972. Author: Metapolitics—From the Romantics to Hitler, 1941. Terror and Decorum; poems, anthology New Directions Ten, 1948, Conservatism Revisited-The Revolt Against Revolt 1815-1949, Strike Through the Mask, New Lyrical Poems, 1950, The First Morning: New Poems, 1952, Shame and Glory of the Intellectuals, 1953, rev. ed., 1978, Dream and Responsibility, The Tension Between Poetry and Society, 1953, The Unadjusted Man; a New Hero for Americans, 1956, Conservatism: From John Adams to Churchill, The Persimmon Tree: poems, 1956, Inner Liberty, The Stubborn Grit in the Machine, 1957, The Tree Witch: A Verse Drama, 1961, New and Selected Poems, 1932-67, 1967, Archer in the Marrow: The Applewood Cycles of 1967-87, 1987; also selections in symposium books Towards a World Community, 1950, Midcentury American Poets, 1950, Arts in Renewal, 1951, The New American Right, 1955, Education in a Free Society, 1958, The Radical Right, 1962, Soviet Policy Making, 1967. Outside Looking In, 1972, A Question of Quality, 1967. BS summa cum laude. Harvard, 1937, MA, 1939, Ph.D., 1942; Henry fellow, Christ Church, Oxford U., Engl., 1937-38; L.H.D., Olivet Coll., 1959. Teaching asst. Harvard, 1941-42, instr. German lit. tutor history and lit. dept., 1946-47; instr. history U.S. Army U., Florence, Italy, 1945; asst.prof. history Smith Coll., 1947- 48, vis. lectr. Russian history, 1948-49; asso. prof. Modern European, Russian history Mt. Holyoke Coll., 1948-55, prof., 1955—; vis. lectr. Am. Culture Oxford U., 1953; Whittal lectr. in poetry Library of Congress, 1954, 63, 79; Fulbright prof. Am. poetry and civilization U. Florence, Italy, 1955; Elliston chair poetry lectr. U. Cin., 1956; vis. lectr. U. Calif. at Berkeley, 1957; Disting. William R. Kenan prof. Mt. Holyoke Coll., 1979;

Charter mem. Council Basic Edn.; vis. poet Russian-Am. cultural exchange program Dept. State, USSR, 1961; vis. research scholar 20th Century Fund, USSR, 1962-63; vis. scholar Rockefeller Study Center at Bellagio, Italy, 1977; vis. artist and scholar Am. Acad. in, Rome, 1978; dir. poetry workshop N.Y. Writers Conf., 1965-67; research fellow Huntington Library, San Marino, Calif. Served with U.S. Army, 1943-45; Africa and Italy. Awarded Tietjens prize for poetry, 1948, Pulitzer prize for poetry, 1949, recipient Most Distinguished Alumnus award Horace Mann School for Boys, 1958; Poetry Translation award Translation Center, Columbia U., 1978; Guggenheim fellow, Rome, 1949-50; Rockefeller Fdn. researcher in history, Germany, summer 1958; NEH sr. research fellow, USSR, 1969; Artists fellow, 1978. Mem. Am. Hist. Assn., Oxford Soc., Poetry Soc. Am., P.E.N., Phi Beta Kappa. Home: 12 Silver St. South Hadley MA 01075

VIEIRA, MICHAEL JOHN, b. Fall River, MA, Oct. 14, 1953; s. Alfred S. and Ethey (Oliveira) V.; m. Audrey A. Martin, June 18, 1977; children—Anne Mary, Jonathan, Michael. Author: In Print: 100 Years of Student Journalism, 1982, A Study of the Relationship between Grades and Extracurricular Activities in a Senior High School, 1987. Ed.: Durfee Chimes, 1979—, Schl. and Commun. Dialogue, 1982—. B.A., Bridgewater State Coll., 1975, M.A.T., 1982; C.A.G.S., R.I. Coll., 1987. Tchr. English and jnlsm. B.M.C. Durfee High Schl., Fall River, 1978—; wrtr. Standard-Times, New Bedford, MA, 1974-85, Providence Jnl., 1985—. Mem. Jnlsm. Educators Assn., NCTE. Home: 4171 N Main St Fall River MA 02720

VILLANI, JIM, b. Youngstown, OH, Nov. 5, 1948; s. Frank Paul and Martha Philomena (Mormile) V. Ed.: Pig Iron, Nos. 1-13; The Stolen House (Remick), Orphan Trees (Peffer and Murcko), Angry Candy (Pauker). BA, Youngstown State U., 1973, MA, 1982; postgrad. U. Pitts., 1983—. Ed./pub. Pig Iron Press, Youngstown, 1973—; poet-in-schs. Ohio Arts Council, 1977—; instr. Youngstown State U., 1981—; teaching fellow U. Pitts., 1983—. Recipient spcl. award Ohio Poetry Day Assn., 1985. Mem. MLA, Sci. Fiction Research Assn., Verse Wrtrs. Guild Ohio. Home: 3306 Hillman St Youngstown OH 44507

VILLARRUBIA, JAN (MARTHA), b. New Orleans, Apr. 11, 1948, d. Forrest David and Audrey Helen (Levy) V.; m. Ernest Charles Merrell, Aug. 18, 1978. Contrbr. poetry: Lit Rvw, Negative Capability, Wind Lit Rvw, Poets On, other lit publs. BA, La. State U., 1970, MA, 1971. Poet-in-schls. program, New Orleans, 1984-85, 85-86, 86-87, 87-88. Winner 1st pl. Poetry Competition, AAP, 1979, 1st pl. Playwrtg. and prodn. Competition, Contemporary Arts Center, New Orleans, 1986. Fellowship for playwrty., La. Div. of the Arts, 1987-88. Mem. P&W, New Orleans Poetry Forum. Home: 38 Crane New Orleans LA 70124

VINACKE, W. EDGAR, (Lewis Card), b. Denver, July 26, 1917; s. Harold M. and Edna L. (Lewis) Vinacke; m. Winifred Ross, Feb. 8, 1947; children—Susan K. Eves, Alan R., Edna M. Evans. Works include: Myths, Fables and Legends for the Young and Old—Tales from a Grandfather, 1985, Readings in General Psychology, 1968, Foundations of Psychology, 1968, The Psychology of Thinking, 1952 (rev. ed., 1974); contrbr. to Nebraska Symposium in Motivation, Encyclopaedia Brittanica; wrkg. on: The Search for Lewis Card (novel). BA, U. of Cincinnati, 1939, PhD, Columbia U., 1942. Served with USNR, 1944-46. Prof., U. of Hawaii, 1946-63; Prof. State U. of NY, Buffalo, 1963-84, prof. emer., 1984—. Awards: Guggenheim Fellow, 1960. Mem. Am. Psych. Assoc., Am. Soc. Assoc., Soc. of Exper. Soc. Psych. Home: 104 Saratoga Rd Buffalo NY 14226

VINCENT, HELEN, b. Elizabeth, NJ; d. James Burline and Eva Harriet (Winter) Vincent. BA with honors, Elmira Coll. Mng. editor True Confessions, Macfadden-Bartell Corp. (NYC), 1954-73; editor, 1973-75, True Story, 1975—. Home: 10 Mohawk Trail Westfield NJ 07090

VINE, JANET DIANA, b. Albany, NY, Apr. 6, 1937, d. Harold Arthur and Dora Mary (Meyer) Vine. Author: Discovering Literature, Reading Guide and Review Tests, 1968, Exploring Literature, Reading Guide and Review Tests, 1968, English, a Comprehensive Review, 1982; contrbr. to Children's Periodicals of the United States, 1984; contrbr. articles to Grit, Early Years, Pegasus, other mags., numerous metro. newspapers. BA, Syracuse U., 1959; MA, SUNY-Albany, 1964. Tchr. public Schls., Kenmore, N.Y., 1959—; tchr. creative writing, adult edn., Amherst, N.Y., 1985. Mem. AG, Natl. League Am. Pen Women, Write Assocs., Assn. Profl. Women Wrtrs., numerous ednl. orgns. Office: Kenmore HS 350 Fries Rd Tonawanda NY 14151

VINING, PEGGY SUE, b. Greenfield, TN, Mar. 4, 1929; d. Clayton Ross and Winnie Mae (Moore) Candle; m. Donald Dent Vining, Sr., Dec. 19, 1948; children—Suzanne Vining Kunkel, Betty Kathryn Vining Moore, Vicky Elaine Vining Crawley, Donald Dent Vining. Jr., Cheri Lynn Vining. Contrbr. articles to Ark. Democrat; articles, poetry to Ark. Gazette; poetry to Ark. Baptist, Voices Intl., Tenn. Voices, anthols., newspapers, church bulltns., others. Wrkg. on collection of poems, children's stories, songs. Tchr.'s Cert., Union U., 1948; B.S. in Elem. Edn., U. Ark., MA, 1984. Tchr. Univ. Kindergarten, Little rock, 1965-70, dir., tchr., 1970-75; deputy dir. U. Ark. Lab Sch., Little Rock, 1975-84, dir., 1984—. Lit. dir. Ark. State Festival of Arts, Little Rock, 1963-76; Ark. Assn. for Children Under Six, Natl. Assn. Young Children's Eds., Southern Assn. Children Under Six, Poet's Roundtable Ark. (pres. 1965-68, 81-83; Sybil Nash Abrams award 1980), Ark. Authors, Composes Artists Soc. (pres. 1982). Home: 6817 Gingerbread Ln Little Rock AR 72204

VINZ, MARK, b. Rugby, ND, Sept. 27, 1942; m. Elizabeth Casler, Jan. 30, 1965; children: Katherine, Sarah. Author: (poems) Climbing the Stairs, 1983; (prose poems) The Weird Kid, 1983; (chapbooks) Winter Promises, 1975, Letters to the Poetry Editor, 1975, Red River Blues, 1977, Songs for a Hometown Boy, 1977, Contingency Plans, 1978, Deep Water, Dakota, 1980; ed. mag. and chapbook series Dacotah Territory, 1971-81. BA, U. Kans., 1964, MA, 1966; postgrad. U. N.Mex., 1966-68. Asst. prof., assoc. prof., prof. English, Moorhead State U., Minn., 1968—. Winner Minn. Voices project competition New Rivers Press, 1983; PEN syndicated fiction project competition PEN/NEA, 1984; NEA poetry fellow, 1974-75. Home: 510 5th Ave S Moorhead MN 56560

VIOLI, PAUL RANDOLPH, b. NYC, July 20, 1944, s. Joseph Theodor and Irma (Francesconi) V.; m. Carol Ann Boylston, June 29, 1969; children—Helen, Alexander. Author: Waterworks, 1972, In Baltic Circles, 1973, Harmatan, 1976, Splurge, 1981. Contrbr. poetry to Harper's, Partisan Rvw, Am. Poetry Rvw. BA, Boston U., 1966. Survey tchr. Peace Corps of Nigeria, 1966-67; managing ed. The Architectural Forum, NY, 1972-74; assoc. prof. NYU., 1982—. Grants, Ingram Merrill Fdn., 1979, Poetry Fellowship, NEA, 1979, 86, Poetry Fellowship, NY St. Council on the Arts, 1978. Home: Rt 4 Box 207 Putnam Valley NY 10579

VIORST, JUDITH STAHL, b. Newark, Feb. 2, 1931; d. Martin Leonard and Ruth June (Ehrenkranz) Stahl; m. Milton Viorst, Jan. 30, 1960; children—Anthony Jacob, Nicholas Nathan, Alexander Noah. Author: children's books Sunday Morning, 1968, I'll Fix Anthony, 1969, Try it Again Sam, 1970, The Tenth Good Thing About Barney, 1971, Alexander and the Terrible Horrible No Good Very Bad Day, 1972, My Mama Says There Aren't Any Zombies, Ghosts, Vampires, Creatures, Demons, Monsters, Fiends, Goblins or Things, 1973, Rosie and Michael, 1974, Alexander, Who Used to Be Rich Last Sunday, 1978; poetry The Village Square, 1965-66, It's Hard to be Hip Over Thirty and Other Tragedies of Married Life, 1968, People and Other Aggravations, 1971, How Did I Get to Be Forty and Other Atrocities, 1976, If I Were in Charge of the World and Other Worries, 1981; (with Milton Viorst) The Washington Underground Gourmet, 1970, Yes Married, 1972, A Visit From St. Nicholas (To a Liberated Household), 1977, Love and Guilt and the Meaning of Life, Etc., 1979; contrbr.: Free to Be—You and Me, 1974; columnist: Redbook mag. BA, Rutgers U., 1952. Research affiliate mem. Washington Psychoanalytic Soc., 1981—. Recipient Emmy award for poems used on Anne Bancroft TV show, 1970, Silver Pencil award, Holland, 1973, Penney-Mo. Mag. award, 1974, Spirit of Achievement award Albert Einstein Coll. Medicine, 1975, GA Children's Picture Storybook award, 1977, Am. Acad. Pediatrics award, 1977, AAUW award for article on older women, 1980. Home: 3432 Ashley Terr NW Washington DC 20008

VIORST, MILTON, b. Paterson, NJ, Feb. 18, 1930; s. Louis and Betty (LeVine) Viorst; m. Judith Stahl, Jan. 30, 1960; children—Anthony, Nicholas, Alexander. Author: Hostile Allies: FDR and deGaulle, 1965, Great Documents of Western Civilization, 1965, Fall from Grace: The Republican Party and the Puritan Ethic, 1968, Hustlers and Heroes, 1971, Fire in the Streets: America in the 1960's, 1980, Making A Difference: The Peace Corps at Twenty-Five, 1986, Sands of Sorrow: Israel's Journey from Independence, 1987; also articles. BA summa cum laude, Rutgers U., 1951; student (Fulbright scholar), U. Lyon, France, 1952; MA, Harvard U., 1955; MS, Columbia U., 1956. Reporter Bergen Record (NJ), 1955-56, Newark Star-Ledger, 1956-57, Washington Post, 1957-61; Washington corr. NY Post, 1961-64; syndicated columnist Washington Evening Star, 1971-75. Chair Fund for Investigative Journalism, 1969-78. Home: 3432 Ashley Terr NW Washington DC 20008

VIRATO, SWAMI, b. Bklyn., Dec. 14, 1938; s. Joseph Charles and Rosalie (Macintovich) Bacanskas. BS, Rutgers U., 1968. Exec. ed. New Frontier Mag., Phila., 1979—. Address: New Frontier 129 N 13th St Philadelphia PA 19107

VISHNISKY, MORRIS IRVING, (Vincent Papp), b. NYC, June 18, 1941, s. Chaim Zadin and Rivka V.; m. Christina Smith, Oct. 1974; children—Christopher, Torrence, Martin. Author: The Search for Value, 1975, Man in War, 1978, Reaching Your Goals, 1981. BS, Yale U., 1964; MS, MIT, 1968. Pres. RPM Enterprises, NYC., 1972—. Served to col. U.S. Army, 1968-72; Vietnam. Office: Rt Holzburg 277 Broadway 1500 New York NY 10007

VITIELLO, JUSTIN, b. NYC, Feb. 14, 1941; s. Michael and Ruth (Weishaupt) V.; divorced; 1 son, Domenic. Translator: Creature of Creatures (Danilo Dolci), 1980, Sicilian Lives (Danilo Dolci), 1982, Flowers and Thorns (Vito Feriante), 1983, The World Is One Creature (Danilo Dolci), 1984, Sicilian Songs (Vito Ferrante), 1986. Contrbr. poems to lit. mags. Completed book of poems, Vanzetti's Fish Cart, accepted for bilingual pubn. in Italy. B.A. in Spanish/English, Brown U., 1963; Ph.D. in Comparative Lit., U. Mich., 1970. Asst. prof. comparative lit. U. Mich., Ann Arbor, 1970-73; asst. to assoc. prof. Italian, Temple U., Phila., 1974—. Home: 1633 E Passyunk Philadelphia PA 19148

VIVANTE, ARTURO, b. Rome, Oct. 17, 1923; came to U.S., 1958; s. Leone and Elena (De Bosis) V.; m. Nancy; children: Lucy, Lydia, Benjamin. Author: (poems) Poesie, 1951; (novels) A Goodly Babe, 1966, Doctor Giovanni, 1969; (short story collections) The French Girls of Killini, 1967, English Stories, 1975, Run to the Waterfall, 1979; Writing Fiction, 1980; (trans.) Essays on Art and Ontology, 1980; also stories in New Yorker mag. and other periodicals and anthologies in U.S. and abroad. BA, McGill U., 1944; MD, Rome U., 1949. Tchr. various Am. Univs., 1968-80, Bennington Coll., Vt., 1980—. Fulbright grantee, 1952; grantee Guggenheim Fdn., 1985, NEA, 1979, Rockefeller Fdn., 1985. Home: Box 817 Wellfleet MA 02667

VIVIAN, DAISY, see Kenyon, Bruce Guy

VOGAN, SARA, b. Pitts., Sept. 20, 1947, d. James Franey and Sarah Elizabeth (Hanna) Vogan. Novelist: In Shelly's Leg, 1981; contrbr. to ZYZZYVA, Cream City Rvw, Antaeus, CutBank, numerous other lit mags and anthologies. MFA, U. Iowa, 1978. Teaching-writing fellow Wrtrs. Workshop, Iowa City, 1977-78; state fiction wrtr. Mont. Arts Council, Missoula, 1978-79; asst. prof. creative writing U. Wis.-Milw., 1980-84; vis. lectr. U. Calif.-Davis, 1984; lectr. San Francisco State U., 1983—; fiction ed. Gilt Edge, New Series, Missoula, 1979-81; ed. Pushcart Prize, NYC, 1981—; grants panelist NEA, Washington, 1982. Recipient NEA fiction award, 1978, U. Wis.-Milw. Fdn. award, 1982, PEN syndicated Fiction award, 1984; Stegner fellow Stanford U., 1979; reviewer Natl. Book Critics Circle. Mem. P&W, AWP. Home: 2559 29th Ave San Francisco CA 94116

VOGEL, PAUL MARK, b. New Brunswick, NJ, July 14, 1968; s. Walter David and Mary Ann (Caputo) V. Ed., Seatbelt, The Scribbler, Images; author: The Last and Least of Men, 1984, The Lost Writings of the Lost Writer, 1984, The Holiday Concept, 1985. Home: 55 Brunswick Ave Spotswood NJ 08884

VOGT, EVON ZARTMAN, JR., b. Gallup, NM, Aug. 20, 1918; s. Evon and Shirley (Bergman) Vogt; m. Catherine Christine Hiller, Sept. 4, 1941; children—Shirley Naneen, Evon Zartman, Eric Edwards, Charles Anthony. Author: Navaho Veterans, 1951, Modern Homesteaders, 1955, (with W.A. Lessa) Reader in Comparative Religion, 1958, (with Ray Hyman) Water Witching U.S.A., 1959, Zinacantan: A Maya Community in the Highlands of Chiapas, 1969 (Harvard Press Faculty prize 1969), The Zinacantecos of Mexico: A Modern Maya Way of Life, 1970, Tortillas for the Gods: A Symbolic Analysis of Zinacanteco Rituals, 1976; editor: Desarrollo Cultural de Los Mayas, 1964, Los Zinacantecos, 1966, People of Rimrock, 1966, Handbook of Middle American Indians, vols. 7, 8, 1969, Aerial Photography in Anthropological Field Research, 1974 (with Richard M. Leventhal) Prehistoric Settlement Patterns, 1983. AB, U. Chgo., 1941, MA, 1946, PhD, 1948. Instr. Harvard, 1948-50, asst. prof., 1950-55, assoc. prof., 1955-59, prof. anthropology, 1959—, dir. Harvard Chiapas project, 1957—, chair dept. anthropology, 1969-73, master Kirkland House, 1974-82, asst. curator Am. ethnology, 1950-59, curator Middle Am. ethnology, 1960—; vis. prof. U. Hawaii, 1972; mem. div. anthropology and psychology NRC, 1955-57. Served from ensign to lt. USNR, 1942-46. Mem. Natl. Acad. Scis. (chair anthropology sect. 1981-84), Am. Acad. Arts and Scis., Soc. Am. Archaeology, Royal Anthrop. Inst. Gt. Britain and Ireland. Home: 14 Chauncy St Cambridge MA 02138

VOIGT, CYNTHIA, b. Boston, Feb. 25, 1942; d. Frederick C. and Elise (Keeney) Voigt; m. 1964 (div. 1972); 2nd m. Walter Voigt, Aug. 30, 1974; children—Jessica, Peter. Author: (children's books) Homecoming, 1981, Tell Me if Lovers are Losers, 1982, Dicey's Song, 1982 (Newbery medal 1983), The Callendar Papers, 1983. BA, Smith Coll., 1963. High Schl. tchr. English (Glen Burnie, MD), 1965-67; tchr. English Key Schl. (Annapolis, MD), 1968-69; Annapolis, MD, 1971-79; tchr., chair Key Schl. (Annapolis), from 1981. Office: Atheneum 597 5th Ave New York NY 10017

VOIGT, ELLEN BRYANT, b. Danville, VA, May 9, 1943, d. Lloyd Gilmore and Missouri Eleanor (Yeatts) Bryant; m. Francis George Wilhelm Voigt, Sept. 5, 1965; children—Jula Dudley, William Bryant. Author: (poems) Claiming Kin, 1976, The Forces of Plenty, 1983; contrbr. poems to The Morrow Anthology of Younger Am. Poets, Norton Anthology of Poetry, Contemporary So. Poetry, Women Working, Ardis Anthology of New Am. Poetry, Twelve Poems, The Pushcart Prize, VIII. BA, Converse Coll., 1964; MFA, U. Iowa, 1966. Tech. wrtr. Coll. Pharmacy, U. Iowa, 1965-66; asst. prof. Iowa Wesleyan Coll., 1966-69; mem. faculty Goddard Coll., Plainfield, Vt., 1970-79, dir. MFA writing program, 1976-79; assoc. prof. MIT, Cambridge, 1979-82; vis. faculty Warren Wilson Coll., Swannanoa, N.C., 1981—. Recipient Discovery award 92d Street YMHA/The Nation, 1976; Poetry in Pub. Places award Am. Intl. Sculptors Symposium, 1977, Pushcart prize, 1983; grantee Vt. Council on Arts, 1975; fellow NEA, 1976, Guggenheim Fdn., 1978, MIT, 1980. Home: Box 16 Marshfield VT 05658

VOILS, GEORGIA ELIZABETH, b. Alton, IL, Dec. 31, 1947; d. George William and Frances Elizabeth (Roberts) Hornsey; m. James B. Voils, Oct. 30, 1970; children—Bonnie, Olivia, Cynthia. Ed., pub.: Sr. Citizen Newspaper of Southern Ill., Godfrey, 1984—. B.A., Southern Ill. U., 1969. Instr. English and writing Lewis & Clark Commun. Coll., Godfrey, 1985—. Home 412 Mercury Dr Godfrey IL 62035

VOKAC, DAVID ROLAND, b. Chgo., June 1, 1940, s. Roland and Helen Peabody (Russell) V. Author: The Great Towns of The West, 1985, The Great Towns of California, 1986, The Great Towns of the Pacific Northwest, 1987. BS in Bus. Adminstrn., U. Ariz., 1962, MA in Geography, 1965. Chief neighborhood planning, City of Denver, 1969-74; chief park devel. San Diego County, 1974-81. Mem. Sigma Xi. Office: West Press Box 99717 San Diego CA 92109

VOLDSETH, BEVERLY ANN, b. Sioux Falls, SD, Oct. 23, 1935, d. Arne Conrad and Gunvor (Fallan) Voldseth; m. Robert Raymond Allers, June 26, 1959; children—Kristin Marlene, Roslyn Ann, Linda Marie. Author: Listening to Voices, 1984, Absorb the Colors, 1985, poetry in A Rich Salt Place, 1986; editor, Rag Mag. BA, Bethel Coll., 1957. Tchr. Goodhue (Minn.) public schls., 1957-59; dir. Northfield Hist. Soc. and Mus., Min., 1984-87; freelance workshops, readings. Mem. CCLM, COSMEP, Intl. Assn. Ind. Pubs. Home: 508 2d Ave Goodhue MN 55027

VOLK, PATRICIA GAY, bNYC, July 16, 1943, d. Cecil Sussman and Audrey Elayne (Morgen) Volk; m. Andrew Blitzer, Dec. 21, 1964; children—Peter Morgen, Polly Volk. Author: The Yellow Banana (short story collection), 1985; contrbr. stories to Quarto Mag., Atlantic, Cosmopolitan, N.Y. Mag.; represented in anthology: Stories About what Happens when Things Fall Apart and What's Left When They Do, 1985. BFA cum laude, Syracuse U., 1964; postgrad. Columbia U., 1977—. Graphic designer Appelbaum & Curtis, NYC, 1964-66; art dir. Seventeen Mag., NYC, 1967-69; sr. v.p., wrtr. Doyle, Dane Bernbach, Inc., NYC, 1969—. Recipient Fiction Book award Word Beat Press, 1984, advt. awards. Office: DDB Needham 437 Madison Ave New York NY 10022

VOLKART, EDMUND HOWELL, b. Aberdeen, MD, Nov. 9, 1919; s. Ernest and Edna Sophia (Ripken) V.; m. Mary Ellen Drew, June 16, 1949; children—Karen Elaine, Kirsten. Author: The Angel's Dictionary: A Modern Tribute to Ambrose Bierce, 1986. Co-editor: Social Behavior and Personality, 1951; (with w. Richard Scott) Medical Care: Readings in the Sociology of Medical Institutions, 1966. B.A., St. John's Coll., 1939; Ph.D., Yale U., 1947. Dean Oreg. State U., Corvallis, 1962-65; exec. officer Am. Sociological Assn., Washington, 1965-70; prof. U. Hawaii, Honolulu, 1970-82, prof. emeritus, 1982—. Recipient Disting. Achievement award Ednl. Press. North Am., 1974. Fellow Am. Assn. Advancement Sci. Home: 750 Ululani St Kailua HI 96734

VON HESS, JOVAK, see Hoeppner, Iona Ruth

VON HOELSCHER, RUSSEL, b. St. Paul, Aug. 10, 1942; s. Clarence William and Francis Irene (Wooldrick) H.; m. Ginger Julian, Dec. 5, 1975 (div. 1980). Author: How to Achieve Total Success, 1983, A Treasury of Home Business Opportunities, 1984, Investment Opportunities for the Mid-1980s, 1985, 36 others. BA, Mesa Coll. Vice-pres. Los Angeles chap. Calif. Right to Read project, 1984. Address: Box 546 El Cajon CA 92022

VON LAUE, THEODORE HERMAN, b. Frankfurt Main, Germany, June 22, 1916 (came to U.S., 1937, naturalized, 1945); s. Max Felix and Magda (Milkau) Von Laue; m. Hildegarde Hunt, Oct. 23, 1943 (div. 1976); children—Christopher, Madeleine, Esther; 2nd m. Angela Turner, Nov. 13, 1976. Author: Leopold Ranke, The Formative Years, 1950, Sergei Witte and the Industrialization of Russia, 1963, Why Lenin? Why Stalin?, 1964, The Global City, 1969: The World Revolution of Westernization, 1987. AB,

Princeton U., 1939, PhD, 1944; cert. Russian Inst., Columbia U., 1948. Asst. prof. history U. Pa. (Phila.) 1948-49, Swarthmore Coll. (PA), 1949-51; lectr. Bryn Mawr Coll. and Swarthmore Coll., 1952-54; asst. prof. history U. Calif. at Riverside, 1955-59; assoc. prof., 1959-60, prof., 1960-64, Washington U. (St. Louis), 1964-70; Francis and Jacob Hiatt prof. history Clark U., 1970-82, Francis and Jacob Hiatt prof. history emeritus, 1983—. Columbia U. Russian Inst. sr. fellow, 1951-52; Fulbright research fellow, Finland, 1954-55; Guggenheim fellow, 1961-62, 74-75; Social Sci. Research Council grantee, 1951-52, 58. Mem. Am. Hist. Assn., Am. Assn. Advancement of Slavic Studies (dir. 1968-71), World Hist. Assoc. Office: Dept Hist Clark U Worcester MA 01610

VON MORPURGO, HENRY, b. San Francisco, Dec. 19, 1909, s. Albert Jurgen and Dorette (Huenecke) von M.; m. Carol Sanborn; children—Carol Patricia, Elizabeth Jane. BA, U. Calif.-Berkeley, 1935. Exec. asst. to chmn. Young & Rubicam, Inc., NYC, 1940-42; exec. asst. to pres. Bechtel Corp., San Francisco, 1942-49; freelance public relations and communications cons., San Francisco and Los Angeles, 1949-62; ed., pub. Chain Merchandiser mag., Piedmont, Calif., 1962—; dir. public affairs and chain merchandising services Globe Publs., Montreal, 1973—. Home: 65 Crocker Ave Piedmont CA 94611

VONNEGUT, KURT, JR., b. Indpls., Nov. 11, 1922; s. Kurt and Edith (Lieber) Vonnegut; m. Jane Marie Cox, Sept. 1, 1945 (div. 1979); children—Mark, Edith, Nanette; adopted nephews—James, Steven and Kurt Adams; 2nd m. Jill Krementz, 1979. Author: novels Player Piano, 1951, Sirens of Titan, 1959, Mother Night, 1961, Cat's Cradle, 1963, God Bless You, Mr. Rosewater, 1964; story collection Welcome to the Monkey House, 1968; novel Slaughterhouse-Five, 1969; play Happy Birthday, Wanda June, 1970; TV script Between Time & Timbuktu or Prometheus-5, 1972; novel Breakfast of Champions, 1973; essays Wampeters, Foma and Granfalloons, 1974; novels Slapstick or Lonesome No More, 1976, Jailbird, 1979; Christmas Story with illustrations by Ivan Chermayeff Sun Moon Star, 1980; autobiographical collage Palm Sunday, 1981; novel Deadeye Dick, 1982; novel Galapagos, 1985; novel Bluebeard, 1987; also short stories, articles, rvws. Student, Cornell U., 1940-42, U. Chgo., 1945-47; MA in Anthropology, U. Chgo., 1971. Reporter Chgo. City News Bur., 1946; pub. relations with Gen. Electric Co., 1947-50; freelance writer, 1950-65; lectr. Writers Workshop, U. Iowa, 1965-67; lectr. in English Harvard, 1970; disting. prof. CCNY, 1973-74. Served with inf. AUS, 1942-45. Mem. Natl. Inst. Arts and Letters (recipient Lit. award 1970). Address: Farber 99 Park Ave New York NY 10016

VON WACKER, ALEXANDER, see Zimmerman, Robert Dingwall

VORBACH, RENEE R., b. Bklyn., Sept. 28, 1946, d. Ford S. and Jeanne (Magill) Relyea III; m. Joseph Robert Vorbach; children—Vanna Jeanne, Cassie Ebba. BA in English, SUNY-New Paltz, 1969, postgrad. Mem. editorial staff Evening News, Newburgh, N.Y., 1969-83, asst. ed. family and food, 1974-83; freelance journalist, photographer, ed., 1983—. Mem. Newspaper Food Eds. and Wrtrs. Assn. (charter). Home: 147 N Beacon St Middletown NY 10940

VOTANO, PAUL ANTHONY, b. Bronxville, NY, Sept. 24, 1929; s. Paul and Mary (Scrima) Votano; m. Joan Jean Basso, Apr. 15, 1961 (div. Mar. 1, 1971); children—Paul, Gregory. Contrbr. to various sports and entertainment mags., 1965—. Asst. sales prom. mgr. US Plywood (NYC), 1962-65; VP Creamer Dickson Basford (NYC), 1965-81; exec. VP Frango-Yuro (White Plains, NY), 1984-85; mgr. mktg. svcs. and corp. commns., ARGO Commns. Corp. (New Rochelle, NY), 1985—. Mem. Publicity Club of NY. Home: 163 Pennsylvania Ave Yonkers NY 10707

VOYLES, J. BRUCE, b. Murphy, NC, June 6, 1953, s. E. R. and Elaine (Walker) V.; m. Debra Graves, Nov. 24, 1972; children—Heather, Vanessa. Author: The Official Price Guide to Pocketknives, 1975, 83, 84, The Official Price Guide to Collector Knives, 1977, 78, 79, 80, 81, 82, Knifemakers: An Official Directory, 1984, The Official Guide to Knives, 1985; contrbr. articles to Gun Week, Knives, Natl. Knife Collector. BA in Journalism, Ga. State U. Ed. Ga. State U. Rev., Atlanta, 1974-75; reporter Community Newspapers, Inc., Murphy, N.C., 1976-77; ed. Knife Collector Mag., Chattanooga, Tenn., 1977-81; ed. Blade mag.,Chattanooga, 1981-85, owner, pub., 1985—. Office: PO Box 22007 Chattanooga TN 37422

VRADENBURGH, MERRY CHRISTINE, b. West Paterson, NJ, Dec. 24, 1963; d. William Edward and Virginia Arden (Kurtzman) Vradenburgh. Wrkg. on book about drug abuse. Ed. Passaic Valley H.S. (Little Falls, NJ); Writer's Digest Schl. of Writing. Mem. Natl. Trust for Historic Preservation, Democratic Natl. Comm. Home: 51 Mary Ave West Paterson NJ 07424

VROMAN, BARBARA FITZ, b. Chgo., Mar. 31; d. William Edwin and Pearl Asenith (Coombs) Fitz; m. Dale Duane Vroman; children—Guy, Kim, Marc, Ryan. Author: Son of Thunder, 1981; co-author: Tomorrow Is a River (with Peggy Hansen Dopp), 1977; published: The Wind will Not Forget (Carolyn Muentner), From Dream to Reality (Arlene Buttles), Skiing into Wisconsin (Jerry Apps), Quest of the Faces (Catherine Geenen). Mem. Wisconsin Authors & Publishers Assoc., Wisc. Regional Wrtrs., Cncl. Wis. Writers. Leslie Cross Award, Cncl. Wis. Wrtrs., 1977, 81. Home: Box 300 Rt 1 Hancock WI 54943

WACHSBERGER, KEN, b. Detroit, July 18, 1949; s. Si and Shirley (Pollack) W.; m. Emily Schuster, Apr. 7, 1979; 1 son, David Joel. Contrbr. poems, articles, short stories to mags., newspapers, political mags. including Lansing Star (MI), Detroit Jewish News, Clev. Mag., Natl. Geneological Soc. Newsletter. Ed., wrtr. (newspaper) Joint Issue, 1969-74. B.S. in Social Sci., Mich. State U., 1978, M.A. in Creative Writing, 1983. Free-lance wrtr., jnlst., 1970—; writing tchr. Mich. State U., East Lansing, 1982-87, Lansing Commun. Coll., Eat Lansing, 1984—; tchr. creative writing East Lansing Arts Workshop, 1983-87; wrtg. tchr. Eastern Mich. Univ., 1987—. Founded Schl. for Compulsive Communicators, 1986. Active Nuclear Weapons Freeze Movement, Lansing, MI, 1984—, La Mariposa, Lansing, 1984—. Mem. NWU, Nat. Genealogical Soc. Home: 4764 Washtenaw B2 Ann Arbor MI 48108

WADDLE, JEFFREY R., Mng. ed. Clifton Mag., 1980; ed. Milacron Monitor, 1981-83, In Great Company, 1984-85, The Meeting Mngr., 1985—. BA in Eng. Lit., U. Cin., 1980. Ed. employee pubs., Cin. Milacron (OH), 1981-83; publicist/ed. JMB Federated Realty, Cin., 1984-85; mgr. communications/ed. Meeting Planners International, Middletown, OH, 1985—. Mem. Cin. Eds. Assn. Office: Mtg Plns 1950 Stemmons Fwy Dallas TX 75207

WADE, CHERYL MARIE, b. Vallejo, CA, Mar. 4, 1948. Contrbr. to various anthols and mags inclg. With The Power of Each Breath, A Disabled Women's Anthology, 1985, Disability Rag., Sinister Wisdom 31, 1986, Calyx 11(1), 1987, Healing From Childhood Sexual Abuse, 1988. MA, U. CA, Berkeley, 1983. Learning disabilities diagnostic assistant & reading tutor counselor/administrator, freelance wrtr. Warner Brown Memorial Award for Research, 1980, PSA Contest Winner, Gov. Commission on Hiring Handicapped, CA, 1984, Scholarship to Workshop, Women's Voices, CA, 1985, Book Grant, Reginald A. Fessenden Ednl. Fund, 1985. Home: 2222 Derby St Berkeley CA 94705

WADE, JOHN STEVENS, see Stevens, C(lysle) J(ulius)

WADE, SETH, b. KY, Nov. 12, 1928; s. Seth Isaac and Ella (Jasper) W.; m. Neslynn Mohani Ramsaran, Dec. 5, 1981. Author: (poems) Mr. Many, 1969, Henry's Wdpile, 1971, The Broken Eye, 1974, Spinoffs, 1976. Contrbr. poems to lit. mags. Editor: Pan Am. Rvw, 1969-85, Funch Press, 1969—. AB, Univ. of Ky., 1952; MA in English, La. State U.-Baton Rouge, 1954. Instr. English, U. Ky.-Northern Ctr., Covington, 1954-55, Ohio State U., Columbus, 1959-60, Western Ky. State Coll., Bowling Green, 1961- 62; asst. prof. English, Pan Am. U., Edinburg, Tex., 1962—. Address: Box 3427 Edinburg TX 78540

WADE, THEODORE EVERETT, JR., b. Pueblo, CO, June 28, 1936; s. Theodore Everett and Zola W.; m. Karen A. Peterson, 1956; children—Timothy, Dorothea, Melvin. Author: With Joy, 1976, 1985 (children's poems), Fun for the Road, 1978, School at Home, 1980, Home School Manual, 1984, 2d ed., 1986, ed. Bubbles: Poetry for Fun and Meaning, 1987, var. corresp. study guides. BA, Union Coll., 1958; MA, U. Nebr., 1962, PhD, 1970. Missionary, Seventh-day Adventist Church, Rwanda & Haiti, 1962-71; dir. curr. dev. Home Study Intl., Washington, 1972-79; prof. Weimar Coll., Weimar, CA, 1980-84; ed. SS Lesson Comments by EW (quarterly), 1986—. Office: Gazelle 5580 Stanley Dr Auburn CA 95603

WADE, TIMOTHY ANDREW, b. Lawton, OK, May 31, 1958; s. Charles Edward and Marjorie Elizabeth (Messinger) W. B.A. in Jnlsm./Public Relations, U. Okla., 1980. Dir. communications PEPCO, Inc., Norman, OK, 1980-85; public relations ed. Lennox Industries Inc., Dallas, 1985—. Home: 4434 Abbott Dallas TX 75205

WADIER, MAX, see Queenan, Joseph Martin, Jr.

WAGGONER, TIMOTHY EDWARD, b. Troy, OH, Mar. 8, 1964; s. Orville Edward, Jr. and Bonnie Jean (Mast) W. Author play: Fob, 1986; columnist: Trotwood Ind., 1986, 87. Contrbr. short story to lit. mag. Ed.: Nexus mag., 1985-86. B.S. in Edn., Wright State U., 1986; postgrad., 1987—. Staff wrtr. Trotwood Ind., Tipp City, Oh, 1986, 87; tutor writing center Wright State U., Dayton, OH, 1984—, English tutor, 1987—. Recipient 2d place for short story Nexus, 1984. Home: 7290 S Mote Rd West Milton OH 45383

WAGNER, CHARLES ABRAHAM, b. NYC, Mar. 10, 1901; s. Morris and Fanny (Haut) Wagner; m. Ruth Warters, 1925 (div., 1927); m. 2d, Celia Bernstein, June 1930; children—Carl, Carol. Author: Poems of the Soil and Sea, 1923, Nearer the Bone: New Poems, 1930; editor: Prize Poems, 1930, Harvard: Four Centuries and Freedoms, a history, 1950. BA, Columbia U., NY, 1923, MA; postgrad., Harvard, 1945. Book rvwr., Brooklyn Times, 1925-27; assoc. ed., NY Daily Mirror, 1932-55; book and art critic, NY Daily Mirror, 1955-63; ed.-in-chief, Mirror Sunday Mag., 1955-63; exec. secy., PSA, 1963-75. Home: 106 Morningside Dr New York NY 10027

WAGNER, DOUGLAS W.E., b. Orange, NJ, Nov. 5, 1938, s. Norman Raphael and Virginia (Taylor) W. AB, Yale U., 1960. Assoc. ed. Med. World News, NYC, 1969-70; assoc. ed. Emergency Medicine, NYC, 1970-76, sr. ed., 1976-81, ed.-in-chief, 1981-87, ed. and pub., Pediatric Therapeutics & Toxicology, Pediatric Trauma, 1987—. Mem. AMWA, Natl. Assn. Sci. Wrtrs. Office: 72 Sussex St Jersey City NJ 07302

WAGNER, JOHN, b. Blue Island, IL, July 14, 1955; s. Edwin Jamesand Diann Iris (Austin) W.; m. Deanna Johnson, July 9, 1983. Contrbr. humorous essays in mags. including English Jnl., Media & Methods, Mainstream Am., Intro.; comedy sketches for local cable TV, improvisational theater. A.S., Thornton Commun. Coll., 1975; B.A. cum laude, Bradley U., 1977; M.A., U. Notre Dame, 1981; Diploma, Players Workshop of the Second City, 1984. English instr. Victor J. Andrew High Sch., Tinley Park, IL, 1978—, (part-time) Coll. of DuPage, Glen Ellyn, IL, 1985—. Home: 2493 Brunswick Circle Woodridge IL 60517

WAGNER, MARYFRANCES CUSUMANO, b. Kansas City, MO Oct. 22, 1947; d. Samuel and Margaret (Passiglia) Cusumano; div. Author: Bandaged Watermelons and Other Rusty Ducks, 1976, Tonight Cicadas Sing, 1981; ed. Mo. Poets: An Anthology, 1983, contrbr. rvws. and poems to New Letters, Voices Intl., Cedar Rock, Circus Maximus, Impact Qtly, Sheba Rvw, Pteranadon, Poetry: People, Pawn Rvw, Poet's Pride, Taurus, Green's Rvw, New Voices, Rebirth of Artemis, others; contrbr. to anthologies: Voices from the Interior, The Dream Book: Anthology of Italian Am Women. BA, U. Mo.-Kansas City, 1965-69, MA, 1970- 74; postgrad. Tchr/model Monza Models, Kansas City, 1967-70; secy. Burns & McDonnell Engring, 1965-70; English tchr. Raytown high schl., 1969—; wrkshop leader Am. Poets Series, 1974-83; poetry improvs with Westport Ballet, 1978-86; poetry outreach mo. Council Arts, 1980-83. Friend, Friends of Art, Nelson Atkins Gallery, Kansas City, 1986; mem. Natl. Audubon Soc., Mo. Conservation. Recipient Excellence in Tchg. Award, Kansas City Star/Chamber of Commerce, 1984. Mem. NCTE, CODA, NEA, Mo NEA. Address: 5907 Northern Raytown MO 64133

WAGNER-STEVENS, TINA MARIE, (Suzanne Stevens), b. West Branch, MI, June 23, 1957; d. Gordon Rodgers and Thelma Lena (Weinberg) Wagner; m. Mike Burgess, Sept. 20, 1975 (div. July 1979); 1 son, Ben Michael; m. Mark Lester Stevens, Nov. 10, 1980. Contrbr. articles to mags. Ed.: Dialog Lit. Mag., 1978-80, Baker's Dozen mag., 1985-87, View from the Boot Closet mag., 1985-86, Myth Makers mag., 1987. Wrkg. on novel, screenplay, feature article. A.A., Delta Coll., 1980; B.S., Eastern Mich. U., 1987, postgrad., 1987—. Promotion asst. Central Bus. District Assn., Detroit, 1984-85; assoc. ed. Alcona Almanac, Lincoln, MI, 1983; wrtr. Eastern Today, Ypsilanti, MI, 1985—; staff wrtr., Business Talk, Ypsilanti, 1987—. Recipient Poetry award ACP, 1979. Mem. WIC (1st place for feature writing 1986). Home: 2127 Golfside A214Y Ypsilanti MI 48197

WAGONER, DAVID RUSSELL, b. Massillon, OH, June 5, 1926; s. Walter Siffert and Rugh (Banyard) Wagoner; m. Patricia Lee Parrott, July 8, 1961 (div. June 1982); 2nd m. Robin Heather Seyfried, July 24, 1982. Author: poetry books, Dry Sun, Dry Wind, 1953, A Place to Stand, 1958, The Nesting Ground, 1963, Staying Alive, 1966, New and Selected Poems, 1969, Working Against Time, 1970, Riverbed, 1972, Sleeping in the Woods, 1974, Collected Poems, 1976, Who Shall Be the Sun?, 1978, In Broken Country, 1979, Landfall, 1981, First Light, 1983; novels, The Man in the Middle, 1954, Money, Money, Money, 1955, Rock, 1958, The Escape Artist (also film 1982), 1965, Baby, Come on Inside, 1968, Where Is My Wandering Boy Tonight?, 1970, The Road to Many a Wonder, 1974, Tracker, 1975, Whole Hog, 1976, The Hanging Garden, 1980; editor: Straw for the Fire: From the Notebooks of Theodore Roethke, 1943-63, 1972. BA in English, Pa. State U., 1947, MA, Ind. U., 1949. Instr. English DePauw U., 1949-50, Pa. State U., 1950-53; asst. prof. U. Wash., 1954-57, assoc. prof., 1958-66, prof., 1966—; Elliston lectr. U. Cin., 1968; editor Poetry Northwest, 1966—; poetry editor Princeton U. Press, 1977-81, Mo. Press, 1983-84. Recipient Morton Dauwen Zabel prize Poetry mag., 1967, Blumenthal-Leviton-Blonder prize, 1974, Tietjens prize, 1977, English-Speaking Union prize, 1980, Sherwood Anderson award, 1980, two Fels prizes CCLM, 1975. Mem. AAP (chancellor 1978—), Soc. Am. Magicians, Natl. Assn. Blackfeet Indians (assoc.). Home: 1918 144th St SE Mill Creek WA 98012

WAGONER, SCOTTIE, see Kaufmann, Sherri Marie

WAHLE, F(REDERICK) KEITH, b. Cin., Nov. 1, 1947, s. Fred Andrew and Mary Avanel (McDaniel) W.; m. Elizabeth Anne Patton, May 26, 1973. Author poetry chapbooks: The Part-Time Arsonist, 1971, The Precious Dead, 1973, The Paper Wedding Ring, 1973, Almost Happy, 1980; contrbr. to Five Cincinnati Poets, 1981; contrbr. poetry, fiction to Abraxas, Anemone, Bitterroot, Gambit, Zahir, numerous other publs. BA, U. Cin., 1969; MFA, U. Iowa, 1974. Library asst. Public Library of Cin. and Hamilton County, 1974-77; first asst. Library for Blind and Physically Handicapped, Cin., 1977—. Ohio Arts Council fellow, 1983; recipient Best Poem of Issue award Cin. Poetry Rvw, 1985, 86. Home: 5307 Eastknoll Ct 511 Cincinnati OH 45239

WAHLGREN, ERICK, b. Chgo., Nov. 2, 1911; s. Oscar G. and Marion I. (Wilkins) Wahlgren; m. Dorothy Sly, Nov. 9, 1939 (div. 1951); children—Nils, Arvid; 2nd m. Beverly Pont, Dec. 18, 1952 (div. 1969); children—Siri, Thor; 3rd m. Helen Gilchrist-Wottring, July 2, 1971; 2 stepchildren. Author: The Kensington Stone: A Mystery Solved, 1958; also several other books, translations and numerous articles on Scandinavian philology. PhB, U. Chgo., 1933, PhD, 1938; MA, U. Neb., 1936. Mem. faculty UCLA, 1938—, prof. Scandinavian langs., 1955-70, prof. Scandinavian and Germanic langs., 1970-77, prof. emeritus, 1977—; vice chair dept. Germanic langs. U. Calif. at Los Angeles (Scandinavian and Germanic langs.), 1963-69; dir. U. Calif. study centers at Univs. Lund (Sweden) and Bergen (Norway), 1972-74; lectr. Uppsala U., also vis. prof. Stockholm Schl. Econs., 1947-48; exchange insstr. U. B.C., summer 1940; vis. prof. Augustana Coll., summer, 1946, U. Calif. at Berkeley, 1968, U. Wash., 1970, Portland State U., 1979-80; U.S. mem. Commn. Ednl. Echange U.S.-Sweden, 1973-74; sr. fellow, cons. Monterey Inst. Fgn. Studies, 1977-78; adv. Natl. Endowment Humanities, 1978—; advisor Oreg. Gov.'s Commn. on Fgn. Langs. and Internat. Study, 1981-83; German lang. dir. Army Specialized Tng. Program, 1943-44. Mem. MLA So., Calif. (exec. bd. 1950-53), MLA Am. (chair Scandinavian sect. 1955, 67). Home: 4243 28th Pl W Seattle WA 98199

WAID, STEPHEN HAMILTON, b. Richmond, VA, Oct. 6, 1948, s. Lewis Carroll and Helen Lois (McCann) W.; m. Margaret Rose Bouldin, Oct. 3, 1970; children—Ann Celeste, Stephan Andrew. BA in Polit. Sci., Old Dominion U., 1970. Sports wrtr. Martinsville (Va.) Bulltn., 1970- 71, Roanoke (Va.) Times-World News, 1971-81; exec. ed. Griggs Pub. Co., Concord, N.C., 1981—; ed. Grand Natl. Scene, 1981—, Grand Nat. Illustrated, 1981—, Indy Car Racing Mag., 1983—, GT Motorsports Mag., 1986—. Mem. Natl. Motorsports Press Assn. (dir., recipient numerous writing awards), Am. Automobile Racing Wrtrs. and Broadcasters Assn. Address: 806 Summerlake Dr Concord NC 28025

WAITE, ROBERT GEORGE LEESON, b. Cartwright, Manitoba, Can., Feb. 18, 1919 (came to U.S., 1929, naturalized, 1943); s. George Lloyd and Alice (Carter) Waite; m. Anne Barnett, Sept. 8, 1943; children—Geoffrey, Peter. Author: Vanguard of Nazism: The Free Corps Movement in Postwar Germany, 1918-23, 1952, The Psychopathic God: Adolf Hitler, 1977; editor, contrbr.: Hitler and Nazi Germany, 1965; editorial bd.: Jnl Modern History, 1957-60; contrbr. to World Book, 1958, Collier's Encyc., 1961, Psychoanalytic Interpretations of History, 1971, Jnl Interdisciplinary History, 1971, Afterword to the Mind of Adolf Hitler, 1972, Human Responses to the Holocaust, 1981; co-translator: (Erich Eyck) A History of the Weimar Republic, 2 vols., 1962, 70. AB Macalester Coll., 1941; MA, U. Minn., 1946, Harvard, 1947, PhD, 1949; postgrad., U. Munich, 1953-54. Teaching asst. Macalester Coll., 1941; Emerton fellow history Harvard, 1947, teaching fellow, 1947-49; asst. prof. history Williams Coll., 1949-53, assoc. prof., 1953-58, prof., 1958—, Brown prof., 1960—, chair dept., 1967-72; dir. History Insts., 1968, 69; staff lectr. Inst. in Humanities (John Hay Fdn.), 1959, 1961-65; staff mem. Natl. Humanities Faculty, 1970—; sr. mem. St. Antony's Coll. Oxford U., 1978, 82. Mem. Am. Hist. Assn., Central European Study Group. Home: Talcott Rd Williamstown MA 10267

WAKEFIELD, DAN, b. Indpls., May 21, 1932; s. Benjamin H. and Brucie (Ridge) W. Creator, story cons.: TV show James at 15, 1977-78, Island in the City: The World of Spanish Harlem, 1959; author: Revolt in the South, 1961, The Addict, an anthology, 1963, Between the Lines, 1966, Supernation at Peace and War, 1968, Going All the Way, 1970, Starting Over, 1973, All Her Children, 1976, Home Free, 1977, Under the Apple Tree, 1982, Selling Out, 1985, Returning: A Spiritual Journey, 1988; (teleplay) The Innocents Abroad (Mark Twain) for PBS 1983; writer coproducer TV movie: The Seduction of Miss Leona, 1980; contrbrg. editor: Atlantic Monthly, 1969—. BA, columbia U., 1955; Nieman fellow, Harvard U., 1963-64. News editor Princeton Packet (NJ), 1955; staff writer The Nation mag.,

1956-59; freelance writer, 1959—; staff Bread Loaf Writers Conf., 1964, 66; vis. lectr. U. Mass., Boston, 1956-66; vis. lectr. journalism U. Ill., 1968. Bernard DeVoto fellow Bread Loaf Writers Conf., 1957. Mem. AG Am., Vestry of King's Chapel. Address: King's Chapel 64 Beacon St Boston MA 02108

WAKEFIELD, KIM STOECKLE, b. New London, CT, Jan. 11, 1953; d. Albert Edward and Frances Rita (Corchinski) Stoeckle; m. Roland A. Wakefield, June 3, 1972; 1 son, Addison Edward. Contrbr. poems to lit. mags., anthols. Student Western Conn. State Coll., 1971-72. Vol., Literacy Vols. of Am., CT, 1986—. Home: 205 Markham St MIddletown CT 06457

WAKIN, EDWARD, b. Bklyn., Dec. 13, 1927, s. Thomas Najem and Josephine (Aziz) W.; m. 2d, Eleanor Kester, Dec. 3, 1967; 1 son, Daniel. Author: A Lonely Minority: The Modern Story of Egypt's Copts, 1963, The Catholic Campus, 1963, At the Edge of Harlem: Portrait of a Middle-Class Negro Family, 1965, The De-Romanization of the American Catholic Church (with J.F. Scheuer), 1966, Controversial Conversations with Catholics, 1969, A Parent's Guide: Religion for Little Children (with Christiane Brusselmans), 1970, Black Fighting Men in U.S. History, 1971, We Were Never Their Age (with James DiGiacomo), 1971, The Battle for Childhood, 1973, Careers in Communication, 1974, Children Without Justice, 1975, Enter the Irish-American, 1976, The Immigrant Experience, 1977, Communications: An Introduction to Media, 1978, You Can Still Change the World (with Richard Armstrong), 1978, Should You Ever Feel Guilty? (with Frank J. McNulty), 1978, Monday Morality: Right and Wrong in Daily Life, 1980, Understanding Teenagers (with James DiGiacomo), 1983, A Catholic Guide to the Mature Years (with Charles Fahey), 1984, Beyond Loneliness (with Sean Cooney), 1985, Trevor's Place: The Story of the Boy Who Brings Hope to the Homeless, 1985; contrbr. numerous articles to Sat. Rvw, Harper's, Sci. Digest, other publs. BA, Fordham U., 1948, PhD, 1973; MSJ, Northwestern U., 1950; MA, Columbia U., 1961. Asst. city ed. Buffalo (N.Y.) Evening News, 1950-52; night city ed., feature ed., Bklyn. city ed. N.Y. World Telegram, 1952-59; mem. faculty Fordham U., Bronx, N.Y., 1960—, now prof. dept. communications, dir. grad. program; lectr. USIS, Africa, Middle East, Far East, 1971, 73; cons. edn. ed. WCBS-TV, 1966-69; cons. to numerous corps., govt. agcys.; contrbg. ed. 50 Plus, Today's Office. Recipient George Polk Meml. award for journalism, 1957; Fund Adult Edn. mass media fellow, 1959-60. Address: 45 Wellington Ave New Rochelle NY 10804

WAKOSKI, DIANE, b. Whittier, CA, Aug. 3, 1937; d. John Joseph and Marie Elvira Cora (Mengel) W.; m. Shepard Sherbell, Sept. 1964 (div. 1966); m. 2nd Michael Watterlond, Feb. 22, 1973 (div. 1975); m. Robert James Turney, Feb. 14, 1983. Author: Coins & Coffins, 1962, Discrepancies and Apparitions, 1966, The George Washington Poems, 1967, Inside the Blood Factory, 1968, The Magellanic Clouds, 1970, The Motorcycle Betrayal Poems, 1973, Dancing on the Grave of a Son of a Bitch, 1973, Trilogy, 1974, Looking for the King of Spain, 1974, Virtuoso Literature for Two and Four Hands, 1975, Waiting for the King of Spain, 1976, The Man Who Shook Hands, 1978, Cap of Darkness, 1980, Toward a New Poetry, 1980, The Magician's Feastletters, 1982, The Collected Greed: Parts I-XIII, 1984, The Rings of Saturn, 1986. Wrkg. on bk-length poem George Washington in the City of Angels. BA, Univ. of Calif., Berkeley, 1960. Wrtr.-in-res. Mich. State Univ., 1976—. Cassandra grant, 1970, NY State Arts Council grant, 1971, Guggenheim grant, 1972, NEA grant, 1973, writer's Fulbright, 1984. Home: 607 Division East Lansing MI 48823

WALATKA, PAMELA PORTUGAL, (Pamela Rainbear Portugal), b. Santa Rosa, CA, July 20, 1942; d. Eugene Jay and Dorothy May (Holmes) Portugal; m. Gerald Anthony Walatka, June 6, 1982; 1 child, Sarah Dorothy. Author: A Place for Human Beings, 1974, 78; illustrator Yoga Card, 1978, 82, 86; ed. CAD Primer: Computer-Aided Design, 1982, 85, 86. Wrkg. on popular anatomy book. BA, U. Calif., Berkeley, 1964. Peace Corps vol., Nepal, 1964-65; yoga tchr. Esalen, Big Sur, Calif., 1967-72; owner Wild Horses Pub. Co., Los Altos Hills, Calif., 1972—. Mem. Peninsula Pubs. (past chmn.). Address: Wild Horses 12310 Concepcion Rd Los Altos Hills CA 94022

WALD, ELFRIEDE, Kristwald-Kallfelz, Elfriede H.

WALDEN, LEA ANN, b. Goodlettsville, TN, Dec. 11, 1964; d. Jimmy Leroy and Carolyn O'lee (Wright) W. Contrbr. poems, short stories to bulltn., mags., anthols. Student U. of South, 1983-84, U. Ala., Huntsville, 1984—. English/Spanish tutor Spcl. Services, Huntsville, 1984-85; English tutor, lectr. Student Devel. Services, Huntsville, 1985—; piano tchr., Huntsville, 1986—. Home: 6500A Whispering Pines Trail Huntsville AL 35806

WALDMAN, ANNE LESLEY, b. Millville, NJ, Apr. 2, 1945; d. John Marvin and Frances (Le Fevre) Waldman; m. Reed Eyre Bye; 1 son—Ambrose. Author: (poetry) Baby Breakdown, 1970, Giant Night, 1970, No Hassles, 1971, Life Notes, 1973, Fast Speaking Woman, 1975, Journals and Dreams, 1976, First Baby Poems, 1983, Makeup on Empty Space, 1984, Invention, 1985, Skin Meat Bones, 1985, (prose) The Romane Thing, 1987; editor: (anthologies) The World Anthology, 1969, Another World, 1972, Talking Poetics From Naropa Institute vol. 1, 1978, vol. 2, 1979; publisher: Angel Hair Books, NYC, Full Court Press, NYC. BA, Bennington Coll., 1966. Dir. The Poetry Project, St. Marks Ch. In-the-Bowery (NYC), 1968-78; co-dir. Jack Kerouac Schl. of Poetics at Naropa Inst. (Boulder, CO), 1974—. Recipient Dylan Thomas Meml. award New Schl., NYC, 1967; CAPS grantee, 1976-77, NEA grantee, 1979-80. Mem. PEN. Office: Naropa Inst 2130 Arapahoe Ave Boulder CO 80302

WALDREP, PHIL, b. Decatur, AL, Sept. 12, 1960; s. Linnes Melton and Bynum Burneu (Kenum) W.; m. Debra Kay Gray, May 25, 1984. Author: How I Found the Will of God, 1987. Contrbg. ed.: Innovations, 1985-86. B.Min., L. Rice Coll., 1981; M.A., 1987. Pres. Phil Waldrep Evangelistic Assn., Trinity, AL, 1980—. Home: Box 148 Trinity AL 35673

WALDROP, ROSMARIE, b Kitzingen, W. Ger., Aug 24, 1935; arr U.S., 1958; d. Josef and Friederike (Wolgemuth) Sebald; m. Bernard Keith Waldrop, Jan. 22, 1959. Author: Against Language?, 1971; poetry: The Aggressive Ways of the Casual Stranger, 1972, The Road Is Everywhere or Stop This Body, 1978, When They Have Senses, 1980, Nothing Has Changed, 1981, Differences for Four Hands, 1984, Streets Enough to Welcome Snow, 1986; novel: The Hanky of Pippin's Daughter, 1986; transl. The Book of Questions by Edmond Jabes, 7 vols.), 1976, 66, 83, 84, The Vienna Group: Six Major Austrian Poets (with Harriett Watts), 1985. Student U. Freiburg, 1954-58; MA, U. Mich.-Ann Arbor, 1960, PhD, 1966. Asst. prof. Wesleyan Univ., Middletown, Conn., 1964-70; vis. lectr. Tufts U., Medford, Mass., 1980-82, Brown Univ., Providence, 1977-78, 83; ed./pub. Burning Deck Press, Providence, 1968—. Recipient Humboldt fellowship, Bonn, W. Ger, 1970-71; Howard Fdn. fellowship, 1974-75; transl. award, Columbia Univ., NYC, 1978; poetry fellowship, NEA, Washington, 1980. Mem. PEN. Address: 71 Elmgrove Providence RI 02906

WALKE, JULIA ANNETTE, b. Elkader, IA, March 9, 1908; d. Niels T. and Anna Marie (Olsen) Nelson; m. Delos Henry Walke, Oct. 30, 1938; children—Gary David, Donna May Walke McLane. Author: (poems) Colored Yarn, 1983. Contrbr. poems to lit. mags., anthols. BS in Comml. Edn., U. Northern Ia., 1932. Secy. Women's Orgn., Los Angeles, 1937, Ch. Bur., Cedar Falls, Ia., 1938. Recipient Book award N. Am. Mentor, 1972, Honors award, 1974, 77, 80; Hon. Mention in genl. div. Ia. Poetry Assn., 1973, 80, Harlan Miller 1st place, 1978; Hon. mention for brochure of poems Ia. Poetry Day Assn., 1973. Mem, Kappa Delta Pi, Pi Omega Pi. Home: 908 N Main St Box 55 Elkader IA 52043

WALKER, ALICE MALSENIOR, b. Eatonton, GA, Feb. 9, 1944; d. Willie Lee and Minnie (Grant) Walker; m. Melvyn R. Leventhal, Mar. 17, 1967 (div. 1977); 1 dau.—Rebecca Walker Leventhal. Author: Once, 1968, The Third Life of George Copeland, 1970, In Love and Trouble, 1973, Langston Hughes, American Poet, 1973, Meridian, 1976, I Love Myself When I Am Laughing, 1979, You Can't Keep a Good Woman Down, 1981, The Color Purple, 1982, In Search of Our Mothers' Gardens, 1983, Good Night, Willie Lee, I'll See You in the Morning, 1979, Revolutionary Petunias, 1974. BA, Sarah Lawrence Coll., 1966. Recipient Lillian Smith award, 1979, Rosenthal award Natl. Inst. Arts and Letters, 1973, Guggenheim Fdn. award, 1979, Am. Book award, 1983, Pulitzer prize, 1983. Office: HB7J Inc 757 3rd Ave New York NY 10017

WALKER, DONALD KNOX, b. Shawnee, OK, Feb. 12, 1943, s. Alwyn and ruth Jane (McCoy) W.; m. Nancetta Joyce Hudson, Aug. 10, 1966; children—Evan Hudson, Jonathan Frederick, Matthew Westmoreland. BFA, U. Okla., 1966. Wrtr. United Illuminating, Hew Haven, 1967-74; staff wrtr. Uniroyal, Inc., Middlebury, Conn., 1974-75; dir. publs., Wire Assn. Intl., Guilford, Conn., 1976-78; mng. dir. Conn. Motor Club, Hamden, ed. Conn. Motorist, 1979-82, ed. F&W Publs., Fairfield, Conn., 1982-86; columnist Artist's Mag.; ed. North Light Mag., 1983-85. Address: 32 Berwick Ct Fairfield CT 06430

WALKER, JEANNE MURRAY, b. Parkers Prairie, MN, May 27, 1944; d. John Gerald and Erna (Aderhold) Murray; m. E. Daniel Larkin, July 16, 1983; children—Molly Juliann Walker, John Edwin Daniel Larkin. Author: Nailing up the Home Sweet Home, 1980, Fugitive Angels, 1984; contrbr. poems to Poetry, American Poetry Rvw, Atlantic Monthly, and other mags. BA, Wheaton College, Wheaton, IL, 1966; PhD, U. of Penn., Phila., 1974. Asst. prof., Haverford College, Pa., 1974-79; assoc. prof., U. of Del., Newark, 1975—. Grants: Del. Arts Cncl., Penn. Arts Cncl., NEA. Mem. MLA, P&W, PEN. Home: 311 North 34th Street Philadelphia PA

19104

WALKER, LOIS VIRGINIA, b. Wheaton, IL, Oct. 23, 1929; d. Earl William and Gertrude Johanna (Wuster) Walker; m. Nicholas N. K. Kittrie, April 20, 1951 (div. 1957). Short story in New Letters, poetry in numerous lit mags inclg. Helicon Nine, West Branch, Small Pond, Dark Tower, Sojourner, Northwoods Journal. Ed. Xanadu, 1979-85, bus. mng. 1985—. BA and BS Ed., U. of Kansas, 1954; student, Columbia U., NYC, 1957-59. Tchr., School Dist. No. 17, Hicksville, NY 1954-86. Mem. PSA, P&W, Long Island Poetry Collective (chair 1980—). Home: 149 Harbor S Amityville NY 11701

WALKER, LOU ANN, b. Hartford City, IN, Dec. 9, 1952; d. Gale Freeman and Doris Jean (Wells) W.; m. Speed Vogel. Author: (children's book) Amy: The Story of a Deaf Child, 1985; A Loss of Words: The Story of Deafness in a Family (Christopher award for humanitarian writing, 1986), 1986. Asst. to mng. ed.: N.Y. Mag., 1976-77; assoc. ed.: Esquire, 1977-79, Diversion Mag., 1980-81; asst. to exec. ed.: Cosmopolitan, 1979-81; ed: Direct Mag., 1981-82. B.A., Harvard U., 1976. Cons. spl. project Museum of Modern Art, N.Y.C., 1982-84. Rockfeller grantee, 1983. Mem. AG. Home: Box 2131 Sag Harbor NY 11963

WALKER, PAMELA, b. Burlington, IA, Apr. 28, 1948; d. Ronald Russell and Helen (Anderson) Walker; m. Edgar Mac Denniston, Nov. 23, 1968 (div. Dec. 1972); m. 2d, Richard Alan Munde, June 30, 1985. Author: (novel) Twyla, 1973. Contrbr. short story to children's mag. BS, Ia. State U., 1970; MFA, U. Ia., 1973. Cons., CBS, NYC, 1979-81, NYC Bd. Edn., 1984; pvt. tutor Riverdale Country Schl., Bronx, N.Y., 1976—. Mem. P&W. Home: 210 W 101st St 4C New York NY 10025

WALKER, ROBERT WAYNE, b. Corinth, MS, Nov. 17, 1948, s. Richard Herman and Janie Elizabeth (McEachern) W.; m. Cheryl Ann Ernst, Sept. 8, 1967; 1 child, Stephen Robert. Author: Sub-Zero, 1979, Daniel Webster Jackson & The Wrongway Railway, 1982, Brain Watch, 1985, Search for the Nile, 1986, Salem's Child, 1987, Aftershock, 1987, Disembodied, 1988. BS in Edn., Northwestern U., 1971, MS in English Edn., 1972. Assoc. registrar Northwestern U., Evanston, Ill., 1972-77; with Am. Dietetic Assn., Chgo., 1977-81; full-time writer, 1981—. Mem. WG of America, Horror Wrtrs of America. Home: Rt 2 Old Market Rd Potsdam NY 13676

WALKER, SUE BRANNAN, b. Montgomery, AL, Apr. 6; d. Louie W. and Katherine (King) Brannan; m. Ronald Walker; children—Wesley, James, Jason. Author: (poems) Traveling My Shadow. Contrbr. poems to anthols., lit. mags. Wrkg. on biography of Jefferson Davis in sonnets. B.S., Univ. of Alabama, 1961; M.A., M.Ed., Tulane U., 1976, ph.D., 1979.Assoc. prof. U. South Ala., Mobile, 1979—; pub. Negative Capability, Mobile, 1981—. Recipient Grand prize Ala. Wrtr.'s Conclave, 1984; Faculty Service award U. South Ala., 1987; named Outstanding Career Woman, Gayfers, Mobile, 1983; fellow Ala. Council on the Arts, 1987. Mem. Natl. League Am. PEN Women (v.p. 1986-87), Ala. State Poetry Soc. (pres. 1986 —), PSA, P&W. Home: 62 Ridgelawn Dr E Mobile AL 36608

WALKER, WILBERT LEE, b. Durham, NC, Jul. 22, 1925; s. James Henry and Nancy Catherine (Herring) Walker; m. Grace Mary Clayborne, Jun. 15, 1951; 1 son—Ronald Lee. Author: We Are Men: Memoirs of World War II and the Korean War, 1972; novels: The Pride of Our Hearts, 1978, Stalemate at Panmunjon, 1980, Servants of All, 1982, The Deputy's Dilemma, (memoir), 1987. BA, Morgan State U., 1950; M Social Work, Howard U., 1954. Field supervisor MD State Dept. of Welfare (Baltimore), 1961-66, coordinator local operations, 1966-73; deputy dir. Dept. of Human Resources (Baltimore), 1973-80; president Heritage Press (Baltimore), 1980—. Bd. mem. Baltimore NAACP. Office: Box 18625 Baltimore MD 21216

WALKINGTON, ETHLYN LINDLEY, b. Fairmount, IN, Oct. 8, 1895; d. Gurney and Adella (Hobson) Lindley; m. Laurence H. Walkington, Nov. 4, 1926 (dec. Oct. 15, 1957); children—James Laurence, William Gurney, Lindley Joseph (dec.). Author: Journey Through a Century, 1966, Gently Down the Stream, 1981. Contrbr. articles to books, mags, newspapers. Student Friends U., Wichita, Kans., 1913-1915; U. Chgo., 1917. Tchr. English high schls. in Ill., Kans., Id., Ariz., 1918-26. Mem. AAUW, Id. Wrtrs. League (2d prize for serious verse 1971, for juvenile fiction 1971, for article 1978, 1st prize for juvenile fiction, 1969, for article 1976, 3rd prize for serious verse, 1984). Home: 470 Ostrander N Twin Falls ID 83301

WALKOWICZ, CHRIS J., b. Rockford, IL, Apr. 20, 1943; d. Roy and Myrtle J. (Nelson) Ippen; m. Edward Walkowicz, May 2, 1964; children—Edward Dean, Teresa Ann Walkowicz Viernow, Michael Mark, Joshua Peter. Author: Successful Dog Breeding: Complete Handbook of Canine Midwifery, 1985, The Bearded Collie, 1987, Atlas of Dog Breeds: Dogs for All Reasons, 1988, Complete Book of Questions and Answers on Dogs, 1988; columnist: Daily Dispatch, Moline, IL, 1980-85. Contrbr. articles to numerous mags., newspapers including Dog Fancy, Am. Kennel Gazette, Capper's Weekly, others. Ed: For Pet's Sake column, 1985-86, Quad City Dog Club Cookbook, 1978, Saintly Salads at Your Request, 1985. Grad. public schls., Rockford. Editorial asst. Today Pubs., Rock Island, IL, 1985-87; free-lance wrtr., ed., 1987—. Asst. librarian Sherrard Public Library, IL, 1978-85. Recipient non-fiction, photography awards Miss. Valley Wrtrs. Conf., 1985, 87. Mem. Dog Wrtrs. Assn. Am. (Book of Yr. award 1985, column and feature awards, 1981, 82, 83, 85, 86, 87), NLAPW. Home: Rt 1 Box CA 33 Sherrard IL 61281

WALL, ISABELLE LOUISE WOOD, (Isa Lou Woods), b. Traphill, NC, Oct. 26, 1909, d. Charlie William and Nelia Elizabeth (Wood) Wood; m. Albert Wall, Feb. 16, 1929; children—Fred Wade, Bernice Adelene Wall Gengo. Author: Time's Beautiful Way, Sandstones of Time, Spiritual Steps, Susan Ahern's Love Letters from Heaven, Theklae of Iconium (40-60 AD); contrbr. to anthologies, newspapers, mags. Wrkg. on "Milestones," and History of Traphill. Mem. Intl. Platform Assoc. for several years, Republican Senatorial Com., pres. and founder Intl. Miracle Fellowship, 1959—. Home: 3231 High Point Rd Winston-Salem NC 27107

WALL, ROBERT EMMET, b. NYC, Apr. 29, 1937; s. Robert Emmet and Sabina (Daly) Wall; m. regina Palasek, Aug. 1, 1959; children—Elizabeth, Nina, Amy, Christopher, Craig. Author: Massachusetts Bay, The Crucial Decade, 1640-1650, 1972, The Canadians, Vol. I (Blackrobe), 1981, Vol. II (Bloodbrothers), 1981, Vol III (Birthright), 1982, Vol. IV (The Patriots), 1982. BA, Holy Cross Coll., 1960; MA, Yale U., 1961, PhD, 1965. Asst. in instrn. Yale U. (New Haven), 1963; instr. history Duke U. (Durham, NC), 1963-65; asst. prof. Mich. State U. (East Lansing), 1965-69, assoc. prof. history, 1970; assoc. prof. Concordia U. (Sir George Williams U.) (Montreal, Que., Can.), 1971-72, prof., 1972-80, chair dept., 1972-77, dean, 1977-80; provost Farleigh Dickinson U. (Rutherford, NJ), 1980—. Office: 217 Montross Ave Rutherford NJ 07070

WALL, THOMAS J. (G. Bear), b. Bayonne, NJ, Mar. 21, 1958; s. Robert Merritt and Anne Marie (Doolan) W. Ed., Scrivener's Review, 1981-83; contbr. arts. to: CARET, 1979-80, Fordham Urban Law Jnl., 1983. BA, Rutgers, 1980; JD, Fordham Law Schl., 1983. Attorney, North Bergen, NJ, 1983—. American Jurisprudence Constitutional Law Award, 1981. Home: 83 West 30th St Bayonne NJ 07002

WALLACE, ALFRED LEON, b. Rome, GA, Apr. 24, 1931; s. Howard Marion and Leola (Corley) W. Poetry in anthologies. Wrkg. on nove letters. Student writing courses. Janitorial supr. Northwest Ga. Regional Hosp., Rome, 1961—. Home: 28 Battey Dr Rome GA 30161

WALLACE, BETTY FRANCES ABERNATHY, b. Gastonia, NC, June 28, 1926, d. Thomas Jackson and Emma Frances (Glenn) Abernathy; m. William Andrew Wallace, Jr., Sept. 4, 1948; children—Rebecca Abernathy, Janet Lynn, William Scott. Author: Through a Time Sieve (Dixie Council of Authors & Jnlsts. "Author of the Yr. Award in Poetry"), 1985; contrbr. poetry: The Wrtr., Lincoln Log, N.Am., New York Herald-Tribune editorial page, 1966. Mentor, numerous other mags.; contrbr. poetry to anthologies including: Book of Charter Year, 1980, Journeys of the Poet/Prophet, 1983, One Score and Two Years of Uncommon Fanfare, 1985, BFA, U. Ga., 1948; postgrad., Ga. State U., 1967-71, West Ga. Coll., 1980-81. Elem. schl. tchr., tchr. of gifted, Ga., 1966—. Recipient awards numerous state poetry socs, First Place, New York Poetry Forum, 1984, Teacher of the Year, Henry County Junior High School, 1986-87, Daniel Whitehead Hicky natl Award, 1983, North American Mentor award, 1983, 1984. Mem. AAUW, Ga. State Poetry Soc. (charter mem.). Home: 30 Woodlawn Ave Hampton GA 30228

WALLACE, GORDON, b. Belle Plaine, KS, Nov. 10, 1909; s. Clarence Blucher and Edna (Wallace) Wallace; m. Florence Evelyn Tidlund, Apr. 8, 1938 (div. June, 1942); 1 son—Roy Neil; 2nd m. Mary Marie Condra, July 2, 1943; children—Barbara Ann, Diane. Author: Random Journey, 1979, The Valiant Heart, 1982; contributor: A Stillness Heard Around the World (author: Stanley Weintraub), 1985. BA, U. of Michigan, 1946; MA, San Francisco State Coll., 1969, Arizona State U., 1976. Registrar-Admissions Prescott Center Coll. (AZ), 1976-77; freelance author, 1978—; publisher Lamplighter Press (Prescott), 1982—. Lt. Col., US Army, 1942-65, Japan, Austria, Germany. Mem. Vets of the Battle of the Bulge. Home: 102 Aztec St Prescott AZ 86301

WALLACE, IRVING, b. Chgo., Mar. 19, 1916; s. Alexander and Bessie (Liss) Wallace; m. Sylvia Kahn, June 3, 1941; children—David, Amy. Freelance writer: articles, short stories, others, 1931-53; author: The Fabulous Originals, 1955, The Square Pegs, 1957, The Fabulous Showman, 1959, The Sins of Philip Fleming, 1959, The Chapman Report, 1960, The Twenty-Seventh Wife, 1961, The Prize, 1962, The Three

Sirens, 1963, The Man (George Washington Carver Inst. 1965), 1964 (Paperback of Year award), The Sunday Gentleman, 1965, The Plot, 1967, The Writing of One Novel, 1968, The Seven Minutes, 1969, The Nympho and Other Maniacs, 1971, The Word, 1972, The Fan Club, 1974 (Popular Culture Assn. award of excellence), The People's Almanac, 1975, The R Document, 1976, The Book of Lists, 1977, The Two, 1978, The People's Almanac 2, 1978, The Pigeon Project, 1979, The Book of Lists 2, 1980, The Second Lady, 1980, The Book of Predictions, 1981, The Intimate Sex Lives of Famous People, 1981, The People's Almanac 3, 1981, The Almighty, 1982, The Book of Lists 3, 1983, Significa, 1983, The Miracle, 1984, The Seventh Secret, 1986, The Celestial Bed, 1987; contrbr. to: Encyc. Brit. Student, Williams Inst., Berkeley, Calif. Served with USAF, Signal Corps, AUS, 1942-46. Mem. AG Am., PEN, Soc. Authors (London). Address: Box 49328 Los Angeles CA 90049

WALLACE, LEW GERALD, b. Covington, KY, Nov. 15, 1946; s. Lew and Alice (Kepler) W.; m. Judith Dayle Gresh, Feb. 28, 1968. Contrbr. numerous features, book rvws., articles to mags., newspapers; ed. residential real estate and automobile sects. in newspapers. BA in Psychology, U. of So. Fla., 1972; M.A. in Psychology, La. State U., 1975. Ed., wrtr., photographer Morning Advocate State Times, Baton Rouge, LA, 1978—. Home: 1663 Keed Ave Baton Rouge LA 70806

WALLACE, ROBERT, b. Springfield, MO, Jan. 10, 1932; s. Roy Franklin and Tincy Pauline (Stough) W.; m. Christine Marie Seidler, May 1, 1982. Author textbook: Writing Poems, 1982; poetry: This Various World, 1957, Views from a Ferris Wheel, 1965, Ungainly Things, 1968, Critters, 1978, Swimmer in the Rain, 1979, Girlfriends and Wives, 1984. BA, Harvard U., 1953; MA, Cambridge U., England, 1955. Instr., Bryn Mawr (PA) Coll., 1957-61; asst. prof. Sweet Briar (VA) Coll., 1961-63, Vassar Coll., Poughkeepsie, NY, 1963-65; prof. Case Western Reserve, Clevelend, 1965—. Individual Artists Grant, NEA, 1984. Home: 2199 Delaware Dr Cleveland OH 44106

WALLACE, RONALD LYNN, b. Gainesville, FL, Dec. 10, 1945, s. Talmadge A. and Katharine (Forman) W.; m. Susan Ann Wallace, Sept. 8, 1978. Author: Those Who Have Vanished: An Introduction to Prehistory, 1983; contrbr. to The History of Juvenile Delinquency, 1986. BA, U. Fla., 1967, PhD, 1975. Assoc. prof. anthropology U. Central Fla., Orlando, 1975—. Served with U.S. Army, 1967-70. Atlantic Center for Arts fellow, 1986. Mem. profl. orgns. Office: Box 25000 Orlando FL 32816

WALLACE, RONALD W., b. Cedar Rapids, IA, Feb. 18, 1945; s. William Edward Wallace and Loretta Martha (Kamprath) Rusch; m. Margaret Elizabeth McCreight, Aug. 3, 1968; 2 daus. Molly Elizabeth, Emily Katherine. Author: Henry James and The Comic Form, 1975, The Last Laugh, 1979, God Be With The Clown, 1984; poetry: Installing the Bees, 1977, Cucumbers, 1978, The Facts of Life, 1979, Plums, Stones, Kisses & Hooks, 1981, Tunes for Bears to Dance To, 1983, The Owl in the Kitchen, 1985, People and Dog in the Sun (poems), 1987. BA, Coll. of Wooster, 1963-67; PhD, U. Mich.-Ann Arbor, 1968-71. Prof. English and dir. Creative Writing Univ. Wis., Madison, 1972—. Recipient Hopwood Award for Poetry, Univ. Mich., Ann Arbor, 1970; Disting. Tchg. Award Univ. Wis., Madison, 1984; Helen Bullis Prize, Poetry Northwest, Seattle, 1985; ACLS Fellowships, 1975, 81. Mem P&W, AWP, Council Wis. Writers. Address: 2220 Chamberlain Ave Madison WI 53705

WALLACE, THOMAS C(HRISTOPHER), b. Vienna, Austria, Dec. 13, 1933; s. Don and Julia (Baer) Wallace; m. Lois Kahn, July 19, 1962; 1 son—George Baer. BA, Yale U., 1955, MA in History, 1957. Editor G.P. Putnam (NYC), 1959-63; with Holt, Rinehart & Winston (NYC), 1963—, editor-in-chief genl. books div., 1968-81; vp, sr. editor Simon & Schuster (NYC), 1981; editor W.W. Norton (NYC), 1982-87; literary agent (NYC), 1987—. Mem. PEN. Home: 45 E 82nd St New York NY 10028

WALLACH, IRA, b. NYC, Jan. 22, 1913; s. Morris David and Rose (Sims) Wallach; m. Devera Sievers, Jan. 25, 1941; 1 dau.—Leah; m. 2d, Lillian Opatoshu, June 4, 1970. Author: The Horn and the Roses, 1947, How to Be Deliriously Happy, 1949, Hopalong-Freud, 1951, Hopalong-Freud Rides Again, 1950, Gutenberg's Folly, 1954, How to Pick a Wedlock, 1956, Muscle Beach, 1959, The Absence of a Cello, 1960, Horatio, 1954, Phoenix 55, 1955, (with A.S. Ginnes) Drink to Me Only, 1958; play Smiling, The Boy Fell Dead, 1961; screenplay Boys' Night Out, 1962, (with George Goodman) The Wheeler-Dealers, Absence of a Cello; play, 1964, (with Peter Ustinov), screenplay Hot Millions (Motion Picture Acad. nomination, 1968, Writers Guild of Gt. Britain award for best Brit. comedy screenplay 1968), Five Thousand Years of Foreplay, 1976. Student, Cornell. Mem. AG Am., DG, WG Am., PEN. Home: 345 W 58th St New York NY 10019

WALLEK, LEE, (The World's Foremost Litcrit), b. Lachine, MN, May 26, 1908; s. Lyman R. and Liza B. (Lee) W.; m. Pearl (Price), Feb. 3, 1933; children—Wayne, Wanda. BA, Augustana Coll., 1931; MA, U. Fla., 1939. Mag. and encyc. ed., Chgo., 1946-58; hrdwr. str. owner, 1959-70; free-lance ed., 1959—; assoc. ed., Candid Press, Chgo., 1970-72; lit. ed. December Mag., 1962—; sr. ed. ABA, 1983-84. Editor: 2 chaps. A Manual of Style (12th ed.). Author: The Forbidden Writings of Lee Wallek (essays), 1977. Wrkg. on story of Torrio and Capone in Chgo. Named Columnist of Yr. (Chgo.), 1971. Served USN 1941-46. Mem. Caxton Club, Club d'Ronde, NWU. Home: Box 302 Highland Park IL 60035

WALLER, GARY F., b. Auckland, N.Z., Jan. 3, 1944, came to U.S., 1983, s. Fred and Joan Elsie (Smythe) W.; m. Jennifer Waller, July 2, 1966 (div. 1980); children—Michael Richard, Andrew Nicholas. Author: The Strong Necessity of Time, 1976, Pamphilia to Amphilanthus, 1977, Mary Sidney Countess of Pembroke, 1977, The Triumph of Death, 1979, Dreaming America, 1979, Sir Philip Sidney and the Interpretation of Renaissance Culture, 1983, Impossible Futures Indelible Pasts, 1983, Sixteenth Century English Poetry, 1986, Reading Texts, 1987, Lexington Introduction to Literature, 1986. BA, U. Auckland, 1965, MA, 1966; PhD, Cambridge (Eng.) U., 1970. Assoc. prof. Dalhousie U., Halifax, N.S., Can., 1972-78; prof., chmn. dept. Wilfrid Laurier U., Waterloo, Can., 1978-83; prof. lit. studies, head English, Carnegie Mellon U., Pitts., 1983—. Office: Eng Carnegie Mellon U Pittsburgh PA 15213

WALLERSTEDT-WEHRLE, JOANNA KATHERINE, b. Columbus, IN, Sept. 14, 1944; d. George Lawrence and Anna Charlotte (Wheeldon) Wallerstedt; m. Jason William Wehrle, June 24, 1979; children: Christina Jo, Michelle Lynn, Gina Rene; grandchildren: Justin Ryan, Ashley Nicole. Author: poems in various anthologies (Words of Praise, Impressions, Heart Songs, others), song lyrics, short articles. Grad. Charlottesville H.S., Charlottesville, IN. Student, Indiana Univ., 1967-69. Social Worker, Columbus, IN., 1975-78; medical aid, Riley Nursing Home, Greenfield, IN, 1978-81; pres. day care ctr., Indpls., 1981-85. Home: 4141 N Elmhurst Dr Indianapolis IN 46226

WALLING, DANA MCNEIL, b. Los Angeles, Jan. 1, 1950, s. Jess Willard and Theresa Fran (Miller) W.; m. Lou Ann Elaine Hill, June 19, 1971; children—Aaron McNeil, Nicole Donise. Contrbg. writer Source mag., 1979-80; book and record rvw. columnist Bread mag., 1980—; contrbg. columnist One mag., 1979-83; contrbr. articles to religious publs. BA, Pasadena Coll., 1972; MRE, Nazarene Theol. Sem., Kansas City, Mo., 1982. Assoc. minister 1st Ch. of Nazarene, Mpls., 1974-77, Boise, Idaho, 1977-80, Westside Ch. of Nazarene, Olathe, Kans., 1980-82; minister Ch. of Nazarene, Carpinteria, Calif., 1982-84; assoc. dean student devel. Point Loma Nazarene Coll., San Diego, 1984—. Home: 3025 Tennyson San Diego CA 92106

WALLIS, WILLIAM GEORGE, b. Eustis, FL, Feb. 13, 1946, s. Ray and Ruth Jean (Crooks) W.; m. Mary Cynthia Doty, Nov. 3, 1968 (div. 1977); m. 2d, Leslie Erin Horn, July 11, 1982; 1 son, Asher David. Author poetry vols. Poems, 1972, Biographer's Notes, 1984; contrbr. to Colo. Qtly, Prairie Schooner, Hanblecheya/The Vision, A Meeting of Cultures, numerous other lit. publs. BA with highest honors in English, So. Ill. U., 1969; PhD, U. Nebr., 1972. Asst. prof. U. Neb., 1972-74; mem. faculty Am. Inst. Mus. Studies, Graz, Austria, 1978-80; postdoctoral study Hannover Conservatory, 1978-80; postdoctoral fellow UCLA, 1983-84; lectr. U. Calif., Santa Barbara, 1984—; engaged as tenor for opera 1980-83 in Hof and Kaiserslautern, concerts in W. Germany and Austria, 1978-83. NDEA fellow, 1969-72; ethnic studies grantee HEW, 1974-76. Mem. Actors Equity. Home: 833 S Stanley Ave Los Angeles CA 90036

WALLS, DWAYNE ESTES, b. Morganton, NC, May 16, 1932; s. William Roy and Dora (Buchanan) Walls; m. Judith Ann Michaels, Sept. 20, 1958; children—Helen Elizabeth, Dwayne Estes. Author: The Chickenbone Special, 1970, The Kidwells, 1980. Student, Lenoir Rhyne Coll., 1950, 53-54, U. NC, 1954-57. Staff writer Durham Sun (NC), 1955, Durham Morning Herald, 1956-58; news editor Chapel Hill Weekly (NC), 1958-60; staff writer Charlotte Observer (NC), 1961-71; freelance writer, 1962—; research assoc. Duke, 1972-73; lectr. NC State U., 1977-79, U. NC at Chapel Hill, 1979—. Served with USAF, 1951-53. Recipient George Polk Meml. Awd., Sidney Hillman Fdn. Awd. Mem. NCCJ, Am. Poli. Sci. Assn., US Office Econ. Opportunity, NC Press Assn., Sigma Delta Chi. Address: Box 25 Bear Creek Rd Pittsboro NC 27312

WALSH, ABIGAIL MARGARET, b. NYC., Aug. 8, 1935; d. Vincent Francis and Teresa Alice (Ward) Walsh; m. Arthur Charles McDonell, Dec. 17, 1955 (div. 1978); 1 dau., Lillian Leslie. Author: Kitty Cat, 1988; contrbr. short stories, articles: Short Story Internat., Bittersweet, Skylark, Maine, others. Wrkg. on children's fiction. BA, Queens Coll., 1969, MS, 1973. Tchr. public schs., Hicksville, N.Y., 1969-80, Machiasport, Me., 1983—. Mem. Soc. Children's Book Wrtrs., NWC, Me. Wrtrs. and Pubs. Alliance, ednl. orgns. Home: RR 1 Box 642 Gouldsboro ME 04607

WALSH, DONALD JAMES, b. Amery, WI, Apr. 3, 1949; s. Donald James and Pearl Josephine (Hecht) W; m. Chery Lynette Leyde, Dec. 28, 1979; children—Brianna Lynn, Colin Patrick. Author, ed.: Current Matters, 1973—, Short Circuits, 1976—, Dairyland Power Annual Reports, 1979—. Contrbr. to outdoor mags., newspapers. Wrkg. on outdoor free lancing. B.A. in Jnlsm., U. Wis., Eau Claire, 1971. Communicaitons ed. Gateway Transportation Co., Inc., LaCrosse, WI, 1971-73; info. specialist Dairyland Power Cooperative, LaCrosse, 1973—, ed., pubs. specialis, 1973—, mgr. employee communications, 1981—; free-lance wrtr., 1969—. Lee Hench Jnlsm. Scholar, U. Wis., 1970; recipient 1st and 2d place Trucking Industry Public Relations Coordinating Com., 1972, 1st place, 1973. Mem. IABC (Gold quill 1980). Home: 3113 S 29th Ct LaCrosse WI 54601

WALSH, DORIS MONTAGUE HUNTLEY, b. Syracuse, d. Lyman Herbert and Eleanor (Montague) Huntley; m. Harold James Walsh, Apr. 25, 1936; children—David, Peter, Laurence, John, Susan (adopted), 22 foster children. Author: God's Children, 1970, Gifts From Above, 1971, 2d ed., 1979, Lucy Lupus Wolf, 1981; ed., pub. "The Recorder," newsletter for Lupus Erythematosis patients and brochures on subject. Wrkg. on poetry, children's story, novel, autobiography. Ed. N.Y. Inst. Journalism. Founder, pres., exec. dir. Central N.Y. Lupus Fdn., Syracuse, 1972-76; columnist Camilus Advocate, Syracuse, Syracuse Post-Standard. Recipient numerous awards for activities in city, state and national Lupus crusade as well as civic and health orgn. vol. efforts. Mem. Nat. League Penwomen (past recording sec., chaplain Central N.Y. chap.), Syracuse Press Club. Home: 200 Bronson Rd Syracuse NY 13219

WALSH, EILEEN CECILE, b. Chgo., Apr. 11, 1914; d. Dennis J. and Emily C. (McMahon) Clifford; m. Ailbe M. Walsh, Feb. 8, 1947 (dec. June 9, 1986); 1 dau., Mary Denise. Contrbr. articles to newspapers including Chgo. Tribune. Ed.: Teen-Mail, 1960-62, Hospital Monthly Mag., 1970-80, Volunteer Pub. at J. F. Kennedy Med. Ctr., at Gottlieb Meml. Hosp. Wrkg. on humorous articles relating to seniors and widowhood. Student Northwestern U., LaSalle Extension U. Dir. volunteers Gottlieb Meml. Hosp., Melrose Park, IL, 1965-68; dir. public relations J. F. Kennedy Med. Ctr., Chgo., 1970-81; now free-lance wrtr. Recipient Gold Medal and Blue Ribbon awards Dartnell Corp., Chgo., 1940-50. Home: 49 N Park Ave 601 Lombard IL 60148

WALSH, GEORGE WILLIAM, b. NYC, Jan. 16, 1931; s. William Francis and Madeline (Maass) Walsh; m. Joan Mary Dunn, May 20, 1961; children—Grail, Simon. Author: Gentleman Jimmy Walker, 1974, Public Enemies, 1980; contrbr. articles to popular mags. BS, Fordham U., 1952; MS, Columbia U., Schl. Journalism, 1953. Copy editor, reporter Cape Cod Standard-Times (Hyannis, MA), 1955; communications specialist IBM (NYC), 1955-58; editorial trainee Time, Inc., 1958-59; writer-reporter Sports Illus. (NYC), 1959-62; book editor, Cosmopolitan (NYC), 1962-65, mng. ed., 1965-74; ed.-in-chief, vp Ballantine Books div. Random House (NYC), 1974-79, Macmillan Pub. Co. (NYC), 1979-85; publishing cons, 1985—. Served with AUS, 1953-55. Mem. Assn. Am. Pubs. Home: 597 4th St Brooklyn NY 11215

WALSH, JOY, b. East Liverpool, OH, May 3, 1935; d. John Richard Staley; m. Thomas James, July 20, 1957; 2 sons, Christopher John, Thomas James Jr. Author poetry: Locating Positions, 1978, The Absent Are Always in the Wrong, 1985, essays: Kerouac: Statement in Brown, 1984; novels: Hymn to Prometheus Transistor, 1985, Driver: Sixteen Gears and Lonely, 1986. BA in English, SUNY-Buffalo, 1975, MA in Humanities, 1979. Ed. and pres. Moody St. Irregs., Inc., Clarence Ctr., N.Y., 1978—. Recipient wrtr.-in-res. awards Allentown Community Ctr., Buffalo, 1984, San Diego State Coll., 1985; arts council publ. grants, Buffalo, 1985, 86, 87. Address: Moody Street Irregulars, Inc. PO Box 157#Clarence Center NY 14032

WALSH, LOREN MELFORD, b. Valparaiso, IN, July 22, 1927; s. Melford Lee and Lois Ada (Beehler) Walsh; m. Shirley B. Hepner, June 21, 1944; children—Lauren Jo, Cindy harper, Robin, Jeannette, Cathy. BA, Valparaiso U., 1951. Quality engr. Stephens Adamson Co. (Aurora, IL), 1951-54, mgr. quality assurance, 1954-59, dir. quality assurance, 1959-68, dir. tech. services, 1968-69; editor Quality Mag., Hitchcock Pub. Co. PhD, Wheaton, IL), 1970—; pres. Hitchcock Pub. Co., 1981—; dir. Aurora Bearing Co. (Batavia, IL). Served with AUS, med. corps, 1945-47. Office: Hitchcock 25 W 550 Geneva Rd Wheaton IL 60188

WALSH, MIKE, b. Limestone, ME, Aug. 17, 1955; s. John Martin Jr. and Bernadette Marie (McCool) W. Editor mag. Expresso Tilt; short stories in Writ (U. Toronto), Fiction '84, Label, Exile & Planet Detroit mag. BA, Temple U., 1978; MA, Colo. State U., 1983. Editor, pub. Expresso Tilt, Philadelphia, PA, 1984—. Home: 737 Wharton St Philadelphia PA 19147

WALT, DICK K., b. Thayer, KS, Nov. 28, 1935; s. Asa Bartlett and Vivian (Russell) Walt; m. Bonnie Gregory, Sept. 15, 1967; 1 dau. by previous marriage—Sarah Margaret. BJ, U. Kan., 1957. With Topeka Daily Capital, 1957-58, 60-61; with Am. Med. News, publ. AMA (Chgo.), 1961—, mng. editor, 1965-71, exec. editor, 1971-82, editor, 1982—. Home: 551 W Deming Pl Chicago IL 60614

WALTERS, CLARA OAKLEY, (Cokey McGee, Hudson McGee), b. Hodgenville, KY, Dec. 5, 1939; d. Samuel McGee and Jessie Bernice (Marcum) W. Contrbr. poems, essays, articles, short stories to mags., anthols., newspapers including Guideposts, Newsweek Mag., others. Wkg. on novel, short story, essay, poetry. A.B. in English and Spanish, Belmont Coll., 1961; M.A. in Comparative Lit., Ind. U., 1972. English/Spanish tchr. public schls., KY, TN, IN, HI, OH, 1961-82. Recipient awards World of Poetry, 1984-87. Address: 7450 Larissa Ct Dayton OH 45414

WALTERS, MARY DAWSON, b. Mitchell County, GA, Oct. 6, 1923; d. William Henry and Carrie Lou (Richardson) Dawson; m. William Gantt, 1977; children by previous marriage—Marjorie, Robert H. McCoy. Published: A Catalog of the Exhibition of Selected Private Presses in the U.S., 1965, Black History Holdings of the Ohio State University Libraries, Afro-Americana, 1969. BSHE, Savannah State Coll., 1949; MS in LS, Atlanta U., 1957; postgrad. in Rusian, Ohio State U., Columbus, 1963. Librarian Carver Jr. High Schl. (Albany, GA), 1956-57; dir. Albany State Coll. Library, 1957-61; vis. prof. Schl. Library Services Atlanta U., 1964; asst. prof. library adminstrn., head div. processing Ohio State U. Library, 1961-71, assoc. prof., head div. processing Ohio State U. Library, 1961-71, assoc. prof., head dept. acquisitions, 1971-74; assoc. librarian, chief acquisitions librarian Calif. State U. at Los Angeles, 1974-77, librarian, collection devel. officer, 1977—. Recipient Dir's. Citation of Merit award Ohio State U. Libraries, 1963. Mem. ALA (councilor at large 1982-86), Calif. Library Assn. Home: 1659 W 81st St Los Angeles CA 90047

WALTERS, RAYMOND JR., b. Bethlehem, PA, Aug. 23, 1912; s. Raymond and Elsie (Rosenberg) Walters. Author: Alexander James Dallas: Lawyer, Politician, Financier, 1943, Albert Gallatin: Jeffersonian Financier and Diplomat, 1957 (named One of Notable Books of Year, ALA), The Virginia Dynasty, 1965, Paperback Talk, 1985. AB, Swarthmore Coll., 1933; postgrad., Princeton U., 1933-35; MA, Columbia U., 1937, PhD, 1942. Editorial staff Current History mag., 1937-39; editorial staff Saturday Rvw., 1946-58, book rvw. editor, 1948-58; editor Encore mag., 1946-48; assoc. editor, columnist NY Times Book Rvw., 1958—; mem. fiction jury Pulitzer Prize adv. bd., 1968. Served with USAF, 1942-46; hist. office hdqrs. USAF, 1943-46. Mem. Am. Hist. Assn., Soc. Am. Historians (vp), PEN. Home: 315 E 68th St New York NY 10021

WALTON, CHELLE KOSTER, b. Dubuque, IA, Mar. 9, 1954; d. Eugene J. and Theresa A. (Luchsinger) Koster; m. Robert W. Walton, July 7, 1984. Contrbr. articles to mags., newspapers including Cricket Mag., Ft. Lauderdale News, Discovery; columnist: Islander Newspaper, 1985—. Ed.: Post-Rvw., North Branch, MN, 1979-80; food ed.: Fort Lauderdale Mag., 1987. B.A., U. Minn, 1976. Dir. public relations MSF Tchrs. Credit Union, St. Paul, 1980-82; freelance wrtr., 1983—. Mem. Fla. Freelance Wrtrs.' Assn. (3d place for humor 1984, 1st place for juvenile non-fiction 1986). Home: 449 Lagoon Sanibel FL 33957

WALTON, CLARENCE, b. Scranton, PA, June 22, 1915; s. Leo and Mary (Southard) Walton; m. Elizabeth Kennedy, June 1, 1946; children—Thomas Michael, Mary Elizabeth. Author: Corporate Social Responsibilities, Big Government and Big Business, 1968, Ethos and The Executive, 1969, Management's Rights and Prerogatives: Quo Warranto; co-author: Conceptual Foundations of Business, 1966, Man and the City of the Future, 1971; editor: Ethics of Corporate Conduct, 1977, Inflation and National Survival, 1979; co-editor: The Business System, 1966, Disorder in Higher Education, 1979. BA, U. Scranton, 1937; MA, Syracuse U., 1938; PhD, Cath. U., 1951. Social Sci. instr. Duquesne U., 1940; prof., chair dept. history and poli. sci. U. Scranton, 1946-53; dean Duquesne U. (Schl. Bus. Administrn.), 1953-58; assoc. dean, prof. Grad. Schl. Bus. Columbia U., 1958-64, dean Schl. Genl. Studies, 1964-69, prof. Grad. Schl. Bus., 1978-80; pres. Cath. U. Am., 1969-78; Charles Lamont Post disting. prof. Am. Coll., 1980—; Penfield fellow Inst. Advanced Intl. Studies (Geneva, Switzerland), 1951-52; dir. Banner Life Ins. Co., Peavey Co. Mem. Scranton Schl. Bd., 1948-52; chair Gov.'s Commn. on Pa. Housing, 1956-57, Pres.'s Panel on Non-Public Edn., 1975-76. Served as lt. USNR, 1942-46. Dir. The Am. Assembly, Rosemount Coll. Home: 1336 Montgomery Ave Rosemont PA 19010

WALTON, CLYDE CAMERON, b. Chgo., Mar. 8, 1925; s. Clyde Cameron and Helen L. (Williams) Walton; m. Anne Hoover, 1946 (div. 1979); children—James R., Jean A., Julia L., 2nd m. Patricia Senn Breivik, July 7, 1979; 1 son—Kenneth A. Breivik. Founder, past editor: Civil War History; editor: Jnl Ill. State Hist. Soc., 1956-67, Indian War of 1864, 1960, An Illinois Gold Hunter in the Black Hills, 1960, John Francis Snyder, Selected Writings, 1962, Behind the Guns: The History of Battery I, 1965, Mr. Lincoln Opens His Mail, 1967, Illinois Reader, 1970. AB, Cornell Coll., Iowa, 1948; AM, U. Chgo., 1950; LittD, Lincoln Coll., 1956. Asst. in charge Serials-Res. Library, State U. Iowa, 1950-51, curator rare books, Univ. archivist, instr. bibliography, 1951-55, head reference dept., asst. prof., 1955-56; state historian Ill. Hist. Library, 1956-67; exec. dir. Ill. Hist. Soc., 1956-67; assoc. prof., dir. libraries No. Ill. U., 1967-77, chair athletic bd., 1969-74; dir. libraries, prof. U. Colo. at Boulder, 1977—; secy. Civil War Centennial Commn. Ill., 1959-65; chair Springfield Hist. Soc., 1956-67; mem. Capitol City Plan Commn., 1965-67, Ill. Historic Sites Adv. Council, 1971-77, chair, 1975-77, Ill. State Archives Adv. Bd., 1973-77. Served with inf. AUS, World War II. Home: 4320 Butler Cr Boulder CO 80303

WALTON, FRANK E., b. Vincennes, IN, Feb. 13, 1909; s. Frank E. and Emma (Miller) W.; m. Carol King Shaw, Aug. 17, 1932. Author: The Sea is My Workshop, 1935, Once They Were Eagles-The Men of the Black Sheep Squadron, 1986; contrbr. articles: TV Guide, Intl. Living, The Outrigger, Air Classics, numerous others. Wrkg. on Vietnam non-fiction, novel. BS in Police Adminstrn., Los Angeles State Coll., 1956, MS in Govt., 1958. With Los Angeles Police Dept., 1938-59, ret. as dep. chief; fgn. service officer U.S. Dept. State, Vietnam, Laos, Thailand, Philippines, Korea, Libya and Washington, 1959-71; freelance wrtr., 1959—; mem. Hawaii Commn. on Culture and Arts. Served to col., USMC, 1942-46; intelligence officer for Black Sheep Squadron, PTO. Decorated Purple Heart, other mil. awards: mem. 1948 U.S. Olympic water polo team. Mem. NWC, numerous profl. and mil. orgns. Home: Colony Surf 2895 Kalakaua Ave Honolulu HI 96815

WALTON, RICHARD EUGENE, b. Pulaski, IA, Apr. 15, 1931; s. Lee Richard and Florence (King) Walton; m. Sharon Claire Doty, Apr. 13, 1952; children—John, Elizabeth, Margaret, Andrew. Author: A Behavioral Theory of Labor Negotiations, 1965, (with R.B. McKersie) The Impact of the Professional Engineering Union, 1961, Managing Human Assets, 1984, Human Resource Management (HRM) Trends and Challenges, 1985, Managing Conflict, 1987, Innovating to Compete, 1987. BS, Purdue U., 1953, MS, 1954; postgrad., Victoria U., New Zealand, 1953; DBA, Harvard, 1959. Served with AUS, 1954-56. Home: 109 Beaver Rd Weston MA 02193

WALTS, ROBERT WARREN, b. New Albany, IN, Apr. 1, 1921; s. William H. and Alma Ethel (Hixon) Walts; m. gloria Halsey Denton, Jan. 22, 1944; children—Robert Denton, Anne Sawyer, Caroline Burns. Author: William Dean Howells and The House of Harper, 1957, Study Guide: The Rise of Silas Lapham, 1963; editor: The American Southwest: Cradle of Literary Art, 1981; contrbr. articles on Howells and Shakespeare to profl. jnls. AB, Rutgers U., 1950, AM, 1951, PhD (Queens fellow), 1953. Mem. faculty U. Mo. (Columbia), 1952-53, U. Ga. (Atlanta), 1953-56, Ga. State Coll., 1953-59; prof. English S.W. Tex. State U. (San Marcos), 1959—, chair dept., 1965-72; Piper prof. State of Tex., 1982. Commr. urban renewal, San Marcos, 1963-69. Served with USNR, 1942-45. Mem. AAUP, MLA, S. Central MLA, Conf. Coll. Tchrs. English (councillor), Coll. English Assn. Home: 408 Sesson Dr San Marcos TX 78666

WALTZ, JON RICHARD, b. Napoleon, OH, Oct. 11, 1929; s. Richard R. and Lenore (Tharp) Waltz. Co-author: The Trial of Jack Ruby, 1965, Cases and Materials on Evidence, 1968, Principles of Evidence and Proof, 1968, Medical Jurisprudence, 1971, Cases and Materials on Law and Medicine, 1980, Evidence: Making the Record, 1981; author: The Federal Rules of Evidence—An Analysis, 1973, Criminal Evidence, 1975, Evidence: A Summary Analysis, 1976, Introduction to Criminal Evidence, 1981; note and comment editor: Yale Law Jnl, 1953-54; mem. editorial adv. bd., Harcourt Brace Jovanovich Law Group, 1978—; contrbr. numerous articles to profl. jnls. BA with honors in Poli. Sci., Coll. Wooster, 1951; JD, Yale U., 1954. Bar: Ohio 1954, Ill. 1965. Assoc. Squire, Sanders & Dempsey (Cleve.), 1954-64; chief prosecutor, City of Willowick (Ohio), 1958-64; assoc. prof. law Northwestern U. Schl. Law (Chgo.), 1964-65, prof. law, 1965-78, Edna B. and Ednyfed H. Williams prof. law, 1978—, instr. med. jurisprudence, 1969—; book critic Washington Post, Chgo. Tribune, others; disting. vis. prof. law Ill. Inst. Tech. Chgo.-Kent Coll. Law, 1974; lectr. Mem. Ill. adv. com. U.S. Commn. on Civil Rights, 1971-74; mem. Ill. Criminal Justice System Policy and Planning Com., 1973-74, Ill. Jud. Inquiry Bd., 1980—; mem. com. med. edn. AMA, 1982-83. Served to capt. AUS, 1955-58. Recipient Disting. Service award Soc. Midland Authors, 1972; Disting. Alumni Award, Coll. of Wooster, 1987. Home: 421 W Melrose Chicago IL 60657

WAMALING, MARK HUNTER, b. Washington, Nov. 24, 1959, s. Charles and Jacqueline W. Author: Fire in the Hole! A Found Poem to Be Read in the Dark, 1985, Vow, 1985. BFA, Frostburg (Md.) State Coll., 1981. Artist asst., Frostburg, Md., 1982; art curator, pub., ed. Newark Press, Adelphi, Md., 1982—; art installation staff Corp. Art Service, Washington, 1985-86. Grantee Handsome Johnson Fdn., Greenwich, Conn., 1984. Office: Newark Press 8123 19th Pl Adelphi MD 20783

WANG, ARTHUR WOODS, b. Port Chester, NY, Oct. 7, 1918; s. Israel and Madolin (Woods) Wang; m. Mary Ellen Mackay, Aug. 13, 1955; 1 son—Michael Anthony. BS, Bowdoin Coll., 1940; postgrad., Columbia U., 1949-51. Advt. research McCann-Erickson, Inc., 1940-41; editor Doubleday & Co., 1942-43, Alfred A. Knopf, Inc., 1943, T.Y. Crowell (Pub.), 1943-47; with E.M. Hale & Co. (Eau Claire, WI), 1947-52; editor A.A. Wyn, Inc., 1952-56; pres., ed.-in-chief Hill & Wang div. Farrar, Straus & Giroux, Inc. (NYC), 1971—, also vp dir. corp. Mem. Am. Book Pubs. Council. Home: 1035 Fifth Ave New York NY 10028

WANGBERG, MARK THOMAS, b. Jacksonville, FL, Sept. 28, 1952; s. Franklin Charles and Jean Ann (Patterson) W.; m. Marguerite Rogers DeLone, Dec. 29, 1984. Author: (chapbooks) Art Poems, 1972, Love Poem, 1972; ed. Pine River Handmade, 1978- 79; contrbr. poetry to Greenfield, Cimarron, S.D. rvws, Abraxas, Folio, Green Horse for Poetry, Poetry Now, Poets On, Pine River, U.S. 1 Worksheets, also others. Wrkg. on love poems. BA, Alma Coll., 1975. Writing artist-in-residence Mich. Council for Arts, Pa. Council on Arts, Pa. Council on Humanities, 1975—; owner, pub. Jack in the Press; play therapist, arts specialist St. Christopher's Hosp. for Children, Phila., 1982-84; founder, instr., vol. writing program Graterford Prison, Pa., 1984—. Cranbook Wrtrs. Conf. scholar, 1978. Mem. P&W. Home: 593 Hansell Rd Wynnewood PA 19096

WANIEK, MARILYN NELSON, b. Cleve., Apr. 26, 1946, d. Melvin M. and Johnnie E. (Mitchell) Nelson; m. Erdmann F. Waniek, 1970 (div. 1979); m. Roger B. Wilkenfeld, 1979; children—Jacob, Dora. Author: For the Body (poems), 1979, The Cat Walked Through the Casserole (with P. Espeland), 1984, Mama's Promises (poems), 1985. Asst. prof. Lane Community Coll., Eugene, Oreg., 1970-72, St. Olaf Coll., Northfield, Minn., 1973-79; asst. prof. U. Conn., Storrs, 1979-80, assoc. prof. dept. English, 1981—; vis. prof. Nissum Seminarium, Denmark, 1972-73. Yaddo poetry resident, 1984; NEA creative writing fellow, 1984. Mem. AWP, Soc. Study of Multi-Ethnic Lit. of U.S. Office: Dept Eng Univ Conn Storrs CT 06268

WANN, DAVID L., b. Chgo., Feb. 26, 1949; s. David L. and Marjorie (Southworth) Wann; m. Julie Anne Bishop, Mar. 10, 1973; children: Colin, Elizabeth. Author poetry: Log Rhythms, 1983; contrbr. to Bloomsbury Rvw, Denver Qtly, NY Qtly, Water and Wastes Engring., Eco-Logos, High County News, Denver Post, Rocky Mountain News, Canyon Courier, Sierra, High Country News, Waste Age. BA in English, De Pauw Univ., Greencastle, Ind.; MS in Environ Sci., U. Colo. Bookstore mgr. Sundial Distbr., Denver, 1974-76; wastewater plant op. Denver Metro, 1976-84; writer EPA, Denver, 1985—. Bd. dirs., Friends of Evergreen Library, Colo.; master gardener, Colo. State Extension Service. Address: 5543 S Santa Clara Indian Hills CO 80454

WANROOY, WILLEM FREDERIK, (Van Waterford), b. Surabaya, Indonesia, June 29, 1925; came to U.S., 1961; m. 2d, Edith Mary Patzer, Dec. 16, 1972; 2 children by previous marriage, 2 step-children. Author: CB & Scan Monitor Merchandising Handbook, 1978, Hear All the Action-Short Wave Listening Handbook, 1978, Radar Detector Handbook, 1978, All About Telephones, 1978, 2d edit., 1983, Guide to Everything Electronic in the Home, 1979, Complete Guide-Handbook to Car Stereo Systems, 1980, The Complete Book of Home Computers, 1982, Computer Controlled Games & Toys and How They Work, 1983, numerous other electronics handbooks. Ed., Indonesia. Served with Dutch Army, 1942-47; Indonesia. Mem. AG, AFTRA, Screen Actors Guild. Home: Box 622 Pahoa HI 96778

WARD, GEOFFREY CHAMPION, b. Newark, OH, Nov. 30, 1940; s. Frederick Champion and Duira Rachel (Baldinger) Ward. Author: Lincoln's Thought and the Present, 1978, Treasures of the Majarajahs, 1983, Before the Trumpet: Young Franklin Roosevelt 1882-1905, 1985; columnist, "Matters of Fact," American Heritage Mag; contrbr, Audubon, Smithsonina, and other periodicals; screenwrtr, Huey Long, Statue of Liberty, 1985. BA, Oberlin Coll., 1962. Sr. picture editor Encyc. Britannica (Chgo.), 1964-68; co-founder, editor Audience mag. (Boston), 1969-73; mng. editor Am. Heritage Mag. (NYC), 1976-78, editor, 1978-82. Home: 1 W 85th St 10E New York NY 10024

WARD, HILEY HENRY, b. Lafayette, IN, July 30, 1929, s. Hiley Lemen and Agnes (Fuller) W.; m. Charlotte Burns; children—Dianne, Carolee,

Marcy, Laurel; m. 2d, Joan Bastel, Aug. 20, 1977. Author: Creative Giving, 1958, Space-Age Sunday, 1960, Documents of Dialogue, 1966, Ecumania, 1968, God and Marx Today, 1968, Prophet of the Black Nation, 1969, Rock 2000, 1969, The Far-Out Saints of the Jesus Communes, 1972, Religion 2101 A.D., 1975, Feeling Good About Myself, 1983, Professional Newswriting, 1985, My Friend's Beliefs, 1987; contrbr. articles, stories, poems to numerous jnls. BA, William Jewell Coll., 1951; MA, Berkeley Bapt. Divinity Schl., 1953, MDiv, McCormick Theol. Sem., 1955; postgrad. Northwestern U., 1948, 56-58, Wayne State U., 1973; PhD in journalism & history, U. Minn., 1977. Wrtr., religion ed. Detroit Free Press, 1960-73; communications educator Mankato (Minn.) State U., 1974-76, Wichita (Kans.) State U., 1976-77, Temple U., Phila., 1977—; founding ed., Media History Digest; exec. ed. Kidbits; ed. Currents publ., United Ch. of Christ; feature wrtr., Travel Wkly; film rvwr, Religious News Service, Natl Christian Reporter. Recipient numerous awards. Address: Dept Jnlsm Temple Uni Philadelphia PA 19122

WARD, L. E., b. Stambaugh, MI, July 5, 1944; s. Leon E. and Lillian E. (Mager) W. Contrbr. film histories and movie criticisms: The Big Reel, Lost Generation Jnl., Classic Images, other periodicals, also Film Book Encyc., 1986; contrbr. poetry: Arulo, Vega, other lit. mags. Contrbr. serial articles: UP Sunday Times, numerous local newspapers. Wrkg. on fiction, non-fiction, film histories, poetry. BA, No. Mich. U., 1966, MA in Lit., 1967. Instr. lit., U. Wis.-Whitewater, 1967-70, Gogebic Community Coll., Ironwood, Mich., 1973-74; freelance wrtr., 1974—. Recipient poetry award Am. Poetry Assn., 1987. Home: Box 107 Iron River MI 49935

WARD, SR., MARK LEE, b. Alexandria, VA, Apr. 8, 1958; s. Jesse Lee Ward, III, and Carolyn Jeanette (Mayo) W.; m. Donna Marie Blackwell, Jan. 5, 1980; children—Mark Lee, Jr., Laura Marie. Ed.: The Subcontractor, 1980-84, Sergeants, 1984-86, Viewpoint, 1984-86, Security Management, 1987. BA, U. VA, 1980. Dir. of publs., Amer. Subcontractors Assn., Alexandria, VA, 1980-84; dir mktg. & communics. Air Force Sgts. Assn., Suitland, MD, 1984-86; ed. Amer. Soc. for Industrial Security, Arlington, VA, 1987—. Feature articles in Trucker's News, Independent Gasoline Marketing, Construction Dimensions, Asbestos Abatement, Painting & Wallcovering Contractor. Mem: Amer. Soc. of Assn. Executives. Home: 3807 Candlelight Ct. Alexandria VA 22310

WARD, NANCY JOAN, b. Dubuque, IA, May 23, 1939; d. John Joseph and Ann Catherine (Schilling) W. Student Clark Coll., Dubuque, 1953-54; BS in Journalism, Northwestern U., 1961. Reporter, Fort Wayne News-Sentinel, 1960-62; reporter, community ed. Canton Daily Ledger, Ill., 1962-66; polit. reporter Pitts. Post Dispatch, Calif., 1967-71; city ed. Tri-Valley Herald, Livermore, Calif., 1971-78; city ed., asst. mng. ed. Contra Costa Times, Walnut Creek, Calif., 1978-84. Recipient 3 Best Investigating Series awards Natl. Suburban Newspapers Assn., 1984. First woman city ed. of a Calif. daily newspaper. Mem. Calif. Pub.-Newspaper Assn. (Best Newspaper in Calif., for Tri-Valley Herald 1972, 73, 76, 78; for Contra Costa Times 1980, 82, 84). Home: Box 66218 Scotts Valley CA 95066

WARD, PENNY L., b. Star Lake, NY, Sept. 20, 1961; d. Winston R. and Louise E. (Marsh) W. Contrbr. poem to anthol. Wrkg. on short stories. Cert. in Fiction, Newspaper Inst. of Am., 1985. Home: Rt 1 Box 21AA NYS Route 3 Oswegatchie NY 13670

WARD, SUSAN BAYER, b. Toledo, Sept. 4, 1944; d. George Franklin and Jane Cowden (Bayer) W. Contrbr. numerous articles to mags., newspapers including Crossroads, AAA Today, Chgo. Tribune, Los Angeles Time. Assoc. ed. to ed.: Going Places Mag., 1981-84; ed.: Chgo. Suburbia Mag., 1979-80; ed., wrtr. film div.: Encyc. Britanica, 1970-72. B.S. in Jnlsm., Northwestern U., 1967. Asst., Wildlife Concepts, Chgo., Orlando, FL, 1972-75; sr. tour mgr. Abercrombie & Kent, Oakbrook, IL, 1976-78; free-lance wrtr., photographer, 1985—. Mem. SATW (2d place for mag. article 1987), Midwest Travel Wrtrs. Assn. (2d place for photo 1987, 3d place for mag. article 1987), AATE, Midwest Wrtrs. Assn. Home: 3500 W Church St Apt 307 Evanston IL 60203

WARD, WM. MICHAEL, B. Sandusky, OH, June 16, 1957; s. William Cranston and Elizabeth W.; m. Tamyan-Sager Ward, June 26, 1982. BA, Otterbein Coll.; postgrad. Bowling Green U. Freelance writer, 1982-83; assoc. ed. Art Material Trade News, Atlanta, 1983-84; ed. The Artist's Mag., Cin., 1984—. Home: 3600 Linwood Ave Cincinnati OH 45226

WARDA, MARK, b. Chgo., Jan. 29, 1952; s. James Alexander and Jennie Ann (Skrebneski) W. Author: Landlords' Rights & Duties in Florida, 1983, How to Start a Business in Florida, 1983, How to Draft Real Estate Contracts, 1984, Land Trusts in Florida, 1984, How to Win in Small Claims Court in Florida, 1985, Brokers Rights and Duties in Florida, 1985, How to Draft Real Estate Leases, 1986. B.A., U. Ill., 1974, J.D., 1978. Bar: Fla., 1978. Sole practice, Clearwater, FL, 1980-86; free-lance wrtr., 1986—. Home: Box 10024 Clearwater FL 34617

WARDLAW, ANITA LOUISE, b. Houston; d. Frederick Mitchell and Lillian Louise Graham; m. Howard Hamilton Wardlaw, Aug. 23, 1980. Var. editorial, writing, design, illus. posits. for Scratch Pad (book), 1971, Iowa State Daily, 1973, Fndns. of Life Sci. (book), 1971, Gib News, 1979-81, The St. Paul News, 1982-84, The Scoop, 1982-84, Newsline, 1982-84, Mgt. Briefing, 1982-84, Mgt. Briefing Live (video), 1982-84, Twin Cities Courier, 1985, Black Enterprise, 1984, Wordspin greeting cards, 1979—; contrbr. num. CPR pubns, 1978—. BS, IA State U., 1975; MA, U. IA, 1977. Var. instr. posits., (Iowa State U, Golden Valley Lutheran Coll, Lowthian Coll). 1977-82; staff writer Prudential, Mpls., 1978-81; sr. communics. spec. The St. Paul (MN) Cos., 1982-84; communics. cons./dir., Wordspin, Coon Rapids, MN, 1985—, Progress Magazine, 1987, Coon Rapids Herald, 1987. Award of excell. in writing, IABC, 1983. Mem. IABC, Twin Cities Freelance Communicators Gp. Address: 300 110th Ln NW Coon Rapids MN 55433

WARE-CAMPBELL, LOUISE, see Campbell, Louise

WARN, EMILY, b. San Francisco, July 16, 1953, d. Jack and Pearl (Appelbaum) Warn. Author: poetry, The Leaf Path, 1982, Highway Suite, 1986, The Book of Esther, 1986; founding ed., mng. ed.: Backbone Mag., 1983-85; contrbr. poetry to Calyx, Xanadu, Hubbub, Rhino, numerous other lit mags. BA, Kalamazoo (Mich.) Coll., 1976; MA in Creative Wrtg., U. Wash., 1981. Tchr. Bush Schl. (Seattle), 1981-82; wrtr.-in-res. Wash. State Arts Commn., Olympia, 1981-86, Idaho State Commn. on Arts, Boise, 1983-84. Recipient Publ. prize in poetry King County Arts Commn., Seattle, 1981, Original Works Project prize in poetry Seattle Arts Commn., 1985; named Outstanding Wrtr. Pushcart Anthology, 1982. Mem. AWP. Home: 1723 27th St Seattle WA 98122

WARNE, CANDICE M., b. Brainerd, MN, June 27, 1945; d. Clarence Emmet and Avis Leota (Cleveland) W.; 1 son, Michael Apland. Ed., The Quenching Quill, 1976-77; contrbr. to Hiram Poetry Rvw., Sou'Wester, Mickle St. Rvw, Voices, Southern Poetry Rvw, Loonfeather, Strong Measures; Midwest Poetry Rvw, Waterways: Poets in the Mainstream, 1983, Nuke-Rebuke Anthol., 1984, others. BA, S.W. State U., 1977. Home: 1247 St Anthony Apt 715 St Paul MN 55104

WARNER, WILLIAM EATON, b. Boston, 1954, s. Sam Bass and Lyle (Lobel) W., Jr. M. Molly Renda. Author: My First Book (As an Adult), 1982, Knute, and Knute Again, 1987; ed., contrbr. ISBN 0-943568-01-3, anthology, 1983. AB, U. Calif., Berkeley, 1976; MFA, Columbia U., 1982. Ed. editorial page Daily Californian, Berkeley, 1975; prodn. ed. Praeger Pubs., NYC, 1976-77; freelance wrtr., 1977—; instr. Bklyn. Coll., 1981-82; reporter Money mag., NYC, 1982-84; mng. ed. N.C. Independent, Durham, 1985—. Office: Box 2690 Durham NC 27705

WARREN, BARBARA LEONARD, b. Fall River, MA, Nov. 3, 1943; d. John Morris and Jeanne Adrienne (Clement) Leonard; m. B. William Warren, Sept. 9, 1972. Author: (book and teaching kit) Capture Creativity: Photographs to Inspire Young Writers, 1982; columnist: Wrtr.'s Guidelines Mag., 1987—, Challenge: Reaching and Teaching the Gifted Child Mag., 1988—. Contrbr. articles to profl. and populr mags. including Am. Girl, Wis. English Jnl., Gifted Child Today, others. Women's ed.: Prescott Courier, AZ, 1972. B.A. in English/Edn., Bridgewater State Coll., 1966; M.A. in English/Edn., Ariz. State U., 1976. Tchr. gifted/jnlsm. Casa Grande Union High Sch., AZ, 1974—. Mem. NWC, NEA, Ariz. Edn. Assn., Casa Grande Edn. Assn., Ariz. Assn. Gifted and Talented, Natl. Assn. Gifted Child, Ariz. English Tchrs' Assn., NCTE. Home: Box 2352 Arizona City AZ 85223

WARREN, JAMES EDWARD, JR., b. Atlanta, Dec. 11, 1908, s. James Edward and Jean Morrison (Mauck) W. Author: (poetry) This Side of Babylon, 1938, Against the Furious Men, 1946, Selected Poems, 1967, Collected Poems, 1980, also 13 chapbooks of poetry, 1964-86; The Teacher of English, 1964, How To Write a Research Paper, 1972, A History of the Lovett School, 1976; contrbr. poems to Atlantic Monthly, Saturday Rvw, Sewanee, So. Poetry, Ga., So. Humanities rvws, Poet Lore, Poetry, Blue Unicorn, Prairie Schooner, Christian Century, others. AB, Emory U., 1930, MAT, 1941. Tchr. English, Atlanta Pub. Schls., 1933-69, head dept., 1964-69; tchr. English, Lovett Schl., Atlanta, 1969-74, head dept., 1971-74, poet-in-residence, 1974-75, schl. historian, 1980—. Served with USAAF, 1942-45. Recipient annl. prize PSA, 1937, lit. achievement award Ga. Wrtrs. Assn., 1967, Writer of Yr. award Atlanta Wrtrs. Club, 1968, Ga. Gov.'s award in poetry, 1980, excellence in teaching award Ga. Assn. Inc. Schls., 1974. Home: 544 Deering Rd NW Atlanta GA 30309

WARREN, JOHNNY WILMER, b. Milledgeville, GA, Sept. 2, 1946; s. Johnnie Linton and Allene (Harden) W.; m. Hannah Lynelle Hall, Aug. 27, 1967; children—Hannah Michelle Dob, Heather Elizabeth Dob. Author: Georgia Magistrate Court Handbook, 1984, rev., 1987, How to Collect Your Small Claim in Georgia, 1987. A.A., Middle Ga. Coll., 1967; B.B.A., Ga. Coll., 1977; J.D., Atlanta Law Sch., 1979. Bar: Ga., 1979. Sole practice, Dublin, GA, 1979—; part-time judge Small Claims Ct., Laurens County, GA, 1979-83, Magistrate Ct., Laurens County, 1983—. Mem. Am. Bar Assn., Am. Trial Lawyers Assn., Ga. Trial Lawyers Assn. Home: 339 Regency Circle Box 775 Dublin GA 31021

WARREN, KATHLEEN JANINE, b. Neenah, WI, Apr. 8, 1942; d. Anton and Charlotte May (Barkofsky) Kuehn; m. Jon Grayson Warren, Aug. 27, 1961; children—Theodore Stuart, Samuel Anthony. Contrbr. articles to mags., newspapers including Spokane Chronicle, Edn. Week, Seed World. BS in Edn. and German, U. Id.-Moscow, 1963, MA in English, 1976. Stringer, Spokane Chronicle & Edn. Week, 1981-82; newswrtr., info. specialist Wash. State U., Pullman, 1983-84, intern coop. edn., 1984-86, instr. journalism, 1984, 86; staff wrtr. U. Id.-Moscow and Wash. State u., 1986; free-lance wrtr., 1981—. Newsletter ed. Patrons of Pub. Edn., Moscow, 1983; bethel tchr. First Presbyn. Ch., Moscow, 1979-83; foster parent Christian Children's Fund, 1976—. Mem. Wash. Press Assn., Coop. Edn. Assn. Home: 2477 W Twin Rd Moscow ID 83843

WARREN, MARGARET LUCILLE, b. Hopkinsville, KY, Jan. 2, 1912; d. Browder Calvin and Mary Lucille (Gray) Warren; divorced; children—Calvin, Janumae, Carolyn Elkins. Contrbr. articles to newspapers, mags. including Chgo. Tribune, Parents, others. Student Murray Coll. Mem. NWC. Home: 144 E Mill St Crofton NY 42217

WARREN, ROBERT PENN, b. Guthrie, KY, Apr. 24, 1905; s. Robert Franklin and Anna Ruth (Penn) Warren; m. Emma Brescia, Sept. 12, 1930 (div. 1950); m. 2d, Eleanor Clark, 1952; children—Rosanna, Gabriel Penn. Author: World Enough and Time, 1950, Brother to Dragons, new version, 1979, Band of Angels, 1955, Segregation, 1956, Promises, 1957, Selected Essays, 1958, The Cave, 1959, You, Emperors and Others, 1960, The Lagacy of the Civil War, 1961, Wilderness, 1961, Flood, 1964, Who Speaks for the Negro, 1965, Selected Poems New and Old, 1923-1966, 1966, Incarnations, 1968, Audubon: A Vision, 1969, Homage to Theodore Dreiser, 1971, Or Else-Poem/Poems, 1968-74, 1975, Democracy and Poetry, 1975, Selected Poems: 1923-75, 1977, A Place to Come to, 1977, Now and Then: Poems, 1976-79, Being Here: Poems, 1978-79, 1980, Rumor Verified, Poems, 1981, chief Joseph of the Nez Perce, a poem, 1983; editor or co-editor other books; a founder and editor: The So. Rvw, 1935-42. BA summa cum laude, Vanderbilt U., 1925; MA, U. Calif., 1927; postgrad., Yale, 1927-28; B.Litt. (Rhodes scholar), Oxford U., 1930. Mem. Fugitive Group of Poets, 1923-25; asst. prof. English Southwestern Coll. (Memphis), 1930-31; acting asst. prof. Vanderbilt U., 1931-34; asst. prof. La. State U., 1934-36, assoc. prof., 1936-42; prof. English Yale, 1961-73; prof. emeritus Yale U., 1973—; chair of poetry Library of Congress, 1944-45; vis. lectr. U. Iowa, 1941: Jefferson lectr. NEH, 1974. Recipient Houghton Mifflin Lit. Fellowship award, 1936, Levinson prize Poetry: A Mag. of Verse, 1936, Caroline Sinkler prize Poetry Soc. SC, 1936, 37, 38, Shelley prize for poetry, 1942, Pulitzer prize for fiction, 1947, Robert Meltzer award Screen Writers Guild, 1949, Sidney Hillman award, 1957, Edna St. Vincent Millay prize PSA, 1958, Natl. Book award for poetry, 1958, Pulitzer prize for fiction 1958, Irita Van Doren Lit. award NY Herald Tribune, 1965, Bollingen prize in poetry Yale U., 1967, Van Wyck Brooks award for poetry, 1970, Natl. medal for Lit., 1970, award for Lit., U. SC, 1973, Emerson-Thoreau award Am. Acad. Arts and Scis., 1975, Copernicus prize Am. Acad. Poets, 1975, Pulitzer prize for poetry, 1979, Harriet Monroe award for poetry, 1979, Commonwealth award, 1980, Prize fellowship McArthur Fdn., 1981, Presdl. Medal of Freedom, 1980, Gold Medal for Poetry, AAAL, 1985, Poet Laureate USA, 1986. Mem. Am. Acad. Arts and Letters, Acad. Arts and Scis., Am. Philo. Soc., AAP (chancellor). Home: 2495 Redding Rd Fairfield CT 06430

WARRICK, JAMES GORDON, b. Roanoke, VA, May 13, 1953; s. Gordon Cole and Virginia Florence (Beheler) W.; m. Constance Marie Rhinaman; July 2, 1977; 1 son, Brandon Robert. Contrbr. articles to The Instrumentalist, The Music Educators Jnl., Jnl. Nat. Assn. Jazz Educators, Jnl. Percussion Arts Soc., Band Dirs. Reference Guide. Contrbg. ed.: The Instumentalist, 1985—. B.Music, Ohio U., 1976; M.Music, 1976. Instr. percussion Marshall U., Huntington, WV, 1976; band dir. Lakewood High Schl., OH, 1977-82, New Trier High Sch., Winnetka, IL, 1982—. Mem. Music Educators Natl. Conf., Natl. Assn. Jazz Educators (Ill. pres.), Am. Fdn. Musicians, Am. Schl. Band. Dir. Assn. Home: 399 Holly Dr Streamwood IL 60107

WARSAW, IRENE, b. Kawkawlin Twp., MI, Nov. 26, 1908; d. Herman August and Auguste (Malzahn) Warsaw. Author: A Word in Edgewise (humorous poetry), 1964 (7th ed.) Warily We Roll Along (humorous poetry), 1979 (2d ed.). Contrbr. poetry: The Lyric, Capper's, Modern Maturity, Scope, Wall St. Jnl., Good Housekeeping, numerous others. Wrkg. on poetry. LittD (hon.), Saginaw Valley State Coll., 1980. Mem. Poetry Soc. Mich., Utah State Poetry Soc., Pa. Poetry Soc., Natl. League Am. Pen Women, Detroit Women Wrtrs., other orgns. Home: 888 N Scheurmann Rd Apt D20 Essexville MI 48732

. **WARSHAW, STANLEY,** b. NYC, Aug. 3, 1929; s. Nathan and Millie W.; m. Leah Esther Stein, June 27, 1954; children—Meryl, Charlene. Author: No Molasses in the Wheat Paste, 1977, How to Become A Financially Successful Paperhanging Entrepreneur, 1981. BBA, CCNY, 1952. Chief exec. officer U.S. School Profl. Paperhanging, Rutland, VT, 1973—. Home: Karen Road Rutland VT 05701

WARTLUFT, DAVID JONATHAN, b. Stouchsburg, PA, Sept. 22, 1938; s. Cleaver Milvard and Dorothy (Stump) Wartluft; m. Joyce Claudia Dittmer, June 15, 1963; children—Elizabeth Marie, Deborah Joy, Rebecca Janet, Andrew Jonathan. Editor: Teamwork, 1970, The Periodical, 1977-82, Luth. Hist. Soc. Eastern PA; author index: Luther in Mid-Career, 1983, Theology in the Old Testament, 1983, The Roots of Anti-Semitism, 1984; contbr. articles to profl. jours. AB (Trexler scholar), Muhlenberg Coll., 1960; Div.M. (Danforth scholar), Lutheran Theol. Sem., 1964; AM (scholar), U. Pa., 1964; MS (Lily Found. scholar), Drexel U., 1968. Asst. chaplain, instr. religion Springfield Coll. (MA), 1962-63; ordained minister Luth. Ch., 1964; pastor Jerusalem Luth. Ch. Luth. Sem. (Phila.), (Allenown, PA), 1964-66; cataloguer & ref. libn. 1966-68, asst. librarian, 1968-77, dir. library and archives, 1977—, chaplain, 1978-79, dir. lst yr. field edn., 1979-81, 82-83; exec. sec. Am. Theol. Library Assn. (Phila.), 1971-81, also editor procs.; archivist Northeastern Pa. Synod, Luth. Ch. Am., 1970—, mem. communications com., 1967-78, sec., 1975-78, mem. conv. com., 1976; vp Luth. Archives Center at Phila., 1979-85, bd. dirs., 1979—. Mem. Southeastern Pa. Theol. Librarians Assn. (sec. 1970-73, chair, 1983-85). Office: 7301 Gemantown Ave Philadelphia PA 19119

WASEGOBOAH, CHARLES, see Smith, Charles

WASHBURN, WILCOMB EDWARD, b. Ottawa, KS, Jan. 13, 1925; s. Harold Edward and Sidsell Marie (Nelson) Washburn; m. Kathryn Cousins, Jan. 2, 1985; children from former marriage—Harold Kitsos, Edward Alexandros. Author: The Governor and the Rebel: A History of Bacon's Rebellion in Virginia, 1957, Red Man's Land/White Man's Law: A Study of the Past and Present Status of the American Indian, 1971, The Assault on Indian Tribalism: General Allotment Law (Dawes Act) of 1887, 1975, The Indian in America, 1975, (with others) The Federal City: Plans and Realities, The Exhibition, 1976; editor: The Indian and the White Man, 1964, Proc. of the Vinland Map Conf., 1971, The American Heritage History of the Indian Wars, 1977. Grad., Phillips Exeter Acad., 1943; AB summa cum laude, Dartmouth Coll., 1948; MA, Harvard U., 1951, PhD, 1955; HHD (hon.), St. Mary's Coll. Md., 1970, Assumption Coll., 1983. Teaching fellow history and lit. Harvard, 1954-55; fellow Inst. Early Am. History and Culture (Williamsburg, VA), 1955-58; instr. Coll. William and Mary, 1955-58; curator div. political history Smithsonian Instn., U.S. Natl. Mus. (Washington), 1958-65, dir. office Am. Studies, 1965—; professorial lectr. Am. U., 1961-63, adj. prof., 1963-69; professorial lectr. in Am. civ. George Washington U., 1966—; cons. in research Grad. Schl. Arts and Scis., George Washington U., 1966—; adj. prof. U. Md., 1976—. Served with USMCR, 1943-46, 51-52. Office: Smithsonian Instn Washington DC 20560

WASHINGTON, TOM F., b. Spokane, WA, Mar. 8, 1949, s. Nat W. and Wanda (Wells) W.; m. Lois W. Mueller, Aug. 11, 1973; children—Timothy A., Daniel T., Molly E., Brian M. Author: Resume Power: Selling Yourself on Paper, 1985. BA, Western Wash. U., 1971; MA, Northeastern Ill. U., 1978. Counselor Career Devel. Center, Seattle, 1979; pres. Career Mgmt. Resources, Bellevue, Wash., 1979—. Office: 1750 112th St. NE Bellevue WA 98004

WASHINGTON, WILLIS, see Briegel, William Eugene

WASIELESKI, DAVID THOMAS, (David Thomas), b. Bklyn., June 4, 1968; s. Eugene B. and Lucy (Renda) W. Editorial asst.: Hard Rock Video mag., 1986; mng. ed.: Hard Rock Video Poster Mag., 1986. Contrbr. articles to Scary Stuff, Nightmare Express. Student Washington U., 1986—. Mem. Natl. Creative Co-op. Home: 5768 Everglades Ln Norcross GA 11204

WASSERMAN, DEBRA, Author: Vegetarianism for the Wrkg. Person, 1986, Healthy Holidays, 1984, I Love Animals and Broccoli, 1985, No Cholesterol Passover Recipes, 1986; contrbr. articles to Jewish Vegetarian (England), Vegetarian Times; ed. Balt. Vegetarians newsletter,

1983-, DC Vegetarian newsletter, 1982-83, Jewish Vegetarian newsletter, 1984—, Vegetarian Jnl, 1985—. Address: PO Box 1463 Baltimore MD 21203

WATERFORD, VAN, see Wanrooy, Willem Frederik

WATERS, CHOCOLATE, b. Aberdeen, MD, Jan. 21, 1949, d. Emory Lee and Pauline Reba (Buller) Waters. Author: To the man reporter from the Denver Post, 1975, revised ed., 1980, Take Me Like A Photograph, 1977, 2nd ed., 1980, Charting New Waters, 1980; represented in Seeds, 1976, Womanthology, 1977, Woman Poet-The West, 1980, Ordinary Women, Extraordinary Lives, 1985; contrbr. to Lips, Motheroot, Focus, Bread & Roses, numerous other lit mags. BA, Lock Haven State Coll., 1971. Dir. Eggplant Press, NYC, 1975—. Mem. NWU, Feminist Wrtrs. Guild, Pi Delta Epsilon. Office: 415 W 44th St 7 New York NY 10036

WATERS, HELEN EUGENIA, b. Davenport, IA, Nov. 18, 1917; d. Charles Hoyle and Lilly Amelia (Grobe) Van Sant; m. Harvey Leon Waters, Mar. 22, 1947; children—Nancy Lea Waters Widger, Cheryl Anne Waters Braun. Coauthor, co-ed.: Mountain Memories, 1981; contrbr. articles: Seventeen mag., Frontier Times, Good Old Days, numerous other publs. Student Dubuque U., 1939-41. Reporter, feature wrtr. Canyon Courier, Evergreen, Colo., 1970-71; ed. Jefferson County Hist. Soc. Newsletter, Evergreen, 1978-79; columnist, feature wrtr. High Timber Time, Conifer, Colo., 1978—; judge Rocky Mountain Wrtrs. Guild, Denver, 1982. Home: 10131 S Deer Creek Rd Littleton CO 80127

WATERS, MICHAEL, b. NYC, Nov. 23, 1949; s. Raymond George and Dorothy (Smith) W.; m. Robin Marie Irwin, May 12, 1972. Author: Fish Light, 1975, Not Just Any Death, 1979, Anniversary of the Air, 1985, The Burden Lifters, 1988. Ed.: Dissolve to Island: On the Poetry of John Logan, 1984. MA, SUNY-Brockport, 1972; MFA, U. Iowa, 1974; PhD, U. Ohio, 1977. Instr. U. Ohio, Athens, 1977-78; assoc. prof. Salisbury State Coll., MD, 1978—; vis. prof. U. Athens, Greece, 1981-82; Banister wrtr.-in-res., Sweet Briar Con., VA, 1987-88. Residency fellow Yaddo, 1978, 80, 83, 84, 87; Pushcart prize, 1984; NEA fellow, 1984; prize for lit. Towson State U., 1985. Home: Box 34 Sweet Briar Va 24595

WATERS, REITA OLITA CLIFTON, b. Statesboro, GA, Dec. 29, 1930; d. George Washington and Sadie Mae (Mixon) Clifton; m. James Carswell Waters, Dec. 21, 1955 (dec. 1983); children—James Jr., George Pierce, Vondesa Mae, Sadeanya Ann. Wrkg. on poetry collection. BS, Ga. So. U. Former tchr. elem. schs. various locations in Ga. Home: Virginia Ave Millen GA 30442

WATKINS, WILLIAM JOHN, b. Coaldale, PA, July 19, 1942, s. Charles William Joseph and Edna Meyers (Pearson) W.; m. Sandra Lee Preno, July 25, 1961; children—Tara, Wade, Chadom. Author: The God Machine, 1973 (Brit. ed. 1975, French ed. 1977, German ed. 1981), Clickwhistle, 1973 (French ed. 1977, German ed. 1981), A Fair Advantage, 1975, What Rough Beast, 1980, The Psychic Experiment Book, 1980, Suburban Wilderness, 1981, Who's Who in New Jersey Wrestling, 1981, The Psychic Diet Book, 1982, Centrifugal Rickshaw Dancer, 1985, Going to See the End of the Sky, 1986; co-author: Ecodeath (with E.V. Snyder), 1972, The Litany of Sh'reev (with Snyder), 1975 (German ed. 1980), Tracker (with Tom Brown), 1978; playwright: Judas Wheel (Per Se award), 1970, A Kind of a Hole, 1974; contrbr. to: Best Sci. Fiction, Best of Isaac Asimov's Sci. Fiction Mag., Space Mail II, other anthologies; contrbr. short stories, articles to Oui, Twilight Zone, Pulpsmith, other publs. BS, Rutgers U., 1964, MEd, 1965. Assoc. prof. Brookdale Community Coll., Lincroft, N.JM., 1970—. Mem. AG, SFWA. Home: 1406 Garven Ave Ocean NJ 07712

WATSON, DONALD RALPH, b. Providence, Sept. 27, 1937; s. Ralph Giles W. and Ethel (Fletcher) Pastene; m. Marja Palqvist, Sept. 8, 1966 (div. Jan. 1984); m. 2d, Judith Obermeyer Criste, Jan. 3, 1986; children—Petrik, Elise. Author: Designing and Building a Solar House, 1977, Energy Conservation through Building Design, 1979, Climatic Design, 1983. AB, Yale U., 1959, B.Arch., 1962, M.Ed., 1969. Architect Peace Corps, Tunisia, 1962-64; archtl. cons. Govt. of Tunisia, 1964-65; pvt. practice architecture, Branford, CT, 1969—; cons. UN, Bhutan, 1976, World Bank, North Yemen, 1979, Dept. of Energy, 1979, Natl. Acad. Scis., 1982. Recipient Honor Design award CT Soc. Architects, 1974, region AIA, 1978, 1st Owens Corning Energy Conservation Bldg. Design Prog., 1983, Am. Pub. Assn. Best Bk. in Arch. & Planning award, 1983; ACSA/AMAX research fellow, 1967-69; research fellow Rockefeller Fdn., 1978. Fellow AIA; mem., editor, Am. Solar Energy Soc. Home: Box 123 Trumbull CT 06611

WATSON, (LOIS) ELAINE, b. Jackson, MI, Oct. 13, 1921; d. William John and Elsie Olive (Feldkamp) Reno; m. William John Watson, Apr. 16, 1949; children—David, Douglas, Diane. Author: We, The Women: Limericks Liberated, 1980; (novels) Anna's Rocking Chair, 1984, To Dwell in the Land, 1985; (verse) Scraps of History, 1985. Contrbr. chpt. to book. Ed.: Echoes from the Moon, 1976. A.B., U. Mich., 1943, M.A., 1951. Tchr., Henry Ford Commun. Coll., Dearborn, MI, 1967-86. Active Bentley Library, Ann Arbor, MI. Recipient cert. of Achievement for article WD, 1986. Mem. Detroit Women Wrtrs. (membership com.), Mich. Poetry Soc. (Humerous Verse award 1977) Home: 1205 Island Dr 102 Ann Arbor MI 48105

WATSON, MARILYN FERN, b. Oklahoma City, July 30, 1934, d. Charles Haddon and Mary Perle (Knotts) Rounds; m. Donald Wayne Watson, Aug. 14, 1954; 1 son, Lyndon Lee. Contrbr. short stories, articles, art: Art Form Mag., N.Mex. Mag., Guideposts, Q23 mag., numerous other publs. Wrkg. on mag. articles, children's book, play, novel. BS magna cum laude in Psychology, Eastern N.Mex. U., 1973, postgrad., 1980-81. Freelance wrtr., artist, Roswell, N.Mex., 1960—. Recipient award Wrtrs. Digest mag., 1959, Guideposts Fdn., 1978. Profl. mem. NWC. Home: 15 Cedar Dr Roswell NM 88201

WATSON, MARSHA JEAN, b. Kansas City, KS, July 18, 1957; d. John Stanley and Doris Jean (Elliott) W. Contrbr. articles on diet, health, self-esteem, edn., short stories to mags. including Family Circle others. Wrkg. on articles. Student U. Mo., Columbia, 1976-79, Kansas City, 1978, 85. Secy., ed. Landauer Assoc., Houston, 1986, data analyst Aldrich Eastman & Waltch, Boston, 1987—. Recipient Honorable Mention, Byline, 1985, 86, 87, 2d place, 84; 4th place Wrtrs. Digest, 1985. Mem. NWC. Home: 47 Rockaway St Apt 3 Lynn MA 01902

WATSON, RICHARD ALLAN, b. New Market, IA, Feb. 23, 1931; s. Roscoe Richard and Daisy Belle (Penwell) W.; m. Patty Jo Andersen, July 30, 1955; 1 dau., Anna Melissa. Author: The Downfall of Cartesianism, 1966, Man and Nature (with Patty Jo Watson), 1969, The Longest Cave (with Roger W. Brucker), 1976, The Philosopher's Diet, 1983, The Breakdown of Cartesian Metaphysics, 1987; novels: Under Plowman's Floor, 1978, The Runner, 1981. BA, U. Iowa, 1953, MA, 1957, PhD, 1961; MS, U. Minn.-Mpls., 1959. Served to 1st lt. USAF, 1953-55; USA. Instr. philo. U. Mich., Ann Arbor, 1961-64; asst. prof. Washington Univ., St. Louis, 1964-67, assoc. prof., 1967-74, prof. philo., 1974—. Home: 756 Harvard Ave St Louis MO 63130

WATSON, ROBERT R., b. St. Louis, July 19, 1963, d. Howard L. and Gloria T. Watson. BJ, U. Mo., 1985. Ed. Jnl. Practical Nursing, St. Louis, 1985—. Mem. St. Louis Bus. Eds. Assn. Home: 7905 Alert Dr St Louis MO 63133

WATSON, ROBERT WINTHROP, b. Passaic, NJ, Dec. 26, 1925; s. Winthrop and Laura Berdan (Trimble) W.; m. Elizabeth Ann Rean, Jan. 12, 1952; children—Winthrop, Caroline. Author: poetry: A Paper Horse, 1962, Advantages of Dark, 1966, Christmas in Las Vegas, 1971, Selected Poems, 1974, Island of Bones, 1977, Night Blooming Cactus, 1980; author novels: Three Sides of the Mirror, 1966, Lily Lang, 1977. BA, Williams Coll., 1946; postgrad. U. Zurich, 1947; MA, Johns Hopkins, 1950, PhD in English, 1955. Instr. English, Williams Coll., 1946, 47-48, 52-53, Johns Hopkins, 1950-52; mem. faculty U. NC, Greensboro, 1952—, prof. English, 1963—; vis. poet, prof. English, CA State U., Northridge, 1968-69. Swiss-Am. exchange fellow, 1947; grantee NEA, 1973; recipient Am. Scholar Poetry prize, 1959, lit. award AAAL, 1977. Office: Dept Eng U NC Greensboro NC 27412

WATTENBERG, BEN J., b. NYC, Aug. 26, 1933; s. Judah and Rachel (Gutman) W.; m. Marna Hade, June 24, 1956 (div. Feb. 1981); children—Ruth, Daniel, Sarah; m. 2d, Diane Abelman, July 10, 1983; 1 dau., Rachel. Narrator, essayist: TV series In Search of Real Am., PBS, 1977-78, Ben Wattenberg's 1980, PBS, 1980; host Ben Wattenberg At Large, PBS, 1981; syndicated columnist United Features, 1981—; author: This U.S.A., 1965 (with R. Scammon), The Real Majority, 1970, The Real America, 1974, Against All Enemies, 1977 (with Ervin Duggan), The Wealth Weapon (with Richard Whalen), 1980, The Good News Is the Bad News Is Wrong, 1984, The Birth Dearth, 1987; co-ed. Public Opinion Mag., 1977—. BA, Hobart Coll., 1955; LLD (hon.), Hobart and William Smith Colls., 1975. Asst. to Pres. Johnson, Washington, 1966-68; bus. cons., Washington, 1968-77; aide to Vice Pres. Hubert Humphrey, Mpls., 1970; co-fdr., chmn. Coalition for a Democratic Majority, 1972—; campaign adviser Senator Henry Jackson, 1972, 76; eminent scholar, prof.-at-large Mary Washington Coll., 1973-74; fellow, trustee Hudson Inst., 1976—; sr. fellow Am. Enterprise Inst., 1977—; mem. presdl. advisory bd. on ambassadorial appts., 1977-80; distinguished vis. prof. U. S. Intl. U., 1978, 79, 87; public mem. U. S. Delegation to Madrid, 1980; vice chmn. Bd. Intl. Broadcasting, 1981, Democracy Program, 1982-83; bd. dirs. Reading Is Fundamental. Office: Am Inst 1150 17th St NW Washington DC 20036

WATTERS, MERELYN JACQUETA, b. Piermont, NH, June 24, 1933; d. Reynold Evan and Marie Phyllis (La Montagne) Adams; m. James Franklin Watters, Nov. 3, 1956; children—James Franklin, Ray Richard. Contrbr. poems to anthols. Recipient Honorable Mention, World of Poetry, 1984, 87, Spcl. Mention award, 1984, Golden Poet award, 1985, 87, Silver Poet award, 1986. Home: HCR 62 Box 63 Macwahoc ME 04451

WATTS, JOHN M., JR., (Jack), b. Mineola, NY, June 3, 1941; s. John M. and Mary Morton (Phelps) W.; m. Judith Ann Geisler, Sept. 3, 1966; children—Robert Judson, Alexis Smith. Ed., Fire Technology, 1983—. BS, FPE, U. MD, 1966; PhD, IE & OR, U. MA, 1978. Asst. prof. U. MD, College Park, 1973-81; visiting academic U. Edinburgh (Scotland), 1979-80; dir. Fire Safety Institute, Middlebury, VT, 1981—. Mem. Soc. Fire Protection Engrs., Ops. Res. Soc. Amer., Soc. Risk Analysis, Intl. Soc. Fire Safety Scientists, Inst. of Industrial Engineers. Office: Box 674 Middlebury VT 05753

WAXMAN, HERBERT J., b. NYC, Jan. 21, 1913; s. Isidore and Alice (Jacobowitz) Waxman; m. Vivian Krischer, May 28, 1939; children—Jill, Jonathan. Author: Where the Worm Grows Fat, 1975; poems in NY Qtly, NY Times, Bitterroot, Alive and Kicking and other lit mags. Student, NY Univ., 1929; CCNY, 1930-38. CPA, own practice, 1940—. Writer on business and taxes., 1940-70. Mem. P&W, Long Island Poetry Collective. Home: 29 Margaret Ct Great Neck NY 11021

WAYBOURN, MARILU M., b. Farmington, NM, Dec. 19, 1931; d. William Ray and Ruth Alice (Torbit) Marshall; m. Jim L. Waybourn, June 13, 1952; children—Connie, Don, Mike. Author: Meet Me at the Fair, 1984. Newspaper computer columnist Farmington Daily Times, 1986—. AA, Stephens Coll., Columbia, Mo., 1951. Supr. pubs. Farmington Daily Times, 1968-82; wrtr., ed. Bur. of Land Mgmt., Farmington, 1985—; free-lance wrtr., 1982—. Home: Box 303 Flora Vista NM 87415

WAYLAN, MILDRED, see Harrell, Irene Burk

WAYNE, HAL, see Dexter, Jerry D.

WAYNE, JANE O., b. St. Louis, MO, Oct. 10, 1938; d. David L. and Frances S. (Rosen) Oxenhandler; m. Sam Wayne, Dec. 21, 1963; children—Ursula, Justine. Author: Looking Both Ways, 1984; poetry in Poetry, The American Scholar, Poetry Northwest, and other lit mags. BA, Washington U., 1964, MA, 1977. Instr., U. of Mo. at St. Louis, 1977-79; lectr., Webster U., St. Louis, Mo., 1981-84. Mem. PSA. Home: 6376 Washington Ave St Louis MO 63130

WEATHERBY, GREGG L., b. Cortland, NY, May 29, 1950; s. Bernard C. and Barbara (Church) W. Contrbr. poetry to New Am. & Can. Poetry, Anteaus, Transition, other lit mags; ed., contrbr. Genesis, Gallery, Spin. Freelance ed./wrtr., actor, until 1979; assoc. ed. Gallery mag., NYC, 1979-82; mng. ed. Genesis mag., NYC, 1982-85, Spin mag., NYC, 1985-86. Mem. ASME. Home: 39 Purdy St Apt 12 Harrison NY 10528

WEATHERSBY, GEORGE BYRON, b. Albany, CA, Dec. 9, 1944; s. Byron and Fannie A. W.; m. Linda Rose W., June 29, 1979; children—Deborah Jane, Geoffrey Byron. Author: Financing Postsecondary Education in the U.S., 1974, Colleges and Money, 1976; contrbr. numerous articles to profl. jnls., 1967—; cons. ed. Jnl Higher Edn., 1974—; exec. ed. Change mag., 1980—. BS, U. CA-Berkeley, 1965, MS, 1966, MBA, 1967; SM, Harvard U., 1968, PhD, 1970. Assoc. dir. analytical studies U. CA-Berkeley, 1969-72, dir. Ford Fdn. research prog., mem. faculty, 1969-72; spcl. asst. to U.S. Secy. of State, Washington, 1972-73; dir. research Natl. Commn. on Financing Higher Edn., Washington, 1973-74; assoc. prof. mgmt. Harvard U., 1974-78; commr. higher edn., IN, 1977-83; mem. steering com. Edn. Commn. of States, 1978-82; bd. dirs. Natl. Ctr. for Higher Edn. Mgmt. Systems, 1980-83; dir. Trng. and Edn. Data Svcs., Inc., 1981—, pres. Curtis Pub. Co., 1983—; vice pres. of finance, dir. Ont. Corp., 1981—; mem. adv. council United Student Aid Funds, Inc. Mem. Am. Council Edn., Ops. Research Soc. Am., Inst. Mgmt. Scis., Econometrica. Office: 123 E Adams St Muncie IN 47302

WEAVER, CLARENCE LAHR, b. Delaware, OH, Nov. 5, 1904; s. Charles Oscar and Maggie Jane (Betz) W.; m. Gertrude Viola Pratt, May 20, 1926; children—Eleanor Janet, Kenneth Harmon, Charles Albert, Carol Lynn; m. 2d, Marjorie Carr MacCready, Nov. 12, 1979. Author: With All My Love, 1936, A Bard's Prayers, 1967, The Quickened Seed, 1981; ed.: The Quickening Seed, 1933-45, Bardic Echoes, 1960-80; compiler Official Author Headings of the State of Mich., 1970. BA, Ohio Wesleyan U., 1926; BS in LS, Western Res. U., 1934; MS in LS, U. Mich., 1959. Proofreader Lakeside Press, Chgo., 1926-31; chief cataloger and edtl. asst. Ohio Hist. Soc. & Library, Columbus, 1935-46; head catalog & order dept. Grand Rapids Public Library, Mich., 1946-69 (ret). Treas., Ohio Poetry Day Assn., Columbus, 1944-45; chaplain, The Bards of Grand Rapids, 1957-66, treas., 1983—; treas. Grand Rapids Friends of the Library, 1983. Mem. ALA (life), Mich. Library Assn., Mich. State Poetry Soc. (v.p., 1977-79). Pres., Theosophical Soc., Grand Rapids, 1971-80; bd. dirs. Kent Philatelic Soc., 1983-84. Home: 125 Somerset Dr NE Grand Rapids MI 49503

WEAVER, GORDON ALLISON, b. Moline, IL, Feb 2, 1937; s. Noble Rodel and Inez Katherin (Nelson) W; m. Judith Lynne Gosnell, Sept. 14, 1961; children: Kristina Katherine, Anna Lynne, Jessica Merle. Author fiction: Count A Lonely Cadence, 1968, The Entombed Man of Thule, 1972, Such Waltzing Was Not Easy, 1975, Give Him a Stone, 1975, Circling Byzantium, 1980, Getting Serious, 1980, Morality Play, 1985, A World Quite Round, 1986; ed. Selected Poems of Father Ryan, 1973, An Artist's Notebook, 1979, The Am. Short Story, 1945-80, 1983; wrkg. on a novel, The Eight Corners of the World. BA, U. Wis.-Milw., 1961; MA, U. Ill.-Urbana, 1962; PhD, U.Denver, 1970. Instr. English Siena Coll., Loudonville, NY, 1963-65; asst. prof. English Marietta Coll., Ohio, 1965-68; asst./assoc. prof. and dir. Center for Writers Univ. S. Miss., Hattiesburg, 1970-75; chmn. English dept. Okla. State Univ., Stillwater, 1975-84, prof, 1984—. Recipient St. Lawrence Award for Fiction, NY, 1973; O. Henry first prize, Doubleday, NYC, 1979; Sherwood Anderson Prize, Mid-Am. Rvw, Bowling Green, Ohio, 1981; Novella Prize, Qtly W, Salt Lake City, 1983. Mem AWP. Address: 2018 W Sunset Dr Stillwater OK 74074

WEAVER, RICHARD L., II, b. Hanover, NH, Dec. 5, 1941; s. Richard L. and Florence B. (Grow) W.; m. Andrea A. Willis; children—R. Scott, Jacquelynn Michelle, Anthony Keith, Joanna Corinne. Author: (with Saundra Hybels) Speech/Communication, 2d ed., 1979, Speech/Communic.: A Reader, 2d ed., 1979, Speech/Communic.: A Student manual, 2d ed., 1979, Understanding Interpersonal Communic., 4th ed., 1987, (with Raymond K. Tucker & Cynthia Berryman-Fink) Research in Speech Communic., 1981, Foundations of Speech Communic.: Perspectives of a Discipline, 1982, Speech Communic. Skills, 1982, Understanding Public Communic., 1983, Readings in Speech Communic., 1985, Understanding Speech Communic. Skills, 1985, Understanding Business Communication, 1985, (with Saundra Hybels) Communicating Effectively, 1986, Skills for Communicating Effectively, 1987; contrbr. to profl jnls. AB, U. MI, 1964, MA, 1965; PhD, Ind. U., 1969. Asst. prof. U. MA, 1968-74; assoc. prof. speech communication Bowling Green State U., 1974-79, prof. interpersonal and public communic., 1979—; dir. basic speech-communication course, 1974—; vis. prof. U. Hawaii-Manoa, 1981-82. Mem. Intl. Communication Assn., Speech Communic. Assn., Central States Speech Assn., Ohio Speech Assn., Intl. Ssoc. Gen. Semantics. Home: 9583 Woodleigh Ct Perrysburg OH 43551

WEAVER, THOMAS, b. Grenville, NM, May 1, 1929; s. Joseph M. and Juanita (Archuleta) W.; m. Dora Edith Martinez, Oct. 21, 1950; children—Thomas Brian, Kathleen, Denise. Author/ed.: Indians in Calif. Rural and Reservation Areas, 1966, Medical Anthropology, 1968, (with A. Magid) Poverty: New Interdisciplinary Perspectives, 1969, Arizona Indian People and Their Relationship to the State's Total Structure, 1971, Political Orgn. and Business Mgt. in the Gila River Indian Community, 1971, (with D. White) The Anthrop. of Urban Environments, 1972, To See Ourselves: Anthrop. and Modern Social Issues, 1973, Indians of Arizona, 1974, Tribal Mgt. Procedures Study of Seven Reservns., 1974, The Douglas Report: The Community Context of Housing and Soc. Probs., 1975, Mexican Migration, 1976, (with E.A. Hoebel) Anthrop. and the Human Experience, 5th ed., 1979. BA, U. NM, 1955, MA, 1960; PhD, U.CA- Berkeley, 1965. Exec. secy. Calif. Commn. on Indian Affairs, Sacramento, 1964; asst. prof. depts. behavioral sci. and anthropology U. KY, 1964-67; asst. prof., Maurice Falk sr. faculty fellow depts. psychiatry and anthrop., U. Pitts., 1967-69; assoc. prof. anthrop. U. AZ, Tucson, 1969-75, prof. 1975—, dir. bur. Ethnic Research, 1969-77; vis. prof. Northwestern U., 1975; vis. Disting. prof. So. Meth. U., summer 1978; cons. Calif. Commn. Indian Affairs, 1965-66. Mem. AAAS, numerous profl. orgns. Home: 6644 Donna Beatrix Cr Tucson AZ 85718

WEBB, BERNICE LARSON, b. Ludell, KS; d. Carl Godfred and Ida Genevieve (Tongish) Larson; m. Ralph Raymond Schear, Aug. 9, 1942 (div. 1956); children: William Carl, Rebecca Rae Schear Gentry; m. Robert MacHardy Webb, July 14, 1961 (dec.). Author: The Basketball Man: James Naismith, 1973 (transl. into Japanese 1980); Beware of Ostriches, 1978; Poetry on the Stage: William Poel, Producer of Verse Drama, 1979; Lady Doctor on a Homestead, 1987; (essay) Critical Survey of Long Fiction, 1983; Ed. Cajun Chatter, 1964-66, The Magnolia, 1967-71; guest ed. New Laurel Rvw., 1976; ed. Louisiana Poets, 1970—; book reviewer Jnl Popular Culture, 1980—, Jnl Am. Culture, 1980—; asst. ed. Asian Basketball Confederation, 1985; contrbr. to Capper's Weekly, Kans. Qtly, Stone Country, Descant, Voices Intl. South Atlantic Qtly., English Jnl, Horn Book Mag., numerous newspapers and other publs. AB, U. Kans., 1956,

MA, 1957, PhD, 1961; postgrad. Univ. of Aberdeen (Scotland), 1959-60. Asst. instr. English, U. Kans., 1958-59, 60-61; asst. prof. English, U. Southwestern La., Lafayette, 1961-67, assoc. prof., 1967-80, prof., 1980—. Recipient Carruth Meml. poetry prizes U. Kans., 1946-81; Seaton award Kans. Qtly., 1980; grantee AAUW Ednl. Fdn., 1978-80, U. Southwestern La., 1980-81, 85-86. Home: 159 Whittington Dr Lafayette LA 70503

WEBB, JAMES EDWARD, b. Grinnell, IA, Sept. 17, 1928; s. James Garfield and Hazel (Pickering) W.; m. Mary Lou Byers, June 10, 1956 (dec. 1974); 1 son, Gregory Scott; m. 2d, Betty Louise Paul, Feb. 4, 1977; stepchildren—Whitney Davis, Sherry Davis. Ed., Grinnel Herald-Register, 1954-67, Pipeline mag., 1970-76, Colleague mag. 1967-82, Hotline nwsltr., 1970-82, Proclaimer nwsltr., 1972-82, Teamwork mag., 1967-82; author: (humorous essays) What If Chicken Little Had Been Right?, 1983, poetry anthol., 1984-85. Student U. IA, 1945-46, 48-50. Ed., Herald-Register Pub. Co., Grinnell, IA, 1954-67; pubns. mgr. Grinnel Mutual Re. Co., Grinnell, 1967-82, dir. pub. relns., 1982—. 1st recipient Sheila V. Meredith Svc. Award, PICA, 1985. Served to Sgt. 1/c, U.S. Army, 1946-48, 50-51. Mem. PICA, PRSA, Natl. Agri-Mktg. Assn. Home: R R 2 Box 20 Gilman IA 50106

WEBB, MELODY, b. Gallup, NM, Apr. 1, 1946; d. Nelden J. Webb and Lorraine Catherine (Overson) Smith; m. David S. Grauman, June 4, 1969 (div. Oct. 1980); m. 2d, Robert M. Utley, Nov. 12, 1980. Author: (book) The Last Frontier: A History of the Yukon Basin of Canada and Alaska, 1985; (report) Big Business in Alaska: The Kennecott Mines, 1898-1938, 1977, Yukon Frontiers: A Historic Resource Study of the Proposed Yukon-Charley National Rivers, 1977, Chronicles of a Cold, Cold War: The Paperwork Battle for Wrangel Island, 1981. BA, U. of Ariz.. 1968; MA in History, San Francisco State U., 1974; Ph.D. in History, U. N.Mex., 1983. Tchr. pub. jr. high schs., New Orleans, 1968-69; free-lance historian, Soldotna, Alaska, 1972-74; archeologist U. Alaska, 1974; research historian Natl. Park Service, Fairbanks, Alaska, 1975-80; Regional Historian Southwest Region, Santa Fe, New Mexico, 1980—. Lt., El Dorado Vol. Fire Dept., Sante Fe, 1983-85, asst. chief, 1986. Recipient (7) Outstanding Performance award Natl. Park Service, Sante Fe, 1979-86; Tom L. Popejoy award U. N.Mex., 1984; Marshall Fdn. scholar, 1964-65. Mem. Orgn. Am. Historians, Western History Assn., Hist. Soc. N.Mex. Home: 5 Vista Grande Ct Sante Fe NM 87505

WEBB, SHARON LYNN, b. Tampa, FL, Feb. 29, 1936, d. William Wesley and Eunice Geraldine (Tillman) Talbott; m. W. Bryan Webb, Feb. 6, 1956; children—Wendy, Jerri, Tracey. Author: RN, 1981, 86, Earthchild, 1982, 83, Earth Song, 1983, 84, Ram Song, 1984, 85, Adventures of Terra Tarkington, 1985, Pestis 18, 1987; contrbr. short stories to mags and anthols. Student, Fla. So. Coll., 1953-56, Miami-Dade Coll., 1972. Freelance wrtr., 1979—. Recipient Phoenix award Deep South Conv., 1985. Mem. AG, AL, SFWA (South/Central regional bd. dirs.). Home: Rt 2 Box 2600 Blairsville GA 30512

WEBBER, GORDON, b. Linden, MI, Oct. 25, 1912; s. Roy Eugene and Dorothea (Boyd) W.; m. Jeanne Carol Curtis, June 29, 1940 (dec.); children—Jacqueline, Dorothea, Laura. Writer TV show I Remember mama, 1950-55; exec. producer TV film The Endless War, 1970; producer Unsell the War natl. campaign, 1971; producer/dir. film The Jogger, 1971 (Cine Golden Eagle, Edinburgh Festival); author: Years of Eden, 1951, the Far Shore, 1954 (citation Friends Am. Writers), What End But Love, 1959 (award Mich. Hist. Soc.), The Great Buffalo Hotel, 1979, Our Kind of People: The Story of The First Fifty Years at Benton & Bowles, 1979, short stories. AB, Jamestown Coll., 1933; MA, U. MI, 1936. Radio, TV writer, NBC, NYC, 1938-48; freelance writer TV plays, 1948-56; with Benton & Bowles, Inc., 1948-75, ret. as sr. v.p., mgr. creative dept., 1975; instr. Parsons Schl. Design, 1975-76. Recipient citation in field of lit. Jamestown Coll., 1959. Mem. PEN, AL. Home: 7 E 86th St New York NY 10028

WEBER, BROM, b. NYC, May 14, 1917; s. Kalman and Nadia (Svonkin) W.; m. Nettie Held, Mar. 21, 1939 (dec. Aug. 1981); children—Eden Elizabeth, Kyle Maxson. Author: Hart Crane: A Biographical and Critical Study, 1948, The Letters of Hart Crane, 1916-32, 1952, Sut Lovingood, 1954, An Anthology of American Humor, 1962, Sherwood Anderson, 1964, The Complete Poems and Selected Letters and Prose of Hart Crane, 1966, Sense and Sensibility in Twentieth-Century Writing, 1970, Hart Crane, 1973, Our Multi-Ethnic Origins and American Literary Studies, 1975; co-ed.: American Vanguard, 1953, American Literature: Tradition and Innovation, 1969; asst. ed. Twice A Year, 1946-48; assoc. ed. Tiger's Eye, 1949-51; adv. ed.: The Lovingood Papers, 1962-67, Modern Fiction Studies, 1957-58, Early Am. Lit., 1966-69, Studies in American Humor, 1973—, MELUS, 1976—; editorial bd. The Hollins Critic, 1965-66. BS, CCNY, 1938; MA, U. WY, 1955; PhD, U.MN, 1957. Writer, ed. Hist. Records Survey, NY, 1938-39; writer, adminr. govt. agcys., Washington & Jersey City, 1940-45; instr. English, CCNY, 1945-50; lectr. lit. and writing New Schl. Soc. Research, NYC, 1948-54; asst. prof. English Purdue U., 1957-58; assoc. prof. English, secy. Am. Studies prog. U. MN, 1958-63; prof. English U. CA-Davis, 1963-76, acting chmn. dept. English, 1964-65, vice chmn. 1965-70, chmn., 1977-78, chmn. Am. studies prog., 1969-70, prof. Am. lit., 1976—; numerous vis. professorships; cons. NEH, 1974-79. Recipient McKnight Humanities award McKnight Fdn., ,62; sr. non-resident fellow Can. Council, 1963; Am. Philo. Soc. grantee, 1976; U. CA Regents humanities fellow, 1976. Mem. MLA, Am. Humor Studies Assn., Soc. for Multi-Ethnic Lit. of U.S. (hon.). Home: 23 Almond Ln Davis CA 95616

WEBER, CHARLES EDWARD, b. NYC, Oct. 30, 1924, s. Walter E. and Clara (Hahr) W.; m. Elizabeth Ridley Woodruff, June 4, 1949; children—David C., Steven W., Kenneth R., Katherine C. Author: Arthritis as a Chronic Potassium Deficiency, 1981, Copper Response in Arthritis, 1985; contrbr. numerous articles to sci. publs. BS in Chemistry, Rutgers U., 1951, MS in Soil Sci., 1956. Analytical chemist State Chem. Office, New Brunswick, N.J., 1951-56; devel. chemist Johns-Manville (N.J.) Co., 1956-57; contractor, Warren, N.J., 1957-82; owner, Kalium, Inc., Warren, 1982-86. Served with USN, 1943-46. Home: 141 Mt Horeb Rd Warren NJ 07060

WEBER, ELIZABETH ANN, b. St. Paul, May 14, 1950, d. Alvin Francis and Eleanor Elizabeth (Smith) Weber; m. William Turner, July 22, 1977 (div. 1980). Author: Small Mercies, 1984; included in anthologies Where We Are: Montana Poets Anthology, 1978, Rain in the Forest, Light in the Trees, 1982; contrbr. to Tendril, Calyx, Scratchgravel Hills, Mont. Rvw, others; ed.: CutBank, 1976, Gilt Edge, New Series, 1979-81. BA, U. Minn., 1973; MFA,U. Mont., 1977. Artist-in-schls. Mont. Arts Council, Helena, 1984-86; instr. N. Mex. State U., Las Cruces, 1986—; PhD candidate and instr. SUNY, Binghamton. Recipient Loring Williams Coll. Poetry prize AAP, 1977, 1st Book award Mont. Arts Council, 1983; Millay Colony for Arts resident, Austerlitz, N.Y., 1984; Milton Kessler Coll. poetry prize AAP, 1987; SUNY Binghamton's Newhouse Award 1986-87. Mem. AWP. Home: 78 Baker St Johnson City NY 13790

WEBER, SAMUEL, b. NYC, July 31, 1926; s. Bernard and Gertrude (Ellenberg) W.; m. Eileen Gloria Hornstein, Mar. 5, 1950; children—Bruce Jay, Robert Matthew. Author: Modern Digital Circuits, 1964, Optoelectronic Devices and Circuits, 1968, Large and Medium Scale Integration, 1974, Circuits for Electronics Engineers, 1977, Electronic Circuits Notebook, 1981. BS in Elec. Engring., VA Poly. Inst., 1947. Engr. N.Y. Bd. Transp., 1948-50, U.S. Naval Shipyard, Bklyn., 1950-52, Barlow Engring. Co., NYC, 1952-54; engring. supr. Curtiss Wright Corp., Woodridge, NJ, 1954-56; electronics engr. Loral Electronics Corp., NYC, 1957-58; staff Electronics Mag., NYC, 1958-67, assoc. mng. ed., 1968-70, exec. ed., 1970-79, ed.-in-chief, 1979—; ed.-in-chief Electrotech. Mag., NYC, 1967. Mem. IEEE. Home: 1 Fieldston Dr Hartsdale NY 10530

WEBER, SHIRLEY ANNE, b. Brownlee, Sask., Can., Oct. 1, 1928; d. Lloyd Wesley Foulston and Grace Francis (Wilkinson) Foulston Cramer; came to U.S., 1946; m. Donald Homer Weber, June 25, 1946 (div. June, 1960); children—Fern Marie Weber Dick, Kenneth Donald, Jo Anne. Author: Blueprint for Building Quality, 1981, reprinted 100,000 copies, 1986; contrbr. to various newspapers and mags. including Sacramento Union, Motor Home Life, Going Places. AA, Am. River Coll., Carmichael, CA, 1974; Jnlsm. BA, CA St. U., Sacramento, 1978. Clerk, CA Dept. of Transp., 1959-64, information officer 1978—; secy. CA General Services Youth Authority, 1964-70, CA Water Resources Control Board, 1970-75; teletypist CA Dept. Motor Vehicles, 1975-77; edn., consultant-wrtr. CA Contractors' License Bd. and CA Dept. Consumer Affairs, Sacramento, 1977-78. Caroline Wakefield Scholarship, CA St. U., 1977. Home: 3672 1B Clairemont Dr San Diego CA 92117

WEBER, SOL, b. Bklyn., Dec. 26, 1933, s. Marcus and Sadie (Mann) W. Contrbr. articles to Cricket mag., Saving Energy, Strategies for Reading series, Bicycling's Best Tours. BEE, CCNY, 1956. Served with U.S. Army, 1957-59. Address: 25-14 37th St Astoria NY 11103

WEBSTER, DIANE LYNN, b. Ontario, OR, Sept. 16, 1954; d. Miles Riley and Elenora (Schlagel) W. Contrbr. to Modern Haiku, Great Lakes Gazette, The Archer, Broken Streets, Up Against the Wall, Mother, Kaleidoscope, Yet Another Small Magazine, other lit mags. Wrkg. on haiku, short stories, poems. AA, Treasure Valley Community Coll., 1974. Janitor, dental office (Ontario, OR), 1973-81; circulation asst., Delta (CO) County Independent, 1982—. Mem. Natl. Wrtrs. Club, Calif. State Poetry Society. Republican. Home: 620 Sloan Delta CO 81416

WEBSTER, GEORGE CALVIN, b. South Haven, MI, July 17, 1924; s. Eugene Homer Webster and Hazel Edna (Empson) Davis; m. Sandra Lee Whitman, Jan. 23, 1960; children—Jeffrey C., Kimberley A. Author: Nitrogen Metabolism in Plants, 1959. Contrbr. chpts. to scientific books, articles o profl. jnls. Wrkg. on novel. B.S., Western Mich. U., 1948; M.S., U. Minn., 1949, Ph.D., 1952. Prof. Ohio State U., Columbus, 1955-61; visiting prof. U. Wis., Madison, 1961-65; chief environmental lab. Space Ctr., Cape Kennedy, FL, 1965-71; head dept., assoc. dean Fla. Inst. of Technology, Melbourne, FL, 1971-85; free-lance wrtr., 1985—. Mem. Am. Assn. Advancement Sci., Am. Soc. Biological Chemists, Am. Soc. Cell Biology. Home: 530 Majorca Ct Satellite Beach FL 32937

WEBSTER, JANI JOHE, b. Johnson City, NY, Nov. 24; d. Lorenzo Frank and Virginia Viola (Boyd) Johe; m. Ogden H. Webster, June 29; children—Jon, Nila. Author: A Spider on the Wall; contrbr. to Calliopes Corner, Inky Trails, Midwest Poetry Rvw, Vega, other lit mags, anthols. BA, Houghton (N.Y.) Coll. Tchr. public schls., Penn Yan, N.Y., Endwell, N.Y. Recipient Best of Issue award Arulo!, Calliopes Corner, Tiotis. Mem. Women Wrtrs. Alliance, Bensalem Assn. Women Wrtrs. Home: 22 Barons Rd Rochester NY 14617

WEBSTER, LEE, b. Oak Park, IL, Jul. 5, 1948; s. Lee and Grace (Holm) Webster; m. Susan Samson, Feb. 22,m 1968 (div. Sept. 1975); 1 dau.—Brooke; 2nd m. Diane Girardi, Mar. 31, 1979; 1 son—Nicholas. Editor: ACM, 1976—, fourteen titles for Thunder's Mouth Press, 1981-85, Curtains (James McManus), 1985. BA, MA, U. of Illinois. Editor/publisher Another Chicago Magazine (Chicago), 1976—; production manager Mobium (Chicago), 1979-84; customer service rep. RR Donnelley (Chicago), 1985—. Board Mem. CCLM. Home: 1152 S East Ave Oak Park IL 60304

WECHSLER, JILL, b. NYC, July 5, 1946; d. Frederick L. and Rhoda (Daum) Wechsler; m. Robert H. Nelson, Dec. 23, 1971; children—Frederick D., Martha I. Columnist: Good Housekeeping, 1980-81. Contrbr. articles to mags., newspapers including Dun's Bus. Month, Cosmopolitan, Washington Post, others. A.B., Vassar Coll., 1968; M.A., Hunter Coll., 1972. Ed. BBP div. Prentice Hall, N.Y.C., 1969-71; ed. Gallagher Report, NYC., 1971-74, Washington ed., Washington, 1974—; mng. ed. Fgn. Bank Focus, Washington, 1986—. Mem. Washington Ind. Wrtrs. (bd. dirs. 1985, 86). Home: 7715 Rocton Ave Chevy Chase MD 20815

WEDGE, GEORGE FRANCIS, III, b. Rochester, NY, Sept. 13, 1927; s. George Francis Wedge and Marie Anne Louise (White) Gardner; m. Margaret Alice Nasmith, Aug. 29, 1953; children—Philip Carter, Louise Elizabeth Pennewell, Alberta Elliott Mayeux. Contrbr. articles to profl. jnls., lit. mags., anthols. Editor: Cottonwood Mag., 1985—; assoc. editor: Critique, 1957-59; adv. editor: Kans. Quarterly, 1971—. Wrkg. on book on alcoholism, novel, collection of poems. AB, Middlebury Coll., 1952; MA, U. Minn.-Mpls., 1955, PhD, 1967. Instr., U. Minn., Mpls., 1955-58; instr. to asst. prof. English and linguistics U. Kans., Lawrence, 1958-68, assoc. prof., 1968—. Bd. dirs. Douglas County Citizens Com. on Alcoholism, Lawrence, 1974—, Kans. Alcoholism Counselors Assn., Topeka, 1982-85. Served with USN, 1945-50. Recipient Seaton award Kans. Quarterly, 1981, 85. Mem. NCTE, MLA, Kansas Wrtrs Assn. Home: 1645 Louisiana St Lawrence KS 66044

WEED, CHERYL ANNE, b. South Hiram, MA, Oct. 21, 1947; d. Archie Orion and Rhoda Levina (Day) Walker; m. Perley Owen Weed, Nov. 1, 1965; children—Webb James, Ira Lee. Contrbr. poems to anthols. Wrkg. on short stories, poems. Diploma in Exec. Secy., Accounting, Westbank Bus. Coll., 1977; student U. Southern Ala., 1965—. Secy. spcl. services Galveston Schl. Dept., TX, 1979-81; payroll clrk. Hydril, Harvey, LA, 1982. Recipient Golden Poet award World of Poetry, 1987, Honorable Mention, 1987. Home: 3004 Olde Gate Rd Mobile AL 36609

WEEKLEY, RICHARD J., b. Grand Junction, CO, Sept. 24, 1945; s. Robert Matthew and Nita Marjorie (Shepherd) W.; m. Calla Darlene, July 1966 (div. 1973); m. 2d Donna Ann, June 21, 1977 (div. May 1985); m. 3rd, Rosalba, May 24, 1985; 1 step-dau., Patty Gonzales. Author: The Adventures of Chef Blake PlasticMan, 1975; author poetry: Mayan Night, 1980, Little Pianos, 1982, Small Diligences, 1988; contrbr. to Poetry/LA, Kansas Quarterly, Queen's Quarterly (Canada), Blue Buildings; co-ed. vol. No. Mag. BS, U. Utah, MS. Teacher, Hart High School, Newhall, CA, 1967—. Winner 1986 Black Bear Publs. Intl Chapbook competition: Not The Subject of Cocktail Parties. Home: 24721 Newhall Ave Newhall CA 91321

WEEKS, ALBERT LOREN, b. Highland Park, MI, Mar. 28, 1923; s. Albert Loren and Vera Grace (Jarvis) W. Author: Reading American History, 1963, The First Bolshevik: A Political Biography of Peter Tkachev, 1968, The Other Side of Coexistence: An Analysis of Russian Foreign Policy, 1970, Richard Hofstadter's The American Political Tradition and the Age of Reform, 1973, Andrei Sakharov and the Soviet Dissidents, 1975, The Troubled Detente, 1976; co-author: (with Herbert I. London) Myths That Rule America, 1980, (with William C. Bodie) War and Peace: Soviet Russia Speaks, 1983; intl. affairs ed.: Def. Sci. 2001, 1982—, Technology Mag.; columnist: Def. Report, 1982—, nat. security ed., N.Y. Tribune, 1982—. Student U. Mich., 1942-43; MA, U. Chgo., 1949; PhD, Columbia U., 1965; cert. Russian Inst., 1960. Rprtr. Chgo. City News Bur., 1946; poli. analyst U.S. Dept. State, 1950-53, Free Europe Com., Inc., 1953-57; lectr. U.S. diplomatic history and Soviet govt. Columbia U., 1951-52; editorial asst. Newsweek Mag., 1957-58; tech. glossary compiler McGraw-Hill Book Co., 1960-61; prof. continuing edn., NYU, NYC, 1959—. Home: 37 Washington Sq W New York NY 10011

WEEKS, ROBERT LEWIS, b. Huntington, WV, July 9, 1924; s. Edwin Francis and Josephine Isabel (Steckel) W.; m. Joanne Parsons, June 7, 1950; children—Robin, Hallam. Books of poetry: The Maker of Globes, 1959, For Those Who Waked Me, 1966. Chapbook—poetry: The Master of Clouds, 1971. Poetry, short stories and rvws in The New Yorker, Mass. Rvw, Prairie Schooner, Beloit Poetry Jnl, Shenandoah, Chgo. Rvw, Poetry Northwest, numerous other pubsl. MA, W.Va. U., 1949; PhD, Ind. U., 1956. Served to T/4 U.S. Army, 1944-46; Philippines. Prof. U. Wis.-Eau Claire, 1954-63, Stephen F. Austin State U., Nacogdoches, Tex., 1963-66, Colo. Women's Coll., Denver, 1966-81. Mem. MLA. Recipient award Best Poems of 1974, Borestone Mountain, 1974. Home: 6767 E Dartmouth Denver CO 80224

WEETMAN, ROBERT RAY, b. Los Angeles, Nov. 23, 1937. Contrbr. numerous poems to anthols. Wrkg. on collection of poetry. B.A. in History, Hofstra U., 1969. Home: 1319 Robertson Rd Anniston AL 36201

WEGLARZ, TERRI MARIE, b. Westchester, IL, May 23, 1965; d. John Erroll and Mariann Joyce (Pensis) W. Grad. Immaculate Heart of Mary Coll. Editorial staff Westchester News, 1978-85; ed. Chgo. Bowler Inc., Westchester, 1981—. Mem. Midwest Bowling Wrtrs. Office: Box 7008 Westchester IL 60153

WEHLITZ, ANNIE LOUISE, (Lou Rogers Wehlitz), b. Hope Mills, NC; d. Duncan Cooper and Nora Lee (Petty) Rogers; m. Hubert Frank Wehlitz, June 4, 1961; step-children—Albert, Lora Wehlitz Shafer. Contrbr. to The Story of Fayetteville; Author: The First Thanksgiving, 1962, Tar Heel Women, (poetry) Memory Is a Star, 1968. Also publ. about 400 sketches of people and poems. AB in Ed. and Jnlsm. U. of NC, 1953. Primary teacher NC pub. schls., 1929-59; asst. ed. NC education (Raleigh), 1943-44; textbook ed. Follett Pub. Co. (Chicago), 1959-62. Mem. Natl. League of Am. Pen Women; NC Poetry Soc., NC Historical & Literary Soc; Alpha Tau Chapter of Delta Kappa Gamma honorary. Home: 310 McAllister St Fayetteville NC 28305

WEICH, PATRICIA GALLANT, b. NYC, July 27, 1945; d. Jack Anson Finke and Gladys (Selverne) Gallant; m. Dr. Martin J. Weich, Aug. 1, 1970; 1 son, Graig Farrell. Articles in various newspapers and mags. Freelance wrtr.. Mem. NWU (mem. edl. collective NY local newsletter), Writers Community. Home: 308 W 104 St New York NY 10025

WEICHEL, KENNETH, b. San Francisco, Oct. 10, 1946; s. Frederich Carl and Isabel (Deschler) W. Author: Paper Pudding, 1971, Androgyne, 1972, Beatitude #27, 1977, Soup, 1980, Ins and Out, 1980, Invisible City, 1980, Chapel Perilous, 1985, also Androgyne Nos. 2-8, 1976-84. BA, San Francisco State U., 1969, MA, 1971. Editor, pub. Androgyne Books, San Francisco, 1971—. Distrbr. Poetry Flash, San Francisco/Berkeley, 1978; coordinator for book fair Intl. Poetry Festival, San Francisco, 1979; book fair organizer Left/Write Conf., San Francisco, 1981; Natl. Poetry Week book fair coord., 1987. Mem. COSMEP, Pacific Ctr. Book Arts. CCLM mag. grantee, 1980. Home: 930 Shields St San Francisco CA 94132

WEIDEMANN, ANTON FREDRICK, b. Tolna, ND, Mar. 26, 1917, s. Jacob and Harriett (Byng) W.; m. Thelma Louise Branson, Nov. 7, 1941; children—Jeanne L. Rollins-Weidemann, Ronald E. Poetry collections: Golden Years of Youth, 1973, Seasons-Seasons, 1974, Through a Poet's Window, 1974, Roses and Thorns, 1976, Sands of Time, 1978, A Far Cry from Heaven, 1984, Green Grows the Grass, 1983; contrbr. poetry to over 100 publs. Student pub. schls., Huntington Beach, Calif. Ranch mgr., Pauma Valley, Calif., 1946—. Recipient award Clover Intl. Poetry Competition, 1974, Diploma D. Beneinevenza, Masters of Modern Poetry, Rome, 1977, M.O.P. Press Award, 1980. Mem. United Amateur Press Assn. Address: 2700 E Valley Pkwy 67 Escondido CA 92027

WEIDMAN, JEROME, b. NYC, Apr. 4, 1913; s. Joseph and Annie (Falkovitz) W.; m. Peggy Wright, 1943; children—Jeffrey, John Whitney. Author: (novels) I Can Get It for You Wholesale, 1937, What's in It for Me?, 1938, I'll Never Go There Any More, 1941, The Lights Around the Shore, 1943, Too Early To Tell, 1946, The Price is Right, 1949, The Hand of the Hunter,

1951, The Third Angel, 1953, Give Me Your Love, 1954, Your Daughter, Iris, 1955, The Enemy Camp, 1958, Before You Go, 1960, The Sound of Bow Bells, 1962, Word of Mouth, 1964, Other People's Money, 1968, The Center of the Action, 1969, Fourth Street East, 1971, Last Respects, 1972, Tiffany Street, 1974, The Temple, 1976, A Family Fortune, 1978, Counsellors-at-Law, 1980 (recipient Antoinette Perry award, Drama Critic Circle award); (short stories) The Horse that Could Whistle Dixie, 1939, The Captain's Tiger, 1947, A Dime A Throw, 1957, My Father Sits In The Dark, 1961, Nine Stories, 1964, The Death of Dickie Draper, 1965; PhD, plays) Fiorello! (NY Drama Critics and Tony awards, co-recipient Pulitzer prize in drama 1960), 1959, Tenderloin, 1961, I Can Get It For You Wholesale, 1962, Ivory Tower, 1969, Asterisk, 1969; (travel) Letter of Credit, 1940; (essays) Traveler's Cheque, 1954, Back Talk, 1963; (memoir) Praying for Rain, 1986. CCNY, 1930-33, Washington Sq. Coll., NYC, 1933-34, NYU Law Schl., 1934-37. Mem. AL. Home: 1966 Pacific Ave San Francisco CA 94109

WEIGEL, ALICE M., b. Harper County, KS, July 29, 1909; d. Franklin Wellington and Dora (Downs) Eggerman; m. Ed. Weigel, June 3, 1930 (dec. 1970); children—Willis, Kenneth, Jan, Phyllis Krueger. Author: Bulwarks of Democracy. Grad. public schls. Jetmore, KS. Home: 509 Mission Mt Hays KS 67601

WEIGEL, TOM, (Harington McGrail), b. NYC, Oct. 14, 1948; s. Thomas McGrail Weigel and Theresa Patricia Harrington-Sheehan. Author: (poems) Little Heart, 1981, Sonnets, 1981; (novels) Audrey Hepburn's Symphonic Salad & The Coming of Autumn, 1980, Twenty Four Haiku After the Japanese, 1980. Student Parsons Coll., NYC, 1967, 77-78. Recipient 3d prize for poetry Ariz. State U., 1969. Mem. P&W, GCLM, Mary Stuart Soc. (Robert Southwell Achievement award 1985, 86). Home: 515 E 6th St C8 New York NY 10009

WEIKEL, DANA ROSE, b. Medford, OR, Oct. 8, 1943; d. Jonathan and Emma Rose (Thornberry) Jackson; m. George Edwin Weikel, Aug. 19, 1961; children—Jonathan, David, Cynthia, George. Author: Death from Child Abuse and No One Heard, 1986, Wrkg. on non-fiction. Feature wrtr. La Femme, Orlando, Fla., 1984-85; freelance wrtr., Orlando, 1985—. Mem. Nat. League Am. Pen Women (treas. Orlando br.), Wrtrs. Group (founder), Fla. Freelance Wrtrs. Assn. Home: 716 Marlowe Ave Olando FL 32809

WEIL, LISE, b. Chgo., Dec. 13, 1950; d. David Maxwell and Aase (Pedersen) Weil. Founder, editor, pub.: Trivia, A. Jnl of Ideas, 1982—. BA summa cum laude, Cornell U., 1972; PhD. comparative Lit., Brown Univ., 1987. Grantee NEA, 1985, 87; Mass. Council on Arts & Humanities Merit Aid grant, 1986-88. Mem. CCLM, Women in German, MLA. Home: Box 70 Montague MA 01351

WEINBERG, ARTHUR, b. Chgo., Dec. 8, 1915; s. Abraham Morris and Anna (Avedon) W.; m. Lila Shaffer, Jan. 25, 1953; children—Hedy Merrill, Anita Michelle, Wendy Clare. Works include: Attorney for the Damned, 1957, (with Lila Weinberg) The Muckrakers, 1961, Verdicts Out of Court, 1963, Instead of Violence, 1963, Passport to Utopia, 1968, Some Dissenting Voices, 1970, Clarence Darrow: Sentimental Rebel, 1980. Free- lance writer. AA, YMCA Coll., Chgo., 1935; diploma jnlsm., Northwestern U., 1938, PhD, 1941. Researcher Ill. Writers Project, Chgo., 1939-41; tech. writer Consol. Aircraft Corp., San Diego, 1941-45; ed. Ft. Lewis (Wash.) Flame, 1946; rprtr. Fairchild Publs., Chgo., 1947-81; midwest bur. chief HFD, 1977-81; midwest ed. Mart mag., 1981—; book reviewer Chgo. Daily News, 1962-76, Chgo. Sunday Tribune, 1976—, Women's Wear Daily, Los Angeles Times; faculty Schl. for New Learning, DePaul, Chgo., 1976—. Recipient social justice award Clarence Darrow Community Center, 1980, Friends of Lit. Chgo. Fdn. Award for best biog., 1980, soc. Midland Authors Award for best biog., 1980, Friends of Midland Authors Award for "Body of Work," 1987. Mem. SMA, ACLU, Press Club, Headline Club. Home: 5421 S Cornell Ave Chicago IL 60615

WEINBERG, GERHARD LUDWIG, b. Hannover, Ger., Jan. 1, 1928; s. Max Bendix and Kate Sarah (Gruenebaum) W.; came to U.S., 1940, naturalized, 1949; m. Wilma Lee Jeffrey, Mar. 29, 1958 (dec. 1985). Author: Guide to Captured German Documents, 1952, Germany and The Soviet Union, 1939-41, 1954, The Foreign Policy of Hitler's Germany, 1933-1936, 1970, The Foreign Policy of Hitler's Germany, 1937-1939, 1980, Behind the Scenes of World War II, 1981; co-author Soviet Partisans in World War II, 1964; ed.: Hitlers zweites Buch, 1961, Transformation of a Continent, 1975; bd. eds.: Jnl Modern History, 1970-72, Central European History, 1976-80. BA, N.Y. State Coll. Tchrs., Albany, 1948; MA, U. Chgo., 1949, PhD, 1951. Research analyst War Documentation project Columbia U., 1951-54; vis. lectr. history U. Chgo., 1954-55, U. KY, Lexington, 1955-56; dir. project microfilming captured German documents Am. Hist. Assn., 1956-57; asst. prof. U. KY, 1957-59; mem. faculty U. MI, Ann Arbor, 1959-74, prof. history, 1963-74, chmn. dept., 1972-73; William Rand Kenan, Jr. prof. history U. NC, Chapel Hill, 1974—; vis. prof. Bonn U., 1983; bd. dirs. Am. Com. History World War II, 1968—; cons. in field. Numerous fellowships inclg. NEH, 1978-79, Guggenheim Fdn., 1971-72. Recipient George Louis Beer prize, Am. Hist. Assn., 1971, Halvorson prize, Western Assn. for German Studies, 1981. Mem. numerous profl. orgns. incl. Am. Hist. Assn., conf. Group Central European History, Am. Commn. on History of Second World War. Home: 331 Azalea Dr Chapel Hill NC 27514

WEINBERG, JONATHAN DAVID, b. Bklyn., July 29, 1967; s. Morton and Sandra (Hirschhorn) W. Ed.: Lincoln Log, 1982-84. A.B. in philosophy, Princeton U., 1988. Bus. mgr. Startone, Brklyn., 1979-85; publisher Princeton Engineer Mag., NJ, 1984—. Home: 523 Laughlin Princeton U Princeton NJ 08544

WEINBERG, LILA SHAFFER, b. Sam and Blanche (Hyman) Shaffer; m. Arthur Weinberg, Jan. 25, 1953; children—Hedy Merrill and Anita Michelle (twins), Wendy Clare. Author: (with Arthur Weinberg) The Muckrakers, 1961, Verdicts Out of Court, 1963, Instead of Violence, 1963, Passport to Utopia, 1968, Some Dissenting Voices, 1970, Clarence Darrow: A Sentimental Rebel, 1980. Editor Ziff-Davis Pub. Co., 1944-53; assoc. chief manuscript ed. jnls. U. Chgo. Press, 1966-80, sr. manuscript ed. books, 1980—; mem. faculty New Schl. for Learning, De Paul U., 1976—., Chgo.; vis. faculty, U. of Chgo., Continuing Edn. Programs. Recipient Friends of Lit. award Chgo. Fdn. Lit., 1980, Social Justice award Darrow Community Ctr., 1980., Soc. Midland Authors Award for best biog., 1980, Friends of Midland Authors Award for "Body of Work," 1987. Mem. SMA, ACLU, YIVO, Pioneer Women, Clarence Darrow Commemorative Com. Home: 5421 S Cornell Ave Chicago IL 60615

WEINBERG, SUSAN CLARE, b. New Haven, Nov. 8, 1959, d. Robert Lester and Patricia Wendy (Yates) Weinberg. Contrbr. short stories: Intro mag., Gargoyle, Sojourner, other publs; contrbr. articles, rvws to Zoogoer mag., Theatre Jnl, Ithaca Jnl; ed. Epoch Qtly, 1985. BA, Boston U., 1982; MFA, Cornell U., 1985. Editorial asst. Theatre Jnl, 1984-85, Friends of the Natl. Zoo, Washington, 1985—. Recipient Annl. Lit. award Antietam Rvw, 1984, Arthur Lynn Andrews prize for fiction, Cornell U., 1985. Mem. P&W, Washington Ind. Wrtrs., Washington Wrtrs.' Center. Home: 5171 N 37th Rd Arlington VA 22207

WEINBROT, HOWARD DAVID, b. Bklyn., May 14, 1936; s. William and Rose (Shapiro) W. Author: The Formal Strain, 1969, Augustus Caesar in Augustan England, 1978, Alexander Pope and the Traditions of Formal Verse Satire, 1982, Eighteenth-Century Satire, 1988; ed. New Aspects of Lexicography, 1972; co-ed. The 18th Century: A Current Bibliography for 1973, 1975; co-ed. Oxford Anthology of Poetry in English, 1987. BA, Antioch Coll., Yellow Springs, OH, 1958; MA with honors, U. chgo., 1959, PhD, 1963. Tchg. fellow U. Chgo., 1962-63; instr. English Yale U., 1963-66; asst. prof., assoc. prof. U. Cal.-Riverside, 1966-69; mem. faculty U. WI, Madison, 1969—, prof. English, 1972-84, Ricardo Quintana Professor, 1984—. Sr. fellow NEH, 1975-76, summer fellow Huntington Lib., 1977, fellow Newberry Lib.-Brit. Acad., 1977-78; Huntington-NEH fellow, 1983; Newberry-NEH fellow, 1985. Mem. Am. & Midwest Socs. 18th Century Studies, Johnson Soc., MLA, Johnsonians. Home: 1505 Wood Ln Madison WI 53705

WEINER, HANNAH A., b. Providence, Nov. 4, 1928, s. Samuel Robert and Ruth (Marks) Finegold; m. Aaron David Weiner, June 19, 1955 (div. June 1959). Author: Sun, June 9, 1975, Clairvoyant Journal, 1978, Little Books Indians, 1980, Nijole's House, 1981, Code Poems, 1982, Sixteen, 1983, Spoke, 1984, Written In, 1985. BA, Radcliffe Coll., 1950. Lingerie designer Kayser Roth Co., NYC, 1959-66, A.H. Schreiber Co., NYC, 1968-73. Copley Fdn. Cassandra grantee, 1968; NEA grant, 1986. Home: 77 E 12th St 2G New York NY 10003

WEINER, MYRON, b. NYC, Mar. 11, 1931; s. Human and Anna (Peretz) W.; m. Sheila Leiman, June 29, 1952; children—Beth, Saul Jeremy. Author: Party Politics in India, 1957, The Politics of Scarcity, 1962, Political Change in South Asia, 1963, Party Building in a New Nation: The Indian National Congress, 1967, Sons of the Soil, 1978, India at the Polls: The Parliamentary Elections of 1977, 1978, India at the Polls—1980, 1983; co- author: Politics of the Developing Areas, 1960, Rapid Population Growth: Consequences and Policy Implications, 1971, Crises and Sequences in Political Development, 1972, Policy Sciences and Population, 1975; ed.: Modernization: The Dynamics of Growth, 1966, Political Parties and Political Development, 1966, State Politics in India, 1968; co-ed.: Indian Voting Behavior, 1963, Electoral Politics in Indian States, 4 vols., 1974-77, The State Religion and Ethnic Politics, 1986, Understanding Political Development, 1987, Competitive Elections in Developing Countries, 1987; editorial bd. Global Political Assessment. BS, CCNY, 1951; MA in Politics, Princeton U., 1953,

PhD, 1955. Instr. Princeton U., 1951-52; asst. prof. U. Chgo., 1956-61; mem. faculty MIT, 1961—; prof. poli. sci. & sr. staff mem. Ctr. Intl. Studies, 1965—, chmn. dept. poli. sci., 1974-77, Ford prof. poli. sci., 1977—, dir. M.I.T. center for Intl Studies, 1987—; mem. Ctr. for Population Studies, schl. Pub. Health, Harvard U., 1973—; co-chmn. joint Harvard/MIT faculty seminar on poli. devel.; vis. prof. Inst. Econ. Growth, Delhi (India) U., 1970; vis. scholar U. Paris, 1966-67, Harry S. Truman Inst., Hebrew U., 1979; chmn. Joint Com. on S. Asia, Am. Council Learned Socs./Social Sci. Research Council, 1980—; secretary American Political Science Assn., 1986; cons. to govt. and fdns. Recipient numerous fellowships. Mem. numerous profl. orgns. incl. AAAS, Council on Fgn. Relations, Natl. Acad. Sci. Home: 1258 Beacon Brookline MA 02146

WEINKAUF, MARY LOUISE S., B. Eau Claire, WI, Sept. 22, 1938; d. Joseph Michael and Marie Barbara (Holzinger) Stanley; m. Alan Dale Winkauf, Oct. 12, 1962 (div. 1986); children: Stephen, Xanti. Author: Early Poems by a Late Beginner, 1976, Mitchell: Centennial History, 1981. New Home, New Hope, 1982, Twentieth Century Science Fiction Writers, 1986; poetry and articles in numerous lit mags, other publs. BA in Edn., U. Wis.-Eau Claire, 1961; MA, U. Tenn., 1962, PhD, 1966. Organist St. John's Luth. Ch., Eau Claire, 1957-61; instr. English, U. Tenn., Knoxville, 1965-66; asst. prof. Adrian Coll., Mich., 1966-69; prof., chmn. dept. Dakota Wesleyan U., Mitchell, S.D., 1969—; organist New Home Luth. Ch., Mitchell, 1983—. Chmn. bd. dirs. Oscar Howe Art Ctr., Mitchell, 1984-86; secy. Republican Women, Mitchell, 1971-73. Named one of Outstanding Educators of Am., Dakota Wesleyan U., 1972, 74. Mem. Sci. Fiction Research Assn., AAUW (state bd. 1986—, Outstanding Mem. award 1984), S.D. State Poetry Soc. (bd. dirs., sec., v.p., pres. 1972—, Perryman-Visser award 1976). Home: 914 University Blvd Mitchell SD 57301

WEINSTEIN, NORMAN, b. Phila., Jan. 26, 1948; s. Emmanuel Weistein and Gertrude (Zamarin) Shafer; m. Julie Hall. Author: Gertrude Stein and the Literature of the Modern Consciousness, 1970, Hanged Man Dances, 1979, Nigredo (Selected Poems 1970-1980), 1982, Albedo, 1984. BA, Bard Coll., 1969; MAT, SUNY-New Paltz, 1975. Coordinator spl. projects Boise State U., Idaho, 1985-86. Mem. Assn. Caribbean Studies. Home: 2301 N 13th Boise ID 83702

WEINSTEIN, ROCIO AITANIA, b. Cordoba, Argentina, Jan. 4, 1943; arrd. USA July 1944; d. Mauricio Leib and Emilia (Barragan) Lasansky; m. Alan Herbert Weinstein, Apr. 4, 1963; children: Rachael Simcha, Anna Chaia, Daniel Aaron, Adam Samuel. Short fiction in Wascana Rvw, Antigonish Rvw, Quarry, West Branch, Salome, Revista/Rvw Interamericana, Kans Qtly, Long Story, Univ. Iowa Museum brochure. BA, U. Iowa, 1970. Pottery instr. Georgian Coll., Ont. Can., 1973-76; co-owner The Barn Collections, Iowa City, 1983. Recipient grant Ontario Arts Council, Toronto, 1982. Mem. AWP, PEN. Address: Box 53 RR5 Iowa City IA 52240

WEINTRAUB, JOSEPH, b. Phila., Dec. 2, 1945. Contrbr. fiction to Motor Sports Jnl, Chgo. Reader, Cream City Rvw, Crosscurrents, Chouteau Rvw, Ascent, Kans. Qtly; contrbr. poetry to Hyperion, Kindred Spirit. BA, U. Pitts., 1966; MA, U. Chgo., 1967 (NYC), 1974. Recipient Ill. Arts Cncl. Fiction award, 1985. Address: 5442 East View Pk Chicago IL 60615

WEINTRAUB, STANLEY, b. Phila., Apr. 17, 1929; s. Ben and Ray (Segal) W.; m. Rodelle Horwitz, June 6, 1954; children—Mark, David, Erica. Author: An Unfinished Novel by Bernard Shaw, 1958, C.P. Snow: A Spectrum, 1963, Private Shaw and Public Shaw, 1963, The War in the Wards, 1964, The Yellow Book: Quintessence of the Nineties, 1974, Reggie, 1965, The Art of William Golding, 1965, The Savoy: Nineties Experiment, 1966, The Court Theatre, 1966, Beardsley, 1967, Biography and Truth, 1967, The Last Great Cause, The Intellectuals and the Spanish Civil War, 1968, Evolution of a Revolt: Early Postwar Writings of T.E. Lawrence, 1968, The Literary Criticism of Oscar Wilde, 1968, Journey to Heartbreak, 1971, Whistler: A Biography, 1974, Lawrence of Arabia: The Literary Impulse, 1975, Four Rossettis: A Victorian Biography, 1977, Aubrey Beardsley: Imp of the Perverse, 1976, The London Yankees: Portraits of American Writers and Artists in England, 1894-1914, 1979, The Unexpected Shaw: Biographical Approaches to G.B.S. and His Work, 1983, A Stillness Heard Round the World: The End of the Great War, 1985, Victoria: An Intimate Biography, 1987 (England: Victoria: Biography of a Queen). Ed.: Shaw: The Annual of Bernard Shaw Studies, 1956—, Shaw: An Autobiography 1856-1898, 1969, Shaw: An Autobiography 1898-1950, 1970, Bernard Shaw's Nondramatic Literary Criticism, 1972, Directions in Literary Criticism, 1973, Saint Joan Fifty Years After: 1923/24-1973/74, 1973. The Portable Bernard Shaw, 1977, (with Anne Wright) Heartbreak House: A Facsimile of the Revised Typescript, 1979, (with Richard Aldington) The Portable Oscar Wilde, 1981, Modern British Dramatists, 1900-1945, 1982, The Playwright and the Pirate: Bernard Shaw and Frank Harris: A Correspondence, 1982, British Dramatists Since World War II, 1983, Bernard Shaw: The Diaries 1885-1897 (2 vols.). BS, West Chester (PA) State Coll., 1949; MA, Temple U., 1951; PhD, PA State U., 1956. Instr. Pa. State U., University Park, 1953-59, asst. prof., 1959-62, assoc. prof., 1962-65, prof. English, 1965-70, research prof., 1970-86, Evan Pugh Prof. of Arts and Humanities, 1986—; dir. Inst. for Arts and Humanistic Studies, 1970—; numerous vis. professorships. Guggenheim fellow 1968-69. Mem. AG. Home: 840 Outer Dr State College PA 16801

WEIR, THERESA ANN, b. Burlington, IA, Oct. 4, 1954; d. Wayne Bernard Stoll and Anna May (Mitchell) Baltz; m. William Ray Weir, Jr., Dec. 13, 1975; children—Neil Alexander, Martha. Author: Untitled Silhouette, 1988, Amazon Lily, 1989. Mem. Romance Wrtrs. Am. Home: RR 1 Box 24 Gladstone IL 61437

WEIR, VIRGINIA LEIGH, b. Iowa City, IA, Jan. 21, 1958; 1 son, Kevin. Contrbg. ed.: Gumbo, 1977; contrbr. poetry to Wrtrs. Forum, Transfer 40, Intro 14, The Best of Intro. BA, San Francisco State U., 1983; postgrad. Warren Wilson Coll. Stockbroker Van Kasper & Co., San Francisco, 1979-81; prin. V. Weir Word Processing, San Francisco, 1983—; typesetter PC World Mag., San Francisco, 1985—. Mem. San Francisco Poetry Center. Home: 1314 De Haro St San Francisco CA 94107

WEISBROD, BURTON ALLEN, b. Chgo., Feb. 13, 1931; s. Leon H. and Idelle (Chernoff) W.; m. Shirley Lindsay, Dec. 23, 1951; children—Glen, Linda. Author: Economics of Public Health, 1961, External Benefits of Public Education, 1964, (with W. Lee Hansen) Benefits, Costs, and Finance of Public Higher Education, 1969, (with Ralph L. Andreano) American Health Policy, 1974, The Voluntary Nonprofit Sector: An Economic Analysis, 1978, (with Joel F. Handler and Neil K. Konesar) Public Interest Law: An Economic and Institutional Analysis, 1978, Economics and Medical Research, 1983, The Nonprofit Economy, 1988; contrbg. author: (with others) Disease and Economic Development: The Case of Parasitic Diseases in St. Lucia, West Indies, 1974; contrbr. numerous articles on econ. of edn., program eval. and health care to profl. jnls.; editorial bd.: Jnl Human Resources, 1966—, Intl. Jnl Social Econ., 1972—, Jnl Public Econs., 1971—; assoc. ed. Public Fin. Qtly, 1972. BS, U. IL, 1951; MA in Economics, Northwestern U., 1952, PhD, 1958. Lectr. econ. Northwestern U., Evanston, IL, 1954-55; instr. econ. Carleton Coll., MN, 1955-57, Washington U., St. Louis, 1957-58, asst. prof. econ., 1958-62, assoc. prof. econ., 1962-64; vis. assoc. prof. Princeton (NJ) U., 1962-63; sr. staff mem. Council of Econ. Advs., Pres. U.S., 1963-64; assoc. prof. dept. econ. U. WI, Madison, 1964-66, prof., 1966—, Evjue-Bascom Prof., 1985—; numerous vis. professorships; mem. research adv. com. Econ. Devel. Admin., U.S. Dept. Commerce, 1967-69; cons. var. fedl. and state govt. agcys., 1964—. Guggenheim fellow, 1969-70; Ford Faculty fellow, 1971-72; sr. research fellow Brookdale Inst., Jerusalem, 1978—. Mem. Am. Econ. Assn., Inst. of Medicine of the Natl. Acad. Scis., AAUP, others. Office: 7422 Soc Sci Bldg Univ Wisc Madison WI 53706

WEISGERBER, DAVID WENDELIN, b. Delphos, OH, May 20, 1938; s. Hubert Louis and Catherine Margaret (Laudick) W.; m. Carole Ann Friemoth, Oct. 23, 1965; children—Jason, Erik. BS, Bowling Green State U., 1960; PhD, U. IL, 1965. Research chemist E.I. duPont de Nemours & Co., Inc., Deepwater, NJ, 1964-69; indexer Chem. Abstracts Service, Columbus, OH, 1969-73, asst. to ed., 1973-77, mgr. chem. substance handling, 1977-79, dir. editorial ops., 1979-82, ed., 1982—. Mem. Am. Chem. Soc., N.Y. Acad. Sci., Am. Soc. Info. Sci. Home: 6178 Middlebury Dr E Worthington OH 43085

WEISHAUS, JOEL, b. Bklyn., July 11, 1939; s. Leo and Sophie (Blonder) W. Editor: Oxherding—A Reworking of the Zen Text, 1971, On the Mesa, 1971, Bits & Snatches, 1973, Woods, Shore Desert (Thomas Merton), 1983. Adj. curator Univ. New Mex. Fine Arts Mus., Albuquerque, 1985—. Served to El, US Army, 1962-63, Ft. Devens, Mass. Recipient PEN Award, NYC, 1971; Mary Robert Reinhart Fdn. Award, NYC, 1977; Helene Wurlitzer Fdn. residency fellowship, 1977-78. Mem. P&W, Albuquerque United Artists. Address: 2812 Garfield SE Albuquerque NM 87106

WEISMAN, ANN E., b. Tulsa, July 26, 1948, d. William Israel and Gertrude (Blend) Weisman. Contrib. poetry to anthologies Where We Are: Montana Poets Anthology, 1978, Point Riders Great Plains Poetry Anthology, 1982, 37 Oklahoma Poets, 1985, others; contrbr. poetry to Nimrod, Chariton Rvw, Kans. Qtly, Borrowed Times, other mags. BA, U. Tulsa, 1971; MFA, U. Mont., 1974. Poet-in-residence Mont. Arts Council, Missoula, 1974-76, State Arts Council Okla., 1985; poet-in-community Arts and Humanities Council Tulsa, 1979-80, poet-in-res., 1985—; mng. ed. Council Oak Books, Tulsa, 1985—. Mem. Ind. Artists Okla, Tulsa Artists' Coalition. Address: 1428 S St. Louis Tulsa OK 74120

WEISMILLER, EDWARD RONALD, b. Monticello, WI, Aug. 3, 1915; s. Jacob and Georgia (Wilson) W.; m. Frances Merewether Power, June 15, 1941; children—Mariana Weismiller Chaffee, Georgia Louise Weismiller Sargeant, Peter Wilson, Charles Edward, Merie Luverne. Author fiction and poetry: The Deer Come Down (Yale Series Younger Poets), 1936, The Faultless Shore, 1946, The Serpent Sleeping, 1962, The Branch of Fire, 1980; contrbr.: The Lyric and Dramatic Milton, 1965, A Milton Encyc., 1978-80; contrbg. ed. A Variorum Commentary on the Poems of John Milton, 6 vols., 1970—. BA, Cornell Coll., 1938, D.Litt., 1953, Merton Coll., Oxford (Eng.) U., 1938-39, 1948-50, D.Phil., 1950; MA, Harvard, 1942. Tchg. fellow English, Harvard, 1940-43; mem. faculty Pomona Coll., 1950-68, prof. English, 1958-68, George Washington U., 1968-80, prof. emeritus, 1981—; Fulbright prof. U. Leiden, Netherlands, 1957-58; mem. Council for Intl. Exchange of Scholars, 1976-79. Rhodes scholar, 1938-39, 48-50; Guggenheim fellow, 1946-47, 47-48; fellow Fund Advancement Edn., Ford Fdn., 1953-54; research award ACLS, 1963, 66, 69, Am. Philo. Soc., 1966, 69; research fellow Folger Lib., 1965, 72-73; spcl. research grantee Rockefeller Fdn., 1965-66; sr. fellow in letters Ctr. Adv. Studies, Wesleyan U., Middletown, CT, 1967-68; research grantee NEH, 1972-73, 77-83. Home: 2400 Virginia Ave NW Washington DC 20037

WEISS, IRVING, b. NYC., Sept. 11, 1921; s. Max and Rose Leah (Kursh) W.; m. Anne du Bois De La Vergne, Dec. 14, 1949; children—Carla, Piera, Bruna, Hugh. Author: (with Anne D. Weiss) American Authors and Books: 1640 to the Present Day, 1972, Thesaurus of Book Digests, 1980. Translator: Plastic Sense (Malcolm de Chazal), 1972, Sens-Plastique (Malcolm de Chazal), 1979. Contrbr. prose, poems, articles to lit. mags., anthols. Humanities ed.: Funk and Wagnalls Standard Reference Encyc., 1957-60. B.A., U. Mich., 1942; M.A., Columbia U., 1949. Asst. prof. English, Fashion Inst. Technology, N.Y.C., 1960-64; prof. English, State U. Coll., New Platz, NY, 1964-85, prof. emeritus, 1985—. Home: 4000 Gypsy Ln 415 Philadelphia PA 19144

WEISS, JAMES MOSES AARON, b. St. Paul, Oct. 22, 1921; s. Louis Robert and Gertrude (Simon) W.; m. Bette Shapera, Apr. 7, 1946; children—Jenny Anne Weiss Ford, Jonathan James. Author: numerous articles in field; ed., co-author Nurses, Patients, and Social Systems, 1968; corr. ed. Jnl Geriatric Psychiatry, 1967—; founding ed., chmn. bd. Jnl Operational Psychiatry, 1970—; editorial adv. Community Mental Health Jnl, 1979—; bd. trustees Mo. Rvw, 1982-83. AB summa cum laude, U. MN, 1941, ScB, 1947, MB, 1949, MD, 1950; MPH with high honors, Yale U., 1951. Tching. asst. psychology St. Thomas Coll., St. Paul, 1941-42; intern USPHS Hosp., Seattle, 1949-50; resident, fellow psychiatry Yale Med. Schl., 1950-53; from instr. to asst. prof. psychiatry Washington U., St. Louis, 1954-60; mem. faculty U. MO, 1959—, prof. psychiatry, 1961—, founding chmn. dept., 1960—, prof. community medicine, 1971—; intl. cons., 1958—; diplomate Am. Bd. Psychiatry and neurology, examiner 1963-83; vis. prof. Inst. Criminology, Cambridge (Eng.) U., 1968-69, All-India Inst. of Medical Sciences and Univ. of Malaya, 1984. Recipient numerous awards inclg. Basic Books award 1974; named Chancellor's Emissary U. MO, 1979. Mem. AAAS and numerous profl. orgs. Research in areas of suicide, homicide, antisocial behavior, aging, social psychiatry. Home: Crow Wing Farm Rt 2 Columbia MO 65201

WEISS, RUTH, (ruth weiss), b. Berlin, June 24, 1928, came to U.S., 1939, d. Oscar and Fani Zlata (Gluck) Weiss. Author: Steps, 1958, Gallery of Women, 1959, South Pacific, 1959, Blue in Green, 1960, Light and Other Poems, 1976, Desert Journal, 1977, Single Out, 1978, 13 Haiku (from All Numbers Work in Time), 1986; The Brink (poetry-jazz film and video); contrbr. to Peace & Pieces anthology, 1973, Contemporary California Women Poets, 1977, 191, an Anthology of San Francisco Poetry, others; contrbr. to Sheaf No. 1, Poetry Score, Semina, Outburst, over 75 lit mags. Home: Box 509 Albion CA 95410

WEISS, SIGMUND, b. Chgo., m. Dora Stoll; 1 dau., Ruth. Author: Poems Written During My Youth Plus, 1976, (with Dora Weiss) Marriage a Dialogue, 1980, Mother Nature Poems, 1984, Poems of a Runaway Boy, 1985. Student pub. schls., Illinois. Actor/poet/thinker/philosopher. Mem. Taproot Sr. Citiz. Writing Workshop, Great South Bay Poetry Coop. Home: 11 Lancaster Pl Stony Brook NY 11790

WEISS, THEODORE RUSSELL, b. Reading, PA, Dec. 16, 1916; s. Nathan and Mollie T. (Weinberg) W.; m. Renee Karol, July 6, 1941. Author: The Breath of Clowns and Kings: Shakespeare's Early Comedies and Histories, 1971, The Man from Porlock, Selected Essays, 1982; (poems) The Catch, 1951, Outlanders, 1960, Gunsight, 1962, The Medium, 1965, The Last Day and the First, 1968, The World Before Us: Poems, 1950-70, 1970, Fireweeds, 1976, Views and Spectacles, Selected Poems, 1978, Views and Spectacles, New and Selected Shorter Poems, 1979, Recoveries, 1982, A Slow Fuse, 1984, From Princeton One Autumn Afternoon: Collected Poems, 1950-86. BA, Muhlenberg Coll., 1938; MA, Columbia Univ., 1940, postgrad., 1940-41. Instr. Eng., Univ. Md., 1941, UNC, 1942-44, Yale, 1944-46; prof. Eng., Bard Coll., 1946-48; poet-in-res., Princeton Univ., 1966-67, prof. Eng. and creative wrtg., 1968—. Editor, pub. Qtly Rvw Lit., 1943—; ed. poetry series Princeton Univ. Press, 1974-78; mem. poetry bd. Wesleyan Univ. Press, 1964-70; juror in poetry for Bollingen Com., 1965; juror Natl. Bk. Awards, 1967. Ford Fdn. fellow, 1957; NEA fellow, 1967; Ingram Merrill Fdn. fellow, 1974, Guggenheim fellow, 1986-87. Home: 26 Haslet St Princeton NJ 08540

WEITZMAN, SARAH BROWN, b. Port Washington, NY, Feb. 6, 1935, d. Philip E. and Mildred (Toole) Brown; m. Arthur H. Weitzman, Nov. 21, 1965. Author: Eve and Other Blasphemy, 1983; poems in Contact II, Kansas Qtly, Arkos Rvw, Manhattan Poetry Rvw, The Smith, other lit mags. BS, NYU, 1956; MA, NYU, 1957. Tchr. of Eng., Seward Park H.S., 1957-63, 1972-74; instr. wrtg., NYU, 1963-67; wrtr./ed., CCP, NYC Bd. of Ed., 1968-72; tchr. Eng., Livingston H.S. (NY), 1974-85; staff development specialist NYCTCC, 1987—. NEA Writing Fellowship, 1984. Mem. PSA, AAP. Home: 301 E 63 St New York NY 10021

WEIXLMANN, JOSEPH NORMAN, b. Buffalo, Dec. 16, 1946; s. Joseph N. and Mary C. (Degenhart) W.; m. Sharron Pollack, Mar. 14, 1982. Author: John Barth: A Descriptive Primary and Annotated Secondary Bibliography, 1976, Am. Short-Fiction Criticism and Scholarship, 1982; ed.: Black Am. Prose Theory (with Chester J. Fontenot), 1984, Belief Versus Theory in Black Am. Lit. Criticism (with Chester J. Fontenot), 1986, Black Am. Lit. Forum, 1976—, co-ed. Studies in Black Am. Lit., 1984—. BA, Canisius Coll., 1968; MA, Kans. State U., 1970, PhD, 1973. Instr. English U. Okla., Norman, 1973-74; asst. prof. Tex. Tech. Univ., Lubbock, 1974-76; asst. prof. English Ind. State U., Terre Haute, 1976-79, assoc. prof., 1979-83, prof., 1983—, assoc. dean of the Coll. of Arts and Sciences, 1987—. Fellow NEH. Mem. MLA (exec. comm. div. Black Am. Lit. and Culture, 1985—), Coll. Lang. Assn., Conf. Learned Jnls. Home: 1601 S Sixth St Terre Haute IN 47802

WELBURN, RON, b. Berwyn, PA, Apr. 30, 1944; 1 son, Elliott. Author: Peripheries: Selected Poems 1966-1968, 1972, Brownup, 1977, The Look in the Night Sky, 1978, Heartland, Selected Poems, 1981. Contrbr. poems, fiction, music rvws., articles to anthols., mags., jnls., newspapers. Mng. editor: The Grackle: Impoverised Music in Transition, 1976-79. BA, Lincoln U., 1968; MA, U. Ariz.-Tucson, 1971; PhD, NYU, 1983. Oral hist. Inst. of Jazz St., Newark, 1980-83; faculty Syracuse U., N.Y., 1970-75; Western Connecticut State U., 1987—; part-time faculty various univs., 1972-75, 77-80, 83-87. Mem. Soc. for Study of Multi-Ethnic Lit. in U.S.; PSA. Home: English Dept. Western Connecticut State U Danbury CT 06810

WELCH, JOHN BUTLER, b. Raymond, NH, Apr. 4, 1940; s. Ai Sawyer and Josephine (Fernald) W. BA, Emerson, 1964. Editor Baker's Plays, Boston, 1976—. Bd. of dir. Boston Shakespeare Co., 1983—; founder and pres. StageSource, Boston, 1984—. Mem. Dramatists Guild. Home: 3 Appleton St Boston MA 02116

WELCH, RICHARD EDWIN, JR., b. Newburyport, MA, June 16, 1924; s. Richard Edwin and Helen (Hale) W.; m. Christina S. Marquand, Sept. 4, 1948; children—Catherine Helen, Richard Edwin III, Christina S., Elizabeth M., Margaret Curzon. Author: Theodore Sedgwick, Federalist: A Political Portrait, 1965, George Frisbie Hoar and The Half-Breed Republicans, 1971, Imperialists vs. Anti-imperialists: The Debate Over Expansionism in the 1890s, 1972, Response to Imperialism: The United States and the Philippine-American War, 1899-1902, 1979, Response to Revolution: The United States and the Cuban Revolution, 1985. AB, Dartmouth, 1948; MA, Harvard, 1949, PhD, 1952. Instr. history Colgate U., 1952-53; asst. prof. Va. Mil. Inst., 1953-58, Lafayette Coll., Easton, Pa., 1958-62, assoc. prof., 1962-70, prof., 1970—, Charles A. Dana prof., 1978—. Mem. Am. Hist. Assn., Orgn. Am. Historians, Soc. Historians of Am. Fgn. Relations. Home: 848 Paxinosa Ave Easton PA 18042

WELLER, SHEILA, b. NYC, Sept. 16, 1945; d. Daniel and Helen (Hover) W.; m. John F. Kelly, Nov. 23, 1982; 1 child, Jonathan. Author: Hansel and Gretel in Beverly Hills (novel), 1978, Rich is Better, 1985, Enticements with Bill Tice, 1985. Contrbr. to McCalls, Redbook, Self, Glamour, Village voice, Family Circle, others. Home: 39 Jane St New York NY 10014

WELLIKOFF, ALAN GABRIEL, b. NYC., May 14, 1946; s. Joseph Leon and Anne (Frimer) W. Author: The American Historical Supply Catalogue: A Nineteenth-Century Sourcebook, 1984, The American Historial Supply Catalogue 2: An Early Twentieth-Century Sourcebook, 1986, (with Denis Boyles and Alan Rose) The Modern Man's Guide to Life, 1987. Contrbr. articles to mags. including Car & Driver, Success Mag., others. B.A. in Am. Studies,

George Washington U., 1968. Asst. ed. Am. Express Hotel Guide, NYC 1980; ed., reporter The Entertainment Cons., NYC., 1981; ed. Southern Calif. Preview, Anaheim, 1982; free-lance jnlst., 1982—. Mem. IMPA. Home: 91 E Park St Springfield MA 01105

WELLMAN, DONALD, b. Nashua, NH, July 7, 1944, s. Donald F. and Frances L. (Bunker) W.; m. Paula J. Westbertg, Sept. 7, 1968 (div. May 1979); 1 child, Tad; m. Irene H. Turner, Jan. 2, 1982; 1 child, Rose. Ed. Coherence, 1981, Perception, 1982, Translations, 1983, 84; contrbr. poetry to Tamarisk, Polis, Hyperion, New Maine Writing, Provincetown Poets, Schist, Maine Rvw, Zahir, others, critical prose to Exquisite Corpse, Polis, Stoney Hills. BA, U. N.H., 1967; DA, U. Oreg., 1975. Tchr. Country Day Schl., St. Croix, V.I., 1975-76; lectr. Boston U., 1978-80, U. Lowell, Mass., 1980-82; asst. prof. Daniel Webster Coll., Nashua, N.H., 1983—; dir. O.ARS, Inc., Cambridge, Mass., 1980—. Served with U.S. Army, 1968-71. Home: Rt 3 Box 225 Weare NH 03281

WELLS, BASIL EUGENE, (Gene Ellerman), b. Springboro, PA, June 11, 1912; s. Carl Harvey and Gertrude Ernestine (Worden) W.; m. Margaret Ellen Hughes, June 10, 1934; children—Hugh Duane, William Carl. Contrbr. fiction to numerous anthols., mags. including Planet Stories, Harper's Weekly, Mike Shayne M.M. Columnist Conneutville Courier, 1976-80. Grad. public schls., Springboro. Owner, Feed-Farm Supplies, Springboro, 1933-38; machine operator, repair mechanic Talon, Inc., Meadville, PA, 1939-74. Home: 7108 Garden St NW Keystone Heights FL 32656

WELLS, JOEL FREEMAN, b. Evansville, IN, Mar. 17, 1930; s. William Jackson and Edith (Strasell) W.; m. Elizabeth Louise Hein, June 5, 1952; children—William, Eugenia, Susan, Steven, Daniel. Author: Grim Fairy Tales for Adults: Parodies of the Literary Lions, 1967, A Funny Thing Happened to the Church, 1969, Under the Spreading Heresy, 1971, The Bad Children's Book, 1972, Second Collection, 1973, Here's to the Family, 1977, How To Survive with Your Teenager, 1982, Coping in the 80s: Eliminating Needless Guilt and Stress, 1986, No Rolling in the Aisles, 1987; ed. Pilgrim's Progress, 1979; co-ed.: Bodies and Souls, 1961, (with Dan Herr) Blithe Spirits, 1962, Bodies and Spirits, ,64, Through Other Eyes, 1965, Moments of Truth, 1966, Contrasts, 1972; contrbr. to Ann Landers Encyc., A to Z, 1978. AB in Jnlsm., U. Notre Dame, 1952. Advt. and promotion dir. Thomas More Assn., Chgo., 1955-64, v.p., 1967—, dir., 1968—; lectr. grad. dept. library sci. Rosary Coll., River Forest, IL, 1964-67; ed. The Critic, Chgo., 1964-80; ed.-in-chief Thomas More Press, Chgo., 1975—; mem. assoc. grad. faculty Loyola U., Chgo., 1984—. Home: 827 Colfax St Evanston IL 60201

WELLS, NANCY MARIE, b. Three Rivers, MI, Mar. 27, 1953; d. Lane T. and Ardena Joyce (Smith) W. Author: Flying Squirrels, 1985. Contrbr. articles to popular mags. including Western Hoseman, N.Y. Conservationist, Smithsonian Mag., others. Ed.: The Living Museum Mag., 1985-87, Impressions newsletter, 1985-87, A View of the Past, 1986, Pleistocene Faunas of the Great Plains, 1987. BS, Zoology, Mich. State Univ., 1975; MA, biology, Western Mich. Univ.; Ph. D., U. Mich., 1987. Ed., sci. wrtr. Ill. State Museum, Springfield, 1985-87; biologist, compiler, ed. U.S. Fish and Wildlife Service, Fort Collins, CO, 1987—. OWAA grantee, 1981, 84. Office U S Fish & Wildlife 1025 Pennock Pl Fort Collins CO 80524

WELLWARTH, GEORGE E., b. Vienna, Austria, June 6, 1932 (arrvd. USA 1946), s. Erwin and Martha (Sobotka) W.; m. Pamela W. Glynn, Apr. 4, 1981. Author: The Theatre of Protest and Paradox, 1964, 2d ed., 1971; Spanish Underground Drama, 1972; ed. The New Wave Spanish Drama, 1970, German Drama between the Wars, 1972, Themes of Drama, 1972, New Generation Spanish Drama, 1976, Three Catalan Dramatists, 1976, Modern Drama and the Death of God, 1986; co-ed. Modern French Theatre, 1964, Post-War German Theatre, 1968, Modern Spanish Theatre, 1968; translator Concise Encyclopedia of Modern Drama, 1964. BA, NYU, 1953; MA, Columbia U., 1954; PhD, U. Chgo., 1957. Asst. prof. English, S.I. Coll., N.Y., 1960-64; assoc. prof. English, Pa. State U., University Park, 1964-70; prof. theatre and comparative lit. SUNY, Binghamton, 1970—. Home: 16 Murray St Binghamton NY 13905

WELSH, JUDITH, b. Patchogue, NY, Feb. 5, 1939; d. Francis William and Muriel (Whitman) Schenck; m. Robert Cooper Welsh, Sept. 16, 1961; children—Derek F., Christopher L. Author: The New Report on Cataract Surgery, 1969, The Second Report on Cataract Surgery, 1971. Contrbr. numerous articles to mags., newspapers. Ed.: Cataract Surgery Now, 1982-84. B.Edn., U. Miami, 1961, M.A., 1968. Ed., Cataract Congress, Miami, 1964-70; communication instr. Bauder Coll., Miami, 1978-80; free-lance wrtr. in health, fitness and travel, 1981—. Recipient 3d place short story NWC, 1982, 3rd place for article, 1982; 1st place for Fla. media Fla. Dental Assn., 1987. Mem. WIC, Wrtrs. & Critics, Fla. Freelance Wrtrs. Assn. Home: 1600 Onaway Dr Miami FL 33133

WELSH, S. PATRICIA, b. Chgo., Aug. 11, 1956 (adopted); 1 dau., Laurie-Jean. Contrbr. poems to anthols., lit. mags. Fairfield U., 1975-80; Norhwestern U., 1986—. Mgr. book dept. Bob's Mag. Stores, Chgo., 1981-84; expense processing coord. Campbell-Mithun Advt., Chgo., 1984—. Recipient Honorable Mention, World of Poetry, 1987. Flower essence practitioner. Mem. Am. Soc. Dowsers, Am. Fdn. Astrologers (Astro Fair assoc.). Home: 6104 N Glenwood Ave Apt 3 Chicago IL 60660

WELSH, WILLIAM FRANCIS ANTHONY, (Edmund Dantes, Bill Burdell), b. Pitts., Aug. 5, 1950, s. William Francis and Mary (Burdell) W. Author: You Can't Get There from Here, 1986; contrbr. to Maelstrom Rvw, Hyperion Poetry Jnl, Nitty Gritty, Interstate, other lit mags. BS, U. Pitts., 1975, MA, 1978. Pres. Acad. Prison Arts, Pitts., 1975—. Grantee NEA, 1975-85, Pa. Council on Arts, 1978-85; winner Best Poem prize King Publs., Washington, 1978. Home: 501 Franklin St East Pittsburgh PA 15112

WELTY, EUDORA, b. Jackson, MS; d. Christian Webb and Chestina (Andrews) W. Author: A Curtain of Green, 1941, The Robber Bridegroom, 1942, The Wide Net, 1943, Delta Wedding, 1946, The Golden Apples, 1949, The Ponder Heart, 1954, The Bride of the Innisfallen, 1955, The Shoe Bird, 1964, Losing Battles, 1970, One Time, One Place, 1971, The Optimist's Daughter, 1972 (Pulitzer prize 1973), The Eye of the Story, 1978, the Collected Stories of Eudora Welty, 1980, One Writer's Beginnings, 1984; contrbr. New Yorker Mag. BA, U. WI, 1929; postgrad. Columbia Schl. Advt., 1930-31. Recipient creative arts medal for fiction, Brandeis U. 1966, Natl. Inst. Arts and Letters Gold medal 1972, Natl. Medal for Lit. 1980. Presdl. Medal of Freedom, 1980. Mem. AAIAL. Home: 1119 Pinehurst St Jackson MS 39202

WENDELL, LEILAH, (Leilah and Haliel)b. Bayshore, NY, Apr. 9, 1958; d. Walter Lyall and Irma (Schwarz) W. Author: (poetry) Threshold, 1978, Twilyte Harvest, 1981, Amethyst and Lampblack, 1985, Songs of the Blue Angel, 1987; (philo.-theol.) The Book of the New Age, 1983, (metaphysical) Infinite Possibilities, 1986; contbr. to Fantasy Book, Amazing Adventures, Owlflight, Elderitch Tales, Jul. of the Brit. Fantasy Soc., Artists Mag., Art Forum, others. Pub. Undinal Songs Mag., NYC, 1979-83; poetry instr. Suffolk Adult Edn., NYC, 1979-82; editor Threshold Assocs., NYC, 1978—; freelance researcher, 1979—; freelance author, artist, art and lit. commentator, 1980—. Recipient N.Am. Mentor Poetry award, 1984, Best Writer of Poetry award SPWAO, 1985. Mem. AG, AL, Am. Artists Profl. League, P&W. Home: 8 Bernstein Blvd Center Moriches NY 11934

WENDT, INGRID DARLENE, b. Aurora, IL, Sept. 19, 1944, d. Edward Julius and Matilda Helen Kathryn (Petzke) Wendt; m. Ralph James Salisbury, Apr. 23, 1969; 1 dau., Erin Marie. Author: Moving the House (poetry), 1980, In Her Own Image: Women Working in the Arts (anthology with Elaine Hedges), 1980, Teaching Guide to accompany "In Her Own Image," 1981, Starting with Little Things: A Guide to Writing Poetry in the Classroom, 1983, Singing the Mozart Requiem (poetry), 1987; contrbr. poetry to Poetry, Poetry Northwest, Poet & Critic, Poetry Now, other lit mags; asst. ed., then mng. ed. Northwest Rvw, 1966-68. BA magna cum laude, Cornell Coll., Mt. Vernon, Iowa, 1966; MFA, U. Oreg., 1968. Asst. prof. Calif. State U., Fresno, 1968-71; adj. instr. U. Oreg., Eugene, 1973-77; wrtr.-in-res. Oreg. Arts Fdn., Portland, 1975—; assoc. ed. Calyx, Corvallis, Oreg., 1981—; presenter poetry readings. D.H. Lawrence fellow U. N.Mex., 1982. Mem. Lane Regional Arts Council (bd. dirs. 1984—), Lane Lit. Guild (bd. dirs. 1984—; pres., 1986-87), PSA, Phi Beta Kappa. Home: 2377 Charnelton St Eugene OR 97405

WENDT, LLOYD, b. Spencer, SD, May 16, 1908; s. Leo L. and Marie (Nylen) W.; m. Helen Sigler, June 16, 1932; 1 dau.—Bette Joan. Author: Gunners Get Glory, 1944, Bright Tomorrow, 1945, Chicago Tribune, The Rise of a Great American Newspaper, 1979, The Wall Street Journal, the Story of Dow Jones and the Nation's Business Newspaper, 1982; co-author wih Herman Kogan: Lord of the Levee, 1943, Bet a Million, 1948, Give the Lady What She Wants, 1952, Big Bill of Chicago, 1953, Chicago: A Pictorial History, 1958. SB, Northwestern U., 1931, SM, 1934. Staff var. nwsprs. 1927-34; rprtr., spl. feature writer mag. sect., ed. Grafic Mag., Sunday ed., Chicago Tribune, 1934-61, assoc. Sunday ed., assoc. ed., 75-77; lectr. fiction writing Norhwestern U., 1946; chmn. fiction div. Medill Sch. Jnlsm., 1950-53; ed. Chgo's Am. nwspr., 1961-69; pub., ed. Chgo. Today, 1969-74; freelance writer, 1977—. Home: 4445 Atwood Cay Circle Sarasota FL 33583

WENDY, see Campbell, Louise

WENNER, JANN S., b. NYC, Jan. 7, 1946; s. Edward and ruth N. (Simmons) W.; m. Jane Ellen Schindelhiem, July 1, 1968; 2 sons, Alexander Jann, Theodore Simon. Author: Lennon Remembers, 1971, Garcia, 1972. Student, U.

CA-Berkeley, 1964-66. Ed., pub. Rolling Stone Mag., San Francisco, 1967—; Look Mag., 1979, Record, NYC, 1981-86; ed.-in-chief Outside Mag., San Francisco, 1977-78; ed.-in-chief, chmn. US Mag., 1985—. Recipient Disting. Achievement award U. So. Calif. Schl. Jnlsm. and Alumni Assn., 1976; Natl. Mag. award, 1970, 77, 86. Mem. ASME. Office: Rolling Stone 745 Fifth Ave New York NY 10151

WENSRICH, MARGARET FRYER, b. Portland, Dec. 9, 1926; d. Ray Barber and Maude Jane (Kilkenny) Fryer. Contrbr. short stories to numerous western and religious mags., 1953-61. BS, Portland State U.; postgrad., Fresno State U., CA, Worchestire Coll., Oxford, England, U. of Aix-en-Provence, France. Tchr., Sacramento City Unified School District, 1966—; freelance book and mag. editor, 1972— pub. Hibiscus Press, 1972—; managing ed. In a Nutshell (lit. mag.), 1975-79; managing ed. Hibiscus Mag., 1985—. Mem. Calif. Writer's Club; Romance Writers Am. Home: Box 22248 Sacramento CA 95822

WENZEL, EVELYN MAKLARY, b. South River, NJ, June 3, 1927; d. Michael Joseph and Mary Ann (Zacharkiewicz) Maklary; m. Albert William Wenzel, Nov. 25, 1948 (dec. 1975); children—Corey William, Kurt Allyn, Kristine Maryann. Contrbr. poetry to periodicals. Wrkg. on poetry. Student public schs., South River. Cook Carmelite Retreat House, Darien, Ill., 1985-87; cook, asst. mgr. St. Francis Retreat House, Oak Brook, Ill., 1987—. Home: 8000 Woodglen Ln Apt 103 Downers Grove IL 60516

WENZEL, LYNN, b. San Francisco, Mar. 22, 1944, d. Ralph Everett and Roberta Frances (Hansen) Shallenberger; m. Jeffrey Bruce Wenzel, June 28, 1964; children—Jennifer Ann, Michael Charles. Contrbr.: N.Y. Times, Newsday, Salome, Bergen Poets 8, Newsweek, Down East Mag., numerous other publs. including The Least You Should Know About English, 1986. Wrkg. on book on Am. popular sheet music. BA magna cum laude, William Paterson Coll., 1975. Freelance graphic artist, 1972—; freelance wrtr., 1978—; ed. Womanspace, 1979—84; presenter poetry readings. Home: 325 Jaeger Ave Maywood NJ 07607

WERNER, FRED H., b. Longmont, CO, Apr. 18, 1908; s. William and Katherine M. (Laber) W.; m. Emma, Jan. 23, 1932; 2 sons, Fred H. Jr., Walter Dean. Author: The Slim Buttes Battle, 1981, The Dull Knife Battle, 1981, The Soldiers Are Coming, 1982, Before the Little Big Horn, 1983, Faintly Sounds the War-Cry, 1983, Meeker—The Story of the Meeker Massacre & Thornburgh Battle, 1985. AB, Colo. State Coll. Edn., 1937, MA, 1942. Tchr. Ariz. State Tchrs. Coll., Tempe, 1942-44; prin. Delta Schl., Greeley, Colo., 1944-47; owner and mgr. Kimbrel Music Co., Greeley, 1947-63; municipal adminstr. City of Greeley, 1963-76; pub. and writer Werner Publs., Greeley, 1976—. Mem. Phi Alpha Theta, Phi Mu Alpha, Am. Hist. Soc. (pres. 1982-83), Greeley Musicians' Assn., Custer Battlefield Hist. & Mus. Assn., Little Big Horn Assocs., Order Indian Wars. Address: 2020 18th Ave Greeley CO 80631

WERNER, HANS-PETER, b. Halle an der Saale, Germany, Nov. 14, 1947; came to U.S., 1953; s. Erich Kurt and Gisela E. (Weszkalnies) W. Ed. Chimera, 1976, Prelude to Fantasy mag., 1978—; contrbr. fiction to Janus, Prelude to Fantasy, Chimera, Copper Toadstool. BA, U. Wis., 1970, MS, 1983. Computer programmer Sperry/Burroughs, Mpls., 1983—. Home: Box 12735 St Paul MN 55112

WERNER, WARREN WINFIELD, b. Alexandria, VA, Feb. 3, 1952; s. Warren William and Helen Cox (Maguire) W.; m. Isabelle Kramer Thompson, Mar. 23, 1985. Author: The Structure of Desire, 1983, The Desire of Loss, 1987; contrbr. to Akros Rvw, Caesura, The Cape Rock, Goddard Jnl, Hiram Poetry Rvw, Lucky Star, Piedmont Lit Rvw, Sonora Rvw, Stardancer, Yarrow, Anthology of Mag Verse and Yearbook Am. Poets, The Chattanhoockie Rfw, Crazy Quilt Rvw, The Montana Rvw, Oregon East, Due South: 20 Auburn Authors. BA, Goddard Coll., 1974; MA, Ohio U., 1979, PhD, 1982. Lectr. Montgomery Coll., Rockville, Md., 1982; instr. Auburn Univ., Ala., 1983-85, asst. prof., 1985—. Mem. AWP, MLA, Assn. Bus. Communications NCTE, Assn of Teachers of Technical Writing. Address: 290 Ivy Ln Auburn AL 36830

WERNLE, HELEN ABIGAIL, b. Crawfordsville, IN, Mar. 20, 1952; d. Robert Frederick and Mary Griffith (Curtis) W. Ed.: Indiana Bus. Mag., 1980-81, Indiana Bus. Jnl, 1984, Endless Vacation, Mag., 1985—. BA, Denison U., 1974. Permissions ed., Curtis Pub. Co., Indpls., 1977-81; Midwest Editing, Indpls., 1982-83; copy ed., spcl. sects. ed., Indpls. Bus. Jnl, 1984; ed. Endless Vacation Mag., Indpls., 1985—. Mem. AATE. Office: Box 80260 Indianapolis IN 46280

WERSHING, SUSAN MEDLER, b. Bklyn., Aug. 9, 1938, d. Edwin L. and E. Frances (Mantyniemi) Medler; m. Francis S. Wershing, Aug. 29, 1959 (div. 1978); children—F. Stephen Jr., Diane Lisa, Gregory Bryce, Cynthia Louise. BA in Journalism, Fairleigh Dickinson U., 1960. Assoc. ed. Med. Econs., Oradell, N.J., 1974-78; sr. ed. Audio Digest Fdn., Glendale, Calif., 1978-79; founder, ed., pub. Dance Tchr. Now, Davis, Calif., 1979—; exec. v.p., dir. Videotape Catalog, Davis, 1985—. Home: 1333 Notre Dame Dr Davis CA 95616

WESLEY, BETH ANN (Ann Wesley), b. Eldorado, IL, Dec. 8, 1957; d. George Robert Wesley and Edna Jean (Beam) Arnold. Author: Trivia AND Technical Manuals, 1984, The Starfleet Graduate School Trivia Manual, 1986, How to Run Your Starfleet Chapter More Effectively, 1986, The Starfleet Engineering Manual, 1986, The Starfleet Graduate School—Command Training Manual, 1986. Entertainment corr.: Petersburg Observer, IL, 1984-85; ed. & pub. Captain's Log, Star Trek sci-fi fanzine. A.A., Springfield Coll., 1977; student Sangamon State U., 1982-84. Chairperson, training officer Starfleet, Newton, IA, 1982—. Home: 817 N 9th Petersburg IL 62675

WESLING, DONALD TRUMAN, b. Buffalo, May 6, 1939, s. Truman Albert Wesling and Helene Marguerite Bullinger; m. Judith Elaine Dulinawka, July 28, 1961; children—Benjamin, Molly, Natasha. Author: Wordsworth and the Adequacy of Landscape, 1970, John Muir: To Yosemite and Beyond, 1980, The Chances of Rhyme: Device and Modernity, 1981, The New Poetries: Poetic Form Since Coleridge and Wordsworth, 1985; ed. Internal Resistances: The Poetry of Edward Dorn, 1985. BA, Harvard U., 1960, PhD, 1965; BA, Trinity Hall, Cambridge U., 1962. Prof. lit dept. U. Calif., San Diego, 1965—. NEH younger humanist fellow, 1973-74. Mem. MLA. Office: Dept Lit U Calif La Jolla CA 92093

WESOLOWSKI, PAUL G, , b. Phila., Oct. 4, 1956; s. Leonard V. and Valerie (Zabczynski) W. Contrbr.: Marx No. 1, 1978, Marx No. 2, 1979; chief researcher: Groucho (Hector Arce), 1978, The Freedonia Gazette 1-16 and Spcl. Issue, 1978-86; contrbr.: Idiot's Digest, 1985. BS, St. Joseph's U., 1978; MBA, Temple U., 1980. Editor, Pub. The Freedonia Gazette, New Hope, Pa., 1978—. Mem. Spcl. Libraries Assn. Club: Natl. Film Soc. Home: Darien 28 New Hope PA 18938

WEST, JEAN, b. Lewis, DE, May 11, 1935; d. Joshua Thomas and Gertrude Elizabeth (Willin) W.; m. Lee A. MacKenzie, June 11, 1955 (div. Aug. 1967); children: Kim, Thor; m. Walter Stephen Phelan, Jan. 20, 1974. Author: Holding the Chariot, 1976; co-ed. Epoch, 1970-72, Epos, 1972-76; contrbr. poems to Epoch, Confrontation, Kaliope, Fla. Rvw, Natl. Forum, others. Wrkg. on collection of poems, novella. AA, Goldey Beacom Coll., Wilmington, Del., 1956; MFA, Cornell U., 1972. Copy wrtr. Cornell U., Ithaca, N.Y., 1967-68; asst. prof. English, Rollins Coll., Winter Park, Fla., 1972-76, assoc. prof., 1976-80, Irving Bacheller prof., 1981—. Fla. Arts Council grantee, 1979. Mem. AAP. Home: 1343 Audubon Rd Maitland FL 32751

WEST, KATHLEENE K., b. Genoa, NE, Dec. 28, d. Alfred N. and Irma N. (Samson) Linnerson. Author: No Warning, 1977, The Armadillo on the Rug and Other Tales, 1978, Land Bound, 1978, The Garden Section, 1982, Water Witching, 1984, Plainswoman, 1985; contrbr. to Woman Poet, the West, Rapunzel, Rapunzel, Great Plains Poetry Anthology, All My Grandmothers Could Sing. AB, U. Nebr., 1967, PhD, 1986; MA, U. Wash., 1975. Tchr. pub. schls., Nebr. and Tex., 1967-71; apprentice Copper Canyon Press, Port Townsend, Wash., 1978-79; poet-in-schls., Wash. and Nebr., 1975-81; teaching asst. U. Nebr., Lincoln, 1985-86. Fulbright scholar, Iceland, 1983-85; Icelandic Govt. scholar, 1983-84. Mem. MLA. Home: Imig 219 Belvedere St Beatrice NE 68508

WEST, MORRIS LANGLO, b. Melbourne, Australia, Apr. 26, 1916; s. Charles Langlo and Florence Guilfoyle (Hanlon) W.; m. Joyce Lawford; children—Christopher, Paul, Melanie, Michael. Author: Gallows on the Sand, 1955, Kundu, 1956, Children of the Sun, 1957, The Crooked Road, 1957, The Concubine, 1958, Backlash, 1958, The Devil's Advocate (Natl. Brotherhood award Natl. Council Christians and Jews 1960, James Tait Black Meml. award 1960, William Heinemann award Royal Soc. 1960, filmed 1977), 1959, The Naked Country, 1960, Daughter of Silence, 1961, The Shoes of the Fisherman, 1963, The Ambassador, 1965, Tower of Babel, 1968, (with R. Francis) Scandal in the Assembly, 1970, The Heretic, A Play in Three Acts, 1970, Summer of the Red Wolf, 1971, The Salamander, 1973, Harlequin, 1974, The Navigator, 1976, Proteus, 1979, The Clowns of God, 1981, The World is Made of Glass, 1983; The World Is Made of Glass (play), 1984. Recipient Intl. Dag Hammarskjold prize, 1978. Fellow Royal Soc. Lit., World Acad. Arts and Scis. Office: Greenbaum et al. 575 Madison Ave New York NY 10022

WEST, PAUL NODEN, b. Eckington, Derbyshire, Eng., Feb. 23, 1930; came to U.S., 1962, naturalized, 1971; s. Alfred Massick and Mildred (Noden) W. Author: Byron and the Spoiler's Art, 1960, I, Said the Sparrow, 1963, The Snow Leopard, 1965, Tenement of Clay, 1965, The Wine of Absurdity, 1966, Alley Jaggers, 1967,

I'm Expecting to Live Quite Soon, 1970, Words for a Deaf Daughter, 1969, Caliban's Filibuster, 1971, Bela Lugosi's White Christmas, 1972, Colonel Mint, 1973, Gala, 1976, The Very Rich Hours of Count von Stauffenberg, 1980, Out of My Depths: A Swimmer in the Univese, 1983, Rat Man of Paris, 1986, Sheer Fiction, 1987, The Universe, and Other Fictions, 1988, From the Canyons to the Stars, 1988. BA, Univ. Birm., 1950; student Oxford U., 1950-52; MA, Columbia U. 1953. Asst. Prof. Engl. Meml. U. NFLD., Can., 1957-58, assoc. prof., 1958-62; faculty Pa. State U., 1963—, prof. English and comparative lit., 1969; disting. writer-in-res., Wichita (Kan.) State U., 1982; fiction judge CAPS Program, NYC, 1974, 81; writer-in-res. U. Ariz., 1984; writer-in-res., Cornell University, 1986; judge Katherine Ann Porter Prize for Fiction, 1984. Recipient Aga Khan Fiction prize, 1973, Hazlett Meml. award for Excellence in Arts (Lit.) 1981; award in Literature from AAIAL, 1985. Served with RAF, 1954-57. Guggenheim fellow, 1962-63; NEA Creative Writing fellow, 1979, 85; Pushcart Prize, 1987; Literary Lion, New York Public Library, 1987. Home: 126 Texas Ln Ithaca NY 14850

WEST, SALLI LOU, (Salli Girard), b. St. George, UT, Feb. 28, 1939; d. E. Penn and Louie (Harris) Smith; divorced; children: Michael, Mary Michelle. Author: (teleplays) Promise Me, 1974, McClure's Run, 1985; (poetry) Required Viewing, 1979; Lady from Santa Fe, 1983; (fiction) Lady from Santa Fe; (non-fiction) B: The Joy—with Computer Files, From Rahma, The Game of Your Lifetime, Oñate; contrbr. articles and short fiction to women's mags. BA in Creative Writing, UCLA, 1966. Wrtr., ed. Roja Mesa Wrtrs. Workshop, Santa Fe, 1981-86; owner, operator, tchr. Roja Mesa Wrtrs. Workshop, Los Angeles, 1975-81. Home: 546 Onate Pl Santa Fe NM 87501

WEST, SANDRA LA VONNE, b. Newark, Jan. 16, 1947. Contrbr. poems to anthols. Ed., pub.: Testimony: A Jnl. of African-Am. Poetry, 1987—; contrbg. ed.: Black Masks Mag., 1986—. Home: Box 495 Montclair NJ 07042

WEST, THOMAS EDWARD, b. Mansfield, OH, May 11, 1954; s. Edward Elden and Doris Miriam (Peat) West; m. Alana Monica Stackhouse, Sept. 10, 1977. Produced plays: The Cloak, 1985, O. Henry's Christmas, 1981, The Inspector General, 1978, others. BA, Ashland Coll., 1975; MFA, Florida State U., 1977. Artistic dir. Asolo Touring Theater (Sarasota, FL), 1977-80; guest prof. Lawrence U. (Appleton, WI), 1981, 83, 85; pres. Rialto Theatrical, Inc. (NYC), 1984-86. Mem. Performing Artists for Nuclear Disarmament (NYC). Home: 326 Columbus Ave 3-I New York NY 10023

WESTBURG, JOHN EDWARD, b. Des Moines, Mar. 24, 1918, s. Lawrence Ray and Harriett May (Hewett) W.; m. Mildred Helen Westaway, Jan. 31, 1933. Ed. more than 30 books and chapbooks, 1964—; contrbr. numerous newspapers and lit. publs. U.S. and Europe. BA, U. S.C., 1949, MA, 1950; MFgnService, U. So. Calif., 1954, MA, 1956, PhD, 1958. Univ. prof. history, poli. sci., English and humanities, 1956-72, 1978-82; sr. ptnr. Westburg Assocs. Pubs., 1964—; ed. N.Am. Mentor mag., 1964—. Served to 1st lt. U.S. Army, 1942-49; ETO, 3 battlestars. Mem. Wis. Fellowship of Poets, Kiwanis Intl., CCLM; bd. dirs. August Derleth Soc. Home: 1745 Madison St Fennimore WI 53809

WESTFALL, RICHARD SAMUEL, b. Fort Collins, CO, Apr. 22, 1924; s. Alfred Rensselaer and Dorothy (Towne) W.; m. Gloria Marilyn Dunn, Aug. 23, 1952; children—Alfred, Jennifer, Kristin. Author: Science and Religion in Seventeenth Century England, 1958, Force in Newton's Physics, 1971, Construction of Modern Science, 1971, Never at Rest: A Biography of Isaac Newton, 1980; ed. (with V.E. Thoren) Steps in the Scientific Tradition, 1969. BA, Yale U., 1948, MA, 1949, PhD, 1955; postgrad. London U., 1951-52. Instr. history Cal. Tech., Pasadena, 1952-53; instr., asst. prof. history State U. Iowa, Iowa City, 1953-57; asst. prof. history Grinnell Coll., 1957-60, assoc. prof., 1960-63; prof. history of science Ind. U., Bloomington, 1963—, prof. history, 1965—, distinguished prof. of history and philosophy of science, 1976—, chmn. dept., 1967-73. Fellow AAAS, Royal Soc. Lit.; mem. Am. Hist. Assn., AAUP, History of Sci. Soc. (Pfizer award 1972, 83; pres. 1977-78), Societe internationale d'Histoire des sciences. Home: 2222 Browncliff Rd Bloomington IN 47401

WESTHEIMER, DAVID, (Z. Z. Smith), b. Houston, Apr. 11, 1917; s. Adolf and Esther (Kaplan) W.; m. Doris Rothstein, Oct. 9, 1945; children—Fred, Eric. Author: (novels) Summer on the Water, 1948, The Magic Fallacy, 1950, Watching Out for Dulie, 1960, A Very Private Island, 1961, This Time Next Year, 1962, Von Ryan's Express, 1964, My Sweet Charlie, 1966, Song of the Young Sentry, 1967, Lighter than a Feather, 1970, Going Public, 1971, Over the Edge, 1972, The Olmec Head, 1974, The Avila Gold, 1974, Rider on the Wind, 1979, Von Ryan's Return, 1980; (with John Sherlock) The Amindra Gamble, 1982; (play) My Sweet Charlie, 1966. Asst. amusement ed., mag. ed, TV ed. The Houston Post, 1939-60, columnist, 1984. BA, Rice U., 1937. Served to lt. col. USAF, 1941-45, 50-53. Mem. PEN, AG, WG. Home: 11722 Darlington 2 Los Angeles CA 90049

WESTHEIMER, MARY HELEN, b. Cin., Apr. 27, 1955; d. Charles Irvin and May (Orton) Westheimer; m. Paul A. Vogel, Feb. 13, 1987. Author: More In Kitchen, 1984. Contrbr. nonfiction, poems to mags., newspapers including PC Week, Phoenix Mag., Am. West Airline Mag., numerous others. Assoc. ed.: Newservice Mag., Poenix, 1983; contrbr., ed.: PWS, 1983—. A.A.A. in Jnlsm., Morehead State U., 1982. Coord., D.I.N. Radio Network, Phoenix, 1983. Mem. Natl. Assn. Women Bus. Owners (co-chair public relations com. 1986-87), Ariz. Authors Assn. (acting exec. dir., 1987), Valley Epson Uses Group (v.p. 1985). Home: 811 E Port au Prince Phoenix AZ 85022

WESTLAKE, DONALD EDWIN EDMUND, b. NYC, July 12, 1933; s. Albert Joseph and Lillian Marguerite (Bounds) W.; m. Abigail Adams, May 18, 1979; children—Sean, Steven, Tod, Paul; stepchildren—Adrienne, Patrick, Katharine. Author 50 novels inclg.: God Save the Mark (Edgar award for best novel MWA 1966), Up Your Banners, 1969, The Hot Rock, 1970, Adios, Scheherazade, 1970, I Gave At The Office, 1971, Help I Am Being Held Prisoner, 1974, Jimmy The Kid, 1975, Two Much, 1975, Brothers Keepers, 1976, Dancing Aztecs, 1976, Enough, 1977, Castle in the Air, 1980 Kahawa, 1982, Why Me, 1983, Good Behavior, 1986. Student, SUNY, Plattsburgh and Binghamton. Office: Burger 39 1/2 Washington Sq S New York NY 10012

WESTON, SUSAN B., b. Lewisburg, PA, Oct. 5, 1943; d. Charles and Margaret (Beck) Brown; m. John H. Weston, Jan. 7, 1968; children—Stephen, Nathaniel. Author: Wallace Stevens: An Intro to the Poetry, 1977; Children of the Light, 1985; contrbr. articles to Criticism, Iowa Rvw, Phantasm; poetry in Beloit Poetry Jnl, Jam Today, Poetry Hawaii. MA, Columbia U., 1968, PhD, 1974. Asst. prof. Univ. Hawaii, Honolulu, 1972-79; presently self-employed writer. Mem. Edn. for Social Responsibility, Boston; North Sub. Peace Initiative, Evanston; League of Women Voters, Soc. Midland Authors. Address: 2019 Colfax St Evanston IL 60201

WESTRICK, ELSIE MARGARET, b. Fort William, Ontario, Canada, Nov. 12, 1910, came to U.S., 1944; d. Melchoir Franz and Clara Alvina (Beese) Beyer; widowed; children—Elvina, Alice, Elsie, Clara, Emily; stepchildren—Clayton, Mildred, George. Contrbr. numerous poems to anthols. Wrkg. on poems, adult short story, children's story. Recipient 3d prize/Honorable Mention, Clover Intl. Poetry Assn., 1971, lifetime membership award, 1973, 6th prize, 1974. Home: 3751 Wheeler Rd Snover MI 48472

WESTRUM, DEXTER, b. Albert Lea, MN, Dec. 6, 1944; s. Lyle R. and Marian R. (Porter) W.; m. Jane Ann Nelson, Dec. 28, 1967. Contrbr. 25 Minn. Writers, Sex and Love in Motion Pictures, James Welch; to lit mags Green River Rvw, Ball State Forum, Event, Free Passage, Storystone, Fallout, Minn. Monthly, No. Lit. Qtly, Sez, Ariz. Qtly, Great River Rvw, San Jose Studies. BA, Sioux Falls Coll., 1967; PhD, U. Minn., 1985. Tchr. assoc. Univ. Minn., Mpls., 1980-85; asst. prof. English Ottawa Univ., Kans., 1985—. Mem. Western Lit. Assn., NCTE. Address: Ottawa Univ Box 57 Ottawa KS 66067

WETZEL, ELIZABETH, b. Wilkinsburg, PA, Aug. 18, 1930; d. Gerald A. and Clare M. (Logsdon) Breen; m. John H. Wetzel, May 21, 1960; children—Stephen, Thomas, Barbara. Author: A Is for Aggravation, 1983. Contrbr. articles to mags., newspapers including Good Housekeeping, Catholic Digest, others. B.S. in Edn., Marquette U., 1953; postgrad. John Caroll U., 1956. Tchr. writing Wooster Bus. Coll., Medina, OH, 1977-79; free-lance wrtr., 1974—. Mem. Medina County Wrtrs. Club (coordinator), Akron Manuscript Club, NWC, Intl. Women's WG. Home: 311 W Washington St Medina OH 44256

WEWER, MILDRED ELIZABETH, (Mildred Phillips Wewer), b. South Pasadena, CA, May 26, 1927; d. Harry Robert and Ida Miles (Plummer) Phillips; m. Robert Earle Williams, June 7, 1960 (div. Apr. 1964); children—Robert Harry, John Stephen; m. Theodore Edward Wewer, May 23, 1975. Author play The Best Christmas Gift, 1974. Contrbr. articles, poem to newspapers, mags. Contrbr., ed.: C.A. Witness, 1945, Pahrump Valley News, 1963, 64. Wrkg. on novels, children's stories, gospel songs, lyrics and melody. Student Mohave Commun. Coll., 1975-87. Info. operator Citizen's Utilities, Kingman, AZ, 1980. Home: 3018 Ames Ave Kingman AZ 86401

WEXLER, NORMAN, b. New Bedford, MA, Aug. 6, 1926; s. Harry and Sophia (Brisson) W.; children—Erica, Merin. Author screenplays: Joe, 1970, Serpico, 1973, Mandingo, 1975, Drum, 1976, Saturday Night Fever, 1977. Student harvard U., 1948. NSF grantee. Mem. DG, WG West, AMPAS. Address: Writers Guild 8955 Beverly Blvd Los Angeles CA 90048

WEXLER, PHILIP, b. NYC, Nov. 20, 1950, s. Harold and Yetty W. Contrbr. poetry to Poet Lore, Tar River Poetry, Kavitha, Widener Rvw, Still Night Writings, others. BS, Poly. Inst. N.Y., 1972; MLS, Rutgers U., 1978. Tech. info. specialist Natl. Library of Medicine, Bethesda, Md., 1978—. Home: 9208 Chanute Drive Bethesda MD 20814

WHALEN, PHILIP GLENN, b. Portland, OR, Oct. 20, 1923; s. Glenn Henry and Phyllis (Bush) W. Author: (poetry) Three Satires, 1951, Self-Portrait, From Another Direction, 1959, Like I Say, 1960, Memoirs of an Inter-Glacial Age, 1960, Every Day, 1965, Highgrade, 1966, On Bear's Head, 1969, Severance Pay, 1971, Scenes of Life at the Capitol, 1971, The Kindness of Strangers, 1975, Enough Said, 1980, Heavy Breathing, 1983; (novels) You Didn't Even Try, 1967, Imaginary Speeches for a Brazen Head, 1972; (interviews) Off the Wall, 1978; (prose text) The Diamond Noodle, 1980; (juvenile) The Invention of the Letter, 1967. BA, Reed Coll., 1951. Lectr., tchr., 1955—. Recipient Poet's Fdn. award 1962, V.K. Ratcliff award 1964, Morton Dauwen Zabal award for poetry, AAIAL, 1986. AAAS grantee-in-aid 1965, Com. on Poetry grantee 1968, 70, 71. Ordained Zen Buddhist priest 1973. Office: Box 31190 San Francisco CA 94131

WHALEN, RICHARD JAMES, b. NYC, Sept. 23, 1935; s. George C. and Veronica (Southwick) W.; m. Joan Marie Giuffe, Oct. 19, 1957; children—Richard Christopher, Laura, Michael. Author: The Founding Father: The Story of Joseph P. Kennedy, 1964, A City Destroying Itself, 1965, Catch the Falling Flag, 1972, Taking Sides, 1974, The Wealth Weapon, 1980; ed.: The Report of The President's Commission on an All-Volunteer Armed Force, 1970, Report of the Pres.'s Commn. on Financial Struct. and Regulation, 1971. BA, Queen's Coll., 1957. Assoc. ed. Richmond (VA) News Leader, 1957-59; contrbg. ed. Time Mag., 1959-60; editorial writer Wall St. Jnl, 1960-62; assoc. ed. Fortune Mag., 1962-66, sr. ed., 1966; writer-in-res. Ctr. Strategic Studies, Georgetown U., Washington, 1966-70; cons. State Dept. 1970-72; sr. policy adviser to Ronald Reagan, 1978-80; chmn. Worldwide Info. Resources, Ltd. Mem. Council of Fgn. Relations. Home: 3220 Volta Pl NW Washington DC 20007

WHALEN, THOMAS DOUGLAS, (Tom Whalen), b. Texarkana, AR, Oct. 28, 1948; s. Ralph Shipley and Louise Francis (Davis) W.; m. Jane Francis Garner, May 1, 1973 (div. 1976). Author: The Eustachia Stories, 1986; ed. Lowlands Rev., 1975-81; contrbr. poetry, articles and short stories to Panache, Chgo. Rvw, Ploughshares, Telescope, Hollins Critic, other lit mags. BA, U. Ark., 1970; MA, Hollins Coll., 1971. Tchr. English and creative writing St. Maria Goretti High Schl., Lake Arthur, La., 1971-72; vis. lectr. McNeese State U., Lake Charles, La., 1973-76; dir. writing program New Orleans Ctr. for Creative Arts, New Orleans, 1977—. La. Div. Arts fellow in lit., 1985. Mem. AWP. Home: 6109 Magazine New Orleans LA 70118

WHALEY, CHARLOTTE T., b. Pitts., June 21, 1925; d. Charles Regnier and Elizabeth (Dunn) Totebusch; m. Gould Whaley, Aug. 24, 1951; children—John Gould, Robert Dunn. Work contrbtd. to Dallas Morning News, 1973-80, Southwest Rvw, Sunstone Review. BA, Southern Methodist U., 1970, MA, 1976. Editorial asst., SMU Press-SW Review, Dallas, 1971-72, asst. ed., 1972-74, assoc. ed., 1974-81, ed. & asst. dir., 1981-84; ed./pub. Still Point Press, Dallas, 1984—. Mem. Book Pubs. Assn. of Texas, No. Texas Assn., Phi Beta Kappa. Home: 4222 Willow Grove Rd Dallas TX 75220

WHALLON, WILLIAM, b. Richmond, IN, Sept. 24, 1928; s. Arthur J. and Adelaide (Wheeler) W.; m. Joanne Holland, Aug. 22, 1957; children—Andrew, Nicholas. Author: Formula, Character, and Context, 1969, Problem and Spectacle, 1980, Inconsistencies, 1983. BA, McGill U., 1950; PhD, Yale U., 1957. Faculty Reed Coll., 1957-62, Mich. State U., East Lansing, 1963—, now prof. comp. lit.; Fulbright prof. comp. lit. U. Bayreuth, 1984-85. Fellow for Ctr. Hellenic Studies, 1962-63. Home: 1532 Parkvale Ave East Lansing MI 48823

WHAM, DAVID BUFFINGTON, b. Evanston, IL, May 25, 1937; s. Benjamin Wham and Virginia (Buffington) Tennant; m. Joan Field Wilber, Mar. 3, 1968 (div. May 1972); children—Benjamin, Rachel. Fiction in numerous lit mags including Woodwind, Story Quarterly, December. BA, Harvard, 1959; postgrad., U. of Iowa, 1962-63. Instr., NW Community College, Powell, Wyo., 1963-65; instr., Southern Il. U., Carbondale, 1965-67; staff wrtr., Bur. of Soc. Sci., Washington, DC, 1967-69; legsltv. asst., U.S. Congress, Washington, 1969-79; with sales and promo. dept., Wisdom Bridge Theatre, Chgo., 1985—. Home: 823 Dobson St Evanston IL 60202

WHARTON, CLIFTON REGINALD JR., b. Boston, Sept. 13, 1926; m. Dolores Duncan, 1950; children: Clifton, Bruce. Co-author: Patterns for Lifelong Learning, 1973; editor: Subsistence Agriculture and Economic Development, 1969; contbr. articles to profl. jnls. B.A., Harvard U., 1947; M.A., U. Chgo., 1956, Ph.D. inEcons, 1958; Pres. Mich. State U., 1970-78; chancellor SUNY System, 1978-87; chmn. & CEO, TIAA-CREF. Address: TIAA-CREF 730 Third Ave New York NY 10017

WHATLEY, JAMES WALLACE, b. Huntsville, AL, March 11, 1945; s. James Wallace and Virginia (Prince) Whatley; m. Carol Adam, Aug. 31, 1966; children—Harold Prince, Julian Leslie. Author: Hardwood, 1984; stories and poems in Images, Kansas Quarterly, Plainsong, Road Apple Review, other lit mags. MFA, UNC-Greensboro, 1972. Instr., Auburn U., Auburn, Ala., 1972-78; prof., Tuskegee Inst., Tuskegee, Ala., 1981-84; prof., Columbus College, Columbus, GA., 1985-86. Mem. AAP, AWP, PSA, P&W. Home: 826 Tullahoma Auburn AL 36830

WHEALDON, EVERETT WHITTIER, b. Naselle, WA, Sept. 5, 1910; s. Joseph Alfred Whealdon and Emma Margaret (Matthews) Whealdon Robarts; m. Marie Emma Sawatzky, June 1935; children—Charlotte, Ann, Jenny Patricia, Joseph Alfred. Author: (novel) Cape Disappointment, 1978, The Green Chain, 1980; (chapbook) Blanket Bill, 1979; (novelette) The Legend of Parker's Cave, 1983, Depression Candle, 1985; The Green Chain and Other Stories of the Great Depression, 1986. Contrbr. short stories, poems, rvws. to lit. mags. Wrkg. on novel of prehistoric human migrations in primitive sea-going crafts. Student Willamette U., 1933-39. U.S. Fish & Wildlife Service, Anderson, CA, 1957-64, Beulah, WY, 1964-65, La Crosse, WI, 1965-71, retired. Home: 314 Logan St Port Townsend WA 98368

WHEATCROFT, JOHN STEWART, b. Phila., July 24, 1925; s. Allen Stewart and Laura Irene (Daniel) W.; m. Joan Michell Osborne, Nov. 10, 1950 (div. 1985); children—Allen, David, Rachel. Author novel: Edie Tells, 1975, Catherine, Her Book, 1983; poetry: Death of a Clown, 1964, Prodigal Son, 1967, A Voice From The Hump, 1977, Ordering Demons, 1981; play: Ofoti, 1966, NET Playhouse TV production, remade as The Boy Who Loved Trolls, 1984; short stories: Slow Exposures, 1986. BA, Bucknell U., Lewisburg, PA, 1948-49; MA, Rutgers U., 1950, PhD, 1960. Instr., U. KS, 1950-52; asst. prof.-presidential prof. Bucknell U., 1952—. Served USN, 1943-46. Natl. Playwriting Award, Children's Community Theatre of Kansas City, 1964, Alcoa Playwriting Award, 1965, Natl. Ednl. TV Award, 1966, Resident fellow, Yaddo, MacDowell Colony, VA Center for the Creative Arts, 1972, 74, 78, 80, 82, 85. Mem. PSA, PEN, College English Assn. Home: 55 N 8th St Lewisburg PA 17837

WHEELER, DANIEL SCOTT, b. Richmond, VA, Apr. 23, 1947; s. Arthur Bruce and Lavinia (Akers) W.; m. Marlene Rae McElfresh, July 27, 1985; children—Matthew, Jamie, Beth, Jennifer. Contrbr. to All Hands Mag., Listen, Compton Encyc., Direction Mag. Student, VA Commonwealth U., Richmond, 1966-69. Jnlst., U.S. Navy, All Hands Mag., Washington, DC, 1974-79; ed. Amer. Legion Mag., Indpls., 1980-85, pub., 1985—. Served to E-6 USN, 1971-79. Mem. SPJ, AEA. Home: 3828 Clubhouse Ct Greenwood IN 46142

WHEELER, SUSAN, b. Pittsburgh, PA, July 16, 1955; d. Ray Barton and Grace Louise (Skeen) Wheeler. Contrbr. to Shenandoah, Sulfur, Massachusetts Rvw, Helicon Nine, Chicago Tribune, others. BA, Bennington College, 1977; grad. student, U. of Chgo., 1979-81. Dir. of Public Programs, School of the Art Institute, 1981-85; dir., Printed Matter, Inc., NYC, 1985—. Recipient Grolier Poetry Prize, 1987. Mem. PSA. Address: Prtd Matter 7 Lispenard St New York NY 10013

WHEELER, THOMAS HUTCHIN, b. West Point, NY, Dec. 15, 1947, s. Lester Lewes and Dorothy (Hutchin) W.; m. Anne Lowe, Jan. 8, 1983; 2 sons, Daniel Lowe, Matthew Lowe. Author: The Guitar Book: A Handbook for Acoustic & Electric Guitarists, 1974, rev. ed., 1978, American Guitars: An Illustrated History, 1982. BA, UCLA; JD, Loyola U.-Los Angeles. Asst. ed. Guitar Player Mag., Cupertino, Calif., 1977-78, assoc. ed., 1978-79, mng. ed., 1979-80, ed., 1980—. Office: GPI 20085 Stevens Creek Blvd Cupertino CA 95014

WHEELER, TRENT H., b. Detroit, Apr. 28, 1959; s. Wayne Benjiman and Sybil Marie W.; m. Victoria Elizabeth Moore, Dec. 15, 1984; 1 son, Tristan Wallace. Ed.: Doctrinal Errors of the Hierarchical Discipleship Movement, 1986, In Remembrance of Me, 1986, Woman's Role in the Church, 1986; contrbr. articles to religious publs.; contrbg. ed.: Gospel Advocate, Nashville, Firm Foundation, Pensacola, Fla., Christian Family, Dallas, Sound Words, Kileen, Tex., Speak as the Oracles, Lansing, Mich. BA, Harding U., 1981. Youth minister Bell Shoals Ch. of Christ, Brandon, Fla., 1981-84; minister Alachua Ch. of Christ, Fla., 1985-86, Wesconnett Ch. of Christ, Jacksonville Fla., 1986—; ed. Proclaimer, Detroit, 1984-85; owner, ed. Beacon Publ., Jacksonville, 1986—. Office Beacon 5225 Wesconnett Blvd Jacksonville FL 32210

WHEELWRIGHT, BETTY, b. Bend, OR, Mar. 7, 1947, d. Richard John and Ora Leone (Alt) Coon. Author: Seaward (poetry), 1978; contrbr. to Tunnel Rd., Across the Generations, Calyx, other publs. BA, Pomona Coll., 1969; PhD, Ind.

U., 1974. Instr. English Gettysburg (Pa.) Coll., 1974-75, Diablo Valley Coll., Pleasant Hill, Calif., 1977—; lect. Stanford U., Palo Alto, Calif., 1984-85, Dominican Coll., San Rafael, Calif., 1985. Bay Area Writing Project fellow U. Calif., Berkeley, 1982. Mem. Berkeley Poets Coop. Home: Box 43 San Geronimo CA 94963

WHELCHEL, SANDRA, b. Denver, May 31, 1944; d. Ralph Earl and Janette Isabelle (March) Everitt; m. Andrew Jackson Whelchel, June 27, 1965; children—Andrew Jackson, Anita Earlyn. Co-author: Your Air Force Academy, 1985; author: (coloring books) A Day in Blue, 1984, A Day at the Cave, 1985, Pro Rodeo Hall of Champions and Museum of the American Cowboy, 1985, Pikes Peak Country, 1986, Mile High Denver, 1987; library columnist Parker Press, CO, 1973-78; history columnist Parker Trail, CO, 1985-87. Contrbr. articles to popular mags. including Jack and Jill, Children's Digest, others. B.A. in Edn., U. Norhern Colo., 1966. Stringer, Douglas County Express, Castle Rock,CO, 1979-81; zone wrtr. Denver Post, 1979-81; writing tchr., 1982—. Mem. NWC (treas. Metro-Denver chpt. 1986, v.p. membership, 1987), Parker Area Hist. Soc. (pres. 1987). Home: 11844 N Delbert Rd Parker CO 80134

WHITBREAD, THOMAS BACON, b. Bronxville, NY, Aug. 22, 1931; s. Thomas Francis and Caroline Nancy (Bacon) W. Author: (poetry) Four Infinitives, 1964, Whomp and Moonshiver, 1982; contrbr.: Prize Stories, 1962, The O. Henry Awards, 1962; ed. Seven Contemporary Authors, 1966. BA, Amherst Coll., 1952; AM, Harvard U., 1953, PhD, 1959. Instr. English, U. Tex. at Austin, 1959-62, asst. prof. 1962-65, assoc. prof., 1965-71, prof. 1971—; vis. assoc. prof. Rice U., 1969-70; mem. lit. adv. panel Tex. Commn. on Arts and Humanities, 1972-76. Recipient third Aga Khan prize for fiction Paris Rvw, 1960, Lit. Anthology Program award NEA, 1968. Mem. MLA, AAUP, Tex. Inst. Letters (Poetry award 1965, 1983). Home: 1014 E. 38th St Austin TX 78705

WHITE, ANN, b. NYC, Aug. 4, 1916; d. Joseph Kaufman and Mary Elcovitz; m. Lawrench White, Dec. 3, 1939 (dec. Apr. 6, 1987); children—Philip, Renee, Kenneth, Charles. Author: Parents and Other Strangers, 1985, Poetry, Drama and the Visual Arts as Therapy, 1970; syndicated columnist For Arts Sake; awardwining poetry in lit mags. Drama critic: Levittown Tribune, 1964-72. Wrkg. on anthol. of poetry, plays. Student Hofstra U., 1970-72; B.A., CCNY, 1939. Assoc. prof. U. Northern Ind., 1960-65; instr. Farmingdale U., NY, 1965-67, Broward Commun. Coll., Pompano Beach, FL, 1977—; supvr. Spl. Recreation, N.Y.C., 1967-77. Named Outstanding Women of Yr., WIC, 1983. Fellow Intl. Inst. Creative Communication; mem. NAPT (regional dir.), Woman's Showcase (founder, dir.). Home: 5266 Gate Lake Rd Fort Lauderdale FL 33319

WHITE, BARBARA BUCKMAN, b. Bklyn., Dec. 25, 1943, d. Robert Francis and Gladys (Orchanian) Buckman; m. Donald Hamilton White, Jr., Aug. 13, 1966; children—Cherilyn Anne, Donald Hamilton III, Jonathan Garthright, Daniel Alexander. Author inspirational poetry booklets: May We Be So Inspired, 1985, An Upward Reach, 1985. BA, Good Counsel Coll., 1965. Real estate salesperson Hometown Real Estate, Homer, N.Y., 1980— Home: 923 Alfred Ln Homer NY 13077

WHITE, CLAIRE NICOLAS, b. Schoorl, Holland, June 18, 1925, came to U.S., 1940, d. Joep and Suzanne (Nys) Nicolas; m. Robert Winthrop White, Aug. 12, 1947; children—Sebastian, Christian, Stephanie, Natalie (dec.). Author: The Death of the Orange Trees (novel), 1963, Biography and Other Poems, 1981, Joep Nicolas (biography), 1979; translator: Time of our Lives (by Martine Rouchaud), 1946, The Assault (by Harry Mulisch), 1985; guest ed.: Mother and Daughters, 1982. BA, Smith Coll., Northampton, Mass., 1946. Mem. PEN. Home: RFD 1 Moriches Rd Box 5 St James NY 11780

WHITE, CURTIS KEITH, b. Oakland, CA, Jan. 24, 1951; s. Earl and Wilma (Foster) W.; 1 dau., Megan. Author: Heretical Songs, 1981, Metaphysics in the Midwest, 1988. Editor: American Made, 1986; Ill. Wrtrs. Rvw., 1984—. BA, U. San Francisco, 1973; MA, Johns Hopkins U., 1974; PhD, U. Ia., 1979. Assoc. prof. Ill. State U., Normal, 1980—. Office: IL State U Dept of Eng Normal IL 61761

WHITE, CYNTHIA, b. NYC, Mar. 19, 1932; d. Carl Leslie and Lillian Poppy (Gruskin) Cannon; m. Robert Ogden White, Sept. 17, 1960 (div. June 1964). BA, Middlebury Coll., 1953. Editorial asst. Doubleday & Co., NYC, 1959; lit agt. Music Corp. Am., NYC, 1959-61; sr. editor Pocket Books-Simon Schuster, NYC, 1962-77, Ballantine Books, 1977-79; exec. editor Dell Pub. Co., NYC, 1979—. Home: 30 East End Ave New York NY 10028

WHITE, DALE ANDREW, b. Jacksonville, FL., Feb. 17, 1958; s. John Andrew and Jeannelle Corinne (Brown) W. Contrbr. short fiction: Scholastic Scope, Published!, GAS, Z Miscellaneous; contrbr. article: St. Petersburg Time, Orlando Sentinel, Gainesville Sun, Writing!, The Shakespeare Newsletter, Ampersand, Quill and Scroll, numerous others; contrbr. interviews of celebrities Tennessee Williams, Andy Warhol, Richard Adams, Bel Kaufman, Bo Diddley, Henny Youngman, numerous other to various publs. BA in Journalism, U. Fla. Intern, reporter Home News, Hialeah, Fla., 1976, UPI, Miami, Fla., 1980, Orlando (Fla.) Sentinel, 1981; reporter Ind. Fla. Alligator, Gainesville, 1976-81; corr. Fla. Times-Union, Jacksonville, 1981-82; columnist, reporter Sarasota (Fla.) Herald-Tribune, 1983—. Home: Box 1695 Bradenton FL 34206

WHITE, EDMUND VALENTINE, b. Cin., Jan. 13, 1940; s. Edmund Valentine and Delilah (Teddlie) W. Author: Forgetting Elena, 1973, Nocturnes for the King of Naples, 1978, A Boy's Own Story, 1982, Caracole, 1985, The Beautiful Room Is Empty, 1988, The Darker Proof (stories), 1988; States of Desire, 1980 (non-fiction). BA, U. Mich., 1962. Writer Time-Life Books, NYC, 1962-70; sr. ed. Saturday Rvw, NYC, 1972-73; asst. prof. writing seminars Johns Hopkins U., Balt., 1977-79; adj. prof. Columbia U. Schl. of Arts, NYC, 1981-83; exec. dir. N.Y. Inst. for Humanities, NYC, 1982-83. Ingram Merrill fellow, 1978; Guggenheim fellow, 1983. Home: 434 Lafayette St New York NY 10003

WHITE, HARRISON COLYAR, b. Washington, Mar. 21, 1930; s. Joel Jesse and Virginia (Armistead) W.; m. Cynthia Alice Johnson, Sept. 10, 1955; children—Elizabeth, John, Benjamin. Author: An Anatomy of Kinship, 1963, (with Cynthia White) Canvases and Careers, 1965, Opportunity Chains, 1970. PhD in Physics, M.I.T., 1955, Princeton U., 1960; MA (hon.), Harvard U., 1963. Ops. analyst Ops. Research Office, Johns Hopkins U., Balt., 1955-56; fellow Ctr. for Advanced Study Behavioral Scis., Stanford U., CA, 1956-57; asst. prof. Carnegie Inst. Tech., 1957-59, U. Chgo., 1959-63; mem. faculty Harvard U., Cambridge, MA, 1963—, prof. sociology, 1968—, chmn. dept., 1975-78; dir., chmn. research com. Urban Systems Research and Engring., Inc., 1970—; vis. prof. U. Edinburgh, 1973-74. Guggenheim fellow, 1973, fellow Am. Sociol. Assn. (Sorokin award 1970, Stouffer award 1975). Mem. AAAS, Natl. Acad. Scis. Home: 62 Dana St Cambridge MA 02138

WHITE, JAMES BOYD, b. Boston, July 28, 1938; s. Benjamin Vroom and Charlotte Green (Conover) W.; m. Mary Louise Fitch, Jan. 1, 1979; children—Emma Lillian, Henry Alfred; children by previous marriage: Catherine Conover, John Southworth. Author: The Legal Imagination, 1973 (with Scarboro) Constitutional Criminal Procedure, 1976, When Words Lose Their Meaning, 1984, Heracles' Bow, 1985. AB, Amherst Coll., 1960; AM, Harvard U., 1961, LLB, 1964. Assoc. Foley, Hoag, & Eliot, Boston, 1964-67; assoc. prof. and prof. law U. Colo., 1967-75, prof. law U. Chgo., 1975-82; prof. law and English, U. MI, Ann Arbor, 1982—; vis. assoc. prof. Stanford U., 1972. Sinclair Kennedy Traveling fellow, 1964-65; NEH fellow, 1979—. Office: U Mich Law School Ann Arbor MI 48109

WHITE, JAMES M., b. Athens, AL, June 26, 1921; s. Lester S. and Willie May Phillips; m. Constance Bie, May 26, 1949; children—James M. White, Jr., Melissa. Student, Auburn, 1941. Space sales, Good Housekeeping Mag., NYC, 1946-51; reg. rep. Life Mag., NYC, 1952-58; pub. Cosmopolitan Mag., NYC, 1958-63, Hiloday Mag., NYC, 1964-66; pub., ed.-in-chief Promenade Mag., NYC, 1967—. Office: Promenade 45 E 45th St New York NY 10017

WHITE, JOAN ELLEN, b. Hammond, IN, Dec. 5, 1945; d. John W. and Daisy (McMurray) W.; m. John H. Schwertfeger, May, 1967 (div. June 1974); 1 son—Geoffrey William Schwertfeger. Wrkg. on: The Portrait, The Reunion, An Unlikely Friend, A Different Time, A Journey Through Vietnam. BA in Psych., Purdue U., 1986. Co-ed., Wiser Lifestyles, Inland Steel, E. Chgo., IN, 1983; ed. AASECT, Hammond, IN, 1984-86; ed.-in-chief Skylark, Hammond, 1985-86. Sigrid Stark Lit. Awards: 1983, Research, 1984, Short Story, 1985, First Place Poetry, 1987, First Place, Novel in Progress, Purdue. Office: Purdue University Hammond IN 46323

WHITE, JOHN IRWIN, b. Washington, Apr. 12, 1902; s. Harry Bateman W. and Grace Allen Brewer; m. Augusta Braxton Postles, Oct. 4, 1930; children—Jonathan Postles White, Jennifer Postles White Fischer; six grandchildren. Author: Am. Vignettes: A Collection of Footnotes to Hist., 1976, Git Along Little Dogies: Songs and Songmakers of the Am. West, 1975; contrbr. to Am. Heritage, The Am. West, Am. Hist. Illustd., Highlights for Children, Yankee, Ariz. Highways, Jnl Am. Folklore, Montana, Old Farmer's Almanac. BA, U. MD, 1924. Sports writer, Washington Star, 1925-26; travel cnslr. Genl. Drafting Co. Inc., NYC, 1927, writer, ed., salesman, 1927-65; freelance writer, 1965—. Honored by Rutgers U. for signif. contrib. to Am. folk music, 1984. Home: Ward Homestead Maplewood NJ 07040

WHITE, JOHN WARREN, b. NYC., Aug. 16, 1939; s. Robert Paul and Jane (Zobel) W.; m. Barbara M. Devin, June 17, 1961; children—

Sandra, Thomas, Sharon, Timothy. Author: Pole Shift, 1980, A Practical Guide to Death and Dying, 1980, The Christmas Mice, 1984. Ed.: The Highest State of Consciousness, 1972, What Is Meditation?, 1974, Frontiers of Consciousness, 1974, Psychic Exploration, 1975, Other Worlds, Other Universes, 1975, Relax, 1976, Future Science, 1977, Kundalini, Evolution and Enlightenment, 1979, What Is Enlightenment?, 1985. B.A., Dartmouth Coll., 1961; M.A.T., Yale U., 1969. Dir. edn. Ins. Noetic Scis., Palo Alto, CA, 1972-74; pres. Alpha Logics, Inc., Bristol, CT, 1979-81; communications specialist Northeast Utilities, Berlin, CT, 1981—.; free-lance wrtr., ed., 1974-79. Mem. AG. Home: 60 Pound Ridge Rd Cheshire CT 06410

WHITE, JON MANCHIP, b. Cardiff, Wales, June 22, came to U.S., 1967, s. Gwilym Manchip and Eva Elizabeth (Ewbank) W.; m. Valerie Leighton, Jan. 14, 1946; children—Bronwen, Rhiannon. Author: 14 novels, 3 biographies, 2 travel books, 4 poetry books, 4 archaeology-anthropology books, numerous films and television plays. MA, Cambridge (Eng.) U., 1948. Sr. exec. officer U.K. Fgn. Service, 1952-56; freelance author, contract screenwrtr., film co. story ed., 1957-67; prof. English, U. Tex., El Paso, 1967-77; Lindsay Young chair of English, U. Tenn., Knoxville, 1977—. Home: 96 Cherokee Bluff Knoxville TN 37920

WHITE, JUDITH ANN, b. Jersey City, NJ, May 2, 1953; d. James Francis and Ermalinda (Russo) W. Contrbr. to Hormones & Behavior, Seventeen, Writing!, McCall's, American Orchid Soc. Bulletin. BS in Chem. & Cell Biol. and Animal Sci., Rutgers U., 1975. Research biochemist Dow Chemical Co., Midland, MI, 1976-78; Realtor/admin. sales Jas. F. White Realty Co., Union, NJ, 1978-85; freelance writer, 1980—. Dillon/Peterson Memorial Essay prize, Am. Orchid Soc., 1986. Mem. AG, NWC. Home: 1844 Cider Mill Rd Union NJ 07083

WHITE, LORELEI ANNETTE, b. LaCrosse, WI, Jan. 15, 1962, d. Raymond and Joyce (Calverley) White. Contrbr. poetry to World of Poetry, CSS Publs. Wrkg. on children's poetry book, short story. Student U. Wis.-LaCrosse. Mem. Am. Poetry Assn. Home: 123 Nina St Apt 1 Saint Paul MN 55102

WHITE, MARY JANE, b. Charlotte, NC, June 14, 1953; d. Thomas Boyette and Jane Eve (Odil) W. Author: The Work of the Icon Painter, 1979, Russian Poetry the Modern Period, 1979, Starry Sky to Starry Sky (poems and translations), 1987. Contrbr. to Am. Poetry Rvw, Cyphers (Dublin, Ireland), Crazy Horse, Iowa Rvw, New Eng. Rvw, New Directions Anthology No. 46. BA, Reed Coll., 1973; MFA, U. Iowa, 1977, JD, 1979. Pvt. practice law, Decorah, Iowa, 1979—. Poetry fellow NEA, 1979, trans. fellow, NEA. 1986. Home: Box 159-A RR 2 Decorah IA 52101

WHITE, MORTON GABRIEL, b. NYC, Apr. 29, 1917; s. Robert and Esther (Levine) Weisberger; m. Lucia Perry, Aug. 29, 1940; children—Nicholas Perry, Stephen Daniel. Author: The Origin of Dewey's Instrumentalism, 1943, Social Thought in America, 1949, The Age of Analysis, 1955, Toward Reunion in Philosophy, 1956, Religion, Politics, and the Higher Learning, 1959, (with Lucia White) The Intellectual Versus the City, 1962; ed.: (with Arthur M. Schlesinger, Jr.) Paths of American Thought, 1963, Foundations of Historical Knowledge, 1965, Science and Sentiment in America, 1972, Documents in the History of American Philosophy, 1972, Pragmatism and the American Mind, 1973, The Philosophy of the American Revolution, 1978, What Is and What Ought to Be Done, 1981, (with Lucia White) Journeys to the Japanese, 1986, Philosophy, The Federalist, and the Constitution, 1987. BS, CCNY, 1936; AM, Columbia U., 1938, PhD, 1942; LHD, CUNY, 1975. Instr. philo. Columbia U., 1942-46; instr. physics CCNY, 1942-43; asst. prof. philo. U. PA, 1946-48, Harvard U., 1948-50, assoc. prof. 1950-53, prof. 1953-70, chmn. dept. 1954-57, acting chmn. 1967-69; prof. Inst. Advanced Study, Princeton, 1970—. Guggenheim fellow, 1950-51; fellow Ctr. Advanced Study Behavioral Scis., 1959-60; fellow ACLS, 1962-63. Mem. AAAS, Am. Philo. Soc. Office: Inst for Advanced Study Princeton NJ 08540

WHITE, NELSON HENRY, (Frater Zarathustra), b. Balt., Oct. 29, 1938; s. Thomas R. and Edith (Eyre) W.; m. Anne Saint-Germain, Aug. 29, 1972. Author: Introduction to Magick, 1972, Magic and the Law, 1980-83, Liber Baal, 1983, Liber Vassago, 1984, Working High Magick, 1981, Selected Conjurations from the Legmeton, 1981, The Wizard's Apprentice, 1982, Collected Rituals from the T. O. T., 1982, Index to the Spirits Given in Honorius, 1983, others. AA, San Bernardino Valley Coll., 1961; BA, U. Redlands, 1968, postgrad., 1969; teaching credentials UCLA 1970. Field service rep. Lockheed Aircraft, Burbank, Calif., 1963; calibration lab. technician RCA Aircraft Equipment, Los Angeles, 1966-67; instr. electronics Calif. Schl. for Deaf, Riverside, 1969-70; co-founder Ch. of the Hermetic Scis., Pasadena, 1970; insp. gen. Ordo Templi Ashtart, Pasadena, 1970-73; lodge master Temple of Truth, Pasadena, 1973—; founder Light of Truth Ch., Pasadena, 1973, pres., chmn. bd., minister, 1973—, bishop, 1974; editor of The White Light, 1973—. Served with USN, 1956-58. Mem. Natl. Rifle Assn., Mensa. Knight of the Grand Cross & Rosette, The Order of St. Andrew of Scotland, 1983; Knight of the Free Templar Order, 1983. Address: Box 93124 Pasadena CA 91109

WHITE, PERRY ELVERADO, b. Oklahoma City, OK, Mar. 25, 1926; s. Jesse Perry and Helen Linnie (Boyd) White; m. Helen Caroline Juedeman, June 28, 1948; children—Keith Perry, Cynthia Gaye White Brooks. Contrbr. numerous articles to mags., newspapers. B.A. in Jnlsm., U. Okla., 1950, M.Liberal Studies, 1976. Advt. mgr., assoc. ed. Frederick Press, OK, 1950-52; ed., pub., owner Big Pasture News, Grandfield, OK, 1954-76; religion ed. Daily Oklahoman, Oklahoma City, 1976—; adj. prof. Oklahoma City U., 1985—. Served with U.S. Navy, 1944-46. Recipient numerous awards for Grandfield newspaper, Okla. Education Assn., 1954-74. Mem. Okla. Press Assn. (numerous awards 1954-76), Oklahoma City Wrtrs. Home: 1601 Willow Brook Moore OK 73160

WHITE, RITA ALEXANDRA, b. Chgo., July 6, 1941, d. Yasha and Anne (Hall) Nikogossoff; children—Daniel, Shawne. Ed. med. newsletters; contrbr. poetry to anthols; author children's poetry and short stories. Wrkg. on screenplays, novels, poetry collection. Student pub. schls., Lake Charles, La. Bookkeeper, office mgr. various firms, 1959-84; controller, prtnr. Biotechnology Search Assocs., Inc., Los Angeles, 1985—; feature wrtr., columnist Agawam (Mass.) Advertiser/News, 1978-83.Publicity chmn. Agawam Arts and Humanities Council, 1982-83, Juvenile Diabetes Fdn., Agawam, 1982-83. Mem. Women Wrtrs. West (v.p. 1985-86), Artists and Wrtrs. Workshop, Soc. Children's Book Wrtrs., Mensa. Home: 930 Westbourne Dr 109 Los Angeles CA 90069

WHITE, SAXON N., b. Cambridge, ID, Nov. 8, 1921, d. Arthur Alfred and Alice Frances (Meade) White; m. Leslie Earl Taylor, Nov. 8, 1939 (div. 1960; children—Janis Dawn, Robert Arthur; m. 2d, Pete A. Uberuaga, Oct. 10, 1965 (div. 1975); m. 3d, Robert E. Kessinger, Sr., June 15, 1979. Contrbr. poetry to The Guild Anthol., Velvet Paws in Print Anthology, Laudamus Te Anthology, Swordsman Rvw, Mendocino Robin, The Muse, Fine Arts Discovery, The Nutmegger, numerous other lit publs.; contrbr. feature articles to The Idaho Statesman, Incredible Idaho; contrbr. articles to numerous mags. and newspapers. Wrkg. on poetry, travel articles, photography. Ed., U. Idaho, Boise State U. Bus. mgmt. Asst. Boise Natl. Forest, 1961-81. Mem. Idaho Wrtrs. League (pres. Caldwell chap. 1970, 71; competition winner 1969), Idaho Press Women. Home: 3921 Kessinger Ln Boise ID 83703

WHITE, STEVE, b. Boston, May 3, 1954; s. Ernest Francis and Alyce Katherine (O'Connell) W.; m. Claire Theresa Collins, Oct. 25, 1981; 1 dau., Jocelyn Noelle. Columnist: The Boston Herald, 1984—, Quincy Patriot Ledger, MA, 1984—, North Shore Mag., MA, 1985—, Worcester Telegram, MA, 1987—. Contrbr. numerous articles to mags., newspapers including Boston Herald Sunday Mag., Metrowest Bus. Rvw., others. B.S. in Jnlsm., Suffolk U., 1976. Ed., The Griffin Report, Weymouth, MA, 1986-87; free-lance wrtr., 1978—. Mem. NWU. Home: 7 Utica St Quincy MA 02169

WHITE, STEVEN FORSYTHE, b. Abingdon, PA, June 25, 1955, s. Robert Francis and Diane (Forsythe) W.; m. Nancy Ellen Pierce, July 21, 1984. Author: Poets of Nicaragua: 1918-1979, 1982, Burning the Old Year, 1984, Las constelaciones de la historia, 1983, Poets of Chile: 1965-1985, 1985, Culture and Politics in Nicaragua, 1985, For the Unborn, 1986, Pablo Antonio Cuadra: Selected Poems, 1987, Federico Garciá Lorca: Poet in New York, 1987. BA, Williams Coll., 1977; MA, U. Oreg., 1982; PhD, Univ. Oregon, 1987. Recipient prize AAP, 1975, 77; Hubbard Hutchinson fellow, 1977-79; Fulbright fellow, 1983. Mem. ALTA, Lane Lit. Guild (pres. 1985), PSA. Home: 95 East Main St Canton NY 13617

WHITE, SUSAN WALTZ, b. Lawton, OK, Sept. 26, 1945; d. Jack L. and Nellie Jane (Geusen) Waltz; m. Dean Kincaid White, June 17, 1967; 1 son, Adam White. Ed.: Town Squire Mag., Kansas City, MO, 1967-70, Indpls. Mag., 1970-72. TV critic Lexington newspapers. B.A., U. Okla., 1967. Home: 1928 Lakes Edge Dr Lexington KY 40502

WHITE, TERRY DALE, b. Kittanning, PA, Dec. 3, 1942; s. E. M. and Helen (Hooks) W.; m. Sharon Auxt, Apr. 16, 1965; children—Jamie, Jonathan. Illustrator, photographer Today's Handbook of Bible Times & Customs, 1984. Contrbr. articles to mags., jnls. Mem. adv. com. Standard Mag., 1985-1989. BME, Grace Coll., Winona Lake, Ind., 1964; MME, Ind. U., 1967. Licensed to ministry Baptist Genl. Conf., 1981. Dir. pub. relations Grace Coll./Sem., 1966-69, assoc. prof., 1971-77; assoc. prof. journalism St. Paul Bible Coll., St. Bonifacius, Minn., 1977-81; assoc. pastor Wooddale Ch., Eden Prairie, Minn., 1981—; faculty Decision Schl. of Christian Writing, St. Paul, 1979—; founder Twin Cities Christian newspaper, 1978; co-founder, ed.

Bus. Life mag., 1984—. Mem. Minn. Christian WG (pres. 1978-80), Evang. Press Assn. (gen. chmn. conv. 1983), Natl. Assn. Ch. Bus. Administrn. (pres. chpt. 1985-86). Home: 6812 Sugar Hill Circle Eden Prairie MN 55344

WHITE, WILLIAM HENRY, b. Glendale, CA, Sept. 9, 1924; s. William Henry and Esther Ruth (Engel) W.; m. Virginia S. Stockton, Jan. 27, 1950; children—Victoria, Deborah. BA, Columbia U., 1948, MS in Jnlsm., 1949. Rprtr. N.Y. Times, 1948-49; book ed. Look, Quick, Flair mags., Cowles Mags., Inc., 1949-51; med. and sci. ed. Look Mag., NYC, 1951-54; med. ed. Sports Illustrated, 1954-55; mng. ed. Med. News, 1956-59; exec. ed. Med. World News, 1959-68; pre., ed. Family Health mag., 1969-74; editorial dir. Med. Opinion mag., 1974-77; pres. Newspaper—books, 1974-78, Scarsdale Inquirer, 1980—, Hartsdale Inquirer, 1981—; ed./pub. Cost Containment Newsletter, 1978—; pub. P.C. Advisor, 1981—, Tufts U. Diet and Nutrition Letter, Cornell U. Animal Health Letter; intl. exec. ed. World Med., Eng., Medicine Mondiale, France; free-lance writer field med. and sci. Mem. NASW. Home: 265 E 65th St New York NY 10021

WHITE, W. ROBIN, b. Madras, India, July 12, 1928, came to U.S., 1944, s. Emmons Eaton and Ruth Esther (Parker) W.; m. Marian Lucille Biesterfeld, Feb. 3, 1948 (dec. 1983); children—Christopher, Parker, Shelley; m. 2d, Doris Mae Baldwin, Aug. 10, 1985. Author: House of Many Rooms, 1958, Elephant Hill, 1959, Men and Angels, 1961, Foreign Soil, 1962, All in Favor Say No, 1964, His Own Kind, 1968, Be Not Afraid, 1972, The Special Child, 1978, Moses the Man, 1981, Troll of Crazy Mule Camp, 1979; ed.: Per/Se Intl. Qtly, vols. 1-4, 1966-69; contrbr. to anthologies. BA, Yale U., 1950; Stegner fellow, Stanford U., 1956-57. Lectr. Scripps Coll., Claremont, Calif., 1984, Calif. State Poly. U., Pomona, 1985-88, instr. UCLA, 1986-88. Recipient Curtis prize Yale U., 1950, Harper prize Harper & Row, 1959, O. Henry award, 1960, Achievement award Ednl. Press, 1974, Regional Center, Ukiah, Calif., 1978, Fulbright nomination, 1987. Mem. AG. Home: 329 E Auburn Way Claremont CA 91711

WHITE, WILLMON LEE, b. Lamesa, TX, mar. 10, 1932; s. Aubrey F. and Jewel (Henderson) W.; m. Carol A. Nelson, Nov. 2, 1957 (div.); children—Tracy, Wrenn, Gehrig, Bob; m. 2d, Barbara K. Kelly, Sept. 16, 1977; 1 dau.—Theresa. BA, McMurry Coll., Abilene, TX, 1953; MA, U. TX, 1956. Rprtr. Abilene Reporter-News (TX), 1953; intern Newsweek Mag., 1954; pub. relations writer Tex. Ins. Adv. Assn., Austin, 1955-56; asst. ed. Humble Way Mag., Humble Oil and Refining Co. (Exxon), Houston, 1956-65; assoc. ed., news ed. Together Mag., Methodist Church, Park Ridge, IL, 1965-69; sr. ed. World Book Encyc., Chgo., 1969-70; asst. ed. then assoc. ed. The Rotarian Mag., Evanston, IL, 1970-74, ed., 1974—, mgr. communications div., under secy., 1979—. Mem. ASME, MPA, ASAE. Office: One Rotary Center 1560 Sherman IL 60201

WHITECLOUD, , see Homesley, Horace Edward

WHITEHEAD, MARGARET HAROLD, b. Aug. 18, 1928; Author juvenile book series Daddy Is a Doctor, 1965. AB, U. Chattanooga, 1950. Ed., pub. series Award Winning Art, 1960-70, New Woman Mag., Palm Beach, FL, 1971-84. Office: Box 189 Palm Beach FL 33480

WHITEHEAD, WILLIAM GRANT, b. Wilmington, NC, Sept. 19, 1943; s. Allen Hallett and Alice London (Boatwright) W. BA magna cum laude, Princeton U., 1965. Coll. traveller Doubleday & Co., Washington, 1966-68, asst. ed., NYC, 1968-70, ed., 1970-73; sr. ed. Doubleday-E.P. Dutton Inc., NYC, 1973-83; ed.-in-chief E.P. Dutton Inc., NYC, 1983—. Home: Hotel Chelsea 222 W 23rd St New York NY 10011

WHITEHOUSE, ANNE CHERNER, (Anne Cherner), b. Birmingham, AL, Jan. 30, 1954; s. Marvin and Leona (Roth) Cherner; m. Stephen Compton Whitehouse, June 24, 1979. Author: (poems) The Surveyor's Hand, 1981. Contrbr. poems to numerous lit. mags., anthols. BA magna cum laude in Social Studies, Harvard Coll., 1976; MFA in Creative Writing, Columbia U., 1979. Recipient Hackney award Ala. Arts Festival, Birmingham, 1976, 79, Joan Grey Untermeyer award Radcliff Coll., 1976, Poetry prize Mademoiselle mag., 1976. Mem. P&W, PSA, AAP. Home: 301 W 108 St New York NY 10025

WHITELAW, NANCY EATON, b. New Bedford, MA., Aug. 29, 1933, d. Joseph March and Mildred Pauline (Pehrson) Eaton; m. David L. Whitelaw, Feb. 19, 1954; children—Katharine, Patricia. Author: Zaner-Bloser Vocabulary Building Books 4 and 5; contrbg. ed.: Early Years; contrbr. articles to McCalls, Working Mother, USA Today, other publs. BA, Tufts U., 1954; MEd, U. Buffalo, 1968. Tchr. public schls., Malden, Mass., 1954-55; tchr. Kiz Koleji, Izmir, Turkey, 1955-58, Sweet Home Schls., Amherst, N.Y., 1967—. Recipient Excellence in Teaching Writing award, N.Y. State Dept. Edn., 1985, Excellence in Writing award Freedom Fdn., Valley Forge, Pa., 1986. Mem. Am. League Penwomen (v.p.), ASJA, Soc. Children's Book Wrtrs. Home: 328 Bramblewood St East Amherst NY 14051

WHITING, ESTELLE LOUISE, b. NYC; d. Paul Lawrence Dunbar and Gertrude Jane (Smith) Whiting. Contrbr. to Travel Agent Mag., Travel Wkly., Zambia Airlines public relations, Essence, Scandinavian Airlines, News and Information, others. BS in Community Health Ed. Hunter Coll., 1975. Health Consultant Human Resources Admin. (NYC), 1982-83; specializes in travel, theater, and health articles; theater critic for Washington (D.C.) Living mag.▶avel wrtr. Chocolate Singles Mag. (Jamaica, NY), 1981—. Chair Intl. Comm., Natl. Cncl. of Negro Wmn., 1982-84. Home: 1172 Anderson Ave Bronx NY 10452

WHITLEY, MARY ANN, b. Flint, MI, Oct. 7, 1951; d. Herson Lamont and Amelia (Leffler) Whitley; m. Patrick A. Sebrey, Sept. 16, 1972 (div. Jan. 7, 1983); m. Craig Steven Sanders, Nov. 9, 1985. Juvenile novels: A Circle of Light, 1983, A Sheltering Tree, 1985. B.S., U. Fla., 1973. Feature wrtr. Gainesville Sun, FL, 1973-75; reporter, photographer Corydon Democrat, IN, 1975-81; feature wrtr., ed. Herald-Telephone, Bloomington, IN, 1981-85; free-lance wrtr. AP, Evansville, IN, 1985-86; copy ed. Indpls. Star, 1986—. Recipient numerous writing awards Hoosier State Press Assn., 1976-81, 1st place for feature writing Natl. Newspaper Assn., 1985. Mem. Woman's Press Club of Ind. (numerous writing and headline writing awards 1982-87). Home: 812 S Stull Ave Apt 6 Bloomington IN 47401

WHITMAN, RUTH, b. NYC, May 28, 1922, d. Meyer David and Martha Harriet (Sherman) Bashein; m. Cedric Whitman, Oct. 13, 1941(dec. Oct. 1958); children—Rachel, Leda; m. 2d, Firman Andrews Houghton, July 23, 1959 (dec. Sept. 1963); 1 son, David; m. 3d, Morton L. Sacks, Oct. 6, 1966. Author: Blood and Milk Poems, 1963, An Anthology of Modern Yiddish Poetry, 1966, The Marriage Wig and Other Poems, 1968, The Selected Poems of Jacob Glatstein, 1972, The Passion of Lizzie Borden: New and Selected Poems, 1973, Tamsen Donner: A Woman's Journey, 1977, Permanent Address: New Poems, 1973-80, Becoming a Poet, 1982, The Testing of Hanna Senesh, 1986. BA, Radcliffe Coll., 1944; MA, Harvard U., 1947. Editor, Harvard U. Press, 1949-60; poetry instr. Cambridge Center for Adult Ed., Mass., 1964-68; poetry lectr. Radcliffe Seminars, 1969—, Harvard wrtg. prog., 1979-84; Fulbright wrtr-in-res., Hebrew U., Jerusalem, 1984-85; wrtr-in-res., Centre Coll., Kentucky, 1987. Alice Fay di Castagnola Award, PSA, 1968; Bunting Inst. Award, Radcliffe Coll., 1968, 70; NEA fellowship, 1975, R.I. State Council on the Arts, 1981. Mem. PSA, New England Poetry Club, PEN, AG, Phi Beta Kappa. Home: 40 Tuckerman Ave Middletown RI 02840

WHITMER, MELVIN HOWARD, b. Mnpls., Jan. 20, 1928; s. Howard Oscar and Anna Rebecca (Hedemann) W.; m. Sophia Ubert, Nov. 8, 1947 (div. Sept. 19, 1983); children—Christine, Kathleen; m. Connie Elizabeth Oldham, May 3, 1985; children—James, Denise, Paul, Richard. Author: Servicing Industrial Electronics, 1962, Servicing Closed Circuit Television, 1967. Contrbr. articles to electronics mags.; author technical lessons. Corr. ed., lesson wrtr. Indst. Technical Inst., 1955-60. Student U. Chgo., 1949-50, Elgin Commun. Coll., 1986-87. Corr. ed. Indsl. Technical Inst., Chgo., 1955-60; contract administr. Admiral Corp., Chgo., 1960-68; assoc. ed. Nuclear-Chgo., Des Plaines, IL, 1968-72; pres. Ad-Tek, Maringo, IL, 1972-74; radio engineer Com/Rad Inc., Des Plaines, 1974-79; instr. Lake County Vocational Schl., Grayslake, 1979-86; technical wrtr. Allen Bradley, Framingham, MA, 1986—. Served with U.S. Navy, 1946-48. Home: 11 Rollingwood Dr Oxford MA 01540

WHITNEY, DAVID CHARLES, b. Salina, KS, Mar. 8, 1921; s. William R. and Jerusha F. (McCartney) W.; m. Elizabeth J. West, Jan. 31, 1943 (dec. 1978); children—Anne G., Katherine W., Jane P. (dec.), West Martin (dec.), Peter A., Lynn McC.; m. 2d, Merrie Robin Vaughn, Feb. 23, 1980. Author: Founders of Freedom, Vol. I, 1964, Vol. II, 1965, The American Presidents, 1967, 69, 75, 78, 82, Two Dynamic Decades, 1968, Colonial Spirit of '76, 1974, The American Legacy, 1975, Discovering the Computer, 1984, Refware Thesaurus: Nouns, Refware Thesaurus: Adjectives, Refware Thesaurus: Builder, Refware Rewriter, 1981, 83 (computer assisted edn. programs), 20 children's books; ed. Reader's Digest Almanac, 1974—; inventor Cycloteacher teaching machine, 1961; developer early childhood edn. curriculums Discovery Program, 1969, Educare System, 1970-72. AB, U. KS, 1942; student, Columbia U., 1946. Rprtr., asst. ed. Douglas Cty. (KS) Outlook), 1940-41, Topeka Daily Capital, 1942; rprtr. U.P.I., 1945-47, asst. copy ed., 1947-49, NYC overnight bur. mgr. and news ed., 1949-51; asst. to mng. ed. World Book Encyc., Chgo., 1952-54, mng. ed., 1954-64; v.p., ed.-in-chief Encyc. Americana, 1964-65; pres., ed. Cowles Edn. Corp., NYC, 1965-68; v.p. ednl. systems Universal Edn. Corp., 1969-72; pres., ed. David C. Whitney Assocs., Inc., 1972—. Benjamin Franklin fellow

Royal Soc. Arts. Mem. Am. Soc. Curriculum Devel., Friends of Library, AG. Trustee W. Deerfield (IL) Twp. Pub. Lib., 1953-59; mem. Library bd. trustees, chappaqua, NY, 1975-80. Address: 160 Princess Dr Madison CT 06446

WHITNEY, J. D., b. Pasadena, CA, Sept. 23, 1940; s. John Keshishyan and Nathalie Adams (Crane) W.; children: Barbara, Joanne, Roger; m. 2d, Judy Ann Weyenberg, Jan 30, 1970; children: David, Douglas, Suzanne, Michael. Author poetry: Hello, 1965 (2d ed., 1967), wu-shih, 1967, Tracks, 1969, The Nabisco Warehouse, 1971, sd, 1973, Some, 1975, Tongues, 1976, Mother, 1981, Word of Mouth, 1986, sd, 1987. BA, U. Mich., 1962, MA, 1966. English Tchr. Allen Park (Mich.) high schl., 1962-66; instr. Wis. State Univ., Platteville, 1962-69; prof. English Univ. Wis., Wausau, 1969—. Recipient writing fellowship, Wis. Arts Bd., 1976. Address: 3851 Henry St Wausau WI 54401

WHITNEY, KAYLA, see Jennings, Jennifer Angelene

WHITNEY, RUTH REINKE, b. Oshkosh, WI, July 23, 1928; d. Leonard G. and Helen (Diestler) Reinke; m. Daniel A. Whitney, Nov. 19, 1949; 1 son—Philip R. BA, Northwestern U., 1949. Copy writer edn. dept. of circulation div. Time, Inc., 1949-53; ed.-in-chief Better Living Mag., 1953-56; assoc. ed. Seventeen mag., 1956-62, exec. ed., 1962-67; ed.-in-chief Glamour mag., 1967—. Mem. ASME, Women in Communications (Matrix award 1980), Women in Media, Fashion Group. Home: Riverview Rd Irvington-on- Hudson NY 10533

WHITTEN, LESLIE HUNTER, JR., b. Jacksonville, FL, Feb. 21, 1928; s. Leslie Hunter and Linnora (Harvey) W.; m. Phyllis Webber, Nov. 11, 1951; children—Leslie Hunter III, Andrew, Daniel, Deborah Gordon. Author: Progeny of the Adder, 1965, Moon of the Wolf, 1967, Pinion, The Golden Eagle, 1968, The Abyss, 1970, F. Lee Bailey, 1971, The Alchemist, 1973, Conflict of Interest, 1976, Sometimes a Hero, 1979, Washington Cycle, 1979, A Killing Pace, 1983, A Day Without Sunshine, 1985. BA in Jnlsm. and English magna cum laude, Lehigh U., 1950. Newsman Radio Free Europe, 1952-57, I.N.S., 1957-58, U.P.I., 1958, Washington Post, 1958-63; with Hearst Newspapers, 1963-66, asst. bur. chief, Washington, 1966-69; sr. investigator Jack Anderson's Washington Merry-Go-Round, 1969—; vis. assoc. prof. Lehigh U., 1967-69. Recipient hon. mention pub. svc. Washington Newspaper Guild, 1963, Edgerton award ACLU, 1974. Home: 114 Eastmore Dr Silver Spring MD 20901

WHIZ, WALTER RAIMU, b. Rockford, IL, May 26, 1918; s. Jules Muraire and Verna Mary (Stevens) W.; m. four times. Author: Success at Law, 1972, Justice Delayed, 1976, Justice Denied, 1983, Justice?, 1985. BS, Northwestern U., 1940; JD, Chgo.-Kent Coll. Law, 1949. Admitted to Ill. bar, 1949; mem. Watts, Whiz, Greene & Payton, 1949—. Served to lt. USAAF, 1943-45, PTO. Mem. ABA, NWU. Office: Box 302 Highland Park IL 60035

WHYTE, WILLIAM HOLLINGSWORTH, b. West Chester, PA, Oct. 1, 1917; s. William Hollingsworth and Louise (Price) W.; m. Jenny Bell Bechtel, Oct. 1964; 1 dau.—Alexandra. Author: Is Anybody Listening?, 1952, The Organization Man, 1956, Open Space Action, 1962, Cluster Development, 1964, The Last Landscape, 1968, The Social Life of Small Urban Spaces, 1980. BA cum laude, Princeton U., 1939. With Vick Chem. Co., 1939-41; writer Fortune Mag., NYC, 1946-51, asst. mng. ed., 1951-59; disting. prof. Hunter Coll., CUNY, 1970-71. Mem. Pres.'s Task Force Natural Beauty, 1964-65; co.-dir. White House Conf. Natural Beauty; bd. dirs. N.Y. Landmarks Conservancy. Recipient Benjamin Franklin mag. writing award, 1953, Liberty and Justice Book award ALA, 1957. Home: 175 E 94th St New York NY 10028

WICK, CARTER, see Wilcox, Collin M.

WICKER, NINA A., b. Caswell County, NC, Oct. 31, 1927; d. Robert Elisha and Martha Frances (Walker) Apple; m. Julian Talmadge Wicker, July 6, 1951; children: Julian Turner, Robert Dale, Wynne Wicker Fields, Mark Allen. Author haiku: October Rain On My Window, 1984; ed. Manna Mag, 1980—; contrbr. to Davidson Misc., St. Andrews Press, Soundings/East, Pembroke Mag, Progressive Farmer, Inc., Farm Jnl., Modern Haiku, Wind Chimes. Teletype op. Western Union, Sanford, NC; credit clrk. Sears Roebuck, Sanford, Tax lister Lee County. Address: 4318 Minter School 1 Rd Sanford NC 27330

WICKES, DIANA C., b. Pitts., Jan. 2, 1930, d. William B. Scott and Calista Cassidy (Wedemier) Grabow; m. Thomas A. Wickes, Aug. 26, 1950; children—Thomas Leslie (dec.), Aeron Dean, Brian G., Lisa Diana. Ed.: Magnetic News-Pioneer Magnetics, 1984-85, Rockwell Intl. employee newsletter, 1982-83; contrbr. to The Toastmaster, Rockwell News, Quality Circles Jnl. BA in Psychology, U. Mont., Missoula, 1956; MSS, Case-Western Res. U., 1973; Cert. Engr., Calif. State U.-Northridge, 1982. Clin. social worker several orgns., Cleve., Los Angeles, 1971-79; quality circle adminstr. Rockwell Intl., El Segundo, Calif., 1982-84; dir. trng. Pioneer Magnetics Co., Santa Monica, Calif., 1984-85; field rep. Rand Corp., Santa Monica, 1986—; lectr. Santa Monica Coll., 1985. Home: 640 Lorna Ln Los Angeles CA 90049

WICKES, GEORGE, b. Antwerp, Belgium, Jan. 6, 1923; s. Francis Cogswell and Germaine (Attout) W.; came to U.S., 1923; m. Louise Westling, Nov. 8, 1975; children by previous marriage—Gregory, Geoffrey, Madeleine (dec.), Thomas, Jonathan. Ed., Lawrence Durrell and Henry Miller Corresp., 1963; author: Henry Miller, 1966, Americans in Paris, 1969, The Amazon of Letters, 1976; trans.: The Memoirs of Frederic Mistral, 1986; adv. ed. Northwest Rvw, 1972—. BA, U. Toronto, Ont., Can., 1944; MA, Columbia U., 1949; PhD, U. Calif.-Berkeley, 1954. Asst. secy. Belgian Am. Ednl. Fdn., NYC, 1947-49; exec. dir. U.S. Ednl. Fdn. in Belgium, 1952-54; instr. Duke U., Durham, NC, 1954-57; asst. prof. to prof. Harvey Mudd Coll. and Claremont Grad. Schl., Calif., 1957-70; prof. English and comp. lit. U. Oreg., Eugene, 1970—, chmn. English Dept., 1976-83; lectr. U.S. Info. Svc., Europe, 69, Africa, 1978, 79; vis. prof. U. Rouen, France, 1970, U. Tubingen, W. Ger., 1981. Fulbright lectr., France, 1962-63, 66, 78; sr. fellow Ctr. for Twentieth Century Studies, U. WI- Milw., 1971; recipient Creative Writing fellowship, NEA, 1973. Office: Eng Dept U OR Eugene OR 97403

WICKLUND, MILLIE MAE, (M. Trap), b. Providence, Jan 1, 1936; d. Carl Leonard and Ellen Linnea (Carlson) Wicklund. Author: The Parachutist and Her One Work of Art, 1983, Hallmark Piece or The Suicide Book, 1983, The History of My Parachute, 1986, White, 1986-87 (serialized). BEd, RI Coll., 1962; postgrad, U. Iowa, 1962-63, 68; Jr. high schl. tchr., Coventry, RI, 1963-64, high schl. tchr., 1965; tchr. West Warick Jr. High, RI, 1968. Mem. Am. Council for Arts, Smithsonian, RI State Poetry Soc. Address: 105 Concord Ave Cranston RI 02910

WICKSTROM, LOIS JUNE, b. Boston, Aug. 14, 1948, d. Robert Louis and Joan (Hirsch) Sinsheimer; m. Eric Wickstrom, July 1, 1967; children—Erica Lorraine, Eileen Anitra. Author: Food Conspiracy Cookbook, 1974, Oliver, 1978, Ladybugs for Loretta, 1978; ed. Pandora mag., 1978—. AA, Pasadena City Coll., 1968; BA, U. Colo., 1977. Reporter Denver Clarion, 1975-77; poet-in-schls. Tampa (Fla.) Arts Council, 1983; tchr. Hillsborough County Schls., Tampa, 1984-85; teaching asst. U. S. Fla., Tampa, 1985—. Winner 1st place fiction Natl. Fan Fantasy Fedn., 1980, U. S. Fla., 1983. Mem. Fla. Freelance Wrtrs. Assn. Home: 10612 Altman St Tampa FL 33612

WIDGERY, JAN, see Widgery, Jeanne-Anna

WIDGERY, JEANNE-ANNA, (Jan Widgery), b. Upland, PA, May 18, 1920, d. Eugene Edmond and Carol Cooke (Meeser) Ayres; m. Rolande Carpenter Widgery, Mar. 29, 1948; children—Carolyn Gail, Catherine Darcy, Claudia Joan. Author: The Adversary, 1966, Trumpet at the Gates, 1970; articles and short stories. BA, Chatham Coll., Pitts., 1941; MA, Radcliffe Coll., 1945. Mem. faculty Chatham Coll., Pitts., 1946-50, Ellis Schl., Pitts., 1956-60, Winchester-Thurston Schl., Pitts., 1960-75; lectr. U. Houston, 1976; tchr. Duchesne Acad., Houston, 1978-83. Recipient fellowship Ossabaw Island, Ga., 1975. Mem. Houston Wrtrs. Workshop, AAUW. Home: 225 Stoney Creek St Houston TX 77024

WIEBE, DALLAS EUGENE, b. Newton, KS, Jan. 9, 1930; s. John Phillip and Otillie Marie (Becker) Wiebe; m. Virginia Margaret Schroeder, Jul. 24, 1951; children—Garth, Ericka. Novel: Skyblue the Badass, 1969; book of short stories: The Transparent Eye-Ball and Other Stories, 1982; co-editor: Cincinnati Poetry Rvw, 1975-83, editor, 1983—. BA, Bethel Coll., 1954; PhD, U. of Michigan, 1960. English instr. U. of Wisconsin (Madison), 1960-63; prof. U. of Cincinnati (OH), 1963—. Aga Khan Fiction Prize, Paris Rvw, 1978; Pushcart Prize, 1979. Mem. AAP, AWP, CCLM. Home: 582 McAlpin Ave Cincinnati OH 45220

WIEDER, LAURANCE, b. NYC, June 28, 1946, s. Herbert Wieder and Gloria (Cohen) Sinclair; m. Andrea Korotky, Aug. 8, 1982; 1 dau., Aiah Rachel Korotky. Author: The Coronet of Tours (poetry), 1972, No Harm Done (poetry), 1975, Man's Best Friend (prose, with William Wegman), 1982; contrbr. poetry, prose to New Yorker, Little Mag., Poetry in Motion, Scripsi, Boulevard, Camera Arts, Village Voice, other publs. BA, Columbia Coll., 1968; MA, Cornell U., 1970. Assoc. ed. Am. Craft mag., NYC, 1978-80, Camera Arts mag., NYC, 1980-82; freelance wrtr., NYC, 1982-84; founder, ed., pub. Brightwaters Press, NYC, 1984, Nimbus Books, Bklyn., 1985—. Poetry grantee Ingram Merrill Fdn., 1974; recipient Natl. Mag. award ASME, 1982. Mem. PEN, PSA. Home: 37 7th Ave Brooklyn NY 11217

WIENER, FERDINAND JOSEPH, b. Royalton, MN, Sept. 3, 1904; s. Martin Andrew and Rosalia (Trettel) W.; m. Mary Ann Gibney, June 17, 1941 (dec. Mar., 1973); children—Ferdinand Eugene, Karen Ann, Maureen Rose. Writer monthly series Lives of the Founders, Am. rev., 1977-78; contrbr. to Better Homes & Gardens, Gardeners Chronicle; transl. wks. from German, incl. Alexa, Through Dark Pathways, also wks. of Albert Dahlem. Self-taught. Horticulturist, florist, landscape designer, 1943-57; ed./pub. Time & Tide, 1968-69. Internatl. Clover poetry award, 1973. Home: 723 5th Ave S Saint Cloud MN 56301

WIENER, MARVIN S., b. NYC, Mar. 16, 1925; s. Max and Rebecca (Dodell) W.; m. Sylvia Bodek, Mar. 2, 1952; children—David Hillel, Judith Rachel. Ed.: Natl. Acad. Adult Jewish Studies Bulln., 1958-78, Past and Present: Selected Essays (Israel Friedlaender), 1961, Jewish Tract Series, 1964-78, Adult Jewish Edn., 1958-78, Talmudic Law and the Modern State (Moshe Silberg), 1973. BS, CCNY, 1944, MS, 1945; BHL, Jewish Theol. Sem. Am., 1947, MHL, Rabbi, 1951, DD (hon.), 1977. Registrar, secy. faculty Rabbinical Schl., Jewish Theol. Sem. Am., 1951-57; cons. Frontiers of Faith TV Series, NBC, 1951-57; dir., instr. liturgy Cantors Inst.-Sem. Coll. Jewish Music, J.T. S.A., 1954-58; faculty coordr. Sem. Schl. and Women's Inst., 1958-64; dir. Natl. Acad. for Adult Jewish Studies, United Synagogue Am., NYC, 1958-78; ed. Burning Bush Press, 1958-78, United Synag. Rvw, 1978-86; co-chmn. Jewish Bible Assn., 1960-64; chmn. bd. rvw. Natl. Council Jewish Audio-Visual materials, 1968-69; mem. exec. bd., editorial adv. bd, vice-pres., Jewish Book Council; cons., Community Relations and Social Action, 1981-1982; dir., com. on congregational standards, United Synagogue of America, 1976-86; Profl. staff, Joint Retirement Board, 1986—; Chmn., Intl Conf. on Adult Jewish Edn, Jerusalem, 1972. Mem. Am. Acad. Jewish Research, Assn. Jewish Studies, N.Y. Bd. Rabbis, Rabbinical Assembly. Home: 67-66 108th St Forest Hills NY 11375

WIER, ALLEN, b. San Antonio, Sept. 9, 1946, s. Ralph A. and George Ann (Marrs) W.; m. Dara Ann Dixon, Apr. 2, 1969 (div. 1983); m. 2d, Ladonice Holloway, Jan. 5, 1984. Author: Blanco (novel), 1978, Things About to Disappear (stories), 1978, Departing As Air (novel), 1983; ed. Voicelust, 1985; contrbr. to So. Rvw, Ga. Rvw, Intro, Ploughshares, other lit mags. BA, Baylor U., 1968; MA, La. State U., 1971; MFA, Bowling Green State U., 1974. Mem. faculty dept. English Longwood Coll., Farmville, Va., 1970-72, Carnegie-Mellon U., Pitts., 1974-75, Hollins (Va.) Coll., 1975-80; prof., vis. wrtr. U. Tex., Austin, 1983, Fla. Intl. U., Miami, 1984-85; prof. U. Ala., Tuscaloosa, 1980—. NEA fellow, 1975, Guggenheim fellow, 1980. Mem. Tex. Inst. Letters (Best Short Fiction award 1978), WG, AWP, PEN. Office: Drawer AL Tuscaloosa AL 35486

WIER, DARA, b. New Orleans, Dec. 30, 1949, d. Arthur Joseph and Grace Cecile (Barrois) Dixon; m. Michael Pettit; children—Emily Caitlin, Guy Gerard. Author: Blood Hook & Eye, 1977, The 8-Step Grapevine, 1980, All You Have in Common, 1984, The Book of Knowledge, 1988; contrbr. poetry to Three Rivers Poetry Jnl, Cimarron Rvw, Morrow Anthology of Younger American Poets, American Poetry Rvw, North American Rvw, others; ed. Ala. Poetry Series. MFA, Bowling Breen U., 1974. Asst. prof. Hollins (Va.) Coll., 1975-80; assoc. prof. U. Ala., Tuscaloosa, 1980-85, U. Mass., Amherst, 1985—; vis. wrtr. U. Utah, Salt Lake City, 1980, U. Tex. Austin, 1983; dir. MFA program in writing, Univ. of Mass. NEA creative wrtg. fellow, 1981. Mem. PEN, AWP, PSA. Home: 504 Montague Rd Amherst MA 01002

WIESE, MICHAEL, b. Champaign, IL, Jul. 12, 1947; s. B.B. Wiese; m. Morgan Smith, Jun. 1, 1980. Author: Independent Film and Videomakers Guide, 1986, Film and Video Budgets, 1985; Home Video: Producing for the Home Market, 1986. Exec. producer: The Beach Boys: An American Band, 1985, New Wave Comedy, 1986, Amazing Masters of the Martial Arts, 1986, Academy Award Winners: Animated Short Films, 1985. Producer: Radiance, 1976, Hardware Wars, 1979, Dolphin, 1979. MFA in Cinematography San Francisco Art Inst., 1969. National Seminar Leader American Film Inst. (Los Angeles), 1980—; director, production Showtime/The Movie Channel (NYC), 1982-83; vp. non-theatrical programming Vestron Video (Stamford, CT), 1984—. Independent Film Grant, American Film Inst., 1976. Home: Box 406 Westport CT 06881

WIESEL, ELIE, b. Sighet, Romania, Sept. 30, 1928; came to U.S., 1956, naturalized, 1963; s. Shlomo and Sarah (Feig) W.; m. Marion Erster Rose, 1969; 1 son, Shlomo Elisha. Author: Night, 1960, Dawn, 1961, The Accident, 1962, The Town Beyond the Wall, 1964, The Gates of the Forest, 1966, The Jews of Silence, 1966, Legends of Our Time, 1968, A Beggar in Jerusalem, 1970, One Generation After, 1971, Souls on Fire, 1972, The Oath, 1973, Ani Maamin, a cantata, 1973, Five Biblical Portraits, 1981, Somewhere a Master: Further Tales of the Hasidic Masters, 1982, Zalmen or the Madness of God; play, 1975, Messengers of God, 1976, A Jew Today, 1978, Four Hasidic Master, 1978, The Trial of God, 1979, The Testament (France's Prix Livre-Inter 1980), 1981 (Prix des Bibliothequaires 1981), Images from the Bible, 1980, 1980, Paroles d'etranger, 1982, The Golem, 1983, The Fifth Son, 1985, Signes d'exode, 1985, Against Silence: The Voice and Vision of Elie Wiesel, Collected Shorter Writings (ed. Irving Abrahamson), 1985, Le Crépuscule, Au Loin, 1987. Student, Sorbonne, Paris, France, 1947-50. Address: Boston U 745 Commonwealth Ave Boston MA 02215

WIESELTIER, LEON, b. Bklyn., June 14, 1952; s. Marke and Stella (Backenroth) W. Author: Nuclear War, Nuclear Peace, 1983; co-translator: (Robert Klein) Form and Meaning, Essays in Renaissance and Modern Art, 1978. BA, Columbia Coll., 1974; postgrad., Balliol Coll., Oxford, Eng., 1976; MA, harvard U., 1979. Sr. editor The New Republic, Washington, 1982-83, lit. editor, 1983—; cons. editor Partisan Rvw, Boston, 1981—. Kellett fellow, 1974-76. Home: 2011 Hillyer Pl NW Washington DC 20009

WIGGS, TERRY ALLEN, b. Princeton, IN, Sept. 24, 1946, s. Maurice Jerald and Lillie Marie (Hayes) W.; m. Patti Lee Jurena, Aug. 10, 1985. Contrbr. poetry, stories to Tilted Planet Tales, vol. 2, N.Mex. Humanities Rvw. BA, U. Ill., 1972; MA, Southwest Tex. State U., 1984. Lectr. Southwest Tex. State U., San Marcos, 1984—. Served with U.S. Army, 1966-69. Mem. Tex. Assn. Creative Writing Tchrs., NCTE, Conf. Coll. Tchrs. English. Home: 918 Chisholm Trail Cu Round Rock TX 78681

WIGHT, DORIS TERESA, b. Harvey, IL, Jan 26, 1929; d. William Preston and Gabrielle Juliet (Begnoche) Senesac; m. Douglas Allen Wight, June 17, 1950; 3 sons, Jeremy, Russell, Sterling. Author: Bird Wings; contrbr, more than 400 poems to 140 publs.; fiction to Miss. Valley Rvw, natl. mags; pedagogy in James Joyce Qtly, Claflin Rvw, Colby Library Qtly, Iowa English Rvw, Jnl English Tchg. Techs, Seeking Promethean Woman in the New Poetry—Stein, Vallejo, Artaud, Rimbaud, Eliot, Jacob, others. PhD in Comp. Lit., U. Wis.-Madison. Creative writing tchr. Univ. Wis. Baraboo, 1974-79; tchr. creative wrtg. Madison Area tech. Coll., U. of Wis. Extension, 1985-86, lectr. in comparative lit., Univ. of Wisc.-Madison. Mem. MLA, PEW, Women's Wrte. Guild, Midwest MLA. Address: 122 Eighth Ave Baraboo WI 53913

WILBERT, FELICIA FIBO, (Anna Lewis), b. Santa Fe, NM, Aug. 25, 1959; d. Lester Martin and Elizabeth (Laws) Libo; m. Paul David Wilbert, June 12, 1982; 1 dau., Emily. Author: Working at Home: The Wave of the Future, 1987, Computer Literacy Primer, 1987; columnist: The Durango Herald, 1986—. Contrbr. articles to mags. newspapers, including Weight Watchers Mag., others. B.L.A. in Landscape Architecture, U. Oreg., 1982. Word processor The Word Processor, Durango, CO, 1983—, instr., 1983—; theater critic The Durango Herald, 1986—. Home: Box 1336 Durango CO 81302

WILBUR, RICHARD PURDY, b. NYC, Mar. 1, 1921; s. Lawrence L. and Helen (Purdy) W.; m. Mary Charlotte Hayes Ward, June 20, 1942; children—Ellen Dickinson, Christopher Hayes, Nathan Lord, Aaron Hammond. Author: The Beautiful Changes, 1947, Ceremony, 1950, A Bestiary, 1955, Moliere's Misanthrope, translation, 1955, Things of This World, 1956, Poems 1943-56, 1957, Candide; (with Lillian Hellman) comic opera, 1957, Advice to a Prophet, 1961, Tartuffe, transl. from Moliere, 1963 (co-recipient Bollingen Transl. prize 1963), Poems of Richard Wilbur, 1963, Loudmouse; juvenile, 1963, Walking to Sleep; poems, 1969; transl. from Moliere The School for Wives, 1971, Opposites; juvenile, 1973, The Mind-Reader; poems, 1976, Responses; criticism, 1976; transl.: The Learned Ladies (Moliere), 1978, Seven Poems, 1981, Andromache (Racine), 1982, Phaedra (Racine), 1986, Lying and other poems, 1987; editor: Complete Poems of Poe, 1959, Poems of Shakespeare, 1966, Selected Poems of Witter Bynner, 1978; cantata for the Statue of Liberty, On Freedom's Ground (music by William Schuman, first performed by the philharmonic in October, 1986). AB, Amherst Coll., 1942, AM, 1952, D.Litt., 1967; AM, Harvard U., 1947, LHD, Lawrence Coll., 1960. Writer-in-residence Smith Coll., 1977-86. Recipient Harriet Monroe prize Poetry mag., 1948; Edna St. Vincent Millay Meml. award, 1957; Natl. Book award, 1957; Pulitzer prize, 1957; Prix de Rome Am. Acad. Arts and Letters, 1954; Brandeis U. Creative Arts award, 1971; Harriet Monroe Poetry award, 1978; numerous others. Guggenheim fellow, 1952-53, 63; Ford fellow, 1960-61. Mem. Am. Acad. Arts and Scis., Natl. Inst. Arts and Letters, AAIAL (pres. 1974-76, chancellor 1977-78, 80-81), AAP (chancellor). Home: Dodwells Rd Cummington MA 01026

WILCOCK, JOHN, b. Eng. Author: The Autobiography and Sex Life of Andy Warhol, 1971, (with Elizabeth Pepper) The Witch's Almanac, 1970-78 and Magical Mystical Sites, 1977, An Occult Guide to South America, 1976, Occult Guide to Britain, 1976, Traveling in Venezuela, 1979; numerous $$-a day guidebooks worldwide; columnist: High Times mag. Former staff writer Daily Mirror, London; former staff writer UP, Can.; a founder, organizer underground newspapers The Village Voice, NYC, The East Village Other, Other Scenes; formerly asst. ed., travel writer N.Y. Times Travel Section. Address: BM-Nomad London WCIV 3XX England

WILCOX, COLLIN M., (Carter Wick), b. Detroit, Sept. 21, 1924; s. Harlan Collin and Lucile Armina (Spangler) W.; m. Beverley Buchman, Dec. 20, 1954; children—Christopher, Jeffrey. Author: The Black Door, 1967, The Third Figure, 1968, The Lonely Hunter, 1969, The Disappearance, 1970, Dead Aim, 1971, Hiding Place, 1972, Long Way Down, 1972, Aftershock, 1973, The Faceless Man, 1974; pseudonym Carter Wick: The Third Victim, 1975, Doctor, Lawyer, 1975, The Watcher, 1976, (with Bill Pronzini) Twospot, 1977, Power Plays, 1978, Mankiller, 1980, Spellbinder, 1981, Stalking Horse, 1982, Swallow's Fall, 1983, Victims, 1985, Night Games, 1986. BA, Antioch Coll., 1948. Copywriter, 1951-53; mystery and suspense novelist, 1967—. Served with USAAF, 1943-44. Mem. MWA (dir.). Home: 4174 26th St San Francisco CA 94131

WILCOX, JACKSON BURTON, b. Altadena, CA, June 16, 1918; s. Phillip Burton and Ethel Ruth (Jackson) Wilcox; m. Marjorie Viole Robbins, Sept. 8, 1940; children—Judith Altermatt, John Mark, Deborah Altermatt, Carol Giddings. Editor/publisher: Silver Wings Press and Silver Wings, quarterly since 1983; editor: Hollywood Free Paper, 1975-79; cartoon collection: Merrylee, 1981. BA, U. of Redlands, 1940; BD, Colgate-Rochester, 1944. Pastor American Baptist Churches, 1941—; freelance cartoonist/wrtr. 1943—. Home: 15832 Mossdale Ave Lancaster CA 93535

WILCOX, LAIRD MAURICE, b.San Francisco, Nov. 28, 1942; s. Laird and AuDeene (Stromer) W.; children—Tony, Elizabeth, Carrie. Ed.: Guide to the American Left, 1985, Guide to the American Right, 1985, Wilcox Report Newsletter, Civil Liberties Rvw. Wrkg. on book on the psychology of ideological belief systems. Dir. Editorial Research Serv., Kansas City, Mo., 1981—. Mem. ACLU, Natl. Council Against Censorship, Free Press Assn.; found. Wilcox Collection Contemporary Political Movements, Spencer Library, Univ. Kans., Lawrence. Recipient Taylor Book Collection award Univ. Kans., Lawrence, 1964. Office: Box 2047 Olathe KS 66061

WILCOX, MARY ANN, b. Youngstown, OH, May 9, 1946; d. Robert Thomas Bruce and Mary Elizabeth Erskin Atha; m. Claude H. Wilcox, Jr., Oct. 5, 1968; 1 son, Alvin Joseph. Contrbr. short stories to anthols. Cert. Tchr. Aide, Ill. Commun. Coll., 1985. Aide writing to read public schs., Pekin, IL, 1986—. Home: 709 Park Ave Pekin IL 61554

WILCOX, PATRICIA ANNE, (E. V. Austin) b. Douglasville, GA, Oct. 12, 1932; d. Glenn and Mattilu (Dailey) Florence; m. John Thomas Wilcox, Sept. 2, 1955; children: Benjamin E., Nathaniel T., Adam A. Author: A House by the Side of the Road (as E. V. Austin), 1975, (poems) A Public and Private Hearth, 1978, An Exile from Silence: Poems to God, 1981; editor/pub.: The Broken Juke (Don Revell), 1975, Ann (John Vernon), 1976, George Scarbrough: New and Selected Poems, 1977, The Drum Concerto (Emily Katharine Harris), 1979, Through Glass (Henry Alley), 1979. BA in English, Emory U., 1956. With promotion dept. Scott, Foresman, Atlanta, 1952-54; English tchr. Atlanta pub. high schls., 1962-63; dir., editor Roberson Ctr. for Arts and Scis. Poetry Studio, Binghamton, N.Y., 1976-78; editor, pub. Iris Press, Inc., Binghamton, 1975—; adj. lectr. creative writing SUNY-Binghamton, 1985. Founder, dir. Roberson Poetry Studio, Binghamton, 1976-78. Mem. Phi Beta Kappa. Home: 27 Chestnut St Binghamton NY 13905

WILD, JAKE, see Draime, Charles Douglas

WILDE, ALAN, b. NYC, May 26, 1929, s. Joseph and Dora (Cohen) W. Author: Art and Order: A Study of E.M. Forster, 1965, Christopher Isherwood, 1971, Horizons of Assent: Modernism, Postmodernism and the Ironic Imagination, 1981; ed.: Critical Essays on E.M. Forster, 1985; Middle Grounds: Studies in Contemporary American Fiction, 1987. BA, NYU, 1950, MA, 1951; PhD, Harvard U., 1958. Asst. prof. Williams Coll., Williamstown, Mass., 1961-64; assoc. prof. Temple U., Phila., 1964-67, prof., 1967—, chmn. grad. studies, 1975-85. Fulbright fellow, 1952-53; recipient Disting. Teaching award Lindback Fdn., 1975, Best Essay of Yr. award Ariz. Qtly, 1984, Guggenheim fellow, 1986-87. Mem. MLA, AAUP. Home: 410 Clarksville Rd Princeton Junction NJ 08550

WILDE, DAVIS STEWART, b. Manistique, MI, Sept. 8, 1937; s. Edward Everett Hale and Dorothy (Harbeson) W.; 1 dau., Emily Takeuchi. B.A. in Jnlsm., Ohio State U., 1969. Reporter, photographer The Willard Times, OH, 1970-82; co-founded, published, edited Prism mag. (area arts & letters), 1980-81; founder, pub., ed. The Willard Junction, 1982-85, ed., 1985—. Recipient Genl. Excellence award for newspaper Ohio Newspaper Assn., 1986. Home: 13 W Maple St Willard OH 44890

WILDE, LARRY, b. Jersey City, NJ, Feb. 6, 1928, s. Selig and Gertrude (Schwartzwald) Wildman; m. Mary Ruth Poulos, June 2, 1974. Author: The Great Comedians Talk about Comedy, 1968 (revised ed. 1973), How the Great Comedy Writers Create Laughter, 1976, The Complete Book of Ethnic Humor, 1978, over 40 joke books; contrbr. to Coronet, Genesis, Penthouse, Gallery. BA, U. Miami. Performance comedian; lectr. ednl. and bus. orgns. on humor. Served as cpl. USMC, 1946-48. Mem. Screen Actors Guild, AFTRA. Home: Box 86 Sea Ranch CA 95497

WILDE, ROBERT EUGENE, b. Ames, IA, Nov. 4, 1923, s. Ivan C. and Dorothy H. (Tillinghast) W.; m. Mary Elizabeth Duff, Dec. 27, 1952; children—Catherine Alice, Patricia Ann. Author: Practical and Decorative Concrete, 1977. BS, Iowa State U., 1949. Assoc. ed. Jnl. Am. Concrete Inst., Detroit, 1949-51, mng. ed., 1952-60; assoc. ed. Rock Products Mag., Chgo., 1951-52; dep. exec. dir. Am. Concrete Inst., Detroit, 1960—; ed. Concrete Abstracts, Detroit, 1973-83; ed., pub. Concrete Intl.: Design & Constrn., Detroit 1979—. Mem. Soc. Profl. Journalists. Home: 19242 Warwick St Birmingham MI 48009

WILDER, CATHERINE, see Foy, Catherine Mary

WILDER, JOHN RICHARD, (formerly Richard Lee Collett Jr.), b. Council Bluffs, IA; s. Richard Lee and Wanda Louise (Carr) Collett; m. Laura Jean Hathaway, Jan. 18, 1983 (div. Nov. 14, 1979); children—Rebecca Elizabeth, Laura Marie, Sara Beth. Contrbr. articles and poetry to var. publs.; sr. ed. Writers House Press. Student Writers Workshop, U. Iowa, 1980-82; MFA in Poetry, Sythesis Schl. Social Research, 1984, PhB, 1982, Master Organizational Design and Adminstrn., 1982, Master Poli. Sci., 1986. Free-lance political lectr. 1976-79; editorial rvw. bd. Univ. Iowa, Iowa City, 1982; governing bd. Windhover Press, Iowa City, 1982; dir. Community Writers Assn., Iowa City, 1982—; sr. ed. Writers House Press, Iowa City, 1983—; poli. corr. The People's Press, San Diego, Calif., 1985—. Served to Alc USAF, 1974-76, Southeast Asia. Membership chmn. Citizens Party Iowa, 1983-84, natl. comm. mem., 1983-84; coord. Sonia Johnson for Pres. campaign, Iowa, 1984; adv. Ctr. for Social Justice, Iowa City, 1984—; bd. dirs. Ray of Hope Ministries. Grantee Univ. Iowa, 1983-84, The Kaltenborn Fdn., 1985; recipient Outstanding Small Press award Pushcart Press, 1983-84, 86-87. Fellow The Inst. for Human Potential; mem. Natl. Psychiatric Assn, Pew. Office: Box 3071 Iowa City IA 52244

WILDGRUBE, IRENE W., (Irene Rose), b. NYC., May 27, 1932; d. John Louis and Theresa Stefi (Nemethy) Wacula; m. Erich Otto Wildgrube, Feb. 12, 1955; children—Erich, Richard, Janet, Nancy. Political reporter Hopewell Valley News, Hopewell, NJ, 1985—. Wrkg. on children's book, fictional account of life among Slovak people. Home: 102 State Hwy 31 Pennington NJ 08534

WILDMAN, EUGENE, b. NYC, Sept. 18, 1936. Author: Montezuma's Ball, 1970, Nuclear Love, 1972. Editor: Chgo. Rvw., 1965-67, Anthology of Concretism, 1969, Experiments in Prose, 1970. M.A., U. Chgo., 1964. Tchr., Northwestern U., Evanston, Ill., 1967-70; U. Ill., Chgo., 1970—. Recipient Fiction awards Ill. Arts Council, 1976, 77, 84, 85. Home: 2705 N Mildred Ave Chicago IL 60614

WILEY, ROBERT F., (Rob), b. E. St. Louis, IL, June 29, 1946; s. Robert Franklin and Lorene Virginia (Matthews) W.; m. Deborah K. McAlexander, June 20, 1970; children—Brian Richard, Melissa Anne. BA with honors in English, Memphis State U., 1975. Sports writer Arkansas Democrat, Little Rock, AR, 1976-78, Log Cabin Democrat, Conway, AR, 78-79, Daily Oklahoman, Oklahoma City, OK, 79-80; freelance writer, Memphis, 1980—; ed. Custom Applicator Mag., Memphis, 1981—; bi-monthly media column for MEMPHIS mag. Recipient Midwest Agrcl. Chemls. Assn. Media Award for Disting. Achievment, 1986. Served to E/5, USN, 1968-72. Mem. SPJ, Sigma Delta Chi. Home: 4448 Castle Heights Memphis TN 38115

WILK, MAX, b. NYC, July 3, 1920; s. Jacob Wilk and Eva Zalk; m. Barbara, Oct. 27, 1949; children—David, Richard, Mary Frances. Author books, 1960—, latest being Don't Raise the Bridge (Lower the Water), 1960, A Tough Act to Follow, 1986, American Treasure Hunt, 1986. Contrbr. articles to mags., TV scripts, sketches, film scripts. BA, Yale U., 1941. Served to cpl. U.S. Army, 1942-46. Bd. dirs. New Dramatists, Inc., NYC, 1986—. Recipient Emmy, 1960, award ASCAP, 1974. Home: 29 Surf Westport CT 06880

WILKENS, GEORGE ROBERT, b. Wilkes-Barre, PA, Mar. 6, 1949; s. Fred and Florence Elizabeth (Erickson) W. Contrbr. articles to Tampa Tribune, Ocala Star-Banner. Mng. ed.: Pasco News, Dade City, FL, 1973-78. Student U. Kans., 1967-72. Staff wrtr. Ocala Star-Banner, FL, 1978-80, Tampa Tribune, 1980—. Mem. Fla. Press Club (pres.), SPJ. Home: Box 2353 Inverness FL 32651

WILKENS, STEVEN A., b. Freeport, IL, Jan. 29, 1957; s. Eugene Paul and Barbara Lynn (Kock) W.; m. Becky Ann Hewitt, Sept. 30, 1979; children: Christine Nichol, Brittany Ann. Author: articles in Sea Classics, 1987, Marshall

Advisor, 1984, 86, 87; working on historical novel. Attended Highland Coll., Freeport. Binder operator, Cable Prtg., Mt. Morrris, Ill., 1974-76; owner Steve's Antiques, Freeport, Ill., 1974-79; deputy sheriff, Stephenson Cty., Ill., 1978-79; sales rep., Sav-a-Stop Inc., Sarasota, Fla., 1979-80; sales/advg. mgr., Dreamers Furniture, Marshall, Mich., 1980—; freelance photographer/wrtr., 1983—. Home: 333 N Main St Ceresco MI 49033

WILKERSON, MICHAEL N., b. Franklin, IN, Oct. 12, 1955, s. William Richard and Anne Margaret (Cooley) W.; m. Deborah L. Galyan, Dec. 22, 1980. Contrbr. stories to TriQtly, Iowa Rvw, Negative Capability, other lit mags; essay to The Progressive; contrbg. ed.: Poet & Critic; asst. ed.: the Landlocked Heart: Poems from Indiana. BGS, Ind. U., 1977, MA, Johns Hopkins U., 1980. News ed., wrtr. Herald-Telephone, Bloomington, Inc., 1971-78; asst. to v.p. Ind. U., Bloomington, 1980-83; founding ed. Ind. Rvw, Bloomington, 1981-82; vis. asst. prof. U. Wis.-Madison, 1983; founder U. of Wis. Inst. for Creative Wrtg., 1986. Address: 317 Oliver Dr Bloomington IN 47401

WILKES, KENNETTE HARRISON, b. San Antonio; d. Charle Noel Douglas and Josephine Rose (Hamilton) Harrison; m. William Warren Wilkes, June 18, 1966; children—Grace, Lisa, Wesley. Contrbr. articles to mags., newspapers; poems to anthols. English ed.: Alington Rvw., 1962; mng. ed.: New Plains Rvw., 1986-87. B.A. in English, U. Tex., Artlington, 1963; M.A. in English, Central State U., 1986. Tchr. public schls., Chgo., London, Edinburgh, Houston, 1967-83. Recipient Edgar Lee Masters prize for poem Okla. State U., 1987, awards Okla. Wrtrs. Conf., 1986. Mem. Poetry Therapy Assn. Office: Box 4131 Edmond OK 73083

WILKES, PENNY F., b. Pasadena, CA, Aug. 8, 1946, d. Wesley Innis and Margaret Ferance (Lewis) Dumm; m. Michael B. Wilkes, June 29, 1968. Ed.: The Elkhounder, 1975-77; contrbr. Natl. Dog Mag., Northern Dog News, Am. Jnl Orthodontics. BA in Anthropology, U. So. Calif., Los Angelles, 1968. Dir. publs. The Bishop's Schl., La Jolla, Calif., 1973-78; editorial coordinator Am. Jnl Orthodontics, La Jolla, 1978-85; owner, operator Creative Communications, La Jolla, 1985— contrbg. ed., INNSIDER, 1986—; freelance wrtr on Americana and country inns, travel, carousel art. Recipient Best Bull. award Dog Wrtrs.' Assn. Am., 1975, Best Series award Northern Dog News, 1979. Mem. AMWA, AG, San Diego Wrtrs/Eds Guild, NLAPW, archivist, Natl Carousel Assn. Home: Box 2201 La Jolla CA 92038

WILKINS, FREDERICK C., b. Lynn, MA, May 23, 1935; s. Charles Hadley and Celia W. Editor: The Eugene O'Neill Newsletter, 1977—. AB, Bowdoin Coll., 1957; MA, U. of Iowa, 1958, PhD, 1965. Asst. prof. English Northeastern U. (Boston), 1969-70; assoc. prof. English Suffolk U. (Boston), 1970-77, prof./chair English, 1978—. Mem. MLA; Pres. Eugene O'Neill Soc., 1986-87. Address: 57 Fairview Rd Lynfield MA 01940

WILKINSON, ROSEMARY, (Rosemary Regina Challoner), b. New Orleans, Feb. 21, 1924; d. William Lindsay and Julia Regina (Sellen) Challoner; m. Henry Bertram Wilkinson, Oct. 15, 1949; children: Denis James, Marian Regina, Paul Francis, Richard Challoner. Author: An Historical Epic, 1974; (poetry) A Girl's Will, 1973, California Poet, 1976, Earth's Compromise, 1977, It Happened To Me, 1978, I Am Earth Woman, 1979, The Poet and the Painter, 1981, Poetry & Arts, 1982, Gems Within, 1984, Nature's Guest, 1984, In the Pines, 1985, Longing For You, 1986. Life poetry teaching credential San Francisco State U., 1978. Poet, author, poetry workshop tchr., lectr., 1978—. Recipient cert. of merit Am. Poets Fellowship Soc., 1973. Fellow World Lit. Acad. (founder); mem. AG, AL Am., Natl. League Am. Pen Women (v.p.), Natl. Fedn. State Poetry Socs, The Ina Coolbrith Circle. Home: 1239 Bernal Ave Burlingame CA 94010

WILL, GEORGE F., b. Champaign, IL, 1941. Author: The Pursuit of Happiness and Other Sobering Thoughts, 1979, The Pursuit of Virtue and Other Tory Notions, 1982, Statecraft as Soulcraft: What Government Does, 1982. Attended, Trinity Coll., Oxford (Eng.) U., Princeton U. Washington editor Natl. Rvw, 1972; political columnist Washington Post, Newsweek mag. Recipient Pulitzer prize for commentary, 1977. Address: Wash Post 1150 15th St NW Washington DC 20071

WILLAND, LOIS CARLSON, b. Mpls., July 17, 1935; d. Theo W. and Lois Gertrude (Davis) Carlson; m. Jon L. Willand, July 22, 1967; children: Tona, Martha. Author: The Use-It-Up Cookbook: A Guide for Using Up Perishable Foods, 1979, reprinted as The Use-It-Up Cookbook: A Guide for Minimizing Food Waste, 1985; contrbr. mag. articles to Family Food Garden, Consumer Digest, Family Circle. BA, St. Olaf Coll., 1957; BS, U. Minn., 1963. Social worker Hennepin County, Mpls., 1959-63; tchr. elem. schls. St. Paul-Bloomington Pub. Schls., 1963-74; self-employed wrtr., 1974—. Mem. AG, COSMEP, Ind. Pubs. Assn. Home: 145 Malcolm Ave SE Minneapolis MN 55414

WILLARD, TIMOTHY HOLMES, b. Washington, Aug. 31, 1951; s. DeVoe Holmes and Martha (Daniels) W. BA, Bard Coll., 1973. Ed., Metrop. Acad. of Ballet Newsletter, Bethesda, MD, 1975; ed. Movers Journal, Arlington, VA, 1978-83; managing ed. The Futurist, Bethesda, 1983—. Home: 1515 Red Oak Dr Silver Spring MD 20910

WILLIAMS, ALBERTA NORINE, (A. Norine, Sonia Davis), b. Olos, Alta., Can., Apr. 22, 1908; d. Albert Emmett and Leola Bell (Myers) Suedekum; m. Billy D. Williams, Sept. 4, 1928 (dec. 1984); children—Neppie Rebecca, Billy Dee Jr. Author: Pearls of a Lady (poetry), 1976, numerous poems, stories, plays, and local histories; poetry in anthologies. Wrkg. on fiction. Mem. Nat. League Am. Pen Women, Poetry Soc. Colo. Home: Lascar Rt Box 75 Rye CO 81069

WILLIAMS, BARBARA JOANN, b. Bonner Springs, KS, Oct. 8, 1933; d. Joseph Howard and Clarice Caudill; m. Levi Dwight Williams; Oct. 4, 1953; children—Timothy Dwight, Melaney, Adrienne, Julia. Contrbr. short story to jnl., poem to anthol., chpt. to book, travel articles to Idaho Statesman. Wrkg. on Gothic mystery novel, short stories, modern Western novel. BA, Boise State U., 1978; grad. Famous Wrtrs. School, 1971. Mem. Delta Delta Delta Sorority, Contralto Boise Master Chorale. Home: 1185 Hampton Rd Boise ID 83704

WILLIAMS, BILL, b. Chgo., Jan. 31, 1939; s. Maynard A. Jr. and Roberta Mary (Sims) W.; m. Barbara J. Smith, Jan. 3, 1959; children—Brian, Barbara, Maynard, Ronna, Kenis, James. Author bus. books, trng. systems materials including: Managing Your Megabytes, 1986, Internal Cash Mgnt. for Banks, 1986, Profitable Equipment Leasing (with Terry Winders), 1987, Bank Branch Management, 1987, Effective Loan Review, 1988; contrbr. short fiction to numerous publs. Wrkg. on novels, short stories. Sudent MacMurray Coll., 1957-59, Ind. U.-South Bend, 1960-61. Wrtr., mag. ed. Asocs. Investment Co., South Bend, 1961-65; wrtr., ed. Litton Instrnl. Materials, Anaheim, Calif., 1966; wrtr., ed., producer Trainex Corp., Westminster, Calif., 1966-67, Pictorial Pubs., Indpls., 1967-69; pres., wrtr., ed. The Wordshop, Inc., Carmel, Ind., 1969—. Home: Box 1038 Carmel IN 46032

WILLIAMS, CHARLES KENNETH, b. Newark, NJ, Nov. 4, 1936; s. Paul Bernard and Dossie (Kasdin) Williams; m. Sarah Jones, 1966; 1 dau., Jessica Anne; m. 2d, Catherine Mauger; 1 son, Jed Mauger. Author: A Day for Anne Frank, 1968, Lies, 1969, I Am the Bitter Name, 1972, With Ignorance, 1977, The Lark, the Thrush, the Starling, 1983, Tar, 1983, Flesh and Blood, 1987; trans., Women of Trachis, 1978. BA, U. of Penn. Prof., George Mason U., 1982—. Awards: Guggenheim fellowship, 1974; NEA fellowship, 1985. Mem. PEN, PSA. Home: 90 Eighth Ave Brooklyn NY 11215

WILLIAMS, DIANE, b. Chgo. Contrbr. fiction to Ascent, Four Quarters, Malahat Rvw, Ohio Rvw, other lit jnls; fiction ed.: Story Qtly, 1985—. Wrkg. on fiction. Office: Box 1416 Northbrook IL 60065

WILLIAMS, D.J., see Worth, Dorothy Janis

WILLIAMS, EDWARD F. III, b. NYC, Jan. 3, 1935, s. E. Foster Jr. and Ida (Richards) W.; m. Sue O. Williams, June 5, 1960; children—Cecile Elizabeth, Alexander H. Author: Early Memphis and its River Rivals, 1968, Fustest with the Mostest, 1970, Confederate Victories at Ft. Pillow, 1973; contrbr. articles to Tenn. Conservationist mag., West Tenn. Hist. Soc., Egyptians Ann., Monitor, Confederate Vet. Mag., other publs. BS in Mech. Engring., Auburn U., 1956; MA in History, Memphis State U., 1974. Corr. Montgomery (Ala.) Advertiser, 1954-56; Sports ed., mng. ed., Auburn Plainsman, 1954-56; ed Environ. Control News for Southern Industry, Memphis, 1971—; pres. E. F. Williams & Assocs., Inc., environ. engrs., 1980—; rep. Tenn. Ho. of Reps., 1970-78. Mem. Am. Hist. Assn., Natl. Soc. Profl. Engineers. Office: 3637 Park Ave 224 Memphis TN 38111

WILLIAMS, EDWARD G., b. Fayetteville, NC, Nov. 3, 1929; s. Alonza S. and Blanche E. (Beebe) W. Author: Not Like Niggers, 1969; contrbr. short stories to A Galaxy of Black Writing, 1970. Wrkg. on hist. novel about Shaka, founder of the Zulu nation. BA, CCNY, 1969. Served with USN, 1950-54. NEA grantee, 1978. Mem. PEN. Home: 20 St James Pl Brooklyn NY 11205

WILLIAMS, IRENE E. G., b. Marion, SC, Feb. 24, 1951; d. Theodore and Dorethea (Leonard) Gurley; m. Hezekiah Williams, Dec. 3, 1969; children—Hezerena, Hezekiah, Derwin, Perry, James Moses, Clinton Martin. Contrbr. articles to newspaper. Religious ed.: Pee Dee Observer, Marion, SC, 1981-86. Wrkg. on children's books, Bubble-Gum Girl, Here Comes Smug! Diploma, Inst. Children's Lit., 1983. Mem. NWC. Home: 503 S Pine St Marion SC 29571

WILLIAMS, IRENE MAE, (Nei-Nei), b. Mercedes, TX, Mar. 12, 1943. Author: Prayer

Feather, 1983, 84, Ind'yan Women, 1984, Understanding, 1984, The Kachina Will Come, 1984, Ancient One, 1984, Carry Away With Me, 1984, Pai Aganti, 1984, The People, 1984, Lizard, Lizard, 1985, Whispered Thoughts Forever, 1985. BA, U. Redlands, Calif., 1976; MA, Calif. State U., San Bernardino, 1982. Tchr., coordinator Riverside County schls., Indio, Calif., 1972-74; tchr., resource specialist Desert Sands Unified Schl. Dist., Indio, 1974-82; adminstrv. asst. Palm Desert Town Ctr., Calif., 1983-86; owner The Desert Indian, 1986—. Recipient merit certs., World of Poetry, 1984-86, Golden Poet award, 1985, 86. Mem. Collectors Natl. Am. Orations. Home: Box 74 La Quinta CA 92253

WILLIAMS, JOAN, b. Memphis, TN, Sept. 26, 1928, d. Priestly Howard and Maude (Moore) Williams; m. Ezra Bowen, Mar. 3, 1954 (div. 1969); children—Ezra Drinker, Matthew Williams. Novelist: The Morning and the Evening, Old Powder Man, The Wintering, County Woman; author: Pariah and Other Stories. BA, Bard Coll., 1950; MA, Fairfield (Conn.) U., 1986. Recipient Marquand 1st Novel award Book-of-the-Month Club, 1961; grantee in lit. Natl. Inst. Arts and Letters, 1962; Guggenheim fellow, 1984. Mem. PEN, AG. Home: 29 Olmstead Hill Wilton CT 06897

WILLIAMS, JOHN A., b. Jackson, MS, 1925; m. Lorrain Isaac; 1 son, Adam; children by previous marriage: Gregory, Dennis. Author: The Angry Ones, 1960, Night Song, 1961, Sissie, 1963, The Man Who Cried I Am, 1967, Sons of Darkness, Sons of Light, 1969, Captain Blackman, 1972, Mothersill and the Foxes, 1975, The Junior Bachelor Society, 1976, The Berhama Account, 1985, Jacob's Ladder, 1987; also 7 vols. of non-fiction, vol. of poems; !Click Song, 1982 (Before Columbus Fdn. Am. Book award 1983); 2 anthologies. Grad., Syracuse U.; LL.D., Southeastern Mass. U., 1978. Home: 693 Forest Ave Teaneck NJ 07666

WILLIAMS, KIMMIKA LYVETTE HAWES, b. Phila., Jan. 7, 1959; d. Samuel Stanford and Lillian Yvonne (Curry) Hawes; m. Charles Carter Williams, May 23, 1980; children—Essence, Tenasha. Author poems: God Made Men Brown, 1982, It Ain't Easy to be Different, 1986. Contrbr. poems to anthols. B.A. in Jnlsm., Howard U., 1980. Reporter, Phila. Tribune, 1984-86; creative writing instr. Penn. Prison Soc., Phila., 1985—; script wrtr. GLA Communications, Phila., 1986—, KYVA Productions, Berlin, NJ, 1987—; cons. Blushing Zebra, Phila., 1987—; playwright, performance poet Bushfire Theate, Phila., 1985—. Poet-in-residence West Phila. Regional Library, 1986—. Recipient Outstanding Jnlsm. award Veteran's Administration, 1986. Home: 331 N Redfield St Philadelphia PA 19139

WILLIAMS, MICHAEL EDWARD, b. Lynn, MA, Dec. 31, 1954, s. Edward James and Barbara Alberta (Patterson) W. Contrbr. articles: Musicians Guide, Lighting Dimensions Mag. Reporter, ed. Daily Evening Item, Lynn, Mass., 1974-84; ed. Lighting Dimensions Mag., Laguna Beach, Calif., 1984-86, N.Y.C., 1986—. Recipient awards New Eng. UPI, 1976, 82. Office: Lighting Mag 135 Fifth Ave New York NY 10010

WILLIAMS, MILLER, b. Hoxie, AR, Apr. 8, 1930, s. Ernest Burdette and Ann Jeanette (Miller) W.; m. Lucille Fern Day, Dec. 31, 1951 (div.); children—Lucinda, Robert, Karyn; m 2d, Rebecca Jordan Hall, Apr. 11, 1969. Author: A Circle of Stone (poems), 1964, Recital (poems), 1965, At The Fair (poems), 1968, The Achievement of John Ciardi, 1968, The Only World There Is (poems), 1971, The Poetry of John Crowe Ransom, 1971, Contemporary Poetry in America, 1972, Halfway from Hoxie: New and Selected Poems, 1973, How Does a Poem Mean?, 1974, Why God Permits Evil (poems), 1977, A Roman Collection, 1980, Distractions (poems), 1981, Ozark, Ozark: A Hillside Reader, 1981, The Boys on Their Bony Mules, 1983, Imperfect Love (poems), 1986, Patterns of Poetry: An Encyclopedia of Forms, 1986; translator: 19 Poetas de Hoy en Los Estados Unidos, 1966, Poems & Antipoems, 1967, Chile: An Anthology of New Writing, 1968, Emergency Poems, 1972, Sonnets of Giuseppe Belli, 1981; co-author: Southern Writing in the Sixties: Poetry (with J.W. Corrington), 1966, Southern Writing in the Sixties: Fiction (with Corrington), 1966, Railroad (with James McPherson), 1976. BS, Ark. State Coll., 1951; MS, U. Ark., 1952. Prof. English and fgn. langs., U. Ark., Fayetteville, 1971—, dir. U. of Ark. Press, 1980—. Recipient Henry Bellaman Poetry award Harvard U., 1957, Arts Fund Award in Poetry, Arts Fund Fdn. N.Y., 1973, Prix de Rome, AAIAL, 1976. Mem. Am. Lit. Translators Assn. Home: 1111 Valley View Dr Fayetteville AR 72701

WILLIAMS, RUTH ARLENE, (Arlene Gommel), b. Washington, Sept. 25, 1956; d. William Raymond and Vivian (Pherigo) Gommel; m. Kenneth Eugene Barden, July 17, 1977 (div. 1982); m. 2d, Stephen Williams, Dec. 8, 1984; 1 son, Matthew Gene. Ed., contrbr.: Tusitala, 1976; contrbr. articles o local newspaper. Wrkg. on poetry, children's articles. BA, U. Indpls. Chemist Ind. Dept. Hwys., Indpls., 1977-86, Ind. Dept. Environ. Mgmt., Indpls., 1986—. Home: 681 Lakeview Dr Noblesville IN 46060

WILLIAMS, S. BRADFORD, JR., b. Grand Rapids, MI, Aug. 28, 1944; s. S. Bradford and Nancy Jane (Luton) W.; m. Connie Kay Kuipers, Feb. 24, 1964; children—S. Bradford Williams, III, Jonathon Tade Williams. Author: Caress Softly Thy Love, 1982, Sunshine Grows the Day, 1983, A Reason for Being—The Philosophy of Monodeitism, 1984, The Easiest Diet in the World, 1986. BA in English, BA in psychology, Grand Valley State Coll., 1967. Dist. supr. Mich. Dept. of Social Services, Jackson, MI, 1968—; pres./pub./ed. The Copper Orchid Pub. Co., Jackson, 1979—; tchr. Jackson Comm. Coll; licensed Social Worker; Mem. Poetry Resource Ctr. of Mich., Poetry Soc. of Mich. Home: 1966 Westbrook Dr Jackson MI 49201

WILLIAMS, STEPHEN ARTHUR, b. Milw., Aug. 3, 1952, s. Kenneth Wynne and Joan (Gibbs) W. Playwright: Beauty and the Beast (adaptation), 1972, BUGS! (musical), 1973, Johnnie Cake (musical), 1974, Liberty! (musical, 1975, In Contempt, 1977, The Emperor's New Clothes (adaptation, musical), 1977, Whimsical Grimm, 1978, The Last Laugh, 1984, A Christmas Carol (adaptation), 1986. Wrkg. on play. BA, Miami U., Oxford, Ohio, 1974, postgrad., 1975-77. Playwright-in-res. BUGS Prodns., Hamilton, Ohio, 1974-77, ART of Cin., 1977-79; freelance wrtr., stage mgr., NYC, 1980—; staff wrtr. VASA H.R.D. Recipient awards Am. Theatre Assn., 1974, Am. Coll. Theatre Festival, 1977, Natl. Playwright's Showcase, 1984. Mem. Actors Equity Assn. Home: 446 W 46th St 14 New York NY 10036

WILLIAMS, THOMAS (ALONZO), b. Duluth, MN, Nov. 15, 1926; s. Thomas Alonzo and Charlotte Clara (Marvin) W.; m. Elizabeth Mae Blood, May 26, 1951; children—Peter Alonzo, Ann Joslin. Author: Ceremony of Love, 1955, Town Burning, 1959, The Night of Trees, 1961, A High New House, 1963, Whipple's Castle, 1969, The Hair of Harold Roux, 1974, Tsuga's Children, 1977, The Followed Man, 1978, The Moon Pinnace, 1986. Student, U. Chgo., 1945, 48-49; BA, U. N.H., 1950, MA, 1958; postgrad., U. Paris, 1950-51, U. Ia., 1956-58. Served to cpl. AUS, 1944-46. Guggenheim fellow, 1963; Dial fellow Fiction, 1963; recipient Roos/Atkins Literary award, 1963, Rockefeller grantee Fiction, 1969, Natl. Book Award fiction, 1975. Mem. AG. Home: 13 Orchard Dr Durham NH 03824

WILLIAMSON, GERALD NEAL, (J N. Williamson), b. Indpls., Apr. 17, 1932; s. Lynn Jordan and Maryesther (Mendenhall) W.; m. Mary Theresa Cavanaugh Welhoelter, July 29, 1960; children—Scott Anthony, John Keith; 4 stepchildren. Author: The Ritual, 1979, The Houngan, 1981, The Evil One, 1983, Ghost, 1984, The Longest Night, 1985, Wards of Armegeddon, 1986, Evil Offspring, 1987, others. Contrbr. stories to Night Cry, Twilight Zone, Ellery Queen's. Editor: masques, 1984 (World Fantasy award runner-up for best anthol./ collection 1985), Masques II, 1987, How to Write Tales of Horror, Fantasy & SF, 1987. Student Butler U., Indpls., 1951-53. Asst. pub. relations Indpls Motor Speedway 500 Mile Race, 1951; ed.-in-chief McConnell & Son Pub., Indpls., 1963-66,, Internat. Computer Programs, Inc., Indpls., 1972-76; free-lance wrtr., 1976—; instr. Wrtr.'s Digest Schl., Cincinnati, 1984—. Recipient Morley-Montgomery award for best essay Baker St. Jnl., N.Y.C., 1961, Bronze medal for best fantasy novel West Coast Rvw of Books, 1981. Mem. Baker St. Irregulars (life), secy.-treas., Horror Wrtrs. Am., SFWA, AG, Small Press Wrtrs. Artists Orgn. (Dale Donaldson Meml. award for service 1985). Home: Box 26117 Indianapolis IN 46226

WILLIAMSON, J. N., see Williamson, Gerald N.

WILLIAMSON, RICHARD, (Adam Ralston), b. Sidney, OH, May 30, 1946; s. Richard and Bertha Marie (Bates) W. Contrbr. articles to mags., newspapers. Wrkg. on novel: In Black and White, Justin, Story about Deprivation and Child Abuse; mystical prose: The Preceptor. B.S. in Electonics Technology, DeVry Inst. Technology, 1967; M.B.A., Ohio State U., 1982. Sr. technical wrtr. Copeland Corp., Sidney, OH, 1970-74, BF Goodrich Co., Troy, OH, 1974-83, Technology/Scientific Inc., Fairborn, OH, 1984-85, Systems Research Labs, Beavercreek, OH, 1986—; technical ed., wrtr. Corning Glass Works, NY, 1983-84; outdoor wrtr. Piqua Daily Call, OH, 1985—. Recipient Achievement award Am. Acad. Sci., 1978. Mem. STC. Home: 90 Crestwood Dr Troy OH 45373

WILLINGHAM, CALDER BAYNARD, JR., b. Atlanta, Dec. 23, 1922; s. Calder Baynard and Eleanor (Willcox) W.; m. Helene Rothenberg; m. Jane Marie Bennett, 1953; 4 sons, 2 daus. Author: End as a Man, 1947, Geraldine Bradshaw, 1950, Reach to the Stars, 1951, The Gates of Hell, 1951, Natural Child, 1952, To Eat a Peach, 1955, Eternal Fire, 1963, Providence Island, 1969, Rambling Rose, 1972, The Big Nickel, 1975, The Building of Venus Four, 1977; movies Thieves Like Us; play End as a Man. Ed., The Citadel, 1940-41, U. Va., 1941-43. Address: Vanguard 424 Madison Ave New York NY 10017

WILLIS, BETTY JO, b. McConnell, WV, Apr. 24, 1942; d. Chester A. and Geraldine (Adkins) Sexton; m. Dale Eugene Willis, Mar. 22, 1969; children—Edgar Daniel, Larry Eugene. Contrbr. poems to anthols. Ed. cassette tapes: Eddie's Prayer, 1985, Father They're Hurting Me, 1985, The Greatest Gift, 1985, The Empty Throne, 1985, Beyond the Sky, 1986, His Rainbow Flowed Red, 1986. Wrkg. on poems, new cassette. Diploma as Licensed Practical Nurse, Huntington (WV) East Vocational Schl., 1967. Charge nurse Arcadia Nursing Home, Coolsville, OH, 1974-77; free-lance wrtr., 1960—. Recipient Spcl. Mention award World of Poetry, 1984, Honorable Mention, 1983-87, Golden Poet award, 1985, 86, 87. Home: 47810 Greenwood Rd Racine OH 45771

WILLIS, JOHN ALVIN, b. Morristown, TN, Oct. 16, 1916; s. John Bradford and George Ann (Myers) W.; m. Claire Olivier, Sept. 25, 1960 (div.); m. 2d, Marina Sarda, Jan. 26, 1978. Asst. editor Theatre World, NYC, 1945-65, editor, 1965—; asst. editor Screen World, NYC, 1948-65, editor, 1965—, Dance World, 1966-80; asst. editor Opera World, 1952-54, Great Stars of Am. Stage, 1952, Pictorial History of Silent Screen, 1953, Pictorial History of Opera in America, 1959, Pictorial History of the American Theatre, 1950, 60, 70, 75, 80, 85. BA cum laude, Milligan Coll., 1938; MA, U. Tenn., 1941; postgrad., Ind. U., Harvard U. Served to lt. USNR, 1943-45. Mem. Actors Equity Assn., former mem. N.Y. Drama Desk, Outer Critics Circle, Natl. Bd. Rev. Motion Pictures (bd. dirs.). Home: 190 Riverside Dr New York NY 10024

WILLIS, JUDITH LAURA LEVINE, b. Bklyn., May 24, 1941, d. Abraham Solomon and Ida (Erdberg) Levine; m. Ronald J. Willis, May 2, 1965 (dec. 1975); 1 dau., Heidi. Contrbr. articles to Woman's Day, Chgo. Tribune, other publs.; contrbr. poetry, prose to WomanSpirit, Broomstick (under penname Judith Laura). Wrkg. on novel, short stories. BS in Journalism, Ohio U., 1963. Reporter Trenton (N.J.) Times, 1963-64; public info. specialist Natl. Clearinghouse for Smoking and Health, Washington, 1966-67; ed. Woodwind, Washington, 1968-70; owner, operator Judith Willis, the Traveling Ed., Arlington, Va., 1967-75; asst. dir. public affairs Fairfax Hosp. Assn., Falls Church, Va., 1975-79; ed. FDA Drug Bulltn., Rockville, Md., 1979—. Recipient awards for articles, page makeup. Mem. Washington Ind. Wrtrs., Wrtrs. Center, Women in Communications. Office: FDA 5600 Fishers Ln Rockville MD 20857

WILLIS, MEREDITH SUE, b. Clarksburg, WV, May 31, 1946, d. Glenn Ernest and Lucille (Meredith) Willis; m. Andrew Bruce Weinberger, May 9, 1982; 1 son, Joel. Author: A Space Apart, 1979, Higher Ground, 1981, Personal Fiction Writing, 1984, Only Great Charges, 1985. BA, Barnard Coll., 1969; MFA, Columbia U., 1972. Cons. Tchrs. and Wrtrs. Collaborative, NYC, 1971—; adj. prof. Pace U., NYC, 1980-84, NYU, 1982—, Pratt Inst., NYC, 1986-87. NEA creative writing fellow, 1978. Mem. AG. Home: 311 Prospect Street South Orange NJ 07079

WILLMOT, WILLIAM CLARENCE, b. Elizabeth, NJ, June 26, 1925; s. Clarence William and Caroline Wienges (Sherman) W.; m.Florence Camilla Veverka, May 22, 1948. Contrbr. articles: The Taro Leaf, The Relay, The Technical Writer, Orlando Sentinel and publs. of USCG Aux. Wrkg. on memoirs of World War II. BGS, Rollins Coll., 1967; MS, Fla. Inst. Tech., 1970; MEd, Stetson U., 1972. Tech. wrtr. U.S. Army Ordnance, Dover, N.J., 1961-62; tech. wrtr. NASA, Kennedy Space Center, Fla., 1962-64, supr., tech. ed., 1964-67, emergency preparedness officer, 1971-79; sr. tech. ed. Pan Am World Services, Patrick AFB, Fla., 1983—; news ed. No. N.J. sect. Inst. Radio Engrs., 1961-62, assoc. ed., 1962; news ed. Sparks Jnl., Soc. Wireless Pioneers, 1982-83, asst. ed., 1986—. Served with U.S. Army, 1943-46; PTO. Mem. Assn. Tchrs. Tech. Writing, Space Coast Wrtrs. Conf. Home: 1630 Venus St Merritt Island FL 32593

WILLOUGHBY, DORIS MELLOTT, b. Easton, PA, June 29, 1936; d. Harold Elton and Margaret Rosetta (Smith) Koerner; m. D. Curtis Willoughby, June 24, 1967. Author: Your School Includes a Blind Student, 1974, rev. ed. 1981, A Resource Guide for Parents and Educators of Blind Children, 1979; contrbr. to: The Balance Sheet, Future Reflections. BA, Grinnell Coll., 1957; postgrad., endorsement to tch. blind, U. MN, 1969. Elementary tchr. Cedar Rapids (IA) Schs., 1957-68; resource tchr., blind, Cedar Rapids, 1969-72; itinerant tchr., blind, Heartland Edn. Agency, Johnston, IA, 1976—. Mem. Council for Exceptl. Child.; Parents Div., Natl. Fedn. Blind. Home: 2711 54th St Des Moines IA 50310

WILLOUGHBY, STEPHEN SCHUYLER, b. Madison, WI., Sept. 27, 1932; s. Alfred and Elizabeth France (Cassell) W.; m. Helen Sali Shapiro, Aug. 29, 1954; children: Wendy Valentine, Todd Alan. Author: Contemporary Teaching of Secondary School Mathematics, 1967, Probability and Statistics, 1968, Teaching Mathematics: What is Basic, 1981, Real Math, 1981, 85. AB, Harvard U., 1953, AM in Teaching, 1955; Ed.D. (Clifford Brewster Upton fellow), Columbia U., 1961. Home: 13 Dingletown Rd Greenwich CT 06830

WILLS, DAVID ARTHUR, b. Arlington, MA, Mar. 24, 1952; m. Delmadean Wills, Feb. 14, 1977. Contrbr. articles to mags., newspapers. Ed.: Exchange, 1986-87, The New Alchemy Quarterly, 1987; asst. ed.: The Rvw. Mg., 1987. Wrkg. on collection of mystery-suspense short stories. B.A., Bridgewater State Coll., 1981; M.S.M., Lesley Coll., 1985. Communications specialist Mass. Adoption Resource Exchange, Boston, 1986-87; pubs. mgr. New Alchemy Inst., Hatchville, MA, 1987—. Mem. NWC, Pofl. Wrtrs. Cape Cod. Home: 5 Orchard Way Sandwich MA 02563

WILLS, GARRY, b. Atlanta, May 22, 1934; s. John and Mayno (Collins) W.; m. Natalie Cavallo, May 30, 1959; children—John, Garry, Lydia. Author: Chesterton, 1961, Politics and Catholic Freedom, 1964, Roman Culture, 1966, Jack Ruby, 1967, Second Civil War, 1968, Nixon Agonistes, 1970, Bare Ruined Choirs, 1972, Inventing America, 1978, At Button's, 1979, Confessions of a Conservative, 1979, Explaining America, 1980, The Kennedy Imprisonment, 1982, Lead Time, 1983, Cincinnatus, 1984, Reagan's America, 1987. BA, St. Louis U., 1957; MA, Xavier U., Cin., 1958, Yale U., 1959, PhD, 1961; LittD, Coll. Holy Cross, 1982, Columbia Coll., 1982. Newspaper columnist Universal Press Syndicate, 1970—. Recipient Natl. Book Critics Circle award, Merle Curti award; others. Address: Dept Hist Northwestern U Evanston IL 60201

WILLSON, ROBERT, b. Mertzon, TX, May 28, 1912, s. James Thomas and Birdie Alice (Blanks) W.; m. Margaret Emma Bosshardt, May 30, 1981; 1 son, Mark Joseph. Author: Concept in Clay (textbook), 1967, College Level Art Curriculum in Glass, 1968, various museum catalogs. Wrkg. on editing Am. Indian poetry books. BA, U. Tex.-Austin, 1934; MFA, U. Bellas Artes, Mex., 1941. Coll. art educator, Tex. Wesleyan Coll., Ft. Worth, 1940-48, U. Miami, Fla., 1952-77; ed. Tejas Art Press, San Antonio, 1977—; ed.: The Ancient Songs of Quetzalcoatl, 1980, All the Wondrousness (poetry), 1980, One More Shiprock Night (poetry), 1981. Active sculptor in glass, with working studio in Venice; exhibits sculptor and watercolors internationally. Grantee U.S. Dept. Edn., 1956. Mem. Tex. Watercolor Soc., San Antonio Poetry Group, Tex. Circuit Book Distbrs., Natl. Glass Art Soc. Home: Terrell Rd San Antonio TX 78209

WILLSON, ROBERT FRANK, b. Detroit, Jan. 12, 1939; s. Robert Frank and Viola Bernice (Coleman) W.; m. Barbara Pearl Benson, Aug. 26, 1961; children—Robert Christopher, Rebecca Elizabeth. Author: Their Form Confounded, 1975, Shakespeare's Opening Scenes, 1977; editor: Landmarks of Shakespeare Crit., 1978, The Macmillan Handbook of English, 1975 (7th ed., 1982), Writing: Analysis and Application, 1978; Landmarks of Crit., The Shakespeare Newsletter; contrbr. articles to Shakespeare Qtly, Shakes. Studies, Shakes. Jahrbuch, Shakes. on Film Newsletter; Hamlet Studies, The Upstart Crow, Cahiers Elisabethians; poetry to Carleton Misc., Take One, New Letters, English Record. BA in English, Wayne State U., 1957-61; MA, U. Wis., 1961, PhD, 1965. Asst. prof. English Temple Univ., Phila., 1965-66, Univ. Mich., Ann Arbor, 1966-73; assoc. prof. Univ. Mo., Kans. City, 1973-75, prof., 1975—, chmn. dept. English, 1975—. Recipient tchg. award All Student Assn., Univ. Mo., 1976; Folger Shakespeare Exhibit award, NEH, 1980. Mem. Shakespeare Assn. Am., Intl. Shakespeare Assn., NCTE. Address: 525 E 54th St Kansas City MO 64110

WILLS-RAFTERY, DOROTHY, b. Glendale, NY, Sept. 26, 1959, d. Earl Larry and Dorothy Ann (Gennewein) Wills; m. Thomas Joseph Raftery, Jr., Sept. 27, 1981. Contrbr. poetry toanthologies: Our World's Most Beautiful Poems, Our World's Best Loved Poems, also Ulster County Gazette, Published!, others. Wrkg. on novels, teleplays. Student Ulster County Coll., 1984. Mem. NWC (founder, pres. Ulster County chap.), Romance Wrtrs. Am., IWWG, Am. Film Inst., Ulster County Council for Arts. Home: RD 2 Box 115G Accord NY 12404

WILOCH, THOMAS, b. Detroit, Feb. 3, 1953, s. Joseph and Jane W.; m. Denise Gottis, Oct. 10, 1981. Ed.: Grimoire mag., 1982-85, Directory of Michigan Literary Publishers (with Leonard Kniffel), 1982. Author: (poems) Stigmata Junction, 1985, Paper Mask, 1987; contrbr. to Elsewhere, 1982, Voices for Peace Anthology, 1983, A Bell Ringing in the Empty Sky, 1985, Serendipity Caper, 1986, All the Devils Are Here, 1986, The Luminous Boat, 1987, Tales By Moonlighting II, 1988, Kayak, Wormwood Rvw, Pinchpenny, numerous other lit mags. BA, Wayne State U., 1978. Editorial asst. Gale Research Co., Detroit, 1977-78, asst. ed., 1978-81, sr. asst. ed., 1981-85, sr. wrtr., 1985—. Recipient Poet Hunt award Schoolcraft Coll., 1985. Home: 43672 Emrick Dr Canton MI 48187

WILSON, ALLISON, b. York, SC, Mar. 14, 1953; d. John J. and Reola S. (Whitworth) Biggers; m. Rodger E. Wilson, Apr. 9, 1971. Columnist: The South/West Guide, 1974. Contrbr. articles to popular mags., profl. jnls., anthols.;

contrbr. poems to lit. mags., anthols. BA, Winthrop Coll., Rock Hill, S.C., 1971; M.S. in Edn., Jackson State U., 1972, MATchg, 1973; Ed.D., Columbia U., 1979. Lectr. in English, Jackson State U., Miss., 1979-80, asst. prof. English, 1980-86, assoc. prof. English, 1986—; reader Phi Kappa Phi Jnl, 1976-79. Coordinator, Writing Workshop for Children, Jackson, 1980-83. Recipient Sr. Essay award Miss. Arts Commn., 1973, 74, Fiction award Wrtr.'s Digest, 1973, Poetry award Ky. State Poetry Soc., 1974, Terre Haute (Ind.) Study Club, 1974, Miss. Fdn. Creative Writing, 1974, Sr. Essay award Greenwood (Miss.) Found. Arts, 1974, Poetry award AAP, 1976, Julia Collier Juvenile Fiction award Deep South Wrtrs' Conf., 1986, Short Story award Natl. Fantasy Fan Fedn., 1986, Juvenile Fiction award Florida State Writing Competition, 1987. Mem conf. Basic Writing Skills, CCCC, MLA. Office: Dept Eng Jackson State U Jackson MS 39217

WILSON, CHERYL LEE, (Cheryl Hoyer Wilson), b. Great Lakes, IL, Feb. 6, 1956; d. Donn William and Jean Elizabeth (Franz) Hoyer; m. Robert Henry Wilson, Aug. 5, 1978; children—Michael Henry, Joshua David. Author: Tattle-Tale Robin and the Huckleberry Pie, 1984, Jeeter and the Adventure, 1985, A Case of Stagefright, 1985, Twister!, 1985, Johnnie Sue and Her Tin Teeth, 1985, The Green Ribbon Race, 1986. B.S. in Edn., U. Central Ark., 1978, M.S. in Edn., 1984. Tchr. Harrison Jr. High Schl., AR, 1979-80, Eagle Heights Elem. Schl., Harrison, 1980–87, Central Elem. Schl., Harrison, 1987—. Mem. NEA, Ark. Edn. Assn. Home: 1605 Crestwood Dr Harrison AR 72601

WILSON, DELBERT RAY, (D. Ray Wilson), b. Riverdale, CA, Jan. 16, 1926; s. Elmer Ray and Hanna Marie (Pelto) W.; m. Beatrice Joy Daffer, Oct. 5, 1947; children: Jeri Rae, Vicky Joy, Juli Anne, Margaret Erin. Author: The Folks, 1974; Fort Kearny on the Platte, 1980; Episode on Hill 616, 1982; Nebraska Historial Tour Guide, 1983; Wyoming Historical Tour Guide, 1984; Iowa Historical Tour Guide, 1986; Missouri Hist. Tour Guide, 1987; Kansas Hist. Tour Guide, 1987. AA/AS, Elgin Community Coll., 1976; BS, No. Ill. U., 1980; LittD (hon.), Judson Coll., 1985. Ed. Crowe Newspapers, Dos Palos, Calif., 1954-55, Holtville Tribune, Calif.,57, Evening Star-News, Culver City, Calif., 1966-70, Daily Courier-News, Elgin, Ill., 1970—; mgr. Desert Newspapers, Glendale, Ariz., 1957-59; advt. rep. Union-Tribune, San Diego, 1959-66. Served with USN, 1943-45; PTO. Mem. Sigma Delta Chi. Home: 1507 Laurel Ct Dundee IL 60118

WILSON, DONALD DOUGLAS, (Don D. Wilson), b. NYC, Jul. 16, 1930; s. Arthur Douglas and Elizabeth Henrietta (Dibble) Wilson; m. Marliese E. Hahne, Sept. 15, 1951 (div. Mar., 1961); children—Donna L. Wilson Rodriguez, Roanne E.; 2nd m. Carolyn Ann Bliss, Jul. 13, 1968; 1 son—Gregory A. Author: Sean O'Casey's Tragi-Comic Vision, 1976, Lucretilis: Pleasant Hill of Horace, 1982, Milk Like Wine, 1986. Verse translations in Amelia, Ararat, Ba Shiru, Milkweed Chronicle, Dimension, Poetry East, Sackbut Rvw, other lit mags; contrbr. to Rhetoric Society Qtly, Anthology of Magazine Verse, Dictionary of American Biography, Cliffs Notes, Robinson Jeffers Newsletter, Paideuma, Editor, Singular Speech Press, Canton, CT. BA, Wagner Coll., 1952; MS, 1957; CAS in lit., Wesleyan U., 1971; PhD in English, St. John's U., 1978. English tchr. several NY, CT, NJ high schls., 1962-65, 1974-77; English adjunct several universities inclg. Rutgers, Seton Hall, 1977-80; asst. prof. Hartford State Tech. Coll. (CT), 1980—; lectr. advanced and creative wrtg., U. Conn. and U. Hartford, 1981-86. Lt. j.g. US Navy, 1952-54. NEH Fellow, Yale U., 1982; NEH Fellow, Harvard U., 1987. Charter mem. American Literary Translators Assn.; Rhetoric Soc. of Am. Mem. NWU. Home: Ten Hilltop Dr Canton CT 06019

WILSON, ERIC, b. Nebraska City, NE, Nov. 23, 1938, s. William Lewis and Annabel (Abbott) W. Author: Es geht weiter (German textbook), 1977; pub. in: Prize Stories 1985: The O. Henry Awards; contrbr. short stories to Mass. Rvw, Epoch, Carolina Qtly, Crosscurrents, other lit mags. BA, Stanford U., 1960, MA, 1963, PhD, 1966. Asst. prof. German, UCLA, 1965-69, Pomona Coll., Claremont, Calif., 1969-73; freelance wrtr.., translator German, Swedish, Danish, Norwegian, 1973—; instr. wrtr.'s program UCLA Extension, Los Angeles, 1978—. Mem. PEN, Ind. Wrtrs. So. Calif. Home: 1319 Pearl St Santa Monica CA 90405

WILSON, HAROLD CHARLES, b. South Boston, MA, June 5, 1931; s. Harold Charles and Mary Catherine (Stemer) W.; m. Janet Catherine Barton, July 27, 1957 (div. Dec. 1976); children—Susan, Joanna; m. 2d, Louise Marie Napoli, Oct. 6, 1979. Author: Those Pearly Isles, 1973, Virgin Gorda Splendor, 1983, Captain Bartholomew Gosnold, 1987. Contrbr. poems, articles to lit. mags. B.S., U. Mass.-Amherst, 1960; M.A., Boston U., 1964. Tchr. sci., history, and psychology pub. schs., Billerica, Belmont and New Bedford, Mass., 1960-79, St. Paul's Schl., Garden City, N.Y., 1970-86. Served with USCG, 1952-56. Chmn., Cape Cod Wrtrs. Conf. Com., Craigville, Mass., 1969; dir. discovery program St. Paul's Schl., 1985-86. Recipient Cert. of Merit for poems on Thoreau, N.Am. Mentor Mag., 1985, poem, Morning Glory, 1986. Home: 295 Stewart Ave Garden City NY 11530

WILSON, IRENE K., b. Boston; m. Edward O. Wilson, Oct. 30, 1955; 1 dau., Catherine. Author: (poems) Wildflowers of the Mind, 1981. Contrbr. poems to lit. mags., anthols. Recipient Poetry awards Midwest Poetry Rvw., 1986; Cicada, Poets for Africa, 1986; Golden Poet Award, 1987. Mem. AAP, MWA, PSA, PEN, Mass.State Poetry Soc., Intl. Platform Assn. Home: 9 Foster Rd Lexington MA 02173

WILSON, JEAN AVIS, b. Hillsdale, MI, June 23, 1924; d. Clyde James and Frances June (Dibble) Avis; m. Richard Christian Wilson, July 16, 1949; children—Richard Avis, Christy Wilson Klim. Author: The Garden Zoo (children's poetry), 1986. Wrkg. on children's poetry. Student U. Mich.,1942-44; BBA, Webber Coll., 1946. Home: 805 Mt Pleasant St Ann Arbor MI 48103

WILSON, KEITH CHARLES, b. Clovis, NM, Dec. 26, 1927, s. Earl Charles and Marjory Valentine (Edwards) W.; m. Heloise Brigham, Feb. 15, 1958; children—Roxanne, Kathleen, Kristin, Kerrin, Kevin. Author: poetry books: Sketches for a New Mexico Hill Town, 1967, II Sequences, 1967, The Old Car, 1967, Graves Registry & Other Poems, 1969, Homestead, 1969, Rocks, 1971, The Shadow of Our Bones, 1971, The Old Man & Others: Some Faces for America, 1971, Psalms for Various Voices, 1972, Midwatch, 1972, Thantog: Songs of a Jaguar Priest, 1977, The Shaman Deer, 1979, While Dancing Feet Shatter the Earth, 1978, Desert Cenote, 1978, The Streets of San Miguel, 1979, Retablos, 1981, Stone Roses: Poems from Transylvania, 1983, Lovesongs & Mandalas, 1984, Meeting in Jal (with Theodore Enslin), 1985; contrbr. poetry, short stories to Descant, Salthouse Miscellany, Prairie Schooner, Kayak, Weed, numerous other lit mags, anthols. BS, U.S. Naval Acad., 1950; MA, U.N.Mex., 1958. Prof., poet-in-res. N.Mex. State U., Las Cruces, 1965—. Served to lt. (j.g.), USN, 1950-54; Korea. Recipient PEN Am. Ctr. award, 1972; D.H. Lawrence writing fellow, U. N.Mex., Taos, 1972; NEA fellow, 1974; Fulbright-Hays sr. fellow, 1974. Mem. AWP, Rio Grande Inst., Rio Grande Wrtrs. Assn. Home: 1500 S Locust St Las Cruces NM 88001

WILSON, LUTHER, b. Pineville, KY, Feb. 2, 1944; s. Luther and Lillian R. (Lee) W.; married; 1 son, Eric Thomas. Editor sociology and poli. sci., NYC., 1970-72; editor Cambridge U. Press, NYC., 1972-76; editor-in-chief U. Okla. Press., 1976-80; dir. U. N. Mex. Press, 1980-85; Syracuse U. Press, 1985—. Oakland U., 1964. Address: 1600 Jamesville Ave Syracuse NY 13244

WILSON, MAROLYN CALDWELL, (Marolyn Caldwell-Wilson) b. Manhattan, KS, Apr. 21, 1934; d. Marion John and Lucile (Laessig) Caldwell; m. L. Davant Mull, June 10, 1955 (div. 1976); children—David L., Richard C. (dec.), Steven D.; m. Robert Wilson, Jan. 1, 1980. Author: Flight into Danger, 1984, Whirlwind, 1985. Wrkg. on mystery novel, An Ill Wind. B.A. in English, U. Md., 1981. Dir., Washington Romance Wrtrs., 1984-85, pres., 1985-86. Mem. Washington Ind. Wrtrs., Wrtr.'s Center. Address: Box 5834 Rockville MD 20855

WILSON, MILES SCOTT, b. Belle Fourche, SD, Dec. 6, 1943; children—Brittany, Clare, Bren. Fiction and poetry in Kans. Qtly, Tex. Rvw, Writers Forum, NM Humanities Rvw, Ind. Rvw, NY Qtly, Anthology of Mag Verse and Yearbook of Am. Poetry, 1984. BA, Pomona Coll., 1966, MFA, Univ. Ore., 1968. Asst. prof. Eng. Central Ore. Comm. Coll., Bend, 1968-73; lectr. in English SW Tex. State Univ., San Marcos, 1980—. Recipient Ione Burden award first prize novel, Deep South Writers' competition, Univ. So. La., 1981, Pushcart Prize, 1982, winner Emerging Wrtrs Competition, Passages North, 1987. Mem. AWP, Tex. Assn. Creative Writing Tchrs. Address: 941 Sycamore St San Marcos TX 78666

WILSON, MINTER LOWTHER, JR., b. Morgantown, WV, Aug. 19, 1925; s. Minter Lowther and Mary Mildred (Friend) W.; m. Helen Hope Sauerwein, June 18, 1946; children—Mary Florence, Barbara Ann, Karen Lee, Stephen David. Ed., The Retired Officer Mag., 1972—. BS in Mil. Sci. & Engr., U.S. Mil. Acad., West Point, 1946; MS in Jnlsm., U. WI, 1963. Var. command, staff & instr. posits. to Colonel, U.S. Army, U.S., Europe, and Far East, 1946-67; G-1 and acting chief staff, 1st armd. div., Ft. Hood, TX, 1967-68; commanding officer 1st Brigade, 1st armd. div., Ft. Hood, 1968-69; chief pub. info. Supreme Hdqrs. Allied Powers Europe, Belgium, 1969-72; dir. communics. The Retired Officers Assn., Alexandria, VA, 1972—. Mem. Pub. Relns. Soc. Amer., Assn. U.S. Army, Amer. Soc. Assn. Execs. Office: Ret Off Assn 201 N Washington St Alexandria VA 22314

WILSON, PATRICIA ANN, (Pat Ryan, Patti Leeper, Kay Fletcher) b. Columbus, OH, Dec. 14, 1937; d. Marion Downs and Eithel Winifred (Jeffrey) Leeper; m. Thomas Francis Ryan, June 6, 1959 (div. 1972); children—Stephen Thomas, Mary Teresa; m. Richard Walter Wilson, Dec.

13, 1974; 1 dau., Jennifer Ann. Contrbr. articles to numerous mags., reports, newsletters, pubs. including Fiesta Mag., Fla. Life Mag., Boca Star, others. Social ed., contrbr. Deerfield Observer, Deerfield Beach, FL, 1978-79, 79—; ed.: Banner News, Boca Raton, FL, 1970-72, 74-78; newsletter ed.: Fla. State Assn. NLAPW, 1986. Elem. edn. cadet cert., Muskigum Coll., 1957. Dir. Communications Century Village East, Deerfield Beach, 1977-78, Chamber of Commerce, Boca Raton, 1975-77, 79—. Recipient Congressional Award U.S. Congress, 1985; named Outstanding Young Woman of Am. from Fla., 1968, Jr. Woman of Yr., Jr. Woman's Club, 1970. Mem. NLAPW (founder, past pres. Boca Raton Pro-Arts branch), Am. Chamber of Commerce Researcher's Assn., Am. Chamber of Commerce Exec.'s Communications Council. Home: 400 NE 44th St Boca Raton FL 33431

WILSON, PHYLLIS STARR, b. New Orleans, Feb. 11, 1928; d. Daniel Davis and Anita (Garripy) S.; m. Hugh Hamilton Wilson, Dec. 24, 1958. Ed.-in-chief Self Mag., 1977-86.BA in English, Tulane U., 1949. Secy. Conde Nast Pubns., NYC, 1951-55; researcher, writer Vogue Mag., NYC, 1955-62; writer, ed. Glamour Mag., NYC, 1962-67, sr. copy ed., featrs., 1967-71, mng. ed., 1971-77; editorial dir. Conde Nast Collections and Founding Ed. Self Mag. 1987—. Mem. ASME. Office: Self Mag 350 Madison Ave New York NY 10017

WILSON, RICK D., b. Storm Lake, IA, Apr. 7, 1948; m. Barbara Hall; Children—Maria, Molly. Contrbr. articles to QEX Mag., Communications Mag., Toastmaster Mag. Ed. numerous technical manuals. B.A., U. Iowa, 1971; M.B.A., U. Mo.-KC, 1981. Mgr. technical pubs. Quintron, Quincy, IL, 1981—. Home: 2221 Maple St Quincy IL 62301

WILSON, ROBERT ANTON, b. Bklyn., Jan. 18, 1932; s. John Joseph and Elizabeth Loretta (Milli) W.; m. Arlen Riley, Jan. 4, 1959; children—Karuna, Jyoti, Graham. Author: Playboy's Book of Forbidden Words, 1972, Sex and Drugs, 1973, The Book of the Breast, 1974, Cosmic Trigger, 1977, The Illuminati Papers, 1980, The Schrodinger's Cat Trilogy, 1979-81, Masks of Illumanti, 1981, Right Where You Are Sitting Now, 1982, The Earth Will Shake, 1982, Prometheos Rising, 1983, The Widow's Son, 1985, The New Inquisition, 1987, Natural Law, 1987, Wilhelm Reich in Hell, 1987; co-author: The Illuminatus Trilogy, 1975, Neuropolitics, 1977. Student, NYU, 1956; PhD, Paideia U., 1979. Assoc. editor Playboy mag., 1965-71; freelance wrtr., 1971—. Address: Zuckerman 21 W 26th St New York NY 10010

WILSON, ROBERT EDWARD, (R. Edward Gatheridge), b. Yonkers, NY, Apr. 30, 1951; s. Edward Norval and Eleanor Elizabeth (Walzer) W.; m. Judy Marie Holly, Sept. 15, 1972 (div. 1978); 1 dau., Jessica; m. Kathryn Angela Williams, June 13, 1981; 1 dau., Elizabeth. Contrbr. poems, articles to anthols., mags., newspapers including N.Y. Times, Fla. Travel Suppl., others. Contrbg. ed.: Recommend Travel Mag., 1983—; ed.: Government Programs and Projects Directory, 1983-84, Encyc. of Med. Organizations and Agcys., 1986, Consumer Sourcebook, 1987. Student William Paterson Coll., 1969-72, 74-75. Ballplayer N.Y. Yankees, 1972-74; reporter Press-Chronicle, Johnson City, TN, 1976-80, Ridgewood Newspapers, Inc., NJ, 1981; ed. Gale Research Co., Ft. Lauderdale, 1982—. Office: Gale 1700 E Las Olas Blvd Fort Lauderdale FL 33301

WILSON, ROBLEY CONANT, JR., b. Brunswick, ME, June 15, 1930; s. Robley Conant and Dorothy May (Stimpson) W.; m. Charlotte A. Lehon, Aug. 20, 1955; children—Stephen, Philip. Author: The Pleasures of Manhood, 1977, Living Alone, 1978, Dancing for Men, 1983 (Drue Heinz 1982). BA, Bowdoin Coll., 1957; MFA, U. Iowa, 1968. Reporter Raymondville Chronicle Tex., 1950-51. Editor: N. Am. Rvw, 1969—. Bd. dirs. AWP, 1983—. Served with USAF, 1951-55; ETO. Guggenheim fellow, 1983-84. Mem. ASME. Home: Box 527 Cedar Falls IA 50613

WILSON, TODD DORIAN, b. Flint, MI, Apr. 22, 1953; s. Charles Richard and Doris Gerel-dine (Urquhart) W. Author: The Poetry of Todd Dorian Wilson, 1981, Selected Poems of Todd Dorian Wilson, Briefly haiku Poems of Todd Dorian Wilson. Contrbr. poems to anthols. Student Mott Jr. Coll., 1971-73. Clrk., U.S. Justice Dept., Washington, 1972-73; assembler Genl. Motors, Flint, 1976—. Recipient Honorable Mention, Rainbow Books, 1981, 82, cert. of Merit, Pomporir Intl., 1982. Home: 109 E Foss Ave Flint MI 48505

WILSON, WILBURN MARTIN, (Willie Wilson), b. Cerulean, KY, Mar. 13, 1930; s. Robert Estill and Veryda Marie (Shanks) W.; m. Jo Ann Campbell, May 23, 1954; children—Donna Jo and Deborah Gay (twins). Contrbr. short stories to mags. Grad. public schls., Cadiz, KY. Program dir. Sta. WPKY, Princeton, KY, 1955-65; genl. mgr. Sta WKDZ, Cadiz, 1966-86; pvt agcy, Wilson's Ideas, 1986—. Mem. Ky. Broadcasters Assn. (bd. dirs.). Home: Rt 6 Box 224 Cadiz KY 42211

WILSON, WILLIAM S., b. Balt., Apr. 7, 1932, s. William S. and May A. (Grubert) W., Jr.; children—Katherine, Ara Ann, Andrew. Author: (short fiction) Why I don't writer like Franz Kafka, 1977, (novel) Birthplace: moving into nearness, 1982. BA, U. Va., 1953; PhD, Yale U., 1961. Prof. English, Queens Coll., NYC, 1961—. Home: 458 W 25th St New York NY 10001

WINANS, ALLAN DAVIS, b. San Francisco, Jan. 12, 1936; s. Allan Davis and Claire Edith (Grierson) W. Author: Carmel Clowns, 1972, Straws of Sanity, 1975, North Beach Poems, 1977, All the Grafitti on All the Bathroom Walls in the World Can't Hide These Scars of Mine, 1977, The Reagan Psalms, 1985; contrbr. Green Isle in the Sea, 1986; short stories and poetry in City Lights Jnl, New York Qtly, Kansas Qtly, Beatitude, Greenfield Rvw, others. BA, San Francisco State U., 1962. Editor-wrtr., San Francisco Arts Commission, 1975-80; editor-publisher, Second Coming Press, SF, 1972—. Awards: Carnegie Fdn. grant, 1980; NEA publishing fellowship, 1975, 1977, 1980. Mem. PSA, PEN. Home: 118 Laidley St San Francisco CA 94131

WIND, MARLISE WABUN, b. Newark, NJ, Apr. 5, 1945; s. Bernard and Anne (Roberts) J.; m. Thomas Wind, July 5, 1986. Pub: The People's Lawyers, 1973, The Bear Tribe's Self-Reliance Book, 1977, The Medicine Wheel Book, 1980, Sun Bear: The Path of Power, 1983. BA, George Washington U., 1967; MA in jnlsm., Columbia U., 1986. Bd. dirs. of the Bear Tribe, Spokane, Wash.; Pres. Wind Communications, Des Moines, Iowa. Address: Wind Commun. 4029 Lincoln Pl Dr Des Moines IA 50312

WINDER, BARBARA DIETZ, b. NYC, Oct. 14, 1927, d. Arthur Orrie and Sarah (Gamsu) Dietz; m. Alvin Eliot Winder, June 18, 1949; children—Mark, Joshua, Sarah, Susan. Contrbr. poems to Yankee, Coll. English, N.Mex. Humanities Rvw, Poetry Tex., Gravida, Calyx, Poet and Critic, Red Fox Rvw, Poet Lore, Poetry of Horses, Traveling Am. with Today's Poets, Bear Crossings, Saturday's Women, Windflower Almanac, others. BA, U. Chgo., 1948; MFA, U. Mass., 1971; DA, SUNY, Albany, 1981. Tchr. English Chicopee Comprehensive High Schl., Mass., 1964-68; instr. Northampton Jr. Coll., Mass., 1969-71; prof. Western Conn. State U., Danbury, 1974—. Recipient 1st prize Wilory Farm Poetry Contest, 1981, 2d prize N.E. States Poetry Contest, 1983. Mem. NCTE. Home: Box 36 Newtown CT 06470

WINDHAM, REVISH, b. Panola, AL, May 31, 1949; s. Ike and Lillie (Green) Windham; m. Hon. Janice L. Bowman, Sept. 22, 1985. Author: Shades of Black, 1970, Shades of Anger, 1972; contrbr. to Living Lyrics, 1967, Ashes to Ashes, 1984, Am. Poetry Anthology, 1985, Reach Out, Creative Rvw, Black Creations, Essence, other mags; ed.-in-chief: Black Forum Mag., 1975-80. BA, Morris Brown Coll., 1962. Vocational Specialist, 1970—; youth counselor NYC Div. for Youth, 1970-84. Home: 800 Grand Concourse Bronx NY 10451

WINDJAMMER, TEE, see Moone, Joseph Leanders

WING, JASPER, see Ewing, Jack

WININGER, DEBORAH KAY, b. New Albany, IN, Aug. 30, 1950; d. Robert Carl Longest and Eula Mae (Jewel) Greenwood; m. Gary Ray Robinson, Sept. 5, 1970 (div.); 1 son, Steven Michael; m. Jack Leslie Wininger, Mar. 5, 1977; 1 son, Derek Justin. Contrbr. poems to anthols. Student Ivy Technical Coll., 1973-74. Recipient award of Merit, World of Poetry, 1984, 85, Silver Poet award, 1986, Golden Poet award, 1987. Home: 318 Vest Rd Box 132 Henryville IN 47126

WINKLES, STUART, see Worowski, Steven

WINOKUR, JON, b. Detroit, Aug. 5, 1947; s. Martin M. and Elinor (Balamut) W. Edit., Master Tips, 1985, Writers on Writing, 1986. BA, Temple U., 1970; JD, U. of W. Los Angeles, 1980. Address: Box 1117 Pacific Palisades CA 90272

WINSOR, KATHLEEN, b. Olivia, MN; d. Harold Lee and Myrtle Belle (Crowder) W.; m. Robert John Herwig (div.); m. Paul A. Porter, June 26, 1956 (dec. Nov. 1975). Author: Forever Amber, 1944, Star Money, 1950, The Lovers, 1952, America, with Love, 1957, Wanderers Eastward, Wanderers West, 1965, Calais, 1979, Jacintha, 1984. AB, U. Calif., 1938. Mem. AG. Address: Abelman 1271 Ave of Americas New York NY 10020

WINSTON, LENA, see Chaffin, Lillie D.

WINSTON, SARAH, (Sarah E. Lorenz), b. NYC, Dec. 15, 1912, d. Henry and Esther (Lorenz) Rosenblum; m. Keith Winston, June 11, 1932 (dec.); children—Neil Robert, David Lorenz. Author: And Always Tomorrow (as Sarah E. Lorenz), 1963, Everything Happens for the Best (1st prize Natl. League Am. Pen Women 1970), 1969, Our Son, Ken (as Sarah E. Lorenz) (1st prize Natl. League Am. Pen Women 1972), 1969, Not Yet Spring (poetry), 1976; ed., author preface V-MAIL: Letters of A World War Two Combat Medic, 1985; contrbr. to numerous newspapers and mags. Wrkg. on novel. Student NYU, 1929-30. Fellow Natl. League Am. Pen Women. Home: 1838 Rose Tree Ln Havertown PA 19083

WINSTON, STEPHEN EDWARD, b. NYC, Nov. 1, 1949, s. Ralph and Irene (Sochrin) W. Contrbr. articles to newspapers, mags. in U.S., Can., Europe and Middle East including Newsday, Miami Herald, Fodor's Travel Guides, Irish Times, Travel-Holiday, Bride's. BA in Poli. Sci., C. W. Post Coll., 1971. Freelance wrtr., Syosset, N.Y., 1972-75; features ed. Tarter Communications, Manhasset, N.Y., 1975-77; wrtr. Hartford (Conn.) Inst. Criminal and Social Justice, 1977—78; reporter Palm Beach Times, West Palm Beach, Fla., 1978-79; ed. Halsey Pub. Co., North Miami, Fla., 1979-87, editorial dir., 1985-87; ed. dir. Intl Voyager Publs., Miami Beach, Fla., 1987—; prin. MW pub. co., Miami. Mem. SATW, Am. Assn. Travel Eds., Fla. Mag. Assn. Office: Intl Voyager 777 Arthur Godfrey Rd Miami Beach FL 33140

WINTER, CARYL, b. Bklyn., Feb. 14, 1944; d. Irving and Eva (Berger) Yellin; m. Robert C. Shaw, Aug. 10, 1980. Author: Present Yourself with Impact, 1983. BA, Am. U., 1965; MA, NY U., 1968. Management analyst Cedars-Sinai Med. Center, Los Angeles, 1976-79; asst. vp, communications City Natl. Bank, Beverly Hills, CA, 1979; instr. UCLA, 1976—; owner Presentations with Impact, Beverly Hills, CA, 1979—. Mem. AG, Women in Business, Women's Natl. Book Assoc. Office: Presntns 400 S Beverly Dr 312 Beverly Hills CA 90212

WINTEROWD, WALTER ROSS, b. Salt Lake City, Jan. 24, 1930, s. Harold Ross and Henrietta Ethel (Fike) W.; m. Norma Graham, Aug. 2, 1952; children—Geoffrey Ross, Anthony Gordon. Author: Rhetoric and Writing, 1965, Rhetoric: A Synthesis, 1969, Structure, Language and Style, 1969, The Contemporary Writer, 1975, Contemporary Rhetoric, 1975, English Writing and Language Skills 6 vols. (with P. Murray), 1984, English: Writing and Skills 6 vols. (with P. Murray), 1986; ed.: The Relevance of Rhetoric (with E.V. Stackpoole), 1966, Themes and Variations (with C. Preston), 1985. BS, Utah State U., 1952; PhD, U. Utah, 1965. Assoc. prof. U. So. Calif., Los Angeles, 1966-70, prof., 1970-76, McElderry prof., 1976—. Served with U.S. Army, 1953-55. Mem. NCTE, MLA, AAUP. Home: 17551 San Roque Ln Huntington Beach CA 92647

WINTERS, ANNE K., b. St. Paul, Oct. 13, 1937; d. Warrington Woodruff Winters and Helen Elvecack. Author: (poems) The Key to the City, 1985; translator: Salamander: Selected Poems of Robert Marteau, 1979; contrbr. poetry to Beloit Poetry Jnl, Kenyon Rvw, Salmagundi, Poetry, Chelsea, Va. Qtly Rvw. BA, NYU, 1961; MA, Columbia U., 1963. Instr. English lit. and composition, Boston State U., 1966-69; assoc. in creative writing MIT, Cambridge, 1982; assoc. in comparative lit. U. Calif., Davis, 1983-85; instr. comparative lit. St. Mary's Coll., Moraga, Calif., 1985—. Recipient Jacob Glatstein Meml. prize Poetry mag., 1979; Woodrow Wilson fellow, 1961; Ingram Merrill Fdn. grantee, 1981-82, NEA grant, 1987. Mem. MLA. Home: 1411 Josephine St Berkeley CA 94703

WINTERS, JANET LEWIS, (Janet Lewis), b. Chgo., Aug. 17, 1899, d. Edwin Herbert and Elizabeth Loxley (Taylor) Lewis; m. Yvor Winters, June 22, 1926 (dec. Jan. 25, 1968); children—Joanna, Daniel. Novelist: The Invasion, 1932, The Wife of Martin Guerre, 1941, Against a Darkening Sky, 1943, 85, The Trial of Soren Qvist, 1947, The Ghost of Monsieur Scarron, 1959, 86, Keiko's Bubble (juvenile), 1961); author poetry books: The Earth-Bound, 1946, Poems 1924-1944, 1950, Poems Old and New, 1981; libretti: The Wife of Martin Guerre, Bergsma, 1957, Mulberry Street, 1981, The Ancien Ones, 1983, The Swans, 1986, The Legend, 1987. AA, Lewis Inst., Chgo., 1918; PhB, U., Chgo., 1920. Tchr. Lewis Inst., Chgo., 1921, Stanford (Calif.) U., 1960, 68, 69, 70, U. Calif.-Berkeley, 1978. Recipient Shelley Meml. Award, 1948, PEN (West) Award, Robert Hirsh Award Los Angeles Times, 1985; Horace Gregory Award, Guggenheim Fdn. fellow, 1950. Mem. PEN, NAACP, ASCAP. Home: 143 W Portola Ave Los Altos CA 94022

WINTERS, SHIRLEY ROYCE, b. Olympia, WA, Sept. 27, 1922; d. Walter Fred Winters and Royce Adel (Crane) Whitten. Contrbr. poems to anthols. Author: (play) They Have a Place, 1949. B.A., Church of Religious Science, 1960. Home: 917 So Trident St Anaheim CA 92804

WINTHROP, ELIZABETH, see Mahony, Elizabeth Alsop

WINTON, CALHOUN, b. Ft. Benning, GA, Jan. 21, 1927, s. George Peterson and Dorothy (Calhoun) W.; m. Elizabeth Jefferys Myers, June 30, 1948; children—Jefferys H., William Calhoun. Author: Captain Steele, 1964, Sir Richard Steele, M.P., 1970; ed.: The Plays of Aaron Hill, 1981; contrbr. articles, essays and rvws to Philol. Qtly, Sewanee Rvw, Greene Centennial Studies, numerous other publs. BA, U. of the South, 1948; MA, Vanderbilt U., 1950; MA, Princeton U., 1954, PhD, 1955. Assoc. prof., coordinator Winterthur Program U. Del., 1960-67; prof., chmn. dept. English U. S.C., Columbia, 1967-75; prof. U. Md., College Park, 1975—. Served to capt. USNR, World War II, Korea. Grantee Am. Philo. Soc., 1960, ACLS, 1963; Guggenheim Fdn., 1965; Folger Shakespeare Library, 1970. Mem. MLA, South Atlantic MLA, Am. Soc. 18th-Century Studies. Office: Dept Eng U Md College Park MD 20742

WIRTHS, CLAUDINE GIBSON, b. Covington, GA, May 9, 1926; d. Count Dillon and Julia Turner (Thompson) Gibson; m. Theodore William Wirths, Dec. 28, 1945; children-William, David. Author: (with Richard H. Williams) Lives Through the Years: A Study of Successful Aging, 1965; (with Mary Bowman-Kruhm) I Hate School: How to Hang in and When to Drop Out, 1987, I Need a Job, 1988, Where's My Other Sock? An Organization Book for Teens, 1989. Contrbr. articles to popular mags., profl. jnls. A.B. in Social Work, English, U. Ky., 1946, M.A. in Clinical Psychology, 1948; M.Ed. in Spcl. Edn., Am. U., 1980; postgrad. U. N.C., 1949-52. Spcl. edn. tchr. Gaithersburg High Schl., MD, 1979-81, coord. learning center, 1981-84; adj. faculty Frederick Commun. Coll., MD, 1987—. Recipient award Md.-Del.-DC Press Assn., 1978. Address: Box 335 Braddock Heights MD 21714

WISE, DAVID, b. NYC, May 10, 1930; s. Raymond L. and Karena (Post) W.; m. Joan Sylvester, Dec. 16, 1962; children—Christopher James, Jonathan William. Author: The Politics of Lying: Government Deception, Secrecy, and Power, 1973, The American Police State: The Government Against the People, 1976, Spectrum, 1981, The Children's Game, 1983, The Samarkand Dimension, 1987, (with Thomas B. Ross) The U-2 Affair, 1962, The Invisible Government, 1964, The Espionage Establishment, 1967, (with Milton C. Cummings, Jr.) Democracy Under Pressure: An Introduction to the American Political System, 1971, 5th ed., 1985; contrbg. author: The Kennedy Circle, 1961, None of Your Business: Government Secrecy in America, 1974, The CIA File, 1976; contrbr. articles to natl. mags. BA, Columbia Coll., 1951. Reporter N.Y. Herald Tribune, 1951-66, chief bur., Albany, N.Y., 1956-57, mem. Washington bur., 1958-66, chief Washington bur., 1963-66; fellow Woodrow Wilson Intl. Center for Scholars, 1970-71. Recipient George Polk Meml. award, 1974; Page One award Newspaper Guild N.Y., 1969. Mem. Washington Ind. Writers. Address: Sterling Lord Agcy 660 Madison Ave New York NY 10021

WISE, EDMUND ALLEN JR., (E. A. Wise), b. Brockton, MA, Mar. 19, 1967; s. Edmund Allen and Linda Shirley (Simmons) W. Contrbr. poems to anthols. Student Bridgewater Coll., 1987—. Shipper, receiver Positive Components, Avon, MA, 1986—. Recipient Honorable Mention, World of Poetry, 1987, Golden Poet award, 1987. Home: 436 Warren Ave Brockton MA 02401

WISE, ERBON WILBUR, b. Leesville, LA, Aug. 14, 1920; s. Edmond Wesley and Eula E. (Bridwell) W.; m. Willie Marie Norris, July 7, 1942; children: Bonnie Marie (Mrs. Jimmie Everett), Edmond Wesley, Edna Ann, Larry Hunt. Author: Wise Family of Louisiana, 1960, Bob, 1965, The Bridwell Family of America, 1968, Tall Pines, The story of Vernon Parish, 1971, '29 Was a Good Year In Vernon Parish, 1975, '40 Was A Good Year In Vernon Parish, 1976, '31 Was A Good Year In Vernon Parish, 1977, "Bold As A Lion" Country Journalism, 1977, Huey P. Long and Vernon Parish, 1977, Brimstone! The History of Sulphur, Louisiana, 1981, Sweat Families of the South, 1983. BS, Northwestern State U., 1941. Served with USAAF, 1941-46; ETO. Home: Sam Dunham Rd Sulphur LA 70663

WISE, K. KELLY, b. New Castle, IN, Dec. 1, 1932, s. John Kenneth Wise and Geraldine (Kelly) Edwards; m. Sybil Anahid Zulalian, Aug. 15, 1959; children—Jocelyn Anne, Adam Kelly, Lydia Louise. Author: Still Points, 1977, A Church, A People, 1981; ed.: The Photographers' Choice, 1975, Lotte Jacobi, 1978, Portrait: Theory, 1981, Photo Facts and Opinions, 1981, City Limits, 1987; contrbr. Octave of Prayer, 1972, Private Realities, 1974, SX-70 Art, 1979, New American Nudes, 1981. BS, Purdue U., 1955; MA, Columbia U., 1959. Photography cons. Natl. Humanities Faculty, Concord, Mass., 1970-74, Polaroid Corp., Cambridge, Mass., 1974-77; photography critic Boston Globe, 1982—; art commentator Natl. Public Radio, 1986—; instr. English, dean of faculty Phillips Acad., Andover, Mass., 1966—. Recipient Kenan grant Phillips Acad., 1983-84, 84-85; grantee Polaroid Corp., 1977, 85. Mem. Soc. Photographic Edn., Photographic Resource Center. Home: 19 School St Andover MA 01810

WISEMAN, THOMAS LYNN, b. Tillamook, OR, Aug. 13, 1944, s. Charles Joseph and Lucille Ellen (Matheny) W.; m. Rachel W. Lott, Mar. 3, 1969; children—Eric Andrew, Kyle Thomas. Editor: Forest Farmer Manual, 23rd-25th eds., 1980-85; Beetles Can Kill Your Ornamental Pines (USDA), 1979, (5 other USDA handbooks). Wrkg. on novel, technical manual, poems, technical writing textbook. BA, Pa. State U., 1971; MA, PhD, Tulane U. Wrtr., ed. U.S. Forest Service, New Orleans, 1977-79; ed., cons.

Forest Farmer mag., Atlanta, 1979—; asst. prof. So. Tech. Inst., Marietta, Ga., 1986—. Mem. Southeastern Outdoor Press Assn. (div.), Soc. Tech. Communicators, MLA, Ga. State Poetry Soc. Home: 3095 Nappa Trail Stone Mountain GA 30087

WITHERUP, WILLIAM ALLEN, b. Kansas City, MO, Mar 24, 1935; s. Mervyn Clyde and Nita Rosemond (Allen) W.; m. Donna Severance, 1962 (div. 1970); children—Gwendolyn Rosemond Witherup, Amber Witherup Allen. Author: (poems) (with Stephan Torre) Horsetails, 1970; The Sangre de Cristo Mountain Poems, 1970; Love Poems, 1971; Private & Public Poems, 1972; Bixby Creek & Four from Kentucky, 1977; Black Ash, Orange Fire, Collected Poems 1959-1985, 1986; co-translator (with Serge Echeverria): This Endless Malice (Enrique Lihn), 1969 and Arctic Poems (Vicente Huidobro), 1974; (with Carmen Scholis) I Go Dreaming Roads (Antonio Machado), 1972; editor: (with Joseph Bruchac) Words from the House of the Dead, 1974. Wrkg. on long poem of bombing of Nagasaki. Student Willamette U., Salem, Ore., 1953-54, U. Ore., 1956-57. Instr. creative writing and performing arts Inst. Am. Indian Arts, Santa Fe, 1963-64; instr. creative writing Soledad Correctional Facility, Soledad, Ca., 1970-1971; Monterey Peninsula Coll, Ca., 1970-75. Creative writing fellow in poetry NEA, 1976. Address: Box 750575 Petaluma CA 94975

WITOMSKI, THEODORE RAYMOND, b. Jersey City, NJ, Sept. 9, 1953; s. Theodore Joseph and Stella Ann (Miekoski) W. Author: Hot Living, 1985, Wads, 1985, Orgasms, 1985, Gay Life, 1986, Stories of the Plague Years, 1987. Contrbr. articles to mags. Editor: Pillow Talk mag., 1981-83, The Connection, 1983-85. Wrkg. on novel. Mem. NWU, Gay and Lesbian Press Assn. Home: 41 Bonaire Dr Toms River NJ 08757

WITSMAN, KARL ROBERT, b. Danville, IL, Nov. 15, 1959; s. Walter Gene and Florence Louise (Petty) W.; m. Amy Elizabeth Howell, May 5, 1982 (div. May 20, 1986); 1 dau., Laura Kathleen. Author: Shape Up Your Memory, 1986. Contrbr. articles to newspapers, mags. Wrkg. on The Secret Memory Training Handbook, sci. fiction book, Of Men and Mice. A.A., Danville Area Commun. Coll., 1979; B.S., U. Ill., 1981. Mental health technician Vermilion Mental Health, Danville, IL, 1983-85; rehabilitation programmer Rehab Products & Services, Danville, 1985-87; rehabilitation counselor Dept. of Rehabilitation Services, Danville, 1987—. Recipient Media Cooperation award Am. Assn. Cross Country Coaches, 1979. Mem. Ill. Rehabilitation Assn., Natl. Rehabilitation Assn. Home: 206 N Scott Oakwood IL 61858

WITT, HAROLD VERNON, b. Santa Ana, CA, Feb. 6, 1923; s. Oscar Solomon and Blanche Ethel (Talcott) Witt; m. Beth Ann Hewitt, Sept. 8, 1948; children—Emily, Eric, Jessamyn. Works include: Flashbacks and Reruns, 1985, The Snow Prince, 1982, Winesburg By the Sea, 1979, Surprised by Others at Fort, Cronkhite, 1975, Now, Swim, 1974, Beasts in Clothes, 1961, The Death of Venus, 1958. Contrbr. to numerous anthologies and mags., including The New York Times, The New Republic, and The New Yorker. BA, U.C. Berkeley, 1943, BLS, 1953; MA, U. of Mich., Ann Arbor, 1947. Freelance wrtr., 1959—; co-editor, Calif. State Poetry Quarterly, 1976; cons. edit., Poet Lore, 1976—; co-edit., Blue Unicorn, 1977—. Winner: Emily Dickinson Award, PSA, 1972. Mem. PSA. Home: 39 Claremont Ave Orinda CA 94563

WITT, SANDRA LEA, b. Parkersburg, IA, Apr. 16, 1949, d. Paul and Wilhelmena (Viel) Adelmund; m. William George Witt, June 10, 1972. Author: (with Mark Rae and David Sessions) Edith and Baby, 1970; contrbr. poetry to Mont. Rvw, Colo. Qtly, Seven Mag., others; fiction to N.Am. Rvw. BA, U. No. Iowa, 1973; MFA, U. Mont., 1980. Tech. wrtr. U. Mont., 1978-80; writing specialist Learning Skills Ctr., U. No. Iowa, Cedar Falls, 1980-81, instr. English, 1981—; mng. ed. N.Am. Rvw, Cedar Falls, 1985; vis. poet-in-schls. Iowa Arts Council, 1986—. Recipient 2d place hist. div. Mississippi Valley Poetry Contest, 1982. Mem. AWP, MLA, Iowa Council Tchrs. English. Home: 313 Lincoln St Cedar Falls IA 50613

WITTREICH, JOSEPH ANTHONY, JR., b. Cleve., July 23, 1939; s. Joseph Anthony and Mamie (Pucel) W. Author: The Romantics on Milton, 1970, Calm of Mind, 1971, Blake's Sublime Allegory, 1973, Milton and the Line of Vision, 1975, Angel of the Apocalypse, 1975, Visionary Poetics, 1979, Composite Orders, 1983, The Apocalypse in English Renaissance Thought and Literature, 1984, Image of That Horror, 1984, Interpreting Samson Agonistes, 1986, Feminist Milton, 1987. BA, U. Louisville, 1960, MA, 1961; PhD, Western Res. U., 1966. NEH grantee, 1974, 86; NEH Huntington Library grantee, 1976; Guggenheim fellow, 1978. Mem. Renaissance Soc. Am., Milton Soc. Am. (pres. 1979), MLA. Home: 320 S 16th St Philadelphia PA 19102

WIXSON, DOUGLAS CHARLES, b. Tulsa, Aug. 9, 1933, s. Douglas Charles Wixson and Evelyn (McElhinney) Newman; m. Suzanne Chamier, Mar. 21, 1970. Transl.: Perspectives in Quantum Theory, 1971; ed.: The Weed King & Other Stories by Jack Conroy, 1985; contrbr. to Encyc. Am. Humorists, 1986, Am. Lit. Mags., 1986; contrbr. articles to Modern Drama, French Am. Rvw, Mo. Folklore Soc. Jnl, Mid-Am. Folklore, Contemporary Lit. Criticism, Midwest Miscellany, Poesie-USA, Mid-Am. VIII, Classical and Modern Lit., Shakespeare Studies, Studies in the Humanities, Book Forum, New Letters, Jnl. Material Culture, Mid-Am. IX, Tradition, N.D. Qtly. Wrkg. on lit. study. BS, MIT, 1955; MS, Stanford U., 1960; PhD, U. N.C., 1971. Educator, 1962—, Fulbright lectr. Universite de St. Etienne, France, 1971-72, maitre de conferences Universite de Savoie, Chambery, France, 1972-74; assoc. prof. English U. Mo., Rolla, 1976—. Grantee Folger Shakespeare Library, 1969, NEH, 1983-84, Weldon-Spring Hum. fellowship, 1984-85; recipient thomas Jefferson award U. Mo., 1983. Mem. Soc Study Midwestern Lit., MLA, Midwest MLA, Mo. Folklore Soc. Home: 1104 Mimosa St Rolla MO 65401

WOERDEHOFF, VALORIE ANNE, b. Kansas City, MO, July 5, 1954, d. Frank Spencer and Dorothy Mae (Conrad) Broadhurst; m. William Vance Breyfogle, Jr., Nov. 9, 1973 (div. 1983); children—Johanna Christine, Matthew James, Christopher William; m. Thomas Alan Woerdehoff, July 5, 1986. Contrbr. Cottonwood Rvw, Frog Pond, Poetic Justice, Spoon River Qtly, numerous others. BA, Loras Coll., Dubuque, IA, 1982, postgrad., 1984—. Mem. staff U. Dubuque, 1983—, dir. univ. relations, 1984—. Grant recipient Iowa Arts Council and NEA, 1986. Mem. PW, AWP. Home: 3666 Pennsylvania Ave Dubuque IA 52001

WOJCIECHOWSKA, MAIA (RODMAN), b. Warsaw, Aug. 7, 1927; came to U.S., 1942; d. Zygmunt R. and Zofia S. (Rudakowska) W.; m. Selden Rodman, 1950 (div. 1957); 1 child, Oriana; m. Richard Larkin, 1970 (div. 1972); 1 child Leonora Wojciechowska. Author: Shadow of a Bull, 1964, Odyssey of Courage, 1965, A Kingdom in a Horse, 1966, The Hollywood Kid, 1967, A Single Light, 1968, Tuned Out, 1969, Hey, What's Wrong with This One?, 1970, Don't Play Dead before You Have To, 1970, The Rotten Years, 1971, The Life and Death of a Brave Bull, 1972, Through the Broken Mirror with Alice, 1972, Till the Break of Day, 1973, How God Got Christian into Trouble, 1985, The People in His Life, 1980. Student Immaculate Heart Coll., Los Angeles, 1945-47. Translator Radio Free Europe, NYC, 1950-51; tennis prof., 1949-84; undercover detective Wm. J. Burns Agy., 1955; editor various mags., publicity agt., freelance writer, 1965—. Recipient Newbery award Newbery, 1965, Ga. Children's Book award U. Ga., 1973; named to N.J. Lit. Hall of Fame, N.J. Inst. Tech., 1985. Home: 122 N Railroad Ave Mahwah NJ 07430

WOLF, FRANCES, see Nauman, Frances Irma

WOLF, SHEILA, b. Stretford, England, Jan. 28, 1934, came to U.S., Apr. 23, 1955, naturalized, 1958; d. James Patrick and Margaret (Glynn) Byrne; m. Kenneth Lamar Wolf, May 8, 1955; children—Donna Lynn, Todd Lamar, Lee Scott. Contrbr. poems to anthols. Wrkg. on collection of poems. Radiologic Technologist, Natl. Coll. Chiropractic, 1983. Free-lance chiropractic asst., 1975—, radiologic technologist, 1983—. Recipient Silver Poet award World of Poetry, 1986, Golden Poet award, 1987, 4th place, 1987. Home: 1155 Sutton Rd Adrian MI 49221

WOLF, STEPHEN MICHAEL, b. Chgo., Sept. 18, 1947. Author: The Visible Man, 1972, The Legacy of Beau Kremel, 1978, The Victorian, 1982, Final Season, 1987, Cutting Bait, 1987. Contrbr. articles to popular mags. Home: 35 E 1st St New York NY 10003

WOLF, VIRGINIA SIMMONS, (Anne Faubion, Virginia Anne Simmons), b. Portland, Feb. 3, 1915; d. Grover Cleveland and Mildred Lydia (Faubion) Simmons; m. Harry Edward Wolf, Apr. 30, 1938; children—Robert Peter, Catherine Swan. Contrbr. articles to profl. jnls., short story to mag.; poems to anthols. Wrkg. on novel, For Freedom's Sake, book of short stories. B.A., Reed Coll., 1936; postgrad. Okla. U., 1940-41. Ed. Agricultural Research Services, Beltsville, MD, 1960-66; free-lance ed., 1966-85; free-lance wrtr., 1985—. Home: 7218 Dockside Ln Columbia MD 21045

WOLFE, (JAMES) DIGBY, b. Harrow, Middlesex, Eng., June 4, 1932, came to U.S., 1964, s. Leslie Herbert and Winifred Julia (Withers) W.; m. Madeleine Simone Macquart, Sept. 6, 1958 (div. 1968). TV critic Sydney (Australia) Morning Herald, 1981-82, contrbr. feature wrtr., 1985—; TV critic Natl. Cath. Reporter, Santa Barbara News and Rvw. Ed., Eng. Free-lance wrtr., variety, rvw. and drama, BBC-TV, Granada-TV, ATV, all in Eng., 1950-58, NBC-TV, CBS-TV and ABC-TV, 1964-85, ATN-TV, Sydney, Australia, 1959-63; tchr., sr. lectr. Minorities' Wrtrs. Workshop, U. So. Calif., Los Angeles, 1968-85. Recipient Emmy award for TV program Laugh-In, 1968. Mem. WG, Australian WG. Home: 1642 N Beverly Dr Beverly Hills CA 90210

WOLFE, THOMAS KENNERLY, JR., b. Richmond, VA, Mar. 2, 1931; s. Thomas Kennerly and Helen (Hughes) W.; m. Sheila Wolfe; 1 dau., Alexandra. Author: The Kandy-Kolored Tangerine-Flake Streamline Baby, 1965, The Electric Kool-Aid Acid Test, 1968, The Pump House Gang, 1968, Radical Chic and Mau-mauing the Flak Catchers, 1970, The New Journalism, 1973, The Painted Word, 1975, Mauve Gloves and Madmen, Clutter and Vine, 1976, The Right Stuff, 1979, In Our Time, 1980, From Bauhaus to Our House, 1981; The Bonfire of Vanities (novel), 1987. AB, Washington and Lee U., 1951. Reporter Springfield (Mass) Union, 1956-59; reporter Latin Am. corr. Washington Post, 1959-62; reporter, mag. writer N.Y. Herald Tribune, 1962-66; mag. writer N.Y. World Jnl. Tribune, 1966-67; contrbg. editor New York mag., 1968-76, Esquire Mag., 1977—. Recipient Front Page awards for humor and fgn. news reporting Washington Newspaper Guild, 1961; award of excellence ASME, 1970; Va. laureate for lit., 1977; Harold D. Vursell Meml. award AAIAL, 1980; Am. Book award for genl. non-fiction, 1980; Columbia Journalism award, 1980. Address: FS&G 19 Union Sq W New York NY 10003

WOLFF, DANIEL J., m. Marta Renzi, June 1, 1984. Author: The Real World (poetry), 1981; contrbr. poetry to Paris Rvw, Shenandoah, Threepenny Rvw, Ploughshares, other lit publs.; Contrbr. essays to Grand Street, The Nation, Sulfur, others; presented in Anthology of Magazine Verse and Yearbook of American Poetry, 1984, 85, Strong Measures, 1985. Assoc. ed. Rock & Roll Confidential, Maywood, N.J., 1985-86. Grantee Conn. Commn. on Arts, 1977, NYC Public Art Fund, 1978; wrtr.-in-residence N.Y. State Council on Arts, 1984-85. Mem. NWU. Home: 12 Castle Heights Ave Upper Nyack NY 10960

WOLFF, GEOFFREY ANSELL, b. Los Angeles, Nov. 5, 1937; s. Arthur Saunders III and Rosemary (Loftus) W.; m. Priscilla Bradley Porter, Aug. 21, 1965; children—Nicholas Hinckley, Justin Porter. Author: Bad Debts, 1969, The Sightseer, 1974, Black Sun, 1976, Inklings, 1978, The Duke of Deception, 1979 Providence, 1986. Grad., Choate Schl., 1955; grad. Princeton Univ., Summa cum laude, A.B., 1961, student, Eastbourne (Eng.) Coll., Cambridge (Eng.) U., 1963-64. Book editor: Washington Post, 1964-69, Newsweek mag., 1969-71, New Times mag., 1974-79; book critic: Esquire mag., 1979-81; New England Monthly, 1986—; founder Golden Horn, lit mag. 1962; contrbr. to Esquire; others. Woodrow Wilson fellow, 1961-62, 63-64; Fulbright fellow, 1963-64; Guggenheim fellow, 1972-73, 77-78; NEH sr. fellow, 1974-75; NEA fellow, 1979-80, 1986-87; ACLS fellow, 1983-84. Mem. PEN. Home: 175 Narragansett Ave. Jamestown RI 02835

WOLFF, TOBIAS, b. Birmingham, AL, June 19, 1945, s. Arthur Saunders Wolff and Rosemary (Loftus) Hutchins; m. Catherine Dolores Spohn, Nov. 1, 1975; children—Michael, Patrick. Author: In the Garden of the North American Martyrs (stories), 1981, The Barracks Thief (novel), 1984, Back in the World (stories), 1985. BA, Oxford (Eng.) U., 1972; MA, Stanford U., 1978. Wrtr.-in-residence Stanford (Calif.) U., 1975-78, Ariz. State U., Tempe, 1978-80, Syracuse (N.Y.) U., 1980—. NEA fellow, 1978, 84; recipient St. Lawrence award for fiction, 1982; Guggenheim fellow, 1983. PEN/Faulkner award, 1985. Mem. AG. Home: 514 Kensington Rd Syracuse NY 13210

WOLFORD-BARNARD, EILEEN JOYCE, b. Greenwich, OH, July 12, 1938; d. Willment Wendall and Laura Leona (Doty) Wolford; m. Julian W. Barnard, Jr., Nov. 6, 1968; 1 dau., Laura Joan Barnard. Writer; shed. Tuby Talk, 1961—; contrbr. to FiberArts mag., Handmade mag., Dialogue mag. Student, Oberlin Coll. Mgr. communics. Ohio Steel Tube Co., Shelby, OH, 1957—. Mem. IABC, Ohio Designer Craftsmen. Home: Box 226 Rt 2 Rock Rd Shelby OH 44875

WOLITZER, HILMA, b. Bklyn., Jan. 25, 1930; d. Abraham Vlictor and Rose (Goldberg) Liebman; married, Sept. 7, 1952; children: Nancy J., Margaret R. Author: Ending, 1974 (Gt. Lakes Coll. Assn. Best New Novel award 1975), In the Flesh, 1977, Hearts, 1980, In the Palomar Arms, 1984; (novels for young readers) Introducing Shirley Braverman, 1975, Out of Love, 1976, Toby Lived Here, 1978. Student, Bklyn. Mus. Art Schl. Vis. lectr. Iowa U. Writers Workshop, spring 1978, fall 1979, fall 1983; adj. prof. writing program Columbia U., fall 1978, spring 1979; mem staff Bread Loaf Writers Conf., 1977, 78, 80, 81, 82, 83. Recipient Lit. award AAIAL, 1981; Bread Loaf fellow, 1974; Guggenheim fellow, 1976-77; NEA fellow, 1978. Mem. PEN, AG, WG Am. Address: 11 Ann Dr Syosset NY 11791

WOLK, HOWARD MARVIN, b. Chgo., Apr. 20, 1920; s. Edward H. and Adele (Marks) W.; m. Sylvia Grade, Sept. 12, 1945. Contrbr. poems to lit. mags., anthols. Attended Wright Jr. Coll., 1941. Corp. v.p. Edward H. Wolk Co., Chgo., 1942-80. Recipient prize Pushcart Press, 1980; Longfellow Poetry award, 1980; Honorable Mention, Sunshine Pres, 1980, Rhyme Time, 1983; cert. of Merit, Nashville Newsletter, 1981; Merit award World of Poetry, 1984, 87, Golden Poet award, 1986, 87; 3d place Prairie State Competition, 1984; Appreciation award Creative Enterprises, 1987; named Poet of Month, Ed.'s Desk, 1983, 87. Mem. Am. Philatelic Soc. Home: 6007 N Sheridan Rd Chicago IL 60660

WOLKOMIR, JOYCE ROGERS, b. Canandaigua, NY, July 20, 1942; d. Arthur Frederick and Ruth Mary (Hogle) Rogers; m. Richard Wolkomir, June 19, 1964. Contrbr. articles to popular mags. including McCalls, Playboy, Vermont Life. BA, Syracuse U., 1964. Editorial asst. Church Woman Mag., NYC, 1964-65; wrtr. Scholastic Mag., NYC, 1965-66; info. specialist Montpelier Schls., Vt., 1966-75; dir. pub. info. Vt. Health Policy Corp., Waterbury, 1977-82; dir. pub. affairs Vt. Dept. Edn., Montpelier, 1982-86; free-lance wrtr., Montpelier, 1975-77, 1986—. Bd. dirs. Project Ind., Barre, Vt., 1980-82; mem. Unified Sch. Dist. High Schl. Human Services Adv. Council, East Montpelier, Vt., 1979-83. Mem. Natl. Assn. State Edn. Dept. Info. Officers (v.p. 1985-86; Excellence award for pubs. 1983, 84, 85; Distinction award for pubs. 1983, 84, 85), Nat. Sch. Pub. Relations Assn., Theta Sigma Phi. Home: Calais Stage Montpelier VT 05602

WOLKOMIR, RICHARD, b. Athens, NY, Jan. 7, 1943; s. Benjamin and Dorothy (Edelhartz) W.; m. Joyce Rogers, June 19, 1964. Contrbr. chpts., articles, essays, short stories to anthols., books, popular mags. including Smithsonian, Rdrs Digest, McCall's, Glamour, Sat. Evening Post, Natl. Wildlife. Reporter: Catskill Daily Mail, N.Y., 1963. BA, Syracuse U., 1964. Ed., wrtr. McGraw-Hill Pub. Co., NYC, 1964-66; dir. pubs. Vt. Edn. Assn., Montpelier, Vt, 1966-70; free-lance wrtr., 1970—. Recipient Disting. Sci. Writing award in mags. AAAS and Westinghouse Corp., 1985. Home: Calais Stage Montpelier VT 05602

WOLKSTEIN, DIANE, b. NJ, d. Harry and Ruth (Barenboim) Wolkstein; 1 dau., Rachel. Author: 8,000 Stones, 1972, The Cool Ride in the Sky: A Black-American Folk Tale, 1973, The Visit, 1976, Squirrel's Song: A Hopi Indian Story, 1975, Lazy Stories, 1973, The Red Lion: A Persian Sufi Tale, 1977, The Magic Orange Tree and Other Haitian Folk Tales, 1978, White Wave: A Tao Tale, 1979, The Banza: A Haitian Folk Tale, 1981, Inanna, Queen of Heaven and Earth, Her Stories and Hymns from Summer, 1983, The Magic Wings, 1983, The Legend of Sleepy Hollow, 1987; contrbr.: Parabola, Quadrant, Horn Book, other publs. BA, Smith Coll., 1964; MA, Bank St. Coll., 1967. Home: 10 Patchin Pl New York NY 10011

WOLLHEIM, DONALD ALLEN, b. NYC, Oct. 1, 1914; s. Jacob Lewis and Rose (Grinnell) W.; m. Elsie Balter, June 25, 1943; 1 dau., Elizabeth Rosalind. Author: Mike Mars series, 1961-65, Biography of Lee deForest, 1962; (lit. criticism) The Universe Makers, 1971; pub. over 50 anthologies including 1st sci. fiction anthology The Pocket Book of Science Fiction, 1943; continuing anthol. series, Annual World's Best Science Fiction, 1965—. BA, NYU, 1935. Editor Ace mags., 1942-47, Avon Books, 1947-52; editorial v.p. Ace Books, 1952-71; pres., publisher DAW Books, Inc., NYC, 1971—. Recipient Hugo award, 1964, Com. award Melbourne Sci. Fiction Conv., 1975, Fritz Leiber award for contrbn. to adult fantasy, 1978, Jules Verne awd., 1986. Mem. SFWA, MWA, WWA, Am. Booksellers Assn., Brit. Sci. Fiction Assn. (dir. 1977—), World Sci. Fiction (pres.'s award 1984). Home: 66-17 Clyde St Rego Park NY 11374

WOLOTKIEWICZ, MARIAN MARGARET, b. Camden, NJ, Apr. 22, 1954; d. Edward J. and Rita J. (Zawitkowski) Wolotkiewicz; m. Paul J. Sagan, Mar. 31, 1984. Author: (with Sonya Nersessian) Handbook of Massachusetts Women Attorneys, 1983-84. Mng. ed.: Mass. Bar Assn. Tax Newsletter, 1978-83; ed.: Women's Bar Assn. Newsletter, 1979-83. Wrkg. on Yes! You Can Write; 2 novels, editing bus. and legal books. B.A., Mt. Holyoke Coll., 1976; J.D., Suffolk U., 1979. Ed., Little, Brown & Co., Boston, 1979-84; pres. Barrister Pub. Inc., Stow, MA, 1981—; free-lance wrtr., ed., 1985—. Mem. NWC. Office: 21 Dunster Dr Stow MA 01775

WOLSHAW, DORENE LEE, see Shaw, Dorene Lee

WOMACK, ERIC, b. Newark, Feb. 26, 1959; s. Donald and Joan (Nash) W. Author: Come Back Home Daddy Ain't Mad With You, 1978, You Are A New Person Altogether, 1984, Earth, Wind, and Fire, 1984, God's Provisions Are Abundant-Prosperity, 1985, How to Develop a Children's Church, 1985, How to Develop a Standard of Ethics in the Church, 1986.Bachelor's Degree in Bible Theology, InH. Bible Inst., 1986; MTheol, Trinity Coll. & Theol. Seminary, Newburgh, Ind. Radiologic technologist Overlook Hosp., Summit, NJ, 1977-80; deacon Faith Temple of Victory, Newark, 1977-80; mortuary of sci. diener Newark Beth Israel Med. Ctr., 1977-84; music tchr. Calvary Christian Sch., Newark, 1985-86; minister & instr. Christian Bible Ctr., Newark, 1984—. Mem. Natl. Board Dirs., Natl. Outreach Bible Inst. Home: 15 Gregory Ave West Orange NJ 07052

WONDRA, JANET C., b. Van Nuys, CA, Sept. 20, 1952, d. Gerald Lloyd and Elizabeth Ellen (Rau) Wondra. Contrbr. poetry to Emerging Island Cultures: A Collection of Stories and Poems, 1984, Quarry West, Mich. Qtly Rvw, Berkeley Poetry Rvw, other publs. BA in Philosophy, UCLA, 1975; MA in English, Creative Wrtg., San Francisco State U., 1983. Lectr. San Francisco State U., 1983—, U. San Francisco, 1983-86; poet, cons. San Francisco Mus. Modern Art, Fine Arts Museums of San Francisco, 1985—; poet, tchr. Calif. poets-in-schls., 1983—; co-pub., ed. Emerging Island Cultures Press, San Francisco, 1984—, lectr. San Jose City Coll., 1987—; lectr. Skyline Coll., 1987—. Winner 1st prize AAP, San Francisco State U., 1982, grant recipient Fleishhacker Fan, 1987; Phi Beta Kappa. Home: 1212 Versailles Ave Alameda CA 94501

WONG, NANCY, b. Canton, China, Mar. 22, 1949, came to U.S., 1956, d. Yau-Tai and Helen (Lau) Hwang. Contrbr. to: L'Orient le Jour, The Daily Star. BA in Psychology, U. Mich., 1971. Freelance photographer, San Francisco. Home: 780 Chestnut St Apt 3 San Francisco CA 94133

WONG, NELLIE, b. Oakland, CA, Sept. 12, 1934, d. Seow Hong and Suey Ting (Yee) Gee. Author: (poetry) Dreams in Harrison Railroad Park, 1977, The Death of Long Steam Lady, 1986; contrbr. to Five Fingers Rvw, Working Classics, Real Fiction, Women Wrtrs. Calendar, Between Ourselves, Ikon No. 4, This Bridge Called My Back, Writings by Radical Women of Color, Hurricane Alice, A Feminist Review. Exec. secy. Bethlehem Steel Corp., San Francisco, 1964-82; adminstrv. asst. U. Calif., San Francisco, 1983—. First organizer Women Wrtrs. Union, meml. Nat. Women Studies Assn., vis. prof. in women's studies, U. Minn., 1985. Address: 690 Spruce St Oakland CA 94610

WOOD, CURTIS L., b. Traphill, NC; s. Charley William and Nelia Elizabeth W.; m. Mary Edith Byrd, Oct. 8, 1947; children—Dennis, Dalton, Mary Woods Triplett. Author: Touched by the Master's Hand (poetry), 1978, Tumbleweed (poetry), 1985; contrbr. poetry: Lyricist mag., Cross Stitch, other publs.; wrtr. gospel and country songs. Wrkg. on book. BBA, Clevenger Coll., 1950. Self-employed accountant, North Wilkesboro, N.C., 1950—. Mem. Country Music Assn., Gospel Music Assn., Broadcast Music Assn. Address: Box 701 North Wilkesboro NC 28659

WOOD, HARVEY JOSEPH, b. Phila., Oct. 4, 1919; s. William H. and Sallie (Tatem) W.; m. Christine Joan Masino, Nov. 23, 1940; 1 son., Harvey J. Author: Industrial Engineering Management, 1959, Conflict in Management, 1970, Principles of Supervision, 1970; (humorous hist. novel) The Goldbrick, 1987. B.S. in Indsl. Engineering, Rutgers U., 1952. Genl. mgr. RCA, Camden, NJ, 1948-66; management cons. H.J.W. Assoc., Penn, NJ, 1966-71; dir. administr. Alfred Angelo, Inc., Willow Grove, PA, 1971-84, retired. Home: 6801 NW 29th Ct Margate FL 33063

WOOD, RENATE, b. Berlin, Germany, Feb. 5, 1938, came to U.S., 1961; d. Joachim and Renate (Badenmuller) Hartisch; m. William Barry Wood, June 30, 1961; children—Oliver H., Christopher B. Author: (poems) Points of Entry, 1981, (chapbook winner Poets of the Foothills Art Ct., Golden, Colo., 1981). Contrbr. poems to lit. mags., anthols. Assoc. editor: Colo. Quarterly, 1978-79. BA, Univ. of Cologne, 1959; PhD, Stanford U., 1970; MFA, Warren Wilson Coll., Swannanoa, N.C., 1985. Instr. Young People's Preparatory Schl. for Musik & Ctr. for the Performing Arts, Boulder, Colo., 1979-82, artist-in-edn. Colo. Council on the Arts & Humanities, Denver, 1981-83; instr., CU Boulder, Div. of Continuing Ed., 1986. Mem. Poets of the Foothills Art Ctr., AWP. Home: 1900 King Ave Boulder CO 80302

WOOD, RICHARD WORTHEN, b. Groveland, MA, Feb. 18, 1923; s. Ralph Clifton and Marian Estelle (Worthen) Wood; m. Barbara Lillian Regan, Aug. 25, 1945 (div. Sept. 1951); children—John Hudson, Kathleen Ann Jendrick; 2nd m. Kathleen Helen Lounsbury, Dec. 31, 1952; children—Richard Worthen, Cheryl Ann Harris. Attended Southwestern College. Ed. Reminder Newspapers (Imperial Beach, CA), 1974-76; ed. several weekly newspapers (Imperial Beach), 1977-84; ed. FRA Monthly News (Imperial Beach), 1981—. Chief Journalist, USN, 1942-70. Freelance wrtr. Journalist of the Year, US Navy, 1966. Home: 1477 Saturn Blvd 101 San Diego CA 92154

WOODFORD, BRUCE POWERS, b. Astoria, OR, Sept. 22, 1919, s. Edwin Stevens and Alice Marion (Powers) W.; m. Xanta Grisogono, Nov. 19, 1955. Author poetry collections: Twenty One Poems and a Play, 1958, Love and other Weathers, 1966, A Suit of Four, 1973, Indiana Indiana, 1976, The Edges of Distance, 1977; contrbr. numerous poems and short stories to lit mags. BA, U. Denver, 1948, MA, 1949, PhD, 1955. Served with US Army, 1943-45. Home: 140 Mesa Vista Santa Fe NM 87501

WOODHAMS, STEPHEN VANCE, b. Tacoma, WA, Feb 16, 1955; s. Wilbur Charles and Margaret Lucille (Coleman) W. Contrbr. to Fiction Monthly, Transfer, The San Francisco Chronicle. BA, San Francisco State U., 1981, MA, 1984. Rvwr. San Francisco Chronicle, 1983—; fiction ed. Fiction Monthly, San Francisco, 1983-85, FM Five, 1985—; lectr. in creative writing, San Francisco State Univ., 1985-86. Address: 2741 Clay St San Francisco CA 94115

WOODIWISS, KATHLEEN ERIN, b. Alexandria, LA, June 3, 1939; d. Charles Wingrove, Sr. and Gladys (Coker) Hogg; m. Ross Eugene Woodiwiss, July 20, 1956; children—Sean Alan, Dorren James, Heath Alexander. Author: The Flame and the Flower, 1972, The Wolf and the Dove, 1974, Shanna, 1977, Ashes in the Wind, 1979, A Rose in Winter, 1982. Student pub. schls., La. Office: Avon Bks 1790 Broadway New York NY 10019

WOODMAN, ALLEN, b. Montgomery, AL, Dec. 21, 1954; s. F. A. (Sandy) and Inez (Holman) W. Author: Stories About How Things Fall Apart and What's Left When They Do, 1985, The Shoebox of Desire and Other Tales, 1987; contrbr. more than 30 stories to N. Am. Rvw, Epoch, Carolina Qlty, other lit mags. Pub. Word Beat Press, Flagstaff, Ariz., 1982—, ed. Apalachee Qtly, 1982-86, ed. Sun Dog, 1982-84, reader Studies in Popular Culture, 1983. PhD, Fla. State Univ., 1986. Asst. prof. creative wrtg., Northern Ariz. U. Recipient citations Best Am. Short Stories, Pushcart Prize series. Address: Box 22310 Flagstaff AZ 86002

WOODS, ALFRED LLOYD, b. Pell City, AL, Feb. 29, 1944; s. Willie Lloyd Woods and Mary Lois (Wrencher) Jack. Author: Handbook of Black Librarianship, 1977; (chapbook) Be Born Again, 1979, Winter Only Last All Day, 1980, Manish, 1984. Contrbr. poems to lit. mags., anthols. Wrkg. on collection of poetry, novels, play. B.A. in English Lit., U. Ill., Chgo., 1971, M.L.S., Champaign, 1972. Exec. dir. Ill. Library Assn., Chgo., 1978-80, South Side Commun. Center, Chgo., 1980-85; art cons. Cousins & Assoc., Chgo., 1985—. Mem. advisory bd. Ill. Literacy Heritage Com., Springfield, 1980-81. Served to sgt. u.S. Air Force, 1964-68. Carnegie fellow, 1971; grantee Ill. Arts Council, 1987; recipient Poetry award U.S. Air Force, 1967, Chgo. Office of Fine Arts, 1987. mem. Ill. Wrtrs., Chgo. Book Clinic, African-Am. Arts Alliance, Chgo. Caucus Black Librarians (pres. 1975-76), Ill. Arts Alliance (sec. 1987-87). Home: 5612 S Maryland Chicago IL 60637

WOODS, ISA LOU, see Wall, Isabelle Louise

WOODS, KENNETH, b. Richmond, VA, Aug. 23, 1954; s. John and Rosie Lee W.; m. Brenda Lee Roberts, Feb. 26, 1983; children—Michael Antonne, Kasey Tennille, and Damion Louis Jackson. Author: Education Is Attitude, 1984, Life Goes On, 1982, Women in General, 1987. Student, Va. State Coll., 1972-77. Tchr. Richmond Public Schls., 1976-81; public relations dir. Our Mag., Atlanta, 1981-85; profl. speaker Woods Unlimited, Atlanta, 1985—. Recipient Golden Poet award World of Poetry, 1987. Office: 1312 S Indian Creek Dr Stone Mountain GA 30083

WOODS-SMITH, SYBIL, b. Townsend, VT, Feb. 3, 1954, d. Marshall Kitchener and Lois Marie (Baker) Smith; m. Frank Joseph Woods, Jr., June 20, 1982; 1 dau., Cecelia Jane. Contrbr. to The Wings, The Vines, 1983; poetry in Southern Poetry Rvw, Worcester Rvw, Cumberland Poetry Rvw, New England Rvw/Bread Loaf Qtly, The Poetry Rvw, and numerous other lit mags. BA, Middlebury College, 1977, MS, Pace U., 1981. R.N. Cooley Dickinson Hosp., Northampton, MA, 1981-82; nurse-prac., Woodland Health Center, Woodland, MS, 1982-83, R.N., Providence Hosp., Anchorage, AK, 1983-84; R.N., St. Luke's Hosp., Columbus, NC, 1984—. Mem. PSA. Home: Box 727 Norwich VT 05055

WOODWARD, C(OMER) VANN, b. Vanndale, AR, Nov. 13, 1908; s. Hugh Allison and Bess (Vann) W.; m. Glenn Boyd MacLeod, Dec. 21, 1937 (dec.); 1 child, Peter Vincent (dec.). Author: Tom Watson: Agrarian Rebel, 1938, The Battle for Leyte Gulf, 1947, Origins of the New South (1877-1913), 1951 (Bancroft prize), Reunion and Reaction, 1951, The Strange Career of Jim Crow, 1955, The Burden of Southern History, 1960, American Counterpoint, 1971, Thinking Back, 1986, Responses of the Presidents to Charges of Misconduct, 1974, Mary Chesnut's Civil War, 1981 (Pulitzer prize 1982); co-editor: The Private Mary Chestnut, 1984. Ph.B., Emory U., 1930; M.A., Columbia U., 1932; Ph.D., U. N.C., 1937. Served as lt. USNR, 1943-46. Recipient Nat. Inst. Arts and Lettrs Lit. award, 1954; Guggenheim Found. fellow, 1946-47, 60-61. Mem. Natl. Inst. Arts and Letters, Am. Acad. Arts and Scis., Brit. Academy. Home: 83 Rogers Rd Hamden CT 06517

WOODWARD, HELEN DE LONG, b. Owosso, MI, May 26, 1896; d. Thomas Elvin and Pauline Marie (Barkhardt) DeLong; children—Mary Louise, Florence May, Raymond, Pearl Emma, Helen Agnes, Joseph Fredrick. Author: Song of Exultation, 1957. Contrbr. poems to anthols., mags. Student Central Mich. U., 1915. Recipient (17) Merit award World of Poetry, Golden Poet award, 1985, 86. Home: 1920 4th Ave S Apt 1404 Minneapolis MN 55404

WOODWARD, PATRICIA BEAL, b. Berlin, PA, June 4, 1949; d. Clifford Lloyd and Alice (Burney) Beal; m. James T. Woodward, Apr. 20, 1974; 1 son, Jeffrey Todd. Author: Today's Stars in Country Music, 1988. A.S., Manatee Jr. Coll., 1969. Customer service representative Sunbeam Outdoor Co., Manning, SC, 1976-77; bd. dirs. secy. Woodward Produce Co. Inc., Huntsville, AL, 1984—. Active Hunstville Museum of Arts, 1985—, Historic Huntsville Assn., 1985—. Home: 4012 Devon St Huntsville AL 35802

WOODWARD, ROBERT UPSHUR, b. Geneva, IL, Mar. 26, 1943; s. Alfred E. and Jane (Upshur) W. Author: (with Carl Bernstein) All the President's Men, 1974; The Final Days, 1976; (with Scott Armstrong) The Brethren, 1979; Wired; 1984; Veil, 1987. B.A., Yale U., 1965. Reporter Montgomery County (Md.) Sentinel, 1970-71; reporter Washington Post, 1971-78, met. editor, 1979-81, asst. mng. editor, 1981—. Served with USNR, 1965-70. Decorated Navy Commendation medal; recipient George Polk Meml. award, 1972, Drew Pearson Fdn. award, 1973, Heywood Broun award, 1973, Sidney Hillman award, 1973. Office: 1150 15th St NW Washington DC 20005

WOODWORTH, RALPH LEON, b. Lima, OH, Dec. 17, 1933; s. Robert William, Sr. and Naomi (Males) W.; m. Erma Jean Miller, Aug. 20, 1955; children—Steven Edward, Timothy Bruce. Author: Light in a Dark Place, 1978. Contrbr. chap., lesson plans to books, feature articles, fiction, editorials to mags. Editor: Union Gospel Press, 1972-74. BA,Roberts Wesleyan Coll., 1957; BD, Asbury Theol. Seminary, 1959; MA, Southern Ill. U., 1981, PhD, 1983. Ordained to ministry Free Methodist Ch., 1961. Pastor, Free Meth. Ch., Ohio, Mich., Ill., Wis., 1959-72, Rockford, Ill., 1974-80; prof. journalism St. Paul Bible Coll., St. Bonifacius, Minn., 1983—; free-lance wrtr., ed., 1970—. Recipient Editorial Contest prize Laymen's Nat. Bible Com., NYC, 1982; Dissertation Research award Southern Ill. U., 1983; Mel Larson scholar Natl. Assn. Evangelicals, 1982-83. Mem. Evang. Press Assn., Assn. Edn. Journalism Mass Communication, Minn. Christian WG. Home: 6 Riverside Terr Watertown MN 55388

WOOLERY, GEORGE WILLIAM, b. Los Angeles, Jan. 25, 1931, s. George Calvin and Leotia Pearl (Sutton) W. Author: Children's Television: The First Thirty-Five Years, 1946-1981, part I, 1983, part II, 1985, Complete Directory to Animated TV Specials, 1962-Present, 1988; contrbr. to Am. Cinematographer, Film World, Westways, numerous other publs.; TV columnist Brentwood (Calif.) News, 1959-61; scriptwrtr. The Wonderful World of Paul Bunyan (animated film), 1967. BA, U. So. Calif., Los Angeles, 1951; MA in Communications, Annenberg Schl. Communications-U. So. Calif., 1976. Promotion, Columbia/UPA Pictures, Hollywood, CA, 1955-56; organizer, dir. public relations film festivals Screen Cartoonists Guild, 1959-61; Intl. Broadcasting Awards, Los Angeles. 1960-74; dir. public relations Playhouse Pictures, Hollywood, Calif., 1956-63, scriptwrtr., public relations cons. Bill Metendez Prodns., others, Los Angeles, 1963-75; historian, lectr., cons. on film animation and children's TV, 1977—. Mem. Hollywood Television and Radio Soc. Address: Box 3804 Orange Olive Sta Orange CA 92665

WOOLEVER, NAOMI LOUISE, b. Williamsport, PA, Sept. 17, 1922; d. Samuel Bruce and Kathryn Elizabeth (Schmidt) W. Contrbr.: PA Nwspr. Pubs. Assn. Bulletin, National Railway Assn. Bulletin, Now and Then Quarterly. BS, PA State U., 1944, MA, 1966. Woman's ed. Gazette & Bulletin, Williamsport, PA, 1944-53, Sun-Gazette, 1953-72; assoc. city ed., Sun-Gazette, 1972-74; prof. of jnlsm., Wmspt. Community Coll. (PA), 1974-76; national ed. Grit Pub. Co., Wmspt., 1976-81; ed.-in-chief, National GRIT, Wmspt., 1981—. Dir. (1956) Natl. Fedn. of Press Women. PA Newswoman of the Year, PA Women's Press Assn., pres. 1956. Home: 326 Montour St Montoursville PA 17754

WORKMAN, GALE ANN, b. Huntington, WV, Apr. 5, 1954; d. Garth Dalmain and Deloris Twila (Rash) Workman; m. Kenneth Reid Schilling, Dec. 28, 1985. Contrbr. articles to jnls., newspapers including Ind. Fla. Alligator, Educator, Communication Arts Jnl., others. B.S. in Jnlsm., U. Fla., 1975, M.A., 1978; Ph.D. in Ednl. Leadership, Fla. State U., 1988. Food ed. Clearwater Sun, FL, 1975-77; info. specialist U. Fla., Gainesville, 1977-79; copy ed. Gainesville Chamber of COmmerce, 1980-81; info. officer Council for Fla. Libraries, Tallahassee, 1981; asst. features ed. Tallahassee Democrate, 1981-84; asst. prof. U. West Fla., Pensacola, 1984—. Mem. West Fla. Press Assn. (Pres.'s award 1985). Home: 7535 South-pointe Pl Pensacola FL 32514

WORLEY, JEFF ROBERT, b. Wichita, KS, July 10, 1947, s. Robert Warren and Peggy Joyce (Lancaster) W.; m. Linda Elizabeth Kraus, Jan. 10, 1982. Contrbr. poetry to Coll. English, Kan. Qtly, Poetry N.W., Cottonwood Rvw, other lit mags. BA in English, Wichita State U., 1971, MFA in Creative Writing, 1975. Instr. European div. U. Md., 1975-83, U. Cin., 1983-84; asst. prof. English, Pa. State U., Altoona, 1984-86; freelance ed., wrtr, 1986—. Wichita State U. Endowment Assn. fellow, 1974-75. Home: 136 Shawnee Pl Lexington KY 40503

WORMHOUDT, ARTHUR LOUIS, b. Pella, IA, June 17, 1917, s. Cornelius Hendrik and Esther Melissa (Maasdam) W.; m. Pearl Arlene Shinn, Nov. 25, 1948; 1 son, Joda Cornelius. Author: 85-vol. Arab Translation Series, 1968—. MA, Harvard U., 1940; PhD, State U. Iowa, 1943. Prof. English and fgn. lang., William Penn Coll., Oskaloosa, Iowa, 1958-79, prof. emeritus, 1979—. Served as sgt. U.S. Army, 1943-45; ETO. Mem. Am. Assn. Tchrs. Arabic, ALTA, Phi Beta Kappa. Home: 1818 Kemble Dr Oskaloosa IA 52577

WOROWSKI, STEVEN, (Stuart Winkles), b. Bklyn., June 26, 1952; s. Edward and Sophie (Czys) W. Author music records rvws.: RPM Mag., 1982-86; record rvws., columnist vintage music: Big Eye Mag., 1980-83; record rvws., features: Goldmine Mag., 1982-86. Wrkg. on screenplay, record rvws., hist. overviews. Home: 901 Mountain Ave Middlesex NJ 08846

WORRALL, MARGARET HOWARD, b. Balt., Apr. 25, 1942; d. Henry Otto deFries and Mary Katherine (Sheppard) Sappington; m. Douglas Geoffrey Worrall; children—Caroline Howard, Patrick Field. Contrbr. numerous articles to mags. Ed.: The History of the Maryland Horse Show Association, 1985, Hampton National Historic Site Guidebook, 1986, Views from the Cupola, 1985—, Steeplechasing Guide, 1983-87. B.A., U. Md., 1964. English tchr. Garrison Forest Schl., MD, 1964-67; salesperson Bryant Realty, Towson, MD, 1966-70; contrbg. ed. Md. Horse Mag., Timonium, 1980—; dir. public relations Fair Hill Races, Elkton, MD, 1987—; free-lance wrtr., 1980—. Mem. Balt. Wrtrs. Alliance. Home: 3021 Black Rock Rd Glyndon MD 21071

WORSHAM, FABIAN, b. Macon, GA, July 11, 1952; d. O. L., Jr. and Virginia (Briley) Clements; m. Gary Steven Worsham, Mar. 22, 1974; 1 son, Austen Winfield. Author: The Green Kangaroo, 1978, Aunt Erma's Country Kitchen & Bordello, 1985. Contrbr. poems to lit. mags., anthols. Editor: Sun Dog, 1978-79, F.S.U. Chapbook Series, 1983-84. B.F.A., U. Ga.-Athens, 1974; M.A., Fla. State U., 1977. Ph.D., 1982. Instr. English, Ga. State U., Atlanta, 1980, Fla. State U., Tallahassee, 1980-84, Auburn U., Ala., 1984—. Recipient 1st prize for poetry Fine Arts Council of Fla. and U. Central Fla., 1976, Honorable Mention award Fla. State U. and AAP, 1982, Poetry Chapbook Competition award Signpost Press, 1984. Mem. AWP, South Atlantic MLA. Home: 255-B Oak St Auburn AL 36830

WORSLEY, C. DALE, b. Baton Rouge, LA, Nov. 3, 1948, s. Ashley C. and Bessie Jane (Sheene) W. Author: The Focus Changes of August Previco, 1980, Lives at Sea, 1982, Cold Harbor; contrbr. to Tchrs. & Wrtrs. Mag. Recipient Word Magic award Natl. Fedn. Community Broadcasters, 1982, NEA grant, 1986. Home: 422 E 9th St 7 New York NY 10009

WORTH, DOROTHY JANIS, (Dorothy Jannis, D.J. Williams), b. Centralhatchee, GA., Dec. 28, 1939; d. John Elbert and Ela Mae (Bagwell) Williamson; m. Roy Eugene Worth, Aug. 29, 1965; 1 son, John Eugene. Ed.: The Reach of Song, Book 5, 1985; contrbr.: Chattahoochee Rvw., Contempo, The Village Wrtr., The Sancutters, numerous other lit. mags. and anthologies. BA, West Ga. Coll., 1967; MA, Ga. State U., 1975. Instr. dept. fgn. lang. Ga. State U., Atlanta, 1978—. Winner numerous natl., state and regional poetry competitions. Mem. Atlanta Wrtrs. Club (Carolyn Wyatt award 1987), Southeastern Wrtrs. Assn. (bd. dirs.), Ga. State Poetry Soc. (past pres.), The Village Wrtrs. Group (bd. dirs.), Poetry Atlanta, Atlanta Writing Resources Center. Home: 1399 Vista Leaf Dr Decatur GA 30033

WORTH, DOUGLAS GREY, b. Phila., Mar. 14, 1940, s. C. Brooke and Merida (Grey) W.; m. Karen Louise Weisskopf, May 2, 1969; children—Colin, Daniel. Author: (poems) Of Earth, 1974, Invisibilities, 1977, Triptych, 1979, From Dream, From Circumstance: New & Selected Poems, 1963-83, 1984, Once Around Bullough's Pond, 1987; contrbr. poems to N.Y. Times, The Nation, Saturday Rvw, Seventeen, Mass. Rvw, Prairie Schooner, also anthologies The Logic of Poetry, New Am. Poetry, The Windflower Home Almanac of Poetry. BA, Swarthmore Coll., 1962; MA, Columbia U., 1964. Tchr. English, Allen-Stevenson Schl., NYC, 1965-67, Rudolf Steiner Schl., NYC, 1967-69, Friends Sem., NYC, 1969-70, Brown Jr. High Schl., Newton, Mass., 1970—. Recipient outstanding acad. book award ALA, 1977, 1st prize Sri Chinmoy Intl. Awards, 1981; Artists Fdn. poetry fellow, 1979; Mass. Arts Council poetry grantee, 1983; Kim Wrtr.-in-res. at The Master School in New York, 1986. Home: 66 Grove Hill Ave Newton MA 02160

WORTH, GEORGE JOHN, b. Vienna, Austria, June 11, 1929; came to U.S., 1940, naturalized, 1945; s. Adolph and Theresa (Schmerzler) W.; m. Carol Laverne Dinsdale, Mar. 17, 1951; children—Theresa Jean, Paul Dinsdale. Author: James Hannay: His Life and Work, 1964, William Harrison Ainsworth, 1972, Dickensian Melodrama, 1978, Thomas Hughes,

1984, Great Expectations: An Annotated Bibliography, 1986; editor: (with Harold Orel) Six Studies in Nineteenth Century English Literature and Thought, 1962, The Nineteenth Century Writer and His Audience, 1969, (with Edwin Eigner) Victorian Criticism of the Novel, 1985. AB, U. Chgo., 1948, MA, 1951; PhD, U. Ill., 1954. Mem. MLA, Dickens Fellowship, Dickens Soc. Address: 3208 Riverview Rd Lawrence KS 66044

WOUK, HERMAN, bNYC, May 27, 1915; s. Abraham Isaac and Esther (Levine) W.; m. Betty Sarah Brown, Dec. 9, 1945; children—Abraham Isaac (dec.), Nathaniel, Joseph. Author: Aurora Dawn, 1947 (Book of the Month club selection for May); The City Boy, 1948, The Traitor, 1949, The Caine Mutiny, 1951 (Pulitzer Prize fiction 1952), The Caine Mutiny Court-Martial, 1953, Marjorie Morningstar, 1955, Nature's Way, 1957, This is My God, 1959, Youngblood Hawke, 1962, Don't Stop the Carnival, 1965, The Winds of War, 1971, War and Remembrance, 1978; screenplay for TV serial The Winds of War, 1983, (novel) Inside, Outside, 1985. Student, Townsend Harris Hall, 1927-30; AB with genl. honors, Columbia U., 1934. Radio programs writer for various comedians, NYC, 1935; asst. Fred Allen, radio comedian, in writing weekly radio scripts, 1936-41. Served as deck officer USNR, 1942-46; aboard destroyer-minesweeper, 3 yrs; Pacific; exec. officer U.S.S. Southard, 1945. Decorated 4 campaign stars, Unit Citation. Mem. DG, AG. Office: BSW Lit Agcy 3255 N St NW Washington DC 20007

WOZNICKI-LIKAVEC, MARIE ELAINE, b. Detroit, Nov. 8, 1952; d. Alphonse John and Helen (Genacanyon) Woznicki; m. David John Lidavec, Oct. 5, 1985; children: Gabrielle Lauren, David John Jr., Rodney Chester. Student Wayne State U., 1970-74. Editorial asst. Henry Ford Hosp. Med. Jnl., Detroit, 1983-85; reporter Ogemaw County Herald, West Branch, Mich., 1986—. Home: 1375 W Sage Lake Rd West Branch MI 48661

WRAY, RONALD EDMONDS, b. Terre Haute, IN, Feb. 20, 1949; s. Donald Washington and Katherine Elizabeth (Edmonds) W. Author: Kathleen & The Col-Fair Poems, 1978, Tracks, 1980, To Change Places, 1980. Contrbr. poetry and fiction to numerous anthols., mags., newspapers. Editor: Primer mag. and press, 1976-80. BA, Purdue U., 1971. Dir., Free the Forms, Indpls., 1976-78, Deer Track Arts Festival, South Bend, Ind., 1979-81, Ragdale Found., Lake Forest, Ill., 1984—M; exec. dir. Century Productions, South Bend, 1978-79; coordinator pubs./lit. arts Chgo. Council on Fine Arts, 1981-83. Panelist lit. arts panel Ind. Arts Council, 1981, Ill. Arts Council, Chgo., 1984-86; judge poetry Chgo. Coalition for Arts in Edn., 1982, Chgo. Poets' Award Chgo. Office of Fine Arts, 1985. Illinois Poet Laureate's Award, 1987. Mem. Fund for Artists' Colonies (bd. dirs.). Home: 1230 N Green Bay Rd Lake Forest IL 60045

WREDE, BARBARA, b. Middletown, CT, Oct. 15, 1931. Author: Make It Clear, 1985; contrbr. articles to pet mags.; wrtr. audio cassettes on Management Sales. BS, Central Ct U., New Britain, 1954; MA, Wesleyan U., Middletown, CT, 1964. Tchr., 1954-80; owner/consultant Take Charge, Fortuna, CA, 1980—. Woman of the Year, Commission on the Status of Women, Humboldt County, CA, 1978. Home: 5107 Hillras Way Fortuna CA 95540

WREDE, PATRICIA COLLINS, b. Chgo., Mar. 27, 1953, d. David Merrill and Monica Marie (Buerglar) Collins; m. James M. Wrede, July 24, 1976. Author: Shadow Magic, 1982, Daughter of Witches, 1983, The Seven Towers, 1984, Talking to Dragons, 1985, The Harp of Imach Thyssel, 1985; contrbr. to Liavek (anthology), 1985, Liavek: The Players of Luck (anthology), 1986. AB in biology, Carleton Coll., 1974; MBA, U. Minn., 1977. Fin. analyst B. Dalton Bookseller, Mpls., 1978-80; sr. fin. analyst Dayton Hudson Corp., Mpls., 1980-83, sr. acct., 1983-85; cons., freelance wrtr., 1985—. Works named on Books for Young Adults list, U. Iowa, 1984, 85. Mem. Scribblies, SFWA. Home: 4900 W 60th St Edina MN 55424

WREGE, BETH MARIE, (Marie Ackley), b. Ashland, WI, Oct. 5, 1954; d. Virgil Carl and LaVerne E. (Ackley) Wrege; m. C. Timothy Hanna, June 26, 1981. Contrbr. articles, chpts. to profl. jnls., books. B.S. in Biology, U. Wis.-Superior, 1978, B.A. in Geology, 1979. Geologist Conservation Div., U.S. Geological Service, Casper, WY, 1979-81, Water Resources Div., St. Paul, 1981-83, Hydrologist, Phoenix, 1983—. Mem. Natl. Water Well Assn., Am. Assn. Petroleum Geologist, Sports Car Club Am. Home: 1301 E Dava Dr Tempe AZ 85283

WRIGHT, A(MOS) J(ASPER) III, b. Gadsden, AL, Mar. 3, 1952; s. Amos Jasper, Jr. and Carolyn (Shores) Wright; m. Nancy Thompson, Jun., 1975 (div. Oct. 1977); 2nd m. Dianne Vargo, Jun. 14, 1980; 1 son—Amos Jasper IV. Author: Frozen Fruit (poetry), 1981, After the Fall: Use of Surplus Capacity in an Academic Library Automation System, 1983, No More Free Lunch, 1983. BA, Auburn U., 1973; MLS, U. of AL, 1982. Library asst. Auburn U. (AL), 1973-81; cataloger Tuscaloosa Public Libr. (AL), 1982-83; clinical librarian Dept. of Anesthesiology U. of Alabama (Birmingham), 1983—. Mem. AG, PSA, Medical Library Assoc. Home: 617 Valley View Dr Pelham AL 35124

WRIGHT, AUSTIN M., b. Yonkers, NY, Sept. 6, 1922; s. John Kirtland and Katharine Wolcott (McGiffert) W.; m. Sara Hull, June 24, 1950; children—Katharine Edith, Joanna Louise, Margaret Hull. Author: The American Short Story in the Twenties, 1961, Camden's Eyes, 1969, First Persons, 1973, The Morley Mythology, 1977, The Formal Principle in the Novel, 1982. A.B., Harvard U., 1943; M.A., U. Chigo., 1948, Ph.D., 1959. Asst. prof. U. Chgo., 1960-62; asst. prof. to assoc. prof. U. Cin., 1962-69, prof. English, 1969—. Served to 1st lt. U.S. Army, 1943-46. Recipient Dolly Cohen award for tchg. U. Cin., 1967, George A. Rieveschl award, 1973; Whiting Wrtrs. award Mrs. Giles Whiting Fdn., 1985, Mem. MLA, AG, PEN, AAUP. Home: 3454 Lyleburn Pl Cincinnati OH 45220

WRIGHT, C.D. (CAROLYN), b. Mountain Home, AR., Jan. 6, 1949, d. Ernie Edward and Alyce Erline (Collins) Wright; m. J. Forest Gander, Apr. 2, 1983. Author: Alla Breve Loving, 1976, Room Rented by a Single Woman, 1977, Terrorism, 1978, Translations of the Gospel Back into Tongues, 1982, Further Adventures with You, 1986. BA in French, Memphis State U., 1972; MFA in Poetry, U. Ark., 1976. Ind. cons. Ark. Arts & Humanities, Little Rock, 1976-78; adj. faculty San Francisco State U., 1979-82; co-ed. Lost Roads Pubs., Providence, 1979—; asst. prof. English Brown U., Providence, 1983—. NEA creative wrtg. fellow, 1981; recipient Witter Bynner prize for poetry AAIAL, 1986. Mem. PSA, AWP, Poetry Center, San Francisco State U. Home: 409 Montgomery Ave Providence RI 02905

WRIGHT, CELESTE TURNER, b. St. John, N.B., Can., Mar. 17, 1906, d. George Howard and Viola (Kelley) Turner (parents U.S. citizens); m. Vedder Allen Wright, June 26, 1933; 1 son, Vedder Allen Jr. Author: Anthony Mundy: An Elizabethan Man of Letters, 1928, Etruscan Princess and Other Poems, 1964, A Sense of Place (poems), 1973, Seasoned Timber (poems), 1977, University Woman (memoir), 1981; contrbr. articles to Philol. Qtly, Ariz. Qtly, numerous other scholarly publs.; contrbr. poetry to Beloit Poetry Jnl, Harper's, Lyric, Cimarron Rvw, Poet Lore, Yale Rvw, Prairie Schooner, numerous other lit mags and anthologies. AB, UCLA, 1925; MA, U. Calif., Berkeley, 1926, PhD, 1928; mem. faculty U. Calif.-Davis from 1928, chmn. dept. English, 1955, prof. emeritus, 1973—. Winner grand prize Ina Coolbrith Circle poetry competition, 1961, 65, 70; U. Calif. Inst. Creative Arts fellow, 1966-67. Mem. PSA (Reynolds Lyric prize 1963), AAP, MLA, Phi Beta Kappa, Renaissance Soc. Am. Home: 1001 D St Davis CA 95616

WRIGHT, CHARLES PENZEL, JR., b. Pickwick Dam, TN, Aug. 25, 1935; s. Charles Penzel and Mary Castleman (Winter) W.; m. Holly McIntire, Apr. 6, 1969; 1 son, Luke Savin Herrick. Author: The Dream Animal, 1968, The Grave of the Right Hand, 1970, The Venice Notebook, 1971, Hard Freight, 1973, Bloodlines, 1975, Colophons, 1977, China Trace, 1977, Wright: A Profile, 1979, The Southern Cross, 1981, Country Music: Selected Early Poems, 1983, The Other Side of the River, 1984, Zone Journals, 1988; transl.: The Storm and Other Poems by Eugenio Montale, 1978 (recipient Edgar Allan Poe award AAP, 1976, Acad.-Inst. award AAIAL, 1977, PEN transl. prize 1979). BA, Davidson (N.C.) Coll., 1957; MFA, U. Iowa, 1963; postgrad., U. Rome, 1963-64. Served with AUS, 1957-61. Recipient Am. Book award for poetry, 1983; Fulbright scholar, 1963-65; Guggenheim fellow, 1976; Ingram Merrill fellow, 1980. Home: 940 Locust Ave Charlottesville VA 22901

WRIGHT, CHARLOTTE HUGHES, b. Youngstown, OH, May 13, 1939; d. Fredrick Tennery and Edith (Davis) Hughes; children—Becky Ellwood, Amy Pope, Randall, Fredrick. Ed. contrbr. to (newsletter) The Green Sheet, Indiana Univ., Indpls., 1984—, Mid-States Newspapers, Brownsburg, IN, 1979-81. Contrbr., columnist, photographer, ed. (newspaper) The Guide, 1970-75; columnist, photographer, mng. ed., ed. (newspaper) The Courier, Brownsburg, IN, 1975-79; columnist contrbr. articles, ed. (newsppaper) The Times, 1979-80. Wrkg. on book, essays, short stories. A.Genl. Studies, Ind. U., 1985. Recipient CASPER Commun. Council, Indpls., 1975, William T. Garrett award Ind. U.-Purdue U., Indpls., 1982, cert. of Appreciaiton of U.S. Army ROTC, Indpls., 1984, 85, Arts Insight 1st place for article Arts Commn. Mag. for Ind., 1985. Home: 7619 Crawfordsville Rd Indianapolis IN 46214

WRIGHT, ELLEN MARIE, b. Phila., June 12, 1953; d. Charles Henry and Regina Marie (Knoll) Zopfi; m. Edward William Smith, Apr. 15, 1977 (div. May, 1984); 1 dau., Danielle Kimberly Smith; m. 2d, Donald Parker Wright, Oct. 28, 1984; 1 step-dau., Kristina Anne Wright. Ed., contrbr.: Forward, 1971, Literary Mag., 1969-71, Cairn, 1973-74, St. Mary of the Angels Acad.

Yrbk. The Grapevine; author articles, short stories, curriculum guides for in-district use. BA, Stonehiill Coll., 1975; MEd, Trenton State Coll., 1977, EdS, 1979. Head tchr., childhood spelst. Kingsway Lrgn. Ctr., Haddonfield, NJ, 1974-78; dir. spec. svcs., Runnemede (NJ) Pub. Schls., 1978-79; lrng. disability tchr./cons. Hammonton (NJ) Pub. Schs., 1979-80; lrng. disability spec. Ventnor (NJ) Pub. Schs., 1981-82, Ocean City (NJ) Pub. Schls., 1982—. Mem. NAEYC, NJ Assn. Lrng. Consultants. Home 120 Sunset Rd Box 886 Rd 2 Woodbine NJ 08270

WRIGHT, HARDY, see Wright, Linsey Hardy

WRIGHT, HUGH ELLIOTT, JR., b. Athens, AL, Nov. 20, 1937; s. Hugh Elliott and Martha Angeline (Shannon) W. Author: (with R. Lecky) Can These Bones Live, 1969, The Big Little School, 1971, (with R. Lynn) Go Free, 1973, Challenge to Mission, 1973, (with Juanita Wright) Viewers Guide to Six American Families, 1977, (with Howard Butt) At the Edge of Hope, 1978, (with Douglas McGaw) A Tale of Two Congregations, 1980, Holy Company: Christian Heroes and Heroines, 1980; editor: with Douglas McGaw) Black Manifesto: Religion, Racism and Reparations, 1969. AB, Birmingham-So. Coll., 1959; MDiv, Vanderbilt U., 1962, DMinistry, 1967; postgrad., Harvard U., 1963. Editorial asst. Motive mag., Nashville, 1965-67; Protestant-Orthodox editor Religious News Service, NYC, 1967-75; editor project on mediating structures and public policy Am. Enterprise Inst., 1979-80; vp Natl. Conf. Christians and Jews, 1983—. Recipient award Birmingham Council Indsl. Editors, 1959, Religious Heritage of Am. award in journalism, 1972, Assoc. Ch. Press Feature Article award, 1980. Mem. AL, AG, Religion Newswriters Assn. Office: 71 5th Ave New York NY 10003

WRIGHT, JAMES BOWERS, b. Phila., July 10, 1950; s. John Samuel and Margaret Lucille (Bowers) W.; 1 dau., Coriell Shane. Author: Bobby Clarke, 1977, Mike Schmidt, 1979; coauthor: The Video Book, 1981; contrbr. article to Country Living. BA in Journalism and English, Syracuse U., 1972. Editor Lakeland (N.J.) Record, Wayne, N.J., 1972; exec. editor Rudder mag., NYC, 1973-76; asst. editor Bergen Record, Hackensack, N.J., 1976—. Home: Box 97 Bellvale NY 10912

WRIGHT, JEANNE ELIZABETH JASON, b. Washington, June 24, 1934; d. Robert Stewart and Elizabeth (Gaddis) Jason; m. Benjamin Hickman Wright, Oct. 30, 1965; stepchildren—Benjamin, Deborah, David, Patricia. Genl. mgr. Black Media, Inc. (advt. rep. co.), NYC, 1970-74, pres., 1974-75, Black Resources, Inc., also pres., exec. editor Natl. Black Monitor, NYC, 1975—; also syndicator weekly editorial features. BA, Radcliffe Coll., 1956; MA, U. Chgo., 1958. Recipient 2d Annl. Freedom's Jnl. award Journalism Students and Faculty of U. D.C. Dept. Communicative and Performing Arts, 1979. Mem. Natl. Assn. Media Women, Newswomen's Club N.Y., Inc. Office: 410 Central Park W Penthouse C New York NY 10025

WRIGHT, JOSEPH S, b. NYC, July 7, 1914, s. Isidore and Rebecca W.; m. Rose Halperin, June 19, 1938; children—Steven, Ellen, Deborah. Author: The Faith of an American (poems), Mordecai at the Gate (one-act play); contrbr. articles, short stories to The Smith, Aim Mag., Adolescence Mag., Listen Mag., other publs. MA in Math. Edn., CCNY, 1968. Tchr. maths. several high schls., colls. in N.Y., 1967-82. Mem. NWC, numberous math. orgns. Home: 8 Waring Row Yonkers NY 10701

WRIGHT, KATHARINE MIRANDA, (Katharine Kennish); b. London, Mar. 22, 1945; came to U.S., 1969; naturalized, 1974; d. Peter Forbes and Jacqueline (Saix) Kennish; m. Neil Morrison Wright, Sept. 11, 1970 (div. Mar. 23, 1982); children—Aneurin, Lydia. Author: The Mountain House, 1981. Wrkg. on archtl. books, fitness book, emigrant novel. Cert. in Architecture, Polytechnic of Central London, 1970. Freelance bookkeeper, Ketchum, Id., 1982-83; instr. fitness RMO Fitness, Kettchum, 1983-85; sec., draftsman J. Jarvis, A.I.A., Ketchum, 1985—. Home: Box 155 Ketchum ID 83340

WRIGHT, LINSEY HARDY, (Lin) (Hardy Wright, Lin H. Wright); b. Memphis, Mar. 27, 1928; s. Erastus Rhinehart and Dorothea Florence (Birkhead) W.; divorced. Author: (with J. N. Lipscomb) Lipscomb's Little Book of Tall Tales, 1975; The First One Hundred Years: Mississippi State University, 1978; (with Gloria C. Correro and James S. Turner) A Plan for Mississippi Kindergartens. Contrbr. short stories to mags., jnls. including Scholastic scope, Ark. Democrat Sunday Mag., Gone Soft, Miss. Arts & Letters. Contrbr. articles to mags. including Golf Digest, Hist. Soc. Quarterly, Miss. State Univ. Alumnus mag., others. BA in Journalism, Harding U., Searcy, Ark., 1952. Reporter, Ark. Gazette, Little Rock, 1950-53; sports ed. Pine Bluff Comml., Ark., 1953-54; tchr. English-journalism pub. schls., Dekalb, St. Joseph, Mo., 1954-56; info. supvr. U. Ark., Fayetteville, 1956-69; owner, pres. Lin H. Wright & Assocs., Fayetteville, 1970-74; ed., assoc. dir. Miss. State U., Starkville, 1974—. Chmn. Higher Edn. Week in Miss., 1986. Recipient 2d place for pub. category Reader's Digest, 1978, Lantern award of excellence Southern Pub. Relations Assn., 1979, award of excellence Natl. Schl. Pub. Relations Assn., 1979. Mem. Coll. Pub. Relations Assn. Miss. (past pres.), Council Advancement Support of Edn. (Exceptional Achievement award 1983), Greater Beaver Lake Assn. (pub. relations counselor 1967-69), Fayetteville C. of C. (pub. relations counselor 1970-74), Starkville C. of C. (pub. relations com. 1980—), Sigma Delta Chi (minority affairs com.). Home: 501 N Montgomery Starkville MS 39759

WRIGHT, NANCY MEANS, b. Glen Ridge, NJ, Oct. 18; d. Robert Thomas and Jessie Washington (Thomson) Means; m. Spencer Victor Wright, Oct. 14; children—Gary, Lesley, Donald, Catharine. Author: (novel) The Losing, 1973, Down the Strings, 1982; (non-fiction) Make Your Own Change, 1985, Vermonters at Their Craft, 1987. Contrbr. short stories, articles, rvws. to listings such as Second Wave, Sojourner, and to popular mags. including Redbook, Seventeen, Family Circle, Woman's World, Yankee. AB, Vassar Coll., MA, Middlebury Coll., 1965. Instr. English and French, Proctor Acad., Andover, N.H., 1958-72; owner, mgr. Cornwall Crafts, Vt., 1972-84; part-time instr. Burlington Coll., Vt., 1985—, U. of Vt. Continuing Ed., Burlington, 1979—; free-lance wrtr., 1972—. Dir., mem. Middlebury Community Players, Vt., 1974—, Middlebury Community Chorus, Middlebury, 1974—, Frog Hollow State Craft Ctr., Middlebury, 1974—. Mem. League Vt. Wrtrs. (past pres., bd. dirs.), AL, Soc. Children's Book Wrtrs. Home: RD 2 Box 620 Middlebury VT 05753

WRIGHT, NATHALIA, b. Athens, GA, Mar. 29, 1913; d. Hilliard Carlisle and Elizabeth (MacNeal) W. Author: The Inner Room, 1938, Melville's Use of the Bible, 1949, 69, Horatio Greenough, First American Sculptor, 1963, American Novelists in Italy: The Discoverers, 1965 (with Harold Orton) Questionnaire for the Investigation of American English, 1972, A Word Geography of England, 1974; also articles; intros. Horatio Greenough, The Travels, Observations and Experience of a Yankee Stonecutter, 1958, John Galt, The Life of Benjamin West, 1959, Washington Allston, Lectures on Art and Poems and Monaldi, 1967, Mary N. Murfree, In the Tennessee Mountains, 1970, The Miscellaneous Writings of Horatio Greenough, 1975; editor: Washington Irving, Journals and Notebooks, Vol. 1, 1969, Letters of Horatio Greenough, American Sculptor, 1972. BA, Maryville Coll., 1933; MA, Yale U., 1938, PhD, 1949. Mem. editorial bd., MLA, 1970-75. Recipient Albert Stanburrough Cook prize in poetry, 1937; grantee Am. Philos. Soc., 1952; Guggenheim fellow, 1953; AAUW fellow, 1959. Mem. MLA, Melville Soc. Home: 713 Court St Maryville TN 37801

WRIGHT, STEPHEN, b. NYC, Nov. 30, 1922; married, 1954 (div. 1960). Author: Crime in the Schools (novel), 1959; editor (and author of intro.): Different: An Anthology of Homosexual Short Stories, 1974; author: Brief Encyclopedia of Homosexuality, 1978; editor, pub. Stephen Wright's Mystery Notebook (quarterly jnl.); also numerous articles in mags; author: (novel) The Adventures of Sandy West, Private Eye. BA, L.I. Univ., 1949; MA, NYU, 1950. Served with USN, 1943-46, PTO. Mem. AG, DG (assoc.), MWA, P & W, Crime Writers Assn. (London). Address: Box 1341 FDR Sta New York NY 10150

WRIGHT, TERRY ALAN, b. Yankton, SD, June 16, 1952, s. Keith L. and Elizabeth (Weir) W.; m. Ann Ashley Pharr, Oct. 1, 1977. Author chapbook: Fun and No Fun, 1984; contrbr. poems to Sequoia, Pig Iron, San Fernando Poetry Jnl, other lit mags. MA, U. Ark., Fayetteville, 1981; MFA, Bowling Green (Ohio) State U., 1983. Instr. U. Ark., Little Rock, 1983-85, U. Central Ark., Conway, 1983—. Mem. P&W, AWP. Home: 6419 R St Little Rock AR 72207

WRIGLEY, ROBERT ALAN, b. East St. Louis, Feb. 27, 1951; s. Arvil William and Betty Ann (Feutsch) W.; m. Vana Lynn Berry, May 29, 1971 (div. 1981); 1 son, Philip Robert; m. Kim Marie Barnes, July 20, 1983. Author: The Sinking of Clay City, 1979, The Glow, 982, In the Dark Pool, 1986, Moon in a Mason Jar, 1986. BA, So. Ill. U., 1974; MFA, U. Mont., 1976. Instr. So. Ill. U., Edwardsville, 1976-77; prof. Lewis Clark State Coll., Lewiston, Idaho, 1977—; writer-in-residence State of Idaho, 1986—. Served as pfc. U.S. Army, 1971. NEA fellow, 1978, 84, 85. Mem. AAP, PSA. Home: 623 7th Avenue Lewiston ID 83501

WROLSEN, JEAN LOSEE, b. Cumberland, MD, Jan. 28, 1920; d. Armour Curry and Clara Vernon (Wiebel) Anderson; m. Berthel Wrolsen (dec.), Sept. 29, 1949. Author and illus: Lambs of the Catskills, 1974, Woodweave, 1980; author: Island Images, 1986. Student, Corcoran School of Art, Washington, DC, 1942-43; student, Arts Students League of NY, NYC, 1944-45; student, Bard Coll., Annandale-on-Hudson, NY, 1947-48. Columnist, Old Dutch Post Star, Saugerties, NY, 1977—; instr., Woodstock School of Art, NY, 1983—; freelance wrtr. and illus. Mem. PSA. Home: 3168 Glasco Tpk Saugerties NY 12477

WU, WILLIAM LUNG-SHEN, (You Ming Wu), b. Hangzhou, Zhejiang, People's Republic of China, Sept. 1, 1921 (arrd. USA June 30, 1941); s. Sing-Chih (Chung-Zao—honorary) and Mary Ju-Mei (Sun) W. Author: 8 books on space flight, colonization of space, over 100 papers in profl. jnls. AB, Stanford, 1943, MD, 1946; MS, in basic chemistry, Tulane, 1955. Tchg. faculty, internal medicine, Tulane, 1948-54; design spclst. (engineer), General Dynamics Corp., San Diego, 1958-64; bioastronautics spclst., Lovelace Fdn., Albuquerque, 1965-65; "creative" science wrtr., ed., foreign intelligence analyst, scientific/technological (theoretical) consultant, "circuit" lectr., 1958-64, 1979—. Address: 219 Corinthian Hs 250 Budd Ave Campbell CA 95008

WUNDERLICH, RAY C(HARLES) JR., b. St. Petersburg, FL, Aug. 11, 1929, s. Ray Charles and Myrtle Ruth (Parr) W.; m. Elinor Howell; children—Mary, Janet, Ray III, David. Author: Kids, Brains and Learning, 1970, Allergy, Brains and Children Coping, 1973, Improving Your Diet, 1976, Fatigue, 1976, Sugar and Your Health, 1982, Nourishing Your Child, 1984, Candida Albicans, 1984, Overweight, 1986, Infection, 1986, The Imagined Yeast Connection, 1985, Allergies, 1985. BS, U. Fla., 1951; MD, Columbia U., 1955. Practice medicine, St. Petersburg, Fla., 1961—. Served to capt. USAF, 1957-59. Mem. Am. Coll. Nutrition, Acad. Orthomolecular Medicine, Am. Soc. Environ. Medicine. Home: 1620 Serpentine Dr S St Petersburg FL 33712

WURSTER, MICHAEL, b. Moline, IL, Aug. 8, 1940. Contrbr. 5 AM, Flipside, Religious Humanism, Sunrust, numerous other lit mags. BA, Dickinson Coll., 1962. Founding mem. Pitts. Poetry Exchange, 1974—; dir. poetry programs Famous Rider Cultural Ctr., Pitts., 1981-86; coord. Carson Street Gallery Poetry Series, Pitts., 1986—. Home: 159 S 16th St Pittsburgh PA 15203

WURSTER, RALPH, b. Elmhurst, IL, Feb. 6, 1930; s. John Edward and Mary Elizabeth (Boyle) W. BS, Northern IL U. Statistical analyst, Caterpillar Tractor Co., Aurora, IL, 1972-73; quality engr., Natl. Electronics, Geneva, IL, 1973-75; tech. ed. Quality Mag., Wheaton, IL, 1975-80, mng. ed., 80-81, ed., 81-86; Quality Management Handbook. Served to SO1, USN, 1950-54. Mem. profl. orgns. Address: Perry Rd Wolverine MI 49799

WYATT-BROWN, BERTRAM, b. Harrisburg, PA, Mar. 19, 1932; s. Hunter and Laura Hibbler (Little) Wyatt-B.; m. Anne Jewett Marbury, June 30, 1962; children—Laura (dec.), Natalie. Author: Lewis Tappan and the Evangelical War Against Slavery, 2d ed., 1971, Southern Honor: Ethics and Behavior in the Old South, 1982, Yankee Saints and Southern Sinners, 1985, Violences and Honor in the Old South, 1987; editor: The American People in the Antebellum South, 1973. BA, U. of South, 1953, King's Coll., Cambridge (Eng.) U., 1956, MA, 1961; PhD, Johns Hopkins U., 1963. Taught Colo. State U., 1962-64; U. Colo., 1964-66; Case Western Res., 1966-83; U. Wis., Madison, 1969-70; Richard J. Milbauer Prof. History, U. Fla., 1983—. Served to lt. USNR, 1953-55. Grantee Am. Philo. Soc., 1968-69, 72-73, NEH, 1975, 85-86, Guggenheim fellow, 1974-75; fellow Davis Center Princeton U., 1977-78. Mem. Soc. Am. Historians. Home: 3201 NW 18th Ave Gainesville FL 32605

WYCKOFF, JULIE ANN, b. Benton Harbor, MI, Aug. 15, 1952; d. Christian Louis and Charlotte Julia (Schmidt) Blough; m. Theodore Lee Wyckoff, June 29, 1974; children—Nicholas M., Peter C., Catherine J. Author: (with Roger Hamlin) Hydropower Redevelopment: A Manual Emphasizing Utilizaiton of Employment and Training Resources, 1979; columnist: Mich. Assn. Nurserymen mag., 1984—; author slides/taps, ednl. films. Contrbr. articles to mags. including Working Mother. Baby Talk, New Shelter, others. Ed.: The Voice of M.A.N. magazine; Guide to Graduate Education in Urban and Regional Planning, 1978. B.A., Mich. State U., 1974, M. Urban Planning, 1980. Women's ed., photographer The Daily Mining Gazette, Houghton, MI, 1976-77; administr., research asst. Mich. State U., East Lansing, 1977-78; media specialist Proaction Inst., Okemos, MI, 1978-81; sr. energy auditor Volt Energy Systems, Lansing, MI, 1981-84; wrtr., producer Wyckoff Productions, East Lansing, 1975—; dir. communications Mich. Assn. Nurseryman, Lansing, 1984—. Recipient Bronze Tusker award World Wildlife Fedn., 1980. Home: 16961 S Nichols Rd East Lansing MI 48823

WYDRA, FRANK THOMAS, b. Republic, PA, May 11, 1939; s. Frank Thoms and Anne (Kois) W.; m. Karen Sylvia Branch, June 24, 1961; children—Denise, Sheri, Tom. Author: Learner Controlled Instruction, 1980; (management games) Performulations, 1978, Dynamics of Power and Authority, 1981. Contrbr. to books, articles to trade mags. B.S., U. Ill., 1961. Vice pres. personnel Allied Supermakets, Detroit, 1967-75; sr. v.p. Harper Grace Hosps., Detroit, 1975-85; pres. Radius Health System, Inc., Detroit, 1983-85; cons., 1985—. Recipient Communications award Mich. Hosp. Personnel Assn., 1981, 82. Home: 1001 W Glengarry Circle Birmingham MI 48010

WYLIE, KENNETH MILLAR, JR., b. Connellsville, PA, May 26, 1927, s. Kenneth Millar and Dorothy Irene (Sundy) W.; m. Sarah Brightman Hibbard, Apr. 24, 1954; children—Clarissa Dale, Mary Barr, Jennifer Sundy. Ed.: Basic Marketing: A Managerial Approach (by Jerome McCarthy), 3d ed., 1968, Operations Research and the Management of Mental Health Systems, 1968, Automation and Illinois, 1969, The Flutist's Progress (by Walfrid Kujala), 1970, The Drummer: Man (by Gordon B. Peters), 1975; contrbr. articles, chaps. to Indsl. Research mag., Encyc. of Aviation and Space Scis., The Life Cycle Library for Young People, New Home Med. Encyc. BS in Journalism, Northwestern U., 1951, MS in Journalism, 1952. Midwestern ed. Popular Sci. Monthly, Chgo., 1953-55; feature ed. Sci. and Mechanics, Chgo., 1955-57; publs. supvr. Ill. Inst. Tech., Chgo., 1957-60; publs. mgr. Northwestern U., Evanston, Ill., 1960-63; freelance ed., 1963-70; mgr. public relations and advt. Soiltest, Inc., Evanston, 1970-82; owner, ed. Evanston Editorial, 1983—. Mem. Sigma Delta Chi. Home: 2517 Thayer St Evanston IL 60201

WYNDHAM, HARALD P., b. Munich, W. Germany, July 23, 1946; came to U.S., 1948; s. Charles P. and Henny (Schmidt) W.; m. Jane Sue Battles, June 18, 1966; children: Jennifer Rene, Jonathon Russell. Author: (poetry) Rain Wakening, 1970, Epithalmion, 1971, Love and Marriage: A Sonnet Cycle, 1973, From the Asylum, 1975, Pebble Creek, 1978, The Exile's Pilgrimage at Christmastide, 1979, Exile in a Cold Country, 1980, Cheap Mysteries, 1981, Homeland, 1984, Ohio Gothic, 1985; (songs) Down Home Ballads, 1974, Strong in the Spirit, 1983, (anthology) Famous Potatoes: Southeast Idaho Poetry, 1986. MA in Am. Lit., Bowling Green U., 1969; MFA in Creative Writing, 1971. Graphic arts Idaho State U., Pocatello, Idaho, 1971-73; prodn. control mgr. Gould-AMI, Pocatello, 1973—. Deacon (chmn.) Presbyn. Ch., Pocatello, 1982—. Home: 243 S 8th Ave Pocatello ID 83201

WYNN, JOE ALLEN, b. Frederick, OK, Feb. 18, 1953; s. Daniel Bruce and Mary Lois (Edwards) W. Contrbr. articles to newspapers, profl. jnls. Ed.: Wings, 1985-87. Wrkg. on devel. schl. pubs. B.A. in English, Okla. Baptist U., 1975; M.Edn., Southwestern Okla. State U., 1985. Tchr., Frederick Publics Schls., OK, 1976—, public info. dir., 1981—; part-time reporter Frederick Daily Leader, 1976-79. Bd. dirs. Frederick Arts and Humanities Council, 1980-83. mem. NEA, Okla. Edn. Assn. (communications com.), Okla. Schl. Public Relations Assn. (past v.p.), Okla. Council Tchrs. English (past v.p.). Home: 504 S 11 Frederick IK 73542

WYNN, J(OHN) (CHARLES), b. Akron, OH, Apr. 11, 1920, s. John Francis and Esther (Griffith) W.; m. Rachel Linnell, Aug. 27, 1943; children—Mark, Martha Wynn Borland, Maryan Wynn Ainsworth. Author: Sermons on Marriage and Family Life, 1956, Pastoral Ministry to Families (book club selection), How Christian Parents Face Family Problems, 1955, Families in the Church: A Protestant Survey (book club selection), 1961, Sex, Family and Society in Theological Focus (book club selection), 1966, Sexual Ethics and Christian Responsibility, 1970, Christian Education for Liberation and Other Upsetting Ideas, 1977, Family Therapy in Pastoral Ministry (book club selection), 1982, The Family Therapist, 1987. BD, Yale U., 1944; BA, Wooster (Ohio) Coll., 1944; DD (hon.), Davis & Elkins Coll., Elkins, W.Va., 1958; MA, Columbia U., 1963, EdD, 1964. Ordained to ministry Presbyn. Ch. USA, 1944; pastor various chs., Ill. and Kans., 1944-50; family research dir., Presbyn. Ch. USA, 1950-59; faculty Colgate Rochester (N.Y.) Div. Schl., 1959-85; emeritus, 1985—. Named for Best Book Religious Edn., Religious News Service, 1977. Office: Div Schl 1100 S Goodman St Rochester NY 14620

WYNNE, BRIAN, see Garfield, Brian Wynne

WYNNE, ELISE MARCIA, see Newson, Eula Mae

WYNNE, FRANK, see Garfield, Brian Wayne

WYSOCKI, NANCY, b. Marshfield, WI Apr. 16, 1940; d. Theodore Bernard and Emily Lenore (Kujawa) W. Contrbr. poem to anthol. Wrkg. on peotry, descriptive prose, biographies. Diploma, Middle-Technical Institute, 1964. Sr. proofreader Worzalla Pub. Co., Stevens Point, WI 1965-68; hinge maker Tee-Nee Factory, Stevens Point, 1968-69. Home: 25 S Wheeler 1A Saint Paul MN 55105

WYSOCKI, SHARON ANN, b. Detroit, Feb. 20, 1955, d. Arthur Leonard and Casmira (Suchorab) Wysocki. Ed., pub. The Wire, grassroots alternative arts periodical, 1981—; contrbr. to Jnl Art, Ariadne's Thread, other lit publs. Workg. on screenplays, media book. BS, Eastern Mich. U., 1977; mem. student exchange program, Warwick (Eng.) U., Sept. to Dec., 1975. Work represented at Mus. Modern Art, NYC. Mem. Buckham Fine Arts Project. Office: Prog Press 7320 Colonial St Dearborn Heights MI 48127

WYSOR, BETTIE, b. VA. Author: The Lesbian Myth, 1974, To Remember Tina, 1975, A

Stranger's Eyes, 1981, Echoes, 1983; contrbr. articles to Town & Country, Harper's Bazaar, Vogue, The New Woman, numerous other publs. Ed. Va. Intermont Coll., Coll. of William and Mary. Advt. copywrtr. numerous agcys., 1956-65; script reader, evaluator, Am. Playhouse; producer, wrtr. John Moses Assocs., NYC; dialogue wrtr. daytime series, ABC, NBC, also story ed. CBS, coordinator; resident playwright Barter Theatre Va.; ed. Dramatists Guild Newsletter, 1976-77. Recipient Merit award Advt. Wrtrs. Assn. N.Y., 1963, 1st and 2nd place Am. Television Comml. Festival award, 1964. Address: Box 103 Wainscott Long Island NY 11075

YAFFE, JAMES, b. Chgo., Mar. 31, 1927, s. Samuel and Florence (Scheinman) Y.; m. Elaine Gordon, Mar. 1, 1964; children—Doborah Ann, Rebecca Elizabeth, Gideon Daniel. Author: Poor Cousin Evelyn and Other Stories, 1951, The Good-for-Nothing (novel), 1953, What's the Big Hurry (novel), 1954, Nothing but the Night (novel), 1957, Mr. Margolies (novel), 1962, Nobody Does You Any Favors (novel), 1966, The American Jews (non- fiction), 1968, The Voyage of the Franz Joseph (novel), 1970, So Sue Me! (non-fiction), 1972, Saul and Morris, Worlds Apart (novel), 1982, My Mother, The Detective (short stories), 1980; playwright: The Deadly Game, 1966, Ivory Tower (with Jerome Weidman), 1969, Cliffhanger, 1985. BA, Yale U., 1948. Prof. English Colo. Coll., Colorado Springs, 1967—, also wrtr.-in-residence, dir. genl. studies, 1982—. Mem. PEN, MWA, WG, DG, AAUP. Home: 1215 N Cascade St Colorado Springs CO 80903

YAGER, CINDA, b. Oneonta, NY, Oct. 21, 1954; d. James Kenneth and Alice Ruth (Kane) Yager. BA, Dickinson College, 1976; cert., Minn. School of Business, 1977. Freelance wrtr./editor, Minneapolis, 1980—; freelance copywrtr. specializing in the arts, Minneapolis, 1984—; writing tchr., Southwest Community School, Minneapolis, 1983-86. Home: 2629 West 43rd St 305 Minneapolis MN 55410

YAKOS, BARBARA VERLEE, b. Biggsville, IL, June 7, 1912; d. Clyde and Bird Marie (Jones) Dixon; m. Howard Arthur Perrin, Dec. 31, 1936 (dec. 1943); 1 son, Roger Howard; m. Anton Yakos, June 25, 1949. Contrbr. articles, short stories to mags., anthols. B.S. in Edn., U. Ill., Champaign, 1946; M.S. in Edn., Washington U., 1956. Tchr. public schs., Alexis, IL, 1931-37, Staunton, IL, 1946-74. Mem. Library Board, Staunton, 1974-80. Mem. Zeta Phi Eta, Kappa Delta Pi. Home: 525 N Franklin St Staunton IL 62088

YALKOVSKY, RAFAEL, (Don Rafael), b. Chgo., Oct. 11, 1917, s. Samuel and Elizabeth Isabelle (Lamb) Y. Contrbr. poetry, articles, short stories to Mont. Almanac, Venture Mag., Neptune, Am. Poetry Anthology, Jnl Geology Sci., Jnl Am. Phys. Union. Wrkg. on history of Iberian oceanography, poetry, short story. MS, U. Chgo., 1955, PhD, 1956. Assoc. geol. engr. Crane Co., Chgo., 1954-56; asst. prof. U. Mont., Missoula, 1956-61; prof. geology Buffalo State Coll., 1962-84, emeritus, 1984—; mem. press corps, UN Law of Sea Confs., NYC and Geneva, 1973-81, non- govtl. observer, Geneva, 1975. Winner short story award Adult Edn., Santa Barbara, Calif., 1953, 54; grantee NSF, 1956-68; vis. scholar U. London, 1974. Mem. NASW, Intl. Sci. Wrtrs. Assn. Address: Box 398 Grand Island NY 14072

YAMADA, MITSUYE MAY, b. Fukuoka, Japan, July 5, 1923 (arrvd. USA 1927), d. Jack Kaichiro and Hide Yasutake; m. Yoshikazu Yamada, Aug. 26, 1950; children—Jeni, Stephen, Kai, Hedi. Author: Camp Notes, 1976, This Bridge Called My Back, 1981, Women Poets of the World, 1983; co-ed. The Webs We Weave, 1986; contrbr. to anthologies So. Calif. Women Wrtrs. & Artists, Arrangements in Lit. BA, NYU, 1947; MA, U. Chgo., 1953. Prof. English, Fullerton Coll., Calif., 1966-69, Cypress Coll., Calif., 1969-85. Recipient lit. arts award Orange County Arts Alliance, 1980, Vesta award for writing The Woman's Bldg., Los Angeles, 1982; Yaddo wrtr.'s fellow, 1984. Mem. Multiethnic Lit. of U.S. (exec. officer), Multicultural Women Wrtrs. (founder). Home: 6151 Sierra Bravo Rd Irvine CA 92715

YAMAGUCHI, ELLEN DIANE, b. Chula Vista, CA, Mar. 21, 1957, d. Daniel Hiroshi and Mary Sanaye (Doi) Yamaguchi. Contrbr. articles, columns to The Southwestern Sun, 1983-84. AA, Southwestern Coll., Chula Vista, Calif., 1981. Newswriter KTTY-TV, Chula Vista, 1985-86. Home: 108 Landis Ave Chula Vista CA 92010

YANCEY, PHILIP DAVID, b. Atlanta, Nov. 4, 1949; s. Marshall Watts and Mildred Sylvania (Diem) Y.; m. Janet Elenor Norwood, June 2, 1970. Author: After The Wedding, 1976, Where Is God When It Hurts? 1977 (Gold Medallion award Evang. Christian Pubs. Assn. 1978), Growing Places, 1978, Unhappy Secrets of the Christian Life, 1979, Fearfully and Wonderfully Made, 1980 (Gold Medallion award), Open Windows, 1982, Insight, 1982, In His Image, 1984 (Gold Medallion award), The Student Bible, 1987 (Gold Medallion award); also articles. BA magna cum laude, Columbia (S.C.) Bible Coll., 1970; MA with highest honors, Wheaton (Ill.) Coll., 1972. Writer, then mng. editor Campus Life mag., Wheaton, 1970-75, editor, 1974-79, ed.-at-large, Christianity Today, 1980—. Mem. Evang. Press Assn. Home: 657 W Wellington Ave Chicago IL 60657

YANKAUER, ALFRED, b. NYC, Oct. 12, 1913, s. Alfred and Teresa (Loewy) Y.; m. Marian Wynn, May 21, 1948; children—Douglas, Kenneth. Author manuals, handbooks; contrbr. articles, editorials, rvws. to pediatric, medical and public health publs.; ed.: Am. Jnl Public Health, 1975. BA, Dartmouth Coll., 1934; MD, Harvard U., 1938, MPH, Columbia U., 1947. Med. educator, official numerous orgns., 1950—; vis. prof. child health WHO, Madras (India) Med. Coll., 1957-59, regional adviser maternal and child health Pan Am. Health Orgn., Washington, 1961-66; prof. dept. community and family medicine U. Mass., Worcester, 1973—; cons., lectr. in field. Mem. Council Biology Eds., numerous med. orgns. Office: Med Schl U Mass Worcester MA 01605

YARMAL, ANN, b. NYC, Jan. 1, 1933; d. Roland Whitney and Kathleen Honor (Leonard) Robbins; children—Kathleen Moore, Cynthia Rubbo. Contrbr. to Connecticut Libraries, 1978, Conn. River Rvw, 1979-86; poetry in Embers, Calliope, Bean Feast and many other lit mags. BA, Southern Ct. State U., New Haven, 1977; MS, Columbia U., NYC, 1979. Libr., Howard Whittemore Mem. Library, Naugatuck, Ct., 1970-79; libr. the Ferguson Library, Stamford, Ct. 1979-82; libr., U.S. Peace Corps, St. Lucia, W.I., 1982-84; libr., Wintonbury Branch Library, Bloomfield, Ct., 1984—. Mem. PSA, CT Poetry Soc. Home: 20 Revere Dr 2 Bloomfield CT 06002

YARYURA-TOBIAS, JOSE A., b. Buenos Aires, Argentina, Feb. 11, 1934; came to U.S., 1963; s. Felipe and Emilia (Tobias) Yaryura; m. Roberta Duncan, Apr. 1, 1961 (div. July 1975); children: Anna Maria, Ricardo, Andrea, Adriana, Roberto; m. Fugen Nezirogiu. Contrbr. poetry to publs. in Can. and Argentina, med. articles to profl. jnls. MD, Buenos Aires U., Med. dir. Bio-Behavioral Psychiatry, Great Neck, N.Y., 1979—. Recipient Federico Garcia Lorca award, 1983. Mem. L.I. Poetry Soc. Office: Bio-Behav 560 Northern Blvd Great Neck NY 11021

YATES, SAMUEL, b. Savannah, GA, May 10, 1919; m. Mae B., Apr. 5, 1941; children—Joy, James Allen, Jean Linda. Author: Prime Period Lengths, 1975, Repunits and Repetends, 1982; contrbr. articles to Mathematics Mag., The Surveyor, Det Kongelige Norske Videnskabers Selskab Skrifter (Norway), Jnl Recreational Math. BA in math., Geo. Wash. U., 1952; MS in Elec. Engring., U. Pa., 1962. Engring. aid., cost acct. Post Engr., Ft. Dix, N.J., 1940-45; asst. chief surveyor, photogrammetry Aero Ser. Corp., Phila., 1945-47, 52-59; geodetic engr. Interam. Geodetic Survey, Mex. and Central Am., 1947-51, U.S. Army Map Serv. Washington, 1951-52; leader sci. programming R.C.A., Moorestown, N.J.,1959-72; vis. prof. Indian Inst. Sci., Bangalore, India, 1978-79. Mem. Math. Assn. Am. Home: 157 Capri-D Kings Pt Delray Beach FL 33484

YEAGER, PHYLLIS DIANE, b. Chattanooga, TN, July 17, 1949; d. Kenneth Gordon O'Rear and Billie Jean (Hilliard) Faulkner; m. James Robert Shelton, Feb. 12, 1972 (div. Feb. 1979); 1 son, James Robert; m. Bobby Dane, June 15, 1984. Contrbr. poems to lit. mags. Student West Ga. Coll., 1987—. Artist, Printed Fabrics, Carrollton, GA, 1972-84. Mem. Nat. Trust Hist. Preservation, Musical Heritage Soc. Home: 16 Garrett Ln Carrollton GA 30117

YEATMAN, TREZEVANT PLAYER III, (Ted P.), b. Nashville, Dec. 16, 1951; s. Trezevant Player and Nancy Lee (McDearman) Y. Author: Jesse James and Bill Ryan at Nashville, 1981, 82; ed. The Big Springs Library Network Directory of Social Services, 1978; contrbr. to Timeless Tennesseans (book), 1984, Book of Days 1987 (book), 1987, articles to numerous publs. inclg. True West, Civil War Times Illustrated, North/South Trader, Qtly of the Natl. Assn. and Ctr. for Outlaw and Lawman History, The James Farm Jnl. BA, Peabody Coll., 1976, MLS, 1977. Feature writer WLAC-AM radio, Nashville, 1971; asst. librarian Current River Regional Library, Van Buren, Mo., 1977-80; freelance writer, researcher, photog., Nashville, 1981—; non-fiction ed. Depot Press, Nashville, 1981—. Bd. advs. Carter County Arts Soc., Van Buren, 1978-79, policy adv. bd. Carter County Office Economic Opportunity, 1978-80. Mem. ALA, Friends of the James Farm, Tenn. Western History and Folklore Soc., J. Frank Dalton Meml. Soc. Home: 5099 Linbar Dr J-170 Nashville TN 37211

YEFIMOV, IGOR, (Andrei Moscovit), b. Moscow, Aug. 8, 1937, came to U.S., 1978, s. Mark Y. and Anna (Melnikova) Y.; m. Marina Rachko, May 29, 1959; children—Leana, Natasha. Author: (in Russian) Metapolitics, 1978, Practical Metaphysics, 1980, Without Bourgeoises, 1979, As One Flesh (novel), 1981, The Judgement Day Archives (novel), 1982; (in English) Our Choice and History, 1985; Kennedi, Osval'd, Kastro, Khrushchev, 1987; contrbr. articles: Mich. Qtly Rvw, Geo, Russian Lit. TriQtly, Kontinent,

Russia, other publs. in USSR, U.S. Wrkg. on book on Kennedy assassination. Ed. Moscow Inst. Lit., Leningrad Poly. Inst. Wrtr. Wrtr.'s Union, Leningrad, 1965-78; ed. Ardis pub. house, Ann Arbor, Mich., 1978-81; mem. AAASS and AATSEEL, 1982—; dir. Hermitage Pubs., Tenafly, N.J., 1981—. Office: Box 410 Tenafly NJ 07670

YENSEN, ARTHUR, b. Lowell, NE, Dec. 3, 1898; s. Harden Joseph Yensen and Ida Fancis Gibson; widowed; children—Eric Arthur, Nicholas Pat, Robert Maynard. Author: I Saw Heaven, 1955 (six editions), Santa's 13 Years in a Shopping Mall, 1982, Santa's Life Story, 1984, How the Wagon Was Painted, 1986, The War Log of an Under Dog, 1986, The Fun Way to Live. BA, U. Mont.-Missoula, (year graduated) 1924. Served as wagoner, Eng. armed forces, 1917-19. Named Disting. Citizen of Id., 1975. Home: Box 369 Parma ID 83660

YERBY, FRANK, b. Augusta, GA, Sept. 5, 1916; s. Rufus Garvin and Willie (Smythe) Y.; m. Flora H. Claire Williams, Mar. 1, 1941 (div.); children: Jacques Loring, Nikki Ethlyn, Faune Ellena, Jan Keith; m. Blanquita Calle-Perez, 1956. Author: The Foxes of Harrow, 1946, The Vixens, 1947, The Golden Hawk, 1948, Prides Castle, 1949, Floodtide, 1950, A Woman Called Fancy, 1951, The Saracen Blade, 1952, The Devil's Laughter, 1952, Bride of Liberty, 1953, Benton's Row, 1954, The Treasure of Pleasant Valley, 1955, Captain Rebel, 1956, Fair Oaks, 1957, The Serpent and the Staff, 1958, Jarrett's Jade, 1959, Gillian, 1960, The Garfield Honor, 1961, Griffin's Way, 1962, The Old Gods Laugh, 1964, An Odor of Sanctity, 1965, Goat Song, 1967, Judas, My Brother, 1968, Speak Now, 1969, The Dahomean, 1970, The Girl from Storyville, 1971, The Voyage Unplanned, 1974, Tobias and the Angel, 1975, A Rose For Ana Maria, 1976, Hail the Conquering Hero, 1977, A Darkness at Ingraham's Crest, 1979, Western: A Saga of the Great Plains, 1982, Devilseed, 1984, McKenzie's Hundred, 1985. AB, Paine Coll., Augusta, 1937; MA, Fisk U., 1938; postgrad., U. Chgo. Recipient O. Henry Meml. award for best first short story, 1944. Address: Avenida de America 37 Apt 710 Madrid Spain 2

YIM, VERA S. W., b. Honolulu, Feb. 23, 1950; d. Henry Y.C. Lung and Loretta (Young) Lung Ijima; 1 child—Napualani H.H. Freelance advt., public relations wrtr., 1979—; poet, wrtr., ed. Color Your World Oahu (Pele award 1983), Honolulu Advt. Fedn., 1982-83; wrtr., ed. Hawaii and World Entertainment News, 1984; wrtr., illustrator greeting cards; wrtr. Rainbow Records Co., Hollywood, Calif., 1983—. Wrkg. on poetry collection, adult fable series, lyrics. Home: Box 2311 Honolulu HI 96804

YODER, CAROLYN PATRICIA, b. Greenwich, CT, July 2, 1953; d. Rufus Wayne and Kathryn Louise (Mulhollen) Y. BA, Washington U., St. Louis, 1975; MA, U. Iowa-Iowa City, 1979. Editorial asst. D.C. Heath & Co., Lexington, 1979-81; publs. asst. Intl. Human Resources Devel. Corp., Boston, 1981-82, prodn. editor, 1982-83; asst. editor Cobblestone Pub., Inc., Peterborough, N.H., 1983, editor, 1983-84, editor-in chief, 1984—; editor-in-chief Faces, 1984—, editor-in-chief Classical Calliope, 1984—. Contbr. illustrations to Sojourner, Women, Lake Hope, Off Our Backs. Mem. Bookbuilders of Boston (prodn. coordinator winning book and cover New England Book Show 1983), Assn. Earth Sci. Editors. Greater Boston Rights and Permissions Grp., Soc. Scholarly Pub., Ednl. Press Assn. Am. Address: Box 139 Henniker NH 03242

YODER, EILEEN RHUDE, b. Evergreen Park, IL, Aug. 20, 1946; d. Howard V. and Diana Joan (Lemon) Rhude; m. Bernard J. Yoder, Oct. 9, 1965 (dov. Nov. 1985); children: Laura, Patricia. Author: How To Start an Elimination Diet, 1981; How To Start a Rotation Diet, 1981; Allergy Free Cooking, 1982; Aspartame, the New Nutritive Sweetener, 1982; Cooking with Natural Sweeteners, 1983; Corn Free Cooking, 1983; Food Allergies and Special Occasions, 1983, The Food Allergy Cookbook, 1987; contrbr. chpt. to Handbook of Food Allergies, 1986. MS in Health Sci., Columbia Pacific U., 1984, PhD in Nutrition, 1984. Dir. E. Yoder & Assocs., Goshen, Ind., 1966-75; pres. Healthful Living Co., N.Y.C., 1975-83, Med. Diet Systems, Inc., Tinley Park, Ill., 1983—. Office: Box 1124 Tinley Park IL 60477

YORK, JOHN THOMAS, b. Winston-Salem, NC, Dec. 13, 1953; s. L.E. (Buck) and Edith Rose (Spencer) Y.; m. Jane McKinney Dec. 26, 1979; children: Elizabeth, Kathryn. Author chapbook: Picking Out, 1982; contrbr. poetry to The Arts Jnl, Cold Mtn. Rvw, Coraddi, Hemlocks & Balsams, The Lyricist, Greensboro Rvw, others. BA in English, Wake Forest U., 1977, MA in Tchg., Duke U., 1979, MFA in Writing, U. NC-Greensboro, 1985. Tchr. high schl., JT Hoggard Schl., Wilmington, NC, 1978-82; tchg. asst. Univ. NC, Greensboro, 1982-84; part-time tchr., Jamestown, 1984-85; tchr. Stoneville Schl., NC, 1985—. Recipient first prize poetry contest, Charlotte Writers Club, 1978; grand prize, Coraddi, 1985; lit. award Greensboro Rvw, 1985; 1987 National Fellow for Independent Study in the Humanities; Mellon Fellow, 1987-88, the U. of North Carolina at Chapel Hill. Address: 2600 Duck Club Rd Greensboro NC 27410

YOSELOFF, MARTIN, b. Sioux City, IA, July 26, 1919; s. Morris and Sarah (Rosansky) Y. Author: No Greener Meadows, 1946, The Family Members, 1948, The Girl in the Spike-Heeled Shoes, 1949, The Magic Margin, 1954, Lily and the Sergeant, 1957, A Time to Be Young, 1967, Remember Me to Marcie, 1973, What Are Little Girls Made of?, 1979, The Wednesday Game, 1988; also narrative for sketch books City of the Mardi Gras, City on the Potomac, 1946. BA, State U. Iowa, 1941. Writer various Iowa newspapers; editorial staff pub. houses, NYC1941-43, 47-49; contrbg. writer Bank Street Coll. publs. Served with AUS, 1943-46. Mem. AL Am., PEN. Home: 139 W 15th St New York NY 10011

YOSELOFF, THOMAS, b. Sioux City, IA, Sept. 8, 1913; s. Morria and Sarah (Rosansky) Y.; m. Sara Rothfuss, Apr. 30, 1938; children—Julien David, Mark Laurence; m. Lauretta Sellitti, Apr. 23, 1964; 1 dau., Tamar Rachel. Author: A Fellow of Infinite Jest, 1946, (with Lillian Stuckey) Merry Adventures of Till Eulenspiegel, 1944, Further Adventures of Till Eulenspiegel, pub. 1957, The Time of My Life, 1979; Editor: Seven Poets in Search of an Answer, 1944, Voyage to America, 1961, Comic Almanac, 1963. AB, U. Iowa, 1934; Litt.D. (hon.), Bucknell U., 1982, L.H.D., Fairleigh Dickinson U., 1982. Pres., chmn bd. Rosemont Pub. & Printing Corp., 1969—; chmn. Associated Univ. Presses, 1969—. Home: 68 Cedar Dr Colts Neck NJ 07722

YOUMANS, RICH, b. Phila., Aug. 3, 1960; s. Richard Earl and Nancy (Callaghan) Y. Contrbr. to Brussels Sprout, Cicada, Dragonfly, Frogpond, Jam To-Day, Inkstone, Jnl of NJ Poets, Modern Haiku, other lit mags. BA, La Salle U. Ast. ed. Ocean County Reporter, Toms River, NJ, 1983; writer Visual Edn., Princeton Junction, NJ, 1983-84; assoc. ed. Coast Mag, Bay Head, NJ, 1984—. Recipient 1st place prize Keystone Press award, Pa. Newspaper Pubs Assn., 1982; co-winner Red Pagoda Broadside Series, 1986. Mem. Ocean County Poets Collective (pres. 1985), Haiku Soc Am. Address: 37B Church St. Lambertville, NJ 08530

YOUNG, ALBERT JAMES, (Al Young), b. Ocean Springs, Miss., May 31, 1939, s. Ernest Albert James and Mary Nettie Bell (Campbell) Y.; 1 son, Michael. Poetry collections: Dancing, 1969, The Song Turning Back Into Itself, 1971, Geography of the Near Past, 1976, The Blues Don't Change: New and Selected Poems, 1982, Heaven: Collected Poems, 1958-88; novels: Snakes, 1970, Who Is Angelina, 1975 (transl. to Chi E Angelina? 1983), Ask Me Now, 1980, Sitting Pretty, 1976 (transl. to Parla Sitting Pretty 1985), Seduction By Light, 1988; non-fiction: Bodies & Soul, 1981, Kinds of Blue, 1984, Things Ain't What They Used to Be, 1987; co-ed. Anthologies: Yardbird Lives, 1978; co-wrtr. screenplays: A Piece of the Action, 1977, Bustin' Loose, 1981, The Stars & Their Courses, 1984. Student U. Mich., 1957-61; BA in Spanish, U. Calif., Berkeley, 1969. Joseph Henry Jackson fellow San Francisco Fdn., 1966, Stegner Writing fellow Stanford U., 1969, Guggenheim Fdn. fellow, NYC, 1974, NEA writing fellow, 1975, Fulbright fellow Council for Intl. Exchange of Scholars, 1984. Address: 514 Bryant St Palo Alto CA 94301

YOUNG, ALLEN, b. Liberty, NY, June 30, 1941, s. Louis and Rae (Goldfarb) Y. Co-ed. (with Karla Jay): Out of the Closets: Voices of Gay Liberation, 1972, After You're Out: Personal Experiences of Gay Men and Lesbian Women, 1975, Lavender Culture, 1979; author (with Jay) The Gay Report, 1979; Gays Under the Cuban Revolution, 1981, North of Quabbin: A Guide to Nine Massachusetts Towns, 1983; editor: More than Sand and Sea: Images of Cape Cod, 1985, Millers River Reader, 1987. AB, Columbia U., 1962, MS in Journalism, 1964; MA, Stanford U., 1963. Reporter Washington Post, 1967; staff mem. Liberation News Service, NYC, 1967-70; partner, Butterworth Corp. map pub., 1971-74; reporter, asst. ed. Athol (Mass.) Daily News, 1978—; owner, pub., ed. Millers River Pub. Co., Athol, 1983—. Office: Box 159 Athol MA 01331

YOUNG, CAROL ANN MORIZOT, (Anna Mahanaim), b. Shreveport, LA, Sept. 21, 1944, d. Russell Edgar and Catherine Eugenia (McClusky) Beeman; m. Donald C. Morizot, Sept. 29, 1975 (div. 1982); m. 2d, Bruce Lynn Young, Sept. 7, 1982; children—Timothy Scott Morizot, David Martin Morizot. Author: Survivors and Other Poems, 1977, Just This Side of Madness: Creativity and the Drive to Create, 1978, 1988; contrbg. ed. Not Everything We Eat Is Curry: A Guide to Bengali Cuisine, 1978; contrbr. poems and articles to Art & Lit. Mag., The Smith, N.Am. Qtly, Haiku Highlights, Orphic Lute, other lit mags. BA, Northeast La. U., 1966, BS, 1971. Wrtr., poet, 1972—; pub., ed. Harold House, Houston, 1977-79; poet-in-schls., Ark. Arts Council, 1979-80. Recipient Mary B. Patton award Am. Fdn. for Blind, 1963, Roberts Intl. Editorial award Roberts Inst. Alcoholism Studies, Ontario, Que., Can., 1963, 1986 Arkansas Democrat Poem of the Year award. Home: 623 South Pine Apt A Little Rock AR 72205

YOUNG, DAVID POLLOCK, b. Davenport, IA, Dec. 14, 1936; s. Cecil T. and Mary Ella (Pollock) Y.; m. Chloe Hamilton, June 17, 1963; children—Newell Hamilton, Margaret Helen. Author: Something of Great Constancy: The Art of "A Midsummer Night's Dream", 1966, Sweating Out the Winter, 1969, The Heart's Forest: Shakespeare's Pastoral Plays, 1972, Boxcars, 1973, Work Lights: 32 Prose Poems, 1977, Rilke's Duino Elegies, 1978, The Names of A Hare in English, 1979, (with Stuart Friebert) A Field Guide to Contemporary Poetry and Poetics, 1980, Four T'ang Poets, 1980, (with Stuart Friebert and David Walker) Valuable Nail: Selected Poems of Gunter Eich, 1981, (with Dana Habova) Interferon, or On Theater, Poems by Miroslav Holub, 1982, Foraging, 1986, Troubled Mirror: A Study of Yeats's 'The Tower,' 1987, Rilke, Sonnets to Orpheus, 1987. Editor: (with Stuart Friebert and David Walker) Field: Contemporary Poetry and Poetics, (with Stuart Friebert) The Longman Anthology of Contemporary Am Poetry, 1983; contrbr. poetry to lit publs. BA, Carleton Coll., 1958; MA, Yale, 1959, PhD, 1965. Recipient U.S. award Intl. Poetry Forum, 1969, Guggenheim Fellow, 1979, NEA Fellow, 1982. Office: Dept Eng Oberlin Coll Oberlin OH 44074

YOUNG, ELISABETH LARSH, b. San Francisco, Aug. 3, 1910; d. Herbert Gladstone and Florence Annette (Lipsher) Larsh; m. James Philip Young, Aug. 13, 1937 (dec. 1976); children—David, Eve Young Visconti. Author: Family Afoot, 1978; (with Jim Young) Bicycle Built for Two, 1940. Contrbr. short stories (Best Am., 1960), articles to mags., newspapers including Quixote, N.Am. Mentor Mag.; columnist, editor: Sunset Mag., 1935-38; mng. editor: Calif. Mag. of the Pacific, 1939-42. Cedar Rapids Gazette; novella to anthol. Travel BA in English Lit., Stanford U., 1931, M.A. in English Lit., 1933; M.A. in Music Theory, Coe Coll., 1962. Home: 202 20th St NE Cedar Rapids IA 52402

YOUNG, FRANK, JR., b. Charlotte, NC, Mar. 14, 1925; s. Frank and Florine (Kelly) Young. Poems published by National Soc. of Published Poets, 1978-80; Night Songs from a Dungeon, 1986. Mailroom super. Robert Eastman (NYC), 1969-73; law clerk Moses & Singer (NYC), 1973-75; quality control mgr. Star-Brite Press (NYC), 1975-79. Mem. NAACP, Urban League. Hon. Ment. Natl. Soc. of Poets, 1980. Comubia U. (NYC), 1951-52, Fordham U. (NYC), 1981-82. Home: 67 Gates Ave Central Islip NY 11722

YOUNG, GARY EUGENE, b. Santa Monica, Calif., Sept. 8, 1951; s. Claude Eugene and Jeanne (Ewing) Y.; m. Tina Bucuvalas, June 22, 1974, (div. 1983); m. 2d, Peggy Orenstein, April 19, 1986. Author: Hands, 1979, 6 Prayers, 1984, In the Durable World, 1985. Editor: The Fugitive Vowels (D. J. Waldie), 1976. The Dreams of Mercurius (John Hall), 1977, House Fires (Peter Wild), 1977, Thirteen Ways of Deranging an Angel (Stephen Kessler), 1978, Short Voyages (Michael Watterlond), 1978, Jack the Ripper (John Hall), 1978, Any Minute (Laurel Blossom), 1979, By Me By Any, Can and Can't Be Done (Killarney Calry), 1979, Yes (Timothy Sheehan), 1979, Begin, Distance (Sherod Santos), 1980, Limits of Resurrection (Brad Crenshaw), 1983, Subconscious Comics (Time Eagan), 1984. BA, U. Calif.-Santa Cruz, 1973; MFA, U. Calif.-Irvine, 1975. Ed., Greenhouse Rvw Press, Santa Cruz, 1976—; assoc. ed. Brandenburg Press, Santa Barbara, Calif., 1981—; v.p. AE Fdn., Soquel, Calif., 1983—. Recipient James D. Phelan Lit. award San Francisco Fdn., 1983; creative writing fellow NEA, 1981. Home: 3965 Bonny Doon Rd Santa Cruz CA 95060

YOUNG, GLORIA ROSE, b. Lake Charles, LA, Aug. 8, 1947; d. James Ware and Rose Mae (Fruge) Farque; m. Donald Ray Young, Aug. 17, 1970; children—Jamie Kris, Donna Renee, Clint Ray, Wesley James, Derrick Ware. Contrbr. poems to anthols. File clrk. Am. Insurance Co., Lake Charles, 1966-71; free-lance wrtr. Recipient Poet Laurate, World of Poetry, 1985, 86, 87, Golden Poet award, 1985, 86, 87. Home: Rt 1 Box 838 Ragley LA 70657

YOUNG, JORDAN R., b. Los Angeles, 1950. Author-illustrator: A Night in the Hard Rock Cafe and Other Poems, 1980; author: How to Become A Successful Freelance Writer, 1980, revised ed., 1983, Spike Jones and his City Slickers: An Illustrated Biography, 1984, Reel Characters, 1986; research assoc., ed.: Laurel and Hardy: The Magic Behind the Myth, 1986; contrbr. non-fiction to N.Y. Times, Los Angeles Times, Christian Sci. Monitor, Millimeter mag., other periodicals, also The People's Almanac, 1975; contrbr. poetry to Electrum, Alura, The Archer, other lit mags. Wrkg. on novel, scripts. BA, Calif. State U., Fullerton, 1973. Freelance wrtr., Los Angeles, 1973—; editorial dir. Moonstone Press, Beverly Hills, Calif., 1980—; tchr. jnlsm. Calif. State U., Long Beach, 1985—. Mem. Orange County Poets (dir. 1981-83), Pubs. Mktg. Assn. So. Calif., Toastmasters Intl. Address: Box 661 Anaheim CA 92805

YOUNG, MARY LOUISE, b. Wilmington, MA, Aug. 5, 1920; d. Philip Burnham and Rhoda Helen (White) Buzzell; m. Franklin Henkel Young, Jan. 21, 1951 (dec. Nov. 4, 1971); children—Philip F., Ruth A., Susan L., Mary J. Contrbr. articles to mags. A.B., Vassar Coll., 1941; B.S., Simmons Coll., 1943; M.S., Columbia U., 1944. Reporter, Cumberland News, MD, 1944-50, 79—; newsletter ed. Regional Edn. Service Agy., Cumberland, 1978-80. Home: Rt 6 Box 109 Cumberland MD 21502

YOUNG, M. CLEMEWELL, b. Rockford, IL, Dec. 21, 1925, d. John Walter and Mary Clemewell (Hinchliff) Harriman; m. Robert Charles Young, Jan. 29, 1949; children—Martha, Sara, Johanna. Author: Rages, Celebrations (poetry), 1975; contrbr. poetry to Chgo. Tribune, Christian Sci. Monitor, Bitterroot, Poet Lore, Embers, Light Years 1984, 85; contrbr. prose to Hartford Courant, N.Y. Times. BA, Syracuse U., N.Y., 1948; MA, U. Conn., Storrs, 1972. Reporter Manchester (Conn.) Herald, 1963-70; prof. English Manchester (Conn.) Herald, 1963-70; prof. English Manchester Community Coll., 1972—, consulting editor Poet Lore, Washington, 1968—. Leader poetry workshop Manchester Community Coll., 1975—. Recipient Descriptive Poetry prize, Poet Lore, 1968. Mem. PSA, Phi Beta Kappa. Home: 123 Notch Rd Bolton CT 06040

YOUNG, NOEL B., b. (Leon Elder), b. San Francisco, Dec. 25, 1922; s. Ralph Willard and Gladys Claudine (Small) Y.; m. Margaret Walters, Feb. 15, 1944 (div. 1965); children—Hilary, Caitilin, Aaron; m. 2d, Judith Purl, Sept. 28, 1966; 1 dau., Molly Amity. Author: Hot Tubs, 1972, Free Beaches, 1975, Waitress, 1985. Student, Stanford U., 1942-43. Owner, Noel Young Printer, Santa Barbara, CA, 1948-69; editor-in-chief Capra Press, Santa Barbara, 1969-m. Panel mem. NEA Lit. Program, Washington, 1985. Office: Box 2068 Santa Barbara CA 93120

YOUNG, RUBY JEAN, b. Haskell, OK, Mar. 13, 1923; d. Leonard and Lucille Carolyn (Nash) Christian; m. Robert Riley Young, May 20, 1947 (dec. May 27, 1983); children—Joanna, Paula, Robert, Betty, Patty. Columnist: Edmond Evening Sun, 1985—. Contrbr. poems to anthols. Student Central State U., 1970-71. Secy. public schls., Edmond, OK, 1964-78, retired. Recipient Golden Poet award World of Poetry, 1985, 86, 87. Mem. Edmond Showcase Poets, Poetry Soc. Okla. Home: 236 Southern Pl Edmond OK 73013

YOUNG, VIRGINIA BRADY, b. NYC, Dec. 2, 1918, d. Joseph and Anna (Meagher) Brady; widowed; stepchildren—Mary E. Young, Robert M. Young. Author poetry collections: The Clooney Beads, 1970, Double Windows, 1972, Circle of Thaw (award Haiku Soc. Am. 1979), 1978, Shedding the River, 1982, Waterfall (haiku), 1984. Student Columbia U. Sr. ed. Conn. River Rvw, 1982-85. Mem. PSA, AAP, Haiku Soc. Am. (pres. Columbia U. chap. 1984-86). Home: 184 Centerbrook Rd Hamden CT 06518

YOUNG, WILHELMINA G., b. Phila., May 1, 1938, d. Charles W. and Grace (Boyajian) Young; m. Khurshid Ahmad (div. 1976); children—Ali Charles, Kareem Alexander. Contrbr.: Rewrites, Stockpot, Ararat Qtly., other lit mags. Wrkg. on poetry collection, one-act play, short stories. BA in English, Glassboro State Coll., 1961; MS in Edn., U. Pa., 1965; postgrad. Stockton Coll. Tchr. Oakcrest High Sch., Mays Landing, N.J., 1963-64; learning disability cons. Ewing Twp. Schs., Trenton, N.J., 1965-69; instr. Wright State U., Dayton, Ohio, 1970-78; owner, mgr. The Rare Rug, Dayton, 1976—, N.J.; freelance wrtr. Home: 5 N. Martindale Ave. Ventnor, NJ 08406

YOUNGER, J. C., see Craig, James Duhadway

YOUNGERT, BARBARA ANN, (Barbara Meerschaert Youngert), b. Detroit, Jan. 1, 1938; d. Hector Achiel and Marie Frances (Campbell) Meerschaert; m. George Stephen Youngert, Jr., Feb. 27, 1960; children—Marie Bernadette, Patricia Mary, Peter George, Phillip Barry. Author, ed.: Together alone, 1985. Contrbr. poems to anthols., newsletter. Student private schls., Detroit. Office mgr. Automotive Industry Action Group, Southfield, MI, 1983-87, project team administr., 1987—. Home: 20567 Pinecrest Taylor MI 48180

YOUNT, JOHN ALONZO, b. Boone, NC, July 3, 1935; s. John Luther and Veera (Sherwood) Y.; m. Susan Childs, Sept. 7, 1957 (div. Jan. 1986); children—Jennifer Sherwood, Sarah Chlds. Author: (novel) Wolf at the Door, 1967, The Trappers Last Shot, 1973, Hardcastle, 1980, Toots in Solitude, 1984. BA, Vanderbilt U., 1960; MFA, U. Ia., 1962. Prof., U. N.H., Durham, 1973—. Served to cpl. U.S. Army, 1953-55. Recipient Disting. Recognition award Friends of Am. Wrtr.'s Assn., 1981. Home: 9CRiver St Apt 31 Newmarket NH 03857

YOURA, DANIEL GEORGE, b. Two Rivers, WI, Dec. 22, 1944, s. Daniel Joseph and Ruth Ella (Beaton) Y. Ed.: Current Thought on Peace and War, 1966-70, Television and the Future of Higher Education, 1971, Global Village Exhibit, 1972, Washington 2000, 1972; pub., ed.: Cosmic Mechanix, 1973, Olympic Mag: Guide to Washington's Olympic Peninsula, 1984—; pub., illustrator: Solar Alcohol: The Fuel Revolution, 1979, Oswald Hoot: The Owl Who Was Scared of the Dark, 1982, I Love Hot Dogs, 1982; author, pub.:

Traveling Around Mt. St. Helens, 1981. BA, U. Wis., Oshkosh, 1967; postgrad., Ohio State U., 1970. Mng. ed. Current Thought on Peace and War, UN, NYC, 1970; ed. Pride, San Juan, P.R., 1971; ednl. planner Council on Higher Edn., Olympia, Wash., 1971-72; research analyst Wash. State Library, Olympia, 1972-73; mgr. Employment Security, Port Townsend, Wash., 1973-76; pub., ed. Olympic Pub. Co., Port Ludlow, Wash., 1977—; pub. Wash. State Expo 86 Official Guidebook, 1986. Office: Box 353 Port Ludlow WA 98365

YU, TIMOTHY PAN, b. Evanston, IL, Aug. 23, 1974; s. Philip H.C. and Linda (Pan) Y. Contrbr. poetry to lit. mags., anthol. Recipient Poet Laureate award Gwendolyn Brooks, U. Chgo., 1983, 2d place for scariest story Pioneer Press, 1984, cert. of Merit, Ill. Mathematics League, 1986, Recognition award Midwest Talent Search, Northwestern U., 1986, 87. Mem. Mensa. Home: 2105 Pioneer Ln Wilmette IL 60091

YUND, THEODORE JOSEPH, b. Troy, NY, June 1, 1947, s. Theodore Joseph and Grace Barbara (Healey) Y.; m. Rosario Garcia de Alba, Aug. 25, 1978; children—Juan Carlos, Luis Gerardo, Rosario Marcela. Contrbr. poetry: Negative Capability, Midwest Poetry Rev., various anthologies. Wrkg. on poetry book. BA in English, Siena Coll., 1972; MD, U. Guadalajara, Mex., 1977. Practice medicine, Amsterdam, N.Y., 1984—. Winner Northeastern States Poetry Contest, 1984, Poetry Press competition, 1985. Home: 196 Guy Park Ave Amsterdam NY 12010

YUP, PAULA ANNE, b. Phoenix, Apr. 5, 1957, d. Bing Lin and Edna Yup; m. Dean Martin Jacobson, May 4, 1985. Contrbr. poems to Southwest: A Contemporary Anthology, The Third Woman: Minority Women Writers of the U.S., Occidental Community Rvw, Echoes from Gold Mountain, Yet Another Small Mag., Passages North, Stone Lion Rvw, Blue Buildings. Author: (chapbook) Love Poems, 1986. BA, Occidental Coll., 1981; MFA, Vt. Coll., 83. Mem. AWP. Home: 41 Damon St Falmouth MA 02540

YURICK, SOL, b. NYC, Jan. 18, 1925, s. Samuel and Florence (Weinstein) Y.; m. Adrienne L. Yurick, Nov. 10, 1958; 1 dau., Susanna. Author: Fertig, 1966, The Warriors, 1965, The Bag, 1968, Someone Just Like You, 1972, An Island Death, 1974, Richard A., 1982, Metatron, 1985. BA, NYU, 1951; MA, Bklyn. Coll., 1961. Served with AUS, 1944-45. Guggenheim Fdn. fellow, 1974. Mem. PEN. Home: 190 Rutland Rd Brooklyn NY 11225

ZACHARIAS, LELA ANN, (Lee Zacharias), b. Chgo., Dec. 1, 1944; d. Joseph Ryan and Dorothine Edna (Hurley) Ives; m. Richard Kirk Zacharias, Oct. 29, 1966 (div. 1976); m. 2d, Michael George Gaspeny, Aug. 15, 1982; 1 son, Max Nathan Gaspeny. Author: Helping Muriel Make it Through the Night, 1976; Lessons, 1981. Editor: A History of Finnish Literature (Jaakko Ahokas), 1973; (with others) Intro, 1980. AB, Ind. U.-Bloomington, 1966; MA, Hollins Coll., 1973; MFA, U. Ark.-Fayetteville, 1976. Lectr., U. N.C., Greensboro, 1975-76, asst. prof., 1976-81, assoc. prof., 1981—, coordinator writing program, 1977—, ed. The Greensboro Rvw., 1977—; asst. dir. pubs. research ctr. for lang. scis. Ind. U., Bloomington, 1967-70; visiting lectr. Princeton U., N.J., 1980-81. Recipient Sir Walter Raleigh award N.C. Dept. Cultural Resources, 1982; fellow NEA, N.C. Arts Council. Mem. AWP. Address: Eng Dept U NC Greensboro NC 27412

ZACHARY, FAY N., b. Pitts., June 3, 1931; d. Harry A. and Rose (Taksa) Bortz; m. Joseph Zachary, Aug. 22, 1954; children—Karen, Janet, Michael. Novelist: Fertility Rights, 1987; contrbr. short story: Ariz. Lit. Mag. BS in Nursing, U. Pitts., 1957; MS in Nursing, U. Pa., 1979. Home: 6317 E Aire Libre Ln Scottsdale AZ 85254

ZACHMANN, VIRGINIA JOYCE, b. Kintyre, ND, May 9, 1933; d. Lewis Roy and Mary Elizabeth (Grove) Lesher; m. Carl Joseph Zachmann, Apr. 23, 1955; children—Linda, Jeffrey, Joyce, Patricia, Barbara. Contrbr. articles and short stories to newspapers, mags. including The New Brighton Bulltn., Woman's World, Wallstreet Jnl. Author seminar for nurses on cardiac pacemakers, 1981, orientation guidebook for hosp., 1978, nurses in-services, script for Mystery Weekend, 1985. RN, St. Alexius Hosp. Schl. Nursing, Bismark, N.D., 1954; BA, Met. State U., St. Paul, 1980. Supr. obstetrics St. Alexius Hosp., Bismark, 1954-55; nurse delivery rm. North Meml. Med. Ctr., Robbinsdale, Minn., 1955-60; staff nurse, asst. head nurse, staff educator Unity Med. Ctr., Fridley, Minn., 1966-81; coordinator obstetrics program Golden Valley Health Ctr., Minn., 1981-82; free-lance wrtr., 1982—. Judge White Bear Arts Council, White Bear Lake, Minn, 1984. Mem. MWA, Loft, NWC. Home: 5059 Eastwood Rd New Brighton MN 55112

ZACHRESON, NICK (NICHOLAS) BERNARD, b. San Diego, Mar. 14, 1952; s. Bernard Ernest and Marjory Bess (McElvania) Z. Author: The San Joaquin Valley, 1979, How Manx Raspberry Won the War, 1984; editor: Talking to the Blindman, 1976, The Myths Do Not Tell Us, 1978, The Trees Along This Road, 1980, Vanishing, 1982, Sun Rose, 1985. Editor, Cypress Publs., Bakersfield, Calif., 1971-75; coeditor Valley Press, Fresno, Calif., 1979-83; editor Blackwells Press, Watsonville, Calif., 1976—; artist-in-residence Calif. Arts Council, Watsonville, 1983-86. Home: 2925 B Freedom Blvd Watsonville CA 95076

ZAGRODNIK, DIANE JEANNE, b. Milw., Oct. 28, 1950; d. Eugene Paul and Margaret Forsyth (Zimmerman) Zagrodnik. Poetry in anthologies. Home: 344 Shawmut Ave Apt 5 Boston MA 02118

ZAHN, CURTIS LENGELIER, b. Detroit, Nov. 12, 1912, s. Oswald Francis and Edith (Langalier) Z.; m. Betty Hale, 1941 (div. 1950). Playwright: Reactivated Man, Plight of Sawyer Cricket, Origin of Species, Albino Kind of Logic, Conditioned Reflex; contrbr. poetry to Electrum, Yellow Silk, Xanadu, other lit mags. Education: U of CA, LA, San Diego State, San Francisco State. Mem. DG, Calif. State Fedn. Poets. Recipient 6 Golden Globe awards, 1965-66. Home: 1352 Miller Dr Los Angeles CA 90069

ZAHRA, SUSAN GORE, b. St. Louis, Mar. 15, 1950; d. Edward William and Lois Jean (Dodge) Gore; m. Raymond Joseph Zahra, Aug. 2, 1975; children—Michael Sorkis, Andrew Kahlil, Matthew Jameel, Kathryn Nicole. Contrbr. articles to mags., newspapers including Mothers Today, Nurse's Link, others. B.A., Southern Ill. U., 1972; postgrad. U. Iowa, 1973-74. Wrtr., editorial asst. Ednl. Research Corp., Marion, IL, 1985-86; free-lance wrtr., 1980—. Recipient Honorable Mention, Wrtr.'s Digest, 1986. Home: Rt 1 Box 145 Goreville IL 62939

ZAHORCHAK, MICHAEL, b. Erie, PA, Nov. 13, 1929; s. Paul and Anna (Macik(Z.; m. Lois Catherine Becker, Nov. 27, 1954. Author: The Art of Low Risk Investing, 1972, 2d ed., 1977, 3d ed., 1987; Favorable Executions, The Wall Street Specialist and the Auction Market, 1974; Climate: The Key to Understanding Business Cycles, 1983; The Principle of Unity: A Guide to Understanding the Process of Change, 1987. BS in Econ. and Fin., U. Pitts., 1950; MA in Fin. and Investments, Baruch Schl., CUNY, 1960. Asst. controller Macmillan Pub. Co., NYC, 1960-62; v.p. Am. Stock Exchange, NYC, 1962-78; exec. dir. Found. for Study of Cycles, Pitts., 1978-80; pres. Tide Press, Linden, N.J., 1980—. Served with inf., U.S. Army, 1951-53; Korea. Home: 1230 S Wood Ave Linden NJ 07036

ZALAZNICK, SHELDON, b. Bronx, NY, Aug. 6, 1928; s. Samuel and Esther Leah (Schneiderman) Z.; m. Vera Altobelli, Apr. 4, 1953; 1 dau., Andrea. Assoc. editor Newsweek mag., 1952-56; v.p. Manning Pub. Relations Co., 1956-59; sr. editor Forbes mag., 1959-63, mng. editor, 1976—; founding editor New York mag. sect. N.Y. Herald Tribune, NYC, 1963-64; Sunday editor N.Y. Herald Tribune, 1964-66; staff writer Genl. Learning Corp., 1966-67; assoc. editor Fortune Mag., 1967-69; v.p., editorial dir. New York mag., 1969-76. Home: 458 W 246th St Bronx NY 10471

ZALBEN, JANE BRESKIN, b. NYC, Apr. 21, 1950; d. Murry and Mae (Kirshbloom) Breskin; m. Steven Zalben, Dec. 25, 1969; children: Alexander, Jonathan. Author: (juveniles) Cecilia's Older Brother, 1973; Lyle and Humus, 1974; Jeremiah Knucklebones, 1974; Basil and Hillary, 1975; An Invitation to the Butterfly Ball: A Counting Rhyme by Jane Yolen, 1976; Penny and the Captain, 1977; Jabberwocky, 1977; All in the Woodland Early: ABC, 1979; Norton's Nighttime, 1979; Will You Count the Stars Without Me?, 1979; Oliver and Alison's Week, 1980; A Perfect Nose for Ralph, 1980; "Oh, Simple!," 1981; Porcupine's Christmas Blues, 1982; Maybe It Will Rain Tomorrow, 1982; Here's Looking at You, Kid, 1984; The Walrus and the Carpenter, 1986; Water from the Moon, 1987; Starlight and Moonshine: Poetry of the Supernatural, 1987 (Shakespeare). Wrkg. on 1st adult novel. BA in Art, Queens Coll., 1971; postgrad. Pratt Graphics Ctr., NYC, 1971-72. Asst. art dir. Dial Press, NYC, 1971-72; designer Ty Crowell, NYC, 1973-74; art dir. Scribners, NYC, 1975-76; lectr. Schl. Visual Arts, N.Y.C., 1976—. Address: Curtis Brown 10 Astor Pl New York NY 10003

ZALL, PAUL MAXWELL, b. Lowell, MA, Aug. 3, 1922; s. Nathan and Bertha (Rubin) Z.; m. Elisabeth Ruth Weisz, June 21, 1948; children—Jonathan, Barnaby, Andrew. Author: Elements of Technical Report Writing, 1962, Hundred Merry Tales, 1963, Nest of Ninnies, 1970, Literary Criticism of William Wordsworth, 1966, (with John Durham) Plain Style, 1967, Simple Cobler of Aggawam in America, 1969, (with J.R. Trevor) Proverb to Poem, 1970, Selected Satires of Peter Pindar, 1971, Comical Spirit ofSeventy-Six, 1976, Ben Franklin Laughing, 1980, (with J.A.L. Lemay) Autobiography of Benjamin Franklin, 1981, Norton Critical Edition of Franklin's Autobiography, 1983, Abe Lincoln Laughing, 1983. BA, Swarthmore Coll., 1948; AM, Harvard U., 1950, PhD, 1951. Research editor Boeing Co., 1956-57; cons. in report writing, proposal preparation and brochures to industry and govt. agcys., 1957—.

Served with USAAF, 1942-45; ETO. Am. Philo. Soc. fellow, 1964, 66; John Carter Brown Library research grantee; Huntington Library research grantee. Home: 1911 Leman St South Pasadena CA 91030

ZALLER, ROBERT MICHAEL, b. NYC, Mar. 19, 1940, s. Abraham Morris and Sylvia (Borenstein) Z.; m. Angeliki Lili Bita, Jan. 19, 1968; stepsons—Philip, Kimon. Author: The Year One, 1969, The Parliament of 1621, Lives of the Poet, 1974, The Cliffs of Solitude, 1983, Europe in Transition, 1660-1815, 1984; ed.: A Casebook on Anais Nin, 1974, Biographical Dictionary of British Radicals in the Seventeenth Century (with others), 3 vols., 1982, 83, 84; contrbr.: Critical Essays on Samuel Beckett. BA, Queens Coll.-CUNY, 1960; MA, Washington U., 1963, PhD, 1968. Lectr. history Queens Coll., NYC, 1967-68, adj. asst. prof., 1970-72; asst. prof. to prof. history U. Miami, Coral Gables, Fla., 1972-87; prof. of history and head, dept. of history and politics, Drexel U., 1987—. Guggenheim fellow, 1985-86. Home: 326 Bryn Mawr Ave. Bala Cynwyd, PA 19004

ZAMORA, MARIA HELENA PALUCH, b. Tuste, Poland, Jan. 10, 1906, came to U.S., 1950, naturalized, 1956; d. Josef and Helena (Pleczynska) Paluch; m. Antoni Zamora, July 14, 1939 (dec. Apr. 22, 1987). Author plays: The Promise, 1942, For You, My Poland, 1943, Excursion, 1946, Frances & Flowers, 1957, Christmas Play, 1970, New Year's Vigil, 1943 (all in Polish; produced in Hungary, Germany, France, Chicago). Contrbr. poems to mags., anthols.; ednl. articles to newspapers. Tchr., dir. Polish Schl., Chgo., 1951-61; ednl. pub. Scott Foresman & Co., Glenview, IL, 1953-71; retired. Mem. NWC. Home: 5540 N Lotus Ave Chicago IL 60630

ZANCA, MINERVA MARTINEZ, b. Bronx, NY, Nov. 14, d. Bill and Maria Martinez; m. Steven Anthony Zanca, may 8, 1983; 1 dau., Veronica. Contrbr. to Manhattan Cable TV, Capital Air Employee Newsletter, Inter Press Service, Teen Mag., other publs. BA, Marymount Coll., NYC, 1979; MA in Journalism, Columbia U., 1987. Public relations asst. Manhattan Cable TV, NYC, 1977-79; corr. UN, NYC, 1980—; ed. Personal Fitness & Bodywork Profls., NYC, 1986—. Home: 73-44 Austin St Forest Hills NY 11375

ZARA, LOUIS, b. NYC, Aug. 2, 1910; s. Benjamin and Celia (Glick) Rosenfeld; m. Bertha Robbins, Sept. 23, 1930; children—Paul, Philip, Daniel; m. Marlene Brett, Mar. 22, 1958; m. Helen Dillman, Aug. 7, 1987. Author: Blessed Is the Man, 1935, Give Us This Day, 1936, Some for the Glory, 1937, This Land Is Ours, 1940, Against This Rock, 1943, Ruth Middleton, 1946, In the House of the King, 1952, Rebel Run, 1951, Blessed Is the Land, 1954, Dark Rider, 1961; non-fiction Jade, 1969, Locks and Keys, 1969; also stories, scenarios, radio scripts, dramas, ABC radio-television show Stump the Authors; scripts Scattergood Baines; contrbr. fiction, essays and articles to mags. and anthologies. Ed., Crane Jr. Coll., 1927-30, U. Chgo., 1930-31. Vice-pres. Ziff Davis Pub. Co., Chgo., NYC, 1946-61, ed.-in-chief, Masterpieces; dir. genl. book div., 1959-61; pres. Pub.'s Cons., Inc., NYC, 1955-56; editor-in-chief genl. trade div. Follett Pub. Co., NYC, 1962-65; editor-in-chief Mineral Digest, 1969-77. Recipient prose award Chgo. Fdn. Lit., 1940, Daroff Meml. fiction award, 1955. Fellow Royal Numis. Soc., Am. Numis. Soc.; mem. Author's Guild, Melville Soc., Overseas Press Club, Mineralogical Soc. Am.; life mem., Natl. Commn. Anti-Defamation League, V.P. Appraisers Assn. of Am. Home: 141 E 56th St New York NY 10022

ZASLOW, EDMUND MORRIS, (Pennant, Edmund), b. NYC, April 28, 1917; s. Herman and Pauline (Gross) Zaslow; m. Doris Kahn, Sept. 1, 1940; children—Susanna Malloy, Martha Stanton, Sara Abigail. Author: I, Too, Jehovah, 1952, Dream's Navel, 1982, Misapprehensions and Other Poems, 1984; poetry in Saturday Rvw, Christian Science Monitor, NY Times, numerous other mags. BS, CCNY, NYC, 1938; MS, New School for Social Research, 1940. Tchr., NYC publ. schls., 1947-56, principal, 1956-77. Adj. prof., Adelphi U., Garden City, NY, 1978—. With US Army, 1943-46. Awards: Kreymborg Memorial Award, 1982 and Carolyn Davies Award, 1982 (PSA), fellowship, the MacDowell Colony. Mem. PSA, PEN, P&W, MLA. Home: 2902 210 St Bayside NY 11360

ZATZ, ARLINE, b. Bklyn., May 2, 1937; d. Joseph and Belle (Israel) Baer; m. Joel L. Zatz, Nov. 4, 1956; children—Robert Jay, David Alan. Contrbr. to Natl. Geog. World Mag., The New York Times, N.Y. Daily News, N.Y. Post, Asbury Park Press, Bucks County Courier Times, Trailer Life Mag., Family Motor Coach Mag., Motor Home Mag., N.J. Outdoors Mag. BA in Jnlsm., Rutgers U., 1977. Consumer affairs officer Borough of Highland Pk., NJ, 1968-71; asst. dir. consumer affairs State of NJ, Newark, 1971-75; freelance writer, 1977—. Writer of Year award, PA Travel Council, 1985. Mem. AAUW. Home: 77 Woodside Ave Metuchen NJ 08840

ZAVRIAN, SUZANNE OSTRO, b. Balt., Feb. 29; d. Marcus and Ethel (Greenspon) Ostro; m. Jacques Zavrian, Sept. 11, 1957 (div. 1983). Author: Demolition Zone, 1976, Dream of the Whale, 1982. BA, NYU, 1952. Managing ed. Pocket Books, NYC, 1962-69; co- publisher, Extensions, 1968-76; asst. dir. CCLM, NYC, 1976-78; exec. ed. Am. Book Review, NYC, 1976-79; co-ordr. NY Book Fair, NYC, 1975—; pub. SZ Press, NYC, 1983—; proprietor Pomander Bookshop, NYC, 1986—. Home: 321 West 94th St New York NY 10025

ZEBAUERS, VLADIMIRS VALDIS, b. Perm, Russia, June 30, 1903, came to U.S., 1949, naturalized, 1969; s. Eduards and Karolina (Zeberg) Z.; m. Midrza Natalija Kapostins, Sept. 22, 1934 (dec. Aug. 31, 1985); children—Baiba, Valdis, Liga. Author: America: Oasis of Freedom, 1980, two Latvian titles. Contrbr. chpt. to Dictionary of Latvian Technical Terminology, 1983. Wrkg. on sequel to America: Oasis of Freedom-Oasis America, and Latvian book. M.Arch., U. Latvia, 1934. Asst. prof. rural architecture Agricultural Acad., Jelgava, Latvia, 1941-44; cons. architect, Denver, 1950-74, retired; free-lance wrtr., 1974—. Fellow Latvian Architects Assn.; mem. Latvian Am. Assn. of Univ. Profs. and Scientists. Home: 3360 S Bellaire St Denver CO 80222

ZEBLEY, JOSEPH WILDMAN JR., b. Appleton, MD, July 9, 1914; s. Joseph Wildman and Annie May (Benjamin) Z.; m. Edith Sophie Schubel, July 4, 1947 (dec. 1972); children—Joseph W. III, Charles Schubel. Author: Childhood Days at Clover Valley, 1972, Family (zublin ou zobel) Zebley in America, 1736-1976, 1976, Our Indian Visitor, 1976, Our Clover Valley Farm, 1978, Scribbling with my pen: A Collection of Prose & Poems, 1980, Mud Cakes & Cherry Sand Pies, 1983, Appleton Country Fair, 1983, The Drift Bird Hunt, 1984; contrbr. articles, reports to numerous publs. Wrkg. on children's fiction, genealogy, other non-fiction. AA, U. Balt., 1947, LLB, 1949, BS in Indsl. Mgmt., 1964, JD, 1970; BS in Mil. Studies, U. Md., 1964; MEd, Johns Hopkins U., 1973, cert. Advanced Studies in Studies, Ed., 1978; PhD in Human Behavior, Newport U., 1984. Owner, operator Clover Valley Farms, Elkton, Md., 1935—; adminstr. Balt. City Public Schs., 1965-82; adj. prof. Balt. Coll. Commerce (now merged with U. Balt.), 1965-70. Served to maj., U.S. Army, 1941-63; NATOUSA, ETO. Mem. Phi Delta Kappa (ed. Johns Hopkins U. Chap. Bulltn. 1979-83), other ednl. orgns. Home: 3810 Juniper Rd Baltimore MD 21218

ZEGERS, KIP, b. Chgo., Oct. 16, 1943, s. Bernard and Alice (Swartz) Z. Author: Backyard (poems), 1975, Tell Me a Story, 1981, The Street that Teaches Everything, 1983, The Promise Is (new and selected poems), 1985. BA, John Carroll U., 1965; MA, Northwestern U., 1966. Tchr. Hunter College High Schl., NYC. Home: 681 President St Brooklyn NY 11215

ZEHRING, JOHN WILLIAM, b. Phila., Sept. 9, 1947; m. Donna Taber, Aug. 3, 1968; children—Micaela, Jeremiah. Author: Preparing for Work, 1981, Working Smart, 1983, Work Smarter Not Harder, 1986, Get Your Career in Gear, 1976, Careers in State and Local Government, 1980, Implications, 1979. Contrbr. numerous articles to mags. B.A., Eastern Coll., 1969; M.A. Rider Coll., 1971; M.A., Princeton Theol. Seminary, 1971; M.Div., Earlham Schl. Religion, 1981. Spcl. asst. to pres. Earlham Coll., Richmond, IN, 1975-83; v.p. development Bangor Theol. Seminary, ME, 1983—. Home: 90 Saratoga Ave Bangor ME 04401

ZEIDNER, LISA A., b. Washington, Mar. 27, 1955, d. Joseph and Dorothy Zeidner. Author: Customs, 1981, Talking Cure, 1982, Alexandra Freed, 1983. BA, Carnegie Mellon U., 1977; MA, Johns Hopkins U., 1978. Assoc. prof. Rutgers U., Camden, N.J., 1979—. Office: Rutgers Univ Camden NJ 08102

ZEIGER, LILA L, (L.L. Zeiger), b. NYC, Dec. 6, 1927; d. Benjamin Hersch and Sara (Dornbrand) Leichtling; m. David Zeiger, Nov. 24, 1949; children: Sara Ellen, Arnold William. Author: (poetry) The Way to Castle Garden, 1982; contrbr. to numerous mags. and anthologies, including Paris Rvw, Kayak, Poetry Now, New Republic, N.Y. Times. MA, Cornell U., 1949; MLS, Pratt Inst., 1956. Tchr. English N.Y.C. high schls., 1949-79; freelance tchr. writing; active Poets in Schls. Program, 1979-84. Recipient Fels award CCLM, 1975; MacDowell Colony fellow, 1977, 79, 83; N.Y. State Arts Council on Arts grantee, 1983-84. Mem. PSA (exec. com.; Claytor award 1978, Kreymborg award 1980, Hemley award 1979), P&W. Home: 9 4th Rd Great Neck NY 11021

ZEILIG, NANCY MEEKS, b. Nashville, Apr. 28, 1943; d. Edward Harvey and Nancy Evelyn (Self) Meeks; m. Lanny Kenneth Fielder, Aug. 20, 1964 (div. Dec. 21, 1970); m. 2d, Charles Elliott Zeilig, Jan. 6, 1974; 1 dau., Sasha Rebecca. Ed., 102 Years, a centennial hist. of the Vanderbilt U. School of Engring, 1975; author numerous articles pubd. in Denver mag., 1977-80; mng. ed. and co-pub. WomanSource, 1982, 84. BA, Birmingham-Southern Col., 1964; postgrad., Vanderbilt U., 1971-73. Editorial asst. Reuben H. Donnelley, NYC, 1969-70; asst. ed. Vanderbilt U., Nashville, 1970-74; ed. U. Minn.,

St. Paul, 1975; asst. ed. McGraw-Hill, Mpls., 1975-76; mng. ed. Denver Mag. (CO), 1976-80; ed. Am. Water Works Assocn., Denver, 1981—. Subject of NBC TV documentary, Women Like Us, 1980. Office: Am WW 6666 W Quincy Ave Denver CO 80235

ZEITNER, JUNE CULP, b. Bay City, MI, Feb. 7.; d. Vernon H. and Pearl (Ailes) Culp; m. C. Albert Zeitner, June 25, 1941. Author: Midwest Gem Trails, 1956, Appalachian Mineral and Gem Trails, 1968, Southwest Mineral and Gem Trails, 1972, Borglum's Unfinished Dream, 1976, How to Carve Jade & Gems, 1987. Contrbr. articles, editorials, columns, book rvws. to numerous mags. Contrbg. editor: Earth Sci. Mag., 1962-67; contrbg. editor: Lapidary Jnl, 1967-77, spcl. asst. editor, 1977—; contrbg. editor: Keystone Mkgt., 1983—. BSc, Northern State Coll., Aberdeen, S.D., 1937. Lectr. intl. gem and jewelry shows, 1967—. Bd. dirs. Rockhound and Lapidary Hall of Fame. Named Disting. Alumni, Northern State Coll., 1976, First Lady of Gems, Intl. Gem Shows Inc., 1976, S.D. Press Woman of Achievement, 1976; elected to Mount Rushmore Natl. Meml. Soc., 1986. Mem. Badlands Sandhill Earth Sci. Club (pres. 1967-68), Midwest Fedn. Mineral. Soc. (pres. 14 states 1969, hon. life), Natl. Bulltn. Eds. (chmn. 1967, Am. Fedn. Mineral. Soc. (Chmn. 1973-74, past dir.), Soc. Vertebrate Paleontologists, Geol. Soc. Am., Intl. Gem Guild (bd. dirs.). Home: 5203 S Canyon Rd Rapid City SD 57702

ZEKOWSKI, ARLENE, b. NYC, May 13, 1922; d. Harry and Belle (Sargoy) Z.; m. Stanley Berne, July 1952. Author: (poetry) Thursday's Season, 1950; (fiction) (with Stanley Berne) A First Book of the Neo-Narrative, 1954, (criticism) (with Stanley Berne) Cardinals & Saints, 1958; (fiction) Concretions, 1962; Abraxas, 1964; Seasons of the Mind, 1969; (drama) The Age of Iron and Other Interludes, 1973; (criticism) Image Breaking Images: A New Mythology of Language, 1977; (fiction) Histories and Dynasties, 1982; contrbr. to anthologies. BA in French and English, Bklyn. Coll., 1944; MA in French and Spanish, Duke U., 1945; Sorbonne, 1950. Grad. fellow in English, La. State U., Baton Rouge, 1958-63; assoc. prof. English, Eastern N.Mex. U., Portales, 1963-80, research prof. English, 1980—. host, co-producer TV series Future Writing Today, Sta. KENW-TV, PBS, 1984-85. Recipient lit. research awards Eastern N.Mex. U., 1966-76; L'Etincelle grad. French scholar award, 1944; Duke U. grad. Romance Lang. fellow, 1944-45. Mem. PEN, COSMEP, Western Ind. Pubs., New Eng. Small Press Assn., Rio Grande Wrtrs. Assn., Santa Fe Wrtrs. Coop. Address: Box 4595 Coronado Sta Santa FE NM 87502

ZELAZNY, ROGER JOSEPH, b. Cleve., May 13, 1937; s. Joseph Frank and Josephine Flora (Sweet) Z.; m. Judith Alene Callahan, Aug. 20, 1966; children—Devin, Trent, Shannon. Author: This Immortal, 1966, Lord of Light, 1967, Creatures of Light and Darkness, 1969, Damnation Alley, 1969, Nine Princes in Amber, 1970, The Guns of Avalon, 1972, To Die in Italbar, 1973, Sign of the Unicorn, 1975, My Name Is Legion, 1976, The Hand of Oberon, 1976, The Courts of Chaos, 1978, The Chronicles of Amber (2 vols.), 1979, The Changing Land, 1981; numerous others; also contrbr. numerous short stories and articles to mags., anthologies. BA, Case Western Res. U., 1959; MA, Columbia U., 1962. Profl. writer, 1969—. Recipient Hugo sci. fiction awards, 1966, 68, 76, 82, 86; Nebula award Sci. Fiction Writers, 1966, 76; others. Address: McCauley Ltd 432 Park Ave So Suite 1509 New York NY 10016

ZELDIN, JESSE, b. NYC, Apr. 8, 1923; s. Isidor and Dorothy (Kaufman) A.; m. Mary-Barbara Kauffman (dec. Apr. 21, 1981), 1 dau., Xenia Valerie. Author: Nikolai Gogol's Selected Passages with Friends, 1969, Lit. and Natl. Identity (with Paul Debreczeny), 1970, Poems and Poli. Letters of F.I. Tyuchev, 1973, Nikolai Gogol's Quest for Beauty, 1978; contrbr.: Western Philo. Systems in Russian Lit., 1979, Norton Critical Ed. of Dead Souls, 1985; articles to Canadian-Am. Slavic Studies, Russian Rvw, Slavic Rvw, Acta Slavica Iaponica, Sobornost, Esprit createur, South Atlantic Qtly; wrkg. on annotated trans. (and intro.) from the orig. Russian and French of articles, poems and letters of A.S. Khomyakov. BA, NYU, 1947; MA, Columbia U., 1948, PhD, 1953. Intelligence analyst DOA, Salzburg, Austria, 1951-52; instr. Hollins Coll., Roanoke, Va., 1953-55, asst. prof., 1955-62, assoc. prof., 1962-70, prof., 1970—. Served to Sgt. AAF, 1943-46, PTO. Recipient sr. lectr., Fulbright/Hays Comm., Hong Kong, 1965-66; vis. scholar, Hokkaido Univ., Sapporo, Japan, 1982-83; sr. scholar award, So. Conf. Slavic Studies, 1985. Mem. Am. Assn. for the Advancement of Slavic Studies, So. Conf. on Slavic Studies (pres., 1970-71). Address: Box 9645 Hollins College VA 24020

ZELEVANSKY, PAUL, b. Bklyn., Sept. 10, 1946; s. Joseph and Elaine (Edelberg) Z.; m. Lynn Hurwitz, Feb. 6, 1968; children: Claudia, Nora. Author: The Book of Takes (named in Best Books of 1977 Am. Inst. Graphic Artists), 1976, Sweep: The Exploration of a Word in Multiple Directions, 1979, The Case for the Burial of Ancestors Book One, 1981, Book Two, 1986. BFA, Carnegie Inst. Tech., 1967; MA, U. Iowa, 1970. Grantee N.Y. State Council on Arts, 1980-81, 83-84, NEA, 1982-83. Mem. P&W. Home: 333 West End Ave New York NY 10023

ZELTINS, TEODORS, b. Riga, Latvia, Oct. 27, 1914; s. Karlis and Antonija (Praulins) Z.; m. Velta Linde, Sept. 30, 1939; 1 child, Inese. Freelance writer, columnist Laiks, 1955-80; author poetry, short stories, essays, novels, inclg. Rigas Gimnazisit, 1939, Slazda, 1952, Rozu Gaitenis, 1958, Melnas Avis, 1958, Pazudusa Paaudze, 1959, Drupu Republika, 1960, Trilogy: Antins Amerika, 1963-70, Mtlestibas Maize, 1971, Nu Ir Ta Stunda, 1975, Lellu Meistars Engelis, 1976, Leopolds Maurs Atztstas, 1978, Septini Srulrieta, 1980. Stud. lit., U. Latvia, 1933-40. Mem. editorial staff Jaunakas Zinas (nwspr.) Riga, Latvia, 1936-40; freelance writer, columnist Laiks (Latvian nwspr.), Bklyn., 1955-80. Num. Latvian Fdn. awards. Mem. Intl. PEN Latvian Centre. Address: 495 Passaic Ave Chatham NJ 07928

ZELVER, PATRICIA, b. Long Beach, CA, Sept. 28, 1923, d. Frank Parnell and Mabel Katherine (Robinson) Farrell; m. Alvin Prescott Zelver, Jan. 8, 1949; children—Nicholas, Michael. Author: The Honey Bunch (novel), 1969, The Happy Family (novel), 1972, A Man of Middle Age & Twelve Stories, 1981; contrbr. short stories: Atlantic Monthly, Ascent, Shenandoah, Three Penny Rvw, other lit mags and popular publs. AB, Stanford U., 1946, MA, 1948. Recipient O. Henry Prize Stories award, 1972, 73, 74, 77, 79, 81, Pushcart Prize, 1980. Home: 280 S Castanya St Portola Valley CA 94025

ZELVIN, ELIZABETH, b. NYC, Apr. 15, 1944, d. Joseph and Edith Judith (Friedman) Lapidus; m. Joseph Zelvin, Dec.2, 1967 (div. 1977); 1 son, Alexander; m. Brian P. Daly, Sept. 12, 1981. Author: I Am the Daughter, 1981. BA, Brandeis U., 1964; MS, Columbia U., 1985. CAPS poetry fellow, N.Y. State Council on Arts, 1983. Home: 115 W 86th St New York NY 10024

ZENTELLA, YOLY GABRIELA, (Gabriela Cerda), b. NYC, Feb. 27, 1949; d. Jose de la Cruz and Isabel (Bolanos) Zentella. Ed. Notebook: A Little Magazine, 1985—. Wrkg. on an historical novel on St. Francis of Assisi. BA, CCNY, 1976, MA in History, 1983. Elementary tchr. Mem. CCLM, Medieval Acad. Am. Office: Box 26B43 Los Angeles CA 90026

ZERKIN, E(DMUND) LEIF, b. Ann Arbor, MI, Mar. 10, 1949, s. Milton and Claire Matilde (Engelberg) Z. Author: Who Took the Drugs?, 1979, Our Chemical Culture: Drug Use and Misuse, 1975, A Comprehensive Guide to the English-Language Literature on Cannabis (Marijuana), 1969; ed.: Hallucinogenic Drug Research: Impact on Science and Society, 1970, Super Me/Super Yo: A Bilingual Drug Abuse Prevention Activity Book for Young Children, 1975, PCP: Problems and Prevention, 1982, Substance Abuse in the Workplace, 1984; ed. Jnl Psychedelic Drugs, 1975-80, Jnl Psychoactive Drugs, 1981—. Student, Beloit (Wis.) Coll., 1966-69; BS, U. Wis., Madison, 1972. Dir., Haight-Ashbury Publs., San Francisco, 1981—; founder, dir. Stash Press, Beloit, Wis., 1967-71; dir. communications U. Wis. Drug Info Center, Madison, 1971-72; mng. ed. TVBE Mag., Madison, 1972-73; publs. dir. Natl. Coordinating Council on Drug Edn., Washington, 1974-75. Mem. AMWA, Soc. Scholarly Pub. Office: Psych Drugs 409 Clayton St San Francisco CA 94117

ZETTLEMOYER, AVE JEANNE, (ave jeanne), b. Phila., Dec. 7, 1953; d. John J. and Evelyn (Scarpello) Ventresca; m. Ron Zettlemoyer; children: Ron Michael, Eric, Mark, Matthew. Author, pub.: Bittersweet, 1984, Moon Moves, 1985, One Edge, Then the Other (haiku), 1985, Scents: Cricket & Crow, 1986, Concrete under My Chin, 1986, Under Black Hat & Madness, 1987, Nine Blind Alleys, 1987; ed.: Black Bear Rvw, Poets eleven . . . audible; contrbr. to lit mags. including Deros, Poetic Justice, The Archer, Alura, Orphic Lute, Phila. Poets, Taurus, Tempest, Calliopes Corner, others. "SureThing" col. in Kindred Spirit Mag. Home: 1916 Lincoln St Croydon PA 19020

ZIAVRAS, CHARLES EFTHEMIOS (JARVIS), b. Lowell, MA, Dec. 15, 1921; s. Efthemois and Panagiota (Neofotistos) Z.; m. Rena Belkakis, Sept. 11, 1948; 1 son, Paul. Author: Visions of Kerouac, 1974, Zeus Has Two Urns, 1976, The Tyrants, 1977, Titanic Interlude, 1984, The Monastery, 1985. BS, Boston U., 1949, MA, 1950. Tchr. High Schl., Hialeah, Fla., 1954-55, Jr. High Sch., Lowell, 1955-56; prof. Univ. of Lowell, 1956—. Fulbright fellow in Greece, 1964-65. Office: Box 853 Lowell MA 01853

ZIEGLER, BETTE J., b. NYC, Jan. 5, 1940, d. Jack and Jeanne (Schwartz) Flaks; m. Herman Ziegler; children—Scott, Laurie. Author: An Affair for Tomorrow (novel), 1978, Older Women/Younger Men (nonfiction), 1979. BA, Fairleigh Dickinson U., 1972. Playwright, N.Y. and N.J., 1971-74; tchr., workshop leader in creative writing, N.J., 1975-79; leader stress-reduction workshops, tchr. meditation, N.Y., 1983—. Mem. Dramatists Guild, AG, P&W. Home: 425 E 58th St New York NY 10022

ZIELINSKI, LESZEK, b. Sochaczew, Warsaw, Poland, Apr. 17, 1948, came to U.S., 1975, s. Henryk and Janina (Wozniak) Z. Author: Fire and Fear (poetry in Polish), 1981, Wounded Day (poetry in Polish), 1982, Thunder (poetry in English), 1983, Burned River (poetry in Polish), 1984, Illusions (poetry in Polish), 1987; co-ed. 75 lat w sluzbie Polski i Polonii (anniversary book of Polish weekly Gwiazda Polarna), 1983, Voice of the Teacher (Polish Qtly.), 1987; ed. Almanach Gwiazdy Polarnej (collection of excerpts), 1985. Ed-in-chief Gwiazda Polarna, 1985-87. Edn. in Poland. Travel agent, Warsaw, 1971-75; ed. Gwiazda Polarna, Stevens Point, Wis., 1981-85, ed.-in-chief, 1985—. Mem. PSA, Polish Wrtrs. Assn. in Exile (Lit. Achievement award 1985), Polish Journalists Assn. Foreign Press Assn. Address: Box 21 Plover WI 54467

ZIGAL, THOMAS, b. Galveston, TX, Oct. 20, 1948. Author: (novel) Playland, 1982; (short stories) Western Edge, 1982. Editor: Perspectives on Photography, 1982, Perspectives on Music, 1985, The Eric Gill Collection, 1982, Joyce at Texas, 1983, Gone With the Wind: A Legend Endures, 1983, Lewis Carroll at Texas, 1985, WCW & Others, 1985; ed. Pawn Revw, 1977-85. BA in English, U. Tex.-Austin, 1970; MA in Creative Writing, Stanford U., 1974. Instr. English, Diablo Valley Coll., Pleasant Hill., Calif., 1975-76; ed. Ednl. Devel. Corp., Menlo Park, Calif., 1972-75, Steck-Vaughn Co., Austin, 1979-80, Humanities Research Ctr., Austin, 1980-86. Recipient Short Story award Tex. Inst. of Letters, 1983. Home: 143 Lone Pine Rd 1051 Aspen CO 81611

ZIMMER, ELIZABETH ANN, b. Rogers City, MI, Oct. 16, 1940; d. Anthony Emil and Marjorie Leona (Greka) Kowalski; m. Gerald Edward Zimmer, Jan. 5, 1982; children by previous marriage: Robert Anthony Wojtaszek, Leita Lynn Smith Altman. Author: My Best Loved Poems, 1985; contrbr. poetry to numerous publs. Wrkg. on book of poetry. Student public schs., Rogers City. Porter, second cook maritime fleet, Interlake Steamship Co., Cleve., 1978-84; owner taxicab bus., Rogers City, Mich., 1985-87. Home: 355 E Woodward St Rogers City MI 49779

ZIMMER, PAUL J., b. Canton, OH, Sept. 18, 1934; s. Jerome Francis and Louise Celina (Surmont) Z; m. Suzanne Jane Koklauner, Apr. 4, 1959; children: Erik, Justine. Author: The Ribs of Death, 1967, The Republic of Many Voices, 1969, The Zimmer Poems, 1976, With Wanda: Town and Country Poems, 1980, The Ancient Wars, 1981, Earthbound Zimmer, 1983, Family Reunion, 1983, The American Zimmer, 1984. BA, Kent State U., 1959. Clrk. Dean Witter, San Francisco, 1959-60; tech. writer Am. Auto Service, San Francisco, 1960-61; salesman Los Angeles News Co., 1961-63; mgr. Macy's Book Depts., San Francisco, 1963-67; assoc. dir. Univ. Pitts. Press, 1967-78; dir. Univ. Ga. Press, Athens, 1978-84, Univ. Iowa Press, Iowa City, 1984—. Served to Pfc, US Army, 1952-54, US. Recipient NEA fellowship, Washington, 1974, 81; Creative Achievement award, AAIIAL, 1985. Mem. Assn. Am. Univ. Presses, AWP. Address: 204 Lexington Ave Iowa City IA 52240

ZIMMERMAN, BILLY RAYMOND, b. Beaumont, TX, Jan. 11, 1941; s. William Franklin and Georgia Lee (Knowles) Z.; m. Evelia Gil, May 9, 1964; 1 child: Robin Ray. Contrbr. poetry to anthologies. Wrkg. on poetry, short stories, non-fiction. BS in Pharmacy, U. Ariz., 1964. Pharmacist, Canoga Park, Calif., 1964-76, Mesa, Ariz., 1976—. Home: 2575 N Val Vista Rd Apache Junction AZ 85219

ZIMMERMAN, JOHNNIE SUE, b. Aiken County, SC, Feb. 18, 1953. Contrbr.: Many Voices/Many Lands, Hollywood Gold, Music of America, Country Your Way. Poetry in anthologies. Wrkg. on biog. Active youth orgns., Phoenix. Home: 8140 W Clarendon Ave Phoenix AZ 85033

ZIMMERMAN, JOSEPH FRANCIS, b. Keene, NH, June 29, 1928; s. John Joseph and May Veronica (Gallagher) Z.; m. Margaret Bernardette Brennan, Aug. 2, 1958; 1 dau., Deirdre Ann. Author: State and Local Government, 1962, The Massachusetts Town Meeting: A Tenacious Institution, 1967, The Federated City: Community Control in Large Cities, 1972, Pragmatic Federalism, The Reassignment of Functional Responsibility, 1976, (with Frank W. Prescott) The Politics of the Veto of Legislation in New York, 1980, The Government and Politics of the Empire State, 1981, Local Discretionary Authority, 1981, The Politics of Subnational Governance, 1983, (with Deirdre A. Zimmerman) State-Local Relations: A Partnership Approach, 1983 (CHOICE award as outstanding acad. book 1984), Participatory Democracy: Populism Revived, 1986; contrib. ed., Natl. Civic Rvw. BA, U. N.H., 1950; MA, Syracuse U., 1951, PhD, 1954. Served to capt. USAF, 1951-53. Mem. Am. Poli. Sci. Assn. (chair, Representation and Electoral Systems sect.). Home: 82 Greenock Rd Delmar NY 12054

ZIMMERMAN, MARGARET CATHERINE, b. Phil., PA, Nov, 13, 1915; d. Lawrence William and Margaretta Catherine (Heim) Beggs; m. Christian Andrew Zimmerman, March 16, 1940. Works include: Verses of Cheer, 1950, Poetic Reveries, 1951, Aureole Glow, 1957, There's Always Light, 1955, My Name Is Mary, 1958, The Gospel Story in Rhyme, 1957, My Lucky Cat, 1958, Rambling Rhyme, 1959. articles, fiction, and poetry in numerous lit and pop. mags. Student, Kensington, PA pub. schls. 1921-32. Mem. United Amateur Press. Home: 2534 E Norris St Philadelphia PA 19125

ZIMMERMAN, ROBERT DINGWALL, (Alexander von Wacker), b. Chgo., Aug. 23, 1952, s. Charles Wacker and Elizabeth (Ellis) Z. Author: The Case of the Software Spy, 1983, The Case of the Starship Movie, 1983, The Case of the Mysterious Dognapper, 1983, The Case of the Video Game Smugglers, 1983, The Case of the Chocolate Snatcher, 1983, The Secret of the Long Lost Cousin, 1983, The Cross & The Sickle, 1984, The Red Encounter, 1986, Blood Russian, 1987. Wrkg. on adult thriller, juvenile mysteries. Student, Macalester Coll., St. Paul, 1971-73; BA in Russian, Mich. State U., 1976. Interpreter, guide USIA, Washington and USSR, 1978; advt. copywrtr., Mpls., 1979-81. Mem. MWA. Home: 3337 Irving Ave So Minneapolis MN 55408

ZIMMERMAN, WILLIAM EDWIN, b. Bklyn., Feb. 2, 1941; s. George Zimmerman and Ruth Eva (Edelbaum) Strauss; m. Teodorina Greggoria Bello, Dec. 13, 1969; 1 dau, Carlota Pastora. Author: How to Tape Instant Oral Bios., 1979, A Book of Questions to Keep Thoughts and Feelings, 1984, Make Beliefs, 1987. BA, Queens Coll, 1962. Ed. Am. Banker, NYC, Banking Week, 1962—; pres. Guarionex Press, NYC, 1979—. Mem. Oral History Assn., Austin, Tex. 1980. Address: 201 W 77th St New York NY 10024

ZIMMERMAN, WINONA ESTELLE, b. Mankato, MN, Nov. 19, 1941, d. James Harold Matson Sr. and Edna Florence Martha (Fischer) Wandersee; m. Steven Ross Sharits, Apr. 18, 1960; chidlren—Rachelle De, Timothy Ross; m. 2d, Philip Carl Zimmermman, Feb. 6, 1977. Contrbr.: Draft Horse Jnl., Horse Scope, Guide, The Evener, other publs. Wrkg. on children's books, reference book. Edn. Mankato State Coll., The Inst., Redding Ridge, Conn. Freelance wrtr., 1978—; MHBA state reporter/columnist, 1980—filiate wrtr., reporter, photographer, City News Svc., 1986—. corr. Support Our Servicemen, 1984-85. Mem. numerous draft horse orgns., United Way Bd. Mem., 1987. Home: Le Center MN 56057

ZIMROTH, EVAN, b. Phila., Feb. 24, 1943; d. Lester and Janet Nurick; m. Peter L. Zimroth, June 20, 1965 (div.); m. 2d, Henry Wollman, Oct. 29, 1977; children—Lilly, Else. Author: (poems) Giselle Considers Her Future, 1978. Contrbr. poems to lit mags. Editor: Poesic Vincennes, 1975-76, The Little Mag., 1978-80. BA, Barnard Coll., 1965; PhD, Columbia U., 1972. Assoc. prof. English, CUNY-Queens Coll., Flushing, N.Y., 1972—, Fellow, N.Y. Fdn. for the Arts, 1985-86; grantee CUNY, 1982. Mem. P&W, PSA. Home: 367 Molino Ave Mill Valley CA 94941

ZINDEL, PAUL, b. S.I., NY, May 15, 1936; s. Paul and Betty (Frank) Z.; m. Bonnie Hildebrand, Oct. 25, 1973. Author: plays The Effect of Gamma Rays On Man-In-The-Moon Marigolds, 1965, And Miss Reardon Drinks A Little, 1967, Let Me Hear You Whisper; TV, 1969, The Secret Affairs of Mildred Wild, 1972, Ladies at the Alamo, 1976; screenplays Mame, 1974, Up the Sandbox, 1972; novels for teenagers The Pigman, 1968, My Darling, My Hamburger, 1969, I Never Loved Your Mind, 1970, Pardon Me, You're Stepping on My Eyeball, 1976, Confessions of a Teen-Age Baboon, 1977, The Undertaker's Gone Bananas, 1978; for children I Love My Mother, 1975; (with wife) book A Star for the Latecomer, 1980; The Pigman's Legacy, 1980, The Girl Who Wanted a Boy, 1981, Ya Novel-The Amazing and Death-defying Diary of Eugene Dingman, 1987. Hairy and Hortense and Hormone High, 1985. BS, Wagner Coll., 1958, MS, 1959, HHD, 1971. Recipient Drama Critics Circle award for Best Am. Play, 1970, Obie award for Best Am. Play, 1970, Drama Desk award for Most Promising Playwright, 1970, Pulitzer prize in Drama for Marigolds, 1971; Ford Fdn. grantee Alley Theatre, 1967. Office: H&R Inc 10 E 53d St New York NY 10022

ZINK, JOSEPH PAUL III, b. Pittsburgh, PA, Sept. 10, 1945; s. Joseph Paul and Cecelia Dorothy (Feldmeier) Zink; m. Kern Walsh Zink, Dec. 17, 1966; 1 son—Joseph Paul. Author: Building Positive Self-Concept in Kids, 1981, Motivating Kids, 1983, Champions on the School Bus, 1982, Champions in the Library, 1982, Champions in the Making, 1983, Ego States, 1986. MA, U. of Detroit, 1970, PhD, 1973. Pediatric Hypnotherapist (Manhattan Beach, CA), 1975—. Profl. ednl. cons. to 2000 school districts in US, Canada and Mexico in the field of child discipline, 1975—. Counselor of the Year, CA Assoc. of Licensed Educational Psychologists, 1984. Office: 1147 Highway Ave Manhattan Beach CA 90266

ZINNES, HARRIET F., b. Boston, d. Assir and Sara Lena (Goldberg) Fich; m. Irving I. Zinnes, Sept. 24, 1943 (dec. 1979); children—Clifford, Alice. Author: (poetry) Waiting and Other

Poems, 1964, An Eye for an I, 1966, I Wanted To See Something Flying, 1976, Entropisms (prose poems), 1978, Book of Ten, 1981; Blood and Feathers: Selected Poems of Jacques Prevert, translator, 1987; ed.: Ezra Pound and the Visual Arts, 1980. Wrkg. on collection of short stories, new collection of poems. PhD, NYU, 1953. Ed. Raritan Arsenal Publs., Metuchen, N.J., 1942-43; assoc. ed. Harper's Bazaar, NYC, 1944-46; tutor Hunter Coll., NYC, 1946-49; asst. prof., assoc. prof., prof. Queens Coll., Flushing, N.Y., 1949—; vis. prof. Am. lit. U. Geneva, Switzerland, spring 1970. MacDowell fellow, 1972, 73, 74, 77; Yaddo fellow, 1978, 81; grantee ACLS, 1978, CUNY, 1979, 81, 86. Mem. PEN, PSA, AAP, Natl. Book Critics Circle. Home: 25 W 54th St New York NY 10019

ZIOLKOWSKI, THEODORE JOSEPH, b. Birmingham, AL, Sept. 30, 1932; s. Miecislaw and Cecilia (Jankowski) Z.; m. Yetta Bart Goldstein, Mar. 26, 1951; children—Margaret Cecilia, Jan Michael, Eric Josef. Author: Hermann Broch, 1964, The Novels of Hermann Hesse, 1965, Hermann Hesse, 1966, Dimensions of the Modern Novel, 1969, Fictional Transfigurations of Jesus, 1972 (James Russell Lowell prize for criticism), Disenchanted Images, 1977, Der Schriftsteller Hermann Hesse, 1979, The Classical German Elegy, 1980, Varieties of Literary Thematics, 1983; also articles; Editor: Hermann Hesse, Autobiographical Writing, 1972, Hermann Hesse, Stories of Five Decades, 1972, Hesse: A Collection of Critical Essays, 1973, Hermann Hesse, My Belief: Selected Essays, 1974, Hermann Hesse, Tales of Student Life, 1976, Hermann Hesse, Pictor's Metamorphoses and Other Fantasies, 1982. AB, Duke U., 1951, AM, 1952; student, U. Innsbruck, Austria, 1952-53; PhD, Yale, 1957. Mem. editorial bd.: Germanic Rvw, 1964—, publs. MLA, 1971-75, Princeton U. Press, 1972-75; translator: The Poetics of Quotation (Herman Meyer), 1968, Hermann Hesse: A Pictorial Biography, 1975. Fulbright research grantee, 1958-59; grantee Am. Philo. Soc., 1959; Natl. Endowment for Humanities grantee, 1978; Guggenheim fellow, 1964-65; Am. Council Learned Socs. fellow, 1972, 76. Mem. Am. Comparative Lit. Assn., MLA, Am. Acad. Arts and Scis. Am. Philosophical Society, Göthingan Acad. of Scis. Home: Wyman Hs 50 Springdale Rd Princeton NJ 08540

ZIROS, CHRISTOS KONSTANTINOS, see Mirtsopoulos, Christos

ZJAWIN, DOROTHY ARLENE, b. Jersey City, NJ, Sept. 25, 1945; d. John Charles and Lillian (Yankielun) Z. Author: Teaching Ideas for the Come-Alive Classroom, 1980. B.A.; M.A., Kean Coll., Union, N.J., 1971; Ed.D., Rutgers U.-New Brunswick, N.J., 1983. Elem. tchr. Jersey City pub. schs., N.J., 1968-76; asst. prof. edn. SUNY, Plattsburg, 1977; free-lance wrtr., N.Y.C., 1978—; adj. instr. William Paterson Coll., Wayne, N.J., 1980, Mercy Coll., Dobbs Ferry, N.Y., 1981—. Mem. AG, Natl. Council Tchrs. Math. Home: 61 W Colfax Ave Roselle Park NJ 07204

ZOLOTOW, CHARLOTTE SHAPIRO, b. Norfolk, VA, June 26, 1915; d. Louis J. and Ella F. (Bernstein) Shapiro; m. Maurice Zolotow, Apr. 14, 1938 (div. 1969); children—Stephen, Ellen. Author: The Park Book, 1944, Big Brother, 1960, The Sky Was Blue, 1963, The Magic Words, 1952, Indian Indian, 1952, The Bunny Who Found Easter, 1959, In My Garden, 1960, Not a Little Monkey, 1957, The Man With The Purple Eyes, 1961, Mr. Rabbit and the Lovely Present, 1962, The White marble, 1963, A Rose, A Bridge and A Wild Black Horse, 1964, Someday, 1965, When I Have a Little Girl, 1965, If it Weren't for You, 1966, Big Sister, Little Sister, 1966, All That Sunlight, 1967, When I Have A Son, 1967, My Friend John, 1968, Summer Is, 1968, Some Things Go Together, 1969, The Hating Book, 1969, The New Friend, 1969, River Winding, 1970, 79, Lateef and His World, 1970, Yani and His World, 1970, You and Me, 1971, Wake Up and Goodnight, 1971, William's Doll, 1972, Hold My Hand, 1972, The Beautiful Christmas Tree, 1972, Janie, 1973, An Overpraised Season, 1973, My Grandson Lew, 1974, The Summer Night, 1974, The Unfriendly Book, 1975, It's Not Fair, 1976, Someone New, 1978, Say It, 1980, If You Listen, 1980, The New Friend, 1981, One Step, Two..., 1981, The Song, 1982, I Know a Lady, 1984, Early Sorrow, 1986. Student, U. Wis., 1933-36. Editor children's book dept. Harper & Row, NYC, 1938-44, sr. editor, 1962-70; v.p., assoc. pub. Harper Jr. Books, 1976-81; editorial cons., editorial dir. Charlotte Zolotow Books, 1981—; tchr. U. Colo. Writers Conf. on Children's Books, U. Ind. Writers Conf.; also lectr. children's books. Mem. PEN19 AL. Home: 29 Elm Pl Hastings-on-Hudson NY 10706

ZOLTOK-SELTZER, HARRIET, b. Los Angeles, d. Nathan and Ida (Kaplan) Zoltok; 1 son, Steven Mark Seltzer. Contrbr. poetry to Phoenix Fires, Am. Mosaic. Student public schls., NYC. Comml. artist Arkwright, Inc., NYC, 1965—. Mem. Bronx Poets and Wrtrs. Alliance (program dir.), Artists Equity, P&W. Home: 2625 Grand Concourse Bronx NY 10468

ZOOK, AMY JO SCHOONOVER, b. Glen Ellyn, IL, Apr. 25, 1937; d. John Dale and Alice R (Fletcher) Schoonover; m. Boyd W McCarty (div 1972); children: Michael, Deborah, Dale; m. 2d, Samuel J Zook Jr, July 15, 1972. Author: A Sonnet Sampler, 1979, 81; contbr chpts to The Study and Writing of Poetry, 1983; contbr more than 700 poems to more than 100 pubs. inclg. Oreg Rvw, Great Lakes Rvw, Laurel Rvw, Descant, Windless Orchard, Roanoke Rvw, Spoon River Qtly, Negative Capability. BA in English, Wittenberg U., 1969; MA in English, W. VA U., 1982. Part-time tchr. Champaign County schls., Urbana, Oh., 1961-66, Clark County schls., Springfield, Oh., 1972-80; English tchr. Mechanicsburg jr high schl., Ohio, 1966-67, Riverside high schl., De Graff, Ohio, 1968-70, Greenon high schl., Enon, Ohio, 1970-72; tchg. asst. W. Va. Univ., Morgantown, 1981-82, 84-85; Eng. instr., Urbana U., Oh., 1986—. Mem. NLAPW (Ohio state pres), Verse Writers Guld Ohio (treas), Nat Fedn State Poetry Socs (contest chmn), Ohio Poetry Day Assn (contest chmn), Soc. for Study of Midwestern Lit., PSA. Address: 3520 State Rt 56 Mechanicsburg OH 43044

ZUCKER, JACK S., b. Brooklyn, Jan. 23, 1935; s. Morris and Elsie (Wachtel) Z.; m. Helen Goldberg, Jan. 19; children—Laurie, Elizabeth. Author: Critical Thinking (comp. anthol.), 1969; Beginnings (poems), 1982; contrbr. poems, essays, short stories to Ann Arbor Rvw, Esquire, Poetry Northwest, Lit Rvw, Epos, other lit mags, periodicals. BA, CCNY, 1957; MA, NYU, 1961. Asst. prof. English, Newark (now Kean) State Coll., 1962-65; asst. prof., Babson Coll., Wellesley, 1965-68; asst. prof., Marietta Coll., 1968-70; tchr., Phillips Academy, Andover, 1970-76; Roeper City and Country Schl., 1976-83; spcl. lectr., Oakland Univ., 1983—; tchr., Wayne State Univ., 1985. AUS, 1957-63. Mem. PSA, New England Poetry Club (1971-76). Home: 14050 Vernon St Oak Park MI 48237

ZUCKER, NAOMI FLINK, b. NYC., Aug. 6, 1938; d. Salomon J. and Florence Judith (Rothman) Flink; m. Norman L. Zucker, June 25, 1961; children: Sara Deborah, George Samuel. Co-author (with Norman L. Zucker): The Coming Crisis in Israel: Private Faith and Public Policy, 1973, The Guarded Gate: The Reality of American Refugee Policy, 1987; contrbr.: N.Y. Times, Present Tense, Annals of Am. Acad. Polit. and Social Sci., others. Wrkg. on book on refugees in Central America. BA, Douglass Coll., 1959; MA, U. R.I., 1982. Copy ed. Houghton Mifflin Co., Boston, 1961-64; freelance ed., 1964-80; lectr. U. R.I., Kingston, 1978—. Home: 25 Locust Dr Kingston RI 02881

ZUCKER, NORMAN LIVINGSTON, b. NYC, Aug. 1, 1933; s. George Meyer and Beatrice Lillian (Livingston) Z.; m. Naomi Judith Flink, June 25, 1961; children—Sara, George. Author: George W. Norris: Gentle Knight of American Democracy, 1966, The American Party Process, 1968, The Coming Crisis in Israel: Private Faith and Public Policy, 1973, The Guarded Gate: The Reality of American Refugee Policy, 1987; contrbr. articles and rvws. to profl. jnls, chpts. to books. BA, Rutgers U., 1954, MA, 1956, PhD, 1960. Wurzweiler Fdn. grantee, 1963; Am. Philo. Soc. grantee, 1964; Rockefeller Fdn. fellow in human rights, 1980. Home: 25 Locust Dr Kingston RI 02881

ZUCKERMAN, ANNA ELAINE, b. Los Angeles, Oct. 3, 1958, d. Edward Kenneth and Ola (Gronsky) Zuckerman. Author: A Voyage to Adventure—Antarctica, 1985, Project Northwest Passage Log Book, 1985. BA, Princeton U. Vice-pres. AEZ Land Co., Santa Monica, Calif., 1980-84; pres. Eye on the World Pub. Co., Santa Monica, 1984—. Home: 972 Hilgard Ave 208 Los Angeles CA 90024

ZUCKERMAN, MARILYN, b. NYC, Mar. 26, 1925, d. Benjamin Zion and Hannah (Goldstein) Sherman; m. Irwin A. Zuckerman, Dec. 12, 1946 (div. 1979); children—Sam, Anne, Edward. Author: Personal Effects (with Helena Minton and Robin Becker), 1976, Monday Morning Movie (poems), 1981; contrbg. author: Dear Winter (poem), 1985, Tribe of Dina (fiction), 1986; contrbr. poetry to N.Y. Qtly, Little Mag., Greenhouse, Women's Qtly Rvw, others. BA, Sarah Lawrence Coll., 1971; MA, Goddard Coll., 1974. Poet-in-schls. N.H. Council Arts, 1975-76; poet-in-res. Mass. Fdn. for Arts and Humanities, 1976-79; mem. field faculty Goddard Cambridge, Mass., 1979; dir. artist colony Windmill House, Wellfleet, Mass., 1980-84; tchr. Emmanuel Coll. Women's Center, Boston, 1985, Center for Women and Change, Arlington, Mass., 1985-86. Recipient Syndicated Fiction Award PEN-NEA, 1985. Mem. Alice James Poetry Coop. Home: 153 Medford St Arlington MA 02174

ZUCKROW, EDWARD, b. NYC, Mar. 19, 1941, s. Leon and Naomi (Kane) Z.; m. Marti Lechow, June 17, 1965; children—Aviva, Deborah. Author: The Death of Horn & Hardart, 1971, Slowly, Out of Stones, 1980. BA, Bklyn. Coll., 1969. Caseworker NYC Dept. Social Services, Bklyn. Recipient Dov Herschel award Bitterroot Mag., 1984. Mem. P&W. Home: 303 Marcy Ave Brooklyn NY 11211

ZUKIN, JANE, b. Detroit, Sept. 20, 1948; d. Samuel and Lama (Charnes) Shetzer; m. Stanley Zukin, June 1, 1969; children—David, Eric, Renee. Author: Milk-Free Diet Cookbook, 1982, Dermatology-Dermatological Surgery, 1985, More Milk-Free Recipes, 1986, Living with Lactose Intolerance, 1986. Pub. qtly. newsletter about lactose intolerence. Student U. Mich., 1966-69; BA, Wayne State U., 1970. Copywriter, saleswoman WQRS radio, Detroit, 1969; ed. program content Storer Broadcasting Co., Detroit, 1970; v.p. Starmakers Inc., Detroit, 1977-84; pres. Comml. Writing Service, Detroit and Iowa City, Ia., 1984—; free-lance wrtr., 1969—. Bd. dirs. young adult div. Jewish Welfare Fedn., 1969-77, mem. pub. relations com., 1969-77. Mem. Univ. Club (wrtr.'s group 1985—); profl. mem. Natl. Writer's Club, Am. Medical Writer's Assn., Am Businesswomen's Assn. Home: 12 Arbury Dr Iowa City IA 52240

ZULU, ITIBARI MASEKELA, b. Oakland, CA, Apr. 24, 1953; m. Simone N. Koivogui, Aug. 9, 1980. BA, Calif. State U.-Hayward, 1976; MLS, San Jose Stae U., 1987. Author: Afro-American Studies Information Workbook: An Afrocentric Perspective, 1985, Marcus Garvey: A Man of Vision, 1985, African Naming Ceremony, 1986; editor, Uhuru Na Umoja, Calif. State U. Fresno, 1979; assoc. ed.: The Jnl of Pan African Studies, 1986; contrbr. Black Times, 1976. Librarian, Fresno County Library, Calif., 1984-85; coll. advisor San Jose State U., Calif., 1985; tchr. Fresno Unified Schl. Dist., 1981—; dir. Calif. Inst. Pan African Studies, Fresno, 1982—; dir. 1986 Pan African Film Festival, Fresno, Calif. Recipient Cert. of Award, Black Educators of Fresno, 1979; Jomo Kenyatta award African Students Union, Calif. State U.-Fresno, 1984; Civic Projects and Cultural Arts award City of Fresno, 1985; Calif. State Library scholar, 1984-85. mem. Calif. Black Faculty and Staff Assn., Black Caucus of ALA, Natl. Council Black Studies. Home: 1046 N 11th St Fresno CA 93702

ZUMWALT, JUDITH ANN ATKINS, b. Willisville, AR, Oct. 2, 1939; d. Robert Garner and Mildred Avis (Bailey) Atkins; m. Henry Arthur Zumwalt, Apr. 15, 1960; children—Amelia Jean, John Garner, Linda Ruth, Victoria Ann, James Arthur. Author: (poetry) Scribbles: My First Thirty Years, 1987. Grad. public schls., Willisville. Home: Rt 1 Box 131 Hope AR 71801

ZWEIG, ELLEN, b. Chgo., Jan. 27, 1947, d. Samuel and Florence (Devin) Zweig. Ed.: (with Stephen Vincent) The Poetry Reading, 1980; author: Impressions of Africa: Part IV: The Play, 1985. MFA, Columbia U., 1970; PhD, U. Mich., 1980. Lectr. Interarts Center, San Francisco State U., 1980-87; bd. dirs. Intersection for the Arts, San Francisco, 1985—; vis. artist Minneapolis Coll. of Art and Design, 1987. Grantee Marin Interarts, 1985, NEA, 1985. Mem. P&W, MLA, College Art Assn. Home: 9530 N. Harding Evanston IL 60203

Geographical Index

Humphrey, Edwin Lowell
Samperi, Frank V.
Tempe
Brownson, Charles
Burns, Patricia Henrietta
Carson, Ronald Frank
Cosner, Shaaron Louise
Donelson, Kenneth L.
Dove, Rita Frances
Ney, James Walter Ed Colby
Wrege, Beth Marie
Tombstone
Leonard, Phyllis G(rubbs)
Tucson
Ali, Agha Shahid
Anderson, Jon
Brady, Steven Roy
Brennan, Karen
Brooks, Ben
Carter, Mary Arkley
Clark, Laverne Harrell
Deloria, Vine Victor, Jr.
Ekstrom, Molly Anne
Garcia, Ignacio Molina
Garrett, Edward Cortez
Gold, Joe
Ingalls, Jeremy
Inman, Will
Kent, Rolly
Mairs, Nancy Pedrick
Momaday, Navarre Scott
Orlen, Steve
Penner, Jonathan David
Prust, Susan Luzader
Rattee, Michael Dennis
Rivera, Miquela Carleen
Rosenblatt, Paul
Rusk, Nance J.
Shelton, Richard
Smiley, Terah Leroy
Sowell, Carol Ann
Speer, Laurel
Weaver, Thomas
Tucson
Quimby, William Robert (Bill)
Tuscon
Nelms, Sheryl Lynne
Willcox
Paradiso, K. L.
Winslow
Rankin, Susan Jewel

Arkansas
Austin
Fincher, Wanda Faye
Bonnerdale
Newman, Ruby M.
Dardanelle
Jaggers, Annielaura Mixon
El Dorado
Strickland, Judy Evelyn
Elkins
Carr, Pat
Fayetteville
Alsbrook, Joseph David
Duval, John Tabb
Jones, Douglas Clyde
Lycan, Kelly G.
Simpson, Ethel Chachere
Williams, Miller
Harrison
Wilson, Cheryl Lee
Hope
Zumwalt, Judith Ann Atkins
Hot Springs
Hall, D. Elaine
Jonesboro
Lavers, Norman
Lott, Rick
Little Rock
Andrews, Mary Anita
Apple, William Marlan
Beggs-Uema, Marck Lewis
Brown, Dee Alexander
Camp, Marcia Claire
Drennan, Janice S.
Herrmann, John
Hollensworth, Mayme Stevens
Hollis Kimball, Stewart
Jauss, David Russell
Libhart, Bonni
Mc Math, Phillip H.
Mook, James
Morgan, James
Rice, Clovita
Ritchey, David
Tudor, Jim Patrick
Vining, Peggy Sue
Wright, Terry Alan
Young, Carol Ann Morizot
Lynn
Howard, Betty Ruth
Mountain Home
Jensen, Maxine Elizabeth
Mountain View
Budy, Andrea Hollander
Newport
Boyce, Wayne
North Little Rock
Clark, Dixie Dugan
Steele, Robert Bainum Jr.
Paragould
Ross, Lee A.
Pine Bluff
Greenberg, Paul
Rogers
Beal, Winnona Marie
Russellville
Almand, J.D.
Salem
Satter, Marlene Yvonne
Siloam Springs
Guinn, Gary Mark
Springdale
Oelschlaeger, Renee Louise
Walnut Ridge
Bagley Tarantino, Alice Marie

California
Albany
Lopez, Raymond Michael
Los Angeles
Lange, Gerald William
Alameda
Chalip, Alice Grace
Mc Brearty, Robert Garner
Samuelson, Georgia Jamie
Wondra, Janet C.
Albany
Abbott, Keith George
Logan, John Burton
Meyers, Carole Terwilliger
Rensberry, Richard J.
Tannenbaum, Judith Nettie
Albion
Cirino, Leonard John
Weiss, Ruth
Almeda
Tafoya, Cathy Jo
Altadena
Burden, Jean (Prussing)
Burkin, Mary
Shectman, Robin
Sterling, Gary Campbell
Amador City
Beilke, Marlan
Anaheim
Dexter, Jerry D. (Hal Wayne)
Singer, Kurt Deutsch
Winters, Shirley Royce
Young, Jordan R.
Anaheim Hills
Smith, Leon L., Sr.
Aptos
Cecil, Paula B.
Evans, John Wayne
Arcadia
Belnap, David Foster
Gabor, Georgia Miriam
Arcata
Carranco, Lynwood
Day, Richard Cortez
Hamby, James A.
Minty, Judith
Atherton
Horowitz, Lenore Wisney
Atwater
Coe, Joe Ann
Auburn
Wade, Theodore Everett, Jr.
Bakersfield
Raborg, Frederick Ashton, Jr.
Bayside
Campa, Joseph Frank
Benicia
Chicago, Judy
Rauch, Irmengard
Berkeley
Alta
Arguelles, Ivan
Bagdikian, Ben Haig
Basart, Ann Phillips
Beloof, Robert Lawrence
Benson, Steve
Boisclair, Joan
Boston, Bruce
Bradley, Marion Zimmer
Callenbach, Ernest
Canan, Janine Burford
Castaneda, Carlos
Clark, Thomas Willard
Covina, Gina
Covino, Michael
Crews, Frederick Campbell
Edwards, J.M.B.
Egan, Ferol
Ellis, Ella Thorp
Entrekin, Charles Edward, Jr.
Ewing, Jeanne Bunderson
Fabilli, Mary
Fisher, Thomas Michael
Foldvary, Fred E.
Fowler, Gene
Frym, Gloria Lynn
Frym, Gloria Lynn
Gawryn, Marvin
Geoffrey Arthur, Cook
Gitlin, Todd
Goldberg, Alan (Howard)
Gray, Alice Wirth
Harris, Kevin J.
Jensen, Dale Alan
Lesser, Wendy Celia
Litwack, Leon Frank
Mackey, Mary
Marine, Gene
Meltzer, David
Meyer, Margaret H.
Milosz, Czeslaw
Miner, Valerie
Moody, R. Bruce
Moser, Norman Calvin
O'Gara, Elaine Janet
Ostrander, (Willis) Frederick
Parkinson, Thomas Francis
Pinsky, Robert Neal
Policoff, Susan Lewis
Polsby, Nelson Woolf
Ratch, Jerry
Rawlins, Susan Elizabeth
Salas, Floyd Francis
Schafer, Edward Hetzel
Senti, R. Richard
Shaddock, David Robert
Simon, John Oliver
Smelser, Neil Joseph
Sonenberg, Maya
Staff, La Vada Falkner
Stone, Jennifer
Thomas, Joyce Carol
Wade, Cheryl Marie
Winters, Anne K.
Bethel Island
Avery, William P.
Beverly Hills
Bugliosi, Vincent T.
Cosby, Bill
Cousins, Norman
Davis, Kevin R.
Davis Aspinwall, Gail Ann
Haley, Alex Palmer
High, Monique Raphel
Lehan, Richard D'aubin
Livingston, Myra Cohn
Mc Kuen, Rod
Neumeyer, Kathleen
Niven, Laurence Van Cott
Shulman, Irving
Singleton, Joan Vietor
Stambler, Irwin
Winter, Caryl
Wolfe, (james) Digby
Big Bear Lake
Pfeiffer, J(ohn) Douglas
Bishop
Shaw, Dorene Lee
Bonita
Stegeman, William H.
Boyes Hot Springs
Hinkle, Richard Paul
Brentwood
Barnes, Mary Jane
Brentwood Los Angeles
Kennedy, John M.
British Columbia
Kinsella, W.
Burbank
Smallenburg, Harry Rus.
Burlingame
Wilkinson, Rosemary
Byron
Alexander, Frank Scott
Calabasas
Treece, Patricia
Calistoga
Endemann, Carl T.
Camarillo
Spencer, Jean W.
Campbell
Martin, Jim
Smith, Cheryl S.
Wu, William Lung-Shen
Canoga Park
Hart, Joan
Matson, John William II
Mc Auley, Milton Kenneth
Canyon Country
Brown, Scott Keith
Capitola
Peterson, Robert
Cardiff
Arnold, Craig Glen
Carmel
Campbell, R(obert) Wright
Hughes-Calero, Heather
Castro Valley
Archer, Myrtle Lilly
Cedar Ridge
Hotchkiss, Bill
Cerritos

Anderson, Moira Katharine
Chico
Hill, Dorothy J.
Keithley, George
Smith, Kellie Michelle
Chula Vista
Carter, Joyce Lee
Yamaguchi, Ellen Diane
Citrus Heights
Enroth, Theresa Louise
Claremont
Barnes, Dick
Koeninger, Kay
Levy, Leonard Williams
Phillips, Edwin Allen
Rana, Kiranjit S., II
Roth, John King
Sellery, J'nan Morse
White, W. Robin
Clayton
Doskey, John Stanley
Ray, Shirley G.
Compton
Hoffman, Ercell H.
Corona del Mar
Umphenour, Jillian Darrelyn
Costa Mesa
Angle, Roger, R.
Balsiger, David Wayne
Jensen, Gerald Randolph
Miller, Shirley Casey
Soler, Dona K.
Cromberg
Kolb, Kenneth Lloyd
Cucumonga
Allen, Blair H.
Culver City
Apple, Jacki
Pacheco, Javier Barrales
Cupertino
Bayard, Jean
Wheeler, Thomas Hutchin
Daly City
Batlin, Alfred Robert
Shortridge, Charles Emil
Danville
Lambert, Georgia Lynn
Reed, John Theodore
Davis
Daunt, Jon
Gold, Seymour Ma(urray)
Hurley, Lucille Shapson
Mc Pherson, Sandra Jean
Mikesell, Suzanne D.
Reed, Ishmael Scott
Thorpe, Stephen J.
Weber, Brom
Wershing, Susan Medler
Wright, Celeste Turner
Del Mar
Antin, David
Feldman, Joseph David
Del Rey
Masumoto, David Mas
Del mar
Brown, Jack
Diablo
Baender, Margaret Woodruff
Diamond Bar
Smith, Wilma Janice
El Cajon
Sanderlin, George
Sanderlin, Owenita Harrah
Thomas, Jesse James
Von Hoelscher, Russel
El Cerrito
Blum, Geoffrey Carl
Bogue, Lucille Maxfield
Nelson, Ray Faraday
Price, Mauricia
El Dorado Hills
Pine, John Christopher
Elk
Koepf, Michael
Emeryville
London, Jack
Encinitas
Ashley, Rosalind Minor
Harden, Michele Louise
Roecker, W(illiam) A(lan)
Rothenberg, Jerome Dennis
Encino
De Kovner-Mayer, Barbara
Fisher, Jerry Saul
Sludikoff, Stanley Robert
Escondido
Kubler-Ross, Elisabeth
Purviance, Donald Gene
Weidemann, Anton Fredrick
Eureka
Pitt, Suzanne Frances
Fair Oaks
Fletcher, Aaron
Schmidt, Tom V.
Fairfax
Bertolino, Rosaleen
Heaphy, James Cullen, III
Fairfield
Moore, Frances F.
Fillmore
Bly, Stephen Arthur
Folsom
Scott-Drennan, Lynne Ellen
Fontana
Boudreau, Edna Mae
Forestville
Hurley, Maureen Viola
Fortuna
Wrede, Barbara
Fountain Valley
Gardner, Joyce D.
Thorstad, Bruce
Fremont
Pickerell, Rodney R.
Reynolds, Lorraine Phyllis
Fresno
Browning, Elizabeth
Hanzlicek, Charles George
Levine, Philip
Rose, Wendy (Bronwen)
Thomas James, Brucie
Zulu, Itibari Masekela
Fullerton
Musso, Laurie Duston
Garden Grove
Ade, Ginny
Michels, Michael E.
Pomeroy, Ira Lewis
Tomkiel, Judith Irene
Gardena
Burley, Kathleen Mary
Georgetown
Lengyel, Cornel Adam
Gilroy
Duerr, Paula Cumming
Morgan, W. Robert
Myer, Charles B(ernard)
Glen Ellen
Schain, Richard
Glendale
Mc Closkey, Mark
Mc Kee, Gerald
Glendora
Hellbusch, Jay Jay
Mahoney, Eugene Frederick
Marshall, Sally Ann
Goleta
Gonder, Budd Eli
Kirscht, Judith Mary (Kenyon)
Mayes, Kathleen
Poynter, Daniel Frank
Pratt, Paul W.
Ramsdale, David Alan
Solter, Aletha Lucia
Granada Hills
Ko, Sung-Won
Grass Valley
Matthews, Joseph Ronald
Graton
London, Jonathan Paul
Greenbrae
Topkins, Katharine
Groveland
Cole, Ruth Elena
Grover City
Musafia, Judith N
Guerneville
Barrio, Raymond
Halcyon
Kempton, Karl
Half Moon Bay
Bonham, George Wolfgang
Happy Camp
Brown, Barbara Black
Brown, Duart Vinson
Hayward
Mc Aulay, Sara W.
Palumbo, Michael Nicholas
Healdsburg
Blocksma, Mary
Thompson, Thomas Dwight
Hermosa Beach
Andrews, Michael Duane
Mitchell, Betty Jo
Highland Beach
Crobaugh, Emma Adelia
Hillsborough
Abrahams, William Miller
Hollywood
Babb, Sanora
Eberts, Michael Albert
Lamparski, Richard
Nauman, Frances Irma
Ogilvie, Lloyd John
Rubenstein, Sharon Lynn
Svehla, John John
Van Vogt, Alfred Elton
Honeydew
Asher, Dustin T.
Huntington Beach
Allen, Carolyn Sessions
Anthony, Joseph
Billiter, William Overton, Jr.
Bryant, Kathy Ann
Criner, John Lawrence
Glenn, Peggy
Green, Raleigh E., II
Huntington, Cynthia
Null, Kathleen "Casey"
Peters, Robert
Winterowd, Walter Ross
Inverness
Dewey, Barbara
Mathews, Keith Rowland
Irvine
Divok, Mario J.
Jones, Pamela Lorraine
Koch, Karen Jean
Martin, Jay (Herbert)
Miller, Joseph Hillis
Obstfeld, Raymond
Yamada, Mitsuye May
Isla Vista
Reese, Harry Eugene
Jan Jose
Silva, Beverly
Kensington
Hillman, Brenda Lynn
Iodice, Ruth Genevieve Work
Michaels, Leonard
Nathan, Leonard Edward
Knightsen
Richeson, Cena Golder
La Canada
Mc Anally, Don
La Honda
Riordan, Michael
La Joll
Pearce, Roy Harvey
La Jolla
Iddings, Kathleen Ann
Kenyon, Karen Beth
Morgan, Neil
Nelson, Mildred
Newmark, Leonard Daniel
Pfeiffer, John William
Schiller, Herbert I.
Wesling, Donald Truman
Wilkes, Penny F.
La Mesa
Bumpus, Jerry Don
La Puente
Hayes, Richard Alan
La Quinta
Williams, Irene Mae
Lafayette
Cortinovis, Dan
Rafferty, Larry E.
Shurtleff, William Roy
Tumpane, John D.
Laguna Beach
Benford, Gregory Albert
Kennedy, Terry
Krieger, Murray
Rubenstein, Elaine J.
Taylor, Theodore Langhans
Laguna Hills
Broida, Helen
Laguna Niguel
Decker, Mary Locher
Mc Dargh-Elvins, Eileen
Lakeside
Herschler, Dale C.
Lakewood
Gates, Reginald D.
Lancaster
Wilcox, Jackson Burton
Lawndale
Thompson, Gary Allen
Loma Linda
Rozenstain, S(hefrah) Ann
Long Beach
Brander, John Morran
Cooper, Sandra Lenore
Lloyd, David Hubert
Rimmer, Christine L.
Snider, Clifton Mark
Long Beach
Dieckmann, Ed(ward) Jr.
Los Altos
Clark, Mason Alonzo
Smith, Shirley Mae
Winters, Janet Lewis
Los Altos Hills
Stegner, Wallace Earle
Walatka, Pamela Portugal
Los Angeles
Aberbach, Joel D(avid)
Adams, Fay
Alexander, Diane
Armstrong, Alice Catt
Bartlett, Helen Buck
Bensink, John Robert
Berges, Marshall William
Berry, John
Bishop, Anne
Bloch, Robert Albert
Boddington, Craig Thornton
Bogen, Laurel Ann
Bombeck, Erma Louise

Boyarsky, Benjamin William
Braudy, Leo Beal
Brown, Sharon
Byron, Stuart
Camron, Roxanne
Caram, Eve
Carpenter, Ben
Carrie, Jacques Felix
Chervin, Ronda
Clothier, Peter D.
Cohan, Anthony Robert
Coleman, Wanda
Cram, Donald James
Crichton, John Michael
Curtis, Hallie Vea
Dahl, Bard
Elkins, Merry Catherine
Exler, Andrew Ross
Fenady, Andrew John
Fisher, Mary Ann
Fonda, Jane
Friedman, Dorothy
Gabbard, Dana Chester
Garrett, Beatrice
Gary, Madeleine Sophie
Gerstler, Amy
Gillette, Paul
Grapes, Marcus Jack
Greeenberg, Marilyn Werstein
Greene, Donald Johnson
Greene, Lorna
Greene, Carla
Gullans, Charles (Bennett)
Harris, Mark Jonathan
Hart, William
Hayden, Dolores
Hertz, Uri L.
Hess, Loretta Rooney
Hill, Millicent Elizabeth
Humphry, Derek John
John, Donas
Johnson, Jean V.
Kemper, Troxey
Kierulff, Stephen
Kierulff, Charles Taylor
King, Carol Soucek
Korn, Henry
La Palma, Marina De Bellagente
Langguth, A.J.
Lanham, Richard Alan
Lawbaugh, Penelope
Leedom-Ackerman, Joanne
Leonard, Elmore John
Levenson, Jordan
Lond, Harley Weldon
Maclaine, Shirley
Marion, Douglas Welch
Martines, Lauro Rene
Matcha, Jack
Mc Dowell, Michael Gerald
Messerli, Douglas
Miles, John Russiano
Morris, Robert Mcquary
Muske, Carol Anne
Northen, Helen
Nyerges, Christopher John
Perry, Susan
Ragan, James
Reed, David Stuart
Rich, Alan
Rivers, Joan
Robbins, Doren Richard
Rogers, Pauline Bonnie
Schlachter, Gail Ann
Schwarz, Joyce A.
Seidenbaum, Art David
Shaw, Stanford Jay
Shideler, Ross Patrick
Shore, Herbert
Shulman, Max
Siatos, Thomas John
Simon, Roger Mitchell
Sklar, George
Smith, Christina Ann
Smith, Chester Leo
Smith, Jack Clifford
Stein, Julia A.
Straus, Austin Guy
Thomas, Robert Dickinson
Trinidad, David Allen
Vangelisti, Paul Louis
Vaughan, Marilou Taylor
Wallace, Irving
Wallis, William George
Walters, Mary Dawson
Westheimer, David
Wexler, Norman
White, Rita Alexandra
Wickes, Diana C.
Zahn, Curtis Lengelier
Zentella, Yoly Gabriela
Zuckerman, Anna Elaine

Los Osos
Hannon, Thomas Michael
Miller, Bruce Winsterd III

Lower Lake
Feuerstein, Georg

Malibu
Levitt, Peter
Moore, Brian
Roloff, Michael
Steinberg, Bernhard Evanbar

Manhattan Beach
Lee, Anthony Asa (Tony Lee)
Zink, Joseph Paul III

Manteca
Hellman, Donna Lee

Marina
Hopper, Jeannette M.

Marina Del Rey
Berg, David

Mendocino
Azrael, Judith Anne
Larsen, Kenneth Marshall
Tarbell, James

Menlo Park
Medeiros, Prisca D. Bicoy
Nanfria, Linda Jean
Phillips, Meredith Bowen

Middletown
Carter, Darle Lynn

Mill Valley
Broughton, James
Dillon, Richard Hugh
Hirshfield, Jane
Mihaly, Eugene Bramer
Moreno, Catherine Hartmus
Patler, Louis
Snyder, Zilpha Keatley
Zimroth, Evan

Mojave
Bergeron, Kathleen Yvonne

Monterey
Dehmler, Mari Lynch

Montrose
Momsen, Wiliam Laurence

Moorpark
Bollinger, Taree

Mount Shasta
Kennett, Jiyu

Mountain View
Ballentine, Lee Kenney
Benyo, Richard Stephen
Martin, (margery) Lee
Pilgrim-Guracar, Genevieve

Mt Shasta
Light, Will

Mt. Baldy
Simon, Maurya

N Hollywood
Mc Gee, Dennis Albert

Napa
Harvey, Julia (Juley)
Leggett, John Ward

Nevada City
Ninkovich, Thomas
Sanfield, Steve
Snyder, Gary Sherman

Newark
Kite, L. Patricia (Pat)

Newbury Park
Kerr, Leslie Ann

Newhall
Weekley, Richard J.

Newport Beach
Brazelton, Eugenia Louise
Du Chemin, Audrey May
Harris, Mac Donald
Mallory, Lee W.
Mitchell, Paul David
Morey, Kathleen Johnson

No Hollywood
Gompertz, Rolf

North Hollywood
Bagai, Eric Paul
Baizer, Eric Wyatt
Brommer, Gerald F(rederick)
Houlihan, Brian T.
Millasich, Hazel Ashton
Miller, M. Hughes

Northridge
Maxwell, Bruce David
Posnansky, Merrick

Norwalk
Henderson, Victor Maurice

Novato
Hanna, Thomas Louis
Hedley, Leslie Woolf
Moore, Rosalie
Schuler, Ruth Wildes

Oakland
Frank, Thaisa
Green, Theo
Hill, Crag A.
Jakubowsky, Frank R.
Lieberson, Stanley
Lockett, Reginald Franklin
Maynard, Robert Clyve
Mc Cann, Cecile Nelken
Mellender, John Clifford
Mitford, Jessica
Narell, Irena Penzik
Nimnicht, Nona Vonne
Painter, Charlotte
Rolfe, Bari
Silverberg, Robert
Tipton, Carolyn Louise
Vance, John Holbrook, (Jack)
Wong, Nellie

Oceanside
Leitmeyer, Walter James Jr.

Ocotillo
Harris, Merry

Ojai
Ponicsan, Darryl

Olympic Valley
Richnak, Barbara M.

Ontario
Rhodes, David Mark

Orange
Rafferty, Kevin Patrick
Woolery, George William

Orangevale
Boyle, John David

Orinda
Lyford, Joseph Philip
Witt, Harold Vernon

Oroville
Aihara, Cornellia
Aihara, Herman
Richards, Carolyn Baxter

Pacific Grove
Domac, Dragutin Charles

Pacific Palisades
Lee, Lance
Rosenau, James Nathan
Strauch, Ralph E.
Winokur, Jon

Pacifica
Miller, Lynn Ruth
Schwirian, Ann
Stanley, John W.

Palm Desert
Kleiner, Richard Arthur

Palm Springs
Bowart, Walter Howard
Hostrop, Richard Winfred

Palmdale
Baumgartner, Daniel Benton

Palo Alto
Finch, Annie Ridley Crane
Mick, Colin Kennedy
Mills, Dan Sam Paxton
Ploeger, Katherine Marie
Robinson, Kathleen Shelley
Smith, Genny Hall
Young, Albert James

Palos Verdes Estates
Bach, Marcus
Moloney, Terrence Patrick
Peter, Laurence Johnston

Panorama City
Robinson, Marcela

Paradise
Fulton, Len

Pasadena
Atchity, Kenneth J.
Bloom, Edward Alan
Bunting, Anne Evelyn
Feynman, Richard Phillips
Hoffberg, Judith A.
House, Richard Calvin
Mandel, Oscar
Post, Jonathan Vos
Renwick, Gloria Rainey
Sperry, Roger Wolcott
Stromberger, Theodore Leo
Thorpe, James
White, Nelson Henry
Zall, Paul Maxwell

Pebble Beach
Craig, James Duhadway

Penngrove
Haslam, Gerald William

Penryn
Anderson, David Charles

Petaluma
Witherup, William Allen

Piedmont
Von Morpurgo, Henry

Pioneer
Robinson, Kaylaine

Pittsburg
Astle, Thora Myrlene
Raner, Bertha Frances

Placentia
Miller, Kathy Collard

Pomona
Smith, Richard Keane

Porterville
Meredith, Marilyn

Portola Valley
Zelver, Patricia

Poway
Dollen, Charles Joseph

Rancho Cucamongo
Mc Coy, Robin Renee

Rancho Palos Verdes
Fifield, William
Haynes, Lincoln Murray

Snodgrass, Tod John
Rancho Santa Fe
Gruenwald, George Henry
Krueger, Caryl Waller
Rancho Temecula
Levine, Samuel Paul
Redlands
Cox, Jack R.
Hall, Christie Lea
Redondo Beach
Battles, (Roxy) Edith
Gilliam, Elizabeth M.
Redwood City
Barry, John Abbott
Ma Hood, James Herbert
Swigart, Rob
Reseda
Dultz, Ron William
Richmond
Johnston, Cicely Anne
King, Rey Reginald
Minnfee, Edna Mae
Munoz, Carlos, Jr.
Ridgecrest
Merrill, Mimi
Riverside
Barricelli, Jean-Pierre
Beatty, Patricia Jean
Chilcote, Ronald H.
Gaustad, Edwin Scott
Mc Queen, Marjorie
Olson, Richard George
Sampson, Carol Ann
Steadman, John Marcellus, III
Stotzfus, Ben Frank
Rohnert Park
Babula, William
Rosemead
Flores, Jose Obed
Roseville
Lourie, Iven B.
Ross
Brett, Peter D.
Sacramento
Blazek, Douglas David
Bottel, Helen Alfea
Burgess, Edward Francis, VIII
Coggins, Kathleen Bobrich
Hartley, Jean Ayres
Housen, Sevrin
Peppers-Johnson, Mary Lynne
Perri, Carol Sue
Schmitz, Dennis
Schrag, Peter
Stenzel, Larry G.
Wensrich, Margaret Fryer
Saint Helena
Strong, Janet Konhaus
Salinas
Robertson, Phil
San Anselmo
Gores, Joseph Nicholas
Hart, John
Montgomery, John Mcvey
San Bernadino
Dolan, G. Keith
San Bernardino
Reginald, Robert
San Carlos
Funge, Robert
San Clemente
Lewis, Jack (Cecil Paul Lewis)
San Diego
Armantrout, (Mary) Rae
Barnett, Bill Marvin
Bartlett, Elizabeth
Bell, Charlotte Dorothy
Berman, Ronald Stanley
Boggs, Marcus Livingstone, Jr.
Brashers, (Howard) Charles
Brenner, Robert Charles
Cassady, Marsh Gary
Cathcart, Margaret E.
Coleman, James N.
Deal, Shirley Mae Herd
Duemer, Joseph
Emry, Douglas Kriss
Field, Stanley
Freilicher, Melvyn S.
Gallup, Stephen Edmonds
Grigsby, Daryl Russell
Jacobs, Horace
Jaffe, Harold
Jaffe, Maggie
Jakes, John William
Jovanovich, William
Kaonis, Donna Christine
Kowit, Steve Mark
Lorrance, Arleen
Morgenstern, Frieda Homnick
Panofsky, Hans Arnold
Rateaver, Bargyla
Savren, Shelley
Self, Edwin Forbes
Stewart, Sharon Diane
Vokac, David Roland
Walling, Dana Mcneil
Weber, Shirley Anne
Wood, Richard Worthen
San Francisco
Jaffer, Frances E.
Addonizio, Kim Theresa
Andrews, Marcia Stephanie
Baker, William Radcliffe
Barletta, Joseph Francis
Beauford, Fred
Bell, Michael Steven
Belli, Melvin Louron
Benet, Thomas Carr
Bermant, Charles Mark
Berry, Linden Farrar
Brady, Dan Phillip
Brodine, Karen Harriet
Burch, Mariel Rae
Burger, Robert Eugene
Caulfield, Carlota
Chin, Marilyn Mei Ling
Conn, Carol
Cooney, Ellen
Curzon, Daniel
Cutler, Jane
D'arpino, Tony
David, Martin A.
Di Prima, Diane
Diaman, N. A.
Dillon, Millicent
Donovan, Diane C.
Dybeck, Dennis Joseph
Evans, Rose Mary
Ferlinghetti, Lawrence
Florsheim, Stewart Jay
Fox, Connie T.
Frank, Darlene
Freed, Lynn Ruth
Fuller, Blair Fairchild
Gach, Gary Gregory
Gallup, Dick
Gold, Herbert
Grinker, Morton
Grzanka, Leonard
Gunn, Thom
Hall, Jerome
Heffernan, Thomas (Carroll, Jr.)
Hession, Joseph Michael
Heymont, George
Johns, Roy
Johnson, Ronald
Johnson, Diane
Joseph, Jennifer
Juba, Robert David
Judd, Ralph Waverly
Kirchner, Elizabeth Ann
Kleinschmidt, Edward Joseph
Kovar, Milo
Langton, Daniel J.
Lanier, Geraldine Fe
Lappe, Frances Moore
Lateiner, Bonnie
Lindahl, Roger Mathews
Lippert, Ronald Steven
Loeffler, Carl Eugene
Lohmann, Jeanne Ruth Ackley
Lurie, Toby
Maisel, Eric Richard
Mallen, Ronald Edward
Marcus, Adrianne Maris
Masarik, Albert E.
Mc Cunn, Ruthanne Lum
Mc Goon, Clifford
Mcmillan, Peter Aidan
Meyer, George Ira
Middlebrook, Diane Wood
Miller, Thomas Eugene
Monroe, Mary
Morris, Richard W.
Murphy, Patrice Ann
Mycue, Edward Delehant
Myers, Gail Elizabeth
Nayer, Louise Bedford
Olsen, Tillie
Ortiz, Roxanne Dunbar
Oswald, Ernest John
Perlman, Susan Gail
Posamentier, Evelyn
Reed, Paul
Rice, Stanley Travis, Jr.
Rogow, Zack
Schramm, Darrell G.h.
Sevandal, Marciana Asis Sagun
Shaw, Li Kung
Silliman, Ron
Silver, David Francis
Singer, Norman
Stafford, Jan
Stahl, Jayne Lyn
Stetler, Russell Dearnley, Jr.
Strauss, David Levi
Strauss, Sally
Szerlip, Barbara L.
Taylor, (Paul) Kent
Terris, Susan
Tolleson, Evangeline W.
Tong, Benjamin Robert
Turkington, Gregg Mcpatrick
Tuttle, Judith Aurre
Vartnaw, William R.
Vogan, Sara
Weichel, Kenneth
Weidman, Jerome
Weir, Virginia Leigh
Whalen, Philip Glenn
Wilcox, Collin M.
Winans, Allan Davis
Wong, Nancy
Woodhams, Stephen Vance
Zerkin, E(dmund) Leif
San Geronimo
Griff, Bernard Matthew
Wheelwright, Betty
San Jose
Barker, James
Brown, Diana
Fox, George H.
Gilligan, Roy
Holyer, Erna Maria
Hood, Philip Boyce
Hruska, Elias Nicolas
Kennedy, Jon Reid
Kusler, Rex Ernest
Paul, William Bruce
Soos, Richard A. Jr.
Trisler, Henry Franklin, Jr.
San Luis Obispo
Barrett, James Lee
San Luis Rey
Funk, Virginia B.
San Marino
Middlekauff, Robert Lawrence
Rolle, Andrew
Tolles, Martha
San Mateo
Thomson, Virginia Winbourn
San Pedro
Basil, Douglas Constantine
Grimes, Nikki
San Rafael
Brady, Holly Wheeler
Hart, Jeanne
Hill, Hyacinthe
Murphy, Winifred Lee
San Ysidro
Martin, Alexander Stella
Santa Ana
Clements, Fred Preston
Santa Barbara
234 S Voluntario St F, Stone
Beckwith, Merle Ray
Bock, Russell Samuel
Bukowski, Charles
Carlisle, Joyce Ellen
Cunningham, Julia Woolfolk
Demaris, Ovid
Fish, Lilian Mann
Frost, David Duane
Garrison, Thomas S.
Hernadi, Paul
Hillman, Aaron Waddell
Kimbrell, Grady Ned
Lazarus, Keo Felker
Lazarus, A(rnold) L(eslie)
Lynds, Dennis
Mccarty, Jesse Louis Henry
Moir, Alfred Kummer
Norris, Wayne Bruce
Rettie, John Garner
Rose, Mark Allen
Stephens, Kathryn Lyle
Sullivan, John Patrick
Tracy, Frank William, Jr.
Young, Noel B.
Santa Clara
Brown, James Michael
Crouse, Karen Jean
Douthwaite, Graham
Driessel, A. Berkley
Jimenez, Francisco
Mc Alister, Thomas Allen
Smith, Sheryl L.
Santa Cruz
Albert, David H.
Archer, Jules
Atkinson, Charles Ora
Hall, James Byron
Hitchcock, George Parks
Houston, James D
Jorgensen, Richard Edward
Marcus, Morton Jay
Mcdowell, Robert A.
Olson, Clayton Leo
Raymond, Mark Wesley
Spivak, Melvin Ezra
Stegner, Stuart Page
Steinberg, David
Swanger, David
Sward, Robert S.
Young, Gary Eugene
Santa Maria
Gamboa, Reymundo
Santa Monica
Adamson, Joe

Arsone, Sarah
Bettleheim, Bruno
Boyd, Malcolm
Cross, Ronald Anthony
Fleischman, Albert Sidney
Guthrie, Sally Record
Hayden, Tom
Johnson, Earl, Jr.
Kessler, Jascha Frederick
Lally, Michael David
Leaf, Paul
Lewis, Thomasine Elizabeth
Loomis, Jan
Mc Donell, Marcella Ann
Penn, Jean Cox
Richmond, Steven Allan
Steele, Timothy Reid
Stern, Arthur Charles
Wilson, Eric
Saratoga
Rosenus, Alan Harvey
Saskatoon Saskatchewan
Porter,
Sausalito
Andersdatter, KarlaBrand, Stewart
Connell, Evan Shelby, Jr.
Shrodes, Caroline
Scotts Valley
Graham, Lola Amanda Beall
Ward, Nancy Joan
Sea Ranch
Wilde, Larry
Seal Beach
Logsdon, Thomas S(tanley)
Mc Eathron, Margaret
Seaside
Lapham, Constance Sumner
Linser, Paul William
Saleh, Dennis
Sebastopol
Bromige, David M.
Grant, J. B.
Sherman Oaks
Corsi, Pietro
Dassanowsky-Harris, Robert
Dubuque, Cheryl Anne
Ellison, Harlan Jay
Feather, Leonard Geoffrey
Nevius, Blake Reynolds
Shingle Springs
Mc Cord, Catherine Gumm
Sierra Madre
Dewey, Donald William
Solana Beach
Kelly, Mary Lee
Sonoma
Kizer, Carolyn Ashley
Pronzini, Bill John
South Lake Tahoe
Langford, Rick C.
South Pasadena
Angel, Ralph Michael
Buscaglia, (Felice) Leo(nardo)
Koertge, Ronald Boyd
Spring Valley
Baldridge, Charlene
Schwartz, Terry Walter
Stanford
Guerard, Albert Joseph
Hendrickson, Jo Ann Elizabeth
L'heureux, John Clarke
Lindenberger, Herbert Samuel
Lipset, Seymour Martin
Montgomery, David Bruce
Orgel, Stephen (Kitay)
Traugott, Elizabeth Closs
Stockton
Kahn, Sy Myron
Lamm, Michael
Schedler, Gilbert Walter
Studio City
Landes, William-Alan
Mathews, Beverly
Parrott, Wanda Sue
Peters, Vickie Jann
Suisun
Gonzalez-Mena, Janet
Sunnyvale
Larson, Randall D.
Ley, James M.
Tetreault, Wilfred F.
Towner, George Rutherford
Susanville
Shrum, Christine Ruth
Sylmar
Begalla, Patricia
Tahoe City
Cutter, Ralph Frederick
Tarzana
Mayer, Jane S.
Terra Bella
Mc Daniel, Bonny Elizabeth
Thousand Oaks
Ames, Steven Edmund
Collings, Michael Robert
Sohl, Jerry
Toluca Lake
Karshner, Roger Kay
Topanga Canyon
Metzger, Deena Posy
Tujunga
Daly, Saralyn R.
Union City
Sawyer, Barbara Jean
Upland
Cassingham, Randy C.
Vacaville
Sander, Lawrence D.
Van Nuys
Blair, Diana
Erbe, Jack Rudolph
Rosenberg, Eva
Sheahen, Allan
Spingarn, Lawrence Perreira
Venice
Itzin, Charles Francis
Mac Arthur, Loren
Mc Laughlin, Michael
Oandasan, William
Sullivan, Larry Michael
Ventura
Mc Auliffe, Frank Malachi
Verdugo City
Parque, Richard Anthony
Viejo
Lewis, Linda Ward
Walnut Creek
Drellich, Karen Kinney
Parker, Pat
Vicker, Ray
Watsonville
Hansen, Elizabeth J.
Reader, Dennis Joel
Zachreson, Nick (Nicholas) Bernard
West Hollywood
Groppa, Carlos G.
Kennedy, Adele Pattin
Terschluse, Marilyn Ann
Westlake Village
Brown Michelson, Linda
Whitethorn
Elder, Gary Michael
Whittier
Call, Jack Stanley
Hewitt, Jerene Cline
Johnson, Peter Christopher
Studebaker, Michael John
Wildomar
Brunsting, Melody Ann
Willits
Mc Cabe, Margaret E.
Rhoades, Jacqueline Jo
Winters
Peattie, Noel Roderick
Woodacre
Giles, Molly
Woodland Hills
Santomauro, Mary Elizabeth
Yorba Linda
O'Rourke, Sheila Anne

Colorado
Arvada
Glann, Elizabeth Jane,
Aspen
Chamberlain, Karen
Zigal, Thomas
Aurora
Deimer, Lorena Ruth Murrill
Eikenberry, Arthur Raymond
Mau, Ernest Eugene
Austin
Marshall, Muriel
Boulder
Cuzzort, R. P.
Eaton, Robert Charles
Fields, Rick D.
Harjo, Joy
Katz, Steve Robert
Kleinberg, Fredric Laufer
Krysl, Marilyn
Lindsey, William Fuselle (Billy)
Macy, Mark H.
Major, Clarence Lee
Mandel, Siegfried
Mc Intyre, Maureen Anne
Michelson, Peter F.
Monnett, John Hamilton
Pearn, Victor
Pereira, Teresinha Alves
Pois, Robert August
Redenius, Mary Palmer
Rogers, Faith Elaine
Sable, Barbara Kinsey
Schoeck, Richard Joseph
Starr, William J.
Steiner, Barbara Annette
Strange, Cathy Lee
Studer, Constance Elaine
Van Itallie, Jean-Claude
Waldman, Anne Lesley
Walton, Clyde Cameron
Wood, Renate
Brighton
Burns, Phyllis Ann
Kroekel, Juliette Ann
Buena Vista
Heilman, M. Grant
Calhan
Rawe, Francis Anthony
Colorado Springs
Doray, Andrea Wesley
Kuyper, Vicki Jean
Leaper, Eric John
Miller, Barbara Ann
Moody, Roberta Lynn
Nelson, Kent
Rogerson, Lynda Gail
Schroeder, Mike F.
Spencer, Dick III
Stone, Joan Elizabeth
Uphoff, Joseph Anthony, Jr.
Yaffe, James
Crestone
Thompson, William Irwin
Delta
Ulrich, Ann Carol
Webster, Diane Lynn
Webster, Diane Lynn
Denver
Blomster, Adelheid
Bryant, Edward Winslow, Jr.
Casewit, Curtis W.
Collins, Peggy Ann
Cordner, Denise Francoise
Dawson, Mary Martha
De Ford, Sara Whitcraft
Downard, Bob Hanson
Dunning, Lawrence
Epstein, Seymour
Fasel, Ida
Frost, Faye Juanita
Graf, Jess D.
Graf, Gary R.
Hamilton, Marcella Denise
Holmes, Marilyn Adams
Horrigan, Patricia Ann
Howell, Dean Myral
Keuning, Patricia Dubrava
Konrad, G. Gregory
Leckenby, Nancy L.
Mangan, Jean
Mc Cabe, Victoria
Mc Gaughey, Kathryn Elizabeth
Mendelsohn, Harold
Nigg, Joseph Eugene
Oliver-Pickett, Cheryl Kay
Omura, James Matsumoto
Omura, James Matsumoto
Pascoe, Patricia Hill
Pehrson, Barbara J.
Raffel, Burton Nathan
Rothman, Howard
Shroeder, Gary Steven
Smith, Sue Frances
Steward, Hal David
Stewart, Eugene Joel
Uchill, Ida Libert
Weeks, Robert Lewis
Zebauers, Vladimirs Valdis
Zeilig, Nancy Meeks
Dever
Milofsky, David
Dillon
Osborne, Maggie Ellen
Post, Rick Alan
Durango
Wilbert, Felicia Fibo
Englewood
Chalmers, Catherine Faye
Morrow, William L
Ramey, Diane Elfriede
Estes Park
Torosian, Jeanne Wylie
Fleming
Hoeppner, Iona Ruth
Florence
Geer, Galen Lee
Fort Collins
Grabill, James Roscoe, Jr.
Nanncy Jean, Steward
Pratt, John Clark
Schwartz, Steven R.
Stephens, Martha T.
Tremblay, William Andrew
Wells, Nancy Marie
Fort Morgan
Brower, Cheryl Diane
Golden
Crowley, Carol Lee
Dubois, Jean Charlotte
Greenberg, Joanne
Grand Junction
Foutz, Dell R.
Greeley
Jones, Don
Trainer, Orvel Leroy
Werner, Fred H.
Idledale
Hogan, Linda K.

Indian Hills
Wann, David L.
Kersey
Bond, Virginia F.
Lafayette
Miullo, Nathaniel Jerome
Lakewood
Costa, Helen Marie
Hutchison, Joseph G., Jr.
Schmitt, Betty J.
Littleton
Crandall, John Karl
Freilinger, Ida M. W.
Hoffman, Cindy Jane
Nelson, Michelle Hoghland
Porter, Margaret Evans
Reese, Deborah Decker
Settles, Cheryl Lynne
Sikes, Avid Glenn
Tom, Creighton Harvey
Waters, Helen Eugenia
Livermore
Hill, Cherry Lynn
Longmont
Battles, Brian James
Loveland
Ide, Patricia Louise
Larson, Marjorie Marie
Patterson, Veronica Shantz
Lyons
Hart, Lois Borland
Manitou Springs
Harris, Madalene Ruth
Merino
Propst, Nell Brown
Parachute
Dougherty, Samuel Allen
Dougherty, Samuel Allen
Parker
Whelchel, Sandra
Pueblo
Bonomelli, Charles James
Buchanan, Hubert A.
Kramer, Philip Earl
Shomaker, Gordon Alexander Jr.
Pueblo West
Hoots, Helen Hardin
Red Feather Lakes
Douglas, Lalette (Hammett Lale)
Rye
Williams, Alberta Norine
Saguache
Ross, Marilyn Ann (Markham)
Salida
Coonfield, Ed
Shovald, Arlene Elizabeth
Steamboat Springs
Kramer, Keith
Veronica Elizabeth, Blake
Sterling
Christian, Roland Carl
USAF Academy
Liotta, Peter Hearns
Westcliffe
Tichy, Susan Elizabeth
Wheat Ridge
Beckstead, Lucille

Connecticut
Bethany
Sewall, Richard Benso
Bloomfield
Coleman, Rosa Lee
Yarmal, Ann
Bolton
Young, M. Clemewell
Bridgeport
Chambers, John Darby
Hill, Judith
Canton
Holdt, David M.
Wilson, Donald Douglas
Chaplin
Daigon, Ruth
Cheshire
White, John Warren
Chester
Cromwell, Sharon Lee
Clinton
Malone, Michael Christopher
Mellow, James Robert
Colchester
Kobelski, Irene Catherine
Colebrook
Mc Neill, William Hardy
Cornwall
Barnes, Robert Goodwin
Brecher, Edward Moritz
Cos Cob
Barnard, Charles Nelson
Coventry
De Garmo, Sherly Frances
Danbury
Bartow, Stuart Allen, Jr.
Muller, Georgene K.
Smith, Alan Harvey
Toland, John Willard
Welburn, Ron
Darien
Anson-Weber, Joan E.
Sonnenblick, Edmund H.
Devon
Ulisse, Peter James
Durham
Galvin, Brendan James
East Hartford
Brennan, David Daniel
East Norwalk
Paterson, Lin Richter
Easton
Hornstein, Harold
Hubbell, Patricia Ann
Ellington
Lyons, Chopeta C.
Enfield
Gergely, Arpad Jozsef
Lepore, Dominick James
Essex
Laffal, Florence
Fairfield
Barone, Rose Marie Pace
Clark, Eleanor
Mortimer, William John
Rinaldi, Nicholas Michael
Russ, Lawrence
Sodaro, Robert J.
Walker, Donald Knox
Warren, Robert Penn
Falls Village
Van Doren, Charles
Farmington
Mann, Ned
Gales Ferry
Mann, Jim
Schultz, Michael Edward
Georgetown
May, Barbara L.
Glastonbury
Mc Nulty, John Bard
Goshen
L'engle, Madeleine
Greens Farms
Straub, Peter Francis
Greenwich
Bonnett, Kendra R.
Mc Cauley, Carole Spearin
Willoughby, Stephen Schuyler
Groton
Lane, Carolyn Blocker
Naillon, Valerine
Guilford
Bryan, Courtlandt Dixon
Holly, Carl Stevens
Lewin, Leonard C.
Van Tassel, Katrina
Guliford
Peters, William
Hamden
Fitzgerald, Robert
Gallagher, Mary Beth
Gay, Peter
Magoveny, Dianne Jeanne
Olson, Jane Virginia
Riker, Leigh Bartley
Smith, John Edwin
Taylor, Paul J.
Woodward, C(omer) Vann
Young, Virginia Brady
Hartford
Baird, Thomas (P.)
Bloom, Lary Roger
Calip, Roger E.
Cohn, Jan Kadetsky
Leventhal, Ann Z.
Pfeil, John Frederick
Jewett City
Buffin, Carol
Kent
Brownell, James Garland
Moore, Honor
MIddletown
Wakefield, Kim Stoeckle
Madison
Falk, Peter Hastings
Whitney, David Charles
Manchester
Cohen, Lila Beldock
Sheftel, Beatrice K.
Manhester
Gorman, Judy
Meriden
Antignani, Bonnie Provenzano
Middle Haddam
Olson, Lawrence
Middletown
Bardeck, Walter Peter
Carroll, Patricia L
Connor, John Anthony
Manchester, William
Ohmann, Richard Malin
Reed, Lillian Craig
Reed, Kit
Reed, Joseph Wayne, Jr
Rose, Phyllis
Slotkin, Richard Sidney
Stevenson, John Edward
Mount Carmel
Douskey, Franz Thomas
Mystic
Thompon, Louise Saari
Thompson, Sue Ellen
New Britain
Carrier, Constance Virginia
Kurtz, Patti Joan
New Canaan
Eskesen, Bennet Hallum (Hal) Jr.
Hutter, Donald Stephen
Moore, Geoffrey Hoyt
Packard, Vance Oakley
Sharpe, Myron Emanuel
New Haven
Bloom, Harold
Brennan, Joseph Payne
Gilman, Richard
Langille-Mattei, Suzanne Yvonne
Lewis, Richard W Baldwin
Macmanus, Yvonne Cristina
Mattei, Loren Neal
Metlitzki, Dorothee
Natanson, Maurice Alexander
Raymond, (Myrtle) Roby
Russel, Carol Ann Marie
Schecter, Joel R.
Tufte, Edward Rolf
New London
Meredith, William
New Milford
Merkling, Frank
Scrimgeour, James Richard
New Preston
Biancolli, Louis
Newington
Kemper, Steven Edward
Newtown
Taylor, Robert Lewis
Winder, Barbara Dietz
Niantic
Erpenbeck, Mary-Lou Brockett
Noroton
Brooke, Avery Rogers
North Haven
Brumbaugh, Robert Sherrick
Norwalk
Ferguson, Dorothy Margueritte
Goodner, John Ross, Jr.
Lance, Jeanne Louise
Oakdale
Luddie, Walter Joseph
Old Greenwich
Morris, William
Morris, Mary Elizabeth
Old Lyme
Urdang, Laurence
Old Saybrook
Holmes, John Clellon
Petry, Ann
Orange
Davis, Jon Edward
Frohman, Howard Loeb
Portland
Marteka, Vincent James, Jr.
Preston
Gibson, Margaret Ferguson
Mc Kain, David W.
Quaker Hill
Deedy, Joyce
Redding
Carroll, Theodus Catherine
Riverside
Koehn, Ilse Charlotte
Mc Curdy, Patrick Pierre
Rocky Hill
Iaacs, Mark D.
Sharp, Arthur Glynn
Rowayton
Seitz, Nicholas Joseph
Roxbury
Feldstein, Albert B.
Gurney, Albert Ramsdell, Jr.
Styron, William
Simsbury
Mc Quilkin, Robert Rennie
Minot, Stephen
South Norwalk
Partch, Kenneth Paul
South Windsor
Salvatore, Michael Joseph
Southbury
Maloff, Saul
Tebbel, John
Southington
Criniti, Mary Pauline
Stamford
Aylesworth, Thomas Gibbons
Barry, Edward William
Beason, Robert Gayle
Berry, John Nichols, III
Bodek, Norman
Crane, Teresa Yancey
Gershman, Elizabeth Gibson

Jaben, Jan Elaine
Pinchot, Ann
Siverd, Bonnie
Stonington
Merrill, James
Storrs
Charters, Ann D.
Hall, Joan Joffe
Kostiner, Eileen T.
Ladd, Everett Carll, Jr.
Sabatine, Jean Ann
Thorson, Robert Mark
Waniek, Marilyn Nelson
Stratford
Krause, Nina
St. Cyr, Napoleon Joseph
Thompson, Rebecca
Taftville
Bonini, Victor Louis
Thomaston
Newton, Debra Irwin
Thompson
Burns, Gerald Patrick
Trumbull
Allen, Richard Stanley
Berry, Henry Arnold, Jr.
Romano, Nick Joseph
Watson, Donald Ralph
W Redding
Ford, Sarah Litsey
Wallingford
Kowalski, John
Washington
Toffler, Alvin
Waterbury
Daddona, Patricia Ann
Florian, John S.
Mitchell, Barbara Joanne
Smith, Jeanette Goates
Waterford
Commire, Anne
West Hartford
Barone, Dennis
Cohn, Janet Stone
Gallo, Donald Robert
Glixon, David M(orris)
Steier, Rodney Dean
Trecker, Janice Law
West Haven
Hall, Theodore Dana
Harris, Frank, III
Weston
Goulart, Ron(ald Joseph)
Harms, Valerie
Lardner, Ring Wilmer, Jr.
Shaw, Fran Weber
Westport
A'hearn, Joan M.
Bernhard, Arnold
Brink, William Joseph, Jr.
De Vries, Peter
Heinrich, Peggy
Krauss, Janet
Martin, Ralph Guy
Peyre, Henri Maurice
Rose, Reginald
Safran, Claire
Wiese, Michael
Wilk, Max
Wethersfield
Clede, Emile William, Jr.
Kulvinskas, Victor P.
Williamantic
Scully, James Joseph
Willimantic
Butterick, George F.
Scully, James Joseph
Taylor, Alexander Douglas
Vernon, Sidney
Wilton
Harrington, Geri
Morgan, Robert B.
Williams, Joan
Windsor
Butler, Robert Francis
Woodbridge
Hamilton, Linda Kay
Hollander, John

Delaware
Hockessin
Casey, Gerald Wayne
Nolan, Agnes Peters
Lewes
Mc Brine, Ava Jean
Lincoln
Harris, Edna Mae
Newark
Binkley, Janet Ramage
Brown, Natalie Joy
Jackson, Fleda Brown
Kline, Lloyd Warfel
Micklos, John Joseph, Jr.
Ruark, Gibbons
Scott, Patricia Jeanne
Snodgrass, W. D.
Venezky, Richard Lawrence
Wilmington
Karl, Jean Edna
Miller, Raymond Russell Jr.
Nollet, Lois Sophia
Nollet, Lois Sophia
Richards, Mary Fallon

District of Columbia
Washington
Aksyonov,Allen, Martha Leslie
Alperovitz, Gar
Backlund, Ralph Theodore
Bailey, Charles Waldo
Baker, Norman Lee
Baker, Carolyn Croom
Baldwin, Deidra B.
Bandow, Douglas Leighton
Barnet, Richard Jackson
Bedini, Silvio A.
Bessom, Malcolm Eugene
Betchkal, James Joseph
Biddle, Livingston
Blake, John Ballard
Blough, Glenn Orlando
Blumenson, Martin
Boorstin, Daniel J.
Boots, Sharon G.
Boyle, John E. Whiteford
Bradford, Marjorie Odell
Bradlee, Benjamin C.
Breen, Ann E.
Broyles, William Dodson, Jr.
Buchwald, Art
Burnham, Sophy
Cavalieri, Grace
Chafetz, Marion Claire
Claire, William
Cline, Tim
Cochrane, Shirley Graves
Colson, Charles Wendell
Combs, Maxine Ruth Solow
Curran, Charles (edward)
Daniels, Hope Mary
Deane, James Garner
Des Marais, Louise Mercier
Downie, Leonard, Jr.
Dumouchel, J. Robert
Epstein, Joseph
Evans, Harold Matthew
Falk, Diane M.
Ferebee, Gideon, Jr.
Flynn, Richard Mc Donnell
Fox, Michael Wilson
Foxhall, Kathryn
Garrett, Wilbur Eugene (Bill)
Geyer, Georgie Anne
Glang, Gabriele
Goldstein, Alan
Goulden, Joseph Chesley
Greenfield, Eloise Little
Griffith, Patricia Browning
Grossman, Andrew Joseph
Grumbach, Doris
Hamarneh, Sami Khalaf
Hamilton, James
Hardison, Osborne Bennett, Jr.
Harrington-Hughes, Kathryn
Hassett, Joseph Malk
Hay, (George) Austin
Hecht, Anthony Evan
Hellinger, Douglas A(lan)
Hellinger, Stephen H(enry)
Hill, Patricia Susan
Hope Ridings, Miller
Johnsen, Gretchen Lynne
Kalaski, Robert John
King, Alvin Thomas
King, Kathryn Elizabeth
Kiplinger, Austin Huntington
Kirkpatrick, Jeane Duane Jordan
Lane, Mark
Lawrence, Jean Hope
Lehrer, James Charles
Leighton, Frances Spatz
Lewis, Douglas
Lewy, Guenter
Licht, Lilla Giles Mcknight
Longley, Laura Ann
Macdonald, William Lloyd
Macdougall, William Lowell
Mackey, Howard Hamilton Jr.
Magarrell, Elaine
Markun, Patricia Maloney
Martin, Judith
Mc Kenzie, Malroy Bernard
Mc Namara, Robert Strange
Michaud, Michael Alan George
Miller, Nathan
Moser, Donald Bruce
Nader, Ralph
Nail, Dawson B.
Nisbet, Robert A
Nordhaus, Jean
Novak, Michael (John), Jr.
Ntube, Dominic Kwang
Ogilvie, Fan S.
Oleshansky, David Sam
Orfalea, Gregory Michael
Owen, Mary Jane
Parker, Joyce Cave
Payton, Randolph Randi
Pertschuk, Michael
Poteete, Robert Arthur
Pryde, Marion Jackson
Quinn, Sally
Rapoport, Daniel
Richards, Jeff
Ridgeway, James Fowler
Rifkin, Jeremy Chicago
Rigby, Richard Norris
Riley, Millie Willett
Rosenthal, Douglas Eurico
Rosenzweig, Phyllis D.
Rowan, Carl Thomas
Safire, William
Sargent, Robert Strong
Schoenbaum, Samuel
Shanks, Hershel
Sheehan, Neil
Shih, Joan Chung-Wen
Shipler, David Karr
Shreve, Susan Richards
Silver, Marc S.
Simon, Paul
Slappey, Mary Mc Gowan
Smith, Terence Fitzgerald
Smith, Robert Ellis
Starke, Linda
Stern, Philip Maurice
Swift, Mary Howard Davidson
Szulc, Tad
Talbot, Strobe
Taquey, Charles Henri
Tauke, Beverly Hubble
Toledano, Ralph De
Tomich, Nancy Ellen
Tucker, Kay Hartman
Tully, Andrew Frederick, Jr.
Viorst, Milton
Viorst, Judith Stahl
Washburn, Wilcomb Edward
Wattenberg, Ben J.
Weismiller, Edward Ronald
Whalen, Richard James
Wieseltier, Leon
Will, George F.
Woodward, Robert Upshur
Wouk, Herman

Florida
Altamonte Springs
Atwood, JeffreyPasternak, Ceel
Altoona
Dill, Edith Palliser
Alva
Schroeder, Robert Engle
Apollo Beach
O'Brien, Susan Barbara
Bay Harbor Isles
Kocin, Sidney
Belleair Beach
Fuentes, Martha Ayers
Belleview
Pellegrini, Ruby Louise
Beverly Hills
Ogden, Prokopov Georgine Lucile
Blountstown
Anderson, Irma Louise
Boca Raton
Augerson, Scott William
Bartley, Shirley Kay
Brown, Drollene Mae
Clarke, John R.
Freiburger, Betsey
Gerson, Noel Bertram
Nathan, Norman
Sandler, Roberta
Schramm, Rachel Fleischamnn
Senz, Laurie S.
Wilson, Patricia Ann
Boynton Beach
Faeder, Gustav S.
Heckelmann, Charles Newman
Bradenton
Furlong, Marcella Lee
Madigan, Grace Evelyn
Mc Millan, Leona Pearl
Pellington, J. Richard
White, Dale Andrew
Brandon
Rae, Michelle Lauren
Casselberry
Stap, Donald L.
Clearwater
Bozza, Linda Susan
Brady, Henry
Carlson, Natalie Savage
Chaffin, Lillie D.
Dunlap, Joe Everett
Shepherd, Catherine
Van Meer, Mary Ann
Warda, Mark
Cocoa

Hayton, Richard Neil
Cocoa Beach
Canfield, Deborah Ann
Quinn, John Collins
Coconut Creek
Schein, Jerome
Coral Gables
Eppes, William David
Hester-Mitch, Louis John
Schwartz, Kessel
Coral Springs
Krulik, Stephanie Miriam
Crawfordville
Petty, Anne C.
Davie
Cooke, Audrey
Farley, Stacey Jeanne
Grayson, Richard
Daytona Beach
Purens, Ilmars Uldis
Delray Beach
James Donald Cary, Crockett-Smith
Mc Cabe, James Victor
Yates, Samuel
Destin
Lanius, Gloria Helene
Dunedin
Dupes, Martha Gail
Dunnellon
Konkle, Janet Marie Everest
East Fort Lauderdale
Mabe, Chauncey
Englewood
Akashah, Mary Scoboria
Albrecht, Peggy Stoddard
Cussen, June
Eustis
Boris, Robert Elliot
Fort Lauderdale
Cassell, Dana Kay
Chamberlain, Donna Jon
Corll, Vivian Morgan
Davis, Kevin Adam
Dougher, Colleen Marie
O'Hanlon, Alvin Merle
Reardon, Edward Hyland
White, Ann
Wilson, Robert Edward
Fort Myers
Barbour, William Rinehart, Jr.
Brown, Robert Hugh
Clark, Margaret Goff
Heckler, Jonellen Beth
Powell, Richard Pitts
Richard Chester, Allen
Sand, George X.
Fort Myers Beach
Schell, Rolfe Finch
Fort Walton Beach
Aldridge, Ray
Frostproof
Noland, Charles Eugene
Ft Lauderdale
Kilgus, Edward John
Koperwas, Sam Earl
Ft Myers
O'Hara, William F., Jr.
Ft. Lauderdale
Moore, Mona
Ft. Lauderdale
Luxner, Morton Bennett
Gainesville
Crews, Harry Eugene
Goldhurst, William
Haldeman, Joe William
Harris, Marvin
Justice, Donald Rodney
Mc Carthy, Kevin Michael
Meeker, Darcy Sue
Mozinski, Cathlee Rae
Pickard, John Benedict
Salchert, Brian Arthur (St. Cloud)
Shomer, Enid
Smith, Jo Anne
Wyatt-Brown, Bertram
Haines City
Stevens, Christine Hyde
Hallandale
Miltner, Emily R.
Havana
Grier, Barbara G.
Hialeah
Fournier, Carlos
Martinez, Georgina V. (Percie Blu)
Hillsboro Beach
Browne, Morgan Trew
Hollywood
Cymet, Tyler Childs
Fell, Frederick Victor
Nightingale, Barbra
Thorne, Rick Joseph
Indialanitic
Perry, Robin L.
Indialantic
Lewis, Richard Stanley
Indian Rocks Beach
Johnson, Marty Jo
Inverness
Wilkens, George Robert
Jacksonville
Baron, Mary Kelley
Fore, Robert Clifford
Harrell, Lori O'Mel
Murray, Ruth Mildred
Perry, Beth
Poyer, David
Register, Victoria Smith
Wheeler, Trent H.
Jacsonville
Sherwood, Evelyn Ruth
Jensen Beach
Pratt, Marjorie Jean
Kenneth City
Hickok, Floyd A.
Key Biscayne
Rona, Donna C.
Key West
Hersey, John
Russell, Sandra Little
Keystone Heights
Wells, Basil Eugene
Kissimmee
Tyrrell, Calvin E.
Lantana
Hughes, Richard Glynne
Largo
Brewster, Bernadette Heidt
Funkhouser, Eileen
Longboat Key
Gorkin, Jess
Longwood
Mc Millan, Patricia Ann
Lutz
Koehler, Jo Ann M.
Maitland
West, Jean
Marathon
Mc Kinlay, Eleanor Grantham
Margate
Strom-Paikin, Joyce Elizabeth
Wood, Harvey Joseph
Melbourne
Abbott, Robert Tucker
Forrester, Susan Annette
Merritt Island
Caporale, Patricia Jeane
Kircher, Joyce Megginson
Smith, Patrick D.
Smith, Patrick Davis
Willmot, William Clarence
Miami
Batten, James Knox
Baxter, Michael John
Berkman, Harold W(illiam)
Bita, Lili
Blais, Madeleine Helena
Brown, Cherri Louise
Bulnes, Sara Maria
Fink, Barbara (Bobbie) Arlene
Gootnick-Bruce, Stephanie
Gorman, John Andrew
Innes, Ruth
Jackson, Rosa Catherine
Johnson, Dorothy Strathman Gullen
Kahn, Hannah
Macado, Mary Stanley
Macarthur, Gloria
Morgan, Marabel
Perry, Nina Diamond
Rivero, Andres
Rockstein, Morris
Tobias, Andrew Previn
Welsh, Judith
Miami Beach
Alschuler, Al
Prange, Marnie
Rauzin, Erica Meyer
Winston, Stephen Edward
Miami Lakes
Penzer, Mark
Ruben, Ann Moliver
Miramar
Friedland, Susan Helen
Naples
Layton, Thomas Ralph
Montgomery, Ruth Shick
Sherwin, James Leland (Lanny)
New Port Richey
Gilbert, Jack
North Fort Myers
Gersdorf, Antoinette Graham
O'Halloran, Judy Mackenzie
Seath, Olga Winnifred Hanna
North Ft Myers
Hughes, Helen Ruth
North Miami
Miller, Harriett Puffer
North Miami Beach
Arkin, Joseph
Edelson, Judith White
Hettich, Michael
Stern, Aaron
North Palm Beach
Leaf, Mindy Glass
Ocala
Bradley, Florence Frances
Olando
Weikel, Dana Rose
Opa Locka
Cline, Richard Allan
Orlando
Blankenship, J. Randall
Christopherson, Leroy Omar
French, E(mma) Yulee
Hemschemeyer, Judith
Mattox, Lewis E.
Mead, Harriet Councill
Owens, Christopher G.
Piquette, Marice Ann
Standish, Craig Peter
Wallace, Ronald Lynn
Ormond Beach
Parente, Audrey
Oviedo
Poole, Kathleen Zada
Palm Beach
Ness, Evaline
Pryor, Hubert
Smith, Kathleen Keer Mcgowan
Whitehead, Margaret Harold
Palmetto
Hunt, Annice Elizabeth
Pensacola
Bowden, Jesse Earle
Robinson, James Arthur
Workman, Gale Ann
Pinellas Park
Jakes, Jean Ann
Plantation
Cleary, Michael
Randi, James
Port Charlotte
Matranga, Frances Carfi
Seale, Joseph Lloyd
Snook, Herbert Edgar
Port St Joe
Biggs, Margaret Key
Port St Lucie
Roorbach, Douglas E.
Port St. Joe
Bedard, Patrick Joseph
Quincy
Boyles-Sprenkel, Carolee Anita
Redington Shores
Tait, Elizabeth Leeds
Riverview
Prance, June E.
Rockledge
Hutcheson, Carolyn Pirtle
Moseley, William
Rotonda West
Kemp, Nettie Emmerine
Safety Harbor
Burden, Nancy Caswell
Saint Augustine Shores
Detjen, Gustav Heinrich
Saint Petersburg
Barnes, Andrew Earl
Coe, Marian (Zipperlin)
Essock, Cyd Pauline
Gillette, Ethel Perry
Radcliffe, Eleanor Schroeder
Rood, Frank William
Schuck, Marjorie Massey
Sanibel
Greenberg, Margaret H.
Walton, Chelle Koster
Sanibel Island
Hallstead, William Finn III
Sarasota
Burke, Edgar Patrick
Burrell, Nancy Bradbury
Cantor, Eli
Forer, Bernard
Hayes, Joseph
Johnson, James Blair
Mc Ilwain, William Franklin
Middleton, Norman G.
Tausch, Gerry Margaret
Wendt, Lloyd
Satellite Beach
Webster, George Calvin
Seminole
Brobst, William Keplinger
Hoagland, Guy Whitney
Shalimar
Colgan, William B.
St Petersburg
Benbow, Charles Clarence
Johnson, A. Paul
Meinke, Peter
Petty, Milana Mc Lead
Rose, Patricia Anthone
Thompson, Sandra Jean
Wunderlich, Ray C(harles) Jr.
Sugarloaf Shores
Kaufelt, David A.
Summerfield
Northacker, Alfred Austin
Sun City Center

Ellison, Glenn
Sunrise
Corseri, Gary Steven
Stirnemann, S. A.
Tallahassee
Bailey, Reubena Winona
Burroway, Janet Gay
Caswell, Donald Eugene
Fowler, Douglas R.
Fox, Vernon Brittain
Hawkins, Hunt
Horvath, John
Macesich, George
Mc Crimmon, James Mcnab
Murphy, Thomas Jay
Rutkovsky, Paul Michael
Shaara, Michael Joseph, Jr.
Stiff, Robert Martin
Tarver, David Paul
Thomson, Sarah Elizabeth
Tampa
Battle, Jean Allen
Cook, Eileen Marie
Dunn, Hampton
Gregory, Patricia Diane
Harkness, Donald Ray
Kent, Richard Vincent
Martin, Dean Frederick
Stearns, Jon Rod
Tinnell, (Marvin) Al(len)
Tompkins, Ralph Joel
Van Spanckeren, Kathryn
Wickstrom, Lois June
Tarpon Springs
Holt, Rochelle Lynn
Pyros, John
Tavares
Prater, Ruby Marian
Temple Terrace
Fuson, Robert Henderson
Titusville
Cummings, Betty Sue
Freeman, Pat S.
Venice
Biniek, Joseph Paul
Briggs, Charlie Irwin
Vero Beach
Martin, Patricia Stone
Moulton, Virginia Nodine
Waldo
Hughes, Walter Jay Sr.
Wesley Chapel
Taylor, Joe W.
West Palm Beach
Gibson, De Marchia
Hardy, C. Colburn
Mainster, Donna Marie
Thomas, Evelyn F.
Wewahitchka
Bass, Eloise
Wilton Manors
Stumpo, Carmine De Rogatis
Winter Park
Blackwell, Linda Christine
Davis, Margaret A.
Winter Springs
Hess, Marie Elizabeth

Georgia
Albany
Champion, Elizabeth Hollis
Sobleskie, Patricia Angela
Alpharetta
Esposito, Donna J.
Snyder, Nancy Ellen
Americus
Alston, Mary Elizabeth
Athens
Andrews, Raymond
Cofer, Judith Ortiz
Coleman, Mary Ann
Corey, Stephen Dale
Gruner, Charles Ralph
Lindberg, Stanley William
Nigro, Felix Anthony
Atlanta
Abugel, Jeffrey
Ali, Shahrazad
Bisher, James Furman
Blankenship, John L.
Browne, Alice Pauline
Byrd, William Aaron, Jr.
Conroy, Donald Patrick
Dorsey, James Wilkinson, Jr.
Drake, Christine Spata
Ferris, Abbott Lamoyne
Gallant, James T.
Galphin, Bruce Maxwell
Gibson, James Riley, Jr.
Hayes, Sarah Hall
Hood, James Byron
Hutchins, Jeane M.
Jurczyk, Irene Donohue
Kristwald-Kallefelz, Elfriede Hildegarde
Martin, Harold Harber
Mellichamp, Josephine Weaver
Mickens, Ronald Elbert
Nelson, Liza
Pryor, Mark Wayne
Purcell, Paul E.
Rubin, Larry Jerome
Sullivan, P(atricia) Lance
Sutherland, Raymond Carter
Vickers, Edward Davin
Warren, James Edward, Jr.
Augusta
Fleming, Berry
Avondale Estates
Carroll, Jane Hammond
Blairsville
Webb, Sharon Lynn
Blakely
Kornegay, Robert Madrid
Carrollton
Yeager, Phyllis Diane
Cave Spring
Muse, Helen Elizabeth
Clarkesville
Luke, Dorothy Rawls
Clarkston
Coker, William R.
Cleveland
Shippey, Juanita Waters
Columbus
Blaker, Charles William
Luckett, Karen Beth
Lummus, Marion Morris
Mc Cumber, Marie Mc Hargue
Riccinto, Patrick John Jr.
Conyers
Raatz, Patricia Anne Tirrell
Cordele
Drinnon, Doris Jean
Crawford
Montgomery, Marion
Dawsonville
Mc Brayer, Nellie K.
Decatur
Austin, Phylis Ann
Hudson, Ellen Matilda
Johnson, Greg
Knight, Nancy Carol
Major, James Russell Richards
Pair, Joyce Morrow
Robb, Thomas Bradley
Worth, Dorothy Janis
Douglasville
Callico, Jeff Scott
Lunsford, M. Rosser
Dublin
Warren, Johnny Wilmer
Dunwoody
Cerny, Janice Louise
East Point
Griffin, Walter
Eastman
Jones, Jack Payne
Epworth
Jones, Ethelene Dyer
Gainesville
Kerley, Gary Lee
Varnum-Gallant, Billie Mae
Gainsville
Oglesby, Theodore Nathaniel Jr.
Griffin
Carter, Curtis Harold, Jr.
Hampton
Wallace, Betty Frances Abernathy
Hapeville
Stebbins, Esther Signe
Jesup
Mosley, Sandra Sherrill
Jonesboro
Skipper, Donald Bruce
LaGrange
Naglee, David Ingersoll
Lawrenceville
Lynn, Thomas Edward
Lilburn
Brock, Jayne
Sewell, Joan Marshall
Lithonia
Sarden, Claudia
Macon
Drinnon, Elizabeth Mccants
Ennis, Lamar Wallace
Jenkins, John Tierce
Jones, Seaborn Gustavus, Jr.
Marietta
Dunwoody, Kenneth Reed
Mc Moy, John H.
Pallotta, Gail Cassady
Martinez
Morgan, Janet Marie Fain
Milledgeville
Lane, Lois M. White
Millen
Waters, Reita Olita Clifton
Norcross
Damon, Constance Tiffany
Maivald, James John
Wasieleski, David Thomas
Oakwood
Strickland, William Bradley
Patteson
Lucas, Ouida La Forrest
Peachtree City
Epps, William David
Quitman
Addison, Era Scott
Rome
Hershey, Jonathan Richard
Wallace, Alfred Leon
Roswell
Kennedy, Sandra Hays
Peterson, Donald Robert
Saint Marys
Kennedy, Bula Bernice
Saint Simons Island
Sanchez, Nancy Eileen
Sandersville
Smith, Wm. Hovey
Savannah
Styles, Teresa Jo
Smyrna
Smith, Harold Lee
Statesboro
Nichols, James Richard
Stone Mountain
Friese, Helen Marie
Morrison, Marvin L.
Newton, James John
Wiseman, Thomas Lynn
Woods, Kenneth
Summerville
Millwood, Pamela Evelyn
Thomasville
Homesley, Horace Edward
Tifton
Tillman, Kayla Linn
Tucker
Stone, John
Valdosta
Davis, Ronald Wayne
Tait, Irene Grayson
Wrightsville
Mc Afee, Virginia Thurston
Young Harris
Moore, Janice Townley
Sellers, Bettie Mixon

Hawaii
Captain Cook
Hoose Quincey, Shelle
Hawaii Honolulu
Kicknosway, Faye
Honalulu
Edel, (Joseph) Leon
Honolulu
Ariyoshi, Rita Clare
Buswink, Anthony Allen
Carr, Albert Bernard
Char, Carlene Mae
Ching, Chauncey T. K.
Chock, Eric Edward
Corsini, Raymond Joseph
Goldsberry, Steven.
Kau, Lawrie Elizabeth
Knowlton, Edgar Colby, Jr.
Kwock, Laureen C.
Lum, Darrell H.Y.
Martin, Robert Bernard
Nakatsuka, Lawrence Kaoru
Newby, Idus Atwell
Porter, Janet Kay
Quagliano, Anthony John
Rho, Lorraine Therese
Sanders, Debra Faye
Schrichte, Dellzell
Sinclair, Marjorie Putnam
Unterecker, John Eugene
Walton, Frank E.
Yim, Vera S. W.
Kailua
Volkart, Edmund Howell
Kailua Kona
Freed, Ray Forrest
Kamuela
Mc Pherson, Michael Mac Kenzie
Rizzuto, James Joseph
Kaneohe
Lindsey, Johanna
Maui
Briley, John Marshall, Jr.
Mililani Town
Allen, James Lovic, Jr.
Na'alehu
Clark, Albert Carl Vernon
Pahoa
Wanrooy, Willem Frederik
Wailuku
Medwid, Stephen
Waipau
Tanouye, Elyse Toshie

Idaho
Boise
Ardinger, Richard Kirk
Chatterton, Roylance Wayne

Crow, Donna Fletcher
Ewing, Jack
Geston, Mark Symington
Hatcher, Robin Lee
Hoot, Patricia Lynch
Longeteig, Iver J.
Lundquist, Richard D.
Marks, Ruth Antoinette
Weinstein, Norman
White, Saxon N.
Williams, Barbara Joann
Caldwell
Gipson, Gordon
Knight, June Elizabeth
Coeur d' Alene
Hutton, Linda Jo
Coeur d'Alene
Mc Leod, James Richard
Emmett
Silva, Joan Yvonne
Fairfield
Reedy, Penelope Michal
Hope
Rolofson, Kristine Nancy
Idaho City
Grimmett, Gerald Glen
Idaho Falls
Janes, Steven M.
Sandifer, Linda Prophet
Spencer, James Richardson
Tetley, Arthur Russell
Ketchum
Wright, Katharine Miranda
Lewiston
Schmadeka, Delores
Wrigley, Robert Alan
Meridian
Balch, Glenn
Dudley, Sherri Denise
Sadler, Norma Jean
Middleton
Kirk, Pearl Louise
Moscow
Warren, Kathleen Janine
Nampa
Mills, Margaret Ann
Parma
Yensen, Arthur
Pocatello
Parker, Barry Richard
Wyndham, Harald P.
Rexburg
Erickson, Donna Mary
Hunter, Donnell Walker
Rigby
Campbell, Patricia Ann
Roberts
Lindstrom, Joyce Leah Evans
Rupert
Jones, Nancy Joy
Sandpoint
Richardson, Linda F.
Tetonia
Commins, Michael William
Twin Falls
Studebaker, William Vern
Walkington, Ethlyn Lindley
Weiser
Fuller, Margaret Cathcart

Illinois
Algonquin
Gardiner, Wayne Jay
Alton
Schlafly, Phyllis Stewart
Altona
Beetler, Dianne Lynn
Anna
Bigler, Mary Jayn
Arlington Heights
Anderson, Joan Wester
Head, Evelyn Harris-Shields
Tidd, Cynthia Ann
Auburn
Knoepfle, John
Aurora
Murr, Danny Lee
Settles, William Frederick
Batavia
Jeffers, Avanella Carmen
Kosinski, Dennis Steven
Beecher
Gold Franke, Paula Christine
Belleville
Chapman, Carolyn Nelson
Jones, Russell Eugene
Berwyn
Miller, Bonnie Mary
Boody
Gault, Seth R.
Bourbonnais
Basu, Tapendu Kumar
Broadview
Barker, Stanley Anthony
Cambridge
Carlson, Lanette Anne
Carbondale
Mohlenbrock, Robert Herman, Jr
Russo, Richard
Shepherd, Gary Kevin
Sprague, Brenda Lee
St. Clair, Philip
Tolley, Tresa Gail
Trescott, Paul Barton
Carol Stream
Lewis, Gregg Allan
Carpentersville
Hopkins, James D.
Miller, Martin Jessee
Cedarville
Parker, Edna Mae
Champaign
Barker, Barry W.
Bridgford, Kim Suzanne
Dowling, James Stephen
Pursifull, Carmen Maria
Rogers, Robert Wentworth
Thomas, Mark Ellis
Charleston
Carr, Gerald Francis
Radavich, David Allen
Chgo
Connelly, Robert Bourke
Silesky, Barry
Chicago
Agnew, Jim
Ahlstroem, G (oesta) W(erner)
Anderson, Mary Jane
Anderson, Annethea Elizabeth
Armah, Ayi Kwei
Arthur, Elizabeth Aldrich
Bard, Susan M.
Barnidge, Mary Shen
Bell, William Joseph
Bellow, Saul
Bennett, Lerone, Jr.
Bernstein, Sidney Ralph
Bevington, David Martin
Bike, William Stanley
Blakely, Robert John
Brannon, Jean Marilyn
Brawley, Paul Holm
Brewer, John Isaac
Brooks, Gwendolyn
Bruce, Debra
Brummel, Mark Joseph
Buchek, Kathleen A.
Bugbee, Helen Louise
Choyke, Phyllis May
Colter, Cyrus
Conn, Sandra
Cooper, Judith
Curry, David Lee
De La Rosa, Edna Elnore
Dikmen, Ned F.
Doherty, John Patrick
Ebert, Roger Joseph
Elitzik, Paul
Esler, William Christopher
Fellowes, Peter
Flory, Joyce V.
Frell, Ellen Frances
Friedberg, Martha A.
Friedrich, Paul William
Gallaher, Cynthia
Gallup, Grant Morris
Gans, Bruce Michael
Gardner, Gerald Faye
Gertz, Elmer
Gilbert, Herman Cromwell
Goetz, John Bullock
Goodwin, Francis Maurice
Graham-Henry, Diane Michelle
Granger, Bill
Greeley, Andrew Moran
Greenberg, Nancy Jean
Greene, Robert Bernard, Jr.
Harmet, A(rnold) Richard
Hellie, Richard
Hemmes, Michael
Highberger, Craig Bender
Ives, Kenneth Holbrook
Johnstone, David Moore
Jones, Richard Andrew
Jones, J. Nicholas
Jones, Peter D'alroy
Jorden, Doris Marie
Jorden, Doris Marie
Kanabus, Henry
Keene, Irene
Kolb, Gwin Jackson
Lach, Alma
Larkin, Emmet
Larson, Daniel William
Leahy, William Joseph
Leavitt, William D.
Lehrman, Nat
Lerman, Albert
Levinsohn, Florence Hamlish
Lewis, Sylvia
Litweiler, John Berkey
Mack, James Melvin
Magida, Phyllis Rose
Mann, Arthur
Marks, Frank Henry
Matthews, Pearl Parkerson
Mc Daniel, Charles-Gene
Mc Gee, Patrick Edgar
Miller, Anita
Miller, James Edwin, Jr.
Miller, Pamela B.
Mills, Ralph Joseph, Jr
Mills, Barbara Kleban
Mitchell, W.J.T.
Moore, Phyllis Lee
Nawrocki, Tom L.
Neugarten, Bernice Levin
Nie, Norman H.
Nims, John Frederick
Nipp, Francis Stuart
Norris, Eileen C.
O'Mara, Deborah Lynn
Overend, Robert Benjamin, Jr.
Panozzo, Michael Edward
Parisi, Joseph (Anthony)
Philipson, Morris
Plotnik, Arthur
Poe, Katrine Laura
Powell, Enid Levinger
Powers, John R.
Prucha, Christine A.
Ramanujan, Molly
Rasmus, John A.
Reed, Sally Ann
Reedy, Jerry Edward
Renshaw, Chalres Clark, Jr.
Reynolds, Pamela C S
Ring, Margaret R.
Rollings, Alane
Rosemont, Franklin
Royko, Mike
Sachs, Edward K.
Salantrie, Frank
Saunders, Doris Evans
Sautter, R. Craig
Sawyers, June
Schmidt, George Neil
Seward, Doyle Adam Jr.
Shulvass, Moses Avigdor (Meyerson)
Sloan, James Park
Solwitz, Sharon Dee
Stern, Richard Gustave
Stewart, Joffre Lamar
Stone, Marie Kirchner
Stuhlman, Daniel D.
Sturdivant, Frederick David
Telser, Lester Greenspan
Terkel, Studs Louis
Tomme, John Carlin
Vertreace, Martha Modena
Walt, Dick K.
Waltz, Jon Richard
Weinberg, Arthur
Weinberg, Lila Shaffer
Weintraub, Joseph
Welsh, S. Patricia
Wildman, Eugene
Wolk, Howard Marvin
Woods, Alfred Lloyd
Yancey, Philip David
Zamora, Maria Helena Paluch
Chicago Heights
Barton, Roger
Clarendon Hills
Craig, Mary Francis Shura
Cyganowski, Carol Klimick
Crystal Lake
Granger, Dennis Lee
Shea, Gerald James
DeKalb
Buehrer, Beverley Bare
Van Steenburgh, Barbara Jean
Deerfield
Andries, Dorothy Delacoma
Haller, Terry
Stupple, Donna-Marie Kathleen
Dekalb
Burchard, Rachael C.
Des Plaines
Ganas, Jane Andrew
Kachmar, Jessie K.
Schuldt, Michael Bruce
DesPlaines
Ashton, Robin G.
Downers Grove
De Vita, Sharon Louise
Feinstein, Robert N (Orman)
Wenzel, Evelyn Maklary
Dundee
Wilson, Delbert Ray
East Peoria
Reed, Dalpha Mae
Edwardsville
Bryant, Tamera Sue
Manning, Lillian O'Neal
Richardson, Betty Joyce
Spurgeon, Dickie Allen
Elburn
Etter, Dave
Elgin

Bayler, Lavon Ann Burrichter
Beers, Victor Gilbert
Cook, David Charles, III
Foster, R(obert) J(ames)
Plazyk, Judy Lynn
Shadwell, Delvenia Gail
Elmhurst
Geannopulos, Nick George
Elmwood Park
O'Brien, John Thomas
Elmwood Pk
Biardo, John Charles
Evanston
Baker, Robert Leon
Bergl, Nancy
Breen, Timothy Hall
Cole, Douglas
Dickson, John
Fox, Edward Inman
Gibbons, (William) Reginald
Graber, Doris Appel
Herbert, Michael Kinzly
Kinzie, Mary
Lipking, Lawrence
Nebel, Henry Martin, Jr.
Northway, Martin
Pritchard, Melissa Brown
Roose, Christina
Seaman, Barbara
Stein, Roberta Katchen
Sussman, Susan
Taylor, Morris
Ver Steeg, Clarence Lester
Ward, Susan Bayer
Wells, Joel Freeman
Weston, Susan B.
Wham, David Buffington
Wills, Garry
Wylie, Kenneth Millar, Jr.
Zweig, Ellen
Evergreen Park
Kuenster, John Joseph
Flossmoor
Bloom, Herbert
Fox Lake
Thurmann, Hollis (Holly Leigh)
Freeport
Putman, Karen Florence
Galena
Eilts, Karin Lynn
Galesburg
Baylor, Murray
Geneva
Nagel, Richard
Gladstone
Weir, Theresa Ann
Glen Ellyn
Agnihotri, Newal K.
Cools, Alta Marie
Mc Kuen, Pamela Dittmer
Glen Flyn
Malone, Michael Patrick
Glencoe
Esarey, Melvin M.
Golin, Milton
Lebovitz, Donna Rudnick
Sabin, Arthur J.
Glendale Heights
Hrascinski, Jo Anne Victoria
Kerner, Deborah Ann
Glendale Hts
Ewald, Heather H.
Glenview
Fleischer, Denise M.
Sherman, Robert T.
Glenwood
Meyer, Clarence
Godfrey
Voils, Georgia Elizabeth
Golconda
Dunning, Ethel Flo
Goreville
Zahra, Susan Gore
Grayslake
Green, Larry Allen
Gurnee
Bodey, Richard Allen
Davis, Marc I.
Hughes, Kim Knox
Hamilton
Graham, Joe Michael
Hawthorn Woods
Mc Comiskey, Bruce Thomas
Hickory Hills
Peyton, Helen E.
Highland Park
Breur, Lester Mons
Feldman, Ruth Duskin
Johnson, Curtis Lee
Kelson, Allen Howard
Locksmith, Joseph Louis
Schmidt, Diane Joy
Tabin, Janet Hale
Wallek, Lee
Hillside
Lommatzsch, Ruth Myrtle
Hinsdale
Kolar, John Joseph
Homewood
Havey, Elizabeth A.
Hoopeston
Moore, Marilyn M.
Jacksonville
Seator, Lynette Hubbard
Jerseyville
Daniels, Gladys Roberta Steinman
Joliet
Belfield, Judith Ann
Miller, Sharon Charlotte
Kenilworth
Mitchell, Maria
Stein, Murray Walter
Kewanee
Bushno, Lila Joan
Kildeer
Collins, Gary Ross
La Grange
Anania, Michael Angelo
Lake Bluff
Whiz, Walter Raimu
Lake Forest
Beck, Joan Wagner
Conway, Alice Frances
Fuller, Mary Margaret Stiehm
Januz, Lauren Robert
Lazar, Paul
Myers, Roger W.
Schulze, Franz, Jr.
Wray, Ronald Edmonds
Lawrenceville
Chunn, Leona Hayes
Lemont
Capek, Antoinette A.
Lewistown
Johnson, Joan E. Stout
Libertyville
Dillmann, Nancy Cameron
Leasure, Janet Lynn
Lincolnwood
Austin, Nancy Elizabeth
Lane, Marc J(ay)
Lisle
Nicholson, Susan Jane Brown
Litchfield
Nelson, Virginia (Gini) L.
Lombard
Walsh, Eileen Cecile
Long Grove
Leeds, Robert X.
Madison
Mc Daniel, Robbie Lee
Mahomet
Rinkel, Margaret Elizabeth
Markham
El, Yusuf Ali
Maywood
Ruffin, Mark Anthony
McHenry
Barton, Colleen
Melrose Park
Valentino, Tina
Moline
Collins, David Raymond
Gerstner, John J.
Morton Grove
Park, Chung I.
Mt Prospect
Hess, Mary Barbara
Mulkeytown
Edwards, Kevin Dale
Mundelein
De Vore, Sheryl Lynn
Roddin, Michael Ian
Naperville
Armstrong, Patricia Kay
Brabec, Barbara
Holloway, Glenna Preston
Kosinsky, Barbara Timm
Phillips, Susan Elizabeth
Raccah, Dominique Marcelle
Niles
Meier, Kay
Normal
Sutherland, Robert D
White, Curtis Keith
Northbrook
Coombe, Jack D.
Huhta, Richard S.
Markham, Marion M.
Williams, Diane
Northfield
Kreader, Barbara Barlow
Oak Lawn
Abusharif, Ibrahim Naseem
Oak Park
Anderson, Paul Dale
Bowman, James Henry
Dominowski, Roger Lynn
Follett, Robert John Richard
Gannello, Alfreda Mavis
Hardy, John Edward
Jacob, John C.
Maxson, Noel Tope
Mines, Jeanette Marie
Murray, Gerald Edward
Sengpiehl, June Shirley
Shaw, Leroy Robert
Webster, Lee
Oakwood
Witsman, Karl Robert
Oswego
Swanson, Laurence Albert
Palatine
Pohl, Frederik
Palestine
Fritchie, Hazel M.
Park City
Poole, Carolyn Ann
Park Forest
Jacobsen, Laura Beth
Putnam, Robert E.
Park Ridge
James, Diane Louise
Soffer, Alfred
Pekin
Wilcox, Mary Ann
Peoria
Farmer, Philip Jose
Orr, Edward Carl
Stauffer, Dorothy Hubbell
Peoria Heights
Grebner, Bernice May Prill
Petersburg
Wesley, Beth Ann (Ann Wesley)
Plainville
Hall, Sandra Jean
Pleasant Plains
Black, Sandra Kay
Quincy
Wilson, Rick D.
Rantoul
Bergamino-Frey, Gina Marie
Richton Park
Godbout, Pamela Sue
River Forest
Heimburger, Donald James
Saunders, Catherine Ruggie
Rochester
Ross, Dorthy Marcussen
Rock Island
Carter, Erskine
Rockford
Diamond, Olivia Harriet
Hartje, Judy Ann
Mc Millan, Karen Alice
Velasco, Kathy Lynn
Rolling Meadows
Fisher, Hal Dennis
Leece, William Joseph
Regnier, Stephen Joseph
Roselle
Lassiter, Isaac Steele
Sandwich
Heller, Janet Ruth
Schaumburg
Rogers, Donald Joseph
Sheridan
Fuchs, Laurel Bernice
Sherrard
Walkowicz, Chris J.
Sidney
Kerr, Kathryn Ann
Skokie
Darack, Arthur J.
Gerstner, Lillian Polus
Henry, Marguerite
Kellman, Jerold L.
Pelzer, David Alan
Sleepy Hollow
Rabe, Berniece Louise
Springfield
Bartlett, Byron Allan
Browning, Tamara Nadine
Schneider, Virginia Dee
St. Charles
Holinger, Richard
Staunton
Kuethe, Peggy Sue
Yakos, Barbara Verlee
Sterling
Brooks, Terry
Stump, Call Alden
Streamwood
Warrick, James Gordon
Streator
Gross, Marilyn Agnes
Sycamore
Plucker, Charlotte Ann
Taylorville
Crites, Dorothy Adele
Griffin, Rachel
Tinley Park
Franzen, Richard B.
Yoder, Eileen Rhude
Tuscola
Porter, Harlan David
Urbana
Bial, Raymond Steven
Chamberlain, Donald William
Friedman, Paul Alan

Haile, H. G.
Hale, Allean Lemmon
Lieberman, Laurence
Osgood, Charles Egerton
Schacht, Richard Lawrence
Schlipf, Frederick A.
Van Walleghen, Michael J(ospeh)
Warenville
Schanstra, Carla Ross
Warrenville
Sennett, John Patrick
Wataga
Mc Curry, James Patrick
Westchester
Weglarz, Terri Marie
Wheaton
Long, Charles Franklin
Muck, Terry Charles
Walsh, Loren Melford
Wheeling
Stewart, June Gary
Wilmette
Appel, Alfred, Jr.
Brindel, June Rachuy
Nash, Jay Robert III
Olsztynski, James C.
Richter, Frank
Yu, Timothy Pan
Winfield
Kliebhan, Jerome L.
Winnetka
Adorjan, Carol Madden
Giffin, Mary Elizabeth
Mc Manus, James
Rauterkus, Mark
Woodridge
Wagner, John
Yates City
Edwards, Linda Ann
Zion
Beem, Jane A.
Jenkins, Jerry Bruce

Indiana

Kerrigan, (Thomas) Anthony
Anderson
Jenkins, Glenna Glee
Bath
Arthur, Elizabeth
Bauer, Steven Albert
Bennington
Kern, Ellyn R.
Beverly Shores
Ruzic, Neil Pierce
Bloomington
Barnstone, Willis
Barton, Thomas Frank, Sr.
Byrnes, Robert Francis
Cecil, Richard Thomas
Dorr, James Suhrer
Ferrell, Robert Hugh
Frommer, Sara Hoskinson
Jacobi, Peter Paul
Mc Graw, Erin
Mitchell, Roger
Pfingston, Roger Carl
Phillips, Michael Joseph
Purcell, Royal
Sanders, Scott Russell
Sebeok, Thomas Albert
Serpento, B. James
Silveus, Mari L.
Stanton, Maura
Thom, James Alexander
Westfall, Richard Samuel
Whitley, Mary Ann
Wilkerson, Michael N.
Brook
Hoffman, Daniel Paul
Campellsbury
Blazek, Joseph Lawrence
Carmel
Williams, Bill
Centerville
Bailey, Jackson Holbrook
Chesterton
Petrakis, Harry Mark
Columbus
Smith, Jeff David
Crown Point
Diddle, Deborah Kay
Daleville
Koontz, Thomas Wayne
Dublin
Callis, Victoria D.
Elkhart
Bartlett, Bruce Allen
Gilbert, Christina Ida
Mc Coy, Easton Whitney
Schmidt, Andrea Gertrud
Evansville
Durham, Marilyn Jean (Wall)
Humpert, John E.
Mc Cutchan, Kenneth Peva
Moriarty, Morgan Johanna
Thomas, Gregory E.
Floyds Knobs
Andrews, Billy F.
Fort Wayne
Briegel, William Eugene
Elliott, Joyce Whitehead
Novak, Robert Lee
Frankfort
Milon, Ella Mae
Gary
Balog, Betty Enocksen
Bennett, Patricia Ann Work
Goshen
Swartley, David Warren
Grabill
Rostky, Duane A. (Dewey Roth)
Greenfield
Hoover, Jesse Wilbert
Greenwood
Wheeler, Daniel Scott
Hammond
Black, Harry George
Kacoha, Margie
White, Joan Ellen
Henryville
Wininger, Deborah Kay
Highland
Bourne, Daniel Carter
Hobart
Ammer, Donald Scott
Macchia, Donald Dean
Indianapolis
Albright, Nancy Eggelhof
Benjamin, Robert L.
Best, Mary Sue
Born, Emily Marie
Buchwald, Sara P.
Couts, Shirley Ashley
Dwyer, Nancy Jean
Evans, Mari
Friman, Alice
Johnson, Ora Mae
Leary, Edward Andrew
Lutholtz, M William
Mason, David Stewart
Meister, Shirley Vogler
Moore, Ercelle
Ragan, Roy Allen
Ramsey, Frank B.
Rasley, Alicia Todd
Riggs, Lynn Spencer
Snow, Robert Lawrence
Sprague, William Leigh
Travis, R(osemarie) L.
Vaughn, James Michael
Wallerstedt-Wehrle, Joanna Katherine
Wernle, Helen Abigail
Williamson, Gerald Neal
Wright, Charlotte Hughes
Indpls
Carter, Jared
Kokomo
Blacklidge, Richard Henry
Gilstad, June Russell
La Porte
Miller, Marguerite Elizabeth
LaPorte
Chesrow, Cathleen Gwen
Lafayette
Hamilton, Rosemary Ann
Lawrenceburg
Gondosch, Linda Ann
Madison
Alphin, Elaine Marie
Hensley, Joe L.
Ries, Richard Raymond
Townsend, Guy Mannering
Monticello
Blanchette, Rita T. Billings
Mount Vernon
Sorenson, Sharon O.
Muncie
Elliott, Margaret (Peg) Johnson
Hayashi, Tetsumaro
Mathis-Eddy, Darlene Fern
Richey, Rodney Paul
Weathersby, George Byron
New Delhi
Seth, Vikram
New Palestine
Van Scyoc, Linda Ja *Noblesville*
Williams, Ruth Arlene
Notre Dame
Christman, Elizabeth A.
Nugent, Walter Terry King
O'Rourke, William Andrew
Rice, (Ethel) Ann
Plainfield
Bill, J(ohn) Brent
Plymouth
Applegate, Debra Annette
Moore, Roberta Lynn
Reaker, Beth Ann
Portage
Pilac, Pamela Ann
Richmond
Fell, Mary Elizabeth
Rockville
Carrington, Elizabeth Ellen
Shelbyville
Losey, Jeanne K.
South Bend
Gernes, Sonia Grace
Plantinga, Alvin
Smith, Jane Davis
Vasta, Edward
Stilesville
Burdsall, Clarice W.
Swayzee
Moorman, Rosemary Lucille
Terre Haute
Edwards, Helen Jean
Weixlmann, Joseph Norman
Valparaiso
Blake, Robert James
Olson, Lynn
Veedersburg
Immel, Mary Blair
Velpen
Lemond, Alan Roy
West Baden
Tolbert, Cledith Cassidy
West Lafayette
Boruch, Marianne
Garfinkel, Alan
Gottfried, Leon Albert
Smith, R(obert) E., Jr.
Stafford, William Talmadge
Wolcott
James, Frank William

Iowa

Albia
Faber, Inez Mc Alister
Ames
Carmen, Marilyn Elaine
Fox, Karl August
Hathaway, Kathy R. Moore
Martone, Michael
Nakadate, Neil Edward
Paradis, Philip M.
Pett, Stephen
Silag, Bill
Swander, Mary Lynch
Ankeny
Naylor, Lois Anne Mc Crea
Schnepf, Max Owen
Bloomfield
Runkle, Mary Arvella
Cambridge
Colvin, Thomas Stuart
Cedar Falls
Klinkowitz, Jerome
Mc Graw, Karen Kay
Salterberg, Susan Kay
Wilson, Robley Conant, Jr.
Witt, Sandra Lea
Cedar Rapids
Carlson, Wendell R.
Murray, John Joseph
Sherer, Billee Jean
Young, Elisabeth Larsh
Central City
Hendricks, Kathleen
Charles City
Davis, A. Jann
Krieger, Theodore Kent
Cherokee
Schleef, Helen Ida
Council Bluffs
Everhart, Robert Phillip
Creston
Christian, Rebecca Anne
Cumberland
Pearce, Floyd Earl
Davenport
Kelleher, James P.
Mc Donald, Julie J.
Nickolas, George Tom
Savoie, Terrence Maurice
Decorah
White, Mary Jane
Des Moines
Amice, Carol Rizzardi
Bryant, David Ernest
Burns, Stuart L
Canfield, Joan Giltner
Clinton, Dorothy Louise
Doty, Ruth
Gildner, Gary
Hirsch, Mary Tone
Miller, Maureen
Moore, Virginia Blanck
Newgaard, Patricia Ann
Tarnopolsky, Rafael
Willoughby, Doris Mellott
Wind, Marlise Wabun
Dubuque
Tigges, John Thomas
Woerdehoff, Valorie Anne
Elkader
Walke, Julia Annette
Fairfield
Kremer, John Frederick

Forest City
Rollefson, Anna Mae Maxine
Gilman
Webb, James Edward
Hudson
Pellett, Kent Louis
Indianola
Lieber, Tood Michael
Iowa City
Aydelotte, William Osgood
Becker, Leslee Ann
Buchan, Vivian Eileen
Campion, Daniel Ray
Engle, Paul Hamilton
Gerber, John Christian
Holland, Stephen Thomas
Johnson, Nicholas
Kottick, Gloria
Longinovic, Tomislav Z.
Mc Cullough, Ken
Mc Pherson, James Allen
Miller, Jane Ruth
Morice, David Jennings
Penick, John Edgar
Rogers, Thomas N.r.
Sayre, Robert Freeman
Sklar, Morty E.
Spires, Elizabeth
Vernon, David Harvey
Weinstein, Rocio Aitania
Wilder, John Richard
Zimmer, Paul J.
Zukin, Jane
Johnston
Gorden, Nancy D.
Kamrar
Losure, Joyce Nelma
Keokuk
Smith, Donnetta Kay
Knoxville
Rank, Maureen Joy
Marengo
Almquist, Mary Rebecca
Mason City
Hendrickson, Carol Follmuth
Moravia
Baty, Vicki Louise
Mount Etna
Sparks, (Theo) Merrill
Moville
Ceynar, Marvin Emil
Nashua
Nebel, Laurie Jean
New Sharon
Roets, Lois Schelle
Oskaloosa
Wormhoudt, Arthur Louis
Pella
Ratzlaff, Keith Alan
Polk City
Drumm, Chris
Raymond
Knudslien, Dewey Victor
Rolfe
Block, Janet Lou
Sergeant Bluff
Johnston, Carole Anne
Shenandoah
Hensleigh, Sarah Esther
Morgans, James Patrick
Sioux Center
Schaap, James Calvin
Stanley
Ingamells, Julia Irene
Victor
Rohrer, Lila Borg
Vinton
Almquist, Sharon Kristina
Wadena
Cavaiana, Mabel
Washington
Leyden, Joan Marie
West Branch
Dennis, (mary) Ruth
Duer, David Edward
West Burlington
Bied, Dan
Wever
Carlson, Arthur Bruce
Wheatland
De Wulf, Kathryn Colleen
Dillon, Debra Jean
Winterset
Hanson, Dick Vincent

Kansas
Leawood Rd
Schudy, Patricia Hellin
Ashland
Mercer, Ethel Viola
Atwood
Kane, William L.
Berryton
Herrmann, Duane Lawrence
Dodge City
Hubbs, Galen Jay
Downs
Smith, Bernita Louise
El Dorado
Sullivan, Gladys Ann
Ellsworth
Belton, Betty Rose
Emporia
Coldsmith, Don(ald Charles)
Scheel, Mark W.
Fairway
Trudeau, Garry B.
Garden
Nichols, Sarah How-Ree
Gardner
Morrison, Susan Gaynelle
Goddard
Hinson, Jerry Lee
Goodland
Stinnette, Carlene Rosalee
Haviland
Jay, Thelma Gertrude Allen
Hays
Weigel, Alice M.
Hiawatha
Barnes, Jerry Neal
Hutchinson
Buzbee, Richard Edgar
Independence
Carroll, Judith Ann
Tranbarger, Ossie Elmo
Kansas City
Mann, Richard Dale
Scott, Jonnie Melia Dean
Kiowa
Brown, Jean Mc Brayer
Lawrence
Burnham, Crispin Reed
Collins, Joseph Thomas
Doty, Carolyn House
Gunn, James Edwin
Low, Denise Lea
Navon, Robert
Orel, Harold
Salkind, Neil Joseph
Seaver, James Everett
Smetzer, Michael Bernie
Wedge, George Francis, III
Worth, George John
Leavenworth
Cherry, Ethel Johnnson
Novak, Michael Paul
Leonardville
Sikes, Shirley Ruth
Lindsborg
Oman, Elizabeth Ann
Peterson, Chester, Jr.
Maize
Bliss, Ronald Gene
Manhattan
Clift, G.W.
Dept Eng Kans State U, Stewart
Fateley, William Gene
Higham, Robin
Holden, Jonathan
Moses, William Robert
Ponte, Joseph Gonsalves Jr.
McPherson
Holloway, Judy A.
Meade
Stacy, Pauline French
Milford
Moore, Nancy Lorene
Newton
Girard, James Preston
Olathe
Wilcox, Laird Maurice
Oskaloosa
Brumme, Marjorie Vivian
Ottawa
Reiter, Lora K.
Westrum, Dexter
Overland Park
Burger, Henry G.
Carter, William Jay
Grimshaw, Thomas Drysdale
Overland Pk
Sharat Chandra, G.S.
Phillipsburg
Berney, Betty Lou
Pittsburg
De Gruson, Gene
Heffernan, Michael Joseph
Meats, Stephen
Schick, James Baldwin Mc Donald
Prairie Village
Clouston, Judith Kay
Severy
Drummond, La Vena May
Shawnee Mission
Bernstein, Mashey Maurice
Peck, Marie Johnston
Stemme, Fred George
St John
Hathaway, Michael Jerry
Sterling
Buckman, Repha Joan
Topeka
Averill, Thomas Fox
Crader, Rebecca Jane
Daniels, Celia Annette
Franklin, Miriam Anna
Harvey, Dorothy May
Mallory, Aileen Lucile
Nichols, Elizabeth L.
Pederson, Cynthia Sue
Tremmel, Robert Arnold
Wamego
Raines, Kathleen Jane
Wichita
Cloud, David Eugene
Cutler, Bruce
Francis, Betty Joe
Harrison, Edna (Lucella) Brigham
Klaassen, Carol S.
Lightburn, Jeffrey Caldwell
Mechem, James Harlan
Montgomery, Cathie Marion
Sobin, Anthony

Kentucky
Ashland
Chere Lynn, Stewart
Berea
Barker, Garry G.
Betsy Layne
Hall, Aileen
Bowling Green
Hall, Betty Kathleen
Miller, Jim Wayne
Minton, John Dean
Cadiz
Wilson, Wilburn Martin
Catlettsburg
Smith, Sharon Kay
Crescent Springs
Crout, Teresa Elizabeth Kochmar
East Bernstadt
Tischler, Monte Maurice
Faubush
Johnson, Mary Lou
Florence
Barth, R(obert) L(awrence)
Fort Thomas
Rhode, Robert Thomas
Frankford
Baker, Joseph Edward
Frankfort
Richey, Bruce Radford
Scott, Walter Ray
Stone, Susan Gail
Stone, Michael Robert
Georgetown
Emmons, Marguerite Atteberry
Hartford
Johnson, Robert Thomas
Hodgenville
O'Dell, Mary Ernestine
Hopkinsville
Dean, Cynthia Bailey
Hyden
Lewis, Judy Jones
Jeffersontown
Koppel, Sheree Powers
Lebanon
Jordan, Paul Richard
Lebanon Junction
Mc Cafferty, Barbara Taylor
Lexington
Black, Creed Carter
Bush, John Charles
Davenport, Guy Mattison
Hollingsworth, Kent
Kerfoot, Glenn Warren
Lyon, George Ella
White, Susan Waltz
Worley, Jeff Robert
Louisville
Bingham, Sallie
Blake, Jane Salley
Davenport, Gwen
Freibert, Lucy M.
Hammon, Arthur Christopher
Hollander, Ella H.
Hughes, Patricia Saddler
Jonas, Ann
Miller, Louis Adam
Morris, Marna Jay
Nash, Alanna K.
Naslund, Alan Joseph
Richardson, Ken Edgar
Schardein, Sandra Wild (Kath Selby)
Tippett, Virginia Monroe
Madisonville
Arnold, Edgar Frank, Jr.
Mayfield
Rice, Patricia Anne
Murray
Lorrah, Jean
Turner, Carolyn Ann
Paducah
Henderson, Kathleen Hayden
Paris
Crump, Judy Gail
Park Hills

Black, Brady Forrest
O'Connor, Dennis Patrick
Port Royal
Berry, Wendell
Prestonsburg
Lowe, Douglas Hayse
Richmond
Branson, Branley Allen
Burkhart, Robert Edward
Siegel, Carolyn Lee
Sutton, Dorothy Moseley
Salem
Stegall, Pauline M
Science Hill
Spaw, June
Thornton
Collins, Jenny Lou Galloway
Trappist
Hart, Patrick Joseph
Waynesburg
Hamilton, Doris Jean
Williamsburg
Nelson-Humphries, Tessa
Olsen, Humphrey Adoniram
Wilmore
Frese, Millie Kay

Louisiana
Avondale
Laird, Elizabeth W.
Baker
Dawson, George Amos
Baton Rouge
Biggers, Ann Peeples
Codrescu, Andrei
Crawford, Gary William
Dobbs, Rosalyne Brown
Fogel, Daniel Mark
Kamenetz, Rodger Lee
Kelly, Mary Jo
Lane, Pinkie Gordon
Madden, David
Meriwether, Nell W.
Meyerer, Margaret Christine
Mistric, Mary Ann
Olney, James
Owen, Sue Ann
Phillabaum, Leslie Ervin
Raby, Elaine Miller
Stanford, Donald Elwin
Wallace, Lew Gerald
BatonRouge
East, Charles
Boyce
Upton, Robert Chapman, Jr.
Carencro
Gallassero, Hilda Kilmer
Chalmette
Molero, Wilson Joseph
Church Point
Daigle, Pierre Varmon
Eunice
Matt, Linda Ann
Franklinton
Aycock, Don Milton
Gretna
Montelius, Susan Ann
Hammond
Nesom, Ruth Evelyn
Homer
Signer, Billie Touchstone
Houma
Malbrough, Ray Thomas
Jefferson
Cooley, Peter John
Mosier, John
Rizzuto, Sharida Ann
Lafayette
Edmonds, David Carson
Nolan, Paul Thomas
Webb, Bernice Larson
Lake Charles
Butler, Robert Olen
German, Norman
Nelson, Curtis Scott
Stokesbury, Leon
Lockport
Le Blanc, Joy Comeaux
Metairie
Ales, Beverly Gloria
Clement, Gregory Vance
Shannon, Don Michael
Strevinsky, Christine Maria
Monroe
Brown, Charline Hayes
Dunnihoo, Dale Russell
Herrington, Terri
Mcdougall, Jo Garot
Rowe, Myra
New Iberia
Raphael, Morris Charles
Thornton, Donald Ray
New Orleans
Adamo, Ralph
Assensoh, Akwasi B.
Barton, Fredrick Preston
Beeler, Myrton Freeman
Biguenet, John Joseph
Bonner, Thomas, Jr.
Brosman, Catharine Savage
Corrington, John William
Dalton, Louisiana
Fennelly, Tony
Gery, John Roy Octavius
Griffin, Emilie Russell Dietrich
Grue, Lee Meitzen
Hannon, Brian Owens
Henricksen, Bruce Conley
Holditch, W. Kenneth
Jacobsen, Norman Howard
Jacobson, Sid
Joseph, Fred, Jr.
Mc Ferren, Martha Dean
Murphy, Kay Ann
Pernoll, Martin Lester
Pizer, Donald
Speer, Garry Wayne
Villarrubia, Jan (Martha)
Whalen, Thomas Douglas
Pineville
Dufour, Darlene
Ponchatoula
Gautreaux, Tim Martin
Ragley
Young, Gloria Rose
Ruston
Ramsey, Michael Kirby
Saint Landry
Blood, Opal Sue
Shreveport
Ewing, Sondra Darlene
Meacham, Arthur Paul
Sulphur
Wise, Erbon Wilbur
hreveport
Brandt, Andrew Curtis

Maine
Augusta
Mc Kenna, James A., III
Tapley, Lance E.
Vanderweide, Harry
Bangor
Zehring, John William
Bath
Hayes, James Russell
Longley, Diane Gene
Belfast
Porter, Bern
Rimm, Virginia Mary
Bowdoinham
Stanley, Charles J.
Brunswick
Coursen, H. R.
Dodd, Anne Wescott
Koller, James Anthony
Camden
Dareff, Hal
Simon, Jo Ann (Joanna Campbell)
Struckhoff, Roger Stephen
Thomas, (Charles) Davis
Canton
Goodine, Francena White
Cape Elizabeth
Deming, Alison Hawthorne
Casco Village
Dibner, Martin
Castine
Booth, Philip
Hoople, Sally Crosby
Mc Carthy, Mary
Damariscotta
Chaney, Debora Anne
Dresden
Bolte, Charles Guy
East Holden
Pollet, Sylvester
Eastport
Mc Hugh, Heather
Ellsworth
Stocking, Marion Kingston
Farmington
Ross, Leona Curtis
Freedom
Brugger, Heidi Nack
Gardiner
Lyons, Richard E.
Gouldsboro
Walsh, Abigail Margaret
Hancock Point
Bell, Harrison Bancroft
Harrington
Lipton, William Lawrence
Harrison
Chase, Otta Louise
Lewiston
Tagliabue, John
Litchfield
Krupinsky, Jacquelyn Stowell
Macwahoc
Watters, Merelyn Jacqueta
Mexico
Farrington, Esther Elizabeth
Mexico City
Benjamin, Robert
Milbridge
Enslin, Theodore Vernon
Ford, Elaine
Moody
Gerald, John Bart
N Vassalboro
Sadoff, Ira
New Harbor
Morrison, April Dawn
New Sharon
Kruchkow, Diane
Nobleboro
Lawless, Gary Cameron
Northeast Harbor
Hansen, Gunnar
Orland
Grenfell, Clarine Coffin
Orono
Simpson, Geddes Wilson
Phippsburg
Mc Lanathan, Richard
Portland
Benington, George Beaubien
Gesner, Elsie Miller
O'Brien, Katharine
Preston, John
Sholl, Elizabeth (Betsy) Neary
Rangeley
Behrman, Daniel
Rumford
Fallon, Tom
South Casco
Benjamin, Mary Lynn
Stockton Springs
Carpenter, William
Thomaston
Olmsted, Robert Walsh
Thorndike
Loeb, Timothy Allan
Waldoboro
Creeley, Robert White
Waterville
Keim, Kathie Marie
Weld
Stevens, C(lysle) J(ulius)
West Peru
Davis, Gregory Todd
Wilton
Emerson, Kathy Lynn
York Beach
Foerster, Richard A.
York Harbor
Smith, Mark Richard

Maryland

Purdon, Eric Sinclaire
Adelphi
Wamaling, Mark Hunter
Annapolis
Crandall, Gilbert Albert
Oppenheim, Lucy Linda
Tapper, Joan Judith
Baltimore
Barth, John Simmons
Bell, Madison Smartt
Berrigan, Philip Francis
Blank, Franklin
Brandt, Edward Newman, Jr.
Clay, Diskin
Dixon, Stephen
Dunn, Jonah Marshall
Epstein, Daniel Mark
Frasier, Thomas Daniel
Goodwin, Bill, Jr.
Govig, Valerie Cowls
Gragasin, Jose Valliente
Green, Jean Susanne
Himes, Geoffrey
Kanigel, Robert
Kenner, William Hugh
Lamberg, Walter Jerome
Livingstone, Harrison Edward
Lord, Walter
Murray, Lee Winslow
Rector, Liam
Reynolds, Benjamin James
Rosenburg, Robert Kemper
Silverman, Albert James
Stahler, Charles
Strausbaugh, John R.
Sullivan, William Joseph
Tansill, Mel
Taylor, James Robert, III
Truesdell, Clifford Ambrose III
Tyler, Anne
Vernon, Harriet Dorothy
Walker, Wilbert Lee
Wasserman, Debra
Zebley, Joseph Wildman Jr.
Berkshire
Puglisi, Angela Aurora
Bethesda
Arlen, Gary O'Hara
Beveridge, George David Jr.

Breggin, Peter Roger
Cornish, Edward Seymour
Goldberg, Barbara June
Jellema, Rod(erick) Hartigh
Joseph, Frank Samuel
Larkin, Mary Ann
Lefcowitz, Barbara F.
Lystad, Mary Hanemann
Manheim, Jarol B(ruce)
Martineau, Francis (Frank) Edward
Morris, Elizabeth J.
Mujica, Barbara Louise
Naylor, Phyllis Reynolds
Neumann, Robert Gerhard
Peabody, Richard Myers
Phillips, Kevin Price
Ross-Breggin, Virginia (Ginger) Faye
Sulkin, Sidney
Tolchin, Martin
Wexler, Philip
Braddock Heights
Wirths, Claudine Gibson
Brandywine
Dougherty, Jay Edwin
California
Cihlar, Christine Carol
Camp Springs
Barlow, Lolete Falck
Catonsville
Gloria Catherine, Oden
Centreville
Robinett, Robena Delite
Charlotte Hall
Foster, Grace Elizabeth
Chester
Dalrymple, Ronald Gerald
Dalrymple, Ronald Gerald
Chevy Chase
Alenier, Karren Lalonde
Bacon, Donald Conrad
Barbiero, Daniel C.
Breitman, Richard D(avid)
Darr, Ann Russell
Fluty, Steven Jay
Gomery, Douglas
Grigg, William
Harney, Kenneth Robert
Levine, Herbert Malcolm
Marine, Michael Ray
O'Rourke, Lawrence Michael
Rogers, Robert Willis
Wechsler, Jill
College Park
Moses, Claire Goldberg
Panichas, George Andrew
Winton, Calhoun
Colora
Merrill, Joan Carolyn
Columbia
Beckenstein, Myron
Venn, Jonathan
Wolf, Virginia Simmons
Crofton
Klyman, Anne Griffiths
Crownsville
Boetig, Donna Byrnes
Cumberland
Young, Mary Louise
Ellicott City
Kress, Agnes Irene
Neil, Fred Applestein
Testerman, Jean Leighton
Emmitsburg
Grisez, Germain G.
Fort Washington
Peele, Roger
Frederick
Gordon, Paul Perry
Hummer, Paul Jacob, Jr.
Frostburg
Bramann, Jorn K.
Gaithersburg
Blate, Samuel Robert
Classon, Louise Laurette
Conroy, Cathryn Devan
Fickling, Amy Leigh
Fratz, Donald Dougals
Germantown
Hoof, David Lorne
Moline, Judith Ann
Glen Arm
Kauffmann, Lane
Glen Burnie
Smith, Debbi Lynn
Glyndon
Worrall, Margaret Howard
Grantsville
Bender, Esther Louise
Greenbelt
Carrington, Grant Clark
Hagerstown
Coffen, Richard Wayne
Hancock
Knox, Ann Brewer
Highland
Comberiate, Josephine Bertolini
Thorman, Richard
Hyattsville
Bode, Carl
Kerr, Walter H.
Rodgers, Mary Columbro
Indian Head
McGuigan, Kathleen Bailey
Jessup
Poellot, Raymond Albert
Kensington
Raffa, Joseph
Ricketts, Mary Jane Gnegy
Kirksville
Hickman, Irene
Lanham
Bussey, Charles David
Laurel
Gregory, Josephine Lane
Scheidhauer, Lynn Irene
Lutherville
Berman, Edgar Frank
Monkton
Booth, Diane Elizabeth
Mount Airy
Chaffee, C. David
Mount Rainier
Inman, Peter T.
New Carrollton
Reno, Susan Bennekemper
Oakland
Parker, Iola B.
Owings Mills
Holdridge, Barbara
Oxon Hill
Atwater, Richard Merlin
Potomac
Daniels, George Goetz
Derricotte, Toi M.
Jason, Philip Kenneth
Molitor, Graham Thomas Tate
Pastan, Linda
Rohrbach, Peter Thomas
Valuchek, Andrew J.
Randallstown
Sachs, Blanche
Reisterstown
Franz, Jeffrey Brian
Silver-Lillywhite, Eileen
Rockville
Absolon, Karel B.
Bennett, Gary Lee
Benson, Clara Mays
Braden, Dennis Ray
Broderick, John Caruthers
Floyd, Camille Maxine
Hegyeli, Ruth Ingeborg Johnsson
Hoover, Carol Faith
Kruger, Mollee (Coppel)
Siegel, Martin
Willis, Judith Laura Levine
Wilson, Marolyn Caldwell
Saint Mary's City
Glaser, Michael S.
Salisbury
Rickards, Catherine Isabella
Silver Spring
Armitage, Barri June
Avery, Helen Palmer
Banes, Daniel
Biggs, Wellington Allen
Boone, Lalia Phipps
Cotterill, Sarah L.
Kessel, Jeffrey Brian
Lasky, Janet Louise
Llediaith, Rhiannon Marie
Mooney, James Hugh
Popkin, Roy Sandor
Ulrich, Homer
Vaughn, Phoebe Juanita
Whitten, Leslie Hunter, Jr.
Willard, Timothy Holmes
Silver spring
Mercer, Linda Lou
Sparks
Freehling, William Wilhartz
St. Michael's
Michener, James Albert
Sykesville
Leister, Mary Mcfarland
Takoma Park
Joy, Perihan Dursun
Ladenheim, Kala Evelyn
Orr, Elaine L.
Temple Hills
Grogan, Earlean Stanley
Towson
Diorio, Margaret Toarello
Eveleth, Janet Stidman
Lott, Clarinda Harriss
Waldorf
Rivera, Vicki Laura
Wheaton
Hotz, Herman

Massachusetts
Allston
Mark, Angela S.
Standing, Sue
Amesbury
Donavel, David Frank
Amherst
Acze, Tamas
Clayton, John J.
Cuomo, George (Michael)
Darling, William Ritchie
Demott, Benjamin Hailer
Fetler, Andrew
Gow, Ellen B.
Katzenbach, John Strong Miner
Langland, Joseph Thomas
Lester, Julius B.
Michelson, Richard
Mcclung, Robert M(arhall)
Neugeboren, Jay
Partee, Barbara Hall
Pettit, Michael Edwin
Strong, Bethany J.
Wier, Dara
Andover
Hall, Ann Louise
Wise, K. Kelly
Arlington
Mc Intyre, Cathryn
Velten, Kathleen Ann
Zuckerman, Marilyn
Athol
Young, Allen
Auburndale
Lindgren, Charlotte Holt
Stein, Dona Luongo
Barnstable
Bunnell, Paul Joseph
Barre
Sullivan, James Edward
Bedford
Kennedy, X.J.
Mendelsohn, Jack
Schmuhl, Marian Hobbs
Belchertown
Ruhl, Steven
Belmont
Fowler, Anne Carroll
Moore, Harrison Lyman
Moore, Mark Harrison
Moore, Richard
Ruocchio, Patricia Jeanne
Berkshire
Smith, David Lionel
Billerica
Merrill, Tom
Bolton
Aastrup, Rondi Suzanne
Boston
Alabiso, Angelo
Angelou, Maya
Battin, Wendy J.
Bell, James Adrian
Cassells, Cyrus Curtis
Davison, Peter Hubert
Dellinger, David
Elliott, Thomas Morrow
Fallows, James Mackenzie
Fast, Howard
Fein, Leonard
Galvin, Maryanne
Gibson, Barry Joseph
Gold, Ivan
Hebbard, Neysa Stanley
Holaday, Susan Mirles
Infante, Christine Marie
Karagianis, Maria Elizabeth
Kaufman, Amy Rebecca
Kikel, Rudy John
Kinsman, Lawrence Charles
Lourie, Dick
Macauley, Robie Mayhew
Manuel, Frank Edward
Mason, Charles Ellis III
Morton, Anne Marie Judith
Nottle, Diane
O'Dell, Scott
O'Dell, Scott
O'donnell-Leach, Karen
O'Kirwan, Seamus
Peterfreund, Stuart Samuel
Pynchon, Thomas
Robbins, Tom
Roby, Kinley Edmund
Sargeant, Nancy Reardon
Spahl, Gary Michael
Sultan, Stanley
Teagan, Mark Tilden
Terrill, Ross Gladwin
Wakefield, Dan
Welch, John Butler
Wiesel, Elie
Zagrodnik, Diane Jeanne
Boxford
Hennessy, Madeleine Joyce
Bradford
Glasser, Perry
Brighton
Gregory, Carolyn Holmes
Brockton

Verrette, Louise Madeleine
Wise, Edmund Allen Jr.
Brookline
Arrowsmith, William Ayres
Beatty, Jack J.
Brox, Eleanor Andrea
Burack, Sylvia E. Kamerman
Cann, Rachel P.
Connors, Thomas E.
Digges, Deborah Lea
Epstein, Leslie Donald
Erick, Miriam A.
Goldwyn, Robert M.
Greene, Bette
Harakas, Stanley Samuel
Ice, Ruth
Jack, Alex
Radford, Richard Francis, Jr.
Vendler, Helen Hennessy
Weiner, Myron
Buzzards Bay
Margeson, Hector
Cambridge
Abt, Clark C(laus)
Alazraki, Jaime
Alexander, Pamela
Alfred, William
Aronson, Michael Andrew
Ayer, Anne
Barnes, Jane Ellen
Bartkowech, Raymond A.
Bate, Walter Jackson
Bernays, Anne
Bonina, Mary
Brustein, Robert Sanford
Buckholts, Claudia
Chase, Naomi Feigelson
Clausen, Wendell Vernon
Collins, Martha
Davis, Hope Hale
Der Hovanessian, Diana
Engel, Monroe
Erickson, David Burdette
Farren, Pat
Feldman, Ruth (Wasby)
Galbraith, John Kenneth
Gardner, Geoffrey
Gilbert, Celia
Goodman, William Beehler
Hamilton, Elissa Lynn Alkoff
Haviaras, Stratis
Hyde, Lewis
Janeway, Michael Charles
Jenks, Carolyn Boyd
Kaplan, Justin
Kearney, Lawrence Michael
Lant, Jeffrey Ladd
Leland, Christopher Towne
Lyon, David William
Mattill, John Isham
May, Ernest Richard
Mazlish, Bruce
Mazur, Gail Beckwith
Mc Wey, Michael
Millman, Lawrence B.
O'Neil, Wayne
Pawlak, Mark Joseph
Pipes, Richard Edgar
Raymond, Monica E.
Schreiber, Ron
Sekler, Eduard Franz
Siever, Raymond
Thernstrom, Stephan Albert
Vernon, Raymond
Vogt, Evon Zartman, Jr.
White, Harrison Colyar
Canton
Donchess, Barbara M.
Locke, Edward
Cataumet
Morse, Margaret Patricia
Centerville
Kimball, Charles Arthur
Chatham
Hatch, Patricia M.
Thorndike, Joseph Jacobs Jr.
Chelsea
Shaw, Martha L.
Chester
Metcalf, Paul C.
Chestnut Hill
Phillis, Yannis Anastasios
Tosteson, Heather
Cohasset
Foell, Earl William
Concord
Coles, Robert
Palay, Sanford Louis
Tapply, William George
Conway
Jenkins, Paul R.
Merriam, Robert Loring
Cummington
Wilbur, Richard Purdy
Dedham
Homburger, Freddy
Deerfield
Garland, Joanne Marie
Dorchester
Corkery, Christopher Jane
Millis, Christopher
Dover
Hinsley-Loeber, Charles Ernest
Duxbury
Brinnin, John Malcolm
East Brewster
Baker, Donald Whitelaw
Easthampton
Metras, Gary
Edgartown
Treat, Lawrence
Fall River
Vieira, Michael John
Falmouth
Yup, Paula Anne
Fitchburg
Cabrinety, Patricia Butler
Florence
Kasper, Michael
Framingham
Cullen, Margaret
Johnson, Christopher Ralph
Nargi, Janice Mary
Gloucester
Ferrini, Vincent
Great Barrington
Hunt, William
Greenfield
Hunter, Sheryl Lynn
Hanover
Kemmett, William J.
Harwich Port
Gilbertson, B(ernice) Charlotte
Hatfield
Coffey, Michael John
Haverhill
Rambach, Peggy Diane
Haydenville
Okrent, Daniel
Todd, Samuel Richard, Jr.
Hingham
Shaner, Richard Clark
Holden
Beck, Robert Nelson
Holyoke
Bartman, Jeffrey
Overton, Jane Taylor
Hyannis
Cook, Petronelle Mary
Lunn, Jean
Jamaica Plain
Baehr, Timothy James
Lake Pleasant
Abel, Robert Halsall
Lenox
Shirer, William Lawrence
Leominster
Cormier, Robert Edmund
Lexington
Benson, Larry Dean
Chomsky, Avram Noam
Glenn, Nancy Noyes
Job, Donald D.
Kenealy, Patrick
Kotelly, George Vincent
Moskow, Shirley Blotnick
Rosenthal, Robert
Trefethen, Florence
Wilson, Irene K.
Lincoln
Squires, James Robert
Littleton
Bracken, Jeanne Munn
Lowell
Sollov, Jacques
Ziavras, Charles Efthemios
Lynfield
Wilkins, Frederick C.
Lynn
Nicholson, F.C. (Frances Costley)
Watson, Marsha Jean
Lynnfield
Bollen, Peter Douglas
Curran, Madeline Mc Grath
Malden
Hill, Carlene Bay
Manchester
Kenny, Herbert A.
Mansfield
Brady, Philip
Marblehead
Kalechofsky, Roberta
Kemelman, Harry
Marlboro
D'elia, Michael Joseph
Marshfield
Boggs, Robert Newell
Mandell, Patricia Athena
Medford
Gordett, Marea Beth
Melrose
Bond, Harold Herant
Kemske, Floyd Steven
Menemsha
Neeld, Judith
Methuen
Laverriere, Lorraine Moreau
Millbury
Driscoll, Mary Harris
Millers Falls
Burdick, Ariane Neiman
Milton
Higgins, George Vincent
Levine, Janet
Tatelbaum, Brenda Loew
Montague
Mariani, Paul Louis
Weil, Lise
N Easton
Phelan, Francis J.
Nahant
Barron, Ray
Natick
Gardiner, Linda
Needham
Littlefield, Bill
Nowak, Edward, Jr.
New Bedford
Almada, Manuel
Concaison, John Silva
Newbury
Ozment, Steven
Newburyport
Cavan, Ann M.
Newton
Angoff, Marion Brenda
Bennett, Bernice Spitz
Montgomery, John Dickey
Moss, Rose
Perlmutter, Philip
Worth, Douglas Grey
Newton Centre
Greenberg, Barbara Levenson
Robinson, Susan Hand
Newton Upper Falls
Pessolano, Linda
Newtonville
Baranczak, Stanislaw
North Amherst
Gibson, Mary Elizabeth G.
North Andover
Buthmann, Ednah Jones
North Brookfield
Neal, Avon
North Egremont
Le Comte, Edward Semple
Northampton
Addelson, Kathryn Pyne
Horowitz, Shel A.
Horowitz, Shel Alan
Kotker, Norman Richard
Kotker, Zane
Long, Robert Hill
Mandell, Richard S.
Milne, Teddy (Margaret)
Newman, Leslea
Skochlas, John
Oxford
Whitmer, Melvin Howard
Peabody
Kelly, Robert E.
Pelham
Huetteman, Susan Ann Bice
Tate, James
Pittsfield
Giannini, David
Valenti, Dan
Pittsvield
Bass, Milton Ralph
Provincetown
Broumas, Olga
Gebelein, Robert Seaver
Lapidus, Jacqueline
Oliver, Mary
Speicher, Rita L.
Quincy
White, Steve
Randolph
Stuart, Anne Elizabeth
Reading
Fowler, William Morgan, Jr.
Rehoboth
Rose, Daniel Asa
Richmond
Sternlieb, Barry F.
Rochester
Finkelstein, Caroline
Rockland
Masterson, Patricia O'Malley
Rockport
Deedy, John Gerard, Jr.
Roslindale
Goldwitz, Susan
Salem
Gallant, Pamela L.
Kessler, Rod
Sandwich
Russell, Francis
Wills, David Arthur
Saxonville

Casper, Leonard Ralph
Shutesbury
Kim, Richard E.
So Hadley
Martin, Valerie Metcalf
Somerville
Blatner, Barbara Ann
Kano, Susan Leslie
Schultz, Nancy Lusignan
Schwartz, Lloyd
Templeman, Kristine Hofgren
Sommerville
Cates, Edward William
South Amherst
Moebius, William
South Deerfield
Lenson, David
South Easton
Chichetto, James William
South Hadley
Bliss, Corinne Demas
Mc Feely, William Shield
Reid, Benjamin Lawrence
Viereck, Peter
South Yarmouth
Boerstler, Richard William
Broadcorens, Yvonne Ramaut
Springfield
Enderlin, Lee
Lasonde, Marilynn Joy
Le Blanc, Catherine Anne
Mozzer, Alanna Jean
Wellikoff, Alan Gabriel
St Lawrence
Grenda-Lukas, John Michael
Stoughton
Litchfield, Ada Bassett
Stow
Wolotkiewicz, Marian Margaret
Truro
Burr, Gray
Vineyard Haven
Just, Ward Swift
Waban
Hazzard, Mary Dwight
Matthews, John Floyd
Waltham
Binstock, Robert Henry
Wareham
Nyman, Mary Mallon
Watertown
Henry, De Witt P.
Pilibosian, Helene Rose
Spivack, Kathleen
Wayland
Callanan, Joseph Alfred
Kirk, Norman Andrew
Wellesby
Mc Mahon, Thomas Arthur
Wellesley
Bouvard, Marguerite Gusman
Somerfield, Neil
Wellesley Center
Costley, Bill
Wellfleet
Galt, Thomas F. Jr
Piercy, Marge
Vivante, Arturo
West Roxbury
Butler, Joseph Patrick
Robbins, Martin
West Tisbury
Riggs, Dionis Coffin
Westborough
Adams, Constance Althea
Westfield
Escandell, Noemi
Kaufman, Martin
Westford
Fallier, Jeanne Hanway
Weston
Burnes, Carol Ganson
Caso, Adolph
Smith, Richard Jay
Tagiuri, Renato
Walton, Richard Eugene
Westwood
Di Nicola, Albert
Williamstown
Millhauser, Steven
Waite, Robert George Leeson
Wilmington
Prentiss, Tina M.
Winthrop
Mc Niff, Thomas Alfred Jr.
Paul George, Farquhar
Woburn
Sorensen, Camey
Worcester
Ferguson, William R.
Gilbert, Christopher
Grilli, Chloe Lenore
Koelsch, William Alvin
La Joie, Raymond Albert
Siegel, William Mordecai
Von Laue, Theodore Herman
Yankauer, Alfred
Wrentham
Ryan, Michael Joseph

Michigan
Bad Axe
Riegle, Karen Dewald
Ada
Middleton, James Franklin
Adrian
Wolf, Sheila
Albion
Powell, Cynthia Anne
Ann Arbor
Aldridge, John Watson
Baker, Sheridan
Bell-Teneketzis, Barbara
Brodsky, Iosif Alexandrovich
Carpenter, John Randell
Clark, Walter H.
Coffin, Lyn
Delbanco, Nicholas F.
Duffy, Yvonne Helen Patricia
Eby, Cecil Degrotte
Feuerwerker, Albert
Fraser, Russell Alfred
Goldstein, Laurence Alan
Green, Elizabeth Adine Herkimer
Holinger, William
Jones, Alan Hedrick
Lewis, David Lanier
Lindenberg, Arthur Jay
Mayman, Martin
Mc Bee, Denis
Press, Simone Naomi Juda
Proffer, Ellendea Catherine
Rice, William C.
Shy, John Willard
Squires, (James) Radcliffe
Starr, Chester
Steinhoff, William Richard
Taylor, Keith
Tillinghast, Richard Williford
Wachsberger, Ken
Watson, (Lois) Elaine
White, James Boyd
Wilson, Jean Avis
Athens
Frye Hoffman, Lois
AuGres
Hinds, Sallie Ann
Baroda
Keller, Robin Kuykendall
Belleville
Stoyenoff, Norma Jeanne Davis
Belmont
Abramowski, Dwain Martin
Benton Harbor
Dandrea, Carmine
Hart, (Jill) Alison
Siebert, Shirley E.
Berrien Springs
Allen, Buck
Big Rapids
Brownell, Joyce E. Tarrier
Foster, Linda Nemec
Kaverman, Donald Lee
Reece, Wayne Gail
Birmingham
Annett, Bruce James, Jr.
Goldwasser, Judith Wax
Hillert, Margaret
Hooper, Patricia
Shipley, Thomas E. Jr.
Smith, David Charles
Wilde, Robert Eugene
Wydra, Frank Thomas
Bloomfield Hills
Buzan, Norma Jeanne Stephens
King, Elizabeth Chiu
Monk, Sean Charles
Boyne City
Paulie
Brighton
Opre, Thomas Edward
Brohman
Mc Feely, Laramie J.
Calumet
Kowacic, Joseph Peter
Kowacic, Joseph Peter
Canton
Wiloch, Thomas
Ceresco
Wilkens, Steven A.
Charlevoix
Faculak, Mary Helen
Ratigan, William
Comstock Park
Eggleston, Alan Earl
Crystal Falls
Hall, Grace
Dearborn
Marsh, Richard Philip
Dearborn Heights
Wysocki, Sharon Ann
Delton
Erskine, Frances Elaine
Mainone, Robert Franklin
Detroit
Abel, Ernest Lawrence
Crittenden, Toya Cynthia
Donovan, Mark
Evans, Karolyn E.
Goodin, Michael Anthony
Madgett, Naomi Long
Markowski, Benedict Stephen
Mc Arthur, Barbara Jean
Morrow, Sheila Ann
Moss, Grave Yard
Rusiniak, Yvonne Lubov
Tarrant, Mary Theresa
Toledo-Pereyra, Luis Horacio
Tye, Henry Jr.
E Lansing
Johnson, Markham P. III
East Detroit
Mielke, Wayne Joseph
East Lansing
Ditchoff, Pamela Jane
Finifter, Ada W(eintraub)
Fox, Hugh Bernard
Freedman, Eric
Paul, Doris Jessie
Thomas, F(ranklin) Richard
Wakoski, Diane
Whallon, William
Wyckoff, Julie Ann
Elberta
Beauregard-Bezou, Marion Joseph
Essexville
Warsaw, Irene
Evart
Marsh, Judith Ann
Farmington
Hund, Robert Arthur
Farmington Hills
Hunt, Deborah Lee
Farwell
Hardin, Kenneth Lee
Flint
Gipson, Angela Christina
Kangas, James Richard
Kearns, Josephine Anna
Matuzak, Joseph Matthew
Morgan, Lanier Vernon
Palmer, Charlene Noel
Palmer, David Walter
Simms, Ami
Wilson, Todd Dorian
Flushing
Fishkin, Howard S.
Mosey, Caron Lee
Fowler
Upton, Lee
Frankfort
Gibson, Keiko Matsui
Gibson, Morgan
Franklin
Heron, Jacqueline Brenda
Fremont
Gerber, Daniel Frank
Glennie
Reglier, Anna Lee Katherine
Grand Haven
Lystra, Helen Percy
Grand Rapids
Anderson, Marie Barbara
Bridges, Patricia Ann
Dillingham, Daniel Jay
Koehler, Ronald E.
Moore, Dianne-Jo
Vander Molen, Robert L.
Weaver, Clarence Lahr
Grandville
Cope, David Edge
Harbor Springs
Lyle, William David
Harper Woods
Rilly, Cherlyl Ann
Haslett
Burns, Virginia Law
Lawder, Douglas Ward, Jr.
Hell
Gaertner, Kenneth Clark
Holland
Franken, Darrell
Ridl, Jack Rogers
Houghton
Ringler, Sharon Mattila
Howell
Carpenter, Patricia
Hudson
Kauffman, Janet
Inkster
Daniel, Hardie William
Interlochen
Delp, Michael W.
Driscoll, Jack
Iron River
Ward, L. E.
Jackson
Williams, S. Bradford, Jr.
Jeddo
Griffith, Geraline Moeller

Jenson
Frye, Della Mae
Kalamazoo
Bowman, Mary Ann
Cline, Charles (William)
Cooley, John R.
Dybek, Stuart John
Galligan, Edward L.
Gideon, Nancy Ann
Gordon, Jaimy
Grossman, Martin Allen
Hilberry, Conrad Arthur
Johnston, William Arnold
Miller, Thomas Bentley
Palmatier, Robert Allen
Laingsburg
Spevak, Teryl A.
Lake Leelanau
Harrison, James Thomas
Lake Linden
Hoheisel, Peter F.
Lansing
Arnink, Donna Jean
Daniels Weinert, Patti Marie
Donally, Keith
Lowe, Kenneth Stephen
Singh, Swayam Prabha
Lapeer
Ferris, Kimberlee Robin
Lathrup Village
Hoover, Mae Morgan
Lawton
Dunham, Sherrie Ann
Lewiston
Morrison, Susan Orinda
Linden
James, David L.
Ludington
Trebilcock, Dorothy Warner
Mackinac Island
Mc Cabe, John Charles, III
Madison Heights
Martinson, A. Denise
Manistee
Leggett, Stephen Charles
Marquette
Chubb, Hilkka Aileen
Heldreth, Leonard Guy
Johnson, Ronald Leroy
Legler, Philip
Reynolds, (Marjorie) Moira Davison
Mecosta
Arnett, Carroll (Gogisgi)
Kirk, Russell Amos
Metamora
Blass, Gerhard Alois
Midland
Levy, Larry
Muskegon
Allison, Alden Gary
Erickson, Neil Le Roy, II
Stone, Julie Lynn
New Baltimore
Mc Partlin, John
North Beach Pentwater
Mc Keown, Tom
Northport
Dame, Edna Genevieve Otto
Minshull, Ruth Ellen
Northville
Jones, Vicki Sue
Oak Park
Livingston-White, Deborah Joyce HalemahZucker, Jack S.
Onaway
Vermilya, Claire (Szala)
Paw Paw
Kuehn, Aaron S.
Peck
Arnold, Jackie Smith
Pentwater
Johnson, Walter
Pleasant Ridge
Chopp-Scheuermann, Joan Janet
Eisenstein, Paul Allan
Pontiac
Beeman, Marsha Lynn
Port Huron
Treleaven, John Waterloo
Potterville
Roose-Church, Lisa Ann
Pullman
Parkhurst, Lolita
Rapid River
Benedict, Elinor Divine
Reed City
Pekrul, Kimberly Ann
Rochester
Coppola, Carlo
Fitzsimmons, Thomas
Schwartz, Roberta Christine
Rochester Hills
Kingery, Lionel Bruce
Rogers City
Hopp, James Lee
Zimmer, Elizabeth Ann
Romeo
Morrisey, Thomas
Roscommon
Schicker, Glenn Earl
Roseville
Clem, Wendy Lee
Royal Oak
Pike, Lawrence
Saginaw
Jones, Timothy Dale
Sandusky
Henderson, Kathleen Susan
Sault Ste Marie
Thomas, Peter D.
Schoolcraft
Laymon, Harold James
Snover
Westrick, Elsie Margaret
Southfield
Carman, Juanita Chenault
Hirschel, Lieselotte Anne
Spelman, Philip Ohel
Southgate
Schuff, Karen Elizabeth
Schuff, Karen Elizabeth
Spring Lake
Cummings, Jean
Deur, Lynne A.
Stambaugh
Carli, Audrey Marilyn
Standish
Bugh, Mary Lou
Stephenson
Silver, Gary Lee
Sterling Heights
Neiger, Michael Alan
Swartz Creek
Meinstein, Crystal Ann
Three Rivers
Boughan, Thomas Robert
Traverse City
Lindenau, Judith Wood
Ross, Raymond Samuel
Troy
Lloyd, Linda Marie
Union
Schneider, C. Rex
Union Lake
Newbound, Betty J.
Vicksburg
Myers, Sue Ann
Warren
De Land, Michelle Karen
Washington
Buzzelli, Elizabeth Kane
West Branch
Woznicki-Likavec, Marie Elaine
Williamston
Landis, Elwood Winton
Wolverine
Wurster, Ralph
Wurtsmith AFB
Jennings, Jennifer Angelene
Ypsilanti
Eshleman, Clayton
Fulton, Alice
Smith, Clara May Freeman
Wagner-Stevens, Tina Marie

Minnesota
Anoka
Medin, Donna Mae
Apple Valley
Schaaf, Richard Edmund
Barnum
Eller, Dawn-Marie
Bemidji
Angell, Valentine Chauncey
Madson, Jerry
Mc Cormick, Patrick M. J.
Sorsoleil, Lori Marie
Benedict
Browne, Michael Dennis
Bloomington
Hess, Karen Jo Matison
Verby, Jane Crawford
Brooklyn Park
Cheng, Fred Nai-Chung
Browerville
Olsen, Donald D.
Burnsville
Firchow, Peter Edgerly
Lindo, David Kenneth
Chatfield
Calvert, Patricia
Collegeville
Hassler, Jon (Francis)
Coon Rapids
Wardlaw, Anita Louise
Cottage Grove
Henriksen, Mary Jo
Crookston
Selzler, Bernard John
Deephaven
Lansky, Vicki Lee
Duluth
Homstad, Gary Duane
Maiolo, Joseph
Skafte, Marjorie Doris
Eden Prairie
Ellis, Joyce K.
White, Terry Dale
Edina
Esbensen, Barbara Juster
Strudwick, Dorothy J.
Wrede, Patricia Collins
Ely
Vickery, Jim Dale
Eyota
Schaefer, Vernon Joseph
Fridley
Nee, Kay Bonner
Frost
Stokes
Golden Valley
Hammer, Roger A.
Sherman, James Richard
Goodhue
Voldseth, Beverly Ann
Grey Eagle
Rylander, Edith May
Hartland
Batt, Allen Edward
Hutchinson
Davis, Terry Michael
Janesville
Studer-Johnson, Marian Kaye
Jordan
Andre, Paul Dean
Markfort, Anne Marie
La Crescent
Servais, Donna J.
Le Center
Zimmerman, Winona Estelle
Litchfield
Nolen, William Anthony
Little Falls
Jewell, Richard
Luverne
Manfred, Frederick Feikema
Mankato
Robbins, Richard Leroy
Ude, Wayne Richard
Maple Grove
Blacik, Stephen Mark
Maple Plain
Bailey, Kathrine E.
Marshall
Dacey, (John) Philip
Minneapolis
Adams, Harold B
Alfs, Matthew Gerd
Almen, Lowell Gordon
Anderson, Brian E.
Appel, Marcia Faye
Axelrod, Mark Richard
Batson, Larry Floyd
Bly, Mark John
Braman, Sandra
Crozier, Ouida G.
Dahlberg, Joyce Karen
Engman, John Robert
Fenick, Barbara Jean
Fischer, Lynn Henry
Fitzpatrick, Kevin John
Freivalds, John
Gagliardi, Annette Jane
Garey, Terry A.
Gordon, Jack Marshall
Greene, Pat Ryan
Hammond, Ruth Elizabeth
Hampl, Patricia
Johnson, James Holbrook
Kyle, Mary J.
Marks, Ada Greiner
Mc Grath, Thomas
Mc Umber, Keith Darren
Niemi, Nicole
Nitso, Evelyn Agnes
Pedoe, Daniel
Ramirez, Joan E.
Robinett, Betty Wallace
Roth, Martha (Vanceburg)
Schaar, Frances Elizabeth
Seagull, Samantha Singer
Shetterly, William Howard
Simon, Werner
Swanson, Gladys Irene
Tarachow, Michael
Toth, Susan Erickson Allen
Truedson, Gail Van Horn
Vecoli, Rudolph John
Veninga, Robert Louis
Willand, Lois Carlson
Woodward, Helen De Long
Yager, Cinda
Zimmerman, Robert Dingwall
Minnetonka
Berman, Sanford
Morrow, George Telford II
Olson, Kay Melchisedech
Moorhead
Callaway, Kathy Jean
Henderson, Julie K.

Martinson, David Keith
Vinz, Mark
Moose Lake
Bly, Robert Elwood
Mpls
Burns, Alan
Heath, Lyn Barrett
New Brighton
Zachmann, Virginia Joyce
Northfield
Klug, Ronald Allan
Rolloff Langworthy, Carol Lemay
Swanson, Stephen Olney
Oronoco
Carney, Charles Seymour
Pequot Lakes
Clark, Viola Anna
Plymouth
Swenson, Grace Stageberg
Rochester
Aho, Kathleen Gail
Parkhurst, Louis Gifford, Jr.
Quinn, Bernetta Viola
Siekert, Robert George
Tilton, Rafael
Saint Cloud
Meissner, William Joseph
Wiener, Ferdinand Joseph
Saint Francis
Schroeder, Cheryl Ann
Saint Joseph
Henn, Sister Mary Ann
Saint Louis Park
Pinkham, Mary Ellen
Saint Paul
Dosedel, James Anthony
Greenberg, Alvin David
Hollabaugh, Mark
Lindahl, Helen Gertrude
Patton, Michael Quinn (Halcolm)
Tracy, James Donald
White, Lorelei Annette
Wysocki, Nancy
Sandstone
Langseth, Muriel Avonne
Santa Fe
Bradford, Richard Roark
Shoreview
Fishwick, Nina Marie
Side Lake
Leschak, Peter Max
South Minneapolis
Farrell, James Joseph
St Cloud
Goenner, Judith Mary
Reyerson, Dennis Orville
Ross, Roseanna Gaye
St Paul
Chamberlain, Marisha Anne
Feroe, Paul James
Helmes, L. Scott
Ingram, Alyce M.
Kaeter, Margaret
Koskenmaki, Rosalie M.
Lexau, Henry
Minczeski, John
Noble, David Watson
Reinhardt, Madge
Slowinski, Emil John
Warne, Candice M.
Werner, Hans-Peter
St. Paul
Deyo, Steven Mark
Miller, Donald Larry
Stillwater
Beattie, Melody Lynn
Sturgeon Lake
Bly, Carol Mclean
Trace
Mueller, Loraine Dorothy
Warroad
Spina, Angela Marie
Watertown
Maravelas, Paul
Woodworth, Ralph Leon
West Aurora
Mulari, Mary Elizabeth
West St Paul
Dahms, Janet H.
Winona
Lund, Orval A., Jr.
Marg, Caroline Catherine
Zumbrota
Thomford, Arline Gesine

Mississippi
Blue Mountain
Cissom, Mary Jo *Brooklyn*
Gerald, Carolyn
Christian
Bettersworth, John Knox
Clinton
Chapman, Cindy Lorraine Farr
Columbus
Smith, Louise Hamilton
Gautier
Lebow-Shepard, Jeanne Swift
Gregory
Glen Allan
Barnes, Nancy Carol
Gulfport
Roberts, Jim Joseph
Smoke, Judith Mccoll
Hattiesburg
Ball, Angela
Fortson, Sanna
Inness-Brown, Elizabeth Ann
Sims, James Hylbert
Hazlehurst
Lowenkamp, William Charles Jr.
Houlka
Hill, Patricia
Jackson
Barry, Mimi Neal
Welty, Eudora
Wilson, Allison
Madison
Saxton, La Verne Young
Natchez
Gee, F. Denise
North Biloxi
Cooper, Billy Norman
Ocean Springs
Howse, Harold D.
Murphy, Diana Sue Grogan (Dim)
Oxford
Flesher, Dale Lee
Nelson, Charles Lamar
Pascagoula
Mc Ingvale, James Wesley (Jim)
Pass Christian
Hillyer, Carter Sinclair
Pearl
Bright, Nancy Elizabeth
Picayune
Clingan, Robert Keith
Starkville
Wright, Linsey Hardy
State Line
Bennett, Carl Edward
Terry
Fuller, Mike Andrew
Tougaloo
Cox, Carol Moore
University
O'Neal, Winston James, Jr.
Waveland
Ling, Edwin Rodger

Missouri
Anderson
Childress, William Dale *Arnold*
Goodridge, Georgia Esther
Summers, Anthony J.
Bonnots Mill
Nunn, Wilfred (Bill)
Branson
Dailey, Janet
Bridgeton
Swan, Frances E (Mueller Swan)
Bronson
Gianoli, Paul Louis
Cape Girardeau
Hecht, Harvey E.
Carthage
Aschwanden, Richard Josef
Chesterfield
Cooper, Kenneth Carlton
Mc Avoy, William Charles
Columbia
Bender, Eleanor M.
Bonetti, Kay Jacqueline
Camargo, Martin J.
Hongo, Garrett Kaoru
Hostetler, Sheri Ann
Killoren, Robert
Lago, Mary Mcclelland
Miller, Leslie Adrienne
Morgan, Speer
Santos, Sherod
Sapp, Eva Jo
Swan, Gladys
Swan, Gladys
Weiss, James Moses Aaron
Des Peres
Diomede, Matthew
Florissant
Bernard, David Kane
Fulton
Karr, Jay Miles
Golden City
Norgard, Elizabeth Ann
Independence
Myers, Bob
Jefferson City
Kinney Hanson, Sharon D.
Kansas City
Banks, Stanley Eugene
Beasley, Conger, Jr.
Damon, Valerie Hubbard
Feiffer, Jules
Goldsmith, Larry Dean
Gusewelle, C. W.
Hoffman, Gloria L.
Londre, Felicia Hardison
Ray, Suzanne Judy
Ray, David Eugene
Tiley, Sharon Kay
Willson, Robert Frank
Kirkwood
Cargas, Harry J(ames)
Liberty
Houghton, Timothy Dane
Macon
Barnes, Jim Weaver
Maryville
Trowbridge, William L.
Moberly
Conroy, Jack
Tatlow, Marilyn Rose
O'fallon
Polette, Nancy (Jane)
Pt Lookout
Christianson, Kevin Earl
Raytown
Wagner, Maryfrances Cusumano
Rocheport
Delon, Floyd G(urney)
Rolla
Wixson, Douglas Charles
Saint Louis
Finkel, Donald
Gass, William H.
Ibur, Jane Ellen
Lipman, David
Merrell, James Lee
Metz, Jerred
Springfield
Borich, Michael
Coy, David Lavar
Lederer, Katherine Gay
Prosser, Harold Lee
St Joseph
Gilgun, John Francis
St Louis
Bauman, George Duncan
Davis, Irvin
Guenther, Charles (John)
Hadas, Pamela White
Holloway, Marcella Marie
Klotzer, Charles Lothar
Lebowitz, Albert
Meyer, M. Yvonne
Moog, Florence Emma
Murphy, Michael
Stang, Richard
Troy, Mary Delphine
Van Duyn, Mona Jane
Watson, Richard Allan
Watson, Robert R.
Wayne, Jane O.
St. Louis
Castro, Jan Garden
Nemerov, Howard
Sweet Springs
Long, Helen Halter
University City
Elkin, Stanley Lawrence
Webster Groves
Olson, Clarence Elmer, Jr.
Schapiro, Nancy

Montana
Big Fork
Blumberg, Nathan(iel) Be
Bigfork
Jones, Margaret Bridwell
Billings
Gilliland, Hap
Bozeman
Lair, Jesse K.
Peavy, Linda
Emigrant
Dowbenko, Uri
Florence
Alcosser, Sandra B.
Glendive
Hackett, Suzanne Frances
Great Falls
Pankowski, Elsie Marie
Missoula
Blauner, Laurie Ann
Brusin, Joyce Helena
Crumley, James
Goedicke, Patricia
Koch, James Verch
Robinson, Leonard Wallace
Ross, Robert E. (Bob)

Nebraska
Beatrice
West, Kathleene K.
Bellevue
Gray, Patrick Worth
Lincoln
Deal, Susan Strayer
Magorian, James Irvin
Raz, Hilda
Scheele, Roy Martin
Omaha

Duggin, Lorraine Jean
Herman, Michelle
Riverdale
Dittmer, Stevan W.

Nevada
Dyer
Hunt, Timothy A.
Henderson
Okins, Elliott Eugene
Las Vegas
Irsfeld, John Henry
Leon, Steve
Liu, Stephen Shu-Ning
Shaw, Arnold
Speer, Betty Jean
Stevens, A(rthur) Wilber, Jr.
Oasis Wells
Paulsen, Norman Deitrich
Pahrumb
Reul, Richard Philip
Reno
Dallman, Elaine Gay
Malott, Adele Renee
Marshall-Nadel, Nathalie
Reid, Randall
Savoy, Douglas Eugene
Townley, John Mark

New Hampshire
Antrim
Kurz, Ron
Ashuelot
Carr, Daniel Paul
Barrington
Harris, Marie
Canaan
Lelchuk, Alan
Center Harbor
Bennett, Norman E.
Concord
Drown, Merle
Cornish Flat
Lawton, Thomas Gerard Samuel
Danbury
Hall, Donald
Dublin
Abbe, George Bancroft
Hale, Judson Drake
Durham
Allbery, Debra L.
Bruce, Robert Vance
Pritchard, Parm Frederick
Williams, Thomas (Alonzo)
East Kingston
Garand, Pierre Arthur
East Sullivan
Morressy, John
Fitzwilliam
Kennedy, James Harrington
Francestown
Milton, Edith
Hampton Falls
Beeler, Thomas Taylor, III
Hancock
Older, Julia D.
Sherman, Steve Barry
Hanover
Bien, Peter Adolph
Eberhart, Richard
Schley, James Powrie
Henniker
Oppenheimer, Joel Lester
Yoder, Carolyn Patricia
Jefferson
Leiper, Esther M.
Keene
Brooks, Virginia K.
Meredith
Simony, Maggy
Nashua
Krutenat, Richard Carroll
Newmarket
Yount, John Alonzo
Penacook
Blakeman, Beth Renee
Peterborough
Gibbs, Barbara Francesca
Portsmouth
Jebb, Robert Dudley
Robinson, John Delyn
Rindge
Burness, Don
Salem
Romano, Frank J.
Seabrook
Cook, Rodney Edwin Sr.
Strafford
Merz, Rollande
Simic, Charles
Stratham
Stuart, Virginia Elaine
Walpole
Gooding, Judson
Warner
Kumin, Maxine
Weare
Wellman, Donald

New Jersey
Allendale
De Vinck, Jose M.
Basking Ridge
Moore, Donald John
Teague, Burton William
Bayonne
Font, David James, Sr.
Silverman, Herschel
Wall, Thomas J. (G. Bear)
Bayville
Sharp, Donna Lee
Beach Haven Terrace
Miller, Ronald R.
Bedminster
Patterson, Timothy Dale
Belle Mead
La Plante, J. Duncan
Belleville
Bridge, Peter J.
Packie, Susan
Bergenfield
Phelan, Thomas Anthony
Berlin
Buehler, Robin Marie
Bloomfield
Amabile, Anthony A.
Gariepy, Henry
Branchville
Eastby, Allen Gerhard
Brick Township
Anstett, Robert Emory
Bricktown
Hubscher, William Donald
Jannicelli, Matteo
Schroeder, Kathleen Audrey
Busking Ridge
Gauch, Patricia Lee
Califon
Mittelmark, Abraham
Camben
Kelly, Armandine Frances
Camden
Zeidner, Lisa A.
Cedar Grove
Mahler-Sussman, Leona Julia
Mandel, Charlotte
Mattingly, Richard E. (Rick)
Chatham
Forde, Joyce P.
Zeltins, Teodors
Cherry Hill
Borowsky, Ben A.
Burgess, Craig E.
Cinnaminson
Schnurr, Constance Burke
Schnurr, William Bernhardt
Clarksburg
Arias-Misson, Alain August
Clifton
Adams-Jacobson, Nancy
Groves, Catherine
Guttman, Dena Ann
Hannum, Susan Michelle
Nemirow, Jill Karin
Collingswood
Holmes, Barbara Ware
Staton, Johanna Bilbo
Colts Neck
Yoseloff, Thomas
Cranbury
Lee, Maurice (du Pont) Jr.
Cresskill
Nelson, Robin Coleman
Dayton
Kennedy-Verbel, Jeanne Marie
Dover
Shadovitz, David Jay
Dumont
Arcella, Lisa
East Brunswick
Caccavale, Judith Lansdowne
Lipman, Burton E.
Richardson, James
East Windsor
Michaels, Carol Ann
Richman, Steven Mark
Edison
Di Pasquale, Emanuel (Paul)
Mercer, Charles
Rubin, Diana Kwiatkowski
Elizabeth
Turner, Jean-Rae
Fair Lawn
Barnes, Jill
Van Houten, Lois M.
Fanwood
Higginson, William J.
Kenny, Adele M.
Far Hills
Atthowe, Jean Fausett
Florham Park
Derham, Matthew Joseph
Forked River
Cudworth, Marsha Elizabeth
Fort Lee
Messer, Andrea Elyse
Freehold
Northart, Leo Joseph
Schwartzman, Lois Phoebe
Frenchtown
Mc Coy, Joseph Jerome, Jr.
Glen Rock
Noah, Hope E.
Green Brook
Simcoe, Annell Lacy
Green Village
Hudgins, Barbara
Riemer, Ruby
Guttenberg
Bell, Harrison B.
Boss, Laura
Hackettstown
Peterson, Charlotte A.
Haddonfield
Kelly, Joseph John
Hasbrouck Heights
Alger, Derek S.
Haworth
Biggs, Mary
Hawthorne
Gillan, Maria Mazziotti
Hazlet
Holland, Susan Palmieri
Highland Park
O'Neill, William Lawrence
Highlands
Smith, Muriel Joan
Hillside
Bickel, William Jon
Hilltop
Rania, Albert Nunzio
Hoboken
Ruggia, James Charles
Hopewell
Hollander, Jean
Jackson
Modica, Terry Ann
Jersey City
Hagan, Marty
Jerrett, Cathy Louise
Lyons, Edward Timothy
Russell, Helen Ross
Shot, Danny
Wagner, Douglas W.E.
Keasbey
Certo, Dominic Nicholas
Kingston
Kolodziej, Krysia
Kinnelon
Maxfield, Maria Ursula
Lake Hopatcong
Tomlinson, Gerald (Arthur)
Lakehurst
Bavota, Michael Francis
Lakewood
Reinman, Jacob J.
Lambertville
Youmans, Rich
Landing
Ludy, Andrew William
Leonia
Hellman, Sheila Almer
Hellman, Hal
Kaye, Evelyn
Klass, Sheila Solomon
Mac Namara, Donal E. J.
Malone, Pamela Altfeld
Ross, Steven Sander
Linden
Rixon, Robert N.
Zahorchak, Michael
Little Silver
Farrell, Pamela Barnard
Livingston
Margulis, Jerry
Ratkovic, Margaret Jeanne
Long Branch
Lagowski, Barbara Jean
Madison
Cummins, Walter (Merrill)
Mc Mullen, Edwin Wallace, Jr.
Norris, Roger Henry
Shippey, Frederick Alexander
Magnolia
Lattany, Kristin Eggleston
Mahwah
Johnson, Roger N.
Wojciechowska, Maia (Rodman)
Mantua
Ranieri, Lorraine Mary
Manville
Strozeski, Charles
Maplewood
Melick, Arden Davis
Rohrs, Wilhelm Hermann
White, John Irwin
Marlton
Brant, William Morton
Mays Landing
Cutter, Margaret Mead

Maywood
Wenzel, Lynn
Mendham
Huemer, Joseph Wilson
Merchantville
Calore, James John
Metuchen
Zatz, Arline
Middlesex
Worowski, Steven
Middletown
Jersild, Arthur T(homas)
Levine, Vicki Lucille
Middleville
Menkus, Belden (Alfred Julian)
Milltown
Jakubowski, Donna Marie
Millville
Kane, Patricia
Schaaf, Frederick Carl
Montclair
Barry, Jan
De Palma, Anthony Robert
Linett, Deena
Simon, Harold
West, Sandra La Vonne
Moorestown
Schepp, Brad Jeffrey
Morganville
Richman, Alan
Morris Plains
Braun, Claire S.
Farre, Thomas R.
Morristown
Cecala, Kathy Petersen
Keyishian, M. Deiter
Klein, Kenneth D.
Mc Crae, Sharon Elizabeth
Ross, Theodore John
Mount Arlington
Rowe, William Morford, Jr.
Mount Ephraim
Shellenberger, Verna S
Mt Holly
Little, Geraldine Clinton
New Brunswick
Baranow, Joan Marie
Catala, Rafael Enrique
Katz, Eliot
New Providence
Simpson, Winifred Rouse
Newark
Mahoney, John Thomas Fitzsimmons
Reeder, Hubert
North Bergen
Tapellini, Donna Lynn
North Brunswick
Heller, Marlene Ann
Tuitt, Ron S.
North Wildwood
Bishop, Stephen Richard
Nutley
Ferraro, Bernadette A.
Oakland
Guston, David H.
Ocean
Watkins, William John
Ocean City
Koob, Raymond Joseph
Smith, Frank Kingston
Oceanport
Masterman-Smith, Virginia
Oradell
Kaplan, Milton
Reynolds, James A.
Paramus
Avakian, Mary
Freericks, Mary Avakian
Parkertown
Henne, Nancy Diane
Parlin
Berger, Amy H.
Passaic
Sanchez, Francisco P.
Pemberton
Sussman, Ocie Jones
Pennington
Groth, Patricia Celley
Smith, Carol Sturm
Wildgrube, Irene W.
Pennsauken
Briggs, John Gurney, Jr.
Peqaunnock
Lumpkin, Kenneth Charles
Perth Amboy
Kananowitz, Anna Gilson
Phillipsburg
De Paolis, Rosemary
Pine Beach
Finale, Frank Louis
Plainfield
Dunkel, Tom Richard
Evans, Alice Mc Donald
Plainsboro
Manulkin, Dena
Pleasantville
Jenkins, Marjorie C.
Port Republic
Dunn, Stephen Elliott
Princeton
Ball, George Wildman
Bowersock, Glen Warren
Brokaw, R. Miriam
Brombert, Victor Henri
Burt, Nathaniel
Davidson, Robert Lee III
Frank, Joseph Nathaniel
Gossman, Lionel
Horowitz, Irving Louis
Jacobowitz, Judah L.
Jaffee, Annette Williams
Keeley, Edmund
Kostar, Ronald Edward
Litz, Arthur Walton, Jr.
Mac Innes, Mairi
Martin, John Rupert
Mc Cleery, William Thomas
Mc Guire, William
Moynahan, Julian Lane
Murphy, Walter Francis
Oates, Joyce Carol
Ostriker, Alicia
Pagels, Elaine Hiesey
Parker, Arri Sendzimir
Pouncy, Mattie Hunter
Roberts, Janet Marie
Segal, Charles Paul
Socolow, Elizabeth A.
Steward, D. E.
Udovitch, Abraham Labe
Uitti, Karl David
Weinberg, Jonathan David
Weiss, Theodore Russell
White, Morton Gabriel
Ziolkowski, Theodore Joseph
Princeton Junction
Wilde, Alan
Rahway
Fink, R. Cullen
Levitt, Susan B.
Vache, Warren Webster
Ramsey
Avgerinos, Cecily Terese
Jacobsen, Michael A.
Randolph
Dugger, Julia Burns
Readington
Long, G. Gordon
Red Bank
Dunlevy, Marion B.
Maxwell, Alice S.
Peterson, Eric Clinton
Sackett, Donna C.
Ridgewood
Johnson, Douglas W(ayne)
Riverton
Suplee, Carol Janet Cunningham
Rocky Hill
Schott, Penelope Scambly
Roosevelt
Keller, David M.
Roselle
Ponticello, Matthew
Roselle Park
Zjawin, Dorothy Arlene
Ruitherford
Petrie, Ferdinand Ralph
Rumson
Robinson, William Wheeler
Rutherford
Guldner, Mary Ellen
Wall, Robert Emmet
Saddle Brook
Buttaci, Sal St. John
Claire, Elizabeth
Saddle River
Roes, Nicholas A.
Saddlebrook
Macebuh, Sandy
Sayreville
Rapp, Lea Bayers
Scotch Plains
Estrin, Herman A.
Harter, Penny
Secaucus
Kliewer, Warren
Sewell
Karpacs, Joanne Mary
Short Hills
Carter, Laura Stephenson
Sicklerville
Ackley, Danielle Renee
Hudgins, William Freeman, Jr.
Skillman
Kortepeter, Carl Max
Prestbo, John Andrew
Somerville
Atkinson, Lucy Jo
Klein, Virginia S.
Kolumban, Nicholas
Mc Laughlin, J. Richard
South Orange
Gale, William A.
Reynolds, John Dana
Willis, Meredith Sue
South Plainfield
Moore, Harry E., Jr
South River
Abbott, John B., Jr.
Sparta
Gray, Carol Lippert
Nersesian, Robert S.
Spotswood
Vogel, Paul Mark
Springfield
Bostwick, Burdette Edwards
Godin, H. Richard
Stockton
Gysi, Charles L., III
Ramsey, Charles Frederic, Jr.
True, June Audrey
Summit
Luberoff, Benjamin J.
Margie, Joyce Daly
Teaneck
Berck, Martin Gans
Miller, Ira
Roth, June Doris Spiewak
Williams, John A.
Tenafly
Anderson, David Poole
Flegler, Joel B.
Gardner, Richard Alan
Lefevere, Patricia Ann
Raeff, Marc
Vaughan, Samuel Snell
Yefimov, Igor
Toms River
Garrett, Susan Mary
Matlaga, Joan
Witomski, Theodore Raymond
Totowa
Marchitti, Elizabeth Van Houten
Trenton
Bienen, Leigh Buchanan
Sayko, Gene J.
Union
Albright, Glen Patrick
Ellis Taylor, Emily
Piatnochka, Ruth Ann
White, Judith Ann
Union Beach
Eben, Lois Ellen
Upper Montclair
Bailey, James Martin
Tiger, Madeline Joan
Unger, Burton
Upper Saddle River
Lally, Garvin E.
Ventnor
Young, Wilhelmina G.
Verona
Henderson, Bruce Raymond
Warren
Weber, Charles Edward
Weehawken
Manejias, Sergio
Scherman, Susan Louise
Wenonah
Gannon, Dee
West Milford
Genader, Ann Marie
West New York
Cordasco, Francesco
West Orange
Fillingham, Patricia
Lauren, Linda
Osborne, John Walter
Womack, Eric
West Paterson
Vradenburgh, Merry Christine
Westfield
Bernstein, Jane
Vincent, Helen
Westmont
Barkhamer, Josephine Rita
Westwood
Diernisse, Villy
Wharton
Brandt, Alvin George
Whiting
Dunetz, Lora E.
Willingboro
Eiferman, Sharon Rees
Taube, Lester S.
Woodbine
Wright, Ellen Marie
Woodbury
Morris, Cecelia Maltby
Woodcliff Lake
Cordner, Jacqueline Willingham,
Yardville
Kilbourne, Clara Anne
Petzinger, William Charles

New Mexico
Alamogordo
Mitchell, Robert Wa
Albuquerque
Alexander, Floyce

Anaya, Rudolfo A.
Aranda, Charles
Bacon, Phillip
Bernell, Sue
Burbank, James Clarke
Burris, Thelma Ruth
Crawford, John F.
Currey, Richard
De Lilla, Celina S.
Dunn, Julia
Durant, Penny Lynne Raife
Frazier, Kendrick Crosby
Ginsburg, Carl S.
Gravel, Clifford Richard Hilaire
Herron, Robert Lane
Hillerman, Tony
Hutton, Paul Andrew
John, Betty
Karni, Michaela Jordan
Long, Frank Weathers
Mc Clernon, Crystal Dawn
Mc Phail, Gordon John
O'Riley, Patrick Adelbert
Price, V. B.
Richter, Harvena
Robbins, Catherine Codispoti
Ruppert, James K.
Thompson, Phyllis Hoge
Toomey, Jeanne Elizabeth (Gray)
Weishaus, Joel

Bloomfield
Seiferle, Rebecca Ann

Chama
Tarrant, Mae Cross

Corrales
Brandi, John
Casteel, Bette
Gottstein, Karen

Deming
Ball, Ivern Imogene
Cress, Floyd Cyril
Gottschalk, Asher M.
Johnson, Donna M.
Moore, Harvielee Ann Offutt

Dixon
Grant, Robert L.

El Prado
Querry, Ronald Burns

Espanola
Salazar, Barbara M.

Flora Vista
Waybourn, Marilu M.

Las Cruces
Jaycox, Elbert Ralph
Priestley, Opal Lee
Wilson, Keith Charles

Los Alamos
Anderson, Karen L.

Mesilla Park
Duran, Natividad Perez

Mimbres
Russell, Sharman Apt

Peralta
Trujillo, Paul Edward

Placitas
Bartlett, Lee Anthony
Goodell, Larry
Pearlman, William D.

Portales
Oldknow, Antony

Rio Rancho
Lacey, Joan Mary
Mcilhaney, Sam Carl

Roswell
Watson, Marilyn Fern

Sant Fe
Sagan, Miriam Anna

Santa FE
Zekowski, Arlene

Santa Fe
Apodaca, Rudy Samuel
Bell, Charles Greenleaf
Berne, Stanley
Berssenbrugge, Mei-Mei
Challem, Jack Joseph
Clow, Barbara Hand
Ehrlichman, John Daniel
Hamilton, Donald Bengtsson
Hocks, Paula Jeanne
Hollon, William Eugene
Holmes, Janet Alice
Lamb, Elizabeth Searle
Levering, Donald Warren
Martin, George Raymond Richard
Murphy, Joy Waldron
Noyes, Stanley (Tinning)
Riccards, Michael Patrick
Shapiro, Erin Pizzey
West, Salli Lou
Woodford, Bruce Powers

Sante Fe
Bashinsky, Sloan Young, II
Huber, Robert Edger
Myers, J. Jay
O'Mara Mc Mahon, Peggy Norreen
Phillips, Aileen Paul
Reeve, Agnesa Lufkin
Webb, Melody

Shiprock
Holmsten, Victoria Lynn

Socorro
Du Bois, Barbara Rattray
Mc Kee, John De Witt
Thompson, Lou Ann

Taos
Bacon, Wallace Alger
Mac Naughton, Anne L.

Tesuque
Hausman, Gerald Andrews
Tarn, Nathaniel

Tohatchi
Dorsett, Martha Janette
Dorsett, Mary Janeen

New York

APO New York
Beckstead, Robert D

Accord
Wills-Raftery, Dorothy

Albany
Anaporte-Easton, Jean Boehlke
Halloran, Daniel F.
Johnson, Judith Evelyn
Kennedy, William
Lunde, Diane S.
Mc Namee, Dardis
Mccoy, Maureen Ellen
Persico, Joseph Edward
Rossiter, Charles M.

Alfred
Howard, Benjamin W.
Martin, Diane D.

Alligerville High Falls
Tetlow, Edwin

Amagansett
Cedering, Siv
Roueché, Berton

Amityville
Walker, Lois Virginia

Amsterdam
Yund, Theodore Joseph

Annandale-on-Hudson
Kelly, Robert

Astoria
Mirtsopoulos, Christos
Spina, Vincent
Weber, Sol

Averill Park
Cardillo, Joe

Babylon
Maggio, Loida Weber

Baldwin
Bram, Elizabeth
Lee, Robert E. A.

Ballston Spa
Barba, Harry

Barrytown
Corman, Cid
Higgins, Richard Carter

Bay Terrace
Gassman, Jayne Dana

Bayshore
Leon, Judene Marie

Bayside
Skemer, Arnold Marius
Zaslow, Edmund Morris

Bayville
Corrody, Carol Ann

Bedford
Petzal, David Elias

Beechhurst
Shainis, Murray J.

Bellport
Bernstein, Herbert J.

Bellvale
Wright, James Bowers

Berkshire
Nizalowski, Edward Michael
Nizalowski, John Anthony

Binghamton
Clements, Arthur L.
Dann, Jack M.
Kessler, Milton
Starzak, Michael Edward
Stein, George Henry
Wellwarth, George E.
Wilcox, Patricia Anne

Bklyn
Swenson, Karen

Blooming Grove
Solonche, Joel R.

Blossvale
Lockhart, Anita May

Boonville
Fedchak, Gregg George

Brentwood LI
Silvers, Vicki

Brockport
Heyen, William H.
Piccione, Anthony
Poulin, A., Jr.

Bronx
Botshon, Ann
Burton, Mary Alice
De Jongh, James Laurence
Dimler, George Richard
Fletcher, Harry George, III
Fortuné, Monique Joan
Grant, Claude De Witt
Hall, Phil
Manesse, Daniel Arthur
Mc Glynn, Brian James
Melino, Eugene Anthony
Mungin, Horace L.
Pollan-Cohen, Shirley
Sacks, Oliver (Wolf)
Schaller, George Beals
Schulman, Mary
Tusiani, Joseph
Whiting, Estelle Louise
Windham, Revish
Zalaznick, Sheldon
Zoltok-Seltzer, Harriet

Bronx New York
Cox, Joseph Mason Andrew

Bronxville
Barnhart, Clarence Lewis
Forester, Bruce Michael
Maiorana, Ronald
Swann, Lois

Brooklyn
Altman, Nathaniel
Armer, Sondra Schecter
Baumbach, Jonathan
Benedetto, Donna A.
Bloom, Pauline
Brown, Kenneth H.
Censabella, Laura Maria
Clarke, La Verne Alexis Evans
Cohen, Robert L.
Contursi, Paul
D'ambrosio, Vinnie-Marie
Dame, Enid
Detz, Joan Marie
Doria, Charles
Eubanks Cuny, Jackie Karen
Fisk, Margaret Cronin
Fleming, James Klein
Frauenglas, Robert Alan
Friedman, Jeffrey H.
Gargan, William Michael
Garner-Lipman, Karen Lee
Georgakas, Dan
Getz, Mike
Harris, William J.
Harvey, Edmund Huxley, Jr.
Hebald, Carol
Henes, Donna
Henning, Barbara J.
Hershon, Robert Myles
Jackanin, Albina Veronica
Kaminsky, Marc
Kraner, Madeline R.
Kutz, Myer Paul
Lerner, Linda
Lesser, Rika Ellen
Luczun, Mary Ellen Teresa
Martin, R. William
Martin, Julian S. S.
Mayer, Ira
Mc Carthy, Rosemary P.
Mc Nerney, Joan
Mernit, Susan
Messing, Robin
Moncrieffe, Hyachinth Williams
Muesing-Ellwood, Edith Elizabeth
Newbauer, John Arthur
Norris, Carole Veronica
Nurkse, Alan D.
Offsey, Sol
Paris, Matthew Lionel
Pessen, Edward
Pochoda, Philip M.
Poindexter, Joseph Boyd
Price, William
Purdy, James
Rutsky, Lester
Sands, Edith Sylvia Abeloff
Sanford, David Boyer
Scarino, Marianne Cannava
Schaeffer, Susan Fromberg
Silverton, Michael John
Sirof, Harriet Toby
Sivack, Denis
Sobczynska, Danuta
Soldo, John J.
Sostchen, Cindy
Spector, Robert Donald
Tarzik, Jack
Teisler, David A.
Tomasson, Verna
Uhrman, Esther
Van Sickle, John Babcock
Vargas, Laura Dennison
Walsh, George William
Wieder, Laurance
Williams, Edward G.
Williams, Charles Kenneth
Yurick, Sol
Zegers, Kip

Zuckrow, Edward
Brooklyn Heights
Gioseffi, Daniela
Buffalo
Ainsworth, Catherine Harris
Andrzejewski, Margaret Rusek
Carrubba, Sandra J. Mcpherson
Daley, John
De Loach, Allen Wayne
Efron, Arthur
Feldman, Irving
Fiedler, Sally A.
Fiedler, Leslie Aaron
Levenson, Fred Barry
Matte, James Allan
Mazzaro, Jerome Louis
Plaut, Martin Edward
Polite, Carlene Hatcher
Ruhland, Elizabeth A.
Storr, John Frederick
Valone, Thomas Francis
Vinacke, W. Edgar
Caledonia
Shaughnessy, Phyllis B.
Camillus
Gebman, Eva Urlish
Canton
Bellamy, Joe David
Shields, David J.
Van De Water, John Ward
White, Steven Forsythe
Carmel
Mc Dermott, Michael James
Cazenovia
Lerman, Rhoda
Center Brunswick (Troy)
Hemming, George Fred
Center Moriches
Hutchins, Shirley M.
Wendell, Leilah
Centereach
Attard, Janet
Centerport
Troise, Fred
Central Islip
Anazagasty, Anita Dolores
Mc Gowan, Harold
Young, Frank, Jr.
Chappaqua
Brownstone, David M.
Friedman, Roy Bennis
George, Jean Craighead
Lieberman, Herbert H.
Lundberg, Ferdinand Edgar
Sugar, Bert Randolph
Chatham
Diggs, Elizabeth Francis
Mc Cully, Emily Arnold
Circleville
Clyne, Patricia Edwards
Clarence Center
Facklam, Margery (Metz)
Clarence Center
Walsh, Joy
Clifton Park
Kleinschrod, Walter Andrew
Clinton
Mulford, Philippa Greene
Simon, Robert L.
Clinton Corners
Reifler, Samuel
Cohocton
O'Brien, Beatrice Marie
College Point
Priore, Frank Vincent
Commack
Talan, Jamie Lynn
Corning
Hope, Akua Lezli
Cornwall-on-Hudson
Toombs, Jane Ellen
Corona
Baley, Geneve
Cortland
Kaminsky, Alice R.
Crestwood
Charney, David H.
Crofton
Warren, Margaret Lucille
Croton on Hudson
Bluestein, Daniel Thomas
Croton-on-Hudson
Henderson, Harry Brinton, Jr.
Kahn, Roger
Merrill, Susan Lee
Needham, Richard Lee
Delmar
Rothstein, Marilyn E.
Squire, Rochelle Brener
Zimmerman, Joseph Francis
Dobbs Ferry
Teison, Herbert J.
East Amherst
Whitelaw, Nancy Eaton
East Aurora
Perry, Marion J.h.
Steck, Carol R.
East Elmhurst
Kaiser, Ernest Daniel
East Greenbush
Nepo, Mark Evan
East Hampton
Claiborne, Craig
Goldman, Martin Raymond Rubin
Ignatow, David
Tillich, Hannah
East Northport
Harrington-Connors, Erin
Israeloff, Roberta
East Norwich
Meyerowitz, Steven A.
East Rockaway
Schneider, Yvette E.
East Setauket
Overton, Ronald Ernest
East Syracuse
Holston, James Eugene
Eastchester
Gottschall, Edward Maurice
Easthampton
Long, Robert
Edmeston
Blackman, Dorothy Loyte
Ellenville
Rosenstock, Francyne N.
Ellicottville
Frank, Tracy Steven Scott
Elmhurst
Barbato, Joseph Allen
Elmira
Hill, Emily Katharine
Tifft, Ellen
Elmont
Barci, Robert John
Elmsford
Coleman, Ellen Schneid
Milne, Robert Scott
Endicott
Joseph, Ronald K.
Endwell
O'Brien, Penny
Reavis, Charles G.
Fairport
Michelucci, Katherine Coralee Burch
Farmingdale
Fishman Suny, Charles
Rozakis, Robert H.
Flushing
Espaillat, Rhina Polonia
Friedman, Norman
Gellis, Barrie Fabian
Goldsmith, Howard
Hesselbach, Bruce William
Landsman, Samuel N.B.
Singer, Frieda
Taylor, Conciere Marlana
Forest Hills
Kozer, Jose
Malin, Irving
Moise, Edwin Evariste
Wiener, Marvin S.
Zanca, Minerva Martinez
Forestville
Lunde, David Eric
Fredonia
Maloney, Dennis Michael
Saveth, Edward Norman
Freehold
O'Neill, Peter J.
Freeport
Sobel, Lester Albert
Swanson, Eleanora
Terris, Virginia Rinaldy
Freeville
Morgan, Robert Ray
Fresh Meadows
Gold, Doris Bauman
Gansevoort
Cackener, Helen Elizabeth Lewis
Garden City
De Mille, Nelson Richard
Grimsley, Will Henry
Hatch, Dorothy L.
Holt, Victoria
Katopes, Peter James
Wilson, Harold Charles
Gardiner
Mabee, Carleton
Garnerville
Allen, David Dudley
Garrison
Barnhart, David Knox
Geneseo
Bachem-Alent, Rose Marie
Beale, Irene Alleman
Harding, Walter
Kelly, David Michael
Kelly, Sylvia Hayden Neahr
Richard, Michel Paul
Geneva
Tall, Deborah
Glen Cove
Tucker, Martin
Glendale
Urbaniak, George Carl
Glenfield
Mihalyi, Louis Leonard
Glenford
Perkins, Michael
Glens Falls
Berbrich, Joan D.
Crosby Metzger, Lisa M.
Metivier, Donald Anthony
Rikhoff, Jean.
Gowanda
Korbar, Marcia Marie
Grand Island
Yalkovsky, Rafael
Grand View-on-Hudson
Hamilton, Patricia Wardley
Great Neck
Eysman, Harvey A.
Gross, Theodore Lawrence
Hurwitz, Johanna
Mc Quade, Walter
Rostky, George Harold
Spanier, Muriel
Waxman, Herbert J.
Yaryura-Tobias, Jose A.
Zeiger, Lila L
Greenwood
Sekoll, June Louise
Guilderland
Felsen, Karl Edwin
Ryan, Nancy Marie
Hall
Shail, Linda Grace
Hamburg
Peterson, Karen Lynn
Ritz, Joseph P.
Stratton, Thomas William
Hamilton
Balakian, Peter
Rexine, John Efstratios
Hamlin
Robertson, Mary E.
Hampton Bays
Bennett, Anna Elizabeth
Harrison
Weatherby, Gregg L.
Hartsdale
Davenport, Karen Odom
Ross, David
Weber, Samuel
Hasting-on-Hudson
Gioia, (Michael) Dana
Hastings on Hudson
Kingston, Cecelia M.
Hastings-On-Hudson
Stephens, Christopher P.
Hastings-on-Hudson
Higgins, Paula Elizabeth
Lehner, Christine Reine
Mc Cullough, Frances Monson
Zolotow, Charlotte Shapiro
Hauppauge
Jacko, Diane Newell
Hempstead
Dillard, Emil Lee
Hewlett LI
Belcher, Grace (Ruth) Daley
Hinsdale
Soucy, Barbara Marie
Homer
Howlett, Joan Gail
White, Ann
Honeoye Falls
Lemperle, Virginia Maxine
Howard Beach
Badillo-Sciortino, Olga Esther
Huntington
Bendiner, Robert
Byrnes, Frederick Joseph
Connor, Robert J.
Damon, John D(rew)
De Masi, Jack Bernard
J. Robert, Connor
Knorr, Judith R.
Huntington Sta
Keremes, Constance Andrea
Huntington Station
Pape, Sharon Barbara
Irvington
Scott-McBride, Nancy Forsyth
Irvington-on-Hudson
Whitney, Ruth Reinke
Ithaca
Ackerman, Diane
Ammons, Archie Randolph
De Laurentis, Louise Budde
Elledge, Scott Bowen
Goldwyn, Craig D.
Hower, Edward
Janowitz, Phyllis
Kendler, Bernhard
Lurie, Alison
Mackin, Jeanne A.
Mc Clane, Kenneth Anderson Jr.
Moore, Robert Laurence
Muratori, Fred

Orear, Jay
Redding, Jay Saunders
Rishel, Mary Ann Malinchak
Sagan, Carl Edward
Sale, Marilyn Mills
Schumacher, Julie Alison
Slatoff, Walter Jacob
Stallworthy, Jon Howie
Summers, Robert Samuel
Tarr, Curtis W.
West, Paul Noden
Jackson Heights
Brodey, Jim
Kimmelman, Burt Joseph
Kuttner, Paul
Murray, Hugh T. Jr.
Jacksonville
Culler, Jonathan Dwight
Jamaica
Brewster, Townsend Tyler
Faust, Naomi Flowe
Keel-Williams, Mildred Yvonne
Kelly, George Anthony
Paolucci, Anne (Attura)
Jamestown
Furlong, Maurice B.
Martin, Janette Gould
Jamesville
Decrow, Karen
Jeffersonville
Nadler, Dorothy (Dot) Luria
Jericho
Axinn, Donald Everett
Johnson City
Weber, Elizabeth Ann
Johnstown
Nilsen, Richard Haldor
Katonah
Allman, John
Frye, John
Phillips, Robert Schaeffer
Thompson, Edward Thorwald
Kenmore
Mc Peters, Sharon Janese
Kenoza Lake
Berg, Abby Marvin
Kew Gardens
Loughlin, Richard L(awrence)
Kings Point
Shor, Cynthia Lynch
Kingston
Fleischer, Leslie
Lake Success
Imperato, Pascal James
Lansing
Lehman, David
Larchmont
Block, Julian
Brown, Lester L.
Greenberg, Alfred Henry
Kerr, Jean
Mayerson, Philip
Larchmont Manor
Kerr, Walter F.
Levittown
Cullem-Kristian, Florence Mary
Lewiston
Laurie, Margaret Sanders
Lindenhurst
Nolin, Lillian Renee
Purdy, Susan
Livingston Manor
Starmer, Ronnie
Livonia
Southworth, Miles F.
Locke
Mc Caull, Julian Lincoln
Locust Valley
Friedrich, Otto Alva
Long Beach
Caplan, Judith Shulamith Langer
Hession, Eileen Melia
Tana, Patti
Long Island
Mccall, Mabel Bunny
Wysor, Bettie
Long Island City
Pantzer, Alfred Kivu
Rosenstein, Ira
Loudonville
Ferguson, Joan M.
Hannay, Margaret Patterson
Lyons Falls
Morrison, Denise Annette
Mahopac
Horvath, Elemer (George)
Mamaroneck
Fitch, Charles Marden
Heilman, Joan Rattner
Perlman, John Niels
Mamaronock
Baker, Samm Sinclair
Manhasset Hills
Rachlin, Harvey
Marlboro
Miller, Mark Dawson
Maspeth
Kwiatkowski, Diana J.
Massapequa
Tinghitella, Stephen
Melrose
Purves, Alan Carroll
Merrick
Kaufman, Stuart J.
Patterson, Raymond Richard
Middletown
Borenstein, Emily Ruth
Borenstein, Emily Schwartz
Vorbach, Renee R.
Miller Place
Kronenberg, Mindy H.
Millwood
Hunt, Morton M(agill)
Hunt, Bernice (Kohn)
Mineola
Danna, Carl
Stillwell
Mohawk
Vercz, Carol Ann
Monroe
Gocek, Matilda Arkensout
Monsey
Bingham, Hiram A.
Katz, Susan A.
Montauk
Rotzinger-Padden, Karin Marie
Montgomery
Lonigan, Paul Raymond
Mount Kisco
Nelson, Milo Gabriel
Mountainville
Mc Carthy, Gerald A.
Mt Vernon
Blackmon, Antonia A.
New york
Field, Edward
New Hyde Park
Lehrer, Stanley
New Paltz
De Cormier-Shekerjian, Regina
Mc Pherson, Bruce Rice
Munsterberg, Hugo
Uschuk, Pamela Marie
New Rochelle
Forster, Arnold
Rosen, Norma
Saunders, Rubie Agnes
Shelton, Nicolina (Nikki)
Sigel, Efrem
Wakin, Edward
New Windsor
Harrison, Charles Edward
New York
Abrams, Linsey
Achtert, Walter Scott
Adams, Alice
Addams, Charles Samuel
Adler, Margot Susanna
Albee, Edward Franklin
Aldan, Daisy
Alexander, Charlotte Anne
Alexander, Shana
Allen, Roberta
Ameen, Mark Joseph
New York
Amory, Cleveland
Anderegg, Karen Klok
Anderson, Jack Warren
Anderson, Curtiss Martin
Anderson, Poul William
Anderson, Alexandra C.
Anderson, Jack Northman
Andre, Michael
Angell, Roger
Anger, Kenneth
Anglesey, Zoe R.
Arlen, Michael J.
Aronson, Arnold P.
Aryeh, Neier
Ashton, Dore
Asimov, Isaac
Astor, Mrs. Vincent
Atlas, James Robert
Attaway, Le Roy
Auchincloss, Louis Stanton
Auel, Jean M(arie)
Augustine, Jane
Axthelm, Pete
Bahr, Laren S.
Bain, Geri Rhonda
Bainbridge, John
Bakal, Carl
Baker, Elizabeth Calhoun
Baker, Russell Wayne
Balakian, Nona Hilda
Balderston, Jean Merrill
Balk, Alfred William
Ballantine, Ian
Balliett, Whitney
Barber, Benjamin R
Barkhorn, Jean Cook
Barlow, William Edward
Barnes, Wade
Barnouw, Erik
Baron, Carolyn
Barthelme, Donald
Bartley, Robert Leroy
Barwood, Jacques
Barzun, Jacques
Bassett, Elizabeth Ewing
Baughman, J. Ross
Bayer, Cary Stuart
Beattie, Ann
Beaufort, John David
Beck, James (Henry) Beck
Beebe, F. Lisa
Begell, William
Beim, Norman
Bel Geddes, Joan
Bell, Jane Matlack
Benchley, Peter Bradford
Bender, Thomas
Benderson, Bruce
Benedikt, Michael
Bentley, Eric
Bercovitch, Hanna Margareta
Berge, Carol
Berger, Thomas Louis
Berger, Eric
Berkow, Ira Harvey
Berkwitt, George Joseph
Berlitz, Charles Frambach
Berman, Ann Muriel
Bernard, Kenneth
Bernstein, Carl
Bernstein, Robert Louis
Bernstein, Charles
Bernstein, Burton
Bernuth, Ernest Patrick, Jr.
Berrigan, Daniel
Berry, Joyce Cha
Biewen, Robert L.
Birmingham, Stephen
Birnbaum, Stephen Norman
Birnstein, Ann
Birsh, Arthur Thomas
Bissell, Leclair
Black, Cathleen Prunty
Black, Hillel Moses
Blacker, Harriet
Blackwell, Earl
Blair, Clay Drewry
Blaise, Clark Lee
Blaser, Cathy B.
Blatty, William Peter
Bleiberg, Robert Marvin
Bleiweiss, Herbert Irving
Bliven, Bruce, Jr.
Block, Lawrence
Bloomingdale, Teresa
Blos, Joan W.
Bluh, Bonnie
Blume, Judy Sussman
Blyth, Myrna Greenstein
Bohle, Bruce William
Bourdon, David
Bourjaily, Vance
Bowles, Paul
Bowser, James William
Boylan, Roger Brendan
Boyle, Kay
Bradbury, Ray Douglas
Brady, Frank R
Brady, Mary Gerard
Brawley, Ernest Charles
Breslin, Jimmy
Brill, Ernest
Brisby, Stewart Paul
Brittain, Rasa
Brody, Jacqueline
Brody, Jane Ellen
Brooks, John
Brown, Rita Mae
Brown, David
Brown, Helen Gurley
Brown, Bernard E(dward)
Brownmiller, Susan
Bryant, Gay
Bryk, William
Buckler, Beatrice
Buckley, Virginia Laura
Buckley, Priscilla Langford
Buckley, William Frank Jr.
Buhagiar, Marion
Burket, Harriet
Burness, Wallace B(inny)
Burroughs, William Seward
Burstein, John
Bylinsky, Gene Michael
Borchardt 136 E 57th, Steinbach
Cabral, Olga Marie
Calisher, Hortense
Cameron, Eleanor Frances
Cameron, Lou
Campbell, Liberty
Caputo, Philip Joseph
Carroll, Jonathan
Caws, Peter James
Chang-Rodriguez, Eugenio
Chapman, Constance Ann

Chin, Daryl
Christman, Henry Max
Christopher, Maurine Brooks
Chute, Marchette
Ciabattari, Jane Dotson
Clampitt, Amy Kathleen
Clark, Mary Higgins
Clark, Matt
Cleaver, Vera Allen
Cohen, Ira H.
Colburn, Robert Dickinson
Cole, Richard
Como, William Michael
Cooper, Arthur Martin
Cooperman, Hasye
Corman, Avery
Corn, Alfred Dewitt
Corso, Gregory Nunzio
Cousins, Linda
Crandall, Charles Jordan
Crandall, Norma Rand
Crase, Douglas
Crowdus, Gary Alan
Cullinan, Elizabeth
Curley, Thomas F.
Currelley, Lorraine
Curry, Jane Louise
Dahlberg, Rlene H
Daly, Janet Morgan
Danto, Arthur Coleman
Davis, Susan Jean
Davis, Christopher
Davis, Allen, III
Dawkins, Cecil
De Haven, Tom
De Vito, Joseph Anthony
Decter, Midge
Del Rey, Lester
Demby, Betty J.
Didion, Joan
Dillard, Annie
Dobell, (Eleanor) Mercy
Dobell, Byron Maxwell
Doctorow, Edgar Lawrence
Donaldson, Stephen Reeder
Donath, Robert E.
Doren, Konstantin (Corky)
Dorset, Gerald Henry
Drennen, Marcia Simonton
Drew, Derek C.
Drury, Allen Stuart
Duberstein, Helen Laura
Dunne, John Gregory
Eady, Cornelius Robert
Eakins, Patricia
Edelman, Elaine
Einbond, Bernard Lionel
Elizabeth, Burke
Elliott, Sumner Locke
Emshwiller, Carol Fries
Espy, Willard R.
Farley, Walter Lorimer
Faust, Irvin
Fein, Cheri
Feirstein, Frederick
Feiwel, Jean Leslie
Fertig, Howard
Finkelstein, Miriam
Finnegan, Pamela Anne
Fiori, Pamela Anne
Fisher, Arthur
Fitzgerald, Frances
Fleming, Thomas James
Follett, Kenneth Martin
Foner, Eric
Foote, Horton
Ford, Gertrude
Ford, Richard C.
Forer, Anne Ruth
Foster, Barbara
Fox, Susan Christine
Fox, Eleanor Mae Cohen
Fox, John
Frady, Marshall Bolton
Frank, Peter (Solomon)
Frank, Reuven
Frank, Gerold
Frankel, Ellen
Frankel, Max
Fraser, Bruce Wickersham
Frederick, Dawn Hildred Ruth
Freedman, Helen Rosengren
Freeman, Cynthia
French, Marilyn
Frenkel, Karen A.
Friday, Nancy
Fried, Philip Henry
Friedan, Betty
Friedman, Betty
Friedman, B(ernard) H(arper)
Frumkes, Lewis Burke
Furlotte, Nicolas
Furnas, Joseph Chamberlain
Gaddis, William
Gaines, Ernest J.
Galassi, Jonathan
Gallagher, Patricia Cecilia
Gangemi, Kenneth
Gardner, Nancy Bruff
Garfield, Brian Wynne
Gasner, Anne
Gelb, Arthur
Gelber, Jack
Gentz, William Howard
Gerhardt, Lillian Noreen
Gibbs, Jamie
Gilbert, Ilsa
Gill, Brendan
Gilmore, Clarence Percy
Ginsberg, Allen
Ginzburg, Ralph
Giovanni, Nikki
Gittelson, Natalie Leavy
Glen, Emilie
Glimm, Adele
Gluckson, James Andrew
Gold, Patricia Mc Manus
Goldemberg, Isaac
Goldsmith, Arthur Austin
Goldsmith, Barbara
Golson, George Barry
Golub, Marcia Helene
Goreau, Angeline W.
Gorey, Edward St. John
Gould, Jean Rosalind
Gould, Lois
Gray, Spalding
Gray, Francine Du Plessix
Green, Gerald
Green, Ashbel
Greenburg, Dan
Gregor, Arthur
Griffo, Lynn Jennifer
Gross, Carol Cott
Groth, Brian Joseph
Guest, Judith Ann
Guest, Barbara
Gunderson, Joanna
Gitlin Agcy 7 W 51st, Stevenson
Haberman, Daniel
Hadas, Rachel
Halberstam, David
Halpern, Daniel
Halsey, William Darrach
Hamill, Pete
Hancock, Niel Anderson
Hanff, Helene
Hannibal, Edward L.
Hardwick, Elizabeth
Harnack, Curtis
Harper, Douglas C.
Harrington, Michael
Harris, T. George
Harris, Marie-Therese
Harrison, Harry (Max)
Harrison, William Neal
Hatvary, George Egon
Haukeness, Helen Liza
Hauss, Deborah
Hazzard, Shirley
Hedges, Dan
Heilbrun, Carolyn Gold
Heinlein, Robert Anson
Heller, Joseph
Hellew, Joyce Virginia
Hemsing, Albert E.
Henderson, Erskine D.
Henderson, Safiya (Sharon)
Hentoff, Nathan Irving
Hentoff, Margot
Herman, Grace G.
Herzog, Arthur, III
Heymann, Clemens Claude
Highwater, Jamake
Himmelfarb, Gertrude
Hirsch, George Aaron
Hite, Shere D.
Hoagland, Edward
Holland, Barbara
Holman, Bob
Hoover, Susan Frantz
Horowitz, David Joel
Howard, Richard
Howard, Jane Temple
Howard-Howard, Margo Chanler
Howe, Irving
Howell, Barbara Miles
Humphreys, John Richard Adams
Hunter, Evan
Hunter-Gault, Charlayne
Hutchison, Michael S.
Hutchison, David A.
Hyams, Joe
Inez, Colette
Irving, John Winslow
Isaacs, Florence
Iverson, Lucille Karin
Jacker, Corinne Litvin
Jaffe, Rona
Janeway, Elizabeth Hall
Janowitz, Tama
Jarvis, Frederick Gordon
Jekel, Pamela L.
Jhabvala, Ruth Prawer
Johnson, Trebbe
Johnson, Evelyne
Jones, Ann (Maret)
Jones, Di Anna Lynn
Jong, Erica Mann
Kael, Pauline
Kail, Robert Lee
Kaplan, Stuart R(onald)
Kash, Wyatt Keith
Katz, William Loren
Katz, Colleen Burke
Kauffmann, Stanley Jules
Kaufman, Bel
Kavaler, Rebecca
Kazin, Alfred
Keating, John Roderick
Keenan, Gerard Patrick
Kehrer, Daniel M.
Kennedy, Margaret Swierz
Kenyon, Bruce Guy
Kern, Edith
Keyes, Daniel
Kimball, Robert Eric
King, Stephen Edwin
Kissick, Gary Richard
Klahr, Myra Blossom
Klein, William Harry
Klein, Norma
Knobler, Peter Stephen
Koch, Kenneth
Koning, Hans
Kono, Toshihiko
Korda, Michael Vincent
Kosinski, Jerzy Nikodem
Kostelanetz, Richard
Kozol, Jonathan
Kraman, Cynthia
Kramer, Jane
Krementz, Jill
Kriegel, Leonard
Krim, Seymour
Kroesen, Jill Anne
Kuehl, John Richard
L'amour, Louis Dearborn
Lachenbruch, David
Lader, Lawrence
Lahr, John
Lamont, Corliss
Landau, Annette Henkin
Landau, Peter Edward
Landsman, Joseph K.
Landsmann, Leanna
Lane, Nancy
Lapham, Lewis Henry
Larrabee, Eric
Larsen, Wendy Wilder
Lauritsen, John P.
Lawrence, Arthur Peter
Lay, Nancy Duke S.
Le Shan, Lawrence L(ee)
Le Shan, Eda J(oan)
Leavitt, Caroline Susan
Lehmann-Haupt, Christopher Charles
Leiber, Fritz
Leibowitz, Herbert Akiba
Leinster, Colin Ronald
Lemay, Harding
Lerch, Sharon
Lesniak, Rose
Levertov, Denise
Levi, Jan Heller
Levi, Toni Mergentime
Levin, Amy Beth
Levin, Ira
Levine, Mark Leonard
Levitas, Gloria B(arach)
Levy, Stephen
Levy, Carol
Levy, Robert Jeffrey
Lewin, Rebecca
Lewis, Harry
Liberman, Alexander
Lifton, Robert Jay
Lilly, Doris
Lindfors, Viveca
Linney, Romulus
Linzner, Gordon
Lippard, Lucy Rowland
Lish, Gordon Jay
Litt, Iris
Littledale, Freya Lota
Lobel, Arnold Stark
Lollar, Coleman Aubrey
Longland, Jean Rogers
Loomis, Sabra
Lopatin, Judy
Lopez, Barry Holstun
Lopez, Sharon Yolanda
Lord, Robert Wilder
Love, Nancy
Lovelace, Carey
Lubar, Robert
Ludlum, Robert
Luntz, Perry
Lynes, (Joseph) Russell, (Jr.)
Maas, Peter

Mac Afee, Norman
Machlin, Milton Robert
Mackenzie, Ginny Lee
Mahony, Elizabeth Alsop
Mailer, Norman
Malanga, Gerard Joseph
Malefakis, Edward E.
Mamet, David Alan
Mandell, Mel
Mano, D. Keith
Mantell, Suzanne
Marcus, Steven
Markson, David M.
Markus, Julia
Martin, Scott D.
Martin, Denise Belisle
Martin, Ann Matthews
Martin, George (Whitney)
Martin, Stephen-Paul
Mason, Bobbie Ann
Mathis, Sharon Bell
Matthews, William
Maule, Hamilton Bee
Maxwell, William
Mayer, Martin Prager
Mayes, Herbert Raymond
Mayhall, Jane Francis
Mc Cann, Michael F.
Mc Clatchy, Joseph Donald
Mc Clure, Michael Thomas
Mc Corduck, Pamela
Mc Cormick, Kenneth Dale
Mc Cracken, Daniel Delbert
Mc Crie, Robert Delbert
Mc Darrah, Fred William
Mc Donell, Robert Terry
Mc Ginniss, Joe
Mc Gonigle, Thomas
Mc Grath, Lee Parr
Mc Guane, Thomas Francis, III
Mc Keown, William Taylor
Medina, Kathryn Bach
Meglin, Nick
Mehta, Ved (Parkash)
Melhem, D(iana) H(elen)
Melman, Seymour
Meltzer, Milton
Menashe, Samuel
Mendini, Douglas A.
Meredith, Scott
Merriam, Eve
Merton, Robert K.
Metz, Robert Roy
Metzroth, Jane Porvancher
Meyer, Susan E.
Meyer, Pucci
Michaels, James Walker
Michel, Trudi
Middendorf, John Harlan
Middleton, Drew
Miller, Walter James
Miller, Arthur
Miller, Roberta Davis
Millett, Katherine Murray
Mills, Paul Lance
Mills, James Spencer
Milton, Barbara
Minahan, John English
Mirabella, Grace
Mirsky, Mark Jay
Mitgang, Herbert
Moffitt, John
Molnar, Thomas
Monaco, James
Moore, Robert Lowell, Jr
Moreno, Eusebio Carlos
Morgan, (George) Frederick
Morgenstern, Dan Michael
Moritz, Charles Fredric
Morris, Edmund
Morris, Wright
Morris, Mary
Morrison, Laura Mary
Morrison, Frank
Morrison, Toni
Morrison, Lillian
Morton, Frederic
Mozeson, Isaac Elchanan
Mullins, Helene
Mullins, Ronald Gift
Murray, Charles (Alan)
Nathan, Robert Stuart
Navasky, Victor Saul
Nemetz, Christine Arax
Nestle, Joan
Neville, Emily Cheney
Newman, Richard Alan
Newman, Rachel
Newson, Eula Mae
Nicholas, Nancy
Nicklaus, (Charles) Frederick
Nickson, Richard
Nissenson, Hugh
Nocerino, Kathryn M.
Nolte, Judith Ann
North, Charles Laurence
Novello, Don
O'Donnell, Laurence Gerard
O'Gorman, Ned
Oatman, Eric Furber
Offit, Sidney
Oisteanu, Valery
Oldham, Joe
Olds, Sharon
Olsen, Richard Ellison
Orrmont, Arthur
Osterman, Susan
Ozick, Cynthia
Paden, Roberta Lee
Padgett, Ron
Paglio, Lydia Elizabeth
Paley, Grace
Parker, Nancy Winslow
Parker, Maynard Michael
Patterson, Charles Wilson
Patty, Ann Elizabeth
Paugh, Thomas Francis
Paul, Sandra K.
Peacock, Molly
Pearlson, Fredda S.
Peck, Richard Wayne
Peper, George Frederick
Persky, Mordecai (Mort)
Persky, Robert Samuel
Peters, Joan Karen
Pett, Saul
Phillips, Louis James
Phillips, William
Picano, Felice
Piel, Gerard
Piirto-Navarre, Jane Marie
Pilcer, Sonia Hanna
Pilpel, Robert H.
Pilpel, Harriet Fleischl
Pirsig, Robert Maynard
Pisar, Samuel
Pitts, Eugene, III
Plimpton, George Ames
Pochoda, Elizabeth Turner
Podhoretz, Norman
Pogrebin, Letty Cottin
Poirier, Richard
Pollak, Richard
Pollet, Elizabeth
Pollitt, Katha
Pomerantz, Charlotte
Porter, Sylvia
Porter, Donald
Porter, Andrew Brian
Potoker, Edward Martin
Powers, Thomas Moore
Powers, James Farl
Prashker, Betty A.
Price, Richard
Purcell, Henry
Puzo, Mario
Queenan, Joseph Martin, Jr.
Quirk, Lawrence Joseph
Rachlin, Nahid
Rackow, Sylvia
Raphael, Phyllis
Raskin, Ellen
Rass, Rebecca Rivka
Ratner, Rochelle
Reed, Rex
Rehns, Marsha Lee
Reich, Herb
Reilly, Nancy O.
Reis, Robert M.
Reiss, Timothy James
Reiss, James
Replansky, Naomi
Reuther, David Louis
Rewald, John
Rhodes, Norman Leonard
Rhodes, Richard Lee
Rice, Carolyn J.
Rich, Adrienne
Rich, Frank Hart
Richards, Elizabeth Glazier
Richardson, Midge Turk
Rinard, Sally Stedman
Rinzler, Carol Gene Eisen
Ritter, Jeffrey Michael (Jeff)
Rivera, Louis Reyes
Roadarmel, Paul Douglas
Robbins, Harold
Roberts, Janet Louise
Robins, Corinne
Robins, Natalie
Robinson, Katherine Woodroofe
Robinson, Raymond Kenneth
Rochon, Edwin Waterbury
Rogers, Rosemary
Rogin, Gilbert Leslie
Rollyson, Carl
Rooney, Andrew Aitken
Rorem, Ned
Rosberg, Rose
Rose, Joel
Rose, Louise Blecher
Rosenberg, John David
Rosenblatt, Ruth
Rosengarten, David
Rosenstiel, Leonie
Rosenthal, David H.
Rosenthal, Jacob
Rosenthal, Abraham Michael
Ross, Andrea Patricia
Rosset, Lisa Krug
Rossner, Judith
Roth, Philip
Rovner, Arkady
Rowe, Beverly Hope
Rubin, David M.
Rudin, Arnold James
Rudin, Marcia Ruth
Rudman, Mark
Rugoff, Milton
Sagan, Kathyrne V.
Sahgal, Pavan
Said, Edward W.
Sainer, Arthur
Saint-Jacques, Alfred Joseph
Salinger, Jerome David
Salinger, Pierre Emil George
Sanders, Ronald
Sanders, Lawrence
Sandler, Lucy Freeman
Sandler, Irving Harry
Santini, Rosemarie
Sarris, Andrew George
Saul, John Woodruff, III
Saunders, Dero Ames
Savage, Thomas U.
Savicky, Randolph Philip
Saxton, Mark
Schaap, Richard Jay
Schachter, Hindy Lauer
Schappes, Morris U(rman)
Schell, Jonathan Edward
Schickel, Richard
Schieffelin, Laurie Graham
Schimmel, Caroline Fearey
Schlesinger, Arthur (Meier), Jr.
Schneebaum, Tobias
Schneemann, Carolee
Schoell, William
Schoenberger, Nancy
Schor, Lynda
Schulberg, Budd
Schulman, Sarah M.
Schultz, Philip (Arnold)
Schuyler, James Marcus
Schwartz, Tony (Anthony)
Schwartz, Lynne Sharon
Schwed, Peter
Schwerin, Doris
Scobie, Itha
Scoppettone, Sandra Valerie
Seaman, Sylvia Sybil
Segal, Jonathan Bruce
Segal, Erich
Segal, Lore
Seidel, Frederick Lewis
Seidensticker, Edward George
Seidman, Hugh
Selig, Karl-Ludwig
Seligman, Daniel
Selsam, Milicent Ellis
Sendak, Maurice Bernard
Shange, Ntozake
Shaplen, Robert Modell
Sheehy, Gail Henion
Shelby, Joyce Young
Sheldon, Sidney
Sherry, James Terence
Shestack, Melvin Bernard
Shnayerson, Robert Beahan
Shuldiner, Herbert
Shulevitz, Uri
Shyre, Paul
Silber, Joan Karen
Silberman, Charles Eliot
Silbert, Layle
Silbey, Paula J.
Silverman, Kenneth Eugene
Silvers, Robert B.
Silverstein, Shelby
Simmons, Shirley J(oyce Leslie)
Singer, Isaac Bashevis
Sklar, Robert Anthony
Smeraldi, Florence G. Stark
Smith, Liz
Smith, Robert Letton
Smith, William Jay
Smith, Anne Mollegen
Snow, Bonnie
Sobol, Donald J.
Solotaroff, Ted
Solzhenitsyn, Alexander
Sonnenberg, Ben
Sorrentino, Gilbert
Sourian, Peter
Spielberg, Peter
Spieler, Francis Joseph
Stanger, Ila
Stanton, Priscilla Anne
Steel, Danielle Fernande
Stern, Richard Martin

Philip, A.g. Davis
Pilcher, Edith
Ricci, Naomi C.
Seltzer, Joanne
Scotia
Lewis, Ricki
Scottsville
Clune, Henry W.
Sea Cliff
Swenson, May
Seaford
Luber, Elliot B.
Selden
Di Franco, Anthony M.
Setauket
Rawson, Eleanor S.
Slatkin, Marcia
Shelter Island
Alpert, Hollis
Sherburne
Busch, Frederick
Shirley
La Veglia, Geri
Shoreham
Ganz, Alice
Silver Creek
Sager, Donna Layne (Layne)
Smithtown
Kneitel, Thomas Stephen
Snyder
Holender, Barbara D.
Sound Beach
Cooper, Jeffrey B.
South New Berlin
Hausrath, Ralph Allan
Southampton
Goldowsky, Barbara
Knowles, John
Loening, Sarah (Elizabeth) Larkin
Parlatore, Anselm
Sparkill
Lukas, Susan
Spencerport
Humphrey, Paul
Spring Glen
Katz, Menke
Spring Valley
Blauvelt, Ralph
Madri, Alberta Maria
Springfield Gardens
Lewis, Harriet (Hattie)
St James
White, Claire Nicolas
Staten Island
Beidel, Hyun Sook
Kibler, Wallace Edward
Lorde, Audre Geraldin
Porter, Darwin Fred
Schwerner, Armand
Thompson, Jacqueline
Stone Ridge
Gould, Roberta
Stoneybrook
Elman, Richard
Stony Brook
Semmel, Bernard
Stuart, Kiel
Weiss, Sigmund
Suffern
Gall, Sally Moore
Rosenthal, M.l.
Shor, Murray
Syosset
Wolitzer, Hilma
Syracuse
Bharati, Agehananda
Carruth, Hayden
Chayat, Sherry
Gallagher, Tess
Goldleaf, Steven
Hoey, Allen S.
Jensen, Dwight William
La Rue, Arlene Catherine
Stephens, Edward Carl
Unger, Douglas Arthur
Walsh, Doris Montague Huntley
Wilson, Luther
Wolff, Tobias
Tarrytown
Capossela, James P.
Tenafly
Rudy, Dorothy L.
Tonawanda
Tucker, Melvin Jay
Vine, Janet Diana
Troy
Biskin, Miriam Marcia
Lemke, Carlton Edward
Mayer, Susan M.
Trumansburg
Mc Conkey, James R.
Taylor, Richard
Upper Nyack
Wolff, Daniel J.
Valhalla
Alvarez, Raymond P.
Valley Cottage
De Lima, Sigrid
Valley Stream
Rosenbaum, Sylvia P.
Vestal
Mitchell, Loften
Wading River
Heinz, Brian James
Wainscott
Henderson, William Charles
Wantagh
Rabiner, Susan
Warwick
Buell, Frederick Henderson
Waterford
Bartel, Pauline C.
Watervliet
Cerri, Lawrence J.
Webster
Smiley, Virginia Kester
Wellsville
Fanton, Roland Benjamin
West Hempstead
Pollio, Ralph Thomas
West Hurley
Brady, Maureen
West Nyack
Cunneen, Joseph
West Point
Kaufmann, Joseph Gregory, Jr.
West Seneca
Albarella, Joan Katherine
West Shokan
Bruner, Richard Wallace
Westbury
Dobrin, Arthur Barry
Levy, Robert
Lundquist, Carl
Westhampton
Billman, Irwin Edward
Westhampton Beach
De'pazzi, Ellen E
White Plains
Bock, Gordon Honold
Ellenbogen, Milton Joseph
Goodman, Walter
Lang, Miriam
Lewis, Marjorie
Rosenberg, Maurice
Silverman, Al
Whitesboro
Epley-Shuck, Barbara Jeanne
Williamsbridge Sta
Johnston, Gary
Williamsville
Blackburn, Barbara Ann
Hartman, Elizabeth Ann
Woodbury
Buckvar, Felice
Woodmere
Abramson, Martin
Woodside
Campbell, Sharon Lynn
Cohen, Barbara Ann
Fax, Elton Clay
Veuhoff, Heinz
Woodstock
Boundy, Donna J.
Godwin, Gail Kathleen
Gordon, Harris A.
Hood, Robert Eric
Michaels, Joanne
Ober, Stuart A.
Rafalsky, Stephen Mark
Yonkers
Flemming, Kay Estelle
Kalian, Robert P.
Lardas, Konstantinos N.
Maguire, Cecilia Gertrude
Papaleo, Joseph
Rosenberg, Nancy Sherman
Tiktin, Carl
Votano, Paul Anthony
Wright, Joseph S
Yorktown
Hanlon, Emily
Yorktown Heights
Blumberg, Leda
Friedman, Stanley P.
Lombardo, Irene E.
Meade, Walter Wathen

North Carolina
Albemarle
Moose, Ruth Morr
Asheville
Brittain, William E.
Hopes, David Brendan
Bakersville
Kuhne, Sharon Anglin
Banner Elk
Speer, Allen Paul III
Bath
Marsh, Carole
Benson
Holmes, Helen Juanita
Black Mountain
Skoyles, John
Blowing Rock
Buxton, Barry Miller
Boone
Lubetsky, Elsie
Sharp, Sharon Annette Andrews
Brevard
Hicks, Clifford Byron
Burnsville
Morgan, Ernest
Carrboro
Bain, Robert Addison
Hogan, Judy Fordham
Chapel Hill
Adams, Elie Maynard
Best, Winfield Judson
Betts, Doris June Waugh
Coulter, N(orman) Arthur, Jr.
Drake, David Allen
Eaton, Charles Edward
Garfunkel, Joseph M.
Hopper, Virginia Shearer
Jones, Paul M.
Malone, Elmer Taylor II Jr.
Munsat, Stanley Morris
Ravenel, Shannon
Rosenberg, Jay Frank
Safransky, Sy
Stadter, Philip Austin
Utiger, Robert David
Van Seters, John
Weinberg, Gerhard Ludwig
Charlotte
Brody, Harry Philip
Knauth, Stephen Craig
Ludvigson, Susan Gayle
Mc Millan, Sally Hill
Newman, P(aul) B(aker)
Smith, Bertie Reece
Tool, Dennis Casler
Chrlotte
Mager, Donald Northrop
Clinton
Kathryn Bright, Gurkin
Concord
Waid, Stephen Hamilton
Cullowhee
Brasfield, James
Byer, Kathryn Stripling
Paulk, William (Eston)
Davidson
Davidson, Chalmers Gaston
Denver
Gleasner, Diana Cottle
Durham
Applewhite, James William
Behn, Robert Dietrich
Bevington, Helen S.
Ebel, Charles William
Elliot, Jeffrey M.
Fish, Stanley Eugene
Franklin, John Hope
Grace, Eugene Vernon
Kaufman, Debra Jane
Mc Fee, Michael Alan
O'Barr, Jean Fox
Orr, Linda
Petroski, Catherine
Petroski, Henry
Porter, Joe Ashby
Price, Reynolds
Sanford, Terry
Shipley, Robert Hopkins
Warner, William Eaton
E Flat Rock
Dayton, Irene Catherine
Fayetteville
Wehlitz, Annie Louise
Goldsboro
Dotson, Raymond Paul
Roberts, Diane Hill
Greensboro
Benfey, Otto Theodor
Bixby, Robert Jay
Chamlee, Kenneth D.
Chappell, Fred
Deagon, Ann
Flynt, Candace
Fragola, Anthony Nicholas
Gates, Nancy Gotter
Gilbert, Marie Rogers
Hester, Martin Luther
Sewell, Elizabeth
Watson, Robert Winthrop
York, John Thomas
Zacharias, Lela Ann
Zacharias, Lela Ann
Greenville
Makuck, Peter
Nischan, Gerda M.
Hayesville
Simpson, Nancy Carolyn
Hillsborough
Gilbo, Anna-Carolyn
Lincoln, C(harles) Eric
Little, Loyd Harry, Jr.
Jamestown

Rosson-Davis, Barbara Ann
Jefferson
Franklin, Robert Mcfarland
Laurinburg
Bayes, Ronald Homer
Liberty
Neese, Ruby S.
Lincolnton
Nixon, Sallie White
Linden
Pack, Lola Kathryn Lee
Macclesfield
Bynum, Cheryl Dianne
Marion
Duncan, Julia Erin Nunnally
New Bern
Baskervill, Jane Gibbs
Pisgah Forest
Mock, Jesse Alexander, Jr
Pittsboro
Walls, Dwayne Estes
Raleigh
Adcock, Elizabeth Sharp
Buckner, Sally Beaver
Miller, Robert James
Moore, Lenard Duane
Payne, Peggy
Reynolds, Sidney Rae
Tucker, Helen W.
Sanford
Thomas, Hazel Foster
Wicker, Nina A.
Southern Pines
Ragan, Samuel Talmadge
Stephenson, Shelby
Sylva
Bridgers, Sue Ellen
Wallace
Overman, Marjorie Moore
Walstonburg
Beaman, Joyce Proctor
Wilkesboro
Wood, Curtis L.
Wilmington
Bache, Ellyn
Sher, Steven J.
Wilson
Harrell, Irene Burk
Johnston, Hugh Buckner
Shackleford, Ruby P.
Taylor, Roy G.
Winston-Salem
Ehle, John
Hanes, Frank Borden
Hart, Bobby Sidna
Schoolfield, Henry Palmer Jr. (Hank)
Shaw, Bynum Gillette
Street, Julia Montgomery
Wall, Isabelle Louise Wood
Winterville
Fay, Julie

North Dakota
Bismarck
Murray, William Sta *Fargo*
Nelson, Rodney
Grand Forks
Borden, William Vickers
Meek, Jay

Ohio
Lake Milton
Huzvar, Barbara Jo
Toledo
Mortemore, Lenore Mary
Ada
De Vore, Mary Alice
Dornbusch, Joan Louise Falquet
Akron
Lally, Margaret M.
Montgomery, Catherine Ann
Andover
Britton, Janet Lorene
Ashtabula
Pitt, Christine A.
Athens
Bugeja, Michael Joseph
Matthews, Jack
Schneider, Duane Bernard
Summers, Hollis
Avon Lake
Miltner, Robert Francis
Batavia
Tausch, Susan Diane
Bay Village
Pascarella, Perry James
Beachwood
Kovel, Terry Horvitz
Kovel, Ralph M.
Stadtler, Beatrice Horwitz
Bedford Heights
Dinardo, Marilynn
Bluffton
Naylor, Ruth Eileen
Bowling Green
Karbowiak, Carol Jean
Mc Cord, Howard Lawrence
Messer, Richard E.
Mott, Michael Charles Alston
O'Connor, Philip F.
Pallister, Janis Louise
Ritchie, Michael Karl
Brecksville
Neuman, Stephanie Sellors
Brunswick
Bryan, Joseph J.
Bucyrus
Polak, Julie Stark
Cambridge
Hickman, Jeannine Frances
Kiplinger, Christina Louise
Canfield
Creager, Maureen
Canton
Carpathios, Neil Emmanuel
Chagrin Falls
Skala, Mary Jane
Chardon
Butcher, Grace
Ortiz, Eugene Denis
Chesterland
Abbott, Robert Alvin
Cincinati
Justice, Jack Ronald
Cincinatti
Hilliard, Garrison Lee
Cincinnati
Arner, Robert David
Biggart, Eleanor Marie
Bogen, Don
Braley, Robert Bruce
Brohaugh, William Edward
Fredette, Jean Marie
Gilman, Julia M.
Hall, Jeannine D.
Harrison, Jeffrey Woods
Hershey, Daniel
Hudgins, Andrew
Hughes, Jon Christopher
Irwin, Miriam Owen
Miller, Kathryn Schultz
Patrick, Sam J.
Polking, Kirk
Reitz, Michelle Mastruserio
Robinson, James Keith
Sanberg, Paul Ronald
Schreiber, Suzanne E.
Schreiber, Mark
Schrier, Arnold
Somers, Margaret Lee
Stephens
Stokes, Terry
Thomas, Norman Carl
Wahle, F(rederick) Keith
Ward, Wm. Michael
Wiebe, Dallas Eugene
Wright, Austin M.
Cleveland
Atkins, Russell
Bernauer, Carol Candice
Borowitz, Albert Ira
Cole, E(ugene) R(oger)
Irwin, Mark
Krumhansl, Bernice Rosemary
Mackenzie, Clara Childs
Mc Laughlin, William De Witt
Rypel, Thaddeus Chester
Salm, Peter
Sandburg, Helga
Stein, Herman David
Wallace, Robert
Cleveland Heights
Abbott, Lee Kittredge
Mc Farland, Anne S.
Prosen, Rose Mary
Clinton
Paolano, Mary
Columbus
Becher, Paul Ronald
Bennett, John M.
Boyd, Catherine Emma
Childs, Sister Maryanna
Conn, Christopher
De Board, Janeen Sloan
Fox, Robert R.
Gerardino, William Ernest
Grigsby, Gordon
Hansen, Ann Natalie
Hatton, Robert Wayland
Head, Yvonne
Hoffman, Dean Allen
Hunker, T(racy) Allen
Landis, Brenda Reinhart
Lense, Edward Louis
Mitchell, Enid
Myers, George, Jr.
Nasar, Jack Leon
Orth, Kevin Robert
Rosen, Gerald Robert
Rosen, Michael J.
Stevens, Andrew
Thomas, Beverly Phyllis
Tracy, Stephen V(ictor)
Curtice
Gaich, Sharon Denise
Cuyahoga Falls
Kindel, Robert James
Dayton
Barrett, Harold Francis, Jr.
Coleman, Stephen M.
Egnor-Brown, Rose Marie
Elliott, John Gibson
Martin, Herbert Woodward
Mitchner, Gary L.
Morse, Carmel Lei
Privette, William Herbert
Walters, Clara Oakley
Delaware
Murrie, Michael Howard
Dublin
Jacob, Mary Ellen L.
E Worthington
Weisgerber, David Wendelin
Enon
Ark, Connie Eileen
Fairborn
Szucs, Andrew Eric
Fairfield
Bastian, Lisa Ann
Findlay
Kendig, Diane Lyn
Lafferty, Susan Lee
Freeport
Bear, (Clara) Ann
Fremont
Fields, Susan Louise
Gahanna
Marlowe, Jeanne
Galion
Miller, Linda Dianne
Galloway
Boiarski, Philip S.
Grafton
O'Donnell, Richard Michael
Granville
Bennett, Paul (Lewis)
Grove City
Schnitzer, Christine A.
Hamilton
O'Reilly, Sue Ann
Hebron
Haugh, Barbara Ann
Holgate
Helberg, Barbara Anne
Huron
Smith, Larry R.
Jackson
Simpson, Edwin L.
Kent
Beckett, Thomas L.
Hassler, Donald M.
Kerman, Judith Berna
Meier, August
Tener, Robert L.
Lakewood
Bottiglier, Janet Ellen
Boughner, Howard Robert
Glaefke, Deborah S.
Koco, Linda Gale
Mackey, Vaino Ilmar
Monte, Bryan Robert
Thomas, Arthur Lawrence
Lancaster
Hoff, B. J.
Lebanon
Cowley, Joseph Gilbert
Lorain
Holp, Carolyn Elaine
Lyn-Dhurst
Kastner, Christine Kriha
Lyndhurst
Marsh, Florence Gertrude
Macedonia
Borton, Jeanette
Malvern
Bell, Victor Leray
Mayfield Heights
Buettner, Deborah Anne
McArthur
Smith, Charles
Mechanicsburg
Zook, Amy Jo Schoonover
Medina
Wetzel, Elizabeth
Mentor-On-The-Lake
Shiplett, June Elizabeth Lund
Miamisburg
Foster, Vickie Lynn
Middletown
Turner, Denise Dunn
Minerva
Reynolds, Denise Annette
Mount Vernon
Rice, Donald Lee
Schwartz, William Jeffrey
New Concord
Bates, Laura Mae
Klaiber, Teresa Lynn Martin
New Knoxville
Hallett, Lewellyn

New Plymouth
Sands, Melody Gail
New Richmond
Bennett, Libbie Ann
New Washington
Norris, Diane Lee
North Fairfield
Knight, Becky
Knight, Rebecca R.
North Lawrene
Augusta Ann (Lewis), Lange
North Olmsted
Berkov, Walter
Briedis, Laura Marija
North Royalton
Guion-Shipley, Joyce
Norton
Frederick, Linda Lenore
Oberlin
Hernton, Calvin C.
Turner, Alberta T.
Young, David Pollock
Olmsted Township
Drahos, Leslie Ann
Koran, Connie Jean
Ottawa
Pierman, Carol J.
Oxford
Pratt, William Crouch, Jr.
Throne, Marilyn Elizabeth
Painesville
Modic, Stanley John
Pataskala
Bone, Brenda Kay
Pemberville
Vaughn, Bonnie Jean
Perrysburg
Mc Millen, William Earl
Neal, James Edward Jr.
Weaver, Richard L., II
Pickerington
Gurvis, Sandra Jane
Plymouth
Smith, Francine Denise
Portsmouth
Hubler, H. Clark
Liddle, Catherine Diane
Lodwick, Teresa Jane
Racine
Willis, Betty Jo
Ravenna
Lewis, Lois Fuller
Reynoldsburg
Conkle, Donald Steven
Rock Creek
Sundberg, Norma Jean
Rocky River
Massé, Mark Henry
Masse, Peggy Hart
Schulze, Kenneth W.
Roseville
Ashford, Mary Jane
Sagamore Hills
Sell, Jill
Salem
Reeves, Timothy Scott
Shaker Heights
Kuby, Lolette Beth
Magner, James Edmund Jr.
Mendel, Roberta Joan
Ornstein, Robert
Shelby
Wolford-Barnard, Eileen Joyce
Sherrodsville
Gilbaugh, No June
Sidney
Stevens, Robert Jay
Solon
Filchock, E.
Grabowski, William J(ohn)
Springfield
Reck, W(aldo) Emerson
Schuller, Mary Ann
Stow
Townsend, Cheryl Ann
Sylvania
De Bruin, Jerome Edward
Terrace Park
Rauth, Ruth Binkley
Tiffin
Shevin, David A.
Toledo
King, Marcia Louise
Lipman, Joel Abelman
Metress, Seamus P.
Muska, Nick
Ried, Glenda E.
Troy
Williamson, Richard
Twinsburg
David, Bruce Edward
Warren
Cross, Mary Frances
Prokop, Michael Stephen
West Milton
Waggoner, Timothy Edward
Westerville
Canzoneri, Robert
Citino, David John
Westlake
Meluch, Rebecca M.
Willard
Wilde, Davis Stewart
Williamsport
Stevens, Andrew L.
Wooster
Mc Coy, Karen Kawamoto
Worthington
Dutta, Prabhat Kumar II
Lockridge, Ernest Hugh
Xenia
Taylor, Dorothy Jean
Yellow Springs
Bixler, Paul
Dungey, Joan Marie
Hamilton, Virginia
Jerome, Judson
Youngstown
Greenway, William Henry, Jr.
Lemon, George Edward
Polite, Frank C.
Villani, Jim

Oklahoma
Bartlesville
Sattler, Helen Rone *Bethany*
Harlan, Ross
Binger
Cart, Dorothy Cariker
Calumet
Condry, Dorothea June
Choctaw
Glover, Lyndia Ruth
Duncan
Guido, Jo Ann
Edmond
Gorrell, Dena Ruth
Preston, Marcia
Rees, Eloise Rodkey
Ross, Glen Ernest
Wilkes, Kennette Harrison
Young, Ruby Jean
Henryetta
Campbell, Louise
Lawton
Mynatt, Cecil Ferrell
Reddout, Donna Jane
Spencer, Mark Morris
Mangum
Gilmer, Mary Elizabeth
McAlester
Marshall, John
Midwest City
Hamilton, Carol Jean
Moore
White, Perry Elverado
N Owasso
Ramsay, Ethel Davis
Norman
Economou, George
Fleer, Marilyn June
Menzie, Donald E.
Morrison, Madison
Owens, Rochelle
Parman, James Frank
Samuels, Alfred Putnam
Sellars, Nigel Anthony
Oklahoma City
Allen, Henry Muriel
Bremkamp, Gloria Howe
Broughton, Pamela Kay
Gammill, William
Harrison, John Devereux, Jr.
Luecke, Janemarie
O'Herin, Timothy Patrick
Price, S. David
Pauls Valley
Magoteaux, Cheryl Ann
Poteau
Lannigan, Julie Beth
Seminole
Trudell, Sharon
Shawnee
Gravley, Ernestine Hudlow
Mitchell, William Richard
Stillwater
Archer, Nuala Miriam
Mize, Joe Henry
Pickens, Kel Norris
Rohrberger, Mary
Shirley, Glenn Dean
Weaver, Gordon Allison
Tulsa
Brite, Mary Alice
Dawkins, Vickie Lynn
Dennison, Sally Elizabeth
Fielding, Peggy Lou Moss
Glancy, Diane
Grabo, Norman Stanley
Greer, Germaine
Hale, Richard Lee
Haralson, Carol Louise
Hauger, Leslie Starr
Kosbab, F(rederic) Paul
Langlais, Patricia Ann
Marder, Daniel
Marshall, Myrna Estey
Mcanally, Mary E(llen)
Misfeldt, Terry C.
O'Brien, Darcy
Powders, Donna Jo
Preston, Sondra Kay
Weisman, Ann E.
Waukomis
Hairs, Hugh Michael
Wynnewood
Fulmer, Sandra Lee
Yukon
Darrow, Terri Lynn
Mc Mullen, Leon F.
Mc Mullen, Betty A.

Oregon
Ashland
Anderson, Michael James
Breakey, Jeffrey M.
Hart, Rosana L.
Beaverton
Dickinson, Janet
Bend
Thompson, David James
Coquille
Miller, Marilee Lois
Corvallis
Alexander, Thomas F.
Donnelly, Margarita Patricia
Robert Joseph, Frank
Runciman, Lex
Eugene
Alley, Henry Melton
Baker, Alton Fletcher
Davis, Walter
Helm, Mike
Langdon, Larry
Lyons, Richard M.
Moody, Rodger
Patterson, Scot G.
Robertson, Howard Wayne
Salisbury, Ralph James
Varley, John Herbert
Wendt, Ingrid Darlene
Wickes, George
Forest Grove
Davies, Robert Allan
Gold Beach
Kosoff, Flora May
Grants Pass
Olafson, Harlan Nestor
Sackett, Ernest L.
Halsey
Carey, Margaret Standish
Hillsboro
Dimeo, R. Steven
Jacksonville
Reiss, Alvin
Junction City
Deemer, Bill
La Grande
Venn, George Andrew
Lake Oswego
Tevlin, Michael F.
Lebanon
Howard, David H.
Medford
Shinn, Duane
Milwaukie
Mc Coy, Miles Edward
Myrtle Creek
Lorts, Jack E.
Newport
Kennedy, Richard Jerome
Oswego
Stafford, William Edgar
Pleasant Hill
Kesey, Ken Elton
Portland
Anderson, Richard
Barrington, Judith M.
Canniff, Kiki
Carlile, Henry David
Cornyn-Selby, Alyce P.
Doulis, Thomas John
Farah, Madelain
Gogol, John Michael
Hecker, Helen Jean
Henderson, Michael Douglas
Hoefling, John Erwin
Le Guin, Ursula Kroeber
Matrazzo, Donna J.
Morrison, J. Ken
Nelson, Vera Joyce
Pavlich, Walter David
Raphael, Dan Ambrose
Reyes, Carlos
Richards, Jerrold Allen
Rutsala, Vern
Shugrue, James Leonard
Smario, Thomas Michael
Steinman, Lisa Malinowski
Rogue River

Draime, Charles Douglas
Salem
Ackerson, Duane Wright, Jr.
Bartlett, Steven James
Mainwaring, William Lewis
Sandy
Knight-Weiler, Rene Margaret
Stayton
Horvat, Martin Michael
Union
Gildemeister, Jerry
West Linn
Smith, Susan Ross
Wilsonville
Bittler, Kerry Andrew
Zig Zag
Stein, Joseph

Pennsylvania
Allentown
Bricklin, Mark Har
Mc Cullagh, James Charles
Avoca
Gougeon, Len Girard
Bala-Cynwyd
Sellin, Eric
Beaver Falls
Bennett, Irving
Bellefonte
Gannon, Robert Haines
Bethel Park
Livingston, Patrick Murray
Bethlehem
Pearson, Jean Elizabeth
Biglerville
Medcalf, Robert Randolph, Jr.
Bloomsburg
Pelton, Timothy John
Bradford
Linda, Leshinski
Bryn Mawr
Beaudet, Eugene (Gene)
Stapleton, Katharine Laurence
California
Knight, Arthur Winfield
Camp Hill
Prescott, Steve
Chadds Ford
Mahoney, William Francis
Chalfont
Baker, Frederick Waller
Chester
Panitt, Merrill
Clarks Summit
Fraustino, Daniel Victor
Coraopolis
Dudley, Bobby G.
Croydon
Everett, Joann Marie
Zettlemoyer, Ave Jeanne
Cynwyd
Caine, Shulamith W.
Cynwyd
Zaller, Robert Michael
Dallastown
Springer, Nancy Connor
Doylestown
Fabian, R. Gerry
Drexel Hill
Alexander, Lloyd Chudley
Comey, James Hugh
Lent, John Anthony
Dunmore
Gilroy, William Gerard
East Pittsburgh
Welsh, William Francis Anthony
Easton
Moss, Mark Doublas
Welch, Richard Edwin, Jr.
Emmaus
Beldon, Sanford T.
Erie
Androla, Ron
Davis, J(ames) Madison (Jr.)
King, Phil John
Fogelsville
Crooker, Barbara
Fox Chapel
Goodenough, Judith B.
Furlong
Thompson, Carol Lewis
Gibbon Glade
Cunningham, Marcia Lynn
Harrisburg
Motier, Donald
Randolph, John Denson
Swaim, Alice Mackenzie
Hatboro
Burns, Richard Keith
Haverford
Corrigan, Cfx, John Thomas
Havertown
Winston, Sarah
Hawley
Brenner, Barbara Johnes
Mc Gouey, Robert
Hellertown
Roberts, Leonard Robert
Honesdale
Ballentine, Rudolph M.
Brown, Kent Louis, Jr.
Hummelstown
Markowski, Michael A.
Indiana
Murphy, Patrick Dennis
Jenkintown
Seid, Ruth
Krumsville
Smith, C. Ray
Lancaster
Fluck, Sandra Squire
Henderson, Mildred K.
Pinsker, Sanford Sigmund
Riley, Michael David
Landisburg
Keys, Kerry Shawn
Laughlintown
Shelton, Mark Logan
Lewisburg
Holzberger, William George
Payne, Michael David
Wheatcroft, John Stewart
Mansfield
Hood, Gwenyth Elise
McMurray
Holmes, Marjorie Rose
Mechanicsburg
Miner, Robert Gordon
Merion
Jackson, Thomas H.
Potok, Chaim
Mifflinburg
Cooper, John Charles
Taylor, Robert Love, Jr.
Millersville
Irion, Mary Jean
Sheaffer, M.p.a.
Milton
Lu, David John
Montoursville
Woolever, Naomi Louise
Murrysville
Hardenbrook, Yvonne Imogene
Narberth
Beck, Alan M(arshall)
Steinbrink, Jerold C.
New Columbia
Fletcher, Pauline Charlotte
Fletcher, Pauline Charlotte
New Hope
Wesolowski, Paul G
New Wilmington
Perkins, James Ashbrook
Oreland
Smith, Gordon Ross
Paoli
Santarlasci, Stephen M.
Philadelphia
Asante, Molefi K(ete)
Ashanti, Baron James
Barr, Tina
Beerman, Herman
Benner, Mary D.
Binzen, Peter Husted
Bradley, David Henry, Jr.
Braun, Henry
Brown, Mary Oliver
Cappello, Rosemary C.
Cohen, Marion Deutsche
Cory, Jim
Ehrhart, William Daniel
Farley, Joseph
Fisher, James Abner, Jr.
Hacthoun, Augusto
Henderson, Maurice Brian
Hoffman, Daniel
Javers, Ron
Lee, Audrey (M.)
Livingston, J.A.
Mangione, Jerre Gerlando
Margolis, Joseph
Marion, John Francis
Mc Kee, Louis
Nichols, Stephen George, Jr.
Olson, Toby
Ott, Gil
Pak, Hyung Woong
Peebles, Marvin L.
Polec, Stanley Walter
Rosenberg, Charles Ernest
Ross, James Francis
Saunders, Sally Love
Sherman, William David
Slavitt, David Rytman
Smith, Barbara Herrnstein
Utada, Beth Brown
Virato, Swami
Vitiello, Justin
Walker, Jeanne Murray
Walsh, Mike
Ward, Hiley Henry
Wartluft, David Jonathan
Weiss, Irving
Williams, Kimmika Lyvette Hawes
Wittreich, Joseph Anthony, Jr.
Zimmerman, Margaret Catherine
Phoenixville
Lukacs, John Adalbert
Pittsburg
Thompson, Gerald Luther
Pittsburgh
Calhoun, Harry L.
Daniels, Jim
Evans, Larry Fredric
Evernden, Margery Elizabeth
Harris, Mark
Hayes, Ann Louise
Kaplan, David Michael
Kinder, Charles Alfonso, II
Masters, Hilary Thomas
Miller, Catherine Diane
Musinsky, Gerald
Nordan, Lewis Alonzo
Oresick, Peter Michael
Perlman, Mark
Petesch, Natalie L M
Roffman, Rosaly De Maios
Schwartz, Jeffrey
Scott, Elizabeth Ann
Shelnutt, Eve B.
Tarr, Joel Arthur
Van Wyngarden, Bruce
Waller, Gary F.
Wurster, Michael
Plymouth Meeting
Mc Kendrick, Joseph Edward, Jr.
Radnor
Sendler, David A.
Smith, Robert Clarke
Reading
Vazakas, Byron
Ridley Park
Metzger, Diane Hamill
Riegelsville
Panshin, Alexel
Rosemont
Walton, Clarence
Secane
Newlin, Margaret Rudd
Selinsgrove
Fincke, Gary W.
Sewickley
Tarasovic, Marcia Margaret
Shelocta
Ochester, Ed
Shippensburg
Taggart, John P(aul)
Slippery Rock
Curry, Elizabeth R.
State College
Asbell, Bernard
Downs, Robert C. S.
Mordecai, Carolyn L.
Raymond, Ilene Helen
Weintraub, Stanley
Strafford
Schweitzer, Darrell Charles
Stroudsburg
Flammonde, Paris
Lee, Hamilton Hangtao
Meyer, Theodore E. (Ted)
Swarthmore
Heald, Jane Dewey
Keyes, Ralph Jeffry
North, Helen Florence
Rose, Gilbert Paul
Rosier, James Louis
Snyder, Susan Brooke
Tannersville
Coddington, Joseph, Jr.
Tannery
Hedges, James
University Park
Lima, Robert
Nelsen, Hart Michael
Rush, Jeffrey S.
Schneeman, Peter Henry
Upper Darby
Hollis, Jocelyn
Villanova
De Camp, L(yon) Sprague
Delaura, David Joseph
Salmon, John Hearsey Mc Millan
Washington Crossing
Martino, Maria Linda
Wayne
Berg, Jean Horton
Kitchin, Rosemarie A.
Waynesburg
Anderson, Maggie
West Chester
Croes, Keith John
Westtown
Mc Cartney, Dorothy Wilson
Williamsport
Cave, George Patton
Wyncote
O'Connell, Richard
Wyndmoor
Paul, David Tyler

Wynnewood
Brooks, Frank Pickering
Wangberg, Mark Thomas
Zionsville
Gibb, Robert

Rhode Island
Adamsville
Cumming, Patricia
Cranston
Wicklund, Millie Mae
Jamestown
Potter, Clarkson Nott
Wolff, Geoffrey Ansell
Kingston
Letcher, Tina H
Tyler, Robert L.
Zucker, Naomi Flink
Zucker, Norman Livingston
Middletown
Whitman, Ruth
Newport
Day, George R.
Providence
Ahern, Thomas Francis
Cassill, Ronald Verlin
Cassill, Karilyn
Cloutier, David Edward
Cook, Albert Spaulding
Corbett, (Winfield) Scott
Gander, Forrest
Harleman, Ann
Hawkes, John
Honig, Edwin B.
Kahn, Paul
Rosenberg, Bruce Alan
Rutherford, Brett
Schevill, James Erwin
Spilka, Mark
Sullivan, Janet Wright
Waldrop, Rosmarie
Wright, C.d. (Carolyn)
Tiverton
Davis, Edward Joseph Jr.
Westerly
Smith, Michael Townsend

South Carolina
Aiken
Bodie, Idella Fallaw
Harris, Joseph Herbert
Miller, Phillip Edward
Anderson
Ilg, Ruth Merkle
Beaufort
Ogburn, Charlton
Bishopville
Studebaker, III, Joseph Elizah
Blythewood
Roberts, Delmar L.
Robertson, Thomas Patrick, Jr.
Central
Steadman, Mark S.
Charleston
Graddick, Richard Adolph
Hamill, Paul J.
Platt, Eugene
Rigney, James Oliver, Jr.
Simson, Joanne (Pascoe)
Clemson
Sawyer, Corinne Holt
Clinton
Moone, Joseph Leanders
Columbia
Asnen, Alan Richard
Bagnal, Kimberly Baughman
Boylston, Samuel Lionel
Bruccoli, Matthew Joseph
Creed, Nellie Anne
Geckle, George Leo, III
Jowers, Lawrence Victor
Lewis, Steven Richard
Mc Kinney, Donald Lee
Meriwether, James Babcock
Rone, William Eugene, Jr.
Smith, Wilbur Stevenson
Edgemoor
Newcomb, Wilburn Wendell
Florence
Harllee, John Thomas
Fripp Island
King, Cynthia Bregman
Garden City
Miller, Jay Earl
Greenville
Baker, David Alan
Long-Tims, Marilyn Virginia
Lowe, Jonathan F.
Greenwood
Cumming, Robert
Olsen, W. Scott
Skelton, Ira Steven
Sullivan, Janice Calhoun
Greer
Poston, David L.
Hardeeville
Cooler, Amanda Jeffers
Hartsville
Browning, Pamela
Hilton Head Island
Bottari, George L.
Hill, Isaac William
Male, Roy Raymond
Irmo
Gardner, Stephen Leroy
Marion
Larrimore, Gloria Dean
Williams, Irene E. G.
Mount Pleasant
Cooper, Barbie Perkins
Lott, Bret
Myrtle Beach
Guy, Carol Ann
Newberry
Farley, Myron Foster
Perry, Thomas Kennedy
Pawley's Island
Cretzmeyer, Stacy Megan
Piedmondt
Cooper, Kathy Nelle
Quinby
Parham, Robert Randall
Rock Hill
Bristow, Robert O'Neil
Casada, James Allen
Christopher, Matthew Frederick
Salley
Bass, Deborah Livingston
Seneca
Curry, Mary Earle Lowry
Spartanburg
Trakas, Deno
Starr
Okenson, Lois Wiley
Summerville
Hager, Jimmy Nelson
Harris, Melanie Gause
Mc Millan, Elma Joyce
Sumter
Amanuddin, Syed
Taylors
Calnon, Guin Corinne
Traveler's Rest
Powell, Evan Arnold
Travelers Rest
Allen, Gilbert Bruce
Union
Greene, Deborah

South Dakota
Brookings
Evans, David Allan
Bryant
Cramer, Marian H.
Deadwood
Goble, Paul
Eden
Johnson, Norma Alice
Hermosa
Hasselstrom, Linda M.
Lemmon
Norris, Kathleen
Mitchell
Weinkauf, Mary Louise S.
Rapid City
Zeitner, June Culp
Sioux Falls
Leih, Grace Janet
Sanford, Geraldine A.
Stevens, Barbara Constance
Vermillion
Milton, John Ronald
Waubay
Lohan, William Denis (Bill)

Tennessee
Knoxville
Moser, Harold Dean
Brentwood
Reed, Alison Touster
Chattanooga
Jackson, Richard Paul
Meacham, Ellis Kirby
Voyles, J. Bruce
Columbia
Bell, Linda R.
Franklin
James Andrew, Crutchfield
Germantown
Conner, Cindy Dixon
Knoxville
Fine, Elsa Honig
Froula, James
Garrett, Leslie
Kelly, Richard
Mynatt, Elaine Simpson
Pobo, Kenneth George
Sorrells, Robert Taliaferro
White, Jon Manchip
Lookout Mountain
Davis, Ann-Marie
Martin
Graves, Roy Neil
Maryville
Wright, Nathalia
Memphis
Bensko, John
Foote, Shelby
Glaser, Isabel Joshlin
Haney, David P.
Page, William Howard
Parish, Barbara Shirk
Rosenthal, Abby Jane
Russell, Thomas Lyon
Share, Donald Seth
Tickle, Phyllis Alexander
Wiley, Robert F.
Williams, Edward F. III
Murfreesboro
Herring, Robert H(erschel)
Nashville
Battle, William Robert
Cheatham, Karyn Elizabeth
Cornwell, Ilene Jones
Egerton, John Walden
Elick, Catherine Lilly
Flynn, John David
Ford, Jesse Hill
Gafford, Charlotte Kelly
Gore, Jeanne Guerrero
Longhurst, Suzanne Elizabeth
Moran, John Charles
Richards, Ramona Pope
Sherburne, Donald Wynne
Shockley, Ann Allen
Smith, Jessie Carney
Summerville, James
Yeatman, Trezevant Player III
Oak Ridge
Scarbrough, George Addison
Sewanee
Bates, Scott
Spears, Monroe Kirk
Spring City
Roe, Ina Lea
Waynesboro
Christian, Paula

Texas
Amarillo
Mojtabai, Ann Grace
Rackley, Audie Neal
Arlington
Chester, Edward William
Floyd, Wayne
Garner, Stanton Berry
Mc Linden, Stephen Kerry
Art
Lindemann, Jo Ann
Austin
Abzug, Robert Henry
Billings, Harold Wayne
Bird, Sarah Ann
Cody, James Marion
Cravey, Robin T.
Davis, Rod
Dugger, Ronnie E.
Farrell, Edmund James
Flowers, Betty Sue
Furman, Laura
Gilmore, Michael
Haining, James Howard
Hawley, Donald Springer
Kelley, Kate
Kent, Carol
La Salle, Peter
Lehmann, Ruth Preston Miller
Louis, William Roger
Lynn, Sandra Dykes
Osborn, Carolyn Culbert
Pickle, Hal B(rittain)
Polome, Edgar Charles
Prigogine, Ilya
Rafferty, Carolyn Banks
Rosenfeld, Arnold Solomon
Ross, Stanley Robert
Satterfield, Ben
Seung, Thomas Kaehao
Skrabanek, Donald W.
Sledd, James Hinton
Sutherland, William Owen Sheppard
Talmadge, Jeffrey D.
Taylor, Charles Bruce
Todd, William Burton
Veninga, James Frank
Whitbread, Thomas Bacon
Azle
Coomer, Joe
Beaumont
Gwynn, R(obert) S(amuel)
Bedford
Norman, Jackie Delois
Bryan
Christensen, Paul
Cedar Park
Oliphant, Dave
Cisco
Lewis, Monte Ross
College Station
Anderson, James E(lliott)

Cole, Ann Marie
Jones, Roger Walton
Mccann, Janet
Poole, Jay Martin
Rosen, David Henry
Unterberger, Betty Miller
Commerce
Tarpley, Fred Anderson
Conroe
Flora, Philip Craig
Dallas
Avery, Neil Francis
Blair, Samuel Rufus
Davis, Stephen W.
Durham, Kenneth M.
Freeman, Marcus A., Jr.
Hale, A. Dean
Hendricks, Thomas Manley
Marcus, Stanley
Maxwell, Otis Allen
Myers, Jack Elliott
Reid, Janet Kay
Schulze, Enika Hermine
Spiegelman, Willard Lester
Timmins, Lois Fahs
Tucker, Charles Christopher
Waddle, Jeffrey R.
Wade, Timothy Andrew
Whaley, Charlotte T.
Denton
Linebarger, James Morris
Spaar, Lisa Russ
Edinburg
Wade, Seth
El Paso
Byrd, Robert J.
Hughes, Lenore Harris
Leach, Joseph Lee
Olvera, Joe
Flower Mound
Holnick, Catherine Sigmund
Fort Worth
Breeze, Grace Wilkie
Reuter, Frank Theodore
Sanders, Leonard Marion, Jr.
Glen Rose
Graves, John Alexander
Grand Prairie
Katz, Amnon
Hearne
Campbell, Ewing
Houston
Berles, James John
Brown, Steven Ford
Chase, Elaine Raco
Dante, Robert David
Diebel, Donald Ray
Edelson, Morris
Hallsten Mc Garry, Susan Joan
Henderson, Archibald
Hirsch, Edward
Langham, Barbara Dee
Macdonald, Cynthia
Miele, Angelo
Orfield, Olivia Fuller
Robinson, Cora Guinn
Rottman, Gordon Leroy
Segerstrom, Jane Archer
Simon, Jacqueline Ann
Van Woerkom, Dorothy O'Brien
Widgery, Jeanne-Anna
Huntsville
Ruffin, Paul Dean
Lubbock
Connor, Seymour Vaughan
Higdon, David Leon
Mc Donald, Walter Robert
Rushing, Jane Gilmore
Lufkin
Bowman, Bob
McAllen
Brinkley, William Clark
Seale, Jan Epton
McKinney
Schulte, Rainer
Nevada
Tobias, Ronald Benjamin
New Boston
Gabbard, Gregory N.
Orange
Mc Bride, Ella Andrepont
Plano
Finley, Glenna
Quinlan
Kieninger, Richard George
Rice Univ Houston
Norbeck, Edward
Richardson
Sapiro, Leland
Round Rock
Wiggs, Terry Allen
San Anonio
Montalvo, Jose Luis
San Antonio
Ashcroft, Shelley Alane
Barnett Scharf, Lauren Ileene
Castillo, Rafael C.
Garcia, Julian S.
Gomez, Rogelio Roberto
Johnson, Sammye La Rue
Neidigh, Kim Lee
Nye, Naomi Shihab
Reposa, Carol Coffee
Sanchez, Ricardo
Sonenschein, David Walter
Talal, Marilynn Carole Glick
Valys, Susan Patricia
Willson, Robert
San Marcos
Galvan, Robert A.
Walts, Robert Warren
Wilson, Miles Scott
Spring
Hamilton, William Roger
Stafford
Chance, Jane
Rogers, Pattiann
Texas City
Allen, William Dean
Victoria
Behlen, Charles William
Hamilton, Leona
Waco
Barcus, James Edgar
Davis, William Virgil
Hunt, Maurice Arthur
Lemaster, Jimmie Ray
Long, Eugene Hudson
Wichita Falls
Hoggard, James Martin
Wimberley
Nelson, Bobby Jack

Utah
Bountiful
Flack, Dora D(utson)
Shields, Steven Layne
Hildale
Jessop, Dorothy Emma
Logan
Brewer, Kenneth Wayne
Hansen, Gary B(arker)
Ogden
Smith, V. La Monte
Orem
Lewis, John (Earl)
Paragonah
Lee, William David
Park City
Poster, Carol
Provo
Hart, Edward Leroy
Lyon, Ted
Salt Lake City
Altman, Irwin
Chertkow, Fern
Cooper, Wyn
Garlington, Jack O'Brien
Ghiselin, Brewster
Lueders, Edward George
Ruffus, Stephen
Snodgrass, Ann A.
Strand, Mark
Sylvester, Janet
Thayne, Emma Lou Warner
Sevier
Baker, Jeannine Ann
Springville
Ruff, Howard Joseph

Vermont
Bennington
Belitt, Ben
Brattleboro
George, Barbara
Burlington
Broughton, T. Alan
Guma, Greg
Huddle, David
Page, Ruth W.
Chelsea
Mc Carriston, Linda
Cornwall
Pack, Robert M.
Derby Line
Mahoney, John Marquis
Essex Junction
Gojmerac-Leiner, Georgia
Fair Haven
Gabriel, Mark A.
Guilford
Arnold, Bob
Marshfield
Voigt, Ellen Bryant
Middlebury
Margolis, Gary Francis
Watts, John M., Jr.
Wright, Nancy Means
Montgomery
Sherman, Joe
Montpelier
Facos, James
Kennedy, Thomas Eugene
Wolkomir, Richard
Wolkomir, Joyce Rogers
Mt Holly
Reeve, F.d.
Murray
Redford, Roberta Carly
No Bennington
Brownell, David Wheaton
North Bennington
Sandy, Stephen Merrill
Norwich
Woods-Smith, Sybil
Peacham
Lederer, William Julius
Plainfield
Dranow, John Theodore
Gluck, Louise Elisabeth
Pownal
Howes, Barbara
Putney
Berry, Betsy E.
Helminski, Edmund Richard
Rohmann, Paul Henry
Randolph
Martin, Don Roger
Richford
Clifton, Merritt Robin
Rutland
Warshaw, Stanley
Sheffield
Kinnell, Galway
Strafford
Moraff, Barbara
Taftsville
Jennison, Peter Saxe
Winooski
Nahra, Nancy Ann

Virginia
Afton
Hornig, Douglas
Alexandria
Anderson, John Charles
Antonazzi, Frank Joseph, Jr.
Ball, Robert M.
Barnett, David Leon
Beltz, William Albert
Ellis, Barbara Williams
Loveless, William Edward
Render, Sylvia Lyons
Ward, Sr., Mark Lee
Wilson, Minter Lowther, Jr.
Alexandria
Berliner, Don
Annandale
Hubler, David Elliot
Arlington
Arnold, Gary Howard
Bierbrier, Doreen
Broder, David Salzer
Elsberg, John William
Goldberg, Hilary Tham
Greenwood, John Edson
Jaffe, David
Mc Aleavey, David Willard
Neuharth, Allen Harold
Orben, Robert
Pogue, Forrest Carlisle
Strahan, Bradley R.
Weinberg, Susan Clare
Blacksburg
Aiken, William Minor
Alton, John G.
Falco, Edward
O'Donohoe, Nicholas Benjamin
Bridgewater
Bittel, Lester Robert
Chantilly
Corsi, Deborah Eranda
Charlotte Courthouse
Hoffman, Henry William
Charlottesville
Bierstedt, Robert
Blackford, Staige D.
Casey, John Dudley
Decker, Virginia Ann
Desmond, Walter Thomas, Jr.
Ford, Kathleen
Garrett, George Palmer, Jr.
Grohskopf, Bernice
Hale, Nancy
Lang, Cecil Yelverton
Langbaum, Robert Woodrow
Latta, John Alex
Levin, David
Moore, John Norton
O'Connell, Jeffrey
Shattuck, Roger Whitney
Taylor, Peter Hillsman
Vandersee, Charles Andrew
Wright, Charles Penzel, Jr.
Chesapeake
Alexander, E. Curtis
Fairfax
Bausch, Richard Carl
Cary, Emily Pritchard
Farrant, Elizabeth

Klappert, Peter
Lewis, Roger
Lister, Marilyn J.
Falls Church
Lomask, Milton Nachman
Roth, Judith Paris
Fincastle
Davis, James Paxton
Fredericksburg
Olson, Mark William
Halifax
Conner, Don R.
Hampden-Sydney
O'Grady, Thomas Joseph
Hampton
Romjue, John Lawson
Herndon
Graff, J. William
Hillsboro
Farwell, Byron Edgar
Hollins
Moore, John Rees
Hollins College
Larsen, Jeanne Louise
Zeldin, Jesse
James Store
Cox, Willis Franklin
Lexington
Balazs, Mary W.
Ballard, Edward Goodwin
Mollenhoff, Clark Raymond
Stuart, Dabney
Lincoln
Taylor, Henry Splawn
Lynchburg
Davis, Sarah Irwin
Madison Heights
Bryant, Sylvia Leigh
Manassas
Holloman, Hugh Jerry
McLean
Church, John Irwin
Oehser, Paul Henry
Rosenberger, Francis Coleman
Middleburg
Bills, Sheryl Jean
Mc Clary, Jane Mc Ilvaine
Midlothian
Smith, David Jeddie
Urofsky, Melvin Irving
Newport News
Paul, Jay Snyder
Norfolk
Barry, Richard Francis, III
Batten, Frank
Kennedy, William S.
Settle, Mary Lee
Petersburg
Morant, Mack Bernard
Portsmouth
Mapp, Alf Johnson, Jr.
Radford
Gallo, Louis Jacob
Hayes, Charles Leonard
Reston
Blehert, (Maurice) Dean
Matthews, Allan Freeman
Rice
Bass, Dorothy Elizabeth
Richmond
Brown, Aubrey Neblett, Jr.
Byrd, Odell Richard, Jr.
Donovan, Gregory Edward
Feine, Paul Money
Freeman, Anne Hobson
Gehman, Christian
Haley, Vanessa Leigh
Pendleton, James Dudley
Satchell, Carol Alexis
Troubetzkoy, Dorothy Ulrich
Roanoke
Bess, Robert Wade
Drewry, Guy Carleton
Hankla, Cathryn
Rheinheimer, Kurt
Salem
Bays, Edrie Hill
Springfield
Evans, Norene Russell (Rusti)
Tucker, Nancy Meredith
Staunton
Lembke, Janet
Sterling
Sanfelici, Arthur Hugo
Sweet Briar
Smart, William Edward Jr.
Waters, Michael
Vienna
Frieseke, Frances
Goodwin, Stephen
Kilmer, Kenton
Virginia Beach
Bouchard, Lynda M.
King, Karen Jeanne
Rosenman, John Brown
Seward, William Ward, Jr.
Smith, A. Robert
Volney
Newman, Charles
Warrenton
Lynskey, Edward C.
Williamsburg
Delaune, (jewel) Lynn
Bloom, Lynn Marie Zimmerman
Esler, Anthony James
Hart, Henry Walker
Mc Giffert, Michael
Woodbridge
Ayres, Ed
Mc Vay, Barry Lee
Woodville
Mc Carthy, Eugene Joseph

Washington
Seattle
Dubois, Christine
Anacortes
Berst, Barb Jo
Bertojames D., Gene
Bertolino, James D.
Auburn
Safford, Dan Scott
Bainbradge Island
Macdonald, Kathryn Elizabeth
Bainbridge Island
Beagle, Peter Soyer
Snydal, James Matthew
Bellevue
Pyle, Kenneth Birger
Washington, Tom F.
Bellingham
Anderson, Carol Jean
Becker, George Joseph
Johnson, Ellwood G.
Kalpakian, Laura Anne
Skinner, Knute (Rumsey)
Bremerton
Edwards, Jane Elizabeth
Burton
Burnham, Gregory Alan
Cheney
Cook-Lynn, Elizabeth
Edmonds
Hundman, Robert Louis
Ellensburg
Bennett, John J.
Halperin, Mark Warren
Powell, Joseph Edward
Everett
Owen, Eileen Edmunds
Friday Harbor
Miller, Jerome K.
Kirkland
Fletcher, Barbara Rainbow
Meredith, Ted Jordan
Longview
Jaeger, Brenda Kay
Lopez Isle
Mahr, Douglas James
Lynnwood
Meyer, Linda D.
Medical Lake
Keeble, John Robert
Trueman, Terry Earl
Mill Creek
Wagoner, David Russell
Naselle
Grimm-Richardson, Anna Louise
Olympia
Nesbit, Robert Carrington
Power, Marjorie
Port Ludlow
Youra, Daniel George
Port Townsend
Bangs, Carol Jane
Cady, Jack
Ransom, Bill
Whealdon, Everett Whittier
Pt Angeles
Carver, Raymond
Pullman
Simonsmeier, Larry Marvin
Puyallup
Harvey, Kenneth Ricardo
Redmond
Rind, Sherry
Richland
Partridge, Dixie Lee
San Juan Island
Gann, Ernest Kellogg
Seattle
Ames, Patrick W.
Bentley, Sean Singer
Bierds, Linda Louise
Bosworth, David
Bourasaw, Noel V.
Bryan, Sharon
Carnevall, Doris L(orrain)
Charles Winfield, Nolte
Clifton, Linda Jane
D'ambrosio, Charles A.
Defrees, Madeline
Dill, Michele Andrus
Fitzgerald, Roger J.
Gormezano, Keith Stephen
Green, Lewis
Hancock, Alexander Digiulio
Handy, Mary Nixeon Civille
Ives, Rich Lee
Kronenberg, Susan L.
Litewka, Jack
Lumsdaine, Arthur Allen
Mc Elroy, Colleen Johnson
Mc Farland, John Bernard
Mc Intyre, Vonda Neel
Mcnamara, Robert James
Murray, Steven T.
Nelson, Jo Ann
Niatum, Duane
Olson, Kirby
Orlock, Carol E.
Potterfield, Peter Lounsbury
Rodieck, Patricia Anna
Russ, Joanna
Ryan, Mary Elizabeth
Simkin, Penelope Payson
Singer, Sarah Beth
Souder, Mark Stephen
Stablein, Marilyn Estelle
Stirling, Dale Alexander
Wahlgren, Erick
Warn, Emily
Selah
Clement, Dallas Brent
Spokane
Bear, Sun
Blewett, Stephen Douglas
Brock, Randall J.
Conoley, Gillian
Crutcher, Christopher C.
Crutcher, Christopher C.
Gurian, Michael W.
Hegi, Ursula Johanna
Stansberry, Domenic Joseph
Sultan
Harris, Jana N.
Tacoma
Andrews, Heber J.
Baker, Elbert Hall
Eklund, Gordon Stewart
Fukuyama, Betty M.
Haller, Amelia Jane
Jensen, Laura Linnea
Jones, R(ichard) P(reston)
Thorp
Nourse, Alan E(dward)
Wahougal
Moore, Raymond S.
Waldron
Aliesan, Jody
Waldron Island
Green, Samuel Leonard
Walla Walla
Potts, Charles
Washougal
Moore, Dorothy N(elson)

West Virginia
Alderson
Head, Robert
Belington
Mc Kinney, Irene
Bethany
Sykes, Robert H.
Charleston
Holsaert, Faith S.
Fairmont
Colander, Valerie Nieman
Glenville
Faulkner, Ronnie Wayne
Huntington
Mc Kernan, Llewellyn Teresa
Mc Kernan, John Joseph
Kearneysville
Naylor, Robert L.
Morgantown
Jones, Mary Holmes
Richwood
Baber, Robert Henry
South Charleston
Gallagher, Karen
Weirton
Russell, Timothy

Wisconsin
Amherst Jct
Sroda, George
Appleton
Dintenfass, Mark
Halla, Robert Christian
Kleinhans, Theodore John
Schneider, Ben Ross, Jr.
Schutte, William Metcalf
Baraboo
Brice, Janet Kay
Wight, Doris Teresa
Beloit
Mc Cown, John Clinton
Rich, Mark David
Brookfield

Lessiter, Frank Donald
Schwanz, H. Lee
Delafield
Behrendt, David Frogner
Dodgeville
Meudt, Edna Kritz
Eau Claire
Lauber, Peg Carlson
Taylor, Bruce
Elm Grove
Morgan, David Page
Fennimore
Dannenmann, Otto Karl
Westburg, John Edward
Glidden
Patitz, Dolores Rose
Green Bay
Bennett, John Frederic
Hudson, Marcus Allan
Hancock
Vroman, Barbara Fitz
Hartland
Plath, James Walter
Howards Grove
Elder, Karl Curtis
Iola
Gunnell, John A.
Mishler, Clifford Leslie
La Crosse
Schirm, Karen Marie
LaCrosse
Becker, Scott Randal
Gardiner, Harry Walter
Walsh, Donald James
Madison
Baeumer, Max Lorenz
Bird, Robert Byron
Cherry, Kelly
Chow, Tse-Tsung
Clayton, Jay
Feraca, Jean Stephanie
Lerner, Gerda
Marth, Elmer Herman
Miller, Stephen M.
Miller, Robert James
Moon, Warren G.
Moore, Lorrie (Marie L.)
Mosse, George L.
Moy, James S.
Osterweil, Wendy
Perkins, Merle Lester
Pollak, Felix
Rideout, Walter Bates
Riley, Jocelyn Carol
Rothstein, Eric
Ruffolo, Lisa M.
Shapiro, Naomi K.
Shaw, Janet
Singer, Marcus George
Spiess, Robert Clayton
Steingass, David Herbert
Stokes, William Forest
Swanberg, Ingrid
Taylor, Charles Andrew (Chuck)
Wallace, Ronald W.
Weinbrot, Howard David
Weisbrod, Burton Allen
McFarland
Knoll, Erwin
Menasha
Dalton, Dorothy
Menomonie
Schuler, Robert Jordan
Mequon
Schwartz, Joseph
Swanson, Roy Arthur
Milwaukee
Berry, Richard Lewis
Cohen, Keith
Cooper, Barbara Mary
Egleson, Janet Frank
Harrold, William Eugene
Hassan, Ihab Habib
Hazard, James Arthur
Key, Donald
Liddy, James
Livingston, Jay Carl
Mooney, Michael Morse
Neuman, Donald Bernard
Peckenpaugh, Angela J.
Poniewaz, Jeff
Powers, Anne
Reedy, George Edward
Shea, Donald Richard
Siegel, Robert Harold
Montello
Burns, Robert Edward
New Glarus
Kubly, Herbert Oswald
Oregon
Cox, James Andrew
Oshkosh
Bennett, Allyson Joy
Cox, Justin Brantlin (Jack)
Flaherty, Doug
Hodgell, Patricia Christine
Platteville
Route, Deborah, A.
Plover
Zielinski, Leszek
Plymouth
Stiefel, Janice J.
Racine
Du Priest, Travis Talmadge
Lindquist, Barbara Louise
Shorewood
Clinton, Lloyd Dewitt
Rosenblum, Martin Jack
Sister Bay
Johnson, Frederick William
Stevens Point
Behm, Richard H
Kallas, Phillip G
Missey, James Lawrence
Stoughton
Danky, James Philip
Verona
Otto, Wayne Raymond
Washburn
Merrill, Augustus Lee
Waukesha
Aman, Reinhold Albert
Wausau
Whitney, J. D.
Wauwatosa
Hachey, Thomas Eugene
West Allis
Mc Martin, Paula J.
Whitewater
Shoemaker, Lynn Henry

Wyoming
Buffalo
Romtvedt, David William
Casper
Eisenhauer, Gale Ann
Levendosky, Charles Leonard
Nichols, Sharon D.
Cheyenne
Moore, Maurine
Jackson
Spence, Gerald Leonard
Jelm
Jones, Jean R.
Laramie
Boresi, Arthur Peter
Fleck, Richard Francis
Mills
Jozwik, Francis Xavier